Hot Off of the VideoHound Newswire...

VIDEOHOUND MULTIMEDIA*

The *Hound* goes around on CD-ROM, bringing the sights and sounds of Hollywood to your search for reviews of 52,000 videos—more than 20,000 movies plus TV shows, cartoons, sports, music, fitness and more. Biographies of contemporary stars, thousands of photos, and more! Windows™—capable multimedia PC required. **$79.95.**

VIDEOHOUND'S CHOICE FOR PCS*

It's the pick-of-the-pooch on diskette for video searching on your personal computer. Prowl through *VideoHound's* vault of 10,000 of the world's most memorable, most-watched and most-wanted videos (including some classic cinema "dogs"). Windows™—capable PC required. **$39.95.**

See ad on inside back cover for more details.

VIDEOHOUND CLUB

For those who want to stay up on new video releases and other *VideoHound* news throughout the year. For more information, please check the appropriate box on the response card. Then mail card in and await big news!

Windows is a trademark of Microsoft Corporation.

Other Visible Ink Titles of Interest:

VideoHound's
GOLDEN
MOVIE
RETRIEVER

VideoHound's GOLDEN MOVIE RETRIEVER

VISIBLE INK PRESS

DETROIT • WASHINGTON, D.C. • LONDON

CREDITS

EDITORS:
Martin Connors
Julia Furtaw

CONTRIBUTING EDITORS:
Beth A. Fhaner
Christine Tomassini
Maria L. Sheler
Richard Lawson
Kristine Carl

PROGRAMMER:
David Trotter

ASSISTANT TO THE PROGRAMMER:
Tricia Seidler

TYPESETTER:
Michael Boyd,
Atlis Publishing Services, Inc.

ART DIRECTOR:
Cynthia Baldwin

COVER DESIGN:
Sheila Young Tomkowiak

PAGE DESIGN:
Kathleen A. Hourdakis

ILLUSTRATIONS:
Terry Colon

PRODUCTION:
Mary Beth Trimper
Dorothy Maki
Evi Seoud
Mary Kelley

DATA ENTRY:
Kenneth D. Benson, Jr.
Gwen Tucker

ASSISTANT TO THE EDITORS:
Jane P. Connors

CATERING:
Britt's Cafe

COSTUMES:
Dayton Hudson

RESEARCH:
Chuck Lewis

PUBLICITY:
Jenny Sweetland, Cheryl McDonald

MARKETING MANAGER:
Lauri Taylor

A Cunning Canine Production

CONTENTS

INTRODUCTION

Welcome to the 1994 edition of *VideoHound's Golden Movie Retriever*, a big, weighty tome useful for bonking bugs, propping doors open, and smoothing the wrinkles out of your clothes overnight. *VideoHound 1994* is your faithful companion to the amazing, astounding world of video, or, more accurately, the great, the good, the bad, and the definitely ugly. For this edition, we've reviewed almost 1,500 new videos, revised and expanded several thousand other reviews, added laserdisc and alternate title indexes, and tweaked any number of other items.

What's *VideoHound* all about? It's both a comprehensive video guide (22,000 videos and counting, or several thousand more than the average guide) and a multifaceted movie reference tool (hundreds of useful indexes make the video quest a walk in the park). And we do enjoy our walks in the park. Our mission is to create the best video guide available, one that scans the movie universe and provides an array of advanced video tracking devices (AVTDs) to help you quickly find needed information. Because for the certified video buff, finding a fact or locating a favorite video is a pleasure in itself. And for the more casual viewer, the choices available at the local video store can be overwhelming and/or under utilized. True to his retriever nature, *VideoHound* is a handy, wide-ranging movie detective, helping you make the most of your limited leisure time. That's four bones and a hearty bark for good, clean fun.

This 1,600-page husky is not your ordinary video guide—it's virtually a private movie database, with a full list of options (incidentally, *VideoHound* is now available on CD-ROM and diskette). Those features include:

- Thousands and thousands of video reviews
- Monumental cast index
- Stupendous director index
- Totally amazing category index
- Extremely entertaining kibbles and series indexes
- Quality driven awards of the world index
- Spiffy laserdisc index
- Sensational alternate title index
- Intellectually pleasing foreign movie index
- Very handy closed caption index
- Perfectly orchestrated music video guide
- Super sleuthhound video distributor guide

That's a lot of parts. While expanding the range of information, we've also tried to make *VideoHound* easier to use. We've improved the so-called explanatory materials and rearranged the contents in our never-ending quest to make *VideoHound* obey your every command (except maybe "sit" and "roll over"). We've flipped several of the indexes to the front of the book so that you can find them faster. The humongous cast and director index is now two, more petite indexes. At the very least, the *Hound* is confident that some items are in a place different from where you last found them.

Also new to *VideoHound* is an improved alphabetic arrangement for listing movie titles (see **Using VideoHound** for details). And the pooch with a nose for film has gone out on a cinematic limb to preview theatrical releases not yet on video but likely to become available during the year.

Much of the impetus to improve comes from readers who write. During the past 12 months we've read the mail (thanks to the hundreds who sent in the little cards in the back of the book and the 17 who wrote long, single-spaced letters with sometimes hard-to-discern handwriting—we share your passion and please write again). Many suggested new topics for the category index, helping us come up with more than 50 new lists. Mr. E.D. of Nebraska, Ms. C.M. of Alberta, and Charles from Ohio all suggested we add screenwriters to the reviews. And we listened. With this edition, *VideoHound* has begun the very large job of noting who wrote the screenplay.

Mrs. A.G. from North Carolina and Jane C. from Michigan suggested we add composers and lyricists. Ditto on that. Somebody in California and a Mr. Billy D. in Texas wanted *VideoHound* to list the songs from musicals. Now we're singing the same song. S.A. from Orlando and Nigel of London desired that *VideoHound* indicate Academy Award nominees as well as Oscar winners. Their wish is our command, alakazeem, alakazaam.

The quest to bring you the best doggone guide to videos doesn't stop here, however; we have plenty of additions and improvements in mind for the next edition. So please, keep those cards and letters coming in, letting us know what you like and don't like about the *Hound*. For general correspondence, write *VideoHound*, **Visible Ink Press, P.O. Box 33477, Detroit, MI 48232-5477.**

USING VIDEOHOUND

More than 1,000 movies are released annually to video. Thousands more are already out on video, with a fraction carried by the average video store. No wonder it's easy to draw a blank when searching for the right video. **VideoHound's Golden Movie Retriever** possesses two simple strengths that enable the reader to make the most of their video knowledge—from the obscure to the box-office hits, the **Hound** lists nearly everything in movieland available on video. Plus, with ten indexes, **VideoHound** enables you to find a video when chewing on only the slightest morsel of information. Less time wasted, more time for fun. That's our motto. That, and keep the cat from the chow and avoid the bath at all costs.

Perhaps you remember the star of a movie you truly would like to rent, but the video title escapes you. Or during a sudden fit of nostalgia you recall that a nameless "B" matinee of long ago featured a flying lizard greatly enlarged by nuclear fall-out that spends its leisure time descending upon hapless Japanese suffering chronic communication breakdowns caused by unsynchronized dialogue. What is the name of that movie? With a wag of the tail, **VideoHound** is on the trail. Or suddenly your weekend plans take a turn for the more domesticated and you've got 48 hours of uninterrupted video bliss ahead. You decide to hold a film festival featuring your favorite director. But you're not quite sure what comprises his or her collected works. Where to look for that information? The **Hound** is back in a flash with the answer, your slippers, and some unidentified thing from under the couch.

ALPHABETIZATION

VideoHound alphabetically arranges titles on a word-by-word basis, including articles and prepositions. Leading articles (*A, An, The*) are ignored in English-language titles. The equivalent foreign articles are not ignored, however: *The Abyss* appears under "A" while *Les Miserables* appears under "L." A short demonstration:

The Monster
Monster
Monster a Go-Go!
The Monster and the Stripper
The Monster Club
The Monster Demolisher
Monster Dog
Monster from Green Hell
Monster from the Ocean Floor
Monster High

Monster in a Box
Monster in the Closet
The Monster Maker
The Monster of London City
The Monster of Piedras Blancas
The Monster Squad
The Monster that Challenged the World
The Monster Walks
Monsters Crash the Pajama Party

Other points to keep in mind:

- Acronyms appear alphabetically as if regular words. For example *C.H.U.D.* is alphabetized as "Chud"; *M*A*S*H* as "Mash."
- Common abbreviations in titles file as if they are spelled out, so *St. Elmo's Fire* will be found under "Saint Elmo's Fire" and *Mr. Baseball* will be alphabetized as "Mister Baseball."
- Proper names in titles are alphabetized beginning with the individual's first name; for instance, *Monty Python's The Meaning of Life* is under "M;" *Richard Pryor: Live on the Sunset Strip* under "R."
- Titles with numbers (*2001: A Space Odyssey*) will be alphabetized as if the number was spelled out under the appropriate letter, in this case "Two Thousand One." When numeric titles gather in close proximity to each other (*2000 Year Old Man, 2001, 2069: A Sex Odyssey*), the titles will be arranged in a low (*2000*) to high (*2069*) numeric sequence.

LASERDISC INDEX

The growing interest in and increasing number of titles available on laserdisc has led *VideoHound* to create a master list of more than 5,000 videos available in this format. And we continue to annotate each video review to indicate type of format available, from beta to VHS to laserdisc.

ALTERNATE TITLE INDEX

Given the trend in video to release movies, particularly older releases, under variant titles, the *Hound* has come up with a list of 3,600 alternate titles that refers back to the primary titles as listed in the review section. The alternate titles are also noted within the review.

CAST/DIRECTOR INDEXES

One of the highlights of *VideoHound* has been the Cast and Director Index, which listed thousands of actors and directors with full video credits. To make this very large index more manageable, we've split it in two: a Cast Index, with some 26,000 actors listed, and a Director Index, with close to 6,000 names. Looking for anything by a particular star or director? Turn here and review at a glance everything available on video. Several other video guides selectively index stars and directors. *VideoHound* is the only guide that indexes every actor and director listed in the cast section of the review. From minor stars to cult directors to box office giants, *VideoHound* has 'em covered (like his favorite backyard bone). Although listed in a first name, last name sequence, the names are alphabetized by last name. Film titles, complete with initial year of release, are arranged in alphabetic order.

CATEGORY INDEX

With nearly 400 terms ranging from the orthodox (*romantic comedy*) to slightly eccentric (*killer appliances*) and many (like *frame-ups, race against time,* and *roommates from hell*) new to this edition, the Category Index permits you to video sleuth from broad type to significant themes to signature scenes. The mix, arranged alphabetically by category, includes hundreds of traditional film genres and sub-genres as well as a feast of *VideoHound* exclusives like *beach blanket bingo, genies,* and *war between the sexes.* Preceding the index is a list of definitions and cross-references. No one list is inclusive; we're continually reclassifying, adding, and subtracting movies. *VideoHound* invites readers to join in the fun by sending in new titles for existing categories, as well as suggestions on new categories.

KIBBLES INDEX

Still a puppy but growing fast, Kibbles is where the miscellaneous heart of the *Hound* lies. Nearly 300 categories are presented, spanning the literary side of movie-making (adapted from a play, Hemingway on video) to a new list of Amy Fisher bio epics (somebody had to do it). Other new items include a list of letterboxed films and more than 130 new author and playwright lists.

Kibbles also covers everything from producers (including Roger Corman and Steven Spielberg) to special effects masters (Rick Baker, Ray Harryhausen) to composers such as John Barry and John Williams. Plus it provides lists of annual box-office winners (that are now on video) since 1939, classic movies, four-bone delights, trash films, modern Shakespeare, Disney fare, Special FX extravaganzas, and of course, bottom of the barrel *Woof!* features, some of which are terrible enough to provide an amusing evening. A complete list of the categories precedes the index. We'll be carefully scanning the mail for new categories that will add to this big pup.

SERIES INDEX

Your favorite continuing sagas are covered here. The Series Index provides 60 concise listings of major movie series ranging from James Bond to National Lampoon to Godzilla to the *Raiders of the Lost Ark.* Recurring cinematic collaborations of note are also listed, including the Marx Brothers, Monty Python, Hope & Crosby, Abbott & Costello, and Turner & Douglas. The full list of series and film partners precedes the index. We're open to suggestions.

AWARDS INDEX

Care to watch an award winner tonight? The Awards Index lists 2,000 films honored by 12 national and international award bodies, representing some 90 categories of competition. This information is also contained in the review following the credits. **Only features available on video and reviewed in the main section are listed in this index; movies not yet released on video are not covered.**

As award-winning films find their way to video, they will be added to the review section and covered in this index. Awards listed include the American Academy Awards; Australia Film Institute; British Academy of Film and Television Arts; Cannes Film Festival; French Cesar; Canadian Genie; Golden Globe; Directors Guild of America; Edgar Allan Poe Awards; Independent Spirit; Montreal Film Festival; and the MTV Awards.

FOREIGN FILM INDEX

Here the *Hound* classifies 4,300 movies by the country/countries of record in which the feature was financed (and not necessarily filmed). Since the producers of a specific film may hail from more than one country, some videos will be listed under more than one country. The foreign codes also appear in the review immediately following the color or black and white designation.

CAPTIONED INDEX

VideoHound identifies more than 3,000 videos available with captioning for hearing impaired viewers provided by either the National Captioning Institute (Falls Church, VA) or the Caption Center (Los Angeles, CA).

MUSIC VIDEO GUIDE

VideoHound alphabetically lists the titles of more than 4,000 music videos and music performance recordings. Due to space limitations and the remarkable sameness of most of the reviews (Music star sings, dances, songs include...), these videos are not covered elsewhere in the book. Music videos are typically prefaced by the name of the artist for quick identification. *VideoHound* has added **distributor codes** to the music video listings, so that you cross-check availability quickly in the **Distributor Guide**.

DISTRIBUTOR GUIDE

Each video review has at least one and as many as three distributor codes. In the reviews, these are located immediately before the critical rating at the bottom of the review. The full address and phone, toll-free, and fax numbers of the 360 distributors listed can be found in the Distributor Guide in the very back of *VideoHound*. A caution: a small number of distributors adhere to a nomadic life-style that includes frequent address changes. A tiny minority on the list in any given year will also go out of business. *VideoHound* lists up to three distributors in order to give you more choice. If you do come upon address changes or other distributor information that we should be aware of, please contact *VideoHound*.

In the main section, those reviews with the code **OM** are on moratorium (distributed at one time, though not currently). Since a title enjoying such status was once distributed, it may well linger on your local video store shelf. When the distributor is not known, the code **NO** appears. For new releases to the theater that have not yet made it to video (but likely will in the coming year), the code **NYR** (not yet released) appears.

SAMPLE REVIEW

Each *VideoHound* review contains up to 18 items of information, ranging from the title to the review to awards received to the critical rating. Information of interest to the film buff or casual viewer includes precise length of the video, whether in color or black and white, availability in VHS or Beta formats (as well as laserdisc), year first released, and list price. The review also contains information on colorized versions, alternate titles, sequels, remakes, sources of adaptations, songs (for most musicals), cast, and directors. Many reviews also identify writers, composers, and lyricists.

1 Aladdin 2 Boy meets princess, loses princess, finds princess, has trouble with evil prince and his nasty parrot. Another stellar effort from Disney centering on Aladdin, a streetwise teenager whose life radically changes after he uncorks a magic lamp and lets loose a large loveable genie who grants him three wishes. He chooses to become a prince to impress the princess Jasmine but finds himself competing with the nasty Jafar, who wants Jasmine as his bride. Williams is truly phenomenal as the big blue genie in what may be his best film role to date. The animators capitalized on his talent for ad-lib and transformed the genie accordingly, resulting in lots of celebrity spoofs and even a few pokes at Disney itself. The storyline is average, but the superb animation sets new standards—a lifelike carpet is one highlight. Coupled with Williams' performance and delightful songs, "Aladdin" soars to the same level as previous efforts. Kane and Salonga are responsible for the singing voices of Aladdin and Jasmine; Gottfried is a riot as Jafar's obnoxious parrot sidekick. Three of the songs are the late Ashman's final legacy. For all ages: adults will enjoy the 1,001 Williams impersonations while kids will get a kick out of the genie, the romantic storyline, and the songs. Be forewarned: very small children may be frightened by some of the scarier sequences. **3** ♫ A Whole New World; Prince Ali; Friend Like Me; One Jump Ahead; Arabian Nights. **4** AKA: The Robin Williams Show.

5 1992 **6** (G) **7** 90m **8** C **9** GB **10** V: Robin Williams, Scott Weinger, Linda Larkin, Jonathan Freeman, Frank Welker, Gilbert Gottfried, Douglas Seale, Brad Kane, Lea Salonga **11** W/D: Ron Clements, John Musker **12** W: Ted Elliot, Terry Rossio **13** M: Alan Menken, Howard Ashman, Tim Rice **14** Academy Awards '92: Best Original Score, Best Song ("A Whole New World") Nominations: Best Sound, Best Sound Effects Editing, Best Song ("Friend Like Me"); MTV Movie Awards '93: Best Comedic Performance (Williams). **15** VHS **16** $24.95 **17** DIS **18** ♫♫♫♫

1 Title	**11 Director** (W/D: indicates writer/director)	
2 Description/review	**12 Writers**	
3 Songs	**13 Composers/Lyricists**	
4 Alternate title (we made this up)	**14 Awards** (Oscar nominations follow Academy Award winners)	
5 Year released		
6 MPAA Rating	**15 Format** (Beta, VHS, and/or LV-laserdisc)	
7 Length	**16 Price** (at highest retail level)	
8 Black and white (B) **or color** (C)	**17 Distributor code**	
9 Country produced in (we made this up too)	**18 One- to four-bone rating** (or *Woof!*)	
10 Cast (V: indicates voiceovers; also includes cameos)		

THE RATING SCALE: ONE DOG'S OPINION

Woof! **(No bones)**
Junk-food video—nothing but empty calories. May be redeemed by stretches so bad they hold interest, like a freeway accident at rush hour.

(One bone)
Poor use of camera, film, sets, script, actors, and studio vehicles.

(One bone and a half)
Toying with respectability, while still lurching in gutter. Often lacking in standard cinematic devices, like plot and performances.

(Two bones)
May be perfectly delightful for certain tastes. A waste of time for others.

(Two bones and a half)
Technically well-made but often standard fare, worth a view if you're in the mood.

(Three bones)
Good story, fine acting provide decent entertainment return on video investment. Might recommend to family members.

(Three bones and a half)
Memorable cinematic fare with flair, verve, polish, sheen, and panache. Easily able to recommend to friends.

(Four bones)
Masterful cinematic expression. Flawless or nearly so. Will want to recommend to everyone you meet.

VideoHound generally doesn't rate nonfeatures, including cartoon shorts and television series.

Movies are rated by genre and sub-genre, so that movies of a certain type (say teen sex comedies) are comparatively rated. For intance, *Weekend at Bernie's 2* is not rated in the same way as the *Godfather*. *Bernie* is appreciative, we're sure.

VideoHound's
GOLDEN
MOVIE
RETRIEVER

The **LASERDISC INDEX** includes 5,000 titles available in the increasingly popular laserdisc format. Titles are arranged alphabetically.

Abbott and Costello Meet Captain Kidd
Abbott and Costello Meet Frankenstein
Abbott and Costello Meet the Killer, Boris Karloff
The Abominable Dr. Phibes
About Last Night...
Above the Law
Abraham Lincoln
Absence of Malice
The Absent-Minded Professor
Absolute Beginners
Absolution
The Abyss
The Accidental Tourist
The Accused
Aces: Iron Eagle 3
Aces Wild
Act of Piracy
Action Jackson
Actors and Sin
Adam's Rib
The Addams Family
Adios Amigo
Adventures in Babysitting
Adventures in Dinosaur City
The Adventures of Baron Munchausen
The Adventures of Buckaroo Banzai Across the Eighth Dimension
Adventures of Captain Marvel
Adventures of Don Juan
Adventures of Eliza Fraser
The Adventures of Ford Fairlane
The Adventures of Ichabod and Mr. Toad
The Adventures of Mark Twain
The Adventures of Milo & Otis
The Adventures of Robin Hood
The Adventures of the Wilderness Family
The Adventures of Tom Sawyer
The Adventurous Knights
Aelita: Queen of Mars
Affair in Trinidad
An Affair to Remember
The Affairs of Annabel
Afraid of the Dark
Africa Screams

African Dream
The African Queen
After Dark, My Sweet
After Hours
Afterburn
Against All Flags
Against All Odds
Agnes of God
The Agony and the Ecstasy
Air America
Airplane!
Airplane 2: The Sequel
Airport
Airport '77
Akira
Akira Kurosawa's Dreams
The Alamo
Alamo Bay
Alan & Naomi
Alexa: A Prostitute's Own Story
Alexander Nevsky
Alexander the Great
Alice
Alice Adams
Alice Doesn't Live Here Anymore
Alice in Wonderland
Alien
Alien 3
Alien from L.A.
Alien Intruder
Alien Nation
Alienator
Aliens
All About Eve
All-American Murder
All Dogs Go to Heaven
All I Want for Christmas
All of Me
All Quiet on the Western Front
All That Jazz
All the King's Men
...All the Marbles
All the Right Moves
All the Vermeers in New York
All This and Tex Avery, Too!
All You Need Is Cash
Allegheny Uprising
Allegro Non Troppo
Alligator 2: The Mutation
All's Fair
...Almost
Almost an Angel
Almost Pregnant

Aloha Summer
Alpine Fire
Alsino and the Condor
Altered States
Alvin Purple
Always
Amadeus
Amazing Grace & Chuck
The Amazing Spider-Man
Amazing Stories
Amazing Stories, Book 2
Amazing Stories, Book 3
Amazing Stories, Book 4
Amazing Stories, Book 5
Amazon
Amazon Women on the Moon
Ambition
The Ambushers
America at the Movies
The American Angels: Baptism of Blood
American Anthem
American Blue Note
American Boyfriends
American Eagle
American Flyers
The American Friend
American Friends
American Gigolo
American Gothic
American Graffiti
An American in Paris
American Me
American Ninja 2: The Confrontation
American Ninja 3: Blood Hunt
American Ninja 4: The Annihilation
American Roulette
American Samurai
An American Tail
An American Tail: Fievel Goes West
An American Werewolf in London
The Americanization of Emily
The Amityville Horror
Amityville 2: The Possession
Amityville 3: The Demon
The Amityville Curse
Amityville 1992: It's About Time
Among the Cinders
Amor Bandido
Amos and Andrew

The Amsterdam Kill
Amsterdamned
Anastasia
Anatomy of a Murder
Anchors Aweigh
And God Created Woman
And Justice for All
And Now for Something Completely Different
And the Ship Sails On
And Then There Were None
The Anderson Tapes
The Andersonville Trial
Android
The Andromeda Strain
Andy and the Airwave Rangers
Andy Hardy Meets Debutante
Andy Warhol's Bad
Angel 3: The Final Chapter
Angel and the Badman
Angel Heart
Angel of H.E.A.T.
Angelo My Love
Angels Die Hard
Angels Over Broadway
Angels with Dirty Faces
Anguish
Animal Behavior
Animal Crackers
Animal Farm
Anna
Anna Karenina
Anne of Avonlea
Anne of Green Gables
Annie
Annie Hall
Another Chance
Another Country
Another 48 Hrs.
Another Time, Another Place
Another Woman
Another You
Any Man's Death
Any Which Way You Can
Apache Chief
Apache Rose
The Apartment
Apartment Zero
Aphrodite
Apocalypse Now
The Appaloosa
The Applegates
Appointment with Death
Appointment with Fear

Apprentice to Murder
April Fool's Day
Arabian Nights
Arachnophobia
Arena
Armed and Dangerous
Armed Response
Army of Darkness
Around the World in 80 Days
Around the World in 80 Ways
The Arrival
Arrowhead
Arsenic and Old Lace
The Art of Dying
Arthur
Arthur 2: On the Rocks
Article 99
As You Like It
As You Were
Aspen Extreme
The Asphalt Jungle
Assassin
Assassination
Assassination of Trotsky
Assault and Matrimony
Asylum
At Close Range
At Play in the Fields of the Lord
At Sword's Point
At the Circus
Atlantic City
Attack of the 50 Foot Woman
Au Revoir Les Enfants
Auntie Lee's Meat Pies
Auntie Mame
Autobiography of a Princess
Autumn Sonata
Avalon
Avenging Angel
Avenging Force
Awakenings
The Awful Truth
Babar: The Movie
The Babe
Babes in Arms
Babes in Toyland
Babes on Broadway
Babette's Feast
Baby Boom
Baby It's You
Baby on Board
Baby, the Rain Must Fall
Baby...Secret of the Lost Legend

Dance

Dance with Death
Dancers
Dances with Wolves
Dandy in Aspic
Danger Zone
Dangerous
Dangerous Game
Dangerous Liaisons
Dangerous Life
Dangerous Moves
Dangerous Pursuit
Dangerous When Wet
Danton
Darby O'Gill & the Little
People
Dark Age
The Dark Backward
Dark Before Dawn
The Dark Crystal
Dark Habits
Dark Passage
Dark Side of the Moon
Dark Star
Dark Tower
Dark Victory
Dark Waters
Darkest Africa
Darkman
Darling
D.A.R.Y.L.
Das Boot
Date with an Angel
A Date with Judy
David and Bathsheba
David and Lisa
David Copperfield
Davy Crockett and the River
Pirates
Dawn of the Dead
The Day After
A Day at the Races
Day of the Dead
The Day of the Dolphin
The Day of the Jackal
The Day of the Locust
Day of the Triffids
The Day the Earth Stood Still
Day Time Ended
Days of Heaven
Days of Thunder
Days of Wine and Roses
D.C. Cab
The Dead
Dead Again
Dead Aim
Dead Bang
Dead Calm
Dead End
Dead Heat
Dead Man Out
Dead Men Don't Wear Plaid
Dead of Night
Dead of Winter
Dead Poets Society
The Dead Pool
Dead Reckoning
Dead Ringers
Dead Space
Dead Zone
Deadbolt
Deadline
Deadlock
Deadly Bet
Deadly Companions
Deadly Dreams
Deadly Friend
Deadly Illusion
Deadly Possession
Deadly Rivals
The Deadly Trackers
Deadtime Stories
Deal of the Century
Dealers
Death Becomes Her
Death Before Dishonor
Death Dreams

Death Hunt
Death of a Salesman
Death of a Scoundrel
Death of an Angel
Death on the Nile
Death Ring
Death Warrant
Death Watch
Death Wish
Death Wish 3
Death Wish 4: The
Crackdown
Deathrow Gameshow
Deathstalker
Deathstalker 2: Duel of the
Titans
Deathstalker 3
The Decameron
The Deceivers
December
Deceptions
Decline of Western Civilization
1
Decoration Day
The Deep
Deep Cover
Deepstar Six
The Deer Hunter
Def by Temptation
Defending Your Life
Defense of the Realm
Defenseless
Deja Vu
The Delicate Delinquent
Delicatessen
Delirious
Deliverance
Delta Force
Delta Force 2: Operation
Stranglehold
Delta Force 3: The Killing
Game
Delusion
Demetrius and the Gladiators
A Demon in My View
Demon Seed
Demon Wind
Demonic Toys
Demons
Demonstone
Denial: The Dark Side of
Passion
Descending Angel
Desert Bloom
The Desert Fox
Desert Hearts
Desert Kickboxer
Desert Phantom
Designing Woman
Desire and Hell at Sunset
Motel
Desire Under the Elms
Desiree
Desk Set
Desperate Hours
Desperate Motives
Desperately Seeking Susan
Destination Moon
Destroyer
Destry Rides Again
The Detective
Detour
The Devil & Daniel Webster
The Devil at 4 O'Clock
Devil in the Flesh
Devil Monster
The Devil's Commandment
Devil's Rain
Devlin
Diabolique
Dial "M" for Murder
Diamond Head
Diamond Run
The Diamond Trap
Diamonds are Forever

Diane
Diary of a Chambermaid
Diary of a Hitman
Diary of a Lost Girl
The Diary of Anne Frank
Dick Tracy
Dick Tracy Returns
Dick Tracy vs. Crime Inc.
Die Hard
Die Hard 2: Die Harder
Die, Monster, Die!
Diggstown
Dillinger
Dim Sum: A Little Bit of Heart
Diner
Dinner at Eight
Diplomaniacs
Diplomatic Immunity
Dirt Bike Kid
Dirty Dancing
The Dirty Dozen
Dirty Harry
Dirty Mary Crazy Larry
Dirty Rotten Scoundrels
The Discreet Charm of the
Bourgeoisie
A Disney Christmas Gift
Disorderlies
Disorderly Orderly
Disorganized Crime
Distant Thunder
Distant Voices, Still Lives
The Distinguished Gentleman
Disturbed
Diva
The Dive
Divine Madness
Do or Die
Do the Right Thing
D.O.A.
Doc Hollywood
The Doctor
Dr. Alien
Dr. Caligari
Dr. Cyclops
Doctor Detroit
Doctor Doolittle
Doctor Duck's Super Secret
All-Purpose Sauce
Dr. Giggles
Dr. Jekyll and Mr. Hyde
Dr. No
Dr. Strangelove, or: How I
Learned to Stop Worrying
and Love the Bomb
Doctor X
Doctor Zhivago
Dodge City
Dodsworth
Does This Mean We're
Married?
Dog Day Afternoon
Dogfight
The Dogs of War
Doll Face
Dollar
Dollars
Dollman
The Dolls
A Doll's House
Dolly Dearest
Dominick & Eugene
Domino
Don Juan
Don Juan, My Love
Don Q., Son of Zorro
Dona Flor and Her Two
Husbands
Dona Herlinda & Her Son
Donovan's Brain
Donovan's Reef
Don't Look Back
Don't Look Now
Don't Mess with My Sister!
Don't Tell Her It's Me

Don't Tell Mom the
Babysitter's Dead
The Doors
The Doors: Soft Parade, a
Retrospective
Doppelganger: The Evil Within
Dorf on Golf
Double-Crossed
Double Exposure: The Story
of Margaret Bourke-White
Double Impact
Double Indemnity
Double Jeopardy
Double Trouble
Down Among the Z Men
Down and Out in Beverly Hills
Down Argentine Way
Down the Drain
Down to Earth
Downhill Racer
Downtown
Dracula
Dracula Blows His Cool
Dragnet
Dragonslayer
Dream a Little Dream
Dream Machine
The Dream Team
Dreams
Dreamscape
Dressed to Kill
The Dresser
Dressmaker
The Drifter
Drifting Weeds
Drive-In Massacre
Driving Force
Driving Me Crazy
Driving Miss Daisy
Drop Dead Fred
Drowning by Numbers
Drugstore Cowboy
Drums
Drums Along the Mohawk
A Dry White Season
The Duchess and the
Dirtwater Fox
Duck Soup
DuckTales the Movie:
Treasure of the Lost Lamp
Dudes
Duel of Hearts
The Duellists
Dumbo
Dune
Dune Warriors
The Dunera Boys
Dungeonmaster
Dynamite and Gold
The Eagle
Early Frost
An Early Frost
Earth Girls are Easy
Earth vs. the Flying Saucers
Earthquake
East of Eden
Easter Parade
Easy Living
Easy Money
Easy Rider
Easy Wheels
Eat a Bowl of Tea
Eating
Echo Park
Echoes of Paradise
Eddie and the Cruisers
Eddie and the Cruisers 2:
Eddie Lives!
Eddie Macon's Run
Eddie Murphy "Delirious"
Eddie Murphy: Raw
The Eddy Duchin Story
Edge of Sanity
Educating Rita
Edward Scissorhands
Egg

Egg and I
The Egyptian
The Eiger Sanction
8 1/2
Eight Men Out
8 Million Ways to Die
18 Again!
84 Charing Cross Road
84 Charlie Mopic
Eijanaika
El Amor Brujo
El Cid
El Dorado
Electra Glide in Blue
Electric Dreams
The Electric Horseman
Elena and Her Men
Eleni
Elephant Boy
The Elephant Man
Elmer Gantry
Elusive Corporal
Elvira Madigan
Elvira, Mistress of the Dark
Elvis Memories
Elvis on Tour
Elvis: One Night with You
Elvis: The Lost Performances
The Emerald Forest
Emissary
Emmanuelle in the Country
Emmanuelle, the Joys of a
Woman
Emperor Jones
Empire of the Air: The Men
Who Made Radio
Empire of the Sun
The Empire Strikes Back
Enchanted April
The Enchanted Cottage
The Enchanted Forest
Encounter at Raven's Gate
The End
End of the Line
Endless Descent
Endless Love
Endless Night
The Endless Summer
Enemies, a Love Story
Enemy Mine
The Enforcer
Enigma
Enormous Changes
Enrapture
Enter the Dragon
Equus
Eraserhead
Erik the Viking
Ernest Goes to Jail
Ernest Saves Christmas
The Erotic Adventures of
Pinocchio
The Errand Boy
Escape Artist
Escape from Alcatraz
Escape from New York
Escape from the Planet of the
Apes
Escape to Witch Mountain
E.T.: The Extra-Terrestrial
Eternal Evil
Ethan Frome
Eve of Destruction
An Evening with Robin
Williams
Evergreen
Eversmile New Jersey
Every Girl Should Be Married
Every Time We Say Goodbye
Every Which Way But Loose
Everybody Wins
Everybody's All American
Everybody's Dancin'
Everybody's Fine

Golden

The Golden Seal
Golden Voyage of Sinbad
Goldfinger
Goldilocks & the Three Bears
Goliath Awaits
Gone with the Wind
Gonza the Spearman
Good Guys Wear Black
Good Morning, Babylon
Good Morning, Vietnam
The Good Mother
Good News
The Good, the Bad and the Ugly
The Good Wife
Goodbye Columbus
The Goodbye Girl
Goodbye, Mr. Chips
Goodbye, My Lady
Goodbye, New York
The Goodbye People
Goodfellas
The Goonies
Gorgo
The Gorgon
The Gorilla
Gorillas in the Mist
Gorky Park
Gospel According to St. Matthew
Gotcha!
Gotham
Gothic
The Graduate
Graffiti Bridge
Grand Hotel
Grand Illusion
Grand Isle
Grand Prix
Grand Tour: Disaster in Time
Grandma's House
The Grapes of Wrath
The Grass is Greener
Grave of the Fireflies
Grave Secrets
Graveyard Shift
Grease
Grease 2
Great Balls of Fire
The Great Caruso
The Great Dictator
The Great Escape
Great Expectations
The Great Gatsby
The Great Lie
The Great McGinty
The Great Mouse Detective
Great Movie Stunts & the Making of Raiders of the Lost Ark
The Great Muppet Caper
The Great Outdoors
Great Race
The Great Train Robbery
The Great Waldo Pepper
A Great Wall
The Great Ziegfeld
The Greatest Show on Earth
The Greatest Story Ever Told
Greed
The Green Berets
Green Card
Green for Danger
Green Ice
Greetings
Gremlins
Gremlins 2: The New Batch
The Grey Fox
Greystoke: The Legend of Tarzan, Lord of the Apes
Griffith Biograph Program
The Grifters
Grim Prairie Tales
The Grim Reaper
Gross Anatomy
Grotesque

Ground Zero
Groundhog Day
Guadalcanal Diary
The Guardian
Guess Who's Coming to Dinner
Guilty as Charged
Guilty by Suspicion
Gulliver's Travels
The Gumshoe Kid
Gun Fury
The Gun in Betty Lou's Handbag
Guncrazy
Gunfight at the O.K. Corral
Gunfighter
The Gunfighters
Gunfire
Gung Ho
Gunga Din
The Gunrunner
Guns
Guns of Justice
The Guns of Navarone
Gus
Guys and Dolls
Gypsy
Hail Mary
Hair
Hairspray
Half Moon Street
The Hallelujah Trail
Halloween
Halloween 2: The Nightmare Isn't Over!
Halloween 3: Season of the Witch
Halloween 4: The Return of Michael Myers
Halloween 5: The Revenge of Michael Myers
Hamburger Hill
Hamburger...The Motion Picture
Hamlet
The Handmaid's Tale
Hang 'Em High
Hangfire
Hangin' with the Homeboys
Hanky Panky
Hannah and Her Sisters
Hanna's War
Hanoi Hilton
Hanover Street
Hans Christian Andersen
Hansel and Gretel
Hanussen
Happy Birthday to Me
The Happy Hooker
The Happy Hooker Goes Hollywood
Happy Hour
Happy Together
Hard Country
Hard Day's Night
Hard Promises
Hard Times
Hard to Hold
Hard to Kill
The Hard Way
Hardbodies
Hardbodies 2
Hardcore
The Harder They Come
Hardware
Harem
Harlem Nights
Harley Davidson and the Marlboro Man
Harmagedon
Harold and Maude
Harper
Harry & Son
Harry and the Hendersons
Harry & Walter Go to New York

Harvey
The Harvey Girls
Hat Box Mystery
Hatari
Haunted Honeymoon
The Haunted Palace
Haunted Summer
The Haunting
Haunting of Sarah Hardy
Havana
Having It All
Having Wonderful Crime
Hawaii
Hawk the Slayer
Hawken's Breed
Hawks
The Hawks & the Sparrows
He Said, She Said
Head
Headhunter
Heart Condition
Heart Like a Wheel
The Heart of Dixie
Heart of Midnight
Heart of the Stag
Heartaches
Heartbreak Hotel
The Heartbreak Kid
Heartbreak Ridge
Heartbreaker
Heartburn
Hearts of Fire
Hearts of the World
Heat
Heat and Sunlight
Heat of Desire
Heat Wave
Heathers
Heaven
Heaven Can Wait
Heaven Help Us
Heaven is a Playground
Heaven's Gate
Heavy Petting
The Heiress
Hell Comes to Frogtown
Hell in the Pacific
Hell is for Heroes
Hellbound: Hellraiser 2
Hellfighters
Hellgate
Hellhole
Hello Again
Hello, Dolly!
Hello Mary Lou: Prom Night 2
Hellraiser
Hellraiser 3: Hell on Earth
Hell's Harbor
Help!
Henry V
Henry & June
Henry: Portrait of a Serial Killer
Her Alibi
Herbie Rides Again
Hercules
Hercules Unchained
Here Comes Mr. Jordan
Here Comes the Groom
Here's Looking at You, Warner Bros.
Hero
Hero and the Terror
Hexed
Hey, Babu Riba
Hey There, It's Yogi Bear
Hi-Jacked
The Hidden
Hidden Agenda
The Hidden Fortress
Hidden Obsession
Hide and Go Shriek
Hider in the House
High & Low
High Anxiety
High Frequency

High Noon
High Plains Drifter
High Road to China
High Season
High Sierra
High Society
High Spirits
High Stakes
High Tide
Higher and Higher
The Highest Honor
Highlander
Highlander 2: The Quickening
Highpoint
Highway 13
The Hills Have Eyes
The Hindenburg
Hips, Hips, Hooray
His Majesty O'Keefe
History is Made at Night
History of the World: Part 1
The Hit
The Hit List
Hit the Deck
Hitcher
The Hitchhiker
Hitchhiker 2
Hitchhiker 3
Hitchhiker 4
The Hitchhiker's Guide to the Galaxy
The Hitman
Hobson's Choice
Hoffa
The Holcroft Covenant
A Hole in the Head
Holiday
Holiday Affair
Holiday Inn
Holiday Rhythm
Hollywood Hot Tubs 2: Educating Crystal
Hollywood Outtakes & Rare Footage
Hollywood Shuffle
Hollywood Varieties
Hollywood Vice Sqaud
Hombre
Home Alone
Home Alone 2: Lost in New York
Home from the Hill
Home is Where the Hart is
Home Movies
Home of the Brave
Homeboy
Homeboys
Homer and Eddie
Homeward Bound: The Incredible Journey
Homework
Homicide
Honey, I Blew Up the Kid
Honey, I Shrunk the Kids
Honeymoon Academy
Honeymoon in Vegas
Honeymoon Killers
Honeysuckle Rose
Honkytonk Man
Hook
Hook, Line and Sinker
Hooper
Hoosiers
Hope and Glory
Hoppity Goes to Town
Hopscotch
Horror Chamber of Dr. Faustus
The Horror of Dracula
Horror Planet
Horrors of Burke & Hare
Horse Feathers
Horseplayer
The Horse's Mouth
The Hostage Tower
Hostile Guns

Hostile Takeover
Hot Chocolate
Hot Pursuit
The Hot Rock
The Hot Spot
Hot Stuff
Hot Target
Hot to Trot!
Hotel Colonial
The Hotel New Hampshire
The Hound of the Baskervilles
House
House 2: The Second Story
House 4: Home Deadly Home
House Calls
House of Games
The House of Usher
House of Wax
The House on Carroll Street
House on Haunted Hill
The House on Sorority Row
House Party
House Party 2: The Pajama Jam
Houseboat
The Householder
The Housekeeper
Housesitter
How I Got into College
How I Won the War
How the West was Won
How to Get Ahead in Advertising
How to Marry a Millionaire
How to Succeed in Business without Really Trying
How U Like Me Now?
Howard the Duck
Howard's End
The Howling
Howling 2: Your Sister is a Werewolf
Howling 3: The Marsupials
Howling 4: The Original Nightmare
Howling 5: The Rebirth
Howling 6: The Freaks
Hud
Hudson Hawk
Hugh Hefner: Once Upon a Time
The Human Comedy
The Human Shield
Humoresque
The Hunchback of Notre Dame
The Hunger
Hunk
The Hunt for Red October
The Hunt for the Night Stalker
The Hunter
Hunter in the Dark
Hunter's Blood
Hurricane
Husbands and Wives
Hush, Hush, Sweet Charlotte
Hussy
The Hustler
Hyper-Sapien: People from Another Star
Hysterical
I Am the Law
I Come in Peace
I Confess
I Could Go on Singing
I Died a Thousand Times
I Love Lucy
I Love N.Y.
I Love You Again
I Love You, Alice B. Toklas
I Love You to Death
I, Madman
I Married a Centerfold
I Married a Witch
I Married a Woman
I Never Sang For My Father

I Posed for Playboy
I Remember Mama
I Shot Billy the Kid
I Spit on Your Grave
I Vitelloni
I Walked with a Zombie
I Wanna Hold Your Hand
I Want to Live!
I Was a Teenage Zombie
Ice Pirates
Ice Station Zebra
Iceman
Identity Crisis
Idiot's Delight
Idolmaker
If...
If It's Tuesday, This Must Be Belgium
If Looks Could Kill
If You Could See What I Hear
Ike
Ikiru
I'll Cry Tomorrow
I'll Get You
Ilsa, Harem Keeper of the Oil Sheiks
Ilsa, She-Wolf of the SS
Ilsa, the Wicked Warden
I'm Dancing as Fast as I Can
I'm Gonna Git You Sucka
I'm the One You're Looking For
Imagemaker
Immediate Family
The Immortalizer
Impromptu
Improper Channels
Impulse
In Cold Blood
In Country
The In Crowd
In Harm's Way
The In-Laws
In Like Flint
In Love and War
In Name Only
In Person
In Praise of Older Women
In Search of Historic Jesus
In the Cold of the Night
In the Good Old Summertime
In the Heat of Passion
In the Heat of the Night
In the Mood
In the Navy
In the Soup
The Incident
Incident at Channel Q
The Incredible Hulk
The Incredible Hulk Returns
The Incredible Mr. Limpet
The Incredible Sarah
The Incredible Shrinking Man
The Incredible Shrinking Woman
Incubus
Indecency
The Indian Runner
Indiana Jones and the Last Crusade
Indiana Jones and the Temple of Doom
Indio
The Informer
Inherit the Wind
The Inner Circle
Inner Sanctum
Innerspace
Innocent Blood
An Innocent Man
Inside Daisy Clover
Inside Information
Inside Moves
Inside the Third Reich
Insignificance
Intent to Kill

Interceptor
Interiors
Intermezzo
Internal Affairs
International House
The Interns
Intimate Power
Into the Fire
Into the Homeland
Into the Night
Into the Sun
Into Thin Air
Intolerance
Intrigue
Intruder
Invaders from Mars
Invasion Earth: The Aliens Are Here!
Invasion of the Body Snatchers
Invasion U.S.A.
The Invisible Kid
The Invisible Man
The Invisible Ray
Irezumi
Irma La Douce
Iron & Silk
Iron Eagle
Iron Eagle 2
The Iron Mask
Iron Maze
The Iron Triangle
Ironweed
Irreconcilable Differences
Ishtar
The Island
Islands in the Stream
Isle of the Dead
Istanbul
It
It Came from Beneath the Sea
It Came from Hollywood
It Couldn't Happen Here
It Happened One Night
It Should Happen to You
It's A Gift
It's a Great Feeling
It's a Mad, Mad, Mad, Mad World
It's a Wonderful Life
It's Always Fair Weather
It's in the Bag
It's My Turn
Ivan the Terrible, Part 1
Ivan the Terrible, Part 2
I've Always Loved You
I've Heard the Mermaids Singing
Izzy & Moe
J. Edgar Hoover
Jabberwocky
Jack & the Beanstalk
Jack the Giant Killer
Jacknife
Jack's Back
Jacob's Ladder
The Jagged Edge
Jailhouse Rock
Jakarta
Jake Speed
James Dean Story
The James Dean 35th Anniversary Collection
Jane Eyre
The January Man
Jason and the Argonauts
Jaws
Jaws 2
Jaws 3
Jaws: The Revenge
Jazz Singer
Jean de Florette
Jennifer 8
Jeremiah Johnson
The Jerk
Jesse James

Jesus Christ, Superstar
Jesus of Montreal
Jet Pilot
A Jetson Christmas Carol
The Jetsons Meet the Flintstones
The Jetsons: Movie
The Jewel of the Nile
Jezebel
Jezebel's Kiss
JFK
The JFK Conspiracy
The Jigsaw Man
Jo Jo Dancer, Your Life is Calling
Joan of Arc
Joe
Joe Kidd
Joe Versus the Volcano
John & Yoko: A Love Story
John F. Kennedy
Johnny Angel
Johnny Be Good
Johnny Come Lately
Johnny Got His Gun
Johnny Guitar
Johnny Handsome
Jolson Sings Again
The Jolson Story
Jour de Fete
Journey into Fear
Journey of Honor
Journey of Hope
The Journey of Natty Gann
Journey to the Center of the Earth
Joy of Living
Joy Sticks
Joyless Street
Ju Dou
Jubal
The Judge and the Assassin
Judgment at Nuremberg
Judgment in Berlin
Judith of Bethulia
Jules and Jim
Julia
Julia and Julia
Juliet of the Spirits
Julius Caesar
Jumpin' at the Boneyard
Jumpin' Jack Flash
June Night
Jungle
Jungle Book
The Jungle Book
Jungle Bride
Jungle Fever
Jungle Goddess
Jupiter's Darling
Just a Gigolo
Just One of the Guys
K-9
Kafka
Kandyland
Kansas
The Karate Kid
The Karate Kid: Part 2
The Karate Kid: Part 3
Katherine
Keaton's Cop
The Keep
Keep 'Em Flying
Keep the Change
Keeper of the City
Keeping Track
Keetje Tippei
Kelly's Heroes
Kentucky Fried Movie
Kentucky Jubilee
Kentucky Kernels
The Key
Key Largo
The Keys of the Kingdom
The KGB: The Secret War
Khartoum

Kickboxer
Kickboxer 2: The Road Back
Kickboxer 3: The Art of War
Kid
Kid from Brooklyn
Kid from Gower Gulch
Kidnapped
Kill Cruise
The Kill Reflex
Kill Slade
Killcrazy
The Killer Elite
Killer Klowns from Outer Space
Killer Tomatoes Eat France
The Killer's Edge
The Killing
A Killing Affair
The Killing Fields
Killing Floor
Killing in a Small Town
The Killing Time
Killpoint
Kind Hearts and Coronets
Kindergarten Cop
The Kindred
The King and I
King Creole
King David
King Dinosaur
King Kong
King Kong Lives
King of Comedy
The King of Hearts
The King of Kings
King of New York
King of the Gypsies
King of the Rocketmen
King Ralph
The King's Whore
Kinjite: Forbidden Subjects
Kismet
The Kiss
A Kiss Before Dying
Kiss Me a Killer
Kiss Me Deadly
Kiss Me Kate
Kiss Me, Stupid!
Kiss of the Spider Woman
Kiss Tomorrow Goodbye
The Kitchen Toto
Klute
Knife in the Water
Knight Moves
Knights of the Round Table
Knock on Any Door
Koyaanisqatsi
Kramer vs. Kramer
The Krays
Kriemhilde's Revenge
Kronos
Krull
Krush Groove
Kuffs
Kwaidan
La Bamba
L.A. Bounty
La Cage aux Folles
La Cage aux Folles 2
La Cage aux Folles 3: The Wedding
La Chienne
La Dolce Vita
La Lectrice
La Nuit de Varennes
La Passante
L.A. Story
La Strada
Labyrinth
Labyrinth of Passion
The Lacemaker
The Ladies' Man
Lady and the Tramp
Lady Beware
Lady Chatterley's Lover
The Lady Eve

Lady for a Day
The Lady from Shanghai
The Lady in Question
The Lady in White
Lady Jane
Lady Mobster
Lady on the Bus
Lady Sings the Blues
The Lady Vanishes
Lady Vanishes
Ladyhawke
Ladykiller
L'Age D'Or
Laguna Heat
The Lair of the White Worm
Lake Consequence
Lambada
The Land Before Time
Land of the Pharaohs
Landslide
Lantern Hill
Laser Mission
Laserblast
Lassie, Come Home
Lassiter
The Last Boy Scout
Last Bullet
Last Dance
The Last Detail
The Last Emperor
Last Exit to Brooklyn
The Last Fling
The Last Hour
Last House on the Left
Last Hurrah
The Last Metro
The Last of England
The Last of His Tribe
Last of the Clintons
The Last of the Finest
The Last of the Mohicans
Last of the Red Hot Lovers
The Last Picture Show
The Last Radio Station
Last Resort
The Last Riders
Last Rites
The Last Starfighter
Last Tango in Paris
The Last Temptation of Christ
The Last Time I Saw Paris
The Last Tycoon
The Last Unicorn
The Last Waltz
The Last Warrior
Late for Dinner
The Late Show
Latino
Lauderdale
Laura
The Lavender Hill Mob
L'Avventura
Law of Desire
Law of the Sea
The Lawnmower Man
Lawrence of Arabia
Le Boucher
Le Chat
Le Complot
Le Crabe Tambour
Le Grand Chemin
Le Mans
Leader of the Band
A League of Their Own
Lean on Me
Leap of Faith
Leather Jackets
Leatherface: The Texas Chainsaw Massacre 3
Leave It to the Marines
Leaving Normal
Legacy of Lies
Legal Eagles
Legend
The Legend of Hell House
The Legend of Hillbilly John

Legend

Silent

Silent Night, Deadly Night 4: Initiation
The Silent Partner
Silent Rage
Silent Running
The Silk Road
Silk Stockings
Silkwood
Silver Bandit
Silver Bullet
The Silver Streak
Silverado
Simba
Simple Men
Sinatra
Sinbad and the Eye of the Tiger
Sinbad of the Seven Seas
Sinbad the Sailor
Since You Went Away
Sincerely Charlotte
Sincerely Yours
Sinful Life
Sing
Singin' in the Rain
Single White Female
Singles
Sins of Jezebel
Sirocco
Sister Act
Sister Kenny
Sister, Sister
The Sisterhood
Six Weeks
Sixteen Candles
'68
Sizzle Beach U.S.A.
Skeleton Coast
Sketch Artist
Ski Patrol
Ski School
Skin Deep
Sky High
Sky Liner
Skyline
Slamdance
Slammer Girls
Slap Shot
Slapstick of Another Kind
Slaughter
Slaughterhouse Five
Slave Girls from Beyond Infinity
Slaves of New York
Sleepaway Camp 3: Teenage Wasteland
Sleeper
Sleeping Beauty
The Sleeping Car
Sleeping with the Enemy
Sleepwalk
Sleepwalkers
Sleuth
Slipping into Darkness
Slipstream
The Slugger's Wife
Slugs
Slumber Party '57
Slumber Party Massacre 2
Small Change
Small Sacrifices
Smash Palace
Smile
Smiles of a Summer Night
Smithereens
Smokescreen
Smokey and the Bandit
Smokey and the Bandit, Part 2
Smokey and the Bandit, Part 3
Smooth Talk
Sneakers
Sniper
Snoopy, Come Home

Snow White and the Seven Dwarfs
So Dear to My Heart
Soapdish
S.O.B.
Social Error
Sodom and Gomorrah
Solar Crisis
Solarbabies
Solaris
Soldier of Orange
A Soldier's Story
Soldier's Tale
Solomon and Sheba
Some Came Running
Some Kind of Hero
Some Kind of Wonderful
Some Like It Hot
Somebody Has to Shoot the Picture
Someone Behind the Door
Someone to Love
Someone to Watch Over Me
Something Special
Something to Sing About
Something Wicked This Way Comes
Something Wild
Sometimes They Come Back
Somewhere in Time
Sommersby
Son of Dracula
Son of Frankenstein
Son of Kong
The Son of Monte Cristo
Son of Paleface
Son of the Morning Star
Son of the Sheik
The Song of Bernadette
Song of the Islands
A Song to Remember
Songwriter
Sonny Boy
Sons of Katie Elder
Sophie's Choice
Sorcerer
Sorority Babes in the Slimeball Bowl-A-Rama
Sorry, Wrong Number
S.O.S. Coast Guard
Soul Man
Soultaker
The Sound of Music
Sounder
South Central
South of Reno
South Pacific
Southern Comfort
Souvenir
Soylent Green
Space: 1999
Spaceballs
SpaceCamp
Spaced Invaders
Spacehunter: Adventures in the Forbidden Zone
Spaceways
The Spanish Main
Sparrows
Spartacus
The Spawning
Speaking Parts
A Special Day
Spectre of the Rose
Speed Zone
Spellbound
Spellcaster
Spetters
Spiders
Spies
Spies, Lies and Naked Thighs
Spies Like Us
Spike of Bensonhurst
The Spiral Staircase
Spirit of '76
Spirit of the Beehive

Spirit of the Eagle
The Spirit of West Point
Spite Marriage
Splash
Splendor in the Grass
Split Decisions
The Spoilers
Spontaneous Combustion
Spookies
Spring Break
Springtime in the Rockies
Spy
Spy in Black
The Spy Who Came in from the Cold
The Spy Who Loved Me
Square Dance
Square Dance Jubilee
The Squeeze
Squeeze Play
Squirm
Stacking
Stage Door Canteen
Stage Fright
Stage Struck
Stagecoach
Stakeout
Stalag 17
Stalin
Stalking Danger
Stand and Deliver
Stand By Me
Stanley and Iris
The Star Chamber
Star Crash
Star 80
A Star is Born
Star of Midnight
Star Quest
Star Slammer
Star Trek: The Motion Picture
Star Trek 2: The Wrath of Khan
Star Trek 3: The Search for Spock
Star Trek 4: The Voyage Home
Star Trek 5: The Final Frontier
Star Trek: The Cage
Star Trek the Next Generation: Encounter at Farpoint
Star Wars
Starchaser: The Legend of Orin
Stardust Memories
Starlight Hotel
Starman
Stars and Bars
Starting Over
State of Grace
State of Siege
State of the Union
State of Things
Static
Stay Awake
Stay Hungry
Stay Tuned
Staying Alive
Staying Together
Steal the Sky
Stealing Heaven
Stealing Home
Steamboat Bill, Jr.
Steel
Steel and Lace
Steel Dawn
The Steel Helmet
Steel Magnolias
Steele Justice
Steele's Law
Stella
Stella Dallas
Step Lively
The Stepfather

Stepfather 2: Make Room for Daddy
Stepfather 3: Father's Day
Stephen King's Golden Years
Stephen King's It
Steppenwolf
Stepping Out
The Sterile Cuckoo
Steve Martin Live
Stewardess School
Stick
Sticky Fingers
Still of the Night
The Sting
The Sting 2
Stir Crazy
A Stolen Face
Stone Cold
The Stone Killer
Stop Making Sense
Stop! or My Mom Will Shoot
Stop That Cab
Stormy Monday
Stormy Weather
Story of Adele H.
The Story of Boys & Girls
The Story of O
The Story of O, Part 2
The Story of Vernon and Irene Castle
Storyville
Stranded
The Strange Affair of Uncle Harry
Strange Brew
Strange Invaders
The Strange Love of Martha Ivers
A Stranger Among Us
The Stranger and the Gunfighter
Stranger on the Third Floor
Stranger than Paradise
Strangers
Strangers on a Train
Strapless
Strategic Air Command
Straw Dogs
Strays
Streamers
Street Asylum
Street Crimes
Street Hunter
Street Knight
Street Smart
Street Soldiers
A Streetcar Named Desire
Streets of Fire
Streets of Gold
Streetwalkin'
Streetwise
Strike It Rich
Strike Up the Band
Stripes
Stroke of Midnight
Strong Man
Student Bodies
A Study in Terror
Stuff Stephanie in the Incinerator
The Stunt Man
Subspecies
Suburban Commando
Suburbia
Subway
Success is the Best Revenge
Sucker Money
Sudden Death
Sudden Impact
Suddenly, Last Summer
Suds
Sugar Cane Alley
The Sugarland Express
The Suicide Club
Sullivan's Travels
Summer

Summer and Smoke
Summer Camp Nightmare
Summer Heat
Summer Job
Summer Lovers
Summer of '42
The Summer of Miss Forbes
A Summer Place
Summer Rental
Summer School
Summer Stock
Summer's Games
Summertime
Sunday, Bloody Sunday
Sunday in the Park with George
Sundown Riders
The Sundowners
Sunset
Sunset Boulevard
Sunset Strip
The Sunshine Boys
Supergirl
Superman: The Movie
Superman 2
Superman 3
Superman 4: The Quest for Peace
The Sure Thing
Surrender
The Survivalist
Survivor
Survivors
Susan Slept Here
Suspect
Suspicion
Suspiria
Swamp Thing
The Swan
Swashbuckler
Swedenhielms
Sweeney Todd: The Demon Barber of Fleet Street
Sweet Bird of Youth
Sweet Charity
Sweet Country
Sweet Dreams
Sweet Hearts Dance
Sweet Liberty
Sweet Smell of Success
Sweet Talker
Sweethearts
Sweetie
Swept Away...
Swimmer
Swimming to Cambodia
The Swindle
Swing Kids
Swing Shift
Swing Time
The Swiss Family Robinson
Switch
Switching Channels
Swoon
The Sword & the Rose
Sword & the Sorcerer
The Sword in the Stone
The Swordsman
Sylvester
Sylvia Scarlett
T Bone N Weasel
T-Men
Table for Five
Taffin
Tai-Pan
Tailspin: Behind the Korean Airline Tragedy
Take Me Out to the Ball Game
Take the Money and Run
Take Two
Takin' It Off
Taking Care of Business
The Taking of Beverly Hills
The Taking of Flight 847: The Uli Derickson Story
The Tale of the Frog Prince

A Tale of Two Chipmunks
Talent for the Game
Tales from the Crypt
Tales from the Darkside
Tales from the Darkside: The
  Movie
Tales of Robin Hood
Tales of the Unexpected
Talk of the Town
Talk Radio
The Tall Guy
Tall in the Saddle
Tall Lie
Tall Story
Tall Texan
Talons of the Eagle
The Taming of the Shrew
Tampopo
Tango and Cash
Tank
Tanner '88
Tap
Tapeheads
Taras Bulba
Target
Tartuffe
Tarzan and His Mate
Tarzan, the Ape Man
A Taste for Killing
Tatie Danielle
Taxi Driver
A Taxing Woman
A Taxing Woman Returns
Tea and Sympathy
The Teacher
Teachers
The Teahouse of the August
  Moon
Teamster Boss: The Jackie
  Presser Story
Teen Wolf
Teenage Mutant Ninja Turtles:
  The Movie
Teenage Mutant Ninja Turtles
  3
The Telephone
Tell Them Willie Boy Is Here
The Tempest
10
The Ten Commandments
Ten Little Indians
10 Rillington Place
Ten to Midnight
Ten Wanted Men
Tender Mercies
The Tender Trap
The Tenth Man
Tequila Sunrise
Terminal Bliss
Terminal Exposure
Terminal Force
The Terminator
Terminator 2: Judgment Day
Terms of Endearment
Terror by Night
Terror in Beverly Hills
Terror in the Swamp
Terror Street
Terror Train
Tess
Testament
Tex
Tex Avery's Screwball
  Classics, Vol. 1
The Texas Chainsaw
  Massacre
Texas Chainsaw Massacre,
  Part 2
Texas Guns
Texasville
Thank Your Lucky Stars
That Hamilton Woman
That Obscure Object of Desire
That Sinking Feeling
That Summer of White Roses
That Touch of Mink

That Was Then...This Is Now
That'll Be the Day
That's Dancing!
That's Entertainment
That's Entertainment, Part 2
That's Life!
That's Singing: The Best of
  Broadway
Theatre of Blood
Thelma & Louise
Them!
There's No Business Like
  Show Business
There's Nothing Out There
These Three
They All Laughed
They Came to Cordura
They Got Me Covered
They Live
They Live by Night
They Made Me a Criminal
They Never Come Back
They Shoot Horses, Don't
  They?
They Were So Young
They Won't Believe Me
Thief
The Thief of Baghdad
Thief of Baghdad
Thief of Hearts
Thieves of Fortune
The Thin Blue Line
The Thin Man
The Thing
Things Change
The Things of Life
Think Big
Third Degree Burn
The Third Man
Third Solution
The 39 Steps
'38: Vienna Before the Fall
This Could Be the Night
This Gun for Hire
This is Spinal Tap
This Island Earth
This Land is Mine
This Property is Condemned
Thompson's Last Run
Thoroughly Modern Millie
Those Magnificent Men in
  Their Flying Machines
Thousand Pieces of Gold
Thousands Cheer
Three Amigos
The Three Caballeros
Three Days of the Condor
Three Days to a Kill
The Three Faces of Eve
Three for the Road
Three Fugitives
The 317th Platoon
Three Legionnaires
Three Men and a Baby
Three Men and a Cradle
Three Men and a Little Lady
The Three Musketeers
Three Musketeers
3 Ninjas
Three O'Clock High
The Three Penny Opera
3:10 to Yuma
The Three Worlds of Gulliver
Throne of Blood
Throw Momma from the Train
Thumbelina
Thunder & Mud
Thunder in the Pines
Thunderball
Thunderbolt & Lightfoot
Thunderground
Thunderheart
Thursday's Game
THX 1138
Tie Me Up! Tie Me Down!
Tiger Claws

Tiger Warsaw
A Tiger's Tale
Tightrope
The Tigress
Till Marriage Do Us Part
Till the Clouds Roll By
Till the End of Time
Tillie's Punctured Romance
Time After Time
Time Bandits
The Time Guardian
The Time Machine
A Time of Destiny
Time of the Gypsies
Time Runner
A Time to Die
Time to Kill
Timebomb
Timerider
Times of Harvey Milk
Tin Men
Tiny Toon Adventures: How I
  Spent My Vacation
To Be or Not to Be
To Catch a Killer
To Catch a Thief
To Die for
To Die Standing
To Have & Have Not
To Joy
To Kill a Mockingbird
To Kill a Priest
To Live & Die in L.A.
Toast of New York
Tobor the Great
Toby McTeague
Togetherness
Tokyo Joe
Tokyo Olympiad
Tokyo Pop
Toll of the Desert
Tom, Dick, and Harry
Tom Jones
tom thumb
Tomb of Ligeia
Tomcat: Dangerous Desires
Tommy
Too Many Girls
Too Much Sun
Tootsie
Top Gun
Top Hat
Top Secret!
Topaz
Topaze
Topper Returns
Tora! Tora! Tora!
Torch Song
Torch Song Trilogy
Torchlight
Torn Curtain
Torrents of Spring
Torture Garden
Total Exposure
Total Recall
Touch and Go
Touch of Evil
Tough Assignment
Tough Guys
Tough Guys Don't Dance
Tour of Duty
Tourist Trap
The Towering Inferno
Toxic Avenger
Toxic Avenger, Part 2
The Toy
Toy Soldiers
Traces of Red
Trading Hearts
Trading Places
Trail of Terror
Trail of the Mounties
Trail of the Pink Panther
Train Robbers
Train to Tombstone
Trancers

Trancers 2: The Return of
  Jack Deth
Trancers 3: Deth Lives
Transformations
Transmutations
Transylvania 6-5000
Trap on Cougar Mountain
Trapper County War
Travels with My Aunt
Treasure Island
Treasure of Monte Cristo
Treasure of the Sierra Madre
A Tree Grows in Brooklyn
The Tree of Wooden Clogs
Tremors
Trespass
Tribute
Tricks of the Trade
Trinity is Still My Name
The Trip to Bountiful
Tripods: The White Mountains
Tripwire
Triumph of the Spirit
Troll
Tron
Troop Beverly Hills
Tropical Snow
Trouble Bound
Trouble in Mind
The Trouble with Angels
The Trouble with Harry
True Believer
True Blood
True Colors
True Confessions
True Grit
True Love
True Stories
Trust
Trust Me
Truth or Dare
Truth or Die
Tucker: The Man and His
  Dream
Tuff Turf
Tumbleweeds
Tune in Tomorrow
Tunes of Glory
The Tunnel
The Tunnel of Love
The Turn of the Screw
Turner and Hooch
Turtle Diary
Tusks
The Tuttles of Tahiti
Twelfth Night
Twelve Angry Men
Twelve Chairs
Twelve O'Clock High
Twenty-One
20 Million Miles to Earth
20,000 Leagues Under the
  Sea
Twice Dead
Twice in a Lifetime
Twilight of the Cockroaches
The Twilight Zone
Twilight Zone: The Movie
Twilight's Last Gleaming
Twin Peaks
Twin Peaks: Fire Walk with
  Me
Twins
Twisted Obsession
Twister
Two Evil Eyes
Two for the Road
Two for the Seesaw
Two Girls and a Sailor
2 Idiots in Hollywood
The Two Jakes
Two Minute Warning
Two Moon Junction
Two of a Kind
Two Rode Together
2001: A Space Odyssey

2010: The Year We Make
  Contact
Two Weeks in Another Town
Tycoon
Ugetsu
UHF
Ulysses
Ulzana's Raid
Umberto D
The Unbearable Lightness of
  Being
The Unbelievable Truth
The Unborn
Uncaged
Uncle Buck
Uncommon Valor
The Undefeated
Under Capricorn
Under Fire
Under Siege
Under Suspicion
Under the Biltmore Clock
Under the Boardwalk
Under the Cherry Moon
Under the Earth
Under the Gun
Under the Volcano
Undersea Kingdom
Understudy: The Graveyard
  Shift 2
Underwater
Unfaithfully Yours
The Unforgiven
Unforgiven
The Unholy
Unholy Four
The Uninvited
Union City
Universal Soldier
Unlawful Entry
The Unnamable
The Unnamable 2: The
  Statement of Randolph
  Carter
Unnatural Causes
Unsettled Land
The Unsinkable Molly Brown
Untamed Heart
Until The End of The World
The Untouchables
Up Periscope
Up the Creek
Up Your Alley
Uranus
Urban Cowboy
Urusei Yatsura 2: Beautiful
  Dreamer
Used Cars
Used People
Utilities
Vagabond
Valentino Returns
Valet Girls
Valley Girl
The Valley of Gwangi
Valley of the Lawless
Valmont
Vamp
Vampire Princess Miyu
Vampire's Kiss
Vanishing Point
Varieties on Parade
The Velvet Vampire
Vengeance
Vengeance Is Mine
Vera Cruz
The Verdict
Verne Miller
Vertigo
A Very Old Man with
  Enormous Wings
V.I. Warshawski
Vice Academy
Vice Squad
Vice Versa
Victim of Love

CAPTIONED INDEX

The **CAPTIONED INDEX** identifies 3,000 videos available with captioning for hearing-impaired viewers provided by either the National Captioning Institute (Falls Church, VA) or the Caption Center (Los Angeles, CA). Titles are arranged alphabetically.

Above the Law
The Abyss
Acceptable Risks
The Accidental Tourist
The Accused
Act of Vengeance
Action Jackson
Adam
The Addams Family
The Adventurers
Adventures in Babysitting
Adventures In Dinosaur City
Adventures in Spying
The Adventures of an American Rabbit
The Adventures of Baron Munchausen
The Adventures of Buckaroo Banzai Across the Eighth Dimension
The Adventures of Ford Fairlane
The Adventures of Milo & Otis
The Adventures of Robin Hood
The Adventures of Sherlock Holmes
An Affair in Mind
An Affair to Remember
Afraid of the Dark
After Dark, My Sweet
After Hours
After Midnight
After Pilkington
After the Shock
Afterburn
Against All Odds
Age Old Friends
Agnes of God
Air America
Air Force
Aladdin
Aladdin and His Wonderful Lamp
The Alamo
Alamo Bay
The Alamo: Thirteen Days to Glory
Alfredo, Alfredo
Alias Billy the Kid
Alice
Alice in Wonderland
Alien 3
Alien Intruder
Alien Nation

Aliens
All-American Murder
All Creatures Great and Small
All Dogs Go to Heaven
All That Jazz
All the Kind Strangers
All the Right Moves
All Through the Night
Allan Quartermain and the Lost City of Gold
Allegheny Uprising
All's Fair
Almost an Angel
Almost Partners
Almost Pregnant
Almost You
Always
Amazing Grace & Chuck
The Amazing Spider-Man
Amazing Stories, Book 2
Amazing Stories, Book 4
Ambition
The American Angels: Baptism of Blood
American Anthem
American Dreamer
American Flyers
American Ninja
American Ninja 2: The Confrontation
American Samurai
American Shaolin: King of the Kickboxers 2
An American Summer
An American Tail
An American Tail: Fievel Goes West
Amityville 1992: It's About Time
Amos and Andrew
Anchors Aweigh
And a Nightingale Sang
And You Thought Your Parents Were Weird!
Andy Hardy Meets Debutante
Anguish
Animal Instincts
Anna
Anne of Avonlea
Anne of Green Gables
Annie
Annie Oakley
Another 48 Hrs.
Another Thin Man
Another Time, Another Place

Another Woman
Another You
Antarctica
Antonia and Jane
Apache Uprising
The Apple Dumpling Gang
The Applegates
Appointment with Death
Apprentice to Murder
April Fool's Day
Arachnophobia
Are You Lonesome Tonight
Arena
Armed and Dangerous
Armed for Action
Around the World in 80 Days
Arrivederci, Baby!
Arrowhead
Arsenic and Old Lace
Arthur
Arthur 2: On the Rocks
Article 99
Artists and Models
Ash Wednesday
Aspen Extreme
Assassination
The Assassination Bureau
Assault and Matrimony
Assault on a Queen
At Close Range
At Play in the Fields of the Lord
The Atomic City
The Attic: The Hiding of Anne Frank
Avalon
Avenging Angel
Avenging Force
Awakenings
The Babe
Babe Ruth Story
Baby Boom
The Baby Doll Murders
Baby It's You
Baby of the Bride
Baby on Board
Baby, Take a Bow
Babycakes
Bachelor Party
Back to Bataan
Back to School
Back to the Beach
Back to the Future
Back to the Future, Part 2
Back to the Future, Part 3

Backdraft
Backfield in Motion
Backstab
Backtrack
The Bad and the Beautiful
Bad Channels
Bad Dreams
Bad Lieutenant
Bad Medicine
Bagdad Cafe
The Ballad of the Sad Cafe
Bambi
Bandolero!
Barbarian and the Geisha
Bare Essentials
Barfly
The Baron and the Kid
Basic Instinct
Basket Case 2
Basket Case 3: The Progeny
The Bastard
Bat 21
Batman
Batman Returns
Battle Circus
Battle Cry
Battle for the Planet of the Apes
Battle of Britain
Battle of the Bulge
Battleground
The Bay Boy
B.C.: The First Thanksgiving
Beach Boys: An American Band
The Bear
The Beast
The Beast with Five Fingers
Beastmaster 2: Through the Portal of Time
Beat the Devil
The Beautiful Blonde from Bashful Bend
Beautiful Dreamers
Beauty and the Beast
Beauty and the Beast: Though Lovers Be Lost
Bebe's Kids
Becoming Colette
Bed & Breakfast
The Bedroom Window
Beer
Beethoven
Beethoven Lives Upstairs
Beetlejuice

Being There
The Believers
Belizaire the Cajun
The Bells of St. Mary's
Ben-Hur
Beneath the Planet of the Apes
Benji the Hunted
Benny & Joon
Bernard and the Genie
Bert Rigby, You're a Fool
Best Defense
Best of Chevy Chase
Best of Comic Relief
Best of Eddie Murphy
Best of the Best 2
The Best of the Two Ronnies
The Best of Times
Betrayed
Betsy's Wedding
Better Off Dead
Betty Blue
Beverly Hills Brats
Beverly Hills Cop
Beverly Hills Cop 2
Beyond Darkness
Beyond Justice
Beyond the Door
Beyond the Door 3
Beyond Therapy
The Big Blue
Big Business
The Big Chill
The Big Easy
Big Girls Don't Cry...They Get Even
Big Jake
Big Jim McLain
The Big Picture
Big Shots
The Big Sky
Big Top Pee Wee
Big Trail
Big Trouble in Little China
Biggles
The Bikini Car Wash Company
The Bikini Car Wash Company 2
Bill & Ted's Bogus Journey
Bill & Ted's Excellent Adventure
Bill Cosby, Himself
A Bill of Divorcement
Billy Bathgate

King Kong
King Kong Lives
King of New York
The King of the Kickboxers
King Ralph
Kings Row
The King's Whore
Kismet
A Kiss Before Dying
Kiss Me Deadly
Kiss of Death
Kiss of the Spider Woman
Kiss Shot
The Kissing Place
The Kitchen Toto
The Klansman
Knight Moves
Knights & Emeralds
Kramer vs. Kramer
The Krays
Krull
Krush Groove
K2: The Ultimate High
Kuffs
La Balance
La Bamba
L.A. Law
L.A. Story
Labyrinth
The Ladies' Man
Ladies of the Chorus
Ladies They Talk About
Lady by Choice
Lady Dragon
The Lady in White
Lady Jane
Lady Killer
Lady Mobster
Lady of the Lake
Ladybugs
Ladyhawke
Ladykiller
Ladykillers
Lake Consequence
Lambada
The Land Before Time
Land of the Pharaohs
Landslide
Lantern Hill
Laser Mission
The Last Boy Scout
The Last Days of Patton
Last Days of Pompeii
The Last Dragon
The Last Emperor
The Last of His Tribe
The Last of Mrs. Cheyney
The Last of the Finest
The Last Picture Show
Last Plane Out
Last Rites
The Last Safari
Last Song
The Last Unicorn
The Last Voyage
The Last Waltz
The Late Show
Latino
Laughing Policeman
The Law and Jake Wade
The Lawnmower Man
Lawrence of Arabia
Le Mans
A League of Their Own
Lean on Me
Leap of Faith
Leather Jackets
Leave 'Em Laughing
Leaving Normal
Legacy of Lies
Legal Eagles
Legend
Legend of Billie Jean
The Legend of Hell House
The Legend of Sleepy Hollow
The Legend of Wolf Mountain

The Lemon Sisters
Lenny
Leonard Part 6
Less Than Zero
Let It Ride
Lethal Lolita—Amy Fisher: My Story
Lethal Weapon
Lethal Weapon 2
Let's Dance
Let's Get Harry
Let's Make it Legal
Letter to Brezhnev
Leviathan
Liberty & Bash
License to Kill
Lies
Lies Before Kisses
Life is Sweet
A Life of Sin
Life Stinks
Lifeboat
The Lighthorseman
The Lightning Incident
Lightning: The White Stallion
The Lightship
Li'l Abner
Lili
Lilies of the Field
Limit Up
The Linguini Incident
Link
Lionheart
Lisa
Listen to Me
Little Big Man
The Little Colonel
Little Dorrit, Film 1: Nobody's Fault
Little Dorrit, Film 2: Little Dorrit's Story
The Little Drummer Boy
The Little Drummer Girl
Little Lord Fauntleroy
Little Man Tate
The Little Match Girl
The Little Mermaid
Little Miss Broadway
Little Monsters
Little Nikita
The Little Princess
Little Red Riding Hood
Little Shop of Horrors
Little Treasure
Little Women
The Littlest Rebel
Live Wire
Livin' Large
The Living Daylights
Local Hero
Lock Up
London Kills Me
Lonely in America
Lonesome Dove
The Long Gray Line
The Long, Hot Summer
The Long, Long Trailer
The Long Walk Home
Look Who's Talking
Look Who's Talking, Too
The Lookalike
Looker
Looking for Miracles
Loose Cannons
Lord of the Flies
Lorenzo's Oil
Lost Angels
The Lost Boys
The Lost Capone
Lost in America
Love Among the Ruins
Love and Bullets
Love at Large
The Love Bug
Love Field
Love Finds Andy Hardy

Love Hurts
A Love in Germany
Love in the Afternoon
Love is a Many-Splendored Thing
Love Kills
Love, Lies and Murder
Love Me or Leave Me
Love or Money?
Love Potion #9
Love with the Proper Stranger
Lovelines
The Lover
Loverboy
Lower Level
Lucas
Lucy and Desi: Before the Laughter
Lust in the Dust
Mac and Me
Macaroni
Mad at the Moon
Mad Dog and Glory
Mad Max Beyond Thunderdome
Madam Satan
Made for Each Other
Made in Heaven
Madhouse
The Magnificent Ambersons
The Maid
Major League
Malcolm X
Malibu Bikini Shop
Malone
The Maltese Falcon
The Mambo Kings
A Man and a Woman
A Man Called Horse
A Man Called Peter
A Man for All Seasons
The Man in the Gray Flannel Suit
The Man in the Iron Mask
The Man in the Moon
Man of the West
Man Trouble
The Man Who Loved Women
The Man Who Would Be King
The Man with One Red Shoe
The Manchurian Candidate
Mandroid
Manhunter
Maniac Cop 2
Maniac Cop 3
Mannequin
Mansfield Park
Map of the Human Heart
Mario
Marked for Death
Marked Woman
Maroc 7
Married to the Mob
The Marrying Man
Martial Law 2: Undercover
Martin's Day
Marty
Mary Poppins
Mascara
Mask
Masquerade
Mass Appeal
Masters of the Universe
The Matchmaker
Matewan
Matinee
Matters of the Heart
Maurice
Max and Helen
Max Headroom, the Original Story
Max Maven's Mindgames
May Wine
McBain
The McConnell Story
McQ

Me and Him
Mean Streets
Meatballs
Meatballs 2
Meatballs 4
Mediterraneo
Meet the Hollowheads
Melody in Love
Memoirs of an Invisible Man
Memories of Me
Memphis
Memphis Belle
Men at Work
Men Don't Leave
Men of Respect
Meridian: Kiss of the Beast
Mermaids
Messenger of Death
Miami Blues
Micki & Maude
A Midnight Clear
The Mighty Ducks
The Mighty Pawns
Mikey
Mildred Pierce
Miles from Home
Millenium
Miller's Crossing
Million Dollar Mystery
Millions
Milo & Otis
Mindwalk
Mindwarp
Miracle Down Under
Miracle Mile
Miracle on 34th Street
Mirrors
Mischief
Misery
Mishima: A Life in Four Chapters
Miss Firecracker
Miss Rose White
The Mission
Mission of Justice
Mississippi Burning
Mississippi Masala
Mrs. Soffel
Mr. & Mrs. Bridge
Mr. Baseball
Mr. Billion
Mr. Corbett's Ghost
Mr. Destiny
Mr. Frost
Mr. Hobbs Takes a Vacation
Mister Johnson
Mr. Love
Mr. Lucky
Mr. Mom
Mr. Music
Mr. North
Mr. Saturday Night
Mistress
Misty
Mo' Better Blues
Mobsters
Moby Dick
Modern Love
The Mole People
Mom
Mom and Dad Save the World
The Money Pit
Monkey Shines
Monsieur Beaucaire
Monster in a Box
Monster in the Closet
Montana
Monte Carlo
Monte Walsh
Monty Python Live at the Hollywood Bowl
Monty Python's Life of Brian
Monty Python's Parrot Sketch Not Included
Moon 44
Moon Over Miami

Moonlighting
Moonraker
Moonstruck
More American Graffiti
Morituri
Morning After
Mortal Passions
Mortal Sins
Mortal Thoughts
Moscow on the Hudson
The Mosquito Coast
Mother Goose Rock 'n' Rhyme
The Mountain
Mountains of the Moon
Moving
Moving Violations
The Mummy's Hand
Munchie
The Muppet Christmas Carol
Muppets Take Manhattan
Murder by Moonlight
Murder in New Hampshire: The Pamela Smart Story
A Murder is Announced
Murder 101
Murder Ordained
Murder Over New York
Murderers Among Us: The Simon Wiesenthal Story
Murderous Vision
Murders in the Rue Morgue
Murphy's Law
Murphy's Romance
The Music Man
My Beautiful Laundrette
My Best Friend Is a Vampire
My Blue Heaven
My Cousin Vinny
My Darlin' Clementine
My Darling Clementine
My Fair Lady
My Father is Coming
My Favorite Blonde
My Friend Irma
My Geisha
My Girl
My Grandpa is a Vampire
My Heroes Have Always Been Cowboys
My Little Pony: The Movie
My Man Adam
My Own Private Idaho
My Samurai
My Stepmother Is an Alien
Mysterious Island
Mystery Date
Mystic Pizza
Nadine
Nails
The Naked Edge
The Naked Gun: From the Files of Police Squad
Naked Gun 2 1/2: The Smell of Fear
Naked Lunch
The Name of the Rose
Narrow Margin
National Lampoon's Christmas Vacation
National Lampoon's European Vacation
National Velvet
Native Son
Nativity
The Natural
Navy SEALS
Necessary Roughness
Nemesis
Neon City
Neptune Factor
Neptune's Daughter
Netherworld
Never Forget
Never on Tuesday
Never Say Never Again

Never

FOREIGN FILM INDEX

The **FOREIGN FILM INDEX** classifies some 4,300 movies by the country of record in which they were produced, and not necessarily filmed. Since the feature may have been financed or produced by more than one country, some videos will appear with more than one country of origin. The codes appear in the review immediately following the color or black and white designation near the top of the review.

Key to Country Origination Tags

AL Algerian	**CH** Chinese	**GR** Greek	**LI** Lithuanian	**SA** South African
AR Argentinean	**CZ** Czech	**HK** Hong Kong	**MX** Mexican	**SP** Spanish
AT Austrian	**DK** Danish	**HU** Hungarian	**NZ** New Zealand	**SW** Swedish
AU Australian	**NL** Dutch	**IN** Indian	**NI** Nicaraguan	**SI** Swiss
BE Belgian	**PH** Filipino	**IR** Irish	**NO** Norwegian	**TU** Turkish
BR Brazilian	**FI** Finnish	**IS** Israeli	**PL** Polish	**TW** Taiwanese
GB British	**FR** French	**IT** Italian	**PT** Portuguese	**YU** Yugoslavian
CA Canadian	**GE** German	**JP** Japanese	**RU** Russian	

Algerian
The Battle of Algiers

Argentinean
Camila
The Devil's Possessed
The Enchanted Forest
Eversmile New Jersey
Far Away and Long Ago
Fridays of Eternity
Funny, Dirty Little War
La Boca del Lobo
Made in Argentina
Man Facing Southeast
Miss Mary
The Official Story
The Stranger
Tango Bar
Time for Revenge
Times to Come
Two to Tango
Veronico Cruz

Australian
ABC's of Love & Sex,
 Australia Style
Air Hawk
Alice to Nowhere
Alison's Birthday
All the Rivers Run
...Almost
Alvin Purple
Alvin Rides Again
American Roulette
Anzacs: The War Down Under
Archer's Adventure
Around the World in 80 Ways
Attack Force Z
Backlash
Barnaby and Me
Barry McKenzie Holds His
 Own
Between Wars
The Black Planet
Black Robe
Bliss
Blood Money
Bloodmoon
Blue Fin
Breaker Morant
Breakfast in Paris
Burke & Wills

Cactus
Camel Boy
Careful, He Might Hear You
Carry Me Back
The Cars That Ate Paris
The City's Edge
The Clinic
The Club
The Coca-Cola Kid
Color Me Dead
Contagion
Crocodile Dundee
The Crossing
A Cry in the Dark
Dangerous Summer
Dark Age
Dark Forces
Dead Calm
Dead Easy
Dead End Drive-In
Deadly Possession
Demonstrator
The Devil's Playground
Dogs in Space
Don's Party
Dot & the Bunny
Dot & the Whale
The Dreaming
The Dunera Boys
Dusty
Earthling
Echo Park
Echoes of Paradise
The Efficiency Expert
The Empty Beach
Endplay
Escape 2000
The Everlasting Secret Family
Fantasy Man
Fast Talking
Father
Fatty Finn
The Fire in the Stone
Fists of Blood
Flirting
For Love Alone
Fortress
Forty Thousand Horsemen
Fran
Frenchman's Farm
The Fringe Dwellers
Gallagher's Travels
Gallipoli
The Getting of Wisdom
The Good Wife

Grendel, Grendel, Grendel
Ground Zero
Hard Knocks
Heatwave
High Rolling in a Hot Corvette
High Tide
The Highest Honor
Howling 3: The Marsupials
I Live with Me Dad
An Indecent Obsession
Inn of the Damned
Innocent Prey
The Irishman
Kangaroo
Killing of Angel Street
Kitty and the Bagman
Lady Stay Dead
The Last Bastion
The Last Days of Chez Nous
The Last Wave
The Lighthorseman
Lonely Hearts
Long John Silver
Mad Dog Morgan
Mad Max Beyond
 Thunderdome
Magee and the Lady
Malcolm
Man of Flowers
The Mango Tree
Mesmerized
Midnight Dancer
Miracle Down Under
Money Movers
Monkey Grip
Moving Targets
My First Wife
Newsfront
Next of Kin
No Room to Run
Norman Loves Rose
Now and Forever
The Odd Angry Shot
Overlanders
Palm Beach
Panic Station
Patrick
Phar Lap
Picnic at Hanging Rock
Plumber
Poor Girl, A Ghost Story
Prince and the Great Race
Prisoner Cell Block H
Prisoners of the Sun
Proof

Puberty Blues
Puzzle
Queen of the Road
The Quest
Quigley Down Under
Race to the Yankee Zephyr
Razorback
Rebel
Return of Captain Invincible
Return to Snowy River
Ride a Wild Pony
The Right Hand Man
Rikky and Pete
Road Games
Run, Rebecca, Run
Sara Dane
Savage Attraction
Second Time Lucky
Shame
Silver City
Sky Pirates
Smuggler's Cove
Squizzy Taylor
Starstruck
Strangers
Strictly Ballroom
Summer City
Sunday Too Far Away
Survivor
Sweet Talker
Sweetie
The Tale of Ruby Rose
Tearaway
A Test of Love
Three's Trouble
Thundering Forest
Tim
Torn Allegiance
Touch & Go
A Town Like Alice
Travelling North
Typhoon Treasure
Under Capricorn
Vincent: The Life and Death of
 Vincent van Gogh
The Wacky World of Wills &
 Burke
Walk into Hell
Warm Nights on a Slow-
 Moving Train
Waterfront
Who Killed Baby Azaria?
The Wild Duck
Windrider
The Winter of Our Dreams

A Woman's Tale
A Yank in Australia
The Year My Voice Broke
The Year of Living
 Dangerously
Young Einstein

Austrian
The Hands of Orlac
Heidi
Time Troopers

Belgian
Daughters of Darkness
The Devil's Nightmare
Dust
Les Rendez-vous D'Anna
Man Bites Dog
Mascara
The Music Teacher
One Sings, the Other Doesn't
Rabid Grannies
Toute Une Nuit
A Wedding in Galilee

Brazilian
Amor Bandido
Black God & White Devil
Black Orpheus
Bye Bye Brazil
The Dolphin
Dona Flor and Her Two
 Husbands
Earth Entranced
Gabriela
Hour of the Star
I Love You
Killer Fish
Kiss of the Spider Woman
Lady on the Bus
Luzia
Opera do Malandro
Pixote
Quilombo
The Story of Fausta
Subway to the Stars
Women in Fury

British
Abdulla the Great

British

Mohammed: Messenger of
God
Mona Lisa
The Monster Club
A Month in the Country
Monty Python and the Holy
Grail
Monty Python Live at the
Hollywood Bowl
Monty Python Meets Beyond
the Fringe
Monty Python's Flying Circus
Monty Python's Life of Brian
Monty Python's The Meaning
of Life
The Moon Stallion
Moonlight Sonata
Moonlighting
The Moonraker
Moonraker
Morgan!
Morons from Outer Space
The Mouse That Roared
Much Ado About Nothing
The Mummy
The Muppet Movie
Murder
Murder at the Baskervilles
Murder by Moonlight
Murder in the Footlights
Murder in the Old Red Barn
A Murder is Announced
Murder of a Moderate Man
Murder on the Campus
Murder on the Orient Express
Murders at Lynch Cross
Murphy's War
The Music Lovers
My Son, the Vampire
Mysterious Island
The Naked Edge
The Naked Truth
Nancy Astor
Nasty Habits
Ned Kelly
Negatives
Never Let Go
Next Victim
Nice Girl Like Me
Nicholas Nickleby
Night Ambush
Night and the City
Night Beat
Night Caller from Outer Space
The Night Has Eyes
Night of the Laughing Dead
Night Train to Munich
The Night Visitor
Night Watch
The Nightcomers
Nine Days a Queen
1984
99 Women
No Comebacks
No Love for Johnnie
No Surrender
No Trace
Norman Conquest
The Norman Conquests, Part
1: Table Manners
The Norman Conquests, Part
2: Living Together
The Norman Conquests, Part
3: Round and Round the
Garden
Northanger Abbey
Nothing But the Night
Number 1 of the Secret
Service
Nuts in May
O Lucky Man
The Oblong Box
The Obsessed
Octopussy
The Odd Job
Odd Man Out

The Odessa File
Of Human Bondage
The Offence
Office Romances
Oh, Alfie
Oh, Mr. Porter
O.H.M.S.
The Old Curiosity Shop
Old Mother Riley's Ghosts
Old Spanish Custom
Oliver!
Oliver Twist
On Approval
On Her Majesty's Secret
Service
One Day in the Life of Ivan
Denisovich
One-Eyed Soldiers
One of Our Aircraft Is Missing
One Wish Too Many
Only Two Can Play
Open All Hours
Order of the Black Eagle
Othello
Out of Season
Overture
Paid to Kill
Paper Marriage
Paper Mask
Paper Tiger
Paperhouse
Party! Party!
Pascali's Island
A Passage to India
The Passing of the Third Floor
Back
Passport to Pimlico
Paul and Michelle
The People That Time Forgot
Performance
Permission To Kill
Personal Services
The Persuaders
Peter's Friends
Phantom Fiend
The Phantom Light
Philby, Burgess and MacLean:
Spy Scandal of the Century
The Pickwick Papers
Pimpernel Smith
Pink Floyd: The Wall
The Pink Panther
The Pink Panther Strikes
Again
Pink Strings and Sealing Wax
Playing Away
A Pocketful of Rye
The Pope Must Diet
Porridge
Portrait of a Lady
Postmark for Danger
Postmark for Danger/
Quicksand
Power
Power Play
Prick Up Your Ears
Pride and Prejudice
Priest of Love
The Prime of Miss Jean
Brodie
The Prince and the Pauper
The Prisoner
The Prisoner: Arrival
A Private Function
Private Life of Don Juan
The Private Life of Henry VIII
The Private Life of Sherlock
Holmes
The Private Secretary
Privates on Parade
Promise Her Anything
The Promoter
Providence
Psychomania
Psychopath
Pulp

Puppet on a Chain
The Pure Hell of St. Trinian's
Pursuit of the Graf Spee
Pygmalion
Quadrophenia
Quartet
Quatermass 2
Quatermass Conclusion
The Quatermass Experiment
Queen of Hearts
The Queen of Spades
Quest for Love
Race for Life
Railway Children
The Rainbow
Rattle of a Simple Man
Reach for the Sky
The Red Shoes
Redneck
Reilly: Ace of Spies
Rembrandt
Rentadick
Repulsion
Return of the Soldier
Revenge
Revolution
Rhodes
Rich and Strange
Richard II
Richard III
Richard's Things
The Riddle of the Sands
Riff Raff
The Ring
Ring of Bright Water
Ripping Yarns
Rita, Sue & Bob Too
Road to 1984
Roadhouse Girl
Robbery
Robbery Under Arms
Robin and Marian
Robin Hood: The Movie
Robin Hood...The Legend:
Herne's Son
Robin Hood...The Legend:
Robin Hood and the
Sorcerer
Robin Hood...The Legend:
The Swords of Wayland
Robin Hood...The Legend:
The Time of the Wolf
Roboman
Rogue's Yarn
Romance with a Double Bass
Romantic Englishwoman
Romeo and Juliet
Room at the Top
Room to Let
A Room with a View
The Ruling Class
Rumpole of the Bailey
Rumpole of the Bailey:
Rumpole's Return
The Runaway Bus
Running Blind
Ryan's Daughter
Saigon: Year of the Cat
Sailing Along
The Sailor Who Fell from
Grace with the Sea
The Saint
Salaam Bombay!
The Salamander
Sammy & Rosie Get Laid
Sanders of the River
Sapphire
The Satanic Rites of Dracula
Saturn 3
Say Hello to Yesterday
Scandal
The Scarlet Pimpernel
The Scars of Dracula
School for Scandal
Scotland Yard Inspector
Scott of the Antarctic

Scream and Scream Again
Scream of Fear
Scrooge
Scrubbers
Scum
Sea Devils
Sea Wolves
Seance on a Wet Afternoon
Seaside Swingers
Sebastian
Second Best Secret Agent in
the Whole Wide World
Second Chance
The Secret Adversary
The Secret Agent
The Secret Four
The Secret Garden
The Secret of the Loch
Secret Places
The Secret Policeman's Other
Ball
Secret Policeman's Private
Parts
Secrets
The Sender
Sense & Sensibility
A Sense of Freedom
The Servant
The 7 Brothers Meet Dracula
Sev ith Veil
Sexton Blake and the Hooded
Terror
Shadey
The Shadow
The Shadow Man
Shadowlands
Shaka Zulu
Shattered
Sherlock Holmes and the
Incident at Victoria Falls
Shirley Valentine
The Shooting Party
A Shot in the Dark
The Shout
Shout at the Devil
Sidewalks of London
The Sign of Four
Silas Marner
The Silent Enemy
The Silent Mr. Sherlock
Holmes
The Silent Passenger
Silent Scream
Simba
Sinbad and the Eye of the
Tiger
The Sinful Bed
Singleton's Pluck
Sister Dora
Six Wives of Henry VIII
Skin Game
Slayground
Slipstream
The Smallest Show on Earth
The Snake Woman
Someone at the Door
Song of Freedom
S.O.S. Pacific
Space: 1999
Space: 1999—Alien Attack
The Spaniard's Curse
Spellbound
Spiral Staircase
Spitfire
Split Second
Spy in Black
Spy of Napoleon
The Spy Who Loved Me
Spy with a Cold Nose
Spymaker: The Secret Life of
Ian Fleming
Stage Fright
The Stars Look Down
Starship
The Statue
Staying On

Stealing Heaven
Steaming
Stevie
A Stolen Face
Storm in a Teacup
Strange Awakening
Stranger in Town
Straw Dogs
The Stud
A Study in Terror
Subterfuge
Success is the Best Revenge
Sudden Terror
A Summer Story
Sunday, Bloody Sunday
Supergirl
Supergrass
Suspended Alibi
Svengali
Sweeney Todd: The Demon
Barber of Fleet Street
Sweet William
Sword of Lancelot
Sword of Sherwood Forest
Sword of the Valiant
Taffin
A Tale of Two Cities
Tales from the Crypt
Tales of Beatrix Potter
Tales That Witness Madness
A Taste of Honey
Taste the Blood of Dracula
The Tell-Tale Heart
The Tempest
The Temptress
Ten Little Indians
10 Rillington Place
Terronauts
The Terror
Terror Ship
The Terrornauts
Tess
That Sinking Feeling
Theatre of Blood
There's a Girl in My Soup
Things Happen at Night
Things to Come
Think Dirty
Thirteenth Day of Christmas
30 Is a Dangerous Age,
Cynthia
The 39 Steps
The Thirty-Nine Steps
This Happy Breed
This Lightning Always Strikes
Twice
This Sporting Life
Those Daring Young Men in
Their Jaunty Jalopies
Those Fantastic Flying Fools
Those Glory, Glory Days
Those Magnificent Men in
Their Flying Machines
Threads
Three of a Kind
Three Stops to Murder
The Three Weird Sisters
Thunder in the City
Thunderball
Tiger Bay
Time Bandits
Time for Murder
Time Lock
Tintorera...Tiger Shark
To See Such Fun
To Sir, with Love
Tom Brown's School Days
Tom Jones
tom thumb
Tomb of Ligeia
Tomb of the Undead
Too Many Crooks
Torture Garden
Touch Me Not
Tough Guy
Tower of Evil

Danish

Twist & Shout
The Wolf at the Door
A World of Strangers
You Are Not Alone

Dutch

Amsterdamned
Army Brats
The Assault
Broken Mirrors
Cold Blood
Dear Boys
Egg
Fatal Error
A Flight of Rainbirds
The 4th Man
In for Treatment
Katie's Passion
Keetje Tippei
The Lift
The Man Inside
My Nights With Susan,
    Sandra, Olga, and Julie
On Top of the Whale
The Pointsman
Question of Silence
Rembrandt—1669
Soldier of Orange
Spetters
To Play or To Die
Turkish Delights
The Vanishing

Filipino

Beast of the Yellow Night
Beyond Atlantis
Blind Rage
Brides of the Beast
Caged Fury
Circle of Fear
The Deadly and the Beautiful
Devil Woman
Horror of the Blood Monsters
Macho Dancer
Night of the Cobra Woman
Once Before I Die
Perfumed Nightmare
Raw Force
Stickfighter
Stryker
Terror is a Man
The Thirsty Dead
Turumba
Twilight People
The Vampire Hookers
The Vampire People

Finnish

Ariel
The Day the Earth Froze
Leningrad Cowboys Go
    America
The Match Factory Girl

French

Act of Aggression
Adorable Julia
After the Fall of New York
Akermania, Vol. 1
Alice in Wonderland
Alphaville
The American Friend
And God Created Woman
And Hope to Die
And Now My Love
Andy Warhol's Dracula
Andy Warhol's Frankenstein
Angele
Another Man, Another Chance
As If It Were Raining
Assassination of Trotsky

The Associate
Asterix vs. Caesar
Atlantic City
Attack of the Robots
Au Revoir Les Enfants
The Avenger
Babette's Feast
Back to the Wall
The Baker's Wife
Band of Outsiders
Basileus Quartet
The Battle of Austerlitz
The Battle of El Alamein
Baxter
The Bear
Beatrice
Beau Pere
Beauty and the Beast
Beethoven
Beethoven's Nephew
Bernadette
The Best Way
Betty Blue
The Big Grab
Bilitis
Bim/Dream of the Wild Horses
Bizarre Bizarre
Black and White in Color
Black Orpheus
Black Tights
Blood and Black Lace
The Blood of Others
Blood Relatives
Blue Country
Blue Jeans
Bluebeard
Bob le Flambeur
Bonjour Tristesse
Borsalino
Boudu Saved from Drowning
Boy Meets Girl
Boyfriends & Girlfriends
The Brain
Breathless
The Bride Is Much Too
    Beautiful
The Bride Wore Black
Buffet Froid
By the Blood of Others
Caged Women
Camille Claudel
Candy Mountain
Captain Blackjack
Carnival in Flanders
Cartouche
Castle of Blood
Castle of the Living Dead
Cat and Mouse
The Cat o' Nine Tails
Catch Me a Spy
Catherine & Co.
Cathy's Curse
Cesar
Cesar & Rosalie
The Chambermaid's Dream
Charles et Lucie
Charlie Bravo
Children of Paradise
Chloe in the Afternoon
Choice of Arms
Christ Stopped at Eboli
Chronopolis
Circle of Love
Circus Angel
City of Joy
Claire's Knee
Cleo from 5 to 7
The Clockmaker
Cobra
A Coeur Joie
Cold Sweat
Confidentially Yours
The Conformist
Conquest of Mycene
Contempt
Conversation Piece

Coup de Grace
Coup de Torchon
Cousin, Cousine
The Cousins
Crainquebille
Crazy for Love
The Crazy Ray
The Crime of Monsieur Lange
Cross My Heart
Cyrano de Bergerac
Damage
Dangerous Liaisons
Danton
Daughters of Darkness
The Day and the Hour
Day for Night
A Day in the Country
The Day the Sky Exploded
The Daydreamer
Deadly Sting
The Deadly Trap
Death Watch
The Decameron
Delicatessen
Delusions of Grandeur
Devil in the Flesh
The Devil's Commandment
The Diabolical Dr. Z
Diabolically Yours
Diabolique
Diary of a Chambermaid
Diary of a Country Priest
Dirty Dishes
Dirty Hands
The Discreet Charm of the
    Bourgeoisie
Diva
Dog Day
Donkey Skin
Dos Cruces en Danger Pass
Double Agents
Double Identity
The Double Life of Veronique
Dracula & Son
Dressmaker
Duke of the Derby
Dust
The Earrings of Madame De...
Edith & Marcel
The Eighties
The Elegant Criminal
Elena and Her Men
Elle Voit des Nains Partout
Elsa, Elsa
Emmanuelle
Emmanuelle 4
Emmanuelle 5
Emmanuelle & Joanna
Emmanuelle in Bangkok
Emmanuelle in Soho
Emmanuelle in the Country
Emmanuelle on Taboo Island
Emmanuelle, the Joys of a
    Woman
Empty Canvas
End of Desire
Enigma
Entr'acte
Entre-Nous
Erendira
Erotic Escape
Et La Tenoresse?...Bordel!
Eternal Return
The Eyes, the Mouth
Fahrenheit 451
Fanny
Fantastic Planet
Fatal Fix
The Favor, the Watch, & the
    Very Big Fish
Fellini's Roma
Femmes de Paris
Fernandel the Dressmaker
Field of Honor
The Fire Within
First Name: Carmen

Forbidden Games
Four Adventures of Reinette
    and Mirabelle
Four Bags Full
The 400 Blows
France/Tour/Detour/Deux/
    Enfants
Frantic
Franz
French Can-Can
The French Detective
The French Touch
The French Way
From Hell to Victory
Full Moon in Paris
The Game is Over
Gervaise
Get Out Your Handkerchiefs
The Gift
Girl in His Pocket
A Girl on Her Own
Godard/Truffaut Shorts
Godson
Going Places
The Golden Coach
Goliath and the Dragon
Grain of Sand
Grand Illusion
The Great War
The Green Room
Hail Mary
The Hairdresser's Husband
The Hands of Orlac
Hanna K.
Happy New Year
Harem
Harvest
Head of the Family
Head Over Heels
Heart of a Nation
Heat of Desire
Hercules Against the Moon
    Men
High Heels
Hiroshima, Mon Amour
The Holes
Holiday Hotel
Honor Among Thieves
Horror Chamber of Dr.
    Faustus
The Horse of Pride
Hothead
Howling 2: Your Sister is a
    Werewolf
The Hurried Man
I Killed Rasputin
I Love All of You
I Sent a Letter to My Love
Icy Breasts
In the Realm of the Senses
Infernal Trio
The Invaders
Investigation
Invitation au Voyage
Is Paris Burning?
Istanbul
It Happened in the Park
It Means That to Me
Italian Straw Hat
J'Accuse
Jacko & Lise
Jailbird's Vacation
Je Tu Il Elle
Jean de Florette
Jenny Lamour
Jesus of Montreal
Josepha
Jour de Fete
Journey Beneath the Desert
Journey to the Lost City
The Joy of Knowledge
Judex
The Judge and the Assassin
Jules and Jim
Jupiter's Thigh
Just Another Pretty Face

Kapo
The Killing Game
The King of Hearts
The Klutz
La Balance
La Bete Humaine
La Boum
La Cage aux Folles
La Cage aux Folles 2
La Cage aux Folles 3: The
    Wedding
La Chevre
La Chienne
La Chute de la Maison Usher
La Femme Nikita
La Jetee/An Occurrence at
    Owl Creek Bridge
La Lectrice
La Marseillaise
La Nuit de Varennes
La Passante
La Petite Sirene
La Ronde
La Symphonie Pastorale
La Truite
La Vengeance d'une Femme
The Lacemaker
L'Addition
Lady Chatterley's Lover
L'Age D'Or
The Last Metro
Last Tango in Paris
The Last Winters
Last Year at Marienbad
L'Atalante
Le Bal
Le Beau Mariage
Le Beau Serge
Le Bonheur
Le Boucher
Le Bourgeois Gentilhomme
Le Cas du Dr. Laurent
Le Cavaleur
Le Chat
Le Complot
Le Corbeau
Le Crabe Tambour
Le Dernier Combat
Le Doulos
Le Gentleman D'Epsom
Le Grand Chemin
Le Joli Mai
Le Jour Se Leve
Le Magnifique
Le Million
Le Petit Amour
Le Plaisir
Le Repos du Guerrier
Le Secret
Le Sex Shop
L'Ecole Buisoniere
Leon Morin, Priest
Leonor
Les Assassins de L'Ordre
Les Biches
Les Carabiniers
Les Comperes
Les Enfants Terrible
Les Grandes Gueules
Les Miserables
Les Mistons
Les Rendez-vous D'Anna
Les Violons du Bal
Les Visiteurs du Soir
L'Etat Sauvage
Letters from My Windmill
Letters to an Unknown Lover
L'Homme Blesse
License to Kill
Life and Nothing But
Light Years
Liliom
The Little Thief
Little World of Don Camillo
Lola
Lola Montes

German

Italian

Sonny and Jed
Sonny Boy
Sotto, Sotto
Spaghetti House
A Special Day
The Spider's Stratagem
Spirits of the Dead
The Squeeze
Star Crash
Stateline Motel
The Station
The Stolen Children
The Story of Boys & Girls
Stranger in Paso Bravo
Stromboli
Submission
Summer Affair
Summer Night
Summer Night with Greek
  Profile, Almond Eyes &
  Scent of Basil
Superargo
Suspiria
Sweet Smell of Woman
Swept Away...
The Swindle
The Sword of El Cid
The Taming of the Shrew
The Tempter
Tentacles
10th Victim
Teorema
Teresa Venerdi
Terror Creatures from the
  Grave
Terror of Rome Against the
  Son of Hercules
Terror of the Steppes
They Call Me Trinity
Thief of Baghdad
Third Solution
Three Brothers
Throne of Fire
Thunder Warrior 2
Tiger of the Seven Seas
Tigers in Lipstick
Till Marriage Do Us Part
Time of Indifference
Time Out for Love
'Tis a Pity She's a Whore
To Forget Venice
Together
Torso
Torture Chamber of Baron
  Blood
The Tragedy of a Ridiculous
  Man
Tramplers
The Tree of Wooden Clogs
Trinity is Still My Name
Tristana
Triumph of the Son of
  Hercules
12 Plus 1
Twitch of the Death Nerve
Two Evil Eyes
Two Nights with Cleopatra
2020 Texas Gladiators
Two Women
Tyrant of Lydia Against the
  Son of Hercules
L'Udienza
Ulysses
Umberto D
Uncle Tom's Cabin
Unsane
Ursus in the Valley of the
  Lions
Vanina Vanini
Variety Lights
Venus Against the Son of
  Hercules
Verdi
A Very Old Man with
  Enormous Wings
Viking Massacre

The Violation of Laura
Violent Breed
Violent Professionals
The Virgin of Nuremberg
Volere Volare
The Wanton Contessa
War Bus Commando
War Victims
The Warning
Warriors of the Wasteland
Watch Me When I Kill
Waterloo
We All Loved Each Other So
  Much
We the Living
Web of the Spider
Wedding in Blood
Weekend
Werewolf in a Girl's Dormitory
When Women Had Tails
When Women Lost Their Tails
Where the Hot Wind Blows
Where's Piccone
White Nights
Wifemistress
Wild, Wild Planet
The Witch
A Woman of Rome
Woman Times Seven
Women in Cell Block 7
Women's Prison Massacre
The Wonders of Aladdin
Yesterday, Today and
  Tomorrow
Yor, the Hunter from the
  Future
Zombie

Japanese

The Adventures of Milo & Otis
Akira
Akira Kurosawa's Dreams
Antarctica
Attack of the Mushroom
  People
Attack Squadron
An Autumn Afternoon
Baby Cart 4: Heart of a
  Parent...Heart of a Child
The Bad Sleep Well
The Ballad of Narayama
The Battle of the Japan Sea
Black Lizard
Black Magic Terror
Black Rain
Body Snatcher from Hell
The Burmese Harp
The Bushido Blade
The Castle of Cagliostro
The Crucified Lovers
The Cruel Story of Youth
Crystal Triangle
The Day and the Hour
Dersu Uzala
Destroy All Monsters
Destroy All Planets
Dodes 'ka-den
Double Suicide
Drifting Weeds
Drunken Angel
Early Summer
Eijanaika
The Empire of Passion
Equinox Flower
Face of Another
The Family Game
Fires on the Plain
Forest of Little Bear
47 Ronin, Part 1
47 Ronin, Part 2
Fugitive Alien
The Funeral
Galaxy Express
The Gambling Samurai

Gamera, the Invincible
Gamera vs. Barugon
Gamera vs. Gaos
Gamera vs. Guiron
Gamera vs. Zigra
Gammera the Invincible
Gappa the Trifibian Monster
Gate of Hell
Ghidrah the Three Headed
  Monster
The Ghost of Yotsuya
The Go-Masters
Godzilla, King of the Monsters
Godzilla 1985
Godzilla on Monster Island
Godzilla Raids Again
Godzilla vs. Biollante
Godzilla vs. Gigan
Godzilla vs. Megalon
Godzilla vs. Monster Zero
Godzilla vs. Mothra
Godzilla vs. the Cosmic
  Monster
Godzilla vs. the Sea Monster
Godzilla vs. the Smog
  Monster
Godzilla's Revenge
Golden Demon
Gonza the Spearman
Gorath
Grave of the Fireflies
The Green Slime
H-Man
Half Human
Harmagedon
Heaven & Earth
The Hidden Fortress
High & Low
Himatsuri
Hiroshima, Mon Amour
Human Beasts
The Human Condition: A
  Soldier's Prayer
The Human Condition: No
  Greater Love
The Human Condition: Road
  to Eternity
The Human Vapor
Hunter in the Dark
I Give My All
I Live in Fear
Ikiru
The Imperial Japanese Empire
Imperial Navy
In the Realm of the Senses
The Insect Woman
Irezumi
The Island
Kagemusha
Kamikaze
King Kong Versus Godzilla
Kojiro
Kwaidan
Late Chrysanthemums
Late Spring
Life of Oharu
Love and Faith
The Lower Depths
MacArthur's Children
Madox-01
The Makioka Sisters
The Manster
The Men Who Tread on the
  Tiger's Tail
Merry Christmas, Mr.
  Lawrence
Mistress
Mother
Mothra
Murder in the Doll House
The Mysterians
Nanami, First Love
No Regrets for Our Youth
Nomugi Pass
Odd Obsession
One-Eyed Swordsman

Onibaba
Osaka Elegy
Phoenix
The Pornographers
Port Arthur
Princess Yang Kwei Fei
Proof of the Man
Ran
Rashomon
Red Beard
Red Lion
Revenge of a Kabuki Actor
Riding Bean
Rikisha-Man
Rikyu
Rodan
Saga of the Vagabond
Samurai 1: Musashi Miyamoto
Samurai 2: Duel at Ichijoji
  Temple
Samurai 3: Duel at Ganryu
  Island
Samurai Reincarnation
Sandakan No. 8
Sanjuro
Sanshiro Sugata
Sansho the Bailiff
Sea Prince and the Fire Child
The Secret of the Telegian
Seven Samurai
She and He
Shin Heike Monogatari
Shinobi Ninja
Shiokari Pass
Shogun Assassin
The Silk Road
Sisters of Gion
Snow Country
Son of Godzilla
Station
The Story of the Late
  Chrysanthemum
Stray Dog
Street of Shame
Summer Vacation: 1999
Sword of Doom
Sword of Fury I
Sword of Fury II
Sword of Heaven
Swords of Death
Tampopo
Tattooed Hit Man
A Taxing Woman
A Taxing Woman Returns
Terror Beneath the Sea
Terror of Mechagodzilla
Tetsuo: The Iron Man
Throne of Blood
Tidal Wave
Time of the Apes
Tokyo Olympiad
Tokyo Story
Traitors of the Blue Castle
Twenty-Four Eyes
Twilight of the Cockroaches
Ugetsu
The Ultimate Teacher
Urotsukidoji: Legend of the
  Overfiend
Urusei Yatsura 1: Only You
Urusei Yatsura 2: Beautiful
  Dreamer
Urusei Yatsura 3: Remember
  My Love
Varan the Unbelievable
Vengeance Is Mine
Violence at Noon
Virus
War in Space
War of the Gargantuas
Warning from Space
Warriors of the Wind
What's Up, Tiger Lily?
When a Woman Ascends the
  Stairs
The White Sheik

The Wolves
Woman in the Dunes
X from Outer Space
Yog, Monster from Space
Yojimbo
Zatoichi: Master Ichi and a
  Chest of Gold
Zatoichi: The Blind
  Swordsman and the Chess
  Expert
Zatoichi: The Blind
  Swordsman's Vengeance
Zatoichi vs. Yojimbo
Zero Pilot

Lithuanian

Adomas Nori Buti Zmogumi
Velnio Nuotaka (The Devil's
  Bride)

Mexican

Amenaza Nuclear
Anita de Montemar
Arizona
Attack of the Mayan Mummy
Bellas de Noche
Black Pit of Dr. M
The Bloody Vampire
The Brainiac
Bring Me the Vampire
The Brute
By Hook or Crook
Caches de Oro
Calacan
Camelia
Children of Sanchez
Con Mi Mujer No Puedo
Conexion Mexico
Conquest
The Craving
Creature of the Walking Dead
The Criminal Life of
  Archibaldo de la Cruz
Crossfire
The Curse of the Aztec
  Mummy
The Curse of the Crying
  Woman
Curse of the Devil
Curse of the Stone Hand
Dance of Death
Despedida de Casada
Diamante, Oro y Amor
Dona Herlinda & Her Son
Dos Esposas en Mi Cama
Dos Postolas Gemelas
El
El Ametralladora
El Aviador Fenomeno
El Aviso Inoportuno
El Bruto
El Ceniciento
El Ciclon
El Cuarto Chino
El Derecho de Comer
El Fin del Tahur
El Forastero Vengador
El Fugitivo
El Gallo de Oro
El Gavilan Pollero
El Gendarme Desconocido
El Hombre Contra el Mundo
El Hombre de la Furia
El Libro de Piedra
El Mariachi
El Penon de las Animas
El Profesor Hippie
El Rey
El Robo al Tren Correo
El Sabor de la Venganza
El Tesoro de Chucho el Roto
El Zorro Blanco
El Zorro Vengador

Emiliano Zapata
Emilio Varela vs. Camelia La
  Texana
Erendira
The Exterminating Angel
Face of the Screaming
  Werewolf
The Fear Chamber
Fearmaker
Fever Mounts at El Pao
Flor Silvestre
Foxtrot
Frontera Sin Ley
Garbancito de la Mancha
Genie of Darkness
Gente Violenta
The Great Madcap
Guitarras Lloren Guitarras
Guns for Dollars
Hay Muertos Que No Hacen
  Ruido
House of Evil
The Illusion Travels by
  Streetcar
Invasion of the Vampires
Invasion of the Zombies
Jungle Warriors
Justicia para los Mexicanos
La Bella Lola
La Carcel de Laredo
La Casa de Madame Lulu
La Casa del Amor
La Chamuscada
La Choca
La Corona de un Campeon
La Diosa Arrodillada
La Fuerza Inutil
La Fuga del Rojo
La Generala
La Hlfa Sin Padre
La Justicia Tiene Doce Anos
La Mansion de la Locura
La Marchanta
La Mentira
La Montana del Diablo
La Pachange
La Trinchera
La Venganza del Kung Fu
La Venganza del Rojo
Lagrimas de Amor
Las Doce Patadas Mortales
  del Kung Fu
Like Water for Chocolate
The Living Coffin
The Living Head
Los Amores de Marieta
Los Apuros de Dos Gallos
Los Asesinos
Los Caciques
Los Cacos
Los Caifanes
Los Dos Hermanos
Los Hermanos Centella
Los Hermanos Diablo
Los Olvidados
Los Sheriffs de la Frontera
Los Tres Amores de Losa
Los Tres Calaveras
Los Vampiros de Coyacan
Macario
The Man and the Monster
Manos Torpes
Marcados por el Destino
Maria
Maria Candelaria
Mariachi
Mexican Bus Ride
Mision Suicida
Misterios de Ultratumba
The Monster Demolisher
Murderer in the Hotel
Musico, Poeta y Loco
Narda or The Summer
Nazarin
The Neighborhood Thief
Neutron and the Black Mask

Neutron vs. the Amazing Dr.
  Caronte
Neutron vs. the Death Robots
Neutron vs. the Maniac
The New Invisible Man
Ni Chana Ni Juana
Nido de Aguilas
Night of a Thousand Cats
Night of the Bloody Apes
Nosotros
Orlak, the Hell of Frankenstein
Pancho Villa Returns
Para Servir a Usted
Patsy, Mi Amor
The Pearl
The Robot vs. the Aztec
  Mummy
Samson in the Wax Museum
Samson vs. the Vampire
  Women
Santa Claus
Santa Sangre
Savagel
Semaforo en Rojo
Sexo Y Crimen
Siempre Hay una Primera Vez
Simon Blanco
Sin Salida
The Sinister Invasion
Sisters of Satan
The Snake People
Somos Novios
Soy un Golfo
Spiritism
Susana
Swamp of the Lost Monster
Tacos al Carbon
Target Eagle
Temporada Salvaje
Thor el Conquistador
Tintorera...Tiger Shark
Torero
The Treasure of the Amazon
Triumphs of a Man Called
  Horse
The Vampire
The Vampire's Coffin
Viridiana
Viva Chihuahua (Long Live
  Chihuahua)
Vivo o Muerto
Warlook Moon
Witches' Mountain
The Witch's Mirror
A Woman Without Love
World of the Vampires
Wrestling Women vs. the
  Aztec Ape
Wrestling Women vs. the
  Aztec Mummy
Wuthering Heights
Y Donde Esta el Muerto?
  (And... Where Is the Dead)
Yanco

New Zealand

Among the Cinders
An Angel at My Table
Bad Blood
Bad Taste
Beyond Reasonable Doubt
The Bridge to Nowhere
Came a Hot Friday
Dangerous Orphans
Dark of the Night
Goodbye Pork Pie
Heart of the Stag
Hot Target
Iris
Mesmerized
Nate and Hayes
The Navigator
Never Say Die
Nutcase

The Quiet Earth
Race to the Yankee Zephyr
Second Time Lucky
Shaker Run
The Silent One
Sleeping Dogs
Smash Palace
Starlight Hotel
Sylvia
Tearaway
Utu
Vigil
Wild Horses

Nicaraguan

Alsino and the Condor

Norwegian

One Day in the Life of Ivan
  Denisovich
Pathfinder
Shipwrecked

Polish

Ashes and Diamonds
Baritone
Border Street
A Brivele der Marnen
Casimir the Great
Colonel Wolodyjowski
Danton
Der Purimshpiel
Dr. Judym
The Double Life of Veronique
The Dybbuk
Enigma Secret
Fever
First Spaceship on Venus
Foul Play
A Generation
Greta
Hands Up
Hero of the Year
In an Old Manor House
In Desert and Wilderness
The Interrogation
Kanal
Karate Polish Style
Knife in the Water
Leper
Mamele
Man of Marble
Moonlighting
Mother of Kings
Nights and Days
Paper Marriage
The Peasants
Pharaoh
The Singing Blacksmith
Train to Hollywood
The Unapproachable
W Hour
Without Love
A Woman and a Woman
Year of the Quiet Sun
Yidl Mitn Fidl

Portuguese

Black Orpheus
In the White City
Life is Beautiful
Return of the Evil Dead
Tombs of the Blind Dead

Russian

Adomas Nori Buti Zmogumi
Aelita: Queen of Mars
Alexander Nevsky
The Amphibian Man
Andrei Rublev

Arsenal
Autumn Marathon
Ballad of a Soldier
Baltic Deputy
The Battleship Potemkin
Bed and Sofa
Burglar
Chapayev
The Cigarette Girl of
  Mosselprom
Come and See
Commissar
The Cranes are Flying
Crime and Punishment
The Day the Earth Froze
Dersu Uzala
Don Quixote
Early Russian Cinema, Vol. 1:
  Beginnings
Early Russian Cinema, Vol. 2:
  Folklore & Legend
Early Russian Cinema, Vol. 3:
  Starewicz's Fantasies
Early Russian Cinema, Vol. 4:
  Provinoial Variations
Early Russian Cinema, Vol. 5:
  Chardynin's Pushkin
Early Russian Cinema, Vol. 6:
  Class Distinctions
Early Russian Cinema, Vol. 7:
  Evgenii Bauer
Early Russian Cinema, Vol. 8:
  Iakov Protazanov
Early Russian Cinema, Vol. 9:
  High Society
Early Russian Cinema, Vol.
  10: The End of an Era
Earth
A Forgotten Tune for the Flute
Freedom is Paradise
Freeze-Die-Come to Life
Fury is a Woman
The General Line
The Girl with the Hat Box
The Golem
Guerilla Brigade
Happiness
Incident at Map-Grid 36-80
The Inspector General
Ivan the Terrible, Part 1
Ivan the Terrible, Part 2
Jazzman
Kindergarten
Kino Pravda/Enthusiasm
The Lady with the Dog
The Legend of Suram
  Fortress
Little Vera
The Magic Voyage of Sinbad
The Man with a Movie Camera
The Mirror
Moscow Does Not Believe in
  Tears
Mother
My Apprenticeship
My Childhood
My Name is Ivan
My Universities
No Greater Love
Oblomov
October
The Overcoat
The Patriots
Peter the First: Part 1
Peter the First: Part 2
Planet Burg
Private Life
Que Viva Mexico
Rasputin
Repentance
Shadows of Forgotten
  Ancestors
Sideburns
A Slave of Love
Solaris
Solo Voyage: The Revenge

Stalker
Storm Over Asia
Strike
A Summer to Remember
Sword & the Dragon
Taxi Blues
The Tsar's Bride
An Unfinished Piece for a
  Player Piano
War and Peace
Waterloo
Zvenigora

South African

African Rage
City of Blood
Deadly Passion
Emissary
The Evil Below
House of the Living Dead
Kill Slade
Place of Weeping
Stay Awake

Spanish

Anguish
Any Gun Can Play
Attack of the Robots
Autopsy of a Ghost
Ay, Carmela!
Bad Man's River
Benjamin Argumedo
Bestia Nocturna
Black Beauty
The Black Pirate
The Blood Spattered Bride
Blood Wedding
Brandy Sheriff
Bromas S.A.
Brujo Luna
Bullet for Sandoval
Cada Noche un Amor
Camila
Cancion en el Alma
Carmen
The Castle of Fu Manchu
Cauldron of Blood
Chimes at Midnight
The Christmas Kid
The City and the Dogs
City of the Walking Dead
Como Dos Gotas de Agua
Conquest
Count Dracula
Cria
The Criminal Life of
  Archibaldo de la Cruz
Curse of the Devil
Danzon
Dark Habits
Dawn of the Pirates
Demons in the Garden
Departamento Compartido
Desde el Abismo
Desperados
Details of a Duel: A Question
  of Honor
The Devil's Possessed
The Diabolical Dr. Z
Dias de Ilusion
Dr. Jekyll and the Wolfman
Dr. Orloff's Monster
Don Juan, My Love
Don Quixote
Donde Duermen
  Dos...Duermen Tres
Dos Chicas de Revista
Dracula vs. Frankenstein
Dracula's Great Love
Duel of Champions
Duelo en el Dorado
El Barbaro
El Cochecito

Spanish

El Condor
El Cristo de los Milagros
El Diputado
El Muerto
El Norte
El Preprimido
El Super
El: This Strange Passion
Endless Descent
Escape from El Diablo
Esposa y Amante
Esta Noche Cena Pancho
Exorcism's Daughter
Expertos en Pinchazos
The Exterminating Angel
Exterminators of the Year 3000
The Fable of the Beautiful Pigeon Fancier
Fangs of the Living Dead
Fin de Fiesta
Fotografo de Senoras
Frida
From Hell to Victory
Frontera
Fuerte Perdido
Furia Pasional
The Fury of the Wolfman
The Garden of Delights
Garringo
Gemidos de Placer
Gladiators 7
Goliath Against the Giants
Gran Valor en la Facultad de Medicina
Grandes Amigos (Great Friends)
Graveyard of Horror
Great Adventure
The Green Wall
Half of Heaven
The Hanging Woman
Hatchet for the Honeymoon
Hawk of the Caribbean
Hellbenders
High Heels
The Holy Innocents
Honey
Horror Express
Horror of the Zombies
Horror Rises from the Tomb
The House of 1000 Dolls
House of Psychotic Women
Human Beasts
The Hunt
I'm the One You're Looking For
In a Glass Cage
In Memoriam
Inquisition
The Invincible Gladiator
It Happened at Nightmare Inn
Johnny Barrows, El Malo
Jornada de Muerte
Kashmiri Run
King of Kong Island
La Hija del General
La Hora 24
La Ley del Revolver
La Nueva Cigarra
La Red del Egano
La Virgen de Guadalupe
Labyrinth of Passion
Last Day of the War
The Last Supper
Law of Desire
The Legend of Blood Castle
Leonor
Letters from the Park
Lightning Bolt
The Lion's Share
Los Hombres Piensan Solo en Solo
Lovers: A True Story
Mama Turns a Hundred
Man of Legend

The Man Who Wagged His Tail
Marianela
Matador
Mayalunta
Miracle in Rome
Mission Stardust
Mr. Superinvisible
The Mummy's Revenge
Murder Mansion
Navajo Joe
The Nest
Night of the Death Cult
Night of the Howling Beast
Night of the Zombies
99 Women
Oasis of the Zombies
On the Line
Orgy of the Vampires
Pancho Villa
Passion for Power
Pepi, Luci, Bom and Other Girls on the Heap
Pieces
Princess Cinderella
Pulsebeat
Red Sun
Return of the Evil Dead
Ricco
The Rue Morgue Massacres
The Saga of the Draculas
Satanik
Savage Island
The Scarlet Letter
The Scorpion's Tail
The Screaming Dead
The Sea Serpent
Skyline
Son of Captain Blood
Sound of Horror
Spirit of the Beehive
The Stilts
Stormquest
The Summer of Miss Forbes
Superargo
Supersonic Man
The Sword of El Cid
Target Eagle
That Obscure Object of Desire
Tie Me Up! Tie Me Down!
Tombs of the Blind Dead
A Town Called Hell
Treasure of the Four Crowns
Tristana
Una Vez en la Vida
Under the Earth
Under the Sheets
The Uprising
Ursus in the Valley of the Lions
Vengeance of the Zombies
A Very Old Man with Enormous Wings
The Violation of Laura
Virgin Among the Living Dead
Viridiana
The Werewolf vs. the Vampire Woman
When the Screaming Stops
A Witch Without a Broom
Women on the Verge of a Nervous Breakdown
Yellow Hair & the Fortress of Gold
Zombie Lake

Swedish

The Adventures of Picasso
After the Rehearsal
The Assignment
The Atonement of Gosta Berling
Autumn Sonata
Brink of Life

The Count of the Old Town
Cries and Whispers
The Devil's Eye
Devil's Wanton
The Doll
Dollar
Dreams
Elvira Madigan
Face to Face
Fanny and Alexander
Flight of the Eagle
From the Life of the Marionettes
Gorilla
The Great Adventure
Hour of the Wolf
I Am Curious (Yellow)
Inga
The Inside Man
Intermezzo
Invasion of the Animal People
Istanbul
June Night
Killing Heat
Lesson in Love
The Magic Flute
The Magician
Maid in Sweden
The Match Factory Girl
Miss Julie
Monika
Montenegro
The Mozart Brothers
My Life as a Dog
Night Is My Future
Ninja Mission
Only One Night
The Outlaw and His Wife
The Ox
The Passion of Anna
Pelle the Conqueror
Persona
The Phantom Chariot
Pippi Goes on Board
Pippi in the South Seas
Pippi Longstocking
Pippi on the Run
Port of Call
The Sacrifice
Sawdust & Tinsel
Scenes from a Marriage
Secrets of Women
The Seventh Seal
The Shame
The Silence
Smiles of a Summer Night
Summer Interlude
Swedenhielms
Thomas Graal's Best Film
Three Strange Loves
Through a Glass Darkly
To Joy
Torment
The Touch
Treasure of Arne
Unmarried Mothers
The Virgin Spring
The Visitors
Walpurgis Night
Wardogs
Wild Strawberries
The Winter Light
Witchcraft Through the Ages
A Woman's Face

Swiss

After Darkness
Alpine Fire
Big Bluff
The Boat is Full
Candy Mountain
The Castle
Chimes at Midnight
Dangerous Moves

Drachenfutter
A Dream of Passion
First Love
Foxtrot
Hail Mary
Heidi
In the White City
Jonah Who Will Be 25 in the Year 2000
Journey of Hope
King Lear
The Lacemaker
Nouvelle Vague
The Pedestrian

Taiwanese

The Association
The Outcasts

Turkish

Baba
The Horse
Istanbul
Midnight Express
The Wall
Yol

Yugoslavian

The Battle of Austerlitz
Battle of Neretva
Battleforce
Cave of the Living Dead
The Great Battle
Guns of War
Hey, Babu Riba
Innocence Unprotected
Kapo
The Love Affair, or The Case of the Missing Switchboard Operator
Man is Not a Bird
One-Eyed Soldiers
Operation Cross Eagles
Romance of a Horsethief
The She-Beast
Son of Samson
Stealing Heaven
Sweet Movie
Time of the Gypsies
Track of the Vampire
Uncle Tom's Cabin
Ward Six
When Father was Away on Business

The **AWARDS INDEX** lists 2,000 films honored by 12 national and international award bodies, representing some 90 categories of competition. This information is also contained in the review following the credits. **Only features available on video and reviewed in the main section are listed in this index; movies not yet released on video are not covered.** As award-winning films find their way to video, they will be added to the review section and covered in this index. The awards covered include:

American Academy Awards
Australia Film Institute
British Academy of Film
and Television Arts
Cannes Film Festival

French Cesar
Canadian Genie
Golden Globe
Directors Guild of America
Edgar Allan Poe Awards

Independent Spirit
Montreal Film Festival
MTV Movie Awards

ACADEMY AWARDS

ACTOR

1928
Emil Jannings
Last Command

1930
George Arliss
Disraeli

1931
Lionel Barrymore
A Free Soul

1932
Wallace Beery
The Champ
Fredric March
Dr. Jekyll and Mr. Hyde

1933
Charles Laughton
The Private Life of Henry VIII

1934
Clark Gable
It Happened One Night

1935
Victor McLaglen
The Informer

1936
Paul Muni
The Story of Louis Pasteur

1937
Spencer Tracy
Captains Courageous

1938
Spencer Tracy
Boys Town

1939
Robert Donat
Goodbye, Mr. Chips

1940
James Stewart
The Philadelphia Story

1941
Gary Cooper
Sergeant York

1942
James Cagney
Yankee Doodle Dandy

1943
Paul Lukas
Watch on the Rhine

1944
Bing Crosby
Going My Way

1945
Ray Milland
The Lost Weekend

1946
Fredric March
The Best Years of Our Lives

1947
Ronald Colman
A Double Life

1948
Laurence Olivier
Hamlet

1949
Broderick Crawford
All the King's Men

1950
Jose Ferrer
Cyrano de Bergerac

1951
Humphrey Bogart
The African Queen

1952
Gary Cooper
High Noon

1953
William Holden
Stalag 17

1954
Marlon Brando
On the Waterfront

1955
Ernest Borgnine
Marty

1956
Yul Brynner
The King and I

1957
Alec Guinness
The Bridge on the River Kwai

1958
David Niven
Separate Tables

1959
Charlton Heston
Ben-Hur

1960
Burt Lancaster
Elmer Gantry

1961
Maximilian Schell
Judgment at Nuremberg

1962
Gregory Peck
To Kill a Mockingbird

1963
Sidney Poitier
Lilies of the Field

1964
Rex Harrison
My Fair Lady

1965
Lee Marvin
Cat Ballou

1966
Paul Scofield
A Man for All Seasons

1967
Rod Steiger
In the Heat of the Night

1968
Cliff Robertson
Charly

1969
John Wayne
True Grit

1970
George C. Scott
Patton

1971
Gene Hackman
The French Connection

1972
Marlon Brando
The Godfather

1973
Jack Lemmon
Save the Tiger

1974
Art Carney
Harry and Tonto

1975
Jack Nicholson
One Flew Over the Cuckoo's Nest

1976
Peter Finch
Network

1977
Richard Dreyfuss
The Goodbye Girl

1978
Jon Voight
Coming Home

1979
Dustin Hoffman
Kramer vs. Kramer

1980
Robert De Niro
Raging Bull

1981
Henry Fonda
On Golden Pond

1982
Ben Kingsley
Gandhi

1983
Robert Duvall
Tender Mercies

1984
F. Murray Abraham
Amadeus

1985
William Hurt
Kiss of the Spider Woman

1986
Paul Newman
The Color of Money

1987
Michael Douglas
Wall Street

1988
Dustin Hoffman
Rain Man

1989
Daniel Day-Lewis
My Left Foot

1990
Jeremy Irons
Reversal of Fortune

1991
Anthony Hopkins
The Silence of the Lambs

1992
Al Pacino
Scent of a Woman

ACTOR— SUPPORTING

1936
Walter Brennan
Come and Get It

1937
Joseph Schildkraut
The Life of Emile Zola

1939
Thomas Mitchell
Stagecoach

1940
Walter Brennan
The Westerner

1941
Donald Crisp
How Green was My Valley

1942
Van Heflin
Johnny Eager

1943
Charles Coburn
The More the Merrier

ACTOR— SUPPORTING
▶cont.

1944
Barry Fitzgerald
Going My Way

1945
James Dunn
A Tree Grows in Brooklyn

1946
Harold Russell
The Best Years of Our Lives

1947
Edmund Gwenn
Miracle on 34th Street

1948
Walter Huston
Treasure of the Sierra Madre

1949
Dean Jagger
Twelve O'Clock High

1950
George Sanders
All About Eve

1951
Karl Malden
A Streetcar Named Desire

1952
Anthony Quinn
Viva Zapata!

1953
Frank Sinatra
From Here to Eternity

1954
Edmond O'Brien
The Barefoot Contessa

1955
Jack Lemmon
Mister Roberts

1956
Anthony Quinn
Lust for Life

1957
Red Buttons
Sayonara

1958
Burl Ives
Big Country

1959
Hugh Griffith
Ben-Hur

1960
Peter Ustinov
Spartacus

1961
George Chakiris
West Side Story

1962
Ed Begley, Sr.
Sweet Bird of Youth

1963
Melvyn Douglas
Hud

1964
Peter Ustinov
Topkapi

1965
Martin Balsam
A Thousand Clowns

1966
Walter Matthau
The Fortune Cookie

1967
George Kennedy
Cool Hand Luke

1969
Gig Young
They Shoot Horses, Don't They?

1970
John Mills
Ryan's Daughter

1971
Ben Johnson
The Last Picture Show

1972
Joel Grey
Cabaret

1973
John Houseman
The Paper Chase

1974
Robert De Niro
The Godfather, Part 2

1975
George Burns
The Sunshine Boys

1976
Jason Robards, Jr.
All the President's Men

1977
Jason Robards, Jr.
Julia

1978
Christopher Walken
The Deer Hunter

1980
Timothy Hutton
Ordinary People

1981
John Gielgud
Arthur

1982
Louis Gossett, Jr.
An Officer and a Gentleman

1983
Jack Nicholson
Terms of Endearment

1984
Haing S. Ngor
The Killing Fields

1985
Don Ameche
Cocoon

1986
Michael Caine
Hannah and Her Sisters

1987
Sean Connery
The Untouchables

1988
Kevin Kline
A Fish Called Wanda

1989
Denzel Washington
Glory

1990
Joe Pesci
Goodfellas

1991
Jack Palance
City Slickers

1992
Gene Hackman
Unforgiven

ACTRESS

1928
Janet Gaynor
Sunrise

1929
Mary Pickford
Coquette

1930
Norma Shearer
The Divorcee

1931
Marie Dressler
Min & Bill

1932
Helen Hayes
The Sin of Madelon Claudet

1933
Katharine Hepburn
Morning Glory

1934
Claudette Colbert
It Happened One Night

1935
Bette Davis
Dangerous

1936
Luise Rainer
The Great Ziegfeld

1937
Luise Rainer
The Good Earth

1938
Bette Davis
Jezebel

1939
Vivien Leigh
Gone with the Wind

1940
Ginger Rogers
Kitty Foyle

1941
Joan Fontaine
Suspicion

1942
Greer Garson
Mrs. Miniver

1943
Jennifer Jones
The Song of Bernadette

1944
Ingrid Bergman
Gaslight

1945
Joan Crawford
Mildred Pierce

1947
Loretta Young
The Farmer's Daughter

1948
Jane Wyman
Johnny Belinda

1949
Olivia de Havilland
The Heiress

1950
Judy Holliday
Born Yesterday

1951
Vivien Leigh
A Streetcar Named Desire

1952
Shirley Booth
Come Back, Little Sheba

1953
Audrey Hepburn
Roman Holiday

1954
Grace Kelly
Country Girl

1955
Anna Magnani
The Rose Tattoo

1956
Ingrid Bergman
Anastasia

1957
Joanne Woodward
The Three Faces of Eve

1958
Susan Hayward
I Want to Live!

1959
Simone Signoret
Room at the Top

1960
Elizabeth Taylor
Butterfield 8

1961
Sophia Loren
Two Women

1962
Anne Bancroft
The Miracle Worker

1963
Patricia Neal
Hud

1964
Julie Andrews
Mary Poppins

1965
Julie Christie
Darling

1966
Elizabeth Taylor
Who's Afraid of Virginia Woolf?

1967
Katharine Hepburn
Guess Who's Coming to Dinner

1968
Barbra Streisand
Funny Girl
Katharine Hepburn
The Lion in Winter

1969
Maggie Smith
The Prime of Miss Jean Brodie

1970
Glenda Jackson
Women in Love

1971
Jane Fonda
Klute

1972
Liza Minnelli
Cabaret

1973
Glenda Jackson
A Touch of Class

1974
Ellen Burstyn
Alice Doesn't Live Here Anymore

1975
Louise Fletcher
One Flew Over the Cuckoo's Nest

1976
Faye Dunaway
Network

1977
Diane Keaton
Annie Hall

1978
Jane Fonda
Coming Home

1979
Sally Field
Norma Rae

1980
Sissy Spacek
Coal Miner's Daughter

1981
Katharine Hepburn
On Golden Pond

1982
Meryl Streep
Sophie's Choice

1983
Shirley MacLaine
Terms of Endearment

1984
Sally Field
Places in the Heart

1985
Geraldine Page
The Trip to Bountiful

1986
Marlee Matlin
Children of a Lesser God

1987
Cher
Moonstruck

1988
Jodie Foster
The Accused

1989
Jessica Tandy
Driving Miss Daisy

1990
Kathy Bates
Misery

1991
Jodie Foster
The Silence of the Lambs

1992
Emma Thompson
Howard's End

ACTRESS— SUPPORTING

1936
Gale Sondergaard
Anthony Adverse

1938
Fay Bainter
Jezebel

1939
Hattie McDaniel
Gone with the Wind

1940
Jane Darwell
The Grapes of Wrath

1941
Mary Astor
The Great Lie

1942
Teresa Wright
Mrs. Miniver

1944
Ethel Barrymore
None But the Lonely Heart

1945
Anne Revere
National Velvet

1946
Anne Baxter
The Razor's Edge

1947
Celeste Holm
Gentleman's Agreement

1948
Claire Trevor
Key Largo

1949
Mercedes McCambridge
All the King's Men

1950
Josephine Hull
Harvey

1951
Kim Hunter
A Streetcar Named Desire

1952
Gloria Grahame
The Bad and the Beautiful

1953
Donna Reed
From Here to Eternity

1954
Eva Marie Saint
On the Waterfront

1955
Jo Van Fleet
East of Eden

1956
Dorothy Malone
Written on the Wind

1957
Miyoshi Umeki
Sayonara

1958
Wendy Hiller
Separate Tables

1959
Shelley Winters
The Diary of Anne Frank

1960
Shirley Jones
Elmer Gantry

1961
Rita Moreno
West Side Story

1962
Patty Duke
The Miracle Worker

1963
Margaret Rutherford
The V.I.P.'s

1964
Lila Kedrova
Zorba the Greek

1965
Shelley Winters
A Patch of Blue

1966
Sandy Dennis
Who's Afraid of Virginia Woolf?

1967
Estelle Parsons
Bonnie & Clyde

1968
Ruth Gordon
Rosemary's Baby

1969
Goldie Hawn
Cactus Flower

1970
Helen Hayes
Airport

1971
Cloris Leachman
The Last Picture Show

1972
Eileen Heckart
Butterflies Are Free

1973
Tatum O'Neal
Paper Moon

1974
Ingrid Bergman
Murder on the Orient Express

1975
Lee Grant
Shampoo

1976
Beatrice Straight
Network

1977
Vanessa Redgrave
Julia

1978
Maggie Smith
California Suite

1979
Meryl Streep
Kramer vs. Kramer

1980
Mary Steenburgen
Melvin and Howard

1981
Maureen Stapleton
Reds

1982
Jessica Lange
Tootsie

1983
Linda Hunt
The Year of Living Dangerously

1984
Peggy Ashcroft
A Passage to India

1985
Anjelica Huston
Prizzi's Honor

1986
Dianne Wiest
Hannah and Her Sisters

1987
Olympia Dukakis
Moonstruck

1988
Geena Davis
The Accidental Tourist

1989
Brenda Fricker
My Left Foot

1990
Whoopi Goldberg
Ghost

1991
Mercedes Ruehl
The Fisher King

1992
Marisa Tomei
My Cousin Vinny

ART DIRECTION

1957
Sayonara

1958
Gigi

1967
Camelot

1968
Oliver!

1969
Hello, Dolly!

1970
Patton

1971
Nicholas and Alexandra

1972
Cabaret

1973
The Sting

1974
The Godfather, Part 2

1975
Barry Lyndon

1976
All the President's Men

1977
Star Wars

1978
Heaven Can Wait

1979
All That Jazz

1980
Tess

1981
Raiders of the Lost Ark

1982
Gandhi

1983
Fanny and Alexander

1984
Amadeus

1985
Out of Africa

1986
A Room with a View

1987
The Last Emperor

1988
Dangerous Liaisons

1989
Batman

1990
Dick Tracy

1991
Bugsy

1992
Howard's End

ART DIRECTION (B & W)

1947
Great Expectations

1948
Hamlet

1949
The Heiress

1950
Sunset Boulevard

1951
A Streetcar Named Desire

1952
The Bad and the Beautiful

1953
Julius Caesar

1954
On the Waterfront

1955
The Rose Tattoo

1956
Somebody Up There Likes Me

1959
The Diary of Anne Frank

1960
The Apartment

1961
The Hustler

1962
To Kill a Mockingbird

1964
Zorba the Greek

1965
Ship of Fools

1966
Who's Afraid of Virginia Woolf?

ART DIRECTION (COLOR)

1947
Black Narcissus

1948
The Red Shoes

1949
Little Women

1950
Samson and Delilah

1951
An American in Paris

1952
Moulin Rouge

1953
The Robe

1954
20,000 Leagues Under the Sea

1955
Picnic

1956
The King and I

1959
Ben-Hur

1960
Spartacus

1961
West Side Story

1962
Lawrence of Arabia

1963
Cleopatra

1964
My Fair Lady

1965
Doctor Zhivago

1966
Fantastic Voyage

CINEMATOGRAPHY

1928
Sunrise

1931
Tabu: A Story of the South Seas

1933
A Farewell to Arms

1934
Cleopatra

1935
A Midsummer Night's Dream

1936
Anthony Adverse

1937
The Good Earth

1967
Bonnie & Clyde

1968
Romeo and Juliet

1969
Butch Cassidy and the Sundance Kid

1970
Ryan's Daughter

1971
Fiddler on the Roof

1972
Cabaret

1973
Cries and Whispers

1974
The Towering Inferno

CINEMATOGRAPHY
▶cont.

1975
Barry Lyndon

1976
Bound for Glory

1977
Close Encounters of the Third Kind

1978
Days of Heaven

1979
Apocalypse Now

1980
Tess

1981
Reds

1982
Gandhi

1983
Fanny and Alexander

1984
The Killing Fields

1985
Out of Africa

1986
The Mission

1987
The Last Emperor

1988
Mississippi Burning

1989
Glory

1990
Dances with Wolves

1991
JFK

1992
A River Runs Through It

CINEMATOGRAPHY (B & W)

1939
Wuthering Heights

1940
Rebecca

1941
How Green was My Valley

1942
Mrs. Miniver

1943
The Song of Bernadette

1944
Laura

1945
Picture of Dorian Gray

1947
Great Expectations

1948
The Naked City

1949
Battleground

1950
The Third Man

1951
A Place in the Sun

1952
The Bad and the Beautiful

1953
From Here to Eternity

1954
On the Waterfront

1955
The Rose Tattoo

1956
Somebody Up There Likes Me

1958
The Defiant Ones

1959
The Diary of Anne Frank

1961
The Hustler

1962
The Longest Day

1963
Hud

1964
Zorba the Greek

1965
Ship of Fools

1966
Who's Afraid of Virginia Woolf?

CINEMATOGRAPHY (COLOR)

1939
Gone with the Wind

1941
Blood and Sand

1943
Phantom of the Opera

1944
Wilson

1946
The Yearling

1947
Black Narcissus

1948
Joan of Arc

1949
She Wore a Yellow Ribbon

1950
King Solomon's Mines

1951
An American in Paris

1952
The Quiet Man

1953
Shane

1954
Three Coins in the Fountain

1955
To Catch a Thief

1956
Around the World in 80 Days

1957
The Bridge on the River Kwai

1958
Gigi

1959
Ben-Hur

1960
Spartacus

1961
West Side Story

1962
Lawrence of Arabia

1963
Cleopatra

1964
My Fair Lady

1965
Doctor Zhivago

1966
A Man for All Seasons

COSTUME DESIGN

1948
Joan of Arc

1957
Les Girls

1958
Gigi

1967
Camelot

1968
Romeo and Juliet

1969
Anne of the Thousand Days

1970
Cromwell

1971
Nicholas and Alexandra

1972
Travels with My Aunt

1973
The Sting

1974
The Great Gatsby

1975
Barry Lyndon

1977
Star Wars

1978
Death on the Nile

1979
All That Jazz

1980
Tess

1981
Chariots of Fire

1982
Gandhi

1983
Fanny and Alexander

1984
Amadeus

1985
Ran

1986
A Room with a View

1987
The Last Emperor

1988
Dangerous Liaisons

1989
Henry V

1990
Cyrano de Bergerac

1991
Bugsy

1992
Bram Stoker's Dracula

COSTUME DESIGN (B & W)

1948
Hamlet

1949
The Heiress

1951
A Place in the Sun

1952
The Bad and the Beautiful

1953
Roman Holiday

1954
Sabrina

1955
I'll Cry Tomorrow

1959
Some Like It Hot

1961
La Dolce Vita

1963
8 1/2

1964
The Night of the Iguana

1965
Darling

1966
Who's Afraid of Virginia Woolf?

COSTUME DESIGN (COLOR)

1949
Adventures of Don Juan

1950
Samson and Delilah

1951
An American in Paris

1952
Moulin Rouge

1953
The Robe

1954
Gate of Hell

1955
Love is a Many-Splendored Thing

1956
The King and I

1959
Ben-Hur

1960
Spartacus

1961
West Side Story

1962
The Wonderful World of the Brothers Grimm

1963
Cleopatra

1964
My Fair Lady

1965
Doctor Zhivago

1966
A Man for All Seasons

DIRECTOR

1930
Lewis Milestone
All Quiet on the Western Front

1933
Frank Lloyd
Cavalcade

1934
Frank Capra
It Happened One Night

1935
John Ford
The Informer

1936
Frank Capra
Mr. Deeds Goes to Town

1937
Leo McCarey
The Awful Truth

1938
Frank Capra
You Can't Take It with You

1939
Victor Fleming
Gone with the Wind

1940
John Ford
The Grapes of Wrath

1941
John Ford
How Green was My Valley

1942
William Wyler
Mrs. Miniver

1943
Michael Curtiz
Casablanca

1944
Leo McCarey
Going My Way

1945
Billy Wilder
The Lost Weekend

1946
William Wyler
The Best Years of Our Lives

1947
Elia Kazan
Gentleman's Agreement

1948
John Huston
Treasure of the Sierra Madre

1949
Joseph L. Mankiewicz
A Letter to Three Wives

1950
Joseph L. Mankiewicz
All About Eve

1951
George Stevens
A Place in the Sun

1952
John Ford
The Quiet Man

1953
Fred Zinneman
From Here to Eternity

1954
Elia Kazan
On the Waterfront

1955
Delbert Mann
Marty

1956
George Stevens
Giant

1957
David Lean
The Bridge on the River Kwai

1958
Vincente Minnelli
Gigi

1959
William Wyler
Ben-Hur

1960
Billy Wilder
The Apartment

1961
Robert Wise
West Side Story

1962
David Lean
Lawrence of Arabia

1963
Tony Richardson
Tom Jones

1964
George Cukor
My Fair Lady

1965
Robert Wise
The Sound of Music

1966
Fred Zinneman
A Man for All Seasons

1967
Mike Nichols
The Graduate

1968
Carol Reed
Oliver!

1969
John Schlesinger
Midnight Cowboy

1970
Franklin J. Schaffner
Patton

1971
William Friedkin
The French Connection

1972
Bob Fosse
Cabaret

1973
George Roy Hill
The Sting

1974
Francis Ford Coppola
The Godfather, Part 2

1975
Milos Forman
One Flew Over the Cuckoo's Nest

1976
John G. Avildsen
Rocky

1977
Woody Allen
Annie Hall

1978
Michael Cimino
The Deer Hunter

1979
Robert Benton
Kramer vs. Kramer

1980
Robert Redford
Ordinary People

1981
Warren Beatty
Reds

1982
Richard Attenborough
Gandhi

1983
James L. Brooks
Terms of Endearment

1984
Milos Forman
Amadeus

1985
Sydney Pollack
Out of Africa

1986
Oliver Stone
Platoon

1987
Bernardo Bertolucci
The Last Emperor

1988
Barry Levinson
Rain Man

1989
Oliver Stone
Born on the Fourth of July

1990
Kevin Costner
Dances with Wolves

1991
Jonathan Demme
The Silence of the Lambs

1992
Clint Eastwood
Unforgiven

FILM

1927
Wings

1929
Broadway Melody

1930
All Quiet on the Western Front

1931
Cimarron

1932
Grand Hotel

1933
Cavalcade

1934
It Happened One Night

1935
Mutiny on the Bounty

1936
The Great Ziegfeld

1937
The Life of Emile Zola

1938
You Can't Take It with You

1939
Gone with the Wind

1940
Rebecca

1941
How Green was My Valley

1942
Mrs. Miniver

1943
Casablanca

1944
Going My Way

1945
The Lost Weekend

1946
The Best Years of Our Lives

1947
Gentleman's Agreement

1948
Hamlet

1949
All the King's Men

1950
All About Eve

1951
An American in Paris

1952
The Greatest Show on Earth

1953
From Here to Eternity

1954
On the Waterfront

1955
Marty

1956
Around the World in 80 Days

1957
The Bridge on the River Kwai

1958
Gigi

1959
Ben-Hur

1960
The Apartment

1961
West Side Story

1962
Lawrence of Arabia

1963
Tom Jones

1964
My Fair Lady

1965
The Sound of Music

1966
A Man for All Seasons

1967
In the Heat of the Night

1968
Oliver!

1969
Midnight Cowboy

1970
Patton

1971
The French Connection

1972
The Godfather

1973
The Sting

1974
The Godfather, Part 2

1975
One Flew Over the Cuckoo's Nest

1976
Rocky

1977
Annie Hall

1978
The Deer Hunter

1979
Kramer vs. Kramer

1980
Ordinary People

1981
Chariots of Fire

1982
Gandhi

1983
Terms of Endearment

1984
Amadeus

1985
Out of Africa

1986
Platoon

1987
The Last Emperor

1988
Rain Man

1989
Driving Miss Daisy

1990
Dances with Wolves

1991
The Silence of the Lambs

1992
Unforgiven

FEATURE DOCUMENTARY

1942
Prelude to War

1954
Vanishing Prairie

1963
Tom Jones

1964
My Fair Lady

1965
The Sound of Music

1966
A Man for All Seasons

1967
In the Heat of the Night

1968
Oliver!

1969
Midnight Cowboy

1970
Patton

1971
The French Connection

1972
The Godfather

1973
The Sting

1974
The Godfather, Part 2

1975
One Flew Over the Cuckoo's Nest

1976
Rocky

1977
Annie Hall

1978
The Deer Hunter

1979
Kramer vs. Kramer

1980
Ordinary People

1981
Chariots of Fire

1982
Gandhi

1983
Terms of Endearment

1984
Amadeus

1985
Out of Africa

1986
Platoon

1987
The Last Emperor

1988
Rain Man

1989
Driving Miss Daisy

1990
Dances with Wolves

1991
The Silence of the Lambs

1992
Unforgiven

1961
The Sky Above, the Mud Below

1970
Woodstock

1971
Hellstrom Chronicle

1972
Marjoe

1973
Great American Cowboy

1975
The Man Who Skied Down Everest

1976
Harlan County, U.S.A.

1983
Times of Harvey Milk

1989
Common Threads: Stories from the Quilt

FILM EDITING

1935
A Midsummer Night's Dream

1936
Anthony Adverse

1937
Lost Horizon

1938
The Adventures of Robin Hood

1939
Gone with the Wind

1941
Sergeant York

1942
The Pride of the Yankees

1943
Air Force

1944
Wilson

1945
National Velvet

1946
The Best Years of Our Lives

1947
Body and Soul

1948
The Naked City

1949
Champion

1950
King Solomon's Mines

1951
A Place in the Sun

1952
High Noon

1953
From Here to Eternity

1954
On the Waterfront

1955
Picnic

1956
Around the World in 80 Days

FILM EDITING
►cont.

1957
The Bridge on the River Kwai

1958
Gigi

1959
Ben-Hur

1960
The Apartment

1961
West Side Story

1962
Lawrence of Arabia

1963
How the West was Won

1964
Mary Poppins

1965
The Sound of Music

1966
Grand Prix

1967
In the Heat of the Night

1968
Bullitt

1969
Z

1970
Patton

1971
The French Connection

1972
Cabaret

1973
The Sting

1974
The Towering Inferno

1975
Jaws

1976
Rocky

1977
Star Wars

1978
The Deer Hunter

1979
All That Jazz

1980
Raging Bull

1981
Raiders of the Lost Ark

1982
Gandhi

1983
The Right Stuff

1984
The Killing Fields

1985
Witness

1986
Platoon

1987
The Last Emperor

1988
Who Framed Roger Rabbit?

1989
Born on the Fourth of July

1990
Dances with Wolves

1991
JFK

1992
Unforgiven

FILM—FOREIGN LANGUAGE

1949
The Bicycle Thief

1951
Rashomon

1952
Forbidden Games

1954
Gate of Hell

1955
Samurai 1: Musashi Miyamoto

1956
La Strada

1957
Nights of Cabiria

1958
Mon Oncle

1959
Black Orpheus

1960
The Virgin Spring

1961
Through a Glass Darkly

1962
Sundays & Cybele

1963
8 1/2

1964
Yesterday, Today and Tomorrow

1965
The Shop on Main Street

1966
A Man and a Woman

1967
Closely Watched Trains

1968
War and Peace

1969
Z

1971
Garden of the Finzi-Continis

1972
The Discreet Charm of the Bourgeoisie

1973
Day for Night

1974
Amarcord

1975
Dersu Uzala

1976
Black and White in Color

1977
Madame Rosa

1978
Get Out Your Handkerchiefs

1979
The Tin Drum

1980
Moscow Does Not Believe in Tears

1981
Mephisto

1983
Fanny and Alexander

1984
Dangerous Moves

1985
The Official Story
When Father was Away on Business

1986
The Assault

1987
Babette's Feast

1988
Pelle the Conqueror

1989
Cinema Paradiso

1990
Journey of Hope

1991
Mediterraneo

MAKEUP

1981
An American Werewolf in London

1982
Quest for Fire

1984
Amadeus

1985
Mask

1986
The Fly

1987
Harry and the Hendersons

1988
Beetlejuice

1989
Driving Miss Daisy

1990
Dick Tracy

1991
Terminator 2: Judgment Day

1992
Bram Stoker's Dracula

MUSIC

1934
One Night of Love

1935
The Informer

1936
Anthony Adverse

1938
The Adventures of Robin Hood

1939
Stagecoach
The Wizard of Oz

1940
Pinocchio

1941
Dumbo

1942
Now, Voyager
Yankee Doodle Dandy

1943
The Song of Bernadette
This is the Army

1944
Cover Girl
Since You Went Away

1945
Anchors Aweigh
Spellbound

1946
The Best Years of Our Lives
The Jolson Story

1947
A Double Life

1948
Easter Parade
The Red Shoes

1949
The Heiress
On the Town

1950
Sunset Boulevard

1951
An American in Paris
A Place in the Sun

1952
High Noon

1953
Lili

1954
Seven Brides for Seven Brothers

1955
Love is a Many-Splendored Thing
Oklahoma!

1956
Around the World in 80 Days
The King and I

1957
The Bridge on the River Kwai

1958
Gigi

1959
Ben-Hur

1960
Exodus
Song Without End

1961
Breakfast at Tiffany's
West Side Story

1962
Lawrence of Arabia
The Music Man

1963
Irma La Douce
Tom Jones

1964
Mary Poppins
My Fair Lady

1965
Doctor Zhivago
The Sound of Music

1966
Born Free
A Funny Thing Happened on the Way to the Forum

1967
Camelot
Thoroughly Modern Millie

1968
The Lion in Winter
Oliver!

1969
Butch Cassidy and the Sundance Kid
Hello, Dolly!

1970
Let It Be
Love Story

1971
Fiddler on the Roof
Summer of '42

1972
Cabaret

1973
The Sting
The Way We Were

1974
The Godfather, Part 2
The Great Gatsby

1975
Barry Lyndon
Jaws

1976
Bound for Glory
The Omen

1977
A Little Night Music
Star Wars

1978
The Buddy Holly Story
Midnight Express

1979
All That Jazz
A Little Romance

1980
Fame

1981
Chariots of Fire

1982
E.T.: The Extra-Terrestrial
Victor/Victoria

1983
The Right Stuff
Yentl

1984
A Passage to India
Purple Rain

1985
Out of Africa

1986
Round Midnight

1987
The Last Emperor

1988
The Milagro Beanfield War

1989
The Little Mermaid

1990
Dances with Wolves

1991
Beauty and the Beast

1992
Aladdin

SONG

1934
"The Continental"
The Gay Divorcee

1936
"The Way You Look Tonight"
Swing Time

1939
"Over the Rainbow"
The Wizard of Oz

1940
"When You Wish Upon a Star"
Pinocchio

1941
"The Last Time I Saw Paris"
Lady Be Good

1942
"White Christmas"
Holiday Inn

1944
"Swinging on a Star"
Going My Way

1945
"It Might as Well Be Spring"
State Fair

1946
"On the Atchison, Topeka and Santa Fe"
The Harvey Girls

1948
"Buttons and Bows"
The Paleface

1949
"Baby It's Cold Outside"
Neptune's Daughter

1951
"In the Cool, Cool, Cool of the Evening"
Here Comes the Groom

1952
"High Noon (Do Not Forsake Me, Oh My Darlin')"
High Noon

1953
"Secret Love"
Calamity Jane

1954
"Three Coins in the Fountain"
Three Coins in the Fountain

1955
"Love Is a Many-Splendored Thing"

Love is a Many-Splendored Thing

1956
"Whatever Will Be, Will Be (Que Sera, Sera)"
The Man Who Knew Too Much

1958
"Gigi"
Gigi

1959
"High Hopes"
A Hole in the Head

1960
"Never on Sunday"
Never on Sunday

1961
"Moon River"
Breakfast at Tiffany's

1962
"Days of Wine and Roses"
Days of Wine and Roses

1963
"Call Me Irresponsible"
Papa's Delicate Condition

1964
"Chim Chim Cher-ee"
Mary Poppins

1965
"The Shadow of Your Smile"
The Sandpiper

1966
"Born Free"
Born Free

1967
"Talk to the Animals"
Doctor Doolittle

1968
"Windmills of Your Mind"
Thomas Crown Affair

1969
"Raindrops Keep Fallin' on My Head"
Butch Cassidy and the Sundance Kid

1970
"For All We Know"
Lovers and Other Strangers

1971
"Theme from Shaft"
Shaft

1972
"The Morning After"
The Poseidon Adventure

1973
"The Way We Were"
The Way We Were

1974
"We May Never Love Like This Again"
The Towering Inferno

1975
"I'm Easy"
Nashville

1976
"Evergreen"
A Star is Born

1977
"You Light Up My Life"
You Light Up My Life

1978
"Last Dance"
Thank God It's Friday

1979
"It Goes Like It Goes"
Norma Rae

1980
"Fame"
Fame

1981
"Arthur's Theme"
Arthur

1982
"Up Where We Belong"
An Officer and a Gentleman

1983
"Flashdance...What a Feeling"
Flashdance

1984
"I Just Called to Say I Love You"
The Woman in Red

1985
"Say You, Say Me"
White Nights

1986
"Take My Breath Away"
Top Gun

1987
"(I've Had) The Time of My Life"
Dirty Dancing

1988
"Let the River Run"
Working Girl

1989
"Under the Sea"
The Little Mermaid

1990
"Sooner or Later"
Dick Tracy

1991
"Beauty and the Beast"
Beauty and the Beast

1992
"A Whole New World"
Aladdin

SOUND

1933
A Farewell to Arms

1934
One Night of Love

1935
Naughty Marietta

1936
San Francisco

1937
Hurricane

1938
The Cowboy and the Lady

1940
Strike Up the Band

1941
That Hamilton Woman

1942
Yankee Doodle Dandy

1943
This Land is Mine

1944
Wilson

1945
The Bells of St. Mary's

1946
The Jolson Story

1947
The Bishop's Wife

1948
The Snake Pit

1949
Twelve O'Clock High

1950
All About Eve

1951
The Great Caruso

1953
From Here to Eternity

1954
The Glenn Miller Story

1955
Oklahoma!

1956
The King and I

1957
Sayonara

1958
South Pacific

1959
Ben-Hur

1960
The Alamo

1961
West Side Story

1962
Lawrence of Arabia

1963
How the West was Won

1964
My Fair Lady

1965
The Sound of Music

1966
Grand Prix

1967
In the Heat of the Night

1968
Oliver!

1969
Hello, Dolly!

1970
Patton

1971
Fiddler on the Roof

1972
Cabaret

1973
The Exorcist

1974
Earthquake

1975
Jaws

1976
All the President's Men

1977
Star Wars

1978
The Deer Hunter

1979
Apocalypse Now

1980
The Empire Strikes Back

1981
Raiders of the Lost Ark

1982
E.T.: The Extra-Terrestrial

1983
The Right Stuff

1984
Amadeus

1985
Out of Africa

1986
Platoon

1987
The Last Emperor

1988
Bird

1989
Glory

1990
Dances with Wolves

1991
Terminator 2: Judgment Day

1992
The Last of the Mohicans

WRITING

1931
Cimarron

1932
The Champ

1933
Little Women

1934
It Happened One Night

1935
The Informer

1936
The Story of Louis Pasteur

1937
The Life of Emile Zola
A Star is Born

1938
Boys Town
Pygmalion

1939
Gone with the Wind
Mr. Smith Goes to Washington

1940
The Great McGinty
The Philadelphia Story

1941
Citizen Kane
Here Comes Mr. Jordan

1942
Mrs. Miniver
Woman of the Year

1943
Casablanca
The Human Comedy

1944
Going My Way
Wilson

1945
The Lost Weekend

1946
The Best Years of Our Lives
Seventh Veil

1947
The Bachelor and the Bobby-Soxer
Miracle on 34th Street

1948
The Search
Treasure of the Sierra Madre

1949
Battleground
A Letter to Three Wives

1950
All About Eve
Panic in the Streets
Sunset Boulevard

1951
An American in Paris
A Place in the Sun

1952
The Bad and the Beautiful
The Greatest Show on Earth
The Lavender Hill Mob

1953
From Here to Eternity
Roman Holiday

1954
Broken Lance
Country Girl
On the Waterfront

1955
Love Me or Leave Me
Marty

1956
Around the World in 80 Days
The Brave One
The Red Balloon

1957
The Bridge on the River Kwai
Designing Woman

1958
The Defiant Ones
Gigi

1959
Pillow Talk
Room at the Top

1960
The Apartment
Elmer Gantry

1961
Judgment at Nuremberg
Splendor in the Grass

1962
Divorce—Italian Style
To Kill a Mockingbird

1963
How the West was Won
Tom Jones

1964
Becket
Father Goose

1965
Darling
Doctor Zhivago

1966
A Man and a Woman
A Man for All Seasons

1967
Guess Who's Coming to Dinner

1968
The Lion in Winter
The Producers

1969
Butch Cassidy and the Sundance Kid
Midnight Cowboy

1970
*M*A*S*H*
Patton

1971
The French Connection
The Hospital

1972
The Candidate
The Godfather

1973
The Exorcist
The Sting

1974
Chinatown
The Godfather, Part 2

1975
Dog Day Afternoon
One Flew Over the Cuckoo's Nest

1976
All the President's Men
Network

1977
Annie Hall
Julia

1978
Coming Home
Midnight Express

1979
Breaking Away
Kramer vs. Kramer

1980
Melvin and Howard
Ordinary People

1981
Chariots of Fire
On Golden Pond

1982
Gandhi
Missing

1983
Tender Mercies
Terms of Endearment

1984
Amadeus
Places in the Heart

1985
Out of Africa
Witness

1986
Hannah and Her Sisters
A Room with a View

1987
The Last Emperor
Moonstruck

1988
Dangerous Liaisons
Rain Man

1989
Dead Poets Society
Driving Miss Daisy

1990
Dances with Wolves
Ghost

1991
The Silence of the Lambs
Thelma & Louise

1992
The Crying Game
Howard's End

AUSTRALIAN FILM INSTITUTE

ACTOR

1974
Jack Thompson
Sunday Too Far Away

1975
John Meillon
Fourth Wish

1976
Nick Tate
The Devil's Playground
Simon Burke
The Devil's Playground

1978
Bill Hunter
Newsfront

1979
Mel Gibson
Tim

1980
Jack Thompson
Breaker Morant

1981
Mel Gibson
Gallipoli

1983
Norman Kaye
Man of Flowers

1984
John Hargreaves
My First Wife

1986
Colin Friels
Malcolm

1987
Leo McKern
Travelling North

1988
Sam Neill
A Cry in the Dark

1990
Max von Sydow
Father

1991
Hugo Weaving
Proof

ACTOR— SUPPORTING

1991
Russell Crowe
Proof

1992
Barry Otto
Strictly Ballroom

ACTRESS

1977
Pat Bishop
Don's Party

1980
Tracey Mann
Hard Knocks

1981
Judy Davis
The Winter of Our Dreams

1982
Noni Hazlehurst
Monkey Grip

1983
Wendy Hughes
Careful, He Might Hear You

1985
Noni Hazlehurst
Fran

1986
Judy Davis
Kangaroo

1987
Judy Davis
High Tide

1988
Meryl Streep
A Cry in the Dark

1990
Julia Blake
Father

1991
Sheila Florance
A Woman's Tale

1992
Lisa Harrow
The Last Days of Chez Nous

ACTRESS— SUPPORTING

1992
Pat Thomsen
Strictly Ballroom

DIRECTOR

1991
Jocelyn Moorhouse
Proof

1992
Baz Luhrmann
Strictly Ballroom

FILM

1974
Sunday Too Far Away

1976
The Devil's Playground

1978
Newsfront

1979
My Brilliant Career

1980
Breaker Morant

1981
Gallipoli

1982
Lonely Hearts

1983
Careful, He Might Hear You

1985
Bliss

1986
Malcolm

1987
The Year My Voice Broke

1988
The Navigator

1990
Flirting

1991
Proof

1992
Strictly Ballroom

BRITISH ACADEMY OF FILM AND TELEVISION ARTS

ACTOR

1952
Marlon Brando
Viva Zapata!

1953
Marlon Brando
Julius Caesar
John Gielgud
Julius Caesar

1954
Kenneth More
Doctor in the House
Marlon Brando
On the Waterfront

1955
Ernest Borgnine
Marty
Laurence Olivier
Richard III

1956
Francois Perier
Gervaise

1957
Alec Guinness
The Bridge on the River Kwai
Henry Fonda
Twelve Angry Men

1958
Sidney Poitier
The Defiant Ones
Trevor Howard
The Key

1959
Peter Sellers
I'm All Right Jack
Jack Lemmon
Some Like It Hot

1960
Jack Lemmon
The Apartment

1961
Paul Newman
The Hustler
Peter Finch
No Love for Johnnie

1962
Burt Lancaster
Birdman of Alcatraz
Peter O'Toole
Lawrence of Arabia

1963
Marcello Mastroianni
Divorce—Italian Style
Dirk Bogarde
The Servant

1964
Richard Attenborough
*Seance on a Wet
Afternoon*
Marcello Mastroianni
*Yesterday, Today and
Tomorrow*

1965
Lee Marvin
Cat Ballou
Dirk Bogarde
Darling

1966
Rod Steiger
Pawnbroker
Richard Burton
*Who's Afraid of Virginia
Woolf?*

1967
Rod Steiger
In the Heat of the Night
Paul Scofield
A Man for All Seasons

1968
Spencer Tracy
*Guess Who's Coming to
Dinner*

1969
Dustin Hoffman
Midnight Cowboy

1970
Robert Redford
*Butch Cassidy and the
Sundance Kid*

1971
Peter Finch
Sunday, Bloody Sunday

1972
Gene Hackman
The French Connection

1973
Walter Matthau
Pete 'n' Tillie

1974
Jack Nicholson
Chinatown
Jack Nicholson
The Last Detail

1975
Al Pacino
Dog Day Afternoon

1976
Jack Nicholson
*One Flew Over the
Cuckoo's Nest*

1977
Peter Finch
Network

1978
Richard Dreyfuss
The Goodbye Girl

1979
Jack Lemmon
The China Syndrome

1980
John Hurt
The Elephant Man

1981
Burt Lancaster
Atlantic City

1982
Ben Kingsley
Gandhi

1983
Michael Caine
Educating Rita
Dustin Hoffman
Tootsie

1984
Haing S. Ngor
The Killing Fields

1985
William Hurt
Kiss of the Spider Woman

1986
Bob Hoskins
Mona Lisa

1987
Sean Connery
The Name of the Rose

1988
John Cleese
A Fish Called Wanda

1989
Daniel Day-Lewis
My Left Foot

1990
Philippe Noiret
Cinema Paradiso

1992
Anthony Hopkins
The Silence of the Lambs

1993
Robert Downey, Jr.
Chaplin

ACTOR— SUPPORTING

1971
Edward Fox
The Go-Between

1972
Ben Johnson
The Last Picture Show

1973
Arthur Lowe
O Lucky Man

1974
John Gielgud
*Murder on the Orient
Express*

1975
Fred Astaire
The Towering Inferno

1976
Brad Dourif
*One Flew Over the
Cuckoo's Nest*

1977
Edward Fox
A Bridge Too Far

1978
John Hurt
Midnight Express

1979
Robert Duvall
Apocalypse Now

1981
Ian Holm
Chariots of Fire

1982
Jack Nicholson
Reds

1983
Denholm Elliott
Trading Places

1984
Denholm Elliott
A Private Function

1985
Denholm Elliott
Defense of the Realm

1986
Ray McAnally
The Mission

1987
Daniel Auteuil
Jean de Florette

1988
Michael Palin
A Fish Called Wanda

1989
Ray McAnally
My Left Foot

1990
Salvatore Cascio
Cinema Paradiso

1992
Alan Rickman
*Robin Hood: Prince of
Thieves*

1993
Gene Hackman
Unforgiven

ACTRESS

1952
Vivien Leigh
A Streetcar Named Desire
1953
Leslie Caron
Lili
Audrey Hepburn
Roman Holiday
1955
Katie Johnson
Ladykillers
Betsy Blair
Marty
1956
Anna Magnani
The Rose Tattoo

1958
Simone Signoret
Room at the Top

1959
Shirley MacLaine
Ask Any Girl
Audrey Hepburn
The Nun's Story

1960
Shirley MacLaine
The Apartment

1961
Sophia Loren
Two Women

1962
Anne Bancroft
The Miracle Worker

1963
Patricia Neal
Hud
Rachel Roberts
This Sporting Life

1964
Audrey Hepburn
Charade

1965
Julie Christie
Darling
Patricia Neal
In Harm's Way

1966
Elizabeth Taylor
*Who's Afraid of Virginia
Woolf?*

1967
Anouk Aimee
A Man and a Woman

1968
Katharine Hepburn
*Guess Who's Coming to
Dinner*

1969
Maggie Smith
*The Prime of Miss Jean
Brodie*

1970
Katharine Ross
*Butch Cassidy and the
Sundance Kid*

1971
Glenda Jackson
Sunday, Bloody Sunday

1972
Liza Minnelli
Cabaret

1973
Delphine Seyrig
*The Discreet Charm of the
Bourgeoisie*

1974
Joanne Woodward
*Summer Wishes, Winter
Dreams*

1975
Ellen Burstyn
*Alice Doesn't Live Here
Anymore*

1976
Louise Fletcher
*One Flew Over the
Cuckoo's Nest*

1977
Diane Keaton
Annie Hall

1978
Jane Fonda
Julia

1979
Jane Fonda
The China Syndrome

1980
Judy Davis
My Brilliant Career

1981
Meryl Streep
*The French Lieutenant's
Woman*

1982
Katharine Hepburn
On Golden Pond

1983
Julie Walters
Educating Rita

1984
Maggie Smith
A Private Function

1985
Peggy Ashcroft
A Passage to India

1986
Maggie Smith
A Room with a View

1987
Anne Bancroft
84 Charing Cross Road

1988
Maggie Smith
*The Lonely Passion of
Judith Hearne*

1989
Pauline Collins
Shirley Valentine

1990
Jessica Tandy
Driving Miss Daisy

1992
Jodie Foster
The Silence of the Lambs

1993
Emma Thompson
Howard's End

ACTRESS— SUPPORTING

1961
Dora Bryan
A Taste of Honey

1969
Celia Johnson
*The Prime of Miss Jean
Brodie*

1970
Susannah York
*They Shoot Horses, Don't
They?*

1971
Margaret Leighton
The Go-Between

1972
Cloris Leachman
The Last Picture Show

ACTRESS—SUPPORTING
►cont.

1973
Valentina Cortese
Day for Night

1974
Ingrid Bergman
Murder on the Orient
Express

1975
Diane Ladd
Alice Doesn't Live Here
Anymore

1976
Jodie Foster
Taxi Driver

1977
Jenny Agutter
Equus

1978
Geraldine Page
Interiors
Vanessa Redgrave
Julia

1979
Rachel Roberts
Yanks

1982
Rohini Hattangady
Gandhi
Maureen Stapleton
Reds

1983
Jamie Lee Curtis
Trading Places

1984
Liz Smith
A Private Function

1985
Rosanna Arquette
Desperately Seeking
Susan

1986
Judi Dench
A Room with a View

1987
Susan Wooldridge
Hope and Glory

1988
Judi Dench
A Handful of Dust

1989
Michelle Pfeiffer
Dangerous Liaisons

1990
Whoopi Goldberg
Ghost

1992
Kate Nelligan
Frankie and Johnny

DIRECTOR

1955
Laurence Olivier
Richard III

1968
Mike Nichols
The Graduate

1969
John Schlesinger
Midnight Cowboy

1970
George Roy Hill
Butch Cassidy and the
Sundance Kid

1971
John Schlesinger
Sunday, Bloody Sunday

1972
Bob Fosse
Cabaret

1973
Francois Truffaut
Day for Night

1974
Roman Polanski
Chinatown

1975
Stanley Kubrick
Barry Lyndon

1976
Milos Forman
One Flew Over the
Cuckoo's Nest

1977
Woody Allen
Annie Hall

1978
Alan Parker
Midnight Express

1979
Francis Ford Coppola
Apocalypse Now

1980
Akira Kurosawa
Kagemusha

1981
Louis Malle
Atlantic City

1982
Richard Attenborough
Gandhi

1983
Bill Forsyth
Local Hero

1984
Wim Wenders
Paris, Texas

1986
Woody Allen
Hannah and Her Sisters

1987
Oliver Stone
Platoon

1988
Louis Malle
Au Revoir Les Enfants

1989
Kenneth Branagh
Henry V

1990
Martin Scorsese
Goodfellas

1992
Alan Parker
The Commitments

1993
Clint Eastwood
Unforgiven

FILM

1947
The Best Years of Our
Lives
Odd Man Out

1948
The Fallen Idol
Hamlet

1949
The Bicycle Thief
The Third Man

1950
All About Eve
The Blue Lamp

1951
La Ronde
The Lavender Hill Mob

1953
Forbidden Games
Genevieve

1954
Hobson's Choice
Wages of Fear

1955
Richard III

1956
Gervaise
Reach for the Sky

1957
The Bridge on the River
Kwai

1958
Room at the Top

1959
Ben-Hur
Sapphire

1960
The Apartment

1961
Ballad of a Soldier
The Hustler
A Taste of Honey

1962
Lawrence of Arabia

1963
Tom Jones

1964
Dr. Strangelove, or: How I
Learned to Stop Worrying
and Love the Bomb

1965
The Ipcress File
My Fair Lady

1966
The Spy Who Came in
from the Cold
Who's Afraid of Virginia
Woolf?

1967
A Man for All Seasons

1968
The Graduate

1969
Midnight Cowboy

1970
Butch Cassidy and the
Sundance Kid

1971
Sunday, Bloody Sunday

1972
Cabaret

1973
Day for Night

1975
Alice Doesn't Live Here
Anymore

1976
One Flew Over the
Cuckoo's Nest

1977
Annie Hall

1978
Julia

1979
Manhattan

1980
The Elephant Man

1981
Chariots of Fire

1982
Gandhi

1983
Educating Rita

1984
The Killing Fields

1985
The Purple Rose of Cairo

1986
A Room with a View

1987
Hope and Glory
Jean de Florette

1988
The Last Emperor

1989
Dead Poets Society

1990
Goodfellas

1992
The Commitments

1993
Unforgiven

CANNES

ACTOR

1946
Ray Milland
The Lost Weekend

1949
Edward G. Robinson
House of Strangers

1951
Michael Redgrave
The Browning Version

1952
Marlon Brando
Viva Zapata!

1953
Charles Vanel
Wages of Fear

1955
Spencer Tracy
Bad Day at Black Rock

1958
Paul Newman
The Long, Hot Summer

1961
Anthony Perkins
Goodbye Again

1962
Murray Melvin
A Taste of Honey

1963
Richard Harris
This Sporting Life

1964
Saro Urzi
Seduced and Abandoned

1965
Terence Stamp
The Collector

1966
Per Oscarsson
Hunger

1969
Jean-Louis Trintignant
Z

1971
Riccardo Cucciolla
Sacco & Vanzetti

1973
Giancarlo Giannini
Love and Anarchy

1974
Jack Nicholson
The Last Detail

1978
Jon Voight
Coming Home

1979
Jack Lemmon
The China Syndrome

1981
Ugo Tognazzi
The Tragedy of a
Ridiculous Man

1982
Jack Lemmon
Missing

1984
Alfredo Landa
The Holy Innocents
Francisco Rabal
The Holy Innocents

1985
William Hurt
Kiss of the Spider Woman

1986
Michel Blanc
Menage
Bob Hoskins
Mona Lisa

1987
Marcello Mastroianni
Dark Eyes

1988
Forest Whitaker
Bird

1989
James Spader
sex, lies and videotape

1990
Gerard Depardieu
Cyrano de Bergerac

1991
John Turturro
Barton Fink

1992
Tim Robbins
The Player

ACTRESS

1946
Michele Morgan
La Symphonie Pastorale

1951
Bette Davis
All About Eve

1952
Lee Grant
Detective Story

1953
Shirley Booth
Come Back, Little Sheba

1956
Susan Hayward
I'll Cry Tomorrow

1957
Giulietta Masina
Nights of Cabiria

1958
Eva Dahlbeck
Brink of Life
Bibi Andersson
Brink of Life
Ingrid Thulin
Brink of Life

1959
Simone Signoret
Room at the Top

1960
Melina Mercouri
Never on Sunday

1961
Sophia Loren
Two Women

1962
Katharine Hepburn
Long Day's Journey into Night
Rita Tushingham
A Taste of Honey

1965
Samantha Eggar
The Collector

1966
Vanessa Redgrave
Morgan!

1967
Pia Degermark
Elvira Madigan

1969
Vanessa Redgrave
Isadora

1971
Kitty Winn
Panic in Needle Park

1973
Joanne Woodward
The Effect of Gamma Rays on Man-in-the-Moon Marigolds

1974
Marie-Jose Nat
Les Violons du Bal

1975
Valerie Perrine
Lenny

1976
Dominique Sanda
The Inheritance

1978
Jill Clayburgh
An Unmarried Woman
Isabelle Huppert
Violette

1979
Sally Field
Norma Rae

1981
Isabelle Adjani
Quartet

1982
Jadwiga Jankowska Cieslak
Another Way

1984
Helen Mirren
Cal

1985
Cher
Mask
Norma Aleandro
The Official Story

1987
Barbara Hershey
Shy People

1988
Barbara Hershey
A World Apart
Jodhi May
A World Apart
Linda Mvusi
A World Apart

1989
Meryl Streep
A Cry in the Dark

1991
Irene Jacob
The Double Life of Veronique

DIRECTOR

1951
Luis Bunuel
Los Olvidados

1955
Jules Dassin
Rififi

1957
Robert Bresson
A Man Escaped

1958
Ingmar Bergman
Brink of Life

1959
Francois Truffaut
The 400 Blows

1969
Voltech Jasny
All My Good Countrymen

1976
Ettore Scola
Down & Dirty

1978
Nagisa Oshima
The Empire of Passion

1979
Terence Malick
Days of Heaven

1982
Werner Herzog
Fitzcarraldo

1984
Bertrand Tavernier
A Sunday in the Country

1985
Andre Techine
Rendez-vous

1986
Martin Scorsese
After Hours

1989
Emir Kusturica
Time of the Gypsies

1990
Pavel Lounguine
Taxi Blues

1991
Joel Coen
Barton Fink

1992
Robert Altman
The Player

FILM

1946
The Lost Weekend

1949
The Third Man

1951
Los Olvidados
Miracle in Milan
Miss Julie

1952
Othello
White Mane

1953
Wages of Fear

1954
Gate of Hell

1955
Marty

1957
Friendly Persuasion

1958
The Cranes are Flying

1959
Black Orpheus

1960
La Dolce Vita

1961
Viridiana

1964
Umbrellas of Cherbourg

1966
A Man and a Woman

1967
Blow-Up

1969
If...

1970
*M*A*S*H*

1971
The Go-Between

1973
Scarecrow

1974
The Conversation

1976
Taxi Driver

1977
Padre Padrone

1978
The Tree of Wooden Clogs

1979
Apocalypse Now
The Tin Drum

1980
Kagemusha

1982
Missing
Yol

1983
The Ballad of Narayama

1984
Paris, Texas

1985
Dance with a Stranger
When Father was Away on Business

1986
The Mission

1987
Under Satan's Sun

1988
Pelle the Conqueror

1989
sex, lies and videotape

1990
Overseas: Three Women with Man Trouble
Wild at Heart

1991
Barton Fink

CESAR

ACTOR

1978
Jean Rochefort
Le Crabe Tambour

1979
Michel Serrault
La Cage aux Folles

1981
Gerard Depardieu
The Last Metro

1983
Philippe Leotard
La Balance

1984
Coluche
Tchao Pantin

1986
Christopher Lambert
Subway

1987
Daniel Auteuil
Jean de Florette

1988
Richard Bohringer
Le Grand Chemin

1990
Philippe Noiret
Life and Nothing But

1991
Gerard Depardieu
Cyrano de Bergerac

ACTOR— SUPPORTING

1977
Claude Brasseur
Pardon Mon Affaire

1978
Jacques Dufilho
Le Crabe Tambour

1979
Jacques Villeret
Robert et Robert

1980
Jean Bouise
Hothead

1984
Richard Anconina
Tchao Pantin

1986
Michel Boujenah
Three Men and a Cradle

1989
Patrick Chesnais
La Lectrice

1991
Jacques Weber
Cyrano de Bergerac

ACTRESS

1978
Simone Signoret
Madame Rosa

1981
Catherine Deneuve
The Last Metro

1982
Isabelle Adjani
Possession

1983
Nathalie Baye
La Balance

1984
Isabelle Adjani
One Deadly Summer

1985
Sabine Azema
A Sunday in the Country

1986
Sandrine Bonnaire
Vagabond

1988
Anemone
Le Grand Chemin

1989
Isabelle Adjani
Camille Claudel

1990
Carol Bouquet
Too Beautiful for You

1991
Anne Parillaud
La Femme Nikita

1970
John Wayne
True Grit

1971
George C. Scott
Patton

1972
Gene Hackman
The French Connection

1973
Marlon Brando
The Godfather

1974
Al Pacino
Serpico

1975
Jack Nicholson
Chinatown

1976
Jack Nicholson
*One Flew Over the
Cuckoo's Nest*

1977
Peter Finch
Network

1978
Richard Burton
Equus

1979
Jon Voight
Coming Home

1980
Dustin Hoffman
Kramer vs. Kramer

1981
Robert De Niro
Raging Bull

1982
Henry Fonda
On Golden Pond

1983
Ben Kingsley
Gandhi
Robert Duvall
Tender Mercies

1984
Tom Courtenay
The Dresser

1985
F. Murray Abraham
Amadeus

1986
Jon Voight
Runaway Train

1987
Bob Hoskins
Mona Lisa

1988
Michael Douglas
Wall Street

1989
Dustin Hoffman
Rain Man

1990
Tom Cruise
Born on the Fourth of July

1991
Jeremy Irons
Reversal of Fortune

1992
Nick Nolte
The Prince of Tides

1993
Al Pacino
Scent of a Woman

ACTOR— MUSICAL/COMEDY

1951
Fred Astaire
Three Little Words

1953
Donald O'Connor
Singin' in the Rain

1954
David Niven
Moon is Blue

1955
James Mason
A Star is Born

1956
Tom Ewell
The Seven Year Itch

1957
Cantinflas
*Around the World in 80
Days*

1958
Frank Sinatra
Pal Joey

1960
Jack Lemmon
Some Like It Hot

1961
Jack Lemmon
The Apartment

1962
Glenn Ford
Pocketful of Miracles

1963
Marcello Mastroianni
Divorce—Italian Style

1965
Rex Harrison
My Fair Lady

1966
Lee Marvin
Cat Ballou

1967
Alan Arkin
*The Russians are
Coming, the Russians are
Coming*

1968
Richard Harris
Camelot

1969
Ron Moody
Oliver!

1970
Peter O'Toole
Goodbye, Mr. Chips

1971
Albert Finney
Scrooge

1972
Chaim Topol
Fiddler on the Roof

1974
George Segal
A Touch of Class

1975
Art Carney
Harry and Tonto

1976
Walter Matthau
The Sunshine Boys

1977
Kris Kristofferson
A Star is Born

1978
Richard Dreyfuss
The Goodbye Girl

1979
Warren Beatty
Heaven Can Wait

1980
Peter Sellers
Being There

1981
Ray Sharkey
Idolmaker

1982
Dudley Moore
Arthur

1983
Dustin Hoffman
Tootsie

1984
Michael Caine
Educating Rita

1985
Dudley Moore
Micki & Maude

1986
Jack Nicholson
Prizzi's Honor

1987
Paul Hogan
Crocodile Dundee

1988
Robin Williams
Good Morning, Vietnam

1989
Tom Hanks
Big

1990
Morgan Freeman
Driving Miss Daisy

1991
Gerard Depardieu
Green Card

1992
Robin Williams
The Fisher King

1993
Tim Robbins
The Player

ACTOR— SUPPORTING

1945
Barry Fitzgerald
Going My Way

1947
Clifton Webb
The Razor's Edge

1948
Edmund Gwenn
Miracle on 34th Street

1949
Walter Huston
*Treasure of the Sierra
Madre*

1950
James Whitmore
Battleground

1952
Peter Ustinov
Quo Vadis

1954
Frank Sinatra
From Here to Eternity

1955
Edmond O'Brien
The Barefoot Contessa

1957
Earl Holliman
The Rainmaker

1958
Red Buttons
Sayonara

1959
Burl Ives
Big Country

1960
Stephen Boyd
Ben-Hur

1961
Sal Mineo
Exodus

1962
George Chakiris
West Side Story

1963
Omar Sharif
Lawrence of Arabia

1964
John Huston
The Cardinal

1965
Edmond O'Brien
Seven Days in May

1966
Oskar Werner
*The Spy Who Came in
from the Cold*

1967
Richard Attenborough
The Sand Pebbles

1968
David Attenborough
Doctor Doolittle

1970
Gig Young
*They Shoot Horses, Don't
They?*

1971
John Mills
Ryan's Daughter

1972
Ben Johnson
The Last Picture Show

1973
Joel Grey
Cabaret

1974
John Houseman
The Paper Chase

1975
Fred Astaire
The Towering Inferno

1976
Richard Benjamin
The Sunshine Boys

1977
Laurence Olivier
Marathon Man

1978
Peter Firth
Equus

1979
John Hurt
Midnight Express

1980
Robert Duvall
Apocalypse Now
Melvyn Douglas
Being There

1981
Timothy Hutton
Ordinary People

1982
John Gielgud
Arthur

1983
Louis Gossett, Jr.
*An Officer and a
Gentleman*

1984
Jack Nicholson
Terms of Endearment

1985
Haing S. Ngor
The Killing Fields

1986
Klaus Maria Brandauer
Out of Africa

1987
Tom Berenger
Platoon

1988
Sean Connery
The Untouchables

1989
Martin Landau
*Tucker: The Man and His
Dream*

1990
Denzel Washington
Glory

1991
Bruce Davison
Longtime Companion

1992
Jack Palance
City Slickers

1993
Gene Hackman
Unforgiven

ACTRESS— DRAMA

1944
Jennifer Jones
The Song of Bernadette

1945
Ingrid Bergman
Gaslight

1946
Ingrid Bergman
The Bells of St. Mary's

ACTRESS— DRAMA ▶cont.

1947
Rosalind Russell
Sister Kenny

1949
Jane Wyman
Johnny Belinda

1950
Olivia de Havilland
The Heiress

1951
Gloria Swanson
Sunset Boulevard

1953
Shirley Booth
Come Back, Little Sheba

1954
Audrey Hepburn
Roman Holiday

1955
Grace Kelly
Country Girl

1956
Anna Magnani
The Rose Tattoo

1957
Ingrid Bergman
Anastasia

1958
Joanne Woodward
The Three Faces of Eve

1959
Susan Hayward
I Want to Live!

1960
Elizabeth Taylor
Suddenly, Last Summer

1961
Greer Garson
Sunrise at Campobello

1962
Geraldine Page
Summer and Smoke

1963
Geraldine Page
Sweet Bird of Youth

1966
Samantha Eggar
The Collector

1967
Anouk Aimee
A Man and a Woman

1969
Joanne Woodward
Rachel, Rachel

1970
Genevieve Bujold
Anne of the Thousand Days

1971
Ali MacGraw
Love Story

1972
Jane Fonda
Klute

1974
Marsha Mason
Cinderella Liberty

1975
Gena Rowlands
A Woman Under the Influence

1976
Louise Fletcher
One Flew Over the Cuckoo's Nest

1977
Faye Dunaway
Network

1978
Jane Fonda
Julia

1979
Jane Fonda
Coming Home

1980
Sally Field
Norma Rae

1981
Mary Tyler Moore
Ordinary People

1982
Meryl Streep
The French Lieutenant's Woman

1983
Meryl Streep
Sophie's Choice

1984
Shirley MacLaine
Terms of Endearment

1985
Sally Field
Places in the Heart

1986
Whoopi Goldberg
The Color Purple

1987
Marlee Matlin
Children of a Lesser God

1988
Sally Kirkland
Anna
Sigourney Weaver
Gorillas in the Mist

1989
Jodie Foster
The Accused
Shirley MacLaine
Madame Sousatzka

1990
Michelle Pfeiffer
The Fabulous Baker Boys

1991
Kathy Bates
Misery

1992
Jodie Foster
The Silence of the Lambs

1993
Emma Thompson
Howard's End

ACTRESS— MUSICAL/COMEDY

1951
Judy Holliday
Born Yesterday

1955
Judy Garland
A Star is Born

1956
Jean Simmons
Guys and Dolls

1957
Deborah Kerr
The King and I

1958
Kay Kendall
Les Girls

1959
Rosalind Russell
Auntie Mame

1960
Marilyn Monroe
Some Like It Hot

1961
Shirley MacLaine
The Apartment

1963
Rosalind Russell
Gypsy

1964
Shirley MacLaine
Irma La Douce

1965
Julie Andrews
Mary Poppins

1966
Julie Andrews
The Sound of Music

1967
Lynn Redgrave
Georgy Girl

1968
Anne Bancroft
The Graduate

1969
Barbra Streisand
Funny Girl

1971
Carrie Snodgress
Diary of a Mad Housewife

1972
Twiggy
The Boy Friend

1973
Liza Minnelli
Cabaret

1974
Glenda Jackson
A Touch of Class

1975
Raquel Welch
Three Musketeers

1976
Ann-Margret
Tommy

1977
Barbra Streisand
A Star is Born

1978
Diane Keaton
Annie Hall
Marsha Mason
The Goodbye Girl

1979
Maggie Smith
California Suite

Ellen Burstyn
Same Time, Next Year

1980
Bette Midler
The Rose

1981
Sissy Spacek
Coal Miner's Daughter

1982
Bernadette Peters
Pennies From Heaven

1983
Julie Andrews
Victor/Victoria

1984
Julie Walters
Educating Rita

1985
Kathleen Turner
Romancing the Stone

1986
Kathleen Turner
Prizzi's Honor

1987
Sissy Spacek
Crimes of the Heart

1988
Cher
Moonstruck

1989
Melanie Griffith
Working Girl

1990
Jessica Tandy
Driving Miss Daisy

1991
Julia Roberts
Pretty Woman

1992
Bette Midler
For the Boys

1993
Miranda Richardson
Enchanted April

ACTRESS— SUPPORTING

1945
Agnes Moorehead
Mrs. Parkington

1946
Angela Lansbury
Picture of Dorian Gray

1947
Anne Baxter
The Razor's Edge

1948
Celeste Holm
Gentleman's Agreement

1949
Ellen Corby
I Remember Mama

1950
Mercedes McCambridge
All the King's Men

1951
Josephine Hull
Harvey

1952
Kim Hunter
A Streetcar Named Desire

1953
Katy Jurado
High Noon

1954
Grace Kelly
Mogambo

1956
Marisa Pavan
The Rose Tattoo

1957
Eileen Heckart
The Bad Seed

1958
Elsa Lanchester
Witness for the Prosecution

1959
Hermione Gingold
Gigi

1960
Susan Kohner
Imitation of Life

1961
Janet Leigh
Psycho

1962
Rita Moreno
West Side Story

1963
Angela Lansbury
The Manchurian Candidate

1964
Margaret Rutherford
The V.I.P.'s

1965
Agnes Moorehead
Hush, Hush, Sweet Charlotte

1966
Ruth Gordon
Inside Daisy Clover

1967
Jocelyn Lagarde
Hawaii

1968
Carol Channing
Thoroughly Modern Millie

1969
Ruth Gordon
Rosemary's Baby

1970
Goldie Hawn
Cactus Flower

1971
Maureen Stapleton
Airport
Karen Black
Five Easy Pieces

1972
Ann-Margret
Carnal Knowledge

1973
Shelley Winters
The Poseidon Adventure

1974
Linda Blair
The Exorcist

1975
Karen Black
The Great Gatsby

1976
Brenda Vaccaro
Once is Not Enough

1977
Katharine Ross
Voyage of the Damned

1978
Vanessa Redgrave
Julia

1979
Dyan Cannon
Heaven Can Wait

1980
Meryl Streep
Kramer vs. Kramer

1981
Mary Steenburgen
Melvin and Howard

1982
Joan Hackett
Only When I Laugh

1983
Jessica Lange
Tootsie

1984
Cher
Silkwood

1985
Peggy Ashcroft
A Passage to India

1986
Meg Tilly
Agnes of God

1987
Maggie Smith
A Room with a View

1988
Olympia Dukakis
Moonstruck

1989
Sigourney Weaver
Working Girl

1990
Julia Roberts
Steel Magnolias

1991
Whoopi Goldberg
Ghost

1992
Mercedes Ruehl
The Fisher King

1993
Joan Plowright
Enchanted April

BEST FILM— DRAMA

1944
The Song of Bernadette

1945
Going My Way

1946
The Lost Weekend

1947
The Best Years of Our Lives

1948
Gentleman's Agreement

1949
Johnny Belinda
Treasure of the Sierra Madre

1950
All the King's Men

1951
Sunset Boulevard

1952
A Place in the Sun

1953
The Greatest Show on Earth

1954
The Robe

1955
On the Waterfront

1956
East of Eden

1957
Around the World in 80 Days

1958
The Bridge on the River Kwai

1959
The Defiant Ones

1960
Ben-Hur

1961
Spartacus

1962
The Guns of Navarone

1963
Lawrence of Arabia

1964
The Cardinal

1965
Becket

1966
Doctor Zhivago

1967
A Man for All Seasons

1968
In the Heat of the Night

1969
The Lion in Winter

1970
Anne of the Thousand Days

1971
Love Story

1972
The French Connection

1973
The Godfather

1974
The Exorcist

1975
Chinatown

1976
One Flew Over the Cuckoo's Nest

1977
Rocky

1978
The Turning Point

1979
Midnight Express

1980
Kramer vs. Kramer

1981
Ordinary People

1982
On Golden Pond

1983
E.T.: The Extra-Terrestrial

1984
Terms of Endearment

1985
Amadeus

1986
Out of Africa

1987
Platoon

1988
The Last Emperor

1989
Rain Man

1990
Born on the Fourth of July

1991
Dances with Wolves

1992
Bugsy

1993
Scent of a Woman

BEST FILM— MUSICAL/COMEDY

1952
An American in Paris

1955
Carmen Jones

1956
Guys and Dolls

1957
The King and I

1958
Les Girls

1959
Gigi

1960
Some Like It Hot

1961
The Apartment
Song Without End

1962
West Side Story

1963
The Music Man
That Touch of Mink

1964
Tom Jones

1965
My Fair Lady

1966
The Sound of Music

1967
The Russians are Coming, the Russians are Coming

1968
The Graduate

1969
Oliver!

1971
*M*A*S*H*

1972
Fiddler on the Roof

1973
Cabaret

1974
American Graffiti

1975
The Longest Yard

1976
The Sunshine Boys

1977
A Star is Born

1978
The Goodbye Girl

1979
Heaven Can Wait

1980
Breaking Away

1981
Coal Miner's Daughter

1982
Arthur

1983
Tootsie

1984
Yentl

1985
Romancing the Stone

1986
Prizzi's Honor

1987
Hannah and Her Sisters

1988
Hope and Glory

1989
Working Girl

1990
Driving Miss Daisy

1991
Green Card

1992
Beauty and the Beast

1993
The Player

DIRECTOR

1944
Henry King
The Song of Bernadette

1945
Leo McCarey
Going My Way

1946
Billy Wilder
The Lost Weekend

1947
Frank Capra
It's a Wonderful Life

1948
Elia Kazan
Gentleman's Agreement

1949
John Huston
Treasure of the Sierra Madre

1950
Robert Rossen
All the King's Men

1951
Billy Wilder
Sunset Boulevard

1953
Cecil B. DeMille
The Greatest Show on Earth

1955
Elia Kazan
On the Waterfront

1956
Joshua Logan
Picnic

1957
Elia Kazan
Baby Doll

1958
David Lean
The Bridge on the River Kwai

1959
Vincente Minnolli
Gigi

1960
William Wyler
Ben-Hur

1962
Stanley Kramer
Judgment at Nuremberg

1963
David Lean
Lawrence of Arabia

1965
George Cukor
My Fair Lady

1966
David Lean
Doctor Zhivago

1967
Fred Zinneman
A Man for All Seasons

1968
Mike Nichols
The Graduate

1969
Paul Newman
Rachel, Rachel

1971
Arthur Hiller
Love Story

1972
William Friedkin
The French Connection

1973
Francis Ford Coppola
The Godfather

1974
William Friedkin
The Exorcist

1975
Roman Polanski
Chinatown

1976
Milos Forman
One Flew Over the Cuckoo's Nest

1977
Sidney Lumet
Network

1978
Herbert Ross
The Turning Point

DIRECTOR ▶cont.

1979
Michael Cimino
The Deer Hunter

1980
Francis Ford Coppola
Apocalypse Now

1981
Robert Redford
Ordinary People

1982
Warren Beatty
Reds

1983
Richard Attenborough
Gandhi

1984
Barbra Streisand
Yentl

1985
Milos Forman
Amadeus

1986
John Huston
Prizzi's Honor

1987
Oliver Stone
Platoon

1988
Bernardo Bertolucci
The Last Emperor

1989
Clint Eastwood
Bird

1990
Oliver Stone
Born on the Fourth of July

1991
Kevin Costner
Dances with Wolves

1992
Oliver Stone
JFK

1993
Clint Eastwood
Unforgiven

DIRECTORS GUILD OF AMERICA

1948
Joseph L. Mankiewicz
A Letter to Three Wives

1949
Carol Reed
The Third Man

1950
Joseph L. Mankiewicz
All About Eve

1951
George Stevens
A Place in the Sun

1952
John Ford
The Quiet Man

1953
Fred Zinneman
From Here to Eternity

1954
Elia Kazan
On the Waterfront
Billy Wilder
Sabrina

1955
Delbert Mann
Marty

1956
George Stevens
Giant

1957
David Lean
The Bridge on the River Kwai

1958
Vincente Minnelli
Gigi

1959
William Wyler
Ben-Hur

1960
Billy Wilder
The Apartment

1961
Robert Wise
West Side Story
Jerome Robbins
West Side Story

1962
David Lean
Lawrence of Arabia

1963
Tony Richardson
Tom Jones

1964
George Cukor
My Fair Lady

1965
Robert Wise
The Sound of Music

1966
Fred Zinneman
A Man for All Seasons

1967
Mike Nichols
The Graduate

1968
Anthony Harvey
The Lion in Winter

1969
John Schlesinger
Midnight Cowboy

1970
Charles Jarrott
Anne of the Thousand Days
Franklin J. Schaffner
Patton

1971
William Friedkin
The French Connection

1972
Francis Ford Coppola
The Godfather

1973
George Roy Hill
The Sting

1974
Francis Ford Coppola
The Godfather, Part 2

1975
Milos Forman
One Flew Over the Cuckoo's Nest

1976
John G. Avildsen
Rocky

1977
Woody Allen
Annie Hall

1978
Michael Cimino
The Deer Hunter

1979
Robert Benton
Kramer vs. Kramer

1980
Robert Redford
Ordinary People

1981
Warren Beatty
Reds

1982
Richard Attenborough
Gandhi

1983
James L. Brooks
Terms of Endearment

1984
Milos Forman
Amadeus

1985
Steven Spielberg
The Color Purple

1986
Oliver Stone
Platoon

1987
Bernardo Bertolucci
The Last Emperor

1988
Barry Levinson
Rain Man

1989
Oliver Stone
Born on the Fourth of July

1990
Kevin Costner
Dances with Wolves

1991
Jonathan Demme
The Silence of the Lambs

1992
Clint Eastwood
Unforgiven

EDGAR ALLAN POE AWARDS

WRITING

1945
Murder, My Sweet

1947
Crossfire

1949
The Window

1950
The Asphalt Jungle

1951
Detective Story

1953
Big Heat

1954
Rear Window

1955
Desperate Hours

1957
Twelve Angry Men

1958
The Defiant Ones

1959
North by Northwest

1960
Psycho

1963
Charade

1964
Hush, Hush, Sweet Charlotte

1965
The Spy Who Came in from the Cold

1966
Harper

1967
In the Heat of the Night

1968
Bullitt

1969
Z

1971
The French Connection

1972
Sleuth

1973
The Last of Sheila

1974
Chinatown

1975
Three Days of the Condor

1976
Family Plot

1977
The Late Show

1981
Cutter's Way

1982
The Long Good Friday

1983
Gorky Park

1984
A Soldier's Story

1985
Witness

1986
Something Wild

1987
Stakeout

1988
The Thin Blue Line

1989
Heathers

INDEPENDENT SPIRIT AWARDS

ACTOR

1986
M. Emmet Walsh
Blood Simple

1987
James Woods
Salvador

1988
Dennis Quaid
The Big Easy

1989
Edward James Olmos
Stand and Deliver

1990
Matt Dillon
Drugstore Cowboy

1991
Danny Glover
To Sleep with Anger

1992
River Phoenix
My Own Private Idaho

1993
Harvey Keitel
Bad Lieutenant

ACTOR— SUPPORTING

1988
Morgan Freeman
Street Smart

1989
Lou Diamond Phillips
Stand and Deliver

1990
Max Perlich
Drugstore Cowboy

1991
Bruce Davison
Longtime Companion

1992
David Strathairn
City of Hope

1993
Steve Buscemi
Reservoir Dogs

ACTRESS

1986
Geraldine Page
The Trip to Bountiful

1987
Isabella Rossellini
Blue Velvet

1988
Sally Kirkland
Anna

1989
Jodie Foster
Five Corners

1990
Andie MacDowell
sex, lies and videotape

1991
Anjelica Huston
The Grifters

1992
Judy Davis
Impromptu
Diane Ladd
Rambling Rose

1993
Fairuza Balk
Gas Food Lodging

ACTRESS—SUPPORTING

1988
Anjelica Huston
The Dead

1989
Rosana De Soto
Stand and Deliver

1990
Laura San Giacomo
sex, lies and videotape

1991
Sheryl Lee Ralph
To Sleep with Anger

1993
Alfre Woodard
Passion Fish

CINEMATOGRAPHY

1986
Trouble in Mind

1987
Platoon

1988
Matewan

1989
The Unbearable Lightness of Being

1990
Drugstore Cowboy

1991
Wild at Heart

1992
Kafka

1993
Night on Earth

DIRECTOR

1986
Martin Scorsese
After Hours
Joel Coen
Blood Simple

1987
Oliver Stone
Platoon

1988
John Huston
The Dead

1989
Ramon Menendez
Stand and Deliver

1990
Steven Soderberg
sex, lies and videotape

1991
Charles Burnett
To Sleep with Anger

1992
Martha Coolidge
Rambling Rose

1993
Carl Franklin
One False Move

FILM

1986
After Hours

1987
Platoon

1988
River's Edge

1989
Stand and Deliver

1990
sex, lies and videotape

1991
The Grifters

1992
Rambling Rose

1993
The Player

FIRST FEATURE

1988
Dirty Dancing

1989
Mystic Pizza

1990
Heathers

1991
Metropolitan

1992
Straight Out of Brooklyn

1993
The Waterdance

MUSIC

1993
Twin Peaks: Fire Walk with Me

WRITING

1986
The Trip to Bountiful

1987
Platoon

1988
River's Edge

1989
Stand and Deliver

1990
Drugstore Cowboy

1991
To Sleep with Anger

1992
My Own Private Idaho

1993
The Waterdance

MONTREAL WORLD FILM FESTIVAL

ACTOR

1979
Giuliano Gemma
Corleone

1980
Robert Duvall
The Great Santini

1983
Gerard Depardieu
Danton

1985
Armin Mueller-Stahl
Angry Harvest

1987
Leo McKern
Travelling North

1989
Daniel Day-Lewis
My Left Foot

ACTOR—SUPPORTING

1986
Dennis Hopper
Blue Velvet

ACTRESS

1978
Glenda Jackson
Stevie

1988
Udvaros Dorottya
Oh, Bloody Life!

DIRECTOR

1992
Maurizio Nichetti
Volere Volare

FILM

1980
The Stunt Man

1982
Brimstone & Treacle
Time for Revenge

1983
The Go-Masters

1988
La Lectrice

1989
Freedom is Paradise

MTV MOVIE AWARDS

ACTION SEQUENCE

1992
Terminator 2: Judgment Day

1993
Lethal Weapon 3

ACTOR

1992
Arnold Schwarzenegger
Terminator 2: Judgment Day

1993
Denzel Washington
Malcolm X

ACTRESS

1992
Linda Hamilton
Terminator 2: Judgment Day

1993
Sharon Stone
Basic Instinct

BREAKTHROUGH PERFORMANCE

1992
Edward Furlong
Terminator 2: Judgment Day

1993
Marisa Tomei
My Cousin Vinny

COMEDIC PERFORMANCE

1992
Billy Crystal
City Slickers

1993
Robin Williams
Aladdin

FILM

1992
Terminator 2: Judgment Day

1993
A Few Good Men

KISS

1992
Macaulay Culkin/Anna Chlumsky
My Girl

1993
Christian Slater/Marisa Tomei
Untamed Heart

MOST DESIRABLE FEMALE

1992
Linda Hamilton
Terminator 2: Judgment Day

1993
Sharon Stone
Basic Instinct

MOST DESIRABLE MALE

1992
Keanu Reeves
Point Break

1993
Christian Slater
Untamed Heart

NEW FILMMAKER

1992
John Singleton
Boyz N the Hood

1993
Carl Franklin
One False Move

ON-SCREEN DUO

1992
Mike Myers/Dana Carvey
Wayne's World

1993
Mel Gibson/Danny Glover
Lethal Weapon 3

SONG

1992
"(Everything I Do) I Do for You"
Robin Hood. Prince of Thieves

1993
"I Will Always Love You"
The Bodyguard

VILLAIN

1992
Rebecca DeMornay
The Hand that Rocks the Cradle

1993
Jennifer Jason Leigh
Single White Female

ALTERNATE TITLES INDEX

The **ALTERNATE TITLE INDEX** lists 3,600 variant titles for movies, including foreign titles. Titles are listed in alphabetical order followed by a cross-reference to the appropriate title as listed in the main video review section.

A-009 Missione Hong Kong See Code Name Alpha (1967)

Abar, the First Black Superman See In Your Face (1977)

Abbott and Costello in the Navy See In the Navy (1941)

Abbott and Costello Meet the Ghosts See Abbott and Costello Meet Frankenstein (1948)

ABC Murders See The Alphabet Murders (1965)

Abdullah's Harem See Abdulla the Great (1956)

Abismos de Pasion See Wuthering Heights (1953)

Absent-Minded See The Daydreamer (1975)

Absinthe See Madame X (1966)

The Accused See The Mark of the Hawk (1957)

Ace See The Great Santini (1980)

Ace Drummond See Squadron of Doom (1936)

Act of Violence See Deadline Assault (1990)

Adam Wants to Be a Man See Adomas Nori Buti Zmogumi (1959)

Addict See Born to Win (1971)

Addio, Fratello, Crudele See 'Tis a Pity She's a Whore (1973)

Adorable Idiot See Ravishing Idiot (1964)

The Adventure See L'Avventura (1960)

Adventure for Two See The Demi-Paradise (1943)

The Adventure of Lyle Swan See Timerider (1983)

Adventures at Rugby See Tom Brown's School Days (1940)

The Adventures of Chatran See The Adventures of Milo & Otis (1989)

The Adventures of Hercules See Hercules 2 (1985)

The Adventures of Jack London See Jack London (1944)

The Adventures of the Great Mouse Detective See The Great Mouse Detective (1986)

The Adventuress See I See a Dark Stranger (1946)

Aerobicide See Killer Workout (1986)

An Affair of the Heart See Body and Soul (1947)

An Affair of the Heart See The Love Affair, or The Case of the Missing Switchboard Operator (1967)

African Fury See Cry, the Beloved Country (1951)

After Jenny Died See Revenge (1971)

Afurika Monogatari See Green Horizon (1983)

Against All Odds See Kiss and Kill (1968)

Agatha Christie's Endless Night See Endless Night (1971)

Agatha Christie's Ten Little Indians See Ten Little Indians (1989)

Age of Gold See L'Age D'Or (1930)

Agent 38-24-36 See Ravishing Idiot (1964)

The Agitators See The Fix (1984)

Agoniya See Rasputin (1985)

Agostino di Ippona See Augustine of Hippo (1972)

Aimez-Vous Brahms See Goodbye Again (1961)

Airport '79 See The Concorde: Airport '79 (1979)

Akage See Red Lion (1969)

Akahige See Red Beard (1965)

Al Di La Della Legge See Beyond the Law (1968)

Al-Ris-Alah See Mohammed: Messenger of God (1977)

L'Albero Degli Zoccoli See The Tree of Wooden Clogs (1978)

Alem Da Paixao See Happily Ever After (1986)

Alfie Darling See Oh, Alfie (1975)

Alias Bulldog Drummond See Bulldog Jack (1935)

Alien P.I. See Alien Private Eye (1987)

Alien Terror See The Sinister Invasion (1968)

Alien Thunder See Dan Candy's Law (1973)

The Alien's Return See The Return (1980)

Alive by Night See Evil Spawn (1987)

All Good Citizens See All My Good Countrymen (1968)

All in Place See All Screwed Up (1974)

All Night Long See Toute Une Nuit (1982)

All That Money Can Buy See The Devil & Daniel Webster (1941)

All This and Glamour Too See Vogues of 1938 (1937)

All Weekend Lovers See The Killing Game (1967)

Alley of Nightmares See She-Freak (1967)

Almost Human See Shock Waves (1977)

Alone Together See Crisscross (1992)

Alphaville, a Strange Case of Lenny Caution See Alphaville (1965)

Alphaville, Une etrange Aventure de Lenny Caution See Alphaville (1965)

Alter Ego See Murder by the Book (1987)

Amanti d'Oltretomba See Nightmare Castle (1965)

The Amazing Quest of Ernest Bliss See Amazing Adventure (1937)

Amazon Women See Gold of the Amazon Women (1979)

Amazonia: The Catherine Miles Story See White Slave (1986)

American Nightmares See Combat Shock (1984)

American Rickshaw See American Tiger (1989)

American Warrior See American Ninja (1985)

The American Way See Riders of the Storm (1988)

Ami de Mon Ami See Boyfriends & Girlfriends (1988)

Amityville 3D See Amityville 3: The Demon (1983)

The Amityville Horror: The Evil Escapes, Part 4 See Amityville 4 (1989)

Amok See Schizo (1977)

The Amorous General See Waltz of the Toreadors (1962)

The Amorous Sex See Sweet Beat (1962)

Amour de Poche See Girl in His Pocket (1962)

And Comes the Dawn...But Colored Red See Web of the Spider (1970)

And Once Upon a Love See Fantasies (1973)

And Then There Were None See Ten Little Indians (1975)

And Woman...Was Created See And God Created Woman (1957)

Anderson's Angels See Chesty Anderson USN (1976)

Andrews' Raiders See The Great Locomotive Chase (1956)

Andy Colby's Incredibly Awesome Adventure See Andy and the Airwave Rangers (1989)

Angel in Red See Uncaged (1991)

Angel of Vengeance See Ms. 45 (1981)

Angel of Vengeance See WarCat (1988)

An Angel Passed Over Brooklyn See The Man Who Wagged His Tail (1957)

Angel Street See Gaslight (1939)

Angels for Kicks See Wild Riders (1971)

Animal House See National Lampoon's Animal House (1978)

Anita—Tanze des Lasters See Anita, Dances of Vice (1987)

Blazing Magnums *See* Strange Shadows in an Empty Room (1976)

Bless 'Em All *See* The Act (1982)

Blind Alley *See* Perfect Strangers (1984)

The Blind Dead *See* Tombs of the Blind Dead (1972)

Blind Man's Bluff *See* Cauldron of Blood (1967)

Blind Terror *See* See No Evil (1971)

Blonde Bombshell *See* Bombshell (1933)

The Blonde From Peking *See* The Peking Blond (1968)

A Blonde in Love *See* Loves of a Blonde (1965)

Blood and Sand *See* Sand and Blood (1987)

Blood Bath *See* Track of the Vampire (1966)

Blood Beast from Outer Space *See* Night Caller from Outer Space (1966)

Blood Brides *See* Hatchet for the Honeymoon (1970)

The Blood Brother *See* Texas Pioneers (1932)

Blood Brothers *See* Bloody Fist (1977)

Blood Castle *See* The Blood Spattered Bride (1972)

Blood Ceremony *See* The Legend of Blood Castle (1972)

Blood Couple *See* Black Vampire (1973)

Blood Creature *See* Terror is a Man (1959)

The Blood Crowd *See* The McMasters (1970)

The Blood Cult of Shangri-La *See* The Thirsty Dead (1974)

Blood Demon *See* The Torture Chamber of Dr. Sadism (1969)

Blood Doctor *See* Mad Doctor of Blood Island (1969)

The Blood Drinkers *See* The Vampire People (1966)

Blood Feast *See* Night of a Thousand Cats (1972)

Blood Fiend *See* Theatre of Death (1967)

Blood for Dracula *See* Andy Warhol's Dracula (1974)

Blood Hunger *See* Vampyres (1974)

Blood In...Blood Out *See* Bound by Honor (1993)

Blood is My Heritage *See* Blood of Dracula (1957)

Blood Mad *See* The Glove (1978)

Blood Moon *See* The Werewolf vs. the Vampire Woman (1970)

Blood Oath *See* Prisoners of the Sun (1991)

Blood of Frankenstein *See* Dracula vs. Frankenstein (1971)

Blood of Fu Manchu *See* Kiss and Kill (1968)

Blood of the Man Devil *See* House of the Black Death (1965)

Blood of the Undead *See* Schizo (1977)

Blood On His Lips *See* Hideous Sun Demon (1959)

The Blood Seekers *See* Cain's Cutthroats (1971)

Blood Splash *See* Nightmare (1982)

Blood Suckers *See* Gallery of Horror (1967)

Blood Thirst *See* Salem's Lot (1979)

Bloodline *See* Sidney Sheldon's Bloodline (1979)

Bloodsilver *See* Beyond the Law (1968)

The Bloody Bushido Blade *See* The Bushido Blade (1980)

Bloody Pom Poms *See* Cheerleader Camp (1988)

Bloomfield *See* The Hero (1971)

Blue and the Gold *See* The Annapolis Story (1955)

Blue Heat *See* The Last of the Finest (1990)

Blue Manhattan *See* Hi, Mom! (1970)

Blue Sierra *See* Courage of Lassie (1946)

Blues for Lovers *See* Ballad in Blue (1966)

Blues La-Chofesh Ha-Godol *See* Late Summer Blues (1987)

The Boat *See* Das Boot (1981)

Bodas de Sangre *See* Blood Wedding (1981)

The Body Stealers *See* Invasion of the Body Stealers (1969)

Bogus Bandits *See* The Devil's Brother (1933)

The Bold Cavalier *See* The Bold Caballero (1936)

Bolero: An Adventure in Ecstasy *See* Bolero (1984)

Bombsight Stolen *See* Cottage to Let (1941)

The Border *See* Frontera (19??)

Border Heat *See* Deadly Stranger (1988)

Born to Kill *See* Cockfighter (1974)

Bosambo *See* Sanders of the River (1935)

Boss Nigger *See* Boss (1974)

Boudu Sauve des Eaux *See* Boudu Saved from Drowning (1932)

Bourbon St. Shadows *See* The Invisible Avenger (1958)

A Bout de Souffle *See* Breathless (1959)

The Boxer *See* Counter Punch (1971)

The Boyfriend School *See* Don't Tell Her It's Me (1990)

Boyichi and the Supermonster *See* Gamera vs. Gaos (1967)

The Boys from Brooklyn *See* Bela Lugosi Meets a Brooklyn Gorilla (1952)

The Brain Machine *See* Mind Warp (1972)

The Brainsnatchers *See* The Man Who Lived Again (1936)

Branded *See* Bad Boy (1939)

Brandy Ashore *See* Green Grow the Rushes (1951)

The Brave and the Beautiful *See* The Magnificent Matador (1955)

The Brave Young Men of Weinberg *See* Up the Academy (1980)

Break In *See* Loophole (1983)

Breakdance *See* Breakin' (1984)

Breakdance 2: Electric Boogaloo *See* Breakin' 2: Electric Boogaloo (1984)

Brenn, Hexe, Brenn *See* Mark of the Devil (1969)

Brennendes Geheimnis *See* Burning Secret (1989)

Bride of the Atom *See* Bride of the Monster (1956)

The Bride of the Lake *See* Lily of Killarney (1934)

Brides of Blood *See* Brides of the Beast (1968)

Bridge Across Time *See* Terror at London Bridge (1985)

Broken Hearts and Noses *See* Crimewave (1985)

Bronenosets Potemkin *See* The Battleship Potemkin (1925)

Bronx Warriors *See* 1990: The Bronx Warriors (1983)

Brothel 8 *See* Sandakan No. 8 (1974)

Brotherhood of the Yakuza *See* The Yakuza (1975)

Bruce Lee's Game of Death *See* Game of Death (1979)

The Brute *See* El Bruto (1952)

Buck Rogers *See* Destination Saturn (1939)

Buckaroo Banzai *See* The Adventures of Buckaroo Banzai Across the Eighth Dimension (1984)

Bud Abbott and Lou Costello In Hollywood *See* Abbott and Costello in Hollywood (1945)

Build My Gallows High *See* Out of the Past (1947)

A Bullet from God *See* God's Gun (1975)

Bullfighter *See* Torero (1956)

Bump in the Night *See* The Final Terror (1983)

The Bunny Caper *See* Games Girls Play (1975)

Burn Out *See* Journey into Fear (1974)

Burn, Witch, Burn *See* Mark of the Devil (1969)

Burning Cross *See* The Klansman (1974)

Burning Hearts *See* Kolberg (1945)

The Burning Man *See* Dangerous Summer (1982)

The Butcher *See* Le Boucher (1969)

The Butcher *See* Psycho from Texas (1983)

Butcher Baker (Nightmare Maker) *See* Night Warning (1982)

The Butterfly Revolution *See* Summer Camp Nightmare (1986)

Bvongiorno, Elefante *See* Pardon My Trunk (1952)

By Hook or By Crook *See* I Dood It (1943)

By Rocket to the Moon *See* Woman in the Moon (1929)

Cabiria *See* Nights of Cabiria (1957)

Caccia Ai Violenti *See* One Step to Hell (1968)

Cactus Jack *See* The Villain (1979)

Cafe of the Seven Sinners *See* Seven Sinners (1940)

The Cage *See* My Sister, My Love (1978)

Caged Females *See* Caged Heat (1974)

Cain's Way *See* Cain's Cutthroats (1971)

Calhoun *See* Nightstick (1987)

The California Dolls *See* ...All the Marbles (1981)

California Holiday *See* Spinout (1966)

California Hot Wax *See* The Bikini Car Wash Company (1990)

California in 1878 *See* Fighting Thru (1930)

California Man *See* Encino Man (1992)

The Californian *See* The Gentleman from California (1937)

Call Harry Crown *See* 99 & 44/100 Dead (1974)

Call it Murder *See* Midnight (1934)

Call of the Savage *See* Savage Fury (1933)

Call the Cops *See* Find the Lady (1975)

The Calling *See* Murder by Phone (1982)

Calling Wild Bill Elliot *See* Western Double Feature 1: Wild Bill & Sunset Carson (194?)

Campanadas a Medianoche *See* Chimes at Midnight (1967)

Camper John *See* Gentle Savage (1973)

Campsite Massacre *See* The Final Terror (1983)

Canicule *See* Dog Day (1983)

Cannibal Orgy, or the Maddest Story Ever Told *See* Spider Baby (1964)

Cannibals in the City *See* Invasion of the Flesh Hunters (1982)

Cannibals in the Streets *See* Invasion of the Flesh Hunters (1982)

Capitaine Morgan *See* Morgan the Pirate (1960)

Captain Mephisto and the Transformation Machine *See* Manhunt of Mystery Island (1945)

Captain Midnight *See* On the Air Live with Captain Midnight (1979)

Captain Yankee *See* Jungle Raiders (1985)

Captive Women 3: Sweet Sugar *See* Sweet Sugar (1972)

Caravans West *See* Wagon Wheels (1934)

The Card *See* The Promoter (1952)

Cardigan's Last Case *See* State's Attorney (1931)

Carnival of Fools *See* Death Wish Club (1983)

Carnival of Thieves *See* Caper of the Golden Bulls (1967)

Carquake *See* Cannonball (1976)

The Cars That Eat People *See* The Cars That Ate Paris (1974)

Cartagine in Fiamme *See* Carthage in Flames (1960)

Cartes sur Table *See* Attack of the Robots (1966)

Carthage en Flammes *See* Carthage in Flames (1960)

The Case of Jonathan Drew *See* The Lodger (1926)

The Case of the Hillside Stranglers *See* The Hillside Strangler (1989)

Case of the Missing Switchboard Operator *See* The Love Affair, or The Case of the Missing Switchboard Operator (1967)

Cash *See* If I Were Rich (1933)

Cassanova and Co. *See* Sex on the Run (1978)

Castle in the Sky *See* Yidl Mitn Fidl (1936)

Castle of Doom *See* Vampyr (1931)

Castle of Terror *See* Castle of Blood (1964)

Castle of Terror *See* The Virgin of Nuremberg (1965)

Castle of the Living Dead *See* The Virgin of Nuremberg (1965)

The Castle of the Spider's Web *See* Throne of Blood (1957)

Castle of the Walking Dead *See* The Torture Chamber of Dr. Sadism (1969)

The Cat *See* Le Chat (1975)

C.A.T. Squad *See* Stalking Danger (1988)

C.A.T. Squad: Python Wolf *See* Python Wolf (1988)

Catchfire *See* Backtrack (1989)

Catholic Boys *See* Heaven Help Us (1985)

Cathy Tippel *See* Katie's Passion (1975)

Cauchemares *See* Cathy's Curse (1977)

Cavalleria Commandos *See* Cavalry Command (1963)

The Cave Dwellers *See* One Million B.C. (1940)

Cave Man *See* One Million B.C. (1940)

Cavegirl *See* Cave Girl (1985)

C.C. & Company *See* Chrome Hearts (1970)

Cell Block Girls *See* Women's Prison Escape (19??)

Cemetary Girls *See* The Vampire Hookers (1978)

Cemetary Girls *See* The Velvet Vampire (1971)

Cento Dollari D'Odio *See* Uncle Tom's Cabin (1969)

Ceremonia Sangrienta *See* The Legend of Blood Castle (1972)

A Certain Mr. Scratch *See* The Devil & Daniel Webster (1941)

Cet Obscur Objet Du Desir *See* That Obscure Object of Desire (1977)

Chaingang Girls *See* Sweet Sugar (1972)

The Challenge *See* It Takes a Thief (1959)

Chamber of Fear *See* The Fear Chamber (1968)

Champ d'Honneur *See* Field of Honor (1987)

Champion Charlie *See* The Champion/His New Job (1915)

A Change of Face *See* Cambio de Cara (1971)

Chaos-Kaos *See* Kaos (1985)

Chastnaya Zhizn *See* Private Life (1982)

The Chautauqua *See* The Trouble with Girls (and How To Get Into It) (1969)

Che? *See* Diary of Forbidden Dreams (1973)

Cheaters *See* Tricheurs (1984)

Chernobyl: The Final Warning *See* Final Warning (1990)

Chevy Van *See* The Van (1977)

Cheyenne Takes Over *See* Western Double Feature 9: LaRue & Beery (194?)

The Chief Wants No Survivors *See* No Survivors, Please (1963)

Chikamatsu Monogatari *See* The Crucified Lovers (1954)

Chikyu Boelgun *See* The Mysterians (1958)

The Child *See* Kill and Go Hide (1976)

Child of Satan *See* To the Devil, A Daughter (1976)

Child of the Night *See* What the Peeper Saw (1972)

Childish Things *See* Confessions of Tom Harris (1972)

China 9, Liberty 37 *See* Gunfire (1978)

Chinchero *See* The Last Movie (1971)

The Chinese Room *See* El Cuarto Chino (1971)

The Chosen *See* Holocaust 2000 (1983)

Christmas Evil *See* Terror in Toyland (1985)

A Christmas Memory *See* ABC Stage 67: Truman Capote's A Christmas Memory (1966)

The Christmas Tree *See* When Wolves Cry (1969)

Christmas Vacation *See* National Lampoon's Christmas Vacation (1989)

Chuck Norris vs. the Karate Cop *See* Slaughter in San Francisco (1981)

Ciaol Manhattan *See* Edie in Ciao! Manhattan (1972)

Cica Tomina Koliba *See* Uncle Tom's Cabin (1969)

The Circle *See* The Vicious Circle (1957)

The Circle *See* Woman in Brown (1948)

Circle of Power *See* Brainwash (1982)

Citadel of Crime *See* Wheel of Fortune (1941)

Citizen's Band *See* FM (1978)

The City Jungle *See* The Young Philadelphians (1959)

The City of the Dead *See* Horror Hotel (1960)

City of the Living Dead *See* Gates of Hell (1983)

The Clairvoyant *See* The Evil Mind (1934)

The Clairvoyant *See* Killing Hour (1984)

The Clansman *See* The Birth of a Nation (1915)

Class of '86 *See* National Lampoon's Class of '86 (1986)

Class Reunion *See* National Lampoon's Class Reunion (1982)

Claude *See* Two of Us (1968)

Clean Slate *See* Coup de Torchon (1981)

Cleo de 5 a 7 *See* Cleo from 5 to 7 (1961)

Clickety Clack *See* Dodes 'ka-den (1970)

Clinton & Nadine *See* Blood Money: The Story of Clinton and Nadine (1988)

The Closest of Kin *See* All the Lovin' Kinfolk (1989)

Club Dead *See* Terror at Red Wolf Inn (1972)

Coast of Terror *See* Summer City (1977)

Coastwatcher *See* The Last Warrior (1989)

Cobweb Castle *See* Throne of Blood (1957)

Code Name: Operation Crossbow *See* Operation Crossbow (1965)

Code Name: Trixie *See* The Crazies (1973)

Code 645 *See* G-Men Never Forget (1948)

Codename: The Soldier *See* The Soldier (1982)

Coffin of Terror *See* Castle of Blood (1964)

Collision Course *See* The Bamboo Saucer (1968)

Colonel Blimp *See* The Life and Death of Colonel Blimp (1943)

Colorado Ranger *See* Guns of Justice (1950)

Come Back to Me *See* Doll Face (1946)

Come Dance with Me *See* Voulez-Vous Danser Avec Moi? (1959)

Come 'n' Get It *See* Lunch Wagon (1981)

Coming Attractions *See* Loose Shoes (1980)

Comizi d'Amore *See* Love Meetings (1964)

Communion *See* Alice Sweet Alice (1976)

Como Agua para Chocolate *See* Like Water for Chocolate (1993)

The Company of Strangers *See* Strangers in Good Company (1991)

Computer Killers *See* Horror Hospital (1973)

The Con Man *See* The Con Artists (1980)

Concerto *See* I've Always Loved You (1946)

Concrete Cowboys *See* Ramblin' Man (1979)

Confession *See* Repentance (1987)

The Confession *See* Quick, Let's Get Married (1971)

Confessions of A Peeping John *See* Hi, Mom! (1970)

Confidential Report *See* Mr. Arkadin (1955)

The Conflict *See* Catholics (1973)

The Conspiracy *See* Le Complot (1973)

Contamination *See* Alien Contamination (1981)

Continuavamo A Chiamarlo Trinita *See* Trinity is Still My Name (1975)

Convention City *See* Sons of the Desert (1933)

Coonskin *See* Streetfight (1975)

Cop Killers *See* Corrupt (1984)

The Corpse *See* Crucible of Horror (1969)

The Cosmic Man Appears in Tokyo *See* Warning from Space (1956)

Cosmo 2000: Planet Without a Name *See* Cosmos: War of the Planets (1980)

Count Dracula and His Vampire Bride *See* The Satanic Rites of Dracula (1973)

Count Dracula's Great Love *See* Dracula's Great Love (1972)

Country Music *See* Las Vegas Hillbillys (1966)

Country Music Daughter *See* Nashville Girl (1976)

Coup de Foudre *See* Entre-Nous (1983)

Coup de Tete *See* Hothead (1978)

Courage *See* Raw Courage (1984)

The Courage of Kavik, the Wolf Dog *See* Kavik the Wolf Dog (1984)

Court Martial *See* Carrington, V.C. (1954)

The Courtneys of Curzon Street *See* The Courtney Affair (1947)

Crack *See* Strike Force (1975)

Cradle of Crime *See* Dead End (1937)

Crash of Silence *See* Mandy (1953)

The Crawling Monster *See* Creeping Terror (1964)

Crazy for You *See* Vision Quest (1985)

Crazy Horse *See* Friends, Lovers & Lunatics (1989)

Crazy House *See* Night of the Laughing Dead (1975)

Crazy Jack and the Boy *See* Silence (1973)

Crazy Streets *See* Forever, Lulu (1987)

Created to Kill *See* Embryo (1976)

The Creature Wasn't Nice *See* Spaceship (1981)

Creatures *See* From Beyond the Grave (1973)

Creatures of the Prehistoric Planet *See* Horror of the Blood Monsters (1970)

Creatures of the Red Planet *See* Horror of the Blood Monsters (1970)

The Creature's Revenge *See* Brain of Blood (1971)

The Creeper *See* Dark Side of Midnight (1986)

The Creeper *See* Rituals (1979)

The Creepers *See* Assault (1970)

The Creepers *See* Island of Terror (1966)

The Creeping Unknown *See* The Quatermass Experiment (1956)

Creeps *See* Bloody Birthday (1980)

The Cricket *See* La Cicada (1983)

Crime Boss *See* New Mafia Boss (1972)

Crime et Chatiment *See* Crime and Punishment (1935)

Crimes in the Wax Museum *See* Nightmare in Wax (1969)

Crimes, Inc. *See* Gangs, Inc. (1941)

The Crimes of Dr. Mabuse *See* Testament of Dr. Mabuse (1962)

The Criminal *See* The Concrete Jungle (1982)

The Crimson Altar *See* The Crimson Cult (1968)

Crimson Executioner *See* The Bloody Pit of Horror (1965)

The Crimson Ghost *See* Cyclotrode "X" (1946)

Crooks in Clover *See* Penthouse (1933)

Crossed Swords *See* The Prince and the Pauper (1978)

Crossing the Line *See* The Big Man: Crossing the Line (1991)

The Crown Caper *See* Thomas Crown Affair (1968)

Cruel Swamp *See* Swamp Women (1955)

Crying Out Loud *See* Cotton Queen (1937)

Crypt of Dark Secrets *See* Mardi Gras Massacre (1978)

C.S. Lewis Through the Shadowlands *See* Shadowlands (1985)

Csillagosok, Katonak *See* The Red and the White (1968)

Cuba Crossing *See* Sweet Dirty Tony (1981)

Cuban Rebel Girls *See* Assault of the Rebel Girls (1959)

Cult of the Dead *See* The Snake People (1968)

Cupid in the Rough *See* Aggie Appleby, Maker of Men (1933)

Curley and His Gang in the Haunted Mansion *See* Who Killed Doc Robbin? (1948)

Curse of Dark Shadows *See* Night of Dark Shadows (1971)

The Curse of Demon Mountain *See* Shadow of Chikara (1977)

Curse of Melissa *See* The Touch of Satan (1970)

Curse of the Blood-Ghouls *See* The Slaughter of the Vampires (1962)

Curse of the Crimson Altar *See* The Crimson Cult (1968)

Curse of the Living Dead *See* Kill, Baby, Kill (1966)

Curse of the Mushroom People *See* Attack of the Mushroom People (1963)

Curses of the Ghouls *See* The Slaughter of the Vampires (1962)

Cutter and Bone *See* Cutter's Way (1981)

Cybele *See* Sundays & Cybele (1962)

Da Bancarella a Bancarotta *See* Peddlin' in Society (1947)

Daddy's Deadly Darling *See* Pigs (1973)

Dagboek Van Een Oude Dwaas *See* Diary of a Mad Old Man (1988)

Dagora *See* Dagora, the Space Monster (1965)

Dai Koesu Yongkari *See* Yongkari Monster of the Deep (1967)

Daibosatsu Toge *See* Sword of Doom (1967)

Daikaiju Baran *See* Varan the Unbelievable (1961)

Daikaiju Gamera *See* Gamera, the Invincible (1966)

Daikyoju Gappa *See* Gappa the Trifibian Monster (1967)

Dalle Ardenne All'Inferno *See* Dirty Heroes (1971)

Dance of Death *See* House of Evil (1968)

Dance of the Dwarfs *See* Jungle Heat (1984)

Dance of the Vampires *See* The Fearless Vampire Killers (1967)

Danger Rides the Range *See* Three Texas Steers (1939)

Dangerous Charter *See* Creeping Terror (1964)

Dangerous Female *See* The Maltese Falcon (1931)

A Dangerous Friend *See* The Todd Killings (1971)

Dangerous Love Affairs *See* Dangerous Liaisons (1960)

Danielle Steel's Fine Things *See* Fine Things (1990)

Danny Travis *See* The Last Word (1980)

Dans la Ville Blanche *See* In the White City (1983)

Dans les Griffes du Maniaque *See* The Diabolical Dr. Z (1965)

Danza Macabra *See* Castle of Blood (1964)

Daoma Zei *See* The Horse Thief (1987)

Dark Angel *See* I Come in Peace (1990)

The Dark Avenger *See* The Warriors (1955)

Dark Eyes *See* Demon Rage (1982)

Dark Eyes of London *See* Dead Eyes of London (1961)

Dark Eyes of London *See* The Human Monster (1939)

Dark Sands *See* Jericho (1938)

D'Artagnan *See* The Three Musketeers (1916)

Das Bildnis des Dorian Gray *See* Dorian Gray (1970)

Das Blaue Licht *See* The Blue Light (1932)

Das Phantom von Soho *See* The Phantom of Soho (1964)

Das Schlangenei *See* The Serpent's Egg (1978)

Das Schloss *See* The Castle (1968)

Das Ungeheuer von London City *See* The Monster of London City (1964)

The Daughter of Frankenstein *See* Lady Frankenstein (1972)

Day of the Woman *See* I Spit on Your Grave (1977)

The Day the Hot Line Got Hot *See* The Hot Line (1969)

The Day the Screaming Stopped *See* The Comeback (1977)

The Day They Gave the Babies Away *See* All Mine to Give (1956)

Daybreak *See* Le Jour Se Leve (1939)

De Aanslag *See* The Assault (1986)

De la Part des Copains *See* Cold Sweat (1974)

De Sable et de Sang *See* Sand and Blood (1987)

De Stilte Rond Christine M *See* Question of Silence (1983)

De Wisselwachter *See* The Pointsman (1986)

Dead Aim *See* Born in America (1990)

Dead Kids *See* Strange Behavior (1981)

Dead of Night *See* Deathdream (1972)

Dead on Course *See* Wings of Danger (1952)

Dead or Alive *See* A Minute to Pray, A Second to Die (1967)

Dead or Alive *See* The Tracker (1988)

Dead People *See* Messiah of Evil (1974)

Deadly Companion *See* The Double Negative (1980)

Deadly Desire *See* Maybe I'll Be Home in the Spring (1970)

Deadly Desires *See* Home for the Holidays (1972)

Deadly Encounter *See* The Meal (1975)

Deadly is the Female *See* Gun Crazy (1949)

The Deadly Rays From Mars *See* Flash Gordon: Mars Attacks the World (1938)

Deadly Sting *See* Evil Spawn (1987)

Deadly Strike *See* Young Hero (1969)

The Deadly Three *See* Enter the Dragon (1973)

The Deadly Tower *See* Sniper (1975)

Deadly Treasure of the Piranha *See* Killer Fish (1979)

Dear Inspector *See* Dear Detective (1978)

Death and the Green Slime *See* The Green Slime (1968)

Death Bite *See* Spasms (1982)

Death Collector *See* Family Enforcer (1976)

Death Corps *See* Shock Waves (1977)

Death Dimension *See* Kill Factor (19??)

Death From Outer Space *See* The Day the Sky Exploded (1957)

Death Game *See* Seducers (1977)

Death House *See* Silent Night, Bloody Night (1973)

Death of a Hooker *See* Who Killed Mary What's 'Er Name? (1971)

The Death of Richie *See* Richie (1977)

Death Ride to Osaka *See* Girls of the White Orchid (1985)

Death Scream *See* The Deadly Trap (1971)

Death Trap *See* Eaten Alive (1976)

Death Vengeance *See* Fighting Back (1982)

The Death Wheelers *See* Psychomania (1973)

Deathstalker 3: The Warriors From Hell *See* Deathstalker 3 (1989)

Debajo del Mundo *See* Under the Earth (1986)

The Debt *See* Veronico Cruz (1987)

Decoy for Terror *See* Playgirl Killer (1966)

Dedee *See* Dedee d'Anvers (1949)

Delta Pi *See* Mugsy's Girls (1985)

Dem Khann's Zindl *See* The Cantor's Son (1937)

Demanty Noci *See* Diamonds of the Night (1964)

Dementia *See* Daughter of Horror (1955)

Demon *See* God Told Me To (1976)

The Demon *See* Onibaba (1964)

Demon Master *See* Craze (1974)

The Demon Planet *See* Planet of the Vampires (1965)

Demoni *See* Demons (1986)

Demonios En El Jardin *See* Demons in the Garden (1982)

The Deputy *See* El Diputado (1978)

Der Amerikanische Soldat *See* The American Soldier (1970)

Der Blaue Engel *See* The Blue Angel (1930)

Der Chef Wuenscht Keine Zeugen *See* No Survivors, Please (1963)

Der Fluch Der Gruenen Augen *See* Cave of the Living Dead (1965)

Der Fussgaenger *See* The Pedestrian (1973)

Der Hauptmann von Koepenick *See* The Captain from Koepenick (1956)

Der Henker Von London *See* The Mad Executioners (1965)

Der Himmel Uber Berlin *See* Wings of Desire (1988)

Der Joker *See* Lethal Obsession (1987)

Der Kongress Tanzt *See* Congress Dances (1931)

Der Letzte Mann *See* The Last Laugh (1924)

Der Morder Dimitri Karamasoff *See* The Brothers Karamazov (1958)

Der Prozess *See* The Trial (1963)

Der Schweigende Stern *See* First Spaceship on Venus (1960)

Der Toderspringer *See* The Jumper (1985)

Der Verlone *See* The Lost One (1951)

The East Side Kids Meet Bela Lugosi *See* Ghosts on the Loose (1943)

Easy Go *See* Free and Easy (1930)

Eaten Alive by Cannibals *See* Emerald Jungle (1980)

Ebirah, Terror of the Deep *See* Godzilla vs. the Sea Monster (1966)

Eboli *See* Christ Stopped at Eboli (1979)

Edgar Allan Poe's Conqueror Worm *See* The Conqueror Worm (1968)

Edgar Allen Poe's The Oblong Box *See* The Oblong Box (1969)

The Edge of Hell *See* Rock 'n' Roll Nightmare (1985)

Edipo Re *See* Oedipus Rex (1967)

Ein Mann wie Eva *See* A Man Like Eva (1983)

Eine Liebe in Deutschland *See* A Love in Germany (1984)

Einer Frisst den Anderen *See* Dog Eat Dog (1964)

Ekstase *See* Ecstasy (1933)

El Ataud Del Coffin *See* The Vampire's Coffin (1958)

El Ataud Del Vampiro *See* The Vampire's Coffin (1958)

El Buque Maldito *See* Horror of the Zombies (1974)

El Cazador de la Muerte *See* Deathstalker (1983)

El Cobra *See* The Cobra (1968)

El Coleccionista de Cadaveres *See* Cauldron of Blood (1967)

El Dedo En El Gatillo *See* Finger on the Trigger (1965)

El Espiritu de la Colmena *See* Spirit of the Beehive (1973)

El Grito de la Muerte *See* The Living Coffin (1958)

El la Nave Va *See* And the Ship Sails On (1983)

El Mas Fabulosi Golpe del Far West *See* The Boldest Job in the West (1971)

El Pirata Negro *See* The Black Pirate (1965)

El Rapto de las Sabinas *See* The Rape of the Sabines (1961)

El Retorno de la Walpurgis *See* Curse of the Devil (1973)

El Robot Humano *See* The Robot vs. the Aztec Mummy (1959)

El Rubio de las dos Caras *See* The Hot Line (1969)

El Sonido de la Muerte *See* Sound of Horror (1964)

El Tesoro del Amazones *See* The Treasure of the Amazon (1984)

El, This Strange Passion Torments *See* El (1955)

El Verano de la Senora Forbes *See* The Summer of Miss Forbes (1988)

Electric Boogaloo "Breakin' 2" *See* Breakin' 2: Electric Boogaloo (1984)

The Electric Monster *See* The Electronic Monster (1957)

Elena et les Hommes *See* Elena and Her Men (1956)

Elevator to the Gallows *See* Frantic (1958)

Emergency Landing *See* Robot Pilot (1941)

Emil Und Die Detektive *See* Emil and the Detective (1964)

Emma Mae *See* Black Sister's Revenge (1976)

The Emperor of Peru *See* The Odyssey of the Pacific (1982)

Empire of Passion *See* In the Realm of Passion (1980)

The Empress Yang Kwei Fei *See* Princess Yang Kwei Fei (1955)

En Effeuillant la Marguerite *See* Mademoiselle Striptease (1957)

En Enda Natt *See* Only One Night (1942)

En Kvinnas Ansikte *See* A Woman's Face (1938)

En Lekiton i Karlek *See* Lesson in Love (1954)

The Enchanted Island *See* La Isla Encantada (1984)

End of the Rainbow *See* Northwest Outpost (1947)

End of the World *See* Panic in the Year Zero! (1962)

End of the World (in Our Usual Bed in a Night Full of Rain) *See* A Night Full of Rain (1978)

Enemies of the Public *See* Public Enemy (1931)

Enemy from Space *See* Quatermass 2 (1957)

Enemy Round-Up *See* Hillbilly Blitzkrieg (1942)

Enid is Sleeping *See* Over Her Dead Body (1991)

Enormous Changes at the Last Minute *See* Trumps (1988)

Ensayo de un Crimen *See* The Criminal Life of Archibaldo de la Cruz (1955)

Entebbe: Operation Thunderbolt *See* Operation Thunderbolt (1977)

Enter the Devil *See* The Eerie Midnight Horror Show (1982)

Entre Tinieblas *See* Dark Habits (1984)

Episoda Del Mare *See* La Terra Trema (1948)

Ercole al Centro Della Terra *See* Hercules in the Haunted World (1964)

Ercole Alla Conquista di Atlantide *See* Hercules and the Captive Women (1963)

Ercole Contro Molock *See* Conquest of Mycene (1963)

Ercole e la Regina de Lidia *See* Hercules Unchained (1959)

Erik the Conqueror *See* The Invaders (1963)

Ernest Hemingway's the Killers *See* The Killers (1964)

Escapade *See* Utopia (1951)

Escape from the Dark *See* The Littlest Horse Thieves (1976)

Escape If You Can *See* St. Benny the Dip (1951)

The Escape of Megagodzilla *See* Terror of Mechagodzilla (1978)

Escape Route *See* I'll Get You (1953)

Escape to Freedom *See* Judgment in Berlin (1988)

Escapement *See* The Electronic Monster (1957)

Escort Girl *See* Half Moon Street (1986)

Espiritismo *See* Spiritism (1961)

Et Dieu Crea la Femme *See* And God Created Woman (1957)

Et Mourir de Plaisir *See* Blood and Roses (1961)

Etat de Siege *See* State of Siege (1973)

European Vacation *See* National Lampoon's European Vacation (1985)

Every Day's a Holiday *See* Seaside Swingers (1965)

Every Home Should Have One *See* Think Dirty (1970)

Every Man For Himself *See* The Ruthless Four (1970)

Every Night a New Lover *See* Cada Noche un Amor (1975)

Every Woman's Man *See* The Prizefighter and the Lady (1933)

Everybody's Cheering *See* Take Me Out to the Ball Game (1949)

Evil Dead 3 *See* Army of Darkness (1992)

Evil in the Swamp *See* All the Kind Strangers (1974)

Ewiger Walzer *See* The Eternal Waltz (1959)

Except For Me and Thee *See* Friendly Persuasion (1956)

Expedition Moon *See* Rocketship X-M (1950)

Exploring the Kinsey Report *See* One Plus One (1961)

Expose *See* The House on Straw Hill (1976)

Extase *See* Ecstasy (1933)

Extreme Close-Up *See* Sex Through a Window (1972)

An Eye for an Eye *See* Psychopath (1973)

An Eye for an Eye *See* Talion (1966)

Eyes of Hell *See* The Mask (1961)

Eyes Without a Face *See* Horror Chamber of Dr. Faustus (1959)

Eyewitness *See* Sudden Terror (1970)

Fabula de la Bella Palomera *See* The Fable of the Beautiful Pigeon Fancier (1988)

The Fabulous Baron Munchausen *See* The Original Fabulous Adventures of Baron Munchausen (1961)

Face of a Stranger *See* The Promise (1978)

Face the Music *See* Black Glove (1954)

The Faceless Monsters *See* Nightmare Castle (1965)

Fakebook *See* American Blue Note (1989)

Falcon's Gold *See* Robbers of the Sacred Mountain (1983)

Fall Break *See* The Mutilator (1985)

The Fall Guy *See* What's Up Front (1963)

The Fall of the House of Usher *See* La Chute de la Maison Usher (1928)

False Face *See* Scalpel (1976)

False Faces *See* Let 'Em Have It (1935)

Falstaff *See* Chimes at Midnight (1967)

Fanatic *See* Die! Die! My Darling! (1965)

The Fanatic *See* The Last Horror Film (1982)

Fangelse *See* Devil's Wanton (1949)

Fanny by Gaslight *See* Man of Evil (1948)

Fanny Och Alexander *See* Fanny and Alexander (1983)

Farewell, Friend *See* Honor Among Thieves (1968)

Farewell, My Love *See* Murder, My Sweet (1944)

The Farm *See* The Curse (1987)

Farm Girl *See* The Farmer's Other Daughter (1965)

Farm of the Year *See* Miles from Home (1988)

Fashions *See* Fashions of 1934 (1934)

Fast Fortune *See* 11 Harrowhouse (1974)

Fatal Assassin *See* African Rage (1978)

Fatal Woman *See* Femme Fatale (1990)

The Father *See* Baba (1973)

Father Brown *See* The Detective (1954)

Father Damien: The Leper Priest *See* Damien: The Leper Priest (1980)

The Father Kino Story *See* Mission to Glory (1980)

Father Master *See* Padre Padrone (1977)

Father, Son and the Mistress *See* For Richer, For Poorer (1992)

Faustrecht der Freiheit *See* Fox and His Friends (1975)

Fear *See* Night Creature (1979)

The Fear *See* Gates of Hell (1983)

Fear Eats the Soul *See* Ali: Fear Eats the Soul (1974)

Fear in the City of the Living Dead *See* Gates of Hell (1983)

Fear in the Night *See* Dynasty of Fear (1972)

Feast of Flesh *See* Blood Feast (1963)

Federico Fellini's 8 1/2 *See* 8 1/2 (1963)

Federico Fellini's Intervista *See* Intervista (1987)

Feel the Heat *See* Catch the Heat (1987)

Female *See* The Violent Years (1956)

The Female Butcher See The Legend of Blood Castle (1972)

A Few Days in the Life of I.I. Oblomov See Oblomov (1981)

The Fiend with the Atomic Brain See Blood of Ghastly Horror (1972)

The Fiend with the Electronic Brain See Blood of Ghastly Horror (1972)

Fiendish Ghouls See Mania (1960)

Fierce See Fighting Mad (1977)

The Fifth Chair See It's in the Bag (1945)

The Fighting Phantom See The Mysterious Rider (1933)

The Fighting Pimpernel See The Elusive Pimpernel (1950)

The Fighting Seventh See Little Big Horn (1951)

Film d'Amore et d'Anarchia See Love and Anarchy (1973)

Filofax See Taking Care of Business (1990)

The Final Crash See Steelyard Blues (1973)

Finally, Sunday See Confidentially Yours (1983)

Fine and Dandy See The West Point Story (1950)

Fire Festival See Himatsuri (1985)

Fire in Eden See Tusks (1989)

Fire Maidens of Outer Space See Fire Maidens from Outer Space (1956)

The First Great Train Robbery See The Great Train Robbery (1979)

The First Hello See High Country (1981)

The First of the Few See Spitfire (1942)

The First Rebel See Allegheny Uprising (1939)

The First Time See The Fighter (1952)

First Woman Into Space See Space Monster (1964)

A Fist Full of Chopsticks See They Call Me Bruce? (1982)

Fist of Fury See Chinese Connection (1973)

Fist Right of Freedom See Fox and His Friends (1975)

Five Bloody Days to Tombstone See Gun Riders (1969)

Five Bloody Graves See Gun Riders (1969)

Five Day Lover See Time Out for Love (1961)

Five Days See Paid to Kill (1954)

Flash Gordon's Trip to Mars See Flash Gordon: Mars Attacks the World (1938)

Flatbed Annie See Flatbed Annie and Sweetiepie: Lady Truckers (1979)

The Flesh and the Fiends See Mania (1960)

The Flesh Creatures See Horror of the Blood Monsters (1970)

Flesh Creatures of the Red Planet See Horror of the Blood Monsters (1970)

Flesh for Frankenstein See Andy Warhol's Frankenstein (1974)

The Flight See The Taking of Flight 847: The Uli Derickson Story (1988)

The Flight of the White Stallions See The Miracle of the White Stallions (1963)

Flipper and the Pirates See Flipper's New Adventure (1964)

Floating Weeds See Drifting Weeds (1959)

Flying Aces See The Flying Deuces (1939)

Fog See A Study in Terror (1966)

Folies Bourgeoises See Twist (1976)

The Folks at Red Wolf Inn See Terror at Red Wolf Inn (1972)

Follow That Bird See Sesame Street Presents: Follow That Bird (1985)

Follow the Hunter See Fangs of the Wild (1954)

Follow Your Dreams See Independence Day (1983)

Fontane Effi Briest See Effi Briest (1974)

For a Few Bullets More See Any Gun Can Play (1967)

For Better or For Worse See Honeymoon Academy (1990)

For Love or Money See If I Were Rich (1933)

For Men Only See Tall Lie (1953)

For We Too Do Not Forgive See Death is Called Engelchen (1963)

Forbidden Alliance See The Barretts of Wimpole Street (1934)

Forbidden Love See Freaks (1932)

Forbidden Paradise See Hurricane (1979)

Forbidden Passions See The Sensuous Teenager (1970)

Forbidden Son See Bulldance (1988)

The Forbin Project See Colossus: The Forbin Project (1970)

Forbrydelsens Element See The Element of Crime (1985)

Ford Fairlane See The Adventures of Ford Fairlane (1990)

The Forest Primeval See The Final Terror (1983)

Forgotten Prisoners: The Amnesty Files See Forgotten Prisoners (1990)

The Forsyte Saga See That Forsyte Woman (1950)

Fort Lost See Fuerte Perdido (1978)

Fortune in Diamonds See The Adventurers (1951)

47 Samurai See 47 Ronin, Part 1 (1942)

Forward March See Doughboys (1930)

The Four Just Men See The Secret Four (1940)

A Fourth for Marriage See What's Up Front (1963)

4...3...2...1...Morte See Mission Stardust (1968)

F.P. 1 Antwortet Nicht See F.P. 1 Doesn't Answer (1933)

Fra Diavolo See The Devil's Brother (1933)

Frage 7 See Question 7 (1963)

Frankenstein '88 See The Vindicator (1985)

Frankenstein Meets the Spacemen See Frankenstein Meets the Space Monster (1965)

Frasier the Lovable Lion See Frasier the Sensuous Lion (1973)

Fraternally Yours See Sons of the Desert (1933)

The Freak From Suckweasel Mountain See Geek Maggot Bingo (1983)

Free to Live See Holiday (1938)

Frenzy See Torment (1944)

Freylekhe Kabtsonim See The Jolly Paupers (1938)

The Fright See Visiting Hours (1982)

The Frightened Lady See The Case of the Frightened Lady (1939)

Friz Freleng's Looney Looney Looney Bugs Bunny Movie See Looney Looney Looney Bunny Movie (1981)

The Frog Prince See The French Lesson (1986)

From a Whisper to a Scream See The Offspring (1987)

From Broadway to Cheyenne See Broadway to Cheyenne (1932)

From the Mixed-Up Files of Mrs. Basil E. Frankweiler See The Hideaways (1973)

Frontier Horizon See The New Frontier (1935)

Fruhlingssinfonie See Spring Symphony (1986)

The Fruit Machine See Wonderland (1988)

Fukkatsu no Hi See Virus (1982)

The Fulfillment of Mary Gray See Fulfillment (1989)

The Fun House See Last House on Dead End Street (1977)

Fun Loving See Quackser Fortune Has a Cousin in the Bronx (1970)

Fuoco Fatuo See The Fire Within (1964)

Furankenshutain No Kaijusanda Tai Gailah See War of the Gargantuas (1970)

Fury of Samson See The Fury of Hercules (1961)

Fury of the Succubus See Demon Rage (1982)

Fury of the Vikings See The Invaders (1963)

Future Cop See Trancers (1985)

Galaxy Express 999 See Galaxy Express (1982)

Gambara vs. Barugon See Gamera vs. Barugon (1966)

Gamblin' Man See Cockfighter (1974)

Game of Survival See Tenement (1985)

Gamera See Gamera, the Invincible (1966)

Gamera Tai Barugon See Gamera vs. Barugon (1966)

Gamera Tai Gaos See Gamera vs. Gaos (1967)

Gamera Tai Guiron See Gamera vs. Guiron (1969)

Gamera Tai Shinkai Kaiju Jigara See Gamera vs. Zigra (1971)

Gamera the Invincible See Gammera the Invincible (1966)

Gamera vs. Gyaos See Gamera vs. Gaos (1967)

Gamera vs. the Deep Sea Monster Zigra See Gamera vs. Zigra (1971)

Gamma 693 See The Chilling (1989)

Gamma 693 See Night of the Zombies (1981)

Gamma Sango Uchu Daisakusen See The Green Slime (1968)

Gammera See Gamera, the Invincible (1966)

Gang War See Odd Man Out (1947)

Gangs of Sonora See Western Double Feature 6: Rogers & Trigger (1950)

Ganja and Hess See Black Vampire (1973)

The Gardener See Seeds of Evil (1976)

The Gargon Terror See Teenagers from Outer Space (1959)

Garou Garou le Passe Muraille See Mr. Peek-A-Boo (1950)

Gas-s-s-s... or, It May Become Necessary to Destroy the World in Order to Save It See Gas-s-s-s! (1970)

Gasu Ningen Daiichigo See The Human Vapor (1968)

A Gathering of Old Men See Murder on the Bayou (1991)

Gatto Rossi In Un Labirinto Do Vetro See Eyeball (1978)

The Gay Divorce See The Gay Divorcee (1934)

The Gay Mrs. Trexel See Susan and God (1940)

Gebroken Spiegels See Broken Mirrors (1985)

Geheimecode Wildganse See Codename: Wildgeese (1984)

Georgia's Friends See Four Friends (1981)

Gestapo See Night Train to Munich (1940)

Get Down and Boogie See Darktown Strutters (1974)

Get Well Soon See Visiting Hours (1982)

Getting Even See Utilities (1983)

Gharbar See The Householder (1963)

Ghare Baire See The Home and the World (1984)

Ghidora, The Three-Headed Monster See Ghidrah the Three Headed Monster (1965)

Ghidorah Sandai Kaiju Chikyu Saidai No Kessan See Ghidrah the Three Headed Monster (1965)

Ghidrah *See* Ghidrah the Three Headed Monster (1965)

Ghost Crazy *See* Ghost Crazy (1944)

The Ghost Creeps *See* Boys of the City (1940)

The Ghost of John Holling *See* Mystery Liner (1934)

The Ghost Steps Out *See* The Time of Their Lives (1946)

Ghost Story *See* Madhouse Mansion (1974)

Ghosts in the Night *See* Ghosts on the Loose (1943)

Ghosts on the Loose *See* Spooks Run Wild (1941)

The Ghoul in School *See* Werewolf in a Girl's Dormitory (1961)

The Giant Leeches *See* Attack of the Giant Leeches (1959)

Gigantis, the Fire Monster *See* Godzilla Raids Again (1959)

Gill Woman *See* Voyage to the Planet of Prehistoric Women (1968)

Gill Women of Venus *See* Voyage to the Planet of Prehistoric Women (1968)

Gingerbread House *See* Who Slew Auntie Roo? (1971)

Girl in Pawn *See* Little Miss Marker (1934)

Girl in the Moon *See* Woman in the Moon (1929)

Girl in the Park *See* Sanctuary of Fear (1979)

Girl in the Street *See* London Melody (1937)

The Girl Was Young *See* Young and Innocent (1937)

Girls For Rent *See* I Spit on Your Corpse (1974)

Girls in Uniform *See* Maedchen in Uniform (1931)

Giro City *See* And Nothing But the Truth (1982)

Giu la Testa *See* A Fistful of Dynamite (1972)

Giulietta Degli Spiriti *See* Juliet of the Spirits (1965)

Gladiatorerna *See* The Gladiators (1970)

The Glass Cage *See* Glass Tomb (1955)

Gli Indifferenti *See* Time of Indifference (1964)

Gli Invasori *See* The Invaders (1963)

Glory at Sea *See* The Gift Horse (1952)

The Glove: Lethal Terminator *See* The Glove (1978)

Glump *See* Please Don't Eat My Mother (1972)

G'mar Giviya *See* Cup Final (1992)

Gnaw: Food of the Gods 2 *See* Food of the Gods: Part 2 (1988)

Go and See *See* Come and See (1985)

The Goat *See* La Chevre (1981)

Godzilla Fights the Giant Moth *See* Godzilla vs. Mothra (1964)

Godzilla on Monster Island *See* Godzilla vs. Gigan (1972)

Godzilla Versus the Bionic Monster *See* Godzilla vs. the Cosmic Monster (1974)

Godzilla vs. Hedora *See* Godzilla vs. the Smog Monster (1972)

Godzilla vs. Hedora *See* Godzilla vs. the Smog Monster (1972)

Godzilla vs. Mechagodzilla *See* Godzilla vs. the Cosmic Monster (1974)

Godzilla vs. the Giant Moth *See* Godzilla vs. Mothra (1964)

Godzilla vs. the Thing *See* Godzilla vs. Mothra (1964)

Godzilla's Counter Attack *See* Godzilla Raids Again (1959)

Going Ape *See* Where's Poppa? (1970)

Gojira *See* Godzilla, King of the Monsters (1956)

Gojira no Musuko *See* Son of Godzilla (1966)

Gojira Tai Hedora *See* Godzilla vs. the Smog Monster (1972)

Gojira Tai Megaro *See* Godzilla vs. Megalon (1976)

Gojira Tai Meka-Gojira *See* Godzilla vs. the Cosmic Monster (1974)

Goke, Body Snatcher from Hell *See* Body Snatcher from Hell (1969)

Goke the Vampire *See* Body Snatcher from Hell (1969)

Gokiburi *See* Twilight of the Cockroaches (1990)

Golden Hands of Kurigal *See* Federal Agents vs. Underworld, Inc. (1949)

The Golden Heist *See* Inside Out (1975)

The Golden Hour *See* Pot O' Gold (1941)

Golden Ivory *See* White Huntress (1957)

The Golden Rooster *See* El Gallo de Oro (1965)

The Golden Trail *See* Riders of the Whistling Skull (1937)

Goliat Contra Los Gigantes *See* Goliath Against the Giants (1963)

Goliath and the Giants *See* Goliath Against the Giants (1963)

Goliath and the Golden City *See* Samson and the 7 Miracles of the World (1962)

Goliath Contro I Giganti *See* Goliath Against the Giants (1963)

Gomar the Human Gorilla *See* Night of the Bloody Apes (1968)

Good Luck, Miss Wyckoff *See* The Shaming (1971)

A Good Marriage *See* Le Beau Mariage (1982)

Good Morning Babilonia *See* Good Morning, Babylon (1987)

A Good Time, A Bad Girl *See* Good Time with a Bad Girl (1967)

Good to Go *See* Short Fuse (1988)

Goodbye Bruce Lee: His Last Game of Death *See* Game of Death (1979)

Goodbye, Children *See* Au Revoir Les Enfants (1987)

Goodbye Gemini *See* Twinsanity (1970)

Goodbye to the Hill *See* Paddy (1970)

Gordon il Pirata Nero *See* The Black Pirate (1926)

Gorilla *See* Nabonga (1944)

Gosta Berling's Saga *See* The Atonement of Gosta Berling (1924)

Gotter der Pest *See* Gods of the Plague (1969)

Gran Amore del Conde Dracula *See* Dracula's Great Love (1972)

The Grand Highway *See* Le Grand Chemin (1987)

The Grass is Singing *See* Killing Heat (1984)

The Grasshopper *See* The Passing of Evil (1970)

Grave Desires *See* Brides of the Beast (1968)

Grave Robbers from Outer Space *See* Plan 9 from Outer Space (1956)

Graveyard Tramps *See* Invasion of the Bee Girls (1973)

The Great Adventure *See* The Adventurers (1951)

Great American Bugs Bunny-Road Runner Chase *See* The Bugs Bunny/Road Runner Movie (1979)

The Great Balloon Adventure *See* Olly Olly Oxen Free (1978)

The Great Day *See* A Special Day (1977)

Great Friends *See* Grandes Amigos (197?)

The Great Georgia Bank Hoax *See* Great Bank Hoax (1978)

The Great Lester Boggs *See* Hootch Country Boys (1975)

The Great Manhunt *See* The Doolins of Oklahoma (1949)

Great Monster Yongkari *See* Yongkari Monster of the Deep (1967)

The Great Schnozzle *See* Palooka (1934)

The Great Spy Mission *See* Operation Crossbow (1965)

The Great Wall is a Great Wall *See* A Great Wall (1986)

The Greatest Battle *See* The Great Battle (1979)

The Greatest Battle on Earth *See* Ghidrah the Three Headed Monster (1965)

The Greatest Love *See* Europa '51 (1952)

The Greeks Had a Word for Them *See* Three Broadway Girls (1932)

Green Monkey *See* Blue Monkey (1987)

The Green Ray *See* Summer (1986)

Greta the Mad Butcher *See* Ilsa, the Wicked Warden (1978)

Grey Matter *See* Mind Warp (1972)

Gridlock *See* Great American Traffic Jam (1980)

Grijpstra and de Gier *See* Fatal Error (1983)

Grine Felder *See* Green Fields (1937)

Gringo *See* Gun Fight at Red Sands (1963)

The Grip of the Strangler *See* The Haunted Strangler (1958)

Gruner Felder *See* Green Fields (1937)

Gruppo di Famiglia in un Interno *See* Conversation Piece (1975)

Guardian of the Wilderness *See* Mountain Man (1977)

Gun Man from Bodie *See* Gunman from Bodie (1941)

Gun Moll *See* Jigsaw (1949)

Guney's The Wall *See* The Wall (1983)

Gunpoint *See* At Gunpoint (1955)

Guns in the Afternoon *See* Ride the High Country (1962)

Guns, Sin and Bathtub Gin *See* Lady in Red (1979)

Gwendoline *See* The Perils of Gwendoline (1984)

Gycklarnas Afton *See* Sawdust & Tinsel (1953)

Haakon Haakonsen *See* Shipwrecked (1990)

Hab Og Karlighed *See* Twist & Shout (1984)

Habricha el Hashemesh *See* Escape to the Sun (1972)

Hadaka No Shima *See* The Island (1961)

Hail to the Chief *See* Hail (1973)

Half Slave, Half Free 2 *See* Charlotte Forten's Mission: Experiment in Freedom (1985)

Hallelujah, I'm a Tramp *See* Hallelujah, I'm a Bum (1933)

Hallucination Generation *See* Hallucination (1967)

Ha'Matarah Tiran *See* Sinai Commandos (1968)

The Hammond Mystery *See* The Undying Monster (1942)

Hand of Night *See* Beast of Morocco (1966)

Handgun *See* Deep in the Heart (1983)

Handle With Care *See* Citizens Band (1977)

Handle with Care *See* Citizens Band (1977)

Hands of a Killer *See* Planets Against Us (1961)

The Hands of Orlac *See* Mad Love (1935)

Hands of the Strangler *See* The Hands of Orlac (1960)

Handsome Serge *See* Le Beau Serge (1958)

The Hangover *See* The Female Jungle (1956)

Happiness *See* Le Bonheur (1965)

Happy Go Lucky *See* Hallelujah, I'm a Bum (1933)

Happy Mother's Day, Love, George *See* Run, Stranger, Run (1973)

How To Steal a Diamond in Four Easy Lessons *See* The Hot Rock (1970)

Huggers *See* Crazy Moon (1987)

The Human Beast *See* La Bete Humaine (1938)

The Human Tornado *See* Dolemite 2: Human Tornado (1976)

Hunchback *See* Hunchback of Notre Dame (1982)

Hungry Pets *See* Please Don't Eat My Mother (1972)

Hungry Wives *See* Season of the Witch (1973)

Hunt to Kill *See* The White Buffalo (1977)

The Hunted *See* Touch Me Not (1974)

Hunter of the Apocalypse *See* The Last Hunter (1980)

Hunters Are For Killing *See* Hard Frame (1970)

Hustler Squad *See* The Doll Squad (1973)

I Accuse *See* J'Accuse (1937)

I Am a Fugitive From the Chain Gang *See* I Am a Fugitive from a Chain Gang (1932)

I Bambini Ci Guardano *See* The Children Are Watching Us (1944)

I Became a Criminal *See* They Made Me a Criminal (1939)

I Call First *See* Who's That Knocking at My Door? (1968)

I Changed My Sex *See* Glen or Glenda (1953)

I Cinque Della Vendetta *See* Five Giants from Texas (1966)

I Coltelli Del Vendicatore *See* Viking Massacre (197?)

I Corpi Presentano Tracce Di Violenza Carnale *See* Torso (1973)

I Crossed the Line *See* The Black Klansman (1966)

I Giorni Dell'Inferno *See* Days of Hell (1984)

I Hate Your Guts *See* Shame (1961)

I Have a New Master *See* Passion for Life (1948)

I Have Lived *See* After Midnight (1933)

I Led Two Lives *See* Glen or Glenda (1953)

I Love to Kill *See* Impulse (1974)

I Married Too Young *See* Married Too Young (1962)

I Nuovi Barbari *See* Warriors of the Wasteland (1983)

I Pianeti Contro di Noi *See* Planets Against Us (1961)

I Skiachtra *See* The Enchantress (1985)

I Tre Volti della Paura *See* Black Sabbath (1964)

I, Vampiri *See* The Devil's Commandment (1956)

I Want Her Dead *See* W (1974)

I Was a Teenage Boy *See* Something Special (1986)

I You She He *See* Je Tu Il Elle (1974)

Ich und Er *See* Me and Him (1989)

Identikit *See* Driver's Seat (1973)

Idi i Smotri *See* Come and See (1985)

Ieri, Oggi E Domani *See* Yesterday, Today and Tomorrow (1964)

If You Feel Like Singing *See* Summer Stock (1950)

Ike: The War Years *See* Ike (1979)

Il Bidone *See* The Swindle (1955)

Il Buco *See* Night Watch (1972)

Il Castello de Morti Vivi *See* Castle of the Living Dead (1964)

Il Cobra *See* The Cobra (1968)

Il Conformist *See* The Conformist (1971)

Il Crudeli *See* Hellbenders (1967)

Il Diario di una Cameriera *See* Diary of a Chambermaid (1964)

Il Diavolo in Corpo *See* Devil in the Flesh (1987)

Il Dio Chiamato a Dorian *See* Dorian Gray (1970)

Il Disprezzo *See* Contempt (1964)

Il Figlio del Capitano Blood *See* Son of Captain Blood (1962)

Il Fiume Del Grande Caimano *See* The Great Alligator (1981)

Il Generale Della-Rovere *See* Generale Della Rovere (1960)

Il Giardino Del Finzi-Contini *See* Garden of the Finzi-Continis (1971)

Il Gigante Di Metropolis *See* The Giant of Metropolis (1961)

Il Giorno e L'Ora *See* The Day and the Hour (1963)

Il Gladiatore Di Roma *See* Gladiator of Rome (1963)

Il Gladiatore Invincible *See* The Invincible Gladiator (1963)

Il Ladro Di Bagdad *See* Thief of Baghdad (1961)

Il Ladro di Bambini *See* The Stolen Children (1993)

Il Lago di Satana *See* The She-Beast (1965)

Il Mio Nome e Nessuno *See* My Name is Nobody (1974)

Il Mondo Di Yor *See* Yor, the Hunter from the Future (1983)

Il Montagna di Dio Cannibale *See* Slave of the Cannibal God (1979)

Il Mulino Delle Donne di Pietra *See* Mill of the Stone Women (1960)

Il Natale Che Quasi Non Fu *See* The Christmas That Almost Wasn't (1966)

Il Pianeta Degli Uomini Spenti *See* Battle of the Worlds (1961)

Il Portiere de Notte *See* The Night Porter (1974)

Il Processo *See* The Trial (1963)

Il Re Dei Criminali *See* Superargo (1967)

Il Roso Segmo Della Pollias *See* Hatchet for the Honeymoon (1970)

Il Sicario *See* The Hit Man (1961)

Il Sigillo de Pechino *See* The Corrupt Ones (1967)

Il Terror Dei Baraberi *See* Goliath and the Barbarians (1960)

Il Tigre *See* Tiger and the Pussycat (1967)

Il Treno *See* The Train (1965)

Il Vangelo Secondo Matteo *See* Gospel According to St. Matthew (1964)

Ill Met By Moonlight *See* Night Ambush (1957)

Illicit Interlude *See* Summer Interlude (1950)

Ilsa, the Absolute Power *See* Ilsa, the Wicked Warden (1978)

Ilya Mourometz *See* Sword & the Dragon (1956)

Im Stahlnetz Des Dr. Mabuse *See* The Return of Dr. Mabuse (1961)

Immediate Disaster *See* The Stranger from Venus (1954)

The Important Story of Alcoholism *See* One Too Many (1951)

Impossible Object *See* The Story of a Love Story (1973)

In Bed with Madonna *See* Truth or Dare (1991)

In Love *See* Falling in Love Again (1980)

In Love and Engaged *See* Somos Novios (1968)

In Old Oklahoma *See* War of the Wildcats (1943)

In the Devil's Garden *See* Assault (1970)

In the Grip of the Spider *See* Web of the Spider (1970)

In the Woods *See* Rashomon (1951)

Incense For the Damned *See* The Bloodsuckers (1970)

Incident at Victoria Falls *See* Sherlock Holmes and the Incident at Victoria Falls (1991)

The Incredible Invasion *See* The Sinister Invasion (1968)

The Incredible Praying Mantis *See* The Deadly Mantis (1957)

The Incredible Torture Show *See* Bloodsucking Freaks (1975)

The Incredibly Strange Creatures *See* Incredibly Strange Creatures Who Stopped Living and Became Mixed-Up Zombies (1963)

Indian Love Call *See* Rose Marie (1936)

Indiscretion *See* Christmas in Connecticut (1945)

Indiscretion *See* Indiscretion of an American Wife (1954)

The Infernal Idol *See* Craze (1974)

The Infra Superman *See* Infra-Man (1976)

Inn of the Frightened People *See* Revenge (1971)

Innocence is Bliss *See* Miss Grant Takes Richmond (1949)

The Innocent and the Damned *See* Girls' Town (1959)

The Insect *See* The Insect Woman (1963)

Inseminoid *See* Horror Planet (1980)

L'Insoumis *See* Fight for Us (1989)

Interlude *See* Intermezzo (1936)

Intermezzo: A Love Story *See* Intermezzo (1939)

The Intruder *See* Shame (1961)

The Invader *See* Old Spanish Custom (1936)

The Invaders *See* The Forty-Ninth Parallel (1941)

Invasion Earth 2150 A.D. *See* Daleks—Invasion Earth 2150 A.D. (1966)

Invasion Force *See* Hangar 18 (1980)

Invasion of Planet X *See* Godzilla vs. Monster Zero (1968)

Invasion of the Astro-Monsters *See* Godzilla vs. Monster Zero (1968)

Invasion of the Astros *See* Godzilla vs. Monster Zero (1968)

Invasion of the Flying Saucers *See* Earth vs. the Flying Saucers (1956)

An Investigation of Murder *See* Laughing Policeman (1974)

The Invisible Creature *See* House on Marsh Road (1960)

The Invisible Horror *See* The Invisible Dr. Mabuse (1962)

Iron Hand *See* Goetz von Berlichingen (1980)

The Iron Hand *See* Chinese Connection (1973)

The Iron Kiss *See* Naked Kiss (1964)

Island of Monte Cristo *See* Sword of Venus (1953)

Island of the Burning Damned *See* Island of the Burning Doomed (1967)

Island of the Fishmen *See* Screamers (1980)

Island of the Living Horror *See* Brides of the Beast (1968)

Isle of Lost Women *See* 99 Women (1969)

Isle of the Living Dead *See* The Snake People (1968)

Isle of the Snake People *See* The Snake People (1968)

Isn't Life A Bitch? *See* La Chienne (1931)

Istanbul, Keep Your Eyes Open *See* Istanbul (1990)

It Comes Up Murder *See* The Honey Pot (1967)

It Happened at Lakewood Manor *See* Ants (1977)

It Happened in Paris *See* The Lady in Question (1940)

It Happened One Summer *See* State Fair (1945)

It Hurts Only When I Laugh *See* Only When I Laugh (1981)

It Lives By Night *See* The Bat People (1974)

It Only Take Five Minutes *See* Five Minutes to Love (1963)

It Stalked the Ocean Floor *See* Monster from the Ocean Floor (1954)

It! The Vampire From Beyond Space *See* It! The Terror from Beyond Space (1958)

It Won't Rub Off, Baby *See* Sweet Love, Bitter (1967)

The Italian Connection *See* Manhunt (1973)

It's Hot in Hell *See* Un Singe en Hiver (1962)

It's My Life *See* My Life to Live (1962)

It's Only Money *See* Double Dynamite (1951)

Ivan's Childhood *See* My Name is Ivan (1962)

Jack Kerouac's America *See* Kerouac (1984)

Jack London's Klondike Fever *See* Klondike Fever (1979)

Jackals *See* American Justice (1986)

Jackie Chan's Police Story *See* Jackie Chan's Police Force (1985)

Jack's Wife *See* Season of the Witch (1973)

Jacqueline Susann's Once is Not Enough *See* Once is Not Enough (1975)

Jail Birds *See* Pardon Us (1931)

Jailbirds' Vacation *See* Les Grandes Gueules (1965)

The Janitor *See* Eyewitness (1981)

Japan Sinks *See* Tidal Wave (1975)

Jatszani Kell *See* Lily in Love (1985)

Jaws 3-D *See* Jaws 3 (1983)

Jayne Mansfield: A Symbol of the '50s *See* The Jayne Mansfield Story (1980)

J.C. *See* Iron Horsemen (1971)

Je Vous Salue Marie *See* Hail Mary (1985)

Jean de Florette 2 *See* Manon of the Spring (1987)

Jeder Fur Sich Und Gott Gegen Alle *See* Every Man for Himself & God Against All (1975)

Jennie *See* Portrait of Jennie (1948)

Jennifer (The Snake Goddess) *See* Jennifer (1978)

The Jester *See* Der Purimshpiler (1937)

Jesus de Montreal *See* Jesus of Montreal (1989)

Jeu de Massacre *See* The Killing Game (1967)

Jew Suss *See* Power (1934)

The Jewish Jester *See* Der Purimshpiler (1937)

The Jezebels *See* Switchblade Sisters (1975)

Jigokumen *See* Gate of Hell (1954)

Jim Buck *See* Portrait of a Hitman (1977)

Job Lazadasa *See* The Revolt of Job (1984)

Joe Palooka *See* Palooka (1934)

Johnnie Mae Gibson: FBI *See* Johnnie Gibson F.B.I. (1987)

Johnny Vagabond *See* Johnny Come Lately (1943)

A Joke of Destiny *See* A Joke of Destiny, Lying in Wait Around the Corner Like a Bandit (1984)

Joker's Wild *See* Body Trouble (1992)

Jonas—Qui Aura 25 Ans en l'an 2000 *See* Jonah Who Will Be 25 in the Year 2000 (1976)

Joseph Sold by His Brothers *See* Joseph & His Brethren (1960)

Journey into Autumn *See* Dreams (1955)

J.R. *See* Who's That Knocking at My Door? (1968)

A Judgement in Stone *See* The Housekeeper (1986)

Jules et Jim *See* Jules and Jim (1962)

Jules Verne's Rocket to the Moon *See* Those Fantastic Flying Fools (1967)

Julie Darling *See* Daughter of Death (1982)

July Pork Bellies *See* For Pete's Sake (1974)

Jumbo *See* Billy Rose's Jumbo (1962)

Jungfrukallan *See* The Virgin Spring (1959)

Jungle Gold *See* Perils of the Darkest Jungle (1944)

Jungle Woman *See* Nabonga (1944)

Just Another Day at the Races *See* Win, Place, or Steal (1972)

Just Ask for Diamond *See* Diamond's Edge (1988)

Justice Rides Again *See* Destry Rides Again (1939)

Kaiju Daisenso *See* Godzilla vs. Monster Zero (1968)

Kaiju Soshingeki *See* Destroy All Monsters (1968)

Kaitei Daisenso *See* Terror Beneath the Sea (1966)

Kakushi Toride No San Akunin *See* The Hidden Fortress (1958)

Kamakazi *See* Attack Squadron (197?)

Karamazov *See* The Brothers Karamazov (1958)

Katherine *See* The Radical (1975)

Keetje Tippel *See* Katie's Passion (1975)

Kenny Rogers as the Gambler *See* The Gambler (1974)

The Kent Chronicles *See* The Bastard (1978)

The Key *See* Odd Obsession (1960)

KGOD *See* Pray TV (1980)

Kid Auto Races at Venice *See* Kid's Auto Race/Mabel's Married Life (1915)

The Kidnap of Mary Lou *See* Almost Human (1979)

Killbots *See* Chopping Mall (1986)

Killer Bait *See* Too Late for Tears (1949)

Killer Bats *See* The Devil Bat (1941)

The Killer Behind the Mask *See* Savage Weekend (1980)

Killer Grizzly *See* Grizzly (1976)

Killer of Killers *See* The Mechanic (1972)

Killer With a Label *See* One Too Many (1951)

The Killers *See* Pigs (1973)

The Killer's Edge *See* Blood Money (1991)

Killers of the Wild *See* Children of the Wild (1937)

Kimono No Kiroku *See* I Live in Fear (1955)

Kin Folk *See* All the Lovin' Kinfolk (1989)

Kinfolk *See* All the Lovin' Kinfolk (1989)

King Cobra *See* Jaws of Satan (1981)

King Gun *See* The Gatling Gun (1972)

King Kong Tai Godzilla *See* King Kong Versus Godzilla (1963)

King Oedipus *See* Oedipus Rex (1957)

King of Africa *See* One Step to Hell (1968)

The King of Criminals *See* Superargo (1967)

King of the Jungleland *See* Darkest Africa (1936)

Kings Ransom *See* Devastator (1985)

Kisenga, Man of Africa *See* Men of Two Worlds (1946)

A Kiss from Eddie *See* The Arousers (1970)

Kiss My Butterfly *See* I Love You, Alice B. Toklas (1968)

KKK *See* The Klansman (1974)

The Kneeling Goddess *See* La Diosa Arrodillada (1947)

Knives of the Avenger *See* Viking Massacre (197?)

The Knock-Out Cop *See* Flatfoot (1978)

Koks I Kulissen *See* Ladies on the Rocks (1983)

Komissar *See* Commissar (1968)

Koneko Monogatari *See* The Adventures of Milo & Otis (1989)

Konjiki Yasha *See* Golden Demon (1953)

Kootenai Brown *See* Showdown at Williams Creek (1991)

Kopek and Broom *See* Find the Lady (1975)

Krasnaya Palatka *See* Red Tent (1969)

Kronos *See* Captain Kronos: Vampire Hunter (1974)

Kumonosujo, Kumonosu-djo *See* Throne of Blood (1957)

Kung Fu Master *See* Le Petit Amour (1987)

Kunisada Chuji *See* The Gambling Samurai (1960)

Kuroi Ame *See* Black Rain (1988)

Kvinn odrom *See* Dreams (1955)

Kvinnors Vantan *See* Secrets of Women (1952)

Kyuketsuki Gokemidoro *See* Body Snatcher from Hell (1969)

La Banda J.&S. Cronaca Criminale del Far West *See* Sonny and Jed (1973)

La Belle et Laete *See* Beauty and the Beast (1946)

La Bestia Uccide a Sangue Freddo *See* Slaughter Hotel (1971)

La Cabeza Viviente *See* The Living Head (1959)

La Camara Del Terror *See* The Fear Chamber (1968)

La Casa Con La Scala Nel Buio *See* A Blade in the Dark (1983)

La Casa Del Terror *See* Face of the Screaming Werewolf (1959)

La Casa Dell' Exorcismo *See* Lisa and the Devil (1975)

La Casa Embrujada *See* The Curse of the Crying Woman (1961)

La Casa Nel Parco *See* House on the Edge of the Park (1984)

La Case de L'Oncle Tom *See* Uncle Tom's Cabin (1969)

La Caza *See* The Hunt (1967)

La Chambre Verte *See* The Green Room (1978)

La Chiesa *See* The Church (1990)

La Ciociara *See* Two Women (1961)

La Ciudad y los Perros *See* The City and the Dogs (1985)

La Commare Secca *See* The Grim Reaper (1962)

La Decima Vittima *See* 10th Victim (1965)

La Dentielliere *See* The Lacemaker (1977)

La Diagonale du Fou *See* Dangerous Moves (1984)

La Dixieme Victime *See* 10th Victim (1965)

La Donna E Donna *See* A Woman is a Woman (1960)

La Double Vie de Veronique *See* The Double Life of Veronique (1991)

La Dueda Interna *See* Veronico Cruz (1987)

La Famiglia *See* The Family (1987)

La Femme d'a Cote *See* The Woman Next Door (1981)

La Femme De Mon Pote *See* My Best Friend's Girl (1984)

La Femme du Boulanger *See* The Baker's Wife (1933)

La Femme Mariee *See* A Married Woman (1965)

La Fiancee du Pirate *See* A Very Curious Girl (1969)

La Figlia di Frankenstein *See* Lady Frankenstein (1972)

La Fille Du Puisatier *See* Well-Digger's Daughter (1946)

La Folle des Grandeurs *See* Delusions of Grandeur (1976)

La Francaise et L'Amour *See* Love and the Frenchwoman (1960)

La Furia Di Ercole *See* The Fury of Hercules (1961)

La Gloire de Mon Pere *See* My Father's Glory (1991)

La Grande Guerre *See* The Great War (1959)

La Grande Guerre *See* The Great War (1959)

La Grieta *See* Endless Descent (1990)

La Historia Oficial *See* The Official Story (1985)

La Horriplante Bestia Humana *See* Night of the Bloody Apes (1968)

La Illusion en Travnia *See* The Illusion Travels by Streetcar (1953)

La Invasion de Los Vampiros *See* Invasion of the Vampires (1961)

La Isla Del Tersoro *See* Treasure Island (1972)

La Kermesse Heroique *See* Carnival in Flanders (1935)

La Legge *See* Where the Hot Wind Blows (1959)

La Ley del Deseo *See* Law of Desire (1986)

La Linea Del Cielo *See* Skyline (1984)

La Loi *See* Where the Hot Wind Blows (1959)

La Lune Dans le Caniveau *See* Moon in the Gutter (1984)

La Mala Ordina *See* Manhunt (1973)

La Maldicion de a Llorona *See* The Curse of the Crying Woman (1961)

La Maldicion de la Momia Azteca *See* The Curse of the Aztec Mummy (1959)

La Marca del Muerto *See* Creature of the Walking Dead (1960)

La Mariee Etait en Noir *See* The Bride Wore Black (1968)

La Mitad del Cielo *See* Half of Heaven (1986)

La Momia Azteca Contra el Robot Humano *See* The Robot vs. the Aztec Mummy (1959)

La Morte Vestita di Dollar *See* Dog Eat Dog (1964)

La Morte Viene Dalla Spazio *See* The Day the Sky Exploded (1957)

La Motocyclette *See* The Girl on a Motorcycle (1968)

La Muerte Viviente *See* The Snake People (1968)

La Nipote del Vampiro *See* Fangs of the Living Dead (1968)

La Noche de Los Mil Gatos *See* Night of a Thousand Cats (1972)

La Noche dell Terror Ciego *See* Tombs of the Blind Dead (1972)

La Noia: L'Ennui Et Sa Diversion, L'Erotisme *See* Empty Canvas (1964)

La Notte Che Evelyn Usca Dalla Tomba *See* The Night Evelyn Came Out of the Grave (1971)

La Novia Esangentada *See* The Blood Spattered Bride (1972)

La Nuit Americaine *See* Day for Night (1973)

La Nuit de Generaux *See* Night of the Generals (1967)

La Nuit Des Espions *See* Double Agents (1959)

La Passante du Sans Souci *See* La Passante (1983)

La Passion Beatrice *See* Beatrice (1988)

La Permission *See* The Story of a Three Day Pass (1968)

La Planete Sauvage *See* Fantastic Planet (1973)

La Poupee *See* The Doll (1962)

La Prise de Pouvoir Par Louis XIV *See* The Rise of Louis XIV (1966)

La Romana *See* A Woman of Rome (1956)

La Ruee Des Vikings *See* The Invaders (1963)

La Secta de los Tughs *See* Dawn of the Pirates (19??)

La Spada del Cid *See* The Sword of El Cid (1962)

La Spina Dorsale del Diavolo *See* Ride to Glory (1971)

L.A. Streetfighters *See* Ninja Turf (1986)

La Strega in Amore *See* The Witch (1966)

La Tatiche de Ercole *See* Hercules (1958)

La Tragedia di un Uomo Ridicolo *See* The Tragedy of a Ridiculous Man (1981)

La Vendetta De Ercole *See* Goliath and the Dragon (1961)

La Vergine de Norimberga *See* The Virgin of Nuremberg (1965)

La Victoire en Chantant *See* Black and White in Color (1976)

La Vie Devant Soi *See* Madame Rosa (1977)

La Vie est Rien d'Autre *See* Life and Nothing But (1989)

La Vie Privee *See* A Very Private Affair (1962)

Laberinto de Pasiones *See* Labyrinth of Passion (1982)

Labyrinth *See* A Reflection of Fear (1972)

Ladri di Biciclette *See* The Bicycle Thief (1948)

Ladri di Saponette *See* The Icicle Thief (1989)

Lady Beware *See* 13th Guest (1932)

The Lady Dances *See* The Merry Widow (1934)

The Lady Dracula *See* Lemora, Lady Dracula (1973)

Lady Hamilton *See* That Hamilton Woman (1941)

Lady in the Fog *See* Scotland Yard Inspector (1952)

Lady Jane Grey *See* Nine Days a Queen (1934)

The Lady Killers *See* Ladykillers (1955)

Lady of Deceit *See* Born to Kill (1947)

Lady of the Shadows *See* The Terror (1963)

L'Amant de Lady Chatterley *See* Lady Chatterley's Lover (1955)

The Lament of the Path *See* Pather Panchali (1954)

L'Amour en Fuite *See* Love on the Run (1978)

The Lamp *See* The Outing (1987)

Lancelot and Guinevere *See* Sword of Lancelot (1963)

Landru *See* Bluebeard (1963)

L'Anee Derniere a Marienbad *See* Last Year at Marienbad (1961)

Larceny Lane *See* Blonde Crazy (1931)

Larsen, Wolf of the Seven Seas *See* The Legend of the Sea Wolf (1958)

Lasky Jedne Plavovlasky *See* Loves of a Blonde (1965)

L'Associe *See* The Associate (1982)

The Last Adventurers *See* Down to the Sea in Ships (1922)

The Last Battle *See* Le Dernier Combat (1984)

Last Chance For a Born Loser *See* Stateline Motel (1975)

The Last Days of Man on Earth *See* The Final Programme (1973)

The Last Days of Sodom and Gomorrah *See* Sodom and Gomorrah (1962)

The Last Great Treasure *See* Mother Lode (1982)

Last House on the Left, Part 2 *See* Twitch of the Death Nerve (1972)

Last Message From Saigon *See* Operation C.I.A. (1965)

Last of the Cowboys *See* Great Smokey Roadblock (1976)

The Last Page *See* Man Bait (1952)

Last Rites *See* Dracula's Last Rites (1979)

The Last Victim *See* Forced Entry (1975)

The Last Warrior *See* The Final Executioner (1983)

The Last Will of Dr. Mabuse *See* Testament of Dr. Mabuse (1962)

The Late Edwina Black *See* The Obsessed (1951)

Latin Love *See* Greek Street (1930)

Latin Quarter *See* Frenzy (1946)

Laughterhouse *See* Singleton's Pluck (1984)

Laura *See* Shattered Innocence (1979)

The Law *See* Where the Hot Wind Blows (1959)

Law Breakers *See* Les Assassins de L'Ordre (1971)

The Law of the Gun *See* La Ley del Revolver (1978)

Lazy Bones *See* Hallelujah, I'm a Bum (1933)

Le Blonde de Pekin *See* The Peking Blond (1968)

Le Caporal Epingle *See* Elusive Corporal (1962)

Le Carrosse D'Or *See* The Golden Coach (1952)

Le Cerveau *See* The Brain (1969)

Le Charme Discret de la Bourgeoisie *See* The Discreet Charm of the Bourgeoisie (1972)

Le Chateau de Ma Mere *See* My Mother's Castle (1991)

Le Cheval D'Orgeuil *See* The Horse of Pride (1980)

Le Crime de Monsieur Lange *See* The Crime of Monsieur Lange (1936)

Le Danger Vient de l'Escape *See* The Day the Sky Exploded (1957)

Le Declin De L'Empire Americain *See* The Decline of the American Empire (1986)

Le Dejeuner Sur l'Herbe *See* Picnic on the Grass (1959)

Le Dernier Metro *See* The Last Metro (1980)

Le Desert des Tartares *See* The Desert of the Tartars (1976)

Le Diable au Corps *See* Devil in the Flesh (1946)

Le Distrait *See* The Daydreamer (1975)

Le Fantome de la Liberte *See* Phantom of Liberty (1968)

Le Feu Follet *See* The Fire Within (1964)

Le Geant de la Vallee Das Rois *See* Son of Samson (1962)

Le Gentleman D'epsom *See* Duke of the Derby (1962)

Le Grand Bleu *See* The Big Blue (1988)

Le Grand Blond Avec Une Chassure Noire *See* The Tall Blond Man with One Black Shoe (1972)

Le Grand Meaulnes *See* The Wanderer (1967)

Le Jour et L'Heure *See* The Day and the Hour (1963)

Le Journal d'un Cure de Campagne *See* Diary of a Country Priest (1950)

Le Journal d'une Femme de Chambre *See* Diary of a Chambermaid (1964)

Le Juge et L'assassin *See* The Judge and the Assassin (1975)

Le Locataire *See* The Tenant (1976)

Le Maitre de Musique *See* The Music Teacher (1988)

Le Mepris *See* Contempt (1964)

Le Meraviglie Di Aladino *See* The Wonders of Aladdin (1961)

Le Mur *See* The Wall (1983)

Le Neveu de Beethoven *See* Beethoven's Nephew (1988)

Le Nottie de Cabiria *See* Nights of Cabiria (1957)

Le Pays Bleu *See* Blue Country (1977)

Le Peau Douce *See* The Soft Skin (1964)

Le Petit Monde de Don Camillo *See* Little World of Don Camillo (1951)

Le Plus Vieux Metier du Monde *See* Oldest Profession (1967)

Le Proces *See* The Trial (1963)

Le Rayon Vert *See* Summer (1986)

Le Regle du Jeu *See* The Rules of the Game (1939)

Le Roi de Coeur *See* The King of Hearts (1966)

Le Rouble a Deux Faces *See* The Hot Line (1969)

Le Rouge aux Levres *See* Daughters of Darkness (1971)

Le Rouge et le Noir *See* The Red and the Black (1957)

Le Salaire De La Peur *See* Wages of Fear (1955)

Le Sang d'un Poete *See* The Blood of a Poet (1930)

le Sant de l'Ange *See* Cobra (1971)

Le Sauvage *See* Lovers Like Us (1975)

Le Train *See* The Train (1965)

Le Trou *See* Night Watch (1972)

Le Vieil Homme Et L'Enfant *See* Two of Us (1968)

Le Voleur De Bagdad *See* Thief of Baghdad (1961)

Leader of the Pack *See* Unholy Rollers (1972)

L'eclisse *See* The Eclipse (1966)

L'Ecole Buissonniere *See* Passion for Life (1948)

Legacy of Blood *See* Blood Legacy (1973)

The Legacy of Maggie Walsh *See* The Legacy (1979)

The Legend *See* James Dean (1976)

Legend in Leotards *See* Return of Captain Invincible (1983)

Legend of Cougar Canyon *See* The Secret of Navajo Cave (1976)

The Legend of Gosta Berling *See* The Atonement of Gosta Berling (1924)

The Legend of Machine Gun Kelly *See* Melvin Purvis: G-Man (1974)

Legend of the Bayou *See* Eaten Alive (1976)

Legend of the Seven Golden Vampires *See* The 7 Brothers Meet Dracula (1973)

Legend of Witch Hollow *See* The Witchmaker (1969)

Legenda Del Rudio Malese *See* Jungle Raiders (1985)

Legenda Suramskoi Kreposti *See* The Legend of Suram Fortress (1985)

The Legendary Curse of Lemora *See* Lemora, Lady Dracula (1973)

Legion of the Damned *See* Battle of the Commandos (1971)

L'Enfant Sauvage *See* The Wild Child (1970)

Leona Helmsley: The Queen of Mean *See* The Queen of Mean (1990)

Lepassager de la Pluie *See* Rider on the Rain (1970)

L'Eredita Ferramonti *See* The Inheritance (1976)

Les Amities Particulieres *See* This Special Friendship (1967)

Les Bas Fonds *See* The Lower Depths (1936)

Les Choses De La Vie *See* The Things of Life (1970)

Les Corrompus *See* The Corrupt Ones (1967)

Les Cousins *See* The Cousins (1959)

Les Deux Anglaises et le Continent *See* Two English Girls (1972)

Les Deux Rivales *See* Time of Indifference (1964)

Les Diabolique *See* Diabolique (1955)

Les Dimanches de Ville d'Arvay *See* Sundays & Cybele (1962)

Les Enfants du Paradise *See* Children of Paradise (1944)

Les Felins *See* Joy House (1964)

Les Femmes *See* The Women (1969)

Les Gaspards *See* The Holes (1972)

Les Grandes Personnes *See* Time Out for Love (1961)

Les Innocents aux Mains Sales *See* Dirty Hands (1976)

Les Jeux Interdits *See* Forbidden Games (1952)

Les Liaisons Dangereuses *See* Dangerous Liaisons (1960)

Les Liens de Sang *See* Blood Relatives (1978)

Les Louves *See* Letters to an Unknown Lover (1984)

Les Mille Et Une Nuits *See* The Wonders of Aladdin (1961)

Les Mongols *See* The Mongols (1960)

Les Noces de Papier *See* A Paper Wedding (1989)

Les Nuits De La Pleine *See* Full Moon in Paris (1984)

Les Parapluies De Cherbourg *See* Umbrellas of Cherbourg (1964)

Les Ripoux *See* My New Partner (1984)

Les Somnambules *See* Mon Oncle D'Amerique (1980)

Les Vacances de Monsieur Hulot *See* Mr. Hulot's Holiday (1953)

Les Valseuses *See* Going Places (1974)

Les Yeux Noirs *See* Dark Eyes (1987)

Les Yeux Sans Visage *See* Horror Chamber of Dr. Faustus (1959)

Lesbian Twins *See* The Virgin Witch (1970)

L'Ete Meurtrier *See* One Deadly Summer (1983)

L'Ete Prochain *See* Next Summer (1984)

L'Eternel Retour *See* Eternal Return (1943)

Lethal *See* The KGB: The Secret War (1986)

A Letter to Mother *See* A Brivele der Mamen (1938)

Letyat Zhuravit *See* The Cranes are Flying (1957)

L'Evangile Selon Saint-Matthieu *See* Gospel According to St. Matthew (1964)

L'Histoire d'Adele H. *See* Story of Adele H. (1975)

Libido *See* The Sensuous Teenager (1970)

Licensed to Kill *See* Second Best Secret Agent in the Whole Wide World (1965)

The Life and Adventures of Nicholas Nickleby *See* Nicholas Nickleby (1946)

The Life and Loves of Beethoven *See* Beethoven (1936)

Life at Stake *See* The Key Man (1957)

Life in the Food Chain *See* Age Isn't Everything (1991)

Life of Brian *See* Monty Python's Life of Brian (1979)

The Life of Jack London *See* Jack London (1944)

The Light Fantastic *See* Love is Better Than Ever (1952)

Lights of Variety *See* Variety Lights (1951)

Like a Crow on a June Bug *See* Sixteen (1972)

Like Father, Like Son *See* The Executioner (1978)

Like Two Drops of Water *See* Como Dos Gotas de Agua (197?)

Lila *See* Mantis in Lace (1968)

Lilacs in the Spring *See* Let's Make Up (1955)

L'Inafferrabile Invincible *See* Mr. Superinvisible (1973)

L'Innocente *See* The Innocent (1976)

The Lion's Den *See* La Boca del Lobo (1989)

L'Isola Degli Uomini Pesce *See* Screamers (1980)

The Little Martyr *See* The Children Are Watching Us (1944)

Little Mother *See* Mamele (1938)

Little Pal *See* Healer (1936)

The Little Sister *See* The Tender Age (1984)

Live a Little, Steal a Lot *See* Murph the Surf (1975)

Live to Love *See* The Devil's Hand (1961)

The Liver Eaters *See* Spider Baby (1964)

Ljubarni Slucaj *See* The Love Affair, or The Case of the Missing Switchboard Operator (1967)

Lo Chiamavano Trinita *See* They Call Me Trinity (1972)

Lo Que Vendra *See* Times to Come (1981)

Lo Sbarco di Anzio *See* Anzio (1968)

Lo Scatenato *See* Catch as Catch Can (1968)

Lo Sceicco Bianco *See* The White Sheik (1952)

Lo Spettro *See* The Ghost (1963)

Lo Strano Vizio Della Signora Wardh *See* Next Victim (1971)

Lo Zio Indegno *See* The Sleazy Uncle (1989)

Loaded Weapon 1 *See* National Lampoon's Loaded Weapon 1 (1993)

Lock Your Doors *See* The Ape Man (1943)

The Lodger: A Case of London Fog *See* The Lodger (1926)

L'Oeuvre au Noir *See* The Abyss (1989)

The Lone Troubador *See* Two-Gun Troubador (1937)

The Lonely Hearts Killers *See* Honeymoon Killers (1970)

Lonely Man *See* Gun Riders (1969)

The Loner *See* Ruckus (1981)

The Long Arm *See* The Third Key (1957)

The Long, Dark Night *See* The Pack (1977)

Long John Silver Returns to Treasure Island *See* Long John Silver (1953)

The Long Ride *See* Brady's Escape (1984)

The Long Shot *See* African Rage (1978)

Look Down and Die *See* Steel (1980)

Loonies On Broadway *See* Zombies on Broadway (1944)

Loose Joints *See* Flicks (1985)

The Loot *See* The Bloody Tattoo (19??)

Looters *See* Trespass (1992)

L'Opera De Quat'Sous *See* The Threepenny Opera (1931)

Lords of Treason *See* Secret Honor (1985)

L'Oro Di Napoli *See* The Gold of Naples (1954)

L'Orribile Segreto Del Dr. Hichcock *See* The Horrible Dr. Hichcock (1962)

Los Ambiciosos *See* Fever Mounts at El Pao (1959)

Los Despiadados *See* Hellbenders (1967)

Los Ojos Azules de la Muneca Rota *See* House of Psychotic Women (1973)

Los Santos Inocentes *See* The Holy Innocents (1984)

Los Tigres del Desierto *See* The Desert Tigers (19??)

Loser Take All *See* Strike It Rich (1990)

The Lost Glory of Troy *See* The Avenger (1962)

The Lost Illusion *See* The Fallen Idol (1949)

Lost Women *See* Mesa of Lost Women (1952)

Lost Women of Zarpa *See* Mesa of Lost Women (1952)

The Loudest Whisper *See* The Children's Hour (1961)

Louis L'Amour's "The Shadow Riders" *See* The Shadow Riders (1982)

The Love Cage *See* Joy House (1964)

Love Eternal *See* Eternal Return (1943)

The Love Factor *See* Alien Women (1969)

Love in Las Vegas *See* Viva Las Vegas (1963)

Love is Blind See Love at First Sight (1976)

The Love Maniac See Blood of Ghastly Horror (1972)

Love Trap See Curse of the Black Widow (1977)

Love You to Death See Deadly Illusion (1987)

Lover of the Great Bear See Smugglers (1975)

Lover, Wife See Wifemistress (1979)

Lovers From Beyond the Tomb See Nightmare Castle (1965)

Lovers Must Learn See Rome Adventure (1962)

Loves of a Scoundrel See Death of a Scoundrel (1956)

The Loves of Isadora See Isadora (1968)

The Loyal 47 Ronin See 47 Ronin, Part 1 (1942)

L'Ucello dalle Plume di Cristallo See The Bird with the Crystal Plumage (1970)

Luci Del Varieta See Variety Lights (1951)

The Lucifer Project See Barracuda (1978)

Lucky Boots See Gun Play (1936)

Lucky 13 See Running Hot (1983)

The Lullaby See The Sin of Madelon Claudet (1931)

L'Ultimo Uomo Della Terra See The Last Man on Earth (1964)

Lunch on the Grass See Picnic on the Grass (1959)

Lunch Wagon Girls See Lunch Wagon (1981)

L'Une Chante L'Autre Pas See One Sings, the Other Doesn't (1977)

L'Uomo Dalle Due Ombre See Cold Sweat (1974)

Lust of the Vampires See The Devil's Commandment (1956)

Lusty Night in Rome See La Notte Brava (1959)

Lycanthropus See Werewolf in a Girl's Dormitory (1961)

Lynching See Linchamiento (1968)

M. Hire See Monsieur Hire (1989)

Ma Nuit Chez Maud See My Night at Maud's (1969)

Macabra See Demonoid, Messenger of Death (1981)

Macabre Serenade See Dance of Death (1969)

Maccheroni See Macaroni (1985)

Maciste Alla Corte Del Gran Khan See Samson and the 7 Miracles of the World (1962)

Maciste at the Court of the Great Khan See Samson and the 7 Miracles of the World (1962)

Maciste la Regina di Samar See Hercules Against the Moon Men (1964)

Maciste, L'Eroe Piu Grande Del Mondo See Goliath and the Sins of Babylon (1964)

Maciste Nella Terra dei Ciclopi See Atlas in the Land of the Cyclops (1961)

Mad Dog See Mad Dog Morgan (1976)

The Mad Hatter See Breakfast in Hollywood (1946)

Mad Magazine's Up the Academy See Up the Academy (1980)

Mad Trapper of the Yukon See Challenge To Be Free (1976)

Mad Wednesday See The Sin of Harold Diddlebock (1947)

Madagascar Landing See Aventure Malgache (1944)

Madame De See The Earrings of Madame De... (1954)

Madame Frankenstein See Lady Frankenstein (1972)

Mademoiselle France See Reunion in France (1942)

Madmen of Mandoras See They Saved Hitler's Brain (1964)

Madonna Truth or Dare See Truth or Dare (1991)

Mafia Junction See Super Bitch (1989)

The Mafu Cage See My Sister, My Love (1978)

The Magnificent Seven See Seven Samurai (1954)

The Magnificent Showman See Circus World (1964)

Making It See Going Places (1974)

Mako: The Jaws of Death See Jaws of Death (1976)

Malenka, the Vampire See Fangs of the Living Dead (1968)

Malenkaya Vera See Little Vera (1988)

Malice in Wonderland See The Rumor Mill (1986)

Malizia See Malicious (1974)

Man and His Mate See One Million B.C. (1940)

A Man Betrayed See Wheel of Fortune (1941)

Man-Eater See Shark! (1968)

The Man From C.O.T.T.O.N., Purlie Victorious See Gone are the Days (1963)

Man from Music Mountain See Texas Legionnaires (1943)

Man from Music Mountain See Western Double Feature 1 (1938)

The Man From Nevada See The Nevadan (1950)

Man from Utah See Western Double Feature 5 (1935)

Man in a Cocked Hat See Carlton Browne of the F.O. (1959)

A Man in Mommy's Bed See With Six You Get Eggroll (1968)

Man in the Middle See 48 Hours to Live (1960)

Man Looking Southeast See Man Facing Southeast (1986)

Man of Bronze See Jim Thorpe: All American (1951)

Man of Fury See El Hombre de la Furia (1965)

Man of the Hour See Colonel Effingham's Raid (1945)

Man on the Move See Jigsaw (1971)

The Man Who Changed His Mind See The Man Who Lived Again (1936)

The Man Who Watched Trains Go By See Paris Express (1953)

The Man With The Deadly Lens See Wrong is Right (1982)

The Man with the Synthetic Brain See Blood of Ghastly Horror (1972)

The Man With the X-Ray Eyes See X: The Man with X-Ray Eyes (1963)

The Man with the Yellow Eyes See Planets Against Us (1961)

Manhattan Project: The Deadly Game See The Manhattan Project (1986)

Manhunt See The Italian Connection (1973)

Maniac See Ransom (1984)

The Maniacs Are Loose See The Thrill Killers (1965)

Manon des Sources See Manon of the Spring (1987)

The Manster—Half Man, Half Monster See The Manster (1959)

Marching Along See Stars and Stripes Forever (1952)

Margaret Bourke-White See Double Exposure: The Story of Margaret Bourke-White (1989)

Maria Marten See Murder in the Old Red Barn (1936)

Marie See Maria (1971)

Marie Walewska See Conquest (1932)

Marijuana the Devil's Weed See Wild Weed (1949)

Marijuana: The Devil's Weed See Marihuana (1936)

Marilyn See Roadhouse Girl (1953)

Marine Issue See Instant Justice (1986)

Mark of Terror See Drums of Jeopardy (1931)

Mark of the Avenger See The Mysterious Rider (1938)

Mark of the Claw See Dick Tracy's Dilemma (1947)

Mark of the Vampire See The Vampire (1957)

Mark Twain See The Adventures of Mark Twain (1985)

Married in Haste See Consolation Marriage (1931)

Mars Invades Puerto Rico See Frankenstein Meets the Space Monster (1965)

The Marseille Contract See The Destructors (1974)

Marusa No Onna See A Taxing Woman (1987)

Marusa No Onna II See A Taxing Woman Returns (1988)

The Marx Brothers at the Circus See At the Circus (1939)

Masculin Feminin See Masculine Feminine (1966)

Mask of Dust See Race for Life (1955)

Mask of Fury See First Yank into Tokyo (1945)

Massacre at Fort Holman See A Reason to Live, A Reason to Die (1973)

Massacre Hill See Eureka Stockade (1949)

Massacre Mafia Style See The Executioner (1978)

The Master See Master Ninja (1978)

Master Dolorosa See The Torture of Silence (1917)

Matango See Attack of the Mushroom People (1963)

The Mating of the Sabine Women See The Rape of the Sabines (1961)

Matt Riker See Mutant Hunt (1987)

Mauri See Big Mo (1973)

Mausoleum See One Dark Night (1982)

The Mayfair Bank Caper See The Big Scam (1979)

Mazel Tov Ou le Mariage See Marry Me, Marry Me (1969)

Mazes and Monsters See Rona Jaffe's Mazes & Monsters (1982)

McKlusky See White Lightning (1973)

The McMasters...Tougher Than the West Itself See The McMasters (1970)

Meachorei Hasoragim See Beyond the Walls (1984)

The Medicine Hat Stallion See Peter Lundy and the Medicine Hat Stallion (1977)

Meet Miss Marple See Murder She Said (1962)

Meet the Applegates See The Applegates (1989)

Meet Whiplash Willie See The Fortune Cookie (1966)

The Meetings of Anna See Les Rendez-vous D'Anna (1978)

Mekagojira No Gyakushu See Terror of Mechagodzilla (1978)

Melody of Youth See They Shall Have Music (1939)

Men in Tights See Robin Hood: Men in Tights (1993)

Men of Steel See Steel (1980)

The Mercenaries See Sweet Dirty Tony (1981)

Mery per Sempre See Forever Mary (1989)

The Message See Mohammed: Messenger of God (1977)

Metempsycose See Tomb of Torture (1965)

Meurtre en 45 Tours See Murder at 45 R.P.M. (1965)

Mi Revolver es la Ley See Colt is My Law (19??)

Mickey Spillane's Margin for Murder See Margin for Murder (1981)

Microscopia See Fantastic Voyage (1966)

Midnight at Madame Tussaud's *See* Midnight at the Wax Museum (1936)

Midnight Heat *See* Sunset Heat (1992)

The Mighty Peking Man *See* Goliathon (1979)

The Mighty Thunder *See* Tundra (1936)

The Mighty Ursus *See* Ursus in the Valley of the Lions (1962)

Mignonne *See* Your Turn Darling (1963)

Mikan No Taikyoku *See* The Go-Masters (1982)

Mikres Aphrodites *See* Young Aphrodites (1963)

Milagro en Roma *See* Miracle in Rome (1988)

Milczaca Gwiazda *See* First Spaceship on Venus (1960)

Mile a Minute Love *See* Roaring Speedboats (1937)

Milou en Mai *See* May Fools (1990)

Milou in May *See* May Fools (1990)

Mind Games *See* The Agency (1981)

Mindwarp: An Infinity of Terror *See* Galaxy of Terror (1981)

The Miracle of Fatima *See* Miracle of Our Lady of Fatima (1952)

Miracle of Life *See* Our Daily Bread (1934)

Miracolo a Milano *See* Miracle in Milan (1951)

Miss Europe *See* Prix de Beaute (1930)

Miss Muette *See* The Diabolical Dr. Z (1965)

Mr. Ashton was Indiscreet *See* The Senator was Indiscreet (1947)

Mr. Bug Goes to Town *See* Hoppity Goes to Town (1941)

Mr. Celebrity *See* Turf Boy (1942)

Mr. Fox of Venice *See* The Honey Pot (1967)

Mr. Invisible *See* Mr. Superinvisible (1973)

Mr. Quilp *See* The Old Curiosity Shop (1975)

Mr. Sebastian *See* Sebastian (1968)

Mister V *See* Pimpernel Smith (1942)

Mr. Wrong *See* Dark of the Night (1985)

Misterios del Ultratumba *See* Black Pit of Dr. M (1958)

Mit Eva Fing Die Sunde An *See* The Bellboy and the Playgirls (1962)

Mitt Liv Som Hund *See* My Life as a Dog (1985)

The Model Killer *See* The Hollywood Strangler Meets the Skid Row Slasher (1979)

Model Massacre *See* Color Me Blood Red (1964)

A Modern Bluebeard *See* Boom in the Moon (1946)

A Modern Hero *See* Knute Rockne: All American (1940)

Mogliamante *See* Wifemistress (1979)

The Mogul *See* Ratings Game (1984)

Mondo Pazzo *See* Mondo Cane 2 (1964)

A Monkey in Winter *See* Un Singe en Hiver (1962)

Monkey Shines: An Experiment in Fear *See* Monkey Shines (1988)

Monsieur Hulot's Holiday *See* Mr. Hulot's Holiday (1953)

Monster *See* Humanoids from the Deep (1980)

The Monster Baran *See* Varan the Unbelievable (1961)

Monster from a Prehistoric Planet *See* Gappa the Trifibian Monster (1967)

Monster Maker *See* Monster from the Ocean Floor (1954)

Monster of Monsters *See* Ghidrah the Three Headed Monster (1965)

Monster of Terror *See* Die, Monster, Die! (1965)

The Monster Show *See* Freaks (1932)

The Monster Walked *See* The Monster Walks (1932)

The Monster with Green Eyes *See* Planets Against Us (1961)

Monster Yongkari *See* Yongkari Monster of the Deep (1967)

Monster Zero *See* Godzilla vs. Monster Zero (1968)

The Monsters Are Loose *See* The Thrill Killers (1965)

Monsters From the Moon *See* Robot Monster (1953)

Monsters from the Unknown Planet *See* Terror of Mechagodzilla (1978)

Monstrosity *See* The Atomic Brain (1964)

Monte Carlo or Bust *See* Those Daring Young Men in Their Jaunty Jalopies (1969)

Montenegro—Or Pigs and Pearls *See* Montenegro (1981)

Morgan: A Suitable Case for Treatment *See* Morgan! (1966)

Morgan il Pirata *See* Morgan the Pirate (1960)

Morgen Grauen *See* Time Troopers (1989)

The Mormon Peril *See* Trapped by the Mormons (1922)

Morning Terror *See* Time Troopers (1989)

Mortal Sins *See* Dangerous Obsession (1988)

Morte a Venezia *See* Death in Venice (1971)

Morton of the Mounted *See* Timber Terrors (1935)

Moscow Distrusts Tears *See* Moscow Does Not Believe in Tears (1980)

Moscow Nights *See* I Stand Condemned (1936)

Moskwa Sljesam Nje Jerit *See* Moscow Does Not Believe in Tears (1980)

Mosura Tai Goira *See* Godzilla vs. Mothra (1964)

Motel *See* Pink Motel (1982)

Motel Vacancy *See* Talking Walls (1985)

Mother Goose A Go-Go *See* The Unkissed Bride (1966)

Mother Riley Meets the Vampire *See* My Son, the Vampire (1952)

Mothra vs. Godzilla *See* Godzilla vs. Mothra (1964)

Mountain of Cannibal Gods *See* Slave of the Cannibal God (1979)

Movie Struck *See* Pick a Star (1937)

The Moving Target *See* Harper (1966)

Mud *See* The Stick-Up (1977)

Mujeres al Borde de un Ataque de Nervios *See* Women on the Verge of a Nervous Breakdown (1988)

Mumsy, Nanny, Sonny, and Girly *See* Girly (1970)

Murder by Mail *See* Schizoid (1980)

Murder by Proxy *See* Blackout (1954)

The Murder in Thorton Square *See* Gaslight (1944)

Murder, Inc. *See* The Enforcer (1951)

Murder on Diamond Row *See* The Squeaker (1937)

Murder One *See* Death Sentence (1974)

The Murderer Dmitri Karamazov *See* The Brothers Karamazov (1958)

Muriel, Or the Time of Return *See* Muriel (1963)

Muriel, Ou le Temps d'Un Retour *See* Muriel (1963)

Murph the Surf *See* Live a Little, Steal a Lot (1975)

The Murri Affair *See* La Grande Bourgeoise (1974)

Music in Darkness *See* Night Is My Future (1947)

Mussolini: The Decline and Fall of Il Duce *See* Mussolini & I (1985)

Mutant *See* Forbidden World (1982)

The Mutation *See* The Freakmaker (1973)

Mutations *See* The Freakmaker (1973)

The Mutilator *See* The Dark (1979)

Mutter Kusters Fahrt Zum Himmel *See* Mother Kusters Goes to Heaven (1976)

My Brother, the Outlaw *See* My Outlaw Brother (1951)

My Darling Shiksa *See* Over the Brooklyn Bridge (1983)

My Father, My Master *See* Padre Padrone (1977)

My Favourite Year *See* My Favorite Year (1982)

My Girlfriend's Boyfriend *See* Boyfriends & Girlfriends (1988)

My Gun is Jammed *See* Bare Hunt (1963)

My Hero *See* A Southern Yankee (1948)

My Love Letters *See* Love Letters (1983)

My Name is John *See* The Legend of Hillbilly John (1973)

My Night with Maud *See* My Night at Maud's (1969)

My Son Alone *See* American Empire (1942)

My Teenage Daughter *See* Teenage Bad Girl (1959)

My Uncle *See* Mon Oncle (1958)

My Uncle, Mr. Hulot *See* Mon Oncle (1958)

Mystere Alexina *See* The Mystery of Alexina (1986)

Mysterious Invader *See* The Astounding She-Monster (1958)

The Mysterious Satellite *See* Warning from Space (1956)

The Mystery of Kaspar Hauser *See* Every Man for Himself & God Against All (1975)

Mystery of the Black Jungle *See* The Black Devils of Kali (1955)

The Mystery of the Marie Celeste *See* The Mystery of the Mary Celeste (1937)

Na Komete *See* On the Comet (1968)

Nagooa *See* Drifting (1982)

The Naked Goddess *See* The Devil's Hand (1961)

Naked Island *See* The Island (1961)

The Naked Night *See* Sawdust & Tinsel (1953)

The Naked Temptress *See* The Naked Witch (1964)

Naked Under Leather *See* The Girl on a Motorcycle (1968)

Naked Youth *See* The Cruel Story of Youth (1960)

Nankai No Kai Ketto *See* Godzilla vs. the Sea Monster (1966)

Nara Livet *See* Brink of Life (1957)

Narayama-Bushi-Ko *See* The Ballad of Narayama (1983)

Nathaniel Hawthorne's "Twice Told Tales" *See* Twice-Told Tales (1963)

Nattvardsgaesterna *See* The Winter Light (1962)

Nature's Mistakes *See* Freaks (1932)

The Navy Steps Out *See* A Girl, a Guy and a Gob (1941)

Necromancy *See* The Witching (1972)

Ned Kelly, Outlaw *See* Ned Kelly (1970)

Neil Simon's Biloxi Blues *See* Biloxi Blues (1988)

Neil Simon's Brighton Beach Memoirs *See* Brighton Beach Memoirs (1986)

Neil Simon's Broadway Bound *See* Broadway Bound (1992)

Neil Simon's Lost in Yonkers *See* Lost in Yonkers (1993)

Neil Simon's The Slugger's Wife *See* The Slugger's Wife (1985)

Nella Stretta M Orsa Del Ragno *See* Web of the Spider (1970)

The Neptune Disaster *See* Neptune Factor (1973)

Neskolko Dnel iz Zhizni I.I. Oblomov *See* Oblomov (1981)

Never Cry Devil *See* Night Visitor (1989)

Never Give an Inch *See* Sometimes a Great Notion (1971)

The New Adventures of Don Juan *See* Adventures of Don Juan (1949)

New Adventures of Tarzan *See* Tarzan and the Green Goddess (1938)

The New Barbarians *See* Warriors of the Wasteland (1983)

New Girl in Town *See* Nashville Girl (1976)

New Wine *See* Melody Master (1941)

The Newcomers *See* The Wild Country (1971)

The Next Man *See* The Arab Conspiracy (1976)

The Next Victim *See* Next Victim (1971)

Night Beauties *See* Bellas de Noche (19??)

The Night Caller *See* Night Caller from Outer Space (1966)

Night Comes Too Soon *See* The Ghost of Rashmon Hall (1947)

Night Encounter *See* Double Agents (1959)

Night Hair Child *See* What the Peeper Saw (1972)

Night Legs *See* Fright (1971)

The Night of San Lorenzo *See* Night of the Shooting Stars (1982)

Night of the Beast *See* House of the Black Death (1965)

Night of the Big Heat *See* Island of the Burning Doomed (1967)

Night of the Bloodsuckers *See* The Vampire Hookers (1978)

Night of the Claw *See* Island Claw (1980)

Night of the Dark Full Moon *See* Silent Night, Bloody Night (1973)

Night of the Demon *See* Curse of the Demon (1957)

Night of the Demon *See* The Touch of Satan (1970)

Night of the Doomed *See* Nightmare Castle (1965)

Night of the Eagle *See* Burn Witch, Burn! (1962)

Night of the Flesh Eaters *See* Night of the Living Dead (1968)

Night of the Seagulls *See* Night of the Death Cult (1975)

Night of the Silicates *See* Island of Terror (1966)

Night of the Wehrmacht Zombies *See* Night of the Zombies (1981)

Night Shadows *See* Mutant (1983)

The Night They Invented Striptease *See* The Night They Raided Minsky's (1969)

Night Train *See* Night Train to Munich (1940)

Night Walk *See* Deathdream (1972)

Nightingale *See* The Young Nurses (1973)

A Nightingale Sang in Berkeley Square *See* The Big Scam (1979)

Nightmare *See* City of the Walking Dead (1983)

Nightmare *See* Nightmare in Badham County (1976)

Nightmare at Shadow Woods *See* Blood Rage (1987)

Nightmare City *See* City of the Walking Dead (1983)

Nightmare House *See* Scream, Baby, Scream (1969)

Nightmare Island *See* The Slayer (1982)

Nightmare Maker *See* Night Warning (1982)

Nightmare on Elm Street 6: Freddy's Dead *See* Freddy's Dead: The Final Nightmare (1991)

Nightriders *See* Western Double Feature 2: Wayne & Hale (198?)

Nights in a Harem *See* Son of Sinbad (1955)

Nikutai No Gakko *See* School for Sex (1969)

1990 I Guerrieri del Bronx *See* 1990: The Bronx Warriors (1983)

1999—Nen No Natsu Yasumi *See* Summer Vacation: 1999 (1988)

Ningen No Joken *See* The Human Condition: Road to Eternity (1959)

Nippon Chiubotsu *See* Tidal Wave (1975)

Nippon Konchuki *See* The Insect Woman (1963)

No Greater Love *See* The Human Condition: Road to Eternity (1959)

No Knife *See* The Frisco Kid (1979)

No Man's Land *See* No Man's Range (1935)

No Place Like Homicide *See* What a Carve-Up! (1962)

Nobi *See* Fires on the Plain (1959)

Noce In Galilee *See* A Wedding in Galilee (1987)

Nocturna, Granddaughter of Dracula *See* Nocturna (1979)

Norman Rockwell's Breaking Home Ties *See* Breaking Home Ties (1987)

North Sea Hijack *See* ffolkes (1980)

The Northfield Cemetery Massacre *See* Northville Cemetery Massacre (1976)

Northwest Frontier *See* Flame Over India (1960)

Nosferatu, A Symphony of Horror *See* Nosferatu (1922)

Nosferatu, A Symphony of Terror *See* Nosferatu (1922)

Nosferatu, Eine Symphonie des Grauens *See* Nosferatu (1922)

Nosferatu, The Vampire *See* Nosferatu (1922)

Not Against the Flesh *See* Vampyr (1931)

Not Wanted *See* Streets of Sin (1949)

Nothing in Order *See* All Screwed Up (1974)

Nowhere to Hide *See* Fatal Chase (1977)

Noz w Wodzie *See* Knife in the Water (1962)

Nuclear Run *See* Chain Reaction (1980)

Nuclear Terror *See* Golden Rendezvous (1977)

Nude in His Pocket *See* Girl in His Pocket (1962)

Numbered Days *See* Cycle Psycho (19??)

Nuovo Cinema Paradiso *See* Cinema Paradiso (1988)

Nurse Sherri *See* Hospital of Terror (1978)

Nyoka and the Lost Secrets of Hippocrates *See* Nyoka and the Tigermen (1942)

Obch Od Na Korze *See* The Shop on Main Street (1965)

Obsession *See* The Hidden Room (1949)

Occhi Senza Volto *See* Horror Chamber of Dr. Faustus (1959)

Oci Ciornie *See* Dark Eyes (1987)

October *See* Ten Days That Shook the World (1927)

Odio le Bionde *See* I Hate Blondes (1983)

Office Party *See* Hostile Takeover (1988)

The Official History *See* The Official Story (1985)

The Official Version *See* The Official Story (1985)

Oh, Charlie *See* Hold That Ghost (1941)

Okasan *See* Mother (1952)

The Old and the New *See* The General Line (1929)

The Old Corral *See* Song of the Gringo (1936)

Old Greatheart *See* Way Back Home (1932)

Old Heidelberg *See* The Student Prince in Old Heidelberg (1927)

The Old Man and the Boy *See* Two of Us (1968)

Old Mother Riley Meets the Vampire *See* My Son, the Vampire (1952)

Old Shatterhand *See* Apaches Last Battle (1964)

Olelkezo Tekintetek *See* Another Way (1982)

Omar Mukhtar *See* Lion of the Desert (1981)

The Omen 3 *See* Final Conflict (1981)

On the Great White Trail *See* Renfrew on the Great White Trail (1938)

On the Road Again *See* Honeysuckle Rose (1980)

Once Upon a Texas Train *See* Texas Guns (1990)

One Born Every Minute *See* Flim-Flam Man (1967)

One Cup of Coffee *See* Pastime (1991)

One For All *See* The President's Mystery (1936)

One for Sorrow, Two for Joy *See* Signs of Life (1989)

One Horse Town *See* Small Town Girl (1953)

One Hundred Percent Pure *See* The Girl from Missouri (1934)

One-Man Mutiny *See* The Court Martial of Billy Mitchell (1955)

One Plus One *See* Sympathy for the Devil (1970)

Onkel Toms Hutte *See* Uncle Tom's Cabin (1969)

Only the French Can! *See* French Can-Can (1955)

Onna Ga Kaidan O Agaru Toki *See* When a Woman Ascends the Stairs (1960)

Operacione Paura *See* Kill, Baby, Kill (1966)

Operation Kid Brother *See* Secret Agent 00 (1967)

Operation Overthrow *See* Power Play (1981)

Operation Serpent *See* Fer-De-Lance (1974)

Operation Undercover *See* Report to the Commissioner (1974)

Operazione Goldman *See* Lightning Bolt (1967)

Opium Connection *See* The Poppy is also a Flower (1966)

The Oracle *See* The Horse's Mouth (1958)

Orazi e Curiazi *See* Duel of Champions (1961)

Orca—Killer Whale *See* Orca (1977)

Order of Death *See* Corrupt (1984)

Orfeu Negro *See* Black Orpheus (1958)

Orgasmo *See* Paranoia (1969)

Orlak, El Infierno de Frankenstein *See* Orlak, the Hell of Frankenstein (1960)

Orphee *See* Orpheus (1949)

Oru Kaiju Daishingeki *See* Godzilla's Revenge (1969)

Osenny Marafon *See* Autumn Marathon (1979)

Other People's Business *See* Way Back Home (1932)

The Other Side of Paradise *See* Foxtrot (1976)

Otto E Mezzo *See* 8 1/2 (1963)

Our Daily Bread *See* City Girl (1930)

Our Girl Friday *See* The Adventures of Sadie (1955)

Ourselves Alone *See* River of Unrest (1937)

Out California Way *See* Western Double Feature 8: Hale & Carradine (194?)

Out of Rosenheim *See* Bagdad Cafe (1988)

Out of the Darkness *See* Night Creature (1979)

Out of the Darkness *See* Teenage Caveman (1958)

Out of the Night *See* Strange Illusion (1945)

Out of the Shadow *See* Murder on the Campus (1952)

Out on Probation *See* Daddy-O (1959)

Outer Reach *See* Spaced Out (1980)

Outlaw Gun *See* A Minute to Pray, A Second to Die (1967)

Outside In *See* Red, White & Busted (1975)

The Outsider *See* Fatal Error (1983)

Outsider in Amsterdam *See* Fatal Error (1983)

The Outsiders *See* Band of Outsiders (1964)

The Pace That Kills *See* Cocaine Fiends (1936)

Panga *See* Curse 3: Blood Sacrifice (1990)

Panic *See* Panique (1947)

Panic at Lakewood Manor See Ants (1977)

Panic on the Trans-Siberian Express See Horror Express (1972)

Panico en el Transiberiano See Horror Express (1972)

Paper Bullets See Gangs, Inc. (1941)

The Parasite Murders See They Came from Within (1975)

Pardon Me, Your Teeth are in My Neck See The Fearless Vampire Killers (1967)

Paris Brule-T-II? See Is Paris Burning? (1968)

Paris Does Strange Things See Elena and Her Men (1956)

Paris is Ours See Paris Belongs to Us (1960)

Paris Nous Appartient See Paris Belongs to Us (1960)

Paris Qui Dort See The Crazy Ray (1922)

Park Plaza See Norman Conquest (1953)

Paroxismus See Venus in Furs (1970)

Parts: The Clonus Horror See The Clonus Horror (1979)

Party Girls See Party Incorporated (1989)

Pasqualino Settebellezze See Seven Beauties (1976)

Pasqualino: Seven Beauties See Seven Beauties (1976)

Passages from "Finnegans Wake" See Finnegan's Wake (1963)

Passages from James Joyce's "Finnegans Wake" See Finnegan's Wake (1963)

The Passerby See La Passante (1983)

The Passion Flower Hotel See Boarding School (1983)

Passion Play See Love Letters (1983)

Passione d'Amore See Passion of Love (1982)

Passions See The Passing of Evil (1970)

Passport to Shame See Room 43 (1958)

The Patsy See Caged Heart (1985)

Patterns of Power See Patterns (1956)

Patton: A Salute to a Rebel See Patton (1970)

Patton—Lust for Glory See Patton (1970)

Pauline a la Plage See Pauline at the Beach (1983)

Paura Nella Citta Dei Morti Viventi See Gates of Hell (1983)

The Peace Game See The Gladiators (1970)

Peacemaker See The Ambassador (1984)

Peau d'Ane See Donkey Skin (1970)

The Peking Medallion See The Corrupt Ones (1967)

Penn of Pennsylvania See The Courageous Mr. Penn (1941)

People Toys See Devil Times Five (1974)

People's Enemy See Prison Train (1938)

Peopletoys See Devil Times Five (1974)

Pepi, Luci, Bom y Otras Chicas del Monton See Pepi, Luci, Bom and Other Girls on the Heap (1980)

Percy's Progress See It's Not the Size That Counts (1974)

Peril en la Demeure See Peril (1985)

Perils from Planet Mongo See Flash Gordon: Rocketship (1936)

The Perils of Gwendoline in the Land of the Yik-Yak See The Perils of Gwendoline (1984)

Perils of Nyoka See Nyoka and the Tigermen (1942)

Persecution See The Graveyard (1974)

Persecution and Assassination of Jean-Paul Marat as Performed by the Inmates of the Asylum of Charenton Under the Direction of the Marquis De Sade See Marat/Sade (1966)

Perseus the Invincible See Medusa Against the Son of Hercules (1962)

Personal Property See Personal Property (1937)

Peter Rabbit and Tales of Beatrix Potter See Tales of Beatrix Potter (1971)

Petersen See Jock Petersen (1974)

Petroleum Girls See Legend of Frenchie King (1971)

The Phantom Empire See Radio Ranch (1935)

Phantom Fiend See The Return of Dr. Mabuse (1961)

The Phantom of Terror See The Bird with the Crystal Plumage (1970)

Phantom of the Air See The Phantom Broadcast (1933)

Phantom of the Plains See Western Double Feature 7: Wild Bill & Crabbe (1945)

The Phantom Ship See The Mystery of the Mary Celeste (1937)

Phar Lap: Heart of a Nation See Phar Lap (1984)

Philo Vance Returns See Infamous Crimes (1947)

Phoebe See Zelly & Me (1988)

The Phoenix See War of the Wizards (1981)

Pickup on 101 See Where the Eagle Flies (1972)

The Pilot See Danger in the Skies (1979)

Pinball Pick-Up See Pick-Up Summer (1979)

Pinball Summer See Pick-Up Summer (1979)

Pioneers See Pioneer Woman (1973)

Pippi Langstrump Pa de Sju Haven See Pippi in the South Seas (1974)

Piranha 2: Flying Killers See Piranha 2: The Spawning (1982)

Pirate's Fiancee See A Very Curious Girl (1969)

The Pizza Connection See The Sicilian Connection (1985)

The Plains of Heaven See Panic Station (1982)

Planet of Horrors See Galaxy of Terror (1981)

Planet of the Lifeless Men See Battle of the Worlds (1961)

The Plants Are Watching See The Kirlian Witness (1978)

Players See The Club (1981)

Playgirl Gang See Switchblade Sisters (1975)

The Playgirls and the Bellboy See The Bellboy and the Playgirls (1962)

Playing for Keeps See Lily in Love (1985)

Please! Mr. Balzac See Mademoiselle Striptease (1957)

Plein Sud See Heat of Desire (1984)

Pluck of the Irish See Great Guy (1936)

Pocomania See The Devil's Daughter (1939)

Poe's Tales of Terror See Tales of Terror (1962)

Pokayaniye See Repentance (1987)

Police Connection See The Mad Bomber (1972)

Police Force See Jackie Chan's Police Force (1985)

The Police Story See Jackie Chan's Police Force (1985)

Poncomania See The Devil's Daughter (1939)

Pony Express See Peter Lundy and the Medicine Hat Stallion (1977)

Pookie See The Sterile Cuckoo (1969)

Poor Albert and Little Annie See I Dismember Mama (1974)

The Poor Outlaws See The Round Up (1966)

The Pope Must Die See The Pope Must Diet (1991)

Popiol i Diament See Ashes and Diamonds (1958)

Poppies Are Also Flowers See The Poppy is also a Flower (1966)

Porte Aperte See Open Doors (1989)

Portrait of a Woman, Nude See Nudo di Donna (1983)

Portrait of Alison See Postmark for Danger (1956)

Portrait of Maria See Maria Candelaria (1946)

Potemkin See The Battleship Potemkin (1925)

Practice Makes Perfect See Le Cavaleur (1978)

Prairie Outlaws See Wild West (1946)

Prairie Rustlers See Western Double Feature 7: Wild Bill & Crabbe (1945)

Pratidwandi See The Adversary (1971)

The Prehistoric Sound See Sound of Horror (1964)

Prehistoric World See Teenage Caveman (1958)

Prenom: Carmen See First Name: Carmen (1983)

Preparez Vous Mouchoirs See Get Out Your Handkerchiefs (1978)

Preppies See Making the Grade (1984)

The President's Women See Foreplay (1975)

Pride of Kentucky See The Story of Seabiscuit (1949)

Priority Red One See Delta Force Commando 2 (1990)

Prison See Devil's Wanton (1949)

The Prisoner See Cold Room (1984)

The Private Life of Paul Joseph Goebbels See Enemy of Women (1944)

The Private Lives of Elizabeth and Essex See Elizabeth, the Queen (1968)

Private Snuffy Smith See Snuffy Smith, Yard Bird (1942)

The Private Wore Skirts See Never Wave at a WAC (1952)

Profession: Reporter See The Passenger (1975)

The Profile of Terror See The Sadist (1963)

Profumo di Donna See Sweet Smell of Woman (1975)

Profundo Rosso See Deep Red: Hatchet Murders (1975)

Prom Night 2 See Hello Mary Lou: Prom Night 2 (1987)

Promise Her Anything See Promises! Promises! (1963)

A Proposito Luciano See Lucky Luciano (1974)

The Protectors, Book One See Angel of H.E.A.T. (1982)

Proud, Damned, and Dead See The Proud and the Damned (1972)

Przesluchanie See The Interrogation (1982)

Psycho a Go Go! See Blood of Ghastly Horror (1972)

Psycho-Circus See Circus of Fear (1967)

Psycho Killers See Mania (1960)

Psycho Puppet See Delirium (1977)

Psycho Sisters See The Sibling (1972)

Psychotic See Driver's Seat (1973)

Ptang, Yang, Kipperbang See Kipperbang (1982)

Public Be Damned See The World Gone Mad (1933)

The Public Be Hanged See The World Gone Mad (1933)

Puo Una Morta Rivivere Per Amore? See Venus in Furs (1970)

The Purim Player See Der Purimshpiler (1937)

Purple Death from Outer Space See Flash Gordon Conquers the Universe (1940)

The Purple Riders See Purple Vigilantes (1938)

Pursuit See Apache Blood (1975)

Q Planes See Clouds Over Europe (1939)

Quai des Orfevres See Jenny Lamour (1947)

Quando De Donne Avevando La Coda *See* When Women Had Tails (1970)

Que He Hecho Yo Para Merecer Estol? *See* What Have I Done to Deserve This? (1985)

Que La Bete Meure *See* This Man Must Die (1970)

Queen of Blood *See* Planet of Blood (1966)

Queen of Broadway *See* Kid Dynamite (1943)

Queen of the Cannibals *See* Doctor Butcher M.D. (1980)

Queen of the Gorillas *See* The Bride & the Beast (1958)

The Queen's Husband *See* The Royal Bed (1931)

Quei Temerari Sulle Loro Pazze, Scatenate, Scalcinate Carriole *See* Those Daring Young Men in Their Jaunty Jalopies (1969)

Quella Villa Accanto Al Cimitero *See* The House by the Cemetery (1983)

Quelqu' Un Derriere la Porte *See* Someone Behind the Door (1971)

Quemimada! *See* Burn! (1970)

The Quest *See* The Longest Drive (1976)

Quien Sabe? *See* A Bullet for the General (1968)

A Quiet Place to Kill *See* Paranoia (1969)

Quoi De Neuf, Pussycat? *See* What's New Pussycat? (1965)

Race For the Yankee Zephyr *See* Treasure of the Yankee Zephyr (1983)

Radon *See* Rodan (1956)

Radon the Flying Monster *See* Rodan (1956)

Rafferty and the Highway Hustlers *See* Rafferty & the Gold Dust Twins (1975)

Rage *See* Rabid (1977)

Rage of the Buccaneers *See* The Black Pirate (1926)

Ragged Angels *See* They Shall Have Music (1939)

The Raging Moon *See* Long Ago Tomorrow (1971)

Raging Waters *See* The Green Promise (1949)

Rags to Riches *See* Callie and Son (1981)

Raiders of the Doomed Kingdom *See* After the Fall of Saigon (1988)

Rainbow on the River *See* It Happened in New Orleans (1936)

Ramrodders *See* The Ramrodder (1969)

Ransom *See* Maniac (1978)

The Rape of Richard Beck *See* Broken Badge (1985)

Rasputin: The Mad Monk *See* Rasputin and the Empress (1932)

The Rats *See* Deadly Eyes (1982)

The Raven *See* Le Corbeau (1943)

RE: Lucky Luciano *See* Lucky Luciano (1974)

The Reader *See* La Lectrice (1988)

The Rebel *See* The Bushwackers (1952)

Rebel of the Road *See* Hot Rod (1979)

Rebel with a Cause *See* The Loneliness of the Long Distance Runner (1962)

Record of a Living Being *See* I Live in Fear (1955)

Red Dragon *See* Code Name Alpha (1967)

Red Dragon *See* Manhunter (1986)

The Red Hangman *See* The Bloody Pit of Horror (1965)

The Red Head *See* Poil de Carotte (1931)

Red Hot Tires *See* Racing Luck (1935)

Red on Red *See* Scarred (1984)

Red River Valley *See* Man of the Frontier (1936)

The Red Tide *See* Blood Tide (1982)

Redneck County *See* Hootch Country Boys (1975)

The Refugee *See* Three Faces West (1940)

Rehearsal for a Crime *See* The Criminal Life of Archibaldo de la Cruz (1955)

Rejuvenatrix *See* The Rejuvenator (1988)

The Remarkable Mr. Kipps *See* Kipps (1941)

Remembrance of Love *See* Holocaust Survivors...Remembrance of Love (1983)

Remorques *See* Stormy Waters (1941)

Renegade Girls *See* Caged Heat (1974)

Renfrew of the Royal Mounted on the Great White Trail *See* Renfrew on the Great White Trail (1938)

Reprieved *See* Sing Sing Nights (1935)

Requiem fur Dominic *See* Requiem for Dominic (1991)

The Rescue *See* Let's Get Harry (1987)

The Resurrection Syndicate *See* Nothing But the Night (1972)

Retaliator *See* Programmed to Kill (1986)

Retik, the Moon Menace *See* Radar Men from the Moon (1952)

Return from the Past *See* Gallery of Horror (1967)

The Return of Maxwell Smart *See* The Nude Bomb (1980)

The Return of Mr. H. *See* They Saved Hitler's Brain (1964)

Return of the Badmen *See* Return of the Bad Men (1948)

Return of the Blind Dead *See* Return of the Evil Dead (1975)

The Return of the Giant Monsters *See* Gamera vs. Gaos (1967)

Return of the Living Dead *See* Messiah of Evil (1974)

Return of the Magnificent Seven *See* Return of the Seven (1966)

Reunion *See* Reunion in France (1942)

Revenge *See* Blood Feud (1979)

The Revenge of Dracula *See* Dracula vs. Frankenstein (1971)

The Revenge of Milady *See* The Four Musketeers (1975)

The Revenge of the Blood Beast *See* The She-Beast (1965)

Revenge of the Dead *See* Night of the Ghouls (1959)

Revenge of the Innocents *See* South Bronx Heroes (1985)

Revenge of the Living Dead *See* Children Shouldn't Play with Dead Things (1972)

Revenge of the Screaming Dead *See* Messiah of Evil (1974)

Revenge Squad *See* Hit & Run (1982)

Rhodes of Africa *See* Rhodes (1936)

Rhosyn A Rhith *See* Coming Up Roses (1987)

Rhythm on the Ranch *See* Rootin' Tootin' Rhythm (1938)

Rich, Young, and Deadly *See* Platinum High School (1960)

Riches and Romance *See* Amazing Adventure (1937)

Richie *See* The Death of Richie (1976)

Ride a Dark Horse *See* Man & Boy (1971)

Riffraff *See* Riff Raff (1935)

The Right to Eat *See* El Derecho de Comer (1987)

Ripped Off *See* Counter Punch (1971)

Risate de Gioia *See* Passionate Thief (1960)

The Rise of Catherine the Great *See* Catherine the Great (1934)

The Rise of Helga *See* Susan Lenox: Her Fall and Rise (1931)

Rising to Fame *See* Susan Lenox: Her Fall and Rise (1931)

Riso Amaro *See* Bitter Rice (1949)

Rites of Summer *See* White Water Summer (1987)

Rivals *See* Deadly Rivals (1972)

The Road *See* La Strada (1954)

Road to Frisco *See* They Drive by Night (1940)

Roaring Timber *See* Come and Get It (1936)

Rob Roy *See* Rob Roy—The Highland Rogue (1953)

Robinson Crusoeland *See* Utopia (1951)

Rocco et Ses Freres *See* Rocco and His Brothers (1960)

Rocket to the Moon *See* Cat Women of the Moon (1953)

Rocky Mountain Mystery *See* The Fighting Westerner (1935)

Rodrigo D.: No Futuro *See* Rodrigo D.: No Future (1991)

Roger Corman's Frankenstein Unbound *See* Frankenstein Unbound (1990)

Roma *See* Fellini's Roma (1972)

Roma, Citta Aperta *See* Open City (1945)

Romance and Riches *See* Amazing Adventure (1937)

Romance da Empregada *See* The Story of Fausta (1988)

Romauld et Juliet *See* Mama, There's a Man in Your Bed (1989)

Rome, Open City *See* Open City (1945)

Romeo in Pyjamas *See* Parlor, Bedroom and Bath (1931)

Romeo, Julia a Tma *See* Sweet Light in a Dark Room (1960)

Romeo, Juliet and Darkness *See* Sweet Light in a Dark Room (1960)

Rommel—Desert Fox *See* The Desert Fox (1951)

Rona Jaffe's Mazes and Monsters *See* Mazes and Monsters (1982)

The Rook *See* Something for Everyone (1970)

Rookies *See* Buck Privates (1941)

Rookies Come Home *See* Buck Privates Come Home (1947)

The Rose and the Sword *See* Flesh and Blood (1985)

Rosemary's Killer *See* The Prowler (1981)

The Rotten Apple *See* Five Minutes to Love (1963)

Rouge Baiser *See* Red Kiss (1985)

Rough Company *See* The Violent Men (1955)

Round Up Time in Texas *See* Western Double Feature 4 (1937)

Rudyard Kipling's Jungle Book *See* Jungle Book (1942)

Rue Cases Negres *See* Sugar Cane Alley (1983)

Rumpo Kid *See* Carry On Cowboy (1966)

Run, Simon, Run *See* Savage Run (1970)

The Runaways *See* South Bronx Heroes (1985)

Running Hot *See* Makin' It (19??)

Russicum *See* Third Solution (1989)

Rustler's Roundup *See* Rustler's Hideout (1944)

The Saboteur *See* Morituri (1965)

Saboteur: Code Name Morituri *See* Morituri (1965)

The Sabre and the Arrow *See* Last of the Comanches (1952)

Sabrina Fair *See* Sabrina (1954)

Sacco e Vanzetti *See* Sacco & Vanzetti (1971)

Sadko *See* The Magic Voyage of Sinbad (1952)

The Saga of Dracula *See* The Saga of the Draculas (1972)

The Saga of Gosta Berling *See* The Atonement of Gosta Berling (1924)

The Saga of the Road *See* Pather Panchali (1954)

Saikaku Ichidai Onna *See* Life of Oharu (1952)

St. Martin's Lane *See* Sidewalks of London (1940)

Sakima and the Masked Marvel *See* The Masked Marvel (1943)

Salerno Beachhead *See* A Walk in the Sun (1946)

The Salute of the Jugger *See* The Blood of Heroes (1989)

Salvation! Have You Said Your Prayers Today? *See* Salvation! (1987)

Sam Cooper's Gold *See* The Ruthless Four (1970)

Sam Marlowe, Private Eye *See* The Man with Bogart's Face (1980)

Sanda Tai Gailah *See* War of the Gargantuas (1970)

Sandakan House 8 *See* Sandakan No. 8 (1974)

The Sandpit Generals *See* Defiant (1970)

Sans Toit Ni Loi *See* Vagabond (1985)

Sansho Dayu *See* Sansho the Bailiff (1954)

Santa Claus Defeats the Aliens *See* Santa Claus Conquers the Martians (1964)

Santa Fe Saddlemates *See* Western Double Feature 1: Wild Bill & Sunset Carson (194?)

Santo en el Museo de Cera *See* Samson in the Wax Museum (1963)

Santo in the Wax Museum *See* Samson in the Wax Museum (1963)

Satan's Claw *See* The Blood on Satan's Claw (1971)

Satan's Daughters *See* Vampyres (1974)

Satan's Dog *See* Play Dead (1981)

Satan's Mistress *See* Demon Rage (1982)

Satan's Satellites *See* Zombies of the Stratosphere (1952)

Satan's Skin *See* The Blood on Satan's Claw (1971)

Satellite of Blood *See* First Man into Space (1959)

Satin Vengeance *See* Naked Vengeance (1985)

Saturday Island *See* Island of Desire (1952)

Satyricon *See* Fellini Satyricon (1969)

Saul e David *See* Saul and David (1968)

The Savage *See* Lovers Like Us (1975)

Savage Apocalypse *See* Invasion of the Flesh Hunters (1982)

Savage Beasts *See* The Wild Beasts (1985)

Savage Season *See* Temporada Salvaje (1987)

The Savage State *See* L'Etat Sauvage (1978)

Scaramouche *See* Loves & Times of Scaramouche (1976)

Scared Stiff *See* Treasure of Fear (1945)

The Scaremaker *See* Girls Night Out (1983)

Scarface: The Shame of a Nation *See* Scarface (1931)

Scarlet Buccaneer *See* Swashbuckler (1976)

The Scarlet Buccaneer *See* Swashbuckler (1984)

Scent of a Woman *See* Sweet Smell of Woman (1975)

Schloss Vogelod *See* The Haunted Castle (1921)

School of Love *See* School for Sex (1969)

The School That Ate My Brain *See* Zombie High (1987)

The Scotland Yard Mystery *See* The Living Dead (1936)

Scoundrel in White *See* High Heels (1972)

Scream *See* The Night God Screamed (198?)

Scream and Die *See* The House that Vanished (1973)

Scream Free! *See* Free Grass (1969)

Screwface *See* Marked for Death (1990)

Scrooge *See* A Christmas Carol (1951)

Scum of the Earth *See* Poor White Trash 2 (1975)

Search for the Mother Lode *See* Mother Lode (1982)

Searchers of the Voodoo Mountain *See* Warriors of the Apocalypse (1985)

Season of Dreams *See* Stacking (1987)

Second Chances *See* Probation (1932)

The Second Coming *See* Messiah of Evil (1974)

Seconds to Live *See* Viva Knievel (1977)

Secret File: Hollywood *See* Secret File of Hollywood (1962)

Secret Honor: A Political Myth *See* Secret Honor (1985)

Secret Honor: The Last Testament of Richard M. Nixon *See* Secret Honor (1985)

The Secret of Dr. Mabuse *See* The Thousand Eyes of Dr. Mabuse (1960)

The Secret of Dorian Gray *See* Dorian Gray (1970)

Secret Paper WB1 *See* Geheimakte WB1 (1942)

The Secret Stranger *See* Rough Riding Rangers (1935)

Secret Weapon *See* Sherlock Holmes and the Secret Weapon (1942)

Secrets of the Red Bedroom *See* Secret Weapons (1985)

Sedotta e Abbandonata *See* Seduced and Abandoned (1964)

The Seducers *See* Death Game (1976)

The Seductress *See* The Teacher (1974)

Seed of Innocence *See* Teen Mothers (1980)

Seed of Terror *See* Grave of the Vampire (1972)

The Seekers *See* Land of Fury (1955)

Seishun Zanoku Monogatari *See* The Cruel Story of Youth (1960)

Sengoku Gunto-Den *See* Saga of the Vagabond (1959)

Sensations *See* Sensations of 1945 (1944)

Senso *See* The Wanton Contessa (1955)

Sensuous Vampires *See* The Vampire Hookers (1978)

Separate Beds *See* The Wheeler Dealers (1963)

Sept Fois Femme *See* Woman Times Seven (1967)

Sergeant Steiner *See* Breakthrough (1978)

The Serpent *See* Night Flight from Moscow (1973)

Seryozha *See* A Summer to Remember (1961)

Sette Volte Donna *See* Woman Times Seven (1967)

Seven Bad Men *See* Rage at Dawn (1955)

Seven Different Ways *See* Quick, Let's Get Married (1971)

Seven Graves for Rogan *See* Time to Die (1983)

Seven Sisters *See* The House on Sorority Row (1983)

Sex Play *See* Games Girls Play (1975)

The Sex Racketeers *See* Man of Violence (1971)

Sex Through a Window *See* Extreme Close-Up (1973)

The Sexorcists *See* The Eerie Midnight Horror Show (1982)

The Shadow Versus the Thousand Eyes of Dr. Mabuse *See* The Thousand Eyes of Dr. Mabuse (1960)

The Shadow Warrior *See* Kagemusha (1980)

Shadows in an Empty Room *See* Strange Shadows in an Empty Room (1976)

Shadows of Our Ancestors *See* Shadows of Forgotten Ancestors (1964)

Shadows of Our Forgotten Ancestors *See* Shadows of Forgotten Ancestors (1964)

Shadows of the Peacock *See* Echoes of Paradise (1986)

Shalimar *See* Deadly Thief (1978)

Shame of the Sabine Women *See* The Rape of the Sabines (1961)

Shark Reef *See* She Gods of Shark Reef (1956)

Shatter *See* Call Him Mr. Shatter (1974)

Shatterhand *See* Apaches Last Battle (1964)

She Devil *See* Drums O'Voodoo (1934)

She Drives Me Crazy *See* Friends, Lovers & Lunatics (1989)

She Got What She Asked For *See* Yesterday, Today and Tomorrow (1964)

She Knew No Other Way *See* Last Resort (1986)

She Monster of the Night *See* Frankenstein's Daughter (1958)

She Shoulda Said No *See* Wild Weed (1949)

Sheba *See* The Graveyard (1974)

She'll Be Sweet *See* Magee and the Lady (1978)

Shenanigans *See* Great Bank Hoax (1978)

Sheriff of Wichita *See* Western Double Feature 4: Rogers & Evans (194?)

Sherlock Holmes *See* The Adventures of Sherlock Holmes (1939)

Sherlock Holmes and the Scarlet Claw *See* Scarlet Claw (1944)

Sherlock Holmes and the Spider Woman *See* Spider Woman (1944)

Sherlock Holmes and the Woman in Green *See* The Woman in Green (1945)

Sherlock Holmes Grosster Fall *See* A Study in Terror (1966)

Sherlock Holmes Und Das Halsband des Todes *See* Sherlock Holmes and the Deadly Necklace (1962)

Shichinin No Samurai *See* Seven Samurai (1954)

Shinju Ten No Amijima *See* Double Suicide (1969)

The Ship was Loaded *See* Carry On Admiral (1957)

Shivers *See* They Came from Within (1975)

Shock *See* Beyond the Door 2 (1979)

Shocked *See* Mesmerized (1984)

Shogun Island *See* Raw Force (1981)

Shoot the Pianist *See* Shoot the Piano Player (1962)

The Shop on High Street *See* The Shop on Main Street (1965)

The Shuttered Room *See* Blood Island (1968)

Sidney Sheldon's Windmills of the Gods *See* Windmills of the Gods (1988)

Siegfried's Death *See* Siegfried (1924)

Siegfrieds Tod *See* Siegfried (1924)

Signe Charlotte *See* Sincerely Charlotte (1986)

The Silent Flute *See* Circle of Iron (1978)

Silent Night, Evil Night *See* Black Christmas (1975)

The Silent One *See* El Callao (197?)

Silken Skin *See* The Soft Skin (1964)

Silver Blaze *See* Murder at the Baskervilles (1937)

Silver Devil *See* Wild Horse (1931)

Silver Spurs *See* Western Double Feature 8: Hale & Carradine (194?)

The Sin *See* The Shaming (1971)

Sinai Commandos: The Story of the Six Day War *See* Sinai Commandos (1968)

Sinister House *See* Who Killed Doc Robbin? (1948)

Sisters *See* Some Girls (1988)

The Sixth of June *See* D-Day, the Sixth of June (1956)

Skate! *See* Blades of Courage (1988)

Ski Lift to Death *See* Snowblind (1978)

Skipper *See* The Todd Killings (1971)

Skyggen Af Emma *See* Emma's Shadow (1988)

The Slammer *See* Short Eyes (1979)

The Slasher *See* Cosh Boy (1961)

Slasher in the House *See* Home Sweet Home (1980)

The Slaughterers *See* Invasion of the Flesh Hunters (1982)

Slave Girls *See* Prehistoric Women (1950)

Slaves of the Invisible Monster *See* The Invisible Monster (1950)

Slay It Again, Sam *See* Codename: Foxfire (1985)

Slip Slide Adventures *See* Water Babies (1979)

Small Town Massacre *See* Strange Behavior (1981)

Smart Alec *See* Movie Maker (1986)

Smokey and the Bandit Ride Again *See* Smokey and the Bandit, Part 2 (1980)

Smorgasbord *See* Cracking Up (1983)

Smultron-Stallet *See* Wild Strawberries (1957)

Snow White and the Three Clowns *See* Snow White and the Three Stooges (1961)

Snuffy Smith *See* Snuffy Smith, Yard Bird (1942)

So Evil, My Sister *See* The Sibling (1972)

Sodome et Gomorrhe *See* Sodom and Gomorrah (1962)

Soldier Duroc *See* Soldat Duroc...Ca Va Etre Ta Fete! (196?)

Soldier In Skirts *See* Triple Echo (1977)

The Soldier Who Declared Peace *See* Tribes (1970)

The Soldiers *See* Les Carabiniers (1963)

Solomon Northrup's Odyssey *See* Half Slave, Half Free (1985)

Sombra, the Spider Woman *See* The Black Widow (1947)

Some Like it Cool *See* Sex on the Run (1978)

Someone is Killing the Great Chefs of Europe *See* Who is Killing the Great Chefs of Europe? (1978)

Someone's Killing the World's Greatest Models *See* She's Dressed to Kill (1979)

Something is Out There *See* Day of the Animals (1977)

Something Like the Truth *See* The Offence (1973)

Something to Hide *See* Shattered (1972)

Something Waits in the Dark *See* Screamers (1980)

Somewhere in France *See* The Foreman Went to France (1942)

Sommarnattens Leende *See* Smiles of a Summer Night (1955)

Son of My Life *See* Hijazo de Mi Vidaza (197?)

Song from the Heart *See* Cancion en el Alma (19??)

The Song of the Road *See* Pather Panchali (1954)

Song of the Sierra *See* Springtime in the Sierras (1947)

Sons of the Legion *See* Sons of the Desert (1933)

Sons of the Musketeers *See* At Sword's Point (1951)

Sophie's Place *See* Crooks & Coronets (1969)

Soul *See* Earth (1930)

Sound From a Million Years Ago *See* Sound of Horror (1964)

Sound of Fury *See* Try and Get Me (1950)

Soup to Nuts *See* Waitress (1981)

Sous le Soleil de Satan *See* Under Satan's Sun (1987)

Sous les Toits de Paris *See* Under the Roofs of Paris (1929)

South of Panama *See* Panama Menace (1941)

South Sea Woman *See* Pearl of the South Pacific (1955)

Southwest to Sonora *See* The Appaloosa (1966)

Space 2074 *See* Star Quest (1989)

The Space Amoeba *See* Yog, Monster from Space (1971)

Space Avenger *See* Alien Space Avenger (1991)

Space Invasion from Lapland *See* Invasion of the Animal People (1962)

Space Invasion of Lapland *See* Invasion of the Animal People (1962)

Space Men *See* Assignment Outer Space (1961)

Space Men Appear in Tokyo *See* Warning from Space (1956)

Space Mission of the Lost Planet *See* Horror of the Blood Monsters (1970)

Space Monster Dagora *See* Dagora, the Space Monster (1965)

Space Mutants *See* Planet of the Vampires (1965)

Space Soldiers *See* Flash Gordon: Rocketship (1936)

Spaceship to the Unknown *See* Flash Gordon: Rocketship (1936)

Spara Forte, Piu Forte...Non Capisco *See* Shoot Loud, Louder, I Don't Understand! (1966)

The Specter of Freedom *See* Phantom of Liberty (1968)

Speed Brent Wins *See* Breed of the Border (1933)

The Spell of Amy Nugent *See* Spellbound (1941)

Spell of the Hypnotist *See* Fright (1956)

Spettri *See* Specters (1987)

The Spider *See* Earth vs. the Spider (1958)

Spider Baby, or the Maddest Story Ever Told *See* Spider Baby (1964)

Spider-Man *See* The Amazing Spider-Man (1977)

Spies-A-Go-Go *See* Nasty Rabbit (1964)

Spies, Lies, and Alibis *See* Code Name: Chaos (1990)

Spinal Tap *See* This is Spinal Tap (1984)

Spione *See* Spies (1928)

Spirit of Tattoo *See* Irezumi (1983)

Spirit of the Dead *See* The Asphyx (1972)

Spirit of the People *See* Abe Lincoln in Illinois (1940)

The Spiritualist *See* The Amazing Mr. X (1948)

Spivs *See* I Vitelloni (1953)

The Split *See* The Manster (1959)

The Spooky Movie Show *See* The Mask (1961)

Spoorloos *See* The Vanishing (1988)

Spot *See* Dog Pound Shuffle (1975)

Spymaker *See* Spymaker: The Secret Life of Ian Fleming (1990)

Stacey and Her Gangbusters *See* Stacey (1973)

Stand and Deliver *See* Bowery Blitzkrieg (1941)

Stand Easy *See* Goon Movie (1953)

Stanno Tutti Bene *See* Everybody's Fine (1990)

Star Child *See* Space Raiders (1983)

Star Packer *See* Western Double Feature 2 (1933)

Stardust *See* Mad About Money (1930)

Starlight Slaughter *See* Eaten Alive (1976)

The Statutory Affair *See* Lola (1969)

Stella Star *See* Star Crash (1978)

Stephen King's Graveyard Shift *See* Graveyard Shift (1990)

Stephen King's Silver Bullet *See* Silver Bullet (1985)

Still Smokin' *See* Cheech and Chong: Still Smokin' (1983)

Storia de Ragazzi e di Ragazze *See* The Story of Boys & Girls (1991)

Stormy Crossing *See* Black Tide (1956)

Story of a Marriage *See* On Valentine's Day (1986)

The Story of an Artist's Studio Secrets *See* Artist's Studio Secrets (1964)

The Story of Gosta Berling *See* The Atonement of Gosta Berling (1924)

The Story of Joseph and His Brethren *See* Joseph & His Brethren (1960)

The Story of Robin Hood *See* The Story of Robin Hood & His Merrie Men (1952)

A Story of the Cruelties of Youth *See* The Cruel Story of Youth (1960)

The Story Without A Name *See* Without Warning (1952)

Straight Jacket *See* Dark Sanity (1982)

Straight on Till Morning *See* Dressed for Death (1974)

Strange Adventure *See* Wayne Murder Case (1938)

The Strange Adventure of David Gray *See* Vampyr (1931)

The Strange Case of Madeleine *See* Madeleine (1950)

Strange Deception *See* The Accused (1948)

Strange Incident *See* The Ox-Bow Incident (1943)

Strange Interval *See* Strange Interlude (1932)

Strange Journey *See* Fantastic Voyage (1966)

The Strange Ones *See* Les Enfants Terrible (1950)

The Strange World of Planet X *See* The Cosmic Monsters (1958)

The Stranger *See* Shame (1961)

Stranger in Our House *See* Summer of Fear (1978)

Stranger in the House *See* Black Christmas (1975)

A Stranger Walked In *See* Love from a Stranger (1947)

Strangler's Morgue *See* The Crimes of Stephen Hawke (1936)

Street Gang *See* Vigilante (1983)

Street Legal *See* The Last of the Finest (1990)

Street Lovo *See* Scarred (1984)

Street of Shadows *See* The Shadow Man (1953)

Streets of New York *See* The Abe Lincoln of Ninth Avenue (1939)

Strictly Confidential *See* Broadway Bill (1934)

Strictly for Pleasure *See* Perfect Furlough (1959)

Striking Back *See* Search and Destroy (1981)

Strip Poker *See* The Big Switch (1970)

Striptease Lady *See* Lady of Burlesque (1943)

The Stu Erwin Show *See* The Trouble with Father (1950)

The Submersion of Japan *See* Tidal Wave (1975)

Subspecies 2 *See* Bloodstone: Subspecies 2 (1993)

Succubus *See* The Devil's Nightmare (1971)

Such Men are Dangerous *See* The Racers (1955)

Suicide Run *See* Too Late the Hero (1970)

Suicide Squadron *See* Dangerous Moonlight (1941)

A Suitable Case for Treatment *See* Morgan! (1966)

The Sullivans *See* The Fighting Sullivans (1942)

Summer Madness *See* Summertime (1955)

Summer of Innocence *See* Big Wednesday (1978)

Summer with Monika *See* Monika (1952)

Summerplay *See* Summer Interlude (1950)

Summertime Killer *See* Ricco (1974)

Sumurun *See* One Arabian Night (1921)

The Sun Demon *See* Hideous Sun Demon (1959)

Suna No Onna *See* Woman in the Dunes (1964)

Sunburst *See* Slashed Dreams (1974)

Sunless *See* Sans Soleil (1982)

Sunrise—A Song of Two Humans *See* Sunrise (1927)

Sunset of a Clown *See* Sawdust & Tinsel (1953)

Super Dragon *See* Secret Agent Super Dragon (1966)

Super Fly T.N.T. *See* Superfly T.N.T. (1973)

The Super Inframan *See* Infra-Man (1976)

Superargo the Giant *See* Superargo (1967)

Superfantagenio *See* Aladdin (1986)

Superman and the Strange People *See* Superman & the Mole Men (1951)

Supersnooper *See* Super Fuzz (1981)

Surf 2: The End of the Trilogy *See* Surf 2 (1984)

Suspected Alibi *See* Suspended Alibi (1956)

Swamp Diamonds *See* Swamp Women (1955)

Sweeney Todd: The Demon Barber of Fleet Street *See* Demon Barber of Fleet Street (1936)

Sweet Candy *See* Candy Stripe Nurses (1974)

Sweet Kill *See* The Arousers (1970)

Sweet Revenge *See* Code of Honor (1984)

Sweet Violence *See* Sweet Ecstasy (1962)

Swept Away...By an Unusual Destiny in the Blue Sea of August *See* Swept Away... (1975)

Swing it Buddy *See* Swing It, Professor (1937)

Swing, Teacher, Swing *See* College Swing (1938)

Switchboard Operator *See* The Love Affair, or The Case of the Missing Switchboard Operator (1967)

Swords of Blood *See* Cartouche (1962)

Sylvia and the Ghost *See* Sylvia and the Phantom (1945)

Symphony of Love *See* Ecstasy (1933)

Szegenylegenyek Nehezeletuck *See* The Round Up (1966)

T & A Academy *See* H.O.T.S. (1979)

T & A Academy 2 *See* Gimme an F (1985)

Tacones Lejanos *See* High Heels (1991)

Tainted Money *See* Show Them No Mercy (1935)

A Tale of Africa *See* Green Horizon (1983)

Tale of the Cock *See* Confessions of Tom Harris (1972)

A Talent for Loving *See* Gun Crazy (1969)

Tales from the Crypt II *See* Vault of Horror (1973)

Tanner: A Political Fable *See* Tanner '88 (1988)

Target: Embassy *See* Embassy (1972)

Target in the Sun *See* The Man Who Would Not Die (1975)

Target of an Assassin *See* African Rage (1978)

Tartu *See* The Adventures of Tartu (1943)

Taste of Fear *See* Scream of Fear (1961)

Tears in Florence *See* Traenen in Florenz (1984)

Teen Kanya *See* Two Daughters (1961)

Teenage Monster *See* Meteor Monster (1957)

The Teenage Psycho Meets Bloody Mary *See* Incredibly Strange Creatures Who Stopped Living and Became Mixed-Up Zombies (1963)

Tell It To the Marines *See* Here Come the Marines (1952)

Tell Your Children *See* Reefer Madness (1938)

Tempo di Uccidere *See* Time to Kill (1989)

Ten Days That Shook The World *See* October (1927)

Tendre Poulet *See* Dear Detective (1978)

Tenebrae *See* Unsane (1982)

Tengoku To Jigoku *See* High & Low (1962)

Tenue de Soiree *See* Menage (1986)

Terminal Station Indiscretion *See* Indiscretion of an American Wife (1954)

Terminus Station *See* Indiscretion of an American Wife (1954)

Terra em Transe *See* Earth Entranced (1966)

Terreur dans l'Espace *See* Planet of the Vampires (1965)

Terror Castle *See* The Virgin of Nuremberg (1965)

Terror Eyes *See* Night School (1981)

Terror From the Sun *See* Hideous Sun Demon (1959)

Terror Hospital *See* Hospital of Terror (1978)

Terror House *See* The Night Has Eyes (1942)

Terror House *See* Terror at Red Wolf Inn (1972)

Terror in Space *See* Planet of the Vampires (1965)

Terror in the Midnight Sun *See* Invasion of the Animal People (1962)

Terror of Sheba *See* The Graveyard (1974)

The Terror Strikes *See* The War of the Colossal Beast (1958)

Terror under the House *See* Revenge (1971)

Texas in Flames *See* She Came to the Valley (1977)

Texas Road Agent *See* Road Agent (1926)

Texas Serenade *See* Old Corral (1936)

Teyve der Milkhiker *See* Tevye (1939)

That Man Mr. Jones *See* Fuller Brush Man (1948)

That Others May Live *See* Border Street (1948)

That They May Live *See* J'Accuse (1937)

That's the Way of the World *See* Shining Star (1975)

Therese Und Isabell *See* Therese & Isabelle (1968)

They Call Me Hallelujah *See* Guns for Dollars (1973)

They Don't Wear Pajamas at Rosie's *See* The First Time (1972)

They Loved Life *See* Kanal (1956)

They Made Me a Fugitive *See* They Made Me a Criminal (1939)

They Passed This Way *See* Four Faces West (1948)

They're Coming to Get You *See* Dracula vs. Frankenstein (1971)

Thin Air *See* Invasion of the Body Stealers (1969)

The Thing From Another World *See* The Thing (1951)

Thirst *See* Three Strange Loves (1949)

The Thirteen Chairs *See* 12 Plus 1 (1970)

The Thirty-Sixth Chamber *See* Master Killer (1984)

Thomas Crown and Company *See* Thomas Crown Affair (1968)

Thoroughbred *See* Run for the Roses (1978)

Thou Shall Not Kill *See* Avenging Conscience (1914)

Thou Shalt Honour Thy Wife *See* Master of the House (1925)

Three Bad Men in the Hidden Fortress *See* The Hidden Fortress (1958)

Three Crazy Legionnaires *See* Three Legionnaires (1937)

Three For the Money *See* Win, Place, or Steal (1972)

Three Rascals in the Hidden Fortress *See* The Hidden Fortress (1958)

The Three Skeletons *See* Los Tres Calaveras (1964)

Three Steps to the Gallows *See* White Fire (1953)

The Threepenny Opera *See* Mack the Knife (1989)

Through the Looking Glass *See* The Velvet Vampire (1971)

Thunder *See* Thunder Warrior (1985)

Thunder Mountain *See* Shadow of Chikara (1977)

Thunder on the Trail *See* Thundering Trail (1951)

Thursday the 12th *See* Pandemonium (1982)

Tidal Wave *See* Portrait of Jennie (1948)

Tierra Bru Tal *See* Savage Guns (1968)

The Tiger *See* Tiger Warsaw (1987)

Tiger in the Sky *See* The McConnell Story (1955)

Tiger of Bengal *See* Journey to the Lost City (1958)

The Tiger Woman *See* Perils of the Darkest Jungle (1944)

Tigers Don't Cry *See* African Rage (1978)

Tight Little Island *See* Whiskey Galore (1948)

Til Dawn Do Us Part *See* Dressed for Death (1974)

Timber Tramps *See* The Big Push (1975)

Time Flyers *See* The Blue Yonder (1986)

A Time For Caring *See* Generation (1969)

The Time of Return *See* Muriel (1963)

Time Raiders *See* Warriors of the Apocalypse (1985)

Time Trap *See* The Time Travelers (1964)

Time Warp Terror *See* Bloody New Year (1987)

Timeslip *See* The Atomic Man (1956)

The Timid Bachelor *See* El Preprimido (197?)

Tini Zabutykh Predkiv *See* Shadows of Forgotten Ancestors (1964)

Tintorera *See* Tintorera...Tiger Shark (1978)

Tintorera...Bloody Waters *See* Tintorera...Tiger Shark (1978)

Tirez sur le Pianiste *See* Shoot the Piano Player (1962)

Titan Find *See* Creature (1985)

To Be a Man *See* Cry of Battle (1963)

To Catch a Spy *See* Catch Me a Spy (1971)

To Elvis, With Love *See* Touched by Love (1980)

To Love a Vampire *See* Lust for a Vampire (1971)

Today We Live *See* The Day and the Hour (1963)

A Toi De Faire *See* Your Turn Darling (1963)

Tomb of the Cat *See* Tomb of Ligeia (1964)

Tomb of the Living Dead *See* Mad Doctor of Blood Island (1969)

Too Many Chefs *See* Who is Killing the Great Chefs of Europe? (1978)

Too Pretty to Be Honest *See* Trop Jolie pour Etre Honette (196?)

The Tormented *See* The Eerie Midnight Horror Show (1982)

Torture Zone *See* The Fear Chamber (1968)

Toto the Hero *See* Toto le Heros (1991)

The Touch of Melissa *See* The Touch of Satan (1970)

Tower of Terror *See* Assault (1970)

A Town Called Bastard *See* A Town Called Hell (1972)

The Town That Cried Terror *See* Maniac (1978)

T.P. Sloane *See* Death Race 2000 (1975)

Train of Terror *See* Terror Train (1980)

Train 2419 *See* The Return of Casey Jones (1934)

Traitement de Choc *See* Shock Treatment (1981)

Transport Z Raje *See* Transport from Paradise (1965)

The Transvestite See Glen or Glenda (1953)

Tras el Cristal See In a Glass Cage (1986)

Travels with Anita See Lovers and Liars (1981)

The Tree of Hands See Innocent Victim (1990)

Tree of Liberty See The Howards of Virginia (1940)

Trial by Combat See Choice of Weapons (1976)

Trigger, Jr. See Western Double Feature 6: Rogers & Trigger (1950)

A Trip with Anita See Lovers and Liars (1981)

Triple Trouble See Kentucky Kernels (1934)

Tristan and Isolde See Lovespell (1979)

Trois Hommes et un Couffin See Three Men and a Cradle (1985)

The Trollenberg Terror See The Crawling Eye (1958)

Tromba See Tromba, the Tiger Man (1952)

Trop Belle Pour Toi See Too Beautiful for You (1988)

Trottie True See The Gay Lady (1949)

Trouble at 16 See Platinum High School (1960)

Trouble Chaser See Li'l Abner (1940)

The Troubles of Two Roosters See Los Apuros de Dos Gallos (1969)

The Trout See La Truite (1983)

Truman Capote's A Christmas Memory See ABC Stage 67: Truman Capote's A Christmas Memory (1966)

Truman Capote's The Glass House See The Glass House (1972)

Try and Find It See Hi Diddle Diddle (1943)

Tsarskaya Nevesta See The Tsar's Bride (1966)

Tsubaki Sanjuro See Sanjuro (1962)

Tudor Rose See Nine Days a Queen (1934)

Tueur de Ch icago See Scarface Mob (1962)

Tulitkkutehtaan Tytto See The Match Factory Girl (1991)

Tulsa Kid See Western Double Feature 9: LaRue & Beery (194?)

The Tunnel See Transatlantic Tunnel (1935)

Turkey Shoot See Escape 2000 (1981)

Twelve Miles Out See Second Woman (1951)

Twice Bitten See The Vampire Hookers (1978)

Twilight in the Sierras See Western Double Feature 3: Rogers & Allen (1950)

Twilight of the Dead See Gates of Hell (1983)

Twinkle, Twinkle, Killer Kane See The Ninth Configuration (1979)

Twinky See Lola (1969)

The Twisted Road See They Live by Night (1949)

2 Cries in the Night See Funeral Home (1982)

Two Minds for Murder See Someone Behind the Door (1971)

Two Weeks in September See A Coeur Joie (1967)

Tystnaden See The Silence (1963)

U-238 and the Witch Doctor See Jungle Drums of Africa (1953)

Uccellacci e Uccellini See The Hawks & the Sparrows (1967)

Uccidero Un Uomo See This Man Must Die (1970)

Uchu Daikaiiju Dogora See Dagora, the Space Monster (1965)

Uchudai Dogora See Dagora, the Space Monster (1965)

Uchujin Tokyo Ni Arawaru See Warning from Space (1956)

Ugetsu Monogatari See Ugetsu (1953)

Ukigusa See Drifting Weeds (1959)

Ulica Graniczna See Border Street (1948)

Ulisse See Ulysses (1955)

The Ultimate Chase See The Ultimate Thrill (1974)

The Ultimate Solution of Grace Quigley See Grace Quigley (1984)

Ultimi Giorni di Pompeii See The Last Days of Pompeii (1960)

The Umbrella Woman See The Good Wife (1986)

Un Amour De Swann See Swann in Love (1984)

Un Amour En Allemagne See A Love in Germany (1984)

Un Angelo e Sceso a Brooklyn See The Man Who Wagged His Tail (1957)

Un Arma de Dos Filos See Shark! (1968)

Un Autre Homme, Une Autre Chance See Another Man, Another Chance (1977)

Un Chapeau de Paille d'Italie See Italian Straw Hat (1927)

Un Complicato Intrigo Di Donne, Vicoli E Delitti See Camorra: The Naples Connection (1985)

Un Condamne a Mort s'est Echappe See A Man Escaped (1957)

Un, Deux, Trois, Quatre! See Black Tights (1960)

Un Dimanche a la Campagne See A Sunday in the Country (1984)

Un Elephant a Trompe Enormement See Pardon Mon Affaire (1976)

Un Grand Amour de Beethoven See Beethoven (1936)

Un Homme Amoureux See A Man in Love (1987)

Un Homme Est Mort See The Outside Man (1973)

Un Homme et Un Femme See A Man and a Woman (1966)

Un Homme Et Une Femme: Vingt Ans Deja See A Man and a Woman: 20 Years Later (1986)

Un Minuto Per Pregare, Un Istante Per Morire See A Minute to Pray, A Second to Die (1967)

Un Senor Muy Viejo Con Unas Alas Enormes See A Very Old Man with Enormous Wings (1988)

Un Trem Para as Estrelas See Subway to the Stars (1987)

Un Uomo da Rispettare See Master Touch (1974)

Un Zoo, La Nuit See Night Zoo (1987)

Una Bruja Sin Escoba See A Witch Without a Broom (1968)

Una Giornata Speciale See A Special Day (1977)

Una Hacka Para la Luna de Miel See Hatchet for the Honeymoon (1970)

Una Ragione Per Vivere e Una Per Morire See A Reason to Live, A Reason to Die (1973)

Unakrsna Vatra See Operation Cross Eagles (1969)

Uncle Harry See The Strange Affair of Uncle Harry (1945)

Uncle Silas See Inheritance (1947)

Unconventional Linda See Holiday (1938)

Under California Skies See Under California Stars (1948)

Under Mexicali Stars See Western Double Feature 3: Rogers & Allen (1950)

Under the Clock See The Clock (1945)

Under the Sun of Satan See Under Satan's Sun (1987)

Underground See The Lower Depths (1936)

An Underwater Odyssey See Neptune Factor (1973)

Underworld See Transmutations (1986)

Underworld After Dark See Big Town After Dark (1947)

Une Femme Est Une Femme See A Woman is a Woman (1960)

Une Femme ou Deux See One Woman or Two (1985)

Une Histoire Simple See A Simple Story (1979)

Une Partie de Campagne See A Day in the Country (1946)

The Unearthly Stranger See The Unearthly Stranger (1964)

Ungus of Terror See Attack of the Mushroom People (1963)

Unknown Satellite Over Tokyo See Warning from Space (1956)

Untel Pere et Fils See Heart of a Nation (1943)

The Unvanquished See Aparajito (1958)

Uomo Dalla Pelle Dura See Counter Punch (1971)

Up in the Cellar See Three in the Cellar (1970)

Up the Chastity Belt See Naughty Knights (1971)

The Upstate Murders See Savage Weekend (1980)

Ursus See Ursus in the Valley of the Lions (1962)

The Usual Unidentified Thieves See Big Deal on Madonna Street (1958)

Utah See Western Double Feature 1 (1938)

Vacation See National Lampoon's Vacation (1983)

Vagabond Violinist See Broken Melody (1934)

Valborgmassoafton See Walpurgis Night (1941)

The Valdez Horses See Chino (1975)

Valdez the Half Breed See Chino (1975)

Valley of Fear See Sherlock Holmes and the Deadly Necklace (1962)

The Vampire See Vampyr (1931)

The Vampire and the Robot See My Son, the Vampire (1952)

The Vampire-Beast Craves Blood See Blood Beast Terror (1967)

Vampire Men of the Lost Planet See Horror of the Blood Monsters (1970)

Vampire Over London See My Son, the Vampire (1952)

Vampire Playgirls See The Devil's Nightmare (1971)

Vampire's Night Orgy See Orgy of the Vampires (1973)

Vampyr, Der Traum Des David Gray See Vampyr (1931)

Vampyr, Ou L'Etrang e Aventure De David Gray See Vampyr (1931)

Vampyres, Daughters of Dracula See Vampyres (1974)

Vasectomy See Vasectomy: A Delicate Matter (1986)

The Vegas Strip Wars See Las Vegas Strip War (1984)

The Veil See Haunts (1977)

Velvet House See Crucible of Horror (1969)

Vendetta: Secrets of a Mafia Bride See A Family Matter (1991)

Vengeance See The Brain (1962)

Vengeance: The Story of Tony Cimo See Vengeance (1989)

Venus in Peltz See Venus in Furs (1970)

The Venusian See The Stranger from Venus (1954)

Vessel of Wrath See Beachcomber (1938)

The Veteran See Deathdream (1972)

The Vicious Circle See Woman in Brown (1948)

Victims of the Beyond See Sucker Money (1934)

Vindicator See Wheels of Fire (1984)

Violence et Passion See Conversation Piece (1975)

Violent Journey See The Fool Killer (1965)

Violent Midnight See Psychomania (1963)

Violent Rage See Fearmaker (1989)

You Can't Steal Love *See* Live a Little, Steal a Lot (1975)

You Don't Need Pajamas at Rosie's *See* The First Time (1969)

The Young and the Damned *See* Los Olvidados (1950)

The Young and the Immortal *See* The Sinister Urge (1960)

The Young and The Passionate *See* I Vitelloni (1953)

Young Commandos *See* Delta Force 3: The Killing Game (1991)

The Young Cycle Girls *See* Cycle Vixens (1979)

Young Dracula *See* Andy Warhol's Dracula (1974)

Young Dracula *See* Son of Dracula (1943)

Young Hearts *See* Promised Land (1988)

Young Hellions *See* High School Confidential (1958)

Young Invaders *See* Darby's Rangers (1958)

Young Scarface *See* Brighton Rock (1947)

The Youngest Spy *See* My Name is Ivan (1962)

Your Past is Showing *See* The Naked Truth (1958)

Your Red Wagon *See* They Live by Night (1949)

Your Witness *See* Eye Witness (1949)

Youth Takes a Hand *See* Behind Prison Walls (1943)

Zabudnite na Mozarta *See* Forget Mozart (1985)

Zamri Oumi Voskresni *See* Freeze-Die-Come to Life (1990)

Zato Ichi To Yojimbo *See* Zatoichi vs. Yojimbo (1970)

Zatoichi Meets Yojimbo *See* Zatoichi vs. Yojimbo (1970)

Zayn Vaybs Lubovnik *See* His Wife's Lover (1931)

Zazie in the Subway *See* Zazie dans le Metro (1961)

Zazie in the Underground *See* Zazie dans le Metro (1961)

Zee & Co. *See* X, Y & Zee (1972)

Zeisters *See* Fat Guy Goes Nutzoid (1986)

Zemiya *See* Earth (1930)

Zerkalo *See* The Mirror (1975)

Zero de Conduit *See* Zero for Conduct (1933)

Zeta One *See* Alien Women (1969)

Zombie *See* I Eat Your Skin (1964)

Zombie Creeping Flesh *See* Night of the Zombies (1983)

Zombie Flesh Eaters *See* Zombie (1980)

Zombies *See* I Eat Your Skin (1964)

Zombies of the Stratosphere *See* Satan's Satellites (1958)

Zormba *See* Zorba the Greek (1964)

Z.P.G. *See* Zero Population Growth (1972)

Zuckerbaby *See* Sugarbaby (1985)

VIDEOHOUND'S GOLDEN MOVIE RETRIEVER

Aaron Loves Angela Puerto Rican girl falls in love with a black teen amidst the harsh realities of the Harlem ghetto. "Romeo and Juliet" meets "West Side Story" in a cliched comedy drama. Music by Jose.
1975 (R) 99m/C Kevin Hooks, Irene Cara, Moses Gunn, Robert Hooks, Jose Feliciano; **D:** Gordon Parks Jr. VHS, Beta $59.95 COL 🏃🏃

Abbott and Costello in Hollywood Bud and Lou appear as a barber and porter of a high class tonsorial parlor in Hollywood. A rather sarcastic look at backstage Hollywood, Abbott & Costello style. Ball makes a guest appearance. **AKA:** Bud Abbott and Lou Costello In Hollywood.
1945 111m/B Bud Abbott, Lou Costello, Frances Rafferty, Warner Anderson, Lucille Ball; **D:** Sylvan Simon. VHS, Beta $19.98 MGM, CCB 🏃🏃

Abbott and Costello Meet Captain Kidd With pirates led by Captain Kidd on their trail, Abbott and Costello follow a treasure map. Bland A&C swashbuckler spoof with a disinterested Laughton impersonating the Kidd. One of the duo's few color films.
1952 70m/C Bud Abbott, Lou Costello, Charles Laughton, Hillary Brooke, Fran Warren, Bill Shirley, Leif Erickson; **D:** Charles Lamont. VHS, Beta, LV $29.95 NOS, UHV 🏃🏃

Abbott and Costello Meet Dr. Jekyll and Mr. Hyde Abbott and Costello take on evil Dr. Jekyll, who has transformed himself into Mr. Hyde, and is terrorizing London. A lame attempt at recapturing the success of "Abbott and Costello Meet Frankenstein."
1952 77m/B Bud Abbott, Lou Costello, Boris Karloff, Craig Stevens, Helen Westcott, Reginald Denny; **D:** Charles Lamont. VHS, Beta $14.95 MCA 🏃🏃

Abbott and Costello Meet Frankenstein Big-budget A&C classic with subsequent big box office. Tells the sad story of Chick and Wilbur, two unsuspecting baggage clerks delivering to a wax museum a crate containing the last but not quite dead remains of Dracula and Dr. Frankenstein's monster. There the fiends are revived, with the help of the vampire's assistant who feigns love for Lou but secretly wants to implant his brain in Frankie Big Shoes. Seems the monster has become too intelli-

gent, so Dracula is seeking to downsize his synapses to make him more controllable. Enter Lou. The Wolf Meister makes a special appearance to warn Chick and Wilbur that trouble looms. Last film to use the Universal creature pioneered by Karloff in 1931, and one of A&C's best efforts. **AKA:** Abbott and Costello Meet the Ghosts.
1948 83m/B Bud Abbott, Lou Costello, Lon Chaney Jr., Bela Lugosi, Glenn Strange, Lenore Aubert, Jane Randolph; **D:** Charles T. Barton; **V:** Vincent Price. VHS, Beta, LV $14.95 MCA 🏃🏃🏃

Abbott & Costello Meet the Invisible Man Abbott and Costello play newly-graduated detectives who take on the murder case of a boxer (Franz) accused of killing his manager. Using a serum that makes people invisible, the boxer helps Costello in a prizefight that will frame the real killers, who killed the manager because the boxer refused to throw a fight. Great special effects and hilarious gags make this one of the best from the crazy duo.
1951 82m/B Bud Abbott, Lou Costello, Nancy Guild, Adele Jergens, Sheldon Leonard, William Frawley, Gavin Muir, Arthur Franz; **D:** Charles Lamont. VHS $14.98 MCA 🏃🏃🏃

Abbott and Costello Meet the Killer, Boris Karloff Unremarkable Abbott and Costello murder mystery. Karloff plays a psychic who tries to frame Lou for murder. Pleasant enough but not one of their best.
1949 84m/B Bud Abbott, Lou Costello, Boris Karloff, Lenore Aubert, Gar Moore, Donna Martell, Alan Mowbray, James Flavin, Roland Winters; **D:** Charles T. Barton. VHS, Beta, LV $9.95 MCA 🏃🏃

Abbott and Costello Scrapbook Rare glimpses of the comedy duo from screen tests, previews, and flubs.
197? 60m/B Bud Abbott, Lou Costello. VHS, Beta $29.95 DVT 🏃🏃

ABC Stage 67: Truman Capote's A Christmas Memory A television drama special narrated by Capote about his remembered childhood experience of baking dozens of fruitcakes for friends at Christmas with his elderly distant cousin, Miss Sook Faulk (Page). She is quiet, lovely and true in this sensitive portrait of why we give and what we have to be thankful for. Adapted

from a Capote short story by Capote and Eleanor Perry. **AKA:** Truman Capote's A Christmas Memory; A Christmas Memory.
1966 51m/B Geraldine Page, Donnie Melvin; **D:** Frank Perry. VHS, Beta, 8mm $24.99 MOV, VYY 🏃🏃

ABC's of Love & Sex, Australia Style An Australian-made sex-education parody.
1986 87m/C AU Brigittia Almsrom, Rettima Borel, Ian Broadbent VHS, Beta $19.95 ACA 🏃

Abducted A woman jogger is abducted by a crazed mountain man in the Canadian Rockies. Weird and unbelievably tedious film is nevertheless highlighted by some spectacular wilderness footage of the Vancouver area, a travelogue bonus for those in the mood.
1986 (PG) 87m/C CA Dan Haggerty, Roberta Weiss, Lawrence King Phillips; **D:** Boon Collins. VHS, Beta $79.95 PSM 🏃½

Abduction Exploitative account of the Patty Hearst kidnapping loosely adapted from a novel by Harrison James written before the kidnapping. A young woman from a wealthy capitalist family is kidnapped by black radicals and held for an unusual ransom. Oh, and she tangles with lesbians, too.
1975 (R) 100m/C Judith-Marie Bergan, David Pendleton, Gregory Rozakis, Leif Erickson, Dorothy Malone, Lawrence Tierney; **D:** Joseph Zito. VHS, Beta $59.95 MED 🏃½

The Abduction of Allison Tate Rich developer takes land belonging to a group of Native Americans. Three young tribe members retaliate by kidnapping the developer's daughter. But when their plans go awry and one of the trio is killed, Allison finds herself sympathizing more with them than with her father's ambitions.
1992 (R) 95m/C Leslie Hope, Bernie White; **D:** Paul Leder. VHS $79.95 MNC 🏃½

The Abduction of Kari Swenson An account of the true-life (it really happened) kidnapping of Olympic biathlon hopeful Swensen by a pair of mischievous Montana mountain men with matrimony in mind. The movie details the abduction of Swenson by the scruffy father and son duo and the massive manhunt. As the put-upon Kari, Pollan exceeds script expectations in this

made-for-television exercise in stress avoidance.
1987 100m/C Joe Don Baker, M. Emmet Walsh, Ronny Cox, Michael Bowen, Geoffrey Blake, Dorothy Fielding, Tracy Pollan; *D:* Stephen Gyllenhaal. VHS **$79.95** VMK *⅟₂*

Abduction of St. Anne An almost interesting made-for-television mystical thriller about a detective and a bishop trying to track down a gangster's daughter, who may have nifty supernatural healing powers the Church would be very interested in having documented.
1975 78m/C Robert Wagner, E.G. Marshall, William Windom, Lloyd Nolan; *D:* Harry Falk. VHS, Beta **$49.95** WOV, GKK *⅃⅃*

The Abductors Caffaro's super-agent takes on international white slavery, a worthy target for any exploitation effort. While the novelty is a tough and intelligent on-screen heroine, sufficient sleaze and violence bring it all down to the proper level of swampland video. Sequel to the never-to-be-forgotten "Ginger."
1972 (R) 90m/C Cheri Caffaro, William Grannell, Richard Smedley, Patrick Wright, Jennifer Brooks; *D:* Don Schain. VHS, Beta **$39.95** MON *⅃*

Abdulla the Great A dissolute Middle Eastern monarch falls for a model, who spurns him for an army officer. While distracted by these royal shenanigans, the king is blissfully unaware of his subjects' disaffection—until they revolt. Dares to lampoon Egypt's dead King Farouk, going against conventional Hollywood wisdom ("Farouk in film is box office poison"). *AKA:* Abdullah's Harem.
1956 89m/C *GB* Gregory Ratoff, Kay Kendall, Sydney Chaplin; *D:* Gregory Ratoff. VHS, Beta **$29.95** VYY *⅃⅃*

Abe Lincoln in Illinois Massey considered this not only his finest film but a part he was "born to play." Correct on both counts, this Hollywood biography follows Lincoln from his log cabin days to his departure for the White House. The Lincoln-Douglass debate scene and Massey's post-presidential election farewell to the citizens of Illinois are nothing short of brilliant. Written by Sherwood from his Pulitzer-Prize winning play. Contrasted with the well-known "Young Mr. Lincoln" (Henry Fonda), its relative anonymity is perplexing. *AKA:* Spirit of the People.
1940 110m/B Raymond Massey, Gene Lockhart, Ruth Gordon, Mary Howard, Dorothy Tree, Harvey Stephens, Minor Watson, Alan Baxter, Howard da Silva, Maurice Murphy, Clem Bevans, Herbert Rudley; *D:* John Cromwell; *W:* Robert Sherwood. VHS, Beta **$19.95** MED, RKO, TTC *⅃⅃⅃⅃*

The Abe Lincoln of Ninth Avenue All-American tale of a poor young man making good in New York. His role model is Abraham Lincoln. Cooper is exceptional, supported by effective performances by the rest of the cast. *AKA:* Streets of New York.
1939 68m/B Jackie Cooper, Martin Spelling, Marjorie Reynolds, Dick Purcell, George Cleveland, George Irving; *D:* William Nigh. VHS, Beta, 8mm **$29.95** VYY *⅃⅃⅟₂*

Abigail's Party Steadman plays the hostess for a very ill-fated dinner party, especially when she realizes her husband has just died on her new carpet.
1977 105m/C *GB* Alison Steadman; *D:* Mike Leigh. VHS **$79.95** WBF, BTV *⅃⅃*

Abilene Town In a post-Civil War Kansas town far from the freeway, Scott is the tough marshall trying to calm the conflict between cattlemen and homesteaders. He also finds time to participate in a romantic triangle with dance hall vixen Dvorak and heart-of-gold Fleming. Snappy pace keeps it interesting. Based on a novel by Ernest Haycox.
1946 90m/B Randolph Scott, Ann Dvorak, Edgar Buchanan, Rhonda Fleming, Lloyd Bridges; *D:* Edwin L. Marin. VHS, Beta, 3/4U, **Special order formats $9.95** NEG, MRV, NOS *⅃⅃⅃*

The Abominable Dr. Phibes After being disfigured in a freak car accident that killed his wife, an evil genius decides that the members of a surgical team let his wife die and shall each perish by a different biblical plague. High camp with the veteran cast in top form.
1971 (PG) 90m/C *GB* Vincent Price, Joseph Cotten, Hugh Griffith, Terry-Thomas, Virginia North, Susan Travers, Alex Scott, Caroline Munro; *D:* Robert Fuest. VHS, Beta, LV **$14.98** VES, LIV *⅃⅃⅃*

The Abomination After a 5,000-year-old creature possesses him during a nightmare, a boy goes on an eye-gouging frenzy. Only the audience gets hurt.
1988 (R) 100m/C Van Connery, Victoria Chaney, Gaye Bottoms, Suzy Meyer, Jude Johnson, Blue Thompson, Scott Davis; *D:* Max Raven. VHS, Beta DMP *⅃*

About Last Night... Semi-realistic comedy-drama which explores the ups and downs of one couple's relationship. Mostly quality performances, especially Perkins and Belushi as friends of the young lovers. Based on David Mamet's play "Sexual Perversity in Chicago," but considerably softened so that more people would buy tickets at the box office, the film acts as a historical view of contemporary mating rituals before the onset of the AIDS crisis.
1986 (R) 113m/C Rob Lowe, Demi Moore, Elizabeth Perkins, James Belushi; *D:* Edward Zwick. VHS, Beta, LV **$14.95** COL *⅃⅃⅃*

Above Suspicion MacMurray and Crawford are American honeymooners (poor Fred!) asked to assist an international intelligence organization. They engage the Nazis in a tense battle of wits. Well-made and engaging.
1943 91m/B Joan Crawford, Fred MacMurray, Conrad Veidt, Basil Rathbone, Reginald Owen; *D:* Richard Thorpe. VHS **$19.98** MGM *⅃⅃⅃*

Above the Law In his debut, Seagal does his wooden best to portray a tough Chicago police detective planning an enormous drug bust of one of the biggest felons in the state. Unfortunately, the FBI has ordered him to back off and find another bust. The reasons are almost as complex as Seagal's character, and like most details of the flick, stupid. However, people don't watch these movies for the acting or the plot, but for the fight scenes, which are well-choreographed and violent. Watch it with someone you love.
1988 (R) 99m/C Steven Seagal, Pam Grier, Henry Silva, Sharon Stone, Ron Dean, Daniel Faraldo; *D:* Andrew Davis. VHS, Beta, LV, 8mm **$19.95** WAR, TLF, PIA *⅃⅃*

Above Us the Waves During WWII, the British navy immobilizes a huge German battleship off the coast of Norway. Effectively dramatizes the British naval preparations for what seemed a suicidal mission: using midget submarines to plant underwater explosives on the hull of the German vessel and detonating them before the Germans could detect the danger.

1956 92m/C *GB* John Mills, John Gregson, Donald Sinden, James Robertson Justice, Michael Medwin, James Kenney, O.E. Hasse, William Russell, Thomas Heathcote, Lee Patterson, Theodore Bikel, Lyndon Brook, Anthony Newley; *D:* Ralph Thomas. VHS REP *⅃⅃⅃*

Abraham Lincoln Griffith's first talking movie takes Abraham Lincoln from his birth through his assassination. This restored version includes the original slavery sequences which were believed to be lost, but obviously were not. Musical score included.
1930 97m/B Walter Huston, Una Merkel, Kay Hammond, E. Allen Warren, Hobart Bosworth, Fred Warren, Henry B. Walthall, Russell Simpson; *D:* D.W. Griffith. VHS, Beta, LV, 3/4U, **Special order formats $19.95** NOS, MRV, CCB *⅃⅃⅟₂*

Abraxas: Guardian of the Universe Good space cop versus bad space cop with an ecological twist. Good-guy Abraxas (Ventura) has the task of stopping planets from destroying their environments and fighting senseless wars. His ex-partner Secundas (Ole-Thorsen) has his own mission, seeking an anti-life power which could destroy the universe. They decide to fight it out, using Earth as the battleground.
1990 (R) 90m/C Jesse Ventura, Sven Ole-Thorsen; *Cameos:* James Belushi. VHS **$89.95** PSM *⅃⅟₂*

Abroad with Two Yanks Two Marine buddies on furlough exhibit slapstick tendencies while competing for the same girl. Along the way a big chase ensues with the two soldiers in drag. Typical wartime shenanigans likely to incite only weak chuckling or inspired snoozing.
1944 81m/B William Bendix, Dennis O'Keefe, Helen Walker, John Loder, George Cleveland, Janet Lambert, James Flavin, Arthur Hunnicutt; *D:* Allan Dwan. VHS, Beta **$12.95** LIV *⅃⅃*

Absence of Malice High-minded story about the harm that the news media can inflict. Field is the earnest reporter who, after being fed some facts by an unscrupulous federal investigator, writes a story implicating Newman in a murder he didn't commit. Field hides behind journalistic confidentiality privilege to put off the outraged Newman, who loses a friend to suicide during the debacle. Interesting performances by Field and Newman.
1981 (PG) 116m/C Paul Newman, Sally Field, Bob Balaban, Melinda Dillon, Luther Adler, Barry Primus, Josef Sommer, John Harkins, Don Hood, Wilford Brimley; *D:* Sydney Pollack. VHS, Beta, LV **$14.95** COL *⅃⅃⅟₂*

The Absent-Minded Professor Classic dumb Disney fantasy of the era. A professor accidentally invents an anti-gravity substance called flubber, causing inanimate objects and people to become airborne. Great sequence of the losing school basketball team taking advantage of flubber during a game. MacMurray is convincing as the absent-minded genius in this newly colored version. Followed by "Son of Flubber."
1961 97m/C Fred MacMurray, Nancy Olson, Keenan Wynn, Tommy Kirk, Leon Ames, Ed Wynn; *D:* Robert Stevenson. VHS, Beta, LV **$19.99** DIS *⅃⅃⅃⅟₂*

Absolute Beginners Fervently stylish camp musical exploring the lives of British teenagers in the 1950s never quite gets untracked, although MTV video moments fill out a spare plot line. Based on a novel by Colin MacInnes. ♫Absolute Beginners; That's Motivation; Volare; Killer Blow; Have You Ever Been Blue?; Quiet Life; Having It All; Selling Out; Va Va Voom; The Naked and

the Dead; Better Git It In Your Soul (The Hot and the Cool); Boogie Stop Shuffle (The Rough and the Smooth); Rodrigo Bay; Riot City; Ted Ain't Dead; Napoli; Cool Napoli; Little Cat; Landlords and Tenants; Santa Lucia; So What?; Hey Little Schoolgirl; Rock Baby Rock; Scorpio; Switching It Off; Hancock's Half Hour; Here Comes the Bride; My Mammy; Sleep Lagoon; Teddy Bears Picnic; Rocking at the 21's; Bongo Rock; Great Balls of Fire; Heat Doesn't Bother Me.
1986 (PG) 107m/C *GB* David Bowie, Ray Davies, James Fox, Eddie O'Connell, Patsy Kensit, Anita Morris, Sade Adu; *D:* Julien Temple. **VHS, Beta, LV $79.95** *HBO* 𝄇𝄇

Absolution Two English boys trapped in a Catholic boarding school conspire to drive a tyrannical priest over the edge of sanity. As a result, bad things (including murder) occur. Burton is interesting in sadistic character study. Not released in the U.S. until 1988 following Burton's death, maybe due to something written in the will.
1981 (R) 105m/C *GB* Richard Burton, Dominic Guard, Dai Bradley, Andrew Keir, Billy Connolly, Willoughby Gray; *D:* Anthony Page. **VHS, Beta, LV $9.95** *SIM, TWE, FCT* 𝄇𝄇

The Abyss Underwater sci-fi adventure about a team of oil-drilling divers pressed into service by the navy to locate and disarm an inoperative nuclear submarine. A high-tech thriller with fab footage underwater and pulsating score. The laserdisc version contains 27 extra minutes of footage. *AKA:* L'Oeuvre au Noir.
1989 (PG-13) 140m/C Ed Harris, Mary Elizabeth Mastrantonio, Todd Graff, Michael Biehn, John Bedford Lloyd, J.C. Quinn, Leo Burmester, Kidd Brewer Jr., Kimberly Scott, Adam Nelson, George Robert Kirk, Chris Elliott; *D:* James Cameron. Academy Awards '89: Best Visual Effects; Nominations: Best Cinematography, Best Sound. **VHS, Beta, LV $14.98** *FXV* 𝄇𝄇𝄇

Accatone! Accatone (Citti), a failure as a pimp, tries his luck as a thief. Hailed as a return to Italian neo-realism, this is a gritty, despairing, and dark look at the lives of the street people of Rome. Pasolini's first outing, adapted by the director from his novel, "A Violent Life." Pasolini served as mentor to Bernardo Bertolucci, listed in the credits as an assistant director.
1961 116m/B *IT* Franco Citti, Franca Pasut, Roberto Scaringelli, Adele Cambria, Paolo Guidi, Silvana Corsini; *D:* Pier Paolo Pasolini. **VHS $79.95** *WBF, APD, TAM* 𝄇𝄇𝄇

Acceptable Risks Toxic disaster strikes when a plant manager is ordered to cut costs and sacrifice safety at the Citichem plant. Predictable plot stars Dennehy as the plant manager who risks all and fights politicians to reinstate the safety standards. Meanwhile, Tyson is the city manager who tries to warn the town of a possible chemical accident that could have devastating effects on the community. Made for television drama that shamelessly preys on audience fears.
1986 (R) 97m/C Brian Dennehy, Cicely Tyson, Kenneth McMillan, Christine Ebersole, Beah Richards, Cindy Gilliland; *D:* Rick Wallace. **VHS, Beta $79.95** *PSM* 𝄇½

Access Code Government agents attempt to uncover a private organization that has gained control of nuclear weapons for the purpose of world domination. A ragged patchwork of disconnected scenes meant to test the virtue of patience.
1984 90m/C Martin Landau, Michael Ansara, MacDonald Carey; *D:* Mark Sobel. **VHS, Beta $79.95** *PSM* 𝄇

Accident A tangled web of guilt, remorse, humor and thwarted sexuality is unravelled against the background of the English countryside in this complex story of an Oxford love triangle. An inside view of English repression at the university level adapted for the screen by Pinter from the novel by Nicholas Mosley. Long-winded but occasionally engrossing character study with interesting performances.
1967 100m/C *GB* Dirk Bogarde, Michael York, Stanley Baker, Jacqueline Sassard, Delphine Seyrig, Alexander Knox, Vivien Merchant, Freddie Jones, Harold Pinter; *D:* Joseph Losey; *W:* Harold Pinter. **VHS, Beta $59.95** *HBO* 𝄇𝄇½

Accident Skate for your life. A hockey game turns into a nightmare when the roof over the arena collapses under the weight of too much ice and snow. One of the few hockey disaster films.
1983 104m/C Terence Kelly, Fiona Reid, Frank Perry; *D:* Donald Britnain. **VHS, Beta $59.95** *TWE* 𝄇½

The Accidental Tourist A bittersweet and subtle story, adapted faithfully from Anne Tyler's novel, of an introverted, grieving man who learns to love again after meeting an unconventional woman. After his son's death and subsequent separation from wife Turner, Macon Leary (Hurt) avoids emotional confrontation, burying himself in routines with the aid of his obsessive-compulsive siblings. Kooky dog-trainer Muriel Pritchett (an exuberant Davis) wins his attention, but not without struggle. Hurt effectively uses small gestures to describe Macon's emotional journey, while Davis grabs hearts with her open performance. Outstanding supporting cast.
1988 (PG) 121m/C William Hurt, Geena Davis, Kathleen Turner, Ed Begley Jr., David Ogden Stiers, Bill Pullman, Amy Wright; *D:* Lawrence Kasdan; *M:* John Williams. Academy Awards '88: Best Supporting Actress (Davis); Nominations: Best Adapted Screenplay, Best Picture, Best Original Score; New York Film Critics Awards '88: Best Film. **VHS, Beta, LV, 8mm $19.98** *WAR, BTV* 𝄇𝄇𝄇½

Accidents A scientist discovers that his invention has been stolen and is going to be used to cause worldwide havoc. He becomes concerned and spends the remainder of the movie trying to relieve himself of anxiety.
1989 (R) 90m/C Edward Albert, Leigh Taylor-Young, Jon Cypher; *D:* Gideon Amir. **VHS, Beta $79.75** *TWE* 𝄇½

Accomplice Plodding whodunit with Arlen as a shy, bookish private eye hired by his old flame to locate her missing husband. His investigations uncover several murders and long after the viewers have put 2 + 2 together, the P.I. smells a rat. The missing husband was a ruse to divert him from the real scam-a bank heist. Painfully low-level excitement.
1946 66m/B Richard Arlen, Veda Ann Borg, Tom Dugan, Michael Branden, Francis Ford; *D:* Walter Colmes. **VHS $19.95** *NOS* 𝄇½

Accused Married dancers Fairbanks and Del Rio are working in a Parisian revue when the show's sultry leading lady (Desmond) makes a pass at Fairbanks. Though he's turned her down, through a series of misunderstandings Del Rio believes the worst and the two women get into a vicious argument. When the star is found dead guess who gets the blame? Del Rio is lovely, Desmond is spiteful, and Fairbanks serves as a fine object of two women's affections.

1936 83m/B *GB* Douglas Fairbanks Jr., Dolores Del Rio, Florence Desmond, Basil Sydney, Athole Stewart, Esme Percy, Googie Withers, Cecil Humphreys; *D:* Thornton Freeland. **VHS** *HCV* 𝄇𝄇½

The Accused Young is cast against character in this story of a college professor who is assaulted by one of her students and kills him in self-defense. A courtroom drama ensues, where Young is defended by the dead man's guardian. Film noir with nice ensemble performance. *AKA:* Strange Deception.
1948 101m/B Loretta Young, Robert Cummings, Wendell Corey, Sam Jaffe, Douglas Dick, Sara Allgood, Ann Doran; *D:* William Dieterle. **VHS, Beta $89.95** *PAR* 𝄇𝄇½

The Accused Provocative treatment of a true story involving a young woman gang raped in a bar while onlookers cheer. McGillis is the assistant district attorney who takes on the case and must contend with the victim's questionable past and a powerful lawyer hired by a wealthy defendant's parents. As the victim with a past, Foster gives an Oscar-winning performance that won raves for its strength and complexity.
1988 (R) 110m/C Jodie Foster, Kelly McGillis, Bernie Coulson, Steve Antin, Leo Rossi; *D:* Jonathan Kaplan. **VHS, Beta, LV, 8mm $14.95** *PAR, FCT, BTV* 𝄇𝄇𝄇

Ace Crawford, Private Eye Bumbling private eye struggles with confusing murder and somehow manages to solve the case.
19?? 71m/C Tim Conway, Billy Barty, Bill Henderson. **VHS** *MCG* 𝄇𝄇

Ace Drummond The complete 13-chapter serial about a murder organization that tries to stop several countries from forming a worldwide clipper ship air service.
1936 260m/B John "Dusty" King, Jean Rogers, Noah Beery Jr.; *D:* Ford Beebe. **VHS, Beta $29.95** *NOS, HHT, VCN* 𝄇𝄇

Ace High Spaghetti western about a ruthless outlaw named Cat Stevens trying to save himself from the noose. Patterned after the famous Sergio Leone-Clint Eastwood westerns, with less of a budget and more camp tendencies.
1968 120m/C *IT* Eli Wallach, Terence Hill, Bud Spencer, Brock Peters, Kevin McCarthy; *D:* Giuseppe Colizzi. **VHS, Beta $14.95** *PAR, FCT* 𝄇½

Ace of Aces An American sculptor is reviled, particularly by his girlfriend, when he does not join fellows in enlisting in what becomes WWI. Out to prove he's not lacking testosterone, he becomes a pilot in France, but is embittered by his experiences. Dated but well-acted war melodrama.
1933 77m/B Richard Dix, Elizabeth Allan, Theodore Newton, Ralph Bellamy, Joseph Sawyer, Frank Conroy, William Cagney; *D:* J. Walter Ruben. **VHS, Beta $19.98** *TTC* 𝄇𝄇

Ace of Hearts A seedy story about a rich guy in the South Pacific who pays heavily to have himself killed.
1985 90m/C Mickey Rooney, Chris Robinson, Pilar Velasquez. **VHS, Beta $39.95** *VCD* 𝄇

Aces and Eights Standard western detailing the final days of Wild Bill Hickok, who was holding aces and eights when shot in the back (he never did finish the game). McCoy does his usual best as the sanitized Billy.
1936 62m/B Tim McCoy, Jimmy Aubrey, Luana Walters, Wheeler Oakman, Earle Hodgins, Frank Glennon; *D:* Sam Newfield. **VHS $19.95** *NOS, DVT, RXM* 𝄇𝄇

Aces: Iron Eagle 3 Colonel "Chappy" Sinclair returns once again in this air adventure. He's been keeping busy flying in air shows when he stumbles across the nefarious activities of a Peruvian drug baron working out of a remote village. Sinclair recruits a team of maverick air circus pilots and they "borrow" a fleet of WWII vintage aircraft to raid the village, coming up against a fellow Air Force officer who turns out to be another villain. Lots of action and a stalwart cast.
1992 (R) 98m/C Louis Gossett Jr., Rachel McLish, Paul Freeman, Horst Buchholz, Christopher Cazenove, Sonny Chiba, Fred Dalton Thompson, Mitchell Ryan, Robert Estes, J.E. Freeman; *D:* John Glen. **VHS, LV** $19.95 COL *羽*

Aces Wild Another poker title. Outlaws menace an honest newspaper until the lawmen show up and send them on their way.
1937 62m/B Harry Carey Sr., Gertrude Messinger, Edward Cassidy, Roger Williams; *D:* Harry Fraser. **VHS, Beta, LV** NO *羽* ½

The Acid Eaters Straight-laced desk jockeys spend their weekends exploring the realm of the senses. Includes nudity.
1967 62m/C Buck Kartalian, Pat Barringer; *W/D:* B. Ron Elliott; *W:* Carl Monson; *M:* Billy Allen. **VHS** $23.00 SMW *羽*

Acorn People An unemployed teacher takes a summer job at a camp for handicapped children and learns sensitivity. Made-for-television weeper adapted by Tewkesbury from the book by Ron Jones.
1982 97m/C Ted Bessell, Cloris Leachman, LeVar Burton, Dolph Sweet, Cheryl Anderson; *D:* Joan Tewkesbury. **VHS, Beta** TLF *羽*

Acqua e Sapone A young innocent model goes to Rome under the watchful eyes of an appointed priest-chaperon, but finds love, fun and other sinful things. Sudsy/romantic comedy.
1983 (PG) 100m/C *IT* Carlo Verdone, Natasha Hovey, Florinda Bolkan, Elena Bolkan; *D:* Carlo Verdone. **VHS, Beta** $59.95 RCA, TAM *羽* ½

Across 110th Street Gritty, violent cop thriller in the blaxploitation genre. Both the Mafia and the cops hunt down three black hoods who, in a display of extremely bad judgement, knocked over a mob-controlled bank while disguised as police. Lots of bullets create buckets of blood. Filmed on location in Harlem.
1972 (R) 102m/C Anthony Quinn, Yaphet Kotto, Anthony (Tony) Franciosa, Paul Benjamin, Ed Bernard, Antonio Fargas, Tim O'Connor; *D:* Barry Shear. **VHS, Beta** $14.95 MGM, FOX *羽*

Across the Bridge A man on the run from Scotland Yard for stealing a fortune flees to Mexico, in the process killing a man and assuming his identity. An ironic twist and his love for a dog seal his final destiny. Steiger's psychological study as the fugitive is compelling. Based on a novel by Graham Greene.
1957 103m/B *GB* Rod Steiger, David Knight, Marla Landi, Noel William, Bernard Lee; *D:* Ken Annakin. **VHS, Beta** LCA *羽* ½

Across the Great Divide Two orphans must cross the rugged snow-covered Rocky Mountains in 1876 in order to claim their inheritance—a 400-acre plot of land in Salem, Oregon. Pleasant coming-of-age tale with majestic scenery.
1976 (G) 102m/C Robert F. Logan, George Flower, Heather Rattray, Mark Hall; *W/D:* Stewart Raffill; *M:* Angelo Badalamenti. **VHS, Beta** $9.98 MED *羽* ½

Across the Pacific Classic Bogie and Huston made on the heels of "The Maltese Falcon." Bogie is an American Army officer booted out of the service on false charges of treason. When no other military will accept him, he sails to China (via the Panama Canal) to offer his services to Chiang Kai-Shek. On board, he meets a variety of seedy characters who plan to blow up the canal. Huston again capitalizes on the counterpoint between the rotundly acerbic Greenstreet, who plays a spy, and stiff-lipped Bogart, who's wooing Astor. Great Bogie moments and fine direction make this an adventure classic. When he departed for the service just prior to filming the final scenes, Huston turned over direction (with Bogie reportedly in an impossible situation) to Vincent Sherman, who did his best to resolve it. Also available colorized.
1942 97m/B Humphrey Bogart, Mary Astor, Sydney Greenstreet, Charles Halton, Victor Sen Yung, Roland Got, Keye Luke, Richard Loo; *D:* John Huston. **VHS** $19.98 MGM, FCT *羽羽* ½

Across the Plains Predictable oater about two brothers who are raised separately after their parents are murdered by outlaws. One is brought up by Indians, the other by the outlaws responsible for wiping out the folks, who tell the boy that Indians did in his ma and pa. Eventually the brothers meet and fight. Odds favor the good one winning, aided by Indian pals.
1939 59m/B Jack Randall, Frank Yaconelli, Joyce Bryant, Hal Price, Dennis Moore, Glenn Strange, Bud Osborne; *D:* Spencer Gordon Bennet. **VHS, Beta** $19.95 NOS, GPV, DVT *羽* ½

Across the Tracks Two brothers, one a juvie-home rebel, the other a straight-A jock, are at odds when the black sheep is pressured into selling drugs. In an attempt to save his brother from a life of crime, the saintly one convinces his brother to join him on the school track team, and the brothers are forced to face off in a big meet. Fairly realistic good guy/bad guy who's really a good guy teen drama. Also available in an "R" rated version. Music by Joel Goldsmith; written by director Tung.
1989 (PG-13) 101m/C Rick Schroder, Brad Pitt, Carrie Snodgress; *W/D:* Sandy Tung; *M:* Joel Goldsmith. **VHS** $19.95 ACA *羽*

Across the Wide Missouri Pioneer epic stars Gable as a rugged fur trapper who marries an Indian woman (Marques) so he can trap beaver pelts on her people's rich land. On the journey to the Indian territory however, the trapper truly falls in love with his bride. Superior historical drama is marred slightly by the use of narration (provided by Howard Keel). Look for lively performances from Menjou as a French tippler and Naish as the quirky Indian Chief. Beautiful scenery filmed in the spectacular Rocky Mountains.
1951 78m/C Clark Gable, Ricardo Montalban, John Hodiak, Adolphe Menjou, Maria Elena Marques, J. Carroll Naish, Jack Holt, Alan Napier; *D:* William A. Wellman. **VHS, Beta** $19.98 MGM, CCB *羽羽* ½

The Act A muddled satire about political double dealing and union corruption further muddled by a twangy musical score manufactured by folksy John Sabastian. *AKA:* Bless 'Em All.
1982 (R) 90m/C Jill St. John, Eddie Albert, Pat Hingle, Robert Ginty, Sarah Langenfeld, Nicolas Surovy; *D:* Sig Shore. **VHS, Beta** $69.95 VES *羽*

Act of Aggression When a Parisian man finds his wife and daughter murdered at a summer resort, he takes the law into his own hands, with predictable results.
1973 (R) 100m/C *FR* Jean-Louis Trintignant, Catherine Deneuve, Claude Brasseur. **VHS, Beta** $59.95 FCT *羽*

Act of Passion: The Lost Honor of Kathryn Beck A woman meets a man at a party and has the proverbial one-night stand. Her privacy is shattered when she discovers that he's a terrorist under surveillance by the police and press. Strong performances by Thomas and Kristofferson help turn this into an interesting American television remake of the German "Lost Honor of Katharina Blum," based loosely on a novel by Heinrich Boll.
1983 100m/C Marlo Thomas, Kris Kristofferson, George Dzundza, Jon DeVries; *D:* Simon Langton. **VHS, Beta** $69.95 VMK *羽羽* ½

Act of Piracy A bankrupt contractor reunites with his estranged wife to track down the brutal terrorists who have kidnapped their son.
1989 (R) 105m/C Ray Sharkey, Gary Busey. **VHS, Beta, LV** $89.98 WAR *羽* ½

Act of Vengeance A group of women band together to hunt down and exact revenge on the man who raped them. Exploitative action-filled thriller. Also called "Rape Squad."
1974 (R) 90m/C Jo Ann Harris, Peter Brown, Jennifer Lee, Lisa Moore, Connie Strickland, Pat Estrin; *D:* Bob Kelljan. **VHS, Beta** $19.99 HBO *羽*

Act of Vengeance Drama about Jock Yablonski, a United Mine Workers official who challenged the president, Tony Boyle. Made for cable, based on fact, showing the events that led up to the murder of Yablonski and his family. Intriguing story lacking cinematic drive.
1986 97m/C Charles Bronson, Ellen Burstyn, Wilford Brimley, Hoyt Axton, Robert Schenkkan, Ellen Barkin; *D:* John MacKenzie. **VHS, Beta** $19.99 HBO *羽羽* ½

Action for Slander A British army officer sporting the typical stiff upper lip is accused of cheating during a card game, and the slander mars his reputation until the case is taken to court. Dryly earnest and honest in its depiction of class differences in pre-war England. Based on a novel by Mary Borden.
1938 84m/B *GB* Clive Brook, Ann Todd, Margaretta Scott, Ronald Squire, Francis L. Sullivan, Felix Aylmer, Googie Withers; *D:* Tim Whelan. **VHS, Beta, 8mm** $29.95 VYY *羽羽* ½

Action in Arabia A newsman uncovers a Nazi plot to turn the Arabs against the Allies while investigating a colleague's murder in Damascus. The desert teems with spies, double agents, and sheiks as suave Sanders goes about his investigative business. Quintessential wartime B-movie.
1944 75m/B George Sanders, Virginia Bruce, Lenore Aubert, Gene Lockhart, Robert Armstrong, H.B. Warner, Alan Napier, Michael Ansara; *D:* Leonide Moguy. **VHS, Beta** $19.98 RKO, TTC *羽*

Action in the North Atlantic Massey and Bogart are the captain and first mate of a Merchant Marine vessel running the lone supply route to the Soviet Union. Eventually they wind up locking horns with a Nazi U-boat. Plenty of action and strenuous flag waving in this propagandorama. Gordon fans won't want to miss her as Massey's wife. Also available colorized.
1943 126m/B Humphrey Bogart, Raymond Massey, Alan Hale Jr., Julie Bishop, Ruth Gordon, Sam Levene, Dane Clark; *D:* Lloyd Bacon. **VHS** $19.98 MGM, FCT *羽*

Action Jackson Power-hungry auto tycoon Nelson tries to frame rebellious black police sergeant Weathers for murder. Being a graduate of Harvard and a tough guy, the cop doesn't go for it. Nelson eats up the screen as the heavy with no redeeming qualities, while Weathers is tongue-in-cheek as the resourceful good guy who keeps running afoul of the law in spite of his best efforts. Lots of action, violence, and a few sexy women help cover the plot's lack of common sense.
1988 (R) 96m/C Carl Weathers, Vanity, Craig T. Nelson, Sharon Stone; **D:** Craig R. Baxley. **VHS, Beta, LV** $19.98 LHV, WAR ⅃⅃

Action U.S.A. A young woman witnesses the murder of her boyfriend by gangsters, who then pursue her to make sure she will never tell what she saw. Throughout Texas she rambles with the mob sniffing at her heels, grateful for the opportunity to participate in numerous stunts and car crashes.
1989 90m/C Barri Murphy, Greg Cummins, William Knight, William Smith, Cameron Mitchell; **D:** John Stewart. **VHS, Beta** $79.95 IMP ⅃½

Actor: The Paul Muni Story Musical biography of Paul Muni, from his beginnings as a traveling actor in Hungary to his New York theatre and movie career.
1978 105m/C Herschel Bernardi, Georgia Brown, Harold Gould. **VHS, Beta** $39.95 LIV ⅃⅃

Actors and Sin Two-part film casting a critical eye toward actors and Hollywood. "Actor's Blood" is the melodramatic story of Shakespearean actor Robinson and his unhappy actress daughter. She commits suicide and he sets out to prove it was murder. Heavy going. Lighter and more entertaining is "Woman of Sin," which relates a Hollywood satire involving a theatrical agent and his newest client, a precocious nine-year-old.
1952 82m/B Edward G. Robinson, Eddie Albert, Marsha Reed, Alan Reed, Dan O'Herlihy, Tracey Roberts; **D:** Lee Games, Ben Hecht. **VHS, LV** $19.95 SVS, COL, HEG ⅃⅃½

Adam Television docu-drama based on a tragic, true story. John and Reve Williams (Travanti and Williams) desperately search for their 6-year-old son abducted during an outing. During their long search and struggle, they lobby Congress for use of the FBI's crime computer. Eventually their efforts led to the creation of the Missing Children's Bureau. Sensitive, compelling performances by Travanti and Williams as the agonized, courageous parents.
1983 100m/C Daniel J. Travanti, JoBeth Williams, Martha Scott, Richard Masur, Paul Regina, Mason Adams; **D:** Michael Tuchner. **VHS, Beta** NO ⅃⅃⅃½

Adam at 6 A.M. Douglas is a young college professor who decides to spend a summer laboring in Missouri, where life, he thinks, is simpler. Of course, he learns that life in the boonies has its own set of problems, but unfortunately it takes him the entire movie before he catches the drift.
1970 (PG) 100m/C Michael Douglas, Lee Purcell, Joe Don Baker, Charles Aidman, Marge Redmond, Louise Latham, Grayson Hall, Dana Elcar, Meg Foster, Richard Derr, Anne Gwynne; **D:** Robert Scheerer. **VHS, Beta** $59.98 FOX ⅃⅃

Adam Had Four Sons Satisfying character study involving the typical turn-of-the-century family nearly consumed by love, jealousy, and hatred. In the early part of the century, a goodly governess (Bergman in her second U.S. film) watches sympathetically over four sons of an American businessman after their mother dies. Economic necessity separates Bergman from the family for sev-

eral years. Upon her return, she tangles with scheming bride-to-be Hayward, a bad girl intent on dividing and conquering the family before walking down the aisle with one of the sons. Based on a novel by Charles Bonner.
1941 81m/B Ingrid Bergman, Warner Baxter, Susan Hayward, Fay Wray, Richard Denning, June Lockhart, Robert Shaw; **D:** Gregory Ratoff. **VHS, Beta** $59.95 COL ⅃⅃½

Adam's Rib Classic war between the sexes cast Tracy and Hepburn as married attorneys on opposite sides of the courtroom in the trial of blonde bombshell Holliday, charged with attempted murder of the lover of her philandering husband. The battle in the courtroom soon takes its toll at home as the couple is increasingly unable to leave their work at the office. Sharp, snappy dialogue by Gordon and Kanin with superb direction by Cukor. Perhaps the best of the nine movies pairing Tracy and Hepburn. Also available colorized.
1950 101m/B Spencer Tracy, Katharine Hepburn, Judy Holliday, Tom Ewell, David Wayne, Jean Hagen, Hope Emerson, Polly Moran, Marvin Kaplan, Paula Raymond, Tommy Noonan; **D:** George Cukor; **W:** Garson Kanin, Ruth Gordon. **VHS, Beta, LV** $19.95 MGM, VYG, HMV ⅃⅃⅃⅃

The Addams Family The positively ooky family, based on the characters created by cartoonist Charles Addams, appear in the original, uncut television episodes. Two episodes per tape. This volume includes "The Addams Family Goes to School" and "Morticia and the Psychiatrist."
1964 50m/B John Astin, Carolyn Jones, Jackie Coogan, Ted Cassidy, Blossom Rock, Ken Weatherwax, Lisa Loring, Felix Silla. **VHS** $9.95 WOV, MOV ⅃⅃⅃⅃

The Addams Family Everybody's favorite family of ghouls hits the big screen, but something is lost in the translation. An imposter claiming to be long-lost Uncle Fester (Lloyd), who says he was in the Bermuda Triangle for 25 years, shows up at the Addams' home to complete a dastardly deed—raid the family's immense fortune. Although Fester's plan is foiled, a series of plot twists highlight the ghoulish family's eccentricities. Darkly humorous but eventually disappointing: Julia, Huston, and Ricci are great in their roles and the sets look good, but the plot is thin. Much closer to the original comic strip by Charles Addams than the popular TV show ever was.
1991 (PG-13) 102m/C Anjelica Huston, Raul Julia, Christopher Lloyd, Dan Hedaya, Elizabeth Wilson, Judith Malina, Carel Struycken, Dana Ivey, Paul Benedict, Christina Ricci, Jimmy Workman, Christopher Hart, John Franklin; **Cameos:** Marc Shaiman; **D:** Barry Sonnenfeld; **W:** Larry Thompson, Caroline Thompson; **M:** Marc Shaiman. **VHS, Beta, LV** $19.95 PAR ⅃⅃

Adios Amigo Offbeat western comedy has ad-libbing Pryor hustling as a perennially inept con man. Script and direction (both provided by Williamson) are not up to Pryor's level, although excessive violence and vulgarity are avoided in a boring attempt to provide good clean family fare.
1975 (PG) 87m/C Fred Williamson, Richard Pryor, Thalmus Rasulala, James Brown, Robert Philip, Mike Henry; **W/D:** Fred Williamson. **VHS, LV** $9.95 SIM, VMK ⅃⅃

Adios Gringo Routine oater in which a young rancher is swindled in a cattle deal and forced to kill in self defense.
1965 ?m/C Montgomery Wood, Evelyn Stewart. **VHS** $16.95 SNC ⅃½

Adios, Hombre An innocent man who was imprisoned for murder escapes from prison and seeks revenge. You'll be saying adios as well.
1968 90m/C IT Craig Hill, Giulia Rubini; **D:** Mario Caiano. **VHS, Beta** $49.95 UNI ⅃

The Adjuster Questions of identity surround the lives of two couples in this surreal black comedy. Noah Render is an insurance adjuster whose clients look to him for all sorts of comfort, so much so that his own identity has become a blurred reflection of their tragedies. His wife Hera is a film censor who secretly tapes the pornographic videos she watches at work. Their carefully organized lives are invaded by Bubba and Mimi, a wealthy couple who pass themselves off as filmmakers who want to use the Render house as a movie set. They are instead looking to involve the Renders in their latest and most elaborate erotic fantasy.
1992 (R) 102m/C CA Elias Koteas, Arsinee Khanjian, Maury Chaykin, Gabrielle Rose; **W/D:** Atom Egoyan. **VHS** $19.98 ORI ⅃⅃⅃

The Admiral Was a Lady Four ex-GIs try to get by in life without going to work. Hendrix walks into their lives as a winning ex-Wave gifted with a knack for repartee who is disgusted by their collective lack of ambition. Nevertheless, she is pursued by the zany quartet with predictable results.
1950 87m/B Edmond O'Brien, Wanda Hendrix, Rudy Vallee, Steve Brodie; **D:** Albert Rogell. **VHS, Beta** $14.98 NOS, FRH, VHE ⅃⅃

Adomas Nori Buti Zmogumi Soviet Lithuanian feature in its original form, with dialogue in Lithuanian. A young worker scrapes together money for a ticket to Buenos Aires, but the money is stolen by the manager of the travel office. **AKA:** Adam Wants to Be a Man.
1959 90m/B RU LI **D:** V. Zhalakyavichus. **VHS, Beta** IHF ⅃⅃

Adoption The third of Meszaros's trilogy, involving a middle-aged Hungarian woman who longs for a child and instead forms a deep friendship with a 19-year-old orphan. In Hungarian with English subtitles. Hungarian title: "Orkobefogadas."
1975 89m/B HU **D:** Marta Meszaros. **VHS, Beta** $69.95 KIV, TAM ⅃⅃⅃

The Adorable Cheat A low-budget, late-silent melodrama about a young woman who tries to get involved in the family business, despite her father's refusal of her help. Once in the business, she finds love.
1928 76m/B Lila Lee, Cornelius Keefe, Burr McIntosh; **D:** Burton King. **VHS, Beta, 8mm** $16.95 GPV, VYY ⅃⅃

Adorable Julia When an actress takes on a lover many years younger than herself, the laughs begin to fly in this sex comedy based on W. Somerset Maugham's novel.
1962 97m/C FR Lilli Palmer, Charles Boyer; **D:** Alfred Weidenmann. **VHS** $29.95 FCT, TIM, VEC ⅃

The Adultress When a husband and wife cannot satisfy their desire to have a family, they hire a young man to help them in this dumb made-for-television melodrama.
1977 (R) 85m/C Tyne Daly, Eric Braeden, Gregory Morton; **D:** Norbert Meisel. **VHS, Beta** NO ⅃

Adventure Island En route to Australia, a small ship stops at a remote island for supplies. The crew is greeted by a crazed, tyrannical leader who makes their lives difficult. Dull low-budget remake of 1937's "Ebb Tide."

1947 66m/C Rory Calhoun, Rhonda Fleming, Paul Kelly, John Abbott; D: Peter Stewart. VHS, Beta $16.95 SNC ✓✓½

Adventure of the Action Hunters
A dying sailor leaves a tourist couple a message leading to a treasure, and they vie for it along with gangsters, mercenaries and other unsavory types.
1987 (PG) 81m/C Ronald Hunter, Sean Murphy, Joe Cimino; D: Lee Bonner. VHS, Beta NO ✓

The Adventurer
An escaped convict saves two wealthy women from death. They mistake him for a gallant sportsman and bring him home. Early Chaplin silent with music track.
1917 20m/B Charlie Chaplin; D: Charlie Chaplin. VHS, Beta, 3/4U, Special order formats CAB ✓✓½

The Adventurers
At the turn of the century, two Boers and an English officer set out to recover stolen jewels hidden in the jungles of South Africa. On the way, greed and anger take their toll a la "The Treasure of Sierra Madre," only on a less convincing scale. AKA: Fortune in Diamonds; The Great Adventure.
1951 82m/B GB Dennis Price, Jack Hawkins, Siobhan McKenna, Peter Hammond, Bernard Lee; D: David MacDonald. VHS, Beta $19.95 NOS ✓✓

The Adventurers
Sleazy Harold Robbins novel retains its trashy aura on film. Unfortunately, this turkey is also long and boring. Set in South America, it tells the tale of a rich playboy who uses and destroys everyone who crosses his path. His vileness results from having seen his mother murdered by outlaws, but his obsession is to avenge his father's murder. Blood, gore, revolutions, and exploitive sex follow him everywhere. Watch and be amazed at the big-name stars who signed on for this one.
1970 (R) 171m/C Candice Bergen, Olivia de Havilland, Bekim Fehmiu, Charles Aznavour, Alan Badel, Ernest Borgnine, Leigh Taylor-Young, Fernando Rey, Thommy Berggren, John Ireland, Sydney Tafler, Rossano Brazzi, Anna Moffo, Christian Roberts, Yorgo Voyagis, Angela Scoular, Yolande Donlan, Ferdinand "Ferdy" Mayne, Jaclyn Smith, Peter Graves, Roberta Haynes; D: Lewis Gilbert. VHS $29.95 PAR Woof!

Adventures Beyond Belief
An irreverent motorcyclist is chased across Europe for a murder he didn't commit. Firmly within the boundaries of belief. Alternative title, "Neat and Tidy."
1987 95m/C Elke Sommer, Jill Whitlow, Graham Stark, Stella Stevens, Larry Storch, Thick Wilson, Skyler Cole, Edie Adams, John Astin; D: Marcus Thompson. VHS, Beta $79.95 SVS ✓

Adventures in Babysitting
A babysitter and her charges leave peaceful suburbia for downtown Chicago in order to rescue a friend in desperate trouble. After having a flat tire on the freeway, trouble takes on new meaning. The group survives encounters with gangsters and prostitutes and a trip through a blues bar and the office building where their parents are having a party. But will they ever make it home?
1987 (PG-13) 102m/C Elisabeth Shue, Keith Coogan, Anthony Rapp, Calvin Levels, Vincent D'Onofrio, Penelope Ann Miller, George Newbern, John Ford Noonan; D: Chris Columbus; M: Michael Kamen. VHS, Beta, LV, 8mm $89.95 TOU ✓✓½

Adventures in Dinosaur City
A group of modern-day pre-teens are transported back in time to the stone age. There they hook up with a group of partying,

leather-clad dinosaurs and help them solve prehistoric crimes.
1992 (PG) 88m/C Omri Katz, Shawn Hoffman, Tiffanie Poston, Pete Koch, Megan Hughes; D: Brett Thompson. VHS, LV $89.98 REP ✓✓

Adventures in Spying
Brian McNichols is just trying to enjoy his summer vacation when he discovers that a notorious drug lord is living in his neighborhood. After realizing there is a $50,000 reward for his capture, he enlists the help of his friend (Schoelen) to get the man's picture for the police. Fun, action-packed viewing for the whole family.
1992 (PG-13) 92m/C Jill Schoelen, Bernie Coulson, Seymour Cassel, G. Gordon Liddy. VHS $89.95 NLC ✓✓

Adventures of a Plumber's Helper
Seems this stud-muffin plumber's helper is no Maytag man when it comes to house calls: when he stumbles on some stolen moolah whilst romping in the boudoir, he finds his chosen profession to be even more lucrative than the trade school brochures promised.
19?? 72m/C VHS $29.95 ACA ✓

Adventures of a Private Eye
A self-mocking British detective farce about an inept private eye who takes his time tracking down a beautiful girl's blackmailer, bedding down with all the women he meets along the way.
1987 96m/C GB Christopher Neil, Suzy Kendall, Irene Handl; D: Stanley Long. VHS, Beta $29.95 ACA ✓

Adventures of a Taxi Driver
Cabbie finds sex, crime, sex, adventure and sex on the road in this off-duty comedy.
1976 89m/C GB Barry Evans, Judy Geeson, Adrienne Posta, Diana Dors, Liz Fraser; D: Stanley Long. VHS, Beta $29.95 ACA Woof!

The Adventures of an American Rabbit
Animated adventure of an unassuming young rabbit who finds himself the sole heir of the Legacy. Before he knows it, he has become the mighty, patriotic protector of animals the world over.
1986 85m/C VHS $14.98 KRT Woof!

The Adventures of Baron Munchausen
From the director of "Time Bandits," "Brazil," and "The Fisher King" comes an ambitious, imaginative, chaotic, and under-appreciated marvel based on the tall (and often confused) tales of the Baron. Munchausen encounters the King of the Moon, Venus, and other odd and fascinating characters during what might be described as an circular narrative in which flashbacks dovetail into the present and place is never quite what it seems. Wonderful special effects and visually stunning sets occasionally dwarf the actors and prove what Gilliam can do with a big budget.
1989 (PG) 126m/C John Neville, Eric Idle, Sarah Polley, Valentina Cortese, Oliver Reed, Uma Thurman, Sting, Jonathan Pryce, Bill Paterson, Peter Jeffrey, Alison Steadman, Charles McKeown, Dennis Winston, Jack Purvis; Cameos: Robin Williams; D: Terry Gilliam. VHS, Beta, LV, 8mm $19.95 COL, CRC ✓✓✓½

The Adventures of Buckaroo Banzai Across the Eighth Dimension
A man of many talents, Buckaroo Banzai (Weller) travels through the eighth dimension in a jet-propelled Ford Fiesta to battle Planet 10 aliens led by the evil Lithgow. Buckaroo incorporates his vast knowledge of medicine, science, music, racing, and foreign relations to his advantage. Offbeat and often humorous cult sci-fi trip. AKA: Buckaroo Banzai.

1984 (PG) 100m/C Peter Weller, Ellen Barkin, Jeff Goldblum, Christopher Lloyd, John Lithgow, Lewis Smith, Rosalind Cash, Robert Ito, Pepe Serna, Vincent Schiavelli, Dan Hedaya, Yakov Smirnoff, Jamie Lee Curtis; D: W.D. Richter. VHS, Beta, LV $9.99 VES, LIV ✓✓✓

The Adventures of Bullwhip Griffin
A rowdy, family-oriented comedy-adventure set during the California Gold Rush. Light Disney farce catches Russell at the tail end of his teenage star days. Pleshette and McDowall embark upon an ocean trip from Boston to San Francisco to find her brother, Russell, who's out west digging for gold. Assorted comedic adventures take place.
1966 110m/C Roddy McDowall, Suzanne Pleshette, Karl Malden, Harry Guardino; D: James Neilson. VHS, Beta $69.95 DIS ✓✓½

Adventures of Captain Fabian
When the captain of the "China Sea" learns that a beautiful woman has been falsely imprisoned, he comes to her rescue. Not one of Flynn's better swashbucklers, with typically low-quality Republic production.
1951 100m/B Errol Flynn, Vincent Price, Agnes Moorehead, Micheline Presle; D: William Marshall. VHS, Beta $39.95 NO ✓✓½

Adventures of Captain Marvel
A 12-episode cliff-hanging serial based on the comic book character. Details the adventures of klutzy Billy Batson, who transforms into superhero Captain Marvel by speaking the magic word, "Shazam!"
1941 240m/B Tom Tyler, Frank "Junior" Coghlan, Louise Currie; D: William Witney. VHS, LV $29.98 VCN, REP, MLB ✓✓½

Adventures of Don Juan
Flynn's last spectacular epic features elegant costuming and loads of action. Don Juan saves Queen Margaret from her evil first minister. He then swashbuckles his way across Spain and England in an effort to win her heart. Grand, large-scale fun and adventure with Flynn at his self-mocking best. Special laserdisc edition includes the original trailer. AKA: The New Adventures of Don Juan.
1949 111m/C Errol Flynn, Viveca Lindfors, Robert Douglas, Romney Brent, Alan Hale Jr., Raymond Burr, Aubrey Mather, Ann Rutherford; D: Vincent Sherman. Academy Awards '49: Best Costume Design (Color); Nominations: Best Art Direction/Set Decoration (Color). VHS, Beta, LV $19.98 MGM, PIA, MLB ✓✓✓½

Adventures of Eliza Fraser
A young shipwrecked couple move from bawdy pleasures to cannibalism after being captured by aborigines.
1976 114m/C Susannah York, Trevor Howard, Leon Lissek, Abigail, Noel Ferrier, Carole Skinner; D: Tim Burstall. VHS, Beta, LV $19.95 STE, NWV ✓✓½

The Adventures of Ford Fairlane
The Diceman plays an unusual detective specializing in rock 'n' roll cases. When a heavy metal singer dies on stage, he takes the case in his own inimitable fashion, pursuing buxom gals, sleazy record executives and even his ex-wife. Not surprisingly, many of his stand-up bits are worked into the movie. Clay, the ever-so-controversial comic in his first (and likely last) starring role haplessly sneers his way through this rock 'n roll dud of a comedy thriller. A quick effort to cash in on Clay's fading star. Forget about it. AKA: Ford Fairlane.
1990 (R) 101m/C Andrew Dice Clay, Wayne Newton, Priscilla Presley, Morris Day, Lauren Holly, Maddie Corman, Gilbert Gottfried, David Patrick Kelly, Brandon Call, Robert Englund, Ed O'Neill, Sheila E, Kari Wuhrer, Tone Loc; D: Renny Harlin. VHS, Beta, LV $19.98 FXV Woof!

The Adventures of Frank and Jesse James The bad brothers of the Wild West are trying to make good for rip-offs committed in their names, so they're hoping to hit pay-dirt with a silver mine. Double cassette.
19?? 180m/B VHS $29.98 REP Woof!

The Adventures of Frontier Fremont A rough and tumble story of a man who leaves the city, grows a beard, and makes the wilderness his home (and the animals his friends). Mountain life, that's the life for me. Almost indistinguishable from Haggerty's "Grizzly Adams," with the usual redeeming panoramic shots of majestic mountains.
1975 95m/C Dan Haggerty, Denver Pyle; **D:** Richard Friedenberg. **VHS, Beta $41.00** UHV, LME �ღ½

The Adventures of Gallant Bess The time-honored story of a rodeo man torn between his girl and his talented horse (the Bess of the title).
1948 73m/C Cameron Mitchell, Audrey Long, Fuzzy Knight, James Millican; **D:** Lew Landers. **VHS** VEC, TIM, HEG ✗✗

The Adventures of Hairbreadth Harry Three short spoofs of the early melodramas cranked out by the movie industry. Includes "Sawdust Baby," "Fearless Harry," and "Rudolph's Revenge."
192? 65m/B Billy West. **VHS, Beta** GPV ✗✗

The Adventures of Huck Finn Decent Disney attempt at adapting an American favorite by Mark Twain. Mischievious Huck and runaway slave Jim travel down the muddy Mississippi, working on life and friendship and getting into all sorts of adventures in the pre-Civil War era. Fast-paced and amusing with good performances by Wood (in the title role) and Broadway trained Vance (as Jim). Racial epithets and minstrel show dialect have been eliminated in this version. Some material, including Jim's close call with a lynch mob and Huck's drunken, brutal father may be too strong for immature children.
1993 (PG) 106m/C Elijah Wood, Courtney B. Vance, Robbie Coltrane, Jason Robards Jr., Ron Perlman, Dana Ivey; **D:** Stephen Sommers; **W:** Stephen Sommers; **M:** Bill Conti. **VHS** NYR ✗✗✗

The Adventures of Huckleberry Finn Mark Twain's classic story about a boy who runs away and travels down the Mississippi on a raft, accompanied by a runaway slave, is done over in MGM-style. Rooney is understated as Huck (quite a feat), while the production occasionally floats aimlessly down the Mississippi. An entertaining follow-up to "The Adventures of Tom Sawyer."
1939 89m/B Mickey Rooney, Lynne Carver, Rex Ingram, William Frawley, Walter Connolly; **D:** Richard Thorpe. **VHS, Beta $19.98** MGM, VID, HMV ✗✗✗

The Adventures of Huckleberry Finn A lively adaptation of the Twain saga in which Huck and runaway slave Jim raft down the Mississippi in search of freedom and adventure. Miscasting of Hodges as Huck hampers the proceedings, but Randall shines as the treacherous King. Strong supporting cast includes Keaton as a lion-tamer and boxing champ Moore as Jim.
1960 107m/C Tony Randall, Eddie Hodges, Archie Moore, Patty McCormack, Neville Brand, Mickey Shaughnessy, Judy Canova, Andy Devine, Sherry Jackson, Buster Keaton, Finlay Currie, Josephine Hutchinson, Parley Baer, John Carradine, Royal Dano, Sterling Holloway, Harry Dean Stanton; **D:** Michael Curtiz. **VHS, Beta $19.98** MGM, FCT ✗✗½

The Adventures of Huckleberry Finn The classic adventure by Mark Twain of an orphan boy and a runaway slave done again as a TV movie and starring F-Troop. Lacks the production values of earlier versions.
1978 100m/C Forrest Tucker, Larry Storch, Kurt Ida, Mike Mazurki, Brock Peters; **D:** Jack B. Hively. **VHS, Beta $9.98** VID ✗✗

The Adventures of Huckleberry Finn An animated version of the Mark Twain classic novel about the friendship between a young boy and a runaway slave.
1984 48m/C D: Peter Hunt. **VHS, Beta $29.98** SUE ✗✗

The Adventures of Huckleberry Finn An adaptation of the Mark Twain story about the adventures encountered by Huckleberry Finn and a runaway slave as they travel down the Mississippi River. Top-notch cast makes this an entertaining version. Originally made for television in a much longer version for PBS's "American Playhouse."
1985 121m/C Sada Thompson, Lillian Gish, Richard Kiley, Jim Dale, Barnard Hughes, Patrick Day, Frederic Forrest, Geraldine Page, Butterfly McQueen; **D:** Peter Hunt. **VHS, Beta $19.95** MCA ✗✗½

The Adventures of Ichabod and Mr. Toad Disney's wonderfully animated versions of Kenneth Grahame's "The Wind in the Willows" and "The Legend of Sleepy Hollow" by Washington Irving. Rathbone narrates the story of Mr. Toad, who suffers from arrogance and eventually must defend himself in court after being charged with driving a stolen vehicle (Disney did take liberties with the story). Crosby provides all the voices for "Ichabod," which features one of the all-time great animated sequences—Ichabod riding in a frenzy through the forest while being pursued by the headless horseman. A treat for all ages.
1949 68m/C D: Clyde Geronomi, James Algar; **V:** Jack Kinney, Bing Crosby. **VHS, LV** DIS, WTA ✗✗✗½

Adventures of Kit Carson Television western, which ran from 1951-1955, set in the 1880s about the famed frontiersman who kept the peace with the help of Mexican sidekick El Toro. Two episodes per tape.
1951 50m/C Bill Williams, John Hamilton, Bill Diamond. **VHS, Beta $19.99** MOV, MVC ✗✗✗½

The Adventures of Mark Twain A clay-animated fantasy based on, and radically departing from, the life and work of Mark Twain. Story begins with Twain flying into outer space in a blimp with stowaways Huck Finn, Tom Sawyer and Becky Thatcher and takes off from there. Above average entertainment for kids and their folks. **AKA:** Mark Twain.
1985 (G) 86m/C D: Will Vinton; **V:** James Whitmore. **VHS, Beta, LV** KRT ✗✗✗

The Adventures of Milo & Otis Delightful Japanese children's film about a farm-dwelling dog and cat and their odyssey after the cat is accidentally swept away on a river. Notable since no humans appear in the film. Well received by U.S. children. Narrated by Moore. **AKA:** Koneko Monogatari; The Adventures of Chatran.
1989 (G) 89m/C JP **D:** Masanori Hata. **VHS, Beta, LV $19.95** COL, RDG, HMV ✗✗✗

The Adventures of Nellie Bly Made for television "Classics Illustrated" story of Nellie Bly, a strong-willed female reporter doing her best to expose wrongdo-

ings in the late 19th century. A decent performance by Purl is overshadowed by the general lack of direction.
1981 100m/C Linda Purl, Gene Barry, John Randolph, Raymond Buktencia, J.D. Cannon, Elayne Heilveil, Cliff Osmond; **D:** Henning Schellerup. **VHS, Beta** NO ✗

The Adventures of Ozzie & Harriet Each volume in this 12-set series contains 4 episodes of the Nelsons' hit TV show from 1953-1964. Vol. 1 features 17-year-old Mary Tyler Moore doing the commercials. Vol. 2 features Mamie Van Doren as the housemother of Ricky's fraternity (some housemother!). The program was the prototype of family sitcoms. Original commercials included. Tapes are available for purchase individually.
195? 56m/B Ozzie Nelson, Harriet Hilliard Nelson, Ricky Nelson, David Nelson; **D:** Ozzie Nelson. **VHS $19.99** MOV ✗

The Adventures of Picasso A Swedish satire on the life of Picasso, dubbed in English. Don't look for art or facts here, or, for that matter, many laughs.
1980 88m/C SW Gosta Ekman, Lena Nyman, Hans Alfredson, Margareta Krook, Bernard Cribbins, Wilfrid Brambell; **D:** Tage Danielsson. **VHS, Beta** NO ✗✗

Adventures of Prince Achmed Three years in the making using the cutout/silhouette animation method. Based on the Arabian Nights stories.
1927 50m/C D: Lotte Reiniger. **VHS, Beta** GVV ✗✗

Adventures of Red Ryder The thrills of the rugged West are presented in this twelve-episode serial. Based on the then-famous comic strip character.
1940 240m/B Donald (Don "Red") Barry, Noah Beery Sr.; **D:** William Witney. **VHS, Beta $80.00** VCN, MLB ✗✗

The Adventures of Rex & Rinty An adventure serial in 12 chapters, featuring one of the last appearances by the original Rin-Tin-Tin.
1935 156m/B Kane Richmond, Harry Woods, Rin Tin Tin Jr; **D:** Ford Beebe, B. Reeves Eason. **VHS, Beta $49.95** NOS, VCN, DVT ✗✗

The Adventures of Rin Tin Tin Chronicles the adventures of that crime-fighting dog, Rin-Tin-Tin.
1947 65m/B Rin Tin Tin, Robert (Bobby) Blake. **VHS $9.99** CCB ✗✗½

The Adventures of Robin Hood A great, rollicking, Technicolor version of the legendary outlaw, following the justice-minded Saxon knight as he battles the Normans, outwits the evil Prince John, and gallantly romances Maid Marian. With grand castle sets and lush forest photography, "Adventures" displays ample evidence of its huge (at the time) budget of $2 million plus and why it's regarded as the swashbuckler standard-bearer. Just entering his prime, Flynn enthusiastically performs most of his own stunts, including intricate sword play and various forms of advanced tree and wall climbing. Flynn, fresh from fencing his way through "Captain Blood," brings to life a Robin brimming with charm and bravura, the enthusiastic protector of poor Saxons everywhere and the obvious undeclared king of Sherwood forest. The rest of the cast likewise attacks with zest, ranging from de Havilland as the cold but eventually sympathetic Maid Marian to Rains' fey performance as the dastardly Prince John (the direct predecessor to Alan Rickman's over-the-top spin on the Sheriff in Costner's remake) to Rathbone's conniving Sir Guy to Robin's

band of very merry men (led by Hale's Little John and Pallette as Friar Tuck). Based on various Robin Hood legends as well as Sir Walter Scott's "Ivanhoe" and the opera "Robin Hood" by De Koven-Smith. Also available in letter-boxed format.
1938 102m/C Errol Flynn, Olivia de Havilland, Basil Rathbone, Alan Hale Jr., Una O'Connor, Claude Rains, Patric Knowles, Eugene Pallette, Herbert Mundin, Melville Cooper, Ian Hunter, Montagu Love; **D:** Michael Curtiz; **W:** Norman Reilly, Seton I. Miller; **M:** Erich Wolfgang Korngold. Academy Awards '38: Best Film Editing, Best Interior Decoration, Best Original Score; Nominations: Best Picture. **VHS, Beta, LV $19.98** MGM, FOX, CRC 🎞🎞🎞🎞

The Adventures of Robin Hood Filmed on location in England and starring Greene as the legendary outlaw/hero, with Pleasance as the evil Prince John. Two episodes per tape. Volume 1 features "The Highlander" and "Tables Turned." Additional episodes are available.
1955 60m/C Richard Greene, Donald Pleasence. **VHS, Beta $19.95** MVC, MOV 🎞🎞🎞🎞

The Adventures of Sadie Collins is stranded on a desert island with three men, two of whom continuously chase her around. Naturally, she falls for the guy who ignores her. Obvious sex comedy which plays on Collins' scantily-clad physical assets. Based on the novel "The Cautious Amorist" by Norman Lindsay. **AKA:** Our Girl Friday.
1955 87m/C *GB* Joan Collins, George Cole, Kenneth More, Robertson Hare, Hermione Gingold, Walter Fitzgerald; **W/D:** Noel Langley. **VHS** NO 🎞🎞½

The Adventures of Sherlock Holmes The immortal Sherlock Holmes and his assistant Dr. Watson conflict with Scotland Yard as they both race to stop arch-criminal Professor Moriarty. The Yard is put to shame as Holmes, a mere amateur sleuth, uses his brilliant deductive reasoning to save the damsel in distress and to stop Moriarty from stealing the Crown Jewels. Second in the series and the last of Rathbone's appearances as the brilliant detective. **AKA:** Sherlock Holmes.
1939 83m/B Basil Rathbone, Nigel Bruce, Ida Lupino, George Zucco, E.E. Clive, Mary Gordon; **D:** Alfred Werker. **VHS, Beta $14.95** FOX 🎞🎞½

The Adventures of Sherlock Holmes: Hound of the Baskervilles Holmes tackles the mysterious and long-lived curse of the Baskervilles. Made for British television. Fine acting, detailed production. A pleasure.
1989 120m/C *GB* Jeremy Brett, Edward Hardwicke. **VHS $39.95** MPI 🎞🎞🎞

The Adventures of Sherlock Holmes' Smarter Brother The unknown brother of the famous Sherlock Holmes takes on some of his brother's more disposable excess cases and makes some hilarious moves. Written, directed, and starring Wilder, with moments of engaging farce borrowing from the Mel Brooks school of parody (and parts of the Brooks ensemble as well).
1978 (PG) 91m/C Gene Wilder, Madeline Kahn, Marty Feldman, Dom DeLuise, Leo McKern, Roy Kinnear, John Le Mesurier, Douglas Wilmer, Thorley Walters; **W/D:** Gene Wilder. **VHS, Beta** FOX 🎞🎞🎞

The Adventures of Sinbad The adventures of the Arabian mythic hero in an animated film version.
1979 47m/C **VHS, Beta $29.98** MGM, LIV, WTA 🎞🎞🎞

The Adventures of Sinbad the Sailor Sinbad receives a map to a treasure island where fabulous stores of jewels are hidden, and, in his search, falls in love with the King's daughter. Animated adventure.
1973 88m/C **VHS, Beta $59.98** LIV, FHE, WTA 🎞🎞🎞

Adventures of Smilin' Jack World War II flying ace Smilin' Jack Martin comes to life in this action-packed serial. Character from the Zack Moseley comic strip about air force fighting over China.
1943 90m/B Tom Brown, Sidney Toler; **D:** Ray Taylor. **VHS, Beta $26.95** SNC, NOS, VAN 🎞🎞🎞

The Adventures of Superman (1942-1943) Seven cartoons from 1942 and 1943 are included in this package: "Underground World," "Terror on the Midway," "Volcano," "Destruction Inc.," "Secret Agent," "Billion Dollar Limited," and "Showdown." Some black and white.
1943 55m/C **VHS, Beta $9.95** VYY 🎞🎞🎞

The Adventures of Tartu A British secret agent, sent to blow up a Nazi poison gas factory in Czechoslovakia, poses as a Romanian. One of Donat's lesser films, in the style of "The 39 Steps." **AKA:** Tartu.
1943 103m/C *GB* Robert Donat, Valerie Hobson, Glynis Johns; **D:** Harold Bucquet. **VHS, Beta $19.95** HHT, VCN, TIM 🎞🎞🎞

The Adventures of Tarzan The screen's first Tarzan in an exciting jungle thriller. Silent.
1921 153m/B Elmo Lincoln. **VHS, Beta $27.95** VYY 🎞🎞

The Adventures of the Flying Cadets Early aerial war adventure serial in thirteen complete chapters.
1944 169m/B Johnny Downs, Regis Toomey; **D:** Ray Taylor, Lewis D. Collins. **VHS, Beta $49.95** NOS, VCN, VYY 🎞½

The Adventures of the Little Rascals Six classic "Our Gang" comedies featuring the Little Rascals. Each short is presented in its original form.
193? 100m/B **VHS** REP 🎞½

The Adventures of the Masked Phantom The adventures of the Masked Phantom.
1938 56m/B Monte Rawlins, Betty Burgess, Larry Mason, Sonny Lamont, Jack Ingram; **D:** Charles Abbott. **VHS, Beta $19.95** NOS, VYY, RXM 🎞½

The Adventures of the Wilderness Family The story of a modern-day pioneer family who becomes bored with the troubles of city life and heads for life in the wilderness. There, they find trouble in paradise. Family-oriented adventure offering pleasant scenery. Followed by "The Wilderness Family, Part 2."
1976 (G) 100m/C Robert F. Logan, Susan Damante Shaw; **D:** Stewart Raffill. **VHS, Beta, LV $9.98** MED 🎞🎞

The Adventures of Tom Sawyer The vintage Hollywood adaptation of the Mark Twain classic, with music by Max Steiner and art direction by William Cameron Menzies. Not a major effort from the Selznick studio, but quite detailed and the best Tom so far.
1938 91m/C Tommy Kelly, Walter Brennan, Victor Jory, May Robson, Victor Kilian, Jackie Moran, Donald Meek, Anne Gillis, Marcia Mae Jones, Clara Blandick, Margaret Hamilton; **D:** Norman Taurog. **VHS, Beta, LV $14.98** FOX, FCT, MLB 🎞🎞🎞

The Adventures of Tom Sawyer Tom Sawyer is a mischievous Missouri boy who gets into all kinds of trouble in this white-washed, made for TV adaptation of the Mark Twain classic.
1973 76m/C Jane Wyatt, Buddy Ebsen, Vic Morrow, John McGiver, Josh Albee, Jeff Tyler. **VHS, Beta $39.95** MCA 🎞🎞½

The Adventures of Ultraman The adventures of Ultraman, a futuristic hero from a distant planet who is able to get quite large when necessary.
1981 90m/C **VHS, Beta $24.95** FHE 🎞🎞½

The Adventures of Walt Disney's Alice Three early Disney shorts featuring Lewis Carroll's cast of characters: "Alice's Egg Plant," "Alice's Orphan," and "Alice the Toreador." Silent.
1925 35m/B **VHS, Beta $29.95** JEF 🎞🎞½

The Adventurous Knights An athlete learns he is the heir to a Transylvanian throne.
1935 60m/B David Sharpe, Mary Kornman, Mickey Daniels, Gertrude Messinger; **D:** Edward Roberts. **VHS, Beta, LV** NO Woof!

The Adversary A young man must quit college because of his father's death. He struggles to find employment in Calcutta but his hardships are magnified by the impersonal society. In Bengali with English subtitles. **AKA:** Pratidwandi.
1971 110m/C *IN* **W/D:** Satyajit Ray. **VHS $39.95** FCT 🎞🎞½

Advise and Consent An interesting political melodrama with a fascinating cast, based upon Allen Drury's novel. The President chooses a candidate for the Secretary of State position which divides the Senate and causes the suicide of a senator. Controversial in its time, though somewhat turgid today. Laughton's last film.
1962 139m/B Don Murray, Charles Laughton, Henry Fonda, Walter Pidgeon, Lew Ayres, Burgess Meredith, Gene Tierney, Franchot Tone, Paul Ford, George Grizzard, Betty White, Peter Lawford, Edward Andrews; **D:** Otto Preminger. **VHS, Beta $14.95** QNE, KAR 🎞🎞🎞

Aelita: Queen of Mars Though the title has blockbuster potential, "Aelita" is a little-known silent Soviet sci-fi flick destined to remain little known. After building a rocket to fly to Mars, a Russian engineer finds its no Martian holiday on the fourth planet from the sun, with the Martians in the midst of a revolution. Silent, with a piano score.
1924 113m/B *RU* **D:** Iakov Protazanov. **VHS, LV $29.95** KIV, FCT, SNC 🎞🎞

The Affair Songwriter/polio victim Wood falls in love for the first time with attorney Wagner. Delicate situation handled well by a fine cast in this television movie.
1973 74m/C Natalie Wood, Robert Wagner, Bruce Davison, Kent Smith, Frances Reid, Pat Harrington; **D:** Gilbert Cates. **VHS, Beta** NO 🎞🎞🎞

An Affair in Mind British television movie about a professional writer who falls in love with a beautiful woman who tries to convince him to assist her in murdering her husband.
1989 88m/C *GB* Amanda Donohoe, Stephen Dillon, Matthew Marsh, Kean-Laurent Cochot; **D:** Michael Baker. **VHS, Beta $39.98** FOX 🎞🎞🎞

Affair in Trinidad Fun in the tropics as nightclub singer Hayworth enlists the help of brother-in-law Ford to find her husband's murderer. The trail leads to international thieves and espionage in a romantic thriller that reunites the stars of "Gilda." Hayworth sings (with Jo Ann Greer's voice) "I've Been Kissed Before."

1952 98m/B Rita Hayworth, Glenn Ford, Alexander Scourby, Torin Thatcher, Valerie Bettis, Steve Geray; *D:* Vincent Sherman. **VHS, LV, SVS** $19.95 *COL, PIA, CCB* ♂♂

The Affair of the Pink Pearl The husband-and-wife private investigation team of Tommy and Tuppence must find within 24 hours the culprit who stole a valuable pink pearl. Based on the Agatha Christie series of short stories. Made for British television.
1984 60m/C *GB* James Warwick, Francesca Annis; *W:* Agatha Christie. **VHS, Beta** $14.95 *PAV* ♂♂½

An Affair to Remember A nightclub singer and wealthy bachelor fall in love on an ocean liner and suffer bad luck later on when they try to get together on shore. Lesser melodramatic remake of McCarey's "Love Affair."
1957 115m/C Cary Grant, Deborah Kerr, Richard Denning, Cathleen Nesbitt, Neva Patterson; *D:* Leo McCarey; *W:* Leo McCarey, Delmer Daves. **VHS, Beta, LV** $19.98 *FOX* ♂♂½

The Affairs of Annabel The first of the popular series of Annabel pictures Lucy made in the late 1930s. Appealing adolescent is zoomed to movie stardom by her press agent's stunts. A behind-the-scenes satire on Hollywood, stars, and agents.
1938 68m/B Lucille Ball, Jack Oakie, Ruth Donnelly, Fritz Feld, Bradley Page; *D:* Ben Stoloff. **VHS, Beta, LV** $29.95 *CCB, RKO, IME* ♂♂½

Afraid of the Dark Convoluted psycho-thriller from a child's point of view. Young Lucas is fearful for his blind mother. It seems a vicious slasher has been attacking blind women and Lucas' father, a policeman, has yet to apprehend the criminal. But...Lucas it seems has a problem with reality. With his fantasies and realities mixed, all the people in his life also play entirely different roles. Characters are so detached and unreal that a viewer is prevented from a clear understanding of anything that may, or may not, be going on. Directorial debut of Peploe.
1992 (R) 91m/C Ben Keyworth, James Fox, Fanny Ardant, Paul McGann, Clare Holman, Robert Stephens; *D:* Mark Peploe. **VHS, LV** $89.95 *COL, NLC* ♂♂

Africa Screams Abbott and Costello go on an African safari in possession of a secret map. Unheralded independent A&C film is actually quite good in the stupid vein, with lots of jungle slapstick, generally good production values and a supporting cast of familiar comedy faces.
1949 79m/B Lou Costello, Bud Abbott, Shemp Howard, Hillary Brooke, Joe Besser, Clyde Beatty; *D:* Charles T. Barton. **VHS, Beta, LV, 3/4U, Special order formats** $9.95 *KAR, MRV, NEG* ♂♂½

Africa Texas Style An East African rancher hires an American cowboy and his Navajo sidekick to help run his wild game ranch. Decent family adventure which served as the pilot for the short-lived TV series "Cowboy in Africa." Features lots of wildlife footage and a cameo appearance by Hayley Mills.
1967 109m/C Hugh O'Brian, John Mills, Nigel Green, Tom Nardini; *Cameos:* Hayley Mills; *D:* Andrew Marton. **VHS** $19.98 *REP* ♂♂

African Dream A period tale about a black man and a white woman fighting against repression in South Africa.
1990 (R) 94m/C Kitty Aldridge, John Kani, Dominic Jephcott, John Carson, Richard Haines, Joy Stewart Spence; *D:* John Smallcombe. **VHS, Beta, LV** $29.95 *HMD, HBO, IME* ♂½

African Journey A moving, cross-cultural drama of friendship. A young black American goes to Africa for the summer to be with his divorced father who is working in the diamond mines. There he meets a young black African like himself; they overcome cultural clashes and learn respect for one another. Beautiful scenery, filmed in Africa. Part of the "Wonderworks" series.
1989 174m/C Jason Blicker, Pedzisai Sithole. **VHS** $79.95 *PME, HMV, BTV* ♂♂½

The African Queen After Hepburn's missionary brother is killed by Germans in World War I Africa, a hard-drinking steamer captain (Bogart) offers the bible-thumping spinster safe passage. Not satisfied with sanctuary, she persuades the dissolute captain to try to destroy a German gunboat blocking the British advance. Only thing is, they have to navigate down uncharted rivers to reach the gunboat, anchored in a large central Africa lake. When not battling myriad aquatic obstacles, the two spend more time fighting each other than they do the Germans. Time alone on an African river in the middle of nowhere has a way of changing a man and a woman (as many philosophers have noted), and Bogie and Hepburn are no exceptions. Mistrust and aversion turn to love, a transition effectively counterpointed by the continuing suspense of their daring mission. A classic that earned Bogart his second Academy Award. Huston and Agee adapted the screenplay, which makes wonderful use of natural dialogue and humor, from C.S. Forester's novel. Shot on location in Africa.
1951 105m/C Humphrey Bogart, Katharine Hepburn, Robert Morley, Theodore Bikel, Peter Bull, Walter Gotell; *W/D:* John Huston; *W:* James Agee. Academy Awards '51: Best Actor (Bogart); Nominations: Best Actress (Hepburn), Best Director (Huston), Best Screenplay. **VHS, Beta, LV** $19.98 *FOX, FCT, TLF* ♂♂♂♂

African Rage Little known release about an aging male nurse (yes, Quinn) who discovers he's dying of an incurable disease. With nothing left to lose, he plans the kidnapping of an African leader, hoping that the ransom will support his family. Meanwhile, another man is plotting the same leader's death. Decent performances help move along the improbable plot. *AKA:* Tigers Don't Cry; The Long Shot; Target of an Assassin; Fatal Assassin.
1978 90m/C *SA* Anthony Quinn, John Phillip Law, Simon Sabela, Ken Gampu, Marius Weyers, Sandra Prinsloo; *D:* Peter Collinson. **VHS, Beta** $9.95 *MPI, SIM* ♂♂

Afrita Hanen A rare Egyptian fantasy starring the famous Mid-Eastern actor, Farrid El Atrache. In Arabic with titles.
1947 97m/B Farrid El Atrache. **VHS, Beta** $39.95 *FCT* ♂♂♂

After Dark, My Sweet A troubled young man in search of a little truth ends up entangled in a kidnapping scheme. Muddled direction is overcome by above average performances and gritty realism. Based on the novel by Jim Thompson.
1990 (R) 114m/C Jason Patric, Rachel Ward, Bruce Dern, George Dickerson, James Cotton, Corey Carrier, Rocky Giordani; *D:* James Foley. **VHS, LV** $89.95 *LIV* ♂♂♂

After Darkness Slow-moving psycho-suspenser about a man obsessed with trying to remedy his twin brother's schizophrenia.
1985 104m/C *SI GB* John Hurt, Julian Sands, Victoria Abril, Pamela Salem; *D:* Dominique Othenin-Girard. **VHS, Beta** $19.95 *CEL* ♂

After Hours An absurd, edgy black comedy that's filled with novel twists and turns and often more disturbing than funny. An isolated uptown New York yuppie (Dunne) takes a late night stroll downtown and meets a sexy woman in an all-night coffee shop. From there he wanders through a series of threatening and surreal misadventures, leading to his pursuit by a vigilante mob stirred by ice cream dealer O'Hara. Something like "Blue Velvet" with more Catholicism and farce. Or similar to "Something Wild" without the high school reunion. Great cameos from the large supporting cast, including Cheech and Chong as burglars. A dark view of a small hell-hole in the Big Apple.
1985 (R) 97m/C Griffin Dunne, Rosanna Arquette, John Heard, Teri Garr, Catherine O'Hara, Verna Bloom, Linda Fiorentino, Dick Miller, Bronson Pinchot; *Cameos:* Cheech Marin, Thomas Chong; *D:* Martin Scorsese. **VHS, Beta, LV** $19.98 *WAR, PIA, KIV* ♂♂♂½

After Julius Twenty years after Julius Grace's death, his memory still hovers over his wife's and daughters' lives. British soap opera moves with glacier-like speed. Adapted from the book by Elizabeth Jane Howard.
1978 150m/C *GB* Faith Brook, John Carson, Cyd Hayman, Cyd Hayman; *D:* John Glenister. **VHS** $59.95 *SVS* ♂♂

After Midnight An aspiring playwright tries to get his work produced, only to meet with dead ends. Eventually, he hooks up with a talented young actress with whom he finds romance and success. *AKA:* I Have Lived.
1933 69m/B Alan Dinehart, Anita Page, Allen Vincent, Gertrude Astor; *D:* Richard Thorpe. **VHS, Beta** $16.95 *SNC* ♂

After Midnight Suspended in a central story about an unorthodox professor who preys upon the deepest fears of his students, a trio of terror tales come to life. From the writers of "The Fly II" and "Nightmare on Elm Street, Part IV." Some chills, few thrills.
1989 (R) 90m/C Marg Helgenberger, Marc McClure, Alan Rosenberg, Pamela Segall, Nadine Van Der Velde, Ramy Zada, Jillian McWhirter, Billy Ray Sharkey; *D:* Jim Wheat. **VHS, Beta** $89.98 *FOX, MGM* ♂♂

After Pilkington British television thriller about an uptight Oxford professor who runs into his bewitching childhood sweetheart after many years. She persuades him to help search for a missing archaeologist.
1988 100m/C *GB* Bob Peck, Miranda Richardson; *D:* Christopher Morahan. **VHS, Beta** $39.98 *FOX* ♂♂

After School Sex is prominent as a priest and one of his students find forbidden love while he prepares for a televised debate with an atheist. It could happen.
1988 (R) 90m/C Sam Bottoms, Edward Binns, Page Hannah, Renee Coleman, Dick Cavett; *D:* William Olsen. **VHS, Beta** $79.95 *ACA* ♂♂

After the Fall of New York Dimwitted post-apocalyptic tale set in New York after the fall of the "Big Bomb." A man, driven to search for the last normal woman, has reason to believe she is frozen alive and kept in the heart of the city. His mission: locate her, thaw her, engage in extremely limited foreplay with her, and repopulate the planet. A poorly dubbed dating allegory.
1985 (R) 95m/C *IT FR* Michael Sopkiw, Valentine Monnier, Anna Kanakis, Roman Geer, Edmund Purdom, George Eastman; *D:* Martin Dolman. **VHS, Beta** $79.98 *VES, LIV* Woof!

After the Fall of Saigon Soldiers in Vietnam go on a killing rampage. Dubbed; country of origin isn't known. *AKA:* Raiders of the Doomed Kingdom.

1988 100m/C Danny Aswatep, Peter Ramwa, Rayak Ramnate, Krao Spartacus. VHS, Beta NO *I*

After the Fox Sellers is a con artist posing as a film director to carry out a bizarre plan to steal gold from Rome. Features occasional backhand slaps at Hollywood, with Mature turning in a memorable performance as the has-been actor starring in Sellers' movie. Though the screenplay was co-written by Neil Simon, the laughs are marginal. Italian title is "Caccia alla Volpe."
1966 103m/C *GB IT* Peter Sellers, Victor Mature, Martin Balsam, Britt Ekland; *D:* Vittorio De Sica; *W:* Neil Simon. VHS, Beta $14.95 *MGM, FOX II*

After the Promise During the Depression, a poor carpenter tries to regain custody of his four sons following the death of his wife. Maudlin television melodrama based on a true story.
1987 100m/C Mark Harmon, Diana Scarwid, Rosemary Dunsmore, Donnelly Rhodes, Mark Hildreth, Trey Ames, Richard Billingsley; *D:* David Greene. VHS $19.95 *STE, NWV II*

After the Rehearsal Two actresses, one young, the other at the end of her career, challenge their director with love and abuse. Each questions his right to use them on stage and off. A thoughtful discussion of the meaning and reason for art originally made for Swedish television. Swedish with English subtitles.
1984 (R) 72m/C *SW* Erland Josephson, Ingrid Thulin, Lena Olin; *D:* Ingmar Bergman. VHS, Beta $59.95 *COL, TAM III*

After the Revolution A struggling novelist decides to write his next book from the viewpoint of his cat. In Hungarian with English subtitles.
1990 82m/C *HU D:* Andras Szirtes. VHS $59.95 *FCT II*

After the Shock Documentary-like dramatization of the San Francisco-Oakland earthquake of October, 1989 and, of course, its aftermath. Incorporates actual footage of the disaster. Written by director Sherman. Made for cable.
1990 (PG) 92m/C Yaphet Kotto, Rue McClanahan, Jack Scalia, Scott Valentine; *W/D:* Gary Sherman. VHS, Beta $79.95 *PAR II*

After the Thin Man Second in a series of six "Thin Man" films, this one finds Nick, Nora and Asta, the lovable terrier, seeking out a murderer from Nora's own blue-blooded relatives. Fast-paced mystery with a witty script and the popular Powell/Loy charm. Sequel to "The Thin Man," followed by "Another Thin Man."
1936 113m/B William Powell, Myrna Loy, James Stewart, Elissa Landi, Joseph Calleia, Jessie Ralph, Alan Marshal; *D:* Woodbridge S. Van Dyke. VHS, Beta $19.98 *MGM III*

Afterburn When Ted, her Air Force pilot husband, is killed in a crash of his F-16 fighter, Janet Harduvel learns the official explanation is pilot error. Convinced that something was wrong with his plane, Janet sets out to investigate, and eventually sue, military contractor General Dynamics. Dern turns in a great performance as the tough widow determined to clear her husband's name. Based on a true story; made for cable television.
1992 (R) 103m/C Laura Dern, Robert Loggia, Vincent Spano, Michael Rooker; *D:* Robert Markowitz. VHS, LV $89.99 *HBO, FCT II*

Aftermath Three astronauts return to Earth and are shocked to discover that the planet has been ravaged by a nuclear war. Quickly they make new plans.

1985 96m/C Steve Barnett, Larry Latham; *D:* Ted V. Mikels. VHS, Beta $9.99 *STE, PSM II 1/2*

Aftershock A beautiful alien and a mysterious stranger battle the Earth's repressive, evil government.
1988 (R) 90m/C Jay Roberts Jr., Elizabeth Kaitan, Chris Mitchum, Richard Lynch, John Saxon, Russ Tamblyn, Michael Berryman, Chris De Rose, Chuck Jeffreys; *D:* Frank Harris. VHS, Beta $79.95 *PSM II 1/2*

Afterward Made-for-British-television horror story about a family that moves into a supposedly haunted house with deadly results.
1985 60m/C *GB* Michael J. Shannon, Kay Harper, John Grillo. VHS, Beta $59.95 *PSM I*

Against A Crooked Sky A young boy sets out with an elderly trapper to find his sister, who was captured by the Indians. Similiar story to "The Searchers," but no masterpiece.
1975 (G) 89m/C Richard Boone, Stewart Peterson, Clint Ritchie, Geoffrey Land, Jewel Blanch; *D:* Earl Bellamy. VHS, Beta $29.95 *VES, CTP II*

Against All Flags An enjoyable Flynn swashbuckler about a British soldier slashing his way through the Spanish fleet at the turn of the 18th century. Though the story has been told before, tight direction and good performances win out. O'Hara is a tarty eyeful as a hot-tempered pirate moll.
1952 81m/C Errol Flynn, Maureen O'Hara, Anthony Quinn, Mildred Natwick; *D:* George Sherman. VHS, Beta, $14.95 *KRT, MCA III*

Against All Odds An interesting love triangle evolves when an ex-football player, played by Bridges, travels to Mexico to find his good friend's girlfriend. Contains complicated plot, numerous double crosses, sensual love scenes, and a chase scene along Sunset Boulevard. As the good friend sans conscience, Woods stars. A remake of 1947's "Out of the Past."
1984 (R) 122m/C Jeff Bridges, Rachel Ward, James Woods, Alex Karras, Jane Greer, Richard Widmark, Dorian Harewood, Swoosie Kurtz, Bill McKinney, Saul Rubinek; *D:* Taylor Hackford. VHS, Beta, LV, 8mm $12.95 *COL II 1/2*

Against the Drunken Cat Paws A blind young martial arts student seeks to regain her sight and avenge the death of her father.
1975 94m/C Chia Ling, Ou-Yang Ksiek. VHS, Beta $39.95 *UNI I*

Against the Wind A motley crew is trained for a mission into Nazi Germany to blow up records and rescue a prisoner. The first half of the film focuses on the group's training, but despite its intensity they win only a pyrrhic victory. A well-done production with solid performances from the cast.
1948 96m/B Robert Beatty, Jack Warner, Simone Signoret, Gordon Jackson, Paul Dupuis, Peter Illing; *D:* Charles Crichton. VHS $19.95 *NOS, TIM, VEC II 1/2*

Agatha A speculative period drama about Agatha Christie's still unexplained disappearance in 1926, and a fictional American reporter's efforts to find her. Beautiful but lackluster mystery. Unfortunately, Hoffman and Redgrave generate few sparks.
1979 (PG) 98m/C Dustin Hoffman, Vanessa Redgrave, Timothy Dalton, Helen Morse, Tony Britton, Timothy West, Celia Gregory; *D:* Michael Apted. VHS, Beta $64.95 *WAR II 1/2*

Age Isn't Everything An appalling clumsy comedy about a recent college graduate who abruptly becomes an old man while retaining his youthful exterior. He looks the same, but walks slowly and talks with a thick

Yiddish accent, get it? The cast just marks time until an inexplicable ending. *AKA:* Life in the Food Chain.
1991 (R) 91m/C Jonathan Silverman, Robert Prosky, Rita Moreno, Paul Sorvino, Rita Karin, Robert Cicchini, Brian Williams, Dee Hoty; *Cameos:* Dr. Joyce Brothers, Bella Abzug; *W:* Douglas Katz. VHS $89.99 *VES II*

Age Old Friends Crusty octogenarian Cronyn must choose. His daughter (played by real-life offspring Tandy) wants him to move out of a retirement home and into her house. But he's struggling to keep neighbor and increasingly senile friend Gardenia from slipping into "zombieland." An emotional treat with two fine actors deploying dignity and wit in the battle against old age. Originally adapted for HBO from the Broadway play, "A Month of Sundays" by Bob Larbey.
1989 89m/C Vincent Gardenia, Hume Cronyn, Tandy Cronyn, Esther Rolle, Michelle Scarabelli; *D:* Allen Kroeker. VHS, Beta $79.99 *HBO III 1/2*

The Agency An advertising agency attempts to manipulate public behavior and opinion through the use of subliminal advertising. A good premise is bogged down by a dull script and plodding performances by all concerned. Based on a Paul Gottlieb novel. *AKA:* Mind Games.
1981 (R) 94m/C *CA* Robert Mitchum, Lee Majors, Valerie Perrine, Saul Rubinek, Alexandra Stewart, George Kaczender; *D:* George Kaczender. VHS, Beta $69.95 *VES, MTX, SIM II*

Agent on Ice Hockey team is stalked by lawyers. No, wait. An ex-CIA agent is stalked for cover-up purposes by the agency and the mob. One slippery fellow.
1986 (R) 96m/C Tom Ormeny, Clifford David, Louis Pastore, Matt Craven; *D:* Clark Worswick. VHS, Beta $19.95 *STE, NWV II*

Aggie Appleby, Maker of Men A wimpy society boy transforms himself into a tough guy, all for the love of a dame. Based on a play by Joseph O. Kesserling. Very slight comedy. *AKA:* Cupid in the Rough.
1933 73m/B Charles Farrell, Wynne Gibson, William Gargan, ZaSu Pitts; *D:* Mark Sandrich. VHS $19.98 *FCT II 1/2*

Agnes of God Stage to screen translation of John Pielmeier's play loses something in the translation. Coarse chain-smoking psychiatrist Fonda is sent to a convent to investigate whether young nun Tilly is fit to stand trial. Seems that the nun may have given birth to and then strangled her baby, although she denies ever having sexual relations and knows nothing about an infant. Naive Fonda is frightened by probing Fonda, while worldly mother-superior Bancroft is distrusting. Melodramatic stew of Catholicism, religious fervor, and science features generally good performances, although Fonda often seems to be acting (maybe it's the cigarettes).
1985 (PG-13) 99m/C Jane Fonda, Anne Bancroft, Meg Tilly, Anne Pitoniak, Winston Reckert, Gratien Gelinas; *D:* Norman Jewison. Academy Awards '85 Nominations: Best Actress (Bancroft), Best Supporting Actress (Tilly), Best Original Score; Golden Globe Awards '86: Best Supporting Actress (Tilly). VHS, Beta, LV $12.95 *COL II*

The Agony and the Ecstasy A big-budget ($12 million, still a lot of money in 1965) adaptation of the Irving Stone book, recounting the conflict between Michelangelo and Pope Julius II after His Holiness directs the artist to paint the Sistine Chapel. We follow the tortured artist through the unpredictable creative process and the hours (it seems literal due to movie length) of painting flat on his back. Heston exudes quiet strength in his sincere interpretation of the genius artist who was homosexual and of course short, while Harrison has a fling as the Pope. The slow script is not up to the generally fine performances. A disappointment at the box office, but certainly worth a look on the small screen for the sets alone. **1965 136m/C** Charlton Heston, Rex Harrison, Harry Andrews, Diane Cilento, Alberto Lupo, Adolfo Celi; **D:** Carol Reed. **VHS, Beta, LV** **$19.98** FOX, IGP ✠✠½

Agony of Love An unhappy homemaker rents a nearby apartment to live out her wildest fantasies and bring some excitement into her otherwise dull life. **1966 ?m/C VHS $20** SMW ✠✠½

Aguirre, the Wrath of God Herzog at his best, combining brilliant poetic images and an intense narrative dealing with power, irony, and death. Spanish conquistadors in 1590 search for the mythical city of gold in Peru. Instead, they descend into the hell of the jungle. Kinski is fabulous as Aguirre, succumbing to insanity while leading a continually diminishing crew in this compelling, extraordinary drama shot in the jungles of South America. Both English- and German-language versions available. **1972 94m/C** GE Klaus Kinski, Ruy Guerra, Del Negro, Helena Rojo, Cecilia Rivera, Peter Berling, Danny Ades; **W/D:** Werner Herzog. **VHS $59.95** NYF, APD, TAM ✠✠✠½

Ah, Wilderness! Delightful tale of a teen boy coming of age in small town America. Watch for the hilarious high school graduation scene. Based on the play by Eugene O'Neill. Remade in 1948 as "Summer Holiday," a musical with Mickey Rooney in the lead. **1935 101m/B** Wallace Beery, Lionel Barrymore, Aline MacMahon, Eric Linden, Cecilia Parker, Spring Dyington, Mickey Rooney, Charley Grapewin, Frank Albertson; **D:** Clarence Brown. **VHS $19.98** MGM, BTV ✠✠✠½

Ain't No Way Back Two hunters stumble upon a feudin' bunch of moonshiners and must leave their city ways behind if they plan to survive. **1989 90m/C VHS, Beta** NO ✠

Air America It's the Vietnam War and the CIA is operating a secret drug smuggling operation in Southeast Asia to finance the effort. Flyboys Gibson and Downey drop opium and glib lines all over Laos. Big-budget Gibson vehicle with sufficient action but lacking much of a story, which was adapted from a book by Christopher Robbins. **1990 (R) 113m/C** Mel Gibson, Robert Downey Jr., Marshall Bell, Nancy Travis, David Marshall Grant, Tim Thomerson, Lane Smith; **D:** Roger Spottiswoode. **VHS, Beta, LV $19.95** LIV, IME ✠✠

Air Force One of the finest of the WWII movies, Hawks' exciting classic has worn well through the years, in spite of the Japanese propaganda. It follows the hazardous exploits of a Boeing B-17 bomber crew who fight over Pearl Harbor, Manila, and the Coral Sea. Extremely realistic dogfight sequences and powerful, introspective real guy interfacing by the ensemble cast are masterfully combined by Hawks. **1943 124m/B** John Garfield, John Ridgely, Gig Young, Arthur Kennedy, Charles Drake, Harry Carey Sr., George Tobias; **D:** Howard Hawks. Academy Awards '43: Best Film Editing; Nominations: Best Black and White Cinematography, Best Original Screenplay. **VHS** FOX ✠✠✠½

Air Hawk Australian made for TV release details the adventures of an outback pilot involved with stolen diamonds.

1984 90m/C AU Eric Oldfield, Louise Howitt, Ellie MacLure, David Robson, David Baker; **D:** David Baker. **VHS, Beta $59.95** VCD ✠

Air Raid Wardens Laurel & Hardy play a couple of small-town failures who become the local air raid wardens during WWII. They even manage to make a mess of this but redeem themselves when they overhear a spy plot and save the town's munitions factory from a German spy ring. A so-so effort from the comic duo. **1943 67m/B** Stan Laurel, Oliver Hardy, Edgar Kennedy, Jacqueline White, Stephen McNally, Russell Hicks, Howard Freeman, Donald Meek, Henry O'Neill; **D:** Edward Sedgwick. **VHS $19.98** MGM ✠✠½

Airplane! A classic lampoon of disaster flicks that's both dumb and hysterical. Remember, without this, there'd be no "Naked Gun." A former pilot who's lost both his girl (she's the attendant) and his nerve takes over the controls of a passenger plane when the crew is hit with food poisoning. The passengers become increasingly crazed and ground support more surreal as our hero struggles to land the plane. Clever, extremely fast, and often very funny parody mangles every Hollywood cliche within reach. The word and sight gags are so furiously paced that if one bombs, you'll scarcely notice. Cameos worth watching include Beaver's mom and Kareem Abdul-Jabbar. The film that launched Leslie Nielsen's second career as a comic actor (now it can be told). And it ain't over till it's over: don't head for the refrigerator or bathroom until the end of the amusing final credits. Followed in 1982 by "Airplane II: The Sequel," which was just as dumb but not as funny. **1980 (PG) 86m/C** Robert Hays, Julie Hagerty, Lloyd Bridges, Peter Graves, Robert Stack, Leslie Nielsen, Stephen Stucker, Ethel Merman; **Cameos:** Kareem Abdul-Jabbar, Barbara Billingsley; **D:** Jerry Zucker, Jim Abrahams. **VHS, Beta, LV, 8mm $14.95** PAR, PIA ✠✠✠½

Airplane 2: The Sequel Not a Zucker, Abrahams and Zucker effort, and sorely missing their slapstick and script finesse. The first passenger space shuttle has taken off for the moon and there's a mad bomber on board. Given the number of stars mugging, it's more of a loveboat in space than a fitting sequel to "Airplane." Nonetheless, some funny laughs and gags. **1982 (PG) 84m/C** Robert Hays, Julie Hagerty, Lloyd Bridges, Raymond Burr, Peter Graves, William Shatner, Sonny Bono, Chuck Connors, Chad Everett, Stephen Stucker, Rip Torn, Ken Finkleman, Sandahl Bergman; **D:** Ken Finkleman. **VHS, Beta, LV $14.95** PAR, PIA ✠✠

Airport Old-fashioned disaster thriller built around an all-star cast, fairly moronic script, and an unavoidable accident during the flight of a passenger airliner. A box-office hit that paved the way for many lesser disaster flicks (including its many sequels) detailing the reactions of the passengers and crew as they cope with impending doom. Considered to be the best of the "Airport" series and adapted by director Seaton from the Arthur Hailey novel. **1970 (G) 137m/C** Dean Martin, Burt Lancaster, Jean Seberg, Jacqueline Bisset, George Kennedy, Helen Hayes, Van Heflin, Maureen Stapleton, Barry Nelson, Lloyd Nolan; **W/D:** George Seaton. Academy Awards '70: Best Supporting Actress (Hayes); Nominations: Best Adapted Screenplay, Best Art Direction/Set Decoration, Best Cinematography, Best Costume Design, Best Film Editing, Best Picture, Best Sound, Best Supporting Actress (Stapleton), Best Original Score; Golden Globe Awards '71: Best Supporting Actress (Stapleton). **VHS, Beta, LV $14.95** MCA, BTV ✠✠✠

Airport '75 After a mid-air collision, a jumbo 747 is left pilotless. Airline attendant Black must fly da plane. She does her cross-eyed best in this absurd sequel to "Airport" built around a lesser "all-star cast." Safe on the ground, Heston tries to talk the airline hostess/pilot into landing, while the impatient Kennedy continues to grouse as leader of the foam-ready ground crew. A slick, insincere attempt to find box office magic again (which unfortunately worked, leading to two more sequels). **1975 (PG) 107m/C** Charlton Heston, Karen Black, George Kennedy, Gloria Swanson, Helen Reddy, Sid Caesar, Efrem Zimbalist Jr., Susan Clark, Dana Andrews, Linda Blair, Myrna Loy; **D:** Jack Smight. **VHS, Beta $59.95** GKK ✠✠

Airport '77 A converted passenger jet owned by billionaire Stewart is filled with priceless art and sets off to Palm Beach for a museum opening. Stewart and friends are joined by an uninvited gang of hijackers. Lemmon takes over the driving from Heston. The plane crash-lands in the ocean and all aboard must fight for survival. Twist to this in-flight disaster is that the bad time in the air occurs underwater, a novel (and some might say, desperate) twist to the old panic in the plane we're all gonna die formula. With a cast of familiar faces, some of them stars and some of them just familiar faces, this is yet another sequel to "Airport" and another box-office success, leading to the last of the series in 1979. **1977 (PG) 114m/C** Jack Lemmon, James Stewart, Lee Grant, Brenda Vaccaro, Joseph Cotten, Olivia de Havilland, Darren McGavin, Christopher Lee, George Kennedy, Kathleen Quinlan; **D:** Jack Smight. **VHS, Beta, LV $14.98** MCA ✠✠

Akermania, Vol. 1 This compilation of director Akerman's shorter works includes "I'm Hungry, I'm Cold," the story of two Belgian girls on the loose in Paris, and "Saute Ma Ville," Akerman's first film. Both are in French with English subtitles. Also included is "Hotel Monterey," a silent experimental film. **1992 89m/C** FR Maria De Medeiros, Pascale Salkin, Chantal Akerman; **D:** Chantal Akerman. **VHS $59.95** WAC, TAM ✠✠✠

Akira Secret government experiments on children with ESP go awry, resulting in an atomic bomb drop on Tokyo. The city in turn builds itself up into a Megalopolis and the experiments continue. Combines animation with live-action. In Japanese with English subtitles or dubbed. **1989 124m/C** JP **D:** Katsuhiro Otomo. **VHS, LV $29.95** WTA, STP, TAM ✠✠

Akira Kurosawa's Dreams An anthological lesson regarding the simultaneous loss of humanity and nature that threatens us all from the renowned Japanese director. Although the startling and memorable imagery is still present, Kurosawa's lessons are strangely trite and consequently lack the power that is normally associated with his work. With English subtitles. **AKA:** Dreams. **1990 (PG) 120m/C** JP Meiko Harada, Akira Terao; **W/D:** Akira Kurosawa. **VHS, LV $89.95** TAM, WAR, FCT ✠✠½

Al Capone Film noir character study of one of the most colorful gangsters of the Roaring Twenties. Sort of an underworld "How to Succeed in Business." Steiger chews scenes and bullets as they fly by, providing the performance of his career. Plenty of gangland violence and mayhem and splendid cinematography keep the fast-paced period piece sailing.

1959 104m/C Rod Steiger, Fay Spain, Murvyn Vye, Nehemiah Persoff, Martin Balsam, James Gregory, Joe De Santis; *D:* Richard Wilson. **VHS, Beta** $14.98 *FOX, FCT* 🎃🎃🎃

Alabama's Ghost Musician steals a dead master magician's secrets, incurring the wrath of the paranormal underworld. **1972** (PG) 96m/C Christopher Brooks, E. Kerrigan Prescott; *D:* Fredric Hobbs. **VHS, Beta** $29.95 *LIV* 🎃½

Aladdin A comedic Italian modernization of the Aladdin fable. *AKA:* Superfantagenio. **1986** (PG) 97m/C *IT* Bud Spencer, Luca Venantini, Janet Agren, Julian Voloshin, Umberto Raho; *D:* Bruno Corbucci. **VHS, Beta** $9.95 *MED* 🎃

Aladdin Boy meets princess, loses princess, finds princess, has trouble with evil prince and his nasty parrot. Another stellar effort from Disney centering on Aladdin, a streetwise teenager whose life radically changes after he uncorks a magic lamp and lets loose a large loveable genie who grants him three wishes. He chooses to become a prince to impress the Princess Jasmine but finds himself competing with the nasty Jafar, who wants Jasmine as his bride. Williams is truly phenomenal as the big blue genie in what may be his best film role to date. The animators capitalized on his talent for ad-lib and transformed the genie accordingly, resulting in lots of celebrity spoofs and even a few pokes at Disney itself. The storyline is average, but the superb animation sets new standards—a lifelike carpet is one highlight; coupled with Williams' performance and delightful songs, "Aladdin" soars to the same level as previous efforts. Kane and Salonga are responsible for the singing voices of Aladdin and Jasmine; Gottfried is a riot as Jafar's obnoxious parrot sidekick. Three of the songs are the late Ashman's final legacy. For all ages: adults will enjoy the 1,001 Williams impersonations while kids will get a kick out of the genie and the songs. Be forewarned: very small children may be frightened by some of the scarier sequences. 🎵A Whole New World; Prince Ali; Friend Like Me; One Jump Ahead; Arabian Nights. **1992** (G) 90m/C *W/D:* Ron Clements, John Musker; *W:* Ted Elliot, Terry Rossio; *M:* Alan Menken, Howard Ashman, Tim Rice; *V:* Robin Williams, Scott Weinger, Linda Larkin, Jonathan Freeman, Frank Welker, Gilbert Gottfried, Douglas Seale, Brad Kane, Lea Salonga. Academy Awards '92: Best Song ("A Whole New World"), Best Original Score; Nominations: Best Song ("Friend Like Me"), Best Sound, Best Sound Effects Editing; MTV Movie Awards '93: Best Comedic Performance (Williams). **VHS** $24.95 *DIS, BTV* 🎃🎃🎃🎃

Aladdin and His Wonderful Lamp The story of Aladdin, a young man who finds a magical oil lamp while he is trapped in a tiny cave. From the "Faerie Tale Theatre" series and director of "Beetlejuice" and "Batman" Tim Burton. **1984** 60m/C Valerie Bertinelli, Robert Carradine, Leonard Nimoy, James Earl Jones; *D:* Tim Burton. **VHS, Beta** $14.98 *KUI, FOX, FCT* 🎃🎃½

Alakazam the Great! A Japanese animated film about an arrogant monkey who is sent on a mission to learn about life. **1961** 84m/C *D:* Lee Kresel; *V:* Frankie Avalon, Dodie Stevens, Jonathan Winters, Arnold Stang, Sterling Holloway. **VHS** *NEG* 🎃🎃½

The Alamo Wayne's directorial effort is an old-fashioned patriotic battle epic recounting the real events of the 1836 fight for independence in Texas. The usual band of diverse and somewhat contentious personalities, including Wayne as a coonskin-capped Davy Crockett, defend a small fort against a very big Mexican raiding party outside of San Antonio. Before taking on the Mexicans and meeting mythic death, the men in the besieged fort fight with each other, learn the meaning of life, and ultimately come to respect each other. Just to make it more entertaining, Avalon sings. The big-budget production features an impeccable musical score by Dmitri Tiomkin and an impressive 7,000 extras for the Mexican army alone. Wayne reportedly received directorial assistance from John Ford, particularly during the big massacre finale. **1960** 161m/C John Wayne, Richard Widmark, Laurence Harvey, Frankie Avalon, Richard Boone, Carlos Arruza, Chill Wills; *D:* John Wayne. Academy Awards '60: Best Sound; Nominations: Best Color Cinematography, Best Film Editing, Best Picture, Best Song ("The Green Leaves of Summer"), Best Supporting Actor (Wills), Best Original Score. **VHS, Beta, LV** $29.98 *MGM, FOX, TLF* 🎃🎃🎃

Alamo Bay A slow-moving but sincere tale of contemporary racism. An angry Vietnam veteran and his red-neck buddies feel threatened by Vietnamese refugees who want to go into the fishing business. Set in Texas, with Texas-sized characters, and based on a true Texas story, as interpreted by the French Malle. **1985** 99m/C Ed Harris, Ho Nguyen, Amy Madigan, Donald Moffatt, Cynthia Carle; *D:* Louis Malle. **VHS, Beta, LV** $79.95 *COL* 🎃🎃½

The Alamo: Thirteen Days to Glory The legendary Davy Crockett (Keith), Colonel William Travis (Baldwin), and Jim Bowie (Arness) overcome personal differences to unite against the Mexican Army, vowing to hold down the fort or die. It takes a true Texan to fully appreciate the merits of this rather pedestrian retelling of a familiar story, but the battle scenes are pretty heady (although they lose some of their froth on the small screen). If nothing else, the ever-versatile Julia is worth seeing as Santa Anna in this made-for-TV rendering of J. Lon Tinkle's "Thirteen Days to Glory." You may not want to remember the Alamo this way. **1987** 180m/C James Arness, Lorne Greene, Alec Baldwin, Brian Keith, Raul Julia; *D:* Peter Werner. **VHS, Beta** $24.98 *FRH* 🎃🎃

Alamut Ambush A federal agent is stalked by assassins, and decides to hunt them in return. Sequel to "Cold War Killer." **1986** 94m/C *GB* Terence Stamp, Michael Culver; *D:* Ken Grieve. **VHS, Beta** *WWV* 🎃

Alan & Naomi In 1944, 14-year-old Alan Silverman is more concerned with his Brooklyn stickball team than the war raging across Europe. This changes when his upstairs neighbor offers refuge to a French-Jewish mother and her young daughter and he is asked to befriend the girl. Naomi witnessed the brutal death of her father by the Nazis and retreated into a world of her own. Together the two build a sweet, if unlikely, friendship. Fine performances save this average coming of age tale. Based on the novel by Myron Levoy. **1992** (PG) 95m/C Lukas Haas, Vanessa Zaoui, Michael Gross, Amy Aquino, Kevin Connolly, Zohra Lampert; *D:* Sterling Van Wagenen. **VHS, LV** $89.95 *COL* 🎃🎃½

The Alaska Wilderness Adventure The tale of a family struggling for survival in the Arctic wilderness. Baby, it's cold out there. **1978** 90m/C **VHS, Beta** *PGN* 🎃🎃

Alberto Express Alberto suffers from a peculiar family tradition. It seems now that he is married and about to be a father himself, he is expected by his father to pay back every cent spent on his own upbringing. The poor and panicky Alberto hops on a train from Paris to Rome and endeavors to raise the necessary cash by preying, in a series of increasingly bizarre ways, on his fellow passengers before he faces his father once again. In French and Italian with English subtitles. **1992** 90m/C *IT* Sergio Castellitto, Nino Manfredi, Marie Trintignant, Jeanne Moreau, Michel Aumont, Dominique Pinon, Marco Messeri, Eugenia Marruzzo; *W/D:* Arthur Joffe. **VHS** $89.95 *FXL* 🎃🎃½

Albino Albino chief leads African terrorists to murder white settlers, one of whom is an ex-policeman's fiancee. So the ex-cop pursues the bad guys, who are fairly easy to identify (just look for the big group hanging with the albino). Danning, Lee, and Howard only briefly show faces and collect checks. **1976** (R) 85m/C Christopher Lee, Trevor Howard, Sybil Danning, Horst Frank, James Faulkner; *D:* Jurgen Goslar. **VHS, Beta** $54.95 *MED* Woof!

The Alchemist See humans transformed into murderous zombies! A bewitched man seeks revenge upon the evil magician who placed a curse on him, causing him to live like an animal. Painfully routine, with a few chills along the way. Amonte is an alias for Charles Band. Filmed in 1981 and released four years later. **1981** (R) 86m/C Robert Ginty, Lucinda Dooling, John Sanderford, Viola Kate Stimpson, Bob Glaudini; *D:* James Amonte. **VHS, Beta** $79.98 *VES, LIV* Woof!

Alex in Wonderland A semi-autobiographical and satirical look at Hollywood from the standpoint of a young director who's trying to follow up his recent hit (in real life, "Bob & Carol & Ted & Alice") with a picture of some integrity that will keep the mass audience away. The confused plot provides obvious parallels to Fellini (who appears in a cameo) and some sharp, often bitter insights into the Hollywood of the early '60s. Strong performances by Sutherland and Burstyn compensate somewhat for the patience-trying self-indulgent arty whining of the script, written by Mazursky and producer Larry Tucker. **1971** (R) 109m/C Donald Sutherland, Ellen Burstyn, Jeanne Moreau, Paul Mazursky; *Cameos:* Federico Fellini; *D:* Paul Mazursky. **VHS, Beta** *MGM* 🎃🎃½

Alexa: A Prostitute's Own Story A prostitute falls for a playwright and decides she wants to change careers. Doesn't sound like much of a switch to us. **1988** (R) 81m/C Christine Moore, Kirk Baily, Ruth Collins; *D:* Sean Delgado. **VHS, Beta, LV** $29.95 *ACA* 🎃

Alexander Nevsky A story of the invasion of Russia in 1241 by the Teutonic Knights of Germany and the defense of the region by good old Prince Nevsky. Eisenstein's first completed project in nearly ten years, it was widely regarded as an artistic disappointment upon release and as pro-war propaganda against the looming conflict with the Nazis. Fabulous Prokofiev score illuminates the classic battle scenes, which used thousands of Russian army regulars. Dubbed in English. **1938** 107m/B *RU* Nikolai Cherkassov, N.P. Okholopkov, Al Abrikossov; *D:* Sergei Eisenstein. **VHS, Beta, LV, 8mm, 3/4U** $29.95 *MVD, MRV, NOS* 🎃🎃½

Alexander the Great A lavish epic about the legendary Greek conqueror of the fourth century B.C., which provides Burton a rare chance at an adventure role. Here we find Alexander is the product of a dysfunctional royal family who hopes to create an idealized world modeled after Greek culture to make up for the love he lacks from daddy. This he does by conquering everything before dying at the age of 33. The great cast helps to overcome the sluggish pacing of the spectacle, while numerous battle scenes featuring loads of spears and arrows are staged effectively. **1955 135m/C** Richard Burton, Fredric March, Claire Bloom, Harry Andrews, Peter Cushing, Danielle Darrieux; **D:** Robert Rossen. **VHS, Beta, LV** $59.95 *MGM, FCT* ♂♂½

Alexander: The Other Side of Dawn Tired made-for-television sequel to the television movie "Dawn: Portrait of a Teenage Runaway." A young man turns to prostitution to support himself on the street of Los Angeles. **1977 100m/C** Leigh McCloskey, Eve Plumb, Earl Holliman, Juliet Mills, Jean Hagen, Loni Chapman; **D:** John Erman. **VHS** *MOV* ♂♂

Alfie What's it all about, Alfie? Caine, in his first starring role, carried along the fairly routine story and made this a box office hit. As the British playboy out of control in mod London, Caine/Alfie is a despicable, unscrupulous and vile sort of guy who uses woman after woman to fulfill his basic needs and then casts them aside until...tragedy strikes. Though it was seen as a sophisticated take on current sexual mores upon release, it now seems a dated but engaging comedy, notable chiefly for its performances. From the Bill Naughton play and reflective of its stage roots. The title song "Alfie," written by Hal David and Burt Bacharach and sung by Dionne Warwick, was a top ten hit. **1966 (PG) 113m/C** *GB* Michael Caine, Shelley Winters, Millicent Martin, Vivien Merchant, Julia Asher; **D:** Lewis Gilbert. Academy Awards '66 Nominations: Best Actor (Caine), Best Adapted Screenplay, Best Picture, Best Song ("Alfie"), Best Supporting Actress (Merchant); Golden Globe Awards '67: Best Foreign Film; National Board of Review Awards '66: 10 Best Films of the Year, Best Supporting Actress (Merchant). **VHS, Beta** $59.95 *PAR* ♂♂♂

Alfredo, Alfredo Hoffman plays a mild-mannered bank clerk who regrets marrying a sexy woman. Lightweight domestic comedy. In Italian with English subtitles (Hoffman's voice was dubbed). **1972 97m/C** *IT* Dustin Hoffman, Stefania Sandrelli, Carla Gravina, Clara Colosimo, Daniela Patella, Duilio Del Prete; **D:** Pietro Germi. **VHS** *PAR* ♂♂

Algiers Nearly a scene-for-scene Americanized remake of the 1937 French "Pepe Le Moko" about a beautiful rich girl (Lamarr) who meets and falls in love with a notorious thief (Boyer, then a leading sex symbol). Pursued by French police and hiding in the underworld-controlled Casbah, Boyer meets up with Lamarr in a tragically fated romance done in the best tradition of Hollywood. Boyer provides a measured performance as Le Moko, while Lamarr is appropriately sultry in her American film debut (which made her a star). Later remade as the semi-musical "Casbah." **1938 96m/B** Charles Boyer, Hedy Lamarr, Sigrid Gurie, Gene Lockhart, Joseph Calleia, Alan Hale Jr.; **D:** John Cromwell. **VHS, Beta, 3/4U, Special order formats** $9.95 *NEG, MRV, NOS* ♂♂

Ali: Fear Eats the Soul A widow cleaning woman in her sixties has a love affair with a Moroccan man 30 years her junior. To no one's surprise, both encounter racism and moral hypocrisy in West Germany. Serious melodrama from Fassbinder, who wrote it and appears as the squirmy

son-in-law. In German with English subtitles. **AKA:** Fear Eats the Soul. **1974 68m/C** *GE* Brigitte Mira, El Hedi Ben Salem, Irm Hermann; **D:** Rainer Werner Fassbinder. **VHS** $79.95 *NYF, FCT, TAM* ♂♂♂

Alias Billy the Kid Western adventure with Carson posing as a famous outlaw to find out who's behind the scam involving the Denton City cattle trade. **19?? 54m/B** Sunset Carson. **VHS** $9.98 *REP* ♂♂

Alias John Law The Good Guy fights for oil rights against the bad guys. Confused program western with an especially convoluted plot. **1935 54m/B** Bob Steele; **D:** Robert North Bradbury. **VHS, Beta** *NO* ♂

Alias John Preston Yet another one of those pseudo-psychological to sleep perchance to dream movies. Lee plays a man haunted by dreams in which he's a murderer, and soon starts to question whether his dreams might not imitate life. It's been done before, it's been done since, and it's been done better. **1956 66m/B** *GB* Betta St. John, Alexander Knox, Christopher Lee, Sandra Dorne, Patrick Holt, Betty Ann Davies, John Longden, Bill Fraser, John Stuart; **D:** David MacDonald. **VHS** $19.98 *SNC* ♂½

Alice A twist on the "Alice in Wonderland" tale. Alice witnesses an attempted murder, faints, and awakens in a weird, yet strangely familiar environment. Adapted from the stage production. **1986 80m/C** Sophie Barjae, Susannah York, Jean-Pierre Cassel, Paul Nicholas. **VHS** $59.95 *LHV, WAR* ♂♂

Alice An acclaimed surreal version of Lewis Carroll's already surreal "Alice in Wonderland," with the emphasis on Carroll's obsessiveness. Utilizing animated puppets and a live actor for Alice, Czech director Svankmajer injects grotesque images and black comedy into Wonderland. Not for the kids. **1988 84m/C** *GB* Kristina Kohoutova; **D:** Jan Svankmajer. **VHS, 3/4U** *WTA, TAM* ♂♂♂½

Alice Farrow is "Alice," a woman plagued with doubts about her lifestyle, her religion, and her happiness. Her perfect children, husband, and apartment don't prevent her backaches, and she turns to an Oriental "herbalist" for aid. She finds his methods unusual and the results of the treatments surprising. Lightweight fairytale of Yuppiedom gone awry. Fine performances, beautiful to look at, and lovely music, but superficial and pointed story that may leave the viewer looking for more. (Perhaps that's Allen's point.) **1990 (PG-13) 106m/C** Mia Farrow, William Hurt, Joe Mantegna, Keye Luke, Alec Baldwin, Cybill Shepherd, Blythe Danner, Gwen Verdon, Bernadette Peters, Judy Davis; **W/D:** Woody Allen. Academy Awards '90 Nominations: Best Original Screenplay; National Board of Review Awards '90: Best Actress (Farrow). **VHS, Beta, LV** $94.98 *ORI, FCT* ♂♂♂

Alice Adams Based on the classic Booth Tarkington novel about a poor girl from a small Midwestern town who falls in love with a man from the upper level of society. She tries desperately to fit in and nearly alienates her family and friends. The sets may be dated, but the insight on human behavior is timeless. **1935 99m/B** Katharine Hepburn, Fred MacMurray, Evelyn Venable, Hattie McDaniel, Fred Stone; **D:** George Stevens. Academy Awards '35 Nominations: Best Actress (Hepburn), Best Picture; National Board of Review Awards '35: 10 Best Films of the Year. **VHS, Beta, LV** $14.98 *CCB, MED, NOS* ♂♂½

Alice Doesn't Live Here Anymore Scorcese marries road opera with pseudo-feminist semi-realistic melodrama and produces uneven but interesting results. A woman's husband dies suddenly, leaving her to care for their eleven-year-old son. On her way to a new life in California, she runs out of money and is stranded in Phoenix. Down to her last few dollars, she takes a job as a waitress in a diner where she meets kindly rancher Kristofferson. In addition to its female point of view, it's notable for being the basis of the once popular television show "Alice," which took the basic structure ("woman works in diner, has no husband and struggles for self-respect, while being victimized by annoying youngster threatening to sprout to pubescence") into sitcom land of no return. Burstyn and Ladd lend key performances, while Kristofferson is typically kinda wooden. **1974 (PG) 105m/C** Ellen Burstyn, Kris Kristofferson, Diane Ladd, Jodie Foster, Harvey Keitel, Vic Tayback, Billy Green Bush; **D:** Martin Scorsese. Academy Awards '74: Best Actress (Burstyn); Nominations: Best Original Screenplay, Best Supporting Actress (Ladd); British Academy Awards '75: Best Actress (Burstyn), Best Film, Best Supporting Actress (Ladd). **VHS, Beta, LV** $19.98 *WAR, PIA, FCT* ♂♂½

Alice Goodbody Sex spoof of a lonely girl's misadventures in Hollywood. **1974 (R) 83m/C** Sharon Kelly, Daniel Kauffman, Keith McConnell, Arem Fisher, Norman Fields, C.D. LaFleure; **D:** John Sturges. **VHS, Beta** $19.95 *MED* ♂

Alice in the Cities American and German culture are compared and contrasted in this early Wenders road work about a German journalist in the USA on assignment who suddenly finds himself custodian to a worldly nine-year-old girl abandoned by her mother. Together they return to Germany and search for the girl's grandmother. Along the way they learn about each other, with many distinctive and graceful Wenders moments. **1974 110m/B** Ruediger Vogler, Yella Rottlaender, Elisabeth Kreuzer, Edda Kochi; **D:** Wim Wenders. **VHS, Beta** $29.95 *PAV, FCT, APD* ♂♂♂½

Alice in Wonderland Another version of the Lewis Carroll classic which combines the usage of Lou Bunin's puppets and live action to tell the story. Released independently to cash in on the success of the Disney version. Takes a more adult approach to the story and is worth viewing on its own merits. **1950 83m/C** *FR* Carol Marsh, Stephen Murray, Pamela Brown, Felix Aylmer, Ernest Milton; **D:** Dallas Bower. **VHS, Beta** $39.95 *MON,* *WTA* ♂♂½

Alice in Wonderland Classic Disney dream version of Lewis Carroll's famous children's story about a girl who falls down a rabbit hole into a magical world populated by strange creatures. Beautifully animated with some startling images, but served with a strange disapssion warmed by a fine batch of songs, including "I'm Late," "A Very Merry Un-Birthday," and the title song. Wynn's Mad Hatter and Holloway's Cheshire Cat are among the treats in store. **1951 (G) 75m/C** **D:** Clyde Geronomi; **V:** Kathryn Beaumont, Ed Wynn, Sterling Holloway, Jerry Colonna, Hamilton Luske, Wilfred Jackson. **VHS, Beta, LV** $24.99 *DIS, FCT, KUI* ♂♂♂

Alice in Wonderland Musical version of the Lewis Carroll's classic tale performed by the Children's Theatre Company and School.

1982 81m/C Annie Enneking, Solvieg Olsen, Wendy Lehr, Jason McLean, Gary Briggle, Elizabeth Fink. **VHS, Beta** $39.95 *MCA* ✍✍½

Alice Sweet Alice Mediocre, gory who-killed-her, best remembered as the debut of Shields (in a small role). *AKA:* Holy Terror; Communion.
1976 (R) 112m/C Brooke Shields, Linda Miller, Paula Sheppard; *D:* Alfred Sole. **VHS, Beta** $29.95 *REP, MRV, BTV* ✍½

Alice Through the Looking Glass Based on Lewis Carroll's classic adventure. Follows the further adventures of young Alice. After a chess piece comes to life, it convinces Alice that excitement and adventure lie through the looking glass.
1966 72m/C Judi Rolin, Ricardo Montalban, Nanette Fabray, Robert Coote, Agnes Moorehead, Jack Palance, Jimmy Durante, Tom Smothers, Roy Castle, Richard Denning; *D:* Alan Handley. **VHS, Beta** $14.98 *SUE, NEG, KAR* ✍½

Alice to Nowhere Concerns a running argument in the Outback over a fortune in gems unknowingly carried by a young woman. Made for Australian television and based on a novel by Evan Green.
1986 210m/C *AU* Rosie Jones, Steve Jacobs, John Waters, Ruth Cracknell; *D:* John Power. **VHS, Beta** $59.95 *PAR* ✍✍

Alice's Adventures in Wonderland Musical adaptation of Lewis Carroll's timeless fantasy of a young girl who meets new friends when she falls into a rabbit hole.
1972 96m/C *GB* Fiona Fullerton, Michael Crawford, Ralph Richardson, Flora Robson, Peter Sellers, Robert Helpmann, Dudley Moore, Michael Jayston, Spike Milligan, Michael Hordern; *W/D:* William Sterling; *M:* John Barry. **VHS, Beta** *VES* ✍✍

Alice's Restaurant Based on the popular and funny 20-minute Arlo Guthrie song "Alice's Restaurant Massacre" about a Flower Child during the Last Big War who gets hassled for littering, man. Step back in time and study the issues of the hippie era, including avoiding the draft, dropping out of college, and dealing with the local pigs. Sort of a modern movie in the cinematic ambling genre, in that nothing really happens.
1969 (PG) 111m/C Arlo Guthrie, James Broderick, Pat Quinn, Geoff Outlaw; *D:* Arthur Penn. **VHS, Beta** $19.95 *MVD, MGM* ✍✍½

Alien Terse direction, stunning sets and special effects, and a well-seasoned cast save this from being another "Slimy monster from Outerspace" story and instead create a grisly rollercoaster of suspense and fear (and a huge box office hit). An intergalactic freighter's crew is invaded by an unstoppable carnivorous alien life-form intent on picking off the crew one by one. While the cast has nothing much to do other than bitch and banter while awaiting the horror of their imminent departure, Weaver is exceptional as Ripley, a self-reliant survivor who goes toe to toe with the Big Ugly. The futuristic, in the belly of the beast visual design creates a vivid sense of claustrophobic doom enhanced further by Jerry Goldsmith's ominous score. Oscar-winning special effects include the classic baby alien busting out of the crew guy's chest routine, a rib-splitting ten on the gore meter. Successfully followed by "Aliens" and "Alien 3."
1979 (R) 116m/C Tom Skerritt, Sigourney Weaver, Veronica Cartwright, Yaphet Kotto, Harry Dean Stanton, Ian Holm, John Hurt; *D:* Ridley Scott; *M:* Jerry Goldsmith. Academy Awards '79: Best Visual Effects; Nominations: Best Art Direction/Set Decoration. **VHS, Beta, LV** $19.98 *FOX* ✍✍✍½

Alien 3 Takes up where "Aliens" left off as Ripley crash lands on Fiorina 161, a planet that serves as a penal colony for 25 celibate but horny men who smell bad. Ripley is forced to shave her head because of the planet's lice problem, and she sets out to survive on the cold, unfriendly planet until a rescue ship can come for her. Fending off sexual advances from the men, Ripley soon discovers she wasn't the only survivor of the crash—the alien survived too and has somehow implanted her with an alien of her own. As the baby alien grows inside her, Ripley fights the mother alien to make the world safe again. Dark and disturbing, filled with religious allegories, and a universe removed from the two earlier Aliens. Intended as the final installment of the series. Weaver received quite a bit of publicity for shaving her head for her role.
1992 (R) 135m/C Sigourney Weaver, Charles S. Dutton, Charles Dance, Paul McGann, Brian Glover, Ralph Brown, Danny Webb, Christopher John Fields, Holt McCallany, Lance Henriksen; *D:* David Fincher. **VHS, LV** *FXV* ✍✍

Alien Contamination Tale of two astronauts who return to Earth from an expedition on Mars carrying some deadly bacterial eggs. Controlled by a Martian intent on conquering the world, the eggs squirt a gloppy juice that makes people explode on contact (a special effect). A cheap and sloppy attempt to cash in on the success of "Alien" written and directed by Cozzi. Dubbed. *AKA:* Contamination.
1981 (R) 90m/C *IT* Ian McCulloch, Louise Monroe, Martin Mase, Samuel Rauch, Lisa Hahn; *D:* Lewis (Luigi Cozzi) Coates. **VHS, Beta** *PGN Woof!*

Alien Dead The teenage victims of a bizarre meteor crash reincarnate as flesh-eating ghouls anxious for a new supply of human food in this extremely low-budget sleep inducer.
1985 (R) 87m/C Buster Crabbe, Linda Lewis, Ray Roberts; *D:* Fred Olen Ray. **VHS, Beta** $19.95 *ACA, GHV* ✍

The Alien Factor Another low-budget crazed critter from outerspace dispatch, this one featuring multiple aliens, one of whom is good, who have the misfortune of crash landing near Baltimore. The grotesque extra-terrestrials jolt a small town out of its sleepy state by wreaking havoc (except for the good one, of course). Decent special effects.
1978 (PG) 82m/C Don Leifert, Tom Griffith, Mary Mertens, Dick Dyszel; *D:* Donald M. Dohler. **VHS, Beta** $59.95 *UHV* ✍✍

Alien from L.A. Awesomely inept comedy about a California girl who unwittingly stumbles onto the famed continent of Atlantis and can't find a yogurt stand. Weakly plotted and acted and filmed. Like, really.
1987 (PG) 88m/C Kathy Ireland, Thom Mathews, Don Michael Paul, Linda Kerridge, William R. Moses; *D:* Albert Pyun. **VHS, Beta, LV** $79.95 *MED Woof!*

Alien Intruder What happens when an evil demon appears before the soldiers of the future in the guise of a beautiful woman? Futuristic trash B-movie emerges from the depths.
1993 (R) 90m/C Billy Dee Williams, Tracy Scoggins, Maxwell Caulfield; *D:* Ricardo Jacques Gale. **VHS, Beta** $89.95 *PMH* ✍✍

Alien Massacre One of the worst films of all time—five short horror stories about zombies and vampires. Inexplicably retitled here, it is more commonly known as "Dr. Terror's Gallery of Horrors" or "Return from the Past" or "The Blood Suckers."

1967 77m/C Lon Chaney Jr., John Carradine, Rochelle Hudson, Roger Gentry, Mitch Evans; *D:* David L. Hewitt. **VHS, Beta** *NO Woof!*

Alien Nation A few hundred thousand alien workers land accidentally on Earth and slowly become part of its society, although widely discriminated against. One of the "newcomers" teams with a surly and bigoted human cop to solve a racially motivated murder. An inconsistent and occasionally transparent script looks at race conflicts and includes some humorous parallels with contemporary American life. Basis for the television series. Producer Hurd was also the force behind "The Terminator" and "Aliens."
1988 (R) 89m/C James Caan, Mandy Patinkin, Terence Stamp, Kevyn Major Howard, Peter Jason, Jeff Kober; *D:* Graham Baker. **VHS, Beta, LV** $19.98 *FOX* ✍✍

Alien Predators Three friends encounter a malevolent alien in this dull reworking of the plot of "The Andromeda Strain" with laughable special effects tossed in for those outwitted by the script.
1980 (R) 92m/C Dennis Christopher, Martin Hewitt, Lynn-Holly Johnson, Luis Prendes; *D:* Deran Sarafian. **VHS, Beta** $79.95 *VTR Woof!*

Alien Prey Two lesbians are making love when they are unexpectedly devoured by a hungry and indiscreet alien. No safe sex there. Graphic sex, violence, and cannibalism abound. Interesting twist to the old eat 'em and leave 'em genre.
1983 85m/C Barry Stokes, Sally Faulkner; *D:* Norman J. Warren. **VHS, Beta** $39.98 *CGH* ✍½

Alien Private Eye An extraterrestrial detective searches Los Angeles for a missing magic disk while investigating an intergalactic crime ring. *AKA:* Alien P.I.
1987 90m/C Nikki Fastinetti; *D:* Nik Rubenfeld. **VHS** *NO* ✍✍

Alien Seed Aliens kidnap a woman and impregnate her. Estrada is the government scientist hot on her trail. (How far could a woman carrying alien offspring wander?)
1989 88m/C Erik Estrada, Heidi Paine, Steven Blade; *D:* Bob James. **VHS** $79.95 *AIP* ✍

Alien Space Avenger A spaceship piloted by four alien convicts crash lands in New York City. Stalked by an intergalactic bounty hunter whose job is to kill them, the aliens attack and hide inside human bodies to avoid discovery. It's a race against time as the preservation of the human race depends on the avenger's ability to seek and destroy the alien invaders. Bland ripoff of "Aliens" with more gore and violence. Shot with the old 3-strip Technicolor method. *AKA:* Space Avenger.
1991 88m/C Robert Prichard, Mike McClerie, Charity Staley, Gina Mastrogiacomo, Kick Fairbanks Fogg, Angela Nicholas, Marty Roberts, James Gillis; *W/D:* Richard W. Haines; *W:* Linwood Sawyer; *M:* Richard Fiocca. **VHS** $89.95 *AIP* ✍✍

Alien Warrior An extraterrestrial fights a street pimp to save a crime-ridden Earth neighborhood. Low-brain rip-off of Superman.
1985 (R) 92m/C Brett Clark, Pamela Saunders; *D:* Edward Hunt. **VHS, Beta** $79.98 *VES, LIV Woof!*

Alien Women A soft-core British science fiction yarn about scantily clad alien babes and the special agent who's trying to uncover their secret. It's all very sketchy, silly and campy, though pleasantly cast with plenty of lovely British actresses. *AKA:* Zeta One; The Love Factor.

1969 (R) 86m/C *GB* James Robertson Justice, Charles Hawtrey, Robin Hawdon, Anna Gael, Brigitte Skay, Dawn Addams, Valerie Leon, Yutte Stensgaard, Wendy Lingham, Rita Webb, Caroline Hawkins; *D:* Michael Cort. **VHS, Beta** $59.95 PSM, SNC ℤ

Alienator In the improbable future, an unstoppable android killer is sent after an intergalactic villain. An intentional "Terminator" rip-off.
1989 (R) 93m/C Jan-Michael Vincent, John Phillip Law, Ross Hagen, Dyana Ortelli, Dawn Wildsmith, P.J. Soles, Teagan Clive, Robert Clarke, Leo Gordon, Robert Quarry, Fox Harris, Hoke Howell, Jay Richardson; *D:* Fred Olen Ray. **VHS, Beta, LV** $79.95 PSM ℤ

Aliens The bitch is back, 50 some years later. The popular sequel to "Alien" amounts to non-stop, ravaging combat in space. Contact with a colony on another planet has mysteriously stopped. Fresh from deep space sleep, Ripley and a slew of pulsar-equipped Marines return to the planet where the deadly alien was first found and confront the mother alien at her nest, which is also inhabited by a whole bunch of the nasty critters spewing for a fight. Something's gotta give, and the Oscar-winning special effects are especially inventive (and messy) in the alien demise department. Dimension (acting biz talk) is given to our hero Ripley, as she discovers maternal instincts lurking within her space suit while looking after a young girl, the lone survivor of the colony, abandoned in the monsters' wake. A special tension-filled gore blaster. Followed by "Aliens 3."
1986 (R) 138m/C Sigourney Weaver, Michael Biehn, Lance Henriksen, Bill Paxton, Paul Reiser, Carrie Henn, Jenette Goldstein; *D:* James Cameron. Academy Awards '86: Best Sound Effects Editing, Best Visual Effects; Nominations: Best Actress (Weaver), Best Art Direction/Set Decoration, Best Film Editing, Best Sound, Best Original Score. **VHS, Beta, LV** $19.98 FOX ℤℤ½

Aliens Are Coming A spaceship crash lands on Earth, and its devious denizens begin invading human bodies. TV movie that's a dull echo of "Invasion of the Body Snatchers."
1980 100m/C Tom Mason, Melinda Fee, Max Gail, Eric Braeden, Matthew Laborteaux; *D:* Harvey Hart. **VHS, Beta** $9.95 WOV, GKK ℤ½

Aliens from Spaceship Earth Are strange, celestial forces invading our universe? If they are, is man prepared to defend his planet against threatening aliens of unknown strength? Lame docudrama featuring the Hurdy Gurdy man himself, Donovan.
1977 107m/C Donovan, Lynda Day George; *D:* Don Como. **VHS, Beta** $59.95 GEM ℤ½

Alison's Birthday A teenage girl learns that some of her family and friends are Satan worshipers at a terrifying birthday party. Meanwhile, the ghost of her dad hovers about, asking for more lines.
1979 99m/C *AU* Joanne Samuel, Lou Brown, Bunny Brooke; *D:* Ian Coughlan. **VHS, Beta** $19.98 VID ℤℤ

Alive Recounts the true-life survival story of a group of Uruguayan rugby players in the 1970's. After their plane crashes in the remote, snowy Andes (in a spectacular sequence) they're forced to turn to cannibalism. Marshall doesn't focus on the gruesome idea, choosing instead to focus on all aspects of their desperate quest for survival. The special effects are stunning, but other parts of the film are never fully realized, including the final scene. Based on the nonfiction book by Piers Paul Read.
1993 (R) 125m/C Ethan Hawke, Vincent Spano, Josh Hamilton, Bruce Ramsay, John Haymes Newton, David Kriegel, Kevin Breznahan, Sam Behrens, Illeana Douglas, Jack Noseworthy, Christian Meoli; *Cameos:* John Malkovich; *D:* Frank Marshall; *W:* John Patrick Shanley; *M:* James Newton Howard. **VHS** NYR ℤℤ½

All About Eve One of the wittiest (and most cynical) flicks of all time follows an aspiring young actress (Baxter) as she ingratiates herself with a prominent group of theater people so that she may become known on Broadway without the years of work usually required. The not-so-innocent babe becomes secretary to aging star Davis and ruthlessly uses everyone around her in her climb to the top, much to Davis' initial disbelief and eventual displeasure. A satirical, darkly funny view of the world of the theater with an all-star cast featuring exceptional work by Davis, Sanders, and Ritter. Knowing of what he wrote, Mankiewicz penned the screenplay, which was based on "The Wisdom of Eve" by Mary Orr. Later staged as the musical "Applause."
1950 138m/B Bette Davis, Anne Baxter, George Sanders, Celeste Holm, Gary Merrill, Thelma Ritter, Marilyn Monroe, Hugh Marlowe, Gregory Ratoff, Eddie Fisher; *W/D:* Joseph L. Mankiewicz. Academy Awards '50: Best Director (Mankiewicz), Best Picture, Best Screenplay, Best Sound, Best Supporting Actor (Sanders); Nominations: Best Film Editing; Academy Awards '50: Best Actress (Baxter), Best Actress (Davis), Best Art Direction/Set Decoration (B & W), Best Black and White Cinematography, Best Supporting Actress (Holm, Ritter), Best Original Score; Cannes Film Festival '51: Best Actress (Davis); Directors Guild of America Awards '51: Best Director (Mankiewicz); National Board of Review Awards '50: 10 Best Films of the Year; New York Film Critics Awards '50: Best Actress (Davis), Best Director (Mankiewicz), Best Film. **VHS, Beta, LV** $19.98 FOX, BTV, HMV ℤℤℤ

All-American Murder A rebellious young man is enrolled in a typical, all-American college for one last shot at mainstream life. Things start out okay, as he meets an attractive young coed. Hours later, he finds himself accused of her grisly murder. The youth is then given 24 hours to prove his innocence by a canny homicide detective. Average performances highlight this film, which isn't able to rise above the mediocre.
1991 (R) 94m/C Christopher Walken, Charlie Schlatter, Josie Bisset, Joanna Cassidy, Richard Kind, Woody Watson, J.C. Quinn, Amy Davis; *D:* Anson Williams; *W:* Barry Sandler. **VHS, Beta, LV** $89.95 PSM ℤℤ

All Creatures Great and Small Taken from James Herriot's best selling novels, this is a delightful, quiet drama of a veterinarian's apprentice in rural England. Fine performance by Hopkins. Followed by "All Things Bright and Beautiful" and a popular British television series.
1974 92m/C *GB* Simon Ward, Anthony Hopkins, Lisa Harrow, Brian Stirner, Freddie Jones, T.P. McKenna; *D:* Claude Whatham. **VHS, Beta** $29.97 RDG, FOX, HMV ℤℤℤ

All Dogs Go to Heaven Somewhat heavy-handed animated musical (Reynolds sings) about a gangster dog who is killed by his partner in business. On the way to Heaven, he discovers how to get back to Earth to seek his revenge. When he returns to Earth, he is taken in by a little girl and learns about something he missed in life the first time around: Love. Expertly animated, but the plot may not keep the grown-ups engrossed, and the kids may notice its lack of charm.
1989 (G) 85m/C *D:* Don Bluth; *V:* Burt Reynolds, Judith Barsi, Dom DeLuise, Vic Tayback, Charles Nelson Reilly, Melba Moore, Candy Devine, Loni Anderson. **VHS, Beta, LV, 8mm** $24.98 MGM, RDG, WTA ℤℤ

All Fall Down A young man (de Wilde) idolizes his callous older brother (Beatty) until a tragedy forces him to grow up. Saint plays the older woman taken in by the brothers' family, who is seduced and abandoned. When she finds herself pregnant and alone, she commits suicide causing the younger brother, who loved her from afar, to vow to kill his older sibling. A well-acted melodrama. Also available colorized.
1962 111m/B Eva Marie Saint, Brandon de Wilde, Warren Beatty, Karl Malden, Angela Lansbury, Constance Ford, Barbara Baxley; *D:* John Frankenheimer; *W:* William Inge. **VHS** $19.98 MGM ℤℤ½

All God's Children Made for television drama about the controversial forced busing issue and two families who must face it. Topnotch cast is occasionally mislead by meandering script attempting to stay true to a sensitive issue.
1980 100m/C Richard Widmark, Ned Beatty, Ossie Davis, Ruby Dee, Mariclare Costello, George Spell, Trish Van Devere, Ken Swofford; *D:* Jerry Thorpe. **VHS, Beta** NO ℤℤ½

All I Want for Christmas Low-budget, sappy holiday tale of a young girl (Birch) who wants to reunite her divorced parents. Determined to fulfill her Christmas wish, Hallie seeks out the Santa Claus at Macy's department store to tell him the one thing she truly wants for Christmas. Birch is charming as are Bacall as her grandmother and Neilsen as Santa but the story is too squishy and bland to be believable.
1991 (G) 92m/C Thora Birch, Leslie Nielsen, Lauren Bacall, Jamey Sheridan, Harley Jane Kozak, Ethan Randall, Kevin Nealon, Andrea Martin; *D:* Robert Lieberman; *W:* Richard Kramer, Thom Eberhardt, Gail Parent; *M:* Neal Israel, Bruce Broughton. **VHS, LV** PAR ℤℤ

All in a Night's Work The founder of a one-man publishing empire is found dead with a smile on his face. His nephew inherits the business and finds himself caught in a series of big and small business misunderstandings. He's also falling in love with the woman he suspects was responsible for his uncle's grin. Nicely paced sex and business comedy with warm performances.
1961 94m/C Dean Martin, Shirley MacLaine, Cliff Robertson, Charlie Ruggles; *D:* Joseph Anthony. **VHS, Beta** $19.95 STE, FOX ℤℤ½

All Mine to Give Sad saga of a Scottish family of eight who braved frontier hardships, epidemics, and death in the Wisconsin wilderness more than a century ago. Midway through, mom and dad die, leaving the oldest child struggling to keep the family together. A strange, though often effective, combination of pioneer adventures and tearjerking moments that avoids becoming hopelessly soapy due to fine performances. Unless you're pretty weathered, you'll need some hankies. Based on the reminiscences of Dale and Katherine Eunson as detailed in a "Cosmopolitan" magazine article. *AKA:* The Day They Gave the Babies Away.
1956 102m/C Glynis Johns, Cameron Mitchell, Rex Thompson, Patty McCormack, Ernest Truex, Hope Emerson, Alan Hale Sr., Royal Dano, Reta Shaw, Rita Johnson, Ellen Corby, Jon Provost; *D:* Allen Reisner; *M:* Max Steiner. **VHS, Beta** $15.95 UHV ℤℤ½

All My Good Countrymen A lyrical, funny film about the eccentric denizens of a small Moravian village soon after the socialization of Czechoslovakia in 1948. Completed

during the Soviet invasion of 1968 and immediately banned. In Czech with English subtitles. *AKA:* All Good Citizens.
1968 115m/C *CZ* Vladimir Mensik, Radoslav Brozobohaty, Pavel Pavlovsky; *D:* Voltech Jasny. VHS, Beta $59.95 *FCT, AUD* ✔✔½

All My Sons A wealthy family is distraught when their eldest son is listed as missing-in-action during WWII. They must cope with guilt, as well as grief, because the father's business reaped profits from the war. Adapted for television from the acclaimed Arthur Miller play.
1986 122m/C James Whitmore, Aidan Quinn, Joan Allen, Michael Learned; *D:* John Power. VHS, Beta $39.95 *MCA* ✔✔✔

All Night Long Offbeat middle-age crisis comedy about a burned-out and recently demoted drugstore executive in L.A. who leaves his wife, takes up with his fourth cousin by marriage, and begins a humorous rebellion, becoming an extremely freelance inventor while joining the drifters, weirdos and thieves of the night. An obscure, sometimes uneven little gem with Hackman in top form and an appealing supporting performance by Streisand. Scripted by W.D. Richter, who also wrote "Invasion of the Body Snatchers" and highlighted by delightful malapropisms and sataric inversion of the usual cliches.
1981 (R) 100m/C Gene Hackman, Barbra Streisand, Diane Ladd, Dennis Quaid, Kevin Dobson, William Daniels; *D:* Jean-Claude Tramont. VHS, Beta $14.95 *GKK* ✔✔✔

All Night Long/Smile Please Two classic comedies by the most overlooked of the great silent clowns, both produced by slapstick progenitor Mack Sennett.
1924 66m/B Harry Langdon, Natalie Kingston, Jack Cooper, Alberta Vaughn. VHS, Beta $29.95 *VYY* ✔✔✔

All of Me A wealthy woman (Tomlin) dies and her guru accidentally transfers her soul to the right side of her lawyer's body, a modern version of existential hell. Lawyer Martin indulges in some funny slapstick as he discovers that his late client is waging an internal war for control of his body. Flat and cliched at times, but redeemed by the inspired clowning of Martin and witty Martin/Tomlin repartee. Based on the novel "Me Too" by Ed Davis.
1984 (PG) 93m/C Steve Martin, Lily Tomlin, Victoria Tennant, Madolyn Smith, Richard Libertini, Dana Elcar, Selma Diamond; *D:* Carl Reiner. VHS, Beta $19.98 *HBO, FCT* ✔✔½

All Over Town Two vaudevillians with a trained seal find themselves involved in a murder when they are kidnapped by a gang of thugs. A lesser Olsen and Johnson comedy with scattered funny moments.
1937 52m/B Ole Olsen, Chic Johnson, Mary Howard, Franklin Pangborn, James Finlayson; *D:* James W. Horne. VHS, Beta $19.95 *NOS, MRV, VYY* ✔✔½

All Quiet on the Western Front Extraordinary anti-war epic based upon the Erich Maria Remarque novel realistically follows seven patriotic German youths as they go together from school to the battlefields of World War I. There they experience the horrors of war first-hand, stuck in the trenches and facing gradual extermination. The story centers around the experiences of one of the youths, Paul Baumer, who changes from enthusiastic war endorser to an extremely battle-weary veteran in an emotionally exact performance by Ayres. Made with a gigantic budget (for the time) of $1.25 million, it features more than 2,000 extras swarming about battlefields set up on ranchland in California. Relentless in its anti-war message and emotionally draining, it startles with both graphic shots and haunting visual poetry. Extremely controversial in the U.S. and Germany upon release, the original version was 140 minutes long (some versions are available with restored footage) and featured ZaSu Pitts as Ayres mother (later reshot with Mercer replacing her). Remarque, who had fought and been wounded on the Western Front, was eventually forced to leave Germany for the U.S. due to the film's ongoing controversy.
1930 103m/B Lew Ayres, Louis Wolheim, John Wray, Slim Summerville, Russell Gleason, Raymond Griffith, Ben Alexander, Beryl Mercer; *D:* Lewis Milestone. Academy Awards '30: Best Director (Milestone), Best Picture; Nominations: Best Cinematography, Best Writing; National Board of Review Awards '30: 10 Best Films of the Year. VHS, Beta, LV $19.95 *MCA, FCT, GLV* ✔✔✔✔

All Quiet on the Western Front A big-budget television remake of the 1930 masterpiece starring John Boy. Sensitive German youth Thomas plunges excitedly into WWI and discovers its terror and degradation. Nowhere near the original's quality.
1979 150m/C Richard Thomas, Ernest Borgnine, Donald Pleasence, Patricia Neal; *D:* Delbert Mann. VHS, Beta, LV $14.95 *FOX, FCT* ✔✔½

All Screwed Up A group of young immigrants come to Milan and try to adjust to city life; they soon find that everything is in its place, but nothing is in order. Wertmuller in a lighter vein than usual. *AKA:* All in Place; Nothing in Order.
1974 104m/C *IT* Luigi Diberti, Lina Polito; *D:* Lina Wertmuller. VHS, Beta *FOX* ✔✔✔

All-Star Cartoon Parade A collection of popular vintage cartoons, starring such favorites as Little Lulu, Casper the Friendly Ghost, Betty Boop and Raggedy Ann and Andy.
19?? 54m/C VHS $29.98 *REP, WTA* ✔✔✔

All That Jazz Fosse's autobiographical portrait with Schneider fully occupying his best role as the obsessed, pill-popping, chain-smoking choreographer/director dancing simultaneously with love and death. But even while dying, he creates some great dancing. Vivid and imaginative with exact editing, and an eerie footnote to Fosse's similar death almost ten years later. Egocentric and self-indulgent for sure, but that's entertainment. ♫On Broadway; Everything Old is New Again; After You've Gone; There'll Be Some Changes Made; Some of These Days; Bye Bye Love.
1979 (R) 120m/C Roy Scheider, Jessica Lange, Ann Reinking, Leland Palmer, Cliff Gorman, Ben Vereen, Erzebet Foldi, John Lithgow, Wallace Shawn, Sandahl Bergman, Nicole Fosse, Keith Gordon, Ben Masters, Theresa Merritt; *D:* Bob Fosse. Academy Awards '79: Best Art Direction/Set Decoration, Best Costume Design, Best Film Editing, Best Original Score; Nominations: Best Actor (Scheider), Best Cinematography, Best Director (Fosse), Best Original Screenplay, Best Picture. VHS, Beta, LV $19.98 *FOX, FCT* ✔✔✔½

All the Kind Strangers Traveling photographer Keach picks up a young hitchhiker and takes him to the boy's home. He discovers six other children there who want him as a father, his alternative being death. He and "Mother" Eggar plot their escape from the dangerous orphans. Made-for-television thriller short on suspense. *AKA:* Evil in the Swamp.
1974 72m/C Stacy Keach, Robby Benson, John Savage, Samantha Eggar; *D:* Burt Kennedy. VHS, Beta $59.98 *FOX* ✔✔

All the King's Men Set in the Depression, a grim and graphic classic which follows the rise of a Louisiana farm-boy from angry and honest political hopeful to powerful but corrupt governor. Loosely based on the life (and death) of Huey Long and told by a newsman who's followed his career (Ireland). Willy Stark (Crawford, in his break-through role) is the politician who, while appearing to improve the state, rules dictatorially, betraying his friends and constituents, proving once again that power corrupts. In her first major role, McCambridge delivers a powerful award-winning performance as the cunning political aide. A potent morality play based on the Robert Penn Warren book, with a script by Rossen, who also produced and directed.
1949 109m/B Broderick Crawford, Mercedes McCambridge, John Ireland, Joanne Dru, John Derek, Anne Seymour, Sheppard Strudwick; *W/D:* Robert Rossen. Academy Awards '49: Best Actor (Crawford), Best Picture, Best Supporting Actress (McCambridge); Nominations: Best Director (Rossen), Best Film Editing, Best Screenplay, Best Supporting Actor (Ireland); New York Film Critics Awards '49: Best Actor (Crawford), Best Film. VHS, Beta, LV $19.95 *COL, BTV* ✔✔✔✔

All the Lovin' Kinfolk Two recent Hillbilly High graduates decide to take on the big city, but find themselves in dire situations. For those with time to kill. *AKA:* Kin Folk; Kinfolk; The Closest of Kin.
1989 (R) 80m/C Mady Maguire, Jay Scott, Anne Ryan, John Denis, Donna Young; *D:* John Hayes. VHS *NO* ✔

...All the Marbles A manager of two beautiful lady wrestlers has dreams of going to the top. Aldrich's last film, and an atypical one, with awkward pacing and a thin veil of sex exploitation. Falk provides needed grace and humor as the seedy manager, with Young contributing his usual competent bit as a hustling promoter dabbling in criminal activity. One of the few tag-team women wrestling pictures, it builds to a rousing finale match in the "Rocky" tradition, although the shift in tone and mounting cliches effectively body slam the intent. *AKA:* The California Dolls.
1981 (R) 113m/C Peter Falk, Burt Young, Richard Jaeckel, Vicki Frederick; *D:* Robert Aldrich. VHS, Beta, LV *MGM, OM* ✔✔

All the President's Men Based on the best-selling book by Washington Post reporters Bob Woodward and Carl Bernstein, this is the true story of the Watergate break-in that led to the political scandal of the decade. The politically based plot and investigation provides for an intriguing, terse thriller that will keep you on the edge of your seat even though you know the ending. Expertly paced by Pakula with a script by William Goldman. Features standout performances by Hoffman and Redford as the reporters who slowly uncover and connect the seemingly isolated facts leading to criminal indictments of the Nixon Administration. Deep Throat Holbrook and Robards as executive editor Ben Bradlee lend more authenticity to the endeavor, which realistically portrays the stop and go of journalistic investigations.
1976 (PG) 135m/C Robert Redford, Dustin Hoffman, Jason Robards Jr., Martin Balsam, Jane Alexander, Hal Holbrook, F. Murray Abraham, Stephen Collins, Lindsay Crouse; *D:* Alan J. Pakula; *W:* William Goldman. Academy Awards '76: Best Adapted Screenplay, Best Art Direction/Set Decoration, Best Sound, Best Supporting Actor (Robards); Nominations: Best Director (Pakula), Best Film Editing, Best Picture, Best Supporting Actress (Alexander); New York Film Critics Awards '76: Best Director (Pakula),

Best Film, Best Supporting Actor (Robards). **VHS, Beta $19.98** *WAR, BTV* 🎬🎬🎬½

All the Right Moves Cruise is the high school football hero hoping for a scholarship so he can vacate pronto the dying Pennsylvania mill town where he grew up. At least he thinks that's what he wants to do. Further mixing up his own mixed feelings are his pushy, ambitious coach (Nelson, doing what he does best), his understanding dad (Cioffi) and supportive girlfriend (Thompson, in a notable early role). Strong performances push the relatively cliched melodrama into field goal range. Cinematographer Chapman's directorial debut. **1983 (R) 90m/C** Tom Cruise, Lea Thompson, Craig T. Nelson, Christopher Penn; *D:* Michael Chapman. **VHS, Beta, LV $14.98** *FOX, FXV* 🎬🎬½

All the Rivers Run First made-for-cable miniseries. A young Australian girl spends her inheritance on a river boat and becomes the first female river captain in Australian history. Directed by George Miller of "Man from Snowy River" fame. Four parts. **1984 400m/C** *AU* Sigrid Thornton, John Waters, Diane Craig, Charles Tingwell, Gus Mercurio; *D:* George Miller, Pina Amenta. **VHS $79.95** *HBO* 🎬🎬½

All the Vermeers in New York A stressed-out Wall Street broker flees to the soothing recesses of the Metropolitan Museum's Vermeer Room. There he meets a beautiful, manipulative French actress dreaming of success in Manhattan. Amidst the opulent art world of New York, the two pursue their relationship to an ultimately tragic end. Jost offers an inside look at the collision of commerce and art and the corrupt underside of New York in this elegant contemporary film. **1991 87m/C** Emmanuelle Chaulet, Stephen Lack, Grace Phillips; *D:* Jon Jost. **VHS, LV $89.98** *WAC, TAM* 🎬🎬🎬

All the Way, Boys Two inept adventurers crash-land a plane in the Andes in the hope of discovering slapstick, but find none. "Trinity" cast up to no good. **1973 (PG) 105m/C** *IT* Terence Hill, Bud Spencer, Cyril Cusack, Michel Antoine; *D:* Giuseppe Colizzi. **VHS, Beta $59.98** *SUE* 🎬½

All the Way Down A ski chalet in the Alps is the setting for much fireside cavorting. **1987 80m/C** Judith Fritsch, Franz Muxeneder. **VHS, Beta $29.95** *MED* 🎬

All the Young Men Fairly powerful men-uniting-in-battle story with an interesting cast, highlighted by Poitier in an early role. A tiny marine squadron overrun by the Chinese in the Korean War attempts to resist the numerous attackers. In their spare time, the men confront racial prejudice when a black man (guess who) takes command. Written and directed by Bartlett. **1960 86m/B** Alan Ladd, Sidney Poitier, James Darren, Glenn Corbett, Mort Sahl; *D:* Hall Bartlett. **VHS, Beta $14.99** *COL* 🎬

All This and Heaven Too When a governess arrives at a Parisian aristocrat's home in the 1840s, she causes jealous tension between the husband and his wife. The wife is soon found murdered. Based on Rachel Field's best-seller. **1940 141m/B** Charles Boyer, Bette Davis, Barbara O'Neil, Virginia Weidler, Jeffrey Lynn, Helen Westley, Henry Daniell, Harry Davenport; *D:* Anatole Litvak. **VHS, Beta $19.95** *MGM* 🎬🎬🎬

All This and Tex Avery, Too! Fourteen cartoons from the great Tex Avery are featured here, including "What Price Freedom," "Doggone Tired," "Wags to

Riches," "The Screwy Truant," "King-Size Canary," "House of Tomorrow" and eight others. **1992 120m/C** *D:* Tex Avery. **LV $34.98** *MGM* 🎬🎬🎬

All Through the Night A very funny spy spoof as well as a thrilling crime story with Bogart playing a gambler who takes on a Nazi spy ring. Features memorable double-talk and a great auction scene that inspired the one with Cary Grant in "North by Northwest." Suspense builds throughout the film as Lorre appears in a sinister role as Pepi and Veidt gives a fine performance as the spymaster. **1942 107m/B** Humphrey Bogart, Conrad Veidt, Karen Verne, Jane Darwell, Frank McHugh, Peter Lorre, Judith Anderson, William Demarest, Jackie Gleason, Phil Silvers, Barton MacLane, Martin Kosleck; *D:* Vincent Sherman. **VHS $19.98** *MGM* 🎬🎬🎬

All You Need Is Cash "The Rutles" star in this parody of The Beatles' legend, from the early days of the "Pre-Fab Four" in Liverpool to their worldwide success. A marvelous pseudo-documentary, originally shown on NBC-TV and with various SNL alumni (including Weiss), that captures the development of the Beatles and '60s rock with devastating effect. Served as the inspiration for "This Is Spinal Tap." **1978 70m/C** Eric Idle, Neil Innes, Rikki Fataar, Dan Aykroyd, Gilda Radner, John Belushi, George Harrison, Gary Weiss; *D:* Eric Idle. **VHS, Beta, LV $14.95** *MVD, PAV, MLT* 🎬🎬🎬

Allan Quartermain and the Lost City of Gold While trying to find his brother, Quartermain discovers a lost African civilization, in this weak adaptation of an H. Rider Haggard adventure. An ostensible sequel to the equally shallow "King Solomon's Mines." **1986 (PG) 100m/C** Richard Chamberlain, Sharon Stone, James Earl Jones; *D:* Gary Nelson. **VHS, Beta $9.99** *FHE, MED* 🎬½

Allegheny Uprising Set in 1759, the story of a frontiersman who clashes with a British military commander in order to stop the sale of firearms to Indians. The stars of "Stagecoach" are back on board in this lesser effort. Also available colorized. *AKA:* The First Rebel. **1939 81m/B** John Wayne, Claire Trevor, George Sanders, Brian Donlevy, Chill Wills, Moroni Olsen; *D:* William A. Seiter. **VHS, Beta, LV $14.98** *RKO, CCB, TTC* 🎬🎬½

Allegro Non Troppo An energetic and bold collection of animated skits set to classical music in this Italian version of Disney's "Fantasia." Watch for the evolution of life set to Ravel's Bolero, or better yet, watch the whole darn movie. Features Nichetti (often referred to as the Italian Woody Allen, particularly by people in Italy) in the non-animated segments, who went on to write, direct, and star (he may have sold concessions in the lobby as well) in "The Icicle Thief." **1976 (PG) 75m/C** *IT* Maurizio Nichetti; *D:* Bruno Bozzetto. **VHS, LV $29.95** *BMG, IME, TAM* 🎬🎬🎬

Alley Cat Woman uses martial arts to fight back against a street gang that attacked her. **1984 (R) 82m/C** Karin Mani, Robert Torti, Brit Helfer, Michael Wayne, Jon Greene; *D:* Edward Victor. **VHS, Beta $69.98** *VES, LIV* 🎬

Alligator Dumped down a toilet 12 long years ago, lonely alligator Ramon resides in the city sewers, quietly eating and sleeping. In addition to feasting on the occasional stray human, Ramon devours the animal remains

of a chemical plant's experiment involving growth hormones and eventually begins to swell at an enormous rate. Nothing seems to satisfy Ramon's ever-widening appetite: not all the people or all the buildings in the whole town, but he keeps trying, much to the regret of the guilt-ridden cop and lovely scientist who get to know each other while trying to nab the gator. Mediocre special effects are only a distraction in this witty eco-monster take penned by John Sayles. **1980 (R) 94m/C** Robert Forster, Lewis Teague, Jack Carter, Henry Silva, Robin Riker, Dean Jagger; *D:* Lewis Teague; *W:* John Sayles. **VHS, Beta $14.98** *LIV* 🎬🎬🎬

Alligator 2: The Mutation Not a sequel to 1980's surprisingly good "Alligator," but a bland rehash with a decent cast. Once again a toxic alligator grows to enormous size and menaces a community. A Donald-Trump-like villain and pro wrestlers (!) bring this up to date, but it's all on the level of a TV disaster movie; even the PG-13 rating is a bit too harsh. **1990 (PG-13) 92m/C** Steve Railsback, Dee Wallace Stone, Joseph Bologna, Woody Brown, Bill Daily, Brock Peters. **VHS, LV $89.95** *COL, NLC* 🎬

Alligator Alley When two young divers witness a major drug deal, they become entangled in a web of danger they never expected. **1972 92m/C** Steve Alaimo, John Davis Chandler, Willie Pastrano, Jeremy Slate, Cece Stone; *D:* William Grefe. **VHS, Beta $79.95** *PSM* 🎬

Alligator Eyes A stranger wearing trouble like a cheap perfume enters the midst of a vacationing trio of New Yorkers. The three travelers, who include a boozy, recently jilted young Lothario and an estranged couple attempting to kindle a reconciliation on the road, have their vulnerabilities exposed by a young hitchhiker sporting a slinky polka dot ensemble and way cool sunglasses. Not until the hitchhiker has insinuated herself into their vacation plans (not to mention their private lives) do the three realize the woman is blind and full of manipulative and vindictive tricks, thanks to the usual brutal childhood. A psycho-sexo-logical thriller with some fine performances. Begins promisingly before fizzling into celluloid cotton candy. **1990 (R) 101m/C** Annabelle Larsen, Roger Kabler, Mary McLain, Allen McCullough, John MacKay; *W/D:* John Feldman. **VHS $19.95** *ACA* 🎬🎬½

The Allnighter A college coed searches through the hypersexed beach-party milieu of her senior year for Mr. Right. Bangle Hoffs is directed by her mom, to no avail. **1987 (PG-13) 95m/C** Susanna Hoffs, John Terlesky, Joan Cusack, Michael Ontkean; *D:* Tamar Simon Hoffs. **VHS, Beta $79.95** *MCA* 🎬

Allonsanfan Early Taviani, in which a disillusioned Jacobin aristocrat in 1816, after Napoleon has fallen, struggles with his revolutionary ideals and his accustomed lifestyle. In Italian with English subtitles. Exciting score by Ennio Morricone. **1973 115m/C** *IT* Marcello Mastroianni, Laura Betti, Renato de Carmine, Lea Massari, Mimsy Farmer, Claudio Cassinelli; *D:* Paolo Taviani; *M:* Ennio Morricone. **VHS, Beta $59.95** *FCT, WBF, TAM* 🎬🎬🎬

All's Fair Silly and predictable comedy about executives who take on their spouses at weekend war games. An unfortunate waste of a good cast. **1989 89m/C** George Segal, Sally Kellerman, Robert Carradine, Jennifer Edwards, Jane Kaczmarek, John Kapelos, Lou Ferrigno; *D:* Rocky Lane. **VHS, Beta, LV $79.95** *MED* 🎬

Almos' a Man Richard Wright's story of a black teenage farm worker in the late 1930's who must endure the pains of growing up. From the "American Short Story" series.
1978 (G) 51m/C Madge Sinclair, Robert Dogui, LeVar Burton. **VHS, Beta** $24.95 MON, MTI, KAR *I*

...Almost Arquette plays a curiously giddy bookworm with a vivid imagination. When her husband disappears on their anniversary, the man of her dreams shows up to sweep her off her feet. Is he real or is he simply another daydream? Almost a good time. *AKA:* Wendy Cracked a Walnut.
1990 (PG) 87m/C *AU* Rosanna Arquette, Bruce Spence; *D:* Michael Pattinson. **VHS, LV** NO *II*

Almost an Angel Another in a recent spat of angels and ghosts assigned back to earth by the head office. A life-long criminal (Hogan) commits a heroic act and finds himself a probationary angel returned to earth to gain permanent angel status. He befriends a wheelchair-bound man, falls in love with the guy's sister, and helps her out at a center for potential juvenile delinquents. Melodramatic and hokey in places, relying too much on Hogan's crocodilian charisma.
1990 (PG) 98m/C Paul Hogan, Linda Kozlowski, Elias Koteas, Doreen Lang, Charlton Heston; *D:* John Cornell; *W:* Paul Hogan. **VHS, LV** $14.95 PAR, PIA *I* ½

Almost Angels Two boys romp in Austria as members of the Vienna Boys Choir. Lesser sentimental Disney effort that stars the actual members of the Choir; not much of a draw for today's Nintendo-jaded young viewers.
1962 85m/C Vincent Winter, Peter Weck, Hans Holt; *D:* Steve Previn. **VHS, Beta** $69.95 DIS *II*

Almost Human An Italian Mafia gorefest about a second-class don who kidnaps a businessman's daughter, and then has trouble trying to collect a ransom. For aficionados of Italian Mafia gorefests only (check your weapons at the door). *AKA:* The Kidnap of Mary Lou.
1979 (R) 90m/C *IT* Henry Silva, Tomas Milian, Laura Belli; *D:* Umberto Lenzi; *M:* Ennio Morricone. **VHS, Beta** $79.95 PSM Woof!

Almost Partners Grandpa's ashes are in trouble. His urn and remains have been stolen. Fortunately, his teenage granddaughter and a detective are on the case. From the PBS "Wonderworks" television series.
1987 58m/C Paul Sorvino, Royana Black, Mary Wickes; *D:* Alan Kingsberg. **VHS** $29.95 PME, HMV Woof!

An Almost Perfect Affair Taxing romantic comedy about an ambitious independent American filmmaker who, after finishing a movie about an executed murderer, travels to the Cannes festival and proceeds to fall in love or lust with the wife of an Italian producer. Numerous inside jokes and capable performances nearly overcome script lethargy.
1979 (PG) 92m/C Keith Carradine, Monica Vitti, Raf Vallone, Christian de Sica, Dick Anthony Williams; *D:* Michael Ritchie. **VHS, Beta** $59.95 PAR *II*

Almost Pregnant Linda Anderson (Roberts) desperately wants a baby, but her husband, Charlie (Conaway) is unable to get her pregnant. Dead set against artificial insemination, Linda decides to take a lover. Charlie doesn't want to lose her, so he goes along with her idea. Linda falls in love with the new guy; discovers he's had a vasectomy and takes yet another lover while continuing to see the other two guys. Hilarious

complications abound in her outrageous quest for a baby. An unrated version containing explicit scenes is also available.
1991 (R) 90m/C Tanya Roberts, Jeff Conaway, Joan Severance, Dom DeLuise; *D:* Michael DeLuise; *W:* Fred Stroppel. **VHS, LV** $89.95 COL *II* ½

Almost Royal Family All kinds of problems arise when a family inherits an island on the St. Lawrence River embargoed by the United States and Canada.
1984 52m/C Sarah Jessica Parker, John Femia. **VHS, Beta** $39.95 WAR *I*

Almost You Normal marital conflicts and uncertainties grow exponentially when a wealthy New York City thirty-something couple hires a lovely young nurse to help care for the wife after a car accident. An unsentimental marital comedy with a good cast that still misses.
1985 (R) 91m/C Brooke Adams, Griffin Dunne, Karen Young, Marty Watt, Christine Estabrook, Josh Mostel, Laura Dean, Dana Delany, Miguel Pinero, Joe Silver, Suzzy Roche, Spalding Gray; *D:* Adam Brooks. **VHS, Beta** $79.98 FOX *II*

Aloha, Bobby and Rose A mechanic and his girlfriend in L.A. become accidentally involved in an attempted robbery and murder and go on the run for Mexico, of course. Semi-satisfying drama in the surf, with fine location photography.
1974 (PG) 90m/C Paul LeMat, Dianne Hull, Robert Carradine, Tim McIntire, Edward James Olmos, Leigh French; *D:* Floyd Mutrux. **VHS, Beta** $49.95 MED *II* ½

Aloha Summer Six surfing teenagers of various ethnic backgrounds learn of love and life in 1959 Hawaii while riding the big wave of impending adulthood, with a splash of Kung Fu thrown in for good measure. Sensitive and bland.
1988 (PG) 97m/C Chris Makepeace, Lorie Griffin, Don Michael Paul, Sho Kosugi, Yuji Okumoto, Tia Carrere; *D:* Tommy Lee Wallace. **VHS, Beta, LV** $19.98 WAR, LHV *II*

Alone Against Rome A muscle-bound warrior takes on the forces of Rome to avenge himself against a scornful woman.
1962 100m/B *IT* Lang Jeffries, Rossana Podesta, Phillippe LeRoy; *D:* Herbert Wise. **VHS, Beta** $16.95 SNC *I* ½

Alone in the Dark Slash and dash horror attempt featuring four escaped patients from a mental hospital who decide that they must kill their doctor because they don't like him. Conveniently, a city-wide blackout provides the opportunity, as the good doctor defends home and family against the aging stars intent on chewing up as much scenery as possible.
1982 (R) 92m/C Jack Palance, Donald Pleasence, Martin Landau, Dwight Schultz; *D:* Jack Sholder. **VHS, Beta** $19.95 NLC, COL *II*

Alone in the Neon Jungle A glamorous big-city police captain is assigned to clean up the most corrupt precinct in town. Pleshette is untypically cast but still manages to make her role believable in a serviceable TV cop drama with more dialogue than action.
1987 90m/C Suzanne Pleshette, Danny Aiello, Georg Stanford Brown, Frank Converse, Joe Morton; *D:* Georg Stanford Brown. **VHS** $19.95 COL, NLC *II*

Alone in the T-Shirt Zone A maniacal T-shirt designer lands in a mental institution.
1986 81m/C Michael Barrack, Taylor Gilbert, Bill Barron. **VHS, Beta** $19.95 STE, NWV *I*

Along Came Jones Cowboy Cooper, who can't handle a gun and is saddled with grumpy sidekick Demarest, is the victim of mistaken identity as both the good guys and the bad guys pursue him thinking he is a vicious killer. Young is the woman who rides to his defense. Cooper produced and Nunnally Johnson scripted this offbeat and charming western parody based on a novel by Alan le May.
1945 93m/B Gary Cooper, Loretta Young, Dan Duryea, William Demarest; *D:* Stuart Heisler. **VHS, Beta** $59.98 FOX *III*

Along the Great Divide A U.S. marshal and his deputy battle pursuing vigilantes and the untamed frontier to bring a falsely accused murderer to trial (and of course, find the real bad guy). Douglas' first western has the usual horse opera cliches supported by excellent cinematography.
1951 88m/B Kirk Douglas, John Agar, Walter Brennan, Virginia Mayo; *D:* Raoul Walsh. **VHS, Beta** $19.98 WAR, TLF *II*

Along the Sundown Trail Standard western escapades as cowboy G-men round up the villains.
1942 59m/B William Boyd, Art Davis, Lee Powell, Julie Duncan, Kermit Maynard, Charles King; *D:* Sam Newfield. **VHS, Beta** VGN *I* ½

Alpha Beta A stage production set to film studying the break-up of a marriage, where all the husband and wife have in common is the children. Finney and Roberts efficiently carry the load.
1973 70m/C Albert Finney, Rachel Roberts; *D:* Anthony Page. **VHS, Beta** $49.95 NO *II* ½

The Alpha Incident Time-worn doomsday drama about an alien organism with the potential to destroy all living things. Government works hard to cover up.
1976 (PG) 86m/C Ralph Meeker, Stafford Morgan, John Goff, Carol Irene Newell, John Alderman; *D:* Bill Rebane. **VHS, Beta** $9.95 MED *I* ½

Alphabet City A drug kingpin who runs New York's Lower East Side has decided to turn over a new leaf, but first he must survive his last night as a criminal while figuring out a way to pay off his large debts. Very stylish and moody, but light on content and plot.
1984 (R) 85m/C Vincent Spano, Michael Winslow, Kate Vernon, Jami Gertz, Zohra Lampert, Ray Serra, Kenny Marino, Daniel Jordano, Miguel Pinero; *D:* Amos Poe. **VHS, Beta** $79.98 FOX *II*

The Alphabet Murders Picture this: Randall playing Agatha Christie's famous Belgian sleuth, Hercule Poirot, and Rutherford—in a cameo—as Miss Marple. As if that wouldn't be enough to make Dame Agatha roll over in her grave, there's plenty of cloying wisecracking and slapsticking throughout. An adaptation of "The ABC Murders" in which Poirot stalks a literate killer who snuffs out his victims in alphabetical order. Hardly a must-see, unless you're hellbent on viewing the entire Randall opus. *AKA:* ABC Murders.
1965 90m/B Tony Randall, Anita Ekberg, Robert Morley, Maurice Denham, Guy Rolfe, Sheila Allen; *Cameos:* Margaret Rutherford; *D:* Frank Tashlin; *W:* Agatha Christie. **VHS, Beta** $19.98 MGM, FCT *II*

Alphaville Engaging and inimitable Godard attempt at science fiction mystery. P.I. Lemmy Caution searches for a scientist in a city (Paris as you've never seen it before) run by robots and overseen by a dictator. The futuristic techno-conformist society must be upended so that Caution may save the scientist as well as nonconformists everywhere. In French with subtitles. *AKA:* Alpha-

A

ville, a Strange Case of Lenny Caution; Alphaville, Une etrange Aventure de Lenny Caution.
1965 100m/B *FR* Eddie Constantine, Anna Karina, Akim Tamiroff; **D:** Jean-Luc Godard. **VHS, Beta $24.95** *NOS, SNC, MRV ⅛⅛⅛*

Alpine Fire Coming of age story about an adolescent girl and her deaf-mute brother living an isolated life in the Swiss Alps. When life on the mountain overwhelms them, they turn to each other for love. Sharply observed with a naturalistic style, elevating the proceedings above mere voyeurism.
1989 119m/C *SI* Thomas Knock, Johanna Lier, Dorothea Moritz, Rolf Illig; **D:** Fredi M. Murer. **VHS, Beta, LV $79.98** *VES, LIV ⅛⅛ ½*

Alsino and the Condor An acclaimed Nicaraguan drama about a young boy, caught in war-torn Nicaragua between the Somoza government and the Sandinista rebels, who dreams of flying above the human strife. In Spanish with English subtitles.
1982 (R) 89m/C *NI* Dean Stockwell, Alan Esquivel; **D:** Miguel Littin. **VHS, Beta, LV $29.95** *PAV, FCT, TAM ⅛⅛⅛*

Altered States Obsessed with the task of discovering the inner man, Hurt's ambitious researcher ignores his family while consuming hallucinogenic drugs and floating in an immersion tank. He gets too inner, slipping way back through the evolutionary order and becoming a menace in the process. A confusing script by Paddy Chayefsky (alias Sidney Aaron) based upon a confusing novel by Chayefsky is supported by great special effects and the usual self-indulgent, provocative, and confusing Russell direction (aided by a $15 million budget). Chayefsky eventually washed his hands of the project after artistic differences with the producers. Others who departed from the film include initial director William Penn and special effects genius John Dkystra (relieved ably by Bran Ferren). Hurt's a solemn hoot in his first starring role.
1980 (R) 103m/C William Hurt, Blair Brown, Bob Balaban, Charles Haid, Dori Brenner, Drew Barrymore; **D:** Ken Russell; **W:** Paddy Chayefsky. **VHS, Beta, LV $14.95** *WAR ⅛⅛⅛*

Alternative A female magazine editor finds herself unmarried and quite pregnant. She is caught in a tug-of-war between the baby's father and her current lover. Dated liberated woman and career snoozer.
1976 90m/C Wendy Hughes, Peter Adams, Mary Mackie, Carla Hoogeveen, Tony Bonner. **VHS, Beta** *NO ⅛*

Alvarez Kelly Offbeat western with Holden as the Mexican-Irish Kelly who has just sold a herd of cattle to the North during the Civil War. Confederate officer Widmark kidnaps Holden in an effort to have the cattle redirected to the South. Aided by the traditional women in the midst of men intent on double-crossing each other, a fierce hatred develops between the two, erupting into violence. Sleepy performance by Holden is countered by an intensive Widmark. Based on a true Civil War incident, the script occasionally wanders far afield with the cattle, who cleverly heighten the excitement by stampeding.
1966 116m/C William Holden, Richard Widmark, Janice Rule, Patrick O'Neal, Harry Carey Jr.; **D:** Edward Dmytryk. **VHS, Beta $12.95** *GKK ⅛⅛ ½*

Alvin Purple Pedestrian comedy about a Mr. Purple, an ordinary Aussie who sells waterbeds and is for some reason constantly being pursued by throngs of sexually insatiable women. Fortunately, he too enjoys sex, even though complications abound. Sexual situations, double entendres, and a script

that aims for cleverness (but rarely attains it) somehow made the lust romp a hit in its native Australia, while worldwide it helped establish a market for Down Under cinema. Written by playwright Alan Hopgood, shot in Melbourne, and followed by "Alvin Rides Again."
1973 (R) 97m/C *AU* Graeme Blundell, George Whaley, Ellie MacLure, Jacki Weaver; **D:** Tim Burstall. **VHS, Beta $19.95** *STE, NWV ⅛ ½*

Alvin Rides Again The sexually insatiable Alvin Purple is asked to impersonate an American gangster who was accidentally killed. Another Aussie sex farce co-written by Tim Burstall, Alan Hopgood, and Alan Finney, who conspire to create a decent sequel to "Alvin Purple," with much of the same cast and crew.
1974 89m/C *AU* Robin Copping, Graeme Blundell, Alan Finney, Brionny Behets, Frank Thring, Jeff Ashby; **D:** David Bilcock. **VHS, Beta $19.95** *STE, NWV ⅛⅛*

Always Jaglom fictionally documents his own divorce and reconciliation with Patrice Townsend: set in the director's home and starring his friends and family, the film provides comic insight into the dynamics of married/about-to-be-married/and used-to-be-married relationships. Set at a Fourth of July barbecue, this bittersweet romantic comedy is a veritable feast for Jaglom fans, but not everyone will find the director's free-form narrative to their taste.
1985 105m/C Henry Jaglom, Patrice Townsend, Bob Rafelson, Melissa Leo, Andre Gregory, Michael Emil, Joanna Frank; **D:** Henry Jaglom. **VHS, Beta, LV $79.98** *VES, LIV ⅛⅛⅛*

Always A hotshot pilot (Dreyfuss) meets a fiery end and finds that his spirit is destined to become a guardian angel to the greenhorn fire-fighting flyboy (Johnson) who steals his girl's heart. Warm remake of "A Guy Named Joe," one of Spielberg's favorite movies. Sparks between Dreyfuss and Hunter eventually ignite, but Goodman delivers the most heat. Hepburn makes an appearance as the angel who guides Dreyfuss. An old-fashioned tree-burner romance that includes actual footage of the 1988 Yellowstone fire.
1989 (PG) 123m/C Holly Hunter, Richard Dreyfuss, John Goodman, Audrey Hepburn, Brad Johnson, Marg Helgenberger, Keith David, Roberts Blossom; **D:** Steven Spielberg; **W:** Jerry Belson; **M:** John Williams. **VHS, Beta, LV $19.95** *MCA, FCT ⅛⅛ ½*

Amadeus An entertaining adaptation by Peter Shaffer of his play about the intense rivalry between 18th century composer Antonio Salieri and Wolfgang Amadeus Mozart. Abraham's Salieri is a man who desires greatness but is tortured by envy and sorrow. His worst attacks of angst occur when he comes into contact with Hulce's Mozart, an immature, boorish genius who, despite his gifts, remains unaffected and delighted by the beauty he creates while irking the hell out of everyone around him. Terrific period piece filmed on location in Prague, with an excellent musical score, beautiful sets, nifty billowy costumes, and realistic American accents for the 18th century Europeans. ♫Concert No. 27 for Pianoforte and Orchestra in B Flat Major; Ave Verum Corpus; A Quintet For Strings in E Flat; A Concerto for Clarinet and Orchestra in A Major; Number 39 in E Flat Major; Number 40 in G Minor; Number 41 in C Major.
1984 (PG) 158m/C F. Murray Abraham, Tom Hulce, Elizabeth Berridge, Simon Callow, Roy Dotrice, Christine Ebersole, Jeffrey Jones, Kenny L. Baker, Cynthia Nixon, Vincent Schiavelli; **D:** Milos Forman. Academy Awards '84: Best Actor (Abraham), Best Adapted Screenplay, Best Art

Direction/Set Decoration, Best Costume Design, Best Director (Forman), Best Makeup, Best Picture, Best Sound; Nominations: Best Actor (Hulce), Best Cinematography, Best Film Editing; Cesar Awards '85: Best Foreign Film; Directors Guild of America Awards '84: Best Director (Forman); Golden Globe Awards '85: Best Actor—Drama (Abraham), Best Director (Forman), Best Film—Drama. **VHS, Beta, LV $19.99** *HBO, GLV, BTV ⅛⅛⅛ ½*

Amarcord Semi-autobiographical Fellini fantasy which takes place in the village of Rimini, his birthplace. Focusing on the young Zanin's impressions of his town's colorful slices of life, Fellini takes aim at facism, family life, and religion in 1930's Italy. Visually ripe, delivering a generous, occasionally uneven mix of satire, burlesque, drama, and tragicomedic lyricism. Considered by people in the know as one of Fellini's best films and the topic of meaningful discussions among art film students everywhere.
1974 (R) 124m/C *IT* Magali Noel, Bruno Zamin, Pupella Maggio, Armando Brancia; **D:** Federico Fellini. Academy Awards '74: Best Foreign Language Film; Nominations: Best Director (Fellini), Best Original Screenplay; National Board of Review Awards '74: 5 Best Foreign Films of the Year; New York Film Critics Awards '74: Best Director (Fellini), Best Film. **VHS, Beta** *APD ⅛⅛⅛ ½*

The Amateur Computer technologist for the CIA dives into a plot of international intrigue behind the Iron Curtain when he investigates the death of his girlfriend, murdered by terrorists. Confused and ultimately disappointing spy drama cursed with a wooden script written by Robert Littell and Diana Maddox and based on a novel by Littell.
1982 (R) 112m/C John Savage, Christopher Plummer, Marthe Keller, Arthur Hill, Ed Lauter; **D:** Charles Jarrott. **VHS, Beta $59.98** *FOX ⅛ ½*

Amateur Night Sloppy musical comedy about the backstage bickering occuring during the amateur night at a famous nightclub.
1985 91m/C Geoffrey Deuel, Dennis Cole, Allen Kirk. **VHS, Beta $69.98** *VES, LIV ⅛*

Amazing Adventure A millionaire wins a bet when he rises from a chauffeur's position to the executive board room without using his wealth. Though not particularly amazing, lightweight English comedy has Grant working hard to charm over and above the demands of the dated formula, a performance he undertook during a vacation from Hollywood. Adapted from a novel by E. Phillips Oppenheim. *AKA:* Romance and Riches; The Amazing Quest of Ernest Bliss; Riches and Romance.
1937 63m/C Cary Grant, Mary Brian, Henry Kendall, Leon M. Lion, Ralph Richardson; **D:** Alfred Zeisler. **VHS, Beta $19.95** *NOS, KRT, DVT ⅛⅛*

The Amazing Colossal Man A standard '50s sci-fi film about atomic radiation. Colonel Manning is exposed to massive doses of plutonium when an experiment backfires (literally). The former good-guy grows to seventy feet and starts taking out his anger on a helpless Las Vegas. Can anything stop his murderous rampages? Followed by "War of the Colossal Beast."
1957 79m/B Glenn Langan, Cathy Downs, William Hudson, James Seay, Russ Bender, Lyn Osborn; **D:** Bert I. Gordon. **VHS $9.95** *COL ⅛⅛*

The Amazing Dobermans Family-oriented pooch performance piece featuring Astaire in one of his lesser roles. Ex-con man Astaire and his five trained Dobermans assist an undercover agent in foiling a small-time criminal's gambling and extortion racket. The

last in a series that includes "The Daring Dobermans" and "The Doberman Gang."
1976 (G) 96m/C Fred Astaire, Barbara Eden, James Franciscus, Jack Carter, Billy Barty; **D:** Byron Ross Chudnow. **VHS, Beta** $9.95 MED ✠✠

Amazing Grace Some righteous mothers led by Moms Mabley go up against corrupt city politics in this extremely dated comedy that was cast with a sense of the absurd.
1974 99m/C Moms Mabley, Slappy White, Moses Gunn, Rosalind Cash, Dolph Sweet, Butterfly McQueen, Stepin Fetchit; **D:** Stan Lathan. **VHS** NO ✠

Amazing Grace & Chuck Perhaps the only anti-war/sports feature ever made. Upon visiting a Minuteman missile site in Montana, a 12-year-old Little Leaguer (Chuck) learns of the dangers of nuclear arms. The concerned youth begins a protest against nuclear weapons by refusing to play until the nations come to a peace agreement. Upon hearing of the young man's stand for his beliefs, pro-basketball star Amazing Grace Smith (Denver Nugget English) quits the team and joins the boy in protest. Turned on by Amazing Grace's sudden surge of social conscience, sports players across the country and the world soon show their support by also refusing to play and by moving into the boy's barn to organize the protest. The movement escalates, forcing the leaders, including President Peck, to take notice. Capra fantasy with good intentions but lacking coherency and plausibility. Big-budget score by Elmer Bernstein.
1987 (PG) 115m/C Jamie Lee Curtis, Gregory Peck, William L. Petersen, Joshua Zuehlke, Alex English; **D:** Mike Newell. **VHS, Beta, LV** $19.99 HBO ✠✠

Amazing Howard Hughes Reveals the full story of the legendary millionaire's life and career, from daring test pilot to inventor to Hollywood film producer to isolated wealthy paranoiac with a germ phobia. Lingers on the rich guy with big problems theme. Big-budget, made for television drama with a nice performance by Jones.
1977 119m/C Tommy Lee Jones, Ed Flanders, James Hampton, Tovah Feldshuh, Lee Purcell; **D:** William A. Graham. **VHS, Beta** $19.95 HBO, FCT ✠✠ ½

Amazing Mr. Blunden Solid kidvid about two youngsters aided by a ghost who travel back in time to save the lives of two murdered children. Adapted by Jeffries from Antonia Barber's novel, "The Ghosts."
1972 (G) 100m/C Laurence Naismith, Lynne Frederick, Garry Miller, Marc Granger, Rosalyn London, Diana Dors; **D:** Lionel Jeffries. **VHS, Beta** $19.95 MED ✠✠ ½

The Amazing Mr. X When a woman's husband dies, she tries to contact him via a spiritualist. Things are not as they seem however, and the medium may just be part of an intricate scheme to defraud the woman. **AKA:** The Spiritualist.
1948 79m/B Turhan Bey, Lynn Bari, Cathy O'Donnell, Richard Carlson, Donald Curtis, Virginia Gregg; **D:** Bernard Vorhaus. **VHS, Beta** $19.95 NOS, SNC, RXM ✠✠ ½

The Amazing Spider-Man The Marvel Comics superhero's unique powers are put to the test when he comes to the rescue of the government by preventing an evil scientist from blackmailing the government for big bucks. The wall-walking web-slinger has his origins probed (a grad student bit by a radioactive spider gains super-human powers) in his live-action debut, which was made for television and led to a short-lived series. **AKA:** Spider-Man.

1977 94m/C Nicholas Hammond, David White, Lisa Eilbacher, Michael Pataki; **D:** E.W. Swackhamer. **VHS, Beta, LV** $24.98 FOX, IME ✠✠

Amazing Stories From the Steven Spielberg produced television series. "The Mission" sees a World War II tail gunner trapped in an unusual predicament. In "The Wedding Ring," a man gives his wife a strange ring and bizarre situations ensue.
1985 70m/C Kevin Costner, Casey Siemaszko, Kiefer Sutherland, Danny DeVito, Rhea Perlman; **D:** Danny DeVito, Steven Spielberg. **VHS, LV** $79.95 MCA, FCT, MOV ✠✠

Amazing Stories, Book 2 Two episodes from the short-lived "Amazing Stories" television series. In "Go To the Head of the Class" (1986), a cruel English teacher is subjected to black magic by a pair of vengeance-minded students. "Family Dog" (1987), is an animated feature designed by Tim Burton about the life of a suburban family from the canine perspective.
1986 71m/C Christopher Lloyd, Scott Coffey, Mary Stuart Masterson; **D:** Robert Zemeckis, Brad Bird; **V:** Stan Freberg, Annie Potts, Mercedes McCambridge. **VHS, LV** $79.95 MCA, WTA ✠✠

Amazing Stories, Book 3 Three stories from the short-lived series produced by Stephen Spielberg. In "Life on Death Row," Patrick Swayze is a criminal who acquires a great new power. Gregory Hines is "The Amazing Falsworth," a nightclub psychic who uncovers a mass murderer by accident. Then an army outcast, played by Charlie Sheen, performs a miracle to save his fellow soldiers from certain death in "No Day at the Beach."
1986 73m/C Patrick Swayze, James Callahan, Gregory Hines, Richard Masur, Charlie Sheen, Ralph Seymour, Philip McKeon, Steven Gethers, Tom Hodges; **D:** Mick Garris, Peter Hyams, Lesli Linka Glatter. **VHS, LV** $79.95 MCA, PIA ✠✠

Amazing Stories, Book 4 Three fantastic tales from the Spielberg-produced television show. "Mirror, Mirror" (1985; directed by Martin Scorsese) finds a director of horror films tormented by the very monsters he created. "Blue Man Down" (1986; directed by Paul Michael Glaser) tells of a cop who is helped by a mysterious young woman after his partner is shot dead. In "Mr. Magic" (1985; directed by Donald Petrie), an aging magician has his powers revitalized thanks to a strange deck of cards.
1985 71m/C Sam Waterston, Helen Shaver, Dick Cavett, Max Gail, Kate McNeil, Chris Nash, Sid Caesar, Leo Rossi; **D:** Martin Scorsese, Paul Michael Glaser, Donald Petrie. **VHS, LV** $79.95 MCA, PIA ✠✠

Amazing Stories, Book 5 More Spielberg produced tales from the television series. "The Pumpkin Competition" is a comedy about a parsimonious widow who enters a pumpkin growing contest. A young girl vanishes for two decades in "Without Diana," and a gang of space travellers collide head on with a trio of high school students working on a science project in "Fine Tuning."
1985 73m/C June Lockhart, Polly Holliday, J.A. Preston, Billy Green Bush, Dianne Hull, Gennie James, Matthew Laborteaux, Gary Riley, Jimmy Gatherum, Milton Berle; **D:** Norman Reynolds, Lesli Linka Glatter, Bob Balaban. **VHS, LV** $79.95 MCA ✠✠

The Amazing Transparent Man A mad scientist makes a crook invisible in order to steal the radioactive materials he needs. The crook decides to rob banks instead. Shot at the Texas State Fair for that elusive futuristic look. For Ulmer fans only.

1960 58m/B Douglas Kennedy, Marguerite Chapman, James Griffith, Ivan Triesault; **D:** Edgar G. Ulmer. **VHS** $16.95 NOS, SNC Woof!

The Amazing Transplant A sleaze-bag psycho has a "love enhancing" transplant, much to the pleasure of his sexual partners. Much to their and our dismay, however, he then kills them and bores us.
1970 90m/C Juan Fernandez, Linda Southern; **D:** Doris Wishman. **VHS, Beta** NO Woof!

Amazon An adventure movie filmed in the Brazilian rainforest with an environmental message. A businessman being chased by the police in the Amazon jungle is rescued by a bush pilot who dreams of mining the Amazon's riches. A Brazilian woman enters the picture and persuades the businessman to help save the rainforest. Portions of the proceeds from the sale of this film go to the Rainforest Action Network.
1990 (R) 88m/C Kari Vaananen, Robert Davi, Rae Dawn Chong; **D:** Mika Kaurismaki. **VHS, LV** $89.98 LIV ✠✠

Amazon Jail Scantily clad women go over the wall and promptly get caught by devil worshiping men in the jungle. They should have known better. Redeemed only by lingerie selection.
1985 94m/C Elisabeth Hartmann, Mauricio Do Valle, Sondra Graffi; **D:** Oswald De Oliveira. **VHS, Beta** NO ✠

Amazon Women on the Moon A plotless, irreverent media spoof, depicting the programming of a slipshod television station as it crams weird commercials and shorts around a comical '50s' science fiction film. Inconsistent, occasionally funny anthology hangs together very loosely. Produced by Landis, with the usual amount of in-joke cameos and allusions to his other works of art.
1987 (R) 85m/C Rosanna Arquette, Steve Guttenberg, Steve Allen, B.B. King, Michelle Pfeiffer, Arsenio Hall, Andrew Dice Clay, Howard Hesseman, Lou Jacobi, Carrie Fisher, Griffin Dunne, Sybil Danning, Henny Youngman, Monique Gabrielle, Paul Bartel, Kelly Preston; **D:** John Landis, Joe Dante, Carl Gottlieb, Peter Horton, Robert Weiss. **VHS, Beta, LV** $79.95 MCA ✠✠

The Amazons Goofy made for television drama about a beautiful doctor who discovers an underground organization of Amazon-descended women bent on taking over the world or at least making life hard for men while investigating a Congressman's mysterious death.
1984 100m/C Tamara Dobson, Jack Scalia, Stella Stevens, Madeleine Stowe, Jennifer Warren; **D:** Paul Michael Glaser. **VHS, Beta** WWV ✠½

Amazons Tall, strong women who occasionally wander around nude search for a magical talisman that will overthrow an evil magician.
1986 (R) 76m/C Windsor Taylor Randolph, Penelope Reed, Joseph Whipp, Willie Nelson, Danitza Kingsley; **D:** Alex Sessa. **VHS, Beta** $79.95 MGM ✠

The Ambassador An American ambassador (Mitchum) is sent to the Middle East to try to solve the area's deep political problems. He quickly becomes the target of terrorist attacks, and is blamed for the nation's unrest. To make matters worse, his wife is having an affair with a PLO leader. The President ignores him, forcing the ambassador to fend for himself. Talk about your bad days. Hudson's last feature. Based on Elmore Leonard's "52 Pickup," and remade a year later under its own title. **AKA:** Peacemaker.

1984 97m/C Robert Mitchum, Ellen Burstyn, Rock Hudson, Fabio Testi, Donald Pleasence; **D:** J. Lee Thompson. VHS, Beta $79.95 *MGM* 🐾🐾½

Ambassador Bill An Oklahoma rancher is appointed ambassador to a country in revolt. Rogers, of course, saves the day with his rustic witticisms. Based on the story "Ambassador from the United States" by Vincent Sheean.
1931 68m/B Will Rogers, Marguerite Churchill, Greta Nissen; **D:** Sam Taylor. VHS $19.98 *FOX, FCT* 🐾🐾

The Ambassador's Daughter The Parisian adventures of an American ambassador's daughter De Havilland and soldier Forsythe, who, unaware of her position, falls in love with her. Faltering comedy written by Krasna is supported by an expert cast (although nearly 40, De Havilland is charming as the young woman) with especially good performances from Menjou and Loy.
1956 102m/C Olivia de Havilland, John Forsythe, Myrna Loy, Adolphe Menjou, Edward Arnold, Francis Lederer, Tommy Noonan, Minor Watson; **D:** Norman Krasna. VHS *MOV* 🐾🐾

Amber Waves Credible made for television drama about a generation-gap conflict between a Midwestern farmer (Weaver) and an irresponsible male model (Russell) who has coasted through life on con and charm.
1982 98m/C Dennis Weaver, Kurt Russell; **D:** Joseph Sargent. VHS, Beta *TLF* 🐾🐾½

Ambition Scriptwriter/star Phillips gets a bone for chutzpah by taking an unsavory lead role; his character torments a paroled psycho so that the killer will kill again and inspire a true-crime bestseller. The plot looks good on paper, but onscreen it's padded and unconvincing.
1991 (R) 99m/C Lou Diamond Phillips, Clancy Brown, Cecilia Peck, Richard Bradford, Willard Pugh, Grace Zabriskie, Katherine Armstrong, John Cullum, Haing S. Ngor; **D:** Scott Goldstein; **W:** Lou Diamond Phillips; **M:** Leonard Rosenman. VHS, Beta, LV $92.98 *FXV, MED* 🐾🐾½

The Ambulance A New York cartoonist witnesses a mysterious ambulance at work and decides to investigate. His probings uncover a plot to sell the bodies of dying diabetics. A surprisingly good no-money feature from low-budget king Cohen. Includes an appearance by Marvel Comics' Stan Lee as himself.
1990 ?m/C Eric Roberts, James Earl Jones, Megan Gallagher, Red Buttons, Eric Braeden, Laurene Landon, Jill Gatsby; **W/D:** Larry Cohen. VHS *COL* 🐾🐾½

Ambush at Tomahawk Gap Three released prisoners go in search of hidden loot and tempers rise when the goods don't turn up. Then the Apaches show up.
1953 73m/C John Hodiak, John Derek, David Brian, Maria Elena Marques, Ray Teal; **D:** Fred F. Sears. VHS, Beta *GKK* 🐾🐾

The Ambush Murders True story of a stalwart white attorney defending a black activist accused of killing two cops. Not the compelling television it could be, but still enjoyable. From Ben Bradlee, Jr.'s novel.
1982 100m/C James Brolin, Dorian Harewood, Alfre Woodard, Louis Giambalvo, John McLiam, Teddy Wilson, Antonio Fargas, Amy Madigan; **D:** Steven Hilliard Stern. VHS, Beta $49.95 *FRH, LIV* 🐾🐾½

Ambush Trail Stranger-in-town Steele metes out justice to help local ranchers while sidekick Saylor leaves 'em laughing.
1946 60m/B Bob Steele, Syd Saylor, I. Stanford Jolley, Lorraine Miller, Charles King, Kermit Maynard; **D:** Harry Fraser. VHS $19.95 *NOS* 🐾🐾

The Ambushers Martin's third Matt Helm farce finds him handling a puzzling case involving the first United States spacecraft. When the craft is hijacked with Rule on board, it's Matt to the rescue, regaining control before unfriendly forces can take it back to Earth. Tired formula seems to have worn Martin out while the remainder of the cast goes to camp. Followed by "The Wrecking Crew."
1967 102m/C Dean Martin, Janice Rule, James Gregory, Albert Salmi, Senta Berger; **D:** Henry Levin. VHS, Beta, LV $14.95 *COL* Woof!

Amenaza Nuclear A Mexican farce about two idiots who try to stop mysterious Chinamen from stealing nuclear arms.
19?? 106m/C *MX* Emeterio Y. Felipes, Lydia Zamora, Ki Jeong Lee. VHS, Beta $59.95 *MAD* 🐾

America New York cable station receives worldwide fame when their signal bounces off of the moon. Uninspired piece of fluff from otherwise talented director Downey.
1986 (R) 83m/C Zack Norman, Tammy Grimes, Michael J. Pollard, Monroe Arnold, Richard Belzer, Liz Torres, Howard Thomashefsky, Laura Ashton, Robert Downey Jr.; **D:** Robert Downey. VHS $79.95 *SVS* 🐾🐾

America at the Movies Scenes from more than 80 of the finest American motion pictures fly by in an effort to tell the story of the cinema and provide a portrait of America as it has been seen on screen for half a century. Scenes from "The Birth of a Nation," "Citizen Kane," "Dr. Strangelove," "East of Eden," "The French Connection," and "From Here to Eternity," are among the many included. Some black and white scenes; produced by the American Film Institute.
1976 116m/C John Wayne, Orson Welles, Peter Sellers, James Dean, Gene Hackman, Burt Lancaster, Julie Harris, Deborah Kerr, Al Pacino, Robert De Niro. VHS, Beta, LV $59.95 *COL, IME* 🐾🐾½

America First A group of seven travelers try to build an "Eden" with the inhabitants of an Appalachian hollow.
1970 90m/C Michael Kennedy, Walter Keller, Pat Estrin, Lois McGuire. VHS, Beta *NO* 🐾½

America/The Fall of Babylon A double feature containing abridged versions; in "America," a Boston patriot and the daughter of an aristocratic Virginia Tory fall in love during the Revolutionary War; "The Fall of Babylon" is one of the stories in D.W. Griffith's "Intolerance." Silent.
1924 56m/B Neil Hamilton, Lionel Barrymore, Constance Talmadge, Elmer Clifton, Alfred Paget. VHS, Beta $29.98 *CCB* 🐾🐾🐾

America 3000 Hundreds of years in the holocaust-torn future, men rebel against a brutal, overpowering race of women, with predictable results.
1986 (PG-13) 94m/C Chuck Wagner, Laurene Landon; **D:** David Engelbach. VHS, Beta $79.95 *MGM* 🐾

The American Angels: Baptism of Blood Three beautiful young women, each with a personal dream, strive to make it in the world of professional wrestling. Hackneyed plot devices, but those simply watching for the wrestling scenes won't be disappointed.
1989 (R) 99m/C Jan MacKenzie, Tray Loren, Mimi Lesseos, Trudy Adams, Patricia Cavoti, Susan Sexton, Jean Kirkland, Jeff Lundy, Lee Marshall; **D:** Beverly Sebastian, Ferd Sebastian. VHS, Beta, LV $79.95 *PAR* 🐾

American Anthem A young gymnast must choose between family responsibilities or the parallel bars. Olympic gymnast Gaylord makes his movie debut but doesn't get the gold. Good fare for young tumblers, but that's about it. Followed by two of the films' music videos and tape-ads featuring Max Headroom.
1986 (PG-13) 100m/C Mitch Gaylord, Janet Jones, Michelle Phillips, Michael Pataki; **D:** Albert Magnoli. VHS, Beta, LV $19.98 *LHV, WAR* 🐾

American Aristocracy A silent comic romp in which Fairbanks, an old moneyed dandy, wreaks havoc on an island resort whose clientele is composed of the nouveau well-to-do.
1917 52m/B Douglas Fairbanks Sr., Jewel Carmen, Albert Parker; **D:** Lloyd Ingraham. VHS, Beta $16.95 *GPV* 🐾🐾

American Autobahn A low-budget independent actioner about a journalist who discovers an underworld weapons ring that hits the highway in pursuit of him.
1984 90m/C Jan Jalenak, Michael von der Goltz, Jim Jarmusch; **D:** Andre Degas. VHS, Beta $79.95 *SVS* 🐾½

American Blue Note Loosely plotted, bittersweet account of a struggling jazz quartet in the early 1960s, as its leader (MacNicol) must decide if their fruitless tours of sleazy bars and weddings are still worth it. The debut of director Toporoff. *AKA:* Fakebook.
1989 (PG-13) 96m/C Peter MacNicol, Carl Capotorto, Tim Guinee, Bill Christopher-Myers, Jonathan Walker, Charlotte d'Amboise, Louis Guss, Zohra Lampert, Trini Alvarado, Sam Behrens; **D:** Ralph Toporoff; **W:** Gilbert Girion, Larry Schanker. VHS, LV $89.95 *COL, BTV* 🐾🐾

American Born Murder Inc. returns to the dismay of one idealist who embarks on a battle he doesn't intend to lose. The mob had better look out.
1989 90m/C Joey Travolta, Andrew Zeller. VHS *PMH* 🐾½

American Boyfriends An ostensible sequel to "My American Cousin," in which two Canadian girls go to California and discover innocent romance and friendship.
1989 (PG-13) 90m/C *CA* Margaret Langrick, John Wildman, Jason Blicker, Lisa Repo Martell; **D:** Sandy Wilson. VHS, Beta, LV $79.95 *LIV* 🐾🐾

An American Christmas Carol Charles Dickens' classic story is retold with limited charm in a made for television effort. This time a greedy American financier (Winkler) learns about the true meaning of Christmas.
1979 98m/C Henry Winkler, David Wayne, Dorian Harewood; **D:** Eric Till. VHS, Beta $14.98 *VES, LIV* 🐾🐾

American Commandos An ex-Green Beret slaughters the junkies who killed his son and raped his wife, and then joins his old buddies for a secret, Rambo-esque mission in Vietnam providing a tired rehash of Vietnam movie cliches. *AKA:* Hitman.
1984 (R) 96m/C Chris Mitchum, John Phillip Law, Franco Guerrero; **D:** Bobby Suarez. VHS, Beta $79.98 *LIV* 🐾

American Dream A midwestern family leaves the suburbs and moves into a Chicago inner-city neighborhood. Good TV-movie pilot for the short-lived series that was Emmy nominated for direction and writing.
1981 90m/C Stephen Macht, Karen Carlson, John Karlen, Andrea Smith, John Malkovich, John McIntire; **D:** Mel Damski. VHS, Beta $29.95 *UNI* 🐾🐾🐾

American Dreamer A housewife wins a trip to Paris as a prize from a mystery writing contest. Silly from a blow on the head, she begins living the fictional life of her favorite literary adventure. Sporadic comedy with a good cast wandering about courtesy of a clumsy screenplay.
1984 (PG) 105m/C JoBeth Williams, Tom Conti, Giancarlo Giannini, Coral Browne, James Staley; *D:* Rick Rosenthal. **VHS, Beta $19.98** FOX 𝙕𝙕

American Drive-In A guffaw-laden teenage comedy about a suburban drive-in theater. The movie being shown at the theater looks suspiciously like the director's previous film, "Hard Rock Zombies." Never released theatrically, for good reason.
1988 92m/C Emily Longstreth, Joel Bennett, Giancarlo Giannini, Pat Kirton, Rhonda Snow; *D:* Krishna Shah. **Beta $79.98** VES, LIV 𝙕

American Eagle A veteran goes crazy and seeks sadistic, bloody revenge on his war buddies. Now his war buddies are the only ones who can stop him.
1990 (R) 92m/C Asher Brauner, Robert F. Lyons, Vernon Wells, Kai Baker; *D:* Robert J. Smawley. **VHS, LV $89.95** VMK 𝙕½

American Empire Two Civil War heroes struggle to build a cattle empire in Texas and are hampered by rustlers, one of whom was their partner. A fine, veteran cast and a tight script keep things moving, including the cattle. *AKA:* My Son Alone.
1942 82m/B Preston Foster, Richard Dix, Frances Gifford, Leo Carrillo; *D:* William McGann. **VHS, Beta, 3/4U, Special order formats $19.95** NOS, MRV, DVT 𝙕𝙕½

American Fabulous The posthumously released autobiography of an eccentric homosexual who lived life in the fast lane. Jeffrey Strouth performs his monologue from the back seat of a 1957 Cadillac, where the images of small-town America are seen to contrast sharply with his flamboyant style. His grotesque and candid recollections include his alcoholic Elvis-impersonator father, a stint as a teenage prostitute, drag queen friends, and drug addiction in New York. Strouth puts a comic twist on even the most brutal of his memories. He died of AIDS at the age of 33 in 1992.
1992 105m/C Jeffrey Strouth; *D:* Reno Dakota; *W:* Jeffrey Strouth. **VHS $59.95** FRV 𝙕𝙕

American Flyers Two competitive brothers train for a grueling three-day bicycle race in Colorado while tangling with personal drama, including the spector that one of them may have inherited dad's tendency for cerebral aneurisms and is sure to drop dead during a bike race soon. Written by bike movie specialist Steve Teisch ("Breaking Away") with a lot of the usual cliches (the last bike ride, battling bros, eventual understanding), which are gracefully overridden by fine bike-racing photography. Interesting performances, especially Chong as a patient girlfriend and Amos as the trainer.
1985 (PG-13) 113m/C Kevin Costner, David Grant, Rae Dawn Chong, Alexandra Paul, John Amos, Janice Rule, Robert Townsend, Jennifer Grey; *D:* John Badham. **VHS, Beta, LV $19.98** WAR 𝙕𝙕½

The American Friend A tribute to the American gangster film that helped introduce Wenders to American moviegoers. A young Hamburg picture framer who thinks he has a terminal disease is set up by American expatriate (Hopper) to become a hired assassin in West Germany. The lure is a promise of quick money that the supposedly dying man can then leave his wife and child. After the first assasination, the two bond. Hopper is the typical Wenders protagonist, a strange man in a strange land looking for a connection, in this case the picture framer and his family. A great, creepy thriller from the acclaimed director adapted from Patricia Highsmith's novel "Ripley's Game." Fuller and Ray (better known as directors) appear briefly as gangsters.
1977 127m/C GE FR Bruno Ganz, Dennis Hopper, Lisa Kreuzer, Gerard Blain, Jean Eustache, Samuel Fuller, Nicholas Ray, Wim Wenders; *W/D:* Wim Wenders. **VHS, Beta, LV $29.95** PAV, FCT, GLV 𝙕𝙕½

American Friends Genteel story masquerading as high comedy has Palin starring as a fussy middle-aged Oxford classics tutor. He goes off on a Swiss holiday and meets American Hartley (Booth) and her adopted daughter, Elinor (Alvarado). Both women are immensely attracted to the don (for reasons that are none too clear) and follow him back to Oxford, where he's engaged in a battle of succession with his rival, Oliver Syme (Molina). The dismal screenplay, lacking in logic and urgency, makes it very hard to care about the story or the characters. The script is said to have been inspired by an incident in the life of Palin's great-grandfather. If this sounds like your cup of tea, save your money and wait for the next Merchant-Ivory production.
1993 (PG) 95m/C GB Michael Palin, Connie Booth, Trini Alvarado, Alfred Molina; *D:* Tristam Powell; *W:* Michael Palin, Tristam Powell. **VHS, LV $92.95** VMK 𝙕𝙕

The American Gangster Documentary look at the beginnings of organized crime and the rise of the gangster in American society. Includes vintage film and photographs. Profiles include Bugsy Siegel, Al Capone, John Dillinger, Pretty Boy Floyd, and Lucky Luciano.
1992 45m/C VHS $14.95 COL 𝙕𝙕

American Gigolo A Los Angeles loner who sexually services the rich women of Beverly Hills becomes involved with the wife of a California state senator and is then framed for a murder he did not commit. A highly stylized but empty view of seamy low lives marred by a contrived plot, with decent romp in the hay readiness displayed by Gere.
1979 (R) 117m/C Richard Gere, Lauren Hutton, Hector Elizondo, Paul Schrader; *D:* Paul Schrader. **VHS, Beta, LV $59.95** PAR 𝙕𝙕

American Gothic Three couples headed for a vacation are instead stranded on an island and captured by a demented family headed by Steiger and De Carlo, a scary enough proposition in itself. Even worse, Ma and Pa have three middle-aged moronic offspring who still dress as children and are intent on killing the thwarted vacationers (who are none too bright themselves) one by bloody one. A stultifying career low for all involved. *AKA:* Hide and Shriek.
1988 (R) 89m/C Rod Steiger, Yvonne De Carlo, Michael J. Pollard, Sarah Torgov, Fiona Hutchinson, Willaim Wright; *D:* John Hough. **VHS, Beta, LV $89.95** VMK Woof!

American Graffiti Lucas' poignant autobiographical take on the early '60s is an atmospheric, episodic look at growing up in the innocence of America before the Kennedy assassination and the Vietnam War. It all takes place on one hectic but typical night in the life of a group of Californian high school friends who've just graduated and are unsure of what the next big step in life is. So they spend their time cruising, girl chasing, listening to Wolfman Jack, and meeting at the drive-in. Successfully creates a slice-of-life for the era with a prudent script, great set design, authentic soundtrack, and consistently fine performances by the young cast, many of whom went on to stardom. Garnered five Oscar nominations but strangely did not win any, although responsible for catapulting Dreyfuss to immediate stardom, branding Lucas a hot directorial commodity with enough leverage to launch "Star Wars," and leading Howard and Williams to find continued age-of-innocence nirvana on "Happy Days." A box-office success that created a minor industry for '60s inspired flicks (including "Diner" and 1979's "More American Graffiti," which had some of the same cast but was not Lucas led). Produced by Francis Ford Coppola and Gary Kurtz and written by Lucas, Gloria Katz, and William Huyck.
1973 (PG) 112m/C Richard Dreyfuss, Ron Howard, Cindy Williams, MacKenzie Phillips, Paul LeMat, Charles Martin Smith, Suzanne Somers, Candy Clark, Harrison Ford, Bo Hopkins, Joe Spano, Kathleen Quinlan, Wolfman Jack; *D:* George Lucas. Academy Awards '73 Nominations: Best Director (Lucas), Best Film Editing, Best Picture, Best Story & Screenplay, Best Supporting Actress (Clark); Golden Globe Awards '74: Best Film—Musical/Comedy. **VHS, Beta, LV $14.95** MCA, FCT 𝙕𝙕𝙕½

An American in Paris Lavish and imaginative musical production scripted by Lerner, with a sweeping score by the Gershwins and knockout choreography by Kelly. Kelly is an ex-G.I. who stays on in Paris after the war to study painting. Rich American Foch decides to support his efforts, in the hopes of acquiring a little extra attention. But Kelly falls for lovely French lady Caron, who unfortunately is scheduled to marry an older gent. Kelly tries desperately (while dancing up a storm) to win her heart. Highlight is an astonishing 17-minute ballet choreographed by Kelly, holding the record for longest movie dance number (and one of the most expensive at more than a half million for a month of filming). For his efforts, the dance king won a special Oscar citation. While it sure looks like Paris, most of it was filmed in MGM studios. ♫S'Wonderful; I Got Rhythm; Embraceable You; Love Is Here To Stay; Tra-La-La; I'll Build a Stairway to Paradise; Nice Work If You Can Get It; By Strauss; Concerto in F (3rd Movement); An American in Paris; Piano Concerto in F.
1951 113m/C Gene Kelly, Leslie Caron, Oscar Levant, Nina Foch, Georges Guetary; *D:* Vincente Minnelli; *W:* Alan Jay Lerner; *M:* George Gershwin, George Gershwin, Ira Gershwin. Academy Awards '51: Best Art Direction/Set Decoration (Color), Best Color Cinematography, Best Costume Design (Color), Best Picture, Best Story & Screenplay, Best Score; Nominations: Best Director (Minnelli), Best Film Editing; Golden Globe Awards '52: Best Film—Musical/Comedy; National Board of Review Awards '51: 10 Best Films of the Year. **VHS, Beta, LV, 8mm $19.98** MGM, TLF, BTV 𝙕𝙕𝙕𝙕

American Justice Two cops, one of whom looks suspiciously like a Simon of "Simon and Simon" fight political corruption and white slavery near the Mexican border. The chief white slaver bears a full resemblance to the other Simon. Sufficient action but less than original. *AKA:* Jackals.
1986 (R) 96m/C Jameson Parker, Gerald McRaney, Wilford Brimley, Jack Lucarelli; *D:* Gary Grillo. **VHS, Beta $79.98** LIV 𝙕𝙕

American Kickboxer 1 Barrett stars as B.J. Quinn, a down on his luck kickboxing champion who spends much of his time onscreen aimlessly wandering (apparently searching for the meaning of his life.) Lackluster script and performances will make this one trying —even for kickboxing fans. Barrett is Chuck Norris' former workout partner, but there isn't enough action often enough for him to show off his formidable skills. **1991 (R) 93m/C** John Barrett, Keith Vitali, Brad Morris, Terry Norton, Ted Leplat; *D:* Frans Nel; *W:* Emil Kolbe; *M:* Frank Becker. **VHS, Beta $89.99** CAN ⅟₂

American Me Violent and brutal depiction of more than thirty years of gang wars and drugs in East Los Angeles. Santana has founded and led a street gang since his teenage years. He's spent the last 18 years in Folsom State Prison, where he and his cohorts are the bosses of the so-called Mexican Mafia, which includes the drugs, scams, murders, and violence that are an everyday fact of prison life. Released from Folsom, Santana goes back to his old neighborhood and attempts to distance himself from his old life but finds his gang ties are stronger than any other alliance. Unsparing and desolate. Directorial debut from Olmos. **1992 (R) 119m/C** Edward James Olmos, William Forsythe, Pepe Serna, Danny De La Paz, Evelina Fernandez, Sal Lopez, Daniel Villarreal, Cary-Hiroyuki Tagawa; *D:* Edward James Olmos. **VHS, LV $19.98** MCA ⅟₂⅟₂

American Nightmare Young man searches for his missing sister against a background of pornography, drug peddling, and prostitution in the slums of a city. The usual titillating squalid urban drama. **1981 85m/C** Lawrence S. Day, Lora Staley, Lenore Zann, Michael Ironside, Alexandra Paul; *D:* Don McBrearty. **VHS, Beta $54.95** MED ⅟₂

American Ninja American Dudikoff is G.I. Joe, a martial-arts expert stationed in the Philippines who alienates most everyone around him (he's a rebel). Deadly black-belt war begins with Joe confronting the army which is selling stolen weapons to the South American black market. Aided by one faithful pal, Joe uses his head-kicking martial arts skills to stop hundreds of ninja combatants working for the corrupt arms dealer. In his spare time he romances the base chief's daughter. Efficient rib-crunching chop-socky action wrapped in no-brainer plot and performed by nonactors. Cannon epic mercilessly followed by at least three sequels. *AKA:* American Warrior. **1985 (R) 96m/C** Michael Dudikoff, Guich Koock, Judie Aronson, Steve James; *D:* Sam Firstenberg. **VHS, Beta $14.95** MGM ⅟⅟

American Ninja 2: The Confrontation Soldiers Dudikoff and James are back again using their martial arts skills (in lieu of any acting) to take on a Caribbean drug-lord. Apparently he has been kidnapping Marines and taking them to his island, where he genetically alters them to become fanatical ninja assassins eager to do his dirty work. The script by actors Conway and James Booth hardly gets in the way of the rib-crunching action, but is an improvement upon Ninja Number One. **1987 (R) 90m/C** Michael Dudikoff, Steve James, Larry Poindexter, Gary Conway; *D:* Sam Firstenberg. **VHS, Beta, LV $19.95** MED ⅟⅟

American Ninja 3: Blood Hunt Second sequel in the American Ninja series. Bradley replaces Dudikoff as the martial arts good guy fighting the martial arts bad guys on a Caribbean island. He's pursued by ex-evangelist Marjoe, who wants to inject him with a nasty virus before unloading the germs to bad buys worldwide. Less ninjutsu; more uninspired martial arts. **1989 (R) 90m/C** David Bradley, Steve James, Marjoe Gortner, Michele Chan, Calvin Jung; *D:* Cedric Sundstrom; *W:* Paul DeMielche. **VHS, Beta, LV $14.95** MGM, CAN Woof!

American Ninja 4: The Annihilation Dudikoff returns after noticeable absence in last sequel. He should have stayed away from #4—its a rehash of tired ideas that never gets off the ground. Forget this and see ''American Ninja 2: The Confrontation,'' the best of this series. **1991 (R) 99m/C** Michael Dudikoff, David Bradley, James Booth, Dwayne Alexandre, Robin Stille, Ken Gampu; *D:* Cedric Sundstrom; *W:* David Geeves; *M:* Nicolaas Tenbroek. **VHS, Beta, LV $89.99** CAN Woof!

American Pluck Before he can inherit anything, a playboy millionaire's son must go out into the world and prove he can make his own way. He meets a beautiful princess, who is pursued by a villainous count. Walsh, as the dashing hero, was the younger brother of director Raoul. Silent with original organ music. **1925 91m/B** George Walsh, Wanda Hawley, Frank Leigh, Sidney De Grey; *D:* Richard Stanton. **VHS, Beta, 8mm $29.99** VYY ⅟⅟

American Roulette Garcia is the exiled president of a Latin American country living in London in this thin political thriller. A plot riddled with weaknesses and poor direction make this potentially interesting film dull and lifeless. **1988 (R) 102m/C** GB AU Andy Garcia, Kitty Aldridge, Robert Stephens, Al Matthews, Susannah Kaye; *D:* Maurice Hatton. **VHS, LV** NO ⅟

American Samurai Drew is the adopted son of a Japanese samurai, who gives him the family's sacred sword. This gesture angers his stepbrother who gets involved with Japanese gangsters and illegal live-blade fighting, and who also vows revenge on this American upstart. Lots of sword play to go with the chop-socky action. **1992 (R) 89m/C** David Bradley, Mark Dacascos, John Fujioka, Valarie Trapp; *D:* Sam Firstenberg; *W:* John Corcoran. **VHS, LV $89.99** WAR, PMS ⅟₂

The American Scream An innocent family vacationing in the mountains stumbles onto a satanic cult. And that can really ruin a vacation. **1987 85m/C** Jennifer Darling, Pons Marr, Blackie Cammett, Kimberly Kramer, Jean Sapienza, Kevin Kaye, Matt Borlenghi, James Cooper; *D:* Mitchell Linden. **VHS, Beta $59.95** GHV ⅟₂

American Shaolin: King of the Kickboxers 2 When Drew gets his butt kicked in a karate tournament he decides to head to China and learn some fight-winning moves from a group of warrior monks. **1992 (PG-13) 103m/C** Reese Madigan, Trent Bushy, Daniel Dae Kim, Billy Chang, Cliff Lenderman, Zhang Shi Yen, Kim Chan, Alice Zhang Hung; *D:* Lucas Lowe. **VHS $89.95** ACA ⅟₂

The American Soldier Fassbinder's homage to the American gangster film tells the story of Ricky, a charismatic hit man. Ricky always wears a gun in a shoulder holster, sports a fedora and a white double-breasted suit, and drinks Scotch straight from the bottle. He also carries out his assigned murders with complete efficiency and no emotion. In German with English subtitles. *AKA:* Der Amerikanische Soldat. **1970 80m/C** GE Karl Scheydt, Elga Sorbas, Jan George; *W/D:* Rainer Werner Fassbinder. **VHS $79.95** NYF, TAM ⅟₂⅟₂

An American Summer A Chicago kid spends a summer with his aunt in beach-rich Los Angeles in this coming-of-age tale filled with '90s teen idols. **1990 100m/C** Brian Austin Green, Joanna Kerns, Michael Landes. **VHS $89.95** SVS ⅟⅟

An American Tail While emigrating to New York in the 1880s, a young Russian mouse (Fievel) is separated from his family. He matures as he learns to live on the Big Apple's dirty boulevards. The bad guys are of course cats. Excellent animation and a high-minded though sentimental and stereotypical plot keep it interesting for adults. Produced by Spielberg and the first big hit for the Bluth factory, a collection of expatriate Disney artists. Aggressively marketed upon release in the hopes of creating Fievel Fever, the flick includes the platinum selling song ''Somewhere Out There.'' Knowing better than to let a money-making mouse tale languish, Bluth followed with ''An American Tale: Fievel Goes West.'' **1986 (G) 81m/C** *D:* Don Bluth; *M:* James Horner; *V:* Dom DeLuise, Madeline Kahn, Phillip Glasser, Christopher Plummer, Nehemiah Persoff, Will Ryan. **VHS, Beta, LV $24.98** MCA, PIA, WTA ⅟⅟½

An American Tail: Fievel Goes West Fievel and the Mousekewitz family continue their pursuit of the American dream by heading West, where the intrepid mouse seeks to become a famous lawman while his sister looks to make it big as a dance hall singer. Songs are ''Somewhere Out There,'' ''Way Out West,'' ''Rawhide,'' ''Dreams to Dream,'' and ''The Girl I Left Behind,'' all performed by the London Symphony Orchestra. Unfortunately released at the same time as ''Beauty and the Beast,'' ''Fievel Goes West'' suffers from comparison. Worthwhile viewing for the whole family, but it won't ever reach the heights of ''B&B.'' The laser edition is letterboxed and features chapter stops. **1991 (G) 75m/C** *D:* Phil Nibbelink, Simon Wells; *W:* Flint Dille; *M:* James Horner; *V:* John Cleese, Dom DeLuise, Phillip Glasser, Amy Irving, Jon Lovitz, Cathy Cavadini, Nehemiah Persoff, Erica Yohn, James Stewart. **VHS, Beta, LV $24.98** MCA ⅟⅟

American Tickler A thigh-slappin' (or is it head-whacking?) series of satirical pastiches in the grand style of ''Kentucky Fried Movie,'' only more sophomoric. A tasteless collection of yearning to be funny sketches about American institutions. *AKA:* Draws. **1976 (R) 77m/C** W.P. Dromak, Joan Sumner, Marlow Ferguson, Jeff Alin; *D:* Chuck Vincent. **VHS, Beta $59.95** GEM ⅟⅟

American Tiger The collegiate hero of ''American Tiger'' is, like so many college students, framed for murder, and he applies himself to clearing his sullied name. Somewhere during this process, he finds himself in the middle of a battle between good and evil on a football field. About what you'd expect from a supernatural kung-fu teen-action drama. *AKA:* American Rickshaw. **1989 (R) 93m/C** Mitch Gaylord, Donald Pleasence, Daniel Greene, Victoria Prouty; *D:* Martin Dolman. **VHS $19.95** ACA ⅟⅟

An American Werewolf in London Although not widely popular with American film critics, this strange and darkly humorous retelling of the classic man-into-wolf horror tale became a cult hit. It follows two American college students (Naughton and Dunne) backpacking through England. One night, they land at the Slaughtered Lamb Pub, where they are attacked viciously by a werewolf when they leave. Dunne is killed and Naughton seriously wounded. While recovering with the aid of a friendly nurse, Naughton is visited by his decomposing friend, who presents him with warnings of impending werewolfdom when the moon is full; Dunne advises suicide. Seat-jumping

horror and gore, highlighted by intensive metamorphosis sequences orchestrated by Rick Baker, are offset by wry humor, though the shifts in tone don't always work. Landis being Landis, also manages to mangle a great many automobiles for no particular reason. Great moon songs permeate the soundtrack, including CCR's "Bad Moon Rising" and Van Morrison's "Moondance." Naughton may seem familiar as the first Who's a Pepper We're A Pepper Dr. Pepper Guy.
1981 (R) 97m/C David Naughton, Griffin Dunne, Jenny Agutter, Frank Oz, Brian Glover; *D:* John Landis. **VHS, Beta, LV $29.98** *LIV, VES* ♫♫♫

Americana A troubled Vietnam vet tries to restore himself by rebuilding a merry-go-round in a small midwestern town, while dealing with opposition from the local residents. Offbeat, often effective post-Nam editorial that was produced and directed in 1973 by Carradine and then shelved. Hershey and Carradine were a couple back then.
1981 (PG) 90m/C David Carradine, Barbara Hershey, Bruce Carradine, John Blythe Barrymore, Michael Greene; *D:* David Carradine. **VHS, Beta $69.98** *VES, LIV* ♫♫½

The Americanization of Emily A happy-go-lucky American naval officer (Garner) with no appetite for war discovers to his horror that he may be slated to become the first casualty of the Normandy invasion as part of a military PR effort in this black comedy-romance. Meanwhile, he spreads the charisma in an effort to woo and uplift Emily (Andrews), a depressed English woman who has suffered the loss of her husband, father, and brother during the war. A cynical, often funny look at military maneuvers and cultural drift that was adapted by Paddy Chayefsky from William Bradford Huie's novel. Also available colorized.
1964 117m/B James Garner, Julie Andrews, Melvyn Douglas, James Coburn, Joyce Grenfell, Keenan Wynn, Judy Carne, Liz Fraser, Edward Binns; *D:* Arthur Hiller; *W:* Paddy Chayefsky. **VHS, LV $19.95** *MGM* ♫♫♫

The Americano Ever-suave Fairbanks frees a South American politician locked in a dungeon, returns him to political success, and captures the heart of his beautiful daughter. Based on Eugene P. Lyle, Jr.'s "Blaze Derringer."
1917 58m/B Douglas Fairbanks Sr., Alma Rubens, Spottiswoode Aitken, Lillian Langdon, Carl Stockade, Tom Wilson; *D:* John Emerson. **VHS, Beta $16.95** *GPV* ♫♫½

Americano A cowboy travelling to Brazil with a shipment of Brahma bulls discovers the rancher he's delivering them to has been murdered. An odd amalgam of western cliches and a South American setting.
1955 85m/C Glenn Ford, Frank Lovejoy, Abbe Lane, Cesar Romero; *D:* William Castle. **VHS $19.98** *REP* ♫♫

The Americano/Variety The two silent classics in abridged form: "The Americano," (1917) about a soldier-of-fortune who aids a revolt-ridden Caribbean country, and "Variety," (1925) a classic German masterpiece about the career of a trapeze artist .
1925 54m/B Douglas Fairbanks Sr., Emil Jannings; *D:* John Emerson, E.A. Dupont. **VHS, Beta $39.95** *CCB* ♫♫

Americathon It is the year 1998 and the United States is almost bankrupt, so President Chet Roosevelt decides to stage a telethon to keep the country from going broke. Interesting satiric premise with a diverse cast, but a poor script and slack pacing spoil all the fun. The soundtrack features music by The Beach Boys and Elvis

Costello while the narration is by George Carlin. Tommy LaSorda and Peter Marshall do the cameo thing.
1979 (PG) 85m/C Peter Riegert, John Ritter, Nancy Morgan, Harvey Korman, Fred Willard, Meatloaf, Elvis Costello, Chief Dan George, Howard Hesseman, Jay Leno; *Cameos:* Tommy Lasorda, Peter Marshall; *D:* Neal Israel. **VHS, Beta $59.95** *LHV, WAR Woof!*

Amin: The Rise and Fall Excessively violent and ultimately pointless dramatization of Idi Amin's eight-year reign of terror in Uganda, which resulted in the deaths of a half million people and the near ruin of a nation.
1982 101m/C Joseph Olita, Geoffrey Keen; *D:* Sharad Patel. **VHS, Beta $59.95** *EMI, HBO Woof!*

The Amityville Horror Sometimes a house is not a home. Ineffective chiller that became a box-office biggie, based on a supposedly real-life occurrence in Amityville, Long Island. The Lutz family moves into the house of their dreams only to find it full of nightmares. Once the scene of a grisly mass murder, the house takes on a devilish attitude, plunging the family into supernatural terror. Pipes and walls ooze icky stuff, flies manifest in the strangest places, and doors mysteriously slam while exorcist Steiger staggers from room to room in scene-chewing prayer. Based on the Jay Anson book and followed by a number of sequels.
1979 (R) 117m/C James Brolin, Margot Kidder, Rod Steiger, Don Stroud, Murray Hamilton, Helen Shaver, Amy Wright; *D:* Stuart Rosenberg. **VHS, Beta, LV** *WAR, OM* ♫♫

Amityville 2: The Possession More of a prequel than a sequel to "The Amityville Horror" (1979). Relates the story of the house's early years as a haven for demonic forces intent on driving a father to beat the kids, a mother to prayer, and a brother to lust after his sister (before he murders them all). Young etc. portray an obnoxious family that you're actually glad to see wasted by the possessed son. A stupid, clumsy attempt to cash in on the success of the first film, which was also stupid and clumsy but could at least claim novelty in the bad housing development genre. Followed by "Amityville III: The Demon" in 1983.
1982 (R) 110m/C James Olson, Burt Young, Andrew Prine, Moses Gunn, Rutanya Alda; *D:* Damiano Damiani. **VHS, Beta, LV $9.98** *SUE Woof!*

Amityville 3: The Demon America's worst real-estate value dupes another funky buyer. The infamous Amityville house is once again restless with terror and gore, though supported with even less plot than the usual smidgin. Cynical reporter Roberts moves in while trying to get to the bottom of the story by way of the basement. Courtesy of 3-D technology, monsters sprang at theater patrons but the video version is strictly two-dimensional, forcing the viewer to press his or her face directly onto the television screen in order to derive similar effect. *AKA:* Amityville 3D.
1983 (R) 98m/C Tony Roberts, Tess Harper, Robert Joy, Candy Clark, John Beal, Leora Dana, John Harkins, Lori Loughlin, Meg Ryan; *D:* Richard Fleischer. **VHS, Beta, LV $79.98** *VES, LIV* ♫½

Amityville 4 It's an unusual case of house-to-house transference as the horror from Amityville continues, now lodged in a Californian residence. The usual good house gone bad story has the place creating a lot of unusual creaks and rattles before deciding to use its inherited powers to attack and possess a little girl. Special effects from Richard

Stutsman ("The Lost Boys" and "Jaws"). Made for television. *AKA:* The Amityville Horror: The Evil Escapes, Part 4.
1989 (R) 95m/C Patty Duke, Jane Wyatt, Norman Lloyd, Frederic Lehne, Brandy Gold; *D:* Sandor Stern. **VHS $89.95** *VMK* ♫½

The Amityville Curse The possessed house is yet again purchased by a pathetically uninformed family. The usual ghostly shenanigans occur with low-budget regularity in this fifth film in the series. Never released theatrically, for good reason.
1990 (R) 91m/C *CA* Kim Coates, Dawna Wightman, Helen Hughes, David Stein, Anthony Dean Rubes, Cassandra Gava, Jan Rubes; *D:* Tom Berry. **VHS, LV $89.95** *VMK Woof!*

Amityville 1992: It's About Time Time is of the essence in the sixth installment of the Amityville flicks. A vintage clock (from Amityville, of course), causes creepy goings-on in a family's house. Actually a halfway decent horror film with high-grade special effects, and much, much better than previous Amityville sequels, which isn't saying much.
1992 (R) 95m/C Stephen Macht, Shawn Weatherly, Megan Ward, Damon Martin, Nita Talbot, Dick Miller; *D:* Tony Randel. **VHS, LV $14.98** *REP* ♫♫

Among the Cinders Sometimes interesting coming of age drama about a sixteen-year-old New Zealand boy who runs away to his grandfather's farm to forget about his friend's accidental death. At the farm, he meets an older woman and compromises his virtue.
1983 103m/C *GE NZ* Paul O'Shea, Derek Hardwick, Rebecca Gibney, Yvonne Lawley, Amanda Jones; *D:* Rolf Haedrich. **VHS, Beta, LV $9.95** *NWV, STE* ♫♫

Amor Bandido When cab drivers in Rio are turning up dead, a young prostitute is torn between her detective father and her prime suspect boyfriend. Drama based on a true story.
1979 95m/C *BR* Paulo Gracindo, Cristina Ache, Paulo Guarniero; *D:* Bruno Barreto. **VHS, LV $79.95** *FXL, IME, TAM* ♫♫½

Amore Rossellini's tribute to actress Magnani consists of the short films "The Human Voice" and "The Miracle." In "The Human Voice," Magnani is shown alone, speaking to her lover on the telephone. Based on Jean Cocteau's one-act drama. In "The Miracle," she is a simple peasant girl who believes her illegitimate child is acutally the new Messiah. In Italian with English subtitles.
1948 78m/B *IT* Anna Magnani; *D:* Roberto Rossellini. **VHS $59.95** *FCT, TAM* ♫♫♫

The Amorous Adventures of Moll Flanders An amusing romp set in 18th century England focusing on a poor orphan girl who seeks wealth. Moll plots to get ahead through an advantageous series of romances and marriages. Her plan is ruined when she falls in love and he turns out to be a wanted highwayman, landing her in prison. Not surprisingly, love (and money) conquers all. Based on the novel by Daniel Defoe. Novak tries in this female derivative of "Tom Jones," but this period piece isn't her style.
1965 126m/C Kim Novak, Richard Johnson, Angela Lansbury, Vittorio De Sica, Leo McKern, George Sanders, Lilli Palmer; *D:* Terence Young. **VHS $19.95** *PAR* ♫♫

Amos Douglas is Amos, an aging baseball coach confined most reluctantly to a nursing home. He's disturbed by recent suspicious events there, his concern causing him to take on Montgomery, the staunch head nurse.

Well-acted drama produced by Douglas's son Peter, offering an echo of "One Flew Over the Cuckoo's Nest," which Dad starred in on Broadway and son Michael helped produce as a movie classic.
1985 100m/C Kirk Douglas, Elizabeth Montgomery, Dorothy McGuire, Pat Morita, James Sloyan, Ray Walston; **D:** Michael Tuchner. **VHS $29.95** SVS ♪♪½

Amos and Andrew Embarrassing attempt at comedy stops short of endorsing the stereotypes it tries to parody. Prizewinning African-American author Andrew Sterling (Jackson) is seen moving into a house on an island previously reserved for the uptight white, and the neighbors call the cops, assuming he's a thief. Chief of police (Coleman) eagerly gets into the act, then exploits drifter Amos (Cage) in a cover-up attempt when he realizes his mistake. Talented cast can't overcome lame jokes and transparent plot that serves as an opportunity to bring black and white together for a "see how much we have in common" bonding session.
1993 (PG-13) 96m/C Nicolas Cage, Samuel L. Jackson, Michael Lerner, Margaret Colin, Giancarlo Esposito, Dabney Coleman, Bob Balaban, Aimee Graham, Brad Dourif; **D:** E. Max Frye; **W:** E. Max Frye; **M:** Richard Gibbs. **VHS, LV** NLC, IME ♪♪½

The Amphibian Man What does a scientist do once he's created a young man with gills? Plunge him in the real world of aqua pura to experience life and love, albeit underwater. Trouble is, the protagonist, who's come to be known as the Sea Devil, takes a dive for a pretty he's snatched from the jaws of death. A 60's Soviet sci-fi romance originally seen on American television.
1961 96m/C RU K. Korleniev, M. Vllznuskaya, D. Y. Kasancki. **VHS $19.98** SNC ♪♪

The Amsterdam Connection Film company acts as a cover for prostitution and drug smuggling, with the girls acting as international couriers.
1977 90m/C HK Chen Shing, Kid Sherrif, Yeung Sze, Jason Pai Piu, Fang Mui San; **D:** Fang Mui San, Lo Ke. **VHS, Beta** NO ♪

The Amsterdam Kill A washed-up ex-agent of the U.S. Drug Enforcement Agency is hired by a desperate U.S. Drug Enforcement Agency to hunt down the kingpin of a narcotics syndicate in Hong Kong. Tedious pace with occasional spells of violence fails to awaken somnambulent Mitchum. Shot on location in Hong Kong.
1978 (R) 93m/C HK Robert Mitchum, Richard Egan, Keye Luke, Leslie Nielsen, Bradford Dillman; **D:** Robert Clouse. **VHS, Beta, LV $9.95** GKK ♪♪

Amsterdamned A crime thriller taking place on the canals of Amsterdam featuring a serial skindiver killer who surfaces periodically to slash and splash. A steely detective fishes for clues. Dubbed.
1988 (R) 114m/C NL Monique Van De Ven, Huub Stapel; **D:** Dick Maas. **VHS, Beta, LV $89.98** VES, LIV ♪♪

Amy Set in the early 1900s, the story follows the experiences of a woman after she leaves her well-to-do husband to teach at a school for the deaf and blind. Eventually she organizes a football game between the handicapped kids and the other children in the neighborhood. Good Disney family fare.
1981 (G) 100m/C Jenny Agutter, Barry Newman, Kathleen Nolan, Margaret O'Brien, Nanette Fabray, Chris Robinson, Lou Fant; **D:** Vincent McEveety. **VHS, Beta $69.95** DIS ♪♪½

The Amy Fisher Story Amy Fisher wishes she looked this good. Perhaps if she did, she could be acting in made-for-television movies like Barrymore instead of providing fodder for them. The ABC account draws from a variety of sources to dramatize the relationship between Amy and her married, ahem, friend, and Amy's subsequent attack on his wife. Although it tries not to take sides, it does include some pretty hot sex scenes which could be why this docudrama garnered the highest ratings of the three network productions released on TV.
1992 96m/C Drew Barrymore, Anthony John Denison, Harley Jane Kozak, Tom Mason, Laurie Paton; **D:** Andy Tennant; **W:** Janet Brownell. **VHS $89.98** ABC ♪♪

Anastasia Bergman won her second Oscar, and deservedly so, for her classic portrayal of the amnesia victim chosen by Russian expatriate Brynner to impersonate Anastasia, the last surviving member of the Romanoff dynasty. As such, she becomes part of a scam to collect millions of rubles deposited in a foreign bank by her supposed father, the now-dead Czar. But is she just impersonating the princess? Brynner as the scheming White General and Hayes as the Grand Duchess who needs to be convinced turn in fine performances as well. Based on Marcelle Maurette's play.
1956 105m/C Ingrid Bergman, Yul Brynner, Helen Hayes, Akim Tamiroff; **D:** Anatole Litvak. Academy Awards '56: Best Actress (Bergman); Nominations: Best Original Score; Golden Globe Awards '57: Best Actress—Drama (Bergman). **VHS, LV** TCF ♪♪♪½

Anastasia: The Mystery of Anna Irving stars as Anna Anderson, a woman who claimed to be the Grand Duchess Anastasia, the sole surviving daughter of Russian Czar Nicholas II. A powerful epic reliving her experience of royalty, flight from execution, and struggle to retain her heritage. The story of Anastasia remains as one of the greatest dramatic mysteries of the 20th century. Adapted from the book "Anastasia: The Riddle of Anna Anderson" by Peter Kurth; originally broadcast on cable television.
1986 190m/C Amy Irving, Olivia de Havilland, Jan Niklas, Nicolas Surovy, Susan Lucci, Elke Sommer, Edward Fox, Claire Bloom, Omar Sharif, Rex Harrison; **D:** Marvin J. Chomsky. **VHS $79.95** CAF ♪♪½

Anatomy of a Murder Tersely and cleverly directed despite its length. Considered by many to be the best courtroom drama ever made, with a score by Duke Ellington to boot. A small-town lawyer in northern Michigan faces an explosive case as he defends an army officer who has killed a man he suspects was his philandering wife's rapist. A realistic, cynical portrayal of the court system not especially concerned with the guilt or innocence of the officer, but instead focusing on the interplay between the various courtroom characters. It's a classic performance by Stewart as the down home but brilliant defense lawyer who matches wits with Scott, the sophisticated prosecutor. Though tame by today's standards, the language used in the courtroom was controversial for its time. Filmed in upper Michigan and based on the bestseller by Robert Traver, who was a judge in the area.
1959 161m/B James Stewart, George C. Scott, Arthur O'Connell, Ben Gazzara, Lee Remick, Eve Arden, Orson Bean, Kathryn Grant, Murray Hamilton, Joseph Welch; **Cameos:** Duke Ellington; **D:** Otto Preminger; **W:** Wendell Mayes; **M:** Duke Ellington. Academy Awards '59 Nominations: Best Actor (Stewart), Best Adapted Screenplay, Best Black and White Cinematography, Best Film Editing, Best Picture,

Best Supporting Actor (O'Connell, Scott); National Board of Review Awards '59: 10 Best Films of the Year; New York Film Critics Awards '59: Best Director (Stewart). **VHS, Beta, LV $19.95** RCA, COL ♪♪♪♪

Anatomy of a Psycho A man plans to avenge his gas chambered brother by committing mass murder. Very cheaply and poorly produced.
1961 75m/B Ronnie Burns, Pamela Lincoln, Darrell Howe, Russ Bender; **D:** Brooke L. Peters. **VHS, Beta $16.95** SNC, TIM ♪

Anatomy of a Seduction Television formula melodrama of a middle-aged divorcee's affair with her son's best friend. Age knows no boundaries when it comes to television lust.
1979 100m/C Susan Flannery, Jameson Parker, Rita Moreno, Ed Nelson, Michael Le Clair; **D:** Steven Hilliard Stern. **VHS, 8mm $79.99** HBO ♪♪

Anatomy of Terror A made for television drama about an army vet going bonkers (what? really?) and revealing espionage secrets in his home life.
1974 73m/C Paul Burke, Polly Bergen, Dinsdale Landen, Basil Henson. **VHS, Beta $29.95** LIV ♪

Anchors Aweigh Snappy big-budget (for then) musical about two horny sailors, one a girl-happy dancer and the other a shy singer. While on leave in Hollywood they return a lost urchin to his sister. The four of them try to infiltrate a movie studio to win an audition for the girl from maestro Iturbi. Kelly's famous dance with Jerry the cartoon Mouse (of "Tom and Jerry" fame) is the second instance of combining live action and animation. The young and handsome Sinatra's easy crooning and Grayson's near operatic soprano are blessed with music and lyrics by Jule Styne and Sammy Cahn. Lots of fun, with conductor-pianist Iturbi contributing and Hollywood-style Little Mexico also in the brew. ♪♪We Hate to Leave; I Fall in Love Too Easily; The Charm of You; The Worry Song; Jalousie; All of a Sudden My Heart Sings; I Begged Her; What Makes the Sun Set?; Waltz Serenade.
1945 139m/C Frank Sinatra, Gene Kelly, Kathryn Grayson, Jose Iturbi, Sharon McManus, Dean Stockwell, Carlos Ramirez, Pamela Britton; **D:** George Sidney. Academy Awards '45: Best Score; Nominations: Best Actor (Kelly), Best Color Cinematography, Best Picture, Best Song ("I Fall in Love Too Easily"). **VHS, Beta, LV $19.98** MGM ♪♪♪

And a Nightingale Sang World War II England is the scene of this sweet romance, a sad and humorous tale of a woman who gives everything for the war effort. Stunning recreation of the final days of the Blitzkreig. Originally produced for Masterpiece Theatre.
1991 90m/C Joan Plowright, Tom Watt, Phyllis Logan, John Woodvine. **VHS $19.95** PBS ♪♪♪

And Baby Makes Six An unexpected pregnancy creates new challenges for a couple with grown children. Dewhurst is excellent as usual. A television film, scripted by Shelley List. Followed by "Baby Comes Home."
1979 100m/C Colleen Dewhurst, Warren Oates, Maggie Cooper, Mildred Dunnock, Timothy Hutton, Allyn Ann McLerie; **D:** Waris Hussein. **VHS, 8mm $79.99** HBO ♪♪½

And God Created Woman Launching pad for Bardot's career as a sex siren, as she flits across the screen in a succession of scanty outfits and hangs out at the St. Tropez beach in what is euphemistically known as a swimsuit while turning up the heat for the males always in attendance. The plot concerns an 18-year-old nymphomaniac

who is given a home by a local family with three handsome young sons. A cutting-edge sex film in its time that was boffo at the box office. In French with English subtitles. *AKA:* And Woman...Was Created; Et Dieu Crea la Femme.
1957 (PG) 93m/C *FR* Brigitte Bardot, Curt Jurgens, Jean-Louis Trintignant, Christian Marquand; *D:* Roger Vadim. **VHS, Beta $29.95** VES ♫♫ ½

And God Created Woman Loose, dull remake by Vadim of his own 1957 softcore favorite about a free-spirited woman dodging men and the law while yearning for rock and roll stardom. DeMornay is a prisoner who hopes to marry one of the local hunks (Spano) so she can be paroled. They marry, she strips, he frets, while political hopeful Langella smacks his lips in anticipation. Available in an unrated 100-minute version.
1988 (R) 98m/C Rebecca DeMornay, Vincent Spano, Frank Langella, Donovan Leitch, Judith Chapman, Thelma Houston; *D:* Roger Vadim. **VHS, Beta, LV $89.98** VES, LIV ♫♫

And God Said to Cain Another Biblically titled western from the prolific Kinski, about a put-upon gunman who must fight for his life.
196? 95m/C Klaus Kinski. **VHS, Beta $29.95** UNI ♫

And Hope to Die Moody, muddled crime drama with a good cast about a fleeing Frenchman who joins a gang of hardened criminals in Canada. They go ahead with their plans to kidnap a retarded girl even though she is already dead. Standard caper film is enhanced by arty camera work and some unusual directorial touches.
1972 95m/C *FR* Robert Ryan, Jean-Louis Trintignant, Aldo Ray, Tisa Farrow; *D:* Rene Clement. **VHS, Beta** NO ♫♫ ½

And I Alone Survived Made-for-television adaptation of the true story of a woman who survives a leisure-plane crash in the Sierra Nevadas and her struggle to get to the village below. Brown does her best to elevate the proceedings above the usual I-hope-I-don't-die cliches.
1978 90m/C Blair Brown, David Ackroyd, Vera Miles, G.D. Spradlin; *D:* William A. Graham. **VHS, Beta $79.95** PSM ♫♫

And Justice for All Extremely earnest attorney Pacino questions the law and battles for justice in and out of the courtroom. He's hired to defend a detested judge on a rape charge, while dealing with a lost-soul caseload of eccentric and tragedy-prone clients (the suicidal transvestite, the young man sent to prison for a minor traffic violation, etc.). Overly melodramatic, with an odd mix of satire, cynicism, and seemingly sincere drama that tends to use a club when a stick will do. Working with a script by Barry Levinson and Valerie Curtin, Jewison aims for a black surrealism, permitting both Pacino and Warden (portraying a judge losing his sanity) to veer into histrionics, to the detriment of what is essentially a gripping behind-the-scenes story. An excellent cast creates sparks, including Lahti in her film debut. And Baltimore never looked lovelier.
1979 (R) 120m/C Al Pacino, Jack Warden, Christine Lahti, Thomas G. Waites, Craig T. Nelson, John Forsythe, Lee Strasberg; *D:* Norman Jewison; *W:* Barry Levinson, Valerie Curtin. **VHS, Beta, LV, 8mm $14.95** COL ♫♫ ½

And Nothing But the Truth A multinational corporation is out to ruin the investigative television report team trying to do a story on the company. *AKA:* Giro City.

1982 90m/C *GB* Glenda Jackson, Jon Finch, Kenneth Colley, James Donnelly; *D:* Karl Francis. **VHS, Beta** NO ♫♫ ½

And Now for Something Completely Different A compilation of skits from BBC-television's "Monty Python's Flying Circus" featuring Monty Python's own weird, hilarious brand of humor. Sketches include "The Upper Class Twit of the Year Race," "Hell's Grannies" and "The Townswomen's Guild Reconstruction of Pearl Harbour." A great introduction to Python for the uninitiated, or a chance for the converted to see their favorite sketches again.
1972 (PG) 89m/C *GB* John Cleese, Michael Palin, Eric Idle, Graham Chapman, Terry Gilliam, Terry Jones; *D:* Ian McNaughton. **VHS, Beta, LV $19.95** COL ♫♫♫

And Now Miguel Plodding tale of a young boy who wants to take over as head shepherd of his family's flock. Filmed in New Mexico, but the over-long outdoor shots make it drag a bit in spite of Cardi's competent performance.
1966 95m/C Pat Cardi, Michael Ansara, Guy Stockwell, Clu Gulager, Joe De Santis, Pilar Del Rey, Buck Taylor; *D:* James B. Clark. **VHS $24.95** NOS ♫♫

And Now My Love A French couple endeavor to maintain their romance despite interfering socio-economic factors—she's a millionaire and he's an ex-con filmmaker. Keller plays three roles spanning three generations, as Lelouch invests autobiographical details to invent a highly stylized, openly sentimental view of French folks in love with love. Along the way he comments on social mores and changing attitudes through the years. Dubbed in English.
1974 (PG) 121m/C *FR* Marthe Keller, Andre Dussollier, Carla Gravina; *D:* Claude Lelouch. **VHS, Beta $19.95** COL, TAM, SUE ♫♫ ½

And Now the Screaming Starts The young bride-to-be of the lord of a British manor house is greeted by bloody faces at the window, a severed hand, and five corpses. Then Cushing shows up to investigate. Good-looking, sleek production with genuine chills.
1973 (R) 87m/C *GB* Peter Cushing, Herbert Lom, Patrick Magee, Ian Ogilvy, Stephanie Beacham, Geoffrey Whitehead, Guy Rolfe; *D:* Roy Ward Baker. **VHS, Beta $79.95** PSM, MED ♫♫ ½

And Soon the Darkness One of two vacationing young nurses disappears in France where a teenager was once murdered and the search is on. Predictable, ineffective suspenser.
1970 (PG) 94m/C *GB* Pamela Franklin, Michele Dotrice, Sandor Eles, John Nettelton, Claire Kelly, Hanna-Marie Pravda; *D:* Robert Fuest. **VHS, Beta $59.99** HBO ♫♫

And the Ship Sails On On the eve of WWI, a group of devoted opera lovers take a luxury cruise to pay their respects to a recently deceased opera diva. Also on board is a group of fleeing Serbo-Croation freedom fighters. A charming and absurd autumnal homage-to-life by Fellini shot entirely in the studio. *AKA:* E la Nave Va.
1983 (PG) 130m/C *IT* Freddie Jones, Barbara Jefford, Janet Suzman, Peter Cellier; *D:* Federico Fellini. **VHS, Beta, LV $59.95** COL, APD, TAM ♫♫♫

And Then There Were None An all-star cast makes up the ten colorful guests invited to a secluded estate in England by a mysterious host. What the invitations do not say, however, is the reason they have been specifically chosen to visit—to be murdered, one by one. Cat and mouse classic based on

Agatha Christie's book with an entertaining mix of suspense and black comedy. Remade in 1966 and again in 1975 as "Ten Little Indians," but lacking the force and gloss of the original.
1945 97m/C Louis Hayward, Barry Fitzgerald, Walter Huston, Roland Young, C. Aubrey Smith, Judith Anderson, Mischa Auer, June Duprez; *D:* Rene Clair; *W:* Agatha Christie. **VHS, Beta, LV $19.95** NOS, UHV ♫♫♫ ½

And Then You Die An intense crime drama about a Canadian drug lord who amasses a fortune from the cocaine and marijuana trade. His empire is threatened as the Mafia, Hell's Angels, and the police try to bring him down.
1988 (R) 115m/C *CA* Kenneth Welsh, R.H. Thompson, Wayne Robson, Tom Harvey, George Bloomfield, Graeme Campbell; *D:* Francis Mankiewicz. **VHS, Beta $79.95** VMK ♫♫♫

And When She Was Bad... A young vamp gets her stepdad and his girlfriend involved in sexual misadventures. Softcore.
1984 90m/C Heather Vale, Lyllah Torena. **VHS, Beta $29.95** MED ♫ ½

And You Thought Your Parents Were Weird! A pair of introverted, whiz kid brothers invent a lovable robot to provide fatherly guidance as well as companionship for their widowed mother. Surprisingly charming, sentimental film is only slightly hampered by low-budget special effects.
1991 (PG) 92m/C Marcia Strassman, Joshua Miller, Edan Gross, John Quade, Sam Behrens, Susan Gibney; *W/D:* Tony Cookson; *M:* Randall Miller; *V:* Alan Thicke, Richard Libertini. **VHS $92.95** VMK ♫♫

The Anderson Tapes Newly released from prison, an ex-con assembles his professional pals and plans the million-dollar robbery of an entire luxury apartment house on NYC's upper east side. Of course, he's unaware that a hoard of law men from federal, state, and local agencies are recording their activities for a wide variety of reasons, though none of the surveillance is coordinated and it has nothing to do with the planned robbery. Based on the novel by Lawrence Sanders, the intricate caper is effectively shaped by Lumet, who skillfully integrates broad satire with suspense. Score by Quincy Jones and shot on location in New York City. Walken is The Kid, his first major role.
1971 (PG) 100m/C Sean Connery, Dyan Cannon, Martin Balsam, Christopher Walken, Alan King, Ralph Meeker, Garrett Morris, Margaret Hamilton; *D:* Sidney Lumet. **VHS, Beta, LV $9.95** GKK, COL ♫♫♫

The Andersonville Trial Details the atrocities experienced by captured Union soldiers who were held in the Confederacy's notorious Andersonville prison during the American Civil War. Provides an interesting account of the war-crimes trial of the Georgia camp's officials, under whom more than 14,000 prisoners died. Moving, remarkable television drama based on the Pulitzer-honored book by MacKinlay Kantor.
1970 150m/C Martin Sheen, William Shatner, Buddy Ebsen, Jack Cassidy, Richard Basehart, Cameron Mitchell; *D:* George C. Scott. **VHS, Beta, LV $59.95** LIV ♫♫♫ ½

Andrei Rublev A 15th-century Russian icon painter must decide whether to record history or participate in it as Tartar invaders make life miserable. During the black and white portion, he becomes involved in a peasant uprising, killing a man in the process. After a bout of pessimism and a vow of silence, he goes forth to create artistic beauty as the screen correspondingly blazes

with color. A brilliant historical drama censored by Soviet authorities until 1971, it was co-written by acclaimed director Tarkovsky and Mikhalkov-Kontchalovsky.
1966 185m/C *RU* Anatoli Solonitzin, Ivan Lapikov, Nikolai Grinko, Nikolai Sergueiev; *W/D:* Andrei Tarkovsky; *W:* Andrej Mikhalkov-Kontchalovsky. VHS $59.99 *TAM, NOS, FCT* ⅛⅛⅛⅛

Androcles and the Lion Stagebound Hollywood version of the George Bernard Shaw story about a tailor in Imperial Rome who saves Christians from a hungry lion he had previously befriended. Sharp dialogue and a plot that's relatively (within the bounds of Hollywood) faithful help a great play become a semi-satisfying cinematic morsel. Harpo Marx was originally cast as Androcles, but was fired by producer Howard Hughes five weeks into the shooting.
1952 105m/B Jean Simmons, Alan Young, Victor Mature, Robert Newton, Maurice Evans; *D:* Chester Erskine. VHS, Beta $19.95 *COL, SUE* ⅛⅛½

Android When an android who has been assisting a quirky scientist in space learns that he is about to be permanently retired, he starts to take matters into his own synthetic hands. Combines science fiction, suspense and cloned romance. A must for Kinski fans.
1982 (PG) 80m/C Klaus Kinski, Don Opper, Brie Howard; *D:* Aaron Lipstadt. VHS, Beta, LV $69.95 *MED* ⅛⅛½

The Andromeda Strain A satellite falls back to earth carrying a deadly bacteria that must be identified in time to save the population from extermination. The tension inherent in the bestselling Michael Crichton novel is talked down by a boring cast. Also available in letter-box format.
1971 (G) 131m/C Arthur Hill, David Wayne, James Olson, Kate Reid, Paula Kelly; *D:* Robert Wise. VHS, Beta, LV $59.95 *MCA* ⅛⅛⅛

Andy and the Airwave Rangers Andy is whisked into the TV!! He finds adventure and excitement—car chases, intergalactic battles, and cartoons. *AKA:* Andy Colby's Incredibly Awesome Adventure.
1989 75m/C Dianne Kay, Vince Edwards, Bo Svenson, Richard Thomas, Erik Estrada; *D:* Deborah Brock. VHS, LV $79.95 *COL* ⅛⅛

Andy Griffith Show Life in Mayberry with smalltown sheriff Andy (Griffith), inept deputy Barney Fife (Knotts), Andy's son Opie (Howard), Aunt Bee (Bavier) and all the other townsfolk in the first of the rural comedy series. Two episodes: "Barney's Sidecar" and "The Darlings Are Coming." Additional episodes are available.
1960 52m/B Andy Griffith, Don Knotts, Ron Howard, Jim Nabors, Francis Bavier, George Lindsey, Howard McNear, Hal Smith, Howard Morris. VHS, Beta *MOV* ⅛⅛

Andy Hardy Gets Spring Fever Andy falls for a beautiful acting teacher, and then goes into a funk when he finds she's engaged. Judge Hardy and the gang help heal the big wound in his heart. A lesser entry (and the seventh) from the popular series.
1939 88m/B Mickey Rooney, Lewis Stone, Ann Rutherford, Fay Holden, Cecilia Parker, Sara Haden, Helen Gilbert; *D:* Woodbridge S. Van Dyke. VHS, Beta $19.95 *MGM* ⅛⅛

Andy Hardy Meets Debutante Seems like there should be an article in that title. Garland's second entry in series, wherein Andy meets and falls foolishly for glamorous debutante Lewis with Betsy's help while family is on visit to New York. Judy/Betsy sings "I'm Nobody's Baby" and "Singing in Rain." Also available with "Love Finds Andy Hardy" on laser disc.

1940 86m/B Mickey Rooney, Judy Garland, Lewis Stone, Ann Rutherford, Fay Holden, Sara Haden, Cecilia Parker, Diana Lewis, Tom Neal; *D:* George B. Seitz. VHS, Beta, LV $19.95 *MGM* ⅛⅛½

Andy Hardy's Double Life In this entertaining installment from the Andy Hardy series, Andy proposes marriage to two girls at the same time and gets in quite a pickle when they both accept. Williams makes an early screen splash.
1942 91m/B Mickey Rooney, Lewis Stone, Ann Rutherford, Fay Holden, Sara Haden, Cecilia Parker, Esther Williams, William Lundigan, Susan Peters, Robert (Bobby) Blake; *D:* George B. Seitz. VHS, Beta $19.95 *MGM, MLB* ⅛⅛½

Andy Hardy's Private Secretary After Andy fails his high school finals he gets help from a sympathetic faculty member. As the secretary, Grayson makes a good first impression in one of her early screen appearances. The Hardy series was often used as a training ground for new MGM talent.
1941 101m/b Mickey Rooney, Kathryn Grayson, Lewis Stone, Fay Holden, Ian Hunter, Gene Reynolds, Sara Haden; *D:* George B. Seitz. VHS, Beta $19.95 *MGM* ⅛⅛

Andy Warhol's Bad In the John Waters' school of "crime is beauty," a Queens housewife struggles to make appointments for both her home electrolysis clinic and her all-female murder-for-hire operation, which specializes in children and pets (who are thrown out of windows and knived, respectively). Her life is further complicated by a boarder (King) who's awaiting the go-ahead for his own assignment, an autistic child unwanted by his mother. One of Warhol's more professional-appearing films, and very funny if your tastes run to the tasteless.
1977 (R) 100m/C Perry King, Carroll Baker, Susan Tyrrell, Stefania Cassini; *D:* Jed Johnson. VHS, Beta, LV $59.95 *SUE, MLB* ⅛⅛⅛

Andy Warhol's Dracula Sex and camp humor, as well as a large dose of blood, highlight Warhol's treatment of the tale. As Dracula can only subsist on the blood of pure, untouched maidens ("weregins"), gardener Dallesandro rises to the occasion in order to make as many women as he can ineligible for Drac's purposes. Very reminiscent of Warhol's "Frankenstein," but with a bit more spoofery. Look for Roman Polanski in a cameo peek as a pub patron. *AKA:* Blood for Dracula; Young Dracula.
1974 (R) 106m/C *IT FR* Udo Kier, Arno Juergling, Maxine McKendry, Joe Dallesandro, Vittorio De Sica; *Cameos:* Roman Polanski; *D:* Paul Morrissey. VHS, Beta $79.95 *TRI, GEM, TAM* ⅛⅛⅛

Andy Warhol's Frankenstein A most outrageous parody of Frankenstein, featuring plenty of gore, sex, and bad taste in general. Baron von Frankenstein (Kier) derives sexual satisfaction from his corpses (he delivers a particularly thought-provoking philosphy on life as he lustfully fondles a gall bladder); his wife seeks her pleasure from the monster himself (Dallesandro). Originally made in 3-D, this is one of Warhol's campiest outings. *AKA:* Flesh for Frankenstein.
1974 (R) 95m/C *GE FR IT* Udo Kier, Dalia di Lazzaro, Monique Van Vooren, Joe Dallesandro; *D:* Paul Morrissey. VHS, Beta $79.95 *TRI, MLB* ⅛⅛½

Angel Low-budget leerer about a 15-year-old honor student who attends an expensive Los Angeles private school during the day and by night becomes Angel, a streetwise prostitute making a living amid the slime and sleaze of Hollywood Boulevard. But wait, all

is not perfect. A psycho is following her, looking for an opportunity.
1984 (R) 94m/C Donna Wilkes, Cliff Gorman, Susan Tyrrell, Dick Shawn, Rory Calhoun, John Diehl, Elaine Giftos, Ross Hagen; *D:* Robert Vincent O'Neil. VHS, Beta $19.95 *STE, HBO* ⅛½

Angel 3: The Final Chapter Former hooker Angel hits the streets to save her newly discovered sister from a life of prostitution. Trashy sequel with a better cast to tepid "Avenging Angel," which was the inept 1985 follow-up to 1984's tasteless "Angel."
1988 (R) 100m/C Maud Adams, Mitzi Kapture, Richard Roundtree, Mark Blankfield, Kin Shriner, Tawny Fere, Toni Basil; *D:* Tom De Simone. VHS, Beta, LV $19.95 *STE, NWV, IME* Woof!

Angel and the Badman When notorious gunslinger Wayne is wounded during a shoot-out, a pacifist family takes him in and nurses him back to health. While he's recuperating, the daughter in the family (Russell) falls for him. She begs him not to return to his previous life. But Wayne, though smitten, thinks that a Duke's gotta do what a Duke's gotta do. And that means finding the dirty outlaw (Cabot) who killed his pa. Predictable but nicely done, with a good cast and script. Wayne provides one of his better performances (and also produced).
1947 100m/B John Wayne, Gail Russell, Irene Rich, Harry Carey Sr., Bruce Cabot; *W/D:* James Edward Grant. VHS, LV $19.98 *REP, NEG, MRV* ⅛⅛⅛

An Angel at My Table New Zealand television mini-series chronicling the life of Janet Frame, New Zealand's premiere writer/poet. At once whimsical and tragic, the film tells of how a mischievous, free-spirited young girl was wrongly placed in a mental institution for eight years, yet was ultimately able to cultivate her incredible storytelling gifts, achieving success, fame and happiness. Adapted from three of Frame's novels: "To the Is-land," "An Angel at My Table," and "The Envoy From Mirror City." Highly acclaimed the world over, winner of over 20 major international awards.
1989 (R) 157m/C *NZ* Kerry Fox, Alexia Keogh, Karen Fergusson, Iris Churn, K.J. Wilson, Martyn Sanderson; *D:* Jane Campion; *W:* Laura Jones. VHS $19.95 *COL, TAM, NLC* ⅛⅛⅛⅛

Angel Baby A mute girl struggles to redefine her faith when she is cured by preacher, but then sees him fail with others. Fine performances all around, notably Reynolds in his screen debut, with cinematography by Haskell Wexler. Adapted from "Jenny Angel" by Elsie Oaks Barber.
1961 97m/B George Hamilton, Salome Jens, Mercedes McCambridge, Joan Blondell, Henry Jones, Burt Reynolds; *D:* Paul Wendkos, Hubert Cornfield. VHS *NO* ⅛⅛½

Angel City A Florida labor camp is the setting for this made-for-TV drama. A family of rural West Virginia migrant workers find themselves trapped inside the camp and exploited by the boss-man. Adapted from Patricia Smith's book by scriptwriter James Lee Barrett.
1980 90m/C Ralph Waite, Paul Winfield, Jennifer Warren, Jennifer Jason Leigh, Mitchell Ryan; *D:* Philip Leacock. VHS $59.95 *XVC* ⅛⅛½

Angel City An experimental parody of film mysteries where a detective investigates the nature of visual truth in and about Hollywood.
1984 75m/C Bob Glaudini; *D:* Jon Jost. VHS, Beta *FCT* ⅛⅛

An Angel for Satan Steele plays a dual role in her last major, Italian horror film. She gives a strong performance as a woman obsessed by the spirit of a statue. In Italian with no subtitles.
1966 ?m/C *IT* Barbara Steele, Anthony Steffen. VHS $16.95 SNC *1/2*

Angel Heart An exotic and controversial look at murder, voodoo cults, and sex in 1955 New Orleans that enabled Bonet to defiantly shed her image as a young innocent (no more Cosby Show for you, young lady). Rourke is marginal NYC private eye Angel, hired by the devilish DeNiro to track a missing big band singer who violated a "contract." His investigation leads him to the bizarre world of the occult in New Orleans, where the blood drips to a different beat. Visually stimulating, with a provocative sex scene between Bonet and Rourke, captured in both R-rated and unrated versions. Adapted by Parker from "Falling Angel" by William Hjortsberg.
1987 (R) 112m/C Mickey Rourke, Robert De Niro, Lisa Bonet, Charlotte Rampling; *W/D:* Alan Parker. VHS, Beta, LV $14.95 LIV, FCT *11/2*

Angel in a Taxi A six-year-old boy in an orphanage decides to choose his own mother, a beautiful ballerina he sees in a magazine, when an ugly couple try to adopt him. Italian film dubbed in English.
1959 89m/B *IT* Wera Cecova, Ettore Manni, Vittorio De Sica, Marietto, Gabriel Ferzetti. VHS, Beta, 8mm $29.95 VYY, FCT *11*

Angel of Death A small mercenary band of Nazi hunters attempt to track down Josef Mengele in South America. Stupid entry in the minor "let's find the darn Nazi before he really causes trouble" genre. Director Franco is also known as A. Frank Drew White.
1986 (R) 92m/C Chris Mitchum, Fernando Rey, Susan Andrews; *D:* Jess (Jesus) Franco. VHS, Beta $19.95 STE, NWV Woof!

Angel of H.E.A.T. Porn-star Chambers is Angel, a female super-agent on a mission to save the world from total destruction. Sex and spies abound with trashy nonchalance.
AKA: The Protectors, Book One.
1982 (R) 90m/C Marilyn Chambers, Mary Woronov, Steve Johnson; *D:* Helen Sanford, Myrl A. Schreibman. VHS, Beta, LV $69.95 VES Woof!

Angel on My Shoulder A murdered convict makes a deal with the Devil (Rains) and returns to earth for revenge as a respected judge who's been thinning Hell's waiting list. Occupying the good judge, the murderous Muni has significant problems adjusting. Amusing fantasy with Muni in a rare and successful comic role. Co-written by Harry Segall, who scripted "Here Comes Mr. Jordan," in which Rains played an angel. Remade in 1980.
1946 101m/B Paul Muni, Claude Rains, Anne Baxter, Onslow Stevens; *D:* Archie Mayo. VHS, Beta, 3/4U, Special order formats $9.95 NEG, MRV, NOS *111*

Angel on My Shoulder A small-time hood wrongfully executed for murder comes back as district attorney. He owes the devil, but he's finding it tough to be evil enough to repay his debt. Okay television remake of the better 1946 film starring Paul Muni.
1980 96m/C Peter Strauss, Richard Kiley, Barbara Hershey, Janice Paige; *D:* John Berry. VHS, Beta $69.98 SUE *11*

Angel Square A Canadian production from the director of the acclaimed "Bye Bye Blues." When the father of a neighborhood boy is brutally attacked, the community bands together to search for the culprit.
1992 106m/C *CA* Ned Beatty; *D:* Anne Wheeler. VHS CGV *11*

Angel Town A foreign exchange student, who happens to be a champion kick-boxer, is forced into combat with LA street gangs.
1989 (R) 90m/C Olivier Gruner, Theresa Saldana, Frank Aragon, Tony Valentino, Peter Kwong, Mike Moroff; *D:* Eric Karson. VHS, Beta $89.95 IMP *1*

Angel with the Trumpet Depressing character study of a woman who marries to please her family, rather than herself. When the Gestapo finds out about her Jewish ancestry, she must make the most important decision of her life.
1950 98m/B *GB* Eileen Herlie, Basil Sydney, Norman Wooland, Maria Schell, Olga Edwards, Oskar Werner, Anthony Bushell, Wilfrid Hyde-White; *D:* Anthony Bushell. VHS $24.95 NOS, TIM *11*

Angela Twisted love story about a young man (Railsback) who jumps the bones of an older woman, unaware that she is the mother he's been separated from for 23 long years. Seems that way back when, the boy was kidnapped by crime boss Huston from mom Loren, an ex-prostitute, who then turned in the boy's dad, who was something of a criminal. Mom thought son was dead, dad vowed revenge from prison, and son went about his unwitting business. It all comes together insipidly, at the expense of the cast and viewer.
1977 91m/C *CA* Sophia Loren, Steve Railsback, John Huston, John Vernon; *D:* Boris Sagal. VHS, Beta $69.98 SUE, SIM *1*

Angele A lovely, naive country girl is lured to the city by a cunning pimp who knows that she wants to escape her oppressive father. With her illegitimate baby, she's discovered in a whorehouse and taken in disgrace back home to dad, who promptly locks her in the barn. One special guy, however, appreciates her purity and plots to rescue her. What he lacks in material resources he makes up for in character. An overlong but moving story of lost innocence and intolerence. In French with English subtitles. Based on the novel "Un de Baumugnes" by Jean Giono.
1934 130m/B *FR* Orane Demazis, Fernandel, Henri Puopon, Edouard Delmont; *D:* Marcel Pagnol. VHS $59.95 INT, TAM *111*

Angelo My Love Compassionate docudrama about New York's modern gypsy community. Follows the adventures of 12-year-old Angelo Evans, the streetwise son of a fortune teller, who, with a fresh view, explores the ups and downs of his family's life. Duvall financed the effort and cast nonprofessional actors in this charming tale of reality and fairy-tale.
1983 (R) 91m/C Angelo Evans, Michael Evans, Steve "Patalay" Tsiginoff, Cathy Kitchen, Millie Tsiginoff; *D:* Robert Duvall; *M:* John Williams. VHS, Beta, LV $59.95 COL *111*

Angel's Brigade Seven models get together to stop a big drug operation. Drive-in vigilante movie fare fit for a rainy night.
1979 (PG) 97m/C Jack Palance, Peter Lawford, Jim Backus, Arthur Godfrey; *D:* Greydon Clark. VHS, Beta $19.98 *11*

Angels Die Hard Novel biker story with the cyclists as the good guys intent on helping a town during a mining disaster. Grizzly Adams makes an early film appearance.

1984 (R) 86m/C Tom Baker, R.G. Armstrong, Dan Haggerty, William Smith; *D:* Richard Compton. VHS, Beta, LV $19.95 STE, NWV *11*

Angels from Hell Early application in the nutso 'Nam returnee genre. Disillusioned Vietnam veteran forms a massive biker gang for the sole purpose of wreaking havoc upon the Man, the Establishment and anyone else responsible for sending him off to war. The big gang invades a town, with predictably bloody results. Sort of a follow-up to "Hell's Angels on Wheels."
1968 86m/C Tom Stern, Arlene Martel, Ted Markland, Stephen Oliver, Paul Bertoya, James Murphy, Jack Starrett, Pepper Martin, Luana Talltree; *D:* Bruce Kessler. VHS NO *1*

Angels Hard as They Come Opposing Hell's Angels leaders clash in a hippie-populated ghost town. A semi-satiric spoof of the biker genre's cliches co-written and produced by Demme. Features an early Glenn appearance and Busey's film debut.
1971 (R) 86m/C Gary Busey, Scott Glenn, James Inglehart, Gary Littlejohn, Sharon Peckinpah; *D:* Joe Viola; *W:* Jonathan Demme. VHS, Beta $24.98 SUE *11*

Angels of the City What's a girl got to do to join a sorority? A house prank turns vicious when two coeds take a walk on the wild side and accidentally observe a murder, making them the next targets. Credible exploitation effort, if that's not an oxymoron.
1989 90m/C Lawrence Hilton-Jacobs, Cynthia Cheston, Kelly Galindo, Sandy Gershman; *D:* Lawrence Hilton-Jacobs. VHS, Beta $29.95 PMH *11*

Angels One Five A worm's-eye view of British air power in WWII. There little "excitement" there is, is generated by flashing lights, plotting maps and status boards. Hawkins and Denison are the only bright spots.
1954 97m/B Jack Hawkins, Michael Denison, Dulcie Gray, John Gregson, Cyril Raymond, Veronica Hurst, Harold Goodwin, Geoffrey Keen, Vida Hope. VHS $19.95 NOS *11*

Angels Over Broadway Slick, fast-paced black comedy about con man Fairbanks, who plans to hustle suicidal thief Qualen during a poker game, but has a change of heart. With the help of call-girl Hayworth and drunken playwright Mitchell, he helps Qualen turn his life around. Ahead of its time with an offbeat morality, but a delight in the '90s.
1940 80m/B Douglas Fairbanks Jr., Rita Hayworth, Thomas Mitchell, John Qualen, George Watts; *D:* Ben Hecht, Lee Garmes. VHS, Beta, LV $19.95 RCA, FCT, COL *111*

Angels' Wild Women From the man who brought you "Dracula vs. Frankenstein" comes an amalgamation of hippies, motorcycle dudes, evil desert gurus and precious little plot.
1972 85m/C Kent Taylor, Regina Carrol, Ross Hagen, Maggie Bemby, Vicki Volante; *D:* Al Adamson. VHS VID Woof!

Angels with Dirty Faces Rousing classic with memorable Cagney twitches and the famous long walk from the cell to the chair. Two young hoodlums grow up on NYC's lower East Side with diverse results—one enters the priesthood and the other opts for crime and prison. Upon release from the pen, Cagney sets up shop in the old neighborhood, where Father O'Brien tries to keep a group of young toughs (the Dead End Kids) from idolizing the famed gangster and following in his footsteps. Bogart's his unscrupulous lawyer and Bancroft a crime boss intent on double-crossing Cagney. Reportedly they were blasting real bullets during the big

shootout, no doubt helping Cagney's intensity. Score by Max Steiner and adapted by Wexley and Duff from a story by Rowland Brown.
1938 97m/B James Cagney, Pat O'Brien, Humphrey Bogart, Ann Sheridan, George Bancroft, Billy Halop, Leo Gorcey, Huntz Hall, Bobby Jordan, Dan Jesse, Gabriel Dell, J. Frank Burke, William Tracy, Bernard Punsley; **D:** Michael Curtiz; **W:** John Wexley, Warren Duff. VHS, Beta, LV $19.98 MGM, FOX, MLB 𝆕𝆕𝆕

AngKor: Cambodia Express An American journalist travels back to Vietnam to search for his long lost love.
1981 96m/C Robert Walker Jr., Christopher George; **D:** Lek Kitiparaporn. VHS, Beta $69.98 VES, LIV 𝆕

The Angry Dragon A martial arts guy seeks revenge on the underworld pimps for the murder of his girlfriend's father.
1979 (R) 96m/C VHS, Beta GEM 𝆕

Angry Harvest During the World War II German occupation of Poland, a gentile farmer shelters a young Jewish woman on the run, and a serious, ultimately interdependent relationship forms. Acclaimed; Holland's first film since her native Poland's martial law imposition made her an exile to Sweden. In German with English subtitles. Contains nudity and violence. **AKA:** Bittere Ernte.
1985 102m/C GE Armin Mueller-Stahl, Elisabeth Trissenaar, Wojciech Pszoniak; **D:** Agnieszka Holland. Academy Awards '85 Nominations: Best Foreign Language Film; Montreal World Film Festival '85: Best Actor (Mueller-Stahl). VHS, Beta $69.95 FCT, GLV, TAM 𝆕𝆕𝆕

Angry Joe Bass Contemporary Native American Joe Bass faces government officials who continually usurp his fishing rights. Something like "Billy Jack" without the intelligence.
1976 82m/C Henry Bal, Molly Mershon; **D:** Thomas G. Reeves. VHS, Beta PGN 𝆕

The Angry Red Planet An unintentionally amusing sci-fi adventure about astronauts on Mars fighting off aliens and giant, ship-swallowing amoebas. Filmed using bizarre "Cinemagic" process, which turns almost everything pink. Wild effects have earned the film cult status.
1959 83m/C Gerald Mohr, Les Tremayne, Jack Kruschen; **D:** Ib Melchoir. VHS, Beta $19.95 HBO 𝆕𝆕

Anguish Well-done horror thriller about a lunatic who, inspired to duplicate the actions of an eyeball-obsessed killer in a popular film, murders a movie audience as they watch the movie. Violence and gore abound.
1988 (R) 85m/C SP Zelda Rubenstein, Michael Lerner, Talia Paul; **D:** Bigas Luna. VHS, Beta, LV $79.98 FOX 𝆕𝆕½

Animal Behavior An animal researcher and a music professor fall in love on a college campus. Jenny Bowen's (the director's real name) comedy was filmed in 1985 and edited/shelved for over 4 years, with good reason.
1989 (PG) 79m/C Karen Allen, Armand Assante, Holly Hunter, Josh Mostel, Richard Libertini; **D:** Riley H. Anne. VHS, Beta, LV $89.99 HBO 𝆕

Animal Called Man Two crooked buddies join a big western gang in pillaging a small town and get in too deep.
1987 83m/C Vassilli Karis, Craig Hill. VHS, Beta $59.95 TWE 𝆕

Animal Crackers The second and possibly the funniest of the thirteen Marx Brothers films, "Animal Crackers" is a screen classic. Groucho is a guest at the house of wealthy matron Margaret Dumont and he, along with Zeppo, Chico, and Harpo, destroy

the tranquility of the estate. Complete with the Harry Ruby music score—including Groucho's "Hooray for Captain Spaulding" with more quotable lines than any other Marx Brothers film: "One morning I shot an elephant in my pajamas. How he got into my pajamas, I'll never know." Based on a play by George S. Kaufman.
1930 (G) 98m/B Groucho Marx, Chico Marx, Harpo Marx, Zeppo Marx, Lillian Roth, Margaret Dumont, Louis Sorin, Hal Thompson, Richard Greig; **D:** Victor Neerman; **W:** Morrie Ryskind. VHS, Beta, LV $19.95 MCA, FCT 𝆕𝆕𝆕

Animal Farm An animated version of George Orwell's classic political satire about a barnyard full of animals who parallel the growth of totalitarian dictatorships. Not entirely successful, but probably best translation of Orwell to film.
1955 73m/C **D:** John Halas, Joy Batchelor. VHS, Beta, LV, 8mm, 3/4U, Special order formats $29.98 KUI, VYY, VCN 𝆕𝆕𝆕

Animal Instincts A woman takes a prescription drug that makes her a nymphomaniac, and her police officer husband discovers that he's turned on by videotaping her in bed with other men and women. One of the many in her constant stream of lovers is a politician whose campaign is based on shutting down all the town's sex clubs. Another in the string of sexual thrillers riding on the coattails of "Basic Instinct."
1992 (R) 94m/C Maxwell Caulfield, Jan-Michael Vincent, Mitch Gaylord, Shannon Whirry, Delia Sheppard, John Saxon, David Carradine; **D:** Alexander Gregory Hippolyte. VHS $89.95 ACA 𝆕

The Animal Kingdom A romantic triangle develops when Howard, married to Loy, has an affair with Harding. The problem is Harding acts more like a wife and Loy a mistress. Intelligently written and directed, with a marvelous performance from veteran character actor Gargan. **AKA:** The Woman in His House.
1932 95m/B Ann Harding, Leslie Howard, Myrna Loy, Neil Hamilton, William Gargan, Henry Stephenson, Ilka Chase; **D:** Edward H. Griffith; **W:** Horace Jackson. VHS $29.95 RKO, FCT, HEG 𝆕𝆕

Animation Wonderland A collection of rarely seen cartoons including "The Early Birds," "The Tinder Box," "Petroushka," "The Chocolate Princess," "King Midas" and many others.
1990 62m/C VHS $9.95 SIM 𝆕𝆕𝆕

Animators from Allegro Non Troppo Live action is combined with Bruno Bozzetto's animation in this feature-length parody of Disney's Fantasia.
1979 70m/C VHS, Beta NO 𝆕𝆕𝆕

Anita, Dances of Vice German avant-garde film celebrates Anita Berber, the "most scandalous woman in 1920s Berlin." Berber was openly bisexual, used drugs, and danced nude in public. In von Praunheim's film, she rises from the dead and creates yet more scandal. **AKA:** Anita—Tanze des Lasters.
1987 85m/C GE Lotti Huber, Ina Blum, Mikhael Honesseau; **D:** Rosa von Praunheim. VHS, Beta, 3/4U $49.95 ICA, GLV, TAM 𝆕𝆕

Anita de Montemar A man is torn between his wife and his child-bearing girlfriend.
196? 127m/C MX Amparo Rivelles, Fernando Soler. VHS, Beta $59.95 UNI 𝆕

The Ann Jillian Story Jillian stars as herself in this television melodrama recounting her battle with breast cancer. Several musical numbers are included.

1988 96m/C Ann Jillian, Tony LoBianco, Viveca Lindfors, Leighton Bewley; **D:** Corey Allen. VHS, Beta NO 𝆕½

Ann Vickers A dashing young army captain wins over the heart of a dedicated social worker. Okay adaptation of a Sinclair Lewis novel, with Dunne suffering more than usual.
1933 76m/B Irene Dunne, Walter Huston, Bruce Cabot, Conrad Nagel, Edna May Oliver; **D:** John Cromwell. VHS, Beta $19.95 RKO, TTC 𝆕𝆕½

Anna Age, envy, and the theatrical world receive their due in an uneven but engrossing drama about aging Czech film star Anna, making a sad living in New York doing commercials and trying for off-Broadway roles. She takes in Krystyna, a young Czech peasant girl who eventually rockets to model stardom. Modern, strongly acted "All About Eve" with a story partially based on a real Polish actress. Kirkland drew quite a bit of flak for shamelessly self-promoting for the Oscar. She still lost.
1987 (PG-13) 101m/C Sally Kirkland, Paulina Porizkova, Robert Fields; **D:** Yurek Bogayevicz. Academy Awards '87 Nominations: Best Actress (Kirkland); Golden Globe Awards '88: Best Actress—Drama (Kirkland); Independent Spirit Awards '88: Best Actress (Kirkland). VHS, Beta, LV $79.98 VES, LIV 𝆕𝆕𝆕

Anna and Bella Two elderly sisters spend an afternoon pouring over the family photo album.
1986 8m/C VHS, Beta, 3/4U $150.00 DCL 𝆕𝆕𝆕

Anna Christie Garbo is the ex-prostitute who finds love with sailor Bickford. Bickford is unaware of his lover's tarnished past and she does her best to keep it that way. Garbo's first sound effort was advertised with the slogan "Garbo Talks." Adapted from the classic Eugene O'Neill play, the film is a slow but rewarding romantic drama.
1930 90m/B Greta Garbo, Marie Dressler, Charles Bickford, George F. Marion; **D:** Clarence Brown. VHS, Beta $19.98 MGM 𝆕𝆕½

Anna Karenina Cinomatic Tolstoy with Garbo as the sad, moody Anna willing to give up everything to be near Varonsky (March), the cavalry officer she's obsessed with. A classic Garbo vehicle with March and Rathbone providing excellent support. Interestingly, a remake of the Garbo and John Gilbert silent, "Love."
1935 85m/B Greta Garbo, Fredric March, Freddie Bartholomew, Maureen O'Sullivan, May Robson, Basil Rathbone, Reginald Owen, Reginald Denny; **D:** Clarence Brown. VHS, Beta $19.98 NOS, MGM, HEG 𝆕𝆕𝆕½

Anna Karenina Stiff version of Tolstoy's passionate story of illicit love between a married woman and a military officer. In spite of exquisite costumes, and Leigh and Richardson as leads, still tedious.
1948 123m/C GB Vivien Leigh, Ralph Richardson, Kieron Moore; **D:** Julien Duvivier. VHS, LV $39.95 GKK, FCT, MRV 𝆕𝆕½

Anna Karenina Made for television version of Tolstoy's novel of betrayal, intrigue, and forbidden love. Anna, defying all social practices of the time, falls into the arms of a dashing count. Features an excellent performance from Paul "A Man For All Seasons" Scofield.
1985 (PG) 96m/C Jacqueline Bisset, Christopher Reeve, Paul Scofield; **D:** Simon Langton. VHS, Beta, LV $89.95 VES 𝆕𝆕

Anna to the Infinite Power Sci fi based on the book of the same name follows a young girl with telepathic powers. When the girl discovers that she has sisters as the result of a strange scientific experiment, she

sets out to find them, drawing on her own inner strength.
1984 101m/C Dina Merrill, Martha Byrne, Mark Patton; *D:* Robert Wiemer. **VHS, Beta** $59.95 COL 🎞🎞½

Annabel Takes a Tour/Maid's Night Out
A delightful comedy double feature. In "Annabel Takes a Tour," a fading movie star falls in love with a writer while on a tour to boost her career, and in "Maids Night Out," an heiress and a millionaire fall in love.
1938 131m/B Lucille Ball, Jack Oakie, Ruth Donnelly, Joan Fontaine, Allan "Rocky" Lane, Hedda Hopper; *D:* Lew Landers. **VHS, Beta** $34.95 RKO, MLB, TTC 🎞🎞½

Annapolis
Life's in the pink for two guys at the U.S. naval academy until jealousy rears its loathsome head when they fall for the same gal. Just when it's beginning to look like love and honor is an either-or proposition, the lovelorn rivals find that although love transcends all, a guy's gotta do what a guy's gotta do, even if it means sticking up for his romantic nemesis. Lots of sub-par male bonding.
1928 63m/B Johnny Mack Brown, Hugh Allan, Hobart Bosworth, William Bakewell, Charlotte Walker, Jeanette Loff; *D:* Christy Cabanne. **VHS, Beta** $19.95 GPV, FCT 🎞

The Annapolis Story
Cliche-ridden WWII drama about two naval cadets romancing the same lucky girl. Low-rent time for director Siegel which wastes a decent cast. *AKA:* Blue and the Gold.
1955 81m/C John Derek, Kevin McCarthy, Diana Lynn, Pat Dooley, L.Q. Jones; *D:* Don Siegel. **VHS, Beta** $19.98 FOX 🎞½

Anne of Avonlea
Equally excellent mini-series sequel to "Anne of Green Gables" in which the romantic heroine grows up and discovers romance. Two tapes lavishly filmed on picturesque Prince Edward Island. Based on the characters from L.M. Montgomery's classic novels "Anne of Avonlea," "Anne of the Island," and "Anne of Windy Poplars." CBC, PBS, and Disney worked together on this "Wonderworks" production. *AKA:* Anne of Green Gables: The Sequel.
1987 224m/C *CA* Megan Follows, Colleen Dewhurst, Wendy Hiller, Frank Converse, Patricia Hamilton, Schuyler Grant, Jonathan Crombie, Rosemary Dunsmore; *W/D:* Kevin Sullivan; *M:* Hagood Hardy. **VHS, Beta, LV** $29.95 KUI, BVV, DIS 🎞🎞½

Anne of Green Gables
A lonely Canadian couple adopts an orphan who keeps them on their toes with her animated imagination, and wins a permanent place in their hearts. Warm (but loose) adaptation of Lucy Maud Montgomery's popular novel is entertaining although 1985 remake is far superior. Followed by "Anne of Windy Poplars."
1934 79m/B Anne Shirley, Tom Brown, O.P. Heggie; *D:* George Nichols. **VHS, Beta** $19.98 RKO, TTC 🎞🎞

Anne of Green Gables
Splendid production of the famous Lucy Maud Montgomery classic about a young orphan girl growing to young adulthood with the help of a crusty brother and sister duo. The characters come to life under Sullivan's direction, and the movie is enhanced by the beautiful Prince Edward Island scenery and wonderful costumes. One of the few instances where an adaptation lives up to (if not exceeds) the quality of the original novel. A WonderWorks presentation that was made with the cooperation of the Disney channel, CBC, and PBS. Followed by "Anne of Avonlea." On two tapes.

1985 197m/C *CA* Megan Follows, Colleen Dewhurst, Richard Farnsworth, Patricia Hamilton, Schuyler Grant, Jonathan Crombie, Marilyn Lightstone, Charmion King, Rosemary Radcliffe, Jackie Burroughs; *W/D:* Kevin Sullivan; *W:* Joe Weisenfeld; *M:* Hagood Hardy. **VHS, Beta, LV** $29.95 KUI, BVV, IGP 🎞🎞½

Anne of the Thousand Days
Lavish re-telling of the life and loves of Henry the VIII. Henry tosses aside his current wife for the young and devastatingly beautiful Anne Boleyn. Burton's performance of the amoral king garnered him an Oscar nomination. Watch for Elizabeth Taylor as a masked courtesan at the costume ball.
1969 (PG) 145m/C Richard Burton, Genevieve Bujold, Irene Papas, Anthony Quayle, John Colicos, Michael Hordern; *D:* Hal B. Wallis. Academy Awards '69: Best Costume Design; Nominations: Best Actor (Burton), Best Actress (Bujold), Best Adapted Screenplay, Best Art Direction/Set Decoration, Best Cinematography, Best Picture, Best Sound, Best Supporting Actor (Quayle), Best Original Score; Directors Guild of America Awards '70: Best Director (Jarrott); Golden Globe Awards '70: Best Actress—Drama (Bujold), Best Film—Drama. **VHS** $59.95 MCA 🎞🎞🎞½

Annie
Stagy big-budget adaption of the Broadway musical, which was an adaptation of the comic strip. A major financial disaster upon release, still it's an entertaining enterprise curiously directed by Huston and engagingly acted by Finney and Quinn. ♫Tomorrow; It's the Hard Knock Life; Maybe; I Think I'm Gonna Like It Here; Little Girls; We Got Annie; Let's Go to the Movies; You're Never Fully Dressed Without a Smile; Easy Street; I Don't Need Anything But You.
1982 (PG) 128m/C Aileen Quinn, Carol Burnett, Albert Finney, Bernadette Peters, Ann Reinking, Tim Curry; *D:* John Huston. **VHS, Beta, LV, 8mm** $19.95 COL, FCT, MLT 🎞🎞

Annie Hall
Planned originally to be based strictly on Allen's life, but expanded upon at the advice of editor Rosenblum, this is the acclaimed coming-of-cinematic-age film for Allen. His love affair with Hall/Keaton is chronicled as an episodic, wistful comedy commenting on family, love, loneliness, communicating, maturity, driving, city life, careers, and various other topics. Abounds with classic scenes, including Goldblum at his mantra at a cocktail party; Allen and the lobster pot; and Allen, Keaton, a bathroom, a baseball bat, and a spider. The film operates on many levels, as does Keaton's wardrobe, which started a major fashion trend. Bit parts to look for include Weaver as Woody's date. Expertly shot by Gordon Willis and cowritten by Brickman.
1977 (PG) 94m/C Woody Allen, Diane Keaton, Tony Roberts, Paul Simon, Shelley Duvall, Carol Kane, Colleen Dewhurst, Christopher Walken, Janet Margolin, John Glover, Jeff Goldblum, Sigourney Weaver, Marshall McLuhan, Beverly D'Angelo, Shelley Hack; *W/D:* Woody Allen; *W:* Marshall Brickman. Academy Awards '77: Best Actress (Keaton), Best Director (Allen), Best Original Screenplay, Best Picture; Nominations: Best Actor (Allen); British Academy Awards '77: Best Actress (Keaton), Best Director (Allen), Best Film; Directors Guild of America Awards '77: Best Director (Allen); Golden Globe Awards '78: Best Actress—Musical/Comedy (Keaton); National Board of Review Awards '77: 10 Best Films of the Year, Best Actress (Keaton); National Society of Film Critics Awards '77: Best Actress (Keaton), Best Film. **VHS, Beta, LV** $19.98 MGM, FOX, VYG 🎞🎞🎞

Annie Oakley
Energetic biographical drama based on the life and legend of sharpshooter Annie Oakley and her on-off relationship with Wild Bill Hickok. Stanwyck

makes a great Oakley. Later musicalized as "Annie Get Your Gun."
1935 90m/B Barbara Stanwyck, Preston Foster, Melvyn Douglas, Pert Kelton, Andy Clyde; *D:* George Stevens. **VHS, Beta** $19.98 RKO, MED, NOS 🎞🎞🎞

Annie Oakley
This biography of the acclaimed shooting star covers her career from age 15 to retirement, including some actual silent footage of Miss Oakley filmed by Thomas Edison in 1923. Made for television. From the "Tall Tales & Legends" series by Shelly Duvall.
1985 52m/C Jamie Lee Curtis, Cliff DeYoung, Brian Dennehy; *D:* Michael Lindsay-Hogg. **VHS, Beta** $19.98 FOX 🎞🎞🎞

The Annihilators
A group of Vietnam vets band together in an extremely violent manner to protect their small town from a gang of thugs.
1985 (R) 87m/C Gerrit Graham, Lawrence Hilton-Jacobs, Paul Koslo, Christopher Stone, Andy Wood, Sid Conrad, Dennis Redfield; *D:* Charles E. Sellier. **VHS, Beta** $9.95 NWV, STE Woof!

Another Chance
Girl-crazy bachelor is returned from heaven for a second chance and has to choose between a "bad" girl and a "good" girl. What a choice!
1988 (R) 99m/C Bruce Greenwood, Frank Annese, Jeff East, Anne Ramsey, Barbara Edwards; *D:* Jerry Vint. **VHS, LV** $9.98 REP, PIA 🎞🎞

Another Country
Julian Mitchell's adaptation of his play about the true story of two English boarding school friends who wind up as spies for the Soviet Union. Based on the lives of Guy Burgess and Donald MacLean, whose youth is rather fancifully depicted in this loving recreation of 1930s English life. Although the film is inferior to the award-winning play, director Kanievska manages to transform a piece into a solid film, and Rupert Everett's performance as Guy Burgess is outstanding.
1984 90m/C *GB* Rupert Everett, Colin Firth, Michael Jenn, Robert Addie, Anna Massey, Betsy Brantley, Rupert Wainwright, Cary Elwes; *D:* Marek Kanievska. **VHS, Beta, LV** $24.98 SUE 🎞🎞½

Another 48 Hrs.
Continuing chemistry between Nolte and Murphy is one of the few worthwhile items in this stodgy rehash. Any innovation by Murphy seems lost, the story is redundant of any other cop thriller, and violence and car chases abound. Pointlessly energetic and occasionally fun for only the true devotee.
1990 (R) 98m/C Eddie Murphy, Nick Nolte, Brion James, Kevin Tighe, Bernie Casey, David Anthony Marshall, Ed O'Ross; *D:* Walter Hill. **VHS, Beta, LV, 8mm** $14.95 PAR 🎞½

Another Man, Another Chance
Remake of Lelouch's "A Man and a Woman," set in the turn-of-the-century American West, pales by comparison to the original. Slow-moving tale casts widow Bujold and widower Caan as lovers. *AKA:* Un Autre Homme, Une Autre Chance.
1977 (PG) 132m/C *FR* James Caan, Genevieve Bujold, Francis Huster, Jennifer Warren, Susan Tyrrell; *D:* Claude Lelouch. **VHS, Beta** NO 🎞🎞

Another Pair of Aces: Three of a Kind
Nelson and Kristofferson team up to clear the name of Taylor, a Texas Ranger accused of murder. Made for television; some scenes deemed too racy for TV were added to the video version. Sequel to "A Pair of Aces."
1991 93m/C Willie Nelson, Kris Kristofferson, Joan Severance, Rip Torn, Dan Kamin, Ken Farmer; *D:* Bill Bixby. **VHS** $89.95 VMK 🎞🎞🎞

Another Stakeout:
See Stakeout 2

Another Thin Man Powell and Loy team up for the third in the delightful "Thin Man" series. Slightly weaker series entry takes its time, but has both Powell and Loy providing stylish performances. Nick Jr. is also introduced as the newest member of the sleuthing team. Sequel to "After the Thin Man;" followed by "Shadow of the Thin Man."
1939 105m/B William Powell, Myrna Loy, Virginia Grey, Otto Kruger, C. Aubrey Smith, Ruth Hussey; *D:* Woodbridge S. Van Dyke. VHS $24.95 *MGM* ♫♫½

Another Time, Another Place Sappy melodrama about an American journalist who suffers an emotional meltdown when her married British lover is killed during WWII. So she heads for Cornwall to console the widow and family.
1958 98m/B *GB* Lana Turner, Barry Sullivan, Glynis Johns, Sean Connery, Terrence Langdon; *D:* Lewis Allen. VHS, Beta $19.95 *KRT, PAR* ♫♫

Another Time, Another Place Bored young Scottish housewife married to an older fella falls in love with an Italian prisoner-of-war who works on her farm during WWII. Occasionally quirky, always finely crafted view of wartime Britain and the little-known life of POWs in England.
1983 (R) 101m/C *GB* Phyllis Logan, Giovanni Mauriello, Gian Luca Favilla, Paul Young, Tom Watson; *D:* Michael Radford. VHS, Beta, LV $24.98 *SUE* ♫♫♫

Another Way The director of 1971's much-lauded "Love" sets this politically charged love story in Hungary in 1958. Opening with a view of a female corpse, the story flashes backward to look at the woman's journalistic career and her relationship with a women colleague. Candid love scenes between women in Hungary of 1958, considered a cinematic novelty in many places outside Hungary. In Hungarian with English subtitles. *AKA:* Olelkezo Tokintetek.
1982 100m/C *HU* Jadwiga Jankowska Cieslak, Grazyna Szapolowska, Josef Kroner, Hernadi Judit, Andorai Peter; *D:* Karoly Makk. VHS, Beta $59.95 *EVD, FCT, TAM* ♫♫♫

Another Woman The study of an intellectual woman whose life is changed when she begins to eavesdrop. What she hears provokes her to examine every relationship in her life, finding things quite different than she had believed. Heavy going, with Rowlands effective as a woman coping with an entirely new vision of herself. Farrow plays the catalyst. Although Allen's comedies are more popular than his dramas, this one deserves a look.
1988 (PG) 81m/C Gena Rowlands, Gene Hackman, Mia Farrow, Ian Holm, Betty Buckley, Martha Plimpton, Blythe Danner, Harris Yulin, Sandy Dennis, David Ogden Stiers, John Houseman; *D:* Woody Allen. VHS, Beta, LV $89.98 *ORI* ♫♫♫

Another You Con man Wilder takes pathological liar Pryor under his care and decides to use his talents to his fullest advantage. Posing as successful businessmen, the duo initiate a scam so complicated that they may end up being double-crossed or worse yet, dead! Can the pair see their plan through without losing their lives? Sad to see how far these two gifted comedians have fallen. Their collaboration is tired and the movie generally dreadful.
1991 (R) 98m/C Richard Pryor, Gene Wilder, Mercedes Ruehl, Vanessa Williams, Stephen Lang; *D:* Maurice Phillips. VHS, LV, 8mm $19.95 *COL* ♫

Antarctica Due to unfortunate circumstances, a group of scientists must leave their pack of huskies behind on a frozen glacier in the Antarctic. The film focuses on the dogs' subsequent struggle for survival. Dubbed. Music by Vangelis.
1984 112m/C *JP* Ken Takakura, Masako Natsume, Keiko Oginome; *D:* Koreyoshi Kurahara. VHS, Beta $59.98 *FOX* ♫♫

Anthony Adverse March is a young man in the 19th century who searches for manhood across America and Mexico. He grows slowly as he battles foes, struggles against adversity and returns home to find his lover in this romantic swashbuckler. A star-studded cast, lush costuming, and an energetic musical score. Highly acclaimed in its time, but now seems dated. Based on the novel by Hervey Allen.
1936 141m/B Fredric March, Olivia de Havilland, Anita Louise, Gale Sondergaard, Claude Rains, Louis Hayward; *D:* Mervyn LeRoy. Academy Awards '36: Best Cinematography, Best Film Editing, Best Supporting Actress (Sondergaard), Best Score; Nominations: Best Interior Decoration, Best Picture. VHS, Beta $19.98 *MGM, BTV, FHE* ♫♫½

Antonia and Jane Enjoyable film tells the story of a longstanding, heavily tested friendship between two women. From the very beginning, they are a study in contrasts—Jane as rather plain, frumpy, and insecure; Antonia as glamorous, elegant, and successful. Both believe that each other's lives are more interesting and exciting than their own. Kidron, who directed this smart witty comedy for British television, offers an honest look into the often complex world of adult friendships.
1991 (R) 75m/C *GB* Imelda Staunton, Saskia Reeves, Patricia Leventon, Alfred Hoffman, Maria Charles, John Bennett, Richard Hope, Alfred Marks, Lila Kaye, Bill Nighy; *D:* Beeban Kidron; *W:* Marcy Kahan; *M:* Rachel Portman. VHS, Beta *PAR* ♫♫♫

Antonio A Texas millionaire on the run from his wife and her divorce lawyer alights in a small Chilean village and turns it upside down.
1973 89m/C Larry Hagman, Trini Lopez, Noemi Guerrero, Pedro Becker; *D:* Claudio Guzman. VHS, Beta *TIM, HEG* ♫♫

Antonio Das Mortes Antonio is a savage mercenary hired to kill rebels against the Brazilian government. Belatedly he realizes he sympathizes with the targets and turns his guns the other way for an incredible shootout finale. A visually lavish political polemic, espousing revolutionary guerrilla action within the format of a South American western. In Portuguese with English subtitles.
1968 100m/C Mauricio Do Valle, Odete Lara; *W/D:* Glauce Rocha. VHS $59.95 *FST, TAM* ♫♫½

Antony and Cleopatra Heston wrote, directed, and starred in this long, dry adaptation of the Shakespeare play that centers on the torrid romance between Mark Antony and Cleopatra.
1973 (PG) 150m/C Charlton Heston, Hildegarde Neff, Fernando Rey, Eric Porter; *D:* Charlton Heston. VHS, Beta $24.98 *SUE* ♫♫

Ants A mad bug parable for the planet-obsessed 90s. Insecticide-infected ants turn militant and check into a local hotel to vent their chemically induced foul mood on the unsuspecting clientele. The guest register includes a gaggle of celebrities who probably wish they'd signed on the Love Boat instead. Made for television (an ant farm would probably be just too horrible on the big

screen). *AKA:* Panic at Lakewood Manor; It Happened at Lakewood Manor.
1977 100m/C Suzanne Somers, Robert Foxworth, Myrna Loy, Lynda Day George, Gerald Gordon, Bernie Casey, Barry Van Dyke, Karen Lamm, Anita Gillette, Moosie Drier, Steve Franken, Brian Dennehy, Bruce French, Stacy Keach, Rene Enriquez, James Storm; *D:* Robert Scheerer. VHS, Beta *LIV* ♫½

Any Gun Can Play Typical spaghetti western. Three men (banker, thief, and bounty hunter) compete for a treasure of gold while wandering about the Spanish countryside. *AKA:* For a Few Bullets More.
1967 103m/C *IT SP* Edd Byrnes, Gilbert Roland, George Hilton, Kareen O'Hara, Pedro Sanchez, Gerard Herter; *D:* Enzo G. Castellari. VHS *HHE* ♫

Any Man's Death Savage is a globe-trotting reporter on the trail of a worldwide conspiracy who accidentally uncovers a Nazi war criminal in Africa. Well-meaning but confused tale.
1990 (R) 105m/C John Savage, William Hickey, Mia Sara, Ernest Borgnine, Michael Lerner; *D:* Tom Clegg. VHS, Beta, LV *PSM* ♫♫

Any Wednesday Okay sex farce about powerful industrialist Robards' use of his mistress's apartment as a tax write-off. When a young company executive learns of the "company" apartment, he meets Robards' nonchalant wife for a tryst of their own. Based on Muriel Resnik's Broadway play; similar to the 1960 "The Apartment." *AKA:* Bachelor Girl Apartment.
1966 110m/C Jane Fonda, Jason Robards Jr., Dean Jones, Rosemary Murphy; *D:* Robert Ellis Miller. VHS, Beta $19.98 *WAR* ♫♫½

Any Which Way You Can Bad brawler Philo Beddoe and his buddy Clyde, the orangutan, are back again in the sequel to "Every Which Way But Loose." This time Philo is tempted to take part in a big bout for a large cash prize. Clyde steals scenes, brightening up the no-brainer story.
1980 (PG) 116m/C Clint Eastwood, Sondra Locke, Ruth Gordon, Harry Guardino; *D:* Buddy Van Horn. VHS, Beta, LV $19.98 *WAR* ♫♫

Anything for a Thrill Two kids save a cameraman's career, make friends with a millionairess, and foil some crooks.
1937 59m/B Frankie Darro, Kane Richmond; *D:* S.A. Grandi. VHS $24.95 *NOS, DVT, HEG* ♫

Anzacs: The War Down Under Well-made Australian TV miniseries about the Australian & New Zealand Army Corps during WWI. Follows the men from the time they enlist to the campaigns in Gallipoli and France.
1985 165m/C *AU* Paul Hogan, Andrew Clarke, Jon Blake, Megan Williams; *D:* George Miller. VHS, Beta $19.95 *CEL* ♫♫♫

Anzio The historic Allied invasion of Italy during WWII as seen through the eyes of American war correspondent Mitchum. Fine cast waits endlessly to leave the beach, though big battle scenes are effectively rendered. Based on the book by Wynford Vaughan Thomas. *AKA:* The Battle for Anzio; Lo Sbarco di Anzio.
1968 117m/C Robert Mitchum, Peter Falk, Arthur Kennedy, Robert Ryan, Earl Holliman, Mark Damon, Reni Santoni, Patrick Magee; *D:* Edward Dmytryk. VHS, Beta $9.95 *RCA* ♫♫

Apache Lancaster is the only Indian in Geronimo's outfit who refuses to surrender in this chronicle of a bitter battle between the Indians and the U.S. cavalry in the struggle for the West. First western for Aldrich is a thoughtful piece for its time that had the original tragic ending reshot (against Al-

drich's wishes) to make it more happy. Adapted from "Bronco Apache" by Paul I. Wellman.
1954 91m/C Burt Lancaster, John McIntire, Jean Peters; **D:** Robert Aldrich. **VHS, Beta $19.98** *MGM, FOX, FCT* 🎬🎬½

Apache Blood An Indian Brave, the lone survivor of an Indian massacre by the U.S. Army, squares off with a calvary scout in the forbidding desert. **AKA:** Pursuit.
1975 (R) 92m/C Ray Danton, DeWitt Lee, Troy Nabors, Diane Taylor, Eva Kovacs, Jason Clark; **D:** Thomas Quillen. **VHS $19.99** *PSM* 🎬½

Apache Chief Two Apache tribe leaders, one good, the other evil clash. Ultimately, and perhaps predictably, they face each other in hand-to-hand combat and peace prevails.
1950 60m/B Alan Curtis, Tom Neal, Russell Hayden, Carol Thurston; **D:** Frank McDonald. **VHS, Beta, LV** *NO* 🎬

Apache Kid's Escape The Apache Kid leads the cavalry on a wild chase across the plains in this saga of the old west.
1930 60m/B Jack Perrin, Buzz Barton. **VHS, Beta $19.95** *NOS, DVT* 🎬

Apache Rose Gambling boat owner plots to gain control of oil found on Vegas Ranch. Roy and Dale oppose the idea. First of the series in color; the original, unedited version of the film.
1947 75m/B Roy Rogers, Dale Evans, Olin Howland, George Meeker; **D:** William Witney. **VHS, Beta, LV $9.99** *FOX, NOS, VCN* 🎬🎬

Apache Uprising A standard western with Calhoun as the lawman up against gunfighters and stagecoach robbers as well as the usual Indians.
1966 60m/C Rory Calhoun, Corinne Calvet, DeForest Kelley, John Russell, Lon Chaney Jr., Gene Evans, Richard Arlen, Robert Harris, Arthur Hunnicutt, Jean Parker, Johnny Mack Brown; **D:** R.G. Springsteen. **VHS** *PAR* 🎬½

Apache Woman Bridges stars as a government agent sent to investigate some crimes committed by a group of Apache Indians. As he tries to calm the townspeople, Bridges discovers that the group is made up of white people led by an educated half-breed. He instigates the help of the half-breed's sister (and also Bridges' love interest) to stop the gang. Some good action, but lots of dull spots.
1955 82m/C Lloyd Bridges, Joan Taylor, Lance Fuller, Morgan Jones, Paul Birch, Jonathan Haze, Paul Dubov, Lou Place; **D:** Roger Corman. **VHS $19.95** *COL, FCT* 🎬½

Apaches Last Battle A boundary scout discovers the ward of an Apache chief has been framed for murder by a cavalry officer who wants to start an Indian war in this exciting Euro western. **AKA:** Old Shatterhand; Shatterhand.
1964 ?m/C Lex Barker, Guy Madison, Pierre Brice. **VHS $16.95** *SNC* 🎬

Aparajito The second of the Apu trilogy, about a boy growing up in India, after "Pather Panchali," and before "The World of Apu." Apu is brought to Benares and his education seriously begins. The work of a master; in Bengali with English subtitles. **AKA:** The Unvanquished.
1958 108m/B *IN* Pinaki Sen Gupta, Karuna Banerjee, Kanu Banerjee, Ramani Sen Gupta; **D:** Satyajit Ray. **VHS, Beta $29.95** *FCT, MRV, TIM* 🎬🎬🎬½

The Apartment A lowly insurance clerk tries to climb the corporate ladder by "loaning" his apartment out to executives having affairs. Problems arise, however, when he unwittingly falls for the most recent girlfriend

of the boss. Highly acclaimed social satire and winner of five Academy Awards. Co-written by Wilder and I.A.L. Diamond (who also wrote "Some Like It Hot").
1960 125m/B Jack Lemmon, Shirley MacLaine, Fred MacMurray, Ray Walston, Jack Kruschen, Joan Shawlee, Edie Adams, Hope Holiday, David Lewis; **D:** Billy Wilder. Academy Awards '60: Best Art Direction/Set Decoration (B & W), Best Director (Wilder), Best Film Editing, Best Picture, Best Story & Screenplay; Nominations: Best Actor (Lemmon), Best Actress (MacLaine), Best Black and White Cinematography, Best Sound, Best Supporting Actor (Kruschen); British Academy Awards '60: Best Actor (Lemmon), Best Actress (MacLaine), Best Film; Directors Guild of America Awards '60: Best Director (Wilder); Golden Globe Awards '61: Best Actor—Musical/Comedy (Lemmon), Best Actress—Musical/Comedy (MacLaine), Best Film—Musical/Comedy; National Board of Review Awards '60: 10 Best Films of the Year; New York Film Critics Awards '60: Best Director (Wilder), Best Film. **VHS, Beta, LV $19.98** *MGM, BTV* 🎬🎬🎬½

Apartment Zero A decidedly weird, deranged psychological drama about the parasite/host-type relationship between two roommates in downtown Buenos Aires: one, an obsessive British movie nut, the other, a sexually mesmerizing stud who turns out to be a cold-blooded psycho.
1988 (R) 124m/C *GB* Hart Bochner, Colin Firth, Fabrizio Bentivoglio, Liz Smith; **D:** Martin Donovan. **VHS, Beta, LV $14.95** *ACA, FCT, IME* 🎬🎬🎬

The Ape When his daughter dies of a crippling disease, Karloff becomes fixated with the mission to cure paralysis. Obviously distraught, he begins donning the hide of an escaped circus ape whose spinal fluid is the key to the serum. Hide-bedecked, he slays unknowing townspeople to tap them of their spinal fluid and cure his latest patient.
1940 62m/B Boris Karloff, Maris Wrixon, Henry Hall, Gertrude Hoffman; **D:** William Nigh. **VHS, Beta $19.95** *NOS, SNC, TIM* 🎬🎬

A*P*E* A*P*E* is thirty-six feet tall and ten tons of animal fury who destroys anything that comes between him and the actress he loves. Cheap rip-off of Kong.
1976 (PG) 87m/C Rod Arrants, Joanna DeVarona, Alex Nicol; **D:** Paul Leder. **VHS, Beta $19.95** *STE, NWV Woof!*

The Ape Man With the aid of a secret potion, a scientist turns himself into a murderous ape. The only way to regain his human side is to ingest human spinal fluid. Undoubtedly inspired by Boris Karloff's 1940 film, "The Ape." **AKA:** Lock Your Doors.
1943 64m/B Wallace Ford, Bela Lugosi; **D:** William Beaudine. **VHS, Beta, 3/4U, Special order formats $19.95** *NOS, MRV, SNC* 🎬½

Aphrodite Steamy drama based on Pierre Louy's masterpiece of erotic literature.
1983 89m/C Valerie Kaprisky; **D:** Robert Fuest. **VHS, Beta, LV $69.98** *VES, LIV* 🎬

Apocalipsis Joe A lonely gunfighter looks to kick an evil criminal out of a small town.
1965 90m/C Eduardo Fajardo, Mary Paz Pondal, Fernando Ceruli, Fernando Bilbao. **VHS, Beta $34.90** *MAD* 🎬🎬½

Apocalypse Now Its merits still the object of debate, Coppola's $40 million epic vision of the Vietnam War was inspired by Joseph Conrad's novella "Heart of Darkness." Disillusioned Army captain Sheen travels upriver into Cambodia to assassinate overweight renegade colonel Brando. His trip is punctuated by surrealistic battles and a terrifying descent into a land where human rationality seems to have slipped away. Considered by some to be the

definitive picture of war in its overall depiction of chaos and primal bloodletting; by others, over-wrought and unrealistic. A cinematic experience that may not translate as well to the small screen, yet worth seeing if for nothing more than Duvall's ten minutes of scenery chewing as a battle-obsessed major ("I love the smell of napalm in the morning!"), a study in manic machismo. Stunning photography by Vittorio Storaro, awe-inspiring battle scenes, and effective soundtrack montage. Both Sheen and Coppola suffered emotional breakdowns during the prolonged filming, and that's a very young Fishburne in his major film debut. Available in widescreen format on laserdisc and in a remastered version in letterbox on VHS with a remixed soundtrack that features Dolby Surround stereo. In 1991 a documentary detailing the making of the film, "Hearts of Darkness: A Filmmaker's Apocalypse," was released.
1979 (R) 153m/C Marlon Brando, Martin Sheen, Robert Duvall, Frederic Forrest, Sam Bottoms, Scott Glenn, Albert Hall, Larry Fishburne, Harrison Ford, G.D. Spradlin, Dennis Hopper, Colleen Camp, Tom Mason; **W/D:** Francis Ford Coppola; **W:** John Milius. Academy Awards '79: Best Cinematography, Best Sound; Nominations: Best Adapted Screenplay, Best Art Direction/Set Decoration, Best Director (Coppola), Best Film Editing, Best Picture, Best Supporting Actor (Duvall); British Academy Awards '79: Best Director (Coppola), Best Supporting Actor (Duvall); Golden Globe Awards '80: Best Director (Coppola), Best Supporting Actor (Duvall); National Society of Film Critics Awards '79: Best Supporting Actor (Forrest). **VHS, Beta, LV $29.95** *PAR* 🎬🎬🎬🎬

Apology A psychotic killer stalks Warren, an experimental artist, in Manhattan while a detective stalks the killer. Made for cable, so expect a little more sex and violence than network TV movies. Written by Mark Medhoff, author of "Children of a Lesser God."
1986 98m/C Lesley Ann Warren, Peter Weller, John Glover, George Loros, Jimmie Ray Weeks, Christopher North, Harvey Fierstein; **D:** Robert Bierman. **VHS $19.95** *HBO* 🎬🎬

The Appaloosa A lamenting loner who decides to begin anew by breeding Appaloosas is ripped off by a desperate woman who steals his horse in order to get away from her abusive amour. Brando falls in love with the girl and the two amazingly survive a wealth of obstacles in their battle against Mexican bandits. **AKA:** Southwest to Sonora.
1966 99m/C Marlon Brando, Anjanette Comer, John Saxon; **D:** Sidney J. Furie. **VHS, Beta, LV $14.95** *MCA* 🎬🎬½

Appassionata Titillating Italian drama about a dentist with a helplessly neurotic wife. He's seduced by his daughter and her best friend. Dubbed.
1974 100m/C *IT* Ornella Muti, Gabriel Ferzetti, Valentina Cortese, Elenora Giorgi; **D:** Gian Luigi Calderone. **VHS, Beta $59.95** *MED* 🎬🎬

Applause Morgan plays a down-and-out burlesque star trying to protect her fresh from the convent daughter. Definitely dated, but a marvelous performance by Morgan. Film buffs will appreciate this early talkie.
1929 78m/B Helen Morgan, Joan Peers, Fuller Mellish Jr., Henry Wadsworth, Dorothy Cumming; **D:** Rouben Mamoulian. **VHS** *PAR* 🎬🎬🎬

The Apple Futuristic musical filmed in Berlin that features a young, innocent, folk-singing couple who nearly become victims of the evil, glitzy record producer who tries to recruit the couple into a life of sex and drugs.
1980 (PG) 90m/C Catherine Mary Stewart, Alan Love, Grace Kennedy, Joss Ackland; **D:** Menahem Golan. **VHS, Beta** *PGN* 🎬½

The Apple Dumpling Gang Three frisky kids strike it rich and trigger the wildest bank robbery in the gold-mad West. Unmistakably Disney, a familial subplot and a wacky duo are provided. Mediocre yet superior to its sequel, "The Apple Dumpling Gang Rides Again."
1975 (G) 100m/C Bill Bixby, Susan Clark, Don Knotts, Tim Conway, David Wayne, Slim Pickens, Harry Morgan; *D:* Norman Tokar. VHS, Beta $19.99 *DIS ＊＊*

The Apple Dumpling Gang Rides Again Two lovable hombres terrorize the West in their bungling attempt to go straight. Fans of Conway or Knotts may appreciate this sequel to Disney's "The Apple Dumpling Gang."
1979 (G) 88m/C Tim Conway, Don Knotts, Tim Matheson, Kenneth Mars, Harry Morgan, Jack Elam; *D:* Vincent McEveety. VHS, Beta $69.95 *DIS ＊＊*

The Applegates Bugs-on-a-rampage flick cross-meshing with the "there's something rotten in suburbia" genre from the director of "Heathers." A bunch of ecologically correct insects in the Amazon are more than a little miffed about the slash-and-burn tactics in the wild, and they decide to implement a plan to establish a kinder, gentler habitat. The head bug orders Begley and his brood to transform into an average American family, set up house in Ohio, and annihilate a neighboring atomic energy generating station. Trouble is, the bug-people find they've grown accustomed to their decadent Homo sapien ways: even insects aren't immune to the lure of sex, drugs, and cable shopping networks. Altogether an imaginative, often quite funny mono joker that should've been shorter. Sometimes you'll wonder whether the screenwriters were given to bouts of narcolepsy. Screenplay by director Lehmann and Redbeard Simmons. *AKA:* Meet the Applegates.
1989 (R) 90m/C Ed Begley Jr., Stockard Channing, Dabney Coleman, Cami Cooper, Bobby Jacoby; *D:* Michael Lehmann. VHS, Beta, LV $89.98 *MED, FOX ＊＊½*

The Appointment A supernatural force enters the bodies and minds of people and suddenly everyone begins going crazy.
1982 90m/C Edward Woodward, Jane Merrow; *D:* Lindsey C. Vickers. VHS, Beta, 8mm $39.95 *SVS Woof!*

Appointment in Honduras An adventurer goes on a dangerous trek through the Central American jungles to deliver funds to the Honduran President.
1953 79m/C Glenn Ford, Ann Sheridan, Zachary Scott; *D:* Jacques Tourneur. VHS, Beta *NO ＊＊*

Appointment with Crime After serving a prison sentence, an ex-con sets out to avenge himself against the colleagues who double crossed him. Well done, highlighted by superior characterizations. Based on the story by Michael Leighton.
1945 91m/B *GB* William Hartnell, Raymond Lovell, Robert Beatty, Herbert Lom, Joyce Howard, Alan Wheatley, Cyril Smith; *W/D:* John Harlow. VHS, Beta $16.95 *SNC ＊＊½*

Appointment with Death Disappointing Agatha Christie mystery with Hercule Poirot solving the murder of a shrewish widow in 1937 Palestine. Music by Pino Donaggio.
1988 (PG) 103m/C Peter Ustinov, Lauren Bacall, Carrie Fisher, John Gielgud, Piper Laurie, Hayley Mills, Jenny Seagrove, David Soul; *D:* Michael Winner; *W:* Agatha Christie. VHS, Beta, LV $19.98 *WAR, FCT ＊½*

Appointment with Fear A tough detective investigates a murder and all of the clues lead him mysteriously to a comatose asylum inmate.
1985 (R) 95m/C Michael Wyle, Michelle Little, Garrick Dowhen; *D:* Alan Smithee. VHS, Beta, LV $14.95 *LIV ＊*

Apprentice to Murder A small Pennsylvania Dutch town is shaken by a series of murders, thought to be associated with a bizarre local mystic and healer. Based on a true story, sort of.
1988 (PG-13) 97m/C Donald Sutherland, Mia Sara, Chad Lowe, Eddie Jones; *D:* Ralph L. Thomas. VHS, Beta, LV $19.95 *STE, NWV, HHE ＊＊*

The Apprenticeship of Duddy Kravitz Young Jewish man in Montreal circa 1948 is driven by an insatiable need to be a "somebody." Everybody has always told him he will be. A series of get-rich-quick schemes backfire in different ways, and he becomes most successful at driving people away. Young Dreyfuss is at his best. Made in Canada with thoughtful detail, and great cameo performances. Script by Mordecai Richler, from his novel.
1974 (PG) 121m/C *CA* Richard Dreyfuss, Randy Quaid, Denholm Elliott, Jack Warden, Micheline Lanctot, Joe Silver; *D:* Ted Kotcheff. Academy Awards '74 Nominations: Best Adapted Screenplay; Berlin International Film Festival '74: Golden Berlin Bear. VHS, Beta $69.95 *PAR ＊＊＊½*

April Fools A bored stockbroker falls in love with a beautiful woman who turns out to be married to his boss. Marvin Hamlisch's score resounds.
1969 (PG) 95m/C Jack Lemmon, Catherine Deneuve, Sally Kellerman, Peter Lawford, Charles Boyer, Myrna Loy, Harvey Korman; *D:* Stuart Rosenberg. VHS, Beta $19.98 *FOX ＊＊*

April Fool's Day College kids vacationing at a secluded island home are systematically murdered by an unknown assailant.
1986 (R) 90m/C Jay Baker, Pat Barlow, Lloyd Berry, Deborah Foreman; *D:* Fred Walton. VHS, Beta, LV $19.95 *PAR ＊*

April in Paris Dynamite Jackson (Day), a chorus girl accidentally sent by the State Department to perform in Paris, meets S. Winthrop Putnam (Bolger), a timid fellow trapped in an unpleasant marriage. They eventually sing and dance their way to warm feelings as they begin a lifelong romance and live happily ever after.
1952 100m/C Doris Day, Ray Bolger, Claude Dauphin, Eve Miller, George Givot, Paul Harvey; *D:* David Butler. VHS $19.98 *WAR, CCB ＊＊*

The Arab Conspiracy Sharpe plays a hit-woman conspiring with assassins from all over the world to kill Arab leaders. One problem—she falls in love with Saudi Arabian ambassador Connery as he tries to gain peace with Palestine. *AKA:* The Next Man; Double Hit.
1976 (R) 108m/C Sean Connery, Cornelia Sharpe, Albert Paulsen, Adolfo Celi, Charles Cioffi; *D:* Richard Sarafian. VHS $9.95 *SIM, QVD ＊＊*

Arabesque A college professor is drawn into international espionage by a beautiful woman and a plot to assassinate an Arab prince. Stylish and fast moving, with music by Henry Mancini. From the novel "The Cipher" by Gordon Votler.
1966 105m/C Gregory Peck, Sophia Loren, George Coulouris; *D:* Stanley Donen. VHS, Beta $14.95 *MCA, FCT ＊＊½*

Arabian Nights The third of Pasolini's epic, explicit adaptations of classic portmanteau, featuring ten of the old Scheherazade favorites adorned by beautiful photography, explicit sex scenes and homoeroticism. In Italian with English subtitles; available dubbed.
1974 130m/C *IT* Ninetto Davoli, Franco Merli, Ines Pellegrini, Luigina Rocchi; *D:* Pier Paolo Pasolini; *M:* Ennio Morricone. VHS, Beta, LV $11.95 *WBF, TAM, APD ＊＊＊*

Arachnophobia Erstwhile Spielberg producer Frank Marshall's directorial debut is a mega-budget thrill-com version of a big bug horror story. Lethal bugs—South American spiders this time—wind up in a white picket fence California community somewhere off the beaten track. There they wreak eight-legged antenna-less havoc on their two-legged antagonists, including an utterly arachnophobic town doctor (Daniels) and a gung-ho insect exterminator (Goodman). The script's a bit yawn-inspiring but the cast and effects will keep you from dozing off. Screenplay by Don Jakoby and Wesley Strick, based on a story by Jakoby and Al Williams.
1990 (PG-13) 109m/C Jeff Daniels, John Goodman, Harley Jane Kozak, Julian Sands, Roy Brocksmith; *D:* Frank Marshall. VHS, Beta, LV $19.99 *HPH ＊＊½*

Arch of Triumph In Paris, an Austrian refugee doctor falls in love just before the Nazis enter the city. Big-budget box-office loser featuring fine cast but sluggish pace. Co-written by Milestone and Harry Brown. Based on the Erich Maria Remarque novel and remade for television.
1948 120m/B Ingrid Bergman, Charles Boyer, Charles Laughton, Louis Calhern; *D:* Lewis Milestone. VHS $129.98 *REP ＊＊＊*

Arch of Triumph A refugee doctor falls in love with a mystery woman as the Nazis enter Paris. Made for television remake of the 1948 film.
1985 95m/C Anthony Hopkins, Lesley-Anne Down, Donald Pleasence; *D:* Waris Hussein. VHS $19.95 *FCT ＊＊½*

Archer: The Fugitive from the Empire A young warrior battles the forces of evil in this television movie. Lots of strange names to learn even if you already know who's going to win the final battle.
1981 97m/C Lane Caudell, Belinda Bauer, George Kennedy, Victor Campos, Kabir Bedi, George Innes, Marc Alaimo, Allen Rich, John Hancock, Priscilla Pointer, Richard Dix, Sharon Barr; *D:* Nick Corea. VHS, Beta $39.95 *MCA ＊*

Archer's Adventure An Australian family film based on a true story. A horsetrainer's young apprentice delivers a prize racehorse to Melbourne, through 600 miles of tough frontier, devious bush rangers, and disaster.
1985 120m/C *AU* Brett Climo; *D:* Denny Lawrence. VHS, Beta $14.95 *NWV, STE ＊½*

Are Parents People? Lighthearted silent comedy about a young girl's successful attempts to reunite her feuding parents. It all begins as she runs away and spends the night in the office of a doctor she has grown to like. After a frantic night of searching, her parents are reunited through their love for her.
1925 60m/B Betty Bronson, Adolphe Menjou, Florence Vidor. VHS $16.95 *GPV, PAR ＊＊*

Are You in the House Alone? Made for television adaptation of Richard Peck's award-winning novel. Story of a high school coed who becomes the target of a terror campaign.

1978 100m/C Blythe Danner, Kathleen Beller, Tony Bill, Scott Colomby; **D:** Walter Grauman. **VHS, Beta** $49.95 *WOV, GKK* 🎬🎬

Are You Lonesome Tonight Suspense thriller casts Seymour as a wealthy socialite who discovers her husband is having an affair with a phone-sex girl. His sudden and mysterious disapppearance forces her to hire a private detective (Stevenson) to track him down, with only the taped conversations as clues. Average made for cable television fare.
1992 (PG-13) 91m/C Jane Seymour, Parker Stevenson, Beth Broderick, Joel Brooks, Robert Pine; **D:** E.W. Swackhamer; **W:** Wesley Moore. **VHS, Beta** $19.95 *PAR* 🎬🎬½

Arena Remember old boxing melodramas about good-natured palookas, slimy opponents, gangsters and dames? This puts those cliches in a garish sci-fi setting, with handsome Steve Armstrong battling ETs and the astro-mob to be the first human pugilistic champ in decades. A really cute idea (from the screenwriters of "The Rocketeer"), but it conks out at the halfway point. Worth a look for buffs.
1988 (PG-13) 97m/C *IT* Paul Satterfield, Claudia Christian, Hamilton Camp, Marc Alaimo, Armin Shimerman, Shari Shattuck, Jack Carter; **D:** Peter Manoogian. **VHS, LV** $14.95 *COL, PIA* 🎬🎬

Aria Ten directors were given carte blanche to interpret ten arias from well-known operas. Henry and D'Angelo star in Julian Temple's rendition of Verdi's "Rigoletto." In Fonda's film debut, she and her lover travel to Las Vegas and eventually kill themselves in the bathtub, just like "Romeo & Juliet." Jarman's piece (a highlight) shows an aged operatic star at her last performance remembering an early love affair. "I Pagliacci" is the one aria in which the director took his interpretation in a straightforward manner.
1988 (R) 90m/C *GB* Theresa Russell, Anita Morris, Bridget Fonda, Beverly D'Angelo, Buck Henry, John Hurt; **D:** Ken Russell, Charles Sturridge, Robert Altman, Bill Bryden, Jean-Luc Godard, Bruce Beresford, Nicolas Roeg, Franc Roddam, Derek Jarman, Julien Temple. **VHS, Beta** $29.95 *ACA, FCT* 🎬🎬

Ariel Refreshing, award-winning offbeat Finnish comedy by much-praised newcomer Kaurismaki (who earlier directed "Leningrad Cowboys Go American"). Hoping to find work in Southern Finland, an out-of-work miner from Northern Finland (Pajala) jets off in his white Cadillac convertible given to him in a cafe by a friend, who promptly shoots himself. There's no linear progression toward a happy ending, although antiheroic subject does find employment and romances a meter maid. Mostly, though, he's one of those it's hell being me guys who wouldn't have any luck if it weren't for bad luck. Strange slice-of-life sporting film noir tendencies, although essentially anti-stylistic. Kaurismaki also scripted.
1989 74m/C *FI* Susanna Haavisto, Turo Pajala; **D:** Aki Kaurismaki. **VHS** $79.95 *KIV, FCT, TAM* 🎬🎬🎬

Arizona A group of illegal aliens struggle for survival after they cross the border into the harsh desert.
1986 94m/C *MX* Roberto "Flaco" Guzman, Juan Valentin. **VHS, Beta** *MED* 🎬½

Arizona Badman There is a bad man in Arizona, and he must be gotten rid of.
1942 60m/B Reb Russell; **D:** S. Roy Luby. **VHS, Beta** $19.95 *NOS, DVT* 🎬½

Arizona Bound Mesa City is infested with a villain and our "Rough Rider" trio must rid the town of him.

1941 57m/B Buck Jones, Tim McCoy, Raymond Hatton, Dennis Moore, Luana Walters; **D:** Spencer Gordon Bennet. **VHS, Beta** $19.95 *NOS, VCN, DVT* 🎬

Arizona Bushwackers Routine western that has Confederate spy Keel taking job as sheriff in small Arizona town. Once there, he has to straighten out a few bad guys who have been selling weapons to the Apaches. Notable for presence of old western-movie veterans Ireland, Donlevy, Brady, and MacLane. Based on a story by Steve Fisher.
1967 87m/C Howard Keel, Yvonne De Carlo, John Ireland, Marilyn Maxwell, Scott Brady, Brian Donlevy, Barton MacLane; **D:** Lesley Selander. **VHS** $14.95 *PAR* 🎬½

Arizona Cowboy An ex-G.I., now the rodeo's big attraction, gets involved in a robbery.
1949 57m/B Rex Allen, Gordon Jones, Roy Barcroft; **D:** R.G. Springsteen. **VHS, Beta** $29.95 *DVT* 🎬

Arizona Days Cowboys join a minstrel group and rescue the show when a group of toughs try to break it up.
1937 56m/B Tex Ritter, Eleanor Stewart, Syd Saylor, Snub Pollard; **D:** John English. **VHS, Beta** $19.95 *NOS, UHV, VDM* 🎬½

Arizona Gangbusters Below-average oater has real-life cowboy McCoy fighting city hall in order to fight other baddies.
1940 57m/B Tim McCoy, Pauline Hadden, Forrest Taylor, Julian Rivero, Curly Dresden; **D:** Peter Stewart. **VHS** $19.95 *DVT, HEG* 🎬

Arizona Gunfighter A young cowhand seeks revenge against the man who murdered his father in this western.
1937 60m/B Bob Steele, Ted Adams; **D:** Sam Newfield. **VHS, Beta** $19.95 *NOS, DVT* 🎬

Arizona Heat A violent cop is teamed up with a tough, but tender female cop in this all-too-familiar tale of two cops chasing a cop killer.
1987 (R) 91m/C Michael Parks, Denise Crosby, Hugh Farrington; **D:** John Thomas. **VHS** $79.98 *REP* 🎬🎬

Arizona Kid Another sagebrush saga featuring Roy in singin' and fightin' action.
1939 54m/B Roy Rogers, Dale Evans; **D:** Horace Carpenter. **VHS, Beta** $9.99 *NOS, DVT, MLB* 🎬

Arizona Raiders Arizona rangers hunt down killers who have been terrorizing the territory.
1965 88m/C Audie Murphy, Buster Crabbe, Gloria Talbott; **D:** William Whitney. **VHS, Beta** $19.95 *NOS, UHV, VCN* 🎬🎬

Arizona Roundup Good vs. bad amid tumbleweed, bleached-white chaps, bloodless shoot-outs and happy endings.
1942 54m/B Tom Keene, Sugar Dawn, Jack Ingram; **D:** Robert Tansey. **VHS, Beta** $19.95 *NOS, VDM* 🎬½

Arizona Stagecoach The Range Busters set out to bust a notorious, guiltless, devil-may-care outlaw gang.
1942 58m/B Ray Corrigan, Max Terhune, Kermit Maynard, Charles King, John "Dusty" King; **D:** S. Roy Luby. **VHS, Beta** $19.95 *NOS, TIM* 🎬

Arizona Terror Our hero is on a quest for vengeance, seeking the posse that killed his partner.
1931 64m/B Ken Maynard. **VHS, Beta** *VCN* 🎬½

Arizona Whirlwind Our intrepid heroes must battle torrents of gunfire in order to prevent a stage hold-up in this western saga.
1944 59m/B Ken Maynard, Hoot Gibson, Bob Steele. **VHS, Beta** $19.95 *NOS, DVT* 🎬

Ark of the Sun God Another adventurer battles the Nazis and nutsies for a 2000-year-old ark buried in the Sahara.
1982 95m/C David Warbeck, John Steiner, Susie Sudlow, Alan Collins, Riccardo Palacio; **D:** Anthony M. Dawson. **VHS, Beta** $59.95 *TWE* 🎬

Armed and Dangerous Candy and Levy are incompetent security guards assigned to a do-nothing job. Things get spiced up when a mobster tries to run a crime ring under their nose. Candy catches on and winds up in a full-fledged chase. Not as funny as it sounds, though occasionally has moments of genuine comedy.
1986 (PG-13) 88m/C John Candy, Eugene Levy, Kenneth McMillan, Brion James, Robert Loggia, Meg Ryan, Don Stroud, Jonathan Banks, Steve Railsback, Bruce Kirby, Tony Burton, Larry Hankin, Judy Landers, David Wohl; **D:** Mark L. Lester; **W:** Harold Ramis, Peter Torokvei, James Keach, Brian Grazer. **VHS, Beta, LV** $14.95 *COL* 🎬🎬

Armed for Action Routine action thriller casts Estevez as Sgt. Phil Towers who gets more than he bargained for when his prisoner, Mafia hitman David Montel, escapes while en route from New York to Los Angeles. When he finally catches up with them, Towers leads a small army of locals on a brutal assault.
1992 88m/C Joe Estevez, Rocky Patterson, Barri Murphy, David Harrod, J. Scott Guy; **D:** Shane Spaulding. **VHS** $89.95 *AIP* 🎬

Armed Response Carradine leads a group of mercenaries in a battle against Chinatown mobsters. They race to locate a priceless jade statue before it can fall into the wrong hands.
1986 (R) 86m/C David Carradine, Lee Van Cleef, Mako, Lois Hamilton, Ross Hagen, Brent Huff; **D:** Fred Olen Ray. **VHS, Beta, LV** $12.95 *RCA* 🎬🎬

Armored Car Robbery Talman and his buddies plot to rob an armored car but are foiled by McGraw and his crimefighters. Surprisingly good B-crime drama.
1950 68m/B Charles McGraw, Adele Jergens, William Talman, Steve Brodie; **D:** Richard Fleischer. **VHS** *RKO* 🎬🎬

Armored Command A beautiful German spy infiltrates an American outpost during the Battle of the Bulge. Tepid WWII fare made too long after the fact.
1961 105m/B Burt Reynolds, Tina Louise, Howard Keel, Earl Holliman, Warner Anderson, Carleton Young; **D:** Byron Haskin. **VHS, Beta** $19.98 *FOX, FCT* 🎬½

Army Brats In this Dutch film a military family goes bloodily and comically to war with itself. Even in a welfare state, parents can't control their wee ones.
1984 105m/C *NL* Akkemay, Frank Schaafsma, Peter Faber; **D:** Ruud Van Hemert. **VHS, Beta** $59.95 *WAR* 🎬½

Army of Darkness Campbell returns for a third "Evil Dead" round as the square-jawed, none too bright hero, Ash in this comic book extravaganza. He finds himself hurled back to the 14th-century through the powers of an evil book. There he romances a babe, fights an army of skeletons, and generally causes all those Dark Age knights a lot of grief, as he tries to get back to his own time. Raimi's technical exuberance is apparent and, as usual, the horror is graphic but still tongue-in-cheek. The "March of the Dead" theme is by composer Danny Elfman. *AKA:* Evil Dead 3.
1992 (R) 77m/C Bruce Campbell, Embeth Davidtz; *Cameos:* Bridget Fonda; **D:** Sam Raimi; **W:** Ivan Raimi, Sam Raimi; **M:** Joseph Lo Duca. **VHS, Beta, LV** *MCA* 🎬🎬🎬

Arnold Outrageous black comedy involving a woman who marries a cadaver to gain his large inheritance. Lots of bizarre and creative deaths in this horror spoof. Unusual wedding scene is a must-see.
1973 (PG) 96m/C Stella Stevens, Roddy McDowall, Elsa Lanchester, Victor Buono, Bernard Fox, Farley Granger, Shani Wallis; **D:** Georg Fenady. **VHS, Beta $69.98** LTG, LIV *♂♂½*

Around the World Kyser leads a USO-like tour to entertain troops. Interesting only in a historical sense. ♫Doodle-Ee-Doo; He's Got a Secret Weapon; Candlelight and Wine; Great News in the Making; They Chopped Down the Old Apple Tree; A Moke from Shamokin.
1943 80m/B Kay Kyser, Ish Kabibble, Ginny Simms, Joan Davis, Mischa Auer; **D:** Allan Dwan. **VHS, Beta $19.98** TTC *♂♂½*

Around the World in 80 Days Niven is the unflappable Victorian Englishman who wagers that he can circumnavigate the earth in four-score days. With his faithful manservant Cantinflas they set off on a spectacular journey. A perpetual favorite providing ample entertainment. Star-gazers will particularly enjoy the more than 40 cameo appearances by many of Hollywood's biggest names. Written by James Poe, John Farrow, and S.J. Perelman from the Jules Verne novel.
1956 (G) 178m/C David Niven, Shirley MacLaine, Cantinflas, Robert Newton, Charles Boyer, Joe E. Brown, Martine Carol, John Carradine, Charles Coburn, Ronald Colman; *Cameos:* Melville Cooper, Noel Coward, Andy Devine, Reginald Denny, Fernandel, Marlene Dietrich, Hermione Gingold, Cedric Hardwicke, Trevor Howard, Glynis Johns, Buster Keaton, Evelyn Keyes, Peter Lorre, Mike Mazurki, Victor McLaglen, John Mills, Robert Morley, Jack Oakie, George Raft, Cesar Romero, Gilbert Roland, Red Skelton, Frank Sinatra, Ava Gardner; **D:** Michael Anderson Sr.; **M:** Victor Young. Academy Awards '56: Best Adapted Screenplay, Best Color Cinematography, Best Film Editing, Best Picture, Best Original Score; Nominations: Best Art Direction/Set Decoration (Color), Best Costume Design (Color), Best Director (Anderson); Golden Globe Awards '57: Best Actor—Musical/Comedy (Cantinflas), Best Film—Drama; National Board of Review Awards '56: 10 Best Films of the Year; New York Film Critics Awards '56: Best Film. **VHS, Beta, LV $29.98** WAR, BTV, HMV *♂♂♂*

Around the World in 80 Ways Sometimes clever, sometimes crude Australian comedy about an aging man rescued from a nursing home and taken on a phony trip around the world by his sons. Odd, but genuinely funny at times.
1986 (R) 90m/C AU Philip Quast, Alan Penney, Diana Davidson, Kelly Dingwall, Gosia Dobrowolska; **D:** Stephen MacLean. **VHS, LV $19.98** SUE, NLC *♂♂½*

Around the World Under the Sea Bunch of men and one woman scientist plunge under the ocean in an experiment to predict earthquakes. They plant earthquake detectors along the ocean floor and discover the causes of tidal waves. They have men-women battles. They see big sea critters.
1965 111m/C David McCallum, Shirley Eaton, Gary Merrill, Keenan Wynn, Brian Kelly, Lloyd Bridges; **D:** Andrew Marton. **VHS, Beta $59.95** MGM *♂♂*

The Arousers Cult item starring hunk Hunter as a handsome California psycho. Tab travels the coast searching for a woman he is able to make love to; those who fail to arouse him come to tragic, climactic ends. Definitely underground and moderately interesting. *AKA:* Sweet Kill; A Kiss from Eddie.
1970 (R) 85m/C Tab Hunter, Nadyne Turney, Roberta Collins, Isabel Jewell, John Aprea, Angel Fox; **D:** Curtis Hanson. **VHS, Beta $24.98** SUE *♂♂½*

The Arrangement Veteran advertising executive Douglas attempts suicide and then sets out to search for the meaning of life. Along the way he attempts to patch up his "arrangements" with his wife, his mistress and his father. Forced, slow, and self-conscious, though well acted. Adapted by Kazan from the director's own novel.
1969 (R) 126m/C Kirk Douglas, Faye Dunaway, Deborah Kerr, Richard Boone, Hume Cronyn, Elia Kazan; **D:** Elia Kazan. **VHS, Beta $59.95** WAR *♂½*

Arrest Bulldog Drummond Captain Drummond is accused of killing the inventor of a futuristic detonator machine and must track down the real killers. Part of the "Bulldog Drummond" series.
1938 57m/B John Howard, Heather Angel, George Zucco, H.B. Warner, E.E. Clive, Reginald Denny, John Sutton; **D:** James Hogan. **VHS, Beta $16.95** PAR, RXM, SNC *♂♂*

The Arrival An never-seen alien parasite turns an old man into a vampiric young stud after female blood. Plot and characterizations never do arrive. Horror director Stuart Gordon cameos as a hairy biker.
1990 (R) 107m/C John Saxon, Joseph Culp, Robert Sampson, Michael J. Pollard; *Cameos:* David Schmoeller; **W/D:** David Schmoeller. **VHS, LV $79.95** PSM *♂*

Arrivederci, Baby! An unfunny sex comedy with Curtis as a modern Bluebeard who weds rich women and kills them for their money. His last mate plans to turn the tables and kill him first.
1966 100m/C Tony Curtis, Rosanna Schiaffino, Lionel Jeffries, Zsa Zsa Gabor, Nancy Kwan, Fenella Fielding, Anna Quayle, Warren Mitchell, Mischa Auer; **W/D:** Ken Hughes. **VHS** PAR *♂*

Arrowhead A long-running argument between a tough Cavalry scout and an Apache chief pits the cowboys against the Indians in this western fantasy. The personal battles that become all-out wars turn back to fist-fights before the matter is finally settled.
1953 105m/C Charlton Heston, Jack Palance, Katy Jurado, Brian Keith, Milburn Stone; **D:** Charles Marquis Warren. **VHS, Beta, LV $14.95** PAR *♂♂½*

Arrowsmith A small-town medical researcher battles his conscience as he juggles his selfish and unselfish motivations for the work he does. He travels to the West Indies to confront the issues of his life and come to terms with himself once and for all. A talented cast takes their time. Based on the classic Sinclair Lewis novel. Two edited versions available (99 and 89 minutes), both of which delete much of Loy.
1931 95m/B Ronald Colman, Helen Hayes, Myrna Loy; **D:** John Ford. **VHS, Beta $19.98** SUE *♂♂½*

Arsenal Classic Russian propagandist drama about strikes affecting the Russian home front during WWI, marking Dovshenko's first great achievement in the realm of Eisenstein and Pudovkin. Silent.
1929 70m/B RU Semyon Svashenko; **D:** Alexander Dovzhenko. **VHS, Beta, 3/4U $24.95** NOS, MRV, IHF *♂♂♂*

The Arsenal Stadium Mystery Inspector Banks of Scotland Yard tracks down the killer of a football star in this clever but unassuming murder mystery.
1939 85m/B GB Leslie Banks, Greta Gynt, Ian MacLean, Liane Linden, Anthony Bushell, Esmond Knight; **D:** Thorold Dickinson. **VHS $16.95** SNC *♂♂½*

Arsenic and Old Lace Set-bound but energetic adaptation of the classic Joseph Kesselring play about easy-going drama critic Grant caught in a sticky situation when he learns of his aunts' favorite pastime. Apparently the kind, sweet, lonely spinsters lure gentlemen to the house and serve them elderberry wine with a touch of arsenic. Even more devastating to Grant is that the women have been burying the bodies in the cellar—a cellar which also serves as the Panama Canal for Grant's crazy cousin who thinks he's Theodore Roosevelt. Massey and Lorre excel in their sinister roles. One of the best madcap black comedies of all time—a must-see. Shot in 1941 and released a wee bit later, and written by the team of Julius J. and Philip G. Epstein. Available colorized.
1944 158m/B Cary Grant, Josephine Hull, Jean Adair, Raymond Massey, Jack Carson, Priscilla Lane, John Alexander, Edward Everett Horton, John Ridgely, James Gleason, Peter Lorre; **D:** Frank Capra. **VHS, Beta, LV $19.95** MGM, VYG, FOX *♂♂♂½*

The Art of Crime A gypsy/detective is drawn into a homicide case when one of his fellow antique dealers is charged with murder. That certain gypsy feeling provides an atmospheric edge over others of the crime art genre. A pilot for a prospective television series based on the novel "Gypsy in Amber." (Script by Bill Davidson and Martin Smith.)
1975 72m/C Ron Leibman, Jose Ferrer, David Hedison, Jill Clayburgh; **D:** Richard Irving; **W:** Bill Davidson, Martin Smith. **VHS** MOV *♂♂½*

The Art of Dying A loony videophile decides to start staging productions of his all-time favorite film scenes. Trouble is, his idea of a fabulous film moment calls for lots of blood and bile as he lures teenage runaways to his casting couch. Director Hauser stars as the cop who's none too impressed with the cinematic remakes, while cult favorite Pollard is his partner. If you like a little atmosphere and psychological depth in your slashers, you'll find this to be the stuff that populates film noir nightmares.
1990 90m/C Wings Hauser, Michael J. Pollard, Sarah Douglas, Kathleen Kinmont, Sydney Lassick; **D:** Wings Hauser. **VHS, LV $19.95** PMH *♂♂♂*

Arthur Spoiled, alcoholic billionaire Moore stands to lose everything he owns when he falls in love with a waitress. He must choose between wealth and a planned marriage, or poverty and love. Surprisingly funny, with an Oscar for Gielgud as Moore's valet, and great performance from Minnelli. Music by Burt Bacharach, whose title song won an Oscar, too. Arguably the best role Moore's ever had, and he makes the most of it, taking the one-joke premise to a nomination for Oscar actor.
1981 (PG) 97m/C Dudley Moore, Liza Minnelli, John Gielgud, Geraldine Fitzgerald, Stephen Elliott, Jill Eikenberry, Lou Jacobi; **D:** Steve Gordon. Academy Awards '81: Best Song ("Arthur's Theme"), Best Supporting Actor (Gielgud); Nominations: Best Actor (Moore), Best Original Screenplay. **VHS, Beta, LV, 8mm $19.98** WAR, FCT, BTV *♂♂♂*

Arthur 2: On the Rocks When Arthur finally marries his sweetheart, it may not be "happily ever after" because the father of the girl he didn't marry is out for revenge. When Arthur discovers that he is suddenly penniless, a bit of laughter is the cure for the blues and also serves well when the liquor runs out. A disappointing sequel with few laughs.

1988 (PG) 113m/C Dudley Moore, Liza Minnelli, John Gielgud, Geraldine Fitzgerald, Stephen Elliott, Ted Ross, Barney Martin, Jack Gilford; *D:* Bud Yorkin. VHS, Beta, LV, 8mm $19.98 WAR, FCT ♂♂½

Arthur's Hallowed Ground A cricket field caretaker battles the board of directors over the fate of his favorite plot of sod.
1984 75m/C Jimmy Jewel, Jean Bolt, Michael Elphick; *D:* Freddie Young. VHS, Beta $59.95 MGM ♂

Article 99 Doctors in a Kansas City Veteran's Administration hospital try to heal patients while putting up with bureaucratic red tape and a stingy administrator. When rogue physician Sturgess (Liotta) is dismissed, the patients hold a siege. Sort of sort of "Mash" (Big Daddy Sutherland did Hawkeye) that gets its title from a fictional rule that says veterans can be treated only for conditions related to military service. Erstwhile cast labors to combine comedic and dramatic intentions of script.
1992 (R) 100m/C Ray Liotta, Kiefer Sutherland, Forest Whitaker, Lea Thompson, John C. McGinley, John Mahoney, Keith David, Kathy Baker, Eli Wallach, Noble Willingham, Julie Bovasso, Troy Evans, Lynne Thigpen, Jeffrey Tambor, Rutanya Alda; *D:* Howard Deutch. VHS, LV $92.98 ORI ♂♂

Artists and Models Martin is a struggling comic book artist and Lewis his idiot roommate. The pair become mixed up in both romance and intrigue when Lewis begins talking in his sleep about spys and such. One of the duo's more pleasant cinematic outings. ♫Inamorata; Lucky Song; You Look So Familiar; Why You Pretend.
1955 109m/C Dean Martin, Jerry Lewis, Shirley MacLaine, Dorothy Malone, Eddie Mayehoff, Eva Gabor, Anita Ekberg, George Winslow, Jack Elam, Herbert Rudley, Nick Castle; *D:* Frank Tashlin. VHS $14.95 PAR, MLB ♂♂½

Artist's Studio Secrets An artist from Greenwich Village only gets aroused by clothed models, so his wife jealously arranges for him to only work with nude women. *AKA:* The Story of an Artist's Studio Secrets; Artist Nude Secrets.
1964 78m/B VHS, Beta $19.95 VDM ♂

As If It Were Raining Constantine gets involved in an embezzlement scheme in Spain in this espionage thriller.
1963 85m/C FR Eddie Constantine, Henri Cogan, Elisa Montes, Jose Nieto, Silvia Solar; *D:* Jose Monter. VHS $16.95 SNC ♂

As Is Two gay New Yorkers deal with a troubled romance and AIDS. A cable television adaptation from the William M. Hoffman play.
1985 86m/C Jonathan Hadary, Robert Carradine; *D:* Michael Lindsay-Hogg. VHS, Beta $19.98 LHV, WAR ♂♂½

As Summers Die Louisiana attorney Glenn fights in the late 1950s to protect the rights of a black family, against the wishes of a powerful local clan. Glenn finds support in surprising places, though. From Winston Groom's acclaimed novel. A cable television movie.
1986 100m/C Scott Glenn, Jamie Lee Curtis, Penny Fuller, Bette Davis, John Randolph, Beah Richards, Ron O'Neal, John McIntire; *D:* Jean-Claude Tramont. VHS, Beta $14.95 NEG ♂♂

As You Desire Me Garbo plays an amnesia victim who returns to a husband she doesn't even remember after an abusive relationship with a novelist. An interesting, if not down-right bizarre movie, due to the pairing of the great Garbo and the intriguing von Stroheim. An adaption of Luigi Pirandello's play.
1932 71m/B Greta Garbo, Melvyn Douglas, Erich von Stroheim, Owen Moore, Hedda Hopper; *D:* George Fitzmaurice. VHS, Beta $19.98 MGM, FCT ♂♂½

As You Like It A Duke's banished daughter poses as a man to win the attentions of one of her father's attendants in this highly stylized Shakespearean comedy adapted by J.M. Barrie and Robert Cullen. Early Shakespearean Olivier.
1936 96m/B GB Elisabeth Bergner, Laurence Olivier, Henry Ainley, Felix Aylmer; *D:* Paul Czinner; *W:* J.M. Barrie, Robert Cullen. VHS, Beta, LV, 3/4U, Special order formats $19.95 NOS, MRV, VYY ♂♂½

As You Like It Shakespeare's lighthearted comedy about all kinds of love—physical and intellectual, sentimental and cynical, enduring love between friends, and romantic love at first sight. Play features the "Seven Ages of Man" speech. Part of the television series "The Shakespeare Plays."
1979 150m/C GB Helen Mirren, Brian Stirner, Richard Pasco. VHS, Beta TLF ♂♂♂

As You Were A girl with a photographic memory enlists in the Army, becoming both a nuisance and comedic victim to her sergeant.
1951 57m/B Joe Sawyer, William Tracy, Sondra Rogers, Joan Vohs. VHS, Beta, LV NO ♂

As Young As You Feel A 65-year-old man is forced to retire from his job. He poses as the head of the conglomerate and convinces them to repeal their retirement policy. He then gains national publicity when he makes a speech about the dignity of man. Watch for Monroe as the boss's secretary. Fine comic performances enhance the script; based on a story by Paddy Chayefsky.
1951 77m/C Monty Woolley, Thelma Ritter, David Wayne, Jean Peters, Constance Bennett, Marilyn Monroe, Allyn Joslyn, Albert Dekker, Clinton Sundberg, Minor Watson; *D:* Harmon Jones. VHS $14.98 FXV ♂♂

Ash Wednesday Taylor endures the pain of cosmetic surgery in an effort to rescue her floundering union with Fonda. Another undistinguished performance by Liz. Fonda is especially slimy as the philandering husband, but only appears in the latter stages of the film.
1973 (R) 99m/C Elizabeth Taylor, Henry Fonda, Helmut Berger, Keith Baxter, Margaret Blye, Maurice Teynac, Monique Van Vooren; *D:* Larry Peerce. VHS $14.95 PAR, FCT, CCB ♂

Ashanti, Land of No Mercy Caine of the week movie with Michael portraying a doctor acting as a missionary in South Africa who finds himself alone in a battle to rescue his wife from a band of slave traders. The chase spans many Middle Eastern countries and begins to look bleak for our man. Talented cast and promising plot are undone by slow pace. Based on the novel "Ebano" by Alberto Vasquez-Figueroa. *AKA:* Ashanti.
1979 117m/C Michael Caine, Omar Sharif, Peter Ustinov, Rex Harrison, William Holden, Beverly Johnson; *D:* Richard Fleischer. VHS, Beta $19.98 TWE ♂

Ashes and Diamonds In the closing days of WWII, a Polish resistance fighter assassinates the wrong man, tries to find love with the right women, and questions the meaning of struggle. A seminal Eastern European masterpiece that defined a generation of pre-solidarity Poles. Available in Polish with English subtitles or dubbed into English. The last installment of the trilogy that includes "A Generation" and "Kanal" and based on a novel by Jerzy Andrzewski. *AKA:* Popiol i Diament.
1958 105m/B PL Zbigniew Cybulski, Eva Krzyzewska, Adam Pawlikowski, Bogumil Kobiela, Waclaw Zastrzezynski; *D:* Andrzej Wajda. VHS, Beta $19.95 TAM, SUE, MRV ♂♂♂½

Ashes and Embers A black Vietnam vet in Los Angeles has trouble fitting into society, eventually running afoul of the police. Ethiopian-born director Gerima endows vital subject matter with a properly alienated mood.
1982 120m/C John Anderson, Evelyn Blackwell; *D:* Haile Gerima. VHS $59.95 FCT ♂♂

Ask Any Girl Lighthearted fluff about a small-town girl who moves to Manhattan. MacLaine plays the bright Meg who gets a job at an ad agency and decides to set her sights on marrying her boss (Young). She asks his older brother's (Niven) help in her quest and the inevitable happens.
1959 101m/C Shirley MacLaine, David Niven, Gig Young, Rod Taylor, Jim Backus, Claire Kelly, Elisabeth Fraser; *D:* Charles Walters. VHS $19.98 MGM, MOV ♂♂½

Aspen Extreme Former Aspen ski instructor writes and directs a movie on (what else?) ski instructors in (where?) Aspen! Long on ski shots and short on plot, this movie never leaves the bunny hill. Two Detroiters leave Motown for Snowtown to pursue a life on the slopes. T.J (Gross) soon has his hands full with two beautiful women (Polo and Hughes) who encourage his dream of becoming a writer. His friend Dexter (Berg), however, acquires a few bad habits, and the whole movie just goes downhill from there.
1993 (PG-13) 128m/C Paul Gross, Peter Berg, Teri Polo, Finola Hughes; *W/D:* Patrick Hasburgh. VHS, Beta, LV $94.95 HPH, BVV ♂

The Asphalt Jungle An aging criminal emerges from his forced retirement (prison) and assembles the old gang for one final heist. A very realistic storyline and a superb cast make this one of the best crime films ever made. Highly acclaimed; based on the work of W.R. Burnett.
1950 112m/B Sterling Hayden, Louis Calhern, Jean Hagen, James Whitmore, Sam Jaffe, John McIntire, Marc Lawrence, Barry Kelley, Anthony Caruso, Teresa Celli, Marilyn Monroe; *D:* John Huston; *W:* Ben Maddow; *M:* Miklos Rozsa. Academy Awards '50 Nominations: Best Black and White Cinematography, Best Director (Huston), Best Screenplay, Best Supporting Actor (Jaffe); Edgar Allan Poe Awards '50: Best Screenplay; National Board of Review Awards '50: 10 Best Films of the Year, Best Director (Huston). VHS, Beta, LV $19.98 MGM, VYG ♂♂♂♂

The Asphyx Nineteenth century doctor Stephens is studying death when he discovers The Asphyx, an aura that surrounds a person just before they die. Stephens delves deeper into his research and finds the keys to immortality. However, his irresponsibility in unleashing the obscure supernatural power on the world brings a swarm of unforeseen and irreversible troubles. High-class sci fi. *AKA:* Spirit of the Dead.
1972 (PG) 98m/C GB Robert Stephens, Robert Powell, Jane Lapotaire, Alex Scott, Ralph Arliss, Fiona Walker, John Lawrence; *D:* Peter Newbrook. VHS, Beta $19.95 UHV, MED ♂♂♂

Assassin Mongolian hordes try to invade China and wind up getting kicked for their efforts.
1979 96m/C VHS, Beta $29.95 UNI ♂

Assassin Athletic karate fighter poses as an underworld figure and infiltrates the largest gang in Japan where he is hired as a hit man.

1979 86m/C Sonny Chiba. VHS, Beta $59.98 *FOX ✗*

Assassin Made for TV drama about a mad scientist who creates a bionic killer for a bizarre plot to take over the world. He programs the cyborg to assassinate the President and other key people to help carry out his plan. A retired CIA operative emerges to stop the scientist by trying to destroy the robot.
1986 (PG-13) 94m/C Robert Conrad, Karen Austin, Richard Young, Jonathan Banks, Robert Webber; *D:* Sandor Stern. VHS, Beta $29.95 *ACA ✗✗*

Assassin Fairly lame thriller about a CIA agent protecting a Senator who falls under suspicion when his charge is shot by an assassin. In investigating the killing the agent discovers the usual governmental conspiracy.
1989 (R) 92m/C Steve Railsback, Nicholas Guest, Xander Berkeley, Elpidia Carrillo; *D:* Jon Hess. VHS, Beta, LV $79.99 *HBO ✗✗*

Assassin of Youth Girl is introduced to marijuana and soon becomes involved in "the thrills of wild parties," and the horrors of the "killer weed." Camp diversion.
1935 70m/B Luana Walters, Arthur Gardner; *D:* Elmer Clifton. VHS, Beta $16.95 *SNC, NOS, TIM ✗½*

Assassination A serious threat has been made to First Lady Ireland and no one is taking it lightly. Secret Service agent Bronson has been called as Ireland's personal bodyguard and suddenly they are both the target of terrorist attacks. Strangely though, the attacks seem to be directed from inside the White House. Bronson as you've seen him many times before.
1987 (R) 93m/C Charles Bronson, Jill Ireland, Stephen Elliott, Michael Ansara, *D:* Peter Hunt. VHS, Beta, LV $9.98 *MED ✗*

The Assassination Bureau Set in Victorian-era London, this amusing farce concerns a society of international assassins lead by the charming Reed. Rigg is an intrepid reporter who pays Reed to have his own organization try to kill him. Reed in turn will try to get them first. A cross-European chase ends in a battle aboard a Zepplin. Tongue-in-cheek whimsy with a fine cast. Based on a short story by Jack London.
1969 106m/C GB Oliver Reed, Diana Rigg, Telly Savalas, Curt Jurgens, Philippe Noiret, Warren Mitchell, Beryl Reid, Clive Revill, Kenneth Griffith, Vernon Dobtcheff, Annabella Incontrera; *D:* Basil Dearden. VHS *PAR ✗✗*

Assassination of Trotsky Middling attempt to dramatize the last days of the Russian Revolutionary leader in Mexico before he's done in with an ice pick.
1972 113m/C FR GB IT Richard Burton, Alain Delon, Romy Schneider, Valentina Cortese, Jean Desailly; *D:* Joseph Losey. VHS, Beta, LV $19.98 *REP, PIA, FCT ✗✗*

The Assassination Run A retired British spy is involved against his will in an intricate plot of terrorism, counter-terrorism and espionage.
1980 111m/C GB Malcolm Stoddard, Mary Tamm; *D:* Ken Hannam. VHS, Beta $59.98 *FOX ✗*

Assault Violent sex murders in a girl's school have the police baffled. The school's pretty art teacher offers to act as bait in order to catch the murderer. *AKA:* In the Devil's Garden; Tower of Terror; The Creepers.

1970 89m/C GB Suzy Kendall, Frank Finlay, Freddie Jones, James Laurenson, Lesley-Anne Down, Tony Beckley; *D:* Sidney Hayers. VHS, Beta $59.95 *SUE ✗½*

The Assault Powerful and disturbing drama about a Dutch boy who witnesses the arbitrary murder of his family by Nazis. The memory tortures him and leaves him empty as he matures. Years later he meets other victims and also the perpetrators of the incident, each of them changed forever by it. Thought-provoking consideration of WWII and the horrors of living in Nazi Germany from many points of view. Based on a novel by Harry Mulisch. Dutch language dubbed into English. *AKA:* De Aanslag.
1986 (PG) 149m/C NL Derek De Lint, Marc Van Uchelen, Monique Van De Ven; *D:* Fons Rademakers. VHS, Beta $19.98 *MGM, TAM, SWC ✗✗✗½*

Assault and Matrimony Real-life married people Tucker and Eikenberry play a married couple fighting tooth and nail. Lots of slapstick and general nonsense. Television film based on James Anderson's novel.
1987 100m/C John Hillerman, Michelle Phillips, Joe Cortese, Michael Tucker, Jill Eikenberry; *D:* James Frawley. VHS, Beta, LV $89.95 *VMK ✗½*

The Assault of Final Rival A young beggar learns the art of kung-fu and that the inner strength actually lies in the hair. So when a rival cuts his hair, the beggar must strengthen his kung-fu skills so his hair will grow back.
1985 87m/C VHS, Beta $14.95 *NEG ✗½*

Assault of the Killer Bimbos Five foolish girls manage to seduce, then kill, a town's criminal element.
1987 90m/C Karen Nielsen, Debi Thibeault, Lisa Schmidt, Simone; *D:* Gorman Bechard. Beta *NO ✗½*

Assault of the Party Nerds Nerds throw a wild party to try and attract new members to their fraternity, while a jock frat plots against them. Sound familiar? Little more than a ripoff of "Revenge of the Nerds" made especially for video.
1989 (R) 82m/C Linnea Quigley, Troy Donahue, Richard Gabai, C. Paul Demsey, Marc Silverberg, Robert Mann, Richard Rifkin, Deborah Roush; *D:* Richard Gabai. VHS, Beta $79.95 *PSM ✗*

Assault of the Rebel Girls A reporter gets involved with smuggling in Castro's Cuba. Flynn's last film, saving the worst for last. *AKA:* Cuban Rebel Girls; Attack of the Rebel Girls.
1959 66m/B Errol Flynn, Beverly Aadland, John McKay, Jackie Jackler, Marie Edmund; *D:* Barry Mahon; *W:* Errol Flynn. VHS, Beta $59.95 *MED ✗½*

Assault on a Queen Stupid Sinatra vehicle about a group of con men who plot together to rob the Queen Mary on one of her trips. Their attack vessel is a renovated World War II German U-boat. The producers tried to capitalize on the popularity of "Ocean's Eleven," but they didn't even come close. Based on a novel by Jack Finney.
1966 106m/C Frank Sinatra, Virna Lisi, Anthony (Tony) Franciosa, Richard Conte, Reginald Denny; *D:* Jack Donohue; *W:* Rod Serling. VHS $14.95 *PAR ✗*

Assault on Agathon Amid the scenic Greek isles, an "executed" WWII guerilla leader returns to lead a revolution, and bloodshed and bombings ensue.
1975 (PG) 95m/C GB IT Nina Van Pallandt, Marianne Faithfull, John Woodvine, Nico Minardos; *D:* Laslo Benedek. VHS, Beta $59.95 *GEM, MRV, PSM ✗✗*

Assault on Precinct 13 Urban horror invades LA. A sleepy police station in Los Angeles is suddenly under siege from a violent youth gang. Paranoia abounds as the police are attacked from all sides and can see no way out. Carpenter's musical score adds much to the setting of this unique police exploitation story that somehow stands as Carpenter's adaptation of Howard Hawks' "Rio Bravo." Semi-acclaimed and very gripping.
1976 91m/C *D:* John Carpenter, John Carpenter, John Carpenter. VHS, Beta $54.95 *MED ✗✗✗*

Assault with a Deadly Weapon When the police budget is cutback, crime runs rampant in an unnamed American city.
1982 86m/C Sandra Foley, Richard Holliday, Lamont Jackson; *D:* Arthur Kennedy. VHS, Beta $39.95 *LIV ✗*

The Assignment The assassination of a high-ranking officer in an uneasy Latin American nation spurs violence and political instability. A Swedish diplomat is assigned the tremendous task of restoring peace and stability between the political factions.
1978 92m/C SW Christopher Plummer, Thomas Hellberg, Carolyn Seymour, Fernando Rey; *D:* Mats Arehn. VHS, Beta $19.95 *STE, NWV ✗✗*

Assignment Outer Space A giant spaceship with bytes for brains is on a collision course with Earth. A team of astronauts is sent to save the world from certain peril. Seems they take the task lightly, though, and their mission (and hence the plot) revolves more around saving sexy sultress Farinon from certain celibacy. If you're into stultifying Italian space operas with a gratuitous sex sub-plot then look up this assignment, but don't say we didn't warn you. Narrated by Jack Wallace; director Margheriti is also known as Anthony Davies. *AKA:* Space Men.
1961 79m/B IT Rik von Nutter, Gabriella Farinon, Archie Savage, Dave Montresor, Alan Dijon; *D:* Antonio Margheriti. VHS $19.98 *NOS, SNC ✗*

Assignment Skybolt When terrorists get their hands on a hydrogen bomb, a special mission is detached to stop them before they start WWIII.
198? 109m/C *D:* Greg Tallas. VHS, Beta $19.99 *BFV ✗½*

The Assisi Underground True but boringly told story of how the Catholic Church helped to save several hundred Italian Jews from being executed by the Nazis during the 1943 German occupation of Italy. Edited from 178 minutes, a good-will gesture from the producers.
1984 115m/C James Mason, Ben Cross, Maximilian Schell, Irene Papas; *D:* Alexander Ramati. VHS, Beta $79.95 *MGM, IGP ✗✗*

The Associate A French farce about a penniless financial consultant who invents a fictitious partner in order to get his business rolling. English subtitles. *AKA:* L'Associe.
1982 (R) 93m/C FR Michel Serrault, Claudine Auger, Catherine Alric, Julien Pardot; *D:* Rene Gainville. VHS, Beta $39.98 *SUE ✗✗*

The Association A man and a woman go undercover to bust an international white slavery ring.
198? 92m/C TW Carter Huang, Angela Mao; *D:* Cheung Wo Chang. VHS, Beta $59.98 *CGH ✗½*

Assunta Spina A very early, very rare Italian epic about ancient Rome, the prototype for the Italian silent epics to come.
1915 70m/B IT VHS, Beta $39.98 *FCT ✗✗*

A

Asterix vs. Caesar Asterix and his trusty pal Obelix do battle once again with Caesar and the Romans, with the Romans coming out worse for wear. Adapted from a French comic strip. *AKA:* Asterix et la Surprise de Cesar.
1985 79m/C *FR D:* Paul Brizzi, Gaetan Brizzi; *V:* Roger Carel, Pierre Tornade. **VHS $39.95** *CEL, WTA ✓✓*

The Astounding She-Monster How can you not love a movie with a title like this? A bad script and snail-paced plot are a good start. A geologist wanting only to be left alone with his rocks survives a brush with the kidnappers of a wealthy heiress only to happen upon an alien spacecraft that's crashed nearby. At the helm is a very tall, high-heeled fem-alien in an obligatory skin-tight space outfit. Excellent, our rock jock thinks, but it seems she kills with the slightest touch. For connoisseurs of truly bad movies. *AKA:* Mysterious Invader.
1958 60m/B Robert Clarke, Kenne Duncan, Marilyn Harvey, Jeanne Tatum, Shirley Kilpatrick, Ewing Miles Brown; *D:* Ronnie Ashcroft. **VHS $19.98** *SNC, MRV, CNM* *Woof!*

The Astro-Zombies A contender as one of the worst movies of all time. Carradine plays a mad scientist creating zombies who eat people's guts. Cult favorite Tura Satana stars. Co-written and co-produced by Wayne Rogers of "M*A*S*H" fame.
1967 83m/C Tura Satana, Wendell Corey, John Carradine, Tom Pace, Joan Patrick, Rafael Campos; *W/D:* Ted V. Mikels; *W:* Wayne Rogers. **VHS, Beta $49.95** *UHV* *Woof!*

Asylum Four strange and chilling stories weave together in this film. A murderer's victim seeks retribution. A tailor seems to be collecting his bills. A man who makes voodoo dolls...only to become one later on. A woman plagued by a double. A doctor visiting the asylum tells each tale. Horrifying and grotesque, not as humorless as American horror films. *AKA:* House of Crazies.
1972 (PG) 100m/C *GB* Peter Cushing, Herbert Lom, Britt Ekland, Barbara Parkins, Patrick Magee, Barry Morse; *D:* Roy Ward Baker. **VHS, Beta, LV $9.99** *STE, PSM, MED ✓✓½*

Asylum of Satan A beautiful concert pianist is savagely tortured by a madman in the Asylum of Satan. Filmed on location in Louisville, Kentucky.
1972 87m/C Charles Kissinger, Carla Borelli, Nick Jolly, Sherry Steiner; *W/D:* William Girdler. **VHS, Beta $19.95** *UHV ✓*

At Close Range Based on the true story of Bruce Johnston Sr. and Jr. in Brandywine River Valley, Pennsylvania. Father, Walken, tempts his teen-aged son, Penn, into pursuing criminal activities with talk of excitement and high living. Penn soon learns that his father is extremely dangerous and a bit unstable, but he's still fascinated by his wealth and power. Sometimes overbearing and depressing, but good acting and fancy camera work. A young cast of stars includes Masterson as the girl Penn tries to impress. Features Madonna's "Live to Tell."
1986 (R) 115m/C Sean Penn, Christopher Walken, Christopher Penn, Mary Stuart Masterson, Crispin Glover, Kiefer Sutherland, Candy Clark, Tracy Walter; *D:* James Foley. **VHS, Beta, LV $79.98** *VES, LIV ✓✓✓*

At Gunpoint A store owner becomes the town hero when, by accident, he shoots and kills a bank robber. *AKA:* Gunpoint.
1955 81m/C Fred MacMurray, Dorothy Malone, John Qualen, Walter Brennan; *D:* Alfred Werker. **VHS, Beta $39.95** *REP, HHE ✓✓*

At Gunpoint A no-account bank robber spends his six-year stint in the slammer plotting his revenge. Having gone thoroughly stir-crazy, the vengeful criminal stalks the lawman who put him away, like so many vengeful criminals before him. Director Harris also scripted this run-of-the-mill addition to big list of bad guy hunting for revenge flicks.
1990 90m/C Frank Kanig, Tain Bodkin, Scott Claflin; *W/D:* Steven Harris. **VHS $79.95** *CAF ✓½*

At Play in the Fields of the Lord A thoughtful epic that never quite lives up to its own self-importance—or length. Two yankee missionary couples try to evangelize a fearsome tribe of Brazilian rain-forest dwellers. One of the Christian families suffers a crisis of faith that's well-acted but not as powerful as a co-plot regarding a modern American Indian (Berenger) who joins the jungle natives with calamitous results. Based on the novel by Peter Matthiessen.
1991 (R) 186m/C Tom Berenger, Aidan Quinn, Kathy Bates, John Lithgow, Daryl Hannah, Tom Waits, Stenio Garcia, Nelson Xavier, Jose Dumont, Niilo Kivirinta; *W/D:* Hector Babenco; *W:* Jean-Claude Carriere; *M:* Zbigniew Preisner. **VHS, Beta, LV $19.98** *MCA ✓✓✓*

At Sword's Point Adventure tale based on Alexandre Dumas' "The Three Musketeers," wherein the sons of the musketeers vie to save their queen from the evil plots of Duke Douglas. *AKA:* Sons of the Musketeers.
1951 81m/C Cornel Wilde, William Smith, Micheline Lanctot, Maureen O'Hara, Henry Beckman, Brian Patrick Clark, John McFadyen, Ken James; *D:* Paul Lynch, Lewis Allen. **VHS, Beta, LV $19.95** *MED, TTC, FCT ✓✓*

At the Circus Marx Brothers invade the circus to save it from bankruptcy and cause their usual comic insanity, though they've done it better before. Beginning of the end for the Marxes, a step down in quality from their classic work, though frequently darn funny. ♫Lydia the Tattooed Lady; Step Up and Take a Bow; Two Blind Loves; Blue Moon. *AKA:* The Marx Brothers at the Circus.
1939 87m/B Groucho Marx, Chico Marx, Harpo Marx, Margaret Dumont, Kenny L. Baker, Florence Rice, Eve Arden, Nat Pendleton, Fritz Feld; *D:* Edward Buzzell. **VHS, Beta, LV $19.95** *MGM ✓✓*

At the Earth's Core A Victorian scientist invents a giant burrowing machine, which he and his crew use to dig deeply into the Earth. To their surprise, they discover a lost world of subhuman creatures and prehistoric monsters. Based on Edgar Rice Burrough's novels.
1976 (PG) 90m/C *GB* Doug McClure, Peter Cushing, Caroline Munro; *D:* Kevin Connor. **VHS, Beta** *WAR, OM ✓✓*

At War with the Army Serviceable comedy from Martin and Lewis in their first starring appearance, as the recruits get mixed up in all kinds of wild situations at their army base. Based on the play by James Allardice.
1950 93m/B Dean Martin, Jerry Lewis, Polly Bergen, Mike Kellin; *D:* Hal Walker. **VHS, Beta, 3/4U, Special order formats $24.95** *NOS, MRV, CAB ✓✓*

Atalia Relates the love between Atalia, a war widow, and the younger man she loves. The problem stems from the fact that she lives in a Kibbutz, and the lifestyle contradicts sharply from that of her beliefs in love, forcing her to eventually make a momentous decision.
1985 90m/C Michal Bat-Adam, Yftach Katzur, Dan Toren; *D:* Akiva Tevet. **VHS $79.95** *ERG ✓✓*

Athena Two sisters (Powell and Reynolds) from an eccentric, health-faddist family fall in love with their opposites. Purdom is the stuffy Boston lawyer who goes off with Powell and Reynolds entices a TV crooner (Damone). Routine romance with routine songs. Reeves, who would become a star as a movie muscleman, appears in a brief role. ♫Love Can Change the Stars; The Girl Next Door; Imagine; Venezia; Chacun le Sait; I Never Felt Better; Vocalize.
1954 96m/C Jane Powell, Debbie Reynolds, Edmund Purdom, Vic Damone, Louis Calhern, Evelyn Varden, Linda Christian, Virginia Gibson, Nancy Kilgas, Dolores Starr, Jane Fischer, Cecile Rogers, Steve Reeves; *D:* Richard Thorpe; *W:* William Ludwig, Leonard Spigelgass; *M:* Hugh Martin, Ralph Blane. **VHS $19.98** *MGM ✓✓½*

Atlantic City A small-time, aging Mafia hood falls in love with a young clam bar waitress, and they share the spoils of a big score against the backdrop of Atlantic City. Wonderful character study that becomes something more, a piercing declaration about a city's transformation and the effect on the people who live there. Lancaster, in a sterling performance, personifies the city, both of them fading with time. *AKA:* Atlantic City U.S.A.
1981 (R) 104m/C *CA FR* Burt Lancaster, Susan Sarandon, Kate Reid, Michel Piccoli, Hollis McLaren; *D:* Louis Malle. Academy Awards '81 Nominations: Best Actor (Lancaster), Best Actress (Sarandon), Best Director (Malle), Best Original Screenplay, Best Picture; British Academy Awards '81: Best Actor (Lancaster), Best Director (Malle); National Society of Film Critics Awards '81: Best Film. **VHS, Beta, LV $14.95** *PAR ✓✓✓½*

Atlantis, the Lost Continent If anything could sink the fabled lost continent of Atlantis it's this cheap fantasy flick. A greek sailor saves a princess and takes her back to her Atlantis home where he's promptly enslaved by the island's evil ruler. But this hero won't put up with any nonsense so he leads his fellow slaves in a revolt and gains his freedom before sinking both evil ruler and island (using atomic power no less!).
1961 90m/C Anthony Hall, Joyce Taylor, John Dall, Bill Smith, Edward Platt, Frank DeKova; *D:* George Pal. **VHS $19.98** *MGM ✓*

Atlas The mighty Atlas takes on massive armies, one of which includes director Corman, in a bid to win the hand of a princess. About as cheap as they come, although it is one of the few Sword & Sandal epics that isn't dubbed.
1960 84m/C Michael Forest, Frank Wolff, Barboura Morris, Walter Maslow; *D:* Roger Corman; *W:* Charles B. Griffith. **VHS $19.95** *DVT, SNC, HEG ✓*

Atlas in the Land of the Cyclops Atlas takes on a hideous one-eyed monster to save a baby from an evil queen. Not a divorce custody drama. *AKA:* Atlas Against the Cyclops; Maciste Nella Terra dei Ciclopi.
1961 100m/C *IT* Mitchell Gordon, Chelo Alonso, Vira Silenti; *D:* Antonio Leonuiola. **VHS $19.98** *SNC, TIM* *Woof!*

Atom Age Vampire Mad scientist doing research on Japanese nuclear bomb victims falls in love with a woman disfigured in an auto crash. To remove her scars, he treats her with a formula derived from the glands of freshly killed women. English dubbed. Not among the best of its kind (a low-rent district if ever there was one), but

entertaining in a mischievous, boy-is-this-a-stupid-film sort of way.
1961 71m/B *IT* Alberto Lupo, Susanne Loret, Sergio Fantoni; **D:** Albert Magnoli. **VHS, Beta** **$16.95** *SNC, NOS, VYY* Woof!

Atomic Attack Nuclear bomb is dropped on New York City and a family living 50 miles away must escape. Gentlemen, start your engines.
1950 50m/B Walter Matthau. **VHS, Beta, 3/4U** **$29.95** *IHF* ☆

The Atomic Brain An old woman hires a doctor to transplant her brain into the body of a beautiful young girl. Of the three girls who are abducted, two become homicidal zombies and the third starts to act catty when she is given a feline brain. A must-see for bad-brain movie fans. **AKA:** Monstrosity.
1964 72m/B Frank Gerstle, Erika Peters, Judy Bamber, Marjorie Eaton, Frank Fowler, Margie Fisco; **D:** Joseph Mascelli. **VHS $19.98** *NOS, SNC* Woof!

The Atomic Cafe A chillingly humorous compilation of newsreels and government films of the 1940's and 1950's that show America's preoccupation with the A-Bomb. Some sequences are in black and white. Includes the infamous training film "Duck and Cover," which tells us what to do in the event of an actual bombing.
1982 92m/C **D:** Kevin Rafferty. **VHS, Beta** **$29.95** *HBO* ☆☆☆

The Atomic City Barry plays a nuclear physicist at Los Alamos whose son is kidnapped by terrorists who want his bomb-making formulas. The bad guys hide out in the nearby mountains which at least makes for some pleasant scenery in this average thriller.
1952 84m/B Gene Barry, Lee Aaker, Michael Moore, Lydia Clarke, Nancy Gates, Milburn Stone; **D:** Jerry Hopper. **VHS** *PAR* ☆☆½

The Atomic Kid A man survives an atomic blast because of a peanut butter sandwich he was eating. As a result, he himself becomes radioactive and discovers that he has acquired some strange new powers which get him into what pass for hilarious predicaments. Screenplay by Blake Edwards.
1954 86m/B Mickey Rooney, Robert Strauss, Elaine Davis, Bill Goodwin; **D:** Leslie Martinson; **W:** Blake Edwards. **VHS $19.98** *REP* ☆☆½

The Atomic Man Owing to radioactive experimentation, a scientist exists for a short time in the future. Once there, both good and evil forces want to use him for their own purposes. **AKA:** Timeslip.
1956 78m/B *GB* Gene Nelson, Faith Domergue, Joseph Tomelty, Peter Arne; **D:** Ken Hughes. **VHS $16.95** *NOS, SNC* ☆½

Atomic Submarine Futuristic sci fi plots government agents against alien invaders. The battle, however, takes place in the ocean beneath the Arctic and is headed by an atomic-powered submarine clashing with a special alien underwater saucer. We all live on the atomic sub for devotees: fun for devotees.
1959 80m/C Arthur Franz, Dick Foran, Bob Steele, Brett Halsey, Joi Lansing; **D:** Spencer Gordon Bennet. **VHS, Beta $39.95** *SNC* ☆

The Atonement of Gosta Berling A priest, forced to leave the priesthood because of his drinking, falls in love with a young married woman. Garbo shines in the first role which brought her critical acclaim; Hanson's performance also makes this a memorable drama. Adapted from the novel by Selma Lagerlof. **AKA:** Gosta Berling's Saga; The Legend of Gosta Berling; The

Story of Gosta Berling; The Saga of Gosta Berling.
1924 91m/B *SW* Lars Hanson, Greta Garbo, Ellen Cederstrom, Mona Martenson, Jenny Hasselquist, Gerda Lundequist; **D:** Mauritz Stiller. **VHS** *VYY, MRV, DVT* ☆☆☆

Ator the Fighting Eagle Styled after "Conan The Barbarian" this mythical action fantasy stars O'Keeffe as Ator, son of Thorn. Ator must put an end to the tragic Dynasty of the Spiders, thereby fulfilling the legend of his family at the expense of the viewer. Goofy low-budget sword and sandal stuff. Followed by "The Blade Master."
1983 (PG) 98m/C *IT* Miles O'Keeffe, Sabrina Siani, Ritza Brown, Edmund Purdom, Laura Gemser; **D:** David Hill. **VHS, Beta $69.99** *HBO* Woof!

Attack Force Z An elite corps of Australian military is Force Z. Volunteers are chosen for a dangerous mission: find the plane that crashed somewhere in the South Pacific and rescue the defecting Japanese government official on board, all before the end of WWII and the feature. Talented cast is effectively directed in low-key adventure featuring young Gibson.
1984 84m/C *AU* Sam Neill, Chris Haywood, Mel Gibson, John Phillip Law, John Waters; **D:** Tim Burstall. **VHS, Beta $19.99** *MCG, MTX* ☆☆

Attack from Outer Space Explores the possibility of extraterrestrial life, particularly on the set.
1980 90m/C VHS, Beta $9.95 *UHV, MRV* Woof!

Attack of the Beast Creatures The survivors of a wrecked ocean liner are stranded on a desert island overrun by savage creatures. This makes them anxious.
1985 82m/C Robert Nolfi, Robert Langyel, Julia Rust, Lisa Pak; **D:** Michael Stanley. **VHS, Beta** *WWV* Woof!

Attack of the 50 Foot Woman A beautiful, abused housewife has a frightening encounter with a giant alien, causing her to grow to an enormous height. Then she goes looking for hubby. Perhaps the all-time classic '50s sci fi, a truly fun movie highlighted by the sexy, 50-foot Hayes in a giant bikini. Has intriguing psychological depth and social commentary done in a suitably cheezy manner. Also available with "House on Haunted Hill" on laser disc.
1958 72m/B Allison Hayes, William Hudson, Roy Gordon; **D:** Nathan Hertz. **VHS, Beta, LV $14.98** *FOX, FCT* ☆☆½

Attack of the Giant Leeches Cheapo Corman fare about giant leeches in a murky swamp who suddenly decide to make human flesh their new food supply. Perturbed inn keeper plays along by forcing his wife and lover into the murk. Leeches frolic. Sometimes tedious, sometimes chilling, always low budget and slimy. Although the special effects aren't top notch, this might be a fine choice for a late night scare/laugh. **AKA:** The Giant Leeches.
1959 62m/B Ken Clarke, Yvette Vickers, Gene Roth, Bruno Ve Sota; **D:** Bernard L. Kowalski. **VHS $19.95** *NOS, SNC* ☆

Attack of the Killer Refrigerator Chiller featuring a group of sleazy college students having a wild party. In the process, they abuse a hapless refrigerator. Fed up, the vengeful appliance goes on a rampage of murder and destruction. Certain to make you view kitchen appliances in a new light. Planned sequels in the newfound kitchen-utility horror genre include "Refrigerator II: Brutally Defrosted" and "Bloody, Bloody Coffee Maker."
1990 ?m/C VHS *BFA* Woof!

Attack of the Killer Tomatoes Candidate for worst film ever made, deliberate category. Horror spoof that defined "low budget" stars several thousand ordinary tomatoes that suddenly turn savage and begin attacking people. No sci-fi cliche remains untouched in this dumb parody. A few musical numbers are performed in lieu of an actual plot. Followed by "Return of the Killer Tomatoes."
1977 87m/C **D:** John DeBello. **VHS, Beta** **$19.95** *MED* Woof!

Attack of the Mayan Mummy A greedy doctor gets his patient to channel her former self so that she can show him where to find an ancient tomb that is filled with treasure. Good idea.
1963 77m/B *MX* Richard Webb, Nina Knight, Norman Burton, Steve Conte; **D:** Jerry Warren. **VHS $16.95** *NOS, LOO, SNC* Woof!

Attack of the Mushroom People A secluded island is the sight where people eating mysterious mushrooms have been turning into oversized, killer 'shrooms' themselves. Trouble is, the only witness to this madness has gone insane. Will anyone believe him before it's too late? **AKA:** Matango; Ungus of Terror; Curse of the Mushroom People.
1963 70m/B *JP* Akira Kubo, Kenji Sahara, Yoshio Tsuchiya, Hiroshi Koizumi; **D:** Inoshiro Honda. **VHS $20.00** *SMW* ☆☆

Attack of the Robots Silly spy spoof about powerful government officials who are being killed off by a mad scientist's robots. Interpol agent Lemmy Caution comes to the rescue. Written by Jean-Claude Carriere. **AKA:** Cartes sur Table.
1966 88m/B *FR* Eddie Constantine, Fernando Rey; **D:** Jess (Jesus) Franco. **VHS, Beta $29.95** *VYY* ☆½

Attack of the Super Monsters Group of prehistoric monsters are developing dastardly plots below the earth to ruin the human race.
1984 85m/C VHS, Beta $39.95 *TWE* ☆

Attack of the Swamp Creature A deranged scientist transforms himself into a swamp critter and terrorizes a small town.
1975 96m/C Frank Crowell, David Robertson; **D:** Arnold Stevens. **VHS, Beta $29.95** *LIV* Woof!

Attack Squadron Story of Japan's suicidal WWII pilots. **AKA:** Kamakazi.
197? 105m/C *JP* **VHS, Beta** *NO* ☆½

The Attic Psycho-drama about an overbearing invalid father and his insecure and unmarried daughter. The girl learns to escape her unhappy life by hiding in the attic. Not horrifying, but a clear analytical look into the game of control.
1980 (R) 92m/C Carrie Snodgress, Ray Milland, Rosemary Murphy, Ruth Cox, Francis Bay, Marjorie Eaton; **D:** George Edwards. **VHS, Beta $59.95** *FOX, MON* ☆☆½

The Attic: The Hiding of Anne Frank Steenburgen shines in the true story of Miep Gies, the Dutch woman who hid Otto Frank, her employer, and his family from the Nazis. Unusual because it is told from Gies' perspective, rather than from the more familiar Anne Frank story. Based on Gies' book, "Anne Frank Remembered." Made for television.
1988 95m/C Mary Steenburgen, Paul Scofield, Eleanor Bron, Ronald Pickup, Huub Stapel, Lisa Jacobs; **D:** John Erman. **VHS $79.95** *CAF* ☆☆½

Attica Tense made for television depiction of the infamous Attica prison takeover in 1971 and the subsequent bloodbath as state troops were called in. Although edited due to

the searing commentary by Rockefeller, it remains powerful and thought-provoking. Adapted from the Tom Wicker bestseller ''A Time to Die.''
1980 97m/C George Grizzard, Charles Durning, Anthony Zerbe, Roger E. Mosley; **D:** Marvin J. Chomsky. **VHS, Beta** $9.98 *SUE, NLC* 🎞🎞🎞

Au Revoir Les Enfants During the Nazi occupation of France in the 1940s, the headmaster of a Catholic boarding school hides three Jewish boys among the other students by altering their names and identities. Two of the students, Julien (Manesse) and Jean (Fejto), form a friendship that ends tragically when Jean and the other boys are discovered and taken away by the Gestapo. Compelling and emotionally wrenching coming of age tale based on an incident from director Malle's childhood is considered to be his best film to date and quite possibly the best he will ever make. In French with English subtitles. *AKA:* Goodbye, Children.
1987 (PG) 104m/C *FR* Gaspard Manesse, Raphael Fejto, Francine Racette, Stanislas Carre de Malberg, Philippe Morier-Genoud, Francois Berleand, Peter Fitz, Francois Negret, Irene Jacob; **W/D:** Louis Malle; **M:** Franz Schubert, Camille Saint-Saens. Academy Awards '87 Nominations: Best Foreign Language Film, Best Original Screenplay; British Academy Awards '88: Best Director (Malle); Cesar Awards '88: Best Director (Malle), Best Film; Los Angeles Film Critics Association Awards '87: Best Foreign Film; Venice Film Festival '87: Best Film. **VHS, Beta, LV** $19.98 *TAM, ORI, FCT* 🎞🎞🎞🎞

Audrey Rose Parents of a young girl are terrified when their darling daughter is having dreadful dreams. Mysterious friend Hopkins cements their fears when he declares that his dead daughter has been reincarnated in their child. The nightmares continue suggesting that none other than Lucifer could be at work. Good cast is hampered by slow-moving take-off on ''The Exorcist'' with a weak staged ending. Adapted by Frank DeFelitta from his novel.
1977 (PG) 113m/C Marsha Mason, Anthony Hopkins, John Beck, John Hillerman; **D:** Robert Wise; **W:** Frank DeFelitta. **VHS, Beta** $59.95 *MGM* 🎞🎞

Augustine of Hippo One of Rossellini's later historical epics, depicting the last years of St. Augustine and how they exemplify the growing conflicts between Church and State, Christian ethic and societal necessity. In Italian with subtitles. *AKA:* Agostino di Ippona.
1972 120m/C *IT* **D:** Roberto Rossellini. **VHS, Beta** $59.95 *FCT* 🎞🎞🎞

Auntie Entertainer must dress and act like his madam aunt who has died, in order to fool her former employees in a house of prostitution.
1980 (R) 85m/C **VHS, Beta** $24.95 *NO Woof!*

Auntie Lee's Meat Pies Auntie Lee's meat pie business is booming thanks to her five beautiful nieces. They help keep their aunt supplied with the secret ingredient—gorgeous young men! Four Playboy Playmates are featured in this cannibalistic horror comedy.
1992 (R) 100m/C Karen Black, Pat Morita, Pat Paulsen, Huntz Hall, Michael Berryman, David Parry, Stephen Quadros; **D:** Joseph F. Robertson. **VHS, LV** $79.95 *COL* 🎞½

Auntie Mame A young boy is brought up by his only surviving relative—flamboyant and eccentric Auntie Mame. Mame is positive that ''life is a banquet and most poor suckers are starving to death.'' Based on the Patrick Dennis novel about his life with ''Auntie Mame.'' Part of the ''A Night at the Movies''

series, this tape simulates a 1958 movie evening, with a Road Runner cartoon, ''Hook, Line and Stinker,'' a newsreel and coming attractions for ''No Time for Sergeants'' and ''Chase a Crooked Shadow.''
1958 161m/C Rosalind Russell, Patric Knowles, Roger Smith, Peggy Cass, Forrest Tucker, Coral Browne; **D:** Morton DaCosta. Academy Awards '58 Nominations: Best Actress (Russell), Best Art Direction/Set Decoration, Best Color Cinematography, Best Film Editing, Best Picture, Best Supporting Actress (Cass); Golden Globe Awards '59: Best Actress—Musical/Comedy (Russell). **VHS, Beta, LV** $19.95 *HNB, WAR* 🎞🎞🎞

The Aurora Encounter Aliens surreptitiously infiltrate a small town in 1897, and spread benevolence everywhere. Family fare.
1985 (PG) 90m/C Jack Elam, Peter Brown, Carol Bagdasarian, Dottie West, George ''Spanky'' McFarland; **D:** Jim McCullough. **VHS, Beta** $14.95 *NWV, STE, HHE* 🎞🎞

Author! Author! Sweet, likable comedy about playwright Pacino who is about to taste success with his first big hit. Suddenly his wife walks out, leaving him to care for her four children and his own son. His views shift as he begins to worry about who will watch the obnoxious kids on opening night. He soon learns to juggle being father and writer without compromising either one. Written by Israel Horovitz.
1982 (PG) 100m/C Al Pacino, Tuesday Weld, Dyan Cannon, Alan King, Andre Gregory; **D:** Arthur Hiller. **VHS, Beta** $14.98 *FOX* 🎞🎞½

Autobiography of a Princess A brief character study shot by Merchant-Ivory in six days. An East Indian princess, living in self-enforced exile in London, invites her father's former tutor to tea. They watch old movie footage of royal India together and dream of a happier past.
1975 59m/C James Mason, Madhur Jaffrey; **D:** James Ivory; **W:** Ruth Prawer Jhabvala. **VHS, LV** $29.95 *FCT, TAM, LUM* 🎞🎞🎞

The Autobiography of Miss Jane Pittman The history of blacks in the South is seen through the eyes of a 110-year-old former slave. From the Civil War through the Civil Rights movement, Miss Pittman relates every piece of black history, allowing the viewer to experience the injustices. Tyson is spectacular in moving, highly acclaimed television drama. Received nine Emmy awards; adapted by Tracy Keenan Wynn from the novel by Ernest J. Gaines.
1974 110m/C Cicely Tyson, Odetta, Joseph Tremice, Richard Dysart, Michael Murphy, Katherine Helmond; **D:** John Korty. **VHS, Beta** *PSM* 🎞🎞🎞½

Autopsy Rash of unexplainable, spontaneous suicides cause a college student to become emotionally upset. Dubbed, with music by Ennio Morricone.
1978 (R) 89m/C *IT* Mimsy Farmer, Barry Primus, Angela Goodwin, Ray Lovelock; **D:** Armando Crispino. **VHS, Beta** $19.95 *MPI, PSM* 🎞½

Autopsy A young gold-digger and a millionaire marry, and then cheat on each other, provoking blackmail and murder.
197? 90m/C Fernando Rey, Gloria Grahame, Christian Hey. **VHS, Beta** *NO* 🎞

Autopsy A war correspondent in Vietnam discovers the gruesome secret behind the doctors' autopsy methods at a military hospital.
1986 90m/C **VHS, Beta** *NO* 🎞½

Autopsy of a Ghost Comedy/horror film stars Rathbone as a ghost and Mitchell as a mad scientist. Notable as Rathbone's last screen appearance. In Spanish with no subtitles.
1967 ?m/C *SP* Basil Rathbone, John Carradine, Cameron Mitchell. **VHS** $16.95 *SNC* 🎞½

An Autumn Afternoon Ozu's final film is a beautiful expression of his talent. In postwar Tokyo, an aging widower loses his only daughter to marriage and begins a life of loneliness. A heart-wrenching tale of relationships and loss. In Japanese with English subtitles.
1962 112m/C *JP* Chishu Ryu, Shima Iwashita, Shin-Ichiro Mikami, Mariko Okada, Keiji Sada; **W/D:** Yasujiro Ozu. **VHS** $69.95 *NYF, TAM* 🎞🎞🎞½

Autumn Born Young heiress is abducted by her guardian and imprisoned while she's taught to obey his will. Ill-fated ex-Playmate Dorothy Stratton's first film.
1979 (R) 76m/C Dorothy Stratten. **VHS, Beta** $39.95 *MON* 🎞½

Autumn Leaves Crawford plays a middle-aged typist grasping at her last chance for love. She marries a younger man who's been romancing her, then finds him more and more unstable and violent. Weak story material that could turn melodramatic and tawdry, but doesn't because of Crawford's strength.
1956 108m/B Cliff Robertson, Joan Crawford, Vera Miles, Lorne Greene; **D:** Robert Aldrich. **VHS, Beta** $9.95 *GKK* 🎞🎞½

Autumn Marathon To say that this is one of the better Russian movies of the past three decades is sort of faint praise, given the state of Soviet cinema. Written by playwright Alexander Volodin, it's just another paint-by-number version of the philandering man who's really an OK Joe who loves his kids comedy. In Russian with English subtitles. *AKA:* Osenny Marafon.
1979 100m/C *RU* Oleg Basilashvili, Natalia Gundareva, Marina Neyelova; **D:** Georgi Daniela. **VHS** $59.95 *KIV, AUD* 🎞🎞🎞

Autumn Sonata Nordic family strife as famed concert pianist Bergman is reunited with a daughter she has not seen in years. Bergman's other daughter suffers from a degenerative nerve disease and had been institutionalized until her sister brought her home. Now the three women settle old scores, and balance the needs of their family. Excellent performance by Bergman in her last film.
1978 97m/C *SW* Ingrid Bergman, Liv Ullmann, Halvar Bjork, Lena Nyman, Gunnar Bjornstrand; **D:** Ingmar Bergman. Academy Awards '78 Nominations: Best Actress (Bergman), Best Original Screenplay; Golden Globe Awards '79: Best Foreign Film; National Board of Review Awards '78: 5 Best Foreign Films of the Year, Best Actress (Bergman), Best Director (Bergman); National Society of Film Critics Awards '78: Best Actress (Bergman). **VHS, Beta, LV** *FOX* 🎞🎞🎞

Avalanche Disasterama as vacationers at a new winter ski resort find themselves at the mercy of a monster avalanche leaving a so-called path of terror and destruction in its wake. Talented cast is buried by weak material, producing a snow-bound adventure yawn.
1978 (PG) 91m/C Rock Hudson, Mia Farrow, Robert Forster, Rick Moses; **D:** Corey Allen. **VHS, Beta** $9.98 *SUE* 🎞½

Avalanche Express Marvin is a CIA agent who uses a defector (Shaw) to lure a scientist (Schell), specializing in biological warfare, aboard a European train. Marvin wants to eliminate Schell but all plans go awry when the snow begins to fall. Ineffec-

tive thriller. Director Robson's and actor Shaw's last film—much of Shaw's dialogue was dubbed due to his death before the film's soundtrack was completed. Based on a novel by Colin Forbes.
1979 (PG) 89m/C Lee Marvin, Robert Shaw, Maximilian Schell, Linda Evans, Mike Connors, Joe Namath, Horst Buchholz, David Hess; *D:* Mark Robson; *W:* Abraham Polonsky. **VHS $19.98** *WAR* ⬚

Avalon Powerful but quiet portrait of the break-up of the family unit as seen from the perspective of a Russian family settled in Baltimore at the close of WWII. Initally, the family is unified in their goals, ideologies and social lives. Gradually, all of this disintegrates; members move to the suburbs and television replaces conversation at holiday gatherings. Levinson based his film on experiences within his own family of Russian Jewish immigrants.
1990 (PG) 126m/C Armin Mueller-Stahl, Aidan Quinn, Elizabeth Perkins, Joan Plowright, Lou Jacobi, Leo Fuchs, Elijah Wood, Eve Gordon, Kevin Pollak; *W/D:* Barry Levinson; *M:* Randy Newman. **VHS, Beta, LV, 8mm $19.95** *COL, PIA, FCT* ⬚⬚⬚

Avenged A vigilante saga of no special merit. Crude thugs violate and kill a young girl. Acquitted as a result of a slip in the arrest, they hit the streets again, thinking they are home free. However, the victim's brother shows up demanding they pay dearly for what they have done. His technique of penance is indeed outside the law.
19?? 90m/C VHS *NO* ⬚⬚

The Avenger The story of a criminal who cuts off the heads of people and mails them off makes for a shocker. Graphic violence will appeal to those who like a good mail-order gorefest and are not employed by the post office.
1960 102m/B *GE* Ingrid van Bergen, Heinz Drache, Ina Duscha, Mario Litto, Klaus Kinski; *D:* Karl Anton. **VHS $16.95** *SNC* ⬚⬚½

The Avenger This time muscleman Reeves plays Aeneas and leads the Trojans in battle against the Greeks. Its supposedly an adaptation of ''The Aeneid'' by Virgil. *AKA:* The Lost Glory of Troy.
1962 108m/C *IT FR* Steve Reeves, Giacomo ''Jack'' Stuart, Carla Marlier, Gianno Garko, Liana Orfei; *D:* Giorgio Rivalta. **VHS $19.95** *SNC, NOS, VYY* ⬚

Avenging Angel Law student Molly ''Angel'' Stewart is back on the streets to retaliate against the men who killed the policeman who saved her from a life of prostitution. Worthless sequel to 1984's ''Angel,'' exploiting the original's exploitative intent. Followed listlessly by ''Angel III: The Final Chapter.''
1985 (R) 94m/C Betsy Russell, Rory Calhoun, Susan Tyrrell, Ossie Davis, Barry Pearl, Ross Hagen, Karin Mani, Robert Tessier; *D:* Robert Vincent O'Neil. **VHS, Beta, LV $14.95** *NWV, STE* Woof!

Avenging Conscience An early eerie horror film, based on tales of Edgar Allan Poe. D.W. Griffith's first large-scale feature. Silent. *AKA:* Thou Shall Not Kill.
1914 78m/B Henry B. Walthall, Blanche Sweet; *D:* D.W. Griffith. **VHS, Beta $29.95** *VYY, GPV, LSV* ⬚⬚

Avenging Disco Godfather Moore parodies the ''Godfather'' and martial arts movies. *AKA:* Avenging Godfather.
1976 (R) 93m/C Rudy Ray Moore, Lady Reed, Carol Speed, Jimmy Lynch; *D:* Rudy Ray Moore. **VHS, Beta** *NO* ⬚⬚½

Avenging Force Okay actioner about retired CIA agent Dudikoff returning to the force to help colleague James run for political office. A group of right-wing terrorists called ''Pentangle'' threatens James, so Dudikoff adds his name to their wanted list. Conflict leads to a forest manhunt where the avenging force does its avenging.
1986 (R) 104m/C Michael Dudikoff, Steve James, John P. Ryan; *D:* Sam Firstenberg. **VHS, Beta, LV $19.95** *MED* ⬚⬚

The Avenging Hand Leaden suspense story about a hotel filled with thieves all searching for stolen loot.
1943 56m/B Noah Beery Jr., Kathleen Kelly, Louis Borell, James Harcourt, Charles Oliver, Reginald Long; *D:* Victor Hanbury. **VHS** *HCV* ⬚1½

Avenging Ninja A martial arts expert goes on a destructive rampage in Paris when his father and daughter are kidnapped by a European crime syndicate. Dubbed.
198? 83m/C John Liu. **VHS, Beta** *NO* ⬚

Aventure Malgache Hitchcock worked with the Moliere Players on this propaganda piece about the French Resistance. He based this story on the experiences of the actor Clarousse. Working for the Resistance in occupied Madagascar Clarousse is betrayed and sent to prison by the Vichy government. Rescued by the British he returns to resume his work. In French with English subtitles. *AKA:* Madagascar Landing.
1944 31m/B *D:* Alfred Hitchcock. **VHS** *MIL* ⬚

The Average Woman Gritty journalist consults plain Jane for ''Modern Woman'' story and finds a major rewrite in order when he falls with a thud for Miss Jane.
1924 52m/B Pauline Garon, David Powell, Burr McIntosh, Harrison Ford, De Sacia Mooers; *D:* William Cabanne. **VHS, Beta $14.95** *GPV* ⬚⬚

The Aviator Pilot Reeve, haunted by the memory of a fatal crash, tries to find a new line of work. Large sums of money persuade him to transport spoiled Arquette to Washington. When the biplane crashes in the mountain wilderness, the two fall in love between scavenging for food and fighting wild animals. From the director of ''Man From Snowy River.''
1985 (PG) 98m/C Christopher Reeve, Rosanna Arquette, Jack Warden, Tyne Daly, Marcia Strassman, Sam Wanamaker, Scott Wilson; *D:* George Miller. **VHS, Beta $14.95** *MGM* ⬚⬚

The Awaken Punch Wherever there's rape, murder, or anything else that demands vengeance, human weapon Young will be there.
19?? ?m/C Yu Young, Shiue Jia Ian, Ou Yang Pey Shan. **VHS $16.50** *OCE* ⬚

Awakening An archeologist discovers the tomb of a murderous queen, but upon opening the coffin, the mummy's spirit is transferred to his baby daughter, born at that instant. They call that bad luck.
1980 (R) 101m/C Charlton Heston, Susannah York, Stephanie Zimbalist; *D:* Mike Newell. **VHS, Beta $19.95** *WAR* ⬚1½

Awakening of Candra Based on a real 1975 incident, a young couple honeymooning in the mountains is assaulted by a lunatic fisherman. The psycho kills the husband and rapes the girl, then he brainwashes poor Candra into thinking it was all an accident. Intense subject matter should be horrifying, but falls short of the mark in this television flop.
1981 96m/C Blanche Baker, Cliff DeYoung, Richard Jaeckel; *D:* Paul Wendkos. **VHS, Beta $59.95** *GEM* Woof!

Awakenings Belatedly following the success of ''Big,'' Marshall's first non-comedic film is based on the true account of Dr. Oliver Sacks. The story details the doctor's experimentation with the drug L-dopa in the chronic care ward of a Bronx hospital, which inspired the ''awakening'' of a number of catatonic patients, some of whom had been in a sleeping state for as long as thirty years. Although guilty of lapsing into over-sentimentality, the story provides a poignant look at both the ''awakened'' patients—who find themselves confronted with lost opportunities and faded youth—and at the doctor who awakened them, only to watch their exquisite suffering as they slip back into their illness. De Niro's performance as Leonard Lowe, the youngest of the group and first to awaken, is heart-rending. Williams offers a subdued and moving performance as the Doctor. At once heart-breaking and uplifting, calculated to provoke thought rather than knee-jerk emotionalism. Based on Sack's book of the same title. Production design by the late Anton Furst, best known for his illusionist production work on ''Batman'' and laser effects for ''Star Wars'' and ''Alien.'' Music by Randy Newman.
1990 (PG-13) 120m/C Robin Williams, Robert De Niro, John Heard, Julie Kavner, Penelope Ann Miller, Max von Sydow, Anne Meara; *D:* Penny Marshall; *M:* Randy Newman. **VHS, Beta, LV, 8mm $19.95** *COL, FCT* ⬚⬚⬚½

Away All Boats The true story of one Captain Hawks, who led a crew of misfits to victory in WWII Pacific aboard transport USS Belinda. Battle scenes are well done; look for early (and brief) appearance by young Clint Eastwood.
1956 114m/B Jeff Chandler, George Nader, Richard Boone, Julie Adams, Keith Andes, Lex Barker; *D:* Joseph Pevney. **VHS, Beta $19.95** *MCA* ⬚⬚½

The Awful Truth After discarding their marriage made in heaven, a young couple (Grant and Dunne in their first screen match) go their separate ways in search of happiness. Meticulously sabotaging each others' new relationships, they discover that, underneath it all, they were made for each other. One of the great screwball comedies; master of comic timing Grant is at his most charming while Dunne is brilliant as his needling ex-wife. The scene in which Dunne poses as Grant's prodigal declasse fan-dancing sister who pays a surprise cocktail-hour visit to the family of his stuffy, haute-mondain bride-to-be is among the most memorable screwball vignettes of all time. And don't miss the custody battle they have over the family dog (Asta of ''The Thin Man'' fame). Screenplay, based on Arthur Richman's play, by Delmar. Preceded by 1925 and 1929 versions and remade in 1953 as ''Let's Do it Again.''
1937 92m/B Irene Dunne, Cary Grant, Ralph Bellamy, Alexander D'Arcy, Cecil Cunningham, Molly Lamont, Esther Dale, Joyce Compton, Robert Allen, Robert Warwick, Mary Forbes; *D:* Leo McCarey; *W:* Vina Delmar. Academy Awards '37: Best Director (McCarey); Nominations: Best Actress (Dunne), Best Film Editing, Best Picture, Best Screenplay, Best Supporting Actor (Bellamy). **VHS, Beta, LV $19.95** *MLB, BTV, COL* ⬚⬚⬚⬚

Ay, Carmela! During the Spanish Civil War, two traveling entertainers with strong anti-Franco views are captured by Franco forces and sentenced to execution. They are reprieved when a theater-loving Lieutenant offers to spare their lives if they will entertain the troops. But, will Carmela perform in order to save her life—if it means betraying her beliefs?

1990 105m/C *SP IT* Carmen Maura, Andres Pajares, Gabino Diego, Maurizio De Razza, Miguel Rellan, Edward Zentara, Jose Sancho, Antonio Fuentes; *D:* Carlos Savrat. **VHS $89.98** *HBO, TAM* 🐾🐾🐾

Baba A poor boatman agrees to be the fall guy in a murder in exchange for the actual murderer supporting his family. But after 24 years in prison, the boatman finds all his sacrificing has been in vain. His daughter has become a prostitute and his son is working as one of the murderer's henchman. In Turkish with English subtitles. *AKA:* The Father.
1973 95m/C *TU D:* Yilmaz Guney. **VHS $39.95** *FCT, HEG* 🐾🐾🐾

Babar: The Movie The lovable Babar, king of the elephants, must devise a plan to outwit an angry hoard of attacking rhinos. Based on the characters of Jean and Laurent de Brunhoff.
1988 (G) 75m/C *W/D:* Alan Bunce; *V:* Gavin Magrath, Gordon Pinsent, Sarah Polley, Chris Wiggins. **VHS, Beta, LV, 8mm $24.95** *FHE, IME, WTA* 🐾🐾½

Babe! A fine television movie about the life of one of America's most famous woman athletes, Babe Didrickson. Adapted by Joanna Lee from Didrickson's autobiography, "The Life I've Led." The movie was nominated for Outstanding Special of 1975-76 and Clark won an Emmy for her work.
1975 120m/C Susan Clark, Alex Karras, Slim Pickens, Jeanette Nolan, Ellen Geer, Ford Rainey; *D:* Buzz Kulik; *M:* Jerry Goldsmith. **VHS** *NO* 🐾🐾🐾½

The Babe Follows the life of legendary baseball player Babe Ruth, portrayed as a sloppy drunkard whose appetites for food, drink, and sex were as large as he was. Alvarado and McGillis do well as the Babe's first and second wives, but this is Goodman's show from start to finish. He's excellent as Ruth, and looks the part, but his fine performance can't make up for a lackluster script filled with holes.
1992 (PG) 115m/C John Goodman, Kelly McGillis, Trini Alvarado, Bruce Boxleitner, Peter Donat, J.C. Quinn, Richard Tyson, James Cromwell, Joe Ragno, Bernard Kates, Stephen Caffrey, Michael McGrady; *D:* Arthur Hiller. **VHS, LV $19.98** *MCA* 🐾🐾½

Babe Ruth Story An overly sentimental biography about the famed baseball slugger. Bendix is miscast as the Bambino, but the actual film clips of the Babe are of interest. A movie to be watched during those infrequent bouts of sloppy baseball mysticism.
1948 107m/B William Bendix, Claire Trevor, Charles Bickford, William Frawley, Sam Levene, Gertrude Niesen; *D:* Roy Del Ruth. **VHS, Beta $19.98** *FOX* 🐾🐾

Babes in Arms The children of several vaudeville performers team up to put on a show to raise money for their financially impoverished parents. Loosely adapted from the Rodgers and Hart Broadway musical of the same name; features some of their songs as well as new additions. ♫Babes in Arms; I Cried for You; Good Morning; You Are My Lucky Star; Broadway Rhythm; Where or When; Daddy Was a Minstrel Man; I'm Just Wild About Harry; God's Country.
1939 91m/B Judy Garland, Mickey Rooney, Charles Winninger, Guy Kibbee, June Preisser; *D:* Busby Berkeley; *M:* Richard Rodgers, Lorenz Hart. **VHS, Beta, LV $19.98** *MGM* 🐾🐾

Babes in Toyland A lavish Disney production of Victor Herbert's timeless operetta, with Toyland being menaced by the evil Barnaby and his Bogeymen. Yes, Annette had a life after Mickey Mouse and before the

peanut butter commercials. Somewhat charming, although the roles of the lovers seem a stretch for both Funicello and Kirk. But the flick does sport an amusing turn by Wynn.
1961 105m/C Annette Funicello, Ray Bolger, Tommy Sands, Ed Wynn, Tommy Kirk; *D:* Jack Donohue. **VHS, Beta $19.99** *DIS* 🐾🐾

Babes in Toyland A young girl must save Toyland from the clutches of the evil Barnaby and his monster minions. Bland TV remake of the classic doesn't approach the original. Music by Leslie Bricusse.
1986 96m/C Drew Barrymore, Pat Morita, Richard Mulligan, Eileen Brennan, Keanu Reeves, Jill Schoelen, Googy Gress; *D:* Clive Donner. **VHS, LV $14.98** *ORI* 🐾🐾

Babes on Broadway Mickey and Judy put on a show to raise money for a settlement house. Nearly the best of the Garland-Rooney series, with imaginative numbers staged by Berkeley. ♫Babes on Broadway; Anything Can Happen in New York; How About You?; Hoe Down; Chin Up! Cheerio! Carry On!; Mama Yo Quiero; F.D.R. Jones; Waiting for the Robert E. Lee.
1941 118m/B Mickey Rooney, Judy Garland, Fay Bainter, Richard Quine, Virginia Weidler, Ray Macdonald, Busby Berkeley; *D:* Busby Berkeley. **VHS, Beta, LV $19.98** *MGM* 🐾🐾½

Babette's Feast A simple, moving pageant-of-life fable. A group of religiously zealous villagers are taught love and forgiveness through a lavish banquet prepared by one of their housemaids, who turns out to be a world-class chef. Adapted from a tale by Isak Dinesen. In French and Danish with English subtitles.
1987 102m/C *DK FR* Stephane Audran, Bibi Andersson, Bodil Kjer, Birgitte Federspiel, Jean-Philippe LaFont, Ebbe Rode, Jarl Kulle; *D:* Gabriel Axel. **VHS, Beta, LV $19.98** *ORI, FCT, APD* 🐾🐾🐾½

The Baby Bizarre story of a social worker who resorts to swinging an ax to cut the apron strings of "baby," a retarded man-child, from his over-protective and insane (bad combination) mother and sisters. Low-budget production looks and feels like a low-budget production, but any movie featuring a grown man wandering about in diapers can't be all bad.
1972 (PG) 85m/C Anjanette Comer, Ruth Roman, Marianna Hill, Suzanne Zenor, David Manzy, Michael Pataki; *D:* Ted Post. **VHS, Beta $39.95** *WWV* 🐾🐾

The Baby and the Battleship The old baby out of (on the?) water plot. While on liberty in Italy, a sailor, after a series of complications, becomes custodian of a baby and attempts to hide the tyke aboard his battleship (hence the title). More complications ensue. Some funny moments. Great cast.
1956 96m/C *GB* John Mills, Richard Attenborough, Andre Morell, Bryan Forbes, Lisa Gastoni, Michael Hordern, Lionel Jeffries, Gordon Jackson, John Le Mesurier; *D:* Jay Lewis. **VHS $19.95** *NOS, MOV, TIM* 🐾🐾½

Baby Boom When a hard-charging female executive becomes the reluctant mother of a baby girl (a gift from a long-lost relative), she adjusts with great difficulty to motherhood and life outside the rat race and New York City (and Sam Shepard as the love interest). A fairly harmless collection of cliches bolstered by Keaton's usual nervous performance as a power-suited yuppie ad queen saddled with a noncareer-enhancing baby, moving from manic yuppie ad maven to jelly-packing Vermont store-owner/mom. To best appreciate flick, see it with a bevy of

five- and six-year-olds (a good age for applauding the havoc that a baby creates).
1987 (PG) 103m/C Diane Keaton, Sam Shepard, Harold Ramis, Sam Wanamaker, James Spader; *D:* Charles Shyer. **VHS, Beta, LV $19.95** *FOX, FCT* 🐾🐾½

Baby Cart 4: Heart of a Parent...Heart of a Child Fourth in a series of six. A man (Wakayama) pushes his son (Tomikawa) across Japan in a baby cart loaded with deadly accessories including built-in guns and switchblades. Copious amounts of bloodshed. In Japanese with English subtitles in a letterbox format.
1972 80m/C *JP* Tomisaburo Wakayama, Akihiro Tomikawa; *D:* Buichi Sato. **VHS $27.90** *VSM* 🐾

Baby Doll Suggestive sex at its best, revolving around the love of cotton in Mississippi. Nubile Baker is married to slow-witted Malden, who runs a cotton gin. His torching of Wallach's cotton gin begins a cycle of sexual innuendo and tension, brought to exhilarating life on screen, without a single filmed kiss. Performers and sets ooze during the steamy exhibition, which was considered highly erotic when released. Excellent performances from entire cast, with expert pacing by director Kazan. Screenplay is based on Tennessee Williams' "27 Wagons Full of Cotton."
1956 115m/B Eli Wallach, Carroll Baker, Karl Malden, Mildred Dunnock, Rip Torn; *D:* Elia Kazan; *W:* Tennessee Williams. Academy Awards '56 Nominations: Best Actress (Baker), Best Adapted Screenplay, Best Black and White Cinematography, Best Supporting Actress (Dunnock); Golden Globe Awards '57: Best Director (Kazan). **VHS, Beta $19.98** *WAR, FCT* 🐾🐾🐾

The Baby Doll Murders Someone in L.A. is killing beautiful young women and then leaving a broken baby doll at the scene of the crime. The gruesome murderer manages to elude everyone, until Detective Benz discovers a link between the victims and a pattern begins to form. He also discovers that his partner's wife is going to be the next victim unless he can stop this ruthless serial killer from striking again.
1992 (R) 90m/C Jeff Kober, Melanie Smith, John Saxon, Tom Hodges; *W/D:* Paul Leder. **VHS $89.98** *REP* 🐾🐾

Baby Face A small town girl moves to the city when her father dies. There she gets a job at a bank and sleeps her way to the top of the business world, discarding used men left and right. The Hays Office was extremely upset with the then risque material and forced Warner to trim the first cut.
1933 70m/B Barbara Stanwyck, George Brent, Donald Cook, John Wayne, Henry Kolker, Margaret Lindsay, Douglas Dumbrille, James Murray; *D:* Alfred E. Green. **VHS, Beta $19.98** *MGM, FCT* 🐾🐾

Baby Face Harry Langdon Two silent shorts by the limpid-eyed comedian: "Saturday Afternoon" (1926), and "Lucky Stars" (1925). Both were written by Frank Capra and Arthur Ripley.
1926 60m/B Harry Langdon, Alice Ward, Natalie Kingston, Vernon Dent, Harry Edwards; *D:* Harry Edwards; *W:* Frank Capra, Arthur Ripley. **VHS, Beta, 8mm $24.95** *VYY* 🐾🐾½

Baby Face Morgan Poor comedy about gangsters who attempt to take advantage of the FBI's preoccupation with saboteurs and spies by muscling in on an insurance firm.
1942 60m/B Mary Carlisle, Richard Cromwell, Robert Armstrong, Chick Chandler, Charles Judels, Warren Hymer, Vince Barnett, Ralf Harolde; *D:* Arthur Dreifuss. **VHS $16.95** *SNC* 🐾🐾

Baby Girl Scott Hurt and Lithgow play the parents of an extremely premature infant who is being kept alive by technology. They make a heartrending decision and then must battle doctors and the system to let their daughter die with dignity. Made for television.
1987 97m/C John Lithgow, Mary Beth Hurt, Linda Kelsey, John Korty. VHS $59.98 LIV ♫♫½

Baby Huey the Baby Giant A compilation of the Baby Huey cartoons.
1962 60m/C VHS, Beta $5.99 WOV ♫♫½

Baby It's You The relationship of a smart, attractive Jewish girl who yearns to be an actress and a street-smart Catholic Italian boy puzzles their family and friends. Arquette's Jill Rosen is headed for college while Spano's the Shiek is busy dropping out of high school and looking for something that looks like a future. Set in New Jersey, "Baby" is about listening to your heart as well as your head. It all works due to Arquette's strong acting and Sayles' script, which explores adolescent dreams, the transition to adulthood, class differences, and the late 1960s with insight and humor. Interesting period soundtrack (Woolly Bully and, for some reason, Bruce Springsteen) helps propel the film, a commercial job which helped finance Sayles' more independent ventures.
1982 (R) 105m/C Rosanna Arquette, Vincent Spano, Jack Davidson, Joanna Merlin, Nick Ferrari, Leora Dana, Robert Downey Jr., Tracy Pollan, Matthew Modine; D: John Sayles. VHS, Beta, LV $79.95 PAR ♫♫♫

Baby Love A softcore fluff-fest about a trollop seducing a doctor's family. The doctor may or may not be her father. Hayden tantalizes the doctor, the doctor's son, and the doctor's wife, as well as the neighbors, leaving only those in adjoining communities untouched. Based on the novel by Tina Chad Christian.
1969 (R) 98m/C GB Ann Lynn, Keith Barron, Linda Hayden, Derek Lamden, Diana Dors, Patience Collier; D: Alastair Reid. VHS, Beta $59.95 NLC Woof!

Baby Love Nerds get revenge against the freshmen who run the local frat house.
1983 80m/C VHS, Beta $59.95 MGM Woof!

The Baby Maker A couple who cannot have children because the wife is sterile decides to hire a woman to have a child for them. However, the relationship between the husband and the surrogate progresses beyond what either of them wanted. Hershey stars as the free-love surrogate mama (just before she underwent the supreme 60s transformation into Barbara Seagull) and Bridges makes his directorial debut. Flick is interesting as a combo critique/exploitation of those wild and groovy 1960s.
1970 (R) 109m/C Barbara Hershey, Collin Wilcox-Horne, Sam Groom, Scott Glenn, Jeannie Berlin; D: James Bridges. VHS $59.95 WAR ♫♫

Baby of the Bride Follow-up to "Children of the Bride," has McClanahan settling into wedded bliss with younger husband Shackleford when she discovers she's pregnant. Not only is she unsure about wanting to be a mom again at her age but then grown—and single—daughter McNichol announces she is also pregnant. The sheer silliness of this made-for-television fare makes it fun to watch.
1991 93m/C Rue McClanahan, Ted Shackleford, Kristy McNichol, John Wesley Shipp, Anne Bobby, Conor O'Farrell; D: Bill Bixby; W: Bart Baker. VHS $89.98 TTC ♫♫½

Baby on Board Kane plays the wife of a Mafia bookkeeper who is accidentally killed in a gangland murder. Out for revenge, she tracks her husband's killer to JFK airport with her four-year old daughter in tow. Just as she pulls the loaded gun from her purse and takes aim, a pickpocket snatches her purse, accidentally firing the gun. Now she's on the run and she jumps into the first cab she can find, driven by Reinhold. New York City is turned upside down as mother, daughter, and cabbie try to elude the mob in this funny but predictable comedy.
1992 (PG) 90m/C Carol Kane, Judge Reinhold, Geza Kovacs, Errol Slue, Alex Stapley, Holly Stapley; D: Francis Schaeffer. VHS, Beta, LV $89.95 PSM ♫♫

Baby Snakes: The Complete Version Concert footage of Zappa is interspersed with clay animation by Bruce Bickford.
1979 166m/C Frank Zappa, Joey Psychotic, Ron Delsener, Donna U. Wanna; D: Frank Zappa. VHS, Beta $79.95 MVD, MPI ♫♫

Baby, Take a Bow Temple's first starring role. As a cheerful Pollyanna-type she helps her father, falsely accused of theft, by finding the true thief.
1934 76m/B Shirley Temple, James Dunn, Claire Trevor, Alan Dinehart; D: Harry Lachman. VHS, Beta $19.98 FOX ♫♫

Baby, the Rain Must Fall A rockabilly singer, paroled from prison after serving time for a knifing, returns home to his wife and daughter, but his outbursts of violence make the reunion difficult. Unsentimental with realistic performances, but script is weak (although written by Foote, based on his play, "The Traveling Lady"). Theme song was a Top 40 hit.
1964 100m/B Steve McQueen, Lee Remick, Don Murray; D: Robert Mulligan; W: Horton Foote Jr. VHS, Beta, LV $9.95 COL, MOV ♫♫

Babycakes A marshmellow romance between an overweight mortuary attendant who decides to follow her heart when she falls for a hunky ice skater. Can she make him appreciate her inner beauty instead of just her not-the-normal-beauty-standard outward appearance? (Happy ending guaranteed.) A made for television remake of the darker German film "Sugarbaby."
1989 94m/C Ricki Lake, Craig Sheffer, Paul Benedict, Betty Buckley, John Karlen; D: Paul Schneider. VHS $89.98 TTC ♫♫½

Babyface Morgan The son of a racketeer is made gang leader by his father's old mob in this crime-comedy.
1942 ?m/B Richard Cromwell, Mary Carlisle. VHS $16.95 SNC ♫♫

The Babylon Story from "Intolerance" Lavishly produced vignette from Griffith's film "Intolerance" as it was released on its own in 1919, in order to recoup the studio losses incurred by that grandest of cinematic follies. Silent with organ score, tinted color.
1916 25m/C Constance Talmadge, Alfred Paget; D: D.W. Griffith. VHS, Beta $19.95 VYY ♫♫♫½

Baby...Secret of the Lost Legend A sportswriter and his paleontologist wife risk their lives to reunite a hatching brontosaurus with its mother in the African jungle. Although this Disney film is not lewd in any sense, beware of several scenes displaying frontal nudity and some violence.
1985 (PG) 95m/C William Katt, Sean Young, Patrick McGoohan, Julian Fellowes; D: B.W.L. Norton. VHS, Beta, LV $79.95 TOU ♫♫

The Babysitter A family hires the mysterious but ingratiating Johanna (Zimbalist) as live-in help without checking on her references (who'd all checked out). The babysitter is the answer to all their problems—Mom's an alcoholic, Dad's a workaholic, and their daughter's just plain maladjusted—but once Johanna's gained their trust (or, in Dad's case, lust), she sets out to manipulate and exploit the family for her own psychotic purposes. Houseman plays the nosy neighbor who's on to her evil plan. Fair made-for-TV treatment of a common suspense plot.
1980 96m/C William Shatner, Patty Duke, Stephanie Zimbalist, Quinn Cummings, John Houseman, David Wallace; D: Peter Medak. VHS, Beta, LV $19.99 HBO ♫♫

Bacall on Bogart Bacall talks about her life with her husband, Humphrey Bogart. Copious film clips are interspersed, most in black and white.
1988 87m/C Humphrey Bogart, Lauren Bacall, Katharine Hepburn, John Huston. VHS, Beta $59.98 RKO, TTC ♫♫

The Bacchantes Poorly dubbed account of a ballerina, her life and loves. Based on the play by Euripides.
1963 100m/B IT Taina Elg, Pierre Brice, Alessandra Panaro, Alberto Lupo, Akim Tamiroff; D: Giorgio Ferroni. VHS $39.95 FCT, TIM ♫♫

The Bachelor Beautiful, seductive period drama about a shy and solitary physician who is forced into a new life when a family tragedy changes everything he once took for granted. Richardson and Carradine give brilliant performances in this provocative story of one man's sexual awakening. Based on a novel by Arthur Schnitzler.
1990 106m/C Keith Carradine, Miranda Richardson, Mari Torocsik, Max von Sydow, Kristin Scott Thomas, Sarah-Jane Fenton, Franco Diogene; W/D: Roberto Faenza; W: Ennio de Concini, Hugh Fleetwood; M: Ennio Morricone. VHS $89.95 TRI ♫♫♫

The Bachelor and the Bobby-Soxer Playboy Grant is brought before Judge Loy for disturbing the peace and sentenced to court her teen-age sister Temple. Cruel and unusual punishment? Maybe, but the wise Judge hopes that the dates will help Temple over her crush on handsome Grant. Instead, Loy and Grant fall for each other. Oscar winning screenplay by Sidney Sheldon. AKA: Bachelor Knight.
1947 95m/B Cary Grant, Myrna Loy, Shirley Temple, Rudy Vallee, Harry Davenport, Ray Collins; D: Irving Reis. VHS, Beta, LV $19.95 CCB, MED, RKO ♫♫♫

Bachelor Apartment Once at the leading edge of the bachelor on the loose genre, this one's hopelessly dated. The scandalous womanizing of a wealthy thirties Lothario just doesn't have the same impact on the men just don't understand generation. Nevertheless, as vintage if-the-walls-could-talk fluff, it's good for a giggle.
1931 77m/B Lowell Sherman, Irene Dunne, Norman Kerry, Claudia Dell, Noel Francis, Charles Coleman; D: Lowell Sherman. VHS $19.98 TTC, FCT ♫♫½

Bachelor Bait A marriage license clerk who's tired of just handing out licenses opens a matrimonial service for men.
1934 75m/B Stuart Erwin, Rochelle Hudson, Pert Kelton, Skeets Gallagher. VHS, Beta CCB ♫½

Bachelor Mother A single salesgirl causes a scandal when she finds an abandoned baby and is convinced by her boss to adopt the child. Smart, witty comedy with nice performance by Rogers.

1939 82m/B Ginger Rogers, David Niven, Charles Coburn; *D:* Garson Kanin. **VHS, Beta, LV $19.98** *CCB, MED, FCT* ♪♪♪

Bachelor of Hearts Sophomoric British comedy set at Cambridge University, with a German exchange student whose difficulty with English brings him to date several women in one evening. Notable for horror fans as the debut of femme fright fave Barbara Steele.
1958 94m/C *GB* Hardy Kruger, Sylvia Syms, Ronald Lewis; *D:* Wolf Rilla. **VHS $19.95** *NOS* ♪♪

Bachelor Party He's silly, cute, and poor. She's intelligent, beautiful, and rich. It must be a marriage made in heaven, because no one in their right mind would put these two together. All is basically well, except that her parents hate him and his friends dislike her. Things are calm until right before the big event, when bride-to-be Kitaen objects to Hank's traditional pre-nuptial partying. Light and semi-entertaining with scattered laughs.
1984 (R) 105m/C Tom Hanks, Tawny Kitaen, Adrian Zmed, George Grizzard, Robert Prescott, William Tepper, Wendie Jo Sperber, Barry Diamond, Michael Dudikoff, Deborah Harmon, John Bloom, Toni Alessandra, Monique Gabrielle, Angela Aames, Rosanne Katon; *D:* Neal Israel. **VHS, Beta, LV $14.98** *FXV, FOX* ♪♪

Back Door to Heaven Traces the path of a young boy who is born into a poor family and the reasons for his turning to a life of crime. A grim and powerful drama with many convincing performances.
1939 85m/B Wallace Ford, Aline MacMahon, Stuart Erwin, Patricia Ellis, Kent Smith, Van Heflin, Jimmy Lydon; *D:* William K. Howard. **VHS $19.95** *NOS, MOV* ♪♪♪½

Back from Eternity Eleven survivors of a plane crash are stranded in a headhunter region of South America's jungle. Remake of "Five Came Back" (1939), which was also directed by Farrow.
1956 97m/B Robert Ryan, Rod Steiger, Anita Ekberg, Phyllis Kirk, Keith Andes, Gene Barry; *D:* John Farrow. **VHS, Beta, LV $19.95** *UHV* ♪♪

Back in the USSR Danger follows two lovers caught up in the Moscow underworld. When young American touring Russia unwittingly gets involved with a beautiful art thief. Lots of fast-paced action in an otherwise muddled film. The first American film shot entirely on location in Moscow.
1992 (R) 87m/C Frank Whaley, Natalia Negoda, Roman Polanski, Claudia Robinson, Dey Young, Andrew Divoff, Brian Blessed, Ravil Issyanov; *D:* Deran Sarafian. **VHS $19.98** *FXV* ♪½

Back Roads Southern hooker meets a down-on-his-luck boxer and both head out for a better life in California, finding love along the way. Ritter road trip lacks any comedic rhythm and survives on Field and Jones working to entertain.
1981 (R) 94m/C Sally Field, Tommy Lee Jones, David Keith; *D:* Martin Ritt. **VHS, Beta $69.98** *FOX* ♪♪

Back Street The forbidden affair between a married man and a beautiful fashion designer carries on through many anxious years to a tragic end. The lavish third film version of the Fanny Hurst novel.
1961 107m/C Susan Hayward, John Gavin, Vera Miles; *D:* David Miller. **VHS, Beta $14.98** *MCA, MLB* ♪♪

Back to Back A beautiful young vigilante embarks on a rampage to clear her family's name and make her town's redneck crooks pay for their crimes. Never released in theaters.

1990 (R) 95m/C Bill Paxton, Todd Field, Apollonia, Luke Askew, Ben Johnson, David Michael-Standing, Susan Anspach, Sal Landi; *D:* John Kincade. **VHS, Beta $79.95** *MGM* ♪

Back to Bataan Colonel forms guerrilla army to raid Japanese in the Philippines and to help Americans landing on Leyte. Also available in a colorized version.
1945 95m/B John Wayne, Anthony Quinn, Beulah Bondi, Fely Franquelli, Richard Loo, Philip Ahn, Lawrence Tierney; *D:* Edward Dmytryk. **VHS, Beta, LV $19.98** *TTC* ♪♪½

Back to Hannibal: The Return of Tom Sawyer and Huckleberry Finn Mark Twain's characters Tom Sawyer and Huckleberry Finn are reunited as adults to solve a murder mystery.
199? 92m/C Raphael Sbarge, Mitchell Anderson, Megan Follows, Paul Winfield. **VHS $19.99** *DIS* ♪♪½

Back to School Dangerfield plays an obnoxious millionaire who enrolls in college to help his wimpy son, Gordon, achieve campus stardom. His motto seems to be "if you can't buy it, it can't be had." At first, his antics embarrass his shy son, but soon everyone is clamoring to be seen with the pair as Gordon develops his own self confidence.
1986 (PG-13) 96m/C Rodney Dangerfield, Keith Gordon, Robert Downey Jr., Sally Kellerman, Burt Young, Paxton Whitehead, Adrienne Barbeau, M. Emmet Walsh, Severn Darden, Ned Beatty, Sam Kinison, Kurt Vonnegut Jr., Robert Picardo, Danny Elfman; *D:* Alan Metter. **VHS, Beta, LV $19.98** *HBO* ♪♪½

Back to the Beach Frankie and Annette return to the beach as self-parodying, middle-aged parents with rebellious kids, and the usual run of sun-bleached, lovers' tiff comedy ensues. Plenty of songs, and guest appearances from television past.
1987 (PG) 92m/C Frankie Avalon, Annette Funicello, Connie Stevens, Jerry Mathers, Bob Denver, Barbara Billingsley, Tony Dow, Pee-Wee Herman, Edd Byrnes, Dick Dale, Don Adams, Lori Loughlin; *D:* Lyndall Hobbs. **VHS, Beta, LV $19.95** *PAR* ♪½

Back to the Future When the neighborhood mad scientist constructs a time machine from a DeLorean, his youthful companion, Marty, accidentally transports himself to 1955. There, Marty must do everything he can to bring his parents together, elude the local bully, and get back...to the future. The soundtrack features Huey Lewis and the News. Lloyd sparkles and Fox is well-cast as the boy out of his element. Nice close with Fox introducing rock 'n roll to the '50s high schoolers. Followed by two sequels.
1985 (PG) 116m/C Michael J. Fox, Christopher Lloyd, Lea Thompson, Crispin Glover, Wendie Jo Sperber, Marc McClure, Thomas F. Wilson, James Tolkan, Casey Siemaszko, Billy Zane, Courtney Gains; *Cameos:* Huey Lewis; *D:* Robert Zemeckis. Academy Awards '85 Nominations: Best Original Screenplay, Best Song ("Power of Love"), Best Sound; People's Choice Awards '86: Best Film. **VHS, Beta, LV $19.95** *MCA, FCT, TLF* ♪♪♪

Back to the Future, Part 2 The Doc and Marty are time-hopping again. The Doc has discovered that the future has changed because of the time-traveling done in the past. Three generations of Marty's family are visited by the pair while they try to set things straight in the present, past, and future. Just trying to catch your breath between the scenes is difficult as you are led to a cliff-hanger ending, the setting for Part III.

1989 (PG) 107m/C Michael J. Fox, Christopher Lloyd, Lea Thompson, Thomas F. Wilson, Harry Waters Jr., Charles Fleischer,. Joe Flaherty, Elisabeth Shue, James Tokan, Casey Siemaszko, Jeffrey Weissman, Flea; *D:* Robert Zemeckis. **VHS, Beta, LV $19.95** *MCA* ♪♪

Back to the Future, Part 3 The young time-traveling hero reads an article about his friend Doc Brown's death, and goes back to the Wild West to warn him. Filmed at the same time as Part II, with music by Alan Silvestri and ZZ Top. Complete trilogy is available as a boxed set.
1990 (PG) 118m/C Michael J. Fox, Christopher Lloyd, Mary Steenburgen, Thomas F. Wilson, Lea Thompson, Elisabeth Shue, Matt Clark, Richard Dysart, Pat Buttram, Harry Carey Jr., Dub Taylor, James Tolkan; *D:* Robert Zemeckis. **VHS, Beta, LV $19.95** *MCA* ♪♪♪

Back to the Wall Moreau is an adulterous wife whose web of deceit results in a suspenseful tail of murder and blackmail.
1956 94m/B *FR* Jeanne Moreau, Gerard Oury, Claire Maurier; *D:* Edouard Molinaro. **VHS $29.95** *FCT, TAM* ♪♪

Backdraft High action story of Chicago firemen has some of the most stupendous incendiary special effects ever filmed. But then there's that plot, B-movie hokum about a mystery arsonist torching strategic parts of the community with the finesse of an expert and a brother-against-brother conflict. Straight-forward performances from most of the cast in spite of the weak storyline. Writer Widen wrote from experience—he used to be a firefighter; real-life Chicago firefighters were reportedly very happy with the realistic and intense fire scenes. Forget the plot and watch the fires in this one. Also available in a letterboxed version.
1991 (R) 135m/C Kurt Russell, William Baldwin, Robert De Niro, Donald Sutherland, Jennifer Jason Leigh, Scott Glenn, Rebecca DeMornay, Jason Gedrick, J.T. Walsh, Tony Mockus Sr., Clint Howard, David Crosby; *D:* Ron Howard; *W:* Gregory Widen; *M:* Hans Zimmer. **VHS, Beta, LV $19.98** *MCA, PIA* ♪♪½

Backfield in Motion Silly but harmless comedy about a widowed mom who tries to get closer to her high-schooler son by organizing a mother-son football game. But it's the boys' football coach who really wants to get close—to mom. Made for television movie debut of both Arnolds.
1991 95m/C Roseanne (Barr) Arnold, Tom Arnold, Colleen Camp, Conchata Ferrell, Johnny Galecki; *D:* Richard Michaels. **VHS, Beta** *TTC* ♪♪½

Backfire If you're gonna rob a bank, you shouldn't let anyone hear you plan it, and if you're not gonna rob a bank, you shouldn't let anyone hear you plan one. This vintage "Lightning" Carson crime western has Carson and friend suspected of bank robbery because someone heard them planning one. The sheriff follows their every footstep as they search for the real perpetrators.
1922 56m/B Jack Hoxie, George Sowards, Lew Meehan, Florence Gilbert; *D:* Alvin J. Neitz. **VHS, Beta $9.95** *GPV* ♪♪

Backfire A mysterious stranger enters the lives of a disturbed 'Nam vet and his discontented wife, setting a pattern of murder and double-cross in motion.
1988 (R) 90m/C Karen Allen, Keith Carradine, Jeff Fahey, Bernie Casey, Dinah Manoff, Dean Paul Martin; *D:* Gilbert Cates. **VHS, Beta, LV $29.95** *VMK* ♪♪

Background to Danger A suspenseful WWII actioner about American agent Raft who travels to Turkey to receive secret documents from the soon-to-be-murdered

Massen. Greenstreet is the Nazi master spy who also wants the documents as do Russian spies, Lorre and Marshall. Somewhat confusing plot but fast-paced. Based on the thriller "Uncommon Danger" by Eric Ambler. This film was Warner Brothers' follow-up to "Casablanca" with Raft in the Bogie role he had turned down in that cinema classic. **1943 80m/B** George Raft, Sydney Greenstreet, Peter Lorre, Brenda Marshall, Osa Massen, Turhan Bey, Kurt Katch, Raoul Walsh. **VHS $19.98** *MGM, MOV* 🎬🎬🎬

Backlash An aborigine barmaid is raped. When her assailant turns up dead, she's charged with murder and winds up in the custody of two police officers on a trip across the outback. Holes in the plot undermine this interesting, although graphic, drama with racial overtones. **1986 (R) 88m/C** *AU* David Argue, Gia Carides, Lydia Miller, Brian Syron, Anne Smith; **D:** Bill Bennett. **VHS, Beta $79.95** *MCG* 🎬🎬½

Backstab A spellbinding tale of work, lust, and murder. Architect Brolin finds himself unable to get over the death of his wife, until a seductive and mysterious woman helps him over his grief. They spend the night together, engulfed in passion, but in the morning he wakes to find himself sleeping with the corpse of his boss. Only the first twist in this intriguing thriller. **1990 (R) 91m/C** James Brolin, Meg Foster, Isabelle Truchon; **D:** Jim Kaufman. **VHS, LV $89.98** *MED* 🎬🎬½

Backstairs An obscure German silent film about urban degradation and familial strife. **1921 44m/B** *GE* Henny Porten, Fritz Kortner, William Dieterle; **D:** Leopold Jessner. **VHS, Beta $39.95** *TAM, NOS, DVT* 🎬🎬

Backstreet Dreams The young parents of an autistic child find themselves torn apart due to their feelings of guilt. The father has an affair with a specialist hired to help the boy, causing further strife. Interesting story possibilities never get far. **1990 (R) 104m/C** Brooke Shields, Jason O'Malley, Sherilyn Fenn, Tony Fields, Burt Young, Anthony (Tony) Franciosa, Nick Cassavetes, Ray "Boom Boom" Mancini; **D:** Rupert Hitzig; **M:** Bill Conti. **VHS, LV $79.98** *VMK* 🎬🎬

Backtrack Foster co-stars in this thriller about an artist who accidentally witnesses a mob hit. The mob puts a hitman (Hopper) on her trail, and after studying his background and listening to audio tapes she recorded, he finds himself falling in love. Originally intended for a theatrical release, it hit the European screens in a different cut as "Catchfire;" Hopper restored his original version and it was released on cable TV in the U.S. *AKA:* Catchfire. **1989 (R) 102m/C** Dennis Hopper, Jodie Foster, Dean Stockwell, Vincent Price, John Turturro, Fred Ward, G. Anthony Sirico, Julie Adams, Frank Gio, Sy Richardson, Helena Kallianiotes, Bob Dylan; *Cameos:* Charlie Sheen, Joe Pesci; **D:** Dennis Hopper. **VHS $19.98** *LIV* 🎬🎬🎬

Backwoods Two campers wish they had never encountered a mountain man when he begins to stalk them with murder in mind. **1987 (R) 90m/C** Jack O'Hara, Dick Kreusser, Brad Armacot; **D:** Dean Crow. **VHS, Beta** *NO* 🎬🎬🎬

The Bad and the Beautiful The story of a Hollywood producer, told from the eyes of an actress, a writer, and a director. Featuring what some consider Turner's best performance ever. Winner of five Oscars, a splendid drama. **1952 118m/B** Kirk Douglas, Lana Turner, Dick Powell, Gloria Grahame, Barry Sullivan, Walter Pidgeon, Gilbert Roland; **D:** Vincente Minnelli. Academy Awards '52: Best Art Direction/Set Decoration (B & W), Best Black and White Cinematography, Best Costume Design (B & W), Best Screenplay, Best Supporting Actress (Grahame); Nominations: Best Actor (Douglas). **VHS, LV $19.98** *MGM, BTV* 🎬🎬🎬½

Bad Blood The true story of Stan Graham, who went on a killing spree in the New Zealand bush when his farm was foreclosed and his life ruined. **1987 104m/C** *NZ* Jack Thompson, Carol Burns, Dennis Lill; **D:** Mike Newell. **VHS, Beta $29.95** *ACA* 🎬🎬

Bad Boy A country boy goes to the big city, and succumbs to urban evils and temptations, but is eventually saved by motherly love. *AKA:* Branded. **1939 60m/B** John Downs, Helen MacKellar, Rosalind Keith, Holmes Herbert; **D:** Kurt Neumann. **VHS, Beta, LV** *NO* 🎬½

Bad Boys When a gang member's little brother is killed in a rumble, the teen responsible (Penn, who else?) goes to a reformatory, where he quickly (though somewhat reluctantly) takes charge. Meanwhile, on the outside, his rival attacks Penn's girlfriend (Sheedy, in her feature film debut) in retaliation, is incarcerated, and ends up vying with Penn for control of the cell block. Backed into a corner by their mutual hatred and escalating peer pressure, the two are pushed over the brink into a final and shattering confrontation. Not as violent as it could be, to its credit; attempts to communicate a message. **1983 (R) 123m/C** Sean Penn, Esai Morales, Reni Santoni, Jim Moody, Eric Gurry, Ally Sheedy, Clancy Brown; **D:** Rick Rosenthal. **VHS, Beta, LV $14.99** *HBO* 🎬🎬🎬

Bad Bunch A white liberal living in Watts tries to befriend a ruthless black street gang, but is unsuccessful. **1976 82m/C** Greydon Clark, Tom Johnigam, Pamela Corbett, Jacqulin Cole, Aldo Ray, Jock Mahoney; **D:** Greydon Clark. **VHS, Beta $59.95** *UHV* 🎬🎬

B.A.D. Cats Two members of a police burglary auto detail team chase after a group of car thieves who are planning a million-dollar gold heist. **1980 74m/C** Asher Brauner, Michelle Pfeiffer, Vic Morrow, Jimmie Walker, Steve Hanks, LaWanda Page; **D:** Bernard L. Kowalski. **VHS, Beta, LV $59.95** *LHV* 🎬

Bad Channels Radio goes awry when female listeners of station KDUL are shrunk and put into specimen jars by a way-out disc jockey and a visiting alien, who plans to take the women back to his planet. Mildly amusing comedy features ex-MTV J Quinn and a soundtrack composed and performed by Blue Oyster Cult. Also available with Spanish subtitles. **1992 (R) 88m/C** Paul Hipp, Martha Quinn, Aaron Lustig, Ian Patrick Williams, Charlie Spradling; **D:** Ted Nicolaou; **W:** Jackson Barr. **VHS, Beta** *PAR* 🎬🎬

Bad Charleston Charlie Dud of a gangster comedy with terrible acting. A comedy? **1973 (PG) 91m/C** Ross Hagen, John Carradine; **D:** Ivan Nagy. **VHS** *NO* Woof!

Bad Company Thoughtful study of two very different Civil War draft dodgers roaming the Western frontier and eventually turning to a fruitless life of crime. Both the cast and script are wonderful in an entertaining film that hasn't been given the attention it's due. **1972 (PG) 94m/C** Jeff Bridges, Barry Brown, Jim Davis, John Savage; **D:** Robert Benton. **VHS, Beta, LV $14.95** *PAR* 🎬🎬🎬½

Bad Day at Black Rock Story of a one-armed man uncovering a secret in a Western town. Wonderful performances from all concerned, especially Borgnine. Fine photography, shot using the new Cinemascope technique. Based on the novel by Howard Breslin. **1954 81m/C** Spencer Tracy, Robert Ryan, Anne Francis, Dean Jagger, Walter Brennan, John Ericson, Ernest Borgnine, Lee Marvin; **D:** John Sturges. Academy Awards '54 Nominations: Best Actor (Tracy), Best Director (Sturges); Cannes Film Festival '55: Best Actor (Tracy). **VHS, LV $19.98** *MGM, VYG, CRC* 🎬🎬🎬

Bad Dreams The only surviving member of a suicidal religious cult from the '60s awakens in 1988 from a coma. She is pursued by the living-dead cult leader, who seeks to ensure that she lives up (so to speak) to the cult's pact. Blood begins flowing as her fellow therapy group members begin dying, but the only bad dreams you'd get from this flick would be over the money lost on the video rental. **1988 (R) 84m/C** Bruce Abbott, Jennifer Rubin, Richard Lynch, Harris Yulin, Dean Cameron, Elizabeth Daily, Susan Ruttan, Charles Fleischer; **D:** Andrew Fleming. **VHS, Beta, LV $89.98** *FOX* 🎬½

Bad Georgia Road A New Yorker inherits a moonshine operation from her uncle, and fights off the syndicate for its profits. **1977 (R) 85m/C** Gary Lockwood, Carol Lynley, Royal Dano, John Wheeler, John Kerry; **D:** John Broderick. **VHS, Beta $49.95** *UHV* 🎬

Bad Girls Do Cry Unbelievably bad exploitation film. Idiotic plot with long scenes of girls stripping down to their undies. Although an American film, the voice track was dubbed in later. **1954 ?m/C** Bill Page, Misty Ayers, Heather English, Ben Frommer. **VHS $16.95** *SNC* Woof!

Bad Girls Dormitory At the New York Female Juvenile Reformatory, suicide seems a painless and welcome escape. Utilizes standard genre identifiers, including rape, drugs, soapy showers, bad docs, and desperate young women trapped in a web of frustration and desire. Cheap and mindless titillation. **1984 (R) 95m/C** Carey Zuris, Teresa Farley; **D:** Tim Kincaid. **VHS, Beta $49.95** *AHV* 🎬🎬

Bad Girls from Mars "B" movie sleaze-o-rama in which everyone is murdered, either before, after, or during sex, just like in real life. When the director of the film within this film hires an actress who is, shall we say, popular, to be the heroine of his latest sci-fier, the fun, slim as it is, begins. **1990 (R) 86m/C** Edy Williams, Brinke Stevens, Jay Richardson, Oliver Darrow; **D:** Fred Olen Ray; **W:** Sherman Scott, Mark Thomas McGee. **VHS $89.95** *VMK* Woof!

Bad Girls Go to Hell From the sultana of sleaze, Wishman, comes this winning entry into Joe Bob Briggs' "Sleaziest Movies in the History of the World" series. A ditsy-but-sexy housewife accidentally commits murder and what follows is a plethora of perversion involving hirsute men and gender-bending women who are hell-bent on showing her how hot it is where bad girls go. **1965 98m/B** **W/D:** Doris Wishman. **VHS $19.98** *SVI* Woof!

Bad Girls in the Movies A compilation of film clips depicting sleazy, criminal, female characters from women's prison films and other seedy sub-genres.
1986 56m/C David Carradine, Gene Autry, Yvonne De Carlo. **VHS, Beta** $19.98 *LIV ✗*

Bad Guys A goulash western about the outlaw days of Hungary in the 1860s. A gang of bandits terrorizes the Transdanubian countryside. In Hungarian with English subtitles. For those seeking the Eastern European Wild West experience.
1979 93m/C *HU* Janos Derzsi, Djoko Rosic, Mari Kiss, Gyorgy Dorner, Laszlo Szabo, Miklos Benedek; *D:* Gyorgy Szomjas. **VHS** $69.95 *EVD, FCT, TAM ✗✗*

Bad Guys An inane comedy about two ridiculous policemen who decide to take the wrestling world by storm after being kicked off the police force. Featuring scenes with many of the world's most popular wrestlers.
1986 (PG) 86m/C Adam Baldwin, Mike Jolly, Michelle Nicastro, Ruth Buzzi, James Booth, Gene LeBell, Norman Burton; *D:* Joel Silberg. **VHS** $79.95 *LIV ✗*

Bad Influence A lackluster effort in the evil-doppelganger school of psychological mystery, where a befuddled young executive (Spader) is led into the seamier side of life by a mysterious stranger (Lowe).
1990 (R) 99m/C Rob Lowe, James Spader, Lisa Zane, Christian Clemenson, Kathleen Wilhoite; *D:* Curtis Hanson. **VHS, Beta, LV** $14.95 *COL ✗✗*

Bad Jim A cowpoke buys Billy the Kid's horse and, upon riding it, becomes an incorrigible outlaw himself. First feature film for Hollywood legend Clark Gable's son.
1989 (PG) 110m/C James Brolin, Richard Roundtree, John Clark Gable, Harry Carey Jr., Ty Hardin, Pepe Serna, Rory Calhoun; *D:* Clyde Ware. **VHS, Beta, LV** $79.95 *COL ✗ 1/2*

Bad Lands A small cowboy posse finds themselves trapped by a band of Apache Indians in the Arizona desert. A remake of "The Lost Patrol."
1939 70m/B Robert Barratt, Guinn Williams, Douglas Walton, Andy Clyde, Addison Richards, Robert Coote, Paul Hurst, Noah Beery Jr.; *D:* Lew Landers. **VHS, Beta** $19.98 *TTC ✗✗ 1/2*

Bad Lieutenant Social chaos and degeneration characterize story as well as nameless loner lieutenant Keitel, who is as corrupt as they come. Assigned to a case involving a raped nun, he's confronted by his own lagging Catholic beliefs and the need for saving grace. From cult filmmaker Ferrara ("Ms. 45") and filled with violence, drugs, and grotesque sexual situations. Tense, over-the-top, urban drama is not intended for seekers of the subtle and should not be viewed on a double bill with "Aladdin." Instead, rent it with "Reservoir Dogs" and prepare yourself for a long tense evening of top-rated Keitel and screen-splitting violence. "R" rated version is also available at 91 minutes.
1992 (NC-17) 98m/C Harvey Keitel, Brian McElroy, Frankie Acciario, Peggy Gormley, Stella Keitel, Victor Argo, Paul Calderone, Leonard Thomas, Frankie Thorn; *D:* Abel Ferrara. **VHS, LV** $92.98 *LIV ✗✗✗*

Bad Man of Deadwood A man-with-a-past joins a circus as a sharp-shooter, and is threatened with disclosure.
1941 54m/B Roy Rogers, George "Gabby" Hayes. **VHS, Beta** $24.95 *DVT, NOS, RXM ✗*

Bad Manners When an orphan is adopted by a wealthy but entirely selfish couple, a group of his orphan friends try to free him from his new home and lifestyle.
1984 (R) 85m/C Martin Mull, Karen Black, Anne De Salvo, Murphy Dunne, Pamela Segall, Edy Williams, Susan Ruttan, Richard Deacon; *D:* Bobby Houston. **VHS, Beta** $19.95 *STE, HBO ✗*

Bad Man's River A Mexican revolutionary leader hires a gang of outlaws to blow up an arsenal used by the Mexican Army.
1972 92m/C *IT SP* Lee Van Cleef, James Mason, Gina Lollobrigida; *D:* Gene Martin. **VHS, Beta** $24.95 *WWV ✗✗*

Bad Medicine A youth who doesn't want to be a doctor is accepted by a highly questionable Latin American school of medicine. Remember that it was for medical students like these that the U.S. liberated Grenada.
1985 (PG-13) 97m/C Steve Guttenberg, Alan Arkin, Julie Hagerty, Bill Macy, Curtis Armstrong, Julie Kavner, Joe Grifasi, Robert Romanus, Taylor Negron, Gilbert Gottfried; *D:* Harvey Miller. **VHS, Beta** $79.98 *FOX Woof!*

The Bad News Bears Family comedy about a misfit Little League team that gets whipped into shape by a cranky, sloppy, beer-drinking coach who recruits a female pitcher. O'Neal and Matthau are top-notch. The kids' language is rather adult, and very titillating for younger viewers. Spawned two sequels and a television series.
1976 (PG) 102m/C Walter Matthau, Tatum O'Neal, Vic Morrow, Joyce Van Patten, Jackie Earle Haley; *D:* Michael Ritchie. **VHS, Beta, LV, 8mm** $14.95 *PAR ✗✗✗*

The Bad News Bears Go to Japan The second sequel, in which the famed Little League team goes to the Little League World Series in Tokyo. Comic adventure features Curtis as a talent agent out to exploit the team's fame.
1978 (PG) 102m/C Tony Curtis, Jackie Earle Haley, Tomisaburo Wakayama, George Wyner; *D:* John Berry. **VHS, Beta, LV** $19.95 *PAR ✗*

The Bad News Bears in Breaking Training With a chance to take on the Houston Toros for a shot at the little league baseball Japanese champs, the Bears devise a way to get to Texas to play at the famed Astrodome. Disappointing sequel to "The Bad News Bears"; followed by "The Bad News Bears Go to Japan" (1978).
1977 (PG) 105m/C William Devane, Clifton James, Jackie Earle Haley, Jimmy Baio; *D:* Michael Pressman. **VHS, Beta, LV** $14.95 *PAR ✗ 1/2*

Bad Ronald No, not a political biography of Ronald Reagan... Fascinating thriller about a disturbed teenager who kills a friend after being harassed repeatedly. The plot thickens after the boy's mother dies, and he is forced to hide out in a secret room when an unsuspecting family with three daughters moves into his house. The story is accurately recreated from the novel by John Holbrook Vance.
1974 78m/C Scott Jacoby, Pippa Scott, John Larch, Dabney Coleman, Kim Hunter, John Fiedler; *D:* Buzz Kulik. **VHS** $49.95 *LIV ✗✗✗*

The Bad Seed A mother makes the tortuous discovery that her cherubic eight-year-old daughter harbors an innate desire to kill. Based on Maxwell Anderson's powerful Broadway stage play. Remade for television in 1985.
1956 129m/B Patty McCormack, Nancy Kelly, Eileen Heckart, Henry Jones, Evelyn Varden, Paul Fix; *D:* Mervyn LeRoy. Academy Awards '56 Nominations: Best Actress (Kelly), Best Black and White Cinematography, Best Supporting Actress (Heckart, McCormack); Golden Globe Awards '57: Best Supporting Actress (Heckart). **VHS, Beta** $59.95 *WAR ✗✗ 1/2*

The Bad Seed Television remake of the movie with the same name. Story about a sadistic little child who kills for her own evil purposes. Acting is not up to par with previous version.
1985 100m/C Blair Brown, Lynn Redgrave, David Carradine, Richard Kiley, David Ogden Stiers, Carrie Wells; *D:* Paul Wendkos. **VHS** $59.95 *NO ✗✗*

The Bad Sleep Well Japanese variation of the 1940 Warner Brothers crime dramas. A tale about corruption in the corporate world as seen through the eyes of a rising executive.
1960 135m/B *JP* Toshiro Mifune, Masayuki Kato, Masayuki Mori, Takashi Shimura, Akira Nishimura; *D:* Akira Kurosawa. **VHS, Beta** $24.95 *SVS, APD, TAM ✗✗✗ 1/2*

Bad Taste A definite pleaser for the person who enjoys watching starving aliens devour the average, everyday human being. Alien fast-food manufacturers come to earth in hopes of harvesting all of mankind. The earth's fate lies in the hands of the government who must stop these rampaging creatures before the whole human race is gobbled up. Terrific make-up jobs on the aliens add the final touch to this gory, yet humorous cult horror flick.
1988 90m/C *NZ* Peter Jackson, Pete O'Herne, Mike Minett, Terry Potter, Craig Smith, Doug Wren, Dean Lawrie; *D:* Peter Jackson. **VHS, LV** *NO ✗✗✗*

The Badge After many failed attempts at a career, a young man finally joins the police force to appease his domineering father.
1990 30m/C *D:* Robert Spara. **VHS** $59.95 *CIG ✗ 1/2*

Badge of the Assassin A television movie based on the true story of a New York assistant DA who directed a campaign to catch a pair of cop-killers from the '70s.
1985 96m/C James Woods, Yaphet Kotto, Alex Rocco, David Harris, Pam Grier, Steven Keats, Richard Bradford, Rae Dawn Chong; *D:* Mel Damski. **VHS, Beta, LV** $29.95 *VMK ✗✗*

Badge 373 In the vein of "The French Connection," a New York cop is suspended and decides to battle crime his own way.
1973 (R) 116m/C Robert Duvall, Verna Bloom, Eddie Egan; *D:* Howard W. Koch. **VHS, Beta** $14.95 *PAR ✗ 1/2*

The Badlanders A western remake of the crime drama "The Asphalt Jungle." Ladd and Borgnine plan a gold robbery against Smith, who cheated them out of their share in a gold mine. Cross and double-cross follow the partners as does romance.
1958 85m/C Alan Ladd, Ernest Borgnine, Kent Smith, Katy Jurado, Claire Kelly, Nehemiah Persoff, Adam Williams; *D:* Delmer Daves. **VHS** $19.98 *MGM ✗✗✗*

Badlands Based loosely on the Charlie Starkweather murders of the 1950s, this impressive debut by director Malick recounts a slow-thinking, unhinged misfit's killing spree across the midwestern plains, accompanied by a starry-eyed 15-year-old schoolgirl. Sheen and Spacek are a disturbingly numb, apathetic, and icy duo.
1974 (PG) 94m/C Martin Sheen, Sissy Spacek, Warren Oates; *D:* Terence Malick. **VHS, Beta, LV** $39.98 *WAR ✗✗✗ 1/2*

Badman's Territory A straight-shooting marshal has to deal with such notorious outlaws as the James and Dalton boys in a territory outside of government control.
1946 79m/B Randolph Scott, Ann Richards, George "Gabby" Hayes, Steve Brodie; *D:* Tim Whelan. **VHS, Beta** $19.98 *RKO, TTC ✗✗✗*

Badmen of Nevada Badmen roam Nevada in the early days before law and order.
1933 57m/B Kent Taylor, Gail Patrick. **VHS, Beta** $29.95 VCN ♫♫½

Baffled Nimoy is a race car driver who has visions of people in danger. He must convince an ESP expert (Hampshire) of the credibility of his vision, and then try to save the lives of the people seen with his sixth sense. Made for television.
1972 90m/C Leonard Nimoy, Susan Hampshire, Vera Miles, Rachel Roberts, Jewel Blanch, Christopher Benjamin; **D:** Philip Leacock. **VHS** FOX ♫♫½

Bagdad Cafe A large German woman, played by Sagebrecht, finds herself stranded in the Mojave desert after her husband dumps her on the side of the highway. She encounters a rundown cafe where she becomes involved with the off-beat residents. A hilarious story in which the strange people and the absurdity of their situations are treated kindly and not made to seem ridiculous. Spawned a short-lived TV series with Whoopi Goldberg. **AKA:** Out of Rosenheim.
1988 (PG) 91m/C GE Marianne Sagebrecht, CCH Pounder, Jack Palance; **D:** Percy Adlon. Academy Awards '88 Nominations: Best Song ("Calling You"); Cesar Awards '89: Best Foreign Film. **VHS, Beta** NO ♫♫♫

Bahama Passage Trite story of one lady's efforts to win the affection of a macho Bahamas stud.
1942 83m/C Madeleine Carroll, Sterling Hayden, Flora Robson, Leo G. Carroll; **D:** Edward H. Griffith. **VHS** PAR, MLB ♫♫½

Bail Jumper A story of love and commitment against incredible odds; some of which happen to be a swarm of locusts, a tornado, and falling meteorites. Joe and Elaine are small-time hoods escaping their dreary lives in Murky Springs Missouri by heading for that great bastion of idyllism and idealism—New York City. But even as the world starts to crumble around them, get the message that love prevails.
1989 90m/C Eszter Balint, B.J. Spalding, Tony Askin, Joie Lee; **D:** Christian Faber. **VHS, Beta** $79.95 FXL ♫♫

Bail Out Three bounty hunters, armed to the teeth, run a car-trashing police gauntlet so they may capture a valuable crook.
1990 (R) 88m/C David Hasselhoff, Linda Blair, John Vernon, Tom Rosales, Charles Brill; **D:** Max Kleven. **VHS, Beta, LV** $89.98 VES, LIV ♫

Bail Out at 43,000 Movie about the lifestyles and love affairs of your average, everyday parachutist.
1957 80m/B John Payne, Karen Steele, Paul Kelly; **D:** Francis D. Lyon. **VHS** MGM ♫♫

Baja Oklahoma A made-for-cable-television film about a country barmaid with dreams of being a country singer. Songs by Willie Nelson, Emmylou Harris and Billy Vera.
1987 110m/C Lesley Ann Warren, Peter Coyote, Swoosie Kurtz, Willie Nelson, Julia Roberts; **D:** Bobby Roth. **VHS, Beta, LV** $89.95 LHV ♫

Baker's Hawk A young boy befriends a red-tailed hawk and learns the meaning of family and caring.
1976 98m/C Clint Walker, Diane Baker, Burl Ives; **D:** Lyman Dayton. **VHS, Beta** $39.95 BPG, HHE ♫♫

The Baker's Wife There's a new baker in town, and he brings with him to the small French village an array of tantalizing breads, as well as a discontented wife. When she runs off with a shepherd, her loyal and naive husband refuses to acknowledge her infidelity; however, in his loneliness, the baker can't

bake, so the townspeople scheme to bring his wife back. Panned as overly cute Marcel Pagnol peasant glorification, and hailed as a visual poem full of wit; you decide. In French with subtitles. Also available for French students without subtitles; a French script booklet is also available. **AKA:** La Femme du Boulanger.
1933 101m/B FR Raimu, Ginette LeClerc, Charles Moulton, Charpin, Robert Vattier; **D:** Marcel Pagnol. **VHS, Beta** $39.95 INT, MRV, DVT ♫♫♫½

Bakery/Grocery Clerk A package of shorts featuring crazy comedian Larry Semon, getting tangled up in mayhem and molasses. Silent with piano score.
1921 55m/B Larry Semon, Oliver Hardy, Lucille Carlisle; **D:** Larry Semon. **VHS, Beta** $19.98 CCB ♫♫

Balboa Set on sun-baked Balboa Island, this is a melodramatic tale of high-class power, jealousy, and intrigue. Never-aired pilot for a television mini-series, in the night-time soap tradition (even features Steve Kanaly from TV's "Dallas"). Special appearance by Cassandra Peterson, also known as horror hostess Elvira; and if that interests you, look for Sonny Bono, as well.
1982 92m/C Tony Curtis, Carol Lynley, Chuck Connors, Sonny Bono, Steve Kanaly, Jennifer Chase, Lupita Ferrer, Martine Beswick, Henry Jones, Cassandra Peterson; **D:** James Polakof. **VHS, Beta** $69.98 VES, LIV Woof!

The Balcony A film version of the great Jean Genet play about a surreal brothel, located in an unnamed, revolution-torn city, where its powerful patrons act out their fantasies. Scathing and rude.
1963 87m/B Peter Falk, Shelley Winters, Lee Grant, Kent Smith, Peter Brocco, Ruby Dee, Jeff Corey, Leonard Nimoy, Joyce Jameson; **D:** Joseph Strick. **VHS, Beta, LV** $29.95 MFV, TAM ♫♫♫

Balkan Express A crew of unlikely slobs become heroes in war-ravaged Europe.
1983 102m/C **VHS, Beta** $19.95 STE, NWV ♫½

Ball of Fire A gang moll hides out with a group of mundane professors, trying to avoid her loathsome boyfriend. The professors are busy compiling an encyclopedia and Stanwyck helps them with their section on slang in the English language. Cooper has his hands full when he falls for this damsel in distress and must fight the gangsters to keep her. Stanwyck takes a personal liking to naive Cooper and resolves to teach him more than just slang.
1941 111m/B Gary Cooper, Barbara Stanwyck, Dana Andrews, Gene Krupa, Oscar Homolka, Dan Duryea, S.Z. Sakall, Henry Travers; **D:** Howard Hawks; **W:** Billy Wilder, Charles Brackett. **VHS, Beta, LV** $19.98 SUE ♫♫♫

Ballad in Blue Real life story of Ray Charles and a blind child. Tearjerker also includes some of Charles' hit songs. ♫I Got a Woman; What'd I Say?. **AKA:** Blues for Lovers.
1966 89m/B GB Ray Charles, Tom Bell, Mary Peach, Dawn Addams, Piers Bishop, Betty McDowall; **D:** Paul Henreid. **VHS, Beta** $39.95 LIV ♫♫

Ballad of a Gunfighter A feud between two outlaws reaches the boiling point when they both fall in love with the same woman.
1964 84m/C Marty Robbins, Bob Barron, Joyce Redd, Nestor Paiva, Laurette Luez; **D:** Bill Ward. **VHS, Beta** $9.99 FHE, PSM ♫

Ballad of a Soldier As a reward for demolishing two German tanks, a nineteen-year-old Russian soldier receives a six-day pass so he can see his mother; however, he meets another woman. Well directed and photographed, while avoiding propaganda.
1960 88m/B RU Vladimir Ivashov, Shanna Prokhorenko; **D:** Grigori Chukrai. Academy Awards '61 Nominations: Best Story & Screenplay; British Academy Awards '61: Best Film. **VHS, Beta, 3/4U** $35.95 HTV, NOS, HHT ♫♫♫½

Ballad of Cable Hogue A prospector, who had been left to die in the desert by his double-crossing partners, finds a waterhole. A surprise awaits his former friends when they visit the remote well. Not the usual violent Peckinpah horse drama, but a tongue-in-cheek comedy romance mixed with tragedy. Obviously offbeat and worth a peek.
1970 (R) 122m/C Jason Robards Jr., Stella Stevens, David Warner, L.Q. Jones, Strother Martin, Slim Pickens; **D:** Sam Peckinpah; **M:** Jerry Goldsmith. **VHS, Beta, LV** $19.90 WAR ♫♫♫

Ballad of Gregorio Cortez Tragic story based on one of the most famous manhunts in Texas history. A Mexican cowhand kills a Texas sheriff in self-defense and tries to elude the law, all because of a misunderstanding of the Spanish language. Olmos turns in a fine performance as Cortez.
1983 (PG) 105m/C Edward James Olmos, James Gammon, Tom Bower, Alan Vint, Barry Corbin, Rosana De Soto, Bruce McGill, Brion James, Pepe Serna, William Sanderson; **D:** Robert M. Young. **VHS, Beta, LV** $14.98 SUE, TAM, NLC ♫♫♫

The Ballad of Narayama Director Imamura's subtle and vastly moving story takes place a vague century ago. In compliance with village law designed to control population among the poverty-stricken peasants, a healthy seventy-year-old woman must submit to solitary starvation atop a nearby mountain. We follow her as she sets into motion the final influence she will have in the lives of her children and grandchildren, a situation described with detachment and without imposing a tragic perspective. In Japanese with English subtitles. **AKA:** Narayama-Bushi-Ko.
1983 129m/C JP Ken Ogata, Sumiko Sakamota, Takejo Aki, Tonpei Hidari, Shoichi Ozawa; **W/D:** Shohei Imamura. **VHS** $59.95 HMV, FCT ♫♫♫♫

The Ballad of Paul Bunyan The good-humored, legendary American giant is pitted against a powerful lumber camp boss who likes to pick on the little guy.
1972 30m/C **D:** Arthur Rankin Jr., Jules Bass. **VHS** $6.95 STE, PSM ♫♫♫

The Ballad of the Sad Cafe An unusual love story starring Redgrave as Miss Amelia, an outcast in a small Southern town during the Depression. A distant relation of Miss Amelia's unexpectedly shows up and the everyday lives of the townspeople are suddenly transformed. When Miss Amelia's one-time husband of ten days returns to town with revenge on his mind, tragedy follows. A moving story that tries to portray both sides of love and its power to enhance and destroy simultaneously. Emotion never seems to come to life in a movie that's nice to watch, but is ultimately disappointing. Adapted from the play by Edward Albee, which was based on the critically acclaimed novella by Carson McCullers. A British/U.S. co-production.

1991 (PG-13) 100m/C *GB* Vanessa Redgrave, Keith Carradine, Cork Hubbert, Rod Steiger, Austin Pendleton, Beth Dixon, Lanny Flaherty, Mert Hatfield, Earl Hindman, Anne Pitoniak; *D:* Simon Callow; *W:* Michael Hirst; *M:* Richard Robbins. VHS, LV *NO* ♫♫½

Ballbuster Cops take on gangs in an all-out high-stakes battle to win back the streets.
19?? 100m/C Ivan Rogers, Bonnie Paine, W. Randolph Galvin, Bill Shirk, Brenda Banet; *W/D:* Eddie Beverly Jr. VHS $39.95 *XVC* ♫♫½

Ballet Shoes The classic children's tale of three sisters living a very sheltered life with their guardian Sylvia, who is working to support all four of them. A story of hope and possibilities. From the BBC Television network.
19?? 120m/C *GB* VHS $29.95 *BFS, HMV* ♫♫

The Balloonatic/One Week "The Balloonatic" (1923) features Keaton in several misadventures. In "One Week" (1920), Keaton and his new bride, Seely, receive a new home as a wedding gift—the kind you have to assemble yourself. Silent.
1923 48m/B Buster Keaton, Phyllis Haver, Sybil Seely; *D:* Buster Keaton. VHS, Beta $17.95 *CCB* ♫♫

Ballyhoo Baby When a couple traveling cross-country pick up a young hitchhiker, the sexual tension between the three builds to a frightening climax.
1990 30m/C *D:* Paul Young. VHS $59.95 *CIG* ♫½

Baltic Deputy An early forerunner of Soviet historic realism, where an aging intellectual deals with post-revolution Soviet life. In Russian with subtitles.
1937 95m/B *RU* Nikolai Cherkassov; *D:* Yosif Heifitz. VHS, Beta, 3/4U $35.95 *FCT, IHF* ♫♫♫½

The Baltimore Bullet Two men make their living traveling through the country as pool hustlers, bilking would-be pool sharks. Features ten of the greatest pool players in the world.
1980 (PG) 103m/C James Coburn, Omar Sharif, Bruce Boxleitner, Ronee Blakley, Jack O'Halloran; *D:* Robert Ellis Miller. VHS, Beta $9.98 *SUE, NLC* ♫♫

Bambi A true Disney classic, detailing the often harsh education of a newborn deer and his friends in the forest. Proves that Disney animation was—and still is—the best to be found. Thumper still steals the show and the music is delightful, including "Let's Sing a Gay Little Spring Song," "Love is a Song," "Little April Shower," "The Thumper Song," and "Twitterpated." Stands as one of the greatest children's films of all time; a genuine perennial from generation to generation. Based very loosely on the book by Felix Salten.
1942 (G) 69m/C *D:* David Hand; *W:* Larry Morey; *M:* Frank Churchill, Edward Plumb; *V:* Bobby Stewart, Peter Behn, Stan Alexander, Cammie King, Donnie Dunagan, Hardie Albright, John Sutherland, Tim Davis, Sam Edwards, Sterling Holloway, Anne Gillis, Perce Pearce. VHS, Beta, LV $26.99 *DIS, APD, RDG* ♫♫♫♫

Bambi Meets Godzilla A spoof on endless film credits, after which the title bout lasts about six seconds. Must be seen to be appreciated.
1969 2m/B *D:* Marv Newland. VHS, Beta $9.95 *PYR* ♫♫½

Bambi Meets Godzilla and Other Weird Cartoons Bambi meets Godzilla, plus many classic animated shorts, including "Crazy Town" with Betty Boop, and Max Fleischer creations.
1987 30m/B VHS $9.95 *RHI* ♫♫½

The Bamboo Saucer Russian and American scientists race to find a U.F.O. in Red China. *AKA:* Collision Course.
1968 103m/C Dan Duryea, John Ericson, Lois Nettleton, Nan Leslie; *D:* Frank Telford. VHS $19.98 *REP* ♫½

Bananas Intermittently hilarious pre-"Annie Hall" Allen fare is full of the director's signature angst-ridden philosophical comedy. A frustrated product tester from New York runs off to South America, where he volunteers his support to the revolutionary force of a shaky Latin-American dictatorship and winds up the leader. Don't miss cameos by Stallone and Garfield. Wittily scored by Marvin Hamlisch.
1971 (PG) 82m/C Woody Allen, Louise Lasser, Carlos Montalban, Howard Cosell, Charlotte Rae, Conrad Bain; *Cameos:* Sylvester Stallone, Allen Garfield; *D:* Woody Allen. VHS, Beta, LV $19.98 *FOX, FCT* ♫♫♫

Bananas Boat A captain takes a man and his daughter away from the collapsing government of their banana republic. The cast and director take a few risks but fail in this would-be comedy. *AKA:* What Changed Charley Farthing.
1978 91m/C *GB* Doug McClure, Hayley Mills, Lionel Jeffries, Dilys Hamlett, Warren Mitchell; *D:* Sidney Hayers. VHS $79.95 *UHV* Woof!

Band of Outsiders A woman hires a pair of petty criminals to rip off her aunt; Godard vehicle for exposing self-reflexive comments on modern film culture. In French with English subtitles. *AKA:* Bande a Part; The Outsiders.
1964 97m/B *FR* Sami Frey, Anna Karina, Claude Brasseur, Louisa Colpeyn; *D:* Jean-Luc Godard. VHS, Beta $49.95 *TAM, NOS, MRV* ♫♫½

Band of the Hand A "Miami Vice" type melodrama about five convicts who are trained to become an unstoppable police unit. The first feature film by Glaser, last seen as Starsky in "Starsky & Hutch."
1986 (R) 109m/C Stephen Lang, Michael Carmine, Lauren Holly, Leon Robinson; *D:* Paul Michael Glaser. VHS, Beta, LV $79.95 *RCA* ♫

The Band Wagon A Hollywood song-and-dance man finds trouble when he is persuaded to star in a Broadway musical. Charisse has been called Astaire's most perfect partner, perhaps by those who haven't seen Rogers. ♫That's Entertainment; Dancing in the Dark; By Myself; A Shine On Your Shoes; Something to Remember You By; High and Low; I Love Louisa; New Sun in the Sky; I Guess I'll Have to Change My Plan; Louisiana Hayride; Triplets; The Girl Hunt.
1953 112m/C Fred Astaire, Cyd Charisse, Oscar Levant, Nanette Fabray, Jack Buchanan; *D:* Vincente Minnelli; *M:* Arthur Schwartz, Jason James Richter. VHS, Beta, LV $19.98 *MGM, FCT* ♫♫♫

Bandera Bandits An escaped convict, while evading a ruthless sheriff, marries a young girl and together they romp off into the sunset.
19?? 98m/C Telly Savalas, Susan George. VHS, Beta $59.95 *TWE* Woof!

Bandit Queen Spanish girl forms a band to stop seizure of Spanish possessions by lawless Californians.
1951 71m/B Barbara Britton, Willard Parker, Philip Reed, Jack Perrin; *D:* William Berke. VHS, Beta *RXM* ♫½

Bandits Three cowboys team up with a band of Mexican outlaws to fight a Mexican traitor.
1973 83m/C Robert Conrad, Jan-Michael Vincent, Roy Jenson; *D:* Robert Conrad, Alfredo Zacharias. VHS, Beta $19.95 *UNI* ♫½

Bandits of Orgosolo An acclaimed, patient drama about a Sardinian shepherd who shelters a band of thieves from the police. When one of the cops is killed the shepherd panics and flees into the hills for survival. Dubbed in English. *AKA:* Banditi a Orgosolo.
1961 98m/B *IT* Michele Cossu, Peppeddu Cuccu; *D:* Vittorio de Seta. VHS, Beta $24.95 *NOS, FCT, VYY* ♫♫½

Bandolero! In Texas, Stewart and Martin are two fugitive brothers who run into trouble with their Mexican counterparts.
1968 (PG) 106m/C James Stewart, Raquel Welch, Dean Martin, George Kennedy, Will Geer, Harry Carey Jr., Andrew Prine; *D:* Andrew V. McLaglen; *M:* Jerry Goldsmith. VHS, Beta $19.98 *FOX* ♫♫½

Bang Bang Kid A western spoof about a klutzy gunfighter defending a town from outlaws. *AKA:* Bang Bang.
1967 (G) 78m/C Tom Bosley, Guy Madison, Sandra Milo; *D:* Stanley Prager. VHS, Beta $59.95 *WWV* ♫♫

Bang the Drum Slowly The original television adaptation of a Mark Harris novel about baseball. A ball player stricken by a terminal illness strikes an unlikely friendship with a teammate. Interesting role for an actor (Newman) who claims to have been driven to acting by running away from the sporting goods business.
1956 60m/B Paul Newman, George Peppard, Albert Salmi. VHS $14.95 *NOS, WKV* ♫♫

Bang the Drum Slowly The touching story of a major league catcher who discovers that he is dying of Hodgkins disease and wants to play just one more season. De Niro is the weakening baseball player and Moriarty is the friend who helps him see it through. Based on a novel by Mark Harris.
1973 (PG) 97m/C Robert De Niro, Michael Moriarty, Vincent Gardenia, Phil Foster, Ann Wedgeworth, Heather MacRae, Selma Diamond, Danny Aiello; *D:* John Hancock. Academy Awards '73 Nominations: Best Supporting Actor (Gardenia); National Board of Review Awards '73: 10 Best Films of the Year; New York Film Critics Awards '73: Best Supporting Actor (De Niro). VHS, Beta, LV $14.95 *PAR, FCT* ♫♫♫

The Bank Dick W.C. Fields wrote the screenplay (using an alias) and stars in this zany comedy about a man who accidentally trips a bank robber and winds up as a guard. Fields' last major role is a classic, a worthy end to his great career. Side two of the laserdisc is in CAV format, which allows single frame access to the frenetic cops and robbers chase sequence. *AKA:* The Bank Detective.
1940 73m/B W.C. Fields, Cora Witherspoon, Una Merkel, Mahatma Kane Jeeves, Jack Norton, Jessie Ralph, Franklin Pangborn, Shemp Howard, Grady Sutton, Russell Hicks, Richard Purcell, Reed Hadley; *D:* Eddie Cline; *W:* Evelyn Del Rio. VHS, Beta, LV $29.95 *MCA* ♫♫♫♫

Bank Shot Hilarious comedy about a criminal who plans to rob a bank by stealing the entire building. Based on the novel by Donald Westlake, and the sequel to "The Hot Rock."
1974 83m/C George C. Scott, Joanna Cassidy, Sorrell Booke, G. Wood, Clifton James, Bob Balaban, Bibi Osterwald; *D:* Gower Champion. VHS, CV *NO* ♫♫♫

The Banker A cop, played by Forster, suspects a wealthy, highly influential banker of brutal serial killings.
1989 (R) 90m/C Robert Forster, Jeff Conaway, Leif Garrett, Duncan Regehr, Shanna Reed, Deborah Richter, Richard Roundtree, Teri Weigel, E.J. Peaker; *D:* William Webb. VHS, Beta, LV *NO* ♫♫

Banzai Runner A cop whose brother was killed in an exclusive desert-highway race decides to avenge by joining the race himself.
1986 88m/C Dean Stockwell, John Shepherd, Charles Dierkop; *D:* John Thomas. **VHS, Beta** $19.95 *VMK* 🎗️🎗️

Bar-20 Stage hold-ups and jewel robberies abound in this Hopalong Cassidy western.
1943 54m/B George Reeves, Douglas Fowley, William Boyd, Andy Clyde, Robert Mitchum, Victor Jory; *D:* Lesley Selander. **VHS, Beta** $19.95 *NOS, MRV, GVV* 🎗️½

Barabbas Barabbas, a thief and murderer, is freed by Pontius Pilate in place of Jesus. He is haunted by this event for the rest of his life. Excellent acting, little melodrama, lavish production make for fine viewing. Based on the novel by Lagerkvist.
1962 144m/C Anthony Quinn, Silvana Mangano, Arthur Kennedy, Jack Palance, Ernest Borgnine, Katy Jurado; *D:* Richard Fleischer. **VHS, Beta, LV** $59.95 *COL* 🎗️🎗️½

Barbarella Based on the popular French sci-fi comic strip drawn by Jean-Claude Forest, this cult classic details the bizarre adventures of a space nymphette (Fonda) encountering fantastic creatures and super beings. You'll see sides of Fonda you never saw before (not even in the workout videos). Notorious in its day; rather silly, dated camp now. Don't miss the elbow-sex scene. Terry Southern contributed to the script. *AKA:* Barbarella, Queen of the Galaxy.
1968 (PG) 98m/C Jane Fonda, John Phillip Law, David Hemmings, Marcel Marceau, Anita Pallenberg, Milo O'Shea; *D:* Roger Vadim. **VHS, Beta, LV** $59.95 *PAR* 🎗️🎗️½

Barbarian and the Geisha The first US diplomat in Japan undergoes culture shock as well as a passionate love affair with a geisha, circa 1856. Music by Hugo Friedhofer.
1958 104m/C John Wayne, Eiko Ando, Sam Jaffe, So Yamamura; *D:* John Huston. **VHS, Beta** $19.98 *FOX* 🎗️🎗️

Barbarian Queen Female warriors led by beauteous babe seek revenge for the capture of their men in this sword-and-sorcery epic. Low-budget rip-off "Conan the Barbarian" is laughable. Also available in an unrated version. Followed by "Barbarian Queen 2: The Empress Strikes Back."
1985 (R) 71m/C *IT* Lana Clarkson, Frank Zagarino, Katt Shea Ruben, Dawn Dunlap, Susana Traverso; *D:* Hector Olivera. **VHS, Beta, LV** $29.98 *VES, LIV* 🎗️

Barbarian Queen 2: The Empress Strikes Back Apparently one movie wasn't enough to tell the beautiful Princess Athalia's story. This time she fights her evil brother Ankaris. He throws her in prison, she escapes, joins a band of female rebels, and leads them into battle. No better than the first attempt.
1989 (R) 87m/C *IT* Lana Clarkson, Greg Wrangler, Rebecca Wood, Elizabeth Jaegen, Roger Cundy; *D:* Joe Finley. **VHS** $89.98 *LIV* 🎗️

The Barbarians Two bodybuilder siblings in animal skins battle wizards and warlords in this dumb-but-fun U.S./Italian co-production. *AKA:* The Barbarians and Co.
1987 (R) 88m/C *IT* David Paul, Peter Paul, Richard Lynch, Eva LaRue, Virginia Bryant, Sheeba Alahani, Michael Berryman; *D:* Ruggero Deodato. **VHS, Beta, LV** $19.95 *MED* 🎗️

Barbarians at the Gate In the "greed is good" financial climate of the 80's, this made-for-cable movie chronicles the $25 billion dollar battle in 1988 for RJR Nabisco, which at the time was working on developing a "smokeless cigarette." Garner is CEO F. Ross Johnson, who is confident that their "smokeless cigarette" will boost the stock's value—until he gets the test-marketing results. Unwilling to risk the product's failure, Johnson decides to buy the company and is challenged by master dealer Kravis (Pryce). Fascinating social commentary on the nastiest mega-deal in history. Based on the book by Bryan Burrough and John Helyar.
1993 (R) 107m/C James Garner, Jonathan Pryce, Peter Riegert, Joanna Cassidy, Fred Dalton Thompson, Leilani Ferrer, Matt Clark, Jeffrey DeMunn; *D:* Glenn Jordan; *W:* Larry Gelbart; *M:* Richard Gibbs. **VHS** *HBO* 🎗️🎗️🎗️½

Barbarosa Offbeat western about an aging, legendary outlaw constantly on the lam who reluctantly befriends a naive farmboy and teaches him survival skills. Nelson and Busey are a great team, solidly directed. Lovely Rio Grande scenery.
1982 (PG) 90m/C Willie Nelson, Gilbert Roland, Gary Busey, Isela Vega; *D:* Fred Schepisi. **VHS, Beta, LV** $19.95 *FOX* 🎗️🎗️🎗️

Barbary Coast A ruthless club owner tries to win the love of a young girl by building her into a star attraction during San Francisco's gold rush days.
1935 90m/B Edward G. Robinson, Walter Brennan, Brian Donlevy, Joel McCrea, Donald Meek, David Niven, Miriam Hopkins; *D:* Howard Hawks. **VHS, Beta, LV** *NO* 🎗️🎗️🎗️

The Barbary Coast A turn-of-the-century detective sleuths the streets of San Francisco in this average made-for-television movie.
1974 100m/C William Shatner, Dennis Cole, Lynda Day George, John Vernon, Charles Aidman, Michael Ansara, Neville Brand, Bill Bixby; *D:* Bill Bixby. **VHS** *SUE, ORI* 🎗️🎗️

The Barber Shop Fields portrays the bumbling, carefree barber Cornelius O'Hare, purveyor of village gossip and problem solver. Havoc begins when a gangster enters the shop and demands that Cornelius change his appearance.
1933 21m/B W.C. Fields, Elise Cavanna, Harry Watson, Dagmar Oakland, Frank Yaconelli. **VHS, Beta** $24.98 *CCB* 🎗️🎗️🎗️

The Barcelona Kill When a journalist and her boyfriend get in too deep with the Barcelona mob, their troubles begin.
1977 86m/C Linda Hayden, John Austin, Simon Andrew, Maximo Valverde; *D:* Jose Antonio De La Loma. **VHS, Beta** *NO* 🎗️½

Bare Essentials Made for TV yuppie Club Med nightmare in which a high-strung couple from New York find themselves marooned on a desert isle with only two other inhabitants. With no cellular telephoning ability and an absence of large-ticket consumer goods to purchase, the two turn their reluctant sights on each other, focusing on the bare essentials, as it were. Great soul-searching scenes for the inarticulate.
1991 (PG) 94m/C Gregory Harrison, Lisa Hartman, Mark Linn-Baker, Charlotte Lewis; *D:* Martha Coolidge. **VHS** $89.98 *REP* 🎗️

Bare Hunt Detective Max T. Unimportant is dragged into the underground world of prospective nude actresses in this supposedly funny "nudie." *AKA:* My Gun is Jammed; The Bear Hunt.
1963 69m/B VHS, Beta $19.95 *VDM* 🎗️

Bare Knees A woman causes a scandal in her family when she arrives at her sister's birthday party with bare knees, cigarettes, and other flapper items. The quintessential flapper movie.

1928 61m/B Virginia Lee Corbin, Donald Keith, Jane Winton, Johnnie Walker, Forrest Stanley, Maude Fulton; *D:* Erle C. Kenton. **VHS, Beta** $17.95 *GPV* 🎗️🎗️

Bare Knuckles The adventures of a low-rent bounty hunter.
1977 (R) 90m/C Robert Viharo, Sherry Jackson, Michael Heit, Gloria Hendry, John Daniels; *D:* Don Edmonds. **VHS, Beta** $59.95 *TWE* 🎗️

The Barefoot Contessa The story, told in flashback, of a Spanish dancer's rise to Hollywood stardom, as witnessed by a cynical director. Shallow Hollywood self-examination also written by Mankiewicz, well-performed.
1954 128m/C Ava Gardner, Humphrey Bogart, Edmond O'Brien, Valentina Cortese, Rossano Brazzi; *D:* Joseph L. Mankiewicz. Academy Awards '54: Best Supporting Actor (O'Brien); Nominations: Best Story & Screenplay; Golden Globe Awards '55: Best Supporting Actor (O'Brien). **VHS, Beta** $19.98 *MGM, FOX, FCT* 🎗️🎗️🎗️

The Barefoot Executive A mailroom boy who works for a national television network finds a chimpanzee that can pick hit shows in this Disney family comedy.
1971 92m/C Kurt Russell, John Ritter, Harry Morgan, Wally Cox, Heather North; *D:* Robert Butler. **VHS, Beta** *DIS, OM* 🎗️🎗️

Barefoot in Athens Television presentation from "George Schaefer's Showcase Theatre" chronicles the last years of the philosopher Socrates who, barefoot and unkempt, an embarrassment to his wife, and a dangerous critic to the corrupt Athenian leaders, nevertheless believes that democracy and truth are all-important in his city.
1966 76m/C Peter Ustinov, Geraldine Page, Anthony Quayle; *D:* George Schaefer. **VHS, Beta** *FHS* 🎗️🎗️

Barefoot in the Park Neil Simon's Broadway hit translates well to screen. A newly wedded bride (Fonda) tries to get her husband (Redford, reprising his Broadway role) to loosen up and be as free-spirited as she is.
1967 106m/C Robert Redford, Jane Fonda, Charles Boyer, Mildred Natwick; *D:* Gene Saks; *W:* Neil Simon. **VHS, Beta, LV** $14.95 *PAR* 🎗️🎗️🎗️

Barfly A semi-autobiographical screenplay by Charles Bukowski. A talented writer chooses to spend his time as a lonely barfly, hiding his literary abilities behind glasses of liquor. Dunaway's character is right on target as the fellow alcoholic.
1987 (R) 100m/C Mickey Rourke, Faye Dunaway, Alice Krige, Frank Stallone, J.C. Quinn; *D:* Barbet Schroeder. **VHS, Beta, LV, 8mm** $19.98 *WAR, FCT* 🎗️🎗️🎗️

The Bargain Hart's first feature, in which he portrays a bandit desperately trying to go straight. Original titles with musical score.
1915 50m/B William S. Hart. **VHS, Beta** $19.95 *NOS, GPV, DVT* 🎗️½

Baring It All A group therapy collective shares their fantasies and arouses each other.
1985 78m/C Paul Bartel. **VHS, Beta** $29.95 *MED* Woof!

Baritone Concerned Polish drama about a prominent opera singer who promises to deliver a grand concert upon returning to his small town, only to lose his voice just before the show is to start. Proof positive that the opera ain't over 'til the fat lady sings.
1985 100m/C *PL* Zbigniew Zapassiewicz; *D:* Janusz Zaorski. **VHS** $49.95 *FCT* 🎗️🎗️

The Barkleys of Broadway The famous dancing team's last film together; they play a quarreling husband/wife showbiz team. 🎵They Can't Take That Away From

Me; The Sabre Dance; Swing Trot; Manhattan Downbeat; A Weekend in the Country; My One and Only Highland Fling; You'd Be Hard to Replace; Bouncin' the Blues; Shoes With Wings On; Piano Concerto in B-flat Minor.
1949 109m/C Fred Astaire, Ginger Rogers, Gale Robbins, Oscar Levant, Jacques Francois, Billie Burke; *D:* Charles Walters; *W:* Adolph Green, Betty Comden; *M:* Harry Warren, Ira Gershwin. **VHS, Beta, LV $19.98** *MGM* 𝒵𝒵𝒵

Barn of the Naked Dead Prine plays a sicko who tortures women while his radioactive monster dad terrorizes the Nevada desert. Rudolph's first film, directed under the pseudonym Gerald Cormier. Also on video as "Terror Circus" and "Nightmare Circus."
1973 86m/C Andrew Prine, Manuella Thiess, Sherry Alberoni, Gylian Roland, Al Cormier, Jennifer Ashley; *D:* Alan Rudolph. **VHS** *NO* Woof!

Barnaby and Me Australian star Barnaby the Koala Bear joins an international con-man in this romantic adventure. The mob is chasing the con-man when he meets and falls for a lovely young woman and her daughter.
1977 90m/C *AU* Sid Caesar, Juliet Mills, Sally Boyden; *D:* Norman Panama. **VHS, Beta $14.95** *ACA* 𝒵𝒵

Barnum P.T. Barnum's life is focused upon in this biography about the man who helped to form "The Greatest Show On Earth."
1986 100m/C Burt Lancaster, Hanna Schygulla, Jenny Lind, John Roney; *D:* Lee Philips. **VHS, Beta, LV $29.95** *ACA* 𝒵𝒵½

The Baron Vengeance is the name of the game when an underworld boss gets stiffed on a deal. Fast-paced no-brainer street drama.
1988 88m/C Calvin Lockhart, Charles McGregor, Joan Blondell, Richard Lynch, Marlene Clark; *D:* Philip Fently. **VHS $14.99** *PGN* 𝒵½

The Baron and the Kid A pool shark finds out that his opponent at a charity exhibition game is his long-lost son. Based on Johnny Cash's song. Made for TV.
1984 100m/C Johnny Cash, Darren McGavin, June Carter Cash, Richard Roundtree; *D:* Gary Nelson. **VHS, Beta $59.98** *FOX* 𝒵

Baron Munchausen The German film studio UFA celebrated its 25th anniversary with this lavish version of the Baron Munchausen legend, starring a cast of top-name German performers at the height of the Third Reich. Filmed in Agfacolor; available in English subtitled or dubbed versions.
1943 120m/C *GE* Hans Albers, Kaethe Kaack, Hermann Speelmans, Leo Slezak; *D:* Josef von Baky. **VHS, Beta $59.95** *TAM, VCD, GLV* 𝒵𝒵𝒵

Baron of Arizona Land office clerk almost succeeds in convincing the U.S. that he owned the state of Arizona.
1951 99m/B Vincent Price, Ellen Drew, Beulah Bondi, Reed Hadley, Vladimir Sokoloff; *D:* Samuel Fuller. **VHS, Beta** *RXM* 𝒵𝒵

Barracuda Lots of innocent swimmers are being eaten by crazed killer barracudas. *AKA:* The Lucifer Project.
1978 (R) 90m/C Wayne Crawford, Jason Evers, Roberta Leighton; *D:* Harry Kerwin. **VHS, Beta $19.98** *VID* Woof!

The Barretts of Wimpole Street The moving, almost disturbing, account of poetess Elizabeth Barrett, an invalid confined to her bed, with only her poetry and her dog to keep her company. She is wooed by poet Robert Browning, in whose arms she finds true happiness and a miraculous recovery.

Multi-faceted drama expertly played by all. *AKA:* Forbidden Alliance.
1934 110m/B Fredric March, Norma Shearer, Charles Laughton, Maureen O'Sullivan, Katherine Alexander, Una O'Connor, Ian Wolfe; *D:* Sidney Franklin. **VHS, LV $19.98** *MGM, CCB* 𝒵𝒵𝒵

Barry Lyndon Ravishing adaptation of the classic Thackeray novel about the adventures of an Irish gambler moving from innocence to self-destructive arrogance in the aristocracy of 18th Century England. Visually opulent. Kubrick received excellent performances from all his actors, and a stunning display of history, but the end result still overwhelms. O'Neal has seldom been better.
1975 (PG) 185m/C Ryan O'Neal, Marisa Berenson, Patrick Magee, Hardy Kruger, Guy Hamilton; *D:* Stanley Kubrick. Academy Awards '75: Best Art Direction/Set Decoration, Best Cinematography, Best Costume Design, Best Original Score; Nominations: Best Adapted Screenplay, Best Director (Kubrick), Best Picture; British Academy Awards '75: Best Director (Kubrick); National Board of Review Awards '75: 10 Best Films of the Year, Best Director (Kubrick). **VHS, Beta, LV $29.95** *WAR, PIA* 𝒵𝒵𝒵½

Barry McKenzie Holds His Own In this sequel to "The Adventures of Barry McKenzie," we find that after a young man's aunt is mistaken for the Queen of England, two emissaries of Count Plasma of Transylvania kidnap her to use as a Plasma tourist attraction. Based on the 'Private Eye' comic strip, this crude Australian film is as disappointing as the first of the Barry McKenzie stories.
1974 93m/C *AU* Barry Humphries, Barry Crocker, Donald Pleasence; *D:* Bruce Beresford. **VHS, Beta $14.98** *VID*

Bartleby A new version of the classic Herman Melville short story. McEnery is Bartleby the clerk, who refuses to leave his job even after he's fired; Scofield is his frustrated boss.
1970 79m/C Paul Scofield, John McEnery, Colin Jeavons, Thorley Walters; *D:* Anthony Friedman. **VHS, LV $29.95** *WST* 𝒵𝒵½

Barton Fink This eerie comic nightmare comes laden with awards (including the Palme D'Or from Cannes) but only really works if you care about the time and place. Fink is a trendy New York playwright staying in a seedy Hollywood hotel in the 1940s, straining to write a simple B-movie script. Macabre events, both real and imagined, compound his writer's block. Superb set design from Dennis Gassner complements an unforgettable cast of grotesques.
1991 (R) 116m/C John Turturro, John Goodman, Judy Davis, Michael Lerner, John Mahoney, Tony Shalhoub, Jon Polito, Steve Buscemi, David Warrilow, Richard Portnow, Christopher Murney; *W/D:* Joel Coen; *W:* Ethan Coen; *M:* Carter Burwell. Academy Awards '91 Nominations: Best Art Direction/Set Decoration, Best Costume Design, Best Supporting Actor (Lerner); Cannes Film Festival '91: Best Actor (Turturro), Best Director (Coen), Best Film; Los Angeles Film Critics Association Awards '91: Best Supporting Actor (Lerner); New York Film Critics Awards '91: Best Supporting Actress (Davis). **VHS $19.98** *FXV, CCB* 𝒵𝒵𝒵

The Bashful Bachelor Yokel joker Abner trades his delivery car for a race horse, hoping to win a big race.
1942 78m/B Chester Lauck, Norris Goff, ZaSu Pitts, Grady Sutton, Louise Currie, Irving Bacon, Earle Hodgins, Benny Rubin; *D:* Malcolm St. Clair. **VHS $24.95** *NOS, RXM* 𝒵𝒵

Basic Instinct Controversial thriller that had tongues wagging months before its theatrical release. Douglas is a burnt-out detective who falls for a beautiful and mani-

pulative murder suspect. Stone is perfectly cast as the bisexual ice queen who may or may not have killed her (male) lover with an ice pick. Noted for highly erotic sex scenes and a very expensive (3 million bucks) script; ultimately the predictable plot is disappointing. Gay activists tried to interrupt filming because they objected to the depiction of Stone's bisexual character but only succeeded in generating more free publicity. The American version is less explicit than the European version—it was edited to avoid an "NC-17" rating. The director's version includes footage cut from the original release, the theatrical trailer, and interviews with Verhoeven, Stone, and Douglas. Stone and writer Eszterhas teamed up again in "Sliver."
1992 (R) 123m/C Michael Douglas, Sharon Stone, George Dzundza, Jeanne Tripplehorn, Denis Arndt, Lelani Sarelle, Bruce A. Young, Chelcie Ross, Dorothy Malone, Wayne Knight, Stephen Tobolowsky; *D:* Paul Verhoeven; *W:* Joe Eszterhas; *M:* Jerry Goldsmith. Academy Awards '92 Nominations: Best Film Editing, Best Original Score; MTV Movie Awards '93: Best Actress (Stone), Most Desirable Female (Stone). **VHS, Beta $49.98** *LIV, PMS* 𝒵𝒵½

Basic Training Three sexy ladies wiggle into the Pentagon in their efforts to clean up the government.
1986 (R) 85m/C Ann Dusenberry, Rhonda Shear, Angela Aames, Walter Gotell; *D:* Andrew Sugarman. **VHS, Beta $79.98** *LIV, VES* Woof!

Basileus Quartet The replacement for a violinist in a well-established quartet creates emotional havoc. Beautiful music, excellent and evocative photography.
1982 118m/C *FR IT* Pierre Malet, Hector Alterio, Omero Antonutti, Michel Vitold, Alain Cuny, Gabriel Ferzetti, Lisa Kreuzer; *D:* Fabio Carpi. **VHS, LV** *NO* 𝒵𝒵𝒵

Basket Case A gory horror film about a pair of Siamese twins—one normal, the other gruesomely deformed. The pair is surgically separated at birth, and the evil disfigured twin is tossed in the garbage. Fraternal ties being what they are, the normal brother retrieves his twin—essentially a head atop shoulders—and totes him around in a basket (he ain't heavy). Together they begin twisted and deadly revenge, with the brother-in-a-basket in charge. Very entertaining, if you like this sort of thing. Followed by two sequels, if you just can't get enough.
1982 89m/C Kevin Van Hentenryck, Terri Susan Smith, Beverly Bonner; *D:* Frank Henenlotter. **VHS, Beta, LV $19.95** *MED* 𝒵𝒵𝒵

Basket Case 2 Surgically separated teenage mutant brothers Duane and Belial are back! This time they've found happiness in a "special" family—until they're plagued by the paparazzi. Higher production values make this sequel slicker than its low-budget predecessor, but it somehow lacks the same charm.
1990 (R) 90m/C Kevin Van Hentenryck, Annie Ross, Kathryn Meisle, Heather Rattray, Jason Evers, Ted Sorel; *D:* Frank Henenlotter. **VHS, Beta, LV $89.95** *IME* 𝒵𝒵½

Basket Case 3: The Progeny In this sequel to the cult horror hits "Basket Case" and "Basket Case 2," Belial is back and this time he's about to discover the perils of parenthood as the mutant Mrs. Belial delivers a litter of bouncing mini-monsters. Everything is fine until the police kidnap the little creatures and chaos breaks out as Belial goes on a shocking rampage in his newly created mechanical body. Weird special effects make this a cult favorite for fans of the truly outrageous.

1992 (R) 90m/C Annie Ross, Kevin Van Hentenryck, Deo Biggers, Gil Roper; **W/D:** Frank Henenlotter. **VHS** $19.98 *MCA* 🎦🎦½

Bass on Titles Academy Award winner Saul Bass translates the themes of major motion pictures into graphic animation. **1977 32m/C VHS, Beta** *PYR* 🎦

The Bastard Dashing (but alas, illegitimate) nobleman roams Europe on futile, Roots-like search, then settles for America during the Revolutionary War in this long-winded television adaptation of John Jakes' equally cumbersome bestseller (part of his popular Bicentennial series). Stevens stars, along with many supporting performers merely keeping active. Followed by "The Rebels" and "The Seekers." **AKA:** The Kent Chronicles. **1978 189m/C** Andrew Stevens, Tom Bosley, Kim Cattrall, Buddy Ebsen, Lorne Greene, Olivia Hussey, Cameron Mitchell, Harry Morgan, Patricia Neal, Eleanor Parker, Donald Pleasence, William Shatner, Barry Sullivan, Noah Beery Jr., William Daniels, Keenan Wynn; **D:** Lee H. Katzin. **VHS** $29.98 *MCA* 🎦🎦½

The Bat A great plot centering around a murderer called the Bat, who kills hapless victims by ripping out their throats when he isn't busy searching for a million dollars worth of securities stashed in the old house he is living in. Adapted from the novel by Mary Roberts Rinehart. **1959 80m/B** Vincent Price, Agnes Moorehead, Gavin Gordon, John Sutton, Lenita Lane, Darla Hood; **D:** Crane Wilbur. **VHS, Beta** $16.95 *NOS, SNC, DVT* 🎦🎦

The Bat People Less-than gripping horror flick in which Dr. John Bech is bitten by a bat while on his honeymoon. He then becomes a sadistic bat creature, compelled to kill anyone who stumbles across his path. The gory special effects make for a great movie if you've ever been bitten by that sort of thing. **AKA:** It Lives By Night. **1974 (R) 95m/C** Stewart Moss, Marianne McAndrew, Michael Pataki, Paul Carr; **D:** Jerry Jameson. **VHS, Beta** $14.95 *HBO* 🎦

Bat 21 Hackman, an American officer, is stranded in the wilds of Vietnam alone after his plane is shot down. He must rely on himself and Glover, with whom he has radio contact, to get him out. Glover and Hackman give solid performances in this otherwise average film. **1988 (R) 112m/C** Gene Hackman, Danny Glover, Jerry Reed, David Marshall Grant, Clayton Rohner, Erich Anderson, Joe Dorsey; **D:** Peter Markle. **VHS, Beta, LV** $19.98 *MED* 🎦🎦

The Bat Whispers A masked madman is stalking the halls of a creepy mansion; eerie tale that culminates in an appeal to the audience to keep the plot under wraps. Unusually crafted film for its early era. Comic mystery based on the novel and play by Mary Roberts Rinehart and Avery Hopwood. **1930 82m/B** Chester Morris, Chance Ward, Richard Tucker, Wilson Benge, DeWitt Jennings, Una Merkel, Spencer Charters; **W/D:** Roland West. **VHS, LV** $24.95 *NOS, DVT, MLB* 🎦🎦½

Bataan A rugged war-time combat drama following the true story of a small platoon in the Philippines endeavoring to blow up a pivotal Japanese bridge. Also available in a colorized version. **1943 115m/B** Robert Taylor, George Murphy, Thomas Mitchell, Desi Arnaz Sr., Lee Bowman, Lloyd Nolan, Robert Walker; **D:** Tay Garnett. **VHS, Beta** $59.95 *MGM, TLF* 🎦🎦½

Bathing Beauty This musical stars Skelton as a pop music composer with the hots for college swim teacher Williams. Rathbone is a music executive who sees the romance as a threat to Skelton's career and to his own profit margin. Full of aquatic ballet, Skelton's shtick, and wonderful original melodies. The first film in which Williams received star billing. 🎵I Cried for You; Bim, Bam, Boom; Tico-Tico; I'll Take the High Note; Loch Lomond; By the Waters of Minnetonka; Magic is the Moonlight; Trumpet Blues; Hora Staccato. **1944 101m/C** Red Skelton, Esther Williams, Basil Rathbone, Bill Goodwin, Jean Porter, Carlos Ramirez, Donald Meek, Ethel Smith, Helen Forrest; **D:** George Sidney; **M:** Xavier Cugat. **VHS** $19.98 *MGM, TTC, FCT* 🎦🎦½

Batman Holy television camp, Batman! Will the caped crusader win the Bat-tle against the combined forces of the Joker, the Riddler, the Penguin, and Catwoman? Will Batman and Robin save the United World Security Council from dehydration? Will the Bat genius ever figure out that Russian journalist Miss Kitka and Catwoman are one and the same? Biff! Thwack! Socko! Don't confuse this with the Michael Keaton version of the Dark Knight; this is the pot-bellied Adam West Batman, teeming with Bat satire. **1966 104m/C** Burt Ward, Adam West, Burgess Meredith, Cesar Romero, Frank Gorshin, Lee Meriwether; **D:** Leslie Martinson. **VHS, Beta, LV** $19.98 *FOX* 🎦🎦½

Batman The blockbuster fantasy epic that renewed Hollywood's faith in media blitzing. The Caped Crusader is back in Gotham City, where even the criminals are afraid to walk the streets alone. There's a new breed of criminal in Gotham, led by the infamous Joker. Their random attacks via acid-based make-up are just the beginning. Keaton is surprisingly good as the dual personality hero though Nicholson steals the show. Marvelously designed and shot. Music by Prince and Danny Elfman. Much better on the big screen. Followed in 1992 by "Batman Returns." **1989 (PG-13) 126m/C** Michael Keaton, Jack Nicholson, Kim Basinger, Robert Wuhl, Tracy Walter, Billy Dee Williams, Pat Hingle, Michael Gough, Jack Palance, Jerry Hall; **D:** Tim Burton; **W:** Sam Hamm, Warren Skaaren. **VHS, Beta, LV, 8mm** $19.98 *FOX, WAR* 🎦🎦🎦½

Batman Returns More of the same from director Burton, with Batman more of a supporting role overshadowed by provocative villains. DeVito is the cruely misshapen Penguin who seeks to rule over Gotham City; Pfeiffer is the exotic and dangerous Catwoman—who has more than a passing purrsonal interest in Batman; Walken is the maniacal tycoon Max Shreck. Pfeiffer fares best in her wickedly sexy role and second-skin costume (complete with bullwhip). Plot is secondary to special effects and nightmarish settings. Despite a big budget, this grandiose sequel is of the love it or leave it variety. **1992 (PG-13) 126m/C** Michael Keaton, Danny DeVito, Michelle Pfeiffer, Christopher Walken, Michael Gough, Michael Murphy, Cristi Conaway, Pat Hingle, Vincent Schiavelli, Jan Hooks, Paul Reubens; **D:** Tim Burton; **W:** Daniel Waters; **M:** Danny Elfman. **VHS** $24.98 *WAR* 🎦🎦½

*batteries not included As a real estate developer fights to demolish a New York tenement, the five remaining residents are aided by tiny metal visitors from outer space in their struggle to save their home. Each resident gains a renewed sense of life in this sentimental, wholesome family film produced by Spielberg. Cronyn and Tandy keep the schmaltz from getting out of hand. Neat little space critters. **1987 (PG) 107m/C** Hume Cronyn, Jessica Tandy, Frank McRae, Michael Carmine; **D:** Matthew Robbins. **VHS, Beta, LV** $19.95 *MCA* 🎦🎦½

Battle Beneath the Earth The commies try to undermine democracy once again when American scientists discover a Chinese plot to invade the U.S. via a series of underground tunnels. Perhaps a tad jingoistic. **1968 112m/C** *GB* Kerwin Mathews, Peter Arne, Viviane Ventura, Robert Ayres; **D:** Montgomery Tully. **VHS, Beta** $59.95 *MGM* 🎦🎦

Battle Beyond the Stars The planet Akir must be defended against alien rapscallions in this intergalactic Roger Corman creation. John Sayles authored the screenplay and co-authored the story on which it was based. **1980 (PG) 105m/C** Richard Thomas, Robert Vaughn, George Peppard, Sybil Danning, Sam Jaffo, John Saxon, Darlanne Fluegel; **D:** Jimmy T. Murakami; **W:** John Sayles. **VHS, Beta, LV** $19.98 *VES, LIV* 🎦🎦½

Battle Beyond the Sun Former Russian movie "Nebo Zowet" is Americanized. Everyone is trying to send a mission to Mars. Roger Corman was the producer, Thomas Colchart is a pseudonym for Francis Ford Coppola. **1963 75m/C** Edd Perry, Arla Powell, Bruce Hunter, Andy Stewart; **D:** Francis Ford Coppola. **VHS** $16.95 *NOS, SNC* 🎦🎦

Battle Circus Sappy drama casts Bogart as a surgeon at a M*A*S*H unit during the Korean War. Allyson is a combat nurse who finds love amongst the harsh reality of a war zone. Bogart was badly miscast and his performance proves it. Weak script and uninspired performances don't help this depressing story. **1953 90m/B** Humphrey Bogart, June Allyson, Keenan Wynn, Robert Keith, William Campbell; **W/D:** Richard Brooks. **VHS** $19.98 *MGM* 🎦½

Battle Cry A group of U.S. Marines train, romance, and enter battle in World War II. Based on the novel by Leon Uris. Part of the "A Night at the Movies" series, this tape simulates a 1955 movie evening, with a cartoon, "Speedy Gonzales," a newsreel, and coming attractions for "Mr. Roberts" and "East of Eden." **1955 169m/C** Van Heflin, Aldo Ray, Mona Freeman, Tab Hunter, Dorothy Malone, Anne Francis, James Whitmore, Raymond Massey; **D:** Raoul Walsh. **VHS, Beta, LV** $69.95 *WAR, PIA* 🎦🎦🎦

Battle for the Planet of the Apes A tribe of human atomic bomb mutations are out to make life miserable for the peaceful ape tribe in the year 2670 A.D. Final chapter in the five-movie simian saga. **1973 (G) 96m/C** Roddy McDowall, Lew Ayres, John Huston, Paul Williams, Claude Akins, Severn Darden, Natalie Trundy; **D:** J. Lee Thompson. **VHS, Beta** $19.98 *FOX* 🎦🎦

Battle Hell The true story of how a British ship was attacked by the Chinese Peoples Liberation Army on the Yangtze River in 1949. **AKA:** Yangtse Incidents. **1956 112m/B** *GB* Richard Todd, Akim Tamiroff, Keye Luke; **D:** Michael Anderson Sr. **VHS, Beta** $19.98 *VID* 🎦🎦

The Battle of Algiers Famous, powerful, award-winning film depicting the uprisings against French Colonial rule in 1954 Algiers. A seminal documentary-style film which makes most political films seem ineffectual by comparison in its use of non-

professional actors, gritty photography, realistic violence, and a boldly propagandistic sense of social outrage.
1966 123m/B AL IT Yacef Saadi, Jean Martin, Brahim Haggiag, Tommaso Neri, Samia Kerbash, Fawzia el Kader, Michele Kerbash, Mohamed Ben Kassen; **D:** Gillo Pontecorvo; **W:** Franco Solinas; **M:** Ennio Morricone. Academy Awards '66 Nominations: Best Foreign Language Film; Academy Awards '68: Best Director (Pontecorvo), Best Story & Screenplay; Venice Film Festival '66: Best Film. **VHS, Beta, LV, 3/4U $29.95** *TAM, IHF* 🎬🎬🎬½

The Battle of Austerlitz Ambitious but numbing costume drama about the events leading up to the epic battle between Napoleon and the overwhelming forces of the Czar and the Austrian Emperor at Austerlitz. Napoleon won. Film has been drastically cut from original 166 minute release. Watch director Gance's silent version, "Napoleon," for a truly epic experience. **AKA:** Austerlitz.
1960 (PG) 123m/C FR IT YU Claudia Cardinale, Martine Carol, Leslie Caron, Vittorio De Sica, Jean Marais, Ettore Manni, Jack Palance, Orson Welles; **D:** Abel Gance. **VHS $69.95** *LIV* 🎬🎬

The Battle of Blood Island Two G.I.s, one Christian and one Jewish, face death at the hands of the Japanese during WWII. Still, they bicker incessantly before finally pulling together to save themselves.
1960 64m/B Richard Devon, Ron Kennedy; **D:** Joel Rapp. **VHS, Beta $16.95** *NOS, SNC* 🎬

Battle of Britain A powerful retelling of the most dramatic aerial combat battle of World War II, showing how the understaffed Royal Air Force held off the might of the German Luftwaffe.
1969 (G) 132m/C Michael Caine, Laurence Olivier, Trevor Howard, Kenneth More, Christopher Plummer, Robert Shaw, Susannah York, Ralph Richardson, Curt Jurgens, Michael Redgrave, Nigel Patrick, Edward Fox; **D:** Guy Hamilton. **VHS, Beta, LV $19.98** *MGM, FOX* 🎬🎬½

Battle of China A look at the people, culture, and industry of China, and Japan's total commitment to conquer the country during World War II, through authentic newsreel footage.
1944 67m/B D: Frank Capra. **VHS, Beta $19.98** *MPI, MRV, HHT* 🎬🎬½

The Battle of El Alamein Action filled movie about the alliance of Italy and Germany in a war against the British, set in a North African desert in the year 1942.
1968 105m/C IT FR Frederick Stafford, Ettore Manni, Robert Hossein, Michael Rennie, George Hilton, Ira Furstenberg; **D:** Calvin Jackson Padget. **VHS, Beta $59.95** *PSM, MRV, GEM* 🎬🎬

Battle of Elderbush Gulch An ancient pioneering western short famous for innocently employing the now-established cliches of bad guy, good guy, and helpless frontier heroine. One of Gish's first films.
1913 22m/B Lillian Gish; **D:** D.W. Griffith. **VHS, Beta $29.95** *VCN, PYR* 🎬🎬

Battle of Neretva During WWII, Yugoslav partisans are facing German and Italian troops and local Chetniks as they battle for freedom. Big budget war film lost continuity with U.S. cut.
1969 106m/C YU Yul Brynner, Curt Jurgens, Orson Welles, Hardy Kruger, Franco Nero, Sergei Bondarchuk; **D:** Veljko Bulajic. **VHS $39.98** *TAM, REP* 🎬🎬

The Battle of Russia Hitler's forces are victorious in Moscow and Leningrad but are thoroughly defeated at the battle of Stalingrad. Authentic newsreel footage.
1944 83m/B D: Frank Capra. **VHS, Beta $19.98** *HHT, MRV, CCB* 🎬🎬

The Battle of San Pietro John Huston's powerful documentary about the famous battle in Italy's Liri Valley, stressing the number of losses sustained in taking this military objective. The film was almost suppressed by the U.S. government, because it was considered to be too strong for general release.
1944 43m/B John Huston. **VHS, Beta, 3/4U $19.98** *IHF, WFV, FUS* 🎬🎬

Battle of the Bulge A recreation of the famous offensive by Nazi Panzer troops on the Belgian front during 1944-45, an assault that could have changed the course of World War II.
1965 141m/C Henry Fonda, Robert Shaw, Robert Ryan, Dana Andrews, Telly Savalas, Ty Hardin, Pier Angeli, George Montgomery, Charles Bronson; **D:** Ken Annakin. **VHS, Beta, LV $59.95** *WAR* 🎬🎬

Battle of the Bullies A made-for-television special about an unsalvageable nerd who plots a high-tech revenge upon a slew of high school bullies.
1985 45m/C Manny Jacobs, Christopher Barnes, Sarah Inglis. **VHS, Beta $19.95** *NWV Woof!*

Battle of the Commandos A tough Army colonel leads a group of convicts on a dangerous mission to destroy a German-built cannon before it's used against the Allied Forces. **AKA:** Legion of the Damned.
1971 94m/C IT Jack Palance, Curt Jurgens, Thomas Hunter, Robert Hunter; **D:** Umberto Lenzi. **VHS $39.98** *REP* 🎬

Battle of the Eagles Follows the true adventures of the "Partisan Squadron," the courageous airmen known as the "Knights of the Sky" during WWII in Yugoslavia.
1981 102m/C Bekim Fehmiu, George Taylor, Gloria Samara, Frank Phillips; **D:** Tom Raymonth. **VHS, Beta** *PGN* 🎬½

The Battle of the Japan Sea A Japanese epic, dubbed in English, centering around the historic WWII battle between Japan and Russia.
1970 (G) 120m/C JP Toshiro Mifune. **VHS, Beta $69.95** *VCD* 🎬🎬

The Battle of the Sexes Sophisticated British comedy has mild-mannered Sellers trying to prevent a business takeover by the brash American Cummings. A good supporting cast and the impeccable Sellers make this one unique. Adapted from the James Thurber short story "The Catbird Seat."
1960 88m/B GB Peter Sellers, Robert Morley, Constance Cummings, James B. Clark; **D:** Charles Crichton. **VHS, Beta** *MRV* 🎬🎬🎬

Battle of the Worlds Typical low-budget science fiction. A scientist tries to stop an alien planet from destroying the Earth. Even an aging Rains can't help this one. Poorly dubbed in English. **AKA:** Il Pianeta Degli Uomini Spenti; Planet of the Lifeless Men.
1961 84m/C IT Claude Rains, Maya Brent, Bill Carter, Marina Orsini, Jacqueline Derval; **D:** Anthony M. Dawson. **VHS, CV $16.95** *SNC, MRV* 🎬🎬🎬

Battle of Valiant Thundering hordes of invading barbarians trample the splendor of ancient Rome beneath their grimy sandals.
1963 90m/C Gordon Mitchell, Ursula Davis, Massimo Serato; **D:** John Gentil. **VHS, Beta** *NO* 🎬

Battle Shock Painter is accused of murdering a cantina waitress while on his honeymoon in Mexico. **AKA:** A Woman's Devotion; War Shock.
1956 88m/C Ralph Meeker, Janice Rule, Paul Henreid; **D:** Paul Henreid. **VHS $39.95** *REP* 🎬½

Battleforce Exciting battle scenes lose their power in the confusion of this mixed-up WWII film about Rommel's last days. Dubbed sequences, news-reel vignettes and surprise performances by big name stars are incomprehensibly glued together. **AKA:** The Battle of the Mareth Line.
1978 97m/C GE YU Henry Fonda, Stacy Keach, Helmut Berger, Samantha Eggar, Giuliano Gemma, John Huston; **D:** Umberto Lenzi. **VHS $9.99** *QVD* 🎬

Battleground A tightly-conceived post-World War II character drama, following a platoon of American soldiers through the Battle of the Bulge. Available in a Colorized version.
1949 118m/B Van Johnson, John Hodiak, James Whitmore, George Murphy, Ricardo Montalban, Marshall Thompson, Jerome Courtland, Don Taylor, Bruce Cowling, Leon Ames, Douglas Fowley, Richard Jaeckel; **D:** William A. Wellman; **W:** Robert Pirosh. Academy Awards '49: Best Black and White Cinematography, Best Story & Screenplay; Nominations: Best Film Editing; Academy Awards '49: Best Director (Wellman), Best Picture, Best Supporting Actor (Whitmore); Golden Globe Awards '50: Best Supporting Actor (Whitmore). **VHS, Beta, LV $19.98** *MGM* 🎬🎬🎬

The Battleship Potemkin Eisenstein's best work documents mutiny aboard the Russian battleship Potemkin in 1905 which led to a civilian uprising against the Czar in Odessa, and the resulting crackdown by troops loyal to the Czar. Beautiful cinematography, especially the use of montage sequences, changed filmmaking. In particular, a horrifying sequence depicting the slaughter of civilians on an Odessa beach by soldiers coming down the stairs leading to it is exceptional; many movies pay homage to this scene including "The Untouchables" and "Love and Death." Viewers should overlook obvious Marxist overtones and see this film for what it is: a masterpiece. **AKA:** Potemkin; Bronenosets Potemkin.
1925 71m/B RU Alexander Antonov, Vladimir Barsky, Grigori Alexandrov, Mikhail Gomorov, Sergei Eisenstein; **D:** Sergei Eisenstein. **VHS, Beta, LV $19.98** *REP, MRV, NOS* 🎬🎬🎬🎬

Battlestar Galactica Plot episode of the sci-fi television series which was later released in the theaters. The crew of the spaceship Galactica must battle their robot enemies in an attempt to reach Earth. Contains special effects designed by John "Star Wars" Dykstra. Individual episodes of the series are also available.
1978 (PG) 125m/C Lorne Greene, Dirk Benedict, Karen Jensen, Jane Seymour, Patrick Macnee, Terry Carter, John Colicos, Richard A. Colla, Laurette Spang, Richard Hatch; **D:** Richard A. Colla. **VHS, Beta, LV $19.95** *MCA, MOV* 🎬🎬½

Battling Amazons Spandex-bedecked women fight, kick-boxing style, though not very well.
1981 60m/C VHS, Beta $19.95 *AHV* 🎬🎬½

Battling Bunyon A wily youngster becomes a comedy boxer for profit, and eventually gets fed up and battles the champ. Silent.
1924 71m/B Chester Conklin, Wesley Barry, Molly Malone, Jackie Fields. **VHS, Beta $16.95** *GPV, VYY* 🎬½

Battling Butler Rich young Keaton tries to impress a young lady by impersonating a boxer. All goes well until he has to fight the real thing. Mostly charming if uneven; one of Keaton's more unusual efforts, thought to be somewhat autobiographical. Silent.

1926 70m/B Buster Keaton, Sally O'Neil, Snitz Edwards, Francis McDonald, Mary O'Brien, Tom Wilson, Walter James; *D:* Buster Keaton. **VHS** *NO* 🎬🎬½

Battling Marshal Fast-moving action western starring Carson.
1948 52m/B Sunset Carson, Lee Roberts; *D:* Oliver Drake. **VHS, Beta** $29.95 *VCN* 🎬½

Battling Outlaws Western featuring the American cowboy Bob Steele.
194? 64m/B Bob Steele. **VHS, Beta** $19.95 *NOS, VCN* 🎬½

Battling with Buffalo Bill Twelve episodes of the vintage serial concerning the exploits of the legendary Indian fighter.
1931 180m/B Tom Tyler, Rex Bell, Franklin Farnum. **VHS, Beta** $29.95 *VCN* 🎬½

The Bawdy Adventures of Tom Jones An exploitive extension of the Fielding novel about the philandering English lad, with plenty of soft-core skin and lewdness.
1976 (R) 89m/C *GB* Joan Collins, Trevor Howard, Terry-Thomas, Arthur Lowe, Murray Melvin; *D:* Cliff Owen. **VHS, Beta** $59.95 *MCA* 🎬½

Baxter A bull terrier lives his life with three different sets of masters. He examines all of humankind's worst faults and the viewer quickly realizes that Baxter's life depends on his refusal to obey like a good dog should. Based on the novel by Ken Greenhall. Funny, sometimes erotic, quirky comedy. In French with English subtitles.
1989 82m/C *FR* Lisa Delamare, Jean Mercure, Jacques Spiesser, Catherine Ferran, Jean-Paul Roussillon, Sabrina Leurquin; *D:* Jerome Boivin. **VHS, LV** $89.95 *FXL, PMS* 🎬🎬½

The Bay Boy Set in the 1930s in Nova Scotia, this period piece captures the coming-of-age of a rural teenage boy. Young Sutherland's adolescent angst becomes a more difficult struggle when he witnesses a murder, and is tormented by the secret.
1985 (R) 107m/C *CA* Liv Ullmann, Kiefer Sutherland, Peter Donat, Matthieu Carriere, Joe MacPherson, Isabelle Mejias, Alan Scarfe, Chris Wiggins, Leah K. Pinsent; *D:* Daniel Petrie. **VHS, Beta, LV** $79.98 *ORI* 🎬🎬½

Bay of Blood Four vacationing youngsters are relentlessly pursued by a homicidal maniac bent on decapitation. Known also as "Last House on the Left Part II," "Carnage," or "Twitch of the Death Nerve." Supposedly the inspiration for "Friday the 13th;" very violent and gory.
1971 (R) 85m/C *IT* Claudine Auger, Isa Miranda, Claudio Volonte, Chris Avran, Luigi Pistilli; *D:* Mario Bava. **VHS, Beta** *MPI* 🎬

Bayou Romance Painter inherits a Louisiana plantation, moves in, and falls in love with a young gypsy.
1986 90m/C Annie Potts, Michael Ansara, Barbara Horan. **Beta** $14.95 *PSM* 🎬

B.C. Rock A cave man learns how to defend himself and has some prehistoric fun with a tribe of female amazons. Animated.
1984 (R) 87m/C VHS, Beta $69.98 *LIV, VES* 🎬🎬

B.C.: The First Thanksgiving The caveman B.C. and his friends are trying to find a turkey to flavor their rock soup in this animated featurette.
1984 25m/C VHS, Beta, LV $14.98 *SUE, NLC* 🎬🎬

Be My Valentine, Charlie Brown The Peanuts gang endures the follies of the heart on St. Valentine's Day. Animated.
1975 30m/C *D:* Phil Roman. **VHS, Beta** $9.98 *MED, VTR, WTA* 🎬🎬

Beach Blanket Bingo A group of sun-worshipping teens who are fascinated by skydiving and sizzling beach parties become involved in a kidnapping plot.
1965 (G) 96m/C Frankie Avalon, Annette Funicello, Linda Evans, Don Rickles, Buster Keaton, Paul Lynde, Harvey Lembeck; *D:* William Asher. **VHS, Beta, LV** $19.99 *HBO* 🎬

Beach Boys: An American Band An in-depth look at the lives and music of the Beach Boys with a soundtrack that features over forty of their songs.
1985 (PG-13) 103m/C Brian Wilson, Carl Wilson, Dennis Wilson, Mike Love, Al Jardine, Bruce Johnson; *D:* Malcolm Leo. **VHS, Beta, LV** $29.95 *MVD, LIV, VES* 🎬

Beach Girls Three voluptuous coeds intend to re-educate a bookish young man and the owner of a beach house.
1982 (R) 91m/C Debra Blee, Val Kline, Jeana Tomasina, Adam Roarke; *D:* Patrice Townsend. **VHS, Beta, LV** $39.95 *PAR* 🎬

The Beach Girls and the Monster Here's one on the cutting edge of genre bending: while it meticulously maintains the philosophical depth and production values of sixties beach bimbo fare, it manages to graft successfuly with the heinous critter from the sea genre to produce a hybrid horror with acres o' flesh. All that, and music by Frank Sinatra, Jr.
1965 70m/B Jon Hall, Sue Casey, Walker Edmiston; *D:* Jon Hall; *M:* Frank Sinatra Jr. **VHS** $19.98 *SNC* 🎬

Beach House In this boring comedy, adolescents frolic on the beach, get inebriated, and listen to rock 'n' roll.
1982 76m/C Kathy McNeil, Richard Duggan, Ileana Seidel, John Cosola, Spence Waugh, Paul Anderson, John A. Gallagher. **VHS, Beta** $59.99 *HBO* 🎬

Beach Party Scientist studying the mating habits of teenagers intrudes on a group of surfers, beach bums, and bikers, to his lasting regret. Typical beach party bingo, with sand, swimsuits, singing, dancing, and not much in way of plot. Historic beginning of five-pic Funicello and Avalon beach epic. Look for assorted Playmates, Peter Falk as motorcyclist, and Beach Boy Brian Wilson surfing, as well as walk-on by Vincent Price. Music contributed by Frankie, Annette, and Dick Dale and the Deltones.
1963 101m/C Frankie Avalon, Annette Funicello, Harvey Lembeck, Robert Cummings, Dorothy Malone, John Ashley; *D:* William Asher. **VHS, Beta** $19.98 *NO* 🎬🎬½

Beachballs From band to beach to dreamgirl's bed, this film chronicles the aspirations of a beach guy.
1988 (R) 79m/C Phillip Paley, Heidi Helmer. **VHS, Beta** $79.95 *MED* Woof!

Beachcomber Comedy set in the Dutch East Indies about a shiftless beachcomber (Laughton) who falls in love with a missionary's prim sister (Lanchester), as she attempts to reform him. The real-life couple of Laughton and Lanchester are their usual pleasure to watch. Remade in 1954. Story by W. Somerset Maugham. *AKA:* Vessel of Wrath.
1938 88m/B *GB* Charles Laughton, Elsa Lanchester, Robert Newton, Tyrone Guthrie; *D:* Erich Pommer. **VHS, Beta, 3/4U, Special order formats** $19.95 *NOS, MRV, DVT* 🎬🎬🎬

Beaches Based on the novel by Iris Rainer Dart about two girls whose friendship survived the test of time. The friendship is renewed once more when one of the now middle-aged women learns that she is dying slowly of a fatal disease.

1988 (PG-13) 123m/C Bette Midler, Barbara Hershey, John Heard, Spalding Gray, Lainie Kazan, James Read; *D:* Garry Marshall. **VHS, Beta, LV, 8mm** $19.99 *TOU, JCF* 🎬🎬🎬½

Beaks: The Movie Two television reporters try to figure out why birds of prey are suddenly attacking humans. Owes nothing to Hitchcock's "The Birds." *AKA:* Birds of Prey.
1987 (R) 86m/C Christopher Atkins, Michelle Johnson; *D:* Rene Cardona Jr. **VHS, Beta** $14.95 *LIV* Woof!

The Bear Breathtaking, effortlessly entertaining family film about an orphaned bear cub tagging after a grown male and dealing with hunters. The narrative is essentially from the cub's point of view, with very little dialogue. A huge money-maker in Europe. Based on a novel by James Oliver Curwood.
1989 (PG) 92m/C *FR* Jack Wallace, Tcheky Karyo, Andre Lacombe; *D:* Jean-Jacques Annaud; *W:* Gerard Brach. **VHS, Beta, LV** $14.95 *COL, RDG, HMV* 🎬🎬🎬

Bear Island Group of secret agents cleverly disguising themselves as U.N. weather researchers converge upon Bear Island in search of a Nazi U-Boat. Looks like rain.
1980 (PG) 118m/C Donald Sutherland, Richard Widmark, Barbara Parkins, Vanessa Redgrave, Christopher Lee, Lloyd Bridges; *D:* Don Sharp. **VHS, Beta** $19.95 *STE* 🎬½

The Bears & I A young Vietnam vet helps Indians regain their land rights while raising three bear cubs. Beautiful photography in this Disney production.
1974 (G) 89m/C Patrick Wayne, Chief Dan George, Andrew Duggan, Michael Ansara; *D:* Bernard McEveety. **VHS** $69.95 *DIS* 🎬🎬

The Beast Violent and cliche-driven war drama notable for its novel twist: wild Russian tank officer becomes lost in the Afghanistan wilderness while being tracked by Afghan rebels with revenge in mind. Filmed in the Israel desert and adapted by William Mastrosimone from his play. *AKA:* The Beast of War.
1988 (R) 93m/C George Dzundza, Jason Patric, Steven Bauer, Stephen Baldwin; *D:* Kevin Reynolds. **VHS, Beta** $89.95 *COL* 🎬🎬½

The Beast from Haunted Cave Gold thieves hiding in a wilderness cabin encounter a spiderlike monster. Surprisingly good performances from Sinatra (Frank's nephew) and Carol. Produced by Gene Corman, Roger's brother.
1960 64m/B Michael Forest, Sheila Carol, Frank Wolff, Richard Sinatra, Wally Campo; *D:* Monte Hellman; *W:* Charles B. Griffith. **VHS** $19.98 *DVT, MRV, SNC* 🎬

The Beast from 20,000 Fathoms Atomic testing defrosts a giant dinosaur in the Arctic; the hungry monster proceeds onwards to its former breeding grounds, now New York City. Oft-imitated saurian-on-the-loose formula is still fun, brought to life by Ray Harryhausen special effects. Based loosely on the Ray Bradbury story "The Foghorn."
1953 80m/B Paul Christian, Paula Raymond, Cecil Kellaway, Kenneth Tobey, Donald Woods, Lee Van Cleef, Steve Brodie, Mary Hill; *D:* Eugene Lourie. **VHS, Beta, LV** $19.95 *WAR, PIA, FCT* 🎬🎬½

Beast in the Cellar Every family has something to hide, and in the case of two spinster sisters, it's their murderous inhuman brother, whom they keep chained in the cellar. Like all brothers, however, the "beast" rebels against his sisters' bossiness and escapes to terrorize their peaceful English countryside. The sisters' (Reid and

Robson) performances aren't bad, but rest of effort is fairly disappointing. *AKA:* Are You Dying Young Man?.
1970 (R) 85m/C *GB* Beryl Reid, Flora Robson, T.P. McKenna; *D:* James Kelly. **VHS, Beta** $59.95 *PGN* 🐾½

Beast of Morocco Interesting vampire film about a Morrocan vampire princess who sets her sights on seducing a noted archaeologist. Of course his girlfriend ends up being abducted by the vampire's servant. *AKA:* Hand of Night.
1966 ?m/C *GB* William Sylvester, Alizia Gur, Terence de Marney. **VHS** $16.95 *SNC* 🐾🐾

Beast of the Yellow Night A dying soldier sells his soul to Satan at the close of World War II. Years later, existing without aging, he periodically turns into a cannibal monster. Although the first half is tedious, the monster turns things around when he finally shows up. Decent gore effects.
1970 (R) 87m/C *PH* John Ashley, Mary Wilcox, Eddie Garcia, Vic Diaz; *D:* Eddie Romero. **VHS, Beta** $19.95 *NOS, UHV, INC* Woof!

The Beast of Yucca Flats A really cheap, quasi-nuclear protest film. A Russian scientist is chased by communist agents into a nuclear testing area and is caught in an atomic blast. As a result, he turns into a club-weilding monster. Voice over narration is used in lieu of dialogue as that process proved too expensive.
1961 53m/B Tor Johnson, Douglas Mellor, Larry Aten, Barbara Francis; *W/D:* Coleman Francis. **VHS** $12.95 *SNC, CNM, MLB* Woof!

The Beast with Five Fingers After a pianist mysteriously dies and leaves his fortune to his private nurse, the occupants of his villa are terrorized by a creature that turns out to be the pianist's hand which was severed by his personal secretary (Lorre). Lorre is also terrorized by hallucinations of the hand, and no matter what he does to stop it (nail it to a desk, throw it in the fire, etc.), nothing can keep the hand from carrying out its mission. A creepy thriller with inventive shots of the severed hand.
1946 88m/B Robert Alda, Andrea King, Peter Lorre, Victor Francen, J. Carroll Naish, Charles Dingle; *D:* Robert Florey. **VHS** $19.98 *MGM* 🐾🐾½

The Beast Within Young woman has the misfortune of being raped by an unseen creature in a Mississippi swamp. Seventeen years later, her son conceived from that hellish union begins to act quite strange, developing a penchant for shedding his skin before turning into an insect-like critter with a cannibalistic appetite. First film to use the air "bladder" type of prosthetic make-up popularized in later, and generally better, horror films. Contains some choice cuts in photo editing: the juxtaposition of hamburger and human "dead meat" is witty. Based on Edward Levy's 1981 novel.
1982 (R) 98m/C Ronny Cox, Bibi Besch, L.Q. Jones, Paul Clemens, Don Gordon; *D:* Philippe Mora. **VHS, Beta** $69.95 *MGM* 🐾🐾

Beastmaster Adventure set in a wild and primitive world. The Beastmaster is involved in a life-and-death struggle with overwhelming forces of evil. Campy neanderthal flesh flick.
1982 (PG) 119m/C Marc Singer, Tanya Roberts, Rip Torn, John Amos, Josh Milrad, Billy Jacoby; *D:* Don A. Coscarelli. **VHS, Beta, LV** $19.95 *MGM* 🐾🐾

Beastmaster 2: Through the Portal of Time This time the laughs are intentional as the Beastmaster follows an evil monarch through a dimensional gate to mo-

dern-day L.A., where the shopping is better for both trendy clothes and weapons. Fun for genre fans, with a behind-the-scenes featurette on the tape.
1991 (PG-13) 107m/C Marc Singer, Kari Wuhrer, Sarah Douglas, Wings Hauser, James Avery, Robert Fieldsteel, Arthur Malet, Robert Z'Dar, Michael Berryman, Larry Dobkin; *D:* Sylvio Tabet. **VHS, LV** $14.98 *REP* 🐾½

Beasts A young couple's plans for a romantic weekend in the Rockies are slightly changed when the pair are savagely attacked by wild beasts.
1983 92m/C Tom Babson, Kathy Christopher, Vern Potter. **VHS, Beta** $49.95 *PSM* 🐾

The Beat Unrealistic film about a bookish new kid who intercedes in the tension between two rival street gangs, changing their lives in his literary way.
1988 101m/C John Savage, Kara Glover, Paul Dillon, David Jacobson, William McNamara; *D:* Peter Mones. **VHS, Beta, LV** $79.98 *LIV, VES* 🐾

Beat Girl An architect's rebellious teenage daughter sinks to the bottom and gets involved in murder along the way. *AKA:* Wild For Kicks.
1960 85m/B *GB* David Farrar, Noelle Adam, Christopher Lee, Gillian Hills, Shirley Anne Field, Oliver Reed; *D:* Edmond T. Greville; *M:* John Barry. **VHS** $29.95 *SNC, FCT, TIM* 🐾🐾

Beat Street This quasi-documentary about break dancing features the music of Ruben Blades, Afrika Bambaata and the Soul Sonic Force, and Grand Master Melle Mel and the Furious Five. ♫Beat Street Breakdown; Baptize the Beat; Stranger in a Strange Land; Beat Street Strut; Us Girls; This Could be the Night; Breakers Revenge; Tu Carino (Carmen's Theme); Frantic Situation.
1984 (PG) 106m/C Rae Dawn Chong, Leon Grant, Saundra Santiago, Robert Taylor, Guy Davis, Jon Chardiet, Duane Jones, Kadeem Hardison; *D:* Stan Lathan. **VHS, Beta, LV** $79.98 *VES, LIV* 🐾🐾½

Beat the Devil Each person on a slow boat to Africa has a scheme to beat the other passengers to the uranium-rich land that they all hope to claim. An unusual black comedy which didn't fare well when released, but over the years has come to be the epitome of spy-spoofs.
1953 89m/C Humphrey Bogart, Gina Lollobrigida, Peter Lorre, Robert Morley, Jennifer Jones; *D:* John Huston. **VHS, Beta, LV** $9.95 *NEG, MRV, NOS* 🐾🐾🐾

Beatlemania! The Movie Boring look at the Fab Four! Not the real Beatles, but impersonators who do a very inadequate job. Based on the equally disappointing stage show. *AKA:* Beatlemania.
1981 86m/C Mitch Weissman, Ralph Castelli, David Leon, Tom Teeley; *D:* Joseph Manduke. **VHS, Beta, LV** *IME* 🐾

The Beatniks Story about the dark secrets of the beat generation in which a man is promised fame and fortune by an agent, but his dreams are dashed when his friend commits murder. A big waste of time.
1960 78m/B Tony Travis, Peter Breck, Karen Kadler, Joyce Terry; *D:* Paul Frees. **VHS** $16.95 *SNC* 🐾

Beatrice In France during the Middle Ages, a barbaric soldier of the Hundred Years' War returns to his estate that his daughter has maintained, only to brutalize and abuse her. In French with English subtitles. *AKA:* La Passion Beatrice.
1988 (R) 132m/C *FR* Julie Delpy, Barnard Pierre Donnadieu, Nils Tavernier; *D:* Bertrand Tavernier. **VHS, Beta, LV** *NO* 🐾🐾🐾½

Beau Brummel The famous silent adaptation of the Clyde Fitch play about an ambitious English dandy's rise and fall.
1924 80m/B John Barrymore, Mary Astor, Willard Louis, Irene Rich, Carmel Myers, Alec B. Francis, William Humphreys; *D:* Harry Beaumont. **VHS, Beta** $19.95 *NOS, HHT, VYY* 🐾🐾½

Beau Brummel Lavish production has Granger in the role of the rags-to-riches dandy who becomes the chief adviser to the Prince of Wales. Born into a life of poverty, George Bryan Brummell uses his wit and intelligence to meet the vain Prince and ingratiate himself to the future king (George IV). He also manages to catch the eye of Taylor, who falls in love with him. The cinematography, sets, and costuming for this period piece are outstanding. Shot on location in England's beautiful countryside, many of the interior shots were taken inside a 15th-century mansion, Ockwell Manor, located near Windsor Castle. Remake of the 1924 silent film starring John Barrymore. Based on the play by Clyde Fitch.
1954 113m/C Stewart Granger, Elizabeth Taylor, Peter Ustinov, Robert Morley, James Donald, James Hayter, Rosemary Harris, Paul Rogers, Noel Willman, Peter Dyneley, Charles Carson; *D:* Curtis Bernhardt; *W:* Karl Tunberg. **VHS** $19.98 *MGM* 🐾🐾🐾

Beau Geste The classic Hollywood adventure film based on the Percival Christopher Wren story about three brothers who join the Foreign Legion after nobly claiming responsibility for a jewel theft they didn't commit. Once enlisted, they must face desert wars and the most despicable commanding officer ever, before clearing their family name. A rousing, much-copied epic.
1939 114m/B Gary Cooper, Ray Milland, Robert Preston, Brian Donlevy, Donald O'Connor, J. Carroll Naish, Susan Hayward, James Stephenson; *D:* William A. Wellman. **VHS, Beta** $29.95 *MCA* 🐾🐾🐾½

Beau Pere Bittersweet satiric romp from Blier about the war zone of modern romance, wherein a 30-year-old widower falls madly in love with his 14-year-old stepdaughter. Sharp-edged and daring. In French with subtitles.
1981 125m/C *FR* Patrick Dewaere, Nathalie Baye, Ariel Besse, Maurice Ronet; *D:* Bertrand Blier. **VHS, Beta** $59.95 *MED, TAM* 🐾🐾🐾

Beau Revel Critically acclaimed romantic drama of the silent era. A passionate dancing girl played by Vidor, one of the twenties' more prolific romantic leads (and erstwhile wife of director King Vidor) is the object of romantic interest of a father and son, which leaves the threesome lovelorn, suicidal, and emotionally scarred. You might recognize Stone from his later role as Judge Hardy in the MGM "Hardy Family" series.
1921 70m/B Lewis Stone, Florence Vidor, Lloyd Hughes, Katherine Kirkham, William Conklin; *D:* John Wray. **VHS, Beta** $24.95 *GPV, FCT* 🐾🐾🐾½

Beauties and the Beast Young nymphomaniacs seek the company of an unlikely suitor—a giant, lonely ape-creature. The real predators, however, are revealed in this comedy.
19?? 83m/C **VHS** *NO* 🐾🐾🐾½

The Beautiful Blonde from Bashful Bend Charming comedy-western gets better with age. Grable is the pistol packing mama mistaken for the new school teacher. Fun performances by all, especially Herbert.
1949 77m/C Betty Grable, Cesar Romero, Rudy Vallee, Olga San Juan, Hugh Herbert, Porter Hall, Sterling Holloway, El Brendel; *D:* Preston Sturges. **VHS, LV** $19.98 *FOX* 🐾🐾½

Beautiful Dreamers Maurice Bucke is a young Canadian physician who runs the London Insane Asylum. After a chance meeting with poet Walt Whitman, both men discover their mutual outrage for current treatment of the mentally ill. Bucke persuades Whitman to visit his asylum in order to try Whitman's theory of human compassion on the asylum's inmates. However, Bucke runs into opposition from the local townspeople, scandalized by Whitman's radical reputation. Fairly humdrum with a larger-than-life performance by Torn as Whitman. Based on Whitman's visit to Canada in 1880. **1992 (PG-13) 108m/C** *CA* Rip Torn, Colm Feore, Wendel Meldrum, Sheila McCarthy, Colin Fox; **W/D:** John Kent Harrison. **VHS, LV $89.95** *HMD, FCT* �′✓1/2

Beauty and the Beast The classic medieval fairy tale is brought to life on the big screen for the first time. Beauty takes the place of her father after he is sentenced to die by the horrible Beast and falls in love with him. Cocteau uses the story's themes and famous set-pieces to create a cohesive and captivating surreal hymn to romantic love that is still the definitive version of B&B. In French with subtitles. *AKA:* La Belle et Laete. **1946 90m/B** *FR* Jean Marais, Josette Day, Marcel Andre, Mila Parely, Nane Germon, Michel Auclair, Georges Auric; **D:** Jean Cocteau. **VHS, Beta, LV $19.95** *TAM, SUE, MLB* ✓✓✓✓

Beauty and the Beast From "Faerie Tale Theatre" comes the story of a Beauty who befriends a Beast and learns a lesson about physical appearance and true love. **1983 60m/C** Susan Sarandon, Klaus Kinski; **D:** Roger Vadim. **VHS, Beta, LV $14.98** *FOX.* *FCT* ✓✓✓1/2

Beauty and the Beast Includes the pilot episode of the fantasy television series, "Once Upon a Time in New York" and the episode "A Happy Life." A young lawyer who has been attacked and left for dead awakens in a society of outcasts who live under the New York City subway system. She has been rescued and befriended by one of them, a charismatic man/beast named Vincent. **1987 100m/C** Linda Hamilton, Ron Perlman. **VHS, Beta, LV $14.98** *REP* ✓✓✓✓

Beauty and the Beast Wonderful Disney musical combining superb animation, splendid characters, and lively songs about a beautiful girl, Belle, and the fearsome and disagreeable Beast. In true fairy tale fashion, the Beast is a handsome prince who is under a terrible curse. Time is running out because if he doesn't find true love soon he will be doomed to life as a beast forever. Belle agrees to be the Beast's companion if he will set his prisoner, her eccentric father, free. With Belle's arrival, the castle servants (a delightful bunch of household objects) work to turn their grisly master into a civilized object of Belle's affections. Notable as the first animated feature to be nominated for the Best Picture Oscar. Features the awarding-winning title song as well as other Menken/Ashman tunes. Destined to become a classic, beloved by generations of children. The deluxe video version features a work-in-progress rough film cut, a compact disc of the soundtrack, a lithograph depicting a scene from the film, and an illustrated book. ♫Beauty and the Beast; Belle; Something There; Be Our Guest. **1991 (G) 84m/C** **D:** Kirk Wise, Gary Trousdale; **M:** Alan Menken, Howard Ashman; **V:** Paige O'Hara, Robby Benson, Rex Everhart, Richard White, Jesse Corti, Angela Lansbury, Jerry Orbach, David Ogden Stiers, Bradley Michael

Pierce, Jo Anne Worley, Kimmy Robertson. Academy Awards '91: Best Song ("Beauty and the Beast"), Best Score; Nominations: Best Picture, Best Song ("Belle", "Be Our Guest"), Best Sound; Golden Globe Awards '92: Best Film—Musical/Comedy. **VHS $24.99** *DIS,* *OM* ✓✓✓✓

Beauty and the Beast: Once Upon a Time in New York When socialite attorney Catherine Chandler is brutally attacked in New York, Vincent, a mysterious man/beast, rescues and befriends her, taking her to his fantastical subterranean world. Pilot for the popular television series. Additional episodes are available. **1987 48m/C** Ron Perlman, Linda Hamilton, Roy Dotrice, Ray Wise. **VHS, LV $14.98** *REP,* *MOV* ✓✓✓✓

Beauty and the Beast: Though Lovers Be Lost The love affair of Vincent and Catherine takes a tragic turn when she is kidnapped by a crime lord. Feature-length drama from the television series. **1989 90m/C** Linda Hamilton, Ron Perlman. **VHS, LV $19.98** *REP* ✓✓✓✓

Beauty for the Asking It sounds like a workable Lucille Ball vehicle—a beautician develops a bestselling skin cream—and even the title sounds like something you'd like to love Lucy in. But somehow the numerous plot implausibilities managed to get by the story's five writers, and the idea of a jilted woman making millions while being financed by her ex's wife just doesn't fly (perhaps it was an idea ahead of its time). Die-hard Lucy fans may find this interesting. **1939 68m/B** Lucille Ball, Patric Knowles, Donald Woods, Frieda Inescort, Frances Mercer; **D:** B.P. Fineman. **VHS $19.98** *TTC, FCT* ✓

Beauty on the Beach A comedy about a mad psychologist, his bizarre experiments with women, and his eventual descent into insanity. In Italian with English subtitles. **196? 90m/C** *IT* Valeria Fabrizi. **VHS, Beta** *NO* ✓

Bebe's Kids When ladies' man Robin falls for the lovely Jamika, he gets some unexpected surprises when he takes her out on a first date to an amusement park. It seems Jamika has a little boy and she is also babysitting for her neighbor Bebe's three trouble-making kids. What follows is a day of torment as the children try to sabotage Robin's romantic intentions. Animated comedy takes some funny pot-shots at black culture, white people, and Disneyland. The children are amusing, especially baby Pee-Wee, a tot with chronically dirty diapers and Tone Loc's gravelly voice. Based on characters created by the late comedian Robin Harris. The video includes the seven-minute animated short "Itsy Bitsy Spider." **1992 (PG-13) 74m/C** **D:** Bruce Smith; **W:** Reginald Hudlin; **V:** Faizon Love, Vanessa Bell Calloway, Wayne Collins, Jonell Green, Marques Houston, Tone Loc, Nell Carter. **VHS, Beta, LV** *PAR, WTA* ✓✓1/2

Because of the Cats Police inspector uncovers an evil cult within his seaside village while investigating a bizarre rape and burglary. **1974 90m/C** Bryan Marshall, Alexandra Stewart, Alex Van Rooyen, Sylvia Kristel, Sebastian Graham Jones; **D:** Fons Rademakers. **VHS, Beta $49.95** *PSM* ✓1/2

Because You're Mine Lanza plays an opera star who is drafted and falls in love with Morrow, his top sergeant's sister. Plenty of singing—maybe too much at times, but Lanza's fans will enjoy it nonetheless.

1952 103m/C Mario Lanza, James Whitmore, Doretta Morrow, Dean Miller, Paula Corday, Jeff Donnell, Spring Byington; **D:** Alexander Hall. **VHS $19.98** *MGM* ✓✓

Becket The adaptation of Jean Anouilh's play about the tumultuous friendship between Henry II of England and the Archbishop of Canterbury Thomas Becket. Becket views his position in the church of little relation to the sexual and emotional needs of a man, until he becomes archbishop. His growing concern for religion and his shrinking need of Henry as friend and confidant eventually cause the demise of the friendship and the resulting tragedy. Flawless acting from every cast member, and finely detailed artistic direction make up for the occasional slow moment. Sound, and Costume Design. **1964 148m/C** Richard Burton, Peter O'Toole, John Gielgud, Donald Wolfit; **D:** Peter Glenville; **W:** Edward Anhalt. Academy Awards '64: Best Adapted Screenplay; Nominations: Best Actor (Burton), Best Actor (O'Toole), Best Art Direction/Set Decoration (Color), Best Color Cinematography, Best Costume Design (Color), Best Director (Glenville), Best Film Editing, Best Picture, Best Sound, Best Supporting Actor (Gielgud), Best Original Score; Golden Globe Awards '65: Best Actor—Drama (O'Toole), Best Film—Drama; National Board of Review Awards '64: 10 Best Films of the Year. **VHS, Beta, LV $59.95** *MPI, UHV, TVC* ✓✓✓

Becky Sharp This premiere Technicolor film tells the story of Becky Sharp, a wicked woman who finally performs one good deed. **1935 83m/C** Miriam Hopkins, Frances Dee, Cedric Hardwicke, Billie Burke, Nigel Bruce, Pat Nixon; **D:** Rouben Mamoulian. **VHS, Beta $19.95** *NOS, MRV, HEG* ✓✓1/2

Becoming Colette Tedious flashbacking bio of French writer Colette, from her innocent days in the country to her (bad) marriage to writer/publisher Willy and on and on to her own growing career as a writer. She begins writing stories, using an alter-ego character, Claudine, which detail her sexual escapades. Lots of naked flesh but little passion. A postscript notes that Colette wrote "Gigi" and was the first woman to receive the French Legion of Honor. **1992 (R) 97m/C** Mathilda May, Klaus Maria Brandauer, Virginia Madsen, Paul Rhys, Jean-Pierre Aumont, John van Dreelen, Lucienne Hamon; **D:** Danny Huston; **W:** Ruth Graham; **M:** John Scott. **VHS $89.95** *ACA* ✓✓

Bed & Breakfast Three generations of women—Mother-in-law Ruth, daughter-in-law Claire, and granddaughter Cassie—lead quiet lives while running a failing Nantucket bed and breakfast. All three women need to break away to lead their own lives but seem destined to remain together. That is, until a mystery man washes up on their beach. Beach guy Adam charms the ladies and romances Claire. It seems, however, that he has a past that could endanger everyone. Lightweight final role for Dewhurst, though she provides some sparks as the strong and loving matriarch. Gentle romantic comedy skims the surface, but is still enjoyable. **1992 (PG-13) 97m/C** Roger Moore, Talia Shire, Colleen Dewhurst, Nina Siemaszko; **D:** Robert Ellis Miller; **W:** Cindy Myers. **VHS, LV $59.95** *HMD* ✓✓1/2

Bed and Sofa Adultery, abortion, and women's rights are brought about by a housing shortage which forces a man to move in with a married friend. Famous, ground-breaking Russian silent. **1927 73m/B** *RU* Nikolai Batalov, Vladimar Fogel; **D:** Abram Room. **VHS, Beta, 3/4U $49.95** *TAM, IHF* ✓✓✓1/2

Bedazzled In the process of hanging himself, Stanley, a short-order cook is approached by the devil with an offer: seven wishes in exchange for his soul. Each of Stanley's wishes is granted with surprising consequences. Cult comedy is a sometimes uneven, but thoroughly entertaining and funny retelling of the Faustian story.
1968 (PG) 107m/C *GB* Dudley Moore, Peter Cook, Eleanor Bron, Michael Bates, Raquel Welch; *D:* Stanley Donen. **VHS, Beta, LV** *FOX* 🐾🐾🐾

Bedford Incident The U.S.S. Bedford discovers an unidentified submarine in North Atlantic waters. The Bedford's commander drives his crew to the point of exhaustion as they find themselves the center of a fateful controversy.
1965 102m/B Richard Widmark, Sidney Poitier, James MacArthur, Martin Balsam, Wally Cox, Donald Sutherland, Eric Portman; *D:* James B. Harris. **VHS, Beta, LV $14.95** *COL, IME* 🐾🐾½

Bedknobs and Broomsticks A novice witch and three cockney waifs ride a magic bedstead and stop the Nazis from invading England during World War II. Celebrated for its animated art.
1971 (G) 117m/C Angela Lansbury, Roddy McDowall, David Tomlinson, Bruce Forsyth, Sam Jaffe; *D:* Robert Stevenson. Academy Awards '71: Best Visual Effects; Nominations: Best Art Direction/Set Decoration, Best Costume Design, Best Song ("The Age of Not Believing"), Best Original Score. **VHS, Beta, LV $24.99** *DIS, WTA* 🐾🐾½

Bedlam Val Lewton produced this creeper set in the famed asylum in 18th-century London. A woman, wrongfully committed, tries to stop the evil doings of the chief (Karloff) of Bedlam, and endangers herself. A fine horror film co-written by Lewton.
1945 79m/B Jason Robards Sr., Ian Wolfe, Glenn Vernon, Boris Karloff, Anna Lee, Billy House, Richard Fraser; *D:* Mark Robson. **VHS, Beta, LV $19.95** *TTC, MED, FCT* 🐾🐾🐾

Bedroom Eyes A successful businessman becomes a voyeur by returning nightly to a beautiful woman's window, until she is killed and he is the prime suspect. Part comic, part disappointing thriller.
1986 (R) 90m/C Kenneth Gilman, Dayle Haddon, Christine Cattall; *D:* William Fruet. **VHS, Beta, LV $29.95** *FOX* 🐾🐾

Bedroom Eyes 2 After discovering his wife has had an affair, a stockbroker takes a lover. When she turns up dead, he and his wife become murder suspects. Provides some suspenseful moments.
1989 (R) 85m/C Wings Hauser, Kathy Shower, Linda Blair, Jane Hamilton, Jennifer Delora; *D:* Chuck Vincent. **VHS, LV $89.95** *VMK, IME* 🐾🐾

The Bedroom Window During an illicit liaison with her husband's co-worker (Guttenberg), a beautiful woman (Huppert) witnesses an assault on another woman (McGovern) from his bedroom window. To keep the affair secret, he reports it as his own account. Since it is secondhand, his story is flawed, and he becomes a suspect. Then a short distance away the body of a woman is found. Now he's in really big trouble. Only her truth or his finding of the assailant can clear him. Semi-tight thriller in the Hitchcock mode.
1987 (R) 113m/C Steve Guttenberg, Elizabeth McGovern, Isabelle Huppert, Wallace Shawn, Paul Shenar; *D:* Curtis Hanson. **VHS, Beta, LV $9.99** *FHE, VES, LIV* 🐾🐾½

Bedtime for Bonzo A professor adopts a chimp to prove that environment, not hereditary, determines a child's future. Fun, lighthearted comedy that stars a future president. Followed by "Bonzo Goes to College."
1951 83m/B Ronald Reagan, Diana Lynn, Walter Slezak, Jesse White, Bonzo the Chimp; *D:* Fred de Cordova. **VHS, Beta $14.95** *MCA, FCT* 🐾🐾½

Bedtime Story Two con artists attempt to fleece an apparently wealthy woman and each other on the French Riviera. Re-made in 1988 as "Dirty Rotten Scoundrels." One of Brando's thankfully few forays into comedy.
1963 99m/C Marlon Brando, David Niven, Shirley Jones, Dody Goodman, Marie Windsor; *D:* Ralph Levy. **VHS, Beta $59.95** *MCA* 🐾🐾

Beer A female advertising executive devises a dangerous sexist campaign for a cheap beer, and both the beer and its nickname become nationwide obsessions. Not especially amusing.
1985 (R) 83m/C Loretta Swit, Rip Torn, Dick Shawn, David Alan Grier, William Russ, Kenneth Mars, Peter Michael Goetz; *D:* Patrick Kelly. **VHS, Beta $19.99** *HBO* 🐾

The Bees Sting of a poor movie is painful. A strain of bees have ransacked South America and are threatening the rest of the world. The buzz is that no one is safe. Cheap rip-off of "The Swarm," which is saying something.
1978 (PG) 93m/C John Saxon, John Carradine, Angel Tompkins, Claudio Brook, Alicia Encinas; *D:* Alfredo Zacharias. **VHS, Beta $29.98** *WAR* Woof!

Beethoven Startling biography of the musical genius, filled with opulent, impressionistic visuals. *AKA:* Beethoven's Great Love; The Life and Loves of Beethoven; Un Grand Amour de Beethoven.
1936 116m/B *FR* Harry Baur, Jean-Louis Barrault, Marcel Dalio; *W:* Abel Gance. **VHS $59.95** *CVC, TAM* Woof!

Beethoven An adorable St. Bernard puppy escapes from dognappers and wanders into the home of the Newtons, who, over dad's objections, adopt him. Beethoven grows into a huge, slobbering dog who sorely tries dad's patience. To make matters worse, two sets of villains also wreak havoc on the Newton's lives. Evil veterinarian Dr. Varnick plots to steal Beethoven for lab experiments, and yuppie couple Brad and Brie plot to take over the family business. Enjoyable cast, particularly Grodin as dad and Chris as Beethoven enable this movie to please more than the milk and cookies set.
1992 (PG) 89m/C Charles Grodin, Bonnie Hunt, Dean Jones, Oliver Platt, Stanley Tucci, Nicholle Tom, Christopher Castile, Sarah Rose Karr, David Duchovny, Patricia Heaton, Laurel Cronin; *D:* Brian Levant; *W:* Edmond Dantes, Amy Holden Jones. **VHS, LV $19.98** *MCA, FCT* 🐾🐾½

Beethoven Lives Upstairs In 19th century Vienna 10 year-old Christoph's life is turned upside-down when the family's eccentric new tenant turns out to be composer Ludwig Van Beethoven. In time, Christoph comes to appreciate the beauty of the music and the tragedy of the composer's deafness. Features more than 25 excerpts of Beethoven's works.
1992 52m/C Neil Munro, Illya Woloshyn, Fiona Reid, Paul Soles, Sheila McCarthy; *D:* David Devine. **VHS $19.98** *BMG, MVD* 🐾🐾½

Beethoven's Nephew A tepid pseudo-historical farce about Beethoven's strange obsession with his only nephew. Directed by erstwhile Warhol collaborator Morrissey. *AKA:* Le Neveu de Beethoven.
1988 103m/C *FR* Wolfgang Reichmann, Ditmar Prinz, Jane Birkin, Nathalie Baye; *D:* Paul Morrissey. **VHS, Beta, LV $9.99** *NWV, STE* 🐾½

Beetlejuice The after-life is confusing for a pair of ultra-nice novice ghosts who are faced with chasing an obnoxious family of post-modern art lovers who move into their house. Then they hear of a poltergeist who promises to rid the house of all trespassers for a price. Things go from bad to impossible when the maniacal Keaton (as the demonic "Betelgeuse") works his magic. The calypso scene is priceless. A cheesy, funny, surreal farce of life after death with inventive set designs popping continual surprises. Ryder is striking as the misunderstood teen with a death complex, while O'Hara is hilarious as the yuppie art poseur.
1988 (PG) 92m/C Michael Keaton, Geena Davis, Alec Baldwin, Sylvia Sidney, Catherine O'Hara, Winona Ryder, Jeffrey Jones, Dick Cavett; *D:* Tim Burton. **VHS, Beta, LV, 8mm $19.98** *WAR, FCT, TLF* 🐾🐾🐾½

Before I Hang When a doctor invents a youth serum from the blood of a murderer, he'll stop at nothing to keep his secret. Karloff himself stands the test of time, and is satisfying as the mad scientist, giving this horror flick its appeal.
1940 60m/B Boris Karloff, Evelyn Keyes, Bruce Bennett, Edward Van Sloan; *D:* Nick Grinde. **VHS, Beta $59.95** *COL* 🐾🐾🐾

Before Morning Police officer poses as a blackmailer to find out which of the two women in the murder victim's life are guilty.
1933 68m/B Leo Carrillo, Lora Baxter, Taylor Holmes. **VHS, Beta** *NO* 🐾½

Before the Revolution One of Bertolucci's first films. Love and politics are mixed when a young man who is dabbling in communism is also flirting with his young aunt. Striking and powerful film that has yet to lose its effect despite the times.
1965 115m/C *IT* Francesco Barilli, Adrianna Asti, Alain Midgette, Morando Morandini, Domenico Alpi; *W/D:* Bernardo Bertolucci; *M:* Ennio Morricone. **VHS $59.95** *NYF, TAM* 🐾🐾

Beggars in Ermine A handicapped, impoverished man organizes all the beggars in the world into a successful corporation. Unusual performance from Atwill.
1934 70m/B Lionel Atwill, Henry B. Walthall, Betty Furness, Jameson Thomas, James Bush, Astrid Allwyn, George "Gabby" Hayes; *D:* Phil Rosen. **VHS, Beta $16.95** *SNC* 🐾🐾

Beginner's Luck A young man convinces his neighbors to engage in swinging activities, leading to predictable and raunchy situations.
1984 (R) 85m/C Sam Rush, Riley Steiner, Charles Homet, Kate Talbot; *D:* Frank Mouris. **VHS, Beta $19.95** *STE, NWV* Woof!

Beginning of the End Produced the same year as "The Deadly Mantis," Gordon's effort adds to 1957's harvest of bugs on a rampage "B"-graders. Giant, radiation-spawned grasshoppers attack Chicago causing Graves to come to the rescue. Easily the best giant grasshopper movie ever made.
1957 73m/B Peggy Castle, Peter Graves, Morris Ankrum, Richard Benedict, James Seay; *D:* Bert I. Gordon. **VHS** *VTR* 🐾🐾½

The Beguiled During the Civil War a wounded Union soldier is taken in by the women at a girl's school in the South. He manages to seduce both a student and a teacher, and jealousy and revenge ensue. Decidedly weird psychological melodrama from action vets Siegel and Eastwood.
1970 (R) 109m/C Clint Eastwood, Geraldine Page, Elizabeth Hartman; *D:* Don Siegel. **VHS, Beta, LV $19.95** *MCA* 🐾🐾🐾

Behave Yourself! A married couple adopts a dog who may be the key for a million-dollar hijacking setup by a gang of hoodlums.
1952 81m/B Shelley Winters, Farley Granger, William Demarest, Lon Chaney Jr., Hans Conried, Elisha Cook Jr., Francis L. Sullivan; *D:* George Beck. VHS, Beta $15.95 *NOS, UHV, TIM* ♪♪½

Behind Enemy Lines Special Forces soldier goes on a special mission to eliminate a possible Nazi spy. Made for television.
1985 (R) 83m/C Hal Holbrook, Ray Sharkey, David McCallum, Anne Twomey, Robert Patrick; *D:* Sheldon Larry. VHS, Beta $79.95 *MED* ♪♪½

Behind Locked Doors A journalist fakes mental illness to have himself committed to an asylum, where he believes a crooked judge is in hiding. A superior "B" mystery/suspense feature, with some tense moments.
1948 61m/B Lucille Bremer, Richard Carlson, Tor Johnson, Douglas Fowley, Herbert Heyes, Ralf Harolde; *D:* Budd Boetticher. VHS $19.95 *VDM* ♪♪½

Behind Office Doors Astor stars as the secretarial "power behind the throne" in this look at who really wields power in an office. Her boss takes her for granted until things go wrong.
1931 82m/B Mary Astor, Robert Ames, Ricardo Cortez, Charles Sellon; *D:* Melville Brown. VHS $19.95 *NOS, TIM, HEG* ♪♪

Behind Prison Walls A steel tycoon and his son are sent to prison, and the son tries to convert his dad to socialism. A fun, light-hearted film, the last for veteran Tully. *AKA:* Youth Takes a Hand.
1943 64m/B Alan Baxter, Gertrude Michael, Tully Marshall, Edwin Maxwell, Jacqueline Dalya, Matt Willis; *D:* Steve Sekely. VHS $16.95 *SNC* ♪♪

Behind the Front Two friends tumble in and out of trouble in this comic Army film. One of the most profitable films of the late twenties.
1926 60m/B Wallace Beery, Raymond Hatton, Richard Arlen, Mary Brian, Chester Conklin; *D:* Edward Sutherland. VHS *GPV* ♪♪½

Behind the Rising Sun A Japanese publisher's political views clash with those of his American-educated son in 1930s Japan. Well done despite pre-war propaganda themes.
1943 88m/B Tom Neal, J. Carroll Naish, Robert Ryan, Mike Mazurki, Margo, Gloria Holden, Don Douglas; *D:* Edward Dmytryk. VHS, Beta $19.98 *RKO* ♪♪½

Behold a Pale Horse A Spanish police captain attempts to dupe Peck into believing that his mother is dying and he must visit her on her deathbed. Loyalist Spaniard Peck becomes privy to the plot against him, but goes to Spain anyway in this post Spanish Civil War film.
1964 118m/B Gregory Peck, Anthony Quinn, Omar Sharif, Mildred Dunnock; *D:* Fred Zinneman. VHS, Beta $9.95 *GKK* ♪♪½

The Being People in Idaho are terrorized by a freak who became abnormal after radiation was disposed in the local dump. Another dull monster-created-by-nuclear-waste non-event. Of limited interest is Buzzi. However, you'd be more entertained (read: amused) by Troma's "The Toxic Avenger," which takes itself much (much!) less seriously.
1983 (R) 82m/C Ruth Buzzi, Martin Landau, Jose Ferrer; *D:* Jackie Kong. VHS, Beta $19.99 *HBO* ♪

Being There A feeble-minded gardener, whose entire knowledge of life comes from watching television, is sent out into the real world when his employer dies. Equipped with his prize possession, his remote control unit, the gardener unwittingly enters the world of politics and is welcomed as a mysterious sage. Sellers is wonderful in this satiric treat adapted by Jerzy Kosinski from his novel.
1979 (PG) 130m/C Peter Sellers, Shirley MacLaine, Melvyn Douglas, Jack Warden, Richard Dysart, Richard Basehart; *D:* Hal Ashby. Academy Awards '79 Nominations: Best Actor (Sellers); Golden Globe Awards '80: Best Actor—Musical/Comedy (Sellers), Best Supporting Actor (Douglas); National Board of Review Awards '79: 10 Best Films of the Year, Best Actor (Sellers). VHS, Beta, LV $19.98 *FOX, FCT, WAR* ♪♪♪½

Bela Lugosi Meets a Brooklyn Gorilla Two men who look like Dean Martin and Jerry Lewis (but aren't) get lost in the jungle, where they meet mad scientist Lugosi. Worse than it sounds. Real Jerry sued for unflattering imitation. *AKA:* The Boys from Brooklyn.
1952 74m/B Bela Lugosi, Duke Mitchell, Sammy Petrillo; *D:* William Beaudine. VHS, Beta $19.95 *NOS, SNC, AOV* Woof!

Bela Lugosi Scrapbook A compilation of Lugosi appearances, outtakes, flubs, and trailers.
197? 60m/B Bela Lugosi. VHS, Beta $29.95 *DVT, RXM* ♪♪½

Belfast Assassin A British anti-terrorist agent goes undercover in Ireland to find an IRA assassin who shot a British cabinet minister.
1984 130m/C Derek Thompson, Ray Lonnen. VHS, Beta $49.95 *PSM* ♪

The Believers Tense horror mystery set in New York city about a series of gruesome, unexplained murders. A widowed police psychologist investigating the deaths unwittingly discovers a powerful Santeria cult that believes in the sacrifice of children. Without warning he is drawn into the circle of the "Believers" and must free himself before his own son is the next sacrifice. Gripping (and grim), unrelenting horror.
1987 (R) 114m/C Martin Sheen, Helen Shaver, Malick Bowens, Harris Yulin, Robert Loggia, Jimmy Smits, Richard Masur, Harley Cross, Elizabeth Wilson, Lee Richardson; *D:* John Schlesinger. VHS, Beta, LV $19.99 *HBO* ♪♪½

Belizaire the Cajun 19th-century Louisiana love story. White prejudice against the Cajuns is rampant and violent, but that doesn't stop sexy faith healer Assante from falling in love with the inaccessible Cajun wife (Youngs) of a rich local. Made with care on a tight budget. Worthwhile, though uneven.
1986 (PG) 103m/C Armand Assante, Gail Youngs, Will Patton, Stephen McHattie, Michael Schoeffling, Robert Duvall; *D:* Glen Pitre. VHS, Beta $79.98 *FOX* ♪♪½

Bell, Book and Candle A young witch makes up her mind to refrain from using her powers. When an interesting man moves into her building, she forgets her decision and enchants him with a love spell.
1958 106m/C James Stewart, Kim Novak, Jack Lemmon, Elsa Lanchester, Ernie Kovacs, Hermione Gingold; *D:* Richard Quine. VHS, Beta, LV $19.95 *COL, FCT, MLB* ♪♪½

Bell Diamond A study by the experimental filmmaker of a Vietnam vet surviving in a bankrupt mining town. Created without a script using non-professional actors.
1981 96m/C *D:* Jon Jost. VHS, Beta *FCT* ♪♪

Bell from Hell A tale of insanity and revenge, wherein a young man, institutionalized since his mother's death, plots to kill his aunt and three cousins.
1974 80m/C Viveca Lindfors, Renaud Verley, Alfredo Mayo; *D:* Claudio Guerin Hill. VHS, Beta $49.95 *UNI* ♪

The Bell Jar Based on poet Sylvia Plath's acclaimed semi-autobiographical novel, this is the story of a young woman who becomes the victim of mental illness. Not for the easily depressed and a disjointed and disappointing adaptation of Plath's work.
1979 (R) 113m/C Marilyn Hassett, Julie Harris, Barbara Barrie, Anne Bancroft, Robert Klein, Anne Jackson; *D:* Larry Peerce. VHS, Beta $29.98 *VES* ♪½

Bell Ringer of Antigua Inspirational story by Royer, one of Hollywood's pioneering women. Shot on location in Guatemala.
1946 ?m/C *W/D:* Fanchon Royer. VHS $15.95 *LOO* ♪½

Bellamy Murderous madman massacres masseuses, and Bellamy is the cop out to get him.
1980 92m/C John Stanton, Timothy Elston, Sally Conabere; *D:* Colin Eggleston, Pina Amenta. VHS, Beta *PGN* ♪

Bellas de Noche A Mexican pimp gets in trouble with the mob. In Spanish. *AKA:* Night Beauties.
197? 110m/C *MX MX* Jorge Rivero, Lalo El Mimo, Rafael Inclan, Sasha Montenegro. VHS, Beta $53.95 *MAD* ♪

The Bellboy Lewis makes his directorial debut in this plotless but clever outing. He also stars as the eponymous character, a bellboy at Miami's Fountainbleau Hotel. Cameos from Berle and Winchell are highlights.
1960 72m/B Jerry Lewis, Alex Gerry, Bob Clayton, Sonny Sands; *Cameos:* Milton Berle, Walter Winchell; *W/D:* Jerry Lewis. VHS, Beta, LV $59.95 *LIV* ♪♪½

The Bellboy and the Playgirls Early Coppola effort adds new film footage to a 1958 German movie. Stars Playboy playmate June "The Body" Wilkinson, with other centerfolds of the time. *AKA:* The Playgirls and the Bellboy; Mit Eva Fing Die Sunde An.
1962 93m/C June Wilkinson; *W/D:* Francis Ford Coppola. VHS $59.95 *SVS* Woof!

The Belle of New York A turn-of-the-century bachelor falls in love with a Salvation Army missionary in this standard musical. ♪Naughty But Nice; Baby Doll; Oops; I Wanna Be a Dancin' Man; Seeing's Believing; Bachelor's Dinner Song; When I'm Out With the Belle of New York; Let a Little Love Come In.
1952 82m/C Fred Astaire, Vera-Ellen, Marjorie Main, Keenan Wynn, Alice Pearce, Gale Robbins, Clinton Sundberg; *D:* Charles Walters. VHS, Beta $19.98 *MGM, FHE* ♪♪

Belle of San Fernando During the era of Spanish brutality in the California colonies, a Spanish spitfire and Irish immigrant fall in love.
1948 74m/B Donald Woods, Gloria Warren. VHS, Beta, LV *NO* ♪

Belle Starr Story The career of Wild West outlaw Belle Starr is chronicled.
197? 90m/C Elsa Martinelli, Robert Wood; *D:* Lina Wertmuller. VHS, Beta *NO* ♪½

The Belles of St. Trinian's Sim is priceless in a dual role as the eccentric headmistress of a chaotic, bankrupt girls' school and her bookie twin brother who scheme the school into financial security. The first in a series of movies based on a popular

British cartoon by Ronald Searles about a girls' school and its mischievous students. Followed by "Blue Murder at St. Trinian's," "The Pure Hell of St. Trinian's," and "The Great St. Trinian's Train Robbery."

1953 86m/B *GB* Alastair Sim, Joyce Grenfell, Hermione Baddeley, George Cole, Eric Pohlmann, Renee Houston, Beryl Reid; *D:* Frank Launder. **VHS, Beta $39.95** *HBO, HMV* 🎞🎞🎞

Bellhop/The Noon Whistle Two comedic shorts back to back, separately featuring the famous comics Laurel and Hardy.

1922 46m/B Stan Laurel, Oliver Hardy. **VHS, Beta $49.95** *CCB* 🎞🎞🎞

Bellissima A woman living in an Italian tenement has unrealistic goals for her plain but endearing daughter when a famous director begins casting a role designed for a child. The mother's maternal fury and collision with reality highlight a poignant film. English subtitles.

1951 130m/B *IT* Anna Magnani; *D:* Luchino Visconti; *W:* Luchino Visconti, Cesare Zavattini, Francesco Rosi, Suso Cecchi D'Amico. **VHS, 3/4U, Special order formats $49.95** *CIG, APD* 🎞🎞🎞

Bellissimo: Images of the Italian Cinema A panoramic film history of Italian cinema, featuring film clips, behind-the-scenes footage and interviews with the industry's leading figures. Clips from "Open City," "Divorce Italian Style," "8 1/2," and "Seven Beauties" are included. In English, and Italian with subtitles.

1987 110m/C *IT* Sophia Loren, Marcello Mastroianni, Bernardo Bertolucci, Dino de Laurentiis, Marco Ferreri, Roberto Rossellini, Vittorio De Sica, Pier Paolo Pasolini, Franco Zeffirelli, Federico Fellini, Lina Wertmuller, Monica Vitti, Giancarlo Giannini, Toto, Anna Magnani; *D:* Gianfranco Mingozzi. **VHS, Beta $59.95** *WBF, FCT, TAM* 🎞🎞🎞

Bellman and True Rewarding, but sometimes tedious character study of a mild mannered computer whiz who teams with a gang of bank robbers. Fine performances, especially subtle dangerous gang characters.

1988 (R) 112m/C *GB* Bernard Hill, Kieran O'Brien, Richard Hope, Frances Tomelty, Derek Newark; *D:* Richard Loncraine. **VHS, Beta $14.95** *MGM, CAN, VES* 🎞🎞½

Bells are Ringing A girl who works for a telephone answering service can't help but take an interest in the lives of the clients, especially a playwright with an inferiority complex. Based on Adolph Green and Betty Comden's Broadway musical. Special letter-boxed edition along with the original trailer available on laserdisc format. 🎵Just in Time; The Party's Over; It's a Perfect Relationship; Do It Yourself; It's a Simple Little System; Better Than a Dream; I Met a Girl; Drop That Name; I'm Going Back.

1960 126m/C Judy Holliday, Dean Martin, Fred Clark, Eddie Foy Jr., Jean Stapleton; *D:* Vincente Minnelli. **VHS, Beta, LV $19.98** *MGM, PIA* 🎞🎞🎞

Bells of Coronado Rogers and Evans team up to expose the murderer of a profitable uranium mine. A gang of smugglers trying to trade the ore to foreign powers is thwarted. The usual thin storyline, but filled with action and riding stunts.

1950 67m/B Roy Rogers, Dale Evans, Pat Brady, Grant Withers; *D:* William Witney. **VHS $12.98** *REP* 🎞🎞

Bells of Death A young martial arts student infiltrates the gang that killed his family and kidnapped his sister, finishing them off one by one.

1990 91m/C Chun Ping, Chang Yi, Chao Hsin Yen; *D:* Yueh Fung. **VHS** *NO* 🎞½

Bells of Rosarita Roy helps foil an evil plan to swindle Evans out of the circus she inherited. All-star western cast under the big top.

1945 54m/B Roy Rogers, Dale Evans, George "Gabby" Hayes, Sunset Carson, Adele Mara, Grant Withers, Roy Barcroft, Addison Richards; *D:* Frank McDonald. **VHS, Beta, 3/4U, Special order formats $19.95** *NOS, MRV, VCN* 🎞🎞½

The Bells of St. Mary's An easy-going priest finds himself in a subtle battle of wits with the Mother Superior over how the children of St. Mary's school should be raised. It's the sequel to "Going My Way." Songs include the title tune and "Aren't You Glad You're You?" Also available in a colorized version.

1945 126m/B Bing Crosby, Ingrid Bergman, Henry Travers; *D:* Leo McCarey. Academy Awards '45: Best Sound; Nominations: Best Actress (Bergman); Academy Awards '45: Best Actor (Crosby), Best Director (McCarey), Best Film Editing, Best Picture, Best Song ("Aren't You Glad You're You"), Best Original Score; Golden Globe Awards '46: Best Actress—Drama (Bergman); New York Film Critics Awards '45: Best Actress (Bergman). **VHS, Beta, LV $19.98** *REP, IGP* 🎞🎞🎞½

Bells of San Angelo Roy foils thieves' attempts to steal a girl's inherited ranch.

1947 54m/C Roy Rogers, Dale Evans; *D:* William Witney. **VHS, Beta $19.95** *NOS, DVT* 🎞

Bells of San Fernando An Irish craftsman and evil Spanish ranch overseer fight for the right to marry a young girl in old California.

1947 75m/B Donald Woods, Gloria Warren, Monte Blue, Byron Foulger. **VHS, Beta, 8mm $19.95** *NOS, VYY, HEG* 🎞

The Belly of an Architect A thespian feast for the larger-than-life Dennehy as blustering American architect whose personal life and health both crumble as he obsessively readies an exhibition in Rome. A multi-tiered, carefully composed tragicomedy from the ideosyncratic filmmaker Greenaway, probably his most accessible work for general audiences.

1991 (R) 119m/C *GB IT* Brian Dennehy, Chloe Webb, Lambert Wilson; *W/D:* Peter Greenaway. **VHS, LV $19.95** *HMD* 🎞🎞🎞½

Beloved Enemy A romantic tragedy set in Civil War-torn Ireland in the 1920s. A rebel leader and a proper English lady struggle to overcome the war's interference with their burgeoning relationship.

1936 86m/B David Niven, Merle Oberon, Brian Aherne, Karen Morley, Donald Crisp; *D:* H.C. Potter. **VHS, Beta, 3/4U, Special order formats $19.95** *NOS, CAB* 🎞🎞🎞

The Beloved Rogue Crosland—who gained a reputation for innovation, having directed "Don Juan" the previous year (noted for the debut of synchronized music), and "The Jazz Singer" the following year (noted for the first talkie bits)—mounted this well-designed and special effect-laden medieval costumer. Barrymore (whom Crosland had directed through 127 kisses in "Don Juan") is in high profile as a swashbuckling caricature of French poet Francois Villon, who battles mightily (and verbally) with Louis XI (played by Veidt, in his first US film). Marked by the excesses typical of Barrymore's prestige days, it flouts history, taking generous poetic license when the facts ain't fab enough. In short, it's great entertainment.

1927 110m/B John Barrymore, Conrad Veidt, Marceline Day, Henry Victor, Mack Swain, Slim Summerville; *D:* Alan Crosland. **VHS, Beta, LV $27.95** *GPV, FCT, VYG* 🎞🎞🎞

Below the Belt Almost interesting tale of street-smart woman from New York City who becomes part of the blue-collar "circus" of lady wrestlers. Ex-wrestling champ Burke plays herself.

1980 (R) 98m/C Regina Baff, Mildred Burke, John C. Becher; *D:* Robert Fowler. **VHS, Beta $59.99** *HBO* 🎞🎞

Below the Border The Rough Riders go undercover to straighten out some cattle rustlers.

1942 57m/B Buck Jones, Tim McCoy, Raymond Hatton, Linda Brent, Roy Barcroft, Charles King; *D:* Howard Bretherton. **VHS, Beta $9.99** *NOS, DVT, VDM* 🎞½

Below the Deadline A man framed for embezzlement is set free and allowed to clear his name by a sympathetic detective.

1929 79m/B Frank Leigh, Barbara Worth, Arthur Rankin, Walter Merrill; *D:* J.P. McGowan. **VHS $16.95** *SNC, VYY* 🎞🎞

The Belstone Fox Orphaned fox goes into hiding, and is hunted by the hound he has befriended and his former owner.

1973 103m/C Eric Porter, Rachel Roberts, Jeremy Kemp; *D:* James Hill. **VHS, Beta** *SUE* 🎞🎞

Ben Sequel to "Willard" finds police Detective Kirtland still on the hunt for a killer rat pack led by Ben, king of the rodents. Title song by young Michael Jackson hit the top of the charts.

1972 (PG) 95m/C Joseph Campanella, Lee Montgomery, Arthur O'Connell, Rosemary Murphy, Meredith Baxter Birney; *D:* Phil Karlson. **VHS, Beta, LV $14.95** *PSM, PAR* 🎞½

Ben-Hur Second film version of the renowned story of Jewish and Christian divisiveness in the time of Jesus. Battle scenes and chariot races still look good, in spite of age. Problems lingered on the set and at a cost of over $4,000,000 it was the most expensive film of its time and took years to finish. A hit at the box office, it still stands as the all-time silent classic. In 1931, a shortened version was released. Based on the novel by Lewis Wallace.

1926 148m/B Ramon Novarro, Francis X. Bushman, May McAvoy, Betty Bronson, Claire McDowell, Carmel Myers, Nigel de Brulier, Ferdinand P. Earle; *D:* Fred Niblo. **VHS, Beta, LV $29.95** *MGM* 🎞🎞🎞🎞

Ben-Hur The third film version of the Lew Wallace classic stars Heston in the role of a Palestinian Jew battling the Roman empire at the time of Christ. Won a record 11 Oscars. The breathtaking chariot race is still one of the best screen races today. Perhaps one of the greatest pictures of all time. Also available in letterbox format.

1959 212m/C Charlton Heston, Jack Hawkins, Stephen Boyd, Haya Harareet, Hugh Griffith, Martha Scott, Sam Jaffe, Cathy O'Donnell, Finlay Currie, Karl Tunberg; *D:* William Wyler; *M:* Miklos Rozsa. Academy Awards '59: Best Actor (Heston), Best Art Direction/Set Decoration (Color), Best Color Cinematography, Best Costume Design (Color), Best Director (Wyler), Best Film Editing, Best Picture, Best Sound, Best Special Effects, Best Supporting Actor (Griffith), Best Original Score; Nominations: Best Adapted Screenplay; British Academy Awards '59: Best Film; Directors Guild of America Awards '59: Best Director (Wyler); Golden Globe Awards '60: Best Director (Wyler), Best Film—Drama, Best Supporting Actor (Boyd). **VHS, Beta, LV $29.98** *MGM, APD, BTV* 🎞🎞🎞🎞

Ben Turpin: An Eye for an Eye Two silent Ben Turpin comedies: "He Looked Crooked, or Why Ben Bolted" (1917) and "Ten Dollars or Ten Days" (1924).

1924 77m/B Ben Turpin, Harry Gribbon. **VHS, Beta, 8mm $29.95** *VYY* 🎞🎞🎞🎞

Bend of the River A haunted, hardened guide leads a wagon train through Oregon territory, pitting himself against Indians, the wilderness and a former comrade-turned-hijacker. *AKA:* Where the River Bends.
1952 91m/C James Stewart, Arthur Kennedy, Rock Hudson, Harry Morgan, Royal Dano; *D:* Anthony Mann. VHS, Beta $19.95 MCA *III*

Beneath Arizona Skies/Paradise Canyon A package of John Wayne westerns filled with lots of rumble tumble action.
1935 109m/B John Wayne. VHS, Beta $19.95 REP *I 1/2*

Beneath the Planet of the Apes In the first sequel, another Earth astronaut passes through the same warp and follows the same paths as Taylor, through Ape City and to the ruins of bomb-blasted New York's subway system, where warhead-worshipping human mutants are found. The strain of sequelling shows instantly, and gets worse through the next three films; followed by "Escape from the Planet of the Apes."
1970 (G) 108m/C Charlton Heston, James Franciscus, Kim Hunter, Maurice Evans, James Gregory, Natalie Trundy, Jeff Corey, Linda Harrison, Victor Buono; *D:* Ted Post. VHS, Beta, LV $19.98 FOX *II 1/2*

Beneath the 12-Mile Reef Two rival groups of divers compete for sponge beds off the Florida coast. Lightweight entertainment notable for underwater photography and early Cinemascope production, as well as Moore in a bathing suit.
1953 102m/C Robert Wagner, Terry Moore, Gilbert Roland, Richard Boone, Peter Graves, J. Carroll Naish; *D:* Robert D. Webb. VHS, Beta, LV $19.95 NOS, WES, GEM *II*

Beneath the Valley of the Ultra-Vixens Sex comedy retread directed by the man with an obsession for big. Scripted by Roger Ebert, who also scripted the cult classic "Beyond the Valley of the Dolls." Explicit nudity.
1979 90m/C Francesca "Kitten" Natavidad, Ann Marie, Ken Kerr, Stuart Lancaster; *D:* Russ Meyer; *W:* Roger Ebert. VHS $89.95 RMF *I*

The Beniker Gang Five orphans, supported by the eldest who writes a syndicated advice column, work together as a family. A made-for-television film.
1983 (G) 87m/C Andrew McCarthy, Jennie Dundas, Danny Pintauro, Charlie Fields; *D:* Ken Kwapis. VHS, Beta $59.95 WAR *II 1/2*

Benjamin Argumedo A true story of the struggle to survive a revolution, and what a person has to endure after it is over.
1978 97m/C SP Antonio Aguilar, Flor Silvestre, Jose Galvez, Irma Lozano; *D:* Mario Hernandez. VHS, Beta NO *I*

Benji In the loveable mutt's first feature-length movie, he falls in love with a female named Tiffany, and saves two young children from kidnappers. Kiddie classic that was a box office hit when first released. Followed by "For the Love of Benji."
1974 (G) 87m/C Benji, Peter Breck, Christopher Connelly, Patsy Garrett, Deborah Walley, Cynthia Smith; *D:* Joe Camp. VHS, Beta $19.99 VES, VTK, FCT *II*

Benji the Hunted The heroic canine, shipwrecked off the Oregon coast, discovers a litter of orphaned cougar cubs, and battles terrain and predators to bring them to safety.
1987 (G) 89m/C Benji, Red Steagall, Frank Inn; *D:* Joe Camp. VHS, Beta, LV $19.99 DIS *I 1/2*

Benji's Very Own Christmas Story Benji and his friends go on a magic trip and meet Kris Kringle and learn how Christmas is celebrated around the world.

Also included: "The Phenomenon of Benji," a documentary about Benji's odyssey from the animal shelter to international stardom.
1983 60m/C VHS, Beta $14.99 BFV *II*

Benny & Joon Depending on your tolerance for cute eccentrics and whimsy this will either charm you with sweetness or send you into sugar shock. Masterson is Joon, a mentally disturbed young woman who paints and has a habit of setting fires. She lives with her overprotective brother Benny (Quinn) who cares for her while ignoring his own private life (he has a romantic interest in the lovely Moore). Sam (Depp) is the outsider who charms Joon, a dyslexic loner who impersonates his heroes Charlie Chaplin and Buster Keaton with eery accuracy. Depp is particularly fine with the physical demands of his role, Masterson sparkling, and Quinn patience personified but the film's easy dismissal of Joon's mental illness is a serious flaw. The laserdisc version is letterboxed.
1993 (PG) 98m/C Johnny Depp, Mary Stuart Masterson, Aidan Quinn, Julianne Moore, Oliver Platt, CCH Pounder, Dan Hedaya, Joe Grifasi, William H. Macy; *D:* Jeremiah S. Chechik; *W:* Barry Berman; *M:* Rachel Portman. VHS, LV $94.99 MGM *II 1/2*

The Benny Goodman Story The life and music of Swing Era bandleader Benny Goodman is recounted in this popular bio-pic. Covering Benny's career from his child prodigy days to his monumental 1938 Carnegie Hall Jazz Concert, the movie's soggy plot machinations are redeemed by a non-stop music track featuring the real Benny and an all-star lineup. ♫Don't Be That Way; Memories of You; Sing, Sing, Sing; Slipped Disc.
1955 116m/C Steve Allen, Donna Reed, Gene Krupa, Lionel Hampton, Kid Ory, Ben Pollack, Harry James, Stan Getz, Teddy Wilson, Martha Tilton; *D:* Valentine Davies. VHS, Beta $19.95 MCA, FCT *II*

Benny Hill's Crazy World The British comedian delivers some of his best material with the help of "Hill's Angels."
1974 55m/C GB Benny Hill. VHS, Beta $19.99 HBO *II*

Bergonzi Hand Drama about two art scoundrels who are astonished when an immigrant admits to painting a forged "Bergonzi."
1970 62m/C Keith Mitchell, Gordon Jackson, Martin Miller. VHS, Beta $24.95 VYY *I*

The Berlin Affair A sordid tale from "The Night Porter" director about a Japanese woman seducing various parties in pre-World War II Germany.
1985 (R) 97m/C IT GE Mio Takaki, Gudrun Landgrebe, Kevin McNally; *D:* Liliana Cavani. VHS, Beta $79.95 MGM, TAM *II*

Berlin Alexanderplatz Fassbinder's 15 1/2-hour epic follows the life, death, and resurrection of Franz Biberkof, a former transit worker who has just finished a lengthy prison term and must learn to adjust in the harsh social atmosphere of Berlin in the 1920s. Melodramatic parable with Biblical overtones considered by some to be a masterpiece. Based on the novel by Alfred Doblin; originally aired as a miniseries on German television. On eight tapes.
1980 930m/C GE Gunter Lamprecht, Hanna Schygulla, Barbara Sukowa, Gottfried John, Elisabeth Trissenaar, Brigitte Mira, Karin Baal, Ivan Desny; *D:* Rainer Werner Fassbinder. VHS, Beta $400.00 FCT, MGM *III 1/2*

Berlin Blues A nightclub singer is torn between two men.
1989 (PG-13) 90m/C GE Julia Migenes-Johnson, Keith Baxter; *D:* Ricardo Franco. VHS, LV $79.95 CAN *III 1/2*

The Berlin Conspiracy Espionage/action potboiler does an imaginative job of setting its action against the fall of the Berlin Wall and the end of the Cold War. A CIA agent forms a shaky alliance with his East German spymaster rival to prevent germ warfare technology from falling into terrorist hands.
1991 (R) 83m/C Marc Singer, Mary Crosby, Stephen Davies, Richard Leparmentier, Terence Henry; *D:* Terence H. Winkless. VHS, LV $89.95 COL *II*

Berlin Express Battle of wits ensues between the Allies and the Nazis who are seeking to keep Germans divided in post-WWII Germany. Espionage and intrigue factor heavily.
1948 86m/B Robert Ryan, Merle Oberon, Paul Lukas, Charles Korvin; *D:* Jacques Tourneur. VHS, Beta, LV $19.95 MED, TTC, FCT *III 1/2*

Berlin Tunnel 21 Based on the novel by Donald Lindquist, five American soldiers attempt a daring Cold War rescue of a beautiful German girl. The plan is to construct a tunnel under the Berlin Wall. A better-than-average film that was made for television.
1981 150m/C Richard Thomas, Jose Ferrer, Horst Buchholz; *D:* Richard Michaels. VHS, Beta $59.99 HBO *I*

Bernadette A French-made version of the legend of St. Bernadette, who endured persecution after claiming to have seen the Virgin Mary. Beautiful in its simplicity, but overly long.
1990 120m/C FR Sydney Penny, Roland LeSaffre, Michele Simonnet, Bernard Dheran, Arlette Didier; *D:* Jean Delannoy. VHS, Beta IGP *II 1/2*

Bernard and the Genie It seems Bernard Bottle is not going to have a happy Christmas—he's been fired from his job and his girlfriend has left him. But things take a turn for the better when he discovers an antique lamp and its resident Genie. But with the Genie granting his every wish, Bernard's sudden wealth is causing some suspicions among both his greedy ex-employer and the police. Meanwhile, the Genie discovers the delights of modern-day England and poses as a department store Santa to truly fulfill a child's Christmas wish. Amusing family fare.
199? (G) 70m/C GB Alan Cumming, Lenny Henry, Rowan Atkinson. VHS $59.98 FXV, BTV *II 1/2*

Bernice Bobs Her Hair An ugly and shy girl's cousin revamps her into a seductress. From the director of "Chilly Scenes of Winter," part of the American Short Story Collection. Adaptation of the F. Scott Fitzgerald story.
1976 49m/C Shelley Duvall, Henry Fonda, Veronica Cartwright, Bud Cort; *D:* Joan Micklin Silver. VHS, Beta $24.95 MON, KAR *I*

Berserk! A seedy traveling circus is beset by a series of murders. Not heralded as one of Crawford's best pieces.
1967 95m/C Joan Crawford, Diana Dors, Judy Geeson, Ty Hardin; *D:* James O'Connolly. VHS, Beta $19.95 RCA *I 1/2*

Berserker Six camping college students are attacked by a bloodthirsty psychotic out of a Nordic myth, who takes the shape of a badder-than-the-average bear.
1987 (R) 85m/C Joseph Alan Johnson, Valerie Sheldon, Greg Dawson; *D:* Jef Richard. VHS, Beta $9.99 STE, PSM *I*

Bert Rigby, You're a Fool A starstruck British coal miner finds his way to Hollywood singing old showtunes, only to be rebuffed by a cynical industry. Reiner also

wrote screenplay. Available with Spanish subtitles.
1989 (R) 94m/C Robert Lindsay, Robbie Coltrane, Jackie Gayle, Bruno Kirby, Cathryn Bradshaw, Corbin Bernsen, Anne Bancroft; **D:** Carl Reiner. **VHS, Beta, LV** $19.98 *WAR* �láá½

Besame Intrigue, espionage, and romance get mixed together in this movie.
1987 101m/C Sara Montiel, Maurice Ronet, Franco Fabrizi. **VHS, Beta** $53.95 *MAD* áá

Best Buns on the Beach Sexploitation movie about 10 beautiful girls in a bikini contest, that ends up with them going topless. Ridiculous plot, for mature (??) audiences.
1987 60m/C VHS, LV $29.95 *IME* Woof!

The Best Christmas Pageant Ever The meanest kids in town just decided to participate in the town's Christmas pageant and something special happens when the curtain finally goes up.
1986 60m/C Dennis Weaver, Karen Grassle. **VHS** $19.95 *RHV* Woof!

Best Defense A U.S. Army tank operator is sent to Kuwait to test a new state-of-the-art tank in a combat situation. Although the cast is popular, the movie as a whole is not funny and the story frequently is hard to follow.
1984 (R) 94m/C Dudley Moore, Eddie Murphy, Kate Capshaw, George Dzundza, Helen Shaver; **D:** Willard Huyck. **VHS, Beta, LV** $14.95 *PAR* á

Best Enemies An English film about a man suffering the trials of the 1960s, including Vietnam, and how it affects his relationships with his friends and wife.
1986 96m/C *GB* Sigrid Thornton, Paul Williams, Judy Morris, Brandon Burke; **D:** David Baker. **VHS, Beta** $29.95 *ACA* áá½

Best Foot Forward Vintage musical about a movie star who agrees to accompany a young cadet to a military ball. Based on the popular Broadway show. The film debuts of Walker, Allyson, and DeHaven. ♫ Buckle Down, Winsocki; The Three B's (Barrelhouse, Boogie Woogie, and the Blues); Alive and Kicking; Two O'Clock Jump; Ev'ry Time; Three Men on a Base; Wish I May; Shady Lady; My First Promise; You're Lucky.
1943 95m/C Lucille Ball, June Allyson, Tommy Dix, Nancy Walker, Virginia Weidler, Gloria DeHaven, William Gaxton, Harry James; **D:** Edward Buzzell. **VHS, Beta** $19.98 *MGM* áá½

Best Friends A pair of screenwriters decide to marry after years of living and working together. Story based on the lives of screenwriters Barry Levinson and Valerie Curtin.
1982 (PG) 109m/C Goldie Hawn, Burt Reynolds, Jessica Tandy, Barnard Hughes, Audra Lindley, Keenan Wynn, Ron Silver; **D:** Norman Jewison. **VHS, Beta, LV** $19.98 *WAR* áá

Best Kept Secrets A feisty woman discovers corruption and blackmail in the police department where her husband is an officer.
1988 104m/C Patty Duke, Frederic Forrest, Peter Coyote; **D:** Jerrold Freedman. **VHS, Beta** $79.95 *VMK* áá½

Best Legs in the 8th Grade A handsome attorney bumps into the gorgeous homeroom angel who had ignored his nebbishly dull countenance in grade school. Lightweight made for TV comedy.
1984 60m/C Tim Matheson, James Belushi, Annette O'Toole, Kathryn Harrold; **D:** Tom Patchett. **VHS, Beta** *NO* áá

The Best Little Girl in the World Exceptional made for TV tale of an apparently perfect teenager suffering from anorexia. Slow starvation is her only cry for help. Fine performances from Durning and Saint.
1981 96m/C Charles Durning, Eva Marie Saint, Jennifer Jason Leigh, Melanie Mayron, Viveca Lindfors, Jason Miller, David Spielberg, Lisa Pelikan, Ally Sheedy; **D:** Sam O'Steen. **VHS, Beta** *NO* áá

The Best Little Whorehouse in Texas Parton is the buxom owner of The Chicken Ranch, a house of ill-repute that may be closed down unless Sheriff-boyfriend Reynolds can think of a way out. Strong performances don't quite make up for the erratically comic script. Based on the long-running Broadway musical, in turn based on a story by Larry McMurtry. Available in a letterboxed edition on laserdisc.
1982 (R) 115m/C Dolly Parton, Burt Reynolds, Dom DeLuise, Charles Durning, Jim Nabors, Lois Nettleton; **D:** Colin Higgins. **VHS, Beta, LV** $19.95 *MCA, FCT, PIA* áá

The Best Man An incisive, darkly satiric political tract, based on Gore Vidal's play, about two presidential contenders who vie for the endorsement of the aging ex-president, and trample political ethics in the process.
1964 104m/B Henry Fonda, Cliff Robertson, Lee Tracy, Margaret Leighton, Edie Adams, Kevin McCarthy, Ann Sothern, Gene Raymond, Shelley Berman, Mahalia Jackson; **D:** Franklin J. Schaffner; **W:** Gore Vidal. **VHS, Beta** $19.98 *MGM* ááá½

The Best of Abbott & Costello Live A compilation of vintage live-television routines by the duo, naturally including "Who's on First," along with their other celebrated bits.
1954 58m/B Bud Abbott, Lou Costello, George Raft, Charles Laughton. **VHS, Beta** $19.88 *WAR* ááá½

Best of Betty Boop A collection of nine Boop classics, including the immortal "Betty Boop's Ker-choo."
1935 56m/B D: Dave Fleischer; **V:** Mae Questel. **VHS, Beta, 8mm** $29.95 *VYY, WTA* ááá½

Best of Betty Boop, Vol. 1 Sweet Betty Boop sashays through 11 of her classic cartoon adventures in this collection of original shorts. Mastered from the original negatives.
1939 90m/C V: Mae Questel. **VHS** $14.98 *REP, WTA* ááá½

Best of Betty Boop, Vol. 2 Another collection of original cartoons starring the "Boop-Oop-a-Doop" girl, assisted by Bimbo and Koko the Clown. These black-and-white cartoons have been recolored for this release.
1939 85m/C V: Mae Questel. **VHS, Beta** $14.98 *REP, WTA* ááá½

The Best of Bogart A two-cassette gift pack of the Bogie classics "The Maltese Falcon" and "Casablanca."
1943 204m/B Humphrey Bogart, Ingrid Bergman, Mary Astor, Sydney Greenstreet. **VHS, Beta** $39.95 *MGM* ááá

Best of Bugs Bunny & Friends This collection includes classics from great cartoon stars Bugs Bunny, Daffy Duck, Tweetie Pie and Porky Pig. Includes "Duck Soup to Nuts," "A Feud There Was" and "Tweetie Pie."
1940 53m/C D: Friz Freleng, Friz Freleng, Chuck Jones, Robert McKimson. **VHS, Beta** *MGM* ááá

The Best of Chaplin Three Chaplin comedies when he worked with Mutual. Includes "The Rink," "One A.M.," and "The Floorwalker."
1918 60m/B Charlie Chaplin; **D:** Charlie Chaplin. **VHS** $59.95 *MVC, VRS* ááá

Best of Chevy Chase A compilation of Chase's funniest skits and routines from the first season of "Saturday Night Live," including the Land Shark and Chase's Gerald Ford impersonation.
1987 60m/C Chevy Chase, John Belushi, Dan Aykroyd, Bill Murray, Laraine Newman, Gilda Radner, Jane Curtin, Garrett Morris, Richard Pryor, Candice Bergen, Jill Clayburgh. **Beta, LV, Q** $19.98 *LHV, WAR* áá½

Best of Comic Relief All-star comedic array of stand-up acts was taped "live" in concert to raise money for America's homeless and released on cable television.
1986 120m/C Whoopi Goldberg, Robin Williams, Billy Crystal, Carl Reiner, Harold Ramis, Martin Short, Jerry Lewis, Howie Mandel, Eugene Levy, Steve Allen, Doc Severinsen, Sid Caesar, John Candy, George Carlin. **VHS, Beta, LV** $39.95 *LHV, WAR* áá½

Best of Comic Relief '90 More than 40 stars make this two hours a real treat, and the hosts aren't so bad themselves: Whoopi Goldberg, Billy Crystal and Robin Williams. Proceeds from this event, and subsequent tape sales go to Comic Relief, Inc. to benefit the homeless in America. Stars include: Bobcat Goldthwait, Elayne Boosler, George Carlin, Louis Anderson, Dennis Miller, The Simpsons.
1990 120m/C Performed by: Bob Goldthwait, Elayne Boosler, George Carlin, Louie Anderson, Dennis Miller. **VHS, Beta** $29.95 *RHI* áá½

Best of Dan Aykroyd A collection of Aykroyd's funniest skits and characters from his five-year stint on "Saturday Night Live," including the Bass-O-Matic Salesman, Irwin Mainway, Julia Child, E. Buzz Miller, the Coneheads, Leonard Pinth-Garnell, and the Czechoslovakian Brothers.
1986 57m/C Dan Aykroyd, John Belushi, Laraine Newman, Chevy Chase, Steve Martin, Bill Murray, Jane Curtin, Madeline Kahn, Shelley Duvall, Gilda Radner. **VHS, Beta** $19.98 *WAR* áá½

Best of Eddie Murphy A compilation of Murphy's funniest bits from his three seasons of "Saturday Night Live," including appearances as Stevie Wonder, Buckwheat, Bill Cosby and Little Richard.
1989 78m/C Eddie Murphy, Joe Piscopo, Robin Duke, Tim Kazurinsky, Mary Gross, Gary Kroeger, Brad Hall, Julia Louis-Dreyfus. **VHS, Beta** $14.95 *PAR* áá½

Best of Ernie Kovacs A compilation of some of the best moments from Ernie Kovacs' television programs that features such memorable characters as Percy Dovetonsils and the Nairobi Trio.
1956 60m/B Ernie Kovacs, Edie Adams, Ernie Hatrak, Bill Wendell, Peter Hanley. **VHS, Beta** $19.95 *WST, DVT, TVC* áá

Best of George Pal George Pal's "Puppetoon" series produced between 1938 and 1943 is highlighted. Black and white selections include "Sleeping Beauty," "Captain Kidding," "Cavalcade of Music," and "Sky Pirates." In color are "Ship of the Ether," "Phillips Broadcast of 1938," "Tubby the Tuba," "John Henry," "The Little Broadcast," "Jasper in a Jam," and "Jasper in the Haunted House."
1979 75m/C VHS, Beta $19.95 *VDM* ááá

Best of Gilda Radner A posthumously released collection of skits featuring the comedienne from "Saturday Night Live," including appearances as RoseAnn Rosannadanna, Lisa Lupner, Baba Wawa and more.
1989 59m/C Gilda Radner, Dan Aykroyd, John Belushi, Chevy Chase, Jane Curtin, Bill Murray, Garrett Morris, Laraine Newman, Madeline Kahn, Buck Henry, Steve Martin, Candice Bergen. **VHS, Beta $19.98** *WAR* ♪♪♪

Best of John Belushi Compilation of sixteen of John Belushi's funniest "Saturday Night Live" routines including "Samurai Deli," "Godfather Therapy" and "Star Trek."
1985 60m/C John Belushi, Dan Aykroyd, Chevy Chase, Jane Curtin, Rob Reiner, Laraine Newman, Bill Murray, Garrett Morris, Gilda Radner, Elliott Gould, Buck Henry, Robert Klein. **VHS, Beta $19.98** *WAR* ♪♪♪

The Best of John Candy on SCTV Some of Candy's most memorable characters, including Johnny LaRue, Yosh Schmenge, and the grown up Theodore "Beaver" Cleaver, are featured on this compilation of his years on SCTV (Second City Television).
198? 62m/C John Candy, Eugene Levy, Rick Moranis, Catherine O'Hara, Harold Ramis, Martin Short. **VHS, LV $39.95** *COL* ♪♪♪

The Best of Little Lulu Mischief-prone Little Lulu returns in this special collection of cartoon adventures.
19?? 60m/C VHS $19.95 *REP, WTA* ♪♪♪

The Best of Mister Magoo Four of Mister Magoo's most hilarious misadventures, entitled "Bearfooted Flat Foot," "Bungled Bungalow," "Bwana Magoo," and "Destination Magoo."
195? 27m/C VHS, Beta $9.98 *GKK* ♪♪♪

Best of Popeye Eight classic Popeye cartoons are included in this compilation.
1983 56m/C VHS, Beta $29.95 *MGM* ♪♪♪

Best of Terrytoons This is a compilation of cartoons featuring Mighty Mouse, Heckle and Jeckle, Deputy Dawg, Gandy Goose, Dinky Duck, Terry Bears and Little Roquefort.
1983 60m/C VHS, Beta *NO* ♪♪½

Best of the Badmen A whole bunch of outlaws, although seemingly quite nice, are brought together by an ex-Union general who is being framed. Too much talk, not enough action.
1950 84m/B Robert Ryan, Claire Trevor, Jack Buetel, Robert Preston, Walter Brennan, Bruce Cabot, John Archer, Lawrence Tierney; *D:* William D. Russell. **VHS, Beta $19.98** *TTC* ♪♪½

Best of the Best An interracial kickboxing team strives to win a world championship.
1989 (PG-13) 95m/C Eric Roberts, Sally Kirkland, Christopher Penn, Phillip Rhee, James Earl Jones, John P. Ryan, John Dye, David Agresta, Tom Everett, Louise Fletcher, Simon Rhee; *D:* Bob Radler. **VHS, Beta, LV $14.95** *COL, SVS* ♪♪½

Best of the Best 2 Tommy and Alex are coaching Alex's son Walter for a karate tournament when they hear that their friend Travis is about to fight at the Coliseum, a notorious venue owned by the champion fighter Brackus and his manager Weldon. Walter sneaks in to see the match only to watch Travis killed in the no-rules martial-arts battle. When he tells his father and Tommy they set out to avenge their friend's death with Tommy ultimately challenging Brackus in a death match.

1993 (R) 100m/C Eric Roberts, Phillip Rhee, Christopher Penn, Ralph Moeller, Wayne Newton, Edan Gross, Sonny Landham, Meg Foster, Simon Rhee; *D:* Bob Radler; *W:* John Allen Nelson, Max Strom. **VHS, LV $94.98** *FXV* ♪♪½

The Best of the Kenny Everett Video Show Scenes from the popular British late-night television show combining new wave rock music, outrageous dancing and innovative video special effects.
1981 104m/C Kenny Everett. **VHS, Beta $29.98** *HBO* ♪♪½

The Best of the Kids in the Hall Features some of the best clips of the hot Canadian comedy ensemble "The Kids in the Hall." Executive producer Lorne Michaels is best known for producing "Saturday Night Live."
1993 120m/C *CA* Dave Foley, Bruce McCulloch, Kevin McDonald, Mark McKinney, Scott Thompson. **VHS $59.95** *COL* ♪♪½

The Best of the Monsters The Canadian comedy team offers a televised look at movie monsters. There is also plenty of political humor mixed in, which might be difficult or elusive for Americans.
196? 45m/B *CA* Wayne & Shuster. **VHS, Beta $24.95** *NOS, DVT* ♪♪½

The Best of the Two Ronnies A selection of skits from the well-loved BBC comedy series.
1977 45m/C *GB* Ronnie Barker, Ronnie Corbett. **VHS, Beta $14.98** *FOX* ♪♪½

The Best of Times Slim story of two grown men who attempt to redress the failures of the past by reenacting a football game they lost in high school due to a single flubbed pass. With this cast, it should have been better.
1986 (PG) 105m/C Robin Williams, Kurt Russell, M. Emmet Walsh, Pamela Reed, Holly Palance, Donald Moffatt, Margaret Whitton, Kirk Cameron; *D:* Roger Spottiswoode; *W:* Ron Shelton. **VHS, Beta, LV, 8mm $14.98** *SUE, NLC* ♪♪

The Best of Warner Brothers, Vol. 1 Classic cartoons from the Warner Brothers archives featuring Porky Pig, Daffy Duck, Bugs Bunny and the gang. Titles include: "Get Rich Quick," "Robinson Crusoe, Jr.," "Porky's Railroad," "Porky's Preview," "I Wanna Be a Sailor," "An Itch in Time," and "Corny Concerto." (Some black and white).
194? 55m/C *D:* Friz Freleng, Chuck Jones, Robert McKimson. **VHS, Beta $19.95** *NO* ♪♪

The Best of Warner Brothers, Vol. 2 A collection of eight vintage Warner Brothers cartoons featuring Daffy Duck and Porky Pig, all from 1936-1942.
193? 55m/C *D:* Friz Freleng, Chuck Jones, Robert McKimson; *V:* Mel Blanc. **VHS, Beta** *NO* ♪♪

Best of W.C. Fields Three of W.C. Field's Mack Sennett shorts are presented in their complete, uncut form: "The Dentist," "The Fatal Glass of Beer," and "The Golf Specialist."
1933 58m/B W.C. Fields, Elise Cavanna. **VHS $19.95** *REP* ♪♪

Best Revenge Two aging hippies engage in a Moroccan drug deal in order to free a kidnapped friend from a sleazy gangster. They get caught by the police, but escape, searching for the engineers of the frame-up.
1983 (R) 92m/C John Heard, Levon Helm, Alberta Watson, John Rhys-Davies, Moses Znaimer; *D:* John Trent. **VHS, Beta $59.95** *LHV, WAR* ♪♪

Best Seller An interesting, subtext-laden thriller about a cop/bestselling author with writer's block, and the strange symbiotic relationship he forms with a slick hired killer, who wants his own story written. Dennehy is convincing as the jaded cop, and is paired well with the psychotic Woods.
1987 (R) 112m/C James Woods, Brian Dennehy, Victoria Tennant, Paul Shenar, Seymour Cassel, Allison Balson; *D:* John Flynn; *W:* Larry Cohen. **VHS, Beta, LV $14.98** *VES* ♪♪♪

The Best Way Two summer camp counselors discover they might be gay and desirous of each other. Miller's first film; in French with English subtitles.
1982 85m/C *FR* Patrick Dewaere, Patrick Bouchitey, Christine Pascal, Claude Pieplu; *D:* Claude Miller. **VHS, Beta $79.95** *FCT* ♪♪½

The Best Years of Our Lives Three World War II vets return home to try to pick up the threads of their lives. A film that represented a large chunk of American society and helped it readjust to the modern post-war ambience is now considered an American classic. Supporting actor Russell, an actual veteran, holds a record for winning two Oscars for a single role. In addition to his Best Supporting Actor award, Russell was given a special Oscar for bringing home and courage to fellow veterans. Based on the novella by MacKinley Kantor. Remade for television as "Returning Home" in 1975.
1946 170m/B Fredric March, Myrna Loy, Teresa Wright, Dana Andrews, Virginia Mayo, Harold Russell, Hoagy Carmichael, Gladys George, Roman Bohnen, Steve Cochran; *D:* William Wyler; *W:* Robert Sherwood; *M:* Hugo Friedhofer. Academy Awards '46: Best Actor (March), Best Director (Wyler), Best Film Editing, Best Picture, Best Screenplay, Best Supporting Actor (Russell), Best Original Score; Nominations: Best Sound; British Academy Awards '47: Best Film; Golden Globe Awards '47: Best Film—Drama; National Board of Review Awards '46: 10 Best Films of the Year, Best Director (Wyler). **VHS, Beta, LV $14.98** *HBO, SUE, FCT* ♪♪♪♪

Bestia Nocturna A psychopath stalks the freeways, mutilating his victims. He is hunted by one man, who relies on his wits to hunt the madman.
1986 93m/C *SP* Raymundo Capetillo, Laura Flores, Eric Del Castillo, Roberto Canedo; *D:* Humberto Martinez Mijares. **VHS, Beta $79.95** *MED, PMS* ♪

Bethune The life story of a Canadian doctor who started a practice in Communist China.
1977 88m/C Donald Sutherland, Kate Nelligan, David Gardner, James Hong; *D:* Eric Till. **VHS, Beta $59.95** *TWE* ♪♪½

Betrayal Psycho-thriller pits an unhappy widow against her seemingly innocent hired companion. Seems this girl has a boyfriend who has a plan to murder the lonely lady for her money. Routine and predictable.
1974 78m/C Amanda Blake, Dick Haymes, Tisha Sterling, Sam Groom; *D:* Gordon Hessler. **VHS $79.95** *JEF* ♪

Betrayal Telefilm based on the book by Lucy Freeman and Julie Roy about a historic malpractice case involving a psychiatrist and one of his female patients. The doctor convinced the female patient that sex with him would serve as therapy.
1978 95m/C Lesley Ann Warren, Rip Torn, Ron Silver, Richard Masur, Stephen Elliott, John Hillerman, Peggy Ann Garner; *D:* Paul Wendkos. **VHS, Beta** *NO* ♪♪½

Betrayal An unusual adult drama, beginning at the end of a seven-year adulterous affair and working its way back in time to finally end at the start of the betrayal of a

husband by his wife and his best friend. Kingsley and Irons make Pinter's adaptation of his own play work.
1983 (R) 95m/C *GB* Ben Kingsley, Patricia Hodge, Jeremy Irons; *D:* David Jones; *W:* Harold Pinter. VHS, Beta $59.98 *FOX* ♫♫½

Betrayal and Revenge The story of the "Monkey King," a Kung Fu warrior determined to avenge his father's murder.
1989 104m/C VHS, Beta *NO* ♫

Betrayal from the East A carnival barker saves the Panama Canal from the vicious Japanese war machine in this rather silly wartime drama.
1944 82m/B Lee Tracy, Nancy Kelly, Richard Loo, Abner Biberman, Regis Toomey, Philip Ahn, Addison Richards, Sen Yung, Drew Pearson; *D:* William Berke. VHS, Beta $19.98 *TTC* ♫♫

Betrayal of the Dove Slater stars as a divorced woman set-up on a blind date by best friend Le Brock. Zane is the dashing doctor who sweeps Slater off her feet but things are never quite what they seem. He may not be Mr. Right and the best friend has her own hidden agenda.
1992 (R) 93m/C Helen Slater, Kelly Le Brock, Billy Zane, Alan Thicke, Harvey Korman, Stuart Pankin, David Lander; *D:* Strathford Hamilton; *W:* Robby Benson. VHS $89.95 *PSM* ♫♫

Betrayed Bombshell Turner and strongman Gable star in this story of World War II intrigue. Suspected of being a Nazi informer, Turner is sent back to Holland for a last chance at redemption. Her cover as a sultry nightclub performer has the Nazis drooling and ogling (can you spell h-o-t?), but her act may be blown by an informant. Can luscious Lana get out of this one intact?
1954 107m/C Clark Gable, Lana Turner, Victor Mature, Louis Calhern, O.E. Hasse, Wilfrid Hyde-White, Ian Carmichael, Niall MacGinnis, Nora Swinburne, Roland Culver; *D:* Gottfried Reinhardt. VHS, Beta $19.98 *MGM, CCB* ♫♫♫

Betrayed A rabid political film, dealing with an implausible FBI agent infiltrating a white supremacist organization via her love affair with a handsome farmer who turns out to be a murderous racist. Winger is memorable in her role as the FBI agent, despite the film's limitations, and admirers of Costa-Gavras's directorial work and political stances will want to see how the director botched this one.
1988 (R) 112m/C Tom Berenger, Debra Winger, John Mahoney, John Heard, Albert Hall; *D:* Constantin Costa-Gavras; *W:* Joe Eszterhas. VHS, Beta, LV $14.95 *MGM* ♫♫

A Betrayed Man Extremely rare 30's independent film.
1936 ?m/C John Hughes, Smiley Burnette. VHS $15.95 *LOO* ♫♫

The Betsy A story of romance, money, power, and mystery centering around the wealthy Hardeman family and their automobile manufacturing business. Loosely patterned after the life of Henry Ford as portrayed in the Harold Robbins' pulp-tome. Olivier is the redeeming feature. *AKA:* Harold Robbins' The Betsy.
1978 (R) 132m/C Laurence Olivier, Kathleen Beller, Robert Duvall, Lesley-Anne Down, Edward Herrmann, Tommy Lee Jones, Katharine Ross, Jane Alexander; *D:* Daniel Petrie; *M:* John Barry. VHS, Beta $59.98 *FOX* ♫♫

Betsy's Wedding Betsy wants a simple wedding. But her father has other, grander ideas. Then there's the problem of paying for it. Dad tries to take care of that in a not-so-typical manner. Will Betsy make it down the aisle? Watch a fine ensemble cast to find out.

1990 (R) 94m/C Molly Ringwald, Alan Alda, Joey Bishop, Madeline Kahn, Catherine O'Hara, Joe Pesci, Ally Sheedy, Burt Young, Anthony LaPaglia; *W/D:* Alan Alda. VHS, Beta, LV $89.95 *TOU* ♫♫½

Better Late Than Never Fun television tale of senior citizens in revolt at an old-age home. Fine characters portrayed by some of the best in the business.
1979 100m/C Harold Gould, Tyne Daly, Strother Martin, Harry Morgan, Victor Buono, George Gobel, Lou Jacobi, Donald Pleasence, Larry Storch; *D:* Richard Crenna. VHS $59.98 *FOX* ♫♫

Better Late Than Never Two penniless old fools vie for the acceptance of a bratty 10-year-old millionairess, who must choose one as her guardian. Niven's last film.
1983 95m/C David Niven, Art Carney, Maggie Smith, Kimberly Partridge, Catherine Hicks, Melissa Prophet; *D:* Bryan Forbes. VHS, Beta $59.98 *FOX* ♫½

Better Off Dead A compulsive teenager's girlfriend leaves him and he decides to end it all. After several abortive attempts, he decides instead to out-ski his ex-girlfriend's obnoxious new boyfriend. Uneven but funny.
1985 (PG) 97m/C John Cusack, Curtis Armstrong, Diane Franklin, Kim Darby, David Ogden Stiers, Dan Schneider, Amanda Wyss, Taylor Negron; *D:* Steve Holland. VHS, Beta, LV $79.98 *FOX* ♫♫½

Betty Blue A vivid, intensely erotic film about two young French lovers and how their inordinately strong passion for each other destroys them, leading to poverty, violence, and insanity. English subtitles. From the director of "Diva."
1986 (R) 121m/C *FR* Beatrice Dalle, Jean-Hughes Anglade, Gerard Darmon; *D:* Jean-Jacques Beineix. VHS, Beta, LV $79.98 *FOX, TAM* ♫♫♫

Betty Boop Cartoons featuring Betty Boop, Daffy Duck and others are featured here. The titles are "The Hot Air Salesman," "Case of the Missing Hare," "There's Good Boos Tonight," and "Yankee Doodle Daffy."
193? 30m/C *V:* Mae Questel, Mel Blanc. VHS, LV *NEG* ♫♫♫

Betty Boop Cartoon Festival Fleischer produced and directed these cartoons of the 1930s including such titles as "Baby Be Good," "Betty Boop with Grampy," "Betty Boop with Henry," "Candid Candidate," "Ding Dong Doggie," and "Kerchoo." Questel provides the voice of the popular flapper.
193? 55m/B *D:* Max Fleischer; *V:* Mae Questel. VHS, Beta $34.98 *HHT, DVT* ♫♫♫

Betty Boop Classics A compilation of Betty Boop and her cartoon pals most fun-filled escapades.
1939 60m/C *V:* Mae Questel. VHS $19.98 *REP, WTA* ♫♫♫

Betty Boop Festival, Vol. 1 An hour of classic Betty Boop cartoons featuring "Is My Palm Red," "Betty's Rise to Fame," "So Does an Automobile," "SOS," "Making Friends," and more.
193? 60m/B *D:* Max Fleischer; *V:* Mae Questel. VHS, Beta $19.98 *NQ* ♫♫♫

Betty Boop Festival, Vol. 2 A compilation of classic Betty Boop cartoons, including "Baby Be Good," "A Little Soap and Water," "Kerchoo," "Be Human," "Not Now," "Betty and Jimmy," "Betty in Blunderland," and "Crazy Town."
193? 55m/B *D:* Max Fleischer; *V:* Mae Questel. VHS, Beta $19.98 *NO* ♫♫

Betty Boop Festival, Vol. 3 Nine cartoons of the ageless gal with the great voice: "Happy You and Merry Me," "No, No, A Thousand Times No," "My Friend the Monkey," "A Song a Day," "Training Pigeons," "Scared Crows," "Whoop's, I'm a Cowboy," "Musical Mountaineers," and "We Did It."
193? 60m/B *D:* Max Fleischer; *V:* Mae Questel. VHS, Beta $19.95 *NO* ♫♫♫

Betty Boop Program A compilation of five Betty Boop cartoons of the 1930s: "Betty in Blunderland," "Betty and the Little King," "Betty Boop with Henry," "Betty and Little Jimmy," and "Candid Candidate."
193? 50m/B *D:* Max Fleischer; *V:* Mae Questel. VHS, Beta *GVV* ♫♫♫

Betty Boop Special Collector's Edition, Vol. 1 Betty Boop returns in this collection of vintage cartoons, presented in their original black-and-white form, with appearances by jazz stars Cab Calloway and Don Redman.
1935 90m/B *D:* Dave Fleischer, Max Fleischer; *V:* Louis Armstrong, Mae Questel. VHS, LV $19.98 *REP, WTA* ♫♫♫

Betty Boop Special Collector's Edition, Vol. 2 That boop-a-doop girl is back in this collection of classic cartoons that features Cab Calloway and his orchestra.
1937 90m/B *V:* Mae Questel. VHS, LV $19.98 *REP, WTA* ♫♫♫

Between Fighting Men The orphaned daughter of a shepherd is adopted by the cowpoke who caused her father's death. The cowpoke's sons fall in love with, and compete for, the love of the girl.
1932 62m/B Ken Maynard, Ruth Hall, Josephine Dunn, Wallace MacDonald; *D:* Forrest Sheldon. VHS $19.95 *NOS, DVT* ♫½

Between Friends Two women with only their respective divorces in common, meet and become fast friends. The rapport between Burnett and Taylor makes for a touching drama. Adapted for cable television from the book "Nobody Makes Me Cry," by Shelley List, one of the producers.
1983 105m/C Elizabeth Taylor, Carol Burnett; *D:* Lou Antonio. VHS, Beta $69.95 *VES* ♫♫½

Between God, the Devil & a Winchester Violent western with plenty of shooting and dust. Lots of cowboys are hot on the trail of some stolen loot from a church but apparently God isn't on their side since the majority bite the dust and become a snack for the vultures.
1972 98m/C Gilbert Roland, Richard Harrison; *D:* Dario Silvester. VHS, Beta $49.95 *UNI* ♫

Between Heaven and Hell Prejudiced Southern gentleman Wagner finds how wrong his misconceptions are, as he attempts to survive WWII on a Pacific Island. Ebsen is exceptional, making this rather simplistic story a meaningful classic.
1956 94m/C Robert Wagner, Terry Moore, Broderick Crawford, Buddy Ebsen, Robert Keith, Brad Dexter, Mark Damon, Kenneth Clark, Harvey Lembeck, Frank Gorshin, Scatman Crothers; *D:* Richard Fleischer. VHS $14.98 *FXV* ♫♫♫

Between Men A father kills a man he believes killed his son and flees. Later in life, the son meets his father. For father and son, this causes some major concern.
1935 59m/B Johnny Mack Brown, Beth Marion, William Farnum; *D:* Robert North Bradbury. VHS, Beta $19.95 *NOS, DVT* ♫♫

Between the Lines A witty, wonderfully realized ensemble comedy about the staff of a radical post-'60s newspaper always on the brink of folding, and its eventual sell-out.
1977 (R) 101m/C John Heard, Lindsay Crouse, Jeff Goldblum, Jill Eikenberry, Stephen Collins, Lewis J. Stadlen, Michael J. Pollard, Marilu Henner; *D:* Joan Micklin Silver. **VHS, Beta** $69.95 *VES* ✍✍✍½

Between Two Women A television movie about a wife's rocky relationship with her bossy mother-in-law, until the latter has a stroke and needs care. Dewhurst won an Emmy for her portrayal of the mother-in-law.
1986 95m/C Farrah Fawcett, Michael Nouri, Colleen Dewhurst, Steven Hill, Bridgette Anderson, Danny Corkill; *D:* Willis Goldbeck. **VHS, Beta** $19.98 *WAR* ✍✍

Between Wars Young doctor in Australia's Medical Corps encounters conflict when he tries to introduce Freud's principles into his work.
1974 97m/C AU Corin Redgrave, Arthur Dignam, Judy Morris, Patricia Leehy, Gunter Meisner; *D:* Michael Thornhill. **VHS, Beta** $19.98 *VID* ✍✍

Beulah Land A television mini-series about 45 years in the lives of a Southern family, including the Civil War. Based on the novels "Beulah Land" and "Look Away, Beulah Land" by Lonnie Coleman.
1980 267m/C Lesley Ann Warren, Michael Sarrazin, Don Johnson, Meredith Baxter Birney, Dorian Harewood, Eddie Albert, Hope Lange, Paul Rudd; *D:* Virgil W. Vogel, Harry Falk. **VHS, Beta, LV** $29.95 *COL, TVC* ✍½

The Beverly Hillbillies The successful sitcom series, which ran from 1962-1971, features Jed Clampett and his Ozark clan striking oil, getting rich, and heading for the good life in California. Two episodes per tape.
1962 51m/B Buddy Ebsen, Irene Ryan, Donna Douglas, Max Baer, Nancy Kulp, Raymond Bailey, Phil Silvers; *Cameos:* John Wayne. **VHS** $12.98 *FXV, MOV* ✍½

Beverly Hills Bodysnatchers A mad scientist and a greedy mortician plot to get rich, but their plan backfires when they bring a Mafia godfather back to life and he terrorizes Beverly Hills.
1989 (R) 85m/C Vic Tayback, Frank Gorshin, Brooke Bundy, Seth Jaffe, Art Metrano; *D:* Jon Mostow. **VHS, LV** $39.95 *IME* ✍½

Beverly Hills Brats A spoiled, rich Hollywood brat hires a loser to kidnap him, in order to gain his parents' attention, only to have both of them kidnapped by real crooks.
1989 (PG-13) 90m/C Martin Sheen, Burt Young, Peter Billingsley, Terry Moore; *D:* Dimitri Sotirakis. **VHS, Beta, LV** $89.95 *LIV, IME* ✍

Beverly Hills Call Girls This racy picture deals with prostitutes in Beverly Hills and their "respectable" clients.
1986 60m/C **VHS, Beta** $24.95 *AHV* Woof!

Beverly Hills Cop When a close friend of smooth-talking Detroit cop Axle Foley is brutally murdered in L.A., he traces the murderer to the posh streets of Beverly Hills. There he must stay on his toes to keep one step ahead of the killer and two steps ahead of the law. Better than average Murphy vehicle.
1984 (R) 105m/C Eddie Murphy, Judge Reinhold, John Ashton, Lisa Eilbacher, Ronny Cox, Steven Berkoff, James Russo, Jonathan Banks, Stephen Elliott, Bronson Pinchot, Paul Reiser, Damon Wayans, Rick Overton; *D:* Martin Brest. Academy Awards '84 Nominations: Best Original Screenplay; People's Choice Awards '85: Best Film. **VHS, Beta, LV, 8mm** $14.95 *PAR* ✍✍½

Beverly Hills Cop 2 The highly successful sequel to the first profitable comedy, with essentially the same plot, this time deals with Foley infiltrating a band of international munitions smugglers.
1987 (R) 103m/C Eddie Murphy, Judge Reinhold, Juergen Prochnow, Ronny Cox, John Ashton, Brigitte Nielsen, Allen Garfield, Paul Reiser, Dean Stockwell; *D:* Tony Scott. **VHS, Beta, LV, 8mm** $14.95 *PAR* ✍½

Beverly Hills Knockouts A bevy of beautiful boxers pummel each other with both fists.
1989 60m/C **VHS, Beta** $39.95 *CEL* ✍½

Beverly Hills Madam In this routine plot, a stable of elite call girls struggle with their lifestyle and their madam, played by Dunaway. Made for television.
1986 (PG-13) 97m/C Faye Dunaway, Louis Jourdan, Donna Dixon, Robin Givens, Marshall Colt, Melody Anderson, Terry Farrell; *D:* Harvey Hart. **VHS, Beta, LV** $79.98 *ORI* ✍

Beverly Hills 90210 In the pilot episode for the immensely popular series, the world is introduced to the exciting teens who wander the halls of West Beverly High. Join Brandon and Brenda Walsh as they move from Minneapolis to Beverly Hills and experience all the trials and tribulations that come with the new zip code. Includes 25 minutes of previously unseen footage.
1990 90m/C Jason Priestly, Shannen Doherty, Luke Perry, Jennie Garth, Brian Austin Green, Tori Spelling, Ian Ziering, Gabrielle Carteris. **VHS, LV** $19.99 *WOV, MOV* ✍

Beverly Hills 90210: The Graduation The 1993 end-of-the-season episode of the hit tv series finds the group finally getting out of Beverly Hills High. As they graduate the friends share plans for the summer (and the future) and you'll see lots of flashbacks as well as their final graduation prank. Includes interviews with the cast and music videos from the series soundtrack.
1993 90m/C Jason Priestly, Shannen Doherty, Luke Perry, Jennie Garth, Brian Austin Green, Tori Spelling, Ian Ziering, Gabrielle Carteris. **VHS** $14.98 *WOV* ✍

Beverly Hills Vamp A madame and her girls are really female vampires with a penchant for hot-blooded men.
1988 (R) 88m/C Britt Ekland, Eddie Deezen, Debra Lamb; *D:* Fred Olen Ray. **VHS, Beta** $79.95 *VMK* ✍

Beware A black singer saves a college from bankruptcy and makes off with the gym teacher. The photography may be a bit harsh, but the all-black cast made this a pioneering but impressive film.
1946 64m/B Louis Jordan, Frank Wilson, Emory Richardson, Valerie Black, Milton Woods; *D:* Bud Pollard. **VHS** $24.95 *NOS, RXM, TIM* ✍½

Beware, My Lovely Taut chiller. Lonely widow Lupino hires a new handy-man. He's great with screen doors and storm windows, but has a problem with sharp tools. Intense and gripping with fine performances.
1952 77m/B Ida Lupino, Robert Ryan, Taylor Holmes, O.Z. Whitehead, Barbara Whiting, Dee Pollock; *D:* Harry Horner. **VHS, LV** $19.98 *REP* ✍✍½

Beware of Pity A crippled baroness thinks she's found true love with a military officer, but it turns out his marriage proposal grew out of pity for her, not passion. A quality but somber British-made historical drama, based on a novel by Stefan Zweig.
1946 105m/B Lilli Palmer, Albert Lieven, Cedric Hardwicke, Gladys Cooper, Ernest Thesiger, Freda Jackson; *D:* Maurice Elvey. **VHS** $19.95 *NOS* ✍✍½

Bewitched A made-for-British-television horror story about an elderly couple ostensibly plagued by the witch-like conniving of a dead woman.
1985 60m/C GB Eileen Atkins, Alfred Lynch; *D:* Edmund Oboler. **VHS, Beta** $59.95 *PSM* ✍✍½

Beyond a Reasonable Doubt In order to get a behind-the-scenes glimpse at the judicial system, a man plays the guilty party to a murder. Alas, when he tries to vindicate himself, he is the victim of his own folly. Not as interesting as it sounds on paper.
1956 80m/B Dana Andrews, Joan Fontaine, Sidney Blackmer, Philip Bourneuf, Barbara Nichols, Sheppard Strudwick, Arthur Franz, Edward Binns; *D:* Fritz Lang. **VHS** $69.95 *VID* ✍✍

Beyond Atlantis An ancient underwater tribe is discovered when it kidnaps landlubbin' women with which to mate.
1973 (PG) 91m/C PH John Ashley, Patrick Wayne, George Nader; *D:* Eddie Romero. **VHS, Beta** $49.95 *UHV* Woof!

Beyond Darkness When Peter and his family move into their New England home they are immediately beset by some unknown terror. With the help of Father George, Peter learns his house was built upon the graves of twenty witches burned for heresy. The witches have decided to seek revenge by kidnapping Peter's young son and sacrificing him to an evil demon. Can Peter destroy the evil spirits before they destroy his son?
1992 (R) 111m/C Gene Le Brock, David Brandon, Barbara Bingham, Michael Stephenson, Stephen Brown; *D:* Clyde Anderson. **VHS** $89.95 *IMP* ✍½

Beyond Dream's Door A young, All-American college student's childhood nightmares come back to haunt him, making dreams a horrifying reality.
1988 86m/C Nick Baldasare, Rick Kesler, Susan Pinsky, Norm Singer; *D:* Jay Woelfel. **VHS, Beta** $29.98 *VID* ✍

Beyond Erotica After being cut out of his father's will, a sadistic young man takes out his rage on his mother and a peasant girl.
1979 90m/C David Hemmings, Alida Valli, Andrea Rau. **VHS** $59.95 *PSM* ✍

Beyond Evil Relatively dimwitted newlywed couple moves into an old island mansion despite rumors that the house is haunted. Sure enough, wife George becomes possessed by the vengeful spirit of a woman murdered 200 years earlier, and a reign of pointless terror begins. Poor rip-off of hybrid Amityville/Exorcist paranormality. Written by Freed and Paul Ross with music by Pino Donaggio ("Carrie").
1980 (R) 98m/C John Saxon, Lynda Day George, Michael Dante, Mario Milano; *D:* Herb Freed. **VHS, Beta** $49.95 *MED* Woof!

Beyond Fear Compelling drama about a man forced to aid a gang in robbery while they hold his wife and son captive.
1975 92m/C Michael Boquet. **VHS, Beta** $49.95 *PSM* ✍✍½

Beyond Innocence A 17-year-old lusts after a mature married woman. Ostensibly based on Raymond Radiguet's "Devil in the Flesh."
1987 87m/C Keith Smith, Katia Caballero, John Morris; *D:* Scott Murray. **VHS, Beta** $79.95 *SVS* ✍

Beyond Justice High action-adventure with the prolific Hauer starring as an ex-CIA agent who is hired to rescue the kidnapped son of a beautiful executive.

1992 (PG-13) 113m/C Rutger Hauer, Carol Alt, Omar Sharif, Elliott Gould. **VHS, LV** *VMK* 𝄫𝄫

Beyond Obsession The strange relationship between a political prisioner, his daughter, and her obsession with a mysterious American is provocatively explored.
1982 116m/C *IT* Marcello Mastroianni, Elenora Giorgi, Tom Berenger, Michel Piccoli; *D:* Liliana Cavani. **VHS $19.95** *FCT* 𝄫𝄫

Beyond Obsession A melodramatic love triangle between an Italian ex-diplomat imprisoned in North Africa, a tempestuous young girl, and a lustful American.
1989 (R) 116m/C *IT* Marcello Mastroianni, Tom Berenger, Elenora Giorgi; *D:* Liliana Cavani. **VHS, Beta $9.95** *SIM, VID, HHE* 𝄫1/2

Beyond Reason A psychologist uses unorthodox methods by treating the criminally insane with dignity and respect.
1977 88m/C Telly Savalas, Laura Johnson, Diana Muldaur, Marvin Laird, Priscilla Barnes; *D:* Telly Savalas. **VHS, Beta $59.95** *MED* 𝄫

Beyond Reasonable Doubt Chilling true-life murder mystery which shattered the peaceful quiet of a small New Zealand town and eventually divided the country. An innocent farmer (Hargreaves) was convicted of a grisly double murder based on evidence planted by a local cop (Hemmings, in a superb role). It wasn't until Yallop's book questioned the facts of the case that it was reopened. Yallop also wrote the screenplay.
1980 127m/C *NZ* David Hemmings, John Hargreaves, Martyn Sanderson, Grant Tilly, Diana Rowan, Ian Watkin; *D:* John Laing; *W:* David Yallop. **VHS, Beta $69.95** *VID* 𝄫𝄫1/2

Beyond the Bermuda Triangle Unfortunate and flat television flick. Businessman MacMurray, now retired, doesn't have enough to do. He begins an investigation of the mysterious geometric island area when his friends and fiancee disappear. Silly.
1975 78m/C Fred MacMurray, Sam Groom, Donna Mills, Suzanne Reed, Dana Plato, Woody Woodbury; *D:* William A. Graham. **VHS** *NO* 𝄫1/2

Beyond the Call of Duty Renegade U.S. Army Commander Len Jordan (Vincent) is after a particularly deadly Vietcong enemy. Aided by the head of a special forces naval unit he tracks his quarry through the notorious Mekong River Delta. But Jordan's mission may be hindered, both personally and professionally, by a beautiful American journalist after a hot story.
1992 (R) 92m/C Jan-Michael Vincent, Eb Lottimer, Jillian McWhirter. **VHS $89.98** *NHO* 𝄫1/2

Beyond the Carribean Bizarre jungle thriller featuring voodoo and native crucifixion. Also known as "Manhunters of the Carribean."
1932 ?m/B Andre Roosevelt. **VHS $16.95** *SNC* 𝄫

Beyond the Door San Francisco woman finds herself pregnant with a demonic child. One of the first "Exorcist" ripoffs; skip this one and go right to the sequel, "Beyond the Door 2." In Italian; dubbed. *AKA:* Beyond Obsession.
1975 97m/C *IT* Juliet Mills, Richard Johnson, David Colin Jr.; *D:* Oliver Hellman. **VHS, Beta, LV $54.95** *MED, COL* Woof!

Beyond the Door 2 Better treatment of the possession theme, but this time the door is to the home of a new family: Colin (from the original) plays a boy possessed by his dead father, who seeks revenge on his widow and her new husband. The last feature of director Bava, written by Lamberto Bava and Franco Barbieri. *AKA:* Shock.

1979 (R) 90m/C *IT* John Steiner, Daria Nicolodi, David Colin Jr., Ivan Rassimov; *D:* Mario Bava. **VHS, Beta $59.95** *MED* 𝄫𝄫1/2

Beyond the Door 3 Fool American students in Yugoslavia board a hellish locomotive which speeds them toward a satanic ritual. Demonic disaster-movie stuff (with poor miniatures) isn't as effective as the on-location filming; Serbian scenery and crazed peasants impart an eerie pagan aura. What this has to do with earlier "Beyond the Door" movies only the marketing boys can say. Some dialogue in Serbo-Croat with English subtitles.
1991 (R) 94m/C Mary Kohnert, Sarah Conway Ciminera, William Geiger, Renee Rancourt, Alex Vitale, Victoria Zinny, Savina Gersak, Bo Svenson; *D:* Jeff Kwitny. **VHS, LV $89.95** *COL, PIA* Woof!

Beyond the Doors Schlockmeister Buchanan directed this feeble attempt to convince the American public that the American government, in an effort to wipe out rock music, murdered Jimi Hendrix and Janis Joplin, and scared Jim Morrison into hiding. *AKA:* Down on Us.
1983 60m/C Gregory Allen Chatman, Riba Meryl, Brian Wolf, Sandy Kenyon; *D:* Larry Buchanan. **VHS, Beta** *UNI, HHE* 𝄫

Beyond the Forest Camp diva Davis, in her last role for Warner Bros., really turns on the histrionics as a big-city gal married to a small-town guy (Cotten) and bored out of her mind. Although the most memorable line, "What a dump," has become larger-than-life, the film itself is rather small and muddled (interestingly, Vidor directed "The Fountainhead" the same year.) A trashy melodrama full of ennui, envy, unwanted pregnancy, and murder, it's definitely high on camp and low on art.
1949 96m/B Bette Davis, Joseph Cotten, David Brian, Ruth Roman, Minor Watson, Regis Toomey; *D:* King Vidor. **VHS $19.95** *MGM, FCT* 𝄫1/2

Beyond the Law Spaghetti western with Van Cleef as the too smart bad guy. He becomes sheriff, picks up the stack of silver at the depot, and disappears. Humorous and clever, with fine location photography. *AKA:* Bloodsilver; Al Di La Della Legge.
1968 91m/C *IT* Lee Van Cleef, Antonio Sabato, Lionel Stander, Bud Spencer, Gordon Mitchell, Ann Smyrner; *D:* Giorgio Stegani. **VHS $9.99** *QVD, IMP* 𝄫𝄫

Beyond the Limit The story of an intense and darkly ominous love triangle which takes place in the South American coastal city of Corrientes. Based on Graham Greene's novel "The Honorary Consul." *AKA:* The Honorary Consul.
1983 (R) 103m/C Michael Caine, Richard Gere, Bob Hoskins, Elpidia Carrillo; *D:* John MacKenzie. **VHS, Beta $59.95** *PAR* 𝄫𝄫1/2

Beyond the Next Mountain A missionary in China attempts to convert all those he meets. Thin plot and marginal acting will likely make viewers fall asleep.
1987 (PG) 97m/C Alberto Isaac, Jon Lormer, Bennett Ohta, Richard Lineback, Edward Ashley, Barry Foster; *D:* James F. Collier, Rolf Forsberg. **VHS, Beta $79.95** *UHV, VGD* 𝄫

Beyond the Poseidon Adventure A sequel to the 1972 film in which salvage teams and ruthless looting vandals compete for access to the sinking ocean liner. Sinking ships should be abandoned.
1979 (PG) 115m/C Michael Caine, Sally Field, Telly Savalas, Peter Boyle, Jack Warden, Slim Pickens, Shirley Knight, Shirley Jones, Karl Malden, Mark Harmon; *D:* Irwin Allen. **VHS, Beta $19.98** *WAR* 𝄫

Beyond the Silhouette It starts out as another sleazy video sex thriller, as the lawyer heroine discovers her sensuality and poses a lot in her underclothes. Then in the third act it become a hyper-paranoid political-conspiracy assassination-o-rama. Pretty weird, Canadian-made junk, also known as "Ultimate Desires."
1990 90m/C Tracy Scoggins, Marc Singer, Brion James; *D:* Lloyd A. Simandl. **VHS, Beta** *NO* 𝄫

Beyond the Stars A sci-fi adventure directed by the author of "Cocoon," wherein a whiz-kid investigates a NASA cover-up of a deadly accident that occurred on the moon during the Apollo 11 landing. Unfortunately, the interesting cast can't make up for the script.
1989 94m/C Martin Sheen, Christian Slater, Olivia D'Abo, F. Murray Abraham, Robert Foxworth, Sharon Stone; *D:* David Saperstein. **VHS, Beta, LV $89.95** *LIV* 𝄫

Beyond the Time Barrier Air Force test pilot gets more than he bargained for when his high speed plane carries him into the future. There he sees the ravages of an upcoming plague, to which he must return.
1960 75m/B Robert Clarke, Darlene Tompkins, Arianne Arden, Vladimir Sokoloff; *D:* Edgar G. Ulmer. **VHS, Beta $16.95** *SNC, CNM* 𝄫𝄫1/2

Beyond the Valley of the Dolls Sleazy, spirited non-sequel to "Valley of the Dolls." Meyer ("Faster, Pussycat! Kill! Kill!") directed this Hollywood parody ("BVD," as it came to be known) about an all-girl rock combo and their search for stardom. Labeled the first "exploitation horror camp musical"—how can you pass that up? Screenplay by film critic Ebert, from an original story by Ebert and Meyer. Mondo trasho.
1970 (NC-17) 109m/C Edy Williams, Dolly Reed; *D:* Russ Meyer; *W:* Roger Ebert. **VHS, Beta, LV $19.98** *FXV, BTV* 𝄫𝄫

Beyond the Walls The opposing factions of a hellish Israeli prison unite to beat the system. Brutal with good characterizations. Available in both subtitled and dubbed versions. *AKA:* Meachorei Hasoragim.
1984 (R) 104m/C *IS* Arnon Zadok, Muhamad Bakri; *D:* Uri Barbash. Academy Awards '84 Nominations: Best Foreign Language Film; Venice Film Festival '85: Best Film. **VHS, Beta $79.95** *WAR, TAM* 𝄫𝄫1/2

Beyond Therapy A satire on modern psychotherapy, from the play by Christopher Durang, about a confused, crazily neurotic couple and their respective, and not any saner, analysts. Unfortunately, comes off as disjointed and confused.
1986 (R) 93m/C Jeff Goldblum, Tom Conti, Julie Hagerty, Glenda Jackson, Christopher Guest; *D:* Robert Altman. **VHS, Beta $19.95** *STE, NWV* 𝄫1/2

Beyond Tomorrow Young romance is guided from the spirit world during the Christmas season, as two "ghosts" come back to help young lovers.
1940 84m/B Richard Carlson, C. Aubrey Smith, Jean Parker, Charles Winninger, Harry Carey Sr., Maria Ouspenskaya; *D:* Edward Sutherland. **VHS, Beta $16.95** *SNC, NOS, DVT* 𝄫

Bhowani Junction A half-Indian, half-English woman is torn between her country and the British officer she loves in post-colonial India. Great cinematography. Based on a book by John Masters.
1956 110m/C Ava Gardner, Stewart Granger, Bill Travers, Abraham Sofaer, Francis Matthews, Marne Maitland, Peter Illing, Edward Chapman, Freda Jackson, Lionel Jeffries; *D:* George Cukor. **VHS, LV $19.98** *MGM* 𝄫𝄫

The Bible...In the Beginning The book of Genesis is dramatized, including the stories of Adam and Eve, Cain and Abel, and Noah and the flood.
1966 155m/C IT George C. Scott, Richard Harris, Stephen Boyd, John Huston, Peter O'Toole, Franco Nero, Ava Gardner; **D:** John Huston. VHS, Beta, LV $29.98 FOX *??*

The Bicycle Thief A world classic and indisputable masterpiece about an Italian workman who finds a job, only to have the bike he needs for work stolen; he and his son search Rome for it. A simple story that seems to contain the whole of human experience, and the masterpiece of Italian neo-realism. Based on the book by Luigi Bartolini. In Italian with English subtitles. **AKA:** Ladri di Biciclette.
1948 90m/B IT Lamberto Maggiorani, Lianella Carell, Enzo Staiola, Elena Altieri, Vittorio Antonucci, Gino Saltamerenda, Fausto Guerzoni; **D:** Vittorio De Sica; **W:** Cesare Zavattini. Academy Awards '49: Best Foreign Language Film; Nominations: Best Screenplay; British Academy Awards '49: Best Film; Golden Globe Awards '50: Best Foreign Film; National Board of Review Awards '49: 5 Best Foreign Films of the Year, Best Director (De Sica). VHS, Beta, LV $69.95 TAM, NOS, MRV *????*

Big A 13-year-old boy makes a wish at a carnival fortune-teller to be "big." When he wakes up the next morning he finds that he suddenly won't fit into his clothes and his mother doesn't recognize him. Until he finds a cure, he must learn to live in the adult world—complete with job, apartment, and romance. Perkins is wonderful as a warming cynic while Hanks is totally believable as the little boy inside a man's body. Marshall directs with authority and the whole thing clicks from the beginning.
1988 (PG) 98m/C Tom Hanks, Elizabeth Perkins, John Heard, Robert Loggia, Jared Rushton, David Moscow, Jon Lovitz, Mercedes Ruehl; **D:** Penny Marshall. Academy Awards '88 Nominations: Best Actor (Hanks), Best Original Screenplay; Golden Globe Awards '89: Best Actor—Musical/Comedy (Hanks); People's Choice Awards '89: Best Film—Musical/Comedy. VHS, Beta, LV $19.98 FOX, HMV *???*

Big Bad John Some good ol' boys ride around in trucks as they get into a variety of shootouts. The soundtrack includes music by Willie Nelson, The Charlie Daniels Band, and others.
1990 (PG-13) 91m/C Jimmy Dean, Ned Beatty, Jack Elam, Bo Hopkins, Romy Windsor, Doug English. VHS, Beta, LV IME *?1/2*

Big Bad Mama Tough and sexy machine-gun toting mother moves her two nubile daughters out of Texas during the Depression, and they all turn to robbing banks as a means of support while creating sharp testosterone increases among the local men. Wild Palm Dickinson has notable nude scene with Captain Kirk. Corman-produced follow-up to "Bloody Mama" was written by William Norton and Francis Ford. "Big Bad Mama 2" arrived some 13 years later.
1974 (R) 83m/C Angie Dickinson, William Shatner, Tom Skerritt, Susan Sennett, Robbie Lee, Sally Kirkland, Noble Willingham, Royal Dano, Dick Miller; **D:** Steve Carver. VHS, Beta $39.98 NO *??1/2*

Big Bad Mama 2 Belated Depression-era sequel to the 1974 Roger Corman gangster film, where the pistol-packin' matriarch battles a crooked politician with the help of her two daughters.
1987 (R) 85m/C Angie Dickinson, Robert Culp, Danielle Brisebois, Julie McCullough; **D:** Jim Wynorski. VHS, Beta $14.95 MGM *?1/2*

The Big Bet High school sex comedy about a guy who is challenged by the school bully to get the gorgeous new girl into bed. Energetic romp is for adults.
1985 (R) 90m/C Sylvia Kristel, Kimberly Evenson, Ron Thomas; **D:** Bert I. Gordon. VHS, Beta $79.98 CGH *??*

The Big Bird Cage Prison spoof sequel to "The Big Doll House." Horny females incarcerated in a rural jail decide to defy their homosexual guards and plan an escape. They are aided by revolutionaries led by a Brooklynese expatriate and his lover. **AKA:** Women's Penitentiary II.
1972 (R) 93m/C Pam Grier, Sid Haig, Anitra Ford, Candice Roman, Teda Bracci, Carol Speed, Karen McKevic; **D:** Jack Hill. VHS, Beta $39.98 WAR *??*

The Big Blue Vapid, semi-true tale about competing free-divers, who descend deep into the big blue without the aid of any kind of breathing apparatus. Arquette is the ditz who makes them come up for air. **AKA:** Le Grand Bleu.
1988 (PG) 122m/C Rosanna Arquette, Jean Reno, Jean-Marc Barr, Paul Shenar, Sergio Castellitto, Marc Duret, Griffin Dunne; **D:** Luc Besson. VHS, Beta, LV $89.95 COL *?1/2*

Big Bluff Disappointing result from an interesting premise; fatally ill woman finds love, but when she surprisingly recovers, her new husband decides to help her back along the path to death. Uneven and melodramatic. **AKA:** Worthy Deceivers.
1955 70m/B SI John Bromfield, Martha Vickers, Robert Hutton, Rosemary Bowie; **D:** W. Lee Wilder. VHS $19.99 NOS, MOV, HEG *?*

Big Boss A hoodlum climbs to the top of a crime syndicate. An Italian film previously titled "Mr. Scarface."
1977 (R) 90m/C IT Jack Palance, Edmund Purdom, Al Cliver, Harry Baer, Gisela Hahn. Beta NO *?1/2*

The Big Brawl Chicago gangster recruits a martial arts expert to fight in a free-for-all match in Texas.
1980 (R) 95m/C Jackie Chan, Jose Ferrer, Mako, Rosalind Chao; **D:** Robert Clouse. VHS, Beta $19.98 WAR *?1/2*

Big Bus The wild adventures of the world's first nuclear-powered bus as it makes its maiden voyage from New York to Denver. Clumsy disaster-movie parody.
1976 (PG) 88m/C Joseph Bologna, Stockard Channing, Ned Beatty, Ruth Gordon, Larry Hagman, John Beck, Jose Ferrer, Lynn Redgrave, Sally Kellerman, Stuart Margolin, Richard Mulligan, Howard Hesseman, Richard B. Shull; **D:** James Frawley. VHS, Beta $49.95 PAR *??*

Big Business Strained high-concept comedy about two sets of identical twins, each played by Tomlin and Midler, mismatched at birth by a near-sighted country nurse. The city set of twins intends to buy out the factory where the country set of twins work. So the country twins march up to the big city to stop the sale and destruction of their beloved home. Both set of twins stay in the Plaza Hotel and zany consequences ensue. Essentially a one-joke outing with some funny moments, but talented comediennes Midler and Tomlin are somewhat wasted. Great technical effects.
1988 (PG) 98m/C Bette Midler, Lily Tomlin, Fred Ward, Edward Herrmann, Michele Placido, Barry Primus, Michael Gross, Mary Gross, Daniel Gerroll, Roy Brocksmith; **D:** Jim Abrahams. VHS, Beta, LV, 8mm $89.95 TOU *??*

The Big Bust Out Several female convicts escape from prison only to be sold into slavery and face additional torture. Nothing redeeming about this exploitative film.
1973 (R) 75m/C Vonetta McGee, Monica Taylor, Linda Fox, Karen Carter, Gordon Mitchell; **D:** Karen Carter. VHS, Beta $24.98 SUE Woof!

Big Calibre A rancher is inches away from being lynched for his dad's murder before he is found to be innocent.
1935 59m/B Bob Steele, Bill Quinn, Earl Dwire, Peggy Campbell, John Elliott, Georgia O'Dell; **D:** Robert North Bradbury. VHS, Beta $12.95 SNC, DVT, WGE *?*

The Big Cat Mountain valley in Utah is ravaged by a cougar, while two ranchers fuss and feud. Big cat, bickering, help make okay adventure.
1949 75m/C Lon McCallister, Peggy Ann Garner, Preston Foster, Forrest Tucker; **D:** Phil Karlson. VHS, Beta $19.95 NOS, MRV, DVT *??*

Big Chase A rookie cop chases down a mob of payroll thieves in this early action film.
1954 60m/B Glenn Langan, Adele Jergens, Lon Chaney Jr., Jim Davis. VHS, Beta, LV NO *?*

The Big Chill Seven former '60s radicals, now coming upon middle age and middle class affluence, reunite on the occasion of an eighth friend's suicide and use the occasion to re-examine their past relationships and commitments. A beautifully acted, immensely enjoyable ballad to both the counter-culture and its Yuppie descendants. Great period music. Kevin Costner is the dead man whose scenes never made it to the big screen.
1983 (R) 108m/C Tom Berenger, Glenn Close, Jeff Goldblum, William Hurt, Kevin Kline, Mary Kay Place, Meg Tilly, JoBeth Williams; **D:** Lawrence Kasdan. VHS, Beta, LV, 8mm $14.95 COL, VYG, CRC *???1/2*

Big Combo A gangster's ex-girlfriend helps a cop to smash a crime syndicate. Focuses on the relationship between Wilde's cop and the gangster Conte in an effective film noir, with some scenes of torture that were ahead of their time.
1955 87m/B Cornel Wilde, Richard Conte, Jean Wallace, Brian Donlevy, Earl Holliman, Lee Van Cleef, Helen Walker; **D:** Joseph H. Lewis. VHS, Beta $19.95 PSM, WWV *???*

Big Country A sprawling epic in which a sea captain who returns from the Pacific with his wife finds himself without moorings in the midst of a family squall.
1958 (R) 168m/C Gregory Peck, Charlton Heston, Burl Ives, Jean Simmons, Carroll Baker, Chuck Connors; **D:** William Wyler. Academy Awards '58: Best Supporting Actor (Ives); Nominations: Best Original Score; Golden Globe Awards '59: Best Supporting Actor (Ives). VHS, Beta $29.98 MGM, BTV *???*

The Big Crimewave A cast of unknowns in a comedy about a loner who takes a bus to Kansas City (Kansas City?) to become a screenwriter, with comic adventures along the way. A feast of jabs at genre films.
1986 80m/C CA John Paizs, Eva Covacs, Darrel Baran; **D:** John Paizs. VHS, Beta CGH, HHE *??*

Big Deadly Game A vacationing American gets caught up in a complicated espionage plot by helping a mysterious wartime buddy.
1954 63m/B Lloyd Bridges, Simone Silva, Finlay Currie. VHS, Beta, LV NO *?1/2*

Big Deal on Madonna Street A band of inept crooks plan to make themselves very rich when they attempt to rob a jewelry store. Their elaborate plans cause numerous (and hilarious) disasters. In Italian

with English subtitles. Remade as "Crackers." **AKA:** The Usual Unidentified Thieves.
1958 90m/B *IT* Marcello Mastroianni, Vittorio Gassman, Toto, Claudia Cardinale; *D:* Mario Monicelli. **VHS, Beta** $29.95 *TAM, CVC, MRV* ♫♫½

The Big Dis An interracial comedy about a young black soldier on a weekend pass who's looking for a willing sexual partner. His confidence is shattered when 12 possibilities turn him down. Feature debut of Eriksen and O'Brien.
1989 88m/B *D:* Gordon Eriksen, John O'Brien. **VHS** $59.95 *FCT* ♫♫

The Big Doll House Roger Corman-produced prison drama about a group of tormented female convicts who decide to break out. Features vintage Grier, and a caliber of women's-prison sleaziness that isn't equalled in today's films. **AKA:** Women's Penitentiary I; Women in Cages.
1971 (R) 93m/C Judy Brown, Roberta Collins, Pam Grier, Brooke Mills, Pat Woodell, Sid Haig, Christianne Schmidtmer, Kathryn Loder; *D:* Jack Hill. **VHS, Beta** $24.98 *SUE, NLC* ♫♫

The Big Easy A terrific thriller. A slick New Orleans detective uncovers a heroin-based mob war while romancing the uptight assistant DA who's investigating corruption on the police force. An easy, Cajun-flavored mystery, a fast-moving action-comedy, a very sexy romance, and a serious exploration of the dynamics of corruption.
1987 (R) 101m/C Dennis Quaid, Ellen Barkin, Ned Beatty, John Goodman, Ebbe Roe Smith, Charles Ludlum; *D:* Jim McBride. **VHS, Beta, LV** $14.99 *HBO, FCT* ♫♫♫

The Big Fix Private investigator Moses Wine finds himself in an ironic situation: searching for a fugitive alongside whom he'd protested in the 60s. Based on a Roger Simen novel.
1978 (PG) 108m/C Richard Dreyfuss, Susan Anspach, Bonnie Bedelia, John Lithgow, F. Murray Abraham, Fritz Weaver, Mandy Patinkin; *D:* Jeremy Paul Kagan. **VHS, Beta** $59.95 *MCA* ♫♫♫

Big Foot Even genre devotees will be disappointed with this one. Sasquatch, who has procreation on his mind, searches rather half-heartedly for a human mate. A horror flick that forgot to include the horror.
1972 92m/C Chris Mitchum, Joi Lansing, John Carradine, John Mitchum; *D:* Bob Slatzer. **VHS, Beta** $39.95 *WWV* Woof!

The Big Gag An international group of comedians travel the world and pull gags on people. Lame.
1987 (R) 84m/C **VHS, Beta** $79.95 *TWE, HHE* ♫

Big Girls Don't Cry...They Get Even A teenage girl decides to run away from home after she's driven crazy by her eccentric new stepfamily. Comic confusion ensues as various family members set out to find her. Hackneyed script and annoying characters hinder this comedy.
1992 (PG) 98m/C Hillary Wolf, Griffin Dunne, Margaret Whitton, David Strathairn, Ben Savage, Adrienne Shelly, Patricia Kalember; *D:* Joan Micklin Silver. **VHS, LV** *COL, NLC* ♫½

The Big Grab A dark big caper thriller about a couple of aging French thugs determined to rip off a casino at Cannes. In French with English subtitles. Also called "Any Number Can Win."
1963 118m/B *FR* Jean Gabin, Alain Delon, Viviane Romance, Maurice Biraud, Carla Marlier; *D:* Henri Verneuil. **VHS, Beta** $19.95 *FCT* ♫♫½

A Big Hand for the Little Lady Fonda and Woodward, playing two West-headed country bumpkins, get involved in a card game in Laredo against high rollers Robards and McCarthy. Fonda risks their savings, finds himself stuck with a losing hand, and has a bit of heart trouble; that's where the little lady comes in. Fine performances and a nifty twist ending don't entirely compensate for the overly-padded script (which evolved from a 48-minute TV play drafted by Sydney Carroll). **AKA:** Big Deal at Dodge City.
1966 95m/C Henry Fonda, Joanne Woodward, Jason Robards Jr., Charles Bickford, Burgess Meredith, Kevin McCarthy; *D:* Fielder Cook. **VHS, Beta** $59.95 *WAR, FCT* ♫♫½

The Big Hangover Odd story about a man whose allergy to alcohol makes him drunk at the most inopportune moments. Johnson stars as the attorney with the peculiar problem and Taylor plays the boss' daughter who helps him overcome the allergy. Good supporting cast can't help this otherwise boring and predictable film.
1950 82m/B Van Johnson, Elizabeth Taylor, Percy Waram, Fay Holden, Leon Ames, Edgar Buchanan, Selena Royle, Gene Lockhart; *W/D:* Norman Krasna. **VHS** $19.98 *MGM* ♫♫

Big Heat When detective Ford's wife (played by Jocelyn Brando, sister of Marlon) is killed in an explosion meant for him, he pursues the gangsters behind it and uncovers a police scandal. His appetite is whetted after this discovery and he pursues the criminals even more vigorously with the help of gangster moll Gloria Grahame. Definitive film noir.
1953 90m/B Glenn Ford, Lee Marvin, Gloria Grahame, Jocelyn Brando, Alexander Scourby, Carolyn Jones; *D:* Fritz Lang. **VHS, Beta, LV** $59.95 *COL* ♫♫½

The Big Hurt A reporter investigating a bizarre double murder discovers a secret government agency involved in torture and mind-control.
1987 (R) 90m/C David Bradshaw, Lian Lunson, Simon Chilvers, Nick Wateres; *D:* Barry Peak. **VHS, Beta, LV** *NO* ♫½

Big Jake An aging Texas cattle man who has outlived his time swings into action when outlaws kidnap his grandson and wound his son. He returns to his estranged family to help them in the search for Little Jake. O'Hara is once again paired up with Wayne and the chemistry is still there.
1971 (PG) 90m/C John Wayne, Richard Boone, Maureen O'Hara, Patrick Wayne, Chris Mitchum, Bobby Vinton; *D:* George Sherman. **VHS, Beta, LV** $19.98 *FOX* ♫♫

Big Jim McLain Wayne and Arness are federal agents working on behalf of the House Un-American Activities Committee to eliminate communist terrorism in Hawaii. And there's a suspicious psychiatrist, too: Wayne falls for a babe whose boss is a shrink who doesn't quite seem on the level. Definitely not a highpoint in the Duke's career.
1952 90m/C John Wayne, Nancy Olson, James Arness, Veda Ann Borg; *D:* Edward Ludwig. **VHS, LV** $19.98 *WAR, FCT* ♫♫

The Big Knife Palance plays a Hollywood superstar who refuses to renew his studio contract, which enrages studio boss Steiger. It seems Steiger knows a very damaging secret about the star and is willing to go to any lengths to have Palance re-sign or wind up destroying himself. A ruthless, emotional look at fame and power, with excellent performances by all. Based on the play by Clifford Odets.
1955 113m/B Jack Palance, Rod Steiger, Ida Lupino, Shelley Winters, Wendell Corey, Jean Hagen, Ilka Chase, Everett Sloane, Wesley Addy, Paul Langton; *D:* Robert Aldrich. **LV** $34.98 *FCT* ♫♫♫

The Big Lift Two G.I.'s assigned to the Berlin airlift ally themselves in counter-intelligence when they discover that their mutual girlfriend is a spy.
1950 119m/B Montgomery Clift, Paul Douglas, Cornell Borchers, Bruni Lobel, O.E. Hasse; *D:* George Seaton. **VHS, Beta** $19.95 *NOS, MRV, DVT* ♫♫½

The Big Man: Crossing the Line Neeson shines as a down on his luck Scottish miner who loses his job during a union strike. Desperate for cash and unable to resolve his bitterness at being unable to support his family, he's enticed by a Glasgow hood to fight in an illegal bare-knuckled boxing match. What follows is an overlong and extremely brutal fight. Good performances from a talented cast overcome a rather preachy script that doesn't disguise its contempt for the Thatcher government, but also allows a glimpse into the tough times that many Brits suffered during the '80s. Based on the novel by William McIlvanney. **AKA:** Crossing the Line.
1991 (R) 93m/C *GB* Liam Neeson, Joanne Whalley-Kilmer, Ian Bannen, Billy Connolly, Hugh Grant, Maurice Roeves, Rob Affleck; *D:* David Leland; *W:* Don MacPherson; *M:* Ennio Morricone. **VHS, LV** $89.95 *COL* ♫♫♫

Big Man on Campus A modern-day Quasimodo makes his home in a belltower. Of course he falls in love with one of the pretty young co-eds and races out of his tower only to be captured by the psychology department. Really, really bad.
1989 (PG-13) 102m/C Tom Skerritt, Corey Parker, Allan Katz, Cindy Williams, Melora Hardin, Jessica Harper; *D:* Jeremy Paul Kagan. **VHS, Beta, LV** $33.96 *VES* ♫

Big Meat Eater A musical gore-comedy about extraterrestrials using radioactive butcher's discards for ship fuel. Deliberate camp that is so bad its funny!
1985 81m/C *CA* George Dawson, Big Miller, Andrew Gillies; *D:* Chris Windsor. **VHS, Beta** $49.95 *MED* ♫♫

Big Mo True story of the friendship that developed between Cincinnati Royals basketball stars Maurice Stokes and Jack Twyman after a strange paralysis hit Stokes. **AKA:** Maurie.
1973 (G) 110m/C Bernie Casey, Bo Svenson, Stephanie Edwards, Janet MacLachlan; *D:* Daniel Mann. **VHS, Beta** $69.95 *VES* ♫♫

Big Mouth A dopey fisherman gets ahold of a treasure map and is pursued by cops and gangsters. Standard Lewis fare, with the requisite infantile histrionics; must be French to appreciate.
1967 107m/C Jerry Lewis, Jeannine Riley, Harold J. Stone, Charlie Callas, Buddy Lester, Susan Bay; *D:* Jerry Lewis. **VHS, Beta** $49.98 *COL* ♫

Big News Based on the play "For Two Cents" by George S. Brooks, this early talkie uses sound to great advantage. Fired for going after a gangster who's a big advertiser (Hardy), reporter Armstrong nevertheless keeps after the crook. When the intrepid reporter pushes too far, murder enters the picture.
1929 75m/B Robert Armstrong, Carole Lombard, Tom Kennedy, Warner Richmond, Wade Boteler, Sam Hardy, Lew Ayres; *D:* Gregory La Cava. **VHS** $19.95 *NOS, TIM* ♫♫

The Big Parade Wonderful WWI silent, considered to be one of the best war flicks of all time. Gilbert and Adoree are exceptional as lovers torn apart by the conflict. Interesting and thoughtful picture of the trauma and trouble brought to men and their loved ones in wartime. Battle scenes are compelling and intense; Vidor's masterpiece.
1925 141m/B John Gilbert, Renee Adoree, Hobart Bosworth, Claire McDowell, Claire Adams, Karl Dane, Tom O'Brien; *D:* King Vidor. **VHS, LV $29.95** MGM ↪↪↪↪

The Big Picture A hilarious, overlooked comedy by and starring a variety of Second City/National Lampoon alumni, about a young filmmaker who is contracted by a big studio, only to see his vision trampled by formula-minded producers, crazed agents, hungry starlets, and every other variety of Hollywood predator.
1989 (PG-13) 95m/C Kevin Bacon, Jennifer Jason Leigh, Martin Short, Michael McKean, Emily Longstreth, J.T. Walsh, Eddie Albert, Richard Belzer, John Cleese, June Lockhart, Stephen Collins, Roddy McDowall; *D:* Christopher Guest. **VHS, Beta, LV $89.95** COL ↪↪1/2

The Big Push Motley bunch of Alaskan lumberjacks get together to save a poor widow's logging camp from a pair of greedy mill owners. *AKA:* Timber Tramps.
1975 (PG) 98m/C Joseph Cotten, Claude Akins, Cesar Romero, Tab Hunter, Roosevelt Grier, Leon Ames, Stubby Kaye, Patricia Medina; *D:* Tay Garnett. **VHS, Beta $59.95** GEM ↪1/2

The Big Rascal Two brothers grow up, learn martial arts, and protect their village amid much kicking and grunting. Dubbed.
1982 93m/C VHS $29.98 BFV ↪1/2

Big Red Set amid the spectacular beauty of Canada's Quebec Province, an orphan boy protects a dog which later saves him from a mountain lion.
1962 89m/C Walter Pidgeon, Gilles Payant; *D:* Norman Tokar. **VHS, Beta $69.95** DIS ↪↪1/2

The Big Red One Fuller's harrowing, intense semi-autobiographical account of the U.S. Army's famous First Infantry Division in World War II, the "Big Red One." A rifle squad composed of four very young men, led by the grizzled Marvin, cut a fiery path of conquest from the landing in North Africa to the liberation of the concentration camp at Falkenau, Czechoslovakia. In part a tale of lost innocence, the film scores highest by bringing the raw terror of war down to the individual level.
1980 (PG) 113m/C Lee Marvin, Robert Carradine, Mark Hamill, Stephane Audran; *D:* Samuel Fuller. **VHS, Beta, LV $19.98** FOX, WAR ↪↪↪1/2

The Big Scam Criminal mastermind Niven recruits ex-con Jordan to pull off a massive bank heist. *AKA:* A Nightingale Sang in Berkeley Square; The Mayfair Bank Caper.
1979 102m/C Richard Jordan, David Niven, Oliver Tobias, Elke Sommer, Gloria Grahame, Hugh Griffith, Richard Johnson; *D:* Ralph Thomas. **VHS $9.95** SIM, VID ↪↪1/2

Big Score When a policeman is falsely accused and dismissed from the Chicago Police Department, he goes after the men who really stole the money from a drug bust. Script was originally intended to be a Dirty Harry flick; too bad it wasn't.
1983 (R) 88m/C Fred Williamson, John Saxon, Richard Roundtree, Nancy Wilson, Ed Lauter, Ron Dean, D'Urville Martin, Michael Dante, Joe Spinell; *D:* Fred Williamson. **VHS, Beta $69.95** VES ↪

Big Shots Two kids, one naive and white, the other black and streetwise, search for a stolen watch.
1987 (PG-13) 91m/C Ricky Busker, Darius McCrary, Robert Joy, Paul Winfield, Robert Prosky, Jerzy Skolimowski; *D:* Robert Mandel. **VHS, Beta, LV $19.98** LHV, WAR ↪

Big Show A western adventure about the making of a western adventure. Autry jangles spurs aplenty in duel role. *AKA:* Home In Oklahoma.
1937 54m/B Gene Autry, Smiley Burnette; *D:* Mack V. Wright. **VHS, Beta $19.95** NOS, VCN, TIM ↪↪

The Big Showdown A young man uses his martial arts skills against the man who murdered his sister and father.
197? 90m/C Shiang Hwa Chyang, Jin Fu War. **VHS, Beta $29.95** UNI ↪

The Big Sky It's 1830, and a rowdy band of fur trappers embark upon a back breaking expedition up the uncharted Missouri River. Based on the A.B. Guthrie Jr. novel, it's an effortlessly enjoyable and levelheaded Hawksian American myth, with a streak of gentle gallows humor. Also available colorized.
1952 122m/C Kirk Douglas, Dewey Martin, Arthur Hunnicutt, Elizabeth Threatt, Buddy Baer, Steve Geray, Jim Davis; *D:* Howard Hawks. **VHS, Beta $14.98** RKO, FCT, TTC ↪↪↪

The Big Sleep Private eye Philip Marlowe, hired to protect a young woman from her own indiscretions, falls in love with her older sister while uncovering murders galore. A dense, chaotic thriller that succeeded in defining and setting a standard for its genre. The very best Raymond Chandler on film combining a witty script with great performances, especially from Bogart and Bacall.
1946 114m/B Humphrey Bogart, Lauren Bacall, John Ridgely, Martha Vickers, Louis Jean Heydt, Regis Toomey, Peggy Knudsen, Dorothy Malone, Bob Steele, Elisha Cook Jr.; *D:* Howard Hawks; *W:* William Faulkner, Jules Furthman, Leigh Brackett; *M:* Max Steiner. **VHS, Beta, LV $19.98** MGM, FOX, PIA ↪↪↪↪

The Big Sleep A tired remake of the Raymond Chandler potboiler about exhausted Los Angeles private dick Marlowe and his problems in protecting a wild young heiress from her own decadence and mob connections. Mitchum appears to need a rest.
1978 (R) 99m/C Robert Mitchum, Sarah Miles, Richard Boone, Candy Clark, Edward Fox, Joan Collins, John Mills, James Stewart, Oliver Reed, Harry Andrews, James Donald, Colin Blakely, Richard Todd; *D:* Michael Winner. **VHS, Beta, LV $19.98** COL, PIA ↪↪

The Big Slice Two would-be crime novelists want to improve their fiction. One masquerades as a cop, the other as a crook, and they infiltrate the underworld from both ends. Clever comedy premise, but vaudeville-level jokes fall flat.
1990 (R) 86m/C Casey Siemaszko, Leslie Hope, Justin Louis, Heather Locklear, Kenneth Welsh, Nicholas Campbell, Henry Ramer; *W/D:* John Bradshaw; *M:* Michael Danna, Jeff Danna. **VHS, LV $19.95** ACA ↪1/2

The Big Sombrero Autry takes a stand against the marriage between an unsuspecting, wealthy Mexican girl and the fortune-seeking bridegroom who wants her land.
1949 77m/C Gene Autry, Elena Verdugo, Steve Dunne, George Lewis; *D:* Frank McDonald. **VHS $39.98** NO ↪↪1/2

Big Stakes Extremely rare Western feature that has a Texas cowboy falling for a Mexican senorita. Plenty of action as complications ensue.
1922 ?m/B VHS GVV ↪

Big Steal An Army officer recovers a missing payroll and captures the thieves after a tumultuous chase through Mexico.
1949 72m/B Robert Mitchum, William Bendix, Jane Greer, Ramon Novarro, Patric Knowles; *D:* Don Siegel. **VHS, Beta, LV** MED ↪↪↪

Big Store Late Marx Brothers in which they are detectives in a large metropolitan department store, foiling a hostile takeover and preventing a murder. Their last MGM effort, with some good moments between the Tony Martin song numbers which include "If It's You" and the immortal "Tenement Symphony." Groucho also leads the "Sing While You Sell" number.
1941 96m/B Groucho Marx, Harpo Marx, Chico Marx, Tony Martin, Margaret Dumont, Virginia Grey, Virginia O'Brien; *D:* Charles Riesner. **VHS, Beta $19.95** MGM, CCB ↪↪1/2

Big Street A timid busboy, in love with a disinterested nightclub singer, gets to prove his devotion when she is crippled in a fall. Based on a Damon Runyon story, "Little Pinks."
1942 88m/B Henry Fonda, Lucille Ball, Agnes Moorehead, Louise Beavers, Barton MacLane, Eugene Pallette, Ozzie Nelson; *D:* Irving Reis. **VHS, Beta, LV $19.95** MED, RKO, TTC ↪↪1/2

The Big Sweat Maybe you've heard this one before: a man who has been framed by the mob escapes from prison and heads for Mexico. But first, he's got to get past the mobsters and police who are hot on his trail. And maybe you've seen some of it before: some of the same stock footage appears in Lommel's "Cold Heat." Not surprisingly, this one bypassed theaters and went straight to video.
1990 85m/C Robert Z'Dar, Steve Molone, Kevin McBride, William Roebuck, Cheri Caspari, David Rushing, Joanne Watkins, Ken Letner; *D:* Ulli Lommel; *W:* Max Bolt; *M:* John Massari. **VHS $79.95** AIP ↪

The Big Switch Gambler is framed for murder and becomes embroiled in a plot to reinstate an old gangster kingpin. *AKA:* Strip Poker.
1970 (R) 68m/C Sebastian Breaks, Virginia Wetherell, Erika Raffael; *D:* Pete Walker. **VHS, Beta $59.95** MON ↪1/2

Big Top Pee Wee Pee Wee's second feature film following the success of "Pee Wee's Big Adventure." This time Pee Wee owns a farm, has a girlfriend (!) and lives the good life until a weird storm blows a traveling circus onto his property. Cute, but not the manic hilarity the first one was. Music by Danny Elfman.
1988 (PG) 86m/C Pee-Wee Herman, Kris Kristofferson, Susan Tyrrell, Penelope Ann Miller, Pee-Wee Herman; *D:* Randal Kleiser. **VHS, Beta, LV, 8mm $14.95** PAR ↪↪

Big Town A newspaper is saved by a new editor who brings integrity to the once scandalous paper. The editor and his reporters also solve a series of murders. Some action, but weak dialogue and direction hold it back. Based on the radio program of the same name. Also known as "Guilty Assignment."
1947 59m/B Philip Reed, Hillary Brooke, Robert Lowery, Byron Barr, Veda Ann Borg, Nana Bryant, Charles Arnt; *D:* William C. Thomas. **VHS $16.95** SNC ↪

Big Town A farmboy, lucky with dice, hits Chicago to claim his fortune where he meets floozies, criminals, and other streetlife. Look for Lane's strip number.
1987 (R) 109m/C Matt Dillon, Diane Lane, Tommy Lee Jones, Bruce Dern, Tom Skerritt, Lee Grant, Suzy Amis; *D:* Ben Bolt. **VHS, Beta, LV $89.98** VES, LIV ↪↪

Big Town After Dark Daring journalists search for the bottom-line story on a gang of criminals. They find themselves caught behind the firing lines when the sun goes down. Slightly better than average thriller. *AKA:* Underworld After Dark.
1947 69m/B Philip Reed, Hillary Brooke, Richard Travis, Anne Gillis; *D:* William C. Thomas. **VHS** **$16.95** *NOS, SNC, RXM* 🎞🎞

Big Trail This pioneering effort in widescreen cinematography was Wayne's first feature film. A wagon train on the Oregon trail encounters Indians, buffalo, tough terrain, and romantic problems.
1930 110m/B John Wayne, Marguerite Churchill, El Brendel, Tully Marshall, Tyrone Power Sr., Ward Bond, Helen Parrish; *D:* Raoul Walsh. **VHS, Beta $19.98** *FOX* 🎞🎞🎞

Big Trees A ruthless lumberman attempts a takeover of the California Redwood Timberlands that are owned by a group of peaceful homesteaders.
1952 89m/C Kirk Douglas, Patrice Wymore, Eve Miller, Alan Hale Jr., Edgar Buchanan; *D:* Felix Feist. **VHS, Beta, 3/4U, Special order formats $19.95** *NOS, MRV, ONE* 🎞🎞🎞

Big Trouble An insurance broker endeavors to send his three sons to Yale by conspiring with a crazy couple in a fraud scheme that goes awry in every possible manner.
1986 (R) 93m/C Alan Arkin, Peter Falk, Beverly D'Angelo, Charles Durning, Robert Stack, Paul Dooley, Valerie Curtin, Richard Libertini; *D:* John Cassavetes. **VHS, Beta, LV $29.95** *RCA, COL* 🎞🎞

Big Trouble in Little China A trucker plunges beneath the streets of San Francisco's Chinatown to battle an army of spirits. An uproarious comic-book-film parody with plenty of action and a keen sense of sophomoric sarcasm.
1986 (PG-13) 99m/C Kurt Russell, Suzze Pai, Dennis Dun, Kim Cattrall; *D:* John Carpenter. **VHS, Beta, LV $14.98** *FXV, FOX* 🎞🎞½

Big Valley The western television series's two feature-length episodes: "Explosion," and "Legend of a General."
1968 90m/C Richard Long, Linda Evans, Barbara Stanwyck, Lee Majors. **VHS, Beta $69.98** *VID* 🎞🎞½

Big Wednesday Three California surfers from the early sixties get back together after the Vietnam war to reminisce about the good old days and take on the big wave. *AKA:* Summer of Innocence.
1978 (PG) 120m/C Jan-Michael Vincent, Gary Busey, William Katt, Lee Purcell, Patti D'Arbanville; *D:* John Milius. **VHS, Beta, LV $59.95** *WAR, PIA* 🎞🎞½

The Big Wheel Old story retold fairly well. Rooney is young son determined to travel in his father's tracks as a race car driver, even when dad buys the farm on the oval. Good acting and direction keep this a cut above average.
1949 92m/B Mickey Rooney, Thomas Mitchell, Spring Byington, Mary Hatcher, Allen Jenkins, Michael O'Shea; *D:* Edward Ludwig. **VHS** *GPV, UHV, TIM* 🎞🎞½

Big Zapper Violent P.I. Marlowe and masochistic assistant Rock work together in this British comic strip film.
1973 94m/C *GB* Linda Marlowe, Gary Hope, Sean Hewitt, Richard Monette, Penny Irving; *D:* Lindsay Shonteff. **VHS** *VCD* 🎞½

The Bigamist Have you heard the one about the traveling salesman in this movie? He has one wife in Los Angeles, another in San Francisco, and they inevitably find out about each other. A maudlin soap opera with a do-it-yourself ending, only shows why

bigamy was done better as farce in the later "Micki and Maude."
1953 79m/B Edmond O'Brien, Joan Fontaine, Ida Lupino, Edmund Gwenn, Jane Darwell, Kenneth Tobey; *D:* Ida Lupino. **VHS $19.98** *DVT, NOS, TIM* 🎞½

Biggles Time-travel fantasy in which a young businessman from present-day New York City is inexplicably transferred into the identity of a 1917 World War I flying ace. He suddenly finds himself aboard a fighter plane over Europe during World War I. *AKA:* Biggles: Adventures in Time.
1985 (PG) 100m/C *GB* Neil Dickson, Alex Hyde-White, Peter Cushing; *D:* John Hough. **VHS, Beta, LV $19.95** *STE, NWV* 🎞🎞

Bikini Beach The surfing teenagers at Bikini Beach and a visitor, British recording star The Potato Bug, join forces to keep their beach from being turned into a retirement community. Songs include "Bikini Drag," "Love's a Secret Weapon," and "Because You're You."
1964 100m/C Annette Funicello, Frankie Avalon, Martha Hyer, Harvey Lembeck, Don Rickles, Stevie Wonder; *D:* William Asher. **VHS, Beta $9.98** *SUE* 🎞🎞

The Bikini Car Wash Company Babes in bikinis in Los Angeles. A young man is running his uncle's carwash when he meets a business major who persuades him to let her take over the business for a cut of the profits. She decides that a good gimmick would be to dress all the female employees in the tiniest bikinis possible. The story is of course secondary to the amount of flesh on display. Also available in an unrated version. *AKA:* California Hot Wax.
1990 (R) 87m/C Joe Dusic, Neriah Napaul, Suzanne Browne, Kristie Ducati; *D:* Ed Hansen. **VHS $89.95** *IMP* Woof!

The Bikini Car Wash Company 2 Entrepreneur Melissa and the other lovely ladies of the Bikini Car Wash Co. find themselves a big success, so much so that a greedy businessman wants to buy them out. In order to get money to fight the takeover, the ladies take to the airwaves of a cable-access station. Their new business adventure involves selling sexy lingerie which means the flesh quotient is as great as ever. An unrated version is also available.
1992 (R) ?m/C Kristie Ducati, Suzanne Browne, Neriah Napaul, Rikki Brando, Greg Raye, Larry De Russy; *D:* Gary Orona; *W:* Bart B. Gustis; *M:* Michael Smith. **VHS $89.95** *IMP* 🎞

Bikini Island Beautiful swimsuit models gather on a remote tropical island for a big photo shoot, each vying to be the next cover girl of the hottest swimsuit magazine. Before long, scantily clad lovelies are turning up dead and full out madness ensues. Will the mystery be solved before they run out of models, or will the magazine have no choice but to grace its cover with a bikinied cadaver? Low-budget trash that has few, if any, redeeming qualities.
1991 (R) 85m/C Holly Floria, Alicia Anne, Jackson Robinson, Shannon Stiles, Cyndi Pass, Sherry Johnson; *D:* Tony Markes; *W:* Emerson Bixby; *M:* Marc David Deeker. **VHS, Beta $79.95** *PSM* 🎞

Bikini Summer Laughs, music, and skin are the order of the day as two nutty guys and a few beautiful girls form an unlikely friendship on the beach. Konop was Julia Roberts's "Pretty Woman" body double. Sort of the 90's version of the old 60's Frankie and Annette beach parties.

1991 90m/C David Millburn, Melinda Armstrong, Jason Clow, Shelley Michelle, Alex Smith, Kent Lipham, Kelly Konop, Carmen Santa Maria; *W/D:* Robert Veze; *W:* Nick Stone; *M:* John Gonzalez. **VHS, LV $29.95** *PMH* 🎞½

Bikini Summer 2 An eccentric family decides to stage a bikini contest to raise money to help the homeless.
1992 (R) 94m/C Jeff Conaway, Jessica Hahn, Melinda Armstrong, Avalon Anders; *D:* Jeff Conaway. **VHS, LV $19.95** *PMH* 🎞

Bilitis A young girl from a private girls' school is initiated into the pleasures of sex and the unexpected demands of love. One of director Hamilton's exploitative meditations on nudity.
1977 (R) 95m/C *FR* Patti D'Arbanville, Bernard Giraudeau, Mona Kristensen; *D:* David Hamilton. **VHS, Beta $54.95** *MED* 🎞½

Bill A made-for-television movie based on a true story about a mentally retarded man who sets out to live independently after 44 years in an institution. Rooney gives an affecting performance as Bill and Quaid is strong as the filmmaker who befriends him. Awarded Emmys for Rooney's performance and the well written script. Followed by "Bill: On His Own."
1981 97m/C Mickey Rooney, Dennis Quaid, Largo Woodruff, Harry Goz; *D:* Anthony Page. **VHS, Beta $59.95** *LIV* 🎞🎞🎞

Bill and Coo An unusual love story with a villian and hero using an all bird cast.
1947 61m/C *D:* Dean Riesner. **VHS, Beta, 8mm $24.95** *NOS, MRV, VYY* 🎞🎞

Bill & Ted's Bogus Journey The big-budget sequel to B & T's first movie has better special effects but about the same quota of laughs. Non-fans still won't think much of it. Slain by lookalike robot duplicates from the future, the airhead heroes pass through heaven and hell before tricking the Grim Reaper into bringing them back for a second duel with their heinous terminators. A most excellent closing-credit montage.
1991 (PG) 98m/C Keanu Reeves, Alex Winter, William Sadler, Joss Ackland, Pam Grier, George Carlin, Amy Stock-Poynton, Hal Landon Jr., Annette Azcuy, Sarah Trigger, Chelcie Ross, Taj Mahal, Roy Brocksmith, William Shatner; *D:* Pete Hewitt; *W:* Chris Matheson, Edward Solomon; *M:* David Newman. **VHS $14.98** *ORI* 🎞🎞

Bill & Ted's Excellent Adventure Excellent premise: when the entire future of the world rests on whether or not two '80s dudes pass their history final, Rufus comes to the rescue in his time-travelling telephone booth. Bill and Ted share an adventure through time as they meet and get to know some of history's most important figures.
1989 (PG) 105m/C Keanu Reeves, Alex Winter, George Carlin, Bernie Casey, Dan Shor, Robert Barron, Amy Stock-Poynton, Ted Steedman; *D:* Stephen Herek. **VHS, Beta, LV, 8mm $14.95** *COL, SUE, NLC* 🎞🎞½

Bill Cosby, Himself Cosby shares his hilarious observations on marriage, drugs, alcohol, dentists, child-bearing and child-rearing in this performance. Recorded at Toronto's Hamilton Place Performing Arts Center.
1981 (PG) 104m/C Bill Cosby; *D:* Bill Cosby. **VHS, Beta, LV $19.98** *FOX* 🎞🎞½

Bill Murray Live from the Second City Prior to his "Saturday Night Live" stardom, Murray performs a few of his comedy acts with his Second City pals.
197? 60m/C Bill Murray, Tim Kazurinski, Mary Gross, George Wendt, Danny Breen. **VHS, Beta $19.98** *TWE* 🎞🎞½

A Bill of Divorcement Hepburn's screen debut, as the daughter of a shell-shocked World War I vet, who requires her care after her mother decides to divorce him. Creaky early talker.
1932 76m/B John Barrymore, Katharine Hepburn, Billie Burke, Henry Stephenson, David Manners, Paul Cavanagh, Elizabeth Patterson; **D:** George Cukor. VHS, Beta, LV $39.98 FOX 🐾🐾½

Bill: On His Own Rooney is again exceptional in this sequel to the Emmy-winning TV movie ''Bill.'' After 44 years in an institution, a mentally retarded man copes more and more successfully with the outside world. Fine supporting cast and direction control the melodramatic potential.
1983 100m/C Mickey Rooney, Helen Hunt, Teresa Wright, Dennis Quaid, Largo Woodruff, Paul Leiber, Harry Goz; **D:** Anthony Page. VHS $59.95 LIV 🐾🐾🐾

Billie Duke stars as a tomboy athlete who puts the boys' track team to shame. Some amusing but very predictable situations, plus a few songs from Miss Duke. Based on Ronald Alexander's play ''Time Out for Ginger.''
1965 86m/C Patty Duke, Jim Backus, Jane Greer, Warren Berlinger, Billy DeWolfe, Charles Lane, Dick Sargent, Susan Seaforth Hayes, Ted Bessell, Richard Deacon; **D:** Don Weis; **W:** Ronald Alexander. VHS, Beta, LV $19.98 MGM 🐾½

The Billion Dollar Hobo Poor, unsuspecting heir of a multimillion dollar fortune must duplicate his benefactor's experience as a hobo during the Depression in order to collect his inheritance. Slow-moving family stuff.
1978 (G) 96m/C Tim Conway, Will Geer, Eric Weston, Sydney Lassick; **D:** Stuart E. McGowan. VHS, Beta $59.98 FOX 🐾½

A Billion for Boris Boris' TV gives a sneak preview of the future and Boris plans to make some money off of it. Zany comedy in the vein of ''Let It Ride.'' Written by Mary Rogers (author of ''Freaky Friday'').
1990 89m/C Lee Grant, Tim Kazurinsky. VHS, Beta $79.95 IMP 🐾🐾½

Billionaire Boys Club Chilling look at greed in the '80s. Nelson plays Joe Hunt, who gets together with a group of rich, preppie friends to manipulate investments in the commodities markets. When a slick con man (Silver) gets in their way he's murdered to keep their schemes intact. Based on a true story and adapted from the book by Sue Horton. Originally shown on television in two parts, the video version is considerably pared down.
1987 94m/C Judd Nelson, Frederic Lehne, Brian McNamara, Raphael Sbarge, John Stockwell, Barry Tubb, Stan Shaw, Jill Schoelen, Ron Silver, James Sloyan, James Karen; **D:** Marvin J. Chomsky. VHS $79.98 LIV 🐾🐾½

Billy Bathgate Uneven but well acted drama set in 1935 New York. A street-wise young man decides getting ahead during the Depression means gaining the attention of mobster Dutch Schultz and joining his gang. As Billy becomes the confidant of the racketeer he learns the criminal life is filled with suspicion and violence; in order to stay alive he must rely on every trick he's learned. Willis has a small role as a rival mobster who gets fitted for cement overshoes. Kidman garnered a Best Supporting Actress Golden Globe nomination for her role as Dutch's girlfriend while Hill earned a Best Supporting Actor nomination from the New York Film Critics Association for his role as the gang's number man. Based on the novel by E.L. Doctorow.
1991 (R) 107m/C Dustin Hoffman, Nicole Kidman, Loren Dean, Bruce Willis, Steven Hill, Steve Buscemi, Billy Jaye, John Costelloe, Tim Jerome, Stanley Tucci, Mike Starr, Moira Kelly, Katherine Houghton, Rochel York; **D:** Robert Benton; **W:** Tom Stoppard; **M:** Mark Isham. VHS, Beta, LV $92.95 TOU 🐾🐾½

Billy Budd The classic Melville good-evil allegory adapted to film, dealing with a British warship in the late 1700s, and its struggle between evil master-at-arms and innocent shipmate. Stamp's screen debut as the naive Billy who is tried for the murder of the sadistic first mate. Well directed and acted.
1962 123m/B GB Terence Stamp, Peter Ustinov, Robert Ryan, Melvyn Douglas, Paul Rogers, John Neville, Ronald Lewis, David McCallum, John Meillon; **D:** Peter Ustinov; **W:** Peter Ustinov, Robert Rossen. VHS, Beta, LV $59.98 FOX 🐾🐾🐾

Billy Crystal: A Comic's Line Comedian Billy Crystal performs a one-man show, highlighting spoofs, of rock videos and other stand-up comics.
1983 59m/C Billy Crystal. VHS, Beta, LV $19.95 PAR 🐾🐾🐾

Billy Crystal: Don't Get Me Started Crystal hosts a comedy television special featuring his standard routines from ''Saturday Night Live'' and numerous guest stars.
1986 60m/C Billy Crystal, Sammy Davis Jr., Eugene Levy, Christopher Guest, Rob Reiner. VHS, Beta, LV $14.98 VES, LIV 🐾🐾🐾

Billy Crystal: Midnight Train to Moscow Recorded live at Moscow's Pushkin Theatre, Crystal travels to Russia, his ancestral home, and shows that comedy is an international language. A breakthrough in Glasnost.
1989 72m/C Billy Crystal; **D:** Paul Flaherty. VHS $19.98 HBO 🐾🐾🐾

Billy Galvin A bullheaded ironworker tries to straighten out the turbulent relationship he has with his rebellious son.
1986 (PG) 95m/C Karl Malden, Lenny Von Dohlen, Joyce Van Patten, Toni Kalem, Keith Szarabajka, Alan North, Paul Guilfoyle, Barton Heyman; **D:** John Gray. VHS, Beta $79.95 LIV, VES 🐾🐾½

Billy Jack On an Arizona Indian reservation, a half-breed ex-Green Beret with pugnacious martial arts skills (Laughlin) stands between a rural town and a school for runaways. Laughlin stars with his real-life wife Taylor. Features the then-hit song ''One Tin Soldier,'' sung by Coven Editors. The movie and its marketing by Laughlin inspired a ''Billy Jack'' cult phenomenon. A Spanish-dubbed version of this film is also available. Followed by a sequel in 1974, ''Trail of Billy Jack,'' which bombed.
1971 (PG) 112m/C Tom Laughlin, Delores Taylor, Clark Howat; **D:** T.C. Frank. VHS, Beta, LV $19.98 WAR, PIA 🐾🐾🐾

Billy Liar A young Englishman dreams of escaping from his working class family and dead-end job as an undertaker's assistant. Parallels James Thurber's story, ''The Secret Life of Walter Mitty.''
1963 94m/B GB Tom Courtenay, Julie Christie, Finlay Currie; **D:** John Schlesinger. VHS, Beta $39.95 HBO 🐾🐾🐾

Billy: Portrait of a Street Kid A ghetto youngster tries pry himself up and out of his bleak surroundings through education, but complications arise when he gets his girlfriend pregnant.
1977 96m/C LeVar Burton, Tina Andrews, Ossie Davis, Michael Constantine; **D:** Steven Gethers. VHS, Beta $34.95 WOV 🐾🐾

Billy Rose's Jumbo Better-than-average update of the circus picture. Durante and Raye are terrific, as are the Rodgers and Hart songs. Fun, with lively production numbers in the inimitable Berkeley style. 🎵Over and Over Again; Circus on Parade; Why Can't I?; This Can't Be Love; The Most Beautiful Girl in the World; My Romance; Little Girl Blue; What is a Circus; Sawdust, Spangles and Dreams. **AKA:** Jumbo.
1962 125m/C Doris Day, Stephen Boyd, Jimmy Durante, Martha Raye, Dean Jagger; **D:** Charles Walters. VHS, LV $19.98 MGM 🐾🐾🐾

Billy the Kid in Texas The famed outlaw takes on trouble and makes sure the Texans never forget that he has been there.
1940 52m/B Bob Steele. VHS, Beta $19.95 NOS, VCN 🐾½

Billy the Kid Returns While trying to clean up a town of its criminal element, Rogers is mistaken for the legendary Billy. Complications ensue.
1938 60m/B Roy Rogers, George ''Gabby'' Hayes, Smiley Burnette, Lynn (Mary Hart) Roberts; **D:** Joseph Kane. VHS, Beta, 3/4U, Special order formats $19.95 NOS, HHT, VCN 🐾½

Billy the Kid Trapped Billy and his partner are rescued from hanging by an outlaw band.
1942 59m/B Buster Crabbe, Al ''Fuzzy'' St. John, Bud McTaggart, Anne Jeffreys, Glenn Strange; **D:** Sherman Scott. VHS $19.95 NOS, MRV, DVT 🐾½

Billy the Kid Versus Dracula The title says it all. Dracula travels to the Old West, anxious to put the bite on a pretty lady ranch owner. Her fiance, the legendary outlaw Billy the Kid, steps in to save his girl from becoming a vampire herself. A Carradine camp classic.
1966 95m/C Chuck Courtney, John Carradine, Melinda Plowman, Walter Janovitz, Harry Carey Jr., Roy Barcroft, Virginia Christine, Bing Russell; **D:** William Beaudine. VHS, Beta $19.95 NOS, SUE, VYY 🐾🐾

Billyboy Coming of age film with the world of boxing as background. Excellent fight scenes.
1979 94m/C Duane Bobrick, Kim Braden. VHS, Beta BFV 🐾🐾

Biloxi Blues Eugene Morris Jerome has been drafted and sent to boot camp in Biloxi, Mississippi where he encounters a troubled drill sergeant, hostile recruits, and a skillful prostitute. Walken is the drill sergeant from hell. Some good laughs from the ever-wry Broderick. A sequel to Neil Simon's ''Brighton Beach Memoirs'' and adapted by Simon from his play. Followed by ''Broadway Bound.'' **AKA:** Neil Simon's Biloxi Blues.
1988 (PG-13) 105m/C Matthew Broderick, Christopher Walken, Casey Siemaszko, Matt Mulern, Corey Parker, Penelope Ann Miller; **D:** Mike Nichols; **W:** Neil Simon. VHS, Beta, LV $14.95 MCA 🐾🐾½

Bim/Dream of the Wild Horses Two famous French shorts, the first of which is dubbed into English.
1952 110m/B FR VHS, Beta $39.95 TAM, DVT, GVV 🐾🐾½

Bimini Code Two female adventurers accept a dangerous mission where they wind up on Bimini Island in a showdown with the mysterious Madame X.
1984 95m/C Vickie Benson, Krista Richardson, Frank Alexander, Rosanna Simanaitis; **D:** Barry Clark. VHS, Beta $49.95 PSM 🐾🐾

Bingo Mediocre spoof of hero-dog movies. The heroic title mutt roams from Denver to Green Bay in search of his absent-minded master, with numerous absurd adventures en route. Some cute moments, but sometimes Bingo is just lame-o. Good family fare.
1991 (PG) 90m/C Cindy Williams, David Rasche, Robert J. Steinmiller Jr., David French, Kurt Fuller, Joe Guzaldo, Glenn Shadix; **D:** Matthew Robbins; **W:** Jim Strain; **M:** Richard Gibbs. **VHS, LV** $19.95 COL, PIA ♂♂½

Bingo Inferno A short narrative film about a precocious kid who connives to break his mother of a compulsive Bingo addiction.
1987 13m/C Beta NO ♂♂½

Bingo Long Traveling All-Stars & Motor Kings Set in 1939, this film follows the comedic adventures of a lively group of black ball players who have defected from the old Negro National League. The All-Stars travel the country challenging local white teams.
1976 (PG) 111m/C Billy Dee Williams, James Earl Jones, Richard Pryor, Stan Shaw; **D:** John Badham. **VHS, Beta** $49.95 MCA, FCT ♂♂♂

Bio Hazard A toxic monster needs human flesh to survive and consequently goes on a rampage.
1985 (R) 84m/C Angelique Pettyjohn, Carroll Borland, Richard Hench; **D:** Fred Olen Ray. **VHS, Beta** $39.98 MTX ♂

The Bionic Woman Sky-diving accident leaves tennis pro Jaimie Somers crippled and near death. Her bionic buddy, Steve Austin, gets his friends to rebuild her and make her better than she was before. The pilot for the television series.
1975 96m/C Lindsay Wagner, Lee Majors, Richard Anderson, Alan Oppenheimer; **D:** Richard Moder. **VHS, Beta** $39.95 MCA ♂♂

The Birch Interval A chronicle of a young Amish girl growing up and experiencing adult passions and fears when she visits her kin in their isolated Pennsylvania community.
1978 (PG) 104m/C Eddie Albert, Rip Torn, Ann Wedgeworth; **D:** Delbert Mann. **VHS, Beta** $9.95 MED ♂♂

Bird The richly-textured, though sadly one-sided biography of jazz sax great Charlie Parker, from his rise to stardom to his premature death via extended heroin use. A remarkably assured, deeply imagined film from Eastwood that never really shows the Bird's genius of creation. The soundtrack features Parker's own solos re-mastered from original recordings.
1988 (R) 160m/C Forest Whitaker, Diane Venora, Michael Zelniker, Samuel E. Wright, Keith David, Michael McGuire, James Handy, Damon Whitaker, Morgan Nagler; **D:** Clint Eastwood. **VHS, Beta, LV** $19.98 MVD, WAR, FCT ♂♂♂

Bird of Paradise An exotic South Seas romance in which an adventurer is cast onto a remote Polynesian island when his yacht haphazardly sails into a coral reef. There he becomes enamored of an exotic island girl, and nature seems to disapprove.
1932 80m/B Joel McCrea, Dolores Del Rio, Lon Chaney Jr.; **D:** King Vidor. **VHS, Beta, 8mm, 3/4U, Special order formats** $19.95 NOS, MRV, VYY ♂♂½

Bird on a Wire After suddenly being forced to emerge from a prolonged period under the Witness Protection Program, an ex-hood and his ex-girlfriend are pursued by old enemies.

1990 (PG-13) 110m/C Mel Gibson, Goldie Hawn, David Carradine, Bill Duke, Stephen Tobolowsky; **D:** John Badham. **VHS, Beta, LV** $19.98 MCA ♂♂

The Bird with the Crystal Plumage An American writer living in Rome witnesses a murder. He becomes involved in the mystery when the alleged murderer is cleared because the woman believed to be his next victim is shown to be a psychopathic murderer. Vintage Argento mayhem. **AKA:** L'Ucello dalle Plume di Cristallo; The Phantom of Terror.
1970 (PG) 98m/C IT Tony Musante, Suzy Kendall, Eva Renzi; **D:** Dario Argento; **M:** Ennio Morricone. **VHS, Beta, LV** $19.95 UHV, MRV ♂♂♂

Birdman of Alcatraz Robert Stroud, convicted of two murders and sentenced to life imprisonment on the Island, becomes an internationally accepted authority on birds. Lovingly told, with stunning performance from Lancaster, and exceptionally fine work from the supporting cast. The confinement of Stroud's prison cell makes the film seem claustrophobic and tedious at times, just as the imprisonment must have been. Ritter played Stroud's mother, who never stops trying to get him out of prison.
1962 143m/B Burt Lancaster, Karl Malden, Thelma Ritter, Betty Field, Neville Brand, Edmond O'Brien, Hugh Marlowe, Telly Savalas; **D:** John Frankenheimer. Academy Awards '62 Nominations: Best Actor (Lancaster), Best Black and White Cinematography, Best Supporting Actor (Savalas), Best Supporting Actress (Ritter); British Academy Awards '62: Best Actor (Lancaster). **VHS** $19.98 COL, FCT ♂♂♂

The Birds Hitchcock attempted to top the success of "Psycho" with this terrifying tale of Man versus Nature, in which Nature alights, one by one, on the trees of Bodega Bay to stage a bloody act of revenge upon the civilized world. Only Hitchcock can twist the harmless into the horrific while avoiding the ridiculous; this is perhaps his most brutal film, and one of the cinema's purest, horrifying portraits of apocalypse. Based on a short story by Daphne Du Maurier; screenplay by novelist Evan Hunter (aka Ed McBain).
1963 120m/C Rod Taylor, Tippi Hedren, Jessica Tandy, Veronica Cartwright, Suzanne Pleshette; **D:** Alfred Hitchcock. **VHS, Beta, LV** $19.95 MCA ♂♂½

Birds & the Bees A millionaire falls in love with an alluring card shark, and then calls it all off when he learns of her profession, only to fall in love with her again when she disguises herself. A remake - and poor shade - of Preston Sturge's 1941 classic "The Lady Eve."
1956 94m/C Mitzi Gaynor, David Niven, George Gobel, Reginald Gardiner, Hans Conried; **D:** Norman Taurog. **VHS, Beta** $19.95 KRT ♂♂

Birds of Paradise Three attractive women who inherit a yacht travel to the Florida Keys to find romance.
1984 (R) 90m/C VHS, Beta NO Woof!

Birds of Prey Made-for-television action film pits an ex-World War II army pilot against a group of kidnapping thieves in an airborne chopper chase.
1972 81m/C David Janssen, Ralph Meeker, Elayne Heilveil; **D:** William A. Graham. **VHS, Beta** $49.95 PSM ♂♂

Birds of Prey A tough urban cop stalks a breed of cold, ruthless assassins in a large city. In HiFi.
1985 90m/C VHS, Beta $19.95 STE, NWV ♂

Birdy An adaptation of the William Wharton novel about two Philadelphia youths, one with normal interests, the other obsessed with birds, and their eventual involvement in the Vietnam War, wrecking one physically and the other mentally. A hypnotic, evocative film, with a compelling Peter Gabriel soundtrack.
1984 (R) 120m/C Matthew Modine, Nicolas Cage, John Harkins, Sandy Baron, Karen Young, Bruno Kirby; **D:** Alan Parker. **VHS, Beta, LV** $79.95 COL ♂♂♂½

Birgitt Haas Must Be Killed A ruthless secret agent (Noiret) plots to murder a German female terrorist and make it appear that her boyfriend was the killer. Never quite hits the mark, despite novel premise and strong cast.
1983 105m/C Philippe Noiret, Jean Rochefort, Lisa Kreuzer; **D:** Laurent Heynemann. **VHS, Beta** $39.95 WWV, GLV ♂♂½

The Birth of a Nation Lavish Civil War epic in which Griffith virtually invented the basics of film grammar. Gish and Walthall have some of the most moving scenes ever filmed and the masterful battle choreography brought the art of cinematography to new heights. Griffith's positive attitude toward the KKK notwithstanding, this was the first feature length silent, and it brought credibility to an entire industry. Based on the play "The Clansman" and the book "The Leopard's Spots" by Thomas Dixon, it is still a rouser, and of great historical interest. Silent with music score. Also available in a 124 minute version. **AKA:** The Clansman.
1915 175m/B Lillian Gish, Mae Marsh, Henry B. Walthall, Robert Harron, Wallace Reid, Joseph Henabery, Donald Crisp, Raoul Walsh, Erich von Stroheim, Eugene Pallette; **D:** D.W. Griffith. **VHS, LV** $49.95 REP, MRV, VYY ♂♂♂½

Birth Right A cheap cautionary film about VD. "A nighttime of pleasure... a lifetime of regret!!!"
1939 52m/B Ethel Moses, Alec Lovejoy, Carmen Newsome, Laura Bowman. **VHS, Beta** NO Woof!

Birthday Boy A cable comedy about a buffoonish salesman's 30th birthday, on which he takes an ill-fated business trip. Written by Belushi.
1985 33m/C James Belushi; **D:** Claude Conrad. **VHS, Beta** $29.98 VES, LIV ♂♂

The Bishop's Wife An angel comes down to earth at Christmas to help a young bishop, his wife and his parishioners. Excellent performances by the cast make this an entertaining outing.
1947 109m/B Cary Grant, Loretta Young, David Niven, Monty Woolley, Elsa Lanchester, James Gleason, Gladys Cooper, Regis Toomey; **D:** Henry Koster. Academy Awards '47: Best Sound; Nominations: Best Director (Koster), Best Film Editing, Best Picture, Best Original Score. **VHS, Beta, LV** $14.98 HBO, SUE, FCT ♂♂♂

The Bitch High-camp follies are the rule in this lustful continuation of "The Stud" as it follows the erotic adventures of a beautiful divorcee playing sex games for high stakes on the international playgrounds of high society. A collaborative effort by the sisters Collins: written by Jackie, with sister Joan well cast in the title role.
1978 (R) 90m/C GB Joan Collins, Kenneth Haigh, Michael Coby, Ian Hendry, Carolyn Seymour, Sue Lloyd, John Ratzenberger; **D:** Gerry O'Hara. **VHS, Beta** $19.99 HBO Woof!

Bite the Bullet Moralistic western tells of a grueling 600-mile horse race where the participants reluctantly develop respect for one another. Unheralded upon release and shot in convincing epic style by Harry Stradling. Excellent cast.

1975 (PG) 131m/C Gene Hackman, James Coburn, Candice Bergen, Dabney Coleman, Jan-Michael Vincent, Ben Johnson, Ian Bannen, Paul Stewart, Sally Kirkland; **D:** Richard Brooks. **VHS, Beta, LV** $12.95 COL ♫♫♫ ½

Bits and Pieces Crazed mutilating killer strikes fear in the hearts of the city dwellers. **1977** 86m/C **VHS, Beta** $59.95 TWE ♫

Bitter Harvest Emmy-nominated made-for-television movie concerning a dairy farmer frantically trying to discover what is mysteriously killing off his herd. Howard is excellent as the farmer battling the bureaucracy to find the truth. Based on a true story. **1981** 98m/C Ron Howard, Art Carney, Tarah Nutter, Richard Dysart, Barry Corbin, Jim Haynie, David Kneel; **D:** Roger Young. **VHS, Beta** $14.95 FRH, LIV ♫♫

Bitter Rice Mangano became a star with her sultry performance about survival in postwar Italy. She scrapes by, working in the rice fields of the Po Valley, loved by the down-to-earth Vallone, who provides her with little excitement. Gassman is the rotten-to-the-core thief who meets up with Mangano while he's running from the police. He mistreats her, she steals his money and betrays her friends, and both destroy each other. In Italian with English subtitles. **AKA:** Riso Amaro. **1949** 96m/C *IT* Silvana Mangano, Vittorio Gassman, Raf Vallone; **D:** Giuseppe de Santis. **VHS** $29.95 FCT ♫♫♫

Bitter Sweet Tragic tale of a woman who finally marries the man she loves, only to find that he is a compulsive gambler. Written by Noel Coward, adapted from his operetta. **1933** 76m/B *GB* Anna Neagle, Fernand Graavey, Esme Percy, Clifford Heatherly, Hugh Williams; **D:** Herbert Wilcox. **VHS** $19.95 NOS, MRV, DVT ♫♫ ½

Bitter Sweet The second version of the Noel Coward operetta, about young romance in 1875 Vienna. Creaky and overrated, but the lush Technicolor and Coward standards help to compensate. ♫Ziguener; I'll See You Again. **1940** 94m/C Jeanette MacDonald, Nelson Eddy, George Sanders, Felix Bressart, Ian Hunter, Sig Rumann, Herman Bing, Fay Holden, Curt Bois, Edward Ashley; **D:** Woodbridge S. Van Dyke; **W:** Lesser Samuels, Noel Coward. **VHS, Beta** $19.98 MGM ♫♫

The Bitter Tears of Petra von Kant Dark German story of lesbian love, the fashion world, obsession and anger. Claustrophobic settings and slow pace may frustrate some viewers. In German with English subtitles. **AKA:** Die Bitteren Traenen der Petra von Kant. **1972** 124m/C *GE* Margit Carstensen, Hanna Schygulla, Irm Hermann, Eva Mattes; **D:** Rainer Werner Fassbinder. **VHS** $79.95 NYF, FCT, TAM ♫♫ ½

Bittersweet Love Two young people fall in love and marry, only to have the bride's mother and the groom's father confess a 30-year-old affair, disclosing that the two newlyweds are actually half-siblings. **1976** (PG) 92m/C Lana Turner, Robert Lansing, Celeste Holm, Robert Alda, Meredith Baxter Birney; **D:** David Miller. **VHS, Beta** $59.98 SUE ♫♫

Bizarre When a wife escapes her perverse, psychologically threatening marriage, she finds her husband still haunts her literally and figuratively, and plots psychological revenge. Dubbed. **1987** 93m/C *IT* Florence Guerin, Luciano Bartoli, Robert Egon Spechtenhauser, Stefano Sabelli. **VHS, Beta** $79.95 PSM ♫

Bizarre Bizarre A mystery writer is accused of murder and disappears, only to return in disguise to try to clear his name. Along the way, a number of French comedians are introduced with a revue of comedy-farce sketches that include slapstick, burlesque, black humor, and comedy of the absurd. In French with English subtitles. **AKA:** Drole de Drama. **1939** 90m/B *FR* Louis Jouvet, Michel Simon, Francoise Rosay; **D:** Marcel Carne. **VHS, Beta** $24.95 NOS, HHT, FST ♫♫♫

The Black Abbot A mysterious black-hooded figure is seen entering a ruined Abbey tower that leads to a country house with buried treasure. Based on an Edgar Wallace story. **1963** 95m/C *GE* Joachim Fuchsberger, Dieter Borsche, Gritt Bottcher, Eva Scholtz, Franz Gottlieb; **D:** Franz Gottlieb. **VHS** $16.95 SNC ♫♫

Black and White as Day and Night A man's talent for the game of chess becomes a destructive obsession. In German with English subtitles. **1963** ?m/C Bruno Ganz. **VHS** $16.95 SNC ♫♫

Black and White in Color An award-winning satire about a French soldier at an African outpost, who, upon hearing the news of the beginning of World War I, takes it upon himself to attack a neighboring German fort. Calamity ensues. In French, with English subtitles. **AKA:** La Victoire en Chantant. **1976** (PG) 100m/C *FR* Jean Carmet, Jacques Dufilho, Catherine Rouvel, Jacques Spiesser, Dora Doll, Jacques Perrin; **D:** Jean-Jacques Annaud. **VHS, Beta, LV** $39.98 LHV, WAR, TAM ♫♫♫

Black & White Swordsmen A running feud between two families provides impetus for much inspired kicking and chopping. **1985** 92m/C Jiang Bin, Chen Hong Lei. **VHS, Beta** NO ♫

Black Arrow Original adventure film of the famous Robert Louis Stevenson novel. Upon return from 16th century's War of the Roses, a young man must avenge his father's murder by following a trail of clues in the form of black arrows. Well made and fun. **AKA:** Black Arrow Strikes. **1948** 76m/B Louis Hayward, Janet Blair, George Macready, Edgar Buchanan, Paul Cavanagh; **D:** Gordon Douglas. **VHS, Beta** $69.95 DIS ♫♫♫

The Black Arrow Exiled bowman returns to England to avenge the injustices of a villainous nobleman. Made-for-cable version of the Robert Louis Stevenson medieval romp is not as well done as the 1948 adaptation. **1984** 93m/C Oliver Reed, Benedict Taylor, Georgia Slowe, Stephan Chase, Donald Pleasence; **D:** John Hough. **VHS, Beta** $69.95 DIS ♫♫

Black Beauty In this adaptation of Anna Sewell's familiar novel, a young girl develops a kindred relationship with an extraordinary horse. **1946** 74m/B Mona Freeman, Richard Denning, Evelyn Ankers; **D:** Max Nosseck. **VHS, Beta** $9.99 CCB, MED ♫♫

Black Beauty International remake of the classic horse story by Anna Sewell. **1971** (G) 105m/C *GB GE SP* Mark Lester, Walter Slezak; **D:** James Hill. **VHS, Beta, LV** $14.95 PAR, FCT ♫♫

Black Beauty/Courage of Black Beauty Two feature-length films based on Anna Sewell's novel about the love of a child for a black stallion. "Black Beauty" was first released in 1946; "Courage of Black Beauty" in 1957. Excellent for children who love horses, of course. **1957** 145m/C Mona Freeman, Johnny Crawford; **D:** Max Nosseck, Harold Schuster. **VHS, Beta** $12.95 MED ♫♫

Black Belt Two masters of Kung Fu clash when both attempt to steal a shipment of gold bullion. **1973** (R) 92m/C **VHS, Beta** $59.95 HHT ♫

Black Belt Fury Chang Li uses his superior kung fu technique and his pureness of soul to fight the evil forces of darkness. **1981** 85m/C Chang Li. **VHS, Beta** NO ♫

Black Belt Jones Martial arts expert fights the mob to save a school of self-defense in Los Angeles' Watts district. **1974** (R) 87m/C Jim Kelly, Gloria Hendry, Scatman Crothers; **D:** Robert Clouse. **VHS, Beta** $19.98 WAR ♫

Black Bikers from Hell Black gang-members infiltrate and wreak havoc on their rivals. Who can stop these brutal young men? Cast with real bikers and biker chicks. **AKA:** Black Angels. **1970** (R) 87m/C King John III, Des Roberts, Linda Jackson, James Whitworth, James Young-El, Clancy Syrko, Beverly Gardner; **W/D:** Lawrence Merrick. **VHS, Beta** $59.95 TPV, JEF ♫ ½

Black Bird In this satiric "sequel" to "The Maltese Falcon," detective Sam Spade, Jr. searches for the mysterious black falcon statuette that caused his father such trouble. Features appearances by Elisha Cook Jr. and Lee Patrick, who starred in the 1941 classic "The Maltese Falcon" with Humphrey Bogart. **1975** (PG) 98m/C George Segal, Stephane Audran, Lionel Stander, Lee Patrick, Elisha Cook Jr., Connie Kreski; **D:** David Giler. **VHS, Beta** $9.95 GKK ♫♫

Black Box Affair An American secret agent must find a black box lost in a B-52 plane crash before it falls into the wrong hands. **1966** 95m/C Craig Hill, Teresa Gimpera, Luis Martin, Jorge Rigaud. **VHS, Beta** NO ♫ ½

Black Brigade Pryor and Williams star in this low budget movie as leaders of an all-black outfit assigned to a suicide mission behind Nazi lines during World War II. Their force wreaks havoc and earns them the respect of military higher-ups. Lots of action and climactic finish. **1969** 90m/C Richard Pryor, Billy Dee Williams, Stephen Boyd. **VHS** QVD ♫♫

Black Caesar A small-time hood climbs the ladder to the head of a Harlem crime syndicate. Music by James Brown. Followed by the sequel "Hell Up in Harlem." **1973** (R) 92m/C Fred Williamson, Julius W. Harris, Val Avery, Art Lund, Gloria Hendry; **D:** Larry Cohen. **VHS, Beta, LV** $19.98 ORI ♫♫

The Black Cat The first of the Boris and Bela pairings stands up well years after release. Polished and taut, with fine sets and interesting acting. Confrontation between architect and devil worshippers as plot, with strange twists. Worth a look. Also available with "The Raven" (1935) on Laser Disc. **AKA:** House of Doom. **1934** 65m/B Boris Karloff, Bela Lugosi, David Manners, Jacqueline Wells, Lucille Lund, Henry Armetta; **D:** Edgar G. Ulmer. **VHS, LV** $9.95 MED, MLB, MCA ♫♫

The Black Cat Spaghetti splatter-meister Fulci, best known for his unabashed ripoffs "Zombie" and "Gates of Hell," tones down the gore this time in a vaguely Poe-ish

tale of a medium with some marbles loose (Magee) whose kitty provides the temporary habitat for spirits its master calls up. The dreary English village setting and the downright myopic camerawork add up to an oppressive viewing experience. Written by Fulci.
1981 92m/C *IT GB* Patrick Magee, Mimsy Farmer, David Warbeck, Al Cliver, Dagmar Lassander; *W/D:* Lucio Fulci. **VHS $14.98** *MED, RHI* Woof!

Black Cat Another cinematic remake of the Edgar Allan Poe short story. The residents of a small English village are terrorized by a fiendish feline, the deadly pet of a revenge-minded clairvoyant.
1986 93m/C *GB IT* Patrick Magee, Mimsy Farmer, David Warbeck, Al Cliver; *D:* Lucio Fulci. **VHS $19.95** *FCT* ⅛½

Black Cat Filmmakers find lots of action in a haunted house. Chock full of references to the works of spaghetti horror dons Mario Bava and Dario Argento.
1990 ?m/C *IT* Caroline Munro, Brett Halsey; *W/D:* Lewis (Luigi Cozzi) Coates. **VHS, Beta** *COL* ⅛½

Black Christmas A college sorority is besieged by an axe-murderer over the holidays. *AKA:* Silent Night, Evil Night; Stranger in the House.
1975 (R) 98m/C *CA* Olivia Hussey, Keir Dullea, Margot Kidder, John Saxon; *D:* Bob Clark. **VHS, Beta $19.98** *WAR* ⅛⅛½

Black Cobra A lesbian exacts revenge for her lover's snake-bite murder by trapping the guilty party with his own snakes.
1983 (R) 97m/C Laura Gemser, Jack Palance. **VHS, Beta $79.95** *GEM* Woof!

The Black Cobra After photographing a psychopath in the process of killing someone, a beautiful photographer seeks the help of a tough police sergeant to protect her. The leader of the Black Cobras gang gives chase.
1987 (R) 90m/C *IT* Fred Williamson, Karl Landgren, Eva Grimaldi. **VHS, Beta $79.95** *TWE* Woof!

Black Cobra 2 A mis-matched team of investigators tracks a notorious terrorist. They find him holding a school full of children as hostage.
1989 (R) 95m/C Fred Williamson. **VHS $14.95** *HMD* ⅛

Black Cobra 3: The Manila Connection Interpol turns to police lieutenant Robert Malone (Williamson) when a team of high-tech weapons thieves threatens the world. Malone attacks like a cyclone on the terrorists' jungle haven. They won't know what hit 'em!
1990 (R) 92m/C Fred Williamson, Forry Smith, Debra Ward; *D:* Don Edwards. **VHS $14.95** *HMD* ⅛½

The Black Coin A condensation of the "Black Coin" movie serial.
1936 80m/B Ralph Graves, Ruth Mix; *D:* Elmer Clifton. **VHS, Beta $69.95** *DVT, MLB, RXM* ⅛½

Black Devil Doll from Hell This shot-on-video movie deals with a nasty little voodoo doll that likes to kill its owners.
1984 70m/C Shirley Jones, Rickey Roach, Marie Sainvilvs; *D:* Chester Turner. **VHS, Beta $49.95** *HHT* ⅛

The Black Devils of Kali Adventurers in the Indian jungle discover a lost race of idol-worshipping primitives. Racist garbage produced near the end of Republic Pictures' existence. Based on a novel by Emillio Salgari. *AKA:* Mystery of the Black Jungle.
1955 72m/B Lex Barker, Jane Maxwell, Luigi Tosi, Paul Muller; *D:* Ralph Murphy. **VHS $16.95** *SNC, MLB* ⅛

Black Dragon Young farm boy moves to the city and teams up with an undercover narcotics agent to infiltrate and destroy the underworld syndicate.
1974 (R) 93m/C Ron Van Cliff, Jason Rai Pow, Jorge Estraga, Nancy Veronica. **VHS $54.95** *SUN* ⅛

The Black Dragons Weird and fairly stupid war drama involving sabotage by the Japanese. Lugosi is the plastic surgeon who deftly cuts and pastes Japanese face parts to permit agents to pass as Americans. Also available colorized.
1942 62m/B Bela Lugosi, Joan Barclay, George Pembroke, Clayton Moore; *D:* William Nigh. **VHS, Beta, 3/4U, Special order formats $24.95** *NOS, MRV, SNC* ⅛

Black Dragon's Revenge The Black Dragon arrives in Hong Kong to investigate the death of a great kung fu master.
1975 (R) 90m/C Ron Van Cliff, Charles Bonet, Jason Rai Pow. **VHS $52.95** *SUN* ⅛

Black Eagle Pre-Glasnost, anti-Soviet tale of two high-kicking spies. CIA and KGB agents race to recover innovative equipment in the Mediterranean.
1988 (R) 93m/C Bruce Doran, Jean-Claude Van Damme, Sho Kosugi; *D:* Eric Karson. **VHS, Beta** *NO* ⅛⅛

Black Eliminator A black cop struggles to stop a maniacal secret agent who plans to destroy the world.
197? 84m/C Jim Kelly, George Lazenby, Harold Sakata, Bob Minos, Patch MacKenzie, Aldo Ray. **VHS, Beta** *NO* ⅛

Black Emmanuelle Emmanuelle travels to Africa on an assignment, but work turns to play as she becomes a willing partner.
1976 121m/C Karin Schubert, Angelo Infanti, Don Powell. **VHS, Beta $59.98** *FOX* ⅛

Black Eyes A lowly waiter, working in a Moscow restaurant, manages to overhear a number of stock tips from the wealthy patrons and makes a tidy pile of rubles to improve his daughter's life. The daughter already thinks he's a successful businessman and is disillusioned when she discovers dad's true profession. All comes out right in the end.
1939 72m/B *GB* Otto Kruger, Mary Maguire, Walter Rilla, John Wood, Marie Wright; *D:* Herbert Brenon. **VHS** *HCV* ⅛½

Black Force Brothers who fight crime with violent actions, are called for assistance in the recovery of an African artifact. Originally known as "Force Four."
1975 82m/C Malachi Lee, Warhawk Tanzania, Owen Watson, Judie Soriano; *D:* Michael Fink. **VHS, Beta $9.95** *SIM* ⅛⅛

Black Force 2 The brothers are back on the scene in another violent, cartilage-shattering adventure.
1978 (R) 90m/C Terry Carter, James B. Sikking. **VHS $29.95** *SIM* ⅛

Black Fury A coal miner's efforts to protest working conditions earn him a beating by the company goons who also kill his friend. He draws national attention to this brutal plight of the workers when he barricades himself inside the mine. Muri's carefully detailed performance adds authenticity to this powerful drama, but it proved too depressing to command a big box office.
1935 95m/B Paul Muni, Barton MacLane, Henry O'Neill, John Qualen, J. Carroll Naish; *D:* Michael Curtiz. **VHS, Beta $59.95** *FOX* ⅛⅛⅛

Black Gestapo A black-exploitation film about a vigilante army taking over a Los Angeles ghetto, first to help residents, but later to abuse them. Extremely violent.
1975 (R) 89m/C Rod Perry, Charles P. Robinson, Phil Hoover, Ed Gross. **VHS, Beta $59.95** *UNI* Woof!

Black Glove A trumpet star defends himself against charges of murdering a Spanish singer by tracking down the real killer. *AKA:* Face the Music.
1954 84m/B Alex Nicol, Eleanor Summerfield. **VHS, Beta, LV $19.95** *NOS* ⅛

Black God & White Devil Another Brazilan socio-political commentary by Rocha, an oft-incendiary filmmaker whose left-leaning works are steeped in mysticism, obscure folklore, and powerful images. An impoverished man transforms from a religious zealot to a bandit, his tale underscored by conflict between poor masses and wealthy landowners.
1964 102m/C *BR D:* Glauce Rocha. **VHS $59.95** *FST* ⅛⅛

Black Godfather The grueling story of a hood clawing his way to the top of a drug-selling mob. Features an all-black cast.
1974 (R) 90m/C Rod Perry, Damu King, Don Chastain, Jimmy Witherspoon, Diane Summerfield; *D:* John Evans. **VHS, Beta** *NO* ⅛

Black Gold Oil field suspense thriller by "B" movie king Hopton.
1936 ?m/B Frankie Darrow, Roy Mason; *D:* Russell Hopton. **VHS $16.95** *SNC* ⅛⅛

The Black Hand Kelly plays well against character in this atmospheric turn-of-the-century thriller. The evil society of the Black Hand murders his father, and he seeks revenge. Well made drama.
1950 93m/B Gene Kelly, J. Carroll Naish, Teresa Celli, Marc Lawrence, Frank Puglia; *D:* Richard Thorpe. **VHS** *NO* ⅛⅛⅛

Black Hand Unemployed Italian immigrant is drawn into a web of murder and betrayal after he is attacked by an Irish gang.
1976 90m/C Lionel Stander, Mike Placido. **VHS, Beta** *NO* ⅛½

The Black Hole A high-tech, computerized Disney space adventure dealing with a mad genius who attempts to pilot his craft directly into a black hole. Except for the top quality special effects, a pretty creaky vehicle.
1979 (G) 97m/C Maximilian Schell, Anthony Perkins, Ernest Borgnine, Yvette Mimieux, Joseph Bottoms, Robert Forster; *D:* Gary Nelson; *M:* John Barry. **VHS, Beta, LV** *DIS, OM* ⅛½

Black Ice After an affair with a popular politician ends violently, Vanessa (Pacula) realizes her boss set up his death—and she's next in line. She finds the nearest taxi and offers the driver plenty of cash if he can quickly get her out of the country. It's going to be the ride of her life. Also available in an unrated version.
1992 (R) 90m/C Michael Nouri, Michael Ironside, Joanna Pacula; *D:* Neill Fearnley. **VHS, Beta $89.95** *PSM* ⅛

Black King Prejudiced propaganda based on the life of Marcus Garvey, black leader of the '20s, who advocated black superiority and a return to Africa. A black con man takes advantage of fellow blacks by organizing a phony back-to-Africa movement, enriching himself in the process. When one man's girlfriend deserts him for the bogus leader, the jilted one blows the whistle. *AKA:* Harlem Hot Shot.

1932 70m/B A.B. Comethiere, Vivian Baber, Knolly Mitchell, Dan Michaels, Mike Jackson; **D:** Bud Pollard. **VHS** $24.95 FCT, TIM, HEG ⅜½

The Black Klansman A black man masquerades as a white extremist in order to infiltrate the KKK and avenge his daughter's murder. In the interest of racial harmony, he seduces the Klan leader's daughter. As bad as it sounds. **AKA:** I Crossed the Line.
1966 88m/B Richard Gilden, Rima Kutner, Harry Lovejoy; **D:** Ted V. Mikels. **VHS, Beta** $39.95 UNI ⅜

The Black Lash Two lawmen go undercover to break a silver hijacking gang.
1952 55m/B Lash LaRue, Al "Fuzzy" St. John, Peggy Stewart, Kermit Maynard; **D:** Ron Ormond. **VHS, Beta** $19.95 NOS, DVT, GPV ⅜

Black Lemons While in prison, a convict is stalked by the Mafia because of what he knows. He eventually spills the beans to the cops, putting himself in unavoidable jeopardy.
198? 93m/C IT Peter Carsten, Antonio Sabato, Florinda Bolkan; **D:** Camillo Bazzoni. **VHS, Beta** $59.95 UNI ⅜

Black Like Me Based on John Howard Griffin's successful book about how Griffin turned his skin black with a drug and traveled the South to experience prejudice firsthand. Neither the production nor the direction enhance the material.
1964 107m/B James Whitmore, Roscoe Lee Browne, Will Geer, Walter Mason, John Marriott, Clifton James, Dan Priest; **D:** Carl Lerner. **VHS, Beta** $19.95 RHI, UND, PTB ⅜½

Black Lizard A camp spectacle set in the Japanese underworld. The Lizard is the glamorous queen of Tokyo crime who plots to steal a famous diamond by first kidnapping the owner's daughter. Complications arise when she falls for a detective. The Lizard is played by female impersonator Maruyama. Mishima, who wrote the original drama and the screenplay, has a cameo as an embalmed corpse. Style is all. In Japanese with English subtitles.
1968 112m/C JP Akihiro Maruyama, Isao Kimura; **Cameos:** Yukio Mishima; **D:** Kinji Fukasaku; **W:** Yukio Mishima. **VHS** $79.95 CCN, TAM ⅜⅜

Black Magic Cagliostro the magician becomes involved in a plot to supply a double for Marie Antoinette.
1949 105m/B Orson Welles, Akim Tamiroff, Nancy Guild, Raymond Burr; **D:** Gregory Ratoff. **VHS, Beta** $12.95 MED ⅜⅜½

Black Magic Insomniac Alex, haunted by the nightly appearances of his dead cousin Ross, goes to Ross' hometown to see if he can find a way to make the apparition disappear. On the way, he runs into his cousin's ex-girlfriend Lilian and falls in love. Problem is, Lilian's a witch, maybe. Lightweight made for cable TV fare.
1992 (PG-13) 94m/C Rachel Ward, Judge Reinhold, Brion James, Anthony LaPaglia; **W/D:** Daniel Taplitz. **VHS, LV** $89.98 MCA ⅜⅜½

Black Magic Terror Jilted by her lover, the old queen of black magic has everybody under her spell. Trouble starts, however, when she turns her back on one of her subjects.
1979 85m/C JP Suzanna, W.D. Mochtar, Alan Nuary; **D:** L. Sudjio. **VHS, Beta** $59.95 TWE ⅜

Black Magic Woman An art gallery owner has an affair with a beautiful and exotic woman but starts to get cold feet when he's plagued by inexplicable phenomena. Seems that black magic woman has put a voodoo spell on him. Listless companion to director Warren's "Blood Spell" that gives

away the ending, has a wretched script, and poor acting.
1991 (R) 91m/C Mark Hamill, Amanda Wyss, Apollonia, Abadah Viera, Larry Hankin, Victor Rivers, Bonnie Ebson; **D:** Deryn Warren; **W:** Gerry Daly; **M:** Randy Miller. **VHS** $89.95 VMK Woof!

The Black Maid A scantily-clad, sassy black maid cleans, cooks, cusses and drives her rascist employer to the brink of insanity.
1974 90m/C IT **VHS, Beta** NO Woof!

The Black Marble A beautiful policewoman is paired with a policeman who drinks too much, is divorced, and is ready to retire. Surrounded by urban craziness and corruption, they eventually fall in love. Based on the Joseph Wambaugh novel.
1979 (PG) 110m/C Paula Prentiss, Harry Dean Stanton, Robert Foxworth, James Woods, Michael Dudikoff; **D:** Harold Becker. **VHS, Beta** $9.98 SUE, NLC ⅜⅜⅜

Black Market Rustlers The Range Busters are at it again. This time they break up a cattle rustling syndicate.
1943 60m/B Ray Corrigan, Dennis Moore, Max Terhune; **D:** S. Roy Luby. **VHS, Beta** $19.95 VCN, VDM, RXM ⅜

Black Moon Rising Based on an idea by John Carpenter ("Halloween"), this film deals with the theft of a new jet-powered car and its involvement in an FBI investigation. Solid performances and steady action enhance this routine effort.
1986 (R) 100m/C Tommy Lee Jones, Linda Hamilton, Richard Jaeckel, Robert Vaughn; **D:** Harley Cokliss. **VHS, Beta, LV** $19.95 STE, NWV ⅜½

Black Narcissus A group of Anglican nuns attempting to found a hospital and school in the Himalayas confront native distrust and human frailties amid beautiful scenery. Adapted from the novel by Rumer Godden. Stunning cinematography. Crucial scenes were cut from the American release by censors.
1947 101m/C GB Deborah Kerr, David Farrar, Sabu, Jean Simmons, Kathleen Byron, Flora Robson, Esmond Knight; **D:** Michael Powell, Emeric Pressburger. **VHS, Beta, LV** $29.95 VID, VYG, MLB ⅜⅜⅜½

Black Oak Conspiracy Based on a true story, this film deals with a mining company conspiracy discovered by an inquisitive stuntman.
1977 (R) 92m/C Jesse Vint, Karen Carlson, Albert Salmi, Seymour Cassel, Robert F. Lyons; **D:** Bob Kelljan. **VHS, Beta** $59.98 NLC ⅜⅜

Black Orchid A businessman and a crook's widow fall in love and try to persuade their children it can work out.
1959 96m/B Sophia Loren, Anthony Quinn, Ina Balin, Mark Richmond, Jimmie Baird; **D:** Martin Ritt. **VHS, Beta** $14.95 PAR ⅜⅜½

Black Orpheus The legend of Orpheus and Eurydice unfolds against the colorful background of the carnival in Rio de Janeiro. In the black section of the city, Orpheus is a street-car conductor and Eurydice, a country girl fleeing from a man sworn to kill her. Dancing, incredible music, and black magic add to the beauty of this film. Based on the play "Orfeu da Conceica". In Portuguese with English subtitles or dubbed. **AKA:** Orfeu Negro.
1958 103m/C BR FR PT Breno Mello, Marpessa Dawn, Lea Garcia, Fausto Guerzoni, Lourdes De Oliveira; **D:** Marcel Camus; **M:** Antonio Carlos Jobim, Luis Bonfa. **VHS, Beta, LV** $29.95 CVC, FOX, VYG ⅜⅜⅜½

Black Panther True story of psychokiller Donald Neilson, who murdered heiress Lesley Whittle in England in the 1970s.
1977 90m/C Donald Sumpter, Debbie Farrington; **D:** Ian Merrick. **VHS, Beta** $69.95 VES, LIV ⅜½

The Black Pirate A shipwrecked mariner vows revenge on the pirates who destroyed his father's ship. Quintessential Fairbanks, this film features astounding athletic feats and exciting swordplay. Silent film with music score. Also available in color. **AKA:** Rage of the Buccaneers; The Black Buccaneer; Gordon il Pirata Nero.
1926 122m/B IT Douglas Fairbanks Sr., Donald Crisp, Billie Dove; **D:** Albert Parker. **VHS, Beta, LV** $19.95 VYY, MRV, REP ⅜⅜⅜

The Black Pirate Italian pirate yarn dubbed into Spanish. **AKA:** El Pirata Negro.
1965 82m/C SP IT George Hilton, Claude Dantes, Tony Kendall. **VHS, Beta** NO ⅜

Black Pit of Dr. M Pretty gruesome horror film in which the ghost of a doctor who has been unjustly executed for murder seeks revenge on employees of an insane asylum. **AKA:** Misterios del Ultratumba.
1958 ?m/B MX Rafael Bertrand, Mary Cortez, Gaston Santos; **D:** Fernando Mendez; **W:** Raymond Obon. **VHS** $20 SMW ⅜

The Black Planet Distant planet of Terre Verte is rapidly running out of energy. To keep the remaining fuel, warhawks Senator Calhoun and General McNab think their part of the planet should blow up the other part. Will the entire planet be destroyed? Obscure sci-fi.
1982 78m/C AU **D:** Paul Williams. **VHS, Beta** $39.98 SUE ⅜

Black Rain Erstwhile Ozu assistant Imamura directs this powerful portrait of a post-Hiroshima family five years after the bombing. Tanaka plays a young woman who, having been caught in a shower of black rain (radioactive fallout) on an ill-timed visit to Hiroshima, returns to her village to find herself ostracized by her peers and no longer considered marriage-worthy. Winner of numerous awards (including one at Cannes and five Japanese Academy Awards). In Japanese with English subtitles. **AKA:** Kuroi Ame.
1988 123m/B JP Kazuo Kitamura, Yoshiko Tanaka; **D:** Shohei Imamura. **VHS** $79.95 FXL, FCT, TAM ⅜⅜⅜

Black Rain Douglas portrays a ruthless American cop chasing a Japanese murder suspect through gang-controlled Tokyo. Loads of action and stunning visuals from the man who brought you "Blade Runner."
1989 (R) 125m/C Michael Douglas, Andy Garcia, Kate Capshaw, Ken Takakura; **D:** Ridley Scott. **VHS, Beta, LV, 8mm** $14.95 PAR ⅜⅜½

Black Rainbow Surprisingly good thriller that's relatively unknown, haunted by a menacing mood. Robards and Arquette are a father/daughter duo who perform clairvoyance scams at carnival sideshows. Suddenly, without warning, Arquette's former cons become real: she sees murder victims—before their demise. Quirky sleeper filmed on location in North Carolina.
1991 (R) 103m/C Rosanna Arquette, Jason Robards Jr., Tom Hulce, Ron Rosenthal, John Bennes, Linda Pierce; **W/D:** Mike Hodges. **VHS, Beta, LV** $19.98 VTR, FXV, MED ⅜⅜⅜

The Black Raven An action film that combines several plots into one. The Black Raven is an inn that sees more excitement than any other—not the least of which is murder!
1943 64m/B George Zucco, Wanda McKay, Glenn Strange, I. Stanford Jolley; **D:** Sam Newfield. **VHS, Beta** $16.95 SNC, MLB, RXM ⅜½

Black Robe In 1634 a young Jesuit priest journeys across the North American wilderness to bring the word of God to Canada's Huron Indians. The winter journey is brutal and perilous and he begins to question his mission after seeing the strength of the Indian's native ways. Stunning cinematography, a good script, and fine acting combine to make this superb. Portrays the Indians in a realistic manner, the only flaw being that Beresford portrays the white culture with very few redeeming qualities and as the only reason for the Indian's downfall. Moore adapted his own novel for the screen. Winner of six Canadian Genie awards in 1991.
1991 (R) 101m/C AU CA Lothaire Bluteau, Aden Young, Sandrine Holt, August Schellenberg, Tantoo Cardinal, Billy Two Rivers, Lawrence Bayne, Harrison Liu; *D:* Bruce Beresford; *W:* Brian Moore. **VHS, LV** $94.95 VMK, TAM 𝅗𝅥𝅗𝅥𝅗𝅥½

The Black Room As an evil count lures victims into his castle of terror, the count's twin brother returns to fulfill an ancient prophecy. Karloff is wonderful in his dual role as the twin brothers.
1935 70m/B Boris Karloff, Marian Marsh, Robert Allen, Katherine DeMille, John Buckler, Thurston Hall; *D:* Roy William Neill. **Beta, LV, Q** $9.95 GKK, MLB 𝅗𝅥𝅗𝅥𝅗𝅥

The Black Room Couples are lured to a mysterious mansion where a brother and his sister promise to satisfy their sexual desires.
1982 (R) 90m/C Linnea Quigley, Stephen Knight, Cassandra Gaviola, Jim Stathis; *D:* Norman Thaddeus Vane. **VHS, Beta, LV** $69.95 VES, LIV 𝅗𝅥

Black Roses A disgusting band of rockers shows up in a small town, and the local kids start turning into monsters. Coincidence?
1988 (R) 90m/C Carmine Appice, Sal Viviano, Carla Ferrigno, Julie Adams, Ken Swofford, John Martin; *D:* John Fasano. **VHS, Beta** $79.95 IMP 𝅗𝅥

Black Sabbath An omnibus horror film with three parts, climaxing with Karloff as a Wurdalak, a vampire who must kill those he loves. Also available with "Black Sunday" on Laser Disc. *AKA:* I Tre Volti della Paura.
1964 99m/C IT Boris Karloff, Jacqueline Pierreux, Michele Mercier, Lidia Alfonsi, Susy Anderson, Mark Damon, Rika Dialina; *D:* Mario Bava. **VHS, Beta** $16.95 SNC, HBO 𝅗𝅥𝅗𝅥𝅗𝅥

Black Samurai When his girlfriend is held hostage, a martial arts warrior will stop at nothing to destroy the organization that abducted her.
1977 (R) 84m/C Jim Kelly; *D:* Al Adamson. **VHS, Beta** NO 𝅗𝅥

The Black Scorpion Two geologists in Mexico unearth a nest of giant scorpions living in a dead volcano. Eventually one of the oversized arachnids escapes to wreak havoc on Mexico City.
1957 85m/B Richard Denning, Mara Corday, Carlos Rivas; *D:* Edward Ludwig. **VHS** $19.98 WAR, MLB, FRG 𝅗𝅥½

Black Shampoo A black hairdresser on the Sunset Strip fights the mob with a chainsaw.
1976 90m/C John Daniels, Tanya Boyd, Joe Ortiz; *D:* Greydon Clark. **VHS, Beta** $59.95 UHV Woof!

Black Sister's Revenge Poorly selected video title mars this intelligent drama about a young black woman's struggle to adjust to the big city after growing up in the deep South. *AKA:* Emma Mae.
1976 100m/C Jerri Hayes, Ernest Williams II, Charles D. Brook III, Eddie Allen; *D:* Jamaa Fanaka. **VHS, Beta** $59.95 UNI 𝅗𝅥𝅗𝅥

The Black Six Six black Vietnam veterans are out to punish the white gang who killed the brother of one of the black men.
1974 (R) 91m/C Gene Washington, Carl Eller, Lem Barney, Mercury Morris, Joe "Mean Joe" Greene, Willie Lanier, Rosalind Miles, John Isenbarger, Ben Davidson, Maury Wills; *D:* Matt Cimber. **VHS, Beta** $49.90 UNI 𝅗𝅥

The Black Stallion A young boy and a wild Arabian Stallion are the only survivors of a shipwreck, and they develop a deep affection for each other. When rescued, they begin training for an important race. Exceptionally beautiful first half. Rooney plays a horse trainer, again. Great for adults and kids. Music by Carmine Coppola.
1979 (PG) 120m/C Kelly Reno, Mickey Rooney, Teri Garr, Clarence Muse; *D:* Carroll Ballard. Academy Awards '79: Best Sound Effects Editing; Nominations: Best Film Editing, Best Supporting Actor (Rooney). **VHS, Beta, LV** $19.98 MGM, FOX, TLF 𝅗𝅥𝅗𝅥𝅗𝅥½

The Black Stallion Returns Sequel to "The Black Stallion" follows the adventures of young Alec as he travels to the Sahara to search for his beautiful horse, which was stolen by an Arab chieftain. Unfortunately lacks much of the charm that was present in the first film. Adapted from the stories by Walt Farley.
1983 (PG) 103m/C Kelly Reno, Teri Garr, Vincent Spano; *D:* Robert Dalva. **VHS, Beta, LV** $19.98 FOX 𝅗𝅥𝅗𝅥½

Black Starlet A girl from the projects of Chicago travels to Hollywood in search of fame. She winds her way through a world of sleaze and drugs in order to make it to the top. Also on video as "Black Gauntlet."
1974 (R) 90m/C Juanita Brown, Eric Mason, Rockne Tarkington, Damu King, Diane Holden; *D:* Chris Munger. **VHS** $59.95 GEM 𝅗𝅥

Black Sunday Executed one hundred years previously, a witch returns with her vampire servant to do the bidding of Satan. A must see for horror fans; firsts for Steele as star and Bava as director. Also available with "Black Sabbath" on Laser Disc.
1960 83m/B IT Barbara Steele, John Richardson, Ivo Garrani, Andrea Checchi, Arturo Dominici; *D:* Mario Bava. **VHS** $19.98 SNC, MRV, MOV 𝅗𝅥𝅗𝅥𝅗𝅥

Black Sunday An Arab terrorist group plots to steal the Goodyear Blimp and load it with explosives. Their intent is to explode it over a Miami Super Bowl game to assassinate the U.S. president and to kill all the fans. Based on Thomas Harris' novel.
1977 (R) 143m/C Robert Shaw, Bruce Dern, Marthe Keller, Fritz Weaver, Steven Keats, Michael Gazzo, William Daniels; *D:* John Frankenheimer; *M:* John Thaw. **VHS, Beta, LV** $24.95 PAR 𝅗𝅥𝅗𝅥½

Black Terrorist Terrorists take over a ranch and slay the inhabitants. They keep a young boy alive and the mother tries to rescue him.
1985 81m/C Allan Granville, Vera Jones; *D:* Neil Hetherington. **VHS, Beta** NO 𝅗𝅥𝅗𝅥½

Black Tide Suspicions arise that a drowning may have actually been a murder. *AKA:* Stormy Crossing.
1956 ?m/C John Ireland, Derek Bond. **VHS** $16.95 SNC 𝅗𝅥𝅗𝅥

Black Tights Chevalier introduces four stories told in dance by Roland Petit's Ballet de Paris company: "The Diamond Crusher," "Cyrano de Bergerac," "A Merry Mourning," and "Carmen." A keeper for dance fans. Shearer's Roxanne in "Cyrano" was her last

performance before retirement. *AKA:* Un, Deux, Trois, Quatre!.
1960 120m/C FR Cyd Charisse, Zizi Jeanmarie, Moira Shearer, Dirk Sanders, Roland Petit; *D:* Terence Young. **VHS, Beta** $29.95 MVD, NOS, VAI 𝅗𝅥𝅗𝅥½

Black Tower An interesting murder mystery telling the story of a desperately impoverished medical student.
1950 54m/B Peter Cookson, Warren Williams, Anne Gwynne, Charles Calvert. **VHS, Beta** $24.95 VYY 𝅗𝅥𝅗𝅥

Black Vampire Jones plays a professor of African studies who is turned into a vampire by another vampire. He then marries the villain's ex-wife, played by Clark, a veteran of Russ Meyer films. Not much of a story but the acting is actually quite good and there are some creepy moments thanks mainly to an interesting score. *AKA:* Blood Couple; Ganja and Hess; Double Possession.
1973 (R) 83m/C Duane Jones, Marlene Clark, Bill Gunn, Sam Waymon, Leonard Jackson, Candece Tarpley, Mabel King; *W/D:* Bill Gunn. **VHS, Beta** $9.95 SIM, GEM 𝅗𝅥½

A Black Veil for Lisa A man attempts to exact revenge upon his unfaithful wife, but things go horribly awry.
1968 87m/C IT GE John Mills, Lucianna Paluzzi, Robert Hoffman; *D:* Massimo Dallamano. **VHS** REP 𝅗𝅥𝅗𝅥

Black Venus A soft-core epic, starring the former Miss Bahamas, Josephine Jacqueline Jones, about the 18th-century French aristocracy. Laughably based upon the stories of Balzac. European film dubbed in English.
1983 (R) 80m/C Josephine Jacqueline Jones, Emiliano Redondo; *D:* Claude Mulot. **VHS, Beta** $79.95 MGM Woof!

Black Water Gold Television movie about a search for sunken Spanish gold.
1969 75m/C Ricardo Montalban, Keir Dullea, Lana Wood, Bradford Dillman, France Nuyen; *D:* Alan Landsburg. **VHS** NO 𝅗𝅥𝅗𝅥½

Black Werewolf A millionaire sportsman invites a group of men and women connected with bizarre deaths or the eating of human flesh to spend the cycle of a full moon at his isolated lodge. *AKA:* The Beast Must Die.
1975 (PG) 93m/C GB Peter Cushing, Calvin Lockhart, Charles Gray, Anton Diffring; *D:* Paul Annett. **VHS, Beta, LV** $9.95 SIM, MED, PSM 𝅗𝅥𝅗𝅥

The Black Widow A fortune-teller plots to steal scientific secrets and take over the world. Serial in thirteen episodes. *AKA:* Sombra, the Spider Woman.
1947 164m/B Bruce Edwards, Carol Forman, Anthony Warde; *D:* Spencer Gordon Bennet. **VHS** $19.98 VCN, REP, MLB 𝅗𝅥𝅗𝅥

Black Widow A federal agent pursues a beautiful murderess who marries rich men and then kills them, making the deaths look natural. The agent herself becomes involved in the final seduction. The two women are enticing and the locations picturesque.
1987 (R) 97m/C Debra Winger, Theresa Russell, Sami Frey, Nicol Williamson, Terry O'Quinn, Dennis Hopper; *D:* Bob Rafelson. **VHS, Beta, LV** $19.98 FOX 𝅗𝅥𝅗𝅥½

The Black Windmill An English spy is caught between his service and the kidnapping of his family by rival spies.
1974 (PG) 102m/C Michael Caine, Donald Pleasence, Delphine Seyrig, Clive Revill, Janet Suzman, John Vernon; *D:* Don Siegel. **VHS, Beta** $59.95 MCA 𝅗𝅥𝅗𝅥½

Blackbeard the Pirate The 18th-century buccaneer is given the full-blooded, Hollywood treatment.

B

1952 99m/C Robert Newton, Linda Darnell, Keith Andes, William Bendix, Richard Egan; *D:* Raoul Walsh. VHS, Beta, LV $19.98 *RKO, TTC* 🎞🎞

Blackbeard's Ghost Disney comedy in which the famed 18th-century pirate's spirit (Ustinov) summoned to wreak havoc in order to prevent an old family home from being turned into a casino.
1967 107m/C Peter Ustinov, Dean Jones, Suzanne Pleshette, Elsa Lanchester, Richard Deacon; *D:* Robert Stevenson. VHS, Beta, LV $19.99 *DIS* 🎞🎞

Blackbelt 2: Fatal Force A man seeks to avenge his brother's murder by going after his killers.
1992 (R) ?m/C Blake Bahner, Roxanne Baird, Michael Vlastas. VHS $89.98 *NHO* 🎞🎞½

Blackboard Jungle Well-remembered urban drama about an idealistic teacher in a slum area who fights doggedly to connect with his unruly students. Bill Hailey's "Rock Around the Clock" over the opening credits was the first use of rock music in a mainstream feature film. Based on Evan Hunter novel.
1955 101m/B Glenn Ford, Anne Francis, Louis Calhern, Sidney Poitier, Vic Morrow, Richard Kiley, Margaret Hayes, John Hoyt, Warner Anderson; *D:* Richard Brooks. VHS, Beta $19.95 *MGM* 🎞🎞🎞½

Blackenstein Doctor into nouveau experimentation restores a man's arms and legs. But a jealous assistant gives our man a bogus injection, causing him to become "Blackenstein," a large African American with chip on hulking shoulder who enjoys killing people and otherwise causing big trouble. Ripe blaxploitation. *AKA:* Black Frankenstein.
1973 (R) 87m/C John Hart, Ivory Stone, Andrea King, Liz Renay, Joe DiSue; *D:* William A. Levey. VHS, Beta $29.95 *MED Woof!*

Blackjack Las Vegas is the scene for action and excitement as the mob puts the hit on tough guy William Smith!
1978 (R) 104m/C William Smith, Tony Burton, Paris Earl, Damu King, Diane Summerfield, Angela May; *D:* John Evans. VHS *TPV* 🎞🎞

Blackmail This first sound film for Great Britain and director Hitchcock features an early visualization of some typical Hitchcockian themes. The story follows the police investigation of a murder, and a detective's attempts to keep his girlfriend from being involved. Look for Hitchcock's very first on-screen cameo. Made as a silent, this was reworked to become a talkie.
1929 86m/B GB Anny Ondra, John Longdon, Sara Allgood, Charles Paton, Cyril Ritchard; *Cameos:* Alfred Hitchcock; *D:* Alfred Hitchcock. VHS, Beta, LV, 3/4U, Special order formats $9.95 *NEG, MRV, NOS* 🎞🎞🎞

Blackmail Familiar story is given new life in this suspenseful movie originally made for cable TV. Blakely is a lonely woman who succumbs to Midkiff's attentions. She doesn't suspect that he's conning her with the help of his lover, Toussaint. Engaging thriller adapted from a short story by Bill Crenshaw.
1991 (R) 87m/C Susan Blakely, Dale Midkiff, Beth Toussaint, John Saxon, Mac Davis; *D:* Ruben Preuss. VHS, Beta *PAR* 🎞🎞🎞

Blackout Blind man recovers his sight and finds that the brother of his girlfriend, once thought dead, is actually alive and well and running a smuggling ring. Routine.
1950 73m/B GB Maxwell Reed, Dinah Sheridan, Patric Doonan, Eric Pohlmann; *D:* Robert S. Baker. VHS, Beta $16.95 *SNC* 🎞½

Blackout A drunken private eye is offered a murder case, and is subsequently framed for the crime. *AKA:* Murder by Proxy.
1954 87m/B Dane Clark, Belinda Lee, Betty Ann Davies; *D:* Terence Fisher. VHS, Beta, LV $89.98 *MLB* 🎞🎞

Blackout Four killers terrorize an office building during the 1977 New York electrical blackout. Soon the police enter, confront them, and the fun starts. Comic touches provide some relief from the violence here.
1978 (R) 86m/C Jim Mitchum, Robert Carradine, Ray Milland, June Allyson, Jean-Pierre Aumont, Belinda J. Montgomery; *D:* Eddy Matalon. VHS, Beta $59.95 *NLC* 🎞🎞

Blackout Made-for-cable-TV thriller. An aging police chief suspects a disfigured amnesiac is responsible for past killings, in spite of the fact that he now leads a subdued family life.
1985 99m/C Richard Widmark, Keith Carradine, Kathleen Quinlan, Michael Beck; *D:* Douglas Hickox. VHS, Beta $79.95 *MED* 🎞🎞½

Blackout Strange memories from childhood come back to her as a woman fights for her life.
1988 (R) 91m/C Carol Lynley, Gail O'Grady, Michael Keys Hall, Joseph Gian, Joanna Miles; *D:* Doug Adams. VHS, Beta, LV *NO* 🎞🎞

The Blacksmith/The Balloonatic Two Buster Keaton shorts: "The Blacksmith" (1922) features Buster as the local blacksmith's apprentice who suddenly finds himself in charge. "The Balloonatic" (1923) presents Buster trapped in a runaway hot air balloon. Both films include music score.
1923 57m/B Buster Keaton, Virginia Fox, Phyllis Haver; *D:* Buster Keaton. VHS, Beta $29.95 *VYY* 🎞🎞

The Blacksmith/The Cops "The Blacksmith" is a burlesque of Longfellow's famous poem "The Village Blacksmith." In "Cops" Buster tries a new business venture to win his girl's hand. Chaos ensues. Silent comedy at its most adroit.
1922 38m/B Buster Keaton, Virginia Fox. VHS, Beta $19.95 *CCB* 🎞🎞

Blacula The African Prince Mamuwalde stalks the streets of Los Angeles trying to satisfy his insatiable desire for blood. Mildly successful melding of blaxploitation and horror that spawned a sequel, "Scream, Blacula, Scream."
1972 (PG) 92m/C William Marshall, Thalmus Rasulala, Denise Nicholas, Vonetta McGee; *D:* William Crain. VHS, Beta, LV $9.98 *ORI, HBO* 🎞🎞

Blade An honest cop challenges a dirty cover-up in killer-stalked New York.
1972 (PG) 79m/C Steve Landesburg, John Schuck, Kathryn Walker; *D:* Ernie Pintoff. VHS, Beta $59.95 *GEM, MRV* 🎞

Blade in Hong Kong Made-for-TV action outing. Investigator travels to Hong Kong, finds trouble and romance in the underbelly of the city. Pilot for un-sold series.
1985 100m/C Terry Lester, Keye Luke, Mike Preston, Jean-Marie Hon, Leslie Nielsen, Nancy Kwan, Anthony Newley, Ellen Regan; *D:* Reza Badiyi. VHS *NO* 🎞🎞

A Blade in the Dark A young man composing a score for a horror film moves into a secluded villa and is inspired and haunted by the mysterious murder he witnesses. *AKA:* La Casa Con La Scala Nel Buio; House of the Dark Stairway.
1983 99m/C Andrea Occhipinti, Anny Papa; *D:* Lamberto Bava. VHS, Beta $69.98 *VES, LIV* 🎞🎞

Blade Master In this sequel to "Ator the Fighting Eagle," O'Keeffe as Ator is back as the Blade Master. Ator defends his people and his family name in a battle against the "Geometric Nucleus": a primitive bomb. His quest leads him and his small band of men to the castle of knowledge. *AKA:* Ator the Invincible.
1984 (PG) 92m/C Miles O'Keeffe, Lisa Foster; *D:* David Hills. VHS, Beta $19.95 *MED* 🎞½

Blade of the Ripper A madman armed with a razor slashes his way through the lovelies of the international jet set.
1984 90m/C George Hilton, Edwige Fenech. VHS, Beta *NO Woof!*

Blade Runner In Los Angeles of the 29th century, a world-weary cop tracks down a handful of murdering, renegade "replicants" (synthetically produced human slaves who, with only days left of life, search madly for some way to extend their prescribed lifetimes). A moody, beautifully photographed dark thriller with sets from an architect's dream. Music by Vangelis. Based on "Do Androids Dream of Electric Sheep" by Philip K. Dick. Laser edition features restored footage, information about special effects and production sketches. A director's cut, released at 117 minutes, removes Ford's narration and the last scene of the film, which Scott considered too "up," as well as inserting several short scenes, including a dream sequence.
1982 (R) 122m/C Harrison Ford, Rutger Hauer, Sean Young, Daryl Hannah, M. Emmet Walsh, Edward James Olmos, Joe Turkel, Brion James, Joanna Cassidy; *D:* Ridley Scott; *W:* Hampton Fancher, David Peoples. VHS, Beta, LV, SVS, 8mm $9.95 *COL, WAR, SUP* 🎞🎞🎞½

Blades Another junk heap from Troma, dealing with the efforts of three golfers who try to stop a maniacal power mower that's been grinding duffers with regularity.
1989 (R) 101m/C Robert North, Jeremy Whelan, Victoria Scott, Jon McBride. VHS, Beta, LV $79.98 *MED* 🎞

Blades of Courage A made-for-television biography of Olympic skater Lori Larouche. Choreographed by Debbi Wilkes. *AKA:* Skate!.
1988 98m/C CA Lynn Nightingale, Christianne Hirt, Colm Feore, Rosemary Dunsmore; *D:* Randy Bradshaw. VHS, Beta $29.95 *ACA* 🎞🎞

Bladestorm Ultra-cheapo fantasy/warrior rehash.
1986 87m/C VHS, Beta *NO* 🎞

Blaise Pascal Another of Rossellini's later historical portraits, detailing the life and times of the 17th-century philosopher, seen as a man whose scientific ideas conflicted with his own religious beliefs. Made for Italian television. In Italian with subtitles.
1971 131m/C IT *D:* Roberto Rossellini. VHS, Beta $79.95 *FCT* 🎞🎞🎞½

Blake of Scotland Yard Blake, the former Scotland Yard inspector, battles against a villain who has constructed a murderous death ray.
1936 70m/B Ralph Byrd, Herbert Rawlinson, Joan Barclay, Lloyd Hughes; *D:* Robert Hill. VHS, Beta $29.95 *NOS, DVT, VCN* 🎞🎞½

Blake's Seven Freedom-fighter Blake and his crew battle against a totalitarian super-power in this futuristic space adventure series from Great Britain. Created by Terry Nation of "Doctor Who" fame. Each volume contains two episodes and is available individually.

198? 105m/C *GB* Gareth Thomas, Sally Knyvette, Paul Darrow, Michael Keating, David Jackson, Jan Chappell; *D:* Michael E. Briant, Vere Lorrimer. VHS $24.98 *BFS, TVC, MOV* 🎥🎥½

Blame It on Rio A middle-aged man has a ridiculous fling with his best friend's daughter while on vacation with them in Rio de Janeiro. Caine and Johnson are amusing, but the script is somewhat weak. Remake of the French film "One Wild Moment."
1984 90m/C Michael Caine, Joseph Bologna, Demi Moore, Michelle Johnson, Valerie Harper; *D:* Stanley Donen. VHS, Beta, LV $29.95 *VES, LIV* 🎥🎥

Blame It on the Bellboy Wild farce set in Venice about a hotel bellboy who confuses three similarly named visitors—sending the wrong ones to meet corporate bigwigs, date women, or even kill. The brisk loses it paces towards the end and devolves into chase scenes.
1992 (PG-13) 79m/C Dudley Moore, Bryan Brown, Richard Griffiths, Andreas Katsulas, Patsy Kensit, Alison Steadman, Bronson Pinchot, Lindsay Anderson, Penelope Wilton; *W/D:* Mark Herman. VHS, Beta $94.95 *HPH* 🎥🎥½

Blame It on the Night A rock star gets to take care of the military cadet son he never knew after the boy's mother suddenly dies. Mick Jagger helped write the story. Available in VHS and Beta Hi-Fi.
1984 (PG-13) 85m/C Nick Mancuso, Byron Thames, Leslie Ackerman, Billy Preston, Merry Clayton; *D:* Gene Taft. VHS, Beta $79.98 *FOX* 🎥🎥

The Blasphemer A well-crafted, engrossing drama about misfortune that befalls someone who disobeys one of the sacred Commandments. Silent music score.
1921 89m/B VHS, Beta $29.95 *VYY* 🎥🎥

Blastfighter After local hoodlums kill his daughter, an ex-con cop goes on a spree of violence and revenge. Director Bava uses the pseudonym "John Old, Jr.," as his father Mario Bava occasionally credited himself as John Old. Italian film shot in Atlanta.
1985 (R) 93m/C *IT* Michael Sopkiw, Valerie Blake, George Eastman; *D:* Lamberto Bava. VHS, Beta $69.95 *VES, LIV Woof!*

Blat A gangster of Italian-Russian descent tries to pull a sting on merry old England's financial world in this comedy. Made for British television.
19?? 90m/C *GB* Robert Hardy, Adrienne Corri, Alfred Molina. VHS $49.95 *FCT* 🎥½

Blaxploitation Cartoons A collection of seldom seen racist cartoons featuring Amos 'n' Andy, Little Black Sambo and other stereotyped characters. Some black and white sequences.
194? 46m/C VHS, Beta $24.95 *DVT, PTB* 🎥½

Blaze The true story of Louisiana governor Earl Long who became involved with a stripper, Blaze Starr, causing a political scandal of major proportions. Robust, good-humored bio-pic featuring a fine character turn by Newman.
1989 (R) 117m/C Paul Newman, Lolita Davidovich, Jerry Hardin, Robert Wuhl, Gailard Sartain, Jeffrey DeMunn, Richard Jenkins; *D:* Ron Shelton. VHS, Beta, LV $89.95 *TOU* 🎥🎥½

Blaze Starr: The Original The enormously "gifted" soft-porn star of the sixties joins a nudist camp. Wacky exploits ensue.
1963 80m/C VHS $39.95 *FXL* 🎥

Blazing Guns A marshal, masquerading inexplicably as a tenderfoot, enters a lawless town and is immediately hired as a deputy.

1950 54m/B Raymond Hatton, Russell Hayden, Fuzzy Knight, Betty Adams. VHS, Beta, LV $19.95 *NOS, HEG* 🎥

The Blazing Ninja Deadly kung-fu senses-dulling mind-paralyzing experience about master of some martial art versus student of same.
19?? 86m/C *HK* Philip Cheung, Sony Tanaka, Ronny Lee, Tim Chen, Sandy Peng, Godfrey Ho; *D:* Godfrey Ho; *W:* Szeto On. VHS $14.98 *VTR Woof!*

Blazing Saddles Wild, wacky spoof by Brooks of every cliche in the western film genre. Little is Black Bart, a convict offered a reprieve if he will become a sheriff and clean up a nasty frontier town; the previous recipients of this honor have all swiftly ended up in shallow graves. A crazy, silly film with a cast full of loveable loonies including comedy greats Wilder, Kahn, and Korman. Watch for the Count Basie Orchestra. A group writing effort, based on an original story by Bergman. Was the most-viewed movie in its first year of release on HBO cable.
1974 (R) 90m/C Cleavon Little, Harvey Korman, Madeline Kahn, Gene Wilder, Mel Brooks, John Hillerman, Alex Karras, Dom DeLuise, Liam Dunn; *W/D:* Mel Brooks, Alan Uger; *W:* Norman Steinberg, Andrew Bergman, Richard Pryor; *M:* John Morris. VHS, Beta, LV $19.98 *WAR* 🎥🎥🎥½

Blazing Stewardesses The Hound salutes the distributor for truth in advertising, as they stamped this as one of the world's worst videos. Lusty, busty stewardesses relax at a western guest ranch under siege from hooded riders and the aging gags of the Ritz Brothers.
1975 (R) 95m/C Yvonne De Carlo, Bob Livingston, Donald (Don "Red") Barry, The Ritz Brothers, Regina Carrol; *D:* Al Adamson. VHS $14.98 *VID Woof!*

Bleak House The British television miniseries adaptation of the Charles Dickens tome about an interminable lawsuit and the decadent, criminal ruling class of 19th-century England. On three tapes.
1985 391m/C *GB* Denholm Elliott, Diana Rigg, Philip Franks, Peter Vaughan, T.P. McKenna, Charles Drake; *D:* Ross Devenish. VHS, Beta $29.98 *FOX, SIG, TVC* 🎥🎥½

Bless the Beasts and Children A group of six teenage boys at a summer camp attempt to save a herd of buffalo from slaughter at a national preserve. Treacly Kramer backwater. Based on the novel by Glendon Swarthout.
1971 (PG) 109m/C Billy Mumy, Barry Robins, Miles Chapin, Darel Glaser, Bob Kramer, Ken Swofford, Jesse White; *D:* Stanley Kramer. VHS, Beta $14.95 *COL* 🎥🎥½

Blessed Event Fast-moving, entertaining film about a Broadway gossip columnist with a poison pen. Tracy has the role of a lifetime as a Walter Winchell prototype who thinks no one is exempt from his juicy column. Powell makes film debut as a crooner after a brief career as a band singer. Based on a play by Manuel Seff and Forrest Wilson.
1932 77m/B Lee Tracy, Mary Brian, Dick Powell, Allen Jenkins, Ruth Donnelly, Emma Dunn, Walter Miller, Tom Dugan, Isabel Jewell; *D:* Roy Del Ruth; *W:* Howard J. Green. VHS $19.98 *MGM* 🎥🎥🎥

Blind Ambition Television mini-series docu-drama traces the career of John Dean, special counsel to President Richard M. Nixon. Focuses on his fractured personal life and touches on virtually all of the Watergate headlines.
1982 95m/C Martin Sheen, Rip Torn. VHS, Beta *TLF* 🎥🎥½

Blind Date Blind man agrees to have a visual computer implanted in his brain in order to help the police track down a psychopathic killer. Violent scenes may be disturbing to some.
1984 (R) 100m/C Joseph Bottoms, Kirstie Alley, Keir Dullea, James Daughton, Lana Clarkson, Marina Sirtis; *D:* Nico Mastorakis. VHS, Beta, LV $79.95 *VES, LIV* 🎥🎥½

Blind Date A blind date between a workaholic yuppie and a beautiful blonde starts off well, but when she drinks too much at dinner, things get out of hand. In addition to embarrassing her date and destroying the restaurant, she has a jealous ex-boyfriend who must be dealt with.
1987 (PG-13) 95m/C Kim Basinger, Bruce Willis, John Larroquette, William Daniels, George Coe, Mark Blum, Phil Hartman, Stephanie Faracy, Alice Hirson, Graham Stark; *D:* Blake Edwards. VHS, Beta, LV $14.95 *COL* 🎥🎥

Blind Faith Action and adventure take a turn for the horrific when several men find themselves in captivity.
1989 (R) ?m/C Eric Gunn, Kevin Yon, Lynne Browne; *W/D:* Dean Wilson. VHS *HHE* 🎥

Blind Fear A blind woman is stalked by three killers in an abandoned country inn.
1989 (R) 98m/C Shelley Hack, Jack Langedijk, Kim Coates, Jan Rubes, Heidi von Palleske; *D:* Tom Berry. VHS, Beta, LV $29.95 *ACA* 🎥½

Blind Fists of Bruce A rich, idle young man learns the techniques of kung fu from a former warrior.
1977? 92m/C Bruce Li; *D:* Kam Bo. VHS, Beta *NO* 🎥½

Blind Fools A scathing indictment of children neglected by ambitious parents.
1940 66m/B Herbert Rawlinson, Claire Whitney, Russell Hicks, Miriam Battista. VHS, Beta, LV *NO* 🎥½

Blind Fury A blind Vietnam vet enlists the aid of a Zen master and a sharpshooter to tackle the Mafia.
1990 (R) 86m/C Rutger Hauer, Terry O'Quinn, Lisa Blount, Randall "Tex" Cobb, Noble Willingham, Meg Foster, Sho Kosugi; *D:* Phillip Noyce. VHS, Beta, LV $89.95 *COL, FCT* 🎥🎥½

Blind Husbands An Austrian officer is attracted to the pretty wife of a dull surgeon. Controversial in its day, this lurid, sumptuous melodrama instigated many stubborn Hollywood myths, including the stereotype of the brusque, jodhpur-clad Prussian director. This was von Stroheim's first outing as director.
1919 98m/B Erich von Stroheim, Fay Wray; *D:* Erich von Stroheim. VHS, Beta $27.95 *VYY* 🎥🎥½

Blind Justice An innocent man is identified as a rapist, and the accusation ruins his life. Made for television.
1986 94m/C Tim Matheson, Lisa Eichhorn, Mimi Kuzyk, Philip Charles MacKenzie, Tom Atkins; *D:* Rod Holcomb. VHS, Beta $59.98 *FOX* 🎥🎥

Blind Man's Bluff A blind professor is accused of murdering his neighbor, but as he tries to solve the mystery, evidence points to his ex-girlfriend who may have framed him for the murder. Surprisingly suspenseful made for cable TV movie is hampered by a stock Hollywood ending.
1991 (PG-13) 86m/C Robert Urich, Lisa Eilbacher, Patricia Clarkson, Ken Pogue, Ron Perlman; *D:* James Quinn; *W:* Joel Gross. VHS, Beta *PAR* 🎥🎥

Blind Rage When the United States government transports $15 million to the Philippines, five blind kung fu masters want a piece of the action.

1978 (R) 81m/C *PH* D'Urville Martin, Leo Fong, Tony Ferrer, Dick Adair, Darnell Garcia, Leila Hermosa, Fred Williamson; *D:* Efren C. Pinon. **VHS, Beta** $59.95 *MGM* 🎬

Blind Side DeMornay and Silver are a married couple whose Mexican vacation turns into trouble when they get into a hit-and-run accident which they don't report. Back home, they're frightened by the sudden appearance of Hauer, who's also just back from Mexico. They think he's after blackmail but he's really just a run-of-the-mill psycho intrigued by DeMornay, who at least keeps her character in control. Silver and Hauer have a great time chewing scenery. Made for cable television. Also available in an unrated version which run 98 minutes.
1993 (R) 92m/C Rebecca DeMornay, Ron Silver, Rutger Hauer; *D:* Geoff Murphy. **VHS** $79.99 *HBO* 🎬½

Blind Vengeance A man whose son was murdered by white supremacists decides to take his own special revenge when they are acquitted by the local jury. But this isn't your usual bloodbath, instead he plays psychological games with the men, waiting for them to break. Made for cable television.
1990 (R) 93m/C Gerald McRaney, Marg Helgenberger, Thalmus Rasulala, Lane Smith, Don Hood, Grand Bush; *D:* Lee Philips; *W:* Henri Simoun, Curt Allen. **VHS** $79.95 *MCA* 🎬🎬½

Blind Vision Von Dohlen stars as William Dalton, a mail clerk who is in love with his beautiful neighbor Leanne (Shelton). Suffering from extreme shyness, Dalton can only spy on her through a telephoto lens. Things start to get complicated for him when one of Leanne's boyfriends turns up dead outside her apartment. Soon afterwards, their landlady and a local police detective uncover a shocking sexual secret that forces Dalton into a deadly game of obsession and desire.
1991 92m/C Lenny Von Dohlen, Deborah Shelton, Ned Beatty, Robert Vaughn, Louise Fletcher; *D:* Shuki Levy. **VHS, LV** $89.95 *WOV* 🎬½

Blinded by the Light Young woman tries to save her brother from attachment to a quasi-religious cult, The Light of Salvation. Real-life brother and sister McNichol team up in this made-for-television drama, one of the earlier examinations of cult behavior.
1982 90m/C Kristy McNichol, Jimmy McNichol, Anne Jackson, Michael McGuire; *D:* John Alonzo. **VHS, Beta** *TLF* 🎬🎬

Blindside A surveillance hobbyist who owns a motel spies on his tenants until a murder involves him in a big-scale drug war.
1988 (R) 98m/C Harvey Keitel, Lori Hallier, Lolita David, Alan Fawcett, Michael Rudder; *D:* Paul Lynch. **VHS, Beta, LV** $14.98 *NLC* 🎬🎬

Blink of an Eye Special agent Sam Browning (Pare) must use his psychic powers and military skills against the terrorists who have kidnapped the CIA director's daughter.
1992 (R) 90m/C Michael Pare. **VHS, LV** $89.95 *VMK* 🎬🎬½

Bliss A savage, surreal Australian comedy about an advertising executive who dies suddenly for a few minutes, and upon his awakening he finds the world maniacally, bizarrely changed. Based on the Peter Carey novel, and one of the most inspired absurdist films of the decade.
1985 (R) 112m/C *AU* Barry Otto, Lynette Curran, Helen Jones; *D:* Ray Lawrence. **VHS, Beta, LV** $19.95 *NWV, STE* 🎬🎬🎬½

The Bliss of Mrs. Blossom Three's a crowd in this light-hearted romp through the machinations of a brassiere manufacturer (Attenborough) and his neglected wife (MacLaine). Mrs. Blossom finds sewing machine repairman Booth so appetizing that she hides him in the attic of the Blossom home. He reads books and redecorates, until, several plot twists later, Attenborough discovers the truth. Witty and wise, with fine supporting cast and excellent pacing.
1968 93m/C *GB* Shirley MacLaine, Richard Attenborough, James Booth, Freddie Jones, John Cleese; *D:* Joseph McGrath. **VHS** $14.95 *PAR, MOV* 🎬🎬🎬

Blithe Spirit Charming and funny adaptation of Coward's famed stage play. A man remarries and finds his long-dead wife is unhappy enough about it to come back and haunt him. Clever supporting cast, with Rutherford exceptional as the medium. Received Oscar for its Special Effects.
1945 96m/C Rex Harrison, Constance Cummings, Kay Hammond, Margaret Rutherford, Hugh Wakefield, Joyce Carey; *D:* David Lean. **VHS** *MLB* 🎬🎬🎬½

The Blob McQueen's first starring role. Science fiction thriller about a small town's fight against a slimy jello invader from space. McQueen's slightly rebellious character redeems himself when he saves the town with quick action. Low-budget, horror/teen-fantasy that became a camp classic. Other names considered for the movie included "The Glob," "The Glob that Girdled the Globe," "The Meteorite Monster," "The Molten Meteorite," and "The Night of the Creeping Dead." Followed by a worthless sequel in 1972, "Son of Blob" (directed by Larry Hagman), and a worthwhile remake in 1988, LV edition contains an additional fifteen minutes of McQueen interviews and the trailers for both the original and the 1988 remake.
1958 83m/C Steve McQueen, Aneta Corseaut, Olin Howland, Earl Rowe; *D:* Irvin S. Yeaworth Jr. **VHS, Beta, LV** $19.95 *COL, GEM, VYG* 🎬🎬½

The Blob A hi-tech remake of the 1958 camp classic about a small town beset by a fast-growing, man-eating mound of glop shot into space by scientists, irradiated into an unnatural being, and then returned to earth. Well-developed characters make this an excellent tribute to the first film.
1988 (R) 92m/C Kevin Dillon, Candy Clark, Joe Seneca, Shawnee Smith, Donovan Leitch, Jeffrey DeMunn; *D:* Chuck Russell. **VHS, Beta, LV** $89.95 *COL* 🎬🎬🎬

Block-heads Twenty years after the end of World War I, soldier Stan is found, still in his foxhole, and brought back to America, where he moves in with old pal Ollie. Also includes a 1934 Charley Chase short "I'll Take Vanilla."
1938 75m/B Stan Laurel, Oliver Hardy, Billy Gilbert, Patricia Ellis, James Finlayson, Charley Chase; *D:* John Blystone. **VHS, Beta** $19.95 *CCB, MED, MLB* 🎬🎬🎬

Blockhouse Four men are entombed in a subterranean stronghold for six years after the D-Day invasion of Normandy. Encourages claustrophobic feeling in viewer. Based on Jean Paul Cleberts' novel "Le Blockhaus."
1973 88m/C *GB* Peter Sellers, Charles Aznavour, Per Oscarsson, Peter Vaughan, Leon Lissek, Alfred Lynch, Jeremy Kemp; *D:* Clive Rees. **VHS, Beta** $42.95 *PGN Woof!*

Blonde Cobra/The Doctor's Dream Here are two short films by Ken Jacobs: Underground film star Jack Smith reminisces about his career in "Blonde Co-

bra" and a country doctor saves the life of a little girl in "Doctor's Dream."
1984 57m/C **VHS, Beta** *NO Woof!*

Blonde Crazy A charming grifter hooks up with a gorgeous blonde as he works the territory of a big wheel criminal. Escapist fare, with fun performances from Cagney and Blondell. *AKA:* Larceny Lane.
1931 81m/B James Cagney, Joan Blondell, Louis Calhern, Ray Milland, Nat Pendleton; *D:* Roy Del Ruth. **VHS** $19.98 *MGM* 🎬🎬½

Blonde in Black Leather A bored Italian housewife takes up with a leather-clad lady biker, and together they cavort about.
1977 88m/C Claudia Cardinale, Monica Vitti; *D:* Carlo DiPalma. **VHS, Beta** $59.95 *NLC* 🎬½

Blonde Savage Charting African territories, an adventurer encounters a white jungle queen swinging amongst the vines. Essentially a cheap, distaff "Tarzan."
1947 62m/B Leif Erickson, Gale Sherwood, Veda Ann Borg, Douglas Dumbrille, Frank Jenks, Matt Willis, Ernest Whitman; *D:* S.K. Seeley. **VHS, Beta** $16.95 *SNC* 🎬

Blonde Venus A German cafe singer marries an Englishman, but their marriage hits the skids when he contracts radiation poisoning and she gets a nightclub job to pay the bills. Sternberg's and Dietrich's fourth film together, and characteristically beautiful, though terribly strange. Dietrich's cabaret number "Hot Voodoo," in a gorilla suit and blonde afro, attains new heights in early Hollywood surrealism.
1932 92m/B Marlene Dietrich, Herbert Marshall, Cary Grant, Dickie Moore, Hattie McDaniel, Sidney Toler; *D:* Josef von Sternberg. **VHS, Beta** $29.95 *MCA* 🎬🎬🎬½

Blood Alley A seasoned Merchant Marine captain takes on a cargo of refugee Chinese to smuggle through enemy territory. Middling, mid-career Wayne vehicle.
1955 115m/C John Wayne, Lauren Bacall, Paul Fix, Joy Kim, Berry Kroeger, Mike Mazurki, Anita Ekberg; *D:* William A. Wellman **VHS, Beta, LV** $19.98 *WAR, PIA, FCT* 🎬🎬

Blood and Black Lace Beautiful models are being brutally murdered and an inspector is assigned to the case, but not before more gruesome killings occur. Bava is, as usual, violent and suspenseful. Horror fans will enjoy this flick.
1964 90m/C *IT FR GE* Cameron Mitchell, Eva Bartok, Mary Arden; *D:* Mario Bava. **VHS, Beta** $59.95 *MED* 🎬

Blood & Concrete: A Love Story Bizarre, violent and stylish film-noir spoof, definitely not for all tastes. The innocent hero gets drawn into a maelstrom of intrigue over a killer aphrodisiac drug. Beals, an addicted punk rocker, gets to perform a few songs.
1990 (R) 97m/C Billy Zane, Jennifer Beals, Darren McGavin; *W/D:* Jeff Reiner. **VHS, LV** $89.95 *COL* 🎬🎬

Blood and Guns Romance, revenge, and action abound in post-revolutionary Mexico.
1979 (R) 96m/C Orson Welles, Tomas Milian, John Steiner; *D:* Giulio Petroni. **VHS, Beta** *MRV* 🎬½

Blood and Roses A girl who is obsessed with her family's vampire background becomes posessed by a vampire and commits numerous murders. The photography is good, but the plot is hazy and only effective in certain parts. Based on the book "Carmilla" by Sheridan LeFanu. Later remade as "The Vampire Lovers" and "The Blood-Spattered Bride." *AKA:* Et Mourir de Plaisir.

1961 74m/C Mel Ferrer, Elsa Martinelli, Annette Vadim, Marc Allegret; *D:* Roger Vadim. **VHS** *PAR* ✘✘

Blood and Sand Vintage romance based on Vincente Blasco Ibanez's novel about the tragic rise and fall of a matador, and the women in his life. The film that made Valentino a star. Remade in 1941. Silent.
1922 87m/B Rudolph Valentino, Nita Naldi, Lila Lee, Walter Long; *D:* Fred Niblo. **VHS, Beta, 3/ 4U, Special order formats $19.95** *REP, NOS, CAB* ✘✘½

Blood and Sand Director Mamoulian "painted" this picture in the new technicolor technique, which makes it a veritable explosion of color and spectacle. Power is the matador who becomes famous and then falls when he is torn between two women, forsaking his first love, bullfighting. Based on the novel "Sangre y Arena" by Vincente Blasco Ibanez. This movie catapulted Hayworth to stardom, primarily for her dancing, but also for her sexiness and seductiveness (and of course, her acting). Remake of the 1922 silent classic; remade again in 1989.
1941 123m/C Tyrone Power, Linda Darnell, Rita Hayworth, Alla Nazimova, Anthony Quinn, J. Carroll Naish, John Carradine, George Reeves; *D:* Rouben Mamoulian; *W:* Jo Swerling; *M:* Alfred Newman. Academy Awards '41: Best Color Cinematography; Nominations: Best Interior Decoration. **VHS, Beta, LV $29.99** *FOX* ✘✘✘

Blood and Sand A bullfighter on the verge of super-stardom risks it all when he falls under the spell of a sexy, seductive woman. Will she destroy his one opportunity for fame? Interesting for people who actually enjoy watching the "sport" of bullfighting. Originally made in 1922 and remade in 1941.
1989 (R) 96m/C Christopher Rydell, Sharon Stone, Ana Torrent, Jose-Luis De Villalonga, Simon Andrew; *D:* Javier Elorrieta. **VHS, LV $89.95** *VMK* ✘✘

Blood and Sand/Son of the Sheik A double feature containing two abridged versions; in "Blood and Sand," an idolized matador meets another woman just before his wedding; in "Son of the Sheik," a man believes he has been betrayed by a dancing girl, and he abducts her to seek revenge. Silent.
1926 56m/B Rudolph Valentino, Lila Lee, Vilma Banky. **VHS, Beta $29.98** *CCB* ✘✘

Blood at Sundown Routine oater where man returns home after the Civil War to find his wife kidnapped by a group of Mexican outlaws who have also taken over his village.
19?? 92m/C Giuliano Gemma, Hally Hamond, Nieves Navarro, Antonio Casas, Fernando Sancho, George Martin; *D:* Duccio Tessari. **VHS, Beta $59.95** *IMP* ✘½

Blood Avenger Vengeance becomes one man's obsession when he witnesses the brutal rape of his sister and murder of his father.
1984 ?m/C **VHS $29.95** *OCE* ✘½

Blood Beach A group of teenagers are devoured by menacing sand, which keeps people from getting to the water by swallowing them whole. Weak parody with some humorous moments; more silly than scary.
1981 (R) 92m/C David Huffman, Marianna Hill, John Saxon, Burt Young, Otis Young; *D:* Jeffrey Bloom. **VHS, Beta $54.95** *MED* Woof!

Blood Beast Terror An entomologist transforms his own daughter into a Deaths-head Moth and she proceeds to terrorize and drink innocent victims' blood. *AKA:* The Vampire-Beast Craves Blood.

1967 81m/C *GB* Peter Cushing, Robert Flemyng, Wanda Ventham; *D:* Vernon Sewell. **VHS, Beta $39.98** *MON* ✘½

Blood Bride A lonely young woman finally finds happiness with her new husband but her world comes crashing about her with soul-mangling ferocity when she discovers he is actually a bloodthirsty maniac.
19?? 90m/C Ellen Barber, Philip English. **VHS, Beta** *NO* ✘½

Blood Brothers A young man who dreams of becoming a lawyer is disturbed when he discovers that his family has mafia ties.
1974 (R) 148m/C *IT* Claudia Cardinale, Franco Nero, Lina Polito; *D:* Pasquale Squitieri. **VHS, Beta** *NO* ✘✘

Blood Brothers James Grizzly Adams, who lives in the mountains of the American wilderness, relives the story of how he met his Indian blood brother, Nakuma. Beautiful scenery.
1977 50m/C Dan Haggerty. **VHS, Beta $14.98** *MCG* ✘✘

Blood Clan Based on the true story of Katy Bane, daughter of notorious Scottish cult leader, Sawney Bane, in whose lair were found the remains of over 1000 killed and cannibilized followers. When found, Bane's entire family was sentenced to death with the exception of Katy, who left to make a new start in Canada. When a rash of mysterious deaths break out in Katy's new home, she must defend herself from rumors that her father's murderous cult is resurfacing.
1991 (R) 91m/C Gordon Pinsent, Michelle Little, Robert Wisden; *D:* Charles Wilkinson. **VHS $29.95** *MNC, FXL* ✘½

Blood Cult A bizarre series of murder-mutilations take place on a small midwestern campus. Contains graphic violence that is not for the squeamish. This film was created especially for the home video market.
1985 92m/C Chuck Ellis, Julie Andelman, Jim Vance, Joe Hardt. **VHS, Beta $24.95** *UHV* ✘

Blood Debts A father is out for revenge after he saves his daughter from some hunters who raped her and also killed her boyfriend.
1983 91m/C Richard Harrison, Mike Manty, Jim Gaines, Anne Jackson, Anne Milhench; *D:* Teddy Page. **VHS, Beta** *NO* ✘

Blood Diner Two spirit-possessed, diner-owning brothers kill countless young girls for demonic rituals, and serve their corpses as gourmet food in their restaurant. Some funny moments mixed in with the requisite gore. Cult potential.
1987 88m/C Rick Burks, Carl Crew; *D:* Jackie Kong. **VHS, Beta $19.98** *VES, LIV* Woof!

Blood Feast The first of Lewis' gore-fests, in which a demented caterer butchers hapless young women to splice them together in order to bring back an Egyptian goddess. Dated, campy, and gross; reportedly shot in four days (it shows). *AKA:* Feast of Flesh.
1963 70m/C Connie Mason, Thomas Wood, Malcolm Arnold; *D:* Herschell Gordon Lewis. **VHS, Beta $29.95** *RHI, SVI* ✘

Blood Feud In Italy preceding Europe's entry into World War II, a young widow is in mourning over the brutal murder of her husband by the Sicilian Mafia. In the meantime she must contend with the rivalry between Mastroianni as a lawyer and Giannini as a small-time crook both vying for her affections. Dubbed. *AKA:* Revenge.

1979 (R) 112m/C *IT* Sophia Loren, Marcello Mastroianni, Giancarlo Giannini; *D:* Lina Wertmuller. **VHS, Beta $59.95** *FOX* ✘✘

Blood for a Silver Dollar Action-filled western, littered with murder, revenge and romance.
1966 98m/C Montgomery Wood, Evelyn Stewart. **VHS, Beta $29.95** *VYY* ✘½

Blood Freak An absolutely insane anti-drug, Christian splatter film. A Floridian biker is introduced to drugs by a young woman and eventually turns into a poultry-monster who drinks the blood of junkies. Narrated by a chain smoker who has a coughing fit. Don't miss it.
1972 86m/C Steve Hawkes, Dana Culliver, Randy Grinter Jr., Tina Anderson, Heather Hughes; *D:* Steve Hawkes, Brad Grinter. **VHS, Beta** *NO* Woof!

Blood Frenzy Psychologist's patients take a therapeutic trip to the desert. The sun and heat take their toll, and everyone gets violent. This kind of therapy we don't need, and the movie's a waste, as well. Made for video. Loring was Wednesday on TV's "The Addams Family."
1987 90m/C John Montero, Lisa Loring, Hank Garrett, Wendy MacDonald; *D:* Hal Freeman. **VHS, Beta** *NO* ✘

Blood Games Buxom baseball team bats 1000 against the home team and the winning babes find out just how poor losers can be. Diamonds aren't always a girl's best friend.
1990 (R) 90m/C Gregory Cummings, Laura Albert, Shelly Abblett, Luke Shay, Ross Hagen; *D:* Tanya Rosenberg. **VHS, LV $79.95** *COL* Woof!

Blood Hook A self-parodying teenage-slasher film about kids running into a backwoods fishing tournament while on vacation, complete with ghouls, cannibalism and grotesquerie.
1986 85m/C Mark Jacobs, Lisa Todd, Patrick Danz; *D:* James Mallon. **VHS, Beta $14.95** *PSM, PAR* ✘✘

Blood Island A couple inherit an old house on a remote New England island where the woman grew up. They discover that this old house needs more than a paint job to make it livable; seems there's something evil in them there walls. Based on an H.P. Lovecraft story. Greene, who's best known for later directing "Godspell," and the solid cast fail to animate the inert script. *AKA:* The Shuttered Room.
1968 100m/C *GB* Gig Young, Carol Lynley, Oliver Reed, Flora Robson; *D:* David Greene. **VHS $29.98** *ACE* ✘✘

Blood Lake A psychotic killer stalks teenagers, to the detriment of all.
1987 90m/C **VHS $19.95** *UHV* Woof!

Blood Legacy Four heirs must survive a night in a lonely country estate to collect their money; what do you think happens? Average treatment of the haunted house theme. *AKA:* Legacy of Blood.
1973 (R) 77m/C John Carradine, John Russell, Faith Domergue, Merry Anders; *D:* Carl Monson. **VHS, Beta $59.95** *GEM, MRV* ✘✘

Blood Lust Dr. Jekyll returns to London to wreak havoc upon the human race.
198? 90m/C **VHS, Beta** *NO* ✘

Blood Mania A retired surgeon's daughter decides to murder her father to collect her inheritance prematurely, but soon learns that crime doesn't pay as well as medicine. Low-budget, low-interest flick.

1970 (R) 90m/C Peter Carpenter, Maria de Aragon, Alex Rocco; **D:** Robert Vincent O'Neil. **VHS, Beta** $19.95 *UHV* 🎬

Blood Money A dying ex-criminal returns to Australia to redeem his name and die with dignity.
1980 (PG) 64m/C *AU* Bryan Brown, John Flaus, Chrissie James; **D:** Christopher Fitchett. **VHS, Beta** $69.95 *SVS* 🎬½

Blood Money Man battles woman and both battle world as they struggle for the rights to a stash of loot in this lugubrious greedfest. Yet another illustrious entry in the prolific career of Ms. Black. **AKA:** The Killer's Edge.
1991 (R) ?m/C Wings Hauser, Karen Black, Robert Z'Dar. **VHS, LV** $79.95 *PMH* 🎬

Blood Money: The Story of Clinton and Nadine A confusing action/thriller with a good cast. Garcia is a small-time exotic bird smuggler whose gun-running brother has been murdered. He uses high-class hooker Barkin to get close to his brother's contacts, who turn out to be running guns to the Nicaraguan contras and involved in a dangerous government conspiracy. Made for cable television. **AKA:** Clinton & Nadine.
1988 95m/C Andy Garcia, Ellen Barkin, Morgan Freeman; **D:** Jerry Schatzberg. **VHS, Beta** $79.95 *FCT* 🎬🎬½

The Blood of a Poet Cocteau's first film, a practically formless piece of poetic cinema, detailing all manner of surreal events occurring in the instant a chimney falls. In French with English subtitles. **AKA:** Le Sang d'un Poete.
1930 55m/B Jean Cocteau; **D:** Jean Cocteau. **VHS, Beta** $24.95 *NOS, MRV, HHT* 🎬🎬½

Blood of Dracula They don't make 1950s rock'n'roll girls' school vampire movies like this anymore, for which we may be grateful. Hypnotism, an amulet, and a greasepaint makeup job turn a shy female student into a bloodsucker. **AKA:** Blood is My Heritage.
1957 71m/B Sandra Harrison, Louise Lewis, Gail Ganley, Jerry Blaine, Heather Ames, Malcolm Atterbury; **D:** Herbert L. Strock. **VHS** $9.95 *COL, MLB* 🎬½

Blood of Dracula's Castle Couple inherit an allegedly deserted castle but upon moving in, discover Mr. and Mrs. Dracula have settled there. The vampires keep young women chained in the dungeon for continual blood supply. Also present are a hunchback and a werewolf. Awesome Adamson production is highlighted by the presence of the gorgeous Volante. Early cinematography effort by the renowned Laslo Kovacs. **AKA:** Dracula's Castle.
1969 84m/C John Carradine, Alexander D'Arcy, Paula Raymond, Ray Young, Vicki Volante, Robert Dix, John Cardos; **D:** Jean Hewitt, Al Adamson. **VHS, Beta** $29.95 *UHV* 🎬

Blood of Ghastly Horror A young man thinks he has a new lease on life when he is the happy recipient of a brain transplant, but his dreams are destroyed when he evolves into a rampaging killer. This movie is so awful it hides behind numerous but rather creative aliases. **AKA:** The Fiend with the Atomic Brain; Psycho a Go Go!; The Love Maniac; The Man with the Synthetic Brain; The Fiend with the Electronic Brain.
1972 87m/C John Carradine, Kent Taylor, Tommy Kirk, Regina Carrol; **D:** Al Adamson. **VHS** $14.95 *VID, MOV* Woof!

The Blood of Heroes A post-apocalyptic action flick detailing the adventures of a battered team of "juggers," warriors who challenge small village teams to a brutal sport (involving dogs' heads on sticks) that's a cross between jousting and football. **AKA:** The Salute of the Jugger.
1989 (R) 97m/C Rutger Hauer, Joan Chen, Vincent D'Onofrio, Anna Katarina; **D:** David Peoples. **VHS, Beta, LV** $89.99 *HBO* 🎬🎬

Blood of Jesus A sinful husband accidentally shoots his newly-baptized wife, causing an uproar in their rural town. Williams later starred as Andy on the "Amos 'n' Andy" television series.
1941 50m/C Spencer Williams Jr., Kathryn Craviness; **W/D:** Spencer Williams Jr. **VHS** $34.95 *FCT, HEG* 🎬

The Blood of Others A driveling adaptation of the Simone de Beauvoir novel about a young French woman at the outbreak of World War II torn between her absent boyfriend in the Resistance and a kind, wealthy German. Made for French television, it stars Jodie Foster and Michael Ontkean as the Gallic pair.
1984 130m/C *FR* Jodie Foster, Sam Neill, Michael Ontkean, Stephane Audran, Lambert Wilson, John Vernon, Kate Reid, Jean-Pierre Aumont; **D:** Claude Chabrol. **VHS, Beta** $9.99 *STE, PSM* 🎬

Blood of the Dragon This film has martial-arts expert Wang Yu killing everyone he meets. One scene has him fighting 100 men at the same time.
1973 (R) 90m/C Wang Yu. **VHS, Beta** *NO* 🎬

Blood of the Dragon Peril/ Revenge of the Dragon Two oriental action masterworks, together on one tape for the first time.
1981 172m/C **VHS, Beta** $7.00 *VTR* 🎬½

Blood of the Vampire A Transylvanian doctor is executed for being a vampire and his hunchbacked assistant brings him back to life.
1958 84m/C *GB* Donald Wolfit, Vincent Ball, Barbara Shelley, Victor Madden; **D:** Henry Cass; **W:** Jimmy Sangster. **VHS, Beta** $59.95 *MPI, MLB* 🎬½

The Blood on Satan's Claw Graphic tale centering on the Devil himself. Townspeople in an English village circa 1670 find the spirit of Satan taking over their children, who begin to practice witchcraft. Well made with lots of attention to period details. Not for the faint-hearted. **AKA:** Satan's Skin; Satan's Claw.
1971 90m/C *GB* Patrick Wymark, Linda Hayden, Barry Andrews, Michele Dotrice; **D:** Piers Haggard. **VHS, Beta** $59.95 *PGN* 🎬🎬🎬

Blood on the Badge Illegal arms have been stolen from a military arsenal and fall into the hands of Libyan Nationalists who begin a terrorist campaign. Detective Neal Farrow is assigned to stop them.
19?? 92m/C Ramon Estevez, David Harrod, Rocky Patterson, Desiree Laforge, Dean Nolen, Melissa Deleon, Todd Everett; **D:** Bret McCormick. **VHS** $89.95 *AIP* 🎬½

Blood on the Moon Well-acted film about a cowboy's involvement in a friend's underhanded schemes. Based on a Luke Short novel, this dark film revolves around a western land dispute between cattlemen and homesteaders.
1948 88m/B Robert Mitchum, Robert Preston, Walter Brennan, Barbara Bel Geddes; **D:** Robert Wise. **VHS, Beta** $19.95 *MED, TTC* 🎬🎬½

Blood on the Mountain After escaping from prison, Jim plots revenge against his accomplice, only to kill an innocent man instead.
1988 71m/C Stracker Edwards, Tim Jones, Paula Preston, Cliff Turknett, Rich Jury; **D:** Donald W. Thompson. **VHS** *MIV* 🎬

Blood on the Sun Newspaperman in Japan uncovers plans for world dominance as propaganda, violence, and intrigue combine in this action-adventure. Also available colorized.
1945 98m/B James Cagney, Sylvia Sidney, Robert Armstrong, Wallace Ford; **D:** Frank Lloyd. **VHS, LV** $19.95 *NOS, MRV, HHT* 🎬🎬½

Blood on the Sun Martial arts action highlights this tale of adventure.
1975 (R) 81m/C Ching Ching Chang, Peng Tien. **VHS, Beta, LV** $59.95 *GEM* 🎬

Blood Orgy of the She-Devils Exploitative gore nonsense about female demons, beautiful witches, and satanic worship. Some movies waste all their creative efforts on their titles.
1974 (PG) 73m/C Lila Zaborin, Tom Pace, Leslie McRae, Ray Myles. **VHS, Beta** $19.95 *WWV* Woof!

Blood Rage A maniacal twin goes on a murderous rampage through his brother's neighborhood. AKA "Nightmare at Shadow Woods." Only for die-hard "Mary Hartman" fans. **AKA:** Nightmare at Shadow Woods.
1987 (R) 87m/C Louise Lasser, Mike Soper; **D:** John Grissmer. **VHS, Beta** $79.95 *PSM* Woof!

Blood Red In 1895 Northern California, an Italian immigrant and his family give bloody battle to a powerful industrialist who wants their land in wine-growing country. Watch for the scenes involving veteran Roberts and his then-newcomer sister, pretty woman Julia.
1988 (R) 91m/C Eric Roberts, Dennis Hopper, Giancarlo Giannini, Burt Young, Carlin Glynn, Lara Harris, Susan Anspach, Julia Roberts, Elias Koteas, Frank Campanella, Aldo Ray, Horton Foote Jr.; **D:** Peter Masterson. **VHS, Beta, LV, 8mm** $14.95 *COL, SUE* 🎬½

Blood Relations A woman is introduced to her fiance's family only to find out that they, as well as her fiance, are murdering, perverted weirdos competing for an inheritance.
1987 (R) 88m/C *CA* Jan Rubes, Ray Walston, Lydie Denier, Kevin Hicks, Lynne Adams; **D:** Graeme Campbell. **VHS, Beta, LV** $19.98 *SUE, NLC* 🎬½

Blood Relatives Suspenseful thriller with good cast. A family is too close for comfort, expressing familial bonds through murder and incest. Release in the U.S. was delayed until 1981 due to the subject matter. **AKA:** Les Liens de Sang.
1978 (R) 100m/C *CA FR* Donald Sutherland, Lisa Langlois, Donald Pleasence, Laurent Malet, David Hemmings; **D:** Claude Chabrol. **Beta, 8mm, EJ** $79.75 *UAV* 🎬🎬🎬

Blood Ring When Sue's boxer husband goes missing she enlists old friend Max to help find him. They uncover a gambling ring run by drug lords where the kickboxing matches are to the death. Naturally, Max decides to use his expert kickboxing skills to get a violent revenge.
1993 90m/C Dale "Apollo" Cook, Andrea Lamatsch, Don Nakaya Neilsen, Steve Tartalia; **D:** Irvin Johnson; **W:** Ron Davies. **VHS** $89.95 *AIP* 🎬½

Blood Salvage A crazy junkman kidnaps beautiful girls, selling their organs to the highest bidder. He meets his match when a potential target refuses to become a victim in spite of her wheelchair. Interesting plot twists keep this Grade B thriller above average. **1990 (R) 90m/C** Evander Holyfield, Lori Birdsong, Danny Nelson, John Saxon, Roy Walston; **D:** Tucker Johnson. **VHS, Beta, LV** *TTC* 🎬

Blood Screams Nosy people drop in on an old town in Mexico and attempt to uncover the secrets hidden there, but bizarre entities throw out the unwelcome mat and terrorize them. Lots of blood and screaming. **1988 (R) 75m/C** Ran Sands, James Garnett. **VHS, Beta $19.98** *WAR* Woof!

Blood Simple A jealous husband hires a sleazy private eye to murder his adulterous wife and her lover. A dark, intricate, morbid morality tale that deviates imaginatively from the standard murder mystery thriller. Written by Joel and Ethan Coen; their first film. **1985 (R) 96m/C** John Getz, M. Emmet Walsh, Dan Hedaya, Frances McDormand; **D:** Joel Coen. **VHS, Beta, LV $79.95** *MCA* 🎬🎬½

Blood Sisters Sorority babes intend to spend a giggle-strewn night in a haunted house but end up decapitated, butchered, and cannibalized. **1986 (R) 85m/C** Amy Brentano, Marla MacHart, Brigete Cossu, Randy Mooers; **D:** Roberta Findlay. **VHS, Beta $14.95** *COL, SVS* Woof!

Blood Song A patient (yester-decade teen throb Frankie Avalon) escapes into the night from a mental institution after murdering an attendant. He takes his only possession with him, a carved wooden flute. A young woman sees him burying his latest victim, and now he's on a hunt to play his "blood song" for her. Pretty bad, but fun to see Avalon play a less-than-squeaky-clean role. **AKA:** Dream Slayer. **1982 90m/C** Frankie Avalon, Donna Wilkes, Richard Jaeckel, Dane Clark, Antoinette Bower; **D:** Alan J. Levi. **VHS, Beta** *NO* 🎬

The Blood Spattered Bride Newlywed couple honeymoon in a remote castle in southern Spain. They are visited by a mysterious young woman who begins to influence the bride in the ways of lesbian bloodsucking. Okay '70s Euro-eroti-horror based on LeFanu's "Carmilla." **AKA:** Blood Castle; La Novia Esangentada. **1972 82m/C** *SP* Simon Andrew, Maribel Martin, Alexandra Bastedo, Dean Selmier, Rosa Ma Rodriguez, Montserrat Julio; **D:** Vicente Aranda. **VHS, Beta $59.95** *MPI* 🎬

The Blood Suckers Cushing stars in this horror film about vampires invading the Greek island of Hydra. **1971 ?m/C** Peter Cushing, Patrick Macnee. **VHS $16.95** *SNC* 🎬🎬

Blood Thirst Obscure horror film about a woman who stays young by indulging in ritual killings and strange experiments. **1965 ?m/C** Robert Winston, Yvonne Nielson. **VHS $16.95** *SNC* 🎬🎬

Blood Tide A disgusting, flesh-eating monster disrupts a couple's vacation in the Greek isles. Beautiful scenery, good cast, bad movie. **AKA:** The Red Tide. **1982 (R) 82m/C** James Earl Jones, Jose Ferrer. **VHS, Beta** *NO* 🎬

Blood Ties An American naval engineer in Sicily gets involved with the Mob in order to save his father's life. **1987 98m/C** *IT* Brad Davis, Tony LoBianco, Vincent Spano, Barbara de Rossi, Maria Conchita Alonso; **D:** Giacomo Battiato. **VHS, Beta $69.95** *TWE* 🎬½

Blood Tracks A woman kills her abusive husband, then hides out in the mountains with her kids until they turn into cannibalistic savages. Years later, people show up to shoot a music video. Blood runs in buckets. **1986 82m/C** Jeff Harding, Michael Fitzpatrick, Naomi Kaneda; **D:** Mike Jackson. **Beta** *NO* 🎬½

Blood Vows: The Story of a Mafia Wife TV's Laura Ingalls (Gilbert) leaps from the prairie to modern-day mafia in this warped Cinderella story. She meets the man of her dreams, whom she slowly finds is her worst nightmare as she becomes trapped within the confines of her new-found "family." Made for television. **1987 100m/C** Melissa Gilbert, Joe Penny, Eileen Brennan, Talia Shire, Anthony (Tony) Franciosa; **D:** Paul Wendkos. **VHS $39.95** *FRH* 🎬🎬

Blood Voyage A crewman aboard a pleasure yacht must find out who is killing off his passengers one by one. **1977 (R) 80m/C** Jonathon Lippe, Laurie Rose, Midori, Mara Modair; **D:** Frank Mitchell. **VHS, Beta $59.95** *MON* Woof!

Blood Wedding A wonderfully passionate dance film from Saura and choreographed by Gades, based on the play by famed author Federico Garcia Lorca. A young bride runs off with her married lover on her wedding day and her jilted husband comes after them. If you like flamenco, there are two more: "Carmen" and "El Amor Brujo." In Spanish with English subtitles. **AKA:** Bodas de Sangre. **1981 71m/C** *SP* Antonio Gades, Christina Hoyos, Marisol, Carmen Villena; **D:** Carlos Savrat. **VHS, Beta $24.95** *XVC, CTH, MED* 🎬🎬🎬

Bloodbath Drugs, sex and terrorism—Dennis Hopper is typecast as an American degenerate who, along with his expatriate friends, is persecuted by local religious cults who need sacrifices. **19?? 89m/C** Dennis Hopper, Carroll Baker, Richard Todd, Faith Brook, Win Wells; **D:** Silvio Narizzano. **VHS, Beta $79.98** *GHV, HHE* 🎬🎬🎬

Bloodbath at the House of Death Price and his compatriots fight a team of mad scientists in this parody of popular horror films. Fun to see Price spoofing his own genre; die-hard horror camp fans will be satisfied. Best line: "Wanna fork?" **1985 92m/C** *GB* Kenny Everett, Pamela Stephenson, Vincent Price, Gareth Hunt; **D:** Ray Cameron. **VHS, Beta $59.95** *MED* 🎬

Bloodbath in Psycho Town A film crew is marked for death by a hooded man when it enters a remote little village. **1989 (R) 87m/C** Ron Arragon, Donna Baltron, Dave Elliott; **W/D:** Alessandro DeGaetano. **VHS** *NO* 🎬

Bloodbeat A supernatural being terrorizes a family as they gather at their country home to celebrate Christmas. **1985 84m/C** Helen Benton, Terry Brown, Claudia Peyton; **D:** Fabrice A. Zaphiratos. **VHS, Beta $59.98** *TWE* 🎬

Bloodbrothers Portrayal of working-class Italian men's lives—if that's possible without the benefit of Italian writers, producers, or director. Still, lots of cussing and general intensity, as Gere's character struggles between staying in the family construction business and doing what he wants to do—work with children. Re-cut for television and re-titled "A Father's Love." **1978 (R) 120m/C** Richard Gere, Paul Sorvino, Tony LoBianco, Kenneth MacMillan, Marilu Henner, Danny Aiello; **D:** Robert Mulligan. **VHS $69.95** *WAR* 🎬🎬½

Bloodfight Exciting kick-boxing and martial arts tournament turns sour when champ offends the sense of honor of the master. Now the champ must battle the master, and only one will remain standing! **1990 (PG-13) ?m/C** Bolo Yeung. **VHS** *IMP* 🎬

Bloodfist A kickboxer tears through Manila searching for his brother's killer. A Roger Corman production. **1989 (R) 85m/C** Don "The Dragon" Wilson, Rob Kaman, Billy Blanks, Kris Aguilar, Riley Bowman, Michael Shaner; **D:** Terence H. Winkless. **VHS, Beta $14.95** *MGM* 🎬🎬

Bloodfist 2 Six of the world's toughest martial artists find themselves kidnapped and forced to do the bidding of the evil Su. The mysterious recluse stages a series of incredible fights between the experts and his own army of drugged warriors. **1990 (R) 85m/C** Don "The Dragon" Wilson, Maurice Smith, James Warring, Timothy Baker, Richard Hill, Rina Reyes; **D:** Andy Blumenthal. **VHS, Beta $14.95** *MGM* 🎬🎬½

Bloodfist 3: Forced to Fight Just as long as nobody's forced to watch, real-life world champion kickboxer Wilson thrashes his way through another showdown-at-the-arena plot. Better-than-average fight choreography. **1991 (R) 90m/C** Don "The Dragon" Wilson, Richard Roundtree, Laura Stockman, Richard Paul, Rick Dean, Peter "Sugarfoot" Cunningham; **D:** Oley Sassone. **VHS $89.98** *NHO* 🎬

Bloodhounds of Broadway A musical tribute to Damon Runyon, detailing the cliched adventures of an assortment of jazz-age crooks, flappers, chanteuses, and losers. **1989 (PG) 90m/C** Madonna, Rutger Hauer, Randy Quaid, Matt Dillon, Jennifer Grey, Julie Hagerty, Esai Morales, Anita Morris, Josef Sommer, William S. Burroughs, Ethan Phillips, Stephen McHattie, Dinah Manoff, Googy Gress, Tony Azito, Tony Longo; **D:** Howard Brookner. **VHS, Beta, LV $19.95** *COL* 🎬½

Bloodlink A well-to-do doctor has a recurring nightmare about killing an elderly woman. This prompts him to explore his past, discovering that he was separated at birth from a twin brother. Naturally, only by searching frantically for his long-lost sibling can the good doctor hope to solve the mystery of the recurring nightmare. A somnolent tale indeed. **1986 (R) 98m/C** Michael Moriarty, Penelope Milford, Geraldine Fitzgerald, Cameron Mitchell, Sarah Langenfeld; **D:** Alberto De Martino. **VHS, Beta $24.95** *SUE* 🎬½

Bloodlust More teenagers fall prey to yet another mad scientist, who stores their dead bodies in glass tanks. Low-budget ripoff of "The Most Dangerous Game" and other such films. A must for Mike Brady (Robert Reed) fans though. **1959 89m/B** Wilton Graff, June Kenney, Robert Reed, Lilyan Chauvin; **W/D:** Ralph Brooke. **VHS $16.95** *SNC, NOS* 🎬

Bloodmatch A whodunit, martial-arts-style: the "sleuth" kidnaps all the suspects in a corruption case and kickboxes each to death until somebody confesses. Not exactly Agatha Christie, and artsy camera moves fail to exploit the fancy footwork. **1991 (R) 85m/C** Thom Mathews, Michel Qissi, Benny "The Jet" Urquidez, Marianne Taylor, Hope Marie Carlton, Dale Jacoby, Thunder Wolf, Vincent Klyn, Peter "Sugarfoot" Cunningham, Hector Pena; **D:** Albert Pyun; **W:** K. Mannah; **M:** Tony Riparetti. **VHS, LV, Q $19.98** *HBO, PIA* 🎬

Bloodmoon The setting is Australia but the sleazy story's all too familiar: an insane killer employs knives and other sharp objects to prevent sex-crazed students from getting past third base.
1990 104m/C *AU* Leon Lissek, Christine Amor, Ian Patrick Williams, Helen Thomson, Hazel Howson, Craig Cronin, Anya Molina; *D:* Alec Mills; *W:* Richard Brennan; *M:* Briany May. VHS, Beta, LV $89.98 *LIV* Woof!

Bloodshed A psychotic harbors a girl's dead body, and systematically kills anyone who discovers his secret.
1983 (R) 88m/C Laslo Papas, Beverly Ross; *D:* Richard Cassidy. VHS, Beta *NO* ⅛

Bloodspell A student with an evil power unleashes it on those who cross his path.
1987 (R) 87m/C Anthony Jenkins, Aaron Teich, Alexandra Kennedy, John Reno; *D:* Deryn Warren. VHS, Beta $79.98 *MCG* ⅛

Bloodsport American soldier Van Damme endeavors to win the deadly Kumite, an outlawed martial arts competition in Hong Kong. Lots of kick-boxing action and the sound of bones cracking.
1988 (R) 92m/C Jean-Claude Van Damme, Leah Ayres, Roy Chiao, Donald Gibb, Bolo Yeung, Norman Burton, Forest Whitaker; *D:* Newton Arnold. VHS, Beta, LV $19.98 *WAR, TLF, PIA* ⅛½

Bloodstalkers Two vacationers in Florida meet up with a band of slaughtering, swamp-based lunatics.
1976 91m/C Kenny Miller, Celea Ann Cole, Jerry Albert; *D:* Robert W. Morgan. VHS, Beta $39.95 *VMK* Woof!

Bloodstone A couple honeymooning in the Middle East unexpectedly become involved in a jewel heist when they discover a valuable ruby amongst their luggage. Non stop action and humor.
1988 (PG-13) 90m/C Charlie Brill, Christopher Neame, Jack Kohler, Brett Stimely; *D:* Dwight Little. VHS, Beta $79.98 *MCG* ⅛⅛

Bloodstone: Subspecies 2 A gory sequel to "Subspecies" finds Radu the vampire pursuing the luscious Michelle. Radu gets some help from his ghoulish mother and yucky demonic spawn. Filmed on location in Romania. *AKA:* Subspecies II.
1993 (R) 107m/C Anders Hove, Denice Duff, Kevin Blair, Michael Denish, Pamela Gordon, Ion Haiduc; *W/D:* Ted Nicolaou. VHS, LV *PAR* ⅛½

The Bloodsuckers A British horror tale set on a Greek Island. An Oxford don is seduced into an ancient vampire cult. Director Michael Burrowes replaces Hartford-Davis in the credits due to a dispute over post-production editing. *AKA:* Incense For the Damned; Doctors Wear Scarlet.
1970 90m/C *GB* Patrick Macnee, Peter Cushing, Patrick Mower, Edward Woodward; *D:* Robert Hartford-Davis. VHS, Beta $19.98 *SNC* ⅛⅛

Bloodsuckers from Outer Space Via an alien invasion, Texas farmers becoming bloodsucking zombies.
1983 80m/C Thom Meyer, Laura Ellis, Billie Keller, Kim Braden; *D:* Glenn Coburn. VHS, Beta $19.98 *LHV, WAR* Woof!

Bloodsucking Freaks Virtually plotless Troma gagfest full of torture, cannabilistic dwarfs, and similar debaucheries, all played out on a Soho Grand Guignol stage (horror shows that allegedly contained real torture and death). Features "The Caged Sexoids," if that tells you anything (a cage of naked cannibal women tended by a dwarf). Not to mention the woman who has her brain sucked out through a straw. Filmed in "Ghoulovision" and originally rated X. Intolerable for most. *AKA:* The Incredible Torture Show.

1975 (R) 89m/C Seamus O'Brian, Niles McMaster; *D:* Joel M. Reed. VHS, Beta $59.98 *VES* Woof!

Bloodsucking Pharoahs of Pittsburgh Pittsburgh is plagued by crazed cannibals who think eternal life is in Pennsylvania. Two detectives on the case are mystified.
1990 (R) 89m/C Jake Dengel, Joe Sharkey, Suzanne Fletcher, Beverly Penberthy, Shawn Elliott, Pat Logan, Jane Hamilton; *D:* Alan Smithee; *W:* Dean Tschetter. VHS, Beta $79.95 *PAR, FCT* Woof!

Bloody Avenger A trio of detectives search for a murderer in the streets of Philadelphia.
198? 100m/C Jack Palance, George Eastman, Jenny Tamburi; *D:* Al Bradley. VHS, Beta $59.95 *VMK* ⅛

Bloody Birthday Three youngsters, bound together by their eerie birth during an eclipse (you know what that means), kill everyone around them that ever gave them problems. Typical "and the fun continues" ending; standard fare. *AKA:* Creeps.
1980 (R) 92m/C Susan Strasberg, Jose Ferrer, Lori Lethin, Melinda Cordell, Joe Penny, Ellen Geer, Julie Brown, Michael Dudikoff, Billy Jacoby; *D:* Edward Hunt. VHS, Beta $9.99 *STE, PSM* ⅛½

The Bloody Brood Really bad flick about a drug-dealing beatnik gang who commit nasty crimes, like feeding messenger boys hamburgers filled with ground glass. Yuck.
1959 80m/C *CA* Jack Betts, Barbara Lord, Peter Falk, Robert Christie; *D:* Julian Hoffman. VHS $16.95 *SNC* Woof!

Bloody Che Contra Follows rebel leader trying to flee the Bolivian mountains and the threat of government forces and chronicles the danger he and his men encounter.
19?? 89m/C John Ireland, Francisco Rabal. VHS, Beta *NO* ⅛

The Bloody Fight Two young people learn the cost of courage and the high price of justice when they avenge a murderer.
197? 90m/C Alan Tang, Yu In Yin, Tan Chin, Pai Ying, Lui Ran In; *D:* N.G. Tien Tsu. VHS, Beta *NO* ⅛

Bloody Fist Story set in China with martial arts scenes and so on. *AKA:* Blood Brothers.
1977 (R) 90m/C VHS, Beta *NO* ⅛

Bloody Mama Corman's violent and trashy story of the infamous Barker Gang of the 30s, led by the bloodthirsty and sex-crazed Ma Barker (Winters, can't you just picture it?) and backed by her four perverted sons. De Niro is the space cadet sibling, Walden the homosexual ex-con, Stroud the sadistic mama lover, and Kimbrough is the lady killer. They're joined by Walden's prison lover, Dern, who also has a thing for Ma Barker. Winters is a riot in this perverse stew of crime, violence, and, of course, sentimental blood bonding (the family that slays together, stays together). Written by Robert Thom and first of the Corman-produced (and sometimes directed) mama movies, followed by "Big Bad Mama" and "Crazy Mama."
1970 (R) 90m/C Shelley Winters, Robert De Niro, Don Stroud, Pat Hingle, Bruce Dern, Diane Varsi, Robert Walden, Clinton Kimbrough, Scatman Crothers; *D:* Roger Corman. VHS, Beta, LV $69.95 *VES, LIV* ⅛⅛½

Bloody Moon Tourists are being brutally attacked and murdered during a small Spanish village's Festival of the Moon.

1983 84m/C Olivia Pascal, Christopher Brugger; *D:* Jess (Jesus) Franco. VHS, Beta $59.95 *TWE* Woof!

Bloody New Year Corpses stalk the living as a group of teens happen upon an impromptu New Year's Eve party on a deserted island. Auld acquaintance shouldn't be forgot, just this flick. *AKA:* Time Warp Terror.
1987 (R) 90m/C *D:* Norman J. Warren. VHS, Beta $29.95 *ACA* ⅛

The Bloody Pit of Horror While wife Jayne Mansfield was in Italy filming "Primitive Love," bodybuilder Hargitay starred in this sado-horror epic. He owns a castle that is visited by a group of models for a special shoot. While in the dungeon, Hargitay becomes possessed by the castle's former owner, a sadist, and begins torturing the models. Supposedly based on the writings of the Marquis de Sade. *AKA:* Crimson Executioner; The Red Hangman.
1965 87m/B *IT* Mickey Hargitay, Louise Barrett, Walter Brandi, Moa Thai, Ralph Zucker, Albert Gordon; *D:* Max (Massimo Pupillo) Hunter. VHS $19.98 *SNC* ⅛½

The Bloody Tattoo A suspicious woman has a map tattooed on her body telling where a treasure is buried. The robbers who drew the map are now looking for her so they can find the treasure. A story full of killing and greed. *AKA:* The Loot.
19?? 90m/C Ko Fay, David Keung, Tsui Siu Keung, Lily Lee. VHS $49.95 *OCE* ⅛½

Bloody Trail A Union soldier who chooses the recently pummeled South as the venue for postwar R-and-R is, for some reason, pursued by Confederates. And his good ol' boy pursuers don't have a sudden change of heart when he teams up with a former slave. Lots of violence and nudity; little plot and entertainment.
1972 91m/C Paul Harper, Rance Howard, John Mitchum; *D:* Richard Robinson. VHS $19.95 *ACA* ⅛

The Bloody Vampire Atmospheric and chilling Mexican vampire film. Sequel to "Invasion of the Vampires."
1962 ?m/C *MX* Carlos Agosti. VHS $16.95 *SNC* ⅛½

Bloody Wednesday It's sanity checkout time when a hotel caretaker is driven mad by tormentors...or is he driving himself mad? What is it about vacant hotels that make men lose their minds? If you can remove "The Shining" from yours, this flick's worthwhile.
1987 89m/C Raymond Elmendorf, Pamela Baker, Navarre Perry; *D:* Mark Gilhuis. VHS, Beta $79.95 *PSM* ⅛⅛½

Blossoms in the Dust The true story of Edna Gladney is told as she starts the Texas Children's Home and Aid Society of Fort Worth. Major league Garson tear-jerker.
1941 100m/B Greer Garson, Walter Pidgeon, Felix Bressart, Marsha Hunt, Fay Holden, Samuel S. Hinds, Kathleen Howard; *D:* Mervyn LeRoy. Academy Awards '41: Best Interior Decoration; Nominations: Best Actress (Garson), Best Color Cinematography, Best Picture. VHS, Beta $19.98 *MGM* ⅛⅛

The Blot A story about a poorly paid professor and his family, whose lifestyle contrasts with that of an affluent neighbor, a butcher.
1921 55m/B Louis Calhern, Claire Windsor; *D:* Lois Weber. VHS, Beta $19.95 *GPV, GVV, DVT* ⅛⅛

Blow Out When a prominent senator is killed in a car crash, a sound effects engineer becomes involved in political intrigue as he tries to expose a conspiracy with the evidence he has gathered. An intricate mystery and homage to Antonioni's "Blow-Up."
1981 (R) 108m/C John Travolta, Nancy Allen, John Lithgow, Dennis Franz; **D:** Brian DePalma. VHS, Beta, LV *WAR, OM* ✶✶✶

Blow-Up A young London photographer takes some pictures of a couple in the park and finds out he may have recorded evidence of a murder. Though marred by badly dated 1960s modishness, this is Antonioni's most accessible film, a sophisticated treatise on perception and the film-consumer-as-voyeur, brilliantly assembled and wrought.
1966 111m/C *GB IT* David Hemmings, Vanessa Redgrave, Sarah Miles, Jane Birkin, Veruschka; **D:** Michelangelo Antonioni. Academy Awards '66 Nominations: Best Director (Antonioni), Best Story & Screenplay; Cannes Film Festival '67: Best Film; National Society of Film Critics Awards '66: Best Director (Antonioni), Best Film. VHS, Beta, LV $19.98 *MGM, VYG, FCT* ✶✶✶½

Blowing Wild Filmed in Mexico, this Quinn-Stanwyck-Cooper love triangle, set in the early thirties, speaks of lust and vengeance, rashness and greed. Stanwyck, married to oil tycoon Quinn, lusts after one-time lover wildcatter Cooper.
1954 92m/B Gary Cooper, Barbara Stanwyck, Anthony Quinn, Ruth Roman, Ward Bond; **D:** Hugo Fregonese. VHS, LV $19.98 *REP, FCT* ✶✶½

Blown Away A mafia wife goes up against her husband in order to retrieve her kidnapped child.
1990 (R) 92m/C Loni Anderson, John Heard, James Naughton; **D:** Michael Miller. VHS, Beta $29.95 *ACA* ✶

Blue A dull western about an American boy (Stamp) raised by Mexicans who doesn't trust another living soul until he finds himself face to face with his former gang, led by his adoptive father (Montalban).
1968 113m/C Terence Stamp, Joanna Pettet, Karl Malden, Ricardo Montalban, Joe DeSantis, Sally Kirkland; **D:** Silvio Narizzano. VHS *PAR* ✶

The Blue and the Grey Epic television mini-series about love and hate inflamed by the Civil War. Keach plays a Pinkerton's secret service agent in this loosely based historical romance.
1985 295m/C Gregory Peck, Lloyd Bridges, Colleen Dewhurst, Stacy Keach, John Hammond, Sterling Hayden, Warren Oates; **D:** Andrew V. McLaglen. VHS, Beta, LV $29.95 *COL, TVC, FCT* ✶✶

The Blue Angel The tale of a man stripped of his dignity. A film classic filled with sensuality and decay, which made Dietrich a European star and led to her discovery in Hollywood. When a repressed professor (Jannings) goes to a nightclub hoping to catch some of his students in the wrong, he finds that he too is taken by Lola, the sultry singer portrayed by Dietrich. After spending the night with her, losing his job, and then marrying her, he goes on tour with the troupe, peddling indiscreet photos of his wife. Versions were shot in both German and English, with the German version sporting English subtitles. Songs include "Falling in Love Again" and "They Call Me Wicked Lola." *AKA:* Der Blaue Engel.
1930 90m/B *GE* Marlene Dietrich, Emil Jannings, Kurt Gerron, Rosa Valetti, Hans Albers; **D:** Josef von Sternberg; **W:** Robert Lieberman, Karl Vollmoller, Carl Zuckmayer; **M:** Karl Vollmoller. VHS, Beta, 8mm, 3/4U, Special order formats $24.95 *NOS, MRV, KRT* ✶✶✶✶

The Blue Bird A weird, dark fantasy about two children who search for the blue bird of happiness in various fantasy lands, but find it eventually at home. Overlooked and impressively fatalistic.
1940 98m/C Shirley Temple, Gale Sondergaard, John Russell, Eddie Collins, Nigel Bruce, Jessie Ralph, Spring Byington, Sybil Jason; **D:** Walter Lang. VHS, Beta $19.98 *FOX, MLB* ✶✶✶

Blue Blood A demonic butler inflicts nightmares upon a family to gain possession of its mansion.
1973 90m/C *GB* Oliver Reed, Derek Jacobi, Fiona Lewis; **D:** Andrew Sinclair. VHS, Beta *NO* ✶

Blue Canadian Rockies Autry's employer sends him to Canada to discourage his daughter from marrying a fortune hunter. The daughter has turned the place into a dude ranch and wild game preserve. When Autry arrives, he encounters some mysterious killings.
1952 58m/B Gene Autry, Pat Buttram, Gail Davis, Ross Ford, Tom London; **D:** George Archainbaud. VHS, Beta $39.95 *CCB* ✶½

Blue City A young man returns to his Florida hometown to find his father murdered, and subsequently vows to solve and avenge the matter. Based on a Ross MacDonald thriller.
1986 (R) 83m/C Judd Nelson, Ally Sheedy, Paul Winfield, Anita Morris, David Caruso, Julie Carmen, Scott Wilson; **D:** Michelle Manning. VHS, Beta, LV $14.95 *PAR* ✶½

Blue Collar An auto assembly line worker, tired of the poverty of his life, hatches a plan to rob his own union. A study of the working class and the robbing of the human spirit.
1978 (R) 114m/C Richard Pryor, Harvey Keitel, Yaphet Kotto, Ed Begley Jr.; **D:** Paul Schrader; **M:** Jack Nitzsche. VHS, Beta, LV $69.95 *MCA, FCT* ✶✶✶

Blue Country A joyful romantic comedy about a pair of free souls who leave their stagnant lives behind to seek out a more idyllic existence. Subtitled in English. *AKA:* Le Pays Bleu.
1977 (PG) 104m/C *FR* Brigitte Fossey, Jacques Sernas. VHS, Beta $59.95 *COL* ✶✶½

Blue De Ville Two young women buy a '59 Cadillac and journey from St. Louis to New Mexico, having adventures on the way. The rambling, free-spirited movie was a pilot for a prospective series that never set sail—but when "Thelma & Louise" hit big this superficially similar item was hauled out on video.
1986 (PG) 96m/C Jennifer Runyon, Kimberly Pistone, Mark Thomas Miller, Alan Autry, Robert Prescott; **D:** Jim Johnston. VHS $89.98 *VMK* ✶✶

Blue Desert Cox is strong in her performance as Lisa Roberts, a comic book artist who leaves New York City for small town Arizona life after surviving a traumatic rape. Once there, she's befriended by Sheffer and Sweeney, a local cop. Battersby does a good job of keeping the suspense level high (in his directorial debut) as Cox finds that there's danger in small towns, too. Fine performances keep this slightly above average.
1991 (R) 98m/C D.B. Sweeney, Courteney Cox, Craig Sheffer, Philip Baker Hall, Sandy Ward; **W/ D:** Bradley Battersby; **W:** Arthur Collis; **M:** Jerry Goldsmith. VHS $19.95 *ACA* ✶✶½

Blue Fin When their tuna boat is shipwrecked, and the crew disabled, a young boy and his father learn lessons of love and courage as the son tries to save the ship.

1978 (PG) 93m/C *AU* Hardy Kruger, Greg Rowe; **D:** Carl Schultz. VHS, Beta $59.98 *SUE* ✶

Blue Fire Lady The heartwarming story of a young girl and her love of horses which endures even her father's disapproval. Good family fare.
1978 96m/C Cathryn Harrison, Mark Holden, Peter Cummins. VHS, Beta $19.95 *MED* ✶✶

Blue Hawaii A soldier, returning to his Hawaiian home, defies his parents by taking a job with a tourist agency. Presley sings "Can't Help Falling in Love." For Elvis fans.
1962 101m/C Elvis Presley, Angela Lansbury, Joan Blackman, Roland Winters, Iris Adrian, John Archer, Steve Brodie; **D:** Norman Taurog. VHS, Beta, LV $14.98 *FOX, MVD* ✶✶

Blue Heaven A couple struggles through problems with their marriage and alcohol abuse.
1984 100m/C Leslie Denniston, James Eckhouse; **D:** Kathleen Dowdey. VHS, Beta $69.95 *VES, LIV* ✶

Blue Iguana An inept bounty hunter travels south of the border to recover millions from a crooked South American bank, and meets up with sexy women, murderous thugs, and corruption.
1988 (R) 88m/C Dylan McDermott, Jessica Harper, James Russo, Dean Stockwell, Pamela Gidley, Tovah Feldshuh; **D:** John Lafia. VHS, Beta, LV $89.95 *PAR* ✶✶

Blue Jeans A young French boy experiences sexual awakening and humiliation in a British school. In French with English subtitles.
1978 80m/C *FR* **D:** Hugues des Roziers. VHS, Beta $29.95 *FCT* ✶✶½

Blue Jeans and Dynamite A stuntman is hired to lift the "Golden Mask of the Duct Tomb" and is followed on land, water, and air. Great chase scenes and action-filled finale.
198? 90m/C Robert Vaughn, Simon Andrew, Katia Kristine. VHS *NO* ✶✶

The Blue Knight Kennedy brings energy and care to this basically standard story. Policeman waiting for retirement searches for his partner's killer. Unexceptional treatment made palatable by actors. Made for television movie.
1975 72m/C George Kennedy, Alex Rocco, Glynn Turman, Verna Bloom, Michael Margotta, Seth Arnold; **D:** J. Lee Thompson. VHS $49.95 *LIV* ✶✶½

The Blue Lagoon Useless remake of 1949 film of the same name. An adolescent boy and girl marooned on a desert isle discover love (read: sex) without the restraints of society. Not too explicit, but nonetheless intellectually offensive. Gorgeous photography of island paradise is wasted on this Shields vehicle.
1980 (R) 105m/C Brooke Shields, Christopher Atkins, Leo McKern, William Daniels; **D:** Randal Kleiser. VHS, Beta, LV $84.95 *COL* Woof!

The Blue Lamp Action-adventure fans familiar with the hoary plot where a cop must avenge the wrongful death of his partner will appreciate this suspenseful British detective effort. It's one of the very first in the genre to explore buddy cop revenge in a very British sort of way. Also sports a concluding chase scene which has stood the test of time. Led to the long-running British TV series "Dixon of Dock Green."
1949 84m/B *GB* Dirk Bogarde, Jimmy Hanley, Jack Warner, Bernard Lee, Robert Flemyng, Patric Doonan, Bruce Seton, Frederick Piper, Betty Ann Davies, Peggy Evans; **D:** Basil Dearden. VHS $29.95 *FCT* ✶✶✶

The Blue Light Co-written by Riefenstahl and Bela Balazs, a fairy tale love story, based on an Italian fable about a mysterious woman, thought to be a witch, and a painter. Riefenstahl's first film, and it brought her to the attention of Adolf Hitler, who requested she make films glorifying the Nazi Party. In German with English subtitles. *AKA:* Das Blaue Licht.
1932 77m/B *GE* Leni Riefenstahl, Matthias Wieman, Max Holsboer; *W/D:* Leni Riefenstahl. **VHS, Beta $29.95** *NOS, MRV, FCT* 🎬🎬🎬

The Blue Lightning Investigator Elliott travels to Australia to retrieve the priceless Blue Lightening gem. He must fight the crime lord in his Aussie encampment. Nice scenery, but unexceptional television story.
1986 95m/C Sam Elliott, Rebecca Gilling, Robert Culp, John Meillon, Robert Coleby, Max Phipps; *D:* Lee Philips. **VHS $39.95** *FRH* 🎬🎬½

The Blue Max During World War I a young German, fresh out of aviation training school, competes for the coveted "Blue Max" flying award with other members of a squadron of seasoned flyers from aristocratic backgrounds. Based on a novel by Jack D. Hunter.
1966 155m/C George Peppard, James Mason, Ursula Andress; *D:* John Guillermin; *M:* Jerry Goldsmith. **VHS, Beta, LV $29.98** *FOX* 🎬🎬½

Blue Money A wild, comedic caper film about a cab-driving nightclub impressionist who absconds with a briefcase packed with cash and is pursued by everyone, even the I.R.A. Originally made for British television.
1984 82m/C *GB* Tim Curry, Dabby Bishop, Billy Connolly, Frances Tomelty; *D:* Colin Bucksey. **VHS, Beta $39.95** *SVS* 🎬🎬

Blue Monkey A mysterious alien plant impregnates a man, who gives birth to a huge, man-eating insect larva. It subsequently grows up into a giant bug, and roams around a quarantined hospital looking for patients to eat. What made you think it had anything to do with monkeys? *AKA:* Green Monkey.
1987 (R) 97m/C Steve Railsback, Susan Anspach, Gwynyth Walsh, John Vernon, Joe Flaherty; *D:* William Fruet. **VHS, Beta $79.95** *COL* 🎬

Blue Movies A couple of jerks try their hand at making porn films with predictable results.
1988 (R) 92m/C Larry Linville, Lucinda Crosby, Steve Levitt, Darien Mathias, Larry Poindexter; *D:* Paul Koval. **VHS, Beta $29.95** *ACA* Woof!

Blue Murder at St. Trinian's The second of the madcap British comedy series (based on cartoons by Ronald Searle) about an incredibly ferocious pack of schoolgirls. This time they travel to the European continent and make life miserable for a jewel thief. Highlight: fantasy sequence in ancient Rome showing the girls thrown to the lions—and scaring the lions.
1956 86m/B *GB* Joyce Grenfell, Terry-Thomas, George Cole, Alastair Sim, Lionel Jeffries, Thorley Walters; *D:* Frank Launder. **VHS $29.95** *VDM* 🎬🎬🎬

Blue Paradise A depiction of Adam and Eve as they peruse the primal landscape and each other.
1986 90m/C Mark Gregory, Andrea Goldman. **VHS, Beta $59.95** *TWE, MLB* Woof!

Blue Ribbon Babes A filmed record of a female athletic competition in Florida, featuring wet T-shirt contests, mud wrestling, and powder-puff boxing.
1986 60m/C VHS, Beta $24.95 *AHV* Woof!

Blue Skies Again Spunky young woman determined to play major league baseball locks horns with the chauvinistic owner and the gruff manager of her favorite team.
1983 (PG) 91m/C Robyn Barto, Harry Hamlin, Mimi Rogers, Kenneth McMillan, Dana Elcar, Andy Garcia; *D:* Richard Michaels. **VHS, Beta $69.95** *WAR* 🎬½

Blue Steel A young Wayne saves a town from financial ruin by leading the citizens to a gold strike. Also available with "Man From Utah" on Laser Disc.
1934 59m/B John Wayne, George "Gabby" Hayes; *D:* Robert North Bradbury. **VHS, Beta, LV, 3/4U, Special order formats $8.95** *NEG, NOS, MRV* 🎬🎬

Blue Steel Director Bigelow's much-heralded, proto-feminist cop thriller. A serious female rookie's gun falls into the hands of a Wall Street psycho who begins a killing spree. Action film made silly with over-anxious sub-text and patriarchy-directed rage.
1990 (R) 102m/C Jamie Lee Curtis, Ron Silver, Clancy Brown, Louise Fletcher, Philip Bosco, Elizabeth Pena, Tom Sizemore; *D:* Kathryn Bigelow. **VHS, Beta, LV, 8mm $14.95** *MGM* 🎬🎬

Blue Sunshine A certain brand of L.S.D. called Blue Sunshine starts to make its victims go insane.
1978 (R) 94m/C Zalman King, Deborah Winters, Mark Goddard, Robert Walden, Charles Siebert, Ann Cooper, Ray Young, Alice Ghostley; *W/D:* Jeff Lieberman. **VHS, Beta $69.95** *VES* 🎬🎬½

Blue Thunder Police helicopter pilot Scheider is chosen to test an experimental high-tech chopper that can see through walls, record a whisper, and level a city block. Seems anti-terrorist supercopter is needed to ensure security during 1984 Olympics. Bothered by Vietnam flashbacks, Scheider then battles wacky McDowell in the skies over L.A. High-techy police drama with satisfying aerial combat scenes nearly crashes with storyline.
1983 (R) 110m/C Roy Scheider, Daniel Stern, Malcolm McDowell, Candy Clark, Warren Oates; *D:* John Badham. **VHS, Beta, LV $12.95** *COL* 🎬🎬½

Blue Tornado An eerie bright light, emitted from a mountain, makes supersonic jets disappear into thin air. A beautiful researcher and a cocky pilot set out to solve the mystery. Better-than-average aerial sequences don't make up for goofy story and ludicrous dialogue.
1990 (PG-13) 96m/C Dirk Benedict, Patsy Kensit, Ted McGinley, David Warner; *D:* Tony B. Dobb. **VHS $89.95** *VMK* 🎬

Blue Velvet A disturbing, unique exploration of the dark side of American suburbia by Lynch, involving an innocent college youth who discovers a severed ear in an empty lot, and is thrust into a turmoil of depravity, murder, and sexual deviance. Brutal, grotesque, and unmistakably Lynch; an immaculately made, fiercely imagined film that is unlike any other. Mood is enhanced by the Angelo Badalamenti soundtrack. Graced by splashes of Lynchian humor, most notably the movie's lumber theme. Hopper is riveting as the chief sadistic nutcase and Twin Peaks' MacLachlan is a study in loss of innocence. Written by Lynch; cinematography by Frederick Elmes.
1986 (R) 121m/C Kyle MacLachlan, Isabella Rossellini, Dennis Hopper, Laura Dern, Hope Lange, Jack Nance, Dean Stockwell, George Dickerson, Brad Dourif; *D:* David Lynch; *M:* Angelo Badalamenti. Academy Awards '86 Nominations: Best Director (Lynch); Independent Spirit Awards '87: Best Actress (Rossellini); Montreal World Film Festival '86: Best Supporting Actor (Hopper); National Society of

Film Critics Awards '86: Best Director (Lynch), Best Film, Best Supporting Actor (Hopper). **VHS, Beta, LV $19.98** *WAR* 🎬🎬🎬

The Blue Yonder In this made-for-video feature, a young boy travels back in time to meet the grandfather he never knew, risking historical integrity. *AKA:* Time Flyers.
1986 89m/C Art Carney, Peter Coyote, Huckleberry Fox; *D:* Mark Rosman. **VHS, Beta $69.95** *DIS* 🎬

Bluebeard Tormented painter with a psychopathic urge to strangle his models is the basis for this effective, low-budget film. One of Carradine's best vehicles.
1944 73m/B John Carradine, Jean Parker, Nils Asther; *D:* Edgar G. Ulmer. **VHS, Beta, 3/4U, Special order formats $19.95** *NOS, MRV, SNC* 🎬🎬½

Bluebeard Written by Francoise Sagan, this is a French biography of Henri-Desire Landru, who seduced and murdered eleven women and was subsequently beheaded. Dubbed into English. *AKA:* Landru.
1963 108m/C *FR* Charles Denner, Danielle Darrieux, Michele Morgan, Hildegarde Neff; *D:* Claude Chabrol. **VHS, Beta $59.98** *NLC* 🎬🎬🎬

Bluebeard Lady killer Burton knocks off series of beautiful wives in soporific remake of the infamous pirate story.
1972 (R) 128m/C Richard Burton, Raquel Welch, Joey Heatherton, Nathalie Delon, Virna Lisi, Sybil Danning; *D:* Edward Dmytryk; *M:* Ennio Morricone. **VHS $59.95** *LIV* 🎬½

Blueberry Hill While her mother struggles with the grief over husband's death, a young girl in a small town learns about life, music, and her late father from a jazz singer. Good soundtrack.
1988 (R) 93m/C Jennifer Rubin, Carrie Snodgress, Margaret Avery; *D:* Strathford Hamilton. **VHS, Beta $79.98** *FOX* 🎬½

The Blues Brothers As an excuse to run rampant on the city of Chicago, Jake and Elwood Blues attempt to raise $5,000 for their childhood orphanage by putting their old band back together. Good music, and lots of cameos.
1980 (R) 133m/C John Belushi, Dan Aykroyd, James Brown, Cab Calloway, Ray Charles, Henry Gibson, Aretha Franklin, Carrie Fisher, John Candy; *Cameos:* Frank Oz, Steven Spielberg, Twiggy, Pee-Wee Herman, Steve Lawrence, John Lee Hooker; *D:* John Landis. **VHS, Beta, LV $19.95** *MCA* 🎬🎬½

Blues Busters Another entry in the "Bowery Boys" series. When Sach emerges from a tonsillectomy with the velvety voice of a crooner, Slip cashes in by turning Louie's Sweet Shop into a nightclub, the better to showcase his buddy's talents. Sach's singing voice provided by John Lorenz.
1950 68m/B Leo Gorcey, Huntz Hall, Adele Jergens, Gabriel Dell, Craig Stevens, Phyllis Coates, Bernard Gorcey, David Gorcey; *D:* William Beaudine. **VHS $14.98** *WAR* 🎬🎬½

Bluffing It A made-for-television movie about an older man who has been disguising his illiteracy for years.
1987 120m/C Dennis Weaver, Janet Carroll, Michelle Little, Robert Sean Leonard, Cleavant Derricks, Victoria Wauchope; *D:* James Sadwith. **VHS $89.95** *OHC* 🎬🎬

The Blum Affair In post-World War I Germany, a Jewish man is framed for the murder of an accountant and uncovers in his capture and prosecution a rat's nest of corruption and anti-Semitism. In German with English subtitles.
1948 109m/B *GE* Hans-Christian Blech, Gisela Trowe, Kurt Ehrhardt, Paul Bildt, Klaus Becker; *D:* Erich Engel. **VHS, Beta $24.95** *NOS, FCT, APD* 🎬🎬

Blume in Love An ironic comedy/drama about a man who falls hopelessly in love with his ex-wife who divorced him for cheating on her while they were married.
1973 (R) 115m/C George Segal, Susan Anspach, Kris Kristofferson, Shelley Winters, Marsha Mason; *D:* Paul Mazursky. VHS, Beta $19.98 WAR *♪♪♪*

BMX Bandits Three adventurous Aussie teens put their BMX skills to the test when they witness a crime and are pursued by the criminals. Much big air.
1983 92m/C Nicole Kidman, David Argue, John Ley, Angelo D'Angelo; *D:* Brian Trenchard-Smith; *W:* Patrick Edgeworth. VHS $79.95 IMP *♪♪*

Boarding House Residents of a boardinghouse discover sinister doings in the basement. It does not occur to any of them to move to another house.
1983 (R) 90m/C Hank Adly, Kalassu, Alexandra Day; *D:* John Wintergate. VHS, Beta PGN, MRV *♪*

Boarding School Basic teen sex comedy about students at a proper Swiss boarding school for girls who devise a plan to seduce the boys at a nearby school by posing as prostitutes. Kinski stars as the American girl who masterminds the caper. *AKA:* The Passion Flower Hotel.
1983 (R) 100m/C GE Nastassia Kinski; *D:* Andre Farwagi. VHS, Beta $69.95 VES, LIV *♪♪*

Boardinghouse Blues A showbiz musical centered around a borading house with tenant troubles. It's an excuse for popular black entertainers of the day to perform, including Lucky Millinder, Bull Moose Jackson, Una Mae Carlisle, and Stumpy and Stumpy.
1948 90m/C Dusty Fletcher, Moms Mabley; *D:* Josh Binney. VHS $34.95 FCT *♪♪*

The Boat is Full A group of refugees pose as a family in order to escape from Nazi Germany as they seek asylum in Switzerland. Available in German with English subtitles or dubbed into English.
1981 104m/C SI Tina Engel, Curt Bois, Renate Steiger, Mathias Gnaedinger; *D:* Markus Imhoof. Academy Awards '81 Nominations: Best Foreign Language Film; Berlin International Film Festival '81: Best Director (Imhoof). VHS, Beta $34.95 SUE, GLV, JCF *♪♪♪*

The Boatniks An accident-prone Coast Guard ensign finds himself in charge of the "Times Square" of waterways: Newport Harbor. Adding to his already "titanic" problems is a gang of ocean-going jewel thieves who won't give up the ship!
1970 (G) 99m/C Robert Morse, Stefanie Powers, Phil Silvers, Norman Fell, Wally Cox, Don Ameche; *D:* Norman Tokar. VHS, Beta $69.95 DIS *♪♪½*

Bob & Carol & Ted & Alice Two California couples have attended a trendy therapy session and, in an attempt to be more in touch with sexuality, resort to applauding one another's extramarital affairs and swinging. Wacky and well-written, this is a farce on free love and psychospeak. Paul Mazursky's directorial debut.
1969 (R) 104m/C Natalie Wood, Robert Culp, Dyan Cannon, Elliott Gould; *D:* Paul Mazursky. VHS, Beta, LV $9.95 GKK *♪♪½*

Bob le Flambeur Wonderful film noir of a compulsive gambler who decides to take a final fling by robbing the casino at Deauville. In French, subtitled in English. English title is "Bob the Gambler."
1955 106m/B FR Roger Duchesne, Isabel Corey, Daniel Cauchy; *D:* Jean-Pierre Melville. VHS, Beta, LV $59.95 COL, TAM *♪♪♪*

Bob Roberts Pseudo-documentary satire about a 1990 Pennsylvania senatorial race between Robbin's right-wing folk singer/entrepreneur versus Vidal's aging liberal incumbent. Roberts seems like a gee-whiz kinda guy but he'll stop at nothing to get elected and he knows a lot about political dirty tricks and, even more important, manipulating the media to get what he wants. Robbins directorial debut turned out to be very timely in view of the 1992 presidential campaign. Features a number of cameos. Line to remember: "Vote first. Ask questions later."
1992 (R) 105m/C Tim Robbins, Giancarlo Esposito, Ray Wise, Gore Vidal, Rebecca Jenkins, Alan Rickman, Brian Murray, Harry J. Lennix, John Ottavino; *Cameos:* Susan Sarandon, James Spader, John Cusack, Fred Ward, Pamela Reed; *W/D:* Tim Robbins. VHS, LV $92.98 LIV *♪♪♪*

Bobbie Jo and the Outlaw Wonderwoman Carter is a bored carhop who yearns to be a country singer. She becomes involved with Marjoe, who fancies himself as a contemporary Billy the Kid. Together, they do their Bonnie and Clyde thing, to a significantly lesser dramatic effect than the original, though a glut of violence keeps the bodies dropping.
1976 (R) 89m/C Lynda Carter, Marjoe Gortner, Jesse Vint; *D:* Mark L. Lester. VHS, Beta $69.98 VES, LIV *♪♪½*

Bobby Deerfield Cold-blooded Grand Prix driver comes face to face with death each time he races, but finally learns the meaning of life when he falls in love with a critically ill woman. Even with race cars, soap opera stalls.
1977 (PG) 124m/C Al Pacino, Marthe Keller, Anny Duperey, Romolo Valli; *D:* Sydney Pollack. VHS, Beta $19.98 WAR *♪♪*

Bobo Lousy bullfighter tries to lure a gorgeous woman into romance. Filmed in Spain and Italy.
1967 103m/C GB Peter Sellers, Britt Ekland, Rossano Brazzi, Adolfo Celi; *D:* Robert Parrish. VHS, Beta, LV $19.98 WAR, PIA, FCT *♪♪½*

Boccaccio '70 Three short bawdy/comedy/pageant-of-life films inspired by "The Decameron," each pertaining to ironically twisted sexual politics in middle class life. A fourth story, "Renzo and Luciana," by Mario Monichelli, has been cut. Dubbed.
1962 145m/C IT Anita Ekberg, Romy Schneider, Tomas Milian, Sophia Loren; *D:* Vittorio De Sica, Luchino Visconti, Federico Fellini. VHS, Beta FCT, MLB *♪♪*

Body and Soul The first screen appearance of Robeson has him cast in a dual role as a conniving preacher and his good brother. The preacher preys on the heroine, making her life a misery. Objections by censors to the preacher's character caused him to be redeemed and become worthy of the heroine's love.
1924 ?m/B Paul Robeson, Julia Theresa Russell, Mercedes Gilbert; *D:* Oscar Micheaux. VHS $29.95 FCT *♪♪*

Body and Soul A young boxer fights his way unscrupulously to the top. Vintage '40s boxing film that defines the genre. Remade in 1981. *AKA:* An Affair of the Heart.
1947 104m/B John Garfield, Lilli Palmer, Hazel Brooks, Anne Revere, William Conrad, Canada Lee; *D:* Robert Rossen. Academy Awards '47: Best Film Editing; Nominations: Best Actor (Garfield), Best Original Screenplay. VHS, LV $14.98 REP *♪♪♪½*

Body & Soul Interesting remake of 1947 gem about a boxer who loses his perspective in the world of fame, fast cars, and women.

1981 (R) 109m/C Leon Isaac Kennedy, Jayne Kennedy, Peter Lawford, Muhammad Ali, Perry Lang; *D:* George Bowers. VHS, Beta $19.95 MGM *♪♪½*

Body Beat Wild jazz and rock dancers are integrated into a previously classical ballet academy. While the students become fast friends, the teachers break off into two rival factions.
1988 (PG) 90m/C Tony Fields, Galyn Gorg, Scott Grossman, Eliska Krupka. VHS, Beta $29.95 VMK *♪♪*

The Body Beneath A living-dead ghoul survives on the blood of innocents and is still preying on victims today.
1970 85m/C Gavin Reed, Jackie Skarvellis, Susan Heard, Colin Gordon; *D:* Andy Milligan. VHS, Beta $19.95 WVV Woof!

Body Chemistry A married sexual-behavior researcher starts up a passionate affair with his lab partner. When he tries to end the relationship, his female associate becomes psychotic. You've seen it all before in "Fatal Attraction." And you'll see it again in "Body Chemistry 2."
1990 (R) 100m/C Marc Singer, Mary Crosby, Lisa Pescia, Joseph Campanella, David Kagen; *D:* Kristine Peterson. VHS, Beta, LV $19.95 COL *♪*

Body Chemistry 2: Voice of a Stranger An ex-cop (Harrison) obsessed with violent sex gets involved with a talk-radio psychologist (Pescia) whose advice could prove deadly in this erotic sequel.
1991 (R) 84m/C Gregory Harrison, Lisa Pescia, Morton Downey Jr., Robin Riker; *D:* Adam Simon. VHS, LV $89.95 COL *♪½*

Body Count A weird and wealthy family will stop at nothing, including murder and cannibalism, to enhance their fortune. Rather than bodies, count the minutes 'til the movie's over. Also titled "The 11th Commandment."
1987 90m/C Marilyn Hassett, Dick Sargent, Steven Ford, Greg Mullavey, Thomas Ryan, Bernie White; *D:* Paul Leder. VHS, Beta $79.98 MCG *♪½*

Body Double A voyeuristic unemployed actor peeps on a neighbor's nightly disrobing and sees more than he wants to. A grisly murder leads him into an obsessive quest through the world of pornographic films.
1984 (R) 114m/C Craig Wasson, Melanie Griffith, Greg Henry, Deborah Shelton, Guy Boyd, Dennis Franz, David Haskell, Rebecca Stanley, Barbara Crampton; *D:* Brian DePalma. VHS, Beta, LV $14.95 COL *♪♪*

Body Heat During a Florida heat wave, a none-too-bright lawyer becomes involved in a steamy love affair with a mysterious woman and then in a plot to kill her husband. Hurt and Turner (in her film debut) became stars under Kasdan's direction (the three would reunite for "The Accidental Tourist"). Hot love scenes supplement a twisting mystery with a suprise ending. Rourke's arsonist and Danson's soft shoe shouldn't be missed.
1981 (R) 113m/C William Hurt, Kathleen Turner, Richard Crenna, Ted Danson, Mickey Rourke; *D:* Lawrence Kasdan; *M:* John Barry. VHS, Beta, LV $19.98 WAR *♪♪♪½*

The Body in the Library A British television-produced Miss Marple mystery, based on Agatha Christie's 1942 novel, involving the septuagenarian detective investigating the murder of a young woman in a wealthy British mansion.
1987 155m/C GB Joan Hickson; *D:* Silvio Narizzano; *W:* Agatha Christie. VHS, Beta $29.98 FOX, HMV *♪♪*

Body Language A successful businesswoman, with a man problem, hires a super secretary with answers to all life's questions—and a deadly agenda all her own.
1992 (R) 93m/C Heather Locklear, Linda Purl, Edward Albert, James Acheson; *D:* Arthur Seidelman; *W:* Dan Gurskis, Brian Ross. VHS, Beta *PAR* 𝔞𝔞

Body Moves Romantic entanglements heat up the competition when two couples enter a steamy dance contest. Not apt to move you.
1990 (PG-13) 98m/C *IT* Kirk Rivera, Steve Messina, Dianne Granger, Linsley Allen, Philip Spruce, Nicole Kolman, Susan Gardner; *D:* Gerry Lively; *W:* Daniel Steel. VHS, Beta $89.95 *PSM* 𝔞𝔞

Body of Evidence A bad movie with pretensions. This one takes "Basic Instinct" a step farther. Instead of an ice pick and sex, sex itself is used as the weapon in a murder trial featuring Madonna as the defendant, Dafoe as her lawyer, and Mantegna as the prosecutor. It seems Madonna's elderly bedmate has died for love (literally) and now she stands to benefit big-time from his will. The plot is, of course, secondary to the S&M sex scenes which feature hot wax and broken glass. Madonna's lack of performance is the least of the film's problems since everyone involved seems to have forgotten any acting talent they possess. Director Edel fails to direct—the film even looks bad. "Body" was the subject of another NC-17 ratings flap but this film shouldn't be seen by anybody. An unrated version is also available.
1992 (R) 99m/C Madonna, Willem Dafoe, Joe Mantegna, Anne Archer, Michael Forest, Charles Hallahan, Mark Rolston, Richard Riehle, Julianne Moore, Frank Langella, Juergen Prochnow, Stan Shaw; *D:* Uli Edel; *W:* Brad Mirman; *M:* Graeme Revell. VHS, Beta, LV $94.99 *MGM* Woof!

Body of Influence A Beverly Hills psychiatrist gets overly involved with a beautiful female patient. But she not only wants his love—she wants his life. Also available in an unrated version.
1993 (R) 96m/C Nick Cassavetes, Shannon Whirry, Sandahl Bergman, Don Swayze, Anna Karin, Catherine Parks, Diana Barton, Richard Roundtree; *D:* Andrew Garroni; *W:* David Schreiber. VHS $89.95 *ACA* 𝔞𝔞

Body Parts For fans of the demented dismemberer niche, Body Parts, a sleazy skin club, loses some of its star talent when the strippers start turning up in cameo video appearances. Seems there's a psycho killer on the loose who videotapes the dismemberment of his stripper-victims. The police decide they've got to meet this guy when he sends them a sample of his work.
1990 90m/C Teri Lee, Dick Monda, Johnny Mandell. VHS, LV *NO* 𝔞

Body Parts A crime psychologist loses his arm in an auto accident and receives a transplant from an executed murderer. Does the limb have an evil will of its own? Poorly paced horror goes off the deep end in gore with its third act. Based on the novel "Choice Cuts" by French writers Pierre Boileau and Thomas Narcejac, whose work inspired some of the greatest suspense films.
1991 (R) 88m/C Jeff Fahey, Kim Delaney, Lindsay Duncan, Peter Murnik, Brad Dourif, Zakes Mokae, Johnny Walsh, Paul Benevictor; *W/D:* Eric Red; *W:* Norman Snider; *M:* Loek Dikker. VHS, Beta, LV $19.95 *PAR* 𝔞𝔞

Body Rock Brooklyn breakdancer Lamas deserts his buddies to work at a chic Manhattan nightclub. Watching Lamas as the emcee/breakdancing fool is a hoot. ♫Body Rock; Team Work; Why Do You Want to Break My Heart?; One Thing Leads to Another; Let Your Body Rock; Vanishing Point; Sharpshooter; The Jungle; Deliver; The Closest to Love.
1984 (PG-13) 93m/C Lorenzo Lamas, Vicki Frederick, Cameron Dye, Michelle Nicastro, Ray Sharkey, Grace Zabriskie, Carole Ita White; *D:* Marcelo Epstein. VHS, Beta $19.95 *STE, HBO* Woof!

The Body Shop Unorthodox love story in which a man decides to patch up his relationship with his dead wife by piecing together her dismembered body. For lovers only. *AKA:* Doctor Gore; Doctor Gore.
1972 91m/C Pat Patterson, Jenny Driggers, Roy Mehaffey, Linda Faile, Candy Furr; *D:* Pat Patterson. VHS $39.98 *PGN* 𝔞

Body Slam A small-time talent monger hits it big with a rock and roll/ professional wrestling tour. Piper's debut; contains some violence and strong language.
1987 (PG) 100m/C Roddy Piper, Captain Lou Albano, Dirk Benedict, Tanya Roberts, Billy Barty, Charles Nelson Reilly, John Astin, Wild Samoan, Tonga Kid, Barry Gordon; *D:* Hal Needham. VHS, Beta $19.98 *SUE, NLC* 𝔞½

The Body Snatcher Based on Robert Louis Stevenson's story about a grave robber who supplies corpses to research scientists. Set in Edinburgh in the 19th century, this Lewton production is superior. One of Karloff's best vehicles.
1945 77m/B Edith Atwater, Russell Wade, Rita Corday, Boris Karloff, Bela Lugosi, Henry Daniell; *D:* Robert Wise. VHS, Beta, LV $19.95 *MED, RKO, TTC* 𝔞𝔞𝔞½

Body Snatcher from Hell An airliner passes through a mysterious cloud and crashes in a desert. One by one, the passengers are turned into vampires. Some interesting special effects. *AKA:* Goke, Body Snatcher from Hell; Goke the Vampire; Kyuketsuki Gokemidoro.
1969 84m/C *JP* Hideo Ko, Teruo Yoshida, Tomomi Sato, Eizo Kitamura, Masay Takahashi, Cathy Horlan, Kazuo Kato, Yuko Kusunoki; *D:* Hajime Sato. VHS $16.95 *SNC* 𝔞½

Body Trouble After being attacked by sharks while vacationing in the Caribbean, a man washes ashore in Miami and then somehow makes his way to New York City. There he meets Vera Vin Rouge and her friends Cinnamon, Spice, Paprika, and Johnny Zero, a gangster. Zero decides he doesn't like the man, so he chases him back to the Caribbean. Supposedly this all happens in only one day. Hmmm... *AKA:* Joker's Wild.
1992 (R) 98m/C Dick Van Patten, Priscilla Barnes, Frank Gorshin, James Hong, Marty Rackham, Michael Unger, Jonathan Soloman, Brit Helfer, Leigh Clark, Patricia Cardell, Richie Barathy; *W/D:* Bill Milling. VHS $89.95 *TRI* 𝔞½

The Body Vanished Murder mystery featuring a corpse that disappears from the scene of the crime.
1939 ?m/C *GB* Lewis Wilson, Frances Dubay, Dana Wilson. VHS $16.95 *SNC* 𝔞𝔞

Body Waves Beach comedy starring Calvert as a teenager who bets his father that he can raise money on his own. In typical teen movie fashion, he invents a sex cream that drives boys and girls wild. Brain candy featuring lots of skimpy bikinis.
1991 (R) 80m/C Bill Calvert, Leah Lail, Larry Linville, Dick Miller, Jim Wise; *D:* P.J. Pesce. VHS $89.98 *NHO* 𝔞½

The Bodyguard The Yakuza, Japan's mafia, and New York's big crime families face off in this martial arts extravaganza.
1976 (R) 89m/C Sonny Chiba, Aaron Banks, Bill Louie, Judy Lee; *D:* Maurice Sarli. VHS, Beta $29.95 *MED* 𝔞½

The Bodyguard Romantic melodrama revolves around a buttoned-down, ex-Secret Service agent turned private bodyguard and the wildly successful singer/actress he reluctantly takes on as a client. Both are impatient with each other: Frank with Rachel's breezy attitude and Rachel with his endless security precautions, but they find their mutual attraction irresistable. Houston doesn't stretch too far in her acting debut as the over-indulged diva but acquits herself well. Costner has extremely bad hair day but easily handles the role of the tightly wound Frank. Critically trashed, a box office smash, and overlong. Originally scripted by producer Kasdan more than a decade ago, with Steve McQueen in mind for Frank. The killer (and motive) aren't hard to figure out, though occasional sharp dialog and a few action pieces keep things moving. Houston's songs include the hit "I Will Always Love You," which was written and originally performed by Dolly Parton.
1992 (R) 130m/C Kevin Costner, Whitney Houston, Gary Kemp, Bill Cobbs, Ralph Waite, Tomas Arana, Michele Lamar Richards, Mike Starr, Christopher Birt, DeVaughn Nixon, Charles Keating, Robert Wuhl; *Cameos:* Debbie Reynolds; *D:* Mick Jackson; *W:* Lawrence Kasdan. Academy Awards '92 Nominations: Best Song ("I Have Nothing"), Best Song ("Run to You"); MTV Movie Awards '93: Best Song ("I Will Always Love You"). VHS, LV $99.99 *WAR, BTV* 𝔞𝔞

Boeing Boeing A dated but still amusing sex farce about a bachelor newspaperman (Curtis) in Paris, his three stewardess girl-friends, and the elaborate plots he resorts to in trying to keep them from finding out about each other. When the new Boeing jet makes air travel faster all Curtis' schemes may come crashing down. Ritter is fun as the exasperated housekeeper and Lewis amazingly subdued as Curtis' business rival.
1965 102m/C Tony Curtis, Jerry Lewis, Dany Saval, Christianne Schmidtmer, Suzanna Leigh, Thelma Ritter; *D:* John Rich. VHS $14.95 *PAR* 𝔞𝔞½

Bog Boggy beast from the Arctic north awakens to eat people. Scientists mount an anti-monster offensive.
1984 (PG) 90m/C Gloria DeHaven, Marshall Thompson, Leo Gordon, Aldo Ray. VHS, Beta $49.95 *PSM* 𝔞

Boggy Creek II The continuing saga of the eight-foot-tall, 300 pound monster from Texarkana. Third in a series of low-budget movies including "The Legend of Boggy Creek" and "Return to Boggy Creek." *AKA:* The Barbaric Beast of Boggy Creek, Part II.
1983 (PG) 93m/C Charles B. Pierce, Cindy Butler, Serene Hedin; *D:* Charles B. Pierce. VHS, Beta, LV $59.95 *MED* 𝔞½

Bogie Television biography of Humphrey Bogart, populated by almost-lookalikes who can almost act.
1980 100m/C Kevin J. O'Connor, Kathryn Harrold, Ann Wedgeworth, Patricia Barry, Alfred Ryder, Donald May, Richard Dysart, Arthur Franz; *D:* Vincent Sherman. VHS, Beta $14.95 *FRH* 𝔞½

Bohemian Girl The last of Laurel and Hardy's comic operettas finds them as guardians of a young orphan (Hood, famous for her roles in the Our Gang comedies), whom no one realizes is actually a kidnapped princess.
1936 74m/B Stan Laurel, Oliver Hardy, Mae Busch, Darla Hood, Jacqueline Wells, Thelma Todd, James Finlayson; *D:* James W. Horne. VHS, Beta $19.95 *MED, CCB* 𝔞𝔞𝔞

Boiling Point Lawman proves once again that justice always triumphs.
1932 67m/B Hoot Gibson. **VHS, Beta $19.95** *NOS, UHV, DVT* ⅃⅃½

Boiling Point Darkly flavored action drama delves into the personalities of its two main characters before setting up a final confrontation. Treasury agent Jimmy Mercer (Snipes) is trying to solve his partner's murder. He relentlessly pursues the murderers in cold and methodical fashion. Sleazy Red Diamond (Hopper), just out of prison, owes the mob and has one week to pay them back. He and trigger-happy sidekick Ronnie (Mortensen) have some unusual ideas about making money. Red occasionally flares up in bouts of psychotic rage in classic Hopper fashion. Lawman and crook both come home to women (Davidovich and Perrine) graduates of the Hollywood school of female martyrdom, selflessly supportive of their men. Grim but cliched.
1993 (R) 93m/C Wesley Snipes, Dennis Hopper, Lolita Davidovich, Viggo Mortensen, Dan Hedaya, Valerie Perrine, Seymour Cassel, Jonathan Banks, Tony LoBianco; *D:* James B. Harris; *W:* James B. Harris; *M:* Cory Lerios, John D'Andrea. **VHS, Beta, LV** *WAR* ⅃⅃½

The Bold Caballero Rebel chieftain Zorro overthrows oppressive Spanish rule in the days of early California. *AKA:* The Bold Cavalier.
1936 69m/B Bob Livingston, Heather Angel, Sig Rumann, Robert Warwick; *D:* Wills Root. **VHS, Beta $19.95** *NOS, VDM, VCN* ⅃⅃½

The Boldest Job in the West Italian western about bankrobbers who meet to divide their spoils. Problem is, the guys with the loot don't show. Dubbed in English. *AKA:* El Mas Fabulosi Golpe del Far West.
1971 200m/C *IT* Mark Edwards, Frank Sancho, Carmen Sevilla; *D:* Joseph Loman. **VHS, Beta** *NO* ⅃

Bolero Beginning in 1936, this international epic traces the lives of four families across three continents and five decades, highlighting the music and dance that is central to their lives.
1982 173m/C James Caan, Geraldine Chaplin, Robert Hossein, Nicole Garcia, Jacques Villeret; *D:* Claude Lelouch. **VHS, Beta $19.95** *VES* ⅃⅃½

Bolero What sounds like a wet dream come true is really just a good snooze: Bo Derek plays a beautiful young woman who goes on a trip around the world in hopes of losing her virginity; in Spain, she meets a bullfighter who's willing to oblige. Too bad Bo cannot act as good as she looks. *AKA:* Bolero: An Adventure in Ecstasy.
1984 (R) 106m/C Bo Derek, George Kennedy, Andrea Occhipinti, Ana Obregon, Olivia D'Abo; *W/D:* John Derek. **VHS, Beta $19.95** *LIV* Woof!

Bolo The authorities pardon two tough prison inmates, setting the scene for revenge.
197? 90m/C Yang Sze, Mi Hsuen, Tsen Chin Wei; *D:* Bill Raymond. **VHS, Beta** *NO* ⅃

Bomb at 10:10 An American pilot escapes from a German POW camp and plots to assassinate a camp commandant.
1967 87m/C George Montgomery, Rada Popovic, Peter Banicevic; *D:* Charles Damic. **VHS, Beta $14.95** *GEM* ⅃

Bombardier A group of cadet bombardiers discover the realities of war on raids over Japan during World War II. Also available colorized.
1943 99m/B Pat O'Brien, Randolph Scott, Robert Ryan, Eddie Albert, Anne Shirley, Barton MacLane; *D:* Richard Wallace. **VHS, Beta $14.98** *RKO, TTC* ⅃⅃½

Bombay Talkie A naive American novelist visits India for "experience," and gets romantically involved with an Indian movie star.
1970 (PG) 110m/C *IN* Jennifer Kendal, Zia Mohyeddi, Shashi Kapoor, Aparna Sen; *D:* James Ivory. **VHS, Beta $29.95** *TAM, SUE, NLC* ⅃⅃⅃

Bombs Away! An atomic bomb is mistakenly shipped to a seedy war surplus store in Seattle, and causes much chicanery.
1986 90m/C Michael Huddleston, Pat McCormick; *D:* Bruce Wilson. **VHS, Beta $14.95** *COL, NLC* ⅃

Bombshell Wry insightful comedy into the Hollywood of the 1930s. Harlow plays a naive young actress manipulated by her adoring press agent. He thwarts her plans until she finally notices and begins to fall in love with him. Brilliant satire with Harlow turning in perhaps the best performance of her short career. *AKA:* Blonde Bombshell.
1933 96m/B Jean Harlow, Lee Tracy, Pat O'Brien, Una Merkel, C. Aubrey Smith, Franchot Tone; *D:* Victor Fleming. **VHS, Beta $19.98** *MGM, BTV, FCT* ⅃⅃⅃

Bon Voyage One of director Hitchcock's short propaganda pieces filmed as a tribute to the French Resistance. In London an RAF pilot is interrogated by the Free French about his escape from France. He was aided by a Polish agent who was actually working for the Gestapo to learn about the Resistance's movements. Flashbacks show the pilot's adventures from the spy's point-of-view. In French with English subtitles.
1944 26m/B John Blythe; *D:* Alfred Hitchcock. **VHS** *MIL* ⅃⅃⅃

Bon Voyage! A family's long-awaited European "dream" vacation turns into a series of comic misadventures in this very Disney, very family, very predictable comedy.
1962 131m/C Fred MacMurray, Jane Wyman, Deborah Walley, Michael Callan, Tommy Kirk, Jessie Royce Landis; *D:* James Neilson. **VHS, Beta, LV $69.95** *DIS* ⅃½

Bon Voyage, Charlie Brown The "Peanuts" comic strip group becomes exchange students in Europe, led by Charlie Brown, Linus, Peppermint Patty, Marcie, and the irrepressible beagle, Snoopy.
1980 (G) 76m/C Charlie Brown; *D:* Bill Melendez. **VHS, Beta, LV $14.95** *PAR, WTA* ⅃⅃⅃

Bonanza This western series about the Cartwright clan and their Ponderosa ranch ran on TV from 1959-1973, second only to "Gunsmoke." Additional episodes available. In "The Pure Truth" Hoss escapes from jail after being unjustly accused of robbing the bank. An eccentric recluse comes to his aid.
1964 50m/C Lorne Greene, Pernell Roberts, Dan Blocker, Michael Landon, Glenda Farrell. **VHS $14.98** *REP, MOV* ⅃⅃⅃

The Bone Yard A weird mortuary is the setting for strange goings on when a murder is investigated.
1990 (R) 98m/C Ed Nelson, Deborah Rose, Norman Fell, Jim Eustermann, Denise Young, Willie Stratford Jr., Phyllis Diller; *W/D:* James Cummins. **VHS, Beta $89.98** *PSM* ⅃

The Bonfire of the Vanities If you read and liked Tom Wolfe's viciously satirical novel, chances are you won't like De Palma's version at all. If you didn't read the book, chances are you still won't like it. Miscast and stripped of the book's gutsy look inside its characters, the film's sole attribute is Vilmos Zsigmond's photography. Hanks is all wrong as wealthy Wall Street trader Sherman McCoy who, taking a wrong turn, finds himself lost in the back streets of the Bronx, where his panic results in the accidental death of a black youth. Newspapers, lawmakers, and ethnic activists are out to use him for a scapegoat, and he has neither the brains, nor the skullduggery, to protect himself. Willis' drunken journalist/narrator, Griffith's blonde mistress, and Freeman's righteous judge are all awkward and thinly written. If still awake, look for F. Murray Abraham's cameo as the Bronx D.A.
1990 (R) 126m/C Tom Hanks, Melanie Griffith, Bruce Willis, Morgan Freeman, Alan King, Kim Cattrall, Saul Rubinek, Clifton James, Donald Moffat, Richard Libertini, Andre Gregory, Robert Stephens; *Cameos:* F. Murray Abraham; *D:* Brian DePalma; *W:* Michael Cristofer. **VHS, Beta, LV, 8mm $19.98** *WAR, FCT* ⅃⅃

Bongo Originally a part of the Disney cartoon anthology "Fun and Fancy Free." Follows the adventures of a circus bear who flees the big time for the wonders of the forests. Narrated by Dinah Shore. Also available with "Ben and Me" on Laser Disc.
1947 36m/C Bill Roberts, Hamilton Luske; *D:* Jack Kinney. **VHS, Beta $12.99** *DIS, BVV, WTA* ⅃⅃

Bonjour Tristesse An amoral French girl conspires to break up her playboy father's upcoming marriage to her stuffy godmother in order to maintain her decadent freedom. Based on the novel by Francoise Sagan; screenplay by Arthur Laurents. Preminger attempted, unsuccessfully, to use this soaper to catapult Seberg to stardom.
1957 94m/C *FR* Deborah Kerr, David Niven, Jean Seberg, Mylene Demongeot, Geoffrey Horne, Walter Chiari, Jean Kent; *D:* Otto Preminger. **VHS, Beta $69.95** *COL* ⅃⅃⅃

Bonnie & Clyde Based on the biographies of the violent careers of Bonnie Parker and Clyde Barrow, who roamed the Southwest robbing banks. In the Depression era, when any job, even an illegal one, was cherished, money, greed, and power created an unending cycle of violence and fury. Highly controversial and influential, with pronounced bloodshed that spurred mainstream cinematic proliferation. Established Dunaway as a star; produced by Beatty in one of his best performances.
1967 111m/C Warren Beatty, Faye Dunaway, Michael J. Pollard, Gene Hackman, Estelle Parsons; *D:* Arthur Penn. Academy Awards '67: Best Cinematography, Best Supporting Actress (Parsons); Nominations: Best Actor (Beatty), Best Actor (Hackman, Pollard), Best Actress (Dunaway), Best Director (Penn), Best Picture, Best Story & Screenplay; Academy Awards '67: Best Costume Design. **VHS, Beta, LV $19.98** *WAR, BTV* ⅃⅃⅃½

Bonnie Prince Charlie Historical epic opening in 1745 and romanticizing the title pretender to the British throne, who united Scottish clans in a doomed campaign against King George. Talky and rather slow-moving except for stirring battle scenes. A notorious box-office flop in its native Britain, where the original running time was 140 minutes.
1948 135m/C *GB* David Niven, Margaret Leighton, Judy Campbell, Jack Hawkins, Morland Graham, Finlay Currie, Elwyn Brook-Jones, John Laurie; *D:* Anthony Kimmins. **VHS $19.95** *NOS* ⅃⅃½

Bonnie Scotland Laurel & Hardy accidentally join an India-bound Scottish regiment. Laughs aplenty.
1935 81m/B Stan Laurel, Oliver Hardy, James Finlayson, Daphne Pollard, June Lang; *D:* James W. Horne. **VHS, Beta $19.98** *MGM, MLB* ⅃⅃½

Bonnie's Kids Two sisters become involved in murder, sex, and stolen money.

1973 (R) 107m/C Tiffany Bolling, Robin Mattson, Scott Brady, Alex Rocco; *D:* Arthur Marks. **VHS, Beta** *NO* 𝒵𝒵½

Boob Tube Television station KSEX is out to change their audience's viewing habits with their unusual programming.
1975 (R) 74m/C John Alderman, Sharon Kelly, Lois Lane. **VHS, Beta $19.95** *GEM* 𝒵𝒵

The Boogey Man Through the reflection in a mirror, a girl witnesses her brother murder his mother's lover. Twenty years later this memory still haunts her; the mirror is now broken, revealing its special powers. Who will be next? Murder menagerie; see footage from this flick mirrored in "The Boogey Man 2."
1980 (R) 93m/C John Carradine, Suzanna Love, Ron James; *D:* Ulli Lommel. **VHS, Beta, LV $59.95** *UHV, HHE* 𝒵𝒵

Boogey Man 2 The story continues; same footage, new director (but Lommel, the director of the original "Boogey Man," co-wrote this script and appears in the film).
1983 90m/C John Carradine, Suzanna Love, Shannah Hall, Ulli Lommel, Sholto Von Douglas; *D:* Bruce Starr. **VHS, Beta $29.95** *VHE* **Woof!**

Book of Love "Zany" hijinks as a teenager struggles with friendship, girls, and those all-important hormones when he moves to a new neighborhood in the mid-50's. Average rehash of every 50's movie and TV show cliche in existence. Surprise! There's a classic rock 'n' roll soundtrack. Adapted by Kotzwinkle from his novel "Jack in the Box."
1991 (PG-13) 88m/C Chris Young, Keith Coogan, Aeryk Egan, Josie Bisset, Tricia Leigh Fisher, Danny Nucci, Michael McKean, John Cameron Mitchell, Lewis Arquette; *D:* Robert Shaye; *W:* William Kotzwinkle; *M:* Stanley Clarke. **VHS, LV, 8mm $19.95** *COL, PIA* 𝒵𝒵

Boom in the Moon Keaton fares poorly in this sci-fi comedy. He's trapped on a space ship to the moon. Poor production, with uneven direction and acting. *AKA:* A Modern Bluebeard.
1946 83m/C Buster Keaton, Angel Garasa, Virginia Serret, Fernando Soto, Luis Barreiro; *D:* Jaime Salvador. **VHS** *NO* **Woof!**

Boom Town A lively vintage comedy/drama/romance about two oil-drilling buddies competing amid romantic mix-ups and fortunes gained and lost.
1940 120m/B Clark Gable, Spencer Tracy, Claudette Colbert, Hedy Lamarr, Frank Morgan, Lionel Atwill, Chill Wills, Curt Bois; *D:* Jack Conway. **VHS, Beta $19.98** *MGM, CCB* 𝒵𝒵

Boomerang A father rescues his wrongly convicted son from prison. Dubbed.
1976 101m/C *IT* Alain Delon, Carla Gravina, Dora Doll; *D:* Jose Giovanni. **VHS, Beta $59.95** *UNI* 𝒵𝒵½

Boomerang A successful, womanizing marketing executive for a cosmetics company (Murphy) meets his match when he falls for a colleague (Givens) who is as vain and sexually predatory as he is. She treats him the way he treats women (as a sex object), and he's shocked into the arms of a nice girl (Berry). Although it's refreshing to see this sexual role reversal, the typical Murphy-style humor is in play with sexist jokes and a couple of vulgar female characters. Grier and Lawrence are great as Murphy's best friends. Blaustein and Sheffield are the same guys who wrote Murphy's "Coming to America."
1992 (R) 118m/C Eddie Murphy, Halle Berry, Robin Givens, David Alan Grier, Martin Lawrence, Grace Jones, Geoffrey Holder, Eartha Kitt, Chris Rock, Tisha Campbell, John Witherspoon, Melvin Van Peebles; *D:* Reginald

Hudlin; *W:* Barry W. Blaustein, David Sheffield. **VHS, Beta, LV** *PAR, PMS* 𝒵𝒵

The Boost A feverish, messy melodrama about a young couple's spiraling decline from yuppie-ish wealth in a haze of cocaine abuse.
1988 (R) 95m/C James Woods, Sean Young, John Kapelos, Steven Hill, Kelle Kerr, John Rothman, Amanda Blake, Grace Zabriskie; *D:* Harold Becker. **VHS, Beta, LV $19.95** *HBO* 𝒵𝒵½

Boot Hill Two guys mess with western baddies and wild women in spaghetti oater.
1969 (PG) 97m/C *IT* Terence Hill, Bud Spencer, Woody Strode, Victor Buono, Lionel Stander; *D:* Giuseppe Colizzi. **VHS, Beta $9.95** *NO* 𝒵𝒵½

Boot Hill Bandits "Crash" Corrigan fights on the side of right in this classic western as he helps corral Wells Fargo bandits.
1942 58m/B Ray Corrigan, John "Dusty" King, Max Terhune, Jean Brooks, John Merton, Glenn Strange; *D:* S. Roy Luby. **VHS $19.95** *NOS, HEG* 𝒵𝒵½

Boothill Brigade Former footballer Brown rides to the rescue when criminals steal land from homesteaders.
1937 58m/B Johnny Mack Brown, Claire Rochelle, Dick Curtis, Horace Murphy, Frank LaRue, Edward Cassidy, Bobby Nelson, Frank Ball, Steve Clark; *D:* Sam Newfield. **VHS $19.95** *NOS, MRV* 𝒵𝒵

Bootleg A detective is on a case that leads to crooked politics and espionage.
1989 82m/C Ray Meagher; *D:* John Prescott. **VHS $79.95** *AIP* 𝒵

Boots & Saddles A young English lord wants to sell the ranch he has inherited but Autry is determined to make him a real Westerner.
1937 54m/B Gene Autry, Judith Allen, Smiley Burnette; *D:* Joseph Kane. **VHS, Beta $19.95** *NOS, MRV, CCB* 𝒵𝒵

Boots Malone An old down-on-his-luck gambling addict and a young, rich kid fascinated by the sordid atmosphere of the racetrack stumble upon one another and form a symbiotic relationship. All goes well for while, but there'd be no movie unless a collection of obstacles suddenly threatens their success, friendship, and even their lives. A rather melodramatic buddy tale, but Holden and Stewart hold interest.
1952 103m/C William Holden, John Stewart, Ed Begley Sr., Harry Morgan, Whit Bissell; *D:* William Dieterle. **VHS** *GKK* 𝒵𝒵½

Bordello A made-for-television western spoof about cowboys and shady ladies.
1979 90m/C Chuck Connors, Michael Conrad, John Ireland, Isela Vega, George Rivero. **VHS, Beta $79.95** *PSM* 𝒵

The Border A border guard faces corruption and violence within his department and tests his own sense of decency when the infant of a poor Mexican girl is kidnapped. Excellent cast, fine cinematography, unusual Nicholson performance.
1982 (R) 107m/C Jack Nicholson, Harvey Keitel, Valerie Perrine, Warren Oates, Elpidia Carrillo; *D:* Tony Richardson. **VHS, Beta, LV $39.95** *MCA* 𝒵𝒵𝒵

Border Badmen It's just another tired old western, even if it does appropriate the classic mystery-thriller plot; following the reading of a siler baron's will, someone starts killing off the relatives.
1945 59m/B Buster Crabbe, Lorraine Miller, Charles King, Ray Bennett, Archie Hall, Budd Buster, Bud Osborne; *D:* Sam Newfield. **VHS, Beta** *GPV, MRV, TIM* 𝒵½

Border Bandits Plodding oater has Brown going after the bad guys. Not only is it a dirty job, but apparently pretty boring.

1946 57m/B Johnny Mack Brown, Raymond Hatton, John Merton, Frank LaRue, Steve Clark, Charles Stevens, Bud Osborne; *D:* Lambert Hillyer. **VHS $19.95** *DVT, HEG* 𝒵

Border Devils A boy is pursued by a ruthless gang of outlaws, until he is saved by the good guys.
1932 60m/B Harry Carey Sr., Art Mix, George "Gabby" Hayes; *D:* William Nigh. **VHS, Beta, LV** *NO* 𝒵

Border Feud LaRue endeavors to prevent someone who, by instigating a family feud, will claim large gold mine rights.
1947 54m/B Lash LaRue, Al "Fuzzy" St. John, Bob Duncan; *D:* Ray Taylor. **VHS, Beta $12.95** *COL, SVS* 𝒵

Border Heat A man and his female partner try to save a group of Mexican laborers from the horrible working conditions their cruel employers inflict upon them.
1988 93m/C John Vernon, Darlanne Fluegel, Michael J. Moore; *D:* Max Kleven. **VHS, Beta $79.98** *MCG* 𝒵

Border of Tong It was the most heinous killing in the history of Chinatown, and the only suitable response was revenge!
1990 ?m/C David Heavener. **VHS** *PMH* 𝒵

Border Patrol Another installment in the Hopalong Cassidy series. This time there's a villainous owner of a silvermine to reckon with. A man so low he's abducting hapless Mexicans as they cross the border, forcing them to work his mines. Hoppy is saddled with the task of persuading him that the town ain't big enough for the both of them. Robert Mitchum makes his perfectly-forgettable film debut as one of the bad guys. Not one of the best in the series, but plenty of action.
1943 63m/B William Boyd, Andy Clyde, Jay Kirby, Russell Simpson, Claudia Drake, George Reeves, Duncan Renaldo; *D:* Lesley Selander. **VHS $19.95** *NOS* 𝒵𝒵

Border Phantom Steele (whom you might recognize as Canino in "The Big Sleep"), takes on a suave Chinese businessman who heads a mail order business; seems he's smuggling mail-order brides from Mexico in this vintage "B"-grade horse opera.
1937 60m/B Bob Steele, Harley Wood, Don Barclay, Carl Hackett, Horace Murphy, Miki Morita; *D:* S. Roy Luby. **VHS $19.99** *NOS, MRV, MTX* 𝒵𝒵

Border Radio A rock singer decides to steal a car and try to outrun some tough thugs hot on his trail.
1988 88m/C **VHS $19.95** *PAV, FCT* 𝒵𝒵

Border Rangers A man joins the Rangers in order to avenge the murders of his brother and sister-in-law.
1950 57m/B Robert Lowery, Donald (Don "Red") Barry, Lyle Talbot, Pamela Blake; *D:* William Berke. **VHS, Beta, LV** *NO* 𝒵

Border Romance Three Americans have their horses stolen by bandits while riding through Mexico. Trouble with the locals follows in this early sound western.
1930 58m/B Don Terry, Armida, Marjorie Kane. **VHS, Beta $24.95** *VYY* 𝒵½

Border Roundup The "Lone Rider" uncovers a gang of thieving crooks.
1941 57m/B George Houston, Al "Fuzzy" St. John, Dennis Moore; *D:* Sam Newfield. **VHS, Beta $19.95** *VDM* 𝒵

Border Saddlemates A U.S. government agent becomes involved in a crooked deal when he is asked to doctor Canadian silver foxes.
1952 67m/B Rex Allen. **VHS, Beta $29.95** *DVT* 𝒵

Border Shootout A trigger-happy sheriff battles a rich young cattle rustler.
1990 (PG) 110m/C Glenn Ford, Charlene Tilton, Jeff Kaake, Michael Horse, Russell Todd, Cody Glenn, Sergio Calderon, Michael Ansara; *D:* C.T. McIntyre. **VHS, Beta $79.98** *TTC* ✂✂

Border Street This film shows how a group of Polish Jews fought off the German occupation forces in the Warsaw ghetto. In Polish with English subtitles. *AKA:* Ulica Graniczna; That Others May Live.
1948 110m/B *PL* VHS, Beta, 3/4U **$39.95** *IHF* ✂✂½

Border Vigilantes Hoppy and pals try to rid a town of outlaws that even the vigilantes can't run off. The big surprise comes when they find out who the leader of the outlaws is.
1941 61m/B William Boyd, Russell Hayden, Andy Clyde, Victor Jory, Morris Ankrum, Frances Gifford, Ethel Wales, Hal Taliaferro; *D:* Derwin Abrahams. **VHS $19.95** *NOS* ✂✂

Borderline MacMurray and Trevor play undercover agents trying to infiltrate a Mexican drug ring. With their real identities hidden, they fall for each other and make a run for the border. Although the leads work well together, they're hindered by an occasionally confusing script. Unfortunately, director Seiter never decides whether the material is of a comedic or dramatic nature.
1950 88m/B Fred MacMurray, Claire Trevor, Raymond Burr, Roy Roberts, Jose Torvay, Morris Ankrum, Charles Lane, Don Diamond, Nacho Galindo, Pepe Hern, Richard Irving; *D:* William A. Seiter. **VHS** *HEG* ✂✂

Borderline Bronson is a border patrol guard in pursuit of a murderer in this action flick. Meanwhile, he gets caught up in trying to help an illegal alien and her young child.
1980 (PG) 106m/C Charles Bronson, Wilford Brimley, Bruno Kirby, Benito Morales, Ed Harris, Kenneth McMillan; *D:* Jerrold Freedman. **VHS, Beta $59.98** *FOX* ✂✂

Bordertown Gunfighters A cowboy breaks up a vicious lottery racket and falls in love in the process.
1943 56m/B Bill Elliott, Anne Jeffreys. **VHS, Beta $29.95** *DVT* ✂½

Boris and Natasha: The Movie The two inept spies from the classic television cartoon "The Adventures of Rocky and Bullwinkle" star in this mediocre live-action comedy. These nogoodniks are sent by "Fearless Leader" to America and encounter the usual misadventures. For true fun watch the original animated versions. Features cameos by Candy, Travolta, and Smith. Never released theatrically, it aired for the first time on cable television.
1992 (PG) 88m/C Sally Kellerman, Dave Thomas, Paxton Whitehead, Andrea Martin, Alex Rocco, Larry Cedar, Arye Gross, Christopher Neame, Anthony Newley; *Cameos:* John Candy, John Travolta, Charles Martin Smith; *D:* Charles Martin Smith. **VHS $89.95** *NLC* ✂½

B.O.R.N. Hagen uncovers an underground network of doctors who kill people and sell the body parts and organs.
1988 (R) 90m/C Ross Hagen, P.J. Soles, William Smith, Hoke Howell, Russ Tamblyn, Amanda Blake, Clint Howard, Rance Howard, Debra Lamb; *D:* Ross Hagen. **VHS, Beta $79.95** *PSM* ✂½

Born Again This is the filmed adaptation of Charles Colson's biography of why he became a born again Christian.
1978 110m/C Dean Jones, Anne Francis, Dana Andrews, George Brent; *D:* Irving Rapper. **VHS, Beta $59.98** *SUE* ✂½

Born American Pre-Glasnost flick about teenagers vacationing in Finland who "accidentally" cross the Russian border. There they battle the Red Plague. Melodramatic and heavily politicized. Original release banned in Finland. *AKA:* Arctic Heat.
1986 (R) 95m/C Mike Norris, Steve Durham, David Coburn, Thalmus Rasulala, Albert Salmi; *D:* Renny Harlin. **VHS, Beta** *NO* ✂

Born Beautiful Made for TV. Beautiful young women come to New York, hoping to strike it rich in the world of modeling. At the same time, a still beautiful, but older and overexposed model comes to grips with a change in her career. Well-told, but sugar-coated.
1982 100m/C Erin Gray, Ed Marinaro, Polly Bergen, Lori Singer, Ellen Barber, Judith Barcroft, Michael Higgins; *D:* Harvey Hart. **VHS** *WAR* ✂✂½

Born Free The touching story of a game warden in Kenya and his wife raising Elsa the orphaned lion cub. When the cub reaches maturity, they work to return her to life in the wild. Great family entertainment based on Joy Adamson's book. Theme song became a hit.
1966 95m/C Virginia McKenna, Bill Travers; *D:* James Hill; *M:* John Barry. **VHS, Beta, LV $14.95** *COL, HMV* ✂✂✂

Born in America A young orphan is adopted by an undertaker. The boy grows up enveloped by his guardian's business and, when things are slow, works to bring in business himself. *AKA:* Dead Aim.
1990 90m/C James Westerfield, Glen Lee, Virgil Frye, Venetia Vianello; *D:* Jose Antonio Bolanos. **VHS** *NO* ✂

Born in East L.A. Marin brings his Bruce Springsteen-parody song to life as he plays a mistakenly deported illegal alien who struggles to return to the U.S.
1987 (R) 85m/C Cheech Marin, Daniel Stern, Paul Rodriguez, Jan-Michael Vincent, Kamala Lopez, Tony Plana, Vic Trevino; *D:* Cheech Marin. **VHS, Beta, LV $14.95** *MCA, FCT* ✂½

Born in Flames An acclaimed futuristic feminist film about women who band together in an effort to gain control of the state owned media.
1983 90m/C *D:* Lizzie Borden. **VHS, 3/4U** *ICA* ✂

Born Innocent As if "The Exorcist" weren't bad enough, Blair is back for more abuse-on-film, this time as a 14-year-old runaway from a dysfunctional family who lands in a reform school for girls. There, she must struggle to be as brutal as her peers in order to survive. Fairly tame by today's standards, it was controversial at its made-for-TV premiere, chiefly due to a rape scene involving a broom handle. First trip up the river for Blair.
1974 92m/C Linda Blair, Joanna Miles, Kim Hunter, Richard Jaeckel; *D:* Donald Wrye. **VHS, Beta $49.95** *WWV* ✂½

Born Invincible A Kung Fu master avenges the kick-death of a student by randomly kick-killing suspects.
1976 90m/C Lo Lieh, Carter Wong, Nancy Yan; *D:* Joseph Kuo. **VHS, Beta $59.95** *GEM* ✂

Born Killer Teenagers in the woods meet up with murderous escaped convicts.
1989 90m/C Francine Lapensee, Fritz Matthews, Ted Prior, Adam Tucker; *D:* Kimberly Casey. **VHS, Beta $79.95** *AIP* ✂½

Born Losers The original "Billy Jack" film in which the Indian martial arts expert takes on a group of incorrigible bikers bothering some California babes and runs afoul of the law. Drive-in fare produced, directed, and written by Billy Jack Laughlin.
1967 (PG) 112m/C Tom Laughlin, Elizabeth James, Jeremy Slate, William Wellman Jr., Robert Tessier, Jane Russell; *D:* T.C. Frank. **VHS, Beta, LV $59.95** *VES, LIV* ✂✂

Born of Fire A flutist investigating his father's death seeks the Master Musician; his search leads him to the volcanic (and supernatural) mountains of Turkey.
1987 (R) 84m/C Peter Firth, Susan Crowley, Stephan Kalipha; *D:* Jamil Dehlavi. **VHS, Beta, LV $79.95** *VMK* ✂½

Born on the Fourth of July A riveting meditation on American life affected by the Vietnam War, based on the real-life, bestselling experiences of Ron Kovic, though some facts are subtly changed. The film follows him as he develops from a naive recruit to an angry, wheelchair-bound paraplegic to an active antiwar protestor. Well-acted and generally laudable; Kovic co-wrote the screenplay and appears as a war veteran in the opening parade sequence.
1989 (R) 145m/C Tom Cruise, Kyra Sedgwick, Raymond J. Barry, Jerry Levine, Tom Berenger, Willem Dafoe, Frank Whaley, John Getz, Caroline Kava, Bryan Larkin, Abbie Hoffman, Stephen Baldwin, Josh Evans; *D:* Oliver Stone; *M:* John Williams. Academy Awards '89: Best Director (Stone), Best Film Editing; Nominations: Best Actor (Cruise), Best Adapted Screenplay, Best Cinematography, Best Picture, Best Sound, Best Original Score; Directors Guild of America Awards '89: Best Director (Stone); Golden Globe Awards '90: Best Actor—Drama (Cruise), Best Director (Stone), Best Film—Drama. **VHS, Beta, LV, 8mm $14.95** *MCA, FCT, BTV* ✂✂✂½

Born to Be Bad Fontaine, an opportunistic woman who was b-b-born to be b-b-bad, attempts to steal a wealthy business man away from his wife while carrying on an affair with a novelist. Ray's direction (he's best known for "Rebel Without a Cause," filmed five years later) prevents the film from succumbing to standard Hollywood formula.
1950 93m/B Joan Fontaine, Robert Ryan, Zachary Scott, Joan Leslie, Mel Ferrer; *D:* Nicholas Ray. **VHS, Beta, LV $19.98** *TTC* ✂✂½

Born to Be Wild A pair of truck drivers are commissioned to deliver a shipment of dynamite. The dynamite will be used to destroy a dam, preventing the surrounding land from falling into the hands of unscrupulous land barons. Good action picture thanks to the cast.
1938 66m/B Ralph Byrd, Doris Weston, Ward Bond, Robert Emmett Keane, Bentley Hewlett, Charles Williams; *D:* Joseph Kane. **VHS, Beta $16.95** *SNC, RXM* ✂

Born to Boogie A concert, a chronicle, and a tribute, "Born To Boogie" is about Marc Bolan and his band T. Rex. The film, which features concert footage from a 1972 concert at the Wembley Empire Pool in London, chronicles the glitter rock era and the next wave of British rock and roll, and pays tribute to Bolan, who died in 1977 just as he was starting a comeback. Ringo Starr and Elton John join T. Rex in the studio for "Children of the Revolution" and "Tutti-Frutti" as well as a psychedelic soiree where Bolan plays acoustic versions of his hits. This film was never released in the United States.
1972 75m/C Marc Bolan, T. Rex, Elton John, Ringo Starr; *D:* Ringo Starr. **VHS $29.98** *MPI, MVD* ✂✂

Born to Dance A quintessential MGM 1930s dance musical, wherein a beautiful dancer gets a sailor and a big break in a show. Great songs by Cole Porter sung in a less than great manner by a gangly Stewart. Powell's first starring vehicle. ♪♪Love Me

Love My Pekinese; I've Got You Under My Skin; Hey Babe Hey; Easy to Love; Rolling Home; Rap Tap on Wood; Entrance of Lucy James; Swingin' the Jinx Away.
1936 108m/B Eleanor Powell, James Stewart, Virginia Bruce, Una Merkel, Frances Langford, Sid Silvers, Raymond Walburn, Reginald Gardiner, Buddy Ebsen; D: Roy Del Ruth; M: Cole Porter, Cole Porter. VHS, Beta, LV $19.98 MGM, MLB ♫♫½

Born to Kill A ruthless killer marries a girl for her money. Minor tough-as-nails noir exemplifying Tierney's stone-faced human-devil film persona. AKA: Lady of Deceit.
1947 92m/B Lawrence Tierney, Claire Trevor, Walter Slezak, Elisha Cook Jr.; D: Robert Wise. VHS, Beta $19.98 TTC ♫♫♫

Born to Race In the world of competitive auto racing, a beautiful engineer is kidnapped for her new controversial engine design.
1988 (R) 95m/C Joseph Bottoms, George Kennedy, Marc Singer, Marla Heasly; D: James Fargo. VHS, Beta $79.95 FOX ♫

Born to Ride A biker rebel joins the Army prior to World War II in order to escape a prison term after a good ol' boy brush with the law. He shuns Army discipline, but proves himself in action as the leader of a scout troup for the Army's motorcycle calvary brigade. Available with Spanish subtitles.
1991 (PG) 88m/C John Stamos, John Stockwell, Teri Polo, Kris Kamm; D: Graham Baker. VHS, Beta $19.98 WAR ♫♫

Born to Run A young Australian boy dreams of restoring his grandfather's run-down horse farm to its former glory. Filmed on location.
1977 87m/C VHS, Beta $69.95 DVT ♫♫

Born to Win A New York hairdresser with an expensive drug habit struggles through life in this well made comedy drama. Excellent acting from fine cast, well-paced, and interestingly photographed. Not well received when first released, but worth a look. AKA: Addict.
1971 (R) 90m/C George Segal, Karen Black, Paula Prentiss, Hector Elizondo, Robert De Niro, Jay Fletcher; D: Ivan Passer. VHS $9.99 QVD, MGM ♫♫½

Born Yesterday Ambitious junk dealer Harry Brock is in love with smart but uneducated Billie Dawn. He hires newspaperman Paul Verrall to teach her the finer points of etiquette. During their sessions, they fall in love and Billie realizes how she has been used by Brock. She retaliates against him and gets to deliver that now-famous line: "Do me a favor, drop dead." Based on the Broadway play.
1950 103m/B Judy Holliday, Broderick Crawford, William Holden; D: George Cukor. Academy Awards '50: Best Actress (Holliday); Nominations: Best Costume Design (B & W), Best Director (Cukor), Best Picture, Best Screenplay; Golden Globe Awards '51: Best Actress—Musical/Comedy (Holliday). VHS, Beta, LV $19.95 COL, FCT, BTV ♫♫♫½

Born Yesterday Remake of the 1950 classic suffers by comparison, particularly Griffith, with the thankless task of surpassing (or even meeting) Judy Holliday's Oscar-winning mark as the dumb blonde, Billie Dawn. Her intellectual inadequacies are glaring when she hits the political world of D.C. with business tycoon boyfriend (Goodman). To make himself look better, he hooks her up with a journalist (Johnson) willing to coach her in Savvy 101, ala Liza Doolittle. What worked well in post-WWII America seems sadly outdated today; stick with the original.
1993 (PG) 102m/C Melanie Griffith, John Goodman, Don Johnson, Edward Herrmann, Max Perlich, Fred Dalton Thompson, Nora Dunn, Benjamin C. Bradlee, Sally Quinn, Michael Ensign, William Frankfather, Celeste Yarnall, Meg Wittner; D: Luis Mandoki; W: Douglas McGrath; M: George Fenton. VHS NYR ♫♫

The Borrower An exiled unstable mutant insect alien serial killer (you know the type) must switch heads with human beings regularly to survive. This colorful, garish gorefest has humor and attitude, but never develops behind the basic grossout situation.
1989 (R) 97m/C Rae Dawn Chong, Don Gordon, Antonio Fargas, Tom Towles; D: John McNaughton. VHS, LV $19.98 WAR, CAN ♫♫

Borsalino Delon and Belmondo are partners in crime in this seriocomic film about gang warfare in 1930's Marseilles. The costumes, settings, and music perfectly capture the mood of the period. Followed by a sequel "Borsalino and Co." Based on "The Bandits of Marseilles" by Eugene Saccomano.
1970 (R) 124m/C FR Jean-Paul Belmondo, Alain Delon, Michel Bouquet, Catherine Rouvel, Francoise Christophe, Corinne Marchand; D: Jacques Deray. VHS $19.95 PAR ♫♫♫

Boss Blaxploitation western parody with Williamson and Martin as a couple of bounty hunters tearing apart a town to find a fugitive. Williamson wrote the relatively non-violent script. AKA: The Black Bounty Killer; Boss Nigger.
1974 (PG) 87m/C Fred Williamson, D'Urville Martin, R.G. Armstrong, William Smith, Carmen Hayworth, Barbara Leigh; D: Jack Arnold. VHS VTK ♫½

Boss Cowboy A cowboy shows who wears the chaps in his family when he kidnaps his girlfriend to prevent her from moving East.
1935 51m/B Buddy Roosevelt, Frances Morris, Sam Pierce, Fay McKenzie, Lafe McKee; D: Victor Adamson. VHS, Beta NO ♫

Boss Foreman A languorous, entwining comedy of errors about a construction foreman and his misadventures with the mob.
1939 58m/C Henry Armetta. VHS, Beta $24.95 VYY Woof!

The Boss Is Served A mother (Berger) and three daughters, racked with debt, are forced to take in boarders. The lascivious man and teenage son want to be more than just boarders to the lovely Berger. In Italian with English subtitles.
196? 95m/C IT Senta Berger, Maurizio Arena, Bruno Zamin. VHS, Beta NO ♫♫

Boss of Big Town Gangsters try to infiltrate the milk industry in this standard crime drama.
1943 65m/B John Litel, Florence Rice, H.B. Warner, Jean Brooks, John Miljan, Mary Gordon, John Maxwell; D: Arthur Dreifuss. VHS, Beta $16.95 SNC, RXM ♫♫

Boss of Rawhide The Texas Rangers fight for law and order in the old west despite odds against them.
1944 60m/B Dave O'Brien, James Newill. VHS, Beta $19.98 NOS, DVT ♫

Boss' Son Worthwhile coming-of-age tale about a young man who learns more than he bargained for about life when he goes to work for his father in the family carpet business. Dad feels he should work his way up through the ranks and makes him a delivery man. The young man meets reality head on and must deal with the injustices of the world around him. Independently filmed by Roth who also wrote the screenplay.
1979 97m/C Rita Moreno, James Darren. VHS, Beta $69.95 VES, LIV ♫♫½

The Boss' Wife A young stockbroker attempts to fix what's wrong with his life by maneuvering sexually with the boss' wife, and complications set in.
1986 (R) 83m/C Daniel Stern, Arielle Dombasle, Christopher Plummer, Martin Mull, Melanie Mayron, Lou Jacobi; D: Ziggy Steinberg. VHS, Beta $79.98 FOX ♫♫

The Boston Strangler Based on Gerold Frank's bestselling factual book about the deranged killer who terrorized Boston for about a year and a half. Traces events from first killing to prosecution. Curtis, going against type, is compelling in title role.
1968 116m/C Tony Curtis, Henry Fonda, George Kennedy, Murray Hamilton, Mike Kellin, George Voskovec, William Hickey, James Brolin, Hurd Hatfield, William Marshall, Jeff Corey, Sally Kellerman; D: Richard Fleischer. VHS, Beta $19.98 FOX ♫♫½

The Bostonians A faith healer's daughter is forced to choose between the affections of a militant suffragette and a young lawyer in 19th Century Boston. Based on Henry James' classic novel.
1984 (PG) 120m/C Christopher Reeve, Vanessa Redgrave, Madeleine Potter, Jessica Tandy, Nancy Marchand, Wesley Addy, Linda Hunt, Wallace Shawn; D: James Ivory. VHS, Beta, LV $79.98 VES, LIV ♫♫½

Botany Bay A rousing costumer about a convict ship in the 1700s that, after a trying voyage, lands in Australia, wherein a framed doctor conquers the local plague. From the novel by Charles Nordoff.
1953 99m/C Alan Ladd, James Mason, Patricia Medina, Cedric Hardwicke; D: John Farrow. VHS, Beta $19.95 KRT ♫♫

Bottoms Up Three nymphomaniacs seduce a virginal mechanic and turn him into an insatiable womanizer. Skin aplenty.
1987 90m/C Adam Janas, Sparky Abbrams, Kathleen Johnson. VHS, Beta $9.99 STE, PSM Woof!

Boudu Saved from Drowning A suicidal tramp completely disrupts the wealthy household of the man that saves him from drowning. A gentle but sardonic farce from the master filmmaker. Remade in 1986 as "Down and Out In Beverly Hills." AKA: Boudu Sauve des Eaux.
1932 87m/B FR Michel Simon, Charles Grandval, Jean Daste; D: Jean Renoir. VHS, Beta $59.95 INT, MRV, DVT ♫♫♫½

Boulevard Nights A young Latino man tries to escape his neighborhood's street-gang violence, while his older brother is sucked into it. Music by Lalo Schifrin, known for the "Mission: Impossible" theme.
1979 (R) 102m/C Richard Yniguez, Danny De La Paz, Marta DuBois, Carmen Zapata, Victor Millan; D: Michael Pressman. VHS, Beta $19.98 WAR ♫♫

Bound by Honor Three-hour epic about Chicano gang culture focuses on three buddies whose lives evolve into a drug-addicted artist, a narc, and a prison regular. Written by acclaimed poet Baca, the film touches on issues such as poverty, racism, drugs, and violence as they pertain to Hispanic life. Unfortunately, the extreme violence (shootings, stabbings, and garrotings) completely overwhelms the rest of the story. Contains profanity, nudity, and sexual innuendo. Based on a story by Ross Thomas. AKA: Blood In...Blood Out.
1993 (R) 174m/C Damian Chapa, Jesse Borrego, Benjamin Bratt, Enrique Castillo, Victor Rivers, Delroy Lindo, Tom Towles; D: Taylor Hackford; W: Floyd Mutrux; Jimmy Santiago Baca, Jeremy Iacone; M: Bill Conti. VHS ♫½

Bound for Glory The award-winning biography of American folk singer Woody Guthrie set against the backdrop of the Depression. Superb portrayal of the spirit and feelings of the period featuring many of his songs encased in the incidents that inspired them. Haskell Wexler's award-winning camera work is superbly expressive. **1976 (PG) 149m/C** David Carradine, Ronny Cox, Melinda Dillon, Randy Quaid; **D:** Hal Ashby. Academy Awards '76: Best Adapted Score, Best Cinematography; Nominations: Best Adapted Screenplay, Best Costume Design, Best Film Editing, Best Picture; National Board of Review Awards '76: Best Actor (Carradine). **VHS, Beta, LV** $59.95 *MGM* 🐾🐾🐾½

The Bounty A new version of "Mutiny on the Bounty," with emphasis on a more realistic relationship between Fletcher Christian and Captain Bligh—and a more sympathetic portrayal of the captain, too. The sensuality of Christian's relationship with a Tahitian beauty also receives greater importance. **1984 (PG) 130m/C** Mel Gibson, Anthony Hopkins, Laurence Olivier, Edward Fox, Daniel Day-Lewis, Bernard Hill, Philip Davis, Liam Neeson; **D:** Roger Donaldson. **VHS, Beta, LV** $29.98 *VES, LIV* 🐾🐾🐾

Bounty Hunters A man hunts down his friend's killer. **1989 (R) 91m/C** Robert Ginty, Bo Hopkins, Loeta Waterdown; **D:** Robert Ginty. **VHS, Beta** $79.95 *AIP* 🐾🐾

The Bounty Man A bounty hunter brings an outlaw in, robbing him of his freedom and his girlfriend. **1972 74m/C** Clint Walker, Richard Basehart, Margot Kidder, Arthur Hunnicutt, John Ericson, Gene Evans; **D:** John Llewellyn Moxey. **VHS, Beta** $19.98 *FOX* 🐾🐾

Bouquet of Barbed Wire Overlong soaper revolves around a weathly family and their hidden secrets: incest and infidelity. On three tapes. **1976 330m/C** Frank Finlay, Susan Penhaligon, Deborah Grant, Sheila Allen, James Aubrey; **D:** Tom Wharmby. **VHS** $79.95 *SVS* 🐾½

The Bourne Identity Chamberlain stars as an amnesiac trying to piece together the fragments of his memory. Is he U.S. espionage agent Jason Bourne or an international terrorist? Aided by Smith (the kidnap victim who falls in love with her captor), the two traverse Europe trying to escape the spy network out to assassinate the mystery man who knows too little. Exciting adaptation of the Robert Ludlum thriller. Originally a two-part television miniseries. **1988 185m/C** Richard Chamberlain, Jaclyn Smith, Denholm Elliott, Anthony Quayle, Donald Moffatt, Yorgo Voyagis; **D:** Roger Young; **W:** Carol Sobieski. **VHS** $79.99 *WAR, BTV* 🐾🐾🐾

Bowery at Midnight Lugosi plays a man who recycles criminals into zombies that commit crimes for his benefit. Bela and an intense mood can't quite save this pic. **1942 60m/B** Bela Lugosi, Tom Neal, Dave O'Brien, Wanda McKay; **D:** Wallace Fox. **VHS, Beta** $19.95 *NOS, MRV, SNC* 🐾½

Bowery at Midnight/Dick Tracy vs. Cueball On one tape, the vintage Lugosi grade-C thriller about zombies in the Bowery, and a standard Dick Tracy entry. **1942 125m/B** Bela Lugosi, Morgan Conway, Dick Wessel, Skelton Knaggs. **VHS, Beta** *AOV* 🐾½

Bowery Blitzkrieg This lesser "East Side Kids" entry has Gorcey opting to enter the boxing ring rather than turn to crime. Needs more Huntz. *AKA:* Stand and Deliver.

1941 62m/B Leo Gorcey, Huntz Hall, Bobby Jordan, Warren Hull, Charlotte Henry, Keye Luke; **D:** Wallace Fox. **VHS** $19.95 *NOS, VEC, TIM* 🐾

Bowery Buckaroos The Bowery Boys take their act West in search of gold, meeting up with the usual amounts of goofy characters and hilarious misunderstandings. **1947 66m/B** Leo Gorcey, Huntz Hall, Bobby Jordan, Gabriel Dell, Billy Benedict, David Gorcey, Julie Briggs, Bernard Gorcey, Chief Yowlachie, Iron Eyes Cody; **D:** William Beaudine. **VHS** $14.98 *WAR* 🐾🐾

Boxcar Bertha Scorsese's vivid portrayal of the South during the 1930s' Depression casts Hershey as a woman who winds up in cahoots with an anti-establishment train robber. Based on the book "Sister of the Road" by Boxcar Bertha Thomson. **1972 (R) 96m/C** Barbara Hershey, David Carradine, John Carradine; **D:** Martin Scorsese. **VHS, Beta, LV** $69.95 *VES, LIV* 🐾🐾½

Boxcar Blues Bird (Coufos) is a down and out fighter who decides to fight "The Man" (Ventura), a bare knuckle fighter who enjoys beating his opponents to death. On the way to the fight, in New Orleans, he meets up with his girl Casey (Langrick), along with some other shady characters, including a truck driving preacher. **1990 96m/C** Paul Coufos, Margaret Langrick, Jesse Ventura, M. Emmet Walsh, Donny Lalonde; **D:** Damian Lee. **VHS** $79.95 *VHE* 🐾

The Boxer and Death A new-wave Czech film about a boxer in a Nazi concentration camp who interests the boxing-obsessed commandant in a match. In Czech with subtitles. **1963 120m/B** Stefan Kvietik; **D:** Peter Solan. **VHS, Beta** $24.95 *NOS, FCT, DVT* 🐾🐾🐾

A Boy and His Dog In the post-holocaust world of 2024, a young man (Johnson) and his talking canine cohort search for food and sex. They happen upon a community that drafts Johnson to repopulate their largely impotent race; Johnson is at first ready, willing, and able, until he discovers the mechanical methods they mean to employ. Based on a short story by Harlan Ellison. The dog was played by the late Tiger of "The Brady Bunch." **1975 (R) 87m/C** Don Johnson, Suzanne Benton, Jason Robards Jr., Charles McGraw, Alvy Moore; **D:** L.Q. Jones. **VHS, Beta, LV** $9.99 *CCB, MED, MRV* 🐾🐾½

Boy, Did I Get a Wrong Number! A real estate agent gets more than he bargained for when he accidentally dials a wrong number. Zany comedy persists as Hope gets entangled in the life of sexy starlet Sommer. **1966 100m/C** Bob Hope, Phyllis Diller, Marjorie Lord, Elke Sommer, Cesare Danova; **D:** George Marshall. **VHS, Beta** *NO* 🐾

The Boy Friend Russell pays tribute to the Busby Berkeley Hollywood musical. Lots of charming dance numbers and clever parody of plot lines in this adaptation of Sandy Wilson's stage play. Fun! ♫The Boy Friend; I Could Be Happy; Won't You Charleston With Me?; Fancy Forgetting; Sur La Plage; A Room in Bloomsbury; Safety in Numbers; It's Never Too Late to Fall in Love; Poor Little Pierette; Rivera; The You Don't Want To Play With Me Blues; All I Do Is Dream Of You; You Are My Lucky Star; Any Old Iron. **1971 (G) 135m/C** *GB* Twiggy, Christopher Gable, Moyra Fraser, Max Adrian, Vladek Sheybal, Georgina Hale, Tommy Tune; **D:** Ken Russell. **VHS** $19.95 *MGM* 🐾🐾🐾

The Boy God Rocco here describes his trials and everyday shenanigans; he the young demi-God, battling evil on a fantasy land. **1986 100m/C** Nino Muhlach; **D:** Erastheo J. Navda. **VHS, Beta** $39.95 *VCD* 🐾

Boy in Blue A "Rocky"-esque biography of Canadian speed-rower Ned Hanlan, who set aside lackluster pursuits to turn to rowing. **1986 (R) 97m/C** *CA* Nicolas Cage, Christopher Plummer, David Naughton; **D:** Charles Jarrott. **VHS, Beta** $79.98 *FOX* 🐾½

The Boy in the Plastic Bubble Well-made, sensitive television drama about a young man born with immunity deficiencies who must grow up in a specially controlled plastic environment. Travolta is endearing as the boy in the bubble. **1976 100m/C** John Travolta, Robert Reed, Glynnis O'Connor, Diana Hyland, Ralph Bellamy, Anne Ramsey; **D:** Randal Kleiser. **VHS, Beta** $59.95 *PSM* 🐾🐾½

Boy Meets Girl Cagney and O'Brien play screenwriters whose every film is a variation on the boy meets girl theme. Trouble is they're running out of ideas and their scripts get increasingly outlandish. A fading cowboy actor is supposed to star in the duo's next film—if they can ever settle down to work. Then they get the idea to feature their friend Wilson's baby in the movie—and guess who becomes a new star. Good satire on moviemaking and movie moguls, which made fine use of the Warner studio back lots, sound stages, and offices. Based on the play by Bella and Samuel Spewack who also wrote the screenplay. **1938 86m/B** James Cagney, Pat O'Brien, Ralph Bellamy, Dick Foran, Marie Wilson, Frank McHugh, Bruce Lester, Ronald Reagan, Penny Singleton, James Stephenson; **D:** Lloyd Bacon; **W:** Bella Spewack, Samuel Spewack. **VHS** $19.98 *MGM* 🐾🐾🐾

Boy Meets Girl A French Holden Caulfield type character cruises the seamier side of Paris in this acclaimed film. Carax's directoral debut at age 22. In French with English subtitles. **1984 100m/B** *FR* Denis Lavant, Mireille Perrier; **D:** Leo Carax. **VHS** $49.95 *FCT, MGM* 🐾🐾🐾

A Boy Named Charlie Brown Charlie Brown enters the National Spelling Bee in New York and makes the final rounds with one other contestant. Based on Charles Schultz's popular comic strip characters from "Peanuts." Music by the Vince Guaraldi trio is, as always, a treat. **1970 86m/C** **D:** Bill Melendez; **M:** Vince Guaraldi, Rod McKuen. **VHS, Beta, LV** $14.98 *FOX* 🐾🐾🐾

Boy of Two Worlds Because he is of a lineage foreign to his late father's town, a boy is exiled to the life of a junior Robinson Crusoe. **1970 (G) 103m/C** Jimmy Sternman, Edvin Adolphson; **D:** Astrid Henning Jensen. **VHS, Beta** $29.95 *GEM* 🐾½

Boy Takes Girl A little girl finds it hard adjusting to life on a farming cooperative during a summer recess. **1983 93m/C** Gabi Eldor, Hillel Neeman, Dina Limon; **D:** Michal Bat-Adam. **VHS, Beta** $59.95 *MGM* 🐾½

Boy! What a Girl Moore (in drag) is mistaken for a woman, and is fought over by a couple of suitors. **1945 60m/B** Sheila Guyse, Tim Moore, Duke Williams, Sheila Guyse, Beth Mays, Elwood Smith; **D:** Arthur Leonard. **VHS, Beta** $34.95 *FCT, GVV, DVT* 🐾🐾

The Boy Who Could Fly After a plane crash kills his parents, a boy withdraws into a fantasy land where he can fly. The young daughter of a troubled family makes friends with him and the fantasy becomes real. A sweet film for children, charming though melancholy for adults, too. Fine cast, including Savage, Dewhurst, and Bedelia keep this from becoming sappy.
1986 (PG) 120m/C Lucy Deakins, Jay Underwood, Bonnie Bedelia, Colleen Dewhurst, Fred Savage, Fred Gwynne, Louise Fletcher; **D:** Nick Castle. **VHS, Beta, LV** $19.98 LHV, WAR ♼♼♼

The Boy Who Left Home to Find Out About the Shivers From "Faerie Tale Theatre" comes this tale about a boy who learns about fear.
1981 60m/C Peter MacNicol, Christopher Lee, Vincent Price; **D:** Graeme Clifford. **VHS, Beta, LV** $14.98 KUI, FOX ♼♼♼

The Boy Who Loved Trolls Paul's fantastic dreams come true when he meets Ofoeti, a real, live troll. The only problem is Ofoeti only has a day to live, and Paul must find a way to save him. Aired on PBS as part of the "Wonderworks" series.
1984 58m/C Sam Waterston, Susan Anton, Matt Dill; **D:** Harvey Laidman. **VHS** $29.95 PME, HMV ♼♼♼

The Boy with the Green Hair When he hears that his parents were killed in an air raid, a boy's hair turns green. The narrow-minded members of his community suddenly want nothing to do with him and he becomes an outcast. Thought-provoking social commentary.
1948 82m/C Pat O'Brien, Robert Ryan, Barbara Hale, Dean Stockwell; **D:** Joseph Losey. **VHS, Beta, LV** $29.95 IME ♼♼♼

Boyfriends & Girlfriends Another one of Rohmer's "Comedies and Proverbs," in which two girls with boyfriends fade in and out of interest with each, casually reshuffling their relationships. Typical, endless-talks-at-cafes Rohmer, the most happily consistent of the aging French New Wave. In French with subtitles. **AKA:** My Girlfriend's Boyfriend; Ami de Mon Ami.
1988 (PG) 102m/C FR Emmanuelle Chaulet, Sophie Renoir, Eric Viellard, Francois-Eric Gendron; **D:** Eric Rohmer. **VHS, Beta, LV** $79.98 ORI, TAM ♼♼½

The Boys from Brazil Based on Ira Levin's novel, a thriller about Dr. Josef Mengele endeavoring to reconstitute the Nazi movement from his Brazilian sanctuary by cloning a brood of boys from Hitler's genes.
1978 (R) 123m/C Gregory Peck, James Mason, Laurence Olivier, Uta Hagen, Steve Guttenberg, Denholm Elliott, Lilli Palmer; **D:** Franklin J. Schaffner; **M:** Jerry Goldsmith. Academy Awards '78 Nominations: Best Actor (Olivier), Best Film Editing, Best Original Score; National Board of Review Awards '78: Best Actor (Olivier). **VHS, Beta, LV** $59.98 FOX ♼♼½

The Boys from Termite Terrace The animators from Warner Brothers who created Bugs Bunny, Daffy Duck, and Porky Pig are interviewed in this series of two untitled programs.
1975 30m/C **VHS, Beta** CMR, NYS ♼♼½

The Boys in Company C A frank, hard-hitting drama about five naive young men involved in the Vietnam War.
1977 (R) 127m/C Stan Shaw, Andrew Stevens, James Canning, Michael Lembeck, Craig Wasson; **D:** Sidney J. Furie. **VHS, Beta, LV** $59.95 COL ♼♼

The Boys in the Band A group of gay friends get together one night for a birthday party. A simple premise with a compelling depiction of friendship, expectations, and lifestyle. One of the first serious cinematic presentations to deal with the subject of homosexuality. The film was adapted from Mart Crowley's play using the original cast.
1970 (R) 120m/C Frederick Combs, Cliff Gorman, Laurence Luckinbill, Kenneth Nelson, Leonard Frey; **D:** William Friedkin. **VHS, Beta, LV** $59.98 FOX ♼♼½

The Boys Next Door Two California lads kill and go nuts during a weekend in Los Angeles. Sheen overacts as a budding psychotic, not an easy thing to do. Apparently is trying to show what a particular lifestyle can lead to. Violent.
1985 (R) 90m/C Maxwell Caulfield, Charlie Sheen, Christopher McDonald, Hank Garrett, Patti D'Arbanville, Moon Zappa; **D:** Penelope Spheeris. **VHS, Beta, LV** $19.95 STE, NWV ♼♼½

Boys of the City The East Side Kids run amuck in an eerie mansion while trying to solve the murder of a judge. **AKA:** The Ghost Creeps.
1940 63m/B Leo Gorcey, Bobby Jordan; **D:** Joseph H. Lewis. **VHS, Beta** $24.95 NOS, SNC, DVT ♼♼

Boy's Reformatory Brothers are framed. One takes the rap, goes to the title institution, breaks out, and hunts the real bad guys. Creaky and antiquated.
1939 62m/B Frankie Darro, Grant Withers, David Durand, Warren McCollum; **D:** Howard Bretherton. **VHS** $15.95 NOS, LOO ♼½

Boys Town Righteous portrayal of Father Flanagan and the creation of Boys Town, home for juvenile soon-to-be-ex-delinquents.
1938 93m/B Spencer Tracy, Mickey Rooney, Henry Hull, Gene Reynolds, Sidney Miller, Frankie Thomas; **D:** Norman Taurog. Academy Awards '38: Best Actor (Tracy), Best Original Screenplay; Nominations: Best Director (Taurog), Best Picture, Best Screenplay **VHS, Beta, LV** $19.98 MGM, BTV, IGP ♼♼♼½

Boyz N the Hood Singleton's debut as a writer and director is an astonishing picture of young black men, four high school students with different backgrounds, aims, and abilities trying to survive Los Angeles gangs and bigotry. Excellent acting throughout, with special nods to Fishburne and Gooding, Jr. Violent outbreaks outside theaters where this ran only proves the urgency of its passionately nonviolent, pro-family message. Hopefully those viewers scared off at the time will give this a chance in the safety of their VCRs. Singleton was the youngest director ever nominated for an Oscar. The laserdisc version includes two extra scenes and an interview with Singleton.
1991 (R) 112m/C Larry Fishburne, Ice Cube, Cuba Gooding Jr., Nia Long, Morris Chestnut, Tyra Ferrell, Angela Bassett; **W/D:** John Singleton; **M:** Stanley Clarke. Academy Awards '91 Nominations: Best Director (Singleton), Best Original Screenplay; Chicago Film Critics Awards '91: Most Promising Actor (Ice Cube); MTV Movie Awards '92: Best New Filmmaker Award (Singleton); National Board of Review Awards '91: 10 Best Films of the Year. **VHS, Beta, LV, 8mm** $19.95 COL, CRC, FCT ♼♼♼½

Braddock: Missing in Action 3 The battle-scarred, high-kicking 'Nam vet battles his way into the jungles once more, this time to rescue his long-lost Vietnamese family. A family effort, Chuck co-wrote the script; his brother directed.
1988 (R) 104m/C Chuck Norris, Aki Aleong, Roland Harrah III; **D:** Aaron Norris. **VHS, Beta, LV** $9.98 MED, CCB ♼

Brady's Escape American WWII pilot is shot down in the Hungarian countryside and befriended by Hungarian csikos (cowboys) in this made-for-cable television movie. **AKA:** The Long Ride.
1984 92m/C HU John Savage, Kelly Reno; **D:** Pal Gabor. **VHS, Beta, LV** $9.95 CAF ♼♼½

The Brain A scientist learns that a mind isn't always a terrible thing to waste when he finds himself being manipulated by the brain of a dead man he's trying to keep alive. Remake of "Donovan's Brain" (1953). **AKA:** Vengeance.
1962 83m/B GB GE Anne Heywood, Peter Van Eyck, Bernard Lee, Cecil Parker, Jack MacGowran; **D:** Freddie Francis. **VHS, Beta, LV** $19.95 NOS, SNC ♼♼½

The Brain Run of the mill comedy caper has Niven planning to heist millions from a NATO train. The caper begins when lots of other crooks decide to rob the same train. The cast holds this one together. **AKA:** Le Cerveau.
1969 (G) 100m/C FR David Niven, Jean-Paul Belmondo, Bourvil, Eli Wallach, Silvia Monti, Fernand Valois; **D:** Gerard Oury. **VHS** PAR ♼♼

The Brain Dr. Blake, host of a popular TV talk-show, is in league with a power-hungry alien brain. Viewers of his show kill themselves and others in the midst of many special effects. The ratings go down.
1988 (R) 94m/C Tom Breznahan, Cyndy Preston, David Gale; **D:** Edward Hunt. **VHS, Beta** $14.95 LIV ♼½

Brain Damage A tongue-in-bloody-cheek farce about a brain-sucking parasite. The parasite in question, Aylmer, addicts our dubious hero to the euphoria induced by the blue liquid the parasite injects into his brain, paving the way for the bloody mayhem that follows. Poor shadow of Henenlotter's far-superior "Basket Case." In fact, it even includes an inside-joke cameo by Van Hentenryck, reprising his "Basket Case" character; look for him on the subway.
1988 (R) 89m/C Rick Herbst, Gordon MacDonald, Jennifer Lowry; **Cameos:** Kevin Van Hentenryck; **D:** Frank Henenlotter. **VHS, Beta** $14.95 PAR ♼♼

Brain Dead Low-budget but brilliantly assembled puzzle-film about a brain surgeon who agrees to perform experimental surgery on a psychotic to retrieve some corporately valuable data—his first mistake, which begins a seemingly endless cycle of nightmares and identity alterations. A mind-blowing sci-fi feast from ex-"Twilight Zone" writer Charles Beaumont.
1989 (R) 85m/C Bill Pullman, Bill Paxton, Bud Cort, Patricia Charbonneau, Nicholas Pryor, George Kennedy; **D:** Adam Simon. **VHS, Beta** $79.98 MGM ♼♼♼½

Brain Donors Goofy, uneven film starring Turturro as a sleazy lawyer trying to take over the Oglethorpe Ballet Company by sweet-talking its aged patronness. He is helped by two eccentric friends, and together the three crack a lot of bad but witty jokes. The film culminates into a hilarious ballet scene featuring someone giving CPR to the ballerina playing the dying swan, an actor in a duck suit, duck hunters, and a pack of hounds. This trio reminds us of second-rate Marx Brothers (or the Three Stooges) but the movie has enough funny moments to be worth a watch.
1992 (PG) 79m/C John Turturro, Bob Nelson, Mel Smith, Nancy Marchand, John Savident, George De La Pena, Juli Donald, Spike Alexander, Teri Copley; **D:** Dennis Dugan; **W:** Pat Proft. **VHS, Beta, LV** PAR ♼♼½

The Brain Eaters A strange ship from inside the Earth invades a small town, and hairy monsters promptly attach themselves to people's necks in a daring bid to control the planet. The imaginative story compensates somewhat for the cheap special effects. Watch for Nimoy before he grew pointed ears.
1958 60m/B Edwin Nelson, Alan Frost, Jack Hill, Joanna Lee, Jody Fair, Leonard Nimoy; *D:* Bruno Ve Sota. **VHS** $9.95 *NOS, CNM* 🎬🎬

The Brain from Planet Arous Lassie meets Alien when an evil alien brain appropriates the body of a scientist in order to take over planet Earth. His plans are thwarted, however, by a good alien brain that likewise inhabits the body of the scientist's dog. High camp and misdemeanors.
1957 80m/B John Agar, Joyce Meadows, Robert Fuller, Henry Travis; *D:* Nathan Juran. **VHS, Beta, LV** $19.95 *RHI, SNC, CNM* 🎬

The Brain Machine Device that probes thoughts menaces a woman scientist.
1972 90m/C James Best, Barbara Burgess, Gil Peterson, Gerald McRaney, Anne Latham; *D:* Joy Houck Jr. **VHS, Beta** *PGN* 🎬

Brain of Blood Deals with a scientist who transplants the brain of a politician into the body of a deformed idiot. The change is minimal. *AKA:* The Creature's Revenge.
1971 107m/C Kent Taylor, John Bloom, Regina Carrol, Angelo Rossitto, Grant Williams, Reed Hadley, Vicki Volante, Zandor Vorkov; *D:* Al Adamson. **VHS, Beta** *NO Woof!*

The Brain That Wouldn't Die Love is a many-splattered thing when a brilliant surgeon keeps the decapitated head of his fiancee alive after an auto accident while he searches for a suitably stacked body onto which to transplant the head. Absurd and satiric (head talks so much that Doc tapes her/its mouth shut) adding up to major entry in trash film genre; much of the gore was slashed for the video, however. *AKA:* The Head That Wouldn't Die.
1963 92m/B Herb Evers, Virginia Leith, Adele Lamont; *D:* Joseph Green. **VHS, Beta** $19.98 *SNC, MRV, FCT* 🎬🎬½

The Brainiac Sorcerer sentenced for black magic returns to strike dark deeds upon the descendants of those who judged him. He turns himself into a hideous monster, feeding on his victims' brains and blood. Yuck.
1961 75m/B *MX* Abel Salazar, Ariadne Welter, Mauricio Garces, Rosa Maria Gallardo. **VHS, Beta** $54.95 *SNC, MRV, HHT* 🎬½

Brainstorm A husband-and-wife team of scientists invents headphones that can record dreams, thoughts, and fantasies (VCR-style) and then allow other people to experience them by playing back the tape. Their marriage begins to crumble as the husband becomes more and more obsessed with pushing the limits of the technology; things get worse when the government wants to exploit their discovery. Special effects and interesting camerawork punctuate this sci-fi flick. Wood's last film; in fact, she died before production was completed.
1983 (PG) 106m/C Natalie Wood, Christopher Walken, Cliff Robertson, Louise Fletcher; *D:* Douglas Trumbull. **VHS, Beta, LV** $14.95 *MGM* 🎬🎬½

Brainwash Dramatic commentary on the capitalist system and the lengths to which people will go to acquire wealth and power. *AKA:* Circle of Power.

1982 (R) 98m/C *GB* Yvette Mimieux, Christopher Allport, John Considine, Cindy Pickett; *D:* Bobby Roth. **VHS, Beta** $59.95 *MED* 🎬½

Brainwaves A young woman has disturbing flashbacks after her brain is electrically revived following a car accident. Curtis is the demented doctor who jump-starts her.
1982 (R) 83m/C Suzanna Love, Tony Curtis, Keir Dullea, Vera Miles; *D:* Ulli Lommel. **VHS, Beta** $24.98 *SUE* 🎬🎬

Bram Stoker's Dracula This should be known as "Francis Ford Coppola's Dracula" since, of course, it is the director's highly charged view of the vampire classic. Visually stunning, heavy on both eroticism and violence, and unfortunately, weak in plot and performance. Oldman, undergoing a number of amazing transformations, portrays the deadly bloodsucker as a lonely soul determined to be reunited with his long-ago love, now in the guise of the innocent Ryder. Hopkins cheerfully chews the scenery as vampire-nemesis Van Helsing and newcomer Frost is fetching as a provocative victim, but Reeves is lightweight in the thankless role of the fiance-hero. Look for musician/singer Waits, who does very well by the bug-eating madman, Renfield. Filmed entirely on soundstages with beautiful costumes and some amazing visual effects and sets. Laserdisc version also includes the 36-minute documentary "The Making of Bram Stoker's Dracula." *AKA:* Dracula.
1992 (R) 128m/C Gary Oldman, Winona Ryder, Anthony Hopkins, Keanu Reeves, Richard E. Grant, Cary Elwes, Bill Campbell, Sadie Frost, Tom Waits; *D:* Francis Ford Coppola; *W:* Jim V. Hart. Academy Awards '92: Best Costume Design, Best Makeup, Best Sound Effects Editing; Nominations: Best Art Direction/Set Decoration. **VHS, Beta, LV, 8mm** *COL* 🎬🎬🎬

Brand New Life A childless couple in their 40s are unexpectedly confronted by the wife's first pregnancy. Both have careers and well-ordered lives that promise to be disrupted.
1972 74m/C Cloris Leachman, Martin Balsam, Wilfrid Hyde-White, Mildred Dunnock; *D:* Sam O'Steen. **VHS, Beta** *LCA* 🎬

Brand of Hate A good cowboy rustles up a gang of rustlers.
1934 61m/B Bob Steele, George "Gabby" Hayes, Lucille Browne, James Flavin; *D:* Lewis Collins. **VHS, Beta** $19.95 *NOS, RXM* 🎬

Brand of the Outlaws A cowboy becomes an unwitting aid to rustlers in this early western.
1936 56m/B Bob Steele, Margaret Marquis, Virginia True Boardman, Jack Rockwell; *D:* Robert North Bradbury. **VHS, Beta** $19.95 *NOS, DVT* 🎬

Branded Ladd (pre-"Shane") impersonates the long-gone son of rich rancher Bickford, with unusual results. Nicely balanced action and love scenes makes this old Max Brand story a better-than-average western. Filmed in Technicolor.
1950 95m/C Alan Ladd, Mona Freeman, Charles Bickford, Joseph Calleia, Milburn Stone; *D:* Rudolph Mate. **VHS, LV** $14.95 *PAR* 🎬🎬½

Branded a Coward A man whose parents were killed seeks revenge via his trusty six-shooters.
1935 56m/B Johnny Mack Brown, Billie Seward, Yakima Canutt; *D:* Sam Newfield. **VHS, Beta** $19.95 *NOS, DVT* 🎬

Branded Men A couple of oddballs become mixed up in a number of zany, western-type adventures.
1931 60m/B Ken Maynard, June Clyde, Irving Bacon, Billy Bletcher, Charles King, Donald Keith; *D:* Phil Rosen. **VHS** $19.95 *NOS* 🎬🎬

Brandy Sheriff A former outlaw tries to make up for the time he lost in prison. In Spanish.
1978 90m/C *SP* Alex Nicol, Maria Contrera, Antonio Casas. **VHS, Beta** $59.95 *HHT* 🎬½

Brannigan The Duke stars in the somewhat unfamiliar role of a rough and tumble Chicago police officer. He travels across the Atlantic to arrest a racketeer who has fled the States rather than face a grand jury indictment. Humor and action abound.
1975 (PG) 111m/C John Wayne, John Vernon, Mel Ferrer, Daniel Pilon, James Booth, Ralph Meeker, Lesley-Anne Down, Richard Attenborough; *D:* Douglas Hickox. **VHS, Beta** $19.98 *MGM, FOX* 🎬🎬½

Brass First post-Archie Bunker role for O'Connor, who plods through this average police drama at a snail's pace, dragging everything else down with him. Made-for-TV pilot for a series that never aired.
1985 (PG) 94m/C Carroll O'Connor, Lois Nettleton, Jimmie Baird, Paul Shenar, Vincent Gardenia, Anita Gillette; *D:* Corey Allen. **VHS, LV** $19.98 *ORI* 🎬½

Brass Target Hypothetical thriller about a plot to kill George Patton in the closing days of WWII for the sake of $250 million in Nazi gold stolen by his staff. Interesting cast can't find story.
1978 (PG) 111m/C Sophia Loren, George Kennedy, Max von Sydow, John Cassavetes, Patrick McGoohan, Robert Vaughn, Bruce Davison, Edward Herrmann, Ed Bishop; *D:* John Hough. **VHS, Beta, LV** $59.95 *MGM* 🎬½

The Bravados A rough, distressing Western revenge tale, wherein a man is driven to find the four men who murdered his wife. In tracking the perpetrators, Peck realizes that he has been corrupted by his vengeance.
1958 98m/C Gregory Peck, Stephen Boyd, Joan Collins, Albert Salmi, Henry Silva, Lee Van Cleef, George Voskovec, Barry Coe; *D:* Henry King. **VHS, Beta** $39.98 *FOX* 🎬🎬🎬

The Brave Bunch A courageous Greek soldier tries to save his men and country during World War II.
1970 110m/C *GR* Peter Funk, John Miller; *D:* Dacosta Carayan. **VHS, Beta** $39.95 *LIV* 🎬½

The Brave One A love story between a Spanish boy and the bull who saves his life. The animal is later carted off to the bull ring. Award-winning screenplay by the then-blacklisted Dalton Trumbo, as "Robert Rich."
1956 100m/C Michael Ray, Rodolpho Moyos, Joi Lansing; *D:* Irving Rapper. Academy Awards '56: Best Original Screenplay; Nominations: Best Film Editing. **VHS, Beta, LV** $49.95 *UHV* 🎬🎬🎬

Brazil The acclaimed nightmare comedy by Gilliam about an Everyman trying to survive in a surreal paper-choked bureaucratic society. There are copious references to "1984" and "The Trial," fantastic mergings of glorious fantasy and stark reality, and astounding visual design. Gilliam co-scripted with Tom Stoppard ("Rosencrantz and Guildenstern are Dead").
1985 (R) 131m/C *GB* Jonathan Pryce, Robert De Niro, Michael Palin, Katherine Helmond, Kim Greist, Bob Hoskins, Ian Holm, Peter Vaughan, Ian Richardson; *W/D:* Terry Gilliam; *W:* Tom Stoppard. Academy Awards '85 Nominations: Best Art Direction/Set Decoration, Best Original Screenplay; Los Angeles Film Critics Association Awards '85: Best Film. **VHS, Beta, LV** $19.95 *MCA, FCT* 🎬🎬½

Break of Hearts Hepburn marries Boyer, who becomes an alcoholic, and then more troubles arise. Very soapy, but well-made.

1935 78m/B Katharine Hepburn, Charles Boyer, Jean Hersholt, John Beal, Sam Hardy; *D:* Phillip Moeller. VHS, Beta, LV $19.98 *TTC* 🎞🎞½

Breakdown A boxer is set up by his girlfriend's father to take the rap for a murder. Lackluster effort.
1953 76m/B Ann Richards, William Bishop, Anne Gwynne, Sheldon Leonard, Wally Cassell, Richard Benedict; *D:* Edmond Angelo. VHS, Beta $16.95 *NOS, SNC* 🎞

Breaker! Breaker! Convoy of angry truck drivers launch an assault on the corrupt and sadistic locals of a small Texas town. Goofy entry in "mad or sex-crazed trucker armed with a CB radio" genre.
1977 (PG) 86m/C Chuck Norris, George Murdock; *D:* Don Hulette. VHS, Beta $9.98 *SUE* 🎞

Breaker Morant In 1901 South Africa, three Australian soldiers are put on trial for avenging the murder of several prisoners. Based on a true story which was then turned into a play by Kenneth Ross, this riveting, popular antiwar statement and courtroom drama heralded Australia's film renaissance. Rich performances by Woodward and Waters.
1980 (PG) 107m/C *AU* Edward Woodward, Jack Thompson, John Waters, Bryan Brown; *D:* Bruce Beresford. Academy Awards '80 Nominations: Best Adapted Screenplay; Australian Film Institute '80: Best Actor (Thompson), Best Film. VHS, Beta, LV, 8mm $9.99 *CCB, COL, HMV* 🎞🎞🎞½

Breakfast at Tiffany's Truman Capote's amusing story of an endearingly eccentric New York City playgirl and her shaky romance with a young writer. Hepburn lends Holly Golightly just the right combination of naivete and worldly wisdom with a dash of melancholy. A wonderfully offbeat romance with music by Henry Mancini.
1961 114m/C Audrey Hepburn, George Peppard, Patricia Neal, Buddy Ebsen, Mickey Rooney, Martin Balsam, John McGiver; *D:* Blake Edwards; *W:* George Axelrod; *M:* Henry Mancini. Academy Awards '61: Best Song ("Moon River"), Best Original Score; Nominations: Best Actress (Hepburn), Best Adapted Screenplay, Best Art Direction/Set Decoration (Color). VHS, Beta, LV, 8mm $14.95 *PAR, FCT* 🎞🎞🎞½

The Breakfast Club Five students from different cliques at a Chicago suburban high school spend a day together in detention. Rather well done teenage culture study; these characters delve a little deeper than the standard adult view of adolescent stereotypes. One of John Hughes' best movies. Soundtrack features Simple Minds and Wang Chung.
1985 (R) 97m/C Ally Sheedy, Molly Ringwald, Judd Nelson, Emilio Estevez, Anthony Michael Hall; *D:* John Hughes. VHS, Beta, LV $19.95 *MCA, FCT* 🎞🎞🎞

Breakfast in Hollywood Movie about the popular morning radio show of the 1940s hosted by Tom Breneman, a coast-to-coast coffee klatch. *AKA:* The Mad Hatter.
1946 93m/B Tom Breneman, Bonita Granville, Eddie Ryan, Beulah Bondi, Billie Burke, ZaSu Pitts, Hedda Hopper, Spike Jones; *D:* Harold Schuster. VHS, Beta $29.95 *NO* 🎞½

Breakfast in Paris Two American professionals in Paris, both crushed from past failures in the love department, find each other.
1981 85m/C *AU* Rod Mullinar, Barbara Parkins, Jack Lenoir; *D:* John Lamond. VHS, Beta $19.95 *STE, NWV* 🎞½

Breakheart Pass A governor, his female companion, a band of cavalrymen, and a mysterious man travel on a train through the mountains of Idaho in 1870. The mystery man turns out to be a murderer. Based on a novel by Alistair MacLean.
1976 (PG) 92m/C Charles Bronson, Ben Johnson, Richard Crenna, Jill Ireland, Charles Durning, Ed Lauter, Archie Moore; *D:* Tom Gries; *M:* Jerry Goldsmith. VHS, Beta, LV $19.98 *MGM, FOX* 🎞🎞

Breakin' Dance phenomenon break dancing along with the hit songs that accompanied the fad. ♫Tibetan Jam; Heart of the Beat; Breakin...There's No Stopping Us; Street People; Showdown; 99 1/2. *AKA:* Breakdance.
1984 (PG) 87m/C Lucinda Dickey, Adolfo "Shabba Doo" Quinones, Michael "Boogaloo Shrimp" Chambers, Ben Lokey, Christopher McDonald, Phineas Newborn III; *D:* Joel Silberg. VHS, Beta, LV $79.95 *MGM* 🎞🎞

Breakin' 2: Electric Boogaloo Breakdancers hold a benefit concert to preserve an urban community center. ♫Electric Boogaloo; Radiotron; Action; When I.C.U. *AKA:* Breakdance 2: Electric Boogaloo; Electric Boogaloo "Breakin' 2".
1984 (PG) 94m/C Lucinda Dickey, Adolfo "Shabba Doo" Quinones, Michael "Boogaloo Shrimp" Chambers, Susie Bono; *D:* Sam Firstenberg. VHS, Beta, LV $79.95 *MGM* 🎞

Breakin' Through The choreographer of a troubled Broadway-bound musical decides to energize his shows with a troupe of street dancers.
1984 73m/C Ben Vereen, Donna McKechnie, Reid Shelton; *D:* Peter Medak. VHS, Beta $69.95 *DIS* 🎞

Breaking All the Rules Comedy about two teenage lovers who find themselves embroiled in a slapdash jewel robbery at an amusement park during the last day of summer break.
1985 (R) 91m/C *CA* Carolyn Dunn, Carl Marotte, Thor Bishopric, Rachel Hayward; *D:* James Orr. VHS, Beta $14.95 *NWV, STE* 🎞½

Breaking Away A light-hearted coming-of-age drama about a high school graduate's addiction to bicycle racing, whose dreams are tested against the realities of a crucial race. An honest, open look at present Americana with tremendous insight into the minds of average youth; shot on location at Indiana University. Great bike-racing photography. Quaid, Barrie, and Christopher give exceptional performances. Basis for television series.
1979 (PG) 100m/C Dennis Christopher, Dennis Quaid, Daniel Stern, Jackie Earle Haley, Barbara Barrie, Paul Dooley, Amy Wright; *D:* Peter Yates. Academy Awards '79: Best Original Screenplay; Nominations: Best Director (Yates), Best Picture, Best Supporting Actress (Barrie), Best Original Score; Golden Globe Awards '80: Best Film—Musical/Comedy; National Board of Review Awards '79: 10 Best Films of the Year, Best Supporting Actor (Dooley). VHS, Beta, LV $59.98 *FOX, HMV* 🎞🎞🎞½

Breaking Glass A "New Wave" musical that gives an insight into the punk record business and at the same time tells of the rags-to-riches life of a punk rock star.
1980 (PG) 94m/C *GB* Hazel O'Connor, Phil Daniels, Jon Finch, Jonathan Pryce; *D:* Brian Gibson. VHS, Beta $49.95 *PAR* 🎞🎞½

Breaking Home Ties Norman Rockwell's illustration is the basis for this coming of age story set in a small Texas town. A young man is eager to be off to college and lessen his family ties but his mother's serious illness may prevent both. Good performances help overcome the sentimentality. Originally made for television. *AKA:* Norman Rockwell's Breaking Home Ties.
1987 95m/C Jason Robards Jr., Eva Marie Saint, Doug McKeon, Claire Trevor, Erin Gray; *W/D:* John Wilder. VHS $79.95 *CAF* 🎞🎞½

Breaking In A semi-acclaimed comedy about a professional thief who takes a young amateur under his wing and shows him the ropes. Under-estimated Reynolds is especially charming. Script by John ("Brother from Another Planet") Sayles is witty and innovative, with intelligent direction from Forsyth.
1989 (R) 95m/C Burt Reynolds, Casey Siemaszko, Sheila Kelley, Lorraine Toussaint, Albert Salmi, Harry Carey Jr., Maury Chaykin, Stephen Tobolowsky, David Frishberg; *D:* Bill Forsyth; *W:* John Sayles. VHS, Beta, LV $89.99 *HBO* 🎞🎞🎞

Breaking Loose A surfer is on the run from a vicious motorcycle gang that kidnapped his girlfriend, but turns to fight eventually, board in hand.
1990 (R) 88m/C Peter Phelps, Vince Martin, Abigail, David Ngoombujarra; *D:* Rod Hay. VHS $14.95 *HMD* 🎞½

Breaking the Ice Unlikely mixture of Mennonites and a big city ice skating show. Young man leaves the farm to get a job singing at the rink. Musical numbers abound with backing by Victor Young and his Orchestra.
1938 79m/B Bobby Breen, Charlie Ruggles, Dolores Costello, Billy Gilbert, Margaret Hamilton. VHS, Beta $19.95 *NOS, VYY, DVT* 🎞🎞

Breaking the Rules Predictable buddy-road movie with a tearjerking premise and comedic overtones. Rob, Gene, and Phil were best buds growing up in Cleveland but young adulthood has separated them. They are reunited by Phil, who is dying of leukemia, and whose last wish is a cross-country road trip to California so he can appear as a contestant on "Jeopardy." Along the way they meet brassy waitress Mary, who impulsively decides to join them and winds up bringing the trio's shaky friendship back together. Potts does well as the big-haired, big-hearted Mary but the actors must work hard to maintain any dignity given the story's melodrama.
1992 (PG-13) 100m/C Jason Bateman, C. Thomas Howell, Jonathan Silverman, Annie Potts, Kent Bateman; *D:* Neal Israel; *W:* Paul Shapiro. VHS, LV $92.99 *HBO* 🎞🎞½

Breaking Up A woman fights to rediscover her personal identity after her fifteen-year marriage crumbles. Made for television. Emmy nominated.
1978 90m/C Lee Remick, Granville Van Dusen, David Stambaugh; *D:* Delbert Mann. VHS, Beta *TLF* 🎞🎞½

Breaking Up Is Hard to Do Six men leave their wives and shack up together on Malibu for a summer of partying and introspection. Made for television; edited down from its original 201 minute length.
1979 96m/C Billy Crystal, Bonnie Franklin, Ted Bessell, Jeff Conaway, Tony Musante, Robert Conrad, Trish Stewart, David Ogden Stiers, George Gaynes; *D:* Lou Antonio. VHS, Beta, LV $9.99 *VMK, STE* 🎞

Breaking with Old Ideas A film made in the waning years of Mao's Cultural Revolution about the construction of a college of workers. In Chinese with subtitles.
1975 126m/C *CH D:* Li Wen-Hua. VHS, Beta $39.95 *FCT* 🎞🎞

Breakout The wife of a man imprisoned in Mexico hires a Texas bush pilot (Bronson) to help her husband (Duvall) escape.

1975 (PG) 96m/C Charles Bronson, Jill Ireland, Robert Duvall, John Huston, Sheree North, Randy Quaid; **D:** Tom Gries; **M:** Jerry Goldsmith. **VHS, Beta, LV** $64.95 COL 🐾

Breakthrough German soldier, broken at the end of World War II, sets out to negotiate with the Allies. Average at best. **AKA:** Sergeant Steiner.
1978 (PG) 96m/C Richard Burton, Robert Mitchum, Rod Steiger, Michael Parks, Curt Jurgens; **D:** Andrew V. McLaglen. **VHS, Beta** $9.95 WOV 🐾🐾

Breath of Scandal An American diplomat in Vienna rescues a princess when she is thrown off a horse; he falls for her like a ton o' bricks. Viennese politics complicate things. Based on a play by Molnar.
1960 98m/C Sophia Loren, John Gavin, Maurice Chevalier, Angela Lansbury; **D:** Michael Curtiz. **VHS** PAR, KRT 🐾🐾

Breathing Fire A Vietnamese teenager and his American brother find out their ex-GI father is behind an armed bank robbery and murder. They join together to protect the only eyewitness—a young girl—against the ruthless gang of criminals and their own father. Lots of kickboxing action for martial arts fans.
1991 (R) 86m/C Bolo Yeung, Jonathan Ke Quan, Jerry Trimble; **D:** Lou Kennedy. **VHS** $89.98 IMP 🐾🐾

Breathless Godard's first feature catapulted him to the vanguard of French filmmakers. A carefree Parisian crook, who emulates Humphrey Bogart, falls in love with an American girl with tragic results. Wonderful scenes of Parisian life. Established Godard's Brechtian, experimental style. Belmondo's film debut. Mistitled "Breathless" for American release, the film's French title actually means "Out of Breath"; however, the fast-paced, erratic musical score leaves you breathless. French with English subtitles. Remade with Richard Gere in 1983 with far less intensity. **AKA:** A Bout de Souffle.
1959 90m/B FR Jean-Paul Belmondo, Jean Seberg, Daniel Boulanger, Jean-Pierre Melville, Liliane Robin; **W/D:** Jean-Luc Godard. **VHS, Beta** $24.95 NOS, MRV, CVC 🐾🐾🐾🐾

Breathless Car thief turned cop killer has a torrid love affair with a French student studying in Los Angeles as the police slowly close in. Glossy, smarmy remake of the Godard classic that concentrates on the thin plot rather than any attempt at revitalizing the film syntax.
1983 (R) 105m/C Richard Gere, Valerie Kaprisky, Art Metrano, John P. Ryan; **D:** Jim McBride; **M:** Jack Nitzsche. **VHS, Beta, LV** $29.98 VES 🐾🐾

A Breed Apart An on-going battle over a rare eagle's eggs strikes sparks between a reclusive conservationist and a scheming adventurer hired by a billionaire collector.
1984 (R) 95m/C Kathleen Turner, Rutger Hauer, Powers Boothe, Donald Pleasence, Brion James, John Dennis Johnston; **D:** Philippe Mora. **VHS, Beta** $19.95 HMD, HBO 🐾🐾

Breed of the Border Tough-fisted cowboys must take the law into their own hands. **AKA:** Speed Brent Wins.
1933 60m/B Bob Steele, Marion Byron, George "Gabby" Hayes, Ernie Adams; **D:** Robert North Bradbury. **VHS, Beta** $19.95 NOS, DVT 🐾

Brenda Starr Amateurish adaptation of the comic strip by Dale Messick. Shields stars as girl reporter Brenda Starr, who is once again risking her life to get the scoop. She finds herself in the jungles of South America searching for a mad scientist who is creating a rocket fuel that could destroy the world. The most entertaining thing about this film is the costumes designed by Bob Mackie.
1986 (PG) 94m/C Brooke Shields, Timothy Dalton, Tony Peck, Diana Scarwid, Nestor Serrano, Jeffrey Tambor, June Gable, Charles Durning, Eddie Albert, Henry Gibson, Ed Nelson; **D:** Robert Ellis Miller. **VHS** COL 🐾

Brewster McCloud Altman's first picture after M*A*S*H brings back much of the cast, combining fantasy, black comedy, and satire in telling the story of a young man whose head is in the clouds or at least is trying to inhabit the upper reaches of the Houston Astrodome. Brewster (Cort) lives covertly in the Dome and dreams of flying. Not only does he dream, he practices. While his frustrated girlfriend masturbates, he works on his wings. He also has a guardian angel (Kellerman) who watches over him and may actually be killing people who give him a hard time, after splattering the victims with bird crap. Murphy is a cop driving a Trans-Am who is obsessed with catching the killer. He is assisted by Schuck, the world's dumbest assistant. And there's a circus allegory as well. Hard to figure what it all means and offbeat as they come, but for certain tastes, exquisite.
1970 (R) 101m/C Bud Cort, Sally Kellerman, Shelley Duvall, Michael Murphy, William Windom, Rene Auberjonois, Stacy Keach, John Schuck, Margaret Hamilton; **D:** Robert Altman. **VHS, Beta** $69.95 MGM 🐾🐾🐾½

Brewster's Millions If Brewster, an ex-GI, can spend a million dollars in one year, he will inherit a substantially greater fortune. Originally a 1902 novel, this is the fifth of seven film adaptations.
1945 79m/B Dennis O'Keefe, June Havoc, Eddie Anderson, Helen Walker, Gail Patrick, Mischa Auer; **D:** Allan Dwan. **VHS, Beta** $19.95 MED 🐾🐾½

Brewster's Millions An aging minor league baseball player must spend 30 million dollars in order to collect an inheritance of 300 million dollars. He may find that money can't buy happiness. Seventh remake of the story.
1985 (PG) 101m/C Richard Pryor, John Candy, Lonette McKee, Stephen Collins, Jerry Orbach, Pat Hingle, Tovah Feldshuh, Hume Cronyn, Rick Moranis; **D:** Walter Hill. **VHS, Beta, LV** $19.95 MCA 🐾½

Brian's Song The story of the unique relationship between Gale Sayers, the Chicago Bears' star running back, and his teammate Brian Piccolo. The friendship between the Bears' first interracial roommates ended suddenly when Brian Piccolo lost his life to cancer. Made for television. Incredibly well-received in its time.
1971 (G) 74m/C James Caan, Billy Dee Williams, Jack Warden, Shelley Fabares, Judy Pace; **D:** Buzz Kulik. **VHS, Beta, LV** $64.95 COL 🐾🐾🐾🐾

The Bride Re-telling of "The Bride of Frankenstein." Sting's Dr. Frankenstein has much more success in creating his second monster (Beals). She's pretty and intelligent and he may even be falling in love with her. When she begins to gain too much independence, though, the awful truth about her origins comes out. Fans of the two leads will want to see this one, but for a true classic see Elsa Lanchester's bride.
1985 (PG-13) 118m/C Sting, Jennifer Beals, Anthony Higgins, David Rappaport, Geraldine Page, Clancy Brown, Phil Daniels, Veruschka; **D:** Franc Roddam. **VHS, Beta, LV** $9.95 FOX 🐾½

The Bride & the Beast While on an African safari honeymoon, a big game hunter's new bride is carried off by a gorilla. Ludicrous jungle tale penned by Edward D. Wood, Jr. **AKA:** Queen of the Gorillas.
1958 78m/B Charlotte Austin, Lance Fuller, William Justine; **D:** Adrian Weiss. **VHS, Beta** AOV Woof!

The Bride Came C.O.D. Rough'n'tough pilot Cagney is hired by a rich Texas oil man to prevent his daughter (the one with the Bette Davis eyes) from marrying cheesy bandleader Carson. The payoff: $10 per pound if she's delivered unwed. What a surprise when Cagney faces the timeworn dilemma of having to choose between love and money. A contemporary issue of "Time" magazine trumpeted: "Screen's most talented tough guy rough-houses one of screen's best dramatic actresses." That tells you right there it's a romantic comedy. Cagney and Davis—a likely pairing, you'd think—are essentially fish out of water, bothered and bewildered by a weak script. Bette had already been Oscared for her Jezebel, and Cagney was on top of the world as America's favorite "Public Enemy" (although a decade earlier he lamented that he was sick of carrying guns and beating up women).
1941 92m/B Bette Davis, James Cagney, Stuart Erwin, Jack Carson, George Tobias, Eugene Pallette, William Frawley; **D:** William Keighley. **VHS** $19.95 MGM, FCT 🐾🐾

The Bride Is Much Too Beautiful Bardot, playing a French farm girl, becomes a renowned model. Dubbed.
1958 90m/C FR Brigitte Bardot, Louis Jourdan, Micheline Presle, Marcel Amont; **D:** Fred Surin. **VHS, Beta** $29.95 NOS, FCT, HEG 🐾🐾½

The Bride of Frankenstein The classic sequel to the classic original in which Dr. F. seeks to build a mate for his monster. More humor than the first, but also more pathos, including the monster's famous but short-lived friendship with a blind hermit. Lanchester plays both the bride and Mary Shelley in the opening sequence.
1935 75m/B Boris Karloff, Elsa Lanchester, Ernest Thesiger, Colin Clive, Una O'Connor, Valerie Hobson, Dwight Frye, John Carradine, E.E. Clive, O.P. Heggie; **D:** James Whale. **VHS, Beta, LV** $14.95 MCA, MLB 🐾🐾🐾🐾

Bride of Re-Animator Herbert West is back, and this time he not only re-animates life but creates life - sexy female life - in this sequel to the immensely popular "Re-Animator." High camp and blood curdling gore make this a standout in the sequel parade. Available in a R-rated version as well.
1989 99m/C Bruce Abbott, Claude Earl Jones, Fabiana Udenio, Jeffrey Combs, Kathleen Kinmont, David Gale; **D:** Brian Yuzna. **VHS, Beta, LV** $89.95 LIV 🐾🐾½

Bride of the Gorilla Burr travels to the jungle where he finds a wife, a plantation, and a curse in this African twist on the werewolf legend. Chaney is the local policeman on his trail. Burr's physical changes are fun to watch. Siodmak wrote the screenplay.
1951 76m/B Raymond Burr, Barbara Payton, Lon Chaney Jr., Tom Conway, Paul Cavanagh; **D:** Robert Siodmak. **VHS** $16.95 NOS, MRV, SNC 🐾🐾

Bride of the Monster Lugosi stars as a mad scientist trying to create a race of giants. Classic Woodian badness. **AKA:** Bride of the Atom.
1956 70m/B Bela Lugosi, Tor Johnson, Loretta King, Tony McCoy; **D:** Edward D. Wood Jr. **VHS, Beta** $19.95 NOS, SNC, VYY Woof!

Bride Walks Out Newlywed crisis: a woman with rich taste learns how to adjust to living on her husband's poor salary, but not before she samples the life of the wealthy. Interesting in a sociological sort of way.
1936 81m/B Barbara Stanwyck, Gene Raymond, Robert Young, Ned Sparks, Willie Best, Helen Broderick, Hattie McDaniel; *D:* Leigh Jason. **VHS, Beta** $19.98 *RKO, TTC* ♫♫

The Bride Wore Black Truffaut's homage to Hitchcock, complete with Bernard Herrmann score. A young woman exacts brutal revenge on the five men who accidentally killed her husband. Excellent cinematography from Raoul Coutard. *AKA:* La Mariee Etait en Noir.
1968 107m/C *FR* Jeanne Moreau, Claude Rich, Jean-Claude Brialy, Michel Bouquet, Michael Lonsdale; *D:* Francois Truffaut. **VHS, LV** $19.98 *MGM, MLB, TAM* ♫♫♫

The Bride Wore Red Crawford stars as a cabaret singer who masquerades as a socialite in an attempt to break into the upper crust. When a wealthy aristocrat invites her to spend two weeks at a posh resort in Tyrol, Crawford plays her part to the hilt, managing to charm both a rich gentleman and the village postman. Typical "love conquers all" melodrama.
1937 103m/B Joan Crawford, Franchot Tone, Robert Young, Billie Burke, Reginald Owen, Lynne Carver, George Zucco; *D:* Dorothy Arzner. **VHS** $19.98 *MGM* ♫♫

The Brides of Dracula A young French woman unknowingly frees a vampire. He wreaks havoc, sucking blood and creating more of the undead to carry out his evil deeds. One of the better Hammer vampire films.
1960 86m/C *GB* Peter Cushing, Martita Hunt, Yvonne Monlaur, Freda Jackson, David Peel, Mona Washbourne; *D:* Terence Fisher. **VHS, LV** $14.98 *MCA, FCT* ♫♫½

Brides of the Beast Filipino radiation monsters get their jollies by eating beautiful young naked women. Newly arrived research scientist and his bride oppose this custom. First in a series of "Blood Island" horrors. *AKA:* Brides of Blood; Grave Desires; Island of the Living Horror.
1968 85m/C *PH* John Ashley, Kent Taylor, Beverly Hills, Eva Darren, Mario Montenegro; *D:* Eddie Romero, Gerardo (Gerry) De Leon. **VHS, Beta** *NO Woof!*

The Brides Wore Blood Four prospective brides are mysteriously murdered, but one is brought back to life and becomes a vampire's mate.
1984 86m/C **VHS, Beta** *NO Woof!*

Brideshead Revisited The acclaimed British miniseries based on the Evelyn Waugh classic about an Edwardian young man who falls under the spell of a wealthy aristocratic family and struggles to retain his integrity and values. On six tapes.
1981 540m/C *GB* Jeremy Irons, Anthony Andrews, Diana Quick, Laurence Olivier, John Gielgud, Claire Bloom, Stephane Audran, Mona Washbourne, John Le Mesurier; *D:* Charles Sturridge, Michael Lindsay-Hogg. **VHS, Beta** *NO Woof!*

The Bridge at Remagen Based on the true story of allied attempts to capture a vital bridge before retreating German troops destroy it. For war-film buffs.
1969 (PG) 115m/C George Segal, Robert Vaughn, Ben Gazzara, Bradford Dillman, E.G. Marshall; *D:* John Guillermin. **VHS, Beta** *NO* ♫♫½

The Bridge of San Luis Rey A priest investigates the famous bridge collapse in Lima, Peru that left five people dead. Based upon the novel by Thornton Wilder.
1944 89m/B Lynn Bari, Francis Lederer, Louis Calhern, Akim Tamiroff, Donald Woods, Alla Nazimova, Blanche Yurka; *D:* Rowland V. Lee. **VHS, Beta, LV** $19.95 *STE, NWV, IME* ♫♫♫

The Bridge on the River Kwai Award-winning adaptation of the Pierre Bouelle novel about the battle of wills between a Japanese POW camp commander and a British colonel over the construction of a rail bridge, and the parallel efforts by escaped prisoner Holden to destroy it. Holden's role was originally cast for Cary Grant. Memorable too for whistling "Colonel Bogey March."
1957 161m/C *GB* William Holden, Alec Guinness, Jack Hawkins, Sessue Hayakawa, James Donald; *D:* David Lean; *W:* Pierre Boulle. Academy Awards '57: Best Actor (Guinness), Best Adapted Screenplay, Best Color Cinematography, Best Director (Lean), Best Film Editing, Best Picture, Best Original Score; Nominations: Best Supporting Actor (Hayakawa); British Academy Awards '57: Best Actor (Guinness), Best Film; Directors Guild of America Awards '57: Best Director (Lean); Golden Globe Awards '58: Best Actor—Drama (Guinness), Best Director (Lean), Best Film—Drama; National Board of Review Awards '57: 10 Best Films of the Year, Best Actor (Guinness), Best Director (Lean), Best Supporting Actor (Hayakawa). **VHS, Beta, LV** $19.95 *COL, BTV, HMV* ♫♫♫♫

Bridge to Hell A group of allied P.O.W.s try to make their way to the American front during World War II in Yugoslavia. A heavily guarded bridge occupied by Nazi troops stands between them and freedom. A special introduction by Michael Dudikoff doing martial arts.
1987 94m/C Jeff Connors, Francis Ferre, Andy Forrest, Paky Valente; *D:* Umberto Lenzi. **VHS** $59.95 *CAN* ♫½

The Bridge to Nowhere Five city kids go hunting and back-packing in the New Zealand wilderness, and are hunted by a maniacal backwoodsman.
1986 82m/C *NZ* Bruno Lawrence, Alison Routledge, Margaret Umbers, Philip Gordon; *D:* Ian Mune. **VHS, Beta** $19.98 *NLC* ♫♫

Bridge to Silence A young hearing-impaired mother's life begins to crumble following the death of her husband in a car crash. Her mother tries to get custody of her daughter and a friend applies romantic pressure. Made for TV melodrama features Matlin in her first television speaking role.
1989 95m/C Marlee Matlin, Lee Remick, Josef Sommer, Michael O'Keefe, Allison Silva, Candice Brecker; *D:* Karen Arthur. **VHS** $59.95 *FRH* ♫♫

Bridge to Terabithia O'Toole and a young boy learn the joys of friendship in a magic kingdom called Terabithia. Adapted from the novel by Katherine Paterson. Originally aired by PBS for the "Wonderworks" television series.
1985 58m/C Annette O'Toole, Julian Coutts, Julie Beaulieu; *D:* Eric Till. **VHS** $29.95 *PME, HMV* ♫♫

A Bridge Too Far A meticulous recreation of one of the most disastrous battles of World War II, the Allied defeat at Arnhem in 1944. Misinformation, adverse conditions, and overconfidence combined to prevent the Allies from capturing six bridges that connected Holland to the German border.
1977 (PG) 175m/C *GB* Sean Connery, Robert Redford, James Caan, Michael Caine, Elliott Gould, Gene Hackman, Laurence Olivier, Ryan O'Neal, Liv Ullmann, Dirk Bogarde, Hardy Kruger, Arthur Hill, Edward Fox, Anthony

Hopkins; *D:* Richard Attenborough. **VHS, Beta, LV** $29.98 *MGM, FOX* ♫♫

The Bridges at Toko-Ri Based on the James A. Michener novel, the rousing war-epic about a lawyer being summoned by the Navy to fly bombing missions during the Korean War. A powerful anti-war statement. Screenplay by Valentine Davis.
1955 103m/C William Holden, Grace Kelly, Fredric March, Mickey Rooney, Robert Strauss, Earl Holliman, Keiko Awaji, Charles McGraw; *D:* Mark Robson. Academy Awards '55: Best Special Effects; Nominations: Best Film Editing. **VHS, Beta, LV** $14.95 *PAR* ♫♫♫½

Brief Encounter Based on Noel Coward's "Still Life" from "Tonight at 8:30," two middle-aged, middle-class people become involved in a short and bittersweet romance in World War II England. Intensely romantic, underscored with Rachmaninoff's Second Piano Concerto.
1946 86m/B *GB* Celia Johnson, Trevor Howard, Stanley Holloway; *D:* David Lean; *W:* Noel Coward. Academy Awards '46 Nominations: Best Actress (Johnson), Best Director (Lean), Best Screenplay; National Board of Review Awards '46: 10 Best Films of the Year; New York Film Critics Awards '46: Best Actress (Johnson). **VHS, Beta** $19.95 *PAR, TAM, HMV* ♫♫♫♫

A Brief History of Time A stunning documentary about physicist Stephen Hawking, the author of the popular book "Brief History of Time." Crippled by Lou Gehrig's Disease, Hawking narrates the film in the computer-synthesized voice he uses to speak. Interviews with family, friends, and colleagues, bring Hawking's scientific theories to light.
1992 (G) 85m/C *D:* Errol Morris; *M:* Philip Glass. **VHS, Beta** *PAR* ♫♫♫

The Brig A film by Jonas Mekas documenting the Living Theatre's infamous performance of Kenneth H. Brown's experimental play. Designed by Julian Beck.
1964 65m/B Adolfas Mekas, Jim Anderson, Warren Finnerty, Henry Howard, Tom Lillard, James Tiroff, Gene Lipton; *D:* John Mekas. **VHS, Beta** $29.95 *MFV, FCT* ♫♫♫

Brigadoon The story of a magical, 18th century Scottish village which awakens once every 100 years and the two modern-day vacationers who stumble upon it. Main highlight is the Lerner and Loewe score. ♫Brigadoon; Almost Like Being in Love; I'll Go Home With Bonnie Jean; Wedding Dance; From This Day On; Heather on the Hill; Waitin' For My Dearie; Once in the Highlands.
1954 108m/C Gene Kelly, Van Johnson, Cyd Charisse; *D:* Vincente Minnelli; *W:* Alan Jay Lerner; *M:* Frederick Loewe, Alan Jay Lerner. **VHS, Beta, LV, 8mm** $19.98 *MGM, TLF* ♫♫♫

Bright Angel Road movie pairs an unconventional team: George wants to visit his aunt to see if she's heard from his mother who ran off with another man; Luey is a free-spirit trying to free her brother from jail. Good performances by Mulroney, Taylor, & Pullman. Ford adapted two of his short stories, "Childern" and "Great Falls" for the gritty and uncompromising script of life in the modern west.
1991 (R) 94m/C Dermot Mulroney, Lili Taylor, Sam Shepard, Valerie Perrine, Burt Young, Bill Pullman, Benjamin Bratt, Mary Kay Place, Delroy Lindo, Kevin Tighe, Sheila McCarthy; *D:* Michael Fields; *W:* Richard Ford; *M:* Chris Young. **VHS** $92.99 *HBO* ♫♫♫

Bright Eyes Shirley Temple stars as an adorable orphan caught between foster parents.

1934 84m/B Shirley Temple, James Dunn, Lois Wilson, Jane Withers, Judith Allen; **D:** David Butler. **VHS, Beta** $19.98 *FOX, MLT* ⊿⊿

Bright Lights, Big City Based on Jay McInerney's popular novel, Fox plays a contemporary yuppie working in Manhattan as a magazine journalist. As his world begins to fall apart, he embarks on an endless cycle of drugs and nightlife. Fox is poorly cast, and his character is hard to care for as he becomes more and more dissolute. Although McInerney wrote his own screenplay, the intellectual abstractness of the novel can't be captured on film.
1988 (R) 110m/C Michael J. Fox, Kiefer Sutherland, Phoebe Cates, Frances Sternhagen, Swoosie Kurtz, Tracy Pollan, Jason Robards Jr., John Houseman, Dianne Wiest, Charlie Schlatter, William Hickey; **D:** James Bridges. **VHS, Beta, LV** $14.95 *MGM* ⊿⊿

Bright Smiler A made-for-British-television mystery about a writer who retires to her favorite spa and falls into the hands of a malevolent masseuse.
1985 60m/C *GB* Janet Suzman. **VHS, Beta** $59.95 *PSM* ⊿ 1/2

Brighton Beach Memoirs The film adaptation of the popular (and semiautobiographical) Neil Simon play. Poignant comedy/drama about a young Jewish boy's coming of age in Depression-era Brooklyn. Followed by "Biloxi Blues" and "Broadway Bound." **AKA:** Neil Simon's Brighton Beach Memoirs.
1986 (PG-13) 108m/C Blythe Danner, Bob Dishy, Judith Ivey, Jonathan Silverman; **D:** Gene Saks. **VHS, Beta, LV** $19.95 *MCA, FCT* ⊿⊿ 1/2

Brighton Rock Sterling performances highlight this seamy look at the British underworld. Attenborough is Pinkie Brown, a small-time hood who ends up committing murder. He manipulates a waitress to get himself off the hook, but things don't go exactly as he plans. Based on the novel by Graham Greene. **AKA:** Young Scarface.
1947 92m/B *GB* Richard Attenborough, Hermione Baddeley, William Hartnell, Carol Marsh, Nigel Stock, Wylie Watson, Alan Wheatley, George Carney, Reginald Purdell; **D:** John Boulting. **VHS** *DVT, HEG* ⊿⊿⊿

Brighton Strangler An actor who plays a murderer assumes the role of the strangler after suffering from a concussion. Decent psychodrama.
1945 67m/B John Loder, June Duprez, Miles Mander; **D:** Max Nosseck. **VHS, Beta** $34.95 *RKO* ⊿⊿

The Brighton Strangler/Before Dawn A mystery double feature: In "The Brighton Strangler," an actor takes his part too seriously as he murders Londoners at night; in "Before Dawn" a brilliant scientist turns to a life of murderous crime.
1945 128m/B John Loder, June Duprez, Miles Mander, Stuart Oland, Dorothy Wilson. **VHS, Beta** $39.95 *RKO, TTC* ⊿⊿

Brighty of the Grand Canyon The spunky donkey Brighty roams across the Grand Canyon in search of adventure. He finds friendship with a gold-digging old prospector who hits pay dirt.
1967 90m/C Joseph Cotten, Pat Conway, Dick Foran, Karl Swenson; **D:** Norman Foster. **VHS, Beta** $24.95 *AHV, VTK, KAR* ⊿ 1/2

Brimstone & Treacle Weird, obsessive psychodrama written by Dennis Potter, in which a young rogue (who may or may not be an actual agent of the Devil) infiltrates the home of a staid British family caring for their comatose adult daughter.

1982 (R) 85m/C *GB* Sting, Denholm Elliott, Joan Plowright, Suzanna Hamilton; **D:** Richard Loncraine; **W:** Dennis Potter. **VHS, Beta** $14.95 *MGM* ⊿⊿⊿

Bring Me the Head of Alfredo Garcia Peckinpah falters in this poorly paced outing. American piano player on tour in Mexico finds himself entwined with a gang of bloodthirsty bounty hunters. Bloody and confused.
1974 (R) 112m/C Warren Oates, Isela Vega, Gig Young, Robert Webber, Helmut Dantine, Emilio Fernandez, Kris Kristofferson; **D:** Sam Peckinpah. **VHS** $59.95 *MGM* ⊿⊿

Bring Me the Vampire A wealthy baron must endure a night of terror in order to receive an inheritance.
1961 100m/B *MX* Maria Eugenia San Martin, Hector Godoy, Joaquin Vargas. **VHS** $16.95 *SNC, MOV* ⊿

Bringing Up Baby The quintessential screwball comedy, featuring Hepburn as a giddy socialite with a "baby" leopard, and Grant as the unwitting object of her affections. One ridiculous situation after another add up to high speed fun. Hepburn looks lovely, the supporting actors are in fine form, and director Hawks manages the perfect balance of control and mayhem. From a story by Hagar Wilde, who helped Nichols with the screenplay. Also available in a colorized version.
1938 103m/B Katharine Hepburn, Cary Grant, May Robson, Charlie Ruggles, Walter Catlett, Fritz Feld, Jonathan Hale, Barry Fitzgerald; **D:** Howard Hawks; **W:** Dudley Nichols. **VHS, Beta, LV** $19.98 *TTC, HMV* ⊿⊿⊿⊿

Brink of Life Three pregnant women in a hospital maternity ward await the impending births with mixed feelings. Early Bergman; in Swedish with English subtitles. **AKA:** Nara Livet.
1957 82m/B *SW* Eva Dahlbeck, Bibi Andersson, Ingrid Thulin, Babro Ornas, Max von Sydow, Erland Josephson, Gunnar Sjoberg; **D:** Ingmar Bergman. **VHS, Beta** $29.95 *VYY, TAM* ⊿⊿ 1/2

Brink's Job Recreates the "crime of the century," Tony Pino's heist of 2.7 million dollars from a Brink's truck. The action picks up five days before the statute of limitations is about to run out.
1978 (PG) 103m/C Peter Falk, Peter Boyle, Warren Oates, Gena Rowlands, Paul Sorvino, Sheldon Leonard, Allen Garfield; **D:** William Friedkin. **VHS, Beta** $59.95 *MCA* ⊿⊿⊿

Britannia Hospital This is a portrait of a hospital at its most chaotic: the staff threatens to strike, demonstrators surround the hospital, a nosey BBC reporter pursues an anxious professor, and the eagerly-anticipated royal visit degenerates into a total shambles.
1982 (R) 111m/C *GB* Malcolm McDowell, Leonard Rossiter, Graham Crowden, Joan Plowright, Mark Hamill, Alan Bates; **D:** Lindsay Anderson. **VHS, Beta** $69.95 *HBO* ⊿⊿ 1/2

British Intelligence Silly American-made film about British espionage. Boris Karloff plays a butler (who is also a spy) trapped by an agent who visits the home of a British bureaucrat. Half-baked story that doesn't hold up.
1940 62m/B Boris Karloff, Margaret Lindsay, Maris Wrixon, Holmes Herbert, Leonard Mudie, Bruce Lester; **D:** Terry Morse. **VHS** $16.95 *NOS, SNC, MLB* ⊿ 1/2

A Brivele der Mamen A Jewish mother does her best to hold her fragile family together, in spite of the ravages of war and poverty. Her travails take her and her family from the Polish Ukraine to New York

City. In Yiddish with English subtitles. **AKA:** A Letter to Mother.
1938 90m/C *PL* Berta Gersten, Lucy Gehrman, Misha Gehrman, Edmund Zayenda; **D:** Joseph Green. **VHS, Beta** $79.95 *ERG, TAM* ⊿⊿⊿

Broadcast News The acclaimed, witty analysis of network news shows, dealing with the three-way romance between a driven career-woman producer, an ace nebbish reporter and a brainless, popular on-screen anchorman. Incisive and funny, though often simply idealistic. Written by James L. Brooks.
1987 (R) 132m/C William Hurt, Albert Brooks, Holly Hunter, Jack Nicholson, Joan Cusack, Robert Prosky, Lois Chiles, John Cusack; **D:** James L. Brooks. Academy Awards '87 Nominations: Best Actor (Hurt), Best Actress (Hunter), Best Cinematography, Best Film Editing, Best Original Screenplay, Best Picture, Best Supporting Actor (Brooks); National Board of Review Awards '87: 10 Best Films of the Year, Best Actress (Hunter). **VHS, Beta, LV** $19.98 *FOX* ⊿⊿⊿

Broadway Bill A man decides to abandon his nagging wife and his job in her family's business for the questionable pleasures of owning a racehorse known as Broadway Bill. This racetrack comedy was also remade by Frank Capra in 1951 as "Riding High." **AKA:** Strictly Confidential.
1934 90m/C Warner Baxter, Myrna Loy, Walter Connolly, Helen Vinson, Margaret Hamilton; **D:** Frank Capra. **VHS** $19.95 *PAV* ⊿⊿⊿

Broadway Bound The final film in Simon's trilogy (preceded by "Brighton Beach Memoirs" and "Biloxi Blues"). This time the playwright's alter ego, Eugene Morris Jerome, is ready to leave Brooklyn for good, hoping to make it as a comedy writer for a radio show. Meanwhile, his mother decides what to do about his unfaithful father. Made for television. **AKA:** Neil Simon's Broadway Bound.
1992 90m/C Jonathan Silverman, Anne Bancroft, Jerry Orbach, Corey Parker, Hume Cronyn, Michele Lee; **D:** Paul Bogart; **W:** Neil Simon. **VHS** *ABC* ⊿⊿ 1/2

Broadway Danny Rose One of Woody Allen's best films, a hilarious, heart-rending anecdotal comedy about a third-rate talent agent involved in one of his client's infidelities. The film magically unfolds as show business veterans swap Danny Rose stories at a delicatessen. Allen's Danny Rose is pathetically lovable.
1984 (PG) 85m/B Woody Allen, Mia Farrow, Nick Apollo Forte, Sandy Baron, Milton Berle, Howard Cosell; **D:** Woody Allen. **VHS, Beta, LV** $19.98 *VES* ⊿⊿⊿ 1/2

The Broadway Drifter A silent Jazz Age drama about a playboy who repents his decadent ways by opening a girls' health school. Complications ensue.
1927 90m/B George Walsh, Dorothy Hall, Bigelow Cooper, Arthur Donaldson; **D:** Bernard McEveety. **VHS, Beta, 8mm** $29.95 *VYY* ⊿⊿

Broadway Limited Three aspiring actors head for the Great White Way with a baby to use as a prop. Thinking the baby kidnapped, the police make things tough for the trio. McLaglen was wasted on this one, which was apparently made to show off the considerable assets of Woodworth. **AKA:** The Baby Vanishes.
1941 75m/B Victor McLaglen, Marjorie Woodworth, Dennis O'Keefe, Patsy Kelly, ZaSu Pitts, Leonid Kinskey, George E. Stone; **D:** Gordon Douglas. **VHS** $19.95 *NOS, TIM* ⊿⊿

Broadway Melody Early musical in which two sisters hope for fame on Broadway, and encounter a wily song and dance man who traps both their hearts. Dated, but

still charming, with lovely score by Freed and Brown. Considered the great granddaddy of all MGM musicals; followed by three more melodies in 1935, 1937, and 1940. ♫Broadway Melody; Give My Regards to Broadway; Truthful Parson Brown; The Wedding of the Painted Doll; The Boy Friend; You Were Meant For Me; Love Boat; Broadway Babies.
1929 104m/B Bessie Love, Anita Page, Charles King, Jed Prouty, Kenneth Thomson, Edward Dillon, Mary Doran; **D:** Harry Beaumont; **M:** Nacio Herb Brown, Arthur Freed. Academy Awards '29: Best Picture; Nominations: Best Actress (Love), Best Director (Beaumont). **VHS, Beta $19.98** MGM, BTV ♫♫½

Broadway Melody of 1936 Exceptional musical comedy with delightful performances from Taylor and Powell. Benny is a headline-hungry columnist who tries to entrap Taylor by using Powell. Great music by Freed/Brown team. ♫Broadway Melody; Broadway Rhythm; You Are My Lucky Star; I've Got a Feeling You're Fooling; All I Do Is Dream of You; Sing Before Breakfast; On a Sunday Afternoon.
1935 110m/B Jack Benny, Eleanor Powell, Robert Taylor, Una Merkel, Sid Silvers, Buddy Ebsen; **D:** Roy Del Ruth; **M:** Nacio Herb Brown, Arthur Freed. **VHS, Beta $19.98** MGM, MLB, CCB ♫♫♫

Broadway Melody of 1938 Third entry in the melody series lacks the sparkle of "Broadway Melody of 1936" despite the all-star cast. Lots of singing and dancing without much charm. Two bright spots: a young Garland singing the now famous "Dear Mr. Gable" and the always lovely Powell's dance numbers. ♫Broadway Rhythm; Dear Mr. Gable (You Made Me Love You); A New Pair of Shoes; Yours and Mine; I'm Feeling Like a Million; Everybody Sing; Follow in My Footsteps; Your Broadway and My Broadway; Sun Showers; Some of These Days; Toreador Song; Largo al Factotum.
1937 110m/B Eleanor Powell, Sophie Tucker, George Murphy, Judy Garland, Robert Taylor, Buddy Ebsen; **D:** Roy Del Ruth; **M:** Nacio Herb Brown, Arthur Freed. **VHS, Beta $19.98** MGM ♫♫½

Broadway Melody of 1940 The last entry in the melody series features the only screen teaming of Astaire and Powell. The flimsy plot is just an excuse for a potent series of Cole Porter musical numbers. ♫I Concentrate on You; I've Got My Eye on You; Begin the Beguine; I am the Captain; Please Don't Monkey With Broadway; Between You and Me; Il Bacio.
1940 103m/B Fred Astaire, Eleanor Powell, George Murphy, Frank Morgan, Ian Hunter; **D:** Norman Taurog. **VHS, Beta, LV $19.98** MGM, TTC, FCT ♫♫½

Broadway Rhythm A too-long look at Broadway behind-the-scenes. Murphy plays a Broadway producer who hopes to land a Hollywood star for his new show. She rejects his offer in favor of a show being produced by his father. Just a chance to showcase a number of popular vaudeville acts, songs, and the music of Tommy Dorsey and his orchestra. ♫All the Things You Are; That Lucky Fellow; In Other Words; Seventeen; Al In Fun; Brazilian Boogie; What Do You Think I Am?; Somebody Loves Me; Milkman Keep Those Bottles Quiet; Solid Potato Salad; Manhattan Serenade; Pretty Baby; Oh You Beautiful Doll; Amor; Ida, Sweet as Apple Cider.
1944 111m/C George Murphy, Ginny Simms, Charles Winninger, Ben Blue, Lena Horne, Eddie Anderson; **D:** Roy Del Ruth; **W:** Dorothy Kingsley, Harry Clork. **VHS $19.98** MGM ♫♫½

Broadway Serenade Melodramatic musical in which a songwriter (Ayres) and his wife, singer MacDonald, make career choices that destroy their marriage. ♫Broadway Serenade for the Lonely Heart; High Flyin'; One Look at You; Time Changes Everything; Un Bel Di; No Time to Argue; Italian Street Song; Les Filles de Cadiz; Musical Contract.
1939 114m/B Jeanette MacDonald, Lew Ayres, Ian Hunter, Frank Morgan, Wally Vernon, Rita Johnson, Virginia Grey, William Gargan; **D:** Robert Z. Leonard; **W:** Charles Lederer. **VHS $19.98** MGM ♫♫½

Broadway to Cheyenne A group of big city gangsters try to take over a small western town but are opposed by heroic cowboys. **AKA:** From Broadway to Cheyenne.
1932 53m/B Rex Bell, George "Gabby" Hayes, Marceline Day; **D:** Harry Fraser. **VHS, Beta $9.95** GPV, RXM, VDM ♫

Broken Angel Jamie seemed to be such a nice girl, with good looks and great grades—and membership in a notorious street gang. When Jamie disappears, her family discovers her secret activities and dad tries to find his wayward little girl. Melodramatic made for television goo.
1988 94m/C William Shatner, Susan Blakely, Erika Eleniak, Roxann Biggs; **D:** Richard T. Heffron. **VHS $79.99** MGM ♫½

Broken Arrow A U.S. scout befriends Cochise and the Apaches, and helps settlers and Indians live in peace together in the 1870s. Acclaimed as the first Hollywood film to side with the Indians, and for Chandler's portrayal of Cochise.
1950 93m/C James Stewart, Jeff Chandler, Will Geer, Debra Paget, Basil Ruysdael, Arthur Hunnicutt, Jay Silverheels; **D:** Delmer Daves. **VHS, Beta $19.98** FOX ♫♫½

Broken Badge Crenna stars as a macho, chauvinistic cop whose attitude towards rape victims changes dramatically after he himself is raped by a couple of thugs. Excellent TV movie. **AKA:** The Rape of Richard Beck.
1985 100m/C Richard Crenna, Meredith Baxter Birney, Pat Hingle, Frances Lee McCain, Cotter Smith, George Dzundza, Joanna Kerns; **D:** Karen Arthur. **VHS $9.95** SIM, VTR ♫♫♫

Broken Blossoms One of Griffith's most widely acclaimed films, photographed by Billy Bitzer, about a young Chinaman in London's squalid Limehouse district hoping to spread the peaceful philosophy of his Eastern religion. He befriends a pitiful street waif who is mistreated by her brutal father, resulting in tragedy. Silent. Revised edition contains introduction from Gish and a newly-recorded score.
1919 102m/B Lillian Gish, Richard Barthelmess, Donald Crisp; **D:** D.W. Griffith. **VHS, Beta, LV $19.95** NOS, MRV, HHT ♫♫♫½

Broken Lance Western remake of "House of Strangers" that details the dissolution of a despotic cattle baron's family. Beautifully photographed.
1954 96m/C Spencer Tracy, Richard Widmark, Robert Wagner, Jean Peters, Katy Jurado, Earl Holliman, Hugh O'Brian, E.G. Marshall; **D:** Edward Dmytryk; **W:** Philip Yordan. Academy Awards '54: Best Story; Nominations: Best Supporting Actress (Jurado). **VHS, Beta, LV $39.98** FOX ♫♫♫½

The Broken Mask A doctor performs remarkable plastic surgery on a patient, but when the patient becomes attracted to his sweetheart, he throws the Hippocratic oath to the wind, and his patient's spiffy new look

has got to go. A ground-breaker amid plastic surgery-gone-amok pieces.
1928 58m/B Cullen Landis, Barbara Bedford, Wheeler Oakman, James Marcus; **D:** James Hogan. **VHS, Beta $19.95** GPV, FCT ♫♫

Broken Melody An opera singer sent to prison by mistake must escape in order to return to the woman of his dreams. **AKA:** Vagabond Violinist.
1934 62m/B GB John Garrick, Margot Grahame, Merle Oberon, Austin Trevor, Charles Carson, Harry Terry; **D:** Bernard Vorhaus. **VHS $29.95** FCT ♫½

Broken Mirrors A disturbing film which intertwines two stories of violence against women: prostitutes go about their daily business in Amsterdam, while a twisted serial killer who imprisons, photographs, and ultimately destroys his victims, draws near. An independently made chiller with staunch feminist agenda. **AKA:** Gebroken Spiegels.
1985 110m/C NL Lineke Rijxman, Henriette Tol; **W/D:** Marleen Gorris. 3/4U ICA ♫♫½

Broken Strings All-black musical in which a concert violinist must come to terms with himself after an auto accident limits the use of his left hand.
1940 50m/B Clarence Muse, Sybil Lewis, William Washington, Matthew "Stymie" Beard; **D:** Bernard B. Ray. **VHS, Beta $24.95** NOS, VYY, VCN ♫

Bromas S.A. A group of teenagers get into a bunch of funny situations.
1987 104m/C SP Mauricio Garces, Gloria Marin, Manuel Valdez, Hermanos King. **VHS, Beta $54.95** MAD ♫♫

Bronco Billy Eastwood stars as a New Jersey shoe clerk who decides to fulfill his dream of being a cowboy hero by becoming the proprietor of a rag-tag wild west show. Locke's one-note performance as a spoiled rich girl who joins up is a problem and the film's charm is as ragged as the acts. Good if you want to see Eastwood in something other than a shoot-'em-up.
1980 (PG) 117m/C Clint Eastwood, Sondra Locke, Bill McKinney, Scatman Crothers, Sam Bottoms, Geoffrey Lewis, Dan Vadis, Sierra Pecheur; **D:** Clint Eastwood. **VHS, Beta, LV $19.98** WAR, TLF, RXM ♫♫½

Bronson Lee, Champion Kung-fu and karate highlight this action adventure.
1978 (PG) 81m/C Tadashi Yamashita. **VHS, Beta $19.98** NO ♫

Bronson's Revenge Two frontier soldiers face constant danger as they attempt to transport death row prisoners, a large quantity of gold, and a stranded woman across the Rocky Mountains territory.
1979 (R) 90m/C Robert Hundar, Roy Hill, Emma Cohen. **VHS $52.95** SUN ♫½

Bronx Cheers Young Italian-American man returns from WWII, falls prey to the misguidance of a has-been boxer. 1990 Academy Award nominee for Best Live Action Short.
1989 30m/C D: Raymond De Felitta. **VHS $59.95** CIG, BTV ♫½

The Bronx Executioner Android, robot, and human interests clash in futuristic Manhattan and all martial arts hell breaks loose. Special introduction by martial arts star Michael Dudikoff.
1986 88m/C Rob Robinson, Margie Newton, Chuck Valenti, Gabriel Gori; **D:** Bob Collins. **VHS, Beta $59.95** CAN ♫

The Bronx War Rival gangs take to the streets in this film from the director of "Hangin' with the Homeboys." A malicious gang leader tricks his gang into going to war over a girl he wants. Very violent; an unrated version available.

1990 (R) 91m/C Joseph P. Vasquez, Fabio Urena, Charmaine Cruz, Andre Brown, Marlene Forte, Francis Colon, Miguel Sierra, Kim West; **D:** Joseph P. Vasquez. **VHS $19.95** ACA 𝄞

Bronze Buckaroo Director Kahn also scripted this all African-American horse opera in which a cowpoke seeks revenge for his pa's death.

1939 57m/B Herbert Jeffries, Artie Young, Rellie Hardin, Spencer Williams Jr., Clarence Brooks, F.E. Miller; **W/D:** Richard C. Kahn. **VHS $24.95** NOS, MRV, TPV 𝄞𝄞

The Brood Cronenberg's inimitable biological nightmares, involving an experimentally malformed woman who gives birth to murderous demon-children that kill every time she gets angry. Extremely graphic. Not for all tastes.

1979 (R) 92m/C CA Samantha Eggar, Oliver Reed; **D:** David Cronenberg. **VHS, Beta, LV $19.98** SUE 𝄞𝄞½

Broth of a Boy A hungry British producer decides to film a birthday party of the oldest man in the world. The old Irishman wants a portion of the profits. Well made and thought provoking.

1959 77m/B IR Barry Fitzgerald, Harry Brogan, Tony Wright, June Thorburn, Eddie Golden; **D:** George Pollock. **VHS $19.95** NOS, HEG 𝄞𝄞½

The Brother from Another Planet An black alien escapes from his home planet and winds up in Harlem, where he's pursued by two alien bounty hunters. Independently made morality fable by John Sayles before he hit the big time; features Sayles in a cameo as an alien bounty hunter.

1984 109m/C Joe Morton, Dee Dee Bridgewater, Ren Woods, Steve James, Maggie Renzi, David Strathairn; **Cameos:** John Sayles; **D:** John Sayles. **VHS, Beta $19.98** FOX, FCT 𝄞𝄞𝄞

Brother Future T.J., a black, streetsmart city kid who thinks school and helping others is all a waste of time gets knocked out in a car accident. As he's lying unconscious, he is transported back in time to a slave auction block in the Old South. There the displaced urbanite is forced to work on a cotton plantation, and watch the stirrings of a slave revolt. T.J. sees the light and realizes how much opportunity he's been wasting in his own life. He comes to just a few moments later, but worlds away from who he was before. Part of the "Wonderworks" series.

1991 110m/C Phill Lewis, Frank Converse, Carl Lumbly, Vonetta McGee. **VHS $29.95** PME, HMV, BTV 𝄞𝄞𝄞

Brother John An early look at racial tensions and labor problems. An angel goes back to his hometown in Alabama to see how things are going.

1970 (PG) 94m/C Sidney Poitier, Will Geer, Bradford Dillman, Beverly Todd, Paul Winfield; **D:** James Goldstone. **VHS $14.95** COL, FCT 𝄞𝄞𝄞

Brother Orchid Mobster puts a henchman in charge of his gang while he vacations in Europe. Upon his return, he is deposed and wounded in an assassination attempt. Hiding out in a monastary, he plots to regain control of the gang, leading to fish outta water episodes and a change in his outlook on life. Fine cast fans through farce intelligently.

1940 87m/B Edward G. Robinson, Humphrey Bogart, Joan Blondell, Donald Crisp, Ralph Bellamy, Allen Jenkins, Charles D. Brown, Cecil Kellaway; **D:** Lloyd Bacon. **VHS, Beta $19.98** MGM, CCB 𝄞𝄞𝄞

Brother Sun, Sister Moon Post-'60s costume epic depicting the trials of St. Francis of Assisi as he evaluates his beliefs in Catholicism. Music by Donovan.

1973 (PG) 120m/C Graham Faulkner, Judi Bowker, Alec Guinness, Leigh Lawson, Kenneth Cranham, Lee Montague, Valentina Cortese; **D:** Franco Zeffirelli. **VHS, Beta $44.95** PAR, APD, TVC 𝄞𝄞½

The Brotherhood Two hot-headed brothers in a Mafia syndicate clash over old vs. new methods and the changing of the Family's guard. Music by Lalo Schifrin.

1968 96m/C Kirk Douglas, Alex Cord, Irene Papas, Luther Adler, Susan Strasberg, Murray Hamilton; **D:** Martin Ritt. **VHS, Beta, LV $14.95** PAR 𝄞𝄞½

Brotherhood of Death Three black Vietnam veterans return to their southern hometown to get even with the Klansmen who slaughtered all of the townspeople.

1976 85m/C Roy Jefferson, Larry Jones, Mike Bass, Le Tari, Haskell V. Anderson; **D:** Bill Berry. **VHS, Beta $59.95** MPI 𝄞½

Brotherhood of Justice Young men form a secret organization to rid their neighborhood of drug dealers and violence. As their power grows, their propriety weakens, until all are afraid of the "Brotherhood of Justice." Exciting made-for-television feature.

1986 97m/C Keanu Reeves, Kiefer Sutherland, Billy Zane, Joe Spano, Darren Dalton, Evan Mirand, Don Michael Paul; **D:** Charles Braverman. **VHS $89.95** VMK, STE 𝄞𝄞

The Brotherhood of Satan In an isolated southern town, a satanic coven persuades children to join in their devil-may-care attitude. Worthwhile.

1971 (PG) 92m/C Strother Martin, L.Q. Jones, Charles Bateman, Anna Capri, Charles Robinson, Alvy Moore, Geri Reischl; **D:** Bernard McEveety. **VHS, Beta, LV $9.95** GKK, IME 𝄞𝄞½

The Brotherhood of the Rose Too many twists and turns mar the otherwise mediocre plot of this murkey adaption of a book by David (First Blood) Morrell. Strauss and Morse are the C.I.A. agents marked for death and running for their lives after uncovering their boss's (Mitchum) plot of world domination. Though almost every scene takes place in a different country, the movie was in fact filmed entirely in New Zealand. Convoluted and frustratingly difficult to follow.

1989 (PG-13) 103m/C Robert Mitchum, Peter Strauss, Connie Sellecca, James B. Sikking, David Morse, M. Emmet Walsh, James Hong; **D:** Marvin J. Chomsky. **VHS $89.95** VMK 𝄞½

Brotherly Love Good twin/bad twin made-for-TV mystery about an escaped psychopath who's out to get his businessman twin brother (Hirsch in both roles).

1985 94m/C Judd Hirsch, Karen Carlson, George Dzundza, Barry Primus, Lori Lethin; **D:** Jeff Bleckner. **VHS, Beta $59.98** FOX 𝄞½

Brothers in Arms Savage mountainmen have developed a weird religion that requires them to hunt down and mercilessly massacre human prey.

1988 (R) 95m/C Todd Allen, Jack Starrett, Dedee Pfeiffer; **D:** George J. Bloom III. **VHS, LV $79.95** REP, PIA 𝄞𝄞

Brothers in Law Wry British humor in this tale of a rookie lawyer up against a veteran judge who forces him to sink or swim.

1957 94m/B GB Richard Attenborough, Ian Carmichael, Terry-Thomas, Miles Malleson, John Le Mesurier; **D:** Roy Boulting. **VHS $19.95** NOS 𝄞𝄞½

The Brothers Karamazov Hollywood adaptation of the classic novel by Dostoyevsky, in which four 19th-Century Russian brothers struggle with their desires for the same beautiful woman and with the father who brutalizes them. Incredible performances from every cast member, especially Cobb. Long and extremely intense, with fine direction from Brooks. Marilyn Monroe tried desperately to get Schell's part. **AKA:** Karamazov; The Murderer Dmitri Karamazov; Der Morder Dimitri Karamasoff.

1958 147m/C Yul Brynner, Claire Bloom, Lee J. Cobb, William Shatner, Maria Schell, Richard Basehart; **D:** Richard Brooks. **VHS, Beta $24.95** KUI, MGM, TAM 𝄞𝄞𝄞

Brothers Lionheart The Lion brothers fight for life, love and liberty during the Middle Ages.

1985 (G) 120m/C Staffan Gotestam, Lars Soderdahl, Allan Edwall; **D:** Olle Hellbron. **VHS, Beta** PAV 𝄞𝄞

Brothers of the West Cowboy saves his brothers from being lynched by proving the guilt of the real outlaws.

1937 56m/B Tom Tyler, Bob Terry, Lois Wilde, Dorothy Short. **VHS, Beta $19.95** NOS, VCN, DVT 𝄞½

Brothers O'Toole The misadventures of a pair of slick drifters who, by chance, ride into a broken-down mining town in the 1890s.

1973 94m/C John Astin, Steve Carlson, Pat Carroll, Hans Conried, Lee Meriwether; **D:** Richard Erdman. **VHS, Beta $49.95** UHV 𝄞𝄞

The Browning Version A lonely, unemotional classics instructor at a British boarding school realizes his failure as a teacher and as a husband. From the play by Terrence Rattigan.

1951 89m/B GB Michael Redgrave, Jean Kent, Nigel Patrick, Wilfrid Hyde-White, Bill Travers; **D:** Anthony Asquith. **VHS, Beta** MOV 𝄞𝄞𝄞½

Brubaker A sanctimonious drama about a reform warden who risks his life to replace brutality and corruption with humanity and integrity in a state prison farm. Powerful prison drama.

1980 (R) 131m/C Robert Redford, Jane Alexander, Yaphet Kotto, Murray Hamilton, David Keith, Morgan Freeman, Matt Clark, M. Emmet Walsh, Everett McGill; **D:** Stuart Rosenberg. **VHS, Beta, LV $19.98** FOX 𝄞𝄞𝄞

Bruce and Shaolin Kung Fu Bruce wins a Kung Fu match against a general's son and now the father's henchmen are after him.

1988 85m/C Bruce Le. **VHS $14.98** BFV 𝄞

Bruce Is Loose Bruce Le fights the evil Master. More foot-in-the-face follies for fun-loving folks.

1984 76m/C Bruce Le. **VHS, Beta $29.99** BFV 𝄞½

The Bruce Lee Collection A collection of Lee's greatest hits including "Fists of Fury," "Chinese Connection," "Return of the Dragon," and "Game of Death." **AKA:** The Bruce Lee Gift Pack.

19?? 397m/C Bruce Lee. **VHS $79.95** FOX 𝄞½

Bruce Lee: Curse of the Dragon A behind the scenes look at the continuing mystery surrounding the life and untimely death of the martial arts superstar who died in 1973 at the age of 32. Highlights the spectacular fight sequences from Lee's movies as well as footage from his funeral and an interview with his son Brandon Lee, whose own death in 1993 raised further comment about a Lee family curse.

1993 90m/C VHS, Beta, LV WAR 𝄞½

Bruce Lee Fights Back From the Grave Bruce Lee returns from the grave to fight the Black Angel of Death with his feet and to wreak vengeance on the evil ones who brought about his untimely demise.
1976 (R) 97m/C Bruce Lee, Deborah Chaplin, Anthony Bronson; **D:** Umberto Lenzi. **VHS, Beta** $49.95 MED *

Bruce Lee: The Legend Tribute to the king of karate films features rare footage and interviews with many of the star's closest friends.
1984 88m/C Bruce Lee, Steve McQueen, James Coburn. **VHS, Beta** $19.98 FOX *

Bruce Lee: The Man/The Myth A dramatization of the life and times of martial arts master Bruce Lee.
1984 90m/C Bruce Lee. **VHS, Beta** $59.95 VES, LIV, TIM *

Bruce Lee's Ways of Kung Fu Copious head-kicking film in honor of the long-dead star. Brings together the best from Shaolin: White Crane, Wu-Deng, Dragon-Fist, Kwun-Lun, Eagle Claws, Tiger, and Leopard in a fight against the Dragon.
198? 87m/C Bruce Lei, Philip Cheung, Pearl Lin. **VHS, Beta** $39.95 UNI *

Bruce Le's Greatest Revenge Bruce Le, one e. Kung-fu action and martial arts fighting occur when a martial arts student gets involved in a clash between Chinese and a discriminatory European Club.
1980 (R) 94m/C Bruce Le. **VHS, Beta** $24.95 GEM *

Bruce Li in New Guinea Bruce Li, i, not ee. The tribe of a remote island worships the legendary Snake Pearl. Two masters of Kung-fu visit the isle and discover they must defend the daughter of the murdered chief against a cruel wizard.
1980 (PG) 98m/C Bruce Li, Ho Chung Dao, Chen Sing; **D:** C.Y. Yang. **VHS, Beta** $19.95 OCE, GEM, MRV *

Bruce Li the Invincible Cheng, the Kung-Fu killer, is pursued by the vengeance-minded Bruce.
1980 93m/C Bruce Li, Ho Chung Dao, Chen Sing. **VHS** $19.95 OCE, MRV, GEM *

Bruce the Superhero Chop-socky action as the coattails-riding Bruce Le takes on the Black Dragon Society.
1979 88m/C Bruce Le. **VHS, Beta** $19.99 BFV, MRV *

Bruce vs. Bill Bruce is Bruce Le, a minor martial arts hero. Nobody's quite sure who Bill is, but Bruce beats up on him in this movie.
1983 (R) 90m/C Bruce Le, Bill Louie. **VHS, Beta** $19.99 BFV *

Bruce's Deadly Fingers Bruce Lee kept a book of deadly finger techniques for kung fu killing. When a vicious gangster kidnaps the Master's ex-girlfriend, one of his followers must rescue her and maintain the book's integrity.
1980 (R) 90m/C Bruce Le, Lo Lieh, Chan Wai, Nora Miao, Rose Marie, Yuen Man Chi, Chang Leih, Young Zee, Wuk Ma No Hans. **VHS, Beta** $24.95 GEM *

Bruce's Fists of Vengeance Le and Lee guard master Bruce Lee's kicking secrets from an evil adversary.
1984 87m/C Bruce Le, Jack Lee, Ken Watanabe, Romano Kristoff, Don Gordon. **VHS, Beta** $57.95 GEM *

Brujo Luna Evil ritualists kill and eat innocent people. Lots of blood and gore—not for the faint of heart. In Spanish.

19?? 90m/C SP Laurie Walters, Joe Spano. **VHS, Beta** $29.95 UNI Woof!

Brussels Transit The story of a Yiddish family's arrival and adjustment to the new world of Brussels, Belgium, after World War II. In Yiddish with English subtitles.
1980 80m/B **D:** Samy Szlingerbaum. **VHS** $69.95 TAM **

Brutal Glory Set in New York City in 1918 and based on the true story of the boxer known as "The Real McCoy." Fascinating and detailed history of a period, a champion, and the man who made it happen.
1989 96m/C Robert Vaughn, Timothy Brantley, Leah K. Pinsent; **D:** Koos Roets. **VHS** NO **

The Brute A greedy slumlord and his sluttish wife hire a dim-witted man to break up a tenant's strike but he accidentally kills one of the strike leaders. In Spanish with English subtitles.
1952 80m/B MX Pedro Armendariz Sr., Katy Jurado, Andres Soler; **D:** Luis Bunuel. **VHS** $24.95 TAM **½

The Brute Man A young man who had been disfigured by his school mates goes out on a trail of revenge. Hatton is convincing in the title role, as in real life he was afflicted with acromegaly, an ailment that produces an enlargment of the bones in the face, hands, and feet.
1946 62m/B Rondo Hatton, Tom Neal, Jane Adams; **D:** Jean Yarborough. **VHS, Beta, LV** $14.95 SVS, AOV, MLB **

Brutes and Savages A collection of footage of primitive societies surviving in the wild, devised for voyeuristic viewing.
1977 91m/C **D:** Arthur Davis. **VHS, Beta** $79.95 MPI *

The Buccaneer A swashbuckling version of the adventures of pirate Jean LaFitte and his association with President Andrew Jackson during the War of 1812. Remake of Cecille B. DeMille's 1938 production.
1958 121m/C Yul Brynner, Charlton Heston, Claire Bloom, Inger Stevens, Charles Boyer, Henry Hull, E.G. Marshall, Lorne Greene; **D:** Anthony Quinn. **VHS, Beta, LV** $14.95 KRT, FCT, NXM **

Buck and the Preacher A trail guide and a con man preacher join forces to help a wagon train of former slaves who are seeking to homestead out West. Poitier's debut as a director.
1972 (PG) 102m/C Sidney Poitier, Harry Belafonte, Ruby Dee, Cameron Mitchell, Denny Miller; **D:** Sidney Poitier. **VHS, Beta** $14.95 COL **½

Buck Privates Abbott and Costello star as two dim-witted tie salesmen, running from the law, who become buck privates during World War II. The duo's first great success, and the film that established the formula for each subsequent film. **AKA:** Rookies.
1941 84m/B Bud Abbott, Lou Costello, Shemp Howard, Lee Norman, Alan Curtis, The Andrews Sisters; **D:** Arthur Lubin. **VHS, Beta, LV** $14.95 MCA **½

Buck Privates Come Home Abbott and Costello return to their "Buck Privates" roles as two soldiers trying to adjust to civilian life after the war. They also try to help a French girl sneak into the United States. Funny antics culminate into a wild chase scene. **AKA:** Rookies Come Home.
1947 77m/B Bud Abbott, Lou Costello, Tom Brown, Joan Shawlee, Nat Pendleton, Beverly Simmons, Don Beddoe, Don Porter, Donald MacBride; **D:** Charles T. Barton. **VHS** $14.98 MCA **

Buck Rogers Conquers the Universe The story of Buck Rogers, written by Phil Nolan in 1928, was the first science fiction story done in the modern super-hero space genre. Many of the "inventions" seen in this movie have actually come into existence—spaceships, ray guns (lasers), anti-gravity belts—a testament to Nolan's almost psychic farsightedness.
1939 91m/B Buster Crabbe, Constance Moore, Jackie Moran; **D:** Ford Beebe, Saul Goodkind. **VHS, Beta** $29.95 FOX **

Buck Rogers in the 25th Century An American astronaut, preserved in space for 500 years, is brought back to life by a passing Draconian flagship. Outer space adventures begin when he is accused of being a spy from Earth. Based on the classic movie serial. Made for TV movie that began the popular series. Additional series episodes are available.
1979 (PG) 90m/C Gil Gerard, Pamela Hensley, Erin Gray, Henry Silva; **D:** Daniel Haller. **VHS, Beta, LV** $19.95 MCA, MOV **

A Bucket of Blood Cult favorite Dick Miller stars as a sculptor with a peculiar "talent" for lifelike artwork. Corman fans will see thematic similarities to his subsequent work, "Little Shop of Horrors" (1960). "Bucket of Blood" was made in just five days, while "Little Shop of Horrors" was made in a record breaking two days. Corman horror/spoof noted for its excellent beatnik atmosphere.
1959 66m/B Dick Miller, Barboura Morris, Antony Carbone, Julian Burton, Ed Nelson, Bert Convy; **D:** Roger Corman. **VHS, Beta** $19.95 NOS, RHI, SNC ***

Buckeye and Blue A hero turned outlaw, his 14 year-old female sidekick, and a gang known as the McCoys are all on the lam from the law in this western adventure.
1987 (PG) 94m/C Robin Lively, Jeffery Osterhage, Rick Gibbs, Will Hannah, Kenneth Jensen, Patrick Johnston, Stuart Rogers, Michael Horse; **D:** J.C. Compton. **VHS, Beta** $29.95 ACA **½

Buckskin Slow moving western about a marshall protecting townspeople from a greedy, land-grabbing cattle baron.
1968 98m/C Barry Sullivan, Wendell Corey, Joan Caulfield, Lon Chaney Jr., John Russell, Barbara Hale, Barton MacLane, Bill Williams; **D:** Michael Moore. **VHS** PAR **½

Buckskin Frontier Story is built around Western railroad construction and cattle empires in the 1860s.
1943 75m/B Richard Dix, Jane Wyatt, Lee J. Cobb, Albert Dekker, Victor Jory, Lola Lane, Max Baer; **D:** Lesley Selander. **VHS, Beta** $9.95 NOS, MRV, GPV **½

Bucktown A black man who reopens his murdered brother's bar fights off police corruption and racism in a Southern town.
1975 (R) 95m/C Fred Williamson, Pam Grier, Bernie Hamilton, Thalmus Rasulala, Art Lund; **D:** Arthur Marks. **VHS, Beta** $59.98 ORI **½

Bud and Lou Comedy/drama recounts Abbott & Costello's rise in Hollywood. While the story, based on the book by Bob Thomas, is interesting, the two funnymen in the leads can't pull off the old classic skits.
1978 98m/C Harvey Korman, Buddy Hackett, Michele Lee, Arte Johnson, Robert Reed; **D:** Robert C. Thompson. **VHS, Beta, LV** $29.95 JTC **½

Buddha Assassinator Young Kung-Fu enthusiast challenges a Ming dynasty lord to a duel to the death.

1982 93m/C Hwang Jang Lee, Mang Hai, Lung Fei, Chien Yueh Sheng. **VHS, Beta $59.95** *WVE* 🎞️

Buddy Buddy A professional hitman's well-ordered arrangement to knock off a state's witness keeps being interrupted by the suicide attempts of a man in the next hotel room.
1981 (R) 96m/C Jack Lemmon, Walter Matthau, Paula Prentiss, Klaus Kinski; *D:* Billy Wilder. **VHS, Beta $79.95** *MGM* 🎞️🎞️½

The Buddy Holly Story An acclaimed biography of the famed 1950s pop star, spanning the years from his meteoric career's beginnings in Lubbock to his tragic early death in the now famous plane crash. Busey performs Holly's hits himself. 🎵Rock Around the Ollie Vee; That'll Be the Day; Oh, Boy; It's So Easy; Well All Right; Chantilly Lace; Peggy Sue.
1978 (PG) 113m/C Gary Busey, Don Stroud, Charles Martin Smith, Conrad Janis, William Jordan; *D:* Steve Rash; *M:* Joe Renzetti. Academy Awards '78: Best Adapted Score; Nominations: Best Actor (Busey), Best Sound; National Society of Film Critics Awards '78: Best Actor (Busey). **VHS, Beta, LV $19.95** *COL* 🎞️🎞️🎞️½

The Buddy System A tale of contemporary love and the modern myths that outline the boundaries between lovers and friends.
1983 (PG) 110m/C Richard Dreyfuss, Susan Sarandon, Jean Stapleton, Nancy Allen, Wil Wheaton, Ed Winter, Keene Curtis; *D:* Glenn Jordan. **VHS, Beta $59.98** *FOX* 🎞️🎞️

Buddy's Song A 60s coming of age tale, only in this case it's the father and not the son who needs to grow up. Dad (Daltrey) is more interested in hanging out with his no-account musician friends than in looking after his family. Although he's not above meddling in his teenage son's musical career, which could be the success his father's never was. Based on the novel by Nigel Hinton who also did the screenplay. British teen idol Hawkes (in his film debut) had a top ten hit song from the film with "The One and Only."
1991 (R) 106m/C GB Roger Daltrey, Chesney Hawkes; *W:* Nigel Hinton. **VHS, LV $89.95** *VMK, BTV* 🎞️🎞️

Buffalo Bill A light, fictionalized account of the life and career of Bill Cody, from frontier hunter to showman.
1944 89m/C Joel McCrea, Maureen O'Hara, Linda Darnell, Thomas Mitchell, Edgar Buchanan, Anthony Quinn, Moroni Olsen, Sidney Blackmer; *D:* William A. Wellman. **VHS, Beta $39.98** *FOX* 🎞️🎞️

Buffalo Bill & the Indians A perennially underrated Robert Altman historical pastiche, portraying the famous Wild West character as a charlatan and shameless exemplar of encroaching imperialism. Great all-star cast amid Altman's signature mise-en-scene chaos.
1976 (PG) 135m/C Paul Newman, Geraldine Chaplin, Joel Grey, Will Sampson, Harvey Keitel, Burt Lancaster, Kevin McCarthy; *D:* Robert Altman. **VHS, Beta $19.98** *FOX* 🎞️🎞️🎞️

Buffalo Bill Rides Again With an Indian uprising on the horizon, Buffalo Bill is called in. Mr. Bill finds land swindlers pitting natives against ranchers, but there's precious little action or interest here.
1947 68m/C Richard Arlen, Jennifer Holt, Edward Cassidy, Edmund Cobb, Charles Stevens; *D:* Bernard B. Ray. **VHS, Beta** *GPV* 🎞️½

Buffalo Jump An independent woman, working as a lounge singer in Toronto, returns to her home in Alberta when her father dies. To her surprise he has left her the family ranch and, to the surprise of everyone else, she decides to stay and run it. She hires a good-looking local man to help her out and they both discover that they want more than a working relationship. However, the fireworks really start when he proposes a marriage of convenience. Engaging performances and beautiful scenery help raise this romantic tale of opposites above the average.
1990 97m/C CA Wendy Crewson, Paul Gross, Marion Gilsenan, Kyra Harper, Victoria Snow; *D:* Eric Till. **VHS $89.95** *ACA* 🎞️🎞️🎞️

Buffalo Rider An adventure film depicting the real-life experiences of C.J. "Buffalo" Jones who worked to save the American buffalo from extinction.
1978 90m/C Rick Guinn, John Freeman, Pricilla Lauris, George Sager, Rich Scheeland; *D:* George Lauris. **VHS, Beta $39.95** *ATP* 🎞️½

Buffalo Stampede Our heroes are involved in a plot to round up buffalo to sell for meat.
1933 60m/B Randolph Scott, Buster Crabbe, Harry Carey Sr., Noah Beery Sr., Raymond Hatton. **VHS, Beta $19.95** *NOS, VCN, MRV* 🎞️

Buffet Froid Surreal black comedy about a group of bungling murderers. First rate acting and directing make this film a hilarious treat. From the director of "Menage." In French with English subtitles.
1979 95m/C FR Gerard Depardieu, Bernard Blier, Jean Carmet, Genevieve Page, Denise Gence, Carol Bouquet, Jean Benguigui, Michel Serrault; *D:* Bertrand Blier. **VHS, LV $59.95** *INT, TAM* 🎞️🎞️🎞️½

Buffy the Vampire Slayer Funny, near-camp teen genre spoof about a Southern Cal valley girl reluctantly claiming her ancient birthright. Buffy is a typical mall gal concerned with shopping and cheerleading. The mysterious Sutherland arrives one day and proclaims it her destiny to slay the vampires who have suddenly infested Los Angeles. Like, sure. Buffy requires some convincing, but eventually takes up the challenge, fighting off the vamps and their seductive leader Hauer, aided by perpetual guy-in-distress Perry. Climax is the prom from hell. Pee Wee Reubens is unrecognizable and terribly amusing as the vampire king's sinister henchman, engaging in one of the longer death scenes of film history. Swanson is appropriately air headed as the athletically indestructable Buffy.
1992 (PG-13) 98m/C Kristy Swanson, Donald Sutherland, Luke Perry, Paul Reubens, Rutger Hauer; *D:* Fran Rubel Kazui. **VHS, LV $19.98** *FXV, PMS* 🎞️🎞️

Buford's Beach Bunnies Harry Buford has made a fortune selling barbecued rabbit sandwiches served by the sexiest waitresses around. Harry wants to leave the business to his son Jeeter—if Jeeter can overcome his overwhelming fear of women. So three of Harry's waitresses decide to show Jeeter a very good time. Lots of pretty girls in not much clothing.
1992 (R) 90m/C Jim Hanks, Rikki Brando, Monique Parent, Amy Page, Barrett Cooper, Ina Rogers, Charley Rossman, David Robinson; *W/D:* Mark Pirro. **VHS $89.95** *IMP* 🎞️

Bug The city of Riverside is threatened with destruction after a massive earth tremor unleashes a super-race of ten-inch mega-cockroaches that belch fire, eat raw meat, and are virtually impervious to Raid. Produced by gimmick-king William Castle, who wanted to install windshield wiper-like devices under theatre seats that would brush against the patrons' feet as the cockroaches crawled across the screen; unfortunately, the idea was squashed flat.
1975 (PG) 100m/C Bradford Dillman, Joanna Miles, William Castle; *D:* Jeannot Szwarc. **VHS, Beta $19.95** *PAR* Woof!

Bugles in the Afternoon Life in the army during Custer's last days, with a love triangle, revenge and the Little Big Horn for added spice.
1952 85m/C Ray Milland, Hugh Marlowe, Helena Carter, Forrest Tucker, Barton MacLane, George Reeves; *D:* Roy Rowland. **VHS $14.95** *REP, FCT* 🎞️🎞️

Bugs! Seven of the wascally wabbit's finest.
1988 60m/C Bugs Bunny; *V:* Mel Blanc. **VHS $14.95** *MGM, WTA* 🎞️🎞️

Bugs & Daffy: The Wartime Cartoons A compilation of Daffy and Bugs classics made during World War II, often dominated by propaganda and Axis-baiting.
1945 120m/C *D:* Robert McKimson, Chuck Jones, Friz Freleng. **VHS, Beta, LV $19.95** *MGM, WTA* 🎞️🎞️

Bugs & Daffy's Carnival of the Animals A host of favorite animated critters are introduced by the wabbit and the duck.
1989 26m/C Bugs Bunny; *D:* Chuck Jones; *V:* Mel Blanc. **VHS $14.95** *WAR, WTA* 🎞️🎞️

Bugs Bunny & Elmer Fudd Cartoon Festival Seven classic Bugs and Elmer shorts, including "Wabbitt Twouble," "Stage Door Cartoon," and "The Big Snooze."
1944 54m/C *D:* Chuck Jones, Tex Avery, Bob Clampett, Friz Freleng, Robert McKimson. **VHS, Beta $19.95** *MGM* 🎞️🎞️

Bugs Bunny Cartoon Festival The animated antics of the nefarious rabbit in four early cartoons.
1944 34m/C *D:* Bob Clampett, Chuck Jones, Friz Freleng. **VHS, Beta $14.95** *MGM* 🎞️🎞️

Bugs Bunny Cartoon Festival: Little Red Riding Rabbit Five classic Bugs shorts, including "Old Grey Hare," "Jack Wabbit and the Beanstalk" and the title cartoon are featured.
1943 37m/C *D:* Chuck Jones, Friz Freleng. **VHS, Beta $14.95** *MGM* 🎞️🎞️

Bugs Bunny: Hollywood Legend Six episodes featuring the wascally wabbit, including "Hair-Raising Hare," "A Hare Grows in Manhattan," and "Herr Meets Hare."
1990 60m/C *V:* Mel Blanc. **VHS $12.98** *MGM, FCT, WTA* 🎞️🎞️

Bugs Bunny in King Arthur's Court The Looney Tuners spoof Mark Twain's masterpiece of classic American literature.
1989 25m/C Bugs Bunny; *W/D:* Chuck Jones; *V:* Mel Blanc. **VHS $14.95** *WAR, WTA* 🎞️🎞️

The Bugs Bunny/Road Runner Movie A compilation of classic Warner Brothers cartoons, starring Bugs Bunny, Daffy Duck, Elmer Fudd, the Road Runner, Wile E. Coyote, Porky Pig, and Pepe Le Pew, including some all-new animated sequences. Also available with Spanish dubbing. *AKA:* Great American Bugs Bunny-Road Runner Chase.
1979 (G) 98m/C *D:* Phil Monroe, Chuck Jones. **VHS, Beta $19.98** *WAR, WTA, APD* 🎞️🎞️

Bugs Bunny Superstar A collection of nine animated classics starring everybody's favorite "wascally wabbitt." Includes fascinating interviews and behind the scenes moments featuring the men and women who brought Bugs to life.
1975 (G) 91m/C D: Larry Jackson, Bob Clampett, Tex Avery, Friz Freleng; **V:** Mel Blanc. **VHS, LV $19.95** MGM, WTA 🎬🎬

Bugs Bunny's Comedy Classics A collection of classic wabbit tales including "Easter Yeggs," "Racketeer Rabbit," "The Hair-Brained Hypnotist," "Acrobatty Rabbit," "Falling Hare," and "Haredevil Hare."
1988 60m/C V: Mel Blanc. **VHS $12.98** MGM, FCT, WTA 🎬🎬

Bugs Bunny's Hare-Raising Tales Six standouts from the furry varmint's vault of classics; includes "Rabbitson Crusoe" and "Rabbit Hood."
1989 45m/C Bugs Bunny; **D:** Abe Levitow; **W/D:** Chuck Jones, Robert McKimson; **W:** Friz Freleng; **V:** Mel Blanc. **VHS $14.95** WAR, WTA 🎬🎬

Bugs Bunny's Looney Christmas Tales Join Bugs as he and his little nephew re-enact two of the world's most beloved Christmas stories; "A Christmas Carol" and "'Twas the Night Before Christmas."
1979 25m/C D: Chuck Jones, Friz Freleng; **V:** Mel Blanc. **VHS $9.95** WAR, APD, WTA 🎬🎬

Bugs Bunny's 3rd Movie: 1,001 Rabbit Tales A compilation of old and new classic cartoons featuring Bugs, Daffy, Sylvester, Porky, Elmer, Tweety, Speedy Gonzalez and Yosemite Sam.
1982 (G) 74m/C D: Chuck Jones, Robert McKimson, Friz Freleng. **VHS, Beta $19.98** WAR, FCT, WTA 🎬🎬

Bugs Bunny's Wacky Adventures Here is a collection of that rascally rabbit's classic cartoons featuring "Ali Baba Bunny," "Hare Do," "Long Haired Hare," "Bunny Hugged," "The Grey Hounded Hare," "Roman Legion Hare," and "Duck, Rabbit, Duck!"
1957 59m/C D: Chuck Jones, Friz Freleng; **V:** Mel Blanc. **VHS, Beta $12.95** WAR, WTA 🎬🎬

Bugs vs. Elmer Seven of the best Bugs/Elmer battles: "Slick Hare," "Unruly Hare," "Hare Remover," "Stage Door Cartoon," "Wabbit Twouble," "The Big Snooze" and "Fresh Hare."
1953 60m/C D: Frank Tashlin, Chuck Jones, Friz Freleng, Robert McKimson, Bob Clampett. **VHS, Beta, LV $14.95** MGM, WTA 🎬🎬

Bugsy Beatty stars as Benjamin "Bugsy" Siegel, the Forties gangster who built the Flamingo Hotel in Las Vegas when it was nothing but a virtual desert, but which grew to become a gambling mecca. Bening is perfect as Bugsy's moll, Virginia Hill, who inspired him to carry out his dream of building the Flamingo (which was her nickname). "Bugsy" is the tale of a very flamboyant man with an extraordinary vision. Beatty and Bening heat up the screen and their off-screen relationship was no different. Fans anticipated their seemingly imminent marriage almost as much as the release of this movie. Almost nothing mars this film which Toback adapted from a novel by Dean Jennings, "We Only Kill Each Other: The Life and Bad Times of Bugsy Siegel."
1991 (R) 135m/C Warren Beatty, Annette Bening, Harvey Keitel, Ben Kingsley, Elliot Gould, Joe Mantegna, Richard Sarafian, Bebe Neuwirth, Wendy Phillips, Robert Beltran, Bill Graham, Lewis Van Bergen, Debrah Farentino; **D:** Barry Levinson; **W:** James Toback; **M:** Ennio Morricone. Academy Awards '91: Best Art Direction/Set Decoration, Best Costume Design; Nominations: Best Actor (Beatty), Best Cinematography, Best Director (Levinson), Best Original Screenplay, Best Picture, Best Supporting Actor (Keitel, Kingsley), Best Original Score; Chicago Film Critics Awards '91: Best Supporting Actor (Keitel); Golden Globe Awards '92: Best Film—Drama; Los Angeles Film Critics Association Awards '91: Best Director (Levinson), Best Film; National Board of Review Awards '91: 10 Best Films of the Year, Best Actor (Beatty). **VHS, Beta, LV, 8mm $19.95** COL 🎬🎬🎬½

Bugsy Malone An all-children's cast highlights this spoof of 1930s' gangster movies. A musical featuring songs by Paul Williams.
1976 (G) 94m/C GB Jodie Foster, Scott Baio, Florrie Augger, John Cassisi, Martin Lev; **D:** Alan Parker. **VHS, Beta, LV $14.95** PAR 🎬🎬½

Bull Durham A lovable American romantic comedy, dealing with a very minor minor-league team and three of its current constituents: an aging baseball groupie that beds one player each season; a cocky, foolish new pitcher; and the older, weary catcher brought in to wise the rookie up. The scene in which Sarandon tries poetry out on the banal rookie is a hoot. Highly acclaimed, the film sears with Sarandon and Costner's love scenes.
1988 (R) 107m/C Kevin Costner, Susan Sarandon, Tim Robbins, Trey Wilson, Robert Wuhl, Jenny Robertson; **D:** Ron Shelton. **VHS, Beta, LV $19.98** ORI, HMV 🎬🎬🎬½

Bull of the West Cattlemen battle for land in the wide open spaces of the old West.
1989 90m/C Charles Bronson, Lee J. Cobb, Brian Keith, George Kennedy, DeForest Kelley, Doug McClure. **VHS** NO 🎬½

Bulldance At a gymnastic school in Crete, a girl's obsession with Greek mythological ritual leads to murder. **AKA:** Forbidden Son.
1988 105m/C Lauren Hutton, Cliff DeYoung, Renee Estevez; **D:** Zelda Barron. **VHS, Beta** ACA 🎬

Bulldog Courage Young man is out to avenge his father's murder.
1935 66m/B Tim McCoy, Lois January, Joan Woodbury, John Elliott; **D:** Sam Newfield. **VHS, Beta $19.95** NOS, VCN, DVT 🎬🎬

Bulldog Drummond A World War I vet, bored with civilian life, is enlisted by a beautiful woman to help her father in various adventures. The first in the long-standing series, based on the detective novels of Herman Cyril McNeile.
1929 85m/B Ronald Colman, Joan Bennett, Montagu Love; **D:** F. Richard Jones. **VHS, Beta $19.98** SUE, RXM 🎬🎬½

Bulldog Drummond at Bay Drummond searches for a group of foreign agents who are trying to steal the plans for a top-secret warplane. Poor British entry to the "Bulldog Drummond" series.
1937 63m/B GB John Lodge, Dorothy Mackaill, Victor Jory, Claud Allister, Hugh Miller; **D:** Norman Lee. **VHS $16.95** SNC 🎬

Bulldog Drummond Comes Back Drummond, aided by Colonel Nielson, rescues his fiancee from the hands of desperate kidnappers.
1937 119m/B John Howard, John Barrymore, Louise Campbell, Reginald Denny, Guy Standing; **D:** Louis King. **VHS, Beta, 3/4U, Special order formats $16.95** SNC, NOS, DVT 🎬🎬

Bulldog Drummond Escapes Drummond, aided by his side-kick and valet, rescues a beautiful girl from spies. He then falls in love with her.
1937 67m/B Ray Milland, Heather Angel, Reginald Denny, Guy Standing, Porter Hall, E.E. Clive; **D:** James Hogan. **VHS, Beta $16.95** SNC, NOS, VYY 🎬🎬

Bulldog Drummond in Africa/ Arrest Bulldog Drummond Two mid-series Bulldog Drummond films, with two new villains.
1938 115m/B John Howard, H.B. Warner, George Zucco. **VHS, Beta $19.98** SUE, RXM 🎬🎬

Bulldog Drummond's Bride Ace detective Bulldog Drummond has to interrupt his honeymoon in order to pursue a gang of bank robbers across France and England. The last of the Bulldog Drummond film series.
1939 69m/B John Howard, Heather Angel, H.B. Warner, E.E. Clive, Reginald Denny, Eduardo Ciannelli; **D:** James Hogan. **VHS, Beta $14.95** QNE, DVT, MRV 🎬🎬

Bulldog Drummond's Peril Murder and robbery drag the adventurous Drummond away from his wedding and he pursues the villains until they are behind bars. One in the film series.
1938 77m/B John Barrymore, John Howard, Louise Campbell, Reginald Denny, E.E. Clive, Porter Hall; **D:** James Hogan. **VHS, Beta, 3/4U, Special order formats $16.95** SNC, CAB, RXM 🎬🎬

Bulldog Drummond's Revenge The Bulldog Drummond character, created by "Sapper" (Herman Cyril McNeile), underwent a number of different incarnations from twenties' silents through the forties, and even occasionally in the fifties and sixties. A suave ex-British officer (a precursor to the glib shaken-not-stirred gentleman-spy variety), Bulldog has been played by the likes of Ronald Colman, Ralph Richardson and Tom Conway, among others. Bulldog's "Revenge" was made in the late thirties, during the series' heyday, the second to star John Howard as Drummond; John "the Profile" Barrymore revels in the character of Inspector Neilson of Scotland Yard, and Reginald Denny plays Algy. In this typically fast-paced installment, suave sleuth Drummond stalks the master criminal responsible for stealing the formula to an explosive.
1937 55m/B John Barrymore, Louise Campbell, John Howard, Reginald Denny, Frank Puglia, Nydia Westman, Lucien Littlefield; **D:** Louis King. **VHS $16.95** SNC, MOV 🎬🎬

Bulldog Drummond's Revenge/ Bulldog Drummond's Peril Once again, Bulldog Drummond becomes entangled with diamond counterfeiters, secret explosives, and other crime and criminals. Two episodes in a series.
1938 118m/B John Howard, John Barrymore, Louise Campbell, Reginald Denny, E.E. Clive, Porter Hall. **VHS, Beta $19.98** SUE 🎬🎬½

Bulldog Drummond's Secret Police The 15th Drummond film, adapted from Herman Cyril McNeile's famed detective novels featuring a million-pound treasure stashed in the Drummond manor and the murderous endeavors to retrieve it.
1939 54m/B John Howard, Heather Angel, H.B. Warner, Reginald Denny, E.E. Clive, Leo G. Carroll; **D:** James Hogan. **VHS, Beta $16.95** SNC, VYY, RXM 🎬🎬

Bulldog Edition Two newspapers engage in an all-out feud to be number one in the city, even going so far as to employ gangsters for purposes of sabotage.
1936 57m/B Ray Walker, Evelyn Knapp, Regis Toomey, Cy Kendall, Billy Newell, Oscar Apfel, Betty Compson, Robert Warwick; **D:** Charles Lamont. **VHS, Beta $16.95** SNC 🎬🎬

Bulldog Jack Fine entry in the series has Drummond's colleague battling it out with Richardson, the leader of gang of jewel thieves. *AKA:* Alias Bulldog Drummond.
1935 62m/B *GB* Fay Wray, Jack Hulbert, Claude Hulbert, Ralph Richardson, Paul Graetz, Gibb McLaughlin; **D:** Walter Forde. **VHS, Beta $16.95** *NOS, SNC, TIM* 𝄢𝄢𝄢

Bullet for Sandoval An ex-Confederate renegade loots and pillages the north Mexican countryside on his way to murder the grandfather of the woman he loves.
1970 (PG) 96m/C *SP IT* Ernest Borgnine, George Hilton; **D:** Julio Buchs. **VHS, Beta $19.95** *UHV* 𝄢𝄢

A Bullet for the General An American mercenary joins with rebel forces during the Mexican Revolution. *AKA:* Quien Sabe?.
1968 95m/C *IT* Martine Beswick, Lou Castel, Gian Marie Volonte, Klaus Kinski; **D:** Damiano Damiani. **VHS, Beta $14.95** *COL, NLC* 𝄢

A Bullet Is Waiting A diligent sheriff finally catches his man only to be trapped in a blinding snowstorm with the hardened criminal.
1954 83m/C Jean Simmons, Rory Calhoun, Stephen McNally, Brian Aherne; **D:** John Farrow. **VHS, Beta** *GKK* 𝄢𝄢

Bulletproof An unstoppable ex-CIA agent battles to retrieve a high-tech nuclear tank from terrorist hands.
1988 (R) 93m/C Gary Busey, Darlanne Fluegel, Henry Silva, Thalmus Rasulala, L.Q. Jones, R.G. Armstrong, Rene Enriquez; **D:** Steve Carver. **VHS, Beta, LV $14.95** *COL* 𝄢

Bullets or Ballots Tough New York cop goes undercover to join the mob in order to get the goods on them. Old-fashioned danger and intrigue follow, making for some action-packed thrills.
1938 82m/B Edward G. Robinson, Humphrey Bogart, Barton MacLane, Joan Blondell, Frank McHugh, Louise Beavers; **D:** William Keighley. **VHS, Beta $19.98** *MGM, CCB* 𝄢𝄢

Bullfighter & the Lady An American goes to Mexico to learn the fine art of bullfighting in order to impress a beautiful woman.
1950 87m/B Robert Stack, Gilbert Roland, Virginia Grey, Katy Jurado; **D:** Budd Boetticher. **VHS, LV $19.98** *REP, PIA* 𝄢𝄢 ½

Bullfighters Stan and Ollie are in hot pursuit of a dangerous criminal which leads them to Mexico where Stan winds up in a bull ring.
1945 61m/B Stan Laurel, Oliver Hardy, Margo Wood, Richard Lane; **D:** Mal St. Clair. **VHS, Beta $29.98** *FOX, MLB* 𝄢𝄢

Bullies A woodland-transplanted young man decides to fight back against an ornery mountain clan who've raped his mother, tortured his father, and beat up his girlfriend. Brutal and unpalatable.
1986 (R) 96m/C *CA* Janet-Laine Green, Dehl Berti, Stephen Hunter; **D:** Paul Lynch. **VHS, Beta, LV $79.95** *MCA* Woof!

Bullitt A detective assigned to protect a star witness for 48 hours senses danger; his worst fears are confirmed when his charge is murdered. Based on the novel, "Mute Witness" by Robert L. Pike, and featuring one of filmdom's most famous car chases.
1968 (PG) 105m/C Steve McQueen, Robert Vaughn, Jacqueline Bisset, Don Gordon, Robert Duvall, Norman Fell, Simon Oakland; **D:** Peter Yates. Academy Awards '68: Best Film Editing; Nominations: Best Sound; Edgar Allan Poe Awards '68: Best Screenplay. **VHS, Beta, LV $19.98** *WAR* 𝄢𝄢𝄢

Bullseye! Knockabout farce is a letdown considering the talents involved. Shady scientists (Moore and Caine) pursue/are pursued by lookalike con-artists (Caine and Moore), who are pursued in turn by international agents. Full of inside jokes and celebrity cameos, but nothing exceptional.
1990 (PG-13) 95m/C Michael Caine, Roger Moore, Sally Kirkland, Patsy Kensit, Jenny Seagrove, John Cleese; **Cameos:** Lee Patterson, Deborah Barrymore, Mark Burns, Debra Lang, Lynn Nesbitt, Steffanie Pitt, Alexandra Pigg; **D:** Michael Winner. **VHS, LV $89.95** *COL, PIA* 𝄢 ½

Bullshot Zany English satire sends up the legendary Bulldog Drummond. In the face of mad professors, hapless heroines, devilish Huns and deadly enemies, our intrepid hero remains distinctly British.
1983 (PG) 84m/C *GB* Alan Shearman, Diz White, Ron House, Frances Tomelty, Michael Aldridge, Ron Pember, Christopher Good; **D:** Dick Clement. **VHS, Beta $59.99** *HBO* 𝄢𝄢 ½

Bullshot Crummond The Low Moan Spectacular comedy troupe performs this satire that trashes oldtime adventure serials.
1984 90m/C VHS, Beta, LV $39.95 *RKO, TTC* 𝄢𝄢 ½

Bullwhip A man falsely accused of murder saves himself from the hangman's noose by agreeing to a shotgun wedding.
1958 80m/C Guy Madison, Rhonda Fleming, James Griffith, Peter Adams; **D:** Harmon Jones. **VHS $19.98** *REP* 𝄢

Bummer Rock band's wild party turns into tragedy when the bass player goes too far with two groupies. It's a bad scene, man.
1973 (R) 90m/C Kipp Whitman, Dennis Burkley, Carol Speed, Connie Strickland; **D:** William Allen Castleman. **VHS, Beta** NO Woof!

Bunco Two policemen working for the Los Angeles Police Department's Bunco Squad discover a college for con artists complete with tape-recorded lessons and on-the-job training.
1983 60m/C Tom Selleck, Robert Urich, Donna Mills, Will Geer, Arte Johnson, Alan Feinstein. **VHS, Beta $59.95** *LHV, WAR* 𝄢

Bundle of Joy Salesgirl who saves an infant from falling off the steps of a foundling home is mistaken for the child's mother. Remake of 1939's "Bachelor Mother." ♫Bundle of Joy; I Never Felt This Way Before; Lullaby in Blue; Worry About Tomorrow; All About Love; Someday Soon; What's So Good About Morning?; You're Perfect In Every Departmant.
1956 98m/C Debbie Reynolds, Eddie Fisher, Adolphe Menjou; **D:** Norman Taurog. **VHS, Beta, LV $19.95** *UHV* 𝄢𝄢 ½

Bunnicula: Vampire Rabbit Strange things happen to a family after they adopt an abandoned bunny. The family dog and cat team up to prove that their furry friend is a vampire in disguise. An animated tale.
1982 23m/C VHS, Beta $19.95 *WOV, GKK, WTA* 𝄢𝄢 ½

A Bunny's Tale The story of Gloria Steinem's undercover journey into the Playboy Club as a fledgling journalist. It is here that she discovered her dedication as a feminist. Based on the book by Steinem.
1985 97m/C Kirstie Alley, Cotter Smith, Deborah Van Valkenburgh, Joanna Kerns, Delta Burke, Diana Scarwid; **D:** Karen Arthur. **VHS, Beta $79.95** *PSM* 𝄢𝄢

Buona Sera, Mrs. Campbell The lovely Lollobridgida and some fast-paced plot moves are the main highlights of this comedy. Mrs. Campbell convinced her three American World War II lovers that each of them had fathered her daughter. All three have supported mother and child through the years, unbeknowst to each other and their wives. When their 20-year reunion brings them back to Italy, Mrs. Campbell must do some fast-thinking and some quick-stepping to keep everyone happy.
1968 113m/C Gina Lollobrigida, Shelley Winters, Phil Silvers, Peter Lawford, Telly Savalas, Lee Grant, Janet Margolin, Marian Moses; **D:** Melvin Frank. **VHS, LV $19.98** *MGM* 𝄢𝄢 ½

The 'Burbs A tepid satire about suburbanites suspecting their creepy new neighbors of murderous activities. Well-designed and sharp, but light on story.
1989 (PG) 101m/C Tom Hanks, Carrie Fisher, Rick Ducommun, Corey Feldman, Brother Theodore, Bruce Dern, Gale Gordon, Courtney Gains; **D:** Joe Dante; **M:** Jerry Goldsmith. **VHS, Beta, LV $14.95** *MCA, CCB* 𝄢 ½

Burden of Dreams The landmark documentary chronicling the berserk circumstances behind the scenes of Werner Herzog's epic "Fitzcarraldo." Stuck in the Peruvian jungles, the film crew was subjected to every disaster imaginable while executing Herzog's vision, including disease, horrendous accident, warring local tribes and the megalomaniacal director himself. Considered better than "Fitzcarraldo," although both films discuss a man's obsession.
1982 94m/C Klaus Kinski, Mick Jagger, Jason Robards Jr., Werner Herzog; **D:** Les Blank. **VHS, Beta, LV $59.95** *FFM, BTV* 𝄢 ½

Bureau of Missing Persons Comedy-drama about big-city bureau of missing persons, in which the hardened Stone is in charge. O'Brien plays a tough cop who is transferred to the bureau and Davis stars as the mystery woman with whom he gets involved. Although fast-paced and intriguing, the film is somewhat confusing and never stays in one direction for very long.
1933 75m/B Bette Davis, Lewis Stone, Pat O'Brien, Glenda Farrell, Allen Jenkins, Ruth Donnelly, Hugh Herbert; **D:** Roy Del Ruth. **VHS $19.98** *MGM* 𝄢𝄢 ½

Burgess, Philby, and MacLean: Spy Scandal of the Century An intriguing, true spy story about three double agents who were able to infiltrate British Intelligence and pass on U.S. atomic secrets to the Soviet Union. Originally aired on PBS.
1986 83m/C VHS, Beta *MTI* 𝄢𝄢 ½

Burglar Not to be confused with the Whoopi Goldberg vehicle, this Russian film relates a story no less American than apple pie and teenage angst. Senka and would-be punk star Kostya are two neglected and disaffected brothers whose father is a drunken womanizer whose presence mitigates not at all his absentee paternalism. When Howmuch, a serious heavy metalloid, pressures Kostya to steal a synthesizer, brother Senka steps in to steal the Community Center's property himself, with not a little consternation. In Russian with English subtitles, the solid performances hold their own against the heavy musical content. *AKA:* Vzlomschik.
1987 89m/C *RU* Konstantin Kinchev, Oleg Yelykomov; **D:** Valery Orgorodnikov. **VHS $59.95** *FCT, KIV* 𝄢𝄢𝄢

Burglar A cat burglar moves to the right side of the law when he tries to solve a murder case. Whoopi's always a treat, but this movie's best forgotten; fans of Whoopi should watch "Jumpin' Jack Flash" again instead. Co-star Bob "Bobcat" Goldthwaite elevates the comedic level a bit.
1987 (R) 103m/C Whoopi Goldberg, Bob Goldthwait, Lesley Ann Warren, John Goodman; **D:** Hugh Wilson. **VHS, Beta, LV $19.98** *WAR, KIV* 𝄢𝄢

Burial Ground A classically grisly splatter film in which the hungry dead rise and proceed to kill the weekend denizens of an isolated aristocratic mansion.
1985 85m/C Karen Well, Peter Bark; **D:** Andrew Bianchi. **VHS, Beta** $79.95 *VES, LIV* ⚔️

Buried Alive A man is sent to prison on trumped up charges. Only the prison nurse believes he is innocent as a crooked politician strives to keep him behind bars.
1939 74m/C Beverly Roberts, Robert Wilcox, George Pembroke, Ted Osborn, Paul McVey, Alden Chase; **D:** Victor Halperin. **Beta, CV** $16.95 *NOS, MRV, LOO* ⚔️

Buried Alive Director d'Amato reaps his finest gore-fest to date, incorporating the well-established taxidermist gone loony motif in his repertoire of appalling bad taste. Not for the squeamish, this bloodier-than-thou spaghetti spooker is chock full of necrophilia, cannibalism, and more.
1981 90m/C *IT* Kieran Canter, Cinzia Monreale, Franca Stoppi; **D:** Joe D'Amato. **VHS** *NO* ⚔️

Buried Alive Once Ravenscroft Hall was an asylum for the incurably insane. Now, the isolated mansion is a school for troubled teenage girls, run by a charismatic psychiatrist. Captivated by his charm, a young woman joins the staff. Soon, she is tormented by nightmare visions of the long-dead victims of a nameless killer. When the students begin to disappear, she realizes he still lives...and she may be his next victim. Carradine's last role.
1989 (R) 97m/C Robert Vaughn, Donald Pleasence, Karen Witter, John Carradine, Ginger Lynn Allen; **D:** Gerard Kikione. **VHS, LV** $14.95 *COL* ⚔️

Buried Alive One of the many horror flicks entitled "Buried Alive," this one (written by Patrick Carducci, and made for cable) is not bad, injecting a bit of levity into the time-worn genre. Schemestress Leigh and her paramour poison her husband. Or so they think, only to discover that he's not quite dead.
1990 (PG-13) 93m/C Tim Matheson, Jennifer Jason Leigh, William Atherton, Hoyt Axton; **D:** Frank Darabont. **VHS** $79.95 *MCA* ⚔️⚔️½

Burke & Wills A lush, big-budgeted true story of the two men who first crossed Australia on foot, and explored its central region. Popular Australian film.
1985 (PG-13) 120m/C *AU* Jack Thompson, Nigel Havers, Greta Scacchi; **D:** Graeme Clifford. **VHS, Beta, LV** $19.98 *NLC, TAM* ⚔️⚔️½

Burlesque of Carmen A silent pastiche of the Bizet opera, with Charlie as Don Schmose. Interesting early work.
1916 30m/B Charlie Chaplin, Ben Turpin, Edna Purviance; **D:** Charlie Chaplin. **VHS, Beta** $19.95 *NOS, DVT, TIM* ⚔️

The Burmese Harp At the end of World War II, a Japanese soldier is spiritually traumatized and becomes obsessed with burying the masses of war casualties. A searing, acclaimed anti-war statement, in Japanese with English subtitles. Remade by Ichikawa in 1985. *AKA:* Harp of Burma; Birumano Tategoto.
1956 115m/B *JP* Shoji Yasui, Rentaro Mikuni, Tatsuya Mihashi, Tanie Kitabayashi, Yunosuke Ito; **D:** Kon Ichikawa. **VHS, Beta, LV** $29.95 *CVC, TAM, APD* ⚔️⚔️⚔️

Burn! An Italian-made indictment of imperialist control by guerrilla-filmmaker Pontecorvo, depicting the efforts of a 19th century British ambassador to put down a slave revolt on a Portuguese-run Caribbean island. Great Brando performance. *AKA:* Quemimada!.

1970 (PG) 112m/C *IT* Marlon Brando, Evarist Marquez, Renato Salvatori; **D:** Gillo Pontecorvo; **M:** Ennio Morricone. **VHS, Beta, LV** $19.98 *MGM, VYG, CRC* ⚔️⚔️½

Burn 'Em Up Barnes Twelve episodes each depicting the adventures of "Burn 'Em Up" Barnes, a racer, and his buddy, Bobbie.
1934 40m/B Frankie Darro, Lola Lane, Jack Mulhall. **VHS, Beta** $26.95 *SNC, NOS, VCN* ⚔️⚔️½

Burn Witch, Burn! A college professor proudly finds himself rapidly rising in his profession. His pride turns to horror though when he discovers that his success is not due to his own abilities, but to the efforts of his witchcraft practicing wife. Excellent, atmospheric horror with a genuinely suspenseful climax. *AKA:* Night of the Eagle.
1962 87m/B *GB* Peter Wyngarde, Janet Blair, Margaret Johnston, Anthony Nicholls, Colin Gordon, Kathleen Byron, Reginald Beckwith, Jessica Dunning; **D:** Sidney Hayers. **VHS** $18.00 *FRG* ⚔️⚔️⚔️

Burndown Victims of a serial killer in a town with a large nuclear reactor are themselves radioactive, which leads the Police Chief and a beautiful reporter to the truth and the hidden conspiracy.
1989 (R) 97m/C Cathy Moriarty, Peter Firth; **D:** James Allen. **VHS, Beta, LV** *NO* ⚔️

The Burning Story of macabre revenge set in the dark woods of a seemingly innocent summer camp.
1982 (R) 90m/C Brian Matthews, Leah Ayres, Holly Hunter; **D:** Tony Maylam. **VHS, Beta** $19.99 *HBO* ⚔️

Burning Bed A made for television dramatic expose (based on a true story) about wife-beating. Fawcett garnered accolades for her performance as the battered wife who couldn't take it anymore. Highly acclaimed and Emmy-nominated.
1985 95m/C Farrah Fawcett, Paul LeMat, Penelope Milford, Richard Masur; **D:** Robert Greenwald. **VHS, Beta** $79.98 *FOX* ⚔️⚔️½

The Burning Court Unusual horror film involving occultism, possession, and family curses. Dubbed into English. Based on a story by John Dickson Carr.
1962 ?m/C Nadja Tiller, Jean-Claude Brialy, Edith Scob. **VHS** $16.95 *SNC* ⚔️½

The Burning Hills Unexceptional cow flick based on a Louis L'Amour novel. Hunter hides from cattle thieves in a barn and, eventually, in the arms of a half-breed Mexican girl (Wood). Tedious and unsurprising.
1956 94m/C Tab Hunter, Natalie Wood, Skip Homeier, Eduard Franz; **D:** Stuart Heisler. **VHS** *MLB* ⚔️½

Burning Rage A blazing, abandoned coal mine threatens to wreak havoc in the Appalachians. The government sends geologist Mandrell to help prevent a disaster. Made for television.
1984 100m/C Barbara Mandrell, Tom Wopat, Bert Remsen, John Pleshette, Carol Kane, Eddie Albert; **D:** Gilbert Cates. **VHS, LV** *NO* ⚔️

Burning Secret After WWI, a widow in Austria (Dunaway) meets a baron (Brandauer) who has befriended her son. Mutual seduction ensues but the sparks don't fly. Adapted from Stefan Zweig story. *AKA:* Brennendes Geheimnis.
1989 (PG) 107m/C *GB* Faye Dunaway, Klaus Maria Brandauer, Ian Richardson, David Eberts; **D:** Andrew Birkin. **VHS, Beta, LV** $89.98 *VES, IME, LIV* ⚔️⚔️

Burning Vengeance A DEA agent enters the deadly world of drugs and single-handedly annihilates the drug smugglers and destroys their kingpin.
1989 120m/C VHS, Beta *AIP* ⚔️⚔️

The Burns and Allen Show George and Gracie's classic vaudeville routines are a highlight of this sitcom series, with George the perpetually harried husband to the scatterbrained Gracie. Additional episodes are available.
1950 115m/B Gracie Allen, George Burns. **VHS, Beta, LV** *SHO, COL, MOV* ⚔️⚔️

Burnt Offerings A family rents a house for the summer and they become affected by evil forces that possess the house.
1976 (PG) 116m/C Oliver Reed, Karen Black, Bette Davis, Burgess Meredith; **D:** Dan Curtis. **VHS, Beta** $59.95 *MGM* ⚔️⚔️

Bury Me an Angel A female biker sets out to seek revenge against the men who killed her brother.
1971 85m/C Dixie Peabody, Terry Mace, Clyde Ventura, Terry Mace, Stephen Whittaker, Gary Littlejohn; **D:** Barbara Peeters. **VHS, Beta, LV** $19.95 *STE, NWV, HHT* ⚔️

The Bus Is Coming A love story entwined with the problems of blacks in a small town.
1972 95m/C Mike Sims, Stephanie Faulkner, Morgan Jones; **D:** Horace Jackson. **VHS, Beta** *NO* ⚔️⚔️

Bus Station A group of travellers look for sex and adventure while taking a bus trip.
1988 89m/C Lucha Villa, Sergio Ramos, Maribel Fernandez, Guillermo Rivas, Charly Valentino. **VHS, Beta** $79.95 *MED* ⚔️

Bus Stop Don Murray plays a naive cowboy who falls in love with Monroe, a barroom singer, and decides to marry her without her permission. Considered by many to be the finest performance by Marilyn Monroe; she sings "That Old Black Magic" in this one. Very funny with good performances by all. Based on the William Inge play. *AKA:* The Wrong Kind of Girl.
1956 96m/C Marilyn Monroe, Arthur O'Connell, Hope Lange, Don Murray, Betty Field, Casey Adams, Hans Conried, Eileen Heckart; **D:** Joshua Logan. Academy Awards '56 Nominations: Best Supporting Actor (Murray); National Board of Review Awards '56: 10 Best Films of the Year. **VHS, Beta, LV** $14.98 *FOX* ⚔️⚔️⚔️

The Busby Berkeley Disc A collection of the innovative dance director's work at Warner Bros. studio covering 1933-37. Berkeley was known for his elaborate production numbers, beautiful women, military precision, and kaleidoscopic patterns in such films as "42nd Street," "Footlight Parade," and the "Gold Diggers" series.
1992 176m/B LV $39.98 *MGM* ⚔️⚔️⚔️

Bush Mama A hallucinatory film about a black woman on welfare trying to care for her daughter in a Los Angeles ghetto. Street violence varies with fantasy scenes in a loose narrative filled with flashbacks.
1976 100m/C D: Haile Gerima. **VHS** $59.95 *FCT* ⚔️⚔️

The Bushbaby The young Brooks is given a tiny bushbaby while visiting Africa with her father. Because of her pet she misses her ship home and finds herself with former servant Gossett, who agrees to take her to a family friend. Unfortunately, the authorities think he's kidnapped the girl and the two, along with the trouble-causing pet, are pursued by the police. Simple-minded kiddie fare.

1970 100m/C Margaret Brooks, Louis Gossett Jr., Donald Houston, Laurence Naismith, Marne Maitland, Geoffrey Bayldon, Jack Gwillim; **D:** John Trent. VHS $19.98 MGM ⅃ ½

The Busher All-American pitcher's romance is interrupted by a gratuitous Mr. Moneybags. Minor-league conflict with little real hardball.
1919 54m/B Charles Ray, Colleen Moore, John Gilbert. VHS, Beta $19.95 GPV, FCT ⅃ ½

The Bushido Blade An action-packed samurai thriller of adventure and betrayal set in medieval Japan. **AKA:** The Bloody Bushido Blade.
1980 92m/C JP Richard Boone, James Earl Jones, Frank Converse; **D:** Tom Kotani. VHS, Beta $69.99 HBO ⅃⅃ ½

The Bushwackers Ireland plays a veteran of the Confederate army who wishes only to put his violent past behind him. He is forced to reconsider his vow when old-west bullies threaten his family. **AKA:** The Rebel.
1952 70m/B Dorothy Malone, John Ireland, Wayne Morris, Lawrence Tierney, Jack Elam, Lon Chaney Sr., Myrna Dell; **D:** Rod Amateau. VHS $16.95 NOS, LOO, SNC ⅃ ½

Business as Usual A meek boutique manager in Liverpool defends a sexually harassed employee, is fired, fights back, and creates a national furor over her rights as a woman.
1988 (PG) 89m/C Glenda Jackson, Cathy Tyson, John Thaw; **D:** Lezli-Ann Barrett. VHS, Beta $19.98 WAR ⅃⅃

Busted Up A young, hard-luck urban street-fighter battles for the sake of his family and neighborhood against local crimelords.
1986 (R) 93m/C CA Irene Cara, Paul Coufos, Tony Rosato, Stan Shaw, Gordon Judges; **D:** Conrad Palmisano. VHS, Beta $79.95 MCA ⅃

Buster The story of Buster Edwards, the one suspect in the 1963 Great Train Robbery who evaded being captured by police. Collins makes his screen debut as one of Britain's most infamous criminals. Collins also performs on the film's soundtrack, spawning two hit singles, "Two Hearts" and "Groovy Kind of Love."
1988 (R) 102m/C GB Phil Collins, Julie Walters, Larry Lamb, Stephanie Lawrence, Ellen Beaven, Michael Atwell, Ralph Brown, Christopher Ellison, Sheila Hancock; **D:** David Green. VHS, Beta, LV $89.95 HBO ⅃⅃ ½

Buster and Billie Tragedy ensues when a popular high school student falls in love with the class tramp in rural Georgia in 1948. Serious, decently appointed period teen drama.
1974 (R) 100m/C Jan-Michael Vincent, Joan Goodfellow, Clifton James, Pamela Sue Martin, Robert Englund; **D:** Daniel Petrie. VHS, Beta $59.95 COL ⅃ ½

Buster Keaton Festival, Vol. 1 A collection of three Keaton silent shorts from 1921-1922: "Paleface," "The Blacksmith" and "Cops." All shorts have a newly composed musical score.
1922 55m/B Buster Keaton. VHS, Beta $19.95 VDM ⅃ ½

Buster Keaton Festival, Vol. 2 Three rare silent shorts featuring the great comic: "The Boat," "Frozen North," and "Electric House."
1923 55m/B Buster Keaton. VHS, Beta $19.95 VDM ⅃ ½

Buster Keaton Festival, Vol. 3 Three more rare silent shorts with Keaton: "Daydreams," "The Balloonatic," and "The Garage," also featuring Fatty Arbuckle.

1920 54m/B Buster Keaton. VHS, Beta $19.95 VDM ⅃ ½

Buster Keaton Rides Again/The Railroader "The Railroader" is a silent comedy short that returns Buster Keaton to the type of slapstick he made famous in his legendary 1920's films. "Buster Keaton Rides Again" (in black-and-white) is a documentary-style look at Keaton filmed during the making of "The Railroader." Besides scenes of Keaton at work, there is also a capsule rundown of his career.
1965 81m/C Buster Keaton. VHS, Beta, LV $29.95 GPV ⅃ ½

Buster Keaton: The Golden Years Features three classic Buster Keaton silent shorts, "The Pale Face," "Daydreams," and "The Blacksmith," all from 1921.
1921 60m/B Buster Keaton. VHS, Beta $29.95 DVT, HEG ⅃ ½

Buster Keaton: The Great Stone Face Program from the Rohauer Collection contains footage of Buster Keaton in "Fatty at Coney Island," "Cops," "Balloonatics," "Day Dreams," and "The General."
1968 60m/B Buster Keaton. VHS, Beta $57.95 MAS ⅃ ½

Bustin' Loose A fast-talking ex-con reluctantly drives a bus load of misplaced kids and their keeper cross-country.
1981 (R) 94m/C Richard Pryor, Cicely Tyson, Robert Christian, George Coe, Bill Quinn; **D:** Oz Scott. VHS, Beta, LV $14.95 MCA ⅃⅃⅃

Busting Gould and Blake play a pair of slightly off-the-wall L.A. cops. The pair are forced "to bust" local addicts and prostitutes instead of the real crime bosses because much of the police department is on the take. Plenty of comedy and action as well as highly realistic drama.
1974 (R) 92m/C Elliott Gould, Robert (Bobby) Blake, Allen Garfield, Antonio Fargas, Michael Lerner, Sid Haig, Cornelia Sharpe; **D:** Peter Hyams. VHS $14.95 MGM, MCA ⅃⅃ ½

But Not for Me Gable stars as a middled-aged entertainment executive who thinks he can forestall maturity by carrying on with his youthful secretary.
1959 105m/B Clark Gable, Carroll Baker, Lilli Palmer, Lee J. Cobb, Barry Coe, Thomas Gomez, Charles Lane; **D:** Walter Lang. VHS $14.95 PAR ⅃⅃ ½

But Where Is Daniel Wax? At a class reunion, a doctor and a popular singing star reminisce about their youth and Daniel Wax, their one-time hero. Hebrew with English subtitles.
1974 95m/C Lior Yaeni, Michael Lipkin, Esther Zevko; **D:** Avram Heffner. VHS, Beta $79.95 ERG, TAM ⅃⅃

Butch and Sundance: The Early Days Traces the origins of the famous outlaw duo. It contains the requisite shoot-outs, hold-ups, and escapes. A "prequel" to "Butch Cassidy and the Sundance Kid."
1979 (PG) 111m/C Tom Berenger, William Katt, John Schuck, Jeff Corey, Jill Eikenberry, Brian Dennehy, Peter Weller; **D:** Richard Lester. VHS, Beta $19.98 FOX ⅃⅃ ½

Butch Cassidy and the Sundance Kid A couple of legendary outlaws at the turn of the century take it on the lam with a beautiful, willing ex-school teacher. With a clever script, humanly fallible characters, and warm, witty dialogue, this film was destined to become a box-office classic. Featured the hit song, "Raindrops Keep Falling on My Head" and renewed the buddy film industry, as Newman and Redford

trade insult for insult. Look for the great scene where Newman takes on giant Ted Cassidy in a fist fight.
1969 (PG) 110m/C Paul Newman, Robert Redford, Katharine Ross, Jeff Corey, Strother Martin, Cloris Leachman, Kenneth Mars, Ted Cassidy, Sam Elliott; **D:** George Roy Hill; **W:** William Goldman; **M:** Burt Bacharach. Academy Awards '69: Best Cinematography, Best Song ("Raindrops Keep Fallin' on My Head"), Best Story & Screenplay, Best Original Score; Nominations: Best Director (Hill), Best Picture, Best Sound; British Academy Awards '70: Best Actor (Redford), Best Actress (Ross), Best Director (Hill), Best Film. VHS, Beta, LV $19.98 FOX, TLF ⅃⅃ ½

The Butcher's Wife Charming tale of a young psychic who brings romance to a Greenwich Village neighborhood that never quite gets off the ground. Moore stars as the clairvoyant whose mystical powers bring magic into the lives of everyone around her, including the local psychiatrist (Daniels), who falls under her spell. Talented cast is virtually wasted with a script that is lightweight; excepting Steenburger and Dzundza who shine.
1991 (PG-13) 107m/C Demi Moore, Jeff Daniels, George Dzundza, Frances McDormand, Margaret Colin, Mary Steenburgen, Max Perlich, Miriam Margolyes, Christopher Durang, Diane Salinger; **D:** Terry Hughes; **W:** Ezra Litwack, Marjorie Schwartz; **M:** Michael Gore, Michael Gore. VHS, Beta, LV $19.95 PAR ⅃⅃

Butler's Dilemma A jewel thief and a playboy both claim the identity of a butler who never existed, with humorous results.
1943 75m/B GB Richard Hearne, Francis L. Sullivan, Hermione Gingold, Ian Fleming. VHS, Beta $29.95 VYY, TIM ⅃⅃

Butterfield 8 A seedy film of the John O'Hara novel about a prostitute that wants to go straight and settle down. Taylor won an Oscar, perhaps because she was ill and had lost in the two previous years in more deserving roles.
1960 108m/C Elizabeth Taylor, Laurence Harvey, Eddie Fisher, Dina Merrill, Mildred Dunnock, Betty Field, Susan Oliver, Kay Medford; **D:** Daniel Mann. Academy Awards '60: Best Actress (Taylor); Nominations: Best Color Cinematography. VHS, Beta, LV $19.98 MGM, PIA, BTV ⅃⅃⅃

Butterflies Ria, a middle-aged housewife with two lazy sons, is beginning to feel her age, and like a butterfly, feeling like she has too much to do and not enough time. Then Leonard appears in her life—divorced, lonely and romantic. Made for British television.
1975 60m/C GB VHS $29.95 BFS ⅃⅃⅃

Butterflies Are Free Fast-paced humor surrounds the Broadway play brought to the big screen. Blind youth Albert is determined to be self-sufficient. A next-door-neighbor actress helps him gain independence from his over-protective mother (Heckart).
1972 (PG) 109m/C Goldie Hawn, Edward Albert, Eileen Heckart, Michael Glaser; **D:** Milton Katselas. Academy Awards '72: Best Supporting Actress (Heckart); Nominations: Best Cinematography, Best Sound. VHS, Beta $9.95 GKK ⅃⅃⅃

Butterfly Based on James M. Cain's novel about an amoral young woman (Pia, who'd you think?) who uses her beauty and sensual appetite to manipulate the men in her life, including her father. Set in Nevada of the 1930s, father and daughter are drawn into a daring and forbidden love affair by their lust and desperation.

1982 (R) 105m/C Pia Zadora, Stacy Keach, Orson Welles, Edward Albert, James Franciscus, Lois Nettleton, Stuart Whitman, June Lockhart; *D:* Matt Cimber; *M:* Ennio Morricone. **VHS, Beta, LV** $79.95 *VES, LIV* ✂✂ ½

Butterfly Affair Beautiful singer, involved in a scheme to smuggle two million dollars worth of gems, plots to double-cross her partners in crime.
1971 (PG) 75m/C Claudia Cardinale, Henri Charriere, Stanley Baker; *D:* Jean Herman. **VHS, Beta** *PGN* ✂✂ ½

Butterfly Ball This retelling of the 19th century classic combines the rock music of Roger Glover, live action and animation by Halas and Batchelor. Only for the brain-cell depressed.
1976 85m/C *GB* Twiggy, Ian Gillian, David Coverdale; *D:* Tony Klinger. **VHS, Beta** *NO* ✂

Buy & Cell A stockbroker attempts to set up a business while serving a prison sentence. An assortment of amusing inmates doesn't help matters much. Fans of Malcolm McDowell will enjoy his performance as the shady warden.
1989 (R) 95m/C Robert Carradine, Michael Winslow, Malcolm McDowell, Ben Vereen, Lise Cutter, Randall "Tex" Cobb, Roddy Piper; *D:* Robert Boris. **VHS, LV** $19.95 *STE, NWV* ✂ ½

Buying Time Two teenagers are arrested when they try to pry their money away from a dishonest bookie, and the police use their connections to solve a drug-related murder.
1989 (R) 97m/C Dean Stockwell, Jeff Schultz, Michael Rudder, Tony De Santis, Leslie Toth, Laura Cruickshank; *D:* Mitchell Gabourie. **VHS, Beta** $79.95 *FOX* ✂

Buzzy Rides the Range Average "B" western with a kid saving the day.
1940 ?m/C Robert "Buzzy" Henry, Dave O'Brien. **VHS** $15.95 *LOO* ✂

By Dawn's Early Light Made-for-cable-TV thriller about two Air Force pilots who must decide whether or not to drop the bombs that would begin World War III.
1989 100m/C Powers Boothe, Rebecca DeMornay, James Earl Jones, Martin Landau, Rip Torn, Darren McGavin; *D:* Jack Sholder. **VHS, Beta, LV** $89.99 *HBO* ✂✂

By Design Two cohabiting women want to have a baby, so they embark on a search for the perfect stud. Not one of Astin's better performances.
1982 (R) 90m/C *CA* Patty Duke, Sara Botsford; *D:* Claude Jutra. **VHS, Beta** $59.99 *HBO* ✂

By Hook or Crook Zany Mexican comedy/mystery featuring the "Super-Mexican" detective solving a series of high-society murders.
1985 94m/C *MX* Rafael Inclan, Maribel Guardia; *D:* Julio Ruiz Llaneza. **VHS, Beta** $72.95 *MED* ✂

By Love Possessed Can a seemingly typical, quiet, New England town stay quiet when Lana Turner is your neighbor? Vintage romantic melodrama about an attorney who is drawn into an affair when he realizes his home life is not all it could be.
1961 115m/C Lana Turner, Efrem Zimbalist Jr., Jason Robards Jr., George Hamilton, Thomas Mitchell; *D:* John Sturges. **VHS** $14.95 *MGM* ✂✂ ½

By the Blood of Others In a small French town, a psycho holds two women hostage in a farmhouse, and the townspeople try to figure out a solution without getting anyone killed. In French with English subtitles.
1973 90m/C *FR* Mariangela Melato; *D:* Marc Simenon. **VHS, Beta** $59.95 *FCT* ✂✂✂

By the Light of the Silvery Moon The equally old-fashioned sequel to "On Moonlight Bay" finds Day engaged to MacRae, who's just returned from Army service in WWI. He wants to postpone their marriage until he gets financially secure and the waiting causes some jealous misunderstandings (naturally resolved by movie's end). Based on Booth Tarkington's "Penrod" stories. ♫By the Light of the Silvery Moon; I'll Forget You; Your Eyes Have Told Me So; Be My Little Baby Bumble Bee; If You Were the Only Girl in the World; Ain't We Got Fun; King Chanticleer.
1953 101m/C Doris Day, Gordon MacRae, Leon Ames, Billy Gray, Rosemary DeCamp, Mary Wickes, Russell Arms, Maria Palmer; *D:* David Butler; *W:* Robert O'Brien, Irving Elinson; *M:* Max Steiner. **VHS, LV** $59.95 *WAR* ✂✂ ½

Bye Bye Baby Two luscious young women cavort amid lusty Italian men on various Mediterranean beaches.
1988 (R) 80m/C Carol Alt, Brigitte Nielsen, Jason Connery, Luca Barbareschi; *D:* Enrico Oldoini. **VHS, Beta, LV** $79.95 *PSM, PAR* ✂

Bye, Bye, Birdie Energized and sweet film version of the Broadway musical about a teen rock and roll idol (Pearson doing Elvis) coming to a small town to see one of his fans before he leaves for the army. The film that made Ann-Margret a star. ♫Bye Bye Birdie; The Telephone Hour; How Lovely to be a Woman; Honestly Sincere; One Boy; Put on a Happy Face; Kids; One Last Kiss; A Lot of Livin' to Do; Rosie.
1963 112m/C Dick Van Dyke, Janet Leigh, Ann-Margret, Paul Lynde, Bobby Rydell, Maureen Stapleton, Ed Sullivan, Trudi Ames; *D:* George Sidney. **VHS, Beta, LV** $19.95 *COL* ✂✂✂

Bye Bye Blues The lives of the Cooper family are disrupted when the husband is called to service during WWII and is then taken prisoner by the Japanese. In need of money, wife Daisy (Jenkins) joins a local swing band and begins charming all who watch her, especially the band's trombone player (Reilly). A sweet-spirited tale of love, loyalty, and the search for inner strength. Jenkins gives a strong performance as the shy wife who becomes an independent woman during her husband's absence.
1989 (PG) 110m/C *CA* Rebecca Jenkins, Michael Ontkean, Luke Reilly, Stuart Margolin, Robyn Stevan, Kate Reid, Wayne Robson; *W/D:* Anne Wheeler; *M:* George Blondheim. **VHS** $29.95 *MNC* ✂✂ ½

Bye Bye Brazil A changing Brazil is seen through the eyes of four wandering gypsy minstrels participating in a tent show traveling throughout the country. Lots of Brazilian charm. Subtitled in English.
1979 100m/C *BR* Jose Wilker, Betty Faria, Fabio Junior, Zaira Zambello; *D:* Carlos Diegues. **VHS, Beta, LV** $79.95 *FXL, TAM, UWA* ✂✂ ½

The C-Man Customs agent Jagger finds work isn't so dull after all. Murder and theft on an international scale make for a busy week as he follows jewel smugglers from Paris to New York. Docu-style though routine crime story.
1949 75m/B Dean Jagger, John Carradine, Harry Landers, Rene Paul; *D:* Joseph Lerner. **VHS** $16.95 *SNC* ✂

Cabaret Hitler is rising to power, racism and anti-Semitism are growing, and the best place to hide from it all is the cabaret. With dancing girls, androgynous master of ceremonies Grey and American expatriate and singer Minnelli, you can laugh and drink and pretend tomorrow will never come. Minnelli does just that, meanwhile unknowingly sharing her English lover with a homosexual German baron. Face to face with the increasing horrors of Nazism, she persists in the belief that the "show must go on." Based on the John Kander's hit Broadway musical (taken from the Christopher Isherwood stories), the film is even more impressive with excellent direction and cinematography. ♫Cabaret; Wilkommen; Mein Herr; Maybe This Time; Two Ladies; Money, Money; Hieraten; Tomorrow Belongs to Me; If You Could See Her.
1972 (PG) 119m/C Liza Minnelli, Joel Grey, Michael York, Marisa Berenson; *D:* Bob Fosse; *W:* Jay Presson Allen. Academy Awards '72: Best Actress (Minnelli), Best Art Direction/Set Decoration, Best Cinematography, Best Director (Fosse), Best Film Editing, Best Sound, Best Supporting Actor (Grey), Best Score; Nominations: Best Adapted Screenplay, Best Picture; British Academy Awards '72: Best Actress (Minnelli), Best Director (Fosse), Best Film; Golden Globe Awards '73: Best Actress—Musical/Comedy (Minnelli), Best Film—Musical/Comedy, Best Supporting Actor (Grey). **VHS, Beta, LV** $19.98 *FOX, BTV, CCB* ✂✂✂

The Cabin in the Cotton Davis stars as a rich, ruthless Southern belle in this dated melodrama about sharecroppers. Barthelmess is cast as a poor sharecropper who is almost brought to ruin when he falls for the sexy Southern vamp. Contains Davis's most famous line, "Ah'd love t'kiss you, but ah jes washed mah hair."
1932 77m/B Bette Davis, Richard Barthelmess, Dorothy Jordan, Henry B. Walthall, Tully Marshall; *D:* Michael Curtiz; *W:* Paul Green. **VHS** $19.98 *MGM* ✂✂ ½

Cabin in the Sky A poor woman fights to keep her husband's soul out of the devil's clutches. Based on a Broadway show and featuring an all-Black cast. Lively dance numbers and a musical score by Harold Arlen and E.Y. Harburg, with contributions from Duke Ellington. Minnelli's first feature film. ♫Cabin in the Sky; Happiness Is Just a Thing Called Joe; Taking a Chance on Love; Life's Full of Consequence; Li'l Black Sheep; Shine; Honey in the Honeycomb.
1943 99m/C Ethel Waters, Eddie Anderson, Lena Horne, Rex Ingram, Louis Armstrong, Duke Ellington; *D:* Vincente Minnelli. **VHS, Beta, LV** $19.98 *MGM, MLB, FHE* ✂✂✂

The Cabinet of Dr. Caligari A pioneering film in the most extreme expressionistic style about a hypnotist in a carnival and a girl-snatching somnambulist. Highly influential in its approach to lighting, composition, design and acting. Much imitated. Silent.
1919 52m/B *GE* Conrad Veidt, Werner Krauss, Lil Dagover; *D:* Robert Wiene. **VHS, Beta, LV, 3/4U,** Special order formats $16.95 *SNC, REP, MRV* ✂✂✂✂

Cabiria The pioneering Italian epic about a Roman and a slave girl having a love affair in Rome during the Second Punic War. Immense sets and set-pieces; an important influence on Griffith and DeMille. Silent.
1914 123m/B *IT* Giovanni Pastrone; *D:* Giovanni Pastrone. **VHS, Beta, 8mm** $39.95 *KIV, FCT, TAM* ✂✂ ½

Cabo Blanco A bartender and a variety of other characters, including an ex-Nazi and a French woman searching for her lover, assemble in Peru after WWII. Nazi Robards controls police chief Rey, while American Bronson runs the local watering hole and eyes French woman Sanda. Hey, this sounds familiar. Everyone shares a common interest: finding a missing treasure of gold, lost in a ship wreck. Remaking "Casablanca" via "The Treasure of Sierra Madre" is never easy.

1981 (R) 87m/C Charles Bronson, Jason Robards Jr., Dominique Sanda, Fernando Rey, Gilbert Roland, Simon MacCorkindale; **D:** J. Lee Thompson; **M:** Jerry Goldsmith. **VHS, Beta** $59.95 MED ✻✻

Caches de Oro A routine arrest turns into the bloodiest case of a federal judge's career.
19?? 90m/C *MX* Alvaro Zermeno, Fernando Casanova, Tony Bravo, Patsy Pepping. **VHS, Beta** $79.95 MED ✻✻

Cactus Melodrama about a young French woman, separated from her husband, who faces the reality of losing her sight after a car accident. She experiences a growing relationship with a blind man and contemplates the thought of risky surgery which may improve her eyesight or cause complete blindness. Countering all that blindness and tangled romance is a camera that pans lush Australian landscapes and humorously focuses on the small telling details of daily life.
1986 95m/C *AU* Isabelle Huppert, Robert Menzies, Monica Maughan, Sheila Florence; **D:** Paul Cox. **VHS, Beta** $19.98 LHV ✻✻½

Cactus Flower Good cast doesn't quite suffice to make this adaptation of a Broadway hit work. A middle-aged bachelor dentist gets involved with a kookie mistress, refusing to admit his real love for his prim and proper receptionist. Hawn's big leap to stardom.
1969 (PG) 103m/C Walter Matthau, Goldie Hawn, Ingrid Bergman, Jack Weston, Rick Lenz; **D:** Gene Saks. **VHS, Beta, LV** $14.95 COL ✻✻

Cactus in the Snow A virginal Army private serving during the Vietnam War era tries to find sex on a 72-hour leave and instead discovers love. Some guys have all the luck. Melodrama never grabs where it ought to.
1972 90m/C Richard Thomas, Mary Layne, Lucille Benson; **D:** Martin Zweiback. **VHS, Beta, LV** NO ✻½

Cada Noche un Amor A singer is deceived into working as a harem girl for rich Arabs. **AKA:** Every Night a New Lover.
1975 90m/C *SP* Sara Montiel, Fernando Graney. **VHS, Beta** MAD ✻

Caddie Based on an autobiographical story of a woman who leaves her unfaithful husband in 1930s Australia. Struggling to raise her two children, she works as a waitress in a bar where she finds romance with one of the regulars. Average script bolstered by Morse's performance.
1981 107m/C Helen Morse, Jack Thompson; **D:** Donald Crombie. **VHS, Beta** $59.95 HBO ✻✻½

The Caddy Lewis plays frantic caddy prone to slapstick against Martin's smooth professional golfer with a bent toward singing. Mostly a series of Martin and Lewis sketches that frequently land in the rough. Introduces several songs, including a classic Martin and Lewis rendition of "That's Amore." Look for cameos by a host of professional golfers.
1953 95m/C Dean Martin, Jerry Lewis, Donna Reed, Barbara Bates, Joseph Calleia, Marshall Thompson, Fred Clark; **Cameos:** Ben Hogan, Sam Snead, Byron Nelson, Julius Boros, Jimmy Thomson, Harry E. Cooper; **D:** Norman Taurog. **VHS, Beta** $14.95 PAR ✻✻

Caddyshack Inspired performances by Murray and Dangerfield drive this sublimely moronic comedy onto the green. Does for golf what "Major League" tried to do for baseball. The action takes place at Bushwood Country Club, where young clean-cut caddy O'Keefe is bucking to win the club's college scholarship. Characters involved in various sophomoric set pieces include obnoxious club president Knight, a playboy who is too laid back to keep his score (Chase), a loud, vulgar, extremely rich golfer (Dangerfield), and Murray as a filthy gopher-hunting groundskeeper. Occasional dry moments are followed by scenes of pure (and tasteless) anarchy, so watch it with someone immature. Gopher holes will never again be the same.
1980 (R) 99m/C Chevy Chase, Rodney Dangerfield, Ted Knight, Michael O'Keefe, Bill Murray, Sarah Holcomb, Brian Doyle-Murray; **W/D:** Harold Ramis; **W:** Brian Doyle-Murray, Doug Kenney. **VHS, Beta, LV** $19.98 WAR ✻✻✻½

Caddyshack 2 The obligatory sequel to "Caddyshack," although Bill Murray wisely avoided further encroachment of gopher holes and director Harold Ramis opted for screenwriting chores only. Mason is the star of the show as a crude self-made millionaire who tangles with the snobs at the country club. Although it occasionally earns a side-splitting chuckle, "Shack 2" has significantly fewer guffaws than the original, proving once again that funny guys are always undone by lousy scripts and weak direction.
1988 (PG) 103m/C Jackie Mason, Chevy Chase, Dan Aykroyd, Dyan Cannon, Robert Stack, Dina Merrill, Randy Quaid, Jessica Lundy, Jonathan Silverman, Chynna Phillips; **D:** Allan Arkush; **W:** Harold Ramis, Peter Torokvei. **VHS, Beta, LV, 8mm** $19.98 WAR ✻✻

Cadence The directorial debut of actor Martin Sheen, this fitful melodrama stars son Charlie as an unruly trooper on a 1960s army base. Placed in an all-black stockade for punishment, he bonds with his brother prisoners by defying the hardcase sergeant (played by Sheen the elder). Characters and situations are intriguing but not rendered effectively. Based on the novel "Count a Lonely Cadence" by Gordon Weaver.
1989 (PG-13) 97m/C Charlie Sheen, Martin Sheen, Larry Fishburne, Michael Beach, Ramon Estevez; **D:** Martin Sheen. **VHS, LV** $14.98 REP, PIA ✻✻

Cadillac Man Williams is the quintessential low-life car salesman in this rather disjointed comedy. A lesser comedic talent might have stalled and been abandoned, but Williams manages to drive away despite the flat script and direction. One storyline follows his attempt to sell 12 cars in 12 days or lose his job, while another follows his confrontation with a gun-toting, mad-as-hell cuckolded husband. Williams and Robbins are often close to being funny in a hyperkinetic way, but the situations are dumb enough to rob most of the scenes of their comedy. Watch for a movie-stealing bit by the spunky waitress at the local Chinese restaurant.
1990 (R) 95m/C Robin Williams, Tim Robbins, Pamela Reed, Fran Drescher, Zack Norman, Annabella Sciorra, Lori Petty, Paul Guilfoyle; **D:** Roger Donaldson. **VHS, Beta, LV** $14.98 ORI ✻✻

Caesar and Cleopatra Based on the classic George Bernard Shaw play. Caesar meets the beautiful Cleopatra in ancient Egypt and helps her gain control of her life. Remains surprisingly true to Shaw's adaptation, unlike many other historical films of the same era.
1946 135m/C *GB* Claude Rains, Vivien Leigh, Stewart Granger, Flora Robson, Francis L. Sullivan, Cecil Parker; **D:** Gabriel Pascal. **VHS, Beta** $29.95 VID ✻✻½

Cafe Express A con artist (he sells coffee illegally aboard an Italian train) stays one step ahead of the law as he raises money to help his ailing son. As in "Bread and Chocolate," Manfredi is again the put-upon working class hero comedically attempting to find a better way of life in this bittersweet tale.
1983 90m/C *IT* Nino Manfredi, Gigi Reder, Adolfo Celi, Vittorio Mezzogiorno; **D:** Nanni Loy. **VHS, Beta** PGN ✻✻½

Cafe Romeo Sweet story of friendship that revolves around a New York City neighborhood coffeehouse. Stewart is Lia, a waitress who dreams of becoming a fashion designer, but is held back from her aspirations by her small-minded husband.
1991 (R) 93m/C Catherine Mary Stewart, Jonathan Crombie; **D:** Rex Bromfield. **VHS, LV** $89.98 REP ✻

The Cage Gangsters enlist a brain-damaged Vietnam vet played by Ferrigno to participate in illegal "cage fights," enclosed wrestling matches fought to the death. Crude and annoying.
1989 (R) 101m/C Lou Ferrigno, Reb Brown, Michael Dante, Mike Moroff, Marilyn Tokuda, James Shigeta, Al Ruscio; **D:** Hugh Kelley. **VHS, Beta, LV** $14.98 ORI ✻

The Cage Sent to prison for murdering his girlfriend, Jive has no idea what the pen has in store for him. The inmates stage a mock trial, the defendant is found guilty and the sentence is too horrible to imagine. From a stage play by the San Quentin Drama Workshop and co-starring Hayes, author of "Midnight Express."
1990 90m/C Rick Cluchey, William Hayes; **W/D:** Rick Cluchey. **VHS, Beta** NO ✻✻✻

Caged Fear Young Krissie (Cloke) is mistakenly put behind bars in a brutal, high-security prison for a shootout caused by her outlaw husband Tommy (Keith) during their honeymoon. Tommy comes up with an outrageous scheme to rescue her. Not quite as bad as it sounds, but close.
1992 (R) 94m/C David Keith, Deborah May, Ray Sharkey, Loretta Devine, Karen Black, Kristen Cloke; **W/D:** Bobby Houston. **VHS, LV** $89.95 NLC ✻✻½

Caged Fury American women being held captive in Southeast Asia are brainwashed into becoming walking time bombs. Yes, that dame's gonna blow. Made in the Philippines with the best of intentions.
1980 (R) 90m/C *PH* Bernadette Williams, Taffee O'Connell, Jennifer Laine; **D:** Cirio H. Santiago. **VHS, Beta** NO ✻

Caged Fury Two Los Angeles women allegedly commit sexual crimes and are sent to prison. Cheap, exploitive women's prison rehash.
1990 85m/C Erik Estrada, Richie Barathy, Roxanna Michaels, Paul Smith, James Hong, Greg Cummins; **D:** Bill Milling. **VHS, Beta, LV** $79.95 COL ✻

Caged Heart According to some cinematic code, the male lead always gets in lots of trouble whenever he tries to help a beautiful stranger. This time, Berry, as Bruno Windler, winds up arrested for shoplifting when he attempts to help Abril. Jailed and on the verge of parole, Windler unwittingly becomes involved in a prison break and is accused of helping a crime don mastermind the escape and of shooting a guard. That's where that gallic flair for capturing the sadomasochistic underbelly of humanity comes in, as Windler is viciously pursued by the malevolent guard. **AKA:** The Patsy.
1985 (R) 85m/C Richard Berry, Victoria Abril, Richard Bohringer, Farid Chopel, Fabrice Eberhard; **D:** Denis Amar. **VHS, Beta** $19.95 STE, NWV ✻✻½

Caged Heat A low-budget babes-behind-bars film that's been screened by The Museum of Modern Art and the New York Collective for the Living Cinema? And touted as the best sexploitation film of the day, produced by New World, a renowned sex'n'violence shop? Not to mention that it's got a theme dubbed by William ("Naked Lunch") Burroughs as "technological psychiatry;" now that's something wild. Demme scripted and made his directorial debut with this genre-altering installment in Roger Corman's formulaic cellblock Cinderella cycle. What's new isn't the plot—an innocent woman is put behind bars, where she loses some of her innocence—but in the treatment of an historically misogynistic genre (not to mention that this all takes place in the US of A, not some vaguely third world never-neverland). These babes may wear hot pants and gratuitously bare their midriffs, but they're not brainless bimbos whose fate is dictated by he-men. Rather, they're strong individuals who work (brace yourself) together to liberate themselves. Not that Demme didn't make any artistic compromises: there are some major lapses in artistic integrity. But the film owes its cult status to its ability to set the genre akimbo and to its ironic refusal (well, most of the time) to be exploitative. Blues music by John Cale; also known as "Renegade Girls." Cult diva Steele returned to the big screen after a six-year hiatus to play the wheelchair-ridden prison warden, a part written specifically for her. *AKA:* Renegade Girls; Caged Females.
1974 (R) 83m/C Juanita Brown, Erica Gavin, Roberta Collins, Barbara Steele, Ella Reid, Cheryl "Rainbeaux" Smith; **W/D:** Jonathan Demme. **VHS** SUE, NWV 🎬🎬½

Caged in Paradiso A convicted criminal and his wife are dumped onto a remote prisoner's isle to live out their lives. When Cara loses contact with her husband, she must fend for herself. Survival tale boringly told.
1989 (R) 90m/C Irene Cara; **D:** Michael Snyder. **VHS, Beta, LV $79.95** VMK, IME 🎬½

Caged Terror Two urbanites hit the countryside for a weekend and meet a band of crazy rapists who ravage the wife and set the husband raging with bloodthirsty revenge. Squalid stroll through the ruins.
1972 76m/C Percy Harkness, Elizabeth Suzuki, Leon Morenzie. **VHS, Beta $59.95** NWV Woof!

Caged Women Undercover journalist enters a women's prison and gets the usual eyeful. *AKA:* Women's Penitentiary 4.
1984 (R) 97m/C FR IT Laura Gemser, Gabriele Tinti, Lorraine De Selle, Maria Romano; **D:** Vincent Dawn. **VHS, Beta $69.95** VES, LIV, PHX 🎬

Cahill: United States Marshal The aging Duke in one of his lesser moments, portraying a marshal who comes to the aid of his sons. The boys are mixed up with a gang of outlaws, proving that no matter how good a parent you are, sometimes the kids just lean toward the wayward. Turns out, though, that the boys harbor a grudge against the old man due to years of workaholic neglect. Will Duke see the error of his ways and reconcile with the delinquent boys? Will he catch the outlaw leader? Will he go on to star in other Duke vehicles?
1973 (PG) 103m/C John Wayne, Gary Grimes, George Kennedy, Neville Brand, Marie Windsor, Harry Carey Jr.; **D:** Andrew V. McLaglen. **VHS, Beta, LV $19.98** WAR, PIA, TLF 🎬🎬

The Caine Mutiny A group of naval officers revolt against a captain they consider mentally unfit. Bogart is masterful as Captain Queeg, obsessed with cleanliness while onboard and later a study in mental meltdown during the court-martial of a crew member who participated in the mutiny. Based on the Pulitzer-winning novel by Herman Wouk, the drama takes a close look at the pressure-filled life aboard ship during WWII.
1954 125m/C Humphrey Bogart, Jose Ferrer, Van Johnson, Fred MacMurray, Lee Marvin, Claude Akins, E.G. Marshall; **D:** Edward Dmytryk. **VHS, Beta, LV, 8mm $19.95** COL, HMV 🎬🎬🎬🎬

The Caine Mutiny Court Martial A young lieutenant is up for a court-martial after taking control of the U.S.S. Caine in the midst of a typhoon. In order to save him, his lawyer must discredit the paranoid Commander Queeg. As the events of the mutiny unfold, it becomes clear that Queeg's obsession with discipline had become a threat to everyone aboard. Good performances, particularly by Bogosian as the lawyer. Based on the Pulitzer Prize-winning novel by Herman Wouk. Made for television.
1988 (PG) 100m/C Jeff Daniels, Eric Bogosian, Brad Davis, Peter Gallagher, Michael Murphy, Kevin J. O'Connor, Daniel H. Jenkins; **D:** Robert Altman. **VHS, LV $89.95** VMK 🎬🎬🎬

Cain's Cutthroats A former Confederate army captain and a bounty hunting preacher team up to settle the score with soldiers on a gang-raping, murdering spree. *AKA:* Cain's Way; The Blood Seekers.
1971 (R) 87m/C Scott Brady, John Carradine, Robert Dix. **VHS, Beta $19.95** GHV, TIM 🎬

Cajon Pass A group of trains challenges the terrain attempting to go through Cajon Pass into Los Angeles.
1988 60m/C VHS, Beta $49.95 VRL 🎬🎬

Cal A young Catholic man is recruited into the Irish Republican Army. He falls in love with an older Protestant widow, whose husband, a policeman, he helped kill, acting as the get-away driver for his fellow Republicans. Thoughtful and tragic, with excellent performances; set in Northern Ireland. Musical score by Mark Knopfler.
1984 (R) 104m/C IR Helen Mirren, John Lynch, Donal McCann, Kitty Gibson, Ray McAnally, John Kavanagh; **D:** Pat O'Connor. **VHS, Beta $19.98** WAR, FCT, TAM 🎬🎬🎬

Calacan A non-human settlement filled with culture and tradition fears only the living in this family musical.
1979 ?m/C MX Mauro Mendonca, Sylvia Guevara, Dora Montiel. **VHS, Beta** NO 🎬🎬🎬

Calamity Jane In one of her best Warner musicals, Day stars as the rip-snortin', gun-totin' Calamity Jane of Western lore. Her on-again, off-again romance with Wild Bill Hickok is set to the songs of Fain and Webster. ♫Secret Love; Just Blew in From the Windy City; The Black Hills of Dakota; The Deadwood Stage (Whip-Crack-Away!).
1953 101m/C Doris Day, Howard Keel, Allyn Ann McLerie; **D:** David Butler; **M:** Sammy Fain, Paul Francis Webster. Academy Awards '53: Best Song ("Secret Love"); Nominations: Best Sound, Best Original Score. **VHS, Beta, LV $19.98** WAR, PIA, FCT 🎬🎬🎬

Calamity Jane A made-for-television biography of the famous lady crack shot. Alexander is cast as the tough-as-nails woman who considered herself on a par with any man.
1982 96m/C Jane Alexander, Frederic Forrest, Ken Kercheval, Talia Balsam, David Hemmings; **D:** James Goldstone. **VHS, Beta $19.98** FOX 🎬🎬½

Calendar Girl In 1962 three best friends decide to travel to Hollywood to meet their pinup idol, Marilyn Monroe.
1993 (PG-13) 86m/C Jason Priestly, Gabriel Olds, Jerry O'Connell, Joe Pantoliano, Stephen Tobolowsky, Kurt Fuller, Susan Griffiths, J.S. York, Curt Truman; **D:** John Whitesell; **W:** Tom Priestley. **VHS** NYR 🎬🎬

California Casanova Mirthless, semi-musical farce about a nerdy stagehand learning to be a great lover to win a beautiful singer's heart who's being blackmailed by a cruel gangster. Nice cast; nobody's home.
1989 (R) 94m/C Jerry Orbach, Audrey Landers, Tyrone Power Jr., Bryan Genesse, Ken Kercheval, Ted Davis, Joyce Blair; **W/D:** Nathaniel Christian. **VHS $19.95** ACA Woof!

California Dreaming Nerdy young man heads west to California where he tries to fit in with the local beach crowd. Reminiscent of the popular beach movies of the '60s.
1979 (R) 93m/C Dennis Christopher, Tanya Roberts, Glynnis O'Connor, John Calvin, Seymour Cassel; **D:** John Hancock. **VHS, Beta $69.95** VES, LIV 🎬🎬

California Girls Radio station stages a beauty contest and three sexy ladies prove to be tough competition. Features women in little swimsuits, minimal plot, and a soundtrack by the Police, Kool & the Gang, Blondie, Queen, and 10cc.
1984 83m/C Al Music, Mary McKinley, Alicia Allen, Lantz Douglas, Barbara Parks; **D:** Rick Wallace. **VHS, Beta** NO 🎬

California Gold Rush Hays portrays young aspiring writer, Bret Harte, who, in search of adventure in 1849, arrives in Sutter's Fort and takes on a job at the local sawmill. When gold is found, Sutter's Fort is soon overrun with fortune hunters whose greed, violence and corruption threaten to tear apart the peaceful community. Made for television.
1981 100m/C Robert Hays, John Dehner, Dan Haggerty, Ken Curtis; **D:** Jack B. Hively. **VHS, Beta** NO 🎬🎬

California Joe California is being eyed by Confederate sympathizers and also by their leader, who wants it for his own plans. Enter California Joe, a Union officer in disguise, who will save the day. Standard western.
1943 55m/B Donald (Don "Red") Barry, Lynn Merrick, Helen Talbot. **VHS, Beta $24.95** DVT 🎬

California Straight Ahead Denny—whose niche in the twenties was silent action comedies, and who had teamed with director Pollard earlier in the decade to produce "The Leatherpushers" series—stars in this silent actioner which features a cross-country road trip, zoo animals-on-a-rampage, and a car-racing conclusion (sounds like an action formula ahead of its time). Audiences didn't realize until the talkies that the All-American manly man was in fact played by a Brit. For those who revel in trivia, Denny appeared in the 1991 "Batman."
1925 77m/B Reginald Denny, Gertrude Olmsted, Tom Wilson, Lucille Ward, John Steppling; **D:** Harry Pollard. **VHS, Beta $24.95** GPV, FCT 🎬🎬

California Suite The posh Beverly Hills Hotel is the setting for four unrelated Neil Simon skits, ranging from a battling husband and wife to feuding friends. Simonized dialogue is crisp and funny. Jazz score by Claude Bolling.
1978 (PG) 103m/C Alan Alda, Michael Caine, Bill Cosby, Jane Fonda, Walter Matthau, Richard Pryor, Maggie Smith, Elaine May; **D:** Herbert Ross; **W:** Neil Simon. Academy Awards '78: Best Supporting Actress (Smith); Nominations: Best Adapted Screenplay, Best Art Direction/Set

Decoration; Golden Globe Awards '79: Best Actress—Musical/Comedy (Smith). **VHS, Beta, LV** $14.95 COL 🎬🎬🎬

Caligari's Cure Palazzolo's first film is a satiric, non-narrative stab at his Catholic upbringing via German expressionism and modern performance art.
1982 70m/C D: Tom Palazzolo. **VHS, Beta** FCT 🎬🎬🎬

Caligula Infamous, expensive, extremely graphic, and sexually explicit adaptation of the life of the mad Roman emperor, Caligula. Scenes of decapitation, necrophilia, rape, bestiality, and sadomasochism abound. Biggest question is why Gielgud, O'Toole, and McDowell lent their talents to this monumentally abhorred film (not to mention Gore Vidal on the writing end, who didn't want the credit). Adult magazine publisher Bob Guccione coproduced and didn't particularly want to release it. Also available in a censored, "R" rated version.
1980 143m/C IT Malcolm McDowell, John Gielgud, Peter O'Toole, Helen Mirren; **D:** Tinto Brass. **VHS, Beta, LV** $79.95 VES, HHE **Woof!**

Call Him Mr. Shatter A hired killer stalks a tottering Third World president and becomes embroiled in international political intrigue. **AKA:** Shatter.
1974 (R) 90m/C GB Stuart Whitman, Peter Cushing, Anton Diffring; **D:** Michael Carreras. **VHS, Beta** $59.98 NLC 🎬

Call Me Psycho-drama about a lusty young woman who responds positively to an obscene telephone caller until she witnesses him murder another person. Doubt creeps into the relationship.
1988 (R) 98m/C Patricia Charbonneau, Patti D'Arbanville, Sam Freed, Boyd Gaines, Stephen McHattie; **D:** Sollace Mitchell. **VHS, Beta, LV** $79.98 VES 🎬

Call of the Canyon A crooked agent for a local meat packer won't pay a fair price, so Gene goes off to talk to the head man to set him straight.
1942 71m/B Gene Autry, Smiley Burnette, Ruth Terry, Thurston Hall, Pat Brady; **D:** Joseph Santley. **VHS, Beta** $29.98 CCB, VCN, GPV 🎬1/2

Call of the Forest Bobby makes friends with a beautiful wild black stallion which is captured and tamed by his father. The father has found a goldmine, also desired by an villain, and Bobby and his horse must come to his father's aid. Black Diamond (the horse) has the best role.
1949 74m/B Robert Lowery, Ken Curtis, Martha Sherrill, Chief Thundercloud, Charles Hughes; **D:** John F. Link. **VHS** $19.95 NOS, DVT, VYY 🎬1/2

Call of the Rockies Action-packed oater in which Carson and Burnette ride across country to save Placer City's mine from crooked townsmen.
19?? 54m/B Sunset Carson, Smiley Burnette. **VHS** $9.98 REP 🎬🎬

Call of the Wild Jack London's famous story about a man whose survival depends upon his knowledge of the Alaskan wilderness almost comes to life. Filmed in Finland.
1972 (PG) 105m/C Charlton Heston, Michele Mercier, George Eastman; **D:** Ken Annakin. **VHS, Beta** $14.95 KUI, SIM, MPI 🎬🎬

Call of the Wild Adaptation of the Jack London story about a dog's trek across the Alaskan tundra.
1983 68m/C VHS, Beta $29.98 VES, LIV, WTA 🎬🎬

Call Out the Marines A group of army buddies re-enlist to break up a spy ring. Two of the guys fall in love with the same girl, not realizing that she's one of the spies.

McLaglen and Lowe's last comedy together. Mediocre outing isn't redeemed by below average musical numbers. 🎵Call Out the Marines; Zana Zaranda; The Light of My Life; Beware; Hands Across the Border.
1942 67m/B Robert Smith, Frank Ryan, Victor McLaglen, Binnie Barnes, Paul Kelly, Edmund Lowe, Franklin Pangborn; **D:** Frank Ryan. **VHS, Beta** $34.95 RKO 🎬🎬

Call to Glory Pilot for the critically praised television series. An Air Force pilot and his family face turbulent times during the Cuban missile crisis.
1984 96m/C Craig T. Nelson, Cindy Pickett, Gabriel Damon, Keenan Wynn, Elisabeth Shue, G.D. Spradlin. **VHS, Beta, LV** $14.95 PAR 🎬🎬1/2

The Caller A strange man enters the house of a lone woman and sets off a long night of suspense and an almost longer evening of inept movie-making.
1987 (R) 90m/C Malcolm McDowell, Madolyn Smith; **D:** Arthur Seidelman. **VHS, Beta** $89.95 TWE 🎬

Callie and Son Details the sordid story of a waitress who works her way up to become a Dallas socialite and her obsessive relationship with her illegitimate son. Written by Thomas Thompson and made for television. Also known as "Rags to Riches." **AKA:** Rags to Riches.
1981 97m/C Lindsay Wagner, Dabney Coleman, Jameson Parker, Andrew Prine, James Sloyan, Michelle Pfeiffer; **D:** Waris Hussein. **VHS, Beta** $59.95 SVS, WAR, SIM 🎬

Calling Paul Temple The wealthy patients of a nerve doctor have been dying and a detective is called in to investigate.
1948 92m/B GB John Bentley, Dinah Sheridan, Margaretta Scott, Abraham Sofaer, Celia Lipton, Aian Wheatley, Wally Patch; **D:** Maclean Rogers. **VHS, Beta** $16.95 SNC 🎬1/2

Calling Wild Bill Elliott The crooked territorial governor is exposed by hero Elliott and sidekick Hayes and justice is restored in this typical B-western. Elliott's first film for Republic; he went on to star in 16 Red Ryder films as well as other westerns for the studio.
1943 55m/B Wild Bill Elliott, George "Gabby" Hayes, Herbert Heyes, Anne Jeffreys, Fred Kohler Jr., Roy Barcroft, Yakima Canutt; **D:** Spencer Gordon Bennet. **VHS** $9.98 REP 🎬1/2

Cambio de Cara Two reporters investigate corporate corruption. Dubbed into Spanish. **AKA:** A Change of Face.
1971 90m/C IT Adolfo Celi, Geraldine Hooper. **VHS, Beta** NO 🎬

Came a Hot Friday Two cheap conmen arrive in a 1949 southern New Zealand town, run various scams and pursue women.
1985 (PG) 101m/C NZ Peter Bland, Philip Gordon, Billy T. James; **D:** Ian Mune. **VHS, Beta** $19.98 NLC 🎬

Camel Boy True story of a young Arabian boy who befriends a camel and their treacherous trek across the desert.
1984 78m/C AU D: Yoram Gross. **VHS, Beta** $69.95 VES, LIV, WTA 🎬1/2

Camelia After much emotional pain, beautiful Camelia learns to love again from the young, warmhearted Rafael. But her new love will not protect her from fate.
19?? 108m/B MX Maria Felix, Jorge Mistral. **VHS, Beta** $54.95 MED 🎬🎬

Camelot The long-running Lerner and Loewe Broadway musical about King Arthur, Guinevere, and Lancelot was adapted from T.H. White's book, "The Once and Future King." Redgrave and Nero have chemistry as the illicit lovers, Harris is strong as the king struggling to hold together his dream, but

muddled direction undermines the effort. Laserdisc edition contains 28 minutes of previously edited footage, trailers and backstage info. 🎵I Wonder What the King is Doing Tonight; The Simple Joys of Maidenhood; Camelot; C'est Moi; The Lusty Month of May; Follow Me; How To Handle a Woman; Then You May Take Me to the Fair; If Ever I Would Leave You; What Do the Simple Folk Do?; I Loved You Once in Silence; Guenevere.
1967 150m/C Richard Harris, Vanessa Redgrave, David Hemmings, Franco Nero, Lionel Jeffries; **D:** Joshua Logan; **M:** Frederick Loewe, Alan Jay Lerner. Academy Awards '67: Best Art Direction/Set Decoration, Best Costume Design, Best Score; Golden Globe Awards '68: Best Actor—Musical/Comedy (Harris). **VHS, Beta, LV** $29.98 WAR, PIA, RDG 🎬🎬🎬

The Cameraman In 1928, after moving to MGM, Keaton made his first feature with a major studio, giving up the total artistic control he had enjoyed in his previous films. Spared from the vilification of studio politics (as wasn't the case with later Keaton films) "The Cameraman" enjoyed both critical and popular success. Keaton's inept tintype portrait-maker has a heart that pitter-patters for an MGM office girl. He hopes to impress her by joining the ranks of the newsreel photographers. Fortuitously poised to grab a photo scoop on a Chinese tong war, he is forced to return empty-handed when an organ-grinder's monkey absconds with his firsthand footage. Will our hero find both romance and career success? Silent with a musical score.
1928 78m/B Buster Keaton, Marceline Day, Harold Goodwin, Harry Gribbon, Sidney Bracy, Edward Brophy, Vernon Dent, William Irving; **D:** Edward Sedgwick. **VHS, LV** $29.95 MGM, FCT 🎬🎬🎬🎬

Cameron's Closet Every child's nightmare comes true. A young boy is convinced that a monster lives in his closet due to his perverse father's psychological tortures. Only this time the monster is real!
1989 (R) 86m/C Cotter Smith, Mel Harris, Scott Curtis, Chuck McCann, Leigh McCloskey, Kim Lankford, Tab Hunter; **D:** Armand Mastroianni. **VHS, LV** $14.95 COL, SVS 🎬1/2

Camila The true story of the tragic romance between an Argentinean socialite and a Jesuit priest in 1847. The two lovers escape to a small provincial village where they live together as man and wife. Eventually they are recognized and condemned to death. Available in Spanish with English subtitles or dubbed into English.
1984 121m/C AR SP Susu Pecoraro, Imanol Arias, Hector Alterio, Elena Tasisto; **D:** Maria-Luisa Bemberg. **VHS, Beta** $19.95 COL, SUE, AUD 🎬🎬🎬

Camille The classic Alexandre Dumas story about a dying French courtesan falling in love with a shallow young nobleman. A clean, romantic adaptation that somehow escapes the cliches and stands as one of the most telling monuments to Garbo's unique magic and presence on film.
1936 108m/B Greta Garbo, Robert Taylor, Lionel Barrymore, Henry Daniell, Elizabeth Allan, Rex O'Malley, Lenore Ulric, Laura Hope Crews; **D:** George Cukor. Academy Awards '37 Nominations: Best Actress (Garbo); National Board of Review Awards '37: 10 Best Films of the Year; New York Film Critics Awards '36: Best Actress (Garbo). **VHS, Beta** $24.95 MGM 🎬🎬🎬1/2

Camille Claudel A lushly romantic version of the art world at the turn of the century, when art was exploding in new forms and independence for women was

unheard of. Sculptor Claudel's unrequited love for art, Rodin, and independence clash, costing her sanity. Very long, it requires an attentive and thoughtful viewing. Adjani won the French Oscar for her performance. In French with English subtitles.
1989 (R) 149m/C FR Isabelle Adjani, Gerard Depardieu, Laurent Grevill, Alain Cuny; **D:** Bruno Nuytten. Academy Awards '89 Nominations: Best Actress (Adjani), Best Foreign Language Film; Cesar Awards '89: Best Actress (Adjani), Best Film. **VHS, Beta, LV $79.98** ORI, IME, TAM 🎞🎞🎞

Camorra: The Naples Connection A prostitute and an American drug dealer find themselves embroiled in the murders of Neapolitan Mafia heads. Violent, overblown, minor Wertmuller. **AKA:** Un Complicato Intrigo Di Donne, Vicoli E Delitti.
1985 (R) 94m/C IT Harvey Keitel, Angela Molina, Lorraine Bracco, Francisco Rabal; **D:** Lina Wertmuller. **VHS, Beta $79.95** MGM 🎞🎞

Camp Classics #1 Five corny classics spanning four decades make up this collection: "Mystery of the Leaping Fish" with Douglas Fairbanks, "Foreign Press Awards," "Musical Beauty Shop," "Edsel Commercial," and "Nixon's Checkers Speech."
195? 80m/B Douglas Fairbanks Sr. **VHS, Beta $37.00** WFV 🎞🎞

Camp Cucamonga: How I Spent My Summer Vacation Zany antics at summer camp abound when Camp Cucamonga's owner mistakes the new handyman for the camp inspector. Well known stars from TV's "Cheers," "The Jeffersons," "The Wonder Years," and "The Love Boat" are featured in this silly made for television flick.
1990 100m/C John Ratzenberger, Sherman Hemsley, Josh Saviano, Danica McKellar, Chad Allen, Dorothy Lyman, Lauren Tewes, G. Gordon Liddy; **D:** Roger Duchonwny. **VHS $9.99** GKK 🎞

Camp Double Feature Two cautionary anti-pot films, now universally recognized as high camp: "Reefer Madness" and "Marihuana." Both are available individually on video.
1939 120m/B Harley Wood, Hugh McArthur, Paul Ellis, Dave O'Brien, Dorothy Short. **VHS, Beta $34.95** JEF 🎞

Campaign in Poland This documentary chronicles the German invasion of Poland during World War II.
1940 80m/B VHS, Beta $29.95 NOS, DVT, HEG 🎞🎞

The Campus Corpse Young man stumbles into deadly college frat hazing and discovers he and rest of cast are utterly devoid of acting ability.
1977 (PG) 92m/C Charles Martin Smith, Jeff East, Brad Davis; **D:** Douglas Curtis. **VHS, Beta $69.95** VES 🎞

Campus Knights If you're a serious student of the campus caper film, this is one of the earliest (though not one of the best) of the genre (if such a distinction can be made). The story involves twin brothers—one a tweedy high-browed professor, the other a bon vivant man about town—who wreak fraternal chaos on the quads.
1929 70m/B Raymond McKee, Shirley Palmer, Marie Quillen, Jean Laverty, Sybil Grove; **D:** Albert Kelly. **VHS, Beta $24.95** GPV, FCT 🎞

Campus Man An entrepreneurial college student markets a beefcake calendar featuring his best friend, until the calendar's sales threaten his friend's amateur athletic status.

1987 (PG) 94m/C John Dye, Steve Lyon, Kim Delaney, Miles O'Keeffe, Morgan Fairchild, Kathleen Wilhoite; **D:** Ron Casden. **VHS, Beta, LV $14.95** PAR 🎞

Can-Can Lackluster screen adaptation of the Cole Porter musical bears little resemblance to the stage version. MacLaine is a cafe owner who goes to court to try and get the "Can-Can," a dance considered risque in gay Paree at the end of the nineteenth century, made legal. Love interest Sinatra happens to be a lawyer. ♫C'est Manifique; Let's Do It; I Love Paris; You Do Something to Me; It's All Right With Me; Live and Let Live; Come Along With Me; Just One of Those Things.
1960 131m/C Frank Sinatra, Shirley MacLaine, Maurice Chevalier, Louis Jourdan, Juliet Prowse, Marcel Dalio, Leon Belasco; **D:** Walter Lang. **VHS, Beta, LV $19.98** FOX, FCT 🎞🎞

Can I Do It...Till I Need Glasses? More to the point, can you stay awake till the end? Prurient juvenile junk. Brief Williams footage was grafted to this mess during 15 minutes of Mork fame.
1977 72m/C Robin Williams, Roger Behr, Debra Klose, Moose Carlson, Walter Olkewicz; **D:** I. Robert Levy. **VHS, Beta $19.95** MED Woof!

Can She Bake a Cherry Pie? Two offbeat characters meet and fall in love in an odd sort of way. Slow-moving and talky but somewhat rewarding. One of Black's better performances.
1983 90m/C Karen Black, Michael Emil, Michael Margotta, Frances Fisher, Martin Frydberg; **D:** Henry Jaglom. **VHS, Beta $39.95** PAR, FCT 🎞🎞

Can You Feel Me Dancing? Family-happy lightweight entertainment coproduced by Kent Bateman and starring Bateman progeny Jason and Justine as brother and sister, a premise that only a father could love. A blind independence-impaired teenager tries to liberate herself from her overbearing family, and finds the secret to conquering her fears and to standing up for herself when she falls in love. Written by spouse-team Steven and J. Miyoko Hensley.
1985 95m/C Jason Bateman, Justine Bateman. **VHS $79.95** MNC, TPV 🎞🎞

Can You Hear the Laughter? The Story of Freddie Prinze Heartstring tugging biography of the late Puerto Rican comedian whose troubled life lead to suicide in spite of his apparent success. He was most noted for his starring role in "Chico and the Man."
1979 100m/C Ira Angustain, Kevin Hooks, Randee Heller, Devon Ericson, Julie Carmen, Stephen Elliott; **D:** Burt Brinckerhoff. **VHS, Beta $79.95** GEM 🎞🎞

Canadian Capers...Cartoons: Vol. I A collection of innovative animated shorts produced by the National Film Board of Canada. Titles include: "The Great Toy Robbery," "The Animal Movie," "The Story of Christmas," "The Energy Carol," "The Bear's Christmas," "Carousel" and "TV Sale."
19?? 61m/C CA **VHS, Beta $29.95** NO 🎞🎞

Canadian Capers...Cartoons: Vol. II A second collection of thought-provoking cartoons from the National Film Board of Canada, including "Spinnolio," "Doodle Film," "Hot Stuff," "The Cruise," "The Specialists" and "No Apple for Johnny."
19?? 58m/C VHS, Beta $29.95 NO 🎞🎞

Cancel My Reservation New York talk show host Hope sets out for a vacation on an Arizona ranch, but winds up in trouble due to a mysterious corpse, a rich rancher,

and an enigmatic mystic. Even more muddled than it sounds. Based on the novel "Broken Gun" by Louis L'Amour, with pointless cameos by Crosby, Wayne, and Wilson.
1972 (G) 99m/C Bob Hope, Eva Marie Saint, Ralph Bellamy, Anne Archer, Forrest Tucker, Keenan Wynn, Flip Wilson, Pat Morita, Chief Dan George; **Cameos:** John Wayne, Bing Crosby, Doodles Weaver; **D:** Paul Bogart. **VHS, Beta $14.95** COL, FCT 🎞

Cancion en el Alma A talented boy singer is stuck in a greedy custody battle over his potential revenues in the wide world of Puerto Rican entertainment. **AKA:** Song from the Heart.
19?? 70m/C SP Luis Fernando Ramirez, Claudia Osuna. **VHS, Beta** NO 🎞½

The Candidate Realistic, satirical look at politics and political campaigning. A young, idealistic lawyer is talked into trying for the Senate seat and learns the truth about running for office. Ritchie's other efforts include "Downhill Racer" and "Bad News Bears."
1972 (PG) 105m/C Robert Redford, Peter Boyle, Don Porter, Allen Garfield, Karen Carlson, Melvyn Douglas, Michael Lerner; **D:** Michael Ritchie; **W:** Jeremy Larner. Academy Awards '72: Best Story & Screenplay; Nominations: Best Sound; National Board of Review Awards '72: 10 Best Films of the Year. **VHS, Beta, LV $19.98** WAR, PIA 🎞🎞🎞

Candide Moderately engaging BBC production of Voltaire's eighteenth century satire on human aspirations and weaknesses. The eponymous hero learns a lesson in optimism from Professor Pangloss. Everything happens for the best, even mediocre made for television dramas.
1976 95m/C GB Frank Finlay. **VHS, 3/4U, Special order formats** TLF 🎞🎞

Candles at Nine An innocent showgirl must spend a month in her late uncle's creepy mansion in order to inherit it, much to the malevolent chagrin of the rest of the family who want the place and the loot for themselves. Uninspired.
1944 84m/B GB Jessie Matthews, John Stuart, Reginald Purdell; **D:** John Harlow. **VHS, Beta $16.95** SNC, VYY, MLB 🎞½

Candleshoe A Los Angeles street urchin poses as an English matron's long lost granddaughter in order to steal a fortune hidden in Candleshoe, her country estate, where Niven butles. Somewhat slapschticky Disney fare.
1978 (G) 101m/C Vivian Pickles, Helen Hayes, David Niven, Jodie Foster, Leo McKern; **D:** Norman Tokar. **VHS, Beta $19.99** DIS 🎞🎞

Candy Mountain Guitar playin' O'Connor roadtrips across America and Canada in search of a legendary guitar maker Yulin. Occasional interest derives from musician cameos from the likes of Buster Poindexter, Dr. John and Redbone.
1987 (R) 90m/C CA FR SI Kevin J. O'Connor, Harris Yulin, Tom Waits, Bulle Ogier, Roberts Blossom; **Cameos:** David Johansen, Leon Redbone, Joe Strummer, Dr. John, Rita MacNeil, Laurie Metcalf; **D:** Robert Frank; **W:** Rudy Wurlitzer. **VHS $14.98** REP, FCT 🎞🎞

Candy Stripe Nurses Even hard-core Roger Corman fans might find his final installment in the nursing comedy pentad to be a lethargic exercise in gratuitous "sexual situations." Bet those uniforms don't meet hospital standards. The previous films in the series are: "The Student Nurses," "Private Duty Nurses," "Night Call Nurses," and "The Young Nurses." **AKA:** Sweet Candy.

1974 (R) 80m/C Candice Rialson, Robin Mattson, Maria Rojo, Kimberly Hyde, Dick Miller, Stanley Ralph Ross, Monte Landis, Tom Baker; **D:** Allan Holleb. **VHS, Beta $59.95** SUE ♫

Candy Tangerine Man Respectable businessman leads a double life as loving father and LA pimp.
1975 88m/C John Daniels, Tom Hankerson, Eli Haines, Marva Farmer, George Flower; **D:** Matt Cimber. **VHS, Beta $49.95** UNI ♫

Candyman This terrifying tale from horror maven Clive Barker is an effective combination of American gothic, academia, and urban squalor. A search for dissertation material leads graduate student Helen Lyle (Madsen) into gang-infested housing. There she encounters the urban myth of Candyman, the son of a former slave who was lynched and is now back with a hook and a vendetta. Filled with the appropriate amount of yucky stuff, yet successfully employs subtle scare tactics and plausible characters.
1992 (R) 98m/C Virginia Madsen, Tony Todd, Xander Berkeley, Kasi Lemmons, Vanessa Williams, DeJuan Guy, Michael Culkin, Gilbert Lewis, Stanley DeSantis; **D:** Bernard Rose; **W:** Bernard Rose. **VHS, Beta, LV, 8mm** COL ♫♫

Cannery Row Baseball has-been Nolte lives anonymously among the downtrodden in the seamy part of town and carries on with working girl girlfriend Winger. Based on John Steinbeck's "Cannery Row" and "Sweet Thursday."
1982 (PG) 120m/C Nick Nolte, Debra Winger, Audra Lindley, M. Emmet Walsh, Frank McRae, James Keane, Sunshine Parker; **D:** David S. Ward; **M:** Jack Nitzsche. **VHS, Beta $19.98** MGM ♫♫½

Cannibal Campout Crazed orphans with eating disorders make square meal of coed babes getting back to nature.
1988 89m/C Carrie Lindell, Richard Marcus, Amy Chludzinski, Jon McBride; **D:** Jon McBride, Tom Fisher. **VHS, Beta** DMP ♫

Cannibal Women in the Avocado Jungle of Death Tongue-in-cheek cult classic features erstwhile playmate Tweed as feminist anthropologist who searches with ditzy student and mucho macho male guide for lost tribe of cannibal women who dine on their mates.
1989 (PG-13) 90m/C Shannon Tweed, Adrienne Barbeau, Karen Mistal, Barry Primus, Bill Maher; **D:** J.D. Athens. **VHS, Beta, LV $79.95** PAR ♫♫½

Cannon Ball/Eyes Have It Conklin stars in "The Cannon Ball" (1915), as an explosives expert in the Boom Powder Factory. "The Eyes Have It" (1928), stars Turpin involved in another misunderstanding with wife and mother-in-law. Silent.
1915 41m/B Chester Conklin, Ben Turpin, Georgia O'Dell, Helen Gilmore, Jack Lipson. **VHS, Beta $19.98** CCB ♫♫½

Cannon Movie Tales: Red Riding Hood Bright re-telling of the little girl in red and that nasty wolf.
1989 (G) 84m/C Craig T. Nelson, Isabella Rossellini; **D:** Adam Brooks. **VHS** WAR ♫♫½

Cannon Movie Tales: Sleeping Beauty Fairchild stars in this version of the sleeping princess and the evil witch.
1989 (G) 90m/C Morgan Fairchild, Tracy Welch, Nicholas Clay, Sylvia Miles, Kenny L. Baker, David Holliday; **D:** David Irving. **VHS** WAR ♫♫½

Cannon Movie Tales: Snow White The incomparable Rigg stars in this witty retelling of the beautiful girl and her seven little friends.
1989 85m/C Diana Rigg, Sarah Peterson, Billy Barty; **D:** Michael Berz. **VHS** WAR ♫♫♫

Cannon Movie Tales: The Emperor's New Clothes Caesar stars in this version of vain despot and the crafty tailors.
1989 85m/C Sid Caesar, Robert Morse, Clive Revill; **D:** David Irving. **VHS** WAR ♫♫½

Cannonball Assorted ruthless people leave patches of rubber across the country competing for grand prize in less than legal auto race. Not top drawer New World but nonetheless a cult fave. Inferior to Bartel's previous cult classic, "Death Race 2000." Most interesting for plethora of cult cameos, including Scorsese, Dante, and grandmaster Corman. **AKA:** Carquake.
1976 (PG) 93m/C David Carradine, Bill McKinney, Veronica Hamel, Gerrit Graham, Robert Carradine, Sylvester Stallone, Jonathan Kaplan; **Cameos:** Martin Scorsese, Roger Corman, Joe Dante; **D:** Paul Bartel. **VHS, Beta $39.98** NO ♫♫

Cannonball/Dizzy Heights and Daring Hearts Two classic comedies featuring Conklin, the Keystone Kops, and wacky aeroplanes from the irrepressible Sennett.
1916 71m/B Chester Conklin; **D:** Mack Sennett. **VHS, Beta $29.95** VYY ♫♫

Cannonball Run So many stars, so little plot. Reynolds and sidekick DeLuise disguise themselves as paramedics to foil cops while they compete in cross-country Cannonball race. Shows no sign of having been directed by an ex-stuntman. One of 1981's top grossers: go figure. Followed by equally languid sequel "Cannonball Run II."
1981 (PG) 95m/C Burt Reynolds, Farrah Fawcett, Roger Moore, Dom DeLuise, Dean Martin, Sammy Davis Jr., Jack Elam, Adrienne Barbeau, Peter Fonda, Molly Picon, Bert Convy, Jamie Farr; **D:** Hal Needham. **VHS, Beta, LV $29.98** VES ♫½

Cannonball Run II More mindless cross-country wheel spinning with gratuitous star cameos. Director Needham apparently subscribes to the two wrongs make a right school of sequels.
1984 (PG) 109m/C Burt Reynolds, Dom DeLuise, Jamie Farr, Marilu Henner, Shirley MacLaine, Jim Nabors, Frank Sinatra, Sammy Davis Jr., Dean Martin, Telly Savalas, Susan Anton, Catherine Bach, Jack Elam, Sid Caesar, Ricardo Montalban, Charles Nelson Reilly; **Cameos:** Henry Silva, Tim Conway, Don Knotts, Molly Picon; **D:** Hal Needham. **VHS, Beta, LV $19.98** WAR ♫

The Canon Operation An ostensibly true story about Korean War espionage.
1983 90m/C VHS, Beta $59.95 VCD ♫

Can't Buy Me Love Unpopular high school nerd Dempsey buys a month of dates with teen babe Peterson for $1000 in order to win friends and influence people. Previously known as "Boy Rents Girl."
1987 (PG-13) 94m/C Patrick Dempsey, Amanda Peterson, Dennis Dugan, Courtney Gains; **D:** Steve Rash. **VHS, Beta, LV $19.99** TOU ♫½

Can't Stop the Music Retired model invites friends from Greenwich Village to a party to help the career of her roommate, an aspiring composer. Disco inferno that nearly reaches heights of surreal ineptness. Put it in a time capsule and let the people of the future decide what the heck was going on in the seventies. Features two of the top hits by the Village People. ♫Y.M.C.A.; Macho Man; Give Me a Break; The Sound of the City; Samantha; I'm a Singing Juggler; Sophistication; Liberation; I Love You to Death; Magic Night; Milkshake.

1980 (PG) 120m/C Valerie Perrine, Bruce Jenner, Steve Guttenberg, Paul Sand, Leigh Taylor-Young, Village People; **D:** Nancy Walker. **VHS, Beta $29.99** HBO Woof!

A Canterbury Tale Writer-director team Powell and Pressburger have loosely modeled a retelling of Chaucer's famous tale of a pilgrimage to the cathedral in Canterbury. Set in Nazi-threatened Britain in 1944, the story follows the pilgrimage of three Brits and an American GI to the eponymous cathedral. Strange, effective, worth looking at. The 95-minute American version, with added footage of Kim Hunter, is inferior to the 124-minute original.
1944 124m/B GB Eric Portman, Sheila Sim, Dennis Price, Esmond Knight, Charles Hawtrey, Hay Petrie; **D:** Michael Powell, Emeric Pressburger. **VHS $59.95** HMV ♫♫

The Canterbury Tales Four Chaucer tales, most notably "The Merchant's Tale" and "The Wife of Bath," are recounted by travelers, with director Pasolini as the bawdy poet. Deemed obscene by the Italian courts, it's the second entry in Pasolini's medieval "Trilogy of Life," preceded by "The Decameron" and followed by "The Arabian Nights." In Italian with English subtitles.
1971 109m/C IT Laura Betti, Ninetto Davoli, Pier Paolo Pasolini, Hugh Griffith, Josephine Chaplin, Michael Balfour, Jenny Runacre; **D:** Pier Paolo Pasolini. **VHS, Beta $79.95** WBF, TAM, APD ♫

The Canterville Ghost Laughton, a 300-year old ghost with a yellow streak, is sentenced to spook a castle until he proves he's not afraid of his own shadow. American troops stay at the castle during WWII, and, as luck would have it, soldier Young is distantly related to spunky young keeper of the castle O'Brien, ghost Laughton's descendant. Once Young is acquainted with his cowardly ancestor, he begins to fear a congenital yellow streak, and both struggle to be brave despite themselves. Vaguely derived from an Oscar Wilde tale.
1944 95m/B Charles Laughton, Robert Young, Margaret O'Brien, William Gargan, Reginald Owen, Rags Ragland, Una O'Connor, Peter Lawford, Mike Mazurki; **D:** Jules Dassin. **VHS, Beta $19.98** MGM ♫♫½

The Canterville Ghost During a family's vacation in an old English manor, they run into a ghost who is doomed to haunt the place until he can overcome his fears. Problems start when the family tries to scare him away. From the "Wonderworks" family movie series.
1991 58m/C Richard Kiley, Mary Wickes. **VHS $29.95** PME, FCT, HMV ♫♫½

Cantonese Iron Kung Fu The ten tigers of Quon Tung perfect martial arts skills known as Cantonen Iron Kung Fu.
197? 90m/C Liang Jia Ren; **D:** Li Chao. **VHS, Beta $54.95** WVE ♫

The Cantor's Son Real-life story based on Moishe Oysher's life, vaguely influenced by Jolson's "Jazz Singer." Runaway Oysher joins troupe of performers as a youth, travels to the shores of America, and finds fame once his beautiful voice is discovered. Returning to his mother country to celebrate his parents' golden anniversary, he encounters his childhood sweetheart and falls in love, but another woman is written into the plot to complicate matters. Poorly acted, laughable staging. In Yiddish with English subtitles. **AKA:** Dem Khann's Zindl; Dem Khann's Zindl.
1937 90m/B Judith Abarbanel, Florence Weiss, Moishe Oysher, Isadore Cashier; **D:** Ilya Motyleff. **VHS, Beta $79.95** ERG, TAM, HEG ♫½

Canvas: The Fine Art of Crime A ruthless, underhanded art gallery owner recruits a desperate young artist into his art stealing schemes. The artist learns how to steal, but decides he wants out after his burglary partner has a brush with death. The gallery owner, however, wants one last job completed.
1992 (R) 94m/C Gary Busey, John Rhys-Davies, Vittorio Rossi, Nick Cavaiola, Cary Lawrence; **D:** Alain Zaloum. VHS $89.98 *LIV* 🎬🎬

Cape Fear Former prosecutor turned small-town lawyer Peck and his family are plagued by the sadistic attentions of criminal Mitchum, who just finished a six year sabbatical at the state pen courtesy of prosecutor Peck. Taut and creepy; Mitchum's a consummate psychopath. Based on (and far superior to) John MacDonald's "The Executioners." Don't pass this one up in favor of the Scorsese remake.
1961 106m/B Gregory Peck, Robert Mitchum, Polly Bergen, Martin Balsam, Telly Savalas, Jack Kruschen; **D:** J. Lee Thompson. VHS, Beta $19.95 *MCA* 🎬🎬🎬½

Cape Fear Scorsese takes on this terrifying tale of brutality and manipulation (previously filmed in 1961) and cranks it up a notch as a paroled convict haunts the lawyer who put him away. Great cast, a rollercoaster of suspense. Note the cameos by Mitchum, Peck, and Balsam, stars of the first version. Original source material was "The Executioners" by John D. MacDonald. Breath-taking rollercoaster of a film. Elmer Bernstein adapted the original score by Bernard Herrmann.
1991 (R) 128m/C Robert De Niro, Nick Nolte, Jessica Lange, Juliette Lewis, Joe Don Baker, Illeana Douglas, Fred Dalton Thompson; **Cameos:** Robert Mitchum, Gregory Peck, Martin Balsam; **W:** Wesley Strick. Academy Awards '91 Nominations: Best Actor (De Niro), Best Supporting Actress (Lewis); Chicago Film Critics Awards '91: Most Promising Actress (Lewis). VHS, LV $19.98 *MCA* 🎬🎬🎬

Caper of the Golden Bulls Former bank robber Boyd is blackmailed into joining a group of safecrackers who plan to assault the Royal Bank of Spain during the annual Santa Maria bull run. More like siesta of the golden bulls. **AKA:** Carnival of Thieves.
1967 104m/C Stephen Boyd, Yvette Mimieux, Giovanna Ralli, Walter Slezak, Vito Scotti; **D:** Russel Rouse. VHS, Beta $59.98 *NLC* 🎬

Capone This is the story of the gangster after Elliot Ness put him in a Chicago jail. That didn't stop Capone from running his crime empire until a single FBI agent worked to sent the crime boss to Alcatraz, where his power would be useless. Exuberant performances from Sharkey and Carradine. Made for television.
1989 (R) 96m/C Ray Sharkey, Keith Carradine, Debrah Farentino. VHS, LV $89.95 *VMK* 🎬🎬½

Capricorn One Astronauts Brolin, Simpson and Waterston follow Mission Controller Holbrook's instructions to fake a Mars landing on a fabricated soundstage when their ship is discovered to be defective. When they find out they're supposed to expire in outer space so that the NASA scam won't become public knowledge, they flee to the desert, while reporter Gould sniffs out the cover up.
1978 (R) 123m/C Elliott Gould, James Brolin, Brenda Vaccaro, O.J. Simpson, Hal Holbrook, Sam Waterston, Karen Black, Telly Savalas; **D:** Peter Hyams; **M:** Jerry Goldsmith. VHS, Beta, LV $59.98 *FOX* 🎬🎬

Captain America Captain America battles a mad scientist in this fifteen-episode serial based on the comic book character.
1944 240m/B Dick Purcell, Adrian Booth, Lionel Atwill; **D:** John English; **W:** Elmer Clifton. VHS, Beta $109.95 *VCN, MLB* 🎬🎬

Captain America Marvel Comic character steps into feature film and flounders. The patriotic superhero son of WWII hero fights bad guy with contraband nuclear weapon. Made for television. Followed the same year with "Captain America II: Death Too Soon."
1979 98m/C Reb Brown, Len Birman, Heather Menzies, Steve Forrest, Robin Mattson, Joseph Ruskin, Michael McManus; **D:** Rod Holcomb. VHS, Beta $39.95 *MCA* 🎬½

Captain America Based on the Marvel Comics superhero. It's 1941 and Steve Rogers has just been recruited to join a top secret experimental government program after flunking his army physical. Injected with a serum, Steve becomes super strong, fast, and smart but is matched in all three by an evil Nazi counterpart, Red Skull. The two battle to a World War II standstill and while Red Skull goes on with his evil plots, the next 40 years finds Captain America fast frozen in the Alaskan tundra. Finally, our hero is thawed in time to do a final battle with his evil nemesis. This one is ridiculous even by comic book standards but it may amuse the kids.
1989 (PG-13) 103m/C Matt Salinger, Scott Paulin, Ronny Cox, Ned Beatty, Darren McGavin, Melinda Dillon; **D:** Albert Pyun. VHS, LV $89.95 *COL* 🎬½

Captain America 2: Death Too Soon Terrorists hit America where it hurts, threatening to use age accelerating drug. Sequelized superhero fights chronic crow lines and series dies slow, painful death. Made for television.
1979 98m/C Reb Brown, Connie Sellecca, Len Birman, Christopher Lee, Katherine Justice, Lana Wood, Christopher Carey; **D:** Ivan Nagy. VHS, Beta $39.95 *MCA* 🎬

Captain Apache Union intelligence officer Van Cleef investigates murder of Indian commissioner and discovers fake Indian war landscam. As clever as the title.
1971 95m/C Lee Van Cleef, Carroll Baker, Stuart Whitman; **D:** Alexander Singer. VHS, Beta $19.95 *MRV, PSM* 🎬

Captain Blackjack All star cast craps out in wannabe thriller about drug smuggling on the French Riviera. Social butterfly Moorehead directs drug traffic, detective Marshall undercovers as doctor, and Sanders looks bored in a British sort of way. **AKA:** Black Jack.
1951 90m/B FR George Sanders, Herbert Marshall, Agnes Moorehead, Patricia Roc, Marcel Dalio; **D:** Julien Duvivier. VHS *VEC, TIM* 🎬🎬

Captain Blood Sabatini adventure story launched then unknown 26-year old Flynn and 19-year old De Havilland to fame in perhaps the best pirate story ever. Exiled into slavery by a tyrannical governor, Irish physician Peter Blood is forced into piracy but ultimately earns a pardon for his swashbuckling ways. Love interest De Havilland would go on to appear in seven more features with Flynn, who took the part Robert Donat declined for health reasons. Cleverly budgeted using ship shots from silents, and miniature sets when possible. First original film score by composer Korngold. Also available colorized.
1935 120m/B Errol Flynn, Olivia de Havilland, Basil Rathbone, J. Carroll Naish, Guy Kibbee, Lionel Atwill; **D:** Michael Curtiz. VHS, Beta $19.98 *MGM, FCT, MLB* 🎬🎬🎬½

Captain Caution Young girl throws caution to the wind when dad dies during the War of 1812, assisting young Mature to take over the old man's ship to do battle with the British. Watch for then unknown sailor Ladd.
1940 84m/B Victor Mature, Louise Platt, Bruce Cabot, Alan Ladd, Robert Barrat, Vivienne Osborne; **D:** Richard Wallace. VHS, Beta *MED* 🎬🎬

The Captain from Koepenick Popular true life comedy about a Berlin cobbler in 1906 who rebels against military bureaucracy by impersonating a Prussian officer and wreaking havoc on his town, arresting authorities and capturing soldiers, only to enjoy folk herodom when his ruse is discovered. Remake of Richard Oswald's 1931 classic. In German with subtitles. **AKA:** Der Hauptmann von Koepenick.
1956 93m/B GE Heinz Ruehmann, Hannelore Schroth, Martin Held, Erich Schellow; **D:** Helmut Kaeutner. VHS, Beta $24.95 *NOS, FCT, TIM* 🎬🎬½

Captain Horatio Hornblower A colorful drama about the life and loves of the British sea captain during the Napoleonic wars. Peck is rather out of his element as the courageous, swashbuckling hero (Errol Flynn was originally cast) but there's enough fast-paced derring-do to make this a satisfying saga. Based on the novel by C.S. Forester.
1951 117m/C GB Gregory Peck, Virginia Mayo, Robert Beatty, Denis O'Dea, Christopher Lee; **D:** Raoul Walsh. VHS, Beta, LV $59.99 *WAR* 🎬🎬🎬

Captain January Crusty old lighthouse keeper rescues little orphan girl with curly hair from drowning and everyone breaks into cutesy song and dance, interrupted only when the authorities try to separate the two. ♫At the Codfish Ball; Early Bird; The Right Somebody to Love.
1936 74m/B Shirley Temple, Guy Kibbee, Buddy Ebsen, Slim Summerville, Jane Darwell, June Lang, George Irving, Si Jenks; **D:** David Butler. VHS, Beta $19.98 *FOX* 🎬🎬½

Captain Kidd Laughton huffs and puffs and searches for treasure on the high seas, finds himself held captive with rest of cast in anemic swashbuckler.
1945 83m/B Charles Laughton, John Carradine, Randolph Scott, Reginald Owen, Gilbert Roland, Barbara Britton, John Qualen, Sheldon Leonard; **D:** Rowland V. Lee. VHS, Beta, 3/4U, Special order formats $9.95 *NEG, MRV, NOS* 🎬½

Captain Kronos: Vampire Hunter Captain Kronos fences thirsty foes in Hammer horror hybrid. Artsy, atmospheric and atypical, it's written and directed with tongue firmly in cheek by Clemens, who penned many an "Avengers" episode. **AKA:** Kronos.
1974 (R) 91m/C GB Horst Janson, John Carson, Caroline Munro, Ian Hendry, Shane Briant, Wanda Ventham, Ian Hendry; **D:** Brian Clemens. VHS, Beta $44.95 *PAR* 🎬🎬🎬

Captain Newman, M.D. Three army guys visit stiff shrink Peck during the final months of WWII in VA ward for the mentally disturbed. Much guilt and agonizing, with comic relief courtesy of Curtis. Peck is sub par, the direction flounders and there's something unsettling about quicksilver shifts from pathos to parody. Nonetheless touching with fine performance from Darin as guilt ridden hero. Based on the novel by Leo Rosten.
1963 126m/C Gregory Peck, Bobby Darin, Tony Curtis, Angie Dickinson, Eddie Albert, James Gregory, Jane Withers, Larry Storch, Robert Duvall; **D:** David Miller. VHS, Beta $59.95 *MCA* 🎬🎬½

Captain Ron A harried couple (Short and Place) inherit a large boat and, with their two smart-mouthed kids, go to the Caribbean to sail the boat back to the United States. Of course they know nothing about sailing, so they hire Captain Ron (Russell), a one-eyed, Long John Silver-talking boat captain. From there, numerous mishaps occur. Short and Place get stuck in the shower, Short falls overboard (several times), Russell gets lost (many times), pirates steal the boat, and more. Although the premise of the film sounds amusing, this one just sinks. Russell looks great in his teeny-weeny bikini, and the scenery is beautiful, but that's about it.
1992 (PG-13) 104m/C Kurt Russell, Martin Short, Mary Kay Place, Meadow Sisto, Benjamin Salisbury; **W/D:** Thom Eberhardt. **VHS, Beta, LV** **$94.95** *TOU* ✂️½

Captain Scarlett Formulaic swashbuckler has nobleman Greene and highway guy Young fighting nasty French Royalists who've been putting the pressure on impecunious peasants. Runaway Spanish damsel in distress courtesy of Amar. Most novel aspect of the production is that the post-Napoleon French terrain has that vaguely south of the border feel.
1953 75m/C Richard Greene, Leonora Amar, Isobel Del Puerto, Nedrick Young, Manolo Fabregas, Isobel Del Puerto; **D:** Thomas Carr. **VHS, Beta $19.95** *NOS, MRV, WES* ✂️

Captain Sinbad Captain Sinbad must destroy the evil El Kerim, but first he must tackle a many-headed ogre, man-eating fish and crocodiles, a large fist clad in a spiked glove, an invisible monster, and more. To kill the villain, Sinbad must destroy his heart, which is kept in a tower with no entrance. A huge, witty, epic production with lots of special effects. This one is fun.
1963 85m/C Guy Williams, Heidi Bruhl, Pedro Armendariz Sr., Abraham Sofaer, Bernie Hamilton, Helmut Schneider; **D:** Byron Haskin. **VHS** *MGM* ✂️½

Captain Swagger A man on the brink of thievery experiences some changes that keep him on the right side of the law.
1925 50m/B Rod La Rocque, Sue Carol. **VHS, Beta $14.95** *GPV* ✂️½

Captains Courageous Rich brat Bartholomew takes a dip sans life jacket while leaning over an ocean liner railing to relieve himself of the half dozen ice cream sodas imprudently consumed at sea. Picked up by a Portugese fishing boat, he at first treats his mandatory three month voyage as an unscheduled cab ride, but eventually, through a deepening friendship with crewman Tracy, develops a hitherto unheralded work ethic. The boy's filial bond with Tracy, of course, requires that the seaman meet with watery disaster. Based on the Rudyard Kipling novel. Director Fleming went on to "Gone With the Wind" and "The Wizard of Oz."
1937 116m/B Spencer Tracy, Lionel Barrymore, Freddie Bartholomew, Mickey Rooney, Melvyn Douglas, Charley Grapewin, John Carradine, Jack LaRue; **D:** Victor Fleming. Academy Awards '37: Best Actor (Tracy); Nominations: Best Film Editing, Best Picture, Best Screenplay; National Board of Review Awards '37: 10 Best Films of the Year. **VHS, Beta $19.98** *MGM, BMV, BTV* ✂️✂️✂️

Captains of the Clouds Unabashedly patriotic film starring Cagney as a daredevil, independent Canadian bush pilot who makes his own flying rules. When World War II begins he joins the Royal Canadian Air Force but washes out when he can't follow orders. However, he finds a way to prove himself a hero as a civilian pilot ferrying a bomber to England. Cagney's first Technicolor film.
1942 113m/C James Cagney, Dennis Morgan, Brenda Marshall, Alan Hale Sr., George Tobias, Reginald Gardiner, Reginald Denny, Russell Arms, Paul Cavanagh; **D:** Michael Curtiz. **VHS** **$19.98** *MGM* ✂️✂️½

Captain's Paradise Golden Fleece captain Guinness chugs between wives in Gibraltar and North Africa, much to the adulation of chief officer Goldner. While Gibraltar little woman Johnson is homegrown homebody, little woman de Carlo is paint the town red type, allowing Guinness to have cake and eat it too, it seems, except that he's inconveniently positioned in front of a firing squad at movie's start.
1953 89m/B *GB* Alec Guinness, Yvonne De Carlo, Celia Johnson, Miles Malleson, Nicholas Phipps, Ferdinand "Ferdy" Mayne, Sebastian Cabot; **D:** Anthony Kimmins. **VHS, Beta $19.98** *HBO, FCT* ✂️✂️✂️

The Captain's Table Former cargo vessel captain Gregson is given luxury liner to command, and fails to revise his cargo captain style to fit new crew and clientele. British cast saves unremarkable script from mediocrity.
1960 90m/C *GB* John Gregson, Peggy Cummins, Donald Sinden, Nadia Gray; **D:** Jack Lee. **VHS $19.95** *PAR* ✂️✂️

Captive Spoiled heiress is kidnapped by terrorist trio and brainwashed into anti-establishment Hearst-like creature.
1987 (R) 98m/C Oliver Reed, Irina Brook, Xavier DeLuc, Hiro Arai; **D:** Paul Mayersberg. **VHS, Beta** *NO* ✂️½

Captive Heart Czech soldier Redgrave assumes the identity of a dead British officer in order to evade Nazis in WWII. Captured and imprisoned in camp reserved for British POWs, his stalagmates think they smell a spy, but he manages to convince them he's an OK Joe. Meanwhile, he's been writing letters home to the little missus, which means he's got a little explaining to do when he's released from prison. Especially fine Redgrave performance.
1947 86m/B *GB* Michael Redgrave, Basil Radford, Jack Warner, Jimmy Hanley, Rachel Kempson, Mervyn Johns; **D:** Basil Dearden. **VHS, Beta $19.95** *NOS, DVT, VEC* ✂️✂️✂️

Captive Hearts Well frayed story holds cast captive in sushi romance. Two American flyers are shot down and taken prisoner in isolated Japanese mountain village, and one is shot by Cupid's arrow.
1987 (PG) 97m/C Pat Morita, Michael Sarrazin, Chris Makepeace; **D:** Paul Almond. **VHS, Beta $14.95** *MGM, FOX* ✂️

Captive Planet Bargain basement FX and really atrocious acting hold audience captive in routine earth on the verge of obliteration yarn.
1978 95m/C Sharon Baker, Chris Auram, Anthony Newcastle; **D:** Al Bradley. **VHS, Beta** *NO* ✂️

Captive Rage South American general Reed hijacks planeful of girlies to encourage US to release his son, who's in trouble because he swaps money for white powder. Violence lives up to title, all else disappoints.
1988 (R) 99m/C Oliver Reed, Robert Vaughn, Claudia Udy; **D:** Cedric Sundstrom. **VHS, Beta, CV $79.99** *MCG* ✂️

The Captive: The Longest Drive 2 Matheson and Russell play two recently reunited brothers in search of their sister, whom they believe is still a captive of the Cheyenne Indians who also raised Russell. Along the way the two come to the aid of a pioneer woman and her young son. This western was actually a brief television series known as "The Quest," and is a continuation of the pilot episode released on video as "The Longest Drive."
1976 (PG-13) 80m/C Kurt Russell, Tim Matheson. **VHS, LV $89.95** *VMK* ✂️✂️

The Capture Above-average story told in flashback has Ayres hiding out in Mexico because he thought he killed an innocent man. He seeks out the widow to question her about him and they wind up marrying. When he finds the real culprit, the man is killed and the evidence points to Ayres. Ayres and Wright are great, as is the native Mexican musical score.
1950 67m/B Lew Ayres, Teresa Wright, Victor Jory, Jacqueline White, Jimmy Hunt, Duncan Renaldo, William Bakewell; **D:** John Sturges. **VHS $19.95** *NOS, TIM* ✂️✂️✂️

The Capture of Bigfoot Barefoot monster tracks footprints around town after 25 years of peace, and evil businessman attempts to capture creature for personal gain.
1979 (PG) 92m/C Stafford Morgan, Katherine Hopkins, Richard Kennedy, Otis Young, George Flower, John Goff; **D:** Bill Rebane. **VHS, Beta $29.95** *AHV* ✂️

The Capture of Grizzly Adams Framed for murder, Adams and his everfaithful companion Ben the bear must not only clear his name but outwit a band of outlaws who are holding his young daughter captive. Made for television.
1982 96m/C Dan Haggerty, Chuck Connors, June Lockhart, Kim Darby, Noah Beery Jr., Keenan Wynn. **VHS $89.95** *WOV* ✂️½

Captured in Chinatown Dog chases bad guys in Chinatown. Bow wow.
1935 53m/B Marion Shilling, Charles Delaney, Philo McCullough, Robert Ellis; **D:** Elmer Clifton. **VHS, Beta, LV $12.95** *SNC, WGE* ✂️

Car Crash Organized crime hits stock car racing head on to produce crashing bore.
19?? 103m/C Joey Travolta, Anna Obregon, Vittorio Mezzogiorno. **VHS $69.95** *SVS* ✂️

Car 54 Where Are You? The first situation comedy about police officers ran on television from 1961-1963. Join offbeat New York cops Gunther Toody and Francis Muldoon of the beleaguered 53rd Precinct. Each cassette contains two episodes. Eight cassettes.
1961 50m/B Fred Gwynne, Joe E. Ross, Nipsey Russell, Al Lewis; **D:** Stanley Prager, Nat Hiken. **VHS $14.95** *REP, FCT, MOV* ✂️

Car Trouble Young English husband buys new Jaguar and wife's not so minor car trouble causes major marital trouble. Funnybone-tickling pairing of Walters and Charleson.
1986 (R) 93m/C *GB* Julie Walters, Ian Charleson; **D:** David Green. **VHS, Beta, LV $79.95** *MCG* ✂️✂️½

Car Wash L.A. carwash is soap opera-esque setting for disjointed comic bits about owners of dirty cars and people who hose them down for a living. Econo budget and lite plot, but serious comic talent. A sort of disco carwash version of "Grand Hotel." Written by Joel Schumacher, with music by Rose Royce. Director Schultz known for "Cooley High."
1976 (PG) 97m/C Franklin Ajaye, Sully Boyer, Richard Brestoff, George Carlin, Richard Pryor, Melanie Mayron, Ivan Dixon, Antonio Fargas; **D:** Michael Schultz. **VHS, Beta $59.95** *MCA, FCT* ✂️✂️½

Caravaggio Controversial biography of the late Renaissance painter famous for his bisexuality, fondness for prostitute models, violence and depravity. Photography by Gabriel Beristain reproduces the artist's visual style. British-made.
1986 97m/C *GB* Nigel Terry, Sean Bean, Tilda Swinton; *D:* Derek Jarman. **VHS, Beta, LV** $79.95 *FCT, TAM, CCN* 🐾🐾🐾

Caravan to Vaccares French Duke hires young American to sneak Eastern European scientist into the States, and little suspense ensues. Based on Alistair MacLean novel.
1974 (PG) 98m/C David Birney, Charlotte Rampling; *D:* Geoffrey Reeve. **VHS, Beta** $69.95 *MED* 🐾

The Caravan Trail A cowboy becomes marshal in order to bring to justice those who have stolen land and murdered his friend. This was shot in color, which was rare for the 1940s.
1946 53m/C Eddie Dean, Lash LaRue, Emmett Lynn, Jean Carlin, Charles King, Robert Barron, Lloyd Ingraham, Bud Osborne; *D:* Robert Emmett. **VHS** $19.95 *NOS, RXM, HEG* 🐾🐾

Carbon Copy Successful white executive has life turned inside out when his seventeen-year old illegitimate son, who happens to be black, decides it's time to look up dear old dad. Typical comedy-with-a-moral written by Stanley Shapiro.
1981 (PG) 92m/C George Segal, Susan St. James, Jack Warden, Paul Winfield, Dick Martin, Vicky Dawson, Tom Poston, Denzel Washington; *D:* Michael Schultz. **VHS, Beta, LV** $9.95 *COL, SUE* 🐾🐾

Cardiac Arrest Lunatic eviscerates victims in trolley town. They left their hearts in San Francisco.
1974 (PG) 95m/C Garry Goodrow, Mike Chan, Max Gail; *D:* Murray Mintz. **VHS, Beta** $69.95 *MED* 🐾

The Cardinal Priestly young Tryon rises through ecclesiastical ranks to become Cardinal, struggling through a plethora of tests of faith, none so taxing as the test of the audience's patience. Had Preminger excised some sixty minutes of footage, he might have had a compelling portrait of faith under fire, but as it stands, the cleric's life is epic confusion. Fine acting, even from Tryon, who later went on to bookish fame, and from Huston who's normally on the other side of the camera. McNamara's final performance. Based on the Henry Morton Robinson novel.
1963 175m/C Tom Tryon, Carol Lynley, Dorothy Gish, Maggie McNamara, Cecil Kellaway, John Huston, John Saxon, Burgess Meredith; *D:* Otto Preminger. Academy Awards '63 Nominations: Best Art Direction/Set Decoration (Color), Best Color Cinematography, Best Director (Preminger), Best Film Editing, Best Supporting Actor (Huston); Golden Globe Awards '64: Best Film—Drama, Best Supporting Actor (Huston). **VHS, Beta, LV** $59.95 *QNE, IME* 🐾🐾½

The Care Bears Movie The Care Bears leave their cloud home in Care-a-lot to try and teach earthlings how to share their feelings of love and caring for each other.
1984 (G) 75m/C *D:* Arna Selznick; *V:* Mickey Rooney, Georgia Engel, Harry Dean Stanton. **VHS, Beta** $14.98 *LIV, VES, VTR* 🐾🐾

The Care Bears Movie 2: A New Generation A sequel to the sweet adventures of the animated bear family and their new offspring.
1986 (G) 77m/C *D:* Dale Schott; *V:* Maxine Miller, Pam Hyatt, Hadley Key. **VHS, Beta** $14.95 *COL, WTA* 🐾🐾

Career An overwrought, depressing drama about the trials and tribulations of an actor trying to make it on Broadway. He'll try anything to succeed. Good direction, but so-so acting.
1959 105m/B Dean Martin, Anthony (Tony) Franciosa, Shirley MacLaine, Carolyn Jones, Joan Blackman, Robert Middleton, Donna Douglas; *D:* Joseph Anthony. Academy Awards '59 Nominations: Best Art Direction/Set Decoration (B & W), Best Black and White Cinematography, Best Costume Design (B & W); Golden Globe Awards '60: Best Actor—Drama (Franciosa). **VHS** *PAR* 🐾🐾½

Career Opportunities "Home Alone" clone for teenagers from John Hughes' factory. Whaley is an unsuccessful con-artist who finally gets a job as the night janitor of the local department store. He fools around at company expense until he finds the town's beauty (Connelly) asleep in a dressing room. The pair then play make-believe until its time to thwart some small-time thieves. Unexciting and unrealistic in the worst way; no wonder Candy isn't billed—he probably didn't want to be.
1991 (PG-13) 83m/C Frank Whaley, Jennifer Connelly, Dermot Mulroney, Kieran Mulroney, John M. Jackson, Jenny O'Hara, Noble Willingham, Barry Corbin, Denise Galik, William Forsythe; *Cameos:* John Candy; *D:* Bryan Gordon; *W:* John Hughes; *M:* Thomas Newman. **VHS, LV** $19.95 *MCA* 🐾½

Carefree Dizzy radio singer Rogers can't make up her mind about beau Bellamy, so he sends her to analyst Astaire. Seems she can't even dream a little dream until shrink Astaire prescribes that she ingest some funny food, which causes her to dream she's in love with the Fredman. Au contraire, says he, it's a Freudian thing, and he hypnotically suggests that she really loves Bellamy. The two line up to march down the aisle together, and Fred stops dancing just long enough to realize he's in love with Ginger. A screwball comedy with music. 🎵 I Used to be Colorblind; The Night is Filled With Music; Change Partners; The Yam.
1938 83m/B Fred Astaire, Ginger Rogers, Ralph Bellamy, Jack Carson, Franklin Pangborn, Hattie McDaniel; *D:* Mark Sandrich; *M:* Irving Berlin. **VHS, Beta, LV** $14.98 *TTC, RKO, MED* 🐾🐾🐾

Careful, He Might Hear You Abandoned by his father, six-year-old P.S. becomes a pawn between his dead mother's two sisters, one working class and the other wealthy, and his worldview is further overturned by the sudden reappearance of his prodigal father. Set in Depression-era Australia, Schultz's vision is touching and keenly observed, and manages a sort of child's eye sense of proportion. Based on a novel by Sumner Locke Elliott.
1984 (PG) 113m/C *AU* Nicholas Gledhill, Wendy Hughes, Robyn Nevin, John Hargreaves; *D:* Carl Schultz. **VHS, Beta** $59.98 *FOX* 🐾🐾🐾

Caribe Caribbean travelogue masquerades as spy thriller. Arms smuggling goes awry, and neither voodoo nor bikinied blondes can prevent audience from dozing. Never released theatrically.
1987 96m/C John Savage, Kara Glover, Stephen McHattie, Sam Malkin; *D:* Michael Kennedy. **VHS, Beta, LV** $79.98 *LIV, VES* 🐾½

The Cariboo Trail Two prospecting men seek their fortune in British Columbia, the golden West of Canada in the 1890s. But they find themselves opposed by a ruthless rancher and claim-jumpers. Actually filmed in Colorado with excellent cinematography and solid performances from some big names, it's still a run-of-the-mill entry. Made the

same year that the Gabby Hayes' show first aired.
1950 80m/C Angela Douglas, Randolph Scott, George "Gabby" Hayes, Bill Williams, Victor Jory; *D:* Gerald Thomas, Edwin L. Marin. **VHS, LV** *FRH, IME* 🐾🐾

Carlton Browne of the F.O. Bumbling Brit diplomat Thomas visits tiny Pacific island of Gallardia, forgotten by the mother country for some fifty years, to insure tenuous international agreement after the island's king dies. Not sterling Sellers but some shining moments. *AKA:* Man in a Cocked Hat.
1959 88m/C *GB* Peter Sellers, Terry-Thomas, Lucianna Paluzzi, Ian Bannen; *D:* Roy Boulting, Jeffrey Dell. **VHS, Beta** $19.98 *HBO, FCT* 🐾🐾½

Carmen Choreographer casts Carmen and finds life imitates art when he falls under the spell of the hotblooded Latin siren. Bizet's opera lends itself to erotically charged flamenco context. Well acted, impressive scenes including cigarette girls' dance fight and romance between Carmen and Don Jose. In Spanish with English subtitles.
1983 99m/C *SP* Antonio Gades, Laura Del Sol, Paco DeLucia, Christina Hoyos; *D:* Carlos Savrat. **VHS, Beta** $29.98 *CTH, MED, TAM* 🐾🐾🐾

Carmen Jones Bizet's tale of fickle femme fatale Carmen heads South with an all black cast and new lyrics by Hammerstein II. Soldier Belafonte falls big time for factory working belle Dandridge during the war, and runs off with miss thang after he kills his C.O. and quits the army. Tired of prettyboy Belafonte, Dandridge's eye wanders upon prize pugilist Escamillo, inspiring ex-soldier beau to wring her throaty little neck. Film debuts of Carroll and Peters. More than a little racist undertone to the direction. Actors' singing is dubbed. 🎵 Dat's Love; Dere's a Cafe on de Corner; Beat Out Dat Rhythm on a Drum; You Talk Just Like My Maw; Stand Up and Fight; Dis Flower; My Joe.
1954 105m/C Dorothy Dandridge, Harry Belafonte, Pearl Bailey, Roy Glenn, Diahann Carroll, Brock Peters; *D:* Otto Preminger. Academy Awards '54 Nominations: Best Actress (Dandridge), Best Original Score; Golden Globe Awards '55: Best Film—Musical/Comedy. **VHS, LV** *MLB* 🐾🐾🐾

Carmilla An adaptation of the Sheridan Le Fanu lesbian vampire tale. From Shelley Duvall's cable television series "Nightmare Classics."
1989 60m/C Meg Tilly, Ione Skye, Roddy McDowall, Roy Dotrice; *D:* Gabrielle Beaumont. **VHS, Beta** $59.95 *NO* 🐾🐾🐾

Carnage Hungry house consumes inhabitants.
1984 91m/C Leslie Den Dooven, Michael Chiodo, Deeann Veeder; *D:* Andy Milligan. **VHS, Beta** $49.95 *MED* 🐾

Carnal Crimes Well-acted upscale softcore trash about a sensuous woman, ignored by her middle-aged lawyer husband and drawn to a young stud photographer with a shady past and S&M tendencies. Available in a sexy unrated version also.
1991 (R) 103m/C Martin Hewitt, Linda Carol, Rich Crater, Alex Kubik, Yvette Stefens, Paula Trickey; *D:* Alexander Gregory Hippolyte; *W:* Jon Robert Samsel; *M:* Matthew Ross, Jeff Fishman. **VHS** *NO* 🐾½

Carnal Knowledge Carnal knowledge of the me generation. Three decades in the sex-saturated lives of college buddies Nicholson and Garfunkel, chronicled through girlfriends, affairs and marriages. Controversial upon release, it's not a flattering anatomy of Y chromosome carriers. Originally written as a play. Kane's debut.

1971 (R) 96m/C Jack Nicholson, Candice Bergen, Art Garfunkel, Ann-Margret, Rita Moreno, Carol Kane; *D:* Mike Nichols; *W:* Jules Feiffer. Academy Awards '71 Nominations: Best Supporting Actress (Ann-Margret); Golden Globe Awards '72: Best Supporting Actress (Ann-Margret). **VHS, Beta, LV, 8mm $14.98** *SUE, COL, FOX* 👤👤👤

Carnival in Flanders A 17th century Gallic village threatened by Spanish invaders decides to roll over and play dead and throws a carnival to end all carnivals to welcome the vanquishers-to-be. Classic French farce won gold medal at the Venice International Exposition of Cinematography and the Grand Prix Du Cinema Francais. In French with English subtitles. *AKA:* La Kermesse Heroique.
1935 90m/B *FR* Francoise Rosay, Louis Jouvet, Jean Murat, Andre Aleme, Micheline Cheirel; *D:* Jacques Feyder. **VHS, Beta $24.95** *NOS, MRV, HHT* 👤👤👤½

Carnival Lady Silver spooner Vincent is scheduled to tie the knot until little lady-to-be discovers he's a bit out of pocket after the stock market takes a wee dip. Jilted and impecunious, he heads for the big top, where he horns in on the high diver's turf, and it's all downhill from there.
1933 66m/B Patricia "Boots" Mallory, A. Vincent. **VHS, Beta $29.95** *VCN* 👤

Carnival of Blood Boring talky scenes punctuated by Coney Island murder mayhem followed by more boring talky scenes. Young's debut, not released for five years. The question's not why they delayed release, but why they bothered at all. A carnival of cliches.
1971 (PG) 80m/C Earle Edgerton, Judith Resnick, Martin Barlosky, John Harris, Burt Young; *W:* Leonard Kirtman. **VHS, Beta** *NO* 👤

Carnival of Souls Cult-followed zero budget zombie opera has young Hilligoss and girlfriends take wrong turn off bridge into river. Mysteriously unscathed, Hilligoss rents room and takes job as church organist, but she keeps running into dancing dead people, led by director Harvey. Spooky, very spooky. Laserdisc version offers restored picture quality and a refined audio track, as well as introductory feature on the movie's background.
1962 80m/B Candace Hilligoss, Sidney Berger, Frances Feist, Stan Levitt, Art Ellison, Herk Harvey; *D:* Herk Harvey. **VHS, Beta, LV $19.99** *VID, MRV, SNC* 👤👤👤

Carnival Rock Story of love triangular in seedy nightclub. Club owner Stewart loves chanteuse Cabot who loves card playin' Hutton. Who cares? Maybe hard-core Corman devotees. Good tunes from the Platters, the Blockbusters, Bob Luman and David Houston.
1957 80m/B Susan Cabot, Brian Hutton, David J. Stewart, Dick Miller; *D:* Roger Corman. **VHS, Beta $9.95** *RHI, AOV, FCT* 👤½

Carnival Story Yet another melodramatic cliche about love triangular under the big top. German girl joins American-owned carnival and two guys start acting out unbecoming territorial behavior. Filmed in Germany.
1954 94m/C Anne Baxter, Steve Cochran, Lyle Bettger, George Nader; *D:* Kurt Neumann. **VHS, Beta, 3/4U, Special order formats $19.95** *NOS, GEM, DVT* 👤½

The Carnivores The flesh-eaters of the animal kingdom—bears, lions, tigers, and others—and their survival instincts are the focus of this nature documentary.
1983 90m/C VHS, Beta $69.95 *DIS* 👤👤

Carnosaur Straight from the Corman film factory, this exploitive quickie about dinosaurs harkens back to '50s-style monster epics. Predictable plot with extremely cheap effects. Genetic scientist Dr. Jane Tiptree (Ladd) is hatching diabolic experiments with chickens when things go awry. The experiments result in a bunch of lethal prehistoric creatures wrecking havoc among the community.
1993 (R) 82m/C Diane Ladd, Raphael Sbarge, Jennifer Runyon, Harrison Page, Clint Howard, Ned Bellamy; *W/D:* Adam Simon. **VHS** *NHO* 👤👤

Carny Hothead carnival bozo Busey and peacemaker Robertson experience friendship difficulties when runaway Foster rolls in hay with one and then other. Originally conceived as a documentary by "Derby" filmmaker Kaylor, it's a candid, unsavory, behind-the-scenes anatomy. Co-written by "The Band" member Robertson.
1980 (R) 102m/C Gary Busey, Robbie Robertson, Jodie Foster, Meg Foster, Kenneth McMillan, Elisha Cook Jr., Craig Wasson; *D:* Robert Kaylor. **VHS, Beta $19.98** *FOX, WAR* 👤👤👤

Carolina Skeletons As a child in a small southern town Gossett, Jr. watched as his brother was accused of a vicious double murder and quickly tried and executed. Thirty years later, the ex-Green Beret returns home to find the real killer and clear his brother's name. But there are those in the town who will do anything to stop their secrets from being revealed.
1992 (R) 94m/C Louis Gossett Jr., Bruce Dern, Melissa Leo, Paul Robeling, G.D. Spradlin, Bill Cobbs, Henderson Forsythe, Clifton James; *D:* John Erman; *W:* Tracy Keenan Wynn; *M:* John Morris. **VHS** *TRI* 👤👤

Caroline? A wealthy young woman is presumed dead in a plane crash. Now 15 years later a stranger appears at the family home claiming to be Caroline—and wanting her inheritance. Is it possible that what she says is true or is it all an elaborate ruse? An especially good performance by Zimbalist. Made for television as a "Hallmark Hall of Fame" presentation. Based on the novel "Father's Arcane Daughter" by E.L. Konigsburg.
1990 (PG) 100m/C Stephanie Zimbalist, Pamela Reed, George Grizzard, Dorothy McGuire, Patricia Neal; *D:* Joseph Sargent. **VHS, LV $89.98** *REP* 👤👤👤

Carousel Much-loved Rodgers & Hammerstein musical based on Ferenc Molnar's play "Liliom" (filmed by Fritz Lang in 1935) about a swaggering carnival barker (MacRae) who tries to change his life after he falls in love with a good woman. Killed while attempting to foil a robbery he was supposed to help commit, he begs his heavenly hosts for the chance to return to the mortal realm just long enough to set things straight with his teenage daughter. Now indisputably a classic, the film lost $2 million when it was released. 🎵If I Loved You; Soliloquy; You'll Never Walk Alone; What's the Use of Wond'rin; When I Marry Mister Snow; When the Children Are Asleep; A Real Nice Clambake; Carousel Ballet; Carousel Waltz; You're a Queer One, Julie Jordan; Mr. Snow; June is Bustin' Out All Over; Soliloquy.
1956 128m/C Gordon MacRae, Shirley Jones, Cameron Mitchell, Gene Lockhart, Barbara Ruick, Robert Rounseville, Richard Deacon, Tor Johnson; *D:* Henry King; *M:* Richard Rodgers, Oscar Hammerstein. **VHS, Beta, LV $19.98** *FOX, RDG, HMV* 👤👤👤

The Carpathian Eagle Police wonder why murdered victims have hearts ripped out while audience wonders what weird title has to do with anything. Routine evisceration fest, part of Elvira's Thriller Video.
1981 60m/C Suzanne Danielle, Sian Phillips, Pierce Brosnan, Anthony Valentine; *D:* Francis Megahy. **VHS, Beta $29.95** *LIV* 👤

The Carpenter Post-nervous breakdown woman receives nightly visits from guy who builds stuff with wood. Very scary stuff. Also available in slightly longer unrated version.
1989 (R) 85m/C Wings Hauser, Lynne Adams, Pierce Lenoir, Barbara Ann Jones; *D:* David Wellington. **VHS, LV $89.98** *REP, PIA* 👤

Carpet of Horror The city of London is terrorized by a small ball emitting poison gas in this schlock horror film. Death results when the ball is rolled into the living rooms of intended victims.
1964 ?m/C Joachim Berger, Carl Lange, Karin Dor. **VHS $16.95** *SNC* 👤👤

The Carpetbaggers Uncannily Howard Hughesian Peppard wallows in wealth and women in Hollywood in the 1920s and 1930s. Spayed version of the Harold Robbins novel. Ladd's final appearance. Followed by the prequel "Nevada Smith." Introduced by Joan Collins.
1964 (PG) 150m/C George Peppard, Carroll Baker, Alan Ladd, Elizabeth Ashley, Lew Ayres, Martha Hyer, Martin Balsam, Robert Cummings; *D:* Edward Dmytryk. **VHS, Beta $59.95** *PAR* 👤👤

Carrie In a part turned down by Cary Grant, Olivier plays a married American who self destructs as the woman he loves scales the heights to fame and fortune. The manager of a posh epicurean mecca, Olivier deserts wife Hopkins and steals big bucks from his boss to head east with paramour Jones, a country bumpkin transplanted to Chicago. Once en route to thespian fame in the Big Apple, Jones abandons her erstwhile beau, who crumbles pathetically. Adapted from Theodore Dreiser's "Sister Carrie," it's mega melodrama, but the performances are above reproach.
1952 118m/B Laurence Olivier, Jennifer Jones, Miriam Hopkins, Eddie Albert, Basil Ruysdael, Ray Teal, Barry Kelley, Sara Berner, William Reynolds, Mary Murphy; *D:* William Wyler. **VHS, Beta, LV $19.98** *PAR, FCT* 👤👤👤

Carrie Overprotected by religious fanatic mother Laurie and mocked by the in-crowd, shy, withdrawn high school girl Carrie White is asked to the prom. Realizing she's been made the butt of a joke, she unleashes her considerable telekinetic talents. Travolta, Allen, and Irving are teenagers who get what they deserve. Based on the Stephen King novel. Laserdisc version features the original movie trailer, an interview with screenwriter Lawrence D. Cohen, publicity shots, a study of De Palma's film-making techniques, and commentary by film expert Laurent Bouzereau.
1976 (R) 98m/C Sissy Spacek, Piper Laurie, John Travolta, William Katt, Amy Irving, Nancy Allen, Edie McClurg, Betty Buckley; *D:* Brian DePalma. **VHS, Beta, LV $19.95** *FOX, MGM, CRC* 👤👤👤

The Carrier Smalltown Sleepy Rock is ideal family-raising turf until plague mysteriously blights inhabitants, and townspeople are out to exterminate all potential carriers. Silverman is standout as local spiritual leader; well orchestrated crowd scenes. Best park your IQ before watching. Filmed on location in Manchester, Michigan.

1987 (R) 99m/C Gregory Fortescue, Steve Dixon, Paul Silverman; **D:** Nathan J. White. **VHS, Beta** *NO* 𝆕𝆕

Carrington, V.C. British army major Niven is brought up for a court-martial on embezzlement charges because he arranges, without official permission, to be reimbursed for money owed to him. A former war hero, he decides to defend himself in court, and, once an affair comes to light, his vindictive wife joins the opposition. Good cast, superlative Niven performance. **AKA:** Court Martial.
1954 100m/B *GB* David Niven, Margaret Leighton, Noelle Middleton, Laurence Naismith; **D:** Anthony Asquith. **VHS, Beta $39.95** *MON* 𝆕𝆕𝆕

Carry Me Back Two brothers carry dead dad back to Australian ranch in order to inherit mucho dinero.
1982 93m/C *AU* Grant Tilly, Kelly Johnson. **VHS, Beta $39.95** *LIV* 𝆕½

Carry On Admiral Weak British comedy about two friends who get drunk and decide it would be fun to switch identities. One has an easy job as a public relations exec but the other is supposedly the captain of a ship. His lack of sea knowledge causes wacky catastrophes. Unrelated to the "Carry On" series of comedies. **AKA:** The Ship was Loaded.
1957 85m/B *GB* David Tomlinson, Brian Reece, Peggy Cummins, Eunice Gayson, A.E. Matthews, Lionel Murton, Joan Sims; **W/D:** Val Guest. **VHS** *NO* 𝆕½

Carry On at Your Convenience Low-brow humor in and around a toilet factory.
1971 86m/C *GB* Sidney James, Kenneth Williams, Charles Hawtrey, Joan Sims, Kenneth Cope; **D:** Gerald Thomas. **VHS, Beta $19.95** *NO* 𝆕½

Carry On Behind "Carry On" crew heads for archeological dig and find themselves sharing site with holiday caravan.
1975 95m/C *GB* Sid James, Kenneth Williams, Elke Sommer, Joan Sims; **D:** Gerald Thomas. **VHS, Beta $59.98** *SUE* 𝆕𝆕

Carry On Cleo "Carry On" spoof of Shakespeare's "Antony and Cleopatra."
1965 91m/C *GB* Sidney James, Amanda Barrie, Kenneth Williams, Kenneth Connor, Jim Dale, Charles Hawtrey, Joan Sims; **D:** Gerald Thomas. **VHS, Beta $39.99** *HBO* 𝆕𝆕½

Carry On Cowboy "Carry On" Western parody of "High Noon." **AKA:** Rumpo Kid.
1966 91m/C *GB* Sidney James, Kenneth Williams, Jim Dale. **VHS, Beta $69.99** *HBO* 𝆕𝆕

Carry On Cruising "Carry On" gang attacks sailing world with low humor and raunchiness.
1962 89m/C *GB* Sidney James, Kenneth Williams, Liz Fraser; **D:** Gerald Thomas. **VHS, Beta $59.99** *HBO* 𝆕

Carry On Dick What made the seemingly endless "Carry On" series of super-low-budget British farces such a hit is a mystery not to be solved. Low production values, scripts that peter out midway, and manifest humor don't normally a classic make; and yet the gang has its following. "Dick," a detective movie spoof, was preceded by some twenty-odd carryings on; suffice it to say that the series, which began in 1958 with "Carry on Sergeant," has not improved with age in subsequent incarnations.
1975 95m/C *GB* Sid James, Joan Sims; **D:** Gerald Thomas. **VHS** *TPV* 𝆕𝆕

Carry On Doctor British series continues as characters of questionable competence join the medical profession. Hospital staff gets caught in battle over secret weight loss formula.
1968 95m/C *GB* Frankie Howerd, Kenneth Williams, Jim Dale, Barbara Windsor; **D:** Gerald Thomas. **VHS $19.95** *PAR* 𝆕𝆕𝆕

Carry On Emmanuelle Bedroom diplomat Emmanuelle enters international politics by taking on foreign legion. Part of the British "Carry On" series.
1978 104m/C *GB* Suzanne Danielle, Kenneth O'Connor, Kenneth Williams, Beryl Reid; **D:** Gerald Thomas. **VHS, Beta** *PGN* 𝆕

Carry On England Mercifully, the gang didn't carry on much beyond this entry, in which a WWII antiaircraft fleet captain bumbles through the usual pranks and imbroglios.
1976 89m/C *GB* Kenneth Connor, Patrick Mower, Judy Geeson; **D:** Gerald Thomas. **VHS** *NO* 𝆕

Carry On Nurse Men's ward in a British hospital declares war on nurses and the rest of the hospital. The second of the "Carry On" series.
1959 86m/B *GB* Shirley Eaton, Kenneth Connor, Hattie Jacques, Wilfrid Hyde-White; **D:** Gerald Thomas. **VHS, Beta $19.95** *NOS, VYY, HBO* 𝆕𝆕

Carry On 'Round the Bend Williams, who played in the original ("Carry On Sergeant"), and Carry On regulars (charpeimugged James and ever-zaftig Jacques), go 'round the bend in yet another installment of the British spoof.
1972 89m/C *GB* Sid James, Kenneth Williams, Hattie Jacques; **D:** Gerald Thomas. **VHS** *TPV* 𝆕½

Carry On Screaming "Carry On" does horror. A pair of goofy detectives trail monsters suspected in kidnapping.
1966 97m/C *GB* Harry H. Corbett, Kenneth Williams, Fenella Fielding, Joan Sims, Charles Hawtrey, Jim Dale, Angela Douglas, Jon Pertwee; **D:** Gerald Thomas. **VHS $19.98** *MOV* 𝆕𝆕

The Cars That Ate Paris Parasitic town in the Parisian (Australia) outback preys on car and body parts generated by deliberate accidents inflicted by wreck-driving wreckless youths. Weir's first film released internationally, about a small Australian town that survives economically via deliberately contriving car accidents and selling the wrecks' scrap parts. A broad, bitter black comedy with some horror touches. **AKA:** The Cars That Eat People.
1974 (PG) 91m/C *AU* Terry Camilleri, Kevin Miles, John Meillon, Melissa Jaffe; **D:** Peter Weir. **VHS, Beta $19.95** *COL* 𝆕𝆕𝆕

Carson City Kid Typical western which has Rogers trying to exact revenge on the man who killed his brother.
1940 54m/B Roy Rogers, Dale Evans. **VHS, Beta $19.95** *NOS, VCN, MED* 𝆕½

Cartel O'Keeffe, "B" actor extraordinaire, plays the wrong man to pick on in this rancid dope opera. Hounded by drug lord Stroud and framed for murder, pilot O'Keeffe decides the syndicate has gone too doggone far when they kill his sister. Exploitive and otherwise very bad.
1990 (R) 106m/C Miles O'Keeffe. **VHS, LV** *IME Woof!*

Carthage in Flames A graphic portrayal of the destruction of ancient Carthage in a blood and guts battle for domination of the known world. A tender love story is a welcome aside in this colorful Italian-made epic. **AKA:** Cartagine in Fiamme; Carthage en Flammes.
1960 96m/C *IT* Anne Heywood, Jose Suarez, Pierre Brasseur; **D:** Carmine Gallone. **VHS, Beta** *NO* 𝆕𝆕

Cartier Affair A beautiful television actress unwittingly falls in love with the man who wants to steal her jewels. Collins designed her own wardrobe. Made for television.
1984 120m/C Joan Collins, David Hasselhoff, Telly Savalas, Ed Lauter, Joe La Due; **D:** Rod Holcomb. **VHS, Beta $39.98** *LHV, WAR* 𝆕

Cartoon All-Stars to the Rescue Cartoon characters from Winnie the Pooh to the Ninja Turtles help kids understand the dangers of drug abuse.
1990 60m/C VHS *BVV* 𝆕

Cartoon Carnival, Vol. 1 Includes "Song of the Birds" (Max Fleischer), "Jerky Turkey" (MGM), "The Talking Magpies" (Terrytoons), "Jasper in the Haunted House" (George Pal), "It's a Hap Hap Happy Day" (Max Fleischer), "Boy Meets Dog" (Walter Lantz), and "The Friendly Ghost" (Harvey Cartoons).
193? 51m/C VHS, Beta $19.95 *HHT* 𝆕

Cartoon Carnival, Vol. 2 A compilation of 8 classic cartoons: "Pincushion Man," "Mary's Little Lamb" and "Jack Frost," all by Ub Iwerks; Max Fleischer's "Cobweb Hotel;" "Farm Frolics," a Merrie Melodies cartoon; Porky Pig in "Timid Toreador;" "Pantry Panic," starring Woody Woodpecker; and a Looney Tunes cartoon, "Hollywood Capers."
193? 55m/C VHS, Beta $30.00 *HHT* 𝆕

Cartoon Cavalcade Here are three classic cartoons from Burt Gillette and Ub Iwerkes: "Molly Moo Cow and the Indians," "The Three Bears," and "Molly Moo Cow and Rip Van Winkle."
1935 23m/C VHS, Beta $19.98 *CCB* 𝆕

Cartoon Classics Three vintage cartoons, in black & white and color: "Baby Be Good," a Betty Boop classic, "Secret Agent," anti-Nazi Superman agitprop, and "King for a Day," an adventure set in Swift's Lilliput.
1940 30m/C VHS, Beta $59.95 *JEF* 𝆕

Cartoon Classics in Color, No. 1 Eight cartoon classics filled with color, movement and lots of fun comprise this tape: "Little Black Sambo," "Jack Frost," "Sinbad the Sailor," "Simple Simon," "Ali Baba," "Molly Moo Cow and the Butterflies," "The Toonerville Trolley," and "Somewhere in Dreamland." Reflects the social consciousness of the time, which some may find offensive.
193? 60m/C VHS, Beta $24.95 *VYY, WTA* 𝆕

Cartoon Classics in Color, No. 2 Presents eight animated Warner Brothers favorites. Includes: Daffy Duck in "Yankee Doodle Daffy," Porky Pig in "Ali Baba Bound," and Bugs Bunny in "Falling Hare."
194? 60m/C D: Chuck Jones, Robert McKimson, Friz Freleng. **VHS, Beta $24.95** *VYY, WTA* 𝆕

Cartoon Classics in Color, No. 3 Various Warner Bros. Bugs/Daffy/Elmer/etc. cartoons from the war years: "A Corny Concerto," "Foney Fables," "The Wacky," "Fifth Column Mouse," "To Duck Or Not To Duck," "The Early Worm Gets the Bird," and "Daffy the Commando."
1943 60m/C D: Bob Clampett, Chuck Jones, Friz Freleng, Robert McKimson. **VHS, Beta, 8mm $24.95** *VYY, WTA* 𝆕

C

Cartoon Classics in Color, No. 4 Another collection of Warner cartoons, featuring Daffy and Bugs: "The Wabbit Who Came To Supper," "A Tale of," "Wackiki Wabbitt," "Daffy Duck and the Dinosaur," and "Fresh Hare."
1948 54m/C *D:* Chuck Jones, Robert McKimson, Friz Freleng, Bob Clampett. VHS, Beta, 8mm $24.95 *VYY, WTA ♫*

Cartoon Classics, No. 1: Looney Tunes & Merrie Melodies A collection of early sound cartoons each based on an extended jazz number: "The Queen Was in the Parlor," "Freddy the Freshman," "Red Headed Baby," "Battling Bosko," "You're Too Careless with Your Kisses," "It's Got Me Again," "Moonlight for Two," and "You Don't Know What You're Doin'."
1933 56m/B VHS, Beta, 8mm $24.95 *VYY, WTA ♫*

Cartoon Classics, No. 4: Cobweb Hotel A collection of eight classic early cartoons, dating from 1929 to 1942. Porky Pig makes a few of his first appearances.
19?? 55m/B *D:* Friz Freleng, Bob Clampett, Paul Terry. VHS, Beta $9.98 *VYY, WTA ♫*

Cartoon Classics, No. 6: Early Animation Seven early cartoons, including two featuring then-famous comic strip stars Mutt and Jeff ("Invisible Revenge" and "Cramps") and Winsor McCay's famous "Gertie," the first animated short ever. Other titles are: "Dog-Gone," "Goodrich Dirt," "Cowpuncher," "Willi's Nightmare," and "The Animated Grouch Chaser."
1914 56m/B VHS, Beta, 8mm $24.95 *VYY, WTA ♫*

Cartoon Classics of the 1930s Eight cartoon classics of the 1930s, including "Felix the Cat," "Daffy and the Dinosaur," and "Bold King Cole."
193? 58m/C VHS, Beta $29.95 *MED ♫*

Cartoon Collection, No. 3: Coal Black & de Sebben Dwarfs Another package of 16 Warner Bros. cartoons from the 1930s and 40s, featuring Bugs Bunny, Daffy Duck and Porky Pig. Titles include "Coal Black and de Sebben Dwarfs," "Calling Dr. Porky," "Tom Turk and Daffy" and "Daffy Doc."
194? 115m/B *D:* Chuck Jones, Friz Freleng, Robert McKimson. VHS, Beta $24.95 *SHO, WTA ♫*

Cartoon Moviestars: Bugs! Bugs Bunny performs solo. Included are Jones' "Bugs Bunny and the Three Bears," Clampett's "Bugs Bunny Gets the Boid," and McKimson's "Gorilla My Dreams."
1948 60m/C *D:* Bob Clampett, Friz Freleng, Chuck Jones, Robert McKimson. VHS *MGM ♫*

Cartoon Moviestars: Elmer! Follow the progress of Elmer Fudd. High points: Freleng's "The Hare-Brained Hypnotist," Davis' "What Makes Daff Duck?" and Jones' "A Pest in the House."
1948 60m/C *D:* Arthur Davis, Friz Freleng, Chuck Jones. VHS *MGM ♫*

Cartoon Moviestars: Porky! Porky Pig takes the spotlight, and with him are some of the funniest stories of all time. Freleng's "I Haven't Got a Hat," Jones' "My Favorite Duck," Clampett's "Baby Bottleneck," and McKimson's "Daffy Doodles."
1947 60m/C *D:* Tex Avery, Bob Clampett, Friz Freleng, Chuck Jones, Robert McKimson, Frank Tashlin. VHS *MGM ♫*

Cartoon Parade, Vol. 1 A collection of cartoons starring Bugs Bunny, Daffy Duck, Porky Pig, Popeye, Superman, and more.
194? 120m/C *D:* Friz Freleng. VHS, Beta $19.95 *MED, WTA ♫*

Cartoon Parade, Vol. 2 Laugh with some of your favorite cartoon characters. Included are Bugs Bunny in "Wabbit Who Came to Supper," Popeye in "Popeye Meets Ali Baba," Superman in "Terror on the Midway," Little Lulu in "Bored of Education," and many more.
194? 117m/C VHS, Beta $19.95 *MED, WTA ♫*

Cartoon Parade, Vol. 3 A collection of cartoon classics including "Falling Hare" with Bugs Bunny, "Cheese Burglar" starring Herman and Katnip, "Somewhere in Dreamland," "Robin Hood Makes Good," and others.
194? 110m/C VHS, Beta $19.95 *MED ♫*

Cartoon Parade, Vol. 4 Another collection of popular cartoons from the 30's and 40's, featuring Max Fleischer's Bouncing Ball, Little Lulu, Superman, Bugs Bunny, and Porky Pig. Some cartoons are in black and white.
1942 120m/C VHS, Beta *MED ♫*

Cartoonal Knowledge: Confessions of Farmer Gray A collection of 7 silent cartoons by Terry, including "Day at the Park," "The Window Washers," "A Cat's Life," and "Chemistry Lesson."
1923 54m/B *D:* Paul Terry. VHS, Beta $24.95 *VYY, WTA ♫*

Cartoonal Knowledge: Farmer Gray and the Mice Seven vintage silent cartoons featuring the irascible Farmer Gray and his adventures with barnyard beasts. Directed by Paul Terry. Silent.
1929 55m/B VHS, Beta $24.95 *VYY, WTA ♫*

Cartoonal Knowledge: Farmer Gray Looks at Life Directed by Paul Terry, this compilation features seven Gray silent shorts, with a musical score.
1926 55m/B VHS, Beta $24.95 *VYY, WTA ♫♫½*

Cartoonies: Featuring Betty Boop A collection of Max Fleischer's best loved cartoons featuring America's favorite cartoon vamp.
193? 46m/C VHS $14.98 *REP ♫♫½*

The Cartoons Go to War A compilation of cartoons made during World War II, which hilariously propound caricatured propagandistic messages.
1943 58m/C VHS, Beta $29.95 *VIC ♫♫½*

Cartouche A swashbuckling action-comedy set in 18th-century France. Belmondo plays a charming thief who takes over a Paris gang, aided by the lovely Cardinale. When is captured, she sacrifices her life to save him and Belmondo and his cohorts vow to have their revenge. Based on a French legend and a well-acted combination of tragedy, action, and farce. In French with English subtitles.
AKA: Swords of Blood.
1962 115m/C *FR IT* Jean-Paul Belmondo, Claudia Cardinale, Odile Versois, Philippe Lemaire; *D:* Philippe de Broca. VHS $29.95 *FCT ♫♫♫*

Carve Her Name with Pride The true story of Violette Szabo who at age nineteen became a secret agent with the French Resistance in World War II.
1958 119m/B Virginia McKenna, Paul Scofield. VHS, Beta *LCA ♫♫½*

The Cary Grant Collection Three of Cary Grant's most memorable films: "Father Goose," Oscar-winning script; "Indiscreet" (w/ Ingrid Bergman); and "Operation Petticoat" (Tony Curtis and Grant are quite a team in this military comedy! Some great gags.)
1990 336m/C Cary Grant, Ingrid Bergman, Leslie Caron, Trevor Howard, Tony Curtis, Dina Merrill, Gavin McLeod, Madlyn Rhue; *D:* Ralph Nelson, Stanley Donen, Blake Edwards. VHS, Beta $59.95 *REP ♫♫½*

Casablanca Can you see George Raft as Rick? Jack Warner did, but producer Hal Wallis wanted Bogart. Considered by many to be the best film ever made and one of the most quoted movies of all time, it rocketed Bogart from gangster roles to romantic leads as he and Bergman (who never looked lovelier) sizzle on screen. Bogart runs a gin joint in Morocco during the Nazi occupation, and meets up with Bergman, an old flame, but romance and politics do not mix, especially in Nazi-occupied French Morocco. Greenstreet, Lorre, and Rains all create memorable characters, as does Wilson, the piano player to whom Bergman says the oft-misquoted, "Play it, Sam." Without a doubt, the best closing scene ever written; it was scripted on the fly during the end of shooting, and actually shot several ways. Written by the Epsteins and Koch from an unproduced play. See it in the original black and white. The laserdisc edition features restored imaging and sound and commentary by film historian Ronald Haver about the film's production, the play it was originally based on, and the famed evolution of the screenplay on audio track two. The 50th Anniversary Edition contains a restored and remastered print, the original 1942 theatrical trailer, a film documentary narrated by Lauren Bacall, and a booklet.
1942 (PG) 102m/B Humphrey Bogart, Ingrid Bergman, Paul Henreid, Claude Rains, Peter Lorre, Sydney Greenstreet, Conrad Veidt, S.Z. Sakall, Dooley Wilson, Marcel Dalio, John Qualen; *D:* Michael Curtiz; *W:* Julius J. Epstein, Philip C. Epstein, Howard Koch; *M:* Max Steiner. Academy Awards '43: Best Director (Curtiz), Best Picture, Best Screenplay; Nominations: Best Actor (Bogart), Best Black and White Cinematography, Best Film Editing, Best Supporting Actor (Rains), Best Original Score; National Board of Review Awards '45: 10 Best Films of the Year. VHS, Beta, LV, 8mm *MGM, OM ♫♫♫♫*

Casablanca Express Nazi commandos hijack Churchill's train in this action-adventure drama.
1989 90m/C Glenn Ford, Donald Pleasence, Jason Connery; *D:* Sergio Martino. VHS, Beta *NO ♫*

Casanova A comedic romp through the bedrooms of 18th-century Europe with Chamberlain as the legendary lover. Lots of lovely ladies and hammy performances. Made for television.
1987 (PG-13) 122m/C Richard Chamberlain, Faye Dunaway, Sylvia Kristel, Ornella Muti, Hanna Schygulla, Sophie Ward, Frank Finlay, Kenneth Colley; *D:* Simon Langton; *W:* George MacDonald Fraser. VHS, Beta, LV $89.98 *TTC ♫♫*

Casanova '70 Mastroianni plays a handsome soldier who has a knack for enticing liberated women in this comic rendition of the much-cinematized legendary yarn. Trouble is, he's in the mood only when he believes that he's in imminent danger. In Italian with English subtitles.

1965 113m/C *IT* Marcello Mastroianni, Virna Lisi, Michele Mercier, Guido Alberti, Margaret Lee, Bernard Blier, Liana Orfei; *D:* Mario Monicelli. VHS *FOX* 🐾🐾½

Casanova's Big Night Classic slapstick comedy stars Hope masquerading as Casanova to determine the nature of Fontaine's intentions in marrying the real Casanova. The all-star cast provides one hilarious scene after another in this dated film. Price has a cameo as the "real" Casanova. Based on a story by Aubrey Wisberg.
1954 85m/C Bob Hope, Joan Fontaine, Audrey Dalton, Basil Rathbone, Hugh Marlowe, Vincent Price, John Carradine, Raymond Burr; *D:* Norman Z. McLeod; *W:* Hal Kanter, Edmund Hartmann. VHS, LV $14.95 *PAR, CCB* 🐾🐾½

A Case of Deadly Force Based on the true story of a black man wrongfully killed by Boston's Tactical Police Force who mistook him for a robber. The police investigation calls it self-defense but the family and the attorney they hire fight to change the verdict. Excellent cast, great dramatic story. Originally made for television.
1986 95m/C Richard Crenna, John Shea, Lorraine Toussaint, Frank McCarthy, Tom Isbell; *D:* Michael Miller. VHS $79.95 *CAF* 🐾🐾🐾

A Case of Libel A made for television dramatization based on attorney Louis Nizer's account of Quentin Reynolds' libel suit against columnist Westbrook Pegler.
1983 90m/C Daniel J. Travanti, Ed Asner; *D:* Eric Till. VHS, Beta $59.95 *LIV* 🐾🐾🐾

Case of the Baby Sitter A private eye investigates jewel thieves posing as nobility.
1947 40m/B Tom Neal, Allen Jenkins, Pamela Blake. VHS, Beta, LV $16.95 *SNC* 🐾

The Case of the Frightened Lady A homicidal family does its collective best to keep its dark past a secret in order to collect some inheritance money. Watch, if you're still awake, for the surprise ending. *AKA:* The Frightened Lady.
1939 80m/B *GB* Marius Goring, Helen Haye, Penelope Dudley Ward, Felix Aylmer, Patrick Barr; *D:* George King. VHS, Beta $16.95 *CNC* 🐾

The Case of the Lucky Legs Yes, there was a Perry Mason before Raymond Burr. Erle Stanley Gardner's sleuthing litigator's first screen appearance came in 1934 with "The Case of the Howling Dog," which initiated Warner Brothers' "A"-grade (but soon-to-be "B"-grade) series. More akin to Nick Charles than to Gardner's character or to his later TV incarnation, the "Lucky Legs" Perry is a high-living, interminably hungover tippler who winces and wisecracks as he unravels the case of the corpse of a crooked con man. William, who left shortly after the series was downgraded to "B" status, plays the esquire; Tobin plays his smart-mouthed secretary, and Ellis is the tomato suspected of murder. Mayo, by the way, went on to direct "The Petrified Forest" the following year.
1935 76m/B Warren William, Genevieve Tobin, Patricia Ellis, Lyle Talbot, Allen Jenkins, Barton MacLane, Peggy Shannon, Porter Hall; *D:* Archie Mayo. VHS, Beta $16.95 *SNC, RXM* 🐾🐾½

The Case of the Missing Lady A famous Arctic explorer asks Tommy and Tuppence to find his missing fiancee. Based on the Christie story.
1983 51m/C Francesca Annis, James Warwick; *W:* Agatha Christie. VHS, Beta $14.95 *PAV* 🐾½

The Case of the Mukkinese Battle Horn The cast of Britain's "The Goon Show" takes over in a zany, slapdash featurette-length mystery spoof.
1956 27m/C *GB* Peter Sellers, Spike Milligan, Dick Emery. VHS, Beta, 8mm $19.95 *VYY* 🐾🐾

Casey at the Bat From Shelley Duvall's made for cable television "Tall Tales and Legends" series, in which the immortal poem is brought to life. Rousing comedy for the whole family.
1985 52m/C Bill Macy, Hamilton Camp, Elliott Gould, Carol Kane, Howard Cosell; *D:* David Steinberg. VHS, Beta $19.98 *FOX* 🐾🐾

Casey Jones and Fury (Brave Stallion) An episode from each of these early adventure series.
1957 60m/B Alan Hale Jr., Peter Graves. VHS, Beta $24.95 *NOS, DVT* 🐾🐾

Casey's Shadow The eight-year-old son of an impoverished horse trainer raises a quarter horse and enters it in the world's richest horse race.
1978 (PG) 116m/C Walter Matthau, Alexis Smith, Robert Webber, Murray Hamilton; *D:* Martin Ritt. VHS, Beta $59.95 *COL* 🐾🐾

Cash A bankrupt financier uses counterfeit money to promote a new company. Also called "For Love or Money."
1934 63m/B *GB* Robert Donat, Wendy Barrie, Edmund Gwenn; *D:* Zoltan Korda. VHS, Beta $29.95 *NOS, MRV, DVT* 🐾🐾

Casimir the Great A dramatized biography of the popular ruler who was instrumental in Poland's development during the period of transition between ancient and modern times. Presented in two segments. In Polish with English subtitles.
19?? ?m/C *PL* Krzysztof Chamiec, Wladyslaw Hanoza. VHS $69.95 *FCT* 🐾🐾½

Casino A made-for-television thriller about back-stabbings and ritzy romance aboard a high-priced gambling liner.
1980 100m/C Mike Connors, Lynda Day George, Bo Hopkins, Gary Burghoff, Joseph Cotten, Robert Reed, Barry Sullivan; *D:* Don Chaffey. VHS, Beta $79.95 *PSM* 🐾½

Casino Royale The product of five directors, three writers and a mismatched cast of dozens, this virtually plotless spoof of James Bond films can stand as one of the low-water marks for 1960s comedy. And yet, there are some marvelous bits within, scenes of bizarre hilarity. Welles and Sellers literally couldn't stand the sight of one another, and their scenes together were filmed separately, with stand-ins.
1967 130m/C David Niven, Woody Allen, Peter Sellers, Ursula Andress, Orson Welles, Jacqueline Bisset, Deborah Kerr, Peter O'Toole, Jean-Paul Belmondo, Charles Boyer, Joanna Pettet, John Huston, William Holden, George Raft; *D:* John Huston, Ken Hughes, Robert Parrish, Val Guest, Joseph McGrath. VHS, Beta, LV $19.95 *MRV, COL* 🐾

Casper the Friendly Ghost Compilation of classic Casper cartoons from the long-running children's show.
1953 60m/C VHS, Beta $9.95 *WOV, WTA* 🐾

Cass Disenchanted filmmaker returns home to Australia to experiment with alternative lifestyles.
1978 90m/C Michelle Fawden, John Waters, Judy Morris, Peter Carroll. VHS, Beta $19.98 *VID* 🐾

Cass Timberlane Scandalous story of a May-December romance set in a small Midwestern town. Tracy stars as Cass Timberlane, a widowed judge who falls for a voluptuous young girl from the wrong side of the tracks (Turner). They marry and experience problems when she is shunned by his snobbish friends. Good performances, especially from the supporting cast, dominate this fairly predictable film. Based on the novel by Sinclair Lewis.
1947 119m/B Spencer Tracy, Lana Turner, Zachary Scott, Tom Drake, Mary Astor, Albert Dekker, Margaret Lindsay, John Litel, Mona Barrie, Josephine Hutchinson, Rose Hobart, Selena Royle; *Cameos:* Walter Pidgeon; *D:* George Sidney; *W:* Donald Ogden Stewart. VHS $19.98 *MGM* 🐾🐾½

Cassandra A fragile young woman has dreams that foretell the future—specifically, a series of grisly murders.
1987 (R) 94m/C Shane Briant, Brionny Behets, Tessa Humphries, Kit Taylor, Lee James; *D:* Colin Eggleston. VHS, Beta, LV *NO* 🐾

The Cassandra Crossing A terrorist with the plague causes havoc on a transcontinental luxury train. Turgid adventure filmed in France and Italy.
1976 (R) 129m/C *GB* Sophia Loren, Richard Harris, Ava Gardner, Burt Lancaster, Martin Sheen, Ingrid Thulin, Lee Strasberg, John Phillip Law, Lionel Stander, O.J. Simpson, Ann Turkel, Alida Valli; *D:* George P. Cosmatos; *M:* Jerry Goldsmith. VHS, Beta *FOX* 🐾½

Cassie Follows the rise of Cassie, a successful country and western singer, and documents all her trials along the way.
1987 (R) 75m/C Marilyn Chambers; *D:* Godfrey Daniels. VHS, Beta *NO* 🐾

Cast a Deadly Spell A bubbly, flavorful witch's brew of private-eye and horror cliches, set in a fantasy version of 1948 Los Angeles where sorcery and voodoo abound, but gumshoe Harry P. Lovecraft uses street smarts instead of magic to track down a stolen Necronomicon—and if you know what that is you'll want to watch. Wild creatures and f/x wizardry complement this made-for-cable-TV trick and treat.
1991 (R) 93m/C Fred Ward, David Warner, Julianne Moore, Clancy Brown, Alexandra Powers; *D:* Martin Campbell; *W:* Joseph Dougherty, Joseph Dougherty. VHS, LV $89.99 *HBO* 🐾🐾🐾

Cast a Giant Shadow Follows the career of Col. David Marcus, hero of the Arab-Israeli War.
1966 138m/C Kirk Douglas, Senta Berger, Angie Dickinson, John Wayne, James Donald, Chaim Topol, Frank Sinatra, Yul Brynner; *D:* Melville Shavelson. VHS, Beta $59.98 *FOX* 🐾

Cast the First Stone Made for TV soaper based on the true story of a former nun who becomes a small town schoolteacher. After being raped, Diane Martin discovers she's pregnant and when she decides to keep the baby the school board dismisses her. The plot centers around her fight to regain her job and dignity—while trying to convince everybody that she doesn't deserve to lose her job simply because she is an unwed mother. Eikenberry gives a strong performance, but it can't carry this lackluster film.
1989 94m/C Jill Eikenberry, Richard Masur, Joe Spano, Lew Ayres, Holly Palance; *D:* John Korty. VHS, LV $59.95 *COL* 🐾🐾

Castaway Based on the factual account by Lucy Irvine. The story of Michael Wilmington, who placed an ad for a young woman to spend a year on a Pacific atoll with him, and the battle of the sexes that followed.
1987 (R) 118m/C Oliver Reed, Amanda Donohoe, Tony Rickards, Georgina Hale; *D:* Nicolas Roeg. VHS, Beta $19.98 *WAR* 🐾🐾½

The Castaway Cowboy A shanghaied cowboy becomes partners with a widow when she turns her Hawaiian potato farm into a cattle ranch. Good, clean "family fare."
1974 (G) 91m/C James Garner, Robert Culp, Vera Miles; **D:** Vincent McEveety. **VHS, Beta** DIS, OM ♂♂

Casting Call Eighteen would-be Hollywood starlets undress and cavort for the camera, in hopes of getting real film work.
1988 60m/C **VHS, Beta, CV** $19.95 AHV ♂

The Castle A man is summoned by the seemingly invisible occupants of a castle to their village. All his efforts to meet with those inhabiting the castle are futile and the task gradually becomes his obsession. Both wonderfully acted and shot, this is a well-executed adaptation of Franz Kafka's novel. **AKA:** Das Schloss.
1968 90m/C GE SI Maximilian Schell, Cordula Trantow, Trudik Daniel, Helmut Qualtinger; **D:** Rudolf Noelte. **VHS, Beta** $79.98 CGH ♂♂♂

Castle in the Desert Charlie Chan investigates murder and other strange goings-on in a spooky old castle. One of the last in the series.
1942 62m/B Sidney Toler, Arleen Whelan, Richard Derr, Douglas Dumbrille, Henry Daniell, Victor Sen Yung; **D:** Harry Lachman. **VHS** $19.98 FOX ♂♂½

Castle of Blood Staying overnight in a haunted castle, a poet is forced to deal with a number of creepy encounters. Cult favorite Steele enhances this atmospheric chiller. Dubbed in English. **AKA:** Castle of Terror; Coffin of Terror; Danza Macabra.
1964 85m/B IT FR Barbara Steele, George Riviere, Margrete Robsahm, Henry Kruger, Montgomery Glenn, Sylvia Sorente; **D:** Anthony Dawson. **VHS** $16.95 SNC ♂♂

The Castle of Cagliostro An animated Japanese adventure tale featuring a hero named Wolf, who's a thief. Wolf infiltrates the suspicious country of Cagliostro, whose one industry is conterfeiting money, and winds up rescuing a princess. Lots of violence to go with the action. In Japanese with English subtitles.
1980 100m/C JP **VHS** $29.95 WTA, STP ♂♂

Castle of Evil Group of heirs gathers on a deserted isle to hear the reading of the will of your basic mad scientist. One by one, they fall victim to a humanoid created by the loony doc in his own image. Inspired moments of unintentional fun.
1966 81m/C Scott Brady, Virginia Mayo, Lisa Gaye, David Brian, Hugh Marlowe, William Thourlby, Shelly Morrison; **D:** Francis D. Lyon. **VHS** $14.98 REP, FCT Woof!

The Castle of Fu Manchu The final chapter in a series starring Lee as the wicked doctor. This time, Lee has developed a gadget which will put the earth into a deep freeze, and at his mercy. To fine tune this contraption, he enlists the help of a gifted scientist by abducting him. However, the helper/hostage has a bad ticker, so Lee must abduct a heart surgeon to save his life, and thus, the freezer project. Most critics felt this was the weakest installment in the series. **AKA:** Assignment: Istanbul; Die Folterkammer des Dr. Fu Manchu.
1968 (PG) 92m/C GE SP IT GB Christopher Lee, Richard Greene, H. Marion Crawford, Tsai Chin, Gunther Stoll, Rosalba (Sara Bay) Neri, Maria Perschy; **D:** Jess (Jesus) Franco. **VHS** $19.95 MRV ♂

Castle of the Creeping Flesh A surgeon's daughter is brutally murdered. Vowing to bring her back he begins ripping out the organs of innocent people and transplanting them into her body. Has the dubious honor of being one of the few movies to sport actual open heart surgery footage. So bad it's...just bad.
1968 85m/C Adrian Hoven, Janine Reynaud, Howard Vernon; **D:** Percy G. Parker. **VHS, Beta** NO Woof!

Castle of the Living Dead Evil Count Drago's hobbies include mummifying a traveling circus group visiting his castle. Lee is as evil as ever, but be sure to look for Sutherland's screen debut. In a dual role, he plays not only the bumbling inspector, but also a witch, in drag. **AKA:** Il Castello de Morti Vivi.
1964 90m/B IT FR Christopher Lee, Gala Germani, Phillippe LeRoy, Jacques Stanislawsky, Donald Sutherland; **D:** Herbert Wise. **VHS** $16.95 SNC, MRV ♂♂

Casual Sex? Two young women, looking for love and commitment, take a vacation at a posh resort where they are confronted by men with nothing on their minds but sex, be it casual or the more formal black-tie variety. Supposedly an examination of safe sex in a lightly comedic vein, though the comic is too light and the morality too limp. Adapted from the play by Wendy Goldman and Judy Toll.
1988 (R) 87m/C Lea Thompson, Victoria Jackson, Stephen Shellan, Jerry Levine, Mary Gross, Andrew Dice Clay; **D:** Genevieve Robert. **VHS, Beta, LV** $19.95 MCA ♂½

Casualities of Love: The "Long Island Lolita" Story Told from the Buttafuoco's point of view, Amy Fisher was nothing but a wacko fatally attracted teenager who misunderstood Joey's harmless flirtations and deliberately went after his wife with a gun. The Buttafuocos received $300,000 from CBS to tell their side of the story which features Milano, who resembles Amy not in the least, as the lead. One of three competing network television versions of the sordid story.
1993 (PG-13) ?m/C Jack Scalia, Alyssa Milano, Phyllis Lyons, Jack Kehler, Michael Bowen, J.E. Freeman, Nicky Corello; **W/D:** John Herzfeld. **VHS** $59.95 COL ♂♂

Casualities of War A Vietnam war morality play about army private Fox in the bush who refuses to let his fellow soldiers and commanding sergeant (Penn) skirt responsibility for the rape and murder of a native woman. Fox achieves his dramatic breakthrough. Based on the true story by Daniel Lang.
1989 (R) 105m/C Sean Penn, Michael J. Fox, Don Harvey, Thuy Thu Le; **D:** Brian DePalma; **W:** David Rabe; **M:** Ennio Morricone. **VHS, Beta, LV, 8mm** $14.95 COL ♂♂♂

A Casualty of War Made-for-TV adaptation of Frederic Forsyth's thriller about modern-day arms smuggling (Libya to Ireland) and espionage. Well-acted, with the exception of Hack.
1990 (R) 96m/C Shelley Hack, David Threlfall, Richard Hope, Alan Howard, Clarke Peters; **D:** Tom Clegg; **W:** Frederick Forsyth. **VHS** NO ♂♂½

The Cat A boy and a tamed mountain lion become friends on the run from a murderous poacher.
1966 95m/C Peggy Ann Garner, Roger Perry, Barry Coe; **D:** Ellis Kadisan. **VHS, Beta** $14.95 COL, NLC ♂

Cat and Mouse A very unorthodox police inspector is assigned to investigate a millionaire's mysterious death. Who done it? French dialogue with English subtitles.
1978 (PG) 107m/C FR Michele Morgan, Serge Reggiani, Jean-Pierre Aumont; **D:** Claude Lelouch. **VHS, Beta** $59.95 COL ♂♂♂½

The Cat and the Canary A great silent film about the ghost of a madman that wanders nightly through the corridors of an old house. Remade twice, once in 1939 and again in 1979.
1927 70m/B Laura LaPlante, Creighton Hale, Tully Marshall, Gertrude Astor; **D:** Paul Leni. **VHS, Beta** $19.95 NOS, MRV, VYY ♂♂♂

The Cat and the Canary A stormy night, a gloomy mansion, and a mysterious will combine to create an atmosphere for murder. An entertaining remake of the 1927 silent film.
1979 (PG) 96m/C GB Carol Lynley, Michael Callan, Wendy Hiller, Olivia Hussey, Daniel Massey, Honor Blackman, Edward Fox, Wilfrid Hyde-White; **D:** Radley Metzger. **VHS, Beta** COL, OM ♂♂

The Cat and the Fiddle Lovely Jerome Kern-Oscar Hammerstein operetta in which Novarro plays a struggling composer who forces his affections on MacDonald. She sings in response to his romantic proposals. The final sequence is in color. ♫ The Night Was Made for Love; She Didn't Say 'Yes'; A New Love is Old; Try to Forget; One Moment Alone; Don't Ask Us Not To Sing; I Watch the Love Parade; The Breeze Kissed Your Hair; Impressions in a Harlem Flat; Poor Pierrot; The Crystal Candelabra; Ha! Cha Cha.
1934 90m/B Ramon Novarro, Jeanette MacDonald, Frank Morgan, Charles Butterworth. **VHS** $19.98 MGM ♂♂♂

Cat Ballou At the turn of the century, a schoolmarm turns outlaw with the help of a drunken gunman. Marvin played Kid Shelleen and his silver-nosed evil twin Tim Strawn in this cheery spoof of westerns. Cole and Kaye sing the narration in a one of a kind Greek chorus.
1965 96m/C Jane Fonda, Lee Marvin, Michael Callan, Dwayne Hickman, Reginald Denny, Nat King Cole, Stubby Kaye; **D:** Elliot Silverstein. Academy Awards '65: Best Actor (Marvin); Nominations: Best Adapted Screenplay, Best Film Editing, Best Song ("The Ballad of Cat Ballou"), Best Original Score; Berlin International Film Festival '65: Best Actor (Marvin); British Academy Awards '65: Best Actor (Marvin); Golden Globe Awards '66: Best Actor—Musical/Comedy (Marvin); National Board of Review Awards '65: 10 Best Films of the Year, Best Actor (Marvin). **VHS, Beta** $14.95 COL, BTV ♂♂♂½

Cat Chaser Weller walks listlessly through the role of an ex-soldier in Miami who has an affair with the wife of an exiled—but still lethal—military dictator. Surprisingly low-key, sometimes effective thriller that saves its energy for sex scenes, also available in a less steamy, 90-minute "R" rated version. Based on an Elmore Leonard novel.
1990 97m/C Kelly McGillis, Peter Weller, Charles Durning, Frederic Forrest, Tomas Milian, Juan Fernandez; **D:** Abel Ferrara; **M:** Chick Corea. **VHS** $89.98 VES ♂♂

The Cat from Outer Space An extraterrestrial cat named Jake crashes his spaceship on Earth and leads a group of people on endless escapades. Enjoyable Disney fare.
1978 (G) 103m/C Ken Berry, Sandy Duncan, Harry Morgan, Roddy McDowall, McLean Stevenson; **D:** Norman Tokar. **VHS, Beta** DIS, OM ♂♂

C

Cat Girl A young bride on her honeymoon finds she has inherited the family curse—she has a psychic link to a ferocious leopard. Numerous murders ensue. Poor production value and a weak script, despite Shelley's fine acting, make this an unworthwhile film.
1957 69m/B Barbara Shelley, Robert Ayres, Kay Callard, Paddy Webster; **D:** Alfred Shaughnessy. VHS $9.95 *PAR, COL* ⬥

Cat in the Cage A young man finds many things have changed at home while he was in a mental institution. Dad has remarried, the housekeeper is practicing witchcraft, the chauffeur is after his mistress, and the cat is gone. So where'd that cat go?
1968 96m/C Colleen Camp, Sybil Danning, Mel Novak, Frank De Kova; **D:** Tony Zarin Dast. VHS, Beta $24.95 *GHV* ⬥½

The Cat o' Nine Tails A blind detective and a newsman team up to find a sadistic killer. A gory murder mystery with music by Ennio Morricone.
1971 (PG) 112m/C *GE FR IT* Karl Malden, James Franciscus, Catherine Spaak, Cinzia de Carolis, Carlo Alighiero; **D:** Dario Argento; **M:** Ennio Morricone. VHS, 8mm *SIM* ⬥

Cat on a Hot Tin Roof Tennessee Williams' powerful play about greed and deception in a patriarchal Southern family. Big Daddy (Ives) is dying. Members of the family greedily attempt to capture his inheritance, tearing the family apart. Taylor is a sensual wonder as Maggie the Cat, though the more controversial elements of the play were toned down for the film version. Intense, believable performances from Ives and Newman.
1958 108m/C Paul Newman, Burl Ives, Elizabeth Taylor, Jack Carson, Judith Anderson; **D:** Richard Brooks. Academy Awards '58 Nominations: Best Director (Brooks); Academy Awards '58: Best Actor (Newman), Best Actress (Taylor), Best Adapted Screenplay, Best Color Cinematography, Best Picture; National Board of Review Awards '58: 10 Best Films of the Year. VHS, Beta, LV $19.98 *MGM, PIA, FCT* ⬥⬥⬥½

Cat on a Hot Tin Roof In this adaptation of the Tennessee Williams play, fights over the family inheritance tear a family apart.
1984 122m/C Jessica Lange, Tommy Lee Jones, Rip Torn, Kim Stanley; **D:** Jack Hofsiss. VHS, Beta, LV $19.98 *MGM, LIV, VES* ⬥

Cat People A young dress designer is the victim of a curse that changes her into a deadly panther who must kill to survive. A classic among the horror genre with unrelenting terror from beginning to end. First horror film from producer Val Lewton.
1942 73m/B Jane Randolph, Elizabeth Russell, Jack Holt, Alan Napier, Simone Simon, Kent Smith, Tom Conway; **D:** Jacques Tourneur. VHS, Beta, LV $19.95 *MED, RKO, TTC* ⬥⬥⬥

Cat People A beautiful young woman learns that she has inherited a strange family trait—she turns into a vicious panther when sexually aroused. The only person with whom she can safely mate is her brother, a victim of the same genetic heritage. Kinski is mesmerizing as the innocent, sensual woman. Remake of the 1942 film.
1982 (R) 118m/C Nastassia Kinski, Malcolm McDowell, John Heard, Annette O'Toole, Ruby Dee, Ed Begley Jr., John Larroquette; **D:** Paul Schrader. VHS, Beta, LV $14.98 *MCA, FCT* ⬥⬥½

Cat Women of the Moon Scientists land on the moon and encounter an Amazon-like force of skimpily attired female chauvinists. Remade as "Missile to the Moon." Featuring the Hollywood Cover Girls as various cat women. Available in its original 3-D format. *AKA:* Rocket to the Moon.
1953 65m/B Sonny Tufts, Victor Jory, Marie Windsor, Bill Phipps, Douglas Fowley, Carol Brewster, Suzanne Alexander, Susan Morrow; **D:** Arthur Hilton. VHS, Beta $12.95 *RHI, SNC, MWP* ⬥⬥

Cataclysm A swell flick about a sadistic demon who spends his time either finding people willing to join him or killing the people who won't. Also on video as "Satan's Supper."
1981 (R) 94m/C Cameron Mitchell, Marc Lawrence, Faith Clift, Charles Moll; **D:** Tom McGowan, Greg Tallas, Philip Marshak. VHS, Beta $49.95 *FOX, ACA* ⬥⬥½

Catacombs An investigative monk and a beautiful photographer stumble across a mysterious, centuries-old evil power.
1989 (R) 112m/C Timothy Van Patten, Laura Schaefer, Ian Abercrombie, Jeremy West; **D:** David Schmoeller. VHS, Beta $89.95 *TWE* ⬥

The Catamount Killing The story of a small town bank manager and his lover. They decide to rob the bank and run for greener pastures only to find their escape befuddled at every turn.
1974 (PG) 82m/C *GE* Horst Buchholz, Ann Wedgeworth; **D:** Krzysztof Zanussi. VHS, Beta $29.98 *VID* ⬥½

Catch as Catch Can An Italian male model is comically besieged by animals of every type, making a mess of his life and career. Dubbed. *AKA:* Lo Scatenato.
1968 95m/C *IT* Vittorio Gassman, Martha Hyer, Gila Golan; **D:** Franco Indovina. VHS, Beta $59.98 *NLC* ⬥

Catch Me a Spy A foreign agent attempts to lure an innocent man into becoming part of a swap for an imprisoned Russian spy. *AKA:* To Catch a Spy.
1971 94m/C *GB FR* Kirk Douglas, Tom Courtenay, Trevor Howard, Marlene Jobert, Bernard Blier, Patrick Mower, Bernadette LaFont; **D:** Dick Clement. VHS, Beta $59.95 *FGM* ⬥½

Catch Me...If You Can High school class president Melissa doesn't want to see the school torn down. To raise fast cash, she teams up with a drag racer and the fun begins.
1989 (PG) 105m/C Matt Lattanzi, Loryn Locklin, M. Emmet Walch, Geoffrey Lewis; **D:** Stephen Sommers. VHS, LV $89.95 *MCG* ⬥⬥

Catch the Heat Alexander is an undercover narcotics agent sent to infiltrate Steiger's South American drug operation. *AKA:* Feel the Heat.
1987 (R) 90m/C Tiana Alexandra, David Dukes, Rod Steiger; **D:** Joel Silberg. VHS, Beta $79.95 *MED* ⬥

Catch-22 Buck Henry's adaptation of Joseph Heller's black comedy about a group of fliers in the Mediterranean during WWII. A biting anti-war satire portraying the insanity of the situation in both a humorous and disturbing manner. Perhaps too literal to the book's masterfully chaotic structure, causing occasional problems in the "are you following along department?" Arkin heads a fine and colorful cast.
1970 (R) 121m/C Alan Arkin, Martin Balsam, Art Garfunkel, Jon Voight, Richard Benjamin, Buck Henry, Bob Newhart, Paula Prentiss, Martin Sheen, Charles Grodin, Anthony Perkins, Orson Welles, Jack Gilford; **D:** Mike Nichols; **W:** Buck Henry. VHS, Beta, LV $14.95 *PAR* ⬥⬥⬥

The Catered Affair Davis, anti-typecast as a Bronx housewife, and Borgnine, as her taxi-driving husband, play the determined parents of soon-to-be-wed Reynolds set on giving her away in a style to which she is not accustomed. Based on Paddy Chayefsky's teleplay, the catered affair turns into a familial

trial, sharing the true-to-life poignancy that marked "Marty," the Oscar-winning Chayefsky drama of the previous year. Scripted by Vidal, the dialogue rings true, too. *AKA:* Wedding Breakfast.
1956 92m/B Bette Davis, Ernest Borgnine, Debbie Reynolds, Barry Fitzgerald, Rod Taylor, Robert Simon; **D:** Richard Brooks; **W:** Gore Vidal. VHS $19.98 *MGM, FCT, CCB* ⬥⬥⬥

Catherine & Co. Lonely, penniless girl arrives in Paris and "opens shop" on the streets of Paris. As business booms, she takes a cue from the big corporations and sells stock in herself.
1976 (R) 91m/C *FR IT* Jane Birkin, Patrick Dewaere, Jean-Pierre Aumont, Jean-Claude Brialy; **D:** Michel Boisrond. VHS, Beta $59.95 *VID* ⬥½

Catherine the Great Slow but lavish and engrossing British dramatization of the tortured and doomed love affair between Catherine, Empress of Russia, and her irrational, drunken husband Peter. *AKA:* The Rise of Catherine the Great.
1934 88m/B *GB* Douglas Fairbanks Jr., Elisabeth Bergner, Flora Robson; **D:** Paul Czinner. VHS, Beta, LV $14.98 *SUE, KRT, VYY* ⬥⬥½

Catholic Hour A dramatized version of the life story of Thomas Frederick Price who co-founded the Maryknoll Missionaries in the early 1900's.
1960 30m/B Edward Cullen, Arthur Gary. VHS, Beta $19.95 *VYY* ⬥⬥

Catholics A sensitive exploration of contemporary mores and changing attitudes within the Roman Catholic church. Sheen is sent by the Pope to Ireland to reform some priests. Based on Brian Moore's short novel and made for television. *AKA:* The Conflict; The Conflict.
1973 86m/C Martin Sheen, Trevor Howard; **D:** Jack Gold. VHS, Beta *NO* ⬥⬥⬥

Cathy's Curse The spirit of her aunt, who died as a child, possesses a young girl in this Canadian-French collaboration. Tries to capitalize on the popularity of "The Exorcist," but falls seriously short. *AKA:* Cauchemares.
1977 90m/C *CA FR* Alan Scarfe, Beverly Murray; **D:** Eddy Matalon. VHS, Beta *NO* ⬥

Catlow A comedic western with Brynner aiming to steal 2 million dollars in gold from under the nose of his friend, lawman Crenna. Based on the novel by Louis L'Amour.
1971 (PG) 103m/C Yul Brynner, Richard Crenna, Leonard Nimoy, JoAnn Pflug, Jeff Corey, Michael Delano, David Ladd, Bessie Love; **D:** Sam Wanamaker; **W:** Scot Finch, J.J. Griffith. VHS $19.98 *MGM* ⬥⬥½

The Cats and Mice of Paul Terry Seven vintage silent Terrytoon cartoons: "The Wild West," "Short Vacation," "China Doll," "Sunny Italy," "Stars of the Circus," "Sharpshooter" and "Ship Ahoy."
1928 55m/B VHS, Beta, 8mm $24.95 *VYY, WTA* ⬥⬥½

Cat's Eye An anthology of three Stephen King short stories connected by a stray cat who wanders through each tale.
1985 (PG-13) 94m/C Drew Barrymore, James Woods, Alan King, Robert Hays, Candy Clark, Kenneth McMillan, James Naughton; **D:** Lewis Teague. VHS, Beta, LV $19.99 *FOX, FCT* ⬥⬥

Cat's Play A widowed music teacher makes a ceremonial occasion of a weekly dinner with an old flame. Then an old friend from her youth suddenly reappears and begins an affair with the gentleman, causing self-destructive passions to explode. In Hungarian with English subtitles.

1974 115m/C *HU* Margit Dayka, Margit Makay, Elma Bulla; *D:* Karoly Makk. **VHS** $59.95 CVC, TAM 𝒵𝒵

Cattle Queen of Montana Reagan stars as an undercover federal agent investigating livestock rustlings and Indian uprisings.
1954 88m/C Ronald Reagan, Barbara Stanwyck, Jack Elam, Gene Evans, Lance Fuller, Anthony Caruso; *D:* Allan Dwan. **VHS, Beta, LV** NO 𝒵𝒵½

Caught A woman marries for wealth and security and is desperately unhappy. She runs away and takes a job with a struggling physician, and falls in love with him. Her husband finds her, forcing her to decide between a life of security or love.
1949 90m/B James Mason, Barbara Bel Geddes, Robert Ryan, Curt Bois, Natalie Schafer, Art Smith; *D:* Max Ophuls. **VHS** $14.98 REP 𝒵𝒵𝒵

Caught in the Draft Hope's funniest role has him as a Hollywood star trying to evade the draft in WW II, but he ends up accidentally enlisting himself. Lamour plays the daughter of a colonel in the Army whom Hope plans to marry, thinking it will get him out of the service. Very funny military comedy and one of Hope's best. Based on a story by Harry Tugend.
1941 82m/B Bob Hope, Dorothy Lamour, Lynne Overman, Eddie Bracken, Clarence Kolb, Paul Hurst, Ferike Boros, Irving Bacon; *D:* David Butler; *W:* Harry Tugend. **VHS** $14.98 MCA 𝒵𝒵𝒵

Cauldron of Blood Blind sculptor Karloff unwittingly uses human skeletons supplied by his crazed wife Lindfors as the framework of his art pieces. *AKA:* Blind Man's Bluff; El Coleccionista de Cadaveres.
1967 (PG) 95m/C *SP* Boris Karloff, Viveca Lindfors, Jean-Pierre Aumont, Rosenda Monteros, Rueben Rojo, Dianik Zurakowska; *W/D:* Edward Mann. **VHS** $14.98 REP, VDC, FCT 𝒵

Cause for Alarm A jealous husband recovering from a heart attack begins to lose his mind. He wrongly accuses his wife of having an affair and attempts to frame her for his own murder. A fast-paced thriller with a nifty surprise ending.
1951 74m/B Loretta Young, Barry Sullivan, Bruce Cowling, Margalo Gillmore, Irving Bacon, Carl "Alfalfa" Switzer; *D:* Tay Garnett. **VHS** $16.95 NOS, SNC, MGM 𝒵𝒵

Cavalcade Traces the lives of the British Marryot family from the death of Queen Victoria, through World War I, the Jazz Age, and the Depression. A wistful adaptation of the hit play by Noel Coward with its touching portrayal of one family trying to weather good times and bad together.
1933 110m/B Diana Wynyard, Clive Brook, Herbert Mundin, Una O'Connor, Ursula Jeans, Beryl Mercer, Merle Tottenham, Frank Lawton, John Warburton, Margaret Lindsay, Billy Bevan; *D:* Frank Lloyd. Academy Awards '33: Best Director (Lloyd), Best Interior Decoration, Best Picture; Nominations: Best Actress (Wynyard). **VHS** $19.98 FXV 𝒵𝒵𝒵

Cavalcade of the West Typical western with two brothers, separated by a kidnapping, growing up on opposite sides of the law. Much later they meet, and the question is: will the outlaw be reformed and reunited with his happy family?
1936 70m/B Hoot Gibson, Rex Lease, Marion Shilling, Earl Dwire; *D:* Harry Fraser. **VHS, Beta** $19.95 GPV, DVT, VCN 𝒵

The Cavalier Chinese cavalier faces love, danger and intrigue while deploying martial arts skills.
1987 90m/C Tang Wei, Lung Fei, Yeh Yuen, Tseng Tsao. **VHS, Beta** $29.95 UNI 𝒵

Cavalier of the West An Army captain is the only negotiating force between the white man and a primitive Indian tribe.
1931 66m/B Harry Carey Sr., Kane Richmond, George "Gabby" Hayes; *D:* John P. McCarthy. **VHS, Beta, LV** $19.95 NOS 𝒵

Cavalry A Union Army Lieutenant is reunited with his family after the Civil War, bringing them happiness and joy.
1936 60m/B Bob Steele, Frances Grant, Karl Hackett, Hal Price; *D:* Robert North Bradbury. **VHS, Beta** $19.90 NOS, DVT 𝒵𝒵½

Cavalry Command Good will and integrity characterize the U.S. soldiers called into a small village to quiet a guerrilla rebellion. *AKA:* Cavalleria Commandos.
1963 77m/C John Agar, Richard Arlen, Myron Healey, Alicia Vergel, William Phipps, Eddie Infante; *W/D:* Eddie Romero. **VHS, Beta** $59.95 PGN, RHI 𝒵½

Cave Girl After falling through a timewarp during a high-school field trip, a social pariah makes a hit with a pre-historic honey. Sexist teen exploitation film, with few original ideas and a not-so-hot cast. *AKA:* Cavegirl.
1985 (R) 85m/C Daniel Roebuck, Cindy Ann Thompson, Saba Moor, Jeff Chayette; *W/D:* David Oliver. **VHS, Beta, LV** $79.95 COL Woof!

Cave Girls A critically acclaimed experimental short by a group of female filmmakers depicting how a society of stone-age women prior to the evolution of thought processes would interact with each other and relate to their surroundings.
1982 28m/C *D:* Cara Brownell, Kiki Smith, Ellen Cooper; *M:* Bush Tetras, Y Pants. **VHS** $29.95 FCT, MWF Woof!

Cave of the Living Dead Mad professor with a past is up to something in cave under castle. Villagers summon Inspector Doren of Interpol to solve a rash of nasty murders that they've blamed on green-eyed, cave dwelling vampires. He's helped by a witch. A challenge to watch till the end. Filmed in Sepiatone and written by C. Von Rock. *AKA:* Der Fluch Der Gruenen Augen.
1965 87m/B *GE YU* Adrian Hoven, Erika Remberg, Carl Mohner, Wolfgang Preiss, Karin Field, Akos Von Rathony, John Kitzmiller, Carl Mohner; *D:* Akos Von Rathony. **VHS, Beta** $39.95 MSP Woof!

Caveman Starr stars in this prehistoric spoof about a group of cavemen banished from different tribes who band together to form a tribe called "The Misfits."
1981 (PG) 92m/C Ringo Starr, Barbara Bach, John Matuszak, Dennis Quaid, Jack Gilford, Shelley Long, Cork Hubbert; *W/D:* Carl Gottlieb. **VHS, Beta** $14.95 MGM, FOX 𝒵𝒵

CB4: The Movie Falling somewhere between a serious attempt and parody, CB4 tries to do both and succeeds at neither. Written in the key of "Wayne's World" by "Saturday Night Live's" Rock. Starts out as a "rockumentary" (please refer to "This is Spinal Tap"), but quickly turns into a sitcom where Rock and two gangsta rapper pals assume the identity of a local club owner who is jailed. Trouble ensues when a city councilman (Hartman, also of SNL) decides to make a campaign issue out of them. At the same time, the club owner breaks out of jail to seek and destroy the imposters who are exploiting his reputation for fun and profit. After watching all the violence, sexism, and profanity tucked into this wandering plot, you just might feel like you were the one exploited for fun and profit.

1993 (R) 83m/C Chris Rock, Allen Payne, Deezer D, Phil Hartman, Charlie Murphy, Khandi Alexander, Arthur Evans; *D:* Tamra Davis; *W:* Chris Rock, Nelson George, Robert Locash. **VHS, LV** MCA 𝒵½

Cease Fire The story of a troubled Vietnam vet who finds solace in a veterans' therapy group. Adapted from the play by George Fernandez.
1985 (R) 97m/C Don Johnson, Robert F. Lyons, Lisa Blount; *D:* David Nutter. **VHS, Beta** $79.99 HBO 𝒵𝒵

Ceiling Zero Cagney is an irrepressible pilot who does as he pleases and loves to aggravate his soft-hearted boss O'Brien. He falls for aviatrix Travis and neglects his duties to woo her, which leads to tragedy. Naturally, this sobers Cagney up and he volunteers for a dangerous test flight. Lots of fast-paced action and Cagney is at his swaggering best. Based on a play by Frank Wead, who also wrote the screenplay. Remade in 1941 as "International Squadron."
1935 95m/B James Cagney, Pat O'Brien, June Travis, Stuart Erwin, Henry Wadsworth, Isabel Jewell, Barton MacLane; *D:* Howard Hawks; *W:* Frank Wead. **VHS** $19.98 MGM 𝒵𝒵𝒵

Celebrity In this television film, a tragic childhood secret must be confronted by three friends when one is charged with murder. Based on the Thomas Thompson novel.
1985 313m/C Michael Beck, Ben Masters, Joseph Bottoms; *D:* Paul Wendkos. **VHS, Beta** $69.95 RCA 𝒵½

Celeste Adlon (who later made the offbeat comedy "Sugarbaby") directed this longish but finely detailed and beautifully photographed biographical look at French writer Marcel (Remembrance of Things Past) Proust. Based on the memoirs of Proust's housekeeper, Celeste Albaret, an uneducated farmgirl, portraying the woman's devoted relationship ('til death did them part) with the middle-aged, homosexual author. It does so with wit, poignancy, and insight, but is not entirely successful in its attempt to render Proust's verbal literary style into a visual medium. In German with English subtitles.
1981 107m/C *GE* Eva Mattes, Jurgen Arndt, Norbert Wartha, Wolf Euba; *D:* Percy Adlon. **VHS** $79.95 NYF, FCT, APD 𝒵𝒵𝒵

Celia: Child Of Terror Set in the 1950s, this film deals with the awful results of a young girl's inability to handle disappointment.
1989 110m/C Rebecca Smart, Nicholas Eadie, Victoria Longley, Mary-Anne Fahey; *D:* Ann Turner. **VHS, Beta** NO 𝒵𝒵

The Cellar A young boy finds an ancient Comanche monster spirit in the basement of his home. His parents, as usual, don't believe him, so he must battle the monster alone.
1990 (PG-13) 90m/C Patrick Kilpatrick, Suzanne Savoy, Chris Miller, Ford Rainey; *D:* Kevin S. Tenney. **VHS** $14.95 HMD 𝒵½

Cellar Dweller A cartoonist moves into an old house and soon discovers it's haunted by a demonic cartoonist who killed himself thirty years earlier. What a coincidence. Low-budget scare-'em-upper filmed on one set and lit by a floodlamp.
1987 78m/C Pamela Bellwood, Deborah Muldowney, Brian Robbins, Vince Edwards, Jeffrey Combs, Yvonne De Carlo; *D:* John Carl Buechler. **VHS, Beta, LV** $19.95 STE, NWV Woof!

The Cemetery Club Story of three Jewish widows who make weekly visits to their husband's graves and are attempting to cope with their lives. Doris (Dukakis) is loyal

to the memory of her husband and acts as the moral conscience of the trio. Lucille (Ladd) is a merry widow who wears clothes more suitable for younger women. She is trying to forget her age, but she also harbors a painful secret. Esther (Burstyn) struggles with her loneliness until a widowed cab driver begins to woo her. Commendably, the characters are given more dimension than Hollywood usually grants women of a certain age. Based on the play "The Cemetary Club" by Menchell, who also wrote the screenplay.
1993 (PG-13) 114m/C Ellen Burstyn, Olympia Dukakis, Diane Ladd, Danny Aiello, Lainie Kazan, Christina Ricci, Bernie Casey, Alan Mason, Sam Schwartz; **D:** Bill Duke; **W:** Ivan Menchell; **M:** Elmer Bernstein. VHS, Beta, LV $94.95 *TOU, BTV* 🐾🐾½

Cemetery High Beautiful high school girls decide to lure the local boys into a trap and kill them.
1989 80m/C Debi Thibeault, Karen Nielsen, Lisa Schmidt, Ruth Collins, Simone, Tony Kruk, David Coughlin, Frank Stewart; **D:** Gorman Bechard. VHS, Beta $79.95 *UNI, HHE* 🐾

Center of the Web John Phillips is a victim of mistaken identity—someone thinks he's a professional hit man. After surviving an apparent mob attempt on his life, Phillips is persuaded by a CIA operative to go along with the deception in order to capture a potential political assassin. At least that's what Phillips is told, but he soon realizes that the deeper he gets into his new role, the deadlier the plot becomes. Davi is one of the best bad guys around and the fast-paced stunts and plot twists make this watchable.
1992 (R) 88m/C Ted Prior, Robert Davi, Tony Curtis, Charlene Tilton, Bo Hopkins, Charles Napier; **D:** David A. Prior. VHS, LV $89.95 *AIP* 🐾🐾

The Centerfold Girls Microscopic storyline involves a deranged man who is determined to kill all the voluptuous young women who have posed nude for a centerfold.
1974 (R) 93m/C Andrew Prine, Tiffany Bolling, Aldo Ray, Jeremy Slate, Ray Danton, Francine York; **D:** John Peyser. VHS, Beta $54.95 *MED* Woof!

Certain Fury Two timid women go on the lam when they are mistaken for escaped prostitutes who shot up a courthouse. The sooner they get caught, the better.
1985 (R) 88m/C Tatum O'Neal, Irene Cara, Peter Fonda, Nicholas Campbell, Moses Gunn; **D:** Stephen Gyllenhaal. VHS, Beta, LV $14.95 *NWV, STE* 🐾

Certain Sacrifice Nineteen-year-old Madonna expresses herself in her film debut. Seeking revenge on the man who raped her, she murders him in a strange ritualistic manner underneath the Brooklyn Bridge. Poor is the man whose pleasures depend on the permission of another?
1980 60m/C Madonna, Jeremy Pattnosh, Charles Kurtz; **D:** Stephen Lewicki. VHS, Beta *WOV, MVD* 🐾

Cesar This is the third and most bittersweet part of Pagnol's famed trilogy based on his play depicting the lives and loves of the people of Provence, France. Marius returns after a 20-year absence to his beloved Fanny and his now-grown son, Cesariot. The first two parts of the trilogy are "Marius" and "Fanny" and were directed by Alexander Korda and Marc Allegret respectively. In French with English subtitles.
1936 117m/B *FR* Raimu, Pierre Fresnay, Orane Demazis, Charpin, Andre Fouche; **D:** Marcel Pagnol. VHS, Beta, LV $24.95 *NOS, MRV, INT* 🐾🐾🐾🐾

Cesar & Rosalie Acclaimed French comedy depicts the love triangle between a beautiful divorcee, her aging live-in companion and a younger man. Engaging portrait of how their relationship evolves over time. In French with English subtitles.
1972 (PG) 110m/C *FR* Romy Schneider, Yves Montand, Sami Frey, Umberto Orsini; **D:** Claude Sautet. VHS, Beta, LV $29.95 *TAM, AUD* 🐾🐾🐾

Chain Gang Killings Pair of shackled prisoners, one black, the other white, escape from a truck transporting them to prison.
1985 99m/C Ian Yule, Ken Gampu. VHS, Beta *NO* 🐾

Chain Gang Women Sordid violence. Two escaped convicts plunder, rob, and rape until a victim's husband comes looking for revenge.
1972 (R) 85m/C Robert Lott, Barbara Mills, Michael Stearns, Linda York; **D:** Lee Frost. VHS $39.95 *ACN* Woof!

Chain Lightning Bogart stars as a bomber pilot who falls in love with a Red Cross worker (Parker) while fighting in Europe in 1943. They lose touch after the war until Bogie goes to work as a test pilot for the same shady airplane manufacturer (Massey) where Parker works. He is given the chance to test a new plane, which has already cost the life of one of his friends. Bogart has more success, along with rekindling the flames of romance. Average script but the flying sequences are well-done.
1950 94m/B Humphrey Bogart, Eleanor Parker, Raymond Massey, Richard Whorf; **D:** Stuart Heisler. VHS $19.98 *MGM* 🐾🐾

Chain Reaction When a nuclear scientist is exposed to radiation after an accident at an atomic power plant, he must escape to warn the public of the danger. *AKA:* Nuclear Run.
1980 87m/C Steve Bisley, Ross Thompson; **D:** Ian Barry. VHS, Beta, LV *NO* 🐾½

Chained Crawford and Gable star in this love triangle that somehow never sizzles. Crawford, in love with married businessman Kruger, takes a South American cruise to get away from it all, meets Gable, and of course falls in love. Seems simple enough, but wait! Crawford goes back to New York City and marries Kruger (his wife grants him a divorce) and is miserable. But then Gable shows up, further complicating matters. Choices, choices. Predictable script was not helped by half-hearted performances.
1934 73m/B Joan Crawford, Clark Gable, Otto Kruger, Stuart Erwin, Una O'Connor; **D:** Clarence Brown. VHS, Beta $19.98 *MGM, CCB* 🐾🐾½

Chained for Life Daisy and Violet Hilton, real life Siamese twins, star in this old-fashioned "freak" show. When a gigolo deserts one twin on their wedding night, the other twin shoots him dead. The twins go on trial and the judge asks the viewer to hand down the verdict. Exploitative and embarrassing to watch.
1951 81m/B Daisy Hilton, Violet Hilton; **D:** Harry Fraser. VHS, Beta $16.95 *SNC, NOS, RHI* Woof!

Chained Heat Seamy tale of the vicious reality of life for women behind bars. Naive Blair is imprisoned again (after another bad jailhouse gig in "Born Innocent") and has usual assortment of negative experiences with domineering prisoners, degenerative guards, and the creepy warden who maintains a prison bachelor pad equipped with hot tub. Needless to say, she grows up in a hurry. Trashifying, archetypal women-in-prison effort that aims to satisfy full range of low-quality audience demands. Sequel to 1982 "Concrete Jungle."

1983 (R) 97m/C Linda Blair, Stella Stevens, Sybil Danning, Tamara Dobson, Henry Silva, John Vernon, Nita Talbot, Louisa Moritz; **D:** Paul Nicholas. VHS, Beta, LV $29.98 *VES* 🐾🐾

Chains A Chicago gangland feud entraps two couples in its web, and the innocents must take care of themselves when the situation goes from bad to worse.
1989 (R) ?m/C Jim Jordan, Michael Dixon, John L. Eves; **D:** Roger J. Barski. VHS $89.95 *IMP* 🐾🐾

Chains of Gold Kind social worker (Travolta) befriends teen who wants to get out of the crack-dealing gang in which he's involved. He infiltrates the gang and risks his life helping the boy get out. Originally aired on cable television.
1992 (R) 95m/C John Travolta, Marilu Henner, Bernie Casey, Hector Elizondo, Joey Lawrence; **D:** Rod Holcomb. VHS $89.95 *ACA* 🐾🐾

The Chair The penitentiary where an evil superintendent was fried in his own electric chair during an inmate uprising is reopened after two decades. The new warden (Benedict), who used to be a subordinate to the dead man, believes in rigid control of the inmates and locks horns with the big-house shrink (Coco), who on the surface is an intelligent humanitarian, but may have a darker side. This acrimonious dispute takes a back seat, when it appears that the spirit of the late warden has come back to make the inmates pay for his untimely death. *AKA:* Hot Seat.
1987 (R) ?m/C James Coco, Paul Benedict, Stephen Geoffreys, Trini Alvarado, John Bentley; **D:** Waldemar Korzeniowswsky. VHS $89.95 *IMP* 🐾🐾

The Chalk Garden A woman with a mysterious past takes on the job of governess for an unruly 14-year-old girl, with unforseen consequences. An excellent adaptation of the Enid Bagnold play although not as suspenseful as the stage production.
1964 106m/C *GB* Deborah Kerr, Hayley Mills, Edith Evans, John Mills, Elizabeth Sellars, Felix Aylmer; **D:** Ronald Neame. Academy Awards '64 Nominations: Best Supporting Actress (Evans); National Board of Review Awards '64: 10 Best Films of the Year, Best Supporting Actress (Evans). VHS, Beta $14.98 *MCA* 🐾🐾🐾

The Challenge Story of the courageous party of explorers who conquered the Matterhorn. Incredible avalanche scenes.
1938 77m/B Luis Trenker, Robert Douglas. VHS, Beta $19.98 *DVT, VYY, TIM* 🐾🐾🐾

Challenge When his entire family is killed, dad decides to seek revenge with his shotgun. Very bloody and violent and very nearly plotless.
1974 (PG) 90m/C Earl Owensby, William T. Hicks, Katheryn Thompson, Johnny Popwell; **D:** Martin Beck. VHS $59.98 *FOX* Woof!

The Challenge A contemporary action spectacle which combines modern swordplay with the mysticism and fantasy of ancient Samurai legends. John Sayles co-wrote the script with Richard Maxwell.
1982 (R) 108m/C Scott Glenn, Toshiro Mifune; **D:** John Frankenheimer; **M:** Jerry Goldsmith. VHS, Beta $59.95 *FOX* 🐾🐾½

Challenge of a Lifetime Marshall stars as a divorcee whose dream is to compete in the Hawaiian Ironman Triathlon. Cult favorite; Woronov has a substantial supporting role.
1985 100m/C Penny Marshall, Richard Gilliland, Jonathan Silverman, Mary Woronov, Paul Gleason, Mark Spitz, Cathy Rigby; **D:** Russ Mayberry. VHS $59.98 *TTC, MOV* 🐾🐾½

Challenge of McKenna Run-of-the-prairie horse opera has drifter Ireland stumble upon danger and intrigue when he enters a mysterious town.
1983 90m/C John Ireland, Robert Woods. **VHS** PMH ✍✍

Challenge of the Dragon Simple martial-arts tale of a Kung-Fu hero defending a town against bad guys.
1982 (R) 87m/C Tarng Long; *D:* Liou-Xiao Ling. **VHS, Beta** NO ✍

Challenge of the Masters A young Kung-Fu artist wins a new tutor in a contest. Soon he's fighting for a friend to protect his family's honor.
1989 97m/C Liu Chia Hui, Liu Chia-Yung, Chen Kuan-Tai, Chiang Yang; *D:* Lu Chia-Liang. **VHS** $69.95 NO ✍

Challenge the Ninja One talented fighter defends a town from high-kicking hordes. Lots of kung fu action for martial arts fans.
198? 92m/C Bruce Baron, Pierre Tremblay, Richard Berman, Eric Redner. **VHS, Beta** $59.95 TWE ✍

Challenge To Be Free Action adventure geared toward a young audience depicting the struggles of a man being pursued by 12 men and 100 dogs across a thousand miles of frozen wilderness. The last film directed by Garnett, who has a cameo as Marshal McGee. Produced in 1972, the release wasn't until 1976. *AKA:* Mad Trapper of the Yukon.
1976 (G) 90m/C Mike Mazurki, Jimmy Kane; *Cameos:* Tay Garnett; *D:* Tay Garnett. **VHS, Beta** $9.98 MED ✍✍

Challenge to Lassie When Lassie's Scottish master dies, the faithful pup remains at his grave. An unsympathetic policeman orders Lassie to leave the premises, inspiring a debate among the townsfolk as to the dog's fate. Based on a true story (although the original hero was a Skye Terrier; remade as "Greyfriar's Bobby."
1949 76m/C Edmund Gwenn, Donald Crisp, Geraldine Brooks, Reginald Owen, Alan Webb, Henry Stephenson, Alan Napier, Sara Allgood; *D:* Richard Thorpe; *M:* Andre Previn. **VHS, Beta** $19.98 MGM, FCT ✍✍½

Challenge to White Fang A courageous dog prevents a scheming businessman from taking over an old man's gold mine.
1986 (PG) 89m/C Harry Carey Jr., Franco Nero; *D:* Lucio Fulci. **VHS, Beta** $69.95 TWE ✍½

Chamber of Horrors A family is brought together at an English castle to claim a fortune left by an aristocrat. However, there's a catch—seven keys may open the vault with the fortune, or leave the key turner dead. Based on the work by Edgar Wallace. *AKA:* The Door With Seven Locks.
1940 80m/B GB Leslie Banks, Lilli Palmer; *D:* Norman Lee. **VHS, Beta** $16.95 NOS, MRV, SNC ✍✍½

The Chambermaid's Dream Softcore whimsy about young French maid who fantasizes about her employer. In French, dubbed.
1986 86m/C FR Michel Lemoine, Elizabeth Tessier. **VHS, Beta** $29.95 MED ✍

Chameleon A freeform dramatic examination of a day in the life of a Los Angeles pusher.
1981 90m/C Bob Glaudini; *D:* Jon Jost. **VHS, Beta** FCT ✍

Chameleon Street Entertaining fact-based account of William Douglas Street, a Detroit man who successfully impersonated, among others, a Time magazine reporter and a surgeon until he was caught and sent to prison. He escaped and went to Yale, faked his identity as a student, and then returned to Michigan to impersonate a lawyer for the Detroit Human Rights Commission. Harris wrote and directed this insightful look into the man who fooled many people, including the mayor of Detroit, Coleman A. Young, who appears briefly as himself.
1989 (R) 95m/C Wendell B. Harris Jr., Angela Leslie, Amina Fakir, Paula McGee, Mano Breckenridge, Richard Kiley, Anthony Ennis; *W/D:* Wendell B. Harris Jr. **VHS, LV** $89.95 ACA, FCT ✍✍✍

The Champ A washed up boxer dreams of making a comeback and receives support from no one but his devoted son. Minor classic most notorious for jerking the tears and soiling the hankies, this was the first of three Beery/Cooper screen teamings.
1931 87m/B Wallace Beery, Jackie Cooper, Irene Rich, Roscoe Ates, Edward Brophy, Hale Hamilton, Jesse Scott, Marcia Mae Jones; *D:* King Vidor; *W:* Francis Marion. Academy Awards '32: Best Actor (Beery), Best Original Screenplay; Nominations: Best Director (Vidor), Best Picture. **VHS, Beta, LV** $19.98 MGM, FCT, BTV ✍✍✍

The Champ An ex-fighter with a weakness for gambling and drinking is forced to return to the ring in an attempt to keep custody of his son. Excessive sentiment may cause cringing. Earned an Academy Award nomination for Best Score. Remake of the 1931 classic.
1979 (PG) 121m/C Jon Voight, Faye Dunaway, Rick Schroder, Jack Warden, Arthur Hill, Strother Martin, Joan Blondell, Elisha Cook; *D:* Franco Zeffirelli. **VHS, Beta, LV** $59.95 MGM ✍½

Champ Against Champ A one-legged ninja masters the 18 kicks and hops his way to ninja superstardom.
198? 90m/C **VHS, Beta** $39.95 TWE ✍

Champagne A socialite's father fakes bankruptcy to teach his irresponsible daughter a lesson. Early, silent endeavor from Hitchcock is brilliantly photographed.
1928 93m/B GB Betty Balfour, Gordon Harker, Ferdinand von Alten, Clifford Heatherly, Jack Trevor; *D:* Alfred Hitchcock. **VHS** $19.99 GPV, MLB, VEC ✍✍

Champagne for Breakfast Sex comedy follows the fun-filled adventures of "Champagne," a free-spirited beauty living life to the fullest.
1979 (R) 69m/B Mary Carlisle, Hardie Albright, Joan Marsh, Lila Lee, Sidney Toler, Bradley Page, Emerson Treacy; *D:* Melville Brown. **VHS** $49.95 WWV ✍

Champagne for Caesar The laughs keep coming in this comedy about a self-proclaimed genius-on-every-subject who goes on a television quiz show and proceeds to win everything in sight. The program's sponsor, in desperation, hires a femme fatale to distract the contestant before the final program. Wonderful spoof of the game-show industry.
1950 90m/B Ronald Colman, Celeste Holm, Vincent Price, Art Linkletter; *D:* Richard Whorf. **VHS, Beta, LV** $39.95 UHV ✍✍✍

Champion An ambitious prizefighter alienates the people around him as he desperately fights his way to the top. When he finally reaches his goal, he is forced to question the cost of his success. From a story by Ring Lardner. Certainly one of the best films ever made about boxing, with less sentiment than

"Rocky" but concerned with sociological correctness.
1949 99m/B Kirk Douglas, Arthur Kennedy, Marilyn Maxwell, Ruth Roman, Lola Albright; *D:* Mark Robson. Academy Awards '49: Best Film Editing; Nominations: Best Actor (Douglas), Best Black and White Cinematography, Best Screenplay, Best Supporting Actor (Kennedy), Best Original Score. **VHS** $19.98 REP ✍✍✍½

The Champion/His New Job Two classic silent shorts by Chaplin, with music; the first is alternately entitled "Champion Charlie." *AKA:* Champion Charlie.
1915 53m/B Charlie Chaplin, Edna Purviance, Ben Turpin, Gloria Swanson, Mack Swain, Billy Anderson; *D:* Charlie Chaplin. **VHS, Beta, 8mm** $24.95 VYY ✍✍✍

Champion Operation Hong Kong heavies pose as police officers. The action follows them from the slums to the red-light district. Lots of martial arts action.
1987 100m/C Tong Chun Chung, Yu Ka Hei, Tang Ho Kwong. **VHS** $49.95 OCE ✍

Champions Moving but cliched story of Bob Champion, a leading jockey who overcame cancer to win England's Grand National Steeplechase. A true story, no less.
1984 113m/C GB John Hurt, Gregory Jones, Mick Dillon, Ann Bell, Jan Francis, Peter Barkworth, Edward Woodward, Ben Johnson, Kirstie Alley, Alison Steadman; *D:* John Irvin. **VHS, Beta, LV** $9.98 SUE, NLC ✍✍

Chan is Missing Two cab drivers try to find the man who stole their life savings. Wry, low-budget comedy filmed in San Francisco's Chinatown was an art-house smash. The first full-length American film produced exclusively by an Asian-American cast and crew.
1982 80m/B Wood Moy, Marc Hayashi, Laureen Chew, Judy Mihei, Peter Wang, Presco Tabios; *D:* Wayne Wang. **VHS** $79.95 NYF, TAM ✍✍✍

Chance With over a million dollars in diamonds missing, Haggerty and Jacobs throw out all the stops to recover them in this action thriller.
1989 90m/C Dan Haggerty, Lawrence Hilton-Jacobs, Addison Randall, Roger Rudd, Charles Gries, Pamela Dixon; *D:* Addison Randall, Charles Kanganis. **VHS** PMH ✍½

Chances Are After her loving husband dies in a chance accident, a pregnant woman remains unmarried, keeping her husband's best friend as her only close male companion. Years later, her now teenage daughter brings a friend home for dinner, but due to an error in heaven, the young man begins to realize that this may not be the first time he and this family have met. A wonderful love-story hampered only minimally by the unbelievable plot.
1989 (PG) 108m/C Cybill Shepherd, Robert Downey Jr., Ryan O'Neal, Mary Stuart Masterson, Josef Sommer, Christopher MacDonald, Joe Grifasi, James Noble; *D:* Emile Ardolino. **VHS, Beta, LV, 8mm** $19.95 COL, FCT ✍✍✍

Chandu on the Magic Island Chandu the Magician takes his powers of the occult to the mysterious lost island of Lemuri to battle the evil cult of Ubasti. Sequel to "Chandu the Magician" and just as campy.
1934 67m/B Bela Lugosi, Maria Alba, Clara Kimball Young. **VHS, Beta** $19.95 NOS, SNC, VYY ✍✍✍

Chandu the Magician Bad guy searches desperately for the secret of a powerful death ray so he can (surprise!) destroy civilization. Not well received in its day, but makes for great high-camp fun now. One of Lugosi's most melodramatic performances.

1932 70m/B Edmund Lowe, Bela Lugosi, Irene Ware, Henry B. Walthall; **D:** William Cameron Menzies, Marcel Varnel. **VHS, Beta** MLB, RXM ♫♫

Chanel Solitaire Uninspiring biography follows the fabulous (simply fabulous) career of dress designer Gabrielle "Coco" Chanel. Ah, go sew something.
1981 (R) 124m/C Marie-France Pisier, Rutger Hauer, Timothy Dalton, Karen Black, Brigitte Fossey; **D:** George Kaczender. **VHS, Beta** $19.95 MED, FCT ♫♫

Chang: A Drama of the Wilderness A farmer and his family has settled a small patch of ground on the edge of the jungle and must struggle for survival against numerous wild animals. The climactic elephant stampede is still thrilling. Shot on location in Siam.
1927 67m/B **W/D:** Merian C. Cooper, Ernest B. Schoedsack. **VHS** $39.95 MIL ♫♫♫½

Change of Habit Three novitiates undertake to learn about the world before becoming full-fledged nuns. While working at a ghetto clinic a young doctor forms a strong, affectionate relationship with one of them. Presley's last feature film. ♫Change of Habit; Let Us Pray; Rubberneckin'.
1969 (G) 93m/C Elvis Presley, Mary Tyler Moore, Barbara McNair, Ed Asner, Ruth McDevitt, Regis Toomey; **D:** William A. Graham. **VHS, Beta** $14.95 MCA, GKK ♫♫

A Change of Seasons One of them so-called sophisticated comedies that look at the contemporary relationships and values of middle-class, middle-aged people who should know better. The wife of a college professor learns of her husband's affair with a seductive student and decides to have a fling with a younger man. The situation reaches absurdity when the couples decide to vacation together.
1980 (R) 102m/C Shirley MacLaine, Bo Derek, Anthony Hopkins, Michael Brandon, Mary Beth Hurt; **D:** Richard Lang. **VHS, Beta** $59.98 FOX ♫♫

The Changeling A music teacher moves into an old house and discovers that a young boy's ghostly spirit is his housemate. The ghost wants revenge against the being that replaced him upon his death. Scary ghost story with some less than logical leaps of script.
1980 (R) 114m/C CA George C. Scott, Trish Van Devere, John Russell, Melvyn Douglas, Jean Marsh; **D:** Peter Medak. **VHS, Beta, LV** $19.98 VES ♫♫½

Changes A young man leaves home and thumbs across the California coast in order to find himself. On the road again.
1969 (PG) 103m/C Kent Lane, Michele Carey, Jack Albertson, Marcia Strassman; **D:** Hall Bartlett. **VHS, Beta** $79.95 PSM ♫

The Channeler The traditional dopey students probe an old Colorado mine and encounter black-robed, demon whazzits. A spunky cast and nice scenery didn't stop the Hound from switching channels on this one.
1989 90m/C Dan Haggerty, Richard Harrison, Jay Richardson, David Homb, Oliver Darrow, Robin Sims, Charles Solomon; **D:** Grant Austin Waldman. **VHS, Beta** NO ♫

Chapayev Striking propagandist drama dealing with the exploits of a legendary Red Army commander during the 1919 battle with the White Russians. Stunning, and carefully choreographed, battle scenes. Adapted from a biographical novel by Dmitri Furmanov. In Russian with English subtitles.
1934 101m/B RU Boris Babochkin, Leonid Kmit; **D:** Sergei Vasiliev, Gregory Vasiliev. **VHS, Beta, 3/4U** $35.95 IHF, AUD, VYY ♫♫♫

Chaplin The life and career of "The Little Tramp" is chronicled by director Attenborough and brilliantly portrayed by Downey, Jr. as Chaplin. A flashback format traces his life from its poverty-stricken Dickensian origins in the London slums through his directing and acting career, to his honorary Oscar in 1972. Slow-moving at parts, but captures Chaplin's devotion to his art and also his penchant towards jailbait. In a clever casting choice, Chaplin's own daughter from his fourth marriage to Oona O'Neill, Geraldine Chaplin, plays her own grandmother who goes mad.
1992 (PG-13) 144m/C Robert Downey Jr., Dan Aykroyd, Geraldine Chaplin, Kevin Dunn, Anthony Hopkins, Milla Jovovich, Moira Kelly, Kevin Kline, Diane Lane, Penelope Ann Miller, Paul Rhys; **D:** Richard Attenborough; **M:** John Barry. Academy Awards '92 Nominations: Best Actor (Downey), Best Art Direction/Set Decoration, Best Original Score; British Academy Awards '93: Best Actor (Downey). **VHS, LV** $94.98 LIV, MOV ♫♫

Chaplin: A Character Is Born The evolution of Chaplin's "Little Tramp" is shown in scenes from his early classics, "The Pawnshop," "The Rink," and "The Immigrant."
1979 40m/B Charlie Chaplin. **VHS, Beta** NO ♫♫♫

Chaplin: A Character Is Born/ Keaton: The Great Stone Face Wynn narrates "A Character Is Born," with scenes from "Little Champ," "The Pawnshop," "The Rink" and "The Immigrant." Buttons presents "The Great Stone Face" featuring scenes from "Cops," "The Playhouse" "The Boat" and "The General."
19?? 90m/C Charlie Chaplin. **VHS, Beta** NO ♫♫½

Chaplin Essanay Book 1 Two of Chaplin's early shorts: "The Tramp" and "The Champion."
1915 51m/B Charlie Chaplin, Edna Purviance, Ben Turpin. **VHS, Beta** $19.98 CCB ♫♫½

The Chaplin Revue The "Revue," put together by Chaplin in 1958, consists of three of his best shorts: "A Dog's Life" (1918), the World War II comedy "Shoulder Arms" (1918), and "The Pilgrim," in which a convict hides out in a clerical guise (1922). Chaplin added self-composed score, narration, and some documentary on-the-set material.
1958 121m/B Charlie Chaplin, Edna Purviance, Sydney Chaplin, Mack Swain; **D:** Charlie Chaplin. **VHS, Beta** $19.98 FOX ♫♫½

Chapter in Her Life An early silent film by Lois Weber which examines the relationships between an orphaned child and the adults in her life.
1923 87m/B **D:** Lois Weber. **VHS, Beta** $19.95 GVV ♫½

Chapter Two Loosely based on Neil Simon's marriage to Mason and his Broadway hit of the same name. A writer, grief-stricken over the death of his first wife, meets the woman who will become his second. Witty dialogue in first half deteriorates when guilt strikes.
1979 (PG) 124m/C James Caan, Marsha Mason, Valerie Harper, Joseph Bologna; **D:** Robert Moore; **W:** Neil Simon. **VHS, Beta, LV** $69.95 COL ♫♫

Charade Mason and wife Pamela star in this trilogy of love and violence. "Portrait of a Murderer" has a young artist sketching the picture of the man who—unknown to her—has just murdered his girlfriend. "Duel at Dawn" concerns an 1880s Austrian officer who steals a woman from another officer and is then challenged to a duel. "The Midas Touch" revolves around a successful but dissatisfied man who abandons his riches to find the meaning of life. Mason himself had said he hoped "this curiosity" would disappear.
1953 83m/B James Mason, Pamela Mason, Scott Forbes, Paul Cavanagh, Bruce Lester, Sean McClory, Vince Barnett; **D:** Roy Kellino. **VHS** $19.95 NOS ♫♫

Charade After her husband is murdered, a young woman finds herself on the run from crooks and double agents who want the $250,000 her husband stole during WWII. Hepburn and Grant are charming and sophisticated as usual in this stylish intrigue filmed in Paris. Music by Henry Mancini.
1963 113m/C Cary Grant, Audrey Hepburn, Walter Matthau, James Coburn, George Kennedy; **D:** Stanley Donen. Academy Awards '63 Nominations: Best Song ("Charade"); British Academy Awards '64: Best Actress (Hepburn); Edgar Allan Poe Awards '63: Best Screenplay. **VHS, Beta** $8.95 NEG, MRV, MCA ♫♫♫½

The Charge of the Light Brigade A British army officer stationed in India deliberately starts the Balaclava charge to even an old score with Surat Khan, who's on the other side. Still an exciting film, though it's hardly historically accurate. De Havilland is along to provide the requisite romance with Flynn. Also available colorized.
1936 115m/B Olivia de Havilland, Errol Flynn, David Niven, Nigel Bruce, Patric Knowles, Donald Crisp, C. Aubrey Smith, J. Carroll Naish, Henry Stephenson, E.E. Clive; **D:** Michael Curtiz, Jack Sullivan. **VHS, Beta, LV** $19.98 MGM, FCT, FOX ♫♫♫

The Charge of the Model T's Comedy about a WWI German spy who tries to infiltrate the U.S. army.
1976 (G) 90m/C Louis Nye, John David Carson, Herb Edelman, Carol Bagdasarian, Arte Johnson; **D:** Jim McCullough. **VHS, Beta** $9.99 SUE ♫½

Chariots of Fire A lush telling of the parallel stories of Harold Abraham and Eric Liddell, English runners who competed in the 1924 Paris Olympics. One was compelled by a hatred of anti-Semitism, the other by the love of God. Outstanding performances by the entire cast.
1981 (PG) 123m/C GB Ben Cross, Ian Charleson, Nigel Havers, Ian Holm, Alice Krige, Brad Davis, Dennis Christopher, Patrick Magee, Cheryl Campbell, John Gielgud, Lindsay Anderson, Nigel Davenport; **D:** Hugh Hudson; **W:** Colin Welland; **M:** Vangelis. Academy Awards '81: Best Costume Design, Best Original Screenplay, Best Picture, Best Score; Nominations: Best Director (Hudson), Best Supporting Actor (Holm); British Academy Awards '81: Best Film, Best Supporting Actor (Holm). **VHS, Beta, LV** $19.98 WAR, FCT, BTV ♫♫♫½

Charles & Diana: A Palace Divided Trashy scandalous tale of the disintegration of the fairytale romance and marriage of Prince Charles and Princess Diana. Oxenberg stars as Princess Di, a role she played a decade ago in "The Royal Romance of Charles and Diana," and Rees does a fine job playing the conservative Prince Charles. Although the film covers all of the couple's highly-publicized troubles, it's such a quick superficial treatment that it's often hard to follow. Nonetheless, it's a flashingly inviting look into the privileged House of Windsor.
1993 92m/C Roger Rees, Catherine Oxenberg, Benedict Taylor, Tracy Brabin, Amanda Walker, David Quilter, Jane How; **D:** John Power. **VHS** $89.98 TTC ♫♫½

Charles et Lucie A has-been couple are ripped off, pursued, persecuted, and saddled with very bad luck in the South of France. Essentially a character study; semi-acclaimed. In French with subtitles.
1979 96m/C **FR** Daniel Ceccaldi, Ginette Garcin, Jean-Marie Proslier, Samson Fainsilber; **D:** Nelly Kaplan. **VHS, Beta** FCT 🎞🎞🎞

Charleston Renoir's third film, a simple erotic dance fantasy that caused much controversy in its day. Silent, with jazz score and historical introduction.
1926 30m/B Catherine Hessling; **D:** Jean Renoir. **VHS, Beta** FCT 🎞🎞🎞

Charley and the Angel Touching story of a man who changes his cold ways with his family when informed by an angel that he hasn't much time to live. Amusing Disney movie set in the Great Depression.
1973 (G) 93m/C Fred MacMurray, Cloris Leachman, Harry Morgan, Kurt Russell, Vincent Van Patten, Kathleen Cody; **D:** Vincent McEveety. **VHS** DIS, OM 🎞🎞½

Charley Chase Festival, Vol. 1 Six classic Charley Chase comedies: "At First Sight" (1923), "Fighting Fluid" (1924), "Young Oldfield" (1924), "Ten Minute Egg" (1924), "Stolen Goods" (1924), and "Long Fliv the King" (1926).
1923 70m/B Charley Chase. **VHS, Beta** $19.95 VDM 🎞🎞

Charley Varrick Matthau, a small-town hood, robs a bank only to find out that one of its depositors is the Mob. Baker's the vicious hit-man assigned the job of getting the loot back. A well-paced, on-the-mark thriller.
1973 (PG) 111m/C Walter Matthau, Joe Don Baker, Felicia Farr, John Vernon, Sheree North, Norman Fell, Andrew Robinson; **D:** Don Siegel. **VHS, Beta** $49.95 MCA 🎞🎞🎞

Charley's Aunt Amusing Victorian farce in which two young male students convince an older fellow student to dress up as their female chaperon so they can pitch woo to two local lovelies. Fun performances and well-paced direction by Sidney. Based on the Brandon Thomas farce, the movie was re-made in 1930, starring Charles Ruggles, and again in 1941, with Jack Benny.
1925 75m/B Sydney Chaplin, Ethel Shannon, Lucien Littlefield, Alec B. Francis; **D:** Scott Sidney. **VHS, Beta** $24.95 GPV, FCT 🎞🎞½

Charlie and the Great Balloon Chase When a grandfather takes his grandson on a cross-country balloon trip, they are hotly pursued by the boy's mother, her stuffy fiance (who wants the boy in military school), the FBI, a reporter, and the Mafia. Made for television.
1982 98m/C Jack Albertson, Adrienne Barbeau, Slim Pickens, Moosie Drier; **D:** Larry Elikann. **VHS, Beta** $59.95 TLF 🎞🎞

Charlie Boy The new owner of an ancient African idol enters the world of the supernatural when he casts a death spell on six people.
1981 60m/C Leigh Lawson, Angela Bruce, Marius Goring; **D:** Robert M. Young. **VHS, Beta** $29.95 LIV 🎞🎞

Charlie Bravo A commando group is commanded to rescue a captured nurse in Vietnam. Dubbed.
1987 (R) 94m/C **FR** Bruno Pradal, Karen Verlier, Jean-Francois Poron; **D:** Rene Demoulin. **VHS, Beta** $59.95 GEM 🎞

A Charlie Brown Celebration The Peanuts gang in an extended adventure in which Lucy courts Schroeder, Patty goes to obedience school, and Charlie Brown finally kicks the football.

1984 49m/C **D:** Bill Melendez. **VHS, Beta** $14.95 KRT, WTA 🎞

A Charlie Brown Christmas Disillusioned by the commercialization of the holiday season, Charlie Brown sets out to find the true meaning of Christmas.
1965 30m/C **D:** Bill Melendez. **VHS, Beta** $9.95 MED, SHV, VTR 🎞

A Charlie Brown Thanksgiving The Peanuts gang learns that Thanksgiving is more than just turkey and stuffing in this family favorite.
1981 25m/C **D:** Bill Melendez, Phil Roman. **VHS, Beta** $14.95 KRT, KAR, WTA 🎞

Charlie Brown's All-Stars Charlie Brown and the whole Peanuts gang is here to delight young and old alike.
1966 26m/C **D:** Bill Melendez. **VHS** $9.98 MED, VTR, WTA 🎞

Charlie Chan and the Curse of the Dragon Queen The famed Oriental sleuth confronts his old enemy the Dragon Queen, and reveals the true identity of a killer.
1981 (PG) 97m/C Peter Ustinov, Lee Grant, Angie Dickinson, Richard Hatch, Brian Keith, Roddy McDowall, Michelle Pfeiffer, Rachel Roberts; **D:** Clive Donner. **VHS, Beta** $9.95 MED 🎞½

Charlie Chan at the Opera The great detective investigates an amnesiac opera star (Karloff) who may have committed murder. Considered one of the best of the series. Interesting even to those not familiar with Charlie Chan.
1936 66m/B Warner Oland, Boris Karloff, Keye Luke, Charlotte Henry, Thomas Beck, Nedda Harrigan, William Demarest; **D:** H. Bruce Humberstone. **VHS, LV** $19.98 FOX 🎞🎞🎞

Charlie Chan at the Wax Museum Charlie and number one son must find a criminal hiding out in a wax museum. Chills abound when the fugitive heads for the chamber of horrors.
1940 63m/B Sidney Toler, Sen Yung, C. Henry Gordon, Marc Lawrence, Joan Valerie, Marguerite Chapman, Ted Osborn, Michael Visaroff; **D:** Lynn Shores. **VHS, LV** $19.98 FOX 🎞½

Charlie Chan in Paris Chan scours the city of lights to track down a trio of counterfeiters. Top-notch plot and plenty of suspense will please all.
1935 72m/B Warner Oland, Mary Brian, Thomas Beck, Erik Rhodes, John Miljan, Minor Watson, John Qualen, Keye Luke, Henry Kolker; **D:** Lewis Seiler. **VHS, LV** $19.98 FOX 🎞🎞½

Charlie Chan in Rio Local police call on Chan to help solve a double murder. One of the series' weaker entries but with fine setting and music.
1941 60m/B Sidney Toler, Mary Beth Hughes, Cobina Wright Jr., Ted North, Victor Jory, Harold Huber, Sen Yung; **D:** Harry Lachman. **VHS, LV** $19.98 FOX 🎞🎞

Charlie Chan in the Secret Service Toler's Chan is now a government agent who is assigned to find the killer of an inventor. Moreland joins up as Chan's taxi-driving, constantly terrified sidekick. The series moved from 20th-century Fox to low-budget Monogram Pictures with this entry, with an ensuing drop in production quality.
1944 64m/B Sidney Toler, Mantan Moreland, Gwen Kenyon, Arthur Loft, Marianne Quon, Lela Tyler, Benson Fong; **D:** Phil Rosen. **VHS** $19.98 MGM 🎞½

Charlie Chan's Secret Chan must solve the murder of the heir to a huge fortune. A good, logical script with plenty of suspects to keep you guessing.
1935 72m/C Warner Oland, Rosina Lawrence, Charles Quigley, Henrietta Crosman, Edward Trevor, Astrid Allwyn; **D:** Gordon Wiles. **VHS** $19.98 FOX 🎞🎞

Charlie Chaplin Carnival, Four Early Shorts This tape features: "The Vagabond," "The Fireman," "The Count," and "Behind the Screen." Sound effects and music added. Silent.
1916 80m/B Charlie Chaplin. **VHS, Beta** $44.95 HHT, HEG 🎞🎞

Charlie Chaplin Cavalcade, Mutual Studios Shorts A compilation tape which features Chaplin's: "One A.M.," "Pawnshop," "Floorwalker," and "The Rink."
1916 81m/B Charlie Chaplin, Edna Purviance; **D:** Charlie Chaplin. **VHS, Beta** $19.95 VDM, HHT, KIV 🎞🎞

Charlie Chaplin Centennial Collection Chaplin is up to his stunts again in an anthology of comedy shorts.
191? 87m/B Charlie Chaplin; **D:** Charlie Chaplin. **VHS** $19.98 FOX 🎞🎞

Charlie Chaplin Festival This video features four classic Chaplin shorts: "The Immigrant," "The Adventurer," "The Cure," and "Easy Street."
1917 80m/B Charlie Chaplin, Edna Purviance, Henry Bergman, Eric Campbell; **D:** Charlie Chaplin. **VHS, Beta** PSM 🎞🎞

Charlie Chaplin Festival Four Chaplin shorts: "The Immigrant," "The Fireman," "Behind the Screen" and "The Adventurer."
1917 60m/B Charlie Chaplin. **VHS, Beta** $24.95 DVT 🎞🎞

Charlie Chaplin: Night at the Show Chaplin, who wrote and directed, plays two different mugs, both out for a night on the town. Mr. Pest, a sharp-dressed upper-cruster, clings to his disgusting habits, and Mr. Rowdy is his working-class doppleganger. Both obnoxious Chaplins-in-disguise collaborate to wreak havoc on a local theater. Contains original organ score.
1915 ?m/B Charlie Chaplin, Edna Purviance; **W/D:** Charlie Chaplin. **VHS, Beta, Special order formats** VYY 🎞🎞🎞

Charlie Chaplin: Rare Chaplin A collection of three Chaplin shorts: "The Bank," "Shanghaied," and "A Night in the Snow."
1915 60m/B Charlie Chaplin, Edna Purviance, Bud Jamison, Billy Armstrong; **D:** Charlie Chaplin. **VHS, Beta** $29.95 KIV 🎞🎞½

Charlie Chaplin: The Early Years, Vol. 1 This video package includes Chaplin's "The Immigrant," "The Count," and "Easy Street." Silent.
1917 62m/B Charlie Chaplin, Edna Purviance, John Rand, Eric Campbell. **VHS, LV** $19.98 REP, PIA, FCT 🎞🎞½

Charlie Chaplin: The Early Years, Vol. 2 This video package includes Chaplin's "The Pawnshop" (1916), "The Adventurer" (1917), and "One A.M." (1916).
1917 61m/B Charlie Chaplin, Edna Purviance, Eric Campbell, Albert Austin, Henry Bergman, John Rand. **VHS, LV** $19.98 REP, PIA, FCT 🎞🎞½

Charlie Chaplin: The Early Years, Vol. 3 This video package includes Chaplin's "The Cure" (1916), "The Floorwalker" (1916), and "The Vagabond."

1916 64m/B Charlie Chaplin, Edna Purviance, Eric Campbell, Albert Austin. **VHS, LV** $19.98 *REP, PIA, FCT 🐾🐾½*

Charlie Chaplin: The Early Years, Vol. 4 This video package includes Chaplin's "Behind the Screen," "The Fireman" (1916), and "The Rink" (1916).
1916 63m/B Charlie Chaplin, Edna Purviance, Eric Campbell, Lloyd Bacon, Albert Austin. **VHS, Beta, LV** $19.98 *REP, PIA, FCT 🐾🐾½*

Charlie Chaplin...Our Hero! Two shorts from 1915 written and directed by Chaplin, "Night at the Show" and "In the Park," as well as a 1914 film, "Hot Finish," in which Charlie plays the villain.
1915 58m/B Charlie Chaplin, Edna Purviance, Lloyd Bacon, Mabel Normand, Chester Conklin, Mack Sennett; *D:* Charlie Chaplin. **VHS, Beta, 8mm** $24.95 *VYY 🐾🐾½*

Charlie Chaplin's Keystone Comedies #1 Six one-reelers which Chaplin filmed in 1914, his first movie-making year: "Making a Living," Chaplin's first, in which he plays a villain; "Kid Auto Races," in which Charlie now sports baggy pants, bowler hat and cane; "A Busy Day," featuring Charlie in drag; "Mabel's Married Life;" "Laughing Gas;" and "The New Janitor." Silent with musical score.
1914 59m/B Charlie Chaplin, Mabel Normand, Mack Swain. **VHS, Beta** $24.95 *VYY, KIV 🐾🐾½*

Charlie Chaplin's Keystone Comedies #2 Three hilarious early Chaplin shorts, "His Trysting Place," "Getting Acquainted" and "The Fatal Mallet." Silent with musical score.
1914 60m/B Charlie Chaplin, Mabel Normand, Mack Swain, Mack Sennett. **VHS, Beta** $29.95 *VYY, KIV 🐾🐾½*

Charlie Chaplin's Keystone Comedies #3 Three more vintage early Chaplin shorts: "Caught in a Cabaret," "The Masquerader," and "Between Showers." Silent, includes a musical score.
1914 59m/B Charlie Chaplin, Mack Swain, Mabel Normand, Chester Conklin; *D:* Charlie Chaplin. **VHS, Beta** $29.95 *VYY, KIV 🐾🐾½*

Charlie Chaplin's Keystone Comedies #4 Four classic silent shorts featuring Chaplin in 1914, including "Caught in the Rain (in the Park)," "His Million Dollar Job," "Mabel's Busy Day," and "The Face on the Bar Room Floor." With musical score.
1914 54m/B Charlie Chaplin, Mack Swain, Alice Davenport, Fatty Arbuckle, Mabel Normand, Chester Conklin, Slim Summerville, Cecile Arnold, Alice Howell. **VHS, Beta, 8mm** $29.95 *VYY, KIV 🐾🐾½*

Charlie Chaplin's Keystone Comedies #5 Four classic silent features: "Mabel's Strange Predicament," "The Rounders," "Tango Tangles," and "The Star Border."
1914 57m/B Charlie Chaplin; *D:* Charlie Chaplin. **VHS** $24.95 *VYY, KIV 🐾🐾½*

Charlie Chase and Ben Turpin Three silent comedy classics, "All Wet," "Publicity Pays," and "A Clever Dummy."
1921 67m/B Ben Turpin, Charley Chase, Wallace Beery, Juanita Hansen. **VHS, Beta** $29.95 *VYY 🐾🐾½*

Charlie Grant's War The true story of a Canadian businessman who hears of Nazi brutality and determines to save European Jews from persecution during the Holocaust. Not among the more distinguished works of its kind.
1980 130m/C *GB* Jan Rubes, R.H. Thompson. **VHS, Beta** $59.95 *QNE 🐾🐾*

Charlie, the Lonesome Cougar Life for a rugged logger will never be the same after he adopts an orphaned cougar. From the Disney factory.
1967 (G) 75m/C Linda Wallace, Jim Wilson, Ron Brown, Brian Russell, Clifford Peterson; *D:* Winston Hibler. **VHS, Beta** $69.95 *DIS 🐾🐾*

Charlotte Forten's Mission: Experiment in Freedom Fact-based story, set during the Civil War. A wealthy, educated black woman, determined to prove to President Lincoln that blacks are equal to whites, journeys to a remote island off the coast of Georgia. There she teaches freed slaves to read and write. Part of the "American Playhouse" series on PBS. Preceded by "Solomon Northrup's Odyssey." *AKA:* Half Slave, Half Free 2.
1985 120m/C Melba Moore, Mary Alice, Ned Beatty, Carla Borelli, Micki Grant, Moses Gunn, Anna Maria Horsford, Bruce McGill, Glynn Turman, Roderick Wimberly; *D:* Barry Crane. **VHS** $59.95 *FCT, PTB 🐾🐾🐾*

Charlotte's Web E.B. White's classic story of a friendship between a spider and a pig is handled only adequately by Hanna-Barbera studios. Some okay songs.
1979 (G) 94m/C *D:* Charles A. Nichols; *V:* Debbie Reynolds, Agnes Moorehead, Paul Lynde, Henry Gibson. **VHS, Beta, LV** $14.95 *KUI, PAR, FCT 🐾🐾½*

Charly A retarded man becomes intelligent after brain surgery, then romances a kindly caseworker before slipping back into retardation. Moving account is well served by leads Roberston and Bloom. Adapted by Sterling Silliphant from the Daniel Keyes novel "Flowers for Algernon."
1968 103m/C Cliff Robertson, Claire Bloom, Lilia Skala, Leon Janney, Dick Van Patten, William Dwyer; *D:* Ralph Nelson. **VHS, Beta, LV** $19.98 *FOX, BTV 🐾🐾🐾*

Charm of La Boheme A vintage German musical based on the Puccini opera. With English subtitles.
1936 90m/B *GE* Jan Keipura, Martha Eggerth, Paul Kemp; *D:* Geza von Bolvary. **VHS, Beta** $29.95 *NOS, DVT, APD 🐾🐾½*

Charro! Elvis Presley in a straight role as a reformed bandit hounded by former gang members. Western fails on nearly all accounts, with Presley hopelessly acting outside his acting limits. He only sings one song. Score by Hugo Montenegro.
1969 (G) 98m/C Elvis Presley, Ina Balin, Victor French, Lynn Kellogg, Barbara Werle, Paul Brinegar, James B. Sikking; *D:* Charles Marquis Warren. **VHS** $19.98 *WAR 🐾*

The Chase Not realizing that his boss-to-be is a mobster, Cummings takes a job as a chauffeur. Naturally, he falls in love with the gangster's wife (Morgan), and the two plan to elope. Somewhat miffed, the cuckolded mafioso and his bodyguard (Lorre) pursue the elusive couple as they head for Havana. The performances are up to snuff, but the story's as unimaginative as the title, with intermittent bouts of suspense.
1946 86m/B Robert Cummings, Michele Morgan, Peter Lorre, Steve Cochran, Lloyd Corrigan, Jack Holt, Don "The Dragon" Wilson; *D:* Arthur Ripley. **VHS, Beta, LV** $16.95 *NOS, MRV, SNC 🐾🐾½*

The Chase A southern community is undone when rumors circulate of a former member's prison escape and return home. Excellent cast only partially shines. Brando is, as usual, outstanding as the beleaguered, honorable sheriff, and Duvall makes a splash in the more showy role as a cuckold who fears the escapee is returning home to avenge a childhood incident. Reliable Dickin-

son also makes the most of her role as Brando's loving wife. Fonda, however, was not yet capable of fashioning complex characterizations, and Redford is under-utilized as the escapee. Written by Lillian Hellman from the play by Horton Foote. Notorious conflicts among producer, director, and writer kept it from being the winner it could have been.
1966 135m/C Marlon Brando, Robert Redford, Angie Dickinson, E.G. Marshall, Jane Fonda, James Fox, Janice Rule, Robert Duvall, Miriam Hopkins, Martha Hyer; *D:* Arthur Penn; *M:* John Barry. **VHS, Beta, LV** $14.95 *COL 🐾🐾½*

Chase A big-city lawyer returns to her small hometown to defend a killer and ends up at odds with the town, including an ex-lover. Routine made for television drama.
1985 104m/C Jennifer O'Neill, Robert Woods, Richard Farnsworth, Michael Parks; *D:* Rod Holcomb. **VHS, Beta** $59.98 *FOX 🐾½*

The Chase Routine made for television actioner. An ex-con killer leads a ruthless cop and a TV news team on a wild chase. Loosely based on a true story.
1991 (PG-13) 93m/C Casey Siemaszko, Ben Johnson, Gerry Bamman, Robert Beltran, Barry Corbin, Ricki Lake, Megan Follows. **VHS, LV** $89.95 *VMK 🐾🐾*

Chasing Dreams Sickly melodrama about a farmboy who finds fulfillment as a baseball player. Lame film promoted as Costner baseball vehicle, but the star of "Bull Durham" and "Field of Dreams" appears only briefly in a secondary role.
1981 (PG) 96m/C David G. Brown, John Fife, Jim Shane, Lisa Kingston, Matt Clark, Kevin Costner; *D:* Sean Roche, Therese Conte. **VHS, Beta** $79.95 *PSM 🐾½*

Chasing Those Depression Blues Four '30s comedy shorts: "Money on Your Life," "Dental Follies," "Any Day in Hollywood" and "Art in the Raw."
1935 58m/B Danny Kaye, Pinky Lee, Edgar Kennedy, Ben Turpin. **VHS, Beta** $24.95 *VYY 🐾½*

Chaste & Pure A young woman is torn between her blooming sexuality and her vows of chastity. Lesser known Antonelli effort.
1977 90m/C *IT* Laura Antonelli. **VHS, Beta** *NO 🐾*

Chato's Land An Indian is tracked by a posse eager to resolve a lawman's death. Conventional violent Bronson vehicle is bolstered by presence of masterful Palance.
1971 (PG) 100m/C Charles Bronson, Jack Palance, Richard Basehart, James Whitmore, Simon Oakland, Richard Jordan, Ralph Waite, Victor French, Lee Patterson; *D:* Michael Winner. **VHS, Beta** $14.95 *MGM 🐾🐾½*

Chattahoochee A man suffering from post-combat syndrome lands in a horrifying institution. Strong cast, with Oldman fine in the lead, and Hopper memorable in extended cameo. Fact-based film is, unfortunately, rather conventionally rendered.
1989 97m/C Gary Oldman, Dennis Hopper, Frances McDormand, Pamela Reed, Ned Beatty, M. Emmet Walsh, William De Acutis, Lee Wilkof, Matt Craven, Gary Klar; *D:* Mick Jackson. **VHS, LV** $89.99 *HBO, IME, FCT 🐾🐾½*

Chattanooga Choo Choo A football team owner must restore the Chattanooga Choo Choo and make a 24-hour run from Chattanooga to New York in order to collect one-million dollars left to him in a will. The train never leaves the station.
1984 (PG) 102m/C Barbara Eden, George Kennedy, Melissa Sue Anderson, Joe Namath, Bridget Hanley, Christopher McDonald, Clu Gulager, Tony Azito; *D:* Bruce Bilson. **VHS, Beta** $59.99 *HBO 🐾½*

Chatterbox A starlet's life and career are severely altered when her sex organs begin speaking. So why didn't they warn her about movies like this? Plenty of B-queen Rialson on view. Good double bill with "Me and Him."
1976 73m/C Candice Rialson, Larry Gelman, Jean Kean, Perry Bullington; **D:** Tom De Simone. **VHS, Beta $59.98** *LIV, VES* ⅈⅈ

The Cheap Detective Neil Simon's parody of the "Maltese Falcon" gloriously exploits the resourceful Falk in a Bogart-like role. Vast supporting cast—notable Brennan, DeLuise, and Kahn—equally game for fun in this consistently amusing venture.
1978 (PG) 92m/C Peter Falk, Ann-Margret, Eileen Brennan, Sid Caesar, Stockard Channing, James Coco, Dom DeLuise, Louise Fletcher, John Houseman, Madeline Kahn, Fernando Lamas, Marsha Mason, Phil Silvers, Vic Tayback, Abe Vigoda, Paul Williams, Nicol Williamson; **D:** Robert Moore; **W:** Neil Simon. **VHS $19.95** *CSM, COL* ⅈⅈⅈ

Cheap Shots Cheap best describes this. Two guys running a sleazy New York State resort motel plot to videotape patrons having sex, but capture an apparent mob murder instead. More of a character study than sexploitation, but who needs these characters? Not a stellar writing/directing debut for Ureles and Stoeffhaas.
1991 (PG-13) 90m/C Louis Zorich, David Patrick Kelly, Mary Louise Wilson, Michael Twaine, Patience Moore; **W/D:** Jeff Ureles; **W:** Jerry Stoeffhaas; **M:** Jeff Beal. **VHS $89.95** *HMD* ⅈ½

Cheaper to Keep Her Alleged comedy about a private detective hired to track likely alimony dodgers. Loathsome, repellent fare, with Davis hopeless in the lead.
1980 (R) 92m/C Mac Davis, Tovah Feldshuh, Jack Gilford, Rose Marie; **D:** Ken Annakin. **VHS, Beta $54.95** *MED Woof!*

The Cheat Ward plays a frivolous socialite heavily indebted to Hayakawa as the Japanese money lender. Hayakawa makes Ward pay with her honor and her flesh by branding her. A dark and captivating drama. Silent with piano score.
1915 55m/B Fanny Ward, Sessue Hayakawa; **D:** Cecil B. DeMille. **VHS, Beta $14.95** *GPV* ⅈⅈⅈ

The Cheaters A young gambler runs away with his boss's son's girlfriend, and is pursued therein.
1976 (R) 91m/C *IT* Dayle Haddon, Luc Merenda, Lino Troisi, Enrico Maria Salerno; **D:** Sergio Martino. **VHS, Beta $59.95** *PSM* ⅈ

Cheaters Two middle class couples are having affairs with each other's spouses. Complications arise when their respective children decide to marry each other.
1984 103m/C Peggy Cass, Jack Kruschen. **VHS, Beta $39.95** *RKO* ⅈ½

Check & Double Check Radio's original Amos 'n' Andy (a couple of blackfaced white guys) help solve a lover's triangle in this film version of the popular radio series. Interesting only as a novelty. Duke Ellington's band plays "Old Man Blues" and "Three Little Words."
1930 85m/B Freeman Gosden, Charles Correll, Duke Ellington; **D:** Melville Brown. **VHS, Beta, LV $19.95** *NOS, MRV, VYY* ⅈ

Check is in the Mail Lame comedy about a financier determined to make his home entirely independent from the rat-race of capitalist society. Dependables Dennehy and Archer are wasted.
1985 (R) 83m/C Brian Dennehy, Anne Archer, Dick Shawn; **D:** Joan Darling. **VHS, Beta $79.95** *MED* ⅈ½

Check Your Guns A crooked judge and a gang of outlaws team up to prey on law-abiding folk and cause headaches for the new sheriff, who's pushing an unsuccessful Old West version of gun control. Nothing really noteworthy here.
1948 55m/B Eddie Dean, Roscoe Ates, Nancy Gates, George Cheseboro, I. Stanford Jolley, Mikel Conrad, Bill Fawcett; **D:** Ray Taylor. **VHS $19.95** *NOS* ⅈⅈ

Checking Out Black comedy about a manic hypochondriac who is convinced that his demise will soon occur. You'll pray that he's right. Daniels can't make it work, and supporters Mayron and Magnuson also have little chance in poorly conceived roles. Written by Joe Esterhaus.
1989 (R) 95m/C Jeff Daniels, Melanie Mayron, Michael Tucker, Kathleen York, Ann Magnuson, Allen Havey, Jo Harvey Allen, Felton Perry, Alan Wolfe; **D:** David Leland. **VHS, Beta, LV** *NO* ⅈ½

Cheech and Chong: Still Smokin' Not really. More like still trying to make a buck. Veteran marijuana-dazed comedy duo travel to Amsterdam to raise funds for a bankrupt film festival group by hosting a dope-a-thon. Lots of concert footage used in an attempt to hold the slim plot together. Only for serious fans of the dopin' duo. *AKA:* Still Smokin'.
1983 (R) 91m/C Cheech Marin, Thomas Chong; **D:** Thomas Chong. **VHS, Beta, LV $14.95** *PAR* ⅈ½

Cheech and Chong: Things Are Tough All Over Stoner comedy team are hired by two rich Arab brothers (also played by Cheech and Chong in acting stretch) and unwittingly drive a car loaded with money from Chicago to Las Vegas. Tired fourth in the series.
1982 (R) 87m/C Cheech Marin, Thomas Chong, Shelby Fiddis, Rikki Marin, Evelyn Guerrero, Rip Taylor; **D:** Tom Avildsen. **VHS, Beta $9.95** *COL* ⅈⅈ

Cheech and Chong's Next Movie A pair of messed-up bumblers adventure into a welfare office, massage parlor, nightclub, and flying saucer, while always living in fear of the cops. Kinda funny, like. Sequel to "Up in Smoke."
1980 (R) 95m/C Cheech Marin, Thomas Chong, Evelyn Guerrero, Edie McClurg, Pee-Wee Herman; **D:** Thomas Chong. **VHS, Beta, LV $14.95** *MCA* ⅈⅈ

Cheech and Chong's Nice Dreams The spaced-out duo are selling their own "specially mixed" ice cream to make cash and realize their dreams. Third in the series.
1981 (R) 97m/C Cheech Marin, Thomas Chong, Evelyn Guerrero, Stacy Keach, Pee-Wee Herman; **D:** Thomas Chong; Timothy Leary. **VHS, Beta, LV $14.95** *COL* ⅈⅈ

Cheech and Chong's, The Corsican Brothers Wretched swashbuckler features the minimally talented duo in a variety of worthless roles. Dumas would vomit in his casket if he knew about this. Fifth in the series.
1984 (PG) 91m/C Cheech Marin, Thomas Chong, Roy Dotrice, Rae Dawn Chong, Shelby Fiddis, Rikki Marin, Edie McClurg; **D:** Thomas Chong. **VHS, LV $79.98** *LIV Woof!*

Cheech and Chong's Up in Smoke A pair of free-spirited burn-outs team up for a tongue-in-cheek spoof of sex, drugs, and rock and roll. First and probably the best of the dopey duo's cinematic adventures. A box-office bonanza when released and still a cult favorite.

1979 (R) 87m/C Cheech Marin, Thomas Chong, Stacy Keach, Tom Skerritt, Edie Adams, Strother Martin, Cheryl "Rainbeaux" Smith; **D:** Lou Adler. **VHS, Beta, LV $14.95** *PAR* ⅈⅈ½

The Cheerful Fraud Denny, who appeared in some two hundred-odd films in his career, masquerades as a butler to be near the girl he loves. A fool for love is a cheerful fraud. A zanily romantic silent comedy.
1927 64m/B Reginald Denny, Gertrude Olmsted, Emily Fitzroy, Gertrude Astor; **D:** William A. Seiter. **VHS, Beta $24.95** *GPV* ⅈ½

Cheering Section High school football teams compete for the grand prize—the privilege of ravishing the losing school's cheerleaders. Rah, rah, rah.
1973 (R) 84m/C Rhonda Foxx, Tom Leindecker, Gregg D'Jah, Patricia Michelle, Jeff Laine; **D:** Harry Kerwin. **VHS** *NO Woof!*

Cheerleader Camp Nubile gals are stalked by a psychopath while they cavort semi-clad at summer camp. *AKA:* Bloody Pom Poms.
1988 (R) 89m/C Betsy Russell, Leif Garrett, Lucinda Dickey, Lorie Griffin, George Flower, Teri Weigel, Rebecca Ferratti; **D:** John Quinn. **VHS, Beta $14.95** *PSM, PAR Woof!*

The Cheerleaders Dimwitted exploitation effort has the usual suspects—moronic jocks and lamebrained gals—cavorting exuberantly. Followed by "Revenge of the Cheerleaders."
1972 (R) 84m/C Stephanie Fondue, Denise Dillaway, Jovita Bush, Debbie Lowe, Sandy Evans; **D:** Paul Glickler. **VHS, Beta, LV $9.99** *STE, PSM, IME Woof!*

Cheerleaders' Beach Party Goodnatured gals undermine the effectiveness of opposing football teams by sexually bewitching enemy players. By standards of the genre, a near masterpiece.
1977 (R) 85m/C Stephanie Hastings, Linda Jenson, Mary Lou Loredan, Denise Upson; **D:** Alex E. Goiten. **VHS, Beta** *PGN* ⅈ

Cheerleaders' Wild Weekend Group of cheerleaders are held captive by a disgruntled former football star. Pom poms wave.
1985 (R) 87m/C Jason Williams, Kristine DeBell; **D:** Jeff Werner. **VHS, Beta $69.98** *LIV, VES Woof!*

Cheers for Miss Bishop The story of a woman who graduates from college then teaches at the same institution for the next 50 years. Somewhat moving. Based on Bess Streeter Aldrich's novel. Score by Edward Ward.
1941 95m/B Martha Scott, William Gargan, Edmund Gwenn, Sterling Holloway, Rosemary DeCamp; **D:** Tay Garnett. **VHS, Beta $19.95** *NOS, MRV, VYY* ⅈⅈ½

Cheetah Two California kids visiting their parents in Kenya embark on the adventure of their lives when, with the help of a young Masai, they adopt and care for an orphaned cheetah. Usual Disney kids and animals story.
1989 (G) 80m/C Keith Coogan, Lucy Deakins, Collin Mothupi; **D:** Jeff Blyth. **VHS, LV $89.98** *DIS* ⅈⅈ

Cherry Hill High Five teen girls compete for former-virgin status. Pass on this one.
1976 (R) 92m/C Linda McInerney, Carrie Olsen, Nina Carson, Lynn Hastings, Gloria Upson, Stephanie Lawlor; **D:** Alex E. Goiten. **VHS, Beta $59.95** *MCA Woof!*

Cherry 2000 Futuristic flick concerns a man who short-circuits his sex-toy robots and embarks on a search for replacement parts across treacherous territory, only to

C

meet a real female—Griffith. Offbeat, occasionally funny.

1988 (PG-13) 94m/C Melanie Griffith, David Andrews, Ben Johnson, Tim Thomerson, Michael C. Gwynne; **D:** Steve DeJarnatt. **VHS, Beta, LV** $19.98 ORI ⅋⅋

Chesty Anderson USN Ultra-lame sexploitation about female naval recruits. Minimal nudity. **AKA:** Anderson's Angels.

1976 90m/C Shari Eubank, Dorri Thompson, Rosanne Katon, Marcie Barkin, Scatman Crothers, Frank Campanella, Fred Willard; **D:** Ed Forsyth. **VHS, Beta** $49.95 WWV ⅋

Cheyenne Autumn The newly restored version of the ambitious, ultimately hit-and-miss western epic about three hundred Cheyenne Indians who migrate from Oklahoma to their Wyoming homeland in 1878. The cavalry, for once, are not the good guys. Widmark is strong in the lead. Stewart is memorable in his comic cameo as Wyatt Earp. Last film from genre master Ford, capturing the usual rugged panoramas. Based on a true story as told in the Mari Sandoz novel.

1964 156m/C Richard Widmark, Carroll Baker, Karl Malden, Dolores Del Rio, Sal Mineo, Edward G. Robinson, Ricardo Montalban, Gilbert Roland, Arthur Kennedy, John Carradine, Victor Jory, Mike Mazurki, George O'Brien, John Qualen; **Cameos:** James Stewart; **D:** John Ford. **VHS, Beta** $19.98 WAR, FCT ⅋⅋½

Cheyenne Kid Determined bronco buster is up against a gang of bad guys.

1933 40m/B Tom Keene, Mary Mason, Roscoe Ates. **VHS, Beta** $19.95 NOS, DVT ⅋½

Cheyenne Rides Again Cheyenne poses as an outlaw to hunt a gang of rustlers.

1938 60m/B Tom Tyler, Lucille Browne, James Fox. **VHS, Beta** $19.95 NOS, VYY, VCN ⅋½

The Cheyenne Social Club Stewart inherits a brothel and Fonda helps him operate it. Kelly directs, sort of. Some laughs, but this effort is beneath this trio.

1970 (PG) 103m/C Henry Fonda, James Stewart, Shirley Jones, Sue Ann Langdon, Elaine Devry; **D:** Gene Kelly. **VHS** $59.95 WAR ⅋⅋

Cheyenne Takes Over Lash sniffs out the bad guy in the case of a murdered ranch heir.

1947 56m/B Lash LaRue, Al "Fuzzy" St. John, George Cheseboro; **D:** Ray Taylor. **VHS, Beta** $12.95 COL, SVS ⅋

Chicago Joe & the Showgirl A London-based GI befriends a loopy showgirl and helps her in various crimes during WWII. Appealing Lloyd overwhelms Sutherland, who shows only limited acting ability here. Kensit and Pigg are fine in smaller roles.

1990 (R) 105m/C GB Emily Lloyd, Kiefer Sutherland, Patsy Kensit, Keith Allen, Liz Fraser, Alexandra Pigg, Ralph Nossek, Colin Bruce; **D:** Bernard Rose. **VHS, LV** $89.95 LIV, IME ⅋⅋

The Chicken Chronicles An affluent high school dude longs to get horizontal with his dream girl. Set in the 1960s. First feature film appearance for Guttenberg.

1977 (PG) 94m/C Phil Silvers, Ed Lauter, Steve Guttenberg, Lisa Reeves, Meredith Baer; **D:** Francis Simon. **VHS, Beta** $14.95 COL, SUE ⅋

Chiefs A police chief in a Southern town discovers a series of murders concealed by town big wigs. Made for TV film boasts a surprisingly strong cast, but provides otherwise conventional entertainment.

1983 200m/C Charlton Heston, Paul Sorvino, Keith Carradine, Brad Davis, Billy Dee Williams, Wayne Rogers, Stephen Collins, Tess Harper, Victoria Tennant; **D:** Jerry London. **VHS, Beta** $29.95 STE, NWV ⅋⅋

Child Bride An edited version of the mildly infamous exploitation quickie about an Ozark hillbilly and his 12-year-old wife.

1939 52m/B **D:** Harry Revier. **VHS, Beta** $16.95 SNC, NOS, HEG Woof!

Child Bride of Short Creek A young Korean war veteran returns to his community where polygamy is allowed, to find that his father intends to marry again, this time to a 15-year-old. Conflict ensues. Made for television. Based on an actual event that occurred in the 1950s.

1981 100m/C Diane Lane, Conrad Bain, Christopher Atkins, Kiel Martin, Helen Hunt; **D:** Robert Lewis. **VHS, Beta** $59.95 PSM ⅋⅋½

Child in the Night A shaken eight-year old boy is a witness to murder in his family, and a psychologist with plenty of her own problems must get him to testify. Middling TV-movie suspense.

1990 (R) 93m/C Tom Skerritt, JoBeth Williams, Darren McGavin, Season Hubley; **D:** Mike Robe. **VHS, Beta** $79.95 TRI ⅋⅋

A Child is Waiting Poignant and provocative story of teachers in an institution for the mentally retarded. Fine performances include Lancaster as the institution's administrator and Garland as a teacher who cares too much for everyone's good. Cassavetes incorporates footage using handicapped children as extras—not entirely seamlessly—providing a sensitive and candid edge.

1963 105m/B Burt Lancaster, Judy Garland, Gena Rowlands, Steven Hill, Bruce Ritchey; **D:** John Cassavetes. **VHS, Beta** $19.98 MGM ⅋⅋⅋

Child of Darkness, Child of Light A priest is sent to investigate two virgin pregnancies and discovers that one child will be a savior and the other the Anti-Christ. Totally mindless brain candy resembling the "Omen" movies and "Rosemary's Baby." Made for cable television. Adapted from James Patterson's book "Virgin."

1991 (PG-13) 85m/C Anthony John Denison, Brad Davis, Paxton Whitehead, Claudette Nevins, Sydney Penny, Kristin Datillo, Viveca Lindfors, Sela Ward, Alan Oppenheimer, Eric Christmas; **D:** Marina Sargenti; **W:** Brian Taggert. **VHS, Beta** PAR ⅋½

Child of Glass A young boy's family moves into a huge New Orleans mansion, and soon after encounters a young girl's ghost and lost treasure from the Civil War. A Disney made for TV movie.

1978 93m/C Barbara Barrie, Biff McGuire, Anthony Zerbe, Nina Foch, Steve Shaw, Katy Kurtzman, Olivia Barash; **D:** John Erman. **VHS, Beta** $69.95 DIS ⅋½

Child of the Prairie An early Mix film about a young cowboy and his city-loving wife down on their luck in a western town. Silent with music score.

1918 63m/B Tom Mix. **VHS, Beta, 8mm** $29.95 VYY ⅋

The Children Familiar nuclear leak leads to monster mutants done to a novel (though extremely low-budget) turn: after a school bus passes through radioactive fog, the kiddies inside assume the ability to incinerate whoever they hug. They also assume a certain zombie-like demeanor and sport black fingernails. None of this is noted by their uncaring and less-than-observant parents, of whom are enticed into a very warm hug. This may be intended as social satire. Not only are the little microwaves extremely dangerous, the only way to kill them is to chop off their hands, leading to a wild limbless finale.

1980 (R) 89m/C Martin Shaker, Gale Garnett, Gil Rogers; **D:** Max Kalmanowicz. **VHS, Beta** $14.95 VES, FCT, RHI Woof!

The Children Kingsley stars as a middle-aged engineer who finds himself caring for seven children in this touching love story from novelist Edith Wharton. Shot on location in Venice, the cinematography is excellent and the cast is superb, but the film lags in places. A remake of "The Marriage Playground."

1990 90m/C GB GE Ben Kingsley, Kim Novak, Siri Neal, Geraldine Chaplin, Joe Don Baker, Britt Ekland, Donald Sinden, Karen Black, Robert Stephens, Rupert Graves, Rosemary Leach; **D:** Tony Palmer. **VHS** $89.95 HMD ⅋⅋½

The Children Are Watching Us Sobering drama of a family dissolution as seen by a child. Worthy example of Italian neo-realism marks the first collaboration between Zavattini and De Sica. In Italian with subtitles. **AKA:** The Little Martyr; I Bambini Ci Guardano.

1944 92m/B IT Luciano de Ambrosis, Isa Pola, Emilio Cigoli; **W/D:** Vittorio De Sica; **W:** Cesare Zavattini. **VHS, Beta** $79.95 FCT ⅋⅋⅋

Children in the Crossfire When youngsters from war-torn Northern Ireland spend a summer in America with children from the Republic of Ireland, both sides find their nationalistic prejudices falling away. But a great challenge awaits them when they return home from their summer of fun. Nicely done drama made for television.

1984 96m/C Charles Haid, Karen Valentine, Julia Duffy, David Huffman; **D:** George Schaefer. **VHS, LV** $79.98 LIV, VES ⅋⅋½

Children of a Lesser God Based upon the play by Mark Medoff, this sensitive, intelligent film deals with an unorthodox speech teacher at a school for the deaf, who falls in love with a beautiful and rebellious ex-student. Inarguably romantic; the original stage production won the Best Play Tony in 1980. Hurt and Matlin reportedly continued their romance off-screen as well.

1986 (R) 119m/C William Hurt, Marlee Matlin, Piper Laurie, Philip Bosco, E. Katherine Kerr; **D:** Randa Haines. Academy Awards '86: Best Actress (Matlin); Nominations: Best Actor (Hurt), Best Adapted Screenplay, Best Picture, Best Supporting Actress (Laurie); Golden Globe Awards '87: Best Actress—Drama (Matlin). **VHS, Beta, LV, 8mm** $19.95 PAR, BTV, JCF ⅋⅋⅋½

The Children of An Lac Three women attempt to rescue hundreds of Vietnamese orphans before Saigon falls to the communists. The film derives actress Balin's actual wartime experience. Made for television.

1980 100m/C Shirley Jones, Ina Balin, Beulah Quo, Alan Fudge, Ben Piazza, Lee Paul, Kieu Chinh, Vic Diaz. **VHS, Beta** $14.95 FRH ⅋⅋

Children of Divorce Made-for-television drama shows divorce from the children's point of view. Standard fare.

1980 96m/C Barbara Feldon, Lance Kerwin, Stacey Nelkin, Billy Dee Williams; **D:** Joanna Lee. **VHS, Beta** $39.95 LIV ⅋½

Children of Paradise Considered by many to be the greatest film ever made, certainly one of the most beautiful. In the Parisian theatre district of the 1800s an actor falls in love with a seemingly unattainable woman. Although circumstances keep them apart, their love never dies. Produced in France during WWII right under the noses of Nazi occupiers; many of the talent (including the writer, poet Jacques Prevert) were active resistance fighters. Laserdisc version features: interview with director Marcel Carne, production photos, analysis of influences of

French painting on the film, and audio essay by film authority Brian Stonehill. In French with English subtitles. *AKA:* Les Enfants du Paradise.
1944 188m/B *FR* Jean-Louis Barrault, Arletty, Pierre Brasseur, Maria Casares; *D:* Marcel Carne. **VHS, LV $79.95** *HMV, VYG, CRC* 𝄞𝄞𝄞𝄞

Children of Rage High-minded and long-winded drama dealing with the Israeli/Palestinian war and terrorism from the viewpoint of an Israeli doctor yearning for peace.
1975 (PG) 106m/C *GB IS* Simon Ward, Cyril Cusack, Helmut Griem, Olga Georges-Picot; *D:* Arthur Seidelman. **VHS, Beta $69.95** *ACA* 𝄞𝄞½

Children of Sanchez Mexican man attempts to provide for his family with very little except faith and love. U.S./Mexican production based on Oscar Lewis' novel. Music by Chuck Mangione.
1979 (PG) 103m/C *MX* Anthony Quinn, Dolores Del Rio, Katy Jurado, Lupita Ferrer; *D:* Hall Bartlett. **VHS, Beta $39.95** *MON* 𝄞𝄞

Children of the Corn Young couple lands in a small Iowa town where children appease a demon by murderously sacrificing adults. Time to move or dispense with some major spankings. Infrequently scary. Another feeble attempt to translate the horror of a Stephen King book to film.
1984 (R) 93m/C Peter Horton, Linda Hamilton, R.G. Armstrong, John Franklin, Courtney Gains, Robbie Kiger; *D:* Fritz Kiersch. **VHS, Beta, LV $9.98** *SUE, STE* 𝄞½

Children of the Corn 2: The Final Sacrifice Reporter working for a tabloid paper gets more than he bargained for when he decides to do a story on the adults murdered in the town of Gatlin, Nebraska. Gatlin's surviving children, who killed their parents in the first film, are now living in a neighboring town and free to kill again. This youthful satanic cult does in authority figures in a number of sacrificial ways, working ever more smartly to create the prime attraction—blood flow. Not based on anything written by Stephen King.
1992 (R) 93m/C Terence Knox, Paul Scherrer, Rosalind Allen, Christie Clark, Ned Romero, Ryan Bollman, Ted Travelstead; *D:* David F. Price; *W:* Gilbert Adler, A.L. Katz. **VHS** *PAR* 𝄞½

Children of the Damned Six children, who are a sample of what man will evolve to in a million years, are born all around the world with genius IQs, ray-gun eyes, and murderous dispositions. Two investigators bring the children together, and while they are being examined by scientists they escape. The children hide out in a church, but they are doomed because their destiny is to be destroyed to teach a lesson to modern man. A sequel to "Village of the Damned" based loosely on the novel "The Midwich Cuckoos" by John Wyndham.
1963 90m/B *GB* Ian Hendry, Alan Badel, Barbara Ferris, Alfred Burke, Sheila Allen, Clive Powell, Frank Summerscales, Mahdu Mathen, Gerald Delsol, Roberta Rex, Franchesca Lee, Harold Goldblatt; *D:* Anton Leader. **VHS, LV $19.98** *MGM* 𝄞𝄞

Children of the Full Moon A young couple find themselves lost in a forest that is the home of a family of werewolves. Earns praise only for brevity. Even bad movie aficionados will want to skip this howler.
1984 60m/C *GB* Christopher Cazenove, Celia Gregory, Diana Dors, Jacof Witken, Robert Urquhart; *D:* Tom Clegg. **VHS, Beta $29.95** *LIV* 𝄞

Children of the Night Allburg seems like a typically quiet small town far removed from any danger—until a vampire is released from an underground crypt and decides to make the town his bloodthirsty target. When a teacher, whose girlfriend is visiting Allburg, learns of the supernatural goings on he decides to investigate, which may be a deadly mistake.
1992 (R) 92m/C Peter DeLuise, Karen Black, Ami Dolenz; *D:* Tony Randel. **VHS $89.95** *COL* 𝄞½

Children of the Wild Adventure story about a pack of dogs surviving in the Rocky Mountain wilderness. Splendid scenery and some interesting sequences. *AKA:* Killers of the Wild.
1937 65m/B Patsy Moran. **VHS** *VYY* 𝄞𝄞½

The Children of Theatre Street Absorbing documentary follows three children attending the renowned Kirov Ballet School. A show for all ages that may be especially enjoyed by kids who are interested in ballet. Kelly's last film appearance.
1977 92m/C *D:* Robert Dornhelm, Earle Mack; *Performed by:* Kirov Ballet. **VHS, Beta $39.95** *MVD, PBC, KUL* 𝄞𝄞𝄞½

The Children of Times Square A mother pursues her son who has fled home and joined a gang of drug dealers in New York City's seedy Times Square. Ordinary television film despite strong casting of Cassidy and Rollins.
1986 95m/C Joanna Cassidy, Howard E. Rollins Jr., Brandon Douglas, David Ackroyd, Griffin O'Neal, Danny Nucci, Larry B. Scott; *D:* Curtis Hanson. **VHS, Beta $14.95** *FRH* 𝄞𝄞

Children Shouldn't Play with Dead Things A band of foolhardy hippie filmmakers on an island cemetary skimp on special effects by using witchcraft to revive the dead. The plan works. Soon the crew has an island full of hungry ghouls to contend with. Film strives for yucks, frequently succeeds. A late night fave, sporting some excellent dead rising from their grave scenes as well as a selection of groovy fashions. Screenwriter/star Ormsby went on to write the remake of "Cat People," while director Clark would eventually helm "Porky's." *AKA:* Revenge of the Living Dead.
1972 85m/C Alan Ormsby, Valerie Mamches, Jeff Gillen, Anya Ormsby, Paul Cronin, Jane Daly, Roy Engelman, Robert Philip, Bruce Solomon, Alecs Baird, Seth Sklarey; *W/D:* Benjamin (Bob) Clark. **VHS, Beta $19.95** *UHV, MPI* 𝄞𝄞½

Children's Carol The winter solstice brings no special joy to Walton's mountain, with short wave reports indicating the Nazi terror spreading across Europe. But huddled in the glow of Walton's barn, the children rediscover the true meaning of Christmas.
1980 94m/C Judy Norton-Taylor, Jon Walmsley, Mary McDonough, Eric Scott, Kami Cotler, Joe Conely, Ronnie Clare, Leslie Winston, Peggy Rea; *D:* Lawrence Dobkin. **VHS, Beta $59.95** *LHV* 𝄞𝄞

The Children's Hour The teaching careers of two women are ruined when girls begin circulating vicious rumors. Only an occasionally taut drama despite forceful handling of a lesbian theme. Updated version of Lillian Hellman's play (adapted by Hellman) is more explicit, but less suspenseful in spite of excellent performances from the talented cast. Remake of Wyler's own "These Three." *AKA:* The Loudest Whisper.
1961 107m/C Shirley MacLaine, Audrey Hepburn, James Garner, Miriam Hopkins, Veronica Cartwright, Fay Bainter; *D:* William Wyler. **VHS, LV $19.98** *MGM, BTV, FCT* 𝄞𝄞

Children's Island A two-volume saga, sold in one package, about children who, after being shipwrecked on an island during World War II, begin a democratic mini-society.
1984 100m/C VHS, Beta $59.95 *SVS* 𝄞𝄞

Child's Christmas in Wales A film of Dylan Thomas's Christmas story about an old, traditional Christmas in Wales circa 1910.
1988 55m/C Mathonwy Reeves; *D:* Don McBrearty. **VHS, Beta $14.98** *LIV, VES, HMV* 𝄞𝄞

Child's Play A boy discovers that his new doll named Chucky is actually the embodiment of a deranged killer. His initially skeptical mom and a police officer come around after various killings. Exciting, if somewhat moronic, fare, with fine special effects. Followed by "Child's Play 2."
1988 (R) 95m/C Catherine Hicks, Alex Vincent, Chris Sarandon, Dinah Manoff, Brad Dourif; *D:* Tom Holland. **VHS, Beta, LV $19.95** *MGM* 𝄞𝄞½

Child's Play 2 Chuckie lives. The basic doll-on-a-rampage story, a metaphor for the Reagan years, lives on in the sequel (you remember: somehow guy-doll Chuckie made it past the quality control people with a highly inflammable temper). A little dotty from playing with dolls, young Vincent finds himself fostered by two new parents, and plagued by an obnoxious and very animated doll that fosters ill will toward all. What's worse is the doll is transmigratory, craving the boy's body as his next address. Chef d'effects Kevin Yagher's new toy is bad, real bad, and so are the other part two FX. Little Chuckie's saga, however grows a tad tiresome. A bad example for small children.
1990 (R) 84m/C Alex Vincent, Jenny Agutter, Gerrit Graham, Christine Elise, Grace Zabriskie; *D:* John Lafia; *V:* Brad Dourif. **VHS, Beta, LV $19.98** *MCA* Woof!

Child's Play 3 Possessed doll Chucky returns to life again in search of a new child to control, and luckily finds his old pal (Whalin) at a military school filled with the usual stereotypes. Gory sequel in a mostly awful series. "Don't F—- With the Chuck" was its catch phrase; that should indicate the level of this junk.
1991 (R) 89m/C Justin Whalin, Perrey Reeves, Jeremy Sylvers, Peter Haskell, Dakin Matthews, Travis Fine, Dean Jacobson, Matthew Walker, Andrew Robinson; *D:* Jack Bender; *W:* Don Mancini, Cory Lerios; *M:* John D'Andrea; *V:* Brad Dourif. **VHS, Beta, LV $19.98** *MCA* 𝄞

Chill Factor A television reporter for an investigative news show uncovers evidence of an international conspiracy. Plot twists abound.
1990 (R) ?m/C Paul Williams, Patrick Macnee, Andrew Prine, Carrie Snodgress, Patrick Wayne, Gary Crosby; *D:* David L. Stanton. **VHS** *NO* 𝄞𝄞

Chillers Travellers waiting for a bus are besieged by carnivorous zombies and voracious vampires. How this is different from the standard bus trip is unclear.
1988 90m/C Jesse Emery, Marjorie Fitzsimmons, Laurie Pennington, Jim Wolfe, David Wohl; *W/D:* Daniel Boyd. **VHS, Beta $9.95** *SIM, PSM* 𝄞

The Chilling Corpses preserved in a deep freeze come alive and plague Kansas City as flesh-chomping zombies. Utterly worthless film doesn't even provide convincing effects. *AKA:* Gamma 693.
1989 (R) 91m/C Linda Blair, Dan Haggerty, Troy Donahue, Jack A. De Rieux, Ron Vincent; *D:* Deland Nuse, Jack A. Sunseri. **VHS $89.95** *HMD* Woof!

C

Chilly Scenes of Winter Quirky comedy with a cult following about a man obsessed with regaining the love of a former girlfriend who is now married. He must also deal with an insane mom and various other problems. Strong, subtle performances from Heard and Riegert. Hurt is somewhat less satisfying as the supposedly fascinating woman. Released with a different, inferior ending as "Head Over Heels." Adapted by Joan Micklin Silver from Ann Beattie's first novel. Watch for Beattie's cameo as a waitress. *AKA: Head Over Heels.*
1979 (PG) 96m/C John Heard, Mary Beth Hurt, Peter Riegert, Kenneth McMillan, Gloria Grahame, Nora Heflin, Griffin Dunne; *Cameos:* Ann Beattie; *W/D:* Joan Micklin Silver. VHS, Beta $19.98 MGM ♂♂½

Chimes at Midnight Classic tragedy—derived by Welles from five Shakespeare plays—about a corpulent blowhard and his friendship with a prince. Crammed with classic sequences, including a battle that is both realistic and funny. The love scene between massive Welles and a nonetheless willing Moreau also manages to be both sad and amusing. Great performances all around, but Welles understandably dominates. The film's few flaws (due to budget problems) are inconsequential before considerable strengths. This one ranks among Welles', and thus the entire cinema's, very best. *AKA: Falstaff; Campanadas a Medianoche.*
1967 115m/B SP SI Orson Welles, Keith Baxter, Jeanne Moreau, John Gielgud, Marina Vlady, Margaret Rutherford, Norman Rodway, Fernando Rey; *W/D:* Orson Welles. VHS, Beta FCT ♂♂♂♂

China Beach The television movie/pilot that launched the acclaimed series, concerning American military women behind the lines during the chaos of the Vietnam War. Nurse McMurphy has only seven days left on her first tour of duty, and in spite of her hate of the brutality of the war, she has mixed feelings about leaving her friends and her work. A USO singer on a one week tour finds her search for men brings the war too close for comfort. Cherry, a new Red Cross volunteer, shows up at the Beach. Skillfully introduces the viewer to all the characters, their problems and joys, without melodrama or redundancy.
1988 95m/C Dana Dolany, Chloe Webb, Robert Picardo, Nan Woods, Michael Boatman, Marg Helgenberger, Tim Ryan, Concetta Tomei, Jeff Kober, Brian Wimmer; *D:* Rod Holcomb; *W:* John Sacret Young. VHS, Beta $79.95 WAR ♂♂♂

China Cry Based on the true story of Sung Negn Yee who escaped from Communist China to the freedom of Hong Kong in the early '60s. Nickson-Soul gives a good performance as the young woman from a privileged background who witessed some of the atrocities of Mao's government policies.
1991 (PG-13) 103m/C Julia Nickson-Soul, Russell Wong, James Shigeta, France Nuyen; *D:* James F. Collier. VHS $24.95 TAM, IGP ♂♂½

China Gate A band of multi-national troops follows a French officer against a communist stronghold in Indochina. Conventional fare bolstered considerably by director Fuller's flair for action. Weak male leads, but Dickinson shines.
1957 97m/B Gene Barry, Angie Dickinson, Nat King Cole, Paul Dubov, Lee Van Cleef, George Givot, Marcel Dalio; *W/D:* Samuel Fuller. VHS $19.98 REP ♂♂♂

China Girl An Italian-American boy and a Chinese-American girl romance despite a war between gangs in their respective NYC communities. This often violent drama is enriched by director Ferrara's slick, high-energy approach.
1987 (R) 90m/C Richard Panebianco, James Russo, Sari Chang, Russell Wong, David Caruso, Joey Chin; *D:* Abel Ferrara. VHS, Beta, LV $79.98 VES ♂♂½

The China Lake Murders A made for cable crazy cop on the loose fable in which a serial killer disguised as a highway patrolman practices population control on the inhabitants of a small town in the Mojave desert. Meanwhile the local sheriff (Skerritt), unwittingly befriends the killer-patrolman. Written by N.D. Schreiner.
1990 (PG-13) 100m/C Tom Skerritt, Michael Parks, Nancy Everhard, Lauren Tewes, Bill McKinney, Loni Chapman; *D:* Alan Metzger. VHS, Beta $79.95 MCA ♂♂½

China O'Brien Gorgeous police officer with martial arts expertise returns home for a little R & R, but finds she has to kick some major butt instead. Violent, dimwitted action drama proves only that cleavage can be macho too.
1988 (R) 90m/C Cynthia Rothrock, Richard Norton, Patrick Adamson, David Blackwell, Steven Kerby, Robert Tiller, Lainie Watts, Keith Cooke; *D:* Robert Clouse. VHS $89.95 IMP, BTV ♂½

China O'Brien 2 The unbreakable China, now a sheriff, battles the standard-issue Vietnam-vet druglord who invades her little town. Made back-to-back with the first film (note that both pics' bad guys have the same gang of henchman!), and in both films Rothrock is basically invincible, so there's no suspense.
1989 (R) 85m/C Cynthia Rothrock, Richard Norton, Keith Cooke; *D:* Robert Clouse. VHS $89.95 IMP ♂½

China Seas The captain of a commercial steamship on the China route has to fight off murderous Malay pirates, a spurned woman, and a raging typhoon to reach port safely. Fast-moving romantic action taken from Crosbie Garstin's novel.
1935 89m/B Clark Gable, Jean Harlow, Wallace Beery, Rosalind Russell, Lewis Stone, C. Aubrey Smith, Dudley Digges, Robert Benchley; *D:* Tay Garnett. VHS, Beta $19.98 MGM ♂♂♂

China Sky An American doctor fights alongside Chinese guerillas against the Japanese during WWII. Drama, to its credit, often opts for character conflict instead of warfare, but this makes it merely dull instead of cliched. Adapted from a Pearl S. Buck novel.
1944 78m/B Randolph Scott, Ellen Drew, Ruth Warrick, Anthony Quinn, Carol Thurston, Richard Loo, Philip Ahn; *D:* Ray Enright. VHS, Beta, LV $19.98 TTC ♂♂

The China Syndrome A somewhat unstable executive at a nuclear plant uncovers evidence of a concealed accident, takes drastic steps to publicize the incident. Lemmon is excellent as the anxious exec, while Fonda and Douglas are scarcely less distinguished as a sympathetic TV journalist and camera operator, respectively. Tense, prophetic thriller that ironically preceded the Three Mile Island accident by just a few months. Produced by Douglas.
1979 (PG) 123m/C Jane Fonda, Jack Lemmon, Michael Douglas, Scott Brady, James Hampton, Peter Donat, Wilford Brimley, James Karen; *D:* James Bridges. Academy Awards '78 Nominations: Best Actress (Fonda), Best Original Screenplay; Academy Awards '79: Best Actor (Lemmon), Best Art Direction/Set Decoration; British Academy Awards '79: Best Actor (Lemmon), Best Actress (Fonda); National Board of Review Awards '79: 10 Best Films of the Year. VHS, Beta, LV $12.98 COL, PIA ♂♂♂½

China White Violence erupts in the streets of Paris, Amsterdam and Bangkok, when international drug cartels battle over the ownership of China White - premium heroin, its sources and its outlets. Rousing, realistic action.
1991 (R) ?m/C Billy Drago, Russell Wong, Lisa Schrage, Steven Leigh; *D:* Ronny Yu. VHS $89.98 IMP ♂♂♂½

Chinatown A private detective finds himself overwhelmed in a scandalous case involving the rich and powerful of Los Angeles. Gripping, atmospheric mystery excels in virtually every aspect, with strong narrative drive and outstanding performances from Nicholson, Dunaway, and Huston. Director Polanski also appears in a suitable unsettling cameo. Fabulous. A sneaky, snaking delight filled with seedy characters and plots-within-plots. Screenplay by Robert Towne. Followed more than 15 years later by "The Two Jakes."
1974 (R) 131m/C Jack Nicholson, Faye Dunaway, John Huston, Diane Ladd, John Hillerman, Burt Young, Perry Lopez, Darrell Zwerling; *Cameos:* Roman Polanski; *D:* Roman Polanski; *W:* Robert Towne; *M:* Jerry Goldsmith. Academy Awards '74: Best Original Screenplay; Nominations: Best Actor (Nicholson), Best Actress (Dunaway), Best Art Direction/Set Decoration, Best Cinematography, Best Costume Design, Best Director (Polanski), Best Film Editing, Best Picture, Best Original Score; British Academy Awards '74: Best Actor (Nicholson), Best Director (Polanski); Golden Globe Awards '75: Best Actor—Drama (Nicholson), Best Director (Polanski), Best Film—Drama; National Board of Review Awards '74: 10 Best Films of the Year; New York Film Critics Awards '74: Best Actor (Nicholson); National Society of Film Critics Awards '74: Best Actor (Nicholson). VHS, Beta, LV, 8mm $19.95 PAR ♂♂♂♂

Chinatown After Dark Ludicrous, inane melodrama about a white girl raised by the Chinese.
1931 50m/B Rex Lease, Barbara Kent, Carmel Myers; *D:* Ralph M. Like. VHS $12.95 SNC, NOS, DVT ♂

Chinatown Connection For some inexplicable reason, local drug dealers start selling poisoned cocaine. Two renegade cops discover the super-secret organization doing the poisoning, arm themselves heavily, and kill lots of people while putting an end to the poisonings. Violent, foolish film with dull performances.
1990 (R) 94m/C Bruce Ly, Lee Majors, Pat McCormick, Art Camacho, Susan Frailey, Scott Richards; *D:* Jean-Paul Ouellette. VHS $79.95 NO ♂

The Chinatown Kid Chased by attackers in his native Hong Kong, a young man decides to try the safety of San Francisco.
1990 90m/C VHS $69.98 NO ♂

The Chinatown Murders: Man Against the Mob A tough cop is up against the Chinese mafia and his own corrupt police force as he tries to stay alive and find some justice.
1992 (R) 96m/C George Peppard, Charles Haid, Richard Bradford, Ursula Andress. VHS $89.95 VMK ♂♂

Chinese Boxes An American man in Berlin is framed in a murder and becomes caught in an international web of crime and intrigue. Low budget but interesting thriller.
1984 87m/C GE GB Will Patton, Adelheid Arndt, Robbie Coltrane; *D:* Christopher Petit. VHS, Beta $69.98 LIV, VES ♂♂½

The Chinese Cat Poorly scripted formula mystery has the younger Chan smitten with a girl who needs the elder Chan's detective skills in finding her father's killer.

1944 65m/B Sidney Toler, Benson Fong, Mantan Moreland, Weldon Heyburn, Joan Woodbury, Ian Keith, Sam Flint; **D:** Phil Rosen. **VHS** $19.98 *MGM* ⅃

Chinese Connection A martial arts expert tracks sadistic brutes who slew his instructor. Wild action sequences provide a breathtaking view of Lee's skill. Dubbed. *AKA:* Fist of Fury; The Iron Hand.
1973 (R) 90m/C *CH* Bruce Lee, James Tien, Robert Baker; **D:** Lo Wei. **VHS, Beta** $19.98 *FOX, MRV, REP* ⅃⅃½

Chinese Connection 2 A martial-arts expert learns that the school where he trained is now run by an unappealing master. Conflict ensues. Bruce Li is not Bruce Lee, but he is fairly good in action portions of this otherwise dull, sloppy venture.
1984 96m/C Bruce Li. **VHS, Beta** $39.95 *TWE* ⅃⅃

Chinese Gods Animated story of Chinese mythology depicts the battles and rivalries occurring circa 1000 B.C. in the period of the Shang Dynasty between Cruel King Cheo's troops and the Marquis Hsi-pa.
1980 (G) 90m/C **VHS, Beta** $19.95 *GEM* ⅃⅃

Chinese Roulette A host of unappealing characters convene at a country house for sexual shenanigans and a cruel game masterminded by a sadistic crippled girl. Cold effort from German master Fassbinder. In German with English subtitles.
1986 96m/C *GE* Anna Karina, Margit Carstensen, Ulli Lommel, Brigitte Mira; **W/D:** Rainer Werner Fassbinder. **VHS, Beta, LV** $79.95 *CVC, TAM* ⅃⅃½

Chinese Stuntman An American in Hong Kong gets caught up in a web of intrigue, and kicks his way out.
197? 85m/C Bruce Li, Ho Chung Tao, John Ladalski, Dan Inosanto. **VHS, Beta** $39.95 *TWE* ⅃

Chinese Web Spiderman adventure in which Spidey becomes entwined in international intrigue and corrupt officials.
1978 95m/C Nicholas Hammond, Robert F. Simon, Rosalind Chao, Ted Danson; **D:** Donald McDougall. **VHS, Beta** $24.98 *FOX* ⅃

Chino A half-Indian horse rancher struggles to maintain his livelihood in this spaghetti western. Not among Bronson's stronger—that is, more viscerally effective—films. Adapted from Lee Hoffman's novel. *AKA:* Valdez the Half Breed; The Valdez Horses.
1975 (PG) 97m/C *IT* Charles Bronson, Jill Ireland, Vincent Van Patten; **D:** John Sturges. **VHS, Beta** $59.95 *MPI, MRV* ⅃⅃

The Chipmunk Adventure The three animated chipmunks, Simon, Theodore and Alvin, get involved with a diamond smuggling ring. Original songs. In HiFi Stereo.
1987 76m/C **D:** Janice Karman. **VHS, Beta, LV** $79.95 *LHV, WAR, WTA* ⅃⅃

The Chisholms If you're into oaters, here's a high fiber six-hour serial: Chisolm (Preston) leads the family as they head west and find trouble with a capital "T" en route from Virginia to Californ-i-a. Originally a network miniseries, it's now a two-cassette rentable; adapted by Evan Hunter from his novel.
1979 300m/C Robert Preston, Rosemary Harris, Brian Keith, Ben Murphy, Charles Frank; **D:** Mel Stuart. **VHS, Beta** $69.95 *LIV* ⅃⅃½

Chisum Cattle baron faces various conflicts, including a confrontation with Billy the Kid. Lame Wayne vehicle contributes nothing to exhausted western genre.

1970 (G) 111m/C John Wayne, Forrest Tucker, Geoffrey Deuel, Christopher George, Ben Johnson, Bruce Cabot, Patric Knowles, Richard Jaeckel, Glenn Corbett; **D:** Andrew V. McLaglen. **VHS, Beta** $19.98 *WAR, TLF* ⅃⅃½

Chitty Chitty Bang Bang An eccentric inventor spruces up an old car and, in fantasy, takes his children to a land where the evil rulers have forbidden children. Poor special effects and forgettable score stall effort. Loosely adapted by Roald Dahl and Hughes from an Ian Fleming story. ♫Chitty Chitty Bang Bang; Hushabye Mountain; Truly Scrumptious; You Two; Toot Sweet; Me Ol' Bam-Boo; Lovely Lonely Man; Posh; The Roses of Success; Chu-Chi Face; Doll on a Music Box.
1968 (G) 142m/C *GB* Dick Van Dyke, Sally Ann Howes, Lionel Jeffries, Gert Frobe, Anna Quayle, Benny Hill; **D:** Ken Hughes. **VHS, Beta, LV** $19.98 *FOX, MGM, TLF* ⅃⅃½

Chloe in the Afternoon A married man finds himself inexplicably drawn to an ungainly young woman. Sixth of the "Moral Tales" series is typical of director Rohmer's talky approach. Not for all tastes, but rewarding for those who are drawn to this sort of thing. In French with English subtitles.
1972 (R) 97m/C *FR* Bernard Verley, Zouzou, Francoise Verley, Daniel Ceccaldi, Malvina Penne, Babette Ferrier, Suze Randall, Marie-Christine Barrault; **D:** Eric Rohmer. **VHS, Beta** $59.95 *TAM, FCT* ⅃⅃⅃

Chocolat A woman recalls her childhood spent in French West Africa and the unfulfilled sexual tension between her mother and black servant. Vivid film provides a host of intriguing characters and offers splendid panoramas of rugged desert landscapes. Profound, if somewhat personal filmmaking from novice director Denis. In French with English subtitles.
1988 (PG-13) 105m/C Mireille Perrier, Emmet Judson Williamson, Cecile Ducasse, Giulia Boschi, Francois Cluzet, Isaach de Bankole, Kenneth Cranham; **D:** Claire Denis. **VHS, Beta, LV** $79.98 *ORI, TAM* ⅃⅃⅃½

The Chocolate Soldier Dull musical in which an opera star tests his wife's fidelity. Lovers of the musical genre will find that this one has too much talking, not enough singing. Lovers of fine films will realize that more singing would hardly improve things. Based loosely on Molnar's play "The Guardsman."
1941 102m/B Nelson Eddy, Rise Stevens, Nigel Bruce, Florence Bates, Dorothy Gilmore, Nydia Westman; **D:** Roy Del Ruth. **VHS** $19.98 *MGM* ⅃

The Chocolate War An idealistic student and a hardline headmaster butt heads at a Catholic boys' school over an unofficial candy business in this tense, unsettling drama. Glover is notable in his familiar villain role, and Gordon is effective in his first effort as director. Based on the Robert Cormier novel.
1988 (R) 95m/C John Glover, Jenny Wright, Wally Ward, Bud Cort, Ilan Mitchell-Smith; **D:** Keith Gordon. **VHS, Beta, LV** $89.98 *MCG* ⅃⅃⅃

The Choice A young woman must make the choice between aborting or keeping her baby in this fairly insipid television drama.
1981 96m/C Susan Clark, Jennifer Warren, Mitchell Ryan, Largo Woodruff; **D:** David Greene. **VHS, Beta** $39.95 *LIV* ⅃⅃

Choice of Arms A gangster's rural retirement is undone by a dimwitted criminal in this sometimes gripping drama. Montand and Deneuve are serviceable in undemanding roles of the gangster and his glamorous wife; Depardieu is more impressive as the trouble-making punk. In French with English subtitles.

1983 114m/C *FR* Gerard Depardieu, Catherine Deneuve, Yves Montand; **D:** Alain Corneau. **VHS, Beta** $59.95 *TAM, MED* ⅃⅃½

Choice of Weapons Ex-cop trying to solve murders focuses on a curious group of 20th-century men who live within a 12th-century fantasy—jousting for sport and chivalrous honor. Offbeat lance thruster notable for incongruity and all-star cast. *AKA:* A Dirty Knight's Work; Trial by Combat.
1976 88m/C *GB* David Birney, Peter Cushing, Donald Pleasence, Barbara Hershey, John Mills, Margaret Leighton; **D:** Kevin Connor. **VHS, Beta** $42.95 *PGN* ⅃⅃

Choices A hearing-impaired athlete suffers alienation when banned from the football squad. What? Controversial covergirl Moore is a supporting player in this, her first film.
1981 90m/C Paul Carafotes, Victor French, Lelia Goldoni, Val Avery, Dennis Patrick, Demi Moore; **D:** Rami Alon. **VHS, Beta** $49.95 *VHE, HHE* ⅃½

The Choirboys Thoroughly mediocre production about overbearing L.A. cops and their off-hours handling of job stress. Few of the strong cast emerge unscathed. Based on the Joseph Wambaugh novel.
1977 (R) 120m/C Charles Durning, Louis Gossett Jr., Perry King, Clyde Kusatsu, Stephen Macht, Tim McIntire, Randy Quaid, Chuck Sacci, Don Stroud, James Woods, Burt Young, Robert Webber, Barbara Rhoades, Vic Tayback, Blair Brown, Charles Haid, Jim Davis; **D:** Robert Aldrich. **VHS, Beta** $14.98 *MCA* ⅃

Choke Canyon An environmentalist thwarts the henchmen of an industrialist eager to coverup a nuclear dump in a picturesque canyon. Good intentions do not necessarily make for a good movie.
1986 (PG) 95m/C Stephen Collins, Bo Svenson, Lance Henriksen; **D:** Chuck Bail. **VHS, Beta** $79.95 *NO* ⅃⅃

C.H.O.M.P.S. Comedy in which a youthful inventor and a popular robot guard dog become the target of a business takeover. Harmless but unfunny and unfun.
1979 (PG) 90m/C Jim Backus, Valerie Bertinelli, Wesley Eure, Conrad Bain, Chuck McCann, Red Buttons; **D:** Don Chaffey. **VHS, Beta** $19.98 *NO* ⅃½

Choose Me Comedy-drama about sad, lonely, and often quirky characters linked to an unlikely L.A. radio sex therapist. Moody, memorable fare features especially strong playing from Bujold as a sexually inexperienced sex therapist and Warren as one of her regular listeners. Typically eccentric fare from director Rudolph.
1984 (R) 106m/C Keith Carradine, Genevieve Bujold, Lesley Ann Warren, Rae Dawn Chong, John Larroquette, John Considine; **W/D:** Alan Rudolph. **VHS, Beta, LV** $9.98 *MED* ⅃⅃½

Chopper Chicks in Zombietown Tough but sexy Chopper Chicks show up in that American vacation mecca, Zombietown, for a little rest and relaxation. Little do they know that a mad mortician has designs on turning our hot heroines into mindless zombie slaves. Can the buxom biker babes thwart the evil embalmer before it's too late, or will they abandon their Harleys to shuffle about in search of human flesh? From the Troma Team.
1991 (R) 86m/C Jamie Rose, Catherine Carlen, Lycia Naff, Vicki Frederick, Kristina Loggia, Martha Quinn, Don Calfa; **W/D:** Dan Hoskins. **VHS, LV** $79.95 *COL, NLC* ⅃⅃

The Choppers Naw, not a fable about false teeth. Teen punk Hall operates a car theft ring made up of fellow punksters. Rock'n'roll tunes by the Hall-meister include the much-overlooked "Monkey in my Hatband."

1961 66m/B Arch Hall Jr., Marianne Gaba, Robert Paget, Tom Brown, Rex Holman, Bruno Ve Sota; **D:** Leigh Jason. **VHS, Beta $16.95** SNC *♂*

Chopping Mall A freak electric storm unleashes killer security robots on a band of teens trapped inside the mall. Nobody shops. Premise undone by obscure humor, lack of flairful action, or horror. Updated imitation of the 1973 TV movie "Trapped." **AKA:** Kill-bots.
1986 (R) 77m/C Paul Bartel, Mary Woronov, Barbara Crampton, John Terlesky, Dick Miller; **D:** Jim Wynorski. **VHS, Beta $19.98** LIV *♂ 1/2*

A Chorus Line A range of performers reveal their insecurities and aspirations while auditioning before a hardnosed director in this adaptation of the popular, overblown Broadway musical. Singing and dancing is rarely rousing. Director Attenborough probably wasn't the right choice for this one. *♫*Dance 10, Looks 3; What I Did for Love; At the Ballet; I Can Do That; Let Me Dance For You; I Hope I Get It; Nothing; The Music and the Mirror; And...; Hello Twelve, Hello Thirteen, Hello Love; Surprise, Surprise; One.
1985 (PG-13) 118m/C Michael Douglas, Audrey Landers, Gregg Burge, Alyson Reed, Janet Jones, Michael Blevins, Terrence Mann, Cameron English, Vicki Frederick, Nicole Fosse, Michelle Johnson; **D:** Richard Attenborough; **M:** Marvin Hamlisch. **VHS, Beta, LV, SVS, 8mm $14.98** SUE, SUP, NLC *♂♂*

A Chorus of Disapproval Adaptation of prolific Alan Ayckbourn's play about a withdrawn, somewhat dimwitted British widower who attempts social interaction by joining community theater, then finds himself embroiled in romantic shenanigans and theatrical intrigue. Irons is fine in the lead, but Hopkins sparkles in the more spectacular role of the musical production's demanding but beleaguered director. Seagrove is impressive as an amoral sexpot. Sharper focus from director Winner would have improved this one, but the film is fun even when it isn't particularly funny.
1989 (PG) 105m/C GB Jeremy Irons, Anthony Hopkins, Jenny Seagrove, Lionel Jeffries, Patsy Kensit, Gareth Hunt, Prunella Scales, Sylvia Syms, Richard Briers, Barbara Ferris; **W/D:** Michael Winner. **VHS, Beta $19.98** NO *♂ 1/2*

The Chosen Executive of a nuclear power facility realizes that his son is the Anti-Christ bent on the world's destruction. This truly horrible film provides nothing in terms of entertainment. It's rarely even laughably bad. **AKA:** Holocaust 2000.
1977 (R) 102m/C Kirk Douglas, Simon Ward, Agostina Belli, Anthony Quayle, Virginia McKenna; **D:** Alberto De Martino. **VHS, Beta $59.98** FOX Woof!

Christ Stopped at Eboli Subdued work about an anti-Fascist writer exiled to rural Italy in the 1930s. Excellent performances from the lead Volonte and supporting players Papas and Cuny. Slow, contemplative film is probably director Rosi's masterpiece. Adapted from Carlo Levi's book. In Italian with English subtitles. **AKA:** Eboli.
1979 118m/C IT FR Gian Maria Volonte, Irene Papas, Paolo Bonacelli, Francois Simon, Alain Cuny, Lea Massari; **D:** Francesco Rosi. **VHS, Beta $59.95** COL, APD, TAM *♂♂♂♂*

Christabel Condensed version of the BBC mini-series based on the true-life World War II exploits of Christabel Bielenberg, a British woman who battled to save her German husband from the horrors of the Ravensbruck concentration camp.
1989 148m/C GB Elizabeth Hurley, Stephen Dillon, Nigel le Vaillant, Geoffrey Palmer; **W:** Dennis Potter. **VHS, Beta $39.98** FOX, TAM *♂♂*

Christian the Lion The true story of Christian, a lion cub raised in a London zoo, who is transported to Africa to learn to live with other lions. With the principals from "Born Free."
1976 (G) 87m/C GB Virginia McKenna, Bill Travers, George Adamson, James Hill; **D:** Bill Travers. **VHS, Beta $29.95** UNI *♂♂ 1/2*

Christiane F. Gripping, visually impressive story of a bored German girl's decline into drug use and prostitution. Based on a West German magazine article. Sobering and dismal look at a milieu in which innocence and youth have run amok. The film's impact is only somewhat undermined by poor dubbing. Bowie appears in a concert sequence.
1982 (R) 120m/C GE Natja Brunkhorst, Thomas Haustein, David Bowie; **D:** Uli Edel; **M:** David Bowie. **VHS, Beta $69.95** MED, GLV *♂♂♂*

Christina Gloomy suspense fare in which a beautiful woman pays a forlorn fellow $25,000 to marry her, then disappears as he begins to actually fall in love with her. His search takes him to various gothic settings. Intriguing, but not really fulfilling. Parkins, however, is appropriately mysterious in the lead.
1974 (PG) 95m/C CA Barbara Parkins, Peter Haskell; **D:** Paul Krasny. **VHS, Beta $59.95** MPI *♂♂ 1/2*

Christine An unassuming teen gains possession of a classic auto equipped with a murderous will. The car more than returns the care and consideration its owner provides. Are you listening GMC? Based on a novel by Stephen King.
1984 (R) 110m/C Keith Gordon, John Stockwell, Alexandra Paul, Robert Prosky, Harry Dean Stanton, Kelly Preston; **D:** John Carpenter. **VHS, Beta, LV, 8mm $14.95** COL *♂♂ 1/2*

A Christmas Carol An early version of Dickens' classic tale about miser Scrooge, who is instilled with the Christmas spirit after a grim evening with some ghosts. Good playing from Owen as Scrooge and Lockhart as the hapless Bob Cratchett. Scary graveyard sequence too.
1938 70m/B Reginald Owen, Gene Lockhart, Terence Kilburn, Leo G. Carroll, Lynne Carver, Ann Rutherford; **D:** Edwin L. Marin. **VHS, Beta, LV $19.95** MGM *♂♂♂*

A Christmas Carol A fine retelling of the classic tale about a penny-pinching holiday hater who learns appreciation of Christmas following a frightful, revealing evening with supernatural visitors. Perhaps the best rendering of the Dickens classic. "And God bless Tiny Tim!" **AKA:** Scrooge.
1951 86m/B GB Alastair Sim, Kathleen Harrison, Jack Warner, Michael Hordern, Patrick Macnee, Mervyn Johns, Hermione Baddeley, Clifford Mollison, George Cole, Carol Marsh, Miles Malleson, Ernest Thesiger, Hattie Jacques, Peter Bull; **D:** Brian Desmond-Hurst. **VHS, Beta, LV $19.95** MLB, HMV *♂♂♂♂*

A Christmas Carol Musical version of the Dickens' classic about a stingy old man who is visited by three ghosts on Christmas Eve.
1954 54m/B Fredric March, Basil Rathbone, Ray Middleton, Bob Sweeney, Christopher Cook. **VHS, Beta** CFV *♂♂*

A Christmas Carol An animated version of the Charles Dickens classic. Hard to beat the Alastair Sim version, however.
1984 72m/C **VHS, Beta** NO *♂♂*

A Christmas Carol Animated version of Charles Dickens' classic tale. The story of how Ebenezer Scrooge changed from a tyrant to a joyous human being one Christmas Eve.

1984 23m/C **D:** Chuck Jones. **VHS, Beta $19.95** CHI *♂♂*

The Christmas Coal Mine Miracle Syrupy made-for-television story about miners struggling for survival in a collapsed mine on Christmas Eve. Also titled "Christmas Miracle in Caulfield, U.S.A."
1977 98m/C Mitchell Ryan, Kurt Russell, Andrew Prine, John Carradine, Barbara Babcock, Melissa Gilbert, Don Porter, Shelby Leverington; **D:** Judd Taylor. **VHS, Beta $59.98** FOX *♂ 1/2*

Christmas Comes to Willow Creek Mutually antagonistic brothers are enlisted to deliver Christmas gifts to an isolated Alaskan community. Can brotherly love be far off? Two leads played together in the rowdy TV series "Dukes of Hazzard." This is hardly an improvement.
1987 96m/C John Schneider, Tom Wopat, Hoyt Axton, Zachary Ansley, Kim Delaney; **D:** Richard Lang. **VHS, Beta $79.95** JTC *♂♂*

A Christmas Gift Short animated films from Canada about the December holiday. Includes "The Great Toy Robbery," "The Energy Carol," "Christmas Cracker" and more!
1990 65m/C CA **VHS, Beta $29.95** WTA, FCT, EXP *♂♂*

Christmas in Connecticut Lightweight comedy about a housekeeping magazine's successful columnist who isn't quite the expert homemaker she presents herself to be. When a war veteran is invited to her home as part of a publicity gimmick, she must master the ways of housekeeping or reveal her incompetence. Stanwyck is winning in the lead role. Also available in a colorized version. **AKA:** Indiscretion.
1945 101m/B Barbara Stanwyck, Reginald Gardiner, Sydney Greenstreet, Dennis Morgan, S.Z. Sakall, Una O'Connor, Robert Shayne, Joyce Compton; **D:** Peter Godfrey. **VHS, Beta, LV $19.98** MGM, PIA *♂♂♂*

Christmas in Connecticut Cannon hosts a weekly television show as America's favorite homemaker/hostess. A local forest ranger (Kristofferson) becomes a hero by saving a little boy's life and her network stages a media event by inviting him to her home for a traditional Christmas dinner. There's only one problem: she can't cook. Schwarzenegger's directorial debut lacks challenge in this fluffy remake. See the original instead. Made for cable television.
1992 93m/C Dyan Cannon, Kris Kristofferson, Tony Curtis, Richard Roundtree, Kelly Cinnante, Gene Lithgow, Vivian Bonnell; **D:** Arnold Schwarzenegger. **VHS $89.98** TTC *♂♂*

Christmas in July A young man goes on a spending spree when he thinks he's won a sweepstakes. Things take a turn for the worse when he finds out that it was all a practical joke. Powell provides a winning performance in this second film from comic master Sturges.
1940 67m/B Dick Powell, Ellen Drew, Raymond Walburn, William Demarest, Franklin Pangborn; **D:** Preston Sturges. **VHS, Beta, LV $14.98** MCA, PIA, FCT *♂♂♂ 1/2*

The Christmas Kid A desperado struggles to determine his true identity while stopping in a frontier town. Gunplay ensues. Don't bother with this one.
1968 87m/C SP Jeffrey Hunter, Louis Hayward, Gustavo Rojo, Perla Cristal, Luis Prendes; **D:** Sidney Pink. **VHS** NO *♂♂*

Christmas Lilies of the Field This made-for-television sequel to "Lilies of the Field" follows an ex-soldier who returns to the church he helped build. This time he sets out to build an orphanage.

1984 98m/C Billy Dee Williams, Maria Schell, Fay Hauser, Judith Piquet; **D:** Ralph Nelson. VHS, Beta $29.95 *MPI* ♪♪½

The Christmas Messenger Brilliantly-colored animation is used to portray tales of Christmas folklore. A Reader's Digest presentation.
1975 25m/C **V:** Richard Chamberlain. VHS, Beta $195.00 *PYR* ♪♪½

Christmas Raccoons The Raccoons have their very own special animated Christmas story to tell.
1984 30m/C VHS, Beta $24.98 *SUE* ♪♪½

A Christmas Story Unlikely but winning comedy of a boy's single-minded obsession to acquire a Red Ryder BB-gun for Christmas. Particularly great sequence involving an impatient department-store Santa. Fun for everyone. Based on a story by Jean Shepherd.
1983 (PG) 95m/C Peter Billingsley, Darren McGavin, Melinda Dillon, Ian Petrella; **D:** Bob Clark. VHS, Beta, LV $19.95 *MGM* ♪♪♪

The Christmas That Almost Wasn't Loathsome humbug decides to destroy Christmas forever by removing Santa Claus from the North Pole. Crude Italian-made children's film nonetheless remembered fondly by a generation of kids. ♫The Christmas That Almost Wasn't; Christmas is Coming; Hustle Bustle; I'm Bad; Kids Get All the Breaks; The Name of the Song is Prune; Nothing to do But Wait; Santa Claus; Time For Christmas; What Are Children Like When They're Fast Asleep?; Why Can't Every Day Be Christmas?. **AKA:** Il Natale Che Quasi Non Fu.
1966 (G) 95m/C *IT* Rossano Brazzi, Paul Tripp, Lidia Brazzi, Sonny Fox, Mischa Auer; **D:** Rossano Brazzi. VHS, Beta $9.99 *HBO* ♪½

A Christmas to Remember Depression-era Minnesota farmer who has lost his son in WWI brings his city-bred grandson to the farm for a holiday visit. Somber, occasionally poignant film buoyed by Robards presence, and Saint's as well. Made for television.
1978 (G) 96m/C Jason Robards Jr., Eva Marie Saint, Joanne Woodward; **D:** George Englund. VHS, Beta $69.95 *NO* ♪♪½

The Christmas Tree Manipulative sudser about the bond that develops between an extremely wealthy man and his mortally ill son. Not among Holden's better films. Also released as "When Wolves Cry."
1969 (G) 110m/C William Holden, Virna Lisi, Andre Bourvil, Brook Fuller; **D:** Terence Young. VHS, Beta $14.95 *UHV* ♪½

The Christmas Wife A lonely man pays a woman to be his holiday companion at a mountain retreat. Sturdy performances by Robards and Harris manage to keep this one from going to the dogs. Based on a story by Helen Norris. Made for cable television.
1988 73m/C Jason Robards Jr., Julie Harris, Don Francks, Patricia Hamilton, Deborah Grover; **D:** David Jones. VHS, Beta $79.99 *HBO* ♪♪½

A Christmas Without Snow Made-for-television film about a lonely divorced woman finding communal happiness within a local church choir led by a crusty choir master.
1980 96m/C Michael Learned, John Houseman, Ramon Bieri, James Cromwell, Valerie Curtin, Ruth Nelson, Beah Richards, Calvin Levels; **D:** John Korty. VHS, Beta $59.98 *FOX* ♪♪½

Christopher Columbus Step-by-step biography of the fifteenth-century explorer, his discovery of America, the fame that first greeted him, and his last days.

1949 103m/C *GB* Fredric March, Florence Eldridge, Francis L. Sullivan; **D:** David MacDonald. VHS, Beta $19.95 *LCA, IGP* ♪♪½

Christopher Columbus The man who explored the New World is shown in all his flawed complexity in this film that takes a contemporary approach to the discoveries and character of Christopher Columbus. Shot on location in Spain, Malta, and the Dominican Republic, the film features an exact replica of Columbus' flagship, the Santa Maria. Originally aired as a six-hour television miniseries.
1985 128m/C Gabriel Byrne, Faye Dunaway, Oliver Reed, Max von Sydow, Eli Wallach, Nicol Williamson, Jose Ferrer, Virna Lisi, Raf Vallone; **D:** Alberto Lattuada. VHS $89.95 *WAR* ♪♪½

Christopher Columbus: The Discovery The 500th anniversary of Columbus' voyage brought this lame excursion in historical biography to the screen briefly. Columbus is portrayed as a swashbuckling adventurer who finally gets the Queen of Spain to agree to finance his voyage of discovery (which primarily consists of discovering a lot of bare-breasted native women). Story is secondary to the banality of the entire production, including the acting. Brando is briefly seen as Torquemada—another film in which he took his substantial paycheck and ran.
1992 (PG-13) 120m/C Georges Corraface, Rachel Ward, Tom Selleck, Marlon Brando, Robert Davi, Oliver Cotton; **D:** John Glen. VHS, Beta, LV $94.99 *WAR* ♪

Christopher Strong Interesting Hepburn turn as a daredevil aviatrix who falls in love with a married British statesman.
1933 77m/B Katharine Hepburn, Billie Burke, Colin Clive, Helen Chandler; **D:** Dorothy Arzner. VHS, Beta, LV $19.98 *RKO, TTC* ♪♪½

Chrome and Hot Leather A Green Beret is out for revenge after vicious bikers kill his fiance. Conventional, tasteless genre fare notable only as Gaye's first film.
1971 (PG) 91m/C William Smith, Tony Young, Michael Haynes, Peter Brown, Marvin Gaye, Michael Stearns, Katherine Baumann, Wes Bishop, Herbert Jeffries; **D:** Lee Frost. VHS *NO* ♪½

Chrome Hearts Rebel biker rescues a buxom gal from a fate worse than death, than vies for control of the gang. Laughable, with Namath hopeless in his film debut. Redeemed only by Ann-Margaret in continual disarray. **AKA:** C.C. & Company.
1970 (R) 91m/C Joe Namath, Ann-Margret, William Smith, Jennifer Billingsley, Teda Bracci, Greg Mullavey, Sid Haig, Bruce Glover; **D:** Seymour Robbie. VHS, Beta $14.95 *COL, SUE, SIM* ♪

Chrome Soldiers Five Vietnam veterans come together to avenge a friend's murder in a town controlled by drug dealers. Busey, as the murdered man's brother, leads the "Chrome Soldiers" in their battle to expose the killers and end local corruption.
1992 92m/C Gary Busey, Ray Sharkey, William Atherton, Yaphet Kotto, Nicholas Guest, Kim Robillard, Norman Skaggs, D. David Morin; **D:** Thomas J. Wright; **W:** Nick Randall. VHS, Beta *PAR* ♪♪

The Chronicles of Narnia Exceptional BBC production of the C.S. Lewis fantasy about four brave children who battle evil in a mythical land where the animals talk and strange creatures roam the countryside. In three volumes: "The Lion, the Witch, and the Wardrobe," "Prince Caspian and the Voyage of the Dawn Treader," and "The Silver Chair." Aired on PBS as part of the "Wonderworks" family movie series.

1989 180m/C *GB* Barbara Kellerman, Jeffery Perry, Richard Dempsey, Sophie Cook, Jonathan Scott, Sophie Wilcox, David Thwaites, Tom Baker; **D:** Alex Kirby. VHS $29.95 *HMV, PME, TVC* ♪♪

Chronopolis A brilliant animated feature film which was five years in the making. The citizens of Chronopolis are immmortals who relieve the boredom of perpetual existence by creating time. In French with English subtitles.
1982 70m/C *FR* **D:** Piotr Kamler. VHS $49.95 *FCT, WTA* ♪♪♪½

Chu Chu & the Philly Flash A has-been baseball player and a lame dance teacher meet while hustling the same corner; he sells hot watches, she's a one-woman band. A briefcase full of government secrets soon involves them with the feds, the mob, and a motley collection of back-alley bums. Insipid comedy is actually worse than its title, with Burnett and Arkin both trying too hard. Supporters Warden, Aiello, and Glover don't help either.
1981 (PG) 102m/C Alan Arkin, Carol Burnett, Jack Warden, Danny Aiello, Ruth Buzzi, Danny Glover, Lou Jacobi; **D:** David Lowell Rich. VHS, Beta $59.98 *FOX* Woof!

Chuck Amuck: The Movie An in-depth look at legendary animator/director Chuck Jones.
1991 51m/C Chuck Jones. VHS $19.98 *WAR, FCT, WTA* Woof!

Chuck Berry: Hail! Hail! Rock 'n' Roll Engaging, energetic portrait of one of rock's founding fathers, via interviews, behind-the-scenes footage and performance clips of Berry at 60. Songs featured: "Johnny B. Goode," "Roll Over Beethoven," "Maybelline," and more. Appearances by Eric Clapton, Etta James, John and Julian Lennon, Roy Orbison, Linda Ronstadt, Bo Diddley and Bruce Springsteen among others.
1987 (PG) 121m/C Chuck Berry, Eric Clapton, Etta James, Robert Cray, Julian Lennon, Keith Richards, Linda Ronstadt, John Lennon, Roy Orbison, Bo Diddley, Jerry Lee Lewis, Bruce Springsteen, Kareem Abdul-Jabbar; **D:** Taylor Hackford. VHS, Beta $19.95 *MCA, MVD, FCT* ♪♪♪½

C.H.U.D. Cannibalistic Humanoid Underground Dwellers are what it's about. Exposed to toxic wastes, a race of flesh-craving, sewer-dwelling monstrosities goes food shopping on the streets of New York. Don't be fooled by the presence of real actors, this one is inexcusable. Followed by a sequel.
1984 (R) 90m/C John Heard, Daniel Stern, Christopher Curry, Kim Greist, John Goodman; **D:** Douglas Cheek. VHS, Beta, LV $9.98 *MRV* Woof!

C.H.U.D. 2: Bud the Chud Asinine teens steal a corpse that is actually a zombie cannibal capable of passing the trait to anyone it bites (but doesn't eat entirely). Graham excels as the kidnapped corpse, but this horror-comedy is consistently repellent. Contains one of Jagger's few film appearances, a situation of no despair.
1989 (R) 84m/C Brian Robbins, Bill Calvert, Gerrit Graham, Tricia Leigh Fisher, Bianca Jagger, Robert Vaughn, Larry Cedar; **D:** David Irving. VHS, Beta, LV $14.98 *LIV, VES, IME* Woof!

Chuka A gunfighter tries to resolve a conflict between Indians and unlikeable troops while simultaneously romancing the fort's beautiful occupant. Pedestrian western features convincing playing from the always reliable Taylor.

1967 105m/C Rod Taylor, Ernest Borgnine, John Mills, Lucianna Paluzzi, James Whitmore, Angela Dorian, Louis Hayward, Michael Cole, Hugh Reilly; **D:** Gordon Douglas. VHS $14.95 PAR, FCT ♫♫½

A Chump at Oxford Two street cleaners foil a bank robbery and receive an all-expenses-paid education at Oxford as their reward. This loopy Laurel and Hardy vehicle provides regular amusement in detailing the duo's exploits in Britain.
1940 63m/B Stan Laurel, Oliver Hardy, James Finlayson, Wilfrid Lucas, Peter Cushing, Charlie Hall; **D:** Alfred Goulding. VHS, Beta, LV $14.98 MED, CCB, FCT ♫♫½

The Church Italian thrill-meister Dario Argento scripted and produced this ecclesiastical gorefest directed by Michele Soavi. A gargoyle-glutted gothic cathedral which happens to stand on the site of a gruesome mass murder is renovated, and the kirk-cleaning turns into a special-effects loaded demonic epiphany. It'll have you muttering your pater noster. Unrated, it's also available in an R-rated version. **AKA:** La Chiesa.
1990 110m/C IT Tomas Arana, Hugh Quarshine, Feodor Chaliapin; **D:** Michele (Michael) Soavi; **W:** Dario Argento; **M:** Keith Emerson. VHS $89.98 NO ♫♫♫

Churchill and the Generals The true story of how Winston Churchill led England away from the bleak Dunkirk battle and rallied the Allied generals to a D-Day victory. Based upon Churchill's memoirs.
1981 180m/C Timothy West, Joseph Cotten, Arthur Hill, Eric Porter, Richard Dysart. VHS, Beta $14.99 STE, PSM ♫♫

C.I.A.: Code Name Alexa Alexa is the beautiful and deadly protege of Victor, who heads an international crime ring. A CIA agent decides the best way to stop Victor is to turn Alexa against her boss. Lots of action and violence.
1992 (R) 93m/C Kathleen Kinmont, Lorenzo Lamas, Alex Cord, O.J. Simpson, Stephen Quadros, Pamela Dixon, Michael Smith; **D:** Joseph Merhi. VHS, LV $89.95 PMH ♫½

Ciao Federico! Fellini Directs Satyricon A documentary of Frederico Fellini's filming of Petronius' "Satyricon." Portrays the Italian filmmaker's larger-than-life directorial approach and relationship with his actors. In English and Italian, with English subtitles.
1969 60m/C Federico Fellini, Martin Potter, Hiram Keller, Roman Polanski, Sharon Tate; **D:** Gideon Bachmann. VHS, Beta $29.95 MFV, TAM ♫½

The Cigarette Girl of Mosselprom A lowly cigarette girl is thrust into the world of moviemaking in this sharp Russian satire. Silent with orchestral score.
1924 78m/B RU **D:** Yuri Zhelyabuzhsky. VHS $29.95 KIV, FCT, TAM ♫♫½

Cimarron Hopelessly overblown saga of an American frontier family from 1890 to 1915. Hokey, cliched, with only sporadic liveliness. How did this one win an Oscar? An adaptation of Edna Ferber's novel, featuring Dunne in an early major role. Remade in 1960.
1930 130m/B Richard Dix, Irene Dunne, Estelle Taylor, Nance O'Neill, William Collier Jr., Roscoe Ates, George E. Stone, Stanley Fields, Edna May Oliver, Dennis O'Keefe; **D:** Wesley Ruggles. Academy Awards '31: Best Adapted Screenplay, Best Interior Decoration, Best Picture; Nominations: Best Actor (Dix), Best Actress (Dunne), Best Cinematography, Best Director (Ruggles); National Board of Review Awards '31:

10 Best Films of the Year. VHS, Beta $19.98 MGM, BTV ♫♫

The Cincinnati Kid Cardsharks gather for a major stakes poker game, with some romance on the side. Conventional fare helped along by serviceable performances and some stunning cinematography. Sam Peckinpah was dismissed as director from this one. Guess he took the script with him.
1965 104m/C Steve McQueen, Edward G. Robinson, Ann-Margret, Tuesday Weld, Karl Malden, Joan Blondell, Rip Torn, Jack Weston, Cab Calloway; **D:** Norman Jewison. VHS, Beta, LV $19.98 MGM ♫♫½

Cinderella Classic Disney animated fairytale about the slighted beauty who outshines her evil stepsisters at a royal ball, then returns to her grim existence before the handsome prince finds her again. Engaging film, with a wicked stepmother, kindly fairy godmother, and singing mice. ♫Cinderella; Bibbidy-Bobbidi Boo; So This Is Love; A Dream Is a Wish Your Heart Makes; The Work Song; Oh Sing, Sweet Nightingale.
1950 76m/C **D:** Wilfred Jackson; **V:** Ilene Woods, William Phipps, Verna Felton, James MacDonald. Academy Awards '50 Nominations: Best Song ("Bibbidy-Bobbidi-Boo"), Best Sound, Best Original Score; Venice Film Festival '50: Special Jury Prize. VHS, Beta $26.99 DIS, KUI ♫♫♫½

Cinderella A made-for-television rendition of the fairy tale as scored by Rodgers and Hammerstein. Songs include "The Loveliness of Evening," "Ten Minutes Ago" and "Do I Love You (Because You're Beautiful?)."
1964 83m/C Lesley Ann Warren, Ginger Rogers, Walter Pidgeon, Stuart Damon, Celeste Holm; **D:** Charles S. Dubin. VHS, Beta, LV $19.98 FOX, FCT ♫♫

Cinderella A soft-core musical adaptation of the fairy tale. Also available unrated, in a longer and more graphic version. Followed by "Fairy Tales."
1977 (R) 87m/C Cheryl "Rainbeaux" Smith, Kirk Scott, Brett Smiley, Sy Richardson; **D:** Michael Pataki. VHS, Beta $69.98 LIV ♫

Cinderella From the "Faerie Tale Theatre" comes the classic tale of a poor girl who goes to a ball to meet the man of her dreams, despite her nasty stepmother and stepsisters.
1984 60m/C Jennifer Beals, Jean Stapleton, Matthew Broderick, Eve Arden; **D:** Mark Cullingham. VHS, Beta, LV $14.98 KUI, FOX, FCT ♫

Cinderella Liberty Bittersweet romance in which a kindly sailor falls for a brash hooker with a son. Sometimes funny, sometimes moving, with sometimes crude direction overcome by truly compelling performances from Caan and Mason. Story written by Darryl Ponicsan from his novel.
1973 (R) 117m/C James Caan, Marsha Mason, Eli Wallach, Kirk Calloway, Burt Young, Bruce Kirby, Dabney Coleman, Sally Kirkland; **D:** Mark Rydell; **M:** John Williams. Academy Awards '73 Nominations: Best Actress (Mason), Best Song ("You're So Nice to Be Around"), Best Original Score; Golden Globe Awards '74: Best Actress—Drama (Mason). VHS, Beta $59.98 FOX ♫♫♫

Cinderella/Thumbelina Animated versions of these two classic children's stories. The first is about a poor girl transformed into a princess by her fairy godmother. "Thumbelina" is about a little girl who is no bigger than your thumb.
1983 50m/C VHS, Beta $7.00 VTR ♫♫♫

Cinderella 2000 There must be something about the Cinderella story that cries out for a soft-core musical telling of the "if the shoe fits the girl it must be true love" fairy tale (Pataki directed a 1977 Cinderella bawdorama). Or maybe it's only logical that the director of "Brain of Blood" and "Satan's Sadists" should turn his talents to a futuristic song-and-dance version of the Prince Charming story. It's the year 2047 and sex is outlawed, except by computer. Strains of Sparky Sugarman's score, including "Doin' Without" and "We All Need Love," set the stage for Erhardt's Cinderella to meet her Prince Charming at that conventional single prince romance venue, a sex orgy. Trouble is, it wasn't a shoe Cinderella lost before she fled, and the charming one must interface, as it were, with the local pretenders to the throne in order to find his lost princess. Touching.
1978 (R) 86m/C Catharine Erhardt, Jay B. Larson, Vaughn Armstrong; **D:** Al Adamson. VHS NO ♫♫

Cinderfella This twist on the classic children's fairy tale features Lewis as the hapless buffoon guided by his fairy godfather. Somewhat overdone, with extended talking sequences and gratuitous musical interludes. Lewis, though, mugs effectively.
1960 88m/C Jerry Lewis, Ed Wynn, Judith Anderson, Anna Maria Alberghetti, Henry Silva, Count Basie, Robert Hutton; **W/D:** Frank Tashlin. VHS, Beta $59.95 LIV ♫♫½

Cinema Paradiso Memoir of a boy's life working at a movie theatre in small-town Italy after World War II. Film aspires to both majestic sweep and stirring poignancy, but only occasionally hits its target. Still manages to move the viewer, and it features a suitably low-key performance by the masterful Noiret. Autobiographically-inspired script written by Tornatore. The version shown in America is approximately a half-hour shorter than the original Italian form. **AKA:** Nuovo Cinema Paradiso.
1988 123m/C IT Philippe Noiret, Jacques Perrin, Salvatore Cascio, Mario Leonardi, Agnes Nano, Leopoldo Trieste; **W/D:** Giuseppe Tornatore; **M:** Ennio Morricone. VHS, LV, 8mm $89.99 HBO, APD, TAM ♫♫♫

Cinema Shrapnel A tour through the wonderful world of screen hype and bad movies, with scenes from terrible trailers, maudlin fundraising shorts, and glitzy movie premieres.
1987 60m/C VHS, Beta NO ♫♫♫

Cinemagic A compilation of four short horror and science fiction films including "Nightfright," "Dr. Dobermind," "Illegal Alien" and "The Thing in the Basement."
1985 60m/C VHS, Beta $39.95 MPI ♫♫♫

Circle Canyon In a remote canyon two opposing outlaw gangs battle to the death.
1933 48m/B Buddy Roosevelt. VHS, Beta NO ♫

Circle Man A made-for-video action drama about the underground sporting phenomenon, bare-knuckle fighting.
1987 90m/C William Sanderson. VHS, Beta $79.95 ACA ♫

Circle of Death Average formula western about a white boy who is raised as an Indian. Later he falls in love with a white girl and leaves the tribe.
1936 55m/B Monte Montana, Yakima Canutt. VHS, Beta $19.95 NOS, VDM ♫½

Circle of Fear An ex-hitman who worked for the Mob upends the black market for sex and drugs in the Philippines while looking for his daughter who was sold into a sex slave ring. El cheapo exploiter.
1989 (R) 90m/C *PH* Patrick Dollaghan, Welsey Pfenning, Joey Aresco, Vernon Wells; *D:* Clark Henderson. **VHS, Beta $44.98** *MGM* 🐾🐾½

Circle of Iron Plenty of action and martial arts combat abound in this story of one man's eternal quest for truth. Originally written by Bruce Lee, James Coburn, and Stirling Silliphant as a rib-crunching vehicle for Lee, who died before production began and was replaced by Kung-Fu Carradine. A cut above most chop-socky actioners. Filmed in Israel. *AKA:* The Silent Flute.
1978 (R) 102m/C *GB* Jeff Cooper, David Carradine, Roddy McDowall, Eli Wallach, Christopher Lee; *D:* Richard Moore. **VHS, Beta $24.98** *SUE* 🐾🐾½

Circle of Love Episodic melodrama drifts from romance to romance in contemporary Paris. A somewhat pretentious remake of Ophuls classic "La Ronde," which was in turn adapted from Arthur Schnitzler's play. Credible performers are undone by Vadim's strained direction. Written by Jean Anouilh.
1964 110m/C *FR* Jane Fonda, Francine Berge, Marie DuBois, Jean-Claude Brialy, Catherine Spaak, Claude Giraud; *D:* Roger Vadim. **VHS, Beta** *JEF* 🐾🐾

Circle of Two A platonic friendship between an aging artist and a young girl is misunderstood by others. Well, of course they do meet in a porno theater. Pedestrian fare adapted from a story by Marie Therese Baird.
1980 (PG) 90m/C *CA* Richard Burton, Tatum O'Neal, Kate Reid; *D:* Jules Dassin. **VHS, Beta $69.95** *VES* 🐾🐾

Circuitry Man Post-apocalyptic saga of future American life as a woman tries to deliver a briefcase full of computer chips to the underground Big Apple. Along the way she runs into Plughead, a humanoid with electrical outlets that allow him to "plug in" to other people's fantasies. Intelligent retelling of a standard tale with an inspired soundtrack by Deborah Holland. Witty and original.
1990 (R) 85m/C Jim Metzler, Dennis Christopher, Dana Wheeler-Nicholson, Vernon Wells; *W/D:* Steven Lovy; *M:* Deborah Holland. **VHS, LV $19.95** *COL* 🐾🐾½

The Circus Classic comedy silent details the tramp's exploits as a member of a traveling circus, including a romance with the bareback rider. Hilarious, less sentimental than most of Chaplin's feature films. Chaplin won a special Academy Award for "versatility and genius in writing, acting, directing and producing" for this one. Outrageous final scenes.
1919 105m/B Charlie Chaplin, Merna Kennedy; *D:* Charlie Chaplin. **VHS $19.98** *FOX* 🐾🐾🐾½

Circus Angel The renowned director of "The Red Balloon" creates a fantasy about a klutzy burglar transformed by a found nightgown into an angel. He begins to serve the dreams and actions of an odd lot of characters. Subtitled in English.
1965 80m/B *FR* Philippe Avron, Mirielle Negre; *D:* Albert Lamorisse. **VHS, Beta $14.98** *SUE, NLC* 🐾🐾🐾

Circus of Fear A travelling troupe is stalked by a murderer. The unedited version is occasionally scary. *AKA:* Psycho-Circus.
1967 92m/C *GB GE* Christopher Lee, Leo Genn, Anthony Newlands, Heinz Drache, Eddi Arent, Klaus Kinski, Margaret Lee, Suzy Kendall; *D:* John Llewellyn Moxey. **VHS, Beta $19.95** *INC, SNC, NOS* 🐾½

Circus of Horrors Nip 'n tuck horror about a plastic surgeon who takes over a circus to escape a disfigured patient bent on revenge. The circus is staffed by former patients with new faces who, one by one, fall victim in fine circus style. A bloody one-ring extravaganza.
1960 87m/C *GB* Donald Pleasence, Anton Diffring, Erika Remberg, Yvonne Monlaur, Jane Hylton, Kenneth Griffith; *D:* Sidney Hayers. **VHS, Beta $59.99** *HBO* 🐾🐾

Circus World A circus boss tries to navigate a reckless, romancing crew through a European tour while searching for aerialist he loved 15 years before and whose daughter he has reared. Too long and too familiar, but nonetheless well done with an excellent finale. Written by Ben Hecht, Julian Halevy, and James Edward Grant. *AKA:* The Magnificent Showman.
1964 132m/C John Wayne, Rita Hayworth, Claudia Cardinale, Lloyd Nolan, Richard Conte; *D:* Henry Hathaway. **VHS, Beta, LV $29.98** *UHV* 🐾🐾½

The Cisco Kid Renaldo is the heroic Cisco, a do-gooder who, with his sidekick Pancho, championed the poor and downtrodden. The first TV series shown in color. Features two episodes: "Quarterhorse" and "The Postmaster." Additional episodes are available.
1950 60m/C Duncan Renaldo, Leo Carrillo. **VHS** *HEG, MOV* 🐾🐾½

The Citadel From the A.J. Cronin novel, the intelligent and honest Hollywood drama about a young British doctor who is morally corrupted by his move from a poor mining village to a well-off practice treating wealthy hypochondriacs. Somewhat hokey but still consistently entertaining, with Donat fine in the lead.
1938 114m/C *GB* Robert Donat, Rosalind Russell, Rex Harrison, Ralph Richardson, Emlyn Williams, Penelope Dudley Ward; *D:* King Vidor. Academy Awards '38 Nominations: Best Actor (Donat), Best Director (Vidor), Best Picture, Best Screenplay; National Board of Review Awards '38: 10 Best Films of the Year; New York Film Critics Awards '38: Best Film. **VHS, Beta $24.95** *MGM, HMV* 🐾🐾🐾

Citizen Cohn An appallingly fascinating look at a human monster. Told in hallucinatory flashbacks, as he lays dying from AIDS, Roy Cohn is a lawyer and power broker, probably best-remembered as the malevolent sidekick to Communist-hunting Senator Joseph McCarthy. But his contempt also extended to antisemitism and gay-bashing (though Cohn was both homosexual and Jewish), and his past comes, literally, back to haunt him. Woods does an exceptional job in bringing this sociopathic heel to wretched life. Adapted from the biography by Nicholas von Hoffman. Made for cable television.
1992 (R) 112m/C James Woods, Joe Don Baker, Joseph Bologna, Ed Flanders, Frederic Forrest, Lee Grant, Pat Hingle; *D:* Frank Pierson; *W:* David Franzoni. **VHS, LV $89.99** *HBO* 🐾🐾

Citizen Kane Extraordinary film is an American tragedy of a newspaper tycoon (based loosely on William Randolph Hearst) from his humble beginnings to the solitude of his final years. One of the greatest films ever made, and a stunning tour-de-force in virtually every aspect, from its fragmented narration to its breathtaking, deep-focus cinematography; from its vivid soundtrack to its

fabulous ensemble acting. Oscar winning script was written by the 25-year-old Welles and Herman J. Mankiewicz. The Laser edition, a three-disc set, was reproduced from a superior negative and features extensive liner notes and running commentary from film historian Robert J. Carringer.
1941 119m/B Orson Welles, Joseph Cotten, Everett Sloane, Dorothy Comingore, Ruth Warrick, George Coulouris, Ray Collins, William Alland, Paul Stewart, Erskine Sanford, Agnes Moorehead, Alan Ladd, Gus Schilling, Philip Van Zandt, Harry Shannon, Sonny Bupp; *D:* Orson Welles. Academy Awards '41: Best Original Screenplay; Nominations: Best Actor (Welles), Best Black and White Cinematography, Best Director (Welles), Best Film Editing, Best Interior Decoration, Best Picture, Best Sound, Best Original Score; National Board of Review Awards '41: 10 Best Films of the Year; New York Film Critics Awards '41: Best Film. **VHS, Beta, LV, 8mm $19.98** *RKO, VYG, CRC* 🐾🐾🐾🐾

Citizens Band Episodic, low-key comedy about people united by their CB use in a midwestern community. Notable performance from Clark as a soft-voiced guide for truckers passing through. Demme's first comedy is characteristically idiosyncratic. Written by Paul Brickman. *AKA:* Handle With Care
1977 (PG) 98m/C Paul LeMat, Candy Clark, Ann Wedgeworth, Roberts Blossom, Charles Napier, Marcia Rodd, Bruce McGill, Ed Begley Jr., Alix Elias; *D:* Jonathan Demme. **VHS, Beta $59.95** *PAR* 🐾🐾

The City Police desperately search for a psychotic determined to kill a country singer. He shouldn't be too hard to find. Made for television.
1976 78m/C Don Johnson, Robert Forster, Ward Costello, Jimmy Dean, Mark Hamill; *D:* Harvey Hart. **VHS, Beta $49.95** *WOV* 🐾

The City and the Dogs A brutal, cynical adaptation of Mario Vargas Llosa's novel. A young military recruit rebels against the authority establishments around him. In Spanish with English subtitles. *AKA:* La Ciudad y los Perros.
1985 135m/C *SP D:* Francisco J. Lombardi Pery. **VHS, Beta $34.95** *FCT, TAM* 🐾🐾🐾

City for Conquest Two lovers go their separate ways to pursue individual careers. He attempts to become a boxing champ, but is blinded in the ring and ends up selling newspapers. She takes a shot at a dancing career but hooks up with an unscrupulous partner. Will the ill-fated pair find happiness again?
1940 101m/B James Cagney, Ann Sheridan, Frank Craven, Donald Crisp, Arthur Kennedy, Frank McHugh, George Tobias, Anthony Quinn, Blanche Yurka, Elia Kazan, Bob Steele; *D:* Anatole Litvak. **VHS, Beta $19.98** *MGM, CCB* 🐾🐾🐾

City Girl Friedrich Murnau, who directed the silent vampire classic "Nosferatu," was removed from the director's chair before "City Girl" was completed and it shows. But so do the marks of his inimitable camera direction. The story concerns a Minnesota grain grower who visits the Windy City and returns with a waitress as his wife. Frustratingly inconsistent, leading you to wonder what could have been had Murnau remained behind the camera (he died the following year). Silent. *AKA:* Our Daily Bread.
1930 90m/B Charles Farrell, Mary Duncan; *D:* F. W. Murnau. **VHS, Beta $39.95** *GPV, FCT* 🐾🐾½

City Heat A hardnosed cop and a plucky private eye berate each other while opposing the mob in this overdone comedy. Both Eastwood and Reynolds spoof their screen personas, but the results are only slightly

C

satisfactory. Good back-up, though, from Alexander and Kahn as the dames.
1984 (PG) 98m/C Clint Eastwood, Burt Reynolds, Jane Alexander, Irene Cara, Madeline Kahn, Richard Roundtree, Rip Torn, Tony LoBianco, William Sanderson; **D:** Richard Benjamin. **VHS, Beta, LV $19.98** WAR 🎬🎬½

City in Fear Stellar cast lights up a made-for-television drama about a tired newspaper columnist (Janssen) who communicates directly with a murdering psychotic (Rourke), as publisher Vaughn applauds and hypes. Rourke's first role, Janssen's last, and Smithee is actually Jud Taylor.
1980 135m/C David Janssen, Robert Vaughn, Mickey Rourke, William Daniels, Perry King, Susan Sullivan, William Prince; **D:** Alan Smithee. **VHS, Beta $69.98** LIV, HHE 🎬🎬🎬

City in Panic A detective and radio talk show host try to catch a psychotic mass murderer busy offing homosexuals throughout the city. Violent with no redeeming social qualities.
1986 85m/C Dave Adamson, Ed Chester, Leeann Westegard; **D:** Robert Bouvier. **VHS, Beta $19.98** TWE 🎬

City Killer A lunatic tries to blackmail the girl he loves into going out on a few dates by committing huge destructive acts of inner-city terrorism (flowers won't do). Made for television.
1987 120m/C Heather Locklear, Gerald McRaney, Terence Knox, Peter Mark Richman, John Harkins; **D:** Robert Lewis. **VHS, Beta $9.99** STE, PSM 🎬

City Lights Masterpiece that was Chaplin's last silent film. The "Little Tramp" falls in love with a blind flower seller. A series of lucky accidents permits him to get the money she needs for a sight-restoring surgery. One of the most eloquent movies ever filmed, due to Chaplin's keen balance between comedy and tragedy.
1931 86m/B Charlie Chaplin, Virginia Cherrill, Florence Lee, Hank Mann, Harry Myers, Henry Bergman, Jean Harlow; **D:** Charlie Chaplin. **VHS, Beta, LV $19.98** FOX 🎬🎬🎬🎬

City Limits In a post-apocalyptic city, gangs of young people on choppers clash.
1985 (PG-13) 85m/C John Stockwell, Kim Cattrall, Darrell Larson, Rae Dawn Chong, Robby Benson, James Earl Jones, Jennifer Balgobin; **D:** Aaron Lipstadt. **VHS, Beta, LV $79.98** VES, LIV, HHE 🎬

City of Blood A South African doctor is embroiled in mystery with racial overtones when prostitutes are being killed with a spiked club. Packaged as a horror film, this movie actually deals with the questions of South African racial tensions in a sophisticated, ultimately tragic manner.
1988 (R) 96m/C SA Joe Stewardson, Ian Yule, Susan Coetzer; **D:** Darrell Roodt. **VHS, Beta** NO 🎬🎬½

City of Hope The picture that "Bonfire of the Vanities" wanted to be, an eventful few days in the fictional metropolis of Hudson: an ugly racial incident threatens to snowball, the corrupt mayor pushes a shady real-estate deal, and a botched robbery has profound implications. Some of the subplots resolve too easily, but this cynical, crazy-quilt of urban life is worthy of comparison with "American Graffiti" and "Nashville" as pure Americana.
1991 (R) 132m/C Vincent Spano, Tony LoBianco, Joe Morton, Todd Graff, David Strathairn, Anthony John Denison, Barbara Williams, Angela Bassett, Gloria Foster, Lawrence Tierney, John Sayles; **W/D:** John Sayles. **VHS, LV, 8mm** COL 🎬🎬🎬

City of Joy A disillusioned American heart surgeon (Swayze) flees to India after losing a patient. In Calcutta he is beaten by a street gang and loses his money and passport, but finds help from a farmer (Puri) who takes him to a nearby clinic in the City of Joy, one of Calcutta's poorest areas. Collins runs the clinic and recruits the reluctant doctor, who comes to know the inhabitants of the City of Joy and undergoes a life-changing transformation. The squalor of Calcutta is shown, but the city's portrayal as a magical place where problems miraculously disappear is unrealistic. Swayze lacks the emotional range for his part, but Collins and Puri are excellent in their roles. Adapted from the book by Dominique Lapierre.
1992 (PG-13) 134m/C GB FR Patrick Swayze, Pauline Collins, Om Puri, Shabana Azmi, Art Malik, Ayesha Dharker, Santu Chowdhury, Imran Badsah Khan, Shyamanand Jalan; **Cameos:** Sam Wanamaker; **D:** Roland Joffe; **W:** Mark Medoff; **M:** Ennio Morricone. **VHS, LV** COL 🎬🎬

City of Shadows Twins separated at birth are reunited by a criminal mind with evil intentions. Double trouble? Music by Tangerine Dream.
1986 (R) 97m/C John P. Ryan, Paul Coufos, Tony Rosato; **D:** David Mitchell. **VHS, Beta $19.95** STE, NWV 🎬🎬

City of the Walking Dead Eco-misery as a community must contend with prowling, radiation-zapped zombies who enjoy chewing through human flesh. **AKA:** Nightmare City; Nightmare.
1983 92m/C IT SP Mel Ferrer, Hugo Stiglitz, Laura Trotter, Francisco Rabal; **D:** Umberto Lenzi. **VHS** NO 🎬

City of Women Visually stunning, but otherwise thin fantasy/drama about a man smothered with women. A journalist wanders through a feminist theme park replete with a roller rink and screening room. Some worthwhile adventures are mixed in with rather dull stretches. Not among the best from either Mastroianni, who is under utilized, or Fellini, who here seems incapable of separating good ideas from bad. Plenty of buxom babes, but otherwise undistinguished. In Italian with English subtitles.
1981 (R) 140m/C IT Marcello Mastroianni, Ettore Manni, Anna Prucnall, Bernice Stegers; **W/D:** Federico Fellini. **VHS, Beta $79.95** NYF, FCT, TAM 🎬🎬

City on Fire An arsonist starts a fire that could engulf an entire city. Flaming bore.
1978 (R) 101m/C CA Barry Newman, Susan Clark, Shelley Winters, Leslie Nielsen, Henry Fonda, Ava Gardner; **D:** Alvin Rakoff. **VHS, Beta $9.98** SUE Woof!

City Slickers Three men with mid-life crises leave New York City for a cattle-ranch vacation that turns into an arduous, character-building stint. Many funny moments supplied by leads Crystal, Stern, and Kirby, but Palance steals the film as a salty, wise cowpoke. Slater is fetching as the lone gal vacationer on the cattle drive. Box office winner notable for a realistic calf birthing scene, one of few in cinema history. From an idea by Crystal, who also produced. Palance stole the show from Oscar ceremonies host Crystal a second time when he accepted his award and suddenly started doing one-arm pushups, startling the audience into laughter.
1991 (PG-13) 114m/C Billy Crystal, Daniel Stern, Bruno Kirby, Patricia Wettig, Helen Slater, Jack Palance, Noble Willingham, Tracy Walter, Josh Mostel, David Paymer, Bill Henderson, Jeffrey Tambor, Phill Lewis, Kyle Secor, Yeardley Smith, Jayne Meadows; **D:** Ron Underwood; **W:** Lowell Ganz, Babaloo Mandel; **M:** Marc Shaiman. **VHS, Beta, LV, SVS, 8mm $19.95** COL, PIA, NLC 🎬🎬🎬

City That Never Sleeps A Chicago cop must decide whether or not to run off with an entertainer, or continue his life with his family. Decisions, decisions. Moody but dated melodrama that's finely acted and indecisively directed, with good use of dim city lights. Nothing new here.
1953 90m/B Gig Young, Mala Powers, Edward Arnold, Paula Raymond, Chill Wills, Marie Windsor; **D:** John H. Auer. **VHS $19.98** REP 🎬🎬½

The City's Edge A young man becomes involved with the mysterious residents of a boarding house on the edge of the ocean.
1983 86m/C AU **VHS, Beta $59.95** MGM 🎬½

Civil War Diary Too young to go to war, a young man struggles for the survival of his family amidst harsh winters, the devastation of the Civil War and his own personal nightmares. Winner of the International Heritage Award in 1990. Based on the Newberry Award winning young people's novel "Across Five Aprils."
1990 82m/C VHS $79.98 RHI 🎬½

The Civil War, Episode 1: The Cause—1861 The blowout PBS hit mini-series, five years in the making by author and filmmaker Ken Burns, is a staggering historical achievement. Episode 1 focuses on the causes of the Civil War from the schism created by Lincoln's election, John Brown's assault on Harper's Ferry, and the firing on Fort Sumter. Also available as a set for $179.95.
1990 99m/C W/D: Ken Burns. **VHS, 3/4U $79.95** PBS, SIG, KUI 🎬🎬🎬🎬

The Civil War, Episode 2: A Very Bloody Affair—1862 Second in the enormously popular PBS series looks at the unexpectedly extreme costs in human life of the War Between the States.
1990 69m/C W/D: Ken Burns. **VHS, 3/4U $59.95** PBS, SIG, KUI 🎬🎬🎬🎬

The Civil War, Episode 3: Forever Free—1862 Third volume in the PBS Emmy-nominated mini-series covers Antietam, Robert E. Lee and Stonewall Jackson planning Confederate strategy, and Lincoln's decision to free the slaves.
1990 76m/C W/D: Ken Burns. **VHS, 3/4U $19.95** PBS, SIG, KUI 🎬🎬🎬🎬

The Civil War, Episode 4: Simply Murder—1863 Union forces meet disaster at Fredericksburg, and Gen. Lee wins a victory but loses Stonewall Jackson in the fourth episode of the Emmy-nominated PBS mini-series.
1990 62m/C W/D: Ken Burns. **VHS, 3/4U $59.95** PBS, SIG, KUI 🎬🎬🎬🎬

The Civil War, Episode 5: The Universe of Battle—1863 Gettysburg, the battleground which claimed 150,000 American lives, is examined in the 5th episode of the Emmy-nominated PBS mini-series.
1990 95m/C W/D: Ken Burns. **VHS, 3/4U $79.95** PBS, SIG, KUI 🎬🎬🎬🎬

The Civil War, Episode 6: Valley of the Shadow of Death—1864 Profiles of Grant and Lee are offered, plus Sherman's assault on Atlanta, in this volume from the Emmy-nominated PBS mini-series.
1990 70m/C W/D: Ken Burns. **VHS, 3/4U $59.95** PBS, SIG, KUI 🎬🎬🎬🎬

The Civil War, Episode 7: Most Hallowed Ground—1864 The nation re-elects Abraham Lincoln, and the North turns General Lee's mansion into Arlington

National Cemetery in this episode of the Emmy-nominated PBS mini-series.
1990 72m/C **W/D:** Ken Burns. **VHS, 3/4U** $59.95 *PBS, SIG, KUI* 🎬🎬🎬🎬

The Civil War, Episode 8: War is All Hell—1865
Sherman marches to the sea and Lee surrenders to Grant in this episode from the Emmy-nominated PBS mini-series.
1990 69m/C **W/D:** Ken Burns. **VHS, 3/4U** $59.95 *PBS, SIG, KUI* 🎬🎬🎬🎬

The Civil War, Episode 9: The Better Angels of Our Nature—1865
In this final episode of the Emmy-nominated PBS mini-series, Lincoln's assassination is examined, and the central characters of the war are summarized.
1990 68m/C **W/D:** Ken Burns. **VHS, 3/4U** $59.95 *PBS, SIG, KUI* 🎬🎬🎬🎬

Civilization
A silent epic about the horrors and immorality of war as envisioned by the ground-breaking film pioneer Ince, who was later murdered. Famous scene involves Christ walking through body-ridden battlefields.
1916 102m/B Howard Hickman, Enid Markey, Lola May; **D:** Thomas Ince. **VHS, Beta** $27.95 *VYY* 🎬🎬🎬

Claire's Knee
A grown man about to be married goes on a holiday and develops a fixation on a young girl's knee. Another of Rohmer's Moral Tales exploring sexual and erotic obsessions. Lots of talk, little else. You'll either find it fascinating or fail to watch more than 10 minutes. Most, however, consider it a classic. Sophisticated dialogue, lovely visions of summer on Lake Geneva. In French with English subtitles.
1971 105m/C FR Jean-Claude Brialy, Aurora Cornu, Beatrice Romand; **D:** Eric Rohmer. **VHS, Beta, LV** $59.95 *TAM, MED, FCT* 🎬🎬🎬½

Clambake
Noxious Elvis vehicle about a rich man's son who wants success on his own terms, so he trades places with a water-skiing teacher. Inane, even in comparison to other Elvis ventures. ♫Clambake; The Girl I Never Loved; Hey, Hey, Hey; Confidence; Who Needs Money?; A House That Has Everything.
1967 98m/C Elvis Presley, Shelley Fabares, Bill Bixby, James Gregory, Gary Merrill, Will Hutchins, Harold Peary; **D:** Arthur Nadel. **VHS, Beta** $19.95 *MGM* 🎬

The Clan of the Cave Bear
A scrawny cavegirl is taken in by Neanderthals after her own parents are killed. Hannah is lifeless as a primitive gamine, and the film is similarly DOA. Ponderous and only unintentionally funny. Based on the popular novel by Jean M. Auel with a screenplay by John Sayles.
1986 (R) 100m/C Daryl Hannah, James Remar, Pamela Reed, John Doolittle, Thomas G. Waites; **D:** Michael Chapman. **VHS, Beta, LV** $14.98 *FXV, FOX* 🎬½

Clara's Heart
A Jamaican maid enriches the lives of her insufferable, bourgeois employers and their particularly repellent son. A kinder, gentler waste of film and Goldberg; sentimental clap-trap which occasionally lapses into comedy.
1988 (PG-13) 108m/C Whoopi Goldberg, Michael Ontkean, Kathleen Quinlan, Neil Patrick Harris, Spalding Gray, Beverly Todd, Hattie Winston; **D:** Robert Mulligan. **VHS, Beta, LV** $19.98 *WAR, FCT* 🎬

Clarence
Clarence, the benevolent angel from the classic "It's a Wonderful Life" is back, risking his wings for a beautiful young woman. Made for cable.

1991 (G) 92m/C Robert Carradine, Kate Trotter; **D:** Eric Till. **VHS** $79.98 *REP* 🎬🎬½

Clarence Darrow
Riveting one-man stage performance shot for television and based on Darrow's writings, adapted from the play by Irving Stone.
1978 81m/C Henry Fonda; **D:** John Rich. **VHS, Beta, LV** $39.95 *ALL, KAR, IME* 🎬🎬🎬

Clarence, the Cross-eyed Lion
Follows the many adventures of a cross-eyed lion and his human compatriots. Great family viewing from the creator of "Flipper."
1965 98m/C Marshall Thompson, Betsy Drake, Richard Haydn, Cheryl Miller, Rockne Tarkington, Maurice Marsac; **D:** Andrew Marton. **VHS** $19.95 *MGM, FCT* 🎬🎬🎬

Clark & McCullough
The zany duo, a hit in burlesque and night clubs, transferred some of their crazy antics onto film. Their comedy shorts include "Fits in a Fiddle" (1933), "Love and Kisses" (1934), "Alibi Bye Bye" (1935), and a rehearsal of "Mademoiselle from New Rochelle" from "Strike Up the Band" (with George Gershwin on piano).
1933 53m/B Bobby Clark, Paul McCullough, George Gershwin, James Finlayson. **VHS, Beta** $57.95 *GVV, DVT, VYY* 🎬🎬½

Clash by Night
A wayward woman marries a fisherman, then beds his best friend. Seamy storyline is exploited to the hilt by master filmmaker Lang. An utterly unflinching melodrama. Early Monroe shines in a supporting role too. Based on the Clifford Odets play.
1952 105m/B Barbara Stanwyck, Paul Douglas, Marilyn Monroe, Robert Ryan, J. Carroll Naish; **D:** Fritz Lang. **VHS, Beta, LV** $15.95 *UHV* 🎬🎬🎬½

Clash of the Ninja
Evil Occidental ninja runs medical smuggling operation. Interpol ninja sets out to stop him. Wild ninja nonsense includes ninja with rotating head and exploding ninja. Dubbed poorly.
1986 90m/C HK Paul Torcha, Louis Roth, Eric Neff, Bernie Junker, Joe Redner, Klaus Mutter, Eddie Chan, Max Kwan, Tom Allen, Stanley Tong; **D:** Wallace Chan; **W:** Kurt Spielberg. **VHS, Beta** $59.95 *TWE* 🎬½

Clash of the Titans
Mind-numbing fantasy derived from Greek legends about heroic Perseus, who slays the snake-haired Medusa and rescues a semi-clad maiden from the monstrous Kraken. Wooden Hamlin plays Perseus and fares better than more accomplished Olivier and Smith, who seem in need of enemas as they lurch about Mt. Olympus. Only Bloom seems truly godlike in a supporting role. Some good, some wretched special effects from pioneer Harryhausen.
1981 (PG) 118m/C GB Laurence Olivier, Maggie Smith, Claire Bloom, Ursula Andress, Burgess Meredith, Harry Hamlin, Sian Phillips, Judi Bowker; **D:** Desmond Davis. **VHS, Beta, LV** $69.95 *MGM, MLB* Woof!

Class
A prep school student discovers that his mother is the lover whom his roommate has bragged about. Lowe is serviceable as the stunned son of sexy Bisset, who woos McCarthy, even in an elevator. Too ludicrous to be enjoyed, but you may watch just to see what happens next.
1983 (R) 98m/C Jacqueline Bisset, Rob Lowe, Andrew McCarthy, Cliff Robertson, John Cusack, Stuart Margolin, Casey Siemaszko; **D:** Lewis John Carlino. **VHS, Beta, LV** $29.98 *VES* 🎬🎬

Class Act
Rappers Kid 'N' Play team up once again in this role reversal comedy. A straight-laced brain and a partying, macho bully find their school records and identifications switched when they enroll in a new high school. This turns out to be good for the

character of both young men, as the egghead learns to loosen up and the bully learns what it feels like to be respected for his ideas rather than a fierce reputation. Comedy is very uneven but the duo are energetic and likable.
1991 (PG-13) 98m/C Christopher Reid, Christopher Martin, Meshach Taylor, Karyn Parsons, Doug E. Doug, Rick Ducommun, Lamont Jackson, Rhea Perlman; **D:** Randall Miller. **VHS, LV** $19.98 *WAR* 🎬🎬½

Class Action
1960s versus 1990s ethics clash when a father and daughter, both lawyers, wind up on opposing sides of a litigation against an auto manufacturer. Hackman and Mastrantonio give intense, exciting performances, almost surmounting the melodramatic script.
1991 (R) 110m/C Mary Elizabeth Mastrantonio, Gene Hackman, Joanna Merlin, Colin Friels; **D:** Michael Apted; **M:** James Horner. **VHS, Beta, LV** $19.98 *FXV* 🎬🎬🎬

Class of Fear
The new kid in school is having a particularly rough time. He's been framed for murdering a teacher and must prove his innocence before he winds up in prison.
1991 (R) 105m/C Julianne McNamara, Noah Blake. **VHS** $79.99 *MNC, MOV* 🎬½

Class of '44
The sequel to "Summer of '42" finds insufferable boys becoming insufferable men at military school. Worse than its predecessor.
1973 (PG) 95m/C Gary Grimes, Jerry Houser, Oliver Conant, Deborah Winters, William Atherton, Sam Bottoms; **D:** Paul Bogart. **VHS, Beta** $19.98 *WAR* 🎬½

The Class of Miss MacMichael
A dedicated instructor inherits and ultimately inspires a class of high school misfits and malcontents. Derivative venture is beneath considerable talents of Jackson. Based on a novel by Sandy Hutson.
1978 (R) 95m/C GB Glenda Jackson, Oliver Reed, Michael Murphy, Rosalind Cash; **D:** Silvio Narizzano. **VHS, Beta** $9.95 *FOX, MED* 🎬🎬

Class of 1984
Teacher King must face a motley crew of teenagers in the classroom. Ring leader and student psychopath Van Patten leads his groupies on a reign of terror through the high school halls, stopping to gang rape King's wife. Teacher attempts revenge. Bloody and thoughtless update of "Blackboard Jungle." Early Fox appearance. Music by Lalo Schifrin and Alice Cooper. Followed by "Class of 1999."
1982 93m/C CA Perry King, Roddy McDowall, Timothy Van Patten, Michael J. Fox, Merrie Lynn Ross, Stefan Arngrim, Al Waxman; **D:** Mark L. Lester. **VHS, Beta, LV** $29.98 *VES* Woof!

Class of 1999
Freewheeling sci-fi set in the near future where teen gangs terrorize seemingly the entire country. A high school principal determines to enforce law and order by installing human-like robots with rocket launchers for arms. Violent, crude entertainment. Class dismissed. Sequel to "Class of 1984" and available in an unrated version.
1990 98m/C Bradley Gregg, Traci Lin, Malcolm McDowell, Stacy Keach, Patrick Kilpatrick, Pam Grier, John P. Ryan, Darren E. Burrows, Joshua Miller; **D:** Mark L. Lester. **VHS, Beta** *VES, LIV* 🎬🎬

Class of Nuke 'Em High
Team Troma once again experiments with the chemicals, with violent results. Jersey high school becomes a hotbed of mutants and maniacs after a nuclear spill occurs. Good teens Chrissy and Warren succumb, the school blows, life goes on. High camp, low

budget, heavy gore. Followed by "Class of Nuke 'Em High Part 2."
1986 (R) 84m/C Janelle Brady, Gilbert Brenton; **D:** Richard W. Haines. **VHS, Beta $9.98** *MED* ✂️½

Class of Nuke 'Em High, Part 2: Subhumanoid Meltdown The Troma team brings us back into the world of the strange. In this adventure, the evil Nukama-ma Corporation holds secret experiments at their "college" and create sub-humanoids as slave labor, swelling unemployment and wrecking the economy. This does not fare too well with the rest of society, including our heroes Roger the reporter, Professor Holt, and the scantily clad sub-humanoid Victoria.
1991 m/C Lisa Gaye, Brick Bronsky, Leesa Rowland. **VHS, Beta, LV $19.98** *VTR, MED, FXV* ✂️

Class of '63 An unfulfilled woman finally discovers the lover she lost nearly ten years ago at her college reunion. Nearly average made for television drama.
1973 74m/C James Brolin, Joan Hackett, Cliff Gorman, Ed Lauter; **D:** John Korty. **VHS, Beta $59.95** *LHV* ✂️✂️

Class Reunion Sexual highjinks are the order of the day at a 10-year high school reunion. Insipid softcore effort. It's cheaper just to cut out heads from yearbooks and paste 'em to skin mags torsos. Not to be confused with "National Lampoon's Class Reunion," equally bad but nonethelss distinct.
1987 (X) 90m/C Marsha Jordan, Renee Bond, Terry Johnson. **VHS, Beta, LV $29.95** *MED Woof!*

Class Reunion Massacre Typically lame-brained horror about the mysterious deaths of former school jerks who've reconvened for the 10-year reunion. Worthless flick stars someone named Finkbinder. Contains graphic violence that is not for the squeamish. Also titled "The Redeemer."
1977 (R) 87m/C T.K. Finkbinder, Damien Knight, Nick Carter. **VHS, Beta $39.98** *UHV Woof!*

Classic Comedy Video Sampler A collection of classic comedy shorts featuring Amos and Andy, The Three Stooges, and Abbott and Costello.
1940 78m/B Bud Abbott, Lou Costello, Moe Howard, Larry Fine, Curly Howard. **VHS, Beta $29.95** *UHV Woof!*

Claudia A wealthy woman who's part of London's high society falls for a lowly musician while trying to escape her dominating husband. Melodramatic meanderings not likely to move you.
1985 (R) 88m/C Deborah Raffin, Nicholas Ball; **D:** Anwar Kawadri. **VHS $19.95** *TTC* ✂️✂️

Claws A woodsman, a game commissioner and an Indian band together to stop a grizzly bear who is killing residents of a small Alaskan town.
1977 (PG) 100m/C Leon Ames, Jason Evers, Anthony Caruso, Glenn Sipes, Carla Layton, Myron Healey; **D:** Richard Bansbach, R.E. Pierson. **VHS, Beta $59.95** *GEM* ✂️

Claws A lone farmboy is subjected to repeated attacks by feline mutants. Meow, baby.
1985 84m/C Jason Roberts, Brian O'Shaughnessy, Sandra Prinsloo. **VHS, Beta $59.95** *WWV Woof!*

The Clay Pigeon Seaman comes to in the hospital after a long coma and discovers he's about to be court-martialed for treason and murder. Effective suspense as he goes after the man who incriminated him.

1949 63m/B Bill Williams, Barbara Hale, Richard Loo; **D:** Richard Fleischer. **VHS, Beta $34.95** *RKO* ✂️✂️½

Clayton County Line Plucky buddies decide to end a cruel sheriff's reign of terror. Derivative and unredeeming.
198? 80m/C Kelly Bradish, Vince Csapos, Michael Heinz, Donald Kenney, Kathy Kenney, Gregg Schultz, Dan Quine, Steve Szilagyi, Dean Wilson; **D:** Dean Wilson. **VHS** *NO* ✂️

Clean and Sober A drug addict hides out at a rehabilitation clinic and actually undergoes treatment. A serious, subtle, and realistic look at the physical/emotional detox-ification of an obnoxious, substance-abusing real estate broker; unpredictable and powerful without moralizing. Keaton is fine in unsympathetic lead, with both Baker and Freeman excelling in lesser roles. Not for all tastes, but its certainly a worthwhile work. Caron, creator of TV's "Moonlighting," debuts here as director.
1988 (R) 124m/C Michael Keaton, Kathy Baker, Morgan Freeman, M. Emmet Walsh, Claudia Christian, Pat Quinn, Ben Piazza, Brian Benben, Luca Bercovici, Tate Donovan, Henry Judd Baker, Mary Catherine Martin; **D:** Glenn Gordon Caron. **VHS, Beta, LV, 8mm $19.98** *WAR, FCT* ✂️✂️✂️½

Clearcut Progressive lawyer finds his liberalism and his survival skills tested among modern Canadian Indians, when a militant native resorts to kidnapping the businessman who threatens their land. Well-acted, brutal drama that asks tough questions; it includes what purports to be the first authentic sweat-lodge ceremony ever filmed.
1992 (R) 98m/C *CA* Graham Greene, Ron Lea, Michael Hogan; **D:** Richard Bugajski. **VHS $89.95** *ACA* ✂️✂️½

Clearing the Range Hoot wants the bad guy who knocked off his brother so he poses as a cringing coward in the hopes of uncovering the villain. Eilers is the love interest as well as his real-life wife.
1931 64m/B Hoot Gibson, Sally Eilers. **VHS, Beta $19.95** *NOS, VCN, DVT* ✂️½

Cleo from 5 to 7 A singer strolls through Paris for 90 minutes, and reconsiders her life while awaiting the results of medical tests for cancer. Typical documentary-like effort from innovative filmmaker Varda, who constructed the film in real time. Look for a brief appearance of master director Jean-Luc Godard. In French with English subtitles. *AKA:* Cleo de 5 a 7.
1961 90m/B *FR* Corinne Marchand, Antoine Bourseillor, Dorothee Blanck, Michel Legrand, Jean-Claude Brialy, Jean-Luc Godard, Anna Karina, Eddie Constantine, Sami Frey; **D:** Agnes Varda. **VHS, Beta $79.95** *FCT* ✂️✂️½

Cleo/Leo Crude and sexist jerk Leo gets chased into the East River by a gun-toting feminist. Reincarnated, Leo returns as Cleo and endures the same Neanderthal remarks and attitudes that "he" used to dish out. Tasteless, exploitive comedy only cynically explores the sex reversal theme.
1989 (R) 94m/C Jane Hamilton, Scott Thompson Baker, Kevin Thomas, Alan Naggar, Ginger Lynn Allen; **D:** Chuck Vincent. **VHS $19.95** *STE, MED* ✂️

Cleopatra Early Hollywood DeMille version of the Egyptian temptress's lust for Marc Antony after Julius Caesar's death. Intermittently interesting extravaganza. Colbert seems to be enjoying herself in the lead role in this hokey, overdone epic. Includes the original theatrical trailer on laser-track 2. Remade in 1963.

1934 100m/B Claudette Colbert, Henry Wilcoxon, Warren William, Gertrude Michael, Joseph Schildkraut, C. Aubrey Smith; **D:** Cecil B. DeMille. Academy Awards '34: Best Cinematography; Nominations: Best Film Editing, Best Picture, Best Sound. **VHS, Beta, LV $14.95** *MCA* ✂️✂️

Cleopatra And we thought DeMille's version was extravagant. After the death of Julius Caesar, Cleopatra, Queen of Egypt, becomes infatuated with Mark Antony. Costly four-hour epic functions like a blimp-sized, multi-colored sleeping tablet. Historical characters are utterly dwarfed by the film's massive scope, and audiences are benumbed by a spectacle of crowd scenes and opulent, grotesque interiors. Taylor looks and often acts like a sex bomb ruler, while Harrison has some notion of Caesar's majesty. Burton, however, is hopelessly wooden. Hard to believe this came from director Mankiewicz. Oscar nominations for Best Picture, actor Harrison, sound, original score and film editing in addition to the awards it won.
1963 246m/C Elizabeth Taylor, Richard Burton, Rex Harrison, Roddy McDowall, Martin Landau, Pamela Brown, Michael Hordern, Kenneth Haigh, Andrew Keir, Hume Cronyn, Carroll O'Connor; **D:** Joseph L. Mankiewicz. Academy Awards '63: Best Art Direction/Set Decoration (Color), Best Color Cinematography, Best Costume Design (Color), Best Visual Effects; Nominations: Best Actor (Harrison), Best Film Editing, Best Picture, Best Sound, Best Original Score; National Board of Review Awards '63: Best Actor (Harrison). **VHS, Beta, LV $29.98** *FOX* ✂️

Cleopatra Jones Lean and lethal government agent with considerable martial arts prowess takes on loathsome drug lords. Dobson is fetching as the lead performer in this fast-paced, violent flick. Followed by "Cleopatra Jones and the Casino of Gold."
1973 (PG) 89m/C Tamara Dobson, Shelley Winters, Bernie Casey, Brenda Sykes; **D:** Jack Starrett. **VHS, Beta $19.98** *WAR* ✂️✂️

Cleopatra Jones & the Casino of Gold Dobson returns as the lethal, physically imposing federal agent to Hong Kong to take on a powerful druglord in this sequel to "Cleopatra Jones." Watch for sexy Stevens as the Dragon Lady.
1975 (R) 96m/C Tamara Dobson, Stella Stevens, Norman Fell; **D:** Chuck Bail. **VHS, Beta $19.98** *WAR* ✂️✂️

The Clergyman's Daughter A clergyman's daughter calls upon detectives Tommy and Tuppence to investigate some murders at the family's country house. Made for British television and based on the Agatha Christie story.
1984 60m/C *GB* James Warwick, Francesca Annis; **W:** Agatha Christie. **VHS, Beta $14.95** *PAV* ✂️½

Cliffhanger Action-packed thriller starring Stallone as Gabe Walker, an expert climber on the Rocky Mountain Rescue Team, who faces his greatest challenge when criminal mastermind (Lithgow) and his henchman appear o the scene. Turner plays fellow climber and love interest. Lithgow make a particularly convincing, if not downright chilling, murderous thief. Filmed in the Italian Alps with a budget of $70 million-plus, this film boasts stunning cinematography and breathtaking footage of the Italian Alps' Dolomite mountain range. Harlin's expert pacing and direction combine to produce maximum thrills and suspense. Looks like this might be the hit Stallone's been waiting for. Based on a story by Michael France, which was based on a premise by John Long.

C

1993 (R) 112m/C Sylvester Stallone, John Lithgow, Michael Rooker, Janine Turner, Rex Linn, Caroline Goodall, Leon, Paul Winfield, Ralph Waite; *D:* Renny Harlin; *W:* Sylvester Stallone, Michael France; *M:* Trevor Jones. VHS COL *ℐℐℐ*

Clifford A mischievous 10-year old boy creates chaos when he visits his bachelor uncle living in Los Angeles.
1993 (PG) m/C Martin Short, Charles Grodin, Mary Steenburgen, Dabney Coleman, Sonia Jackson; *D:* Paul Flaherty; *W:* Bobby Von Hayes, Jay Dee Rock. VHS ORI *ℐℐℐ*

A Climate for Killing Arizona police are baffled when a woman murdered 16 years earlier is again found dead. Case open? Hunks Bauer and Beck are earnest in leads, and Ross and Sara are foxy. Passable entertainment.
1991 (R) 104m/C Steven Bauer, John Beck, Katharine Ross, Mia Sara; *W/D:* J.S. Cardone. VHS, Beta, LV $89.98 MED *ℐℐ½*

The Climb German mountain climbers attempt to conquer the Himalayan Nanga Parbat, the world's fifth highest peak. Sometimes compelling film based on 1953 expedition in which only one member succeeded in reaching the summit.
1987 (PG) 90m/C Bruce Greenwood, James Hurdle, Kenneth Welsh; *D:* Donald Shebib. VHS, Beta, LV $19.95 IME *ℐℐ½*

The Clinic Day in the life farce follows the sometimes humorous events at a VD clinic featuring a homosexual doctor, assisted by a curious student intern.
1983 95m/C AU Chris Haywood, Simon Burke, Gerda Nicolson, Rona McLeod, Suzanne Raylance, Veronica Lang, Pat Evison; *D:* David Stevens. VHS, Beta $29.98 VID *ℐℐ*

Clipped Wings The Bowery Boys are at their best as they inadvertantly join the army while visiting a friend and in the process of their usual bumblings, uncover a Nazi plot.
1953 62m/B Leo Gorcey, Huntz Hall, Bernard Gorcey, David Condon, Bennie Bartlett, June Vincent, Mary Treen, Philip Van Zandt, Elaine Riley, Jeanne Dean, Lyle Talbot; *D:* Edward L. Bernds. VHS $14.98 WAR *ℐℐ½*

Cloak and Dagger An American physicist joins the secret service during WWII and infiltrates Nazi territory to release a kidnapped scientist who is being forced to build a nuclear bomb. Disappointing spy show with muted anti-nuclear tone. Written by Ring Lardner Jr. and Albert Maltz.
1946 106m/B Gary Cooper, Lilli Palmer, Robert Alda, James Flavin, Vladimir Sokoloff, J. Edward Bromberg, Marc Lawrence, Ludwig Stossel; *D:* Fritz Lang. VHS, LV $19.95 REP, FCT *ℐℐ*

Cloak & Dagger A young boy, last seen befriending E.T., depends upon his imaginary super-friend to help him out when some real-life agents are after his video game. Coleman is particularly fun as both dad and fantasy hero in an interesting family adventure.
1984 (PG) 101m/C Dabney Coleman, Henry Thomas, Michael Murphy, John McIntire, Jeanette Nolan; *D:* Richard Franklin. VHS, Beta, LV $19.95 MCA *ℐℐℐ*

The Clock Appealing romance about an office worker who meets and falls in love with a soldier on two-day leave in New York City. Charismatic Walker and likeable Garland make a fine screen couple, and Wynn is memorable as the drunk. The original theatrical trailer is included on the laserdisc format. *AKA:* Under the Clock.
1945 91m/B Judy Garland, Robert Walker, James Gleason, Marshall Thompson, Keenan Wynn; *D:* Vincente Minnelli. VHS, LV $19.98 BTV, PIA, MGM *ℐℐℐ*

The Clockmaker Contemplative drama about a clockmaker whose life is shattered when his son is arrested as a political assassin. Tavernier regular Noiret excels in the lead. In French with English subtitles.
1976 105m/C FR Philippe Noiret, Jean Rochefort, Jacques Denis, William Sabatier, Christine Pascal; *D:* Bertrand Tavernier. VHS, Beta, LV $34.95 FCT, LUM, PIA *ℐℐℐ½*

Clockwise Monty Python regular Cleese is a teacher preoccupied by punctuality. His neurosis proves his undoing when he falls victim to misadventure while traveling to deliver a speech. Cleese is acceptable, dialogue and story is less so, though sprinkled with a fair amount of humor.
1986 (PG) 96m/C GB John Cleese, Penelope Wilton, Alison Steadman, Stephen Moore, Sharon Maiden; *D:* Christopher Morahan. VHS, LV $79.99 HBO *ℐℐ½*

A Clockwork Orange In the Britain of the near future, a sadistic punk leads a gang on nightly rape and murder sprees, then is captured and becomes the subject of a grim experiment to eradicate his violent tendencies in this extraordinary adaptation of Anthony Burgess's controversial novel. The film is an exhilarating experience, with an outstanding performance by McDowell as the funny, fierce psychopath. Many memorable, disturbing sequences, including a rape conducted while assailant McDowell belts "Singing in the Rain." Truly outstanding, provocative work from master filmmaker Kubrick.
1971 (R) 137m/C GB Malcolm McDowell, Patrick Magee, Adrienne Corri, David Prowse; *W/D:* Stanley Kubrick. Academy Awards '71 Nominations: Best Adapted Screenplay, Best Director (Kubrick), Best Film Editing, Best Picture; New York Film Critics Awards '71: Best Director (Kubrick), Best Film. VHS, Beta, LV $19.98 WAR, PIA, FCT *ℐℐℐℐ*

Clodhopper A farmboy decides to head out for New York where he achieves fame on Broadway for his dance number, the "Clophooper Glide." He stays true to his hometown girl, however, and returns to save his father's farm from financial ruin. Music by R. Cameron Menzies.
1917 47m/B Charles Ray, Margery Wilson; *D:* Victor Schertzinger. VHS, Beta $16.95 GPV, CCB, DVT *ℐℐ*

The Clones A doctor discovers a government experiment engineered to murder him with a perfect clone.
1973 (PG) 90m/C Michael Greene, Gregory Sierra; *D:* Paul Hunt, Lamar Card. VHS, Beta $69.98 LIV, HHE *ℐ*

Clones of Bruce Lee It's a martial arts free-for-all as bold masters from throughout the world duel for supremacy in the realm of self defense. If you like martial arts movies, you'll probably like this one. If you don't know if you like martial arts movies, find out with one of the actual Bruce Lee's flicks.
1980 (R) 87m/C Dragon Lee, Bruce Le, Bruce Lai, Bruce Thai; *D:* Joseph Kong. VHS, Beta $49.95 MED *ℐℐ*

The Clonus Horror A scientist discovers a government plot to clone the population by freezing bodies alive and using their parts in surgery. *AKA:* Parts: The Clonus Horror.
1979 90m/C Tim Donnelly, Keenan Wynn, Peter Graves, Dick Sargent, Paulette Breen; *D:* Robert S. Fiveson. VHS, Beta $69.98 LIV *ℐ½*

Close Encounters of the Third Kind Middle-American strangers become involved in the attempts of benevolent aliens to contact earthlings. Despite the sometimes mundane nature of the characters, this Spielberg epic is a stirring achievement. Studded with classic sequences, and the ending is an exhilarating experience of special effects and peace-on-earth feelings. Dreyfuss and Dillon excel as friends who are at once bewildered and obsessed by the alien presence, and French filmmaker Truffaut is also strong as the stern, ultimately kind scientist. Laserdisc includes: formerly edited scenes, live interviews with Spielberg, special effects man Douglas Trumbull, and composer John Williams, publicity materials, and over 1,000 production photos.
1977 (PG) 152m/C Richard Dreyfuss, Teri Garr, Melinda Dillon, Francois Truffaut, Bob Balaban; *D:* Steven Spielberg; *M:* John Williams. Academy Awards '77: Best Cinematography, Best Sound Effects Editing; Nominations: Best Art Direction/Set Decoration, Best Director (Spielberg), Best Film Editing, Best Sound, Best Supporting Actress (Dillon), Best Original Score; National Board of Review Awards '77: 10 Best Films of the Year. VHS, Beta, LV $14.95 COL, CRC *ℐℐℐℐ*

Close My Eyes A hot, steamy summer arouses vibrant passions in a brother and sister, and neither marriage nor blood relation can halt the inevitable.
1991 (R) 105m/C Alan Rickman, Clive Owen, Saskia Reeves; *D:* Stephen Poliakoff. VHS $89.95 ACA *ℐℐ*

Close to Home A runaway fleeing a home life of abuse and neglect befriends a TV journalist doing a story on similar girls. She turns to him for support after she is arrested and returned home. Merely mediocre.
1986 93m/C CA Daniel Allman, Jillian Fargey, Anne Petrie; *D:* Rick Beairsto. VHS, Beta $79.95 TWE *ℐℐ*

Closely Watched Trains A novice train dispatcher attempts to gain sexual experience in German-occupied Czechoslovakia during WWII. Many funny scenes in this film regarded by some as a classic. Based upon the classic Czech novel by Bohumil Hrabal and subtitled in English.
1966 89m/C CZ Vaclav Neckar, Jitka Bendova, Vladimir Valenta, Josef Somr; *D:* Jiri Menzel. VHS, Beta, LV $59.95 TAM, FXL, COL *ℐℐℐ½*

The Closer Aiello is "The Closer," a high-powered salesman whose world is falling apart. Somewhere between the money and the power, he's lost touch with his family and the truly important things in life. Is it too late to get them back?
1991 (R) 87m/C Danny Aiello, Michael Pare, Joe Cortese, Justine Bateman, Diane Baker, James Karen, Rick Aiello, Michael Lerner; *D:* Dimitri Logothetis. VHS, LV $19.95 ACA *ℐℐ½*

Closet Cases of the Nerd Kind In this comical takeoff on "Close Encounters of the Third Kind," a zany assortment of mortals meet up with extraterrestrials. All of the memorable scenes of the Spielberg film are recreated and spoofed.
1980 12m/C VHS, Beta PYR *ℐℐ½*

Closet Land Severe, stylized political allegory aims high but fails to convincingly distill totalitarian repression into just two characters—a government inquisitor and his captive, a woman subjected to hideous mental and physical torture. Child-molesting emerges as an ill-advised subtheme. A better video on the same subject: "Interrogation," from Poland.
1990 (R) 95m/C Madeleine Stowe, Alan Rickman; *W/D:* Radha Bharadwaj. VHS, Beta, LV $92.98 FXV, VTR *ℐℐ½*

Cloud Dancer A self-absorbed acrobat uses and abuses those around him, including his girlfriend. Carradine and O'Neill fail to distinguish themselves in this mediocre film.

1980 (PG) 107m/C David Carradine, Jennifer O'Neill, Joseph Bottoms, Colleen Camp; **D:** Barry Brown. **VHS, Beta** $9.99 *STE, PSM* ♫♫

Cloud Waltzing The screen version of a Harlequin romance about a journalist who arrives in France to interview a vintner and finds romance and danger. Melodrama bolstered by the presence of photogenic Beller. 1987 103m/C Kathleen Beller, Francois-Eric Gendron, Paul Maxwell, Therese Liotard, Claude Gensac, David Baxt; **D:** Gordon Flemyng. **VHS, Beta** $19.95 *PAR* ♫♫½

Clouds Over Europe A test pilot and a man from Scotland Yard team up to find out why new bomber planes are disappearing. *AKA:* Q Planes. 1939 82m/B Laurence Olivier, Valerie Hobson, Ralph Richardson; **D:** Tim Whelan. **VHS, Beta, LV** $49.95 *SUE* ♫♫♫

Clown A broken-down funny man with a worshipful son obtains one last career opportunity. This "Champ"-derived tearjerker features credible playing from Skelton and Considine as father and son, respectively. 1953 91m/B Red Skelton, Jane Greer, Tim Considine, Steve Forrest; **D:** Robert Z. Leonard. **VHS, Beta** $49.95 *MGM* ♫♫½

Clown House Young brothers are stalked in their home by three demonic clowns. 1988 (R) 95m/C Nathan Forrest Winters, Brian McHugh, Sam Rockwell, Viletta Skillman, Timothy Enos, Tree; **D:** Victor Salva. **VHS, Beta, LV** $89.95 *COL* ♫

Clown Murders Posh Halloween party is undone when a cruel group fakes a kidnapping to ruin a too-prosperous pal's business deal. Awkward thriller boasts little suspense. Candy plays it straight, mostly, in this one. 1983 94m/C John Candy, Al Waxman, Susan Keller, Lawrence Dane; **D:** Martyn Burke. **VHS, Beta** $59.95 *TWE* ♫½

Clowning Around Simon, who has lived in foster homes all his life, dreams of becoming a famous circus clown. When he's sent to a new home, his new foster parents think his idea is silly, so he runs away and joins the circus. There he meets Anatole, a European clown has-been who can no longer perform because of injuries. Simon believes Anatole can teach him about clowning, so he follows Anatole to Paris to help make his dream come true. Part of the "Wonderworks" series. 199? 165m/C VHS $29.95 *PME, HMV, BTV* ♫ ½

The Clowns An idiosyncratic documentary about circus clowns. Director Fellini has fashioned an homage that is sincere, entertaining, and personal. Contains some truly poignant sequences. Made for Italian television with English subtitles. 1971 (G) 90m/C *IT W/D:* Federico Fellini; *M:* Nino Rota. **VHS, Beta** $39.95 *HTV, NOS, MRV* ♫♫♫½

The Club A soccer coach tries to train and motivate a mediocre squad into worthy of playing for—and perhaps even winning—the league cup. Conventional sports story is significantly improved by Thompson's rendering of the coach. *AKA:* Players. 1981 (PG) 99m/C *AU* Jack Thompson, Graham Kennedy, Frank Wilson, John Howard, Alan Cassell; **D:** Bruce Beresford. **VHS, Beta** $19.95 *ACA* ♫♫♫

Club Extinction A near-future thriller in which Berlin is plagued by a wave of suicides. An investigator suspects a spa representative and a media tycoon of being involved. Features a fine international cast, but the film is a lesser venture from prolific master Chabrol. *AKA:* Docteur M.

1989 (R) 105m/C *GE* Alan Bates, Andrew McCarthy, Jennifer Beals, Jan Niklas; **D:** Claude Chabrol. **VHS, Beta** $89.95 *PSM, FCT* ♫♫½

Club Fed A rigid prison warden's plot to impose greater discipline is undone by inmate highjinks. Crude laughs and one-dimensional play from a cast of recognizable names and faces. 1991 (PG-13) 93m/C Judy Landers, Sherman Hemsley, Karen Black, Burt Young, Rick Schmidt, Allen Garfield, Joseph Campanella, Lyle Alzado, Mary Woronov, Debbie Lee Carrington; **D:** Nathaniel Christian. **VHS, Beta** $79.95 *PSM* ♫ ½

Club Havana A benevolent nightclub owner tries to save one of his singers from the depths of despair by reuniting her with her boyfriend. Minor musical with minor musical numbers. ♫Besame Mucho; Tico Tico. 1946 62m/B Tom Neal, Margaret Lindsay, Don Douglas, Isabelita, Dorothy Morris, Ernest Truex; **D:** Edgar G. Ulmer. **VHS, Beta** $16.95 *SNC* ♫½

Club Life A hardened biker finds sex, drugs, and violence on the Hollywood streets. What did he expect? Peace, love, and understanding? 1986 (R) 93m/C Tony Curtis, Dee Wallace Stone, Tom Parsekian, Michael Parks, Jamie Barrett; **D:** Norman Thaddeus Vane. **VHS, Beta** $9.99 *STE, PSM* ♫

Club Med An insecure comedian and his goofy friend try to make the most of a ski vacation. Perhaps your only chance to see Thicke, Killy, and Coolidge together. 1983 (PG) 60m/C Alan Thicke, Jim Carrey, Jean-Claude Killy, Rita Coolidge, Ronnie Hawkins; **D:** David Mitchell, Bob Giraldi. **VHS, Beta** $39.95 *AHV* ♫♫

Club Paradise A Chicago fireman flees the big city for a faltering tropical resort and tries to develop some night life. Somewhat disappointing with Williams largely playing the straight man. Most laughs provided by Martin, particularly when she is assaulted by a shower, and Moranis, who gets lost while windsurfing. 1986 (PG-13) 96m/C Robin Williams, Peter O'Toole, Rick Moranis, Andrea Martin, Jimmy Cliff, Brian Doyle-Murray, Twiggy, Eugene Levy, Adolph Caesar, Joanna Cassidy, Mary Gross, Carey Lowell; **D:** Harold Ramis. **VHS, Beta, LV** $19.98 *WAR* ♫♫½

Clue The popular boardgame's characters must unravel a night of murder at a spooky Victorian mansion. The entire cast seems to be subsisting on sugar, with wild eyes and frantic movements the order of the day. Butler Curry best survives the uneven script and direction. Warren is appealing too. The theatrical version played with three alternative endings, and the video version shows all three successively. 1985 (PG) 96m/C Lesley Ann Warren, Tim Curry, Martin Mull, Madeline Kahn, Michael McKean, Christopher Lloyd, Eileen Brennan, Howard Hesseman, Lee Ving, Jane Wiedlin, Colleen Camp; **D:** Jonathan Lynn. **VHS, Beta, LV** $19.95 *PAR* ♫♫½

The Clutching Hand The Clutching Hand seeks a formula that will turn metal into gold and detective Craig Kennedy is out to prevent him from doing so. A serial in 15 chapters on three cassettes. 1936 268m/B Jack Mulhall, Rex Lease. **VHS, Beta** $26.95 *SNC, NOS, VDM* ♫♫

Coach Sexy woman is unintentionally hired to coach a high school basketball team and mold rookies into lusty young champions. Low-grade roundball fever.

1978 (PG) 100m/C Cathy Lee Crosby, Michael Biehn, Keenan Wynn, Sidney Wicks; **D:** Bud Townsend. **VHS, Beta** $9.95 *MED* ♫½

Coal Miner's Daughter A strong bio of country singer Loretta Lynn, who rose from Appalachian poverty to Nashville riches. Spacek is perfect in the lead, and she even provides acceptable rendering of Lynn's tunes. Band drummer Helm shines as Lynn's father, and Jones is strong as Lynn's downhome husband. Uneven melodrama toward the end, but the film is still a good one. ♫Coal Miner's Daughter; Sweet Dreams of You; I'm a Honky-Tonk Girl; You're Lookin' at Country; One's On the Way; You Ain't Woman Enough to Take My Man; Back in My Baby's Arms. 1980 (PG) 125m/C Sissy Spacek, Tommy Lee Jones, Levon Helm, Beverly D'Angelo; **D:** Michael Apted. Academy Awards '80: Best Actress (Spacek); Nominations: Best Adapted Screenplay, Best Art Direction/Set Decoration, Best Cinematography, Best Film Editing, Best Picture; Golden Globe Awards '81: Best Actress—Musical/Comedy (Spacek), Best Film—Musical/Comedy; Los Angeles Film Critics Association Awards '80: Best Actress (Spacek); National Board of Review Awards '80: 10 Best Films of the Year, Best Actress (Spacek); National Society of Film Critics Awards '80: Best Actress (Spacek). **VHS, Beta, LV** $14.95 *MCA, PIA, BTV* ♫♫♫

The Coast Patrol B. Reeves Eason, responsible for the chariot scene in the silent "Ben Hur" and the action scenes in "The Charge of the Light Brigade," directed Fay in one of her earliest parts, eight years before the role that prompted her to say "I didn't realize that King Kong and I were going to be together for the rest of our lives, and longer..." Much Eason-style high action when smugglers meet the coast patrol. 1925 63m/B Kenneth McDonald, Claire De Lorez, Fay Wray; **D:** B. Reeves Eason. **VHS, Beta** $19.95 *NOS, GPV, FCI* ♫♫½

Coast to Coast A wacky woman escapes from a mental institution and teams with a pugnacious trucker for a cross-country spree. Ostensibly freewheeling comedy is only occasionally worthwhile despite appropriate playing from leads Cannon and Blake, who deserve better. 1980 (PG) 95m/C Dyan Cannon, Robert (Bobby) Blake, Quinn Redeker, Michael Lerner, Maxine Stuart, Bill Lucking; **D:** Joseph Sargent. **VHS, Beta, LV** $49.95 *PAR* ♫♫

Cobra To pay off the debts incurred by his profligate playbuoyance, Valentino takes a job with an antique dealer, falls for the dealer's secretary and arranges an assignation with the dealer's wife, who is inconveniently killed at the designated rendezvous. Complications abound as Valentino finds himself Shiek out of luck. Not a prequel to the flag-wagging Stallone vehicle, this lesser Valentino effort—directed by Henabery (who played Lincoln in "The Birth of a Nation")—was released a year before the famous heartthrob's untimely death, and enjoyed a rather acrid critical reception. Which isn't to say the public didn't flock to see the Italian stallion flare his nostrils. 1925 70m/B Rudolph Valentino, Nita Naldi, Casson Ferguson, Gertrude Olmsted; **D:** Joseph Henabery. **VHS, Beta** $27.95 *GPV, FCT* ♫

The Cobra A tightlipped U.S. agent ogles a voluptuous siren when not fighting opium smugglers from the Middle East. A must for all admirers of Ekberg. *AKA:* Il Cobra; El Cobra. 1968 93m/C Dana Andrews, Anita Ekberg; **D:** Mario Sequi. **VHS** *NO* ♫

Cobra A hired killer destroys most of a mob family and becomes the target of revenge for the lone survivor. Moody thriller boasts an international cast. *AKA:* le Sant de l'Ange. **1971 93m/C** *FR IT* Sterling Hayden, Senta Berger, Jean Yanne; *D:* Yves Boisset. **VHS, Beta $59.95** *UNI* ♂♂½

Cobra A cold-blooded cop protects a model from a gang of deranged killers. Lowbrow, manipulative action fare void of feeling. Truly exploitive, with little expression from the leads. Highlight is the extended chase sequence. **1986 (R) 87m/C** Sylvester Stallone, Reni Santoni, Brigitte Nielsen, Andrew Robinson; *D:* George P. Cosmatos. **VHS, Beta, LV $19.98** *WAR* ♂

Cobra Two martial-arts masters duel to the death. Isn't that what always happens in these chop-sock affairs? **19?? 90m/C** Bruce Lee. **VHS, Beta $19.99** *BFV* ♂

Cobra Against Ninja Once again, two martial arts experts try to kill each other. Can't be many of these fellas left. **198? 88m/C** Jimmy Bosco, Paul Branney, Gary Carter, Alan Friss, Alfred Pears; *D:* Joseph Lai. **VHS $59.95** *IMP* ♂

The Cobra Strikes Nosey thief gets more than he bargained for when he works his way through an inventor's studio. Low-budget and unexceptional. **1948 62m/B** Sheila Ryan, Richard Fraser, Leslie Brooks, Herbert Heyes; *D:* Charles F. Reisner. **VHS $19.95** *NOS, MOV, RXM* ♂½

The Cobweb Shady goings on are uncovered at a psychiatric ward run by a bunch of neurotic administrators. A strong cast, director and producer do not add much to this dull outing. **1955 125m/C** Lauren Bacall, Richard Widmark, Gloria Grahame, Charles Boyer, Lillian Gish, John Kerr, Susan Strasberg, Oscar Levant, Tommy Rettig, Paul Stewart, Adele Jergens, Bert Freed, Sandy Descher, Fay Wray, Virginia Christine; *D:* Vincente Minnelli. **LV $39.98** *MGM* ♂♂

The Coca-Cola Kid A smug sales executive treks to Australia to improve regional sales and becomes embroiled in sexual and professional shenanigans. Roberts is strong in the difficult lead role, and Scacchi is compelling in an awkwardly constructed part. Ambitious satire is somewhat scattershot, with more storylines than it needs. Still, filmmaker Makavejev is usually capable of juggling the entire enterprise. **1984 (R) 94m/C** *AU* Eric Roberts, Greta Scacchi, Bill Kerr; *D:* Dusan Makavejev. **VHS, Beta, LV $19.95** *LIV, VES, FCT* ♂♂♂½

Cocaine Cowboys Lame rockers support themselves between gigs by peddling drugs then find out they've run afoul of the mob. Palance is the only worthwhile aspect of this rambling venture produced at Andy Warhol's home. **1979 (R) 90m/C** Jack Palance, Andy Warhol, Tom Sullivan, Suzanna Love; *D:* Ulli Lommel. **VHS, Beta** *MED, OM* ♂

Cocaine Fiends Drug use leads siblings into a squalid life of addiction, crime, prostitution, and eventually suicide. Ostensibly straight morality tale functions better as loopy camp. Features memorable slang. *AKA:* The Pace That Kills. **1936 74m/B** Lois January, Noel Madison; *D:* W.A. Conner. **VHS, Beta $16.95** *SNC, NOS, MED* ♂♂

Cocaine: One Man's Seduction Made-for-television film documents one man's degeneration into drug addiction. Weaver snorts convincingly in lead. **1983 97m/C** Dennis Weaver, Karen Grassle, Pamela Bellwood, David Ackroyd; *D:* Paul Wendkos. **VHS, Beta $14.95** *FRH, CHI* ♂♂½

Cocaine Wars An undercover U.S. agent kills dozens while trying to rescue his kidnapped girlfriend from an evil South American drug tycoon. Violent, but otherwise unaffecting. **1986 (R) 82m/C** John Schneider, Kathryn Witt, Royal Dano; *D:* Hector Olivera. **VHS, Beta $19.95** *MED* ♂

Cockeyed Cavaliers Wheeler and Woolsey are stockaded for stealing the Duke's horses and carriage. To escape jail they swap clothes with some drunken royalty. **1934 70m/B** Bert Wheeler, Robert Woolsey, Dorothy Lee, Thelma Todd; *D:* Mark Sandrich. **VHS, Beta $34.98** *CCB* ♂♂

Cockfighter A unique, grim portrait of a cockfighting trainer. Oates, in the lead, provides voiceover narrations, but the film otherwise remains silent until the end. Strong support from Stanton. Interesting, violent fare. *AKA:* Gamblin' Man; Born to Kill; Wild Drifters. **1974 (R) 84m/C** Warren Oates, Harry Dean Stanton, Richard B. Shull, Troy Donahue, Millie Perkins; *D:* Monte Hellman. **VHS, Beta $59.98** *SUE* ♂♂♂

Cocktail A smug young man finds fame and fortune as a proficient, flashy bartender, charming the ladies with his bottle and glass juggling act. Slick, superficial film boasts a busy soundtrack and serviceable exchanges between male leads Cruise and Brown. There's less chemistry between Cruise and love interest Shue. Filmed in a high-tech rock video style. **1988 (R) 103m/C** Tom Cruise, Bryan Brown, Elisabeth Shue, Lisa Banes, Laurence Luckinbill, Kelly Lynch, Gina Gershon, Ron Dean, Paul Benedict; *D:* Roger Donaldson. **VHS, Beta, LV, 8mm $19.99** *TOU* ♂♂½

The Cocoanuts In their film debut, the Marx Brothers create their trademark, indescribable mayhem. Stagey, technically crude comedy nonetheless delights with zany, free-for-all exchanges, antics. Includes famous "viaduct" exchange. Songs by Irving Berlin; written by George S. Kaufman and Morrie Ryskind. **1929 96m/B** Groucho Marx, Chico Marx, Harpo Marx, Zeppo Marx, Margaret Dumont, Kay Francis, Oscar Shaw, Mary Eaton; *D:* Robert Florey, Joseph Santley. **VHS, Beta, LV $19.95** *MCA* ♂♂½

Cocoon Humanist fantasy in which senior citizens discover their fountain of youth is actually a breeding ground for aliens. Heartwarming, one-of-a kind drama showcases elderly greats Ameche, Brimley, Gilford, Cronyn, and Tandy. A commendable, recommendable venture. Based on David Saperstein's novel and followed by "Cocoon: The Return." **1985 (PG-13) 117m/C** Wilford Brimley, Brian Dennehy, Steve Guttenberg, Don Ameche, Tahnee Welch, Jack Gilford, Hume Cronyn, Jessica Tandy, Gwen Verdon, Maureen Stapleton, Tyrone Power Jr., Barret Oliver, Linda Harrison. **VHS, Beta, LV $19.98** *FOX, FCT, BTV* ♂♂♂

Cocoon: The Return Old timers who left with aliens in "Cocoon" return to earth and face grave problems. Less compelling sequel misses guiding hand of earlier film's director, Ron Howard. Still, most of cast from the original is on board here, and the film has its moments. **1988 (PG) 116m/C** Don Ameche, Wilford Brimley, Steve Guttenberg, Maureen Stapleton, Hume Cronyn, Jessica Tandy, Gwen Verdon, Jack Gilford, Tahnee Welch, Courteney Cox, Brian Dennehy, Barret Oliver; *D:* Daniel Petrie. **VHS, Beta, LV $19.98** *FOX* ♂

C.O.D. Bosom buddies must develop advertising campaign for brassiere producer or find their careers are bust. Premise milked for all its worth, so you may want to keep abreast of this one. On the other hand, you may not give a hoot. Oh well, tit for tat. **1983 (PG) 96m/C** Chris Lemmon, Olivia Pascal, Jennifer Richards, Corinne Alphen, Teresa Ganzel, Carole Davis; *D:* Chuck Vincent. **VHS, Beta $69.95** *VES, LIV* ♂

Code Name Alpha You don't have to have a federal case of intelligence to figure out where this FBI story's going and how it's going to get there. Someone's smuggling sophisticated electrical components to the communists, and a team of intelligence agents, including Granger and Schiaffino, hike over to Hong Kong to break up the party. *AKA:* Red Dragon; A-009 Missione Hong Kong. **1967 89m/C** *IT GE* Stewart Granger, Rosanna Schiaffino, Harald Juhnke, Paul Klinger, Helga Sommerfeld, Horst Frank; *D:* Ernest Hofbauer. **VHS $14.99** *VTR* ♂♂

Code Name: Chaos A political spoof featuring a group of renegade spies trying to come up with a get-rich-quick scheme. It involves inventing a global crisis in a small Asian country but the plan comes under the scrutiny of a CIA agent who's not in on the scheme. *AKA:* Spies, Lies, and Alibis. **1990 (?) 96m/C** Robert Loggia, Diane Ladd, David Warner, Alice Krige, Brian Kerwin; *D:* Antony Thomas. **VHS $89.98** *LIV, MOV, LIV* ♂♂

Code Name: Dancer A retired spy leaves her peaceful life, husband and family to take care of business in Cuba. Made for television. **1987 93m/C** Kate Capshaw, Jeroen Krabbe, Gregory Sierra, Cliff DeYoung. **VHS $89.95** *VMK* ♂♂

Code Name: Diamond Head In Hawaii, a secret agent is assigned to retrieve a deadly chemical that has been hidden by a master of disguises. Made for television. **1977 78m/C** Roy Thinnes, France Nuyen, Zulu, Ian McShane; *D:* Jeannot Szwarc. **VHS, Beta $49.95** *WOV* ♂

Code Name: Emerald WWII drama in which an American agent must stop an enemy spy with knowledge of impending D-Day invasion. Conventional TV fare boasts a fine performance by von Sydow, but Stolz is hopelessly miscast as an adult. Perhaps the only film featuring both Bucholz and Berger. First feature film by NBC-TV network. **1985 (PG) 95m/C** Ed Harris, Max von Sydow, Eric Stoltz, Horst Buchholz, Helmut Berger, Cyrielle Claire, Patrick Stewart, Graham Crowden; *D:* Jonathan Sanger. **VHS, Beta, LV $79.98** *FOX* ♂

Code Name: Zebra The Zebra Force helps the cops put bad guys away. When the bad guys get out, they want revenge. The result: lots of violence and action. Wasn't released theatrically. **1984 96m/C** Jim Mitchum, Mike Lane, Timmy Brown, Joe Dante, Deana Jurgens, Frank Sinatra Jr.; *D:* Joe Tornatore. **VHS, Beta $79.95** *TWE* ♂½

Code of Honor A young woman vows revenge on the military commanders who caused her brother's demise. Neatly made psychological thriller is surprisingly good for a TV movie. *AKA:* Sweet Revenge.

1984 105m/C Kevin Dobson, Wings Hauser, Alec Baldwin, Merritt Butrick, Kelly McGillis, Alfre Woodard, Savannah Smith, Helen Hunt, Dana Elcar; *D:* David Green. **VHS** $59.95 XVC ✰✰½

Code of Honor Prominent businessman embarks on mission of revenge when police fail to apprehend his wife's rapist. No surprise here. You either enjoy this sort of thing or you lead a reasonably fulfilling life.
1988 90m/C Cameron Mitchell, Mark Sabin. **VHS** NO ✰

Code of Silence A police loner must contend with both a gang war and police department corruption. Hectic, violent action-drama with some wild stunts.
1985 (R) 100m/C Chuck Norris, Henry Silva, Bert Remsen, Molly Hagan, Nathan Davis, Dennis Farina; *D:* Andy Davis. **VHS, Beta, LV** $14.99 HBO, PIA ✰✰

Code of the Fearless A cowboy wins the heart of a beautiful malden while bringing evildoers to justice.
1939 56m/B Fred Scott, Claire Rochelle, John Merton, Harry Harvey, Walter McGrail, Roger Williams; *D:* Raymond K. Johnson. **VHS** $19.95 NOS, DVT ✰

Codename: Foxfire An attractive secret agent is framed for wrongdoing and must clear her name by tracking the enemy spy lurking within the intelligence network. Always interesting Cassidy is an asset, but this by-the-numbers TV film is otherwise a misappropriation of the term "intelligence" in relation to espionage. *AKA:* Slay It Again, Sam.
1985 99m/C Joanna Cassidy, John McCook, Sheryl Lee Ralph, Henry Jones, Luke Andreas; *D:* Corey Allen. **VHS, Beta** $39.95 MCA ✰✰

Codename: Icarus A young mathematical genius, enrolled at a special school for accelerated study uncovers evil government plots to use the students for espionage. Made for British television.
1985 106m/C *GB* Barry Angel, Jack Galloway; *D:* Marilyn Fox. **VHS, Beta** $19.95 FOX, TVC ✰✰

Codename Kyril Edward ("The Equalizer") Woodward plays a British spy pitted against Soviet assassin Kyril (Charleson) who's been sent to England by the KGB to rout out a double agent. Turns out there's more to it than Kyril knows, and nobody loves an assassin. Based on John Trenhaile's "A Man Called Kyril," John Hopkins' script is slow from the gun, but eventually builds something akin to momentum. Made for cable TV.
1991 (R) 115m/C Edward Woodward, Ian Charleson, Denholm Elliott, Joss Ackland, Richard E. Grant; *D:* Ian Sharp. **VHS** $79.98 TTC ✰✰½

Codename: Terminate Title says it all in this tender exploration of the human condition. Jungle-trained mercenaries grab their guns and go after an American pilot shot down behind enemy lines.
1990 84m/C Robert Mason, Jim Gaines. **VHS** NO ✰½

Codename: Vengeance A macho fellow tries to stop a killer holding the shah's wife and son hostage. Dated.
1987 (R) 97m/C Robert Ginty, Cameron Mitchell, Shannon Tweed; *D:* David Winters. **VHS** $79.98 MCG ✰

Codename: Wildgeese The big-name cast of this meandering mercenary macho-rama probably wish they'd been credited under code names; solid histrionics cannot a silly script save. A troop of commandos-for-hire are engaged by the Drug Enforcement Administration to obliterate an opium operation in Asia's infamous Golden Triangle, and

much mindless agitation ensues. *AKA:* Geheimecode Wildganse.
1984 (R) 101m/C *IT GE* Lewis Collins, Lee Van Cleef, Ernest Borgnine, Klaus Kinski, Mimsy Farmer; *D:* Anthony M. Dawson. **VHS** $19.95 STE, NWV ✰½

Cody A former bronco buster wants his son to "take it like a man" when the boy's dog dies. Then a mystical goose arrives to mellow the old man. That's really the plot.
1967 82m/C Tony Becker, Terry Evans. **VHS, Beta** PGN ✰

A Coeur Joie Sixties set piece about a gorgeous woman who must choose between her much older lover or her newfound stud. Bardot and U.K. scenery keep this one from sinking entirely. In French with English subtitles. *AKA:* Two Weeks in September.
1967 100m/C *FR* Brigitte Bardot, Laurent Terzieff; *D:* Serge Bourguignon. **VHS, Beta** $19.95 KRT ✰✰

Coffy A beautiful woman feigns drug addiction to discover and destroy the evil dealers responsible for her sister's death. Grier is everything in this exploitative flick full of violence and nudity.
1973 (R) 91m/C Pam Grier, Booker Bradshaw, Robert DoQui, Allan Arbus; *D:* Jack Hill. **VHS, Beta, LV** $19.98 ORI, FCT ✰✰

Cohen and Tate Two antagonistic mob hitmen kidnap a 9-year-old who witnessed his parent's recent murder by the mob. In order to survive, the boy begins to play one psycho off the other.
1988 (R) 113m/C Roy Scheider, Adam Baldwin, Harley Cross, Cooper Huckabee; *D:* Eric Red. **VHS, Beta, LV** $19.98 SUE, NLC ✰✰

Cold Blood A small dubbed Dutch film about a pair of kidnap victims who turn the tables on their captors.
197? (R) 90m/C *NL* Rutger Hauer. **VHS, Beta** $9.95 SIM, WWV ✰½

Cold Blooded Murder A martial arts master assists the cops in a hunt for a Jack-the-Ripper-style killer. Among Lee's more obscure appearances.
19?? 96m/C Lau Dan, Bruce Lee, Stephen Leung, Chan Wai, Carter Wong; *D:* Albert Law. **VHS** NO ✰

Cold Comfort A father arranges his teen daughter's romance, but finds his plans going awry in this Canadian thriller. Nominated for several Canadian television awards, including Best Actress, Best Actor, Best Picture and Best Musical Score.
1990 (R) 90m/C *CA* Margaret Langrick, Maury Chaykin; *D:* Vic Sarin. **VHS** $89.98 REP ✰✰½

Cold Days Four men await execution for their part in the WWII massacre of Jews and Serbs. Their reminiscences and justifications, if any, are examined. Stunning cinematography and unusual theme for 1960s Hungarian political climate.
1966 102m/C *HU D:* Andras Kovacs. **VHS** $59.95 FCT ✰½

Cold Eyes of Fear A man and his girlfriend are besieged by a raving convict whom his uncle, a judge, had put away years before. Shades of "Cape Fear" on a low budget.
197? 88m/C Fernando Rey, Frank Wolfe, Karin Shubert; *D:* Enzo G. Castellari; *M:* Ennio Morricone. **VHS, Beta** $59.95 TWE ✰

Cold Feet Light romantic comedy about a television director just recovering from a failed marriage and his fall for a lab researcher who just went through a break-up herself.
1984 (PG) 96m/C Griffin Dunne, Marissa Chibas, Blanche Baker, Mark Cronogue; *D:* Bruce Van Dusen. **VHS, Beta** $29.95 FOX ✰✰½

Cold Feet Modern-day western in which a trio of loopy desperados smuggle jewels inside a racehorse's stomach. Quirky comedy offers wild performances from Waits and sex-bomb Kirkland. Could use more laughs, though. Written by Thomas McGuane and Jim Harrison and filmed largely on McGuane's ranch.
1989 (R) 94m/C Keith Carradine, Tom Waits, Sally Kirkland, Rip Torn, Kathleen York, Bill Pullman; *D:* Robert Dornhelm. **VHS, Beta, LV** $89.95 LIV ✰✰½

Cold Front A hired assassin turned serial killer is hunted by two dedicated cops.
1989 (R) 94m/C Martin Sheen, Michael Ontkean, Beverly D'Angelo, Kim Coates; *D:* Paul Bnarbic. **VHS, Beta, LV** $89.99 HBO ✰½

Cold Heat When a custody battle rocks a crime boss' world, he pulls out all the stops in the war against his wife.
1990 85m/C John Phillip Law, Britt Ekland, Robert Sacchi, Roy Summerset, Joanne Watkins, Chance Michael Corbitt; *D:* Ulli Lommel. **VHS, Beta** $79.95 AIP ✰✰

Cold Heaven Alex and Marie Davenport are on vacation when an accident occurs and Alex dies—or does he? The next day his body disappears and his unfaithful wife begins to have paranoid delusions that he is returning to exact retribution for her affair. But these aren't her only visions, for during the past year Marie has also had religious visions she believes are part of a personal battle with God. Harmon does what he can with his role as the alleged corpse but Russell is uncharacteristically whiny and bland. Convoluted story of marriage, death, and spirituality; doesn't pan out on any accounts. Based on a novel by Brian Moore.
1992 (R) 103m/C Theresa Russell, Mark Harmon, James Russo, Talia Shire, Will Patton, Richard Bradford; *D:* Nicolas Roeg; *W:* Allan Scott. **VHS, LV** $92.95 HMD, FCT ✰½

Cold Justice An ex-prizefighter (Daltrey) and his friends welcome an English priest into their tough southside Chicago neighborhood. The good father seems too good to be true as he befriends the locals—even raising funds for the children's hospital. When the funds never make it to the hospital and the neighborhood begins to experience a number of violent tragedies, the residents decide to take their own revenge.
1989 (R) 94m/C Dennis Waterman, Roger Daltrey, Penelope Milford, Ron Dean, Bert Rosario; *W/D:* Terry Green. **VHS, LV** $89.95 COL ✰✰

Cold River An experienced guide takes his two children on an extended trip through the Adirondacks. For the children, it's a fantasy vacation until their father succumbs to a heart attack in the chilly mountains. "Cold River" is a journey of survival, and an exploration of human relationships.
1981 (PG) 94m/C Pat Petersen, Richard Jaeckel, Suzanne Weber; *D:* Fred G. Sullivan. **VHS, Beta** $59.98 FOX ✰✰

Cold Room College student on vacation with her father in East Berlin discovers the horrors hidden in an antiquated hotel room next to hers. Made for cable television. From the novel by Jeffrey Caine. *AKA:* The Prisoner.
1984 95m/C George Segal, Renee Soutendijk, Amanda Pays, Warran Clarke, Anthony Higgins; *D:* James Dearden. **VHS, Beta** $59.95 FOX ✰½

Cold Sassy Tree Endearing romance of a scandalous May-December marriage as perceived by the younger woman's teenage son. Dunaway and Widmark shine, and small town pettiness is vividly rendered. Adapted

from the books by Olive Ann Burns. A superior made-for-cable production.
1989 95m/C Faye Dunaway, Richard Widmark, Neil Patrick Harris, Frances Fisher, Lee Garlington, John M. Jackson; *D:* Joan Tewkesbury. **VHS $14.98** TTC 🎞🎞🎞½

Cold Steel Standard revenge drama about a hardnosed Los Angeles cop tracking his father's disfigured psycho-killer. Cast includes the always intense Davis, ex-pop star Ant, and screen scorchstress Stone. Still it's predictable, low-grade fare.
1987 (R) 91m/C Brad Davis, Jonathan Banks, Adam Ant, Sharon Stone; *D:* Dorothy Ann Puzo. **VHS, Beta $79.95** COL 🎞½

Cold Steel for Tortuga An Italian epic about a mercenary rescuing his woman and his gold from an evil governor. Dubbed.
1965 95m/C *IT* Guy Madison, Rick Battaglia, Ingeborg Schoener; *D:* Luigi Capuano. **VHS, Beta** NO 🎞

Cold Sweat A brutal drug trader takes his ultra-violent revenge after his wife is captured by a drug boss' moronic henchmen. Typical Bronson flick boasts superior supporting cast of Ullman and Mason. Writing and direction, however, are mediocre. *AKA:* L'Uomo Dalle Due Ombre; De la Part des Copains.
1974 (PG) 94m/C *IT FR* Charles Bronson, Jill Ireland, Liv Ullmann, James Mason; *D:* Terence Young. **VHS, Beta $59.95** GEM, MRV 🎞🎞

Cold Turkey Often witty satire about what happens when an entire town tries to stop smoking for a contest. Van Dyke is fine as the anti-smoking minister; newscasters Bob and Ray are riotous; oldtimer Horton's swansong. Wholesome, somewhat tame fare.
1971 (PG) 99m/C Dick Van Dyke, Pippa Scott, Tom Poston, Bob Newhart, Vincent Gardenia, Barnard Hughes, Jean Stapleton, Graham Jarvis, Edward Everett Horton; *D:* Norman Lear. **VHS, Beta, LV $19.95** MGM 🎞🎞

Cold War Killers Soviet and British agents vie for control of prized cargo plane recently retrieved from the sea floor.
1986 (PG) 85m/C *GB* Terence Stamp; *D:* William Brayne. **VHS, Beta $79.95** WWV 🎞½

Coldfire Two rookie cops work to undo the havoc unleashed on the streets of LA because of a deadly new drug sought for its powerful high. Not many surprises here.
1990 90m/C Wings Hauser, Kamar Reyes, Robert Viharo, Gary Swanson; *D:* Wings Hauser. **VHS, LV $19.95** PMH 🎞½

The Colditz Story Prisoners of war from the Allied countries join together in an attempt to escape from Colditz, an allegedly escape-proof castle-prison deep within the Third Reich.
1955 93m/B John Mills, Eric Portman, Lionel Jeffries, Bryan Forbes, Ian Carmichael, Anton Diffring; *D:* Guy Hamilton. **VHS, Beta $59.99** HBO 🎞🎞½

Cole Justice An older man, haunted by the memory of his girlfriend's rape and murder thirty-five years earlier, takes to the streets to protect innocent citizens from lowlife criminals. Somewhat unusual revenge pic filmed in and around Tulsa, Oklahoma.
1989 90m/C Carl Bartholomew, Keith Andrews, Mike Wiles, Nick Zickefoose; *D:* Carl Bartholomew. **VHS, Beta $9.95** SIM 🎞🎞

The Collector Compelling adaptation of the John Fowles novel about a withdrawn butterfly collector who decides to add to his collection by kidnapping a beautiful girl he admires. He locks her in his cellar hoping she will fall in love with him. Chilling, unsettling

drama with Stamp unnerving, yet sympathetic in lead.
1965 119m/C *GB* Terence Stamp, Samantha Eggar, Maurice Dallimore, Mona Washbourne; *D:* William Wyler. Academy Awards '65 Nominations: Best Actress (Eggar), Best Adapted Screenplay, Best Director (Wyler); Cannes Film Festival '65: Best Actor (Stamp), Best Actress (Eggar). **VHS, Beta, LV $59.95** COL 🎞🎞🎞½

Collector's Item Two lovers reunite after 16 years and a flurry of memories temporarily rekindles their passion, which comes dangerously close to obsession. Casting of the physically bountiful Antonelli helps this effective erotic drama.
1989 99m/C *IT* Tony Musante, Laura Antonelli, Florinda Bolkan; *D:* Giuseppe Patroni Griffi. **VHS, Beta** NO 🎞🎞

College A high school valedictorian tries out for every sport in college, hoping to win the girl. Vintage Keaton antics, including disaster as a soda jerk, an attempt to be a track star, and the pole vault through a window to rescue the damsel in distress. Musical score by John Muri.
1927 60m/B Buster Keaton, A. Cornwall, Harold Goodwin; *D:* James W. Horne. **VHS, Beta, LV $19.95** DVT, MRV, CCB 🎞🎞🎞½

College Swing Lightweight, lackluster musical about Allen inheriting a small town college which she turns into a hangout for her vaudeville pals. Top cast is basically wasted performing many forgettable songs and familiar routines. Based on an adaptation by Frederick Hazlitt Brennan from a story by Ted Lesser. ♫College Swing; What Did Romeo Say to Juliet?; I Fall In Love With You Every Day; You're a Natural; The Old School Bell; Moments Like This; How D'ja Like to Love Me?; What a Rumba Does to Romance. *AKA:* Swing, Teacher, Swing.
1938 86m/B George Burns, Gracie Allen, Martha Raye, Bob Hope, Edward Everett Horton, Ben Blue, Betty Grable, Jackie Coogan, John Payne; *D:* Raoul Walsh. **VHS $14.98** MCA 🎞🎞

Collision Course A wise-cracking cop from Detroit teams up with Japan's best detective to nail a ruthless gang leader. Release was delayed until 1992 due to a lawsuit, but it was resolved in time to coordinate the release when Leno's debut as the host of "The Tonight Show." Pretty marginal, but diehard fans of Leno may appreciate it. Filmed on location in Detroit.
1989 (PG) 99m/C Pat Morita, Jay Leno, Chris Sarandon, Al Waxman. **VHS, Beta $89.99** HBO 🎞

The Colombian Connection America's best undercover agent battles a powerful cocaine empire deep in the jungles of the Amazon, where slave labor and political corruption abound.
1991 90m/C Miles O'Keeffe, Henry Silva. **VHS, Beta** NO 🎞🎞

Colonel Effingham's Raid A retired army colonel uses military tactics to keep an old historical courthouse open, while defeating some crooked politicians in the process. *AKA:* Man of the Hour.
1945 70m/B Joan Bennett, Charles Coburn, William Eythe, Donald Meek; *D:* Irving Pichel. **VHS, Beta $19.95** NOS, HEG, TIM 🎞🎞

Colonel Redl Absorbing, intricately rendered psychological study of an ambitious officer's rise and fall in pre-World War I Austria. Brandauer is excellent as the vain, insecure homosexual ultimately undone by his own ambition and his superior officer's smug loathing. Muller-Stahl and Landgrebe are particularly distinguished among the supporting players. The second in the Szabo/Brandauer trilogy, after "Mephisto" and be-

fore "Hanussen." In German with English subtitles.
1984 114m/C *GE HU* Klaus Maria Brandauer, Armin Mueller-Stahl, Gudrun Landgrebe; *D:* Istvan Szabo. **VHS, Beta, LV $29.95** PAV, FCT, GLV 🎞🎞🎞

Colonel Wolodyjowski An adaptation of the monumental novels by Henryk Sinkiewicz chronicling the attack on Poland's eastern border by the Turks in 1668. In Polish with English subtitles.
1969 160m/C *PL* Tadeusz Loniski, Magdalena Zawadzka, Daniel Olbrychski; *D:* Jerzy Hoffman. **VHS $49.95** FCT 🎞🎞½

Color Adventures of Superman Seven cartoon adventures of the Man of Steel animated by the Fleischer Studio between 1941 and 1943. Titles include "Superman," "The Mechanical Monsters," "The Magnetic Telescope," "The Japoteurs," "The Bulleteers," "Jungle Drums," and "The Mummy Strikes."
194? 52m/C **VHS, Beta, 8mm $24.95** VYY 🎞🎞½

Color Me Blood Red Artist decides that the red in his paintings is best rendered with human blood. He even manages to continue his art career—when not busy stabbing and mutilating the unsuspecting citizenry. Short and shoddy. Also known as "Model Massacre."
1964 74m/C Don Joseph, Sandi Conder; *D:* Herschell Gordon Lewis. **VHS, Beta $29.95** NO Woof!

Color Me Dead A victim of an extremely slow-acting poison frantically spends his final days trying to uncover his killer. Another inferior remake of B-thriller "D.O.A." Rent that one instead.
1969 (R) 97m/C *AU* Tom Tryon, Carolyn Jones, Rick Jason, Patricia Connolly, Tony Ward; *D:* Eddie Davis. **VHS** REP, TIM 🎞½

The Color of Money Flashy, gripping drama about former pool hustler Fast Eddie Felsen (Newman) who, after years off the circuit, takes a brilliant but immature pool shark (Cruise) under his wing. Strong performances by Newman as the grizzled veteran, Cruise as the showboating youth, and Mastrantonio and Shaver as the men's worldly girlfriends. Worthy sequel to '50s classic "The Hustler."
1986 (R) 119m/C Paul Newman, Tom Cruise, Mary Elizabeth Mastrantonio, Helen Shaver, John Turturro, Forest Whitaker; *D:* Martin Scorsese. Academy Awards '86: Best Actor (Newman); Nominations: Best Adapted Screenplay, Best Art Direction/Set Decoration, Best Supporting Actress (Mastrantonio). **VHS, Beta, LV $19.95** TOU, BTV 🎞🎞🎞½

The Color Purple Celie is a poor black girl who fights for her self-esteem when she is separated from her sister and forced into a brutal marriage. Spanning 1909 to 1947 in a small Georgia town, the movie chronicles the joys, pains, and people in her life. Adaptation of Alice Walker's acclaimed book features strong lead from Goldberg (her screen debut), Glover, Avery, and talk-show host Winfrey (also her film debut). It's hard to see director Spielberg as the most suited for this one, but he acquits himself nicely, avoiding the facileness that sometimes flaws his pics. Brilliant photography by Allen Davian and musical score by Quincy Jones (who coproduced) compliment this strong film.
1985 (PG-13) 154m/C Whoopi Goldberg, Danny Glover, Oprah Winfrey, Margaret Avery, Adolph Caesar, Rae Dawn Chong, Willard Pugh, Akosua Busia; *D:* Steven Spielberg. Academy Awards '85 Nominations: Best Actress (Goldberg), Best Adapted Screenplay, Best Art Direction/Set Decoration, Best Cinematography, Best Costume Design, Best Makeup, Best Picture, Best Song

("Miss Celie's Blues (Sister)"), Best Supporting Actress (Avery, Winfrey), Best Original Score; Directors Guild of America Awards '85: Best Director (Spielberg); Golden Globe Awards '86: Best Actress—Drama (Goldberg); National Board of Review Awards '85: 10 Best Films of the Year, Best Actress (Goldberg). **VHS, Beta, LV** $19.98 WAR, FCT *XXX*½

Colorado Roy tries to find his brother, a Union deserter, during the Civil War.
1940 54m/B Roy Rogers, George "Gabby" Hayes, Milburn Stone; *D:* Joseph Kane. **VHS, Beta** $9.99 NOS, MED, DVT *X*½

Colorado Serenade Standard oater has Dean, Sharpe and Ates trying to prevent a young outlaw from bullying the local citizenry. Sharpe shows off his athletic prowess, and King provides some laughs. Other than that, it's pretty routine stuff.
1946 68m/C Eddie Dean, David Sharpe, Roscoe Ates, Forrest Taylor, Dennis Moore, Warner Richmond, Bob Duncan, Charles King; *D:* Robert Emmett. **VHS** $19.95 NOS, RXM, HEG *X*

Colorado Sundown A conniving brother and sister attempt to cheat a man out of his inheritance.
1952 67m/B Rex Allen, Mary Ellen Kay, Slim Pickens, June Vincent, Koko; *D:* William Witney. **VHS** $19.95 NOS, DVT, TIM *X*

Colors Vivid, realistic cop drama pairs sympathetic veteran Duvall and trigger-tempered rookie Penn on the gang-infested streets of East Los Angeles. Fine play from leads is one of the many assets in this controversial, unsettling depiction of deadly streetlife. Colorful, freewheeling direction from the underrated Hopper. Rattling rap soundtrack too. Additional footage has been added for video release.
1988 (R) 120m/C Sean Penn, Robert Duvall, Maria Conchita Alonso, Trinidad Silva, Randi Brooks, Grand Bush, Don Cheadle, Rudy Ramos; *D:* Dennis Hopper. **VHS, Beta, LV** $19.98 ORI, FCT *XXX*½

Colossus and the Amazon Queen Idle gladiators are unwillingly recruited for service to Amazons. Doesn't seem like the worst way to make a living. But lead actor Taylor—so notable in comedies, thrillers, and action flicks—is too good for this sort of thing. Dubbed.
1964 94m/C IT Rod Taylor, Dorian Gray, Ed Fury. **VHS, Beta, 8mm** $29.95 VYY *X*½

Colossus of the Arena In 4th century Rome, Forest plays a mighty gladiator who uncovers a plot to imprison a beautiful princess. Through an incredible series of feats and combats, he exposes an evil duke as a traitor.
1960 ?m/C Mark Forest, Scilla Gabel. **VHS** $16.95 SNC *X*

Colossus: The Forbin Project A computer designed to manage U.S. defense systems teams instead with its Soviet equal and they attempt world domination. Wiretight, suspenseful film seems at once dated yet timely. Based on the novel by D.F. Jones. *AKA:* The Forbin Project.
1970 100m/C Eric Braeden, Susan Clark, Gordon Pinsent; *D:* Joseph Sargent. **VHS, Beta** $59.95 MCA *XXX*

Colt Comrades A bad guy's monopoly on water rights is jeopardized when Boyd and Clyde strike water while drilling for oil. Nothing really notable here, except for Bob (Robert) Mitchum and George ("Superman") Reeves in minor roles.
1943 67m/B William Boyd, Andy Clyde, Jay Kirby, George Reeves, Gayle Lord, Earle Hodgins, Victor Jory, Douglas Fowley, Herbert Rawlinson, Robert Mitchum; *D:* Lesley Selander. **VHS** $19.95 NOS *XX*

Colt is My Law Bandits steal a railroad-funding gold shipment, and are pursued relentlessly by mysterious masked men. *AKA:* Mi Revolver es la Ley.
19?? 95m/C Anthony Clark, Lucy Gilly, Michael Martin. **VHS, Beta** NO *X*½

Columbia Pictures Cartoon Classics Eight award-winning films from Columbia Pictures, including "Gerald McBoing-Boing" (1950), "Rooty Toot Toot" (1951), "Madeline" (1952), and "Magoo's Puddle Jumper" (1956).
1952 50m/C *V:* Jim Backus. **VHS, Beta** $19.95 COL *X*½

Columbo: Murder By the Book The rumpled, cigar-smoking television detective investigates the killing of a mystery writer. Scripted by Steven Bochco of "Hill Street Blues" and "L.A. Law" fame.
1971 79m/C Peter Falk, Jack Cassidy, Rosemary Forsyth, Martin Milner; *D:* Steven Spielberg. **VHS, Beta** $39.95 MCA *XX*½

Columbo: Prescription Murder Peter Falk's debut as the raincoat-clad lieutenant investigating the death of a psychiatrist's wife. Rich with subplots. Good mystery fare.
1967 99m/C Peter Falk, Gene Barry, Katherine Justice, William Windom, Nina Foch, Anthony James, Virginia Gregg; *D:* Richard Irving. **VHS, Beta** MCA *XX*

Coma A doctor discovers murder and corpse-nabbing at her Boston hospital, defies her male bosses, and determines to find out what's going on before more patients die. Exciting, suspenseful fare, with Bujold impressive in lead. Based on the novel by Robin Cook.
1978 (PG) 113m/C Genevieve Bujold, Michael Douglas, Elizabeth Ashley, Rip Torn, Richard Widmark, Lois Chiles, Harry Rhodes, Tom Selleck; *D:* Michael Crichton; *M:* Jerry Goldsmith. **VHS, Beta, LV** $14.95 MGM *XXX*

Comancheros Texas Ranger Wayne and his prisoner fight with the Comancheros, an outlaw gang who is supplying guns and liquor to the dreaded Comanche Indians. Elmer Bernstein's musical score adds flavor. Last film by Curtiz.
1961 108m/C John Wayne, Ina Balin, Stuart Whitman, Nehemiah Persoff, Lee Marvin, Bruce Cabot; *D:* Michael Curtiz. **VHS, Beta** $19.98 FOX *XXX*

Combat! Morrow and Jason starred in this gritty series about an Army platoon in Europe during the final years of World War II. In "The Bridge at Chalons" Marvin guest stars as a demolitions expert. Additional episodes available.
1962 50m/B Vic Morrow, Rick Jason, Lee Marvin. **VHS, Beta** $19.95 GKK, MOV *XXX*

Combat Academy Weak comedy about two goofballs sent to a military academy to straighten out, but instead turn the academy on its ear with their antics. Unremarkable.
1986 96m/C Keith Gordon, Jamie Farr, Sherman Hemsley, John Ratzenberger, Bernie Kopell, Charles Moll; *D:* Neal Israel. **VHS, LV** $19.95 STE, NWV *X*

Combat Killers A World War II Army captain grabs for individual glory on the battlefield, and jeopardizes the lives of his platoon.
1980 96m/C Paul Edwards, Marlene Dauden, Claude Wilson; *D:* Ken Loring. **VHS, Beta** $59.95 MED *X*

Combat Shock A Vietnam veteran returns home and decides to rid his city of undesirables by killing them. Familiar plot handled in typically crude, conventional manner. *AKA:* American Nightmares.

1984 (R) 85m/C Ricky Giovinazzo, Nick Nasta, Veronica Stork; *D:* Buddy Giovnazzo. **VHS, Beta** $9.99 STE, PSM *X*

Come Along with Me A made-for-television adaptation of Shirley Jackson's unfinished novel about a woman who sells all and leaves her hometown when her husband dies, determined to start a new career as a seer.
1984 60m/C Estelle Parsons, Barbara Baxley, Sylvia Sidney; *D:* Joanne Woodward. **VHS, Beta** $24.95 MON, KAR *XX*½

Come and Get It A classic adaptation of the Edna Ferber novel about a lumber king battling against his son for the love of a woman. Farmer's most important Hollywood role. *AKA:* Roaring Timber.
1936 99m/B Frances Farmer, Edward Arnold, Joel McCrea, Walter Brennan, Andrea Leeds; *D:* William Wyler, Howard Hawks. Academy Awards '36: Best Supporting Actor (Brennan); Nominations: Best Film Editing. **VHS, Beta** $19.98 HBO, SUE, BTV *XXX*

Come and See Harrowing, unnerving epic which depicts the horrors of war as a boy soldier roams the Russian countryside during the Nazi invasion. Some overwhelming sequences, including tracer-bullets flashing across an open field. War has rarely been rendered in such a vivid, utterly grim manner. Outstanding achievement from Soviet director Klimov. In Russian with English subtitles. *AKA:* Idi i Smotri; Go and See.
1985 142m/C RU Alexei Kravchenko, Olga Mironova, Lubomiras Lauciavicus; *D:* Elem Klimov. **VHS** $59.95 KIV, FCT, TPV *XXXX*

Come Back, Africa A classic documentary about a Zulu family surviving under apartheid in South Africa.
1960 83m/B **VHS, Beta** $29.95 MFV, FCT *XXX*

Come Back Little Reba A semi-educational film about a young black boy and his lovable aging dog.
1986 60m/C **VHS, Beta, LV** PAR, PIA *X*

Come Back, Little Sheba Unsettling drama about a worn-out housewife, her abusive, alcoholic husband and a comely boarder who causes further marital tension. The title refers to the housewife's despairing search for her lost dog. Booth, Lancaster, and Moore are all excellent. Based on the play by William Inge, this film still packs an emotional wallop.
1952 99m/B Burt Lancaster, Shirley Booth, Terry Moore, Richard Jaeckel, Philip Ober, Liza Golm, Walter Kelley; *D:* Daniel Mann. Academy Awards '52: Best Actress (Booth); Nominations: Best Film Editing, Best Supporting Actress (Moore); Cannes Film Festival '53: Best Actress (Booth); Golden Globe Awards '53: Best Actress—Drama (Booth). **VHS, Beta, LV** $19.95 PAR, FCT, BTV *XXX*½

Come Back to the Five & Dime Jimmy Dean, Jimmy Dean Five women convene at a run-down Texas drugstore for a 20-year reunion of a local James Dean fan club. The women recall earlier times and make some stunning revelations. Altman's filming of Ed Graczyk's sometimes funny, sometimes wrenching play proves fine vehicle for the actresses. Cher is probably the most impressive, but Dennis and Black are also memorable.
1982 (PG) 109m/C Sandy Dennis, Cher, Karen Black, Kathy Bates, Sudie Bond, Marta Heflin; *D:* Robert Altman. **VHS, Beta, LV** $19.98 SUE *XXX*

Come Blow Your Horn Neil Simon's first major Broadway success is a little less successful in its celluloid wrapper, suffering a bit from a familiar script. Sinatra's a playboy

who blows his horn all over town, causing his close-knit New York Jewish family to warp a bit. Dad's not keen on his son's pledge of allegiance to the good life, and kid brother Bill would like to be his sibling's understudy in playboyhood.
1963 115m/C Frank Sinatra, Lee J. Cobb, Tony Bill, Molly Picon, Barbara Rush, Jill St. John; **D:** Bud Yorkin. **VHS, Beta $14.95** PAR 🎬🎬🎬

Come On, Cowboys The Three Mesquiteers rescue an old circus friend from certain death. Part of "The Three Mesquiteers" series.
1937 54m/B Bob Livingston, Ray Corrigan. **VHS, Beta $25.00** MED, DVT 🎬 ½

Come On Rangers Also called "Come On Ranger." Rogers and his friends go to Texas to avenge the death of a comrade.
1938 54m/B Roy Rogers, George "Gabby" Hayes. **VHS, Beta $19.95** NOS, DVT, RXM 🎬

Come On Tarzan Maynard and his trusty horse Tarzan save wild horses from the bad guys who want to turn them into dog food.
1932 60m/B Ken Maynard. **VHS, Beta $19.95** NOS, VDM, DVT 🎬 ½

Come See the Paradise Just before WWII, ex-union organizer Jack McGurn (Quaid) takes a job at a movie theatre in Los Angeles' Little Tokyo and falls in love love with Lily (Tomita), the owner's daughter. They marry (out of state because California law prohibited interracial marriages) before the bombing of Pearl Harbor and the subsequent internment of Japanese-Americans. Not a film with much big screen history, but effectively presented for the little theater of the living room. Told in flashback, the story offers a candid look at the racism implicit in the Asian-American relocations and at the hypocrisy that often lurks beneath the surface of the pursuit of liberty and justice for all. British writer-director Parker's most successful efforts (such as "Birdy," "The Commitments" and "Midnight Express") have been those he has directed but not penned. Typically, the "Paradise" script indulges a bit too much in screenwriter's license and concedes to the obvious. Nonetheless, the cast, apart from Quaid's misguided attempt at seriousness, is excellent, and the subject has not yet been cast into the vast bin of Hollywood cliches.
1990 (R) 135m/C Dennis Quaid, Tamlyn Tomita, Sab Shimono; **W/D:** Alan Parker. **VHS, Beta, LV $19.98** FOX, FCT, CCB 🎬🎬🎬

The Comeback A singer attempting a comeback in England finds his wife murdered. **AKA:** The Day the Screaming Stopped.
1977 100m/C GB Jack Jones, Pamela Stephenson, David Doyle, Bill Owen, Sheila Keith, Richard Johnson; **D:** Pete Walker. **VHS, Beta $19.98** LHV 🎬

Comeback The story of a disillusioned rock star, played by Eric Burdon (the lead singer of the Animals), who gives up his life in the fast lane and tries to go back to his roots.
1983 105m/C Eric Burdon; **D:** Christel Bushmann. **VHS, Beta $24.95** MGM 🎬🎬 ½

Comeback Kid An ex-big league baseball player is conned into coaching an urban team of smarmy street youths, and falls for their playground supervisor. Made for television.
1980 97m/C John Ritter, Susan Dey; **D:** Peter Levin. **VHS, Beta $9.98** SUE, NLC 🎬

The Comedians Disturbing and powerful drama of political intrigue set against the murderous dictatorship of "Papa Doc" Duvalier. Burton plays the cynical owner of a

resort hotel with Taylor as his German mistress. Ustinov is great as he does his usual scene-stealing in his role as a South American ambassador married to Taylor. Excellent cast was somewhat held back by sluggish direction and an uninspired script. Based on the novel of the same name by Graham Greene.
1967 148m/C Elizabeth Taylor, Richard Burton, Alec Guinness, Peter Ustinov, Paul Ford, Lillian Gish, Raymond St. Jacques, Zakes Mokae; **D:** Peter Glenville; **W:** Graham Greene. **VHS $19.98** MGM 🎬🎬 ½

Comedy Classics Three early comedy shorts: "Double Trouble," with Pollard; "So and Sew," with Ball; and "Technocrazy," directed by Al Christie.
1935 60m/B Snub Pollard, Oliver Hardy, Lucille Ball, Billy Bevan, Monty Collins. **VHS, Beta $59.95** JEF 🎬🎬 ½

Comedy Classics of Mack Sennett and Hal Roach Three comedy silent films: "Love, Loot and Crash;" "Looking for Trouble;" and "A Desperate Scoundrel."
1915 51m/B VHS, Beta $29.95 VYY 🎬🎬 ½

Comedy Festival #1 Collection of three comic films: "Speed in the Gay Nineties," with Clyde; "Disorder in the Court," with the Three Stooges; "Hail Brother," with Gilbert.
193? 53m/B Andy Clyde, Billy Gilbert, Curly Howard, Moe Howard, Larry Fine. **VHS, Beta $34.95** HHT 🎬🎬 ½

Comedy Festival #2 Collection of comedy films: "Bashful Romeo," with Lamb; "Super Snooper," with Clyde; "Super Stupid," with Gilbert.
193? 53m/B Gil Lamb, Andy Clyde, Billy Gilbert. **VHS, Beta $34.95** HHT 🎬🎬 ½

Comedy Festival #3 Collection of comic films: "Big Flash," with Langdon; "Half A Hero," and "Pardon My Papa," with Temple.
193? 53m/B Harry Langdon, Shirley Temple. **VHS, Beta $34.95** HHT 🎬🎬 ½

Comedy Festival #4 A collection of comic films: "His Weak Moment," "Fainting Lover," and "Shopping with the Wife."
193? 53m/B Andy Clyde. **VHS, Beta $34.95** HHT 🎬🎬 ½

The Comedy of Terrors Comedy in which some deranged undertakers take a hands-on approach to insuring their continued employment. Much fun is supplied by the quartet of Price, Lorre, Karloff, and Rathbone, all veterans of the horror genre.
1964 84m/C Vincent Price, Peter Lorre, Boris Karloff, Basil Rathbone, Joe E. Brown, Joyce Jameson; **D:** Jacques Tourneur; **W:** Richard Matheson. **VHS, LV $79.98** MOV 🎬🎬🎬

Comedy Reel, Vol. 1 Contains three W.C. Fields shorts: "Golf Specialist," "Fatal Glass of Beer," and "The Dentist."
19?? 60m/B W.C. Fields. **VHS, Beta, 3/4U, Special order formats $23.95** CAB 🎬🎬 ½

Comedy Reel, Vol. 2 These comedy shorts feature the Three Stooges in "Disorder in the Court," Edgar Kennedy and Franklin Pangborn in "Next Door Neighbors," and W. C. Fields in "The Barbershop."
19?? 60m/B Moe Howard, Edgar Kennedy, Franklin Pangborn, W.C. Fields. **VHS, Beta, 3/4U, Special order formats $23.95** CAB 🎬🎬 ½

Comes a Horseman Robards is a cattle baron, attempting to gobble up all the oil-rich land his neighbor owns. Neighbor Fonda has the courage to stand up to him, with the help of a World War II veteran and

the local old timer Farnsworth, in this slow-moving but intriguing western drama.
1978 (PG) 119m/C James Caan, Jane Fonda, Jason Robards Jr., George Grizzard, Richard Farnsworth, Jim Davis, Mark Harmon; **D:** Alan J. Pakula. Academy Awards '78 Nominations: Best Supporting Actor (Farnsworth); National Board of Review Awards '78: 10 Best Films of the Year, Best Supporting Actor (Farnsworth). **VHS, Beta** FOX 🎬🎬 ½

Comfort and Joy After his kleptomaniac girlfriend deserts him, a Scottish disc jockey is forced to reevaluate his life. He becomes involved in an underworld battle between two mob-owned local ice cream companies. Another odd comedy gem from Forsyth, who did "Gregory's Girl" and "Local Hero". Music by Dire Straits guitarist Mark Knopfler.
1984 (PG) 93m/C GB Bill Paterson, Eleanor David, C.P. Grogan, Alex Norton, Patrick Malahide, Rikki Fulton, Roberto Berrardi; **D:** Bill Forsyth. **VHS, Beta $69.95** MCA 🎬🎬🎬

The Comfort of Strangers An atmospheric psychological thriller. Mary and Colin (Richardson and Everett), a handsome young British couple, take a Venetian holiday to rediscover the passion in their relationship. Lost in the aqua-riddled labyrinthine city, they chance, it seems, upon Robert (Walken) who wears an impeccable white suit and tells them of his father. A sort of Vergil in an Italian suit, Robert later reappears, and, abetted by his wife Caroline (Mirren), gradually leads the couple on an eerie tour of urbane decadence that hints at danger. Psychologically tantalizing and horrifyingly erotic, the movie's based on Ian McEwan's novel, with an adroit screenplay by Harold Pinter.
1991 (R) 102m/C Christopher Walken, Natasha Richardson, Rupert Everett, Helen Mirren; **D:** Paul Schrader; **W:** Harold Pinter; **M:** Angelo Badalamenti. **VHS, Beta $79.95** PAR, FCT 🎬🎬🎬

The Comic Van Dyke is terrific as a silent screen comedian (a composite of several real-life screen comics) whose ego destroys his career. Recreations of silent films, and the blend of comedy and pathos, are especially effective. Written by Carl Reiner.
1969 (PG) 96m/C Dick Van Dyke, Mickey Rooney, Michele Lee, Cornel Wilde, Nina Wayne, Pert Kelton, Jeannine Riley; **D:** Carl Reiner. **VHS, Beta, LV $59.95** COL 🎬🎬🎬

The Comic In a future police state, a young comedian kills the star and takes his place in the show. His future rises, but who cares?
1985 90m/C Steve Munroe, Bernard Plant, Jeff Pirie; **D:** Richard Driscoll. **VHS, Beta** NO 🎬

Comic Book Kids Two youngsters enjoy visiting their friend's comic strip studio, since they have the power to project themselves into the cartoon stories. Viewers will be less impressed.
1982 (G) 90m/C Joseph Campanella, Mike Darnell, Robyn Finn, Jim Engelhardt, Fay De Witt. **VHS, Beta** GEM 🎬

Comic Cabby A day in the life of an introvert cabby seems to last forever. From "New York City Cab Driver's Joke Book" by Jim Pietsch.
1987 59m/C Bill McLaughlin, Al Lewis. **VHS, Beta $59.95** VES, LIV Woof!

Coming Home A look at the effect of the Vietnam War on the American home front. The wife of a gung-ho Marine officer volunteers as an aide in a Veteran's Hospital, befriends and eventually falls in love with a Vietnam veteran, paraplegic from war injuries. His attitudes, pain, and his first-hand knowledge of the war force her to re-exam-

C

ine her previously automatic responses. Honest look at the everyday life of disabled veterans, unusual vision of the possibilities of simple friendship between men and women. Fonda and Voight are great; Dern's character suffers from weak scriptwriting late in the film. Critically acclaimed. Compelling score from late '60s music.
1978 (R) 130m/C Jane Fonda, Jon Voight, Bruce Dern, Penelope Milford, Robert Carradine, Robert Ginty; **D:** Hal Ashby; **W:** Robert C. Jones. Academy Awards '78: Best Actor (Voight), Best Actress (Fonda), Best Screenplay; Nominations: Best Director (Ashby), Best Film Editing, Best Picture, Best Supporting Actor (Dern), Best Supporting Actress (Milford); Cannes Film Festival '78: Best Actor (Voight); Golden Globe Awards '79: Best Actor—Drama (Voight), Best Actress—Drama (Fonda). **VHS, Beta, LV** $19.98 MGM, FOX, FCT 𝄪𝄪𝄪½

The Coming of Amos A wonderful send-up of all those Fairbanks-style melodramas, with La Rocque as an Aussie on vacation on the French Riviera falling for and eventually rescuing Goudal, as the Russian princess held captive by the lustful Beery.
1925 60m/B Rod La Rocque, Jetta Goudal, Noah Beery Sr., Florence Vidor; **D:** Paul Sloane. **VHS, Beta** NO 𝄪𝄪𝄪

Coming Out Alive Tense thriller about a woman and her hired mercenary who try to rescue her kidnapped son from his estranged father—a radical is involved in an assassination plot. Hylands is especially compelling.
1984 73m/C Helen Shaver, Scott Hylands, Michael Ironside, Monica Parker. **VHS, Beta** $59.95 TWE 𝄪𝄪½

Coming Out of the Ice Engrossing true story of Victor Herman, an outstanding American athlete who worked in Russia in the 1930s. He was imprisoned in Siberia (for 38 years!) for refusing to renounce his American citizenship. Made for television.
1982 (PG) 100m/C John Savage, Willie Nelson, Ben Cross, Francesca Annis, Peter Vaughan; **D:** Waris Hussein. **VHS, Beta** $59.98 FOX 𝄪𝄪𝄪

Coming to America An African prince (Murphy) decides to come to America in search of a suitable bride. He lands in Queens, and quickly finds American women to be more confusing than he imagined. Sometimes overly-cute entertainment relieved by clever costume cameos by Murphy and Hall. Later lawsuit resulted in columnist Art Buchwald being given credit for story.
1988 (R) 116m/C Eddie Murphy, Arsenio Hall, James Earl Jones, John Amos, Madge Sinclair, Shari Headley, Don Ameche, Louie Anderson; **D:** John Landis. **VHS, Beta, LV, 8mm** $14.95 PAR, FCT 𝄪𝄪𝄪

Coming Up Roses Pleasant comedy about the residents of a small mining village in the South of Wales who fight to keep their local movie house from being shut down. In Welsh with English subtitles. **AKA:** Rhosyn A Rhith.
1987 (PG) 95m/C GB Dafydd Hywel, Iola Gregory, Olive Michael, Mari Emlyn, Bill Paterson; **D:** Stephen Bayly. **VHS, Beta** $29.95 PAV, FCT, TAM 𝄪𝄪½

Command Decision Upon realizing he must send his men on missions-of-no-return to destroy German jet production, Gable's WWII flight commander becomes tactically at odds with his political superior, Pidgeon (who's not keen to have his precision bombing plans placed in an unflattering light). Based on the stage hit by William Wister Haines, it's a late war pic by Wood, who earlier directed such diverse efforts as "A Night at the Opera," "The Devil and Miss Jones," and "Our Town." Vintage war-is-hell actioner.

1948 112m/B Clark Gable, Walter Pidgeon, Van Johnson, Brian Donlevy, Charles Bickford, John Hodiak; **D:** Sam Wood. **VHS** $19.98 MGM, FCT 𝄪𝄪½

Commando An ex-commando leader's daughter is kidnapped in a blackmail scheme to make him depose a South American president. He fights instead, and proceeds to rescue his daughter amid a torrential flow of falling bodies. Violent action spiced with throwaway comic lines.
1985 (R) 90m/C Arnold Schwarzenegger, Rae Dawn Chong, Dan Hedaya, Vernon Wells, James Olson, David Patrick Kelly, Alyssa Milano; **D:** Mark L. Lester. **VHS, Beta, LV** $14.98 FXV, TLF 𝄪𝄪𝄪

Commando Attack A tough sergeant leads a group of misfit soldiers to blow up a German radio transmitter the day before D-Day.
1967 90m/C Michael Rennie, Monica Randall, Bob Sullivan. **VHS, Beta** $59.95 UNI 𝄪½

Commando Invasion When an army captain is accused of murder, he hunts down the man he knows is responsible for the crime. Jungle revenge mayhem is confusing. Set in Viet Nam.
1987 90m/C Jim Gaines, Michael James, Gordon Mitchell, Carol Roberts, Pat Vance, Ken Watanabe; **D:** John Gale. **VHS** $59.95 QHV 𝄪

Commando Squad During World War II, soldiers go to battle to prevent the development of a device that re-animates flesh. The script stays dead.
1976 (R) 82m/C Chuck Alford, Peter Owen, April Adams; **D:** Charles Nizet. **VHS, Beta** $24.95 GHV 𝄪

Commando Squad Story of drug agents undercover in Mexico, and a female agent who rescues her kidnapped lover. Firepower is wasted, but Shower is a former "Playboy" Playmate of the Year.
1987 (R) 90m/C Brian Thompson, William Smith, Kathy Shower, Sid Haig, Robert Quarry, Ross Hagen, Mel Welles, Marie Windsor, Russ Tamblyn; **D:** Fred Olen Ray. **VHS, Beta** $79.95 TWE 𝄪

Commandos Commando operation against Rommel's forces in North Africa during WWII. Too much said, not enough action. Also known as "Sullivan's Marauders."
1973 (PG) 100m/C GE IT Lee Van Cleef, Jack Kelly; **D:** Armando Crispino. **VHS, Beta** $49.95 GEM, MRV, PSM 𝄪½

Commandos Strike at Dawn Norwegian villagers, including Muni, fight the invading Nazis, and eventually help the British Navy battle them over an Arctic supply line. Okay script helped along by veteran actors Muni and Gish. Written by Irwin Shaw, based on a C.S. Forester story.
1943 100m/B Paul Muni, Lillian Gish, Cedric Hardwicke, Anna Lee, Ray Collins, Robert Coote, Alexander Knox, Rosemary DeCamp; **D:** John Farrow. **VHS, Beta** $69.95 COL 𝄪𝄪

The Commies are Coming, the Commies are Coming Cult classic will leave viewers red from laughing in disbelief. Webb narrates this anti-communist movie about the Russians taking over the United States. Filmed in a documentary style, it captures the paranoia of the times. Re-released in 1984, just before the Evil Empire collapsed.
1957 60m/B Jack Webb, Andrew Duggan, Robert Conrad, Jack Kelly, Peter Brown; **D:** George Waggner. **VHS, Beta** $39.95 RHI 𝄪𝄪

Commissar Before the Soviet Union ended up in the ashcan of history, this film was labeled as "treason" and shelved in Red Russia. Now, even Americans can view the story of a female Soviet soldier who becomes pregnant during the civil war of 1922. The Soviet military has no policy regarding pregnancy, so the woman is dumped on a family of outcast Jews to complete her pregnancy. This film makes the strong statement that women were just as discriminated against in the U.S.S.R. as were many races or creeds, especially Jews. In Russian with English subtitles. Released in the U.S. in 1988. **AKA:** Komissar.
1968 105m/B RU Nonna Mordyukova, Rolan Bykov; **D:** Alexander Askoldov. **VHS** $59.95 KIV 𝄪𝄪𝄪

The Commitments Convinced that they can bring soul music to Dublin, a group of working-class youth form a band. Based on the book by Roddy Doyle, this high-energy production paints an interesting, unromanticized picture of modern Ireland and refuses to follow standard showbiz cliches, even though its lack of resolution hurts. Honest, whimsical dialog laced with poetic obscenities, delivered by a cast of mostly unknowns. The very successful soundtrack features the music of Wilson Pickett, James Brown, Otis Redding, Aretha Franklin, Percy Sledge and others, and received a Grammy nomination.
1991 (R) 116m/C Andrew Strong, Bronagh Gallagher, Glen Hansard, Michael Aberne, Dick Massey, Ken McCluskey, Robert Arkins, Dave Finnegan, Johnny Murphy, Angeline Ball, Felim Gormley, Maria Doyle; **D:** Alan Parker. Academy Awards '91 Nominations: Best Film Editing; British Academy Awards '92: Best Director (Parker), Best Film. **VHS, Beta, LV** $19.98 FXV, CCB, IME 𝄪𝄪𝄪

Committed The story of stage and screen actress Frances Farmer, who went from stardom to a mental institution and a lobotomy. A more subtle, incisive version of the story than the Hollywood biopic "Frances." An independent production directed by McLaughlin and Tillman.
1984 77m/C D: Sheila McLaughlin, Lynne Tillman. **VHS** $59.95 FCT 𝄪𝄪𝄪

Committed Schlock-meister Levey's latest directorial effort is a step above his earlier "Slumber Party" and "Happy Hooker Goes to Washington," a statement ringing with the faintest of praise. Thinking she's applying for a job at an asylum, a nurse discovers she has committed herself. Try as she may, not even a committed nurse can snake her way out of the pit of madness they call "The Institute."
1991 (R) 93m/C Jennifer O'Neill, William Windom, Robert Forster, Ron Palillo, Sydney Lassick; **D:** William A. Levey. **VHS** $89.98 MED 𝄪½

The Committee Comedy film of the seminal comedy troupe "The Committee," specialists in short, punchy satire. Dated, but of interest to comedy buffs.
1968 (PG) 88m/C Wolfman Jack, Howard Hesseman, Barbara Bosson, Peter Bonerz, Garry Goodrow, Carl Gottlieb; **D:** Jack Del. **VHS, Beta** $59.95 PAV 𝄪𝄪

Common Bonds After being put together in an experimental outreach program, two mismatched partners struggle to break free from a system that threatens to destroy them both.
1991 (PG) 109m/C Rae Dawn Chong, Michael Ironside, Brad Dourif; **D:** Allan Goldstein. **VHS, Beta** $89.95 ACA 𝄪½

Common Law Wife Made-for-the-drive-in flick about a man whose common law marriage is threatened by his niece, who wants his money. Murder and mayhem abound when the man's moonshine is poisoned. Cheap and exploitative.
1963 (R) 81m/B Lacy Kelly, Shugfoot Rainey, Annabelle Lee, Jody Works, Anne MacAdams, George Edgely; *D:* Eric Sayers. VHS $16.95 SNC ✗

Common Threads: Stories from the Quilt The heavily awarded, made-for-cable-TV documentary about the Quilt: an immense 14-acre blanket created by the survivors of AIDS victims as a monument to their loved ones' premature deaths. All proceeds from the sale of this tape go to the NAMES Project Foundation in support of the Quilt and AIDS service providers.
1989 79m/C *D:* Robert Epstein, Jeffrey Friedman. VHS, Beta, LV $49.95 IME, HBO ✗

Communion A serious adaptation of the purportedly nonfictional bestseller by Whitley Strieber about his family's abduction by extraterrestrials. Spacey new age story is overlong and hard to swallow.
1989 (R) 103m/C Christopher Walken, Lindsay Crouse, Frances Sternhagen, Joel Carlson, Andreas Katsulas, Basil Hoffman; *D:* Philippe Mora. VHS, Beta, LV NO ✗✗

Como Dos Gotas de Agua Twin sisters trade places with each other in this limp musical comedy in Spanish. *AKA:* Like Two Drops of Water; Like Two Drops of Water.
197? 104m/C *SP* Pili & Mili, Isabél Garces, Luis Davila, Manolo Moran. VHS, Beta $49.95 MAD ✗

Company Business Sam Boyd is a retired CIA agent who's brought back to swap Pyiotr Grushenko (Baryshnikov), a Russian mole in the State Department, for a U-2 pilot being held in Moscow. The swap is to be made in Berlin and also involves two million dollars of what turns out be to Colombian drug money. When things inevitably go wrong (both intelligence agencies would like them out of the way permanently) the two men find they must depend on each other if they want to stay alive. An unimaginative plot wastes a stalwart cast in this old-fashioned spy drama.
1991 (PG-13) 99m/C Gene Hackman, Mikhail Baryshnikov, Kurtwood Smith, Terry O'Quinn; *W/D:* Nicholas Meyer. VHS $19.98 MGM ✗ 1/2

Company Limited The story of a young Indian sales executive working for a British owned firm, set in contemporary Calcutta. English subtitles.
197? 112m/B *IN* VHS, Beta, 3/4U, Special order formats CIG ✗✗

The Company of Wolves A young girl on the threshold of womanhood listens to her grandmother tell fairy tales and dreams of a medieval fantasy world inhabited by wolves and werewolves. An adult "Little Red Ridinghood" type comedy heavy on Freudian symbolism. Not really for kids.
1985 (R) 95m/C Angela Lansbury, David Warner, Micha Bergese, Tusse Silberg, Sarah Patterson, Brian Glover, Danielle Dax, Graham Crowden, Stephen Rea; *D:* Neil Jordan. VHS, Beta, LV $19.98 VES, LIV ✗✗✗

The Competition Two virtuoso pianists meet at an international competition and fall in love. Will they stay together if one of them wins? Can they have a performance career and love too? Is he trying to distract her with sex, so he can win? Dreyfuss and Irving are fine (they practiced for four months to look like they were really playing the pianos),

and Remick's character has some interesting insights into the world of art.
1980 (PG) 125m/C Richard Dreyfuss, Amy Irving, Lee Remick, Sam Wanamaker, Joseph Cali, Ty Henderson, Priscilla Pointer, James B. Sikking; *D:* Joel Oliansky. VHS, Beta, LV $14.95 COL, TVC ✗✗✗

The Compleat Beatles Music, interviews, film clips, animation and live performances make up this "rockumentary" on the Beatles. New interviews are featured, as well as vintage film clips and studio footage with narration by Malcolm McDowell. The first U.S. press conference, legendary Hamburg footage, and an in-depth interview with George Martin are highlights.
1982 120m/C John Lennon, Paul McCartney, Ringo Starr, George Harrison, George Martin, Brian Epstein, Billy Preston, Milt Oken, Bruce Johnston, Roger McGuinn, Mike McCartney, Mick Jagger; *D:* Patrick Montgomery. VHS, Beta, LV $19.95 MVD, MGM ✗✗✗

The Compleat Tex Avery Every MGM cartoon directed by Avery from 1942 to 1956 is included on this five-disc set.
194? ?m/C *D:* Tex Avery. LV $89.95 MGM, WTA ✗✗✗

The Complete Superman Collection, Vols. 1 & 2 Produced by the legendary Max Fleischer Studios. Contains 19 shorts about the Man of Steel from 1941-1944.
194? ?m/C VHS $22.45 BSV ✗✗✗

Complex Cute tale of a clever dog (aren't they all?) who annoys his swinish, beer-guzzling master by learning how to play chess, speak French, and read Dostoevsky.
1985 12m/C VHS, Beta, 3/4U $160.00 BFA ✗✗✗

Complex World The Heartbreak Hotel is a notorious rock club which may not be around much longer. It seems the young owner's father is an ex-CIA redneck who is running for President and his son's profession is a political liability. Meanwhile, the town's mayor wants to replace the club with a shopping mall. A bomb is planted in the club's basement, terrorists lurk, and a gang of bikers is spoiling for a fight but the crowd at the Heartbreak just rocks on.
1992 (R) 81m/C Dan Welch, Bob Owczarek, Jay Charbonneau, Tilman Gandy Jr., David P.B. Stephens; *W/D:* James Wolpaw. VHS $89.95 HMD ✗ 1/2

Compromising Positions A philandering dentist is killed on Long Island, and a bored housewife begins to investigate, uncovering scandal after scandal. Black comedy mixed unevenly with mystery makes for unsatisfying brew. However, Ivey is a standout as Sarandon's best friend. Screenplay was written by Susan Isaacs, based on her novel of the same title.
1985 (R) 99m/C Susan Sarandon, Raul Julia, Edward Herrmann, Judith Ivey, Mary Beth Hurt, Joe Mantegna, Josh Mostel, Anne De Salvo; *D:* Frank Perry. VHS, Beta, LV $19.95 PAR ✗✗

Computer Beach Party A couple of surf-head college computer hackers foil their mayor's plans to develop their favorite beach. The title, at least, is original.
1988 97m/C Hank Amigo, Stacey Nemour, Andre Chimene; *D:* Gary A. Troy. VHS, Beta $69.98 VES, LIV ✗

Computer Dreams Various computer animated shorts have been compiled, including "Pencil Test," "Mars Rover," and "Nestor Sextone."
1987 60m/C VHS MPI, WTA ✗

Computer Wizard Boy genius builds a powerful electronic device. His intentions are good, but the invention disrupts the town and lands him in big trouble. Not the "Thomas Edison Story."
1977 (G) 91m/C Henry Darrow, Kate Woodville, Guy Madison, Marc Gilpin; *D:* John Florea. VHS, Beta NO ✗

The Computer Wore Tennis Shoes Disney comedy (strictly for the kids) about a slow-witted college student who turns into a genius after a "shocking" encounter with the campus computer. His new brains give the local gangster headaches. Sequel: "Now You See Him, Now You Don't."
1969 (G) 87m/C Kurt Russell, Cesar Romero, Joe Flynn, William Schallert, Allan Hewitt, Richard Bakalayan; *D:* Robert Butler. VHS, Beta DIS, OM ✗✗

Comrades in Arms When an international drug cartel threatens to take over the world, the United States and Russia must set their differences aside and team up to stop them.
1991 (R) 91m/C Lyle Alzado, Rick Washburne, John Christian, Lance Henriksen; *W/D:* J. Christian Ingvordsen. VHS $89.98 REP ✗ 1/2

The Comrades of Summer Mantegna plays big-league baseball coach Sparky Smith, whose fiery temper gets him into big trouble. Out of a job, he discovers the only team willing to take a chance on him happens to be Russian. Sparky finds the players of the Russian National team need a lot of help—and not just with their English. Made for cable television.
1992 (R) 90m/C Joe Mantegna, Natalia Negoda, Michael Lerner; *D:* Tommy Lee Wallace; *W:* Robert Rodat; *M:* William Olvis. VHS, LV $89.99 HBO ✗✗ 1/2

The Con Artists After con man Quinn is sprung from prison, he and his protege set up a sting operation against the beautiful Capucine. Not clever or witty enough for the caper to capture interest. *AKA:* The Con Man.
1980 86m/C *IT* Anthony Quinn, Adriano Celentano, Capucine, Corinne Clery; *D:* Sergio Corbucci. VHS, Beta $19.98 VID, HHE ✗ 1/2

Con Man Robin Mitchell is a small-time con man on the fringes of London's underworld. He witnesses a brutal mob hit, which means they want him dead, and his girlfriend has decided it's just too dangerous being a part of his life. But Mitchell is convinced his luck will change for the better as he puts together a million-dollar long-shot that could secure him for life—if he survives.
1992 91m/C Ian McShane, Gayle Hunnicutt, Keith Barron, Alan Lake, Luan Peters; *D:* Francis Megahy. VHS $59.95 HMD ✗

Con Mi Mujer No Puedo A compulsive Don Juan's wife decides to match her husband's carnal activities tryst for tryst. Naughty boredom.
1987 101m/C *MX* Guillermo Bredeston, Leonor Benedetto, Javier Portales; *D:* Enrique Dawl. VHS, Beta $57.95 UNI ✗ 1/2

Conagher A lyrical, if poorly plotted Western about a veteran cowboy who takes the whole movie to decide to end up in the arms of the pretty widow lady. Cable-TV adaptation of Louis L'Amour's novel doesn't have much intensity, though Elliott captures his character well.
1991 94m/C Sam Elliott, Katharine Ross, Barry Corbin; *D:* Reynaldo Villalobos. VHS, Beta $89.98 TTC ✗✗ 1/2

Conan the Barbarian A fine sword and sorcery tale featuring brutality, excellent production values, and a rousing score. Conan's parents are killed and he's enslaved. But hardship makes him strong, so when he is set free he can avenge their murder and retrieve the sword bequeathed him by his father. Sandahl Bergman is great as The Queen of Thieves, and Schwarzenegger maintains an admirable sense of humor throughout. Jones is dandy, as always. Based on the character created by Robert E. Howard. Sequel: "Conan the Destroyer."
1982 (R) 115m/C Arnold Schwarzenegger, James Earl Jones, Max von Sydow, Sandahl Bergman, Mako, Ben Davidson, Valerie Quennessen, Cassandra Gaviola, William Smith; D: John Milius. VHS, Beta, LV $14.95 MCA ♂♂♂

Conan the Destroyer Conan is manipulated by Queen Tamaris into searching for a treasure. In return she'll bring Conan's love Valeria back to life. On his trip he meets Jones and Chamberlain, who later give him a hand. Excellent special effects, good humor, camp fun, somewhat silly finale. Sequel to the better "Conan the Barbarian."
1984 (PG) 101m/C Arnold Schwarzenegger, Grace Jones, Wilt Chamberlain, Sarah Douglas, Mako, Olivia D'Abo, Jeff Corey; D: Richard Fleischer. VHS, Beta, LV $14.95 MCA ♂♂½

The Concentratin' Kid An unusual horse opera sans shootouts and fisticuffs. Hoot's fiancee is kidnapped and taken to the range so that the renegade cowpokes can, uh, benefit from a female perspective on home decorating. Despite being outnumbered, Hoot concentrates and sets the rescue in motion, taking on the gang of rustlers without firing a shot.
1930 54m/B Hoot Gibson, Katherine Crawford, Duke Lee, Robert E. Homans, James Mason; D: Arthur Rosson. VHS, Beta $9.95 GPV ♂

The Concorde: Airport '79 A supersonic film in the "Airport" tradition has the Concorde chased by missiles and fighter aircraft before it crashes in the Alps. Incredibly far-fetched nonsense with an all-star cast doesn't fly. AKA: Airport '79.
1979 (PG) 103m/C Alain Delon, Susan Blakely, Robert Wagner, Sylvia Kristel, John Davidson, Charo, Sybil Danning, Jimmie Walker, Eddie Albert, Bibi Andersson, Monica Lewis, Andrea Marcovicci, Martha Raye, Cicely Tyson, Mercedes McCambridge, George Kennedy, David Warner; D: David Lowell Rich. VHS, Beta $14.98 MCA ♂

Concrete Angels A poignant glimpse at the influence of rock music in its infancy. A group of deprived teens in Toronto form a band and audition to open for the Beatles. Lack of nostalgia is refreshing, but too much of this is amateurish.
1987 (R) 97m/C CA Joseph Dimambro, Luke McKeehan, Omie Craden, Dean Bosacki. VHS, Beta $29.95 ACA ♂

Concrete Beat A newspaper reporter simultaneously searches for a murderer, tries to win his ex-wife back, and writes front page stories for his editor/ex-father-in-law. Tough assignment. Made for television.
1984 74m/C Kenneth McMillan, John Getz, Darlanne Fluegel, Rhoda Gemignani; D: Robert Butler. VHS, Beta $59.95 PSM ♂½

The Concrete Cowboys Two bumbling backwoodsmen come to the metropolis of Nashville and promptly turn detective to foil a blackmail scheme and locate a missing singer. Barbara Mandrell and Roy Acuff play themselves. Silly made-for-TV pilot of short-lived series.
1979 100m/C Jerry Reed, Tom Selleck, Morgan Fairchild, Claude Akins, Gene Evans, Roy Acuff, Barbara Mandrell; D: Burt Kennedy. VHS FOX ♂½

The Concrete Jungle After being set up by her no-good boyfriend, Bregman is sent to a correctional facility for drug smuggling. There she must learn to fend for herself (or else). Typical prison for gals fare with cute babes in revealing outfits, a topless riot, the bad warden, and a concerned social worker. Followed by "Chained Heat." AKA: The Criminal.
1982 (R) 106m/C Tracy Bregman, Jill St. John, Barbara Luna, Peter Brown, Aimee Eccles, Nita Talbot, Sondra Currie; D: Tom De Simone. VHS, Beta $59.95 COL ♂♂

Condemned to Hell A tough-as-iron street punk gets thrown into a women's prison, where she must fight for her existence. Low-brow violence galore.
198? 97m/C IT Leonor Benedetto. VHS, Beta $59.95 TWE Woof!

Condemned to Live Mild-mannered doctor Ralph Morgan and his fiancee Maxine Doyle seem like your average early 20th Century Middle-European couple...but the doctor's hunchbacked servant Mischa Auer is a tipoff that this is a horror movie of some sort. Like many men, the doctor has suffered from a vampire curse all his life. And, like many men, he is unaware of his blood-sucking habit, thanks to the concealment efforts of his loyal (hunchback) servant. Doyle discovers her fiance's sanguine secret, but not before she finds out she really loves Gleason, anyway. Answers the question: just how do you jilt a vampire?
1935 68m/B Ralph Morgan, Maxine Doyle, Russell Gleason, Pedro de Cordoba, Mischa Auer, Lucy Beaumont, Carl Stockade; D: Frank Strayer. VHS $19.98 SNC, TIM, LSV ♂

Condorman Woody Wilkins, an inventive comic book writer, adopts the identity of his own character, Condorman, in order to help a beautiful Russian spy defect. A Disney film, strictly for the small fry.
1981 (PG) 90m/C Michael Crawford, Oliver Reed, Barbara Carrera, James Hampton, Jean-Pierre Kalfon, Dana Elcar; D: Charles Jarrott. VHS, Beta $69.95 DIS ♂♂½

Conduct Unbecoming Late nineteenth century India is the setting for a trial involving the possible assault of a British officer's wife. Ambitious production based on a British stage play suffers from claustrophobic atmosphere but is greatly redeemed by the first rate cast.
1975 (PG) 107m/C GB Michael York, Richard Attenborough, Trevor Howard, Stacy Keach, Christopher Plummer, Susannah York, James Faulkner, Michael Culver, Persis Khambatta; D: Michael Anderson Sr. VHS CRV ♂♂½

Coneheads Comedy inspired by once popular characters from "Saturday Night Live" coasts in on the coattails of "Wayne's World." Aykroyd and Curtin reprise their roles as Beldar and Prymaat, the couple from the planet Remulak who are just trying to fit in on Earth. Except for speaking in metallic-sounding voices, drinking entire six packs of beer at once, and becoming sexually aroused by tossing fur-covered rings on each other's cones, they're no different than any typical American family. Newman, who created the role of teenage daughter Connie, appears as Connie, while Burke takes over as Connie (toddler Connie is Aykroyd's daughter, in her film debut.) One-joke premise is a decade late and a dime short, though cast of comedy all-stars provide a lift.
1993 ?m/C Dan Aykroyd, Jane Curtin, Laraine Newman, Jason Alexander, Michelle Burke, Chris Farley, Michael Richards, Lisa Jane Persky, Sinbad, Shishir Kurup, Michael McKean, Phil Hartman, David Spade, Dave Thomas, Jan Hooks, Chris Rock, Adam Sandler, Julia Sweeney, Danielle Aykroyd; D: Steven Barron; W: Dan Aykroyd, Tom Davis, Bonnie Turner, Terry Turner. VHS NYR ♂♂½

Conexion Mexico Not-bad actioner about the Mexican police fighting against drug traffickers who are aided by a group of vicious women.
1987 85m/C MX Sergio Goyri, Victor Junco, Silvia Manriquez, Sergio Bustamante. VHS, Beta $75.00 MAD ♂♂½

Conexion Oriental A journalist investigates an Oriental crime syndicate. Not much mystery to the mystery. Dubbed into Spanish. AKA: East Connection.
1970 90m/C Dale Robertson, Lucianna Paluzzi, Callsto Calisti. VHS, Beta NO ♂½

The Confessional A mad priest unleashes a monster from his confessional to wreak havoc upon the world. Pray for your VCR. AKA: House of Mortal Sin.
1975 (R) 108m/C GB Anthony Sharp, Susan Penhaligon, Stephanie Beacham, Norman Eshley, Sheila Keith; D: Pete Walker. VHS, Beta $59.95 PSM ♂

Confessions of a Police Captain A dedicated police captain tries to wipe out the bureaucratic corruption that is infecting his city. Balsam gives a fine performance in a heavy-going tale.
1972 (PG) 104m/C IT Martin Balsam, Franco Nero, Marilu Tolo; D: Damiano Damiani. VHS, Beta $59.98 SUE ♂♂

Confessions of a Vice Baron Vice Baron Lombardo makes it big as a drug dealer and flesh peddler, then loses it all when he falls in love. Sleazy exploitation.
1942 70m/B Willy Castello; D: Harvey Thew. VHS, Beta $16.95 SNC ♂

Confessions of a Young American Housewife Routine sexploiter about a recent divorcee who moves in with two younger couples and experiences sexual liberation.
1978 (R) 85m/C Jennifer Wells, Rebecca Brooke, Chris Jordan. VHS, Beta $29.95 MED ♂

Confessions of Tom Harris Somewhere between all the prize fighting, leg breaking for the mob, and jail terms for rape, Tom Harris finds time for a life-changing encounter with love. Murray wrote the script, based on true story. AKA: Tale of the Cock; Childish Things.
1972 (PG) 90m/C Don Murray, Linda Evans, David Brian, Gary Clarke, Logan Ramsey, Angelique Pettyjohn; D: John Derek, David Nelson. VHS, Beta NO ♂

Confidential A G-man goes under cover to infiltrate a crime ring. Well made and full of action, fun array of character actors. Naish particularly good as nasty killer.
1935 67m/B Donald Cook, Evelyn Knapp, Warren Hymer, J. Carroll Naish, Herbert Rawlinson, Morgan Wallace, Kane Richmond, Theodore von Eltz, Reed Howes; D: Edward L. Cahn. VHS VYY ♂♂½

Confidential A '40s detective tries to solve a decades-old axe murder, only to disappear himself. Horrible fare from our friends north of the border.
1986 (R) 95m/C CA Neil Munro, August Schellenberg, Chapelle Jaffe, Tom Butler; D: Bruce Pittman. VHS, Beta NO Woof!

Confidentially Yours Truffaut's homage to Hitchcock, based on Charles Williams' "The Long Saturday Night." A hapless small-town real estate agent is framed for a rash of murders and his secretary, who is secretly in love with him, tries to clear his name. Truffaut's last film is stylish and entertaining. In French with English subtitles. *AKA:* Vivement Dimanche!; Finally, Sunday.
1983 (PG) 110m/B *FR* Fanny Ardant, Jean-Louis Trintignant, Philippe Morier-Genoud, Philippe Laudenbach, Caroline Sihol; *D:* Francois Truffaut. **VHS, Beta $59.98** FOX, TAM, HMV 🐾🐾🐾

Conflict Bogart falls for his sister-in-law and asks his wife for a divorce. She refuses, he plots her murder, and thinks up the alibi. When the police fail to notify him of her death, Bogart is forced to report his wife missing. But is she dead? Her guilty husband smells her perfume, sees her walking down the street, and discovers the body is missing from the scene of the crime. Suspenseful thriller also features Greenstreet as a psychologist/family friend who suspects Bogart knows more than he's telling.
1945 86m/B Humphrey Bogart, Alexis Smith, Sydney Greenstreet, Rose Hobart, Charles Drake, Grant Mitchell; *D:* Curtis Bernhardt. **VHS $19.98** MGM 🐾🐾🐾

The Conformist Character study of young Italian fascist, plagued by homosexual feelings, who must prove his loyalty by killing his old professor. Decadent and engrossing story is brilliantly acted. Based on the novel by Alberto Moravia, scripted by Bertolucci. *AKA:* Il Conformist.
1971 (R) 108m/C *IT FR GE* Jean-Louis Trintignant, Stefania Sandrelli, Dominique Sanda, Pierre Clementi, Gastone Moschin; *D:* Bernardo Bertolucci. Academy Awards '71 Nominations: Best Adapted Screenplay; National Board of Review Awards '71: 5 Best Foreign Films of the Year; National Society of Film Critics Awards '71: Best Director (Bertolucci). **VHS, Beta, LV $44.95** TAM, PAR, APD 🐾🐾🐾🐾

Congress Dances A rare German musical about a romance in old Vienna. Popular in its day, it was subsequently banned by the Nazis in 1937. In German with English subtitles. *AKA:* Der Kongress Tanzt.
1931 92m/B *GE* Lilian Harvey, Conrad Veidt, Willy Fritsch; *D:* Erik Charell. **VHS, Beta $44.95** TAM, NOS, HHT 🐾🐾🐾

A Connecticut Yankee A charming, if somewhat dated, version of the popular Mark Twain story, "A Connecticut Yankee in King Arthur's Court." Rogers is a radio shop owner who dreams his way back to the Knights of the Round Table. Story rewritten to fit Rogers' amiable style and to make then-current wisecracks. Great cast overcomes weak points in the script.
1931 96m/B Will Rogers, Myrna Loy, Maureen O'Sullivan, William Farnum; *D:* David Butler. **VHS $19.98** FOX, FCT 🐾🐾🐾

A Connecticut Yankee in King Arthur's Court A pleasant version of the famous Mark Twain story about a 19th century man transported to Camelot and mistaken for a dangerous wizard. This was the third film version of the classic, which was later remade as "Unidentified Flying Oddball," a made for television movie and an animated feature. ♫Once and For Always; Busy Doin' Nothin'; If You Stub Your Toe on the Moon; When Is Sometime?; Twixt Myself and Me. *AKA:* A Yankee in King Arthur's Court.
1949 108m/C Bing Crosby, Rhonda Fleming, William Bendix, Cedric Hardwicke, Henry Wilcoxon, Murvyn Vye, Virginia Field; *D:* Tay Garnett. **VHS, Beta, LV $14.98** MCA 🐾🐾½

A Connecticut Yankee in King Arthur's Court An animated version of the classic Mark Twain story.
1970 74m/C *D:* Zoran Janjic. **VHS, Beta $19.95** MGM 🐾🐾

The Connection The Living Theatre's ground-breaking performance of Jack Gelber's play about heroin addicts waiting for their connection to arrive, while a documentary filmmaker hovers nearby with his camera.
1961 105m/B Warren Finnerty, Carl Lee, William Redfield, Freddie Redd Quartet, Roscoe Lee Browne, Garry Goodrow, James Anderson, Jackie McLean; *D:* Shirley Clarke. **VHS, Beta $29.95** MFV, FCT 🐾🐾🐾½

The Connection Durning steps in to work a deal between hotel jewel thieves and the insurance company. Complex plot handled deftly by all concerned. Made for television.
1973 74m/C Charles Durning, Ronny Cox, Dennis Cole, Zohra Lampert, Heather MacRae, Dana Wynter; *D:* Tom Gries. **VHS, Beta $59.95** VMK 🐾🐾½

The Conqueror Wayne in pointed helmet and goatee is convincingly miscast as Genghis Khan in this woeful tale of the warlord's early life and involvement with the kidnapped daughter of a powerful enemy. Rife with stilted, unintentionally funny dialogue, Oriental western was very expensive to make (with backing by Howard Hughes). No matter; it's surreal enough to enable viewer to approximate an out-of-body experience. Written by Oscar Millard and listed in "The Fifty Worst Films of All Time." Even those on the set suffered: filming took place near a nuclear test in Utah and many members of the cast and crew eventually developed cancer.
1956 111m/C John Wayne, Susan Hayward, William Conrad, Agnes Moorehead, Lee Van Cleef, Pedro Armendariz Sr., Thomas Gomez, John Hoyt; *D:* Dick Powell. **VHS, Beta $19.95** MCA Woof!

Conqueror & the Empress Low-budget tale of English explorers who roust an island prince from his throne, motivating him to engage in inspired blood-letting.
1964 89m/C Guy Madison, Ray Danton, Mario Petri, Alberto Farnese. **VHS, Beta** NO Woof!

Conqueror of the World The adventures of a caveman named Bog. Really. Based on the novel by Albert Cavallone. Available in Spanish.
1985 90m/C **VHS, Beta** NO Woof!

The Conqueror Worm Price turns in a fine performance portraying the sinister Matthew Hopkins, a real-life 17th century witch-hunter. No "ham" in this low-budget, underrated thriller. The last of three films from director Reeves, who died from an accidental overdose in 1969. Also available with "Tomb of Ligeia" on Laser Disc. *AKA:* Witchfinder General; Edgar Allan Poe's Conqueror Worm.
1968 95m/C *GB* Vincent Price, Ian Ogilvy, Hilary Dwyer, Rupert Davies, Robert Russell, Patrick Wymark, Wilfrid Brambell; *D:* Michael Reeves. **VHS $59.99** HBO, FCT 🐾🐾🐾

Conquest Garbo, as the Polish countess Marie Walewska, tries to persuade Napoleon (Boyer) to free her native Poland from the Russian Tsar. Garbo, Boyer, and Ouspenskaya are outstanding, while the beautiful costumes and lavish production help, but the script is occasionally weak. "Conquest" was a box office flop in the United States and ended up costing MGM more than any movie

it had made up until that time. *AKA:* Marie Walewska.
1932 90m/B Greta Garbo, Charles Boyer, Reginald Owen, Alan Marshal, Henry Stephenson, Leif Erickson, May Whitty, Maria Ouspenskaya, Vladimir Sokoloff, Scotty Beckett; *D:* Clarence Brown. **VHS, Beta $19.98** MGM, FCT 🐾🐾🐾

Conquest Sword and sorcery tale of two mighty warriors against an evil sorceress who seeks world domination. High point is the score written by Claudio Simonetti, who scores Dario Argento's horror films.
1983 (R) 92m/C *IT SP MX* Jorge Rivero, Andrea Occhipinti, Violeta Cela, Sabrina Siani; *D:* Lucio Fulci. **VHS, Beta $59.95** MED 🐾½

Conquest of Cochise Mediocre oater about a cavalry officer who must stop the war between the Apache and Comanche tribes and a group of Mexicans in the Southwest of the 1850s.
1953 70m/C John Hodiak, Robert Stack, Joy Page; *D:* William Castle. **VHS, Beta $14.99** GKK 🐾🐾

Conquest of Mycene Hercules battles an evil queen and this time he may actually lose! Muscleman mayhem will entertain the kids. *AKA:* Ercole Contro Molock.
1963 102m/C *IT FR* Gordon Scott, Rosalba (Sara Bay) Neri, Jany Clair; *D:* Giorgio Ferroni. **VHS $16.95** SNC 🐾½

Conquest of Space A spaceship sets off to explore Mars in spite of the commander's attempts to sabotage the voyage. He believes the flight is an heretical attempt to reach God. An uneasy mixture of religion and space exploration detracts from the nifty special effects which are the only reason to watch.
1955 81m/C Walter Brooke, Eric Fleming, Mickey Shaughnessy, Phil Foster, William Redfield, William Hopper, Benson Fong, Ross Martin; *D:* Byron Haskin. **VHS** PAR 🐾½

Conquest of the Normans During the Norman invasion of England, Oliver is accused of kidnapping the King. To save his life, Oliver must find the true identity of the abductors. With so much plot, there should have been some suspense.
1962 83m/C Cameron Mitchell. **Beta $39.95** AIP 🐾

Conquest of the Planet of the Apes The apes turn the tables on the human Earth population when they lead a revolt against their cruel masters in the distant year of 1990. Sure, there's plenty of cliches—but the story drags you along. The 4th film in the series. Followed by "Battle for the Planet of the Apes."
1972 (PG) 87m/C Roddy McDowall, Don Murray, Ricardo Montalban, Natalie Trundy, Severn Darden, Hari Rhodes; *D:* J. Lee Thompson. **VHS, Beta, LV $19.98** FOX 🐾🐾½

Conrack The true story of Pat Conroy, who tried to teach a group of illiterate Black children in South Carolina by using common-sense teaching techniques to inspire their interest. Voight is convincing as the earnest teacher. Based on Conroy's novel "The Water Is Wide."
1974 (PG) 111m/C Jon Voight, Paul Winfield, Madge Sinclair, Hume Cronyn, Martin Ritt; *D:* Martin Ritt; *M:* John Williams. **VHS, Beta $59.98** FOX 🐾🐾🐾

Consenting Adults Made for television movie about a distressed family coming to terms with a favorite son's homosexuality. Restrained exploration of the controversial subject. Based on Laura Z. Hobson's novel.

1985 100m/C Marlo Thomas, Martin Sheen, Barry Tubb, Talia Balsam, Ben Piazza, Corinne Michaels; *D:* Gilbert Cates. **VHS** *NO* ♫♫½

Consenting Adults Cookie-cutter thriller capitalizes on popular "psycho-destroys-your-normal-life" theme. Average yuppie couple (Kline and Mastrantonio) are startled and then seduced by the couple moving in next door (Spacey and Miller), who conduct a considerably less-restrained lifestyle. Wife-swapping leads to murder and an innocent man is framed. Plot and characters are underdeveloped yet manage to hold interest through decent performances.
1992 (R) 109m/C Kevin Kline, Mary Elizabeth Mastrantonio, Kevin Spacey, Rebecca Miller, Forest Whitaker, E.G. Marshall; *D:* Alan J. Pakula; *W:* Matthew Chapman. **VHS, Beta, LV** $94.95 *HPH, IME* ♫♫

Consolation Marriage A couple meet and marry after being jilted by others, then must make a choice when their old flames return. Dunne and O'Brien make a charming couple in this early talkie. One of Dunne's early starring roles. *AKA:* Married in Haste.
1931 82m/B Irene Dunne, Pat O'Brien, John Halliday, Matt Moore, Myrna Loy, Lester Vail; *D:* Paul Sloane. **VHS, Beta** $19.98 *TTC* ♫♫½

Conspiracy Defense Secretary William Baine is haunted by a past sexual encounter, and a top secret team moves in to avert any hint of what could become a "sex scandal." Based on a true story.
1989 (R) 87m/C James Wilby, Kate Hardie, Glyn Houston; *D:* Christopher Barnard. **VHS, Beta** $29.95 *ACA* ♫♫

Conspiracy of Hearts A convent of nuns hide Jewish children in 1943 Italy despite threats to their personal safety. Suspenseful tale despite the familiar plot.
1960 113m/B *GB* Lilli Palmer, Yvonne Mitchell, Sylvia Syms, Ronald Lewis; *D:* Ralph Thomas. **VHS, Beta** *LCA* ♫♫♫

A Conspiracy of Love A made-for-television movie about three generations of a divorce-torn family trying to pull itself back together. Sugary domestic tale tries to be uplifting, succeeds in being cliche-ridden.
1987 93m/C Robert Young, Drew Barrymore, Glynnis O'Connor, Elizabeth Wilson, Michael Laurence, John Fujioka, Alan Fawcett; *D:* Noel Black. **VHS** $19.95 *STE, NWV* ♫

Conspiracy of Terror Married detectives investigate a series of murders and unearth a grisly cult in a quiet suburb. Standard fare with a few too cute lines concerning the leads' mixed-faith marriage. Made for television pilot.
1975 78m/C Michael Constantine, Barbara Rhoades, Mariclare Costello, Roger Perry, David Opatoshu, Logan Ramsey; *D:* John Llewellyn Moxey. **VHS** *LIV* ♫

Conspiracy: The Trial of the Chicago Eight Courtroom drama focuses on the rambunctious trial of the Chicago Eight radicals, charged with inciting a riot at the Democratic National Convention of 1968. Dramatized footage mixed with interviews with the defendants. Imaginative reconstruction of history.
1987 118m/C Peter Boyle, Elliott Gould, Robert Carradine, Martin Sheen, David Clennon, David Kagen, Michael Lembeck, Robert Loggia; *D:* Jeremy Paul Kagan. **VHS, Beta** $79.95 *HBO* ♫♫♫

Conspirator Somewhat engrossing drama about a beautiful young girl who discovers that her new husband, a British army officer, is working with the Communists. Elizabeth Taylor stars as the naive American wife and Robert Taylor plays her Russkie

agent husband. Although madly in love with his wife, he is given orders to kill her. Picture falls apart at end due to weak script. Based on the novel by Humphrey Slater.
1949 85m/B *GB* Robert Taylor, Elizabeth Taylor, Robert Flemyng, Harold Warrender, Honor Blackman, Marjorie Fielding, Thora Hird; *D:* Victor Saville; *W:* Sally Benson, Gerard Fairlie. **VHS** $19.98 *MGM* ♫♫½

Consuming Passions A ribald, food-obsessed English comedy about a young idiot who rises within the hierarchy of a chocolate company via murder. You'll never guess what the secret ingredient in his wonderful chocolate is. Based on a play by Michael Palin and Terry Jones (better known as part of the Monty Python troupe), the film is sometimes funny, more often gross, and takes a single joke far beyond its limit.
1988 (R) 95m/C Vanessa Redgrave, Jonathan Pryce, Tyler Butterworth, Freddie Jones, Prunella Scales, Sammi Davis-Voss, Thora Hird; *D:* Giles Foster. **VHS, Beta, LV** *NO* ♫½

Contagion Innocent real estate agent meets a reclusive, eccentric millionaire who offers him unlimited wealth and beautiful women, but only if he kills someone. Interesting ethical premise loses its philosophic purity.
1987 90m/C *AU* John Doyle, Nicola Bartlett, Roy Barrett, Nathy Gaffney, Pamela Hawksford; *D:* Karl Zwicky. **VHS, Beta** $14.95 *SVS* ♫½

Contempt A film about the filming of a new version of "The Odyssey," and the rival visions of how to tell the story. Amusing look at the film business features Fritz Lang playing himself, Godard as his assistant. Bardot is pleasant scenery. Adapted from Moravia's "A Ghost at Noon." *AKA:* Le Mepris; Il Disprezzo.
1964 102m/C *IT FR* Brigitte Bardot, Jack Palance, Fritz Lang, Georgia Moll, Michel Piccoli; *W/D:* Jean-Luc Godard. **VHS, Beta, LV** $19.95 *COL, TAM, SUE* ♫♫♫½

Continental Divide A hard-nosed political columnist takes off for the Colorado Rockies on an "easy assignment"—interviewing a reclusive ornithologist, with whom he instantly falls in love. A city slicker, he first alienates her, but she eventually falls for him, too. But it's not exactly a match made in heaven. Story meanders to a conclusion of sorts. Probably the most normal Belushi ever was on screen. Scripted by Lawrence Kasdan.
1981 (PG) 103m/C John Belushi, Blair Brown, Allen Garfield, Carlin Glynn, Tony Ganios, Val Avery, Tim Kazurinsky; *D:* Michael Apted; *W:* Lawrence Kasdan. **VHS, Beta, LV** $14.95 *MCA, PIA* ♫♫

Contra Company A teenage girl and an embittered ex-terrorist narrowly escape from a terrorist-infested region in this confusing film about politics, drugs, and sinister dealings.
1988 (R) 110m/C **VHS, Beta** *NO* ♫

Contraband The leader of a smuggling gang escapes from an ambush in which his brother was murdered. He searches for a haven of safety while his cronies seek brutal revenge. Average crime yarn lacks much excitement. Dubbed into English.
1986 95m/C *IT* Fabio Testi, Ivana Monti; *D:* Lucio Fulci. **VHS, Beta** *NO* ♫½

Control Tedious tale of fifteen volunteers for a 20-day fallout shelter habitation experiment who become trapped when a real nuclear emergency occurs. Filmed in Rome. Made for cable TV.

1987 83m/C *IT* Burt Lancaster, Kate Nelligan, Ben Gazzara, Andrea Ferreol, Lavinia Segurini, Andrea Occhipinti, Cyrielle Claire, Jean Benguigui, Kate Reid, Erland Josephson, Ingrid Thulin; *D:* Giuliano Montaldo. **VHS, Beta** $79.99 *HBO* ♫½

The Conversation Hackman plays a surveillance expert increasingly uneasy about his job as he begins to suspect he is an accomplice to murder. Powerful statement about privacy, responsibility and guilt. Written by Coppola and one of the best movies of the 70s.
1974 (PG) 113m/C Gene Hackman, John Cazale, Frederic Forrest, Allen Garfield, Cindy Williams, Robert Duvall, Teri Garr, Michael Higgins, Elizabeth McRae, Harrison Ford; *D:* Francis Ford Coppola. Academy Awards '74 Nominations: Best Original Screenplay, Best Picture, Best Sound; Cannes Film Festival '74: Best Film; National Board of Review Awards '74: 10 Best Films of the Year, Best Actor (Hackman), Best Director (Coppola). **VHS, Beta, LV** $14.95 *PAR* ♫♫♫½

Conversation Piece An aging art historian's life is turned upside down when a Countess and her daughters rent out the penthouse in his estate. Sometimes-talky examination of scholarly pretensions. *AKA:* Violence et Passion; Gruppo di Famiglia in un Interno.
1975 (R) 112m/C *IT FR* Burt Lancaster, Silvana Mangano, Helmut Berger, Claudia Cardinale; *D:* Luchino Visconti. **VHS, Beta** $69.99 *HBO* ♫♫♫

Convicted Lean thriller about a woman cleared of a murder charge, but only when a second, identical murder occurs while she is jailed.
1932 57m/B Aileen Pringle, Jameson Thomas, Harry Myers, Dorothy Christy, Richard Tucker; *D:* Christy Cabanne. **VHS, Beta, LV** $19.85 *NOS* ♫♫½

Convicted Solid story of innocent man imprisoned for rape, and his wife's determined efforts to free him. Larroquette does well in unexpected role. Based on a true story. Made for television.
1986 94m/C John Larroquette, Carroll O'Connor, Lindsay Wagner; *D:* David Lowell Rich. **VHS, Beta** $69.98 *TTC* ♫♫½

Convicted: A Mother's Story Jillian embezzles cash from her employer, all for the sake of a bum of a boyfriend, and goes to jail. Odd casting hinders a ho-hum plot. Made for television.
1987 95m/C Ann Jillian, Kiel Martin, Fred Savage, Gloria Loring, Christa Denton; *D:* Richard T. Heffron. **VHS, Beta** $79.95 *JTC* ♫

Convicts at Large An escaped convict steals the clothes of a inept architect. Left with only prison duds, the architect stumbles into the bad side of town and gets involved with the mob. Inane.
1938 58m/B Ralph Forbes, Paula Stone. **VHS, Beta, LV** *NO* ♫

Convoy Life aboard a convoy ship in the North Sea during WWII. The small cruiser is picked on by a German U-Boat. Will a rescuer appear? Noted for technical production values.
1940 95m/B Clive Brook, John Clements, Edward Chapman, Judy Campbell, Edward Rigby, Stewart Granger, Michael Wilding, George Benson; *D:* Pen Tennyson. **VHS** $19.95 *NOS* ♫♫½

Convoy A defiant trucker leads an indestructible truck convoy to Mexico to protect high gasoline prices. Lightweight stuff was inspired by the song "Convoy" by C.W. McCall.

1978 (R) 106m/C Kris Kristofferson, Ali MacGraw, Ernest Borgnine, Burt Young, Madge Sinclair, Franklin Ajaye, Cassie Yates; *D:* Sam Peckinpah. VHS, Beta $79.95 *HBO* ♫♫

Coogan's Bluff An Arizona deputy sheriff (Eastwood) travels to New York in order to track down a killer on the loose. First Eastwood/Siegel teaming is actioner. The television series "McCloud" was based on this film.
1968 (PG) 100m/C Clint Eastwood, Lee J. Cobb, Tisha Sterling, Don Stroud, Betty Field, Susan Clark, Tom Tully; *D:* Don Siegel. VHS, Beta, LV $19.95 *MCA* ♫♫♫

The Cook, the Thief, His Wife & Her Lover An exclusive restaurant houses four disturbing characters. Greenaway's powerful vision of greed, love, and violence may be too strong for some tastes. Available in several different versions: the standard unrated theatrical release, the unrated version in a letterboxed format, an R-rated cut which runs half an hour shorter, and a Spanish-subtitled version.
1990 (R) 123m/C GB Richard Boringer, Michael Gambon, Helen Mirren, Alan Howard, Tim Roth; *D:* Peter Greenaway. VHS $19.95 *VMK* ♫♫♫½

Cookie A light comedy about a Mafia don's daughter trying to smart mouth her way into the mob's good graces. A character-driven vehicle, this plot takes a backseat to casting. Wiest is superb as Falk's moll. The screenplay is by Nora Ephron and Alice Arlen.
1989 (R) 93m/C Emily Lloyd, Peter Falk, Dianne Wiest, Jerry Lewis, Brenda Vaccaro, Ricki Lake, Lionel Stander, Michael Gazzo, Adrian Pasdar, Bob Gunton; *D:* Susan Seidelman; *W:* Alice Arlen, Nora Ephron. VHS, Beta, LV, 8mm $19.95 *WAR* ♫♫½

Cooking Up Trouble The crazy trio become foster dads in this "Stooge" type comedy.
1944 ?m/C Shemp Howard, Billy Gilbert, Maxie Rosenbloom. VHS $1944 *LOO* ♫♫

Cool As Ice "Rapper" Vanilla Ice makes his feature film debut as a rebel with an eye for the ladies, who motors into a small, conservative town. Several so-so musical segments. For teenage girls only.
1991 (PG) 92m/C Vanilla Ice, Kristin Minter, Michael Gross, Sydney Lassick, Dody Goodman, Naomi Campbell, Candy Clark; *D:* David Kellogg. VHS, Beta, LV $79.95 *MCA* ♫

Cool Blue An unsuccessful painter meets the woman of his dreams, has a brief affair, then tries to locate her in the greater Los Angeles metro area. Good luck. Watch for Penn's cameo.
1988 (R) 93m/C Woody Harrelson, Hank Azaria, Ely Pouget, John Diehl; *Cameos:* Sean Penn; *D:* Mark Mullin, Richard Shepard. VHS, Beta, LV $89.95 *COL* ♫½

Cool Hand Luke One of the last great men-in-chains films. A man (Newman) sentenced to sweat out a term on a prison farm refuses to compromise with authority. Martin shines in his supporting role as the oily warden, uttering that now-famous phrase, "What we have here is a failure to communicate." Kennedy's performance as leader of the chain gang won him an Oscar. Based on the novel by Donn Pearce.
1967 126m/C Paul Newman, George Kennedy, J.D. Cannon, Strother Martin, Dennis Hopper, Anthony Zerbe, Lou Antonio, Wayne Rogers, Harry Dean Stanton, Ralph Waite, Joe Don Baker, Richard Davalos, Jo Van Fleet; *D:* Stuart Rosenberg. Academy Awards '67: Best Supporting Actor (Kennedy); Nominations: Best Adapted Screenplay, Best Original Score; Academy Awards '67: Best Actor (Newman). VHS, Beta, LV $19.98 *WAR, BTV* ♫♫♫½

Cool It, Baby A woman's life is ripped apart when she unknowingly appears in a raunchy stag film while under the influence of drugs.
1967 ?m/B VHS $20 *SMW* ♫♫♫½

Cool it Carol A girl and her boyfriend leaves a small town for the excitement of city life. After she works as a prostitute and a model, they return to their quiet home. There's no place like home.
1968 101m/C Robin Askwith, Janet Lynn, Jess Conrad, Stubby Kaye. VHS, Beta $59.95 *MON* Woof!

Cool Mikado A jazzy modernization of the Gilbert-Sullivan operetta, in which an American soldier is kidnapped by the gangster fiance of the Japanese girl he loves.
1963 81m/C GB Stubby Kaye, Frankie Howerd, Dennis Price; *D:* Michael Winner. VHS, Beta $79.95 *JEF* ♫♫

Cool World Underground cartoonist Jack Deebs enters his own adult cartoon "Cool World," lured by his sex-kitten character "Holli Would," who needs him to leave her animated world and become human. Holli's plan is opposed by the only other human to occupy Cool World, a slick detective whose main job is to prevent noids (humans) and doodles (cartoons) from having sex and destroying the balance between the two existences. A mixture of live-action and wild animation. Director Bakshi's creations are not intended for children but this is less explicit than usual, which may be one of the problems. Little humor and a flat script leave this film too uninvolving.
1992 (PG-13) 101m/C Gabriel Byrne, Kim Basinger, Brad Pitt, Michele Abrams, Deidre O'Connell, Carrie Hamilton, Frank Sinatra Jr.; *D:* Ralph Bakshi. VHS, Beta, LV *PAR, PMS, WTA* ♫♫

Cooley High Black high school students in Chicago go through the rites of passage in their senior year during the '60s. Film is funny, smart and much acclaimed. Great soundtrack featuring Motown hits of the era is a highlight. Sequel to the TV series "What's Happening."
1975 (PG) 107m/C Glynn Turman, Lawrence Hilton-Jacobs, Garrett Morris, Cynthia Davis; *D:* Michael Schultz; *W:* Eric Monte. VHS, LV $79.95 *ORI, FCT, PTB* ♫♫♫

Cop Left by his wife and child, a ruthless and work-obsessed detective goes after a twisted serial killer. Woods' exceptional ability to play sympathetic weirdos is diluted by a script—based on James Ellroy's novel "Blood on the Moon"—that warps the feminist theme, is violent, and depends too heavily on coincidence.
1988 (R) 110m/C James Woods, Lesley Ann Warren, Charles Durning, Charles Haid, Raymond J. Barry, Randi Brooks, Annie McEnroe, Victoria Wauchope; *D:* James B. Harris. VHS, Beta, LV $19.95 *PAR* ♫♫½

Cop and a Half Streetwise 8-year-old (Golden) accidentally witnesses a murder and then bullys police into letting him join the force (for a day) when he withholds key information. Enter his partner for the day—hard-edged detective Reynolds, who claims to hate kids, but who we know will learn to love them. Meanwhile, the outlaw (Sharkey) knows Devon saw him and is trying to silence him permanently. Predictable fantasy may appeal to kids, but will make most adults yawn. One of Sharkey's last roles.
1993 (PG) 87m/C Norman D. Golden II, Burt Reynolds, Ruby Dee, Ray Sharkey; *D:* Henry Winkler; *W:* Arne Olsen; *M:* Alan Silvestri. VHS *NYR* ♫½

The Cop & the Girl A cop falls for a teenage runaway, ends up on the lam. Confused story overpowered by camera work. Lots of violence and strong language. Dubbed.
1986 94m/C GE Juergen Prochnow, Annette Von Klier; *D:* Peter Keglevic. VHS, Beta $79.95 *WWV* ♫

Cop in Blue Jeans Undercover cop goes after a mob kingpin in this violent, badly dubbed crime yarn.
1978 92m/C Tomas Milian, Jack Palance, Maria Rosaria Omaggio, Guido Mannari; *D:* Bruno Corbucci. VHS, Beta $24.95 *VMK* ♫

Cop-Out A cop is framed. His brother is mad. Teamed up with a sexy lawyer, he exposes the filth that is corrupting the city. Okay melodrama.
1991 102m/C David Buff, Kathryn Luster, Dan Ranger, Reggie DeMorton, Lawrence L. Simeone; *W/D:* Lawrence L. Simeone. VHS, Beta $79.95 *AIP* ♫♫

Copacabana A shady theatrical agent (Groucho) books a nightclub singer into two shows at the same time at New York's ritzy nightclub. Lots of energy spent trying to enliven a routine script. Also available colorized. ♫Tico Tico; Stranger Things Have Happened; Je Vous Amie; My Heart Was Doing a Bolero; Let's Do the Copacobana; I Haven't Got a Thing to Sell; We've Come to Copa.
1947 91m/B Groucho Marx, Carmen Miranda, Steve Cochran, Gloria Jean, Andy Russell, Earl Wilson; *D:* Alfred E. Green. VHS, LV $19.98 *REP, FCT, MLB* ♫♫

Copenhagen Nights A young Danish girl discovers sex in a local orgy-club. Softcore, dubbed, and retitled.
198? 80m/C DK Lilli Carati, Ajita Wilson. VHS, Beta $29.95 *MED* Woof!

Copkillers Two men desperate for an easy way to make money embark on a murderous shooting spree. Mostly blanks.
1977 (R) 93m/C Jason Williams, Bill Osco. VHS, Beta $59.95 *TWE* Woof!

Copper Canyon Milland plays a Confederate Army officer who heads West after the Civil War, meets up with Lamarr, and sparks a romance. Good chemistry between the leads in this otherwise standard western.
1950 84m/B Ray Milland, Hedy Lamarr, MacDonald Carey, Mona Freeman, Harry Carey Jr., Frank Faylen, Taylor Holmes, Peggy Knudsen; *D:* John Farrow. VHS $14.95 *PAR, FCT* ♫♫½

Copperhead A group of copperhead snakes attack a family who possess a stolen Incan gold necklace. This one bites.
1984 (R) 90m/C Jack Renner, Gretta Ratliff, David Fritts, Cheryl Nickerson. VHS, Beta $59.95 *UHV* ♫

Cops and Robbers Two cops use a Wall Street parade for returning astronauts as a cover for a multi-million dollar heist. Exceptional caper film thanks to the likable leads and genuine suspense.
1973 (PG) 89m/C Joseph Bologna, Dick Ward, Sheppard Strudwick, John P. Ryan, Ellen Holly, Dolph Sweet, Joe Spinell, Cliff Gorman; *D:* Aram Avakian. VHS $14.95 *MGM, WKV* ♫♫½

Cops/One Week Two vintage Keaton shorts, with original organ score.
1922 51m/B Buster Keaton; *D:* Buster Keaton, Eddie Cline. VHS, Beta, 8mm *VYY* ♫♫½

Coquette Pickford's first talkie portrays her as a flirtatious flapper from a well-to-do family who falls in love with a poor man her father despises. So much in fact that daddy kills the young man and then commits sui-

cide, leaving his daughter to face the world alone. Pickford and Brown get to share a melodramatic death scene and audiences flocked to hear "America's Sweetheart" speak onscreen. Based on a play by George Abbott and Anne Preston.
1929 75m/B Mary Pickford, Johnny Mack Brown, Matt Moore, John Sainpolis, Henry Kolker, George Irving, Louise Beavers, William Janney; *D:* Sam Taylor. **VHS $19.98** *MGM* ✽✽½

Cord & Dischords/Naughty Nurse Two vintage silent shorts featuring some lesser known slapstick clowns cavorting in blackface.
1928 50m/B Fred Parker, Jack Cooper, Ella MacKenzie, Spencer Williams Jr. **VHS, Beta $14.95** *VYY* ✽

Cordelia A dramatization of an actual court case in turn-of-the century Quebec, in which an "overly" vivacious woman is accused of "murdering her husband.
1987 115m/C *CA* **VHS, Beta** *NFC* ✽✽

Coriolanus, Man without a Country When the Romans begin to abuse their rights, the Plebians call upon the brave and mighty Coriolanus to lead them into battle against their oppressors. Predictable muscle man outing.
1964 ?m/C *IT* Gordon Scott, Alberto Lupo, Lilla Brignone. **VHS, Beta $16.95** *SNC* ✽✽

Corleone Limp tale about two boyhood friends who grow up to fight the evil landowners who dominate Italy. To accomplish this, one becomes a mobster, the other a politician.
1979 (R) 115m/C *IT* Claudia Cardinale, Giuliano Gemma; *D:* Pasquale Squitieri. **VHS, Beta $79.95** *MGM* ✽

The Corn is Green Touching story of a school teacher in a poor Welsh village who eventually sends her pet student to Oxford. Davis makes a fine teacher, though a little young, while the on-site photography provides atmosphere. Based on play by Emlyn Williams. Music by Max Steiner. Remade in 1979.
1945 115m/B Bette Davis, John Dall, Nigel Bruce, Joan Lorring, Arthur Shields, Mildred Dunnock, Rhys Williams, Rosalind Iven; *D:* Irving Rapper; *M:* Max Steiner. **VHS, Beta $19.95** *MGM, FCT* ✽✽✽

Cornbread, Earl & Me A high school basketball star from the ghetto is mistaken for a murderer by cops and shot, causing a subsequent furor of protest and racial hatred. Superficial melodrama.
1975 (R) 95m/C Moses Gunn, Rosalind Cash, Bernie Casey, Tierre Turner, Madge Sinclair, Keith Wilkes, Antonio Fargas; *D:* Joseph Manduke. **VHS, Beta $59.95** *HBO* ✽✽

Cornered Tough Powell plays an airman released from a German prison camp who pursues a Nazi war criminal to avenge the death of his wife and child.
1945 102m/B Dick Powell, Walter Slezak, Micheline Cheirel, Luther Adler; *D:* Edward Dmytryk. **VHS, Beta, LV $19.98** *RKO, TTC* ✽✽✽

Coroner Creek Scott's fiancee commits suicide during an Indian attack on her stagecoach, and the couple's dowry is stolen. Scott sets out to trace the loot and exact his revenge. A superior production, notable for being one of the first westerns with an adult theme.
1948 89m/B Randolph Scott, Marguerite Chapman, George Macready, Sally Eilers, Edgar Buchanan, Wallace Ford, Forrest Tucker; *D:* Ray Enright. **VHS** *NO* ✽✽½

Corporate Affairs A ruthless business woman climbing her way to the top literally seduces her boss to death.

1990 (R) 92m/C Peter Scolari, Mary Crosby, Chris Lemmon, Ken Kercheval; *D:* Terence H. Winkless. **VHS $79.98** *MGM* ✽✽

The Corpse Grinders Low-budget bad movie classic in which a cardboard corpse-grinding machine makes nasty cat food that makes cats nasty. Sets are cheap, gore effects silly, and cat attacks ridiculous.
1971 (R) 73m/C Sean Kenney, Monika Kelly, Sandford Mitchell; *W/D:* Ted V. Mikels. **VHS, Beta $19.95** *WWV Woof!*

The Corpse Vanishes Lugosi at his chilling best as a diabolical scientist who snatches young brides and drains their blood in an effort to keep his 70-year-old wife eternally youthful. Not for newlyweds!
1942 64m/B Bela Lugosi, Luana Walters, Tristram Coffin, Elizabeth Russell, Vince Barnett, Joan Barclay, Angelo Rossitto; *D:* Wallace Fox. **VHS, Beta, 3/4U, Special order formats $19.95** *NOS, MRV, SNC* ✽✽

Corregidor A love triangle develops between doctors treating the wounded during the World War II battle. A poor propaganda piece which contains only shaky stock footage for its "action" sequences.
1943 73m/B Otto Kruger, Elissa Landi, Donald Woods, Rick Vallin, Frank Jenks, Wanda McKay, Ian Keith; *D:* William Nigh. **VHS $19.95** *NOS, MOV, HEG* ✽✽

Corrida Interdite Slow-motion sequences reveal the beauty of the bullfighting ritual without neglecting the deadly nature of the sport.
1958 10m/C **VHS, Beta** *FLI* ✽✽

The Corridor: Death Two Americans are involved in a car accident in Israel which triggers a debate on the Jewish perspective of death and the afterlife. Filmed on location at Hadassah Hospital on St. Scopus, Jerusalem. The final part of the trilogy preceded by "The Eighth Day: Circumcision" and "The Journey: Bar Mitzvah."
19?? 25m/C **VHS, Beta $39.95** *ERG* ✽✽

Corridors of Blood Karloff is a doctor, in search of a viable anesthetic, who accidently becomes addicted to drugs, then turns to grave robbers to support his habit. Karloff plays usual threatening doctor to perfection. *AKA:* The Doctor from Seven Dials.
1958 86m/C *GB* Boris Karloff, Betta St. John, Finlay Currie, Christopher Lee, Francis Matthews, Adrienne Corri, Nigel Green; *D:* Robert Day. **VHS, Beta $39.95** *MPI* ✽✽½

Corrupt Bad narcotics cop goes after murderer, but mysterious Lydon gets in the way. An acquired taste, best if you appreciate Lydon, better known as Johnny Rotten of the Sex Pistols. *AKA:* Order of Death; Cop Killers.
1984 (PG) 99m/C *IT* Harvey Keitel, John (Johnny Rotten) Lydon, Sylvia Sidney, Nicole Garcia, Leonard Mann; *D:* Roberto Faenza; *M:* Ennio Morricone. **VHS, Beta $69.95** *HBO* ✽✽✽

The Corrupt Ones Everyone's after a photographer who has a medallion that will lead to buried treasure in China. Great characters hampered by pedestrian script. *AKA:* Il Sigillo de Pechino; Die Holle von Macao; Les Corrompus; The Peking Medallion; Hell to Macao.
1967 87m/C Robert Stack, Elke Sommer, Nancy Kwan, Christian Marquand, Werner Peters; *D:* James Hill. **VHS, Beta $49.95** *SUE, NLC* ✽✽½

Corruption Mostly soft-porn. Alleged plot: The Mob is interested in having Shea work for them, and makes it worth his while.
1989 (R) 80m/C Mary McGee, Patrick Shea. **VHS** *NO Woof!*

Corsair Actioner about a gorgeous debutante and a handsome gangster who find themselves caught up with a gang of bootlegging pirates. Todd is always worth watching.
1931 73m/B Chester Morris, Thelma Todd, Frank McHugh, Ned Sparks, Mayo Methot; *D:* Roland West. **VHS, Beta $19.95** *NOS, KRT, RXM* ✽✽

The Corsican Brothers Alexander Dumas' classic about twins who, although separated, remain spiritually tied throughout their various adventures. Fairbanks takes on dual roles in this entertaining swashbuckler. Remade for television in 1984.
1942 111m/B Douglas Fairbanks Jr., Akim Tamiroff, Ruth Warrick, J. Carroll Naish, H.B. Warner, Henry Wilcoxon; *D:* Gregory Ratoff. **VHS, Beta, LV $12.95** *MED* ✽✽½

Corvette Summer After spending a semester restoring a Corvette in his high school shop class, an L.A. student must journey to Las Vegas to recover the car when it is stolen. There he meets a prostitute, falls in love, and steps into the "real world" for the first time. Potts intriguing as the low-life love interest, but she can't save this one. *AKA:* The Hot One.
1978 (PG) 104m/C Mark Hamill, Annie Potts, Eugene Roche, Kim Milford, Richard McKenzie, William Bryant; *D:* Matthew Robbins. **VHS, Beta $59.95** *MGM* ✽

Cosh Boy Vicious male youths stalk women on the streets of London in this low-budget Jack the Ripper rip-off. *AKA:* The Slasher.
1961 90m/B Joan Collins, James Kennedy. **VHS, Beta** *NO Woof!*

The Cosmic Eye Animated tale of three musicians from outer space who come to earth to spread the message of worldwide peace and harmony. A variety of cultural perspectives about the origins and destiny of the Earth are offered. Rather moralizing but the animation is impressive.
1971 71m/C *D:* Faith Hubley; *V:* Dizzy Gillespie, Maureen Stapleton, Benny Carter. **VHS, Beta, LV $59.98** *LTY, WTA, DIS* ✽✽✽

The Cosmic Man An alien arrives on Earth with a message of peace and restraint. He is regarded with suspicion by us nasty Earthlings. Essentially "The Day the Earth Stood Still" without the budget, but interesting nonetheless.
1959 72m/B Bruce Bennett, John Carradine, Angela Greene, Paul Langton, Scotty Morrow; *D:* Herbert Greene. **VHS, Beta $14.95** *RHI, SNC* ✽½

The Cosmic Monsters Scientist accidentally pops a hole in the ionosphere during a magnetism experiment. Then huge, mean insects arrive to plague mankind. Coincidence? You figure it out. *AKA:* The Strange World of Planet X.
1958 75m/B Forrest Tucker, Gaby Andre, Alec Mango, Hugh Latimer, Martin Benson; *D:* Gilbert Gunn. **VHS, Beta $14.95** *RHI, MRV, SNC* ✽½

Cosmo Jones, Crime Smasher Murder mystery based on a forties radio program.
1943 ?m/C *IT* Mantan Moreland, Frank Graham. **VHS $16.95** *SNC* ✽✽

Cosmos: War of the Planets The ultimate battle for survival is fought in outer space, though not very well and on a small budget. Special effects especially laughable. *AKA:* Cosmo 2000: Planet Without a Name; War of the Planets.
1980 (PG) 90m/C *IT* Katia Christine, West Buchanan, John Richardson, Yanti Somer; *D:* Al Bradley. **VHS, Beta** *PGN Woof!*

Cottage to Let Propaganda thriller about a Nazi plot to kidnap the inventor of a new bombsight. Focused cast struggles with lackluster script. *AKA:* Bombsight Stolen.
1941 90m/B *GB* Leslie Banks, Alastair Sim, John Mills, Jeanne de Casalis, Carla Lehmann, George Cole, Michael Wilding, Frank Cellier, Wally Patch, Catherine Lacey; *D:* Anthony Asquith. VHS, Beta $16.95 SNC ℤ½

Cotter A Native American rodeo clown feels responsible for a cowboy's death, returns home to reflect on his life. Fair story, best at the small town feeling.
1972 94m/C *D:* Don Murray, Carol Lynley, Rip Torn, Sherry Jackson; *D:* Paul Stanley. VHS, Beta $39.95 XVC, UHV ℤ

Cotton Candy Follows the faintly interesting trials and tribulations of a high school senior who tries to form a rock band. At first he meets failure, but is ultimately successful with the band and romance. Made for television. Ron Howard, of "Happy Days" fame co-wrote the script with his brother, Clint, and also directed.
1982 97m/C Charles Martin Smith, Clint Howard, Leslie King; *D:* Ron Howard. VHS, Beta TLF ℤℤ

The Cotton Club With $50 million in his pocket, Francis reaches for an epic and delivers: handsome production, lots of dance, bit of singing, confused plot, uneven performances, that last too long. A musician playing at The Cotton Club falls in love with gangster Dutch Schultz's girlfriend. A black tap dancer falls in love with a member of the chorus line who can pass for white. These two love stories are told against a background of mob violence and music. Excellent performances by Hoskins and Gwynne. ♫Minnie the Moocher; Ill Wind; The Mooch; Ring Dem Bells; Drop Me Off in Harlem; Cotton Club Stomp; Truckin; Mood Indigo; Copper Colored Gal; Crazy Rhythm; The Jitter Bug.
1984 (R) 121m/C Diane Lane, Richard Gere, Gregory Hines, Lonette McKee, Bob Hoskins, Fred Gwynne, James Remar, Nicolas Cage, Lisa Jane Persky, Allen Garfield, Gwen Verdon, Joe Dallesandro, Jennifer Grey, Tom Waits, Diane Venora; *D:* Francis Ford Coppola; *M:* John Barry. VHS, Beta, LV, 8mm $14.98 SUE, NLC ℤℤℤ

Cotton Comes to Harlem Cambridge and St. Jacques star as Harlem plainclothes detectives Grave Digger Jones and Coffin Ed Johnson in this successful mix of crime and comedy. They're investigating a suspicious preacher's back-to-Africa scheme which they suspect is a swindle. Directorial debut of Davis. Filmed on location in Harlem, New York. Based on the novel by Chester Himes. Followed by a weak sequel, "Come Back, Charleston Blue."
1970 (R) 97m/C Godfrey Cambridge, Raymond St. Jacques, Calvin Lockhart, Judy Pace, Redd Foxx, John Anderson, Emily Yancy, J.D. Cannon, Teddy Wilson, Eugene Roche, Cleavon Little, Lou Jacobi; *D:* Ossie Davis. VHS $14.95 MGM ℤℤℤ

Cotton Queen Romance and light intrigue plague the children of two rival textile mill owners. *AKA:* Crying Out Loud.
1937 80m/B Will Fyffe, Stanley Holloway; *D:* Joe Rock. VHS, Beta, 8mm $29.95 VYY, FCT ℤ½

The Couch Trip Aykroyd is an escapee from a mental institution who passes himself off as a radio psychologist and becomes a media sensation. There are a few laughs and some funny characters but for the most part this one falls flat.

1987 (R) 98m/C Dan Aykroyd, Walter Matthau, Charles Grodin, Donna Dixon, Richard Romanus, Arye Gross, David Clennon, Mary Gross; *D:* Michael Ritchie. VHS, Beta, LV $19.98 ORI ℤ½

Could It Happen Here? A lurid Italian spectacle about a metropolis thrown into a state of chaotic martial law by terrorism. Dubbed.
198? 90m/C *IT* Luc Merenda, Marcella Michelangeli; *D:* Massimo Pirri. VHS, Beta NO ℤ

The Count Chaplin pretends to be the secretary of his boss, who in turn is posing as a count. Silent with musical soundtrack added.
1916 20m/B Charlie Chaplin; *D:* Charlie Chaplin. VHS, Beta, 3/4U, Special order formats CAB ℤℤ½

Count/Adventurer Two Chaplin two-reelers: "The Count (The Phoney Nobleman)" (1916), in which Charlie impersonates a count at the home of Miss Moneybags, and "The Adventurer" (1917), Chaplin's final film for Mutual, in which he plays an escaped convict with the law relentlessly on his trail. Silent with musical score.
1917 52m/B Charlie Chaplin, Eric Campbell, Edna Purviance, Frank Coleman; *D:* Charlie Chaplin. VHS, Beta $39.95 VYY ℤℤ½

Count Dracula Passable version of the Dracula legend (based on the novel by Bram Stoker) has Lee as the thirsty count on the prowl for fresh blood.
1971 (R) 90m/C *SP GE IT* Christopher Lee, Herbert Lom, Klaus Kinski, Frederick Williams, Maria Rohm, Soledad Miranda; *D:* Jess (Jesus) Franco. VHS $14.98 REP, FCT ℤℤ½

Count Dracula's Great Love European horror superstar Naschy plays Dracula; stylishly done in the Hammer tradition. Considered by many to be Naschy's best horror film.
1972 ?m/C Paul Naschy. VHS $16.95 SNC, SMW ℤℤ

The Count of Monte Cristo One of the first full-length features starring popular stage stars of the day. The first truly American feature, it was based on the classic tale of revenge by Alexander Dumas. Silent. Remade many times.
1912 90m/B James O'Neill. VHS, Beta $19.95 NOS, VYY, DVT ℤℤ½

The Count of Monte Cristo A true swashbuckling revenge tale about Edmond Dantes, who unjustly spends years prison. After escaping, he gains ever so sweet and served quite cold revenge. Adaptation of the Alexandre Dumas classic.
1934 114m/B Robert Donat, Elissa Landi, Louis Calhern, Sidney Blackmer, Irene Hervey, Raymond Walburn, O.P. Heggie; *D:* Rowland V. Lee. VHS, Beta $9.99 CCB, MED ℤℤℤ

The Count of Monte Cristo The Alexander Dumas classic about an innocent man (Chamberlain) who is imprisoned, escapes, and finds the treasure of Monte Cristo, which he uses to bring down those who wronged him. Good version of the historical costumer. Originally shown in theaters in Europe, but broadcast on television in the U.S.
1974 104m/C *GB* Richard Chamberlain, Kate Nelligan, Donald Pleasence, Alessio Orano, Tony Curtis, Louis Jourdan, Trevor Howard, Taryn Power; *D:* David Greene. VHS, Beta $19.98 LIV ℤℤ½

The Count of the Old Town Feisty townsfolk settle the score after a gang of booze smugglers trick them out of their money. In Swedish with English subtitles.
1934 90m/B *SW* Ingrid Bergman. VHS, Beta $29.95 WAC, TAM ℤℤ

Count Yorga, Vampire The vampire Count Yorga is practicing his trade in Los Angeles, setting up a coven and conducting seances. Good update of the traditional character, with Quarry suitably solemn and menacing. Followed by "The Return of Count Yorga." Also available with "Cry of the Banshee" on laserdisc.
1970 (PG) 90m/C Robert Quarry, Roger Perry, Michael Murphy, Michael Macready, Donna Anders, Judith Lang; *D:* Bob Kelljan. VHS, Beta $19.99 HBO ℤℤ½

Countdown Documentary-type fictional look at the first moon mission and its toll on the astronauts and their families. Timely because the U.S. was trying to send a man to the moon in 1968. Interesting as a look at the developing Altman style.
1968 102m/C James Caan, Robert Duvall, Michael Murphy, Ted Knight, Joanna Moore, Barbara Baxley, Charles Aidman, Steve Ihnat, Robert Altman; *D:* Robert Altman. VHS, Beta $19.98 WAR ℤℤ½

Counter Attack Story of murder and insurance fraud takes place on the back lots of the Hong Kong film industry. As good as these get.
1984 105m/C Bruce Li, Dan Inosanto, John Ladalski, Young Kong; *D:* Bruce Li. VHS, Beta WVE ℤ½

Counter Destroyer A woman retreats to a secluded island to write a film script. But then she is attacked by an army of disgruntled Vampire-zombies. Who can work with all that commotion? Fortunately for her, ninja warriors arrive in the nick of time.
1987 90m/C VHS, Beta TWE ℤ

Counter Measures A helicopter pilot stumbles on to a bizarre chain of crimes and disasters.
1987 98m/C Monte Markham; *D:* Gerban Ceth. VHS, Beta PGN ℤ

Counter Punch Blake is a boxer framed for the murder of his manager who sets out to clear his name by finding the killers. Fair rendition of a familiar plot. *AKA:* Ripped Off; The Boxer; Uomo Dalla Pelle Dura.
1971 (R) 72m/C *IT* Robert (Bobby) Blake, Ernest Borgnine, Gabriel Ferzetti, Catherine Spaak, Tomas Milian; *D:* Franco Prosperi. VHS, Beta $9.95 SIM, LIV ℤℤ½

Counterblast A Nazi spy assumes the role of a British scientist in order to gain classified information for the Fatherland. The trouble begins when he refuses to carry out an order to execute a pretty young assistant. Appealing performances distract from the somewhat confusing plot. *AKA:* The Devil's Plot.
1948 99m/B *GB* Robert Beatty, Mervyn Johns, Nova Pilbeam, Margaretta Scott, Sybilla Binder, Marie Lohr, Karel Stepanek, Alan Wheatley; *D:* Paul Stein. VHS, Beta $16.95 SNC, RXM ℤℤ

The Counterfeit Traitor Suspense thriller with Holden playing a double agent in Europe during World War II. Based on the true adventures of Eric Erickson, the top Allied spy of WW II, who was captured by the Gestapo but escaped.
1962 140m/C William Holden, Lilli Palmer, Hugh Griffith, Werner Peters, Eva Dahlbeck; *D:* George Seaton. VHS, Beta $29.95 PAR ℤℤ½

Counterforce A rough group of mercenaries is hired to guard a Mideastern leader being chased by his country's ruling despot. Mild action with predictable story.
1987 (R) 98m/C George Rivero, George Kennedy, Andrew Stevens, Isaac Hayes, Louis Jourdan, Kevin Bernhardt, Hugo Stiglitz, Robert Foster, Susana Dosamantes; *D:* J. Anthony Loma. VHS, Beta, LV $89.95 LIV ℤ

Country Strong story of a farm family in crisis when the government attempts to foreclose on their land. Good performances all around and an excellent portrayal of the wife by Lange. "The River" and "Places In the Heart," both released in 1984, also dramatized the plight of many American farm families in the early 1980s.
1984 (PG) 109m/C Jessica Lange, Sam Shepard, Wilford Brimley, Matt Clark, Therese Graham, Levi L. Knebel; *D:* Richard Pearce. **VHS, Beta, LV $79.95** TOU *♫♫♫*

Country Gentlemen Vaudeville team, Olsen and Johnson, play fast-talking conmen who sell shares in a worthless oil field to a bunch of World War I veterans. What a surprise when oil is actually found there. Not one of the duo's better performances.
1936 54m/B Ole Olsen, Chic Johnson, Joyce Compton, Lila Lee, Ray Corrigan, Donald Kirke, Pierre Watkin; *D:* Ralph Staub. **VHS, Beta $24.95** NOS, MRV, VYY *♫♫*

Country Girl In the role that completely de-glamorized her (and won her an Oscar), Kelly plays the wife of alcoholic singer Crosby who tries to make a comeback with the help of director Holden. One of Crosby's four dramatic parts, undoubtedly one of his best. Seaton won an Oscar for his adaptation of the Clifford Odets play. Remade in 1982. *♫*The Search is Through; Dissertation on the State of Bliss; It's Mine, It's Yours; The Land Around Us.
1954 104m/B Bing Crosby, Grace Kelly, William Holden, Gene Reynolds, Anthony Ross; *D:* George Seaton; *W:* George Seaton. Academy Awards '54: Best Actress (Kelly), Best Screenplay; Nominations: Best Actor (Crosby), Best Black and White Cinematography, Best Director (Seaton), Best Picture; Academy Awards '56: Best Art Direction/Set Decoration (B & W); Golden Globe Awards '55: Best Actress—Drama (Kelly); National Board of Review Awards '54: 10 Best Films of the Year, Best Actress (Kelly). **VHS, Beta $14.95** PAR, BTV *♫♫♫½*

Country Girl Aging, alcoholic actor is desperate for a comeback. His director blames his fiercely loving wife for the downfall. Poor cable TV remake of 1954 version with Bing Crosby.
1982 137m/C Dick Van Dyke, Faye Dunaway, Ken Howard. **VHS, Beta $19.99** HBO *♫*

The Country Kid A freckle-faced teenager and his two brothers are beset by a wicked uncle out to steal their inheritance. One of Barry's best-remembered films.
1923 60m/B Wesley Barry, "Spec" O'Donnell, Bruce Guerin, Kate Price, Helen Jerome Eddy, George Nichols; *D:* William Beaudine. **VHS, Beta** NO *♫♫♫*

Country Lovers, City Lovers Two adaptations of short stories by South African novelist Nadine Gordimer about interracial love.
1972 121m/C VHS, Beta $69.95 MGM *♫♫½*

Countryman A dope-smuggling woman crashes her plane in Jamaica and is rescued by Countryman, a rasta super hero. Not very good, but at least there's great music by Bob Marley and others.
1983 (R) 103m/C Hiram Keller, Kristine Sinclair; *D:* Dickie Jobson. **VHS, Beta $59.95** MVD, MED *♫♫*

County Fair This early silent film is an adaptation of Neil Burgess' play about life in New England.
1920 60m/B Helen Jerome Eddy, David Butler. **VHS, Beta $24.95** NOS, DVT, HEG *♫♫*

Coup de Grace Engaging political satire about a wealthy aristocratic woman in Latvia during the 1919-1920 Civil War, and how she attempts to maintain her lifestyle as German soldiers are housed on her estate. Her unrequited love for a German officer adds to her troubles. In German with English subtitles. Co-written by von Trotta and based on the novel by Marguerite Yourcenar.
1978 96m/B GE FR Margarethe von Trotta, Matthias Habich, Rudiger Kirschstein, Matthieu Carriere; *D:* Volker Schlondorff. **Beta $59.95** COL, APD, GLV *♫♫½*

Coup de Torchon Set in 1938 French West Africa, Noiret plays corrupt police chief Lucien Cordier who is consistently harrassed by his community, particularly by the town pimp. He usually overlooks the pimp's crimes, but when Cordier catches him and a friend shooting at plague victims' bodies floating down the river he decides to murder them in cold blood. Based on the novel "POP 1280" by Jim Thompson. In French with English subtitles. *AKA:* Clean Slate.
1981 128m/C FR Philippe Noiret, Isabelle Huppert, Guy Marchand, Stephane Audran, Eddy Mitchell, Jean-Pierre Marielle; *D:* Bertrand Tavernier. **VHS** NO *♫♫♫*

Coupe de Ville Three brothers are forced by their father to drive mom's birthday present from Detroit to Florida in the summer of '63. Period concerns and music keep it interesting.
1990 (PG-13) 98m/C Patrick Dempsey, Daniel Stern, Arye Gross, Joseph Bologna, Alan Arkin, Annabeth Gish, Rita Taggart, James Gammon; *D:* Joe Roth. **VHS, Beta, LV $19.95** MCA *♫♫½*

Couples and Robbers Rich couple and a poor couple are unexpectedly brought together.
1984 29m/C VHS, Beta DCL *♫*

Courage Based on fact, a television movie about a Hispanic mother in New York City who, motivated by her drug-troubled children, goes undercover and exposes a multi-million-dollar drug ring. Loren is great in a decidedly non-glamorous role.
1986 141m/C Sophia Loren, Billy Dee Williams, Hector Elizondo, Val Avery, Dan Hedaya, Ron Rifkin, Jose Perez; *D:* Jeremy Paul Kagan. **VHS, Beta $29.95** STE, NWV *♫♫♫*

Courage Mountain If you're looking for a good sequel to Johanna Spyri's classic "Heidi" this isn't it. Europe is on the brink of WWI when teenage Heidi leaves her beloved mountain for an exclusive boarding school in Italy. Not surprisingly in a war zone, the military takes over and the kids are sent to an orphanage run by nasties (see also "Oliver!"). The girls escape to the mountains and are saved by none other than Sheen as Heidi's pal Peter (who cast the twentysomething Sheen as a teenager? Bad mistake.) Ridiculous sequel to the classic tale will appeal to kids despite what the critics say.
1989 (PG) 92m/C Juliette Caton, Joanna Clarke, Nicola Stapleton, Charlie Sheen, Jan Rubes, Leslie Caron, Jade Magri, Kathryn Ludlow, Yorgo Voyagis; *D:* Christopher Leitch; *W:* Weaver Webb; *M:* Sylvester Levay. **VHS, Beta, LV $14.95** COL, FCT *♫*

Courage of Black Beauty Another version of the perennial heart warmer about a boy and his horse.
1957 80m/C Johnny Crawford, Mimi Gibson, John Bryant, Diane Brewster, J. Pat O'Malley; *D:* Harold Schuster. **VHS, Beta $12.95** LIV *♫½*

Courage of Lassie Fourteen-year-old Taylor is the heroine in this girl loves dog tale. In this case, the dog is actually called Bill, not Lassie, in spite of the film's title. Bill is found wounded by Taylor and she nurses him back to health. He proves to be loving, loyal, and useful, so much so that, through a complicated plotline, he winds up in the Army's K-9 division and returns home with the doggie version of shell-shock. Taylor's still there to nurse him back to his old kind self again. *AKA:* Blue Sierra.
1946 93m/C Elizabeth Taylor, Frank Morgan, Tom Drake, Selena Royle, Harry Davenport; *D:* Fred M. Wilcox. **VHS $19.98** MGM *♫♫½*

Courage of Rin Tin Tin Rusty and his faithful dog Rin Tin Tin help the cavalry soldiers of Fort Apache keep law and order in a small Arizona town. The perennial kid-pleasing German Shepherd comes through again.
1983 90m/C James Brown, Lee Aaker. **VHS, Beta $24.95** MON *♫*

Courage of the North The Mounties break up a fur-stealing ring with the help of Captain Dog and Dynamite Horse. Bound to set your hair on end.
1935 55m/B John Preston, June Love, William Desmond, Tom London, Jimmy Aubrey, Dynamite Horse, Captain Dog. **VHS, Beta** NO *♫½*

Courageous Avenger A sheriff brings a treacherous ore mine foreman to justice.
1935 59m/B Johnny Mack Brown. **VHS, Beta, LV** MLB *♫*

Courageous Dr. Christian Dr. Christian is faced with an epidemic of meningitis among the inhabitants of a shanty town. Typical entry in the "Dr. Christian" series.
1940 66m/B Jean Hersholt, Dorothy Lovett, Tom Neal, Robert Baldwin, Maude Eburne; *D:* Bernard Vorhaus. **VHS, Beta $19.95** NOS, VYY, DVT *♫♫*

The Courageous Mr. Penn Slow-moving British film, outlining the achievements of William Penn, the Quaker founder of Pennsylvania. *AKA:* Penn of Pennsylvania.
1941 79m/B GB Clifford Evans, Deborah Kerr, Dennis Arundell, Aubrey Mallalieu, D.J. Williams, O.B. Clarence, Charles Carson, Henry Oscar, J.H. Roberts; *D:* Lance Comfort. **VHS, Beta $19.95** NOS, VYY, TIM *♫♫*

The Courier A former drug addict seeks revenge on the dealers who killed his friend. Only thing that saves it are the songs by U2, The Pogues, and Hothouse Flowers. Musical score by Elvis Costello.
1988 (R) 85m/C IR Gabriel Byrne, Ian Bannen, Padraig O'Loingsigh, Cait O'Riordan, Patrick Bergin; *D:* Joe Lee, Frank Deasy. **VHS, Beta, LV $79.98** VES, LIV *♫♫*

Courier of Death A courier is embroiled in a mob war/struggle over a locked briefcase with mysterious contents.
1984 77m/C Joey Johnson, Barbara Garrison; *D:* Tom Shaw. **VHS, Beta $69.95** VES, LIV *♫*

Court Jester Swashbuckling comedy stars Danny Kaye as a former circus clown who teams up with a band of outlaws trying to dethrone a tyrant king. Kaye poses as the court jester so he can learn of the evil king's intentions. Filled with more color, more song, and more truly funny lines than any three comedies put together, this is Kaye's best performance. *♫*They'll Never Outfox the Fox; Baby, Let Me Take You Dreaming; My Heart Knows a Lovely Song; The Maladjusted Jester.
1956 101m/C Danny Kaye, Glynis Johns, Basil Rathbone, Angela Lansbury, Cecil Parker, John Carradine, Mildred Natwick, Robert Middleton; *D:* Norman Panama, Melvin Frank. **VHS, Beta, LV $14.95** PAR *♫♫♫*

The Court Martial of Billy Mitchell Terrific courtroom drama depicts the secret trial of Billy Mitchell, head of the Army Air Service in the 1920s, who predicted the role of airpower in subsequent warfare and the danger of war with Japan. Mitchell incurred the wrath of the military by publicly faulting the lack of U.S. preparedness for invasion. Steiger is outstanding as the attor-

ney; Cooper is great as Mitchell. Debut for Montgomery. **AKA:** One-Man Mutiny.
1955 100m/C Gary Cooper, Charles Bickford, Ralph Bellamy, Rod Steiger, Elizabeth Montgomery, Fred Clark, James Daly, Jack Lord, Peter Graves, Darren McGavin, Robert Simon, Jack Perrin, Charles Dingle; **D:** Otto Preminger. **VHS, LV $19.98** *REP* 🎬🎬🎬

The Court Martial of Jackie Robinson True story of a little known chapter in the life of the famous athlete. During his stint in the Army, Robinson refused to take a back seat on a bus and subsequently faced the possibility of court martial. Originally made for cable television.
1990 (R) 94m/C Andre Braugher, Daniel Stern, Ruby Dee, Stan Shaw, Paul Dooley, Bruce Dern; **D:** Larry Peerce. **VHS, Beta $79.98** *TTC, FCT* 🎬🎬½

The Courtesans of Bombay Gritty docudrama, set in Pavanpul, the poverty-stricken brothel section of Bombay, shows how the women of the area must live.
1985 74m/C *GB* Kareem Samar, Zohra Segal, Saeed Jaffrey; **D:** Ismail Merchant. **VHS, Beta $29.98** *SUE, TAM, NLC* 🎬🎬½

Courtin' Wildcats Early Gibson programmer in which he plays a frail eastern college boy who was sent west by his father to toughen up. Once there, he meets Gilbert and ends up marrying her.
1929 56m/B Hoot Gibson, Eugenia Gilbert, Monte Montague; **D:** Jerome Storm. **VHS $9.95** *GPV* 🎬½

The Courtney Affair An aristocratic young Britisher causes a stir when he marries an Irish maid. As a result, the couple must face terrific social ostracism. Classy soap opera family saga was a big money maker in England. **AKA:** The Courtneys of Curzon Street.
1947 112m/B *GB* Anna Neagle, Michael Wilding, Gladys Young, Michael Medwin, Coral Browne, Jack Watling, Bernard Lee; **D:** Herbert Wilcox. **VHS** *NO* 🎬🎬½

Courtship From renowned playwright Horton Foote comes this touching story about a sheltered, upper-crust young girl who shocks her family and friends by eloping with a traveling salesman. Made for television.
1987 84m/C Hallie Foote, William Converse-Roberts, Amanda Plummer, Rochelle Oliver, Michael Higgins; **D:** Howard Cummings. **VHS, Beta $19.98** *LHV, WAR* 🎬🎬🎬

The Courtship of Eddie's Father A clever nine-year-old boy plays matchmaker for his widowed dad in this rewarding family comedy-drama (the inspiration for the TV series). Some plot elements are outdated, but young Howard's performance is terrific; he would later excel at direction. Based on the novel by Mark Toby.
1962 117m/C Glenn Ford, Shirley Jones, Stella Stevens, Dina Merrill, Ron Howard, Jerry Van Dyke; **D:** Vincente Minnelli. **VHS $19.98** *MGM, FCT* 🎬🎬🎬

Cousin, Cousine Pleasant French comedy about distant cousins who meet at a round of family parties, funerals, and weddings and become friends, but their relationship soon becomes more than platonic. Remade in the U.S. in 1989 as "Cousins." In French with English subtitles.
1976 (R) 95m/C *FR* Marie-Christine Barrault, Marie-France Pisier, Victor Lanoux, Guy Marchand, Ginette Garcin, Sybil Maas; **D:** Jean-Charles Tacchella. Academy Awards '76 Nominations: Best Actress (Barrault), Best Foreign Language Film, Best Original Screenplay; Cesar Awards '76: Best Supporting Actress (Pisier); National Board of Review Awards '76: 5 Best Foreign Films of the Year. **VHS, Beta, LV $29.95** *IME, FOX, APD* 🎬🎬🎬½

The Cousins Set against the backdrop of Parisian student life, two very different cousins (one twisted, the other saintly) vie for the hand of Mayniel. This country mouse, city mouse adult fable ultimately depicts the survival of the fittest. Chabrol's lovely but sad second directorial effort. **AKA:** Les Cousins.
1959 112m/B *FR* Jean-Claude Brialy, Gerard Blain, Juliette Mayniel, Claude Cerval, Genevieve Cluny; **D:** Claude Chabrol. **VHS** *PAR* 🎬🎬🎬

Cousins An American remake of "Cousin, Cousine," in which two distant cousins-by-marriage meet at a wedding and, due to their respective spouses' infidelities, fall into each other's arms. A gentle love story with a humorous and biting look at the foibles of extended families.
1989 (PG-13) 110m/C Isabella Rossellini, Sean Young, Ted Danson, William L. Petersen, Norma Aleandro, Lloyd Bridges, Keith Coogan; **D:** Joel Schumacher. **VHS, Beta, LV $19.95** *PAR, FCT, HMV* 🎬🎬½

Cover Girl A vintage wartime musical about a girl who must decide between a nightclub career and a future as a cover model. Hayworth is beautiful; Kelly dances like a dream; Silvers and Arden are hilarious. Songs by Ira Gershwin and Jerome Kern; cinematography by Rudolph Mate. ♫Cover Girl; Sure Thing; Make Way For Tomorrow; Put Me to the Test; Long Ago and Far Away; That's the Best of All; The Show Must Go On; Who's Complaining?; Poor John.
1944 107m/C Rita Hayworth, Gene Kelly, Phil Silvers, Otto Kruger, Lee Bowman, Jinx Falkenberg, Eve Arden, Edward Brophy, Anita Colby; **D:** Charles Vidor; **M:** Ira Gershwin, Jerome Kern. Academy Awards '44: Best Score; Nominations: Best Color Cinematography, Best Interior Decoration, Best Song ("Long Ago and Far Away"), Best Sound. **VHS, Beta, LV $19.95** *COL* 🎬🎬🎬

Cover Girl Models An action-packed seventies adventure in which beautiful models are forced to fight for survival.
1975 82m/C Lindsay Bloom, Pat Anderson, John Kramer, Rhonda Leigh Hopkins, Mary Woronov; **D:** Cirio H. Santiago. **VHS, Beta** *SUE* 🎬

Cover-Up Terrorist attacks on U.S. military bases in Israel are just a smokescreen for a greater threat. The below-par actioner stands out only for the hokey religious symbolism in its Good Friday climax.
1991 (R) 89m/C Dolph Lundgren, Louis Gossett Jr., John Finn; **D:** Manny Coto. **VHS, LV $39.95** *LIV, IME* 🎬½

The Covered Wagon Prototypical silent Western began the genre. Wagon train moves cross-country, battling weather and wild Indians. By today's standards, somewhat bucolic and uneventful, but the location photography holds up quite well. Big budget film in its day, and enormously popular.
1923 98m/B Warren Kerigan, Lois Wilson, Alan Hale Sr., Ernest Torrence; **D:** James Cruze. **VHS, LV $14.95** *PAR* 🎬🎬½

Covered Wagon Days The Three Mesquiteers set out after silver smugglers who have framed Rico's brother for murder.
1940 54m/B Bob Livingston, Raymond Hatton, Duncan Renaldo, John Merton, Reed Howes; **D:** George Sherman. **VHS $9.95** *REP* 🎬🎬

Covergirl Wealthy man decides to relieve his boredom by molding a young woman into a supermodel. She finds the glamorous life isn't always what it's cracked up to be. TV-type melodrama. **AKA:** Dreamworld.
1983 (R) 98m/C *CA* Jeff Conaway, Irena Ferris, Cathie Shirriff, Roberta Leighton, Deborah Wakeham; **D:** Jean-Claude Lord. **VHS, Beta $19.99** *HBO, STE* 🎬½

Covert Action A drug kingpin who desires to protect his business tries to frame a captain for a crime he did not commit.
1988 85m/C Rick Washburne, John Christian, Stuart Garrison Day, Amanda Zinsser, Johnny Stumper; **D:** J. Christian Ingvordsen. **VHS, Beta $79.98** *MCG* 🎬½

Cow Town A range war results when ranchers begin fencing in their land to prevent cattle rustling. Autry's 72nd film has some good songs and a dependable cast.
1950 70m/B Gene Autry, Gail Davis, Jock Mahoney, Harry Shannon; **D:** John English. **VHS, Beta $29.98** *CCB* 🎬½

Coward of the County A devout pacifist is put to the test when his girlfriend is raped. Good performances by all concerned. Based on the lyrics of Kenny Rogers' hit song of the same name. Made for television.
1981 115m/C Kenny Rogers, Frederic Lehne, Largo Woodruff, Mariclare Costello, Ana Alicia, Noble Willingham; **D:** Dick Lowry. **VHS, Beta $19.98** *LHV, WAR* 🎬🎬½

Cowboy Film chronicling the determination of cattle-herders in the West.
1954 69m/C **VHS, Beta, LV** *RXM* 🎬½

Cowboy & the Ballerina A television movie about an aging rodeo star who falls in love with a petite ballerina defecting from a Russian Dance Company. Good cast makes it watchable.
1984 96m/C Lee Majors, Leslie Wing, Christopher Lloyd, Anjelica Huston, George De La Pena; **D:** Jerry Jameson. **VHS, Beta $79.95** *PSM* 🎬🎬

Cowboy & the Bandit A cowboy comes to the aid of a widow being victimized by outlaws.
1935 58m/B Rex Lease, Bobby Nelson, William Desmond; **D:** Albert Herman. **VHS, Beta $19.95** *NOS* 🎬

The Cowboy and the Lady Oberon plays a madcap heiress who is deposited by her politician father on their Florida estate to keep her out of trouble while he seeks the Presidential nomination. She is bored and decides to go to a local rodeo where she meets cowboy Cooper. Both are instantly smitten and marry on impulse. Cooper doesn't know about her wealth and when her father finds out about the marriage he's appalled that his daughter has married beneath her. Since this is a comedy all comes out right in the end. Good cast, weak story.
1938 91m/B Gary Cooper, Merle Oberon, Patsy Kelly, Walter Brennan, Fuzzy Knight, Mabel Todd, Henry Kolker, Harry Davenport; **D:** H.C. Potter. Academy Awards '38: Best Sound; Nominations: Best Song ("The Cowboy and the Lady"), Best Original Score. **VHS $19.98** *FCT, HBO* 🎬🎬½

Cowboy & the Senorita A cowboy solves the mystery of a missing girl and wins her lovely cousin. The first film that paired Rogers and Evans, who went on to become a winning team, on and offscreen.
1944 56m/B Roy Rogers, John Hubbard, Dale Evans. **VHS, Beta $9.95** *NOS, MRV, DVT* 🎬🎬

Cowboy Commandos Improbable plot has cowboys riding out after Nazi spies, who want to steal valuable ore.
1943 53m/B Ray Corrigan, Dennis Moore, Max Terhune, Budd Buster, John Merton; **D:** S. Roy Luby. **VHS $19.95** *DVT, RXM, HEG* 🎬🎬

Cowboy Counselor Cowboy Hoot Gibson helps an enchanting girl clear her innocent brother's name.
1933 60m/B Hoot Gibson. **VHS, Beta** *UHV* 🎬

Cowboy Millionaire An Englishwoman comes to an American dude ranch and falls in love with one of the ranch hands. Entertaining Western comedy.
1935 65m/B George O'Brien, Evalyn Bostock, Edgar Kennedy, Alden Chase; *D:* Eddie Cline. VHS $19.95 *NOS, DVT, RXM* 🎬🎬½

The Cowboys Wayne stars as a cattle rancher who is forced to hire eleven schoolboys to help him drive his cattle 400 miles to market. Clever script makes this one of Wayne's better Westerns. Carradine's film debut. Inspired the television series.
1972 (PG) 128m/C John Wayne, Roscoe Lee Browne, A. Martinez, Bruce Dern, Colleen Dewhurst, Slim Pickens, Robert Carradine; *D:* Mark Rydell; *M:* John Williams. VHS, Beta $19.98 *WAR, TLF* 🎬🎬🎬

Cowboys Don't Cry When a modern cowboy's wife is killed in an automobile accident, he must change his immature ways and build a solid future with his teenage son or perish in loneliness.
1988 96m/C Rebecca Jenkins, Ron White, Janet-Laine Green. VHS, Beta *MCA* 🎬🎬

Cowboys from Texas The Three Mesquiteers bring about a peaceful settlement to a fight between cattlemen and homesteaders. Part of "The Three Mesquiteers" series.
1939 54m/B Bob Livingston, Raymond Hatton, Duncan Renaldo, Carole Landis. VHS, Beta *MED* 🎬½

Cowboys of the Saturday Matinee The history of B-movie westerns is traced from the beginning of the sound era.
1984 75m/B Gene Autry, Tex Ritter, Roy Rogers. VHS, Beta $19.98 *LHV, FCT, WAR* 🎬½

Coyote Trails Standard western adventure has cowboy Tyler helping a damsel in distress.
1935 68m/B Tom Tyler. VHS, Beta $19.95 *NOS, VCN, RXM* 🎬½

Crack House A man seeks revenge for the murder of a relative by drug dealers. Average exploitation flick.
1989 (R) 91m/C Jim Brown, Richard Roundtree, Anthony Geary, Angel Tompkins, Greg Gomez Thomsen, Clyde R. Jones, Cheryl Kay; *D:* Michael Fischa. VHS, Beta, LV $14.95 *MGM, WAR* 🎬🎬

Crack Shadow Boxers Through a series of misadventures, Wu Lung and Chu San battle to protect the inhabitants of a small village from the onslaught of relentless bandits.
197? 91m/C *HK* Ku Feng, Chou Li Lung, Han Guo Gai; *D:* Weng Yao Hai. VHS, Beta $54.95 *OCE* 🎬

Crack-Up Largely ignored at the time of its release, this tense tale is now regarded as a minor classic of film noir. An art expert suffers a blackout while investigating a possible forgery and must piece together the missing hours to uncover a criminal conspiracy.
1946 70m/B Pat O'Brien, Claire Trevor, Herbert Marshall, Ray Collins, Wallace Ford, Damian O'Flynn, Erskine Sanford; *D:* Irving Reis. VHS, Beta, LV $19.98 *TTC* 🎬🎬½

The Cracker Factory Wood is impressive as a woman committed to a mental institution who attempts to charm her way out of treatment. Made for television.
1979 90m/C Natalie Wood, Perry King, Shelley Long, Vivian Blaine, Juliet Mills, Peter Haskell; *D:* Burt Brickerhoff. VHS, Beta *NO* 🎬🎬½

Crackers The offbeat story of two bumbling thieves who round up a gang of equally inept neighbors and go on the wildest crime spree you have ever seen. A would-be comic remake of "Big Deal on Madonna Street."
1984 (PG) 92m/C Donald Sutherland, Jack Warden, Sean Penn, Wallace Shawn, Larry Riley, Trinidad Silva, Christine Baranski, Charlaine Woodard, Tasia Valenza; *D:* Louis Malle. VHS, Beta, LV $59.95 *MCA* 🎬🎬

Cracking Up Accident-prone misfit's mishaps on the road to recovery create chaos for everyone he meets. Lewis plays a dozen characters in this overboard comedy with few laughs. *AKA:* Smorgasbord.
1983 (PG) 91m/C Jerry Lewis, Herb Edelman, Foster Brooks, Milton Berle, Sammy Davis Jr., Zane Buzby, Dick Butkus, Buddy Lester; *D:* Jerry Lewis. VHS, Beta $19.98 *WAR* 🎬½

The Crackler During the '20s, a husband-and-wife private investigation team (Tommy and Tuppence) set out to find a gang of forgers operating in high society circles. Based on a story by Agatha Christie. Made for British television.
1984 60m/C *GB* James Warwick, Francesca Annis. VHS, Beta $14.95 *PAV* 🎬🎬

The Cradle Will Fall A made-for-television adaptation of the pulpy bestselling mystery by Mary Higgins Clark about a woman who cannot convince anyone she witnessed a murder. The cast of "The Guiding Light" appear. Poor script and poor direction do not a thriller make.
1983 103m/C Lauren Hutton, Ben Murphy, James Farentino, Charita Bauer, Peter Simon; *D:* John Llewellyn Moxey. VHS, Beta $19.98 *LHV, WAR* Woof!

Craig's Wife A classic soap opera about a pitiful woman driven to total ruin by her desire for social acceptance and material wealth. Russell makes her surprisingly sympathetic. Based on a Pulitzer Prize-winning George Kelly play. Remake of a silent film, was also remade as "Harriet Craig."
1936 75m/B Rosalind Russell, John Boles, Alma Kruger, Jane Darwell, Billie Burke; *D:* Dorothy Arzner. VHS, Beta $59.95 *RCA* 🎬🎬🎬

Crainquebille The classic satire based on the Anatole France story about a street merchant in Paris unfairly imprisoned and eventually surviving peacefully as a tramp. Silent.
1923 50m/B *FR* Maurice Feraudy; *D:* Jacques Feyder. VHS, Beta $34.95 *FCT, GPV* 🎬🎬🎬

The Cranes are Flying When her lover goes off to fight during World War II, a girl is seduced by his cousin. Touching love story is free of politics. Filmed in Russia; English subtitles. *AKA:* Letyat Zhuravli.
1957 91m/B *RU* Tatyana Samoilova, Alexei Batalov, Vasily Merkuryev, A. Shvorin; *D:* Mikhail Kalatozov. VHS, Beta, LV, 3/4U $35.95 *IHF* 🎬🎬🎬½

Crash and Burn Rebels in a repressive future police state reactivate a huge, long-dormant robot to battle the establishment's army of powerful androids. Special effects by David Allen make the mayhem interesting.
1990 (R) 85m/C Ralph Waite, Paul Ganus, Eva LaRue, Bill Moseley; *D:* Charles Band. VHS, Beta, LV $19.98 *PAR* 🎬½

The Crash of Flight 401 A plane, full of recognizable TV stars, crashes in the Florida Everglades. "Airport" for a smaller screen. Based on a real event. Made for television.
1978 97m/C William Shatner, Adrienne Barbeau, Eddie Albert, Brooke Bundy, Christopher Connelly, Lorraine Gary, Ron Glass, Sharon Gless, Brett Halsey, George Maharis, Gerald S.

O'Loughlin; *D:* Barry Shear. VHS, Beta $14.95 *FRH* 🎬½

Crashout Six men break out of prison in this entertaining melodrama. Bendix plays the gang's leader to nasty perfection.
1955 82m/B William Bendix, Gene Evans, Arthur Kennedy, Luther Adler, William Talman, Marshall Thompson, Beverly Michaels; *D:* Lewis R. Foster. VHS $19.98 *REP* 🎬🎬½

The Crater Lake Monster The dormant egg of a prehistoric creature hatches after a meteor rudely awakens the dozing dino. He's understandably miffed and begins a revenge campaign. Prehistoric yawner.
1977 (PG) 85m/C Richard Cardella, Glenn Roberts, Mark Siegel, Bob Hyman, Kacey Cobb; *D:* William R. Stromberg. VHS, Beta $19.95 *UHV, MRV* Woof!

The Craving Naschy returns as El Hombre Lobo for the umpteenth time and once again battles a female vampire (see "Werewolf vs. the Vampire Woman"). Although continental Europe's biggest horror star, this film was such a box office disaster that Naschy went bankrupt. He was then forced to turn to Japan for financing (see "The Human Beasts"). Naschy also directed under a pseudonym.
1980 (R) 93m/C *MX* Paul Naschy, Julie Saly; *D:* Jack Molina. VHS, Beta $69.95 *VES, LIV* 🎬

The Crawling Eye Hidden in a radioactive fog on a mountaintop, the crawling eye decapitates its victims and returns these humans to Earth to threaten mankind. Average acting, but particularly awful special effects. Based on a British TV series. *AKA:* The Trollenberg Terror.
1958 87m/B *GB* Forrest Tucker, Laurence Payne, Janet Munro, Jennifer Jayne, Warren Mitchell; *D:* Quentin Lawrence. VHS, Beta, LV $19.95 *SNC, MRV, MED* 🎬

The Crawling Hand An astronaut's hand takes off without him on an unearthly spree of stranglings. Silly stuff is a hands-down loser.
1963 98m/B Alan Hale Jr., Rod Lauren, Richard Arlen, Peter Breck, Kent Taylor, Arline Judge, Allison Hayes; *D:* Herbert L. Strock. VHS, Beta, LV $9.95 *NOS, RHI, GEM* Woof!

Crawlspace Beautiful girls lease rooms from a murdering, perverted doctor who spies on them, then kills. You may find Kinski amusing but not terrifying.
1986 (R) 86m/C Klaus Kinski, Talia Balsam, Joyce Van Patten, Sally Brown, Barbara Whinnery; *D:* David Schmoeller. VHS, Beta $19.98 *VES, LIV* 🎬

Craze Tongue-in-cheek tale of a crazed antique dealer who slays a number of women as sacrifices to an African idol named Chuku. *AKA:* The Infernal Idol; Demon Master.
1974 (R) 96m/C Jack Palance, Diana Dors, Julie Ege, Suzy Kendall, Michael Jayston, Edith Evans, Hugh Griffith, Trevor Howard; *D:* Freddie Francis. VHS, Beta *MRV* 🎬🎬

Crazed Dull plodder about a psychopath who keeps a dead girl's body in his boarding house and kills all intruders to keep his secret.
1982 88m/C Laslo Papas, Belle Mitchell, Beverly Ross; *D:* Richard Cassidy. VHS, Beta $49.95 *TWE* Woof!

Crazed Cop A man's mind snaps when his wife is found raped and murdered, and nothing will stop him on his quest for revenge. Low budget and violent.
1988 85m/C Ivan Rogers, Sandy Brooke, Rich Sutherlin, Doug Irk, Abdulah the Great; *D:* Paul Kyriazi. VHS, Beta $69.95 *UNI* 🎬

The Crazies A poisoned water supply makes the residents of a small town go on a chaotic, murderous rampage. When the army is called into to quell the anarchy, a small war breaks out. Message film about the military is muddled and derivative. *AKA:* Code Name: Trixie.
1973 (R) 103m/C Lane Carroll, W.G. McMillan, Harold W. Jones, Lloyd Hollar, Lynn Lowry; *D:* George A. Romero. **Beta** *NO* ⅄⅄

Crazy Fat Ethel II A fat, hungry, homicidal female psychopath gets released from the asylum and goes on a cannabilistic rampage. Offensive junk. Sequel to "Criminally Insane."
1985 90m/C Priscilla Alden, Michael Flood, Jane Lambert, Robert Copple; *D:* Nick Phillips. **VHS, Beta** *NO Woof!*

Crazy for Love A village idiot stands to inherit the town inn if he can get a diploma within a year. With English subtitles.
1952 80m/B *FR* Brigitte Bardot, Bourvil, Jane Marken, Nadine Basile. **VHS, Beta $24.95** *DVT, TAM, GVV* ⅄⅄½

Crazy from the Heart Sweet made-for-cable TV tale of a high school principal in a small south Texas town who discovers the romance of her life one weekend with a Mexican janitor. Strong, nuanced performances from Lahti and Blades make this chestnut of a story work beautifully, with able help from supporting actors.
1991 104m/C Christine Lahti, Ruben Blades, Mary Kay Place, Brent Spiner, William Russ, Louise Latham, Tommy Muntz, Robin Lively, Bibi Besch, Kamala Lopez; *D:* Thomas Schlamme. **VHS, Beta, LV $89.98** *TTC* ⅄⅄⅄

Crazy Horse and Custer: "The Untold Story" Long before Little Big Horn, two legendary enemies find themselves trapped together in deadly Blackfoot territory. George Armstrong Custer and Crazy Horse are forced to form a volatile alliance in their life-or-death struggle against the murderous Blackfoot Tribe. History takes a back seat to Hollywood scriptwriting.
1990 (R) 120m/C Slim Pickens, Wayne Maunder, Mary Ann Mobley, Michael Dante. **VHS** *NO* ⅄

Crazy in Love Three generations of women live on an island in the home that has been in their family for years. Hunter is wildly in love with her husband, but misses (and doesn't quite trust) him when he is away on business. Enter Sands, who showers her with affection and fills the void in her life. The supporting cast fleshes out the story nicely and illustrates the reasons behind Hunter's insecurity. Enjoyable romantic comedy doesn't throw out anything heavy. Adapted from the novel by Luanne Rice; made for television.
1992 93m/C Holly Hunter, Gena Rowlands, Bill Pullman, Julian Sands, Frances McDormand, Herta Ware; *D:* Martha Coolidge. **VHS, LV $89.98** *TTC* ⅄⅄½

Crazy Kung Fu Master Fighting like you've never seen before as lots and lots of martial arts guys kick and rip 1920s Shanghai to pieces.
1987 90m/C Kent Cheng, Wong Ching, Wang Yu. **VHS, Beta $19.95** *OCE* ⅄

Crazy Mama Three women go on a crime spree from California to Arkansas, picking up men and having a hoot. Crime and comedy in a campy romp. Set in the 1950s and loaded with period kitsch.
1975 (PG) 81m/C Cloris Leachman, Stuart Whitman, Ann Sothern, Jim Backus, Linda Purl; *D:* Jonathan Demme. **VHS, Beta $69.98** *SUE* ⅄⅄½

Crazy Moon A rich high school nerd falls in love with a deaf girl, and must struggle against his domineering father's and older brother's prejudices. The viewer must struggle against the romantic cliches and heavy-handed message to enjoy a basically tender tale of romance. *AKA:* Huggers.
1987 (PG-13) 89m/C Kiefer Sutherland, Vanessa Vaughan, Peter Spence, Ken Pogue, Eve Napier; *D:* Allan Eastman. **VHS, Beta, LV $14.95** *SUE, NLC* ⅄⅄½

Crazy People Advertising exec Emory Leeston (Moore) writes commercials that describe products with complete honesty, and is committed to a mental hospital as a result. He meets a variety of characters at the hospital, including Hannah, with whom he falls in love. A tepid box-office blunder that sounds funnier than it is. We give half a bone for the ad slogans, the funniest part of the movie. Our favorite: "Most of our passengers arrive alive" for an airline.
1990 (R) 91m/C Dudley Moore, Daryl Hannah, Paul Reiser, Mercedes Ruehl, J.T. Walsh, Ben Hammer, Dick Cusack, Alan North, David Paymer, Danton Stone, Doug Yasuda, Bill Smitrovich, Paul Bates, Floyd Vivino, Cliff Eidelman; *D:* Tony Bill; *W:* Mitch Markowitz. **VHS, Beta, LV $14.95** *PAR* ⅄½

The Crazy Ray The classic silent fantasy about a mad scientist who endeavors to put the whole population of Paris in a trance. Vintage Clair nonsense. *AKA:* Paris Qui Dort.
1922 60m/B *FR* Henri Rollan, Albert Prejean, Marcel Vallee, Madeleine Rodrigue; *D:* Rene Clair. **VHS, Beta $16.95** *SNC, FCT, MRV* ⅄⅄⅄

Crazy Streets Cop Baldwin becomes involved in a deadly game of intrigue when a drug deal goes sour.
198? (R) 85m/C Alec Baldwin, Deborah Harry; *W/D:* Amos Kollek. **VHS** *MTX* ⅄⅄⅄

The Creation of the Humanoids Set in the familiar post-holocaust future, this is a tale of humans outnumbered by androids and the resulting struggle for survival. Slow and silly low-budget sets. For some reason, Andy Warhol was reported to love this film.
1962 84m/C Don Megowan, Frances McCann, Erica Elliot, Don Doolittle, Dudley Manlove; *D:* Wesley E. Barry. **VHS, Beta $39.95** *MON, MRV, SNC Woof!*

Creator A Frankenstein-like scientist plans to clone a being based on his wife, who died thirty years ago. As his experiments begin to show positive results, his romantic attention turns towards his beautiful lab assistant. O'Toole as the deranged scientist almost saves this one. Based on a novel by Jeremy Leven.
1985 (R) 108m/C Peter O'Toole, Mariel Hemingway, Vincent Spano, Virginia Madsen, David Ogden Stiers, John Dehner, Karen Kopins, Jeff Corey; *D:* Ivan Passer. **VHS, Beta, LV $69.99** *HBO* ⅄⅄

Creature A two thousand-year-old alien life form is killing off astronauts exploring the planet Titan. "Alien" rip-off has its moments, but not enough of them. Kinski provides some laughs. *AKA:* Titan Find.
1985 (R) 97m/C Klaus Kinski, Stan Ivar, Wendy Schaal, Lyman Ward, Annette McCarthy, Diane Salinger; *D:* William Malone. **VHS, Beta, LV $9.98** *MED* ⅄

Creature from Black Lake Two anthropology students from Chicago travel to the Louisiana swamps searching for the creature from Black Lake. Predictably, they find him. McClenny, incidentally, is Morgan Fairchild's sister.
1976 (PG) 95m/C Jack Elam, Dub Taylor, Dennis Fimple, John David Carson, Bill Thurman, Catherine McClonny; *D:* Joy Houck Jr. **VHS, Beta $59.95** *MRV, VES, LIV* ⅄

Creature from the Black Lagoon An anthropological expedition in the Amazon stumbles upon the Gill-Man, a prehistoric humanoid fish monster who takes a fancy to fetching Adams, a coed majoring in "science," but the humans will have none of it. Originally filmed in 3-D, this was one of the first movies to sport top-of-the-line underwater photography and remains one of the most enjoyable monster movies ever made. The score by Joseph Gershenson became a "Creature Features" standard. Sequels: "Revenge of the Creature" and "The Creature Walks Among Us."
1954 79m/B Richard Carlson, Julie Adams, Richard Denning, Antonio Moreno, Whit Bissell, Nestor Paiva, Ricou Browning; *D:* Jack Arnold. **VHS, Beta, LV $14.95** *MCA, GKK* ⅄⅄⅄

Creature from the Haunted Sea Monster movie satire set in Cuba shortly after the revolution and centering around an elaborate plan to loot the Treasury and put the blame on a strange sea monster. Corman comedy is predictably low budget but entertaining. "Wain" is really Robert Towne, winner of an Oscar for screenwriting. Remake of "Naked Paradise."
1960 76m/B Antony Carbone, Betsy Jones-Moreland, Beach Dickerson, Edward Wain, E.R. Alvarez, Robert Bean; *D:* Roger Corman, Monte Hellman; *W:* Charles B. Griffith. **VHS, Beta $19.95** *NOS, MRV, SNC* ⅄⅄

Creature of Destruction A beautiful young woman is hypnotized and inadvertantly reverted to her past life as a hideous sea monster. Buchanan's remake of his own 1956 production, "The She Creature."
1967 ?m/B Les Tremayne, Aron Kincaid, Pat Delaney, Neil Fletcher, Ann McAdams; *D:* Larry Buchanan. **VHS $19.98** ⅄

Creature of the Walking Dead Scientist brings his grandfather back to life with horrifying results for the cast and the audience. Made cheaply and quickly in Mexico in Mexico in 1960, then released with added footage directed by Warren. *AKA:* La Marca del Muerto.
1960 74m/B *MX* Rock Madison, Ann Wells, George Todd, Willard Gross, Bruno Ve Sota; *D:* Frederic Corte, Jerry Warren. **VHS $16.95** *NOS, MRV, SNC* ⅄½

Creature with the Blue Hand A German horror film based on a passable Edgar Wallace story about a man unjustly convicted of murders actually committed by a lunatic. Dubbed.
1970 92m/C *GE* Klaus Kinski, Harald Leopold, Hermann Leschau, Diana Kerner, Carl Lange, Ilse Page; *D:* Alfred Vohrer. **VHS, Beta** *NO* ⅄⅄

Creatures the World Forgot A British-made bomb about two tribes of cavemen warring over power and a cavewoman. No special effects, dinosaurs, or dialogue.
1970 96m/C Julie Ege, Robert John, Tony Bonner, Rosalie Crutchley, Sue Wilson; *D:* Don Chaffey. **VHS, Beta $69.95** *COL, MLB Woof!*

The Creeper After experimenting with a variety of serums, a doctor turns into a murderous monster with feline paws.
1948 65m/B Eduardo Ciannelli, Onslow Stevens, June Vincent, Ralph Morgan; *D:* Jean Yarborough. **VHS, Beta $14.95** *MLB* ⅄⅄

Creepers A young girl talks to bugs and gets them to follow her instructions, which comes in handy when she battles the lunatic who is killing her school chums. Argento

C

weirdness—and graphic gore—may not be for all tastes.
1985 (R) 82m/C *IT* Jennifer Connelly, Donald Pleasence, Daria Nicolodi, Elenora Giorgi, Dalia di Lazzaro, Patrick Bauchau, Fiore Argento; *D:* Dario Argento. **VHS, Beta $79.95** *MED* ✗✗½

The Creeping Flesh A scientist decides he can cure evil by injecting his patients with a serum derived from the blood of an ancient corpse. Some truly chilling moments will get your flesh creeping.
1972 (PG) 89m/C *GB* Peter Cushing, Christopher Lee, Lorna Heilbron, George Benson; *D:* Freddie Francis. **VHS, Beta, LV $49.95** *COL, IME, MLB* ✗✗½

Creeping Terror Gigantic alien carpet monster (look for the tennis shoes sticking out underneath) devours slow-moving teenagers. Partially narrated because some of the original soundtrack was lost, with lots of bad acting, a worse script, laughable sets, and a ridiculous monster. Beware of the thermometer scene. *AKA:* The Crawling Monster; Dangerous Charter.
1964 81m/B Vic Savage, Shannon O'Neal, William Thourlby, Louise Lawson, Robin James; *D:* Art J. Nelson. **VHS, Beta $54.95** *UHV* Woof!

Creepozoids In the near future, a monster at an abandoned science complex stalks army deserters hiding out there. Violent nonsense done better by others.
1987 72m/C Linnea Quigley, Ken Abraham, Michael Aranda; *D:* David DeCoteau. **Beta, LV** *NO* ✗

Creepshow Stephen King's tribute to E.C. Comics, those pulp horror comic books of the 1950s that delighted in grizzly, grotesque, and morbid humor, the film tells five horror tales. Features King himself in one segment, as a none-too-bright farmer who unknowingly cultivates a strange, alien-origin moss. With despicable heroes and gory monsters, this is sure to delight all fans of the horror vein. Those easily repulsed by cockroaches beware!
1982 (R) 120m/C Hal Holbrook, Adrienne Barbeau, Viveca Lindfors, E.G. Marshall, Stephen King, Leslie Nielsen, Carrie Nye, Fritz Weaver, Ted Danson, Ed Harris; *D:* George A. Romero. **VHS, Beta, LV $19.98** *WAR* ✗✗½

Creepshow 2 Romero adapted three Stephen King stories for this horror anthology which presents gruesome looks at a hit-and-run driver, a wooden Indian, and a vacation gone wrong. Gory and childish stuff from two masters of the genre. Look for King as a truck driver.
1987 (R) 92m/C Lois Chiles, George Kennedy, Dorothy Lamour, Tom Savini, Domenick John, Frank S. Salsedo, Holt McCallany, David Holbrook, Page Hannah, Daniel Beer, Stephen King; *D:* Michael Gornick; *W:* George A. Romero. **VHS, Beta, LV $19.95** *STE, NWV* ✗½

The Cremators A meteorite carrying an alien lands at a seaside resort and everyone begins bursting into flames. Low budget effort from the scripter of ''It Came from Outer Space.''
1972 90m/C Marvin Howard, Maria de Aragon; *D:* Harry Essex. **VHS, Beta $59.95** *WVV* Woof!

Cria The award-winning story of a 9-year-old girl's struggle for maturity in a hostile adult world. In Spanish with English subtitles.
1976 (PG) 115m/C *SP* Geraldine Chaplin, Ana Torrent, Conchita Perez; *D:* Carlos Savrat. **VHS, Beta, LV $59.95** *INT, APD, TAM* ✗✗✗

Cricket on the Hearth An adaptation of Charles Dickens' short story about a mail carrier and his bride, who find the symbol of good luck, a cricket on the hearth, when they enter their new home. Silent with organ score.
1923 68m/B Paul Gerson, Virginia Brown Faire, Paul Moore, Joan Standing. **VHS, Beta $24.98** *CCB* ✗✗

Cries and Whispers As a woman dies slowly of tuberculosis, three women care for her: her two sisters, one sexually repressed, the other promiscuous, and her servant. The sisters remember family love and closeness, but are too afraid to look death in the face to aid their sister. Only the servant can touch her in her dying and only the servant believes in God and his will. Beautiful imagery, focused through a nervous camera, which lingers on the meaningless and whisks away from the meaningful. Absolute mastery of cinematic art by Bergman. *AKA:* Viskingar Och Rop.
1972 (R) 91m/C *SW* Harriet Andersson, Ingrid Thulin, Liv Ullmann, Kary Sylway, Erland Josephson, Henning Moritzen; *W/D:* Ingmar Bergman. Academy Awards '73: Best Cinematography; Nominations: Best Costume Design, Best Director (Bergman), Best Picture, Best Story & Screenplay; National Board of Review Awards '73: 5 Best Foreign Films of the Year, Best Director (Bergman). **VHS, Beta, LV $59.95** *WAR, TAM* ✗✗✗

Crime & Passion Two scheming lovers plan to get rich by having the woman marry a multimillionaire and sue for a quick divorce. The multimillionaire is no patsy, however, and seeks a deadly revenge. Three scripts by six writers were combined to create this story. That explains the many problems.
1975 (R) 92m/C Omar Sharif, Karen Black, Joseph Bottoms, Bernhard Wicki; *D:* Ivan Passer. **VHS, Beta $69.95** *VES, LIV* ✗½

Crime and Punishment Original French production (preceding the American version by just one week) of Dostoyevski's novel, the tale of a young murderer, his crime, and ultimately, his confession. Generally considered better than the American version, the French throw out all that is not dramatic, keeping the psychology and suspense. Remade in 1958. *AKA:* Crime et Chatiment.
1935 110m/B Harry Baur, Pierre Blanchar, Madeleine Ozeray, Marcelle Geniat, Lucienne Lemarchand; *D:* Pierre Chenal. **VHS $59.95** *FCT, TIM* ✗✗✗✗

Crime and Punishment Pared down but well-executed version of the Dostoyevski novel. Lorre is superb as Raskolnikov, who robs and murders an elderly pawnbroker. Believing he has committed the perfect murder, he accepts the invitation of police inspector Porfiry (Arnold) to observe the investigation. Gradually Raskolnikov's conscience begins to overwhelm him as Porfiry slowly works to wring a confession from the killer. Von Sternberg's subdued directorial approach worked well to explore the psychological aspects of guilt, although the melodramatic French film version (released at the same time) scored better with the critics.
1935 88m/B Peter Lorre, Edward Arnold, Marian Marsh, Tala Birell, Elisabeth Risdon, Robert Allen, Douglas Dumbrille, Gene Lockhart; *D:* Josef von Sternberg; *W:* S.K. Lauren, Joseph Anthony. **VHS $19.95** *COL* ✗✗✗

Crime and Punishment Ponderous, excruciatingly long adaptation of the Dostoyevski classic involving a haunted murderer and the relentless policeman who seeks to prove him guilty. In Russian with English subtitles.
1970 200m/B *RU* Georgi Taratorkin, Victoria Fyodorova; *W/D:* Lev Kulijanov. **VHS $59.95** *TAM, DVT, HEG* ✗✗

Crime Busters Two guys attempt to pull off a bank heist but accidentally join the Miami police force instead. Hill and Spencer are enjoyable as usual but the film suffers from poor dubbing. Remake of ''Two Supercops.''
1978 (PG) 114m/C *IT* Terence Hill, Bud Spencer, Laura Gemser, Luciana Catenacci, David Huddleston; *D:* E.B. Clucher. **VHS, Beta $19.98** *WAR* ✗½

Crime Killer Confusing shenanigans about an explosive ex-CIA agent enlisted by the FBI to battle a brutal crime syndicate shipping guns to nasty Arabs.
1985 90m/C George Pan-Andreas, Leo Morrell, Althan Karras; *D:* George Pan-Andreas. **VHS, Beta $19.95** *STE, NWV* ✗

Crime Lords When a pair of cops are suspended from the force for committing a blunder, they travel to Hong Kong to continue their investigation. Little do they know their sleuthing has drawn then into a confrontation with one of largest crime syndicates in the world. Lots of action, beautiful women, and exotic locations keep this basic buddy plot moving well.
1991 (R) 96m/C Wayne Crawford, Martin Hewitt, Susan Byun, Mel Castelo, James Hong; *D:* Wayne Crawford. **VHS $19.95** *ACA* ✗✗

The Crime of Dr. Crespi A doctor takes his revenge on a man who is after his girlfriend by injecting him with suspended animation serum. Extremely campy performance from von Stroheim; Frye's biggest role in terms of screen time.
1935 64m/B Erich von Stroheim, Dwight Frye, Paul Guilfoyle, Harriett Russell, John Bohn; *D:* John H. Auer. **VHS, Beta $16.95** *NOS, SNC, MLB* ✗

Crime of Honor A European executive goes public with his company's corruption, and his family suffers predictable ruin as a result. Based on a true story.
1985 95m/C Maria Schneider, David Suchet; *D:* John Goldschmidt. **VHS, Beta $29.95** *ACA* ✗

The Crime of Monsieur Lange A charming French socialist fantasy written by Jacques Prevert wherein the workers of a publishing company turn the business into a thriving cooperative while their evil boss is gone. When he returns, they plot to kill him. Rather talky, but humorous. In French with subtitles. French script booklet also available. *AKA:* Le Crime de Monsieur Lange.
1936 90m/B *FR* Rene Lefevro, Jules Berry, Florelle, Sylvia Bataille, Jean Daste, Nadia Sibirskaia; *D:* Jean Renoir. **VHS, Beta $29.95** *FCT, INT, APD* ✗✗✗

Crime Story The full-length television pilot for the Michael Mann cop show, about the police cracking down on the Mob in 1940s Chicago. Tough stuff with moody camera-work and original music by Todd Rundgren.
1986 96m/C Dennis Farina, Anthony John Denison, Stephen Lang, Darlanne Fluegel; *D:* Abel Ferrara. **VHS, Beta, LV $14.95** *NWV, STE* ✗✗✗

Crime Story: The Complete Saga All 42 episodes of the 1986-1988 NBC cops-versus-mobsters series set first in Chicago in 1963, and later in Las Vegas. The series was created by Michael Mann, the executive producer of ''Miami Vice.'' Del Shannon updated the lyrics to his hit ''Runaway'' for the series theme. Available as a boxed set of ten tapes or individually.
1986 ?m/C Dennis Farina, Anthony John Denison, Bill Smitrovich, Steve Ryan, Bill Campbell, Paul Butler, Stephen Lang, Darlanne Fluegel. **VHS $14.98** *STE* ✗✗✗

Crime Zone In a totalitarian, repressive, future society, two young lovers try to beat the system and make it on their own. A well-made, if occasionally muddled, low-budget film shot in Peru, of all places.
1988 (R) 93m/C David Carradine, Peter Nelson, Sherilyn Fenn, Orlando Sacha, Don Manor; **D:** Luis Llosa. **VHS** $79.95 *MGM* 🐾🐾½

Crimebusters A man exacts revenge against a government conspiracy that kidnapped his loved ones.
1979 (PG) 90m/C Henry Silva, Anthony Sabato, **D:** Michael Tarantini. **VHS, Beta** *NO* 🐾½

Crimes & Misdemeanors One of Allen's most mature films, exploring a wide range of moral ambiguities through the parallel and eventually interlocking stories of a nebbish filmmaker—who agrees to make a profile of a smug Hollywood television comic and then sabotages it—and an esteemed ophthalmologist who is being threatened with exposure by his neurotic mistress. Intriguing mix of drama and comedy few directors could pull off. Look for Daryl Hannah in an unbilled cameo.
1989 (PG-13) 104m/C Martin Landau, Woody Allen, Alan Alda, Mia Farrow, Joanna Gleason, Anjelica Huston, Jerry Orbach, Sam Waterston, Claire Bloom, Jenny Nichols, Caroline Aaron; **Cameos:** Daryl Hannah; **D:** Woody Allen. **VHS, Beta, LV** $89.98 *ORI* 🐾🐾🐾

Crimes at the Dark House In this campy, melodramatic adaptation of Wilkie Collins's novel "The Woman in White," a man kills his rich wife and puts a disguised mental patient in her place. Later remade using the book's title.
1939 69m/B *GB* Tod Slaughter, Hilary Eaves, Sylvia Marriott, Hay Petrie, Geoffrey Wardwell; **D:** George King. **VHS** $19.95 *NOS, MRV, SNC* 🐾🐾🐾

Crimes of Dr. Mabuse Supernatural horror classic about the evil Dr. Mabuse controlling an underworld empire while confined to an insane asylum. One of the best "mad doctor" movies ever made. Also known as "The Testament of Dr. Mabuse" or "The Last Will of Dr. Mabuse."
1932 120m/B *GE* Rudolf Klein-Rogge, Otto Wernicke, Gustav Diesl, Karl Meixner; **D:** Fritz Lang. **VHS** $16.95 *SNC* 🐾🐾🐾½

Crimes of Passion Vintage whacked-out Russell, not intended for the kiddies. A business-like fashion designer becomes a kinky prostitute at night. A disturbed street preacher makes her the heroine of his erotic fantasies. A dark terrifying vision of the underground sex world and moral hypocrisy. Sexually explicit and violent, with an extremely black comedic center. Music score by Rick Wakeman. Turner's portrayal is honest and believable, Perkins overacts until he nearly gets a nosebleed, but it's all for good effect. Cut for "R" rating to get it in the theatres; this version restores some excised footage. Also available in rated version.
1984 101m/C Kathleen Turner, Anthony Perkins, Annie Potts, John Laughlin, Bruce Davison, Norman Burton; **D:** Ken Russell. **VHS, Beta, LV** $14.95 *NWV, STE* 🐾🐾🐾

The Crimes of Stephen Hawke The world knows Stephen Hawke as a big-hearted money lender. What they don't know is his favorite hobby is breaking peoples' spines. An entertaining thriller set in the 1800s. **AKA:** Strangler's Morgue.
1936 65m/B *GB* Tod Slaughter, Marjorie Taylor, D.J. Williams, Eric Portman, Ben Soutten; **D:** George King. **VHS, Beta** $16.95 *SNC, MRV, HEG* 🐾🐾

Crimes of the Heart Based on Beth Henley's acclaimed play. A few days in the lives of three very strange Southern sisters, one of whom has just been arrested for calmly shooting her husband after he chased her black lover out of town. Spacek as the suicidal sister is a lark. A tart, black comedy that works better as a play than a film.
1986 (PG-13) 105m/C Sissy Spacek, Diane Keaton, Jessica Lange, Sam Shepard, Tess Harper, Hurd Hatfield; **D:** Bruce Beresford. Academy Awards '86 Nominations: Best Actress (Spacek), Best Adapted Screenplay, Best Supporting Actress (Harper); Golden Globe Awards '87: Best Actress—Musical/Comedy (Spacek). **VHS, Beta, LV** $19.98 *LHV, WAR* 🐾🐾½

Crimewave Zany spoof about serial killers co-written by Ethan and Joel Coen and directed by "Darkman" Raimi. Set in Detroit (Raimi's hometown), it's a rhapsody to comic book style, short on plot and long on style. With such credentials you expect more. **AKA:** The XYZ Murders; Broken Hearts and Noses.
1985 (PG-13) 83m/C Louise Lasser, Paul Smith, Brion James, Bruce Campbell, Reed Birney, Sheree J. Wilson, Edward R. Pressman, Julius W. Harris; **D:** Sam Raimi; **W:** Ethan Coen, Joel Coen. **VHS, Beta** $19.98 *NLC* 🐾🐾

Criminal Act A newspaper editor hits the street to prove she's still a tough reporter, but uncovers a dangerous scandal in the process.
1988 94m/C Catherine Bach, Charlene Dallas, Nicholas Guest, John Saxon, Vic Tayback; **D:** Mark Byers. **VHS, Beta** $79.95 *PSM* 🐾½

Criminal Code Aging melodrama about a young man who's jailed for killing in self-defense. His life worsens at the hands of a prison warden when the head guy's daughter falls for him. Remade as "Penitentiary" and "Convicted."
1931 98m/B Walter Huston, Phillips Holmes, Boris Karloff, Constance Cummings, Mary Doran, DeWitt Jennings, John Sheehan; **D:** Howard Hawks. **VHS, Beta** $59.95 *COL, MLB* 🐾🐾½

Criminal Court A man accused of murdering his blackmailer hires the real killer as his attorney. Hard to follow, with an interesting premise that turns flat.
1946 63m/B Tom Conway, Martha O'Driscoll, Robert Armstrong, Addison Richards, June Clayworth, Pat Gleason, Steve Brodie; **D:** Robert Wise. **VHS, Beta** *RKO* 🐾🐾

Criminal Justice A black man is accused of a crime by a woman with whom he was involved. Is it justice or revenge? Strong cast in important story. Made for cable TV.
1990 (R) 92m/C Forest Whitaker, Jennifer Grey, Rosie Perez, Anthony LaPaglia; **W/D:** Andy Wolk. **VHS** $89.95 *HBO* 🐾🐾🐾

Criminal Law An ambitious young Boston lawyer gets a man acquitted for murder, only to find out after the trial that the man is guilty and renewing his killing spree. Realizing he's the only one privy to the killer's trust, the lawyer decides to stop him himself. A white-knuckled thriller burdened by a weak script.
1989 (R) 113m/C Kevin Bacon, Gary Oldman, Karen Young, Joe Don Baker, Tess Harper; **D:** Martin Campbell; **M:** Jerry Goldsmith. **VHS, Beta, LV** $89.98 *HBO* 🐾🐾

The Criminal Life of Archibaldo de la Cruz Seeing the death of his governess has a lasting effect on a boy. He grows up to be a demented cretin whose failure with women leads him to conspire to kill every one he meets, a task at which he also fails. Hilarious, bitter Bunuelian diatribe. In Spanish with English subtitles. **AKA:** Ensayo de un Crimen; Rehearsal for a Crime.
1955 95m/B *MX SP* Ernesto Alonso, Ariadne Welter, Rita Macedo, Rodolfo Landa, Andrea Palma, Miroslava Stern; **D:** Luis Bunuel. **VHS, Beta** $39.95 *FCT, WBF* 🐾🐾🐾

Criminally Insane Authorities release 250 pounds of cleaver-wielding maniacal fury from the loony bin. She seeks food and human blood. They should have known better. Followed by "Crazy Fat Ethel II."
1975 61m/C Priscilla Alden, Michael Flood; **D:** Nick Phillips. **VHS, Beta** $59.95 *WWV* 🐾

Criminals Within A scientist working on a top secret formula is murdered and a detective tries to nail the spy ring responsible. Very confusing, poor usage of some fine female cast members. **AKA:** Army Mystery.
1941 67m/B Eric Linden, Ann Doran, Constance Worth, Donald Curtis, Weldon Heyburn, Ben Alexander; **D:** Joseph H. Lewis. **VHS, Beta** $16.95 *SNC* 🐾

The Crimson Cult Eden and his girlfriend are invited to a mysterious mansion. They discover that Lee is out to enact revenge as his ancestor was burned for witchcraft by Eden's. An all-star horror disaster. Karloff was eighty and confined to a wheelchair. Despite ads claiming this as his last film, he made four more in Mexico. Highlights include the scantily clad Steele in sado-masochistic sequences and a psychedelic party with strippers and body painters. **AKA:** The Crimson Altar; Curse of the Crimson Altar.
1968 (PG) 87m/C *GB* Boris Karloff, Christopher Lee, Mark Eden, Barbara Steele, Virginia Wetherell, Michael Gough, Rupert Davies; **D:** Vernon Sewell. **VHS** $79.98 *MOV* 🐾

The Crimson Ghost The Crimson Ghost plots to enslave the world by stealing an atomic weapon. Serial in twelve episodes. Also available in a 93 minute colorized edition.
1946 100m/B Charles Quigley, Clayton Moore, Linda Stirling, I. Stanford Jolley; **D:** William Witney, Fred Brannon. **VHS** $29.98 *REP, VCN, MLB* 🐾

Crimson Pirate An 18th-century buccaneer pits his wits and brawn against the might of a ruthless Spanish nobleman. Considered by many to be one of the best swashbucklers, laced with humor and enthusiastically paced. Showcase for Lancaster and Cravat's acrobatic talents.
1952 104m/C *GB* Burt Lancaster, Eva Bartok, Torin Thatcher, Christopher Lee, Nick Cravat; **D:** Robert Siodmak. **VHS, Beta, LV** $19.98 *WAR* 🐾🐾🐾½

Crimson Romance Two unemployed American pilots in Europe decide to join the German airforce for want of anything better to do. Conflicts revolve around a warmongering Commandant and his pilot.
1934 70m/B Ben Lyon, Sari Maritza, James Bush, Erich von Stroheim, Jason Robards Sr., Herman Bing, Vince Barnett; **D:** David Howard. **VHS, Beta, 8mm** $19.95 *NOS, VYY, RXM* 🐾

Crisis at Central High A dramatic television recreation of the events leading up to the 1957 integration of Central High in Little Rock, Arkansas. The screenplay is based on teacher Elizabeth Huckaby's journal. Woodward was nominated for an Emmy for her performance as Huckaby.
1980 120m/C Joanne Woodward, Charles Durning, William Ross, Henderson Forsythe; **D:** Lamont Johnson. **VHS, Beta** *NO* 🐾🐾🐾

Criss Cross A classic grade-B film noir, in which an armored car driver is suckered into a burglary by his ex-wife and her hoodlum husband. Multiple back-stabbings and dou-

ble-crossings ensue. Written by Daniel Fuchs.
1948 98m/B Burt Lancaster, Yvonne De Carlo, Dan Duryea, Stephen McNally, Richard Long, Tony Curtis; **D:** Robert Siodmak. **VHS, Beta $59.95** MCA ⅋⅋⅋

Crisscross It's 1969 and Tracy Cross is a divorced mom whose ex-husband is a traumatized Vietnam vet who has left her alone to raise their 12 year-old son Chris during some hard times. She works two jobs, as a waitress and, unbeknownst to her son, as a stripper in a local club. When Chris sneaks into the club and sees her act he takes drastic measures to help out—by selling drugs. Film is sluggish and relies too much on voice-overs to explain thoughts but Hawn gives a convincing and restrained performance as the mother. **AKA:** Alone Together.
1992 (R) 100m/C Goldie Hawn, David Arnott, Arliss Howard, James Gammon, Keith Carradine, J.C. Quinn; **D:** Chris Menges. **VHS, LV $19.98** MGM ⅋⅋½

Critical Condition During a blackout, a criminal masquerades as a doctor in a city hospital. Limp comedy embarrassing for Pryor.
1986 (R) 99m/C Richard Pryor, Rachel Ricotin, Ruben Blades, Joe Mantegna; **D:** Michael Apted. **VHS, Beta, LV $19.95** PAR ⅋

Critters A gang of furry, razor-toothed aliens escapes from its prison ship to Earth with their bounty hunters right behind them. They make it to a small town in Kansas where they begin to attack anything that moves. Not just a thrill-kill epic, but a sarcastic other-worldly thrill-kill epic.
1986 (PG-13) 86m/C Dee Wallace Stone, M. Emmet Walsh, Billy Green Bush, Scott Grimes; **D:** Stephen Herek. **VHS, Beta, LV $14.95** COL ⅋⅋½

Critters 2: The Main Course Sequel to the hit horror-comedy, wherein the voracious alien furballs return in full force to Grovers Bend, Kansas, from eggs planted two years before. Occasionally inspired "Gremlins" rip.
1988 (PG-13) 93m/C Scott Grimes, Liane Curtis, Don Opper, Barry Corbin, Terrence Mann; **D:** Mick Garris. **VHS, Beta, LV $14.95** COL ⅋⅋

Critters 3 The not-so-loveable critters are back, terrorizing the occupants of a tenement building.
1991 (PG-13) 86m/C Francis Bay, Aimee Brooks, Leonardo DiCaprio, Don Opper; **D:** Kristine Peterson. **VHS $89.95** COL, NLC ⅋⅋

Critters 4 The ghoulish critters are back, and this time a strain of genetically engineered mutant critters (what's the difference?) wants to take over the universe.
1991 (PG-13) 94m/C Don Opper, Paul Whitthorne, Angela Bassett, Brad Dourif, Terrence Mann; **D:** Rupert Harvey. **VHS, LV $89.95** NLC, COL ⅋⅋

Crocodile Giant crocodile attacks a beach town, killing and devouring dozens of people. The locals sit around trying to figure a way to stop the critter. Special effects include rear-projected croc. Lots of blood but lacking humor of "Alligator." Filmed in Thailand and Korea.
1981 (R) 95m/C Nat Puvanai, Tiny Tim; **D:** Herman Cohen. **VHS, Beta $59.99** HBO Woof!

Crocodile Dundee New York reporter Sue Charlton is assigned to the Outback to interview living legend Mike Dundee. When she finally locates the man, she is so taken with him that she brings him back to New York with her. There, the naive Aussie wanders about, amazed at the wonders of the city and unwittingly charming everyone he comes in contact with, from high-society transvestites to street hookers. One of the surprise hits of 1986.
1986 (PG-13) 98m/C AU Paul Hogan, Linda Kozlowski, John Meillon, David Gulpilil, Mark Blum; **D:** Peter Faiman. Academy Awards '86 Nominations: Best Original Screenplay; Golden Globe Awards '87: Best Actor—Musical/Comedy (Hogan). **VHS, Beta, LV, 8mm $14.95** PAR ⅋⅋⅋½

Crocodile Dundee 2 In this sequel Mike Dundee, the loveable rube, returns to his native Australia looking for new adventure, having "conquered" New York City. He inadvertently gets involved in stopping a gang of crooks active in Australia and New York. Lacks the charm and freshness of the first film.
1988 (PG) 110m/C Paul Hogan, Linda Kozlowski, Kenneth Welsh; **D:** John Cornell. **VHS, Beta, LV $14.95** PAR ⅋⅋½

Cromwell A lavish British-made spectacle about the conflict between Oliver Cromwell and Charles I, and the British Civil War. History is twisted as Cromwell becomes the liberator of the oppressed. Harris gives a commanding performance and the battle scenes are stunners.
1970 (G) 139m/C GB Richard Harris, Alec Guinness, Robert Morley, Frank Finlay, Patrick Magee, Timothy Dalton; **D:** Ken Hughes. Academy Awards '70: Best Costume Design; Nominations: Best Original Score. **VHS, Beta, LV $19.95** COL, TVC ⅋⅋½

The Crooked Circle More comedy than mystery as slapstick policeman Gleason goes under cover as a swami. Not helped at all by a weak script and poor photography.
1932 69m/B Ben Lyon, ZaSu Pitts, James Gleason, C. Henry Gordon, Raymond Hatton, Roscoe Karns; **D:** H. Bruce Humberstone. **VHS $12.95** SNC, NOS ⅋

Crooked Hearts Dysfunctional family drama means well but lays it on too thick, as a father/son rivalry threatens to sunder the tight-knit Warrens. Based on a novel by Robert Boswell.
1991 (R) 113m/C Peter Coyote, Jennifer Jason Leigh, Peter Berg, Cindy Pickett, Vincent D'Onofrio; **D:** Michael Bortman. **VHS, Beta, LV $89.98** MGM ⅋⅋

Crooked Trail A lawman and bad guy become friends.
1936 58m/B Johnny Mack Brown. **VHS, Beta, LV** NO ⅋

Crooks & Coronets Two-bit crooks plot to rob the country estate of an eccentric British dowager. **AKA:** Sophie's Place.
1969 (PG) 106m/C GB Cesar Romero, Telly Savalas, Warren Oates, Edith Evans; **D:** James O'Connolly. **VHS, Beta $19.98** WAR ⅋½

The Cross & the Switchblade An idealistic priest tries to bring the message of religion to the members of a vicious street gang. They don't wanna listen. Spanish language version available.
1972 (PG) 105m/C Pat Boone, Erik Estrada, Jackie Giroux, Jo-Ann Robinson; **D:** Don Murray. **VHS, Beta $19.95** VGD, VBL, VIS ⅋½

Cross Country Action revolves around the brutal murder of a call girl, with initial suspicion falling on a television advertising director involved with the woman. The story twists and turns from the suspect to investigating detective Ironside without becoming particularly interesting.
1983 (R) 95m/C CA Richard Beymer, Nina Axelrod, Michael Ironside; **D:** Paul Lynch. **VHS, Beta, LV $9.98** SUE, STE, NLC ⅋½

Cross Creek Based on the life of Marjorie Kinnan Rawlings, author of "The Yearling," who, after 10 years as a frustrated reporter/writer, moves to the remote and untamed Everglades. There she meets colorful local characters and receives the inspiration to write numerous bestsellers. Well acted though overtly sentimental at times.
1983 (PG) 115m/C Mary Steenburgen, Rip Torn, Peter Coyote, Dana Hill, Alfre Woodard, Malcolm McDowell; **D:** Martin Ritt. **VHS, Beta $19.99** HBO ⅋⅋½

Cross Examination A boy is charged with his father's murder, and a defense attorney struggles to acquit him.
1932 61m/B H.B. Warner, Sally Blane, Sarah Padden. **VHS, Beta, LV** NO ⅋½

Cross Mission Predictable actioner about a photographer and a soldier who are captured by the enemy. Packed with a bit of ninja, ammo, and occult.
1989 (R) 90m/C Richard Randall; **D:** Al Bradley. **VHS $59.95** CAN ⅋

Cross My Heart Light comedy about two single people with complicated, post-divorce lives who go on a date and suffer accordingly. Will true love prevail?
1988 (R) 91m/C Martin Short, Annette O'Toole, Paul Reiser, Joanna Kerns; **D:** Armyan Bernstein. **VHS, Beta $79.95** MCA ⅋⅋

Cross My Heart A group of school children conspire to hide the death of one of the group's mothers. This will prevent his placement in the state orphanage. Interesting premise is blandly treated by Fansten. Child actors don't seem realistic, photography is without flair. In French with English subtitles.
1991 ?m/C FR Sylvain Copans; **D:** Jacques Fansten. **VHS, Beta** FXL ⅋⅋

Cross of Iron During WWII, two antagonistic German officers clash over personal ideals as well as strategy in combatting the relentless Russian attack. Followed by "Breakthrough."
1976 (R) 120m/C James Coburn, Maximilian Schell, James Mason, David Warner, Senta Berger; **D:** Sam Peckinpah. **VHS, Beta $19.95** MED, MED ⅋⅋½

Crossbar Aaron Kornylo is determined to reach Olympic qualifications in the high jump despite having only one leg. Inspired by a true story, this program dramatically shows how far determination and work can take a person.
1979 77m/C John Ireland, Brent Carver, Kate Reid; **D:** John Trent. **VHS, Beta $49.95** TWE, LCA ⅋

Crossfire A Jewish hotel guest is murdered and three soldiers just back from Europe are suspected of the crime. The first Hollywood film that explored racial bigotry. Due to the radical nature of its plot, the director and the producer were eventually black-listed for promoting "un-American" themes. Loosely based on Richard Brooks' "The Brick Foxhole."
1947 86m/B Robert Young, Robert Mitchum, Robert Ryan, Gloria Grahame, Paul Kelly; **D:** Edward Dmytryk. Academy Awards '46 Nominations: Best Picture; Academy Awards '47: Best Director (Dmytryk), Best Screenplay, Best Supporting Actor (Ryan), Best Supporting Actress (Grahame); Edgar Allan Poe Awards '47: Best Screenplay; National Board of Review Awards '47: 10 Best Films of the Year. **VHS, Beta $19.95** MED ⅋⅋⅋½

Crossfire Two bandits are almost hung in the midst of the Mexican revolution. Released in the U.S. in 1979. **AKA:** The Bandit.

1967 (PG) 82m/C *MX* Robert Conrad, Jan-Michael Vincent, Manuel Lopez Ochoa, Roy Jenson; *D:* Robert Conrad, Alfredo Zacharias. **VHS, Beta** $59.95 *ACA* 🎬

Crossfire A rescue team heads to Vietnam to pick up their MIA comrades. With no help from the government and the enemy at every turn, can they possibly succeed?
1989 (R) 99m/C Richard Norton, Michael Meyer, Daniel Dietrich, Don Pemrick, Eric Hahn, Wren Brown, Steve Young; *D:* Anthony Maharaj. **VHS, LV** $19.98 *SUE* 🎬

The Crossing Powerful coming-of-age story in which Meg, a sheltered young woman, falls in love with an ambitious artist named Sam. When he decides to leave their small town to pursue his career, she turns to his best friend for comfort and companionship. However, when Sam unexpectedly returns, Meg is forced to make a choice that could drastically change all of their lives.
1992 (R) 92m/C *AU* Russell Crowe, Danielle Spencer, Robert Mammone; *W:* Ranald Allan. **VHS, LV** $89.98 *REP* 🎬🎬

Crossing Delancey A Jewish woman (Bozyk), in old world style, plays matchmaker to her independent young granddaughter. Charming modern-day New York City fairy tale that deftly manipulates cliches and stereotypes. Lovely performance from Irving as the woman whose heart surprises her. Riegert is swell playing the gentle but never wimpy suitor. Bozyk was a star on the Yiddish vaudeville stage. Appealing music by the Roches, with Suzzy Roche giving a credible performance as Irving's friend. Adapted for the big screen by Sandler from her play of the same name.
1988 (PG) 97m/C Amy Irving, Reizl Bozyk, Peter Riegert, Jeroen Krabbe, Sylvia Miles, Suzzy Roche, George Martin; *D:* Joan Micklin Silver; *W:* Susan Sandler. **VHS, Beta, LV, 8mm** $19.98 *WAR, FCT, JCF* 🎬🎬🎬

Crossing the Bridge An after-high-school tale of three buddies and their restless lives as they take their uncertain steps towards adulthood. It's 1975 in Detroit and Mort, Danny, and Tim cling to high-school memories as they pass time on petty jobs, drinking, and cruising across the Ambassador Bridge to check out the Canadian strip joints. Their big moment—for better or worse—comes when they are offered the chance to make a lot of quick cash if they'll smuggle hash from Toronto to Detroit. Directorial debut of Binder.
1992 (R) 105m/C Josh Charles, Jason Gedrick, Stephen Baldwin, Cheryl Pollak, Jeffrey Tambor; *W/D:* Mike Binder. **VHS, Beta, LV** $94.95 *TOU* 🎬🎬

Crossing the Line Two motocross racers battle it out for the championship.
1990 (R) 90m/C Jon Stafford, Rick Hearst, Paul Smith, Cameron Mitchell, Vernon Wells, Colleen Morris, John Saxon; *D:* Gary Graver. **VHS, Beta, LV** $79.95 *COL* 🎬

Crossover A devoted male nurse works the graveyard shift in the psychiatric ward and neglects his personal life.
1982 (R) 96m/C James Coburn, Kate Nelligan; *D:* John Guillermin. **VHS, Beta** $69.95 *VES, LIV* 🎬½

Crossover Dreams Actor and musician Blades moves this old story along. Sure that he has at last made the international Big Time, a salsa artist becomes a self-important back-stabber after cutting an album. Great music. Blades's first film. ♫Good For Baby; Liz's Theme; Sin Fe; Todos Vuelven; Libra Timbero; Elegua; Merecumbe; Judy, Part 2; Yiri Yiri Bon.

1985 86m/C Ruben Blades, Shawn Elliott, Elizabeth Pena, Virgilio Marti, Tom Signorelli, Frank Robles, Joel Diamond, Amanda Barber, John Hammil; *D:* Leon Ichaso. **VHS, Beta** $14.95 *HBO, NEG* 🎬🎬½

Crossroads A blues-loving young white man, classically trained at Juilliard, befriends an aging black blues-master. After helping the old man escape from the nursing home, the two hop trains to the South where it's literally a duel with the devil. Fine performances by Macchio, Gertz, and Morton. Wonderful music, mostly by Ry Cooder.
1986 (R) 100m/C Ralph Macchio, Joe Seneca, Jami Gertz, Joe Morton; *D:* Walter Hill. **VHS, Beta, LV** $19.95 *RCA, COL* 🎬🎬½

Crow Hollow A Victorian mansion inhabited by three whacko sisters is the site of a murder committed in an attempt to cash in on an inheritance. When a young woman investigates, eyebrows are raised.
1952 69m/B *GB* Donald Houston, Nastasha Parry, Nora Nicholson, Esma Cannon, Melissa Stribling; *D:* Michael McCarthy. **VHS, Beta** $16.95 *SNC, RXM* 🎬🎬

The Crowd A look at the day-to-day trials of a working-class family set against the backdrop of wealthy society. True-to-life, it's peppered with some happy moments, too. One of the best silent films. Available on laserdisc as a double feature with another '20s classic, "The Wind."
1928 104m/B Eleanor Boardman, James Murray, Bert Roach, Daniel G. Tomlinson, Dell Henderson, Lucy Beaumont; *D:* King Vidor. **VHS, Beta, LV** $29.95 *MGM* 🎬🎬🎬🎬

Crucible of Horror Two women plot the murder of an unsuspecting husband, but he turns the tables on them. *AKA:* Velvet House; The Corpse.
1969 91m/C *GB* Michael Gough, Yvonne Mitchell, Sharon Gurney; *D:* Viktors Ritelis. **VHS, Beta** $59.95 *PGN* 🎬🎬

Crucible of Terror Mad sculptor covers beautiful models with hot wax, then imprisons them in a mold of bronze.
1972 95m/C Mike Raven, Mary Maude, James Bolam. **VHS, Beta** $49.95 *PSM, MRV, GEM* Woof!

The Crucifer of Blood A disappointing Sherlock Holmes yarn, made for cable TV. Heston is adequate as the Baker Street sleuth, but the mystery—about two retired British soldiers who share an accursed secret and a vengeful comrade—unreels clumsily in the form of flashbacks that give away most of the puzzle from the start. Interesting only in that Dr. Watson has a love affair, more or less. Adapted from a play (and looking like it) by Paul Giovanni, inspired by Arthur Conan Doyle's "The Sign of Four."
1991 105m/C Charlton Heston, Richard Johnson, Susannah Harker, John Castle, Clive Wood, Simon Callow, Edward Fox; *D:* Fraser Heston. **VHS, Beta** $89.98 *TTC* 🎬½

The Crucified Lovers A shy scroll-maker falls in love with his master's wife. Excellent Japanese tragedy with fine performances all around. *AKA:* Chikamatsu Monogatari; Chikamatsu Monogatari.
1954 100m/B *JP* Kazuo Hasegawa, Kyoko Kagawa, Yoko Minamida, Eitaro Shindo, Sakae Ozawa; *D:* Kenji Mizoguchi. **VHS** *FCT* 🎬🎬🎬½

Cruel Sea Well-made documentary-like account of a Royal Navy corvette on convoy duty in the Atlantic during WWII.
1953 121m/B *GB* Jack Hawkins, Stanley Baker, Denholm Elliott, Virginia McKenna; *D:* Charles Frend. **VHS, Beta** $29.95 *BVG, HBO, BMV* 🎬🎬🎬

The Cruel Story of Youth A teenage girl and her criminal boyfriend use sex to get money out of rich, middle-aged men in this controversial look at the disillusionment of youth and the breaking of old values and traditions in Japan after World War II. In Japanese with English subtitles. *AKA:* Seishun Zanoku Monogatari; Naked Youth; A Story of the Cruelties of Youth.
1960 96m/C *JP* Yusuke Kawazu, Miyuki Kuwano, Yoshiko Kuga; *W/D:* Nagisa Oshima. **VHS** $79.95 *NYF* 🎬🎬🎬

Cruise into Terror A sarcophagus brought aboard a pleasure cruise ship unleashes an evil force that slowly starts to kill off the ship's passengers, most of whom likely thought they were on the Love Boat. Made for television.
1978 100m/C Ray Milland, Hugh O'Brian, John Forsythe, Christopher George, Dirk Benedict, Frank Converse, Lynda Day George, Stella Stevens; *D:* Bruce Kessler. **VHS, Beta** $49.95 *PSM* Woof!

Cruise Missile Unique task force is on a mission to keep the world from nuclear holocaust.
1978 100m/C Peter Graves, Curt Jurgens, Michael Dante; *D:* Ted V. Mikels. **VHS, Beta** *NO* 🎬

Cruisin' High Two city street gangs battle it out.
1975 (R) 109m/C David Kyle, Kelly Yaegermann, Rhodes Reason. **VHS, Beta** $69.95 *VES, LIV* 🎬

Cruising Rookie cop Pacino is deep undercover investigating the bizarre murders of homosexuals in New York's West Village. Sexually explicit but less than suspenseful mystery. Release was sensationalized, with many gay rights groups voicing loud disapproval of the sordid gay characterization, while others feared copy-cat crimes. Excellent New York City cinematography; music by Jack Nitzsche.
1980 (R) 102m/C Al Pacino, Paul Sorvino, Karen Allen, Powers Boothe; *D:* William Friedkin; *M:* Jack Nitzsche. **VHS, Beta** $19.98 *WAR* 🎬🎬

The Crush Wealthy 14-year-old temptress Silverstone develops an obsessive crush on good-looking 28-year-old Elwes, who's renting her family's guest house. In an attempt to win his heart, she rewrites his poorly composed magazine articles. This doesn't convince him they should mate for life, so she sabotages his apartment to vent her rage. Sound familiar? The plot's lifted right out of "Fatal Attraction" and writer/director Shapiro doesn't offer viewers anything inventively different. He does manage to substitute new methods for the spurned lover to snare her prey. Limp plot would have been exciting if we hadn't seen it so many times before. Silverstone's film debut.
1993 (R) 89m/C Cary Elwes, Alicia Silverstone, Jennifer Rubin, Kurtwood Smith, Gwynyth Walsh, Amber Benson; *D:* Alan Shapiro; *W:* Alan Shapiro; *M:* Graeme Revell. **VHS, Beta, LV** *WAR* 🎬½

Crusoe A lushly photographed version of the Daniel Defoe classic. Crusoe is an arrogant slave trader stranded on a desert island populated by unfriendly natives. Themes of prejudice, fear, and choice appear in this never-padded, thoughtful film. Quinn gives an excellent performance as the stranded slave-trader.
1989 (PG-13) 94m/C Aidan Quinn, Ade Sapara, Jimmy Nail, Timothy Spall; *D:* Caleb Deschanel; *W:* Walon Green. **VHS, Beta, LV** *NO* 🎬🎬½

Cry-Baby An homage and spoof of '50s teen-rock melodramas by the doyen of cinematic Bad Taste, involving a terminal bad-boy high schooler who goes with a square blond and starts an inter-class rumble. Musical numbers, throwaway gags and plenty of knee-bending to Elvis, with a weak story supported by offbeat celeb appearances.
1990 (PG-13) 85m/C Johnny Depp, Amy Locane, Polly Bergen, Traci Lords, Ricki Lake, Iggy Pop, Susan Tyrrell, Patty Hearst, Kim McGuire, Darren E. Burrows, Troy Donahue, Willem Dafoe, David Nelson; **D:** John Waters. **VHS, Beta, LV** $19.95 *MCA ♪♪♪*

Cry Danger A falsely imprisoned man is released from jail, and he searches for those who framed him.
1951 80m/B Dick Powell, Rhonda Fleming, William Conrad, Richard Erdman; **D:** Robert Parrish. **VHS** $19.98 *REP ♪♪♪*

A Cry for Love An amphetamine addict and an alcoholic meet, fall in love, and help each other recover. Based on the best seller by Jill Schary Robinson, "Bedtime Story."
1980 96m/C Susan Blakely, Powers Boothe, Gene Barry, Charles Siebert, Herb Edelman, Fern Fitzgerald, Lainie Kazan; **D:** Paul Wendkos. **VHS, Beta** $14.95 *FRH ♪♪*

Cry Freedom A romantic look at the short life of South African activist Steven Biko, and his friendship with the white news editor, Donald Woods. The film focuses on Woods' escape from Africa while struggling to bring Biko's message to the world. Based on a true story.
1987 (PG) 157m/C Kevin Kline, Denzel Washington, Penelope Wilton; **D:** Richard Attenborough. **VHS, Beta, LV** $14.98 *MCA, KUI, FCT ♪♪ ½*

Cry from the Mountain Heavily religious film about a father and son who go on a kayak trip through Alaska's wilderness so the father can break the news of his impending divorce. A series of events occurs that change their lives, and they meet a mysterious mountain man who relies on his faith in God to get by in the wilderness. Features an appearance by Rev. Billy Graham.
1985 (PG) 78m/C James Cavan, Wes Parker, Rita Walter, Chris Kidd, Coleen Gray, Jerry Ballew, Allison Argo, Glen Alsworth, Myrna Kidd; **D:** James F. Collier. **VHS, Beta, LV** $59.95 *LIV ♪*

A Cry from the Streets Drama about the plight of orphan children and dedicated social workers in England.
1957 100m/C *GB* Max Bygraves, Barbara Murray, Kathleen Harrison, Colin Petersen; **D:** Lewis Gilbert. **VHS** $29.95 *FCT ♪♪*

A Cry in the Dark Tight film story of the infamous Australian murder trial of Lindy Chamberlain, who was accused of killing her own baby, mostly because of the intensely adverse public opinion, aroused by vicious press, that surrounded the case. Chamberlain blamed the death on a wild dingo dog. Near-documentary style, with Streep excellent as the religious, unknowable mother. Based on the book "Evil Angels" by John Bryson and released in Australia under that title. This case was also detailed in the film "Who Killed Baby Azaria?"
1988 (PG-13) 120m/C *AU* Meryl Streep, Sam Neill, Bruce Myles, Charles Tingwell, Nick Tate, Neil Fitzpatrick, Maurice Fields, Lewis Fitzgerald; **D:** Fred Schepisi. Academy Awards '88 Nominations: Best Actress (Streep); Australian Film Institute '88: Best Actor (Neill), Best Actress (Streep); New York Film Critics Awards '88: Best Actress (Streep). **VHS, Beta, LV, 8mm** $19.98 *WAR, FCT ♪♪♪ ½*

A Cry in the Night After Jenny (Higgins Clark) marries an internationally-acclaimed artist, she thinks her life is complete. However, once she and her two daughters move into his country estate, her life takes a tragic turn as she's haunted by the mysterious deaths of her ex-husband and newborn child. King plays the new husband who turns out to have a few psychological quirks of his own. Based on the bestselling novel by Mary Higgins Clark. Actress Higgins Clark is the novelist's daughter. Made for television.
1993 (PG-13) 99m/C Perry King, Carol Higgins Clark; **W/D:** Robin Spry. **VHS** $89.98 *REP ♪♪ ½*

A Cry in the Wild A 14 year old boy must find his way back to civilization when he's the lone survivor of an airplane crash. Strong acting from Rushton, excellent nature photography make this well-used story work again.
1990 (PG) 93m/C Jared Rushton, Ned Beatty, Pamela Sue Martin, Stephen Meadows; **D:** Mark Griffiths. **VHS** $14.95 *MGM ♪♪♪*

Cry of a Prostitute: Love Kills Former prostitute joins with a professional assassin in an effort to pacify rival gangsters in Italy.
1972 (R) 86m/C Henry Silva, Barbara Bouchet; **D:** Andrew Bianchi. **VHS, Beta** $59.95 *PSM ♪*

Cry of Battle Anxious for the challenges of manhood, a well-heeled young man joins a guerrilla militia in the Philippines. **AKA:** To Be a Man.
1963 99m/B Van Heflin, Rita Moreno, James MacArthur; **D:** Irving Lerner. **VHS, Beta** $49.95 *PSM, MRV, FGF ♪♪ ½*

Cry of the Banshee Witch-hunter Price and family are tormented by Satanic powers seeking revenge. Superior horror period piece. Also available with "Count Yorga, Vampire" on Laserdisc.
1970 (PG) 87m/C *GB* Vincent Price, Elisabeth Bergner, Essy Persson, Hugh Griffith, Hilary Dwyer, Sally Geeson, Patrick Mower; **D:** Gordon Hessler. **VHS, Beta** $79.99 *HBO ♪♪ ½*

Cry of the Black Wolves A trapper wrongly accused of murder saves the life of a bounty hunter hired to capture him.
197? 90m/C Ron Ely, Catherine Conti. **VHS, Beta** *NO ♪*

Cry of the Innocent An action-packed thriller about a Vietnam veteran who is out to find a group of Irish terrorists that killed his family.
1980 93m/C Cyril Cusack, Alexander Knox, Rod Taylor, Joanna Pettet, Nigel Davenport; **D:** Michael O'Herlihy. **VHS, Beta** *NO ♪♪♪*

Cry of the Werewolf A beautiful New Orleans gypsy protects her mother's mummified remains by periodically turning into a werewolf and killing people.
1944 63m/B Nina Foch, Stephen Crane, Osa Massen, Blanche Yurka, Barton MacLane, Ivan Triesault, John Abbott, Fritz Leiber; **D:** Henry Levin. **VHS** $14.99 *MOV ♪♪*

Cry Panic A man is thrown into a strange series of events after accidentally running down a man on a highway. Made for television.
1974 74m/C John Forsythe, Anne Francis, Earl Holliman, Claudia McNeil, Ralph Meeker; **D:** James Goldstone. **VHS, Beta** $49.95 *PSM ♪♪*

Cry Terror Two escaped convicts take two beautiful women hostage hoping to gain their own freedom. Only a quick-thinking undercover police officer can save the girls. Made for television.
1974 71m/C *GB* Bob Hoskins, Susan Hampshire, Gabrielle Drake. **VHS, Beta** *NO ♪♪*

Cry, the Beloved Country A black country minister travels to Johannesberg to be with his son after the youth is accused of killing a white man. Through the events of the trial, the horror, oppression, and destruction of South Africa's apartheid system are exposed. Startling and moving, the first entertainment feature set against the backdrop of apartheid. Still trenchant; based on the novel by Alan Paton. **AKA:** African Fury.
1951 111m/B *GB* Canada Lee, Charles Carson, Sidney Poitier, Joyce Carey, Geoffrey Keen; **D:** Zoltan Korda. **VHS** $69.95 *MON, FCT ♪♪♪*

Cry Uncle Comic account of a private eye who investigates a blackmailing case involving a film of orgies in which, much to his chagrin, he participated.
1971 85m/C Allen Garfield, Paul Sorvino; **D:** John G. Avildsen. **VHS, Beta** $79.95 *PSM ♪♪ ½*

Cry Vengeance A falsely-imprisoned detective gets out of jail and searches for the people who framed him and killed his family.
1964 83m/B Mark Stevens, Joan Vohs, Martha Hyer, Skip Homeier; **D:** Mark Stevens. **VHS, Beta** $19.98 *REP ♪♪ ½*

The Crying Game PR lesson in how to launch a small movie into the hypersphere and ensure critical silence on salient characterization. Jordan's gritty drama is a complex blend of violence, love, betrayal, guilt, and redemption and is not about what it seems to be about much of the time. Fergus (Rea) is a soft-hearted IRA volunteer involved in the kidnapping of black British soldier Jody (Whitaker). The two become friendly and Fergus learns of Jody's love for his special friend Dil (Davidson). When the hostage plans goes awry, Fergus escapes his associates' wrath by hiding out in London. Eventually he looks up, and falls for, the exotic Dil. But Fergus can't escape his past, especially when two IRA cohorts track him down, leading to both violence and sacrifice. Wonderful performances by all, including Rea as the appealing, conscience-stricken Fergus; Richardson as the cold, violent IRA moll Jude; and Davidson, in a film debut, as the needy, charismatic Dil. Whitaker is terrific in his 15 minutes of intense screen time. Filled with definite surprises and unexpected pleasures. On a par with Jordan's best, including "Mona Lisa." Title is taken from a top-5 British hit of 1964, three versions of which are heard.
1992 (R) 112m/C *IH* Stephen Rea, Jaye Davidson, Miranda Richardson, Forest Whitaker, Adrian Dunbar, Jim Broadbent, Ralph Brown, Breffini McKenna, Joe Savino, Birdie Sweeney, Andre Bernard; **D:** Neil Jordan; **W:** Neil Jordan. Academy Awards '92: Best Original Screenplay; Nominations: Best Actor (Rea), Best Director (Jordan), Best Film Editing, Best Picture, Best Supporting Actor (Davidson); Chicago Film Critics Awards '92: Best Foreign Film; Independent Spirit Awards '93: Best Foreign Film; Los Angeles Film Critics Association Awards '92: Best Foreign Film; New York Film Critics Awards '92: Best Supporting Actress (Richardson); National Society of Film Critics Awards '92: Best Actor (Rea). **VHS, LV** $94.98 *LIV, MOV, BTV ♪♪♪ ½*

Crypt of Dark Secrets Vietnam veteran recovering from wounds in the Louisiana swamps encounters a friendly Indian spirit who saves him from death.
1976 (R) 100m/C Maureen Chan, Ronald Tanet, Wayne Mack, Herbert G. Jahncke; **D:** Jack Weis. **VHS, Beta** *NO ♪*

Crypt of the Living Dead An undead woman from the 13th century makes life miserable for visitors on Vampire Island.

1973 (PG) 75m/C Andrew Prine, Mark Damon, Teresa Gimpera, Patty Shepard, Francisco (Frank) Brana; *D:* Ray Danton. **VHS, Beta** *NO Woof!*

Crystal Heart A medically isolated songwriter with an incurable disease falls in love with a lovely rock singer.
1987 (R) 103m/C Lee Curreri, Tawny Kitaen, Lloyd Bochner; *D:* Gil Bettman. **VHS, Beta** $19.95 *STE, NWV ♫*

Crystal Triangle An anthropologist seeks a message from God and discovers the Crystal Triangle, which will give him the means to do so. But he isn't the only one who wants the Crystal—because whoever possesses the message of God holds the fate of the world in their hands. Animated; in Japanese with English subtitles.
1987 86m/C *JP* **VHS, LV** $39.95 *CPM, TAM, WTA ♫♫½*

Crystalstone A wooden cross leads a pair of orphans on a dangerous search for the legendary Crystalstone.
1988 (PG) 103m/C Frank Grimes, Kamlesh Gupta, Laura Jane Goodwin, Sydney Bromley; *D:* Antonio Pelaez. **VHS, Beta** $79.98 *MCG ♫♫*

Cthulhu Mansion The oldest-looking juvenile delinquents you've ever seen release evil spirits when they take over a magician's estate. Not very special effects and abominable dialogue; it claims to be based on H.P. Lovecraft stories, but that's a load of dung.
1991 (R) 95m/C Frank Finlay, Marcia Layton, Brad Fisher, Melanie Shatner, Luis Fernando Alves, Kaethe Cherney, Paul Birchard, Francisco (Frank) Brana; *W/D:* J.P. Simon. **VHS** $9.98 *REP Woof!*

Cuba Cynical, satirical adventure/love story. Mercenary soldier rekindles an old affair during the Castro revolution. Charismatic cast and good direction make for an entertaining, if overlooked, Connery vehicle.
1979 (R) 121m/C Sean Connery, Brooke Adams, Jack Weston, Hector Elizondo, Denholm Elliott, Chris Sarandon, Lonette McKee; *D:* Richard Lester. **VHS, Beta** $14.95 *MGM, FOX ♫♫♫*

Cujo A rabid dog goes berserk and attacks a mother and her child who are trapped inside a broken-down Pinto. Frighteningly realistic film is based on Stephen King's bestseller.
1983 (R) 94m/C Dee Wallace Stone, Daniel Hugh-Kelly, Danny Pintauro, Ed Lauter, Christopher Stone; *D:* Lewis Teague. **VHS, Beta, LV** $19.98 *WAR ♫♫*

Cul de Sac A macabre, psychological thriller set in a dreary castle on a small island off the British coast. Pleasance is an eccentric, middle-aged hermit living acrimoniously with his young, nympho wife (Dorleac) when their home is invaded by two wounded gangsters (Stander and MacGowran), who proceed to hold the couple hostage. MacGowran soon dies of his wounds, leaving Stander and Pleasance to fight it out, encouraged by the luscious Dorleac, who finds her fun where she can. A bleak, sinister film considered one of Polanski's best.
1966 111m/C *GB* Donald Pleasence, Francoise Dorleac, Lionel Stander, Jack MacGowran, Jacqueline Bisset; *W/D:* Roman Polanski. **VHS** $29.95 *FCT ♫♫♫*

Culpepper Cattle Co. A young, starry-eyed yokel wants to be a cowboy and gets himself enlisted in a cattle drive, where he learns the harsh reality of the West.
1972 (PG) 92m/C Gary Grimes, Billy Green Bush, Bo Hopkins, Charles Martin Smith, Geoffrey Lewis; *D:* Dick Richards; *M:* Jerry Goldsmith. **VHS, Beta** $19.98 *FOX ♫♫½*

Cult People Interviews and film clips featuring a host of filmmaking's favorite cult personalities.
1989 60m/C Patrick Macnee, Cameron Mitchell, James Karen, Russ Meyer, Curtis Harrington, Waris Hussein, Michael Sarne. **VHS** $19.95 *FCT ♫½*

Cup Final The similarities and contradictions in war and sports, where passions and competition run high, are depicted in this emotional drama. Set in 1982 during Israel's invasion of Lebanon. Cohen is an Israeli soldier passionately interested in the World Cup soccer tournament. When he is taken prisoner by the PLO he discovers his captor Ziad shares his interest in the Italian national team. This common interest brings the two antagonists reluctantly together. In Hebrew and Arabic with English subtitles. *AKA:* G'mar Giviya.
1992 107m/C *IS* Moshe Ivgi, Muhamad Bacri, Suheil Haddad; *D:* Eran Riklis; *W:* Eyal Halfon; *M:* Raviv Gazil. **VHS** $59.95 *ICA, BTV ♫♫*

The Cure Chaplin arrives at a spa to take a rest cure, accompanied by a trunk full of liquor that somehow gets dumped into the water at the resort. Silent with music track.
1917 20m/B Charlie Chaplin, Edna Purviance, Eric Campbell, Albert Austin; *D:* Charlie Chaplin. **VHS, Beta, 3/4U, Special order formats** *VYY, CAB ♫♫*

Curfew A young woman rushes home so she doesn't break her curfew, only to find two killers with time on their hands waiting for her. Violent.
1988 (R) 86m/C John Putch, Kyle Richards, William Wellman Jr., Bert Remsen; *D:* Gary Winick. **VHS, Beta, LV** $19.95 *STE, NWV ♫♫*

Curiosity Kills Young people find more than they bargained for when they begin to investigate the death of a fellow tenant. Tense made-for-cable thriller.
1990 (R) 86m/C Rae Dawn Chong, C. Thomas Howell, Courteney Cox, Paul Guilfoyle, Jeff Fahey; *D:* Colin Bucksey. **VHS** $79.95 *MCA ♫♫*

Curley High-spirited youngsters play pranks on their schoolteacher. A part of the Hal Roach Comedy Carnival.
1947 53m/C Larry Olsen, Frances Rafferty, Eilene Janssen, Walter Abel; *D:* Bernard Carr. **VHS, Beta** $19.95 *DVT, NOS, HHT ♫♫*

Curley & His Gang in the Haunted Mansion Eccentric scientist gets involved in a haunted mansion mystery.
1947 54m/C Larry Olsen. **VHS, Beta** $19.95 *MRV ♫½*

Curly Sue Adorable, homeless waif Porter and her scheming, adoptive father Belushi plot to rip off single, career-minded female attorney Lynch in order to take in some extra cash. Trouble is, all three heartstrings are tugged, and the trio develop a warm, caring relationship. A throwback to the Depression era's Shirley Temple formula films met with mixed reviews. Undiscriminating younger audiences should have a good time, though. Available in widescreen format on laserdisc.
1991 (PG) 102m/C James Belushi, Kelly Lynch, Alison Porter, John Getz, Fred Dalton Thompson; *W/D:* John Hughes. **VHS, Beta, LV, 8mm** $19.98 *WAR, CCB ♫♫*

Curly Top Orphan Temple helps land a husband for her beautiful sister. Along the way, she sings "Animal Crackers in My Soup." Remake of the silent "Daddy Long Legs," which was remade again in 1955.
1935 74m/B Shirley Temple, John Boles, Rochelle Hudson, Jane Darwell, Esther Dale, Arthur Treacher, Rafaela Ottiano; *D:* Irving Cummings. **VHS, Beta** $19.98 *FOX, MLT ♫♫½*

The Curse After a meteorite lands near a small farming community and contaminates the area, a young boy tries to prevent residents from turning into slime-oozing mutants. Remake of "Die, Monster, Die." *AKA:* The Farm.
1987 (R) 92m/C Wil Wheaton, Claude Akins, Malcolm Danare, Cooper Huckabee, John Schneider, David Keith, Amy Wheaton, David Chaskin; *D:* David Keith. **VHS, Beta, LV** $14.95 *MED, VTR, IME ♫*

Curse 2: The Bite Radiation affected snakes are transformed into deadly vipers whose bites change their unsuspecting victims into horrible creatures.
1988 (R) 97m/C Jill Schoelen, J. Eddie Peck, Jamie Farr, Savina Gersak, Bo Svenson; *D:* Fred Goodwin. **VHS, Beta** $89.95 *TWE ♫*

Curse 3: Blood Sacrifice An African sugar cane plantation becomes host to a horrible nightmare when a voodoo curse is placed on the owners. The monstrous God of the Sea is summoned to avenge the accidental death of a baby, and the hellish journey into insanity begins. *AKA:* Panga.
1990 (R) 91m/C Christopher Lee, Jenilee Harrison, Henry Cele; *D:* Sean Barton. **VHS, LV** $79.95 *COL ♫*

Curse 4: The Ultimate Sacrifice Beneath the monastery at San Pietro lies buried the beast of the Apocalypse. For 400 years the secret has been kept and then an American priest and a lovely school teacher unwittingly break the seal and unleash the cursed beast upon an unsuspecting world.
1992 (R) 84m/C Timothy Van Patten, Laura Schaefer, Jeremy West, Ian Abercrombie; *D:* David Schmoeller. **VHS, LV** $79.95 *COL ♫½*

The Curse of Frankenstein Young Victor Frankenstein reenacts his father's experiments with creating life from the dead resulting in a terrifying, hideous creature. The first in Hammer's Frankenstein series and followed by "Revenge of Frankenstein." From the Shelley story. Make-up by Jack Pierce, who also created the famous make-up for Universal's Frankenstein monster.
1957 83m/C *GB* Peter Cushing, Christopher Lee, Hazel Court, Robert Urquhart, Valerie Gaunt; *D:* Terence Fisher; *W:* Jimmy Sangster. **VHS, Beta** $14.95 *WAR, MLB ♫♫½*

The Curse of King Tut's Tomb Made-for-television movie is set in 1922 where archaeologists have just opened Tutankhamen's tomb. The curse of the boy king is unleashed as tragic events bring the adventurers uncommon doom. Oh boy.
1980 98m/C Robin Ellis, Harry Andrews, Eva Marie Saint, Raymond Burr, Wendy Hiller; *D:* Philip Leacock. **VHS, Beta** $9.95 *GKK ♫½*

Curse of the Alpha Stone A professor experiments with an ancient formula on a student, creating a babbling maniac who slaughters freshman girls.
1985 90m/C **VHS, Beta** $49.95 *UHV Woof!*

The Curse of the Aztec Mummy A mad scientist schemes to rob a Mayan pyramid of its treasure but the resident mummy will have none of it. Sequel to "Robot vs. the Aztec Mummy" and followed by "Wrestling Women vs. the Aztec Mummy." *AKA:* La Maldicion de la Momia Azteca.
1959 65m/B *MX* Ramon Gay, Rosita Arenas, Crox Alvarado; *D:* Rafael Portillo. **VHS** $16.95 *SNC Woof!*

Curse of the Aztec Mummy/ Robot vs. the Aztec Mummy Vengeful mummy of an Aztec warrior stalks those who attempt to steal a fabulous treasure. A mad criminal scientist wants the

treasure and uses gangsters and a human robot to get what he wants.
1959 130m/B Ramon Gay, Rosita Arenas, Crox Alvarado, Luis Aceves Cantaneda; *D:* Rafael Portillo. **VHS, Beta** *HHT Woof!*

Curse of the Black Widow An investigator follows a trail of brutal murders to the lair of a supernatural gigantic spider in the middle of Los Angeles. Made for television. *AKA:* Love Trap.
1977 100m/C Patty Duke, Anthony (Tony) Franciosa, Donna Mills, June Lockhart, Sid Caesar, Vic Morrow, June Allyson, Roz Kelly, Jeff Corey; *D:* Dan Curtis. **VHS, Beta** *NO ⬚⬚*

Curse of the Blue Lights Mysterious lights begin appearing at the local romantic spot. Little do the young lovers know, it hails the arrival of a ghoul, intent on raising the dead. Also available in an unedited version. Unfortunately, nothing can resurrect this film.
1988 (R) 93m/C Brent Ritter; *D:* John H. Johnson. **VHS, Beta** *NO Woof!*

Curse of the Cat People A young sensitive girl is guided by the vision of her dead mother. Sequel to "Cat People." Available in a colorized version.
1944 70m/B Simone Simon, Kent Smith, Jane Randolph, Elizabeth Russell, Ann Carter; *D:* Robert Wise, Gunther Von Fristch. **VHS, Beta, LV $19.95** *MED, TTC ⬚⬚⬚*

The Curse of the Crying Woman Unknowing descendant of a witch is lured to her aunt's home to perform the act that will revive the monstrous crying woman and renew a reign of evil. *AKA:* La Maldicion de a Llorona; La Casa Embrujada.
1961 74m/B *MX* Rosita Arenas, Abel Salazar, Rita Macedo, Carlos Lopez Moctezuma. **VHS, Beta $59.95** *SNC, HHT, TIM ⬚1/2*

Curse of the Demon A famous psychologist investigates a colleague's mysterious death and enters a world of demonology and the occult, climaxing in a confrontation with a cult's patron demon. Superb thriller based upon the story "Casting the Runes" by M.R. James. *AKA:* Night of the Demon.
1957 81m/B *GB* Dana Andrews, Peggy Cummins, Niall MacGinnis, Maurice Denham; *D:* Jacques Tourneur. **VHS, Beta, LV $9.95** *GKK, MLB ⬚⬚⬚1/2*

Curse of the Devil This time Naschy is turned into a werewolf by annoyed gypsies whose ancestors were slain by his. *AKA:* El Retorno de la Walpurgis.
1973 (R) 73m/C *MX SP* Paul Naschy, Maria Silva, Patty Shepard, Fay Falcon; *D:* Carlos Aured; *W:* Paul Naschy. **VHS $19.98** *SNC, UHV ⬚1/2*

Curse of the Headless Horseman The headless horseman rides again, bringing terror to all who cross his path!
1972 80m/C Don Carrara, Claudia Dean, B.G. Fisher, Margo Dean, Lee Byers, Joe Cody; *D:* John Kirkland. **VHS** *NO ⬚1/2*

Curse of the Living Corpse A millionaire comes back to rotting life to kill his negligent relatives. Scheider's first film.
1964 84m/C Candace Hilligoss, Roy Scheider, Helen Warren, Margot Hartman; *D:* Del Tenney. **VHS, Beta $39.95** *PSM ⬚*

Curse of the Living Dead Two siblings are forced to eat flesh for eternity after their witch-doctor mother puts a curse on them.
1989 90m/C *D:* Lawrence Foldes. **VHS, Beta** *ELV, HHE ⬚*

Curse of the Pink Panther Clifton Sleigh, an inept New York City detective played by Wass, is assigned to find the missing Inspector Clouseau. His efforts are complicated by an assortment of gangsters and aristocrats who cross paths with the detective. So-so attempt to keep popular series going after Seller's death. Niven's last film.
1983 (PG) 110m/C Ted Wass, David Niven, Robert Wagner, Herbert Lom, Joanna Lumley, Capucine, Robert Loggia, Harvey Korman, Leslie Ash, Denise Crosby; *D:* Blake Edwards. **VHS, Beta $79.95** *MGM ⬚⬚*

Curse of the Queerwolf A man is bitten on the butt by gay werewolf and transforms into the title character. Filmed in Santa Barbara in 8mm; some funny moments. From the director of "A Polish Vampire in Burbank."
1987 90m/C Michael Palazzolo, Kent Butler, Taylor Whitney; *D:* Mark Pirro. **VHS $9.95** *SIM, HHE ⬚⬚*

Curse of the Screaming Dead An unpredictable zombie yarn.
1984 90m/C VHS, Beta *NO Woof!*

Curse of the Stone Hand A pair of stone hands causes folks to do suicidal things. A mutation of a Mexican and a Chilean horror film, each purchased and monster-mashed into one by Warren.
1964 72m/B *MX* John Carradine, Ernest Walch, Sheila Bon, Katherine Victor, Lloyd Nelson; *D:* Jerry Warren. **VHS $15.95** *NOS, LOO Woof!*

Curse of the Swamp Creature A mad scientist in the Everglades attempts to create half human/half alligator monsters. In turn, a geologic expeditional force attempts to stop his experimentation. Low budget thrills courtesy of Larry Buchanan.
1966 80m/C John Agar, Francine York, Shirley McLine, Bill Thurman, Jeff Alexander; *D:* Larry Buchanan. **VHS $19.98** *MOV, VDM ⬚*

The Curse of the Werewolf Horror film about a 19th-century European werewolf that is renowned for its ferocious departure from the stereotypical portrait of the beast.
1961 91m/C *GB* Oliver Reed, Clifford Evans, Yvonne Romain, Catherine Feller, Anthony Dawson, Michael Ripper; *D:* Terence Fisher. **VHS, Beta $14.98** *MCA, TLF, MLB ⬚⬚1/2*

Curse of the Yellow Snake Written by Edgar Wallace, this voluminous yarn features a running battle over an ancient Chinese artifact, with crazed Chinese cultists running through foggy London streets.
1963 98m/C *GE* Joachim Berger, Werner Peters; *D:* Franz Gottlieb. **VHS, Beta $29.95** *VYY ⬚⬚*

Curtain Up "Little theatre" dramatics and the exasperating temperaments of amateur theatricals are exposed in this adaptation of the play "On Monday Next," by Philip King.
1953 82m/C *GB* Robert Morley, Margaret Rutherford, Olive Sloane; *D:* Ralph Smart. **VHS, Beta** *LCA ⬚⬚*

Curtains Director has a clash of wills with a film star that spells "Curtains" for a group of aspiring actresses gathered together at a haunted house for an audition. Hamfest with no thrills, chills, gore, or gratuitous skin. Written by Robert Guza, Jr. and directed by Stryker (Richard Ciupka hiding behind pseudonym).
1983 (R) 90m/C *CA* John Vernon, Samantha Eggar; *D:* Jonathan Stryker. **VHS, Beta $69.95** *VES Woof!*

Custer's Last Fight Re-enactment of the American West period when the Sioux and Cheyenne Indian tribes bitterly opposed the white man. Silent.

1912 50m/B *D:* Francis Ford. **VHS, Beta $19.95** *NOS, DVT ⬚1/2*

Custer's Last Stand Feature-length version of the Mascot serial recounting the last days of the famous General.
1936 70m/B Frank McGlynn, Rex Lease, Nancy Caseell, Lona Andre, William Farnum, Reed Howes, Jack Mulhall, Josef Swickard, Ruth Mix; *D:* Elmer Clifton. **VHS, Beta $69.95** *VCN, GPV, TIM ⬚1/2*

Cut and Run Two journalists follow a lead to the former South American home of Jim Jones, and are instantly captured by local guerrillas.
1985 (R) 87m/C Michael Berryman, Willie Aames, Lisa Blount, Karen Black. **VHS, Beta $19.95** *STE, NWV ⬚*

The Cut Throats Americans stumble upon an isolated Nazi outpost stocked with gold and beautiful women. Exploitation at its worst.
1989 (R) 80m/C Jay Scott, Joanne Douglas, Jeff Letham, Pat Michaels, Barbara Lane; *W/D:* John Hayes. **VHS** *NO ⬚*

Cutter's Way An embittered and alcoholic disabled Vietnam vet and his small-time crook/gigolo friend wrestle with justice and morality when the drifter uncovers a murder but declines to get involved. An unusually cynical mystery from the novel by Newton Thorburg. *AKA:* Cutter and Bone.
1981 (R) 105m/C Jeff Bridges, John Heard, Lisa Eichhorn, Ann Dusenberry, Stephen Elliott, Nina Van Pallandt, George Dickerson; *D:* Ivan Passer; *M:* Jack Nitzsche. **VHS, Beta, LV $69.95** *MGM ⬚⬚1/2*

Cutting Class Murders proliferate in a high school, where a student with a history of mental illness is number one on the suspect list. Tongue-in-cheek mayhem.
1989 91m/C Jill Schoelen, Roddy McDowall, Donovan Leitch, Martin Mull, Brad Pitt; *D:* Rospo Pallenberg. **VHS, LV $9.98** *REP ⬚⬚*

The Cutting Edge Take one spoiled figure skater who can't keep a partner, team her with a cocky ex-hockey player who thinks the only sport on ice IS hockey and you've got a winning combo. Rather thin plot revolves around their quest for Olympic gold and can't be taken too seriously, but the sparks fly between Kelly and Sweeney—the reason this movie works.
1992 (PG) 101m/C D.B. Sweeney, Moira Kelly, Roy Dotrice, Terry O'Quinn, Dwier Brown, Rachelle Ottley, Jo Jo Starbuck; *D:* Paul Michael Glaser. **VHS, LV $19.98** *MGM ⬚⬚1/2*

Cyberpunk Documentary exploring William Gibson's literary and cultural phenomena of Cyberpunk. Includes interviews with Gibson, Jaron Lanier, Timothy Leary and Michael Synergy.
1991 60m/C William Gibson, Timothy Leary, Jaron Lanier, Michael Synergy; *D:* Marianne Trench. **VHS $29.95** *MFV, FCT, TAM ⬚⬚1/2*

Cyborg In a deathly, dirty, post-holocaust urban world, an able cyborg battles a horde of evil mutant thugs. Poorly-made action flick.
1989 (R) 85m/C Jean-Claude Van Damme, Deborah Richter, Vincent Klyn, Dayle Haddon; *D:* Albert Pyun. **VHS, Beta, LV $14.95** *MGM, PIA ⬚*

Cycle Psycho Two girls are abused by a crazed motorcycle gang. *AKA:* Numbered Days.
19?? (R) 80m/C Joe Turkel, Tom Drake, Stephen Oliver. **VHS, Beta $59.95** *ACA Woof!*

Cycle Vixens Three girls jump on their hogs and head from Colorado to California. Much leather, motor revving and other obligatory motorcycle-trash trimmings. *AKA:* The Young Cycle Girls.

1979 (R) 90m/C Loraine Ferris, Daphne Lawrence, Deborah Marcus, Lonnie Pense, Kevin O'Neill, Bee Lechat, Billy Bullet; *D:* Peter Perry. **VHS $9.95** *SIM Woof!*

Cyclone The girlfriend of a murdered scientist must deliver a secretly devised motorcycle into righteous government hands, much to the dismay of evil agents and corrupt officials. Good fun, sparked by a stellar "B" cast.
1987 (R) 89m/C Heather Thomas, Jeffrey Combs, Ashley Ferrare, Dar Robinson, Martine Beswick, Robert Quarry, Martin Landau, Huntz Hall, Troy Donahue, Michael Reagan, Dawn Wildsmith, Bruce Fairbairn, Russ Tamblyn; *D:* Fred Olen Ray. **VHS, Beta, LV $79.95** *COL ⅛*

Cyclone Cavalier A dauntless hero travels through Central America on an adventurous spree.
1925 58m/B Reed Howes; *D:* Albert Rogell. **VHS, Beta $16.95** *GPV ⅛*

Cyclone of the Saddle Typical Western about a range war.
1935 53m/B Rex Lease, Bobby Nelson, William Desmond, Yakima Canutt; *D:* Elmer Clifton. **VHS, Beta** *NO ⅛*

Cyclops When an expedition party searches throughout Mexico for a woman's long lost fiance, they are shocked when they find out that radiation has turned him into a one-eyed monster.
1956 72m/B Tom Drake, Gloria Talbott, Lon Chaney Jr., James Craig; *D:* Bert I. Gordon. **VHS, Beta $29.95** *LIV, MLB ⅛*

Cyclotrode "X" The Crimson Ghost attempts to kidnap the inventor of the title machine, which would enable him to rule the world. Edited from what was originally a 12-part serial. Moore (The Lone Ranger) plays a bad guy. *AKA:* The Crimson Ghost.
1946 100m/B Charles Quigley, Linda Stirling, I. Stanford Jolley, Clayton Moore, Kenne Duncan; *D:* William Witney, Fred Brannon. **VHS, Beta, 3/4U $29.98** *VCN ⅛½*

Cyrano de Bergerac Edmund Rostand's famous story of a large nosed yet poetic cavalier, who finds himself too ugly to be loved. He bears the pain of his devotion to Roxanne from afar, and helps the handsome but tongue-tied Christian to romance her. Ferrer became famous for this role, which won him an Oscar. Also available colorized.
1950 112m/B Jose Ferrer, Mala Powers, William Prince, Elena Verdugo, Morris Carnovsky; *D:* Michael Gordon. **VHS, LV, 3/4U, Special order formats $9.95** *NEG, MRV, NOS ⅛⅛*

Cyrano de Bergerac Edmond Rostand's gallant poet and swordsman, with the extraordinary nose, is well-portrayed by Jacobi in this Royal Shakespeare Company production. Translated and adapted by Anthony Burgess.
1985 177m/C *GB* Derek Jacobi, Sinead Cusack. **VHS $29.95** *TVC, TTC ⅛⅛*

Cyrano de Bergerac Depardieu brings to exhilarating life Rostand's well-loved play about the brilliant but grotesque-looking swordsman/poet, afraid of nothing—except declaring his love to the beautiful Roxanne. One of France's costliest modern productions, a multi-award winner for its cast, costumes, music and sets. English subtitles (by Anthony Burgess) are designed to capture the intricate rhymes of the original French dialogue.
1990 (PG) 135m/C *FR* Gerard Depardieu, Jacques Weber, Anne Brochet, Vincent Perez, Roland Bertin, Josiane Stoleru, Phillipe Volter, Philippe Morier-Genoud, Pierre Maguelon; *D:* Jean-Paul Rappeneau. Academy Awards '90: Best Costume Design; Nominations: Best Actor (Depardieu), Best Art Direction/Set Decoration,

Best Foreign Language Film, Best Makeup; Cannes Film Festival '90: Best Actor (Depardieu); Cesar Awards '91: Best Actor (Depardieu), Best Director (Rappeneau), Best Film, Best Supporting Actor (Weber). **VHS, LV $89.98** *ORI, FCT ⅛⅛⅛*

D-Day on Mars The Purple Monster is Earth's only hope against alien invaders bent on taking over the planet. Originally a 15-part Republic serial titled "The Purple Monster Strikes."
1945 100m/B Dennis Moore, Linda Stirling, Roy Barcroft, James Craven, Bud Geary, Mary Moore; *D:* Spencer Gordon Bennet, Fred Brannon. **VHS $29.98** *REP ⅛*

D-Day, the Sixth of June An American soldier has an affair with a Englishwoman weeks before D-Day, where he unhappily finds himself fighting side by side with her husband. *AKA:* The Sixth of June.
1956 106m/C Richard Todd, Dana Wynter, Robert Taylor, Edmond O'Brien, John Williams, Jerry Paris, Richard Stapley; *D:* Henry Koster. **VHS, Beta $19.98** *FOX ⅛⅛⅛*

Da A middle-aged man returns to Ireland for his father's funeral. As he sorts out his father's belongings, his father returns as a ghostly presence to chat with him about life, death, and their own relationship. Based on the Hugh Leonard play with Hughes recreating his Tony-award winning role.
1988 (PG) 102m/C Barnard Hughes, Martin Sheen; *D:* Matt Clark. **VHS, Beta, LV** *NO ⅛⅛½*

Dad Hoping to make up for lost time, a busy executive rushes home to take care of his father who has just had a heart attack. What could have easily been sappy is made bittersweet by the convincing performances of Lemmon and Danson. Based on the novel by William Wharton.
1989 (PG) 117m/C Jack Lemmon, Ted Danson, Ethan Hawke, Olympia Dukakis, Kathy Baker, Zakes Mokae, J.T. Walsh, Kevin Spacey, Chris Lemmon; *D:* Gary David Goldberg. Academy Awards '89 Nominations: Best Makeup; National Media Owl Awards '90: First Prize. **VHS, Beta, LV $19.95** *MCA ⅛⅛½*

Daddy Long Legs Far from the great musicals, but enjoyable. An eccentric millionaire glimpses a French orphan and becomes her anonymous benefactor. Her musing over his identity spawns some surreal (often inexplicable) dance numbers, but love conquers all, even lesser Johnny Mercer songs. From a story by Jean Webster, also done in 1919 with Mary Pickford, 1931 with Janet Gaynor and 1935 with Shirley Temple as "Curly Top." ♫ Daddy Long Legs; Something's Got To Give; Sluefoot; Dream; History of the Beat; C-A-T Spells Cat; Welcome Egghead.
1955 126m/C Fred Astaire, Leslie Caron, Terry Moore, Thelma Ritter, Fred Clark, Charlotte Austin, Larry Keating; *D:* Jean Negulesco. **VHS, LV $19.98** *FXV, FCT ⅛⅛⅛*

Daddy-O Drag racer Daddy-O traps the killers of his best friend and lands the blonde bombshell Jana. It might seem bad since it's dated, but, hey, it may have been bad in 1959, too! *AKA:* Out on Probation.
1959 74m/B Dick Contino, Sandra Giles; *D:* Lou Place; *W:* David Moessinger. **VHS $9.95** *COL ⅛*

Daddy's Boys Since farming during the Depression is a rather low-paying endeavor, this family turns to thieving instead. But all-for-one and one-for-all is not the credo for one of the sons who decides to branch out on his own. Produced by Roger Corman.
1987 (R) 90m/C Daryl Haney, Laura Burkett, Raymond J. Barry, Dan Shor; *D:* Joe Minion; *W:* Daryl Haney. **VHS, Beta, LV $69.95** *COL ⅛½*

Daddy's Dyin'...Who's Got the Will? Based on the critically acclaimed play, this bittersweet comedy stars Bridges and D'Angelo as two members of the spiteful Turnover clan. When Daddy is on his deathbed, the entire family uses the opportunity to stab each other in the back. Non-stop humor and deep-hearted honesty carries this film quickly from beginning to end. The cast of well-known screen actors makes this a delightful adaptation.
1990 (PG-13) 95m/C Beau Bridges, Beverly D'Angelo, Tess Harper, Judge Reinhold, Amy Wright, Keith Carradine; *D:* Jack Fisk. **VHS, Beta, LV $14.95** *MGM ⅛⅛½*

Daddy's Gone A-Hunting It's an eye for an eye, a baby for a baby in this well-done psychological thriller. A happily married woman is stalked by her deranged ex-boyfriend, whose baby she aborted years before. Now he wants the life of her child as just compensation for the loss of his.
1969 (PG) 108m/C Carol White, Paul Burke, Scott Hylands, Rachel Ames, Mala Powers; *D:* Mark Robson; *M:* John Williams. **VHS $19.98** *WAR ⅛⅛⅛*

Daffy Duck & Company Seven Daffy classics, including a few earlier entries: "To Duck or Not to Duck," "Conrad the Sailor," "Daffy Duck and the Dinosaur," "The Dover Boys," "House Hunting Mice" and "Hep Cat."
1950 60m/C *D:* Chuck Jones, Robert McKimson, Friz Freleng, Bob Clampett; *V:* Jack Benny, Peter Lorre. **VHS, Beta $14.95** *MGM, WTA ⅛⅛⅛*

Daffy Duck Cartoon Festival: Ain't That Ducky There's wacky down-filled humor galore in this compilation tape. The cartoons include "Ain't That Ducky," "Daffy Duck Slept Here," "Hollywood Daffy," "Conrad the Sailor" and "The Wise Cracking Duck." Made between 1942 and 1947.
194? 35m/C *D:* Chuck Jones, Friz Freleng, Robert McKimson, Bob Clampett. **VHS, Beta $14.95** *MGM ⅛⅛⅛*

Daffy Duck Cartoon Festival: Daffy Duck & the Dinosaur Five classic Daffy shorts, including "Plane Daffy," "Nasty Quacks" and the title cartoon are featured.
1945 36m/C *D:* Chuck Jones, Chuck Jones, Robert McKimson, Bob Clampett. **VHS, Beta $14.95** *MGM, MRV ⅛⅛⅛*

Daffy Duck: The Nuttiness Continues... Daffy Duck runs amuck in this collection of cartoon classics that include "Beanstalk Bunny," "Deduce You Say," "Rabbit Fire," "Dripalong Daffy," "Porky's Duck Hunt," "Duck Amuck," "The Daffy Duck," and "The Scarlet Pumpernickel."
1956 59m/C *D:* Chuck Jones, Bob Clampett, Tex Avery. **VHS, Beta $12.95** *WAR, WTA ⅛⅛⅛*

Daffy Duck's Madcap Mania Six of the billed-comedian's best.
1989 45m/C *D:* Chuck Jones; *W/D:* Robert McKimson. **VHS $14.95** *WAR, WTA ⅛⅛⅛*

Daffy Duck's Movie: Fantastic Island A compilation of classic Warner Brothers cartoons, starring Daffy Duck, Speedy Gonzales, Bugs Bunny, Porky Pig, Sylvester, Tweety, Pepe Le Pew, Pirate Sam, Granny, Foghorn Leghorn and the Tasmanian Devil.
1983 (G) 78m/C *D:* Friz Freleng. **VHS, Beta, LV $19.98** *WAR, FCT, WTA ⅛⅛⅛*

Daffy Duck's Quackbusters Daffy, with help from pals Bugs and Porky, sets up his own "ghostbusting" service. Good compilation of old classics such as "Night of the

Living Duck," plus a new feature, "The Duxcorcist." Video is also available in Spanish.

1989 (G) 79m/C Daffy Duck, Bugs Bunny, Porky Pig; **D:** Greg Ford, Terry Lennon; **V:** Mel Blanc. **VHS, Beta, LV $19.98** *WAR, FCT, APD* ♫♫♫

Dagger Eyes A political assassin at work is inadvertently captured on film by a photographer. The assassin's mob employers will go to any lengths to destroy the film. Say cheeeeeese!

198? 84m/C Carol Bouquet, Philip Coccioletti, John Steiner; **D:** Carlo Vanzina. **VHS, Beta** *NO* ♫½

Daggers 8 The Kung Fu masters are back, battling their opponents with deadly daggers.

1980 90m/C VHS, Beta $39.95 *TWE* ♫

Dagora, the Space Monster Giant, slimy, pulsating mass from space lands on Earth and begins eating everything in sight. Scientists join together in a massive effort to destroy the creature. Believe it or not, it's sillier than most of the Japanese sci-fi genre. Written by Shinichi Sekizawa. **AKA:** Dagora; Space Monster Dagora; Uchudai Dogora; Uchu Daikaiju Dogora.

1965 80m/C Yosuke Natsuki, Yoko Fujiyama. **VHS, Beta $29.95** *VYY Woof!*

The Dain Curse In 1928, private eye Hamilton Nash must recover stolen diamonds, solve a millionaire's suicide, avoid being murdered, and end a family curse. Based on the novel by Dashiell Hammett. Made-for-television as a 312-minute miniseries.

1978 118m/C James Coburn, Jason Miller, Jean Simmons, Beatrice Straight, Hector Elizondo; **D:** E.W. Swackhamer. **VHS, Beta $69.98** *SUE, MTX* ♫♫

Daisy Miller Shepherd portrays the title character in this adaptation of the Henry James novella about a naive young American woman travelling through Europe and getting a taste of the Continent during the late 19th century. Though it is intelligently written and has a good supporting cast, the film seems strangely flat, due in large part to Shepherd's hollow performance.

1974 (G) 93m/C Cybill Shepherd, Eileen Brennan, Cloris Leachman, Mildred Natwick; **D:** Peter Bogdanovich. Academy Awards '74 Nominations: Best Costume Design; National Board of Review Awards '74: 10 Best Films of the Year. **VHS, Beta $14.95** *PAR* ♫♫½

Dakota Fine cast becomes embroiled in railroad land dispute. In the meantime, love strikes The Duke. Standard Wayne western saga never quite gets on track.

1945 82m/B John Wayne, Vera Ralston, Walter Brennan, Ward Bond, Ona Munson; **D:** Joseph Kane. **VHS, LV $14.98** *REP, PIA* ♫♫

Dakota A troubled half-breed teenager works for a rancher, romances his daughter, and befriends his crippled 12-year-old son. A well-meaning, but predictable drama.

1988 (PG) 96m/C Lou Diamond Phillips, Dee Dee Norton, Eli Cummins, Herta Ware; **D:** Fred Holmes. **VHS, Beta, LV $89.99** *HBO* ♫♫

Dakota Incident Decent western about stagecoach passengers travelling through Dakota Territory who must defend themselves against an Indian attack.

1956 88m/C Dale Robertson, Ward Bond, Linda Darnell, John Lund; **D:** Lewis R. Foster. **VHS $19.98** *REP* ♫♫

Daleks—Invasion Earth 2150 A.D. A sequel to "Dr. Who and the Daleks," wherein the popular British character endeavors to save the Earth from a robotic threat. **AKA:** Invasion Earth 2150 A.D.

1966 81m/C *GB* Peter Cushing, Andrew Keir, Jill Curzon, Ray Brooks; **D:** Gordon Flemyng. **VHS, Beta $79.99** *HBO* ♫♫½

Dam Busters Well-done and exciting film details the efforts of British scientists trying to devise a method of destroying a strategic dam in Nazi Germany during World War II. Definitely one of the better in the war movie genre.

1955 119m/B *GB* Michael Redgrave, Richard Todd, Ursula Jeans, Basil Sydney; **D:** Michael Anderson Sr. **VHS, Beta $59.99** *HBO, HMV* ♫♫♫½

Damage The elegant Irons portrays Stephen, a middle-aged, married British politician who has always been completely in control of his life, especially where his feelings are concerned. Then he meets Anna (Binoche), his son's less-than-innocent fiance, and immediately begins an obsessive, wildly sexual affair with her. Stephen should have listened to Anna's warning about herself "Damaged people are dangerous, they know they can survive," because their passion leads to betrayal and tragedy. Binoche is more icon than human being but the film still hypnotizes as an exploration of passion. Based on the novel by Josephine Hart. An unrated version is also available.

1992 (R) 111m/C *FR GB* Jeremy Irons, Juliette Binoche, Rupert Graves, Miranda Richardson, Ian Bannen, Leslie Caron, Peter Stormare, Gemma Clark, Julian Fellowes; **D:** Louis Malle; **W:** David Hare. **VHS, LV $89.99** *COL, IME, MOV* ♫♫♫

Dames A millionaire with fanatically religious beliefs tries to stop the opening of a Broadway show. In the last of the grand budget-breaking spectacles before the "production code" came into being, distinguished choreographer Busby Berkeley took his imagination to the limit: watch for the dancing clothes on an ironing board and dancing girls with puzzle pieces on their backs which form the real Keeler. ♫Dames; I Only Have Eyes For You; When You Were a Smile on Your Mother's Lips and a Twinkle in Your Father's Eye; Try To See It My Way; The Girl at the Ironing Board.

1934 95m/B Dick Powell, Joan Blondell, Ruby Keeler, ZaSu Pitts, Guy Kibbee, Busby Berkeley; **D:** Ray Enright; **W:** Delmer Daves. **VHS, Beta, LV $19.98** *MGM, FOX* ♫♫♫

Damien: Omen 2 Sequel to "The Omen" about Damien, a young boy possessed with mysterious demonic powers, who kills those people who anger him. Followed by "The Final Conflict."

1978 (R) 110m/C William Holden, Lee Grant, Lew Ayres, Robert Foxworth, Sylvia Sidney, Lance Henriksen; **D:** Don Taylor; **M:** Jerry Goldsmith. **VHS, Beta, LV $19.98** *FOX* ♫♫

Damien: The Leper Priest True story of a Roman Catholic priest who doomed himself by voluntarily serving on a leper colony one hundred years ago. Somewhat disappointing considering the dramatic material. Originally a vehicle for David Janssen, who died prior to filming. Made for television. **AKA:** Father Damien: The Leper Priest.

1980 100m/C Ken Howard, Mike Farrell, Wilfrid Hyde-White, William Daniels, David Ogden Stiers; **D:** Steven Gethers. **VHS, Beta $59.95** *LIV* ♫♫

Damn the Defiant Adventure abounds when Guinness, as captain of the HMS Defiant during the Napoleonic wars, finds himself up against not only the French but his cruel second-in-command (Bogarde) and a mutinous crew as well. In the end, both a fleet-wide mutiny and a French invasion of England are avoided. Much attention is paid to period detail in this well-crafted film. **AKA:** HMS Defiant.

1962 101m/C *GB* Alec Guinness, Dirk Bogarde, Maurice Denham, Anthony Quayle; **D:** Lewis Gilbert. **VHS, Beta, LV $14.95** *COL, FCT* ♫♫♫

Damn Yankees Musical feature adapted from the Broadway hit. A baseball fan frustrated by his team's lack of success makes a pact with the devil to become the team's new star. Verdon is dynamite as the devil's accomplice. Great Bob Fosse choreography. ♫Whatever Lola Wants; (You Gotta Have) Heart; Shoeless Joe From Hannibal Mo; Goodbye, Old Girl; A Little Brains, a Little Talent; Who's Got the Pain; Two Lost Souls; There's Something About an Empty Chair; Those Were the Good Old Days; Six Months Out of Every Year; Heart. **AKA:** What Lola Wants.

1958 110m/C Gwen Verdon, Ray Walston, Tab Hunter, Jean Stapleton, Russ Brown; **D:** George Abbott, Stanley Donen. **VHS, Beta, LV $19.98** *WAR, FCT, HMV* ♫♫♫

Damnation Alley A warrior, an artist, and a biker jump in tank and set off in search of civilization after Armageddon. They go to Albany instead. So-so attempt to revive the post-nuclear holocaust genre which was more successfully accomplished by the "Mad Max" series. Adapted by Alan Sharp and Lukas Heller from Roger Zelazny's novel.

1977 (PG) 87m/C George Peppard, Jan-Michael Vincent, Paul Winfield, Dominique Sanda, Jackie Earle Haley; **D:** Jack Smight; **M:** Jerry Goldsmith. **VHS, Beta $59.98** *FOX* ♫½

The Damned Depicts the Nazi takeover of a German industrialist family and their descent into greed, lust, and madness. Comes in dubbed or subtitled formats.

1969 (R) 146m/C *IT GE* Dirk Bogarde, Ingrid Thulin, Helmut Griem, Charlotte Rampling, Helmut Berger; **D:** Luchino Visconti. Academy Awards '69 Nominations: Best Story & Screenplay; National Board of Review Awards '69: 5 Best Foreign Films of the Year. **VHS, Beta $59.95** *WAR, APD, TAM* ♫♫½

Damned River Four friends take a guided tour down Zimbabwe's Zambezi River, only to find midway down that their guide is a murderous psycho. Survival becomes a priority.

1989 (R) 93m/C Stephen Shellan, Lisa Aliff, John Terlesky, Marc Poppel, Bradford Bancroft; **D:** Michael Schroeder. **VHS, Beta $89.98** *FOX* ♫½

A Damsel in Distress Astaire falls for an upper-class British girl, whose family wants her to have nothing to do with him. Features memorable songs from the Gershwins. ♫A Foggy Day in Londontown; Nice Work If You Can Get It; Stiff Upper Lip; Put Me to the Test; I Can't Be Bothered Now; The Jolly Tar and the Milkmaid; Things Are Looking Up; Sing of Spring; Ah Che a Voi Perdoni Iddio.

1937 101m/B Fred Astaire, Joan Fontaine, George Burns, Gracie Allen, Ray Noble, Montagu Love, Reginald Gardiner; **D:** George Stevens; **M:** George Gershwin, Ira Gershwin. **VHS, Beta, LV $14.98** *CCB, MED, TTC* ♫♫♫

Dan Candy's Law A Canadian mountie becomes a driven hunter, and then desperate prey, when he tries to track down the Indian who killed his partner. **AKA:** Alien Thunder.

1973 90m/C *CA* Donald Sutherland, Gordon Tootoosis, Chief Dan George, Kevin McCarthy; *D:* Claude Fournier. **VHS, Beta** $79.95 *PSM, SIM* ✂✂½

Dance Two ballet dancers struggle to find love amidst the backstage treacheries and demanding schedules of their profession. 1990 90m/C John Revall, Ellen Troy, Carlton Wilborn, Charlene Campbell; *D:* Robin Murray. **VHS, Beta** *AIP* ✂✂½

Dance Fools Dance Fast-paced drama has Crawford and Bakewell as a pair of spoiled rich kids who are forced to face poverty when the stock market crashes. He meets up with Gable, who's producing liquor illegally, while she gets a job at a newspaper. When Gable arranges something akin to the St. Valentine's Day Massacre, Bakewell's investigative reporting of the situation produces fatal results. The Hays Office had a problem with Crawford and friends appearing in their underwear. Cast notes: Gable was just starting out at MGM, which is why he was billed sixth; the William Holden here is not THE William Holden, and Edwards went on to provide the voice of Jiminy Cricket in "Pinocchio." 1931 82m/B Joan Crawford, Lester Vail, Cliff Edwards, William Bakewell, William Holden, Clark Gable; *D:* Harry Beaumont. **VHS, Beta** $19.98 *MGM, FCT* ✂✂✂

Dance, Girl, Dance The private lives and romances of a wartime nightclub dance troupe. Standard Hollywood potpourri of dance, drama, comedy. ♫Mother, What Do I Do Now?; Jitterbug Bite; Morning Star. 1940 88m/B Maureen O'Hara, Louis Hayward, Lucille Ball, Virginia Field, Ralph Bellamy, Maria Ouspenskaya, Mary Carlisle, Katherine Alexander, Edward Brophy; *D:* Dorothy Arzner. **VHS, Beta, LV** $19.98 *RKO, TTC* ✂✂

The Dance Goes On After the death of an uncle, Keach and his estranged son Almond reunite at the old Quebec family farm left to them. The father is country-bred and appreciates the property but his Los Angeles-reared son wants to sell for a quick profit. Director Almond cast his own son in the starring role as well as ex-wife Bujold, who plays the ambitious showbiz mother. 1992 104m/C James Keach, Matt Almond, Genevieve Bujold, Cary Lawrence; *W/D:* Paul Almond. **VHS** $89.95 *MNC* ✂✂

Dance Hall A Pennsylvania dance hall owner is propelled into romantic confusion with the introduction of a sultry blond dancer into his club. 1941 73m/B Cesar Romero, Carole Landis, William Henry, June Storey; *D:* Irving Pichel. **VHS, Beta** $19.95 *NOS, KRT, TIM* ✂½

Dance Hall Racket A sleazy, stilted expose of dance hall vice featuring a brief appearance by Bruce and his wife, Harlow. 1958 60m/B Lenny Bruce, Honey Harlow; *D:* Phil Tucker. **VHS, Beta** $19.98 *DVT, HEG* ✂✂

Dance Macabre Englund takes on a dual role as a man with a split personality—one of whom is deadly. Jessica, an American ballerina, enrolls in a Russian dance academy and meets mesmerizing choreographer, Anthony. Unfortunately for Jessica she happens to look exactly like Anthony's long-dead lover and he becomes obsessed with her. Also, her fellow dancers are being brutally murdered. Are the events connected? 1991 (R) 97m/C Robert Englund, Michelle Zeitlin, Marianna Moen, Julene Renee, Alexander Sergeyev; *W/D:* Greydon Clark. **VHS, LV** $89.95 *COL* ✂

Dance of Death Just before his death, Karloff agreed to appear in footage for four Mexican cheapies that were practically thrown together. If they had mixed the footage instead of matched it, the flicks couldn't be any worse. This one concerns a lunatic toy-maker whose toys kill and maim his heirs. *AKA:* House of Evil; Macabre Serenade. 1969 89m/C *MX* Boris Karloff, Julissa, Andres Garcia, Jack Hill; *D:* Juan Ibanez. **VHS, Beta** *NO* Woof!

Dance of Death A girl learns kung fu and kills many warriors by kicking them in the ribs and head. 1984 81m/C Mao Ying, Shih Tien, Shiao Bou-Lo, Chien Pay, Chia Kai, Noh Tikki. **VHS, Beta** $39.95 *UNI* ✂

Dance of Life A look at the backstage goings-on at a burlesque theater. A successful entertainer's life goes down the tubes when he hits the bottle. His wife leaves him because of his philandering, but returns when she sees how much he really needs her. One scene of the Ziegfeld Follies uses two-tone Technicolor technology. This was re-made twice: as "Swing High, Swing Low" in 1937 and as "When My Baby Smiles at Me" in 1948. Carroll replaced the stage lead, who was said to have no "name recognition"—Barbara Stanwyck. ♫True Blue Lou; King of Jazzmania; Cuddlesome Baby; Flippity Flop; Ladies of the Dance; The Mightiest Matador; Sweet Rosie O'Grady; In the Gloaming; Sam, the Accordion Man. 1929 115m/B Nancy Carroll, Hal Skelly, Ralph Theadore, Charles D. Brown, Dorothy Revier, Al "Fuzzy" St. John, Oscar Levant; *D:* John Cromwell. **VHS** $19.95 *NOS, MLB, TIM* ✂✂½

Dance of the Damned A case where low-budget isn't synonymous with bomb. Fascinating noir-ish plot concerning a vampire who wants to learn more about the life of his next victim, a deep-thinking stripper, who has lost the will to live it. Surprisingly well-done and acted; above-par for this genre. 1988 (R) 83m/C Cyril O'Reilly, Starr Andreeff; *D:* Katt Shea Ruben. **VHS, Beta, LV** *NO* ✂✂

Dance or Die Just goes to show that in Las Vegas you can't have your dance and drugs too, because if the Mob doesn't get you, the Feds will. Made for video (though maybe it shouldn't have been made at all). In HiFi Stereo. 1987 90m/C Ray Kieffer, Rebecca Barrington; *D:* Richard W. Munchkin. **VHS, Beta** *NO* ✂

Dance with a Stranger The engrossing and factual story of Ruth Ellis who gained notoriety as the last woman hanged in Great Britain. This emotional and sometimes violent film mirrors the sensationalism produced in the 1950s. The film follows Ellis's pre-trial life and her perpetual struggle to maintain her independence. Newcomer Richardson portrays the Marilyn Monroe look-alike barmaid. 1985 (R) 101m/C *GB* Miranda Richardson, Rupert Everett, Ian Holm, Joanne Whalley-Kilmer; *D:* Mike Newell. **VHS, Beta, LV** $19.98 *VES, LIV* ✂✂✂½

Dance with Death When strippers turn up brutally murdered, a young journalist goes undercover to solve the case. 1991 (R) 90m/C Maxwell Caulfield, Barbara Alyn Jones, Martin Mull, Drew Snyder, Catya Sassoon; *D:* Charles Philip Moore. **VHS, LV** $89.98 *HBO* ✂

Dance with Me, Henry When Lou becomes involved with Bud's gambling debts and the local district attorney turns up dead, Lou's not only wanted by the law, but by the mafia as well. This was the great comedy

duo's last picture together and it's clear the pair are not happy about working with each other, even on this mediocre effort. 1956 90m/B Bud Abbott, Lou Costello, Gigi Perreau, Rusty Hamer, Mary Wickes, Ted de Corsia; *D:* Charles T. Barton. **VHS** $19.98 *MGM* ✂½

Dancers During the filming of the ballet "Giselle" in Italy, a famous, almost-over-the-hill dancer (Baryshnikov, ten years after his role in "The Turning Point") coaches a young, inexperienced starlet. He hopes to revitalize his life and his dancing. Features dancers from the Baryshnikov-led American Ballet Theatre. 1987 (PG) 99m/C Mikhail Baryshnikov, Leslie Browne, Julie Kent, Mariangela Melato, Alessandra Ferri, Lynn Seymour, Victor Barbee, Tommy Rall; *D:* Herbert Ross. **VHS, Beta, LV** $19.98 *CTH, WAR, FCT* ✂✂½

Dances with Wolves The story of a U.S. Army soldier, circa 1870, whose heroism in battle allows him his pick of posts. His choice, to see the West before it disappears, changes his life. He meets, understands and eventually becomes a member of a Lakota Sioux tribe in the Dakotas. Costner's first directorial attempt proves him a talent of vision and intelligence. This sometimes too objective movie lacks a sense of definitive character, undermining its gorgeous scenery and interesting perspective on the plight of Native Americans. Lovely music and epic proportions. Adapted by Blake from his novel. 1990 (PG-13) 181m/C Kevin Costner, Mary McDonnell, Graham Greene, Rodney Grant, Floyd Red Crow Westerman, Tantoo Cardinal, Robert Pastorelli, Charles Rocket, Maury Chaykin, Jimmy Herman, Nathan Lee Chasing His Horse; *D:* Kevin Costner; *W:* Michael Blake; *M:* John Barry. Academy Awards '90: Best Adapted Screenplay, Best Cinematography, Best Director (Costner), Best Film Editing, Best Picture, Best Sound, Best Score; Nominations: Best Actor (Costner), Best Art Direction/Set Decoration, Best Costume Design, Best Supporting Actor (Greene), Best Supporting Actress (McDonnell), Best Original Score; Directors Guild of America Awards '90: Best Director (Costner); Golden Globe Awards '91: Best Director (Costner), Best Film—Drama; National Board of Review Awards '90: 10 Best Films of the Year, Best Director (Costner). **VHS, Beta, LV** $9.92 *ORI, FCT, IME* ✂✂✂½

Dancing in the Dark An interesting but slow-moving Canadian film about the perfect housewife who learns that after 20 years of devotion to him, her spouse has been unfaithful. Realizing how her life has been wasted she murders her husband and, in the end, suffers a mental breakdown. 1986 (PG-13) 93m/C *CA* Martha Henry, Neil Munro, Rosemary Dunsmore; *D:* Leon Marr. **VHS, Beta** $19.95 *STE, NWV* ✂✂½

Dancing Lady Rarely seen film is MGM's answer to "42nd Street," with Crawford as a small-time hoofer trying to break into Broadway. The screen debuts of Astaire and Eddy. ♫Everything I Have Is Yours; Heigh-Ho! The Gang's All Here; Hold Your Man; That's the Rhythm of the Day; My Dancing Lady; Let's Go Bavarian; Hey Young Fella. 1933 93m/B Clark Gable, Joan Crawford, Fred Astaire, Franchot Tone, Nelson Eddy, Ted Healy, Moe Howard, Shemp Howard, Larry Fine; *D:* Robert Z. Leonard. **VHS, Beta** $19.98 *MGM, TTC, FCT* ✂✂½

Dancing Man A gigolo romances both mother and daughter and winds up implicated in murder as a result. Dismissable. 1933 65m/B Judith Allen, Reginald Denny, Natalie Moorhead; *D:* Albert Ray. **VHS, Beta, 8mm** $29.95 *VYY* ✂½

Dancing Mothers A fast-living woman becomes involved with her mother's roguish boyfriend in this silent film with accompanying musical score.
1926 85m/B Clara Bow, Alice Joyce; *D:* Herbert Brenon. **VHS, Beta** $19.95 *NOS, MRV, DVT* ♂♂½

Dancing Pirate A Boston dance instructor is kidnapped by pirates and jumps ship in Mexico, where he romances a mayor's daughter. The silly story boasts some Rodgers and Hart tunes, plus the early use of Technicolor, exploited here for all it was worth and then some. ♫Are You My Love?; When You're Dancing the Waltz.
1936 83m/C Charles Collins, Frank Morgan, Steffi Duna, Luis Alberni, Victor Varconi, Jack LaRue; *D:* Lloyd Corrigan. **VHS** $19.95 *NOS, LOO, TIM* ♂♂

The Dancing Princesses When five naughty princesses wear the soles of their slippers out every night, their father the King must foot the bill. He soon tires of this expense and offers a reward to the person who can discover how this happens. A handsome prince becomes invisible to follow the lovely ladies and discover their secret. From the "Faerie Tale Theatre" series. Made for television.
1984 60m/C Lesley Ann Warren, Peter Weller, Sachi Parker, Roy Dotrice; *D:* Peter Medak. **VHS, Beta** $14.98 *KUI, FOX, FCT* ♂♂

Dandelions German soft-core flick starring Hauer in an early role as a man jilted by his wife. To make himself feel better he decides to explore the sleazier side of life. Meaningless film evokes no sympathy but some may appreciate the titillation. Dubbed.
1974 92m/C *GE* Rutger Hauer, Dagmar Lassander; *D:* Adrian Hoven. **VHS, Beta** $79.95 *WWV* ♂

Dandy in Aspic A double-agent is assigned to kill himself in this hard to follow British spy drama. The film is based on Derek Marlowe's novel. Mann died midway through shooting and Harvey finished direction.
1968 (R) 107m/C *GB* Laurence Harvey, Tom Courtenay, Lionel Stander, Mia Farrow, Harry Andrews, Peter Cook, Per Oscarsson; *D:* Anthony Mann. **VHS, Beta, LV** $69.95 *COL* ♂½

Danger Ahead! Comedy short featuring an exciting train chase.
1926 15m/B **VHS, Beta** $49.95 *IUF* ♂½

Danger Ahead Newill stars again as Renfrew of the Mounties—this time he tries to rid the north woods of the baddies who are trying to take over.
1940 57m/B Jim Newill, Dorothea Kent, Guy Usher, Dave O'Brien, Bob Terry; *D:* Ralph Staub. **VHS** $19.95 *DVT, HEG* ♂

Danger: Diabolik A superthief called Diabolik (Law) continuously evades the law while performing his criminal antics. *AKA:* Diabolik.
1968 (PG-13) 99m/C *IT* John Phillip Law, Marisa Mell, Michel Piccoli, Terry-Thomas; *D:* Mario Bava; *M:* Ennio Morricone. **VHS** *PAR* ♂

Danger in the Skies An alcoholic airline pilot tries to straighten out his life when he nearly loses everything while drinking on the job. Made for cable television. *AKA:* The Pilot.
1979 (PG) 99m/C Cliff Robertson, Diane Baker, Dana Andrews, Gordon MacRae, Milo O'Shea, Frank Converse, Edward Binns; *D:* Cliff Robertson. **VHS, Beta** $79.95 *UHV* ♂½

Danger Lights Depicts the railroads and the railroad men's dedication to each other and their trains.
1930 73m/B Jean Arthur, Louis Wolheim, Robert Armstrong; *D:* George B. Seitz. **VHS, Beta** $19.95 *PEN, MRV, NOS* ♂½

Danger Man Great spy stories that inspired the "Secret Agent" series.
1961 120m/B Patrick McGoohan. **VHS** $79.80 *MPI* ♂♂♂½

Danger Man This BBC series is the precursor to the highly popular "Secret Agent" series. McGoohan stars as special agent John Drake in an episode entitled "Bury the Dead." Additional episodes are available.
1961 30m/B *GB* Patrick McGoohan. **VHS** $14.99 *MPI, MOV* ♂♂♂½

Danger on the Air A radio program sponsor—a much-despised misogynist—is murdered, and the sound engineer attempts to solve the mystery. Features Cobb in one of his earliest roles; Garrett also directed "Lady in the Morgue" that year.
1938 70m/B Donald Woods, Nan Grey, Berton Churchill, Jed Prouty, William Lundigan, Skeets Gallagher, Edward Van Sloan, George Meeker, Lee J. Cobb, Johnny Arthur, Linda Hayes, Louise Stanley; *D:* Otis Garrett. **VHS, Beta** $16.95 *SNC* ♂

Danger Trails Rehashed western programmer. Features the hero who must save the rancher's honor as well as the ranch, while fighting detestable hombres with the traditional fare as an arsenal.
1935 55m/B Guinn Williams, Marjorie Gordon, Wally Wales, John Elliott, Ace Cain, Edmund Cobb; *D:* Bob Hill. **VHS** $19.95 *NOS, DVT, GPV* ♂½

Danger UXB During the 1940 London blitz "Danger UXB" was scrawled wherever there was, or thought to be, an unexploded German bomb. This miniseries covers the exploits of the Royal Engineers whose job it was, with little training and lots of nerve, to defuse the bombs. Based on the memoirs of Major A.B. Hartley of the Royal Engineers. On five cassettes. Made for television.
1981 660m/C *GB* Anthony Andrews, Judy Geeson, Maurice Roeves, Kenneth Cranham, Jeremy Sinden, Ian Cuthbertson, George Innes, Norman Chappell, Kenneth Farrington, Gordon Kane, Ken Kitson, Robert Longden, Robert Pugh, Deborah Watling. **VHS** $149.95 *SIG, TVC* ♂♂½

Danger Zone A man is hired to bid for a saxophone at an auction and then has the instrument stolen from him. He discovers it contained stolen jewelry and tries to recover it.
1951 56m/B Hugh Beaumont, Tom Neal, Richard Travis, Virginia Dale. **VHS, Beta, LV** *NO* ♂♂

Danger Zone A low-budget, low-brow flick about an all-female rock band whose bus breaks down in the middle of the desert, leaving the girls to defend themselves against a merciless motorcycle gang. You'll wish this one was a mirage.
1987 (R) 90m/C Robert Canada, Jason Williams, Kriss Braxton, Dana Dowell, Jamie Ferreira; *D:* Henry Vernon. **VHS, Beta** $19.98 *NLC* Woof!

Danger Zone 2 A pernicious biker is released from prison on a technicality and decides to pay a social call to the undercover cop who set him up.
1989 (R) 95m/C Jason Williams, Robert Random; *D:* Geoffrey G. Bowers. **VHS** $79.98 *MCG* ♂

Danger Zone 3: Steel Horse War The "Danger Zone" dude is back and this time he's taken on a bevy of biker-types in a most gruesome battle to make our deserts safe.
1990 (R) 91m/C Jason Williams, Robert Random, Barne Suboski, Juanita Ranney, Rusty Cooper, Giles Ashford; *D:* Douglas Bronco. **VHS, Beta** $79.98 *PMR* ♂

Dangerous Davis won her first Oscar for her rather overdone portrayal of a has-been alcoholic actress reformed by a smitten architect who recognizes her from her days as a star.
1935 72m/B Bette Davis, Franchot Tone, Margaret Lindsay, Alison Skipworth, John Eldridge, Dick Foran; *D:* Alfred E. Green. **VHS, Beta, LV** $19.98 *MGM, BTV* ♂♂½

A Dangerous Age A young girl, hoping to marry her lover, runs away from boarding school.
1957 ?m/C Ben Piazza, Ann Pearson. **VHS** $16.95 *SNC* ♂½

Dangerous Appointment Story of an innocent store clerk accused of theft and attempted murder.
1934 ?m/C Charles Starrett, Dorothy Wilson. **VHS** $16.95 *SNC* ♂

Dangerous Charter A group of fishermen discover a deserted yacht and man its helm. But their good fortune takes a decided turn for the worst as they become caught in mob-propelled danger.
1962 76m/C Chris Warfield, Sally Fraser, Richard Foote, Peter Foster, Wright King; *D:* Robert Gottschalk. **VHS, Beta** $19.95 *NOS, ACA, TIM* ♂½

Dangerous Company Murder, sex, infidelity, and expensive living are highlighted in this made-for-video production. What, you want something more in a film?
1988 (R) 98m/C Cliff DeYoung, Tracy Scoggins, Chris Mulkey; *D:* Ruben Preuss. **VHS, Beta** $29.95 *MCG* ♂

Dangerous Curves Two friends are assigned to deliver a new Porsche to a billionaire's daughter - one of them talks the other into taking a little detour, and the trouble begins. This one went straight to video.
1988 (PG) 93m/C Robert Stack, Tate Donovan, Danielle von Zernaeck, Robert Klein, Elizabeth Ashley, Leslie Nielsen; *D:* David Lewis. **VHS, Beta** $79.98 *VES, LIV* ♂½

Dangerous Game A computer hacker leads his friends through a department store's security system, only to find they can't get out until morning. They soon discover they are not alone when one of the group turns up dead.
1990 (R) 102m/C Miles Buchanan, Sandy Lillingston, Kathryn Walker, John Polson; *D:* Stephen Hopkins. **VHS, Beta, LV** $29.95 *ACD* ♂½

Dangerous Holiday A young violin prodigy would rather be just "one of the boys" than be forced to practice all the time. He decides to run away but has everyone in an uproar thinking he's been kidnapped.
1937 54m/B Hedda Hopper, Guinn Williams, Jack La Rue, Franklin Pangborn, Grady Sutton. **VHS, Beta** $24.95 *VYY* ♂♂

Dangerous Hours An anti-communist propaganda film with Hughes as the innocent young college boy who gets duped by the evil Marxists until he realizes the truth of his all-American upbringing. Silent with original organ score.
1919 88m/B Lloyd Hughes; *D:* Fred Niblo. **VHS, Beta, 8mm** $24.95 *VYY, FCT, GPV* ♂♂

Dangerous Liaisons A couple take each other to the brink of destruction via their insatiable desire for extra-marital affairs. Vadim attempted to repeat his success with Brigitte Bardot by featuring wife Annette as a new sex goddess, but lightning didn't strike twice. *AKA:* Les Liaisons Dangereuses; Dangerous Love Affairs.

1960 111m/B *FR IT* Gerard Philippe, Jeanne Moreau, Jeanne Valeri, Annette Vadim, Simone Renant, Jean-Louis Trintignant, Nikolas Vogel; *D:* Roger Vadim. **VHS, LV $59.95** *INT, APD, TAM* 🎬🎬

Dangerous Liaisons Stylish and absorbing, this adaptation of the Laclos novel and the Christopher Hampton play centers around the relationship of two decadent members of 18th-century French nobility. The two, Close and Malkovich, spend their time testing and manipulating the loves of others. They find love often has a will of its own. Possibly the best of the several versions available. Interesting to comparison-view with director Milos Forman's version of this story, 1989's ''Valmont.''
1988 (R) 120m/C John Malkovich, Glenn Close, Michelle Pfeiffer, Uma Thurman, Keanu Reeves, Swoosie Kurtz, Mildred Natwick, Peter Capaldi; *D:* Stephen Frears. Academy Awards '88: Best Adapted Screenplay, Best Art Direction/Set Decoration, Best Costume Design; Nominations: Best Actress (Close), Best Picture, Best Supporting Actress (Pfeiffer), Best Original Score; British Academy Awards '89: Best Supporting Actress (Pfeiffer); Cesar Awards '90: Best Foreign Film. **VHS, Beta, LV, 8mm $19.98** *WAR, FCT* 🎬🎬🎬

Dangerous Life Explosive drama brings to the screen the story of the Philippine uprising. It shows the horrible events that lead to the fall of Marcos and permitted the rise of Corazon Aquino.
1989 163m/C Gary Busey; *W:* David Williamson. **VHS, Beta, LV** *NO* 🎬🎬

Dangerous Love Advice to the lovelorn: Avoid this one. Female members of a video dating service are being filmed in a death scene—their own.
1987 87m/C Lawrence Monoson, Brenda Bakke, Peter Marc, Elliott Gould, Anthony Geary; *D:* Marty Ollstein. **VHS, Beta $79.95** *MED Woof!*

A Dangerous Man: Lawrence after Arabia At the 1919 Paris Peace Conference, T.E. Lawrence serves as the liaison to the Hashemite delegation in an effort to have the Allies agree to Arab independence. He finds the diplomatic fields more treacherous than anything he encountered during World War I. Fiennes does well in the difficult role of the reluctant, ambivalent hero.
1991 104m/C *GB* Ralph Fiennes. **VHS $29.95** *PBS, PAV* 🎬🎬🎬

Dangerous Mission A young woman witnesses a mob murder in New York and flees to the Midwest, pursued by killers and the police. Good cast couldn't do much with this one.
1954 75m/B Victor Mature, Piper Laurie, Vincent Price, William Bendix; *D:* Louis King. **VHS, Beta $19.95** *MED* 🎬½

Dangerous Moonlight Polish concert pianist becomes a bomber pilot for the British in World War II, though his wife wants him to stay at the piano. Great battle and music sequences; the piece ''Warsaw Concerto'' became a soundtrack hit. *AKA:* Suicide Squadron.
1941 97m/B *GB* Anton Walbrook, Sally Gray, Derrick DeMarney, Cecil Parker, Percy Parsons, Kenneth Kent, Guy Middleton, John Laurie, Frederick Valk; *D:* Brian Desmond Hurst. **VHS, Beta $19.98** *TTC* 🎬🎬🎬

Dangerous Moves A drama built around the World Chess championship competition between a renowned Russian master and a young, rebellious dissident. The chess game serves as both metaphor and background for the social and political tensions it produces. With English subtitles. *AKA:* La Diagonale du Fou.

1984 (PG) 96m/C *SI* Liv Ullmann, Michel Piccoli, Leslie Caron, Alexandre Arbatt; *D:* Richard Dembo. **VHS, Beta, LV $59.95** *LHV, IME* 🎬🎬🎬

Dangerous Obsession A woman kidnaps the doctor she blames for her boyfriend's death and instead of exacting revenge, she makes him her personal sex slave. In the case of this flick, it's really a fate worse than death. *AKA:* Divine Obsession; Mortal Sins.
1988 (R) 81m/C *IT* Corinne Clery, Brett Halsey; *D:* Lucio Fulci. **VHS $79.95** *AIP* 🎬

Dangerous Orphans Not completely awful tale of three brothers, orphaned as boys when their father is murdered before their very eyes, and the vendetta they have against the killer.
1986 (R) 90m/C *NZ* Peter Stevens, Peter Bland, Ian Mune, Ross Girven, Jennifer Ward-Lealand; *D:* John Laing. **VHS, Beta $29.95** *ACA* 🎬½

Dangerous Passage A ne'er-do-well inherits 200 grand but gets in trouble before he can collect it. He ends up falling in with assorted misfits aboard a tramp steamer.
1944 60m/B Robert Lowery, Phyllis Brooks, Jack La Rue, Victor Kilian; *D:* William Berke. **VHS, Beta, 8mm $24.95** *VYY* 🎬🎬

Dangerous Pursuit A woman discovers that a man she slept with years ago is an assassin. Knowing too much, she finds herself next on his hit list. Decent psycho-thriller that was never released theatrically.
1989 95m/C Gregory Harrison, Alexandra Powers, Scott Valentine, Brian Wimmer, Elena Stiteler; *D:* Sandor Stern. **VHS, Beta, LV $89.99** *PAR* 🎬🎬

Dangerous Summer In Australia, an American businessman building a resort is the victim of elaborate arson/murder insurance schemes. *AKA:* The Burning Man.
1982 100m/C *AU* Tom Skerritt, James Mason, Ian Gilmour, Wendy Hughes; *D:* Quentin Masters. **VHS, Beta** *NO* 🎬🎬

Dangerous When Wet A typical Williams water-musical. A farm girl dreams of fame by swimming the English Channel. One famous number pairs Williams with cartoon characters Tom & Jerry in an underwater frolic. 🎵I Got Out of Bed on the Right Side; Ain't Nature Grand; I Like Men; Fifi; In My Wildest Dreams.
1953 96m/C Esther Williams, Fernando Lamas, Charlotte Greenwood, William Demarest, Jack Carson; *D:* Charles Walters; *M:* Arthur Schwartz, Johnny Mercer. **VHS, Beta, LV $19.98** *MGM* 🎬🎬

Dangerously Close A group of anti-crime high school students organize a hall monitoring gang that becomes a group of neo-fascist disciplinarian elite.
1986 (R) 96m/C John Stockwell, Carey Lowell, J. Eddie Peck; *D:* Albert Pyun. **VHS, Beta $9.98** *MED* 🎬½

Daniel The children of a couple who were executed for espionage (patterned after the Rosenbergs) struggle with their past in the dissident 1960s. So-so adaptation of E.L. Doctorow's ''The Book of Daniel.''
1983 (R) 130m/C Timothy Hutton, Amanda Plummer, Mandy Patinkin, Lindsay Crouse, Ed Asner, Ellen Barkin; *D:* Sidney Lumet. **VHS, Beta $59.95** *PAR* 🎬🎬½

Daniel and the Towers Daniel and his friends enjoy making fun of Sam, the man who is building glass towers in Watts, California. But when Daniel must pay for the repairs of a shopkeeper's window, he turns to Sam for help. Sam agrees to fix the windows if Daniel helps him collect glass for the towers. In the process, Sam and Daniel become friends and Sam teaches Daniel valuable lessons about beauty and determi-

nation. Although this story is fictional, the glass towers, built by Sam Rodia, really stand in Watts. A viewers' guide is included. Part of the ''Wonderworks'' series.
199? 55m/C Allan Arbus, Michael McKean, Carmen Zapata, Miguel Alamo. **VHS $29.95** *PME, HMV, BTV* 🎬🎬½

Daniel Boone Daniel Boone guides a party of settlers from North Carolina to the fertile valleys of Kentucky, facing Indians, food shortages and bad weather along the way. O'Brien turns in a fine performance as the early American frontier hero.
1934 75m/B George O'Brien, Heather Angel, John Carradine; *D:* David Howard. **VHS, Beta $19.95** *NOS, MRV, QNE* 🎬½

Daniel Boone: Trail Blazer Low-budget, though surprisingly well-acted rendition of the frontiersman's heroics, filmed in Mexico.
1956 75m/B Bruce Bennett, Lon Chaney Jr., Faron Young, Damian O'Flynn, Fred Kohler Jr., Claudio Brook, Kem Dibbs; *D:* Ismael Rodriguez, Albert C. Gannaway; *W:* John Patrick, John Hubbard. **VHS $19.95** *NOS, MRV, REP* 🎬½

Danny Charming story of a lonely young girl who receives an injured horse that was no longer fit for the spoiled daughter of the rich owners.
1979 (G) 90m/C Rebecca Page, Janet Zarish, Barbara Jean Earhardt, Gloria Maddox, George Luce; *D:* Gene Feldman. **VHS, Beta $59.95** *MON, WOM, HHE* 🎬🎬½

Danny Boy Veteran dog, returning from the war, has difficulty adjusting to life back home. Things get worse for him and his young master when Danny Boy is assumed to be shell-shocked and dangerous. One of the few shell-shocked dog stories ever filmed.
1946 67m/B **VHS, Beta $29.95** *NO* 🎬½

Danny Boy Takes place in Ireland where a young saxaphonist witnesses a murder and, in an effort to understand it, sets out to find the killer. Thought-provoking film is meant to highlight the continuing struggles in Ireland.
1984 (R) 92m/C *IR* Stephen Rea, Veronica Quilligan, Honor Heffernan, Marie Kean, Donal McCann, Ray McAnally; *D:* Neil Jordan. **VHS, Beta $59.95** *COL* 🎬🎬🎬

Dante's Inferno Abandon all hope you who watch this film. A one-time friend sends his ruthless capitalist nemesis a copy of Dante's ''Inferno,'' and the man reads the book and dreams he's gone to hell (would that be the dress circle?) A silent film that was controversial in its day: the body-stockinged actors were believed to be nude (which would have made it the first nudie Comedy).
1924 54m/B Lawson Butt, Howard Gaye, Ralph Lewis, Pauline Starke, Josef Swickard; *D:* Henry Otto. **VHS $10.95** *CNM* 🎬🎬

Dante's Inferno: Life of Dante Gabriel Rossetti The flamboyant life of mid-19th century English Pre-Raphaelite artist/poet Dante Gabriel Rossetti is depicted with the usual Russell flair. The drunken, drug-taking, womanizing Rossetti was part of the leading intellectual group of his age, which included Swinburne, Morris, Ruskin, and Rossetti's sister, the poet Christina Rossetti.
1969 90m/B *GB* Oliver Reed; *D:* Ken Russell. **VHS $39.95** *TAM* 🎬🎬

Danton A sweeping account of the reign of terror following the French Revolution. Focuses on the title character (wonderfully portrayed by Depardieu) and is directed with searching parallels to modern-day Poland by that country's premier filmmaker, Andrzej

Wajda. Well-done period sets round out a memorable film. In French with English subtitles.
1982 (PG) 136m/C *PL FR* Gerard Depardieu, Wojciech Pszoniak, Patrice Chereau, Angela Winkler; *D:* Andrzej Wajda. **VHS, Beta, LV $59.95** *COL, TAM* 𝒵𝒵𝒵𝒵

Danzon Julia (Rojo), a single, working-class mom escapes the drudgery of her simple existence by going to a Mexico City dance hall every Wednesday. There she loses herself to the movement of the danzon, a Haitian dance popular in Cuba. When her partner of six years, Carmelo (Rergis), doesn't show up one night, Julia's life is turned around. She seeks him out in his hometown of Veracruz where, instead of finding him, she makes many new friends and learns that she wasn't searching for Carmelo so much as she was searching for herself. Quiet and restrained, like the ballroom-style danzon at the center of the plot. Applauded at Cannes. In Spanish with English subtitles.
1991 (PG-13) 96m/C *SP* Maria Rojo, Carmen Salinas, Blanca Guerra, Tito Vasconcelos, Victor Carpintero, Victor Vasconcelos; *D:* Maria Novaro; *W:* Maria Novaro, Betriz Novaro. **VHS** *NYR* 𝒵𝒵𝒵½

Darby O'Gill & the Little People Set in Ireland, a roguish old story teller tumbles into a well and visits the land of leprechauns who give him three wishes in order to rearrange his life. When he tries to tell his friends what happened, they think that it is only another one of his stories. A wonderful Disney production (despite its disappointing box-office performance) with wit, charm and an ounce or two of terror.
1959 (G) 93m/C Albert Sharpe, Janet Munro, Sean Connery, Estelle Winwood; *D:* Robert Stevenson. **VHS, Beta, LV $19.99** *DIS* 𝒵𝒵𝒵½

Darby's Rangers World War II pot-boiler with Garner as the leader of a commando team put together for covert operations in North Africa and Italy. Successful battle sequences combine with slow-paced romantic scenes as the soldiers chase women when not chasing the enemy. *AKA:* Young Invaders.
1958 122m/B James Garner, Jack Warden, Edd Byrnes, Peter Brown, Stuart Whitman, David Janssen, Etchika Choreau, Venetia Stevenson, Torin Thatcher, Joan Elan, Corey Allen, Murray Hamilton; *D:* William A. Wellman; *W:* Guy Trosper; *M:* Max Steiner. **VHS $19.98** *WAR* 𝒵𝒵½

Daredevils of the Red Circle Three young men set out to free a man held prisoner by an escaped convict. A serial in twelve chapters.
1938 195m/B Charles Quigley, Herman Brix, Carole Landis; *D:* John English, William Witney. **VHS $59.95** *REP, VCN, MLB* 𝒵𝒵½

Daring Dobermans In this sequel to "The Doberman Gang," the barking bank-robbers have a new set of crime-planning masters. A young Indian boy who loves the dogs enters the picture and may thwart their perfect crime.
1973 (PG) 88m/C Charles Robinson, Tim Considine, David Moses, Claudio Martinez, Joan Caulfield; *D:* Byron Ross Chudnow. **VHS, Beta $59.98** *FOX* 𝒵𝒵

Daring Game A group of scuba divers nicknamed the Flying Fish attempt to rescue a woman's husband and daughter from an island dictatorship. Failed series pilot by producer Ivan Tors, better known for "Sea Hunt" and "Flipper."
1968 100m/C Lloyd Bridges, Brock Peters, Michael Ansara, Joan Blackman; *D:* Laslo Benedek. **VHS, Beta $39.98** *NO* 𝒵𝒵

The Dark A supernatural beast commits a string of gruesome murders. *AKA:* The Mutilator.
1979 (R) 92m/C William Devane, Cathy Lee Crosby, Richard Jaeckel, Keenan Wynn, Vivian Blaine; *D:* John Cardos. **VHS, Beta $9.95** *MED, SIM* 𝒵½

Dark Age An Australian conservationist must track down a rampaging, giant, semi-mythical alligator before it is killed by bounty hunters. Based on the novel (and Aboriginal legend) "Numunwari."
1988 (R) 90m/C *AU* John Jarratt, David Gulpilil, Max Phipps, Ray Meagher, Nikki Coghill, Burnam Burnam; *D:* Arch Nicholson. **VHS, Beta, LV $19.98** *NLC* 𝒵𝒵½

The Dark Angel Maud is the young and innocent heiress to a fortune in this gothic mystery of creeping unease. She is intrigued by the romantic portrait of her youthful and unknown Uncle Silas. But her mysterious uncle is no longer the Byronic hero. What secret wickedness does his ravaged face hide? And what about Maud's drug-addicted governess and the brutish young man in the cemetary? Does Uncle Silas just want Maud's fortune or Maud herself? Watch and see. Excellent performances by O'Toole as the decadent uncle and Edney as the innocent-but-not-stupid Maud. Based on the novel "Uncle Silas" by J.S. Le Fanu. Made for British television.
1991 150m/C *GB* Peter O'Toole, Beatie Edney, Jane Lapotaire, Tim Woodward, Alan MacNaughton, Barbara Shelley, Guy Rolfe; *D:* Peter Hammond. **VHS $89.98** *FXV* 𝒵𝒵𝒵

Dark August A New Yorker drops out and transplants to rural Vermont, where he accidentally kills a young girl and then suffers numerous horrors as a result of a curse put on him by the girl's grandfather.
1976 (PG) 87m/C J.J. Barry, Carole Shelyne, Kim Hunter, William Robertson; *D:* Martin Goldman. **VHS, Beta $59.95** *VES, LIV* 𝒵𝒵

The Dark Backward A dark, subversive comedy about a garbage man who dreams of making it big in show biz as a stand-up comedian. He's terrible until a third arm starts growing out of his back and the sheer grotesqueness of his situation makes him a temporary star. Caan and Newton are interestingly cast, but young, first-time director Rifkin's foray into David Lynch territory was not well received by critics.
1991 (R) 97m/C Judd Nelson, Bill Paxton, Wayne Newton, Lara Flynn Boyle, James Caan, Rob Lowe, Claudia Christian; *W/D:* Adam Rifkin. **VHS, LV $89.95** *COL* 𝒵½

Dark Before Dawn American farmers and Vietnam veterans team up against corrupt government officials and ruthless businessmen in this violent film about the plight of the underdog.
1989 (R) 95m/C Doug McClure, Sonny Gibson, Ben Johnson, Billy Drago, Rance Howard, Morgan Woodward, Buck Henry, Jeffery Osterhage, Red Steagall, John Martin; *D:* Robert Totten. **VHS, Beta, LV $79.98** *VES, LIV* 𝒵½

Dark Command The story of Quantrell's Raiders who terrorized the Kansas territory during the Civil War until one man came along to put a stop to it. Colorful and talented cast add depth to the script. Also available colorized.
1940 95m/B John Wayne, Walter Pidgeon, Claire Trevor, Roy Rogers, Marjorie Main, George "Gabby" Hayes; *D:* Raoul Walsh. **VHS, Beta $14.98** *REP, FCT* 𝒵𝒵𝒵

Dark Corner Gripping, intricate film noir about a detective, already framed once, who may go up the river yet again—this time for the murder of his ex-partner, the guy who framed him the first time. Loyal secretary Ball helps to extricate him from this tangled web.
1946 99m/B Lucille Ball, Mark Stevens, Clifton Webb, William Bendix, Cathy Downs, Reed Hadley, Constance Collier, Kurt Kreuger; *D:* Henry Hathaway. **VHS, Beta $59.98** *FOX* 𝒵𝒵𝒵

The Dark Crystal Jen and Kira, two of the last surviving Gelflings, attempt to return a crystal shard (discovered with the help of a sorceress) to the castle where the Dark Crystal lies, guarded by the cruel and evil Skeksis. Designed by Brian Froud. From the creators of the Muppets.
1982 (PG) 93m/C *D:* Jim Henson. **VHS, Beta, LV $19.99** *HBO* 𝒵𝒵𝒵

Dark Eyes An acclaimed Italian film based on a several short stories by Anton Chekov. Mastroianni is a weak-willed Italian, trapped in a marriage of convenience, who falls in love with a mysterious, also married, Russian beauty he meets in a health spa. He embarks on a journey to find her and, perhaps, his lost ideals. Hailed as Mastroianni's consummate performance. In Italian with English subtitles. *AKA:* Les Yeux Noirs; Oci Ciornie.
1987 118m/C *IT* Marcello Mastroianni, Silvana Mangano, Elena Sofonova, Marthe Keller; *D:* Nikita Mikhalkov. Academy Awards '87 Nominations: Best Actor (Mastroianni); Cannes Film Festival '87: Best Actor (Mastroianni). **VHS, Beta $79.98** *GHV, FOX* 𝒵𝒵𝒵½

Dark Forces A faith-healer promises to help a senator's dying son and finds the politician's wife also desires his assistance. This Australian film is uneven and predictable. Though rated "PG," beware of two rather brief, but explicit, nudity scenes. *AKA:* Harlequin.
1983 (PG) 96m/C *AU* Robert Powell, David Hemmings, Broderick Crawford, Carmen Duncan; *D:* Simon Wincer. **VHS, Beta $9.95** *MED* 𝒵𝒵

Dark Habits An early Almodovar farce about already-demented nuns in a failing convent trying to raise funds with the help of a nightclub singer who is on the run. Although certainly irreverant, it doesn't quite have the zing of his later work. In Spanish with subtitles. *AKA:* Entre Tinieblas.
1984 116m/C *SP* Carmen Maura, Christina Pascual, Julieta Serrano, Marisa Paredes; *D:* Pedro Almodovar. **VHS, Beta, LV $79.95** *TAM, CCN* 𝒵𝒵½

The Dark Half Another flawed chiller based on a novel by Stephen King. Hutton stars as Thad Beaumont, a married writing instructor whose serious novels have been failures. However, writing as George Stark, he has had phenomenal success with grisly horror stories. In a publicity stunt Thad kills off and publicly buries George (who doesn't want to stay dead). Soon everyone who's crossed Thad is brutally murdered. Meanwhile, dead alter ego George resurrects and begins to make his very physical appearances. Hutton acquits himself well in this change of pace dual role. Otherwise, the psychological thrills are few and the gore is plentiful. Pittsburgh serves as location double for King's usual New England territory. Film's release was delayed due to Orion's bankruptcy problems.
1991 (R) 122m/C Timothy Hutton, Amy Madigan, Michael Rooker, Julie Harris, Robert Joy, Kent Broadhurst, Beth Grant, Rutanya Alda, Tom Mardirosian, Chelsea Field, Royal Dano; *D:* George A. Romero; *W:* George A. Romero; *M:* Christopher Young. **VHS** *NYR* 𝒵𝒵

Dark Horse Meyers is a young woman distraught over the death of her mother. She gets into trouble and is assigned to do community service work at a horse farm where she finds herself caring for a prize-winning horse.
1992 (PG) 98m/C Ari Meyers, Mimi Rogers, Ed Begley Jr., Donovan Leitch, Samantha Eggar; **D:** David Hemmings. **VHS $89.98** FCT, MOV, LIV *🟊🟊½*

The Dark Hour Two detectives team up to solve a murder in which multiple suspects are involved. Based on Sinclair Gluck's "The Last Trap."
1936 72m/B Ray Walker, Irene Ware, Berton Churchill, Hedda Hopper, Hobart Bosworth, E.E. Clive; **D:** Charles Lamont. **VHS, Beta $16.95** NOS, LOO, SNC *🟊½*

Dark Journey World War I Stockholm is the setting for a love story between a double agent and the head of German Intelligence. Clever, sophisticated production; Leigh is stunning. **AKA:** The Anxious Years.
1937 82m/B *GB* Vivien Leigh, Conrad Veidt, Joan Gardner, Anthony Bushell, Ursula Jeans; **D:** Victor Saville. **VHS, Beta, 3/4U, Special order formats $19.95** NOS, MRV, CAB *🟊🟊½*

Dark Mirror A psychologist and a detective struggle to determine which twin sister murdered a prominent physician. Good and evil siblings finely-acted by de Havilland.
1946 85m/B Olivia de Havilland, Lew Ayres, Thomas Mitchell, Garry Owen; **D:** Robert Siodmak. **VHS $14.98** REP *🟊🟊🟊*

Dark Mountain A forest ranger rescues his gal from the clutches of a hardened criminal.
1944 56m/B Robert Lowery, Ellen Drew, Regis Toomey, Eddie Quillan, Elisha Cook Jr.; **D:** William H. Pine, William C. Thomas. **VHS $24.95** NOS, DVT, TIM *🟊½*

Dark Night of the Scarecrow Thriller with a moral. Prejudiced townspeople execute a retarded man who was innocently befriended by a young girl. After his death unusual things begin to happen. Slow to start but effective. Made for television.
1981 100m/C Charles Durning, Tanya Crowe, Larry Drake; **D:** Frank DeFelitta. **VHS, Beta $59.98** FOX, HHE *🟊🟊🟊*

Dark Obsession Byrne portrays a husband who lives out his dark erotic fantasies with his wife (Donohoe). Driven by a mysterious guilt, madness slowly begins to take him. Based on a true scandal. Available in an "NC-17" rated version. **AKA:** Diamond Skulls.
1990 (R) 97m/C Gabriel Byrne, Amanda Donohoe, Michael Hordern, Judy Parfitt; **D:** Nick Broomfield. **VHS, Beta $89.95** PSM *🟊🟊½*

Dark of the Night A young woman, new to the city, purchases a used Jaguar and finds she must share it with the car's former owner—a woman murdered inside the Jag. Decent psycho-thriller with some suspenseful and amusing moments. **AKA:** Mr. Wrong.
1985 88m/C *NZ* Heather Bolton, David Letch, Gary Stalker; **D:** Gaylene Preston. **VHS, Beta $79.98** LIV *🟊🟊½*

Dark Passage Bogart plays a convict who escapes from San Quentin to prove he was framed for the murder of his wife. He undergoes plastic surgery and is hidden and aided by Bacall as he tries to find the real killer. Stars can't quite compensate for a far-fetched script and so-so direction.
1947 107m/B Humphrey Bogart, Lauren Bacall, Agnes Moorehead, Bruce Bennett, Tom D'Andrea; **D:** Delmer Daves. **VHS, Beta, LV $19.95** FOX *🟊🟊½*

Dark Past A crazy, escaped convict holds a psychologist and his family hostage, and the two men engage in psychological cat-and-mouse combat. An underrated thriller with off-beat casting.
1949 75m/B William Holden, Lee J. Cobb, Nina Foch, Adele Jergens; **D:** Rudolph Mate. **VHS, Beta $69.95** COL *🟊🟊🟊*

Dark Places Masquerading as a hospital administrator, a former mental patient inherits the ruined mansion of a man who had killed his wife and children and died insane. As he lives in the house, the spirit of its former owner seems to overcome him with a need to repeat the crime. Meanwhile, Lee, Collins, and Lom think the nut is hiding money they would like to get their collective hands on. Low-budget but fairly effective.
1973 (PG) 91m/C *GB* Joan Collins, Christopher Lee, Robert Hardy; **D:** Don Sharp. **VHS, Beta $24.98** SUE *🟊🟊*

The Dark Power Ex-cowboy LaRue and his trusty whip provide this flick with its only excitement. As sheriff, he must deal with the dead Mexican warriors who rise to wreak havoc when a house is built on their burial ground.
1985 87m/C Lash LaRue, Anna Lane Tatum; **D:** Phil Smoot. **VHS, Beta** NO *🟊*

The Dark Ride Lunatic picks up women with the intention of raping and killing them. Ugly thriller based on the evil deeds of serial murderer Ted Bundy.
1984 83m/C James Luisi, Susan Sullivan, Martin Speer; **D:** Jeremy Hoenack. **VHS, Beta $69.95** MED *🟊½*

Dark Rider Dark Rider is a mysterious, motorcycle riding hero who comes to the rescue of a small town. Besieged by a gangster who buys up all their land, the townspeople must abandon their homes and indeed, their very dreams. That is until Dark Rider rolls into to town to enact his own unique brand of vengeance.
1991 94m/C Joe Estevez, Doug Shanklin, Alicia Kowalski, David Shark, Chuck Williams; **W:** Chuck Williams, Bob Ivy. **VHS $79.95** AIP *🟊½*

Dark River: A Father's Revenge When his daughter is killed in a toxic waste dump accident, a man begins revenge on the company and its managers. Tense, with important message.
1990 95m/C Helen Hunt, Mike Farrell, Tess Harper. **VHS $79.98** TTC *🟊🟊*

The Dark Room A disturbed young man becomes obsessed with his father's voluptuous mistress and longs to possess her.
1984 90m/C **VHS, Beta** NO *🟊½*

Dark Sanity Uninvolving attempt at horror has a recently de-institutionalized woman envisioning death and destruction (something you'll wish the film would do) while everyone else just thinks she's losing her marbles. Problem is we don't really care. **AKA:** Straight Jacket.
1982 89m/C Aldo Ray, Kory Clark, Andy Gwyn, Bobby Holt; **D:** Martin Greene. **VHS, Beta $59.95** PSM *Woof!*

The Dark Secret of Harvest Home An urban couple confront a pagan cult in the New England town into which they've moved. Based upon the Thomas Tryon novel. Made for television.
1978 118m/C Bette Davis, Rosanna Arquette, David Ackroyd, Rene Auberjonois, Michael O'Keefe; **D:** Leo Penn. **VHS, Beta $59.95** MCA *🟊🟊½*

Dark Shadows "Dark Shadows" had already been on television for about eight months when the character of Barnabas Collins was introduced. This volume serves to familiarize the viewer with characters and situations that were running on the series at that time. These are the first five episodes that feature Barnabas. Original air dates are April 17 to May 1, 1967. Contains both B&W and color episodes. Additional episodes available.
1967 120m/B Joan Bennett, Kathryn Leigh Scott, John Karien, Alexandre Molthe, Jonathan Frid, David Selby, Kate Jackson; **D:** John Sedwick. **VHS $29.95** MPI, MOV *🟊🟊½*

The Dark Side of Love A young girl gets involved with the rougher side of New Orleans society, gets pregnant, and realizes how she's been degraded.
1979 94m/C James Stacy, Glynnis O'Connor, Jan Sterling, Mickey Rooney. **VHS, Beta $59.95** GEM *🟊½*

Dark Side of Midnight A super-detective tracks down a psychopathic killer. **AKA:** The Creeper.
1986 (R) 108m/C James Moore, Wes Olsen, Sandy Schemmel, Dave Bowling. **VHS, Beta $79.95** PSM *🟊½*

Dark Side of the Moon Members of a space ship sent on a routine mission to the far side of the moon, discover an unknown force that feeds on human emotion and consumes the soul. Lukewarm science fiction/horror.
1990 (R) 96m/C William Bledsoe, Alan Blumenfeld, John Diehl, Robert Sampson, Wendy MacDonald, Camilla More, Joe Turkel; **D:** D.J. Webster. **VHS, LV $89.95** VMK *🟊🟊*

Dark Star John Carpenter's directorial debut is a low-budget, sci-fi satire which focuses on a group of scientists whose mission is to destroy unstable planets. During their journey, they battle their alien mascot (who closely resembles a walking beach ball), as well as a "sensitive" and intelligent bombing device which starts to question the meaning of its existence. Enjoyable early feature from John "Halloween" Carpenter and Dan "Aliens" O'Bannon. Fun, weird, and unpredictable.
1974 (G) 95m/C Dan O'Bannon, Brian Narelle; **D:** John Carpenter. **VHS, Beta, LV $19.95** HHT, IME, UHV *🟊🟊🟊*

Dark Tower Decent cast is wasted in yet another inept attempt at horror. An architect is dismayed to learn that an evil force is inhabiting her building and it might just be the ghost of her dearly departed husband.
1987 (R) 91m/C Michael Moriarty, Jenny Agutter, Theodore Bikel, Carol Lynley, Anne Lockhart, Kevin McCarthy; **D:** Ken Barnett. **VHS, Beta, LV $79.98** IME *🟊*

Dark Victory A spoiled young heiress discovers she is dying from a brain tumor. She attempts to pack a lifetime of parties into a few months, but is rescued by her doctor, with whom she falls in love. Classic final scene with Davis at the top of her form. Bogart plays an Irish stable hand, but not especially well. Also available in a colorized version.
1939 106m/B Bette Davis, George Brent, Geraldine Fitzgerald, Humphrey Bogart, Ronald Reagan, Henry Travers; **D:** Edmund Goulding. **VHS, Beta, LV $19.95** MGM *🟊🟊🟊½*

Dark Waters The drowning death of her parents has left a young woman mentally unstable. She returns to her family home in the backwaters of Louisiana with her peculiar aunt and uncle to serve as guardians. It eventually becomes apparent that someone

D

is trying to drive her insane. This one tends to be rather murky and it's not simply due to the plentiful scenes of misty swampland.
1944 93m/B Merle Oberon, Franchot Tone, Thomas Mitchell, Fay Bainter, Elisha Cook Jr., John Qualen, Rex Ingram; *D:* Andre de Toth. **VHS, Beta, LV $19.95** *STE, NWV* *♂♂*

Darker than Amber John D. MacDonald's houseboat-dwelling detective Travis McGee (Taylor) rescues a girl (Kendall) he's fallen for, and soon discovers that the mugs who thugged her were part of a collection racket. A violent action melodrama upgraded from its original "R" rating.
1970 (R) 96m/C Rod Taylor, Suzy Kendall, Theodore Bikel, Jane Russell, James Booth, Janet MacLachlan, William Smith, Anna Capri, Chris Robinson; *D:* Robert Clouse. **VHS** *CTY* *♂♂*

Darkest Africa Legendary animal trainer Beatty is the hero of this 15 episode cliffhanger serial as he vies with beasts—both animal and human. *AKA:* Batmen of Africa; King of the Jungleland.
1936 270m/B Clyde Beatty, Manuel King, Elaine Shepard. **LV $49.98** *REP, MOV* *♂♂*

Darkman Raimi's disfigured-man-seeks-revenge suspenser is comicbook kitsch cross-pollinated with a strain of gothic horror. Neeson plays a scientist who's on the verge of discovering the key to cloning body parts; brutally attacked by the henchmen of a crooked politico, his lab is destroyed and he's left for dead. Turns out he's not dead—just horribly disfigured and a wee bit chafed—and he stalks his deserving victims from the shadows, using his lab know-how to disguise his rugged bad looks. Exquisitely violent, it's got tunes by hipster Danny Elfman. Montage by Pablo Ferro.
1990 (R) 95m/C Liam Neeson, Frances McDormand, Larry Drake, Colin Friels, Nelson Mashita, Jenny Agutter, Rafael H. Robledo; *D:* Sam Raimi; *M:* Danny Elfman. **VHS, Beta, LV $19.95** *MCA, CCB* *♂♂♂*

Darkroom An unstable young man devises a scheme to photograph his father in bed with his mistress, and then use the pics to blackmail dear ol' dad.
1990 90m/C Jill Pierce, Jeffrey Allen Arbaugh, Sara Lee Wade, Aaron Teich; *D:* Terrence O'Hara **VHS** *NO* *♂½*

The Darkside In this frightening drama, a young prostitute and an innocent cabbie attempt to escape the clutches of a maniacal film producer with a secret he won't let them reveal.
1987 (R) 95m/C Tony Galati, Cyndy Preston; *D:* Constantino Magnatta. **VHS $79.95** *VMK* *♂½*

Darktown Strutters Effort to satirize racial stereotypes is humorless and ineffective. Black female motorcycle gang searches for the kidnapped mother of one of the members. *AKA:* Get Down and Boogie.
1974 85m/C Trina Parks, Roger E. Mosley, Shirley Washington; *D:* William Witney. **VHS, Beta $59.98** *NLC* *♂*

Darling A young amoral model tries to hold boredom at bay by having a number of love affairs. She joins the international jet set and manages to reach the top of European society by marrying a prince. She then learns what an empty life she has. Christie won an Oscar for her portrayal of the disillusioned, cynical young woman. Academy Award winning screenplay by Frederic Raphael.
1965 122m/B *GB* Julie Christie, Dirk Bogarde, Laurence Harvey; *D:* John Schlesinger. Academy Awards '65: Best Actress (Christie), Best Costume Design (B & W), Best Story; Nominations: Best Director (Schlesinger), Best Picture; British Academy Awards '65: Best Actor (Bogarde), Best Actress (Christie); National Board

of Review Awards '65: 10 Best Films of the Year, Best Actress (Christie), Best Director (Schlesinger). **VHS, Beta, LV $19.95** *COL, VYG, BTV* *♂♂♂½*

D.A.R.Y.L. The little boy found by the side of the road is too polite, too honest and too smart. His friend explains to him the necessity of imperfection (If you don't want the grown-ups to bother you too much) and he begins to become more like a real little boy. But the American military has a top-secret interest in this child, since he is in fact the combination of a cloned body and a computer brain. More interesting when it's involved with the human beings and less so when it focuses on science.
1985 (PG) 100m/C Mary Beth Hurt, Michael McKean, Barret Oliver, Colleen Camp; *D:* Simon Wincer. **VHS, Beta, LV $14.95** *PAR* *♂♂*

Das Boot Superb detailing of life in a German U-boat during World War II. Intense, claustrophobic atmosphere complemented by nail-biting action provides a realistic portrait of the stressful conditions that were endured on these submarines. Excellent performances, especially from Prochnow. With English subtitles. Originally a 6-hour special made for German television. Also available in a dubbed version. From the novel by Lothar-Guenther Buccheim. *AKA:* The Boat.
1981 (R) 150m/C *GE* Juergen Prochnow, Herbert Gronemeyer, Klaus Wennemann, Hubertus Bengsch, Martin Semmelrogge, Bernd Tauber, Erwin Leder; *D:* Wolfgang Petersen. **VHS, Beta, LV $19.95** *COL, APD, TAM* *♂♂♂♂*

Das Testament des Dr. Mabuse The third, and only sound, Mabuse film by Lang. The infamous crime lord/megalomaniac plots the world's destruction from the confines of an asylum cell. In German, with English subtitles. Released as "The Last Will of Dr. Mabuse" in the U.S. in 1943.
1933 122m/B *GE* Rudolf Klein-Rogge, Otto Wernicke, Gustav Diesl, Karl Meixner; *D:* Fritz Lang. **VHS, Beta $29.98** *SNC, SUE, GLV* *♂♂♂½*

Date Bait When a teen couple decides—much to their parents' chagrin—to elope, they find themselves on a date with danger when their post-nuptials are plagued by pushers and assorted other bad guys.
1960 71m/B Gary Clarke, Marlo Ryan, Richard Gering, Danny Logan; *D:* O'Dale Ireland. **VHS, Beta $16.95** *SNC* *♂*

Date with an Angel When aspiring musician Knight fishes a beautiful angel out of the swimming pool, he is just trying to rescue her. But the beauty of the angel overwhelms him and he finds himself questioning his upcoming wedding to Cates, a cosmetic mogul's daughter. Too cute and too sentimental, though Beart's beauty is other-wordly.
1987 (PG) 114m/C Emmanuelle Beart, Michael E. Knight, Phoebe Cates, David Dukes, Bibi Besch, Albert Macklin, David Hunt, Michael Goodwin; *D:* Tom McLoughlin. **VHS, Beta, LV $19.99** *HBO* *♂½*

A Date with Judy Standard post-war musical dealing with teenage mix-ups in and around a big high school dance. Choreography by Stanley Donen. ♫Cuanto La Gusto; Strictly on the Corny Side; It's a Most Unusual Day; Judaline; I've Got a Date with Judy; I'm Gonna Meet My Mary; Temptation; Mulligatawny.
1948 114m/C Jane Powell, Elizabeth Taylor, Carmen Miranda, Wallace Beery, Robert Stack, Xavier Cugat, Selena Royle, Leon Ames; *D:* Richard Thorpe. **VHS, Beta, LV $19.98** *MGM, MLB* *♂♂*

Daughter of Death A little mentally off-center since she witnessed the gruesome rape and murder of her mother, a teenage girl doesn't bond well with her new mom when dad remarries. *AKA:* Julie Darling.
1982 (R) 100m/C *CA GE* Anthony (Tony) Franciosa, Isabelle Mejias, Sybil Danning, Cindy Gurling, Paul Hubbard, Benjamin Schmoll; *D:* Paul Nicholas. **VHS $59.99** *FCT* *♂*

The Daughter of Dr. Jekyll The doc's daughter believes she may have inherited her father's evil curse when several of the locals are found dead.
1957 71m/B John Agar, Arthur Shields, John Dierkes, Gloria Talbott; *D:* Edgar G. Ulmer. **VHS, Beta $39.98** *FOX* *♂½*

Daughter of Horror A young woman finds herself involved with a porcine mobster who resembles her abusive father. Trouble is, Dad's dead, and daughter dearest abetted his departure. Obscure venture into expressionism that was initially banned by the New York State Board of Censors. Shot on a low budget (how low was it? So low that McMahon narrated because shooting with sound was too expensive). The 55 minutes tend to lag, although the film should be intriguing to genre enthusiasts and to fans of things pseudo-Freudian. *AKA:* Dementia.
1955 60m/B Adrienne Barrett, Bruno Ve Sota, Ben Roseman; *W/D:* John Parker. **VHS $19.98** *NOS, SNC, MRV* *♂♂*

Daughter of the Dragon Fu Manchu is again on the prowl, this time sending his daughter to murder Fletcher to avenge the death of his wife and son during China's Boxer Rebellion. Based on a Sax Rohmer story.
1931 70m/B Anna May Wong, Warner Oland, Sessue Hayakawa, Bramwell Fletcher, Holmes Herbert; *D:* Lloyd Corrigan. **VHS $19.95** *NOS* *♂♂*

Daughter of the Tong FBI agent gets tong twisted when he tries to put a lid on a smuggling ring headed by a woman (who's beautiful, of course). Something that resembles acting is wasted in a mess of a movie.
1939 56m/B Evelyn Brent, Grant Withers, Dorothy Short, Dave O'Brien; *D:* Raymond K. Johnson. **VHS, Beta $16.95** *NOS, SNC* *♂*

Daughters of Darkness Newlyweds on their way to England stop at a posh French hotel. There they meet a beautiful woman whom the hotel owner swears had been there forty years ago, even though she hasn't aged a bit. When she introduces herself as Countess of Bathory (the woman who bathed in the blood of virgins to stay young) folks begin to wonder. A really superb erotic vampire film charged with sensuality and a sense of dread. *AKA:* Le Rouge aux Levres.
1971 (R) 87m/C *BE GE IT FR* Delphine Seyrig, John Karlen, Daniele Ouimet, Andrea Rau, Paul Esser, Georges Jamin, Joris Collet, Fons Rademakers; *D:* Harry Kumel. **VHS, Beta** *NO* *♂♂♂*

Daughters of Satan Selleck, in an early role as a virile museum buyer, antagonizes a coven of witches when he purchases a painting. His wife, played by Grant, becomes a target of the witches' revenge and salacious shenanigans ensue.
1972 (R) 96m/C Tom Selleck, Barra Grant, Paraluman, Tani Phelps Guthrie; *D:* Hollingsworth Morse. **VHS, Beta** *NO* *♂*

Daughters of the Dust A Gullah family living on the Sea Islands off the Georgia coast in 1902 contemplate moving to the mainland in this emotional tale of change. The Gullah are descendants of West African slaves and their isolation has kept

their superstitions and native dialect (a mixture of Western African, Creole, and English) intact. Five women of the Peazant family reflect on their lives and family as they gather together for a final family picnic. They include 88-year-old Nana, the matriarch of the family; Yellow Mary, a prosperous ex-prostitute who has returned to the family fold; Eula, whose pregnancy may be the result of a rape; Baptist missionary, Viola; and daughter-in-law Haagar, who can't wait to escape what she sees as the backwardness of the island. Family bonds and memories are celebrated with a quiet narrative and beautiful cinematography in Dash's feature-film directorial debut.
1992 113m/C Cora Lee Day, Barbara O, Alva Rogers, Kaycee Moore, Cheryl Lynn Bruce, Adisa Anderson; **W/D:** Julie Dash. **VHS $79.95** KIV, FCT, PMS �△�△✭½

Dave Regular guy Dave Kovic (Kline) happens to impersonate the President for profit. When the real President suffers a stroke from "overstimulation," Dave's job as a lookalike launches him into the White House as part of evil Chief of Staff Langella's plan to stage a coup and put the real prez on ice. No one anticipates, however, just how well Dave will do as the Commander-in-Chief—especially the First Lady (Weaver)—as Dave goes on to prove that sometimes a regular guy can turn out to be more of a "real" President than the President himself. Director/producer Reitman's seamless comedy prompts lots of hearty belly laughs and the feel-good faith that despite the overwhelming odds, everything will turn out just fine. Sturges he ain't, but what the heck. Political cameos abound: look for real-life Senators Alan Simpson, Paul Simon, Howard Metzenbaum, Tom Harkin, and Christopher Dodd as well as the commentators from TV's "The McLaughlin Group," and Stone's hilarious turn on "Larry King Live" as he tries to convince the public of a conspiracy.
1993 (PG-13) 110m/C Kevin Kline, Sigourney Weaver, Frank Langella, Kevin Dunn, Ving Rhames, Ben Kingsley, Charles Grodin, Faith Prince, Anna Deavere Smith; **Cameos:** Oliver Stone, Arnold Schwarzenegger; **D:** Ivan Reitman; **W:** Gary Ross; **M:** James Newton Howard. **VHS** NYR �△✭½

David A haunting portrait of the survival of a Jewish teenager in Berlin during the Nazi reign of terror, based on the novel by Joel Koenig. Universally acclaimed, this was the first film about the Holocaust made in Germany by a German Jew. In German with English subtitles.
1979 106m/C GE Mario Fischel, Walter Taub, Irene Vrkijan, Torsten Hentes, Eva Mattes; **D:** Peter Lilienthal. **VHS, Beta $79.95** KIV, GLV, TAM ✭✭✭½

David and Bathsheba The Bible story comes alive in this lush and colorful Fox production. Peck and Hayward are great together and Peck is properly concerned about the wrath of God over his transgressions. Terrific costumes and special effects, lovely music and a fine supporting cast keep this a notch above other Biblical epics.
1951 116m/C Gregory Peck, Susan Hayward, Raymond Massey, Kieron Moore, James Robertson Justice, Jayne Meadows, John Sutton, Dennis Hoey, Francis X. Bushman, George Zucco; **D:** Henry King. **VHS, LV $19.98** FXV, FOX ✭✭✭

David and Lisa Director Perry was given an Oscar for this sensitive independently-produced film. Adapted from Theodore Isaac Rubin's true case history novel concerning a young man and woman who fall in love while institutionalized for mental ill-

ness. Dullea and Margolin are excellent in the title roles of this sleeper.
1962 94m/B Keir Dullea, Janet Margolin, Howard da Silva, Neva Patterson, Clifton James; **D:** Frank Perry. **VHS, Beta, LV $69.95** COL, MRV ✭✭✭

David Copperfield Superior adaptation of Charles Dickens' great novel. An orphan grows to manhood in Victorian England with a wide variety of help and harm. Terrific acting by Bartholomew, Fields, Rathbone, and all the rest. Lavish production, lovingly filmed.
1935 132m/B Lionel Barrymore, W.C. Fields, Freddie Bartholomew, Maureen O'Sullivan, Basil Rathbone, Lewis Stone; **D:** George Cukor. Academy Awards '35 Nominations: Best Film Editing; Academy Awards '36: Best Picture; National Board of Review Awards '35: 10 Best Films of the Year. **VHS, Beta, LV $19.98** MGM ✭✭✭✭

David Copperfield This British made-for-television production is more faithful to the Dickens classic than any of its predecessors. The added material, however, fails to highlight any one character as had the successful 1935 MGM version. Still, the exceptional (and largely stage-trained) cast do much to redeem the production.
1970 118m/C Richard Attenborough, Cyril Cusack, Edith Evans, Pamela Franklin, Susan Hampshire, Wendy Hiller, Ron Moody, Laurence Olivier; **D:** Delbert Mann. **VHS** FOX ✭✭½

David Copperfield An animated adaptation of the Dickens classic about a young boy growing up in 19th-century England.
1983 72m/C VHS, Beta $24.95 KUI ✭✭✭✭

DaVinci's War Frank DaVinci's sister is murdered and he wants revenge. So he hooks up with a professional killer and a bunch of Vietnam vets and gets the firepower he needs to blow the bad guys away.
1992 (R) 94m/C Joey Travolta, Michael Nouri, Vanity, Richard Foronjy, Branscombe Richmond, Sam Jones, Jack Bannon; **Cameos:** Brian Robbins, James Russo; **W/D:** Raymond Martino; **M:** Jeff Lass. **VHS $89.95** TRI ✭✭

Davy Crockett and the River Pirates Another Disney splice and dice of two episodes from the television series, chronicling the further adventures of our frontier hero. Davy meets up with Mike Fink, the King of the Ohio River, and the two engage in a furious keelboat race, and then unite to track down a group of thieves masquerading as Indians and threatening the peace.
1956 (G) 81m/C Fess Parker, Buddy Ebsen, Jeff York; **D:** Norman Foster. **VHS, Beta, LV** DIS, OM ✭✭½

Davy Crockett, King of the Wild Frontier Three episodes of the popular Disney television series are blended together here to present the life and some of the adventures of Davy Crockett. These include his days as an Indian fighter and his gallant stand in defense of the Alamo. Well-done by a splendid cast, the film helped to spread Davy-mania among the children of the 1950s.
1955 (PG) 93m/C Fess Parker, Buddy Ebsen, Hans Conried, Ray Whiteside, Pat Hogan, William Bakewell, Basil Ruysdael, Kenneth Tobey; **D:** Norman Foster. **VHS, Beta $19.99** DIS ✭✭✭

Dawn! True story of Dawn Fraser, an Olympic champion swimmer and an unfulfilled woman willing to fight for her happiness.
1983 114m/C Bronwyn MacKay-Payne, Tom Richards. **VHS, Beta $19.98** VID ✭✭

Dawn Express Nazi spies infiltrate the U.S. in search of a secret formula designed to enhance the power of gasoline. Another film made to contribute to the war effort that doesn't make much sense.
1942 63m/B Michael Whalen, Anne Nagel, William Bakewell, Constance Worth, Hans von Twardowski, Jack Mulhall, George Pembroke, Kenneth Harlan, Robert Frazer; **D:** Albert Herman. **VHS, Beta $16.95** SNC, TIM ✭✭½

Dawn of the Dead Romero's gruesome sequel to his "Night of the Living Dead." A mysterious plague causes the recently dead to rise from their graves and scour the countryside for living flesh. Very violent, gory, graphic, and shocking, yet not without humor. Gives interesting consideration to the violence created by the living humans in their efforts to save themselves.
1978 126m/C David Emge, Ken Foree, Gaylen Ross; **D:** George A. Romero. **VHS, Beta, LV $14.99** HBO ✭✭✭½

Dawn of the Mummy Lousy plot and bad acting—not to mention gore galore—do this one in. A photographer and a bevy of young fashion models travel to Egypt for a special shoot. They unwittingly stumble upon an ancient tomb, teeming with vengeance-minded mummies.
1982 93m/C Brenda King, Barry Sattels, George Peck, Joan Levy; **D:** Frank Agrama. **VHS, Beta $69.99** HBO Woof!

Dawn of the Pirates An adventurer stumbles upon a murderous tribe of Tughs and the beautiful white woman they captured. **AKA:** La Secta de los Tughs.
19?? 95m/C SP VHS, Beta NO ✭½

Dawn on the Great Divide Jones' last film before his tragic and untimely death trying to save people from a fire at the Coconut Grove in Boston. Wagon train has to battle not only Indians, but bad guys as well. Plot provides more depth than the usual western fare.
1942 57m/B Buck Jones, Tim McCoy, Raymond Hatton, Mona Barrie, Robert Lowery, Betty Blythe, Jane Wiley, Harry Woods, Roy Barcroft; **D:** Howard Bretherton. **VHS, Beta, 3/4U, Special order formats $19.95** NOS, MRV, VCN ✭✭½

Dawn Patrol Flynn plays a flight commander whose nerves are shot in this story of the British Royal Flying Corps during World War I. The focus is on the effects that the pressures and deaths have on all those concerned. Fine performances from all in this well-done remake of the 1930 film.
1938 103m/B Errol Flynn, David Niven, Basil Rathbone, Donald Crisp, Barry Fitzgerald, Melville Cooper; **D:** Edmund Goulding. **VHS, Beta $19.98** FOX, MGM ✭✭✭

Dawn Rider Formula western has all the right ingredients: Wayne as a cowboy out to get revenge on the gang that murdered his father. Features stuntman Canutt in rare acting role.
1935 60m/B John Wayne, Marion Burns, Yakima Canutt; **D:** Robert North Bradbury. **VHS $8.95** NEG, REP, MRV ✭✭

Dawn Rider/Frontier Horizon A double feature of two of Wayne's earliest western films.
1939 114m/B John Wayne, Jennifer Jones, Marion Burns; **D:** Robert North Bradbury, George Sherman. **VHS, Beta $34.95** REP ✭✭

The Dawson Patrol Royal Canadian Mountie dog-sled race turns into a dramatic battle for survival.
1978 75m/C George R. Robinson, Tim Henry, Neil Dainaro, James B. Douglas; **D:** Peter Kelly. **VHS, Beta $49.95** TWE ✭½

D

The Day After Powerful drama graphically depicts the nuclear bombing of a midwestern city and its after-effects on the survivors. Made for television, and very controversial when first shown, gathering huge ratings and vast media coverage.
1983 126m/C Jason Robards Jr., JoBeth Williams, John Lithgow, Steve Guttenberg; **D:** Nicholas Meyer. **VHS, Beta, LV** $9.98 SUE 🐾🐾🐾

The Day and the Hour A woman becomes accidentally involved in the resistance movement during the Nazi occupation of France in World War II. **AKA:** Today We Live; Le Jour et L'Heure; Il Giorno e L'Ora; Viviamo Oggi.
1963 110m/C FR JP Simone Signoret, Stuart Whitman, Genevieve Page, Michel Piccoli, Reggie Nalder, Pierre Dux, Billy Kearns; **D:** Rene Clement. **VHS, Beta** $24.95 TAM, MON 🐾🐾½

A Day at the Races Though it seems labored at times, the brilliance of the brothers Marx still comes through in this rather weak tale of a patient in a sanitorium who convinces horse doctor Groucho to take on running the place. ♫A Message from the Man in the Moon; On Blue Venetian Waters; Tomorrow is Another Day; All God's Chillun Got Rhythm.
1937 111m/B Groucho Marx, Harpo Marx, Chico Marx, Sig Rumann, Douglas Dumbrille, Margaret Dumont, Allan Jones, Maureen O'Sullivan; **D:** Sam Wood. **VHS, Beta, LV** $19.95 MGM, CCB 🐾🐾🐾½

Day for Night A wryly affectionate look at the profession of moviemaking—its craft, character, and the personalities that interact against the performances commanded by the camera. In French with English subtitles. **AKA:** La Nuit Americaine.
1973 (PG) 116m/C FR Jean-Pierre Leaud, Jacqueline Bisset, Jean-Pierre Aumont, Valentina Cortese, Francois Truffaut; **D:** Francois Truffaut. Academy Awards '73: Best Foreign Language Film; Nominations: Best Director (Truffaut), Best Original Screenplay, Best Supporting Actress (Cortese); British Academy Awards '73: Best Director (Truffaut), Best Film, Best Supporting Actress (Cortese); National Society of Film Critics Awards '73: Best Director (Truffaut), Best Film, Best Supporting Actress (Cortese). **VHS, Beta** $19.95 TAM, WAR, APD 🐾🐾🐾🐾

A Day for Thanks on Walton's Mountain Many of the original television-show cast members returned for this sentimental Thanksgiving reunion on Walton's Mountain. Made for television.
1982 97m/C Ralph Waite, Ellen Corby, Judy Norton-Taylor, Eric Scott, Jon Walmsley, Robert Wightman, Mary McDonough, David W. Harper, Kami Cotler, Joe Conley, Ronnie Clair Edwards, Richard Gilliland, Melinda Naud; **D:** Harry Harris. **VHS** $59.99 WAR 🐾🐾

A Day in October Sweeney plays Niels Jensen, a Danish resistance fighter fighting in Copenhagen as the Nazis prepare to invade Denmark in 1943. Injured in a sabotage attempt he is rescued by Sara, a young Jewish woman. Her family reluctantly and fearfully hide the young man as they finally face up to a Nazi reality and decide what to do. Niels and Sara fall in love as he and the other resistance fighters prepare a plan to help the Danish Jews escape annihilation by the Nazis. Based on historical fact. Filmed on location in Denmark.
1992 (PG-13) 96m/C D.B. Sweeney, Kelly Wolf, Tovah Feldshuh, Daniel Benzali, Ole Lemmeke, Kim Romer, Anders Peter Bro, Lars Oluf Larsen; **D:** Kenneth Madsen; **W:** Damian F. Slattery. **VHS** $89.95 ACA, FOX 🐾🐾½

A Day in the Country The son of the famed painter gives us the moving tale of a young woman's sudden and intense love for a man she meets while on a picnic with her family. Beautifully adapted from a story by Guy de Maupassant. Renowned photographer Henri Cartier-Bresson contributed to the wonderful cinematography. In French with English subtitles. **AKA:** Une Partie de Campagne.
1946 40m/B FR Sylvia Bataille, Georges Darnoux, Jane Marken, Paul Temps; **D:** Jean Renoir. **VHS, Beta** $24.95 NOS, MRV, DVT 🐾🐾🐾½

A Day in the Death of Joe Egg Based on the Peter Nichols play, an unlikely black comedy about a British couple trying to care for their retarded/autistic child, nearly destroying their marriage in the process. They begin to contemplate euthanasia as a solution. Well-acted, but potentially offensive to some. Written by David Deutsch.
1971 (R) 106m/C GB Alan Bates, Janet Suzman; Elizabeth Robillard, Peter Bowles, Joan Hickson, Sheila Gish; **D:** Peter Medak. **VHS, Beta** $69.95 COL 🐾🐾🐾

The Day It Came to Earth Completely silly and unbelievable sci-fi flick has meteor crashing into the watery grave of a mobster. The decomposed corpse is revived by the radiation and plots to take revenge on those who fitted him with cement shoes.
1977 (PG) 89m/C Roger Manning, Wink Roberts, Bob Ginnaven, Rita Wilson, Delight de Bruine; **D:** Harry Z. Thomason. **VHS, Beta** PGN Woof!

Day of Judgment A mysterious stranger arrives in a town to slaughter those people who violate the Ten Commandments.
1981 101m/C William T. Hicks, Harris Bloodworth, Brownlee Davis; **D:** C.D.H. Reynolds. **VHS, Beta** $69.99 HBO 🐾½

Day of the Animals Nature gone wild. It seems a depleted ozone layer has exposed the animals to the sun's radiation, turning Bambi and Bugs into brutal killers. A group of backpackers trek in the Sierras, unaware of the transformation. Far-fetched and silly (we hope) **AKA:** Something is Out There.
1977 (PG) 95m/C Christopher George, Leslie Nielsen, Lynda Day George, Richard Jaeckel, Michael Ansara, Ruth Roman, Jon Cedar, Susan Backlinie, Andrew Stevens, Gil Lamb; **D:** William Girdler **VHS** $59.95 MED 🐾

Day of the Assassin A Mideast shah's yacht explodes, sending a huge fortune to the bottom of a murky bay. This sets off a rampage of treasure hunting by a variety of ruthless mercenaries.
1981 94m/C Glenn Ford, Chuck Connors, Richard Roundtree, Henry Silva, Jorge Rivero; **D:** Brian Trenchard-Smith. **VHS, Beta** $79.95 PSM 🐾

Day of the Cobra A corrupt narcotics bureau official hires an ex-cop to find a heroin kingpin on the back streets of Genoa, Italy.
1984 95m/C IT Franco Nero, Sybil Danning, Mario Maranzana, Licinia Lentini, William Berger; **D:** Enzo G. Castellari. **VHS, Beta** $49.95 MED 🐾½

Day of the Dead The third in Romero's trilogy of films about flesh-eating zombies taking over the world. Romero hasn't thought up anything new for the ghouls to do, and the humans are too nasty to care about this time around. For adult audiences.
1985 91m/C Lori Cardillo, Terry Alexander, Joseph Pilato, Jarleth Conroy; **D:** George A. Romero. **VHS, Beta, LV** $19.95 MED, IME 🐾½

The Day of the Dolphin Research scientist, after successfully working out a means of teaching dolphins to talk, finds his animals kidnapped; espionage and assassination are involved. Dolphin voices by Buck Henry, who also wrote the screenplay.
1973 (PG) 104m/C George C. Scott, Trish Van Devere, Paul Sorvino, Fritz Weaver, Jon Korkes, John Dehner, Edward Herrmann, Severn Darden; **D:** Mike Nichols; **W:** Buck Henry. Academy Awards '73 Nominations: Best Sound; National Board of Review Awards '73: 10 Best Films of the Year. **VHS, Beta, LV** $14.98 SUE, NLC 🐾🐾

The Day of the Jackal Frederick Forsyth's best-selling novel of political intrigue is splendidly brought to the screen by Zinnemann. A brilliant and ruthless assassin hired to kill Charles de Gaulle skirts the international intelligence pool, while intuitive police work to stop him. Tense, suspenseful, beautiful location photography. Excellent acting by Fox, Cusack and Britton.
1973 (PG) 142m/C Edward Fox, Alan Badel, Tony Britton, Derek Jacobi, Cyril Cusack, Olga Georges-Picot; **D:** Fred Zinneman. **VHS, Beta, LV** $59.95 MCA 🐾🐾🐾½

The Day of the Locust Compelling adaptation of Nathaniel West's novel concerning the dark side of 1930s' Hollywood. A no-talent amoral actress's affair with a meek accountant leads to tragedy and destruction. Told from the view of a cynical art director wise to the ways of Hollywood.
1975 (R) 140m/C Donald Sutherland, Karen Black, Burgess Meredith, William Atherton, Billy Barty, Bo Hopkins, Richard Dysart, Geraldine Page; **D:** John Schlesinger; **M:** John Barry. Academy Awards '75 Nominations: Best Cinematography, Best Supporting Actor (Meredith); National Board of Review Awards '75: 10 Best Films of the Year. **VHS, Beta, LV** $14.95 PAR 🐾🐾🐾½

Day of the Maniac Psychotic drug addict will stop at nothing to support his growing habit.
1977 (R) 89m/C George Hilton, Susan Scott; **D:** Sergio Martino. **VHS, Beta** $69.95 REP 🐾½

Day of the Panther The Panthers—the world's most formidable martial artists—-are mighty torqued when panther-Linda is pithed, and they're not known to turn the other cheek. Much chop-socky kicking and shrilling.
1988 86m/C John Stanton, Eddie Stazak; **D:** Brian Trenchard-Smith. **VHS, Beta** $79.95 CEL 🐾½

Day of the Triffids The majority of Earth's population is blinded by a meteor shower which also causes plant spores to mutate into giant carnivores. Well-done adaptation of John Wyndham's science fiction classic.
1963 94m/C Howard Keel, Janet Scott, Nicole Maurey, Janet Scott, Kieron Moore, Mervyn Johns; **D:** Steve Sekely. **VHS, Beta, LV** $29.95 MED, MRV, PSM 🐾🐾🐾

Day of Triumph A dynamic version of the life of Christ as seen through the eyes of the apostles Andrew and Zadok, the leaders of the Zealot underground.
1954 110m/C Lee J. Cobb, Robert Wilson, Ralph Freud; **D:** Irving Pichel. **VHS** $39.95 REP 🐾🐾🐾

Day of Wrath An involving psychological thriller based on records of witch trials from the early 1600s. An old woman, burned at the stake as a witch, puts a curse on the local parson and his family. Grim and unrelentingly pessimistic, moving from one horrific scene to another, director Dreyer creates a masterpiece of terror. Based on a play by

Hans Wiers Jenssen. In Danish with English subtitles. *AKA:* Vredens Dag.
1943 110m/B *DK* Thorkild Roose, Sigrid Neiiendam, Lisbeth Movin; *D:* Carl Theodor Dreyer. **VHS, Beta, 3/4U, Special order formats $49.95** *TAM, NOS, SNC* 𝄞𝄞𝄞𝄞

The Day that Shook the World Slow-moving but intriguing account of events surrounding the assassination of Archduke Ferdinand of Austria that triggered World War I. Garnered an R-rating due to some disturbingly graphic scenes.
1978 (R) 111m/C Christopher Plummer, Florinda Bolkan, Maximilian Schell; *D:* Veljko Bulajic. **VHS $29.95** *VID* 𝄞

Day the Bookies Wept Decent yarn about cabbies tricked into buying a "racehorse." Turns out she's old as the hills and hooked on alcohol to boot, but they enter her in the big race anyway.
1939 50m/B Betty Grable, Joe Penner, Tom Kennedy, Richard Lane; *D:* Leslie Goodwins. **VHS, Beta $34.98** *CCB* 𝄞𝄞

The Day the Earth Caught Fire The earth is knocked out of orbit and sent hurtling toward the sun when nuclear testing is done simultaneously at both the North and South Poles. Realistic and suspenseful, this is one of the best of the sci-fi genre.
1962 100m/B Janet Munro, Edward Judd, Leo McKern; *D:* Val Guest. **VHS, Beta $14.95** *NEG, HBO, KAR* 𝄞𝄞𝄞½

The Day the Earth Froze Witch steals the sun because she couldn't have a magical mill that produced grain, salt, and gold. Everything on Earth freezes. Based on a Finnish epic poem.
1959 67m/B *FI RU* Nina Anderson, Jon Powers, Ingrid Elhardt, Paul Sorenson; *D:* Gregg Sebelious. **VHS $16.95** *SNC* 𝄞𝄞

The Day the Earth Stood Still A gentle alien lands on Earth to deliver a message of peace and a warning against experimenting with nuclear power. He finds his views echoed by a majority of the population, but not the ones who are in control. In this account based loosely on the story of Christ, Rennie is the visitor backed by the mighty robot Gort. One of the greatest science fiction films of all time. Score by Bernard Herrmann.
1951 92m/B Michael Rennie, Patricia Neal, Hugh Marlowe, Sam Jaffe, Francis Bavier, Lock Martin, Bobby Gray; *D:* Robert Wise. **VHS, Beta, LV $14.98** *FOX, FCT, MLB* 𝄞𝄞𝄞½

The Day the Sky Exploded Sci-fi disaster drama doesn't live up to the grandiose title, as a runaway rocket ship hits the sun, unleashing an asteroid shower that threatens Earth with tidal waves, earthquakes, heat waves and terrible dialogue. The highlight of this Franco-Italian effort is the cinematography by horror director Mario Bava. *AKA:* Death From Outer Space; La Morte Viene Dalla Spazio; Le Danger Vient de l'Escape.
1957 80m/B *FR IT* Paul Hubschmid, Madeleine Fischer, Fiorella Mari, Ivo Garrani, Dario Michaelis; *D:* Richard Benson. **VHS $29.95** *NOS, FCT, TIM* 𝄞½

The Day the Women Got Even Four suburban homemakers take up the life of vigilantes to save unsuspecting actresses from a talent agent's blackmail scheme. Made for television.
1980 98m/C JoAnn Pflug, Tina Louise, Georgia Engel, Barbara Rhoades, Julie Hagerty, Ed O'Neil; *D:* Burt Brinckerhoff. **VHS, Beta** *TLF* 𝄞½

Day Time Ended A pair of glowing UFO's streaking across the sky and an alien mechanical device with long menacing appendages are only two of the bizarre phenomena witnessed from a lone house in the desert. Good special effects. Also released as "Time Warp" (1978). *AKA:* Vortex.
1980 80m/C Chris Mitchum, Jim Davis, Dorothy Malone; *D:* John Cardos. **VHS, Beta, LV** *MED, MRV* 𝄞𝄞

The Day Will Dawn Suspenseful British-made World War II thriller about a reporter and a young Norwegian girl who plot to sabotage a secret Nazi U-boat base near the girl's town. Co-written by Terence Rattigan. *AKA:* The Avengers.
1942 100m/B *GB* Deborah Kerr, Hugh Williams, Griffith Jones, Ralph Richardson, Francis L. Sullivan, Roland Culver, Niall MacGinnis, Finlay Currie; *D:* Harold French. **VHS, Beta, 8mm $29.95** *VYY* 𝄞𝄞𝄞

Day with Conrad Green Set in 1927, this program presents a somewhat farcical look at a successful Broadway producer as he attempts to cope with a full schedule of personal and business problems on the day of the funeral of his longtime assistant.
1980 60m/C Fred Gwynne. **VHS, Beta** *MTP* 𝄞𝄞𝄞

Daydreamer By combining live action and animation in this delightful feature-length film, young Hans Christian Andersen comes face-to-face with many of the same characters he would later write about. Imaginative and finely-crafted.
1966 98m/C Paul O'Keefe, Ray Bolger, Jack Gilford, Margaret Hamilton; *V:* Jules Bass; Tallulah Bankhead, Boris Karloff, Burl Ives, Terry-Thomas. **VHS, Beta $19.98** *SUE* 𝄞𝄞𝄞

The Daydreamer Richard, who also wrote the screenplay and directed the film, stars as a bumbling fool let loose in the French corporate world with comical results. In French with subtitles. *AKA:* Absent-Minded; Le Distrait.
1975 90m/C *FR* Pierre Richard, Bernard Blier, Maria Pacome, Marie-Christine Barrault; *W/D:* Pierre Richard. **VHS, Beta $19.95** *FCT* 𝄞½

Days and Nights in the Forest Four men living in Calcutta decide to leave the city for a brief vacation. Each has a different emotional experience which will change him forever, including a brief love affair and finding true romance. In Bengali with English subtitles.
1970 120m/C *IN* *D:* Satyajit Ray. **VHS $39.95** *FCT* 𝄞𝄞½

Days of Glory Peck's screen debut finds him as a Russian peasant bravely fighting the Nazi blitzkrieg almost single-handedly.
1943 86m/B Tamara Toumanova, Gregory Peck, Alan Reed, Maria Palmer, Lowell Gilmore, Hugo Haas; *D:* Jacques Tourneur. **VHS, Beta $19.98** *TTC* 𝄞𝄞½

Days of Heaven A drifter (Gere), his younger sister, and a woman he claims is his sister become involved with a Texas sharecropper. Told through the eyes of the younger girl, this is a sweeping vision of the U.S. before the first World War. Loss and loneliness, deception, frustration, and anger haunt these people as they struggle to make the land their own. Deservedly awarded an Oscar for breathtaking cinematography.
1978 (PG) 95m/C Richard Gere, Brooke Adams, Sam Shepard, Linda Manz, Stuart Margolin; *D:* Terence Malick; *W:* Terence Malick; *M:* Ennio Morricone. Academy Awards '78: Best Cinematography; Nominations: Best Costume Design, Best Sound, Best Original Score; Cannes Film Festival '79: Best Director (Malick); National Board of Review Awards '78: 10 Best

Films of the Year; New York Film Critics Awards '78: Best Director (Malick); National Society of Film Critics Awards '78: Best Director (Malick). **VHS, Beta, LV $14.95** *PAR* 𝄞𝄞𝄞½

Days of Hell Forgettable tale of four mercenaries who are hired to rescue a doctor and his daughter held captive by guerrillas somewhere in Afghanistan only to find out they're pawns in an even bigger scheme. *AKA:* I Giorni Dell'Inferno.
1984 90m/C Conrad Nichols, Richard Raymond, Stephen Elliott, Kinako Harada; *D:* Anthony Richmond. **VHS, Beta** *NO* 𝄞

Days of Thrills and Laughter Delightful compilation of clips from the era of silent films, showcasing the talents of the great comics as well as daring stuntman.
1961 93m/B Buster Keaton, Charlie Chaplin, Harold Lloyd, Stan Laurel, Oliver Hardy, Douglas Fairbanks Sr.; *D:* Robert Youngson. **VHS, Beta $29.95** *MPI* 𝄞𝄞𝄞½

Days of Thunder "Top Gun" in race cars! Cruise follows the same formula he has followed for several years now (with the notable exception of "Born on the Fourth of July.") Cruise and Towne co-wrote the screenplay concerning a young kid bursting with talent and raw energy who must learn to deal with his mentor, his girlfriend, and eventually the bad guy. First film that featured cameras that were actually on the race cars. If you like Cruise or race cars then this is the movie for you.
1990 (PG-13) 108m/C Tom Cruise, Robert Duvall, Randy Quaid, Nicole Kidman, Cary Elwes, Michael Rooker, Fred Dalton Thompson; *D:* Tony Scott; *W:* Tom Cruise, Robert Towne; *M:* Hans Zimmer. **VHS, Beta, LV, SVS $14.95** *PAR, SUP* 𝄞𝄞

Days of Wine and Roses The original "Playhouse 90" television version of J.P. Miller's story which was adapted for the big screen in 1962. An executive on the fast track and his young wife, initially only social drinkers, find themselves degenerating into alcoholism. A well-acted, stirring drama.
1958 89m/B Cliff Robertson, Piper Laurie; *D:* John Frankenheimer. **VHS, Beta** *MGM* 𝄞𝄞½

Days of Wine and Roses A harrowing tale of an alcoholic advertising man who gradually drags his wife down with him into a life of booze. Part of the "A Night at the Movies" series, this tape simulates a 1962 movie evening with a Bugs Bunny cartoon, "Martian Through Georgia," a newsreel, and coming attractions for "Gypsy" and "Rome Adventure." Big screen adaptation of the play originally shown on television.
1962 138m/B Jack Lemmon, Lee Remick, Charles Bickford, Jack Klugman, Jack Albertson; *D:* Blake Edwards; *M:* Henry Mancini, Johnny Mercer. Academy Awards '62: Best Song ("Days of Wine and Roses"); Nominations: Best Actor (Lemmon), Best Actress (Remick), Best Art Direction/Set Decoration (B & W), Best Costume Design (B & W). **VHS, Beta, LV $19.98** *WAR, PIA* 𝄞𝄞𝄞½

Dayton's Devils Nielsen is the leader of a motley crew of losers who plan to rob a military base bank in this action-packed heist flick.
1968 107m/C Rory Calhoun, Leslie Nielsen, Lainie Kazan, Hans Gudegast, Georg Stanford Brown; *D:* Jack Shea. **VHS, Beta** *TIM* 𝄞𝄞

D.C. Cab A rag-tag group of Washington, D.C. cabbies learn a lesson in self-respect in this endearing comedy. Though not without flaws, it's charming all the same.
1984 (R) 100m/C Mr. T, Leif Erickson, Adam Baldwin, Charlie Barnett, Irene Cara, Anne De Salvo, Max Gail, Gloria Gifford, Gary Busey, Jill Schoelen, Marsha Warfield; *D:* Joel Schumacher. **VHS, Beta, LV $19.95** *MCA* 𝄞𝄞½

The Dead The poignant final film by Huston, based on James Joyce's short story. At a Christmas dinner party in turn-of-the-century Dublin, a man discovers how little he knows about his wife when a song reminds her of a cherished lost love. Beautifully captures the spirit of the story while providing Huston an opportunity to create a last lament on the fickle nature of time and life. **1987 (PG) 82m/C** *GB* Anjelica Huston, Donal McCann, Marie Kean, Donal Donnelly, Dan O'Herlihy, Helen Carroll, Frank Patterson; *D:* John Huston. Academy Awards '87 Nominations: Best Adapted Screenplay, Best Costume Design; Independent Spirit Awards '88: Best Director (Huston), Best Supporting Actress (Huston); National Society of Film Critics Awards '87: Best Film. **VHS, Beta, LV $89.98** *LIV, VES, TVC* ✍✍✍½

Dead Again Branagh's first film since his brilliant debut as the director/star of "Henry V" again proves him a visionary force on and off camera. As the smart L.A. detective hired to discover the identity of a beautiful, but mute woman, he's realistic, clever, tender and cynical. He finds that he's apparently trapped in a nightmarish cycle of murder begun years before. Literate, lovely to look at, suspenseful, with a sense of humor to match its high style. **1991 (R) 107m/C** Kenneth Branagh, Emma Thompson, Andy Garcia, Lois Hall, Richard Easton, Derek Jacobi, Hanna Schygulla, Campbell Scott; *Cameos:* Robin Williams; *D:* Kenneth Branagh; *W:* Scott Frank; *M:* Patrick Doyle. **VHS, LV $19.95** *PAR, CCB* ✍✍✍½

Dead Ahead: The Exxon Valdez Disaster On March 24, 1989 the oil tanker Exxon Valdez ran aground off Alaska in Prince William Sound. The oil spill reached nearly 11 million gallons and the pollution spread over 1000 miles of Alaskan beaches, killing hundreds of thousands of animals. The film focuses on the first crucial days and portrays the inadequate precautions, incompetence, greed, and petty bureaucracy that made an appalling situation even worse. Lloyd stars as Exxon official Frank Iarossi, in charge of the official cleanup, caught between onsite confusion and corporate bungling while Heard is outraged environmentalist Dan Lawn. News and home videotapes of the actual spill are used to enhance the dramatization. Filmed in Vancouver, British Columbia. Made for cable television. *AKA:* Disaster at Valdez. **1992 (PG-13) 90m/C** Christopher Lloyd, John Heard, Rip Torn, Michael Murphy, Ken Walsh, Bob Gunton, Mark Metcalf, Paul Guilfoyle, David Morse; *D:* Paul Seed; *W:* Michael Baker; *M:* David Ferguson. **VHS $89.95** *IMP* ✍✍✍

Dead Aim A dud about Soviet spies who introduce even more drugs into New York City, ostensibly to bring about the downfall of the U.S. Obviously a completely far-fetched plot. **1987 (R) 91m/C** Ed Marinaro, Isaac Hayes, Corbin Bernsen; *D:* William Vanderkloot. **VHS, LV $89.98** *LIV, HHE* Woof!

Dead and Buried Farentino is the sheriff who can't understand why the victims of some pretty grisly murders seem to be coming back to life. Eerily suspenseful. **1981 (R) 95m/C** James Farentino, Jack Albertson, Melody Anderson, Lisa Blount, Bill Quinn, Michael Pataki; *D:* Gary Sherman. **VHS, Beta $19.98** *VES* ✍✍½

Dead as a Doorman A young writer takes a part-time post as a doorman and becomes the target of a murderous lunatic. **1985 83m/C** Bradley Whitford, Sharon Schlarth, Bruce Taylor; *D:* Gary Youngman. **VHS, Beta $69.98** *LIV, VES* ✍½

Dead Bang A frustrated cop uncovers a murderous white supremacist conspiracy in L.A. Frankenheimer's deft directorial hand shapes a somewhat conventional cop plot into an effective vehicle for Johnson. **1989 (R) 102m/C** Don Johnson, Bob Balaban, William Forsythe, Penelope Ann Miller, Tim Reid, Frank Military, Michael Higgins, Michael Jeter; *D:* John Frankenheimer. **VHS, Beta, LV, 8mm $19.98** *WAR* ✍✍½

Dead Calm A taut Australian thriller based on a novel by Charles Williams. A young married couple is yachting on the open seas when they happen upon the lone survivor of a sinking ship. They take him on board only to discover he's a homicidal maniac. Makes for some pretty suspenseful moments that somewhat make up for the weak ending. **1989 (R) 97m/C** *AU* Sam Neill, Billy Zane, Nicole Kidman; *D:* Phillip Noyce. **VHS, Beta, LV, 8mm $19.98** *WAR, FCT* ✍✍✍

Dead Certain A "Silence of the Lambs" rip-off. Dourif (again specializing in weirdos) is the jailed serial killer providing tantalizing clues to the identity of a new killer on the loose. **1992 (R) 93m/C** Brad Dourif, Francesco Quinn, Karen Russel; *W/D:* Anders Palm. **VHS $89.95** *HMD* ✍

The Dead Don't Die Unbelievable plot set in the 1930s has Hamilton as a detective trying to prove his brother was wrongly executed for murder. He ultimately clashes with the madman who wants to rule the world with an army of zombies. Perhaps if they had cast Hamilton as Master of the Zombies. Made for television. **1975 74m/C** George Hamilton, Ray Milland, Linda Cristal, Ralph Meeker, Joan Blondell, James McEachin; *D:* Curtis Harrington. **VHS, Beta $49.95** *WOV, GKK* ✍

Dead Easy Livin' ain't easy for a Sydney sleaze-club owner, his working-girl girlfriend, and a slandered cop when they're caught between machete-wielding enemy gangs (it seems somebody made the crime boss REALLY mad). The three flee in that quintessential escape vehicle—a two-ton truck—to qualify the effort as an Australian contender for greatest chase scene ever (heavy chassis category). **1982 92m/C** *AU* Scott Burgess, Rosemary Paul; *D:* Bert Deling. **VHS, Beta $59.95** *MCG* ✍✍

Dead End Sidney Kingsley play, adapted for the big screen by Lillian Hellman, traces the lives of various inhabitants of the slums on New York's Lower East Side as they try to overcome their surroundings. Gritty drama saved from melodrama status by some genuinely funny moments. Film launched the Dead End Kids. *AKA:* Cradle of Crime. **1937 92m/B** Sylvia Sidney, Joel McCrea, Humphrey Bogart, Wendy Barrie, Claire Trevor, Allen Jenkins, Marjorie Main, Leo Gorcey; *D:* William Wyler. **VHS, Beta, LV $19.98** *MGM, SUE, MLB* ✍✍✍½

Dead End City Street-wise resident of L.A. organizes fellow citizens into a vigilante force to fight the gangs for control of the city. **1988 88m/C** Dennis Cole, Greg Cummins, Christine Lunde, Robert Z'Dar, Darrell Nelson, Alena Downs; *D:* Peter Yuval. **VHS, Beta $39.95** *AIP* ✍½

Dead End Drive-In In a surreal, grim future a man is trapped at a drive-in theater-cum-government-run concentration camp, where those considered to be less than desirable members of society are incarcerated.

1986 (R) 92m/C *AU* Ned Manning, Natalie McCurray, Peter Whitford; *D:* Brian Trenchard-Smith. **VHS, Beta $19.95** *STE, NWV* ✍✍

Dead End Street Young prostitute attempts to change her self-destructive lifestyle. It's not easy. **1983 86m/C** *IS* Anat Atzman, Yehoram Gaon. **VHS, Beta $59.95** *TWE* ✍½

Dead Eyes of London Blind old German men are dying to lower their premiums in this geriatric thriller: someone (perhaps the director of the home for the blind?) is killing off the clientele for their insurance money, and a Scotland Yard inspector aims to expose the scam. Relatively early vintage Kinski, it's a remake of the eerie 1939 Lugosi vehicle, "The Human Monster" (originally titled "Dark Eyes of London"), adapted from Edgar Wallace's "The Testament of Gordon Stuart." *AKA:* Dark Eyes of London; Die Toten Augen von London. **1961 95m/B** *GE* Joachim Fuchsberger, Karin Baal, Dieter Borsche, Ady Berber, Klaus Kinski, Eddi Arent, Wolfgang Lukschy; *D:* Alfred Vohrer. **VHS $19.98** *SNC* ✍✍½

Dead for a Dollar A Colonel, a con man, and a mysterious woman team up in the Old West to search for the two hundred thousand dollars they stole from a local bank. **197? 92m/C** John Ireland, George Hilton, Piero Vida, Sandra Milo. **VHS, Beta $49.95** *UNI, MOV* ✍½

Dead Girls A rock group whose lyrics focus on suicide goes on vacation. The members find themselves stalked by a serial killer who decides to take matters out of the musicians' hands and into his own. Graphic violence. **1990 (R) 105m/C** Diana Karanikas, Angela Eads; *D:* Dennis Devine. **VHS** *HHE* ✍

Dead Heat Some acting talent and a few funny moments unfortunately don't add up to a fine film, though they do save it from being a complete woofer. In this one even the cops are zombies when one of them is resurrected from the dead to help his partner solve his murder and rid the city of the rest of the undead. **1988 (R) 86m/C** Joe Piscopo, Treat Williams, Lindsay Frost, Darren McGavin, Vincent Price, Keye Luke, Clare Kirkconnell; *D:* Mark Goldblatt. **VHS, Beta, LV $19.95** *STE, NWV* ✍½

Dead Heat on a Merry-Go-Round Coburn turns in a great performance as the ex-con who masterminds the heist of an airport safe. Intricately woven plot provides suspense and surprises. The film is also notable for the debut of Ford in a bit part (he has one line as a hotel messenger). **1966 (R) 108m/C** James Coburn, Camilla Sparv, Aldo Ray, Nina Wayne, Robert Webber, Rose Marie, Todd Armstrong, Marian Moses, Severn Darden, Harrison Ford; *D:* Bernard Girard. **VHS, Beta $69.95** *COL* ✍✍✍

Dead in the Water Brown is Charlie Deegan, a big-time lawyer with a rich wife that he'd rather see dead. Charlie and his mistress plot the perfect murder to dispose of his spouse and collect her money. When plans go awry, he ends up as a suspect for the wrong murder in this story of infidelity and greed. **1991 (PG-13) 90m/C** Bryan Brown, Teri Hatcher, Anne De Salvo, Veronica Cartwright; *D:* Bill Condon; *W:* Eleanor Gaver, Robert Seidenberg, Walter Klenhard. **VHS, Beta $79.95** *MCA* ✍½

Dead Lucky A novice tries gambling and wins a fortune, but his luck leads him into an entanglement with an assassin, a scam artist, and a beautiful woman. Based on the novel "Lake of Darkness."

1960 91m/B *GB* Vincent Ball, Betty McDowall, John Le Mesurier, Alfred Burke, Michael Ripper; **D:** Montgomery Tully. **VHS, Beta $19.98** *FCT* ⊿½

Dead Man Out Both Glover and Blades turn in exceptional performances in this thought-provoking drama. A convict on Death Row (Blades) goes insane and therefore cannot be executed. The state calls in a psychiatrist (Glover) to review the case and determine whether he can be cured so that the sentence can be carried out. Powerful and riveting morality check.
1989 87m/C Danny Glover, Ruben Blades, Tom Atkins, Larry Block, Sam Jackson, Maria Ricossa; **D:** Richard Pearce. **VHS, Beta, LV $89.99** *HBO* ⊿⊿⊿

Dead Man Walking In a post-holocaust future, half the population has been stricken with a deadly plague. Hauser is a mercenary, dying from the disease, who is hired to rescue a young woman who was kidnapped and is being held in the plague zone.
1988 (R) 90m/C Wings Hauser, Brion James, Pamela Ludwig, Sy Richardson, Leland Crooke, Jeffrey Combs; **D:** Gregory Brown. **VHS $9.98** *REP* ⊿

Dead Mate A woman marries a mortician after a whirlwind romance only to discover that, to her husband, being an undertaker is not just a job, it's a way of life.
1988 93m/C Elizabeth Mannino, David Gregory, Lawrence Bockus, Adam Wahl; **D:** Straw Weisman. **VHS, Beta $79.95** *PSM* ⊿

Dead Men Don't Die An anchorman is slain by criminals but resurrected as a shambling voodoo zombie. Few viewers notice the difference in this inoffensive but repetitious farce. The living-dead Gould appears to be having a lot of fun.
1991 (PG-13) 94m/C Elliott Gould, Melissa Anderson, Mark Moses, Philip Bruns, Jack Betts, Mabel King; **W/D:** Malcolm Marmorstein. **VHS $19.95** *ACA* ⊿½

Dead Men Don't Wear Plaid Martin is hilarious as a private detective who encounters a bizarre assortment of suspects while trying to find out the truth about a scientist's death. Ingeniously interspliced with clips from old Warner Brothers films. Features Humphrey Bogart, Bette Davis, Alan Ladd, Burt Lancaster, Ava Gardner, Barbara Stanwyck, Ray Milland and others. Its only flaw is that the joke loses momentum by the end of the film.
1982 (PG) 89m/B Steve Martin, Rachel Ward, Reni Santoni, George Gaynes, Frank McCarthy, Carl Reiner; **D:** Carl Reiner. **VHS, Beta, LV $14.95** *MCA, FCT, HMV* ⊿⊿½

Dead Men Walk A decent, albeit low budget, chiller about twin brothers (Zucco in a dual role); one a nice, well-adjusted member of society, the other a vampire who wants to suck his bro's blood. Sibling rivalry with a bite.
1943 65m/B George Zucco, Mary Carlisle, Dwight Frye, Nedrick Young, Al "Fuzzy" St. John, Dwight Frye; **D:** Sam Newfield. **VHS, Beta $14.95** *NOS, MRV, SNC* ⊿⊿

Dead of Night The template for episodic horror films, this suspense classic, set in a remote country house, follows the individual nightmares of five houseguests. Redgrave turns in a chillingly convincing performance as a ventriloquist terrorized by a demonic dummy. Not recommended for light-sleepers. Truly spine-tingling.
1945 102m/B *GB* Michael Redgrave, Sally Ann Howes, Basil Radford, Naunton Wayne, Mervyn Johns, Roland Culver, Googie Withers, Frederick Valk; **D:** Basil Dearden, Robert Hamer, Alberto

Cavalcanti, Charles Crichton. **VHS, Beta $59.99** *HBO, RXM* ⊿⊿⊿⊿

Dead of Night This trilogy features Richard Matheson's tales of the Supernatural: "Second Chance," "Bobby," and "No Such Thing As a Vampire," all served up by your hostess, Elvira.
1977 76m/C Joan Hackett, Ed Begley Jr., Patrick Macnee, Anjanette Comer; **D:** Dan Curtis. **VHS, Beta, LV $39.95** *LIV* ⊿⊿

Dead of Winter A young actress is suckered into a private screen test for a crippled old director, only to find she is actually being remodeled in the guise of a murdered woman. Edge-of-your-seat suspense as the plot twists.
1987 (R) 100m/C Mary Steenburgen, Roddy McDowall, Jan Rubes, Ken Pogue, William Russ; **D:** Arthur Penn. **VHS, Beta, LV $79.98** *FOX* ⊿⊿⊿

Dead on the Money Adequate made for TV suspenser about a woman who believes her lover plots a dire fate for her cousin. But nothing is what it seems here. Confusing, droopy in spots, but fun.
1991 92m/C Corbin Bernsen, Amanda Pays, John Glover, Eleanor Bergen, Kevin McCarthy; **D:** Mark Cullingham. **VHS, Beta $89.98** *TTC* ⊿⊿½

Dead or Alive Tex and the Texas Rangers pretend to be outlaws in order to join a gang terrorizing a town.
1941 54m/B Tex Ritter, Dave O'Brien, Guy Wilkerson, Charles King, Bud Osborne, Reed Howes; **D:** Elmer Clifton. **VHS, Beta $11.95** *GPV, RXM, VCN* ⊿½

Dead Pit Leave this one in the pit it crawled out of. Twenty years ago a mad scientist was killed as a result of horrible experiments he was conducting on mentally ill patients at an asylum. A young woman stumbles across his experiments, awakening him from the dead.
1989 (R) 90m/C Jeremy Slate, Steffen Gregory Foster; **D:** Brett Leonard. **VHS, Beta $89.95** *IMP* Woof!

Dead Poets Society An idealistic English teacher inspires a group of boys in a 1950s' prep school to pursue individuality and creative endeavor, resulting in clashes with school and parental authorities. Williams shows he can master the serious roles as well as the comic with his portrayal of the unorthodox educator. Big box office hit occasionally scripted with a heavy hand in order to elevate the message. The ensemble cast is excellent.
1989 (PG) 128m/C Robin Williams, Ethan Hawke, Robert Sean Leonard, Josh Charles, Gale Hansen, Kurtwood Smith, James Waterson, Dylan Kussman; **D:** Peter Weir. Academy Awards '89: Best Original Screenplay; Nominations: Best Actor (Williams), Best Director (Weir), Best Picture; British Academy Awards '89: Best Film; Cesar Awards '91: Best Foreign Film. **VHS, Beta, LV, 8mm $19.99** *TOU* ⊿⊿⊿½

The Dead Pool Dirty Harry Number Five features a new twist on the sports pool: a list of celebrities is distributed and bets are placed on who will be first to cross the finish line, literally. Unfortunately someone seems to be hedging their bet by offing the celebs themselves. When Harry's name appears on the list, he decides to throw the game.
1988 (R) 92m/C Clint Eastwood, Liam Neeson, Patricia Clarkson, Evan C. Kim, David Hunt, Michael Currie, Michael Goodwin; **D:** Buddy Van Horn. **VHS, Beta, LV, 8mm $19.98** *WAR, TLF* ⊿½

Dead Reckoning Bogart and Prince are two World War II veterans en route to Washington when Prince disappears. Bogart trails Prince to his Southern hometown and discovers he's been murdered. Blackmail

and more murders follow as Bogie tries to uncover the truth. Suspenseful with good performances from all, especially Bogart.
1947 100m/B Humphrey Bogart, Lizabeth Scott, Morris Carnovsky, Charles Cane, Wallace Ford, William Prince, Marvin Miller; **D:** John Cromwell. **VHS, Beta, LV $19.98** *CCB, COL* ⊿⊿⊿

Dead Reckoning A plastic surgeon and his lovely wife embark on a cruise aboard his new luxury yacht. The intrigue begins with a storm, an isolated island, and the discovery that the captain is the wife's former lover.
1989 (R) 95m/C Cliff Robertson, Susan Blakely, Rick Springfield; **D:** Robert Lewis. **VHS, LV $79.95** *MCA* ⊿½

Dead Right A black man is unjustly put into prison in the Deep South. He manages to escape in order to try and prove his innocence.
1988 111m/C Raymond St. Jacques, Dana Wynter, Kevin McCarthy, Barbara McNair. **VHS, Beta $79.95** *PSM* ⊿½

Dead Ringers A stunning, unsettling chiller, based loosely on a real case and the bestseller by Bari Wood and Jack Geasland. Irons, in an excellent dual role, is effectively disturbing as the twin gynecologists who descend into madness when they can no longer handle the fame, fortune, drugs, and women in their lives. Acutely upsetting film made all the more so due to its graphic images and basis in fact.
1988 (R) 117m/C *CA* Jeremy Irons, Genevieve Bujold, Heidi von Palleske; **D:** David Cronenberg. **VHS, Beta, LV $9.99** *CCB, MED* ⊿⊿⊿

Dead Silence Screenwriter Cliff Morgan has written a classic film noir screenplay... with the money, it seems all Cliff's problems are solved... or are they?
1990 (R) 92m/C Clete Keith, Doris Anne Soyka, Joseph Scott, Craig Fleming; **D:** Harrison Ellenshaw. **VHS $89.95** *SVS* ⊿

Dead Sleep A nurse discovers that comatose patients at a private clinic have been used as guinea pigs by an overzealous doctor. This minor-league chiller from Down Under is said to have been inspired by an actual medical scandal.
1991 (R) 95m/C Linda Blair, Tony Bonner; **D:** Alec Mills. **VHS $89.98** *VES* ⊿⊿

Dead Solid Perfect Quaid stars as a golf pro whose life on the PGA tour is handicapped by his taste for scotch and his eye for the ladies. Based on the book by Dan Jenkins.
1988 97m/C Randy Quaid, Kathryn Harrold, Jack Warden, Larry Riley, Brett Cullen, Corinne Bohrer; **W/D:** Bobby Roth; **W:** Dan Jenkins. **VHS, Beta $79.99** *WAR, BTV* ⊿⊿

Dead Space Dead space lay between the ears of whoever thought we needed this remake of 1982's "Forbidden World." At a lab on a hostile planet an experimental vaccine mutates into a prickly puppet monster who menaces the medicos. Needed: a vaccine against cheapo "Alien" ripoffs.
1990 (R) 72m/C Marc Singer, Laura Tate, Bryan Cranston, Judith Chapman; **D:** Fred Gallo. **VHS, LV $79.95** *COL* ⊿

Dead Women in Lingerie When beautiful models are turning up dead, a detective is called in to solve the mystery. Perhaps they committed suicide to avoid being in this picture any longer than necessary. Title sounds like the next episode of "Geraldo."
1990 (R) 87m/C June Lockhart, Lyle Waggoner, John Romo, Jerry Orbach, Maura Tierney; **D:** Erika Fox. **VHS $79.98** *MNC* Woof!

Dead Wrong Undercover agent falls in love with the drug smuggler she's supposed to bring to justice.
1983 93m/C Britt Ekland, Winston Rekert, Jackson Davies. VHS, Beta $49.95 MED ℐ½

Dead Wrong: The John Evans Story The true story of Evans' life of crime and eventual execution in the electric chair, using footage of an interview taped before his death.
1984 45m/C VHS, 3/4U AFC ℐ½

Dead Zone A man gains extraordinary psychic powers following a near-fatal accident. He is forced to decide between seeking absolute seclusion in order to escape his frightening visions, or using his "gift" to save mankind from impending evil. A good adaptation of the Stephen King thriller.
1983 (R) 104m/C Christopher Walken, Brooke Adams, Tom Skerritt, Martin Sheen, Herbert Lom, Anthony Zerbe, Colleen Dewhurst; *D:* David Cronenberg. VHS, Beta, LV $14.95 PAR ℐℐℐ

Deadbolt Divorced med student Marty Hiller (Bateman) desperately needs a roommate and Alec Danz (Baldwin) seems perfect. Soon they're sharing more than the rent, until Danz kills her friends and imprisons her in the apartment (equipped of course with soundproof walls and bulletproof glass—one wonders why she doesn't bang on the floor to gain attention.) Would be thriller attempts to capitalize on the roommate from hell theme that started with "Single White Female," but isn't as effective. Went straight to video and showed up on network TV several months later.
1992 (R) 95m/C Justine Bateman, Adam Baldwin, Michelle Scarabelli, Chris Mulkey, Cyndi Pass, Isabelle Truchon, Douglas Jackson. VHS, LV $89.95 NLC ℐℐ

The Deadliest Art: The Best of the Martial Arts Films The masters of bare-handed combat team up in this look at the best of the martial arts movies. Action packed.
1990 ?m/C Yuen Biao, Jackie Chan, Samo Hung, Kareem Abdul-Jabbar, Sho Kosugi, Bruce Lee, Angela Mao, Cynthia Rothrock; *W/D:* Sandra Weintraub. VHS $89.98 FXV ℐℐ

Deadline Journalist must find out the truth behind a minor earthquake in Australia.
1981 94m/C Barry Newman, Trisha Noble, Bill Kerr. VHS, Beta $7.50 WOV ℐ½

Deadline Eerie tale of horror writer's life as it begins to reflect his latest story in this play on the "truth is stranger than fiction" adage.
1982 85m/C Stephen Young, Sharon Masters, Cindy Hinds, Phillip Leonard; *D:* Mario Azzopardi. VHS, Beta $42.95 PGN ℐℐ

Deadline Walken is a cynical American journalist assigned to cover the warring factions in Beirut. He finds himself becoming more and more involved in the events he's supposed to report when he falls in love with a German nurse who is aiding the rebel forces. Tense, though sometimes murky drama.
1987 (R) 110m/C GE Christopher Walken, Hywel Bennett, Marita Marschall; *D:* Nathaniel Gutman. VHS, Beta, LV NO ℐℐ

Deadline Assault Kate McSweeny is a beautiful young reporter who is brutally attacked and raped by a gang of savage youths. Kate must now face the unsettling facts; they're still on the streets and they may be stalking her again. *AKA:* Act of Violence.

1990 (R) 90m/C Elizabeth Montgomery, James Sloyan, Sean Frye, Biff McGuire, Michael Goodwin, Linden Chiles; *D:* Paul Wendkos. VHS ELV, HHE ℐ½

Deadline at Dawn Hayward is an aspiring actress who tries to help a sailor (Williams) prove that he is innocent of murder. Screenplay by Clifford Odets was based on a novel by Cornell Woolrich.
1946 82m/B Bill Williams, Susan Hayward, Lola Lane, Paul Lukas, Joseph Calleia; *D:* Harold Clurman. VHS, Beta $19.98 RKO, MLB, TTC ℐℐ

Deadline Auto Theft A fun lovin' guy drives fast cars and meets beautiful women. Nudge, nudge, wink, wink.
1983 90m/C H.B. Halicki, Hoyt Axton, Marion Busia, George Cole, Judi Gibbs, Lang Jeffries Jr.; *D:* H.B. Halicki. VHS, Beta $79.95 IMP ℐ

Deadlock Hauer and Rogers star as inmates in a prison of the future. This prison has no walls, no fences and no guards - and no one EVER escapes. Each prisoner wears an explosive collar that is tuned to the same frequency as one of the other prisoner's. Should the two separate by more than 100 yards, the collars explode. When Rogers convinces Hauer that they are on the same frequency, the two escape. Trouble is, they are being pursued not only by the police, but by Hauer's former partners in crime as well. Can the two find the freedom they are looking for - without losing their heads? Originally made for cable television.
1991 (R) 103m/C Rutger Hauer, Mimi Rogers, Joan Chen, James Remar; *D:* Lewis Teague. VHS, Beta, LV $19.98 VTR, FXV, MED ℐℐ½

Deadly Alliance Two impecunious filmmakers (who happen to be hunks) and a babe (for good measure) poke their noses in where they're not wanted (in the shady business of an international oil cartel). "Deadly Dull" would be a more appropriate moniker.
1978 90m/C Kathleen Arc, Tony de Fonte, Michele Marsh, Walter Prince; *D:* Paul S. Parco. VHS, Beta NO ℐ

The Deadly and the Beautiful Dr. Tsu sends her "deadly but beautiful" task force to kidnap the world's prime male athletes for use in her private business enterprise. *AKA:* Wonder Women.
1973 (PG) 82m/C PH Nancy Kwan, Ross Hagen, Maria de Aragon, Roberta Collins, Tony Lorea, Sid Haig, Vic Diaz, Shirley Washington, Gale Hansen; *D:* Robert Vincent O'Neil. VHS, Beta $29.95 MED ℐ

Deadly Bet A made-for-video saga of a kickboxer who loses his money and his girl when he loses the big match. Lots of fight sequences as he works to regain his career.
1991 (R) 92m/C Jeff Wincott, Charlene Tilton, Steven Leigh; *D:* Richard W. Munchkin. VHS, LV $29.95 PMH ℐ½

Deadly Blessing A young, recently widowed woman is visited in her rural Pennsylvania home by some friends from the city. Something's not quite right about this country life and they become especially suspicious after meeting their friend's very religious in-laws.
1981 (R) 104m/C Maren Jensen, Susan Buckner, Sharon Stone, Ernest Borgnine, Karen Jensen, Jeff East, Lisa Hartman, Lois Nettleton; *D:* Wes Craven. VHS, Beta $24.98 SUE ℐℐ

Deadly Breed Beware your friendly neighborhood cop. A band of white supremacists has infiltrated the local police force, intent on causing violence, not keeping the peace.

1989 90m/C William Smith, Addison Randall, Blake Bahner, Joe Vance; *D:* Charles Kanganis. VHS $29.95 PMH ℐ½

Deadly Business The true story of a man who turned from crime to become a government informant. As a garbage man, he works to stop the illegal dumping of chemicals in New Jersey. An interesting made-for-televison drama.
1986 100m/C Alan Arkin, Armand Assante, Michael Learned, Jon Polito, George Morfogen, James Rebhorn; *D:* John Korty. VHS WOV ℐℐℐ

Deadly Business Hard-nosed collection man for a lethal loan shark finds he is the one with the debt to pay as he's stalked through the city street by hit men.
19?? 95m/C David Peterson, John Lazarus, Leo Gabrowski. VHS, Beta NO ℐ½

Deadly Commando When terrorists begin kidnapping diplomats, only the Deadly Commandos have a chance of saving them.
19?? 88m/C VHS, Beta MOV ℐ

Deadly Companions Keith is an ex-gunslinger who agrees to escort O'Hara through Apache territory in order to make up for inadvertently killing her son. Director Peckinpah's first feature film.
1961 90m/C Maureen O'Hara, Brian Keith, Chill Wills, Steve Cochran; *D:* Sam Peckinpah. VHS, Beta, LV $19.95 STE, NWV ℐℐ½

Deadly Conspiracy Saxon plays a corrupt businessman who kills an employee about to blow the whistle on his shady dealings. Hauser is the good cop, with the bad personal life, who makes it his mission to bring Saxon to justice. The prolific Hauser brings some fast-paced action to this routine story.
1991 92m/C Wings Hauser, John Saxon, Frances Fisher, Patti D'Arbanville, Margaux Hemingway, Greg Mullavey; *D:* Paul Leder. VHS $89.95 MNC ℐℐ

Deadly Dancer It's up to a lone cop to find out who's been offing the hoofers in L.A.
1990 88m/C Adolfo "Shabba Doo" Quinones, Smith Wordes, Walter W. Cox, Steve Jonson; *D:* Kimberly Casey. VHS $79.95 AIP ℐ½

Deadly Darling Muddled, completely awful tale centering on two different rapes with no discernible attempt made to link the two or establish a plot.
1985 91m/C Fonda Lynn, Warren Chan, Bernard Tsui, Cherry Kwok; *D:* Karen Young. VHS, Beta $49.95 UNI Woof!

Deadly Desire Seduced by the beautiful Harrold, security guard Scalia finds himself putting his life on the line when Harrold asks him to help cheat her husband out of millions in an insurance scam. Trouble ensues when they try to outsmart Harrold's powerful entrepreneurial husband.
1991 (R) 93m/C Jack Scalia, Kathryn Harrold, Will Patton, Joe Santos; *D:* Charles Correll. VHS PAR, HHE ℐℐ

Deadly Diamonds Cop is on the trail of diamond smugglers who leave a trail of death in their wake.
1991 90m/C Dan Haggerty, Troy Donahue, Eli Rich, Kathleen Kane, Kenna Grob, Nicholas Mercer; *D:* Thomas Atcheson; *W:* Ron Herbst. VHS, Beta GNS, PHX, HHT ℐ½

Deadly Dreams A young boy's parents are killed by a maniac who then commits suicide. Years later, he dreams that he is being stalked anew by the same killer. Nightmares turn into reality in this decent horror/suspense flick.
1988 (R) 79m/C Mitchell Anderson, Xander Berkeley, Thom Babbes, Juliette Cummins; *D:* Kristine Peterson. VHS, Beta, LV NO ℐℐ

Deadly Embrace Sordid tale of wealthy man (Vincent) who wants to get rid of his wife—permanently. He enlists the aid of a beautiful young coed. Soft-core sleaze with nary a redeemable quality.
1988 82m/C Jan-Michael Vincent, Jack Carter, Ty Randolph, Linnea Quigley, Michelle Bauer, Ken Abraham; *D:* Ellen Cabot. **VHS, Beta** $79.95 *PSM Woof!*

Deadly Encounter Thrilling actioner in which Hagman portrays a helicopter pilot—a former war ace—who allows an old flame to talk him into helping her escape from the mobsters on her trail. Terrific edge-of-your-seat aerial action.
1972 90m/C Larry Hagman, Susan Anspach, Michael C. Goetz, James Gammon; *D:* William A. Graham. **VHS, Beta** *NO ♔♔♔*

Deadly Encounter Lacking any redeemable qualities, this film shows just how low some people go. Merrill hosts a dinner to garner financial support for a budding playwright, but what we get is a look at the lifestyles of the rich and perverse.
1978 (R) 90m/C Dina Merrill, Carl Betz, Leon Ames, Vicki Powers, Mark Rasmussen, Susan Logan; *D:* R. John Hugh. **VHS, Beta** $19.95 *NEG Woof!*

Deadly Eyes After eating grain laced with steroids a group of rats grows to mammoth proportions (dachshunds in rat drag were used). Their appetites grow accordingly—now they crave humans. Amid the nibbling by the giant rat-dogs, romance blooms. Silly adaptation by Charles Eglee of Frank Herbert's "The Rats." *AKA:* The Rats.
1982 (R) 93m/C Sam Groom, Sara Botsford, Scatman Crothers, Lisa Langlois, Cec Linder; *D:* Robert Clouse. **VHS, Beta** $19.98 *WAR ♔ ½*

Deadly Fieldtrip Four female students and their teacher are abducted by a biker gang and held hostage on a deserted farm.
1974 91m/C Zalman King, Brenda Fogarty, Robert Porter; *D:* Earl Barton. **VHS, Beta** $79.95 *MNC ♔ ½*

Deadly Force Ex-cop turned private detective stalks a killer in Los Angeles who has left an "X" carved in the forehead of each of his 17 victims. If he had just signed his name, things could have been tidied up much earlier.
1983 (R) 95m/C Wings Hauser, Joyce Ingalls, Paul Shenar, Al Ruscio, Arlen Dean Snyder, Lincoln Kilpatrick; *D:* Paul Aaron. **VHS, Beta** $14.98 *SUE, NLC ♔ ½*

Deadly Friend A well-meaning horror flick? That's what Wes Craven has tried to provide for us. When the girlfriend of a lonely teenage genius is accidentally killed, he decides to insert his robot's "brain" in her body, though the results aren't entirely successful. The same can be said for the film which was based on Diana Henstell's more effective novel "Friend."
1986 (R) 91m/C Matthew Laborteaux, Kristy Swanson, Michael Sharrett, Anne Twomey, Richard Marcus, Anne Ramsey; *D:* Wes Craven. **VHS, Beta, LV** $14.95 *WAR ♔♔*

Deadly Game A reunion at a remote hotel leads to an ordeal of psychological terror and murderous intrigue.
1982 (R) 108m/C George Segal, Robert Morley, Trevor Howard, Emlyn Williams, Alan Webb; *D:* George Schaefer. **VHS, Beta** $59.98 *SUE ♔♔*

Deadly Game Much-maligned and preyed-upon witness is protected by a weary cop, who speaks with the use of English subtitles.
1983 90m/C GE Mel Ferrer, Helmut Berger, Barbara Sukowa; *D:* Karoly Makk, Dieter Geissler. **VHS, Beta** $39.95 *VCD, GLV ♔ ½*

The Deadly Game East-West intrigue prior to the fall of the Berlin Wall finds a Western operative returning from a dangerous mission, only to walk into a trap set by his own side.
1987? 104m/C GB David Hemmings. **VHS** $59.99 *HBO, FCT, TAM ♔♔*

Deadly Game Horribly burned, a vengeful millionaire invites seven people he believes have wronged him to spend the weekend on his isolated island. He has promised them each a reward for their good deeds, but instead plans to have a big-game hunt with his "guests" as the prey.
1991 (R) 93m/C Roddy McDowall, Jenny Seagrove, Marc Singer, Michael Beck; *D:* Tom Wright. **VHS, Beta** *PAR ♔ ½*

Deadly Games Ineffective plot involving a series of murders in a small town is seemingly played out by the principal characters in a horror board game. Film is saved from being a complete waste by Groom's good performance as the local cop.
1980 94m/C Sam Groom, Jo Ann Harris, Steve Railsback, Dick Butkus, June Lockhart, Colleen Camp; *D:* Scott Mansfield. **VHS, Beta** $39.95 *MON ♔ ½*

Deadly Harvest Scientists' worst fears have been realized—due to ecological abuse and over-development of the land, food has become extremely scarce. This in turn has caused people to become a bit savage. They are particularly nasty to a farmer and his family. Not a bad plot, but a poorly acted film.
1972 (PG) 86m/C Clint Walker, Nehemiah Persoff, Kim Cattrall, David G. Brown, Gary Davies; *D:* Timothy Bond. **VHS, Beta** $19.95 *STE, NWV ♔*

Deadly Hero Gripping tale of a young woman who becomes the prey of a New York City cop after questioning the brutal methods he employed while saving her from being assaulted, ultimately killing her attacker. Williams makes film debut in this chilling suspenser.
1975 (R) 102m/C Don Murray, James Earl Jones, Diahn Williams, Lilia Skala, Conchata Ferrell, George S. Irving, Treat Williams, Josh Mostel; *D:* Ivan Nagy. **VHS, Beta** $39.98 *SUE ♔♔♔*

Deadly Illusion Williams is a private detective who manages to get himself tangled in a complex web of intrigue and winds up framed for murder. Decent outing for all. *AKA:* Love You to Death.
1987 (R) 95m/C Billy Dee Williams, Morgan Fairchild, Vanity, John Beck, Joe Cortese; *D:* William Tannen, Larry Cohen; *W:* Larry Cohen. **VHS, Beta, LV** $79.95 *COL ♔♔*

Deadly Impact Las Vegas casinos are targeted for rip-off by means of a computer. Svenson and Williamson give good performances, but that's not enough to save this one.
1984 90m/C IT Bo Svenson, Fred Williamson, Marcia Clingan, John Morghen, Vincent Conti; *D:* Larry Ludman. **VHS, Beta** $29.98 *LIV, VES ♔ ½*

Deadly Innocence A shy, lonely girl works at an isolated gas station. After her father's death, she takes in a boarder—a mysterious woman being chased by her past.
1988 (R) 90m/C Mary Crosby, Andrew Stevens, Amanda Wyss; *D:* John D. Patterson, Hugh Parks. **VHS** *NO ♔ ½*

Deadly Intent The widow of a murdered archeologist becomes the target of fortune hunters when they try to get their hands on the priceless jewel her husband brought back from a dig.

1988 83m/C Lisa Eilbacher, Steve Railsback, Maud Adams, Lance Henriksen, Fred Williamson, Persis Khambatta; *D:* Nigel Dick. **VHS** $29.95 *FRH ♔♔*

Deadly Intruder Quiet vacation spot is being terrorized by an escapee from a mental institution. So much for a little R and R.
1984 86m/C Chris Holder, Molly Creek. **VHS, Beta** $69.99 *HBO ♔ ½*

Deadly Kick A kick-boxer generously demonstrates his kicking abilities to all.
1986 93m/C VHS, Beta $19.95 *UHV ♔ ½*

The Deadly Mantis A gigantic praying mantis lies in a million-year-old sleep in the frozen reaches of the Arctic. Then a volcanic eruption releases the critter and the flying beastie does it's destructive best on Washington, DC and New York City until the military can gas it into oblivion. Typically silly fifties sci-fi with decent special effects. *AKA:* The Incredible Praying Mantis.
1957 79m/B Craig Stevens, William Hopper, Alix Talton, Pat Conway, Donald Randolph; *D:* Nathan Juran; *W:* Martin Berkeley. **VHS** $14.98 *MCA ♔ ½*

Deadly Matrimony A womanizing mob lawyer (Williams) murders the wife who wants to leave him and dumps her body in a canal to make it seem she's disappeared. When the body is accidentally recovered, tough-but-honest Chicago cop John Reed (Dennehy) works to put the lawyer away. Only the lawyer and his mob connections have a significant number of the police force on the payroll and Jack's investigation may cost him more than his pension. Okay crime-drama with Dennehy and Williams always worth watching. Based on a true story. Made for television.
1992 ?m/C Brian Dennehy, Treat Williams, Embeth Davidtz, Susan Ruttan, John M. Jackson, Lisa Eilbacher, Terry Kinney, George Morfogen. *♔♔ ½*

Deadly Mission Five soldiers in World War II France are convicted of crimes against the Army, only to escape from lock-up and become focal points in a decisive battle.
1978 (R) 99m/C Bo Svenson, Peter Hooten, Fred Williamson. **VHS, Beta** $69.98 *LIV ♔ ½*

Deadly Neighbor New neighbor moves in, dead neighborhood housewives move out. Another neighbor becomes suspicious and investigates.
1991 90m/C Don Leifert, George Stover, Lydia Laurans; *D:* Donald M. Dohler. **VHS** $59.95 *UHV ♔♔*

Deadly Obsession A disfigured lunatic stalks a young co-ed hoping to extort $1 million from the wealthy dean of the school.
1988 (R) 93m/C Jeffrey R. Iorio; *D:* Jeno Hodl. **VHS** $14.98 *REP, FCT ♔ ½*

Deadly Passion A James Cain-like thriller about a private eye getting carnally involved with a beautiful and treacherous woman who is manipulating her late husband's estate through murder and double-crossing.
1985 (R) 100m/C SA Brent Huff, Ingrid Boulting, Harrison Coburn, Lynn Maree; *D:* Larry Larson. **VHS, Beta** $79.98 *LIV ♔ ½*

Deadly Possession A college student plays amateur detective when she tries to clear her ex-husband's name after he is accused of the horrible murder of a fellow student.
1988 99m/C AU Penny Cook, Anna-Maria Winchester, Liddy Clark, Olivia Hamnett; *D:* Craig Lahiff. **VHS, Beta, LV** $79.98 *LIV, VES ♔♔*

D

Deadly Prey Prior is up against a fully outfitted army of bloodthirsty mercenaries who are using innocent people as "live targets" at their secret bootcamp. Plot lifted from "The Most Dangerous Game" has more than its share of gruesome violence.
1987 (R) 87m/C Cameron Mitchell, Troy Donahue, Ted Prior, Fritz Matthews; **W/D:** David A. Prior. **VHS, Beta** $79.95 *SVS Woof!*

Deadly Reactor In a post-nuclear future a lone preacher turns into an armed vigilante to protect the people of a town being terrorized by a vicious motorcycle gang.
1989 88m/C David Heavener, Stuart Whitman, Darwyn Swalve, Allyson Davis; **D:** David Heavener. **VHS, Beta** *AIP ℐℐ*

Deadly Recruits The Russians did it! The Russians did it! Stamp is convinced that the downfall of several top students at Oxford, amid scandal and rumor, is due to a KGB conspiracy.
1986 92m/C *GB* Terence Stamp, Michael Culver, Carmen Du Sautoy, Robin Sachs; **D:** Roger Tucker. **VHS, Beta** $79.95 *WWV ℐ½*

Deadly Revenge Action-adventure pic with not much adventure and even less action. Small-town reporter finds himself up against a mob boss when he takes over the nightclub business of a friend killed by the mobsters. Dubbed.
1983 (R) 90m/C *IT* Rodolfo Ranni, Julio de Grazia, Silvia Montanari, Fred Commoner; **D:** Juan Carlos Sesanzo. **VHS, Beta** $59.95 *UNI ℐ*

Deadly Rivals Quirky tale of a youngster who, in order to deal with his jealousy, plots against the man his mother is going to marry. *AKA:* Rivals.
1972 (R) 103m/C Joan Hackett, Robert Klein, Scott Jacoby; **D:** Krishna Shah. **VHS, Beta** *NO ℐℐ*

Deadly Rivals Stevens plays a laser specialist in Miami for a top-secret weapons conference. A beauty takes a interest in him but then she's first accused of being a spy and then mistaken for a courier in the pay of a ruthless crime boss. Can Stevens find the truth?
1992 (R) 93m/C Andrew Stevens, Cela Wise, Joseph Bologna, Margaux Hemingway, Richard Roundtree, Francesco Quinn, Randi Ingerman; **D:** James Dodson; **W:** Redge Mahaffey; **M:** Ashley Irwin. **VHS, LV** *MCA ℐ*

Deadly Sanctuary Censors stopped production of this film several times. The Marquis de Sade's writings provided the inspiration (though there's nothing inspired about it) for this tale of two recently orphaned young women who get caught up in prostitution, an S&M club, and murder.
1968 92m/C Jack Palance, Mercedes McCambridge, Sylva Koscina, Klaus Kinski, Akim Tamiroff, Romina Power; **D:** Jess (Jesus) Franco. **VHS, Beta** $39.95 *MON Woof!*

Deadly Spygames A special agent for the United States Special Operations Bureau finds himself in deep trouble.
1989 ?m/C Troy Donahue, Tippi Hedren; **W/D:** Jack M. Sell. **VHS** $59.95 *UNI Woof!*

Deadly Sting Silva devises an intricate scheme to gain revenge on the men who cheated him out of his share of a gold bullion heist.
1982 90m/C *FR* Henry Silva, Philip Clay, Andre Pousse; **D:** Jean-Claude Roy. **VHS, Beta** *NO ℐ½*

Deadly Stranger Fluegel's talents could have been put to much better use than as the selfish mistress of a plantation owner who is taking advantage of the migrant workers toiling on his land. Moore is a drifter and hired hand who rallies the workers to stand up to the owner. *AKA:* Border Heat.
1988 93m/C Darlanne Fluegel, Michael J. Moore, John Vernon, Ted White; **D:** Max Kleven. **VHS** *MCG ℐ*

Deadly Strangers Two people meet up on the road and decide to share a ride. We discover that one of them is an insane killer who's escaped from a mental institution. Suspense builds nicely, but the ending is flawed.
1982 89m/C *GB* Hayley Mills, Simon Ward, Sterling Hayden, Ken Hutchison; **D:** Sidney Hayers. **VHS, Beta** *PGN ℐℐ*

Deadly Strike Lee leads a martial arts team to derring-do. A challenge for Lee, but not for the viewer.
1981 92m/C Bruce Lee. **VHS, Beta** $29.99 *BFV, MRV ℐ½*

Deadly Sunday A family's weekly Sunday drive turns terrifying when desperate jewel thieves detour them and hold them hostage.
1982 85m/C Dennis Ely, Henry Sanders, Gylian Roland, Douglas Alexander; **D:** Donald M. Jones. **VHS, Beta** $59.98 *LIV ℐ½*

Deadly Surveillance Two tough policemen investigate a series of drug-related murders and stake out a possible suspect—a beautiful woman who's the lover of one of the lawmen. Tension in this Canadian-made cop opera evaporates in the third act for a standard buddy-buddy action finale. Made for television.
1991 (R) 92m/C Michael Ironside, Christopher Bondy, Susan Almgren, Vlasta Vrana, David Carradine; **D:** Paul Ziller. **VHS** $89.98 *REP ℐℐ*

Deadly Thief A former jewel thief comes out of retirement to challenge those who are now tops in the profession to try and steal the world's most precious ruby from him. Of course all they have to lose is their lives. What could have been an exciting adventure is made curiously boring. *AKA:* Shalimar.
1978 90m/C *IN* Rex Harrison, John Saxon, Sylvia Miles, Dharmendra, Zenat Aman, Shammi Kapoor; **D:** Krishna Shah. **VHS, Beta** $49.95 *PSM ℐℐ*

The Deadly Trackers If gorey oaters are your thing, this one's definitely for you; if not, make tracks. Harris plays a spiteful sheriff who heads south of the border to get his pound of flesh from the outlaws who slew his family in a bank robbery. Overlong revenge-o-rama based on Samuel Fuller's short story, "Riata"; might have been bearable if Fuller hadn't been bumped from the director's chair (as it is, he and other contributors refused to be listed in the credits).
1973 (PG) 104m/C Richard Harris, Rod Taylor, Al Lettieri, Neville Brand, William Smith, Paul Benjamin, Pedro Armendariz Jr.; **D:** Barry Shear. **VHS, LV** $59.95 *WAR, PIA, FCT ℐ*

The Deadly Trap Confusing thriller that couldn't. Dunaway is the mentally unstable wife of an ex-spy. His former employers have targeted him with plans to use her and her fragile state-of-mind to their advantage. *AKA:* Death Scream.
1971 (PG) 96m/C *FR IT* Faye Dunaway, Frank Langella, Barbara Parkins, Maurice Ronet; **D:** Rene Clement. **VHS** *FCT ℐ*

Deadly Twins After being beaten and gang-raped, twin sister singers are out to seek revenge. Nothing new here; don't waste your time.
1985 87m/C Audrey Landers, Judy Landers, Ellie Russell, Wayne Allison; **D:** Joe Oaks. **VHS, Beta** $79.95 *PSM Woof!*

Deadly Vengeance It's strictly low budget as the mob kills Jones's boyfriend, forcing her to mount a vengeful but inexpensive offensive against the crime syndicate's bigwigs.
1981 84m/C Grace Jones, Alan Marlowe, Arthur Roberts. **VHS, Beta** *NO ℐ*

Deadly Weapon It's a bit of nerdish wish fulfillment when 15-year-old geek Eastman finds a secret anti-matter weapon conveniently lost by the military in an Arizona stream. You won't like the kid any more than you'll like the story of this low rent boy-gets-back-at-bullies sci fi fiasco.
1988 (PG-13) 89m/C Rodney Eastman, Gary Frank, Michael Horse, Ed Nelson, Kim Walker; **D:** Michael Miner. **VHS** $79.95 *TWE, HHE ℐ*

Deadly Weapons Chesty Morgan, she of the 73-inch bustline, takes on the mob using only her God-given abilities. One of Joe Bob Briggs' "Sleaziest Movies in the History of the World" series, and he is welcome to it.
1970 (R) 90m/C Chesty Morgan, Harry Reems; **D:** Doris Wishman. **VHS** *NO ℐ*

Deadman's Curve Decent bio pic detailing the lives of Jan Berry and Dean Torrence who, as Jan and Dean, started the surf music wave only to wipe out after an almost-fatal car wreck. Shows how they deal with and recover from the tragedy. Made for television.
1978 100m/C Richard Hatch, Bruce Davison, Pamela Bellwood, Susan Sullivan, Dick Clark, Wolfman Jack; **D:** Richard Compton. **VHS** $59.95 *GEM ℐℐ*

Deadtime Stories Mother Goose it's not. Fairy tales "Little Red Riding Hood" and "Goldilocks and the Three Bears," among others, are presented like you've never before seen them—as low-budget horror tales.
1986 93m/C Michael Mesmer, Brian DePersia, Scott Valentine, Phyllis Craig, Melissa Leo, Nicole Picard; **D:** Jeffrey Delman. **VHS, Beta, LV** *NO ℐ½*

Deadwood In the untamed West, a young cowboy is mistaken for the notorious Billy the Kid. Cinematography by Vilmos Zsigmond.
1965 100m/C Arch Hall Jr., Jack Lester, Melissa Morgan, Robert Dix; **D:** James Landis. **VHS, Beta** $29.95 *RHI, FCT ℐ½*

Deadwood Pass Below-standard fare has Tyler rescuing Monti more times than seems reasonable. Monti was once an all-around helper to W.C. Fields.
1933 62m/B Tom Tyler, Alice Dahl, Wally Wales, Buffalo Bill Jr., Lafe McKee, Bud Osborne, Charles "Slim" Whitaker, Charlotte (Carlotta) Monti; **D:** J.P. McGowan. **VHS** $19.95 *DVT, HEG ℐ*

Deal of the Century A first-rate hustler and his cohorts sell second-rate weapons to third-world nations; unfortunately, their latest deal threatens to blow up in their faces—literally.
1983 (PG) 99m/C Chevy Chase, Sigourney Weaver, Gregory Hines, Richard Libertini, Wallace Shawn; **D:** William Friedkin. **VHS, Beta, LV** $19.98 *WAR ℐ*

Dealers Two money-hungry stock traders mix business and pleasure, then set their sights on one final all or nothing score.
1989 (R) 92m/C *GB* Rebecca DeMornay, Paul McGann, Derrick O'Connor; **D:** Colin Bucksey. **VHS, Beta, LV** $29.95 *ACA, IME ℐ½*

Dear America: Letters Home from Vietnam Acclaimed documentary featuring pictures and film of the war with voice-overs by dozens of Hollywood stars reading the words of American GIs. Initially made for cable television.

1988 (PG) 84m/C D: Bill Couturie. VHS, Beta, 3/4U $89.98 HBO, AMB ♫♫♫½

Dear Boys A stylized film of sexual fantasies and romance between a moody writer and a carefree young man who relentlessly pursues excitement. Based on the novel by Gerald Reve.
1980 90m/C NL Hugo Netsers, Hans Dagelet, Bill Van Dijk, Albert Mol; D: Paul de Lussanet. VHS $69.95 FCT ♫♫

Dear Brigitte A young American kid ("Lost in Space" tyke Mumy) writes a love letter to Brigitte Bardot and travels to Paris to find and meet her in person.
1965 100m/C James Stewart, Billy Mumy, Glynis Johns, Fabian, Cindy Carol, John Williams, Jack Kruschen, Brigitte Bardot, Ed Wynn, Alice Pearce; D: Henry Koster. VHS, Beta $19.98 FOX ♫½

Dear Dead Delilah Moorehead is Delilah, the matriarch of a southern family, who is on her deathbed. Her heirs are fighting to the bitter—and bloody—end to be the first to find Delilah's money, buried somewhere on her land.
1972 90m/C Agnes Moorehead, Will Geer, Michael Ansara, Patricia Carmichael, Dennis Patrick; D: John Farris. VHS, Beta $59.98 SUE ♫½

Dear Detective Vaccaro is the head of the police homicide unit who is trying to track down the killer of several politicians. In the midst of her investigation, she falls for an old friend, a professor of Greek language. Made for television and based on a French television series. AKA: Dear Inspector; Tendre Poulet.
1978 90m/C Brenda Vaccaro, Arlen Dean Snyder, Michael MacRae, John Dennis Johnston, Jack Ging, Stephen McNally, M. Emmet Walsh, Constance Forslund, R.G. Armstrong; D: Dean Hargrove. VHS NO ♫

Dear Murderer A husband suspects his wife of having an affair, and devises an ingenious, if complicated, trap for her. Inspired performances from the leads, but the plot is grim and confusing.
1947 94m/B GB Eric Portman, Greta Gynt, Dennis Price, Jack Warner, Maxwell Reed, Hazel Court, Andrew Crawford, Jane Hylton; D: Arthur Crabtree. VHS, Beta $16.95 SNC ♫♫

Dear Wife Comedy about those ties that bind. Even though her father is runnning for reelection to the State Senate, Freeman wants her brother-in-law (Holden) to run against him. Sequel to "Dear Ruth."
1949 88m/B William Holden, Joan Caulfield, Edward Arnold, Billy DeWolfe, Mona Freeman; D: Richard Haydn. VHS, Beta $19.95 KRT ♫♫½

Death at Love House A screen writer becomes obsessed when he is hired to write the life story of a long dead silent movie queen. Filmed at the Harold Lloyd estate. Made for television.
1975 74m/C Robert Wagner, Kate Jackson, Sylvia Sidney, Joan Blondell, John Carradine; D: E.W. Swackhamer. VHS, Beta $59.95 PSM ♫½

Death Be Not Proud Based on the book by John Gunther detailing the valiant battle fought by his son against the brain tumor that took his life at the age of 17. Wonderfully acted by the three principals, especially Alexander, this film leaves us feeling hopeful despite its subject. Made for television.
1975 74m/C Arthur Hill, Robby Benson, Jane Alexander, Linden Chiles, Wendy Phillips; D: Donald Wrye. VHS, Beta LCA ♫♫♫

Death Beach Karate and judo versus Chinese martial arts. A group of Japanese hoodlums invade a Chinese village in search of a magical herb.
198? 83m/C Chen Kuan-Tai, Chen Sing. VHS, Beta $59.95 SVS ♫½

Death Becomes Her Aging actress Madeline Ashton (Streep) will do anything to stay young and beautiful, especially when her childhood rival Helen Sharp (Hawn) shows up, 200 pounds lighter and out to revenge the loss of her fiance (Willis), now Ashton's husband. She consumes a potion that stops the aging process (and keeps her alive forever), and when her henpecked husband pushes her down the stairs, she becomes part of the living dead. Turns out Hawn has also taken the potion, and the two women are destined to spend the rest of eternity together—that is if their dead bodies don't rot too quickly. Watch for the hilarious party filled with dead celebrities (Elvis, Marilyn Monroe, Andy Warhol, James Dean, Jim Morrison, etc.) who all look as good as the day they died. Great special effects and fun performances by Streep and Hawn playing their glamour-girl roles to the hilt add merit to this biting commentary on Hollywood's obsession with beauty and youth.
1992 (PG-13) 105m/C Meryl Streep, Bruce Willis, Goldie Hawn, Isabella Rossellini, Ian Ogilvy, Adam Storke, Nancy Fish, Sydney Pollack; Cameos: Fabio Lanzoni; D: Robert Zemeckis; W: Martin Donovan, David Koepp. VHS, Beta, LV $95.00 PMS, PMS ♫♫♫

Death Before Dishonor Formula actioner stars Dryer as a tough Marine sergeant who battles ruthless Middle Eastern terrorists after they slaughter his men and kidnap his commanding officer (Keith).
1987 (R) 95m/C Fred Dryer, Brian Keith, Joanna Pacula, Paul Winfield; D: Terry J. Leonard. VHS, Beta, LV $19.95 NWV, STE ♫♫

Death Blow The victims of a violent rapist team together to stop the criminal after he repeatedly skirts conviction.
1987 (R) 90m/C Martin Landau, Frank Stallone, Jerry Van Dyke, Terry Moore, Henry Darrow, Jack Carter, Peter Lapis, Don Swayze, Donna Denton; D: Raphael Nussbaum. VHS, Beta NO ♫½

Death by Dialogue Muddled story of some teenagers who discover an old film script from a project never produced because it was haunted by tragic accidents.
1988 (R) 90m/C Laura Albert, Ken Sagoes; D: Tom Dewier. VHS, Beta NO ♫

Death by Prescription After adjusting his patients' wills to benefit himself, an evil physician sees to their mysterious deaths.
198? 75m/C Timothy West, Nigel Davenport. VHS, Beta $29.95 ACA, MOV ♫½

Death Challenge Gangs battle without weapons, motive or discretion in this kung fu extravaganza.
1980 94m/C Steve Leving, Susan Wong. VHS, Beta $39.95 UNI ♫½

Death Chase An average Joe, just jogging down the street, is thrown into a desperate game of cat-and-mouse when a body lands at his feet.
1987 86m/C William Zipp, Paul Smith, Jack Starrett, Bainbridge Scott; D: David A. Prior. VHS, Beta NO ♫½

Death Code Ninja Ninjas battle each other sword-to-foot for the possession of a map on which the peace of the world depends. El cheapo kung-fu rip.
1987 90m/C HK John Wilford, Mike Abbott, Judy Barnes, Edgar Fox; D: Tommy Cheung; W: Frank Lewis. VHS, Beta $59.95 TWE Woof!

Death Collector In the future, when insurance companies run the world, if you don't pay your premium you die.
1989 (R) 90m/C Daniel Chapman, Ruth Collins; D: Tom Gniazdowski. VHS, Beta NO ♫½

Death Cruise The six winners of a free cruise find that there is a fatal catch to the prize in this made-for-TV movie.
1974 74m/C Kate Jackson, Celeste Holm, Tom Bosley, Edward Albert, Polly Bergen, Michael Constantine, Richard Long; D: Ralph Senesky. VHS, Beta $39.95 AHV ♫½

The Death Curse of Tartu Another aspiring cult classic. (Read: A low-budget flick so bad it's funny). Students accidentally disturb the burial ground of an Indian medicine man who comes to zombie-like life with a deadly prescription.
1966 84m/C Fred Pinero, Doug Hobart, William Grefe. VHS, Beta NO Woof!

Death Dreams Crista thinks she has a perfect life with her wealth, beautiful daughter Jennie, and handsome new husband George. Then Jennie tragically drowns. It appears to be an accident until Jennie contacts her mother from beyond the grave to tell what really happened. Is the tragedy turning Crista's mind or is there truly something sinister going on—something that involves George? Based on the novel by William Katz. Routine suspenser originally appeared on cable television.
1992 94m/C Marg Helgenberger, Christopher Reeve, Fionnula Flanagan; D: Martin Donovan. VHS, LV $89.95 NLC ♫♫

Death Driver In order to make a comeback, a stuntman attempts to do a stunt that was responsible for ending his career ten years earlier. Obviously brave but none too smart.
1978 93m/C Earl Owensby, Mike Allen, Patty Shaw, Mary Ann Hearn; D: Jimmy Huston. VHS, Beta $59.99 HBO ♫½

Death Drug Cliched alarmist film about a talented musician ruining his career by becoming addicted to the drug angel dust.
1983 73m/C Philip Michael Thomas, Vernee Watson, Rosalind Cash; D: Oscar Williams. VHS, Beta $29.95 ACA ♫½

Death Duel of Mantis Martial arts extravaganza featuring Chin Yin Fei, man of many fists in motion.
1984 90m/C VHS, Beta $29.98 UNI ♫½

Death Feud A man tries to save the woman he loves from the man who would destroy her and her former pimp.
1989 98m/C Karen Mayo Chandler, Chris Mitchum, Frank Stallone. VHS, Beta $14.95 HMD ♫½

Death Force When a Vietnam veteran comes to New York City, he becomes a hitman for the Mafia.
1978 (R) 90m/C Jayne Kennedy, Leon Isaac Kennedy, James Iglehardt, Carmen Argenziano; D: Cirio H. Santiago. VHS, Beta NO ♫½

Death from a Distance A reporter and a detective put the moves on a group of astronomers who may be responsible for a murder.
1936 73m/B Russell Hopton, Lola Lane, George F. Marion, John St. Polis, Lee Kohlmar, Lew Kelly, Wheeler Oakman, Robert Frazer, Cornelius Keefe; D: Frank Strayer. VHS, Beta $16.95 SNC ♫♫

Death Game A businessman allows two innocent-looking young women into his home to make a phone call. Once inside, they proceed to wreak havoc on his mind, body, and property. AKA: The Seducers.

1976 (R) 91m/C Sondra Locke, Colleen Camp, Seymour Cassel; *D:* Beth Brickell, Peter S. Traynor. **VHS, Beta $19.95** *UHV* ♂♂½

Death Games Two young men shooting a documentary about an influential music promoter ask too many wrong questions, causing the powers-that-be to want them out of the picture for good.
1982 78m/C Lou Brown, David Clendenning, Jennifer Cluff. **VHS, Beta $29.98** *VID* ♂♂½

Death Goes to School A strangler is loose in a girl's school, and the music teacher has a hunch as to who it is.
1953 65m/B *GB* Barbara Murray, Gordon Jackson, Pamela Allan, Jane Aird, Beatrice Varley; *D:* Stephen Clarkson. **VHS, Beta $16.95** *SNC* ♂½

Death House Kerek Keillor is on Death Row at Townsend State Prison when he discovers a plot to use inmates for scientific experiments in biological warfare. He decides the best way to get out is to volunteer, which means convincing the man who put him in prison that they're now on the same side.
19?? 92m/C Dennis Cole, Anthony (Tony) Franciosa, John Saxon. **VHS $89.95** *AIP* ♂½

Death Hunt A man unjustly accused of murder pits his knowledge of the wilderness against the superior numbers of his pursuers.
1981 (R) 98m/C Charles Bronson, Lee Marvin, Ed Lauter, Andrew Stevens, Carl Weathers, Angie Dickinson; *D:* Peter Hunt. **VHS, Beta, LV $14.98** *FXV, FOX* ♂♂

Death in Deep Water A sensuous woman lures a man into a plot to kill her incredibly rich husband.
1974 71m/C Bradford Dillman, Suzan Farmer. **VHS, Beta $29.95** *LIV* ♂

Death in the Shadows A young woman searches for her mother while trying to avoid a killer. Filmed entirely in Holland.
19?? 96m/C *D:* Vivian Pieters. **VHS** *NO* ♂½

Death in Venice A lush, decadent adaptation of the Thomas Mann novella about an aging and jaded composer, here suggested to be Gustav Mahler, tragically obsessed with ideal beauty as personified in a young boy. Music by Mahler. *AKA:* Morte a Venezia.
1971 (PG) 124m/C *IT* Dirk Bogarde, Mark Burns, Bjorn Andresen, Marisa Berenson, Silvana Mangano; *D:* Luchino Visconti. **VHS, Beta $59.95** *WAR, TAM, PME* ♂♂♂½

Death is Called Engelchen An influential, important work of the Czech new wave. A survivor of World War II remembers his experiences with the SS leader Engelchen in a series of flashbacks. In Czech with subtitles. *AKA:* For We Too Do Not Forgive.
1963 111m/B *CZ D:* Jan Kadar, Elmar Klos. **VHS, Beta $59.95** *FCT* ♂♂♂½

Death Journey Producer and director Williamson portrays private eye Jesse Crowder, hired by the New York D.A. to escort a key witness cross-country. A regular Williamsonfest.
1976 (R) 90m/C Fred Williamson, D'Urville Martin, Bernie Kuby, Heidi Dobbs, Stephanie Faulkner; *D:* Fred Williamson. **VHS, Beta $49.95** *UNI* ♂½

The Death Kiss Creepy thriller about eerie doings at a major Hollywood film studio where a sinister killer does away with his victims while a cast-of-thousands movie spectacular is in production.
1933 72m/B Bela Lugosi, David Manners, Adrienne Ames, Edward Van Sloan, Vince Barnett; *D:* Edwin L. Marin. **VHS, Beta, 8mm, 3/4U, Special order formats $14.95** *NOS, SNC, CAB* ♂♂½

Death Kiss When a man hires a psychopath to murder his wife, his plan doesn't proceed exactly as expected.
1977 90m/C Larry Daniels, Dorothy Moore. **VHS, Beta $49.95** *PSM, LSV* ♂½

Death Machines Young karate student must face the "Death Machines," a team of deadly assassins who are trained to kill on command.
1976 (R) 93m/C Ron Marchini, Michael Chong, Joshua Johnson; *D:* Paul Kyriazi. **VHS, Beta $59.98** *VID* ♂½

Death Magic A group of five ceremonial magicians performs a spell to bring someone back from the dead, but the man they bring back, a soldier from the Civil War, decides to go on a vicious murdering spree to kill the descendants of the people who convicted him of murder in 1875. A suspenseful first entry from director Clinco.
1992 93m/C Anne Coffrey, Keith DeGreen, Jack Dunlap, Danielle Frons, Norman Stone; *W/D:* Paul E. Clinco. **VHS** *NO* ♂½

Death Mask of the Ninja Two princes, separated at birth, reunite and kick everyone in the head. Dubbed.
198? 95m/C Joey Lee, Tiger Tung, Jon Chen. **VHS, Beta $54.95** *MOV* ♂½

The Death Merchant Foundering attempt at a nuclear thriller. A modern mad man hopes to sell a computer chip to third world countries but is thwarted by a secret agent. Confusing, illogical plot highlighted by mediocre performances.
1991 90m/C Lawrence Tierney, Martina Castle, Melody Munyan, Monika Schnarre; *D:* Jim Winburn; *W:* Kari Holman. **VHS $79.95** *AIP* ♂

Death Nurse Fresh from "Crazy Fat Ethel II," aspiring Queen of Camp Alden takes takes up residence in a health care establishment, much to the dismay of the patients who give up their lives in exchange for their money.
1987 80m/C Priscilla Alden, Michael Flood; *D:* Nick Phillips. **VHS $29.98** *VCD* ♂♂

Death of a Bureaucrat A Cuban hero dies, and in tribute, the Communist government buries him with his union card. His widow, however, needs the card in order to collect a pension, and she enlists her nephew's help to retrieve it. The nephew finds himself buried in red tape, and digs himself in ever-deeper as he seeks to disinter his late uncle. A wry satire of the communist bureaucracy in Cuba, brimming with comedic tributes to Harold Lloyd, Buster Keaton and Laurel & Hardy. Alea's film was only briefly released in 1966 and was promptly banned, eventually finding its way to the U.S. in 1979. In Spanish with English subtitles.
1966 87m/B Salvador Wood, Silvia Planas, Manuel Estanillo, Gaspar de Santelices, Carlos Ruiz de la Tejera, Omar Alfonso, Ricardo Suarez, Luis Romay, Elsa Montero; *D:* Thomas Gutierrez Alea. **VHS, Beta $69.95** *NYF, FCT, TAM* ♂♂♂

Death of a Centerfold Drama based on the life and tragic death of Playboy model and actress Dorothy Stratten. More effectively handled in Bob Fosse's "Star 80."
1981 96m/C Jamie Lee Curtis, Bruce Weitz, Robert Reed, Mitchell Ryan, Bibi Besch; *D:* Gabrielle Beaumont. **VHS, Beta $59.95** *MGM* ♂♂

Death of a Gunfighter A western town courting eastern investors and bankers seeks a way to kill their ex-gunslinger sheriff.
1969 (PG) 94m/C Richard Widmark, Lena Horne, Carroll O'Connor, John Saxon, Larry Gates; *D:* Don Siegel; *W:* Robert Totten. **VHS, Beta $9.95** *MCA* ♂♂

Death of a Salesman A powerful made-for-television adaptation of the famous Arthur Miller play. Hoffman won an Emmy (as did Malkovich) for his stirring portrayal of Willy Loman, the aging salesman who realizes he's past his prime and tries to come to grips with the life he's wasted and the family he's neglected. Reid also turns in a fine performance as his long-suffering wife.
1986 135m/C Dustin Hoffman, John Malkovich, Charles Durning, Stephen Lang, Kate Reid, Louis Zorich; *D:* Volker Schlondorff. **VHS, Beta, LV $19.98** *LHV, FCT, WAR* ♂♂♂♂

Death of a Scoundrel A womanizing entrepreneur is murdered and the culprit could be any one of his many jealous romantic conquests. *AKA:* Loves of a Scoundrel.
1956 119m/B George Sanders, Zsa Zsa Gabor, Yvonne De Carlo, Victor Jory; *D:* Charles Martin. **VHS, Beta, LV $15.95** *♂♂½*

Death of a Soldier During World War II, the uneasy U.S.-Australian alliance explodes when a psychotic American soldier murders three Melbourne women. The lawyer hired to defend him has to fight political as well as legal influences. Based on a true story.
1985 (R) 93m/C James Coburn, Reb Brown, Maurie Field, Belinda Darey; *D:* Philippe Mora. **VHS, Beta $79.98** *FOX* ♂♂

The Death of Adolf Hitler British made-for-television film depicting Hitler's last ten days in an underground bunker. Drug-addled, suicidal, and Eva Braun-haunted, he receives the news of the fall of the Third Reich. While the film avoids cliche, it lacks emotional depth.
1984 107m/C *GB* Frank Finlay, Caroline Mortimer; *D:* Rex Firlin. **VHS, Beta $59.95** *LHV, TLF, WAR* ♂♂½

Death of an Angel When her crippled daughter runs away to join a cult in Mexico, a recently ordained priest (Bedelia) follows her, only to become caught up herself with the leader of the group.
1986 95m/C Bonnie Bedelia, Nick Mancuso, Pamela Ludwig, Alex Colon; *D:* Petru Popescu. **VHS, Beta, LV** *NO* ♂½

The Death of Richie Gazzara does a fine job as a father driven to kill his drug-addicted teenage son, portrayed by Benson. Occasionally lapses into melodrama, but all-in-all a decent adaptation of Thomas Thompson's book "Richie" which was based on a true story. *AKA:* Richie.
1976 97m/C Ben Gazzara, Robby Benson, Eileen Brennan, Clint Howard; *D:* Paul Wendkos. **VHS, Beta** *LCA* ♂♂

Death of the Incredible Hulk Scientist David Banner's new job just may provide the clues for stopping his transformation into the monstrous Incredible Hulk. But first there are terrorists after the Hulk who need to be defeated and Banner's new romance to contend with. Made for television.
1990 96m/C Bill Bixby, Lou Ferrigno, Elizabeth Gracen, Philip Sterling; *D:* Bill Bixby. **VHS $79.95** *RHI* ♂½

Death of the Rat A serious/comic meditation on the tragedy of modern technological life.
1975 6m/C *D:* Pascal Aubier. **VHS, Beta** *FFM* ♂½

Death on the Nile Agatha Christie's fictional detective, Hercule Poirot, is called upon to interrupt his vacation to uncover who killed an heiress aboard a steamer cruising down the Nile. Anthony Schaffer's screenplay boasts Ustinov's first stint as the Bel-

gian sleuth. Anthony Powell's costume design won an Oscar.
1978 (PG) 135m/C *GB* Peter Ustinov, Jane Birkin, Lois Chiles, Bette Davis, Mia Farrow, David Niven, Olivia Hussey, Angela Lansbury, Jack Warden, Maggie Smith, George Kennedy, Simon MacCorkindale, Harry Andrews, Jon Finch; *D:* John Guillermin. **VHS, Beta, LV** $19.99 *HBO* 🎬🎬½

Death Promise Ho-hum excuse for a horror flick has murderous landlord trying to evict his tenants using whatever means are necessary.
1978 (R) 90m/C Charles Bonet. **VHS, Beta** *PGN* 🎬

Death Race 2000 In the 21st century, five racing car contenders challenge the national champion of a cross country race in which drivers score points by killing pedestrians. Gory fun. Based on the 1956 story by Ib Melchior, and followed by "Deathsport." Made for television. *AKA:* T.P. Sloane.
1975 (R) 80m/C David Carradine, Simone Griffeth, Sylvester Stallone, Mary Woronov; *D:* Paul Bartel; *W:* Charles B. Griffith, Robert Thom. **VHS, Beta** $19.95 *VDM, MRV* 🎬🎬½

Death Rage A hitman comes out of retirement to handle the toughest assignment he has ever faced: search for and kill the man who murdered his brother. He finds out he's the victim of a Mafia doublecross.
1977 (R) 92m/C *IT* Yul Brynner, Martin Balsam; *D:* Anthony M. Dawson. **VHS, Beta** $14.98 *VID* 🎬½

Death Raiders When an Asian ruler's family is kidnapped it's up to the Death Raiders to kick their way to a peaceful solution.
1987 86m/C VHS, Beta *MOV* 🎬½

Death Ray It's a race to the finish as terrorists threaten to unleash the world's most powerful weapon.
19?? 93m/C Gordon Scott. **VHS, Beta** $19.99 *BFV, MRV* 🎬½

Death Ray 2000 A pair of futuristic spies search out the whereabouts of a stolen military device that could kill all life on Earth. *AKA:* T.P. Sloane.
1981 100m/C Robert F. Logan, Ann Turkel, Maggie Cooper, Dan O'Herlihy; *D:* Lee H. Katzin. **VHS, Beta** $49.95 *WOV* 🎬½

Death Rides the Plains Western with a twist. A man lures prospective buyers to his ranch, kills them, and steals their money. It's up to our heroes to ride to the rescue.
1944 53m/B Bob Livingston, Al "Fuzzy" St. John, Nica Doret, Ray Bennett; *D:* Sam Newfield. **VHS, Beta** $24.95 *VYY, VDM* 🎬🎬

Death Rides the Range Cold war hits the West as Russian spies start a range war to cover a spy operation.
1940 57m/B Ken Maynard, Fay McKenzie, Ralph Peters, Charles King, John Elliott, Kenneth Rhodes, Bud Osborne; *D:* Sam Newfield. **VHS, Beta** $19.95 *NOS, DVT, VCN* 🎬½

Death Ring Basic action/martial arts tale about three men who must battle the bad guys to ensure their own survival.
1993 (R) 91m/C Mike Norris, Chad McQueen, Don Swayze, Billy Drago, Isabel Glasser; *D:* Robert J. Kizer; *W:* George T. LeBrun. **VHS, LV** *COL, NLC* 🎬

Death Row Diner A movie mogul, executed for a crime he didn't commit, is brought back to life by a freak electrical storm. Nothing will stop him from exacting revenge.

1988 90m/C Jay Richardson, Michelle McClellan, John Content, Tom Schell, Dennis Mooney, Frank Sarcinello Sr.., Dana Mason. **VHS, Beta** *NO* 🎬½

Death Scream Drama based on the New York murder of Kitty Genovese, whose cries for help while being assaulted went ignored by her neighbors. Good casting but the pacing deteriorates. Written by Stirling Silliphant. Made for television.
1975 100m/C Raul Julia, John P. Ryan, Lucie Arnaz, Ed Asner, Art Carney, Diahann Carroll, Kate Jackson, Cloris Leachman, Tina Louise, Nancy Walker, Eric Braeden, Allyn Ann McLerie, Tony Dow, Sally Kirkland; *D:* Richard T. Heffron. **VHS** *ACE* 🎬🎬

Death Screams Attractive college coeds have a party and get hacked to pieces for their troubles by a machete-wielding maniac.
1983 (R) 88m/C Susan Kiger, Jennifer Chase, Jody Kay, William T. Hicks, Martin Tucker. **VHS, Beta** *GEM* 🎬

Death Sentence When a woman juror on a murder case finds out that the wrong man is on trial, she is stalked by the real killer. Made for television. *AKA:* Murder One.
1974 74m/C Cloris Leachman, Laurence Luckinbill, Nick Nolte, William Schallert; *D:* E.W. Swackhamer. **VHS, Beta** $49.95 *PSM* 🎬½

Death Ship A luxury liner is destroyed by an ancient, mysterious freighter on open seas, leaving the survivors to confront the ghost ship's inherent evil in this slow-going horror flick.
1980 (R) 91m/C *CA GB* George Kennedy, Richard Crenna, Nick Mancuso, Sally Ann Howes, Saul Rubinek, Kate Reid; *D:* Alvin Rakoff. **VHS, Beta** $19.98 *SUE, NLC* 🎬

Death Shot Two plainclothes detectives (who seem just as sleazy as the criminals they're trying to bust) try to break up a drug ring and find that, with a little coercion, their best sources of information are the pimps and junkies they want to stop. Senseless attempt to make an action pic.
1973 90m/C Richard C. Watt, Frank Himes; *D:* Mitch Brown. **VHS** $59.95 *SVS* 🎬

Death Spa A health club is possessed by the spirit of a vengeful woman. The fitness craze takes on a campy new twist.
1987 (R) 87m/C William Bumiller, Brenda Bakke, Merritt Butrick; *D:* Michael Fischa. **VHS** $79.98 *MPI* Woof!

Death Sport In this sequel to the cult hit "Death Race 2000," a group of humans play a game of death in the year 3000. The object is to race cars and kill as many competitors as possible. Not as good as the original, but still watchable.
1978 (R) 83m/C David Carradine, Claudia Jennings, Richard Lynch, William Smithers, Will Walker, David McLean, Jesse Vint; *D:* Henry Suso, Allan Arkush. **VHS, Beta** *WAR, OM* 🎬🎬

The Death Squad A police commissioner hires an ex-cop to find a group of vigilante cops who are behind a series of gangland-style executions. Good cast, though that's about all this flick has got going for it. Made for television.
1973 74m/C Robert Forster, Melvyn Douglas, Michelle Phillips, Mark Goddard, Bert Remsen, Claude Akins; *D:* Harry Falk. **VHS, Beta** $59.95 *PSM* 🎬½

Death Stalk Dream vacation turns nightmarish for two couples when the wives are taken hostage by several escaped convicts. Made for television.

1974 90m/C Vince Edwards, Vic Morrow, Anjanette Comer, Robert Webber, Carol Lynley, Neville Brand, Norman Fell; *D:* Robert Day. **VHS, Beta** $59.95 *GEM, WWV, HHE* 🎬½

Death Target Three former mercenaries team up for one last mission that gets sidetracked when one of the soldiers-of-fortune falls for a worker with a habit.
1983 72m/C Jorge Montesi, Elaine Lakeman; *D:* Peter Hyams. **VHS, Beta** $49.95 *PSM* 🎬½

Death Tide Hoodlums pirate a ship full of diamonds in this story of death and crime on the high seas.
1958 ?m/C Frank Silvera. **VHS** $16.95 *SNC* 🎬🎬

Death Train Dead man seems to have been struck by a train, but clueless investigator can't figure out where the train came from.
1979 96m/C Hugh Keays-Byrne, Ingrid Mason, Max Meldrum; *D:* Igor Auzins. **VHS, Beta** *PGN* 🎬½

Death Valley Greed turns gold prospectors in Death Valley against each other.
1946 70m/C Robert Lowery, Helen Gilbert, Sterling Holloway; *D:* Lew Landers. **VHS, Beta** $29.95 *TIM* 🎬½

Death Valley Good cast, lousy plot. Youngster (Billingsley) gets caught up with a psycho cowpoke while visiting mom in Arizona.
1981 (R) 90m/C Paul LeMat, Catherine Hicks, Peter Billingsley, Wilford Brimley, Edward Herrmann, Stephen McHattie; *D:* Dick Richards. **VHS, Beta** $79.95 *MCA* 🎬

Death Valley Days: No Gun Behind His Badge Western anthology series which ran on television from 1952-1970 and was noted for its longtime sponsor, 20 Mule Team Borax, as well as its hosts, including Stanley Andrews, Ronald Reagan, Robert Taylor, and Dale Robertson. On this tape: the premiere episode plus "Halo for a Bad Man." Each additional tape contains two episodes.
1965 55m/C Robert Taylor, Ronald Reagan. **VHS** $9.95 *RHI, MOV* 🎬½

Death Valley Manhunt A marshal hired to protect a man's oil wells discovers that the company manager is keeping the profits for himself.
1943 55m/B Bill Elliott, George "Gabby" Hayes, Anne Jeffreys; *D:* John English. **VHS, Beta** $29.95 *DVT* 🎬

Death Valley Rangers The hero pretends to be an outlaw to expose a gang robbing gold-laden stagecoaches.
1944 59m/B Ken Maynard, Hoot Gibson, Bob Steele, Linda Brent, Kenneth Harlan; *D:* Robert Tansey. **VHS** $19.95 *NOS, DVT* 🎬½

Death Warmed Up A crazed brain surgeon turns ordinary people into bloodthirsty mutants, and a small group of young people travel to his secluded island to stop him.
1985 83m/C Michael Hurst, Margaret Umbers, David Letch; *D:* David Blyth. **VHS, Beta** $69.98 *LIV, VES* 🎬½

Death Warrant Van Damme whams and bams a little less than usual in this cop-undercover-in-prison testosterone fest. As a Royal Canadian Mountie undercover in prison—where inmates are perishing under mysterious circumstances—the pectoral-perfect Muscles from Brussels is on the brink of adding two plus two when an inmate transferee threatens his cover. Contains the requisite gratuitous violence, prison bromide, and miscellaneous other Van Dammages.

1990 (R) 111m/C Jean-Claude Van Damme, Robert Guillaume, Cynthia Gibb, George Dickerson, Patrick Kilpatrick; *D:* Deran Sarafian. **VHS, LV** $19.98 *MGM, PIA* 🎞🎞

Death Watch In the future, media abuse is taken to an all time high as a terminally ill woman's last days are secretly filmed by a man with a camera in his head. Intelligent, adult science fiction with an excellent cast. 1980 (R) 128m/C *FR GE* Romy Schneider, Harvey Keitel, Harry Dean Stanton, Max von Sydow; *D:* Bertrand Tavernier. **VHS, LV** $29.98 *SUE* 🎞🎞🎞

Death Weekend A woman is stalked by a trio of murderous, drunken hoodlums who seek to spoil her weekend. *AKA:* House by the Lake. 1976 89m/C *CA* Brenda Vaccaro, Don Stroud, Chuck Shamata, Richard Ayres, Kyle Edwards; *D:* William Fruet. **VHS, Beta** $69.98 *LIV, VES* 🎞½

Death Wish A middle-aged businessman turns vigilante after his wife and daughter are violently attacked and raped by a gang of hoodlums (one is Goldblum in his film debut). He stalks the streets of New York seeking revenge on other muggers, pimps, and crooks, making the neighborhood safer for those less macho. Music by Herbie Hancock. 1974 (R) 93m/C Charles Bronson, Vincent Gardenia, William Redfield, Hope Lange, Jeff Goldblum, Stuart Margolin, Olympia Dukakis; *D:* Michael Winner. **VHS, Beta, LV** $14.95 *MGM, PAR* 🎞🎞½

Death Wish 2 Bronson recreates the role of Paul Kersey, an architect who takes the law into his own hands when his family is victimized once again. Extremely violent sequel to the successful 1974 movie. Followed by "Death Wish 3" (1985) and 4 (1987) in which Bronson continues to torture the street scum and the viewers as well. 1982 (R) 89m/C J.D. Cannon, Charles Bronson, Jill Ireland, Vincent Gardenia, Anthony (Tony) Franciosa; *D:* Michael Winner. **VHS, Beta, LV** $19.98 *WAR, OM Woof!*

Death Wish 3 Once again, Charles Bronson blows away the low lifes who have killed those who were dear to him and were spared in the first two films. 1985 (R) 100m/C Charles Bronson, Martin Balsam, Deborah Raffin, Ed Lauter, Alex Winter, Marina Sirtis; *D:* Michael Winner. **VHS, Beta, LV** $14.98 *MGM* 🎞½

Death Wish 4: The Crackdown The four-times-weary urban vigilante hits crack dealers hard, hard. 1987 (R) 100m/C Charles Bronson, John P. Ryan, Kay Lenz; *D:* J. Lee Thompson. **VHS, Beta, LV** $19.95 *MED* 🎞

Death Wish Club Young woman gets involved in a club with an unusual mission—suicide. *AKA:* Carnival of Fools. 1983 93m/C Meridith Haze, Rick Barns, J. Martin Sellers, Ann Fairchild; *D:* John Carr. **VHS, Beta** *NO* 🎞½

Deathcheaters Australian Secret Service offers two stuntmen a top secret mission in the Philippines. 1976 (G) 96m/C **VHS, Beta** $69.98 *VES* 🎞½

Deathdream In this reworking of the "Monkey's Paw" tale, a mother wishes her dead son would return from Vietnam. He does, but he's not quite the person he used to be. Gripping plot gives new meaning to the saying, "Be careful what you wish for—it might come true." *AKA:* Dead of Night; Night Walk; The Veteran. 1972 98m/C *CA* John Marley, Richard Backus, Lynn Carlin; *D:* Bob Clark; *W:* Alan Ormsby. **VHS, Beta** $59.95 *MPI* 🎞🎞½

Deathhead Virgin An evil virgin spirit is waiting to possess one of two men eager to find a sunken fortune. The fate of the fortunate one is only death! 1974 (R) 94m/C Jock Gaynor, Larry Ward, Diane McBain, Vic Diaz. **VHS, Beta** *NO* 🎞½

Deathmask A four-year-old boy's corpse is found buried in a cardboard box, and a medical examiner—whose daughter met a similar fate—investigates the murder. Could've been done more tastefully. 1969 102m/C Farley Granger, Ruth Warrick, Danny Aiello; *D:* Richard S. Friedman. **VHS, Beta** $69.95 *PSM* 🎞🎞

Deathmoon A businessman plagued by recurring werewolf nightmares goes on a Hawaiian vacation to try to forget his troubles. Made for television. 1978 90m/C Robert Foxworth, Joe Penny, Debralee Scott, Dolph Sweet, Charles Haid; *D:* Bruce Kessler. **VHS, Beta** *NO* 🎞½

Deathrow Gameshow Condemned criminals can either win their freedom or die in front of millions on a new television show that doesn't win the host many friends. 1988 78m/C John McCafferty, Robin Bluthe, Beano, Mark Lasky; *D:* Mark Pirro. **VHS, Beta, LV** *MED* 🎞½

Deathstalker Deathstalker sets his sights on seizing the evil wizard Munkar's magic amulet so he can take over Munkar's castle. The only excuse for making such an idiotic film seems to have been to fill it with half-naked women. Filmed in Argentina and followed by two sequels that were an improvement. *AKA:* El Cazador de la Muerte. 1983 (R) 80m/C Richard Hill, Barbi Benton, Richard Brooker, Victor Bo, Lana Clarkson; *D:* John Watson. **VHS, Beta, LV** $29.98 *LIV, VES Woof!*

Deathstalker 2: Duel of the Titans Campy fantasy comically pits the lead character against an evil wizard. Sword-and-sorcery spoof doesn't take itself too seriously. 1987 85m/C John Terlesky, Monique Gabrielle, John Lazar, Toni Naples, Maria Socas, Queen Kong; *D:* Jim Wynorski. **VHS, Beta, LV** $29.98 *LIV, VES* 🎞🎞

Deathstalker 3 Another humorous entry in the Deathstalker saga. This time there's action, romance, magic and the Warriors From Hell. *AKA:* Deathstalker 3: The Warriors From Hell. 1989 85m/C John Allen Nelson, Carla Herd, Terri Treas, Thom Christopher; *D:* Alfonso Corona. **VHS, Beta, LV** $79.98 *LIV, VES, HHE* 🎞½

Deathstalker 4: Clash of the Titans The sword and sorcery epic continues, with our hero revealing yet more musculature in his efforts to defeat an evil queen and her legion of stone warriors. 1991 (R) 85m/C Richard Hill, Maria Ford, Michelle Moffett, Brent Baxter Clark; *D:* Howard R. Cohen. **VHS** $89.98 *NHO* 🎞

Deathtrap A creatively-blocked playwright, his ailing rich wife, and a former student who has written a surefire hit worth killing for, are the principals in this compelling comedy-mystery. Cross and double-cross are explored in this film based on the Broadway hit by Ira Levin. 1982 (PG) 118m/C Henry Jones, Michael Caine, Christopher Reeve, Dyan Cannon, Irene Worth; *D:* Sidney Lumet. **VHS, Beta** $19.98 *WAR* 🎞🎞

The Decameron Pasolini's first epic pageant in his "Trilogy of Life" series. An acclaimed, sexually explicit adaptation of a handful of the Boccaccio tales. In Italian with English subtitles. 1970 (R) 111m/C *FR IT GE* Franco Citti, Ninetto Davoli, Angela Luce, Patrizia Capparelli, Jovan Jovanovich, Silvana Mangano, Pier Paolo Pasolini; *D:* Pier Paolo Pasolini; *M:* Ennio Morricone. **VHS, Beta, LV** $79.95 *WBF, TAM, APD* 🎞🎞🎞½

Decameron Nights Story of Boccaccio's pursuit of a recently-widowed young women is interwoven amongst the three of the fourteenth-century Italian writer's bawdy tales. 1953 87m/C *GB* Louis Jourdan, Joan Fontaine, Binnie Barnes, Joan Collins, Marjorie Rhodes; *D:* Hugo Fregonese. **VHS, Beta** $19.95 *NOS, MRV, QNE* 🎞🎞½

Deceived A successful career woman with a passionate husband and a young daughter feels she has it all until her husband is apparently killed in a bizarre tragedy. But just how well did she know the man she married? Who was he really and what secrets are hidden in his past? As she struggles to solve these mysteries, her own life becomes endangered in this psychological thriller. 1991 (PG-13) 115m/C Goldie Hawn, John Heard, Ashley Peldon; *D:* Damien Harris; *W:* Mary Agnes Donoghue. **VHS, Beta** $92.95 *TOU* 🎞🎞

The Deceivers A British officer infiltrates a deadly sect in colonial India. The sect murders and robs unwary travelers. Interesting premise falters somewhat due to rather slow pacing. 1988 (PG-13) 112m/C *GB* Pierce Brosnan, Saeed Jaffrey, Shashi Kapoor, Keith Michell; *D:* Nicholas Meyer. **VHS, Beta, LV** $89.95 *WAR* 🎞🎞

December Four prep-school students in New Hampshire must confront the reality of war when the Japanese bomb Pearl Harbor. A touching story of courage and friendship that takes place in one night during the surprise-attack. 1991 (PG) 92m/C Wil Wheaton, Chris Young, Brian Krause, Balthazar Getty, Jason London; *W/D:* Gabe Torres. **VHS, LV** *NO* 🎞🎞

December Flower A young woman arrives at her aunt's estate so she can nurse her back to health, but she finds her aunt a bit down in the mouth: seems someone is trying to kill her, and she could be next in line. 19?? 65m/C Jean Simmons, Mona Washbourne, Bryan Forbes. **VHS** $19.99 *FCT, MOV* 🎞🎞½

December 7th: The Movie Banned for 50 years by the U.S. Government, this planned Hollywood explanation to wartime audiences of the Pearl Harbor debacle offers such "offensive" images as blacks fighting heroically alongside whites, loyal Japanese-Americans, and Uncle Sam asleep on the morning of the attack. The Chief of Naval Operations confiscated the original film, claiming it demeaned the Navy. The battle scenes were so realistic they fooled even documentarians. This isn't the most incisive video on the event—just an unforgettable snapshot. 1991 82m/B Walter Huston, Harry Davenport; *D:* John Ford. **VHS** $19.95 *KIT, CPM, TIM* 🎞🎞½

Deception Davis is a pianist torn between two loves: her intensely jealous sponsor (Rains) and her cellist boyfriend (Henreid). Plot in danger of going over the melodramatic edge is saved by the very effective performances of the stars.

1946 112m/B Bette Davis, Paul Henreid, Claude Rains, John Abbott, Benson Fong; *D:* Irving Rapper. VHS, Beta $19.95 *MGM* 🎞🎞🎞

Deceptions A risque, semi-erotic thriller about a wealthy society woman (Sheridan) who kills her husband. Sheridan claims that she acted in self-defense, but macho cop Hamlin has a different view. He interrogates her, grows increasingly attracted, and is drawn into her web of seduction.
1990 (R) 105m/C Harry Hamlin, Nicolette Sheridan. VHS, LV $89.98 *REP* 🎞🎞

The Decline of the American Empire The critically acclaimed French-Canadian film about eight academic intellectuals who spend a weekend shedding their sophistication and engaging in intertwining sexual affairs. Examines the differing attitudes of men and women in regards to sex and sexuality. In French with English subtitles. *AKA:* Le Declin De L'Empire Americain.
1986 (R) 102m/C *CA* Dominique Michel, Dorothee Berryman, Louise Portal, Genevieve Rioux; *D:* Denys Arcand. Academy Awards '86 Nominations: Best Foreign Language Film; Genie Awards '87: Best Director (Arcand), Best Film, Best Supporting Actor (Arcand), Best Supporting Actress (Portal). VHS, Beta $79.95 *MCA,* *TAM* 🎞🎞🎞

Decline of Western Civilization 1 The L.A. hard core punk scene. Music by X, Circle Jerks, Black Flag, Fear and more.
1981 100m/C *D:* Penelope Spheeris. VHS, Beta, LV $49.95 *MVD, MED* 🎞🎞🎞

Decline of Western Civilization 2: The Metal Years Following Spheeris's first documentary about hardcore punk, she in turn delves into the world of heavy metal rock. We are given a look at some of the early rockers, as well as some of the smaller bands still playing L.A. clubs. Features appearances by Alice Cooper, Ozzy Osbourne, Poison, Gene Simmons and Megadeth.
1988 (R) 90m/C Alice Cooper, Ozzy Osbourne, Gene Simmons, Megadeth, Lizzie Borden, Faster Pussycat; *D:* Penelope Spheeris. VHS, Beta $14.95 *COL, MVD, FCT* 🎞🎞🎞

Decoration Day Garner plays a retired Southern judge who aids an angry childhood friend who has refused to accept his long-overdue Medal of Honor. Investigating the past leads to a decades-old mystery and a tragic secret that has repercussions for everyone involved. Based on the novel by John William Corrington. A Hallmark Hall of Fame presentation.
1990 (PG) 99m/C James Garner, Bill Cobbs, Judith Ivey, Ruby Dee, Larry Fishburne; *D:* Robert Markowitz. VHS, LV $89.95 *REP* 🎞🎞🎞

Dedee d'Anvers A gritty dockside melodrama about a drunken prostitute abused by her pimp. A sailor and a local barkeep don't like it. In French with subtitles. *AKA:* Dedee; Woman of Antwerp.
1949 95m/B Simone Signoret, Marcel Dalio, Bernard Blier, Marcel Pagliero, Jane Marken; *D:* Yves Allegret. VHS, Beta $24.95 *NOS, FCT, TAM* 🎞🎞½

A Dedicated Man A lonely woman agrees to act as a wife for a businessman to lend him credibility. A British "Romance Theater" presentation.
1986 60m/C *GB* Alec McCowen, Joan Plowright; *D:* Robert Knights. VHS $11.95 *PSM* 🎞🎞½

The Deep An innocent couple get involved in an underwater search for a shipwreck, and they quickly find themselves in over their heads. Gorgeous photography manages to keep this slow mover afloat. Famous for Bisset's wet T-shirt scene.

Based on the novel by Peter Benchley. The laserdisc edition offers widescreen format.
1977 (PG) 123m/C Nick Nolte, Jacqueline Bisset, Robert Shaw, Louis Gossett Jr., Eli Wallach; *D:* Peter Yates; *M:* John Barry. VHS, Beta, LV $14.95 *GKK, PIA* 🎞🎞

Deep Cover A man dares to go beyond the walls of a mysterious English manor in order to expose the secrets that lie within the manor.
1988 (R) 81m/C Tom Conti, Donald Pleasence, Denholm Elliott, Kika Markham, Phoebe Nicholls; *D:* Richard Loncraine. VHS, Beta $79.95 *PSM, PAR* 🎞½

Deep Cover Fishburne plays Russell Stevens Jr., a straight-arrow cop who goes undercover to infiltrate a Latin American cocaine cartel. While undercover, he becomes partners with drug dealer David Jason (Goldblum), and undergoes an inner transformation until he realizes he is betraying his cause. Confusing and commercial, yet marked with a moral rage.
1992 (R) 107m/C Larry Fishburne, Jeff Goldblum, Charles Martin Smith, Victoria Dillard, Clarence Williams III, Gregory Sierra, Robert Guenveur Smith, Cory Curtis, Glynn Turman; *D:* Bill Duke; *W:* Michael Tolkin, Henry Bean. VHS, LV $59.95 *COL, NLC* 🎞🎞½

Deep End A 15-year-old boy working as an attendant in a bath house falls in love with a 20-year-old woman in this tragic tale of a young man obsessed. Good British cast and music by Cat Stevens.
1970 88m/C *GB GE* Jane Asher, John Moulder-Brown, Diana Dors; *D:* Jerzy Skolimowski. VHS *FCT* 🎞🎞🎞

Deep in My Heart A musical biography of the life and times of composer Sigmund Romberg, with guest appearances by many MGM stars. 🎵Leg of Mutton; You Will Remember Vienna; Softly, as in a Morning Sunrise; Mr. & Mrs.; I Love to Go Swimmin' with Wimmin; The Road to Paradise; Will You Remember; It; Serenade; One Alone; Your Land and My Land; Lover, Come Back to Me; Stouthearted Men; When I Grow Too Old to Dream; The Desert Song; Goodbye Girls; Fat, Fat Fatima; Jazza, Jazza Doo Do; Miss U.S.A.; Auf Wiedersehn; Leg of Mutton.
1954 132m/C Jose Ferrer, Merle Oberon, Paul Henreid, Walter Pidgeon, Helen Traubel, Rosemary Clooney, Jane Powell, Howard Keel, Cyd Charisse, Gene Kelly, Ann Miller; *D:* Stanley Donen. VHS, Beta $19.98 *MGM* 🎞🎞½

Deep in the Heart When a young teacher is raped at gunpoint on a second date, she takes the law into her own hands. Just-off-the-target film tries to take a stand against the proliferation of guns in the U.S. Thought-provoking all the same. *AKA:* Handgun.
1983 (R) 99m/C *GB* Karen Young, Clayton Day, Ben Jones, Suzie Humphreys; *D:* Tony Garnett. VHS, Beta $69.99 *HBO* 🎞🎞

Deep Red: Hatchet Murders A stylish but gruesome rock music-driven tale of a composer who reads a book on the occult which happens to relate to the sadistic, sangfroid murder of his neighbor. When he visits the book's author, he discovers that she has been horribly murdered as well. *AKA:* The Hatchet Murders; Profundo Rosso; Dripping Deep Red.
1975 100m/C David Hemmings, Daria Nicolodi; *D:* Dario Argento. VHS, Beta $19.99 *HBO, QVD* 🎞🎞½

Deep Six A World War II drama that examines the conflict between pacifism and loyalty. A staunch Quaker is called to active duty as a lieutenant in the U.S. Navy, where

his beliefs put him into disfavor with shipmates.
1958 110m/C Alan Ladd, William Bendix, James Whitmore, Keenan Wynn, Efrem Zimbalist Jr., Joey Bishop; *D:* Rudolph Mate. VHS, Beta $54.95 *UHV* 🎞🎞

Deep Space A flesh-eating alien lands on earth and, after devouring a cop, is stalked by his partner. An "Alien" rip-off. Some humorous moments keep us from thinking too hard about how much the monster resembles our friend from "Alien."
1987 90m/C Charles Napier, Ann Turkel, Ron Glass, Bo Svenson, Julie Newmar; *D:* Fred Olen Ray. VHS, Beta $79.95 *TWE* 🎞½

Deepstar Six When futuristic scientists try to set up an undersea research and missile lab, a group of subterranean monsters get in the way.
1989 (R) 97m/C Taurean Blacque, Nancy Everhard, Greg Evigan, Miguel Ferrer, Matt McCoy, Nia Peeples, Cindy Pickett, Marius Weyers; *D:* Sean S. Cunningham. VHS, Beta, LV $9.99 *CCB, IVE* 🎞½

The Deer Hunter A powerful and vivid portrait of Middle America with three steel-working friends who leave home to face the Vietnam War. Controversial, brutal sequences in Vietnam are among the most wrenching ever filmed; the rhythms and rituals of home are just as purely captured. Neither pro- nor anti-war, but rather the perfect evocation of how totally and forever altered these people are by the war. Emotionally shattering; not to be missed.
1978 (R) 183m/C Robert De Niro, Christopher Walken, Meryl Streep, John Savage, George Dzundza, John Cazale, Chuck Aspegren, Rutanya Alda, Shirley Stoler, Amy Wright; *D:* Michael Cimino; *M:* John Williams. Academy Awards '78: Best Director (Cimino), Best Film Editing, Best Picture, Best Sound, Best Supporting Actor (Walken); Nominations: Best Actor (De Niro), Best Cinematography, Best Original Screenplay, Best Supporting Actress (Streep); Golden Globe Awards '79: Best Director (Cimino); Los Angeles Film Critics Association Awards '78: Best Director (Cimino); New York Film Critics Awards '78: Best Film, Best Supporting Actor (Walken). VHS, Beta, LV $14.95 *MCA, FCT, BTV* 🎞🎞🎞🎞

The Deerslayer Low-budget snoozer based on the classic novel by James Fenimore Cooper. Frontiersman Hawkeye and his Indian companion Chingachgook set out to rescue a beautiful Indian maiden and must fight bands of hostile Indians and Frenchmen along the way.
1978 98m/C Steve Forrest, Ned Romero, John Anderson, Joan Prather; *D:* Richard Friedenberg. VHS, Beta $19.95 *STE, UHV* 🎞½

Def by Temptation A potent horror fantasy about a young black theology student who travels to New York in search of an old friend. There he meets an evil woman who is determined to seduce him and force him to give in to temptation. Great soundtrack.
1990 (R) 95m/C James Bond III, Kadeem Hardison, Bill Nunn, Samuel L. Jackson, Minnie Gentry, Rony Clanton; *D:* James Bond III. VHS, Beta, LV $89.98 *SGE, IME* 🎞🎞

Def-Con 4 Three marooned space travelers return to a holocaust-shaken Earth to try to start again, but some heavy-duty slimeballs are in charge and they don't want to give it up. Good special effects bolster a weak script.
1985 (R) 85m/C Maury Chaykin, Kate Lynch, Tim Choate; *D:* Paul Donovan. VHS, Beta $14.95 *NWV, STE* 🎞½

The Defender CBS "Studio One" presentation of a live courtroom drama. First shown in 1957. Made for television.
1957 112m/B Steve McQueen, William Shatner, Ralph Bellamy, Martin Balsam. **VHS, Beta** $29.95 FCT ⬥⬥½

Defenders of the Law Early action talkie concerned with gang warfare and law enforcement.
1931 64m/B John Holland, Mae Busch, Alan Cooke, Joseph Girard, Edmund Breese, Catherine Dale Owen, Robert Gleckler; **D:** Joseph Levering. **VHS** $9.95 GPV ⬥⬥

Defending Your Life Brooks' cockeyed way of looking at the world travels to the afterlife in this uneven comedy/romance. In Judgement City, where everyone goes after death, past lives are examined and judged. If you were a good enough person (and didn't let your fears control your life) you get to stay in heaven (where you wear funny robes and eat all you want without getting fat). If not, it's back to earth for another go-round. Brooks plays an L.A. advertising executive who crashes his new B.M.W. and finds himself defending his life. When he meets and falls in love with Streep, his interest in staying in heaven multiplies. Occasionally charming, seldom out-right hilarious. A funny premise taken too seriously. Available in widescreen on laserdisc.
1991 (PG) 112m/C Albert Brooks, Meryl Streep, Rip Torn, Lee Grant, Buck Henry; **W/D:** Albert Brooks. **VHS, LV, 8mm** $19.95 WAR ⬥⬥⬥

The Defense Never Rests Perry Mason, the lawyer who never loses a case, aids his friend and secretary, Della Street, in this made-for-television movie.
1990 95m/C Raymond Burr, Barbara Hale, Al Freeman Jr., William Katt, Patrick O'Neal. **VHS, Beta** $29.98 MCG ⬥⬥

Defense of the Realm A British politician is accused of selling secrets to the KGB through his mistress and only a pair of dedicated newspapermen believe he is innocent. In the course of finding the answers they discover a national cover-up conspiracy. An acclaimed, taut thriller.
1985 (PG) 96m/C GB Gabriel Byrne, Greta Scacchi, Denholm Elliott, Ian Bannen, Bill Paterson, Fulton Mackay, Robbie Coltrane; **D:** David Drury. **VHS, Beta, LV** $14.95 COL, SUE ⬥⬥⬥½

Defense Play Two teenagers are unwittingly stuck in the middle of a Soviet plot to steal the plans that created a technologically advanced helicopter.
1988 (PG) 95m/C David Oliver, Susan Ursitti, Monte Markham, William Frankfather, Patch MacKenzie; **D:** Monte Markham. **VHS, Beta** $19.98 TWE ⬥½

Defenseless Hershey tries hard in an unplayable part as a giddy attorney who finds herself trapped in a love-affair/legal case that turns murderous. Good cast and interesting twists contend with a sexist subtext, which proves a woman can't "have it all."
1991 (R) 106m/C Barbara Hershey, Sam Shepard, Mary Beth Hurt, J.T. Walsh, Sheree North; **D:** Martin Campbell. **VHS, LV** $19.98 LIV ⬥⬥

Defiance A former merchant seaman moves into a tenement in a run-down area of New York City. When a local street gang begins terrorizing the neighborhood, he decides to take a stand. Familiar plotline handled well in this thoughtful film.
1979 (PG) 101m/C Jan-Michael Vincent, Art Carney, Theresa Saldana, Danny Aiello; **D:** John Flynn. **VHS, Beta** $69.98 LIV, VES ⬥⬥

Defiant Two rival street gangs clash when one admits a young orphan girl. **AKA:** The Wild Pack; The Sandpit Generals.
1970 93m/C Kent Lane, John Rubinstein, Tisha Sterling; **D:** Hall Bartlett. **VHS, Beta** $69.98 LIV ⬥½

The Defiant Ones Thought-provoking story about racism revolves around two escaped prisoners (one black, one white) from a chain gang in the rural South. Their societal conditioning to hate each other dissolves as they face constant peril together. Critically acclaimed.
1958 97m/B Tony Curtis, Sidney Poitier, Theodore Bikel, Lon Chaney Jr., Charles McGraw, Cara Williams; **D:** Stanley Kramer; **W:** Nathan E. Douglas, Harold Jacob Smith. Academy Awards '58: Best Black and White Cinematography, Best Original Screenplay; Nominations: Best Actor (Curtis), Best Actor (Poitier), Best Director (Kramer), Best Film Editing, Best Picture, Best Supporting Actor (Bikel), Best Supporting Actress (Williams); British Academy Awards '58: Best Actor (Poitier); Edgar Allan Poe Awards '58: Best Screenplay; Golden Globe Awards '59: Best Film—Drama. **VHS, Beta** $19.95 MGM, FOX ⬥⬥⬥½

The Defilers Disturbing, low-budget J.D. movie in which two thugs imprison a young girl in a basement and force her to be their love slave.
1965 (R) ?m/B Byron Mabe, Jerome Eden, Mae Johnson; **D:** David Friedman. **VHS** $16.95 SNC ⬥

Deja Vu A lame romantic thriller about the tragic deaths of two lovers and their supposed reincarnation 50 years later.
1984 (R) 95m/C GB Jaclyn Smith, Nigel Terry, Claire Bloom, Shelley Winters; **D:** Anthony Richmond. **VHS, Beta, LV** $79.95 MGM ⬥

The Deliberate Stranger Harmon is engrossing as charismatic serial killer Ted Bundy, sentenced to death for several Florida murders and suspected in the killings of a least 25 women in several states. After eluding police for five years Bundy was finally arrested in Florida in 1979. His case became a cause celebre on capital punishment as it dragged on for nine years. Bundy was finally executed in 1989. Based on the book "Bundy: The Deliberate Stranger" by Richard W. Larsen. Made for television.
1986 188m/C Mark Harmon, M. Emmet Walsh, Frederic Forrest, John Ashton, George Grizzard, Ben Masters, Glynnis O'Connor, Bonnie Bartlett, Billy Green Bush, Lawrence Pressman; **D:** Marvin J. Chomsky. **VHS, Beta** $69.99 WAR, PMS ⬥⬥⬥

The Delicate Delinquent Lewis's first movie without Dean Martin finds him in the role of delinquent who manages to become a policeman with just the right amount of slapstick.
1956 101m/B Jerry Lewis, Darren McGavin, Martha Hyer, Robert Ivers, Horace McMahon; **D:** Don McGuire. **VHS, Beta, LV** $24.95 PAR ⬥⬥½

A Delicate Thread A collection of four award-winning cartoons from the Hubley Studio, including "Eggs," (1970) "The Hat," (1964) "Children of the Sun," (1960) and "Second Chance: Sea" (1976).
1986 49m/C V: Dudley Moore, Dizzy Gillespie. **VHS, Beta** $49.95 DVT ⬥⬥½

Delicatessen Set in a 21st-century Paris, this hilarious debut from directors Jeunot and Caro focuses on the lives of the oddball tenants of an apartment building over a butcher shop. Although there is a famine, the butcher shop is always stocked with fresh meat—made from the building's tenants. When a new handyman (and intended victim) moves in, he falls for the butcher's daughter and the two team up to stop the carnage. Part comedy, part horror, part romance, this film merges a cacophony of sights and sounds with intriguing results. Watch for the scene involving a symphony of creaking bed springs, a squeaky bicycle pump, a cello, and clicking knitting needles. In French with English subtitles.
1992 (R) 95m/C FR Dominique Pinon, Marie-Laure Dougnac, Jean Claude Dreyfus, Ticky Holgado, Anne Marie Pisani; **D:** Jean-Marie Jeunet, Marc Caro. **VHS, Beta, LV** $89.95 PAR, TAM ⬥⬥⬥

Delightfully Dangerous Often Deadly Dull. A farfetched musical rooted in yesteryear about mismatched sisters, one a 15-year-old farm girl, the other a New York burlesque dancer, in competition on Broadway. ♫I'm Only Teasin'; In a Shower of Stars; Mynah Bird; Through Your Eyes to Your Heart; Delightfully Dangerous; Once Upon a Song.
1945 92m/B Jane Powell, Ralph Bellamy, Constance Moore, Arthur Treacher, Louise Beavers; **D:** Arthur Lubin. **VHS** $19.95 DVT, NOS, VDM ⬥⬥

Delinquent Daughters Slow-paced drama about a high school girl who commits suicide and the cop and reporter who try to find out why so darn many kids are getting into trouble.
1944 71m/B June Carlson, Fifi d'Orsay, Teala Loring; **D:** Albert Herman. **VHS, Beta** $16.95 SNC, VYY ⬥½

Delinquent Parents A wayward girl gives up her baby for adoption. She turns her life around and becomes a juvenile court judge. Years later, who should come up before her for misdeeds but her long-lost daughter. The Hound cannot improve on a contemporary critic who renamed this "Delinquent Producers."
1938 62m/B Doris Weston, Maurice Murphy, Helen MacKellar, Terry Walker, Richard Tucker, Morgan Wallace; **D:** Nick Grinde. **VHS** $15.95 NOS, LOO ⬥½

Delinquent School Girls Three escapees from an asylum get more than they bargained for when they visit a Female Correctional Institute to fulfill their sexual fantasies. Buys into just about every conceivable stereotype. **AKA:** Bad Girls.
1984 (R) 89m/C Michael Pataki, Bob Minos, Stephen Stucker; **D:** Gregory Corarito. **VHS, Beta** $69.98 LIV, VES, SIM Woof!

Delirious A writer for a television soap opera wakes from a bash on the head to find himself inside the story where murder and mayhem are brewing. Can he write himself back to safety, and find romance along the way? Somehow Candy just isn't believeable as a romantic lead and the film has few laughs.
1991 (PG) 96m/C John Candy, Mariel Hemingway, Emma Samms, Raymond Burr, David Rasche, Dylan Baker, Charles Rocket, Jerry Orbach, Renee Taylor, Robert Wagner; **D:** Tom Mankiewicz. **VHS, Beta, LV, 8mm** $94.99 MGM, PIA ⬥½

Delirium Homicidal maniac goes on a killing spree and has just one thing in mind—women. Angry group of citizens inadvertently includes the demonic villain in their vigilante club. Nothing redeeming here. **AKA:** Psycho Puppet.
1977 94m/C Turk Cekovsky, Debi Shanley, Terry Ten Brock; **D:** Peter Maris. **VHS, Beta** $19.95 PGN Woof!

Deliverance A terrifying exploration of the primal nature of man and his alienation from nature, based on the novel by James Dickey, which he adapted for the film (and in which he makes an appearance as a sheriff). Four urban professionals, hoping to get away from it all for the weekend, canoe down a southern river, encounter crazed backwoodsmen, and end up battling for survival. Excellent performances all around, especially by Voight. Debuts for Beatty and Cox. "Dueling Banjos" scene and tune are memorable as is scene where the backwoods boys promise to make the fellows squeal like pigs. **1972 (R) 109m/C** Jon Voight, Burt Reynolds, Ronny Cox, Ned Beatty, James Dickey, Bill McKinney; **D:** John Boorman; **W:** Bill McKinney, Bill McKinney. Academy Awards '72 Nominations: Best Director (Boorman), Best Film Editing, Best Picture; National Board of Review Awards '72: 10 Best Films of the Year. **VHS, Beta, LV $19.98** WAR, FCT 𝄞𝄞𝄞𝄞

Delivery Boys The "Delivery Boys," three breakdancers aiming to win the $10,000 New York City Break-Off, find unusual perils that may keep them from competing.
1984 (R) 94m/C Joss Marcano, Tom Sierchio, Jim Soriero, Mario Van Peebles, Samantha Fox; **D:** Ken Handley. **VHS, Beta $19.95** STE, NWV 𝄞½

Delos Adventure A geological expedition in South America stumbles upon covert Russian activities and must battle to survive in this overly-violent actioner.
1986 (R) 98m/C Roger Kerns, Jenny Neumann, Kevin Brophy; **D:** Joseph Purcell. **VHS, Beta $79.95** TWE 𝄞

Delta Force Based on the true hijacking of a TWA plane in June 1985. Arab terrorists take over an airliner; the Delta Force, led by Lee Marvin and featuring Norris as its best fighter, rescue the passengers in ways that cater directly to our nationalistic revenge fantasies. Average thriller, exciting and tense at times, with fine work from Marvin, Norris, and Forster.
1986 (R) 125m/C Lee Marvin, Chuck Norris, Shelley Winters, Martin Balsam, George Kennedy, Hanna Schygulla, Susan Strasberg, Bo Svenson, Joey Bishop, Lainie Kazan, Robert Forster, Robert Vaughn, Kim Delaney; **D:** Menahem Golan. **VHS, Beta, LV $9.99** MED 𝄞𝄞

Delta Force 2: Operation Stranglehold Delta Force is back with martial artist and military technician Norris at the helm. Action-packed and tense.
1990 (R) 110m/C John P. Ryan, Chuck Norris, Billy Drago, Richard Jaeckel, Paul Perri; **D:** Aaron Norris. **VHS, Beta, LV $89.98** MED, BTV 𝄞½

Delta Force 3: The Killing Game A terrorist mastermind plants an atomic bomb in an American city, and the President has only one choice...call in the Delta Force. The leading men in this lackluster thriller are the sons of Hollywood's biggest stars. **AKA:** Young Commandos.
1991 (R) 97m/C Nick Cassavetes, Eric Douglas, Mike Norris, Matthew Penn, John P. Ryan, Sandy Ward; **D:** Sam Firstenberg. **VHS, LV $89.99** CAN, PIA 𝄞½

Delta Force Commando Two U.S. Fighter pilots fight against terrorism in the deadly Nicaraguan jungle.
1987 (R) 90m/C Fred Williamson, Bo Svenson. **VHS $79.99** VES 𝄞½

Delta Force Commando 2 The celluloid was hardly dry on the first "Delta Force Commando" before the resourceful Italians began grinding out this follow-up, with the lead commando getting the Force entangled in a deadly international conspiracy. **AKA:** Priority Red One.
1990 (R) 100m/C IT Richard Hatch, Fred Williamson, Giannina Facio, Van Johnson; **D:** Frank Valenti. **VHS $89.95** LIV 𝄞

Delta Fox Delta Fox is carrying a million dollars for the mob, but the mob is carrying a grudge and the chase is on.
1977 90m/C Priscilla Barnes, Richard Lynch, Stuart Whitman, John Ireland; **D:** Beverly Sebastian, Ferd Sebastian. **VHS, Beta** NO 𝄞

Delta Heat A new designer drug hits L.A. and detective Mike Bishop (Edwards) follows his partner to the drug's source in Louisiana. When Bishop arrives he discovers his partner has been tortured and murdered in order to keep the drug lord's foes in line. Bishop must then save himself and find justice in the steamy streets of New Orleans. Routine lone guy vs. bad guys actioner.
1992 (R) 91m/C Anthony Edwards, Lance Henriksen, Betsy Russell, Linda Dona, Rod Masterson, John McConnell, Clyde Jones; **D:** Michael Rischa. **VHS $89.95** ACA 𝄞

Deluge Tidal waves causd by earthquakes have destroyed most of New York (though some may think this is no great loss) in this early sci-fi pic.
1933 72m/B Edward Van Sloan, Peggy Shannon, Sidney Blackmer, Fred Kohler Jr., Matt Moore, Samuel S. Hinds, Lane Chandler; **D:** Felix Feist. **VHS, Beta** MWP 𝄞𝄞

Delusion Gothic thriller in which invalid Cotten and family are harassed by a possibly supernatural killer as told by Cotten's nurse. Filmed in 1980. Ending is a let-down. **AKA:** The House Where Death Lives.
1984 (R) 93m/C Patricia Pearcy, David Hayward, John Dukakis, Joseph Cotten, Simone Griffeth; **D:** Alan Beattie. **VHS, Beta $24.98** SUE 𝄞½

Delusion A yuppie with an embezzled fortune is held up in the Nevada desert by a psycho hood with a showgirl lover. But who's really in charge here? The snappy, hip, film-noir thriller takes a few unlikely twists and has an open Lady-or-the-Tiger finale that may infuriate some. Available in a widescreen edition on laserdisc.
1991 (R) 100m/C Jim Metzler, Jennifer Rubin, Kyle Secor, Robert Costanzo, Tracy Walter, Jerry Orbach; **D:** Carl Colpaert. **VHS, LV $89.98** COL 𝄞𝄞½

Delusions of Grandeur A French comedy of court intrigue set in 17th-century Spain. In French with English subtitles. Based loosely on Victor Hugo's "Ruy Blas." **AKA:** La Folle des Grandeurs.
1976 85m/C FR Yves Montand, Louis de Funes, Alice Sapritch, Karin Schubert, Gabriele Tinti; **D:** Gerard Oury. **VHS, Beta $24.95** FCT 𝄞𝄞½

Demented Beautiful and talented woman is brutally gang-raped by four men, but her revenge is sweet and deadly as she entices each to bed and gives them a big dose of their own medicine. All-too-familiar plot offers nothing new.
1980 (R) 92m/C Sallee Elyse, Bruce Gilchrist. **VHS, Beta $54.95** MED 𝄞

Dementia 13 This eerie thriller, set in a creepy castle, is an early Coppola film about the members of an Irish family who are being offed by an axe murderer one-by-one. **AKA:** The Haunted and the Hunted.
1963 75m/B William Campbell, Luana Anders, Bart Patton, Patrick Magee; **W/D:** Francis Ford Coppola. **VHS, Beta, 3/4U, Special order formats $19.95** NOS, MRV, SNC 𝄞𝄞½

Demetrius and the Gladiators A sequel to "The Robe," wherein the holy-robe-carrying slave is enlisted as one of Caligula's gladiators and mixes with the trampy empress Messalina.

1954 101m/C Victor Mature, Susan Hayward, Michael Rennie, Debra Paget, Anne Bancroft, Jay Robinson, Barry Jones, William Marshall, Ernest Borgnine; **D:** Delmer Daves. **VHS, Beta, LV $19.98** FOX 𝄞𝄞½

The Demi-Paradise Tongue-in-cheek look at people's perceptions of foreigners has Olivier as a Russian inventor (?!) who comes to England with some trepidation. Though the Brits are plenty quirky, he manages to find romance with Ward in this charming look at British life. **AKA:** Adventure for Two.
1943 110m/B GB Laurence Olivier, Penelope Dudley Ward, Margaret Rutherford, Wilfrid Hyde-White; **D:** Anthony Asquith. **VHS, Beta $19.95** NOS, VDM, DVT 𝄞𝄞𝄞

Demolition Ex-international courier finds that the "simple" task he has consented to do for his old employers is deceptively hazardous.
1977 90m/C John Waters, Belinda Giblin, Fred Steele, Vincent Ball; **D:** Kevin Dobson. **VHS, Beta $59.95** PGN 𝄞

The Demon A small town may be doomed to extinction, courtesy of a monster's thirst for the blood of its inhabitants.
1981 (R) 94m/C Cameron Mitchell, Jennifer Holmes. **VHS, Beta $14.98** HBO, UHV, VID 𝄞½

Demon Barber of Fleet Street Loosely based on an actual event, this film inspired the 1978 smash play "Sweeney Todd." Slaughter stars as a mad barber who doesn't just cut his client's hair. He happens to have a deal cooked up with the baker to provide him with some nice 'juicy' filling for his meat pies. Manages to be creepy and funny at the same time. **AKA:** Sweeney Todd: The Demon Barber of Fleet Street.
1936 68m/B GB Tod Slaughter, Eve Lister, Bruce Seton; **D:** George King. **Beta $19.95** NOS, MRV, SNC 𝄞𝄞½

The Demon Fighter A mystical super-being suddenly appears to kick, punch and smash anyone who gets in his way. What he wants, no one knows.
1988 ?m/C VHS $29.95 OCE 𝄞𝄞½

Demon for Trouble Outlaws are murdering land buyers in this routine western.
1934 58m/B Bob Steele. **VHS, Beta $19.95** NOS, HEG, RXM 𝄞

Demon Hunter Terror reigns while a deranged killer stalks his next victim.
1988 90m/C George Ellis, Erin Fleming, Marrianne Gordon; **D:** Massey Cramer. **VHS, Beta** NO 𝄞½

A Demon in My View In a role similar to his infamous Norman Bates in "Psycho," Perkins stars as a man who hides a terrible secret—he is a former serial killer. When a fellow tenant in his apartment house accidentally destroys his doll, Perkins' tenuous sanity is shaken and he begins killing again. A smart thriller. Perkins last big-screen role.
1992 (R) 98m/C Anthony Perkins, Sophie Ward, Stratford Johns; **D:** Petra Hafter. **VHS, LV $89.95** VMK, MOV 𝄞½

The Demon Lover Leader of a satanic cult calls forth the devil when he doesn't get his way. Poorly acted and badly produced. Features comic book artists Val "Howard the Duck" Mayerick and Gunnar "Leatherface" Hansen. Also on video as "Devil Master" and "Master of Evil."
1977 (R) 87m/C Christmas Robbins, Val Mayerick, Gunnar Hansen, Tom Hutton, David Howard; **W/D:** Donald G. Jackson, Jerry Younkins. **VHS, Beta $9.95** UNI, PMR Woof!

Demon Lust A couple's lovely country vacation is turned into a nightmare when two drifters terrorize them.
19?? 76m/C *D:* Bernard Buys. **VHS, Beta** **$59.95** *GHV* ⫫

Demon of Paradise Dynamite fishing off the coast of Hawaii unearths an ancient, man-eating lizard-man. Uneven, unexciting horror attempt.
1987 (R) 84m/C Kathryn Witt, William Steis, Leslie Huntly, Laura Banks; *D:* Cirio H. Santiago. **VHS, Beta** **$14.95** *WAR* *Woof!*

Demon Possessed When Tom is critically injured in a snowmobile race in a remote woods, he and his friends find shelter in a deserted children's camp. It turns out the camp was run by a secret religious cult that practiced occult murder and the demon that haunted the place has never left. When Tom dies this satanic spirit finds the perfect host to return to human form and continue its bloody work.
199? (R) 97m/C Dawn Laurrie, Aaron Kjenass, David Fields, Eve Montgomery; *D:* Christopher Webster; *W:* Julian Weaver; *M:* John Tatgenhorst. **VHS** **$89.95** *AIP* ⫫ ½

Demon Queen A vampirish woman seduces, then murders, many men.
1987 70m/C Mary Fanaro, Dennis Stewart, Cliff Dance; *D:* Donald Farmer. **VHS, Beta** *NO* ⫫

Demon Rage Neglected housewife drifts under the spell of a phantom lover. *AKA:* Satan's Mistress; Fury of the Succubus; Dark Eyes.
1982 (R) 98m/C Britt Ekland, Lana Wood, Kabir Bedi, Don Galloway, John Carradine, Sherry Scott; *D:* James Polakof. **VHS, Beta** **$59.95** *HHE* ⫫ ½

Demon Seed When a scientist and his wife separate so he can work on his computer, the computer takes over the house and impregnates the wife. Bizarre and taut.
1977 (R) 97m/C Julie Christie, Fritz Weaver, Gerrit Graham, Berry Kroeger; *D:* Donald Cammell; *V:* Robert Vaughn. **VHS, Beta, LV** **$59.95** *MGM* ⫫⫫⫫

Demon Warrior An Indian shaman curses a land-stealing white man and revenge comes in the form of the Demon Warrior, who can appear but once every ten years.
19?? 82m/C **VHS** **$79.98** *MNC, MOV* ⫫⫫

Demon Wind A gateway to Hell opens up on a secluded farm and various heroic types try to close it. Meanwhile, demons attempt to possess those humans in their midst. Zombies abound in this near-woof.
1990 (R) 97m/C Eric Larson, Francine Lapensee, Rufus Norris; *D:* Charles Philip Moore. **VHS, Beta, LV** **$79.95** *PAR* ⫫ ½

Demon Witch Child A wrongly accused old woman commits suicide and possesses a young girl who takes revenge on everyone.
1975 90m/C **VHS, Beta** **$9.95** *NO* *Woof!*

Demon with a Glass Hand In the vein of "The Terminator," a man goes back two hundred years in time to escape the evil race that rules the planet.
1964 63m/B Robert Culp, Arlene Martel, Abraham Sofaer. **VHS, Beta** **$14.95** *MGM* ⫫ ½

Demonic Toys The possessed playthings attack a bunch of unfortunates in a warehouse, and pumped-up lady cop Scoggins deserves an award for keeping a straight face. Skimpily scripted gore from the horror assembly-line at Full Moon Productions. Far more entertaining are the multiple behind-the-scenes featurettes on the tape.

1991 (R) 86m/C Tracy Scoggins, Bentley Mitchum, Michael Russo, Jeff Weston, Daniel Cerney, Pete Schrum; *D:* Peter Manoogian. **VHS, Beta, LV** *PAR, PIA* ⫫ ½

Demonoid, Messenger of Death Discovery of an ancient temple of Satan worship drastically changes the lives of a young couple when the husband becomes possessed by the Demonoid, which initially takes on the form of a severed hand. Poor script needs hand, producing a number of unintentionally laughable moments. *AKA:* Macabra.
1981 (R) 85m/C Samantha Eggar, Stuart Whitman, Roy Cameron Jenson; *D:* Alfredo Zacharias. **VHS, Beta** **$9.95** *MED* ⫫

The Demons As she slips into death, a tortured woman curses her torturers.
1974 (R) 90m/C Anne Libert, Britt Nichols, Doris Thomas. **VHS, Beta** **$49.95** *UNI* ⫫

Demons A horror film in a Berlin theater is so involving that its viewers become the demons they are seeing. The new monsters turn on the other audience members. Virtually plotless, very explicit. Rock soundtrack by Accept, Go West, Motley Crue, and others. Revered in some circles, blasted in others. Followed by "Demons 2." *AKA:* Demoni.
1986 (R) 89m/C *IT* Urbano Barberini, Natasha Hovey, Paolo Cozza, Karl Zinny, Fiore Argento, Fabiola Toledo, Nicoletta Elni; *D:* Lamberto Bava. **VHS, Beta, LV** **$19.95** *STE, NWV* ⫫ ½

Demons 2 Lamberto Bava's inferior sequel to "Demons" has been compared to the works of Romero, Raimi, and even Cronenberg, but never, ever, favorably. The son of horror-meister Mario Bava, Lamberto collaborated with Italian auteur Dario Argento (who co-wrote and produced) to create a non-sequitur of a sequel (storywise). Although a hit in Italy, "Demons 2" seems to have been edited by some kind of crazed cutting room slasher, and the dubbing is equally hackneyed. We find the residents of a chi-chi high rise watching a documentary about the events of "Demons"—a sort of high-tech play-within-a-play ploy—when a demon emerges from a TV set, spreads his creepy cooties, and causes the tenants to sprout fangs and claws and nasty tempers. Much blood dripping from ceilings, plumbing fixtures and various body parts.
1987 88m/C *IT* David Knight, Nancy Brill, Coralina Cataldi Tassoni, Bobby Rhodes, Asia Argento, Virginia Bryant; *D:* Lamberto Bava. **VHS** **$29.99** *IMP* ⫫ ½

Demons in the Garden Centers on the disintegration of a family after the end of the Spanish Civil War, due to sibling rivalries and a variety of indiscretions. Problems mount as two brothers become involved with their stepsister. Story takes on poignancy in its narration by a young boy. Beautiful cinematography. In Spanish with English subtitles. *AKA:* Demonios En El Jardin.
1982 (R) 100m/C *SP* Angela Molina, Ana Belen, Encarna Paso, Imanol Arias; *D:* Manuel Gutierrez Aragon. **VHS** **$79.95** *CVC, TAM* ⫫⫫⫫

Demons of Ludlow Demons attend a small town's bicentennial celebration intent on raising a little hell of their own.
1975 83m/C Paul von Hauser, Stephanie Cushna, James Robinson, Carol Perry; *D:* Steven Kuether. **VHS, Beta** **$59.95** *TWE* ⫫

Demons of the Mind A sordid psychological horror film about a baron in 19th century Austria who imprisons his children, fearing that mental illness is a family trait. Also on video as "Blood Evil."

1972 (R) 85m/C *GB* Michael Hordern, Patrick Magee, Yvonne Mitchell, Robert Hardy, Gillian Hills, Virginia Wetherell, Shane Briant, Paul Jones; *D:* Peter Sykes. **VHS, Beta** **$59.99** *HBO, ACA, MLB* ⫫⫫

Demonstone A television reporter becomes possessed by a Filipino demon and carries out an ancient curse against the family of a corrupt government official. *AKA:* Heartstone.
1989 (R) 90m/C Lee Ermey, Jan-Michael Vincent, Nancy Everhard; *D:* Andrew Prowse. **VHS, Beta, LV** **$29.95** *FRH* ⫫

Demonstrator A father and son are at odds when dad heads an Asian military coalition and junior protests. Notable for being one of the first major Australian films to use an entirely native cast.
1971 90m/C *AU* Joe James, Irene Inescort, Gerard Maguire, Wendy Lingham, Harold Hopkins; *D:* Warwick Freeman. **VHS** **$19.95** *ACA* ⫫⫫ ½

Demonwarp A vengeance-minded hunter journeys into an evil, primeval forest to kill the monsters that abducted his daughter.
1987 91m/C George Kennedy, Emmett Alston. **VHS, Beta** **$79.95** *VMK* *Woof!*

Dempsey In this made for television film based on Jack Dempsey's autobiography, Williams plays the role of the famed world heavyweight champ. His rise through the boxing ranks as well as his personal life are chronicled. A bit slow-moving considering the pounding fists and other action.
1983 110m/C Treat Williams, Sam Waterston, Sally Kellerman, Victoria Tennant, Peter Mark Richman, Jesse Vint, Bonnie Bartlett, James Noble; *D:* Gus Trikonis. **VHS, Beta** *MED* ⫫⫫

Denial: The Dark Side of Passion A strong-willed woman tries to put a destructive love affair behind her—but if she succeeded there'd be no movie. Torrid stuff with a watchable cast.
1991 (R) 103m/C Robin Wright, Jason Patric, Barry Primus, Christina Harnos, Rae Dawn Chong; *W/D:* Eric Dignam. **VHS, LV** **$89.98** *REP* ⫫⫫

Dennis the Menace Straight from the Hughes kiddie farm comes Kevin McAllister—oops!—Dennis Mitchell (newcomer Gamble), curious, crafty, and blond 5-year-old. Dennis' view of the world is anything but conventional and he dreams and schemes of ways to act out his extraordinary perceptions of life. Each personal expression, however, manages to be a threat to the physical and mental well-being of hot-head neighbor Mr. Wilson (Matthau, perfectly cast as the grump). Lloyd is very nasty as protagonist Switchblade Sam; Plowright, Thompson, and Stanton round out the cast as Mrs. Wilson and the Mitchell parents, respectively. Sure to please young kids, but parents may be less enthralled with this adaptation of the popular '50s comic strip and subsequent TV series.
1993 (PG) 94m/C Walter Matthau, Mason Gamble, Joan Plowright, Christopher Lloyd, Lea Thompson, Robert Stanton, Billie Bird, Paul Winfield, Amy Sakasitz, Kellen Hathaway; *D:* Nick Castle; *W:* John Hughes; *M:* Jerry Goldsmith. **VHS** *NYR* ⫫⫫ ½

The Dentist Fields treats several oddball patients in his office. After watching the infamous tooth-pulling scene, viewers are sure to brush regularly.
1932 22m/B W.C. Fields, Elise Cavanna, Babe Kane, Bud Jamison, Zedna Farley. **VHS, Beta** **$19.98** *CCB* ⫫⫫⫫ ½

The Denver & Rio Grande Action-packed western about two rival railroads competing to be the first to complete a line through the Royal Gorge. Plot is predictable, but the scene featuring two trains crashing into each other is worth it (Haskin used actual trains for this stunt).
1951 89m/C Edmond O'Brien, Sterling Hayden, Dean Jagger, ZaSu Pitts, J. Carroll Naish; **D:** Byron Haskin. VHS PAR ♂♂½

Departamento Compartido A notorious ladies' man and his shy friend become unlikely roommates after their wives kick them out of their homes.
1985 100m/C SP Alberto Olmedo, Tato Bores, Graciela Alfano, Camila Perisse; **D:** Hugo Sofovich. VHS, Beta $29.95 MED ♂

The Deputy Drummer Second-rate early British musical, notable as a later vehicle for silent-era star Lane. He plays a penniless composer who impersonates an aristocrat to attend a party, and catches jewel robbers in the act.
1935 71m/B GB Lupino Lane, Jean Denis, Kathleen Kelly, Wallace Lupino, Margaret Yarde, Syd Crossley. VHS $19.95 NOS ♂½

Deputy Marshall Hall trails a pair of bankrobbers, fights off landgrabbers, and finds romance as well.
1950 75m/B Jon Hall, Frances Langford, Dick Foran. VHS, Beta RXM ♂½

Der Purimshpiler A drifter embarks on a quest for happiness, which takes him to various small towns. In one, he meets and falls in love with a shoemaker's daughter. In Yiddish with English subtitles. **AKA:** The Purim Player; The Jester; The Jewish Jester.
1937 90m/B PL Miriam Kressyn, Zygmund Turkow, Hymie Jacobsen; **D:** Joseph Green. VHS, Beta $79.95 ERG ♂♂½

Deranged Of the numerous movies based on the cannibalistic exploits of Ed Gein ("Psycho," "Texas Chainsaw Massacre," etc.), this is the most accurate. A dead-on performance by Blossom and a twisted sense of humor help move things along nicely. The two directors, Gillen and Ormsby, previously worked together on the classic "Children Shouldn't Play with Dead Things." An added attraction is the early special effect work of gore wizard Tom Savini.
1974 (R) 82m/C CA Roberts Blossom, Cosette Lee, Robert Warner, Marcia Diamond, Brian Sneagle; **D:** Jeff Gillen, Alan Ormsby. VHS $18.00 FRG, MRV ♂♂♂

Deranged A mentally unstable, pregnant woman is attacked in her apartment after her husband leaves town. She spends the rest of the movie engaged in psychotic encounters, real and imagined. Technically not bad, but extremely violent and grim. Not to be confused with 1974 movie of the same name.
1987 (R) 85m/C Jane Hamilton, Paul Siederman, Jennifer Delora, James Gillis, Jill Cumer, Gary Goldman; **D:** Chuck Vincent. VHS $14.95 REP ♂½

Derby The documentary story of the rise to fame of roller-derby stars on the big rink.
1971 (R) 91m/C Charlie O'Connell, Lydia Gray, Janet Earp, Ann Colvello, Mike Snell; **D:** Robert Kaylor. VHS, Beta $49.95 PSM, FFF ♂♂♂

Dersu Uzala An acclaimed, photographically breathtaking film about a Russian surveyor in Siberia who befriends a crusty, resourceful Mongolian. They begin to teach each other about their respective worlds. Produced in Russia; one of Kurosawa's stranger films.
1975 124m/C JP RU Yuri Solomin, Maxim Munzuk; **D:** Akira Kurosawa. VHS, Beta $29.98 SUE ♂♂♂½

Descending Angel The premise is familiar: a swastika-friendly collaborator is forced out of the closet. But the cast and scripting make this made-for-cable there's-a-Nazi-in the-woodwork suspenser better than average, despite its flawed finale. Scott plays a well-respected Romanian refugee—active in the community, in the church, and in Romanian-American activities—whose daughter's fiance (Roberts) suspects him of Nazi collusion.
1990 (R) 96m/C George C. Scott, Diane Lane, Eric Roberts, Mark Margolis, Vyto Ruginis, Amy Aquino; **D:** Jeremy Paul Kagan; **W/D:** George C. Scott. VHS, LV $89.99 HBO ♂♂♂

Desde el Abismo After the birth of her son, a young mother takes to drink while in the throes of post-partum depression. In Spanish.
19?? 115m/C SP Thelma Biral, Alberto Argibay, Olga Zubarry. VHS, Beta $29.95 MED ♂½

Desert Bloom On the eve of a nearby nuclear bomb test, a beleaguered alcoholic veteran and his family struggle through tensions brought on by a promiscuous visiting aunt and the chaotic, rapidly changing world. Gish shines as the teenage daughter through whose eyes the story unfolds. From a story by Corr and Linda Ramy.
1986 (PG) 103m/C Jon Voight, JoBeth Williams, Ellen Barkin, Annabeth Gish, Allen Garfield, Jay Underwood; **D:** Eugene Corr. VHS, Beta, LV $9.95 RCA ♂♂♂

Desert Commandos When the Allies appear to be winning World War II, the Nazis devise a plan to eliminate all of the opposing forces' leaders at once.
196? ?m/C Kenneth Clark, Horst Frank, Jeanne Valeri, Carlo Hinterman, Gianni Rizzo. VHS NO ♂♂

The Desert Fox Big-budgeted portrait of German Army Field Marshal Rommel, played by Mason, focuses on the soldier's defeat in Africa during World War II and his subsequent, disillusioned return to Hitler's Germany. Mason played Rommel again in 1953's "Desert Rats." **AKA:** Rommel—Desert Fox.
1951 87m/B James Mason, Cedric Hardwicke, Jessica Tandy, Luther Adler; **D:** Henry Hathaway. VHS, Beta, LV $19.98 FOX, TLF ♂♂♂

Desert Gold A fierce Indian chief battles a horde of greedy white men over his tribe's gold mine. Based on a novel by Zane Grey.
1936 58m/B Buster Crabbe, Robert Cummings, Marsha Hunt, Tom Keene, Raymond Hatton, Monte Blue, Leif Erickson; **D:** Charles T. Barton. VHS, Beta $19.95 NOS, DVT ♂½

Desert Guns/Six-Shootin' Sheriff Double feature includes a rare Tearle "B" film and a Maynard oater from 1938.
1936 ?m/C Conway Tearle, Ken Maynard. VHS $18 RXM ♂♂

Desert Hearts An upstanding professional woman travels to Reno, Nevada in 1959 to obtain a quick divorce, and slowly becomes involved in a lesbian relationship with a free-spirited casino waitress.
1986 (R) 93m/C Helen Shaver, Audra Lindley, Patricia Charbonneau, Andra Akers, Dean Butler, Jeffrey Tambor, Denise Crosby, Gwen Welles; **D:** Donna Deitch. VHS, Beta, LV $29.98 LIV, VES ♂♂♂

Desert Kickboxer A border guard takes on a cocaine dealer and his henchmen, fighting for gold and, of course, a beautiful woman. Lots of kickboxing action.
1992 (R) 86m/C John Haymes Newton, Judie Aronson, Sam DeFrancisco, Paul Smith; **D:** Isaac Florentine. VHS, LV $89.99 HBO ♂♂

The Desert of the Tartars Story of a young soldier who dreams of war and discovers the real battle for him is with time. **AKA:** Le Desert des Tartares.
1976 (PG) 140m/C Jacques Perrin; **M:** Ennio Morricone. VHS, Beta $59.95 SUE ♂½

Desert Passion Heather and Maggie are two friends who dream of a better life, so they head to Las Vegas to try their luck. When their car breaks down, the duo wind up being kidnapped and taken to an underground fantasyland where they become sexual pawns.
1993 ?m/C Carrie Janisse, Missy Browne, Tony Bond. VHS $79.95 CEL ♂

Desert Phantom Villains threaten to rob a woman of her ranch until a stranger rescues her.
1936 66m/B Johnny Mack Brown. VHS, Beta, LV NO ♂½

The Desert Rats A crusty British captain (Burton) takes charge of an Australian division during World War II. Thinking they are inferior to his own British troops, he is stiff and uncaring to the Aussies until a kind-hearted drunk and the courage of the division win him over. Crack direction from Wise and Newton's performance (as the wag) simply steal the movie. Mason reprises his role as Germany Army Field Marshal Rommel from "The Desert Fox."
1953 88m/B Richard Burton, Robert Newton, Robert Douglas, Torin Thatcher, Chips Rafferty, Charles Tingwell, James Mason; **D:** Robert Wise. VHS, Beta $19.98 FXV, FCT ♂♂♂

Desert Snow Here's a non-formulaic dope opera oater: cowboys 'n' drug runners battle it out for an out-of-the-way, underpopulated western town. About as clever as the title.
1989 (R) 90m/C Frank Capizzi, Flint Carney, Shelley Hinkle, Sam Incorvia, Carolyn Jacobs; **D:** Paul de Cruccio. VHS, Beta VTR ♂♂

The Desert Tigers Allied soldiers escape from a German POW camp and battle for survival across the African deserts. **AKA:** Los Tigres del Desierto.
19?? 95m/C Richard Harrison, Lea Lander. VHS, Beta $39.98 MOV ♂½

Desert Trail Wayne is a championship rodeo rider accused of bank robbery.
1935 57m/B John Wayne, Paul Fix, Mary Kornman; **D:** Robert North Bradbury. VHS, Beta, 3/4U, Special order formats $9.98 REP, COL, MRV ♂½

Desert Warrior Earth becomes a waste site after a nuclear war. Ferrigno stars as a post-nuke hero in this low-budget action film. Very bad acting.
1988 (PG-13) 89m/C Lou Ferrigno, Shari Shattuck, Kenneth Peer, Anthony East; **D:** Jim Goldman. VHS, Beta $79.95 PSM ♂

The Deserters Sergeant Hawley, a Vietnam-era hawk, hunts deserters and draft-dodgers in Canada. There, he confronts issues of war and peace head-on.
198? 110m/C Alan Scarfe, Dermot Hennelly, Jon Bryden, Barbara March. VHS, Beta MOV ♂½

Designing Woman Bacall and Peck star in this mismatched tale of romance. She's a chic high-fashion designer, he's a rumpled sports writer. The fun begins when they try to adjust to married life together. Neither likes the other's friends or lifestyle. Things get even crazier when Bacall has to work with her ex-lover Helmore on a fashion show and Peck's former lover Gray shows up as well. And as if that weren't enough, Peck is being hunted by the mob because of a boxing story he's written. It's a fun, quick,

witty tale that is all entertainment and no message. Bacall's performance is of note because Bogart was dying of cancer at the time.
1957 118m/C Gregory Peck, Lauren Bacall, Dolores Gray, Sam Levene, Tom Helmore, Mickey Shaughnessy, Jesse White, Chuck Connors, Edward Platt, Alvy Moore, Jack Cole; **D:** Vincente Minnelli; **W:** George Wells. **VHS, Beta, LV** $19.98 *MGM* 🎬🎬🎬

Desire and Hell at Sunset Motel Low-budget thriller takes place at the Sunset Motel in 1950s Anaheim. Fenn is the bombshell wife of a toy salesman who's in town for a sales meeting, while she just wants to visit Disneyland. She's soon fooling around with another guy and her husband hires a psychotic criminal to spy on her as her new lover plots to kill hubby. Very confusing plot isn't worth figuring out. Film's only redeeming quality is the imaginative and creative work used in the visuals. Castle's directorial debut.
1992 (PG-13) 90m/C Sheryln Fenn, Whip Hubley, David Hewlett, David Johansen, Paul Bartel; **W/D:** Alien Castle. **VHS, Beta, LV** $89.98 *FXV* 🎬 ½

Desire Under the Elms Ives, the patriarch of an 1840s New England farming family, takes a young wife (Loren) who promptly has an affair with her stepson. Loren's American film debut. Based on the play by Eugene O'Neill.
1958 114m/B Sophia Loren, Anthony Perkins, Burl Ives, Frank Overton; **D:** Delbert Mann. **VHS, Beta, LV** $19.95 *KRT, FCT, PAR* 🎬🎬 ½

Desiree A romanticized historical epic about Napoleon and his 17-year-old mistress, Desiree. Based on the novel by Annemarie Selinko. Slightly better than average historical fiction piece.
1954 110m/C Marlon Brando, Jean Simmons, Merle Oberon, Michael Rennie, Cameron Mitchell, Elizabeth Sellars, Cathleen Nesbitt; **D:** Henry Koster. **Beta, LV, CDV** $19.95 *FOX, IME* 🎬🎬 ½

Desk Set One of the later and less dynamic Tracy/Hepburn comedies, about an efficiency expert who installs a giant computer in an effort to update a television network's female-run reference department. Still, the duo sparkle as they bicker, battle, and give in to love. Based on William Marchant's play. **AKA:** His Other Woman.
1957 103m/C Spencer Tracy, Katharine Hepburn, Joan Blondell, Gig Young, Dina Merrill, Neva Patterson; **D:** Walter Lang. **VHS, Beta, LV** $19.98 *FOX, FCT* 🎬🎬🎬

Despair A chilling and comic study of a victimized chocolate factory owner's descent into madness, set against the backdrop of the Nazi rise to power in the 1930s. Adapted from the Nabokov novel by Tom Stoppard.
1979 120m/C GE Dirk Bogarde, Andrea Ferreol, Volker Spengler, Klaus Lowitsch; **D:** Rainer Werner Fassbinder; **W:** Tom Stoppard. **VHS, Beta** *GLV* 🎬🎬🎬

Despedida de Casada After their divorce, a man and a woman concentrate on making the other's life miserable.
1987 101m/C MX Ana Louisa Peluffo, Mauricio Garces, Hector Suarez. **VHS, Beta** $55.95 *MAD* 🎬🎬

Desperados After the Civil War, a murderous renegade and two of his sons go on a looting rampage, eventually kidnapping the child of the third son who just wants to live in peace. Made in Spain.
1969 (PG) 90m/C SP Jack Palance, Vince Edwards, Christian Roberts, George Maharis, Neville Brand, Sylvia Syms; **D:** Henry Levin. **VHS, Beta** $14.95 *COL* 🎬🎬 ½

The Desperados When a young woman is raped by outlaws robbing her stagecoach, a bevy of western heroes band together to avenge her.
198? 86m/C Keenan Wynn, Henry Silva, Michele Carey, John Anderson, Joe Turkel; **D:** Ron Joy. **VHS** $14.95 *SIM, COL* 🎬 ½

Desperate An honest truck driver witnesses a mob crime and must escape with his wife in this minor film noir. Eventually, the law is on his tail, too.
1947 73m/B Steve Brodie, Audrey Long, Raymond Burr, Jason Robards Sr., Douglas Fowley, William Challee, Ilka Gruning, Nan Leslie; **D:** Anthony Mann. **VHS, Beta** $19.98 *TTC* 🎬🎬 ½

Desperate Cargo Two showgirls stranded in a Latin American town manage to get aboard a clipper ship with hoodlums who are trying to steal the vessel's cargo.
1941 69m/B Ralph Byrd, Carol Hughes, Jack Mulhall. **VHS, Beta** $24.95 *NOS, DVT, HEG* 🎬 ½

Desperate Characters A slice-of-city-life story about a middle-class couple living in a once-fashionable section of Brooklyn, New York, who watch their neighborhood disintegrate around them. Their marriage on remote control, the two find their lives a series of small disappointments, routine work, uncertain friendships, and pervasive violence. Excellent performances, especially by MacLaine as the harried wife, but the film's depressing nature made it a complete box office flop.
1971 (R) 87m/C Shirley MacLaine, Kenneth Mars, Gerald S. O'Loughlin, Sada Thompson, Michael Higgins, Rose Gregorio, Jack Somack, Chris Gampel, Mary Ellen Hokanson, Patrick McVey, Carol Kane; **W/D:** Frank D. Gilroy. **VHS** *PAR* 🎬🎬🎬

Desperate Hours A tough, gritty thriller about three escaped convicts taking over a suburban home and holding the family hostage. Plenty of suspense and fine acting. Based on the novel and play by Joseph Hayes.
1955 112m/B Humphrey Bogart, Fredric March, Martha Scott, Arthur Kennedy, Gig Young, Dewey Martin, Mary Murphy, Robert Middleton, Richard Eyer; **D:** William Wyler. **VHS, Beta** $14.95 *PAR* 🎬🎬🎬

Desperate Hours In this remake of the 1955 thriller, an escaped prisoner holes up in a suburban couple's home, waiting for his lawyer/accomplice to take him to Mexico. Tensions heighten between the separated couple and the increasingly nerve-wracked criminals. Terrific, if not downright horrifying, performance by Rourke. Hopkins, Rogers, Crouse, and Lynch work well in their roles, too.
1990 (R) 105m/C Mickey Rourke, Anthony Hopkins, Mimi Rogers, Kelly Lynch, Lindsay Crouse, Elias Koteas, David Morse; **D:** Michael Cimino. **VHS, Beta, LV** $19.98 *MGM, FHE* 🎬🎬 ½

Desperate Journey Flynn and Reagan are two of five Allied fighters shot down over Nazi occupied Poland. They go through various tight squeezes such as stealing Goering's car in Berlin, and eliminating a few Nazis at a chemical factory to get back to the safety of England. All the while they are hunted by Massey as Nazi Major Otto Baumester, who of course bumbles and fumbles the whole affair. Strictly propaganda intended to keep up morale on the homefront. Flynn was not pleased about having Reagan as his co-star, seeing as he was usually paired with female leads.
1942 108m/B Errol Flynn, Ronald Reagan, Raymond Massey, Nancy Coleman, Alan Hale Jr., Arthur Kennedy; **D:** Raoul Walsh. **VHS, Beta** $19.98 *MGM* 🎬🎬 ½

Desperate Lives High school siblings come into contact with drugs and join their guidance counselor in the war against dope. Average made for TV fare.
1982 100m/C Diana Scarwid, Doug McKeon, Helen Hunt, William Windom, Art Hindle, Tom Atkins, Sam Bottoms, Diane Ladd, Dr. Joyce Brothers; **D:** Robert Lewis. **VHS, Beta** $49.95 *LIV* 🎬🎬

Desperate Living Typical John Waters trash. A mental patient (Stole) is released and becomes paranoid that her family may be out to kill her. After aiding in the murder of her husband (the hefty maid, Hill, suffocates him by sitting on him), Stole and Hill escape to Mortville, a town populated by outcasts such as transsexuals, murderers, and the woefully disfigured.
1977 90m/C Jean Hill, Mink Stole, Edith Massey, Mary Vivian Pearce, Liz Renay, Susan Lowe; **D:** John Waters. **VHS, Beta** $19.95 *COL, NLC* 🎬🎬 ½

Desperate Motives Keith and his fiancee Helgenberger are a charming couple who arrive to stay with Keith's distant cousin (Katt) and his family. Only what the family doesn't realize is that the duo have escaped from an asylum for the criminally insane and want to take over their lives. **AKA:** Distant Cousins.
1992 (R) 92m/C David Keith, Marg Helgenberger, William Katt, Mel Harris, Mary Crosby, Brian Bonsall, Cyndi Pass; **D:** Andrew Lane; **W:** C. Courtney Joyner. **VHS, LV** $89.98 *NLC* 🎬🎬

Desperate Moves An Oregon-transplanted geek in San Francisco sets out to make himself over in order to win his dream girl. Sometimes effective, often sappy treatment of his coming to terms with the big city.
1986 90m/C Isabel Sanford, Steve Tracy, Paul Benedict, Christopher Lee, Eddie Deezen; **D:** Oliver Hellman. **VHS, Beta** $19.98 *TWE* 🎬🎬

Desperate Scoundrel/The Pride of Pikeville Two classic comedy films back to back featuring the best of the early silent comics.
1922 44m/B Ford Sterling, Ben Turpin, The Keystone Cops. **VHS, Beta** $19.98 *CCB* 🎬🎬

Desperate Target Courageous people fight against all odds to survive.
1980 90m/C Chris Mitchum. **VHS, Beta** *PGN* 🎬 ½

Desperate Teenage Lovedolls A trashy view of the formation of a tacky all-girl punk group.
1984 60m/C Jennifer Schwartz, Hilary Rubens, Steve McDonald, Tracy Lea; **D:** David Markey. **VHS, Beta** $28.95 *HHT* 🎬

Desperate Women Made for television western about three unjustly accused female convicts rescued en route to prison by an ex-hired gun.
1978 98m/C Susan St. James, Dan Haggerty, Ronee Blakley, Ann Dusenberry, Susan Myers; **D:** Earl Bellamy. **VHS, Beta** $59.95 *LIV* 🎬 ½

Desperately Seeking Susan A bored New Jersey housewife gets her kicks reading the personals. When she becomes obsessed with a relationship between two lovers who arrange their meetings through the columns, she decides to find out for herself who they are. But when she is involved in an accident the housewife loses her memory and thinks she is Susan, the free-spirited woman in the personals. Unfortunately, Susan is in a lot of trouble with all sorts of unsavory folk and our innocent housewife finds herself caught in the middle. Terrific characters, with special appeal generated by Arquette and Madonna. Quinn winningly plays the romantic interest.

1985 (PG-13) 104m/C Rosanna Arquette, Madonna, Aidan Quinn, Mark Blum, Robert Joy, Laurie Metcalf, Steven Wright, John Turturro, Richard Hell, Annie Golden, Ann Magnuson; **D:** Susan Seidelman. **VHS, Beta, LV** $14.98 HBO, FCT ⅍⅍

Destination Moon Story of man's first lunar voyage contains Chesley Bonstell's astronomical artwork and a famous Woody Woodpecker cartoon. Includes previews of coming attractions from classic science fiction films.
1950 91m/C Warner Anderson, Tom Powers, Dick Wesson, Erin O'Brien Moore; **D:** Irving Pichel. Academy Awards '50: Best Special Effects; Nominations: Best Art Direction/Set Decoration (Color). **VHS, Beta, LV** $19.95 SNC, MED ⅍⅍½

Destination Moonbase Alpha In the 21st century, an explosion has destroyed half the moon, causing it to break away from the Earth's orbit. The moon is cast far away, but the 311 people manning Alpha, a research station on the moon, must continue their search for other life forms in outer space. A thankless task. Pilot for the television series "Space: 1999."
1975 93m/C Martin Landau, Barbara Bain, Barry Morse. **VHS, Beta** FOX ⅍⅍

Destination Saturn Buck Rogers awakens from suspended animation in the twenty-fifth century. **AKA:** Buck Rogers.
1939 90m/B Buster Crabbe, Constance Moore; **D:** Ford Beebe. **VHS, Beta, 3/4U, Special order formats** $19.95 NOS, CAB ⅍⅍

Destination Tokyo A weathered World War II submarine actioner, dealing with the search-and-destroy mission of a U.S. sub sent into Tokyo harbor. Available in a colorized version.
1943 135m/B Cary Grant, John Garfield, Alan Hale Jr., Dane Clark, John Ridgely, Warner Anderson, William Prince, Robert Hutton, Tom Tully, Peter Whitney, Faye Emerson, John Forsythe; **D:** Delmer Daves. **VHS, Beta** $19.98 MGM ⅍⅍

Destroy All Monsters When alien babes take control of Godzilla and his monstrous colleagues, it looks like all is lost for Earth. Adding insult to injury, Ghidra is sent in to take care of the loose ends. Can the planet possibly survive this madness? Classic Toho monster slugfest also features Mothra, Rodan, Son of Godzilla, Angila, Varan, Baragon, Spigas and others. **AKA:** Kaiju Soshingeki.
1968 (G) 88m/C JP Akira Kubo, Jun Tazaki, Yoshio Tsuchiya, Kyoko Ai, Yukiko Kobayashi, Kenji Sahara, Andrew Hughes; **D:** Inoshiro Honda. **VHS** $18.00 FRG ⅍⅍½

Destroy All Planets Aliens whose spaceships turn into giant flying squids are attacking Earth. It's up to Gammera, the flying, fire-breathing turtle to save the day.
1968 ?m/C JP Peter Williams, Kojiro Hongo, Toru Takatsuka. **VHS** $16.95 SNC ⅍⅍

Destroyer Trials and tribulations aboard a WWII destroyer result in tensions, but when the time comes for action, the men get the job done.
1943 99m/B Edward G. Robinson, Glenn Ford, Marguerite Chapman, Edgar Buchanan, Leo Gorcey, Regis Toomey, Edward Brophy; **D:** William A. Seiter. **VHS, Beta** NO ⅍⅍⅍

Destroyer Small-budget film crew goes to an empty prison to shoot, and are stalked by the ghost/zombie remains of a huge serial killer given the electric chair 18 months before.
1988 (R) 94m/C Anthony Perkins, Deborah Foreman, Lyle Alzado; **D:** Robert Kirk. **VHS, Beta, LV** NO ⅍

The Destructors An American narcotics enforcement officer in Paris seeks the help of a hitman in order to catch a druglord. **AKA:** The Marseille Contract.
1974 (PG) 89m/C GB Anthony Quinn, Michael Caine, James Mason, Maureen Kerwin, Alexandra Stewart; **D:** Robert Parrish. **VHS, Beta** $69.98 LIV, VES, HHE ⅍⅍

Destry Rides Again An uncontrollably lawless western town is whipped into shape by a peaceful, unarmed sheriff. A vintage Hollywood potpourri with Dietrich's finest post-Sternberg moment; standing on the bar singing "See What the Boys in the Back Room Will Have." The second of three versions of this Max Brand story. First was released in 1932; the third in 1954. **AKA:** Justice Rides Again.
1939 94m/B James Stewart, Marlene Dietrich, Brian Donlevy, Charles Winninger, Mischa Auer, Irene Hervey, Una Merkel, Billy Gilbert, Jack Carson, Samuel S. Hinds; **D:** George Marshall. **VHS, Beta, LV** $19.95 MCA, FCT ⅍⅍⅍⅍

Details of a Duel: A Question of Honor A butcher and a teacher collide in this comedy, and prodded by the church, militia and town officals, must duel before the entire town. In Spanish with English subtitles.
1989 97m/C SP D: Sergio Cabrera. **VHS** $59.95 TAM, FCT ⅍⅍½

The Detective Based on G.K. Chesterton's "Father Brown" detective stories, a slick, funny English mystery in which the famous priest tracks down a notorious, endlessly crafty antique thief. **AKA:** Father Brown.
1954 91m/B GB Alec Guinness, Peter Finch, Joan Greenwood, Cecil Parker, Bernard Lee; **D:** Robert Hamer; **M:** Jerry Goldsmith. **VHS, Beta** $19.95 COL ⅍⅍⅍

The Detective A New York detective investigating the mutilation murder of a homosexual finds political and police department corruption. Fine, gritty performances prevail in this suspense thriller. Based on the novel by Roderick Thorpe.
1968 114m/C Frank Sinatra, Lee Remick, Ralph Meeker, Jacqueline Bisset, William Windom, Robert Duvall, Tony Musante, Jack Klugman, Al Freeman Jr.; **D:** Gordon Douglas. **VHS, Beta, LV** $59.98 FOX ⅍⅍⅍

Detective Sadie & Son A television movie about an elderly detective and her young son cracking a case.
1984 96m/C Debbie Reynolds, Sam Wanamaker, Brian McNamara. **VHS, Beta** NO ⅍

Detective School Dropouts Since they couldn't pass detective school, are they smart enough to outwit a kidnapper? Find out and get a few laughs at the same time. **AKA:** Dumb Dicks.
1985 (PG) 92m/C Lorin Dreyfuss, David Landsberg, Christian de Sica, George Eastman; **D:** Filippo Ottoni. **VHS, Beta** $79.95 MGM ⅍⅍

Detective Story Intense drama about a New York City police precinct with a wide array of characters led by a disillusioned and bitter detective (Douglas). Excellent casting is the strong point, as the film can be a bit dated. Based on Sydney Kingsley's Broadway play.
1951 103m/B Kirk Douglas, Eleanor Parker, Lee Grant, Horace McMahon, William Bendix, Craig Hill, Cathy O'Donnell, Bert Freed, George Macready, Joseph Wiseman, Gladys George, Frank Faylen, Warner Anderson, Gerald Mohr; **D:** William Wyler. Academy Awards '51 Nominations: Best Actress (Parker), Best Director (Wyler), Best Screenplay, Best Supporting Actress (Grant); Cannes Film Festival '52: Best Actress (Grant); Edgar Allan Poe Awards '51: Best Screenplay. **VHS** PAR ⅍⅍⅍½

Detour Considered to be the creme de la creme of "B" movies, a largely unacknowledged but cult-followed noir downer that's well-designed, stylish, and compelling, if not a bit contrived and sometimes annoyingly shrill. Shot in six days with six indoor sets by "B" film swami Ulmer. Neal plays a down-on-his-luck pianist hitching cross-country to rejoin his singer fiancee after both have abandoned hopes of stardom. His first wrong turn involves the accidental death of the man who picked him up from hitchhiking, and after that, he's en route to Destiny with a capital "D" when he picks up fatal femme Savage, who's as vicious a vixen as ever ruined a pretty good man. Told in flashback, it's also been called the most despairing of all "B"-pictures. It's as noir as they get.
1946 67m/B Tom Neal, Ann Savage, Claudia Drake, Edmund MacDonald; **D:** Edgar G. Ulmer. **VHS, Beta, LV** $19.95 KRT, MRV, SNC ⅍⅍⅍

Detour to Danger Two young men set out on a fishing expedition and run into crooks and damsels in distress. Unintentionally hilarious "acting" by the no-name cast make this a grade-Z "B" movie. Of interest only because it was filmed in the three-color Kodachrome process used primarily in documentaries.
1945 56m/C Britt Wood, John Day, Nancy Brinckman; **D:** Richard Talmadge. **VHS, Beta, 8mm** $24.95 VYY Woof!

Detroit 9000 A pair of Detroit policemen investigate a robbery that occurred at a black congressman's fundraising banquet. Also on video as "Detroit Heat."
1973 (R) 106m/C Alex Rocco, Scatman Crothers, Hari Rhodes, Lonette McKee, Herbert Jefferson Jr.; **D:** Arthur Marks. **VHS, Beta** $69.99 HBO, SIM ⅍½

Deutschland im Jahre Null The acclaimed, unsettling vision of post-war Germany as seen through the eyes of a disturbed boy who eventually kills himself. Lyrical and grim, in German with subtitles.
1947 75m/B GE Franz Gruber; **D:** Roberto Rossellini. **VHS, Beta** $29.95 FCT, GLV ⅍⅍⅍½

Devastator A Vietnam vet exacts violent revenge on the murderer of an old army buddy. **AKA:** Kings Ransom; The Destroyers.
1985 (R) 79m/C Richard Hill, Katt Shea Ruben, Crofton Hardester; **D:** Cirio H. Santiago. **VHS, Beta** $79.95 MGM ⅍

Devi A minor film in the Ray canon, it is, nonetheless, a strange and compelling tale of religious superstition. An Indian farmer becomes convinced that his beautiful daughter-in-law is the reincarnation of the goddess Kali. The girl is then pressured into accepting a worship that eventually drives her mad. In Bengali with English subtitles.
1960 96m/B IN Chhabi Biswas, Sharmila Tagore, Soumitra Chatterjee; **D:** Satyajit Ray. **VHS, Beta** $49.95 TAM, WFV, DVT ⅍⅍⅍½

The Devil The last remaining humans try to fight off demonic lifeforms that need to feed on their flesh.
1984 90m/C **VHS, Beta** $39.95 VCD ⅍

The Devil & Daniel Webster A young farmer, who sells his soul to the devil, is saved from a trip to Hell when Daniel Webster steps in to defend him. This classic fantasy is visually striking and contains wonderful performances. **AKA:** All That Money Can Buy; Here Is a Man; A Certain Mr. Scratch.

1941 109m/B James Craig, Edward Arnold, Walter Huston, Simone Simon, Gene Lockhart, Jane Darwell, Anne Shirley, John Qualen, H.B. Warner; *D:* William Dieterle. **VHS, Beta, LV** $14.95 COL, SUE, VYG ⅋⅋⅋½

Devil & Leroy Basset Keema Gregwolf kills a deputy, breaks from jail with the Basset brothers, hijacks a church bus, kidnaps a family, and gets into other troublesome situations while on a posse-eluding cross-country adventure.
1973 (PG) 85m/C Cody Bearpaw, John Goff, George Flower; *D:* Robert E. Pearso. **VHS, Beta** $59.95 PSM ⅋

The Devil & Max Devlin Good cast wanders aimlessly in Disney family fantasy. The recently deceased Max Devlin strikes a bargain with the devil. He will be restored to life if he can convince three mortals to sell their souls. Music by Marvin Hamlisch.
1981 (PG) 95m/C Elliott Gould, Bill Cosby, Susan Anspach, Adam Rich, Julie Budd; *D:* Steven Hilliard Stern. **VHS, Beta** DIS, OM ⅋½

The Devil & Miss Jones Engaging romantic comedy finds a big business boss posing as an ordinary salesclerk to weed out union organizers. He doesn't expect to encounter the wicked management or his beautiful co-worker, however.
1941 90m/B Jean Arthur, Robert Cummings, Charles Coburn, Edmund Gwenn, Spring Byington, William Demarest, S.Z. Sakall; *D:* Sam Wood. **VHS** $19.98 REP ⅋⅋⅋½

The Devil at 4 O'Clock An alcoholic missionary and three convicts work to save a colony of leper children from a South Seas volcano. Quality cast barely compensates for mediocre script.
1961 126m/B Spencer Tracy, Frank Sinatra, Kerwin Mathews, Jean-Pierre Aumont; *D:* Mervyn LeRoy. **VHS, Beta, LV** $39.95 GKK, IME ⅋⅋½

The Devil Bat Madman Lugosi trains a swarm of monstrous blood-sucking bats to attack whenever they smell perfume. Followed by the sequel "Devil Bat's Daughter." *AKA:* Killer Bats.
1941 67m/B Bela Lugosi, Dave O'Brien, Suzanne Kaaren, Yolande Donlan; *D:* Jean Yarborough. **VHS, Beta** $19.95 NOS, SNC, PSM ⅋⅋

The Devil Bat's Daughter A young woman, hoping to avoid becoming insane like her batty father, consults a psychiatrist when she starts to have violent nightmares. Unsuccessful sequel to "Devil Bats."
1946 66m/B Rosemary La Planche, Michael Hale, John James, Molly Lamont; *D:* Frank Wisbar. **VHS, Beta** $14.95 COL, SVS, MRV ⅋½

Devil Diamond Mystery-suspense yarn about two amateur detectives who find themselves facing danger after tracking down a gang of evil jewel thieves.
1937 ?m/C Kane Richmond, Frankie Darro. **VHS** $16.95 SNC ⅋⅋

Devil Dog: The Hound of Hell A family has trouble with man's best friend when they adopt a dog that is the son of the "Hound of Hell" in this made for television movie.
1978 95m/C Richard Crenna, Yvette Mimieux, Kim Richards, Victor Jory; *D:* Curtis Harrington. **VHS, Beta** NO ⅋

Devil Dogs of the Air Cagney and O'Brien team up in another air drama with Cagney once again the cocky pilot who, this time, joins the Marine Air Corp. O'Brien plays his flying idol (and later rival). Cagney finds all his wisecracking and luck are no match for knowledge and experience but he learns. Good stunt flying; shot on location at the San Diego naval air base.

1935 85m/B James Cagney, Pat O'Brien, Margaret Lindsay, Frank McHugh, Robert Barratt, Russell Hicks, Ward Bond; *D:* Lloyd Bacon. **VHS** $19.98 MGM ⅋⅋½

Devil Doll An escaped convict uses a mad scientist's human-shrinking formula to evil ends—he sends out miniature assassins in the guise of store-bought dolls. Rarely seen horror oldie. Co-written by Erich Von Stroheim.
1936 80m/B Lionel Barrymore, Maureen O'Sullivan, Frank Lawton; *D:* Tod Browning; *W:* Tod Browning, Erich von Stroheim. **VHS, Beta** $19.95 MGM, MLB ⅋⅋⅋

Devil Doll Ventriloquist's dummy, which contains the soul of a former performer, eyes a beautiful victim in the crowd. Newspaper guy senses trouble. Cut above the usual talking, stalking dummy story.
1964 80m/B GB Bryant Holiday, William Sylvester; *D:* Lindsay Shonteff. **VHS, Beta** $59.95 MPI ⅋⅋

Devil Girl from Mars Sexy female from Mars and her very large robot arrive at a small Scottish inn to announce that a Martian feminist revolution has occurred. The distaff aliens then undertake a search of healthy Earth males for breeding purposes. Believe it or not, the humans don't want to go and therein lies the rub. A somewhat enjoyable space farce.
1954 76m/B GB Hugh McDermott, Hazel Court, Patricia Laffan, Peter Reynolds, Adrienne Corri, Joseph Tomelty, Sophie Stewart, John Laurie, Anthony Richmond; *D:* David MacDonald. **VHS, Beta** $16.95 NOS, MRV, SNC ⅋½

Devil Horse A boy's devotion to a wild horse marked for destruction as a killer leads him into trouble. A serial in twelve, thirteen-minute chapters.
1932 156m/B Frankie Darro, Harry Carey Sr., Noah Beery Sr.; *D:* Otto Brower, Richard Talmadge. **VHS, Beta** $49.95 NOS, VCN, DVT ⅋⅋

The Devil in Silk A composer marries a woman, not knowing that she is psychotically jealous. After she commits suicide, he must prove to the police that he did not kill her. Original dialogue in German.
1956 102m/B GE Lilli Palmer, Curt Jurgens, Winnie Markus; *D:* Rolf Hansen. **VHS, Beta** $16.95 NOS, SNC ⅋⅋½

Devil in the Flesh Acclaimed drama about a French soldier's wife having a passionate affair with a high school student while her husband is away fighting in World War I. From the novel by Raymond Radiguet. Dubbed. Updated and remade in 1987. *AKA:* Le Diable au Corps.
1946 112m/B FR Gerard Philippe, Micheline Presle, Denise Grey; *D:* Claude Autant-Lara. **VHS, Beta** $24.95 NOS, FCT, APD ⅋⅋⅋

Devil in the Flesh A angst-ridden, semi-pretentious Italian drama about an obsessive older woman carrying on an affair with a schoolboy, despite her terrorist boyfriend and the objections of the lad's psychiatrist father, who had treated her. In Italian with subtitles. Famous for a graphic sex scene, available in the unrated version. Updated remake of the 1946 French film. *AKA:* Il Diavolo in Corpo.
1987 (R) 110m/C IT Maruschka Detmers, Federico Pitzalis; *D:* Marco Bellochio. **VHS, Beta, LV** $79.98 ORI, TAM ⅋

Devil Kiss Gothic horror including zombies, virgins, sorcery, and the inevitable living dead.
1977 93m/C Oliver Mathews, Evelyn Scott. **VHS, Beta** $59.95 HMV ⅋

Devil Monster A world-weary traveler searches for a girl's fiance in the South Pacific, and is attacked by a large manta.
1946 65m/B Barry Norton, Blanche Mehaffey; *D:* S. Edward Graham. **VHS, Beta, LV** $16.95 SNC ⅋

Devil of the Desert Against the Son of Hercules The grandson of Zeus ventures into the wasteland to take on a feisty foe.
1962 ?m/C IT Kirk Morris, Michele Girardon; *D:* Riccardo Freda. **VHS, Beta** $16.95 SNC ⅋⅋½

Devil on Horseback A miner's son journeys to London to become a jockey in this comedy/drama. As he tries to bully his way into the racing circuit, he succeeds, but not in the way he anticipated.
1954 88m/B GB Googie Withers, John McCallum, Jeremy Spenser, Liam Redmond; *D:* Cyril Frankel. **VHS, Beta, 8mm** $29.95 VYY ⅋⅋

The Devil on Wheels Inspired by his dad's reckless driving, a teenager becomes a hot rodder and causes a family tragedy. A rusty melodrama that can't be described as high-performance.
1947 67m/B James B. Cardwell, Noreen Nash, Darryl Hickman, Jan Ford, Damian O'Flynn, Lenita Love. **VHS** $15.95 NOS, LOO ⅋⅋

Devil Rider A monster from Hell, the Devil Rider, once rode the plains in search of human fodder. In the present day, a pleasure ranch is built on his old territory, and people begin dying in the most horrific manners. Could this mean the return of the Devil Rider?
1991 90m/C VHS NO ⅋½

Devil Riders Unspectacular horse opera has a crooked lawyer trying to get his grubby hands on some choice land. Enter Crabbe to set things straight.
1944 56m/B Buster Crabbe, Al "Fuzzy" St. John, Patti McCarty, Charles King, John Merton, Kermit Maynard, Frank LaRue, Jack Ingram, George Cheseboro, Edward Cassidy; *D:* Sam Newfield. **VHS** $19.95 NOS, MRV, TIM ⅋½

The Devil Thumbs a Ride A naive traveller picks up a hitchhiker, not knowing he's wanted for murder. Will history repeat itself in this interesting noir?
1947 63m/B Ted North, Lawrence Tierney, Nan Leslie; *D:* Felix Feist. **VHS, Beta** $34.95 RKO ⅋⅋⅋

The Devil Thumbs a Ride/ Having Wonderful Crime A mystery double feature. In "Devil Thumbs a Ride," a ruthless killer-bank robber hitches a ride from an inebriated travelling salesman. In "Having Wonderful Crime," a criminal lawyer investigates the disappearance of a magician.
1947 132m/B Lawrence Tierney, Pat O'Brien, George Murphy, Carole Landis, Nan Leslie, George Zucco; *D:* Felix Feist, Edward Sutherland. **VHS, Beta** $39.95 RKO ⅋⅋⅋

Devil Times Five To take revenge for being incarcerated in a mental hospital, five children methodically murder the adults who befriend them. *AKA:* Peopletoys; People Toys; The Horrible House on the Hill.
1974 (R) 87m/C Gene Evans, Sorrell Booke, Shelly Morrison; *D:* Sean McGregor. **VHS, Beta** $54.95 MED ⅋½

Devil Wears White A student's vacation is disrupted when he becomes involved in a war with an insane arms dealer who wants to take over a Latin American Republic.
1986 (R) 92m/C Robert Livesy, Jane Higginson, Guy Ecker, Anthony Cordova; *D:* Steven A. Hull. **VHS, Beta** $79.95 TWE ⅋

D

Devil Woman A Filipino Gorgon-woman seeks reptillian revenge on the farmers who killed her family. Bad news.
1976 (R) 79m/C **PH** Rosemarie Gil; **D:** Albert Yu, Felix Vilars. **VHS** $19.98 SNC *Woof!*

Devilfish A small seaside community is ravaged by berserk manta rays in this soggy saga.
1984 92m/C **IT** **D:** Lamberto Bava. **VHS, Beta** $59.95 VMK *♂*

The Devils In 1631 France, a priest is accused of commerce with the devil and sexual misconduct with nuns. Since he is also a political threat, the accusation is used to denounce and eventually execute him. Based on Aldous Huxley's "The Devils of Loudun," the movie features masturbating nuns and other excesses—shocking scenes typical of film director Russell. Supposedly this was Russell's attempt to wake the public to their desensitization of modern horrors of war. Controversial and flamboyant.
1971 (R) 109m/C **GB** Vanessa Redgrave, Oliver Reed, Dudley Sutton, Max Adrian, Gemma Jones, Murray Melvin; **D:** Ken Russell. **VHS, Beta** $19.98 WAR, TAM *♂♂♂*

Devil's Angels A motorcycle gang clashes with a small-town sheriff. Cheap 'n' sleazy fare.
1967 84m/C John Cassavetes, Beverly Adams, Mimsy Farmer, Salli Sachse, Nai Bonet, Leo Gordon; **D:** Daniel Haller; **W:** Charles B. Griffith. **VHS** NO *♂*

The Devil's Brigade "Dirty Dozen" style film with Holden as the leader of special commando brigade consisting of the usual misfits and oddballs. The team is trained to take on the Nazis in Scandanavia but has their assignment cancelled. Instead, they take them on in the Italian Alps, making for some perilous adventures. Non-acting notables include former football great Alex Hornung and former boxing champ Gene Fullmer.
1968 130m/C William Holden, Cliff Robertson, Vince Edwards, Michael Rennie, Dana Andrews, Gretchen Wyler, Andrew Prine, Claude Akins, Carroll O'Connor, Richard Jaeckel, Jack Watson, Paul Hornung, Jeremy Slate, Don Megowan, Patric Knowles, James Craig, Richard Dawson, Tom Stern, Luke Askew; **D:** Andrew V. McLaglen. **VHS, Beta** $19.98 MGM *♂♂*

The Devil's Brother In one of their lesser efforts, Laurel and Hardy star as bumbling bandits in this comic operetta based on the 1830 opera by Daniel F. Auber. Also available with "Laurel & Hardy's Laughing 20's" on laserdisc. **AKA:** Fra Diavolo; Bogus Bandits; The Virtuous Tramps.
1933 88m/B Stan Laurel, Oliver Hardy, Dennis King, Thelma Todd, James Finlayson, Lucille Browne; **D:** Charles "Buddy" Rogers, Hal Roach. **VHS** $19.98 MGM, MLB, CCB *♂♂*

Devil's Canyon An ex-lawman, serving time in an Arizona prison, is beset by a jailed killer seeking vengeance for his own incarceration. Filmed in 3-D.
1953 92m/B Dale Robertson, Virginia Mayo, Stephen McNally, Arthur Hunnicutt, Robert Keith, Jay C. Flippen, Whit Bissell; **D:** Alfred Werker. **VHS, Beta** $19.98 TTC *♂♂*

The Devil's Cargo When a man is accused of killing a racetrack operator, he calls in the Falcon to clear his name. The master detective finds this to be a most difficult task however, especially when the accused is found poisoned in his cell. One of the final three "Falcon" films, in which Calvert replaced Tom Conway.
1948 61m/B John Calvert, Rochelle Hudson, Roscoe Karns, Lyle Talbot, Tom Kennedy; **D:** John F. Link. **VHS, Beta** $16.95 SNC *♂½*

The Devil's Commandment A lurid melodrama about a Parisian newspaperman's journey into a network of crime and perversion. Cinematography by Mario Bava. **AKA:** I, Vampiri; Lust of the Vampires.
1956 90m/B **FR** Giana Maria Canale, Dario Michaelis, Carlo D'Angelo, Wandisa Guida, Paul Muller, Renato Tontini; **D:** Riccardo Freda. **VHS, Beta, LV** $16.95 WGE, SNC *♂♂*

Devil's Crude Adventurous sailor and a young oil heir uncover a conspiracy within a giant corporation.
1971 85m/C **IT** Franco Nero. **VHS, Beta** $59.95 TWE *♂*

The Devil's Daughter A sister's hatred and voodoo ceremonies play an important part in this all-black drama. **AKA:** Pocomania; Poncomania.
1939 60m/B Nina Mae McKinney, Jack Carter, Ida James, Hamtree Harrington. **VHS, Beta** $16.95 SNC, VYY, DVT *♂½*

The Devil's Daughter Satan, in a desperate bid to take over the planet, orders his minions to flood the earth with horrific evil. Only one woman can prevent the Hell-Master from succeeding, and she may be too late!
1991 (R) 112m/C **IT** Kelly Curtis, Herbert Lom, Maria Angela Giordano, Michel Hans Adatte, Carla Cassola, Angelika Maria Boeck, Tomas Arana; **D:** Michele (Michael) Soavi. **VHS** $89.98 REP *♂½*

The Devil's Disciple Entertaining adaptation of George Bernard Shaw play set during the American Revolution. Standout performances by Douglas as a romantic rogue, Lancaster as a New England pastor, and Olivier as British General Burgoyne. Film suffers from choppy direction, but the excellent cast more than makes up for it.
1959 82m/B **GB** Burt Lancaster, Kirk Douglas, Laurence Olivier, Janet Scott, Eva Le Gallienne, Harry Andrews, Basil Sydney, George Rose; **D:** Guy Hamilton. **VHS** $19.98 MGM *♂♂♂*

The Devil's Eye The devil dispatches Don Juan to tempt and seduce a young virgin bride-to-be, a reverend's daughter, no less. Based on the Danish radio play "Don Juan Returns." **AKA:** Djavulens Oga.
1960 90m/B **SW** Bibi Andersson, Jarl Kulle; **D:** Ingmar Bergman. **VHS, Beta** $29.98 SUE, TAM, NLC *♂♂*

Devil's Gift A young boy's toy is possessed by a demon and havoc ensues.
1984 112m/C Bob Mendlesolin, Vicki Saputo, Steven Robertson; **D:** Kenneth Berton. **VHS, Beta** $69.98 LIV, VES *Woof!*

The Devil's Hand When Alda finds a doll that represents his ideal woman in a curio shop, the shop's owner (Hamilton, aka Commissioner Gordon), tells him the dream girl who modeled for the doll lives nearby. Trouble is, she's part of a voodoo cult, and guess who's head voodoo-man. Big trouble for Alda; big snooze for you. **AKA:** Devil's Doll; The Naked Goddess; Live to Love.
1961 71m/B Linda Christian, Robert Alda, Neil Hamilton, Ariadne Welter; **D:** William Hole Jr. **VHS** $19.98 NOS, SNC, LOO *♂*

The Devil's Harvest A vintage "Reefer Madness"-style cautionary film about pot, the "smoke of Hell."
193? 52m/B **VHS, Beta** NO *Woof!*

The Devil's Mistress A gang of criminals on a pillaging spree murder a man and rape his Indian wife, only to find out she's a she-demon who won't let bygones be bygones. Written by director Wanzer, this monster-oater lacks essential nutrients.

1968 66m/C Joan Stapleton, Robert Gregory, Forrest Westmoreland, Douglas Warren, Oren Williams, Arthur Resley; **W/D:** Orville Wanzer. **VHS** $19.98 SNC *♂½*

The Devil's Nightmare A woman leads seven tourists (representing the seven deadly sins) on a tour of a medieval European castle. There they experience demonic tortures. Lots of creepy moments. Euro-horror/sex star Blanc is fantastic in this otherwise mediocre production. **AKA:** Vampire Playgirls; Succubus; The Devil Walks at Midnight.
1971 (R) 88m/C **BE IT** Erika Blanc, Jean Servais, Daniel Emilfork, Lucien Raimbourg, Jacques Monseau, Colette Emmanuelle, Ivana Novak, Shirley Corrigan, Frederique Hender; **D:** Jean Brismee. **VHS, Beta** $59.95 MON, APP *♂½*

The Devil's Partner Yet another uninspired devil yarn in which an old-timer trades in his senior citizenship by dying and coming back in the form of his younger self. Young again, he takes a new wife and indulges in multiple ritual sacrifices. Noteworthy only by virtue of the cast's later TV notoriety—Buchanan and Foulger would later appear on "Petticoat Junction," Nelson played Dr. Rossi on "Peyton Place," and Crane beached a role on "Hawaiian Eye."
1958 75m/B Ed Nelson, Jean Allison, Edgar Buchanan, Richard Crane, Spencer Carlisle, Byron Foulger, Claire Carleton; **D:** Charles R. Rondeau. **VHS** $19.98 SNC, MRV, CNM *♂½*

Devil's Party A tenement boy's reunion party turns into a night of horror when one of the guests is killed. As a result, the childhood friends band together to uncover the murderer's identity.
1938 65m/B Victor McLaglen, Paul Kelly, William Gargan, Samuel S. Hinds; **D:** Ray McCarey. **VHS, Beta** $24.95 NOS, MRV, DVT *♂♂*

The Devil's Playground Sexual tension rises in a Catholic seminary, distracting the boys from their theological studies. The attentions of the priests only further their sexual confusion. Winner of many Australian film awards. Schepisi wrote the screenplay as well as directed.
1976 107m/C **AU** Arthur Dignam, Nick Tate, Simon Burke, Charles Frawley, Jonathon Hardy, Gerry Dugan, Thomas Keneally; **D:** Fred Schepisi. **Beta** $79.95 ALL *♂♂*

The Devil's Possessed A Middle Ages despot tortures and maims the peasants in his region until they rise up and enact an unspeakable revenge.
1974 90m/C **AR SP** Paul Naschy; **D:** Leon Klimovsky. **VHS, Beta** NO *♂½*

Devil's Rain The rituals and practices of devil worship, possession, and satanism are gruesomely related. Interesting cast.
1975 (PG) 85m/C Ernest Borgnine, Ida Lupino, William Shatner, Eddie Albert, Keenan Wynn, John Travolta, Tom Skerritt; **D:** Robert Fuest. **VHS, Beta, LV** $19.95 UHV *♂½*

The Devil's Sleep When a crusading woman sets out to break up a teen narcotics ring, the threatened thugs attempt to draw her daughter into their sleazy affairs, thus assuring the mother's silence.
1951 81m/B Lita Grey Chaplin, Timothy Farrell, John Mitchum, William Thomason, Tracy Lynn; **D:** W. Merle Connell. **VHS, Beta** $16.95 SNC *♂*

Devil's Son-in-Law A black stand-up comic makes a deal with a devil.
1977 (R) 95m/C Rudy Ray Moore; **D:** Cliff Roguemore. **VHS, Beta** NO *Woof!*

The Devil's Undead When a Scottish orphanage is besieged by a rash of cold-blooded murders, the detectives Lee and Cushing are summoned to investigate. Interesting spin on that old possessed by demons theme.

1975 (PG) 90m/C GB *Christopher Lee, Peter Cushing; D: Peter Sasdy.* **VHS, Beta $59.95** *MON, MLB ♫♫½*

Devil's Wanton A young girl tries to forget an unhappy relationship by beginning a new romance with an equally frustrated beau. Gloomy, but hopeful. *AKA: Fangelse; Prison.*

1949 80m/B SW *Doris Svedlund, Eva Henning, Hasse Ekman; D: Ingmar Bergman.* **VHS, Beta $29.95** *NOS, MRV, DVT ♫♫½*

The Devil's Web A demonic nurse infiltrates, manipulates, and corrupts three beautiful sisters.

1974 (PG) 73m/C *Diana Dors, Andrea Marcovicci, Ed Bishop, Cec Linder, Michael Culver.* **VHS, Beta $29.95** *LIV ♫½*

Devil's Wedding Night An archaeologist and his twin brother fight over a ring that lures virgins into Count Dracula's Transylvanian castle. Vampire queen Bay seduces the dimwit twins and strips at every chance she gets.

1973 (R) 85m/C *Mark Damon, Sara (Rosalba Neri) Bay, Frances Davis; D: Paul Solvay.* **VHS, Beta $49.95** *UHV Woof!*

Devlin Devlin is a tough cop with an alcohol problem and a bad marriage. His father-in-law, Brennan, is a powerful local political boss. When Brennan's son is murdered, Devlin is the fall guy. Seeking to clear himself, he discovers a conspiracy going back thirty years. Made for cable television.

1992 (R) 110m/C *Bryan Brown, Roma Downey, Lloyd Bridges; D: Rick Rosenthal.* **VHS, Beta, LV $89.98** *FXV ♫♫*

Devlin Connection Retired private investigator helps his son learn the ropes as he embarks on a Los Angeles crime fighting career. Hudson's last starring television series, excluding his "Dynasty" role. All thirteen episodes are available separately.

1982 50m/C *Rock Hudson, Jack Scalia, Louis Giambalvo, Leigh Taylor-Young, Jack Kruschen; D: Christian Nyby.* **VHS, Beta $39.95** *TWE ♫♫*

Devonsville Terror Strange things begin to happen when a new school teacher arrives in Devonsville, a town that has a history of torture, murder, and witchcraft. The hysterical townspeople react by beginning a 20th-century witchhunt.

1983 (R) 97m/C *Suzanna Love, Donald Pleasence, Deanna Haas, Mary Walden, Robert Walker Jr., Paul Wilson; D: Ulli Lommel.* **VHS, Beta $9.98** *SUE ♫♫*

Devotion A lovesick British miss disguises herself as a governess so she can be near the object of her affection, a London barrister.

1931 80m/B *Ann Harding, Leslie Howard, Robert Williams, O.P. Heggie, Louise Closser Hale, Dudley Digges; D: Robert Milton.* **VHS $19.98** *TTC ♫♫½*

D.I. A tough drill sergeant is faced with an unbreakable rebellious recruit, threatening his record and his platoon's status. Webb's film features performances by actual soldiers.

1957 106m/B *Jack Webb, Don Dubbins, Jackie Loughery, Lin McCarthy, Virginia Gregg; D: Jack Webb.* **VHS, Beta $59.95** *WAR ♫♫*

The Diabolical Dr. Z When dad dies of cardiac arrest after the medical council won't let him make the world a kinder gentler place with his personality-altering technique, his dutiful daughter—convinced the council brought on dad's demise—is out to change some personalities in a big way. *AKA: Miss Muette; Dans les Griffes du Maniaque.*

1965 86m/B SP FR *Mabel Karr, Fernando Montes, Estella Blain, Antonio J. Escribano, Howard Vernon; D: Jess (Jesus) Franco.* **VHS $19.98** *SNC ♫♫*

Diabolically Yours A French thriller about an amnesiac who struggles to discover his lost identity. Tensions mount when his pretty spouse and friends begin to wonder if it's all a game. Dubbed. *AKA: Diaboliquement Votre.*

1967 94m/C FR *Alain Delon, Senta Berger; D: Julien Duvivier.* **VHS, Beta $59.95** *UNI ♫♫½*

Diabolique The mistress and the wife of a sadistic schoolmaster conspire to murder the man, carry it out, and then begin to wonder if they have covered their tracks effectively. Plot twists and double-crosses abound. In French with English subtitles. Remade for television as "Reflections of Murder." *AKA: Les Diabolique.*

1955 107m/B FR *Simone Signoret, Vera Clouzot, Paul Meurisse, Charles Vanel, Michel Serrault; D: Henri-Georges Clouzot.* **VHS, Beta, LV, 8mm, 3/4U, Special order formats $29.95** *NOS, VYY, SNC ♫♫♫½*

Dial Help A lame Italian-made suspenser about a model plagued by ghostly phone calls.

1988 (R) 94m/C IT *Charlotte Lewis, Marcello Modugno, Mattia Sbragia, Victor Cavallo; D: Ruggero Deodato.* **VHS, Beta $79.95** *PSM ♫½*

Dial "M" for Murder An unfaithful husband devises an elaborate plan to murder his wife for her money, but when she accidentally stabs the killer-to-be, with scissors no less, he alters his methods. Part of the "A Night at the Movies" series, this tape simulates a 1954 movie evening with a Daffy Duck cartoon, "My Little Duckaroo," a newsreel, and coming attractions for "Them" and "A Star Is Born." Filmed in 3-D. Based on the play by Frederick Knotts.

1954 123m/C *Ray Milland, Grace Kelly, Robert Cummings, John Williams, Anthony Dawson; D: Alfred Hitchcock.* **VHS, Beta, LV $19.98** *WAR, PIA, TLF ♫♫♫*

Diamante, Oro y Amor A pair of amateur gangsters find themselves in some crazy situations.

1987 93m/C MX *Julio Aleman, Hilda Aguirre, Hector Suarez, Adriana Roel, Chucho Salinas.* **VHS, Beta $59.95** *MAD ♫♫*

Diamond Head A Hawaiian landowner brings destruction and misery to his family via his stubbornness. Based on the Peter Gilman novel.

1962 107m/C *Charlton Heston, Yvette Mimieux, George Chakiris, France Nuyen, James Darren; D: Guy Green; M: John Williams.* **VHS, Beta, LV $69.95** *COL ♫♫½*

Diamond Ninja Force Non-adventure minimally hosted by Sho Kosugi pitting reluctant ninjas against indifferent mortal enemies with the usual half-hearted revenge motif. Shabby ninja imitator.

198? 90m/C **VHS, Beta $59.95** *TWE Woof!*

Diamond Run A streetwise American expatriate frantically searches for his girl-friend after unwittingly involving her in an assassination plot.

1990 (R) 89m/C *William Bell Sullivan, Ava Lazar, Ayu Azhari, David Thornton, Peter Fox; D: Robert Chappell.* **VHS, Beta, LV** *NO ♫½*

Diamond Trail East Coast jewel thieves bring their operation to the West, trailed by a New York reporter.

1933 58m/B *Rex Bell, Frances Rich, Bud Osborne, Lloyd Whitlock, Norman Feusier; D: Harry Fraser.* **VHS, Beta $19.95** *NOS, DVT, TIM ♫½*

The Diamond Trap A Manhattan detective finds himself in the middle of a diamond heist and involved with a con artist. Made for television.

1991 (PG) 93m/C *Howard Hesseman, Brooke Shields, Ed Marinaro.* **VHS, LV $89.95** *VMK ♫♫*

Diamonds A tense film in which the Israel Diamond Exchange is looted by a motley array of criminal heisters. Shaw plays a dual role as twin brothers.

1972 (PG) 108m/C IS *Robert Shaw, Richard Roundtree, Barbara Hershey, Shelley Winters; D: Menahem Golan.* **VHS, Beta $59.98** *NLC ♫♫*

Diamonds are Forever 007 once again battles his nemesis Blofeld, this time in Las Vegas. Bond must prevent the implementation of a plot to destroy Washington through the use of a space-orbiting laser. Fabulous stunts include Bond's wild drive through the streets of Vegas in a '71 Mach 1. Connery returned to play Bond in this film after being offered the then record-setting salary of one million dollars.

1971 (PG) 120m/C GB *Sean Connery, Jill St. John, Charles Gray, Bruce Cabot, Jimmy Dean, Lana Wood, Bruce Glover, Putter Smith, Norman Burton, Joseph Furst, Bernard Lee, Desmond Llewelyn, Laurence Naismith, Leonard Barr, Lois Maxwell, Margaret Lacey, Joe Robinson, Donna Garrat, Trina Parks; D: Guy Hamilton; M: John Barry.* **VHS, Beta, LV $19.95** *MGM, TLF ♫♫♫½*

Diamond's Edge An adolescent private eye and his juvenescent brother snoop into the affairs of the Fat Man, and find out that the opera ain't over until they find out what's in the Fat Man's mysterious box of bonbons. A genre-parodying kid mystery, written by Anthony Horowitz, based on his novel, "The Falcon's Malteser." *AKA: Just Ask for Diamond.*

1988 (PG) 83m/C *Susannah York, Peter Eyre, Patricia Hodge, Nickolas Grace; D: Stephen Bayly.* **VHS, Beta $79.99** *HBO ♫♫*

Diamonds of the Night A breakthrough masterpiece of the Czech new wave, about two young men escaping from a transport train to Auschwitz and scrambling for survival in the countryside. Surreal, powerfully expressionistic film, one of the most important of its time. In Czech with English subtitles. Accompanied by Nemec's short "A Loaf of Bread." *AKA: Demanty Noci.*

1964 71m/B CZ *D: Jan Nemec.* **VHS, Beta $59.95** *FCT ♫♫♫♫*

Diamonds on Wheels A Disney film about three British teenagers, amid a big road rally, discovering stolen diamonds and getting pursued by gangsters.

1973 84m/C **VHS, Beta $69.95** *DIS ♫*

Diane Overstuffed medieval drama featuring Turner as Diane de Potier, the mistress of a sixteenth century French King. Moore plays the king in his Hollywood debut. Gorgeous sets and costumes couldn't boost this film at the box office, which had disappointing figures in spite of the expense bestowed upon it. Based on the novel "Diane de Poitier" by John Erskine.

1955 110m/C *Lana Turner, Pedro Armendariz Jr., Roger Moore, Marisa Pavan, Cedric Hardwicke, Torin Thatcher, Taina Elg, John Lupton, Henry Daniell, Sean McClory, Michael Ansara; D: David Miller; W: Christopher Isherwood.* **VHS, LV $19.98** *MGM ♫♫*

Diary of a Chambermaid A chambermaid wants to marry a rich man and finds herself the object of desire of a poor servant willing to commit murder for her. Excellent comic drama, but very stylized in direction and set design. Produced during Renoir's years in Hollywood. Adapted from a story by

Octave Mirbeau, later turned into a play. Remade in 1964 by Luis Bumel.
1946 86m/B Paulette Goddard, Burgess Meredith, Hurd Hatfield, Francis Lederer, Judith Anderson, Florence Bates, Almira Sessions, Reginald Owen; **D:** Jean Renoir. **VHS $19.98** *REP, FCT* ⅃⅃⅃

Diary of a Chambermaid Vintage Bunuelian social satire about a young girl taking a servant's job in a provincial French family, and easing into an atmosphere of sexual hypocrisy and decadence. In French with English subtitles. Remake of the 1946 Jean Renoir film. **AKA:** Le Journal d'une Femme de Chambre; Il Diario di una Cameriera.
1964 97m/C *FR* Jeanne Moreau, Michel Piccoli, Georges Geret, Francoise Lugagne, Daniel Ivernel; **D:** Luis Bunuel. **VHS, Beta, LV $19.98** *TAM, APD, IME* ⅃⅃⅃½

Diary of a Country Priest With "Balthazar" and "Mouchette," this is one of Bresson's greatest, subtlest films, treating the story of an alienated, unrewarded young priest with his characteristic austerity and Catholic humanism. In French and English subtitles. **AKA:** Le Journal d'un Cure de Campagne.
1950 120m/B *FR* Claude Layou, Jean Riveyre, Nicole Ladmiral; **D:** Robert Bresson. **VHS, Beta $59.95** *DVT, APD, TAM* ⅃⅃⅃½

Diary of a Hitman A hitman is hired to knock off the wife and child of a commodities broker who claims his wife is a drug addict and the infant is a crack baby and not his. The hired killer wants out of the business, but needs to pull off one more job for a down payment on his apartment. Beset by doubts, he breaks conduct by conversing with the victim and discovers the broker lied. Based on the play "Insider's Price" by Pressman.
1991 (R) 90m/C Forest Whitaker, James Belushi, Sherilyn Fenn, Sharon Stone, Lewis Smith, Lois Chiles; **D:** Roy London; **W:** Kenneth Pressman. **VHS, LV $89.95** *COL* ⅃⅃½

Diary of a Lost Girl The second Louise Brooks/G.W. Pabst collaboration (after "Pandora's Box") in which a frail but mesmerizing German girl plummets into a life of hopeless degradation. Dark and gloomy, the film chronicles the difficulties she faces, from rape to an unwanted pregnancy and prostitution. Based on the popular book by Margarete Boehme. Silent. Made after flapper Brooks left Hollywood to pursue greater opportunities and more challenging roles under Pabst's guidance.
1929 99m/B *GE* Louise Brooks, Fritz Rasp, Josef Rovensky, Sybille Schmitz; **D:** G.W. Pabst. **VHS, Beta, LV $19.95** *GPV, MRV, VDM* ⅃⅃⅃½

Diary of a Mad Housewife Despairing of her miserable family life, a housewife has an affair with a writer only to find him to be even more selfish and egotistical than her no-good husband. Snodgress plays her character perfectly, hearing the insensitive absurdity of her husband and her lover over and over again, enjoying her martyrdom even as it drives her crazy.
1970 (R) 94m/C Carrie Snodgress, Richard Benjamin, Frank Langella; **D:** Frank Perry. Academy Awards '70 Nominations: Best Actress (Snodgress); Golden Globe Awards '71: Best Actress—Musical/Comedy (Snodgress); National Board of Review Awards '70: 10 Best Films of the Year, Best Supporting Actor (Langella). **VHS, Beta $14.95** *GKK* ⅃⅃⅃

Diary of a Mad Old Man A wistful drama about an old man who's lost everything except his desire for his daughter-in-law, which sends him into fits of nostalgia. **AKA:** Dagboek Van Een Oude Dwaas.

1988 (PG-13) 93m/C Derek De Lint, Ralph Michael, Beatie Edney. **VHS, Beta $79.95** *MED* ⅃⅃

Diary of a Madman Price is once again possessed by an evil force in this gothic thriller. Fairly average Price vehicle, based on Guy de Maupassant's story.
1963 96m/C Vincent Price, Nancy Kovack, Chris Warfield, Ian Wolfe, Nelson Olmstead; **D:** Reginald LeBorg. **VHS, Beta** *NO* ⅃⅃

Diary of a Rebel A fictional account of the rise of Cuban rebel leader Che Guevara.
1984 89m/C John Ireland, Francisco Rabal. **VHS, Beta** *NO* ⅃

Diary of a Teenage Hitchhiker Teen girl ignores family restrictions and police warnings about a homicidal rapist stalking the area and continues to thumb rides to her job at a beach resort. One night she's picked up for ride she'll never forget.
1982 96m/C Charlene Tilton, Dick Van Patten; **D:** Ted Post. **VHS, Beta** *NO* ⅃

Diary of a Young Comic New York comedian searches for the meaning of lunacy. He finds it after Improvisation in Los Angeles.
1979 74m/C Stacy Keach, Dom DeLuise, Richard Lewis, Bill Macy, George Jessel, Gary Muledeer, Nina Van Pallandt; **D:** Gary Weis. **VHS, Beta $39.95** *PAV* ⅃⅃

The Diary of Anne Frank In June 1945, a liberated Jewish refugee returns to the hidden third floor of an Amsterdam factory where he finds the diary kept by his youngest daughter, Anne. The document recounts their years in hiding from the Nazis. Based on the actual diary of 13-year-old Anne Frank, killed in a death camp during WWII.
1959 150m/B Millie Perkins, Joseph Schildkraut, Shelley Winters, Richard Beymer, Gusti Huber, Ed Wynn, Lou Jacobi, Diane Baker; **D:** George Stevens. Academy Awards '59: Best Art Direction/Set Decoration (B & W), Best Black and White Cinematography, Best Supporting Actress (Winters); Nominations: Best Costume Design (B & W), Best Director (Stevens), Best Picture, Best Supporting Actor (Wynn), Best Original Score. **VHS, Beta, LV $79.98** *KUI, FOX, BTV* ⅃⅃⅃½

Diary of Forbidden Dreams A beautiful young girl finds herself drawn into bizarre incidents that cause her to go insane. Set on the Italian Riviera, the story is an edited version of Roman Polanski's 1973 film "What?;" it's the most offbeat rendition of "Alice in Wonderland" you're apt to find. Unfortunately, the convoluted plot lessens its appeal. **AKA:** What?; Che?.
1973 (R) 94m/C *IT* Marcello Mastroianni, Hugh Griffith, Sydne Rome, Roman Polanski; **D:** Roman Polanski. **VHS, Beta $19.95** *VDM, TWE* ⅃⅃⅃

Diary of the Dead A newlywed kills his aggravating mother-in-law, only to have her repeatedly return from the grave.
1987 (PG) 93m/C Hector Elizondo, Geraldine Fitzgerald, Salome Jens; **D:** Arvin Brown. **Beta** *NO* ⅃

Dias de Ilusion The fantasy world in which Lucia and her sister live was created for only one reason, and only Lucia's diary has the secret. In Spanish.
1980 94m/C *SP* Andrea Del Boca, Luisina Brando. **VHS, Beta $29.95** *MED* ⅃½

Dick Barton, Special Agent Dick Barton is called in when a mad scientist threatens to attack London with germ-carrying bombs. The first film production for Hammer Studios, later to be known for its horror classics.

1948 70m/B *GB* Don Stannard, Geoffrey Ford, Jack Shaw; **D:** Alfred Goulding. **VHS, Beta $16.95** *SNC* ⅃

Dick Barton Strikes Back "Mr. French" Cabot has a nuclear weapon and is willing to use it; that is, until Dick Barton arrives to put the Frenchman out of commission. Generally considered the best of the Dick Barton film series.
1948 73m/B *GB* Don Stannard, Sebastian Cabot, Jean Lodge; **D:** Godfrey Grayson. **VHS, Beta $16.95** *SNC* ⅃⅃½

Dick Tracy Serial, based on the comic-strip character, in fifteen chapters. Tracy tries to find his kidnapped brother as he faces the fiend "Spider." The first chapter is thirty minutes and each additional chapter is twenty minutes.
1937 310m/B Ralph Byrd, Smiley Burnette, Irving Pichel, Jennifer Jones; **D:** John English. **VHS, Beta, LV $29.95** *SNC, VYY, UHV* ⅃⅃½

Dick Tracy Beatty, wearing the cap of producer, director, and star, performs admirably on all fronts in one of the biggest movies of 1990. Beatty's Tracy is somewhat flat in comparison to the outstanding performances and makeup of the unique villains, especially Pacino, but altogether, the movie is very entertaining. Stylistically, Beatty hits his mark. Shot in only 7 colors, using timeless sets that capture the essence rather than the reality of the city, the film successfully brings the comic strip to life. Madonna turns in a fine performance as the seductive Breathless Mahoney, belting out Stephen Sondheim like she was born to do it. People expecting the gothic technology of "Batman" may be disappointed, but moviegoers searching for a memory made real will be thrilled.
1990 (PG) 105m/C Warren Beatty, Madonna, Charlie Korsmo, Glenne Headly, Al Pacino, Dustin Hoffman, James Caan, Mandy Patinkin, Paul Sorvino, Charles Durning, Dick Van Dyke, R.G. Armstrong, Catherine O'Hara, Estelle Parsons, Seymour Cassel, Michael J. Pollard, William Forsythe, Kathy Bates, James Tolkan; **D:** Warren Beatty; **W:** Jim Cash, Jack Epps Jr.; **M:** Danny Elfman, Stephen Sondheim. Academy Awards '90: Best Art Direction/Set Decoration, Best Makeup, Best Song ("Sooner or Later"); Nominations: Best Cinematography, Best Costume Design, Best Sound, Best Supporting Actor (Pacino). **VHS, Beta, LV $19.99** *TOU, FCT, IME* ⅃⅃⅃

Dick Tracy and the Oyster Caper A collection of cartoons based upon the comic-strip character.
1961 60m/C VHS, Beta $29.95 *MED* ⅃⅃⅃½

Dick Tracy, Detective The first Dick Tracy feature film, in which Splitface is on the loose, a schoolteacher is murdered, the Mayor is threatened, and a nutty professor uses a crystal ball to give Tracy the clues needed to connect the crimes.
1945 62m/B Morgan Conway, Anne Jeffreys, Mike Mazurki, Jane Greer, Lyle Latelle; **D:** William Burke. **VHS, Beta $16.95** *SNC, MED, VYY* ⅃⅃

Dick Tracy, Detective/The Corpse Vanishes On one tape, the first Dick Tracy feature film and Lugosi's minor epic about a mad scientist using virgin's blood to restore youth to an aging countess.
1942 126m/B Bela Lugosi, Morgan Conway, Luana Walters, Tristram Coffin, Mike Mazurki, Jane Greer, Lyle Latelle; **D:** William Burke. **VHS, Beta** *AOV* ⅃½

Dick Tracy Double Feature #1 Mystery-adventure double feature presents Chester Gould's popular comic strip hero in live action. Includes "Dick Tracy, Detective" and "Dick Tracy's Dilemma."

1945 122m/B Ralph Byrd, Lyle Latelle, Morgan Conway, Anne Jeffreys. **VHS, Beta** $54.95 *UHV* ✍️½

Dick Tracy Double Feature #2
Chester Gould's famous comic strip character is personified in "Dick Tracy Meets Gruesome" and "Dick Tracy vs. Cueball," a double-feature videocassette featuring Dick Tracy battling two of his arch-enemies.
1947 127m/B Boris Karloff, Ralph Byrd, Morgan Conway, Anne Jeffreys. **VHS, Beta** $54.95 *UHV* ✍️✍️

Dick Tracy Meets Gruesome
Gruesome and his partner in crime, Melody, stage a bank robbery using the secret formula of Dr. A. Tomic. Tracy has to solve the case before word gets out and people rush to withdraw their savings, destroying civilization as we know it. *AKA:* Dick Tracy's Amazing Adventure; Dick Tracy Meets Karloff.
1947 66m/B Boris Karloff, Ralph Byrd, Lyle Latelle; *D:* John Rawlins. **VHS, Beta** $14.95 *NOS, MRV, SNC* ✍️✍️

Dick Tracy Returns
15-chapter serial. Public Enemy Paw Stark and his gang set out on a wave of crime that brings them face to face with dapper Dick.
1938 100m/B Ralph Byrd, Charles Middleton; *D:* William Witney. **VHS, Beta, LV** $79.95 *UHV, IME, MLB* ✍️✍️

Dick Tracy: The Original Serial, Vol. 1
The first seven parts of the original popular serial. The comic strip character comes to life and tries to stop the spider, a dangerous criminal.
1937 150m/B Ralph Byrd, Smiley Burnette, Kay Hughes, Francis X. Bushman, Lee Van Atta; *D:* Ray Taylor; *W:* Alan James. **VHS, Beta** $24.95 *GKK* ✍️✍️✍️

Dick Tracy: The Original Serial, Vol. 2
The last eight chapters of the highly acclaimed serial. Tracy is still tracking down the Spider in this action-packed adventure.
1937 160m/B Ralph Byrd, Smiley Burnette, Kay Hughes, Francis X. Bushman, Lee Van Atta; *D:* Ray Taylor; *W:* Alan James. **VHS, Beta** $24.95 *GKK* ✍️✍️✍️

Dick Tracy: The Spider Strikes
Dick Tracy, his bumbling sidekick, and his beautiful, brainy assistant go up against the master criminal, The Spider.
1937 60m/B Ralph Byrd, Morgan Conway, Francis X. Bushman. **VHS, Beta** $9.95 *SIM, KAR* ✍️✍️✍️

Dick Tracy vs. Crime Inc.
Dick Tracy encounters many difficulties when he tries to track down a criminal who can make himself invisible. A serial in 15 chapters.
1941 100m/B Ralph Byrd, Ralph Morgan, Michael Owen; *D:* William Witney; *W:* John English. **VHS, Beta, LV** $79.95 *UHV, IME, MLB* ✍️✍️

Dick Tracy vs. Cueball
Dick Tracy has his work cut out for him when the evil gangster Cueball appears on the scene. Based on Chester Gould's comic strip.
1946 62m/B Morgan Conway, Anne Jeffreys; *D:* Gordon Douglas. **VHS, Beta, 3/4U, Special order formats** $14.95 *NOS, QNE, UHV* ✍️✍️

Dick Tracy's Dilemma
The renowned police detective Dick Tracy tries to solve a case involving the Claw. Based on the Chester Gould comic strip. *AKA:* Mark of the Claw.
1947 60m/B Ralph Byrd, Lyle Latelle, Kay Christopher, Jack Lambert, Ian Keith, Jimmy Conlin; *D:* John Rawlins. **VHS, Beta** $14.95 *QNE, MRV, UHV* ✍️✍️

Dick Turpin
In this rare film, Mix plays the famed English highwayman who seeks adventure in historical Britain.
1925 60m/B Tom Mix, Alan Hale Jr.; *D:* John Blystone. **VHS, Beta** $47.50 *GVV* ✍️✍️½

Didn't You Hear?
An alienated college student discovers that dreams have a life of their own when he becomes immersed in his own fantasy world.
1983 (PG) 94m/C Dennis Christopher, Gary Busey, Cheryl Waters, John Kauffman. **VHS, Beta** $49.95 *PSM* ✍️½

Die! Die! My Darling!
A young widow visits her mad ex-mother-in-law in a remote English village, and is imprisoned by the mourning woman as revenge for her son's death. Bankhead's last role. *AKA:* Fanatic.
1965 97m/C *GB* Tallulah Bankhead, Stefanie Powers, Peter Vaughan, Maurice Kaufman, Donald Sutherland, Gwendolyn Watts, Yootha Joyce, Winifred Dennis; *D:* Silvio Narizzano; *W:* Richard Matheson. **Beta** $9.95 *COL, MLB* ✍️½

Die Grosse Freiheit Nr. 7
A man tries to stop his niece's love affair with a sailor. Nazi propaganda minister Goebbels banned this film in Germany, since it showed German soldiers getting drunk and also had Hildebrand cast as a prostitute. After the war, however, it enjoyed great popularity throughout Germany. Albers sings the classic "Auf der Reeperbahn." In German with no English translation.
1945 100m/C *GE* Hans Albers, Hilde Hildebrand. **VHS, Beta, 3/4U** $35.95 *IHF* ✍️½

Die Hard
High-voltage action thriller pits a lone New York cop against a band of ruthless high-stakes terrorists who attack and hold hostage the employees of a large corporation as they celebrate Christmas in a new L.A. high rise. It's just as unbelievable as it sounds, but you'll love it anyway. Rickman, who later charmed audiences as the villain in "Robin Hood: Prince of Thieves," turns in a marvelous performance as the chief bad guy. Based on the novel "Nothing Lasts Forever" by Roderick Thorp.
1988 (R) 114m/C Bruce Willis, Bonnie Bedelia, Alan Rickman, Alexander Godunov, Paul Gleason, William Atherton, Reginald Vel Johnson, De'voreaux White, Hart Bochner, James Shigeta, Mary Ellen Trainor; *D:* John McTiernan; *W:* Jeb Stuart, Steven E. de Souza; *M:* Michael Kamen. **VHS, Beta, LV** $19.98 *FOX* ✍️✍️✍️

Die Hard 2: Die Harder
Fast, well-done sequel brings another impossible situation before the wise-cracking, tough-cookie cop. Our hero tangles with a group of terrorists at an airport under siege, while his wife remains in a plane circling above as its fuel dwindles. Obviously a repeat of the plot and action of the first "Die Hard," with references to the former in the script. While the bad guys lack the fiendishness of their predecessors, this installment features energetic and finely acted performances. Fairly gory, especially the icicle-in-the-eyeball scene. Adapted from the novel "58 Minutes" by Walter Wager and characters created by Roderick Thorp.
1990 (R) 124m/C Bruce Willis, William Atherton, Franco Nero, Bonnie Bedelia, John Amos, Reginald Vel Johnson, Dennis Franz, Art Evans, Fred Dalton Thompson, Bill Sadler, Sheila McCarthy, Robert Patrick, John Leguizamo, Robert Costanzo, Tom Verica; *D:* Renny Harlin; *W:* Doug Richardson, Steven E. de Souza; *M:* Michael Kamen. **VHS, LV** $19.98 *FOX* ✍️✍️✍️

Die Laughing
A cab driver unwittingly becomes involved in murder, intrigue, and the kidnapping of a monkey that has memorized a scientific formula that can destroy the world. Benson wrote, produced, scored, and acted in this supposed comedy.
1980 (PG) 108m/C Robby Benson, Charles Durning, Bud Cort, Elsa Lanchester, Peter Coyote; *D:* Jeff Werner. **VHS, Beta** $19.98 *WAR* Woof!

Die, Monster, Die!
A reclusive scientist experiments with a radioactive meteorite and gains bizarre powers. Karloff is great in this adaptation of H.P. Lovecraft's "The Color Out of Space." *AKA:* Monster of Terror.
1965 80m/C *GB* Boris Karloff, Nick Adams, Suzan Farmer, Patrick Magee; *D:* Daniel Haller. **VHS, LV** $19.99 *HBO* ✍️✍️

Die Screaming, Marianne
A girl is on the run from her father, a crooked judge, who wants to kill her before her 21st birthday, when she will inherit evidence that will put him away for life.
1973 81m/C Michael Rennie, Susan George, Karin Dor; *D:* Pete Walker. **VHS, Beta** $49.95 *UNI* ✍️

Die Sister, Die!
Thriller about a gothic mansion with an eerie secret in the basement features a battle between a senile, reclusive sister and her disturbed, tormenting brother.
1974 88m/C Jack Ging, Edith Atwater, Antoinette Bower, Kent Smith, Robert Emhardt; *D:* Randall Hood. **VHS, Beta** $59.95 *MPI* ✍️

A Different Kind of Love
A romantic novel on tape, in modern settings. Love, frustration, tragedy.
1985 60m/C Joyce Redman. **Beta** $11.95 *PSM* ✍️

Different Story
Romance develops when a lesbian real estate agent offers a homosexual chauffeur a job with her firm. Resorts to stereotypes when the characters decide to marry.
1978 (PG) 107m/C Perry King, Meg Foster, Valerie Curtin, Peter Donat, Richard Bull; *D:* Paul Aaron. **VHS, Beta** $19.95 *SUE, NLC* ✍️✍️½

Digby, the Biggest Dog in the World
Poor comedy-fantasy about Digby, a sheepdog, who wanders around a scientific laboratory, drinks an experimental fluid, and grows and grows and grows.
1973 (G) 88m/C *GB* Jim Dale, Angela Douglas, Spike Milligan, Dinsdale Landen; *D:* Joseph McGrath. **VHS, Beta** $59.95 *PSM* ✍️

Digging Up Business
Johnson tries to save the family funeral home business from financial ruin with some unique interment services. This film needs a decent burial.
1991 (PG) 89m/C Lynn-Holly Johnson, Billy Barty, Ruth Buzzi, Murray Langston, Yvonne Craig, Gary Owens; *D:* Mark Byers. **VHS** $79.95 *MNC* Woof!

Diggstown
A lightweight and good-natured sports comedy about a boxing scam. Con man Gabriel Caine (Woods), fresh out of prison, heads for Diggstown and the unregulated boxing matches arranged by town boss, John Gillon (Dern). The bet is that Caine's one boxer can beat any 10 boxers, chosen by Gillon, in a 24-hour period. So Caine decides to hook up with an old friend, former prizefighter "Honey" Roy Palmer (Gosset Jr.), to run the scam of his life. Dern is sufficiently nasty and Woods his usual nervy self but it's Gossett Jr. who manages to hold everything together as the aging boxer. Based on the novel "The Diggstown Ringers" by Leonard Wise.
1992 (R) 97m/C James Woods, Louis Gossett Jr., Bruce Dern, Oliver Platt, Heather Graham; *D:* Michael Ritchie. **VHS, Beta, LV** $19.98 *MGM* ✍️✍️½

Dillinger John Dillinger's notorious career, from street punk to public enemy number one, receives a thrilling fast-paced treatment. Tierney turns in a fine performance in this interesting account of the criminal life.
1945 70m/C Lawrence Tierney, Edmund Lowe, Anne Jeffreys, Elisha Cook Jr.; **D:** Max Nosseck. **VHS, Beta** $14.98 *FOX, FCT* 🎬🎬🎬

Dillinger The most colorful period of criminality in America is brought to life in this story of bank-robber John Dillinger, "Baby Face" Nelson, and the notorious "Lady in Red."
1973 (R) 106m/C Warren Oates, Michelle Phillips, Richard Dreyfuss, Cloris Leachman, Ben Johnson, Harry Dean Stanton; **D:** John Milius. **VHS, Beta, LV** $69.98 *LIV, VES* 🎬🎬🎬

Dim Sum: A Little Bit of Heart The second independent film from the director of "Chan Is Missing." A Chinese-American mother and daughter living in San Francisco's Chinatown confront the conflict between traditional Eastern ways and modern American life. Gentle, fragile picture made with humor and care. In English and Chinese with subtitles.
1985 (PG) 88m/C Laureen Chew, Kim Chew, Victor Wong, Ida F.O. Chong, Cora Miao, John Nishio, Joan Chen; **D:** Wayne Wang. **VHS, Beta, LV** $29.95 *PAV, FCT, IME* 🎬🎬🎬

Dimples When Shirley's pickpocket grandfather is caught red-handed, she steps in, takes the blame, and somehow ends up in show business. ♫Hey, What Did the Bluebird Say?; He Was a Dandy; Picture Me Without You; Oh Mister Man Up in the Moon; Dixie-Anna; Get On Board; Swing Low Sweet Chariot.
1936 78m/B Shirley Temple, John Carradine, Frank Morgan, Helen Westley, Berton Churchill, Robert Kent, Delma Byron; **D:** William A. Seiter. **VHS, Beta** $19.98 *FOX* 🎬🎬½

Diner A group of old high school friends meet at "their" Baltimore diner to find that more has changed than the menu. A bittersweet look at the experiences of a group of Baltimore post-teenagers growing up, circa 1959. Particularly notable was Levinson's casting of "unknowns" who have since become household names. Features many humorous moments and fine performances.
1982 (R) 110m/C Steve Guttenberg, Daniel Stern, Mickey Rourke, Kevin Bacon, Ellen Barkin, Timothy Daly, Paul Reiser, Michael Tucker; **D:** Barry Levinson. **VHS, Beta, LV** $19.95 *MGM, PIA* 🎬🎬🎬½

Dingaka A controversial drama from the writer and director of "The Gods Must Be Crazy" about a South African tribesman who avenges his daughter's murder by tribal laws, and is then tried by white man's laws. A crusading white attorney struggles to acquit him.
1965 96m/C Stanley Baker, Juliet Prowse, Ken Gampu; **D:** Jamie Uys. **VHS, Beta** $14.95 *COL, NLC, FCT* 🎬🎬½

The Dining Room Six performers play more than 50 roles in this adaptation of A.R. Gurney Jr.'s play set in a dining room, where people live out dramatic and comic moments in their lives. From the "American Playhouse" series.
1986 90m/C Remak Ramsay, Pippa Perthree, John Shea, Frances Sternhagen; **D:** Allan Goldstein. **VHS, Beta** $59.95 *PBS, ACA* 🎬🎬½

Dinner at Eight A social-climbing woman and her husband throw a dinner party for various members of the New York elite. During the course of the evening, all of the guests reveal something about themselves. Special performances all around, especially Barrymore, Dressler, and Harlow. Superb comedic direction by Cukor. Adapted from the play by Edna Ferber and George Kaufman.
1933 110m/C John Barrymore, Lionel Barrymore, Wallace Beery, Madge Evans, Jean Harlow, Billie Burke, Marie Dressler, Phillips Holmes, Jean Hersholt; **D:** George Cukor. **VHS, Beta, LV, 8mm** $24.95 *MGM* 🎬🎬🎬🎬

Dinner at Eight A social-climbing romance novelist throws an elegant dinner party. Made for television remake of the 1933 film does not compare well.
1989 100m/C Lauren Bacall, Charles Durning, Ellen Greene, Harry Hamlin, John Mahoney, Marsha Mason, Tim Kazurinsky; **D:** Ron Lagomarsino. **VHS, Beta** $139.98 *TTC* 🎬🎬

Dinner at the Ritz Daughter of a murdered Parisian banker vows to find his killer with help from her fiance.
1937 78m/B *GB* David Niven, Annabella, Paul Lukas; **D:** Harold Schuster. **VHS, Beta, 3/4U, Special order formats** $19.95 *NOS, MRV, VYY* 🎬🎬½

Dino Social worker joins a young woman in helping a seventeen-year-old delinquent re-enter society.
1957 96m/B Sal Mineo, Brian Keith, Susan Kohner; **D:** Thomas Carr. **VHS, Beta** $39.95 *REP* 🎬½

Dinosaurus! Large sadistic dinosaurs appear in the modern world. They eat, burn, and pillage their way through this film. Also includes a romance between a Neanderthal and a modern-age woman.
1960 85m/C Ward Ramsey, Kristina Hanson, Paul Lukather; **D:** Irvin S. Yeaworth Jr. **VHS, Beta** $9.95 *NWV, STE, SNC* 🎬

Diplomaniacs Wheeler and Woolsey, official barbers on an Indian reservation, are sent to the Geneva peace conference to represent the interests of their tribe. Slim plot nevertheless provides quite a few laughs. Fun musical numbers.
1933 62m/B Bert Wheeler, Robert Woolsey, Marjorie White, Hugh Herbert; **D:** William A. Seiter. **VHS, Beta, LV** $19.98 *CCB, IME, TTC* 🎬🎬½

Diplomatic Courier Cold-war espionage saga has secret agent Power attempting to re-steal sensitive documents from the hands of Soviet agents. Involved and exciting thriller. Michael Ansara, Charles Bronson and Lee Marvin made brief appearances.
1952 97m/B Tyrone Power, Patricia Neal, Stephen McNally, Hildegarde Neff, Karl Malden; **D:** Henry Hathaway. **VHS** *TCF* 🎬🎬

Diplomatic Immunity Vicious killer gets off scot-free due to his diplomatic immunity. That is, until the victim's ex-soldier father follows this low-life to the jungles of Paraguay to exact revenge. A heap o' action.
1991 (R) 95m/C Bruce Boxleitner, Billy Drago, Meg Foster, Robert Forster; **D:** Peter Maris. **VHS, Beta, LV** $89.95 *FRH, IME* 🎬½

Dirkham Detective Agency Three children team up to form the Dirkham Detective Agency and are hired by a veterinarian to recover two dognapped poodles.
1983 60m/C Sally Kellerman, Stan Shaw, John Quade, Gordon Jump, Randy Morton. **VHS, Beta** *NO* 🎬½

Dirt Bike Kid A precocious brat is stuck with a used motorbike that has a mind of its own. Shenanigans follow in utterly predictable fashion as he battles bankers and bikers with his bad bike.
1986 (PG) 91m/C Peter Billingsley, Anne Bloom, Stuart Pankin, Patrick Collins, Sage Parker, Chad Sheets; **D:** Hoite C. Caston. **VHS, Beta, LV, 8mm** $14.95 *COL, NLC* 🎬½

Dirt Gang A motorcycle gang terrorizes the members of a film crew on location in the desert.
1971 (R) 89m/C Paul Carr, Michael Pataki, Michael Forest; **D:** Jerry Jameson. **VHS, Beta** $59.95 *MPI* 🎬

Dirty Dancing An innocent 17-year-old (Grey) is vacationing with her parents in the Catskills in 1963. Bored with the program at the hotel, she finds the real fun at the staff dances. Falling for the sexy dance instructor (Swayze), she discovers love, sex, and rock and roll dancing. An old story, with little to save it, but Grey and Swayze are appealing, the dance sequences fun, and the music great. Swayze, classically trained in ballet, also performs one of the sound-track songs.
1987 (PG-13) 97m/C Patrick Swayze, Jennifer Grey, Cynthia Rhodes, Jerry Orbach, Jack Weston, Jane Brucker, Kelly Bishop, Lonny Price, Charles "Honi" Coles, Bruce Morrow; **D:** Emile Ardolino. **VHS, Beta, LV** $19.98 *LIV, VES* 🎬🎬🎬

Dirty Dishes A French film sardonically examining the fruitless life of the average housewife as she confronts a series of bizarre but pointless experiences during the day. Dubbed and subtitled versions available. The director is the American daughter-in-law of the late Luis Bunuel.
1982 (R) 99m/C *FR* Carol Laurie, Pierre Santini; **D:** Joyce Bunuel. **VHS, Beta** $29.98 *SUE* 🎬🎬🎬

The Dirty Dozen A tough Army major is assigned to train and command twelve hardened convicts offered absolution if they participate in a suicidal mission into Nazi Germany in 1944. Well-made movie is a standout in its genre. Rough and gruff Marvin is good as the group leader.
1967 (PG) 149m/C Lee Marvin, Ernest Borgnine, Charles Bronson, Jim Brown, George Kennedy, John Cassavetes, Clint Walker, Donald Sutherland, Telly Savalas, Robert Ryan, Ralph Meeker, Richard Jaeckel, Trini Lopez; **D:** Robert Aldrich. Academy Awards '67: Best Sound Effects Editing; Nominations: Best Film Editing, Best Sound, Best Supporting Actor (Cassavetes). **VHS, Beta, LV** $19.98 *MGM, TLF* 🎬🎬🎬

The Dirty Dozen: The Next Mission Disappointing made for television sequel to the 1967 hit, with Marvin reprising his role as the leader of the motley pack. In this installment, the rag-tag toughs are sent on yet another suicide mission inside Nazi Germany, this time to thwart an assassination attempt of Hitler.
1985 97m/C Lee Marvin, Ernest Borgnine, Richard Jaeckel, Ken Wahl, Larry Wilcox, Sonny Landham, Ricco Ross; **D:** Andrew V. McLaglen. **VHS, Beta** $79.95 *MGM* 🎬½

Dirty Gertie from Harlem U.S.A. All-black cast performs a variation of W. Somerset Maugham's "Rain." Gertie goes to Trinidad to hide out from her jilted boyfriend.
1946 60m/B Gertie LaRue, Spencer Williams Jr., Francine Everett, Don "The Dragon" Wilson. **VHS, Beta** $24.95 *NOS, DVT, VYY* 🎬🎬

Dirty Hands A woman and her lover conspire to murder her husband. A must for fans of the sexy Schneider. Cinematography provides moments that are both interesting and eerie. *AKA:* Les Innocents aux Mains Sales.
1976 102m/C *FR* Rod Steiger, Romy Schneider, Paul Giusti, Jean Rochefort, Hans-Christian Blech; **D:** Claude Chabrol. **VHS** *FCT* 🎬½

Dirty Harry Rock-hard cop Harry Callahan attempts to track down a psychopathic rooftop killer before a kidnapped girl dies. Harry abuses the murderer's civil rights, however, forcing the police to return the criminal to the streets, where he hijacks a

school bus and Harry is called on once again. The only answer to stop this vicious killer seems to be death in cold blood, and Harry is just the man to do it. Taut, suspenseful direction by Siegel, who thoroughly understands Eastwood's on-screen character. Features Callahan's famous "Do you feel lucky?" line, the precursor to his "Go ahead, make my day."
1971 (R) 103m/C Clint Eastwood, Harry Guardino, John Larch, Andy Robinson, Reni Santoni, John Vernon; **D:** Don Siegel. **VHS, Beta, LV, 8mm $19.98** WAR, TLF 🎬🎬🎬½

Dirty Heroes A band of escaped World War II POWs battle the Nazis for a precious treasure in the war's final days. **AKA:** Dalle Ardenne All'Inferno.
1971 (R) 117m/C John Ireland, Curt Jurgens, Adolfo Celi, Daniela Bianchi, Michael Constantine; **D:** Alberto De Martino; **M:** Ennio Morricone. **VHS, Beta $59.95** VTR, WES 🎬🎬

Dirty Laundry Insipid wreck of a comedy about a klutz who accidentally gets his laundry mixed up with $1 million dollars in drug money. Features Olympians Lewis and Louganis. Never released theatrically.
1987 (PG-13) 81m/C Leigh McCloskey, Jeanne O'Brien, Frankie Valli, Sonny Bono, Carl Lewis, Greg Louganis, Nicholas Worth; **D:** William Webb. **VHS, Beta $79.95** SVS Woof!

Dirty Mary Crazy Larry A racecar driver, his mechanic, and a sexy girl hightail it from the law after pulling off a heist. Great action, great fun, and an infamous surprise ending.
1974 (PG) 93m/C Peter Fonda, Susan George, Adam Roarke, Vic Morrow, Roddy McDowall; **D:** John Hough. **VHS, Beta, LV** FOX 🎬🎬🎬

Dirty Mind of Young Sally Sally's erotic radio program broadcasts from a mobile studio, which must stay one step ahead of the police.
1972 (R) 84m/C Sharon Kelly. **VHS, Beta** NO Woof!

Dirty Partners High-kicking, bone-crunching ninja bank robbers plan to steal a gold bullion shipment.
198? 90m/C VHS, Beta $59.95 SVS 🎬

Dirty Rotten Scoundrels A remake of the 1964 "Bedtime Story," in which two confidence tricksters on the Riviera endeavor to rip off a suddenly rich American woman, and each other. Caine and Martin are terrific, Martin has some of his best physical comedy ever, and Headly is charming as the prey who's always one step ahead of them. Fine direction from Oz, the man who brought us the voice of Yoda in "The Empire Strikes Back."
1988 (PG) 112m/C Steve Martin, Michael Caine, Glenne Headly; **D:** Frank Oz. **VHS, Beta, LV $19.98** ORI 🎬🎬🎬

Dirty Tricks History professor Gould fights with bad guys for a letter written by George Washington. Thoroughly forgettable comedy lacking in laughs.
1981 (PG) 91m/C CA Elliott Gould, Kate Jackson, Arthur Hill, Rich Little; **D:** Alvin Rakoff. **VHS, Beta $14.95** COL, SUE 🎬½

Dirty Work A drug-dealing bail bondsman (Ashton) steals counterfeit money from the mob and then sets up his partner (Dobson) as the fall guy. Can Dobson survive long enough to set things straight?
1992 (R) 88m/C John Ashton, Kevin Dobson, Roxann Biggs, Donnelly Rhodes, Jim Byrnes, Mitchell Ryan; **D:** John McPherson; **W:** Aaron Julien; **VHS, Beta** PAR 🎬

Disappearance A hired assassin discovers an ironic link between his new target and his missing wife.

1981 (R) 80m/C CA Donald Sutherland, David Hemmings, John Hurt, Christopher Plummer, David Warner, Virginia McKenna; **D:** Stuart Cooper. **VHS, Beta $19.95** VES, RHI 🎬🎬

The Disappearance of Aimee Dramatic recreation of events surrounding the 1926 disappearance of evangelist Aimee Semple McPherson. She claimed she was abducted, but her mother insisted she ran away to have an affair. Excellent made for television movie with an exceptional cast. Originally to star Ann-Margret.
1976 110m/C Faye Dunaway, Bette Davis, James Sloyan, James Woods, John Lehne, Lelia Goldoni, Barry Brown, Severn Darden; **W:** Anthony Harvey. **VHS, Beta $59.95** LIV 🎬🎬🎬

Disciple Vintage silent western wherein Hart's unsmiling good-bad guy tries to clean up a lawless town and win back his wife, who has shamelessly fallen in with a corrupt saloon-keeper. Co-scripted by Thomas Ince.
1915 80m/B William S. Hart, Dorothy Dalton, Robert McKim, Jean Hersholt; **D:** William S. Hart. **VHS, Beta, 8mm $29.95** VYY 🎬½

Disciple of Death Raven plays "The Stranger," a ghoul who sacrifices virgins to the Devil.
1972 (R) 82m/C GB Mike Raven, Ronald Lacey, Stephen Bradley, Virginia Wetherell; **D:** Tom Parkinson. **VHS, Beta $49.95** UNI 🎬

Disconnected "Sorry, Wrong Number" is updated, with more than ample doses of sex and violence.
1987 81m/C Mark Walker. **VHS, Beta $7.00** VTR 🎬½

Discontent An early silent film by Lois Weber in which a cantankerous old vet goes to live with his wealthy nephew. The harmonious family life is disrupted by his meddling ways.
1916 30m/B **D:** Lois Weber. **VHS, Beta $42.50** GVV 🎬½

The Discovery Program Four award-winning short films on one video: "Ray's Male Heterosexual Dance Hall," "Greasy Lake," "The Open Window," and "Hearts of Stone." The subjects range from humorous and offbeat to tragic and deadly serious.
1989 106m/C VHS, Beta $79.95 FCT 🎬🎬½

The Discreet Charm of the Bourgeoisie Bunuel in top form, satirizing modern society. These six characters are forever sitting down to dinner, yet they never eat. Dreams and reality, actual or contrived, prevent their feast. **AKA:** Le Charme Discret de la Bourgeoisie.
1972 100m/C FR Fernando Rey, Delphine Seyrig, Jean-Pierre Cassel, Bulle Ogier, Michel Piccoli, Stephane Audran, Luis Bunuel; **W/D:** Luis Bunuel; **W:** Jean-Claude Carriere. Academy Awards '72: Best Foreign Language Film; Nominations: Best Story & Screenplay; British Academy Awards '73: Best Actress (Seyrig); National Board of Review Awards '72: 5 Best Foreign Films of the Year; National Society of Film Critics Awards '72: Best Director (Bunuel), Best Film. **VHS, Beta, LV $59.95** TAM, MED, APD 🎬🎬🎬🎬

Dishonored Lady After her ex-boyfriend is murdered, a female art director finds that she's the number one suspect. When put on trial for the dastardly deed, she takes the fifth in this mediocre melodrama.
1947 85m/B Hedy Lamarr, Dennis O'Keefe, William Lundigan, John Loder; **D:** Robert Stevenson. **VHS, Beta, 3/4U, Special order formats $16.95** SNC, NOS, CAB 🎬½

Disney Beginnings A collection of nine silent Disney cartoons, including "Four Musicians of Bremen," "Puss in Boots," "Great Guns" and "Mechanical Cow."

1920 60m/B VHS, Beta $19.95 VDM 🎬🎬

A Disney Christmas Gift A collection of Christmas scenes from such Disney classics as "Peter Pan," "The Sword in the Stone," and "Cinderella."
1982 47m/C VHS, Beta, LV $12.99 DIS, WTA 🎬🎬

Disney's American Heroes Two Disney tall tales of American folk heroes: "Pecos Bill" and "Paul Bunyan."
1982 39m/C VHS, Beta DIS 🎬🎬

Disney's Halloween Treat Scenes from Disney classics, such as "Snow White and the Seven Dwarfs," "Fantasia," "Peter Pan" and "The Sword and the Stone" are tied together with a Halloween theme.
1984 47m/C VHS, Beta $39.95 DIS 🎬🎬

Disney's Storybook Classics A collection of classic children's fables, featuring "Little Toot" (1948, excerpted from "Melody Time"), the story of a little harbor tugboat; "Chicken Little" (1943); "The Grasshopper and the Ant" (1934, a "Silly Symphony"); and "Peter and the Wolf" (1946, excerpted from "Make Mine Music"), a Disneyized version of Prokofiev's famous concert piece.
1982 121m/C Sterling Holloway, The Andrews Sisters. **VHS, Beta** DIS 🎬🎬

Disorderlies Members of the popular rap group cavort as incompetent hospital orderlies assigned to care for a cranky millionaire. Fat jokes abound with performances by the Fat Boys.
1987 (PG) 86m/C Fat Boys, Ralph Bellamy; **D:** Michael Schultz. **VHS, Beta, LV $19.98** WAR 🎬

Disorderly Orderly When Jerry Lewis gets hired as a hospital orderly, nothing stands upright long with him around. Vintage slapstick Lewis running amuck in a nursing home.
1964 90m/C Jerry Lewis, Glenda Farrell, Everett Sloane, Kathleen Freeman, Susan Oliver; **D:** Frank Tashlin. **VHS, Beta, LV $14.95** PAR 🎬½

Disorganized Crime On the lam from the law, Bernsen attempts to organize a group of his ex-con buddies to pull off the perfect heist. Before the boys can organize, however, the cops are hot on Bernsen's trail, and he must vacate the meeting place. Good cast attempts to lift this movie beyond script.
1989 (R) 101m/C Lou Diamond Phillips, Fred Gwynne, Corbin Bernsen, Ruben Blades, Hoyt Axton, Ed O'Neill, Daniel Roebuck, William Russ; **D:** Jim Kouf. **VHS, Beta, LV $89.95** TOU 🎬🎬

The Displaced Person In this television adaptation of Flannery O'Connor's story, the inhabitants of a 1940s Georgia farm find their lives disrupted by a Polish refugee family. The strong work ethic practiced by the foreigners makes their less-productive, if not lazy, neighbors regard them with caution and contempt. Well-crafted depiction of the prejudice faced by many immigrants aspiring to realize the American dream.
1976 58m/C Irene Worth, John Houseman, Henry Fonda, Shirley Stoler, Lane Smith, Earl Jones; **D:** Glenn Jordan. **VHS, Beta $24.95** MON, KAR 🎬🎬🎬½

Disraeli Arliss deservedly won the Best Actor Oscar for his title role as the famed British prime minister to Queen Victoria. This particular slice of the cunning statesman's life depicts his efforts to secure the Suez Canal for England against the Russians. Arliss' wife also played his screen spouse. One of Warner's earliest and best biographical pictures. Based on a play by Louis Napoleon Parker.

1929 87m/B George Arliss, Joan Bennett, Florence Arliss, Anthony Bushell, David Torrence, Doris Lloyd, Ivan Simpson, Gwendolyn Logan; *D:* Alfred E. Green. Academy Awards '30: Best Actor (Arliss); Nominations: Best Picture, Best Writing. **VHS** $19.98 *MGM* 🐾🐾🐾

Distant Drums A small band of adventurers tries to stop the Seminole War in the Florida Everglades.
1951 101m/C Gary Cooper, Mari Aldon, Robert Barratt, Richard Webb, Ray Teal, Arthur Hunnicutt; *D:* Raoul Walsh. **VHS** $19.98 *REP, FCT* 🐾🐾

Distant Thunder A bitter, unrelenting portrait of a small Bengali neighborhood as the severe famines of 1942, brought about by the "distant thunder" of WWII, take their toll. A mature achievement from Ray; in Bengali with English subtitles.
1973 92m/C *IN* Soumitra Chatterjee, Sandhya Roy, Babita, Gobinda Chakravarty, Romesh Mukerji; *D:* Satyajit Ray. **VHS, Beta** $44.95 *FCT* 🐾🐾🐾½

Distant Thunder A scarred Vietnam vet, who has become a recluse, and his estranged son reunite in the Washington State wilderness, causing him to reflect on his isolation. Strong premise and cast watered down by weak script.
1988 (R) 114m/C *CA* John Lithgow, Ralph Macchio, Kerrie Keane, Janet Margolin, Rick Rosenthal; *D:* Rick Rosenberg. **VHS, Beta, LV** $14.95 *PAR* 🐾🐾

Distant Voices, Still Lives A profoundly executed, disturbing film chronicling a British middle-class family through the maturation of the three children, under the dark shadow of their abusive, malevolent father. An evocative, heartbreaking portrait of British life from World War II on, and of the rhythms of dysfunctional families. A film festival favorite.
1988 87m/C *GB* Freda Dowie, Peter Postlethwaite, Angela Walsh, Dean Williams, Lorraine Ashbourne; *D:* Terence Davies. **VHS, Beta, LV, CDV** $89.95 *LIV* 🐾🐾🐾

The Distinguished Gentleman A small-time con man (Murphy) manages to scam his way into a political career and winds up in Congress. The other characters serve mostly as foils for Murphy's comedic talent. Viewers will laugh despite the story's predictablity.
1992 (R) 122m/C Eddie Murphy, Lane Smith, Sheryl Lee Ralph, Joe Don Baker, Victoria Rowell, Grant Shaud, Kevin McCarthy, Charles S. Dutton; *D:* Jonathan Lynn; *W:* Marty Kaplan. **VHS, LV** $94.95 *BVV* 🐾🐾

Distortions Hussey is a widow whose evil aunt (Laurie) is holding her hostage. What the film lacks in suspense throughout most of the movie is made up for in the end.
1987 (PG) 90m/C Piper Laurie, Steve Railsback, Olivia Hussey, Edward Albert, Rita Gam, Terence Knox; *D:* Armand Mastroianni. **VHS, Beta** $29.95 *ACA* 🐾🐾

Disturbance The two personas of a young schizophrenic get him entangled in a mysterious string of murders.
1989 81m/C Timothy Greeson, Lisa Geoffreion; *D:* Cliff Guest. **VHS, Beta** $79.98 *VID* 🐾½

Disturbed Lusty mental hospital director McDowell meets sex starved and suicidal Gidley in this less-than-stellar erotic creeper. Redeemed only by McDowell's performance and more evidence that the droog's career hasn't been just peachy since "Clockwork Orange." Written by director Winkler.
1990 (R) 96m/C Malcolm McDowell, Geoffrey Lewis, Priscilla Pointer, Pamela Gidley, Clint Howard; *W/D:* Charles Winkler. **VHS, LV** $89.95 *LIV* 🐾

Diva While at a concert given by his favorite star, a young French courier secretly tapes a soprano who has refused to record. The film follows the young man through Paris as he flees from two Japanese recording pirates, and a couple of crooked undercover police who are trying to cover-up for the chief who not only has a mistress, but runs a prostitution ring. Brilliant and dazzling photography compliment the eclectic soundtrack.
1982 (R) 123m/C *FR* Frederic Andrei, Roland Bertin, Richard Bohringer, Gerard Darmon, Jacques Fabbri, Wilhelmenia Wiggins Fernandez, Dominique Pinon; *D:* Jean-Jacques Beineix. **VHS, Beta, LV** $29.95 *MGM, APD* 🐾🐾🐾½

The Dive Two North Sea oil-rig workers are trapped far below the waves when the lifeline to their diving bell snaps in rough seas.
1989 (PG-13) 90m/C Bjorn Sundquist, Frank Grimes, Einride Eidsvold, Michael Kitchen; *D:* Tristan De Vere Cole. **VHS, Beta, LV** *NO* 🐾🐾

Dive Bomber Exciting aviation film that focuses on medical problems related to flying. Flynn stars as an aviator-doctor who conducts experiments to eliminate pilot-blackout. MacMurray, Toomey, and Heydt perform well as three flyboys stationed in Hawaii. Great flying sequences filmed at San Diego's naval base with extra scenes shot at Pensacola. Warner Bros. released this film just months before the Japanese attacked Pearl Harbor. Based on the story "Beyond the Blue Sky" by Frank Wead.
1941 130m/B Errol Flynn, Fred MacMurray, Ralph Bellamy, Alexis Smith, Regis Toomey, Robert Armstrong, Allen Jenkins, Craig Stevens; *D:* Michael Curtiz; *W:* Frank Wead, Robert Buckner. **VHS** $19.98 *MGM* 🐾🐾🐾

Divine Two Divine flicks from Waters. First, Divine plays a naughty girl who, not surprisingly, since this one is titled "The Diane Linkletter Story," ends up a successful suicide. "The Neon Woman" is a rare live performance, with Divine a woman who owns a strip joint and has a slew of problems you won't read about in Dear Abby.
1990 110m/C Divine; *D:* John Waters. **VHS** $29.99 *FCT* 🐾½

The Divine Enforcer A monsignor in a crime-ridden L.A. neighborhood reaches his wit's end in trying to stave off perpetrators of injustice. Fortunately, help arrives in the form of a mysterious priest who is equally handy with his fists, nunchakus, and guns. From then on it's no more mister nice guy, and the criminals haven't a prayer.
1991 90m/C Jan-Michael Vincent, Erik Estrada, Jim Brown, Judy Landers, Don Stroud, Robert Z'Dar, Michael Foley, Carrie Chambers, Hiroko; *D:* Robert Rundle. **VHS, Beta** $79.95 *PSM* 🐾½

Divine Madness Bette Midler is captured at her best in a live concert at Pasadena Civic Auditorium.
1980 (R) 87m/C Bette Midler; *D:* Michael Ritchie. **VHS, Beta, LV** $19.98 *WAR* 🐾½

Divine Nymph Charts the erotic adventures of the beautiful and young Manuela, who is dangerously pursued by two cousins.
1971 100m/C *IT* Laura Antonelli, Marcello Mastroianni, Terence Stamp; *D:* Giuseppe Patroni Griffi; *M:* Ennio Morricone. **VHS, Beta** $59.95 *MPI* 🐾½

Diving In Have you heard the one about the acrophobic diver? It seems a paralyzing fear of heights is the only thing between a young diver and Olympic gold. Much splashing about and heartstring-tugging.
1990 (PG-13) 92m/C Burt Young, Matt Adler, Kristy Swanson, Matt Lattanzi, Richard Johnson, Carey Scott, Yolanda Jilot; *D:* Strathford Hamilton. **VHS, Beta** $89.95 *PAR, FCT* 🐾🐾

Divorce His, Divorce Hers The first half of this drama shows the crumbling of a marriage through the husband's eyes. The second half offers the wife's perspective. Made for television.
1972 144m/C Richard Burton, Elizabeth Taylor; *D:* Waris Hussein. **VHS, Beta** *NO* 🐾🐾

Divorce—Italian Style A middle-aged baron bored with his wife begins directing his amorous attentions to a teenage cousin. Since divorce in Italy is impossible, the only way out of his marriage is murder—and the baron finds a little-known law that excuses a man from murdering his wife if she is having an affair (since he would merely be defending his honor). A hilarious comedy with a twist ending. Available in Italian with English subtitles or dubbed in English. *AKA:* Divorzio All'Italiana.
1962 104m/B *IT* Marcello Mastroianni, Daniela Rocca, Leopoldo Trieste; *D:* Pietro Germi; *W:* Pietro Germi, Ennio de Concini, Alfredo Giannetti. Academy Awards '62: Best Screenplay; Nominations: Best Actor (Mastroianni), Best Director (Germi); British Academy Awards '63: Best Actor (Mastroianni); Golden Globe Awards '63: Best Actor—Musical/Comedy (Mastroianni), Best Foreign Film. **VHS** $39.95 *HTV, TAM* 🐾🐾🐾½

The Divorce of Lady X A spoiled British debutante, in the guise of "Lady X," makes a woman-hating divorce lawyer eat his words through romance and marriage. Based on the play by Gilbert Wakefield.
1938 92m/C *GB* Merle Oberon, Laurence Olivier, Ralph Richardson, Binnie Barnes; *D:* Tim Whelan. **VHS, Beta** $19.95 *NOS, MRV, UNI* 🐾🐾½

The Divorcee Early Leonard film (he'd later directed "The Great Ziegfield" and "Pride and Prejudice") casts Shearer as a woman out to beat her husband at philandering. Married to a journalist, she cavorts with her husband's best friend and a discarded old flame as only a pre-production code gal could. Shearer—who Lillian Hellman described as having "a face unclouded by thought"—grabbed an Oscar. Based on the novel "Ex-Wife" by Ursula Parrott.
1930 83m/B Norma Shearer, Chester Morris, Conrad Nagel, Robert Montgomery, Mary Doran, Tyler Brooke, George Irving, Helen Johnson; *D:* Robert Z. Leonard. Academy Awards '30: Best Actress (Shearer); Nominations: Best Director (Leonard), Best Picture, Best Writing. **VHS** $19.98 *MGM, FCT, BTV* 🐾🐾½

Dixiana A Southern millionaire falls for a circus performer shortly before the start of the Civil War. Part color. ♫Dixiana; Here's to the Old Days; A Tear, a Kiss, a Smile; My One Ambition is You; A Lady Loved a Soldier; Mr. & Mrs. Sippi; Guiding Star.
1930 99m/B Bebe Daniels, Bert Wheeler, Robert Woolsey, Dorothy Lamour, Bill Robinson; *D:* Luther Reed. **VHS, Beta** $24.95 *NOS, DVT, TIM* 🐾½

Dixie: Changing Habits A New Orleans madam and a Mother Superior go head to head in this amusing made-for-television movie. In the end all benefit as the nuns discover business sense and pay off a debt, while the former bordello owner cleans up her act. Above-average scripting and directing for the medium.
1985 100m/C Suzanne Pleshette, Cloris Leachman, Kenneth McMillan, John Considine, Geraldine Fitzgerald, Judith Ivey; *D:* George Englund. **VHS** $59.95 *LIV* 🐾🐾

Dixie Dynamite The two daughters of a Georgia moonshiner set out to avenge the murder of their father. The music is performed by Duane Eddy and Dorsey Burnette.

1976 (PG) 88m/C Warren Oates, Christopher George, Jane Anne Johnstone, Kathy McHaley, R.G. Armstrong, Wes Bishop; **D:** Lee Frost. **VHS, Beta** $49.95 *UHV* ⅛

Dixie Jamboree Low-budget musical has gangster on the lam using an unusual method to escape from St. Louis—the last Mississippi Showboat. ♫Dixie Showboat; No, No, No; If It's a Dream; You Ain't Right with the Lord; Big Stuff.
1944 69m/B Guy Kibbee, Frances Langford, Louise Beavers, Charles Butterworth; **D:** Christy Cabanne. **VHS, Beta** $19.95 *NOS, VYY, DVT* ⅛

Dixie Lanes A relentlessly nostalgic comedy set in a small town at the end of WWII. A woman, troubled by her nephew's restless antics, puts him to work. Unfortunately she adds to his plight, as her business involves the Black Market.
1988 92m/C Hoyt Axton, Karen Black, Art Hindle, John Vernon, Ruth Buzzi, Tina Louise, Pamela Springsteen, Nina Foch; **D:** Don Cato. **VHS, Beta** $79.95 *CEL* ⅛

Django Django is a stranger who arrives in a Mexican-border town to settle a dispute between a small band of Americans and Mexicans.
1968 (PG) 90m/C Franco Nero, Loredana Nusciak, Angel Alvarez; **D:** Sergio Corbucci. **VHS, Beta** *NO* ⅛½

Django Shoots First Spaghetti western with usual amount of action and plot twists.
1974 96m/C Glen Saxson, Evelyn Stewart, Alberto Lupo. **VHS, Beta** $29.95 *VYY* ⅛½

Do or Die Former "Playboy" centerfolds Speir and Vasquez team up as a couple of federal agent babes who take on international crime boss Morita. But the crimelord is ready for our scantily clad heroines with a sick game of revenge—and the stakes are their very lives!
1991 (R) 97m/C Erik Estrada, Dona Speir, Roberta Vasquez, Pat Morita, Bruce Penhall, Carolyn Liu, Stephanie Schick; **W/D:** Andy Sidaris. **VHS, LV** $79.95 *COL* ⅛½

Do the Right Thing An uncompromising, brutal comedy about the racial tensions surrounding a white-owned pizzeria in the Bed-Stuy section of Brooklyn on the hottest day of the summer, and the violence that eventually erupts. Ambivalent and, for the most part, hilarious, Lee's coming-of-age.
1989 (R) 120m/C Spike Lee, Danny Aiello, Richard Edson, Ruby Dee, Ossie Davis, Giancarlo Esposito, Bill Nunn, John Turturro, John Savage, Rosie Perez, Frankie Faison; **W/D:** Spike Lee. **VHS, Beta, LV** $19.95 *MCA, FCT* ⅛⅛½

D.O.A. A man is given a lethal, slow-acting poison. As his time runs out, he frantically seeks to learn who is responsible and why he was targeted for death. Dark film noir scored by Dmitri Tiomkin. Remade in 1969 as "Color Me Dead" and in 1988 with Dennis Quaid and Meg Ryan. Also available colorized.
1949 83m/B Edmond O'Brien, Pamela Britton, Luther Adler, Neville Brand, Beverly Garland; **D:** Rudolph Mate. **VHS, Beta, 3/4U, Special order formats** $16.95 *SNC, NOS, VYY* ⅛⅛½

D.O.A. Well-done remake of the 1949 thriller with Quaid portraying a college professor who is poisoned and has only 24 hours to identify his killer. His search for the suspect is further complicated by the fact that he is being sought by the police on phony charges of murder. Directed by the same people who brought "Max Headroom" to television screens.

1988 (R) 98m/C Dennis Quaid, Meg Ryan, Charlotte Rampling, Daniel Stern, Jane Kaczmarek; **D:** Rocky Morton, Annabel Jankel. **VHS, Beta, LV** $89.95 *TOU* ⅛⅛½

D.O.A.: A Right of Passage Often-depressing documentary about the British punk rock movement of the late '70s. The performance scenes are exciting. Also contains footage of the late Sid Vicious with his girlfriend Nancy Spungen, whom he was later accused of murdering.
1981 (R) 93m/C The Sex Pistols, X-Ray Specs. **VHS, Beta** $54.95 *VES, LIV, MVD* ⅛⅛½

The Doberman Gang Clever thieves train a gang of Dobermans in the fine art of bank robbery. Sequelled by "The Daring Dobermans."
1972 (PG) 85m/C Byron Mabe, Hal Reed, Julie Parrish, Simmy Bow, JoJo D'Amore; **D:** Byron Ross Chudnow. **VHS, Beta** $59.98 *FOX* ⅛⅛

Doc Hollywood A hotshot young physician on his way to a lucrative California practice gets stranded in a small Southern town. Will the wacky woodsy inhabitants persuade the city doctor to stay? There aren't many surprises in this fish-out-of-water comedy, but the cast injects it with considerable charm.
1991 (PG-13) 104m/C Michael J. Fox, Julie Warner, Woody Harrelson, Barnard Hughes, David Ogden Stiers, Frances Sternhagen, Bridget Fonda, George Hamilton, Roberts Blossom, Helen Martin, Macon McCalman; **D:** Michael Caton-Jones. **VHS, Beta, LV, 8mm** $19.98 *WAR, PIA* ⅛⅛½

Doc Savage Doc and "The Amazing Five" fight a murderous villain who plans to take over the world. Based on the novels of Kenneth Robeson.
1975 (PG) 100m/C Ron Ely, Pamela Hensley; **D:** Michael Anderson Sr. **VHS, Beta** $19.98 *WAR* ⅛⅛½

Docks of New York Von Sternberg made his mark in Hollywood with this silent drama about two dockside losers finding love amid the squalor. A rarely seen, early masterpiece. Score by Gaylord Carter.
1928 60m/B George Bancroft, Betty Compson, Olga Baclanova; **D:** Josef von Sternberg. **VHS, Beta** $29.95 *PAR* ⅛

The Doctor A hotshot doctor develops throat cancer and gets treated at his own hospital, an ordeal that teaches him a respect and compassion for patients that he formerly lacked. Potential melodrama is saved by fine acting and strong direction. Based on the autobiographical book "A Taste of My Own Medicine" by Dr. Edward Rosenbaum.
1991 (PG-13) 125m/C William Hurt, Elizabeth Perkins, Christine Lahti, Mandy Patinkin; **D:** Randa Haines. **VHS, Beta, LV** $92.95 *TOU* ⅛⅛½

Dr. Alien Alien poses as beautiful scientist and turns a college freshman into a sex-addicted satyr. Likewise, the cast turns this flick into a dog.
1988 (R) 90m/C Billy Jacoby, Olivia Barash, Stuart Fratkin, Troy Donahue, Arlene Golonka, Judy Landers; **D:** David DeCoteau. **VHS, Beta, LV** $19.95 *PAR* ⅛

The Doctor and the Devils Based on an old screenplay by Dylan Thomas, this is a semi-Gothic tale about two criminals who supply a physician with corpses to study, either digging them up or killing them fresh.
1985 (R) 93m/C GB Timothy Dalton, Julian Sands, Jonathan Pryce, Twiggy, Stephen Rea, Beryl Reid, Sian Phillips, Patrick Stewart; **D:** Freddie Francis. **VHS, Beta** $79.98 *FOX* ⅛⅛½

Doctor at Large A fledgling doctor seeks to become a surgeon at a hospital for the rich. Humorous antics follow. The third of the "Doctor" series.
1957 98m/C GB Dirk Bogarde, Muriel Pavlow, James Robertson Justice, Shirley Eaton, Donald Sinden, Anne Heywood; **D:** Ralph Thomas. **VHS, Beta** $29.95 *VID* ⅛⅛½

Doctor at Sea To escape a troublesome romantic entanglement and the stresses of his career, a London physician signs on a cargo boat as a ship's doctor and becomes involved with French bombshell Bardot. The second of the "Doctor" series.
1956 93m/C GB James Robertson Justice, Dirk Bogarde, Brigitte Bardot; **D:** Ralph Thomas. **VHS, Beta** $29.95 *VID* ⅛⅛½

Dr. Black, Mr. Hyde Not-so-horrifying tale of a black Jekyll who metamorphoses into a white monster with the help of the special potion. Unintended laughs lessen suspense. **AKA:** Dr. Black and Mr. White; The Watts Monster.
1976 (R) 88m/C Rosalind Cash, Stu Gilliam, Bernie Casey, Marie O'Henry; **D:** William Crain. **VHS, Beta** $29.95 *UHV* ⅛

Doctor Blood's Coffin The aptly named doctor performs hideous experiments on the unsuspecting denizens of a lonely village. Good cast in this effective chiller.
1962 92m/C GB Kieron Moore, Hazel Court, Ian Hunter; **D:** Sidney J. Furie. **VHS** $16.95 *SNC, TIM* ⅛⅛½

Doctor Butcher M.D. Mad doctor's deranged dream of creating "perfect people" by taking parts of one person and interchanging them with another backfires as his monstrosities develop strange side effects. The M.D., by the way, stands for "Medical Deviate." Dubbed. **AKA:** Queen of the Cannibals.
1980 (R) 81m/C IT Ian McCulloch, Alexandra Cole, Peter O'Neal, Donald O'Brien; **D:** Frank Martin. **VHS, Beta** $39.98 *PGN, IVE Woof!*

Dr. Caligari The granddaughter of the original Dr. Caligari promotes "better living through chemistry" in her insane asylum while using her patients as guinea pigs in her bizarre sexual experiments. Nothing outstanding here in terms of story or performance, but "Dick Tracy" has nothing on the visually compelling set designs and make-up.
1989 (R) 80m/C Madeleine Reynal, Fox Harris, Laura Albert, Jennifer Balgobin, John Durbin, Gene Zerna, David Parry, Barry Phillips; **D:** Stephen Sayadian. **VHS, LV** *FCT* ⅛⅛

Dr. Christian Meets the Women This entry in the "Dr. Christian" series of films has the small-town physician once again exposing a con man trying to filch the townspeople.
1940 63m/B Jean Hersholt, Edgar Kennedy, Rod La Rocque, Dorothy Lovett; **D:** William McGann. **VHS, Beta, 8mm** $29.95 *VYY* ⅛½

Dr. Cyclops The famous early Technicolor fantasia about a mad scientist miniaturizing a group of explorers who happen upon his jungle lab. Landmark F/X and a slow-moving story.
1940 76m/C Albert Dekker, Janice Logan, Victor Kilian, Thomas Coley, Charles Halton; **D:** Ernest B. Schoedsack. **VHS, Beta, LV** $14.98 *MCA, FCT, MLB* ⅛⅛½

Dr. Death, Seeker of Souls Evil doctor discovers a process for transmigrating his soul into the bodies of people he murdered 1000 years ago. Now he seeks to revive his wife. Final role for 77-year-old "Stooge" Moe Howard.

1973 (R) 93m/C John Considine, Barry Coe, Cheryl Miller, Stewart Moss, Leon Askin, Jo Morrow, Florence Marly, Sivi Aberg, Athena Lorde, Moe Howard; *D:* Eddie Saeta. VHS, Beta $59.95 *PSM* 🎬

Doctor Detroit Aykroyd is funny in thin film, portraying a meek college professor who gets involved with prostitutes and the mob, under the alias "Dr. Detroit." Aykroyd later married actress Donna Dixon, whom he worked with on this film. Features music by Devo, James Brown, and Pattie Brooks.
1983 (R) 91m/C Dan Aykroyd, Howard Hesseman, Donna Dixon, T.K. Carter, Lynn Whitfield, Lydia Lei, Fran Drescher, Kate Murtagh, George Furth, Andrew Duggan, James Brown, Glenne Headly; *D:* Michael Pressman. VHS, Beta, LV $14.95 *MCA* 🎬🎬

Doctor Doolittle An adventure about a 19th century English doctor who dreams of teaching animals to speak to him. Realistic premise suffers from poor script. Based on Hugh Lofting's acclaimed stories. ♫Doctor Dolittle; My Friend the Doctor; Talk to the Animals; I've Never Seen Anything Like It; Beautiful Things; When I Look in Your Eyes; After Today; Fabulous Places; Where Are the Words?; I Think I Like You; Something in Your Smile; The Vegetarian; At the Crossroads; Like Animals.
1967 144m/C Rex Harrison, Samantha Eggar, Anthony Newley, Richard Attenborough, Geoffrey Holder, Peter Bull; *D:* Richard Fleischer. Academy Awards '67: Best Song ("Talk to the Animals"), Best Visual Effects; Nominations: Best Cinematography, Best Sound, Best Original Score; Academy Awards '67: Best Film Editing, Best Picture; Golden Globe Awards '68: Best Supporting Actor (Attenborough); National Board of Review Awards '67: 10 Best Films of the Year. VHS, Beta, LV $19.98 *FOX, FCT, MLT* 🎬🎬

Doctor Doom Conquers the World Spider Man battles the evil Doctor Doom who uses his scientific skills to conquer the world.
1985 90m/C VHS, Beta $9.99 *PSM* 🎬

Doctor Duck's Super Secret All-Purpose Sauce Conglomeration of video, music, and comedy clips directed by the former Monkee done in the style of his popular "Elephant Parts."
1985 90m/C Michael Nesmith, Whoopi Goldberg, Jimmy Buffett, Rosanne Cash, Jay Leno; *D:* Michael Nesmith. VHS, Beta, LV $9.95 *MVD, PAV* 🎬

Doctor Faustus A stilted, stagy, but well-meaning adaptation of the Christopher Marlowe classic about Faust, who sold his soul to the devil for youth and the love of Helen of Troy.
1968 93m/C Richard Burton, Andreas Teuber, Elizabeth Taylor, Ian Marter; *D:* Richard Burton. VHS, Beta $69.95 *COL* 🎬½

Dr. Frankenstein's Castle of Freaks Dr. Frankenstein and his dwarf assistant reanimate a few Neanderthals that are terrorizing a nearby Rumanian village.
1974 (PG) 87m/C IT Rossano Brazzi, Michael Dunn, Edmund Purdom, Christiane Royce; *D:* Robert Oliver. VHS, Beta *SNC* 🎬

Dr. Giggles Drake plays the psycho-genius Dr. Giggles, an escaped mental patient who sets out to avenge the death of his psycho-genius father (dementia runs in the family). He returns to his family home to procure the necessary medical instruments, most notably a hypodermic needle, and starts killing people—on screen with the tools and in the audience with remarkably stupid one-liners.

1992 (R) 96m/C Larry Drake, Holly Marie Combs, Glenn Quinn, Keith Diamond, Cliff DeYoung; *W/D:* Manny Coto; *W:* Graeme Whifler. VHS, Beta, LV *MCA* 🎬

Dr. Goldfoot and the Bikini Machine A mad scientist employs gorgeous female robots to seduce the wealthy and powerful, thereby allowing him to take over the world. Title song by the Supremes.
1966 90m/C Vincent Price, Frankie Avalon, Dwayne Hickman, Annette Funicello, Susan Hart, Kay Elkhardt, Fred Clark, Deanna Lund, Deborah Walley; *D:* Norman Taurog. VHS *AIP* 🎬🎬

Doctor Gore A demented pediatrician tries to assemble a facsimile of his dead wife with pieces of other women.
1975 90m/C J.G. Patterson, Jenny Driggers, Roy Mehaffey; *D:* Pat Patterson. VHS, Beta $19.95 *UHV* Woof!

Dr. Hackenstein A doctor tries to revive his wife by "borrowing" parts from unexpected (and unsuspecting) guests.
1988 (R) 88m/C David Muir, Stacy Travis, Catherine Davis Cox, Dyanne DiRosario, Anne Ramsey, Logan Ramsey; *D:* Richard Clark. VHS, Beta $79.98 *MCG* 🎬½

Dr. Heckyl and Mr. Hype A naughty, comical version of the Jekyll and Hyde story. Exuberantly wicked performances from Reed and Coogan; stellar cast of "B" veterans.
1980 (R) 100m/C Oliver Reed, Sunny Johnson, Maia Danzinger, Mel Welles, Virgil Frye, Kedrick Wolfe, Jackie Coogan, Corinne Calvet, Dick Miller, Lucretia Love; *W/D:* Charles B. Griffith. VHS, Beta *PGN* 🎬🎬

Doctor in Distress Aging chief surgeon falls in love for the first time. His assistant tries to further the romance as well as his own love life. Comedic fourth in the six-film "Doctor" series.
1963 102m/C GB Dirk Bogarde, James Robertson Justice, Leo McKern, Samantha Eggar; *D:* Ralph Thomas. VHS, Beta $29.95 *VID* 🎬🎬½

Doctor in the House Four medical student/roommates seek only to examine lovely women and make lots of cash. In the process, they are also tempted by the evils of drink, but rally to make their grades. A riotous British comedy with marvelous performances all around. Led to six sequels and a television series.
1953 92m/C GB Dirk Bogarde, Muriel Pavlow, Kenneth More, Donald Sinden, Kay Kendall, James Robertson Justice, Donald Houston, Geoffrey Keen, George Coulouris, Shirley Eaton, Joan Hickson, Richard Wattis; *D:* Ralph Thomas. VHS $19.95 *PAR, HMV* 🎬🎬🎬½

Dr. Jack/For Heaven's Sake In "Dr. Jack" (1922) and "For Heaven's Sake" (1926) Lloyd acts respectively as an unorthodox doctor and as a debonair millionaire who falls in love with a poor girl. Silent comedy shorts from Lloyd.
1926 88m/B Harold Lloyd, Jobyna Ralston; *D:* Sam Taylor. VHS, Beta *TLF* 🎬🎬🎬½

Dr. Jekyll and Mr. Hyde The first American film version of Robert Louis Stevenson's horror tale about a doctor's experiments that lead to his developing good and evil sides to his personality. Silent. Kino Video's edition also contains the rarely seen 1911 version of the film, as well as scenes from a different 1920 version.
1920 96m/B John Barrymore, Martha Mansfield, Brandon Hurst, Charles Lane, J. Malcolm Dunn, Nita Naldi; *D:* John S. Robertson. VHS, LV $16.95 *SNC, REP, MRV* 🎬🎬🎬

Dr. Jekyll and Mr. Hyde The hallucinatory, feverish classic version of the Robert Louis Stevenson story, in which the good doctor becomes addicted to the formula that turns him into a sadistic beast. Possibly Mamoulian's and March's best work, and a masterpiece of subversive, pseudo-Freudian creepiness. Eighteen minutes from the original version, lost until recently, have been restored, including the infamous whipping scene.
1931 96m/B Fredric March, Miriam Hopkins, Halliwell Hobbes, Rose Hobart, Holmes Herbert, Edgar Norton; *D:* Rouben Mamoulian. Academy Awards '32: Best Actor (March); Nominations: Best Adapted Screenplay, Best Cinematography; Venice Film Festival '31: Best Actor (March). VHS, Beta, LV $19.98 *MGM, BTV* 🎬🎬🎬

Dr. Jekyll and Mr. Hyde Strangely cast adaptation of the Robert Louis Stevenson story about a doctor's experiment on himself to separate good and evil.
1941 113m/B Spencer Tracy, Ingrid Bergman, Lana Turner, Donald Crisp; *D:* Victor Fleming. VHS, Beta, LV $19.98 *MGM* 🎬🎬🎬

Dr. Jekyll and Mr. Hyde Yet another production of Robert Louis Stevenson's classic story of a split-personality.
1968 90m/C Jack Palance. VHS, Beta $49.95 *LIV* 🎬🎬

Dr. Jekyll and Mr. Hyde Dr. Jekyll discovers a potion that turns him into the sinister Mr. Hyde. Based on the classic story by Robert Louis Stevenson.
1973 90m/C Kirk Douglas, Michael Redgrave, Susan George, Donald Pleasence; *D:* David Winters. VHS, Beta, LV $59.95 *SVS, IME* 🎬🎬

Dr. Jekyll and Sister Hyde A tongue-in-cheek variation on the split-personality theme, which has the good doctor transforming himself into a sultry, knife-wielding woman who kills prostitutes.
1971 (R) 94m/C GB Ralph Bates, Martine Beswick, Gerald Sim; *D:* Roy Ward Baker. VHS, Beta $59.99 *HBO, MLB* 🎬🎬½

Dr. Jekyll and the Wolfman Naschy's sixth stint as El Hombre Lobo. This time he visits a mysterious doctor in search of a cure but ends up turning into Mr. Hyde, a man who likes to torture women. *AKA:* Dr. Jekyll y el Hombre Lobo.
1971 (R) 85m/C SP Paul Naschy, Shirley Corrigan, Jack Taylor; *D:* Leon Klimovsky. VHS $19.98 *SNC* 🎬

Dr. Jekyll vs. the Werewolf A man afflicted with the characteristics of a wolf seeks a cure from Dr. Jekyll's grandson.
1971 ?m/C Paul Naschy, Jack Taylor. VHS $16.95 *SNC* 🎬½

Dr. Jekyll's Dungeon of Death Dr. Jekyll and his lobotomized sister, Hilda, scour the streets of San Francisco looking for human blood to recreate his great-grandfather's secret serum. Also on video as "Dr. Jekyll's Dungeon of Darkness."
1982 (R) 90m/C James Mathers, Dawn Carver Kelly, John Kearney, Jake Pearson; *D:* James Wood. VHS, Beta *GHV* 🎬

Dr. Judym The screen adaptation of writer Stefan Zeromski's story of an impoverished youth who grows up to become an idealistic physician. In Polish with English subtitles.
19?? 94m/C PL *D:* Wlodzimierz Haupe. VHS $49.95 *FCT, MOV* 🎬🎬

Dr. Kildare's Strange Case Dr. Kildare administers a daring treatment to a man suffering from a mental disorder of a dangerous nature. One in the film series.

D

1940 76m/B Lew Ayres, Lionel Barrymore, Laraine Day; **D:** Harold Bucquet. **VHS, Beta** $19.95 *NOS, HHT, DVT* ♫♫

Dr. Mabuse the Gambler The massive, two-part crime melodrama, introducing the raving mastermind/extortionist/villain to the world. The film follows Dr. Mabuse through his life of crime until he finally goes mad. Highly influential and inventive. Lang meant this to be a criticism of morally bankrupt post-World War I Germany. Followed some time later by "Testament of Doctor Mabuse" and "The Thousand Eyes of Dr. Mabuse." Silent. **AKA:** Doktor Mabuse der Spieler.
1922 242m/B *GE* Rudolf Klein-Rogge, Aud Egede Nissen, Alfred Abel, Gertrude Welcker, Lil Dagover, Paul Richter; **D:** Fritz Lang. **VHS, Beta** $16.95 *SNC, MRV, NOS* ♫♫♫½

Dr. Mabuse vs. Scotland Yard A sequel to the Fritz Lang classics, this film features the arch-criminal attempting to take over the world with a mind-controlling camera.
1964 90m/B *GE* Sabine Bethmann, Peter Van Eyck; **D:** Paul May. **VHS, Beta** $29.95 *SNC, VYY, GLV* ♫♫½

Dr. Minx An account of a professor's sleazy, sordid affairs. Noteworthy only for the exceptionally poor acting of Ms. Williams.
1975 (R) 94m/C Edy Williams, Harvey Jason, Marlene Schmidt, Alvy Moore, William Smith; **D:** Hikmet Avedis. **VHS** *NO* ♫

Doctor Mordrid: Master of the Unknown Two immensely powerful sorcerers from the 4th dimension cross over into present time with two very different missions—one wants to destroy the Earth, one wants to save it.
1992 (R) 102m/C Jeffrey Combs, Yvette Nipar, Jay Acovone, Brian Thompson; **D:** Albert Band, Charles Band. **VHS, Beta** *PAR* ♫♫

Dr. No The world is introduced to secret agent James Bond when it is discovered that a mad scientist is sabotaging rocket launchings from his hideout in Jamaica. The first 007 film is far less glitzy than any of its successors but boasts the sexiest "Bond girl" of them all in Andress, and promptly made stars of her and Connery. On laserdisc, the film is in wide-screen transfer and includes movie bills, publicity photos, location pictures, and the British and American trailers. The sound effects and musical score can be separated from the dialogue. Audio interviews with the director, writer, and editor are included as part of the disc.
1962 (PG) 111m/C *GB* Sean Connery, Ursula Andress, Joseph Wiseman, Jack Lord, Zena Marshall, Eunice Gayson, Margaret LeWars, John Kitzmiller, Lois Maxwell, Bernard Lee, Anthony Dawson; **D:** Terence Young; **M:** John Barry. **VHS, Beta, LV** $19.98 *MGM, VYG, CRC* ♫♫♫

Dr. Orloff's Invisible Horror In this horror film, Dr. Orloff creates an invisible ape-monster that escapes and goes on a rampage.
1972 ?m/C Howard Vernon. **VHS** $16.95 *SNC* ♫½

Dr. Orloff's Monster As if "The Awful Dr. Orloff" wasn't awful enough, the doctor is back, this time eliminating his enemies with his trusty killer robot. Awful awful.
1964 88m/B *SP* Jose Rubio, Agnes Spaak; **D:** Jess (Jesus) Franco. **VHS** $19.98 *SNC* Woof!

Dr. Otto & the Riddle of the Gloom Beam Ernest is in your face again. Fresh from the TV commercials featuring "Ernest" comes Varney playing a villain out to wreck the global economy. He also

---

plays all the other characters, too. Way bizarre, "Know whut I mean?"
1986 (PG) 92m/C Jim Varney; **D:** John R. Cherry III. **VHS, Beta** $59.95 *GKK* ♫½

Doctor Phibes Rises Again The despicable doctor contines his quest to revive his beloved wife. Fun, superior sequel to "The Abominable Dr. Phibes."
1972 (PG) 89m/C *GB* Vincent Price, Robert Quarry, Peter Cushing, Beryl Reid, Hugh Griffith, Terry-Thomas; **D:** Robert Fuest. **VHS, Beta** $19.98 *LIV, VES* ♫♫½

Doctor Satan's Robot Indestructible robot is battled by insane Dr. Satan in reedited serial, "Mysterious Dr. Satan."
1940 100m/B Eduardo Ciannelli, Robert Wilcox, William Newell, Ella Neal; **D:** William Whitney, John English. **VHS** $29.95 *VCN* ♫♫½

Dr. Seuss' Grinch Grinches the Cat in the Hat/Pontoffel Pock A Dr. Seuss animated double feature: The Cat in the Hat and the Grinch cross paths in "The Grinch Grinches the Cat in the Hat" and a young man gains his self confidence in "Pontoffel Pock."
1982 49m/C **VHS, Beta** $14.98 *FOX, WTA* ♫♫

Dr. Seuss' Halloween Is Grinch Night Animated tale about a young boy who must muster up enough courage to save his family and town from the nasty Grinch. Based upon the Dr. Seuss story.
1977 25m/C **VHS, Beta** $14.98 *FOX* ♫♫

Doctor Snuggles Animated adventure in which Doctor Snuggles pursues the evil Professor Emerald after a strange series of events occurs.
1984 60m/C **VHS, Beta** $49.95 *SUE* ♫♫½

Dr. Strange A made-for-television pilot based upon the Marvel Comics character who, with the help of a sorcerer, practices witchcraft in order to fight evil.
1978 94m/C Peter Hooten, Clyde Kusatsu, Jessica Walter, Eddie Benton, John Mills; **D:** Philip DeGuere. **VHS, Beta** $39.95 *MCA* ♫

Dr. Strangelove, or: How I Learned to Stop Worrying and Love the Bomb Peter Sellers plays a tour-de-force triple role in Stanley Kubrick's classic black anti-war comedy. While a U.S. President (Sellers) deals with the Russian situation, a crazed general (Hayden) implements a plan to drop the A-bomb on the Soviets. Famous for Pickens' wild ride on the bomb, Hayden's character's "purity of essence" philosophy, Scott's gumchewing militarist, a soft-drink vending machine dispute, and countless other scenes. Classically written by Terry Southern, based on the novel "Red Alert" by Peter George.
1964 93m/B *GB* Peter Sellers, George C. Scott, Sterling Hayden, Keenan Wynn, Slim Pickens, James Earl Jones, Peter Bull; **D:** Stanley Kubrick. Academy Awards '64 Nominations: Best Actor (Sellers), Best Adapted Screenplay, Best Director, Best Picture; British Academy Awards '64: Best Film; New York Film Critics Awards '64: Best Director (Kubrick). **VHS, Beta, LV, 8mm** $19.95 *COL, HMV* ♫♫♫♫

Dr. Syn The story of a seemingly respectable vicar of Dymchurch who is really a former pirate. The last film of George Arliss.
1937 90m/B *GB* George Arliss, Margaret Lockwood, John Loder; **D:** Roy William Neill. **VHS, Beta, 3/4U,** Special order formats $19.95 *NOS, MRV, CAB* ♫♫

Dr. Syn, Alias the Scarecrow A mild-mannered minister is, in reality, a smuggler and pirate avenging King George III's injustices upon the English people. Originally

---

broadcast in three parts on the Disney television show.
1964 (G) 129m/C Patrick McGoohan, George Cole, Tony Britton, Michael Hordern, Geoffrey Keen, Kay Cole; **D:** James Neilson. **VHS, Beta** $69.95 *DIS* ♫♫½

Doctor Takes a Wife A fast, fun screwball comedy wherein two ill-matched career people are forced via a publicity mix-up to fake being married. Co-written by George Seaton and Ken Englund.
1940 89m/B Ray Milland, Loretta Young, Reginald Gardiner, Gail Patrick, Edmund Gwenn, George Metaxa; **D:** Alexander Hall. **VHS, Beta** $69.95 *COL* ♫♫♫

Dr. Tarr's Torture Dungeon A mysterious man is sent to the forest to investigate the bizarre behavior of Dr. Tarr who runs a torture asylum.
1975 (R) 90m/C Claudio Brook, Ellen Sherman, Robert Dumont. **VHS, Beta** *NO* Woof!

Dr. Terror's House of Horrors On a train, six traveling companions have their fortunes told by a mysterious doctor. Little do they realize that their final destination has changed. Creepy and suspenseful, especially the severed-hand chase sequence.
1965 92m/C *GB* Christopher Lee, Peter Cushing, Donald Sutherland; **D:** Freddie Francis. **VHS** $14.95 *REP, MLB* ♫♫½

Doctor Who: An Unearthly Child In the British series' first episode, Doctor Who and his granddaughter travel to prehistoric times to witness the discovery of fire.
1963 98m/B *GB* William Hartnell. **VHS** $19.98 *FXV, MOV* ♫♫½

Doctor Who and the Daleks The Time-Lord and his three grandchildren accidentally transport themselves to a futuristic planet inhabited by the Daleks, who capture the travelers and hold them captive. A feature film version of the long-running British television show.
1965 78m/C *GB* Peter Cushing, Roy Castle; **D:** Gordon Flemyng. **VHS, Beta** $69.99 *HBO* ♫♫

Doctor Who: Brain of Morbius The Doctor and Sarah find a space scientist has kept alive the brain of the evil renegade Time Lord, Morbius, and plans to transplant the brain into a new body.
1975 59m/C *GB* Tom Baker, Elizabeth Sladen; **D:** Christopher Barry. **VHS, Beta** $19.98 *FOX, MOV* ♫

Doctor Who: Cybermen—The Early Years Baker, the 6th Doctor, hosts this look at one of the Time Lord's favorite enemies, the robotic and ruthless Cybermen.
19?? 120m/C *GB* **VHS** $19.99 *FXV, MOV* ♫♫

Doctor Who: Day of the Daleks From the long-running British television show. The Doctor must stop the evil Daleks from gaining control of Earth. Hailed as one of the best episodes by fans.
1972 90m/C *GB* Jon Pertwee; **D:** Paul Bernard. **VHS, Beta** $19.98 *FOX, MOV* ♫♫

Doctor Who: Deadly Assassin On his home planet of Gallifrey the Doctor stands accused of murder before the council of the Time Lords. Can he prove his innocence and battle that arch-fiend "The Master?"
1976 90m/C *GB* Tom Baker; **D:** David Maloney. **VHS, Beta** $19.98 *FOX, MOV* ♫♫

Doctor Who: Death to the Daleks The Doctor and Sarah must battle the Daleks in order to find an antidote to a deadly virus threatening all life in the universe.

1974 90m/C *GB* Jon Pertwee, Elizabeth Sladen; *D:* Michael E. Briant. **VHS, Beta $19.98** *FOX, MOV* 🎦🎦

Doctor Who: Earthshock The Doctor finds himself in the middle of a 26th-century murder mystery on an abandoned planet—and it seems his old enemies the Cybermen are involved!
1980 99m/C *GB* Peter Davison. **VHS $19.99** *FXV, MOV* 🎦🎦

Doctor Who: Pyramids of Mars Join Dr. Who and Sarah Jane as they battle a professor possessed by the God of Darkness who must be stopped before he destroys humankind. From the British television series.
1975 91m/C *GB* Tom Baker, Elizabeth Sladen; *D:* Paddy Russell. **VHS, Beta $19.98** *FOX, MOV* 🎦🎦

Doctor Who: Revenge of the Cybermen The Doctor, Sarah Jane, and Harry must free a space station from the deadly grip of the half-robot, half-human Cybermen.
1975 92m/C *GB* Tom Baker, Elizabeth Sladen; *D:* Michael E. Briant. **VHS, Beta $19.98** *FOX, MOV* 🎦🎦

Doctor Who: Robots of Death The Doctor and new-on-the-scene Leela must solve a series of murders on a planet inhabited by robots.
1976 91m/C *GB* Tom Baker, Louise Jameson; *D:* Michael E. Briant. **VHS, Beta $19.98** *FOX, MOV* 🎦🎦

Doctor Who: Shada The Doctor, Romana, and K-9 seek the help of a Time Lord living incognito on Earth. A six-part Time Lord cycle never aired on television. The story was not completed but the available scenes have been linked with narration by Baker.
1980 110m/C *GB* Tom Baker. **VHS $19.98** *FOX, TVC, MOV* 🎦🎦

Doctor Who: Terror of the Zygons Still more hideous aliens threaten the Earth. Their instrument of destruction? The Loch Ness Monster. Unless of course the Doctor can stop them. From the British television series.
1975 92m/C *GB* Tom Baker, Elizabeth Sladen. **VHS, Beta $19.98** *FOX, MOV* 🎦🎦

Doctor Who: The Ark in Space The Doctor, Sarah Jane, and Harry find the last survivors of Earth living in a giant space ark. They're threatened by insect-like aliens who want to use the humans as host bodies.
1974 90m/C *GB* Tom Baker, Elizabeth Sladen. **VHS, Beta $19.98** *FOX, MOV* 🎦🎦

Doctor Who: The Caves of Androzani A four-part story, the last featuring Davison as Doctor No. 6, has our hero battling wits with android creator Sharaz Jek for control of a mysterious and addictive substance.
1984 101m/C *GB* Peter Davison. **VHS $19.98** *FOX, TVC, MOV* 🎦🎦

Doctor Who: The Curse of Fenric In this adventure, the Doctor's battle with the wolves of Fenric take him beck to World War II Britain.
1989 104m/C *GB* Sylvester McCoy. **VHS $19.98** *FOX, MOV* 🎦🎦

Doctor Who: The Five Doctors Literally the best of the best. The Doctor's five regenerations, numerous companions, lots of bad guys, even the Master, reunite for a spectacular showdown. An exceptional treat for fans.

1983 90m/C *GB* Peter Davison, Jon Pertwee, Patrick Troughton, Tom Baker, Richard Hurndall; *D:* Peter Moffatt. **VHS, Beta $19.98** *FOX, MOV* 🎦🎦

Doctor Who: The Hartnell Years Seventh Doctor McCoy hosts this look at the first three seasons of the long-running program and the first of the Doctors, Hartnell.
1965 88m/B *GB* William Hartnell. **VHS $19.98** *FOX, MOV* 🎦🎦

Doctor Who: The Pertwee Years A compilation of highlights from the 1970s featuring Pertwee's adventures as the Time Lord in the long-running British television series.
197? 88m/C *GB* Jon Pertwee. **VHS $19.98** *FOX, TVC, MOV* 🎦🎦

Doctor Who: The Seeds of Death Martian Ice Warriors plan to infect 21st-century Earth with a deadly fungus carried by seed pods. Can the Doctor and his companions prevent the catastrophe?
1969 137m/B *GB* Patrick Troughton; *D:* Michael Ferguson. **VHS, Beta $19.98** *FOX, MOV* 🎦🎦

Doctor Who: The Talons of Weng-Chiang The Doctor and Leela face off against a murderous time-traveling magician in Victorian London.
1977 140m/C *GB* Tom Baker, Louise Jameson; *D:* Michael E. Briant. **VHS, Beta $19.98** *FOX, MOV* 🎦🎦

Doctor Who: The Three Doctors This 10th-anniversary special highlights three incarnations of the Doctor as they join forces to battle a renegade Time Lord known as Omega.
1973 99m/C *GB* Jon Pertwee, Patrick Troughton, William Hartnell. **VHS $19.98** *FOX, MOV* 🎦🎦

Doctor Who: The Tom Baker Years Baker starred the longest as the Doctor, for seven seasons, and here he looks at his favorite epsiodes and other highlights from the series.
197? 170m/C *GB* VHS **$19.99** *FXV, MOV* 🎦🎦

Doctor Who: The Troughton Years The third Doctor serves as host to highlight the accomplishments of his predecessor in all his adventures.
1967 84m/B *GB* Patrick Troughton. **VHS $19.98** *FOX, MOV* 🎦🎦

Doctor Who: The Twin Dilemma Twins Romulus and Remus are a kidnapped pair of mathematical geniuses about to be used in a scheme for galactic domination. The Doctor must save the day but in his newly-regenerated state his behavior is even more erratic than usual.
1984 99m/C *GB* Colin Baker. **VHS $19.99** *FXV, MOV* 🎦🎦

Doctor Who: The War Games The Doctor, Zoe, and Jamie find themselves involved in an alien-staged, life-sized war simulation using soldiers plucked from different centuries. Can the Time Lord save the day? On two cassettes.
1969 243m/C *GB* Patrick Troughton. **VHS $19.98** *FOX, MOV* 🎦🎦

Doctor Who: Tomb of the Cyberman The Doctor, Jamie, and Victoria visit an archeological dig which unfortunately uncovers the deadly robotic Cybermen.
1967 100m/B *GB* Patrick Troughton. **VHS $19.98** *FOX, TVC, MOV* 🎦🎦

Doctor X An armless mad scientist uses a formula for "synthetic flesh" to grow temporary limbs and commit murder. A classic, rarely seen horror oldie, famous for its very early use of two-color Technicolor.
1932 77m/C Lionel Atwill, Fay Wray, Lee Tracy, Preston Foster; *D:* Michael Curtiz. **VHS, Beta, LV $19.95** *MGM, MLB* 🎦🎦½

Doctor Zhivago A sweeping adaptation of the Nobel Prize-winning Boris Pasternak novel about an innocent Russian poet-intellectual caught in the furor and chaos of the Bolshevik Revolution. Essentially a poignant love story filmed as a historical epic. A panoramic film that popularized the song "Lara's Theme." Overlong, with often disappointing performances, but gorgeous scenery. Lean was more successful in "Lawrence of Arabia," where there was less need for ensemble acting.
1965 197m/C Omar Sharif, Julie Christie, Geraldine Chaplin, Rod Steiger, Alec Guinness, Klaus Kinski, Ralph Richardson, Rita Tushingham, Siobhan McKenna, Tom Courtenay; *D:* David Lean; *W:* Robert Bolt; *M:* Maurice Jarre. Academy Awards '65: Best Adapted Screenplay, Best Art Direction/Set Decoration (Color), Best Color Cinematography, Best Costume Design (Color), Best Original Score; Nominations: Best Director (Lean), Best Film Editing, Best Picture, Best Sound, Best Supporting Actor (Courtenay); Golden Globe Awards '66: Best Actor—Drama (Sharif), Best Director (Lean), Best Film—Drama; National Board of Review Awards '65: 10 Best Films of the Year, Best Actress (Christie). **VHS, Beta, LV $29.97** *MGM, RDG, HMV* 🎦🎦🎦

Doctors and Nurses A children's satire of soap operas wherein the adults play the children and vice-versa.
1982 90m/C Rebecca Rigg, Drew Forsythe, Graeme Blundell; *D:* Maurice Murphy. **VHS, Beta** *VID* 🎦🎦

Doctors' Wives An adaptation of the Frank Slaughter potboiler about a large city hospital's doctors, nurses, and their respective spouses, with plenty of affairs, medical traumas, and betrayals.
1970 (R) 102m/C Dyan Cannon, Richard Crenna, Gene Hackman, Carroll O'Connor, Rachel Roberts, Janice Rule, Diana Sands, Ralph Bellamy, John Colicos; *D:* George Schaefer. **VHS, Beta $69.95** *COL* 🎦½

Dodes 'ka-den In this departure from his samurai-genre films, Kurosawa depicts a throng of fringe-dwelling Tokyo slum inhabitants in a semi-surreal manner. Fascinating presentation and content. *AKA:* Clickety Clack.
1970 140m/C *JP* Yoshitaka Zushi, Junzaburo Ban, Kiyoko Tange; *D:* Akira Kurosawa. **VHS, Beta $19.98** *TAM, SUE* 🎦🎦🎦½

Dodge City Flynn stars as Wade Hutton, a roving cattleman who becomes the sheriff of Dodge City. His job: to run a ruthless outlaw and his gang out of town. De Havilland serves as Flynn's love interest, as she did in many previous films. A broad and colorful shoot-em-up!
1939 104m/C Errol Flynn, Olivia de Havilland, Bruce Cabot, Ann Sheridan, Alan Hale Jr., Frank McHugh, Victor Jory, Henry Travers; *D:* Michael Curtiz. **VHS, Beta, LV $19.98** *MGM, FOX, FCT* 🎦🎦🎦

Dodsworth The lives of a self-made American tycoon and his wife are drastically changed when they take a tour of Europe. The success of their marriage seems questionable as they re-evaluate their lives. Huston excels as does the rest of the cast in this film, based upon the Sinclair Lewis novel.

1936 101m/B Walter Huston, David Niven, Paul Lukas, John Payne, Mary Astor, Ruth Chatterton, Maria Ouspenskaya; **D:** William Wyler. Academy Awards '36: Best Interior Decoration; Nominations: Best Actor (Huston), Best Adapted Screenplay, Best Director (Wyler), Best Picture, Best Sound, Best Supporting Actress (Ouspenskaya). **VHS, Beta, LV $19.98** *HBO, SUE* 🐾🐾🐾½

Does This Mean We're Married? A stand-up comedian is trying to find success in the comedy clubs of Paris but without her green card she may soon be deported. She finds a sleazy marriage broker who fixes her up with a womanizing songwriter who needs money. As usual, immigration officials suspect that the marriage is a fake and the mismatched couple must live together to prove them wrong. **1990 (PG-13) 93m/C** Patsy Kensit, Stephane Freiss; **D:** Carol Wiseman. **VHS, LV $19.95** *COL, NLC* 🐾🐾

Dog Day An American traitor, who is on the lam from the government, and his cronies, takes refuge on a small farm. A surprise awaits him when the farmers come up with an unusual plan to bargain for his life. **AKA:** Canicule. **1983 101m/C** *FR* Lee Marvin, Miou-Miou, Victor Lanoux; **D:** Yves Boisset. **VHS, Beta $79.98** *LIV* 🐾🐾½

Dog Day Afternoon Based on a true story, this taut, yet fantastic thriller centers on a bi-sexual and his slow-witted buddy who rob a bank to obtain money to fund a sex change operation for the ringleader's lover. Pacino is breathtaking in his role as the frustrated robber, caught in a trap of his own devicing. Very controversial for its language and subject matter when released, it nevertheless became a huge success. Director Lumet keeps up the pace, fills the screen with pathos without gross sentiment. **1975 (R) 124m/C** Al Pacino, John Cazale, Charles Durning, James Broderick, Chris Sarandon, Carol Kane, Lance Henriksen, Dick Williams; **D:** Sidney Lumet; **W:** Frank Pierson. Academy Awards '75: Best Original Screenplay; Nominations: Best Actor (Pacino), Best Director (Lumet), Best Film Editing, Best Picture, Best Supporting Actor (Sarandon); British Academy Awards '75: Best Actor (Pacino); National Board of Review Awards '75: 10 Best Films of the Year, Best Supporting Actor (Durning). **VHS, Beta, LV $19.98** *WAR* 🐾🐾🐾½

Dog Eat Dog Centering on a heist scheme by Mitchell, this one has nothing to offer except Mansfield's attributes. **AKA:** Einer Frisst den Anderen; La Morte Vestita di Dollar. **1964 86m/B** Cameron Mitchell, Jayne Mansfield, Isa Miranda; **D:** Ray Nazarro. **VHS, Beta, 8mm $29.99** *VYY, HEG* 🐾

A Dog of Flanders A young Dutch boy and his grandfather find a severely beaten dog and restore it to health. **1959 96m/C** David Ladd, Donald Crisp, Theodore Bikel, Max Croiset, Monique Ahrens; **D:** James B. Clark. **VHS, Beta $14.95** *PAR* 🐾🐾½

Dog Pound Shuffle Two drifters form a new song-and-dance act in order to raise the funds necessary to win their dog's freedom from the pound. Charming Canadian production. **AKA:** Spot. **1975 (PG) 98m/C** *CA* Ron Moody, David Soul; **W/D:** Jeffrey Bloom. **VHS, Beta $59.98** *FOX* 🐾🐾🐾

The Dog Soldier This "video novel" dramatically depicts a state of future events whereby a lone human in flight struggles to preserve his right to be free. **1972 40m/B VHS, Beta** *PCV* 🐾½

Dog Star Man The silent epic by the dean of experimental American film depicts man's spiritual and physical conflicts through Brakhage's characteristically freeform collage techniques. **1964 78m/C** **D:** Stan Brakhage. **VHS, Beta $29.95** *MFV, FCT* 🐾

Dogfight It's 1963 and a baby-faced Marine and his buddies are spending their last night in San Francisco before leaving the U.S. for a tour of duty in Vietnam. They agree to throw a "dogfight," a competition to see who can bring the ugliest date to a party. Birdlace (Phoenix) chooses Taylor, a shy, average-looking waitress who dreams of becoming a folk singer and realizes too late that she doesn't deserve the treatment he's about to subject her to. This quiet film didn't see a wide release, but is worth renting due to an above average script which is held up by the splendid performances of Phoenix and Taylor. **1991 (R) 94m/C** River Phoenix, Lili Taylor, Richard Panebianco, Anthony Clark, Mitchell Whitfield, E.G. Daily, Holly Near, Brendan Fraser, Peg Phillips; **D:** Nancy Savoca; **W:** Bob Comfort. **VHS, Beta, LV, 8mm $19.98** *WAR, PIA* 🐾🐾🐾

Dogs in Space A low-budget Australian film about a clique of aimless Melbourne rock kids in 1978, caught somewhere between post-hippiedom and punk, free love and heroin addiction. Acclaimed. Written by Lowenstein; music by Hutchence, Brian Eno, Iggy Pop, and others. **1987 109m/C** *AU* Michael Hutchence, Saskia Post, Nique Needles, Tony Helou, Deanna Bond; **D:** Richard Lowenstein. **VHS, Beta $79.98** *FOX* 🐾🐾

Dogs of Hell The sheriff of an idyllic resort community must stop a pack of killer dogs from terrorizing the residents. **1983 90m/C** Earl Owensby, Bill Gribble, Jerry Rushing; **D:** Worth Keeter. **VHS, Beta $59.95** *MED* 🐾½

The Dogs of War A graphic depiction of a group of professional mercenaries, driven by nothing but their quest for wealth and power, hired to overthrow the dictator of a new West African nation. Has some weak moments which break up the continuity of the movie. Based on the novel by Frederick Forsyth. **1981 (R) 102m/C** *GB* Christopher Walken, Tom Berenger, Colin Blakely, Paul Freeman, Hugh Millais, Victoria Tennant, JoBeth Williams; **D:** John Irvin. **VHS, Beta, LV $14.95** *MGM* 🐾🐾½

The Dogs Who Stopped the War A Canadian children's film about a dog who puts a halt to an escalating snowball fight between rival gangs. **1984 (G) 90m/C** *CA* **VHS, Beta $79.95** *HBO* 🐾🐾

Doin' Time At the John Dillinger Memorial Penitentiary, the inmates take over the prison under the supervision of warden "Mongo." Silliness prevails. **1985 (R) 80m/C** Jeff Altman, Dey Young, Richard Mulligan, John Vernon, Colleen Camp, Melanie Chartoff, Graham Jarvis, Pat McCormick, Eddie Velez, Jimmie Walker, Judy Landers, Nicholas Worth, Mike Mazurki, Muhammad Ali, Melinda Fee, Francesca "Kitten" Natavidad, Ron Palillo; **D:** George Mendeluk. **VHS, Beta $19.98** *WAR* 🐾

Doin' Time on Planet Earth A young boy feels out of place with his family and is convinced by two strange people (aliens themselves?) that he is really an extraterrestrial. Amusing, aimless fun directed by the son of Walter Matthau.

1988 (PG-13) 83m/C Adam West, Candice Azzara, Hugh O'Brian, Matt Adler, Timothy Patrick Murphy, Roddy McDowall, Maureen Stapleton; **D:** Charles Matthau. **VHS, Beta $19.98** *WAR* 🐾🐾½

Dolemite An ex-con attempts to settle the score with some of his former inmates. He forms a band of kung-fu savvy ladies. Strange combination of action and comedy. **1975 (R) 88m/C** Rudy Ray Moore, Jerry Jones; **D:** D'Urville Martin. **VHS** *XVC* 🐾½

Dolemite 2: Human Tornado Nobody ever said Moore was for everybody's taste. But, hey, when blaxploitation movies were the rage, Rudy the standup comic was out there rapping through a series of trashy movies that, when viewed today, have survived the test of time. This one's just as vile, violent, and sexist as the day it was released. When Rudy is surprised in bed with a white sheriff's wife, he flees and meets up with a madam and a house of kung-fu-skilled girls who are embroiled in a fight with a local mobster. **AKA:** The Human Tornado. **1976 (R) 98m/C** Rudy Ray Moore, Lady Reed. **VHS** *XVC* 🐾½

The Doll A lonely night watchman happens upon two burglars and, in the chase, the thieves knock over a mannequin. The watchman reports the mannequin stolen, brings it home and begins to have conversations with it. Soon, the doll's needs cause him to steal jewelry and clothes, until his brutish neighbor discovers his secrets. In Swedish with English subtitles. **AKA:** La Poupee; He, She or It. **1962 96m/B** *SW* Per Oscarsson, Gio Petre, Tor Isedal, Elsa Prawitz; **D:** Arne Mattson. **VHS $29.95** *FCT, DVT, AUD* 🐾🐾

Doll Face Story of a stripper who wants to go legit and make it on Broadway. Film was adapted from the play "The Naked Genius" by tease queen Gypsy Rose Lee. ♫Dig You Later; Here Comes Heaven Again; Chico-Chico; Somebody's Walkin' In My Dreams; Red Hot and Beautiful. **AKA:** Come Back to Me. **1946 80m/B** Vivian Blaine, Dennis O'Keefe, Perry Como, Carmen Miranda, Martha Stewart, Reed Hadley; **D:** Lewis Seiler. **VHS, Beta, LV $19.99** *NOS, HHT, DVT* 🐾🐾½

The Doll Squad Three voluptuous special agents fight an ex-CIA agent out to rule the world. **AKA:** Hustler Squad. **1973 (PG) 93m/C** Michael Ansara, Francine York, Anthony Eisley, Tura Satana; **D:** Ted V. Mikels. **VHS, Beta $39.95** *GHV, MRV* 🐾

Dollar The actress wife of an industrialist, convinced that he is having an affair, follows him to a ski lodge in attempt to catch him in the act. In Swedish with English subtitles. **1938 74m/B** *SW* Georg Rydeberg, Ingrid Bergman, Kotti Chave, Tutta Rolf, Hakan Westergren, Elsa Burnett, Edvin Adolphson, Gosta Cederlund, Eric Rosen; **D:** Gustaf Molander. **VHS, Beta, LV $29.95** *WAC, TAM* 🐾🐾

Dollars A bank employee and his dizzy call-girl assistant plan to steal the German facility's assets while installing its new security system. Lighthearted fun. Music by Quincy Jones. **AKA:** The Heist. **1971 (R) 119m/C** Warren Beatty, Goldie Hawn, Gert Frobe, Scott Brady, Robert Webber; **D:** Richard Brooks. **VHS, Beta, LV $9.95** *GKK* 🐾🐾🐾

The Dollmaker Excellent made for television adaptation of Harriette Arnow's novel. A strong-willed Kentucky mother of five helps move her family to Detroit in the 1940s. Petrie's direction moves the story along and creates a lovely period vision.

1984 140m/C Jane Fonda, Levon Helm, Geraldine Page, Amanda Plummer, Susan Kingsley; *D:* Daniel Petrie. **VHS, Beta** $79.98 *FOX* 🎬🎬½

Dollman An ultra-tough cop from an Earth-like planet (even swear words are the same) crashes in the South Bronx—and on this world he's only 13 inches tall. The filmmakers squander a great premise and cast with bloody shootouts and a sequel-ready non-ending.
1991 (R) 86m/C Tim Thomerson, Jackie Earle Haley, Kamala Lopez, Humberto Ortiz, Nicholas Guest, Michael Halsey, Eugene Glazer, Judd Omen, Frank Collison, Vincent Klyn; *D:* Albert Pyun. **VHS, Beta, LV** $19.95 *PAR, PIA* 🎬½

The Dolls A tropically located photographer recruits an area beauty into the fashion world with his winning smile and macho charm, only to learn native traditions forbid her to follow him.
1983 96m/C Tetchie Agbayani, Max Thayer, Carina Schally, Richard Seward; *D:* Hubert Frank. **VHS, Beta, LV** $69.98 *LIV, VES Woof!*

Dolls A group of people is stranded during a storm in an old, creepy mansion. As the night wears on, they are attacked by hundreds of antique dolls. Tongue-in-cheek.
1987 (R) 77m/C Ian Patrick Williams, Carolyn Purdy-Gordon, Carrie Lorraine, Stephen Lee, Guy Rolfe, Bunty Bailey, Cassie Stuart, Hilary Mason; *D:* Stuart Gordon. **VHS, Beta** $14.98 *LIV, VES* 🎬🎬½

A Doll's House An all-star cast is featured in this original television production of Henrik Ibsen's classic play about an independent woman's quest for freedom in nineteenth-century Norway.
1959 89m/B Julie Harris, Christopher Plummer, Jason Robards Jr., Hume Cronyn, Eileen Heckart, Richard Thomas. **VHS, Beta** $39.95 *MGM, FCT* 🎬🎬½

A Doll's House Fonda plays Nora, a subjugated 19th-century housewife who breaks free to establish herself as an individual. Based on Henrik Ibsen's classic play; some controversy regarding Fonda's interpretation of her role.
1973 (G) 98m/C Jane Fonda, Edward Fox, Trevor Howard, David Warner, Delphine Seyrig; *D:* Joseph Losey; *M:* John Barry. **Beta** $9.99 *STE, PSM* 🎬🎬½

A Doll's House A Canadian production of the Henrik Ibsen play about a Norwegian woman's search for independence.
1989 (G) 96m/C *CA* Claire Bloom, Anthony Hopkins, Ralph Richardson, Denholm Elliott, Anna Massey, Edith Evans; *D:* Patrick Garland. **VHS, Beta, LV** $9.99 *STE* 🎬🎬🎬

Dolly Dearest Strange things start happening after an American family takes over a run-down Mexican doll factory. They create a new doll called "Dolly Dearest" with deadly results. In the same tradition as the "Chucky" series.
1992 (R) 94m/C Rip Torn, Sam Bottoms, Denise Crosby; *D:* Maria Lease. **VHS, LV** $92.95 *VMK* 🎬½

The Dolphin A dolphin visits a Brazilian fishing village each full moon, turns himself into a man, and casts a spell of seduction over the women. Villagers are both enchanted and angered by the dolphin-man, since his presence creates desire in local women but scares fish from the waters. In Portuguese with English subtitles.
1987 95m/C *BR* Carlos Alberto Riccelli, Cassia Kiss, Ney Latorraca; *W/D:* Walter Lima Junior. **VHS** $79.95 *FXL, TAM* 🎬🎬½

Dominick & Eugene Dominick is a little slow, but he makes a fair living as a garbageman—good enough to put his brother through medical school. Both men struggle with the other's faults and weaknesses, as they learn the meaning of family and friendship. Well-acted, especially by Hulce, never melodramatic or weak.
1988 (PG-13) 96m/C Ray Liotta, Tom Hulce, Jamie Lee Curtis; *D:* Robert M. Young; *W:* Alvin Sargent, Corey Blechman. **VHS, Beta, LV** $19.98 *ORI, FCT* 🎬🎬🎬

Dominique is Dead A woman is driven to suicide by her greedy husband; now someone is trying to drive her mad. AKA Dominique and Avenging Spirit.
1979 (PG) 95m/C Cliff Robertson, Jean Simmons, Jenny Agutter, Simon Ward, Ron Moody; *D:* Michael Anderson Sr. **VHS, Beta** $9.95 *SIM, PSM* 🎬🎬

Domino A beautiful woman and a mysterious guy link up for sex, murder and double-crosses. Dubbed. Tries to be arty and avant-garde, but only succeeds in being a piece of soft-core fluff.
1988 (R) 95m/C *IT* Brigitte Nielsen, Tomas Arana, Daniela Alzone; *D:* Ivana Massetti. **VHS, Beta, LV** $89.95 *LIV* 🎬

The Domino Principle It's got nothing to do with pizza. Viet vet Hackman is a doltish convict sprung from the joint by a government organization to do some dirty work: work as a political assassin. Heavy-handed direction and lack of suspense make it less than it should be. *AKA:* The Domino Killings.
1977 (R) 97m/C Gene Hackman, Candice Bergen, Richard Widmark, Mickey Rooney, Edward Albert, Eli Wallach; *D:* Stanley Kramer. **VHS, Beta** $9.99 *CCB, FOX* 🎬🎬

Don Amigo/Stage to Chino A western double feature: The Cisco Kid and Pancho ride together again in "Don Amigo," and in "Stage to Chino," a postal inspector investigates a gang who robs rival stage lines.
194? 122m/B Duncan Renaldo, Leo Carrillo, George O'Brien, Roy Barcroft; *D:* Edward Killy. **VHS, Beta** $34.95 *RKO, TTC* 🎬½

Don Daredevil Rides Again Don Daredevil flies into danger in this 12-episode serial.
1951 180m/B Ken Curtis. **VHS, Beta** $29.98 *REP, MLB, MED* 🎬

The Don is Dead A violent Mafia saga wherein a love triangle interferes with Family business, resulting in gang wars. *AKA:* Beautiful But Deadly.
1973 (R) 96m/C Anthony Quinn, Frederic Forrest, Robert Forster, Al Lettieri, Ina Balin, Angel Tompkins, Charles Cioffi; *D:* Richard Fleischer; *M:* Jerry Goldsmith. **VHS, Beta** $59.95 *MCA* 🎬½

Don Juan Barrymore stars as the swashbuckling Italian duke with Spanish blood who seduces a castelful of women in the 1500s. Many exciting action sequences, including classic sword fights in which Barrymore eschewed a stunt double. Great attention is also paid to the detail of the costumes and settings of the Spanish-Moor period. Noted for employing fledgling movie sound effects and music-dubbing technology, which, ironically, were responsible for eclipsing the movie's reputation. Watch for Loy as an Asian vamp and Oland as a pre-Charlie Chan Cesare Borgia.
1926 90m/B John Barrymore, Mary Astor, Willard Louis, Estelle Taylor, Helene Costello, Myrna Loy, June Marlowe, Warner Oland, Montagu Love, Hedda Hopper, Gustav von

Seyffertitz; *D:* Alan Crosland. **VHS, LV** $29.95 *MGM, FCT* 🎬🎬🎬½

Don Juan, My Love Sexy comedy finds the ghost of Don Juan given a chance, after 450 years in Purgatory, to perform a good deed and free his soul. In Spanish with English subtitles. *AKA:* Don Juan, Mi Querido Fantasma.
1990 96m/C *SP* Juan Luis Galiardo, Rossy de Palma, Maria Barranco, Loles Leon; *D:* Antonio Mercero. **VHS, LV** $79.95 *FXL, FCT, TAM* 🎬🎬🎬

Don Q., Son of Zorro Zorro's son takes up his father's fight against evil and injustice. Silent sequel to the 1920 classic.
1925 111m/B Douglas Fairbanks Sr., Mary Astor. **VHS, Beta, LV** $19.95 *NOS, WFV, CCB* 🎬🎬

Don Quixote Miguel de Cervantes' tale of the romantic who would rather be a knight in shining armor at night. Chaliapin stars as the knight-errant on his nightly errands, tilting at windmills and charging flocks of sheep. Certain scenes were adapted to fit the pre-World War II atmosphere, as it was filmed during the same time that the Nazis were burning books.
1935 73m/B Feodor Chaliapin, George Robey, Sidney Fox, Miles Mander, Oscar Asche, Emily Fitzroy, Wally Patch; *D:* G.W. Pabst. **VHS** $19.95 *NOS, MLB, VEC* 🎬🎬🎬

Don Quixote The lauded, visually ravishing adaptation of the Cervantes classic, with a formal integrity inherited from Eisenstein and Dovshenko. In Russian with English subtitles.
1957 110m/B *SP RU* Nikolai Cherkassov, Yuri Tobubeyev; *D:* Grigori Kosintsev. **VHS, Beta** $34.95 *FCT, AUD* 🎬🎬🎬½

Don Winslow of the Coast Guard Serial in 13 episodes features comic-strip character Winslow as he strives to keep the waters of America safe for democracy.
1943 234m/B Don Terry, Elyse Knox; *D:* Ford Beebe, Ray Taylor. **VHS, Beta** $49.95 *NOS, MED, VDM* 🎬½

Don Winslow of the Navy Thirteen episodes centered around the evil Scorpion, who plots to attack the Pacific Coast, but is thwarted by comic-strip hero Winslow.
1943 234m/B Don Terry, Walter Sande, Anne Nagel; *D:* Ford Beebe, Ray Taylor. **VHS, Beta** $49.95 *NOS, MED, MLB* 🎬½

Dona Flor and Her Two Husbands A woman becomes a widow when her philandering husband finally expires from drink, gambling, and ladies. She remarries, but her new husband is so boring and proper that she begins fantasizing spouse number one's return. But is he only in her imagination? Remade as "Kiss Me Goodbye." *AKA:* Dona Flor e Seus Dois Maridos.
1978 106m/C *BR* Sonia Braga, Jose Wilker, Mauro Mendonca; *D:* Bruno Barreto. **VHS, Beta, LV** $79.95 *FXL, IME, TAM* 🎬🎬🎬

Dona Herlinda & Her Son A Mexican sex comedy about a mother who manipulates her bisexual son's two lovers (one male, one female), until all four fit together into a seamless unit. In Spanish with English subtitles. Slow, but amusing. *AKA:* Dona Herlinda y Su Hijo.
1986 90m/C *MX* Guadalupe Del Toro, Arturo Meza, Marco Antonio Trevino, Leticia Lupersio; *D:* Jaime Humberto Hermosillo. **VHS, Beta, LV** $79.95 *TAM, CCN* 🎬🎬

Donde Duermen Dos...Duermen Tres A Spanish "Mr. Mom"-flavored domestic comedy.
198? 94m/C *SP* Susana Gimenez, Juan Carlos Calabro. **VHS, Beta** $57.95 *UNI* 🎬

Donkey Skin A charming, all-star version of the medieval French fairy tale about a king searching for a suitable wife in a magical realm after his queen dies. In his quest for the most beautiful spouse, he learns that his daughter is that woman. She prefers Prince Charming, however. In French with English subtitles. *AKA:* Peau d'Ane.
1970 89m/C *FR* Catherine Deneuve, Jean Marais, Delphine Seyrig, Jacques Perrin; *D:* Jacques Demy. **VHS, Beta $19.95** *TAM, SUE* ♂♂♂

Donner Pass: The Road to Survival Tame retelling of the western wagon-train pioneers who were forced to resort to cannibalism during a brutal snowstorm in the Rockies. The tragedy is lightly implied, keeping the film suitable for family viewing.
1984 98m/C Robert Fuller, Diane McBain, Andrew Prine, John Anderson, Michael Callan; *D:* James L. Conway. **VHS, Beta $19.95** *STE, UHV, HHE* ♂♂

Donovan's Brain A scientist maintains the still-living brain of a dead millionaire and begins to be controlled by its powerful force. Based on Curt Siodmak's novel.
1953 85m/B Lew Ayres, Gene Evans, Nancy Davis, Steve Brodie; *D:* Felix Feist. **VHS, Beta, LV $39.95** *IME, MGM, MLB* ♂♂

Donovan's Reef Two World War II buddies meet every year on a Pacific atoll to engage in a perpetual bar-brawl, until a stuck-up Bostonian maiden appears to find her dad, a man who has fathered a brood of lovable half-casts. A rollicking, good-natured film from Ford.
1963 109m/C John Wayne, Lee Marvin, Jack Warden, Elizabeth Allan, Dorothy Lamour, Mike Mazurki, Cesar Romero; *D:* John Ford. **VHS, Beta, LV $19.95** *PAR, TLF* ♂♂♂

Don's Party A rather dark comedy focusing on Australian Yuppie-types who decide to watch the election results on television as a group. A lot more goes on at this party, however, than talk of the returns. Sexual themes surface. Cast members turn fine performances, aided by top-notch script and direction.
1976 90m/C *AU* Pat Bishop, Graham Kennedy, Candy Raymond, Veronica Lang, John Hargreaves; *D:* Bruce Beresford. **VHS, Beta $14.98** *VID, FCT* ♂♂

Don't Answer the Phone Deeply troubled photographer stalks and attacks the patients of a beautiful psychologist talk-show hostess. *AKA:* The Hollywood Strangler.
1980 (R) 94m/C James Westmoreland, Flo Gerrish, Ben Frank; *D:* Robert Hammer. **VHS, Beta $19.95** *MED* ♂

Don't Be Afraid of the Dark A young couple move into their dream house only to find that demonic little critters are residing in their basement and they want more than shelter. Made for TV with creepy scenes and eerie makeup for the monsters.
1973 74m/C Kim Darby, Jim Hutton, Barbara Anderson, William Demarest, Pedro Armendariz Jr.; *D:* John Newland. **VHS, Beta $49.95** *LIV* ♂♂

Don't Bother to Knock As a mentally unstable hotel babysitter, Monroe meets a pilot (Widmark) and has a brief rendezvous with him. When the little girl she is babysitting interrupts, Monroe is furious, and later tries to murder the girl. This is one of Monroe's best dramatic roles. Bancroft's film debut as the Widmark's girlfriend.
1952 76m/B Richard Widmark, Marilyn Monroe, Anne Bancroft, Elisha Cook Jr., Jim Backus, Lurene Tuttle, Jeanne Cagney, Donna Corcoran; *D:* Roy Ward Baker. **VHS $14.98** *FXV* ♂♂½

Don't Change My World To preserve the natural beauty of the north woods, a wildlife photographer must fight a villainous land developer and a reckless poacher. Eco-correct.
1983 89m/C Roy Tatum, Ben Jones. **VHS, Beta $59.98** *LIV* ♂½

Don't Cry, It's Only Thunder A young army medic who works in a mortuary in Saigon becomes involved with a group of Vietnamese orphans and a dedicated army doctor. Based on a true story.
1982 (PG) 108m/C Dennis Christopher, Susan St. James, Roger Brown, Li Lu, Thu Thuy, James Whitmore; *D:* Peter Werner. **VHS, Beta $59.95** *COL* ♂♂½

Don't Drink the Water Based on Woody Allen's hit play, this film places an average Newark, New Jersey, family behind the Iron Curtain, where their vacation photo-taking gets them accused of spying.
1969 (G) 100m/C Jackie Gleason, Estelle Parsons, Joan Delaney, Ted Bessell, Michael Constantine; *D:* Howard Morris. **VHS, Beta $9.95** *COL, SUE* ♂♂½

Don't Go in the House Long-dormant psychosis is brought to life by the death of a young man's mother.
1980 (R) 90m/C Dan Grimaldi, Robert Osth, Ruth Dardick; *D:* Joseph Ellison. **VHS, Beta $54.95** *MED* ♂

Don't Go in the Woods Routine exercise in "don't do that" terror genre (includes warnings about going into houses, answering phones, looking into basements, opening windows, etc.). This time, four young campers are stalked by a crazed killer armed with prerequisite ax.
1981 (R) 88m/C **VHS, Beta $59.98** *VES Woof!*

Don't Go to Sleep After a fatal car crash, a young girl misses mom and dad so much she returns from the grave to take them where they can be one big happy family again. Better than most made-for-TV junkfood fright-fests, written by Keenan Wynn's son, Ned.
1982 93m/C Dennis Weaver, Valerie Harper, Robin Ignico, Kristin Cummings, Ruth Gordon, Robert Webber; *D:* Richard Lang. **VHS $29.95** *UNI* ♂♂

Don't Look Back A famous documentary about Bob Dylan at the beginning of his career: on the road, in performance and during private moments. From the director of "Monterey Pop."
1967 95m/B Bob Dylan, Joan Baez, Donovan; *D:* D.A. Pennebaker. **VHS, Beta, LV $19.98** *WRV, MVD, PAR* ♂♂♂

Don't Look Back: The Story of Leroy "Satchel" Paige Drama of the legendary baseball pitcher who helped break down racial barriers, based on his autobiography. Made-for-TV fare. Gossett hits a home run in the lead, but the overall effort is a ground-rule double.
1981 98m/C Louis Gossett Jr., Beverly Todd, Cleavon Little, Clifton Davis, John Beradino, Jim Davis, Ossie Davis, Hal Williams; *D:* George C. Scott, Richard A. Colla. **VHS** *ABC* ♂♂½

Don't Look in the Attic A couple finds a haunted house with cows in the attic.
1981 90m/C Beba Loncar, Jean-Pierre Aumont; *D:* Carl Ausino. **VHS, Beta** *NO Woof!*

Don't Look in the Basement Things get out of hand at an isolated asylum and a pretty young nurse is caught in the middle. Straight-jacketed by a low budget.
1973 (R) 95m/C Rosie Holotik, Anne MacAdams, William Bill McGhee, Rhea MacAdams, Gene Ross, Betty Chandler, Camilla Carr, Robert Dracup, Jessie Kirby, Hugh Feagin, Harryete

Warren, Jessie Lee Fulton, Michael Harvey; *D:* S.F. Brownrigg. **VHS, Beta $14.98** *VID, MPI* ♂½

Don't Look Now A psychological thriller about a couple's trip to Venice after their child drowns. Notable for a steamy love scene and a chilling climax. Based on the novel by Daphne Du Maurier.
1973 (R) 110m/C Donald Sutherland, Julie Christie, Hilary Mason; *D:* Nicolas Roeg. **VHS, Beta, LV $49.95** *PAR* ♂♂♂

Don't Mess with My Sister! A married, New York junkyard worker falls in love with a belly dancer he meets at a party. The affair leads to murder and subsequently, revenge. An interesting, offbeat film from the director of "I Spit on Your Grave."
1985 90m/C Joe Perce, Jeannine Lemay, Jack Gurci, Peter Sapienza, Laura Lanfranchi; *D:* Mier Zarchi. **VHS, Beta, LV $29.98** *VID* ♂♂½

Don't Open the Door! A young woman is terrorized by a killer located inside her house.
1974 (PG) 90m/C Susan Bracken, Gene Ross, Jim Harrell; *D:* S.F. Brownrigg. **VHS, Beta $24.95** *GEM Woof!*

Don't Open Till Christmas A weirdo murders various Santa Clauses in assorted gory ways. Best to take this one back to the department store.
1984 86m/C *GB* Edmund Purdom, Caroline Munro, Alan Lake, Belinda Mayne, Gerry Sundquist, Mark Jones; *D:* Edmund Purdom. **VHS, Beta $69.98** *LIV, VES Woof!*

Don't Raise the Bridge, Lower the River After his wife leaves him, an American with crazy, get-rich-quick schemes turns his wife's ancestral English home into a Chinese discotheque. Domestic farce that comes and goes; if mad for Lewis, rent "The Nutty Professor."
1968 (G) 99m/C Jerry Lewis, Terry-Thomas, Jacqueline Pearce; *D:* Jerry Paris. **VHS, Beta $59.95** *COL* ♂

Don't Shove/Two Gun Gussie Two early Harold Lloyd shorts feature the comedian's embryonic comic style as a young fellow impressing his date at a skating rink ("Don't Shove") and a city slicker out West ("Two Gun Gussie"). Silent with piano scores.
1919 27m/B Harold Lloyd, Bebe Daniels, Noah Young, Snub Pollard. **VHS, Beta $19.95** *CCB* ♂♂

Don't Tell Daddy Two less-than-virtuous women get the local men to seduce their virginal older sister.
1990 (R) 90m/C Eva Garden, Elina Moon. **VHS, Beta $39.95** *MON* ♂

Don't Tell Her It's Me Guttenberg is determined to win the heart of an attractive writer. With the assistance of his sister, he works to become a dream man. Clever premise, promising cast, lame comedy. From the novel by Sarah Bird. *AKA:* The Boyfriend School.
1990 (PG-13) 101m/C Steve Guttenberg, Jami Gertz, Shelley Long, Kyle MacLachlan; *D:* Malcolm Mowbray; *W:* Sarah Bird. **VHS, Beta, LV $92.99** *HBO, PIA* ♂

Don't Tell Mom the Babysitter's Dead Their mother traveling abroad, the title situation leaves a houseful of teenagers with the whole summer to themselves. Eldest daughter Applegate cons her way into the high-powered business world while the metalhead son parties hardy. Many tepid comic situations, not adding up to very much.
1991 (PG-13) 105m/C Christina Applegate, Keith Coogan, Joanna Cassidy, John Getz, Josh Charles, Concetta Tomei, Eda Reiss Merin; *D:* Stephen Herek. **VHS, Beta, LV, 8mm $19.98** *HBO, PIA* ♂½

The Doolins of Oklahoma Scott is the leader of the last of the southwestern outlaw gangs, pursued by lawmen and changing times with the onset of the modern age. Fast-paced and intelligent. *AKA:* The Great Manhunt.
1949 90m/B Randolph Scott, George Macready, Louise Allbritton, John Ireland, Virginia Huston, Charles Kemper, Noah Beery Jr.; *D:* Gordon Douglas. **VHS, Beta $14.99** *GKK* ⅛⅛ ½

Doom Asylum Several sex kittens wander into a deserted sanatorium and meet up with the grisly beast wielding autopsy instruments. The people involved with this spoof should have been (more) committed.
1988 (R) 77m/C Patty Mullen, Ruth Collins, Kristen Davis, William Hay, Kenny L. Price, Harrison White, Dawn Alvan, Michael Rogan; *D:* Richard S. Friedman. **VHS, Beta $29.95** *ACA Woof!*

Doomed Caravan Hoppy and his pals lend a hand when some villains try to monopolize the wagon train business. Location shooting was done in the valleys of central California.
1941 60m/B William Boyd, Russell Hayden, Andy Clyde, Minna Gombell, Morris Ankrum, Georgia Hawkins, Trevor Bardette, Pat O'Brien; *D:* Lesley Selander. **VHS $19.95** *NOS* ⅛⅛⅛

Doomed Love Love is hell, especially when the object of your affection happens to be deceased. A professor of literature in the throes of unrequited love decides to reunite himself with his lost love. Won awards when released in Berlin.
1983 75m/C Bill Rice; *D:* Andrew Horn. **VHS $59.95** *MWF, FCT* ⅛⅛ ½

Doomed to Die Cargo of stolen bonds leads to a tong war and the murder of a shipping millionaire. Part of Mr. Wong series. Worth a look if only for Karloff's performance.
1940 67m/B Boris Karloff, Marjorie Reynolds, Grant Withers; *D:* William Nigh. **VHS, Beta, 3/4U, Special order formats $19.95** *NOS, MRV, SNC* ⅛⅛

The Doomsday Flight Uneven made-for-television thriller scripted by Rod Serling. O'Brien plants an altitude-triggered bomb on a jet in an effort to blackmail the airline. Search for the bomb provides some suspenseful and well-acted moments.
1966 100m/C Jack Lord, Edmond O'Brien, Van Johnson, John Saxon, Katherine Crawford; *D:* William A. Graham. **VHS, Beta $39.95** *MCA* ⅛⅛

Doomwatch A scientist discovers a chemical company is dumping poison into local waters, deforming the inhabitants of an isolated island when they eat the catch of the day. Unsurprising.
1972 89m/C *GB* Ian Bannen, Judy Geeson, John Paul, Simon Oates, George Sanders; *D:* Peter Sasdy. **VHS, Beta** *MON, SUE* ⅛⅛ ½

Door to Door A made-for-cable comedy about two door-to-door salesmen who race to stay one step ahead of the law and their own company. Fairly lightweight, but it has its moments.
1984 93m/C Ron Leibman, Jane Kaczmarek, Arliss Howard, Alan Austin; *D:* Patrick Bailey. **VHS, Beta $9.95** *MED* ⅛

Door-to-Door Maniac Criminals hold a bank president's wife hostage, unaware that the husband was looking to get rid of her in favor of another woman. Cash's screen debut. Aside from the cast, not particularly worth seeing. Also titled "Five Minutes to Live."
1961 80m/B Johnny Cash, Ron Howard, Vic Tayback, Donald Woods; *D:* Bill Karn. **VHS, Beta $19.95** *VDM* ⅛ ½

Door with the Seven Locks Bizarre Edgar Wallace story of man who leaves seven keys to a treasure vault in his will. Remake of "Chamber of Horrors."
1962 96m/C *GE* Eddi Arent, Heinz Drache, Klaus Kinski, Ady Berber; *D:* Alfred Vohrer. **VHS $16.95** *SNC* ⅛⅛ ½

The Doors Stone first approached Morrison himself with an early incarnation of the Doors docudrama, but it's hard to believe that even the Lizard King could play himself with any more convincing abandon than does Kilmer. He seems inhabited by the beautiful boy, and the film's strength lies in the truth of Kilmer's performance and of the recreation of an era. Trouble is, Morrison's story—one of drugs, abuse, and abject self-indulgence—grows more than a little tiresome, and the audience, with the exception of the not-to-be-ignored ranks of die-hard Doors fans, are bound to lose sight of whatever sympathy they might have had for the drug-addled singer. Ryan is forgettable as Morrison's hippie-chick wife, MacLachlan sports a funny wig and dabbles on the keyboards as Ray Manszarek, and Quinlan is atypically cast as a sado-masochistic journalist paramour.
1991 (R) 138m/C Val Kilmer, Meg Ryan, Kevin Dillon, Kyle MacLachlan, Frank Whaley, Michael Madsen, Kathleen Quinlan; *D:* Oliver Stone. **VHS, LV, 8mm $92.95** *COL, FCT* ⅛⅛ ½

The Doors: Soft Parade, a Retrospective The Doors' final TV appearance in 1969 forms the centerpiece of this concert-video tie-in to the Oliver Stone film. Fans should a-Door previously unreleased backstage interviews and a notable version of "The Unknown Soldier."
1969 50m/C *D:* Ray Manzarek. **VHS, LV $19.95** *MCA, PIA* ⅛⅛ ½

Dope Mania A potpourri of anti-drug propaganda spanning from the '30's to the '60's, campily detailing the degradation thought to result instantly from pot and cocaine.
1986 60m/C **VHS, Beta $29.95** *RHI* ⅛⅛

Doppelganger: The Evil Within Holly Gooding (Barrymore) seems like such a nice girl—until the police suspect her of the brutal murder of her mother. Her new friend Patrick (Newbern) begins to see another side to the vulnerable Holly—a seductress capable of doing anything to get what she wants.
1990 (R) 105m/C Drew Barrymore, George Newbern, Dennis Christopher, Sally Kellerman, Leslie Hope; *W/D:* Avi Nesher. **VHS, LV $89.98** *FXV* ⅛⅛

Dorf and the First Games of Mount Olympus The video comedy character bungles his way through a parody of the ancient Greek Olympics.
1987 30m/C Tim Conway; *D:* Lang Elliott. **VHS, Beta $29.95** *JTC* ⅛⅛

Dorf Goes Auto Racing Wacky "Doozle Dorf" shows us mortals how to race cars through Europe.
1989 30m/C Tim Conway. **VHS, Beta $29.95** *PMR* ⅛⅛

Dorf on Golf Conway's Scandinavian golf expert/moron character gets his own mini-instruction show.
1986 30m/C Tim Conway. **VHS, Beta, LV $19.95** *JTC, VTK, KAR* ⅛⅛

Dorf's Golf Bible Another made-for-tape Dorf golf satire, wherein the pint-sized character mucks up 18 holes as best he can.
1989 45m/C **VHS, Beta $14.95** *JTC, RDG* ⅛⅛

Dorian Gray Modern-day version of the famous tale by Oscar Wilde about an ageless young man whose portrait reflects the ravages of time and a life of debauchery. More sex, less acting with Berger in lead. Not nearly as good as the original version, "The Picture of Dorian Gray." *AKA:* The Secret of Dorian Gray; Il Dio Chiamato a Dorian; Das Bildness des Dorian Gray.
1970 (R) 92m/C *GE IT* Richard Todd, Helmut Berger, Herbert Lom; *D:* Massimo Dallamano. **VHS $14.98** *REP, FCT* ⅛ ½

Dorm That Dripped Blood Five college students volunteer to close the dorm during their Christmas vacation. A series of grisly and barbaric incidents eliminates the youngsters one by one. As the terror mounts, the remaining students slowly realize that they are up against a terrifyingly real psychopathic killer. Merry Christmas.
1982 (R) 84m/C Laura Lopinski, Stephen Sachs, Pamela Holland; *D:* Stephen Carpenter, Jeffrey Obrow. **VHS, Beta $59.95** *MED Woof!*

Dorothy in the Land of Oz The further animated adventures of L. Frank Baum's characters from the "Wizard of Oz."
1981 60m/C **VHS, Beta $29.95** *FHE, PMS Woof!*

Dos Chicas de Revista A former film actor now recovering from a mental breakdown and drug addiction comes across a book written about him when he was bigtime. He meets the girl who wrote the book and they enjoy a happy relationship. In Spanish.
19?? 90m/C *SP* Lina Morgan, Manolo Gomez Bur. **VHS, Beta $19.95** *MED* ⅛ ½

Dos Cruces en Danger Pass Charming fairy tale about a widowed king in search of a beautiful wife. Gorgeous color production. Also known as "Peau D'Ane." In French with English subtitles.
1971 0090m/C *FR* Catherine Deneuve, Jacques Perrin, Jean Marais, Delphine Seyrig; *D:* Jacques Demy. **VHS, Beta $29.98** *SUE* ⅛⅛

Dos Esposas en Mi Cama A man finds himself in trouble when he must choose between his present wife and the wife he thought was dead. In Spanish.
1987 90m/C *MX* Joaquin Cordero, Teresa Velasquez, Hector Lechuga, Roxana Bellini. **VHS, Beta $57.95** *MAD* ⅛

Dos Postolas Gemelas Two teenage girls sing in the old West. In Spanish.
1965 84m/C *MX* Pili & Mili, Sean Flynn, Jorge Rigaud, Beni Deus. **VHS, Beta $49.95** *MAD* ⅛⅛

Dot & the Bunny The adventures of a spunky young red-haired heroine on her quest for a missing baby kangaroo named Joey. A mix of animation and live action with a subtle moral.
1983 79m/C *AU D:* Yoram Gross. **VHS, Beta $14.98** *FOX* ⅛⅛

Dot & the Whale An animated Australian fantasy about a girl who helps a beached whale.
1987 75m/C *AU* **VHS, Beta $14.95** *IVE, FHE, WTA* ⅛ ½

Double Agents Two double agents are sent on a rendezvous to exchange vital government secrets. Dubbed in English. *AKA:* La Nuit Des Espions; Night Encounter.
1959 81m/B *FR* Marina Vlady, Robert Hossein. **VHS, Beta $29.95** *VYY* ⅛

Double Cross Tank Polling (Connery), a British journalist, uses the secrets of an ex-hooker (Donohoe) to get back at a corrupt politician who ruined Polling's life five years earlier. Lots of action and a few graphic murders in this thriller.

1992 (R) 96m/C Amanda Donohoe, Peter Wyngarde, Jason Connery; **D:** James Marcus. **VHS** $79.95 *MNC* ✂✂

Double-Crossed In 1984 Barry Seal agrees to inform on Colombia's Medellin Cartel and its links to the Sandanista government of Nicaragua in exchange for leniency on drug-smuggling charges. Little does he know that the personal consequences will turn deadly when his cover is blown and the government double-crosses him. Hopper's hyped-up performance as drug smuggler turned DEA informant Seal showcases this true-crime tale. 1991 111m/C Dennis Hopper, Robert Carradine, G.W. Bailey, Adrienne Barbeau. **VHS, LV** $79.99 *WAR* ✂✂½

Double Deal An honest man and a gangster are rivals in love. The gangster robs a jewelry store and tries to pin the crime on the good guy. This is a movie with a moral so don't expect him to get away with it. 1939 60m/C Monte Hawley, Jeni Le Gon, Edward Thompson, Florence O'Brien; **D:** Arthur Dreifuss. **VHS** $34.95 *FCT* ✂✂

Double Deal Murder, mayhem, and industrial espionage come into play as parties fight over an oil field. 1950 65m/B Marie Windsor, Richard Denning, Taylor Holmes; **D:** Abby Berlin. **VHS, Beta** $24.95 *DVT* ✂½

Double Deal Unfaithful woman and her lover plot to steal priceless opal from hubby. Lifeless and silly. 1984 90m/C Louis Jourdan, Angela Punch McGregor; **D:** Brian Kavanagh. **VHS, Beta** *NO* ✂⅛

Double Dynamite A bank teller is at a loss when his racetrack winnings are confused with the cash lifted from his bank during a robbery. Forgettable, forgotten shambles. Originally filmed in 1948. *AKA:* It's Only Money. 1951 80m/B Frank Sinatra, Jane Russell, Groucho Marx, Don McGuire, Howard Freeman, Harry Hayden, Nestor Paiva, Lou Nova, Joe Devlin; **D:** Irving Cummings. **VHS, Beta** $19.98 *RKO, TTC* ✂½

Double Edge The Palestinian-Israeli conflict is the focus of this drama about an ambitious reporter (Dunaway). On her first foreign assignment, New Yorker Faye Milano finds herself way out of her depth when she covers a colleague's beat in Jerusalem. Unable to remain a detached observer, Faye instead becomes an active participant, alternating between her affair with an Israeli reserves officer and her friendship with a family of Palestinian intifada leaders. Dunaway and Kollek are unfortunately stiff in their performances but the location (Israel and the West Bank) is interesting and the story surprisingly balanced. 1992 (PG-13) 85m/C *IS* Faye Dunaway, Amos Kollek, Muhamad Bakri, Shmuel Shilo, Makram Khouri, Michael Schneider, Anat Atzman, Ann Belkin; **W/D:** Amos Kollek. **VHS, Beta** $89.99 *WAR* ✂✂

Double Exposure A young photographer's violent nightmares become the next day's headlines. Unsurprising vision. 1982 (R) 95m/C Michael Callan, James Stacy, Joanna Pettet, Cleavon Little, Pamela Hensley, Seymour Cassel; **D:** William B. Hillman. **VHS, Beta** $59.98 *VES* ✂✂

Double Exposure: The Story of Margaret Bourke-White Beautifully shot but slow biography of a woman who became a well-known professional photographer for "Life" magazine during the 1930s and 1940s, as well as the first official female

photojournalist of World War II. Made for cable television. *AKA:* Margaret Bourke-White. 1989 105m/C Farrah Fawcett, Frederic Forrest, Mitchell Ryan, David Huddleston, Jay Patterson, Ken Marshall; **D:** Lawrence Schiller. **VHS, LV** $9.98 *TTC* ✂✂½

Double Face A wealthy industrialist kills his lesbian wife with a car bomb, but she seems to haunt him through pornographic films. 1970 84m/C Klaus Kinski, Annabella Incontrera. **VHS, Beta** $49.95 *UNI* ✂½

Double Identity Former college professor turned criminal Mancuso moves to a corn patch called New Hope in hopes of returning to the straight and narrow. He finds a good woman to stand by him, but, alas, crime, like smoking, is easier to start than to quit. Much intrigue and deceit. 1989 (PG-13) 95m/C *CA FR* Nick Mancuso, Leah K Pinsent, Patrick Bauchau, Anne LeTourneau, Jacques Godin; **D:** Yves Boisset. **VHS** $29.95 *MNC* ✂✂½

Double Impact Van Damme plays twins re-united in Hong Kong to avenge their parents' murder by local bad guys, but this lunkhead kick-em-up doesn't even take advantage of that gimmick; the basic story would have been exactly the same with just one Jean-Claude. Lots of profane dialogue and some gratuitous nudity for the kiddies. 1991 (R) 107m/C Jean-Claude Van Damme, Cory Everson, Geoffrey Lewis; **D:** Sheldon Lettich. **VHS, Beta, LV, 8mm** $19.95 *COL, PIA, CCB* ✂½

Double Indemnity The classic seedy story of an insurance agent seduced by a deadly woman into killing her husband so they can collect together from his company. Terrific, influential film noir, the best of its kind. Co-written by Wilder and Raymond Chandler; music by Miklos Rozsa. Based on the James M. Cain novel. 1944 107m/B Fred MacMurray, Barbara Stanwyck, Edward G. Robinson, Tom Powers, Porter Hall, Jean Heather, Byron Barr; **D:** Billy Wilder. **VHS, Beta, LV** $19.95 *MCA, FCT* ✂✂✂✂

Double Jeopardy Boxleitner stars as a married man who risks his family and life when his sexy ex-lover returns to town. She easily involves him in deception—and murder. A cake-walk for Ward as the femme fatale. Made for cable television. 1992 (R) 101m/C Bruce Boxleitner, Rachel Ward, Sela Ward, Sally Kirkland; **D:** Lawrence Schiller. **VHS, Beta, LV** $89.98 *FXV, PMS* ✂✂

A Double Life Colman plays a Shakespearean actor in trouble when the characters he plays begin to seep into his personal life and take over. Things begin to look really bad when he is cast in the role of the cursed Othello. Colman won an Oscar for this difficult role, and the moody musical score garnered another for Rosza. 1947 103m/B Ronald Colman, Shelley Winters, Signe Hasso, Edmond O'Brien, Ray Collins, Millard Mitchell; **D:** George Cukor; **W:** Ruth Gordon, Garson Kanin; **M:** Miklos Rozsa. Academy Awards '47: Best Actor (Colman), Best Score; Nominations: Best Director (Cukor), Best Original Screenplay; Golden Globe Awards '48: Best Actor—Drama (Colman). **VHS** $14.98 *REP, FCT, BTV* ✂✂✂

The Double Life of Veronique They say everyone has a twin, but this is ridiculous. Two women—Polish Veronika and French Veronique—are born on the same day in different countries, share a singing talent, a cardiac ailment, and, although the two never meet, a strange awareness of each other. Jacob is unforgettable as

the two women, and director Krzysztof creates some spellbinding scenes but the viewer has to be willing to forgo plot for atmosphere. *AKA:* La Double Vie de Veronique. 1991 (R) 96m/C *FR PL* Irene Jacob, Phillipe Volter, Sandrine Dumas, Aleksander Bardini, Louis Ducreux, Claude Duneton, Halina Gryglaszewska, Kalina Jedrusik; **W/D:** Krzysztof Kieslowski. **VHS, Beta** *PAR* ✂✂

The Double McGuffin A plot of international intrigue is uncovered by teenagers—a la the Hardy Boys—when a prime minister and her security guard pay a visit to a small Virginia community. They're not believed, though. Action-packed from the makers of Benji. Dogs do not figure prominently here. 1979 (PG) 100m/C Ernest Borgnine, George Kennedy, Elke Sommer, Ed "Too Tall" Jones, Lisa Whelchel, Vincent Spano; **D:** Joe Camp; **V:** Orson Welles. **VHS, Beta** $69.95 *VES* ✂✂

The Double Negative A photojournalist pursues his wife's killer in a confusing story. Based on Ross MacDonald's "The Three Roads." *AKA:* Deadly Companion. 1980 96m/C *CA* Michael Sarrazin, Susan Clark, Anthony Perkins, Howard Duff, Kate Reid, Al Waxman, Elizabeth Shepherd; **D:** George Bloomfield. **VHS, Beta** *BFV* ✂½

The Double O Kid Lance is a 17-year-old video game master who's interning at the Agency, a covert spy organization. Ordered to rush a package to Los Angeles, Lance discovers that a madman computer virus designer and his henchwoman desperately want what he's carrying. Aided by the prerequisite pretty girl, Lance must avoid all the hazards sent his way. 1992 (PG-13) 95m/C Corey Haim, Wallace Shawn, Brigitte Nielsen, Nicole Eggert, John Rhys-Davies, Basil Hoffman, Karen Black; *Cameos:* Anne Francis; **W/D:** Duncan McLachlan; **W:** Andrea Buck. **VHS, Beta** $89.95 *PSM* ✂✂½

Double Revenge Two men feel they have a score to settle after a bank heist gone sour leaves two people dead. 1989 90m/C Joe Dallesandro, Nancy Everhard, Leigh McCloskey, Richard Rust, Theresa Saldana; **D:** Armand Mastroianni. **VHS** $9.98 *REP* ✂½

Double Standard You'll be less concerned with the plot—a community discovers that a prominent judge has maintained two marriages for nearly twenty years—than with the possibility that such dim-witted myopes might actually have existed in the real world. This made-for-TV slice of bigamy is for fans of the oops-I-forgot-I'm-married genre only. 1988 95m/C Robert Foxworth, Michelle Greene, Pamela Bellwood, James Kee; **D:** Louis Rudolph. **VHS** $14.95 *FRH* ✂½

Double Suicide From a play by Monzarmon Chikamatsu, a tragic drama about a poor salesman in 18th century Japan who falls in love with a geisha and ruins his family and himself trying to requite the hopeless passion. Stylish with Iwashita turning in a wonderful dual performance. In Japanese with subtitles. *AKA:* Shinju Ten No Amijima. 1969 105m/B *JP* Kichiemon Nakamura, Shima Iwashita, Yusuke Takita, Hosei Komatsu; **D:** Masahiro Shinoda. **VHS, Beta** $59.95 *SVS, TAM* ✂✂✂

Double Threat An aging sex star makes her return to the screen opposite a younger actor with whom she is having an affair. When the director wants to include nude sex scenes in the film she agrees to use a younger body-double. Then the actress discovers her lover is involved in off-screen

action with the double as well. This does not please her and she decides to take a deadly revenge. An unrated version is also available.
1992 (R) 94m/C Sally Kirkland, Andrew Stevens, Lisa Shane, Richard Lynch, Anthony (Tony) Franciosa, Sherrie Rose, Chick Vennera; **D:** David A. Prior. **VHS $89.95** AIP ♪♪

Double Trouble When rock star Presley falls in love with an English heiress, he winds up involved in an attempted murder. The king belts out "Long Legged Girl" while evading cops, criminals, and crying women. A B-side.
1967 92m/C Elvis Presley, Annette Day, John Williams, Yvonne Romain, The Wiere Brothers, Michael Murphy, Chips Rafferty; **D:** Norman Taurog. **VHS, Beta $19.95** MGM ♪♪

Double Trouble Twin brothers—one a cop, one a jewel thief—team up to crack the case of an international jewel smuggling ring headed by a wealthy and politically well-connected businessman and his righthand man.
1991 (R) 87m/C David Paul, Peter Paul, James Doohan, Roddy McDowall, Steve Kanaly, A.J. Johnson, David Carradine; **D:** John Paragon. **VHS, LV $89.95** COL ♪

Double Vision Suspense thriller starring Cattrall as Caroline, a medical student who goes to London to check out the strange disappearance of her twin sister, Lisa. Assuming her identity, Caroline gets deeply involved in a kinky lifestyle that may result in murder. Based on a short story by Mary Higgins Clark.
1992 (PG-13) 92m/C Kim Cattrall, Gale Hansen, Christopher Lee; **D:** Robert Knights. **VHS $89.98** REP ♪♪

Double Wedding Madcap comedy starring Powell as a wacky painter who doesn't believe in working and Loy as a workaholic dress designer. Loy has chosen a fiance for her younger sister, Irene, to marry, but Irene has plans of her own. When Irene and her beau meet bohemian Powell, the fun really begins. Script suffers slightly from too much slapstick and not enough wit, although the stars (in their seventh outing as a duo) play it well. Based on the play "Great Love" by Ferenc Molnar.
1937 86m/B William Powell, Myrna Loy, Florence Rice, John Beal, Jessie Ralph, Edgar Kennedy, Sidney Toler, Mary Gordon; **D:** Richard Thorpe; **W:** Jo Swerling. **VHS $19.98** MGM ♪♪♪

Doubting Thomas Rogers' last film, which was in theatres when he was killed in a plane crash. Silly story of a husband and his doubts about his wife and her amateur-acting career. The show goes on in spite of his doubts, her forgotten lines, and wardrobe goofs. Remake of 1922's silent film "The Torch Bearers."
1935 78m/B Will Rogers, Billie Burke, Alison Skipworth, Sterling Holloway; **D:** David Butler. **VHS $19.98** FOX, FCT ♪♪½

Doughboys Keaton's second talkie is a so-so comedy about a rich man who mistakenly enlists in the Army during WWI. He manages to bumble his way through basic training and win the heart of a pretty girl. There are a few bright moments, particularly a musical number between Keaton and "Ukulele Ike" Edwards. **AKA:** Forward March.
1930 80m/B Buster Keaton, Cliff Edwards, Edward Brophy, Sally Eilers, Victor Potel, Arnold Korff, Frank Mayo; **D:** Edward Sedgwick. **VHS $19.98** MGM ♪♪½

Doughnuts & Society Two elderly ladies who run a coffee shop suddenly strike it rich and find that life among the bluebloods is not all it's cracked up to be. No sprinkles.

1936 70m/B Louise Fazenda, Maude Eburne, Eddie Nugent, Ann Rutherford, Hedda Hopper, Franklin Pangborn. **VHS, Beta $29.95** VYY ♪½

The Dove A hilarious short spoof of the Ingmar Bergman films "Wild Strawberries," "The Seventh Seal," and "The Silence." English sub-titles.
1968 15m/B Madeline Kahn; **M:** John Barry. **VHS, Beta** PYR ♪♪♪

The Dove The true story of a 16-year-old's adventures as he sails around the world in a 23-foot sloop. The trip took him five years and along the way he falls in love with a girl who follows him to exotic locales. Photography and scenery are magnificent.
1974 (PG-13) 105m/C Joseph Bottoms, Deborah Raffin, Dabney Coleman, Peter Gwynne; **D:** Charles Jarrott. **VHS, Beta $14.95** PAR ♪♪½

Down Among the Z Men Enlisted man helps a girl save an atomic formula from spies. Funny in spots but weighed down by musical numbers from a female entourage. From the pre-Monty Python comedy troupe "The Goons."
1952 71m/B GB Peter Sellers, Spike Milligan, Harry Secombe, Michael Bentine, Carole Carr; **D:** Maclean Rogers. **VHS, Beta, LV $19.95** PAV ♪♪

Down & Dirty A scathing Italian satire about a modern Roman family steeped in petty crime, incest, murder, adultery, drugs, and arson. In Italian with English subtitles. Italian title: "Brutti, Sporchi, e Cattivi."
1976 115m/C IT Nino Manfredi, Francesco Anniballi, Maria Bosco; **D:** Ettore Scola. **VHS, Beta $59.94** MED, TAM ♪♪♪

Down and Out in Beverly Hills A modern retelling of Jean Renoir's classic "Boudu Sauve des Eaux" with some nice star turns. A spoiled wealthy couple rescue a suicidal bum from their swimming pool. He, in turn, beds the wife, the maid and the daughter, solves the dog's identity crisis, rescues the man and his son from frustration and finds he doesn't like being a bum. A box-office hit.
1986 (R) 103m/C Nick Nolte, Bette Midler, Richard Dreyfuss, Little Richard, Mike the Dog, Elizabeth Pena; **D:** Paul Mazursky. **VHS, Beta, LV $19.95** TOU ♪♪½

Down Argentine Way A lovely young woman falls in love with a suave Argentinian horse breeder. First-rate Fox musical made a star of Grable and was Miranda's first American film. ♫South American Way; Down Argentina Way; Two Dreams Met; Mama Yo Quiero; Sing to Your Senorita.
1940 90m/C Don Ameche, Betty Grable, Carmen Miranda, Charlotte Greenwood, J. Carroll Naish, Henry Stephenson, Leonid Kinskey; **D:** Irving Cummings. **VHS, Beta, LV $19.98** FOX, MLB ♪♪♪

Down by Law In Jarmusch's follow-up to his successful "Stranger than Paradise," he introduces us to three men: a pimp, an out-of-work disc jockey, and an Italian tourist. When the three break out of prison, they wander through the Louisiana swampland with some regrets about their new-found freedom. Slow-moving at times, beautifully shot throughout. Poignant and hilarious, the film is true to Jarmusch form: some will love the film's offbeat flair, and others will find it bothersome. It's a strange and wonderful world. Music by Lurie and Waits.
1986 (R) 107m/C John Lurie, Tom Waits, Roberto Benigni, Ellen Barkin; **D:** Jim Jarmusch. **VHS, Beta $79.94** FOX ♪♪♪

Down Dakota Way Strange coincidence between a recent murder and a fatal cow epidemic. Rogers helps some locals bring the link to light.

1949 67m/C Roy Rogers, Dale Evans, Pat Brady, Monte Montana, Elisabeth Risdon, Byron Barr, James B. Cardwell, Roy Barcroft, Emmett Vogan; **D:** William Witney. **VHS $12.98** REP ♪½

Down Mexico Way Two cowboys come to the aid of a Mexican town whose residents have been hoodwinked by a phony movie company. Very exciting chase on horseback, motorcycle, and in automobiles.
1941 78m/B Gene Autry, Smiley Burnette, Fay McKenzie, Duncan Renaldo, Champion; **D:** Joseph Santley. **VHS, Beta $19.95** CCB ♪♪

Down Texas Way One of the "Rough Riders" series. When one of the boys is accused of murdering his best friend, his two companions search for the real killer.
1942 57m/B Buck Jones, Tim McCoy, Raymond Hatton; **D:** Howard Bretherton. **VHS, Beta $9.99** NOS, VCN ♪♪

Down the Drain A broad-as-a-city-block farce about an unscrupulous criminal lawyer and his assortment of crazy clients. A fine first half but someone pulls the plug in the middle of the bath.
1989 (R) 90m/C Andrew Stevens, John Matuszak, Teri Copley, Joseph Campanella, Don Stroud, Stella Stevens, Jerry Mathers, Benny "The Jet" Urquidez; **D:** Robert C. Hughes. **VHS, Beta, LV $89.95** COL ♪♪

Down to Earth Ever-gallant lover Fairbanks overruns a mental hospital to save his sweetheart. Once inside, he's determined to show the patients that their illness is illusion, and reality is the cure. A quixotic gem from Fairbanks' pre-swashbuckling social comic days. Director Emerson's wife was the scenarist, and Victor Fleming, who went on to direct "The Wizard of Oz" and "Gone with the Wind" (to name a few), was the man behind the camera.
1917 68m/B Douglas Fairbanks Sr., Eileen Percy, Gustav von Seyffertitz, Charles P. McHugh, Charles Gerrard, William H. Keith, Ruth Allen, Fred Goodwine; **D:** John Emerson. **VHS, Beta $24.95** GPV, FCT ♪♪♪

Down to Earth A lackluster musical and box office flop with an impressive cast. Hayworth is the Greek goddess of dance sent to Earth on a mission to straighten out Broadway producer Parks and his play that ridicules the Greek gods. Anita Ellis dubs the singing of Hayworth. A parody of "Here Comes Mr. Jordan," remade in 1980 as "Xanadu."
1947 101m/C Rita Hayworth, Larry Parks, Marc Platt, Roland Culver, James Gleason, Edward Everett Horton, Adele Jergens, George Macready, William Frawley, James Burke, Fred F. Sears, Lynn Merrick, Myron Healey; **D:** Alexander Hall. **VHS, LV $19.95** COL, PIA, CCB ♪♪

Down to the Sea in Ships Bow made her movie debut in this drama about the whalers of 19th-century Massachusetts. Highlighted by exciting action scenes of an actual whale hunt. Silent with music score and original tinted footage. **AKA:** The Last Adventurers.
1922 83m/B Marguerite Courtot, Raymond McKee, Clara Bow; **D:** Elmer Clifton. **VHS, Beta $19.95** NOS, CCB, GPV ♪♪½

Down Twisted A young woman gets involved with a thief on the run in Mexico in this "Romancing the Stone" derivative. The muddled plot deserves such a confusing title.
1989 (R) 89m/C Carey Lowell, Charles Rocket, Trudi Dochtermann, Thom Mathews, Linda Kerridge, Courteney Cox; **D:** Albert Pyun. **VHS, Beta $89.95** MED ♪

Down Under Two gold-hungry beach boys go to Australia looking for riches, and document their adventures on film. Essentially a crudely shot, tongue-in-cheek travelogue narrated by Patrick Macnee.
1986 90m/C Don Atkinson, Donn Dunlop, Patrick Macnee. VHS, Beta $79.95 UHV ℤ

Downhill Racer An undisciplined American skier locks ski-tips with his coach and his new-found love while on his way to becoming an Olympic superstar. Character study on film. Beautiful ski and mountain photography keep it from sliding downhill.
1969 (PG) 102m/C Robert Redford, Camilla Sparv, Gene Hackman, Dabney Coleman; D: Michael Ritchie. VHS, Beta, LV $14.95 PAR ℤℤ½

Downtown Urban comedy about a naive white suburban cop who gets demoted to the roughest precinct in Philadelphia, and gains a streetwise black partner. Runs a routine beat.
1989 (R) 96m/C Anthony Edwards, Forest Whitaker, Joe Pantoliano, Penelope Ann Miller; D: Richard Benjamin. VHS, Beta, LV $89.98 FOX ℤℤ½

D.P. A black orphan attaches to the only other black in post-WWII Germany. From a story by Kurt Vonnegut, Jr. Made for television.
1985 60m/C Stan Shaw, Rosemary Leach, Julius Gordon. VHS $24.95 MON, KAR ℤ½

Drachenfutter Powerful story dealing with a Pakistani immigrant's attempts to enter the Western world. Themes of alienation and helplessness are emphasized. Dialogues occur in 12 languages, predominantly German and Mandarin Chinese; subtitled in English. AKA: Dragon's Food; Dragon Chow.
1987 75m/B GE SI Bhasker, Ric Young, Buddy Uzzaman; D: Jan Schutte. VHS, Beta $69.95 NYF, TAM ℤℤℤ

Dracula Lugosi, in his most famous role, plays a vampire who terrorizes the countryside in his search for human blood. From Bram Stoker's novel. Although short of a masterpiece due to slow second half, deservedly rated a film classic. What would Halloween be like without this movie? Sequelled by "Dracula's Daughter."
1931 75m/B Bela Lugosi, David Manners, Dwight Frye, Helen Chandler, Edward Van Sloan; D: Tod Browning. VHS, Beta, LV $14.95 MCA, TLF, HMV ℤℤℤ

Dracula Count on squinty-eyed Palance to shine as the Transylvanian vampire who must quench his thirst for human blood. A made-for-television adaptation of the Bram Stoker novel that really flies.
1973 105m/C Jack Palance, Simon Ward, Fiona Lewis, Nigel Davenport; D: Dan Curtis. VHS, Beta, LV $29.95 LIV ℤℤ½

Dracula Langella recreates his Broadway role as the count who needs human blood for nourishment. Notable for its portrayal of Dracula as a romantic and tragic figure in history. Overlooked since the vampire spoof "Love at First Bite" came out at the same time.
1979 (R) 109m/C Frank Langella, Laurence Olivier, Kate Nelligan, Donald Pleasence; D: John Badham; M: John Williams. VHS, Beta, LV $19.95 MCA ℤℤ½

Dracula The prince of darkness returns looking for blood in this animated adaptation of Bram Stoker's classic novel.
1984 90m/C VHS, Beta $59.98 LIV, VES, WTA ℤℤ½

Dracula: A Cinematic Scrapbook A look at the blood-sucking monster in both film and legend, featuring rare film trailers and interviews with actors such as Bela Lugosi, Christopher Lee, and Lon Chaney, Jr. In color and B&W.
1991 60m/C W/D: Ted Newsom. VHS, Beta $9.95 RHI, FCT ℤℤ½

Dracula & Son Dracula spoof in which the count fathers a son who prefers girls and football to blood. Poor English dubbing and choppy ending drive a stake through the heart. AKA: Dracula Pere et Fils.
1976 (PG) 88m/C FR Christopher Lee, Bernard Menez, Marie Breillat; D: Edouard Molinaro. VHS, Beta $9.95 GKK ℤ

Dracula Blows His Cool Three voluptuous models and their photographer restore an ancient castle and open a disco in it. The vampire lurking about the castle welcomes the party with his fangs.
1982 (R) 91m/C John Garco, Betty Verges; W/D: Carlo Ombra. VHS, Beta, LV MED ℤ

Dracula/Garden of Eden The abridged version of the chilling vampire film "Nosferatu" is coupled with "The Garden of Eden," in which Tini Le Brun meets her Prince Charming while vacationing with her Baroness friend. Silent.
1928 52m/B Max Schreck, Alexander Granach, Corrine Griffith, Charles Ray, Louise Dressler. VHS, Beta $19.95 CCB ℤℤ

Dracula Has Risen from the Grave Lee's Dracula is foiled by the local priest before he can drain the blood from innocent villagers. Effectively gory. One of the Hammer series of Dracula films followed by "Taste the Blood of Dracula."
1968 (G) 92m/C GB Christopher Lee, Rupert Davies, Veronica Carlson, Barbara Ewing, Barry Andrews, Michael Ripper; D: Freddie Francis. VHS $19.98 WAR ℤℤ½

Dracula Rising A modern-day art historian (Travis) turns out to have been a witch, burned at the stake, in a past life. She was also the blood-drinking Count's lost love. Now Dracula's a monk and when he sees this reincarnated beauty is he going to be able to keep his hands—er, fangs—off her?
1993 (R) ?m/C Christopher Atkins, Stacy Travis; D: Fred Gallo. VHS $89.98 NHO ℤℤ½

Dracula (Spanish Version) Filmed at the same time as the Bela Lugosi version of "Dracula," using the same sets and the same scripts, only in Spanish. Thought to be more visually appealing and more terrifying than the English-language counterpart. The only thing it's missing is a presence like Lugosi. Based on the novel by Bram Stoker.
1931 104m/B Carlos Villarias, Lupita Tova, Eduardo Arozamena, Pablo Alvarez Rubio, Barry Norton, Carmen Guerrero; D: George Melford; W: Garrett Fort. VHS $14.98 MCA ℤℤ½

Dracula Sucks A soft-core edit of a hardcore sex parody about Dracula snacking on the usual bevy of screaming quasi-virgins.
1979 (R) 90m/C James Gillis, Reggie Nalder, Annette Haven, Kay Parker, Serena, Seka, John Leslie; D: Philip Marshak. VHS, Beta UNI, OM ℤ

Dracula: Up in Harlem When the Prince of Darkness gets together with the people of the night, the Pentagon rolls out the heavy metal. This may suck your brain out.
1983 90m/C VHS, Beta NO Woof!

Dracula vs. Frankenstein An alien reanimates Earth's most infamous monsters in a bid to take over the planet. Rennie's last role. Also on video as, "Assignment: Terror."
1969 91m/C IT GE SP Michael Rennie, Paul Naschy, Karin Dor, Patty Shepard; D: Hugo Fregonese, Tulio Demicheli; W: Paul Naschy. VHS $29.95 UAV ℤ

Dracula vs. Frankenstein The Count makes a deal with a shady doctor to keep him in blood. Vampire spoof that's very bad but fun. Last film for both Chaney and Naish. Features a cameo by genre maven Forrest J. Ackerman. AKA: Blood of Frankenstein; They're Coming to Get You; Dracula Contra Frankenstein; The Revenge of Dracula.
1971 (R) 90m/C SP J. Carroll Naish, Lon Chaney Jr., Regina Carrol, Russ Tamblyn, Jim Davis, Anthony Eisley, Zandor Vorkov, John Bloom, Angelo Rossitto; Cameos: Forrest J. Ackerman; D: Al Adamson. VHS $14.98 VID, SVS Woof!

Dracula's Daughter Count Dracula's daughter, Countess Marya Zaleska, heads to London supposedly to find the cure to a mysterious illness. Instead she finds she has a taste for human blood, especially female blood. She also finds a man, falls in love, and tries to keep him by casting a spell on him. A good script and cast keep this sequel to Bela Lugosi's "Dracula" entertaining.
1936 71m/B Gloria Holden, Otto Kruger, Marguerite Churchill, Irving Pichel, Edward Van Sloan, Nan Grey, Hedda Hopper; D: Lambert Hillyer. VHS $14.98 MCA ℤℤℤ

Dracula's Great Love Four travellers end up in Dracula's castle for the night, where the horny Count takes a liking to one of the women. Left out in the sun too long. AKA: Gran Amore del Conde Dracula; Count Dracula's Great Love; Vampire Playgirls; Dracula's Virgin Lovers.
1972 (R) 96m/C SP Paul Naschy, Charo Soriano; D: Javier Aguirre. VHS, Beta $59.95 SNC, MPI Woof!

Dracula's Last Rites Blood-curdling tale of a sheriff and a mortician in a small town who are up to no good. Technically inept: film equipment can be spotted throughout. Don't stick your neck out for this one. AKA: Last Rites.
1979 (R) 86m/C Patricia Lee Hammond, Gerald Fielding, Victor Jorge; D: Domonic Paris. VHS, Beta $59.95 PGN, CAN Woof!

Dracula's Widow Countess Dracula, missing her hubby and desperately in need of a substitute, picks innocent Raymond as her victim. His girlfriend and a cynical cop fight to save his soul from the Countess' damnation. Directed by the nephew of Frances Ford Coppola.
1988 (R) 85m/C Sylvia Kristel, Josef Sommer, Lenny Von Dohlen; D: Christopher Coppola. VHS, Beta $14.99 HBO ℤℤ

Dragnet Sgt. Joe Friday and Officer Frank Smith try to solve a mob slaying but have a rough time. Alexander plays the sidekick in "Dragnet" pre-Morgan days. Just the facts: feature version of the TV show that's suspenseful and well-acted.
1954 88m/C Jack Webb, Ben Alexander, Richard Boone, Ann Robinson; D: Jack Webb. VHS, Beta $14.95 MCA ℤℤ½

Dragnet Detectives Joe Friday and Frank Smith make the streets of Los Angeles safe in this police series which ran from 1951-1959. Two episodes per tape.
195? 55m/C Jack Webb, Ben Alexander. VHS $19.99 MOV, MRV ℤℤ

Dragnet In this semi-parody of the vintage television cop show, Sgt. Joe Friday's straight-laced nephew and his sloppy partner take on the seamy crime life of Los Angeles. Neither Aykroyd nor Hanks can save the big-budget lackluster spoof that's full of holes.

1987 (PG-13) 106m/C Dan Aykroyd, Tom Hanks, Christopher Plummer, Harry Morgan, Elizabeth Ashley, Dabney Coleman; *D:* Tom Mankiewicz. VHS, Beta, LV $14.95 *MCA* ♫♫

The Dragon Fist A young man must avenge the death of his father in this martial arts film.
1980 90m/C Jackie Chan. VHS, Beta *NO* ♫

Dragon Force Korean martial artists fend off Japanese invaders in the 1930s.
1982 101m/C Kangjo Lee; *D:* Key-Nam Nam. VHS, Beta *NEG* ♫½

Dragon from Shaolin The Shaolin monks match wits, chops, and kicks with the brutal Ching government.
197? 90m/C Bruce Lee. VHS, Beta $54.95 *MOV* ♫½

Dragon Lady Ninja/Devil Killer Two Kung-Fu features to shred your sanity, and perhaps your very soul.
19?? 150m/C VHS, Beta *NO* ♫

Dragon Lee vs. the Five Brothers Mr. Lee successfully thwarts an attempted overthrow of the Ching Government with his furiously brutal fighting talents.
1981 89m/C Dragon Lee. VHS, Beta *NO* ♫

The Dragon Lives Again A martial arts adventure that is dedicated to the memory of Bruce Lee.
198? (R) 90m/C Bruce Leong, Alexander Grand. VHS, Beta *NO* ♫♫

Dragon Lord A resident of a small town fights those who would demolish the old ways of life with Kung-Fu.
19?? 90m/C Jackie Chan. VHS, Beta $59.98 *CGH, PEV* ♫

Dragon Princess When the king of karate and his dragon princess confront the blind master of the bloody blades, sparks fly.
197? 90m/C Sonny Chiba, Sue Shiomi. VHS, Beta *NO* ♫

The Dragon Returns A young man desperately kicks and chops to save the woman he loves from slave traders.
19?? 90m/C Bruce Le, Meng Fei, Lo Lieh. VHS, Beta *OCE* ♫

Dragon Rider The Dragon Rider kicks underworld druglords as he goes on a crime-fighting quest.
1985 87m/C Wong Sun. VHS, Beta $39.95 *WWV* ♫

Dragon Seed The lives of the residents of a small Chinese village are turned upside down when the Japanese invade it. Based on the Pearl S. Buck novel. Lengthy and occasionally tedious, though generally well-made with heart-felt attempts to create Oriental characters, without having Asians in the cast.
1944 145m/B Katharine Hepburn, Walter Huston, Agnes Moorehead, Akim Tamiroff, Hurd Hatfield, J. Carroll Naish, Henry Travers, Turhan Bey, Aline MacMahon; *D:* Jack Conway. VHS, Beta $19.98 *MGM, FCT* ♫♫½

The Dragon Strikes Back Chinese immigrant, a master of Kung Fu, stands up to a gang of white toughs who are brutally terrorizing and killing poor Mexican farmers.
1975 (R) 92m/C VHS, Beta $59.95 *HHT* ♫½

The Dragon That Wasn't (Or Was He?) A bear adopts a baby dragon, then has a difficult time returning the reptile to his home in the Misty Mountains once he grows to dragon-like proportions. Animated.
1983 83m/C VHS, Beta $19.95 *MCA, WTA* ♫½

Dragon: The Bruce Lee Story Entertaining and inspiring account of the tragic life of Chinese-American martial-arts legend Bruce Lee. Jason Scott Lee gives a great

performance as the talented artist, exuding Lee's joy of life and gentle spirit. Lee died mysteriously of a brain disorder at the age of 32, just as he was on the verge of becoming a major motion picture star. Even more ironic and eerie, this film's release coincided with his son Brandon's shooting death on a movie set. The martial arts sequences in "Dragon" are extraordinary, but the film offers more than just martial-arts thrills. It offers insight into the life of a unique man and his incredible ambition. Based on the book "Bruce Lee: The Man Only I Knew" by Linda Lee Caldwell.
1993 (PG-13) 121m/C Jason Scott Lee, Lauren Holly, Robert Wagner, Michael Learned, Nancy Kwan, Kay Tong Lim, Sterling Macer, Ric Young; *W/D:* Rob Cohen; *W:* Edward Khmara, John Raffo; *M:* Randy Edelman. VHS ♫♫♫

Dragon the Odds A man named Mo masters Kung Fu "maniac style" in order to repossess the gymnasium that was willed to him.
198? 90m/C VHS, Beta $39.95 *TWE* ♫

Dragon vs. Needles of Death It's a battle to the finish against the unstoppable deadly needles in this Kung-Fu adventure.
1982 86m/C Don Chien, Wong Ting. VHS, Beta *FOX* ♫

Dragonard Slaves on a West Indies island rebel against their cruel masters.
1988 (R) 93m/C Eartha Kitt, Oliver Reed, Annabel Schofield, Patrick Warburton; *D:* Gerard Kikione. VHS, Beta $79.95 *WAR* ♫½

Dragonfight Corporations rule the world and vie for supremacy through gladiator combat in this action-adventure saga set in the near future. Fights are to the death and when the current champ refuses a new challenger the corporate honchos decide to provoke him into battle by having the challenger mow down innocent bystanders. Several execs also decide the slaughter has to stop but they may be the next targets.
1992 (R) 84m/C Robert Z'Dar, Michael Pare, Paul Coufos, Charles Napier, James Hong, Alexa Hamilton, Fawna MacLaren. VHS, Beta $89.99 *WAR* ♫½

Dragonfly Squadron Korean war drama about pilots and their romantic problems. Never gets off the ground.
1954 82m/C John Hodiak, Barbara Britton, Bruce Bennett, Jess Barker; *D:* Lesley Selander. VHS $39.95 *SVS* ♫

Dragon's Claw A young man's parents are murdered, and he trains in shaolin skills in order to exact revenge.
198? 90m/C Jimmy Liu, Hwang Cheng Li; *D:* Joseph Kuo. VHS, Beta $59.95 *GEM* ♫

The Dragon's Showdown After witnessing the brutal decapitations of his parents, a young man learns Kung-Fu to avenge their deaths.
1983 90m/C Dragon Lee; *D:* Godfrey Ho. VHS, Beta $59.95 *SVS, GEM* ♫

Dragonslayer A sorcerer's apprentice suddenly finds himself the only person who can save the kingdom from a horrible, fire-breathing dragon. Extreme violence but wonderful special effects, smart writing, and a funny performance by Richardson.
1981 (PG) 110m/C Peter MacNicol, Caitlin Clarke, Ralph Richardson, John Hallam, Albert Salmi, Chloe Salaman; *D:* Matthew Robbins. VHS, Beta, LV $19.95 *PAR, COL* ♫♫♫

Dragstrip Girl An 18-year-old girl comes of age while burning rubber at the dragstrip—the world of boys, hot rods, and horsepower. A definite "B" movie that may seem dated.

1957 70m/B Fay Spain, Steven Terrell, John Ashley, Frank Gorshin; *D:* Edward L. Cahn. VHS $9.95 *COL* ♫

The Drake Case A slight courtroom drama made during the waning days of the silent era. You'll probably recognize Brit Lloyd from her later career.
1929 56m/B Robert Frazer, Doris Lloyd, Gladys Brockwell. VHS, Beta $19.95 *GPV, FCT* ♫♫

The Draughtsman's Contract A beguiling mystery begins when a wealthy woman hires an artist to make drawings of her home. Their contract is quite unusual, as is their relationship. Everything is going along at an even pace until murder is suspected, and things spiral down to darker levels. A simple story turned into a bizarre puzzle. Intense enough for any thriller fan.
1982 (R) 103m/C *GB* Anthony Higgins, Janet Suzman, Anne Louise Lambert, Hugh Fraser; *D:* Peter Greenaway. VHS $19.99 *MGM, FCT* ♫♫♫

Draw! Two has-been outlaws warm up their pistols again in this old-fashioned Western. Star power and some smart moments make it worthwhile. Made for TV.
1981 98m/C Kirk Douglas, James Coburn, Alexandra Bastedo, Graham Jarvis; *D:* Steven Hilliard Stern. VHS, Beta $69.95 *MED* ♫♫

Dreadnaught The White Tiger goes undercover in a circus troupe to escape from his pursuers.
197? 97m/C Yuen Shun-Yee; *D:* Yuen Woo Ping. VHS, Beta $59.98 *CGH, PEV* ♫

Dreadnaught Rivals A student is taught by his drunken servant how to avenge himself on the culprits who kidnapped his girlfriend. Dubbed.
198? 90m/C Sinon Lin, Kent Ko, Louisa Monk. VHS, Beta $54.95 *MOV* ♫

Dream a Little Dream A strange teen transformation drama about an old man and his wife trying mystically to regain their youth. When they collide bikes with the teenagers down the street, their minds are exchanged and the older couple with the now young minds are transported to a permanent dream-like state. Same old switcheroo made bearable by cast.
1989 (PG-13) 114m/C Corey Feldman, Corey Haim, Meredith Salenger, Jason Robards Jr., Piper Laurie, Harry Dean Stanton, Victoria Jackson, Alex Rocco, Billy McNamara; *D:* Marc Rocco. VHS, Beta, LV $89.98 *LIV, VES, HHE* ♫♫

Dream Chasers A bankrupt old codger and an 11-year-old boy stricken with cancer run away together during the Great Depression.
1984 (PG) 97m/C Harold Gould, Justin Dana. VHS, Beta $79.98 *FOX* ♫

Dream Date Lovely teenager is wooed by hip, playful suitor until trouble ensues when goofball sidekick enters the picture. Family entertainment.
1993 (PG-13) 96m/C Tempestt Bledsoe, Clifton Davis, Kadeem Hardison, Anne-Marie Johnson, Pauly Shore, Richard Moll; *D:* Anson Williams. VHS $89.95 *TRI, PMS* ♫♫½

A Dream for Christmas Earl Hamner, Jr. (best known for writing the "The Waltons") wrote this moving story of a black minister whose church in Los Angeles is scheduled to be demolished. Made for television.
1973 100m/C Hari Rhodes, Beah Richards, George Spell, Juanita Moore, Joel Fluellen, Robert DoQui, Clarence Muse; *D:* Ralph Senesky. VHS $49.95 *LIV* ♫♫♫

Dream Lover Terrifying nightmares after an assault lead McNichol to dream therapy. Treatment causes her tortured unconscious desires to take over her waking behavior, and she becomes a violent schizophrenic. Slow, heavy, and not very thrilling.
1985 (R) 105m/C Kristy McNichol, Ben Masters, Paul Shenar, Justin Deas, Joseph Culp, Gayle Hunnicutt, John McMartin; **D:** Alan J. Pakula. **VHS, Beta** $14.95 *MGM √√*

Dream Machine A childish teen comedy, based on that old urban legend of the lucky kid given a free Porshe by the vengeful wife of a wealthy philanderer. The gimmick is that the husband's body is in the trunk; the murderer is in pursuit. The tape includes an anti-drug commerical—but nothing against reckless driving, which the picture glorifies.
1991 (PG) 88m/C Corey Haim, Evan Richards, Jeremy Slate, Randall England, Tracy Fraim, Brittney Lewis, Susan Seaforth Hayes; **D:** Lyman Dayton. **VHS, LV** $89.95 *LIV, PIA √ ½*

Dream No Evil A mentally disturbed woman is forced to commit bizarre murders to protect her warped fantasy world.
1975 93m/C Edmond O'Brien, Brooke Mills, Marc Lawrence, Arthur Franz; **D:** John Hayes. **VHS, Beta** $19.95 *AHV √ ½*

A Dream of Kings Quinn is exceptional in this Petrakis story of an immigrant working to get his dying son home to Greece. Last film appearance for Stevens before committing suicide at age 36.
1969 (R) 107m/C Anthony Quinn, Irene Papas, Inger Stevens, Sam Levene, Val Avery; **D:** Daniel Mann. **VHS** $59.95 *WAR √√√*

A Dream of Passion A woman imprisoned in Greece for murdering her children becomes the object of a publicity stunt for a production of ''Medea,'' and she and the lead actress begin to exchange personalities. Artificial gobbledygook.
1978 (R) 105m/C *GR SI* Ellen Burstyn, Melina Mercouri, Andreas Voutsinas; **D:** Jules Dassin. **VHS, Beta** $9.98 *NLC √ ½*

Dream Street A weak morality tale of London's lower classes. Two brothers, both in love with the same dancing girl, woo her in their own way, while a Chinese gambler plans to take her by force. Silent with music score. Based on Thomas Burke's ''Limehouse Nights.''
1921 138m/B Tyrone Power Sr., Carol Dempster, Ralph Graves, Charles Mack; **D:** D.W. Griffith. **VHS, Beta** $49.95 *VYY √√*

The Dream Team On their way to a ball game, four patients from a mental hospital find themselves lost in New York City after their doctor is knocked out by murderers. Some fine moments from a cast of dependable comics. Watch for numerous nods to ''One Flew Over the Cuckoo's Nest,'' another Lloyd feature. Keaton fans won't want to miss this one.
1989 (PG-13) 113m/C Michael Keaton, Christopher Lloyd, Peter Boyle, Stephen Furst, Lorraine Bracco, Milo O'Shea, Dennis Boutsikaris, Philip Bosco, James Remar; **D:** Howard Zieff. **VHS, Beta, LV** $19.95 *MCA √√ ½*

Dream to Believe A slice of life of your typical high school coed—mom's dying, stepdad's from hell, sports injury hurts, and, oh yeah, championship gymnastic competitions loom. Designed to make you feel oh-so-good in that MTV kind of way. Reeves is most excellent as the girl's blushing beau.
1985 96m/C Rita Tushingham, Keanu Reeves, Olivia D'Abo; **D:** Paul Lynde. **VHS, Beta** $79.98 *HHE √√*

Dream Trap A young man is obsessed with a girl in his dreams. When he meets a girl who really exists, fantasy louses up every opportunity for the real thing.
1990 90m/C Kristy Swanson, Sasha Jensen, Jeanie Moore; **D:** Hugh Parks; **W/D:** Tom Logan. **VHS** *NO √ ½*

Dreamchild A poignant story of the autumn years of Alice Hargreaves, the model for Lewis Carroll's ''Alice in Wonderland.'' Film follows her on a visit to New York in the 1930s, with fantasy sequences including Wonderland characters created by Jim Henson's Creature Shop invoking the obsessive Reverend Dodgson (a.k.a. Carroll).
1985 (PG) 94m/C *GB* Coral Browne, Ian Holm, Peter Gallagher, Jane Asher, Nicola Cowper; **D:** Gavin Millar; **W:** Dennis Potter. **VHS, Beta** $14.95 *MGM, HBO √√√*

Dreamer The excitement of bowling is exploited for all it's worth in this ''strike or die'' extravaganza. One of a kind.
1979 (PG) 86m/C Tim Matheson, Susan Blakely, Jack Warden, Richard B. Shull; **D:** Noel Nosseck. **VHS** $59.98 *FOX √√*

The Dreaming A young doctor stumbles upon a dimension where reality and fantasy are blurred, and where the supernatural reigns supreme.
1989 87m/C *AU* **VHS, Beta** *NO √*

Dreaming Lips An orchestra conductor's wife falls in love with her husband's violinist friend. Tragedy befalls the couple. Bergner outstanding in a familiar script.
1937 70m/B *GB* Raymond Massey, Elisabeth Bergner, Romney Brent, Joyce Bland, Charles Carson, Felix Aylmer; **D:** Paul Czinner, Lee Garmes. **VHS, Beta** $29.95 *CCB, VYY √√ ½*

Dreaming Out Loud Screen debut of popular radio team Lum 'n Abner. The boys get involved in several capers to bring progress to their small Arkansas town. Rural wisecracks make for pleasant outing. First in film series for the duo.
1940 65m/B Frances Langford, Phil Harris, Clara Blandick, Robert Wilcox, Chester Lauck, Norris Goff, Frank Craven, Bob Watson, Irving Bacon; **D:** Harold Young. **VHS, Beta** $24.95 *NOS, DVT, VYY √√*

Dreams Unfocused film about the lives and loves of two successful women. Subtitled. **AKA:** Kvinn odrom; Journey into Autumn.
1955 86m/B *SW* Harriet Andersson, Gunnar Bjornstrand, Eva Dahlbeck, Ulf Palmo; **D:** Ingmar Bergman. **VHS, Beta, LV** $14.95 *VDM, TAM, SUE √√*

Dreams Come True Silly young comedy-romance about two young lovers who discover the trick of out-of-body travel, and have various forms of spiritual contact while their bodies are sleeping.
1984 (R) 95m/C Michael Sanville, Stephanie Shuford; **D:** Max Kalmanowicz. **VHS, Beta** $59.95 *MED √*

Dreams Lost, Dreams Found A young widow journeys from the U.S. to Scotland in search of her heritage. The third ''Harlequin Romance Movie,'' made for cable television.
1987 102m/C Kathleen Quinlan, Betsy Brantley, Charles Gray; **D:** Willi Patterson. **VHS** $19.95 *PAR √ ½*

Dreams of Desire Engaged couple goes to Hong Kong to enjoy that city's sensual pleasures.
1982 80m/C **VHS, Beta** *PGN √*

Dreamscape When a doctor teaches a young psychic how to enter into other people's dreams in order to end their nightmares, somebody else wants to use this psychic for evil purposes. The special effects are far more convincing than the one man-saves-the-country-with-his-psychic-powers plot.
1984 (PG-13) 99m/C Dennis Quaid, Max von Sydow, Christopher Plummer, Eddie Albert, Kate Capshaw, David Patrick Kelly, George Wendt, Jana Taylor; **D:** Joseph Ruben. **VHS, Beta, LV** $19.99 *HBO, IME √√ ½*

Dreamwood A myth-packed experimental film by James Broughton with muse-figures, angels, flower-children, and the like.
1972 45m/C **D:** James Broughton. **VHS, Beta** $29.95 *MFV √√√*

Dress Gray Very fine and exciting adaptation of the Lucian K. Truscott IV novel about a coverup at an Eastern military academy. Baldwin stars as cadet Slaight, an upper classman who finds more secrets than he can handle when a younger cadet (Cassidy), with whom he had an adversarial relationship, is murdered. The cadet was not only from a social and politically connected family but was gay. Slaight is also romancing his sister and she wants him to investigate. Everyone else advises Slaight to accept the official verdict and keep quiet—for the sake of his career if not his life. Originally a television miniseries.
1986 192m/C Alec Baldwin, Hal Holbrook, Eddie Albert, Lloyd Bridges, Susan Hess, Timothy Van Patten, Patrick Cassidy, Alexis Smith, James B. Sikking, Lane Smith; **D:** Glenn Jordan; **W:** Gore Vidal. **VHS, Beta** *WAR √√√*

Dressed for Death A tale of true love gone bad as a woman is chased and murdered in her castle by the psychopath she loves. **AKA:** Straight on Till Morning; Til Dawn Do Us Part.
1974 (R) 121m/C *GB* Rita Tushingham, Shane Briant, Tom Bell, Annie Ross, Katya Wyeth, James Bolam, Claire Kelly; **D:** Peter Collinson. **VHS, Beta** $19.95 *ACA √ ½*

Dressed to Kill Sherlock Holmes finds that a series of music boxes holds the key to plates stolen from the Bank of England. The plot's a bit thin, but Rathbone/Bruce, in their final Holmes adventure, are always a delight.
1946 72m/B Basil Rathbone, Nigel Bruce, Patricia Morison, Edmund Breon, Tom Dillon; **D:** Roy William Neill. **VHS, LV** $14.98 *NEG, MRV, REP √√ ½*

Dressed to Kill A contemporary thriller merging bombastic DePalma with a tense Hitchcockian flare. A sexually unsatisfied Dickinson ends up in bed with a man who catches her eye in a museum. After leaving his apartment, she is brutally murdered. Dickinson's son soon teams up with a prostitute to track and lure the killer into their trap. Suspenseful and fast paced. Dickinson's museum scene is wonderfully photographed and edited. DePalma was repeatedly criticized for using a stand-in during the Dickinson shower scene; he titled his next film ''Body Double'' as a rebuttal.
1980 (R) 105m/C Angie Dickinson, Michael Caine, Nancy Allen, Keith Gordon, Dennis Franz, David Margulies, Brandon Maggart; **D:** Brian DePalma. **VHS, Beta, LV** $19.98 *WAR, OM √√ ½*

The Dresser The film adaptation of Ronald Harwood's Broadway play about an aging English actor/manager, his dresser, and their theater company touring England during World War II. Marvelous showbiz tale is lovingly told, superbly acted.
1983 (PG) 119m/C Albert Finney, Tom Courtenay, Edward Fox, Michael Gough, Zena Walker, Eileen Atkins, Cathryn Harrison; **D:** Peter Yates. Academy Awards '83 Nominations: Best Actor (Courtenay), Best Actor (Finney), Best Adapted Screenplay, Best Director (Yates), Best Picture; Golden Globe Awards '84: Best Actor—

Drama (Courtenay). **VHS, Beta, LV** $12.95 *COL* �ää ½

Dressmaker French comedian Fernandel stars as a man's tailor who designs dresses in secret so as not to compete with his dressmaker wife. Lightweight but entertaining. English subtitled.
1956 95m/B *FR* Fernandel, Francoise Fabian; **D:** Jean Boyer. **VHS, Beta, LV** $29.95 *NOS, GVV, DVT* ää ½

Dressmaker Two sisters in World War II Liverpool must deal with their young niece's romantic involvement with an American soldier. Plowright and Whitelaw turn in fine performances as the two siblings with very different outlooks on life.
1989 90m/C *GB* Joan Plowright, Billie Whitelaw, Peter Postlethwaite, Jane Horrocks, Tim Ransom; **D:** Jim O'Brien. **VHS** $79.95 *CAP, TAM* ää ½

The Drifter A lumberjack makes sacrifices for the love between his brother and the lumbermill owner's daughter.
1932 56m/B William Farnum, Noah Beery Sr., Phyliss Barrington. **VHS, Beta, LV** $19.95 *NOS, WGE, VYY* ää

The Drifter It's psychos, psychos everywhere as a beautiful young woman learns to regret a one-night stand. A good, low-budget version of "Fatal Attraction." Director Brand plays the cop.
1988 (R) 90m/C Kim Delaney, Timothy Bottoms, Miles O'Keeffe, Al Shannon, Larry Brand; **D:** Larry Brand. **VHS** $79.95 *MGM* ää ½

Drifting A controversial Israeli film about a homosexual filmmaker surviving in modern-day Jerusalem. First such movie to be made in Israel. In Hebrew with English titles. *AKA:* Nagooa.
1982 103m/C *IS* Jonathan Sagalle, Ami Traub, Ben Levine, Dita Arel; **D:** Amos Guttman. **VHS, Beta** $69.95 *FCT* ää ½

Drifting Souls In order to save her father's life, a beautiful young woman marries for money instead of love.
1932 65m/C Lois Wilson, Theodore von Eltz, Shirley Grey, Raymond Hatton, Gene Gowing, Bryant Washburn; **D:** Louis King. **VHS, Beta** *GPV* ää

Drifting Weeds A remake by Ozu of his 1934 silent film about a troupe of traveling actors whose leader visits his illegitimate son and his lover after years of separation. Classic Ozu in his first color film. In Japanese with English subtitles. *AKA:* Floating Weeds; The Duckweed Story; Ukigusa.
1959 128m/B *JP* Ganjiro Nakamura, Machiko Kyo, Haruko Sugimura, Ayako Wakao; **D:** Yasujiro Ozu. **VHS, Beta, LV** $29.95 *FCT, MRV, HEG* äää ½

Driller Killer Frustrated artist goes insane and begins to kill off Manhattan residents with a carpenter's drill. Likewise, the plot is full of holes.
1974 (R) 78m/C Jimmy Laine, Carolyn Marz, Bob DeFrank; **D:** Abel Ferrara. **VHS, Beta** *NO Woof!*

Drive-In A low-budget bomb showing a night in the life of teenage yahoos at a Texas drive-in.
1976 (PG) 96m/C Lisa Lemole, Glen Morshower, Gary Cavagnaro; **D:** Rod Amateau. **VHS, Beta** $69.95 *COL Woof!*

Drive-In Massacre Two police detectives investigate a bizarre series of slasher murders at the local drive-in. Honk the horn at this one.
1974 (R) 78m/C Jake Barnes, Adam Lawrence. **VHS, Beta, LV** *NO Woof!*

Driven to Kill No-name cast assemble in low-rent suspenser portraying the ugly side of love: bent on revenge, a man is out to obliterate the thugs who made his life a horrible experience highlighted by misery and boredom.
1990 ?m/C Jake Jacobs, Chip Campbell, Michele McNeil. **VHS** $79.95 *PMH* ää

The Driver A police detective will stop at nothing to catch "The Driver," a man who has the reputation of driving the fastest getaway car around. Chase scenes win out over plot.
1978 131m/C Ryan O'Neal, Bruce Dern, Isabelle Adjani, Ronee Blakley, Matt Clark; **D:** Walter Hill. **VHS, Beta** $59.98 *FOX* ä ½

Driver's Seat Extremely bizarre film with a cult following that was adapted from the novel by Muriel Spark. Liz stars as a deranged woman trying to keep a rendezvous with her strange lover in Rome. In the meantime she wears tacky clothes and delivers stupid lines. *AKA:* Psychotic; Identikit.
1973 (R) 101m/C *IT* Elizabeth Taylor, Ian Bannen, Mona Washbourne, Andy Warhol; **D:** Giuseppe Patroni Griffi. **VHS, Beta** $24.98 *SUE, SIM Woof!*

Driving Force In an effort to capitalize on the popularity of the "Road Warrior" movies, features a lone trucker battling a gang of roadhogs in another post-holocaust desert. Ultimately, runs off the road.
1988 (R) 90m/C Sam Jones, Catherine Bach, Don Swayze; **D:** A.J. Prowse. **VHS, Beta, LV** $29.95 *ACA* ä

Driving Me Crazy When an East German car inventor comes to America, it's laughs in the fast lane in this all-star comedy.
1991 (PG-13) 88m/C Billy Dee Williams, Thomas Gottschalk, Dom DeLuise, Milton Berle, Steve Kanaly, Michelle Johnson, Richard Moll, Morton Downey Jr., George Kennedy; **D:** Jon Turteltaub. **VHS, LV** $89.95 *SVS* ä ½

Driving Miss Daisy Tender and sincere portrayal of a 25-year friendship between an aging Jewish woman and the black chauffeur forced upon her by her son. Humorous and thought-provoking, skillfully acted and directed, it subtly explores the effects of prejudice in the South. The development of Aykroyd as a top-notch character actor is further evidenced here. Part of the fun is watching the changes in fashion and auto design. Adapted from the play by Alfred Uhry.
1989 (PG) 99m/C Jessica Tandy, Morgan Freeman, Dan Aykroyd, Esther Rolle, Patti LuPone; **D:** Bruce Beresford. Academy Awards '89: Best Actress (Tandy), Best Adapted Screenplay, Best Makeup, Best Picture; Nominations: Best Actor (Freeman), Best Costume Design, Best Film Editing, Best Supporting Actor (Aykroyd); British Academy Awards '90: Best Actress (Tandy); Golden Globe Awards '90: Best Actor—Musical/Comedy (Freeman), Best Actress—Musical/Comedy (Tandy), Best Film—Musical/Comedy; National Board of Review Awards '89: 10 Best Films of the Year, Best Actor (Freeman). **VHS, Beta, LV, 8mm** $19.98 *WAR, FCT, BTV* äää ½

Drop Dead Fred As a little girl, Lizzie Cronin had a manic, imaginary friend named Fred, who protected her from her domineering mother. When her husband dumps her twenty years later, Fred returns to "help" as only he can. Although the cast is fine, incompetent writing and direction make this a truly dismal affair. Plus, gutter humor and mean-spirited pranks throw the whole "heart-warming" premise out the window. Filmed in Minneapolis.

1991 (PG-13) 103m/C Phoebe Cates, Rik Mayall, Tim Matheson, Marsha Mason, Carrie Fisher, Daniel Gerroll, Ron Eldard; **D:** Ate De Jong. **VHS, LV** $92.95 *LIV, PIA Woof!*

Drop-Out Mother A woman gives up her executive position to become a housewife and full-time mom; expected domestic turmoil follows. Standard made for television fare and sort of a sequel to "Drop-Out Father," shown in 1982.
1988 100m/C Valerie Harper, Wayne Rogers, Carol Kane, Kim Hunter, Danny Gerard; **D:** Charles S. Dubin. **VHS** $39.95 *FRH* ää

The Dropkick Erstwhile D.W. Griffith leading man Barthelmess stars in this pigskin whodunnit: a coach's suicide looks like murder, and the prime suspect is the team's most valuable player. Cast includes ten bona fide university football players and Hedda "nobody's interested in sweetness and light" Hopper, while The Duke makes cameo. Webb later went on to direct a musical with Eddie Cantor and Rudy Vallee ("Glorifying the American Girl"). Silent. Based on the story "Glitter" by Katherine Brush.
1927 62m/B Richard Barthelmess, Barbara Kent, Dorothy Revier, Eugene Strong, Alberta Vaughn, Brooks Benedict, Hedda Hopper; *Cameos:* John Wayne; **D:** Millard Webb; **W:** Winifred Dunn. **VHS, Beta** $24.95 *GPV, FCT* äää

Drowning by Numbers Three generations of women, each named Cissie Colpitts, solve their marital problems by drowning their husbands and making deals with a bizarre coroner. Further strange visions from director Greenaway, complemented by stunning cinematography courtesy of Sacha Vierny. A treat for those who appreciate Greenaway's uniquely curious cinematic statements.
1987 (R) 121m/C *GB* Bernard Hill, Joan Plowright, Juliet Stevenson, Joely Richardson; **D:** Peter Greenaway. **VHS, LV** $19.98 *LIV* äää ½

The Drowning Pool Newman returns as detective Lew Harper (of "Harper" by Ross MacDonald) to solve a blackmail case. Uneventful script and stodgy direction, but excellent character work from all the cast members keep this watchable. Title is taken from a trap set for Newman, from which he must escape using most of his female companion's clothing. Adapted from a character created by Ross MacDonald.
1975 (PG) 109m/C Paul Newman, Joanne Woodward, Anthony (Tony) Franciosa, Murray Hamilton, Melanie Griffith, Richard Jaeckel; **D:** Stuart Rosenberg. **VHS, Beta** $19.98 *WAR* ää

Drug Wars 2: The Cocaine Cartel Muddled drama featuring crazy unpredictable DEA agents executing the downfall of Colombia's Medellin drug kingpins. Average sequel to the award-winning miniseries "Drug Wars."
1992 200m/C Alex McArthur, Dennis Farina, Julie Carmen, John Glover, Karen Young, Michele Placido, Gustav Vintas, Geno Silva; **D:** Paul Krasny. **VHS** *MCA* ää

Drugstore Cowboy A gritty, uncompromising depiction of a pack of early 1970s drugstore-robbing junkies as they travel around looking to score. Brushes with the law and tragedy encourage them to examine other life-styles, but the trap seems impossible to leave. A perfectly crafted piece that reflects the "me generation" era, though it tends to glamorize addiction. Dillon's best work to date. Based on a novel by prison inmate James Fogle.
1989 (R) 100m/C Matt Dillon, Kelly Lynch, James Remar, James Le Gros, Heather Graham, William S. Burroughs, Beah Richards, Grace Zabriskie, Max Perlich; **D:** Gus Van Sant. **VHS, Beta, LV** $19.95 *LIV, FCT* äää ½

D

Drum This steamy sequel to "Mandingo" deals with the sordid interracial sexual shenanigans at a Southern plantation. Bad taste at its best.
1976 (R) 101m/C Ken Norton, Warren Oates, Pam Grier, Yaphet Kotto, Fiona Lewis, Isela Vega, Cheryl "Rainbeaux" Smith; *D:* Steve Carver. **VHS, Beta $69.98** *LIV, VES* Woof!

Drum Beat An unarmed Indian fighter sets out to negotiate a peace treaty with a renegade Indian leader. Bronson is especially believable as chief. Based on historical incident.
1954 111m/C Alan Ladd, Charles Bronson, Marisa Pavan, Robert Keith, Rodolfa Acosta, Warner Anderson, Elisha Cook Jr., Anthony Caruso; *D:* Delmer Daves. **VHS, Beta $54.95** *UHV* ♫♫

Drum Taps Maynard saves the day for a young girl who is being pushed off her land by a group of speculators.
1933 55m/B Ken Maynard, Dorothy Dix, Frank "Junior" Coghlan, Kermit Maynard; *D:* J.P. McGowan. **VHS, Beta $19.95** *NOS, VDM, VYY* ♫♫

Drums A native prince helps to save the British army in India from being annihilated by a tyrant. Rich melodrama with interesting characterizations and locale. *AKA:* The Drum.
1938 96m/B *GB* Sabu, Raymond Massey, Valerie Hobson, Roger Livesey, David Tree; *D:* Zoltan Korda. **VHS, Beta, LV $14.95** *SUE* ♫♫ ½

Drums Along the Mohawk Grand, action-filled saga about pre-Revolutionary America, detailing the trials of a colonial newlywed couple as their village in Mohawk Valley is besieged by Indians. Based on the Walter Edmonds novel, and vintage Ford.
1939 104m/C Henry Fonda, Claudette Colbert, Edna May Oliver, Eddie Collins, John Carradine, Dorris Bowdon, Arthur Shields, Ward Bond, Jessie Ralph, Robert Lowery; *D:* John Ford. **VHS, Beta, LV $19.98** *FOX* ♫♫♫ ½

Drums in the Deep South A rivalry turns ugly as two former West Point roommates wind up on opposite sides when the Civil War breaks out. Historical drama hampered by familiar premise.
1951 87m/C James Craig, Guy Madison, Craig Stevens, Barbara Payton, Barton MacLane; *D:* William Cameron Menzies. **VHS, Beta, 3/4U, Special order formats $19.95** *NOS, MRV, VGR* ♫♫

Drums of Fu Manchu Fu Manchu searches for the scepter of Genghis Khan, an artifact that would give him domination over the East. Brandon smoothly evil as the Devil Doctor. Originally a serial in 15 chapters.
1940 150m/B Henry Brandon, Robert Kellard, George Cleveland, Dwight Frye, Gloria Franklin, Tom Chatterton; *D:* William Witney, John English. **VHS, Beta $69.95** *VCN, MLB* ♫♫♫

Drums of Jeopardy A father wanders through czarist Russia and the U.S. to seek revenge on his daughter's killer. Cheap copy of "Dr. Fu Manchu." *AKA:* Mark of Terror.
1931 65m/B Warner Oland, June Collyer, Lloyd Hughes, George Fawcett, Mischa Auer; *D:* George B. Seitz. **VHS $24.95** *NOS, SNC, DVT* ♫

Drums O'Voodoo A voodoo princess fights to eliminate the town bad guy in this all-black feature that is greatly hampered by shoddy production values. *AKA:* She Devil.
1934 70m/B Laura Bowman, J. Augustus Smith, Edna Barr; *D:* Arthur Hoerl. **VHS, Beta $16.95** *SNC* Woof!

Drunken Angel Alcoholic doctor gets mixed up with local gangster. Kurosawa's first major film aided by strong performances. With English subtitles.
1948 108m/B *JP* Toshiro Mifune, Takashi Shimura, Choko Iida; *D:* Akira Kurosawa. **VHS, Beta $39.95** *DVT, MRV, TAM* ♫♫♫

A Dry White Season A white Afrikaner living resignedly with apartheid confronts the system when his black gardener, an old friend, is persecuted and murdered. A well-meaning expose that, like many others, focuses on white people.
1989 (R) 105m/C Donald Sutherland, Marlon Brando, Susan Sarandon, Zakes Mokae, Janet Suzman, Juergen Prochnow, Winston Ntshona; *D:* Euzhan Palcy. **VHS, Beta, LV $19.98** *FOX, FCT* ♫♫♫

Drying Up the Streets Tepid message tale of a police drug squad out to terminate the pattern that has young women turning to a life of prostitution and drugs.
1976 90m/C *CA* Len Cariou, Don Francks, Sarah Torgov, Calvin Butler; *D:* Robin Spry. **VHS, Beta $69.98** *LIV, VES* ♫

Dual Alibi Identical twin trapeze artists murder a colleague for a winning lottery ticket. Lom plays the brothers in a dual role.
1947 87m/B *GB* Herbert Lom, Terence de Marney, Phyllis Dixey, Ronald Frankau, Abraham Sofaer, Harold Berens, Sebastian Cabot; *D:* Alfred Travers. **VHS, Beta $16.95** *NOS, SNC* ♫♫

Dual Flying Kicks Chinese provincial mayor allies himself to a group of bandits amid much high kicking.
1982 95m/C Chen Hsing, Tan Tao Liang. **VHS, Beta** *WVE* ♫

Dubarry Early sound version of the romantic experiences of Madame Dubarry, the alluring French heroine of David Belasco's "DuBarry." Talmadge's last film.
1930 81m/B Norma Talmadge, Conrad Nagel, William Farnum, Hobart Bosworth, Alison Skipworth; *D:* Sam Taylor. **VHS, Beta $24.95** *NOS, DVT, HEG* ♫♫ ½

DuBarry Was a Lady Skelton is a washroom attendant who daydreams that he is King Louis XV of France. Dorsey's band gets to dress in period wigs and costumes. ♫♫DuBarry Was a Lady; Do I Love You, Do I?; Friendship; Well, Did You Evah; Taliostro's Dance; Katie Went to Haiti; Madame, I Love Your Crepes Suzettes; Thinking of You; A Cigarette, Sweet Music and You; Sleepy Lagoon; You Are My Sunshine; I'm Getting Sentimental Over You; Salome; Ladies of the Bath; Get Me a Taxi; On to Combat; No Matter How You Slice It, It's Still Salome.
1943 112m/C Lucille Ball, Gene Kelly, Red Skelton, Virginia O'Brien, Zero Mostel, Dick Haymes, Jo Stafford & the Pied Pipers, Tommy Dorsey & His Orchestra, Rags Ragland, Donald Meek, George Givot, Louise Beavers; *D:* Roy Del Ruth. **VHS, Beta $19.98** *MGM, CCB* ♫♫ ½

Dubeat-E-O A filmmaker races against time to finish making a documentary about the Los Angeles underground hardcore punk scene, and becomes immersed in the subculture. Somewhat of a haphazard exercise in filmmaking that is best appreciated by rock fans.
1984 84m/C Ray Sharkey, Joan Jett, Derf Scratch, Len Lesser, Nora Gaye; *D:* Alan Sacks. **VHS, Beta $59.95** *MVD, MED* ♫ ½

The Duchess and the Dirtwater Fox Period western strung together with many failed attempts at humor, all about a music-hall hooker who meets a bumbling card shark on the make.
1976 (PG) 105m/C George Segal, Goldie Hawn, Conrad Janis, Thayer David; *D:* Melvin Frank. **VHS, Beta, LV $19.98** *FOX* ♫ ½

Duchess of Idaho Williams tries to help her roommate patch up a romance gone bad, but ends up falling in love herself. MGM guest stars liven up an otherwise routine production. ♫Baby Come Out of the Clouds; You Can't Do Wrong Doin' Right; Let's Choo Choo to Idaho; Of All Things; Or Was It Spring; Warm Hands, Cold Heart; Singlefoot Serenade; You Won't Forget Me.
1950 98m/C Esther Williams, Van Johnson, John Lund, Paula Raymond, Amanda Blake, Eleanor Powell, Lena Horne; *D:* Robert Z. Leonard. **VHS $19.98** *MGM* ♫♫

Duck Soup The Marx Brothers satiric masterpiece (which failed at the box office). Groucho becomes the dictator of Freedonia, and hires Chico and Harpo as spies. Jampacked with the classic anarchic and irreverent Marx shtick; watch for the mirror scene. Zeppo plays a love-sick tenor, in this, his last film with the brothers. Screenplay by Bert Kalmar and Holly Ruby.
1933 70m/B Groucho Marx, Chico Marx, Harpo Marx, Zeppo Marx, Louis Calhern, Margaret Dumont, Edgar Kennedy; *D:* Leo McCarey. **VHS, Beta, LV $19.95** *MCA, FCT* ♫♫♫♫

DuckTales the Movie: Treasure of the Lost Lamp Uncle Scrooge et al embark on a lost-ark quest—sans Harrison Ford—for misplaced treasure (i.e., a lamp that can make the sky rain ice cream). Based on the daily Disney cartoon of the same name, it's more like an extended-version Saturday morning sugar smacks'n'milk 'toon. See it with someone young.
1990 (G) 74m/C **VHS, Beta, LV $22.99** *DIS, WTA* ♫♫

Dude Bandit An unscrupulous moneylender tries to gain control of a ranch but Gibson comes to the rescue. Gibson actually plays three roles: the rancher's best friend, an aw-shucks cowpoke disguise in order to find out what's going on, and the title character used to bedevil the crooks.
1932 68m/B Hoot Gibson, Gloria Shea. **VHS, Beta $29.95** *VCN, UHV, VYY* ♫♫

Dude Ranger Well-acted Zane Grey story about an easterner who gets caught up in a range war and cattle rustling when he takes possession of some property out west.
1934 58m/B Smiley Burnette, George O'Brien, Irene Hervey; *D:* Eddie Cline. **VHS, Beta $19.95** *VDM* ♫♫ ½

Dudes Three city kids head for the desert and run afoul of some rednecks. Tired grade-6 revenge story.
1987 (R) 90m/C Jon Cryer, Catherine Mary Stewart, Daniel Roebuck, Flea, Lee Ving, Calvin Bartlett, Pete Willcox, Glenn Withrow; *D:* Penelope Spheeris. **VHS, Beta, LV $9.99** *CCB, IVE* ♫

Duel Spielberg's first notable film, a made-for-television exercise in paranoia penned by Robert Bloch. A docile traveling salesman is repeatedly attacked and threatened by a huge, malevolent tractor-trailer on an open desert highway. Released theatrically in Europe.
1971 (PG) 90m/C Dennis Weaver, Lucille Benson, Eddie Firestone, Cary Loftin; *D:* Steven Spielberg. **VHS, Beta $39.95** *MCA* ♫♫♫

Duel at Diablo An exceptionally violent film that deals with racism in the Old West. Good casting; western fans will enjoy the action.
1966 103m/C James Garner, Sidney Poitier, Bibi Andersson, Dennis Weaver, Bill Travers; *D:* Ralph Nelson. **VHS $19.98** *MGM* ♫♫♫

Duel in the Eclipse A strategically timed eclipse permits a gringo to avenge his brother's murder.

19?? 100m/C Fernando Sancho. **VHS, Beta** $39.95 *TWE ⅃*

Duel in the Sun A lavish, lusty David O. Selznick production of a minor western novel about a vivacious half-breed Indian girl, living on a powerful dynastic ranch, who incites two brothers to conflict. Selznick's last effort at outdoing his epic success with "Gone With the Wind."
1946 130m/C Gregory Peck, Jennifer Jones, Joseph Cotten, Lionel Barrymore, Lillian Gish, Butterfly McQueen, Harry Carey Sr., Walter Huston, Charles Bickford, Herbert Marshall; *D:* King Vidor. **VHS, Beta** $19.98 *FOX ⅃⅃⅃*

Duel of Champions It's ancient Rome, and the prodigal gladiator has come home. Now the family must have a duel to decide who will rule. *AKA:* Orazi e Curiazi.
1961 90m/C *IT SP* Alan Ladd, Francesca Bett; *D:* Ferdinando Baldi. **VHS, Beta** *NO ⅃*

Duel of Fists When the owner of a boxing institute dies, he instructs his son in his will to go searching for his long-lost brother in Thailand. All he can go on is an old photograph and the knowledge that his brother is a Thai boxer.
1989 111m/C David Chiang, Chen Hsing, Ti Lung, Tang Ti. **VHS, Beta** $69.95 *NO ⅃*

Duel of Hearts Beautiful Caroline falls in love with wealthy Lord Vane Brecon, who unfortunately is accused of murder. When Caroline tries to help him clear his name she discovers he's hiding a number of secrets. Based on the romance novel "Duel of Love" by Barbara Cartland. Nothing too inspiring here, although regency romance fans will appreciate the attention to detail. Originally made for cable television.
1992 (PG-13) 95m/C *GB* Alison Doody, Michael York, Geraldine Chaplin, Benedict Taylor, Billie Whitelaw, Virginia McKenna, Richard Johnson, Jeremy Kemp, Beryl Reid, Suzanna Hamilton, Jolyon Baker, Julie Kate; *D:* John Hough. **VHS, Beta, LV** $89.98 *TTC ⅃⅃*

Duel of the Brave Ones A man undertakes a dangerous trek through Japan to search for jewel thieves.
1980 87m/C Chang Wu Lang, Tony Wai Shing. **VHS, Beta** $39.95 *TWE ⅃*

Duel of the Iron Fist Master of the martial arts must do battle with a brutal gang to save his own group from extinction.
1972 (R) 98m/C David Chiang, Ti Lung, Wang Ping, Yu Hui. **VHS, Beta** $59.95 *HHT, UHV ⅃*

Duel of the Masters Two ninja masters fight to the finish and then start again.
1976 95m/C **VHS, Beta** $29.99 *BFV ⅃ 1/2*

Duel of the Seven Tigers Nine of the world's greatest Kung Fu and Karate exponents team up in this martial arts spectacular.
1980 80m/C Cliff Lok, Ka Sa Fa, Chio Chi Ling, Lam Men Wei, Wang Pan Pan, Charlie Chan. **VHS, Beta** $39.95 *TWE ⅃*

The Duellists A beautifully photographed picture about the long-running feud between two French officers during the Napoleonic wars. Based on "The Duel" by Joseph Conrad.
1978 (PG) 101m/C *GB* Keith Carradine, Harvey Keitel, Albert Finney, Edward Fox, Tom Conti, Christina Raines, Diana Quick; *D:* Ridley Scott. **VHS, Beta, LV** $49.95 *PAR ⅃⅃⅃*

Duelo en el Dorado A white man and Indian fight over the custody of an orphan.
19?? 90m/C *SP* Luis Aguilar, Lola Beltran, Emilio Fernandez, German Valdes. **VHS, Beta** $78.95 *MAD ⅃ 1/2*

Duet for One A famous concert violinist learns she is suffering from multiple sclerosis and is slowly losing her ability to play. Convinced that her life is meaningless without music, she self-destructively drifts into bitter isolation. From the play by Tom Kempinski.
1986 (R) 108m/C Julie Andrews, Max von Sydow, Alan Bates, Liam Neeson; *D:* Andrei Konchalovsky. **VHS, Beta** $14.95 *MGM ⅃⅃*

The Duke is the Tops In Horne's earliest existing film appearance, she's off to attempt the "big-time," while her boyfriend joins a traveling medicine show. ♫I Know You Remember.
1938 80m/C Ralph Cooper, Lena Horne, The Basin Street Boys, Rubber Neck Boys, Marie Bryant. **VHS, Beta** $39.95 *NOS, MRV, VCN ⅃⅃ 1/2*

Duke of the Derby A scheming racehorse handicapper bets over his head and ruins his higher-than-means lifestyle. In French with English subtitles. *AKA:* Le Gentleman D'epsom.
1962 83m/C *FR* Jean Gabin; *D:* Gilles Grangier. **VHS, Beta** $19.95 *FCT, DVT, HEG ⅃⅃*

Duke: The Films of John Wayne A gift-pack collection of three of Wayne's finest: "Flying Leathernecks," "Fort Apache," and "She Wore a Yellow Ribbon."
1989 332m/C John Wayne. **VHS** $59.95 *TTC ⅃⅃*

Dumb Waiter A mini-play by Harold Pinter about two hitmen awaiting instructions for a job in an empty boardinghouse, and getting comically mixed messages. Made for television.
1987 60m/C John Travolta, Tom Conti; *D:* Robert Altman; *W:* Harold Pinter. **VHS, Beta** $79.95 *PSM ⅃⅃*

Dumbo Animated Disney classic about a baby elephant growing up in the circus who is ridiculed for his large ears, until he discovers he can fly. The little elephant who could fly then becomes a circus star. Expressively and imaginatively animated, highlighted by the hallucinatory dancing pink elephants sequence. Endearing songs by Frank Churchill, Oliver Wallace, and Ned Washington, including "Baby Mine," "Pink Elephants on Parade," and "I See an Elephant Fly."
1941 63m/C *D:* Ben Sharpsteen; *V:* Sterling Holloway, Edward Brophy, Verna Felton, Herman Bing, Cliff Edwards. Academy Awards '41: Best Score; Nominations: Best Song ("Baby Mine"); National Board of Review Awards '41: 10 Best Films of the Year. **VHS, Beta, LV** $24.99 *DIS, KUI, APD ⅃⅃⅃⅃*

The Dummy Talks When a ventriloquist is murdered, a midget goes undercover as a dummy to find the killer. Watch closely and you might see his lips move.
1943 85m/B *GB* Jack Warner, Claude Hulbert, Beryl Orde, Derna-Hazell, Ivy Benson, Manning Whiley; *D:* Oswald Mitchell. **VHS, Beta** $16.95 *SNC ⅃⅃*

Dune Lynch sci-fi opus based on the Frank Herbert novel boasting great set design, muddled scripting, and a good cast. The story: controlling the spice drug of Arrakis permits control of the universe in the year 10991. Paul, the heir of the Atreides family, leads the Freemen in a revolt against the evil Harkhonens who have violently seized control of Arrakis, also known as Dune, the desert planet. That's as clear as it ever gets. Music by Brian Eno and Toto.
1984 (PG-13) 137m/C Kyle MacLachlan, Francesca Annis, Jose Ferrer, Sting, Max von Sydow, Juergen Prochnow, Linda Hunt, Freddie Jones, Dean Stockwell, Virginia Madsen, Brad Dourif, Kenneth McMillan, Silvana Mangano, Jack Nance, Sian Phillips, Paul Smith, Richard Jordan,

Everett McGill, Sean Young; *D:* David Lynch. **VHS, Beta, LV** $24.95 *MCA, FCT ⅃⅃*

Dune Warriors Earth is a parched planet in the year 2040. Renegade bands cruise the desert, making short shrift of civilized people who band together in remote villages. When peaceful farmer Carradine's family falls prey to the pillagers, surely he and the most evil warlord of all must clash. Good action and stunts, if the dummy plot doesn't get you first.
1991 (R) 77m/C David Carradine, Richard Hill, Luke Askew, Jillian McWhirter, Blake Boyd; *D:* Cirio H. Santiago. **VHS, LV** $89.95 *COL, PIA ⅃ 1/2*

The Dunera Boys Hoskins shines in this story about Viennese Jews who, at the onset of World War II, escape to England where they are suspected as German spies. Subsequently, the British shipped them all to an Australian prison camp, where they re-created in peace their Viennese lifestyle.
1985 (R) 150m/C *AU* Bob Hoskins, Joe Spano, Warren Mitchell, Joseph Furst, Moshe Kedem, Dita Cobb, John Meillon, Mary-Anne Fahey, Simon Chilvers, Steven Vidler; *D:* Sam Lewin. **VHS, Beta, LV** $9.99 *STE, PSM ⅃⅃⅃*

Dungeon of Harrow Unbelievably cheap tale of shipwrecked comrades who encounter a maniacal family on an otherwise deserted island. Not your stranded-on-a-desert-island fantasy come true. Filmed in San Antonio; a harrowing bore.
1964 74m/B Russ Harvey, Helen Hogan, Bill McNulty, Pat Boyette; *D:* Pat Boyette. **VHS** $19.98 *SNC ⅃*

Dungeonmaster A warlord forces a computer wiz to participate in a bizarre "Dungeons and Dragons" styled game in order to save a girl held captive. Save yourself the trouble.
1985 (PG-13) 80m/C Jeffrey Byron, Richard Moll, Leslie Wing, Danny Dick, John Carl Buechler, Charles Band, David Allen, Steven Ford, Peter Manoogian, Ted Nicolaou; *D:* Charles Band, Rosemarie Turko. **VHS, Beta, LV** $29.98 *LIV ⅃ 1/2*

The Dunwich Horror Young warlock acquires a banned book of evil spells, starts trouble on the astral plane. Stockwell hammy. Loosely based on H. P. Lovecraft story.
1970 90m/C Sandra Dee, Dean Stockwell, Lloyd Bochner, Ed Begley Sr., Sam Jaffe, Joanna Moore; *D:* Daniel Haller. **VHS, Beta** $9.98 *SUE ⅃⅃*

Duplicates Harrison and Greist are a married couple whose young son has disappeared. When the boy is found he has no memory of his former life or parents. The couple discover he's the victim of secret experiments which transfer human memories into computer banks. Will they become the next targets?
1992 (PG-13) 92m/C Gregory Harrison, Kim Greist, Cicely Tyson, Lane Smith, William Lucking, Kevin McCarthy; *D:* Sandor Stern. **VHS, Beta** *PAR, PMS ⅃⅃*

Durango Valley Raiders Sheriff is the leader of the outlaws, and a young cowboy finds out.
1938 55m/B Bob Steele; *D:* Sam Newfield. **VHS, Beta** $19.95 *VCN, DVT ⅃ 1/2*

Dust A white woman in South Africa murders her father when he shows affection for a young black servant. Controversial and intense.
1985 87m/C *FR BE* Jane Birkin, Trevor Howard, John Matshikiza, Nadine Uwampa; *W/D:* Marion Hansel. **VHS, Beta** *NO ⅃⅃⅃*

Dust to Dust A short mystery made for British television about an aging gentleman who answers a request for correspondence and discovers ulterior, and evil, motives.
1985 60m/C *GB* Patricia Hodge, Michael Jayston, Judy Campbell. **VHS, Beta $59.95** *PSM* 𝄞𝄞𝄞

Dusty Touching story of a wild dingo dog raised by an Australian rancher amd trained to herd sheep. Filmed in the Australian bush and based on the children's book by Frank Dalby Davison.
1985 89m/C *AU* Bill Kerr, Noel Trevarthen, Carol Burns, Nicholas Holland, John Stanton; *D:* John Richardson. **VHS, Beta $19.95** *MED, FCT* 𝄞𝄞

Dutch Working class boob attempts to pick up his girlfriend's son from boarding school. Their trip together gives them an unexpected chance to connect, if they don't kill each other first. Silly premise from the Hughes factory has little innovation and uses typecasting instead of acting.
1991 (PG-13) 107m/C Ed O'Neill, Ethan Randall, JoBeth Williams; *D:* Peter Faiman. **VHS $19.98** *FXV, IME* 𝄞½

Dutch Girls Muddled mayhem as a horny high school field hockey team travels through Holland, cavorts about, and discovers the meaning of life.
1987 83m/C *GB* Bill Paterson, Colin Firth, Timothy Spall; *D:* Giles Foster. **VHS, Beta $29.95** *ACA Woof!*

Dutch Treat Two nerds con a sultry, all-girl rock band into thinking they're powerful record company execs. Nobody's buying.
1986 (R) 95m/C Lorin Dreyfuss, David Landsberg; *D:* Boaz Davidson. **VHS, Beta $79.95** *MGM* 𝄞

D.W. Griffith Triple Feature A collection of three short D.W. Griffith films including ''The Battle of Elderbush Gulch,'' ''Iola's Promise,'' and ''The Goddess of Sagebrush Gulch.''
1913 50m/B Mae Marsh, Lillian Gish, Mary Pickford, Blanche Sweet, Charles West; *D:* D.W. Griffith. **VHS, Beta $19.95** *KRT, FCT* 𝄞𝄞½

The Dybbuk A man's bride is possessed by a restless spirit. Set in the Polish-Jewish community before WWI and based on the play by Sholom Anski. Considered a classic for its portrayal of Jewish religious and cultural mores. In Yiddish with English subtitles.
1937 123m/B *PL* Abraham Morewski, Isaac Samberg, Moshe Lipman, Lili Liliana, Dina Halpern; *D:* Michal Waszynski. **VHS, Beta $39.95** *IHF, FCT, NCJ* 𝄞𝄞𝄞½

Dying Room Only Travelling through the desert, a woman's husband suddenly disappears after they stop at a secluded roadside diner. Richard Matheson script is a spooker. Made for television.
1973 74m/C Cloris Leachman, Ross Martin, Ned Beatty, Louise Latham, Dana Elcar, Dabney Coleman; *D:* Philip Leacock. **VHS $49.95** *LIV* 𝄞𝄞½

The Dying Truth A wrongfully accused prisoner lies dying in his cell. Trouble is, he can't die in peace until he solves the murder they say he committed. Interesting mix of the supernatural and mystery, although perhaps not one of Carradine's more memorable roles.
1991 80m/C David Carradine, Stephanie Beacham, Stephen Greif, Stephan Chase, Larry Carby, Lesley Dunlop; *D:* John Hough. **VHS** *NO* 𝄞𝄞

Dying Young Muted romance with a wealthy leukemia victim hiring a spirited, unschooled beauty as his nurse. They fall in love, but the film is either too timid or too unimaginative to mine emotions denoted by the title. Nobody dies, in fact; a grim ending (faithful to the Marti Leimbach novel on which this was based) got scrapped after testing poorly with audiences. The actors try their best, photography is lovely, and Kenny G's mellow music fills the soundtrack. Scott is the late Dewhurst's son.
1991 (R) 111m/C Julia Roberts, Campbell Scott, Vincent D'Onofrio, Colleen Dewhurst, Ellen Burstyn, David Selby; *D:* Joel Schumacher; *W:* Richard Friedenberg. **VHS $19.98** *FXV* 𝄞𝄞

Dynamite Romance explodes as two young demolitions experts vie for the same girl. Stand back.
1949 68m/B William Gargan, Virginia Welles, Richard Crane, Irving Bacon; *D:* William H. Pine. **VHS, Beta $24.95** *NOS, DVT, HEG* 𝄞

Dynamite and Gold Nelson and crew embark on a search for lost gold, battling hostile Indians, the Mexican army and assorted bandits along the way. A mediocre television movie. *AKA:* Where the Hell's the Gold?.
1988 (PG) 91m/C Willie Nelson, Delta Burke, Jack Elam, Alfonso Arau, Gregory Sierra, Michael Wren, Gerald McRaney; *W/D:* Burt Kennedy. **VHS, LV $19.95** *ACA* 𝄞𝄞

Dynamite Chicken Melange of skits, songs, and hippie satire is dated. Includes performances by Joan Baez, Lenny Bruce, B.B. King, and others.
1970 (R) 75m/C Joan Baez, Richard Pryor, Lenny Bruce, Jimi Hendrix, Sha-Na-Na; *D:* Ernie Pintoff. **VHS, Beta** *NO* 𝄞𝄞

Dynamite Dan A man knocks out the heavyweight boxing champion after he flirts with his girlfriend and decides to give up his day job to become a championship boxer. He is a success, and in the end he has to face the champion again. Will he win?
1924 62m/B Kenneth McDonald, Frank Rice, Boris Karloff, Eddie Harris, Diana Alden, Harry Woods, Jack Richardson; *D:* Bruce Mitchell. **VHS, Beta $16.95** *GPV, LSV* 𝄞½

Dynamite Pass Offbeat oater about disgruntled ranchers attempting to stop the construction of a new road.
1950 61m/B Tim Holt, Richard Martin, Regis Toomey, Lynn (Mary Hart) Roberts, Denver Pyle; *D:* Lew Landers. **VHS, Beta** *MED* 𝄞𝄞

Dynamite Ranch Ranchers fight tooth and nail to keep their rights and property in this Maynard oater.
1932 60m/B Ken Maynard. **VHS, Beta $19.95** *NOS, UHV, DVT* 𝄞

Dynamo A glamorous advertising executive pursues a kung fu expert to sign a contract with her agency for a kick boxing contest.
1980 (R) 81m/C **VHS, Beta $9.98** *SUE* 𝄞

Dynasty A leader of the Ming Dynasty is killed by evil Imperial Court eunuch and his son the monk sets out to avenge him. In 3-D. Run-of-the-mill kung-fu stunts.
1977 94m/C Bobby Ming, Lin Tashing, Pai Ying, Tang Wei, Jin Gang; *D:* Zhang Meijun. **VHS, Beta $29.95** *BFV* 𝄞𝄞

Dynasty Pulitzer Prize-winning author James Michener creates the usual sweeping saga of a family torn by jealousy, deception, and rivalry in love and business as husband, wife, and brother-in-law seek their fortune in the Ohio frontier of the 1820s.
1982 90m/C Sarah Miles, Harris Yulin, Stacy Keach. **VHS, Beta** *TLF, LME* 𝄞𝄞

Dynasty of Fear Matters get rather sticky at a British boys' school when the headmaster's wife seduces her husband's assistant. Together they conspire to murder her husband and share his fortune. *AKA:* Fear in the Night; Honeymoon of Fear.
1972 (PG) 93m/C *GB* Peter Cushing, Joan Collins, Ralph Bates, Judy Geeson, James Cossins; *D:* Jimmy Sangster. **VHS, Beta $19.95** *ACA, HBO* 𝄞½

E. Nick: A Legend in His Own Mind Satire of videos and magazines designed for adults.
1984 75m/C Don Calfa, Cleavon Little, Andra Akers, Pat McCormick; *D:* Robert Hegyes. **VHS, Beta $39.95** *LIV* 𝄞½

Each Dawn I Die Cagney stars as a reporter who is a ferverent critic of the political system. Framed for murder and imprisoned, he is subsequently befriended by fellow inmate, Raft, a gangster. Once hardened by prison life, Cagney shuns his friend and becomes wary of the system. Despite its farfetched second half and mediocre script, the film makes interesting viewing thanks to a stellar performance from Cagney.
1939 92m/B James Cagney, George Raft, George Bancroft, Jane Bryan, Maxie Rosenbloom, Alan Baxter, Thurston Hall, Stanley Ridges, Victor Jory; *D:* William Keighley. **VHS, Beta $19.95** *MGM* 𝄞𝄞½

The Eagle In this tale of a young Cossack ''Robin Hood,'' Valentino assumes the persona of the Eagle to avenge his father's murder. The romantic rogue encounters trouble when he falls for the beautiful Banky much to the chagrin of the scorned Czarina Dresser. Fine performances from Valentino and Dresser. Silent, based on a Alexander Pushkin story. Released on video with a new score by Carl Davis.
1925 77m/B Rudolph Valentino, Vilma Banky, Louise Dressler, George Nichols, James Marcus; *D:* Clarence Brown. **VHS, Beta, LV, 3/4U, Special order formats $19.95** *NOS, HBO, VYY* 𝄞𝄞𝄞

Eagle Claws Champion A ninja master accidentally kills a friend, goes to prison, gets released and returns to fight again.
198? 90m/C Sho Kosugi. **VHS, Beta $29.98** *TWE* 𝄞

The Eagle Has Landed Duvall, portraying a Nazi colonel in this World War II spy film, commissions Sutherland's Irish, English-hating character to aid him in his mission to kill Prime Minister Winston Churchill. Adapted from the bestselling novel by Jack Higgins. A restored version is available at 134 minutes.
1977 (PG) 123m/C Michael Caine, Donald Sutherland, Robert Duvall, Larry Hagman, Jenny Agutter, Donald Pleasence, Treat Williams, Anthony Quayle; *D:* John Sturges. **VHS, Beta $19.98** *FOX, FCT* 𝄞𝄞

Eagles Attack at Dawn After escaping from an Arab prison, an Israeli soldier vows to return with a small commando force to kill the sadistic warden.
1974 (PG) 96m/C *IS* Rick Jason, Peter Brown, Joseph Shiloal. **VHS, Beta $39.98** *VID* 𝄞½

Eagle's Shadow After a poor orphan boy rescues an aged beggar, the grateful old man tutors the lad in Snake-Fist techniques.
1984 101m/C Jackie Chan, Juan Jan Lee, Simon Yuen, Roy Horan; *D:* Yuen Woo Ping. **VHS, Beta** *WVE* 𝄞𝄞

Eagle's Wing John Briley, screenwriter of the award-winning epic ''Gandhi,'' attempts to weave the threads of allegory smoothly in this white man vs. red man Western from England. The mediocre story finds Native American Waterston dueling white trapper Sheen in a quest to capture an elusive, exotic white stallion.

1979 111m/C *GB* Martin Sheen, Sam Waterston, Harvey Keitel, Stephane Audran, Caroline Langrishe; *D:* Anthony Harvey. VHS, Beta $19.95 MED *ℐℐ*½

Early Cinema Vol. 1 A compendium of early silent shorts, mostly predating 1920, which includes: Melies' "Conquest of the North Pole"; Linder's "Man and the Statue" and "Max's Mother In Law"; Drew's "Auntie's Portrait"; Normand's "Mabel's Dramatic Career"; Mix's "An Angelic Attitude" Sennett and Swain's "Cowboy Ambrose"; Lloyd's "Just Neighbors" and Parrott's "Take the Air."
1919 118m/B Mabel Normand, Harold Lloyd, Sidney Drew, Max Linder, Paul Parrott, Tom Mix, Mack Swain; *D:* Mabel Normand, Harold Lloyd, Max Linder, Georges Melies, Mack Sennett. VHS, Beta FCT *ℐ*½

Early Days A cantankerous, salty, once-powerful politician awaits death.
1981 67m/C Ralph Richardson. VHS, Beta $49.98 FOX *ℐℐ*

Early Films #1 A collection of silent movies from the very early days of the industry, including: "The Great Train Robbery," "1895 Lumiere Films," "Dreams of a Rarebit Fiend," "Trip to the Moon," and "Life of an American Fireman."
1903 45m/B *D:* The Lumiere Brothers, Georges Melies, Edwin S. Porter. VHS, Beta WFV *ℐℐ*

Early Frost Near suspenseful whodunit centering around a simple divorce investigation that leads to the discovery of a corpse.
1984 95m/C Diana McLean, Jon Blake, Janet Kingsbury, David Franklin; *D:* Terry O'Connor. VHS, Beta, LV NO *ℐ*½

An Early Frost Highly praised, surprisingly intelligent made-for-television drama following the anguish of a successful lawyer who tells his closed-minded family that he is gay and dying of AIDS. Sensitive performance by Quinn in one of the first TV films to focus on the devastating effects of HIV. Rowlands adeptly displays her acting talents as the despairing mother.
1985 97m/C Aidan Quinn, Gena Rowlands, Ben Gazzara, John Glover, D.W. Moffett, Sylvia Sidney; *D:* John Erman. VHS, Beta, LV $69.95 COL *ℐℐℐ*½

Early Russian Cinema, Vol. 1: Beginnings Four films from 1908-1911, including a documentary and the first film adaptation of a Chekhov play. English subtitles.
1911 45m/B *RU* VHS $29.95 MIL *ℐℐℐ*½

Early Russian Cinema, Vol. 2: Folklore & Legend Four films from 1909-1912: two depicting typical Russian folktales and two, directed by Goncharov, featuring national and cultural themes of the day. English subtitles.
1912 55m/B *RU* *D:* Vasilii Goncharov. VHS $29.95 MIL *ℐℐℐ*½

Early Russian Cinema, Vol. 3: Starewicz's Fantasies Three films by director Starewicz, known for his use of puppet animation. This selection also includes a live-action fantasy from a Gogol story and an anti-German war allegory. English subtitles.
1915 58m/B *RU* *D:* Wladislaw Starewicz. VHS $29.95 MIL *ℐℐℐ*½

Early Russian Cinema, Vol. 4: Provincial Variations The provincial Latvian film "Wedding Day" highlights Jewish life while the melodrama "Merchant Bashkirov's Daughter" follows a scandal based on an actual murder. English subtitles.
1913 55m/B *RU* VHS $29.95 MIL *ℐℐℐ*½

Early Russian Cinema, Vol. 5: Chardynin's Pushkin Actor-director Chardynin's adaptations of two Pushkin stories. English subtitles.
1913 45m/B *RU* Ivan Mosjoukine; *D:* Petr Chardynin. VHS $29.95 MIL *ℐℐℐ*½

Early Russian Cinema, Vol. 6: Class Distinctions The hardship of rural life and a view of servants and masters are depicted in two films. English subtitles.
1914 94m/B *RU* *D:* Vasilii Goncharov, Evgenii Bauer. VHS $29.95 MIL *ℐℐℐ*½

Early Russian Cinema, Vol. 7: Evgenii Bauer Three films from the prolific director of some 80 films, covering both melodrama and erotic comedy. English subtitles.
1915 95m/B *RU* *D:* Evgenii Bauer. VHS $29.95 MIL *ℐℐℐ*½

Early Russian Cinema, Vol. 8: Iakov Protazanov Two films from director Protazanov, including his controversial film on the last days of Tolstoy which provoked legal action from the writer's family due to its scandalous depiction. English subtitles.
1916 104m/B *RU* *D:* Iakov Protazanov. VHS $29.95 MIL *ℐℐℐ*½

Early Russian Cinema, Vol. 9: High Society Three films covering social and urban topics, including a newsreel on the death of Russia's greatest star of the day. English subtitles.
1919 72m/B *RU* *D:* Evgenii Bauer. VHS $29.95 MIL *ℐℐℐ*½

Early Russian Cinema, Vol. 10: The End of an Era Three films, including Bauer's last film "For Luck" and a fragment with the husband-wife acting team of Lisenko and Mosjoukine before their departure into exile. English subtitles.
1917 72m/B *RU* Ivan Mosjoukine, Natalia Lisenko; *D:* Evgenii Bauer. VHS $29.95 MIL *ℐℐℐ*½

Early Sound Films This series of experimental shorts from throughout the silent era depicts the various methods of devising sound film, prior to "The Jazz Singer" in 1927.
1928 90m/B VHS, Beta $59.50 GVV *ℐℐℐ*½

Early Summer A classic from renowned Japanese director Ozu, this film chronicles family tensions in post-World War II Japan caused by newly-independent women rebelling against the social conventions they are expected to fulfill. Perhaps the best example of this director's work. Winner of Japan's Film of the Year Award. In Japanese with English subtitles. *AKA:* Bakushu.
1951 150m/B *JP* Ichiro Sugai, Setsuko Hara, Chikage Awashima; *D:* Yasujiro Ozu. VHS, Beta $59.95 SVS, FCT, TAM *ℐℐℐ*

Early Warner Brothers Cartoons Eight cartoons from the first days of the Merrie Melodies. Includes "Sinking in the Bathtub," "Lady Play Your Mandolin," "One More Time," "Freddie the Freshman," "You Don't Know What You're Doin'," "Red Headed Baby," "I Love a Parade," and "The Shanty Where Santy Lives."
1931 55m/B VHS, Beta $19.95 VDM *ℐℐℐ*

The Earrings of Madame De... A simple story about a society woman who sells a pair of diamond earrings that her husband gave her, then lies about it. Transformed by Ophuls into his most opulent, overwrought masterpiece, the film displays a triumph of form over content. In French with

English subtitles. *AKA:* Diamond Earrings; Madame De.
1954 105m/C *FR* Charles Boyer, Danielle Darrieux, Vittorio De Sica, Lea di Lea, Jean Debucourt; *D:* Max Ophuls. VHS, Beta $69.95 FCT, MRV, TAM *ℐℐℐℐ*

Earth Classic Russian silent film with English subtitles. Problems begin in a Ukrainian village when a collective farm landowner resists handing over his land. Outstanding camera work. Kino release runs 70 minutes. *AKA:* Zemlya; Soul.
1930 57m/B *RU* Semyon Svashenko, Mikola Nademsy, Stephan Shkurat; *D:* Alexander Dovzhenko. VHS, Beta, 3/4U $24.95 VYY, CCB, IHF *ℐℐℐℐ*

Earth Entranced A complex political lamentation from Rocha, the premiere director of Brazil's own new wave cinema. Here a writer switches his allegiance from one politician to another, only to find that he (and the masses) lose either way. In Portuguese with English subtitles. *AKA:* Terra em Transe.
1966 105m/C *BR* Jose Lewgoy, Paulo Gracindo, Jardel Filho, Glauce Rocha; *W/D:* Glauce Rocha. VHS $59.95 FST *ℐℐ*

Earth Girls are Easy Valley girl Valerie is having a bad week: first she catches her fiancee with another woman, then she breaks a nail, then furry aliens land in her swimming pool. What more could go wrong? When the aliens are temporarily stranded, she decides to make amends by giving them a head-to-toe makeover. Devoid of their excessive hairiness, the handsome trio of fun-loving extraterrestrials set out to experience the Southern California lifestyle. A sometimes hilarious sci-fi/musical, featuring bouncy shtick and a gleeful dismantling of modern culture.
1989 (PG) 100m/C Geena Davis, Jeff Goldblum, Charles Rocket, Julie Brown, Jim Carrey, Damon Wayans, Michael McKean, Angelyne, Larry Linville; *D:* Julien Temple. VHS, Beta, LV $14.98 LIV, VES *ℐℐ*½

Earth vs. the Flying Saucers Extraterrestrials land on Earth and issue an ultimatum to humans concerning their constant use of bombs and missiles. Peace is threatened when the military disregards the extraterrestrials' simple warning. Superb special effects by Ray Harryhausen; written by Curt Siodmak. *AKA:* Invasion of the Flying Saucers.
1956 83m/B Hugh Marlowe, Joan Taylor, Donald Curtis, Morris Ankrum; *D:* Fred F. Sears. VHS, Beta, LV $9.95 COL, MLB *ℐℐ*½

Earth vs. the Spider Man-eating giant mutant (teenage ninja?) tarantula makes life miserable for a small town in general and high school partyers in particular. Silly old drive-in fare is agony for many, camp treasure for a precious few. *AKA:* The Spider.
1958 72m/B Edward Kemmer, June Kennedy, Gene Persson, Gene Roth, Hal Torey, Mickey Finn; *D:* Bert I. Gordon. VHS $9.95 COL, MLB *ℐ*

Earthling A terminally ill Holden helps a young Schroder survive in the Australian wilderness after the boy's parents are killed in a tragic accident. Lessons of life and the power of the human heart are passed on in this panoramic, yet mildly sentimental film.
1980 (PG) 102m/C *AU* William Holden, Rick Schroder, Jack Thompson, Olivia Hamnett, Alwyn Kurts; *D:* Peter Collinson. VHS, Beta $69.98 LIV, VES *ℐℐ*½

Earthquake Less-than mediocre drama centers on a major earthquake in Los Angeles and its effect on the lives of an engineer, his spoiled wife, his mistress, his father-in-law, and a suspended policeman. Filmed in much-hyped Sensurround—a tech-

nique intended to shake up the theater a bit, but which will have no effect on your television set. Good special effects, but not enough to compensate for lackluster script.
1974 (PG) 123m/C Charlton Heston, Ava Gardner, George Kennedy, Lorne Greene, Genevieve Bujold, Richard Roundtree, Marjoe Gortner, Barry Sullivan, Victoria Principal, Lloyd Nolan, Walter Matthau; **M:** John Williams. Academy Awards '74: Best Sound, Best Visual Effects; Nominations: Best Art Direction/Set Decoration, Best Cinematography, Best Film Editing. **VHS, Beta, LV $14.98** MCA *𝄞𝄞*

Earthworm Tractors Ambitious tractor salesman Alexander Botts will do anything to make a sale. Brown excels as the fast-talking lead. Comedy is strengthened by its supporting cast. Based on characters first appearing in the "Saturday Evening Post."
1936 63m/B Joe E. Brown, June Travis, Guy Kibbee, Dick Foran, Carol Hughes, Gene Lockhart, Olin Howland; **D:** Ray Enright. **VHS $19.95** NOS, NXM, HEG *𝄞𝄞1/2*

East and West Morris Brown, a worldly New York Jew, returns home to Galicia with his daughter Mollie for a traditional family wedding. She teaches the young villagers to dance and box but meets her romantic match in a young yeshiva scholar who forsakes tradition to win her heart. Picon shines as the exuberant flapper. With English and Yiddish intertitles.
1923 85m/B Molly Picon, Jacob Kalish, Sidney Goldin; **D:** Sidney Goldin. **VHS $72.00** NCJ *𝄞𝄞𝄞*

East End Hustle High-priced call girl rebels against her pimp and sets out to free other prostitutes as well. Also available in an 88-minute unrated version.
1976 (R) 88m/C VHS, Beta $69.98 LIV, VES *𝄞*

East L.A. Warriors A mobster, Hilton-Jacobs, manipulates Los Angeles gangs in this non-stop action adventure.
1989 90m/C Tony Bravo, Lawrence Hilton-Jacobs, Kamar Reyes, William Smith; **D:** Addison Randall. **VHS, Beta $69.95** PAR *𝄞1/2*

East of Borneo Tropical adventure involving a "lost" physician whose worried wife sets out to find him in the jungle. She locates her love only to discover he has a prestigious new job tending to royalty and didn't want to be found.
1931 76m/B Charles Bickford, Rose Hobart, Georges Renavent; **D:** George Melford. **VHS, Beta, 3/4U, Special order formats $16.95** SNC, DVT, CAB *𝄞1/2*

East of Eden Steinbeck's contemporary retelling of the biblical Cain and Abel story receives superior treatment from Kazan and his excellent cast. Dean, in his first starring role, gives a reading of a young man's search for love and acceptance that defines adolescent pain. Though filmed in the 1950s, this story still rivets today's viewers with its emotional message.
1954 115m/C James Dean, Julie Harris, Richard Davalos, Raymond Massey, Jo Van Fleet, Burl Ives, Albert Dekker; **D:** Elia Kazan. Academy Awards '55: Best Supporting Actress (Van Fleet); Nominations: Best Actor (Dean), Best Director (Kazan), Best Screenplay; Golden Globe Awards '56: Best Film—Drama; National Board of Review Awards '55: 10 Best Films of the Year. **VHS, Beta, LV $19.98** WAR, BTV, HMV *𝄞𝄞𝄞𝄞*

East of Eden Remade into a television mini series, this Steinbeck classic tells the tale of two brothers who vie for their father's affection and the woman who comes between them. Seymour is notable as the self-serving mother who abandons her babies to lead a disreputable life. Rife with biblical symbolism and allusions.

1980 375m/C Jane Seymour, Bruce Boxleitner, Warren Oates, Lloyd Bridges, Anne Baxter, Timothy Bottoms, Soon-Teck Oh, Karen Allen, Hart Bochner, Sam Bottoms, Howard Duff, Richard Masur, Wendell Burton, Nicholas Pryor, Grace Zabriskie, M. Emmet Walsh, Matthew "Stymie" Beard; **D:** Harvey Hart. **VHS, Beta, LV $29.95** STE, LIV *𝄞𝄞1/2*

East of Elephant Rock In 1948, a young first secretary of the British Embassy returns from leave in England to a tense atmosphere in a colony in southeast Asia. Beautiful scenery can't make up for weak plot.
1976 93m/C GB John Hurt, Jeremy Kemp, Judi Bowker, Christopher Cazenove; **D:** Don Boyd. **VHS, Beta $59.98** SUE *𝄞1/2*

East of Kilimanjaro A freelance photographer and a doctor search frantically to find the carrier of a fatal disease near the slopes of the majestic Mt. Kilimanjaro. Routine killer virus flick filmed in Africa. Also know as "The Big Search."
1959 75m/C Marshall Thompson, Gaby Andre, Fausto Tozzi; **D:** Arnold Belgard. **VHS** SUE *𝄞𝄞*

East Side Kids Early East Side kids. A hoodlum wants to prevent his brother from beginning a similar life of crime.
1940 60m/B Leon Ames, Harris Berger, Dennis Moore, Joyce Bryant; **D:** Robert F. Hill. **VHS, Beta $19.95** NOS, MRV, DVT *𝄞𝄞*

East Side Kids/The Lost City The first East Side Kids film introduces some soon-familiar faces. "The Lost City" is a composite of all twelve episodes of the serial; edited for brevity.
1935 135m/B Dennis Moore, Vince Barnett, William Boyd, Kane Richmond. **VHS, Beta** AOV *𝄞𝄞*

East Side, West Side Stanwyck and Mason try hard to make this simple-minded soaper work, with mixed results. A wealthy couple experiences marital woes, aggravated by a ambitious young woman and a soft-hearted man suffering from unrequited love. Based on the popular novel by Marcia Davenport.
1949 110m/B Barbara Stanwyck, James Mason, Ava Gardner, Van Heflin, Gale Sondergaard, William Frawley, Nancy Davis; **D:** Mervyn LeRoy. **VHS $19.98** MGM *𝄞𝄞*

Easter Parade A big musical star (Astaire) splits with his partner (Miller) claiming that he could mold any girl to replace her in the act. He tries and finally succeeds after much difficulty. Astaire and Garland in peak form, aided by a classic Irving Berlin score. ♫Happy Easter; Drum Crazy; It Only Happens When I Dance With You; Everybody's Doin' It; I Want to Go Back to Michigan; Beautiful Faces Need Beautiful Clothes; A Fella With an Umbrella; I Love a Piano; Snookey Ookums; Ragtime Violin; When the Midnight Choo-Choo Leaves for Alabam; Shaking the Blues Away; Steppin' Out With My Baby; A Couple of Swells; The Girl on the Magazine Cover; Better Luck Next Time; Easter Parade.
1948 103m/C Fred Astaire, Judy Garland, Peter Lawford, Ann Miller, Jules Munshin; **D:** Charles Walters; **M:** Johnny Green, Roger Evans. **VHS, Beta, LV $19.98** MGM, HMV *𝄞𝄞𝄞1/2*

Easy Come, Easy Go Elvis, as a Navy frogman, gets excited when he accidentally discovers what he believes is a vast sunken treasure. Music is his only solace when he finds his treasure to be worthless copper coins. ♫Easy Come, Easy Go; The Love Machine; Yoga is as Yoga Goes; Sing, You Children; You Gotta Stop; I'll Take Love.

1967 96m/C Elvis Presley, Dodie Marshall, Pat Priest, Elsa Lanchester, Frank McHugh, Pat Harrington; **D:** John Rich. **VHS, Beta $14.95** PAR *𝄞𝄞*

Easy Kill A man takes the law into his own hands to exact revenge on drug lords.
1989 100m/C Jane Badler, Cameron Mitchell, Frank Stallone; **D:** Josh Spencer. **VHS, Beta** NO *𝄞1/2*

The Easy Life Haunting film about a hedonistic man from a small Italian village who takes a mild-mannered student pleasure-seeking. The ride turns sour and the playboy is ultimately destroyed by his own brutality.
1963 105m/B IT Vittorio Gassman, Catherine Spaak, Jean-Louis Trintignant, Luciana Angiolillo; **D:** Dino Risi. **VHS** FST *𝄞𝄞𝄞*

Easy Living Compromised melodrama about an over-the-hill football player who must cope with his failing marriage and looming retirement. Based on an Irwin Shaw story.
1949 77m/B Victor Mature, Lucille Ball, Jack Paar, Lizabeth Scott, Sonny Tufts, Lloyd Nolan, Paul Stewart; **D:** Jacques Tourneur. **VHS, Beta, LV $19.95** MED, TTC *𝄞𝄞1/2*

Easy Money A basic slob has the chance to inherit $10 million if he can give up his loves: smoking, drinking, and gambling among others. Dangerfield is surprisingly restrained in this harmless, though not altogether unpleasing comedy.
1983 (R) 95m/C Rodney Dangerfield, Joe Pesci, Geraldine Fitzgerald, Jennifer Jason Leigh, Tom Ewell, Candice Azzara, Taylor Negron; **D:** James Signorelli. **VHS, Beta, LV $19.98** VES *𝄞𝄞*

Easy Rider Slim-budget, generation-defining movie. Two young men in late 1960s undertake a motorcycle trek throughout the Southwest in search of the real essence of America. Along the way they encounter hippies, rednecks, prostitutes, drugs, Jack Nicholson, and tragedy. One of the highest-grossing pictures of the decade, this movie undoubtedly influenced two generations of "youth-oriented dramas," which all tried unsuccessfully, to duplicate the original accomplishment. Some psychedelic scenes and a great role for Nicholson are added bonuses. Look for the graveyard dancing scene in New Orleans. Features one of the best 60s rock scores around. In a league that includes "Mean Streets" and "The Wanderers."
1969 (R) 94m/C Peter Fonda, Dennis Hopper, Jack Nicholson, Karen Black, Toni Basil, Robert Walker Jr.; **D:** Dennis Hopper. **VHS, Beta, LV, 8mm $19.95** COL, CCB *𝄞𝄞1/2*

Easy Street Chaplin portrays a derelict who, using some hilarious methods, reforms the residents of Easy Street. Chaplin's row with the town bully is particularly amusing. Silent with musical soundtrack added.
1916 20m/B Charlie Chaplin; **D:** Charlie Chaplin. **VHS, Beta, 3/4U, Special order formats** CAB *𝄞𝄞𝄞*

Easy to Love Williams is in love with her boss, but he pays her no attention until a handsome singer vies for her affections. Set at Florida's Cypress Gardens, this aquatic musical features spectacular water ballet productions choreographed by Busby Berkeley, and the title song penned by Cole Porter. ♫Easy to Love; Coquette; Beautiful Spring; That's What Rainy Day is For; Look Out! I'm Romantic; Didja Ever.
1953 96m/C Esther Williams, Van Johnson, Tony Martin, John Bromfield, King Donovan, Carroll Baker; **D:** Charles Walters. **VHS $19.98** MGM *𝄞𝄞1/2*

Easy Virtue Hitchcock directs this adaptation of a Noel Coward play as a social melodrama. Larita is an unhappily married socialite with a lover. When her husband discovers her infideltiy they divorce and she is marked as a woman of loose morals. Her reputation is not enhanced by her marriage to a younger man whose family diapproves.
1927 79m/B *GB* Isabel Jeans, Ian Hunter, Frank Dyall, Eric Bransby Williams, Robin Irvine, Violet Farebrother; *D:* Alfred Hitchcock. **VHS, Beta** $19.95 *NOS, MRV, GPV* 🐾🐾½

Easy Wheels Like most decent biker movies, "Wheels" is propelled by bad taste and a healthy dose of existentialist nihilism. But there's an unusual plot twist in this parody. A biker named She-Wolf and her gang kidnap female babies and let wolves rear the children. Their elaborate plan is to create a race of super women who will subdue the troublesome male population. But can this "noble" plan succeed?
1989 94m/C Paul LeMat, Eileen Davidson, Marjorie Bransfield, Jon Menick, Mark Holton, Karen Russell, Jami Richards, Roberta Vasquez, Barry Livingston, George Plimpton; *W/D:* David O'Malley. **VHS, Beta, LV** $29.95 *FRH* 🐾🐾½

Easyriders Video Magazine A series based on the popular magazine, ripe with a variety of features from the biker world, including coverage of Daytona Bike Week 89, Rodeo Action, the Wall of Death, Grateful Dead Roadies, the Black Hills Rally, Midwest Ice Racing, Malcom Forbes' Last Ride, David Mann's original Daytona collection, plus wild biker chicks and plenty of good times, biker style.
1991 (NC-17) 60m/C VHS $29.95 *EAS* 🐾🐾½

Eat a Bowl of Tea Endearing light drama-comedy concerning a multi-generational Chinese family. They must learn to deal with the problems of life in America and in particular, marriage, when Chinese women are finally allowed to immigrate with their husbands to the United States following World War II. Adaptation of Louis Chu's story, directed by the man who brought us "Dim Sum." A PBS "American Playhouse" presentation.
1989 (PG-13) 102m/C Cora Miao, Russell Wong, Lau Siu Ming, Eric Tsang, Victor Wong, Jessica Harper; *D:* Wayne Wang; *W:* Judith Rascoe. **VHS, Beta, LV** $19.98 *COL* 🐾🐾½

Eat and Run A bloody comedy about a 400-pound alien with a taste for Italian (people, that is).
1986 (R) 85m/C Ron Silver, R.L. Ryan, Sharon Schlarth; *D:* Christopher Hart. **VHS, Beta** $19.95 *STE, NWV* 🐾

Eat My Dust Teenage son of a California sheriff steals the best stock cars from a race track to take the town's heartthrob for a joy ride. Subsequently he leads the town on a wild car chase. Brainless but fast-paced.
1976 (PG) 89m/C Ron Howard, Christopher Norris, Warren Kemmerling, Rance Howard, Clint Howard, Corbin Bernsen; *D:* Charles B. Griffith. **VHS, Beta** $9.98 *SUE* 🐾🐾

Eat the Peach An idiosyncratic Irish comedy about two young unemployed rebels who attempt to break free from their tiny coast town by becoming motorcycle champs after seeing the Elvis Presley film "Roustabout." Together they create the "wall of death,"—a large wooden barrel in which they can perform various biker feats.
1986 90m/C *IR* Stephen Brennan, Eamon Morrissey, Catherine Byrne, Niall Toibin; *D:* Peter Ormrod. **VHS, Beta** $79.98 *FOX* 🐾🐾½

Eat the Rich A British farce about a group of terrorists who take over the popular London restaurant, Bastard's. Led by a former, disgruntled transvestite employee, they turn diners into menu offerings. Music by Motorhead.
1987 (R) 89m/C *GB* Nosher Powell, Lanah Pellay, Fiona Richmond, Ronald Allen, Sandra Dorne; *Cameos:* Paul McCartney, Bill Wyman, Koo Stark, Miranda Richardson; *D:* Peter Richardson. **VHS, Beta** $89.95 *COL* 🐾

Eaten Alive A Southerner takes an unsuspecting group of tourists into a crocodile death trap. Director Tobe Hooper's follow-up to "The Texas Chainsaw Massacre." Englund is more recognizable with razor fingernails as Freddy Krueger of the "Nightmare on Elm Street" films. *AKA:* Death Trap; Starlight Slaughter; Legend of the Bayou; Horror Hotel Massacre.
1976 (R) 96m/C Neville Brand, Mel Ferrer, Carolyn Jones, Marilyn Burns, Stuart Whitman, Robert Englund; *D:* Tobe Hooper. **VHS, Beta** $59.95 *PSM* 🐾🐾

Eating Set in Southern California, women gather to celebrate birthdays for three of their friends who are turning 30, 40 and 50. As the party commences, women from two generations discuss their attitudes towards food and men...and discover hilarious parallels.
1990 (R) 110m/C Nelly Alard, Frances Bergen, Mary Crosby, Lisa Richards, Gwen Welles, Daphna Kastner, Elizabeth Kemp, Marlena Giovi, Marina Gregory; *W/D:* Henry Jaglom. **VHS, Beta, LV** *PAR* 🐾🐾½

Eating Raoul The Blands are a happily married couple who share many interests: good food and wine, entrepreneurial dreams, and an aversion to sex. The problem is, they're flat broke. So, when the tasty swinger from upstairs makes a pass at Mary and Paul accidentally kills him, they discover he's got loads of money; Raoul takes a cut in the deal by disposing of—or rather recycling—the body. This may just be the way to finance that restaurant they've been wanting to open. Wonderful, offbeat, hilarious comedy.
1982 (R) 83m/C Mary Woronov, Paul Bartel, Buck Henry, Ed Begley Jr., Edie McClurg, Robert Beltran, John Paragon; *D:* Mary Woronov, Paul Bartel. **VHS, Beta** $19.98 *FOX* 🐾🐾🐾½

Ebony Dreams World War II documentary focuses on the experience of female factory workers during and after the war. Five contemporary women relate their personal endeavors and struggles to retain their jobs once the war ended. Excellent use of newsreel footage and interesting interviews with the women.
1980 85m/C Philomena Nowlin; *D:* Bill Brame. **VHS** $19.95 *LPC* 🐾🐾🐾½

Ebony Tower Based on the John Fowles novel about a crusty old artist who lives in a French chateau with two young female companions. They are visited by a handsome young man, thereby initiating sexual tension and recognizably Fowlesian plot puzzles. Made for British television. Features some partial nudity.
1986 80m/C *GB* Laurence Olivier, Roger Rees, Greta Scacchi, Toyah Wilcox; *D:* Robert Knights. **Beta** *NO* 🐾🐾½

Echo Murders A Sexton Blake mystery wherein he investigates a mine owner's mysterious death, opening up a veritable can of murdering, power-hungry worms.
1945 75m/B David Farrar, Dennis Price. **VHS, Beta** $19.95 *NOS, VYY* 🐾½

Echo Park An unsung sleeper comedy about three roommates living in Los Angeles' Echo Park: a body builder, a single-mother waitress, and an itinerant songwriter. Charts their struggles as they aim for careers in showbiz. Offbeat ensemble effort.
1986 (R) 93m/C *AU* Tom Hulce, Susan Dey, Michael Bowen, Cheech Marin, Christopher Walker, Shirley Jo Finney, Cassandra Peterson, Yana Nirvana, Timothy Carey; *D:* Robert Dornhelm. **VHS, Beta, LV** $19.98 *KRT* 🐾🐾½

Echoes A young painter's life slowly comes apart as he is tormented by nightmares that his stillborn twin brother is attempting to murder him.
1983 (R) 90m/C Gale Sondergaard, Mercedes McCambridge, Richard Alferi, Ruth Roman, John Spencer, Nathalie Nell; *D:* Arthur Seidelman. **VHS, Beta** $19.98 *VID* 🐾

Echoes in the Darkness Television mini series based on the true-life Joseph Wambaugh bestseller about the "Main Line" murder investigation in Pennsylvania in 1979. Police are baffled when a teacher is murdered and her children vanish. Suspicion falls on a charismatic coworker and the school's principal. On two tapes.
1987 234m/C Peter Coyote, Robert Loggia, Stockard Channing, Peter Boyle, Cindy Pickett, Gary Cole, Zeljko Ivanek, Alex Hyde-White, Treat Williams; *D:* Glenn Jordan. **VHS** $29.95 *STE, NWV* 🐾🐾½

Echoes of Conflict The turbulent Middle East and Arab-Israeli tensions are spotlighted in three new wave films from Israel. Includes "The Cage," "The Movie," and "Don't Get Involved." In Hebrew with English subtitles. In color and black and white.
1989 91m/C *IS* **VHS** $79.95 *FCT, TAM, KIV* 🐾🐾

Echoes of Paradise After a series of earth-shattering events, a depressed woman journeys to an island where she falls for a Balinese dancer. Soon she must choose between returning home or beginning life anew in paradise. *AKA:* Shadows of the Peacock.
1986 (R) 90m/C *AU* Wendy Hughes, John Lone, Rod Mullinar, Peta Toppano, Steven Jacobs, Gillian Jones; *D:* Phillip Noyce. **VHS, Beta, LV** $14.95 *ACA* 🐾½

The Eclipse The last of Antonioni's trilogy (after "L'Avventura" and "La Notte"), wherein another fashionable and alienated Italian woman passes from one lover to another searching unsuccessfully for truth and love. Highly acclaimed. In Italian with subtitles. *AKA:* L'eclisse.
1966 123m/B *IT* Monica Vitti, Alain Delon, Francisco Rabal, Louis Seigner; *D:* Michelangelo Antonioni. **VHS, Beta** $29.95 *MRV, FCT, APD* 🐾🐾🐾½

Ecstasy A romantic, erotic story about a young woman married to an older man, who takes a lover. Features Lamarr, then Hedy Kiesler, before her discovery in Hollywood. Film subsequently gained notoriety for Lamarr's nude scenes. In Czech with English subtitles. *AKA:* Extase; Ekstase; Symphony of Love.
1933 90m/B *CZ* Hedy Lamarr, Jaromir Rogoz; *D:* Gustav Machaty. **VHS, Beta, 8mm** $29.95 *HTV, NOS, MRV* 🐾🐾½

Ecstasy Soft core fluff about a film director's wife's erotic adventures.
1984 (R) 82m/C Tiffany Bolling, Franc Luz, Jack Carter, Britt Ekland, Julie Newmar. **VHS, Beta** $19.95 *MGM* Woof!

Ecstasy Inc. A husband-wife sex therapist team kill their patients.
1988 86m/C Gabriel River, Christina Andress. **VHS, Beta** $29.95 *MED* 🐾

Eddie and the Cruisers In the early 1960s, rockers Eddie and the Cruisers score with one hit album. Amid their success, lead singer Pare dies mysteriously in a car accident. Years later, a reporter decides to write a feature on the defunct group, prompting a former band member to begin a search for missing tapes of the Cruisers' unreleased second album. Questions posed at the end of the movie are answered in the sequel. Enjoyable soundtrack by John Cafferty and the Beaver Brown Band.
1983 (PG) 90m/C Tom Berenger, Michael Pare, Ellen Barkin, Joe Pantoliano, Matthew Laurance; **D:** Martin Davidson. **VHS, Beta, LV, 8mm** **$14.95** MVD, SUE, NLC ♂♂

Eddie and the Cruisers 2: Eddie Lives! A sequel to the minor cult favorite, in which a rock star believed to be dead emerges under a new name in Montreal to lead a new band. The Beaver Brown Band again provides the music.
1989 (PG-13) 106m/C CA Michael Pare, Marina Orsini, Matthew Laurance, Bernie Coulson; **D:** Jean-Claude Lord. **VHS, Beta, LV** **$9.99** CCB, IVE, IME ♂ ½

Eddie Macon's Run Based on a true story; Eddie Macon has been unjustly jailed in Texas and plans an escape to run to Mexico. He is followed by a tough cop who is determined to catch the fugitive. Film debut of Goodman.
1983 (PG) 95m/C Kirk Douglas, John Schneider, Lee Purcell, John Goodman, Leah Ayres; **D:** Jeff Kanew. **VHS, Beta, LV** **$69.95** MCA ♂♂

Eddie Murphy "Delirious" Murphy raps about life, sex, childhood etc. in this scathing, scatalogical, stand-up performance. Strong language.
1983 (R) 69m/C Eddie Murphy, Richard Tienken, Robert Wachs; **D:** Bruce Gowers. **VHS, Beta, LV** **$14.95** PAR ♂♂ ½

Eddie Murphy: Raw Murphy's second stand-up performance film, featuring many of his woman-bashing observations on life.
1987 (R) 90m/C Eddie Murphy; **D:** Robert Townsend. **VHS, Beta, LV, 8mm** **$14.95** PAR ♂♂

The Eddy Duchin Story Glossy tearjerker that profiles the tragic life of Eddy Duchin, the famous pianist/bandleader of the 30s and 40s. Features almost 30 songs, including classics by Cole Porter, George and Ira Gershwin, Hammerstein, Chopin, and several others.
1956 123m/C Tyrone Power, Kim Novak, Victoria Shaw, James Whitmore, Rex Thompson; **D:** George Sidney; **M:** George Dunning. **VHS, LV** **$19.95** COL, MVD, TVC ♂♂

Eden Eden is a luxury resort designed to cater to personal fantasies and filled with numerous intrigues. Part-owner Eve Sinclair faces a number of professional and personal complications, including the tragic death of her husband, a brother-in-law who's interested in more than business, and an old friend with uncertain motives. Lots of sex in beautiful settings. Made for cable television.
1992 ?m/C Barbara Alyn Woods, Jack Armstrong, Steve Chase, Darcy Demoss, Jeff Griggs; **D:** Victor Lobl; **W:** Stephen Black, Henry Stern. **VHS** **$79.95** UND ♂♂

Eden 2 The continuing saga of the luxury resort Eden. Owner Eve is still having erotic dreams of late husband Grant while fending off the very real advances of his brother Josh and becoming attracted to Paul, her late husband's best friend. The guests are equally caught up in erotic dilemmas involving sexual blackmail. Made for cable television.

1993 ?m/C Barbara Alyn Woods, Jack Armstrong, Steve Chase, Darcy Demoss, Jeff Griggs; **D:** Kristine Peterson; **W:** Stephen Black, Henry Stern. **VHS** **$79.95** UND ♂♂

Edge of Darkness Compelling war-drama about the underground movement in Norway during Nazi takeover of World War II. Flynn plays a Norwegian fisherman who leads the local underground movement and Sheridan is his loyal fiancee. Although several problems occurred throughout filming, this picture earned high marks for its superb performances and excellent camerawork. Based on the novel by William Woods.
1943 120m/B Errol Flynn, Ann Sheridan, Walter Huston, Nancy Coleman, Helmut Dantine, Judith Anderson, Ruth Gordon, John Beal; **D:** Lewis Milestone; **W:** Robert Rossen **VHS** **$19.98** MGM ♂♂♂ ½

Edge of Darkness Originally produced as a mini series for British television, this mystery involves a police detective who investigates his daughter's murder and uncovers a web of espionage and intrigue.
1986 307m/C GB Joe Don Baker, Bob Peck, Jack Woodson, John Woodvine, Joanne Whalley-Kilmer; **D:** Martin Campbell. **VHS, Beta** **$29.95** FOX, TVC ♂♂

Edge of Fury When a businessman is unjustly arrested on a drug charge, he enlists the help of his chauffeur to clear his name.
198? 90m/C Bruce Li, Andrew Sage, Michael Danna, Tommy Lee. **VHS, Beta** NO ♂

Edge of Honor Young Eagle Scouts camping in the Pacific Northwest discover a woodland weapons cache and wage guerilla war against killer lumberjacks out to silence them. A boneheaded, politically correct action bloodbath; you don't have to like the logging industry to disapprove of the broad slurs against its men shown here.
1991 (R) 92m/C Corey Feldman, Meredith Salenger, Scott Reeves, Ken Jenkins, Christopher Neame, Don Swayze; **D:** Michael Spence. **VHS** **$19.95** ACA ♂ ½

Edge of Sanity An overdone Jekyll-Hyde reprise, with cocaine serving as the villainous substance. The coke-created Hyde is posited as a prototype for Jack the Ripper. Not for the easily queasy. Available in a 90 minute, unrated version.
1989 (R) 85m/C GB Anthony Perkins, Glynis Barber, David Lodge, Sarah Maur-Thorp; **D:** Gerard Kikione. **VHS, Beta, LV** NO ♂ ½

Edge of the Axe A small town is held in the grip of terror by a demented slasher.
1989 91m/C Barton Faulks, Christina Marie Lane, Page Moseley, Fred Hollyday; **D:** Joseph Braunstein. **VHS, Beta** **$79.98** MCG ♂ ½

Edge of the World Moody, stark British drama of a mini-society in its death throes, expertly photographed on a six-square-mile island in the Shetlands. A dwindling fishing community of fewer than 100 souls agonize over whether to migrate to the mainland; meanwhile the romance of a local girl with an off-islander takes a tragic course. Choral effects were provided by the Glasgow Orpheus Choir.
1937 80m/B GB Finlay Currie, Niall MacGinnis, Grant Sutherland, John Laurie, Michael Powell; **W/D:** Michael Powell. **VHS** **$19.95** NOS ♂♂♂

Edie in Ciao! Manhattan Real-life story of Edie Sedgwick, Warhol superstar and international fashion model, whose life in the fast lane led to ruin. **AKA:** Ciao! Manhattan.
1972 (R) 84m/C Edie Sedgwick, Baby Jane Holzer, Roger Vadim, Paul America, Viva. **VHS, Beta** **$14.95** PAV, FCT ♂♂

Edison the Man Story of Tommy Edison's early years of experimentation in the basement. The young genious eventually invents light bulbs, motion pictures, and a sound recording device. Well played by Tracy.
1940 108m/C Spencer Tracy, Rita Johnson, Lynne Overman, Charles Coburn, Gene Lockhart, Henry Travers, Felix Bressart; **D:** Clarence Brown. **VHS, Beta** **$19.98** MGM ♂♂ ½

Edith & Marcel A fictionalization of the love affair between chanteuse Edith Piaf and boxer Marcel Cerdan (played by his son, Marcel Cerdan, Jr.). In French, with English subtitles.
1983 104m/C FR Evelyne Bouix, Marcel Cerdan Jr., Charles Aznavour, Jacques Villeret; **D:** Claude Lelouch. **VHS, Beta** **$59.95** MED ♂ ½

Educating Rita Walters and Caine team beautifully in this adaptation of the successful Willy Russell play which finds an uneducated hairdresser determined to improve her knowledge of literature. In so doing, she enlists the aid of a tutor: a disillusioned alcoholic, adeptly played by Caine. Together, the two find inspiration in one another's differences and experiences. Ultimately, the teacher receives a lesson in how to again appreciate his work and the classics as he observes his pupil's unique approach to her studies. Some deem this a "Pygmalion" for the '80s.
1983 (PG) 110m/C GB Michael Caine, Julie Walters, Michael Williams, Maureen Lipman; **D:** Lewis Gilbert. Academy Awards '83 Nominations: Best Actor (Caine), Best Actress (Walters), Best Adapted Screenplay; British Academy Awards '83: Best Actor (Caine), Best Actress (Walters), Best Film; Golden Globe Awards '84: Best Actor—Musical/Comedy (Caine), Best Actress—Musical/Comedy (Walters). **VHS, Beta, LV, 8mm** **$14.95** COL ♂♂♂ ½

The Education of Sonny Carson Chilling look at the tribulations of a black youth living in a Brooklyn ghetto amid drugs, prostitution, crime, and other forms of vice. Based on Sonny Carson's autobiography. Still pertinent some twenty years after its theatrical release.
1974 (R) 104m/C Rony Clanton, Don Gordon, Paul Benjamin; **D:** Michael Campus. **VHS, Beta** **$59.95** MED ♂♂ ½

Edward and Mrs. Simpson Made-for-television dramatic reconstruction of the years leading to the abdication of King Edward VIII, who forfeited the British throne in 1936 so that he could marry American divorcee Wallis Simpson. Originally aired on PBS.
1980 270m/C Edward Fox, Cynthia Harris; **D:** Waris Hussein. **VHS, Beta** **$79.95** HBO, TVC ♂♂

Edward Scissorhands Depp's a young man created by loony scientist Price, who unfortunately dies before he can attach hands to his boy-creature. The boy's "rescued" from his lonely existence outside of suburbia (in a gothic castle, not exurbia) by an indefatigably ingratiating lady from Avon. With scissors in place of hands, he has more trouble fitting into suburbia than would most new kids on the block, and he struggles with being different and lonely in a cardboard-cutout world. Burton co-wrote and directed this visually captivating fairy tale full of splash and color. But toward the end—as if Burton suddenly realized his social satire was failing or that box-office returns dictate creativity—the tale resorts to a Hollywood-prefab denouement, sapping whatever moral fiber might have been.

1990 (PG-13) 100m/C Johnny Depp, Dianne Wiest, Winona Ryder, Alan Arkin, Vincent Price, Anthony Michael Hall; *D:* Tim Burton. **VHS, Beta, LV** $19.98 *FOX, FCT* �⅃⅃

Edward II Jarman's controversial adaptation of Christopher Marlowe's play "The Troublesome Reign of Edward II" portrays the weak-willed monarch as neglecting his kingdom for love. Unfortunately, it's not for his queen but for his commoner male lover. His neglect of both queen and country lead to a swift and brutal downfall. Jarman's use of contemporary anachronisms, stream of conscienceness approach, and heavy symbolism may leave more than one viewer wondering what's going on.
1992 (R) 91m/C *GB* Steven Waddington, Kevin Collins, Andrew Tiernan, John Lynch, Dudley Sutton, Tilda Swinton, Jerome Flynn, Jody Graber, Nigel Terry, Annie Lennox; *W/D:* Derek Jarman. **VHS** $19.95 *COL, TAM* ⅃⅃½

Eegah! Another Arch Hall (Merriwether) epic in which an anachronistic Neanderthal falls in love in '60s California. Reputed to be one of the worst films of all time.
1962 93m/C Marilyn Manning, Richard Kiel, Arch Hall Jr.; *D:* Nicholas Merriwether. **VHS, Beta** $9.95 *RHI, FCT Woof!*

The Eerie Midnight Horror Show A life-size statue of a crucified thief comes to life after being stolen from a church by a female art student. After centuries of chastity, the possessed statue seeks relief. *AKA:* The Sexorcists; The Tormented; Enter the Devil.
1982 (R) 92m/C Stella Carnachia, Chris Auram, Lucretia Love; *D:* Mario Gariazzo. **VHS, Beta** *NO Woof!*

The Effect of Gamma Rays on Man-in-the-Moon Marigolds A wonderful drama based on the Pulitzer Prize winning play by Paul Zindel. The story centers around eccentric young Beatrice and her depressed family. Beatrice is preparing her experiment for the school science fair, determined to beat her competition. Her exhibit shows how radiation sometimes kills the helpless marigolds, but sometimes causes them to grow into even more beautiful mutations. This mirrors Beatrice, who flowers even amidst the drunkenness of her mother and the dullness of her sister.
1973 (PG) 100m/C Joanne Woodward, Nell Potts, Roberta Wallach, Judith Lowry, Richard Venture; *D:* Paul Newman. **VHS** *NO* ⅃⅃⅃

Effi Briest A 19th-century tragedy well-played by Schygulla and empowered with Fassbinder's directorial skills. Effi (Schygulla) is a 17 year-old beauty, unhappily married to a much older man. She drifts into a brief affair, which is not discovered for several years. When her husband does discover her past infidelity, the Prussian legal code permits him a chilling revenge. Based on a popular 19th-century novel by Theodor Fontane. In German with English subtitles. *AKA:* Fontane Effi Briest.
1974 135m/B *GE* Hanna Schygulla, Wolfgang Schenck, Lilo Pempeit, Ulli Lommel; *W/D:* Rainer Werner Fassbinder. **VHS** $79.95 *NYF, TAM, PMS* ⅃⅃⅃½

The Efficiency Expert Lighthearted Australian comedy about a dingy moccasin factory where a rigid efficiency consultant is invited to save the eccentric family-run company from bankruptcy. Predictable ending contains a nevertheless timely message about the importance of the bottom line.
1992 (PG) 97m/C *AU* Anthony Hopkins, Bob Mendelsohn, Alwyn Kurts, Bruno Lawrence, Angela Punch McGregor, Russell Crowe, Rebecca Rigg, Toni Collette; *D:* Mark Joffe; *W:*

Andrew Knight. **VHS, Beta** $89.95 *PAR, BTV* ⅃⅃½

Egg Striking film from Holland chronicles the life of a quiet, middle-aged baker who answers a personal ad from a schoolteacher. After much correspondence, the teacher visits the baker in his village, and the townspeople take great interest in what happens next. In Dutch with English subtitles.
1988 58m/C *NL* Johan Leysen, Marijke Vengelers; *D:* Danniel Danniel. **VHS, LV** $29.95 *KIV, LUM, TAM* ⅃⅃½

Egg and I Based on the true-life adventures of best-selling humorist Betty MacDonald. A young urban bride agrees to help her new husband realize his life-long dream of owning a chicken farm. A dilapidated house, temperamental stove, and suicidal chickens test the bride's perseverance, as do the zany antics of her country-bumpkin neighbors, Ma and Pa Kettle, who make their screen debut. Plenty of old-fashioned laughs.
1947 104m/B Claudette Colbert, Fred MacMurray, Marjorie Main, Percy Kilbride, Louise Allbritton, Richard Long, Billy House, Richard Long, Donald MacBride; *D:* Chester Erskine. **VHS, Beta, LV** $14.95 *MCA, KRT* ⅃⅃⅃

The Egyptian Based on the sword-and-sandal novel by Mika Waltari, this is a ponderous big-budget epic about a young Egyptian in Akhnaton's epoch who becomes physician to the Pharaoh.
1954 140m/C Edmund Purdom, Victor Mature, Peter Ustinov, Bella Darvi, Gene Tierney, Henry Daniell, Jean Simmons, Michael Wilding, Judith Evelyn, John Carradine, Carl Benton Reid; *D:* Michael Curtiz. **VHS, Beta, LV** $19.98 *FOX, IME* ⅃⅃½

The Eiger Sanction An art teacher returns to the CII (a fictionalized version of the CIA) as an exterminator hired to assassinate the killers of an American agent. In the process, he finds himself climbing the Eiger. Beautiful Swiss Alps scenery fails to totally compensate for several dreary lapses. Based on the novel by Trevanian.
1975 (R) 125m/C Clint Eastwood, George Kennedy, Vonetta McGee, Jack Cassidy, Thayer David; *D:* Clint Eastwood; *M:* John Williams. **VHS, Beta, LV** $19.95 *MCA, TLF* ⅃⅃⅃

8 1/2 The acclaimed Fellini self-portrait of a revered Italian film director struggling with a fated film project wanders through his intermixed life, childhood memories, and hallucinatory fantasies. Subtitled in English. *AKA:* Otto E Mezzo; Federico Fellini's 8 1/2.
1963 135m/B *IT* Marcello Mastroianni, Claudia Cardinale, Anouk Aimee, Sandra Milo, Barbara Steele, Rossella Falk; *D:* Federico Fellini. Academy Awards '63: Best Costume Design (B & W), Best Foreign Language Film; Nominations: Best Art Direction/Set Decoration (B & W), Best Director (Fellini), Best Story & Screenplay; National Board of Review Awards '63: 5 Best Foreign Films of the Year; New York Film Critics Awards '63: Best Foreign Film. **VHS, Beta, LV** $69.95 *VES, MRV, MPI* ⅃⅃⅃⅃

Eight Men Out Taken from Eliot Asinof's book, a moving, full-blooded account of the infamous 1919 "Black Sox" scandal, in which members of the Chicago White Sox teamed to throw the World Series for $80,000. A dirge of lost innocence, this is among Sayles's best films. Provides an interesting look at the "conspiracy" that ended "shoeless" Joe Jackson's major-league career. The actual baseball scenes are first-rate, and Straithairn, Sweeney, and Cusack give exceptional performances. Sayles makes an appearance as Ring Lardner. Enjoyable viewing for even the non-sports fan.

1988 (PG) 121m/C John Cusack, D.B. Sweeney, Perry Lang, Jane Alexander, Bill Irwin, Clifton James, Michael Rooker, Michael Lerner, Christopher Lloyd, Studs Terkel, David Strathairn, Charlie Sheen, Kevin Tighe, John Mahoney, John Sayles, Gordon Clapp, Richard Edson, James Reed, Don Harvey; *D:* John Sayles. **VHS, Beta, LV** $19.98 *ORI, FCT* ⅃⅃⅃

8 Million Ways to Die An ex-cop hires himself out to rescue a pimp-bound hooker, and gets knee-deep in a mess of million-dollar drug deals, murder, and prostitution. Slow-moving but satisfying. Based on the book by Lawrence Block.
1985 (R) 115m/C Jeff Bridges, Rosanna Arquette, Andy Garcia, Alexandra Paul; *D:* Hal Ashby; *W:* Oliver Stone. **VHS, Beta, LV** $19.98 *FOX* ⅃⅃

Eight Witnesses Suspense thriller about a man being murdered in front of eight blind witnesses.
1954 ?m/C Peggy Ann Garner. **VHS** $15.95 *LOO* ⅃⅃

18 Again! After a bump on the head, an 81-year-old man and his 18-year-old grandson mentally switch places, giving each a new look at his life. Lightweight romp with Burns in especially good form, but not good enough to justify redoing this tired theme.
1988 (PG) 100m/C George Burns, Charlie Schlatter, Anita Morris, Jennifer Runyon, Tony Roberts, Red Buttons, Miriam Flynn; *D:* Paul Flaherty. **VHS, Beta, LV** $19.95 *STE, NWV* ⅃⅃½

18 Bronzemen Eighteen martial artists band together to defeat evil.
1979 90m/C Polly Kuan, James Tien, Carter Wong; *D:* Joseph Kuo. **VHS, Beta** *NO* ⅃

Eighteen Jade Arhats A kung fu epic with a blind heroine who nevertheless kicks other people in the eyes.
1984 95m/C Chia Ling, Ou-Yang Ksiek, Sun Chia-Lin, Otae Mofo. **VHS, Beta** $57.95 *UNI* ⅃

1860 During the Battle of Calatafimi in May of 1860, Sicilian peasants revolted against the King of Naples' army. The story focuses on four people caught up in the fighting: the spouse of a revolutionary, a foppish intellectual, a rebel priest, and the young shepherd who is sent with a message to Genoa asking for assistance. Blasetti made great use of location filming and natural light. In Italian with English subtitles.
1933 72m/C *IT* *D:* Alexandro Blasetti. **VHS** $29.95 *FCT, TAM* ⅃⅃

The Eighties A comic, pseudo-documentary romp through the making of a musical. Not just another dime-a-dozen song-and-dance flick, but plays with the genre with humor and intelligence, treating us to an insider's view of a performance arranged at a shopping plaza, from the rigorous auditions to the tedium of the production of songs and routines. Treated in a light-hearted, sensitive, just on the verge of laughable manner, it concludes with 30 minutes of song and dance. In French with English subtitles.
1983 86m/C *FR* Aurore Clement, Lio, Magali Noel, Pascale Salkin; *D:* Chantal Akerman; *W:* Chantal Akerman, Jean Gruault. **VHS** $79.95 *WAC, FCT, TAM* ⅃⅃½

84 Charing Cross Road A lonely woman in New York and a book-seller in London begin corresponding for business reasons. Over a twenty-year period, their relationship grows into a friendship, and then a romance, though they communicate only by mail. Based on a true story.
1986 (PG) 100m/C Anne Bancroft, Anthony Hopkins, Judi Dench; *D:* David Jones. **VHS, Beta, LV** $19.95 *COL, TVC, HMV* ⅃⅃⅃

84 Charlie Mopic A widely acclaimed drama about the horrors of Vietnam seen through the eyes of a cameraman assigned to a special front-line unit. Filled with a cast of unknowns, this is an unsettling film that sheds new light on the subject of the Vietnam war. Powerful and energetic; music by Donovan.
1989 (R) 89m/C Richard Brooks, Christopher Burgard, Nicholas Cascone, Jonathon Emerson, Glen Morshower, Jason Tomlins, Byron Thames; **D:** Patrick Duncan. **VHS, Beta, LV $89.95** COL *ÆÆÆ*

Eijanaika A gripping story of a poor Japanese man who returns to his country after a visit to America in the 1860s. Memorable performances make this an above-average film. In Japanese with English subtitles. **AKA:** Why Not?.
1981 151m/C JP Ken Ogata, Shigeru Izumiya; **D:** Shohei Imamura. **VHS, LV $79.95** KIV, FCT, TAM *ÆÆÆ½*

El Bunuel's psychological study of romantic obsession. A wealthy, middle-aged man meets and marries a young woman and develops a paranoid obsession with her supposed infidelities—even to the point of violence. In Spanish with English subtitles. **AKA:** El, This Strange Passion Torments.
1955 100m/C Arturo de Cordova, Delia Garces; **D:** Luis Bunuel. **VHS $59.95** FCT, TAM *ÆÆÆ*

El Ametralladora A retired general tussles with a man known as "The Machine Gun."
1965 90m/C MX Pedro Infante, Margarita Mora, Alfredo Varela. **VHS, Beta $44.95** MAD *ÆÆ*

El Amor Brujo An adaptation of the work of Miguel de Falla, in which flamenco dancers enact the story of a tragic romance.
1986 100m/C Antonio Gades, Christina Hoyos, Laura Del Sol; **D:** Carlos Savrat. **VHS, Beta, LV $29.95** PAV, CTH, FCT *ÆÆÆ*

El Aviador Fenomeno A private eye goes undercover to investigate several murders.
1947 90m/B MX Adalberto "Resortes" Martinez, Maria Eugenia San Martin, David Silva, Pedro de Aguillon. **VHS, Beta $39.95** MAD, PM5 *ÆÆ*

El Aviso Inoportuno Two men journey to Mexico City to become actors, but are unable to find jobs in their chosen field.
1987 121m/C MX Enrique Cuenca, Eduardo Manzano, Carlos Lopez Moctezuma. **VHS, Beta $57.95** MAD *ÆÆ*

El Barbaro In the beginning of civilization, when evil powers rule, a barbarian has two ambitions in life: to seek revenge for his friend's death and to rescue the world from a sorcerer's power.
1984 88m/C SP Andrea Occhipinti, Maria Scola, Violeta Cela, Sabrina Sellers. **VHS, Beta** MED *Æ*

El Bruto A mid-Mexican-period Bunuel drama, about a brainless thug who is used as a bullying pawn in a struggle between a brutal landlord and discontented tenants. In Spanish with English titles. **AKA:** The Brute.
1952 83m/B MX Pedro Armendariz Sr., Katy Jurado, Andres Soler, Rosita Arenas; **D:** Luis Bunuel. **VHS, Beta $59.95** TAM, FCT, APD *ÆÆ½*

El Callao A Puerto Rican gang in New York City searches for their former leader. When they mistakenly kill a priest who looks like him, trouble begins. **AKA:** The Silent One.
1977 90m/C Jose Albar, Olga Agostini. **VHS, Beta** NO *Æ½*

El Ceniciento An innocent man gets into trouble because he can't stop thinking about a beautiful princess.

1947 90m/B MX Tin Tan, Alicia Caro, Andres Soler. **VHS, Beta $48.95** MAD *ÆÆ*

El Ciclon An invincible lawman comes to town, looking to clean things up.
1947 120m/B MX Miguel Aceves Mejia, Flor Silvestre, Sonia Furio, Raul Ramirez. **VHS, Beta $45.95** MAD *ÆÆ*

El Cid Charts the life of Rodrigo Diaz de Bivar, known as El Cid, who was the legendary eleventh-century Christian hero who freed Spain from Moorish invaders. Music by Miklos Roza. Noted for its insanely lavish budget, this epic tale is true to its setting and features elaborate battle scenes.
1961 184m/C Charlton Heston, Sophia Loren, Raf Vallone, Hurd Hatfield, Genevieve Page; **D:** Anthony Mann. **VHS, Beta, LV $29.95** BFV, UHV, FCT *ÆÆÆ*

El Cochecito The great Spanish actor, Jose Isbert, stars as the head of a large family whose closest friends are all joined together in a kind of fraternity defined by the fact that they each use a wheelchair. He feels excluded because he does not have or need one, so he goes to great lengths to gain acceptance in this "brotherhood." In Spanish with English subtitles. **AKA:** The Wheelchair.
1960 90m/B SP Jose Isbert; **D:** Marco Ferreri. **VHS, Beta $69.95** KIV *ÆÆÆ*

El Condor Two drifters search for gold buried in a Mexican fort.
1970 (R) 102m/C SP Jim Brown, Lee Van Cleef, Patrick O'Neal, Marianna Hill, Iron Eyes Cody, Elisha Cook Jr.; **D:** John Guillermin. **VHS $59.95** WAR, SIM *Æ½*

El Cristo de los Milagros After a ruthless thief has a vision of Christ, he changes his criminal ways. In Spanish.
198? 90m/C SP Juan Gallardo, Norma Lazarendo, Claudio Lanuza, Julio Cesar. **VHS, Beta $74.95** MAD *Æ*

El Cuarto Chino A madman terrorizes the ports of Acapulco, Mexico. **AKA:** The Chinese Room.
1971 97m/C MX Cathy Crosby, Guillermo Murray, Carlos Rivas, Regina Torne. **VHS, Beta $69.95** MAD *Æ*

El Derecho de Comer A good natured vagrant finds a purse filled with money and a love letter. **AKA:** The Right to Eat.
1987 86m/C MX Arturo Correa, Findingo, Lissette, Luis Cosme. **VHS, Beta $54.95** MAD *ÆÆ½*

El Diablo A young man finds the West more wild than he expected. He finds "help" in the shape of Gossett as he tries to free a young girl who's being held by the notorious El Diablo. Made for television. Better than average.
1990 (PG-13) 107m/C Louis Gossett Jr., Anthony Edwards, John Glover, Robert Beltran; **D:** Peter Markle. **VHS $89.99** HBO *ÆÆ½*

El Diablo Rides A fierce feud between cattlemen and sheepmen develops, with touches of comedy in between.
1939 57m/B Bob Steele, Carleton Young, Kit Guard. **VHS, Beta $19.95** VDM, VCN, VYY *Æ½*

El Diputado A famous politician jeopardizes his career when he has an affair with a young man. In Spanish. Also available with English subtitles. **AKA:** The Deputy.
1978 111m/C SP Jose Sacristan, Maria Luisa San Jose, Jose Alonso; **D:** Eloy De La Iglesia. **VHS, Beta $79.95** FCT *ÆÆ½*

El Dorado A gunfighter rides into the frontier town of El Dorado to aid a reckless cattle baron in his war with farmers over land rights. Once in town, the hired gun meets up with an old friend—the sheriff—who also happens to be the town drunkard. Switching

allegiances, the gunslinger helps the lawman sober up and defend the farmers. This Hawks western displays a number of similarities to the director's earlier "Rio Bravo" (1959), starring Wayne, Dean Martin, and Ricky Nelson—who charms viewers as the young sidekick "Colorado" much like Caan does as "Mississippi" in El Dorado.
1967 126m/C John Wayne, Robert Mitchum, James Caan, Charlene Holt, Ed Asner, Arthur Hunnicutt, Christopher George, R.G. Armstrong, Jim Davis, Paul Fix, Johnny Crawford, Michele Carey; **D:** Howard Hawks. **VHS, Beta, LV $14.95** PAR, TLF *ÆÆÆ*

El Fego Baca: Six-Gun Law An Arizona DA tackles a seemingly clear-cut murder case. Compiled from Walt Disney television episodes.
1962 77m/C Robert Loggia, James Dunn, Lynn Bari, Annette Funicello. **VHS, Beta $69.95** DIS *Æ½*

El Fin del Tahur An unwed mother falls in love with a gambler who must face a crooked rival.
1987 90m/C MX Luciana, Jaime Moreno, Mario Almada, Gloriella Ruben Benavides. **VHS, Beta $59.95** MAD *ÆÆ*

El Forastero Vengador A man arrives in town and challenges an evil woman dictator.
1965 95m/C MX Jaime Fernandez, Eleazar Garcia Chelelo, Ofelia Guillman. **VHS, Beta $39.95** MAD *ÆÆ*

El Fugitivo A man convicted of a crime he didn't commit waits for the right moment to exact his revenge.
1965 95m/C MX Luis Aguilar, Lucha Villa, Amparo Rivelles, Rita Macedo. **VHS, Beta $58.95** MAD *ÆÆ*

El Gallo de Oro Two rival gamblers bet everything on a big cockfight in Mexico. This film examines the story behind the cockfights and what they mean in Mexican tradition. **AKA:** The Golden Rooster.
1965 94m/C MX Ignacio Lopez Tarso, Lucha Villa, Narciso Busquets. **VHS, Beta $68.00** MAD, APD *ÆÆ*

El Gavilan Pollero A singing man in the West enthralls many a beautiful lady in this western. Packed full with gambling, horse racing, music, and women.
1947 90m/B MX Pedro Infante, Antonio Badu, Lilia Prado. **VHS, Beta $44.95** MAD *ÆÆ*

El Gendarme Desconocido Cantiflas bungles his way into becoming a police officer after accidentally apprehending a gang of criminals in this bumble-filled comedy.
1941 110m/B MX Cantinflas, Mapita Cortes, Gloria Marin, Daniel "Chino" Herrera, Carlos Lopez Moctezuma; **D:** Miguel M. Delgado. **VHS, Beta** NO *ÆÆ*

El Hombre Contra el Mundo A Mexican comic-book hero comes to life so he can battle a variety of evils.
1987 100m/C MX Jorge Rivero, Nadia Milton, Narciso Busquets, Tito Junco. **VHS, Beta $75.95** MAD *ÆÆ½*

El Hombre de la Furia The son of a rancher seeks to avenge his father's death. **AKA:** Man of Fury.
1965 90m/B MX Javier Solis, Dacia Gonzales, Fernando Soto. **VHS, Beta $49.95** MAD *ÆÆ½*

El Libro de Piedra An isolated ranch harbors dark, horrible secrets. There's no telling what could be causing such strange occurrences.
1968 100m/C MX Margo Lopez, Joaquin Cordero; **D:** Carlos Enrique Taboada. **VHS, Beta $59.95** UNI *Æ*

El Mariachi Extremely low-budget but clever mixture of humor and violence in a tale of mistaken identity set in a small Mexican border town. "El Mariachi" is a musician, carrying a guitar case, who wonders why everyone seems to be trying to kill him. He learns a notorious gunslinger, who hides his weapons in a similar case, has escaped from the local jail and wants revenge on the drug dealer who did him wrong. 24-year-old director Rodriguez makes his feature film debut with this $7000 feature, originally intended only for the Spanish-language market. Film festival awards and critical attention brought the work to wider release. In Spanish with English subtitles.
1993 (R) 84m/C MX Carlos Gallardo, Reinol Martinez, Consuelo Gomez, Peter Marquardt; D: Robert Rodriguez; W: Carlos Gallardo, Robert Rodriguez. VHS *NYR* 🎞🎞🎞

El Monte de las Brujas A mad widow burns her daughter alive in a satanistic ritual. In Spanish.
197? 90m/C Patty Shepard. VHS, Beta $57.95 *UNI* 🎞

El Muerto In 19th-century Buenos Aires, a young man flees his home after killing an enemy. Arriving in Montevideo, he becomes a member of a smuggling ring. In Spanish with English subtitles.
1975 103m/C SP Thelma Biral, Juan Jose Camero, Francisco Rabal; D: Hector Olivera. VHS, Beta $24.98 *TAM, MED* 🎞½

El Norte Gripping account of a Guatemalan brother and sister, persecuted in their homeland, who make an arduous journey north ("El Norte") to America. Their difficult saga continues as they struggle against overwhelming odds in an attempt to realize their dreams. Passionate, sobering, and powerful. In English and Spanish with English subtitles. Produced in association with the "American Playhouse" series for PBS. Produced by Anna Thomas who also co-wrote the story with Nava.
1983 (R) 139m/C SP David Villalpando, Zaide Silvia Gutierrez, Ernesto Cruz, Eracio Zepeda, Stella Quan; D: Gregory Nava. VHS, Beta $68.00 *FOX, APD* 🎞🎞🎞🎞

El Paso Stampede Cowboy investigates raids on cattle herds used to feed Americans fighting in the Spanish-American War.
1953 50m/B Allan "Rocky" Lane, Eddy Waller, Phyllis Coates; D: Harry Keller. VHS, Beta $29.95 *VCN* 🎞½

El Penon de las Animas Spanish film features a classic premise—two long-feuding families find complications as their bitter relationship as their children fall in love with one another.
1947 90m/B MX Maria Felix, George Negrete. VHS, Beta $44.95 *MAD* 🎞

El Preprimido A newlywed travels to France to learn about sex before approaching his bride. Upon arrival, however, he finds the prostitutes are on strike. AKA: The Timid Bachelor.
197? 101m/C SP Alfredo Landa, Isabel Garces. VHS, Beta *NO* 🎞

El Profesor Hippie A freewheeling college history professor befriends a group of students, taking them to a far-off part of the country where adventures befall them. In Spanish.
1969 95m/C MX Luis Sandrini, Soledad Silveyra; D: Fernando Ayala. VHS, Beta $29.95 *MED* 🎞🎞

El Rey The story of "The King," a rebel during the Mexican Revolution.
1987 93m/C MX Antonio Aguilar, Carmen Montejo, Pancho Cordova, Gerardo Reyes. VHS, Beta $58.95 *MAD* 🎞🎞

El Robo al Tren Correo A young man must confront a ruthless band of outlaws to prove that he didn't steal a gold shipment.
1947 90m/B MX Carlos Cortez, Noe Murayama, Julissa. VHS, Beta $39.95 *MAD* 🎞🎞

El Sabor de la Venganza A man's wife and son vow to avenge his murder.
1965 92m/C MX Isela Vega, Jorge Luke, Cameron Mitchell, Mario Almada. VHS, Beta $59.95 *MAD* 🎞🎞

El Super A Cuban refugee, still homesick after many years, struggles to make a life for himself in Manhattan as an apartment superintendent. In Spanish with English subtitles; an American production shot on location in New York City.
1979 90m/C SP Raymundo Hidalgo-Gato, Orlando Jiminez-Leal, Zully Montero, Raynaldo Medina, Juan Granda, Hilda Lee, Elizabeth Pena; D: Leon Ichaso. VHS *APD, TAM, NYF* 🎞🎞🎞

El Tesoro de Chucho el Roto A widow with half of a treasure map must fend off thieves while she searches for the other half.
1947 90m/B MX Joaquin Cordero, Ana Berta Lepe, Manuel Lopez Ochoa. VHS, Beta $44.95 *MAD* 🎞🎞

El: This Strange Passion Disturbing drama in which a man, convinced he is cuckolded, slowly descends into madness. Bunuel's surreal, almost Freudian look at the Spanish male's obsession with female fidelity. In Spanish with English subtitles.
1952 82m/B SP Arturo de Cordova, Delia Garces, Luis Beristain, Aurora Walker; D: Luis Bunuel. VHS $59.95 *HTV, FCT* 🎞🎞🎞

El Zorro Blanco A man in a white mask rescues a kidnapped heiress.
1987 90m/C MX Juan Miranda, Hilda Aguirre, Carlos Agosti. VHS, Beta $59.95 *MAD* 🎞🎞

El Zorro Vengador Zorro's best friend is killed and his bride abducted. And, you better believe he's going to make those baddies pay.
1947 90m/B MX Luis Aguilar, Maria Eugenia San Martin. VHS, Beta $39.95 *MAD* 🎞🎞

Eleanor & Franklin An exceptional television dramatization of the personal lives of President Franklin D. Roosevelt and his wife Eleanor. Based on Joseph Lash's book, this Emmy award-winning film features stunning performances by Alexander and Herrmann in the title roles.
1976 208m/C Jane Alexander, Edward Herrmann, Ed Flanders, Rosemary Murphy, MacKenzie Phillips, Pamela Franklin, Anna Lee, Linda Purl, Linda Kelsey, Lindsay Crouse; D: Daniel Petrie; M: John Barry. VHS, Beta $59.95 *SIG, TLF* 🎞🎞🎞½

Eleanor: First Lady of the World Stapleton plays the former first lady after her husband's death as she goes on to work at the United Nations and emerges as even more of an influential public figure. Made for television.
1982 104m/C Jean Stapleton, E.G. Marshall, Coral Browne, Joyce Van Patten, Gail Strickland, Kenneth Kimmins; D: John Erman. VHS $59.95 *COL* 🎞🎞½

Electra Glide in Blue An Arizona motorcycle cop uses his head in a world that's coming apart at the seams. Good action scenes; lots of violence.
1973 (R) 113m/C Robert (Bobby) Blake, Billy Green Bush, Mitchell Ryan, Jeannine Riley, Elisha Cook Jr., Royal Dano; D: James W. Guercio. VHS, LV $14.95 *MGM* 🎞🎞🎞

Electric Dreams A young man buys a computer that yearns to do more than sit on a desk. First it takes over his apartment, then it sets its sights on the man's cello-playing neighbor—the same woman his owner is courting. To win her affections, the over-eager computer tries to dazzle her with a variety of musical compositions from his unique keyboard. Cort supplies the voice of Edgar the computer in this film that integrates a rock-music video format.
1984 (PG) 95m/C Lenny Von Dohlen, Virginia Madsen, Maxwell Caulfield, Bud Cort, Koo Stark; D: Steven Barron. VHS, Beta, LV $79.95 *MGM* 🎞🎞½

The Electric Horseman Journalist Fonda sets out to discover the reason behind the kidnapping of a prized horse by an ex-rodeo star. The alcoholic cowboy has taken the horse to return it to its native environment, away from the clutches of corporate greed. As Fonda investigates the story she falls in love with rebel Redford. Excellent Las Vegas and remote western settings.
1979 (PG) 120m/C Robert Redford, Jane Fonda, John Saxon, Willie Nelson, Valerie Perrine, Wilford Brimley, Nicholas Coster; D: Sydney Pollack. VHS, Beta, LV $19.95 *MCA* 🎞🎞½

The Electronic Monster Insurance claims investigator Cameron looks into the death of a Hollywood starlet and discovers an exclusive therapy center dedicated to hypnotism. At the facility, people vacation for weeks in morgue-like body drawers, while evil Dr. Illing uses an electronic device to control the sleeper's dreams and actions. Eerie. Intriguingly, it is one of the first films to explore the possibilities of brainwashing and mind control. AKA: Escapement; The Electric Monster.
1957 72m/B GB Rod Cameron, Mary Murphy, Meredith Edwards, Peter Illing; D: Montgomery Tully. VHS $16.95 *SNC* 🎞🎞

The Elegant Criminal Based on the true story of France's most infamous killer, Pierre Lacenaire. The film begins with Lacenaire in prison, writing his memoirs, receiving his admirers, and awaiting his execution (in 1836). A series of flashbacks detail his life and the supposed social clime which hindered his better instincts and turned him to the criminal life. However, Auteuil has such a wonderful time playing the charming bad guy that any blame to society fails to convince. In French with English subtitles.
1992 120m/C FR Daniel Auteuil, Jean Poiret, Jacques Weber, Marie-Armelle DeGuy, Maiwenn Le Besco, Patrick Pineau; W/D: Francis Girod; W: George Conchon. VHS $89.95 *FXL, BTV, FCT* 🎞🎞🎞½

The Element of Crime In a monochromatic, post-holocaust future, a detective tracks down a serial killer of young girls. Made in Denmark, this minor festival favorite features an impressive directional debut and awaits cult status. Filmed in Sepiatone. AKA: Forbrydelsens Element.
1985 104m/C DK Michael Elphick, Esmond Knight, Jerold Wells, Meme Lei, Astrid Henning-Jensen, Preben Leerdorff-Rye, Gotha Andersen; D: Lars von Trier. VHS, Beta $79.95 *UNI, TAM* 🎞🎞½

Elena and Her Men The romantic entanglements and intrigues of a poor Polish princess are explored in this enjoyable French film. Beautiful cinematography by Claude Renoir. In French with subtitles. AKA: Paris Does Strange Things; Elena et les Hommes.

E

1956 98m/C *FR* Ingrid Bergman, Jean Marais, Mel Ferrer, Jean Richard, Magali Noel, Pierre Bertin, Juliette Greco; *D:* Jean Renoir. **VHS, Beta, LV** $59.95 *INT, FCT, TAM* 🐾🐾🐾

Eleni The true story of "New York Times" reporter Nicholas Gage and his journey to Athens to discover the truth about his mother's execution by Communists during the Greek rebellion after World War II. Adapted by Steve Tesich from Gage's bestselling book.
1985 (PG) 117m/C John Malkovich, Kate Nelligan, Linda Hunt, Oliver Cotton, Ronald Pickup, Dimitra Arliss, Rosalie Crutchley; *D:* Peter Yates. **VHS, Beta, LV, 8mm** $14.98 *COL, IGP, TAM* 🐾🐾

Elephant Boy An Indian boy helps government conservationists locate a herd of elephants in the jungle. Sabu's first film. Available in digitally remastered stereo.
1937 80m/B *GB* Sabu, Walter Hudd, W.E. Holloway; *D:* Robert Flaherty, Zoltan Korda. **VHS, Beta, LV** $19.98 *HBO, SUE* 🐾🐾🐾

The Elephant Man A biography of John Merrick, a severely deformed man who, with the help of a sympathetic doctor, moved from freak shows into posh London society. Lynch's first mainstream film, shot in black and white, it presents a startlingly vivid picture of the hypocrisies evident in the social moves of the Victorian era. Moving performance from Hurt in title role.
1980 (PG) 125m/B Anthony Hopkins, John Hurt, Anne Bancroft, John Gielgud, Wendy Hiller, Freddie Jones, Kenny Baker; *D:* David Lynch. Academy Awards '80 Nominations: Best Actor (Hurt), Best Art Direction/Set Decoration, Best Costume Design, Best Director (Lynch), Best Film Editing, Best Picture, Best Original Score; British Academy Awards '80: Best Actor (Hurt), Best Film; Cesar Awards '82: Best Foreign Film; National Board of Review Awards '80: 10 Best Films of the Year. **VHS, Beta, LV** $14.95 *PAR* 🐾🐾🐾🐾

Elephant Walk The balmy jungles of Sri Lanka provide the backdrop for a torrid triangular story of love on an agricultural estate in this post-prime Dieterle effort. Taylor, ignored by her wealthy drunkard husband, finds solace in the arms of her spouse's sexy right-hand man. As if keeping the affair secret weren't elephantine task enough, Taylor braves an epidemic of cholera and a pack of vengeful elephants who decide to take an unscheduled tour of her humble home. The lethargic performances of the lead characters make this more of a sleep walk, but Sofaer and Biberman's supporting appearances are worth the price of rental. Taylor replaced Vivian Leigh in the early stages of filming after Leigh fell ill, but the final production includes footage of Leigh in faraway shots.
1954 103m/C Elizabeth Taylor, Dana Andrews, Peter Finch, Abraham Sofaer, Abner Biberman; *D:* William Dieterle. **VHS** $14.95 *PAR, FCT* 🐾🐾½

11 Harrowhouse The Consolidated Selling System at 11 Harrowhouse, London, controls much of the world's diamond trade. Four adventurous thieves plot a daring heist relying on a very clever cockroach. A rather successful stab at spoofing detailed "heist" films. *AKA:* Anything for Love; Fast Fortune.
1974 (PG) 95m/C *GB* Charles Grodin, Candice Bergen, James Mason, Trevor Howard, John Gielgud; *D:* Aram Avakian. **VHS, Beta** $59.98 *FOX* 🐾🐾🐾

Eli Eli An American Yiddish film about a family forced to live apart because of their farm's failure. Lighthearted and fun, with songs by Sholom Secunda. In Yiddish with English titles.

1940 85m/B Esther Feild, Lazar Fried, Muni Serebroff; *D:* Joseph Seiden. **VHS, Beta** $39.95 *FCT, AUD* 🐾🐾½

The Eliminators A cyborgian creature endeavors to avenge himself on his evil scientist creator with help from a kung fu expert and a Mexican. The group uses time travel and other devices to achieve their mission.
1986 (PG) 95m/C Roy Dotrice, Patrick Reynolds, Denise Crosby, Andrew Prine, Conan Lee; *D:* Peter Manoogian. **VHS, Beta** $79.98 *FOX* 🐾

Elizabeth of Ladymead Four generations of a British family live through their experiences in the Crimean War, Boer War, World War I, and World War II. Neagle, playing the wives in all four generations, aptly explores the woman's side of war. Enjoyable performances from husband and wife team Neagle and Wilcox.
1948 97m/C Anna Neagle, Hugh Williams, Bernard Lee, Michael Lawrence, Nicholas Phipps, Isabel Jeans; *D:* Herbert Wilcox. **VHS, Beta** $24.95 *DVT, TIM, VEC* 🐾🐾🐾

Elizabeth, the Queen Historical drama recreates the struggle for power by Robert Devereaux, Earl of Essex, whom the aging Queen Elizabeth I both loved and feared, and whose downfall she finally invoked. Part of "George Schaefer's Showcase Theatre." *AKA:* The Private Lives of Elizabeth and Essex.
1968 76m/C Judith Anderson, Charlton Heston; *D:* George Schaefer. **VHS, Beta** *FHS* 🐾🐾

Eliza's Horoscope A frail Canadian woman uses astrology in her search for love in Montreal, and experiences bizarre and surreal events. An acclaimed Canadian film.
1970 120m/C *CA* Tommy Lee Jones, Elizabeth Moorman; *D:* Gordon Sheppard. **VHS, Beta** $24.95 *AHV* 🐾🐾½

Ella Cinders The American mania for breaking into the movies is satirized in this look at a girl who wins a trip to Hollywood in a small-town beauty contest. Silent with original organ score.
1926 60m/B Colleen Moore, Harry Langdon, Lloyd Hughes, Jed Prouty, Vera Lewis; *D:* Alfred E. Green. **VHS, Beta** $19.95 *NOS, FST, TIM* 🐾🐾½

Elle Voit des Nains Partout A film of France's "Cafe Theatre Show," wherein various fairy tale characters' stories are revised per modern situations. In French with subtitles.
1983 83m/C *FR* *D:* Jean-Claude Sussfeld. **VHS, Beta** $59.95 *FCT* 🐾🐾½

Ellie A murderous widow's stepdaughter tries to save her father from being added to the woman's extensive list of dearly departed husbands.
1984 (R) 90m/C Shelley Winters, Sheila Kennedy, Pat Paulsen, George Gobel, Edward Albert; *D:* Peter Wittman. **VHS, Beta** $79.98 *LIV, VES* 🐾🐾

Elmer Follows the adventures of a temporarily blinded youth and a lovable hound dog who meet in the wilderness and together set off in search of civilization.
1976 (G) 82m/C Elmer Swanson, Phillip Swanson; *D:* Christopher Cain. **VHS, Beta** $59.98 *LIV* 🐾½

Elmer Fudd Cartoon Festival Fussy Elmer Fudd gets little respect and more than his share of torment from "wascals." Includes "An Itch in Time," "Hardship of Miles Standish," "Elmer's Pet Rabbit," and "Back-Alley Operator." Made between 1940 and 1947.
194? 33m/C *D:* Chuck Jones, Robert McKimson, Friz Freleng. **VHS, Beta** $14.95 *MGM* 🐾½

Elmer Fudd's Comedy Capers Eight classic Fudd cartoons, including "Hare Brush," "The Rabbit of Seville," and "What's Opera, Doc?" The latter short finds Fudd crooning "Kill the Wabbit" to the tune of Wagner's popular composition "Die Valkyrie," while "Seville" features the memorable Bugs the Barber using his toes to lather up Fudd's head.
1955 57m/C *D:* Chuck Jones, Robert McKimson, Friz Freleng. **VHS, Beta** $12.95 *WAR, WTA* 🐾½

Elmer Gantry The classic multi-Oscar-winning adaptation of the Sinclair Lewis novel written to expose and denounce the flamboyant, small-town evangelists spreading through America at the time. In the film, Lancaster is the amoral Southern preacher who exacts wealth and power from his congregation, and takes a nun as a mistress. Jones stars as his ex-girlfriend who resorts to a life of prostitution.
1960 146m/C Burt Lancaster, Shirley Jones, Jean Simmons, Dean Jagger, Arthur Kennedy, Patti Page, Edward Andrews, John McIntire, Hugh Marlowe, Rex Ingram; *D:* Richard Brooks. Academy Awards '60: Best Actor (Lancaster), Best Adapted Screenplay, Best Supporting Actress (Jones); Nominations: Best Picture, Best Original Score; National Board of Review Awards '60: 10 Best Films of the Year, Best Supporting Actress (Jones). **VHS, Beta, LV** $19.98 *FOX, MGM, PIA* 🐾🐾🐾½

Elsa, Elsa Satire of moviemaking life finds a scriptwriter-director distracted by the loss of his girlfriend and unable to concentrate on writing a memoir of his career as a child actor. He creates a subplot dealing with his romantic problems, and puts the film in jeopardy. Fine acting and witty dialogue. In French with English subtitles.
1985 85m/C *FR* *D:* Didier Haudepin. **VHS** $49.95 *FCT* 🐾🐾🐾

Elusive Corporal Set in a P.O.W. camp on the day France surrendered to Germany, this is the story of the French and Germans, complete with memories of a France that is no more. *AKA:* Le Caporal Epingle.
1962 108m/B Jean-Pierre Cassel, Claude Brasseur, O.E. Hasse, Claude Rich; *D:* Jean Renoir. **VHS, Beta, LV** $59.95 *INT, VYY, APD* 🐾🐾🐾½

The Elusive Pimpernel Niven sparkles in this otherwise undistinguished adaptation of Baroness Orczy's "The Scarlet Pimpernel." *AKA:* The Fighting Pimpernel.
1950 109m/C *GB* David Niven, Margaret Leighton, Jack Hawkins, Cyril Cusack, Robert Coote, Edmund Audran, Danielle Godet, Patrick Macnee; *W/D:* Michael Powell, Emeric Pressburger. **VHS, Beta** $59.95 *HMV, FCT* 🐾🐾½

Elves A group of possessed, neo-Nazi elves performs serious human harm at Christmas time in this tongue-in-check thriller.
1989 (PG-13) 95m/C Dan Haggerty, Deanna Lund, Julie Austin, Borah Silver; *D:* Jeffrey Mandel. **VHS, Beta** $79.95 *AIP* 🐾

Elvira Madigan Chronicles the 19th-century Swedish romance between a young officer and a beautiful circus tight-rope walker. Based on a true incident. Exceptional direction and photography.
1967 (PG) 89m/C *SW* Pia Degermark, Thommy Berggren; *D:* Bo Widerberg. **VHS, Beta, LV** $34.95 *HBO* 🐾🐾🐾

Elvira, Mistress of the Dark A manic comedy based on Peterson's infamous B-movie horror-hostess character. The mega-busted terror-queen inherits a house in a conservative Massachusetts town and causes double-entendre chaos when she attempts to sell it.

1988 (PG-13) 96m/C Cassandra Peterson, Jeff Conaway, Susan Kellerman, Edie McClurg, Daniel Greene, W. Morgan Shepherd; **D:** James Signorelli. **VHS, Beta, LV** $19.95 STE, NWV *ZZ*

Elvis and Me A TV mini series based on Priscilla Beaulieu Presley's autobiography about her life with the Pelvis. Features many of Presley's biggest hits, sung by country star Ronnie McDowell. Film may aggravate Elvis fans, however, as the King is often depicted negatively from his ex-wife's point of view.
1988 187m/C Dale Midkiff, Susan Walters, Billy Green Bush, Linda Miller, Jon Cypher; **D:** Larry Peerce. **VHS, Beta** $29.95 STE, NWV *ZZ* ½

The Elvis Files Documentary examining the strange details surrounding Elvis's death. Contains some rare footage and interviews in support of Brewer's theory that Elvis's death was faked.
1990 55m/C **VHS** $19.98 MED, TTC *Z* ½

Elvis in the Movies All of the King's movies are covered, complete with scenes and highlights from each. A must for Elvis fans. A must for Elvis impersonators. A must for average Elvis look-alikes. Essentially, a must for fans of all types and ages.
1990 ?m/C Elvis Presley. **VHS** COL *Z* ½

Elvis Memories A video scrapbook of Elvis' career, including concert appearances, home movies, and contemporary interviews.
1985 48m/C Elvis Presley, Priscilla Presley, Cybill Shepherd, Dick Clark. **VHS, Beta, LV** $29.95 MVD, LIV, VES *Z* ½

Elvis on Tour A revealing glimpse of Elvis Presley, onstage and off, during a whirlwind concert tour.
1972 93m/C Elvis Presley; **D:** Pierre Adidge, Robert Abel. **VHS, Beta, LV** $19.95 MGM *Z* ½

Elvis: One Night with You The celebrated crooner performs such memorables as "Heartbreak Hotel," "Blue Suede Shoes," and "Are You Lonesome Tonight" in this unedited performance from his 1968 Christmas Special.
1968 53m/C Elvis Presley. **VHS, Beta, LV** $19.95 MVD, MED, VTK *Z* ½

Elvis Presley's Graceland Elvis' ex-wife (Priscilla Beaulieu Presley) takes the viewer on a tour of Graceland, the famous Memphis, Tennessee, mansion, which was home to the rock star from 1957 until his death in 1977.
1984 60m/C **VHS, Beta** $19.95 NEG, KAR *Z* ½

Elvis: Rare Moments with the King Footage of Elvis from news conferences, his wedding and media newsreels.
1990 60m/B Elvis Presley. **VHS, Beta** $12.95 MVD, GKK *Z* ½

Elvis Stories Collection of humorous shorts dealing with the King, from Mojo Nixon's song "Elvis Is Everywhere" to Cusack as a burger maker who claims to receive messages from Elvis through his patties.
1989 30m/C John Cusack, Ben Stiller, Joel Murray, Mojo Nixon, Rick Saucedo. **VHS, Beta** $14.95 RHI *Z* ½

Elvis: The Echo Will Never Die Celebrities chat about the King and how much they miss him, recounting anecdotes about his rise to fame.
1986 50m/C Tom Jones, B.B. King, Sammy Davis Jr., Casey Kasem, Ursula Andress. **VHS, Beta, 3/4U** $29.95 IHF, MVD, MPI *Z* ½

Elvis: The Lost Performances A video collection of live performances and rehearsal footage that was discovered in MGM's underground vaults in 1986. Includes

outtakes from "Elvis: That's the Way It Is" and "Elvis on Tour." A must for fans and collectors of Elvis memorabilia.
1992 60m/C Elvis Presley. **VHS, LV** $19.98 WAR *Z* ½

Elvis: The Movie A made-for-television biography of the legendary singer, from his high school days to his Las Vegas comeback. Russell gives a convincing performance and lip syncs effectively to the voice of the King (provided by country singer Ronnie McDowell). Also available in 150-minute version.
1979 117m/C Kurt Russell, Season Hubley, Shelley Winters, Ed Begley Jr., Dennis Christopher, Pat Hingle, Bing Russell, Joe Mantegna; **D:** John Carpenter. **VHS, Beta** $69.98 LIV, VES *ZZ* ½

Emanon A coming-of-age tale about a young kid and the Christ-like vagabond, named Emanon (or "no name" if spelled in reverse), he befriends.
1986 (PG-13) 101m/C Stuart Paul, Cheryl Lynn, Jeremy Miller; **D:** Stuart Paul. **VHS, Beta** $19.98 NLC *Z* ½

Embassy In this mediocre espionage thriller, von Sydow is a Soviet defector under asylum at the U.S. embassy in Beirut. Colonel Connors, a Russian spy, penetrates embassy security and wounds von Sydow. He is caught, escapes, is captured, escapes, and is caught again. Great cast, but script is often too wordy and contrived. **AKA:** Target: Embassy.
1972 90m/C GB Richard Roundtree, Chuck Connors, Max von Sydow, Ray Milland, Broderick Crawford, Marie-Jose Nat; **D:** Gordon Hessler. **VHS** $79.95 WVE *ZZ*

Embassy A made-for-television movie about an American family in Rome that unknowingly possesses a secret computer chip, and thus is pursued by ruthless agents.
1985 104m/C Nick Mancuso, Blanche Baker, Eli Wallach, Sam Wanamaker, Richard Gilliland, Mimi Rogers, George Grizzard, Richard Masur, Kim Darby; **D:** Robert Lewis. **VHS, Beta** $79.95 WWV *ZZ*

Embryo An average sci-fi drama about a scientist who uses raw genetic material to artificially produce a beautiful woman, with ghastly results. **AKA:** Created to Kill.
1976 (PG) 108m/C Rock Hudson, Barbara Carrera, Diane Ladd, Roddy McDowall, Ann Schedeen, John Elerick, Dr. Joyce Brothers; **D:** Ralph Nelson. **VHS, Beta** $19.95 STE, LIV *ZZ*

The Emerald Forest Captivating adventure about a young boy who is kidnapped by a primitive tribe of Amazons while his family is traveling through the Brazilian jungle. Boothe is the father who searches 10 years for him. An engrossing look at tribal life in the vanishing jungle. Beautifully photographed and based upon a true story. Features the director's son as the kidnapped youth.
1985 (R) 113m/C Powers Boothe, Meg Foster, Charley Boorman, Dira Pass, Rui Polonah; **D:** John Boorman. **VHS, Beta, LV, SVS, 8mm** $14.98 SUE, SUP, NLC *ZZZ*

Emerald Jungle While searching for her missing sister in the jungle, Agren encounters cannibal tribes and a colony of brain-washed cult followers. Originally titled "Eaten Alive by Cannibals," this Italian feature was cut for its U.S. release. **AKA:** Eaten Alive by Cannibals.
1980 92m/C IT Robert Kerman, Janet Agren, Mel Ferrer, Luciano Martino, Mino Loy; **D:** Umberto Lenzi. **VHS, Beta** NO *Z* ½

Emerald of Artama Anyone viewing the most precious and sought after stone in the history of man does not live to tell about it.
1967 93m/C Rory Calhoun. **VHS** NO *Z*

Emergency Scenes from the Living Theatre's works after their return to America from four years of self-imposed exile, including "Frankenstein," "Mysteries," and "Paradise Now."
1968 29m/C Julian Beck, Judith Malina; **D:** Gwen Brown. **VHS, Beta** $29.95 MFV *ZZZ*

Emil and the Detective A German ten-year-old is robbed of his grandmother's money by gangsters, and subsequently enlists the help of pre-adolescent detectives to retrieve it. Good Disney dramatization of the Erich Kastner children's novel. Remake of the 1931 German film starring Rolf Wenkhaus. **AKA:** Emil Und Die Detektive.
1964 99m/C Walter Slezak, Roger Mobley; **D:** Peter Tewkesbury. **VHS, Beta** $69.95 DIS *ZZ* ½

Emiliano Zapata Zapata was a hero of the Mexican Revolution who sacrificed everything because of the high hopes he had for his country.
1987 139m/C MX Antonio Aguilar, Jaime Fernandez, Mario Almada, Patricia Aspillaga. **VHS, Beta** $59.95 MAD *ZZ*

Emilienne An artistic young couple toys with the sexual possibilities that exist outside of, and within, a marriage.
1978 (X) 94m/C **VHS, Beta** $59.95 VID *ZZ*

Emilio Varela vs. Camelia La Texana A pair of criminals encounter trouble when one tries to reform while the other insists on a life of crime.
1987 110m/C MX Maria Almada, Jorge Russek, Silvia Manriquez. **VHS, Beta** $59.95 MAD *ZZ*

Emily Returning from her exclusive Swiss finishing school, licentious young Emily discovers mama is a prostitute and deals with the scalding news by delving into a series of erotic encounters at the hands of her willing "instructors." Stark's first venture into the realm of soft porn.
1977 87m/C Koo Stark; **D:** Henry Herbert. **VHS, Beta** $59.95 MGM Woof!

Eminent Domain A communist party member wakes up to find himself stripped of power in a Kafkaesque purge, not knowing what he is accused of—or why. A potent premise, indifferently handled despite filming on location in Poland. Based on actual events that befell the family of scriptwriter Androej Krakowski.
1991 (PG-13) 102m/C Donald Sutherland, Anne Archer, Paul Freeman, Bernard Hepton, Francoise Michaud, Jodhi May; **D:** John Irvin. **VHS** $39.95 SVS, IME *ZZ* ½

Emissary An American politician and his wife are blackmailed in Africa by the Russians into revealing state secrets that could spark World War III.
1989 (R) 98m/C SA Robert Vaughn, Ted Leplat, Terry Norton, Andre Jacobs; **D:** Jan Scholtz. **VHS, Beta, LV** NO *ZZ*

Emmanuelle Filmed in Bangkok, a young, beautiful woman is introduced by her husband to an uninhibited world of sensuality. Above-average soft-core skin film, made with sophistication and style. Kristel maintains a vulnerability and awareness, never becoming a mannequin.
1974 92m/C FR Sylvia Kristel, Alain Cuny, Marika Green; **D:** Just Jaeckin. **VHS, Beta** $84.95 COL *ZZ* ½

Emmanuelle 4 Emmanuelle flees a bad relationship and undergoes plastic surgery to mask her identity. Ultimately, she becomes a beautiful young model in the form of a different actress, of course.
1984 (R) 95m/C *FR* Sylvia Kristel, Mia Nygren, Patrick Bauchau; *D:* Francis Giacobetti. **VHS, Beta $79.95** *MGM* 💩

Emmanuelle 5 This time around sexy Emmanuelle is abducted from her yacht at the Cannes Film Festival and forced to join an Arab sheik's harem of slaves. A good example of a series that should have quit while it was ahead.
1987 (R) 78m/C *FR* Monique Gabrielle, Charles Foster; *D:* Steve Barnett, Walerian Borowczyk. **VHS $89.98** *NHO* 💩 1/2

Emmanuelle 6 The saga of the sexy beauty continues. This time Emmanuelle and a group of models head for the paradise of an Amazon jungle where they promptly become the prized captives of a drug lord.
1992 (R) 80m/C VHS **$89.98** *NHO* 💩

Emmanuelle & Joanna A mistreated newlywed bride goes to her sister's whorehouse and stumbles across lots of soft-core antics.
1986 90m/C *FR* Sherry Buchanan, Danielle Dublino. **VHS, Beta $29.95** *MED* 💩

Emmanuelle in Bangkok Emanuelle's exotic, erotic experiences in the Far East include a royal masseuse, suspense, and the Asian art of love.
1978 (R) 94m/C *FR* VHS, Beta **$29.98** *VID* 💩

Emmanuelle in Soho Yet another episode of the sleaze-queen's sexual exploits, this time in London's porn-saturated Soho district.
198? (R) 90m/C *FR* VHS, Beta **$59.95** *PSM* 💩

Emmanuelle in the Country Emmanuelle becomes a nurse in an attempt to bring comfort and other pleasures to those in need.
1978 90m/C *FR* Laura Gemser. **VHS, Beta, LV** *IME* 💩

Emmanuelle on Taboo Island Marooned young man discovers a beautiful woman on his island. This delights him.
1976 (R) 95m/C *FR* Laura Gemser, Paul Giusti, Arthur Kennedy. **VHS, Beta** *PGN* 💩 1/2

Emmanuelle, the Joys of a Woman The amorous exploits of a sensuous, liberated couple take them and their erotic companions to exotic Hong Kong, Bangkok, and Bali.
1976 92m/C *FR* Sylvia Kristel, Umberto Orsini, Catherine Rivet, Frederic Lagache; *D:* Francis Giacobetti. **VHS, Beta, LV, 8mm $69.95** *PAR* 💩

Emmanuelle, the Queen Seeking revenge, Emmanuelle plots the murder of her sadistic husband. The lecherous assassin she hires tries to blackmail her, and she challenges him at his own game of deadly seduction.
1975 90m/C Laura Gemser. **VHS, Beta $29.98** *VID* 💩

Emmanuelle's Daughter A Greek-made thriller in which a vapidly sensuous heroine cavorts amid episodes of murder, blackmail, and rape.
1979 91m/C *GR* Laura Gemser, Gabriele Tinti, Livia Russa, Vagelis Varton, Nadia Neri. **Beta** *NO* 💩

Emma's Shadow In the 1930s, a young girl fakes her own kidnapping to get away from her inattentive family and comes to befriend an ex-convict sewer worker. In Danish with English subtitles. Winner of the Prix de la Jeunesse at Cannes, it was voted

1988's Best Danish Film. *AKA:* Skyggen Af Emma.
1988 93m/C *DK* Bjorje Ahistedt, Kruse Line; *D:* Soeren Kragh-Jacobsen. **VHS $79.95** *FXL, FCT, TAM* 💩💩💩

Emperor Caligula: The Untold Story A raunchy look at the famed Roman's bacchanalian sexual excesses.
198? 100m/C David Cain Haughton, Laura Gemser, Oliver Finch. **VHS, Beta $19.98** *TWE, MOV* Woof!

Emperor Jones Loosely based on Eugene O'Neill's play, film portrays the rise and fall of a railroad porter whose exploits take him from a life sentence on a chain gang to emperor of Haiti. Robeson recreates his stage role in his first screen appearance.
1933 72m/B Paul Robeson, Dudley Digges, Frank Wilson, Fredi Washington, Ruby Elzy; *D:* Dudley Murphy. **VHS, Beta, LV, 3/4U, Special order formats $12.95** *SNC, NOS, HHT* 💩💩 1/2

Emperor Jones/Paul Robeson: Tribute to an Artist A classic, rarely viewed version of the Eugene O'Neill play about a criminal who schemes his way into becoming the king of a Caribbean island. Robeson's only true dramatic film appearance. The film is accompanied by a documentary profile of Robeson, made in 1979.
1933 102m/B Paul Robeson, Dudley Digges, Frank Wilson; *D:* Dudley Murphy. **VHS, Beta $14.95** *COL, SUE* 💩💩 1/2

Emperor of the Bronx A look at crime, sleaze, violence, and the actions of bad guys in the inner-city.
1989 90m/C William Smith. **VHS, Beta $29.95** *HHE* 💩

The Emperor's New Clothes The story of an emperor and the unusual outfit he gets from his tailor. A "Faerie Tale Theatre" presentation.
1984 60m/C Art Carney, Alan Arkin, Dick Shawn; *D:* Peter Medak. **VHS, Beta $14.98** *KUI, FOX, FCT* 💩

The Empire of Passion A peasant woman and her low-life lover kill the woman's husband, but find the future they planned with each other is not to be. The husband's ghost returns to haunt them, and destroy the passionate bond which led to the murder. Oshima's follow-up to "In the Realm of the Senses." In Japanese with English subtitles.
1976 110m/C *JP* Nagisa Oshima, Kazuko Yoshiyuki, Tatsuya Fuji, Takahiro Tamura, Takuzo Kawatani; *D:* Nagisa Oshima. **VHS $89.95** *FCT* 💩💩💩

Empire of Spiritual Ninja Ninja student gone bad encounters his former teacher. Tedious pseudo ninja adventure with more talking than action and more gunplay than chop socky action. Dubbed.
19?? 90m/C *HK* Tom Berlin, Hubert Hays; *D:* Bruce Lambert; *W:* Jerry Sawyer. **VHS $59.95** *TWE* Woof!

Empire of the Air: The Men Who Made Radio Documentary traces the history of radio from 1906-1955 and profiles its three rival creators: Lee de Forest, Edwin Howard Armstrong and David Sarnoff.
1991 120m/C VHS, LV **$19.95** *PBS* Woof!

Empire of the Ants A group of enormous, nuclear, unfriendly ants stalk a real estate dealer and prospective buyers of undeveloped oceanfront property. Story originated by master science-fiction storyteller H. G. Wells.
1977 (PG) 90m/C Joan Collins, Robert Lansing, John David Carson, Albert Salmi, Jacqueline Scott, Robert Pine; *D:* Bert I. Gordon. **VHS, Beta $9.98** *SUE* 💩 1/2

Empire of the Dragon Rip-roaring martial arts adventure featuring standard number of wide-ranging kicks.
198? 90m/C Chen Tien Tse, Chia Kai, Chang Shan. **VHS, Beta** *NO* 💩

Empire of the Sun Spielberg's mature, extraordinarily vivid return to real storytelling, adapted from the best-selling J.G. Ballard novel. Although yearning to be a great film, it experiences occasional flat spots which keep it slightly out of contention. A young, wealthy British boy living in Shanghai is caught in the turbulence when China is invaded by the Japanese at the onset of World War II. Separated from his family, he is thrust into an unfamiliar life of poverty and discomfort when he is interred in a prison camp. A mysterious, breathtaking work, in which Spielberg's heightened juvenile romanticism has a real, heartbreaking context. Written by Tom Stoppard; cinematography by Allen Daviau; cameo by Ballard. Interesting to compare to other films made in 1987 concerning a young boy's recollection of World War II, including Louis Malle's "Au Revoir Les Enfants" and John Boorman's "Hope and Glory."
1987 (PG) 153m/C Christian Bale, John Malkovich, Miranda Richardson, Nigel Havers, Joe Pantoliano, Leslie Phillips; *Cameos:* J.G. Ballard; *D:* Steven Spielberg; *W:* Tom Stoppard; *M:* John Williams. Academy Awards '87 Nominations: Best Art Direction/Set Decoration, Best Cinematography, Best Costume Design, Best Film Editing, Best Sound, Best Original Score; National Board of Review Awards '87: 10 Best Films of the Year, Best Director (Spielberg). **VHS, Beta, LV, 8mm $19.98** *WAR, TAM* 💩💩💩

Empire State When his friend disappears from a posh London nightclub, a young man searches for him and finds more action and intrigue than he can handle. Even so, this movie's still pretty bland.
1987 (R) 102m/C *GB* Cathryn Harrison, Martin Landau, Ray McAnally; *D:* Ron Peck. **VHS, Beta $79.95** *VMK* 💩

The Empire Strikes Back The second film in the epic "Star Wars" trilogy finds young Luke Skywalker and the Rebel Alliance plotting new strategies as they prepare to battle the evil Darth Vader and the forces of the Dark Side. Luke travels to a distant planet to learn the ways of a Jedi knight from master Yoda, while Han and Leia find time for romance and a few adventures of their own. This installment introduces the charismatic Lando Calrissian, the vulgar and drooling Jabba the Hut, and a mind-numbing secret from Vadar. With the same superb special effects and a hearty plot, this movie is a true continuation of the excellent tradition set by 1977's "Star Wars." Followed by "Return of the Jedi" in 1983. Also available on Laserdisc with "The Making of 'Star Wars'."
1980 (PG) 124m/C Mark Hamill, Carrie Fisher, Harrison Ford, Billy Dee Williams, Alec Guinness, David Prowse, Kenny Baker, Frank Oz, Anthony Daniels, Peter Mayhew; *D:* Irvin Kershner; *M:* John Williams; *V:* James Earl Jones. Academy Awards '80: Best Sound, Best Visual Effects; Nominations: Best Art Direction/Set Decoration, Best Original Score; People's Choice Awards '81: Best Film. **VHS, Beta, LV $19.98** *FOX, FCT, RDG* 💩💩💩💩

Employees' Entrance William stars as a ruthless department store manager in this story about commerce and compromise during the Depression. Young gives an excellent performance as the wife of one of his employees. Outrageous, and racy, this pre-Code film was expertly-directed by veteran

craftsman Del Ruth. Based on a play by David Boehm.
1933 74m/B Warren William, Loretta Young, Wallace Ford, Alice White, Allen Jenkins; *D:* Roy Del Ruth; *W:* Robert Presnell. VHS **$19.98** *MGM ♂♂♂*

The Empty Beach A tough private detective investigates the disappearance of a wealthy business tycoon.
1985 87m/C *AU* Bryan Brown, Anna Maria Monticelli; *D:* Chris Thomson. **VHS, Beta $69.98** *LIV ♂ 1/2*

An Empty Bed Award-winning independent production depicting Bill Frayne, an older homosexual, and the challenges of his everyday life. Told mostly in flashbacks as Bill encounters people and places during the course of one day, this is a delicate drama with important statements about homosexuality, aging and honesty.
1990 60m/C John Wylie, Mark Clifford Smith, Conan McCarty, Dorothy Stinnette, Kevin Kelly, Thomas Hill, Harriet Bass; *W/D:* Mark Gasper. **VHS $59.99** *YOC, FCT, TAM ♂♂*

Empty Canvas A spiritually-bankrupt artist becomes obsessively jealous of his mistress who refuses to marry him in the hope that someone better will come along. Based on the Alberto Moravia novel. *AKA:* La Noia: L'Ennui Et Sa Diversion, L'Erotisme.
1964 118m/B *FR IT* Horst Buchholz, Catherine Spaak, Bette Davis; *D:* Damiano Damiani. **VHS, Beta $59.98** *SUE, MLB ♂ 1/2*

Empty Suitcases A woman becomes alienated from society when she commutes between a lover in New York City and a job in Chicago.
1984 55m/C **VHS, Beta** *NO ♂♂*

Enchanted April Two women, tired of their overbearing husbands, rent a villa in Portofino, Italy for a month with two other very different women—a beautiful but bored socialite, and a crusty old woman with an impeccable literary pedigree. The effects of the charming villa, with plenty of wisteria and sunshine, do wonders for the women. A charming and romantic period piece. Based on the 1922 novel by Elizabeth von Arnim.
1992 (PG) 93m/C *GB* Miranda Richardson, Joan Plowright, Josie Lawrence, Polly Walker, Alfred Molina, Jim Broadbent, Michael Kitchen; *D:* Mike Newell; *W:* Peter Barnes; *M:* Richard Rodney Bennett. Academy Awards '92 Nominations: Best Adapted Screenplay, Best Costume Design, Best Supporting Actress (Plowright); Golden Globe Awards '93: Best Actress—Musical/Comedy (Richardson), Best Supporting Actress (Plowright). **VHS, Beta, LV $89.99** *PAR, MOV, WAR ♂♂ 1/2*

The Enchanted Cottage Represents Hollywood's "love conquers all" fantasy hokum, as a disfigured war vet and a homely girl retreat from the horrors of the world into a secluded cottage, where they both regain youth and beauty. A four-tissue heart-tugger. Adopted from the Arthur Pinero play.
1945 91m/B Dorothy McGuire, Robert Young, Herbert Marshall, Mildred Natwick, Spring Byington, Hillary Brooke, Richard Gaines, Robert Clarke; *D:* John Cromwell. **VHS, Beta, LV $19.98** *NOS, RKO, TTC ♂♂ 1/2*

The Enchanted Forest An elderly man teaches a boy about life and the beauty of nature when the boy gets lost in a forest.
1945 78m/C *AR* Harry Davenport, Edmund Lowe, Brenda Joyce; *D:* Lew Landers. **VHS, Beta, LV $19.95** *STE, NOS, NWV ♂♂ 1/2*

Enchanted Island Sailor stops on an island to find provisions and ends up falling in love with a cannibal princess. Thinly based upon Herman Melville's "Typee."

1958 94m/C Jane Powell, Dana Andrews, Arthur Shields; *D:* Allan Dwan. **VHS, Beta $15.95** *UHV ♂ 1/2*

The Enchanted Journey A full-length animated film about a chimpanzee who escapes from a zoo and journeys to freedom.
197? 90m/C *V:* Orson Welles, Jim Backus. **VHS, Beta $29.95** *MED, WTA ♂*

The Enchantress A daring boy experiences his first true loves and passions when he journeys through a mystical land in order to find a beautiful fairy. In Greek with subtitles. *AKA:* I Skiachtra.
1985 93m/C *GR* Alkis Kourkoulos, Sofia Aliberti, Lily Kokodi, Antogone Amanitou, Vicky Koulianou, Nicols Papaconstantinou, Stratos Pachis; *D:* Manoussos Manoussakis. **VHS, Beta $59.95** *FCT ♂ 1/2*

Encino Man Two, like, totally uncool Valley dudes dig up a 10,000-year old caveman in the backyard. After giving him a makeover and teaching him the necessities like the four basic food groups (Milk Duds in the dairy group, Sweet Tarts in the fruit group), they use the gnarly caveman as their ticket to popularity and dates to the prom. Juvenile humor appealing to teens; strictly brain candy. *AKA:* California Man.
1992 (PG) 88m/C Sean Astin, Brendan Fraser, Pauly Shore, Megan Ward, Robin Tunney, Rick Ducommun, Mariette Hartley, Richard Masur, Michael DeLuise; *D:* Les Mayfield; *W:* Shawn Schepps. **VHS, Beta $19.99** *HPH ♂♂*

Encore The third W. Somerset Maugham omnibus (following "Quartet" and "Trio") which includes: "Winter Cruise," "The Ant and the Grasshopper," and "Gigolo and Gigolette."
1952 85m/B *GB* Nigel Patrick, Kay Walsh, Roland Culver, John Laurie, Glynis Johns, Ronald Squire, Noel Purcell, Peter Graves; *D:* Pat Jackson, Anthony Pelissier, Harold French. **VHS, Beta** *NO ♂♂♂*

Encounter at Raven's Gate Punk rockers and extraterrestrials meet amid hard rock and gallons of gore.
1988 (R) 85m/C Eddie Cleary, Steven Vidler; *D:* Rolf de Heer. **VHS, Beta, LV $29.95** *HMD, HBO, IME ♂ 1/2*

Encounter with the Unknown Relates three fully documented supernatural events including a death prophesy and a ghost.
1975 90m/C Rosie Holotik, Gene Ross; *D:* Harry Z. Thomason. **VHS, Beta $29.95** *UHV ♂♂ 1/2*

The End Reynolds plays a young man who discovers he is terminally ill. He decides not to prolonging his suffering and attempts various tried-and-true methods for committing suicide, receiving riotous help from the crazed DeLuise.
1978 (R) 100m/C Burt Reynolds, Sally Field, Dom DeLuise, Carl Reiner, Joanne Woodward, Robby Benson, Kristy McNichol, Norman Fell, Pat O'Brien, Myrna Loy, David Steinberg; *D:* Burt Reynolds. **VHS, Beta, LV $14.95** *MGM, FOX ♂♂ 1/2*

End of August A spinster of New Orleans Creole aristocracy, circa 1900, breaks out of her sheltered life and experiences new sexual and romantic awareness. Adapted from "The Awakening" by Kate Chopin.
1982 (PG) 104m/C Sally Sharp, David Marshall Grant, Paul Roebling; *D:* Bob Graham. **VHS, Beta $59.98** *NLC ♂*

End of Desire Schell discovers that her husband, Marquand, has married her for her money and is having an affair with the maid in this melodrama based on De Maupas-

sant's story, "Une Vie." A period piece that is a little on the slow side. In French with English subtitles.
1962 86m/C *FR* Maria Schell, Christian Marquand, Pascale Petit, Ivan Desny; *D:* Alexandre Astruc. **VHS** *NO ♂*

The End of Innocence In her attempts to please everyone in her life, a woman experiences a nervous breakdown. Written and directed by Cannon.
1990 (R) 102m/C Dyan Cannon, John Heard, George Coe, Viveka Davis, Rebecca Schaeffer, Billie Bird; *W/D:* Dyan Cannon; *M:* Michael Convertino. **VHS, Beta $89.95** *PAR, FCT ♂♂ 1/2*

The End of St. Petersburg A Russian peasant becomes a scab during a workers' strike in 1914. He is then forced to enlist in the army prior to the 1917 October Revolution. Fascinating, although propagandistic film commissioned by the then-new Soviet government. Silent.
1927 75m/B Ivan Chuvelov; *D:* Vsevolod Pudovkin. **VHS, Beta $24.95** *NOS, MRV, WFV ♂♂♂ 1/2*

End of the Line Two old-time railroad workers steal a locomotive for a cross-country jaunt to protest the closing of the local railroad company. Produced by Steenburgen.
1988 (PG) 103m/C Wilford Brimley, Levon Helm, Mary Steenburgen, Kevin Bacon, Holly Hunter, Barbara Barrie, Bob Balaban, Howard Morris, Bruce McGill, Clint Howard, Trey Wilson; *D:* Jay Russell. **VHS, Beta, LV $79.95** *KRT, LHV, WAR ♂♂ 1/2*

End of the Road Keach is a troubled college professor whose bizarre treatment by his psychologist (Jones) produces tragic results. He eventually enters into an affair with the wife of a co-worker. Adapted from John Barth's story, with a confused script cowritten by Terry Southern. Rated X upon release for adult story and nudity. Fascinating, if uneven.
1970 (X) 110m/C Stacy Keach, James Earl Jones, James Coco, Harris Yulin, Dorothy Tristan; *D:* Aram Avakian. **VHS, Beta $59.98** *FOX ♂♂ 1/2*

End of the World A coffee machine explodes, sending a man through a window and into a neon sign, where he is electrocuted. A priest witnesses this and retreats to a convent where he meets his alien double and heads for more trouble with outer space invaders. Interesting premise.
1977 (PG) 88m/C Christopher Lee, Sue Lyon, Lew Ayres, MacDonald Carey, Dean Jagger, Kirk Scott; *D:* John Hayes. **VHS, Beta $29.95** *MED Woof!*

Endangered Species Offbeat thriller with sci-fi leanings about a retired New York cop on vacation in America's West who is drawn into a female sheriff's investigation of a mysterious series of cattle killings. Could it be UFOs? Based on a true story.
1982 (R) 97m/C Robert Urich, JoBeth Williams, Paul Dooley, Hoyt Axton, Peter Coyote, Harry Carey Jr., Dan Hedaya, John Considine; *D:* Alan Rudolph. **VHS, Beta $69.95** *MGM ♂♂ 1/2*

Endgame Grotesquely deformed survivors of World War III fight their way out of radioactive New York City to seek a better life.
1985 98m/C Al Oliver, Moira Chen, Jack Davis, Bobby Rhodes, Jill Elliot; *D:* Steve Benson. **VHS, Beta $59.95** *MED ♂*

Endless Descent At least it seems endless. A group of scientist-types set out in search of a sunken sub, but somehow take a wrong turn into the rift, the deepest chasm at the bottom of the sea. There, they discover unimaginable horrors—that is, if you've nev-

er seen "Alien," or just about any other icky-monster flick. A Spanish film, shot in English, by director Simon, whose other works of art include "Pieces" and "Slugs." *AKA:* La Grieta.
1990 (R) 79m/C *SP* Jack Scalia, Lee Ermey, Ray Wise, Deborah Adair, Ely Pouget; *D:* J.P. Simon. **VHS, Beta, LV $89.95** *LIV* Woof!

The Endless Game Cold War suspenser has British secret-agent-man Finney attempting to solve the murder of his erstwhile fellow agent-lover, much to the dismay of the government. Written by director Forbes, this made-for-cable would-be thriller is a decidedly mediocre waste of a talented cast. Also of note, it was actor-director Sir Anthony Quayle's final appearance.
1989 (PG-13) 123m/C *GB* Albert Finney, George Segal, Derek De Lint, Monica Guerritore, Ian Holm, John Standing, Anthony Quayle, Kristin Scott Thomas; *M:* Ennio Morricone. **VHS $89.95** *PSM, FCT* 🎞🎞

Endless Love Although only 15, David and Jade are in love. Her parents think they are too serious and demand that the two spend time apart. David attempts to win her parents' affection and approval, goes mad in the process, and commits a foolish act (he burns the house down) that threatens their love forever. Based on the novel by Scott Spencer. Of interest only to those with time on their hands or smitten by a love so bad that this movie will seem grand in comparison. Features Cruise's first film appearance.
1981 (R) 115m/C Brooke Shields, Martin Hewitt, Don Murray, Shirley Knight, Beatrice Straight, Richard Kiley, Tom Cruise, James Spader, Robert Moore, Jami Gertz; *D:* Franco Zeffirelli. **VHS, Beta, LV $14.98** *LIV, VES* 🎞🎞

Endless Night An adaptation of an Agatha Christie tale. Focuses on a young chauffeur who wants to build a dream house, and his chance meeting with an American heiress. *AKA:* Agatha Christie's Endless Night.
1971 95m/C *GB* Hayley Mills, Hywel Bennett, Britt Ekland, George Sanders, Per Oscarsson, Peter Bowles; *D:* Sidney Gilliat; *W:* Agatha Christie. **VHS, Beta, LV $19.99** *HBO* 🎞🎞

The Endless Summer Director Bruce Brown follows two young surfers around the world in their search for the perfect wave in this wryly narrated documentary.
1966 90m/C Mike Hynson, Robert August; *D:* Bruce Brown. **VHS, Beta, LV $24.95** *PAV, FCT, HMV* 🎞🎞

Endplay An Australian-made crime/horror drama in which two brothers cover for each other in a series of murders involving blonde hitchhikers. Based on a novel by Russell Braddon.
1975 110m/C *AU* George Mallaby, John Waters, Ken Goodlet, Delvene Delaney, Charles Tingwell, Robert Hewett, Kevin Miles; *D:* Tim Burstall. **VHS $14.95** *ACA* 🎞🎞½

Enemies, a Love Story A wonderfully resonant, subtle tragedy based on the novel by Isaac Bashevis Singer. A post-Holocaust Jew, living in Coney Island, can't choose between three women—his current wife (who hid him during the war), his tempestuous lover, and his reappearing pre-war wife he presumed dead. A hilarious, confident tale told with grace and patience.
1989 (R) 119m/C Ron Silver, Lena Olin, Anjelica Huston, Margaret Sophie Stein, Paul Mazursky, Alan King, Judith Malina, Rita Karin, Phil Leeds, Elya Baskin, Marie-Adele Lemieux; *D:* Paul Mazursky. Academy Awards '89 Nominations: Best Adapted Screenplay, Best Supporting Actress (Huston, Olin); New York Film Critics Awards '89: Best Director (Mazursky), Best

Supporting Actress (Olin). **VHS, Beta, LV $89.98** *MED* 🎞🎞🎞½

Enemy Below Suspenseful World War II sea epic, in which an American destroyer and a German U-Boat chase one another and square off in the South Atlantic.
1957 98m/C Robert Mitchum, Curt Jurgens, David Hedison, Theodore Bikel, Doug McClure, Russell Collins; *D:* Dick Powell. **VHS, Beta $19.98** *FOX, FCT* 🎞🎞🎞

Enemy Mine A space fantasy in which two pilots from warring planets, one an Earthling, the other an asexual reptilian Drac, crash land on a barren planet and are forced to work together to survive.
1985 (PG-13) 108m/C Dennis Quaid, Louis Gossett Jr., Brion James, Richard Marcus, Lance Kerwin; *D:* Wolfgang Petersen. **VHS, Beta, LV $19.98** *FOX* 🎞🎞

Enemy of the Law Texas rangers battle evil in an old frontier town.
1945 59m/B Tex Ritter, Dave O'Brien; *D:* Harry Fraser. **VHS, Beta $19.95** *NOS, VCN, DVT* 🎞🎞½

Enemy of Women Chronicles the life and loves of Nazi propagandist Dr. Joseph Goebbels. *AKA:* The Private Life of Paul Joseph Goebbels.
1944 90m/B Claudia Drake, Paul Andor, Donald Woods, H.B. Warner, Sigrid Gurie, Ralph Morgan, Gloria Stuart; *D:* Alfred Zeisler; *W:* Alfred Zeisler. **VHS, Beta $24.95** *NOS, DVT, GLV* 🎞½

Enemy Territory A handful of citizens trapped in a New York City housing project after dark are stalked by a violent, murderous street gang.
1987 (R) 89m/C Ray Parker Jr., Jan-Michael Vincent, Gary Frank, Frances Foster; *D:* Peter Manoogian. **VHS, Beta $79.98** *FOX* 🎞🎞

Enemy Unseen A bickering squad of mercenaries slog through the African jungle to find a girl abducted by crocodile-worshipping natives. Dull Jungle-Jim-style adventure, notable for the hilariously phony crocs that occasionally clamp onto the characters.
1991 (R) 90m/C Vernon Wells, Stack Pierce, Ken Gampu, Michael McCabe, Angela O'Neill; *D:* Elmo De Witt. **VHS $79.95** *AIP* 🎞

The Enforcer A district attorney goes after an organized gang of killers in this film noir treatment of the real-life "Murder, Inc." case. *AKA:* Murder, Inc.
1951 87m/B Humphrey Bogart, Zero Mostel, Ted de Corsia, Everett Sloane, Roy Roberts, Lawrence Tolan, King Donovan, Bob Steele, Adelaide Klein, Don Beddoe, Tito Vuolo, John Kellogg; *D:* Bretaigne Windust, Raoul Walsh; *W:* Martin Rackin. **VHS, LV $19.95** *REP* 🎞🎞½

The Enforcer Dirty Harry takes on a female partner and a vicious terrorist group that is threatening the city of San Francisco. See how many "punks" feel lucky enough to test the hand of the tough cop.
1976 (R) 96m/C Clint Eastwood, Tyne Daly, Harry Guardino, Bradford Dillman, John Mitchum; *D:* James Fargo. **VHS, Beta, LV $19.98** *WAR* 🎞🎞½

Enforcer from Death Row An ex-con is recruited by a secret international peacekeeping organization to track down and eliminate a band of murderous spies.
1978 87m/C Cameron Mitchell, Leo Fong, Darnell Garcia, Booker T. Anderson, John Hammond, Mariwin Roberts. **VHS, Beta $69.98** *LIV, GHV* 🎞

An Englishman Abroad During the Cold War a British actress visits Moscow and chances to meet a notorious English defector. Behind their gossip and small talk is a tragicomic portrait of the exiled traitor/spy. He was the infamous Guy Burgess; his

actress was Coral Browne, here playing herself in a pointed recreation scripted by Alan Bennett. Made for British TV; nuances may be lost on yank viewers. Winner of several British awards.
1983 63m/C *GB* Alan Bates, Coral Browne, Charles Gray; *D:* John Schlesinger. **VHS $49.95** *PRV, FCT* 🎞🎞🎞

Enid is Sleeping Well-done comedy noir in the now-popular there's a corpse in the closet subgenre. A woman in a mythical New Mexican town tries to hide the body of her sister Enid, who she's accidentally killed. Enid, it turns out, wasn't thrilled to discover her sister sleeping with her police-officer husband. Phillips and Perkins restored the film to its original state after it was ruthlessly gutted by the studio. Written by director Phillips.
1990 ?m/C Elizabeth Perkins, Judge Reinhold; *W/D:* Maurice Phillips. **VHS** *VES* 🎞🎞🎞

Enigma Trapped behind the Iron Curtain, a double agent tries to find the key to five pending murders by locating a Russian coded microprocessor holding information that would unravel the assassination scheme.
1982 (PG) 101m/C *FR GB* Martin Sheen, Brigitte Fossey, Sam Neill, Derek Jacobi, Frank Finlay, Michael Lonsdale; *D:* Jeannot Szwarc. **VHS, Beta, LV $69.98** *SUE* 🎞🎞

Enigma Secret Three Polish mathematicians use their noggins to break the Nazi secret code machine during WWII. Based on a true story; in Polish with English subtitles.
1979 158m/C *PL* Tadeusz Borowski, Piotr Fronczewski, Piotr Garlicki. **VHS $49.95** *FCT* 🎞🎞

Enola Gay: The Men, the Mission, the Atomic Bomb Based on the bestselling book by Gordon Thomas and Max Gordon Witts, this made for television drama tells the story of the airmen aboard the B-29 that dropped the first atomic bomb. Details the events during World War II leading up to the decision to bomb Hiroshima and the concerns of the crew assigned the task.
1980 150m/C Patrick Duffy, Billy Crystal, Kim Darby, Gary Frank, Gregory Harrison, Ed Nelson, Robert Walden, Stephen Macht, Robert Pine, James Shigeta, Henry Wilcoxon; *D:* David Lowell Rich. **VHS, Beta $69.95** *PSM* 🎞🎞

Enormous Changes Three stories about New York City women and their personal relationships. Screenplay co-authored by John Sayles was based on the stories of Grace Paley. Also titled "Enormous Changes at the Last Minute."
1983 115m/C Ellen Barkin, David Strathairn, Ron McLarty, Maria Tucci, Lynn Milgrim, Kevin Bacon; *D:* Mirra Bank. **VHS, Beta, LV $79.95** *VMK* 🎞🎞🎞

Enrapture A chauffeur is the prime suspect when a promiscuous passenger is murdered in his limousine. The driver did it?
1990 (R) 87m/C Ona Simms, Harvey Siegel, Richard Parnes; *D:* Chuck Vincent. **VHS, LV $79.95** *ATL* 🎞½

Ensign Pulver A continuation of the further adventures of the crew of the U.S.S. Reluctant from "Mister Roberts," which was adapted from the Broadway play.
1964 104m/C Walter Matthau, Robert Walker Jr., Larry Hagman, Jack Nicholson, Millie Perkins, James Coco, James Farentino, Burl Ives, Gerald S. O'Loughlin, Al Freeman Jr.; *D:* Joshua Logan. **VHS, Beta $19.98** *WAR* 🎞

Enter Laughing Based on Reiner's semi-autobiographical novel and play, depicts the botched efforts of a Bronx-born schlump to become an actor. Worthwhile, but doesn't live up to the original.

1967 112m/C Reni Santoni, Jose Ferrer, Elaine May, Shelley Winters, Jack Gilford, Don Rickles, Michael J. Pollard, Janet Margolin, Rob Reiner; *D:* Carl Reiner. **VHS, Beta** $59.95 *RCA* ♫♫

Enter the Dragon The American film that broke Bruce Lee worldwide combines Oriental conventions with 007 thrills. Spectacular fighting sequences including Karate, Judo, Tae Kwon Do, and Tai Chi Chuan are featured as Lee is recruited by the British to search for opium smugglers in Hong Kong. *AKA:* The Deadly Three.
1973 (R) 98m/C Bruce Lee, John Saxon, Jim Kelly; *D:* Robert Clouse. **VHS, Beta, LV** $19.98 *WAR* ♫♫♫

Enter the Game of Death Bruce Lee stars in this kung fu epic with mucho head kicking and rib punching.
1980 88m/C Bruce Lee. **VHS, Beta** $29.99 *BFV* ♫ ½

Enter the Ninja First and most serious of the Cannon canon of relatively well-done ninja epics (faint praise) that created original box-office stir for genre (mostly among adolescents needing outlet). Ninja Nero visits old friend in Philippines who's being pressured by ruthless evil guy George to give up the farm. Nero dispatches numerous thugs before indulging in ninja slugfest with Kosugi. Written by Dick Desmond.
1981 (R) 99m/C Franco Nero, Susan George, Sho Kosugi, Christopher George, Alex Courtney; *D:* Menahem Golan. **VHS, Beta** $14.95 *MGM* ♫♫

Enter the Panther Amidst, and regardless of, a double-crossing plot featuring a treacherous family and a sought-after gold mine, a young man kicks heads and punches his way to fame.
1979 91m/C Bruce Li, Tsai Chin, Tse Lan. **VHS, Beta** $24.95 *GEM* ♫

Enter Three Dragons Kung Fu artistry abounds in this head-kicking action-adventure film.
1981 90m/C Dragon Lee, Bruce Lea, Yang Tsze, Samuel Walls, Chang Li, Bruce Li, Jackie Chin. **VHS** *SUN* ♫

The Entertainer Splendid drama of a down and out vaudevillian who tries vainly to gain the fame his dying father once possessed. His blatant disregard for his alcoholic wife and his superficial sons brings his world crashing down around him, and he discovers how self-destructive his life has been. Remade in 1975 for television. Adapted from the play by John Osborne.
1960 97m/B GB Laurence Olivier, Brenda de Banzie, Roger Livesey, Joan Plowright, Daniel Massey, Alan Bates, Shirley Anne Field, Albert Finney, Thora Hird; *D:* Tony Richardson. **VHS** $39.95 *FCT* ♫♫♫ ½

Entertaining Mr. Sloane Playwright Joe Orton's masterpiece of black comedy concerning a handsome criminal who becomes the guest and love interest of a widow and her brother.
1970 90m/C Beryl Reid, Harry Andrews, Peter McEnery, Alan Webb; *D:* Douglas Hickox. **VHS, Beta** $59.99 *HBO* ♫♫ ½

The Entity Supposedly based on a true story about an unseen entity that repeatedly rapes a woman. Hershey the victim whom nobody believes. She eventually ends up at a university for talks with parapsychologist Silver. Pseudo-science to the rescue as the over-sexed creature is frozen dead in its tracks. Exploitative violence, gore, and nudity aplenty, balanced to a degree by Hershey's strong performance. Screenplay by Frank DeFelitta.

1983 (R) 115m/C Barbara Hershey, Ron Silver, Alex Rocco; *D:* Sidney J. Furie. **VHS, Beta** $19.98 *FOX* ♫♫

Entr'acte Clair's famous dada-surrealist classic short, reflecting his sense of humor, as various eccentric characters become involved in a crazy chase. Silent.
1924 21m/B FR *D:* Rene Clair. **VHS, Beta** *MRV, TAM, GVV* ♫♫

Entre-Nous Two attractive, young French mothers find in each other the fulfillment their husbands cannot provide. One of the women was confined in a concentration camp during WWII; the other is a disaffected priest. In French with English subtitles. *AKA:* Between Us; Coup de Foudre.
1983 (PG) 112m/C FR Isabelle Huppert, Miou-Miou, Guy Marchand; *D:* Diane Kurys. **VHS, Beta** $19.98 *MGM, TAM* ♫♫♫ ½

EPIC: Days of the Dinosaurs An animated fable about two babies born into a pack of dingoes in a prehistoric world. They must fight for superiority over the mystical powers of nature.
1987 75m/C *D:* Yoram Gross. **VHS, Beta** $39.95 *IVE, FHE, WTA* ♫ ½

Epic That Never Was A fascinating documentary of the circumstances under which a big-budgeted 1937 adaptation of Graves' ''I, Claudius,'' filmed by Von Sternberg, was shelved after Oberon's auto accident and director/star disagreements. Features both interviews made 30 years later and much of the existing footage, a testament to its unfulfilled potential as a masterpiece.
1965 74m/C Charles Laughton, Flora Robson, Merle Oberon, Emlyn Williams, Robert Newton, Josef von Sternberg, Robert Graves. **VHS, Beta, 8mm** $24.95 *NOS, VYY, VRS* ♫ ½

Epitaph An average American family's life is disrupted by the mother's habitual axe-murdering.
1987 90m/C *D:* Joseph Merhi. **VHS, Beta** *NO* ♫

Equalizer 2000 A warrior in a post-holocaust future plots to overthrow a dictatorship by using a high-powered gun.
1986 (R) 85m/C Richard Norton, Corinne Wahl, William Steis; *D:* Cirio H. Santiago. **VHS, Beta** $79.95 *MGM* ♫

The Equalizer: Memories of Manon Feature-length episode of the popular television crime thriller about an ex-agent who uses guns and espionage tactics to help people who are being persecuted by ruthless villians on the streets of New York City. In this installment, McCall, the Equalizer, learns that he has a daughter and that her life is in peril.
1988 96m/C Edward Woodward, Melissa Sue Anderson, Anthony Zerbe, George DiCenzo, Jon Polito, Robert Lansing, Keith Szarabajka; *D:* Tony Wharmby. **VHS, Beta** $39.95 *MCA* ♫♫ ½

Equinox Young archaeologists uncover horror in a state forest. The ranger, questing for a book of spells that the scientists have found, threatens them with wonderful special effects, including winged beasts, huge apes, and Satan. Though originally an amateur film, it is deemed a minor classic in its genre.
1971 (PG) 80m/C Edward Connell, Barbara Hewitt, Frank Bonner, Robin Christopher, Jack Woods, Fritz Leiber; *D:* Jack Woods. **VHS** *NO* ♫♫♫

Equinox Flower Ozu's first color film tells the sensitive story of two teenage girls who make a pact to protect each other from the traditional prearranged marriages their parents have set up. Lovely film that focuses on the generation gap between young and

old in the Japanese family. In Japanese with English subtitles.
1958 118m/C JP Shin Saburi, Kinuyo Tanaka, Ineko Arima, Miyuki Kuwano, Chishu Ryu; *D:* Yasujiro Ozu. **VHS** $69.95 *NYF, ART, FCT* ♫♫

Equus A psychiatrist undertakes the most challenging case of his career when he tries to figure out why a stable-boy blinded horses. Based upon the successful play by Peter Shaffer, but not well transferred to film.
1977 (R) 138m/C Richard Burton, Peter Firth, Jenny Agutter, Joan Plowright, Colin Blakely, Harry Andrews; *D:* Sidney Lumet. Academy Awards '77 Nominations: Best Actor (Burton), Best Adapted Screenplay, Best Supporting Actor (Firth); British Academy Awards '77: Best Supporting Actress (Agutter); Golden Globe Awards '78: Best Actor—Drama (Burton), Best Supporting Actor (Firth). **VHS, Beta, LV** $69.95 *MGM* ♫♫ ½

Era Notte a Roma An American, Russian, and British soldier each escape from a concentration camp in the waning days of WWII and find refuge in the home of a young woman. Rossellini also co-scripted.
1960 145m/C IT *D:* Roberto Rossellini. **VHS** $79.95 *TPV* ♫♫♫

Eraserhead The infamous cult classic about a numb-brained everyman wandering through what amounts to a sick, ironic parody of the modern urban landscape, innocently impregnating his girlfriend and fathering a pestilent embryonic mutant. Surreal and bizarre, the film has an inner, completely unpredictable logic all its own. Lynch's first feature-length film (he directed, produced, and wrote the screenplay). Stars Jack Nance, who later achieved fame in Lynch's ''Twin Peaks'' as Pete the logger.
1978 90m/B Jack Nance, Charlotte Stewart, Jack Fisk, Jeanne Bates; *D:* David Lynch. **VHS, Beta, LV** *COL, OM* ♫♫♫

Erendira Based on Gabriel Garcia-Marquez's story about a teenage girl prostituting herself to support her witch-like grandmother after accidentally torching the elder's house. The film follows the two as they travel across the desert trying out new and inventive ways to survive. Unusual ending tops off a creative, if not eclectic, movie. In Spanish with English subtitles.
1983 103m/C FR MX GE Irene Papas, Claudia Ohana, Michael Lonsdale, Rufus, Jorge Fegan; *D:* Ruy Guerra. **VHS, Beta** $24.95 *XVC, MED, APD* ♫♫ ½

Eric Made-for-television tear-jerker about a young athlete who fights for his life after he's diagnosed with leukemia. Based on the true-life account written by Eric's mother Doris Lund.
1975 100m/C Patricia Neal, John Savage, Claude Akins, Sian Barbara Allen, Mark Hamill, Nehemiah Persoff, Tom Clancy; *D:* James Goldstone. **VHS, Beta** $39.95 *LIV* ♫♫♫

Erik An ex-government agent working in Central America finds his loyalties divided when he is approached by a female activist and his old CIA friends. They want him to help expose his current boss as a drug smuggler.
1990 90m/C Stephen McHattie, Deborah Van Valkenburgh. **VHS, Beta** *SVS* ♫♫

Erik, the Viking The Norse Warrior discovers not only the New World but traitorous subordinates among his crew, calling for drastic measures.
1972 95m/C Giuliano Gemma, Gordon Mitchell. **VHS, Beta** $59.95 *UNI* ♫

Erik the Viking A mediocre Monty Pythonesque farce about a Viking who grows dissatisfied with his barbaric way of life and decides to set out to find the mythical Asgaard, where Norse gods dwell. Great cast of character actors is wasted.
1989 (PG-13) 104m/C *GB* Tim Robbins, Terry Jones, Mickey Rooney, John Cleese, Imogen Stubbs, Anthony Sher, Gordon John Sinclair, Freddie Jones, Eartha Kitt; *D:* Terry Jones. **VHS, Beta, LV $89.98** *ORI* ✬✬½

Ernest Goes to Camp A screwball, slapstick summer camp farce starring the character Ernest P. Worrell as an inept camp counselor. When progress threatens the camp, Ernest leads the boys on a turtle-bombing, slop-shooting attack on the construction company. Followed by "Ernest Saves Christmas" and "Ernest Goes to Jail."
1987 (PG) 92m/C Jim Varney, Victoria Racimo, John Vernon, Iron Eyes Cody, Lyle Alzado, Gailard Sartain, Daniel Butler, Hakeem Abdul-Samad; *D:* John R. Cherry III. **VHS, Beta $19.99** *TOU* ✬✬½

Ernest Goes to Jail The infamous loon Ernest P. Worrell winds up in the jury box and the courtroom will never be the same again. Jury duty suddenly becomes hard-time in the slammer for poor Ernest when he is mistaken for a big-wig organized crime boss. Sequel to "Ernest Goes to Camp" and "Ernest Saves Christmas."
1990 (PG) 81m/C Jim Varney, Gailard Sartain, Randall "Tex" Cobb, Bill Byrge, Barry Scott, Charles Napier; *D:* John R. Cherry III. **VHS, LV $89.95** *BVV, TOU* ✬✬

Ernest Saves Christmas Ernest P. Worrell is back. When Santa decides that it's time to retire, Ernest must help him recruit a has-been children's show host who is a bit reluctant. For Ernest fans only, and only the most dedicated of those. Second in the series featuring the nimble-faced Varney, the first of which was "Ernest Goes to Camp," followed by "Ernest Goes to Jail."
1988 (PG) 91m/C Jim Varney, Douglas Seale, Oliver Clark, Noelle Parker, Billie Bird; *D:* John R. Cherry III. **VHS, Beta, LV $89.95** *TOU* ✬✬

Ernest Scared Stupid Pea-brained Ernest P. Worrell returns yet again in this silly comedy. When he accidentally releases a demon from a sacred tomb a 200-year-old curse threatens to destroy his hometown, unless Ernest can come to the rescue. Would you want your town depending on Ernest's heroics? Who would have thought that the annoying Ernest P. Worrell could appear in one movie, let alone four?
1991 (PG) 93m/C Jim Varney, Eartha Kitt, Austin Nagler, Jonas Moscartolo, Shay Astar; *D:* John Cherry. **VHS, Beta $14.99** *TOU* ✬✬½

Ernesto A lushly erotic Italian film depicting the troubled relationship between a young, devil-may-care gay youth and his older, cool-ly seducing lover. In Italian with subtitles.
1979 98m/C *IT* Martin Halm, Michele Placido; *D:* Salvatore Samperi. **VHS, Beta $79.50** *FCT* ✬✬½

Ernie Kovacs: Between the Laughter A made for television version of the television comic's life and career, ending with his tragic death in a car accident in 1962. Shows the brand of humor that made Kovacs famous as well as the devastation that he suffered after the tragic kidnapping of his children by his first wife during divorce proceedings. Kovac's second wife, Edie Adams, makes a brief appearance.
1984 95m/C Jeff Goldblum, Cloris Leachman, Melody Anderson, Madolyn Smith, John Glover; *Cameos:* Edie Adams; *D:* Lamont Johnson. **VHS, Beta $79.95** *WWV* ✬✬

The Erotic Adventures of Pinocchio Softcore comedy version of the fairy tale. As the ads say, "it's not his nose that grows!" You'll have to look carefully to spot Danning and Brandt; Ray Dennis Steckler served as cinematographer.
1971 (R) 77m/C Alex Roman, Dyanne Thorne, Karen Smith, Eduardo Ranez, Carolyn Brandt, Sybil Danning; *D:* Corey Allen. **VHS, LV** *NO* ✬✬

Erotic Dreams The Devil tries to persuade a young guy to come to Hell by showing him a tableau of lusty soft-core vignettes.
1987 70m/C **VHS, Beta $59.95** *CEL* Woof!

Erotic Escape Soft-core fun about party girls taking over a small French town. Originally in French, but dubbed in English. Check your brain at the door.
1986 86m/C *FR* Marie-Claire Davy, Pauline Larrieu. **VHS, Beta $29.95** *MED* ✬

Erotic Illusion A strange mother, father and son view a porn film and each becomes obsessed with its heroine. Italian softcore.
1986 90m/C *IT* Silvana Venturelli, Frank Wolff, Paolo Turco. **VHS, Beta $29.95** *MED* ✬

Erotic Images A beautiful psychology teacher publishes her doctoral thesis on sex and becomes a best-selling author, which threatens her marriage.
1985 (R) 93m/C Britt Ekland, Edd Byrnes, John McCann; *D:* Declan Langan. **VHS, Beta $69.98** *LIV, VES* Woof!

The Erotic Three Unusual love triangle is explored.
1983 90m/C **VHS, Beta** *PGN* ✬

Erotic Touch of Hot Skin Sex, murder, false identities, car crashes, and striptease in the Riviera.
1965 78m/B Fabienne Dali, Sophie Hardy, Jean Valmont, Francois Dryek; *D:* Max Pecas. **VHS, Beta $19.95** *VDM* ✬

Erotica: Fabulous Female Fantasies A made-for-video soft-core feature involving the sexual adventures of five women at a resort hotel.
1986 60m/C *D:* Adam Friedman. **VHS, Beta $29.98** *LIV, VES* ✬

The Errand Boy Jerry Lewis' patented babbling schnook hits Hollywood in search of a job. When he lands a position as an errand boy, Hollywood may never be the same again in this prototypical comedy; a must for Lewis fans only.
1961 92m/B Jerry Lewis, Brian Donlevy, Dick Wesson, Howard McNear, Felicia Atkins, Fritz Feld, Sig Rumann, Renee Taylor, Doodles Weaver, Mike Mazurki, Lorne Greene, Michael Landon, Dan Blocker, Pernell Roberts, Snub Pollard, Kathleen Freeman; *D:* Jerry Lewis. **VHS, LV $59.95** *LIV* ✬✬½

Escapade Sons thinking their parents are en route to divorce court create a scheme to achieve peace worldwide. The pacifist father's reaction juxtaposes idealistic youth with the cynicism of adulthood. Adapted from a play by Roger MacDougall.
1955 87m/B *GB* John Mills, Yvonne Mitchell, Alastair Sim, Jeremy Spenser, Andrew Ray, Marie Lohr, Peter Asher; *D:* Philip Leacock. **VHS $29.95** *MOV, VYY* ✬✬✬

Escapade in Florence As two students in Florence paint their way to immortality, an elaborate art-forging ring preys upon their talents.
1962 81m/C Tommy Kirk, Ivan Desny; *D:* Steve Previn. **VHS, Beta $69.95** *DIS* ✬

Escapade in Japan A Japanese youth helps an American boy frantically search the city of Tokyo for his parents. Shot in Japan.

1957 93m/C Cameron Mitchell, Teresa Wright, Jon Provost, Roger Nakagawa, Philip Ober, Clint Eastwood; *D:* Arthur Lubin. **VHS, Beta $15.95** *UHV* ✬

Escape A fun-loving, care-free Irish officer is sent to oversee the toughest POW prison in Scotland. There, he becomes consumed with keeping the facility secure despite the intricate escape plans laid out by a group of rioters.
1990 (PG) 90m/C Brian Keith, Helmut Griem; *D:* Lamont Johnson. **VHS** *NO* ✬✬

Escape A woman attempts to track down her brother's killer and finds an entire town mysteriously controlled by a sadistic and powerful man. Features General Hospital's bad-boy Shriner.
1990 (R) 100m/C Elizabeth Jeager, Kim Richards, Kin Shriner; *D:* Richard Styles. **VHS** *HHE* ✬½

Escape Artist Award-winning cinematographer Deschanel's first directorial effort is this quirky film about a teenage escape artist who sets out to uncover the identity of his father's killers.
1982 (PG) 96m/C Griffin O'Neal, Raul Julia, Teri Garr, Joan Hackett, Desi Arnaz Sr., Gabriel Dell, Huntz Hall, Jackie Coogan; *D:* Caleb Deschanel. **VHS, Beta, LV $79.98** *LIV, VES* ✬✬✬

Escape from Alcatraz A fascinating account of the one and only successful escape from the maximum security prison at Alcatraz in 1962. The three men were never heard from again.
1979 (PG) 112m/C Clint Eastwood, Patrick McGoohan, Roberts Blossom, Fred Ward, Danny Glover; *D:* Don Siegel. **VHS, Beta, LV $14.95** *PAR* ✬✬✬

Escape from Cell Block Three Five escaped female convicts take it on the lam for Mexico and freedom.
1978 82m/C Carolyn Judd, Teri Guzman, Bonita Kalem. **VHS, Beta $9.99** *STE, PSM* ✬

Escape from Death Row Convicted criminal mastermind, sentenced to die, devises a brilliant and daring plan of escape on the eve of his execution.
1976 (R) 85m/C Lee Van Cleef, James Lane, Barbara Moore, Alice Belios. **VHS, Beta** *PGN* ✬

Escape from DS-3 Bostwick and "Police Academy" alumnus Smith team up in a familiar story: framed for a serious crime, a man attempts to escape from a maximum security satellite prison. About as good as you'd expect.
198? 88m/C Jackson Bostwick, Bubba Smith. **VHS $79.99** *MNC, MOV* ✬✬

Escape from El Diablo Two juvenile delinquents harass guards at a Mexican prison. Being from California, they use frisbees and skateboards to help their escape.
1983 (PG) 92m/C *SP GB* Jimmy McNichol, Timothy Van Patten, John Ethan Wayne; *D:* Gordon Hessler. **VHS, Beta $9.95** *MED* ✬

Escape from Galaxy Three A pair of space travelers fight off a bevy of evil aliens.
1976 (G) 90m/C James Milton, Cheryl Buchanan. **VHS, Beta $79.95** *PSM* ✬

Escape from Hell Two scantily clad women escape from a jungle prison and are pursued by their sadistic warden. *AKA:* Hellfire on Ice, Part 2: Escape from Hell.
1989 ?m/C Anthony Steffen, Ajita Wilson; *D:* Edward Muller. **VHS $59.95** *HHE* ✬

Escape from New York The ultimate urban nightmare: a ruined, future Manhattan is an anarchic prison for America's worst felons. When convicts hold the President hostage, a disgraced war hero unwillingly

attempts an impossible rescue mission. Cynical but largely unexceptional sci-fi action, putting a good cast through tight-lipped peril.
1981 (R) 99m/C Kurt Russell, Lee Van Cleef, Ernest Borgnine, Donald Pleasence, Isaac Hayes, Adrienne Barbeau, Harry Dean Stanton, Season Hubley; **D:** John Carpenter. **VHS, Beta, LV** $14.98 SUE, NLC ♫♫½

Escape from Planet Earth A spaceship is damaged deep in space and only a few of the crew can make it back to Earth. But who will decide who lives or dies? Also known as "The Doomsday Machine." **AKA:** The Doomsday Machine.
1967 91m/B Grant Williams, Bobby Van, Ruta Lee, Henry Wilcoxon, Mala Powers, Casey Kasem, Mike Farrell, Harry Hope; **D:** Lee Sholem. **VHS** $59.95 ACA ♫

Escape from Safehaven Brutal slimeballs rule a mad, sadistic world in the post-apocalyptic future, and a family tries to escape them. In very poor taste.
1988 (R) 87m/C Rick Gianasi, Mollie O'Mara, John Wittenbauer, Roy MacArthur, William Beckwith; **D:** Brian Thomas Jones, James McCalmont. **VHS, Beta** $79.95 SVS Woof!

Escape from Sobibor Nail-biting, true account of the largest successful escape from a Nazi prison camp, adapted from Richard Rashke's book. Made for TV.
1987 (PG-13) 120m/C Alan Arkin, Joanna Pacula, Rutger Hauer, Hartmut Becker, Jack Shepherd; **D:** Jack Gold. **VHS** $89.98 LIV ♫♫♫

Escape from the Bronx Invading death squads seek to level the Bronx. Local street gangs cry foul and ally to defeat the uncultured barbarians. Sequel to "1990: The Bronx Warriors."
1985 (R) 82m/C Mark Gregory, Henry Silva, Valeria D'Obici, Timothy Brent, Thomas Moore, Andrea Coppola; **D:** Enzo G. Castellari. **VHS, Beta** $69.95 MED ♫

Escape from the KGB A CIA agent escapes from a Soviet prison, taking plans for a new space installation with him.
1987 99m/C Thomas Hunter, Ivan Desny, Marie Versini, Walter Barns; **D:** Harald Phillipe. **VHS, Beta** NO Woof!

Escape from the Planet of the Apes Reprising their roles as intelligent, English-speaking apes, McDowall and Hunter flee their world before it's destroyed, and travel back in time to present-day America. In L.A. they become the subjects of a relentless search by the fearful population, much like humans Charlton Heston and James Franciscus were targeted for experimentation and destruction in simian society in the earlier "Planet of the Apes" and "Beneath the Planet of the Apes." Sequelled by "Conquest of the Planet of the Apes" and a television series.
1971 (G) 98m/C Roddy McDowall, Kim Hunter, Sal Mineo, Ricardo Montalban, William Windom, Bradford Dillman, Natalie Trundy, Eric Braeden; **D:** Don Taylor; **M:** Jerry Goldsmith. **VHS, Beta, LV** $19.98 FOX ♫♫♫

Escape Me Never Flynn plays a struggling composer in this sappy period piece about poverty-stricken artists in Italy at the turn of the century. Flynn falls for his brother's wealthy fiancee (Parker), although he is married to the faithful Lupino. Atypical role for Flynn and definitely not one of his best. Based on the novel "The Fool of the Family," by Margaret Kennedy and the play "Escape Me Never" by Kennedy.
1947 101m/B Errol Flynn, Ida Lupino, Eleanor Parker, Gig Young, Reginald Denny, Isobel Elsom; **D:** Peter Godfrey; **W:** Thomas Williamson. **VHS** $19.98 MGM ♫½

Escape to Athena A motley group is stuck in a German P.O.W. camp on a Greek island during World War II.
1979 (PG) 102m/C GB Roger Moore, Telly Savalas, David Niven, Claudia Cardinale, Richard Roundtree, Stefanie Powers, Sonny Bono, Elliott Gould, William Holden; **D:** George P. Cosmatos. **VHS, Beta** $19.98 FOX ♫♫½

Escape to Burma A man on the run for a murder he did not commit finds refuge and romance in an isolated jungle home.
1955 86m/C Barbara Stanwyck, Robert Ryan, Reginald Denny; **D:** Allan Dwan. **VHS, Beta** $39.95 DIS, BVV ♫½

Escape to Love Beautiful student helps a famous dissident escape from Poland, only to lose him to another heroic venture.
1982 105m/C Clara Perryman, Louis Jourdan; **D:** Herbert Stein. **Beta** $14.95 PSM ♫½

Escape to Paradise The last of Breen's films for RKO has him as a South American motorcycle-taxi driver acting as a guide for tourist Taylor. When Breen sets Taylor up with Shelton, trouble ensues. ♫Tra-La-La; Rhythm of the Rio; Ay, Ay, Ay.
1939 60m/B Bobby Breen, Kent Taylor, Maria Shelton, Joyce Compton, Rosina Galli, Frank Yaconelli; **D:** Erle C. Kenton. **VHS** $19.95 NOS, RXM ♫½

Escape to the Sun Pair of Russian university students plan to flee their homeland so they can be allowed to live and love free from oppression. **AKA:** Habricha el Hashemesh.
1972 (PG) 94m/C IS Laurence Harvey, Josephine Chaplin, John Ireland, Jack Hawkins, Lila Kedrova, Clive Revill; **D:** Menahem Golan. **VHS, Beta** $39.95 IVE ♫½

Escape to Witch Mountain Two young orphans with supernatural powers find themselves on the run from a greedy millionaire who wants to exploit their amazing gift. Adapted from a novel by Alexander Key.
1975 (G) 97m/C Kim Richards, Ike Eisenmann, Eddie Albert, Ray Milland, Donald Pleasence; **D:** John Hough. **VHS, Beta, LV** $19.99 DIS ♫♫♫

Escape 2000 In a future society where individuality is considered a crime, those who refuse to conform are punished by being hunted down in a jungle. Gross, twisted takeoff of Richard Connell's "The Most Dangerous Game." **AKA:** Turkey Shoot.
1981 (R) 80m/C AU Steve Railsback, Olivia Hussey, Michael Craig; **D:** Brian Trenchard-Smith. **VHS, Beta** $9.98 SUE, STE Woof!

Escapes In the tradition of "The Twilight Zone," Vincent Price introduces five short thrillers featuring time travel, aliens, and telepathy. Produced with computer assistance for sharper, more contrasted images.
1986 72m/C Vincent Price, Jerry Grisham, Lee Canfield, John Mitchum, Gil Reade; **D:** David Steensland. **VHS, Beta** $9.99 STE, PSM ♫♫

Escapist A professional escape artist becomes involved in a perverted corporate plot and must escape to save his life and livelihood.
1983 87m/C Bill Shirk, Peter Lupus; **D:** Eddie Beverly Jr. **VHS, Beta** $69.98 LIV, VES Woof!

Escort Girls The escort girls are a group of actresses, models, and secretaries who really know how to show their clients a good time.
1974 77m/C David Dixon, Maria O'Brien, Marika Mann, Gil Barber, Helen Christie. **VHS, Beta** $59.95 GEM Woof!

E.S.P. A young man is given the amazing power of extra-sensory perception.
1983 96m/C Jim Stafford, George Deaton. **VHS, Beta** BFV Woof!

Esposa y Amante While her daughter contemplates suicide, a mother remembers the happy early years of her marriage, followed by the wrong-doings of her husband which caused her to seek comfort in the arms of an old lawyer friend. Her daughter is now suffering for the problems of her own marriage. In Spanish.
197? 102m/C SP Ramiro Oliveros, Ricardo Merino, Victoria Abril, Frika Wallner. **VHS, Beta** $29.95 MED ♫

Esta Noche Cena Pancho A Spanish comedy about the antics of men at a bachelor party.
1987 90m/C SP Alfonso Zayas, Carmen Salinas, Armando Silvestre, Alberto Rojas; **D:** Victor Manuel Castro. **VHS, Beta** MED ♫

Estate of Insanity An English lord and his second wife become involved in a web of death when a maniac stalks their ancient estate.
1970 90m/C John Turner, Heather Sears, Ann Lynn; **D:** Robert Hartford-Davis. **VHS, Beta** NO ♫

Et La Tenoresse?...Bordel! A French comedy about a color-blind painter and his kinky fashion photographer roommate living in Paris. In French with subtitles.
1984 100m/C FR **D:** Patrick Schulmann. **VHS, Beta** $59.95 FCT ♫♫

E.T.: The Extra-Terrestrial The famous Spielberg fantasy, one of the most popular and highest grossing films in history, portrays a limpid-eyed alien stranded on earth and his special bonding relationship with a young boy. A modern fairy tale providing warmth, humor and sheer wonder.
1982 (PG) 115m/C Henry Thomas, Dee Wallace Stone, Drew Barrymore, Robert MacNaughton, Peter Coyote, C. Thomas Howell, Sean Frye; **D:** Steven Spielberg; **M:** John Williams. Academy Awards '82: Best Sound, Best Visual Effects, Best Original Score; Nominations: Best Film Editing; Academy Awards '82: Best Cinematography, Best Director (Spielberg), Best Picture, Best Sound; Golden Globe Awards '83: Best Film—Drama; People's Choice Awards '83: Best Film. **VHS, Beta, LV** $24.95 MCA, APD, RDG ♫♫♫♫

Eternal Evil A bored television director is taught how to have out-of-body experiences by his devil-worshipping girlfriend. He eventually realizes that when he leaves his body, it runs around killing people.
1987 (R) 85m/C Karen Black, Winston Rekert, Lois Maxwell; **D:** George Mihalka. **VHS, Beta, LV** $79.98 LIV ♫

Eternal Return A lush modern retelling of the Tristan/Isolde legend. A young man falls passionately in love with his aunt, only to die of unrequited love. The script was written by Jean Cocteau. In French with English subtitles. **AKA:** L'Eternel Retour; Love Eternal.
1943 100m/B FR Jean Marais, Madeleine Sologne; **D:** Jean Delannoy; **W:** Jean Cocteau. **VHS, Beta** $29.98 SUE, TAM, NLC ♫♫½

The Eternal Waltz Overly sentimental chronicle of the life of composer Johann Strauss. Only director Verhoeven's touch holds the viewer's interest, though the production values are excellent. **AKA:** Ewiger Walzer.
1959 97m/C Bernhard Wicki, Hilde Krahl, Annemarie Duerringer, Friedl Loor, Eduard Strauss Jr., Gert Frobe, Arnulf Schroeder; **D:** Paul Verhoeven. **VHS** $24.95 NOS ♫♫

Eternally Yours A witty magician's career threatens to break up his marriage.

E

1939 95m/B David Niven, Loretta Young, Hugh Herbert, Broderick Crawford, C. Aubrey Smith, Billie Burke, Eve Arden, ZaSu Pitts; **D:** Tay Garnett. **VHS, Beta, 3/4U, Special order formats** $19.95 *NOS, MRV, HHT* 🎬🎬½

Eternity While trying to uncover corrupt corporate America a television reporter falls in love with a model who works for a media king and puts his credibility on the line. He believes he and the woman shared romance in a past life.
1990 (R) 122m/C Jon Voight, Armand Assante, Wilford Brimley, Eileen Davidson, Kaye Ballard, Lainie Kazan, Joey Villa, Steven Keats, Eugene Roche, Frankie Valli, John P. Ryan; **D:** Steven Paul. **VHS** $14.95 *ACA* 🎬

Ethan A missionary in the Philippines falls in love with a woman and exiles himself for his fall from grace.
1971 91m/C Robert Sampson, Rosa Rosal, Eddie Infante; **D:** Michael DuPont. **VHS, Beta** $24.95 *GHV* 🎬½

Ethan Frome Neeson stars as the lonely, poverty-stricken 19th-century New England farmer who has long and faithfully cared for his bitter, invalid wife. When his wife's distant young cousin comes to take over as house-keeper they both succumb to their forbidden passion with tragic results. The performers carry the burden of the film's sluggish pacing, where the bleak setting of Massachusetts in winter tends to overwhelm the events. Based on the novel by Edith Wharton.
1992 (PG) 107m/C Liam Neeson, Patricia Arquette, Joan Allen, Tate Donovan, Katherine Houghton; **D:** John Madden; **W:** Richard Nelson. **VHS, LV** *TOU* 🎬🎬½

Eubie! The popular Broadway musical revue based on the life and songs of Eubie Blake is presented in a video transfer. Some of Eubie's best known songs, performed here by members of the original cast, include "I'm Just Wild About Harry," "Memories of You," "In Honeysuckle Time" and "The Charleston Rag."
1982 100m/C Gregory Hines, Maurice Hines, Leslie Dockery, Alaina Reed, Lynnie Godfrey, Mel Johnson Jr, Jeffrey V. Thompson; **D:** Julianne Boyd. **VHS, Beta** $19.98 *WAR, OM* 🎬🎬½

Eureka! A bizarre, wildly symbolic slab of Roegian artifice that deals with the dream-spliced life of a rich, bored gold tycoon who becomes tortured over his daughter's marriage and his own useless wealth. Eventually he is bothered by the Mafia and led to the courtroom by business competitors. From the book by Paul Mayersberg.
1981 (R) 130m/C *GB* Gene Hackman, Theresa Russell, Joe Pesci, Rutger Hauer, Mickey Rourke, Ed Lauter, Jane Lapotaire; **D:** Nicolas Roeg. **VHS, Beta** $79.95 *MGM* 🎬🎬½

Eureka Stockade Four early Australian gold prospectors join forces to fight their governor and the police for the rights to dig on the continent. *AKA:* Massacre Hill.
1949 103m/B Chips Rafferty, Peter Finch, Jane Barrett, Peter Illing; **D:** Harry Watt. **VHS, Beta** $24.95 *NOS, DVT, HEG* 🎬🎬

Europa, Europa The incredible, harrowing and borderline-absurdist true story of Solomon Perel, a young Jew who escaped the Holocaust by passing for German at an elite, Nazi-run academy. Such a sharp evocation of the era that the modern German establishment wouldn't submit it for the Academy Awards. In German and Russian with English subtitles.
1991 (R) 115m/C *GE* Marco Hofschneider, Klaus Abramowsky, Michele Gleizer, Rene Hofschneider, Nathalie Schmidt, Delphine Forest; **D:** Agnieszka Holland. Academy Awards '91

Nominations: Best Adapted Screenplay; Golden Globe Awards '92: Best Foreign Film; National Board of Review Awards '91: 5 Best Foreign Films of the Year; New York Film Critics Awards '91: Best Foreign Film. **VHS** $79.98 *ORI, TAM* 🎬🎬🎬½

Europa '51 The despairing portrait of post-war malaise, as an American woman, whose son committed suicide, lives in Rome searching for some semblance of meaning, and ends up in an asylum. One of Bergman & Rossellini's least-loved films. In Italian with subtitles. *AKA:* The Greatest Love.
1952 110m/B Ingrid Bergman, Alexander Knox, Ettore Giannini, Giulietta Masina; **D:** Roberto Rossellini. **VHS, Beta** $59.95 *FCT* 🎬🎬½

The Europeans Henry James's satirical novel about two fortune-seeking expatriates and their sober American relations.
1979 90m/C Lee Remick, Lisa Eichhorn, Robin Ellis, Wesley Addy, Tim Woodward; **D:** James Ivory. Academy Awards '79 Nominations: Best Costume Design; National Board of Review Awards '79: 10 Best Films of the Year. **VHS, Beta** $59.95 *CVC, TAM, LUM* 🎬🎬🎬

Eve of Destruction Hell knows no fury like a cutting-edge android-girl on the war-path. Modeled after her creator, Dr. Eve Simmons, Eve VII has android-babe good looks and a raging nuclear capability. Wouldn't you know, something goes haywire during her trial run, and debutante Eve turns into a PMS nightmare machine, blasting all the good Doctor's previous beaux. That's where military agent Hines comes in, though you wonder why. Dutch actress Soutendijk plays dual Eves in her first American film.
1990 (R) 101m/C Gregory Hines, Renee Soutendijk, Kevin McCarthy; **D:** Duncan Gibbins. **VHS, Beta, LV** $19.95 *COL, NLC, SUE Woof!*

Evel Knievel The life of motorcycle stuntman Evel Knievel is depicted in this movie, as portrayed by George Hamilton. Stunts will be appreciated by Evel Knievel fans.
1972 (PG) 90m/C George Hamilton, Bert Freed, Rod Cameron, Sue Lyon; **D:** Marvin J. Chomsky. **VHS, Beta** $59.95 *MPI* 🎬🎬

Even Angels Fall One of heartthrob singer Humperdinck's scattered dramatic projects, a mystery thriller about a romance novelist moving into a New York brownstone whose previous inhabitant committed suicide—or was it murder?
1990 ?m/C Morgan Fairchild, Engelbert Humperdinck; **D:** Thomas Calabrese. **VHS** *NO* 🎬

An Evening with Robin Williams Robin Williams explodes all over the screen in this live nightclub performance taped at the Great American Music Hall in San Francisco.
1983 92m/C Robin Williams. **VHS, Beta, LV** $14.95 *PAR* 🎬🎬

Evergreen The daughter of a retired British music hall star is mistaken for her mother and it is thought that she has discovered the secret of eternal youth. 🎵Daddy Wouldn't Buy Me a Bow-Wow; When You've Got a Little Springtime in Your Heart; If I Give in to You; Tinkle, Tinkle, Tinkle; Dear, Dear; Dancing on the Ceiling; Just by Your Example; Over My Shoulder.
1934 91m/B *GB* Jessie Matthews, Sonnie Hale, Betty Balfour, Barry Mackay; **D:** Victor Saville; **M:** Richard Rodgers, Harry Woods, Lorenz Hart, Harry Woods. **VHS, Beta, LV, 3/4U, Special order formats** $39.95 *NOS, HMV, VMK* 🎬🎬½

The Everlasting Secret Family Politics and family life make strange bedfellows. A top political figure joins a secret homosexual organization in his search for power.

1988 93m/C *AU* Arthur Dignam, Mark Lee, Dennis Miller, Heather Mitchell; **D:** Michael Thornhill. **VHS** $79.95 *FCT, CCN* 🎬🎬

Eversmile New Jersey A dentist travels through Patagonia, offering dental care and advice to anyone in need, and a young woman, taken with the dental knight, dumps her boyfriend and stows away with him. When he discovers his admirer, he is less than ecstatic, but a chance tooth extraction on the road reveals the young woman's natural dental talents, and the two bond, as it were. Screenplay by Jorge Goldenberg, Roberto Scheuer and Carlos Sorin; from the director of "The Official Story."
1989 (PG) 88m/C *AR* Daniel Day-Lewis, Mirjana Jokovic; **D:** Carlos Sorin; **W:** Jorge Goldenberg, Roberto Scheuer, Carlos Sorin. **VHS, Beta, LV** $89.98 *FXV, MED* 🎬½

Every Girl Should Be Married A shopgirl sets her sights on an eligible bachelor doctor.
1948 84m/B Cary Grant, Betsy Drake, Diana Lynn, Franchot Tone; **D:** Don Hartman. **VHS, Beta, LV** $19.98 *RKO, TTC* 🎬🎬½

Every Girl Should Have One A rambunctious comedy about a chase following a million-dollar diamond theft.
1978 90m/C Zsa Zsa Gabor, Robert Alda, Alice Faye, Sandra Vacey, John Lazar. **VHS, Beta** $59.95 *GEM* 🎬½

Every Man for Himself & God Against All This film tells the story of Kaspar Hauser, a young man who mysteriously appears in a small German town, having been confined since birth. His alternate vision of the world and attempts to reconcile with reality make for a lovely, though demanding film. In German with English subtitles. *AKA:* The Mystery of Kaspar Hauser; Jeder Fur Sich Und Gott Gegen Alle.
1975 110m/C *GE* Bruno S; **D:** Werner Herzog. **VHS, Beta** $59.95 *COL, APD, GLV* 🎬🎬🎬🎬

Every Man's Law A cowboy who poses as a hired gunman is almost lynched by ranchers who think he is a murderer.
1935 60m/B Johnny Mack Brown. **VHS, Beta** $19.95 *VCN* 🎬½

Every Time We Say Goodbye In 1942, Jerusalem, an American flyboy falls in love with a young Sephardic Jewish girl, whose family resists the match.
1986 (PG-13) 97m/C Tom Hanks, Christina Marsillach, Benedict Taylor; **D:** Moshe Mizrahi. **VHS, Beta, LV** $79.98 *LIV* 🎬🎬½

Every Which Way But Loose Fairly pointless Eastwood foray featuring Clint as a beer-guzzling, country-music loving truck driver earning a living as a barroom brawler. He and his orangutan travel to Colorado in pursuit of the woman he loves. Behind him are a motorcycle gang and an L.A. cop. All have been victims of his fists. Sequel is "Any Which Way You Can."
1978 (R) 119m/C Clint Eastwood, Sondra Locke, Geoffrey Lewis, Beverly D'Angelo, Ruth Gordon; **D:** James Fargo. **VHS, Beta, LV** $19.98 *WAR* 🎬🎬

Everybody Sing A down-on-their-luck theatrical family, including Garland (who is kicked out of boarding school for singing Mendelssohn with a swing beat) decides to put on a show in hopes of making a comeback. Dumb plot and boring songs make this one for die-hard Garland fans only. 🎵Swing, Mr. Mendelssohn, Swing; The One I Love; Down on Melody Farms; The Show Must Go On; I Wanna Swing; Never Was There Such a Perfect Day; Quainty Dainty Me; Why? Because; Snooks; Cosi, Cosa; Swing Low, Sweet Chariot.

1938 80m/B Allan Jones, Fanny Brice, Judy Garland, Reginald Owen, Billie Burke, Reginald Gardiner, Lynne Carver, Monty Woolley; *D:* Edwin L. Marin. **VHS $19.98** *MGM, MVD* 🎭🎭

Everybody Wins A mystery-romance about a befuddled private eye trying to solve a murder and getting caught up with the bizarre prostitute who hired him. Arthur Miller based this screenplay on his stage drama "Some Kind of Love Story." Confused and, given its pedigree, disappointing mystery. **1990** (R) 110m/C Nick Nolte, Debra Winger, Will Patton, Jack Warden, Kathleen Wilhoite, Frank Converse, Frank Military, Judith Ivey; *D:* Karel Reisz; *W:* Arthur Miller. **VHS, Beta, LV $89.98** *ORI* 🎭

Everybody's All American Shallow, sentimental melodrama about a college football star and his cheerleader wife whose lives, subsequent to their youthful glories, is a string of disappointments and tragedies. Decently acted and based on Frank Deford's novel. **1988** (R) 127m/C Jessica Lange, Dennis Quaid, Timothy Hutton, John Goodman, Carl Lumbly, Ray Baker, Savannah Smith; *D:* Taylor Hackford. **VHS, Beta, LV, 8mm $89.95** *WAR* 🎭🎭

Everybody's Dancin' A ballroom proprietor's business is marred by random killings in her establishment as the bands play on. 🎵Foolish Tears; Oblivious; Deep Freeze Dinah; I Shook; Rhumba Boogie. **1950** 66m/B Spade Cooley, Dick Lane, Hal Derwin, The Pioneers; *D:* Will Jason. **VHS, Beta, LV** *NO* 🎭½

Everybody's Fine Mastroianni stars in this bittersweet story of a father on a mission to reunite his five grown children. His journey takes him all over Italy as he tries to bring them together in this touching film about enduring family love. In Italian with English subtitles. *AKA:* Stanno Tutti Bene. **1990** (PG-13) 115m/C *IT* Marcello Mastroianni, Salvatore Cascio, Valeria Cavalli, Norma Martelli, Marino Cenna, Roberto Nobile, Salvatore Cascio; *D:* Giuseppe Tornatore; *M:* Ennio Morricone. **VHS, LV $19.95** *COL, TAM* 🎭🎭½

Everything You Always Wanted to Know About Sex (But Were Afraid to Ask) Satiric comical sketches about sex includes a timid sperm cell, an oversexed court jester, a sheep folly, and a giant disembodied breast. Quite entertaining in its own jolly way. Based on the book by Dr. David Reuben. **1972** (R) 88m/C Woody Allen, John Carradine, Lou Jacobi, Louise Lasser, Anthony Quayle, Geoffrey Holder, Lynn Redgrave, Tony Randall, Burt Reynolds, Gene Wilder, Robert Walden, Jay Robinson; *D:* Woody Allen. **VHS, Beta, LV $19.98** *MGM, FOX, PIA* 🎭🎭🎭

The Evictors Young couple moves into an abandoned, haunted farmhouse in a small Louisiana town. Unfortunately, they don't know anything about its horrible bloody history. And the real estate agent acts kinda funny. AIP Amityville scare-a-thon. **1979** (PG) 92m/C Vic Morrow, Michael Parks, Jessica Harper, Sue Ann Langdon, Dennis Fimple; *D:* Charles B. Pierce. **VHS, Beta $59.98** *LIV, VES* Woof!

The Evil A psychologist must destroy an evil force that is killing off the members of his research team residing at an old mansion. **1978** (R) 80m/C Richard Crenna, Joanna Pettet, Andrew Prine, Victor Buono, Cassie Yates; *D:* Gus Trikonis. **VHS, Beta $19.98** *SUE* 🎭🎭

Evil Altar A man controls a small town, but only so long as he offers sacrifices to the devil!

1989 (R) 90m/C William Smith, Robert Z'Dar, Pepper Martin, Theresa Cooney, Ryan Rao; *D:* Jim Winburn. **VHS $89.95** *NO* 🎭

The Evil Below A couple hits the high seas in search of the lost treasure ship "El Diablo," resting on the ocean floor. In the process they trigger an evil curse and then must attempt to thwart it. **1987** 90m/C *SA* June Chadwick, Wayne Crawford; *D:* Jean-Claude Dubois. **VHS, Beta** *NO* 🎭

Evil Clutch A young couple vacationing in the Alps encounter several creepy locals when they find themselves in the midst of a haunted forest. The cinematography is extremely amateurish in this Italian gorefest and the English dubbing is atrocious. However, the special makeup effects are outstanding and the musical score adds a touch of class to this otherwise inept horror film. **1989** (R) 88m/C *IT* Coralina Cataldi Tassoni, Diego Riba, Elena Cantarone, Luciano Crovato, Stefano Molinari; *W/D:* Andreas Marfori. **VHS $79.95** *UND, RHI* 🎭½

Evil Dead Five vacationing college students unwittingly resurrect demons which transform the students into evil monsters. Exuberantly gory low-budgeter followed by two sequels. **1983** 126m/C Bruce Campbell, Ellen Sandweiss, Betsy Baker, Hal Delrich; *D:* Sam Raimi. **VHS, Beta, LV $14.99** *HBO, IME* 🎭🎭½

Evil Dead 2: Dead by Dawn A gory, tongue-in-cheek sequel/remake of the original festival of gag and gore, in which an ancient book of magic invokes a crowd of flesh-snacking, joke-tossing ghouls. Followed by yet a third bloodfest. **1987** (R) 84m/C Bruce Campbell, Sarah Berry, Dan Hicks; *D:* Sam Raimi. **VHS, Beta, LV $14.98** *LIV, VES* 🎭🎭🎭

Evil Judgement A young girl investigates a series of murders and finds the culprit is a psychopathic judge. **1985** 93m/C Pamela Collyer, Jack Langedijk, Nanette Workman; *D:* Claude Castravelli. **VHS, Beta $69.95** *MED* 🎭½

Evil Laugh Medical students and their girlfriends party at an abandoned orphanage, until a serial killer decides to join them. **1986** (R) 90m/C Tony Griffin, Kim McKamy, Jody Gibson, Dominick Brascia; *D:* Dominick Brascia. **VHS $79.95** *CEL* Woof!

The Evil Mind A fraudulent mind reader predicts many disasters that start coming true. *AKA:* The Clairvoyant. **1934** 80m/B *GB* Claude Rains, Fay Wray, Jane Baxter, Felix Aylmer; *D:* Maurice Elvey. **VHS, Beta, 3/4U, Special order formats $16.95** *SNC, NOS, KRT* 🎭🎭½

The Evil of Frankenstein The third of the Hammer Frankenstein films, with the mad doctor once again finding his creature preserved in ice and thawing him out. Preceded by "The Revenge of Frankenstein" and followed by "Frankenstein Created Woman." **1964** 84m/C *GB* Peter Cushing, Duncan Lamont, Peter Woodthorpe, Sandor Eles, Kiwi Kingston, Katy Wild; *D:* Freddie Francis. **VHS, Beta $14.98** *MCA, MLB* 🎭🎭

Evil Spawn A fading movie queen takes an experimental drug to restore her youthful beauty, but it only turns her into a giant silverfish. *AKA:* Deadly Sting; Alive by Night. **1987** 90m/C Bobbie Bresee, John Carradine, Drew Godderis, John Terrance, Dawn Wildsmith; *D:* Kenneth J. Hall. **VHS, Beta** *NO* 🎭

Evil Spirits Boardinghouse tenants are murdered while the crazy landlady cashes their social security checks. This seedy horror cheapie doesn't take itself seriously, and like-minded genre buffs may enjoy the cult-film cast. **1991** (R) 95m/C Karen Black, Arte Johnson, Virginia Mayo, Michael Berryman, Martine Beswick, Bert Remsen, Yvette Vickers, Robert Quarry, Mikel Angel, Debra Lamb; *D:* Gary Graver. **VHS, Beta, LV $79.95** *PSM* 🎭½

The Evil That Men Do A hitman comes out of retirement to break up a Central American government's political torture ring and, in the process, brings a friend's killer to justice. Based on the novel by R. Lance Hill. **1984** (R) 90m/C Charles Bronson, Theresa Saldana, Joseph Maher, Jose Ferrer, Rene Enriquez, John Glover, Raymond St. Jacques, Antoinette Bower, Enrique Lucero, Jorge Luke; *D:* J. Lee Thompson. **VHS, Beta, LV, 8mm $14.95** *COL* 🎭🎭

Evil Toons A quartet of lovely coeds on a cleaning job venture into a deserted mansion. There they accidentally release a vulgar, lustful, animated demon who proceeds to cause their clothes to fall off. Can the girls escape the haunted mansion with their sanity, virtue and wardrobes intact? **1990** (R) 86m/C David Carradine, Dick Miller, Monique Gabrielle, Suzanne Ager, Stacy Nix, Madison Stone, Don Dowe, Arte Johnson, Michelle Bauer; *D:* Fred Olen Ray. **VHS, Beta $79.95** *PSM* 🎭½

Evil Town In this poorly made film, a wandering guy discovers a town overrun with zombies created by a mad doctor. **1987** (R) 88m/C Dean Jagger, James Keach, Robert Walker Jr., Doria Cook, Michele Marsh; *D:* Edward Collins. **VHS, Beta $79.95** *TWE, HHE* 🎭

Evil Under the Sun An opulent beach resort is the setting as Hercule Poirot attempts to unravel a murder mystery. Based on the Agatha Christie novel. **1982** (PG) 102m/C *GB* Peter Ustinov, Jane Birkin, Maggie Smith, Colin Blakely, Roddy McDowall, Diana Rigg, Sylvia Miles, James Mason, Nicholas Clay; *D:* Guy Hamilton; *W:* Agatha Christie. **VHS, Beta, LV $19.99** *HBO* 🎭🎭

Evil's Commandment Original vampire film which started the classic Italian horror cycle. A gorgeous Countess needs blood to stay young, otherwise she reverts to a 200-year-old vampire. **1956** ?m/B *IT* Giana Maria Canale; *D:* Riccardo Freda. **VHS $20** *SMW* 🎭½

Evils of the Night Teenage campers are abducted by sex-crazed alien vampires. Bloody naked mayhem follows. **1985** 85m/C John Carradine, Julie Newmar, Tina Louise, Neville Brand, Aldo Ray, Karrie Emerson, Bridget Hollman; *D:* Mardi Rustam. **VHS, Beta $69.98** *LIV* 🎭

Evilspeak Bumbling misfit enrolled at a military school is mistreated by the other cadets. With the help of his computer, he retaliates with satanic power. Bits, bytes, and gore. **1982** (R) 89m/C Clint Howard, Don Stark, Lou Gravance, Lauren Lester, R.G. Armstrong, Joe Cortese, Claude Earl Jones, Haywood Nelson; *D:* Eric Weston. **VHS, Beta $59.98** *FOX* Woof!

The Ewok Adventure Those adorable, friendly and funny characters from "Return of the Jedi" make the jump from film to television in a new adventure from George Lucas. In this installment, the Ewoks save a miraculous child from harm with the help of a young human. This fun-filled adventure has Lucas's thumbprint all over it and great

special effects. Followed by "Ewoks: The Battle for Endor."
1984 (G) 96m/C Warwick Davis, Eric Walker, Aubree Miller, Fionnula Flanagan; **D:** John Korty. **VHS, Beta, LV $14.95** MGM, FCT ♫♫½

The Ewoks: Battle for Endor A television movie based on the furry creatures from "Return of the Jedi," detailing their battle against an evil queen to retain their forest home. Preceded by "The Ewok Adventure."
1985 98m/C Wilford Brimley, Warwick Davis, Aubree Miller, Sian Phillips, Paul Gleason, Eric Walker; **D:** Jim Wheat, Ken Wheat. **VHS, Beta, LV $14.95** MGM, FCT ♫♫½

Ex-Lady Davis stars as a liberated woman who loves advertising writer Raymond, but doesn't want to marry him. However, she believes living together is the most suitable arrangement. The two open up an ad agency and complications ensue. Remake of "Illicit," which was filmed only two years earlier with Barbara Stanwyck in the lead role.
1933 65m/B Bette Davis, Gene Raymond, Frank McHugh, Claire Dodd, Monroe Owsley, Ferdinand Gottschalk; **D:** Robert Florey. **VHS $19.98** MGM ♫♫

Ex-Mrs. Bradford Amateur sleuth Dr. Bradford teams up with his ex-wife to solve a series of murders at the race track. Sophisticated comedy-mystery; witty dialogue.
1936 80m/B William Powell, Jean Arthur, James Gleason, Eric Blore, Robert Armstrong; **D:** Stephen Roberts. **VHS, Beta, LV $19.95** NOS, MED ♫♫♫

Excalibur A sweeping, visionary retelling of the life of King Arthur, from his conception, to the sword in the stone, to the search for the Holy Grail and the final battle with Mordred. An imperfect, sensationalized version, but still the best yet filmed.
1981 (R) 140m/C Nigel Terry, Nicol Williamson, Nicholas Clay, Helen Mirren, Cherie Lunghi, Paul Geoffrey, Gabriel Byrne, Liam Neeson, Patrick Stewart, Charley Boorman, Corin Redgrave; **D:** John Boorman. **VHS, Beta, LV $19.98** WAR, TVC ♫♫♫½

Excessive Force Routine actioner lives up to its title by offering lots of violence, but little else. Gang leader Young seeks revenge on the cops who he believes ruined a $3 million drug deal. Loner cop Griffith is the only one to survive the grudge killings and goes after Young himself. Talented cast underachieves. Limited theatrical release sent this one almost straight to video.
1993 (R) 87m/C Thomas Ian Griffith, Lance Henriksen, James Earl Jones, Charlotte Lewis, Tony Todd, Burt Young, W. Earl Brown; **D:** Jon Hess; **W:** Thomas Ian Griffith; **M:** Charles Bernstein. **VHS** COL, NLC ♫½

The Execution A made-for-television film about five female friends who discover that the Nazi doctor who brutalized them in a concentration camp during World War II is now living a normal life in California. Together they plot his undoing.
1985 92m/C Loretta Swit, Valerie Harper, Sandy Dennis, Jessica Walter, Rip Torn, Barbara Barrie, Robert Hooks, Michael Lerner; **D:** Paul Wendkos. **VHS, Beta $9.99** STE, PSM ♫½

The Execution of Private Slovik This quiet powerhouse of a TV movie recounts in straightforward terms the case of Eddie Slovik, a WWII misfit who became the only American soldier executed for desertion since the Civil War. The Levinson/Link screenplay (based on the book by William Bradford Huie) ends up deifying Slovik, which some might find hard to take. But there's no arguing the impact of the drama, or of Sheen's unaffected lead performance.

1974 122m/C Martin Sheen, Mariclare Costello, Ned Beatty, Gary Busey, Matt Clark, Ben Hammer, Warren Kemmerling; **D:** Lamont Johnson; **W:** Richard Levinson, William Link. **VHS $79.95** MCA ♫♫♫½

Execution of Raymond Graham The lawyers and family of Raymond Graham struggle to keep him from being executed for murder. Based on a true story; made for television.
1985 104m/C Morgan Freeman, Jeff Fahey, Kate Reid, Laurie Metcalf, Josef Sommer; **D:** Daniel Petrie. **VHS, Beta** NO ♫♫½

The Executioner A thriller wherein a British spy must prove that his former colleague is a double agent. Elements of back-stabbing, betrayal, and espionage abound.
1970 (PG) 107m/C GB Judy Geeson, Oscar Homolka, Charles Gray, Nigel Patrick, George Peppard, Joan Collins, Keith Mitchell; **D:** Sam Wanamaker. **VHS, Beta $9.95** COL, GKK ♫♫

The Executioner A very cheap, very "Godfather"-like story of a mafia family gone awry. Also known as "Like Father, Like Son" and "Massacre Mafia Style." **AKA:** Like Father, Like Son; Massacre Mafia Style.
1978 (R) 84m/C Duke Mitchell, Vic Caesar, Dominic Micelli, John Strong, Jim Williams, Lorenzo Dodo; **W/D:** Duke Mitchell. **VHS, Beta** GEM, MRV ♫

Executioner of Venice Marauding pirates with time on hands swarm in from the Adriatic Sea and attempt to rob the Venetians blind. The Doge and his godson come to the rescue.
1963 90m/C Guy Madison, Lex Barker, Alessandra Panaro; **D:** Louis Capauno. **VHS, Beta** NO ♫

The Executioner, Part 2: Frozen Scream Brutal feud rocks the Mafia, and a crime kingpin's passionate son seeks revenge on his father's slayers. Not a sequel to any other films bearing similar titles. Strange thing is, no "Executioner, Part I" was ever made. Pretty laughable.
1984 (R) 150m/C Chris Mitchum, Aldo Ray, Antoine John Mottet, Renee Harmon; **D:** James Bryant. **VHS, Beta $49.98** GEM ♫

The Executioner's Song European version of the television movie based on Norman Mailer's Pulitzer Prize-winner, recounting the life and death of convicted murderer Gary Gilmore. Features adult-minded footage not seen in the U.S. version.
1982 157m/C Tommy Lee Jones, Rosanna Arquette, Eli Wallach, Christine Lahti, Jenny Wright, Jordan Clark, Steven Keats; **D:** Lawrence Schiller. **VHS, Beta $29.95** STE, LIV ♫♫½

Executive Action Political thriller providing a different look at the events leading to the assassination of JFK. In this speculation, a millionaire pays a professional spy to organize a secret conspiracy to kill President Kennedy. Ryan's final film. Adapted by Dalton Trumbo from Mark Lane's "Rush to Judgement."
1973 (PG) 91m/C Burt Lancaster, Robert Ryan, Will Geer, Gilbert Green, John Anderson; **D:** David Miller. **VHS, Beta, LV $19.98** WAR ♫♫½

Executive Suite One of the first dog-eat-dog dramas about high finance and big business. The plot centers on the question of a replacement for the freshly buried owner of a gigantic furniture company.
1954 104m/B William Holden, June Allyson, Barbara Stanwyck, Fredric March, Walter Pidgeon, Louis Calhern, Shelley Winters, Paul Douglas, Nina Foch, Dean Jagger; **D:** Robert Wise. **VHS, Beta $29.95** MGM ♫♫♫

Exiled in America A Central American freedom fighter (Albert) flees his country for the United States, settling in a small town with his wife. She gets a waitressing job at a local diner, telling the owner her husband died in an accident, and the owner's son winds up falling in love with her. Things get complicated when the death squad, led by a corrupt CIA agent, follows Albert to his hiding place, and the local sheriff threatens to blow his cover.
1990 84m/C Maxwell Caulfield, Edward Albert, Viveca Lindfors, Kamala Lopez, Stella Stevens, Wings Hauser; **W/D:** Paul Leder. **VHS $79.95** PSM ♫♫

Exiled to Shanghai A couple of newsreel men invent a television device that revolutionizes the business.
1937 65m/B Wallace Ford, June Travis, Dean Jagger, William Bakewell, Arthur Lake, Jonathan Hale, William Harrigan, Sarah Padden; **D:** Armand Schaefer. **VHS $24.95** NOS, DVT, HEG ♫♫½

Exit the Dragon, Enter the Tiger Story about the death of karate master Bruce Lee.
1976 84m/C **VHS, Beta $24.95** UHV, TWE ♫½

Exodus Chronicles the post-WWII partition of Palestine into a homeland for Jews; the anguish of refugees from Nazi concentration camps held on ships in the Mediterranean; the struggle of the tiny nation with forces dividing it from within and destroying it from the outside; and the heroic men and women who saw a job to be done and did it. Based on the novel by Leon Uris; filmed in Cyprus and Israel. Preminger battled the Israeli government, the studio, and the novel's author to complete this epic. Cost more than $4 million, a phenomenal amount at the time.
1960 208m/C Paul Newman, Eva Marie Saint, Lee J. Cobb, Sal Mineo, Ralph Richardson, Hugh Griffith, Gregory Ratoff, Felix Aylmer, Peter Lawford, Jill Haworth, John Derek, David Opatoshu, Marius Goring, Alexandra Stewart, Michael Wager, Martin Benson, Paul Stevens, George Maharis; **D:** Otto Preminger; **W:** Dalton Trumbo. Academy Awards '60: Best Original Score; Nominations: Best Color Cinematography, Best Supporting Actor (Mineo); Golden Globe Awards '61: Best Supporting Actor (Mineo). **VHS, Beta, LV $29.98** FOX, SWC ♫♫♫

Exorcism A satanic cult in a small English village commits a series of gruesome crimes that have the authorities baffled.
1974 90m/C Paul Naschy, Maria Perschy; **D:** Juan Bosch. **VHS, Beta $19.95** HHE ♫½

Exorcism's Daughter While running an insane asylum, a man discovers that a woman has lost her mind because as a child, she witnessed her mother's death during an exorcism. Pretty grim but interesting for genre fans. A natural double feature with "House of Psychotic Women." **AKA:** House of Insane Women.
1974 (R) 93m/C SP Amelia Gade, Francisco Rabal, Espartaco Santoni; **D:** Rafael Morena Alba. **VHS $16.95** SNC ♫

The Exorcist Truly terrifying story of a young girl who is possessed by a malevolent demon. Brilliantly directed by Friedkin, with underlying themes of the workings and nature of fate. Impeccable casting and unforgettable, thought-provoking performances. A rare film that remains startling and engrossing with every viewing; it spawned countless imitations and changed the way horror films were made. Based on the bestseller by William Peter Blatty, who won an Oscar for his screenplay. Not for the squeamish. When first released, the film created mass hysteria in theaters, with people fainting and paramedics on the scene.

1973 (R) 120m/C Ellen Burstyn, Linda Blair, Jason Miller, Max von Sydow, Jack MacGowran, Lee J. Cobb, Kitty Winn; **D:** William Friedkin; **W:** William Peter Blatty; **M:** Jack Nitzsche. Academy Awards '73: Best Adapted Screenplay, Best Sound; Nominations: Best Actress (Burstyn), Best Art Direction/Set Decoration, Best Cinematography, Best Director (Friedkin), Best Film Editing, Best Picture, Best Supporting Actor (Miller), Best Supporting Actress (Blair); Golden Globe Awards '74: Best Director (Friedkin), Best Film—Drama, Best Supporting Actress (Blair). **VHS, Beta, LV** $19.98 *WAR* ♫♫♫½

Exorcist 2: The Heretic Unnecessary sequel to the 1973 hit "The Exorcist" which featured extensive recutting by Boorman. After four years, Blair is still under psychiatric care, suffering from the effects of being possessed by the devil. Meanwhile, a priest investigates the first exorcist's work as he tries to help the head-spinning lass. Decent special effects.
1977 (R) 118m/C Richard Burton, Linda Blair, Louise Fletcher, Kitty Winn, James Earl Jones, Ned Beatty, Max von Sydow; **D:** John Boorman; **M:** Ennio Morricone. **VHS, Beta** $14.95 *WAR* ♫♫

The Exorcist 3 Apparently subscribing to the two wrongs make a right school of sequels, novelist Blatty this time sits in the director's chair. The result is slightly better than the first sequel, but still a far cry from the original. It's fifteen years later, and Detective Kinderman (played by Scott) is faced with a series of really gross murders that bear the indubitable mark of a serial killer who was flambeed in the electric chair, it seems, the same night as the exorcism of the pea-soup expectorating devil of the original. With the aid of priests Flanders and Dourif the detective stalks the transmigratory terror without the help of Linda Blair, who was at the time spoofing "The Exorcist" in "Repossessed."
1990 (R) 105m/C George C. Scott, Ed Flanders, Jason Miller, Nicol Williamson, Scott Wilson, Brad Dourif, Nancy Fish, George DiCenzo, Viveca Lindfors; **W:** William Peter Blatty. **VHS, Beta, LV** $19.98 *FOX, CCB* ♫♫

The Expendables A rugged captain turns a platoon of criminals and misfits into a tough fighting unit for a particularly dangerous mission from which they might not return. See the "Dirty Dozen" instead.
1989 (R) 89m/C Anthony Finetti, Peter Nelson, Loren Haynes, Kevin Duffis; **D:** Cirio H. Santiago. **VHS, Beta, LV** $79.95 *MED* ♫½

Experience Preferred... But Not Essential An English schoolgirl gets her first job at a resort where she learns about life. Made for British television.
1983 (PG) 77m/C GB Elizabeth Edmonds, Sue Wallace, Geraldine Griffith, Karen Meagher, Ron Bain, Alun Lewis, Robert Blythe; **D:** Peter Duffell. **VHS, Beta** $59.95 *MGM* ♫♫½

Experiment in Terror A psychopath kidnaps a girl in order to blackmail her sister, a bank teller, into embezzling $100,000. Score by Henry Mancini.
1962 123m/B Lee Remick, Glenn Ford, Stefanie Powers, Ross Martin; **D:** Blake Edwards. **VHS, Beta, LV** $59.95 *COL, IME* ♫♫♫

Experiment Perilous A psychologist and a recently widowed woman band together to find her husband's murderer. An atmospheric vintage mystery.
1945 91m/B Hedy Lamarr, Paul Lukas, George Brent, Albert Dekker; **D:** Jacques Tourneur. **VHS, Beta** $19.95 *MED* ♫♫♫

Expertos en Pinchazos In this comedy from Spain, Albert and George, experts at giving injections to women, inject a patient with venom by mistake. Now they must find her within 48 hours. In Spanish.
1979 100m/C SP Alberto Olmedo, Jorge Porcel. **VHS, Beta** $29.95 *MED* ♫½

The Experts When the KGB needs real Americans for their spies to study, they kidnap two out-of-work New Yorkers who mistakenly believe that they have been hired to open a nightclub in Nebraska. Shot on location in Canada. Sometimes funny and directed by former Second City TV MacKenzie Brother, Dave Thomas.
1989 (PG-13) 94m/C John Travolta, Arye Gross, Charles Martin Smith, Kelly Preston, James Keach, Deborah Foreman, Brian Doyle Murray; **D:** Dave Thomas. **VHS, Beta, LV, 8mm** $14.95 *PAR* ♫♫

Explorers Intelligent family fare involving three young boys who use a contraption from their makeshift laboratory to travel to outer space. From the director of "Gremlins," displaying Dante's characteristic surreal wit and sense of irony.
1985 (PG) 107m/C Ethan Hawke, River Phoenix, Jason Presson, Amanda Peterson, Mary Kay Place, Dick Miller, Robert Picardo; **D:** Joe Dante; **M:** Jerry Goldsmith. **VHS, Beta, LV** $14.95 *PAR* ♫♫½

Explosion Distraught and disturbed young man evades the draft after losing a brother in Vietnam. Arriving in Canada, he meets another draft-dodger with whom he embarks on a murderous rampage.
1969 (R) 96m/C Don Stroud, Gordon Thomson, Michele Chicione, Richard Conte; **D:** Jules Bricken. **VHS, Beta** $59.95 *TWE* ♫½

Exposed High fashion model Kinski falls in with a terrorist gang through a connection with violinist Nureyev. Weak plotting undermines the end of this political thriller. However, Kinski is brilliant, stripping the barrier between performance and audience.
1983 (R) 100m/C Nastassia Kinski, Rudolf Nureyev, Harvey Keitel, Ian McShane, Bibi Andersson; **D:** James Toback. **VHS, Beta** $79.95 *MGM* ♫♫

Exposure A rugged American photographer (Coyote) on assignment in Rio turns vigilante to locate the vicious killer of a young prostitute. Coyote and his girlfriend (Pays) get caught up in the deadly underworld of international arms trading and drug running as they search for the murderer.
1991 (R) 99m/C Peter Coyote, Amanda Pays, Tcheky Karyo. **VHS** $92.99 *HBO* ♫

Express to Terror Passengers aboard an atomic-powered train en route to Los Angeles attempt to kill a sleazy theatrical agent. Pilot for the "Supertrain" series.
1979 100m/C Steve Lawrence, George Hamilton, Vic Morrow, Broderick Crawford, Robert Alda, Don Stroud, Fred Williamson, Stella Stevens, Don Meredith; **D:** Dan Curtis. **VHS, Beta** $49.95 *PSM* ♫½

Exquisite Corpses An Oklahoma hayseed charges to New York with a new, slick image. He meets the wife of a wealthy man, and together they organize a murderous operation.
1988 95m/C Zoe Tamerlaine Lund, Gary Knox, Daniel Chapman, Ruth Collins; **D:** Temistocles Lopez. **VHS, LV** $79.95 *MNC* ♫½

The Exterminating Angel A fierce, funny surreal nightmare, wherein dinner guests find they cannot, for any definable reason, leave the dining room; full of dream imagery and characteristically scatological satire. One of Bunuel's best, in Spanish with English subtitles.
1962 95m/B MX SP Silvia Pinal, Enrique Rambal, Jacqueline Andere, Jose Baviera, Augusto Benedico, Luis Beristain; **D:** Luis Bunuel. **VHS, Beta** $59.95 *TAM, HTV, FCT* ♫♫♫½

Exterminator Vietnam veteran hunts down the gang that assaulted his friend and becomes the target of the police, the CIA and the underworld in this bloody banal tale of murder and intrigue. Followed by creatively titled "Exterminator II."
1980 (R) 101m/C Christopher George, Samantha Eggar, Robert Ginty; **D:** James Glickenhaus. **VHS, Beta, LV** $14.98 *SUE, NLC* ♫

Exterminator 2 The Exterminator battles the denizens of New York's underworld after his girlfriend is crippled, then murdered by the ruthless Mr. X. Violence galore.
1984 (R) 88m/C Robert Ginty, Mario Van Peebles, Deborah Geffner, Frankie Faison; **D:** Mark Buntzman. **VHS, Beta** $79.95 *MGM* ♫

Exterminators of the Year 3000 The Exterminator and his mercenary girlfriend battle with nuclear mutants over the last remaining tanks of purified water on Earth. Low-budget Road Warrior rip-off.
1983 (R) 101m/C IT SP Robert Jannucci, Alicia Moro, Alan Collins, Fred Harris; **D:** Jules Harrison. **VHS, Beta** $69.99 *HBO Woof!*

Extra Girl A silent melodrama/farce about a farm girl, brilliantly played by Normand, who travels to Hollywood to be a star. Once in the glamour capital, she gets used and abused for her trouble. Written by Mack Sennett.
1923 87m/B Mabel Normand, Ralph Graves, Vernon Dent; **D:** F. Richard Jones. **VHS, Beta, 8mm** $29.95 *VYY* ♫

The Extraordinary Adventures of Mr. West in the Land of the Bolsheviks The first achievement from the Kuleshov workshop, a wacky satire on American insularity depicting a naive and prejudiced American visiting Russia and being taken advantage of. Silent.
1924 55m/B Vsevolod Pudovkin, Boris Barnett; **D:** Lev Kuleshov. **VHS, Beta** $29.95 *FCT, TAM, KIV* ♫♫

Extreme Close-Up Drama about spies and their equipment. Screenplay by Crichton. *AKA:* Sex Through a Window.
1973 (R) 80m/C James McMullan, James A. Watson Jr., Kate Woodville, Bara Byrnes, Al Checco, Antony Carbone; **D:** Jeannot Szwarc; **W:** Michael Crichton. **VHS** $69.95 *VES* ♫

Extreme Prejudice A redneck Texas Ranger fights a powerful drug kingpin along the U.S.-Mexican border. Once best friends, they now fight for justice and the heart of the woman they both love.
1987 (R) 104m/C Nick Nolte, Powers Boothe, Maria Conchita Alonso, Michael Ironside, Rip Torn; **D:** Walter Hill; **M:** Jerry Goldsmith. **VHS, Beta, LV** $14.95 *LIV* ♫♫

Extremities An adaptation of the topical William Mastrosimone play about an intended rape victim who turns on her attacker, captures him, and plots to kill him. Violent and exploitive.
1986 (R) 83m/C Farrah Fawcett, Diana Scarwid, James Russo, Alfre Woodard; **D:** Robert M. Young. **VHS, Beta, LV, 8mm** $19.95 *PAR* ♫♫

The Eye Creatures Alien creatures in the form of eyeballs are fought off by a teenager and his girlfriend. A low-budget, gory, science fiction feature.
1965 80m/B John Ashley, Cynthia Hull, Warren Hammack, Chet Davis, Bill Peck; **D:** Larry Buchanan. **VHS** $16.98 *NOS, SNC* ♫

An Eye for an Eye A story of pursuit and revenge with Norris as an undercover cop pitted against San Francisco's underworld and high society.
1981 (R) 106m/C Chuck Norris, Christopher Lee, Richard Roundtree, Matt Clark, Mako, Maggie Cooper; *D:* Steve Carver. **VHS, Beta** $19.98 SUE, NLC ♂♂

Eye of the Demon A couple moves to a small town in Massachusetts and discovers that the area had once been a haven for witchcraft. To their horror, they soon find that old habits die hard, and the spellcasting continues in a nearby graveyard. Made for cable television.
1987 92m/C Tim Matheson, Pamela Sue Martin, Woody Harrelson, Barbara Billingsley, Susan Ruttan; *D:* Carl Schenkel. **VHS** $89.95 VMK ♂

Eye of the Eagle A special task force is given a dangerous assignment during the Vietnam war.
1987 (R) 84m/C Brett Clark, Ed Crick, Robert Patrick, William Steis, Cec Verrell; *D:* Cirio H. Santiago. **VHS, Beta** $79.95 MGM ♂½

Eye of the Eagle 2 When his platoon is betrayed and killed in Vietnam, a surviving soldier joins with a beautiful girl and seeks revenge.
1989 93m/C Todd Field, Andy Wood, Ken Jacobson, Ronald Lawrence; *D:* Carl Franklin. **VHS, Beta** NO ♂

Eye of the Eagle 3 Filipino-made Vietnam-War shoot-em-up, rack-em-up, shoot-em-up again, with U.S. forces pinned down against seemingly overwhelming odds. Violent.
1991 (R) 90m/C Otovo Kanaly, Ken Wright, Peter Nelson, Carl Franklin. **VHS** $89.98 NHO, CGV ♂½

Eye of the Needle Based on Ken Follett's novel about a German spy posing as a shipwrecked sailor on a deserted English island during World War II. Lonely, sad, yet capable of terrible violence, he is stranded on an isolated island while en route to report to his Nazi commander. He becomes involved with an English woman living on the island, and begins to contemplate his role in the war.
1981 (R) 112m/C Donald Sutherland, Kate Nelligan, Ian Bannen, Christopher Cazenove, Philip Brown; *D:* Richard Marquand. **VHS, Beta** $14.95 MGM, FOX ♂♂½

Eye of the Octopus Based on a true story of a boy who traveled to a Pacific Island to learn the ways of the people there.
1982 23m/C **VHS, Beta** JOU ♂

Eye of the Storm At the highway gas station/motel/diner where they live, two young brothers witness their parent's murder. Their younger brother is blinded in the same incident. Ten years later both brothers are still there and the tragedy may have turned one of them psychotic. When the abusive Gladstone and his young and sexy wife are stranded at the gas station it brings out the worst in everyone, with a violent climax during an equally violent thunderstorm.
1991 (R) 98m/C Craig Sheffer, Bradley Gregg, Lara Flynn Boyle, Dennis Hopper, Leon Rippy; *D:* Yuri Zeltser. **VHS** $89.95 NLC ♂♂½

Eye of the Tiger A righteous ex-con battles a crazed, crack-dealing motorcycle gang that terrorized and murdered his wife, and is moving on to infest his town.
1986 (R) 90m/C Gary Busey, Yaphet Kotto, Seymour Cassel, Bert Remsen, William Smith; *D:* Richard Sarafian. **VHS, Beta** $14.95 LIV ♂♂

Eye on the Sparrow A couple (Winningham and Carradine) desperately want to raise a child of their own, but the system classifies them as unfit parents since they are both blind. Together they successfully fight the system in this inspiring made for television movie that was based on a true story.
1991 (PG) 94m/C Mare Winningham, Keith Carradine, Conchata Ferrell; *D:* John Korty. **VHS** $89.98 REP ♂♂½

Eye Witness An American attorney goes abroad to free a friend from the British legal system. A book of poems becomes the necessary device in deducing the whereabouts of the witness testifying to his friend's alibi. *AKA:* Your Witness.
1949 104m/B GB Robert Montgomery, Felix Aylmer, Leslie Banks, Michael Ripper, Patricia Wayne; *D:* Robert Montgomery. **VHS** $16.95 NOS, SNC ♂♂½

Eyeball An intrepid policeman is stumped by a madman who is removing eyeballs from his victims. At least they won't have to watch this movie. *AKA:* Gatto Rossi In Un Labirinto Do Vetro.
1978 (R) 87m/C IT John Richardson, Martine Brochard; *D:* Umberto Lenzi. **VHS, Beta** $59.95 PSM Woof!

Eyes Behind the Stars A news photographer accidentally gets a few pictures of invading aliens, but nobody takes him seriously, particularly the government.
1972 95m/C IT Martin Balsam, Robert Hoffman, Nathalie Delon, Sherry Buchanan; *D:* Roy Garrett. **VHS, Beta** $49.95 NEG ♂

Eyes of a Stranger Terrifying maniac stalks his female prey by watching their every move. Tewes is cast as a journalist, the stronger of the two sisters in this exploitative slasher.
1981 (R) 85m/C Lauren Tewes, John Disanti, Jennifer Jason Leigh; *D:* Ken Wiederhorn. **VHS, Beta** $14.95 WAR Woof!

Eyes of Fire In early rural America, a group of pioneers set up camp in the wilderness and are besieged during the night by Indian witchcraft.
1984 (R) 86m/C Dennis Lipscomb, Rebecca Stanley, Fran Ryan, Rob Paulsen, Guy Boyd, Karlene Crockett; *D:* Avery Crounse. **VHS, Beta, LV** $79.95 VES ♂♂

Eyes of Julia Deep Rare silent film featuring the ill-fated Minter as Julia, a woman who prevents Terry (Forrest) from killing himself. Piano scored.
1918 54m/B Mary Miles Minter, Alan Forrest, Alice Wilson, George Periolat; *D:* Lloyd Ingraham. **VHS** $16.95 GPV ♂♂

Eyes of Laura Mars A photographer exhibits strange powers—she can foresee a murder before it happens through her snapshots. In time she realizes that the person responsible for a series of killings is tracking her. Title song performed by Barbra Streisand.
1978 (R) 104m/C Faye Dunaway, Tommy Lee Jones, Brad Dourif, Rene Auberjonois, Raul Julia, Darlanne Fluegel, Michael Tucker; *D:* Irvin Kershner; *W:* John Carpenter, David Zelag Goodman. **VHS, Beta, LV** $14.95 GKK ♂♂½

Eyes of Texas Bryant, a lawyer who uses a pack of killer dogs to get the land she wants, is pursued by a U.S Marshal played decently by Rogers.
1948 54m/B Roy Rogers, Lynn (Mary Hart) Roberts, Andy Devine, Nana Bryant, Roy Barcroft; *D:* William Witney. **VHS, Beta** $9.99 NOS, VCN, RXM ♂½

The Eyes of the Amaryllis A young girl becomes involved in a mysterious game when she arrives in Nantucket to care for her insane, invalid grandmother. Based on the story by Natalie Babbitt and filmed on location on Nantucket Island.
1982 (R) 94m/C Martha Byrne, Ruth Ford, Guy Boyd, Jonathan Bolt, Katherine Houghton; *D:* Frederick King Keller. **VHS, Beta** $69.98 LIV, VES ♂½

Eyes of the Beholder Janice is a psychopathic serial killer who suffered brain damage from a botched surgical attempt to reverse his insanity. Now he's escaped from the state mental institution, heading straight for the secluded home of the doctor who made him crazier than ever. During a raging storm, Janice stalks the doctor, his wife, and their two hapless dinner guests in a sadistic game of cat-and-mouse.
1992 (R) 89m/C Lenny Von Dohlen, Joanna Pacula, Matt McCoy, George Lazenby, Kylie Travis, Charles Napier; *W/D:* Lawrence L. Simeone; *M:* Greg Turner. **VHS, LV** $92.87 COL ♂♂

Eyes of the Panther One of Shelley Duvall's "Nightmare Classics" series, this adaptation of an Ambrose Bierce story concerns a pioneer girl haunted for years by the animal urges of a wild cat.
1990 60m/C Daphne Zuniga, C. Thomas Howell, John Stockwell; *D:* Noel Black. **VHS, Beta, LV** $59.95 NO ♂♂

Eyes of Turpin Are Upon You! Two early Turpin silent comedies: "Idle Eyes" and "A Small Town Idol."
1921 56m/B Ben Turpin, Ramon Novarro, Marie Prevost, James Finlayson. **VHS, Beta** $24.95 VYY ♂♂

The Eyes of Youth A young woman searches her soul for answers: to marry or not to marry is the question. A little foresight, in the form of a glimpse into the hypothetical future, helps her make the right choice. Very early Valentino fare in which the sheik plays a cad.
1919 78m/B Clara Kimball Young, Edmund Lowe, Rudolph Valentino. **VHS, Beta** $29.95 GPV, FCT, VYY ♂♂

Eyes Right! Based on a story by Ernest Grayman, this portrayal of life in a military prep school has its main character experience struggle, recognition, love, jealousy, and triumph. Silent.
1926 46m/B Francis X. Bushman. **VHS, Beta** $29.95 VYY, GPV ♂♂

The Eyes, the Mouth A young man has an affair with his dead twin brother's fiancee. Happiness eludes them as they are haunted by the deceased's memory and the family's grief. In Italian with English subtitles.
1983 (R) 100m/C FR IT Lou Castel, Angela Molina; *D:* Marco Bellochio. **VHS, Beta** $59.95 COL, TAM ♂♂

Eyewitness When a murder occurs in the office building of a star-struck janitor, he fabricates a tale in order to initiate a relationship with the television reporter covering the story. Unfortunately the killers think he's telling the truth, which plunges the janitor and reporter into a dangerous and complicated position, pursued by both police and foreign agents. Somewhat contrived, but Hurt and Weaver are always interesting. Woods turns in a wonderful performance as Hurt's somewhat-psychotic best friend. *AKA:* The Janitor.
1981 (R) 102m/C William Hurt, Sigourney Weaver, Christopher Plummer, James Woods, Kenneth MacMillan, Pamela Reed, Irene Worth, Steven Hill, Morgan Freeman; *D:* Peter Yates. **VHS, Beta, LV** $14.98 FXV, FOX ♂♂½

F

F. Scott Fitzgerald in Hollywood
Dramatization begins in the late 1930s when Fitzgerald was lured to Hollywood to work in the burgeoning film industry. It covers the period when, with his wife in a mental institution, he lived with Sheila Graham and struggled against alcoholism. Interesting story made dull and depressing by Miller's uninspired performance, but it's almost saved by Weld's portrayal of Zelda. Made for television.
1976 98m/C Jason Miller, Tuesday Weld, Julia Foster, Dolores Sutton, Michael Lerner, James Woods; **D:** Anthony Page. **VHS, Beta** *LME* 🎞️🎞️

F/X
A Hollywood special effects expert is contracted by the government to fake an assassination to protect a mob informer. After completing the assignment, he learns that he's become involved in a real crime and is forced to reach into his bag of F/X tricks to survive. Twists and turns abound in this fast-paced story that was the sleeper hit of the year. Followed by a sequel.
1986 (R) 109m/C Bryan Brown, Cliff DeYoung, Diane Venora, Brian Dennehy, Jerry Orbach, Mason Adams; **D:** Robert Mandel. **VHS, Beta, LV $14.98** *HBO, FCT* 🎞️🎞️🎞️

F/X 2: The Deadly Art of Illusion
Weak follow-up finds the special-effects specialist set to pull off just one more illusion for the police. Once again, corrupt cops use him as a chump for their scheme, an over-complicated business involving a stolen Vatican treasure.
1991 (PG-13) 107m/C Bryan Brown, Brian Dennehy, Rachel Ticotin, Philip Bosco, Joanna Gleason; **D:** Richard Franklin. **VHS, LV $34.95** *ORI, IME* 🎞️🎞️

Fabiola
The first of the big Italian spectacle movies, this one opened the door for a flood of low-budget imitators. Fabiola, the daughter of a Roman senator, becomes a Christian when her father's Christian servants are accused of murdering him. In the meantime, the Emperor Constantine speeds toward Rome to convert it to Christian status. You can bet plenty of Christians will lose their heads, be thrown to the lions and generally burn at the stake before he does.
1948 96m/C *IT* Michel Simon, Henri Vidal, Gino Cervi; **D:** Alexandro Blasetti. **VHS $16.95** *SNC, FCT* 🎞️🎞️

The Fable of the Beautiful Pigeon Fancier
A powerful man who has always gotten what he wanted spies a beautiful young married woman and sets out to make her his own. Based on the Gabriel Gracia Marquee novel "Life in the Time of Cholera." In Spanish with English subtitles.
AKA: Fabula de la Bella Palomera.
1988 73m/C *SP* Ney Lotorraco, Claudia Ohana, Tonia Carrero, Dina Stat, Chico Diaz; **D:** Ruy Guerra. **VHS, LV $79.95** *FXL, FCT, TAM* 🎞️🎞️½

The Fables of Harry Allard
The New England storyteller narrates animated versions of "It's So Nice to Have a Wolf Around the House," and "Miss Nelson Is Missing."
1979 30m/C VHS, Beta $14.95 *NWV* 🎞️🎞️½

Fables of the Green Forest
Johnny Chuck, Peter Cottontail, Chatter the Squirrel and other memorable Thornton W. Burgess characters come to life in "Whose Footprint Is That?" and "Johnny's Hibernation." Available in English and Spanish versions.
1979 55m/C VHS, Beta $14.95 *MED, WTA* 🎞️🎞️½

Fabulous Adventures of Baron Munchausen
The legendary Baron Munchausen, known for his tall tales, relates the story of his trek to the strange and beautiful land of Trukesban in a mixture of live action and animation. Wonderful special effects but a boring storyline. In German with English subtitles.
1961 84m/C *GE* Milos Kopecky, Jana Brejchova, Rudolph Jelinek, Jan Werich; **D:** Karel Zeman. **VHS, Beta $19.98** *LIV, VES* 🎞️🎞️

The Fabulous Baker Boys
Two brothers have been performing a tired act as nightclub pianists for fifteen years. When they hire a sultry vocalist to revitalize the routine, she inadvertently triggers long-suppressed hostility between the "boys." The story may be a bit uneven, but fine performances by the three leading actors, the steamy 1940s atmosphere, and Pfeiffer's classic rendition of "Makin' Whoopee," are worth the price of the rental. Music by Dave Grusin.
1989 (R) 116m/C Michelle Pfeiffer, Jeff Bridges, Beau Bridges, Elie Raab, Jennifer Tilly; **D:** Steven Kloves. Academy Awards '89 Nominations: Best Actress (Pfeiffer), Best Cinematography, Best Film Editing, Best Original Score; Golden Globe Awards '90: Best Actress—Drama (Pfeiffer); Los Angeles Film Critics Association Awards '89: Best Actress (Pfeiffer); National Board of Review Awards '89: Best Actress (Pfeiffer); New York Film Critics Awards '89: Best Actress (Pfeiffer). **VHS, Beta, LV, 8mm $19.95** *LIV, FCT* 🎞️🎞️🎞️

The Fabulous Dorseys
The musical lives of big band leaders Tommy and Jimmy Dorsey are portrayed in this less than fabulous biography that's strong on song but weak on plot. Guest stars include Art Tatum, Charlie Barnet, Ziggy Elman, Bob Eberly and Helen O'Connell. Highlights are the tunes. ♫At Sundown; I'll Never Say Never Again; To Me; Green Eyes; Dorsey Concerto; Art's Blues; Everybody's Doin' It; The Object of My Affection; Runnin' Wild; When You and I Were Young, Maggie; Waitin' at the Gate for Katy; Marie.
1947 91m/B Tommy Dorsey, Jimmy Dorsey, Janet Blair, Paul Whiteman, Sara Allgood, Arthur Shields; **D:** Alfred E. Green. **VHS, LV $19.95** *NOS, MRV, QNE* 🎞️🎞️

Fabulous Joe
A talking dog named Joe gets involved in the life of a hen-pecked husband.
1947 54m/C Walter Abel, Donald Meek, Margot Grahame, Marie Wilson; **D:** Bernard Carr. **VHS, Beta $19.95** *NOS* 🎞️🎞️

The Face at the Window
Melodramatic crime story of a pair of ne'er-do-well brothers who terrorize Paris to conceal their bank robberies.
1939 65m/B Tod Slaughter, Marjorie Taylor, John Warwick, Robert Adair, Harry Terry; **D:** George King. **VHS $14.99** *NOS, MRV, HEG* 🎞️🎞️

A Face in the Crowd
Journalist (Neal) discovers a down-home philosopher (Griffith) and puts him on her television show. His aw-shucks personality soon wins him a large following and increasing influence—even political clout. Off the air he reveals his true nature to be insulting, vengeful, and power-hungry—all of which Neal decides to expose. Marks Griffith's spectacular film debut as a thoroughly despicable character and deserved of Remick as the pretty cheerleader he takes an interest in. Budd Schulburg wrote the screenplay from his short story "The Arkansas Traveler." He and director Kazan collaborated equally well in "On the Waterfront."
1957 126m/B Andy Griffith, Patricia Neal, Lee Remick, Walter Matthau, Anthony (Tony) Franciosa; **D:** Elia Kazan. **VHS, Beta $19.98** *WAR, FCT* 🎞️🎞️🎞️½

A Face in the Fog
Two newspaper reporters set out to solve a number of murders that have plagued the cast of a play. Also interested is the playwright. Good low-budget thriller.
1936 66m/B June Collyer, Lloyd Hughes, Lawrence Gray, Al "Fuzzy" St. John, Jack Mulhall, Jack Cowell, John Elliott, Sam Flint, Forrest Taylor, Edward Cassidy; **D:** Bob Hill. **VHS, Beta $16.95** *NOS, SNC* 🎞️🎞️

Face of Another
A severely burned man gets a second chance when a plastic surgeon makes a mask to hide the disfigurement. Unfortunately this face leads him to alienation, rape, infidelity, and murder. In Japanese with English subtitles.
1966 124m/B *JP* Tatsuya Nakadai, Machiko Kyo; **D:** Hiroshi Teshigahara. **VHS, Beta $59.95** *SVS, TAM* 🎞️🎞️

Face of the Screaming Werewolf
Originally a Mexican horror/comedy that was bought for U.S. distribution by Jerry Warren, who earned his spot in the horror hall of fame with "The Incredible Petrified World" and "Teenage Zombies." A scientist brings a mummy back to life, but when he removes the bandages (gasp), the subject turns out to be of the canine persuasion. Suffers from comic evisceration; not much to scream about. **AKA:** La Casa Del Terror; House of Terror.
1959 60m/B *MX* Lon Chaney Jr., Landa Varle, Raymond Gaylord; **D:** Gilberto Martinez Solares, Jerry Warren. **VHS $16.95** *SNC, MRV* 🎞️½

Face the Music
Ringwald and Dempsey were once stormily married and pursing successful, collaborative careers as singer/songwriters for the movies. But they've abandoned the work, along with the marriage, until a movie producer makes them a very lucrative offer for a new song. Only Dempsey's new girlfriend has some voracious objections.
1992 (PG-13) 93m/C Patrick Dempsey, Molly Ringwald, Lysette Anthony. **VHS $89.98** *LIV* 🎞️½

Face to Face
Dramatic adaptation of two short stories, "The Secret Sharer," by Joseph Conrad, and Stephen Crane's "The Bride Comes to Yellow Sky." The Conrad story features Mason as a sea captain who discovers a fugitive stowaway aboard his ships. The Crane story features Preston as a sheriff threatened by an old-time gunfighter.
1952 92m/B Bretaigne Windust, James Mason, Michael Pate, Robert Preston, Marjorie Steele, Gene Lockhart, Minor Watson; **D:** John Brahm. **VHS** *RKO* 🎞️🎞️½

Face to Face
Bergman's harrowing tale of a mental breakdown. Ullmann has a bravura role as a psychiatrist deciding to vacation at her grandparent's house in the country. Once there she begins to experience depression and hallucinations tied to her past with both her mother and grandmother. Her deeply repressed feelings eventually lead to a suicide attempt, which brings some much needed help. Originally a four-hour series made for Swedish television. In Swedish with English subtitles.
1976 136m/C *SW* Liv Ullmann, Erland Josephson, Gunnar Bjornstrand, Aino Taube-Henrikson, Sven Lindberg; **W/D:** Ingmar Bergman. Academy Awards '76 Nominations: Best Actress (Ullmann), Best Director (Bergman); Golden Globe Awards '77: Best Foreign Film. **VHS** *PAR* 🎞️🎞️🎞️

Faces of Death, Part 2
Mindless sequel to "Faces of Death" further explores violent termination of man by man and by nature in a graphic and grisly gala. Not for the squeamish.
1985 84m/C VHS, Beta $79.95 *MPI Woof!*

Fade to Black Young man obsessed with movies loses his grip on reality and adopts the personalities of cinematic characters (Hopalong Cassidy and Dracula among them) to seek revenge on people who have wronged him. Thoroughly unpleasant, highlighted by clips from old flicks.
1980 (R) 100m/C Dennis Christopher, Tim Thomerson, Linda Kerridge, Mickey Rourke, Melinda Fee; *D:* Vernon Zimmerman. VHS, Beta $9.95 *MED, MLB* Woof!

Fahrenheit 451 Chilling adaptation of the Ray Bradbury novel about a futuristic society that has banned all reading material and the firemen whose job it is to keep the fires at 451 degrees: the temperature at which paper burns. Werner is a fireman who begins to question the rightness of his actions when he meets the book-loving Christie—who also plays the dual role of Werner's TV-absorbed wife. Truffaut's first color and English-language film.
1966 112m/C *FR* Oskar Werner, Julie Christie, Cyril Cusack, Anton Diffring; *D:* Francois Truffaut. VHS, Beta, LV $19.98 *MCA, KUI, MLB 𝄞𝄞𝄞*

Fail-Safe A nail-biting nuclear age nightmare, in which American planes have been erroneously sent to bomb the USSR, with no way to recall them. An all-star cast impels this bitterly serious thriller, the straight-faced flipside of "Dr. Strangelove."
1964 111m/B Henry Fonda, Dan O'Herlihy, Walter Matthau, Larry Hagman, Fritz Weaver, Dom DeLuise; *D:* Sidney Lumet. VHS, Beta, LV $14.95 *COL 𝄞𝄞𝄞½*

Fair Game Hedonistic maniacs roam rural areas killing, looting and raping, until a beautiful woman they capture fights back.
1985 (R) 90m/C Kim Trengove, Kerry Mack, Marie O'Loughlina, Karen West; *D:* Christopher Fitchett. VHS, Beta $79.95 *IMP* Woof!

Fair Game A psychotic but imaginative ex-boyfriend locks his former girlfriend in her apartment with a lethal giant Mamba snake. Understandably uninterested in its serpentine attention, the young woman must trespass against the Hollywood code and keep her wits in the face of danger. Guaranteed not to charm you.
1989 (R) 81m/C Greg Henry, Trudie Styler, Bill Moseley; *D:* Mario Orfini. VHS, LV $89.95 *VMK* Woof!

Fairytales A ribald musical fantasy for adults. In order to save the kingdom, the prince must produce an heir. The problem is that only the girl in the painting of "Princess Beauty" can "interest" the prince and she must be found. Good-natured smut.
1979 (R) 83m/C Don Sparks, Prof. Irwin Corey, Brenda Fogarty, Sy Richardson, Nai Bonet, Martha Reeves; *D:* Harry Tampa. VHS, Beta $39.95 *MED 𝄞𝄞*

Faith When young dancer Faith's parents are killed in an accident she winds up in a frightening foster home. Running away, she meets a gentlemanly mobster who helps her attain her dance dreams. Laughably implausible.
1992 (R) 104m/C Sylvia Seidel, Ami Dolenz, Richard Maldone. VHS, LV $92.95 *VMK 𝄞*

Fake Out Nightclub singer is caught between the mob and the police who want her to testify against her gangland lover. Typical vanity outing for Zadora.
1982 89m/C Pia Zadora, Telly Savalas, Desi Arnaz Jr.; *D:* Matt Cimber. VHS, Beta $69.99 *HBO 𝄞*

Falcon Brave knight battles for the honor of a beautiful maiden; with or without the Falcon's help.

1974 105m/C Franco Nero. VHS, Beta $59.95 *TWE 𝄞*

The Falcon and the Snowman True story of Daulton Lee and Christopher Boyce, two childhood friends who, almost accidentally, sell American intelligence secrets to the KGB in 1977. Hutton and Penn are excellent, creating a relationship we care about and strong characterizations. Pat Metheny and Lyle Mays perform the musical score.
1985 (R) 110m/C Sean Penn, Timothy Hutton, Lori Singer, Pat Hingle, Dorian Harewood, Richard Dysart, Michael Ironside, Jennifer Runyon; *D:* John Schlesinger. VHS, Beta, LV $29.98 *LIV, VES 𝄞𝄞𝄞*

The Falcon in Hollywood The falcon gets caught up with the murder of an actor who was part of a Tinseltown love triangle. The film takes place on RKO's back lot for a behind-the-scenes view of Hollywood. Part of the popular "Falcon" series from the 1940s.
1944 67m/B Tom Conway, Barbara Hale, Veda Ann Borg, Sheldon Leonard, Frank Jenks, Rita Corday, John Abbott; *D:* Gordon Douglas. VHS $59.98 *MED 𝄞𝄞½*

The Falcon in Mexico When paintings from a supposedly dead artist turn up for sale in New York City, the Falcon and the artist's daughter wind up journeying to Mexico to solve the mystery. Part of "The Falcon" series.
1944 70m/B Tom Conway, Mona Maris, Nestor Paiva; *D:* William Berke. VHS, Beta *MED 𝄞½*

Falcon Takes Over/Strange Bargain A mystery double feature. In "The Falcon Takes Over," the Falcon becomes involved in a series of murder and an ex-con's last love, and in "Strange Bargain," an underpaid bookkeeper gets in on an insurance swindle.
1949 131m/B George Sanders, Ward Bond, Allen Jenkins, Martha Scott, Harry Morgan, James Gleason, Anne Revere, Hans Conried; *D:* Irving Reis. VHS, Beta $34.95 *TTC, RKO 𝄞𝄞*

Falcon's Adventure/Armored Car Robbery A mystery double feature: The Falcon uncovers a vicious plot to steal a formula for synthetic diamonds in "The Falcon's Adventure," and four participants in an armored car robbery flee after slaying a policeman in "Armored Car Robbery."
1950 122m/B Tom Conway, Madge Meredith, William Talman, Charles McGraw, Adele Jergens; *D:* William Berke. VHS, Beta $34.95 *TTC, RKO 𝄞½*

The Falcon's Brother Enemy agents intent on killing a South American diplomat are foiled by the Falcon's brothers at a steep personal cost. The plot enabled Sanders' real-life brother Conway to take over the title role in "The Falcon" mystery series, a role which he played nine more times.
1942 64m/B Tom Conway, George Sanders, Keye Luke, Jane Randolph; *D:* Stanley Logan. VHS, Beta *MED 𝄞𝄞*

Fall and Rise of Reginald Perrin 1 Starring Leonard Rossiter, this BBC show has Reginald getting out of the rat race.
1978 107m/C *GB* Leonard Rossiter. VHS $29.95 *BFS, HMV 𝄞𝄞𝄞*

Fall and Rise of Reginald Perrin 2 After part one's escape from the rat race, this time Reginald is back in suburbia.
1978 120m/C *GB* Leonard Rossiter. VHS $29.95 *BFS, HMV 𝄞𝄞𝄞*

Fall from Innocence A girl is driven to a life of prostitution and drugs by the sexual abuse inflicted upon her by her father.

1988 81m/C Isabelle Mejias, Thom Haverstock, Amanda Smith, Rob McEwan; *D:* Carey Connor. VHS $79.95 *MNC 𝄞½*

The Fall of the House of Usher Lord Roderick Usher is haunted by his sister's ghost in this poor adaptation of the Poe classic.
1952 70m/B *GB* Kay Tendeter, Gwen Watford, Irving Steen, Lucy Pavey; *D:* Ivan Barnett. VHS $16.95 *SNC, FCT 𝄞*

The Fall of the House of Usher The moody Roger Corman/Vincent Price filmization, the first of their eight Poe adaptations, depicting the collapse of the famous estate due to madness and revenge. Terrific sets and solid direction as well as Price's inimitable presence. *AKA:* House of Usher.
1960 85m/C Vincent Price, Myrna Fahey, Mark Damon; *D:* Roger Corman. VHS, Beta $19.95 *KUI 𝄞𝄞𝄞*

The Fall of the House of Usher Another version of Edgar Allan Poe's classic tale of a family doomed to destruction. Stray to the Roger Corman/Vincent Price version to see how it should have been done.
1980 (PG) 101m/C Martin Landau, Robert Hays, Charlene Tilton, Ray Walston; *D:* James L. Conway. VHS, Beta $19.98 *UHV, LME 𝄞½*

The Fall of the Roman Empire An all-star, big budget extravaganza set in ancient Rome praised for its action sequences. The licentious son of Marcus Aurelius arranges for his father's murder and takes over as emperor while Barbarians gather at the gate. Great sets, fine acting, and thundering battle scenes.
1964 187m/C Sophia Loren, Alec Guinness, James Mason, Stephen Boyd, Christopher Plummer, John Ireland, Anthony Quayle, Eric Porter, Mel Ferrer, Omar Sharif; *D:* Anthony Mann. VHS, Beta, LV $29.95 *BFV, UHV, KAR 𝄞𝄞𝄞*

Fallen Angel Television movie about a child pornographer and a particular young girl he finds easily exploitable because of her unbalanced home situation. Fine cast, solid direction.
1981 100m/C Dana Hill, Richard Masur, Melinda Dillon, Ronny Cox; *D:* Robert Lewis. Beta $59.95 *COL 𝄞𝄞½*

Fallen Champ: The Untold Story of Mike Tyson Director Kopple's provocative documentary on the boxing champ, from his roots in a Brooklyn ghetto to his conviction for rape in 1991. Tyson is shown as pathetic, vulnerable, and violent—psychologically unprepared for both acclaim and responsibility, as well as easily manipulated by promoters and opportunists. A mixture of ring footage and interviews with sportswriters, promoters, trainers, and others as well as media coverage of Tyson. Made for television.
1993 93m/C *D:* Barbara Kopple. VHS $59.95 *COL 𝄞𝄞½*

The Fallen Idol A young boy wrongly believes that a servant he admires is guilty of murdering his wife. Unwittingly, the child influences the police investigation of the crime so that the servant becomes the prime suspect. Richardson as the accused and Henrey as the boy are notable. Oscar nominated screenplay by Graham Greene from his short story, "The Basement Room." *AKA:* The Lost Illusion.
1949 92m/B *GB* Ralph Richardson, Bobby Henrey, Michele Morgan, Sonia Dresdel, Jack Hawkins, Bernard Lee; *D:* Carol Reed. Academy Awards '49 Nominations: Best Director (Reed), Best Screenplay; British Academy Awards '48: Best Film; National Board of Review Awards '49: 10 Best Films of the Year, Best Actor

(Richardson). **VHS, Beta, LV, 3/4U, Special order formats $19.95** NOS, MRV, PSM ✍✍✍

The Fallen Sparrow Garfield is superb as a half-mad veteran of the Spanish Civil War. Captured and brutalized, he never revealed the whereabouts of a valuable possession. His return to the U.S. continues his torture as Nazi agent Slezak uses the woman Garfield loves to set a trap and finish the job. Solid performances and good plot are highlights.
1943 94m/B John Garfield, Maureen O'Hara, Walter Slezak, Patricia Morison, Martha O'Driscoll, Bruce Edwards, John Miljan, John Banner, Hugh Beaumont; **D:** Richard Wallace. **VHS, Beta $29.95** MED, IME ✍✍

Falling Down Douglas stars as "D-FENS" (taken from his license plate), a normally law-abiding white-collar geek who snaps while stuck in a traffic jam on a hot day in Los Angeles. Like Charles Bronson in "Death Wish," he decides to take matters into his own hands. Unlike Bronson, he is not avenging the attack on his wife by a specific criminal, but raging against whomever gets in his way. Acquiring a bazooka and other high-gauge weaponry, he attracts the attention of a police detective (Duvall) who is on his last day before retirement. Hershey has the thankless role of the ex-wife Douglas contacts. This film is essentially a revenge fantasy and has been vilified by some for catering to the baser emotions.
1993 (R) 112m/C Michael Douglas, Robert Duvall, Barbara Hershey, Rachel Ticotin, Tuesday Weld, Frederic Forrest; **D:** Joel Schumacher; **W:** Ebbe Roe Smith; **M:** James Newton Howard. **VHS $94.99** WAR ✍✍

Falling from Grace Bud Parks (Mellencamp) is a successful country singer who, accompanied by his wife and daughter, returns to his small Indiana hometown to celebrate his grandfather's 80th birthday. He's tired of both his career and his marriage and finds himself taking up once again with an old girlfriend (Lenz), who is not only married to Bud's brother but is also having an affair with his father. Bud believes he's better off staying in his old hometown but the problems caused by his return may change his mind. Surprisingly sedate, although literate, family drama with good ensemble performances. Actor-director debut for Mellencamp.
1992 (PG-13) 100m/C John Cougar Mellencamp, Mariel Hemingway, Kay Lenz, Claude Akins, Dub Taylor, Brent Huff, Deidre O'Connell, Larry Crane; **D:** John Cougar Mellencamp; **W:** Larry McMurtry. **VHS, LV $92.95** COL, FCT ✍✍✍

Falling in Love Two married New Yorkers unexpectedly fall in love after a coincidental meeting at the Rizzoli Book Store. Weak but gracefully performed reworking of "Brief Encounter," where no one seems to ever complete a sentence. An unfortunate re-teaming for Streep and De Niro after their wonderful work in "The Deer Hunter."
1984 (PG-13) 106m/C Robert De Niro, Meryl Streep, Harvey Keitel, Dianne Wiest, George Martin, Jane Kaczmarek, David Clennon; **D:** Ulu Grosbard. **VHS, Beta, LV $19.95** PAR ✍✍½

Falling in Love Again Romantic comedy about middle-aged dreamer Gould and realistic wife York. They travel from Los Angeles to their hometown of New York for his high school reunion, where Gould is suddenly attacked by nostalgia vibes for his youth, seen in countless flashbacks, and prominently featuring Pfeiffer, notable in her film debut. Like watching a home movie about people you don't care about. **AKA:** In Love.

1980 (PG) 103m/C Elliott Gould, Susannah York, Michelle Pfeiffer; **D:** Steven Paul. **VHS, Beta $24.98** SUE ✍½

False Arrest A woman is falsely accused of killing her husband's business partner and winds up in prison where she continues to fight to prove her innocence. Mills does well in this less-than-glamorous role. Based on a true story. Made for television.
1992 102m/C Donna Mills, Steven Bauer, James Handy, Lane Smith, Lewis Van Bergen, Dennis Christopher, Robert Wagner; **D:** Bill L. Norton. **VHS, Beta $89.98** TTC, PMS ✍✍½

False Colors Hopalong Cassidy unmasks a crook posing as a ranch heir. This was the 49th Hopalong Cassidy feature.
1943 54m/B William Boyd, Robert Mitchum, Andy Clyde, Jimmy Rogers; **D:** George Archainbaud. **VHS, Beta $9.99** NOS, MRV, VYY ✍

False Faces A ruthless, money-hungry quack is hounded by the law and the victims of his unscrupulous plastic surgery.
1932 80m/B Lowell Sherman, Peggy Shannon, Lila Lee, Joyce Compton, Berton Churchill, David Landau, Eddie Anderson, Ken Maynard; **D:** Lowell Sherman. **VHS, Beta $29.95** VYY ✍½

False Identity A radio psychologist buys a Purple Heart medal at a garage sale and then tries to find out about the original recipient. But her questions are making a number of folks uneasy, including a potentially dangerous stranger.
1990 (PG-13) 97m/C Genevieve Bujold, Stacy Keach, Veronica Cartwright, Tobin Bell, Mimi Maynard; **D:** James Keach. **VHS, Beta, LV $89.99** PAR ✍½

False Note Against a background of vibrant colors and collages, a little, crippled beggar-musician roams through a modern city, playing his small barrel organ which inevitably emits a sour note. He discovers a kindred spirit in an abandoned carousel horse.
1972 10m/C VHS, Beta IFB ✍½

False Witness A New Orleans district attorney and her lover, a private investigator, find themselves working the same rape-murder case. When their methods disagree both find themselves in danger. Adapted from a novel by Dorothy Uhnak. Made for television.
1989 96m/C Phylicia Rashad, Philip Michael Thomas, Terri Austin, George Grizzard; **D:** Arthur Seidelman. **VHS** STE ✍✍½

Fame Follows eight talented teenagers from their freshmen year through graduation from New York's High School of Performing Arts. Insightful and absorbing, director Parker allows the kids to mature on screen, revealing the pressures of constantly trying to prove themselves. A faultless parallel is drawn between these "special" kids and the pressures felt by high schoolers everywhere. Great dance and music sequences. The basis for the television series. ♫Fame; Red Light; I Sing the Body Electric; Dogs in the Yard; Hot Lunch Jam; Out Here On My Own; Is It OK If I Call You Mine?.
1980 (R) 133m/C Irene Cara, Barry Miller, Paul McCrane, Anne Meara, Joanna Merlin, Richard Belzer; **D:** Alan Parker; **M:** Michael Gore. Academy Awards '80: Best Song ("Fame"), Best Original Score; Nominations: Best Film Editing, Best Film Editing, Best Original Screenplay, Best Song ("Out Here on My Own"), Best Sound. **VHS, Beta, LV $19.99** MGM, FCT ✍✍✍

Fame is the Spur A lengthy but interesting look at the way power corrupts, plus an insight into the Conservative versus Labor dynamics of British government. Redgrave is a poor, idealistic worker who decides to help

his fellow workers by running for Parliament. There, he falls prey to the trappings of office with surprising consequences. Look hard for Tomlinson, who went on to star in "Mary Poppins" and "Bedknobs and Broomsticks" for Disney.
1947 116m/B GB Michael Redgrave, Rosamund John, Bernard Miles, Hugh Burden, Guy Verney, Carla Lehmann, Seymour Hicks, David Tomlinson; **D:** Roy Boulting. **VHS $19.95** NOS, TIM, VEC ✍✍½

The Family As a New Orleans hit-man who resists joining the mob, Bronson initiates an all-out war on the syndicate and its boss, played by Savalas. A poorly dubbed Italian action film.
1973 94m/C IT Charles Bronson, Jill Ireland, Telly Savalas; **D:** Sergio Sollima. **VHS, Beta $59.95** MPI ✍✍½

The Family An 80-year-old patriarch prepares for his birthday celebration reminiscing about his family's past triumphs, tragedies and enduring love. The charming flashbacks, convincingly played, all take place in the family's grand old Roman apartment. In Italian with English subtitles or dubbed. **AKA:** La Famiglia.
1987 128m/C IT Vittorio Gassman, Fanny Ardant, Philippe Noiret, Stefania Sandrelli; **D:** Ettore Scola. **VHS, Beta, LV $19.98** LIV, VES, TAM ✍✍✍

Family Business A bright Ivy Leaguer, impressed by the exploits and vitality of his criminal grandfather, recruits him and his ex-con dad to pull off a high-tech robbery, which goes awry. Caper film, with its interest in family relationships and being true to one's nature. Casting Connery, Hoffman, and Broderick as the three leaves a big believability problem in the family department.
1989 (R) 114m/C Sean Connery, Dustin Hoffman, Matthew Broderick, Rosana De Soto, Janet Carroll, Victoria Jackson, Bill McCutcheon, Deborah Rush, Marilyn Cooper, Salem Ludwig, Rex Everhart, James Tolkan; **D:** Sidney Lumet. **VHS, Beta, LV, 8mm $19.95** COL, FCT ✍✍½

A Family Circus Christmas All the characters of the famous comic strip, "Family Circus," celebrate Christmas with a funny approach. The hysterics begin when one of the children asks Santa for a very unusual present, which he delivers!
1984 30m/C D: Al Kouzel. **VHS, Beta $9.95** FHE, WTA ✍✍½

Family Enforcer A small-time hoodlum is bent on becoming the best enforcer in an underworld society. **AKA:** Death Collector.
1976 (R) 82m/C Joe Cortese, Lou Criscuola, Joe Pesci, Anne Johns, Keith Davis; **D:** Ralph De Vito. **VHS, Beta $19.95** UHV ✍

The Family Game An obsessive satire about a poor, belligerent college student hired by a wealthy contemporary Japanese family to tutor their spoiled teenage son. Provides an all-out cultural assault on the Japanese bourgeoisie. In Japanese with English subtitles.
1983 107m/C JP Yusaku Matsuda, Juzo Itami, Saori Yuki, Ichirota Miyagawa; **D:** Yoshimitsu Morita. **VHS, Beta $59.95** SVS, FCT, TAM ✍✍✍

Family Jewels A spoiled child-heiress has to choose among her six uncles to decide which should be her new father. If you like Jerry Lewis, you can't miss this! In addition to playing all six uncles, Lewis plays the chauffeur, as well as serving as producer, director, and coauthor of the script.
1965 100m/C Jerry Lewis, Donna Butterworth, Sebastian Cabot, Robert Strauss; **D:** Jerry Lewis. **VHS, Beta $19.95** PAR ✍✍

Family Life A portrait of a 19-year-old girl battling her parents to establish her own identity. She is subjected to increasingly vigorous psychological interventions in this documentary-style effort originally made for British television. *AKA*: Wednesday's Child.
1971 108m/C *GB* Sandy Ratcliff, Bill Dean, Grace Cave; *D*: Ken Loach. **VHS, Beta $59.95** COL ⅃⅃½

The Family Man A brief encounter-between a married Manhattanite (Asner) and a much younger single woman (Baxter Birney) is sensitively handled in this film which explores their passionate affair. Made-for-television.
1979 98m/C Ed Asner, Meredith Baxter Birney, Paul Clemens, Mary Joan Negro, Anne Jackson, Martin Short, Michael Ironside; *D*: Glenn Jordan. **VHS, Beta** TLF ⅃⅃

A Family Matter A Mafia chieftain adopts a child whose father was killed by hit men. She grows into a beautiful woman bent on revenge. Melodramatic Italian-American co-production, made for TV. *AKA*: Vendetta: Secrets of a Mafia Bride.
1991 (R) 100m/C Eric Roberts, Carol Alt, Eli Wallach, Burt Young. **VHS, LV $89.95** VMK ⅃⅃

Family Plot Alfred Hitchcock's last film focuses on the search for a missing heir which is undertaken by a phony psychic and her private-eye boyfriend, with all becoming involved in a diamond theft. Campy, lightweight mystery that stales with time and doesn't fit well into Hitchcock's genre. Screenplay by Ernest Lehman.
1976 (PG) 120m/C Karen Black, Bruce Dern, Barbara Harris, William Devane, Ed Lauter, Katharine Helmond; *D*: Alfred Hitchcock; *M*: John Williams. **VHS, Beta, LV $19.95** MCA ⅃⅃½

Family Prayers Coming-of-age drama, set in 1969 Los Angeles, about 13-year-old Andrew and his family troubles. His father Martin (Mantegna) is a compulsive gambler which causes wife Rita (Archer) untold anxiety and constant friction between the two. Tension is heightened by Nan (LuPone), Rita's opinionated older sister who has bailed the family out of their money problems more than once. Meanwhile, Andrew tries to look out for his younger sister and prepare for his bar-mitzvah. A little too much of a nostalgic golden glow surrounds what is essentially a family tragedy.
1991 (PG) 109m/C Tzvi Ratner-Stauber, Joe Mantegna, Anne Archer, Patti LuPone, Paul Reiser, Allen Garfield, Conchata Ferrell, David Margulies; *D*: Scott Rosenfelt; *W*: Steven Ginsburg. **VHS $89.95** COL ⅃⅃½

Family Reunion A young man brings a pretty hitchhiker to his family reunion where they mistake her for his fiancee (who recently dumped him).
1988 97m/C David Eisner, Rebecca Jenkins, Henry Beckman, Linda Sorensen; *D*: Dick Sarin. **VHS, Beta $19.95** MNC ⅃½

Family Secrets A made-for-television drama about a daughter, mother, and grandmother overprotecting and manipulating each other during a weekend together.
1984 96m/C Maureen Stapleton, Stefanie Powers, Melissa Gilbert, James Spader; *D*: Jack Hofsiss. **Beta** NO ⅃⅃½

Family Sins A television movie about a domineering father who dotes on his sports-oriented son while willfully neglecting the other. Eventually this leads to calamity.
1987 93m/C James Farentino, Jill Eikenberry, Andrew Bendarski, Mimi Kuzyk, Brent Spiner, Michael Durrell, Tom Bower; *D*: Jerrold Freedman. **VHS $79.98** REP ⅃⅃

Family Upside Down An aging couple fight their separation after the husband has a heart attack and is put into a nursing home. The fine cast received several Emmy nominations, with Astaire the winner. Made-for-television.
1978 100m/C Helen Hayes, Fred Astaire, Efrem Zimbalist Jr., Patty Duke; *D*: David Lowell Rich. **VHS, Beta $59.95** COL ⅃⅃⅃

Family Viewing Surrealistic depiction of a family—obsessed with television and video—whose existence is a textbook model of home sweet dysfunctional home. An early, experimental film from Canada's Egoyan, it won considerable praise for its social commentary.
1988 92m/C CA Adian Tierney, Gabrielle Rose; *D*: Atom Egoyan. **VHS, LV $79.95** FXL, FCT, TAM ⅃⅃

Famous Five Get Into Trouble Four precocious youngsters and a dog get involved with a criminal plot and cutely wile their way out of it. Scandinavian; dubbed in English.
1987 90m/C Astrid Villaume, Ove Sprogoe, Lily Broberg; *D*: Trine Hedman. **VHS, Beta $69.95** TWE ⅃

The Fan A Broadway star is threatened and her immediate circle cut down when a lovestruck fan feels he has been rejected by his idol. The stellar cast makes this bloody and familiar tale seem better than it is.
1981 (R) 95m/C Lauren Bacall, Maureen Stapleton, James Garner, Hector Elizondo, Michael Biehn, Griffin Dunne; *D*: Edward Bianchi. **VHS, Beta, LV $14.95** PAR ⅃⅃

Fancy Pants Remake of "Ruggles of Red Gap" features Hope, a British actor posing as a butler. Also featuring Ball, an amusing contrast. Fine performances all around. ♫Fancy Pants; Home Cookin'.
1950 92m/C Bob Hope, Lucille Ball, Bruce Cabot, Jack Kirkwood, Lea Penman, Eric Blore, John Alexander, Norma Varden; *D*: George Marshall. **VHS, Beta, LV $14.95** PAR ⅃⅃½

Fandango Five college friends take a wild weekend drive across the Texas Badlands for one last fling before graduation and the prospect of military service. Expanded by Reynolds with assistance from Steven Spielberg, from his student film. Provides a look at college and life during the '60s Vietnam crisis.
1985 (PG) 91m/C Judd Nelson, Kevin Costner, Sam Robards, Chuck Bush, Brian Cesak, Elizabeth Daily, Suzy Amis, Glenne Headly, Pepe Serna; *W/D*: Kevin Reynolds. **VHS, Beta $19.98** WAR ⅃⅃½

Fangoria's Weekend of Horrors A documentary about the making of horror films, featuring interviews with the industry's most scream-invoking artists. Copious film clips.
1986 60m/C Rick Baker, Wes Craven, Tobe Hooper, Robert Englund. **VHS, Beta $9.98** MED ⅃⅃½

Fangs Unfriendly reptile-stomping villagers take the life of Mr. Snakey's favorite serpent. He sends his slithering pets on a vengeful and poisonous spree.
1975 (R) 90m/C Les Tremayne, Janet Wood, Bebe Kelly, Marvin Kaplan, Alice Nunn; *D*: Vittorio Schiraldi. **VHS, Beta $24.95** GEM, MRV ⅃½

Fangs of Fate A gang of bad guys battles the town's new marshal.
1925 67m/B Bill Patton, Dorothy Donald. **VHS, Beta, 8mm $29.95** GPV, VYY ⅃½

Fangs of the Living Dead When a young woman inherits a castle, her uncle, who happens to be a vampire, tries to persuade her to remain among the undead. *AKA*: Malenka, the Vampire; La Nipote del Vampiro.
1968 80m/C SP IT Anita Ekberg, Rossana Yanni, Diana Lorys, Fernando Bilbao, Paul Muller, John Hamilton, Julian Ugarte, Andriana Ambesi; *W/D*: Armando de Ossorio. **VHS $19.98** SNC ⅃½

Fangs of the Wild When a young boy witnesses a murder at his father's hunting lodge, no one but the killer believes him. When the killer decides to get rid of the boy, Buck the Wonder Dog gets involved. *AKA*: Follow the Hunter.
1954 72m/B Charles Chaplin Jr., Onslow Stevens, Margia Dean, Freddy Ridgeway, Phil Tead, Robert Stevenson, Buck the Wonder Dog; *D*: William Claxton. **VHS $19.95** NOS, DVT ⅃⅃

Fanny Second part of Marcel Pagnol's trilogy depicting the lives of the people of Provence, France. The poignant tale of Fanny, a young woman who marries an older man when Marius, her young lover, leaves her pregnant when he goes to sea. Remade several times but the original holds its own very well. "Marius" was first in the trilogy; "Cesar" was third.
1932 128m/B FR Raimu, Charpin, Orane Demazis, Pierre Fresnay, Alida Rauffe; *D*: Marc Allegret. **VHS, Beta, LV $64.95** INT, MRV, HHT ⅃⅃⅃⅃

Fanny A young girl falls in love with an adventurous sailor, and finds herself pregnant after he returns to the sea. With the help of the sailor's parents, she finds, marries and eventually grows to love a much older man, who in turn cares for her and adores her son as if he were his own. When the sailor returns, all involved must confront their pasts and define their futures. Beautifully made, with fine performances and a plot which defies age or nationality. Part of the "A Night at the Movies" series, this tape simulates a 1961 movie evening, with a Tweety Pie cartoon, "The Last Hungry Cat," a newsreel and coming attractions for "Splendor in the Grass" and "The Roman Spring of Mrs. Stone."
1961 148m/C FR Leslie Caron, Maurice Chevalier, Charles Boyer, Horst Buchholz, Lionel Jeffries; *D*: Joshua Logan. Academy Awards '60 Nominations: Best Color Cinematography; Academy Awards '61: Best Actor (Boyer), Best Film Editing, Best Picture, Best Original Score; National Board of Review Awards '61: 10 Best Films of the Year. **VHS, Beta $19.98** NOS, WAR ⅃⅃⅃

Fanny and Alexander The culmination of Bergman's career, this autobiographical film is set in a rural Swedish town in 1907. It tells the story of one year in the lives of the Ekdahl family, as seen by the young children, Fanny and Alexander. Magic and religion, love and death, reconciliation and estrangement are skillfully captured in this carefully detailed, lovingly photographed film. In Swedish with English subtitles. *AKA*: Fanny Och Alexander.
1983 (R) 197m/C SW Pernilla Allwin, Bertil Guve, Gunn Walgren, Allan Edwall, Ewa Froling, Erland Josephson, Harriet Andersson, Jarl Kulle; *D*: Ingmar Bergman. Academy Awards '83: Best Art Direction/Set Decoration, Best Cinematography, Best Costume Design, Best Foreign Language Film; Nominations: Best Director (Bergman), Best Original Screenplay; Cesar Awards '84: Best Foreign Film; Golden Globe Awards '84: Best Foreign Film. **VHS, Beta, LV $39.98** SUE, TAM, NLC ⅃⅃⅃⅃

F

Fanny Hill A softcore adaptation of the racy Victorian classic.
1983 (R) 80m/C *GB* Lisa Raines, Shelley Winters, Wilfrid Hyde-White, Oliver Reed. **VHS, Beta** $79.95 *MGM* 🎬🎬

Fanny Hill: Memoirs of a Woman of Pleasure Sexual exploits of an innocent in bawdy 18th-century London, as directed by notorious "Super Vixen" Meyer (though by Meyer standards, proceedings are fairly innocuous, if inept). Based on the novel.
1964 105m/B Miriam Hopkins, Walter Giller, Alexander D'Arcy, Leticia Roman; *D:* Russ Meyer. **VHS, Beta** *PGN* Woof!

Fantasia Disney's most personal animation feature first bombed at the box office and irked purists who couldn't take the plotless, experimental mix of classical music and cartoons. It became a cult movie, embraced by more liberal generations of moviegoers. Reissue of the original version, painstakingly restored, has ceased because of a planned remake, so get copies while they last. 🎵Toccata & Fugue in D; The Nutcracker Suite; The Sorcerer's Apprentice; The Rite of Spring; Pastoral Symphony; Dance of the Hours; Night on Bald Mountain; Ave Maria; The Cossack Dance.
1940 116m/C Mickey Mouse; *Performed by:* Philadelphia Symphony Orchestra. **VHS, LV** $24.99 *DIS, FCT, RDG* 🎬🎬🎬🎬

Fantasies Teenage lovers Derek and Hooten return to their Greek island home and decide to improve their village by turning it into a tourist haven. First collaboration of the Dereks is a loser, lacking plot, direction, and decent acting. Bo shows no talent but the obvious one and is actually credited as Kathleen Collins. *AKA:* And Once Upon a Love.
1973 (R) 81m/C Bo Derek, Peter Hooten, Anna Alexiades; *D:* John Derek. **VHS, Beta** $59.98 *FOX* Woof!

The Fantasist This sex crime thriller features a deranged killer who makes obscene, yet seductive phone calls to young ladies before murdering them.
1989 (R) 98m/C Timothy Bottoms, Christopher Cazenove; *D:* Robin Hardy. **VHS** $79.98 *REP* 🎬

Fantastic Animation Festival Fourteen award-winning animated shorts are combined into one feature-length program. Included are "Closed Mondays," "The Last Cartoon Man," "French Windows," "Moonshadow," and "Cosmic Cartoon."
1977 (PG) 91m/C **VHS, Beta** *MED, OM* 🎬

Fantastic Balloon Voyage Three men embark on a journey across the equator in a balloon, experiencing myriad adventures along the way. Much hot air.
198? (G) 100m/C Hugo Stiglitz, Jeff Cooper. **VHS, Beta** $29.95 *GEM* 🎬

Fantastic Planet A critically acclaimed French, animated, sci-fi epic based on the drawings of Roland Topor. A race of small humanoids are enslaved and exploited by a race of giants on a savage planet, until one of the small creatures manages to unite his people and fight for equality. *AKA:* La Planete Sauvage.
1973 (PG) 68m/C *FR D:* Rene Laloux; *V:* Barry Bostwick. **VHS, Beta** $39.98 *SNC, MRV, VYY* 🎬🎬🎬

Fantastic Seven The Fantastic Seven is a daredevil team sent to rescue a Hollywood sex symbol who has been kidnapped and held for ransom while shooting on location off the coast of Miami.
1982 96m/C Elke Sommer, Christopher Connelly. **VHS, Beta** *TLF* 🎬1/2

Fantastic Voyage An important scientist, rescued from behind the Iron Curtain, is so severely wounded by enemy agents that traditional surgery is impossible. After being shrunk to microscopic size, a medical team journeys inside his body where they find themselves threatened by the patient's natural defenses. Great action, award-winning special effects. *AKA:* Microscopia; Strange Journey.
1966 100m/C Stephen Boyd, Edmond O'Brien, Raquel Welch, Arthur Kennedy, Donald Pleasence, Arthur O'Connell, William Redfield, James Brolin; *D:* Richard Fleischer. Academy Awards '66: Best Art Direction/Set Decoration (Color), Best Visual Effects; Nominations: Best Color Cinematography, Best Film Editing. **VHS, Beta, LV** $19.98 *FOX, CCB* 🎬🎬🎬

The Fantastic World of D.C. Collins Gary Coleman plays a daydreaming teenager who thinks he is being pursued by mysterious strangers seeking a videotape that was unknowingly slipped to him. Made for television.
1984 100m/C Gary Coleman, Bernie Casey, Shelley Smith, Fred Dryer, Marilyn McCoo, Phillip Abbott, George Gobel, Michael Ansara; *D:* Leslie Martinson. **VHS** $19.95 *STE, NWV* 🎬

Fantasy in Blue The search for the solution to a sexual stalemate results in a couple's strange experimentation.
197? 81m/C **VHS, Beta** *MED, MRV* 🎬

Fantasy Island Three people fly ("De plane, boss!") to an island paradise and get to live out their fantasies for a price. Made for television; the basis for the TV series.
1976 100m/C Ricardo Montalban, Bill Bixby, Sandra Dee, Peter Lawford, Carol Lynley, Hugh O'Brian, Eleanor Parker, Dick Sargent, Victoria Principal; *D:* Richard Lang. **VHS, Beta** $49.95 *PSM* 🎬

Fantasy Man A restless middle-aged man tries to relieve his mid-life crisis with the help of three women.
1984 100m/C *AU* Harold Hopkins, Jeanie Drynan, Kerry Mack, Kate Fitzpatrick; *W/D:* John Meagher. **VHS, Beta** $59.95 *VCD* 🎬1/2

Fantasy Mission Force Dastardly double crossing catches a crack commando unit with its pants down.
198? 90m/C Jackie Chan. **VHS, Beta** *NO* 🎬

Far and Away Meandering old-fashioned epic about Irish immigrants, romance, and settling the American West. Set in the 1890s, Joseph Donelly (Cruise), the son of a tenant farmer, is forced to flee his Irish homeland after threatening the life of his landlord. He emigrates to America in the company of the feisty Shannon Christie (Kidman), the landlord's daughter, and they wind up trying to earn their keep in Boston. What they both want is land of their own— and in the government-sponsored Oklahoma land rush in 1893 they get their chance. Particularly brutal scenes of Cruise earning his living as a bare-knuckled boxer contrast with the expansiveness of the land rush ending. Slow, spotty, and a little too slick for its own good, though real-life couple Cruise and Kidman are an attractive pair. Story was developed by co-producers Dolman and Howard and scripted by Dolman. Filmed in 70-mm Panavision on location in Ireland and Montana. Also available in a letter boxed version.
1992 (PG-13) 140m/C Tom Cruise, Nicole Kidman, Thomas Gibson, Robert Prosky, Barbara Babcock, Colm Meaney, Eileen Pollock, Michelle Johnson, Cyril Cusack, Clint Howard, Rance Howard; *D:* Ron Howard; *W:* Bob Dolman; *M:* John Williams. **VHS, Beta, LV** *MCA* 🎬🎬1/2

Far Away and Long Ago Based on the autobiographical novel by Guillermo Hudson which details the memories which haunted his childhood—the Argentinian pampas, its gauchos, witchcraft, and women. In Spanish with English subtitles.
1974 91m/C *AR* Juan Jose Camero, Leonor Manso; *D:* Manuel Antin. **VHS** $24.98 *TAM* 🎬🎬1/2

Far Country Cattlemen must battle the elements and frontier lawlessness in this classic. Stewart leads his herd to the Yukon in hopes of large profits, but ends up having to kidnap it back from the crooked sheriff and avenging the deaths of his friends. Entertaining and the Yukon setting takes it out of the usual Western arena.
1955 97m/C James Stewart, Ruth Roman, Walter Brennan, Harry Morgan, Corinne Calvet, Jay C. Flippen, John McIntire; *D:* Anthony Mann. **VHS, Beta** $14.95 *KRT* 🎬🎬🎬

Far Cry from Home A battered wife attempts to escape from her domineering husband before it's too late.
1977? 87m/C Mary Ann McDonald, Richard Monette. **VHS, Beta** $49.95 *TWE* 🎬

Far East Two ex-lovers meet in Southeast Asia and join forces to find the woman's missing husband, a reporter.
1985 105m/C Bryan Brown, Helen Morse; *D:* John Duigan. **VHS, Beta** $59.95 *LHV* 🎬1/2

Far from Home Drew Barrymore is the seductive teen being scoped by a psychotic killer while on vacation with her father. Lots of over-the-top performances by the familiar cast.
1989 (R) 86m/C Matt Frewer, Drew Barrymore, Richard Masur, Karen Austin, Susan Tyrrell, Anthony Rapp, Jennifer Jilly, Andras Jones, Dick Miller; *D:* Meiert Avis. **VHS, LV** $89.98 *LIV, VES* 🎬🎬

Far from the Madding Crowd A lavish, long adaptation of Thomas Hardy's nineteenth century classic about the beautiful Bathsheba and the three very different men who love her. Her first love is a handsome and wayward soldier (Stamp), her second the local noble lord (Finch) and her third the ever-loving and long-patient farmer (Bates). Christie is well cast as the much-desired beauty. Gorgeous cinematography by Nicolas Roeg.
1967 (PG) 165m/C *GB* Julie Christie, Terence Stamp, Peter Finch, Alan Bates, Prunella Ransome; *D:* John Schlesinger. Academy Awards '67 Nominations: Best Original Score; National Board of Review Awards '67: 10 Best Films of the Year, Best Actor (Finch). **VHS, Beta, LV** $29.98 *MGM* 🎬🎬🎬

Far Frontier Roy Rogers saves the day by thwarting a band of outlaws who are being smuggled across the border in soybean oil cans. Includes musical numbers and horse tricks.
1948 60m/B Roy Rogers, Andy Devine, Clayton Moore. **VHS** $9.95 *NOS, REP* 🎬🎬

Far North Written by Shepard, this is a quirky comedy about a woman returning to her rural family homestead after her father is seriously injured by a horse and trying to deal with her eccentric family's travails.
1988 (PG-13) 96m/C Jessica Lange, Charles Durning, Tess Harper, Donald Moffatt, Ann Wedgeworth, Patricia Arquette; *D:* Sam Shepard. **VHS, Beta, LV, 8mm** $19.95 *NLC* 🎬🎬1/2

A Far Off Place Self-sufficient and unpretentious, Nonnie (Witherspoon) is an American girl growing up in Africa with her parents, who oversee a game preserve. Winslow (Randall) proves her opposite—a snobbish and obnoxious city boy visiting the preserve with his father. When poachers

slaughter a herd of elephants (a very graphic scene) and then the teens' parents, the duo is forced to trek the Kalahari Desert with the assistance of Xhabbo (Bok), a teenage bushman. Recovering relatively quickly from their parents' assassinations, Winslow and Nonnie find themselves in a romance. Lacking suspense but graphically violent, this is not your typical Disney flick. Based on the books "A Story Like the Wind" and "A Far Off Place" by Laurens van der Post.
1993 (PG-13) 104m/C Reese Witherspoon, Ethan Randall, Sarel Bok, Jack Thompson, Maximilian Schell; **D:** Mikael Salomon; **W:** Robert Caswell, Jonathan Hensleigh, Sally Robinson; **M:** James Horner. **VHS** *NYR* 🐾🐾

Far Out Man An unalterable middle-aged hippie is sent by his worried family and his psychiatrist on a cross-country journey to rediscover himself. The script makes no sense and has very few laughs.
1989 (R) 105m/C Thomas Chong, Rae Dawn Chong, C. Thomas Howell, Shelby Chong, Martin Mull, Paris Chong, Paul Bartel, Judd Nelson, Michael Winslow, Cheech Marin; **D:** Thomas Chong. **VHS, Beta, LV $89.95** *COL* Woof!

The Far Pavilions A British officer falls in love with an Indian princess during the second Afghan War. Cross is appropriately noble and stiff-upper-lipped but Irving is miscast as his ethnic love. Based on the romantic bestseller by M.M. Kaye, this lavish production was made for cable television. *AKA:* Blade of Steel.
1984 108m/C Ben Cross, Amy Irving, Omar Sharif, Benedict Taylor, Rossano Brazzi, Christopher Lee; **D:** Peter Duffell. **VHS, Beta $14.95** *NEG, HBO, KAR* 🐾🐾½

Faraway Fantasy A Texan beds down in a Bavarian hotel with the perky, nubile maids.
1987 86m/C Judith Fritsch, Franz Muxeneder. **VHS, Beta $29.95** *MED* Woof!

Farewell, My Lovely A remake of the 1944 Raymond Chandler mystery, "Murder, My Sweet," featuring private eye Phillip Marlowe hunting for an ex-convict's lost sweetheart in 1941 Los Angeles. Perhaps the most accurate of Chandler adaptations, but far from the best, this film offers a nicely detailed production. Mitchum is a bit too world-weary as the seen-it-all detective.
1975 (R) 95m/C *GB* Robert Mitchum, Charlotte Rampling, Sylvia Miles, John Ireland, Anthony Zerbe, Jack O'Halloran, Harry Dean Stanton, Sylvester Stallone, Cheryl "Rainbeaux" Smith; **D:** Dick Richards. Academy Awards '75 Nominations: Best Supporting Actress (Miles); National Board of Review Awards '75: 10 Best Films of the Year. **VHS, Beta $24.98** *SUE* 🐾🐾🐾

A Farewell to Arms The original film version of Ernest Hemingway's novel about the tragic love affair between an American ambulance driver and an English nurse during the Italian campaign of World War I. The novelist disavowed the ambiguous ending, but the public loved the film. Fine performances and cinematography.
1932 85m/B Helen Hayes, Gary Cooper, Adolphe Menjou, Mary Philips, Jack LaRue, Blanche Frederici; **D:** Frank Borzage. Academy Awards '33: Best Cinematography, Best Sound; Nominations: Best Interior Decoration, Best Picture; National Board of Review Awards '32: 10 Best Films of the Year. **VHS, Beta, LV, 3/4U, Special order formats $9.95** *NEG, MRV, NOS* 🐾🐾🐾

Farewell to the King During World War II, a ship-wrecked American deserter becomes the chief of a tribe of Borneo headhunters until his jungle kingdom is caught between the forces of the U.S. and Japanese. With the help of a British officer he

helps them defend themselves when the Japanese invade. An old-fashioned war epic with beautiful performances and solid if uninspired-performances by the leads.
1989 (PG-13) 114m/C Nick Nolte, Nigel Havers, Marius Weyers, Frank McRae, Marilyn Tokuda, Elan Oberon, William Wise, James Fox; **D:** John Milius. **VHS, Beta, LV $19.98** *ORI* 🐾🐾½

Fargo Express When the kid brother of Maynard's true love is falsely accused of robbing a stagecoach, Maynard works to clear his name. Routine stuff.
1932 60m/B Ken Maynard, Helen Mack, Paul Fix; **D:** Alan James. **VHS, Beta $19.95** *NOS, VCN, DVT* 🐾½

The Farmer Takes a Wife Henry Fonda's first film, recreating his stage role, as a mid-nineteenth century farmer at odds with the Erie canal builders and struggling to court the woman he loves. Remade as a musical in 1953.
1935 91m/B Janet Gaynor, Henry Fonda, Charles Bickford, Slim Summorville, Jane Withers; **D:** Victor Fleming. **VHS** *TCF* 🐾🐾½

The Farmer Takes a Wife Poor musical remake of the 1935 drama, about the trials of a struggling 1850s farmer and the Erie canal boat cook he loves. Contains no memorable music and Robertson can't compete with Henry Fonda's original role as the farmer. ♫We're in Business; On the Erie Canal; We're Doing It for the Natives in Jamaica; When I Close My Door; Today I Love Everybody; Somethin' Real Special; With The Sun Warm Upon Me; Can You Spell Schenectady?.
1953 81m/C Betty Grable, Dale Robertson, Thelma Ritter, John Carroll, Eddie Foy Jr.; **D:** Henry Levin. **VHS, Beta, LV $19.98** *FOX* 🐾🐾

The Farmer's Daughter Young portrays Katrin Holmstrom, a Swedish farm girl who becomes a maid to Congressman Cotten and winds up running for office herself (not neglecting to find romance as well). The outspoken and multi-talented character charmed audiences and was the basis of a television series in the 1960s.
1947 97m/B Loretta Young, Joseph Cotten, Ethel Barrymore, Charles Bickford, Harry Davenport, Lex Barker, James Arness, Rose Hobart; **D:** H.C. Potter. Academy Awards '47: Best Actress (Young); Nominations: Best Supporting Actor (Bickford). **VHS, Beta $59.98** *FOX, BTV* 🐾🐾🐾

The Farmer's Other Daughter A rural comedy about Farmer Brown whose lovely daughter is eyed by all the farmhands. He also has to contend with dastardly Mr. Barksnapper who wants to take his farm away from him until one of his daughter's beaus comes to the rescue. *AKA:* Farm Girl.
1965 84m/C Ernest Ashworth, Judy Pennebaker, Bill Michael; **D:** John Patrick Hayes. **VHS $19.95** *SVS, COL* 🐾🐾

The Farmer's Wife Silent British comedy about a recently widowed farmer searching for a new wife. Meanwhile, his lovely housekeeper would be the perfect candidate. Screenplay written by Hitchcock, based on Eden Philpott's play.
1928 97m/B *GB* Jameson Thomas, Lillian Hall-Davies, Gordon Harker; **D:** Alfred Hitchcock. **VHS $16.95** *NOS, SNC, MLB* 🐾🐾½

Fashions of 1934 A typical, lightweight thirties musical with impressive choreography by Busby Berkeley. Powell plays a disreputable clothing designer who goes to Paris to steal the latest fashion designs and winds up costuming a musical and fall in love. ♫Spin a Little Web of Dreams; Broken Melody. *AKA:* Fashions.

1934 78m/B Bette Davis, William Powell, Frank McHugh, Hugh Herbert, Reginald Owen, Busby Berkeley; **D:** William Dieterle. **VHS, Beta $19.95** *VDM* 🐾🐾

Fass Black Yet another man against the mob flick straight out of Bartlett's familiar plot lines. Amidst gratuitous music and violence, a disco owner locks horns with the syndicate after they try to take over his place. There's a good reason disco is dead.
1977 (R) 105m/C John Poole, Jeanne Bell, Cal Wilson, Harold Nicholas, Nicholas Lewis; **D:** D'Urville Martin. **VHS $39.95** *XVC* 🐾🐾

The Fast and the Furious On the lam after being falsely charged with murder, Ireland picks up a fast car and a loose woman (or is it a loose car and a fast woman?) and makes a run for the border by entering the Pebble Beach race.
1954 73m/B John Ireland, Dorothy Malone, Bruce Carlisle, Iris Adrian; **D:** John Ireland, Edwards Sampson. **VHS $19.95** *NOS, TIM* 🐾🐾

Fast Break New York deli clerk who is a compulsive basketball fan talks his way into a college coaching job. He takes a team of street players with him, with predictable results on and off the court. Kaplan's screen debut.
1979 (PG) 107m/C Gabe Kaplan, Harold Sylvester, Randee Heller; **D:** Jack Smight. **VHS, Beta $19.95** *GKK* 🐾½

Fast Bullets Texas Rangers fight a gang of smugglers and rescue a kidnap victim in this typical western.
1944 52m/B Tom Tyler, Rex Lease. **VHS, Beta $19.95** *NOS, VCN, DVT* 🐾½

Fast Company The life story of champion race car driver Lonnie Johnson including women, money, and the drag racing sponsors.
1978 90m/C William Smith, John Saxon, Claudia Jennings, Nicholas Campbell, Don Francks; **D:** David Cronenberg. **VHS, Beta** *AOV* 🐾🐾

Fast Fists During the reign of the Min Kou Government, the Red Light Net gang of bandits terrorizes the countryside. One fateful evening, the gang's leader attempts to kidnap and kill a famous actress. This is the incredible story of what happened.
19?? 90m/C Jimmy Wang Yu. **VHS, Beta $57.95** *OCE* 🐾

Fast Food A super-cheap, strangulated attempt at low comedy, wherein an entrepreneurial hamburger peddler invents a secret aphrodisiac sauce. Look for former porn-star Traci Lords.
1989 90m/C Clark Brandon, Tracy Griffith, Randal Patrick, Traci Lords, Kevin McCarthy, Michael J. Pollard, Jim Varney; **D:** Michael A. Simpson. **VHS, Beta, LV $29.95** *FRH* 🐾

Fast Forward A group of eight teenagers from Ohio learn how to deal with success and failure when they enter a national dance contest in New York City. A break-dancing variation on the old show business chestnut. ♫Fast Forward; How Do You Do; As Long As We Believe; Pretty Girl; Mystery; Curves; Showdown; Do You Want It Right Now?; Hardrock; Taste.
1984 (PG) 110m/C John Scott Clough, Don Franklin, Tracy Silver, Cindy McGee; **D:** Sidney Poitier. **VHS, Beta, LV $79.95** *COL* 🐾½

Fast Getaway Chases scenes proliferate when a teen criminal mastermind plots bank heists for his outlaw father. Relatively painless adolescent action-comedy, cleverly acted, quickly forgotten.
1991 (PG) 91m/C Corey Haim, Cynthia Rothrock, Leo Rossi, Ken Lerner, Marcia Strassman; **D:** Spiro Razatos. **VHS, LV, 8mm $89.95** *COL, PIA* 🐾🐾

Fast Kill A terrorist plot begins to fall apart when the conspirators fight among themselves.
1973 94m/C Tom Adams, Susie Hampton, Michael Culver, Peter Halliday; **D:** Lindsay Shonteff. **VHS, Beta** $19.95 *GEM* ♫

Fast Lane Fever A drag racer challenges a factory worker to a no-holds-barred race.
1982 (R) 94m/C **VHS, Beta** $69.95 *MGM* ♫

Fast Money Three pals can't resist the temptation of big bucks from flying drugs in from Mexico, but they find danger along the way.
1983 92m/C Sammy Allred, Sonny Carl Davis; **D:** Doug Holloway. **VHS, Beta** $39.95 *LIV* ♫½

Fast Talking The story of a quick-talking, incorrigible, fifteen-year-old Australian boy's humorous though tragic criminal schemes. The young protagonist slides his way through a life marked by a degenerate home life, a brother who forces him to sell drugs, and a future that holds no promise.
1986 93m/C *AU* Steve Bisley, Tracey Mann, Peter Hehir, Dennis Moore, Rod Zuanic, Toni Allaylis, Chris Truswell; **W/D:** Ken Cameron. **VHS, Beta** $19.98 *SUE, NLC* ♫♫

Fast Times at Ridgemont High Teens at a Southern California high school revel in sex, drugs, and rock 'n' roll. A full complement of student types meet at the Mall—that great suburban microcosm percolating with angst-ridden teen trials—to contemplate losing their virginity, plot skipping homeroom, and move inexorably closer to the end of their adolescence. The talented young cast became household names: Sean Penn is most excellent as the California surfer dude who antagonizes teacher, Walston, aka "Aloha Mr. Hand." Based on the best-selling book by Cameron Crowe, it's one of the best of this genre.
1982 (R) 91m/C Sean Penn, Jennifer Jason Leigh, Judge Reinhold, Robert Romanus, Brian Backer, Phoebe Cates, Ray Walston, Scott Thomson, Vincent Schiavelli, Amanda Wyss, Forest Whitaker, Kelli Maroney, Eric Stoltz, Pamela Springsteen, James Russo, Martin Brest, Anthony Edwards; **D:** Amy Heckerling. **VHS, Beta, LV** $14.95 *MCA* ♫♫♫

Fast Walking A prison guard is offered fifty-thousand dollars to help a militant black leader escape from jail, the same man his cousin has contracted to kill.
1982 (R) 116m/C James Woods, Kay Lenz, M. Emmet Walsh, Robert Hooks, Tim McIntire, Timothy Carey, Susan Tyrrell; **D:** James B. Harris. **VHS, Beta** $19.98 *FOX, HHE* ♫♫

Faster Pussycat! Kill! Kill! It doesn't get any better than this! Three sexy go-go dancers get their after-work kicks by hot-rodding in the California desert. They soon find themselves enveloped in murder, kidnapping, lust and robbery after a particular race gets out of hand. Easily the most watchable, fun and funny production to spring from the mind of Russ Meyer. Those who haven't seen this cannot truly be called "cool."
1966 83m/B Tura Satana, Haji, Lori Williams, Susan Bernard, Stuart Lancaster, Paul Trinka, Dennis Busch, Ray Barlow, Mickey Foxx; **D:** Russ Meyer; **W:** Jack Moran. **VHS** $79.95 *RMF, FCT* ♫♫

Fastest Guitar Alive Debut of the Man with a Tear in His Voice is strictly for inveterate fans of the legendary Orbison. Rebel operative/crooner during the Civil War, whose rhythm is good but timing is bad, steals a Union gold supply, but the war ends before he makes it back to the land of Dixie.

Seems that makes him a common thief. Orbison penned seven of the eight songs.
1968 88m/C Roy Orbison, Sammy Jackson, Margaret Pierce, Joan Freeman; **D:** Michael Moore. **VHS, Beta** $14.95 *MGM, MVD* ♫½

The Fat Albert Christmas Special Bill Cosby's famous creations star in this animated Christmas story. And if you're not careful, you just may learn something about yourself.
1977 27m/C **D:** Hal Sutherland; **V:** Bill Cosby, Jan Crawford, Gerald Edwards, Eric Suter. **VHS, Beta** $7.00 *VTR* ♫½

The Fat Albert Easter Special Fat Albert and the Cosby Kids learn lessons and have fun in this animated special.
1982 27m/C **V:** Bill Cosby, Jan Crawford, Eric Suter, Gerald Edwards. **VHS, Beta** $7.00 *VTR* ♫½

The Fat Albert Halloween Special More fun and learning from Fat Albert and the gang.
1977 27m/C **D:** Hal Sutherland; **V:** Bill Cosby, Jan Crawford, Gerald Edwards, Eric Suter, Erika Carroll. **VHS, Beta** $7.00 *VTR* ♫½

Fat and the Lean An early short film from Roman Polanski that satirizes government tyranny and absurdity.
1961 16m/C **D:** Roman Polanski. **VHS, Beta** *IHF, FLI* ♫♫♫

Fat City One of Huston's later triumphs, a seedy, street-level drama based on the Leonard Gardner novel about an aging alcoholic boxer trying to make a comeback and his young worshipful protege. Highly acclaimed. Tyrrell earned an Oscar nomination as the boxer's world-weary lover.
1972 (PG) 93m/C Stacy Keach, Jeff Bridges, Susan Tyrrell, Candy Clark, Nicholas Colasanto; **D:** John Huston. **VHS, Beta** $19.95 *COL* ♫♫♫½

Fat Guy Goes Nutzoid A crude farce about an obese mental patient who escapes from the mental hospital and joins two teenagers on a wild trip to New York City. **AKA:** Zeisters.
1986 85m/C Tibor Feldman, Peter Linari, John MacKay, Joan Allen; **D:** John Golden. **VHS, Beta** $79.95 *PSM* Woof!

Fat Man and Little Boy A lavish, semi-fictional account of the creation of the first atomic bomb, and the tensions between J. Robert Oppenheimer and his military employer, Gen. Leslie Groves. Overlong but interesting. Cusack, whose character never existed, is especially worthwhile as an idealistic scientist.
1989 (PG-13) 127m/C Paul Newman, Dwight Schultz, Bonnie Bedelia, John Cusack, Laura Dern, John C. McGinley, Natasha Richardson; **D:** Roland Joffe; **W:** Bruce Robinson, Tony Garnett. **VHS, Beta, LV, 8mm** $14.95 *PAR, FCT, HMV* ♫♫½

Fatal Attraction Couple meet after an auto accident. They begin an affair which turns dark and bizarre. Fine cast doesn't get far with this peculiar premise, although every one tries hard. **AKA:** Head On.
1980 (R) 90m/C *CA* Sally Kellerman, Stephen Lack, John Huston, Lawrence Dane; **D:** Michael Grant. **VHS, Beta** $29.98 *VES* ♫♫

Fatal Attraction When a very married New York lawyer is seduced by a beautiful blonde associate, the one-night stand leads to terror as she continues to pursue the relationship. She begins to threaten his family and home with possessive, violent acts. An expertly made, manipulative thriller; one of the most hotly discussed films of the 1980s. A successful change of role for Close as the sexy, scorned, and deadly other woman. Music by Maurice Jarre. Also available in a

---

special "director's series" edition, featuring Lyne's original, controversial ending.
1987 (R) 120m/C Michael Douglas, Glenn Close, Anne Archer, Stuart Pankin, Ellen Hamilton-Latzen, Ellen Foley, Fred Gwynne, Meg Mundy, J.J. Johnston; **D:** Adrian Lyne; **W:** James Dearden. Academy Awards '87 Nominations: Best Actress (Close), Best Adapted Screenplay, Best Director (Lyne), Best Film Editing, Best Picture, Best Supporting Actress (Archer); People's Choice Awards '88: Best Film—Drama. **VHS, Beta, LV, 8mm** $14.95 *PAR, FCT, PIA* ♫♫♫

Fatal Beauty A female undercover cop in Los Angeles tracks down a drug dealer selling cocaine (from which the title is taken). Elliott is the mob bodyguard who helps her out. Violent and sensational, the film tries to capitalize on the success of "Beverly Hills Cop" and fails miserably. Goldberg is wasted in this effort and the picture tiptoes around the interracial romance aspects that are implied.
1987 (R) 104m/C Whoopi Goldberg, Sam Elliott, Ruben Blades, Harris Yulin, Cheech Marin, Brad Dourif; **D:** Tom Holland. **VHS, Beta, LV** $14.95 *MGM* ♫½

Fatal Bond Blair plays a small-town hairdresser caught in an obsessive love affair with a drifter. When she suspects her boyfriend is committing a string of rape-murders, will she turn him in or protect him? Or is she next?
1991 (R) 89m/C Linda Blair, Jerome Elhers, Stephen Leeder, Donal Gibson, Caz Lederman, Tao Gerbert, Penny Pederson, Joe Bugner; **D:** Vincent Monton; **W:** Phillip Avalon. **VHS** *COL* ♫½

Fatal Charm There's a serial killer at work in a small town. So far six women have been raped and murdered. But cute-teen Valerie can't believe it when the townspeople accuse that sweet guy Adam, especially since he's the one boy Valerie is so very attracted to.
1992 (R) 90m/C Christopher Atkins, Amanda Peterson, Mary Frann, James Remar, Andrew Robinson, Peggy Lipton; **D:** Alan Smithee; **W:** Nicholas Niciphor. **VHS** $89.95 *ACA* ♫♫

Fatal Chase Van Cleef is a U.S. Marshal assigned to protect ex-hitman Musante from his vengeful former employers. And you thought you didn't get along with your boss. Typical made-for-TV fodder written by Anhalt, who usually manages to be a trifle more entertaining. **AKA:** Nowhere to Hide.
1977 78m/C Lee Van Cleef, Tony Musante, Charles Robinson, Lelia Goldoni, Noel Fournier, Russell Johnson, Edward Anhalt; **D:** Jack Starrett; **W:** Edward Anhalt. **VHS** $9.95 *SIM* ♫♫

Fatal Confinement Wrenching drama finds Crawford, having lived 15 years in seclusion with her young daughter, forced to sell her land to a giant corporation bent on expansion. Interesting also for the similarities to Crawford's real-life "Mommie Dearest" lifestyle.
1964 70m/C *GB* Joan Crawford, Paul Burke, Charles Bickford; **D:** Robert Guest. **VHS** $39.95 *FCT, MOV* ♫♫½

Fatal Error Dutch police thriller about the investigation of a cop killing. Dubbed. **AKA:** Outsider in Amsterdam; The Outsider; Grijpstra and de Gier.
1983 85m/C *NL* Rutger Hauer, Rijk de Gooyer, Willeke Van Ammelrooy, Donald M. Jones; **D:** Wim Verstappen; **M:** Ennio Morricone. **VHS, Beta** $79.95 *WES* ♫½

Fatal Exposure The insatiably sanguinary Jack the Ripper lives on in the form of his great grandson, who avails himself of modern technology to capture those magic moments on videotape. Just goes to show home movies don't have to be bland.

1990 ?m/C Blake Bahner, Ena Henderson, Julie Austin, Dan Schmale, Renee Cline, Gary Wise, Joy Ovington. VHS *TPV, HHE* 🎬🎬

Fatal Exposure A divorcee on vacation with her young sons accidentally picks up the wrong snapshots at the developers'. It turns out she has her hands on some incriminating photos, and the subject will resort to anything, even murder, to keep her quiet. Originally made for television.
1991 (PG-13) 89m/C Mare Winningham, Nick Mancuso, Christopher McDonald, Geoffrey Blake; *D:* Alan Metzger. VHS, Beta *PAR* 🎬🎬

Fatal Fix A French film expose of urban heroin addiction. Music by the Pretenders.
198? 90m/C *FR* Helmut Berger, Corinne Clery; *D:* Massimo Pirri. VHS, Beta *NO* 🎬🎬½

Fatal Games Young female athletes are mysteriously disappearing at the Falcon Academy of Athletics and a crazed killer is responsible.
1984 84m/C Sally Kirkland, Lynn Banashek, Sean Masterson. VHS, Beta $59.95 *MED* 🎬🎬½

The Fatal Glass of Beer Fields' son returns to his home in the north woods after serving a jail term in this slapstick comedy short.
1933 18m/B W.C. Fields, Rosemary Theby, George Chandler, Richard Cramer. VHS, Beta $19.98 *CCB* 🎬🎬½

The Fatal Hour Karloff is enlisted to aid police in solving the murder of a detective. As Karloff is rounding up suspects, three more murders take place. Feeble.
1940 68m/B Boris Karloff, Marjorie Reynolds, Grant Withers, Charles Trowbridge, John Hamilton, Frank Puglia, Jason Robards Sr.; *D:* William Nigh. VHS, Beta, 8mm $16.98 *VYY, SNC, TIM* 🎬🎬½

The Fatal Image A mother and daughter on vacation in Paris inadvertently videotape an international mob hit, making them the target of ruthless assassins. Filmed on location in Paris. Made for television.
1990 96m/C Michele Lee, Justine Bateman, Francois Dunoyer, Jean-Pierre Cassel, Sonia Petrovna; *D:* Thomas J. Wright. VHS $89.95 *WOV* 🎬🎬

Fatal Images A camera mysteriously causes all the models who pose for it to die, prompting the photographer to investigate.
1982 90m/C Lane Coyle. VHS, Beta $49.95 *AHV* 🎬

Fatal Instinct A tough-guy cop trying to solve a murder instead finds himself a victim of sexual obsession in this erotic thriller. Also available in an unrated version. Not to be confused with (but doesn't everything sound familiar) "Basic Instinct."
1992 (R) 93m/C Michael Madsen, Laura Johnson, Tony Hamilton; *D:* John Dirlam. VHS $89.95 *NLC, COL* 🎬½

Fatal Instinct Spoof on erotic thrillers such as "Fatal Attraction" and "Basic Instinct." Assante plays a guy with dual careers—he's busts the bad guys as a cop but then turns around and defends them as an attorney.
1993 (R) ?m/C Armand Assante, Sean Young, Sherilyn Fenn, Kate Nelligan; *D:* Carl Reiner; *W:* David O'Malley. VHS *NYR* 🎬🎬½

Fatal Justice Mars is a topnotch assassin who's been in the business too long and knows too much so the agency he works for decides to kill him off. They send young and beautiful professional Diana to do the job but will she be able to when she discovers Mars is actually her father?
199? 90m/C Joe Estevez. VHS $89.95 *AIP* 🎬

Fatal Mission A Vietnam soldier captures a female Chinese guerilla and uses her as his hostage and guide through the jungle.
1989 (R) 84m/C Peter Fonda, Mako, Tia Carrere. VHS, Beta, LV $79.98 *MED* 🎬

Fatal Pulse Sorority girls are being killed off in grisly ways. Basic slasher/gore.
1988 90m/C Michelle McCormick, Ken Roberts, Joe Phelan, Alex Courtney. VHS, Beta $19.95 *CEL* Woof!

Fatal Skies An evil schemer plots to dump toxic waste in a small town's water supply until a group of teens comes to the rescue.
1990 88m/C Timothy Leary. VHS, Beta $139.95 *AIP* 🎬

Fatal Vision The television film version of Joe McGinniss' controversial book about the murder trial of Dr. Jeffrey MacDonald, the Marine corps physician accused of murdering his whole family and blaming the killings on crazed hippies. McGinniss first believed MacDonald may have been innocent but his subsequent investigation, and his book, proved otherwise. The starring debut for Cole. MacDonald still protests his innocence.
1984 192m/C Gary Cole, Karl Malden, Eva Marie Saint, Andy Griffith, Barry Newman; *D:* David Greene. VHS, Beta, LV $69.95 *COL* 🎬🎬½

Fate Sweet comedy. A young man plans his love-affair carefully, but his biggest problem is meeting the girl of his dreams. Cheerful acting from Lynn and Paul. Stylish and charming.
1990 (PG-13) 115m/C Cheryl Lynn, Stuart Paul, Kaye Ballard, Susannah York; *D:* Stuart Paul. VHS $19.95 *ACA* 🎬🎬½

The Fate of Lee Khan Much blood is shed as a rebellion is led against the Mongols during the Yuan dynasty.
1973 107m/C Roy Chaid, Angela Mao; *D:* Kinghu. VHS, Beta $39.95 *CGH, FCT* 🎬🎬½

Father After World War II, a Hungarian youth makes up stories about his dead father's heroism that enhance his own position. Eventually he becomes obsessed with the facts surrounding his father's death at the hands of the enemy and, learning the truth, lays the past to rest. In Hungarian with English subtitles.
1967 89m/B *HU* Andras Balint, Miklos Gabor; *W/D:* Istvan Szabo. VHS, Beta, LV $175.00 *VYY, DVT, TAM* 🎬🎬

Father A woman receives an anonymous telephone call telling her to watch a television news program and learn the truth about her beloved father. What she sees is her father's face superimposed over that of a young Nazi soldier and an aging, unstable woman accusing her father of war crimes. The daughter fiercely believes her father to be a victim of mistaken identity but questions keep nagging at her. Very similiar in plot to "Music Box" and just as pedestrian in spite of some good performances.
1990 (PG-13) 106m/C *AU* Max von Sydow, Carol Drinkwater, Julia Blake, Steven Jacobs; *D:* John Power. VHS $79.95 *MNC* 🎬

The Father Clements Story The true story of a black priest in Chicago who battled the Roman Catholic hierarchy in order to adopt a troubled teenager. Made for television.
1987 100m/C Louis Gossett Jr., Malcolm Jamal Warner, Carroll O'Connor, Leon Robinson; *D:* Edwin Sherin. VHS *LIV* 🎬🎬½

Father Figure When a divorced man attends his ex-wife's funeral, he discovers that he must take care of his estranged sons. Based on young adult writer Richard Peck's novel; a well-done made-for-television movie.
1980 94m/C Hal Linden; Timothy Hutton, Cassie Yates, Martha Scott, Jeremy Licht; *D:* Jerry London. VHS, Beta *NO* 🎬½

Father Goose During World War II, a liquor-loving plane-spotter stationed on a remote Pacific Isle finds himself stuck with a group of French refugee schoolgirls and their teacher. Some predictable gags, romance, and heroism fill out the running time pleasantly. Scriptwriters Stone and Tarloff, who were competitors, not collaborators on the project, shared an Oscar.
1964 116m/C Cary Grant, Leslie Caron, Trevor Howard; *D:* Ralph Nelson; *W:* Peter Stone, Frank Tarloff. Academy Awards '64: Best Story & Screenplay; Nominations: Best Film Editing, Best Sound. VHS $19.98 *REP* 🎬🎬½

Father Hood Family drama has Swayze playing a small-time criminal whose daughter tracks him down after leaving the foster-care shelter where she and her brother are being abused. The family takes to the road, running from both the police and a journalist (Berry) who wants to expose the corrupt foster-care system.
1993 (PG-13) m/C Patrick Swayze, Halle Berry, Diane Ladd, Brian Bonsall; *D:* Darrell Roodt. VHS 🎬🎬½

Father of the Bride A classic, quietly hilarious comedy about the tribulations of a father preparing for his only daughter's wedding. Tracy is suitably overwhelmed as the loving father and Taylor radiant as the bride. A warm vision of American family life, accompanied by the 1940 MGM short "Wedding Bills." Also available in a colorized version. Followed by "Father's Little Dividend" and later a television series. Remade in 1991.
1950 94m/C Spencer Tracy, Elizabeth Taylor, Joan Bennett, Billie Burke, Leo G. Carroll, Russ Tamblyn, Don Taylor, Moroni Olsen, Russ Tamblyn; *D:* Vincente Minnelli; *W:* Francis Goodrich, Albert Hackett. VHS, Beta, LV $19.98 *MGM, PIA* 🎬🎬🎬½

Father of the Bride Remake of the 1950 comedy classic portrays one of the most overextravagant weddings in recent film history. Martin is believable as the reluctant dad who complains about everything from expenses, to the groom, to the future in-laws, all the while secretly hoping the wedding will be called off. Of course, his griping is a front to hide his struggle to accept the fact that his little girl is growing up and getting married. Predictable plot and characters don't hide any surprises, but nothing detracts from the purpose of the film: to be a nice, charming movie. Keaton is little more than window dressing as the mother of the bride; Short steals several scenes as a pretentious and rather irritating wedding coordinator. Williams pulls off a nice film debut—observant viewers will recognize her as the bride-to-be in a TV ad for Sprint, calling her dad to tell him she's engaged. Adapted from the original screenplay, which was adapted from a novel by Edward Streeter.
1991 (PG) 105m/C Steve Martin, Diane Keaton, Kimberly Williams, Kieran Culkin, George Newbern, Martin Short, B.D. Wong, Peter Michael Goetz, Kate McGregor Stewart, Martha Gehman; *Cameos:* Eugene Levy; *W/D:* Charles Shyer; *W:* Nancy Meyer; *M:* Alan Silvestri. VHS, Beta, LV $94.95 *TOU* 🎬🎬½

Fathers and Sons Max is a brooding, former bad-boy movie director living on the Jersey Shore. His wife's death causes him to rethink his life and deal with his drinking problem. He also tries to get to know his equally brooding teenage son, Ed. Turns out addiction may run in the family as Ed experiments with drugs. Ill-fitting subplot deals a serial killer stalking the community. Goldblum brings an uneasy gentleness to the father's role in an otherwise slow, talky, and obviously symbolic flick.
1992 (R) 100m/C Jeff Goldblum, Rory Cochrane, Mitchell Marchand, Famke Janssen, Natasha Gregson Wagner, Ellen Greene, Samuel L. Jackson, Joie Lee, Rosanna Arquette, Michael Disend; *D:* Paul Mones; *W:* Paul Mones.*COL* 🎞️ 1/2

Father's Little Dividend Tracy expects a little peace and quiet now that he's successfully married off Taylor in this charming sequel to "Father of the Bride." However, he's quickly disillusioned by the news he'll soon be a grandfather - a prospect that causes nothing but dismay. Reunited the stars, director, writers, and producer from the successful first film.
1951 82m/B Spencer Tracy, Joan Bennett, Elizabeth Taylor, Don Taylor, Billie Burke, Russ Tamblyn, Moroni Olsen; *D:* Vincente Minnelli; *W:* Francis Goodrich, Albert Hacket. **VHS, Beta, LV** $9.95 *NEG, MRV, NOS* 🎞️🎞️🎞️

A Father's Revenge Dennehy is the only reason to bother with this average hostage drama. He's the father of a stewardess who's one of a group being held by terrorists. They're scheduled to die in 72 hours unless Dennehy can find a way to rescue them. Made for television.
1988 (R) 93m/C Brian Dennehy, Joanna Cassidy, Ron Silver; *D:* John Herzfeld. **VHS, LV** $89.95 *VMK* 🎞️🎞️1/2

Fatso After the shocking death of his obese cousin, an obsessive overeater struggles to overcome his neurosis with the aid of his sister and a self-help group called "Chubby Checkers." Bancroft's first work as both writer and director.
1980 (PG) 93m/C Dom DeLuise, Anne Bancroft, Ron Carey, Candice Azzara; *D:* Anne Bancroft. **VHS, Beta** $14.98 *FOX* 🎞️1/2

Fatty and Mabel Adrift/Mabel, Fatty and the Law Fatty and Mabel have problems enjoying their wedded bliss in these two silent shorts, which have a newly recorded orchestral score on the soundtrack.
1916 40m/B Fatty Arbuckle, Mabel Normand, Al "Fuzzy" St. John, Minta Durfee, Teddy the Dog. **VHS, Beta** $19.98 *CCB* 🎞️1/2

Fatty Finn A children's gagfest about young kids and bullies during the Depression, based on Syd Nicholls' comic strip.
1984 91m/C *AU* Ben Oxenbould, Bart Newton; *D:* Maurice Murphy. **VHS, Beta** $14.98 *VID* 🎞️1/2

Faust The classic German silent based upon the legend of Faust, who sells his soul to the devil in exchange for youth. Based on Goethe's poem, and directed by Murnau as a classic example of Germanic expressionism. Remade as "All That Money Can Buy" in 1941.
1926 117m/B *GE* Emil Jannings, Warner Fuetterer, Gosta Ekman, Camilla Horn; *D:* F. W. Murnau. **VHS, Beta** $24.95 *NOS, MRV, GPV* 🎞️🎞️🎞️1/2

Faust Joan Sutherland introduces the opera based on Goethe's dramatic poem telling of a man who makes a pact with the devil. Some of the most beautiful moments in French opera are presented. Puppet characters help explain the story and make it accessible to youngsters.
1973 30m/C Joan Sutherland. **VHS, Beta** *BFA* 🎞️🎞️🎞️1/2

The Favor, the Watch, & the Very Big Fish Set in a fairytale version of Paris. Hoskins is a photographer of religious subjects searching for a man to pose as Jesus. He discovers his subject in the hirsute Goldblum, a mad bar pianist who actually thinks he's the savior. Richardson plays the object of Hoskins's shy affections, an actress who does dubbing work by providing the moaning and groaning for porno flicks. Messy attempt at screwball-comedy with some brief humorous moments.
1992 (R) 89m/C *GB FR* Bob Hoskins, Jeff Goldblum, Natasha Richardson, Michel Blanc, Jacques Villeret, Angela Pleasence, Jean-Pierre Cassel, Bruce Altman; *W/D:* Ben Lewin. **VHS, LV** $92.95 *VMK, FCT* 🎞️🎞️

Fawlty Towers Cleese stars as the most obnoxious and inept hotel proprietor on earth in these three comedy episodes from the BBC series: "A Touch of Class," "Hotel Inspectors," and "The Germans," (which features Cleese's extraordinary goose-stepping). Additional episodes available.
1977 90m/C *GB* John Cleese, Prunella Scales, Connie Booth, Andrew Sachs; *W:* John Cleese, Connie Booth. **VHS** $19.98 *FOX, MOV, SIG* 🎞️🎞️🎞️

FBI Girl An FBI clerk is used as bait to trap a murderer and break up a gang. Burr, pre-Perry Mason, plays a bad guy.
1952 74m/B Cesar Romero, George Brent, Audrey Totter, Raymond Burr, Tom Drake; *D:* William Berke. **VHS, Beta, LV** *RXM* 🎞️🎞️

The FBI Murders A fact-based chiller about the bloody 1986 shootout between Miami FBI agents and a pair of violent killers (Soul and Gross playing against type). This made for television drama was shown on TV as "In the Line of Duty: The FBI Murders."
1988 95m/C David Soul, Michael Gross, Ronny Cox, Bruce Greenwood, Doug Sheehan, Teri Copley; *D:* Dick Lowry; *W:* Tracy Keenan Wynn. **VHS** $79.95 *CAF* 🎞️🎞️🎞️

The FBI Story Mr. Stewart goes to Washington in this anatomy of the Federal Bureau of Investigation. If you're a fan of the gangster genre (LeRoy earlier directed "Little Caesar"), and not especially persnickety about fidelity to the facts, this actioner offers a pseudo-factual (read fictional) glimpse—based on actual cases from the 1920s through the 1950s—into the life of a fictitious agent-family man.
1959 149m/C James Stewart, Vera Miles, Nick Adams, Murray Hamilton, Larry Pennell; *D:* Mervyn LeRoy. **VHS, LV** $19.98 *WAR, PIA, FCT* 🎞️🎞️🎞️

Fear An impoverished medical student murders the professor he believes is tormenting him and his life suddenly gets better. He falls in love and gets a scholarship but the police are closing in on his crime. Except...did any of it really happen? Or is he suffering from hallucinations. Low-budget psycho-drama with some good paranoid moments.
1946 68m/B Peter Cookson, Warren William, Anne Gwynne, James B. Cardwell, Nestor Paiva; *D:* Alfred Zeisler. **VHS** *VES* 🎞️🎞️

Fear A vacationing family is plagued by a murderous Vietnam vet and other psychotic cons.
1988 (R) 96m/C Frank Stallone, Cliff DeYoung, Kay Lenz, Robert Factor; *D:* Robert A. Ferretti. **VHS, Beta, LV** *NO* 🎞️

Fear A young psychic (Sheedy) delves into the minds of serial killers and writes novels about her experiences. But what happens when the next killer is also a psychic and decides to play mind-games with her? Above

average suspense sustains this made-for-cable thriller.
1990 (R) 98m/C Ally Sheedy, Lauren Hutton, Michael O'Keefe, Stan Shaw, Dina Merrill, John Agar, Marta DuBois; *D:* Rockne S. O'Bannon; *M:* Henry Mancini. **VHS** $89.98 *VES* 🎞️🎞️1/2

Fear, Anxiety and Depression A neurotic aspiring playwright in New York has various problems with his love life. Sub-Woody Allen comedy attempt, with a few bright spots. The dregs of New York, with all the violence and degradation, are brought to the screen here.
1989 (R) 84m/C Todd Solondz, Stanley Tucci; *W/D:* Todd Solondz. **VHS, Beta** $89.95 *VIR* 🎞️1/2

The Fear Chamber Hardly a Karloff vehicle. Boris shot the footage for this and three other Mexican "horror" films in LA, an unfortunate swan song to his career, though he was fortunate to be quickly written out of this story. The near plot concerns a mutant rock that thrives on human fear. Doctor Karloff and his assistants make sure the rock is rolling in sacrificial victims (women, of course). A prodigious devaluation of the "B"-grade horror flick, it's so bad it's just bad. *AKA:* Torture Zone; Chamber of Fear; La Camara Del Terror.
1968 88m/C *MX* Boris Karloff, Yerye Beirut, Julissa, Carlos East; *D:* Juan Ibanez, Jack Hill. **VHS** $19.99 *SNC, MPI* Woof!

Fear City Two partners who own a talent agency are after the psychopath who is killing off their prized strippers with the aid of a local cop. Sleazy look at Manhattan low life.
1985 (R) 93m/C Billy Dee Williams, Tom Berenger, Jack Scalia, Melanie Griffith, Rae Dawn Chong, Joe Santos, Maria Conchita Alonso, Rossano Brazzi; *D:* Abel Ferrara. **VHS, Beta, LV** $79.99 *HBO* 🎞️1/2

Fear in the City The Sicilian Mafia and a black crime gang battle for control of the streets.
1981 90m/C *IT* Michael Constantine, Fred Williamson, Gianni Manera; *D:* Gianni Manera. **VHS, Beta** *NO* 🎞️

Fear in the Night Suspenseful tale of a murder committed by a man under hypnosis. Fearing his nightmares are real Kelley talks his detective friend into investigating his "crime," which leads them to a mansion, a mirrored room, and a plot that takes some clever and unexpected twists. Remade in 1956 as "Nightmare."
1947 72m/B Paul Kelly, DeForest Kelley, Ann Doran, Kay Scott, Robert Emmett Keane; *D:* Maxwell Shane. **VHS** $59.99 *SNC, HBO* 🎞️🎞️🎞️

The Fear Inside Lahti plays a woman suffering from agoraphobia who, because of her fear, has not left her home in more than a year. To help out, Lahti invites a seemingly charming college student to live with her. When the young woman's equally charming "brother" comes to visit, Lahti discovers the two aren't so charming after all. A standard woman-in-terror film with a better-than-average cast. Made for cable television.
1992 (R) 100m/C Christine Lahti, Jennifer Rubin, Dylan McDermott; *D:* Leon Ichaso. **VHS, Beta, LV** $89.89 *FXV* 🎞️🎞️1/2

Fear No Evil A teenager who is the human embodiment of the demon Lucifer commits acts of demonic murder and destruction. His powers are challenged by an 18-year-old girl, who is the embodiment of the archangel Gabriel. First feature from La Loggia is better than it sounds.
1980 (R) 90m/C Stefan Arngrim, Kathleen Rowe McAllen, Elizabeth Hoffman; *D:* Frank Laloggia. **VHS, Beta** $9.95 *COL, SUE* 🎞️🎞️

Fear Strikes Out Perkins plays Jimmy Piersall, star outfielder for the Boston Red Sox, and Malden, his demanding father, in the true story of the baseball star's battle for sanity. One of Perkins' best screen performances.
1957 100m/B Anthony Perkins, Karl Malden, Norma Moore, Adam Williams, Perry Wilson; **D:** Robert Mulligan. **VHS, Beta, LV** $14.95 PAR ⅃⅃

Fearless An Italian detective has found a Viennese banker's daughter, but continues to pursue the unanswered questions of the case, embroiling himself in a web of intrigue and plotting.
1978 89m/C Joan Collins, Maurizio Merli, Franz Antel. **VHS, Beta** $19.95 STE, NWV ⅃

Fearless Fighters Kung fu action is fast and furious in this film wherein everybody is Kung fu fightin'.
1977 83m/C Lei Peng, Mu Lan. **VHS, Beta** $7.00 VTR ⅃

Fearless Hyena A young man uses his martial arts skills to get revenge against the men who murdered his grandfather.
1979 97m/C Jackie Chan. **VHS, Beta** NO ⅃

Fearless Hyena: Part 2 A happy-go-lucky Yin/Yang clan disciple must abandon his gambling and acrobatic endeavors to kick members of a rival clan in the head.
1986 90m/C Jackie Chan. **VHS, Beta** NO ⅃

The Fearless Vampire Killers Underrated, off-off-beat, and deliberately campy spoof on vampire films in which Tate is kidnapped by some fangy villains. Vampire trackers MacGowran and Polanski pursue the villains to the haunted castle and attempt the rescue. Only vampire movie with a Jewish bloodsucker ("Boy, have you got the wrong vampire," he proclaims to a maiden thrusting a crucifix at him). Inside the castle, Polanski is chased by the count's gay vampire son. Highlight is the vampire ball with a wonderful mirror scene. Many other amusing moments. **AKA:** Pardon Me, Your Teeth are in My Neck; Dance of the Vampires.
1967 98m/C GB Jack MacGowran, Roman Polanski, Alfie Bass, Jessie Robbins, Sharon Tate, Ferdinand "Ferdy" Mayne, Iain Quarrier; **D:** Roman Polanski. **VHS, Beta, LV** $19.98 MGM ⅃⅃⅃

The Fearless Young Boxer A young man trains in martial arts in order to exact revenge for his father's murder.
1973 94m/C **VHS, Beta** $39.95 UNI ⅃

Fearmaker After the mysterious death of her father, the heiress to his fortune is tangled in a web of treachery created by other potential inheritors. **AKA:** House of Fear; Violent Rage.
1989 (PG) 90m/C MX Katy Jurado, Paul Picerni, Sonia Amelio, Carlos East; **D:** Anthony Carras. **VHS, Beta** $59.95 PSM ⅃

Feast for the Devil A woman searches for her missing sister in a mysterious coastal village, only to fall under the occult spell of a mad doctor.
197? 90m/C Krista Nell, Thomas Moore, Teresa Gimpera. **VHS, Beta** NO ⅃½

Federal Agent Lots of cliches fill this crime film about a federal agent chasing foreign spys who are looking for a new explosive.
1936 53m/B William Boyd, Charles A. Browne, Irene Ware, George Cooper, Lentia Lace, Dan Alvarado; **D:** Sam Newfield. **VHS, Beta** $8.95 GPV ⅃⅃

Federal Agents vs. Underworld, Inc. Super G-Man Dave Worth goes up against Nila, a greedy villainess bent on finding the golden hands of Kurigal so she may rule the world. A 12-episode serial edited onto two cassettes. **AKA:** Golden Hands of Kurigal.
1949 167m/B Kirk Alyn, Rosemary La Planche, Roy Barcroft, Carol Forman, James Dale, Bruce Edwards; **D:** Fred Brannon. **VHS** $29.98 REP, MLB ⅃⅃

Feds Two women enter the FBI Academy and take on the system's inherent sexism with feebly comic results.
1988 (PG-13) 82m/C Rebecca DeMornay, Mary Gross, Ken Marshall, Fred Dalton Thompson, Larry Cedar, James Luisi, Raymond Singer; **D:** Dan Goldberg. **VHS, Beta, LV** WAR ⅃½

Feel My Pulse Silent comedy about a rich fanatic who leaves everything in his will to his young niece on the stipulation that she lead a germ-free life; when she reaches 21, she moves into the sanitarium she's inherited, not knowing it has become a base for prohibition-era rum runners.
1928 86m/B Bebe Daniels, Richard Arlen, William Powell; **D:** Gregory La Cava. **VHS, Beta** $27.95 VYY ⅃⅃

Feel the Motion A female auto-mechanic wants to make it big in the music biz. She sees her chance when she slips her demo tape onto a hit TV-music show.
1986 98m/C Sissy Kelling, Frank Meyer-Brockman, Ingolf Locke, Falco, Meatloaf. **VHS, Beta** $69.95 VMK ⅃

Feelin' Screwy A couple of misfit dweebs attempt to rid their town of the local drug dealer in order to impress a couple of babes in this limp coming-of-ager.
1990 90m/C Quincy Reynolds, Larry Gamal, Darin McBride, Hassan Jamal, Marsha Carter, Brooks Morales, Anna Fuentes; **W/D:** Riffat A. Khan. **VHS** NO ⅃

Feelin' Up A young man sells all his possessions to come to New York in search of erotic adventures.
1976 (R) 84m/C Malcolm Groome, Kathleen Seward, Rhonda Hansome, Tony Collado, Charles Douglass; **D:** David Secter. **VHS, Beta** $69.98 LIV, VCS Woof!

Feet First A shoe salesman puts on "upper crust" airs as he begins a shipboard romance with a girl who thinks he's wealthy. Lloyd's second sound film shows him grappling with technique and has scenes that recall highlights of his silent hits.
1930 85m/B Harold Lloyd, Barbara Kent, Robert McWade; **D:** Clyde Bruckman. **VHS, Beta** TLF ⅃⅃½

Feet Foremost A made-for-British-television horror story about an industrialist haunted by the spirit of a teenage girl.
1985 60m/C GB Jeremy Kemp. **VHS, Beta** $59.95 PSM ⅃½

Felicity Upon graduating an exclusive finishing school, a young girl travels to the Orient and has a number of sexual experiences.
1983 (R) 91m/C Jody Hanson, Marilyn Rodgers; **D:** John Lamond. **VHS, Beta** MED ⅃

Felix in Outer Space Felix and Poindexter travel through the galaxy to do battle with the evil duo, the Professor and Rock Bottom.
1985 55m/C **VHS, Beta** $29.95 MED ⅃

Felix the Cat: The Movie Classic cartoon creation Felix returns in a trite feature. The feline and his bag of tricks enter a dimension filled with He-Man/Mutant Ninja Turtles leftovers; new-age princess, comic reptiles, robots and a Darth Vader clone who's defeated with ridiculous ease. Strictly for undemanding kids.
1991 83m/C **VHS, Beta** $19.99 BVV, FCT, WTA ⅃½

Felix's Magic Bag of Tricks The professor is after Felix's Magic Bag of Tricks once again in this collection of cartoon favorites.
1984 60m/C **D:** Joseph Oriolo. **VHS, Beta** $14.95 MED, WTA ⅃½

Fellini Satyricon Fellini's famous, garish, indulgent pastiche vision of ancient Rome, based on the novel "Satyricon" by Petronius, follows the adventures of two young men through the decadences of Nero's reign. Actually an exposition on the excesses of the 1960s, with the actors having little to do other than look good and react to any number of sexual situations. Crammed with excesses of every variety. In Italian with English subtitles. Also available on laserdisc with additional footage and letterboxing. **AKA:** Satyricon.
1969 (R) 129m/C IT Martin Potter, Capucine, Hiram Keller, Salvo Randone, Max Born; **D:** Federico Fellini. **VHS, Beta, LV** $19.98 MGM, VYG, FCT ⅃⅃⅃

Fellini's Roma Fellini reviews his youth in this stream-of-consciousness homage to Rome and Italy. Best left for fervent Fellini fans. **AKA:** Roma.
1972 (R) 128m/C IT FR Peter Gonzales, Britta Barnes, Pia de Doses, Fiona Florence, Marne Maitland, Renato Giovannoli; **W/D:** Federico Fellini; **V:** Federico Fellini. **VHS, Beta** $19.98 MGM, FCT, APD ⅃⅃½

Fellow Traveler Two old friends, an actor and a screenwriter, both successful, get blacklisted for reputed Communist leanings in 1950s Hollywood. Good performances and a literate script. Made for cable television.
1989 97m/C Ron Silver, Hart Bochner, Daniel J. Travanti, Imogen Stubbs, Katherine Borowitz, Jonathan Hyde; **D:** Philip Saville. **VHS, Beta** $89.95 PAR ⅃⅃⅃

Female Feminist look at life in the 30's stars Chatterton as the wealthy president of an auto factory who wines and dines the office men and then gives them the strictly business line the next day. However, she finally meets her match when Brent walks through the door. (The two stars were a real-life married couple at the time.) Funny, role-reversal story directed by Curtiz of "Casablanca" fame. Based on a story by Donald Henderson Clark.
1933 60m/B Ruth Chatterton, George Brent, Philip Reed, Ruth Donnelly, Johnny Mack Brown, Lois Wilson, Gavin Gordon, Ferdinand Gottschalk; **D:** Michael Curtiz, William Dieterle; **W:** Gene Markey, Kathryn Scola. **VHS** $19.98 MGM ⅃½

The Female Bunch The man-free world of an all-woman settlement is shattered by the arrival of a handsome stranger. Some of this garbage was filmed on location at the notorious Charles Manson ranch, and that's the least of its flaws.
1969 (R) 86m/C Jennifer Bishop, Russ Tamblyn, Lon Chaney Jr., Nesa Renet, Geoffrey Land, Regina Carrol; **D:** Al Adamson, John Cardos. **VHS** $16.95 SNC Woof!

The Female Jungle Below-average whocares whodunnit directed by Roger Corman stock-company actor Ve Sota. Police sergeant Tierney is caught between a rock and a hard place. The prime suspect in a murder case, Tierney discovers a series of clues that implicate his friend Carradine. Interesting only for the screen debut of the

nympho-typecast Miss Jayne—of whom Bette Davis said "Dramatic art in her opinion is knowing how to fill a sweater." *AKA:* The Hangover.
1956 56m/B Lawrence Tierney, John Carradine, Jayne Mansfield, Burt Kaiser, Kathleen Crowley, James Kodl, Rex Thorson, Jack Hill; *D:* Bruno Ve Sota. **VHS $9.95** COL, FCT ℐ

Female Trouble Divine leads a troublesome existence in this $25,000 picture. She turns to a life of crime and decadence, seeking to live out her philosophy: "Crime is beauty." Look closely at the Divine rape scene where she plays both rapist and victim. Climax of her deviant ways comes with her unusual night club act, for which the law shows no mercy. Trashy, campy; for die-hard Waters fans.
1975 (R) 95m/C Divine, David Lochary, Mary Vivian Pearce, Mink Stole, Edith Massey, Danny Mills, Cookie Mueller, Susan Walsh; *D:* John Waters. **VHS, Beta $39.98** HHE ℐℐ½

Femme Fatale When a man's new bride disappears he teams up with an artist pal to track her down. Their search takes them to L.A.'s avant-garde art scene—and deeper into deception and mystery. *AKA:* Fatal Woman.
1990 (R) 96m/C Colin Firth, Lisa Zane, Billy Zane, Scott Wilson, Lisa Blount; *D:* Andre Guttfreund. **VHS, LV $89.98** REP, PIA ℐℐ½

Femmes de Paris A funny and risque French musical comedy about the comings and goings of the cast of a naughty nightclub shows. In French with English subtitles.
1953 79m/C FR Robert Dhery, Collette Brosset, Louis de Funes, Bluebell Girls. **VHS, Beta $29.95** NO ℐℐ

Fer-De-Lance A stricken submarine is trapped at the bottom of the sea, with a nest of deadly snakes crawling through the ship. Made for television. *AKA:* Operation Serpent.
1974 120m/C David Janssen, Hope Lange, Ivan Dixon, Jason Evers; *D:* Russ Mayberry. **VHS, Beta $49.95** WOV ℐ½

Fergie & Andrew: Behind Palace Doors More soap-opera from the British royals in this tale of feisty redhead, Sarah Ferguson, and the neglectful Prince Andrew. He's away a lot, she's bored by all the palace propriety and causes too many scandals, and their marriage falls apart. Made for television.
1993 92m/C Pippa Hinchley, Sam Miller, Peter Cellier, Harold Innocent, Edita Brychta; *D:* Michael Switzer. **VHS, Beta $89.98** TTC ℐℐ

Fernandel the Dressmaker Fernandel dreams of designing exquisite dresses, but when the opportunity arises, he finds his cheating partners get in the way. In French with English subtitles.
1957 95m/B FR Fernandel, Suzy Delair, Francoise Fabian, Georges Chamarat; *D:* Jean Boyer. **VHS, Beta, 8mm $29.95** FCT, VYY ℐℐ½

Ferngully: The Last Rain Forest Animated eco-musical follows the adventures of independent-minded flying sprite Crysta, who lives in a rain forest beset by pollution. She discovers the outside world and becomes smitten with the human Zak, who is helping to cut down the forest. Crysta decides to reduce him to her size and show him the error of his ways. She's aided by fellow sprite, Pips, and a crazy bat (Batty Koda with a voice provided by the lively Williams) who's escaped from a research laboratory. But the humans aren't the only bad guys; wandering among the vines is evil woodland spirit Hexxus, a gloppy blob who likes toxic waste. So-so script with politically pristine environmental message may grow tiresome for both adults and children, though

expert animation and brilliant coloring enlivens the tale.
1992 (G) 72m/C *D:* Bill Kroyer; *V:* Samantha Mathis, Christian Slater, Robin Williams, Tim Curry, Jonathan Ward, Grace Zabriskie, Cheech Marin, Thomas Chong, Tone Loc. **VHS $24.98** FXV, MLT ℐℐ½

Ferocious Female Freedom Fighters A typical foreign-made action flick with female wrestlers is spoofed by the L.A. Connection comedy troupe which did the totally ridiculous dubbed dialog.
1988 90m/C Eva Arnaz, Barry Prima. **VHS, Beta, LV** MED, IME ℐ

Ferris Bueller's Day Off It's almost graduation and if Ferris can get away with just one more sick day—it had better be a good one. He sweet talks his best friend into borrowing his dad's antique Ferrari and sneaks his girlfriend out of school to spend a day in Chicago. Their escapades lead to fun, adventure, and almost getting caught. Broderick is charismatic as the notorious Bueller with Gray amusing as his tattle-tale sister doing everything she can to see him get caught. Led to TV series. One of Hughes' more solid efforts.
1986 (PG-13) 103m/C Matthew Broderick, Mia Sara, Alan Ruck, Jeffrey Jones, Jennifer Grey, Cindy Pickett, Edie McClurg, Charlie Sheen; *D:* John Hughes. **VHS, Beta, LV, 8mm $14.95** PAR, TLF ℐℐℐ

Ferry to Hong Kong World-weary, heavy drinking traveler comes aboard the "Fat Annie," a ship skippered by the pompous Captain Hart. The two men clash, until an act of heroism brings them together. Embarrassingly hammy performance by Welles as the ferry skipper.
1959 103m/C Curt Jurgens, Orson Welles, Sylvia Syms; *D:* Lewis Gilbert. **VHS, Beta $9.95** SUE ℐ½

The Feud A wacky comedy about the ultimate "family feud." The Bullards of Millville and the Bealers of Hornbeck engage in a battle of the witless, and no one in either town is safe. A silly, irreverent comedy of the slapstick variety. Based on a novel by Thomas Berger.
1990 (R) 87m/C Rene Auberjonois, Ron McLarty, Joe Grifasi, David Strathairn, Gale Mayron; *D:* Bill D'Elia. **VHS $89.95** VMK ℐℐ

Feud of the Trail A cowboy saves a range family's gold and falls in love with their daughter in the process. Tyler plays both the hero and the villain here.
1937 56m/B Tom Tyler, Harlin Wood, Guinn Williams; *D:* Robert Hill. **VHS, Beta $19.95** NOS, DVT ℐ

Feud of the West Old West disagreements settled with guns in this outing for cowboy star Gibson, here portraying a rodeo performer.
1935 60m/B Hoot Gibson. **VHS, Beta $19.95** NOS, UHV, VCN ℐ½

Fever Controversial Polish film based on Andrzej Strug's novel "The Story of One Bomb." Focusing on a period in Polish history marked by anarchy, violence, resistance, and revolution, it was banned before it won eventual acclaim at the Gdansk Film Festival. In Polish with English subtitles.
1981 115m/C PL *D:* Agnieszka Holland. **VHS $49.95** FCT ℐℐℐ

Fever A once-honest cop trades his good life in for a shot at dealing drugs. Meanwhile, his wife's lover wants to murder him.
1988 (R) 83m/C Bill Hunter, Gary Sweet, Mary Regan, Jim Holt; *D:* Craig Lahiff. **VHS, Beta, LV $14.95** ACA ℐ

Fever An ex-con and a high-powered lawyer join forces to rescue the woman both of them love from a vicious killer. Made for cable television. Available in Spanish.
1991 (R) 99m/C Armand Assante, Sam Neill, Marcia Gay Harden, Joe Spano; *D:* Larry Elikann. **VHS $89.98** HBO ℐℐ

Fever Mounts at El Pao A minor effort from director Bunuel about the regime of a dictator in an imaginary South American country. In Spanish with English subtitles. *AKA:* Los Ambiciosos.
1959 97m/B MX Gerard Philippe, Jean Servais; *D:* Luis Bunuel. **VHS, Beta $24.95** NOS, FCT, FST ℐℐ½

Fever Pitch Sordid story of a sports writer (O'Neal) who becomes addicted to gambling. Very poor script.
1985 (R) 95m/C Ryan O'Neal, Catherine Hicks, Giancarlo Giannini, Bridgette Anderson, Chad Everett, John Saxon, William Smith, Patrick Cassidy, Chad McQueen; *D:* Richard Brooks. **VHS, Beta $79.98** FOX Woof!

A Few Good Men Strong performances by Cruise and Nicholson carry this story of a peacetime military coverup involving the mysterious death of a soldier at a base in Cuba. Cruise is Lt. Kaffee, a wisecracking smart aleck who only incidentally is a Navy lawyer. Sleepwalking through his comfortable career in Washington, he accepts the defense of two soldiers pinned for the murder of their cohort. Unconcerned about their fate, he is about ready to write them off until he performs an obligatory interview with the commanding officer at the base, Colonel Jessup (Nicholson). The tough-as-nails Marine Colonel is the sort of man you'd want defending your country's border, but hope you never get stuck in an elevator with. Transformed by a face-blanching encounter with the brusque Jessup, Lt. Kaffee smells a rat, but Jessup practically dares him to prove it. Lt. Commander (Moore) is another lawyer assigned to the case with Kaffee, though her actual function seems to be holding Kaffee's hand. Intriguing mano-a-mano courtroom battle between Kaffee and Jessup provides the true fireworks. Viewers will make a few tough assessments about the powers of the military. Based on the play by Sorkin, who also wrote the screenplay. The laserdisc version is available in letterbox format.
1992 (R) 138m/C Tom Cruise, Jack Nicholson, Demi Moore, Kevin Bacon, Kevin Pollak, Kiefer Sutherland, James Marshall, J.T. Walsh, Christopher Guest, J.A. Preston, Matt Craven, Wolfgang Bodison, Xander Berkeley, Cuba Gooding Jr.; *D:* Rob Reiner; *W:* Aaron Sorkin; *M:* Marc Shaiman. Academy Awards '92 Nominations: Best Film Editing, Best Picture, Best Sound, Best Supporting Actor (Nicholson); Chicago Film Critics Awards '93: Best Supporting Actor (Nicholson); MTV Movie Awards '93: Best Film; People's Choice Awards '93: Best Film, Best Film—Drama. **VHS, Beta, LV, 8mm $99.99** COL, CRC, MOV ℐℐℐ½

A Few Moments with Buster Keaton and Laurel and Hardy Three short appearances: "The Tree in a Test Tube," a government film with Stan & Ollie about wood's role in the war effort; an episode of "The Ed Sullivan Show," with the duo, and a commercial for Simon Pure Beer featuring Keaton.
1963 17m/B Stan Laurel, Oliver Hardy, Buster Keaton, Ed Sullivan, Pete Smith. **VHS, Beta, 8mm $9.95** VYY ℐℐ

ffolkes Rufus Excalibur Ffolkes is an eccentric underwater expert who is called upon to stop a madman (Perkins, indulging himself) from blowing up an oil rig in the North

Sea. Entertaining farce with Moore playing the opposite of his usual suave James Bond character. **AKA:** Assault Force; North Sea Hijack.
1980 (PG) 99m/C Roger Moore, James Mason, Anthony Perkins, David Hedison, Michael Parks; **D:** Andrew V. McLaglen. **VHS, Beta** $59.95 MCA ♫♫

Fiction Makers Roger Moore stars as Simon Templar, also known as "The Saint," a sophisticated detective who is hired to help Amos Klein. Klein turns out to be an alias for a beautiful novelist who is being threatened by the underworld crime ring. Based on the Leslie Chateris' character.
1967 102m/C Roger Moore, Sylvia Syms. **VHS, Beta** FOX ♫♫

Fictitious Marriage Eldad Ilan, a high school teacher experiencing a mid-life crisis, travels to Israel to get away from his family in order to consider his life's direction. In Hebrew with English subtitles.
1988 90m/C Shlomo Bar-Aba, Irit Sheleg, Ofra Veingarten; **D:** Haim Bouzaglo. **VHS** $79.95 ERG ♫♫

Fiddler on the Roof Based on the long-running Broadway musical. The poignant story of Tevye, a poor Jewish milkman at the turn of the century in a small Ukrainian village, and his five dowry-less daughters, his lame horse, his wife, and his companionable relationship with God. Topol, an Israeli who played the role in London, is charming, if not quite as wonderful as Zero Mostel, the Broadway star. Finely detailed set decoration and choreography, strong performances from the entire cast create a sense of intimacy in spite of near epic proportions of the production. The play was based on the Yiddish stories of Tevye the Dairyman, written by Sholem Aleichem, which have been previously filmed as straight drama. ♫Tradition; Matchmaker, Matchmaker; If I Were a Rich Man; Sabbath Prayer; To Life; Miracle of Miracles; Tevye's Dream; Sunrise, Sunset; Wedding Celebration; Do You Love Me?; Far from the Home I Love; Chava Ballet; Anatevka.
1971 (G) 184m/C Chaim Topol, Norma Crane, Leonard Frey, Molly Picon; **D:** Norman Jewison; **M:** John Williams. Academy Awards '71: Best Cinematography, Best Sound, Best Score; Nominations: Best Actor (Topol), Best Art Direction/Set Decoration, Best Director (Jewison), Best Picture, Best Supporting Actor (Frey); Golden Globe Awards '72: Best Actor—Musical/Comedy (Topol), Best Film—Musical/Comedy. **VHS, Beta, LV** $29.97 FOX, MGM, TLF ♫♫♫½

The Field After an absence from the big screen, intense and nearly over the top Harris won acclaim as an iron-willed peasant fighting to retain a patch of Irish land he's tended all his life, now offered for sale to a wealthy American. His uncompromising stand divides the community in this glowing adaptation of John B. Keane's classic play, an allegory of Ireland's internal conflicts.
1990 (PG-13) 113m/C GB Richard Harris, Tom Berenger, John Hurt, Sean Bean, Brenda Fricker, Frances Tomelty, Sean McGinley, Jenny Conroy; **W/D:** Jim Sheridan. **VHS, Beta, LV** $19.98 LIV, TVC ♫♫♫½

Field of Dreams Based on W. P. Kinsella's novel "Shoeless Joe," this uplifting mythic fantasy depicts an Iowa corn farmer who, following the directions of a mysterious voice that first speaks to him while he's out tending the farm, cuts a baseball diamond in his corn field. "If you build it, he will come," instructs the voice and soon the ball field is inhabited by the spirit of Joe Jackson and the other ballplayers who were caught up and disgraced in the notorious 1919 "Black Sox"

World Series baseball scandal. Jones, portraying a character based on reclusive author J.D. Salinger, is reluctantly pulled into the mystery. It's all about chasing a dream, paying debts, maintaining innocence in spite of adulthood, finding redemption, reconciling the child with the man, and of course, celebrating the mythic lure of baseball. Costner and Madigan are strong, believable characters.
1989 (PG) 106m/C Kevin Costner, Amy Madigan, James Earl Jones, Burt Lancaster, Ray Liotta, Timothy Busfield, Frank Whaley, Gaby Hoffman; **D:** Phil Alden Robinson. **VHS, Beta, LV** $19.95 MCA, FCT, HMV ♫♫♫½

Field of Fire One of America's top military experts has been taken hostage and it's up to a top general to rescue him. But the rescue doesn't come off as planned and all must fight their way through the Cambodian jungle to safety.
1992 (R) 96m/C David Carradine. **VHS, LV** $89.99 HBO ♫♫

Field of Honor A look at the harrowing experience of jungle combat through the eyes of a Dutch infantryman in Korea.
1986 (R) 93m/C Everett McGill, Ron Bradsteder, Hey Young Lee; **D:** Hans Scheepmaker. **VHS, Beta, LV** $19.98 MGM ♫♫

Field of Honor A quiet French anti-war drama set during the Franco-Prussian war in 1869 in which a peasant boy volunteers to fight in place of a rich man's son. He is befriended behind enemy lines by a young boy and both try to avoid capture. In French with English subtitles. **AKA:** Champ d'Honneur.
1987 (PG) 87m/C FR Cris Campion, Eric Wapier, Pascale Rocard, Frederic Mayer; **D:** Jean-Pierre Denis. **VHS, Beta** $19.98 ORI, TAM ♫♫½

The Fiend A religious cultist, already unbalanced, grabs a knife and starts hacking away Jack-the-Ripper style.
1971 (R) 87m/C Ann Todd, Patrick Magee, Tony Beckley, Madeline Hinde, Suzanna Leigh, Percy Herbert; **D:** Robert Hartford-Davis. **VHS, Beta** $39.95 MON ♫

Fiend Glowing supernatural thing flits around graveyard before animating dead guy who needs to kill in order to go on living. Murderous dead guy becomes a small-town music teacher feeding parasitically on his students to satisfy his supernatural hunger. His neighbor suspects some discord. Low-budget time waster.
1983 93m/C Don Leifert, Richard Nelson, Elaine White, George Stover; **D:** Donald M. Dohler. **VHS, Beta** $49.95 PSM Woof!

Fiend Without a Face An isolated air base in Canada is the site for a scientist using atomic power in an experiment to make a person's thoughts materialize. Only his thoughts are evil and reveal themselves as flying brains with spinal cords that suck human brains right out of the skull. Tons of fun for fifties SF fans and anyone who appreciates the sheer silliness of it all.
1958 77m/B Marshall Thompson, Kim Parker, Terence Kilburn, Michael Balfour, Gil Winfield, Shane Cordell; **D:** Arthur Crabtree. **VHS, LV** $19.98 CCB, REP, PIA ♫♫

The Fiendish Plot of Dr. Fu Manchu A sad farewell from Sellers, who in his last film portrays Dr. Fu in his desperate quest for the necessary ingredients for his secret life-preserving formula. Sellers portrays both Dr. Fu and the Scotland Yard detective on his trail, but it's not enough to save this picture, flawed by poor script and lack of direction.

1980 (PG) 100m/C GB Peter Sellers, David Tomlinson, Sid Caesar, Helen Mirren; **D:** Piers Haggard. **VHS, Beta, LV** $19.98 WAR, FCT Woof!

Fiesta A girl comes from Mexico City to her father's hacienda where her old boyfriend awaits her return with a proposal of marriage. Full of authentic Mexican dances and music. ♫Fantasia Mexican; La Bamba; La Luna Enamorada; Miriano; Romeria Vasca.
1947 44m/C Anne Ayars, George Negrete, Armida; **D:** Richard Thorpe. **VHS, Beta** $24.95 VYY, DVT, QNE ♫♫

Fifth Avenue Girl An unhappy millionaire brings home a poor young woman to pose as his mistress to make his family realize how they've neglected him. As this below-par social comedy drones toward its romantic conclusion, the rich folks see the error of their ways and love conquers all.
1939 83m/B Ginger Rogers, Walter Connolly, Tim Holt, James Ellison, Franklin Pangborn; **D:** Gregory La Cava. **VHS, Beta, LV** $29.95 RKO, IME, TTC ♫½

Fifth Day of Peace In the aftermath of the World War I armistice, two German soldiers find themselves wandering around the Italian countryside without direction until they are caught and tried for desertion by their German commander. An interesting plot that is marred by too obvious plot twists. Based on a true story.
1972 (PG) 95m/C IT Richard Johnson, Franco Nero, Larry Aubrey, Helmut Schneider; **D:** Giuliano Montaldo. **VHS, Beta** $19.95 PSM ♫♫

The Fifth Floor College disco dancer overdoses on drugs and winds up in an insane asylum, complete with menacing attendant Hopkins and apathetic doctor Ferrer. Pathetic, exploitative trash written by Meyer Dolinsky and director Avedis.
1980 (R) 90m/C Bo Hopkins, Dianne Hull, Patti D'Arbanville, Mel Ferrer; **D:** Howard Avedis. **VHS, Beta** $59.95 MED Woof!

The Fifth Monkey A man embarks on a journey to sell four monkeys in order to fill a dowry for his bride, but along the way he encounters all sorts of obstacles and adventures. Filmed on location in Brazil.
1990 (PG-13) 93m/C Ben Kingsley; **W/D:** Eric Rochant. **VHS, LV** $89.99 COL, FCT ♫½

The Fifth Musketeer A campy adaptation of Dumas's "The Man in the Iron Mask," wherein a monarch's evil twin impersonates him while imprisoning the true king. A good cast and rich production shot in Austria make for a fairly entertaining swashbuckler. **AKA:** Behind the Iron Mask.
1979 (PG) 90m/C GB Beau Bridges, Sylvia Kristel, Ursula Andress, Cornel Wilde, Ian McShane, Alan Hale Jr., Helmut Dantine, Olivia de Havilland, Jose Ferrer, Rex Harrison; **D:** Ken Annakin. **Beta** $59.95 COL ♫♫

Fifty Fifty Jake and Frenchie are a couple of mercenaries forced by the CIA not only to work together but with a bunch of incompetent guerillas to overthrow a Southeast Asian dictator. Weller handles the violence, Hays handles the comedy, and both get chased a lot.
1993 (R) 101m/C Robert Hays, Peter Weller, Ramona Rahman, Charles Martin Smith; **D:** Charles Martin Smith; **W:** Dennis Shryack, Michael Butler; **M:** Peter Bernstein. **VHS, LV** $92.98 CAN ♫♫

50 of the Greatest Cartoons Join many of your cartoon favorites for this once in a lifetime festival including Bugs Bunny, Casper, Mighty Mouse, Woody Woodpecker and Felix the Cat.
1990 360m/C VHS $14.99 STE ♫♫

$50,000 Reward Maynard's first western finds him being victimized by an unscrupulous banker who wants Maynard's land deeds for property on which a new dam is being built.
1925 49m/B Ken Maynard, Esther Ralston. **VHS, Beta $19.98** *DVT, CCB, HEG* ✓½

52 Pick-Up After a fling, a wealthy industrialist is blackmailed by a trio of repulsive criminals and determines to save himself. First he becomes deeply caught in their web of murder. Based on an Elmore Leonard novel with lots of gruesome violence and good performances.
1986 (R) 111m/C Roy Scheider, Ann-Margret, Vanity, John Glover, Doug McClure, Clarence Williams III, Kelly Preston, Robert Trebor, Lonny Chapman; *D:* John Frankenheimer. **VHS, Beta, LV $19.95** *MED* ✓✓½

55 Days at Peking A costume epic depicting the Chinese Boxer Rebellion and the fate of military Britishers caught in the midst of the chaos. Standard fare superbly handled by director Ray and an all-star cast.
1963 150m/C Charlton Heston, Ava Gardner, David Niven, John Ireland, Flora Robson, Paul Lukas, Jacques Sernas; *D:* Nicholas Ray. **VHS, Beta, LV $29.95** *BFV, UHV, KAR* ✓✓✓

The Fig Tree After her mother passes away, Miranda becomes tormented by the fear of death. Now her aunt must help her cope with this difficult part of life. Aired on PBS as part of the "Wonderworks" family movie series.
1987 58m/C Olivia Cole, William Converse-Roberts, Doris Roberts, Teresa Wright, Karron Graves; *D:* Calvin Skaggs. **VHS $29.95** *PME, FCT, HMV* ✓

Fight for Gold In the frozen wastes of the North, a man becomes embroiled in a violent quest for gold.
1986 107m/C *GE* Doug McClure, Harald Leipnitz, Heinz Reinl, Roberto Bianco, Angelica Ott, Kristina Nel; *D:* Harald Reinl. **VHS $14.95** *ACA* ✓

A Fight for Jenny Miami Viceroy Thomas and Warren play an interracial couple who fight for custody of the wife's child from a previous marriage. Standard made-for-TV meaningful drama (bite-sized issues served with a modicum of melodrama).
1990 (PG) 95m/C Philip Michael Thomas, Lesley Ann Warren, Jean Smart, Lynne Moody, William Atherton; *D:* Gilbert Moses. **VHS $79.95** *PSM* ✓✓

Fight for Survival Young female aspirant of kung fu must recover sacred books that were stolen by disguised kung fu masters.
1977 (R) 101m/C Shangkuan Ling-Feng. **VHS, Beta** *FOX* ✓½

Fight for the Title Benny Leonard's reign as the lightweight boxing champ has just begun when World War II is declared. Against his manager's wishes, Benny decides to enlist.
1957 30m/C Michael Landon, George Brenlin; *D:* Eric Kenton. **VHS $14.95** *FCT, RHI* ✓✓

Fight for Us A social activist, recently released from prison, takes on the death squads terrorizing the countryside in post-Marcos Philippines. In Spanish with English subtitles. *AKA:* L'Insoumis.
1989 (R) 92m/C Phillip Salvador, Dina Bonnevie, Gina Alajar, Benbol Roco. **VHS, Beta, LV $59.95** *NO* ✓½

Fight for Your Life Three escaped convicts—a white bigot, an Asian, and a Chicano—take a black minister's family hostage. After suffering all manner of vicious torture, the family exacts an equally brutal revenge. Shades of "The Desperate Hours"

and "Extremities," but with much more graphic violence and a racial twist.
1979 89m/C *CA* William Sanderson, Robert Judd, Lela Small. **VHS, Beta $59.95** *MON* ✓

Fight to the Death An evil businessman hires a group of deadly assassins to assist with the Japanese invasion of China at the start of World War II. Includes self-defense tips segment.
1983 100m/C Chang Li, Ron Van Cliff. **VHS** *NO* ✓

The Fighter A Mexican patriot, involved in a struggle to overthrow a dictator, falls for a co-revolutionist. Flashbacks show the destruction of his family and village, and his pugilistic expertise, which he uses to fight for a huge purse to help the cause. Adapted from Jack London's "The Mexican." *AKA:* The First Time.
1952 78m/B Richard Conte, Vanessa Brown, Lee J. Cobb, Frank Silvera, Roberta Haynes, Hugh Sanders, Claire Carleton, Martin Garralaga; *D:* Herbert Kline. **VHS** *DVT, HEG* ✓✓

Fighter Attack Story of a WWII pilot, based in Corsica, who is shot down during a mission to destroy a Nazi supply station. He meets with a woman of the Italian underground, and succeeds in destroying his target with her help.
1953 80m/C Sterling Hayden, J. Carroll Naish, Joy Page; *D:* Lesley Selander. **VHS $19.98** *REP* ✓✓

Fightin' Ranch A famous lawman saves his reputation, previously tainted. A Maynard classic.
1930 60m/B Ken Maynard. **VHS, Beta** *UHV* ✓✓

Fighting Ace A young Chinese student sets out to take martial arts revenge on the villains who killed his family. Dubbed.
198? 86m/C Liu Chang Liang, Lung Chun Erl. **VHS, Beta** *NO* ✓

The Fighting American A frat boy proposes to a girl on a brotherly dare, and, unflattered by the fraternal proposal, the girl flees to the Far East to return to the bosom of her family. But it turns out the boy really does love the girl, by golly, and he's got just enough of that fighting American spirit to prove it. Predates Oland's Charlie Chan career by seven years.
1924 65m/B Pat O'Malley, Mary Astor, Raymond Hatton, Warner Oland; *D:* Tom Forman. **VHS, Beta $16.95** *GPV, FCT* ✓

Fighting Back Reactionary tale of an angry resident in a crime-ridden Philadelphia neighborhood who organizes a patrol of armed civilian vigilantes. The police attempt to head off a racial confrontation in this effective drama graced with some fine performances. *AKA:* Death Vengeance.
1982 (R) 96m/C Tom Skerritt, Patti LuPone, Michael Sarrazin, Yaphet Kotto; *D:* Lewis Teague. **VHS, Beta $14.95** *PAR* ✓✓

Fighting Black Kings Martial arts and karate masters appear in this tale of action.
1976 (PG) 90m/C William Oliver, Charles Martin, Willie Williams, Mas Oyama. **VHS, Beta $19.98** *WAR, OM* ✓

Fighting Caballero The Rough Riders effectively handle a gang of mine-harassing outlaws.
1935 60m/B Rex Lease; *D:* Elmer Clifton. **VHS, Beta** *NO* ✓

Fighting Caravans In this early big-budget western, based on a story by Zane Grey, a wagon train sets out west from Missouri. Cooper emerges as the hero after warding off an Indian attack that takes the lives of the original leaders. *AKA:* Blazing Arrows.

1931 80m/B Gary Cooper, Ernest Torrence, Tully Marshall, Fred Kohler Jr., Lili Damita; *D:* Otto Brower, David Burton. **VHS, Beta $19.95** *NOS, MRV, VYY* ✓

Fighting Cowboy Bill settles a tungsten mine dispute with a greedy miner and some outlaws.
1933 50m/B Buffalo Bill Jr.; *D:* Denver Dixon. **VHS, Beta, LV** *NO* ✓

Fighting Devil Dogs Two Marine lieutenants are assigned the task of obtaining a deadly secret weapon controlled by crooks. A serial in twelve chapters.
1943 195m/B Eleanor Stewart, Montagu Love, Hugh Sothern; *D:* William Witney. **VHS $29.98** *REP, VCN, MLB* ✓

Fighting Duel of Death Subculture evildoers threaten a convict and his lady friend. The two fight back with astounding expertise and effective results.
19?? 88m/C Mah Sah, Richard Chui. **VHS $14.99** *NEG* ✓½

Fighting Father Dunne Mega-hokey Hollywood steamroller about a tough priest caring for St. Louis newsboys in the early 1900s. Based on a true story.
1948 92m/B Pat O'Brien, Darryl Hickman, Charles Kemper, Una O'Connor, Arthur Shields, Harry Shannon, Joe Sawyer, Anna Q. Nilsson, Donn Gift, Myrna Dell; *D:* Ted Tetzlaff. **VHS, Beta** *RKO, TTC* ✓✓

Fighting Fists of Shanghai Joe Fearsome fighting man from the Far East engages a vile American land baron in a battle of honor.
1965 94m/C Klaus Kinski, Gordon Mitchell, Carla Romanelli, Robert Hundar, Chen Lee; *D:* Mario Ciano. **VHS, Beta $59.95** *TWE* ✓

Fighting Jack After he saves a girl from a watery death, a man is accused of horse stealing and trespassing.
1926 52m/B Bill Bailey, Hazel Deane, Frona Hale, John Byron, Sailor Sharkey, Herma Cordova; *D:* Louis Chauder. **VHS, Beta $16.95** *GPV* ✓

The Fighting Kentuckian Homeward bound from the Battle of New Orleans in 1814, a Kentucky rifleman lingers in a French settlement in Alabama. His romance with the daughter of a French general is blocked by the father until the American saves the community from an assault by land grabbers. Hardy as a frontiersman is well worth the view. An action-packed, well-photographed hit.
1949 100m/B John Wayne, Oliver Hardy, Vera Ralston, Marie Windsor, Philip Dorn, John Howard, Hugo Haas, Grant Withers; *D:* George Waggner. **VHS $19.98** *MED, REP* ✓✓½

The Fighting Legion Maynard shows his foresight here, making this one of the first westerns to fully exploit sound by adding music and singing. Standard plot has Maynard going after the villain who murdered his brother.
1930 69m/B Ken Maynard, Dorothy Dwan, Ernie Adams, Stanley Blystone, Frank Rice; *D:* Harry J. Brown. **VHS $16.95** *GPV, DVT, HEG* ✓

Fighting Life The tale of two brothers who overcome immense physical and emotional handicaps and become vital members of society. The two stars of the film are both physically handicapped.
1980 90m/C **VHS, Beta** *NO* ✓✓

Fighting Mad A singing Mountie tangles with border-crossing robbers and saves the reputation of a woman they exploit. One of the "Renfrew of the Mounties" series.
1939 57m/B James Newill, Milburn Stone, Sally Blane; *D:* Sam Newfield. **VHS, Beta $39.98** *VDM* ✓½

Fighting Mad A peaceful land owner is driven to violence when he discovers that the business men who want his property are planning to murder two of his family members in order to get it. The local sheriff's apathy forces the man to take the law into his own hands. Unlike other Fonda films of the time which consist of chaotic violence and car crashes, this story is a well performed character study.
1976 (R) 90m/C Peter Fonda, Lynn Lowry, John Doucette, Phil Carey, Scott Glenn, Kathleen Miller; *D:* Jonathan Demme. VHS *CON* 🎬🎬½

Fighting Mad Soldiers leave their buddy for dead in wartime Vietnam. He is alive, but captured by Japanese soldiers who believe they are still fighting in WWII. *AKA:* Fierce.
1977 (R) 96m/C James Iglehart, Jayne Kennedy, Leon Isaac Kennedy; *D:* Cirio H. Santiago. VHS 🎬½

Fighting Marines U.S. Marines are trying to establish an air base on Halfway Island in the Pacific, but are thwarted by the "Tiger Shark," a modern-day pirate. First appeared as a serial.
1936 69m/B Jason Robards Sr., Grant Withers, Ann Rutherford, Pat O'Malley; *D:* Joseph Kane, B. Reeves Eason. VHS, Beta $29.95 *VYY, VCN, VDM* 🎬½

Fighting Parson In order to infiltrate a lawless town Gibson, a gunsliging cowboy, dresses as a revivalist preacher.
1935 65m/B Hoot Gibson, Marceline Day, Robert Frazer, Stanley Blystone, Skeeter Bill Robbins, Charles King; *D:* Harry Fraser. VHS, Beta *UHV, GPV* 🎬

Fighting Pilot Talmadge is a real fighter in this classic talkie. His assignment is to rescue the plans for a secret aircraft from ill fate.
1935 62m/B Richard Talmadge, Victor Mace, Gertrude Messinger, Eddie Davis, Robert Frazer; *D:* Noel Mason. VHS, Beta $24.95 *NOS, DVT, GPV* 🎬

The Fighting Prince of Donegal An Irish prince battles the invading British in 16th Century Ireland. Escaping their clutches, he leads his clan in rescuing his mother and his beloved in this Disney swashbuckler. Based on the novel "Red Hugh, Prince of Donegal" by Robert T. Reilly.
1966 110m/C Peter McEnery, Susan Hampshire, Tom Adams, Gordon Jackson, Andrew Keir; *D:* Michael O'Herlihy. VHS, Beta $69.95 *DIS* 🎬🎬½

Fighting Renegade The search for an Indian burial ground in Mexico prompts two murders and McCoy, disguised as a notorious bandit part of the time, is wrongly accused. Justice triumphs in the end.
1939 60m/B Tim McCoy; *D:* Sam Newfield. VHS, Beta $19.95 *NOS, VCN, DVT* 🎬½

The Fighting Rookie LaRue, better known for playing hoods, is a rookie cop set up and disgraced by the mob. But he fights back to regain his honor and bring the gang to justice.
1934 65m/B Jack LaRue; *D:* Spencer Gordon Bennet. VHS, Beta, 8mm $29.95 *VYY* 🎬½

Fighting Seabees As a hot-tempered construction foreman who battles Navy regulations as well as the Japanese, Wayne emerges as a larger-than-life hero in this action-packed saga of the Pacific theater of World War II. Extremely popular patriotic drama depicts the founding of the Seabees, the naval construction corps, amidst the action and the would-be romance with a woman reporter. Also available colorized.
1944 100m/B John Wayne, Susan Hayward, Dennis O'Keefe, William Frawley; *D:* Edward Ludwig. VHS $19.98 *REP* 🎬🎬½

The Fighting 69th Cornball but entertaining World War I drama with lots of action. Cagney is a Brooklyn street tough who joins the all-Irish 69th New York regiment but could care less about its famed military history. He promptly defies his superiors and barely scrapes through his training. Sent to France the swaggering Cagney turns coward when confronted by the horrors of war but eventually redeems himself. O'Brien is the famed regimental chaplain Father Duffy, while Brent is commander "Wild Bill" Donovan, who would later found the OSS in World War II. Lots of heart-tugging emotion backed with a fine supporting cast.
1940 90m/B James Cagney, Pat O'Brien, George Brent, Jeffrey Lynn, Alan Hale Sr., Frank McHugh, Dennis Morgan, William Lundigan, Dick Foran, Guinn Williams, Henry O'Neill, John Litel, George Reeves; *D:* William Keighley; *W:* Fred Niblo, Norman Reilly Raine, Dean Franklin. VHS $19.98 *MGM* 🎬🎬

The Fighting Stallion Canutt stars as a drifter hired by a rancher who's determined to capture a beautiful wild stallion (played by Boy the Wonder Horse). Silent with original organ score.
1926 76m/B Yakima Canutt, Neva Gerber, Bud Osborne. VHS, Beta, 8mm $16.95 *GPV, VYY* 🎬🎬🎬

The Fighting Sullivans The true story of five brothers killed on the Battleship Juneau at Guadalcanal during World War II. The tale tells of the fury felt by the siblings after Pearl Harbor, their enlistment to fight for their country, and their tragic fate in the heat of battle. Truly a stirring tribute to all lives lost in combat. *AKA:* The Sullivans.
1942 110m/B Anne Baxter, Thomas Mitchell, Selena Royle, Eddie Ryan, Trudy Marshall, James B. Cardwell, Roy Roberts, Ward Bond, Mary McCarty, Bobby Driscoll, Addison Richards, Selmer Jackson, Mae Marsh, Harry Strang, Barbara Brown; *D:* Lloyd Bacon. VHS *IVY, MLB* 🎬🎬🎬½

Fighting Texans An entire town invests in an oil well, on the advice of young salesman Bell, that the bankers are sure is a dud. Imagine their surprise when it turns out to be a gusher.
1933 60m/B Rex Bell, Luana Walters, Betty Mack, Gordon DeMain; *D:* Armand Schaefer. VHS $19.95 *NOS, DVT* 🎬

Fighting Thru Maynard fights off the bad guys and wins the girl after some nifty riding in his first all-talkie western. *AKA:* California in 1878.
1930 60m/B Ken Maynard, Jeanette Loff; *D:* William Nigh. VHS, Beta $19.95 *NOS, DVT* 🎬

The Fighting Trooper Based on the James Oliver Curwood story, "Footprints," this frontier tale presents a Mountie who goes undercover as a trapper in the Northwest. He is out to catch a murderer.
1934 57m/B Kermit Maynard. VHS, Beta $9.95 *NOS, VDM, DVT* 🎬½

Fighting Valley Texas Rangers O'Brien, Newill, and Wilkerson ride off to break up an outlaw gang that is trying to monopolize the ore smelting business. O'Brien later went on to directing for TV and also wrote for Red Skelton.
1943 60m/B Dave O'Brien, Jim Newill, Guy Wilkerson, Patti McCarty, John Merton, Curly Dresden; *W/D:* Oliver Drake. VHS $19.95 *DVT, HEG* 🎬

Fighting Vigilantes A villainous food distributor is terrorizing his rivals until LaRue whips him. Holt and her father put together a committee called "The Vigilantes" to help out. Holt is the daughter of movie good guy Jack Holt.
1947 61m/B Lash LaRue, Al "Fuzzy" St. John, Jennifer Holt, George Cheseboro, Lee Morgan, Russell Arms, Steve Clark; *D:* Ray Taylor. VHS $19.95 *NOS* 🎬🎬

The Fighting Westerner Scott stars as a mining engineer who becomes entangled in mysterious murders. Mrs. Leslie Carter stars in a rare screen role. *AKA:* Rocky Mountain Mystery.
1935 54m/B Randolph Scott, Chic Sale, Ann Sheridan, Charles T. Barton. VHS, Beta, 8mm $24.95 *VYY, MRV* 🎬½

Fighting with Kit Carson Famous guide and Indian fighter lead bands of settlers westward. Action-packed. Twelve chapters, 13 minutes each.
1933 156m/B Johnny Mack Brown, Noah Beery Sr.; *D:* Armand Schaefer, Colbert Clark. VHS, Beta $49.95 *NOS, VCN, VDM* 🎬🎬

Film House Fever A compilation of clips from sleazy, cult-type movies, including "Blood Feast" and "Hot Night at the Go Go Lounge."
1986 58m/C Jamie Lee Curtis, James Keach, Lon Chaney Jr., Harvey Korman. VHS, Beta $59.98 *LIV, VES* 🎬

Films by Peter Thompson Three semi-experimental documentary shorts by Thompson, each using film form to comment on matters of both personal and public history: "Two Portraits," a memoir about Thompson's parents; "Universal Hotel," a meditation on photographs of a Polish POW forced into deep-cold medical experiments in Dachau, and "Universal Citizen," about a Guatemalan smuggler who was once an inmate at Dachau.
1987 74m/C *D:* Peter Thompson. VHS, Beta *FCT* 🎬

Filthy Harry Eastwood and Bronson look-alikes send up the vigilante film.
19?? 90m/C VHS $59.95 *TPV, HHE* 🎬½

Fin de Fiesta When a corpse is found in the swimming pool, the party takes a dive. Spanish pool party fans will lap this one up. In Spanish.
1971 91m/C SP Isela Vega, Hector Suarez, Ana Martin; *D:* Mauricio Walerstein. VHS, Beta $49.95 *MED* 🎬

The Final Alliance A tough loner takes on a vicious motorcycle gang that's terrorizing a small town, and realizes that they're also responsible for his family's death.
1989 (R) 90m/C David Hasselhoff, John Saxon, Bo Hopkins, Jeanie Moore; *D:* Mario Di Leo. VHS, Beta, LV $79.95 *COL* 🎬

Final Analysis Glossy thriller starring Gere as a San Francisco psychiatrist who falls for the glamorous sister of one of his patients. Basinger plays the femme fatale and Thurman is Gere's sexually neurotic patient. Although heavily influenced by "Vertigo," this film never comes close to attaining the depth of Hitchcock's cinematic masterpiece. Roberts gives the most gripping performance in this slick suspense movie as Basinger's sleazy gangster husband.
1992 (R) 125m/C Richard Gere, Kim Basinger, Uma Thurman, Eric Roberts, Paul Guilfoyle, Keith David, Robert Harper, Jolyon Baker, Harris Yulin, Agustin Rodriguez; *D:* Phil Joanou; *W:* Wesley Strick. VHS, LV $94.99 *WAR* 🎬🎬½

Final Approach Test pilot Jason Halsey (Sikking) crashes in the desert and awakens in the office of psychiatrist Dio Gottlieb (Elizondo). Halsey can't remember anything about his past, or his own name for that matter, but through word association games and psychological tests, he begins to remember as Gottlieb tries to pry information from his brain. Showy computer effects are excel-

lent, but they only serve to fill holes in a story that has an unsatisfying ending. Notable as first film mde with digital sound. Also available in a letterboxed version.
1991 (R) 100m/C James B. Sikking, Hector Elizondo, Madolyn Smith, Kevin McCarthy, Cameo Kneuer, Wayne Duvall; **D:** Eric Steven Stahl. **VHS, LV $92.95** VMK ✍✍

Final Assignment A Canadian television reporter agrees to smuggle a dissident Soviet scientist's ill granddaughter out of Russia for treatment along with a videotape documenting tragic experiments on children with steroids. She manages to evade the KGB while carrying on with a Russian press officer, and enlists the support of a Jewish fur trader. Location shooting in Canada instead of Russia is just one pitfall of this production. Also on video as, ''The Moscow Chronicle.''
1980 101m/C CA Genevieve Bujold, Michael York, Burgess Meredith, Colleen Dewhurst; **D:** Paul Almond. **VHS, Beta $69.98** LIV, VES ✍

Final Comedown A black revolutionary attempts to get white radicals behind his war against racism. He fails and starts a racial bloodbath.
1972 (R) 84m/C Billy Dee Williams, D'Urville Martin, Celia Kaye, Raymond St. Jacques, Pamela Jones, R.G. Armstrong; **D:** Oscar Williams. **VHS, Beta $59.98** NLC, SIM ✍

Final Conflict Unwelcomed third installment in the ''Omen'' series, concerning Satan's son Damien. Now 32, and the head of an international conglomerate, he is poised for world domination but fears another savior is born. Several monks and many babies meet gruesome deaths before he gets his comeuppance. The last theatrical release was then followed by a made-for-television movie called ''Omen IV: The Awakening'' (1991). **AKA:** The Omen 3.
1981 108m/C Sam Neill, Lisa Harrow, Barnaby Holm, Rossano Brazzi; **D:** Graham Baker; **M:** Jerry Goldsmith. **VHS, Beta, LV $19.98** FOX ✍½

The Final Countdown A U.S. nuclear-powered aircraft carrier, caught in a time warp, is transported back to 1941, just hours before the bombing of Pearl Harbor. The commanders face the ultimate decision—leave history intact or stop the incident and thus avoid World War II. Excellent photography and a surprise ending.
1980 (PG) 92m/C Kirk Douglas, Martin Sheen, Katharine Ross, James Farentino, Charles Durning; **D:** Don Taylor. **VHS, Beta, LV $19.98** VES ✍✍✍

Final Cut While filming in a secluded swampland, a crew stumbles on a local sheriff's crooked scheme and one by one, the crew members disappear.
1988 92m/C Carla De Lane, T.J. Kennedy, Joe Rainer, Brett Rice, Jordan Williams; **D:** Larry G. Brown. **VHS, Beta $79.95** VMK ✍½

Final Embrace When Laurel's famous sister is murdered she decides to do a little investigating on her own. She's aided by a young cop who just happened to be obsessed with the murdered woman.
1992 (R) ?m/C Robert Rusler, Nancy Valen, Dick Van Patten, Linda Dona; **D:** Oley Sassone; **W:** R.J. Robertson, Jim Wynorski; **M:** Daniel Licht. **VHS $89.98** NHO ✍½

Final Exam Psychotic killer stalks college students during exam week. This one's too boring to be scary. You root for the psycho to off everyone just to have the movie over.
1981 (R) 90m/C Cecile Bagdadi, Joel Rice; **D:** Jimmy Huston. **VHS, Beta $14.95** COL, SUE Woof!

The Final Executioner A valiant man finds a way to stop the slaughter of innocent people in a post-nuclear world. **AKA:** The Last Warrior.
1983 95m/C William Mang, Marina Costa, Harrison Muller, Woody Strode; **D:** Romolo Guerrieri. **VHS, Beta $59.95** MGM ✍

Final Extra Ambitious reporter's career gets a boost when he's assigned to investigate the murder of a rival. Silent with music score.
1927 60m/B Grant Withers, Marguerite de la Motte. **VHS, Beta, 8mm $19.95** NOS, VYY, DVT ✍✍

Final Impact Nick Taylor seeks vengeance on reigning kickboxing champ Jake Gerard through his prodigy, Danny Davis. Will sweet revenge for the wicked beating, suffered at the hands of Gerard years earlier, be his?
1991 99m/C Lorenzo Lamas, Kathleen Kinmont, Mimi Lesseos, Kathrin Lautner, Jeff Langton, Mike Worth; **D:** Joseph Merhi, Stephen Smoke. **VHS $29.95** PMH ✍½

Final Justice A small-town Texan sheriff wages a war against crime and corruption that carries him to Italy and the haunts of Mafia hitmen.
1984 (R) 90m/C Joe Don Baker, Rossano Brazzi, Patrizia Pellegrino; **D:** Greydon Clark. **VHS, Beta $79.95** VES ✍

Final Mission Vengeful one-man army follows the professional hit man who slaughtered his family from L.A. to Laos. His pursuit leads to a jungle showdown. Gee, sounds like ''Rambo, First Blood,'' though obviously less grand and glorious.
1984 101m/C Richard Young, John Dresden, Kaz Garas, Christine Tudor. **VHS, Beta $19.99** HBO ✍

Final Notice A detective tracking a serial killer has as his only evidence a trail of shredded photos of nude women. Not released theatrically.
1989 91m/C Gil Gerard, Steve Landesburg, Jackie Burroughs, Melody Anderson, Louise Fletcher, David Ogden Stiers, Kevin Hicks; **D:** Steven Hilliard Stern; **W:** John Gay; **M:** Tom Scott. **VHS, Beta, LV $59.99** PAR, PIA ✍

The Final Option An agent of England's Special Air Services team goes undercover as one of a band of anti-nuclear terrorists that take over the U.S. Embassy in London. Violent, but unconvincing. **AKA:** Who Dares Wins.
1982 (R) 125m/C GB Lewis Collins, Judy Davis, Richard Widmark, Robert Webber, Edward Woodward, Ingrid Pitt, Kenneth Griffith, Tony Doyle, John Duttine; **D:** Ian Sharp. **VHS, Beta $79.95** MGM ✍

The Final Programme In this futuristic story, a man must rescue his sister—and the world—from their brother, who holds a microfilmed plan for global domination. Meanwhile, he must shield himself from the advances of a bisexual computer programmer who wants to make him father to a new, all-purpose human being. Based on the Michael Moorcock ''Jerry Cornelius'' stories, the film has gained a cult following. **AKA:** The Last Days of Man on Earth.
1973 85m/C GB Hugh Griffith, Harry Andrews, Jon Finch, Jenny Runacre, Sterling Hayden, Patrick Magee, Sarah Douglas; **D:** Robert Fuest. **VHS, Beta $59.95** HBO, SUE ✍✍½

Final Sanction After a nuclear holocaust exhausts their military resources, the U.S. and the Soviets each send one-man armies to battle each other for final control of the world.

1989 90m/C Robert Z'Dar, Ted Prior. **VHS, Beta** AIP, HHE ✍✍½

Final Shot: The Hank Gathers Story Inspirational story of Gathers, who rose from the ghetto to become one of America's top college basketball stars at Loyola Marymount, until tragedy strikes during a game.
1992 92m/C Victor Love, Duane Davis, Nell Carter, George Kennedy. **VHS, Beta $79.95** PSM ✍✍½

The Final Terror Group of young campers is stalked by a mad killer in a desolate, backwoods area. Better-than-average stalked-teens entry is notable for the presence of some soon-to-be stars. **AKA:** Campsite Massacre; Bump in the Night; The Forest Primeval.
1983 (R) 90m/C John Friedrich, Rachel Ward, Adrian Zmed, Daryl Hannah, Joe Pantoliano, Ernest Harden, Mark Metcalf, Lewis Smith, Cindy Harrel, Akosua Busia; **D:** Andrew Davis. **VHS, Beta, LV $29.98** LIV, VES ✍✍

Final Verdict A trial lawyer defends a man he knows is guilty, throwing his life and his family into turmoil. Made for cable television.
1991 93m/C Treat Williams, Glenn Ford, Amy Wright, Olivia Burnette; **D:** Jack Fisk. **VHS, Beta $89.98** TTC ✍✍½

Final Warning A dramatization of actual events surrounding the 1986 melt-down of the nuclear power plant at Chernobyl. Made for television. **AKA:** Chernobyl: The Final Warning.
1990 94m/C Jon Voight, Jason Robards Jr., Sammi Davis-Voss; **D:** Anthony Page. **VHS $79.98** TTC ✍✍½

Find the Lady Candy assumes a supporting role as a bumbling cop who is part of an incompetent police team trying to rescue a kidnapped socialite. **AKA:** Call the Cops; Kopek and Broom.
1975 79m/C CA John Candy, Peter Cook, Mickey Rooney, Lawrence Dane, Alexandra Bastedo; **D:** John Trent. **VHS, Beta** NO ✍½

Finders Keepers A wild assortment of characters on board a train en route from California to Nebraska search for five million dollars hidden in the baggage car.
1984 (R) 96m/C Michael O'Keefe, Beverly D'Angelo, Ed Lauter, Louis Gossett Jr., Pamela Stephenson, Jim Carrey, David Wayne, Brian Dennehy; **D:** Richard Lester. **VHS, Beta $59.98** FOX ✍✍

Fine Gold A false charge of embezzlement leaves a man without home and family, so he decides to turn the tables on those who betrayed him.
19?? 91m/C Andrew Stevens, Ray Walston, Ted Wass, Stewart Granger, Lloyd Bochner, Jane Badler. **VHS, Beta $79.99** MCG ✍✍

A Fine Madness A near-classic comedy about a lusty, rebellious poet thrashing against the pressures of the modern world, and fending off a bevy of lobotomy-happy psychiatrists. Shot on location in New York City, based on Elliot Baker's novel.
1966 104m/C Sean Connery, Joanne Woodward, Jean Seberg, Patrick O'Neal, Colleen Dewhurst, Clive Revill, John Fiedler; **D:** Irvin Kershner. **VHS, Beta $19.98** WAR ✍✍✍

A Fine Mess Two buffoons cash in when one overhears a plan to dope a racehorse, but they are soon fleeing the plotters' slapstick pursuit. The plot is further complicated by the romantic interest of a gangster's wife. The television popularity of the two stars did not translate to the big screen; perhaps it's Edwards' fault.

1986 (PG) 100m/C Ted Danson, Howie Mandel, Richard Mulligan, Stuart Margolin, Maria Conchita Alonso, Paul Sorvino; *D:* Blake Edwards. **VHS, Beta, LV** $19.95 COL 🎦½

A Fine Romance An improbable romance set in Paris features Andrews and Mastroianni as abandoned spouses falling in love. Andrews is the prim English Pamela who has been abandoned by her docter husband. Mastroianni is the irrepresible Cesareo, whose wife has just happened to run off with the aforementioned doctor. They meet to plan how to get their spouses back and wind up with opposites attracting. Not much story and the charm is spread thin. Based on the play "Tchin, Tchin" by Francois Billetdoux.
1992 (PG-13) 83m/C Julie Andrews, Marcello Mastroianni, Ian Fitzgibbon, Jean-Pierre Castaldi, Jean-Jacques Dulon, Maria Machado, Jean-Michel Cannone, Catherine Jarret, Gene Saks; *W:* Ronald Harwood. **VHS** $89.95 ACA 🎦🎦

Fine Things Bernie Fine thinks everything will be dandy now that he has a beautiful new bride and a cute stepdaughter. Then his wife dies and his stepdaughter's unreliable father wants sole custody. What's a nice guy to do? Based on the novel by Danielle Steel. Made for television. *AKA:* Danielle Steel's Fine Things.
1990 145m/C D.W. Moffett, Tracy Pollan, Judith Hoag, Cloris Leachman, Noley Thornton; *D:* Tom Moore; *W:* Peter Lefcourt. **VHS** $89.95 WOV 🎦🎦½

Finessing the King Private eyes Tommy and Tuppence follow a mysterious newspaper notice to a masked ball where a murder is about to occur. Based on the Agatha Christie story. Made for British television.
1984 60m/C *GB* James Warwick, Francesca Annis; *W:* Agatha Christie. **VHS, Beta** $14.95 PAV 🎦🎦½

The Finest Hour Two Navy buddies have a falling out when they both fall for the same woman. But they must put aside their differences when their next mission sends them to Iraq to deal with the deadly threat of biological warfare.
1991 (R) 105m/C Rob Lowe, Gale Hansen, Tracy Griffith, Eb Lottimer; *W/D:* Shimon Dotan. **VHS, LV** $89.95 COL 🎦½

The Finger Man An ex-con cooperates with the feds rather than return to jail. The deal is that he gets the dirt on an underworld crime boss. Solid performances.
1955 82m/B Frank Lovejoy, Forrest Tucker, Peggy Castle, Timothy Carey, Glenn Gordon; *D:* Harold Schuster. **VHS** $19.98 REP 🎦🎦½

Finger on the Trigger Veterans from both sides of the Civil War are after a hidden supply of gold, but find that they must band together to fend off an Indian attack. Routine. *AKA:* El Dedo En El Gatillo.
1965 89m/C Rory Calhoun, James Philbrook, Todd Martin, Silvia Solar, Brad Talbot; *D:* Sidney Pink. **VHS, Beta** $7.00 VTR 🎦🎦

Fingerprints Don't Lie A fingerprint expert pins the murder of the town mayor on an innocent guy, then suspects a frame-up.
1951 56m/B Richard Travis, Sheila Ryan, Tom Neal; *D:* Sam Newfield. **VHS, Beta, LV** NO 🎦

Fingers Keitel is a mobster's son, reluctantly working as a mob debt-collector, all the while dreaming of his ambitions to be a concert pianist. The divisions between his dreams and reality cause him to crack. Toback's first film generates psychological tension and excellent performances.

1978 (R) 89m/C Harvey Keitel, Tisa Farrow, Jim Brown, Michael Gazzo, Danny Aiello, Marian Seldes, James Toback, Tanya Roberts; *D:* James Toback. **VHS, Beta** $49.95 MED 🎦🎦🎦

Finian's Rainbow A leprechaun comes to America to steal back a pot of gold taken by an Irishman and his daughter in this fanciful musical comedy based on a 1947 Broadway hit. Both the sprite and the girl find romance; the share-cropping locals are saved by the cash; a bigot learns the error of his ways; and Finian (Astaire) dances off to new adventures. The fine production and talented cast are not used to their best advantage by the director who proved much better suited for "The Godfather." Entertaining, nonetheless. ♫How Are Things in Glocca Morra?; Look To the Rainbow; That Old Devil Moon; If This Isn't Love; Something Sort of Grandish; The Be-Gat; This Time of Year; The Great Come and Get It Day; When I'm Not Near the Girl I Love; When the Idle Poor Become the Idle Rich; Rain Dance Ballet.
1968 (G) 141m/C Fred Astaire, Petula Clark, Tommy Steele, Keenan Wynn, Al Freeman Jr., Don Francks, Susan Hancock, Dolph Sweet; *D:* Francis Ford Coppola. **VHS, Beta, LV** $19.98 WAR, PIA 🎦🎦🎦

Finish Line A high school track star turns to steroids to enhance his performance after being pushed by an overzealous father. The father-and-son Brolins play the pair. Made for cable.
1989 100m/C James Brolin, Josh Brolin, Mariska Hargitay, Kristoff St. John, John Finnegan, Billy Vera, Stephen Lang; *D:* John Nicolella. **VHS** $139.96 TTC 🎦🎦½

Finishing School Girls' school roommates Rogers and Dee experience heartaches and loves lost while enduring disinterested parents and snobbish peers. Box office bomb when released, despite a strong cast.
1933 73m/B Ginger Rogers, Frances Dee, George Nichols, Beulah Bondi, Bruce Cabot, Billie Burke, John Halliday, Sara Haden, Jack Norton, Joan Barclay, Jane Darwell; *D:* George Nichols. **VHS, Beta** $19.98 TTC 🎦½

The Finishing Touch Someone is stalking L.A.'s most gorgeous women and Detective Sam Stone (Nader) is assigned to the case. Stone discovers his prime suspect is a video artist with a taste for pornography. When Stone's investigation is cut short, his ex-wife, Detective Hannah Stone (Hack) is brought in to take over the case. Unfortunately, she finds herself falling for the suspect in this erotic thriller.
1992 (R) 82m/C Michael Nader, Shelley Hack, Arnold Vosloo, Art Evans, Clark Johnson, Theodore Raimi; *D:* Fred Gallo. **VHS** $89.95 COL 🎦🎦

Finnegan Begin Again A middle-aged schoolteacher and a grouchy, 65-year-old newspaper editor find romance despite their other obligations. Winning performances add charm to this cable TV movie.
1984 112m/C Mary Tyler Moore, Robert Preston, Sam Waterston, Sylvia Sidney, David Huddleston; *D:* Joan Micklin Silver. **VHS, Beta** $14.95 NEG, HBO, KAR 🎦🎦

Finnegan's Wake Portions of the filmed adaptation of James Joyce's novel are shown in this program along with an interview with producer/director Mary Ellen Bute. *AKA:* Passages from "Finnegans Wake"; Passages from James Joyce's "Finnegans Wake".
1963 92m/B **VHS, Beta, 3/4U, EJ, Q** CMR, NYS 🎦🎦

Fire A fire started by an escaped convict rages through Oregon timberland in this suspenseful made-for-television Irwin Allen disaster drama.
1977 98m/C Ernest Borgnine, Vera Miles, Patty Duke, Alex Cord, Donna Mills; *D:* Earl Bellamy. **VHS, Beta** $59.95 WAR 🎦½

Fire Alarm A change of scene for Western star Brown as he portrays a fireman who, in-between his work, romances a career girl.
1938 67m/B Johnny Mack Brown, Noel Francis; *D:* Karl Brown. **VHS, Beta, LV** $19.95 NOS, WGE, VYY 🎦

Fire and Ice An animated adventure film that culminates in a tense battle between good and evil, surrounded by the mystical elements of the ancient past. Designed by Frank Frazetta.
1983 (PG) 81m/C Randy Norton, Cynthia Leake; *D:* Ralph Bakshi; *V:* Susan Tyrrell, William Ostrander. **VHS, Beta, LV** $12.98 COL, WTA 🎦🎦½

Fire and Ice A tale of love on the slopes. Two skiers realize that their feelings for each other are perhaps even stronger than their feelings about skiing. You won't care though, except for some fine ski footage.
1987 (PG) 83m/C Suzy Chaffee, John Eaves; *D:* Willy Bogner. **VHS, Beta, LV** $14.95 SUE 🎦

Fire and Rain Based on the real-life crash of a Delta Airlines plane in Dallas and the rescue efforts made following the disaster. Familiar cast-members turn in decent performance. Made for television.
1989 89m/C Angie Dickinson, Charles Haid, Tom Bosley, David Hasselhoff, Robert Guillaume, Susan Ruttan, John Beck, Patti LaBelle, Dean Jones, Lawrence Pressman, Penny Fuller; *D:* Jerry Jameson; *W:* Gary Sherman. **VHS, Beta, LV** $59.99 PAR, PIA 🎦🎦

Fire and Sword A Cornish knight must choose between loyalty for king and country and the love of an Irish woman in this medieval drama. A not very inspired retelling of the Tristan and Isolde legend.
1982 84m/C *GB* Peter Firth, Leigh Lawson, Antonia Preser, Christopher Waitz; *D:* Veith von Furstenberg. **VHS, Beta** $69.98 LIV 🎦

Fire Birds Army attack helicopters and the people who fly them are used in the war on drugs in South America. Failed to match either the exciting flight sequences, the romantic interest or the box office of "Top Gun." *AKA:* Wings of the Apache.
1990 (PG-13) 85m/C Nicolas Cage, Tommy Lee Jones, Sean Young, Bryan Kestner, Dale Dyo, Mary Ellen Trainor, J.A. Preston, Peter Onorati; *D:* David Green; *W:* Nick Thiel, Paul F. Edwards; *M:* David Newman. **VHS, Beta, LV** $19.99 TOU 🎦

Fire Down Below Hayworth is the been-around-the-block beauty who persuades Mitchum and Lemmon, two small-time smugglers, to take her to a safe haven, no questions asked. Both men fall for her obvious charms, causing them to have a falling out until a life or death situation puts their friendship to the test. An unoriginal melodrama indifferently acted by everyone but Lemmon. Good location work in Trinidad and Tobago.
1957 116m/C *GB* Robert Mitchum, Jack Lemmon, Rita Hayworth, Herbert Lom, Anthony Newley; *D:* Robert Parrish. **VHS, Beta, LV** $19.95 COL, COL, CCB 🎦🎦

Fire, Ice and Dynamite Moore is onscreen only briefly as an eccentric tycoon who fakes suicide to watch several teams of challengers scramble in a madcap wintersports contest for his millions. A German-made avalanche of crazy stunts, bad jokes,

and product plugs for countless European companies, commencing with a literal parade of guests, from astronaut Buzz Aldrin to soul man Isaac Hayes. Numbing; must be seen to be believed.
1991 (PG) 105m/C Roger Moore, Shari Belafonte-Harper, Simon Shepherd, Uwe Ochsenknecht, Marjoe Gortner; *D:* Willy Bogner. **VHS $89.98** VES, LIV 🐾½

Fire in the Night In a small Southern town, a beautiful and sure-footed woman battles the limitless resources of the town's predominant dynastic family.
1985 89m/C Graciela Casillas, John Martin. **VHS, Beta $19.95** STE, NWV 🐾½

Fire in the Sky Disappearance of jogger Walton (Sweeney) in the Arizona desert sparks a criminal investigation into his whereabouts. Sheriff Watters (Garner) questions his jogging companions closely. Walton returns claiming he was abducted by aliens from outer space and though Watters doubts Walton's story, viewers do not, since aliens have already made an appearance. At this point, the story becomes about how Walton tries to convince anyone he was abducted. Perhaps this mirrors what director Lieberman went through while trying to convince backers that the film should be made. He could have benefitted by understanding the difference between what he was telling viewers and what he was showing them. Captivating special effects are one of the story's few bright spots. (The spacecraft looks like a giant orange.) Based on a story that might be true.
1993 (PG-13) 98m/C D.B. Sweeney, Robert Patrick, Craig Sheffer, Peter Berg, James Garner, Henry Thomas; *D:* Robert Lieberman; *W:* Tracy Torme; *M:* Mark Isham. **VHS** PAR 🐾🐾

The Fire in the Stone A young boy discovers an opal mine and dreams of using the treasure to reunite his family. However, when the jewels are stolen from him, he enlists his friends to help get them back. Based on the novel by Colin Thiele.
1985 97m/C AU Paul Smith, Linda Hartley, Theo Pertsindis. **VHS, Beta $39.95** WAR 🐾🐾

Fire Maidens from Outer Space Fire maidens prove to be true to the space opera code that dictates that all alien women be in desperate need of male company. Astronauts on an expedition to Jupiter's thirteenth moon discover the lost civilization of Atlantis, which, as luck would have it, is inhabited by women only. Possibly an idea before its time, it might've been better had it been made in the sixties, when space-exploitation came into its own. *AKA:* Fire Maidens of Outer Space.
1956 80m/B GB Anthony Dexter, Susan Shaw, Paul Carpenter, Harry Fowler, Jacqueline Curtiss, Sydney Tafler, Maya Koumani, Jan Holden, Kim Parker; *W/D:* Cy Roth. **VHS $16.95** CNM, MLB 🐾

Fire Monsters Against the Son of Hercules The son of the muscular one does battle with a hydra-headed monster in this average sword and sandal adventure.
1962 ?m/C Reg Lewis. **VHS $16.95** SNC 🐾🐾

The Fire Next Time In the year 2017, the United States is being ravaged by an ecological holocaust caused by a deadly combination of pollution and global warming. Nelson, Bedelia and their children are forced from their Louisiana home by a natural disaster and decide to head for bettter times in Canada. Their travels aren't easy. Made for television.
1993 195m/C Craig T. Nelson, Bonnie Bedelia, Juergen Prochnow, Richard Farnsworth, Justin Whalin, Charles Haid, Sal Lopez, Shawn Toovey, Ashley Jones; *Cameos:* Odetta; *D:* Tom

McLoughlin; *W:* James Henerson. **VHS $89.95** CAF 🐾🐾½

Fire Over England A young naval officer volunteers to spy at the Spanish court to learn the plans for the invasion of his native England and to identify the traitors among the English nobility. He arouses the romantic interest of his queen, Elizabeth I, one of her ladies, and a Spanish noblewoman who helps with his missions, and later leads the fleet to victory over the huge Spanish Armada. The first on-screen pairing of Olivier and Leigh is just one of the many virtues of this entertaining drama.
1937 81m/B GB Flora Robson, Raymond Massey, Laurence Olivier, Vivien Leigh, Leslie Banks, James Mason; *D:* William K. Howard. **VHS, Beta, 3/4U, Special order formats $19.95** NOS, MRV, VYY 🐾🐾🐾

Fire with Fire A boy at a juvenile detention center and a Catholic school girl fall in love. However, they find themselves on the run from the law when he escapes to be with her. Sheffer and Madsen are appealing in this otherwise unspectacular film.
1986 (PG-13) 103m/C Craig Sheffer, Virginia Madsen, Jon Polito, Kate Reid, Jean Smart; *D:* Duncan Gibbins. **VHS $79.95** PAR 🐾🐾

The Fire Within Ronet plays an alcoholic writer recently released from a sanitorium after a breakdown. Believing his life will only continue its downward spiral, he pays a final visit to friends and calmly plots his suicide. Malle clearly and pitilessly describes a man beyond despair. Based on a novel by Pierre Drieu La Rochelle, which itself fictionalized the suicide of writer Jacques Rigaut. In French with English subtitles. *AKA:* Le Feu Follet; Fuoco Fatuo.
1964 104m/B FR Maurice Ronet, Lena Skerla, Yvonne Clech, Hubert Deschamps, Jean-Paul Moulinot; *W/D:* Louis Malle. **VHS $69.95** NYF, TAM, PMS 🐾🐾🐾

Fireback A Vietnam vet's wife is kidnapped by the mob, causing him to take up arms and spill blood yet again.
1978 90m/C Bruce Baron, Richard Harrison. **VHS, Beta $39.95** LIV 🐾½

Fireball Forward A battalion fighting in France during WWII is having a bad time until Gazzara takes over and turns makes them into a crack fighting team. Uses some battle footage from the movie "Patton." Made for television.
1972 (PG) 100m/C Ben Gazzara, Eddie Albert, Ricardo Montalban, Dana Elcar, L.Q. Jones, Anne Francis; *D:* Marvin J. Chomsky. **VHS $9.99** QVD 🐾🐾½

Fireballs Sexploitaton pic set at a firehouse, where a batch of female recruits turn up the heat for three stud hose-bearers. The title should give you some idea of the intellectual level.
1990 89m/C Mike Shapiro, Goren Kalezik; *D:* Mike Shapiro. **VHS $79.95** ATL 🐾½

Firebird 2015 A.D. Dreary action adventure set in a 21st century society where automobile use is banned because of an extreme oil shortage. Private cars are hunted down for destruction by the Department of Vehicular Control. One over-zealous enforcer decides to make it a package deal and throws in the owners as well. Everyone connected with effort should have been cited for running stop sign.
1981 (PG) 97m/C Darren McGavin, George Touliatos, Doug McClure; *D:* David Robertson. **VHS, Beta $69.98** SUE 🐾

Firecracker Female martial arts expert retaliates against the crooks who murdered her sister.

1971 83m/C Jillian Kesner, Darby Hinton. **VHS, Beta** NO 🐾

Firefight After a nuclear holocaust, convicted criminals endeavor to rule the wasteland.
1987 100m/C James Pfeiffer, Janice Carraher, Jack Tucker; *D:* Scott Pfeiffer. **VHS, Beta $69.95** TWE 🐾

The Firefly Although slow-paced and long, this adaptation of the 1912 Rudolf Friml operetta was one of MacDonald's most popular films. Co-star Jones gets to sing the best song in the film, "Donkey Serenade," while MacDonald sings most of the others. 🎵Love Is Like a Firefly; English March; A Woman's Kiss; He Who Loves and Runs Away; When a Maid Comes Knocking at Your Heart; When the Wine Is Full of Fire; The Donkey Serenade; Giannina Mia; Sympathy.
1937 140m/B Jeanette MacDonald, Allan Jones, Warren William, Billy Gilbert, Henry Daniell, Douglas Dumbrille, George Zucco; *D:* Robert Z. Leonard. **VHS $19.98** MGM 🐾🐾½

Firefox A retired pilot sneaks into the Soviet Union for the Pentagon to steal a top-secret, ultra-sophisticated warplane and fly it out of the country. Best for the low-altitude flight and aerial battle sequences, but too slow on character and much too slow getting started.
1982 (PG) 136m/C Clint Eastwood, Freddie Jones, David Huffman, Warren Clarke, Ronald Lacey, Kenneth Colley, Nigel Hawthorne, Kai Wulff; *D:* Clint Eastwood. **VHS, Beta, LV $19.98** WAR 🐾🐾½

Firehawk Several American soldiers survive the crash of their helicopter into the jungles of Vietnam. They think their only enemy is the Vietcong but when they discover the copter has been sabotaged the hunt is on for the traitor among them.
1992 (R) 92m/C Martin Kove, Matt Salinger, Vic Trevino. **VHS, LV $89.95** LIV 🐾🐾

Firehead A pyrokinetic Soviet defector begins using his powers to destroy American munitions in the name of peace. When a clandestine pro-world organization hears of this, they attempt to capture the man and use him for their own evil purposes.
1990 (R) 88m/C Christopher Plummer, Chris Lemmon, Martin Landau, Gretchen Becker, Brett Porter; *D:* Peter Yuval. **VHS, Beta, LV $89.98** AIP 🐾🐾½

Firehouse Tempers ignite in a lily-white firehouse when a black rookie replaces an expired veteran. March—of "Paper Lion" renown—directed this made-for-TV emergency clone, which ran ever-so-briefly as an adventure series on TV in 1974 (with a largely different cast).
1972 73m/C Richard Roundtree, Vince Edwards, Andrew Duggan, Richard Jaeckel, Sheila Frazier, Val Avery, Paul LeMat, Michael Lerner; *D:* Alex March. **VHS $59.95** XVC 🐾🐾

Firehouse In the style of "Police Academy," three beautiful and sex-starved fire-fighting recruits klutz up an urban firehouse. A softcore frolic.
1987 (R) 91m/C Barrett Hopkins, Shannon Murphy, Violet Brown, John Anderson; *D:* J. Christian Ingvordsen. **VHS, Beta $14.95** ACA 🐾

The Fireman Chaplin portrays a fireman who becomes a hero. Silent with musical soundtrack added.
1916 20m/B Eric Campbell, Edna Purviance, Charlie Chaplin; *D:* Charlie Chaplin. **VHS, Beta, 3/4U, Special order formats $39.95** CAB, VYY 🐾🐾½

The Firemen's Ball A critically acclaimed comedy about a small-town ball held for a retiring fire chief. Plans go amusingly awry as beauty contestants refuse to show themselves, raffle prizes and other items—including the gift for the guest of honor—are stolen, and the firemen are unable to prevent an old man's house from burning down. Forman's second film is sometimes interpreted as political allegory; in Czechoslovakian, with English subtitles.
1968 73m/C *CZ* Vaclav Stockel, Josef Svet; **D:** Milos Forman. **VHS, Beta $59.95** *COL, TAM* ⅛⅛⅛

Firepower Loren blames her chemist husband's death on a rich industrialist and hires hitman Coburn to take care of the matter. Less than compelling.
1979 (R) 104m/C Sophia Loren, James Coburn, O.J. Simpson, Christopher F. Bean; **D:** Michael Winner. **VHS, Beta $59.98** *FOX* ⅛½

Fires on the Plain A grueling Japanese anti-war film about an unhinged private in the Philippines during World War II who roams the war-torn countryside encountering all manner of horror and devastation. In Japanese with English subtitles. *AKA:* Nobi.
1959 105m/B *JP* Eiji Funakoshi, Osamu Takizawa, Mickey Custis, Asao Suno; **D:** Kon Ichikawa. **VHS, Beta $29.98** *SUE, MRV, HHT* ⅛⅛⅛

Fires Within A curiously flat romance with political overtones. After eight years as a political prisoner in Cuba, Nestor (Smits) is released and goes to Miami to be reunited with his wife and daughter. Once there he finds his wife has fallen in love with another man. Now Nestor must choose between his politics and the chance to win back his family. Secondary plot lines fizzle out and a talented cast is largely wasted. Scacchi is beautiful but hardly believable as the Cuban wife.
1991 (R) 90m/C Jimmy Smits, Greta Scacchi, Vincent D'Onofrio; **D:** Gillian Armstrong. **VHS, Beta $89.99** *MGM* ⅛

Firesign Theatre Presents Nick Danger in the Case of the Missing Yolks Firesign characters Nick Danger and Rocky Rococo are featured in this story of a truly interactive family who live through their television set.
1983 60m/C Phil Proctor, Phil Austin, Peter Bergman. **VHS, Beta $29.95** *PAV* ⅛⅛½

Firestarter A C.I.A.-like organization is after a little girl who has the ability to set anything on fire in this filmed adaptation of Stephen King's bestseller. Good special effects help a silly plot.
1984 (R) 115m/C David Keith, Drew Barrymore, Freddie Jones, Martin Sheen, George C. Scott, Heather Locklear, Louise Fletcher, Moses Gunn, Art Carney, Antonio Fargas, Drew Snyder; **D:** Mark L. Lester. **VHS, Beta, LV $19.95** *MCA* ⅛

Firewalker An "Indiana Jones" clone about three mercenaries endeavoring to capture a fortune in hidden gold. Paper-mache sets and a villain with an eye patch that consistently changes eyes are just some of the gaffes that make this one of the worst edited movies in history.
1986 (PG) 106m/C Chuck Norris, Louis Gossett Jr., Melody Anderson; **D:** J. Lee Thompson. **VHS, Beta $19.95** *MED* ⅛

The Firing Line The Central American government hires a mercenary rebel-buster to squash insurgents. Everything's great until he finds out he agrees with the rebel cause, and he trains them to fight the government. Below average renegade-with-a-hidden-heart warpic.
1991 93m/C Reb Brown, Shannon Tweed; **D:** John Gale. **VHS, LV $79.95** *AIP* ⅛

The Firm With a top-flight cast promising a good time, the script based on the top-selling novel of 1991 by John Grisham nearly guarantees it. Cruise is Mitch McDeere, an ambitious, idealistic Ivy League law school grad who accepts a great offer from a small but wealthy Memphis law firm. As with anything that seems too good to be true, he discovers nothing in life is free and the seemingly prestigious firm is really a front for the Mob. Then the FBI wants Mitch to help them set up the bad guys—or take the fall himself. Riveting study of a young man in a no-win situation. Book fans beware: the script is fairly faithful, until the end. The movie rights to this one were snapped up even before the book was published.
1993 (R) ?m/C Tom Cruise, Jeanne Tripplehorn, Gene Hackman, Hal Holbrook, Terry Kinney, Wilford Brimley, Ed Harris, Holly Hunter, David Strathairn, Gary Busey, Steven Hill, Tobin Bell, Barbara Garrick, Jerry Hardin, Karina Lombard, John Beal; **D:** Sydney Pollack; **W:** Robert Towne, David Rayfiel; **M:** Dave Grusin **VHS** *NYR* ⅛⅛⅛

First Affair A made-for-television film about a young innocent girl undergoing the pressures of freshman life at college, including her first love affair, which is with the husband of a female professor.
1983 95m/C Loretta Swit, Melissa Sue Anderson, Joel Higgins; **D:** Gus Trikonis. **VHS, Beta $59.98** *FOX* ⅛⅛⅛

First & Ten A failing football team emphasizes sexual, rather than athletic conquests, under the guidance of their female owner. Made for cable TV and followed by "First & Ten: The Team Scores Again."
1985 88m/C Delta Burke, Geoffrey Scott, Reid Shelton, Ruta Lee, Fran Tarkenton; **D:** Donald Kushner. **VHS, Beta $69.98** *LIV, VES* ⅛

First & Ten: The Team Scores Again A sequel to the made-for-cable-television comedy "First and Ten" about a football team's relationship with their female owner.
1985 101m/C Delta Burke, Geoffrey Scott, Ruta Lee, Reid Shelton, Clayton Landey, Fran Tarkenton. **VHS, Beta $69.98** *LIV, VES* ⅛

First Blood Stallone is a former Green Beret survivor of Vietnam whose nightmares of wartime horrors are triggered by a wrongful arrest in a small town. He escapes into the mountains of the Northwest and leads his pursuers to all manner of bloody ends. Finally, the Army is summoned to crush him. Extremely violent and frequently confused, fueled on the revenge fantasy and not much concerned with the rules of plot realism. A box-office hit that launched the "Rambo" series. Followed by "Rambo: First Blood, Part 2."
1982 (R) 96m/C Sylvester Stallone, Richard Crenna, Brian Dennehy, Jack Starrett; **D:** Ted Kotcheff; **M:** Jerry Goldsmith. **VHS, Beta, LV $14.95** *HBO, LIV, TLF* ⅛

First Born In search of romance, divorced mother Garr finds an intriguing man, Weller. Trouble erupts when her son learns Weller is a cocaine dealer. Talented cast makes most of story.
1984 (PG-13) 100m/C Teri Garr, Peter Weller, Christopher Collet, Corey Haim, Sarah Jessica Parker, Robert Downey Jr.; **D:** Michael Apted. **VHS, Beta, LV $14.95** *PAR* ⅛⅛½

The First Christmas A shepherd boy is miraculously rewarded for his generosity to nuns. Animated, with voices of Angela Lansbury and Cyril Ritchard.
1975 23m/C *V:* Angela Lansbury, Cyril Ritchard. **VHS, Beta $12.95** *WAR, WTA* ⅛⅛½

The First Deadly Sin Police lieutenant Sinatra tracks down a homicidal killer in spite of wife Dunaway's illness and his impending retirement. Read Lawrence Sanders' bestselling novel; it's a lot more exciting than this.
1980 (R) 112m/C Frank Sinatra, Faye Dunaway, David Dukes, Brenda Vaccaro, James Whitmore; **D:** Brian G. Hutton. **VHS, Beta, LV $59.95** *WAR* ⅛½

First Family Flat satire of life in the White House. The humor is weak and silly at best, despite the excellent comedy cast. Henry's first directional effort.
1980 (R) 100m/C Bob Newhart, Madeline Kahn, Gilda Radner, Richard Benjamin; **D:** Buck Henry. **VHS, Beta $19.98** *WAR* ⅛½

First Legion Boyer and Addy are seminarians struggling with their faith when they are confronted with a supposed miracle. Low-key examination of religion and conflict within a religious community.
1951 77m/B Charles Boyer, Barbara Rush, William Demarest, Leo G. Carroll; **D:** Douglas Sirk. **VHS, Beta $59.98** *LIV, LIG* ⅛⅛½

First Love A sixteen year old lad falls in love with a slightly older woman only to have his feelings rejected and to discover that she's his father's mistress. Actor Schell's directorial debut.
1970 (R) 90m/C *GE SI* John Moulder-Brown, Dominique Sanda, Maximilian Schell, Valentina Cortese; **D:** Maximilian Schell. **VHS, Beta $49.95** *NEG* ⅛⅛½

First Love A story of an idealistic college student who takes love (and especially making love) more seriously than the rest of his peers, including his girlfriend. Based on Harold Brodkey's story "Sentimental Education." Darling's directorial debut.
1977 (R) 92m/C William Katt, Susan Dey, John Heard, Beverly D'Angelo, Robert Loggia; **D:** Joan Darling; **M:** John Barry. **VHS, Beta $49.95** *PAR* ⅛½

First Man into Space An astronaut returns to Earth covered with strange space dust and with an organism feeding inside him (shades of "Alien"). The alien needs human blood to survive and starts killing in order to get it. *AKA:* Satellite of Blood.
1959 78m/B Marshall Thompson, Marla Landi, Bill Edwards; **D:** Robert Day. **VHS, Beta $19.98** *DVT, RHI, HEG* ⅛

First Men in the Moon A fun, special effects-laden adaptation of the H. G. Wells novel about an Edwardian civilian spacecraft visiting the moon and the creature found there. Visual effects by Ray Harryhausen. Finch makes a brief appearance.
1964 103m/C *GB* Martha Hyer, Edward Judd, Lionel Jeffries, Erik Chitty, Peter Finch; **D:** Nathan Juran; **W:** Nigel Kneale, Jan Read. **VHS, Beta, LV $19.95** *COL, PIA, MLB* ⅛

First Monday in October A comedy concerning the first woman appointed to the Supreme Court, a conservative, and her colleague, a crusty but benign liberal judge. Though based on a Broadway hit, it ended up seeming to foreshadow the real-life appointment of Sandra Day O'Connor, which occurred at about the time the film was released. The title refers to the date the court begins its sessions.
1981 (R) 99m/C Walter Matthau, Jill Clayburgh, Barnard Hughes, James Stephens, Jan Sterling; **D:** Ronald Neame. **VHS, Beta, LV $84.95** *PAR* ⅛½

The First Movie Cowboy Three shorts featuring the very first movie cowboy, Bronco Billy.
1913 47m/B G.M. Anderson; **D:** G.M. Anderson. **VHS, Beta, 8mm $24.95** *VYY* ⅛½

First Name: Carmen Carmen, although posing as an aspiring filmmaker, really is a bank robber and terrorist. She is also such a femme fatale that during a bank robbery one of the guards decides to run away with her. Gooddard cast himself as Carmen's uncle. Amusing late Godard. *AKA:* Prenom: Carmen.
1983 95m/C *FR* Maruschka Detmers, Jacques Bonaffe, Jean-Luc Godard, Myriem Roussel, Christophe Odent; *D:* Jean-Luc Godard. **VHS, Beta, LV** $79.95 *CVC, TAM* 🎬🎬🎬

The First Nudie Musical A producer tries to save his studio by staging a 1930s style musical, but with a naked cast and risque lyrics. Has attained semi-cult/trash status. ♫The First Nudie Musical; The Lights and the Smiles; Orgasm; Lesbian Butch Dyke; Dancing Dildos; Perversion; Honey, What Ya Doin' Tonight; Let 'Em Eat Cake; I Don't Have to Hide Anymore; Where Is a Man.
1975 (R) 93m/C Cindy Williams, Stephen Nathan, Diana Canova, Bruce Kimmel; *D:* Mark Haggard. **VHS, Beta** $59.95 *MED, HHT* 🎬🎬

The First Olympics: Athens 1896 Recounts the organization and drama surrounding the first modern-day Olympic games when the inexperienced American team shocked the games with their success. Made for television.
1984 260m/C Louis Jourdan, Angela Lansbury, David Ogden Stiers, Virginia McKenna, Jason Connery, Alex Hyde-White, Honor Blackman, Bill Travers; *D:* Alvin Rakoff. **VHS, Beta** $29.95 *COL* 🎬🎬½

The First Power A detective and psychic join forces to track down a serial killer who, after being executed, uses his satanic powers to kill again.
1989 90m/C Lou Diamond Phillips, Tracy Griffith, Jeff Kober, Mykel T. Williamson, Elizabeth Arlen; *W/D:* Robert Resnikoff. **VHS, Beta, LV, 8mm** $14.95 *COL, SUE, NLC* 🎬½

First Spaceship on Venus Eight scientists from various countries set out for Venus and find the remains of a civilization far in advance of Earth's that perished because of nuclear weapons. A sometimes compelling anti-nuclear sci-fi effort made with German and Polish backing. Originally released at 130 minutes. *AKA:* Der Schweigende Stern; Milczaca Gwiazda.
1960 78m/C *GE PL* Yoko Tani, Oldrich Lukes, Ignacy Machowski, Julius Ongewe, Michal Postnikow, Kurt Rackelmann, Gunther Simon, Tang-Hua-Ta, Lucyna Winnicka; *D:* Kurt Maetzig. **VHS, Beta** $19.95 *NOS, MRV, SNC* 🎬🎬🎬

First Strike The United States and the USSR engage in nuclear submarine warfare when the Soviets hijack a U.S. sub and aims its weapons at Arab oil fields.
1985 90m/C Stuart Whitman, Persis Khambatta. **VHS, Beta** $69.95 *VCD* 🎬

The First Time It's pre-Porky's zaniness as a vacationing youth understandably wants to spend his "first time" with Bisset. Other than her presence, this film has little to offer. *AKA:* You Don't Need Pajamas at Rosie's; The Beginners Three; The Beginners; They Don't Wear Pajamas at Rosie's; Doin' It.
1969 (R) 90m/C Jacqueline Bisset, Wes Stern, Rick Kelman, Wink Roberts; *D:* James Neilson. **VHS** *NO* 🎬½

First Time A comedy about a college student who can't quite succeed with women, despite coaching from his roommate and counseling from a psychology professor whose assistance is part of a research project. *AKA:* Doin' It.

1982 (R) 96m/C Tim Choate, Krista Errickson, Marshall Efron, Wallace Shawn, Wendie Jo Sperber, Cathryn Damon; *D:* Charles Loventhal. **VHS, Beta** $19.99 *HBO, SIM* 🎬🎬½

First Turn On Not to be confused with "The Thomas Edison Story," this sex-comedy follows the adventures of several young campers who decide to die happy when an avalanche leaves them trapped in a cave. A longer unrated version is available.
1983 (R) 84m/C Georgia Harrell, Michael Sanville, Googy Gress, Jenny Johnson, Heide Basset, Vincent D'Onofrio, Sheila Kennedy; *D:* Michael Herz, Samuel Weil. **VHS, Beta** $69.98 *LIV* 🎬

First Yank into Tokyo An American army pilot who grew up in Japan undergoes plastic surgery in order to infiltrate Japanese lines and get information from an American scientist. Some last minute editing to capitalize on current events made this the first American film to deal with the atomic bomb. *AKA:* Mask of Fury.
1945 83m/B Tom Neal, Richard Loo, Barbara Hale, Marc Cramer; *D:* Gordon Douglas. **VHS, Beta** $19.98 *RKO, TTC* 🎬🎬

A Fish Called Wanda An absurd, high-speed farce about four criminals trying to retrieve $20 million they've stolen from a safety deposit box and each other. Meanwhile, barrister Cleese falls in love with the female thief (Curtis). There's some sick, but funny, humor involving Palin's problem with stuttering and some very dead doggies. Kline received an Oscar for his dumb and vain character. Written by Cleese and Crichton, who understand that silence is sometimes funnier than speech, and that timing is everything. Wickedly funny.
1988 (R) 98m/C John Cleese, Kevin Kline, Jamie Lee Curtis, Michael Palin, Tom Georgeson, Maria Aitken; *D:* Charles Crichton. Academy Awards '88: Best Supporting Actor (Kline); Nominations: Best Director (Crichton), Best Original Screenplay; British Academy Awards '88: Best Actor (Cleese), Best Supporting Actor (Palin). **VHS, Beta, LV** $19.95 *FOX, BTV, MGM* 🎬🎬🎬

Fish Hawk When an alcoholic Indian, Fish Hawk, meets a young boy in the forest, they strike up a friendship and he attempts to clean up his act. Attempts to be heartwarming.
1979 (G) 95m/C *CA* Will Sampson, Charlie Fields; *D:* Donald Shebib. **VHS, Beta** $19.95 *MED* 🎬½

The Fish that Saved Pittsburgh A floundering basketball team hires an astrologer to try and change their luck. She makes sure all the team members' signs are compatible with their star's Pisces sign (the fish). Produced a disco soundtrack with several Motown groups who also performed in the movie.
1979 (PG) 104m/C Jonathan Winters, Stockard Channing, Flip Wilson, Julius Erving, Margaret Avery, Meadowlark Lemon, Nicholas Pryor, James Bond III, Kareem Abdul-Jabbar, Jack Kehoe, Debbie Allen; *D:* Gilbert Moses. **VHS, Beta** $59.95 *LHV, WAR* 🎬

The Fisher King In derelict-infested Manhattan a down-and-out radio deejay meets a crazed vagabond (Williams) obsessed with medieval history and in search of the Holy Grail. At first the whimsical mix of Arthurian myth and modern urban hell seems amazingly wrongheaded. In retrospect it still does. But while this picture runs it weaves a spell that pulls you in, especially in its quiet moments. Your reaction to the silly ending depends entirely on how well you're bamboozled by a script that equates madness with enlightenment and the homeless with holy

fools. Filmed on the streets of New York, with many street people playing themselves.
1991 (R) 138m/C Robin Williams, Jeff Bridges, Amanda Plummer, Mercedes Ruehl; *D:* Terry Gilliam. Academy Awards '91: Best Supporting Actress (Ruehl); Nominations: Best Actor (Williams), Best Art Direction/Set Decoration, Best Original Screenplay, Best Original Score; Chicago Film Critics Awards '91: Best Supporting Actress (Ruehl); Golden Globe Awards '92: Best Actor—Musical/Comedy (Williams), Best Supporting Actress (Ruehl). **VHS, Beta, LV** $19.95 *COL, CCB* 🎬🎬🎬

Fisherman's Wharf Breen stars as an orphan adopted by a San Francisco fisherman who runs away when his aunt and bratty cousin come to live with them.
1939 72m/B Bobby Breen, Leo Carrillo, Henry Armetta, Lee Patrick, Rosina Galli, Leon Belasco; *D:* Bernard Vorhaus. **VHS** $19.95 *NOS* 🎬½

F.I.S.T. A young truck driver turns union organizer for idealistic reasons, but finds himself teaming with gangsters to boost his cause. His rise to the top of the union comes at the cost of his integrity, as Stallone does a character resembling Jimmy Hoffa.
1978 (R) 145m/C Sylvester Stallone, Rod Steiger, Peter Boyle, David Huffman, Melinda Dillon, Tony LoBianco, Kevin Conway, Peter Donat, Cassie Yates, Brian Dennehy; *D:* Norman Jewison. **VHS, Beta, LV** $79.98 *MGM, FOX* 🎬🎬½

Fist Street fighter battles his way through the urban jungle seeking personal freedom and revenge.
1979 (R) 84m/C Richard Lawson, Annazette Chase, Dabney Coleman. **VHS, Beta** *NO* 🎬

Fist Fighter The ups and downs of a professional bare-knuckle fighter as he avenges a friend's murder.
1988 (R) 99m/C George Rivero, Edward Albert, Brenda Bakke, Mike Connors, Simon Andrew, Matthias Hues; *D:* Frank Zuniga. **VHS, Beta, LV** $9.99 *CCB, IVE* 🎬½

A Fist Full of Talons A sexy maiden, a young warrior, and a goofy thief team up to fight evil in the early Chinese republic.
19?? 100m/C VHS, Beta $34.95 *OCE* 🎬

Fist of Death Two high-kicking kids battle gangs of killers using only their bare fighting skills.
1987 90m/C Jackie Chan, Tong Lung. **VHS, Beta** *NO* 🎬

Fist of Fear, Touch of Death Madison Square Garden is the scene for a high stakes martial arts face-off. Standard kung-fu film highlighted by short clips of the late Bruce Lee.
1977 (R) 90m/C Fred Williamson, Ron Van Cliff, Adolph Caesar, Aaron Banks, Bill Louie; *D:* Matthew Mallinson. **VHS, Beta** $39.95 *LIV* 🎬

Fist of Honor A young boxer seeks to avenge his fiance's death, a beautiful girl squares off against a bad-cop, and two mobster leaders try to take control of the same city. When a member of one family breaks a truce and begins killing rival family members, the violence escalates and old scores will be settled.
1992 (R) 90m/C Sam Jones, Joey House, Harry Guardino, Nicholas Worth, Frank Sivero, Abe Vigoda, Bubba Smith; *D:* Richard Pepin; *W:* Charles Kanganis. **VHS** $89.95 *PMH* 🎬

Fist of Vengeance The East Asia Society hires a samurai to kill a young Chinese officer.
197? 90m/C Shoji Karada, Lu Pi Chen. **VHS, Beta** *NO* 🎬

The Fist, the Kicks, and the Evils A young man who's father is murdered learns kung fu and sets out for revenge.

1980 90m/C Kao Fei, Bruce Liang. VHS, Beta $29.95 OCE ⅜

Fistful of Death Kinski portrays a vengefully violent and desperate cowpoke in the days of the old West.
1967 84m/C Klaus Kinski. VHS, Beta $59.95 TWE ⅜

A Fistful of Dollars The epitome of the "spaghetti western" pits Eastwood as "the man with no name" against two families who are feuding over land. A remake of Kurosawa's "Yojimbo," and followed by Leone's "For a Few Dollars More", and "The Good, The Bad, and The Ugly."
1964 101m/C IT Clint Eastwood, Gian Marie Volonte, Marianne Koch; D: Sergio Leone; M: David Foster. VHS, Beta, LV $19.98 MGM, FCT, TLF ⅜⅜⅜

A Fistful of Dynamite A spaghetti western, with Leone's trademark humor and a striking score by Ennio Morricone. An Irish demolitions expert and a Mexican peasant team up to rob a bank during a revolution in Mexico. AKA: Duck, You Sucker; Giu la Testa.
1972 (PG) 138m/C IT James Coburn, Rod Steiger, Romolo Valli; D: Sergio Leone; M: Ennio Morricone. VHS, Beta, LV $59.95 MGM ⅜⅜⅜

Fists of Blood A martial arts expert seeks revenge on the drug baron who murdered his friend and kidnapped his girl.
1987 90m/C AU Eddie Stazak; D: Brian Trenchard-Smith. VHS, Beta $39.95 CEL ⅜½

Fists of Bruce Lee An undercover cop cracks a drug-smuggling ring by kicking out in all directions.
190? 00m/C Bruce Lee, Lo Lieh; D: Bruce Lee. VHS, Beta NO ⅜

Fists of Dragons Vengeful, sacrificial bloodshed abounds in this Chinese boxing extravaganza.
1969 92m/C Huang I Lung, Ou Ti; D: Yeh Yung Chu. VHS, Beta $29.95 TWE ⅜

Fists of Fury Bruce Lee stars in this violent but charming Kung Fu action adventure in which he must break a solemn vow to avoid fighting in order to avenge the murder of his teacher by drug smugglers. AKA: The Big Boss.
1973 (R) 102m/C Bruce Lee, Maria Yi; D: Lo Wei. VHS, Beta $19.98 FOX ⅜⅜⅜

Fists of Fury 2 Chen Shan must survive the Organizations' onslaughts to kill him. He escapes their perilous plots only to return to battle against them after they kill his mother for her inability to disclose Chen's hiding place. Finally Chen defeats the Evil Organization himself.
1980 (R) 90m/C Bruce Li, Ho Chung Do, Shum Shim Po. VHS, Beta $19.98 GEM ⅜½

Fists of the White Lotus A Shaolin warrior seeks revenge for the killing of his pals by the vicious White Lotus.
198? 95m/C D: Lo Lieh. Beta NO ⅜

Fit for a King A reporter becomes a princess' knight in shining armor when he foils an assassination plot in this screwball romance.
1937 73m/B Joe E. Brown, Leo Carrillo, Helen Mack, Paul Kelly, Harry Davenport; D: Edward Sedgwick. VHS, Beta $24.95 NOS, DVT, HEG ⅜⅜

Fitzcarraldo Although he failed to build a railroad across South America, Fitzcarraldo is determined to build an opera house in the middle of the Amazon jungles and have Enrico Caruso sing there. Based on a true story of a charismatic Irishman's impossible quest at the turn of the century. Of note: No special effects were used in this movie—

everything you see actually occurred during filming, including hauling a large boat over a mountain.
1982 (PG) 157m/C GE Klaus Kinski, Claudia Cardinale, Jose Lewgoy, Miguel Angel Fuentes; D: Werner Herzog. VHS, Beta $69.95 WAR, APD, TAM ⅜⅜⅜

Five Came Back When a plane with twelve passengers crashes in the South American jungle, only five can ride in the patched-up wreck. Since the remainder will be left to face head hunters, intense arguments ensue. Same director remade this as "Back from Eternity" in 1956.
1939 93m/B Lucille Ball, Chester Morris, John Carradine, Wendy Barrie, Kent Taylor, Joseph Calleia, C. Aubrey Smith, Patric Knowles; D: John Farrow. VHS, Beta, LV $29.95 RKO, TTC ⅜⅜

Five Card Stud Five members of a lynching party are being killed one by one, and a professional gambler, who tried to prevent the lynching, attempts to ensnare the killer with the aid of a preacher with a gun. The poor script was based on a novel by Ray Gaulden.
1968 (PG) 103m/C Robert Mitchum, Dean Martin, Inger Stevens, Roddy McDowall, Yaphet Kotto, John Anderson, Katherine Justice; D: Henry Hathaway. VHS, Beta $14.95 PAR ⅜½

Five Corners A quixotic, dramatic comedy about the inhabitants of the 5 Corners section of the Bronx in 1964, centering around a girl being wooed by a psychotic rapist, her crippled boyfriend, and the hero-turned-racial-pacifist who cannot rescue her out of principle.
1988 (R) 92m/C Jodie Foster, John Turturro, Todd Graff, Tim Robbins, Elizabeth Berridge, Rose Gregorio, Gregory Rozakis, Rodney Harvey; D: Tony Bill; W: John Patrick Shanley. VHS, Beta $14.95 MGM ⅜⅜⅜

Five Days One Summer Set in 1932, the story of a haunting and obsessive love affair between a married Scottish doctor and a young woman who happens to be his niece. While on vacation in the Swiss Alps, the doctor must vie for her love with their handsome young mountain climbing guide. Based on a story by Kay Boyle.
1982 (PG) 108m/C Sean Connery, Betsy Brantley, Lambert Wilson; D: Fred Zinneman. VHS, Beta $19.98 WAR ⅜⅜

Five Easy Pieces Nicholson's superb acting brings to life this character study of a talented musician who has given up a promising career and now works on the oil rigs. After twenty years he returns home to attempt one last communication with his dying father and perhaps, reconcile himself with his fear of failure and desire for greatness. Black, Anspach, and Bush create especially memorable characters. Nicholson ordering toast via a chicken salad sandwich is a classic.
1970 (R) 98m/C Jack Nicholson, Karen Black, Susan Anspach, Lois Smith, Billy Green Bush, Fannie Flagg, Ralph Waite; D: Andrien Joyce, Bob Rafelson. Academy Awards '70 Nominations: Best Actor (Nicholson), Best Picture, Best Story & Screenplay, Best Supporting Actress (Black); Golden Globe Awards '71: Best Supporting Actress (Black). VHS, Beta, LV, 8mm $14.95 COL, VYG, WME ⅜⅜⅜⅜

Five Fighters from Shaolin Five high-kicking fighters endeavor to recapture their temple from an evil duke.
1977 88m/C Chang Shen, Lung Kwan, Dhiu Min Shien; D: Ko Shu-How. VHS, Beta $39.95 MPI, MOV ⅜

Five for Hell The army picks five of its meanest men for a suicide mission during WWII. They must go behind German lines and find the plans for the enemy offensive.
1967 88m/C IT Klaus Kinski, John Garko, Nick Jordan, Margaret Lee; D: Frank Kramer. VHS, Beta $59.95 TWE ⅜

Five Giants from Texas El cheapo spaghetti western features Madison, television's former Wild Bill Hickock, as a rancher fighting off displaced Mexican peasants and outlaws. AKA: I Cinque Della Vendetta.
1966 103m/C Guy Madison, Monica Randall; D: Aldo Florio. VHS, Beta $59.95 TWE ⅜

Five Golden Dragons A typical action film about an American running afoul of ruthless gold trafficking in Hong Kong. Even this stellar cast can't help the script.
1967 92m/C GB Robert Cummings, Christopher Lee, Brian Donlevy, Klaus Kinski, George Raft, Dan Duryea, Margaret Lee; D: Jeremy Summers. VHS, Beta $59.98 NO ⅜

The Five Heartbeats Well told story of five black singers in the 1960s, their successes and failures as a group and as individuals. Although every horror story of the music business is included, the story remains fresh and the acting excellent. Music is fine, but secondary to the people. Well written characters with few cliches. Skillfully directed by Townsend (of "Hollywood Shuffle") who did research by talking to the Dells. Less than memorable showing at the box office but fun and entertaining.
1991 (R) 122m/C Robert Townsend, Tressa Thomas, Michael Wright, Harry J. Lennix, Diahann Carroll, Leon, Hawthorne James, Chuck Patterson, Roy Fegan; W/D: Robert Townsend; W: Keenan Ivory Wayans. VHS, Beta, LV $19.95 FXV ⅜⅜⅜

Five Miles to Midnight Brett and Danny have to depend on a photographer (Collins) for help to smuggle a gangster out of Italy. From the British "Persuaders" adventure series. Made for television.
1980 52m/C GB Roger Moore, Tony Curtis, Joan Collins. VHS $39.95 SVS ⅜⅜⅜

Five Minutes to Live Cash (the country singer) stars as a psycho who holds a housewife hostage in hopes of getting a ransom from her wealthy husband. Of interest only for the strange cast ensemble. AKA: Door-to-Door Maniac.
1961 80m/C Johnny Cash, Donald Woods, Cay Forrester, Pamela Mason, Vic Tayback, Ron Howard; D: Bill Karn; W: Cay Forrester. VHS AOV ⅜

Five Minutes to Love McClanahan (one of TV's "Golden Girls") plays a young, sleazy hussy named "Poochie, the girl from the shack." This exploitation schlocker appears to be McClanahan's first film. AKA: The Rotten Apple; It Only Take Five Minutes.
1963 ?m/C Rue McClanahan, Paul Leder. VHS $16.95 SNC ⅜

The Five of Me A man with five personalities finds that livin' ain't easy and seeks professional help. Made for television, based on the autobiography of Henry Hawksworth.
1981 100m/C David Birney, Dee Wallace Stone, Mitchell Ryan, John McLiam, James Whitmore Jr., Ben Piazza; D: Paul Wendkos. VHS $39.95 LIV ⅜⅜½

The Five Pennies Sentimental biography starring Kaye as famed jazzman Red Nichols features performances by legendary musicians Bob Crosby, Bobby Troup, Ray Anthony and Louis Armstrong. This movie marked Weld's film debut. ♫Good Night Sleep Tight; The Five Pennies; Battle Hymn of the Republic; When the Saints Go Marching In; The Music Goes 'Round and Around; Jingle Bells; Carnival of Venice; Paradise. **1959 117m/C** Danny Kaye, Louis Armstrong, Barbara Bel Geddes, Tuesday Weld, Harry Guardino; **W/D:** Melville Shavelson. **VHS, Beta** $14.95 PAR ♪♪½

The 5000 Fingers of Dr. T In Dr. Seuss' only non-animated movie, a boy tries to evade piano lessons and runs right into the castle of the evil Dr. Terwilliger, where hundreds of boys are held captive for piano lessons. Worse yet, they're forced to wear silly beanies with "happy fingers" waving on top. Luckily, the trusted family plumber is on hand to save the day through means of an atomic bomb. Wonderful satire, horrible music, mesmerizing Seussian sets. The skating brothers (who are joined at their beards) are a treat. **1953 88m/C** Peter Lind Hayes, Mary Healy, Tommy Rettig, Hans Conried; **D:** Roy Rowland; **W:** Dr. Seuss, Allan Scott. **VHS, Beta, LV** $59.95 XVC, FCT ♪♪♪

Five Weeks in a Balloon This adaptation of the Jules Verne novel follows the often-comic exploits of a 19th-century British expedition that encounters many adventures on a balloon trek across Africa. Pleasant fluff with a good cast. **1962 101m/C** Fabian, Peter Lorre, Red Buttons, Cedric Hardwicke, Barbara Eden; **D:** Irwin Allen. **VHS, Beta, LV** $19.98 FOX, FCT ♪♪½

The $5.20 an Hour Dream Lavin is a divorced mother and factory worker burdened with debt and determined to get and keep a job on the higher-paying, traditionally all-male assembly line. Lesser feminist drama on the heels of "Norma Rae." Made for television. **1980 96m/C** Linda Lavin, Richard Jaeckel, Nicholas Pryor, Pamela McMyler, Mayf Nutter, Taurean Blacque, Robert Davi, Dennis Fimple, Dana Hill, Ernie Hudson; **D:** Russ Mayberry. **VHS, Beta** TLF ♪♪

The Fix A group of cocaine smugglers get their just desserts as the federal government catches them in a sting operation. **AKA:** The Agitators. **1984 95m/C** Vince Edwards, Richard Jaeckel, Julie Hill, Charles Dierkop, Byron Cherry, Robert Tessier; **D:** Will Zens. **VHS, Beta** $39.95 WWV ♪

The Flame & the Arrow Dardo the Arrow, a Robin Hood-like outlaw in medieval Italy, leads his band of mountain fighters against a mercenary warlord who has seduced his wife and kidnapped his son. Spectacular acrobatics, with Lancaster performing his own stunts, add interest to the usual swashbuckling. Music score by Max Steiner. **1950 88m/C** Burt Lancaster, Virginia Mayo, Aline MacMahon, Nick Cravat, Robert Douglas, Frank Allenby; **D:** Jacques Tourneur. **VHS, Beta, LV** $19.98 WAR ♪♪♪

The Flame is Love A made-for-television adaptation of one of Barbara Cartland's romantic novels. An American heiress falls tragically in love with a Parisian journalist despite her engagement to an Englishman. Takes place at the turn of the century. **1979 98m/C** Linda Purl, Timothy Dalton, Shane Briant; **D:** Michael O'Herlihy. **VHS, Beta** $69.98 LIV ♪½

Flame of the Barbary Coast A rancher from Montana vies with a gambling czar for a beautiful dance hall queen and control of the Barbary Coast district of San Francisco. The great earthquake of 1906 provides the plot with a climax. Also available colorized. **1945 91m/B** John Wayne, Ann Dvorak, Joseph Schildkraut, William Frawley; **D:** Joseph Kane. **VHS** $14.98 MED, REP ♪♪½

Flame of the Islands De Carlo plays a smoldering, passionate chanteuse who struggles with love and gangsters for possession of a Bahamian casino in this tropical heat wave. **1955 92m/C** Yvonne De Carlo, Howard Duff, Zachary Scott, James Arness, Kurt Kasznar, Barbara O'Neil; **D:** Edward Ludwig. **VHS, Beta** $39.98 NO ♪♪

Flame Over India When Moslems lay siege to a British fortress in India, Governess Wyatt (Bacall) and Captain Scott (More) save the Maharaja's son and escape by commandeering a train. Along the way they find treason, adventure and love. **AKA:** Northwest Frontier. **1960 130m/C** GB Kenneth More, Lauren Bacall, Herbert Lom, Wilfrid Hyde-White, I.S. Johar, Ursula Jeans, Ian Hunter, Eugene Deckers, Jack Gwillim, Govind Raja Ross, Frank Olegario; **D:** J. Lee Thompson. **VHS** HEG, SUE, DVT ♪♪♪

Flame to the Phoenix A World War II drama about the Polish cavalry forces' decimation to German Panzer tanks. **1985 80m/C** GB Paul Geoffrey, Ann Firbank, Frederick Treves; **D:** William Brayne. **VHS, Beta** $79.95 WWV ♪½

The Flame Trees of Thika In 1913, a British family travels to East Africa to start a coffee plantation. Seen through the eyes of the young daughter, her childhood consists of the local Masai and Kikuyu tribes, the eccentric and sometimes unhappy English neighbors, and the wild animals that roam the plains. Based on the memoirs of writer Elspeth Huxley. On four cassettes. Shown on PBS "Masterpiece Theatre." **198? 366m/C** GB Hayley Mills, Holly Aird, David Robb, Ben Cross. **VHS** $129.95 SIG, TVC ♪♪♪

Flaming Frontiers A frontier scout matches wits against gold mine thieves. In fifteen episodes. **1938 300m/B** Johnny Mack Brown, Eleanor Hanson, Ralph Bowman; **D:** Ray Taylor. **VHS, Beta** $49.95 NOS, VCN, VYY ♪½

Flaming Lead A hard-drinkin' ranch owner hires a nightclub cowboy to help him get an Army horse contract. **1939 57m/B** Ken Maynard, Eleanor Stewart, Walter Long, Tom London; **D:** Max Alexander. **VHS** $19.95 NOS, DVT, HEG ♪½

Flaming Signal Featuring Flash the Wonder Labrador, this action-packed film deals with a pilot who crash-lands near a Pacific island, just as the natives, provoked by an exploitative German trader, are rising up against the whites. Both Flash and his master manage to rescue the missionary's pretty daughter. **1933 64m/B** Noah Beery Sr., Madeline Day, Carmelita Geraghty, Mischa Auer, Henry B. Walthall. **VHS, Beta, LV** $16.95 SNC, LSV, RXM ♪½

Flaming Star In 1870s Texas, a family with a white father and an Indian mother is caught in the midst of an Indian uprising. The mixed-blood youth, excellently played by Presley, must choose a side with tragic results for all. A stirring, well-written drama of frontier prejudice and one of Presley's best films. **1960 101m/C** Elvis Presley, Dolores Del Rio, Barbara Eden, Steve Forrest, John McIntire, Richard Jaeckel, L.Q. Jones; **D:** Don Siegel. **VHS, Beta** $14.98 FOX, MVD ♪♪♪

The Flaming Teen-Age Schlocky pseudo-documentary demonstrating the evils of drugs and alcohol. Exploitative, and the teenagers look really old. Cheaply made, and it shows. **1956 67m/B** Noel Reyburn, Ethel Barrett, Jerry Frank, Shirley Holmes; **D:** Irvin S. Yeaworth Jr., Charles Edwards. **VHS** $16.95 SNC ♪

The Flaming Urge A small town is plagued by mysterious fires. Could a pyromaniac be on the loose? **1953 67m/B** Harold Lloyd Jr., Cathy Downs. **VHS, Beta** $16.95 SNC ♪

The Flamingo Kid A Brooklyn teenager (Dillon) gets a summer job at a fancy beach club on Long Island. His father is a plumber, who remembers how to dream, but is also aware of how rough the world is on dreamers. Suddenly making lots of money at a mostly easy job, the kid is attracted to the high style of the local sports car dealer and gin rummy king, and finds his father's solid life a bore. By the end of the summer, he's learned the true value of both men, and the kind of man he wants to be. Excellent performances all around, nice ensemble acting among the young men who play Dillon's buddies. Great sound track. Film debut of Janet Jones, who seems a little old for her part as a California college sophomore. **1984 (PG-13) 100m/C** Matt Dillon, Hector Elizondo, Molly McCarthy, Martha Gehman, Richard Crenna, Jessica Walter, Carole Davis, Janet Jones, Fisher Stevens, Bronson Pinchot; **D:** Garry Marshall. **VHS, Beta, LV** $29.98 LIV, VES ♪♪♪

Flamingo Lead Maynard aids a female cavalry horse-raiser amid various western adversities. **1939 57m/B** Ken Maynard. **VHS, Beta** UHV ♪

Flamingo Road A scandalously entertaining melodrama in which Crawford portrays a carnival dancer who intrigues Scott and Brian in a small Southern town where the carnival stops. Crawford shines in a role that demands her to be both tough and sensitive in a corrupt world full of political backstabbing and sleazy characters. Remade as a TV movie and television soap-opera series in 1980. **1949 94m/B** Joan Crawford, Zachary Scott, David Brian, Sydney Greenstreet, Gertrude Michael, Gladys George, Virginia Huston, Fred Clark; **D:** Michael Curtiz; **W:** Edmund H. North, Robert Wilder. **VHS, LV** $19.98 MGM ♪♪♪

Flanagan Boy A prizefighter and his manager's loose wife conspire to drown her husband for more than one reason. Also known as "Bad Blonde." **AKA:** Bad Blonde. **1953 79m/B** GB Barbara Payton, Tony Wright. **VHS, Beta, LV** NO ♪

The Flash When police scientist Barry Allen is accidentally doused by chemicals and then struck by lightening the combination makes him into a new superhero. His super-strength and quickness help his quest in fighting crime in Central City where he's aided by fellow scientist Tina McGee (the only other person to know his secret). In this adventure, the Flash seeks out the violent and mesmerizing leader of a biker gang who caused the death of Barry's brother. Based on the DC comic book character, this is the pilot episode for the short-lived television series. The look is dark and stylized and not played for camp. **1990 94m/C** John Wesley Shipp, Amanda Pays, Michael Nader; **M:** Danny Elfman. **VHS, Beta, LV** $19.98 WAR ♪♪

Flash & Firecat A beautiful blonde and a crazy thief steal and race their way across the country in a dune buggy with the police hot on their trail.
1975 (PG) 90m/C Roger Davis, Tricia Sembera, Dub Taylor, Richard Kiel; *D:* Ferd Sebastian. **VHS, Beta** *NO* 🎬

Flash Challenger Frank Chan fights to reclaim some stolen gold meant to finance a revolution.
1969 90m/C **Beta $29.98** *TWE* 🎬

Flash Gordon Camp version of the adventures of Flash Gordon in outer space. This time, Flash and Dale Arden are forced by Dr. Zarkov to accompany him on a mission to far-off Mongo, where Ming the Merciless is threatening the destruction of Earth. Music by Queen.
1980 (PG) 111m/C Sam Jones, Melody Anderson, Chaim Topol, Max von Sydow, Ornella Muti, Timothy Dalton, Brian Blessed; *D:* Mike Hodges. **VHS, Beta, LV $39.95** *MCA* 🎬🎬

Flash Gordon Battles the Galactic Forces of Evil Flash Gordon returns to battle with Ming the Merciless in this collection of cartoon adventures.
1979 59m/C **VHS, Beta $19.95** *MED* 🎬½

Flash Gordon Conquers the Universe Ravaging plague strikes the earth and Flash Gordon undertakes to stop it. A serial in twelve chapters. *AKA:* Purple Death from Outer Space.
1940 240m/B Buster Crabbe, Carol Hughes, Charles Middleton, Frank Shannon. **VHS, Beta, 3/4U, Special order formats $49.95** *NOS, MRV, SNC* 🎬½

Flash Gordon: Mars Attacks the World The earth is plagued by the evil Ming, but Flash Gordon steps in. From the serial. *AKA:* The Deadly Rays From Mars; Flash Gordon's Trip to Mars.
1938 87m/B Buster Crabbe, Jean Rogers, Charles Middleton. **VHS, Beta, 3/4U, Special order formats $39.95** *CAB* 🎬½

Flash Gordon: Rocketship Re-edited from the original Flash Gordon serial in which Flash and company must prevent the planet Mongo from colliding with Earth. Good character acting and good clean fun. *AKA:* Spaceship to the Unknown; Perils from Planet Mongo; Space Soldiers; Atomic Rocketship.
1936 97m/B Buster Crabbe, Jean Rogers, Frank Shannon, Charles Middleton, Priscilla Lawson, Jack Lipson; *D:* Frederick Stephani. **VHS, Beta, 3/4U, Special order formats $29.95** *VYY, PSM, CAB* 🎬🎬½

Flash Gordon: Space Adventurer Join Flash Gordon, Dale Arden and Dr. Zarkov as they encounter all kinds of adventures while traveling through outer space.
1979 58m/C **VHS, Beta $19.95** *MED* 🎬

Flash Gordon: The Beast Men's Prey Flash and crew take on an alien menace in this brand new adventure from the King Features "Animated Comics" series.
1991 30m/C **VHS $9.99** *BFV* 🎬

Flash Gordon: Vol. 1 Join Flash Gordon and Dale Arden as they struggle to maintain peace in the galaxy in this pair of episodes from the series.
1953 60m/B Steve Holland, Irene Champlin. **VHS, Beta $29.95** *DVT* 🎬

Flash Gordon: Vol. 2 Flash and Dale continue their quest for intergalactic tranquility in this pair of episodes from the series.
1953 60m/B Steve Holland, Irene Champlin. **VHS, Beta $29.95** *DVT* 🎬

Flash Gordon: Vol. 3 The struggle for intergalactic peace continues as Flash Gordon battles Ming the Merciless in this pair of episodes from the series.
1953 60m/B **VHS, Beta $29.95** *DVT* 🎬

A Flash of Green A crooked politician is helping a construction firm exploit valuable waterfront property. He enlists the influence of a hesitant local journalist, who then falls for the woman leading the homeowner's conservation drive against the development plan. Made for American Playhouse and produced by costar Jordon. Based on the work of John D. MacDonald.
1985 122m/C Ed Harris, Blair Brown, Richard Jordan, George Coe; *W/D:* Victor Nunez. **VHS, Beta $59.95** *MED* 🎬🎬

Flashback FBI agent Sutherland's assignment sounds easy: escort aging 1960s radical Hopper to prison. But Hopper is cunning and decides not to go without a fight. He uses his brain to outwit the young Sutherland and to turn him against himself. Good moments between the two leads and with Kane, as a woman who never left the sixties behind.
1989 (R) 108m/C Dennis Hopper, Kiefer Sutherland, Carol Kane; *D:* Franco Amurri. **VHS, Beta, LV $89.99** *PAR* 🎬🎬🎬

Flashdance 18-year-old Alex wants to dance. She works all day as a welder (and has a hot affair going with her boss), dances at a local bar at night, and hopes someday to get enough courage to audition for a spot at the School of Ballet. Glossy music video redeemed somewhat by exciting choreography with Marine Jahan doing the dancing for Beals. Oscar-winning title song sung by Irene Cara. Inspired the torn-sweatshirt trend in fashion of the period. ♫Flashdance...What a Feeling; I Love Rock 'n Roll; Manhunt; Gloria; Lady, Lady, Lady; Seduce Me Tonight.
1983 (R) 95m/C Jennifer Beals, Michael Nouri, Belinda Bauer, Lilia Skala, Cynthia Rhodes, Sunny Johnson, Lee Ving, Kyle T. Heffner, Ron Karabatsos, Robert Wuhl, Elizabeth Sagal; *D:* Franca Pasut. Academy Awards '83: Best Song ("Flashdance...What a Feeling"); Nominations: Best Cinematography, Best Film Editing, Best Song ("Maniac"). **VHS, Beta, LV, 8mm $14.95** *PAR* 🎬🎬

Flashpoint A pair of Texas border patrolmen discover an abandoned jeep that contains a fortune in cash, apparently from the 1960s. As they try to figure out how it got there, they become prey to those who want to keep the secret. With this cast, flick ought to be better.
1984 (R) 95m/C Treat Williams, Kris Kristofferson, Tess Harper, Rip Torn, Miguel Ferrer, Roberts Blossom; *D:* William Tannen. **VHS, Beta, LV $79.99** *HBO* 🎬🎬

Flashpoint Africa When a news team follows a terrorist group's activities it winds up in a power struggle with terrifying consequences.
1984 99m/C Trevor Howard, Gayle Hunnicutt, James Faulkner. **VHS, Beta** *NO* 🎬½

Flat Top The training of Navy fighter pilots aboard "flat top" aircraft carriers during World War II provides the drama here. A strict commander is appreciated only after the war when the pilots realize his role in their survival. The film makes good use of actual combat footage; fast-paced and effective.
1952 85m/C Sterling Hayden, Richard Carlson, Keith Larsen, John Bromfield; *D:* Lesley Selander. **VHS, Beta, LV $9.98** *REP, FCT* 🎬🎬½

Flatbed Annie and Sweetiepie: Lady Truckers A couple of good ol' gals hit the road and encounter a variety of bad guys out to steal their truck. Made for television. *AKA:* Flatbed Annie.
1979 100m/C Annie Potts, Kim Darby, Harry Dean Stanton, Arthur Godfrey, Rory Calhoun, Bill Carter; *D:* Robert Greenwald. **VHS, Beta $79.99** *HBO* 🎬🎬

Flatfoot Tough police officer will let nothing stop him from finding and arresting drug smugglers. Good for laughs as well as lots of action. *AKA:* The Knock-Out Cop.
1978 (PG) 113m/C *IT GE* Bodo, Werner Pochat, Bud Spencer, Enzo Cannavale, Dagmar Lassander, Joe Stewardson; *D:* Steno. **VHS, Beta** *NO* 🎬🎬

Flatliners A group of medical students begin after-hours experimentation with death and out-of-body experiences. Some standard horror film images but Roberts and Sutherland create an energy that makes it worth watching.
1990 (R) 111m/C Kiefer Sutherland, Julia Roberts, William Baldwin, Oliver Platt, Kevin Bacon, Kimberly Scott, Joshua Rudoy; *D:* Joel Schumacher. **VHS, Beta, LV, 8mm $19.95** *COL* 🎬🎬

Fleischer Color Classics A compendium of 8 1930's Max Fleischer cartoons, including "An Elephant Never Forgets," "Dancing on the Moon," "Fresh Vegetable Mystery" and "Greedy Humpty Dumpty."
1939 55m/C **VHS, Beta $19.95** *VDM* 🎬🎬

Flesh An Andy Warhol-produced seedy urban farce about a bisexual street hustler who meets a variety of drug-addicted, deformed, and sexually deviant people. Dallesandro fans will enjoy his extensive exposure (literally).
1968 90m/C Joe Dallesandro, Geraldine Smith, Patti D'Arbanville; *D:* Paul Morrissey. **VHS, Beta** *PAR, FCT* 🎬🎬🎬

Flesh and Blood An unjustly convicted lawyer is released from prison to find out his wife has died. He vows revenge on those who falsely imprisoned him and assumes the disguise of a crippled beggar to begin his plot. Silent with musical score.
1922 75m/B Lon Chaney Sr.; *D:* Irving Cummings. **VHS, Beta, 8mm $16.95** *SNC, VYY, GVV* 🎬🎬

Flesh and Blood A rowdy group of 16th Century hellions makes off with a princess who is already spoken for and pillage and plunder their way to revenge. Hauer leads the motley group through sword fights, raids, and the like. Dutch director Verhoeven's first English language film. Not for children; with rape scenes, nudity, and graphic sex. *AKA:* The Rose and the Sword.
1985 (R) 126m/C Rutger Hauer, Jennifer Jason Leigh, Tom Burlinson, Susan Tyrrell; *D:* Paul Verhoeven. **VHS, Beta, LV $19.99** *LIV, VES, SIM* 🎬🎬½

Flesh and Blood Show Rehearsal turns into an execution ritual for a group of actors at a mysterious seaside theatre. Truth in titling: features blood, gore, and some sex. Shot in part in 3-D. *AKA:* Asylum of the Insane.
1973 (R) 93m/C *GB* Robin Askwith, Candace Glendenning, Tristan Rogers, Ray Brooks, Jenny Hanley, Luan Peters, Patrick Barr; *D:* Pete Walker. **VHS, Beta $59.95** *MON* 🎬

The Flesh and the Devil Classic Garbo at her seductive best as a woman who causes a feud between two friends. Gilbert is an Austrian officer, falls for the married Garbo and winds up killing her husband in a duel. Banished to the African Corps he asks

his best friend (Hanson) to look after his lady love. But Hanson takes his job too seriously, falling for the lady himself. Great silent movie with surprise ending to match. The first Gilbert and Garbo pairing.
1927 112m/B John Gilbert, Greta Garbo, Lars Hanson, Barbara Kent, George Fawcett, Eugenie Besserer; *D:* Clarence Brown. **VHS $29.95** *MGM ℤℤℤ½*

Flesh and the Spur A cowboy tracks the killer of his brother. Future Mannix Mike Connors (nicknamed 'Touch' at the time) joins the search. Unedifying western with oddball touches, notably a theme song by Chipmunks creator Ross Bagdasarian.
1957 78m/C John Agar, Maria English, Mike Connors, Raymond Hatton, Maria Monay, Joyce Meadows, Kenne Duncan; *D:* Edward L. Cahn. **VHS $15.95** *NOS, LOO ℤ½*

The Flesh Eaters A claustrophobic low-budget thriller about a film queen and her secretary who crash-land on an island inhabited by your basic mad scientist. His latest experiment is with tiny flesh-eating sea creatures. Shock ending.
1964 87m/C Martin Kosleck, Rita Morley, Byron Sanders, Barbara Wilkin, Ray Tudor; *D:* Jack Curtis. **VHS, Beta $39.95** *SNC ℤ½*

Flesh Eating Mothers Housewives are transformed into cannibals after a mystery virus hits their town. Their kids must stop the moms from eating any more people.
1989 90m/C Robert Lee Oliver, Donatella Hecht, Valorie Hubbard, Neal Rosen, Terry Hayes; *D:* James Aviles Martin. **VHS, Beta $14.95** *ACA ℤ*

Flesh Feast Classically horrendous anti-Nazi bosh, in which a mad female plastic surgeon (Lake) rejuvenates Hitler and then tortures him to death with maggots to avenge her mother's suffering. Lake's last film, and the sorriest sign-off any actress ever had.
1969 (R) 72m/C Veronica Lake, Phil Philbin, Heather Hughes, Martha Mischon, Yanka Mann, Dian Wilhite, Chris Martell; *D:* Brad F. Ginter. **VHS, Beta $39.95** *WWV Woof!*

Flesh Gordon Soft-core spoof of the "Flash Gordon" series. Flesh takes it upon himself to save Earth from the evil Wang's sex ray; Wang, of course, being the leader of the planet Porno. Lackluster special effects and below par story dull an already ridiculous movie. Look for cameo by real-life porn starlet Candy Samples.
1972 70m/C Jason Williams, Suzanne Fields, Joseph Hudgins, John Hoyt, Howard Zieff, Michael Benveniste; *Cameos:* Candy Samples; *D:* Mike Light. **VHS, Beta, LV $19.98** *MED, IME ℤ*

Fleshburn An Indian Vietnam War veteran escapes from a mental institution to get revenge on the four psychiatrists who committed him.
1984 (R) 91m/C Steve Kanaly, Karen Carlson, Sonny Landham, Macon McCalman; *D:* George Gage. **VHS, Beta $59.95** *MED ℤℤ*

Fletch Somewhat charming comedy. When newspaper journalist Fletch goes undercover to get the scoop on the local drug scene, a wealthy young businessman enlists his help in dying. Something's rotten in Denmark when the man's doctor knows nothing of the illness and Fletch comes closer to the drug scene than he realizes. Throughout the entire film, Chevy Chase assumes a multitude of flippant comic characters to discover the truth. Based on Gregory McDonald's novel.
1985 (PG) 98m/C Chevy Chase, Tim Matheson, Joe Don Baker, Dana Wheeler-Nicholson, M. Emmet Walsh, Kenneth Mars, Geena Davis, Richard Libertini, George Wendt, Kareem Abdul-Jabbar, Alison La Placa; *D:* Michael Ritchie. **VHS, Beta, LV $14.95** *MCA ℤℤ*

Fletch Lives In this sequel to "Fletch," Chase is back again as the super-reporter. When Fletch learns of his inheritance of a Southern estate he is eager to claim it. During his down-home trip he becomes involved in a murder and must use his disguise skills to solve it before he becomes the next victim. Based on the novels of Gregory MacDonald.
1989 (PG) 95m/C Chevy Chase, Hal Holbrook, Julianne Phillips, Richard Libertini, Lee Ermey, Cleavon Little; *D:* Michael Ritchie. **VHS, Beta, LV $14.95** *MCA ℤℤ*

Flicks A compilation of skits parodying the tradition of Saturday afternoon matinees, including coming attractions and a cartoon. Never released theatrically. *AKA:* Hollyweird; Loose Joints.
1985 (R) 79m/C Martin Mull, Joan Hackett, Pamela Sue Martin, Betty Kennedy, Richard Belzer; *D:* Peter Winograd. **VHS, Beta $69.95** *MED ℤℤ*

The Flight A non-narrative view of glider planes as they soar over the countryside and rivers of the Laurentians and Canadian Rockies. Useful in language arts classes.
1989 96m/C Eli Danker, Sandy McPeak, Lindsay Wagner; *D:* Paul Wendkos. **VHS, Beta, LV $79.95** *VES, IME ℤℤ*

Flight from Glory A group of pilots fly supplies over the Andes from their isolated base camp to even more isolated mines. Morris is their leader who watches as, one by one, the men are killed on their dangerous flights. To make a bad situation worse, Heflin arrives as a new recruit - along with his pretty wife.
1937 66m/B Chester Morris, Onslow Stevens, Whitney Bourne, Van Heflin; *D:* Lew Landers. **VHS, Beta** *RKO ℤℤ½*

Flight from Singapore Transporting desperately needed blood to Malaysia, a flight crew is forced to crash land in the jungle. Nicely done if trite.
1962 74m/B *GB* Patrick Allen, Patrick Holt, William Abney, Harry Fowler; *W/D:* Dudley Birch. **VHS, Beta $16.95** *SNC ℤ½*

Flight from Vienna A high-ranking Hungarian security officer, disenchanted with communism, stages a daring escape from his country. In Vienna, he asks the British for political asylum, but is sent back to Hungary to help a scientist escape in order to prove his loyalty. Cold war drama hangs together on strength of Bikel's performance.
1958 54m/B Theodore Bikel, John Bentley, Donald Gray. **VHS, Beta $24.95** *VYY ℤℤ*

Flight of Black Angel Wacked-out F-16 pilot fancies himself an angel of death, and, after annihilating a number of trainees, sets out to make Las Vegas a nuked-out ghost town. Squadron commander Strauss, however, is not pleased with his pilot's initiative. Written by Henry Dominic, the script runs out of gas and heads into a nosedive. Made for cable TV.
1991 (R) 102m/C Peter Strauss, William O'Leary, James O'Sullivan, Michael Keys Hall; *D:* Jon Mostow. **VHS $89.95** *VMK ℤℤ½*

Flight of Dragons This animated tale takes place between the Age of Magic and the Age of Science, in a century when dragons ruled the skies.
1982 98m/C *D:* Arthur Rankin Jr., Jules Bass; *V:* John Ritter, Victor Buono, James Earl Jones. **VHS, Beta $19.98** *WAR, WTA ℤℤ*

A Flight of Rainbirds In a dual role, Krabbe plays a biologist who dreams he must lose his virginity within a week or die and his alter ego who joins him in the search for the perfect woman. In Dutch with English subtitles.
1981 94m/C *NL* Jeroen Krabbe; *D:* Ate De Jong. **VHS, LV $79.95** *TAM ℤℤ*

Flight of the Eagle Based on the actual ill-fated expedition of Salomon Andree who, with two friends, attempted to fly from Sweden to the North Pole in a hydrogen balloon in 1897. The last half of the film drags somewhat as the three struggle to survive in the frozen north after their balloon crashes. Beautifully photographed adventure. In Swedish with English subtitles.
1982 115m/C *SW* Max von Sydow, Goran Stangertz, Clement Harari, Sverre Anker; *D:* Jan Troell. **VHS, Beta, LV $24.95** *AHV ℤℤ½*

Flight of the Grey Wolf A tame, innocent wolf is mistaken for a killer and must run for his life with the help of his boy-owner.
1976 82m/C Bill Williams, Barbara Hale, Jeff East. **VHS, Beta $69.95** *DIS ℤ½*

Flight of the Intruder Vietnam naval pilots aboard an aircraft carrier don't like the way the war is being handled, so they go rogue and decide to go on a mission to bomb an enemy air base in Hanoi. Loads of male bonding.
1990 (PG-13) 115m/C Danny Glover, Willem Dafoe, Brad Johnson, Rosanna Arquette, Tom Sizemore; *D:* John Milius. **VHS, Beta, LV $14.95** *PAR ℤ½*

Flight of the Navigator A boy boards an alien spacecraft and embarks on a series of time-travel adventures with a crew of wisecracking extraterrestrial creatures. When he returns home eight years later, a NASA investigation ensues. Paul Reubens, better known as Pee Wee Herman, provides the voice of the robot.
1986 (PG) 90m/C Joey Cramer, Veronica Cartwright, Cliff DeYoung, Sarah Jessica Parker, Matt Adler, Howard Hesseman; *D:* Randal Kleiser; *V:* Paul Reubens. **VHS, Beta, LV $19.99** *DIS ℤℤ½*

The Flight of the Phoenix A group of men stranded in the Arabian desert after a plane crash attempt to rebuild their plane in order to escape before succumbing to the elements. Big budget, all-star survival drama based on the novel by Elleston Trevor.
1965 147m/C James Stewart, Richard Attenborough, Peter Finch, Hardy Kruger, Dan Duryea, George Kennedy, Ernest Borgnine, Ian Bannen; *D:* Robert Aldrich. **VHS, Beta, LV $19.98** *FOX ℤℤℤ*

Flight to Fury A cheap independent adventure film, featuring the novice Hellman-Nicholson team, about a few assorted mercenaries searching for a horde of diamonds when their plane crashes in the wilderness of the Philippines. Nicholson also wrote the script from a story by the director and producer.
1966 73m/B Jack Nicholson, Dewey Martin, Fay Spain, Vic Diaz, Jacqueline Hellman; *D:* Monte Hellman; *W:* Jack Nicholson. **VHS, Beta $59.95** *WAR ℤ½*

Flight to Mars An expedition crash lands on the red planet and discovers an advanced underground society that wants to invade earth using the U.S. spacecraft. Includes previews of coming attractions from classic science fiction films. First movie of this genre to be shot in color.
1952 72m/C Cameron Mitchell, Marguerite Chapman, Arthur Franz; *D:* Lesley Selander. **VHS, Beta, LV $19.95** *MED, IME ℤℤ*

Flight to Nowhere An FBI agent tracks down a stolen map of atomic bomb source material with the help of a charter pilot and a dizzy blonde. Muddled plot and no discernable acting.
1946 74m/B Alan Curtis, Evelyn Ankers, Jack Holt; *D:* William Rowland. VHS, Beta, LV $16.95 SNC, WGE, VYY *Woof!*

Flights of Fancy The renowned animators, Faith and John Hubley, produced several whimsical short subjects through the '50s and '60s. This tape includes several, including: "The Adventure of an *," "Moonbird," "Windy Day" and "Zuckerkandl."
1986 45m/C Faith Hubley, John Hubley. VHS, Beta $49.95 DIS 🎞🎞🎞

Flim-Flam Man A con man teams up with an army deserter to teach him the fine art of flim-flamming as they travel through small southern towns. Love may lead the young man back to the straight and narrow, but not his reprobate mentor. Scott is wonderful; and the slapstick episodes move at a good pace. *AKA:* One Born Every Minute.
1967 104m/C George C. Scott, Michael Sarrazin, Slim Pickens, Sue Lyon, Jack Albertson, Harry Morgan; *D:* Irvin Kershner; *M:* Jerry Goldsmith. VHS, Beta $59.98 FOX 🎞🎞

The Flintstones The foibles of the two Stone Age families, the Flintstones and the Rubbles, are chronicled in these two animated episodes of the classic series.
1960 50m/C *V:* Alan Reed, Mel Blanc, Jean Vander Pyl, Bea Benadaret. VHS, Beta $29.95 TTC 🎞🎞

The Flintstones: Dino & Juliet When that jerk Loudrock moves next door, he and Fred Flintstone just don't get along! But Dino has goo-goo eyes for the noisy neighbor's poodle. Also includes some Hanna-Barbera trivia!
1989 30m/C *V:* Alan Reed, Mel Blanc, Jean VanDerPyl. VHS, Beta $9.95 TTC, WTA 🎞🎞

The Flintstones Meet Rockula & Frankenstone Fred, Wilma, Barney and Betty win a trip to Rocksylvania and meet up with Count Rockula and his monster, Frankenstone. "Flintstones' New Neighbors!" is also included.
1980 75m/C VHS, Beta, LV $29.95 TTC, WOV, WTA 🎞🎞

Flipper A fisherman's son befriends an injured dolphin, is persuaded to return him to the wild, and earns the animal's gratitude. Prime kids' fare, as its sequels and television series attest.
1963 87m/C Chuck Connors, Luke Halpin, Kathleen Maguire, Connie Scott; *D:* James B. Clark. VHS, Beta $19.98 MVD, MGM 🎞🎞🎞

Flipper's New Adventure Believing they are to be separated, Flipper and Sandy travel to a remote island. Little do they know, a British family is being held for ransom on the island they have chosen. It's up to the duo to save the day. An enjoyable, nicely done family adventure. *AKA:* Flipper and the Pirates.
1964 103m/C Luke Halprin, Pamela Franklin, Tom Helmore, Francesca Annis, Brian Kelly, Joe Higgins, Ricou Browning; *D:* Leon Benson. VHS, Beta $19.98 MGM, FCT 🎞🎞🎞

Flipper's Odyssey Flipper has disappeared and his adopted family goes looking for him, but when one of the boys gets trapped in a cave, Flipper is his only hope.
1966 77m/C Luke Halprin, Brian Kelly, Tommy Norden; *D:* Paul Landres. VHS, Beta $59.95 PSM 🎞🎞

Flirtation Walk West point musical that has cadet Powell falling in love with the general's daughter (Keeler), who is already engaged to lieutenant Eldredge. Some fairly good numbers, including "Mr. and Mrs. Is The Name," and "Flirtation Walk." In an attempt to change her image, Keeler hardly dances at all, which is too bad for the viewer. Based on a story by Lou Edelman and Delmer Daves.
1934 98m/B Dick Powell, Ruby Keeler, Pat O'Brien, Ross Alexander; *D:* Frank Borzage; *W:* Delmer Daves. VHS $19.98 MGM 🎞🎞½

Flirting Set in an Australian boarding school in 1965, this charming film follows the misadventures of the adolescent Danny Embling. Danny has the misfortune to be both bright and sensitive which puts him seriously at odds with his masculine peers. He then finds love with an outcast at the neighboring girls boarding school. Thandiwe is a beautiful, poised black diplomat's daughter from Uganda who's slowly drawn to the awkward Danny. Kidman has a supporting role as a snobbish older boarding school girl, not quite as bad as she seems. Tender and amusing. The second of director Duigan's coming-of-age trilogy, preceded by "The Year My Voice Broke" (the third film is not yet completed).
1989 (R) 100m/C *AU* Noah Taylor, Thandie Newton, Nicole Kidman, Bartholomew Rose, Felix Nobis, Josh Picker, Kiri Paramore, Marc Gray, Joshua Marshall, David Wieland, Craig Black; *W/D:* John Duigan. VHS, LV $94.95 VMK 🎞🎞🎞

Flirting with Fate Early Fairbanks-cum-acrobat vehicle. Having hired a hitman to rub himself out, a young man decides he doesn't want to die, after all. Seems there's a girl involved.
1916 51m/B Douglas Fairbanks Sr., Jewel Carmen, Howard Gaye, William E. Lawrence, George Beranger, Dorothy Hadel, Lillian Langdon; *D:* Christy Cabanne. VHS, Beta $24.95 NOS, GPV, FCT 🎞🎞🎞

Flood! Irwin Allen's first made-for-television disaster film. A dam bursts and devastates a small town, so a helicopter pilot must save the day. Good cast is swept along in a current of disaster-genre cliches.
1976 98m/C Robert Culp, Martin Milner, Barbara Hershey, Richard Basehart, Carol Lynley, Roddy McDowall, Cameron Mitchell, Teresa Wright, Francine York; *D:* Earl Bellamy. VHS, Beta $59.95 WAR 🎞🎞

The Floorwalker Chaplin becomes involved with a dishonest floorwalker in a department store. Silent.
1917 20m/B Charlie Chaplin; *D:* Charlie Chaplin. VHS, Beta, 3/4U, Special order formats CAB 🎞🎞🎞

The Floorwalker/By the Sea Two early Chaplin short comedies, featuring a hilarious scene on an escalator in the first film. Silent.
1915 51m/B Charlie Chaplin, Edna Purviance, Eric Campbell; *D:* Charlie Chaplin. VHS, Beta, 8mm $24.95 VYY 🎞🎞🎞

Flor Silvestre The son of a rich rancher romances a young woman against the background of the Mexican Revolution. *AKA:* Wild Flower.
1958 90m/B *MX* Dolores Del Rio, Pedro Armendariz Sr.; *D:* Emilio Fernandez. VHS, Beta $64.95 MAD 🎞

The Florida Connection An action thriller set in the Florida Swamps with a collection of villains and a vague plot about smuggling.
1974 90m/C Dan Pastorini, June Wilkinson. VHS, Beta $9.95 UNI 🎞

Florida Straits A recently released Cuban prisoner hires a few losers and their boat to return to the island, supposedly to find the girl he loves. The real quest is for gold buried during the Bay-of-Pigs invasion in this none-too-original made-for-cable movie that at least offers a good cast.
1987 (PG-13) 98m/C Raul Julia, Fred Ward, Daniel H. Jenkins, Antonio Fargas; *D:* Mike Hodges. VHS, Beta, LV $19.98 ORI 🎞🎞

Flower Angel The Flower Angel and her friends, a white kitty and a lovable brown dog, are searching for the Flower of Seven Colors. In their travels they help a lonely old man and his beautiful daughter find the love they have for each other.
1980 46m/C VHS, Beta $29.95 FHE 🎞🎞

Flower Drum Song The Rodgers and Hammerstein musical played better on Broadway than in this overblown adaptation of life in San Francisco's Chinatown. Umeki plays the young girl who arrives from Hong Kong for an arranged marriage. Her intended (Soo) is a fast-living nightclub owner already enjoying the love of singer Kwan. Meanwhile Umeki falls for the handsome Shigeta. Naturally, everything comes together in a happy ending. ♫I Enjoy Being A Girl; Don't Marry Me; Grant Avenue; You Are Beautiful; A Hundred Million Miracles; Fan Tan Fanny; Chop Suey; The Other Generation; I Am Going to Like It Here; Love Look Away; Sunday.
1961 133m/C Nancy Kwan, Jack Soo, James Shigeta, Miyoshi Umeki, Juanita Hall; *D:* Henry Koster; *M:* Richard Rodgers, Oscar Hammerstein. VHS, Beta, LV $39.98 MCA, FCT, PIA 🎞🎞

Flowers in the Attic Based on the V.C. Andrews bestseller, a would-be thriller about four young siblings locked for years in their family's old mansion by their grandmother with their mother's selfish acquiescence. A chicken-hearted, clumsy flop that skimps on the novel's trashier themes.
1987 (PG-13) 93m/C Victoria Tennant, Kristy Swanson, Louise Fletcher, Jeb Stuart Adams; *D:* Jeffrey Bloom. VHS, Beta, LV $19.95 NWV, STE 🎞½

The Flowers of St. Francis Rossellini's presentation of St. Francis and his friars' attainment of spiritual harmony. In Italian with English subtitles. This is the British release version, 10-15 minutes longer than the U.S. version.
1950 75m/B *IT* Federico Fellini; *D:* Roberto Rossellini. VHS, Beta $34.95 FCT 🎞🎞🎞

Flush Unorthodox comedy involving funny noises.
1981 90m/C William Calloway, William Bronder, Jeannie Linero; *D:* Andrew J. Kuehn. VHS TPV 🎞🎞

Flush It While working in the honey factory, Harvey finds a clue that leads him on a wild escapade in search of a buried treasure. Surprises abound along the way.
1976 (R) 90m/C VHS, Beta NO 🎞

The Flustered Comedy of Leon Errol The popular Depression-era comedian Errol is showcased in three shorts: "Crime Rave," "Man-I-Cured," and "A Panic in the Parlor."
1939 56m/B Leon Errol, Vivian Tobin, Dorothy Granger, Frank Faylen, Virginia Vale. VHS, Beta, 8mm $24.95 VYY 🎞🎞

The Fly The historic, chillingly original '50s sci-fi tale about a hapless scientist experimenting with teleportation who accidentally gets anatomically confused with a housefly. Campy required viewing; two sequels fol-

lowed, and a 1986 remake which itself has spawned one sequel.
1958 94m/C Vincent Price, David Hedison, Herbert Marshall, Patricia Owens; *D:* Kurt Neumann. **VHS, Beta, LV** $14.98 FOX ✗✗✗

The Fly A sensitive, humanistic remake of the 1958 horror film about a scientist whose flesh is genetically intermixed with a housefly via his experimental transportation device. A thoughtful, shocking horror film, with fine performances from Goldblum and Davis and a brutally emotional conclusion. Followed by "The Fly II" in 1989.
1986 (R) 96m/C Jeff Goldblum, Geena Davis, John Getz; *D:* David Cronenberg. **VHS, Beta, LV** $19.98 FOX ✗✗✗

The Fly 2 Inferior sequel to Cronenberg's opus, in which the offspring of Seth Brundle achieves full genius maturity in three years, falls in love, and discovers the evil truth behind his father's teleportation device and the corporate auspices that backed it.
1989 (R) 105m/C Eric Stoltz, Daphne Zuniga, Lee Richardson, John Getz, Harley Cross; *D:* Chris Walas. **VHS, Beta, LV** $19.98 FOX, CCB ✗✗½

Fly with the Hawk A troubled teenager gets lost in the wilderness for a year, and learns some important things from nature to take back to civilization.
19?? 90m/C Peter Ferri, Peter Snook, Shelley Lynne Speigel; *D:* Robert Tanos. **VHS** NO ✗✗

Flying Blind Foreign agents are thwarted in their attempt to steal a vital air defense secret. Unconvincing espionage plot cobbled into a story about a Los Angeles-Las Vegas puddle jumper.
1941 69m/B Richard Arlen, Jean Parker, Marie Wilson. **VHS, Beta** $24.95 NOS, DVT, TIM ✗✗½

The Flying Deuces Ollie's broken heart lands Laurel and Hardy in the Foreign Legion. The comic pair escape a firing squad only to suffer a plane crash that results in Hardy's reincarnation as a horse. A musical interlude with a Laurel soft shoe while Hardy sings "Shine On, Harvest Moon" is one of the film's highlights. *AKA:* Flying Aces.
1939 65m/B Stan Laurel, Oliver Hardy, Jean Parker, Reginald Gardiner, James Finlayson; *D:* Edward Sutherland. **VHS, Beta, LV, 3/4U, Special order formats** $9.95 NEG, MRV, NOS ✗✗✗

Flying Discman from Mars A Martian warlord battles a brave pilot and his secretary in this exciting serial not seen in 30 years. The original 12 episodes are edited together on two cassettes.
1951 167m/B **VHS** $29.98 REP, MLB ✗✗✗

Flying Down to Rio The first Astaire-Rogers musical, although they are relegated to supporting status behind Del Rio and Raymond. Still, it was enough to make them stars and a team that epitomizes the height of American musical films. The slim story revolves around singer Del Rio's two suitors and receives a splendid, art deco production, featuring Vincent Voumans' score. Showgirls dancing on plane wings in flight provide another memorable moment. ♫Music Makes Me; The Carioca; Orchids in the Moonlight; Flying Down to Rio.
1933 89m/B Fred Astaire, Ginger Rogers, Dolores Del Rio, Eric Blore, Gene Raymond, Franklin Pangborn; *D:* Thornton Freeland. **VHS, Beta** $19.95 MED, TTC ✗✗✗

The Flying Fool Two flying brothers battle for the charms of a sexy singer.
1929 75m/B William Boyd, Marie Prevost, Russell Gleason; *D:* Tay Garnett; *W:* Russell Gleason. **VHS, Beta** RXM, VYY ✗✗

Flying from the Hawk A 12-year-old boy sees something he shouldn't and soon finds that his friends and relatives are mysteriously vanishing.
1986 110m/C John Ireland, Diane McBain. **VHS, Beta** $19.95 NEG ✗½

Flying Karamazov Brothers Comedy Hour The wild and crazy Karamazov brothers show what they can do in this fun-filled video of comedy, acrobatics, and juggling.
1983 59m/C The Flying Karamazov Brothers. **VHS, Beta** $19.98 MCG ✗½

Flying Leathernecks Tough squadron leader Wayne fights with his fellow officer Ryan in Guadalcanal when their leadership styles clash. But when the real fighting begins all is forgotten as Wayne leads his men into victorious battle, winning the admiration and devotion of his fliers. Memorable World War II film deals with war in human terms.
1951 102m/C John Wayne, Robert Ryan, Janis Carter; *D:* Nicholas Ray. **VHS, Beta, LV** $19.98 RKO, VID, TLF ✗✗✗

The Flying Saucer U.S. and Russian scientists clash over their search for a huge flying saucer that is hidden under a glacier. The first movie to deal with flying saucers. The cassette includes animated opening and closing sequences plus previews of coming attractions.
1950 120m/B Mikel Conrad, Pat Garrison, Hanz von Teuffen; *D:* Mikel Conrad. **VHS, Beta** $14.95 RHI, MWP, UHV ✗½

Flying Saucers Over Hollywood: The Plan 9 Companion This documentary looks at what many consider to be the worst film of all time, "Plan 9 from Outer Space," released in 1959. The cult classic, directed by the equally bizarre Edward D. Wood, Jr., is revealed in all its absurdity, including interviews with cast, crew, and fans.
1993 111m/C **VHS** $24.95 ATM ✗½

The Flying Scotsman A fired railroad worker tries to wreck an express train on the engineer's last journey. The daughter of the intended victim saves the day. Silent, with sound added.
1929 60m/B Ray Milland, Pauline Johnson, Moore Marriot; *D:* Castleton Knight. **VHS, Beta** $24.95 NOS, DVT, TIM ✗½

Flying Tigers Salutes the All-American Volunteer Group which flew for China under General Claire Chennault against the Japanese before the U.S. entered World War II. A squadron leader and a brash new recruit both vie for the affections of a pretty nurse in-between their flying missions. Romance and a few comic touches take a back seat to graphic scenes of aerial battles and dramatization of heroic sacrifice in this rousing war film.
1942 101m/B John Wayne, Paul Kelly, John Carroll, Anna Lee, Mae Clarke, Gordon Jones; *D:* David Miller. **VHS, LV** $19.98 REP ✗✗½

Flying Wild A gang of saboteurs is out to steal top-secret airplane blueprints. Who else but the Bowery Boys could conceivably stop them? No Satch in this one.
1941 62m/B Leo Gorcey, Bobby Jordan, Donald Haines, Joan Barclay, David Gorcey, Bobby Stone, Sammy Morrison; *D:* William West. **VHS** $19.95 NOS, LOO, TIM ✗½

FM The disc jockeys at an L.A. radio station rebel in the name of rock'n'roll. Despite the promising cast and setting (Mull makes his movie debut as a memorable space case), this is just disjointed and surprisingly unhip;

one producer took his name off it due to creative difficulties. The decent soundtrack includes concert footage of Jimmy Buffet and Linda Ronstadt. ♫FM; Do It Again; FM Reprise; Livingston Saturday Night; The Key To My Kingdom; Green Grass and High Tides; Life In The Fast Lane; Bad Man; Poor, Poor, Pitiful Me; Love Me Tender; Life's Been Good To Me; Cold As Ice; Feels Like the First Time; Slow Ride; Night Moves; Sentimental Lady; Fly Like An Eagle; Just The Way You Are; Lido Shuffle; Hollywood; Your Smiling Face; We Will Rock You; More Than A Feeling. *AKA:* Citizen's Band.
1978 (PG-13) 104m/C Eileen Brennan, Alex Karras, Cleavon Little, Martin Mull, Cassie Yates, Linda Ronstadt, Jimmy Buffett; *D:* Lamont Johnson. **VHS, LV** $14.98 MCA, PIA ✗✗

The Fog John Carpenter's blustery follow-up to his success with "Halloween." An evil fog containing murderous, vengeful ghosts envelops a sleepy seaside town and subjects the residents to terror and mayhem.
1978 (R) 91m/C Hal Holbrook, Adrienne Barbeau, Jamie Lee Curtis, Janet Leigh, John Houseman; *D:* John Carpenter. **VHS, Beta, LV, 8mm** $14.95 COL, SUE ✗✗

Fog Island Murder and terror lurk after a greedy inventor, who was framed for fraud by his business partner, is released from prison. He plots revenge by inviting his foes to his island home.
1945 72m/B George Zucco, Lionel Atwill, Terry Morse, Jerome Cowan; *D:* Terry Morse. **VHS, Beta** $19.95 NOS, SNC, VCN ✗½

Foghorn Leghorn's Fractured Funnies Eight Leghorn classic shorts, including "Plop Goes the Weasel," "Feather Dusted," and "The Foghorn Leghorn." "I say...I say...boy, let go of my leg."
1952 58m/C *D:* Robert McKimson, Chuck Jones, Friz Freleng, Bob Clampett. **VHS, Beta** $12.95 WAR, WTA ✗✗

Folks! Selleck is a successful Chicago stockbroker who finds his world crashing down on him. His wife and kids have left him, the FBI is after him, and, worst of all, his parents have moved in with him. His parents don't want to be a burden, so Selleck decides that the best way to solve his financial woes is to help his parents commit suicide so he can collect on their insurance policies. The parents help by driving their car into oncoming traffic. In the meantime, Selleck receives numerous injuries, including a black eye, a dog bite, broken fingers, a broken leg, and an amputated toe. Tasteless comedy that makes fun of aging and Alzheimer's Disease. Selleck is too sweet and cuddly for his role, but Ameche is good as the senile father, and Ebersole is great as Selleck's unpleasant sister.
1992 (PG-13) 109m/C Tom Selleck, Don Ameche, Anne Jackson, Christine Ebersole, Wendy Crewson, Robert Pastorelli, Michael Murphy, Kevin Timothy Chevalia, Margaret Murphy; *D:* Ted Kotcheff. **VHS** FXV ✗

Follies Girl There's folly in expecting that this wartime tuner would hold up today. An army private romances a dress designer and a musical show somehow results. ♫Keep the Flag A-Flying; No Man In The House; Someone to Love; I Told A Lie; Shall We Gather at the Rhythm?; Fascination; I Knew Your Father's Son; Thoity Poiple Boids.
1943 74m/B Wendy Barrie, Doris Nolan, Gordon Oliver, Anne Barrett, Arthur Pierson; *D:* William Rowland. **VHS** $15.95 NOS, LOO ✗

Follies in Concert A filmed record of the famed Stephen Sondheim musical play, performed at Lincoln Center in New York with an all-star cast. Songs include "I'm Still

Here,'' ''Losing My Mind,'' ''Broadway Baby'' and ''The Ladies Who Lunch.''
1985 90m/C Carol Burnett, Lee Remick, Betty Comden, Andre Gregory, Adolph Green, Mandy Patinkin, Phyllis Newman, Elaine Stritch, Jim Walton, Licia Albanese. **VHS, Beta, LV $19.95** *MVD, FRH* 🎬🎬

Follow Me Round-the-world odyssey of three moon doggies searching for adventure—and the perfect wave. Spectacular surfing scenes are complemented by songs performed by Dino, Desi, and Billy.
1969 (G) 90m/C Claude Codgen, Mary Lou McGinnis, Bob Purvey; *D:* Gene McCabe. **VHS, 3/4U, Q, Special order formats** *BEI* 🎬🎬

Follow Me, Boys! A Disney film about a simple man who decides to put down roots and enjoy the quiet life, after one year too many on the road with a ramshackle jazz band. That life is soon interrupted when he volunteers to lead a high-spirited boy scout troop.
1966 120m/C Fred MacMurray, Vera Miles, Lillian Gish, Charlie Ruggles, Elliott Reid, Kurt Russell, Luanna Patten, Ken Murray; *D:* Norman Tokar. **VHS, Beta $69.95** *DIS* 🎬🎬🎬

Follow Me Quietly Serial strangler who only kills in the rain is stalked by Lundigan. Very good little thriller which packs a punch in less than an hour.
1949 59m/B William Lundigan, Dorothy Patrick, Jeff Corey, Nestor Paiva, Charles D. Brown, Paul Guilfoyle; *D:* Richard Fleischer. **VHS, Beta $19.95** *TTC, MLB, RXM* 🎬🎬🎬

Follow That Camel Foreign Legion sergeant who invents acts of heroism finally gets a chance to really help out a friend in need. Part of the ''Carry On'' series.
1967 95m/C *GB* Phil Silvers, Kenneth Williams, Anita Harris, Jim Dale; *D:* Gerald Thomas. **VHS, Beta $29.95** *VID* 🎬½

Follow That Car Three southern kids become FBI agents and begin a thigh-slappin', rip-snortin' down-home escapade.
1980 (PG) 96m/C Dirk Benedict, Tanya Tucker, Teri Nunn; *D:* Daniel Haller. **VHS, Beta $59.98** *NLC* 🎬

Follow That Dream Elvis plays a musical hillbilly whose family is trying to homestead on government land along the sunny Florida coast. Based on Richard C. Powell's novel ''Pioneer Go Home.'' The songs-the only reason to see this movie—include ''Angel'', and ''What a Wonderful Life'', and the title track.
1961 111m/C Elvis Presley, Arthur O'Connell, Anne Helm, Simon Oakland, Jack Kruschen, Joanna Moore, Howard McNear; *D:* Gordon Douglas. **VHS, Beta $19.95** *MGM* 🎬🎬

Follow That Rainbow Believing that her long-lost father is a popular touring singer, a young lass pursues him from Switzerland to South Africa.
1966 90m/C Joe Stewardson, Memory Jane, Joan Bickhill. **VHS, Beta** *PGN* 🎬

Follow the Fleet A song-and-dance man joins the Navy and meets two sisters in need of help in this Rogers/Astaire bon-bon featuring a classic score by Irving Berlin. Look for Betty Grable, Lucille Ball, and Tony Martin in minor roles. Hilliard went on to be best known as the wife of Ozzie Nelson in TV's ''The Adventures of Ozzie and Harriet.'' 🎵Let's Face the Music and Dance; We Saw the Sea; I'm Putting All My Eggs In One Basket; Get Thee Behind Me, Satan; But Where Are You?; I'd Rather Lead a Band; Let Yourself Go.
1936 110m/B Fred Astaire, Ginger Rogers, Randolph Scott, Harriet Hilliard Nelson, Betty Grable, Lucille Ball; *D:* Mark Sandrich. **VHS, Beta, LV $29.95** *RKO, MED, TTC* 🎬🎬🎬

Follow the Leader On leave from the Army, Hall and Gorcey discover that one of the gang has been jailed on a trumped-up charge and set about finding the real culprit. 🎵Now and Then; All I Want to Do Play the Drums. *AKA:* East of the Bowery.
1944 65m/B Leo Gorcey, Huntz Hall, Gabriel Dell, Jack LaRue, Joan Marsh, Billy Benedict, Mary Gordon, Sammy Morrison; *D:* William Beaudine; *M:* Gene Austin, Sherrill Sisters. **VHS $19.95** *NOS* 🎬🎬

Food of the Gods On a secluded island giant rats, chickens, and other creatures crave human flesh, blood, bones, etc. This cheap, updated version of the H. G. Wells novel suffers from lousy performances and a lack of imagination.
1976 (PG) 88m/C Marjoe Gortner, Pamela Franklin, Ralph Meeker, Ida Lupino, Jon Cypher; *D:* Bert I. Gordon. **VHS, Beta $19.98** *LIV, VES* Woof!

Food of the Gods: Part 2 The killer beasts and animals of the first film (and of H.G. Wells' classic novel) strike again; gigantic rats maim young girls. Easily as bad as the original. *AKA:* Gnaw: Food of the Gods 2.
1988 (R) 93m/C Paul Coufos, Lisa Schrage; *D:* Damian Lee. **VHS, Beta, LV $9.99** *CCB, IVE* Woof!

Fool for Love Explores the mysterious relationship between a modern-day drifter and his long-time lover, who may or may not be his half-sister, as they confront each other in a seedy New Mexico motel. Adapted by Shepard from his play; music by George Burt.
1986 (R) 108m/C Sam Shepard, Kim Basinger, Randy Quaid, Harry Dean Stanton; *D:* Robert Altman. **VHS, Beta $14.95** *MGM* 🎬🎬

The Fool Killer In the post-Civil War south, a 12 year-old boy learns that a terrifying legend about an axe-murderer may be all too real. Offbeat film with striking visuals and photography. Debut film for Albert and another choice psycho role for Perkins. *AKA:* Violent Journey.
1965 100m/B Anthony Perkins, Edward Albert, Dana Elcar, Henry Hull, Salome Jens, Arnold Moss; *D:* Servando Gonzalez. **VHS $19.98** *REP* 🎬🎬½

A Fool There Was The rocket that blasted Theda Bara to stardom and launched the vamp film genre. One of the few extant Bara films, it tells the now familiar story of a good man whom crumbles from the heights of moral rectitude thanks to the inescapable influence of an unredeemable vamp. Bette Davis described Bara as ''divinely, hysterically, insanely malevolent.'' Much heavy emoting; subtitled (notoriously) ''Kiss Me, My Fool!'' Based on Rudyard Kipling's ''The Vampire.''
1914 70m/B Theda Bara, Edward Jose, Runa Hodges, Clifford Bruce; *D:* Frank Powell. **VHS, Beta $27.95** *GPV, FCT* 🎬🎬½

Foolin' Around An innocent Oklahoma farm boy arrives at college and falls in love with a beautiful heiress. He will stop at nothing to win her over, including crashing her lavish wedding ceremony.
1980 (PG) 101m/C Gary Busey, Annette O'Toole, Eddie Albert, Tony Randall, Cloris Leachman; *D:* Richard T. Heffron. **VHS, Beta $24.98** *SUE* 🎬🎬½

Foolish Wives A remake of Von Stroheim's classic depicting the confused milieu of post-war Europe as reflected through the actions of a bogus count and his seductive, corrupt ways. Comes as close as possible to the original film.

1922 107m/B Erich von Stroheim, Mae Busch, Maude George, Cesare Gravina, Harrison Ford; *D:* Erich von Stroheim. **VHS, Beta, LV $29.95** *KIV, CCB, HHT* 🎬🎬🎬½

Fools Two lonely people—he an aging horror film actor and she a young woman estranged from her husband—start a warm romance when they meet in San Francisco. The husband reacts violently. Good cast seems lost.
1970 (PG) 93m/C Jason Robards Jr., Katharine Ross, Scott Hylands; *D:* Tom Gries. **VHS, Beta $59.95** *PSM* 🎬

Fools of Fortune Adaptation of William Trevor's novel depicting Willie Clinton's childhood and adult experiences of family dramatics played against the backdrop of post-WWI Ireland. During the Irish war for independence, a family is attacked by British soldiers, creating emotional havoc for the survivors. Though well-acted and poignant, it's a rather disjointed and straying shamrock opera.
1990 (PG-13) 104m/C *GB* Mary Elizabeth Mastrantonio, Iain Glen, Julie Christie, Michael Kitchen, Sean McClory, Frankie McCafferty; *D:* Pat O'Connor. **VHS, LV $89.95** *COL, PIA, FCT* 🎬🎬½

Footlight Frenzy The Law Moan Spectacular comedy troupe are at it again as they perform a benefit play where everything goes wrong.
1984 110m/C *GB* Alan Shearman, Diz White, Ron House, Frances Tomelty, Michael Aldridge, Ron Pember. **VHS, Beta $39.95** *RKO* 🎬

Footlight Parade Broadway producer Cagney is out of work. Sound films have scared off his backers until his idea for staging live musical numbers before the cinema features lures them back. Lots of authentic backstage action precedes three spectacular Busby Berkeley-choreographed numbers that climax the film, including the giant water ballet featuring more than 100 performers. 🎵Ah, the Moon is Here; Sittin' on a Backyard Fence; Honeymoon Hotel; By A Waterfall; Shanghai Lil.
1933 104m/B James Cagney, Joan Blondell, Dick Powell, Ruby Keeler, Guy Kibbee, Ruth Donnelly; *D:* Lloyd Bacon. **Beta, LV, Q $19.98** *MGM, FOX* 🎬🎬🎬

Footlight Serenade A boxer falls for a beautiful dancer with whom he's costarring in a Broadway play. Unfortunately, she's secretly married to another of the actors and her husband is becoming jealous of the boxer's intentions. Light, fun musical. One of a series of Grable movies made to boost morale during World War II. 🎵Are You Kidding?; I'm Still Crazy About You; I Hear the Birdies Sing; Living High; I'll Be Marching to a Love Song; Land On Your Feet; I'm Stepping Out With a Memory Tonight.
1942 80m/B Betty Grable, Victor Mature, John Payne, Jane Wyman, Phil Silvers, James Gleason, Mantan Moreland; *D:* Gregory Ratoff. **VHS, Beta $19.98** *FOX* 🎬🎬½

Footloose When a city boy moves to a small Midwestern town, he discovers some disappointing news: rock music and dancing have been forbidden by the local government. Determined to bring some '80s-style life into the town, he sets about changing the rules and eventually enlists the help of the daughter of the man responsible for the law. Rousing music, talented young cast, and plenty of trouble make this an entertaining musical-drama. 🎵Footloose; Let's Hear it for the Boy; The Girl Gets Around; Dancing in the Sheets; Somebody's Eyes; Almost Paradise; I'm Free; Never; Holding Out for a Hero.

1984 (PG) 107m/C Kevin Bacon, Lori Singer, Christopher Penn, John Lithgow, Dianne Wiest, John Laughlin, Sarah Jessica Parker; *D:* Herbert Ross. VHS, Beta, LV, 8mm $14.95 PAR *ℐℐ*½

For a Few Dollars More The Man With No Name returns as a bounty hunter who teams up with a gunslinger/rival to track down the sadistic leader of a gang of bandits. Violent. Sequel to "A Fistful of Dollars" (1964) and followed by "The Good, The Bad, and The Ugly". Letterboxed laserdisc edition features the original movie trailer.
1965 (PG) 127m/C *IT* Clint Eastwood, Lee Van Cleef, Klaus Kinski, Gian Marie Volonte; *D:* Sergio Leone; *M:* Ennio Morricone. VHS, Beta, LV $19.95 FOX, MGM, PIA *ℐℐ*½

For Auld Lang Syne: The Marx Brothers Four classic comedy shorts: "Monkey Business Special," "Gai Dimanche," "Hooks and Jabs," and "For Auld Lang Syne."
1932 46m/B Chico Marx, Groucho Marx, Alan Marx, Harpo Marx. VHS, Beta VYY *ℐℐ*½

For Better and For Worse A nice young couple is planning to have your average nice wedding when one of their friends gets hold of an invitation and decides to jokingly invite the Pope to attend. But the joke is on them when the Pope accepts. Talk about upstaging the bride!
1992 (PG) 94m/C Patrick Dempsey, Kelly Lynch. VHS, LV $89.98 LIV *ℐℐ*½

For Heaven's Sake Lloyd's first film for Paramount has him making an accidental donation to a skid row mission, then marrying the preacher's daughter and converting all the neighborhood tough guys.
1926 60m/B Harold Lloyd, Jobyna Ralston, Noah Young, James Mason, Paul Weigel; *D:* Sam Taylor. VHS NO *ℐℐ*

For Heaven's Sake A bumbling basketball team is lent some heavenly assistance in the form of a meddling angel. But can he hit the jumper? Made for television.
1979 90m/C Ray Bolger, Kent McCord. VHS $49.99 LIV *ℐ*½

For Keeps Two high school sweethearts on the verge of graduating get married after the girl becomes pregnant, and suffer all the trials of teenage parenthood. Written by Tim Kazurinsky and Denise DeClure.
1988 (PG-13) 98m/C Molly Ringwald, Randall Batinkoff, Kenneth Mars; *D:* John G. Avildsen. VHS, Beta, LV $14.95 COL *ℐ*½

For Ladies Only A struggling actor takes a job as a male stripper to pay the rent. Among the leering ladies is Davis, daughter of former President Reagan. Made for television.
1981 100m/C Gregory Harrison, Patricia Davis, Dinah Manoff, Louise Lasser, Lee Grant, Marc Singer, Viveca Lindfors, Steven Keats; *D:* Mel Damski. VHS, Beta NO *ℐℐ*

For Love Alone A young Australian college co-ed in the 1930s falls in love with a handsome, controversial teacher and follows him to London, only to discover he's not her Mr. Right after all.
1986 102m/C *AU* Helen Buday, Sam Neill, Hugo Weaving; *D:* Stephen Wallace. VHS, Beta $69.95 LIV *ℐℐ*

For Love of Ivy Poitier is a trucking executive who has a gambling operation on the side. Ivy is the Black maid of a rich white family who is about to leave her job to look for romance. The two are brought together but the road to true love doesn't run smooth. Based on a story by Poitier.

1968 (PG) 102m/C Sidney Poitier, Abbey Lincoln, Beau Bridges, Carroll O'Connor, Nan Martin; *D:* Daniel Mann. VHS, Beta $19.98 FOX *ℐℐ*

For Love or Money A super-rich hotel owner wants her lawyer to find her three beautiful daughters. However, she doesn't trust him enough not to meddle in the search. Lavish production and a good cast can't overcome the mediocrity of the script and direction.
1963 108m/C Kirk Douglas, Mitzi Gaynor, Thelma Ritter, William Bendix, Julie Newmar, Gig Young, Leslie Parrish, William Windom, Richard Sargent; *D:* Michael Gordon. VHS NO *ℐℐ*

For Love or Money Made-for-television fare about game-show contestants finding money and romance.
1984 91m/C Jamie Farr, Suzanne Pleshette, Gil Gerard, Ray Walston, Lawrence Pressman, Mary Kay Place; *D:* Terry Hughes. VHS, Beta, 3/4U $39.95 IME *ℐ*½

For Love or Money A real estate man with Career on the mind has to choose between the woman in his life and the condo development that stands firmly between them and happily-ever-afterdom.
1988 (PG) ?m/C Timothy Daly, Haviland Morris, Kevin McCarthy. VHS $89.99 HBO *ℐℐ*

For Love or Money Romantic comedy starring Fox as a struggling hotel concierge who wants to open his own elegant hotel, but must first suck up to a slimy entrepreneur (Higgins) who claims he'll finance Fox's endeavors if he carries out certain duties. One of the jobs entails babysitting Higgins' beautiful mistress (Anwar).
1993 (PG) 89m/C Michael J. Fox, Gabrielle Anwar, Isaac Mizrahi, Anthony Higgins, Michael Tucker, Bobby Short, Dan Hedaya, Bob Balaban; *D:* Barry Sonnenfeld; *W:* Mark Rosenthal, Larry Konner; *M:* Bruce Broughton. VHS *ℐℐ*½

For Me and My Gal In his film debut, Kelly plays an opportunistic song-and-dance man who lures a young vaudevillian (Garland) away from her current partners. World War I interrupts both their career and romance, but you can count on them being reunited. Loaded with vintage tunes. ♫For Me and My Gal; They Go Wild, Simply Wild Over Me; The Doll Shop; Oh, Johnny, Oh; Oh, You Beautiful Doll; When You Wore A Tulip; Don't Leave Me Daddy; Do I Love You; By The Beautiful Sea; After You've Gone; Till We Meet Again; Tell Me; We Don't Want The Bacon; Ballin' the Jack; Mademoiselle From Armentieres; What Are You Going to Do to Help the Boys?; How Ya Gonna Keep 'Em Down on the Farm?; Where Do We Go From Here?; Goodbye Broadway, Hello France; Smiles; It's A Long Way to Tipperary; Oh Frenchy; Pack Up Your Troubles; When Johnny Comes Marching Home.
1942 104m/B Gene Kelly, Judy Garland, George Murphy, Martha Eggerth, Ben Blue, Richard Quine, Keenan Wynn, Stephen McNally; *D:* Busby Berkeley. VHS, Beta, LV $19.98 MGM *ℐℐ*½

For Pete's Sake Topsy-turvy comedy about a woman whose efforts to get together enough money to put her husband through school involve her with loan sharks, a madame, and even cattle rustling in New York City. Not one of Streisand's best. *AKA:* July Pork Bellies.
1974 (PG) 90m/C Barbra Streisand, Michael Sarrazin, Estelle Parsons, William Redfield, Molly Picon; *D:* Peter Yates. VHS, Beta $9.95 COL *ℐℐ*

For Richer, For Poorer A very rich, successful businessman notices his son is happy just to sit back and let dad earn all the dough while he waits for his share. In order

to teach his son a lesson, Dad decides to give all his money away. But the plan backfires when both realize that earning a second fortune may not be as easy as they assumed. Below average made for cable fare. *AKA:* Father, Son and the Mistress.
1992 (PG) 90m/C Jack Lemmon, Talia Shire, Joanna Gleason, Jonathan Silverman, Madeline Kahn, George Wyner; *D:* Jay Sandrich. VHS $89.99 HBO *ℐ*½

For the Boys Midler stars as Dixie Leonard, a gutsy singer-comedian who hooks up with Eddie Sparks (Caan) to become one of America's favorite USO singing, dancing, and comedy teams. The movie spans 50 years and three wars—including Korea and Vietnam—and raises such issues as the blacklist and the role of politics in showbiz. Glitzy Hollywood entertainment falters despite Midler's strong performance. ♫Billy-A-Dick; Come Rain or Come Shine; In My Life; Stuff Like That There.
1991 (R) 120m/C Bette Midler, James Caan, George Segal, Patrick O'Neal, Christopher Rydell, Arye Gross, Norman Fell, Rosemary Murphy, Dori Brenner, Bud Yorkin, Jack Sheldon, Melissa Manchester, Brandon Call; *Cameos:* Arliss Howard; *D:* Mark Rydell; *W:* Marshall Brickman, Neal Jimenez, Lindy Laub; *M:* Dave Grusin. Academy Awards '91 Nominations: Best Actress (Midler); Golden Globe Awards '92: Best Actress—Musical/Comedy (Midler). VHS $19.98 FXV *ℐℐ*

For the Love of Angela Pretty and young shop clerk involves herself with both the shopkeeper and his son.
1986 90m/C Louis Jourdan. Beta $14.95 PSM *ℐ*½

For the Love of Benji In this second "Benji" film, the adorable little dog accompanies his human family on a Greek vacation. He is kidnapped to be used as a messenger for a secret code, but escapes, to have a series of comic adventures in this entertaining family tour.
1977 (G) 85m/C Benji, Patsy Garrett, Cynthia Smith, Allen Finzat, Ed Nelson; *D:* Joe Camp. VHS, Beta $19.99 FCT, APD, BFV *ℐℐ*

For the Love of It Television stars galore try to hold together this farce about car chases in California, stolen secret documents, and (of course) true love. Outstandingly mediocre. Made for television.
1980 100m/C Deborah Raffin, Jeff Conaway, Tom Bosley, Norman Fell, Don Rickles, Henry Gibson, Pat Morita, William Christopher, Lawrence Hilton-Jacobs, Adrian Zmed, Barbi Benton, Adam West; *D:* Hal Kanter. VHS, Beta $14.95 FRH *ℐ*½

For Those About to Rock: Monsters in Moscow A tribute to the young people who defended Russia's new freedom during 1991's attempted coup. The first open-air festival-style concert ever to take place in Russia features the music of AC/DC, Metallica, The Black Crowes, Pantera, and Russia's Electro Shock Therapy.
1991 84m/C *D:* Wayne Isham. VHS, Beta, LV $19.98 WAR, MVD, PMS *ℐℐ*½

For Us, the Living The life and assassination of civil rights activist Medgar Evers are dramatically presented in this production of "American Playhouse" for PBS. Insight into the man is given, not just a recording of the events surrounding his life. Adapted from the biography written by Evers' widow.
1988 84m/C Howard E. Rollins Jr., Rocky Aoki, Paul Winfield, Irene Cara; *D:* Michael Schultz. VHS, Beta $79.95 MED, KUI, FCT *ℐℐℐ*

For Your Eyes Only In this James Bond adventure, 007 must keep the Soviets from getting hold of a valuable instrument aboard a sunken British spy ship. Sheds the gadgetry of its more recent predecessors in the series in favor of some spectacular stunt work and the usual beautiful girl and exotic locale. Glen's first outing as director, though he handled second units on previous Bond films. Sheena Easton sang the hit tune.
1981 (PG) 136m/C *GB* Roger Moore, Carol Bouquet, Chaim Topol, Lynn-Holly Johnson, Julian Glover, Cassandra Harris, Jill Bennett, Michael Gothard, John Wyman, Jack Hedley, Lois Maxwell, Desmond Llewelyn, Geoffrey Keen, Walter Gotell, Charles Dance; *D:* John Glen; *M:* Bill Conti. **VHS, Beta, LV $19.98** *MGM, FOX, TLF* ⚜⚜⚜

For Your Love Only A beautiful young student falls in love with her teacher and is blackmailed, leading her to murder her tormentor. Soap opera made for German television. Dubbed in English.
1979 90m/C *GE* Nastassia Kinski, Christian Quadflieg, Judy Winter, Klaus Schwarzkopf; *D:* Wolfgang Petersen. **VHS, Beta $69.00** *PGN, GLV* ⚜⚜

Forbidden In Nazi Germany, a German countess has an affair with a Jewish intellectual, and she winds up hiding him from the S.S. Based on the novel "The Last Jews of Berlin" by Leonard Gross. Slow made-for-cable movie.
1985 116m/C Jacqueline Bisset, Juergen Prochnow, Irene Worth, Peter Vaughan, Amanda Cannings, Avis Bunnage; *D:* Anthony Page. **VHS, Beta $79.95** *IVE, SWC* ⚜⚜½

The Forbidden City San San is a young Chinese maiden who has the misfortune to fall in love with a Western diplomat. After he is sent away on business San San keeps secret the fact she has born her lover a child but her actions are unforgiven by her father, a deposed mandarin.
1918 72m/B Norma Talmadge, Thomas Meighan; *D:* Sidney Franklin. **VHS, Beta $29.95** *PAV, VYY* ⚜⚜

The Forbidden Dance The first of several quickies released in 1990 applying hackneyed plots to the short-lived Lambada dance craze. The nonsensible plot has a Brazilian princess coming to the U.S. in order to stop further destruction of the rain forest. Instead, she winds up falling for a guy, teaching him to Lambada, and going on TV for a dance contest. Features an appearance by Kid Creole and the Coconuts.
1990 (PG-13) 90m/C Laura Herring, Jeff James, Sid Haig, Richard Lynch, Kid Creole & the Coconuts; *D:* Greydon Clark. **VHS, Beta, LV $19.95** *COL* Woof!

Forbidden Games The famous anti-war drama about two French children play-acting the dramas of war amid the carnage of World War II. Fossey is a young refugee who sees her parents and dog killed. She meets a slightly older boy whose family takes the girl in. The children decide to bury the animals they have seen killed in the same way that people are buried—even stealing crosses from the cemetery to use over the animal graves. Eventually they are discovered and Fossey is again separated from her new-found home. Acclaimed; available in both dubbed and English-subtitled versions. *AKA:* Les Jeux Interdits.
1952 90m/B *FR* Brigitte Fossey, Georges Poujouly, Amedee; *D:* Rene Clement. Academy Awards '52: Best Foreign Language Film; Nominations: Best Story, Best Story; British Academy Awards '53: Best Film; National Board of Review Awards '52: 5 Best Foreign Films of the Year; New York Film Critics Awards '52:

Best Foreign Film; Venice Film Festival '52: Best Film. **VHS, Beta, LV $29.98** *NOS, SUE, APD* ⚜⚜⚜⚜

Forbidden Impulse A group of teenage girls set out to seduce older men. Softcore.
1985 80m/C Denise Sexton, Crystal Tillery, Martin Hendler. **VHS, Beta $29.95** *MED* ⚜

Forbidden Love A man in his early 20's falls in love with a woman twice his age, much to the chagrin of her daughters. Made for television.
1982 96m/C Andrew Stevens, Yvette Mimieux, Dana Elcar, Lisa Lucas, Jerry Hauser, Randi Brooks, Lynn Carlin, Hildy Brooks, John Considine; *D:* Steven Hilliard Stern. **VHS, Beta** *NEG* ⚜

Forbidden Passion: The Oscar Wilde Movie A British-made look at Wilde's later years, emphasizing his homosexuality and the Victorian repression that accompanied it.
1987 120m/C *GB* Michael Gambon, Robin Lermitte. **VHS, Beta $79.95** *VMK* ⚜⚜½

Forbidden Planet In 2200 A.D., a space cruiser visits the planet Altair-4 to uncover the fate of a previous mission of space colonists. They are greeted by Robby the Robot and discover the only survivors of the Earth colony which has been preyed upon by a terrible space monster. A classic science fiction version of the Shakespearean classic "The Tempest." Laserdisc features formerly "cut" scenes, production and publicity photos, the original screen treatment, and special effects outtakes.
1956 98m/C Walter Pidgeon, Anne Francis, Leslie Nielsen, Warren Stevens, Jack Kelly, Richard Anderson, Earl Holliman, George Wallace; *D:* Fred M. Wilcox. **VHS, Beta, LV $19.95** *MGM, PIA, VYG* ⚜⚜⚜½

Forbidden Sun An Olympic gymnastics coach and her dozen beautiful students go to Crete to train. When one of them is brutally raped, vengeance is meted out by the girls.
1989 (R) 88m/C Lauren Hutton, Cliff DeYoung, Renee Estevez; *D:* Zelda Barron. **VHS, Beta, LV $14.95** *ACA* ⚜

Forbidden Trails Rough Riders adventure has Silver the horse saving his owner from the vengeance of two outlaws. Two more heroes go under cover to bring the bad guys to justice.
1941 60m/B Buck Jones, Tim McCoy, Raymond Hatton; *D:* Robert North Bradbury. **VHS, Beta $9.95** *NOS, VCN, DVT* ⚜½

Forbidden World Lives of a genetic research team become threatened by the very life form they helped to create: a man-eating organism capable of changing its genetic structure as it grows and matures. Corman-produced quickie follow-up to "Galaxy of Terror" is a graphically violent rip-off of "Alien." *AKA:* Mutant.
1982 (R) 82m/C Jesse Vint, Dawn Dunlap, June Chadwick, Linden Chiles; *D:* Allan Holzman. **VHS, Beta, LV $69.98** *SUE* Woof!

Forbidden Zone A sixth dimension kingdom is ruled by the midget, King Fausto, and inhabited by dancing frogs, bikini-clad tootsies, robot boxers, and degraded beings of all kinds. Original music by Oingo Boingo, and directed by founding member Elfman.
1980 75m/B Herve Villechaize, Susan Tyrrell, Kipper Kids, Viva; *D:* Richard Elfman. **VHS, Beta $39.95** *MED* ⚜½

Force Five A group of ex-cons form an anti-crime undercover force turning their skills toward justice. Nothing new in this made for television pilot.

1975 78m/C Gerald Gordon, Nicholas Pryor, James Hampton, David Spielberg, Leif Erickson, Bradford Dillman; *D:* Walter Grauman. **VHS, Beta $54.95** *MED* ⚜⚜

Force: Five Mercenary gathers a group of like-minded action groupies together to rescue the daughter of a powerful man from a religious cult. All action and no brains.
1981 (R) 95m/C Joe Lewis, Pam Huntington, Master Bong Soo Han; *D:* Robert Clouse. **VHS, Beta $54.95** *MED* ⚜

Force of Evil A cynical attorney who works for a mob boss and for Wall Street tries to save his brother from the gangster's takeover of the numbers operation. The honorable, though criminal, brother refuses the help of the amoral lawyer, and he is finally forced to confront his conscience. Garfield's sizzling performance and the atmospheric photography have made this a film noir classic.
1949 80m/B John Garfield, Thomas Gomez, Marie Windsor, Sheldon Leonard, Ray Roberts; *D:* Abraham Polonsky. **VHS, LV $19.98** *REP* ⚜⚜⚜

Force of Evil A paroled murderer returns to his hometown to brutalize the family that refused to fabricate an alibi for him. Made for television.
1977 100m/C Lloyd Bridges, Eve Plumb, William Watson, Pat Crowley; *D:* Richard Lang. **VHS, Beta, LV $49.95** *WOV, GKK* ⚜

Force of Impulse J.D. schlocker featuring an impressive cast involved with everything from hot rods to robbery to parental problems.
1960 ?m/C J. Carroll Naish, Robert Alda, Tony Anthony, Christina Crawford, Jody McCrea, Lionel Hampton. **VHS $16.95** *SNC* ⚜

Force of One A team of undercover narcotics agents is being eliminated mysteriously, and karate expert Norris saves the day in this sequel to "Good Guys Wear Black."
1979 (PG) 91m/C Chuck Norris, Bill Wallace, Jennifer O'Neill, Clu Gulager; *D:* Paul Aaron. **VHS, Beta $54.95** *MED* ⚜⚜

Force on Thunder Mountain A father and son go camping and encounter ancient Indian lore and flying saucers.
1977 93m/C Christopher Cain, Todd Dutson. **VHS, Beta $19.95** *UHV* ⚜

Force 10 from Navarone So-so sequel to Alistair MacLean's "The Guns of Navarone," follows a group of saboteurs whose aim is to blow up a bridge vital to the Nazi's in Yugoslavia. Keep an eye out for Ford, Nero, and Bach. Lots of double-crosses and action sequences, but doesn't quite hang together.
1978 (PG) 118m/C Robert Shaw, Harrison Ford, Barbara Bach, Edward Fox, Carl Weathers, Richard Kiel, Franco Nero; *D:* Guy Hamilton. **VHS, Beta, LV $19.98** *WAR, OM* ⚜⚜

Forced Entry Psychopathic killer-rapist hesitates over one of his victims, and she murders him instead. *AKA:* The Last Victim.
1975 (R) 92m/C Tanya Roberts, Ron Max, Nancy Allen; *D:* Jim Sotos. **VHS, Beta** *NO* ⚜

Forced March On location in Hungary, an actor portrays a poet who fought in World War II and became a victim of the Holocaust. However, the deeper he gets into his role, the thinner the line between illusion and reality becomes.
1990 104m/C Chris Sarandon, Renee Soutendijk, Josef Sommer, John Seitz; *D:* Rick King. **VHS, Beta, LV $89.99** *SGE, MOV, IME* ⚜⚜½

Forced Vengeance Vietnam vet pits himself against the underworld in Hong Kong. With Norris in the lead, you can take it for granted there will be plenty of martial arts action.
1982 (R) 103m/C Chuck Norris, Mary Louise Weller; *D:* James Fargo. **VHS, Beta $19.95** *MGM ♫♫*

Ford: The Man & the Machine Episodic biography of ruthless auto magnate Henry Ford I from the building of his empire to his personal tragedies. The cast lacks spark and Robertson (Ford) is positively gloomy. The only one appearing to have any fun is Thomas (Ford's mistress). Based on the biography by Robert Lacey.
1987 200m/C Cliff Robertson, Hope Lange, Heather Thomas, Michael Ironside, Chris Wiggins, R.H. Thomson; *D:* Allan Eastman. **VHS $79.95** *CAF ♫♫½*

Foreign Affairs Vinnie Miller (Woodward) is a prim New England college teacher off on a research sabbatical to London. On the flight Vinnie's seatmate is boisterous good-ole-boy Chuck Mumpson (Dennehy), with whom she appears to have nothing in common. Naturally the two middle-aged romantics find a funny, though bittersweet, love together. A rather distracting subplot find's Vinnie's young colleague Fred (Stolz) involved in an affair with an older, eccentric British actress (Beacham). Based on the novel by Alison Lurie. Made for cable television.
1993 120m/C Joanne Woodward, Brian Dennehy, Eric Stoltz, Stephanie Beacham, Ian Richardson, Robert Hands; *D:* Jim O'Brien; *W:* Chris Bryant. **VHS, LV $89.98** *TTC ♫♫♫*

Foreign Body An Indian (played by "Passage to India" star, Banerjee) visiting London pretends to be a doctor and finds women flocking to him. Excellent overlooked British comedy.
1986 (PG-13) 108m/C *GB* Victor Banerjee, Warren Mitchell, Trevor Howard, Geraldine McEwan, Amanda Donohoe, Denis Quilley, Eve Ferret, Anna Massey; *D:* Ronald Neame. **VHS $19.99** *HBO ♫♫½*

Foreign Correspondent A classic Hitchcock tale of espionage and derring-do. A reporter is sent to Europe during World War II to cover a pacifist conference in London, where he becomes romantically involved with the daughter of the group's founder and befriends an elderly diplomat. When the diplomat is kidnapped, the reporter uncovers a Nazi spy-ring headed by his future father-in-law.
1940 120m/B Joel McCrea, Laraine Day, Herbert Marshall, George Sanders, Robert Benchley, Albert Basserman; *D:* Alfred Hitchcock. Academy Awards '40 Nominations: Best Black and White Cinematography, Best Interior Decoration, Best Original Screenplay, Best Picture, Best Supporting Actor (Basserman); National Board of Review Awards '40: 10 Best Films of the Year. **VHS, Beta, LV $59.95** *WAR, PIA ♫♫♫♫*

The Foreigner Secret agent who comes to New York City to meet his contact becomes entrapped in a series of mysterious events revolving around the underground club scene.
1978 90m/B Eric Mitchell, Patti Astor, Deborah Harry; *D:* Amos Poe. **VHS, Beta $59.95** *FCT ♫*

The Foreman Went to France Industrial engineer travels to France during WWII to help prevent secret machinery from falling into the hands of the Nazis and their allies. *AKA:* Somewhere in France.
1942 88m/B *GB* Clifford Evans, Constance Cummings, Robert Morley; *D:* Charles Frend. **VHS, Beta $24.95** *NOS, MRV, DVT ♫♫½*

Foreplay Inane trilogy of comedy segments involving characters with White House connections. Stories are introduced by former President Mostel discussing his downfall in a television interview. Lame rather than risque, wasting talents of all involved. Each segment was scripted and directed by a different team. *AKA:* The President's Women.
1975 100m/C Pat Paulsen, Jerry Orbach, Estelle Parsons, Zero Mostel; *D:* Bruce Malmuth, John G. Avildsen. **VHS, Beta $59.98** *LIV, VES Woof!*

The Forest Spooks and a cannibalistic killer terrorize a group of campers. Nothing that hasn't been done countless times before.
1983 90m/C *D:* Don Jones. **VHS, Beta $59.95** *STE, PSM ♫*

Forest Duel Revenge is sweet in this rural Kung Fu epic.
1985 83m/C VHS, Beta $14.95 *SVS ♫*

Forest of Little Bear A man returns to his impoverished family in 1928 and decides to seek the reward put on the head of a one-eared man-eating bear. He kills the bear but faces a dilemma when he sees the bear left a helpless cub behind. In Japanese with English subtitles.
1979 124m/C *JP D:* Toshio Goto. **VHS $59.95** *FCT ♫*

Forever A teenage girl experiences true love for the first time and struggles with its meaning. Made for television adaptation of Judy Blume's novel.
1978 100m/C Stephanie Zimbalist, Dean Butler, John Friedrich, Beth Raines, Diana Scarwid; *D:* John Korty. **VHS $59.95** *GEM ♫♫½*

Forever and a Day Tremendous salute to British history centers around a London manor originally built by an English admiral during the Napoleonic era and the exploits of succeeding generations. The house even manages to survive the blitz of World War II showing English courage during wartime. Once-in-a-lifetime casting and directing.
1943 104m/B Brian Aherne, Robert Cummings, Ida Lupino, Charles Laughton, Herbert Marshall, Ray Milland, Anna Neagle, Merle Oberon, Claude Rains, Victor McLaglen, Buster Keaton, Jessie Matthews, Roland Young, C. Aubrey Smith, Edward Everett Horton, Elsa Lanchester, Edmund Gwenn; *D:* Rene Clair, Edmund Goulding, Cedric Hardwicke, Frank Lloyd, Victor Saville, Robert Stevenson, Herbert Wilcox, Kent Smith. **VHS $19.95** *HTV, MLB ♫♫♫♫*

Forever Darling Mixed effort from the reliable comedy duo sees Desi playing a dedicated chemist who neglects his wife while pursuing the next great pesticide. Lucy calls on her guardian angel (Mason) to help her rekindle her marriage. He advises her to go with Desi when he tests his new bug killer, and a series of hilarious, woodsy calamities occur. Lucy and Desi are always fun to watch, but '60s TV sitcom fans will enjoy the fact that Mrs. Howell (Schaefer) and Jane Hathaway (Kulp) appear in the same picture.
1956 91m/C Lucille Ball, Desi Arnaz Sr., James Mason, Louis Calhern, John Emery, John Hoyt, Natalie Schafer, Nancy Kulp; *D:* Alexander Hall. **VHS, Beta $19.98** *MGM, CCB ♫♫*

Forever Emmanuelle Sensual young woman finds love and the ultimate erotic experience in the wilds of the South Pacific in this sequel to the porn-with-production-values "Emmanuelle."
1982 (R) 89m/C Annie-Belle, Emmanuelle Arsan, Al Cliver. **VHS, Beta, LV $29.98** *LIV, VES ♫*

Forever Evil The vacationing denizens of a secluded cabin are almost killed off by the cult followers of a mythic god.
1987 107m/C Red Mitchell, Tracey Huffman, Charles Trotter, Howard Jacobsen, Kent Johnson. **VHS, Beta $79.95** *UHV ♫*

Forever Female A bright comedy about show business, egos, and love. Holden is a young playwright whose first play is accepted by stage producer Douglas on the condition that the lead role, featuring a 19-year-old heroine, be rewritten for his ex-wife Rogers. She's an aging leading lady smitten by Holden's charms—as is the ingenue Crowley, who would be perfect for the role as written. Complications and manipulations abound as the play makes its way to production. Adaptation of the Sir James Barrie play "Rosalind."
1953 93m/B Ginger Rogers, William Holden, Paul Douglas, Pat Crowley, James Gleason, Jesse White, George Reeves, Marjorie Rambeau, King Donovan, Vic Perrin, Marion Ross; *D:* Irving Rapper. **VHS** *PAR ♫♫♫*

Forever James Dean A profile of the legendary actor/cult hero, examining his life, short career and remaining legacy. Also includes the original previews of his three feature films. A must for serious Dean fans.
1988 69m/C James Dean, Julie Harris, William Bast, Kenneth Kendall; *D:* Ara Chekmayan. **VHS, Beta $29.98** *WAR, FCT ♫♫♫*

Forever, Lulu A down-on-her-luck novelist winds up involved with the mob and a gangster's girlfriend. Completely laughless comedy with amateurish direction. *AKA:* Crazy Streets.
1987 (R) 86m/C Hanna Schygulla, Deborah Harry, Alec Baldwin, Annie Golden, Paul Gleason, Dr. Ruth Westheimer; *D:* Amos Kollek. **VHS, Beta, LV $79.95** *COL ♫*

Forever Mary A teacher tries to better the lives of the boys sentenced to a reformatory in Palermo, Sicily, when a teenage transvestite prostitute (the title character) is admitted to the school. In Italian with English subtitles. *AKA:* Mery per Sempre.
1989 100m/C *IT* Michele Placido, Alesandro DiSanzo, Francesco Benigno; *D:* Marco Risi. **VHS $79.95** *CCN, TAM ♫♫♫*

Forever Young A young boy immerses himself in Catholicism. Admiring a priest, he is unaware that the priest's friend is involved with his mother. Tangled, but delicate handling of the coming-of-age story. Made originally for British television.
1985 85m/C *GB* James Aubrey, Nicholas Gecks, Alec McCowen; *D:* David Drury. **VHS, Beta $59.95** *MGM ♫♫*

Forever Young Gibson is still adorable, even in predictable movies like this; designed to be a tear-jerker, it serves mostly as a star vehicle. When test pilot Gibson's girlfriend is hit by a car and goes into a coma, he volunteers to be cryogenically frozen for one year. But, oops, he is left frozen for fifty years, until he is accidentally thawed out by a couple of kids. After some bumbling around with nineties-type technology, he is assisted by one of the boys (Wood) and his single mom (Curtis). Then he discovers his one true love didn't die as he thought and the government finds out about him. Through all the schmaltz, the relationship Gibson develops with Wood turns out to be the most authentic and endearing love in the film.
1992 (PG) 102m/C Mel Gibson, Jamie Lee Curtis, Elijah Wood, Isabel Glasser, George Wendt, Joe Morton, Nicolas Surovy, David Marshall Grant; *D:* Steve Miner; *W:* Jeffrey Abrams. **VHS, LV, 8mm $94.99** *WAR, BTV ♫♫½*

Forger of London Edgar Wallace tale in which Scotland Yard investigates a counterfeit ring connected to a prime suspect, an amnesiac playboy.
1961 91m/C *GE* Eddi Arent, Karin Dor, Viktor de Kowa, Hellmut Lange, Robert Graf; *D:* Harald Reinl. VHS $16.95 *SNC* ⅛⅛

Forget Mozart On the day of Mozart's death, the head of the secret police gathers a group together for questioning. They include the composer's wife, his lyricist, the head of a Masonic lodge, and Salieri, Mozart's rival. Each has a different story to tell to the investigator about the composer's life and death. The film makes use of a number of sets and costumes from "Amadeus" and was also filmed on location in Prague. In German with English subtitles. *AKA:* Zabudnite na Mozarta.
1985 93m/C *GE* Armin Mueller-Stahl, Catarina Raacke; *D:* Salvo Luther. VHS $79.95 *WBF* ⅛⅛

The Forgotten After 17 years as POWs, six Green Berets are freed, only to face a treacherous government conspiracy aimed at eliminating them. Produced and written by Carradine, Railsback and James Keach. Made for television.
1989 96m/C Keith Carradine, Steve Railsback, Stacy Keach, Pepe Serna, Don Opper, Richard Lawson; *D:* James Keach. VHS, Beta, LV $59.95 *PAR* ⅛⅛

The Forgotten One An uninspired author and a female reporter become mixed up in a century-old murder and the restless ghost it spawned.
1989 (R) 89m/C Kristy McNichol, Terry O'Quinn, Blair Parker, Elisabeth Brooks; *D:* Phillip Badger. VHS, Beta, LV $14.95 *ACA* ⅛½

Forgotten Prisoners Celluloid proof that conviction and true grit do not always entertainment make. Greenwald—whose credits range from "Xanadu" to "The Burning Bed"—directed this righteous but stationary drama about an Amnesty International official (Silver) who's assigned to look into the incarceration and egregious mistreatment of Turkish citizens. Made for cable TV. *AKA:* Forgotten Prisoners: The Amnesty Files.
1990 (R) 92m/C Ron Silver, Roger Daltrey, Hector Elizondo; *D:* Robert Greenwald; *M:* Brad Fiedel. VHS, Beta $79.98 *TTC, FCT* ⅛⅛

A Forgotten Tune for the Flute A delightful, Glasnost-era romantic comedy. A bureaucrat caught up in a dull, stuffy existence has a heart attack and winds up falling in love with his nurse. He then must decide between his comfortable, cared-for life or the love which beckons him. In Russian with English subtitles.
1988 131m/C *RU* Leonid Filatov, Tatiana Dogileva, Irina Kupchenko; *D:* Edgar Ryazanov. VHS, Beta, LV $29.95 *FRH, TAM* ⅛⅛⅛

Forgotten Warrior Vengeance is the name of the game as a Vietnam vet tracks down the fellow officer who tried to kill him and shot his commander.
1986 76m/C Quincy Frazer, Sam T. Lapuzz, Ron Marchini, Joe Meyer; *D:* Nick Cacas, Charlie Ordonez. VHS, Beta $79.95 *MNC* ⅛½

Forlorn River Nevada and Weary, two law-abiding men, seek to return their hometown to peace by eliminating a gang of outlaws. Based on a novel by Zane Grey.
1937 62m/B Buster Crabbe, June Martel, John D. Patterson, Harvey Stephens, Chester Conklin, Lew Kelly, Syd Saylor; *D:* Charles T. Barton. VHS $19.95 *NOS, DVT, RXM* ⅛½

The Formula Convoluted story about a secret formula for synthetic fuel that meanders it's way from the end of WWII to the present. A U.S. soldier waylays and then joins forces with, a German general entrusted with the formula. Years later, after the American is murdered, his friend, a hard-nosed L.A. cop, starts investigating, meeting up with spies and a reclusive oil billionaire. Scott and Brando have one good confrontation scene but the rest of the movie is just hot air. From the novel by Steve Shagan.
1980 (R) 117m/C Marlon Brando, George C. Scott, Marthe Keller, G.D. Spradlin, Beatrice Straight, John Gielgud, Richard Lynch; *D:* John G. Avildsen. VHS, Beta $19.98 *MGM* ⅛½

Formula for a Murder A very rich but paralyzed woman marries a scheming con artist who plots to kill her and inherit everything.
1985 89m/C Christina Nagy, David Warbeck, Rossano Brazzi. VHS, Beta $69.98 *LIV* ⅛

Forsaking All Others Screwball comedy featuring several MGM superstars. Friends since childhood, Gable has been in love with Crawford for 20 years, but she never realizes it and plans to marry Montgomery. Crawford is very funny in this delightful story of a wacky romantic triangle.
1935 84m/B Joan Crawford, Clark Gable, Robert Montgomery, Charles Butterworth, Billie Burke, Rosalind Russell, Frances Drake; *D:* Woodbridge S. Van Dyke; *W:* Joseph L. Mankiewicz. VHS $19.98 *MGM* ⅛⅛

Fort Apache The first of director Ford's celebrated cavalry trilogy, in which a fanatical general leads his reluctant men to an eventual slaughter, recalling George Custer at Little Big Horn. In residence: Ford hallmarks of spectacular landscapes and stirring action, as well as many vignettes of life at a remote outpost. Don't forget to catch "She Wore a Yellow Ribbon" and "Rio Grande," the next films in the series. Also available in a colorized version.
1948 125m/B John Wayne, Henry Fonda, Shirley Temple, John Agar, Pedro Armendariz Sr., Victor McLaglen, Ward Bond, Anna Lee; *D:* John Ford. VHS, Beta, LV $19.95 *TTC, RKO, VID* ⅛⅛⅛½

Fort Apache, the Bronx A police drama set in the beleaguered South Bronx of New York City, based on the real-life experiences of two former New York cops who served there. Newman is a decent cop who goes against every kind of criminal and crazy and against his superiors in trying to bring law and justice to a downtrodden community.
1981 (R) 123m/C Paul Newman, Ed Asner, Ken Wahl, Danny Aiello, Rachel Ticotin, Pam Grier, Kathleen Beller; *D:* Daniel Petrie. VHS, Beta, LV $9.99 *CCB, VES* ⅛⅛⅛

Fortress A teacher and her class are kidnapped from their one-room schoolhouse in the Australian outback. They must use their ingenuity and wits to save their lives in this violent made-for-cable-television suspense drama.
1985 (R) 90m/C *AU* Rachel Ward, Sean Garlick, Rebecca Rigg; *D:* Arch Nicholson. VHS, Beta $19.99 *HBO* ⅛

Fortress of Amerikka In the not-too-distant future, mercenaries get their hands on a secret weapon that could allow them to take over the USA.
1989 ?m/C Gene Le Brock, Kellee Bradley. VHS $79.99 *IMP* ⅛½

Fortune and Men's Eyes Exploitative and depressing film about life in a Canadian prison. A naive young man is sent to prison for marijuana possession and has

to make a difficult choice—be regularly sodomized by a man who will protect him or be raped by everyone else. Based on the play by John Herbert.
1971 (R) 102m/C Wendell Burton, Michael Greer, Zooey Hall, Danny Freedman; *D:* Harvey Hart; *W:* John Herbert. VHS $19.98 *MGM* ⅛⅛

The Fortune Cookie After receiving a minor injury during a football game, a TV cameraman is convinced by his seedy lawyer brother-in-law to exaggerate his injury and start an expensive lawsuit. A classic, biting comedy by Wilder. First of several Lemmon-Matthau comedies. The letterbox laserdisc version contains the original theatrical trailer. *AKA:* Meet Whiplash Willie.
1966 125m/B Jack Lemmon, Walter Matthau, Ron Rich, Cliff Osmond, Judi West, Lurene Tuttle; *D:* Billy Wilder. Academy Awards '66: Best Supporting Actor (Matthau); Nominations: Best Art Direction/Set Decoration (B & W), Best Black and White Cinematography, Best Story & Screenplay. VHS, Beta, LV $19.95 *FOX, MGM, PIA* ⅛⅛⅛

Fortune Dane Police detective Fortune Dane goes undercover to clear his name after he is framed for murder.
1986 (PG) 83m/C Carl Weathers, Adolph Caesar; *D:* Nicholas Sgarro; *W:* Charles Correll. VHS, Beta $29.95 *VMK* ⅛½

Fortune's Fool A beef king and profiteer marries a younger woman and soon discovers the problems that ambition can cause. Silent.
1921 60m/B *GE* Emil Jannings, Daguey Servaes, Reinhold Schunzel; *D:* Reinhold Schunzel. VHS, Beta $29.95 *NOS, MRV, VYY* ⅛⅛

Fortunes of War British professor Guy Pringle arrives with his bride, Harriet, to take up a teaching post in the Balkans in 1939. The idealistic Guy soon becomes enmeshed in anti-fascist politics and involved with the local members of the British embassy. When threatened by war they travel to Athens and then Cairo, where Guy's increasing involvement in the political situation, and his neglect of Harriet, causes a crisis in their marriage. Slow-moving drama with some self-centered characters is redeemed by the acting skills of those involved. Based on the autobiographial novels of Olivia Manning. Originally shown on "Masterpiece Theater" on PBS.
1987 160m/C *GB* Kenneth Branagh, Emma Thompson, Rupert Graves, Ronald Pickup, Robert Stephens, Charles Kay, James Villers, Harry Burton, Ciaran Madden, Diana Hardcastle, Greg Hicks, Alan Bennett, Jeremy Brundell, Jeremy Sinden; *D:* James Cellan Jones; *W:* Alan Plater. VHS $89.98 *FOX, FCT, TVC* ⅛⅛⅛

Forty Carats Ullmann plays the just-turned forty divorcee who has a brief fling with the half-her-age Albert while on vacation in Greece. She figures she'll never see him again but, back in New York, he turns up on the arm of her beautiful daughter (Raffin). Except he's still interested in mom. The rest of the movie is spent trying to convince Ullmann that love can conquer all. Ullmann's very attractive but not well-suited for the part; Raffin's screen debut. Based on the Broadway hit.
1973 (PG) 110m/C Liv Ullmann, Edward Albert, Gene Kelly, Binnie Barnes, Deborah Raffin, Nancy Walker; *D:* Milton Katselas; *W:* Jay Presson Allen. VHS, Beta $59.95 *COL* ⅛⅛½

Forty Days of Musa Dagh Based on the true story of Armenia's fight for freedom against Turkey in the 1914 uprising and the dreadful cost. From the novel by Franz Werfel.
1985 120m/C Michael Constantine, David Opatoshu. VHS, Beta $69.95 *VCD* ⅛⅛

The Forty-Ninth Parallel Six Nazi servicemen, seeking to reach neutral American land, are trapped and their U-boat sunk by Royal Canadian Air Force bombers, forcing them into Canada on foot, where they run into an array of stalwart patriots. Dated wartime propaganda made prior to the U.S. entering the war; riddled with entertaining star turns. **AKA:** The Invaders.
1941 90m/B *GB* Laurence Olivier, Leslie Howard, Eric Portman, Raymond Massey, Glynis Johns, Finlay Currie, Anton Walbrook; *D:* Michael Powell; *W:* Emeric Pressburger, Rodney Ackland. **VHS, Beta, LV** $29.95 *VID, VYG* ✂✂✂

Forty Thousand Horsemen The story of the ANZACS of Australia, created to fight Germany in the Middle East during World War II. This Australian war drama is full of cavalry charges, brave young lads, and "Waltzing Matilda."
1941 86m/B *AU* Chips Rafferty, Grant Taylor, Betty Bryant, Pat Twohill. **VHS, Beta** $29.95 *FCT, VYY* ✂✂½

42nd Street A Broadway musical producer faces numerous problems in his efforts to reach a successful opening night. Choreography by Busby Berkeley. A colorized version of the film is also available. ♫You're Getting to Be a Habit With Me; Shuffle Off to Buffalo; Young and Healthy; Forty-Second Street; It Must Be June.
1933 89m/B Warner Baxter, Ruby Keeler, Bebe Daniels, George Brent, Dick Powell, Guy Kibbee, Ginger Rogers, Una Merkel, Busby Berkeley; *D:* Lloyd Bacon; *M:* Al Dubin, Harry Warren. **VHS, Beta, LV** $19.98 *MGM, FOX, HMV* ✂✂✂✂

47 Ronin, Part 1 Turn of the 18th-century epic chronicling the samurai legend. The warriors of Lord Asano set out to avenge their leader, tricked into committing a forced seppuku, or hara-kiri. The photography is generously laden with views of 18th century gardens as well as panoramic vistas. This is the largest and most popular film of the Kabuki version of the story by Seika Mayama. In Japanese with English subtitles. **AKA:** The Loyal 47 Ronin; 47 Samurai.
1942 111m/C *JP D:* Kenji Mizoguchi. **VHS** $59.95 *SVS, TAM* ✂✂✂

47 Ronin, Part 2 Second half of the film in which the famous Japanese folklore tale of Lord Asano and his warriors is told. The film follows Asano's samurai as they commit themselves to avenging their leader in 1703. In Japanese with English subtitles.
1942 108m/C *JP D:* Kenji Mizoguchi. **VHS** $59.95 *SVS, TAM* ✂✂✂

48 Hrs. An experienced San Francisco cop (Nolte) springs a convict (Murphy) from jail for 48 hours to find a vicious murdering drug lord. Murphy's film debut is great and Nolte is perfect as his gruff foil.
1982 (R) 97m/C Nick Nolte, Eddie Murphy, James Remar, Annette O'Toole, David Patrick Kelly, Sonny Landham, Brion James, Denise Crosby; *D:* Walter Hill. **VHS, Beta, LV** $14.95 *PAR* ✂✂✂

48 Hours to Live A reporter travels to a nuclear scientist's secluded island to find the scientist held hostage by nuclear weapon-seeking terrorists. **AKA:** Man in the Middle.
1960 86m/B Anthony Steel, Ingemar Johannson, Marlies Behrens. **VHS, Beta** $39.95 *SVS* ✂

Fotografo de Senoras A novice photographer finds himself being mistaken for a rapist when naked women keep popping up in front of his camera.
1985 110m/C *SP* Jorge Porcel, Graciela Alfano, Tristan. **VHS, Beta** *MED* ✂

Foul Play Bearing no similarity to the Goldie Hawn vehicle of the same name, this Polish crimer is based on a true story, and stars two of Poland's Olympic boxers. A young man, accused of theft, is coerced by the Warsaw police to go undercover in return for having the charges against him dropped. With English subtitles.
1976 98m/C *PL* Marek Powowski, Jan Szcepanski, Jerzy Kulej. **VHS** $14.95 *FCT* ✂✂

Foul Play Hawn is a librarian who picks up a hitchhiker which leads to nothing but trouble. She becomes involved with San Francisco detective Chase in an effort to expose a plot to kill the Pope during his visit to the city. Also involved is Moore as an English orchestra conductor with some kinky sexual leanings. Chase is charming (no mugging here) and Hawn both bubbly and brave. A big winner at the box office; features Barry Manilow's hit tune "Ready to Take a Chance Again."
1978 (PG) 116m/C Goldie Hawn, Chevy Chase, Dudley Moore, Burgess Meredith, Billy Barty, Rachel Roberts, Eugene Roche, Brian Dennehy, Chuck McCann, Bruce Solomon; *D:* Colin Higgins. **VHS, Beta, LV, 8mm** $19.95 *PAR* ✂✂✂

Found Alive After a painful divorce, a woman kidnaps her son and steals away into the Mexican jungle, with only the help of her faithful butler.
1934 65m/B Barbara Bedford, Maurice Murphy, Robert Frazer, Edwin Cross; *D:* Charles Hutchinson. **VHS, Beta** $16.95 *SNC* ✂

The Fountainhead Cooper is an idealistic, uncompromising architect who refuses to change his designs. When he finds out his plans for a public housing project have been radically altered he blows up the building and winds up in court defending his actions. Neal is the sub-plot love interest. Based on the novel by Ayn Rand.
1949 113m/C Gary Cooper, Patricia Neal, Raymond Massey, Ray Collins, Henry Hull; *D:* King Vidor. **VHS, Beta** $19.98 *MGM, FOX* ✂✂✂

Four Adventures of Reinette and Mirabelle Small but touching Rohmer tale of the friendship between two women—one a naive country girl (Miquel, as Reinette), the other a sophisticated Parisian (Forde, as Mirabelle)—who share an apartment and a number of experiences, but who have a very different manner of inhabiting those experiences. A thoroughly French human comedy, one of Rohmer's better studies. In French with English subtitles.
1989 95m/C *FR* Joelle Miquel, Jessica Forde; *W/D:* Eric Rohmer. **VHS** $69.95 *NYF, FCT, TAM* ✂✂✂

Four Bags Full A bitter comedy about two smugglers during World War II who try to get a slaughtered pig to the black market under the Nazis' noses. In French with English subtitles.
1956 82m/C *FR* Jean Gabin, Louis de Funes, Bourvil, Jeanette Batti; *D:* Claude Autant-Lara. **VHS, Beta** $14.95 *VDM, FCT* ✂✂½

Four Daughters Classic, three-hankie outing in which four talented daughters of music professor Rains fall in love and marry. Garfield shines, in a role tailor-made for him, as the world-weary suitor driven to extremes in the name of love. Great performances from all. Based on the novel "Sister Act" by Fannie Hurst.
1938 90m/B Claude Rains, John Garfield, May Robson, Priscilla Lane, Lola Lane, Rosemary Lane, Gale Page, Dick Foran, Jeffrey Lynn; *D:* Michael Curtiz. **VHS** $19.98 *MGM, CCB* ✂✂✂

Four Days in July Two couples from Belfast, one Catholic and one Protestant, find they have something in common when they meet in the maternity ward as both couples become first-time parents. Script and dialog were mainly improvised, which provides both dull stretches and the film's charm.
1984 99m/C *GB* Des McAleer, Brid Brennan, Charles Lawson, Paula Hamilton, Shane Connaughton, Eileen Pollock, Stephen Rea; *D:* Mike Leigh. **VHS** $79.95 *WBF, BTV* ✂✂

Four Deuces Gang war is underway between the Chico Hamilton mob and Vic Morano and the Four Deuces during the Depression. Comedy and action combine with elements of strong language, strong sex, and strong violence.
1975 87m/C Jack Palance, Carol Lynley, Warren Berlinger, Adam Roarke; *D:* William H. Bushnell Jr. **VHS, Beta** $59.99 *HBO, TIM* ✂½

Four Eyes and Six Guns In 1882 a New York optometrist, who's a fan of the popular dime-store western novels, moves to Tombstone, Arizona in search of adventure. He's just in time too because Sheriff Wyatt Earp is trying to rid the town of those pesky Doom Brothers but is having a problem with his eyesight (causing his gunshots to go astray). Now if the greenhorn can just get Earp to wear his new glasses. Silly but harmless fluff. Made for cable television.
1993 92m/C Judge Reinhold, Fred Ward, Patricia Clarkson, M. Emmet Walsh. **VHS, Beta** $89.98 *TTC* ✂✂½

Four Faces West McCrea is an honest rancher who nevertheless robs the local bank in order to save his father's ranch from foreclosure. His humanity in helping a diphtheria-ridden family leads to his capture, but the sheriff promises a light sentence, since he is not a typical bad guy. Fine performances strengthen this low-key western. **AKA:** They Passed This Way.
1948 90m/B Joel McCrea, Frances Dee, Charles Bickford; *D:* Alfred E. Green. **VHS** $14.95 *REP* ✂✂½

The Four Feathers A grand adventure from a story by A.E.W. Mason. After resigning from the British Army a young man is branded a coward and given four white feathers as symbols by three of his friends and his lady love. Determined to prove them wrong he joins the Sudan campaign of 1898 and rescues each of the men from certain death. They then take back their feathers as does his girl upon learning of his true courage. Excellent performances by Smith and Richardson.
1939 95m/C *GB* John Clements, Ralph Richardson, C. Aubrey Smith, June Duprez, Donald Gray; *D:* Zoltan Korda. **VHS, Beta, LV** $14.98 *SUE, FCT, HMV* ✂✂✂✂

The Four Feathers Determined to return the symbols of cowardice, four feathers, to his friends and fiancee, a man courageously saves his friends' lives during the British Sudan campaign and regains the love of his lady. Made-for-television movie is the fifth remake.
1978 95m/C Beau Bridges, Jane Seymour, Simon Ward, Harry Andrews, Richard Johnson, Robert Powell; *D:* Don Sharp. **VHS, Beta** $59.99 *HBO* ✂

Four for Texas Perhaps Aldrich's later success with "The Dirty Dozen" can be attributed, in part, to this exercise in how not to make a comic western; poorly made, over long, and far too dependant on the feminine charisma of Ekberg and Andress. Slow-moving Sinatra-Martin vehicle tells the tale of con

men in the Old West who battle bandits and bad bankers for a stash of loot.
1963 124m/C Frank Sinatra, Dean Martin, Anita Ekberg, Ursula Andress, Charles Bronson, Victor Buono, Jack Elam; *D:* Robert Aldrich. **VHS, Beta, LV $59.95** *WAR, FCT ♂♂*

Four Friends The magical good and bad dream of the 1960s is remembered in this story of four friends. A young woman and the three men in love with her first come together in high school and then separate, learning from college, war and drug abuse, and each other in this ambitious movie from Steve Tesich, the writer of "Breaking Away." Good performances by all. *AKA:* Georgia's Friends.
1981 (R) 114m/C James Leo Herlihy, Craig Wasson, Jodi Thelen, Michael Huddleston, Jim Metzler, Reed Birney; *D:* Arthur Penn. **VHS, Beta $19.98** *WAR, OM ♂♂♂*

The Four Hands of Death: Wily Match Two martial artists are the best of friends, in and out of the ring—until they both fall for the same woman!
197? 90m/C Cheung Fu Hung, Jimmy Lee, Mo Man Sau. **VHS, Beta $49.95** *OCE ♂ ½*

The Four Horsemen of the Apocalypse Silent classic and star maker for Valentino concerning an Argentine family torn apart by the outbreak of WWI. Valentino is a painter who moves from his native Argentina to France and is persuaded to enlist by a recruiter who invokes the image of the Biblical riders. His excellence as a soldier, however, proves to be his undoing. The 1962 remake can't hold a candle to original, adapted from a novel by Vicente Blasco-Ibanez.
1921 110m/B Rudolph Valentino, Alice Terry, Pomeroy Cannon, Josef Swickard, Alan Hale Sr., Mabel van Buren, Nigel de Brulier, Bowditch Turner, Wallace Beery; *D:* Rex Ingram. **VHS** *NO ♂♂♂ ½*

The Four Horsemen of the Apocalypse The members of a German family find themselves fighting on opposite sides during World War II. This remake of the vintage Valentino silent failed at the box office, with complaints about its length, disjointed script, and uninspired performances. The title refers to the horrors of conquest, pestilence, war, and death. Adapted from the book by Vincente Blasco-Ibanez.
1962 153m/C Glenn Ford, Charles Boyer, Lee J. Cobb, Paul Henreid, Yvette Mimieux; *D:* Vincente Minnelli. **VHS, Beta $24.95** *MGM ♂♂ ½*

The 400 Blows The classic, groundbreaking semi-autobiography that initiated Truffaut's career and catapulted him to international acclaim, about the trials and rebellions of a 12-year-old French schoolboy. One of the greatest and most influential of films, and the first of Truffaut's career-long Antoine Doinel series. With English subtitles.
1959 97m/B *FR* Jean-Pierre Leaud, Claire Maurier, Albert Remy, Guy Decomble, Georges Flament, Patrick Auffay; *D:* Francois Truffaut. Academy Awards '59 Nominations: Best Story & Screenplay; Cannes Film Festival '59: Best Director (Truffaut); New York Film Critics Awards '59: Best Foreign Film. **VHS, Beta, LV $59.98** *FOX, MRV, APD ♂♂♂♂*

Four in a Jeep In Vienna in 1945, soldiers from different countries are serving as an international military police force. They clash as a result of political demands and their love for the same woman. Shot on location in Austria.
1951 83m/B Ralph Meeker, Viveca Lindfors, Joseph Yadin, Michael Medwin; *D:* Leopold Lindtberg. **VHS, Beta $19.95** *NOS, SVS ♂♂ ½*

Four Infernos to Cross Martial arts mixes with drama in this story of the struggle the Korean people encountered while under Japanese rule before World War II.
197? 90m/C Musung Kwak, Kyehee Kim. **VHS, Beta $39.95** *UNI, MOV ♂*

Four Jacks and a Jill Four musicians are left in the lurch when their band singer leaves them for her gangster boyfriend and they must frantically search for a replacement. Not completely uninteresting, but rather bland and old now. Earlier versions of the story were released as "Street Girl" and "That Girl from Paris." ♫ I'm in Good Shape For the Shape I'm In; You Go Your Way and I'll Go Crazy; I Haven't A Thing to Wear; Wherever You Are; Boogie Woogie Conga.
1941 68m/B Anne Shirley, Ray Bolger, Desi Arnaz Sr., Jack Durant, June Havoc, Eddie Foy Jr., Fritz Feld; *D:* Jack Hively. **VHS, Beta $19.98** *TTC ♂♂*

The Four Musketeers A fun-loving continuation of "The Three Musketeers," reportedly filmed simultaneously. Lavish swashbuckler jaunts between France, England, and Italy, in following the adventures of D'Artagnan and his cohorts. Pictures give an amusing depiction of Lester-interpreted seventeenth-century Europe, with fine performances especially by Dunaway as an evil countess seeking revenge on our heroes and Welch as the scatterbrained object of York's affections. *AKA:* The Revenge of Milady.
1975 (PG) 108m/C Michael York, Oliver Reed, Richard Chamberlain, Frank Finlay, Raquel Welch, Christopher Lee, Faye Dunaway, Jean-Pierre Cassel, Geraldine Chaplin, Simon Ward, Charlton Heston, Roy Kinnear, Nicole Calfan; *D:* Richard Lester. **VHS, Beta** *LIV, OM ♂♂♂*

Four Robbers The ruthless Ma initiates his series of crimes throughout the Far East, somehow staying ahead of the cops. When the final showdown occurs, it's an all out kung fu massacre.
197? 90m/C Lau Chun, Shek Hon, Kong Seng, Lee Wing Shan. **VHS, Beta $49.95** *OCE ♂*

Four Rode Out A Mexican outlaw is pursued by his girlfriend, one-time partner, and the law. Brutal, inferior western.
1969 99m/C Pernell Roberts, Sue Lyon, Leslie Nielsen, Julian Mateos; *D:* John Peyser. **VHS** *NO ♂*

The Four Seasons Three upper-middle-class New York couples share their vacations together, as well as their friendship, their frustrations and their jealousies. Alda's first outing as a film director is pleasant and easy on the eyes.
1981 (PG) 108m/C Alan Alda, Carol Burnett, Sandy Dennis, Len Cariou, Jack Weston, Rita Moreno, Bess Armstrong; *D:* Alan Alda. **VHS, Beta, LV $19.95** *MCA ♂♂ ½*

Four Sided Triangle Two mad scientists find their friendship threatened when they discover that they are both in love with the same woman. So they do what anyone would do in this situation—they invent a machine and duplicate her.
1953 81m/B *GB* James Hayter, Barbara Payton, Stephen Murray, John Van Eyssen, Percy Marmont; *D:* Terence Fisher. **VHS $19.98** *NOS, SNC, MLB ♂*

Four Ways Out Four average guys are fed up by their lot in life and stage a box-office robbery of their local soccer stadium. They don't get to enjoy their ill-gotten gains. In Italian with subtitles or dubbed.
1957 77m/B *IT* Gina Lollobrigida, Renato Baldini, Paul Muller; *D:* Pietro Germi. **VHS $16.95** *SNC ♂♂ ½*

The 4D Man A physicist makes two fateful discoveries while working on a special project that gets out of control, leaving him able to pass through matter and see around corners. He also finds that his touch brings instant death. Cheap but effective sci-fier. Young Duke has a small part.
1959 85m/C Robert Lansing, Lee Meriwether, James Congdon, Guy Raymond, Robert Strauss, Patty Duke; *D:* Irvin S. Yeaworth Jr. **VHS, Beta, LV $19.95** *STE, NWV, MLB ♂♂ ½*

1492: Conquest of Paradise Large-scale Hollywood production striving for political correctness is a drawn-out account of Columbus's (Depardieu) discovery and subsequent exploitation of the "New World." Skillful directing by Ridley Scott and impressive scenery add interest, yet don't make up for a script which chronicles events but tends towards trite dialogue and characterization. Available in both pan-and-scan and letterbox formats.
1992 (PG-13) 142m/C Gerard Depardieu, Sigourney Weaver, Armand Assante, Angela Molina, Fernando Rey, Tcheky Karyo, Frank Langella; *D:* Ridley Scott; *W:* Roselyne Bosch; *M:* Vangelis. **VHS, Beta, LV $95.95** *PAR, BTV ♂♂ ½*

The 4th Man Steeped in saturated colors and jet black comedy, Verhoeven's nouveau noir mystery enjoyed considerable art-house success but was not released in the US until 1984. The story is decidedly nonlinear, the look stylish and symbolic. Krabbe is an alcoholic bisexual Catholic writer who inadvertently becomes the hypotenuse of a love triangle involving Herman, a young man he encounters at a railway station, and his lover Christine, who owns the Sphinx beauty parlor and whose three husbands died, shall we say, mysteriously. Named one of the year's best films by the National Board; atmospheric score by Loek Dikker. In Dutch with English subtitles.
1979 104m/C *NL* Jeroen Krabbe, Renee Soutendijk, Thom Hoffman, Jon DeVries, Geert De Jong; *D:* Paul Verhoeven. **VHS, Beta, LV $24.95** *XVC, MED, TAM ♂♂♂ ½*

The Fourth Protocol Well-made thriller based on the Frederick Forsyth bestseller about a British secret agent trying to stop a young KGB agent from destroying NATO and putting the world in nuclear jeopardy. Brosnan, as the totally dedicated Russkie, gives his best performance to date while Caine, as usual, is totally believable as he goes about the business of tracking down the bad guys.
1987 (R) 119m/C *GB* Michael Caine, Pierce Brosnan, Ned Beatty, Joanna Cassidy, Julian Glover, Ray McAnally, Michael Gough, Ian Richardson; *D:* John MacKenzie. **VHS, Beta, LV $19.98** *LHV, WAR ♂♂♂*

Fourth Story A misfit detective is hired by a beautiful woman to find her missing husband. The investigation reveals some unseemly facts about the gentleman. Characterizations and plot twists keep this made-for-cable mystery interesting.
1990 (PG-13) 91m/C Mark Harmon, Mimi Rogers, Cliff DeYoung, Paul Gleason, M. Emmet Walsh; *D:* Ivan Passer; *W:* Andrew Guerdat. **VHS, Beta, LV $89.98** *MED, IME ♂♂♂*

The Fourth War Scheider and Prochnow are American and Russian colonels, respectively, assigned to guard the West German-Czechoslovakian border against each other. With the end of the cold war looming, these two frustrated warriors begin to taunt each other with sallies into the other's territory, threatening to touch off a major superpower conflict.

1990 (R) 109m/C Roy Scheider, Juergen Prochnow, Tim Reid, Lara Harris, Harry Dean Stanton; **D:** John Frankenheimer. **VHS, Beta, LV** $89.99 *HBO* 🎞🎞

Fourth Wise Man A Biblical Easter story about a rich physician searching for Christ in Persia.
1985 72m/C Martin Sheen, Lance Kerwin, Alan Arkin, Harold Gould, Eileen Brennan, Ralph Bellamy, Adam Arkin, Richard Libertini. **VHS, Beta** $69.95 *LIV, IGP* 🎞🎞

Fourth Wish When a single father learns that his son is dying, he vows to make his son's last months as fulfilling as possible. Bring lots of hankies.
1975 107m/C John Meillon, Robert Bettles, Robyn Nevin; **D:** Don Chaffey. **VHS, Beta** $49.95 *SUE* 🎞

Fowl Play An unlikely threesome encounter various hardships and mishaps on their way to the first cock-fighting Olympics. Let's hope it's the last cock-fighting Olympics.
1983 90m/C Nancy Kwan. **VHS, Beta** *PGN Woof!*

Fox and His Friends Fassbinder's breakthrough tragi-drama, about a lowly gay carnival barker who wins the lottery, thus attracting a devious, exploiting lover, who takes him for everything he has. In German with English subtitles. **AKA:** Faustrecht der Freiheit; Fist Right of Freedom.
1975 123m/C **GE** Rainer Werner Fassbinder, Peter Chatel, Karl-Heinz Boehm, Adrian Hoven, Harry Baer, Ulla Jacobsson, Kurt Raab; **D:** Rainer Werner Fassbinder. **VHS, Beta** $79.95 *FCT, NYF, TAM* 🎞🎞🎞½

Foxes Four young California girls grow up with little supervision from parents still trying to grow up themselves. They rely on each other in a world where they have to make adult choices, yet are not considered grown-up. They look for no more than a good time and no tragic mistakes.
1980 (R) 106m/C Jodie Foster, Cherie Currie, Marilyn Kagan, Scott Baio, Sally Kellerman, Randy Quaid, Laura Dern; **D:** Adrian Lyne. **VHS, Beta** $14.95 *MGM, FOX* 🎞🎞

Foxfire In the role that won her Tony and Emmy awards, Tandy stars as Annie Nations, a woman who has lived her entire life in the Blue Ridge Mountains. Widowed, all she has left are the memories of her beloved husband, with whom she regularly communes. Her son tries to convince her to move, and it becomes a clash of the wills as Annie tries to decide to stay in her past or change her future. Made for television.
1987 (PG) 118m/C Jessica Tandy, Hume Cronyn, John Denver, Gary Grubbs, Harriet Hall; **D:** Judd Taylor. **VHS** $14.98 *REP* 🎞🎞🎞

Foxfire Light A young woman vacationing in the Ozarks is drawn into a romance with a cowboy. But her mother's social ambitions and her own indecesion may tear them apart.
1984 (PG) 102m/C Tippi Hedren, Lara Parker, Leslie Nielsen, Barry Van Dyke; **D:** Allen Baron. **VHS, Beta** $79.95 *PSM* 🎞

Foxstyle A wealthy nightclub owner struggles with his country roots and his city sophistication.
1973 84m/C Juanita Moore, Richard Lawson, John Taylor, Jovita Bush; **D:** Clyde Houston. **VHS, Beta** *MOV* 🎞½

Foxtrap An L.A. courier is hired to find a runaway girl and bringing her in Europe, discovers he's been led into a trap. A low budget Italian co-production.
1985 89m/C **IT** Fred Williamson, Christopher Connelly, Arlene Golonka; **D:** Fred Williamson. **VHS, Beta** $69.95 *VES* 🎞

Foxtrot A wealthy count isolates himself, his wife, and their two servants, on an island but cannot escape his past or the horrors of World War II. Even the good cast can't save the pretentious script and inadequate production. **AKA:** The Other Side of Paradise.
1976 (R) 91m/C **SI MX** Peter O'Toole, Charlotte Rampling, Max von Sydow, Jorge Luke; **D:** Arturo Ripstein. **VHS, Beta** $59.98 *NLC* 🎞🎞

Foxy Brown A bitter woman poses as a prostitute to avenge the mob-backed deaths of her drug dealer brother and undercover cop boyfriend. Extremely violent black exploitation flick.
1974 (R) 92m/C Pam Grier, Terry Carter, Antonio Fargas, Kathryn Loder; **D:** Jack Hill. **VHS, Beta** $19.98 *ORI, FCT* 🎞

F.P. 1 An artifical island (Floating Platform 1) in the Atlantic is threatened by treason. This slow-moving 1930s technothriller is the English-language version of the German "F.P. 1 Antwortet Nicht" ("F.P. 1 Doesn't Answer"). Both were directed at the same time by Hartl, using different casts.
1933 74m/B **GE** Leslie Fenton, Conrad Veidt, Jill Esmond. **VHS** $19.95 *NOS* 🎞🎞

F.P. 1 Doesn't Answer A mid-Atlantic refueling station (Floating Platform 1) is threatened by treason and a pilot sets out to put things right. Features pre-Hollywood vintage Lorre; Albers was Germany's number one box office draw at the time. In German. **AKA:** F.P. 1 Antwortet Nicht.
1933 74m/B **GE** Hans Albers, Sybille Schmitz, Paul Hartmann, Peter Lorre, Hermann Speelmanns; **D:** Karl Hartl. **VHS** $16.95 *SNC, LSV* 🎞🎞

Fraidy Cat This program includes four animated fantasies for children.
1974 45m/C **VHS, Beta** $29.95 *PSM, WTA* 🎞🎞

Frame Up A small town sheriff is trying to investigate a murder tied to a fraternity's initiation. However, he runs into opposition from the most powerful man in town.
1991 (R) 90m/C Wings Hauser, Bobby DiCicco, Frances Fisher, Dick Sargent, Robert Picardo; **D:** Paul Leder. **VHS, LV** $9.98 *REP* 🎞🎞

Framed A nightclub owner is framed for murder, which understandably irks him. He's determined to get paroled and then seek revenge on the crooked cops responsible for his incarceration. This action melodrama features the writer, director and star of "Walking Tall."
1975 (R) 106m/C Joe Don Baker, Gabriel Dell, Brock Peters, Conny Van Dyke, John Marley; **D:** Phil Karlson. **VHS, Beta** $24.95 *PAR* 🎞🎞

Framed An art forger gets tripped up by a beautiful con artist. However, when they meet again he is willingly drawn into her latest swindle.
1990 87m/C Jeff Goldblum, Kristin Scott Thomas, Todd Graff. **VHS, Beta** $89.99 *HBO* 🎞🎞

Fran A young woman is torn between her desperate need for a male companion and the care of her children. Well made, albeit depressing, Australian production.
1985 92m/C **AU** Noni Hazlehurst, Annie Byron, Alan Fletcher; **D:** Glenda Hambly. **VHS, Beta** *NO* 🎞🎞

France/Tour/Detour/Deux/Enfants A twelve-part television series made for French television in which Godard and Mieville chronicle, in their characteristically reflexive fashion, the lives of two French schoolchildren and how their everyday growth is informed by television and the media. In French with English subtitles.
1978 26m/C **FR D:** Jean-Luc Godard, Anne-Marie Mieville. **VHS, Beta** *EAI* 🎞🎞🎞

Frances The tragic story of Frances Farmer, the beautiful and talented screen actress of the 30's and early 40's, who was driven to a mental breakdown by bad luck, drug and alcohol abuse, a neurotic, domineering mother, despicable mental health care, and her own stubbornness. After being in and out of mental hospitals, she is finally reduced to a shadow by a lobotomy. Not nearly as bleak as it sounds, this film works because Lange understands this character from the inside out, and never lets her become melodramatic or weak.
1982 134m/C Jessica Lange, Kim Stanley, Sam Shepard; **D:** Graeme Clifford; **M:** John Barry. **VHS, Beta, LV** $19.99 *HBO* 🎞🎞🎞

The Franchise Affair A teenage girl in need of an alibi accuses two reclusive women of kidnapping and abusing her. It's up to a lawyer to sort out the truth. Based on the novel by Josephine Tey.
1952 149m/C **GB** Michael Denison, Dulcie Gray, Anthony Nicholls, Marjorie Fielding, Athene Seyler, Ann Stephens, Patrick Troughton; **D:** Lawrence Huntington. **VHS** $49.95 *FCT* 🎞🎞

Francis Gary Powers: The True Story of the U-2 Spy A television dramatization of the true experiences of Gary Powers, a CIA spy pilot whose plane was shot down over the Soviet Union in 1960. His capture, trial, and conviction are all portrayed in detail, taken from Power's own reminiscences.
1976 120m/C Lee Majors, Noah Beery Jr., Nehemiah Persoff, Lew Ayres, Brooke Bundy; **D:** Delbert Mann. **VHS, Beta** *WOV* 🎞🎞½

Francis in the Navy The precocious talking mule, Francis, is drafted, and his buddy, played by O'Connor, comes to the rescue. The loquacious beast proves he has the superior grey matter however, and ends up doing all the thinking. Look for Clint Eastwood in his second minor role.
1955 80m/B Donald O'Connor, Martha Hyer, Jim Backus, Paul Burke, David Janssen, Clint Eastwood, Martin Milner; **D:** Arthur Lubin. **VHS** $9.95 *MCA* 🎞

Frank and I A soft-core epic about a Victorian woman who disguises herself as a boy in order to enter the house of a distinguished Englishman.
1983 (R) 75m/C Jennifer Inch, Christopher Pearson; **D:** Gerard Kikione. **VHS, Beta** $79.95 *MGM Woof!*

Frankenhooker Jeffrey Franken is a nice guy; he didn't mean to mow his fiancee down in the front lawn. But sometimes bad things just happen to good people. Luckily Jeff thought to save her head and decides to pair it up with the body of some sexy streetwalkers. Voila! You have Frankenhooker: the girlfriend with more than a heart. The posters say it best, "A Terrifying Tale of Sluts and Bolts." Also available in an "R" rated version.
1990 (R) 90m/C James Lorinz, Patty Mullen, Charlotte J. Helmkamp, Louise Lasser; **D:** Frank Henenlotter. **VHS, LV** *FCT* 🎞½

Frankenstein The definitive expressionistic Gothic horror classic that set the mold. Adapted from the Mary Shelley novel about Dr. Henry Frankenstein, the scientist who creates a terrifying, yet strangely sympathetic monster. Great performance by Karloff as the creation, which made him a monster star. Several powerful scenes, excised from the original version, have been restored. Side two of the laser disc version contains the original theatrical trailer, plus a collection of photos and scenes replayed for study purposes.

1931 71m/B Boris Karloff, Colin Clive, Mae Clarke, John Boles, Dwight Frye, Edward Van Sloan; **D:** James Whale. **VHS, Beta, LV $14.95** MCA, TLF, HMV ✂✂✂✂

Frankenstein A brilliant scientist plays God, unleashing a living monster from the remains of the dead. A TV movie version of the legendary horror story. Good atmosphere provided by producer Dan "Dark Shadows" Curtis.
1973 130m/C Robert Foxworth, Bo Svenson, Willie Aames, Susan Strasberg; **D:** Glenn Jordan. **VHS, Beta $49.95** IVE ✂✂½

Frankenstein A remake of the horror classic, closely following the original story, wherein the creature speaks (and waxes philosophical), the doctor sees him as his dark subconscious, and the two die in an arctic confrontation.
1982 81m/C Robert Powell, Carrie Fisher, David Warner, John Gielgud; **D:** James Ormerod. **VHS, Beta $59.98** LIV ✂✂½

Frankenstein: A Cinematic Scrapbook A behind the scenes look at the world's most infamous monster, featuring interviews with Boris Karloff, Bela Lugosi and Lon Chaney, Jr. Also included are original movie trailers. In color and B&W.
1991 60m/C **W/D:** Ted Newsom. **VHS, Beta $9.95** RHI, FCT ✂✂½

Frankenstein and the Monster from Hell A young doctor is discovered conducting experiments with human bodies and thrown into a mental asylum run by none other than Dr. Frankenstein himself. They continue their gruesome work together, creating a monster who develops a taste for human flesh. This really lame film was the last of the Hammer Frankenstein series.
1974 (R) 93m/C Peter Cushing, Shane Briant, Madeline Smith, David Prowse, John Stratton; **D:** Terence Fisher. **VHS** PAR ✂✂

Frankenstein '80 Guy named Frankenstein pieces together a monster who goes on a killing spree. Bottom of the barrel Italian production with funky music and lots of gore.
1979 88m/C IT GE John Richardson, Gordon Mitchell, Leila Parker, Dada Gallotti, Marisa Travers; **D:** Mario Mancini. **VHS, Beta $59.95** NO Woof!

Frankenstein General Hospital A completely laughless horror spoof wherein the twelfth grandson of the infamous scientist duplicates his experiments in the basement of a modern hospital. A must see for Frankenstein fans; considered by some the worst Frankenstein movie ever made.
1988 90m/C Mark Blankfield, Kathy Shower, Leslie Jordan, Irwin Keyes; **D:** Deborah Roberts. **VHS, Beta, LV** NO Woof!

Frankenstein Island Four balloonists get pulled down in a storm and end up on a mysterious island. They are greeted by one Sheila Frankenstein and encounter monsters, amazons, and other obstacles. Completely inept; Carradine "appears" in a visionary sequence wearing his pajamas.
1981 (PG) 97m/C Cameron Mitchell, Andrew Duggan, John Carradine; **D:** Jerry Warren. **VHS, Beta** NO Woof!

Frankenstein Meets the Space Monster A classic grade-Z epic about a space robot gone berserk among Puerto Rican disco dancers. **AKA:** Mars Invades Puerto Rico; Frankenstein Meets the Spacemen.
1965 80m/B James Karen, Nancy Marshall, Marilyn Hanold; **D:** Robert Gaffney. **VHS, Beta $39.95** PSM Woof!

Frankenstein Meets the Wolfman The two famous Universal monsters meet and battle it out in this typical grade-B entry, the fifth from the series. The Werewolf wants Dr. Frankenstein to cure him, but only his monster (played by Lugosi) remains.
1942 73m/C Lon Chaney Jr., Bela Lugosi, Patric Knowles, Lionel Atwill, Maria Ouspenskaya; **D:** Roy William Neill. **VHS, Beta, LV $14.98** MCA, MLB ✂✂✂

Frankenstein Unbound Corman returns after nearly 20 years with a better than ever B movie. Hurt plays a nuclear physicist time traveler who goes back to the 1800s and runs into Lord Byron, Percy and Mary Shelley and their neighbor Dr. Frankenstein and his monster. Great acting, fun special effects, intelligent and subtle message, with a little sex to keep things going. **AKA:** Roger Corman's Frankenstein Unbound.
1990 (R) 86m/C John Hurt, Raul Julia, Bridget Fonda, Jason Patric, Michael Hutchence, Catherine Rabett; **D:** Roger Corman. **VHS, Beta, LV $89.98** FOX ✂✂✂

Frankenstein's Daughter Demented descendant of Dr. Frankenstein sets a den of gruesome monsters loose, including the corpse of a teenaged girl he revitalizes, as he continues the mad experiments of his forefathers. **AKA:** She Monster of the Night.
1958 85m/B John Ashley, Sandra Knight; **D:** Richard Cunha. **VHS, Beta $9.95** NOS, MRV, RHI ✂

Frankenstein's Great Aunt Tillie An excrutiatingly bad send up of the Frankenstein saga with the good doctor about to be evicted from his estate because of back taxes. Gabor appears for a few seconds in a flashback.
1983 99m/C Donald Pleasence, Yvonne Furneaux, Aldo Ray, June Wilkinson, Zsa Zsa Gabor; **W/D:** Myron J. Gold. **VHS, Beta $59.95** VCD Woof!

Frankenweenie "Frankenweenie" is the tale of a lovable spunky dog named Sparky and his owner, Victor Frankenstein. When Sparky is hit by a car, Victor brings him back to life through the use of electric shock. This affectionate parody of "Frankenstein" launched renowned director Burton's career.
1984 (PG) 27m/B Shelley Duvall, Daniel Stern, Barret Oliver, Paul Bartel; **W/D:** Tim Burton. **VHS, Beta $14.99** BVV Woof!

Frankie and Johnny Based on the song of the same name, famed torch singer Morgan portrays a singer in a bordello who shoots her unfaithful lover. Release was delayed two years by the Hays Office's intervention in how a house of prostitution could be portrayed on screen. Too bad they reached an agreement. Not even Morgan's rendition of the title song redeems this.
1936 68m/B Helen Morgan, Chester Morris; **D:** Chester Erskine. **VHS, Beta $24.98** CCB ✂

Frankie and Johnny Elvis is a riverboat gambler/singer with lousy luck until Kovack changes the odds. This upsets his girlfriend Douglas who shoots him (but not fatally). Elvis wears period costumes, but this is otherwise similar to his contemporary films. ♫When the Saints Go Marching In; Look Out Broadway; Shout It Out; Frankie and Johnny; Chesay; Come Along; Petunia; The Gardner's Daughter; Beginner's Luck; What Every Woman Lives For; Everybody Come Aboard; Hard Luck; Please Don't Stop Loving Me.
1965 88m/C Elvis Presley, Donna Douglas, Harry Morgan, Audrey Christie, Anthony Eisley, Sue Ann Langdon, Robert Strauss, Nancy Kovack; **D:** Fred de Cordova. **VHS, Beta $19.95** MGM ✂✂½

Frankie and Johnny An ex-con gets a job as a short-order cook and falls for a world-weary waitress. She doesn't believe in romance, but finally gives into his pleas for a chance and finds out he may not be such a bad guy after all. Nothing can make Pfeiffer dowdy enough for this role, but she and Pacino are charming together. In a change of pace role, Nelligan has fun as a fellow waitress who loves men. Based on the play "Frankie and Johnny in the Clair de Lune" by McNally who also wrote the screenplay.
1991 (R) 117m/C Al Pacino, Michelle Pfeiffer, Hector Elizondo, Nathan Lane, Kate Nelligan, Jane Morris, Greg Lewis, Al Fann, K. Callan, Phil Leeds, Tracy Reiner, Dey Young; **D:** Garry Marshall; **W:** Terrance McNally; **M:** Marvin Hamlisch. **VHS, LV $19.95** PAR, CCB ✂✂✂

Frantic From Louis Malle comes one of the first French New Wave film noir dramas. A man kills his boss with the connivance of the employer's wife, his lover, and makes it look like suicide. Meanwhile, teenagers have used his car and gun in the murder of a tourist couple and he is indicted for that crime. Their perfectly planned murder begins to unravel into a panic-stricken nightmare. A suspenseful and captivating drama. Director Malle's first feature film. Musical score by jazz legend Miles Davis. **AKA:** Elevator to the Gallows; Ascenseur Pour L'Echafaud.
1958 92m/B Maurice Ronet, Jeanne Moreau, Georges Poujouly; **D:** Louis Malle; **M:** Miles Davis. **VHS, Beta, 8mm $16.95** SNC, NOS, VYY ✂✂✂

Frantic While in Paris, an American surgeon's wife is kidnapped when she inadvertantly picks up the wrong suitcase. Her kidnappers want their hidden treasure returned, which forces the husband into the criminal underground and into unexpected heroism when he seeks to rescue her. Written by Polanski and Gerard Brach; music by Ennio Morricone. Contrived ending weakens on the whole, but Polanski is still master of the dark film thriller.
1988 (R) 120m/C Harrison Ford, Betty Buckley, John Mahoney, Emmanuelle Seigner, Jimmie Ray Weeks, Yorgo Voyagis, David Huddleston, Gerard Klein; **D:** Roman Polanski; **M:** Ennio Morricone. **VHS, Beta, LV $19.98** WAR, FCT ✂✂✂

Franz A French mercenary and an insecure woman struggle with a doomed love affair. In French with English subtitles.
1972 90m/C FR Jacques Brel; **D:** Jacques Brel. **VHS, Beta $19.95** KHI, TAM ✂

Frasier the Sensuous Lion A zoology professor is able to converse with Frasier, a lion known for his sexual stamina and whose potency is coveted by a billionaire (shadow of monkey glands rejuvenation therapy). A fairly typical, if slightly risque, talking critter film. **AKA:** Frasier the Lovable Lion.
1973 (PG) 97m/C Michael Callan, Katherine Justice, Frank De Kova, Malachi Throne, Victor Jory, Peter Lorre Jr., Marc Lawrence; **D:** Pat Shields. **VHS, Beta $9.99** STE, PSM ✂

Fraternity Vacation Two college fraternity men show a nerd the greatest time of his life while he's on vacation in Palm Springs.
1985 (R) 95m/C Stephen Geoffreys, Sheree J. Wilson, Cameron Dye, Leigh McCloskey, Tim Robbins, Matt McCoy, Amanda Bearse, John Vernon, Nita Talbot, Barbara Crampton, Kathleen Kinmont, Max Wright, Julie Payne, Franklin Ajaye, Charles Rocket, Britt Ekland; **D:** James Frawley. **VHS, Beta, LV $9.95** NWV, STE ✂

The Freakmaker Mad professor attempts to breed plants with humans in his lab and has the usual bizarre results. Experiments that fail go to Dunn, a dwarf who runs

a freak show. Shamelessly includes real freaks as if plot was not strange enough. **AKA:** Mutations; The Mutation.
1973 (R) 90m/C *GB* Donald Pleasence, Tom Baker, Brad Harris, Julie Ege, Michael Dunn, Jill Haworth; **D:** Jack Cardiff. **VHS, Beta $19.98** VDC ✗✗

Freaks The infamous, controversial, cult-horror classic about a band of circus freaks that exact revenge upon a beautiful aerialist and her strongman lover after enduring humiliation and exploitation. Based on Ted Robbins story "Spurs." It was meant to out-horror "Frankenstein" but was so successful that it was repeatedly banned. Browning's film may be a shocker but it is never intended to be exploitative since the "Freaks" are the only compassionate, loyal, and loving people around. **AKA:** Nature's Mistakes; Forbidden Love; The Monster Show.
1932 66m/B Wallace Ford, Olga Baclanova, Leila Hyams, Roscoe Ates, Harry Earles; **D:** Tod Browning. **VHS, Beta, LV $59.95** MGM ✗✗✗½

Freaky Friday A housewife and her teenage daughter inadvertently switch bodies and each then tries to carry on the other's normal routine. Mary Rodgers' popular book is brought to the screen with great charm in this above average Disney film.
1976 (G) 95m/C Barbara Harris, Jodie Foster, Patsy Kelly, Dick Van Patten, Ruth Buzzi; **D:** Gary Nelson. **VHS, Beta $19.99** DIS ✗✗½

Freddy's Dead: The Final Nightmare Freddy's daughter journeys to Springwood, Ohio to put a stop to her father's evil ways. Will she be able to destroy this maniac, or is a new reign of terror just beginning? The sixth, and supposedly last, film in the "Nightmare" series. **AKA:** Nightmare on Elm Street 6: Freddy's Dead.
1991 (R) 96m/C Robert Englund, Lisa Zane, Shon Greenblatt, Leslie Deane, Ricky Dean Logan, Breckin Majer, Yaphet Kotto, Elinor Donahue, Roseanne (Barr) Arnold, Johnny Depp, Alice Cooper; **D:** Rachel Talalay. **VHS, LV $19.95** COL, NLC ✗✗

Free Amerika Broadcasting A drama about an alternate reality in which Richard Nixon was assassinated, leaving Spiro Agnew president. As a result, the country turns to violent revolution.
1989 80m/C Brian Kincaid; **D:** Dean Wilson. **VHS** NO ✗✗

Free and Easy Keaton plays the incompetent manager of a beauty contest winner (Page) from Gopher City, Kansas. Page and her overbearing mother, accompanied by Keaton, go to Hollywood to make the girl a star. They gate-crash the MGM studio where all cause havoc and it turns out Keaton is the one who lands in front of the cameras (Page has to settle for romancing Montgomery). Provides a behind-the-scenes look at the MGM studio, with a number of MGM stars making cameo appearances. **AKA:** Easy Go.
1930 92m/B Buster Keaton, Anita Page, Robert Montgomery, Trixie Friganza, Fred Niblo; **Cameos:** Cecil B. DeMille, Jackie Coogan, Lionel Barrymore, William Haines; **D:** Edward Sedgwick. **VHS $19.98** MGM ✗✗½

Free Grass A gang of thoughtless hippie drug smugglers and abusers escape from the police, drink acid-spiked wine, shoot each other, and have love-ins. **AKA:** Scream Free!.
1969 82m/C Russ Tamblyn, Richard Beymer, Casey Kasem, Lana Wood, Warren Finnerty. **VHS, Beta, LV** NO ✗

Free Ride A kooky kid steals a sportscar to impress a girl, and gets involved with local hoods. They chase each other around.

1986 (R) 92m/C Gary Hershberger, Reed Rudy, Dawn Schneider, Peter DeLuise, Brian MacGregor. **VHS, Beta, LV $19.95** LIV ✗

A Free Soul Tippling litigator Barrymore helps low-life mobster Gable beat a murder rap, only to discover the hood has stolen his daughter's heart. Bargaining with his ditzy daughter, he vows to eschew the bottle if she'll stay away from good-for-nothing Gable. Directed by Brown, best known for his work with Garbo, and based on the memoirs of Adela Rogers St. John. The final courtroom scene—a cloak-and-gavel classic—cinched Barrymore's Oscar. Remade with Liz Taylor as "The Girl Who Had Everything" (although, ironically, the earlier version is the racier of the two).
1931 94m/B Norma Shearer, Leslie Howard, Lionel Barrymore, Clark Gable, James Gleason, Lucy Beaumont; **D:** Clarence Brown. Academy Awards '31: Best Actor (Barrymore); Nominations: Best Actress (Shearer), Best Director (Brown). **VHS $19.98** MGM, FCT, BTV ✗✗½

Free to Love Screen idol Bow plays a young woman, fresh out of prison, who is taken in by a kindly, affluent patron. But, as the silent drama axiom would have it, there's no escaping the past, and she's forced to defend her former life when her guardian is murdered.
1925 61m/B Clara Bow, Donald Keith, Raymond McKee; **D:** Frank O'Connor. **VHS, Beta $16.95** GPV, FCT ✗✗

Free, White, and 21 A black motel owner is accused of raping a white civil rights worker. Produced in a "pseudo documentary" form which sometimes drags.
1962 104m/B Frederick O'Neal, Annalena Lund, George Edgely, John Hicks, Hugh Crenshaw, George Russell; **D:** Larry Buchanan. **VHS** NO ✗✗

Free Willy Sentimental story about a 12-year-old runaway (Richter) who befriends a whale. Should appeal to children for its heartwarming story and delightful sea acrobatics. An electronically operated stand-in whale was used for far-off shots; a domesticated performing whale named Keiko for the close-ups. Director Wincer was known to grumble about the temperamental Keiko during shooting. Suggested viewing for students of animal behavior.
1993 (PG) 120m/C Jason James Richter, Lori Petty, Jayne Atkinson, August Schellenberg, Michael Madsen; **D:** Simon Wincer; **W:** Keith A. Walker, Corey Blechman; **M:** Basil Poledouris. **VHS** NYR ✗✗½

Freebie & the Bean Two San Francisco cops nearly ruin the city in their pursuit of a numbers-running mobster. Top-flight car chases and low-level, bigoted humor combine. Watch for Valerie Harper's appearance as Arkin's wife. Followed by a flash-in-the-pan television series.
1974 (R) 113m/C Alan Arkin, James Caan, Loretta Swit, Valerie Harper, Jack Kruschen, Mike Kellin; **D:** Richard Rush. **VHS, Beta, LV $19.98** WAR ✗½

Freedom A young man finds the price of freedom to be very high when he tries to escape from Australian society in a silver Porsche.
1981 102m/C Jon Blake, Candy Raymond, Jad Capelja, Reg Lye, John Clayton; **D:** Joseph Sargent. **VHS, Beta $69.95** VID ✗½

Freedom is Paradise With his mother dead and his father missing, thirteen-year-old Sasha is growing up in a bleak reform school. Every time he runs away he is caught and severely beaten upon his return. When Sasha learns of his father's whereabouts he sets out on a 1,000 mile journey to the gulag-

style prison where is father is being held. Bodrov's directorial debut. In Russian with English subtitles.
1989 75m/C *RU* **D:** Sergei Bodrov. **VHS $69.95** FCT ✗✗✗

Freedom Road A made for television drama about a Reconstruction Era ex-slave, portrayed by heavyweight champion Ali, who is elected to the U.S. Senate and subsequently killed while trying to obtain total freedom for his race. Based on a novel by Howard Fast.
1979 186m/C Ron O'Neal, Edward Herrmann, John McLiam, Ernest Dixon, Alfre Woodard, Kris Kristofferson, Muhammad Ali; **D:** Jan Kadar. **VHS, Beta $69.95** WOV, FCT ✗✗

Freefall A female attorney begins to feel the toll of the '80s when, at the height of her dissatisfaction with her husband and job, an old beau shows up.
1990 28m/C **D:** Liz Leshin. **VHS $59.95** CIG ✗½

Freejack Futuristic thriller set in the year 2009, where pollution, the hole in the ozone layer, and the financial gap between the social classes have grown to such horrific proportions that the rich must pillage the past to find young bodies to replace their own. Estevez stars as a young race car driver whose sudden death makes him an ideal candidate for this bizarre type of surgery. Once transported to the future, he becomes a "Freejack" who must run for his life to escape not only the bounty hunter (Jagger), but also the ruthless tycoon (Hopkins), who puts a price on Freejack's head. Good cast brings this one up slightly.
1992 (R) 110m/C Emilio Estevez, Mick Jagger, Rene Russo, Anthony Hopkins, Jonathan Banks, David Johansen, Amanda Plummer, Grand Bush, Frankie Faison, Esai Morales, John Shea; **D:** Geoff Murphy. **VHS, Beta, LV $19.98** WAR ✗✗½

Freeway A nurse attempts to find the obsessive killer who shot her husband. The murderer phones a radio psychiatrist from his car, using Biblical quotes, while cruising for new victims. Okay thriller, based on the L.A. freeway shootings.
1988 (R) 91m/C Darlanne Fluegel, James Russo, Billy Drago, Richard Belzer, Michael Callan, Steve Franken, Kenneth Tobey, Clint Howard; **D:** Francis Delia. **VHS, Beta, LV $14.98** NWV, STE ✗✗½

The Freeway Maniac A low budget thriller about an escaped convict who ends up on a movie set where he continues his former career: murder. Music by former "Doors" guitarist Robby Krieger.
1988 (R) 94m/C Loren Winters, James Courtney, Shepard Sanders, Donald Hotton; **D:** Paul Winters; **M:** Robby Krieger. **VHS, Beta $79.95** MED ✗

Freeze-Die-Come to Life First feature film from Kanevski, who spent 8 years in a labor camp before glasnost. The story of two children who overcome the crushing poverty and bleakness of life in a remote mining community with friendship and humor. Beautifully filmed images, fine acting, touching but never overly sentimental story. The title comes from a children's game of tag. In Russian with English subtitles. **AKA:** Zamri Oumi Voskresni.
1990 105m/C *RU* Pavel Nazarov, Dinara Drukarova; **D:** Vitaly Kanevski. **VHS $89.95** FXL, ART, BST ✗✗✗½

Freeze Frame Doherty is a high school TV reporter who's determined to capture a biotech conspiracy on video in this funny, fast-paced action flick. Nothing objectionable here.

1992 78m/C Shannen Doherty, Charles Haid, Robyn Douglass, Seth Michaels; **W/D:** William Bindley. VHS, LV $89.95 *COL, NLC* ♫♫½

French Can-Can Dramatically sparse but visually stunning depiction of the can-can's revival in Parisian nightclubs. Gabin plays the theater impressario who discovers laundress Arnoul and decides to turn her into the dancing star of his new revue at the Moulin Rouge. In French with English subtitles. *AKA:* Only the French Can!.
1955 93m/C *FR* Jean Gabin, Francoise Arnoul, Maria Felix, Jean-Roger Caussimon, Edith Piaf, Patachou; **D:** Jean Renoir. VHS, Beta, LV $39.95 *INT, APD, TAM* ♫♫♫

The French Connection Two NY hard-nosed narcotics detectives stumble onto what turns out to be one of the biggest narcotics rings of all time. Cat-and-mouse thriller will keep you on the edge of your seat; contains one of the most exciting chase scenes ever filmed. Hackman's portrayal of Popeye Doyle is exact and the teamwork with Scheider special. Won multiple awards. Based on a true story from the book by Robin Moore. Followed in 1975 by "French Connection 2."
1971 (R) 102m/C Gene Hackman, Roy Scheider, Fernando Rey, Tony LoBianco, Eddie Egan, Sonny Grosso, Marcel Bozzuffi; **D:** William Friedkin. Academy Awards '71: Best Actor (Hackman), Best Adapted Screenplay, Best Director (Friedkin), Best Film Editing, Best Picture; Nominations: Best Cinematography, Best Sound, Best Supporting Actor (Scheider); British Academy Awards '72: Best Actor (Hackman); Directors Guild of America Awards '71: Best Director (Friedkin); Edgar Allan Poe Awards '71: Best Screenplay; Golden Globe Awards '72: Best Actor—Drama (Hackman), Best Director (Friedkin); Best Film—Drama; National Board of Review Awards '71: 10 Best Films of the Year, Best Actor (Hackman). VHS, Beta, LV $19.98 *FOX* ♫♫♫½

French Connection 2 New York policeman "Popeye" Doyle goes to Marseilles to crack a heroin ring headed by his arch nemesis, Frog One, who he failed to stop in the United States. Dour, super-gritty sequel to the 1971 blockbuster, and featuring one of Hackman's most uncompromising performances.
1975 (R) 118m/C Gene Hackman, Fernando Rey, Bernard Fresson; **D:** John Frankenheimer. VHS, Beta, LV $59.98 *FOX* ♫♫♫

The French Detective Two detectives, one an old-time tough guy and the other a young cynic, are after a ruthless politician and his pet hood. Grim but entertaining.
1975 90m/C *FR* Lino Ventura, Patrick Dewaere, Victor Lanoux; **D:** Pierre Granier-Deferre. VHS, Beta $59.95 *COL* ♫♫♫

French Intrigue International agents track drug lords from the U.S. to France in a so-so spy thriller.
19?? (R) 90m/C Jane Birkin, Curt Jurgens. VHS, Beta $19.99 *BFV* ♫♫

The French Lesson A romantic British farce from a screenplay by cartoonist Posy S. Simmonds, dealing with an English girl who goes to school in Paris and finds love. *AKA:* The Frog Prince.
1986 (PG) 90m/C *GB* Alexandre Sterling, Jane Snowdon; **D:** Brian Gilbert. VHS, Beta $69.95 *WAR* ♫♫½

The French Lieutenant's Woman Romantic love and tragedy in the form of two parallel stories, that of an 18th-century woman who keeps her mysterious past from the soldier who loves her, and the lead actor and actress in the film of the same story managing an illicit affair on the set. Extraordinary

performances and beautifully shot. From a Harold Pinter screenplay, based upon the John Fowles novel.
1981 (R) 124m/C Meryl Streep, Jeremy Irons, Leo McKern, Lynsey Baxter; **D:** Karel Reisz. Academy Awards '81 Nominations: Best Actress (Streep), Best Adapted Screenplay, Best Art Direction/Set Decoration, Best Costume Design, Best Film Editing; British Academy Awards '81: Best Actress (Streep); Golden Globe Awards '82: Best Actress—Drama (Streep). VHS, Beta, LV $19.95 *MGM, FOX* ♫♫♫½

The French Line A millionairess beauty travels incognito while trying to sort out which men are after her money, and which ones aren't. The 3-D presentation of Russell's physique in skimpy costumes earned this the condemnation of the Catholic Legion of Decency, which pumped the box office even higher. Lacks the charm of "Gentlemen Prefer Blonds," which it imitates. ♫Comment Allez-Vous; Well, I'll Be Switched; Any Gal From Texas; What Is This That I Feel?; With A Kiss; By Madame Fuelle; Wait Till You See Paris; Poor Andre; The French Line.
1954 102m/C Jane Russell, Gilbert Roland, Craig Stevens, Kim Novak, Arthur Hunnicutt; **D:** Lloyd Bacon. VHS, Beta $19.98 *CCB, TTC* ♫♫

French Postcards Three American students study all aspects of French culture when they spend their junior year of college at the Institute of French Studies in Paris. The same writers penned "American Graffiti" a few years earlier.
1979 (PG) 95m/C Miles Chapin, Blanche Baker, Valerie Quennessen, Debra Winger, Mandy Patinkin, Marie-France Pisier; **D:** Willard Huyck. VHS, Beta $59.95 *PAR* ♫♫

French Quarter A dual story about a young girl in the modern-day French Quarter of New Orleans who is also the reincarnation of a turn-of-the-century prostitute. Everyone gets to play two roles but this film is more curiosity than anything else.
1978 (R) 101m/C Bruce Davison, Virginia Mayo, Lindsay Bloom, Alisha Fontaine, Lance LeGault, Anne Michelle; **D:** Dennis Kane. VHS, Beta $19.95 *UHV* ♫♫½

French Quarter Undercover Two undercover cops in New Orleans thwart a terrorist plot aimed at the World's Fair.
1985 (R) 84m/C Michael Parks, Bill Holiday; **D:** Joe Catalanotto. VHS, Beta $69.95 *LIV* ♫

The French Touch Fernandel stars in this French farce about a shepherd who decides to open his own clip joint as a hairdresser and finds himself a hit among the Parisiennes. Fair to middling comedy.
1954 84m/B *FR* Fernandel, Renee Devillers, Georges Chamarat; **D:** Jean Boyer. VHS $24.95 *NOS* ♫♫½

The French Way One of the legendary Baker's few films, in which she portrays a Parisian nightclub owner playing matchmaker for a young couple. In French with English subtitles.
1940 72m/B *FR* Josephine Baker, Micheline Presle, Georges Marchal; **D:** Jacques de Baroncelli. VHS, Beta $29.95 *VDM, FCT* ♫♫½

The French Woman Soft-core story of blackmail, murder, and sex involving French cabinet ministers mixing passion and politics. From the director of "Emmanuelle."
1979 (R) 97m/C Francoise Fabian, Klaus Kinski; **D:** Just Jaeckin. VHS, Beta $29.98 *VID* ♫

Frenchman's Farm A young woman witnesses a killing at a deserted farmhouse. When she tells the police, they tell her that the murder happened forty years before. Average thriller that probably won't keep you on the edge of your seat.

1987 (R) 90m/C *AU* Tracey Tanish, David Reyne, John Meillon, Norman Kaye, Tui Bow; **D:** Ron Way. VHS, Beta *NO* ♫½

Frenzy A sculptor, pushed over the brink of sanity when he discovers that his wife is having an affair, turns to his art for solace...and seals his wife's corpse in a statue. Creepy story written by director Sewell. *AKA:* Latin Quarter.
1946 75m/B *GB* Derrick DeMarney, Frederick Valk, Joan Greenwood, Joan Seton, Valentine Dyall, Martin Miller; **W/D:** Vernon Sewell. VHS $19.98 *SNC* ♫♫½

Frenzy The only film in which Hitchcock was allowed to totally vent the violence and perverse sexuality of his distinctive vision, in a story about a strangler stalking London women in the late '60s. Finch plays the convicted killer-only he's innocent and must escape prison to find the real killer. McGowen is wonderful as the put-upon police inspector. A bit dated, but still ferociously hostile and cunningly executed.
1972 (R) 116m/C *GB* Jon Finch, Barry Foster, Barbara Leigh-Hunt, Anna Massey, Alec McCowen, Vivien Merchant, Billie Whitelaw, Jean Marsh; **D:** Alfred Hitchcock. VHS, Beta, LV $19.95 *MCA* ♫♫♫

Fresh Horses A wrong-side-of-the-tracks Depression-era romance. McCarthy is the engaged college boy who falls for backwoods girl Ringwald, who turns out to have a destructive secret.
1988 (PG-13) 92m/C Molly Ringwald, Andrew McCarthy, Patti D'Arbanville, Ben Stiller; **D:** David Anspaugh; **M:** David Foster. VHS, Beta, LV $89.95 *COL* ♫♫

Fresh Kill A young guy from Chicago goes to Hollywood, and gets mixed up in drugs and murder. Made for video.
1987 90m/C Flint Keller, Patricia Parks; **D:** Joseph Merhi. VHS, Beta *NO* ♫

The Freshman Country boy Lloyd goes to college and, after many comic tribulations, saves the day with the winning touchdown at the big game and wins the girl of his dreams. This was one of the comedian's most popular films.
1925 75m/B Harold Lloyd, Jobyna Ralston, Brooks Benedict, James Anderson, Hazwel Keener; **D:** Sam Taylor; **W:** Fred Newmeyer. VHS, Beta *TLF* ♫♫♫♫

The Freshman Brando, in an incredible parody of his Don Corleone character, makes this work. Broderick is a college student in need of fast cash, and innocent enough to believe that any work is honest. A good supporting cast and a twisty plot keep things interesting. Sometimes heavy handed with its sight gags, but Broderick and Brando push the movie to hilarious conclusion. Don't miss Burt Parks' musical extravaganza.
1990 (PG) 102m/C Marlon Brando, Matthew Broderick, Penelope Ann Miller, Maximilian Schell, Bruno Kirby, Frank Whaley, Jon Polito, Paul Benedict, Richard Gant, B.D. Wong, Bert Parks; **W/D:** Andrew Bergman; **M:** David Newman. VHS, Beta, LV, 8mm $19.95 *COL, FCT* ♫♫½

Frida The life of controversial Mexican painter Frido Kahlo is told via deathbed flashbacks using the artist's paintings to set the scenes. In Spanish with English subtitles.
1984 108m/C *SP* Ofelia Medina, Juan Jose Gurrola, Max Kerlow; **D:** Paul Leduc. VHS, Beta, LV $79.95 *CVC, IME, APD* ♫♫½

Friday Foster A beautiful, young photographer investigates an assassination attempt and uncovers a conspiracy against black politicians. Based on the Chicago Tribune comic strip.

1975 (R) 90m/C Pam Grier, Yaphet Kotto, Thalmus Rasulala, Carl Weathers, Godfrey Cambridge; D: Arthur Marks. VHS, Beta $59.98 ORI, FCT ✓✓½

Friday the 13th Notable as among the first in a very long series of slasher flicks, with effects by Tom Savini. A New Jersey camp reopens after it's been closed for 20 years after a history of "accidental" deaths. And the horror begins again. Six would-be counselors arrive to get the place ready. Each is progressively murdered: knifed, speared, and axed. Followed by numerous, equally gory sequels.
1980 (R) 95m/C Betsy Palmer, Adrienne King, Harry Crosby, Laurie Bartrarr, Mark Nelsor, Kevin Bacon; D: Sean S. Cunningham. VHS, Beta, LV $14.95 PAR ✓✓

Friday the 13th, Part 2 New group of teen camp counselors are gruesomely executed by the still undead Jason. Equally as graphic as the first installment; followed by several more gorefests.
1981 (R) 87m/C Amy Steel, John Furey, Adrienne King, Betsy Palmer; D: Steve Miner. VHS, Beta, LV $14.95 PAR Woof!

Friday the 13th, Part 3 Yet another group of naive counselors at Camp Crystal Lake fall victim to the maniacal Jason. The 3-D effects actually helped lessen the gory effects, but this is still awful. Followed by more disgusting sequels.
1982 (R) 96m/C Dana Kimmell, Paul Krata, Richard Brooker; D: Steve Miner. VHS, Beta, LV $14.95 PAR Woof!

Friday the 13th, Part 4: The Final Chapter Jason escapes from the morgue to once again slaughter and annihilate teenagers at a lakeside cottage. Preceded by four earlier "Friday the 13th" films, equally as graphic. The title's also a lie since there's several more sequels to look forward to.
1984 (R) 90m/C Erich Anderson, Judie Aronson, Kimberly Beck, Peter Barton, Tom Everett, Corey Feldman, Crispin Glover; D: Joseph Zito. VHS, Beta, LV $14.95 PAR Woof!

Friday the 13th, Part 5: A New Beginning Jason rises from the dead to slice up the residents of a secluded halfway house. The sequels, and the sameness, never stop. See Part 6...
1985 (R) 92m/C John Shepherd, Melanie Kinnaman, Shavar Ross, Richard Young, Juliette Cummins, Corey Feldman; D: Danny Steinmann. VHS, Beta, LV $14.95 PAR Woof!

Friday the 13th, Part 6: Jason Lives One of the few youths not butchered by Jason digs him up and discovers he's not (and never will be) dead. Carnage ensues...and the sequels continue.
1986 (R) 87m/C Thom Mathews, Jennifer Cooke, David Kagen; D: Tom McLoughlin. VHS, Beta, LV $14.95 PAR Woof!

Friday the 13th, Part 7: The New Blood A young camper with telekinetic powers accidentally unchains Jason from his underwater lair with the now-familiar results. There's still another bloody sequel to go.
1988 (R) 90m/C Lar Park Lincoln, Kevin Blair, Susan Blu; D: John Carl Buechler. VHS, Beta, LV $14.95 PAR Woof!

Friday the 13th, Part 8: Jason Takes Manhattan Yet another sequel (so far the last), with the ski-masked walking slaughterhouse transported to New York. Most of the previous action in the movie takes place on a cruise ship. This one is less gruesome than others in the series.
1989 (R) 96m/C Jensen Daggett, Scott Reeves, Peter Mark Richman, Barbara Bingham; W/D: Rob Hedden. VHS, Beta, LV $14.95 PAR ✓

Fridays of Eternity A romantic comedy about loyalty, fidelity, love, and lovers all with a tinge of the supernatural. In Spanish with English subtitles.
1981 89m/C AR Thelma Biral, Hector Alterio; D: Hector Olivera. VHS $24.98 TAM ✓✓

Fried Green Tomatoes Two stories about four women, love, friendship, Southern charm, and eccentricity are untidily held together by wonderful performances. Evelyn Couch (Bates) is an unhappy, middle-aged woman who meets the talkative 83 year-old Ninny Threadgoode (Tandy) while visiting a nursing home. Ninny reminisces about her life in the town of Whistle Stop, Alabama, during the Depression and the two women, Idgie (Masterson) and Ruth (Parker), who ran the local cafe. The more Evelyn hears about how the unconventional duo remade their lives to suit each other so long ago, the more Evelyn finds the confidence to work on her own life. Back-and-forth narrative as it tracks multiple storylines is occasionally confusing, though strong character development holds interest. A surprising box office hit adapted by Fannie Flagg from her novel "Fried Green Tomatoes at the Whistle Stop Cafe."
1991 (PG-13) 130m/C Kathy Bates, Jessica Tandy, Mary Stuart Masterson, Mary Louise Parker, Cicely Tyson, Chris O'Donnell, Stan Shaw, Gailard Sartain, Timothy Scott, Gary Basaraba, Lois Smith, Grace Zabriskie; D: Jon Avnet; W: Fannie Flagg. Academy Awards '91 Nominations: Best Adapted Screenplay, Best Supporting Actress (Tandy); National Media Owl Awards '92: First Prize. VHS, Beta, LV $19.98 MCA ✓✓✓

Frieda An RAF officer brings his German wife home after the war and she is naturally distrusted by his family and neighbors. An interesting look at post-war bigotry.
1947 97m/B GB David Farrar, Glynis Johns, Mai Zetterling, Flora Robson, Albert Lieven; D: Basil Dearden. VHS $19.95 NOS, VYY, TIM ✓✓½

Friendly Fire Based on a true story of an American family in 1970 whose soldier son is killed by "friendly fire" in Vietnam, and their efforts to uncover the circumstances of the tragedy. Touching and powerful, with an excellent dramatic performance by Burnett. Made for television.
1979 146m/C Carol Burnett, Ned Beatty, Sam Waterston, Timothy Hutton; D: David Greene. VHS, Beta $59.98 FOX ✓✓✓

Friendly Persuasion Earnest, solidly acted tale about a peaceful Quaker family struggling to remain true to its ideals in spite of the Civil War which touches their farm life in southern Indiana. Cooper and McGuire are excellent as the parents with Perkins fine as the son worried he's using his religion to hide his cowardice. Based on a novel by Jessamyn West; music by Dimitri Tiomkin. AKA: Except For Me and Thee.
1956 140m/C Gary Cooper, Dorothy McGuire, Anthony Perkins, Marjorie Main; D: William Wyler. Academy Awards '56 Nominations: Best Adapted Screenplay, Best Director (Wyler), Best Picture, Best Song ("Friendly Persuasion (Thee I Love)"), Best Sound, Best Supporting Actor (Perkins); Cannes Film Festival '57: Best Film. VHS, Beta, LV $59.98 FOX ✓✓✓

Friends Ho-hum drama about an orphaned French girl and an unloved English boy who meet, become friends, and decide to run away together, setting up house in a deserted beach cottage. They even have a baby before they're discovered. Provides no insight into the teenagers dilemmas. Followed by "Paul and Michelle."

1971 (R) 101m/C GB Sean Bury, Anicee Alvina, Pascale Roberts, Sady Rebbot, Ronald Lewis; D: Lewis Gilbert; M: Elton John. VHS $14.95 PAR ✓

Friends Forever Conformity, sexuality, and friendship are explored in this coming-of-age drama. Kristian is a shy, conformist sixteen-year-old, starting off at a new school. He finds himself drawn to two different young men who equally dominate his class. Henrik's androgynous sexual charm is equaled by his independence while the moody Patrick is the leader of a band of troublemakers. Kristian gains in self-confidence by their friendship but is tested when he learns Patrick is gay.
1986 95m/C DK D: Stefan Christian Henszelman. VHS $69.95 FCT ✓✓✓

Friends, Lovers & Lunatics A weekend turns into a romantic nightmare/laugh-fest when a man visits his ex-girlfriend and her new "friend", and winds up in a new romance himself. AKA: Crazy Horse; She Drives Me Crazy.
1989 87m/C CA Daniel Stern, Deborah Foreman, Sheila McCarthy, Page Fletcher, Elias Koteas; D: Stephen Withrow. VHS, Beta, LV $29.95 FRH, IME ✓✓½

Fright A woman—convinced that she died in 1889 as part of a suicide pact with Prince Rudolph of Austria—seeks help from a psychiatrist who promptly falls in love with her (didn't Freud say it was supposed to be the other way around?). AKA: Spell of the Hypnotist.
1956 ?m/B Nancy Malone, Eric Fleming, Frank Marth, Humphrey Davis, Ned Glass, Norman Burton; D: W. Lee Wilder. VHS $19.98 SNC ✓

Fright A baby-sitter is menaced by a mental hospital escapee. He turns out to be the father of the boy she is watching. Tense but violent thriller. AKA: Night Legs.
1971 87m/C GB Susan George, Honor Blackman, Ian Bannen, John Gregson, George Cole, Dennis Waterman; D: Peter Collinson. VHS MOV ✓✓

Fright House Two stories of terror. "Fright House" features witches preparing an old mansion for a visit from the Devil. "Abandon" explains the prolonged youth of a teacher to her young student.
1989 (R) 110m/C Al Lewis, Duane Jones; D: Len Anthony. VHS, Beta NO ✓

Fright Night It's Dracula-versus-the-teens time when Charley suspects that his new neighbor descends from Count Vlad's line. He calls in the host of "Fright Night," the local, late-night, horror-flick series, to help de-ghoul the neighborhood. But they have a problem when the vampire discovers their plans (and nobody belives them anyway). Sarandon is properly seductive as the bloodsucker. Followed by sequel.
1985 (R) 106m/C William Ragsdale, Chris Sarandon, Amanda Bearse, Roddy McDowall, Stephen Geoffreys; D: Tom Holland. VHS, Beta, LV $19.95 COL ✓✓½

Fright Night 2 The sequel to the 1985 release "Fright Night," in which the harassed guy from the original film learns slowly that the vampire's sister and her entourage have come to roost around his college. Not quite as good as the original but the special effects are worth a look.
1988 (R) 108m/C Roddy McDowall, William Ragsdale, Traci Lin, Julie Carmen; D: Tommy Lee Wallace. VHS, Beta, LV $14.95 LIV ✓✓

Frightmare A seemingly quiet British couple do indulge in one strange habit—they're cannibals.

1974 (R) 86m/C *GB* Deborah Fairfax, Kim Butcher, Rupert Davies, Sheila Keith; *D:* Pete Walker. **VHS, Beta** $59.98 *PSM* ✰✰½

Frightmare Great horror star dies, but he refuses to give up his need for adoration and revenge.
1983 84m/C Ferdinand "Ferdy" Mayne, Luca Bercovici, Nita Talbot, Peter Kastner; *D:* Norman Thaddeus Vane. **VHS, Beta** $59.95 *VES* ✰

Frightshow Four independent short horror films; "Nightfright," "Thing in the Basement," "Dr. Dobermind," and "Illegal Alien."
1984 60m/C **VHS** $29.98 *MPI* ✰

The Fringe Dwellers An Aborigine family leave their shantytown and move to the white, middle-class suburbs of Australia, encountering prejudice and other difficulties. Well acted and interesting but the ending's a letdown.
1986 (PG) 98m/C *AU* Kristina Nehm, Justine Saunders, Bob Maza, Kylie Belling, Denis Walker, Ernie Dingo; *D:* Bruce Beresford. **VHS, Beta, LV** $79.95 *SVS* ✰✰½

The Frisco Kid An innocent orthodox rabbi (Wilder) from Poland is sent to the wilds of San Francisco during the 1850s gold rush to lead a new congregation. He lands in Philadelphia, joins a wagon train and is promptly robbed and abandoned. He eventually meets up with a not-too-bright robber (Ford) who finds himself unexpectly befriending the man and undergoing numerous tribulations in order to get them both safely to their destination. This isn't a laugh riot and some scenes fall distinctly flat but Wilder is sweetness personified and lends the movie its charm. *AKA:* No Knife.
1979 (R) 119m/C Gene Wilder, Harrison Ford, Ramon Bieri, George DiCenzo, Penny Peyser, William Smith; *D:* Robert Aldrich. **VHS, Beta** $19.98 *WAR* ✰✰

Fritz the Cat Ralph Bakshi's animated tale for adults about a cat's adventures as he gets into group sex, college radicalism, and other hazards of life in the '60s. Loosely based on the underground comics character by Robert Crumb. Originally X-rated.
1972 77m/C *D:* Ralph Bakshi. **VHS, Beta** *WAR, OM* ✰✰✰

Frog A boy adds a frog to his reptile collection but gets the surprise of his life when he finds it's really an enchanted Prince! Followed by "Frogs!" Part of the "Wonderworks" series.
1989 55m/C Paul Williams, Scott Grimes, Shelley Duvall, Elliott Gould, David Grossman. **VHS, Beta, LV** $19.98 *ORI, IME* ✰✰✰

Frogs An environmental photographer working on a small island in Florida interrupts the birthday celebration of a patriarch. He and the folks at the party soon realize that various amphibians animals in the surrounding area are going berserk and attacking humans. One of the first environmentally-motivated animal-vengeance films, and one of the best to come out of the '70s.
1972 (PG) 91m/C Ray Milland, Sam Elliott, Joan VanArk, Adam Roarke, Judy Pace, Lynn Borden, Mae Mercer, David Gilliam, George Skaff; *D:* George McCowan. **VHS, Beta** *WAR, OM* ✰✰½

Frogs! Arlo is almost the most popular boy in school and is hoping to be crowned the king of his school's Spring Fling dance—until he and his friend Gus are turned into frogs by a witch. When Arlo and Gus discover their frog pond is being poisoned, they turn to the geeky Hannah for help. A sequel to "Frog." A viewers' guide is included. Part of the "Wonderworks" series.

1997? 55m/C Shelley Duvall, Elliot Gould, Paul Williams, Scott Grimes, Judith Ivey. **VHS** $29.95 *PME, HMV, BTV* ✰✰½

Frolics on Ice Pleasant comedy-musical about a family man saving to buy the barber shop he works at. Irene Dare is featured in several ice skating production numbers.
1940 65m/B Roscoe Karns, Lynn (Mary Hart) Roberts, Irene Dare, Edgar Kennedy. **VHS, Beta** $29.95 *VYY* ✰✰

From Beyond A gruesome, tongue-in-cheek adaptation of the ghoulish H.P. Lovecraft story. Scientists discover another dimension through experiments with the pineal gland. From the makers of "Re-Animator," and just as funny.
1986 (R) 90m/C Jeffrey Combs, Barbara Crampton, Ted Sorel; *D:* Stuart Gordon. **VHS, Beta, LV** $19.98 *LIV, VES* ✰✰✰

From Beyond the Grave This horror compendium revolves around a mysterious antique shop whose customers experience various supernatural phenomena, especially when they try to cheat the shop's equally mysterious owner. *AKA:* Creatures.
1973 (PG) 98m/C *GB* Peter Cushing, David Warner, Ian Bannen, Donald Pleasence, Margaret Leighton, Lesley-Anne Down, Diana Dors, Ian Ogilvy; *D:* Kevin Connor. **VHS, Beta** $59.95 *WAR* ✰✰

From Broadway to Cheyenne Here is an early western with lots of rip roarin' action, stunts and guns.
1932 60m/B Rex Bell, Robert Ellis, Alan Bridge, Matthew Betz, Marceline Day, George "Gabby" Hayes; *D:* Harry Fraser. **VHS, Beta** $19.95 *NOS, DVT* ✰

From China with Death After a vicious warlord wipes out his family, a young man trains under a martial arts master to prepare himself for revenge.
1973 (R) 90m/C **VHS, Beta** $59.95 *HHT* ✰

From Hell to Borneo A mercenary must defend his secluded island from pirates and gangsters.
1964 (PG) 90m/C George Montgomery, Torin Thatcher, Julie Gregg, Lisa Moreno; *D:* George Montgomery. **VHS, Beta** *NO* ✰½

From Hell to Victory Group of friends of different nationalities vow to meet each year in Paris on the same date but WWII interrupts their lives and friendships. Director Lenzi used the alias Hank Milestone. Good battle scenes but nothing special.
1979 (PG) 100m/C *SP FR* George Peppard, George Hamilton, Horst Buchholz, Jean-Pierre Cassel, Capucine, Sam Wanamaker, Anny Duperey, Ray Lovelock; *D:* Umberto Lenzi. **VHS, Beta** $9.95 *SIM, MED, HHE* ✰✰

From Here to Eternity A complex, hard-hitting look at the on and off-duty life of soldiers (both enlisted and officers) at the Army base in Honolulu in the days before the Pearl Harbor attack. Pruitt wants to be the company bugler but instead is given every dirty detail in camp because he refuses to continue as the company boxer (he won, but also blinded a friend in a fight). His best friend is Maggio, who's always in trouble, and his good-guy top sergeant just happens to be having a torrid affair with the commander's wife. Pruitt, meanwhile, is introduced to a club "hostess" who is a lot more vulnerable than she's willing to admit. This is a movie filled with great performances: Kerr and Reed shine in atypical roles; Clift is sensitive but stubborn; Lancaster, strong and passionate; and Borgnine is the epitome of villainy as a brutal sergeant. Sinatra won an Oscar for his portrayal of the doomed Maggio. Still has the most classic waves-on-the-beach love

scene in filmdom. Based on the novel by James Jones, which was toned down by the censors.
1953 118m/B Burt Lancaster, Montgomery Clift, Frank Sinatra, Deborah Kerr, Donna Reed, Ernest Borgnine, Philip Ober, Jack Warden, Mickey Shaughnessy, George Reeves, Claude Akins; *D:* Fred Zinneman; *W:* Daniel Taradash. Academy Awards '53: Best Black and White Cinematography, Best Director (Zinneman), Best Film Editing, Best Picture, Best Screenplay, Best Sound, Best Supporting Actor (Sinatra), Best Supporting Actress (Reed); Nominations: Best Actor (Clift), Best Actor (Lancaster), Best Actress (Kerr), Best Costume Design (B & W); Golden Globe Awards '54: Best Director (Zinneman); Golden Globe Awards '54: Best Supporting Actor (Sinatra); National Board of Review Awards '53: 10 Best Films of the Year; New York Film Critics Awards '53: Best Actor (Lancaster), Best Director (Zinneman), Best Film. **VHS, Beta, LV, 8mm** $19.95 *COL, PIA, BTV* ✰✰✰✰

From Here to Eternity From here to eternity...and back on the silver screen. Remake of the 1953 classic is based on James Jones' novel about life on a Hawaiian military base just before WWII. Decent actioner, but no Oscar-winner this time around. Made for television.
1979 (PG-13) 110m/C Natalie Wood, Kim Basinger, William Devane, Steve Railsback, Peter Boyle, Will Sampson, Andy Griffith, Roy Thinnes; *D:* Buzz Kulik. **VHS, Beta, LV** $89.95 *VMK, FCT* ✰✰½

From Here to Maternity A made-for-television soap opera-based spoof about modern maternity. Three women want to be pregnant but their significant others aren't interested in paternity.
1985 40m/C Carrie Fisher, Arleen Sorkin, Lauren Hutton, Griffin Dunne, Paul Reiser. **VHS, Beta** $59.95 *LIV, VES* ✰✰½

From Hollywood to Deadwood A beautiful starlet is kidnapped and the private eye searching for her discovers blackmail and danger.
1989 (R) 90m/C Scott Paulin, Jim Haynie, Barbara Schock; *D:* Rex Pickett. **VHS, Beta, LV** $19.95 *MED, FCT, IME* ✰✰

From Noon Till Three A change of pace role for Bronson as a two-bit gunfighter in a spoof of western legends. Bronson has a brief romance with Ireland who, believing him dead, fictionalizes their relationship in a series of books and builds the mediocre Dorsey into a western hero. When he turns up alive no one, including Ireland, believes that he is the real Dorsey and he's gradually driven crazy. Good script, weak direction but Bronson is likeable.
1976 (PG) 99m/C Charles Bronson, Jill Ireland, Douglas Fowley, Stan Haze, Damon Douglas; *W/D:* Frank D. Gilroy. **VHS** $14.95 *MGM* ✰✰½

From Russia with Love Bond is back and on the loose in exotic Istanbul looking for a super-secret coding machine. He's involved with a beautiful Russian spy and has the SPECTRE organization after him, including villainess Rosa Klebb (she of the killer shoe). Lots of exciting escapes but not an over-reliance on the gadgetry of the later films. The second Bond feature, thought by many to be the best. The laserdisc edition includes audio interviews with director Terence Young and others on the creative staff. The musical score and special effects can be separated from the actors' dialogue. The laserdisc also features publicity shots, American and British trailers, on-location photos, and movie posters.

1963 (PG) 125m/C *GB* Sean Connery, Daniela Bianchi, Pedro Armendariz Sr., Lotte Lenya, Robert Shaw, Eunice Gayson, Walter Gotell, Lois Maxwell, Bernard Lee, Desmond Llewelyn, Nadja Regin, Alizia Gur, Martine Beswick, Leila; *D:* Terence Young; *M:* John Barry. **VHS, Beta, LV** $19.98 *MGM, VYG, CRC* ♫♫♫½

From "Star Wars" to "Jedi": The Making of a Saga Using copious amounts of actual footage from the films, this movie follows the production of all three "Star Wars" sagas, concentrating on the special effects involved.
1983 65m/C David Prowse, Harrison Ford, Carrie Fisher, Billy Dee Williams, Alec Guinness; *D:* George Lucas. **VHS, Beta** $19.98 *FOX, FLI*

From the Dead of Night A spooky chiller about a near-death experience. Fashion designer Wagner narrowly escapes death but gets close enough to the other side that six of the dead feel cheated that she didn't join them. They decide to rectify the mistake and Wagner is pursued by the shadowy figures. Based on the novel "Walkers" by Gary Bradner. Made for television.
1989 192m/C Lindsay Wagner, Bruce Boxleitner, Diahann Carroll, Robert Prosky, Robin Thomas; *D:* Paul Wendkos. **VHS** $89.95 *AIP* ♫♫♫

From the Earth to the Moon A mad scientist invents a new energy source and builds a rocket which takes him, his daughter, and two other men for some adventures on the moon. Based on the novel by Jules Verne.
1958 100m/C George Sanders, Joseph Cotten, Debra Paget, Don Dubbins; *D:* Byron Haskin. **VHS, Beta, LV** $15.95 *UHV* ♫♫

From the Earth to the Moon An animated version of the Jules Verne classic about man's first landing on the moon.
1979 50m/C **VHS, Beta** $19.95 *MGM, WTA* ♫♫

From the Hip A young lawyer (Nelson) gets the chance of a lifetime when his office assigns a murder case to him. The only problem is that he suspects his client is very guilty indeed and must discover the truth without breaking his code of ethics. Nelson's courtroom theatrics are a bit out of hand, as he flares his nostrils at every opportunity. The movie is encumbered by a weak script and plot as well as a mid-story switch from comedy to drama.
1986 (PG) 112m/C Judd Nelson, Elizabeth Perkins, John Hurt, Ray Walston; *D:* Bob Clark. **VHS, Beta, LV** $19.98 *LHV, WAR* ♫♫

From the Life of the Marionettes A repressed man in a crumbling marriage rapes and kills a young prostitute. Another look at the powers behind individual motivations from Bergman, who uses black and white and color to relate details of the incident.
1980 (R) 104m/C *SW* Robert Atzorn, Christine Buchegger, Martin Benrath, Rita Russek, Lola Muethel, Walter Schmidinger, Heinz Bennent; *D:* Ingmar Bergman. **VHS, Beta, LV** $39.95 *LIV* ♫♫♫

From the Terrace Newman is a wealthy Pennsylvania boy who goes to New York and marries into even more money and social position when he weds Woodward. He gets a job with her family's investment company and neglects his wife for business. She turns to another man and when he goes home for a visit he also finds a new romance which leads to some emotional soul searching. The explicitness of O'Hara's very long novel was diluted by the censors and Newman's performance is a stilted disappointment. Loy, as

Newman's alcoholic mother, earned the best reviews.
1960 144m/C Paul Newman, Joanne Woodward, Myrna Loy, Ina Balin, Felix Aylmer, Leon Ames, George Grizzard, Patrick O'Neal, Barbara Eden, Mae Marsh; *D:* Mark Robson. **VHS, Beta, LV** $19.98 *FOX* ♫♫½

The Front Woody is the bookmaker who becomes a "front" for blacklisted writers during the communist witch hunts of the 1950s in this satire comedy. The scriptwriter and several of the performers suffered blacklisting themselves during the Cold War. Based more or less on a true story.
1976 (PG) 95m/C Woody Allen, Zero Mostel, Herschel Bernardi, Michael Murphy, Danny Aiello, Andrea Marcovicci; *D:* Martin Ritt. Academy Awards '76 Nominations: Best Original Screenplay; National Board of Review Awards '76: 10 Best Films of the Year. **VHS, Beta, LV** $12.95 *COL* ♫♫♫

The Front Page The original screen version of the Hecht-MacArthur play about the shenanigans of a battling newspaper reporter and his editor in Chicago. O'Brien's film debut here is one of several hilarious performances in this breathless pursuit of an exclusive with an escaped death row inmate.
1931 101m/B Adolphe Menjou, Pat O'Brien, Edward Everett Horton, Mae Clarke, Walter Catlett; *D:* Lewis Milestone. Academy Awards '31 Nominations: Best Actor (Menjou), Best Director (Milestone), Best Picture; National Board of Review Awards '31: 10 Best Films of the Year. **VHS, Beta, 3/4U, Special order formats** $19.95 *NOS, MRV, HHT* ♫♫♫½

The Front Page A remake of the Hecht-MacArthur play about the managing editor of a 1920s Chicago newspaper who finds out his ace reporter wants to quit the business and get married. But first an escaped convicted killer offers the reporter an exclusive interview.
1974 (PG) 105m/C Jack Lemmon, Walter Matthau, Carol Burnett, Austin Pendleton, Vincent Gardenia, Charles Durning, Susan Sarandon; *D:* Billy Wilder; *W:* Billy Wilder, I.A.L. Diamond. **VHS, LV** $89.95 *MCA* ♫♫½

Frontera If you're looking for action, go to the Border! Anything goes on the dangerous, exciting "Frontera." *AKA:* The Border.
19?? ?m/C *SP* Fernando Allende, Daniela Romo. **VHS, Beta** *VVC* ♫½

Frontera Sin Ley The son of Santo fights against local gangsters' crime and abuse in Pueblo Viejo.
19?? ?m/C *MX* Mil Mascaras, Eleazar Garcia Chelelo, Carmen Del Valle, Hijo Del Santo. **VHS, Beta** *NO* ♫

Frontier Days Cody goes undercover to capture the leader of a gang of stagecoach robbers. He also manages to capture a killer along the way.
1934 60m/B Bill Cody, Ada Ince, Wheeler Oakman; *D:* Sam Newfield. **VHS, Beta** $19.95 *NOS, DVT* ♫½

Frontier Fugitives When a trapper is murdered—allegedly by Indians—the Texas Rangers ride in to investigate.
1945 58m/B Tex Ritter, Dave O'Brien, Guy Wilkerson, Lorraine Miller, I. Stanford Jolley, Jack Ingram; *D:* Harry Fraser. **VHS** $19.95 *NOS* ♫½

Frontier Horizon Wayne and the Three Mesquiteers help out ranchers whose land is being bought up by crooked speculators.
1939 55m/B John Wayne, Jennifer Jones, Ray Corrigan, Raymond Hatton; *D:* George Sherman. **VHS, Beta, 3/4U, Special order formats** $19.95 *REP, CAB* ♫♫

Frontier Justice Gibson is the foolish son of a cattle owner who has been forced into an insane asylum because of a battle over water rights. Naturally, he must take on responsibility and rescue his father.
1935 56m/B Hoot Gibson, Richard Cramer; *D:* Robert McGowan. **VHS, Beta** $19.95 *NOS, VCN, DVT* ♫♫

Frontier Outlaws A gang of villains is selling stolen cattle, and Crabbe poses as an interested buyer to catch them in the act. Laughs are provided by Lynn as a judge, and "Fuzzy" St. John as Crabbe's sidekick.
1944 58m/B Buster Crabbe, Al "Fuzzy" St. John, Frances Gladwin, Marin Sais, Charles King, Jack Ingram, Kermit Maynard, Edward Cassidy, Emmett Lynn, Budd Buster; *D:* Sam Newfield. **VHS** $19.95 *NOS, MRV, TIM* ♫♫

Frontier Pony Express Roy and Trigger do their best to help the Pony Express riders who are being attacked by marauding gangs in California during the time of the Civil War. Plenty of action here.
1939 54m/B Roy Rogers; *D:* Joseph Kane. **VHS, Beta** $19.95 *NOS, MED, DVT* ♫♫

Frontier Scout Action-packed western has Wild Bill Hickock, portrayed by former opera singer Houston, forcing Lee's surrender in the Civil War before pursuing cattle rustlers out West.
1938 60m/B George Houston, Mantan Moreland; *D:* Sam Newfield. **VHS, Beta** $19.95 *NOS, DVT, RXM* ♫♫

Frontier Vengeance Barry is falsely accused of murder and works to clear his name while at the same time romancing a stagecoach driver who's trying to win a race with a rival stagecoach line.
1940 54m/B Donald (Don "Red") Barry, Nate Watt. **VHS, Beta** *MED, RXM* ♫½

The Frontiersman Things plod along at the little red schoolhouse until Hoppy and the guys have to take off after some rustlers. Features the members of the St. Brendan Boys Choir as the schoolboys. Unusual for its lack of gunplay until near the end.
1938 71m/B William Boyd, George "Gabby" Hayes, Russell Hayden, Evelyn Venable, Clara Kimball Young, Charles Hughes, Dick Jones, Roy Barcroft, Emily Fitzroy; *D:* Lesley Selander. **VHS** $19.95 *NOS* ♫♫

Frosty the Snowman Classic cartoon about the magic snowman and the children he befriends.
1969 30m/C *D:* Arthur Rankin Jr., Jules Bass; *V:* Billy DeWolfe, Jackie Vernon. **VHS** $14.95 *FHE, BTV, WTA* ♫♫

Frozen Alive A scientist experiments with suspended animation but, wouldn't you know, someone murders his wife while he's on ice. Apparently being frozen stiff does not an alibi make, and he becomes the prime suspect. Much unanimated suspense.
1964 80m/B *GB GE* Mark Stevens, Marianne Koch, Delphi Lawrence, Joachim Hansen, Walter Rilla, Wolfgang Lukschy; *D:* Bernard Knowles. **VHS** $19.98 *MOV* ♫

Frozen Assets Pathetic attempt at comedy from Long and Bernsen. He's an ambitious executive who finds the "bank" of his corporation's latest acquisition deals in sperm and not cash. Still, he expects this acquisition to be a success and comes up with a number of tacky ways, much to the horror of the facility's administrator, to make that profit margin grow.
1992 (PG-13) 93m/C Corbin Bernsen, Shelley Long, Larry Miller, Dody Goodman, Gerrit Graham, Paul Sand, Teri Copley, Matt Clark; *D:* George Miller; *W:* Don Klein, Tom Kartozian. **VHS** $94.98 *FXV* ♫

Frozen Terror A madman resembling both Jack Frost and Jack the Ripper claims victims at random.
1980 93m/C Bernice Stegers; *D:* Lamberto Bava. VHS, Beta $69.95 *LIV, VES ℐ*

Fu Manchu Villainous arch-criminal Fu Manchu plots to enslave the world in "The Golden God" and "The Master Plan," two episodes from the television series.
1956 60m/B Glenn Gordon, Laurette Luez, Clark Howat, Lee Matthews. VHS, Beta $24.95 *DVT ℐ*

Fuerte Perdido Settlers battle for their lives against hostile Indians led by Geronimo. In Spanish. *AKA:* Fort Lost.
1978 90m/C *SP* Esther Rojo, German Cobos, Mario Vidal. VHS, Beta $59.95 *HHT ℐ*

The Fugitive Fonda plays a priest devoted to his God and the peasants under his care. He finds himself on the run when all religion is outlawed in this nameless South-of-the-border dictatorship. Despite the danger of capture, he continues to minister to his flock. His eventual martyrdom unites the villagers in prayer, much to the chagrin of the militia. Considered Fonda's best performance and Ford's favorite film. Shot on location in Taxco, Cholula and Cuernavaca, Mexico. Excellent supporting performances. Based on the Graham Greene novel "The Power and the Glory" although considerably cleaned up for the big screen - Greene's priest had lost virtually all of his faith and moral code. Here the priest character is a genuine Ford hero with no moral ambiguities. A gem.
1948 99m/B Henry Fonda, Dolores Del Rio, Pedro Armendariz Sr., J. Carroll Naish, Leo Carrillo, Ward Bond, Robert Armstrong, John Qualen; *D:* John Ford. VHS, Beta, LV $19.98 *TTC ℐℐℐℐ*

The Fugitive On the run with Dr. Richard Kimble (Janssen) who sees himself convicted of the murder of his wife. Unable to prove his innocence, he takes advantage of a train collision to make good his escape, thus allowing him to pursue the real assailant, a mysterious one-armed man. Two episodes from the classic television series: "The Girl from Little Egypt" and "The End Is but the Beginning." Additional episodes are available.
1963 60m/C David Janssen, Barry Morse, Bill Raisch, Diane Brewster, Ed Nelson, Pamela Tiffin, Andrew Duggan, Barbara Barrie. VHS $19.99 *MOV, HHE ℐℐℐℐ*

The Fugitive Yes, this is the big-screen version of the old '60s TV series, only this time Ford is Dr. Richard Kimble. The story's basically the same—Kimble's wife is murdered, the police think he did it, and he's on the lam trying to find the real killer, the mysterious one-armed man. Jones is appropriately nasty as the relentless federal agent pursuer. Due to illness, Richard Jordan was replaced by Krabbe after production had begun. Alec Baldwin was originally slated to star as Kimble, but backed out and Ford was cast. Sound familiar? Baldwin was also slated to reprise his role as Jack Ryan in "Patriot Games" but was replaced by Ford.
1993 ?m/C Harrison Ford, Tommy Lee Jones, Julianne Moore, Sela Ward, Jeroen Krabbe, Joe Pantoliano, Andreas Katsulas; *D:* Andrew Davis; *W:* David N. Twohy, Jeb Stuart. VHS *NYR ℐℐ½*

Fugitive Alien Alien and Earth forces battle it out. Dubbed for Japanese.
1986 103m/C *JP* VHS, Beta $39.95 *CEL Woof!*

The Fugitive Kind A young drifter walks into a sleepy Mississippi town and attracts the attention of three of its women with tragic results. Based upon the Tennes-

see Williams' play "Orpheus Descending." Good performances but the writing never hangs well-enough together for coherence.
1960 122m/B Marlon Brando, Anna Magnani, Joanne Woodward, Victor Jory, R.G. Armstrong, Maureen Stapleton; *D:* Sidney Lumet. VHS, Beta $19.98 *MGM, FOX ℐℐℐ*

Fugitive Lovers An innocent guy rescues a gangster's beautiful wife from suicide, and invites his wrath by running away with her.
197? (R) 95m/C Steve Oliver, Virginia Mayo, Sondra Currie, John Russell. Beta *NO ℐ*

Fugitive Road The great von Stroheim stars as a crusty but soft-hearted border guard who arbitrarily detains people at the crossing.
1934 69m/B Erich von Stroheim, Wera Engels, Leslie Fenton, Harry Holman; *D:* Frank Strayer. VHS $19.95 *NOS ℐℐ*

Fugitive Samurai A samurai, with his young son, flees a vengeful shogun and seeks the friends who betrayed him.
1984 92m/C Kinnosuke Yorozuya, Katzutaka Nishikawa. VHS, Beta, LV $59.95 *SVS ℐℐ*

The Fugitive: Taking of Luke McVane An early silent western in which Hart upholds the cowboy code of honor.
1915 28m/B William S. Hart, Enid Markey. VHS, Beta $24.95 *VYY ℐℐ*

Fugitive Valley Muddled plot has villains-turned-heroes on the trail of some outlaws and stolen money. Terhune shows off some of his vaudeville skills, and King sings some songs.
1941 61m/B Ray Corrigan, John "Dusty" King, Max Terhune, Julie Duncan, Glenn Strange, Bob Kortman, Tom London, Reed Howes; *D:* S. Roy Luby. VHS $19.95 *NOS, HEG ℐ½*

Fulfillment Ladd stars as Mary Gray, a turn-of-the-century woman comfortably married to good but unexciting farmer, Jonathan (Levine). He's unable to give his wife the child they both desperately want and when his younger brother, Aaron (Smith), visits, the hope is Aaron can be persuaded to help out. The naturally volatile situation is heightened by the fact Mary is very drawn to the handsome Aaron anyway, and the feeling is mutual. Based on the novel "The Fulfillment" by LaVyrle Spencer. Made for television.
AKA: The Fulfillment of Mary Gray.
1989 (PG-13) 96m/C Cheryl Ladd, Ted Levine, Lewis Smith; *D:* Piers Haggard. VHS $89.98 *REP ℐℐ½*

Full Circle Peter Straub wrote this eerie tale about a grief-stricken young woman whose child has recently died. To overcome her loss, she moves into a new house—which is haunted by the ghost of a long-dead child. *AKA:* The Haunting of Julia.
1977 (R) 96m/C *CA GB* Mia Farrow, Keir Dullea, Tom Conti, Jill Bennett, Robin Gammell; *D:* Richard Loncraine. VHS, Beta *MED ℐℐ*

Full Exposure: The Sex Tape Scandals Sleazy drama about a murdered call girl who was blackmailing her clients with sex videos. A cop and his inexperienced female partner are assigned to catch the killer. Made for television.
1989 (R) 95m/C Jennifer O'Neill, Lisa Hartman, Vanessa Williams, Anthony John Denison, Peter Jurasik; *D:* Noel Nosseck; *W:* Stephen Zito; *M:* Dana Kaproff. VHS $89.95 *WOV ℐ½*

Full Fathom Five Central American militants, angered by America's invasion of Panama, hijack a submarine and threaten a nuclear assault on Houston. Boring and dumb.

1990 (PG) 90m/C Michael Moriarty, Maria Rangel, Michael Cavanaugh, John Lafayette, Todd Field, Daniel Faraldo; *D:* Carl Franklin. VHS, Beta $79.98 *MGM ℐℐ½*

Full Hearts & Empty Pockets Follows the happy-go-lucky adventures of a young, handsome, impoverished gentleman on the loose in Rome. Dubbed in English.
1963 88m/B *IT GE* Linda Christian, Gino Cervi, Senta Berger; *D:* Camillo Mastrocinque. VHS, Beta $29.95 *VYY ℐℐ½*

Full Metal Jacket A three-act Vietnam War epic co-written by Kubrick, Michael Herr and the novel's original author, Gustav Hasford, about a single Everyman impetuously passing through basic training then working in the field as an Army photojournalist and fighting at the onset of the Tet offensive. First half of the film is the most realistic bootcamp sequence ever done. Unfocused but powerful.
1987 (R) 116m/C Matthew Modine, Lee Ermey, Vincent D'Onofrio, Adam Baldwin, Dorian Harewood, Arliss Howard, Kevyn Major Howard; *D:* Stanley Kubrick. VHS, Beta, LV, 8mm $19.98 *WAR, FCT ℐℐℐ½*

Full Metal Ninja When his family is kidnapped, a trained martial artist trails their abductors and swears revenge.
1989 90m/C Pat Allen, Pierre Kirby, Sean Odell, Jean Paul, Renato Sala; *D:* Charles Lee. VHS, Beta $59.95 *IMP ℐ*

Full Moon in Blue Water His wife's been dead a year, he owes back taxes on his bar, his father has Alzheimer's, and his only form of entertainment is watching old home movies of his wife: Floyd has problems. Enter Louise, a lonely spinster who feels that it is her personal duty to change his life. If she doesn't do it, the bizarre things that happen after her arrival will.
1988 (R) 96m/C Gene Hackman, Teri Garr, Burgess Meredith, Elias Koteas; *D:* Peter Masterson. VHS, Beta, LV $19.98 *MED ℐℐ½*

Full Moon in Paris A young woman in Paris moves out on her architect lover in order to experience freedom. Through a couple of random relationships, she soon finds that what she hoped for is not what she really wanted. *AKA:* Les Nuits De La Pleine.
1984 (R) 101m/C *FR* Pascale Ogier, Tcheky Karyo, Fabrice Luchini; *D:* Eric Rohmer. VHS, Beta $24.95 *XVC, MED, TAM ℐℐ½*

Full of Life Holliday stars in this domestic comedy about a non-religious young woman who had married, in a civil ceremony, into a strict, Italian-Catholic family. Although she is now eight months pregnant the family still wants the couple to have a church wedding. Holliday is a winning personality and the humor is lightly handled.
1956 91m/C Judy Holliday, Richard Conte, Salvatore Baccaloni, Ester Minciotti; *D:* Richard Quine. VHS $19.95 *FCT ℐℐ½*

The Fuller Brush Girl Lots of slapstick with Ball as a door-to-door saleswoman unexpectedly involved in a murder. She and dim-bulb boyfriend Albert are chased by cops, murderers, and smugglers in this frantic farce. Sequel to Red Skelton's (who has a cameo) 1948 film "The Fuller Brush Man."
1950 84m/B Lucille Ball, Eddie Albert, Carl Benton Reid, Gale Robbins, Jeff Donnell, John Litel, Fred Graham, Lee Patrick; *Cameos:* Red Skelton; *D:* Lloyd Bacon; *W:* Frank Tashlin. VHS $19.95 *COL ℐℐ½*

Fuller Brush Man A newly hired Fuller Brush man becomes involved in murder and romance as he tries to win the heart of his girlfriend. A slapstick delight for Skelton fans. *AKA:* That Man Mr. Jones.

F

1948 93m/B Red Skelton, Janet Blair, Don McGuire, Adele Jergens; **D:** Frank Tashlin. **VHS, Beta, LV** $19.95 COL ♂♂½

Fun & Fancy Free Part-animated, part-live-action feature is split into two segments: "Bongo" with Dinah Shore narrating the story of a happy-go-lucky circus bear; and "Mickey and the Beanstalk"—a "new" version of an old fairy tale.
1947 96m/C Edgar Bergen, Charlie McCarthy, Jiminy Cricket, Mickey Mouse, Donald Duck, Goofy, Dinah Shore. **VHS, Beta** DIS ♂♂½

Fun Down There This smalltown boy-comes-to-the-big city is so bad, it's...bad. A naive—and unsympathetic—gay man from upstate New York moves to Greenwich Village and has fun down there (and they don't mean Australia). Written by director Roger Stigliano and Michael Waite.
1988 89m/C Michael Waite, Nickolas Nagurney, Gretschen Somerville, Martin Goldin, Kevin Och; **D:** Roger Stigliano; **W:** Michael Waite, Roger Stigliano. **VHS** $59.95 WBF, FCT, TAM Woof!

Fun in Acapulco Former trapeze artist Elvis romances two beauties and acts as a part-time lifeguard and night club entertainer. He must conquer his fear of heights for a climactic dive from the Acapulco cliffs. Features ten musical numbers. ♫Fun in Acapulco; Vino, Dinero y Amor; Mexico; The Bullfighter Was A Lady; El Toro; Marguerita; (There's) No Room To Rhumba (In A Sports Car); I Think I'm Going To Like It Here; You Can't Say No In Acapulco; Guadalajara.
1963 97m/C Elvis Presley, Ursula Andress, Elsa Cardenas, Paul Lukas, Alejandro Rey, Larry Domasin, Howard McNear; **D:** Richard Thorpe. **VHS, Beta** $14.98 FOX, MVD ♂♂

Fun with Dick and Jane An upper-middle class couple turn to armed robbery to support themselves when the husband is fired from his job. Though it has good performances, the film never develops its intended bite.
1977 (PG) 104m/C George Segal, Jane Fonda, Ed McMahon; **D:** Ted Kotcheff. **VHS, Beta** $9.95 COL ♂♂

The Funeral A sharp satire of the clash of modern Japanese culture with the old. The hypocrisies, rivalries and corruption in an average family are displayed at the funeral of its patriarch who also happened to own a house of ill repute. Itami's breakthrough film, in Japanese with English subtitles.
1984 112m/C JP Tsutomu Yamazaki, Nobuko Miyamoto, Kin Sugai, Ichiro Zaitsu, Nekohachi Edoya, Shoji Otake; **D:** Juzo Itami. **VHS** $19.98 REP, FCT, TAM ♂♂♂½

Funeral for an Assassin A professional assassin seeks revenge for his imprisonment by the government of South Africa, a former client. Planning to kill all of the country's leading politicians, he masquerades as a black man, a cover which is designed to fool the apartheid establishment.
1977 (PG) 92m/C Vic Morrow, Peter Van Dissel; **D:** Ivan Hall. **VHS, Beta** $59.95 GEM, MRV, VTR ♂½

Funeral Home Terrified teen spends her summer vacation at her grandmother's tourist home, a former funeral parlor. Rip-off of "Psycho." **AKA:** 2 Cries in the Night.
1982 90m/C CA Lesleh Donaldson, Kay Hawtry; **D:** William Fruet. **VHS, Beta** PGN ♂♂½

Funeral in Berlin Second of the Caine-Harry Palmer espionage films (following up "Ipcress File"), in which the deadpan British secret serviceman arranges the questionable defection of a Russian colonel. Good look at the spy biz and postwar Berlin. "Billion Dollar Brain" continues the series.

1966 102m/C Michael Caine, Eva Renzi, Oscar Homolka; **D:** Guy Hamilton. **VHS, Beta, LV** $14.95 PAR ♂♂♂

The Funhouse Four teenagers spend the night at a carnival funhouse, witness a murder, and become next on the list of victims. From the director of cult favorite "Texas Chainsaw Massacre," but nothing that hasn't been seen before.
1981 (R) 96m/C Elizabeth Berridge, Shawn Carson, Cooper Huckabee, Largo Woodruff, Sylvia Miles; **D:** Tobe Hooper. **VHS, Beta, LV** $14.98 MCA ♂♂

Funland In the world's weirdest amusement park a clown goes nuts over the new corporate owners' plans for the place and decides to seek revenge.
1989 (PG-13) 86m/C David Lander, William Windom, Bruce Mahler, Michael McManus; **D:** Michael A. Simpson. **VHS, LV** $79.98 LIV, IME, VES ♂

Funny About Love Fairly absurd tale with dashes of inappropriate black humor about a fellow with a ticking biological clock. Nimoy sheds his Spock ears to direct a star-studded cast in this lame tale of middle-aged cartoonist Wilder who strays from wife Lahti after having problems on the conception end into the welcoming arms of fertile college co-ed Masterson in his quest to contribute to the population count.
1990 (PG-13) 107m/C Gene Wilder, Christine Lahti, Mary Stuart Masterson, Robert Prosky, Stephen Tobolowsky, Anne Jackson, Susan Ruttan, David Margulies; **D:** Leonard Nimoy; **W:** Norman Steinberg, David Frankel. **VHS, Beta, LV, 8mm** $14.95 PAR ♂½

Funny, Dirty Little War An Argentinian farce about the petty rivalries in a small village erupting into a violent, mini-civil war. In Spanish with English subtitles.
1983 80m/C AR Federico Luppi, Julio de Grazia, Miguel Angel Sola; **D:** Hector Olivera. **VHS, Beta** $24.95 XVC, MED, TAM ♂♂½

Funny Face A musical satire on beatniks and the fashion scene also features the May-December romance between Astaire and the ever-lovely Hepburn. He is a high-fashion photographer (based on Richard Avedon); she is a Greenwich Village bookseller fond of shapeless, drab clothing. He decides to take her to Paris and show her what modeling's all about. The elegant musical score features classic Gershwin. The laserdisc includes the original theatrical trailer and is available in widescreen. ♫Let's Kiss and Make Up; He Loves and She Loves; Funny Face; How Long Has This Been Going On?; Clap Yo' Hands; S'Wonderful; Bonjour Paris; On How To Be Lovely; Marche Funebre; Think Pink.
1957 103m/C Fred Astaire, Audrey Hepburn, Kay Thompson, Suzy Parker; **D:** Stanley Donen; **M:** George Gershwin, Ira Gershwin. **VHS, Beta, LV, 8mm** $14.95 PAR, FCT ♂♂♂

The Funny Farm Comedy about a group of ambitious young comics striving to make it in the crazy world of comedy at Los Angeles' famous comedy club, The Funny Farm.
1982 90m/C CA Miles Chapin, Eileen Brennan, Peter Aykroyd; **D:** Ron Clark. **VHS, Beta** $19.95 STE, HBO ♂½

Funny Farm Chevy Chase as a New York sportswriter finds that life in the country is not quite what he envisioned. The comedy is uneven throughout, with the best scenes coming at the end.
1988 (PG) 101m/C Chevy Chase, Madolyn Smith, Joseph Maher, Jack Gilpin, Brad Sullivan, MacIntyre Dixon; **D:** George Roy Hill. **VHS, LV** $19.98 WAR ♂♂

Funny Girl Follows the early career of comedian Fanny Brice, her rise to stardom with the Ziegfeld Follies and her stormy romance with gambler Nick Arnstein in a fun and funny look at back stage music hall life in the early 1900s. Streisand's film debut followed her auspicious performance of the role on Broadway. Score was augmented by several tunes sung by Brice during her performances. Excellent performances from everyone, captured beautifully by Wyler in his musical film debut. Followed by "Funny Lady." ♫My Man; Second Hand Rose; I'd Rather Be Blue Over You; People; Don't Rain On My Parade; I'm The Greatest Star; Sadie, Sadie; His Love Makes Me Beautiful; You Are Woman, I Am Man; If A Girl Isn't Pretty; The Swan; Roller Skate Rag; Funny Girl.
1968 (G) 151m/C Barbra Streisand, Omar Sharif, Walter Pidgeon, Kay Medford, Anne Francis; **D:** William Wyler. Academy Awards '68: Best Actress (Streisand); Nominations: Best Cinematography, Best Film Editing, Best Picture, Best Song ("Funny Girl"), Best Sound, Best Supporting Actress (Medford), Best Original Score; Golden Globe Awards '69: Best Actress—Musical/Comedy (Streisand). **VHS, Beta, LV** $19.95 COL, PIA, BTV ♂♂♂

Funny Lady A continuation of "Funny Girl," recounting Fanny Brice's tumultuous marriage to showman Billy Rose in the 1930s and her lingering affection for first husband Nick Arnstein. One of the rare sequels which are just as good, or at least almost, as the original. ♫How Lucky Can You Get?; Great Day; More Than You Know; Blind Date; So Long, Honey Lamb; Isn't This Better; Let's Hear It For Me; I Like Him/I Like Her; It's Only a Paper Moon; I Found a Million Dollar Baby In a Five and Ten Cent Store; Beautiful Face, Have a Heart; If You Want the Rainbow, You Must Have the Rain; I Caught a Code In My Dose; Am I Blue?; Clap Hands, Here Comes Charley; Me and My Shadow; If I Love Again; Isn't It Better.
1975 (PG) 137m/C Barbra Streisand, Omar Sharif, James Caan, Roddy McDowall, Ben Vereen, Carole Wells, Larry Gates, Heidi O'Rourke; **D:** Herbert Ross; **W:** Jay Presson Allen. **VHS, Beta, LV** $19.95 COL, PIA, FCT ♂♂½

Funny Money Pointed, satirical look at the British habit of financing life with the almighty credit card. Sometimes uneven comedy.
1982 92m/C GB Greg Henry, Elizabeth Daily, Gareth Hunt, Derren Nesbitt, Annie Ross; **D:** James K. Clarke. **VHS, Beta** $69.95 LIV ♂

A Funny Thing Happened on the Way to the Forum A bawdy Broadway farce set in ancient Rome where a conniving, slave plots his way to freedom by aiding in the romantic escapades of his master's inept son. Terrific performances by Mostel and Gilford. Keaton's second-to-last film role. The Oscar-winning score includes such highlights as "Comedy Tonight," "Lovely," and "Everybody Ought to Have a Maid."
1966 100m/C Zero Mostel, Phil Silvers, Jack Gilford, Buster Keaton, Michael Hordern, Michael Crawford, Annette Andre; **D:** Richard Lester; **M:** Ken Thorne. **VHS, Beta, LV** $19.99 FOX, FCT ♂♂½

Furia Pasional A hot, passionate film about a lusty couple in romantic trouble.
197? ?m/C SP Alfonso Muguia, Hilda Cibar, Manuel Cepeda. **VHS, Beta** MAD ♂½

The Furious Bruce Lee fights the forces of a villainous drug dealer known as the Cobra.
1981 (PG) 88m/C Bruce Le. **VHS, Beta** $29.99 BFV ♂

Furious The sister of a young martial arts apprentice is killed by the master, with a great deal of action and special effects.
1983 (PG) 85m/C Simon Rhee, Howard Jackson, Arlene Montano. **VHS, Beta** $49.95 *VHE* ⅃

The Furious Avenger A released convict, on his way to avenging his family's murder, stops a rape and takes on one opponent after another in this rousing kick-fest. Dubbed.
1976 84m/C Hsiung Fei, Fan Ling, Chen Pei Ling, Tien Yeh, Wang Mo Chou. **VHS, Beta** $39.95 *UNI* ⅃

Furious Slaughter In the 1930's, a martial artist risks it all in a bold attempt to obliterate a white slave ring.
197? 90m/C Jimmy Wang Yu. **VHS, Beta** $19.95 *OCE* ⅃

The Further Adventures of Tennessee Buck Mercenary adventurer travels through tropical jungles acting as a guide to a dizzy couple. Along the way, they encounter cannibals, headhunters, and other bizarre jungle things in this lame take on "Indiana Jones." Shot on location in Sri Lanka.
1988 (R) 90m/C David Keith, Kathy Shower, Brant Van Hoffman; *D:* David Keith. **VHS, Beta, LV** $19.98 *MED* ⅃

Further Adventures of the Wilderness Family, Part 2 Also known as the "Further Adventures of the Wilderness Family." Depicts the Robinson family who left civilization for the freedom of the Colorado wild. Predictable retread, but more good family adventure drama from the makers of "Adventures of the Wilderness Family." *AKA:* Wilderness Family, Part 2.
1977 (G) 104m/C Heather Rattray, Ham Larsen, George Flower, Robert F. Logan, Susan Damante Shaw; *D:* Frank Zuniga. **VHS, Beta** $9.98 *MED* ⅃⅃½

Fury Tracy gives an excellent performance as an innocent young man framed for kidnapping and then nearly murdered by a lynch mob. His plans for revenge are thwarted by his girlfriend, who fears that he will turn into the murderer he has been accused of being. Powerful anti-violence message is well-made, with strong ensemble acting. Lang's favorite of his American-made films.
1936 96m/B Spencer Tracy, Sylvia Sidney, Walter Abel, Bruce Cabot, Edward Ellis, Walter Brennan, Frank Albertson; *D:* Fritz Lang. **VHS, Beta** $19.98 *MGM* ⅃⅃⅃½

The Fury The head of a government institute for psychic research finds that his own son is snatched by supposed terrorists who wish to use his lethal powers. The father tries to use another young woman with psychic power to locate him, with bloody results. A real chiller.
1978 (R) 117m/C Kirk Douglas, John Cassavetes, Carrie Snodgress, Andrew Stevens, Amy Irving, Charles Durning, Daryl Hannah; *D:* Brian DePalma; *M:* John Williams. **VHS, Beta** $19.98 *FOX* ⅃⅃

Fury A man and woman meet in the Amazonian jungle and the sparks begin to fly.
198? 75m/C Stuart Whitman, Laura Gemser. **VHS, Beta** *NO* ⅃

Fury in the Shaolin Temple A kung fu master kills the thief who stole his temple's secret by kicking him in the head.
198? 89m/C Liu Chia Hui. **VHS, Beta** *NO* ⅃

Fury is a Woman A Polish version of Shakespeare's Macbeth which ranks with the greatest film translations of his work. In Czarist Russia the passionate wife of a plantation owner begins an affair with a farm hand, and poisons her father-in-law when he finds them out. As her madness grows, she plots the murder of the husband. Letterbox format. In Serbian with English subtitles.
1961 93m/B *RU* Olivera Markovic, Ljuba Tadic, Kapitalina Eric; *D:* Andrzej Wajda. **VHS** $59.95 *HTV, TAM* ⅃⅃⅃½

The Fury of Hercules It's up to the mighty son of Zeus to free an enslaved group of people from an oppressive, evil ruler. Surely all who stand in his way will be destroyed. Another Italian muscleman film. *AKA:* La Furia Di Ercole; Fury of Samson.
1961 95m/C *IT* Brad Harris, Brigitte Corey, Mara Berni, Carlo Tamberlani, Serge Gainsbourg, Elke Arendt, Alan Steel; *D:* Gianfranco Parolini. **VHS** $9.95 *GKK, SNC* ⅃½

Fury of King Boxer The rebel Shaolin warriors fight the evil overlords, as usual.
1983 92m/C Kuo Shu Chung, Wang Yu; *D:* Ting Shan Si. **VHS, Beta** $29.99 *BFV* ⅃

The Fury of the Wolfman A murdering werewolf is captured by a female scientist who tries to cure his lycanthropy with drugs and brain implants. Pretty slow going, but hang in there for the wolfman versus werewoman climax.
1970 80m/C *SP* Paul Naschy, Perla Cristal; *D:* Jose Maria Zabalza; *W:* Paul Naschy. **VHS, Beta** $49.95 *UNI, NLC, LOO* ⅃

Fury on Wheels Tale of men who race cars and wreak havoc and vice versa.
1971 (PG) 89m/C Judd Hirsch, Tom Ligon, Paul Sorvino, Logan Ramsey, Collin Wilcox-Horne. **VHS, Beta** *PGN* ⅃

Fury to Freedom: The Life Story of Raul Ries A young man raised in the volatile world of abusive and alcoholic parents grows into an abusive and violent adult. One night, however, he meets something he can't beat up, and it changes his life.
1985 78m/C Gil Gerard, John Quade, Tom Silardi. **VHS** $29.95 *UHV, VIS* ⅃⅃

Future Cop A hard-nosed, old-fashioned cop is forced to team with the ultimate partner—a robot. Silly made-for-TV movie, but likable leads.
1976 78m/C Ernest Borgnine, Michael J. Shannon, John Amos, John Larch, Herbert Nelson, Ronnie Clair Edwards; *D:* Judd Taylor. **VHS** *PAR* ⅃⅃

Future Force In the crime-filled future cops can't maintain order. They rely on a group of civilian mercenaries to clean up the streets.
1989 (R) 90m/C David Carradine, Robert Tessier, Anna Rapagna, William Zipp. **VHS, Beta** $79.95 *AIP* ⅃

Future Hunters In the holocaust-blitzed future, a young couple searches for a religious artifact that may decide the future of the planet.
1988 96m/C Robert Patrick, Linda Carol, Ed Crick, Bob Schott; *D:* Cirio H. Santiago. **VHS, Beta, LV** $19.98 *LIV, VES* ⅃

Future Kill Anti-nuclear activists battle fraternity brothers in this grim futuristic world. Shaky political alliances form between revenge-seeking factions on both sides.
1985 (R) 83m/C Edwin Neal, Marilyn Burns, Doug Davis; *W/D:* Ronald W. Moore. **VHS, Beta, LV** $19.98 *LIV, VES* ⅃

Future Zone In an attempt to save his father from being murdered, a young man travels backwards in time.
1990 (R) 88m/C David Carradine, Charles Napier, Ted Prior; *D:* David A. Prior. **VHS, LV** $79.95 *AIP* ⅃⅃

Futurekick In the not so distant future, a kickboxer with an attitude and cyborg capabilities must use every ounce of strength in a battle against evil.
1991 (R) 80m/C Don "The Dragon" Wilson, Meg Foster, Christopher Penn, Eb Lottimer; *W/ D:* Damian Klaus. **VHS** *NHO* ⅃½

Futureworld In the sequel to "Westworld," two reporters junket to the new "Futureworld" theme park, where they first support a scheme to clone and control world leaders. Includes footage shot at NASA locations.
1976 (PG) 107m/C Peter Fonda, Blythe Danner, Arthur Hill, Yul Brynner, Stuart Margolin; *D:* Richard T. Heffron. **VHS, Beta** $19.98 *WAR, OM* ⅃⅃

Futz Story from off-Broadway is of a man who loves his pig and the world that can't understand the attraction. Better in original stage production.
1969 90m/C John Pakos, Victor Lipari, Sally Kirkland; *D:* Tom O'Horgan. **VHS, Beta** *NO* ⅃½

Fuzz Reynolds is the Boston cop on the track of a bomber killing policemen, punks setting winos on fire, and some amorous fellow officers. Combines fast action and some sharp-edged humor.
1972 (PG) 92m/C Burt Reynolds, Tom Skerritt, Yul Brynner, Raquel Welch, Jack Weston, Charles Martin Smith; *D:* Richard A. Colla. **VHS, Beta** $14.95 *MGM, FOX* ⅃⅃½

Fyre Young beautiful girl moves from the Midwest to Los Angeles and becomes a prostitute.
1978 (R) 90m/C Allen Garfield, Lynn Theel, Tom Baker, Cal Haynes, Donna Wilkes, Bruce Kirby; *D:* Richard Grand. **VHS, Beta** *MED* ⅃½

"G" Men Powerful story based loosely on actual events that occurred during FBI operations in the early 1930s, with Cagney on the right side of the law, though still given to unreasonable fits of anger. Raised and educated by a well-known crime kingpin, a young man becomes an attorney. When his friend the FBI agent is killed in the line of duty, he joins the FBI to seek vengeance on the mob. But his mob history haunts him, forcing him to constantly prove to his superiors that he is not under its influence. Tense and thrilling classic.
1935 86m/B James Cagney, Barton MacLane, Ann Dvorak, Margaret Lindsay, Robert Armstrong, Lloyd Nolan, William Harrigan, Regis Toomey; *D:* William Keighley. **VHS, Beta** $19.98 *MGM, CCB* ⅃⅃⅃½

G-Men Never Forget Moore, former stunt-man and future Lone Ranger, stars in this 12-part serial about FBI agents battling the bad guys. Lots of action. On two cassettes. *AKA:* Code 645.
1948 167m/B Clayton Moore, Roy Barcroft, Ramsay Ames, Drew Allen, Tommy Steele, Eddie Acuff; *D:* Fred Brannon, Yakima Canutt. **VHS** $29.98 *REP, MLB* ⅃⅃½

G-Men vs. the Black Dragon Reedited serial of "Black Dragon of Manzanar" stars Cameron as Fed who battles Asian Axis agents during WWII. Action-packed.
1943 244m/B Rod Cameron, Roland Got, Constance Worth, Nino Pipitone, Noel Cravat; *D:* William Witney. **VHS, LV** $29.98 *REP, MED, MLB* ⅃⅃½

Gabriel Over the White House Part political satire, part fantasy, and completely fascinating. Huston is a venal politician, completely in thrall to his crooked cohorts, who manages to get elected President. While recuperating from an auto accident Huston thinks he's seen a vision of the

Archangel Gabriel, who essentially tells him to change his crooked ways. From bought man Huston changes to righteous do-gooder, much to the dismay of his criminal companions, who stop at nothing to get rid of the man they think has simply gone insane. Huston gives a powerful performance in this decidedly oddball film.
1933 86m/B Walter Huston, Karen Morley, Arthur Byron, Franchot Tone, Dickie Moore, C. Henry Gordon, David Landau, Samuel S. Hinds, Jean Parker; D: Gregory La Cava. VHS $19.98 MGM, MOV 𝒶𝒶𝒶

Gabriela A sultry romance develops between a Brazilian tavern keeper and the new cook he's just hired. Music by Antonio Carlos. Derived from Jorge Amado's novel. In Portuguese with English subtitles.
1984 (R) 102m/C BR Sonia Braga, Marcello Mastroianni, Nelson Xavier, Antonio Cantafora; D: Bruno Barreto. VHS, Beta $19.98 MGM, TAM 𝒶𝒶

Gaby: A True Story The story of a woman with congenital cerebral palsy who triumphs over her condition with the help of family and loved ones, and ends up a college graduate and acclaimed author. Based on a true story.
1987 (R) 115m/C Rachel Levin, Liv Ullmann, Norma Aleandro, Robert Loggia; D: Luis Mandoki. VHS, Beta, LV $79.95 COL 𝒶𝒶𝒶

Gaiety Explores the lighter side of lion hunting.
1943 40m/B Antonio Moreno, Armida, Anne Ayars. VHS, Beta $14.95 QNE 𝒶𝒶½

Gal Young 'Un Set during the Prohibition era, a rich, middle-aged woman living on her property in the Florida backwoods finds herself courted by a much younger man. She discovers she is being used to help him set up a moonshining business. Unsentimental story of a strong woman. Based on a Marjorie Kinnan Rawlings story.
1979 105m/C Dana Preu, David Peck, J. Smith; D: Victor Nunez. VHS, Beta $29.95 ACA 𝒶𝒶𝒶

Galactic Gigolo An alien descends to earth on vacation, and discovers he's irresistible to human women. Intended as science-fiction satire, but there's more sleaze than humor.
1987 80m/C Carmine Capobianco, Debi Thibeault, Ruth Collins, Angela Nicholas, Frank Stewart; D: Gorman Bechard. Beta NO 𝒶

Galaxina In the 31st century, a beautiful robot woman capable of human feelings is created. Stumbling parody of superspace fantasies features murdered Playmate Stratten in one of few film appearances.
1980 (R) 95m/C Dorothy Stratten, Avery Schreiber, Stephen Macht; D: William Sachs. VHS, Beta, LV $59.95 MCA 𝒶½

Galaxy Express In this animated adventure, a young boy sets out to find immortality by traveling on The Galaxy Express, an ultramodern 35th century space train that carries its passengers in search of their dreams. AKA: Galaxy Express 999.
1982 (PG) 91m/C JP D: Taro Rin; V: Booker Bradshaw, Corey Burton. VHS, Beta $39.98 NO 𝒶𝒶

Galaxy Invader Chaos erupts when an alien explorer crash lands his spacecraft in a backwoods area of the United States.
1985 (PG) 90m/C Richard Ruxton, Faye Tilles, Don Leifert. VHS, Beta $24.95 NEG 𝒶

Galaxy of Terror Astronauts sent to rescue a stranded spaceship get killed by vicious aliens. Big first: Moran (Joanie on "Happy Days") explodes. Inferior Corman-produced "Alien" imitation still manages to shock and displays generous gore. Written by director Clark and Marc Siegler. Followed

by "Forbidden World." AKA: Mindwarp: An Infinity of Terror; Planet of Horrors.
1981 (R) 85m/C Erin Moran, Edward Albert, Ray Walston, Grace Zabriskie, Zalman King; D: B.D. Clark. VHS, Beta, LV $9.98 SUE 𝒶½

Gallagher's Travels A screwball male/female reporting team chase an animal smuggling ring through the wilds of Australia.
1987 94m/C AU Ivar Kants, Joanne Samuel, Stuart Campbell, Jennifer Hagan; D: Michael Caulfield. VHS, Beta $79.95 TWE 𝒶

The Gallant Hours Biography of Admiral "Bull" Halsey (Cagney) covers five weeks, October 18 through December 1, 1942, in the World War II battle of Guadalcanal in the South Pacific. Director Montgomery forgoes battle scenes to focus on the human elements in a war and what makes a great leader. Fine performance by Cagney.
1960 115m/B James Cagney, Dennis Weaver, Ward Costello, Richard/Jaeckel, Les Tremayne, Robert Burton, Raymond Bailey, Karl Swenson, Harry Landers, James T. Goto; D: Robert Montgomery. VHS $19.98 MGM 𝒶𝒶𝒶

Gallery of Horror Five horror stories better left untold. Chaney and Carradine each appear in one segment. AKA: Dr. Terror's Gallery of Horrors; Return from the Past; Blood Suckers.
1967 90m/C Lon Chaney Jr., John Carradine. VHS, Beta $19.95 ACA, MRV 𝒶

Gallipoli History blends with the destiny of two friends as they become part of the legendary World War I confrontation between Australia and the German-allied Turks. A superbly filmed, gripping commentary on the wastes of war. Haunting score; excellent performances by Lee and a then-unknown Gibson. Remake of a lesser 1931 effort "Battle of Gallipoli."
1981 (PG) 111m/C AU Mel Gibson, Mark Lee, Bill Kerr, David Argue, Tim McKenzie; D: Peter Weir. VHS, Beta, LV $19.95 PAR 𝒶𝒶𝒶𝒶

Galloping Dynamite Early western based on a James Oliver Curwood story. A ranger avenges the death of his brother killed for gold.
1937 58m/B Kermit Maynard; D: Harry Fraser. VHS, Beta $19.95 VDM 𝒶½

The Galloping Ghost A 12-chapter serial starring football great "Red" Grange about big games, gambling, and underworld gangs.
1931 226m/B VHS, Beta $49.95 NOS, VDM, VYY 𝒶

Galyon Soldier of fortune is recruited by an oil tycoon to find his daughter and son-in-law who have been kidnapped by terrorists in South America.
1977 (PG) 92m/C Stan Brock, Lloyd Nolan, Ina Balin. VHS, Beta NO 𝒶

Gambit Caine's first Hollywood film casts him as a burglar who develops a "Topkapi"-style scheme to steal a valuable statue with MacLaine as the lure and Lom as the equally devious owner. Once Caine's careful plan is put into operation, however, everything begins to unravel.
1966 109m/C Shirley MacLaine, Michael Caine, Herbert Lom, Roger C. Carmel; D: Ronald Neame. VHS, Beta $59.95 MCA 𝒶𝒶½

The Gamble A young man (Modine) seeks to rescue his father from gambling debts by wagering himself against a lustful countess (Dunaway). When he loses the bet, however, he flees and joins up with a runaway (Beals) with the countess and her henchmen in close pursuit.
1988 (R) 108m/C Matthew Modine, Jennifer Beals, Faye Dunaway; D: Carlo Vanzina. VHS, Beta, LV $89.98 PSM 𝒶𝒶

Gamble on Love Woman returns to her father's Las Vegas casino and falls for the man who manages the gaming room.
1986 90m/C Beverly Garland; D: Jim Balden. Beta $14.95 PSM 𝒶

The Gambler College professor Axel Freed has a gambling problem so vast that it nearly gets him killed by his bookies. He goes to Las Vegas to recoup his losses and wins big, only to blow the money on stupid sports bets that get him deeper into trouble. Excellent character study of a compulsive loser on a downward spiral. AKA: Kenny Rogers as the Gambler.
1974 (R) 111m/C James Caan, Lauren Hutton, Paul Sorvino, Burt Young, James Woods; D: Karel Reisz; W: James Toback. VHS, Beta, LV $69.95 PAR 𝒶𝒶𝒶

The Gambler & the Lady A successful London-based gambler and casino owner endeavors to climb the social ladder by having an affair with a member of the British aristocracy. He not only has to contend with his jilted nightclub singer girlfriend but also with the gangsters who would like to take over his clubs. Dull direction and a mediocre script.
1952 72m/B GB Dane Clark, Naomi Chance, Kathleen Byron; D: Patrick Jenkins. VHS, Beta, LV NO 𝒶½

Gambler's Choice A police lieutenant and his boyhood friend find themselves on opposite sides of the law in this crime drama. Even though both men are romantically involved with the same woman, their friendship remains intact.
1944 66m/B Chester Morris, Nancy Kelly, Russell Hayden, Sheldon Leonard, Lee Patrick, Lloyd Corrigan, Tom Dugan, Lyle Talbot, Charles Arnt; D: Frank McDonald. VHS $19.95 NOS 𝒶𝒶

The Gambling Samurai A samurai returns to his village to find it besieged by a ruthless government. Instead of attacking, he bides his time and works to undermine the government—finally achieving his revenge. In Japanese with English subtitles. AKA: Kunisada Chuji.
1960 101m/C JP Toshiro Mifune, Michiyo Aratama; D: Senkichi Taniguhi. VHS, Beta $59.95 VDA 𝒶𝒶

The Gambling Terror A cowboy goes after a mobster selling protection to hapless ranchers.
1937 53m/B Johnny Mack Brown, Charles King; D: Sam Newfield. VHS, Beta $19.95 NOS, VCN, HEG 𝒶𝒶

The Game Three friends arrange a puzzle-murder-mystery for a selected group of guilty people, with $1 million as the prize—and death for the losers.
1989 91m/C Tom Blair, Debbie Martin. VHS, Beta, LV $69.95 TWE 𝒶

Game for Vultures Racial unrest in Rhodesia is the backdrop for this tale of a black revolutionary who fights racist sanctions. The noble topic suffers from stereotypes and oversimplification.
1986 (R) 113m/C GB Richard Harris, Richard Roundtree, Joan Collins, Ray Milland; D: James Fargo. VHS, Beta $19.98 TWE 𝒶𝒶

The Game is Over A wealthy neglected wife falls in love with her grown stepson, causing her to divorce her husband and shatter her life. A good performance by Fonda, then Vadim's wife. Modern version of Zola's "La Curee."
1966 (R) 96m/C FR Jane Fonda, Peter McEnery, Michel Piccoli; D: Roger Vadim. VHS, Beta $69.95 MED 𝒶𝒶½

A Game of Crime Intriguing murder story with strong horror overtones.

1960 ?m/C John Barrymore Jr., Luisa Rivelli. **VHS $15.95** LOO ✗✗

Game of Death Bruce Lee's final kung fu thriller about a young martial arts movie star who gets involved with the syndicate. Lee died halfway through the filming of this movie and it was finished with out-takes and a double. **AKA:** Goodbye Bruce Lee: His Last Game of Death; Bruce Lee's Game of Death. **1979** (R) 100m/C Bruce Lee, Dean Jagger, Kareem Abdul-Jabbar, Colleen Camp, Chuck Norris; **D:** Robert Clouse; **M:** John Barry. **VHS, Beta, LV $19.98** FOX ✗✗

The Game of Love Olin presides over Henry's bar, the lost and found of lonely hearts and lust, where people go to quench that deep thirst for love. **1990** (PG) 94m/C Ed Marinaro, Belinda Bauer, Ken Olin, Robert Rusler, Tracy Nelson, Max Gail, Janet Margolin, Brynn Thayer; **D:** Bobby Roth. **VHS, LV $19.95** ACA ✗✗

Game of Seduction A murdering, womanizing playboy pursues a single, married woman, and gets caught up in a treacherous cat-and-mouse game. Dubbed. **1986** 81m/C Sylvia Kristel, Jon Finch, Nathalie Delon; **D:** Roger Vadim. **VHS, Beta** NO ✗

Game of Survival A young man from another planet is transported to Earth. Seems he's pitted against six of the most ferocious warriors in the galaxy in a game of survival that will be fought to the death. Violent. **1985** (X) 85m/C Nikki Hill, Cindy Coatman, Roosevelt Miller Jr. **VHS $7.95** SIM ✗

Game of Survival A young rebel warrior from another planet is sent to earth to battle six of the galaxy's most brutal warriors. **1989** 85m/C Nikki Hill, Cindy Coatman, Roosevelt Miller Jr.; **D:** Armand Gazarian. **VHS, Beta** NO ✗

Gamera, the Invincible This Japanese monster flick features the ultimate nuclear super-turtle who flies around destroying cities and causing panic. First in the series of notoriously bad films, this one is cool in black and white and has some impressive special effects. Dubbed in English. **AKA:** Gamera; Gammera; Daikaiju Gamera. **1966** 86m/B JP Brian Donlevy, Albert Dekker, Diane Findlay, John Baragrey, Dick O'Neill, Eiji Funakoshi; **D:** Noriaki Yuasa. **VHS, LV $9.99** JFK, SNC ✗½

Gamera vs. Barugon The monstrous turtle returns to Earth from his outer space prison, now equipped with his famous legjets. He soon wishes he had stayed airborne, however, when he is forced to do battle with 130-foot lizard Barugon and his rainbow-melting ray. Tokyo and Osaka get melted in the process. **AKA:** Gamera Tai Barugon; Gambara vs. Barugon; The War of the Monsters. **1966** 101m/C JP Kojiro Hongo, Kyoko Enami; **D:** Shigeo Tanaka. **VHS, Beta $9.99** JFK ✗½

Gamera vs. Gaos Now fully the good guy, Gamera slugs it out with a bat-like critter named Gaos. Suspense rules the day when Gaos tries to put out the super turtle's jets with his built-in fire extinguisher but luckily for Earth, Gamera has a few tricks of his own up his shell. **AKA:** The Return of the Giant Monsters; Gamera vs. Gyaos; Boyichi and the Supermonster; Gamera Tai Gaos. **1967** 87m/C JP Kojiro Hongo, Kichijiro Ueda, Naoyuki Abe; **D:** Noriaki Yuasa. **VHS, Beta, LV $9.99** JFK ✗½

Gamera vs. Guiron Gamera risks it all to take on an evil, spear-headed monster on a distant planet. Highlight is the sexy, leotard clad aliens who want to eat the little Earth kids' brains. **AKA:** Attack of the Monsters; Gamera Tai Guiron. **1969** 88m/C JP Nobuhiro Kashima, Christopher Murphy, Miyuki Akiyama, Yuko Hamada, Eiji Funakoshi; **D:** Noriaki Yuasa. **VHS, Beta $9.99** JFK ✗

Gamera vs. Zigra Gamera the flying turtle chose an ecological theme for this, his final movie. It seems that the alien Zigrans have come to Earth to wrest the planet from the hands of the pollutive humans who have nearly destroyed it. The aliens kill the staunch turtle, but the love and prayers of children revive him that he may defend Earth once more. **AKA:** Gamera Tai Shinkai Kaiju Jigara; Gamera vs. the Deep Sea Monster Zigra. **1971** 91m/C JP Reiko Kasahara, Mikiko Tsubouchi, Koji Fujiyama, Arlene Zoellner, Gloria Zoellner; **D:** Noriaki Yuasa. **VHS, Beta, LV $9.99** JFK ✗

Games Girls Play The daughter of an American diplomat organizes a contest at a British boarding school to see which of her classmates can seduce important dignitaries. **AKA:** The Bunny Caper; Sex Play. **1975** 90m/C Christina Hart, Jane Anthony, Jill Damas, Drina Pavlovic; **D:** Jack Arnold. **VHS, Beta** NO ✗½

The Gamma People A journalist discovers a Balkan doctor shooting children with gamma rays, creating an army of brainless zombies. Cult-renowned grade-Z tripe. **1956** 83m/B GB Walter Rilla, Paul Douglas, Eva Bartok; **D:** John Gilling. **VHS, Beta $9.95** RCA Woof!

Gammera the Invincible A giant, fire-breathing space turtle terrorizes the earth following an atomic explosion. Good special effects in this juvenile sci-fi movie. **AKA:** Gamera the Invincible. **1966** 88m/C JP Brian Donlevy, Albert Dekker, John Baragrey; **D:** Noriaki Yuasa. **VHS $16.95** SNC ✗✗

Gandhi The biography of Mahatma Gandhi from the prejudice he encounters as a young attorney in South Africa, to his role as spiritual leader to the people of India and his use of passive resistance against the country's British rulers, and his eventual assassination. Kingsley is a marvel in his Academy Award-winning role and the picture is a generally riveting epic worthy of its eight Oscars. **1982** (PG) 188m/C GB Ben Kingsley, Candice Bergen, Edward Fox, John Gielgud, John Mills, Saeed Jaffrey, Trevor Howard, Ian Charleson, Roshan Seth, Athol Fugard, Martin Sheen, Daniel Day-Lewis, Rohini Hattangady; **D:** Richard Attenborough; **W:** John Briley. Academy Awards '82: Best Actor (Kingsley), Best Art Direction/Set Decoration, Best Cinematography, Best Costume Design, Best Director (Attenborough), Best Film Editing, Best Original Screenplay, Best Picture; Nominations: Best Makeup, Best Original Score; British Academy Awards '82: Best Actor (Kingsley), Best Director (Attenborough), Best Film, Best Supporting Actress (Hattangady); Golden Globe Awards '83: Best Actor—Drama (Kingsley), Best Director (Attenborough), Best Foreign Film; New York Film Critics Awards '82: Best Film. **VHS, Beta, LV $29.95** COL, BTV, HMV ✗✗✗½

Gang Bullets Mobster tries to continue his dirty systems in a new town, but finds the legal force incorruptible.

1938 62m/B Anne Nagel, Robert Kent, Charles Trowbridge, Morgan Wallace, J. Farrell MacDonald, Arthur Loft, John Merton; **D:** Lambert Hillyer. **VHS, Beta $16.95** SNC ✗

Gang Busters Prisoners plan a breakout. Slow and uninteresting adaptation of the successful radio series. Filmed in Oregon. **1955** 78m/B Myron Healey, Don Harvey, Sam Edwards, Frank Gerstle; **D:** Bill Karn. **VHS $19.95** NOS, SNC ✗½

Gang War Low-budget gangster film with an all-back cast about two gangs fighting for control of the city's jukebox business. **1940** 60m/B Ralph Cooper, Gladys Snyder, Reggie Fenderson, Lawrence Criner, Monte Hawley, Jesse C. Brooks, Maceo B. Sheffield; **D:** Leo Popkin. **VHS $24.95** NOS, RXM ✗

Gang Wars There's a riot going on as Puerto Rican, Black, and Chinese gangs fight it out for control of the city. **AKA:** Devil's Express. **1975** (R) 82m/C Warhawk Tanzania, Larry Fleishman, Sam DeFazio, Wilfred Roldan, Elsie Roman, Sarah Nyrick; **D:** Barry Rosen. **VHS $9.95** SUN ✗

Gangbusters Men battle crime in the city in this serial In thirteen episodes based on the popular radio series of the same name. **1938** 253m/B Kent Taylor, Irene Hervey, Robert Armstrong. **VHS, Beta, 3/4U, Special order formats $49.95** NOS, CAB, VCN ✗✗

The Gang's All Here Darro joins a trucking firm whose rigs are being run off the road and hijacked by a competitor. Features "Charlie Chan" regulars Luke and Moreland. ♫ Minnie's in the Money; The Lady in the Tutti-Frutti Hat; A Journey to a Star; No Love, No Nothin'; Paducah; The Polka Dot Polka. **1941** 63m/B Frankie Darro, Marcia Mae Jones, Jackie Moran, Mantan Moreland, Keye Luke; **D:** Jean Yarborough. **VHS $19.95** NOS, RXM ✗½

Gangs, Inc. A woman is sent to prison for a hit-and-run accident, actually the fault of a wealthy playboy. When she learns his identity she vows revenge and turns to crime to achieve her evil ends. Okay thriller suffers from plot problems. Ladd has a minor role filmed before he became a star. **AKA:** Crimes, Inc.; Paper Bullets. **1941** 72m/B Joan Woodbury, Lash LaRue, Linda Ware, John Archer, Vince Barnett, Alan Ladd; **D:** Phil Rosen. **VHS, Beta $19.95** NOS, MRV, DVT ✗✗

The Gangster Sullivan plays a small-time slum-bred hood who climbs to the top of the underworld, only to lose his gang because he allows his fears to get the better of him. (There's nothing to fear except when someone knows you're afeared.) Noir crimer with an interesting psychological perspective, though a bit sluggish at times. **1947** 84m/B **VHS $14.98** FOX, FCT ✗✗½

Gangster Wars A specially edited-for-video version of the television mini-series "The Gangster Chronicles." Based on fact, it deals with the growth of organized crime in America from the early days of this century, through the eyes of three ghetto kids who grow up to become powerful mobsters. **1981** 121m/C Michael Nouri, Joe Penny, Brian Benben, Kathleen Lloyd, Madeleine Stowe, Robert Davi; **D:** Richard Sarafian. **VHS, Beta $59.95** MCA ✗✗

Gangsters City is ruled by the mob and nothing can stop their bloody grip except "The Special Squad." **1979** 90m/C IT Michael Gazzo, Tony Page, Vicki Sue Robinson, Nai Bonet; **D:** Mac Ahlberg. **VHS, Beta $39.95** VCD, HHE, MTX ✗

Gangster's Den A gang of renegades scare a woman out of buying a gold-laden piece of land and Billy the Kid comes to her rescue.
1945 56m/B Buster Crabbe, Kermit Maynard, Al "Fuzzy" St. John, Charles King; *D:* Sam Newfield. VHS, Beta $19.95 VDM, TIM *I*

Gangster's Law A look at a seedy gangster's downfall. Filmed on location in Italy. Dubbed.
1986 89m/C Klaus Kinski, Maurice Poli, Susy Anderson, Max Delys; *D:* Siro Marcellini. VHS, Beta $69.95 TWE *Woof!*

Gangsters of the Frontier The people of Red Rock are forced to work in the town mines by two prison escapees until Ritter and his friends ride to the rescue. Part of the "Texas Ranger" series.
1944 56m/B Tex Ritter, Dave O'Brien; *W/D:* Elmer Clifton. VHS, Beta $19.95 NOS, DVT, RXM *I*

Gangway Pat Wayne (Matthews), a London newspaper reporter, is mistaken for a jewel thief and kidnapped by gangsters aboard a New York-bound ocean liner. In the meantime, the real thief is aboard posing as a Hollywood actress (Blakeney), and it's up to Scotland Yard inspector Bob Deering (Mackay) to solve the crime. Matthews was considered by many to be the English equivalent of America's Eleanor Powell. Based on an original story by Dwight Taylor.
1937 90m/B GB Jessie Matthews, Barry Mackay, Olive Blakeney, Liane Ordeyne, Patrick Ludlow, Nat Pendleton, Noel Madison, Alastair Sim, Doris Rogers, Laurence Anderson, Bennie Dorn; *W/D:* Sonnie Hale; *W:* Lesser Samuels. VHS HEG *I* ½

Ganjasaurus Rex Monster spoof about a giant green dinosaur emerging from the pot-laden hills of California. Maybe it's all in your head, man.
1987 (R) 100m/C Paul Bassis, Dave Fresh, Rosie Jones; *D:* Ursi Reynolds. VHS, Beta $59.95 RHI *I*

Gappa the Trifibian Monster Researchers visiting a tropical island find a giant egg and take it back to Tokyo with them, dismaying the egg's giant monster parents. Dubbed. *AKA:* Daikyoju Gappa; Monster from a Prehistoric Planet.
1967 (PG) 90m/C JP VHS, Beta $19.98 ORI *I* ½

The Garbage Pail Kids Movie The disgusting youngsters, stars of bubblegum cards, make their first and last film appearance in this live action dud. The garbage is where it should be thrown.
1987 (PG) 100m/C Anthony Newley, MacKenzie Astin, Katie Barberi; *D:* Rod Amateau. VHS, Beta, LV $14.95 PAR, KRT, IME *Woof!*

Garbancito de la Mancha A child with magic powers takes his goat on a quest to rescue his friends.
1987 70m/C MX VHS, Beta $45.95 MAD *II*

Garbo Talks A dying eccentric's last request is to meet the reclusive screen legend Greta Garbo. Bancroft amusingly plays the dying woman whose son goes to extreme lengths in order to fulfill his mother's last wish.
1984 (PG-13) 104m/C Anne Bancroft, Ron Silver, Carrie Fisher, Catherine Hicks, Steven Hill, Howard da Silva, Dorothy Loudon, Harvey Fierstein, Hermione Gingold; *D:* Sidney Lumet. VHS, Beta $19.98 MGM, FOX *II*

The Garden of Allah Dietrich finds hyper-romantic encounters in the Algerian desert with Boyer, but this terrible secret may doom them both. This early Technicolor production, though flawed, is an absolute

must for Dietrich fans. Yuma, Ariz. substituted for the exotic locale.
1936 85m/C Marlene Dietrich, Charles Boyer, Basil Rathbone, C. Aubrey Smith, Tilly Losch, Joseph Schildkraut, Henry Kleinbach (Brandon), John Carradine; *D:* Richard Boleslawski. VHS, LV $59.98 FOX *III*

The Garden of Delights A wicked black comedy about a millionaire, paralyzed and suffering from amnesia after a car accident. His horrendously greedy family tries to get him to remember and reveal his Swiss bank account number. Acclaimed; in Spanish with English subtitles.
1970 95m/C SP Jose Luis Lopez Vasquez, Lina Canelajas, Luchy Soto, Francisco Pierra, Charo Soriano; *D:* Carlos Savrat. VHS, Beta $68.00 TAM, CVC, FCT *III*

The Garden of Eden Milestone—whose "Two Arabian Nights" had won an Academy Award the previous year, and who went on to direct "All Quiet on the Western Front" and "Of Mice and Men"—directed this sophisticated ersatz Lubitsch sex comedy. Griffith, the so-called "Orchid Lady," is a young girl who dreams of diva-dom but falls deep into the underbelly of the seedy side of Budapest. With the aid of a fallen baroness, however, she finds her way to Monte Carlo and has her turn in the limelight. A handsome production designed by William Cameron Menzies, art director for "Gone With the Wind."
1928 115m/B Corrine Griffith, Louise Dressler, Charles Ray, Lowell Sherman; *D:* Lewis Milestone. VHS, Beta, 8mm $19.95 NOS, VYY, TIM *III*

Garden of the Finzi-Continis Acclaimed film by DeSica about an aristocratic Jewish family living in Italy under increasing Fascist oppression on the eve of World War II. The garden wall symbolizes the distance between the Finzi-Continis and the Nazi reality about to engulf them. Flawless acting and well-defined direction. In Italian with English subtitles or dubbed. *AKA:* Il Giardino Del Finzi-Contini.
1971 (R) 90m/C IT Dominique Sanda, Helmut Berger, Lino Capolicchio, Fabio Testi; *D:* Vittorio De Sica. Academy Awards '71: Best Foreign Language Film; Nominations: Best Adapted Screenplay; Berlin International Film Festival '71: Golden Berlin Bear; National Board of Review Awards '71: 5 Best Foreign Films of the Year. VHS, Beta, LV $39.98 LHV, IME, APD *IIII*

Gardens of Stone A zealous young cadet during the Vietnam War is assigned to the Old Guard patrol at Arlington Cemetery, and clashes with the patrol's older officers and various pacifist civilians. Falls short of the mark, although Jones turns in an excellent performance.
1987 (R) 112m/C James Caan, James Earl Jones, D.B. Sweeney, Anjelica Huston, Dean Stockwell, Lonette McKee, Mary Stuart Masterson, Bill Graham, Sam Bottoms, Casey Siemaszko, Larry Fishburne; *D:* Francis Ford Coppola. VHS, Beta, LV $89.98 FOX *III*

Garringo Lawmen attempt to bring to justice a man who is intent on killing the soldiers responsible for his father's death.
1969 95m/C IT SP Anthony Steffen, Peter Lee Lawrence, Jose Bodalo; *D:* Rafael Romero Marchent. VHS, Beta $44.95 MAD *II*

Gas This dog has tycoon Hayden buying up all the gas stations in town to create a crisis that will make him richer. Everyone in the cast wastes their time, especially Sutherland as a hip DJ reporting on the gas shortage.
1981 (R) 94m/C CA Donald Sutherland, Susan Anspach, Sterling Hayden, Peter Aykroyd, Howie Mandel, Helen Shaver; *D:* Les Rose. VHS, Beta $79.95 PAR *Woof!*

Gas Food Lodging Nora (Adams) is a weary waitress in Laramie, New Mexico, trying her best to raise two teenaged daughters on her own. Trudi (Skye) defiantly sleeps around, disillusioned about love and trying to hurt both her mother and herself. The younger Shade spends most of her time in the escapist, melodrama films playing at the local Spanish-language movie palace. Shade would also like to either reunite her mother with her long-gone father (Brolin) or find her mother a new love, and find out about love herself. A special friend of Shade's is Darius, an eccentric widow dresser, played by Leitch, Skye's brother. Nothing works out quite as intended but multi-dimensional characters, poignant situations, and enormous emotional appeal highlight the directorial debut of Anders. Based on the Richard Peck novel "Don't Look and It Won't Hurt."
1992 (R) 100m/C Brooke Adams, Ione Skye, Fairuza Balk, James Brolin, Rob Knepper, Donovan Leitch; *W/D:* Allison Anders. VHS, LV COL *III*

Gas Pump Girls Comedy about five lovely ladies who manage a gas station and use their feminine wiles to win the battle against a shady oil sheik.
1979 (R) 102m/C Kirsten Baker, Dennis Bowen, Huntz Hall, Steve Bond, Leslie King, Linda Lawrence; *D:* Joel Bender. VHS, Beta, LV VES *I* ½

Gas-s-s-s! A gas main leak in an Alaskan defense plant kills everyone beyond thirty-something and the post-apocalyptic pre-boomer survivors are left to muddle their way through the brume. Trouble is, AIP edited the heck out of the movie, much to Corman's chagrin, and the result is a truncated comedy; Corman was so displeased, in fact, he left to create New World studios. Music by Country Joe and the Fish. *AKA:* Gas-s-s-s... or, It May Become Necessary to Destroy the World in Order to Save It.
1970 (PG) 79m/C Robert Corff, Elaine Giftos, Pat Patterson, George Armitage, Alex Wilson, Ben Vereen, Cindy Williams, Bud Cort, Talia Shire, Country Joe & the Fish; *D:* Roger Corman. VHS, Beta NO *II* ½

Gaslight A forgotten British classic that fell victim to the American production of the same title and theme that was filmed only five years later. Set in late Victorian London, Wynyard is the rich innocent married to the calculating Walbrook, who slowly tries driving his bride insane in order to discover some hidden family jewels. She comes under the protection of a Scotland Yard detective (Pettingell) who suspects Walbrook has already murdered once. An outstandingly eerie psychological thriller. Based on the play "Angel Street" by Patrick Hamilton. *AKA:* Angel Street.
1939 84m/C GB Anton Walbrook, Diana Wynyard, Frank Pettingell, Cathleen Cordell; *D:* Thorold Dickinson. VHS $29.95 FCT *III* ½

Gaslight Lavish remake of the 1939 film, based on the Patrick Hamilton play "Angel Street." A man tries to drive his beautiful wife insane while searching for priceless jewels. Her only clue to his evil acts is the frequent dimming of their gaslights. A suspenseful Victorian era mystery. Lansbury's film debut, as the tarty maid. *AKA:* The Murder in Thorton Square.
1944 114m/B Charles Boyer, Ingrid Bergman, Joseph Cotten, Angela Lansbury, Terry Moore, May Whitty, Barbara Everest, Emil Rameau, Edmund Breon, Halliwell Hobbes, Tom Stevenson; *D:* George Cukor. Academy Awards '44: Best Actress (Bergman), Best Interior Decoration; Nominations: Best Actor (Boyer), Best Black and White Cinematography, Best

Picture, Best Screenplay, Best Supporting Actress (Lansbury); Golden Globe Awards '45: Best Actress—Drama (Bergman). **VHS, Beta, LV** $19.98 *MGM, TIM, BTV* �యయయ ½

The Gate Kids generally like to explore and Dorff and Tripp are no exception. When a large hole is exposed in their backyard, it would be a childhood sin not to see what's in it, right? What they don't know is that this hole is actually a gateway to and from Hell. The terror they unleash includes more than just run-of-the-mill demons. Good special effects. Followed by "Gate 2."
1987 (PG-13) 85m/C Christa Denton, Stephen Dorff, Louis Tripp; *D:* Tibor Takacs. **VHS, Beta, LV** $14.98 *LIV, VES* �యయ

Gate 2 Tripp returns in his role as Terry, a young student of demonology in this lame sequel to "The Gate." Terry and a few of his teen buddies call up a group of demons that have been confined behind a gate for billions of years. The demons are used to grant modest wishes, but the wishes end up having very evil effects. Incredibly weak plot saved only by the special monster effects, which include live action and puppetry.
1992 (R) 90m/C Louis Tripp, Simon Reynolds, Pamela Segall, James Villemaire, Neil Munro, James Kidnie, Andrea Ladanyi; *D:* Tibor Takacs; *W:* Michael Nankin. **VHS, LV** *COL* ✯✯ ½

Gate of Hell Set in 12th-century Japan. A warlord desires a beautiful married woman and seeks to kill her husband to have her. However, he accidentally kills her instead. Filled with shame and remorse, the warlord abandons his life to seek solace as a monk. Heavily awarded and critically acclaimed. In Japanese with English subtitles. *AKA:* Jigokumen.
1954 89m/C *JP* Kazuo Hasegawa, Machiko Kyo; *D:* Teinosuke Kinugasa. **VHS, Beta, 8mm** $29.98 *NOS, SUE, DVT* ✯✯✯ ½

Gates of Hell Salem, Massachusetts, must battle the risen dead in this gorefest that tried to disguise itself under many other titles. *AKA:* Paura Nella Citta Dei Morti Viventi; City of the Living Dead; The Fear; Twilight of the Dead; Fear in the City of the Living Dead.
1983 90m/C Christopher George, Janet Agren, Katherine MacColl, Robert Sampson; *D:* Lucio Fulci. **VHS, Beta** $29.95 *PGN, IGP Woof!*

The Gathering A dying man seeks out the wife and family he has alienated for a final Christmas gathering. James Poe authored this well-acted holiday tearjerker that won the 1977-78 Emmy for outstanding TV drama special.
1977 94m/C Ed Asner, Maureen Stapleton, Lawrence Pressman, Stephanie Zimbalist, Bruce Davison, Gregory Harrison, Veronica Hamel, Gail Strickland; *D:* Randal Kleiser; *M:* John Barry. **VHS, Beta** $49.95 *WOV* ✯✯ ½

A Gathering of Eagles Hudson portrays a hard-nosed Air Force colonel during peacetime whose British wife must adjust to being a military spouse.
1963 115m/C Rock Hudson, Rod Taylor, Mary Peach, Barry Sullivan, Kevin McCarthy, Henry Silva, Leif Erickson; *D:* Delbert Mann; *M:* Jerry Goldsmith. **VHS** *MGM* ✯✯ ½

The Gathering: Part 2 Sequel in which a widow has a Christmas reunion with her family, but conflict arises when she introduces a new man in her life. Not as effective as the original, also made for TV.
1979 98m/C Maureen Stapleton, Efrem Zimbalist Jr., Jameson Parker, Bruce Davison, Lawrence Pressman, Gail Strickland, Veronica Hamel; *D:* Charles S. Dubin. **VHS** *TTC* ✯✯

The Gathering Storm Based on the first book of memoirs from Sir Winston Churchill, this drama examines the pre-World War II years.
1974 72m/C Richard Burton, Virginia McKenna, Ian Bannen; *D:* Herbert Wise. **Beta** $14.95 *PSM* ✯✯

The Gatling Gun Poor tale of the Cavalry, Apache Indians, and renegades all after the title weapon. *AKA:* King Gun.
1972 (PG) 93m/C Guy Stockwell, Woody Strode, Patrick Wayne, Robert Fuller, Barbara Luna, John Carradine, Pat Buttram, Phil Harris; *D:* Robert Gordon. **VHS** *HHE* ✯✯ ½

Gator Sequel to "White Lightning" (1973) follows the adventures of Gator (Reynolds), who is recruited to gather evidence to convict a corrupt political boss who also happens to be his friend. Reynolds in his good ole' boy role with lots of chase scenes. Talk show host Michael Douglas made his film debut in the role of the governor. First film Reynolds directed.
1976 (PG) 116m/C Burt Reynolds, Jerry Reed, Lauren Hutton, Jack Weston, Alice Ghostley, Dub Taylor; *D:* Burt Reynolds. **VHS, Beta** $14.95 *MGM, FOX* ✯✯

Gator Bait The Louisiana swamp is home to the beautiful Desiree, and woe be unto any man who threatens her family. Aims to please fans of the raunchy and violent. Followed by an equally vile sequel.
1973 (R) 91m/C Claudia Jennings, Clyde Ventura, Bill Thurman, Janet Baldwin; *W/D:* Ferd Sebastian, Beverly Sebastian. **VHS, Beta, LV** $19.95 *PAR* ✯ ½

Gator Bait 2: Cajun Justice A city girl comes to the Louisiana swamp and turns violent in an effort to exact revenge on the men who have been tormenting her.
1988 (R) 94m/C Jan MacKenzie, Tray Loren, Paul Muzzcat, Brad Kepnick, Jerry Armstrong, Ben Sebastian; *W/D:* Ferd Sebastian, Beverly Sebastian. **VHS, Beta, LV** $19.95 *PAR* ✯

The Gauntlet A cop is ordered to Las Vegas to bring back a key witness for an important trial—but the witness turns out to be a beautiful prostitute being hunted by killers. Violence-packed action.
1977 (R) 111m/C Clint Eastwood, Sondra Locke, Pat Hingle, Bill McKinney; *D:* Clint Eastwood. **VHS, Beta, LV** $19.98 *WAR, TLF* ✯✯

The Gay Divorcee Astaire pursues Rogers to an English seaside resort, where she mistakes him for the hired correspondent in her divorce case. Based on the musical play "The Gay Divorce" by Dwight Taylor and Cole Porter. The title was slightly changed for the movie because of protests from the Hays Office. ♫Don't Let It Bother You; A Needle in a Haystack; Let's K-nock K-nees; Night and Day; The Continental. *AKA:* The Gay Divorce.
1934 107m/B Fred Astaire, Ginger Rogers, Edward Everett Horton, Eric Blore, Alice Brady, Erik Rhodes, Betty Grable; *D:* Mark Sandrich. Academy Awards '34: Best Song ("The Continental"); Nominations: Best Interior Decoration, Best Picture, Best Sound, Best Score. **VHS, Beta, LV** $29.95 *MED, TTC* ✯✯✯

The Gay Lady Light romantic comedy set in the 1890s about an actress who climbs to stardom in London theater and winds up marrying into the aristocracy. Look for Christopher Lee and Roger Moore in early bit parts. *AKA:* Trottie True.
1949 95m/C *GB* Jean Kent, James Donald, Hugh Sinclair, Lana Morris, Bill Owen, Michael Medwin, Andrew Crawford; *D:* Brian Desmond Hurst. **VHS** *MOV, UNI* ✯✯

Gay Purr-ee Delightful tale of feline romance in the City of Lights. For all ages.

1962 85m/C *D:* Abe Levitow; *W:* Chuck Jones; *M:* Harold Arlen; *V:* Judy Garland, Robert Goulet, Red Buttons, Hermione Gingold, Mel Blanc. **VHS, LV** $19.98 *WAR, FCT, WTA* ✯✯

The Gay Ranchero Rogers, without Dale Evans, in an average tale of old west meets new crooks. Rogers is the sheriff who foils gangsters trying to take over an airport. The action doesn't stop him from singing a duet with leading lady Frazee on "Wait'll I Get My Sunshine in the Moonlight."
1942 55m/B Roy Rogers, Andy Devine, Tito Guizar, Jane Frazee, Estelita Rodriguez; *D:* William Witney. **VHS, Beta, 3/4U, Special order formats** $9.99 *NOS, VCN, CAB* ✯✯

Geek Maggot Bingo It's too bad director Zed waited until mid-"Bingo" to post a sign warning "Leave Now, It Isn't Going Get Any Better!" Conceived by the New York underground's don of the "Cinema of Transgression" to be an off-the-rack cult classic, this horror spoof is too long on in-jokes and short on substance to earn its number in the cult hall of fame. It does, however, boast Death as Scumbalina the vampire queen and Hell as a punk cowboy crooner (before alternative country hit the airwaves). TV horror-meister Zacherle narrates. *AKA:* The Freak From Suckweasel Mountain.
1983 70m/C Richard Hell, Donna Death, John Zacherle; *D:* Nick Zedd. **VHS** $39.99 *MWF, MOV* ✯

Geheimakte WB1 Historical drama centering on the invention of the U-boat by Sergeant Wilhelm Bauer during Denmark's WWII blockade of the ports of Schleswig-Holstein. In German with no subtitles. *AKA:* Secret Paper WB1.
1942 91m/B *GE* Alexander Golling; *D:* Herbert Selpin. **VHS, Beta, 3/4U** $35.95 *IHF* ✯✯

The Geisha Boy Jerry is a floundering magician who joins the USO and tours the Far East. His slapstick confrontations with the troupe leader and an officer who dreams of attending his own funeral provide hearty laughs, plus Lewis finds romance with a Japanese widow after her son claims him as a father. Pleshette's film debut, with an appearance by the Los Angeles Dodgers.
1958 98m/C Jerry Lewis, Marie McDonald, Sessue Hayakawa, Barton MacLane, Suzanne Pleshette, Nobu McCarthy; *D:* Frank Tashlin. **VHS** $14.95 *PAR* ✯✯

Gemidos de Placer A young, sex-obsessed couple get involved with murder. In Spanish.
197? 90m/C *SP* Lina Romay. **VHS, Beta** $57.95 *UNI* ✯

Gemini Affair Two women go to Hollywood to become rich and famous but end up being very disappointed.
198? 88m/C Marta Kristen, Kathy Kersh, Anne Seymour. **VHS, Beta** $49.95 *UNI* ✯

Gene Autry Matinee Double Feature #1 Includes "Blue Canadian Rockies" (1952), where Autry must investigate a series of murders, and "Last of the Pony Riders" (1953), in which the final days of the pony express yield a sinister conspiracy.
1953 117m/C Gene Autry; *D:* George Archainbaud. **VHS** $39.98 *NO* ✯

Gene Autry Matinee Double Feature #2 An exciting western double feature: A cowboy goes after the man who stole his rodeo winnings in "Melody Trail" and a territorial ranger investigates a series of Indian raids in "Winning of the West."

1953 117m/B Gene Autry, Champion, Smiley Burnette, Alan Bridge; *D:* George Archainbaud, Joseph Kane. **VHS, Beta $39.98** *NO ♫*

Gene Autry Matinee Double Feature #3 Gene stars in "Prairie Moon," in which he teaches some tough kids a lesson about life, and "On Top of Old Smokey," which sees a young woman trying to save her small town.
1953 113m/B Gene Autry, Smiley Burnette; *D:* George Archainbaud, Ralph Staub. **VHS, Beta $39.98** *NO ♫*

The Gene Krupa Story The story of the famous jazz drummer and his career plunge after a drug conviction. Krupa recorded the soundtrack, mimed by Mineo, who was too young for a convincing portrayal. Gavin McLeod (of "Love Boat" fame) has a small part as Mineo's dad.
1959 101m/B Sal Mineo, James Darren, Susan Kohner, Susan Oliver, Anita O'Day, Red Nichols; *D:* Don Weis. **VHS, Beta $19.95** *COL, FCT ♫♫½*

The General Keaton's masterpiece and arguably the most formally perfect and funniest of silent comedies. Concerns a plucky Confederate soldier who single-handedly retrieves a pivotal train from Northern territory. Full of eloquent man-vs-machinery images and outrageous sight gags. Remade as "The Great Locomotive Chase" in 1956 with Fess Parker.
1927 78m/B Buster Keaton, Marion Mack; *D:* Buster Keaton; Clyde Bruckman. **VHS, Beta, LV, 8mm, 3/4U, Special order formats $29.95** *NOS, HHT, VYY ♫♫♫♫*

General Della Rovere DeSica is superb as a con-man who is blackmailed into impersonating an executed Italian general. Excellent direction by Rossellini. Based on a novel by Indro Montanelli.
1960 129m/B *IT* Vittorio De Sica, Sandra Milo, Giovanna Ralli, Hannes Messemer; *D:* Roberto Rossellini. **VHS $29.95** *AUD, VEC ♫♫♫½*

The General Died at Dawn A clever, atmospheric suspense film about an American mercenary in Shanghai falling in love with a beautiful spy as he battles a fierce Chinese warlord who wants to take over the country. Playwright-to-be Odets' first screenplay; he, O'Hara and '30s gossip hound Skolsky have cameos as reporters.
1936 93m/B Gary Cooper, Madeleine Carroll, Akim Tamiroff, Dudley Digges, Porter Hall, William Frawley, Philip Ahn; John O'Hara, Clifford Odets, Sidney Skolsky; *D:* Lewis Milestone; *W:* Clifford Odets. **VHS, Beta $14.98** *MCA ♫♫♫*

The General Line Eisenstein's classic pro-Soviet semi-documentary about a poor farm woman who persuades her village to form a cooperative. Transgresses its partyline instructional purpose by vivid filmmaking. The director's last silent film. *AKA:* The Old and the New.
1929 90m/B *RU* Marfa Lapkina; *D:* Sergei Eisenstein. **VHS, Beta, 3/4U $24.95** *NOS, MRV, DVT ♫♫♫♫*

General Spanky The only feature "Our Gang" comedy goofed by transplanting them to a Civil War milieu popular at the time. Confederate kids Spanky and Alfalfa play soldier, ultimately outsmarting Union troops. The rascals are still funny sometimes, but Buckwheat's role as an eager slave is disturbing today.
1936 73m/B George "Spanky" McFarland, Phillips Holmes, Ralph Morgan, Irving Pichel, Rosina Lawrence, Billie "Buckwheat" Thomas, Carl "Alfalfa" Switzer, Louise Beavers; *D:* Fred Newmeyer. **VHS, LV $19.98** *MGM, FCT ♫♫*

Generale Della Rovere A World War II black marketeer is forced by the Nazis to go undercover in a local prison. To find out who the resistance leaders are, he poses as a general. But when prisoners begin to look to him for guidance, he finds the line between his assumed role and real identity diminished, leading to a tragic conclusion. Acclaimed film featuring a bravura lead performance by veteran director De Sica. In Italian with English subtitles. *AKA:* Il Generale Della-Rovere.
1960 139m/B *IT* Vittorio De Sica, Otto Messmer, Sandra Milo; *D:* Roberto Rossellini. **VHS, Beta $29.95** *NOS, CVC, HHT ♫♫♫½*

A Generation During World War II, a young man escapes from the Warsaw Ghetto and finds his way to the Polish Resistance. He falls in love with the leader of the local group and finds the courage to fight for his freedom. Strong directorial debut from Wajda. Scripted by Czeszko from his novel "Pokolenie." In Polish with English subtitles.
1954 90m/C *PL* Tadeusz Lomnicki, Ursula Modrzynska, Zbigniew Cybulski, Roman Polanski; *D:* Andrzej Wajda; *W:* Bohdan Czeszko. **VHS $29.95** *FCT ♫♫♫*

Generation A very pregnant bride informs everyone she'll give birth at home without doctors, and creates a panic. Based on the Broadway play by William Goodhart. *AKA:* A Time For Caring.
1969 109m/C David Janssen, Kim Darby, Carl Reiner, Peter Duel, Andrew Prine, James Coco, Sam Waterston; *D:* George Schaefer; *W:* William Goodhart. **VHS, Beta $69.98** *SUE ♫♫*

Generations: Mind Control-From the Future Max Lang has lost all self-control and is being driven by evil forces beyond time, forced to kill while fleeing total extinction.
1980 54m/C **VHS, Beta** *BEI ♫*

Genevieve A 1904 Darracq roadster is the title star of this picture which spoofs "classic car" owners and their annual rally from London to Brighton. Two married couple challenge each other to a friendly race which becomes increasingly intense as they near the finish line.
1953 86m/C *GB* John Gregson, Dinah Sheridan, Kenneth More, Kay Kendall; *D:* Henry Cornelius. Academy Awards '54 Nominations: Best Story & Screenplay, Best Original Score; British Academy Awards '53: Best Film; Golden Globe Awards '55: Best Foreign Film. **VHS, Beta** *LCA ♫♫♫*

Genie of Darkness The ashes of Nostradamus himself are retrieved in a bid to destroy his vampiric descendent. Edited from a Mexican serial; if you were able to sit through this one, look for "Curse of Nostradamus" and "The Monster Demolisher."
1960 ?m/B *MX* German Robles; *D:* Frederick Curiel. **VHS $16.95** *SNC, NOS, LOO ♫*

Gente Violenta A crook who steals a million dollars worth of diamonds has to flee from both the police and his old gang.
1987 90m/C *MX* Armando Silvestre, Antonio De Hudd, Rebeca Silva, Victor Junco. **VHS, Beta $58.95** *MAD ♫♫*

Gentle Giant An orphaned bear is taken in by a boy and his family and grows to be a 750 pound giant who must be returned to the wild. "Gentle Ben" TV series was derived from this feature.
1967 93m/C Dennis Weaver, Vera Miles, Ralph Meeker, Clint Howard, Huntz Hall; *D:* James Neilson. **VHS $14.98** *REP ♫♫*

Gentle Savage When an Indian is wrongly accused of raping and beating a white woman, the white community seeks revenge. The vengeful mob, led by the victim's step-father, is unaware that it's really their ringleader who is responsible for the crime. When the accused's brother is slain, the Indian community retaliates. Violent but well-crafted. *AKA:* Camper John.
1973 (R) 85m/C William Smith, Gene Evans, Barbara Luna, Joe Flynn; *D:* Sean McGregor. **VHS $29.95** *LIV ♫♫½*

Gentleman Bandit So-so drama about Father Bernard Pagano, a Boston priest mistakenly arrested as a stickup artist. Based on a true story. Made for television.
1981 96m/C Ralph Waite, Julie Bovasso, Jerry Zaks, Joe Grifasi, Estelle Parsons, Tom Aldredge; *D:* Jonathan Kaplan. **VHS, Beta $59.95** *MTI ♫*

The Gentleman from California The dashing son of a Mexican landowner returns home and finds his people's land stolen from them by greedy tax collectors. *AKA:* The Californian.
1937 56m/B Ricardo Cortez, Marjorie Weaver, Katherine DeMille; *D:* Gus Meins. **VHS, Beta, 8mm** *VYY ♫*

Gentleman from Texas Ropin', ridin', and romance figure in this less than dramatic oater.
1946 55m/B Johnny Mack Brown, Raymond Hatton, Claudia Drake, Reno Blair, Christine McIntyre; *D:* Lambert Hillyer. **VHS $19.95** *NOS, DVT ♫*

Gentleman Jim A colorful version of the life of oldtime heavyweight boxing great Jim Corbett, transformed from a typical Warner Bros. bio-pic by director Walsh into a fun-loving, anything-for-laughs donnybrook. Climaxes with Corbett's fight for the championship against the great John L. Sullivan. One of Flynn's most riotous performances.
1942 104m/B Errol Flynn, Alan Hale Jr., Alexis Smith, Jack Carson, Ward Bond, Arthur Shields, William Frawley; *D:* Raoul Walsh. **VHS, Beta, LV $19.98** *MGM, FOX ♫♫♫½*

The Gentleman Killer A man-with-no-name clears a ravaged border town of murdering bandits.
1978 95m/C Anthony Steffen, Silvia Solar. **VHS, Beta $49.95** *UNI ♫*

Gentleman's Agreement A magazine writer (Peck) looks for a new angle for an article on anti-Semitism by pretending to be Jewish. His new identity pervades his life in unexpected ways, almost destroys his relationships, but contributes to the success of his magazine series. This movie was Hollywood's first major attack on anti-Semitism. Controversial in its day, yet still timely.
1947 118m/B Gregory Peck, Dorothy McGuire, John Garfield, Celeste Holm, Anne Revere, June Havoc, Albert Dekker, Jane Wyatt, Dean Stockwell, Nicholas Joy; *D:* Elia Kazan; *W:* Moss Hart. Academy Awards '47: Best Director (Kazan), Best Picture, Best Supporting Actress (Holm); Nominations: Best Actress (McGuire); Academy Awards '47: Best Actor (Peck), Best Film Editing, Best Screenplay, Best Supporting Actress (Revere). **VHS, LV $19.98** *FXV ♫♫♫*

Gentlemen of Titipu Animated version of Gilbert and Sullivan's "The Mikado."
1982 27m/C **VHS, Beta** *PGN ♫♫*

Gentlemen Prefer Blondes Amusing satire involving two show-business girls from Little Rock trying to make it big in Paris. Seeking rich husbands or diamonds, their capers land them in police court. Monroe plays Lorelei Lee, Russell is her sidekick. Despite an occasionally slow plot, the music, comedy, and performances are great fun. Film version of a Broadway adaption of a story by Anita Loos. Followed by (but without Monroe) "Gentlemen Marry Brunettes." ♫A (Two) Little Girl(s) From Little Rock; Bye, Bye

Baby; Ain't There Anyone Here For Love?; When Love Goes Wrong; Diamonds Are A Girl's Best Friend.
1953 91m/C Marilyn Monroe, Jane Russell, Charles Coburn, Elliott Reid, Tommy Noonan, George Winslow; **D:** Howard Hawks. **VHS, Beta, LV** $14.98 *FOX* 🎬🎬🎬

Genuine Risk Gorgeous young woman turns off her crime boss boyfriend bigtime when she seduces his bodyguard. Genuine tripe.
1989 (R) 89m/C Terence Stamp, Michelle Johnson, Peter Berg, M.K. Harris; **D:** Kurt Voss. **VHS, LV** $89.95 *COL* 🎬½

George! A carefree bachelor takes his girlfriend and his 250-pound St. Bernard on a trip to the Swiss Alps where he proves that a dog is not always man's best friend.
1970 (G) 87m/C Marshall Thompson, Jack Mullaney, Inge Schoner; **W/D:** Wallace C. Bennett. **VHS, Beta** $39.95 *UHV* 🎬½

George and the Christmas Star George is dissatisfied with the paper star he cut out to put atop his Christmas tree, so he builds a spaceship and goes to catch a real star. Features songs by Paul Anka.
1985 25m/C Paul Anka; **D:** Gerald Potterton. **VHS, Beta** $12.95 *PAR, WTA* 🎬½

The George McKenna Story Washington stars as the newly appointed principal of George Washington High in Los Angeles. The school is located in South Central, a gang and drug-infested war zone where the students are armed for their own protection. The situation appears hopeless but McKenna refuses to give up. Based on a true story. Made for television.
1986 96m/C Denzel Washington, Lynn Whitfield, Akosua Busia, Richard Masur; **D:** Eric Laneuville; **W:** Charles Eric Johnson; **M:** Herbie Hancock. **VHS** $79.95 *PSM* 🎬🎬½

George Pal Color Cartoon Carnival A collection of eight classic George Pal cartoons: "Jasper in a Jam," "Wolf Wolf," "Mighty Mouse," "Pin Cushion Man," "Mary's Little Lamb," "Molly Moo Coo and Robinson Crusoe," "Little Black Sambo," and "Jasper's Derby."
1944 80m/C **D:** George Pal. **VHS, Beta** $24.95 *DVT* 🎬½

George Washington Slept Here Hilarious side-splitter about a couple who moves from their Manhattan apartment to an old, broken-down country home in Connecticut. It's one catastrophe after another as the couple tries to renovate their home and deal with a grouchy neighbor. Based on the play by George S. Kaufman and Moss Hart.
1942 93m/B Jack Benny, Ann Sheridan, Charles Coburn, Percy Kilbride, Hattie McDaniel, William Tracy; **D:** William Keighley. **VHS** $19.98 *MGM* 🎬🎬🎬

George White's Scandals A lightweight musical comedy look at the show biz world and why the show must go on. Based on White's Broadway extravaganzas. Jazz numbers by Gene Krupa and his band. Preceded by "George White's Scandals" of 1934 and 1935. 🎵Bolero in the Jungle; E.H.S.; Leave Us Leap; I Want to be a Drummer in the Band; How Did You Get Out of My Dreams?; I Wake Up in the Morning; Who Killed Vaudeville?; Scandals; Liza; Os Pintinhos No Perreiro; Wishing; Life is Just a Bowl of Cherries; Bouquet and Lace.
1945 95m/B Joan Davis, Jack Haley, Jane Greer, Phillip Terry, Margaret Hamilton, Martha Holliday; **D:** Felix Feist. **VHS, Beta** $39.98 *CCB* 🎬🎬

George's Island When young George is placed with the worst foster parents in the world, his eccentric grandfather helps him escape. They wind up on Oak's Island, where, legend has it, Captain Kidd's ghost and buried treasure reside. They soon find out the legends are true!
1991 (PG) 89m/C Ian Bannen, Sheila McCarthy, Maury Chaykin, Nathaniel Moreau; **D:** Paul Donovan; **W:** J. William Ritchie; **M:** Marty Simon. **VHS, LV** $19.95 *COL, NLC* 🎬🎬🎬

Georgia, Georgia Sands is a black entertainer on tour in Sweden who falls for a white photographer. Her traveling companion, who hates whites, takes drastic action to separate the lovers. Poor acting, script, and direction. Based on a book by Maya Angelou.
1972 (R) 91m/C Diana Sands, Dirk Benedict, Minnie Gentry; **D:** Stig Bjorkman; **W:** Maya Angelou. **VHS, Beta** $59.95 *PSM* 🎬½

Georgy Girl Redgrave finely plays the overweight ugly-duckling Georgy who shares a flat with the beautiful and promiscuous Meredith (Rampling). Georgy is, however, desired by the wealthy and aging Mason and soon by Meredith's lover (Bates) who recognizes her good heart. When Meredith becomes pregnant, Georgy persuades her to let her raise the baby, leaving Georgy with the dilemma of marrying the irresponsible Bates (the baby's father) or the settled Mason. The film and title song (sung by the Seekers) were both huge hits. Based on the novel by Margaret Foster who also co-wrote the screenplay. Mason, Redgrave, and cinematographer Ken Higgins were Oscar nominees.
1966 100m/B *GB* Lynn Redgrave, James Mason, Charlotte Rampling, Alan Bates, Bill Owen, Claire Kelly, Rachel Kempson; **D:** Silvio Narizzano. Academy Awards '66 Nominations: Best Actress (Redgrave), Best Black and White Cinematography, Best Song ("Georgy Girl"), Best Supporting Actor (Mason); Golden Globe Awards '67: Best Actress—Musical/Comedy (Redgrave); National Board of Review Awards '66: 10 Best Films of the Year; New York Film Critics Awards '66: Best Actress (Redgrave). **VHS, Beta, LV** $19.95 *RCA, FCT, COL* 🎬🎬🎬

Germicide Scientist tries to warn the world of the threat posed by a horrifying bacterial weapon. Terrorists and his mistress hatch plots against him.
1974 90m/C Rod Taylor, Bibi Andersson. **Beta** $59.95 *PSM* 🎬

Geronimo In typical Hollywood casting Connors stars as the Indian leader on the warpath against the cavalry over broken treaties. Lots of action and the Indians are actually the good guys.
1962 101m/C Chuck Connors, Ross Martin, Pat Conway, Kamala Devi, Adam West, Lawrence Dobkin, Denver Pyle, Enid Jaynes, Armando Silvestre, John Anderson; **D:** Arnold Laven. **VHS** $14.95 *MGM* 🎬🎬½

Geronimo's Revenge When Geronimo starts a battle with the settlers, a rancher he has befriended finds himself caught in the middle. The fourth soggy Disney TV oater from the "Tales of Texas John Slaughter" series.
1960 77m/C Tom Tryon, Darryl Hickman; **D:** Harry Keller. **VHS, Beta** *NO* 🎬½

Gertrud The simple story of an independent Danish woman rejecting her husband and lovers in favor of isolation. Cold, dry, minimalistic techniques make up Dreyer's final film. In Danish with subtitles.
1964 116m/B *DK* Nina Pens Rode, Bendt Rothe, Ebbe Rode; **W/D:** Carl Theodor Dreyer. **VHS, Beta** $34.95 *FCT, DVT, HEG* 🎬🎬½

Gervaise The best of several films of Emile Zola's "L'Assommoir." A 19th-century middle-class family is destroyed by the father's plunge into alcoholism despite a mother's attempts to save them. Well acted but overwhelmingly depressing. Music by Georges Auric. In French with English subtitles.
1956 89m/B *FR* Maria Schell, Francois Perier, Suzy Delair, Armand Mestral; **D:** Rene Clement. Academy Awards '56 Nominations: Best Foreign Language Film; British Academy Awards '56: Best Actor (Perier), Best Film; National Board of Review Awards '57: 5 Best Foreign Films of the Year; New York Film Critics Awards '57: Best Foreign Film; Venice Film Festival '56: Best Actress (Schell). **VHS, Beta** $29.95 *DVT, FST, WFV* 🎬🎬🎬

Get Along Gang The Get Along Gang has an opportunity to find the meaning of cooperation and friendship at their annual Scavenger Hunt.
1984 22m/C **M:** John Sebastian. **VHS, Beta** *NO* 🎬½

Get Christie Love! Vintage blaxploitation from the genre's halcyon days, when going undercover meant a carte blanche for skimpy outfits. Based on Dorothy Uhnak's detective novel, the eponymous policewoman goes undercover to bring a thriving drug empire to it knees. The outcome: a TV series. Graves previously appeared on television as one of the "Laugh-In" party girls.
1974 95m/C Teresa Graves, Harry Guardino, Louise Sorel, Paul Stevens, Andy Romano, Debbie Dozier; **D:** William A. Graham. **VHS** $59.95 *XVC* 🎬🎬

Get Crazy The owner of the Saturn Theatre is attempting to stage the biggest rock-and-roll concert of all time on New Year's Eve 1983, and everything is going wrong in this hilarious, off-beat film.
1983 90m/C Malcolm McDowell, Allen Garfield, Daniel Stern, Gail Edwards, Ed Begley Jr., Lou Reed, Bill Henderson; **D:** Allan Arkush. **VHS, Beta, LV** $9.98 *3UE, NLC* 🎬🎬½

Get Out Your Handkerchiefs Unconventional comedy about a husband desperately attempting to make his sexually frustrated wife happy. Determined to go to any lengths, he asks a Mozart-loving teacher to become her lover. She is now, however, bored by them both. Only when she meets a 13-year-old genius at the summer camp where the three adults are counselors does she come out of her funk and find her sexual happiness. Laure is a beautiful character, but Depardieu and Dewaere are wonderful as the bewildered would-be lovers. Academy Award winner for best foreign film. In French with English subtitles. *AKA:* Preparez Vous Mouchoirs.
1978 (R) 109m/C *FR* Gerard Depardieu, Patrick Dewaere, Carole Laure; **D:** Bertrand Blier. **VHS, Beta, LV** $19.98 *WAR, INT, TAM* 🎬🎬🎬½

Get Rita Italian prostitute sets up her gangster boyfriend for a murder she committed and she winds up as mob boss.
19?? 90m/C Sophia Loren, Marcello Mastroianni; **D:** Tom Rowe. **VHS, Beta** $19.95 *CTC* 🎬🎬

Get Smart: The Movie Would you believe Maxwell Smart is back as CONTROL's most incompetent agent? How about Agent 99 as his sidekick? Hymie the robot and those no-good-niks at KAOS? Well, it's all true. This reunion movie from the '60s television show highlights all the wacky gadgetry, including the shoe phone, but fails to find the show's original outlandishness. Made for television.

1989 93m/C Don Adams, Barbara Feldon, Dick Gautier, Bernie Kopell, Kenneth Mars, Harold Gould; **D:** Gary Nelson. **VHS** $89.95 WOV ♫♫½

Get That Man When a cabby is mistaken for the murdered heir to a vast fortune, his life suddenly becomes complex.
1935 57m/B Wallace Ford, Leon Ames, Lillian Miles, E. Allen Warren; **D:** Spencer Gordon Bennet. **VHS, Beta, LV** $19.95 NOS ♫♫

The Getaway McQueen plays a thief released on a parole arranged by his wife (McGraw) only to find out a corrupt politician wants him to rob a bank. After the successful holdup, McQueen finds out his cohorts are actually in the politician's pocket and trying unsuccessfully to double-cross him. McQueen and McGraw are forced into a feverish chase across Texas to the Mexican border, pursued by the politician's henchmen and the state police. This film is a completely amoral depiction of crime and violence with McQueen taciturn as always and McGraw again showing a complete lack of acting skills. Based on a novel by Jim Thompson.
1972 (PG) 123m/C Steve McQueen, Ali MacGraw, Ben Johnson, Sally Struthers, Al Lettieri, Slim Pickens, Jack Dodson, Dub Taylor, Bo Hopkins; **D:** Sam Peckinpah; **W:** Walter Hill; **M:** Quincy Jones. **VHS, Beta** FCT ♫♫

Getting Even A maniac threatens to poison the entire population of Texas with a deadly gas unless he gets $50 million. An adventurous businessman sets out to stop him. **AKA:** Hostage: Dallas.
1986 (R) 90m/C Edward Albert, Joe Don Baker, Audrey Landers; **D:** Dwight Little. **VHS, Beta** $79.95 LIV, VES ♫½

Getting Even Dundee and Evans served together in Vietnam. Fifteen years later they're reunited by the FBI to track a former Marine, who once betrayed Evans to the enemy. Seems he's now a drug traffiker and arms dealer who also gets his sadistic pleasures by killing women. The two ex-Marines find they have one last battle to fight.
1992 (R) 93m/C Richard Roundtree, Michael J. Aronin; **D:** Leandro Lucchetti. **VHS** $89.95 COL ♫♫

Getting It On High school student uses his new-found video equipment for voyeuristic activity.
1983 (R) 100m/C Martin Yost, Heather Kennedy, Jeff Edmond, Kathy Rockmeier, Mark Alan Ferri; **D:** William Olsen. **VHS, Beta** $69.95 LIV, VES ♫

Getting It Right A sweet-natured British comedy about an inexperienced, shy adult male who is quite suddenly pursued by a middle-aged socialite, a pregnant, unstable rich girl, and a modest single mother. Novel and screenplay by Elizabeth Jane Howard.
1989 (R) 101m/C GB Jesse Birdsall, Helena Bonham Carter, Lynn Redgrave, Peter Cook, John Gielgud, Jane Horrocks, Richard Huw, Shirley Anne Field, Pat Haywood, Judy Parfitt, Bryan Pringle; **D:** Randal Kleiser. **VHS, Beta, LV** NO ♫♫½

Getting Lucky A shrinking violet schoolboy is granted his adolescent fantasy by a pandering little leprechaun who makes him the object of desire of a voluptuous pompom girl...Seems it's more complicated than that, though.
1989 (PG-13) ?m/C Lezlie Z. McGraw, Steven Cooke, Rick McDowell; **D:** Michael Paul Girard. **VHS** $59.95 HHE ♫♫

The Getting of Wisdom A 13-year-old girl from the Australian outback tries to establish her identity, and her individuality, within the restricting confines of a Victorian girl's boarding school. Based on the novel by Henry Handel Richardson.

1977 100m/C AU Susannah Fowle, Hilary Ryan, Alix Longman, Sheila Helpmann, Patricia Kennedy, Barry Humphries, John Waters; **D:** Bruce Beresford. **VHS, Beta** FOX ♫♫½

Getting Over A black promoter is hired as a figurehead by a bigoted record company president and proceeds to try to run the company his own way. He develops an all-girl group called "The Love Machine" and gets involved in a singer's kidnapping and a record company run by gangsters. Filled with cliches and stereotypes.
1981 108m/C John Daniels, Gwen Brisco, Mary Hopkins, John Goff, Andrew "Buzz" Cooper; **W/ D:** Bernie Rollins. **VHS, Beta** $59.95 UNI ♫

Getting Physical After being mugged, a secretary decides to get in shape and enters the world of female body building. Crammed with workout scenes and disco music. Made for television.
1984 95m/C Alexandra Paul, Sandahl Bergman, David Naughton; **D:** Steven Hilliard Stern. **VHS, Beta** $59.98 FOX ♫½

Getting Straight A returning Vietnam soldier (Gould) goes back to his alma mater to secure a teaching degree and gets involved in the lives of his fellow students and the turbulence of the end of the '60s, including campus riots. A now-dated "youth" picture somewhat watchable for Gould's performance.
1970 (R) 124m/C Elliott Gould, Candice Bergen, Jeff Corey, Cecil Kellaway, Jeannie Berlin, Harrison Ford, John Rubinstein, Robert F. Lyons, Max Julien; **D:** Richard Rush. **VHS, Beta** $59.95 COL ♫♫

Getting Wasted Set in 1969 at a military academy for troublesome young men, chaos ensues when the cadets meet hippies.
1980 (PG) 98m/C Brian Kerwin, Stephen Furst, Cooper Huckabee. **VHS, Beta** $19.95 UHV ♫½

The Ghastly Ones Three couples must stay in a haunted mansion to inherit an estate, but they're soon being violently killed off. No budget and no talent. Remade as "Legacy of Blood."
1968 81m/C Don Williams, Maggie Rogers, Hal Belsoe, Veronica Redburn; **D:** Andy Milligan. **VHS, Beta** NO Woof!

Ghetto Blaster A Vietnam vet takes on out-of-control street gangs to make his neighborhood safe.
1989 (R) 86m/C R.G. Armstrong, Richard Hatch, Richard Jaeckel, Harry Caesar, Rose Marie; **D:** Alan L. Stewart. **VHS, Beta** $79.95 PSM ♫

Ghetto Revenge An embittered Vietnam vet gets caught between white supremacists and black radical activists in this coming home story. He returns and tries to build a life but succumbs to the desire for vengeance and things are never the same.
19?? ?m/C Mike Sims. **VHS** NO ♫

Ghidrah the Three Headed Monster When a three-headed monster from outer-space threatens the world, humans, having nowhere else to turn, appeal to the friendly Mothra, Rodan, and Godzilla. Rock'em, sock 'em giant thrashing about as Tokyo once again gets trampled. Dependable afternoon monster fare complete with usual dubious dubbing. **AKA:** Ghidorah Sandai Kaiju Chikyu Saidai No Kessan; Ghidora, The Three-Headed Monster; Ghidrah; The Greatest Battle on Earth; The Biggest Right on Earth; Monster of Monsters.
1965 85m/C JP Yosuke Natsuki, Yuriko Hoshi; **D:** Inoshiro Honda. **VHS, Beta** $19.95 HHT, VCN, VHE ♫♫½

The Ghost A woman is driven mad by her supposedly dead husband and their evil housekeeper. Sequel to "The Horrible Dr. Hichcock." **AKA:** Lo Spettro.
1963 96m/C IT Barbara Steele, Peter Baldwin, Leonard Eliott, Harriet White; **D:** Robert Hampton. **VHS, Beta** $14.95 SNC, LPC ♫½

Ghost Zucker, known for overboard comedies like "Airplane!" and "Ruthless People," changed tack and directed this undemanding romantic thriller, which was the surprising top grosser of 1990. Swayze is a murdered investment consultant attempting (from somewhere near the hereafter) to protect his lover, Moore, from imminent danger when he learns he was the victim of a hit gone afoul. Goldberg is the medium who suddenly discovers that the powers she's been faking are real. A winning blend of action, special effects (from Industrial Light and Magic) and romance.
1990 (PG-13) 127m/C Patrick Swayze, Demi Moore, Whoopi Goldberg, Tony Goldwyn, Vincent Schiavelli; **D:** Jerry Zucker. Academy Awards '90: Best Original Screenplay, Best Supporting Actress (Goldberg); Nominations: Best Film Editing, Best Picture, Best Original Score; Golden Globe Awards '91: Best Supporting Actress (Goldberg); People's Choice Awards '91: Best Film—Drama. **VHS, Beta, LV, SVS, 8mm** $89.95 PAR, SUP, FCT ♫♫♫

The Ghost and Mrs. Muir A charming, beautifully directed fantasy about a feisty widow who, with her young daughter, buys a seaside house and refuses to be intimidated by the crabby ghost of its former sea captain owner. When the widow falls into debt, the captain dictates his sea adventures, which she adapts into a successful novel. The ghost also falls in love with the beautiful lady. Tierney is exquisite and Harrison is sharp-tongued and manly. Based on R. A. Dick's novel.
1947 104m/B Gene Tierney, Rex Harrison, George Sanders, Edna Best, Anna Lee, Vanessa Brown, Robert Coote, Natalie Wood, Isobel Elsom; **D:** Joseph L. Mankiewicz; **M:** Bernard Herrmann. **VHS, Beta, LV** $19.98 FOX, HMV ♫♫♫

The Ghost and the Guest Newlyweds spend their honeymoon in a house in the country only to find that gangsters are using the place as a hideout. Chases involving secret passages ensue.
1943 59m/B James Dunn, Florence Rice, Mabel Todd; **D:** William Nigh; **W:** Morey Amsterdam. **VHS, Beta** $16.95 SNC ♫♫½

The Ghost Breakers As a follow-up to the Hope/Goddard 1939 comedy thriller "The Cat and the Canary," this spooky comedy was even better. Lots of laughs and real chills as Hope and Goddard investigate a haunted mansion that she's inherited in Cuba. Effective horror scenes are expertly handled by director Marshall. Remade in 1953 as "Scared Stiff" with Dean Martin and Jerry Lewis. Based on the play by Paul Dickey and Charles Goddard.
1940 83m/B Bob Hope, Paulette Goddard, Richard Carlson, Paul Lukas, Willie Best, Pedro de Cordoba, Noble Johnson, Anthony Quinn; **D:** George Marshall. **VHS** $14.98 MCA ♫♫♫

The Ghost Camera Slight story of a man falsely accused of murder. A photograph taken at the murder scene can prove his innocence if only the missing camera can be discovered.
1933 68m/B GB Henry Kendall, Ida Lupino, John Mills; **D:** Bernard Vorhaus. **VHS** HCV ♫♫½

Ghost Chase A young filmmaker desperate for funds inherits his dead relative's clock, from which issues the ghost of the deceased's butler. The ghostly retainer aids

in a search for the departed's secret fortune. Neither scary nor funny.
1988 (PG-13) 89m/C Jason Lively, Jill Whitlow, Tim McDaniel, Paul Gleason, Chuck "Porky" Mitchell; **D:** Roland Emmerich. **VHS, Beta, LV** *NO* 𝄞½

Ghost Chasers The Bowery Boys become mixed up in supernatural hijinks when a seance leads to the appearance of a ghost that only Sach can see.
1951 70m/B Leo Gorcey, Huntz Hall, Billy Benedict, David Gorcey, Buddy Gorman, Bernard Gorcey, Jan Kayne, Philip Van Zandt, Lloyd Corrigan; **D:** William Beaudine. **VHS $14.98** *WAR* 𝄞𝄞½

Ghost City Our hero must deal with a masked gang that is "haunting" a town.
1932 60m/B Bill Cody, Helen Foster, Ann Rutherford, John Shelton, Reginald Owen; **D:** Harry Fraser. **VHS $19.95** *NOS, DVT, HEG* 𝄞

Ghost Crazy Three wild comedians and a gorilla create mayhem in a haunted house. **AKA:** Ghost Crazy.
1944 ?m/C Shemp Howard, Billy Gilbert, Maxie Rosenbloom. **VHS $15.95** *LOO* 𝄞𝄞

Ghost Dad A widowed workaholic dad is prematurely killed and returns from the dead to help his children prepare for the future. Cosby walks through doors, walls, and other solid objects for the sake of comedy—only none of it is funny.
1990 (PG) 84m/C Bill Cosby, Denise Nicholas, Ian Bannen, Christine Ebersole, Dana Ashbrook, Arnold Stang; **D:** Sidney Poitier; **M:** Henry Mancini. **VHS, Beta, LV $19.95** *MCA* 𝄞

Ghost Dance Sacred Indian burial ground is violated, with grim results.
1983 93m/C Sherman Hemsley, Henry Ball, Julie Amato; **D:** Peter Bufa. **VHS, Beta $49.95** *TWE* 𝄞

Ghost Fever Two bumbling cops try to evict the inhabitants of a haunted house and get nowhere. A bad rip-off of "Ghostbusters." Alan Smithee is a pseudonym used when a director does not want his or her name on a film—no wonder.
1987 (PG) 86m/C Sherman Hemsley, Luis Avalos; **D:** Alan Smithee. **VHS, Beta, LV $19.98** *NLC* Woof!

The Ghost Goes West A brash American family buys a Scottish castle and transports the pieces to the United States along with the Scottish family ghost (Donat). Also along is the ghost's modern-day descendant (also played by Donat) who is the new castle caretaker and in love with the new owner's daughter. It turns out to be up to the ghost to get the two lovers together and find his own eternal rest. A rather lovable fantasy written by Robert Sherwood. Rene Clair's first English film. Available in digitally remastered stereo with original movie trailer.
1936 85m/B *GB* Robert Donat, Jean Parker, Eugene Pallette, Elsa Lanchester; **D:** Rene Clair. **VHS, Beta $19.98** *HBO, SUE* 𝄞𝄞𝄞

Ghost in the Noonday Sun Crew of a treasure-seeking pirate ship sets sail for high sea silliness in this slapstick adventure film. Not a theatrical release for one obvious reason—it's terrible.
1974 90m/C *GB* Peter Sellers, Spike Milligan, Anthony (Tony) Franciosa, Clive Revill, Rosemary Leach, Peter Boyle; **D:** Peter Medak. **VHS, Beta** *NO* Woof!

Ghost Keeper Three girls are trapped in a mansion with an old hag and various supernatural apparitions.
1980 87m/C Riva Spier, Murray Ord, Georgie Collins; **D:** Vernon Sewell. **VHS, Beta $59.95** *NWV* 𝄞

The Ghost of Fletcher Ridge Two friends on a hunting trip run into some backwoodsmen and uncover their moonshining operation. When one of the men is killed, the other flees to the forest in a desperate bid for survival.
198? 90m/C Campbell Scott, Bernie White, Virginia Lantry, Len Lesser; **D:** Michael Bordon. **VHS $9.95** *SIM* 𝄞

Ghost of Hanley House Obscure, low-budget ghost story, shot in Texas.
1968 ?m/B VHS $20 *SMW* 𝄞𝄞

The Ghost of Rashmon Hall Doctor tries to rid his home of the ghosts of a sailor, his wife and her lover. **AKA:** Night Comes Too Soon.
1947 52m/B Valentine Dyall, Anne Howard, Alex Flavorsham, Howard Douglas, Beatrice Marsden, Arthur Brander. **VHS, Beta $16.95** *SNC, MWP* 𝄞

Ghost of the Ninja An evil, masked assassin terrorizes the city but meets his match in the heroic "ghost" ninja.
19?? 114m/C Roy Chiao Hung, Steve Tung-Wai. **VHS, Beta $19.99** *BFV* 𝄞

The Ghost of Yotsuya Based on the Japanese legend of a man who must betray his wife to get the power he seeks. When he does, however, what follows is a horrifying revenge. In Japanese with English subtitles.
1958 100m/C *JP* Shigeru Amachi. **VHS, Beta $59.95** *VDA* 𝄞½

Ghost Patrol A cowboy duo kidnaps the inventor of a ray gun in order to hijack mail planes, but they're stopped by G-Man McCoy and friends. An odd hybrid of science fiction and western, to say the least.
1930 57m/B Tim McCoy, Walter Miller, Wheeler Oakman, Sam Newfield. **VHS, Beta $45.95** *VCN, UHV* 𝄞½

Ghost Rider A lawman is aided in his outlaw-nabbing efforts by the ghost of a gunfighter.
1935 56m/B Rex Lease; **D:** Jack Levine. **VHS, Beta $19.95** *NOS, WGE* 𝄞

Ghost Rider Former footballer Brown rides the range once again, this time with an element of the supernatural nipping at his heels.
1943 58m/B Johnny Mack Brown, Raymond Hatton, Tim Seidel, Beverly Boyd, Milburn Morante; **D:** Wallace Fox. **VHS** *NO* 𝄞

Ghost Ship Young couple is tortured by ghostly apparitions when they move into an old yacht with a dubious past. Grade "b" haunting featuring the murdered wife of the ship's former owner as the poltergeist.
1953 69m/B *GB* Dermot Walsh, Hazel Court, Hugh Burden, John Robinson; **D:** Vernon Sewell. **VHS, Beta $14.95** *NOS, SNC* 𝄞½

Ghost Stories: Graveyard Thriller A compilation of stories with ghosts, vampires and other creatures of the night.
1986 56m/C D: Lynn Silver. **VHS, Beta $59.98** *LIV, VES* 𝄞½

Ghost Story Four elderly men, members of an informal social club called the Chowder Society, share a terrible secret buried deep in their pasts—a secret that comes back to haunt them to death. Has moments where it's chilling, but unfortunately they're few. Based on the best-selling novel by Peter Straub.
1981 (R) 110m/C Fred Astaire, Melvyn Douglas, Douglas Fairbanks Jr., John Houseman, Craig Wasson, Alice Krige, Patricia Neal; **D:** John Irvin. **VHS, Beta, LV $19.95** *MCA* 𝄞𝄞

Ghost Town Good guy Carey saves a mine from claim jumpers, but not before he is mistakenly incarcerated as his friend's murderer, and then proved innocent.
1937 65m/B Harry Carey Sr.; **D:** Harry Fraser. **VHS, Beta, LV $19.95** *WGE, TIM, VDM* 𝄞

Ghost Town Fine sleeper about a modern sheriff who must rid a ghost town of its age-old curse.
1988 (R) 85m/C Franc Luz, Catherine Hickland, Jimmie F. Skaggs, Penelope Windust, Bruce Glover, Blake Conway, Laura Schaefer; **D:** Richard Governor. **VHS, LV $19.95** *STE, NWV* 𝄞𝄞½

Ghost Town Gold The Three Mesquiteers series continues as the trio outwits bank robbers who have hidden their loot in a ghost town.
1936 53m/B Bob Livingston, Ray Corrigan, Max Terhune; **D:** Joseph Kane. **VHS, Beta $19.95** *NOS, DVT* 𝄞

Ghost Town Law The Rough Riders step in to save the day when a group of outlaws defend their hideout by murdering anyone who approaches.
1942 62m/B Buck Jones, Tim McCoy, Raymond Hatton; **D:** Howard Bretherton. **VHS, Beta, 3/4U, Special order formats $9.99** *NOS, VCN, CAB* 𝄞½

Ghost Town Renegades A pair of government agents prevent a crook from gaining control of a mining town.
1947 57m/B Lash LaRue, Al "Fuzzy" St. John, Jennifer Holt; **D:** Ray Taylor. **VHS, Beta $12.95** *COL, SVS* 𝄞

The Ghost Train Passengers stranded at a train station are told tales of a haunted train. Forced to stay at the station overnight, they encounter a number of comically spooky situations.
1941 85m/B *GB* Arthur Askey, Richard Murdock, Kathleen Harrison; **D:** Walter Forde. **VHS, Beta $16.95** *NOS, SNC* 𝄞𝄞

Ghost Valley When Keene and Kennedy inherit land rich in unmined ore, the administrator (Harris) attempts to scare them off. To foil his plan, Keene conceals his identity and takes a job as the administrator's assistant. Based on a story by Adele Buffington.
1932 54m/B Tom Keene, Merna Kennedy, Mitchell Harris, Billy Franey, Harry Bowen, Kate Campbell, Ted Adams, Buck Moulton, Harry Semels, Al Taylor, Charles "Slim" Whitaker; **D:** Fred Allen. **VHS** *HEG* 𝄞𝄞½

The Ghost Walks A playwright has his new masterpiece acted out in front of an unsuspecting producer, who thinks that a real murder has taken place. But when the cast really does start disappearing, who's to blame?
1934 69m/B John Miljan, June Collyer, Richard Carle, Spencer Charters, Johnny Arthur, Henry Kolker; **D:** Frank Strayer. **VHS $12.95** *SNC, NOS, DVT* 𝄞𝄞

Ghost Writer A writer discovers the ghost of a movie star haunting her beach house, and together they solve the dead vamp's murder.
1989 (PG) 94m/C Audrey Landers, Judy Landers, Jeff Conaway, David Doyle, Anthony (Tony) Franciosa, Joey Travolta, John Matuszak, David Paul, Peter Paul; **D:** Kenneth J. Hall. **VHS, Beta $79.95** *PSM* 𝄞

Ghostbusters After losing their scholastic funding, a group of "para-normal" investigators decide to go into business for themselves, aiding New York citizens in the removal of ghosts, goblins and other annoying spirits. This comedy-thriller about Manhattan being overrun by ghosts, contains great special effects, zany characters, and some of the best laughs of the decade. Also

available in a laserdisc version with letterboxing, analysis of all special effects, complete screenplay, and original trailer. Followed by a sequel.
1984 (PG) 103m/C Bill Murray, Dan Aykroyd, Harold Ramis, Rick Moranis, Sigourney Weaver, Annie Potts, Ernie Hudson, William Atherton; **D:** Ivan Reitman. VHS, Beta, LV, 8mm $19.95 COL, PIA, VYG *♫♫♫*

Ghostbusters 2 After being sued by the city for the damages they did in the original "Ghostbusters," the boys in khaki are doing kiddie shows at birthday parties. When a river of slime that is actually the physical version of evil is discovered running beneath the city, the Ghostbusters are back in action. They must do battle with a wicked spirit in a painting or the entire world will fall prey to its ravaging whims.
1989 (PG) 102m/C Bill Murray, Dan Aykroyd, Sigourney Weaver, Harold Ramis, Rick Moranis, Ernie Hudson, Peter MacNicol, David Margulies, Wilhelm von Homburg, Harris Yulin, Annie Potts; **D:** Ivan Reitman. VHS, Beta, LV, 8mm $19.95 COL *♫♫ ½*

Ghosthouse It looks like an average suburban house, but it's haunted by the ghost of a little girl—and when she comes, evil is sure to follow.
1988 91m/C Lara Wendell, Gregg Scott; **D:** Humphrey Humbert. VHS, Beta $79.95 IMP *♫*

Ghostriders One hundred years after their hanging, a band of ghostly outlaws take revenge on the townfolk's descendents.
1987 85m/C Bill Shaw, Jim Peters, Ricky Long, Cari Powell, Mike Ammons, Arland Bishop; **D:** Alan L. Stewart. VHS, Beta $9.99 STE, PSM *♫*

Ghosts Can Do It The Hound doesn't like jumping to conclusions, but is it possible this obscurity was titled to be reminiscent of the more publicized Bo Derek vehicle "Ghosts Can't Do it?" comedy about a man who returns to his sexy wife despite her efforts at killing him.
1990 88m/C Garry McDonald, Pamela Stephenson. VHS $59.95 ATL, HHE *♫ ½*

Ghosts Can't Do It Another wet-shirted, Bo-dacious softcore epic, involving a young woman who would like to have the spirit of her virile, but unfortunately dead, husband return to inhabit a living body.
1990 (R) 91m/C Bo Derek, Anthony Quinn, Don Murray, Leo Damian; **D:** John Derek. VHS, Beta, LV $59.95 COL, TTC *♫*

Ghosts of Berkeley Square The ghosts of two retired soldiers of the early 18th century are doomed to haunt their former home, and only a visit from a reigning monarch can free them.
1947 85m/B Wilfrid Hyde-White, Robert Morley, Felix Aylmer; **D:** Vernon Sewell. VHS, Beta $24.95 VYY *♫♫ ½*

The Ghosts of Hanley House No-budget spooker with no-brain plot. Several unlucky guests spend an evening in a creepy mansion...sound familiar? Shot in Texas.
1968 80m/C Barbara Chase, Wilkie De Martel, Elsie Baker, Cliff Scott. VHS, Beta $16.95 SNC *♫ ½*

Ghosts on the Loose The Bowery Boys stumble into nasty Nazi spy Lugosi in a supposedly haunted mansion. Gardner plays Bowery Boy Hall's sister. **AKA:** The East Side Kids Meet Bela Lugosi; Ghosts in the Night.
1943 67m/B Leo Gorcey, Huntz Hall, Bobby Jordan, Sammy Morrison, Billy Benedict, Stanley Clements, Bobby Stone, Bill Bates, Bela Lugosi, Ava Gardner; **D:** William Beaudine. VHS, Beta, 3/4U, Special order formats $9.95 NEG, MRV, NOS *♫♫*

Ghosts That Still Walk Spooky phenomena occur. The demons possessing a young lad's soul may be responsible.
1977 92m/C Ann Nelson, Matt Boston, Jerry Jenson, Caroline Howe, Rita Crafts; **D:** James T. Flocker. VHS, Beta $29.95 UHV, MRV *♫*

Ghostwarrior A 16th century samurai warrior's ice-packed body is revived and runs amuck in the streets of modern-day Los Angeles.
1986 (R) 86m/C Hiroshi Fujioka, Janet Julian, Andy Wood, John Calvin; **D:** Larry Carroll. VHS, Beta $79.98 VES *♫*

Ghostwriter Based on Philip Roth's best-selling novel, the story is of a writer coming to terms with his past. Roth co-wrote the screenplay. First seen on PBS.
1984 90m/C Sam Wanamaker, Claire Bloom, Rose Arrick, MacIntyre Dixon, Cecile Mann, Joseph Wiseman, Mark Linn-Baker, Paulette Smit; **D:** Tristam Powell. VHS, Beta $69.95 PBS *♫♫*

The Ghoul An eccentric English Egyptologist desires a sacred jewel to be buried with him and vows to come back from the grave if the gem is stolen. When that happens, he makes good on his ghostly promise. A minor horror piece with Karloff only appearing at the beginning and end of the film. This leaves the middle very dull.
1934 73m/B GB Boris Karloff, Cedric Hardwicke, Ernest Thesiger, Dorothy Hyson, Ralph Richardson, Anthony Bushell; **D:** T. Hayes Hunter. VHS $19.95 NOS, SNC, DVT *♫♫ ½*

The Ghoul A defrocked clergyman has a cannibal son to contend with—especially after the drivers in a local auto race begin to disappear. Hurt is the lunatic family gardener.
1975 (R) 88m/C GB Peter Cushing, John Hurt, Alexandra Bastedo, Don Henderson, Stewart Bevan; **D:** Freddie Francis. VHS, Beta $19.95 MED *♫♫*

Ghoul School A spoof of horror films and college flicks, with lots of scantily clad women and bloody creatures in dark hallways.
1990 (R) 90m/C Joe Franklin, Nancy Siriani, William Friedman. VHS $79.95 HHE *♫*

Ghoulies A young man gets more than he bargained for when he conjures up a batch of evil creatures when dabbling in the occult. Ridiculous but successful. Followed by two sequels.
1985 (PG-13) 81m/C Lisa Pelikan, Jack Nance, Scott Thomson, Tamara DeTreaux, Mariska Hargitay, Bobbie Bresee; **D:** Luca Bercovici. VHS, Beta $29.98 LIV, VES, HHE *♫*

Ghoulies 2 Inept sequel to "Ghoulies" (1985), wherein the little demons haunt a failing carnival horror house, whose revenues begin to soar. Followed by a second sequel.
1988 (R) 89m/C Damon Martin, Royal Dano, Phil Fondacaro, J. Downing, Kerry Remsen; **D:** Albert Band. VHS, Beta, LV $14.98 LIV, VES *♫*

Ghoulies 3: Ghoulies Go to College Third in the series has the best special effects and the worst storyline. Not satisfied with ripping off "Gremlins," this one imposes Three Stooges personae upon a trio of demons at large on a beer- and babe-soaked campus.
1991 (R) 94m/C Kevin McCarthy, Griffin O'Neal, Evan Mackenzie; **D:** John Carl Buechler. VHS $89.98 VES, LIV Woof!

G.I. Blues Three G.I.'s form a musical combo while stationed in Germany. Prowse is the nightclub singer Presley falls for. Presley's first film after his military service. ♫Shopping Around; Tonight Is So Right For Love; What's She Really Like?; Frankfurt Special; Didya Ever; Big Boots; Pocketful of Rainbows; Doin' the Best I Can; Blue Suede Shoes; G.I. Blues; Wooden Heart.
1960 104m/C Elvis Presley, Juliet Prowse, Robert Ivers, Leticia Roman, Ludwig Stossel, James Douglas, Jeremy Slate; **D:** Norman Taurog. VHS, Beta, LV $14.98 FOX, MVD *♫♫*

G.I. Executioner An adventure set in Singapore featuring a Vietnam veteran turned executioner. **AKA:** Wit's End; Dragon Lady.
1971 (R) 86m/C Tom Kenna, Victoria Racimo, Angelique Pettyjohn, Janet Wood, Walter Hill; **D:** Joel M. Reed. VHS, Beta $69.95 VES *♫*

G.I. Jane A television producer faints when he gets his draft notice and dreams his company is stranded at a desert post with a company of WACs.
1951 62m/B Jean Porter, Tom Neal, Iris Adrian, Jimmy Lloyd, Mara Lynn, Michael Whalen; **D:** Reginald LeBorg. VHS, Beta, LV NO *♫*

G.I. Joe: The Movie A full-length animated cartoon based on the famous toy character.
1986 90m/C **D:** Don Jurwich; **V:** Don Johnson, Burgess Meredith, Sgt. Slaughter. VHS, Beta $19.95 CEL, WTA *♫ ½*

Giant Based on the Edna Ferber novel, this epic saga covers two generations of a wealthy Texas cattle baron (Hudson) who marries a strong-willed Virginia woman (Taylor) and takes her to live on his vast ranch. It explores the problems they have adjusting to life together, as well as the politics and prejudice of the time. Dean plays the resentful ranch hand (who secretly loves Taylor) who winds up striking oil and beginning a fortune to rival that of his former boss. Dean's last movie—he died in a car crash shortly before filming was completed.
1956 201m/C Elizabeth Taylor, Rock Hudson, James Dean, Carroll Baker, Chill Wills, Dennis Hopper, Rod Taylor, Earl Holliman, Jane Withers, Sal Mineo, Mercedes McCambridge; **D:** George Stevens. Academy Awards '56: Best Director (Stevens); Nominations: Best Actor (Dean), Best Actor (Hudson), Best Adapted Screenplay, Best Art Direction/Set Decoration (Color), Best Costume Design (Color), Best Film Editing, Best Picture, Best Supporting Actress (McCambridge), Best Original Score; Directors Guild of America Awards '56: Best Director (Stevens). VHS, Beta, LV $29.98 WAR, BTV *♫♫♫ ½*

The Giant Claw Giant, winged (and stringed) bird attacks from outer space and scientists Morrow, Corday and Ankrum attempt to pluck it. Good bad movie; Corday was Playboy's Miss October, 1958.
1957 76m/B Jeff Morrow, Mara Corday, Morris Ankrum, Louis D. Merrill, Edgar Barrier, Robert Shayne, Morgan Jones, Clark Howat; **D:** Fred F. Sears. VHS $14.98 MOV *♫ ½*

Giant from the Unknown Giant conquistador is revived after being struck by lightning and goes on a murderous rampage. Unbelievably bad.
1958 80m/B Edward Kemmer, Buddy Baer, Bob Steele, Sally Fraser; **D:** Richard Cunha. VHS, Beta $16.95 NOS, SNC, MWP Woof!

The Giant Gila Monster A giant lizard has the nerve to disrupt a local record hop, foolishly bringing upon it the wrath of the local teens. Rear-projection monster isn't particularly effective, but the film provides many unintentional laughs.
1959 74m/B Don Sullivan, Lisa Simone, Shug Fisher, Jerry Cortwright, Beverly Thurman, Don Flourney, Pat Simmons; **D:** Ray Kellogg. VHS $9.95 NOS, RHI, SNC *♫ ½*

The Giant of Marathon Reeves shrugs off the role of Hercules to play Philippides, a marathoner (who uses a horse) trying to save Greece from invading Persian

hordes. Lots of muscle on display, but not much talent. Cinematography by Mario Bava.
1960 90m/C *IT* Steve Reeves, Mylene Demongeot, Daniela Rocca, Ivo Garrani, Alberto Lupo, Sergio Fantoni; *D:* Jacques Tourneur. **VHS** $16.95 *SNC, MLB* ♭♭

The Giant of Metropolis Muscle-bound hero goes shirtless to take on the evil, sadistic ruler of Atlantis (still above water) in 10,000 B.C. Ordinary Italian adventure, but includes interesting sets and bizarre torture scenes. *AKA:* Il Gigante Di Metropolis.
1961 92m/C *IT* Gordon Mitchell, Roldano Lupi, Bella Cortez, Liana Orfei; *D:* Umberto Scarpelli. **VHS** $19.98 *SNC* ♭♭

The Giant Spider Invasion A meteorite carrying spider eggs crashes to Earth and soon the alien arachnids are growing to humongous proportions. Notoriously bad special effects, but the veteran "B" cast has a good enough time.
1975 (PG) 76m/C Steve Brodie, Barbara Hale, Leslie Parrish, Robert Easton, Alan Hale Jr., Dianne Lee Hart, Bill Williams, Christianne Schmidtmer; *D:* Bill Rebane. **VHS** *MOV* ♭

Giant Steps Williams plays Slate Hopson, a moody jazz legend idolized by a talented young trumpet player. When the two meet Hopson clues the boy into some of life's lessons and rediscovers his own joy at making music.
19?? 94m/C Billy Dee Williams, Michael Mahonen; *M:* Eric Leeds. **VHS** $89.95 *MNC* ♭♭

Giants of Rome Rome is in peril at the hands of a mysterious secret weapon that turns out to be a giant catapult. Ludicrous all around.
1963 87m/C *IT* Richard Harrison, Ettore Manni. **VHS, Beta** $16.95 *SNC* Woof!

The Giants of Thessaly Jason and Orpheus search for the Golden Fleece, encountering and defeating monsters, wizards, and a scheming witch.
1960 86m/C *IT* Roland Carey, Ziva Rodann, Massimo Girotti, Alberto Farnese; *D:* Riccardo Freda. **VHS** $16.95 *SNC* ♭♭

Gideon's Trumpet True story of Clarence Earl Gideon, a Florida convict whose case was decided by the Supreme Court and set the precedent that everyone is entitled to defense by a lawyer, whether or not they can pay for it. Based on the book by Anthony Lewis. Made for television.
1980 104m/C Henry Fonda, Jose Ferrer, John Houseman, Dean Jagger, Sam Jaffe, Fay Wray; *D:* Robert Collins. **VHS, Beta** $14.95 *WOV, VTK* ♭♭½

Gidget A plucky, boy-crazy teenage girl (whose nickname means girl midget) discovers romance and wisdom on the beaches of Malibu when she becomes involved with a group of college-aged surfers. First in a series of Gidget/surfer films. Based on a novel by Frederick Kohner about his daughter.
1959 95m/C Sandra Dee, James Darren, Cliff Robertson, Mary Laroche, Arthur O'Connell, Joby Baker; *D:* Paul Wendkos. **VHS, Beta, LV** $9.95 *COL* ♭♭

Gidget Goes Hawaiian Gidget is off to Hawaii with her parents and is enjoying the beach (and the boys) when she is surprised by a visit from boyfriend "Moondoggie." Sequel to "Gidget" and followed by "Gidget Goes to Rome."
1961 102m/C Deborah Walley, James Darren, Carl Reiner, Peggy Cass, Michael Callan, Eddie Foy Jr.; *D:* Paul Wendkos. **VHS, Beta** $14.95 *COL* ♭♭

Gidget Goes to Rome Darren returns in his third outing as boyfriend "Moondoggies" to yet another actress playing "Gidget" as the two vacation in Rome and find themselves tempted by other romances. Second sequel to "Gidget."
1963 104m/C Cindy Carol, James Darren, Jeff Donnell, Cesare Danova, Peter Brooks, Jessie Royce Landis; *D:* Paul Wendkos; *M:* John Williams. **VHS, Beta** $19.95 *COL, RCA* ♭♭½

The Gift Story of a 55-year-old man who chooses early retirement in the hopes of changing his dull and boring life. Unbeknownst to him, his co-workers arrange the ultimate retirement gift - a woman. Silly French sexual farce.
1982 (R) 105m/C *FR* Pierre Mondy, Claudia Cardinale, Clio Goldsmith, Jacques Francois, Cecile Magnet, Remy Laurent; *D:* Michael Lang. **VHS, Beta** $19.95 *FCT* ♭♭½

The Gift Horse A domineering British officer commands an old battleship but finds both the ship and the crew are still seaworthy after a battle with the Germans. *AKA:* Glory at Sea.
1952 99m/B *GB* Trevor Howard, Richard Attenborough, Sonny Tufts, Bernard Lee; *D:* Compton Bennett. **VHS, Beta** $39.95 *MON, DVT, HEG* ♭♭

The Gift of Love Saccharine, made-for-television adaption of O. Henry's Christmas romance "The Gift of the Magi."
1990 96m/C James Woods, Marie Osmond, Timothy Bottoms, June Lockhart, David Wayne; *D:* Don Chaffey. **VHS** $24.95 *MON, KAR* ♭½

The Gig In this small, independently-made film, a band of middle-aged amateur jazz musicians give up their stable occupations for a once-in-a-lifetime shot at a two-week gig in the Catskills.
1985 95m/C Wayne Rogers, Cleavon Little, Warren Vache, Joe Silver, Daniel Nalbach; *D:* Frank D. Gilroy. **VHS, Beta, LV** $79.95 *LHV, WAR* ♭♭½

Gigi Based on Colette's story of a young Parisian girl (Caron) trained to become a courtesan to the wealthy Gaston (Jourdan). But he finds out he prefers her to be his wife rather than his mistress. Chevalier is Gaston's roguish father who casts an always admiring eye on the ladies, Gingold is Gigi's grandmother and former Chevalier flame, and Gabor amuses as Gaston's current, and vapid, mistress. One of the first MGM movies to be shot on location, this extravaganza features some of the best tributes to the French lifestyle ever filmed. Musical score by Lerner and Loewe includes memorable classics. Winner of nine Academy Awards. ♫Gigi; Ah Yes, I Remember It Well; Thank Heaven For Little Girls; The Night They Invented Champagne; She's Not Thinking of Me; It's a Bore; Gossip; I'm Glad I'm Not Young Anymore; The Parisians; Gaston's Soliloquy; Say A Prayer For Me Tonight; A Toujours.
1958 119m/C Leslie Caron, Louis Jourdan, Maurice Chevalier, Hermione Gingold, Eva Gabor, Isabel Jeans; *D:* Vincente Minnelli; *M:* Frederick Loewe, Alan Jay Lerner. **VHS, Beta, LV, 8mm** $19.98 *MGM, BTV* ♭♭♭♭

Gilda An evil South American gambling casino owner hires young American Ford as his trusted aide, unaware that Ford and his sultry wife Hayworth have engaged in a steamy affair. Hayworth does a striptease to "Put the Blame on Mame" in this prominently sexual film. This is the film that made Hayworth into a Hollywood sex goddess.
1946 110m/B Rita Hayworth, Glenn Ford, George Macready, Joseph Calleia; *D:* Charles Vidor. **VHS, Beta, LV** $19.95 *COL* ♭♭♭½

The Gilded Cage Two brothers are falsely accused of art theft and must find the real crooks in order to clear their names.
1954 77m/B *GB* Alex Nicol, Veronica Hurst, Clifford Evans, Ursula Howells, Elwyn Brook-Jones, John Stuart; *D:* John Gilling. **VHS, Beta** $16.95 *SNC* ♭♭

Gimme an F The handsome cheerleading instructor at Camp Beaver View ruffles a few pom-poms when he discovers that the camp's owner is about to enter into a shady deal with some foreigners. The film certainly deserves an "F" for foolishness if nothing else. *AKA:* T & A Academy 2.
1985 (R) 100m/C Stephen Shellan, Mark Keyloun, John Karlen, Jennifer Cooke; *D:* Paul Justman. **VHS, Beta** $79.98 *FOX, SIM* Woof!

Gimme Shelter The sixties ended as violence occurred at a December 1969 free Rolling Stones concert attended by 300,000 people in Altamont, California. This "Woodstock West" became a bitter remembrance in rock history, as Hell's Angels (hired for security) do some ultimate damage to the spectators. A provocative look at an out-of-control situation.
1970 91m/C Mick Jagger, Keith Richards, Charlie Watts, Bill Wyman, Mick Taylor; *D:* David Maysles. **VHS, Beta, LV** $29.95 *COL, MVD* Woof!

Gin Game Taped London performance of the Broadway play about an aging couple who find romance in an old age home. Two-character performance won awards; touching and insightful.
1984 82m/C Jessica Tandy, Hume Cronyn; *D:* Mike Nichols. **VHS, Beta** $39.95 *RKO, VTK, STS* ♭♭♭

Ginger Fabulous super-sleuth Ginger faces the sordid world of prostitution, blackmail and drugs. Prequel to "The Abductors" and followed eventually by "Girls Are for Loving."
1972 90m/C Cheri Caffaro, William Grannell; *D:* Don Schain. **VHS, Beta** $39.95 *MON* ♭

Ginger Ale Afternoon A smutty comedy revolving around a triangle formed by a married couple and their sexy next-door neighbor. The film tries for fizz but only comes up flat. Music by Willie Dixon.
1989 88m/C Dana Anderson, John M. Jackson, Yeardley Smith; *D:* Rafal Zeilinski. **VHS, Beta, LV** $29.95 *ACA, IME* ♭

Ginger & Fred An acclaimed story of Fellini-esque poignancy about an aging dance team. Years before they had gained success by reverently impersonating the famous dancing duo of Astaire and Rogers. Now, after thirty years, they reunite under the gaudy lights of a high-tech television special. Wonderful performances by the aging Mastroianni and the still sweet Masina. In Italian with English subtitles.
1986 (PG-13) 126m/C *IT* Marcello Mastroianni, Giulietta Masina, Franco Fabrizi; *D:* Federico Fellini. **VHS, Beta** $19.98 *MGM, FCT, APD* ♭♭♭

Ginger in the Morning A salesman is enamored of a young hitchhiker whom he picks up on the road. This is the same year Spacek played the innocent-gone-twisted in "Badlands."
1973 90m/C Sissy Spacek, Slim Pickens, Monte Markham, Susan Oliver, Mark Miller; *D:* Gordon Wiles. **VHS, Beta** *NO* ♭♭

The Girl The first of Meszaros' trilogy, dealing with a young girl who leaves an orphanage to be reunited with her mother, a traditional country peasant. In Hungarian with English subtitles. Meszaros' first film. Followed by "Riddance" (1973) and "Adoption" (1975).
1968 86m/B *HU* *D:* Marta Meszaros. **VHS, Beta** $69.95 *KIV, TAM* ♭♭♭

The Girl A wealthy attorney begins an affair with a young schoolgirl, eventually leading to murder.
1986 (R) 104m/C Franco Nero, Christopher Lee, Bernice Stegers, Clare Powney; *D:* Arne Mattson. **VHS, Beta $19.95** STE, NWV ✍½

A Girl, a Guy and a Gob A shy rich boy falls in love with a girl who has her sights on another. Silly but enjoyable cast. *AKA:* The Navy Steps Out.
1941 91m/B Lucille Ball, Edmond O'Brien, George Murphy, Franklin Pangborn, Henry Travers, Lloyd Corrigan; *D:* Richard Wallace. **VHS, Beta $19.98** RKO, TTC ✍✍

The Girl Can't Help It Satiric rock and roll musical comedy about a retired mobster who hires a hungry talent agent to promote his girlfriend, a wannabe no-talent singer. Mansfield's first starring role. Classic performances by some of the early greats including Eddie Cochran, Gene Vincent, The Platters, Little Richard and Fats Domino.
1956 99m/B Jayne Mansfield, Tom Ewell, Edmond O'Brien, Julie London, Ray Anthony; *D:* Frank Tashlin. **VHS, Beta, LV $59.98** FOX ✍✍½

Girl Crazy A wealthy young playboy is sent to an all-boy school in Arizona to get his mind off girls. Once there, he still manages to fall for a local girl who can't stand the sight of him. The eighth film pairing for Rooney and Garland. ♫Sam and Delilah; Embraceable You; I Got Rhythm; Fascinating Rhythm; Treat Me Rough; Bronco Busters; Bidin' My Time; But Not For Me; Do; When It's Cactus Time in Arizona; Boy, What Love Has Done to Me; Barbary Coast; Could You Use Me?. *AKA:* When the Girls Meet the Boys.
1943 99m/B Mickey Rooney, Judy Garland, Tommy Dorsey & His Orchestra, Nancy Walker, June Allyson; *D:* Norman Taurog; *M:* George Gershwin, Ira Gershwin. **VHS, Beta, LV $19.98** MGM, TTC, FCT ✍✍✍

Girl from Calgary A female rodeo champ ropes her boyfriends much like she ropes her cows, but not without a knock-down, drag-out fight between the two which forces our cowgirl to make the choice she seems to know is fated. Stock rodeo footage is intercut with the heroine riding an obviously mechanical bucking bronc.
1932 66m/B Fifi d'Orsay, Paul Kelly; *D:* Philip H. Whitman. **VHS, Beta, LV $24.95** WGE, VYY ✍

Girl from Chicago In this crime melodrama a secret service agent falls in love while on assignment in Mississippi. When he's back in New York he finds a good friend of his girl's in serious trouble with the numbers racket.
1932 69m/C Starr Calloway, Grace Smith, Eugene Brooks, Frank Wilson; *D:* Oscar Micheaux. **VHS $34.95** FCT ✍½

Girl from Hunan Turn-of-the-century China, a 12-year-old girl is married to a 2-year-old boy in a typical arranged marriage. She grows into womanhood treating her toddler husband with sibling affection, but conducts a secret love affair with a farmer. Intolerant village laws against adultry place her life in jeopardy. In Mandarin with English subtitles.
1986 99m/C Na Renhua, Deng Xiaotuang, Yu Zhang; *D:* Xie Fei. **VHS $79.95** NYF, TAM ✍✍✍

The Girl from Missouri Cute comedy in which Harlow tries to snag a millionaire without sacrificing her virtues. Lots of laughs and hilarious action, especially the scene where Harlow arrives at the yacht in Florida. Kelly is great as Harlow's wise-cracking girlfriend. Witty dialogue by Emerson and Loos, who also wrote "Gentleman Prefer Blondes." *AKA:* One Hundred Percent Pure.
1934 75m/B Jean Harlow, Lionel Barrymore, Franchot Tone, Lewis Stone, Patsy Kelly, Alan Mowbray, Clara Blandick, Russell Hopton; *D:* Jack Conway; *W:* Anita Loos, John Emerson. **VHS $19.98** MGM ✍✍✍

The Girl from Petrovka A high-spirited Russian ballerina falls in love with an American newspaper correspondent. Their romance is complicated by the suspicious KGB. Bittersweet with a bleak ending.
1974 (PG) 103m/C Goldie Hawn, Hal Holbrook, Anthony Hopkins; *D:* Robert Ellis Miller. **VHS, Beta $59.95** MCA ✍½

The Girl from Tobacco Row A Southern slut involved with a cache of stolen cash fools with both a convict and the sheriff.
1966 90m/C Tex Ritter, Rachel Romen, Earl Richards, Tim Ormond, Rita Faye, Ralph Emery; *D:* Ron Ormond. **VHS, Beta $59.95** NO ✍

Girl Happy The King's fans will find him in Fort Lauderdale, Florida this time as the leader of a rock 'n' roll group. His mission: to chaperon the daughter of a Chicago mobster who naturally falls for him. Why not? ♫Girl Happy; Cross My Heart and Hope to Die; Do Not Disturb; Spring Fever; Wolf Call; Do the Clam; Fort Lauderdale Chamber of Commerce; Puppet On a String; I've Got to Find About My Baby; The Meanest Girl in Town; Startin' Tonight.
1965 96m/C Elvis Presley, Harold J. Stone, Shelley Fabares, Gary Crosby, Nita Talbot, Mary Ann Mobley, Jackie Coogan; *D:* Boris Sagal. **VHS, Beta $19.95** MGM ✍✍

Girl Hunters That intrepid private eye, Mike Hammer (played by his creator, Spillane), is caught up with communist spies, wicked women, and a missing secretary. Hammer is his usual judge-and-jury character but the action is fast-paced.
1963 103m/B Mickey Spillane, Lloyd Nolan, Shirley Eaton, Hy Gardner, Scott Peters; *D:* Roy Rowland. **VHS, Beta $16.95** SNC, NOS, DVT ✍✍

A Girl in a Million Williams dumps his verbose wife and seeks peace and quiet in a men-only War Department office. All is well until the arrival of a colonel and his daughter, mute from trauma. Finding her silence appealing, he marries her, but another trauma restores her speech. Sexist comedy may have played better in its day.
1946 90m/B *GB* Hugh Williams, Joan Greenwood, Naunton Wayne, Wylie Watson, Garry Marsh; *D:* Francis Searle. **VHS $19.95** NOS ✍✍

The Girl in a Swing An Englishman impulsively marries a beautiful German girl and both are subsequently haunted by phantoms from her past - are they caused by her psychic powers? Cliche-ridden silliness. Based on the Richard Adams novel.
1989 (R) 119m/C Meg Tilly, Rupert Frazer, Elspet Gray, Lynsey Baxter, Nicholas Le Prevost, Jean Boht; *D:* Gordon Hessler. **VHS, Beta, LV $89.99** HBO ✍✍½

Girl in Black The shy daughter of a once wealthy household gets the chance to escape her genteel poverty when she falls in love with the young man boarding with her family. He is attracted to her but a shocking tragedy changes everything. In Greek with English subtitles.
1956 100m/C *GR* Ellie Lambetti; *D:* Michael Cacoyannis. **VHS, Beta $59.95** FCT ✍✍

Girl in Black Stockings Beautiful women are mysteriously murdered at a remote, Utah hotel. Interesting, little known thriller similar to Hitchcock's "Psycho," but pre-dating it by three years.

1957 75m/B Lex Barker, Anne Bancroft, Mamie Van Doren, Ron Randell, Marie Windsor, John Dehner, John Holland, Diana Van Der Vlis; *D:* Howard W. Koch. **VHS $18.00** FRG ✍✍

The Girl in Blue A lawyer, ill at ease with his current romance, suddenly decides to search for a beautiful woman he saw once, and instantly fell in love with, years before.
1974 (R) 103m/C *CA* Maud Adams, David Selby, Gay Rowan, William Osler, Diane Dewey, Michael Kirby; *D:* George Kaczender. **VHS, Beta $79.95** PSM ✍½

A Girl in Every Port Navy buddies acquire an ailing racehorse and try to conceal it aboard ship along with a healthy horse they plan to switch it with in an upcoming race. Groucho flies without his brothers in this zany film.
1952 86m/B Groucho Marx, William Bendix, Marie Wilson, Don DeFore, Gene Lockhart; *D:* Chester Erskine. **VHS, Beta, LV $19.98** CCB ✍✍½

Girl in Gold Boots Aspiring starlet meets up with a draft evader and a biker on her way to Hollywood where she gets a job as a go-go dancer in a sleazy club. But things don't go smoothly when a murder and a drug theft are revealed. ♫Do You Want to Laugh or Cry?; For You; Hello, Michelle; One Good Time, One Good Place; Lonesome Man; You Gotta Come Down; Everything I Touch Turns to Gold; Cowboy Santa; Wheels of Love; Sin; Minnie Shimmy; Jimmy's Girl; Strange Things.
1969 94m/C Jody Daniels, Leslie McRae, Tom Pace, Mark Herron; *D:* Ted V. Mikels. **VHS, Beta $39.95** WWV ✍

Girl in His Pocket Mad scientist creates a potion that turns things into three-inch statues. He uses it mostly to have trysts with his lab assistant so his fiance won't find out. Based on "The Diminishing Draft" by Waldemar Kaempfert. *AKA:* Amour de Poche; Nude in His Pocket.
1962 82m/C *FR* Jean Marais, Genevieve Page, Agnes Laurent; *D:* Pierre Kast. **VHS $16.95** SNC ✍✍

The Girl in Lover's Lane A drifter falls in love with a small town girl but becomes a murder suspect when she turns up dead. Interesting mainly for Elam's uncharacteristic portrayal of a village idiot.
1960 78m/B Brett Halsey, Joyce Meadows, Lowell Brown, Jack Elam; *D:* Charles R. Rondeau. **VHS, Beta $16.95** SNC ✍✍

The Girl in Room 2A A young woman is trapped in a mansion with the elderly owner and her demented son. Routine horrorfest.
1976 (R) 90m/C Raf Vallone, Daniela Giordano. **VHS, Beta $59.95** PSM Woof!

The Girl in the Picture A mild British comedy about a young photographer who is happy to lose, but then strives to regain, his live-in girlfriend.
1986 (PG-13) 89m/C *GB* John Gordon-Sinclair, Irina Brook, David McKay, Catherine Guthrie, Paul Young; *D:* Cary Parker. **VHS, Beta $79.95** VES ✍✍½

The Girl Most Likely Light musical comedy about a romance-minded girl who dreams of marrying a wealthy, handsome man. She runs into a problem when she finds three prospects. Remake of 1941's "Tom, Dick and Harry" with Ginger Rogers. Choreography by great Gower Champion. ♫The Girl Most Likely; All the Colors of the Rainbow; I Don't Know What I Want; Balboa; We Gotta Keep Up With the Joneses; Crazy Horse.

1957 98m/C Jane Powell, Cliff Robertson, Tommy Noonan, Kaye Ballard, Una Merkel; **D:** Mitchell Leisen. **VHS, Beta, LV** $15.95 *UHV* ⅃⅃ ½

Girl of the Golden West
A musical version of the David Belasco chestnut about a Canadian frontier girl loving a rogue. One of Eddy and MacDonald's lesser efforts but features Ebsen's song and dance talents. ♫Camptown Races; Shadows on the Moon; Soldiers of Fortune; Soldiers of Fortune Reprise; Shadows on the Moon Reprise; The Wind in the Trees; Liebestraum; Ave Maria; Senorita; Who Are We to Say; Who Are We to Say Reprise.
1938 120m/B Jeanette MacDonald, Nelson Eddy, Walter Pidgeon, Leo Carrillo, Buddy Ebsen, Leonard Penn, Priscilla Lawson, Bob Murphy, Olin Howland, Cliff Edwards, Billy Bevan; **D:** Robert Z. Leonard. **VHS, Beta** $19.95 *MGM* ⅃⅃

A Girl of the Limberlost
A young Indiana farmgirl fights to bring her estranged parents back together, in spite of a meddling aunt and the unexplained phenomena that haunt her. Fine acting and beautiful scenery. Originally broadcast on public television as part of the "Wonderworks" family movie series, it's best appreciated by young teens. Adapted from Gene Stratton Porter's much-filmed novel.
1990 120m/C Annette O'Toole, Joanna Cassidy, Heather Fairfield. **VHS** $29.95 *PME, HMV* ⅃⅃

Girl on a Chain Gang
A girl on the run gets caught by police and does her time on a chain gang—an otherwise all-male chain gang. Predictable.
1965 96m/B William Watson, Julie Ange, R.K. Charles; **W/D:** Jerry Gross. **VHS, Beta** $16.95 *SNC Woof!*

The Girl on a Motorcycle
Singer Faithfull is a bored housewife who dons black leather and hops on her motorcycle to meet up with her lover (Delon), all the while remembering their other erotic encounters. **AKA:** Naked Under Leather; La Motocyclette.
1968 (R) 92m/C *GB* Alain Delon, Marianne Faithfull, Roger Mutton; **D:** Jack Cardiff. **VHS, Beta** $59.95 *MLB* ⅃⅃

A Girl on Her Own
A young actress embarking on her first big role in Paris must also deal with family and political considerations in this drama set during the political upheaval of 1935.
1976 112m/C *FR* Sophie Chemineau, Bruno La Brasca; **D:** Philippe Nahoun. **VHS** $49.95 *FCT* ⅃⅃

Girl Rush
Two bad vaudeville comics are stuck in California during the gold rush and are promised sacks of gold if they can persuade some women to come to a rowdy mining town. ♫Annabella's Bustle; Rainbow Valley; If Men Could Only See Us Now; Walking Arm in Arm With Jim.
1944 65m/B Wally Brown, Alan Carney, Frances Langford, Vera Vague, Robert Mitchum, Paul Hurst, Patti Brill, Sarah Padden, Cy Kendall; **D:** Gordon Douglas. **VHS, Beta** *RKO, TTC* ⅃

The Girl Said No
A sleazy bookie poses as a theatrical producer in order to get even with a dance hall floozy who once stiffed him. **AKA:** With Words and Music.
1937 72m/B Robert Armstrong, Irene Hervey; **W/D:** Andrew L. Stone. **VHS, Beta** $19.95 *NOS, DVT, VYY* ⅃ ½

Girl Shy
Harold is a shy tailor's apprentice who is trying to get a collection of his romantic fantasies published. Finale features Lloyd chasing wildly after girl of his dreams.
1924 65m/B Harold Lloyd, Jobyna Ralston, Richard Daniels; **D:** Fred Newmeyer; **W:** Sam Taylor. **VHS, Beta** *TLF* ⅃⅃⅃

A Girl to Kill for
A temptress lures a randy college guy into a plot of murder and betrayal.
1990 (R) 85m/C Sasha Jensen, Karen Austin, Alex Cord, Rod McCary, Karen Medak; **D:** Richard Oliver. **VHS, Beta, LV** $79.95 *COL* ⅃½

Girl-Toy
A nerdy guy is afraid of women until a beautiful motorcyclist sweeps him off his feet. Before they can consummate their relationship, he is kidnapped by a lustful erotic cult who find him irresistible.
1984 86m/C Gerry Sont, Lenita Psillakis, Jon Finlayson. **VHS, Beta** *NO* ⅃

Girl Under the Sheet
A con-man/archaeologist moves into an ancient castle and begins romancing a beautiful resident ghost.
196? 89m/C Chelo Alonso, Walter Chiari. **VHS, Beta** *NO* ⅃

The Girl Who Had Everything
Good melodrama with top cast, intelligent script and smooth direction. Taylor plays the spoiled daughter of a criminal lawyer (Powell) who falls for her father's client (Lamas), a suave, underground syndicate boss. Remake of the 1931 film "A Free Soul," which starred Norma Shearer, Clark Gable, and Lionel Barrymore. Based on the novel of the same name by Adela Rogers St. John.
1953 69m/B Elizabeth Taylor, Fernando Lamas, William Powell, Gig Young, James Whitmore, Robert Burton; **D:** Richard Thorpe. **VHS** $19.98 *MGM* ⅃⅃ ½

The Girl Who Spelled Freedom
A young Cambodian girl, speaking little English, strives to adjust to life in Chattanooga, Tennessee. She faces her challenges by becoming a champion at the national spelling bee. Based on a true story. Made-for-television.
1986 90m/C Wayne Rogers, Mary Kay Place, Jade Chinn; **D:** Simon Wincer. **VHS, Beta** $59.95 *DIS* ⅃⅃⅃

The Girl with the Hat Box
Early Russian production about a poor working girl who's paid with a lottery ticket rather than rubles (an ironic pre-communist theme?). When she strikes it rich in the lottery, her boss gives chase and silent antics ensue. Silent with orchestral score.
1927 67m/B *RU* Anna Sten, Vladimar Fogel, Serafina Birman, Ivan Koval-Samborsky; **D:** Boris Barnett. **VHS** $29.95 *KIV, FCT, TAM* ⅃⅃

Girlfriend from Hell
The Devil inhabits the body of a teenage wallflower and turns her into an uncontrollable vamp.
1989 (R) 95m/C Liane Curtis, Dana Ashbrook, Leslie Deane, James Daughton, Anthony Barrie, James Karen; **W/D:** Daniel M. Peterson. **VHS, Beta, LV** $14.95 *LIV* ⅃

Girlfriends
The bittersweet story of a young Jewish photographer learning to make it on her own. Directorial debut of Weill reflects her background in documentaries as the true-to-life episodes unfold.
1978 87m/C Melanie Mayron, Anita Skinner, Eli Wallach, Christopher Guest, Amy Wright, Viveca Lindfors, Bob Balaban; **D:** Claudia Weill. **VHS, Beta** $19.98 *WAR* ⅃⅃⅃

Girls Are for Loving
Undercover agent Ginger faces real adventure when she battles it out with her counterpart, a seductive enemy agent. Her third adventure following "Ginger" (1970) and "The Abductors" (1971).
1973 90m/C Cheri Caffaro, Timothy Brown; **D:** Don Schain. **VHS, Beta** $39.95 *MON* ⅃

A Girl's Folly
A country girl falls in love with the leading man of a film shooting on location. She wants to become a rich actress, but fails miserably. The actor offers her all the luxuries she will become

his mistress. When she finally agrees, her mother shows up. What will our country maid do now?
1917 66m/B Robert Warwick, Doris Kenyon, June Elvidge, Johnny Hines; **D:** Maurice Tourneur. **VHS, Beta, 8mm** $19.95 *VYY* ⅃⅃ ½

Girls! Girls! Girls!
Poor tuna boat fisherman Elvis moonlights as a nightclub singer to get his father's boat out of hock. He falls for a rich girl pretending to be poor; and after some romantic trials, there's the usual happy ending. ♫The Nearness of You; Never Let Me Go; Girls, Girls, Girls; Return to Sender; We're Coming in Loaded; A Boy Like Me, A Girl Like You; Song of the Shrimp; Earth Boy; The Walls Have Ears; Thanks to the Rolling Sea; Because of You; Where Do We Come From?; We'll Be Together, Mama; I Don't Wanna Be Tied; I Don't Want To.
1962 106m/C Elvis Presley, Stella Stevens, Laurel Goodwin, Jeremy Slate, Benson Fong, Robert Strauss, Ginny Tiu, Guy Lee, Beulah Quo; **D:** Norman Taurog. **VHS, Beta** $14.98 *FOX, MVD* ⅃⅃

Girls in Chains
Girls in a reformatory, a teacher, a corrupt school official, and the detective trying to nail him. There's also a murder with the killer revealed at the beginning of the film.
1943 72m/B Arline Judge, Roger Clark, Robin Raymond, Barbara Pepper, Dorothy Burgess, Clancy Cooper; **D:** Edgar G. Ulmer. **VHS, Beta** $16.95 *NOS, SNC* ⅃

Girls in Prison
Anne Carson is sent to prison for a bank robbery she didn't commit, and although the prison chaplain believes her story, the other prisoners think she knows where the money is hidden. They plan a prison break, forcing Carson to go with them and get the money, but they soon run across the real robber, also searching for the loot. A below-average "B" prison movie, lacking the camp aspects of so many of these films.
1956 87m/B Richard Denning, Joan Taylor, Adele Jergens, Helen Gilbert, Lance Fuller, Jane Darwell, Raymond Hatton; **D:** Edward L. Cahn. **VHS** $9.95 *COL* ⅃ ½

Girls Just Want to Have Fun
An army brat and her friends pull out all the stops and defy their parents for a chance to dance on a national television program. Based loosely upon Cyndi Lauper's song of the same name.
1985 (PG) 90m/C Sarah Jessica Parker, Helen Hunt, Ed Lauter, Holly Gagnier, Morgan Woodward, Lee Montgomery, Shannen Doherty, Biff Yeager; **D:** Alan Mett:tor. **VHS, Beta, LV** $9.95 *NWV, STE* ⅃ ½

Girls Next Door
A bevy of boisterous beauties cavort and cause havoc in buffoon-cluttered suburbia.
1979 (R) 85m/C Kirsten Baker, Perry Lang, Leslie Cederquist, Richard Singer; **D:** James Hong. **VHS, Beta, LV** *NO* ⅃

Girls Night Out
Ex-cop must stop a killer who is murdering participants in a sorority house scavenger hunt and leaving cryptic clues on the local radio station. **AKA:** The Scaremaker.
1983 (R) 96m/C Hal Holbrook, Rutanya Alda, Julia Montgomery, James Carroll; **D:** Robert Deubel. **VHS, Beta** $69.95 *HBO* ⅃

Girls of Don Juan
A nerd finds that every woman he meets somehow falls in love or lust with him.
197? 88m/C Anne Libert, Monica Vitti. **VHS, Beta** $29.95 *MED* ⅃

The Girls of Huntington House
A teacher in a school for unwed mothers finds herself becoming increasingly absorbed in her students' lives. Made for television.

1973 73m/C Shirley Jones, Mercedes McCambridge, Sissy Spacek, William Windom, Pamela Sue Martin, Darrell Larson; **D:** Alf Kjellin. VHS **$59.95** LIV ✓✓

The Girls of Malibu A bevy of girls frolic on the Malibu beaches without clothes.
1986 60m/C VHS, Beta **$24.95** AHV Woof!

Girls of the White Orchid A naive American girl thinks she's getting a job singing in a Japanese nightclub, but it turns out to be a front for a prostitution ring run by the Japanese Yakuza. A made-for-television movie based on real stories, though the producers concentrate on the seamy side. **AKA:** Death Ride to Osaka.
1985 96m/C Ann Jillian, Jennifer Jason Leigh; **D:** Jonathan Kaplan. VHS, Beta **$59.95** LHV ✓

Girls on the Road Two girls are just out for fun cruising the California coast. But that handsome hitchhiker turns out to be a deadly mistake.
1973 (PG) 91m/C CA Kathleen Cody, Michael Ontkean, Dianne Hull, Ralph Waite; **D:** Thomas J. Schmidt. VHS, Beta **$59.95** UNI ✓½

Girls Riot Young, female juvenile delinquents have had enough! They decide to give their warden-like headmistress a taste of her own violence.
1988 100m/C Jocelyne Boisseau, Cornelia Calwer, Angelica Domrose, Ute Freight; **D:** Manfred Purzer. VHS, Beta **$39.95** ACN ✓

Girls School Screamers Six young women and a nun are assigned to spend the weekend checking the contents for sale in a scary mansion bequeathed to their school. Unfortunately, the psychotic killer inhabiting the place doesn't think that's a good idea.
1986 (R) 85m/C Mollie O'Mara, Sharon Christopher, Vera Gallagher; **D:** John P. Finegan. VHS, Beta **$69.98** LIV ✓

Girls' Town Typical bad girls and drag racing fifties flick has Van Doren sent to a correctional institute, run by nuns. This tough girl sees the error of her wicked ways and turns into a goody-two-shoes. **AKA:** The Innocent and the Damned.
1959 90m/B Mamie Van Doren, Mel Torme, Paul Anka, Ray Anthony, Maggie Hayes, Cathy Crosby, Elinor Donahue, Gigi Perreau, Jim Mitchum, Gloria Talbott, Harold Lloyd Jr., Charles Chaplin Jr.; **D:** Charles Haas; **W:** Robert Smith. VHS **$9.98** REP ✓

Girly An English gothic about an excessively weird family that lives in a crumbling mansion and indulges in murder, mental aberration, and sexual compulsion. **AKA:** Mumsy, Nanny, Sonny, and Girly.
1970 (R) 101m/C GB Michael Bryant, Ursula Howells, Pat Heywood, Howard Trevor, Vanessa Howard, Michael Ripper; **D:** Freddie Francis. VHS, Beta **$79.95** PSM ✓

Git! A young runaway and his faithful dog are taken in by a wealthy dog-breeder and trained by him into a crack hunting team.
1965 90m/C Jack Chaplain, Richard Webb, Heather North; **D:** Ellis Kadison. VHS, Beta **$14.95** COL, NLC ✓½

Git Along Little Dogies It's cattle ranchers versus oil men with Autry caught in the middle of the petro/cow war. But Gene still finds a little time to romance the town banker's pretty daughter.
1937 60m/B William Farnum, Gene Autry, Judith Allen, Champion, Smiley Burnette; **D:** Joseph Kane. VHS, Beta **$19.95** NOS, VYY, DVT ✓½

Give a Girl a Break Three talented but unknown babes vie for the lead in a stage production headed for Broadway after the incumbent prima donna quits. After befriending one of the various men associated with the production, each starlet thinks she's a

shoe-in for the part. Entertaining but undistinguished musical with appealing dance routines of Fosse and the Champions. Ira Gershwin, collaborating for the first and only time with Burton Lane, wrote the lyrics to two of the songs. ♫Give the Girl a Break; In Our United State; It Happens Every Time; Nothing is Impossible; Applause, Applause; Challenge Dance.
1953 84m/C Marge Champion, Gower Champion, Debbie Reynolds, Helen Wood, Bob Fosse, Kurt Kasznar, Richard Anderson, William Ching, Larry Keating, Donna Martell; **D:** Stanley Donen. VHS **$19.98** MGM, TTC, FCT ✓✓½

Give 'Em Hell, Harry! James Whitmore's one-man show as Harry S. Truman filmed in performance on stage; Whitmore was nominated for a Tony.
1975 103m/C James Whitmore; **D:** Steve Binder. VHS, Beta **$19.95** WOV ✓✓½

Give My Regards to Broad Street McCartney film made for McCartney fans. Film features many fine versions of the ex-Beatle's songs that accompany his otherwise lackluster portrayal of a rock star in search of his stolen master recordings. ♫Eleanor Rigby; Ballroom Dancing; Good Day, Sunshine; Silly Love Songs; No Values; No More Lonely Nights; Yesterday; Not Such a Bad Boy; The Long and Winding Road.
1984 (PG) 109m/C GB Paul McCartney, Bryan Brown, Ringo Starr, Barbara Bach, Tracy Ullman, Ralph Richardson, Linda McCartney; **D:** Peter Webb. VHS, Beta, LV **$19.95** MVD, FOX ✓✓

Gizmo! A hilarious and affectionate tribute to crackpot inventors everywhere, with footage of dozens of great and not-so-great machines and other creations. Some segments in black-and-white.
1977 77m/C **D:** Howard Smith. VHS, Beta **$19.98** WAR, OM ✓✓½

The Gladiator Brown stars as a mild-mannered collegiate who accidently ingests a serum which turns him into a real he-man. Things take a turn for the funniest when the effects wear off, just as he is to wrestle Man Mountain Dean. Chock-full of Brown's trademark physical humor.
1938 70m/B Joe E. Brown, Man Mountain Dean, June Travis, Dickie Moore, Lucien Littlefield, Robert Kent, Ethel Wales; **D:** Edward Sedgwick. VHS **$19.95** NOS ✓✓✓½

The Gladiator An angry Los Angeles citizen turns vigilante against drunk drivers after his brother is one of their victims. Made for television.
1986 94m/C Ken Wahl, Nancy Allen, Robert Culp, Stan Shaw, Rosemary Forsyth; **D:** Abel Ferrara. VHS, Beta, LV **$19.95** STE, NWV, HHE ✓½

Gladiator When suburban Golden Gloves boxing champion Tommy Riley (Marshall) is forced to move to the inner city because of his father's gambling debts, he becomes involved with an evil boxing promotor who thrives on pitting different ethnic races against each other in illegal boxing matches. Eventually Riley is forced to fight his black friend Lincoln (Gooding), even though Lincoln has been warned that another blow to the head could mean his life. Although this film tries to serve some moral purpose, it falls flat on the mat.
1992 (R) 98m/C Cuba Gooding Jr., James Marshall, Robert Loggia, Ossie Davis, Brian Dennehy, Cara Buono, John Heard, John Seda, Lance Slaughter; **D:** Rowdy Herrington. VHS, LV COL ✓½

Gladiator of Rome A gladiator flexes his pecs to save a young girl from death at the hands of evil rulers. **AKA:** Il Gladiatore Di Roma.

1963 105m/C IT Gordon Scott, Wandisa Guida, Roberto Risso, Ombretta Colli, Alberto Farnese; **D:** Mario Costa. VHS **$16.95** SNC ✓

The Gladiators Televised gladiatorial bouts are designed to subdue man's violent tendencies in a futuristic society until a computer makes a fatal error. **AKA:** The Peace Game; Gladiatorerna.
1970 90m/C Arthur Pentelow, Frederick Danner; **D:** Peter Watkins. VHS, Beta UHV ✓

Gladiators 7 Sparta must be freed from the tyrannical rule of the Romans. In lieu of samurai or cowboys, who better than the Gladiators 7 to do the deed? Plenty of sword-to-sword action and scantily clad Italian babes.
1962 92m/C SP IT Richard Harrison, Loredana Nusciak, Livio Lorenzon, Gerard Tichy, Edoardo Toniolo, Joseph Marco, Barta Barry; **D:** Pedro Lazaga. VHS, Beta **$16.95** SNC ✓½

Glass A normally complacent man is driven to the brink of savagery when a killer begins stalking his employees.
1990 92m/C Alan Lovell, Lisa Peers, Adam Stone, Natalie McCurray. VHS **$59.95** ATL ✓½

The Glass Bottom Boat A bubbly but transparent Doris Day comedy, in which she falls in love with her boss at an aerospace lab. Their scheme to spend time together gets her mistaken for a spy. Made about the time they stopped making them like this anymore; it's innocuous slapstick romance with a remarkable 1960's cast, including a Robert Vaughn cameo as the Man From U.N.C.L.E. Doris sings "Que Sera, Sera" and a few other numbers.
1966 110m/C Doris Day, Rod Taylor, Arthur Godfrey, Paul Lynde, Eric Fleming, Alice Pearce, Ellen Corby, John McGiver, Dom DeLuise, Dick Martin, Edward Andrews; **Cameos:** Robert Vaughn; **D:** Frank Tashlin; **W:** Everett Freeman. VHS, Beta, LV **$19.98** MGM ✓✓

The Glass House Alda stars as a middle-aged college professor, convicted on a manslaugter charge, who is sent to a maximum security prison and must learn to deal with life inside. Filmed at Utah State Prison, real-life prisoners as supporting cast add to the drama. Still has the power to chill, with Morrow particularly effective as one of the inmate leaders. Adapted from a Truman Capote story. Made for television. **AKA:** Truman Capote's The Glass House.
1972 92m/C Alan Alda, Vic Morrow, Clu Gulager, Billy Dee Williams, Dean Jagger, Kristopher Tabori; **D:** Tom Gries. VHS, Beta **$49.95** WWV, MOV, HHT ✓✓✓

The Glass Jungle Will a cab driver save Los Angeles? When armed terrorists and the FBI battle it out in the sunny California city an innocent cabby seems to hold the solution to survival.
1988 94m/C Lee Canalito, Joe Filbeck, Diana Frank, Mark High, Frank Scala; **D:** Joseph Merhi. VHS, Beta **$69.95** HHE ✓✓

The Glass Key The second version of Dashiell Hammet's novel, a vintage mystery movie concerning a nominally corrupt politician (Donlevy) being framed for murder, and his assistant sleuthing out the real culprit. One of Ladd's first starring vehicles; Lake is the mystery woman who loves him, and Bendix a particularly vicious thug.
1942 85m/B Alan Ladd, Veronica Lake, Brian Donlevy, William Bendix, Bonita Granville, Richard Denning, Joseph Calleia, Moroni Olsen, Dane Clark; **D:** Stuart Heisler. VHS, Beta, LV **$29.95** MCA ✓✓✓

The Glass Menagerie An aging Southern belle deals with her crippled daughter Laura, whose one great love is her collection of glass animals. The third film adaptation of the Tennessee Williams classic, which preserves the performances of the Broadway revival cast, is a solid-but-not-stellar adaptation of the play. Music by Henry Mancini with an all-star acting ensemble.
1987 (PG) 134m/C Joanne Woodward, Karen Allen, John Malkovich, James Naughton; **D:** Paul Newman. **VHS, Beta, LV $79.95** KUI, MCA √√√

The Glass Slipper In this version of the "Cinderella" saga, Caron plays an unglamourous girl gradually transformed into the expected beauty. Winwood is the fairy godmother who inspires the girl to find happiness, rather then simply providing it for her magically. The film is highlighted by the stunning dance numbers, choreographed by Roland Petit and featuring the Paris ballet.
1955 93m/C Leslie Caron, Michael Wilding, Keenan Wynn, Estelle Winwood, Elsa Lanchester, Barry Jones, Amanda Blake, Lurene Tuttle; **D:** Charles Walters. **VHS, Beta $19.98** MGM, FCT √√

Glass Tomb At a circus, a man performs the world's longest fast inside a glass cage, and becomes the raison d'etre for murder. **AKA:** The Glass Cage.
1955 59m/B John Ireland, Honor Blackman, Eric Pohlmann, Tonia Bern, Sidney James; **D:** Montgomery Tully. **VHS, Beta, LV** NO √√

Gleaming the Cube A skateboarding teen investigates his brother's murder. Film impresses with its stunt footage only. For those with adolescent interests.
1989 (PG-13) 102m/C Christian Slater, Steven Bauer, Min Luong, Art Chudabala, Le Tuan; **D:** Graeme Clifford. **VHS, Beta, LV $14.98** LIV, VES √√

Glen and Randa Two young people experience the world after it has been destroyed by nuclear war. Early McBride, before the hired-gun success of "The Big Easy."
1971 94m/C Steven Curry, Shelley Plimpton; **D:** Jim McBride; **W:** Rudy Wurlitzer. **VHS, Beta, LV $59.95** UHV, IME √√½

Glen or Glenda An appalling, quasi-docudrama about transvestism, interspersed with meaningless stock footage, inept dream sequences and Lugosi sitting in a chair spouting incoherent prattle at the camera. Directorial debut of Wood, who, using a pseudonym, played the lead; one of the phenomenally bad films of this century. An integral part of the famous anti-auteur's canon. **AKA:** He or She; I Changed My Sex; I Led Two Lives; The Transvestite.
1953 70m/B Bela Lugosi, Edward D. Wood Jr., Lyle Talbot, Donald Woods; **D:** Edward D. Wood Jr. **VHS, Beta $19.95** NOS, MRV, SNC Woof!

Glengarry Glen Ross A seven-character study chronicling 48-hours in the lives of some sleazy real estate men in danger of getting the ax from their hard-driving bosses. A standout cast includes Pacino as the glad-handing sales leader, Lemmon as the hustler fallen on dim prospects, and Baldwin, briefly venomous, as the company hatchet-man. Brutal and hard-edged with very strong language. Mamet scripted from his Tony-award winning Broadway play.
1992 (R) 100m/C Al Pacino, Jack Lemmon, Ed Harris, Alec Baldwin, Alan Arkin, Kevin Spacey, Jonathan Pryce; **D:** James Foley; **W:** David Mamet. Academy Awards '92 Nominations: Best Supporting Actor (Pacino); National Board of Review Awards '93: Best Actor (Lemmon); Venice Film Festival '93: Best Actor (Lemmon). **VHS, LV $94.98** LIV, MOV √√√

The Glenn Miller Story The music of the Big Band Era lives again in this warm biography of the legendary Glenn Miller, following his life from the late '20s to his untimely death in a World War II plane crash. Stewart's likably convincing and even fakes the trombone playing well. ♫Moonlight Serenade; In the Mood; Tuxedo Junction; Little Brown Jug; Adios; String of Pearls; Pennsylvania 6-5000; Stairway to the Stars; American Patrol; I Know Why; Chattanooga Choo-Choo; Bidin' My Time; I Dreamed I Dwelt in Marble Halls; St. Louis Blues March; Basin Street Blues; Over the Rainbow.
1954 (G) 113m/C James Stewart, June Allyson, Harry Morgan, Gene Krupa, Louis Armstrong, Ben Pollack; **D:** Anthony Mann. Academy Awards '54: Best Sound; Nominations: Best Story & Screenplay, Best Original Score. **VHS, Beta, LV $19.95** MCA, RDG √√√

Glitch! Two inept burglars fumble an attempted robbery and somehow wind up with a slew of beautiful models, but in big trouble with the mob.
1988 (R) 88m/C Julia Nickson-Soul, Will Egan, Steve Donmyer, Dan Speaker, Dallas Cole, Ji Tu Cambuka, Dick Gautier, Ted Lange, Teri Weigel, Fernando Carzon, John Kreng, Lindsay Carr; **D:** Nico Mastorakis. **VHS, Beta, LV $29.95** ACA √√½

The Glitter Dome Two policemen discover the sleazier side of Hollywood when they investigate the murder of a pornographer. Based upon the novel by Joseph Wambaugh. Made for television.
1984 90m/C Stuart Margolin, John Marley, James Garner, John Lithgow, Margot Kidder, Colleen Dewhurst; **D:** Stuart Margolin. **VHS, Beta $59.99** HBO √√½

Glitz A Miami cop and an Atlantic City lounge singer team up to investigate a call-girl's death and wind up too close to a drug ring. Based on the novel by Elmore Leonard. Made for television.
1988 96m/C Jimmy Smits, John Diehl, Markie Post, Ken Foree, Madison Mason, Robin Strasser; **D:** Sandor Stein. **VHS, Beta $79.95** WAR √√½

Gloria She used to be a Mafia moll, now she's outrunning the Mob after taking in the son of a slain neighbor. He's got a book that they want, and they're willing to kill to get it. Gritty attempt by director Cassavetes at a mainstream hit.
1980 (PG) 123m/C Gena Rowlands, John Adams, Buck Henry, Julie Carmen; **D:** John Cassavetes. Academy Awards '80 Nominations: Best Actress (Rowlands); Venice Film Festival '80: Best Film. **VHS, Beta, LV $69.95** COL √√½

Glorifying the American Girl Eaton's a chorus girl performing in the Ziegfeld Follies, which lends itself to numerous production numbers. The only film Ziegfeld ever produced. ♫What I Wouldn't Do For That Man; Blue Skies; I'm Just a Vagabond Lover; Baby Face; At Sundown; Beautiful Changes; Sam the Old Accordian Man; There Must Be Someone Waiting For Me.
1930 96m/B Mary Eaton, Dan Healey, Eddie Cantor, Rudy Vallee; **D:** Millard Webb. **VHS, Beta $19.95** NOS, HHT, DVT √√

Glory A racehorse owner finds the money to enter her filly in the Kentucky Derby. No surprises here.
1956 100m/C Margaret O'Brien, Walter Brennan, Charlotte Greenwood; **D:** Dick Butler. **VHS, Beta $15.95** UHV √√

Glory A rich, historical spectacle chronicling the 54th Massachusetts, the first black volunteer infantry unit in the Civil War. The film manages to artfully focus on both the 54th and their white commander, Robert Gould Shaw. Based on Shaw's letters, the film uses thousands of accurately costumed "living historians" (re-enactors) as extras in this panoramic production. A haunting, bittersweet musical score pervades what finally becomes an anti-war statement. Stunning performances throughout, with exceptional work from Freeman and Washington.
1989 (R) 122m/C Matthew Broderick, Morgan Freeman, Denzel Washington, Cary Elwes, Jihmi Kennedy, Andre Braugher, John Finn, Donovan Leitch, John Cullum, Bob Gunton, Jane Alexander, Raymond St. Jacques; **D:** Edward Zwick; **W:** Kevin Jarre. Academy Awards '89: Best Cinematography, Best Sound, Best Supporting Actor (Washington); Nominations: Best Film Editing. **VHS, Beta, LV, 8mm $19.95** COL, FCT, BTV √√√½

Glory Boys A secret agent is hired to protect an Israeli scientist who is marked for assassination by the PLO and IRA.
1984 110m/C Rod Steiger, Anthony Perkins, Gary Brown, Aaron Harris; **D:** Michael Ferguson. **VHS, Beta $59.95** PSM √√½

Glory! Glory! Slashing satire about TV evangelism. Richard Thomas as the meek son of founder of Church of the Champions of Christ brings in lewd female rock singer to save the money-machine ministry from financial ruin. Rock music, sex, and MTV-like camera work make it worth seeing. James Whitmore is a treat.
1990 (R) 152m/C Ellen Greene, Richard Thomas, Barry Morse, James Whitmore; **D:** Lindsay Anderson. **VHS, Beta, LV $59.98** ORI, IME √√√

The Glory Stompers Hopper prepares for his Easy Rider role as the leader of a motorcycle gang who battles with a rival leader over a woman. Very bad, atrocious dialogue, and a "love-in" scene that will be best appreciated by insomniacs.
1967 85m/C Dennis Hopper, Jody McCrea, Chris Noel, Jock Mahoney, Lindsay Crosby, Robert Tessier, Casey Kasem; **D:** Anthony M. Lanza. **VHS** NO Woof!

Glory Years Three old friends find themselves in charge of the scholarship fund at their 20th high school reunion. Unfortunately, they decide to increase the fund by gambling in Las Vegas and lose it all on a fixed fight!
1987 150m/C George Dzundza, Archie Hahn, Tim Thomerson, Tawny Kitaen, Donna Pescow, Donna Denton; **D:** Arthur Seidelman. **VHS, Beta $79.95** HBO √

The Glove Ex-cop turned bounty hunter has his toughest assignment ever. It's his job to bring in a six-and-a-half foot, 250-pound ex-con who's been wreaking havoc with an unusual glove—it's made of leather and steel. **AKA:** The Glove: Lethal Terminator; Blood Mad.
1978 (R) 93m/C John Saxon, Roosevelt Grier, Joanna Cassidy, Joan Blondell, Jack Carter, Aldo Ray; **D:** Ross Hagen. **VHS, Beta $19.95** MED √√

Gnome-Mobile A lumber baron and his two grandchildren attempt to reunite a pair of forest gnomes with a lost gnome colony. Brennan has a dual role as both a human and a gnome grandfather. Wynn's last film. Based on a children's novel by Upton Sinclair.
1967 84m/C Walter Brennan, Richard Deacon, Ed Wynn, Karen Dotrice, Matthew Garber; **D:** Robert Stevenson. **VHS, Beta** DIS, OM √√

Gnomes The gnomes are wily little creatures who are in constant battle with their oversized, underwitted adversaries, the trolls. The books of Wil Huggen and Rien Poortvliet inspired the film.
1980 48m/C **VHS, Beta $225.00** PYR, WTA √√

The Go-Between A wonderful tale of hidden love. A young boy (Guard) acts as a messenger between the aristocratic Christie and her former lover Bates. But tragedy befalls them all when the lovers are discovered. The story is told as the elderly messenger (now played by Redgrave) recalls his younger days as this go-between and builds to a climax when he is once again asked to be a messenger for the lady he loved long ago. Based on a story by L. P. Hartley and adapted by Harold Pinter.
1971 (PG) 116m/C *GB* Julie Christie, Alan Bates, Dominic Guard, Margaret Leighton, Michael Redgrave, Michael Gough, Edward Fox; *D:* Joseph Losey; *W:* Harold Pinter. Academy Awards '71 Nominations: Best Supporting Actress (Leighton); British Academy Awards '71: Best Supporting Actor (Fox), Best Supporting Actress (Leighton). **VHS** *CSM, MGM* 𝄞𝄞𝄞 ½

Go Down Death In this early all-black film, a minister is caught in a moral dilemma literally between Heaven and Hell. Scenes of the afterlife are taken from early silent films.
1941 63m/B Myra D. Hemmings, Samuel H. James, Eddy L. Houston, Spencer Williams Jr., Amos Droughan; *D:* Spencer Williams Jr. **VHS, Beta $29.95** *NOS, DVT, TIM* 𝄞 ½

Go for Broke! Inexperienced officer Johnson heads a special World War II attack force which is made up of Japanese Americans. Sent to fight in Europe, they prove their bravery and loyalty to all. Good, offbeat story.
1951 92m/B Van Johnson, Giana Maria Canale, Warner Anderson, Lane Nakano, George Miki; *D:* Robert Pirosh. **VHS, Beta, 3/4U $19.95** *NOS, MRV, VYY* 𝄞𝄞 ½

Go for Broke Motorcycle stunts, fights, and car chases highlight this action film.
1990 ?m/C **VHS** *VYY* 𝄞𝄞 ½

Go for It Oddball supercops go after a mad scientist—who has created a deadly "K"-bomb—and they encounter killer whales, karate busboys and malevolent Shirley Temple clones along the way.
1983 (PG) 109m/C *IT* Bud Spencer, Terence Hill, David Huddleston; *D:* E.B. Clucher. **VHS, Beta $79.95** *WAR* 𝄞𝄞

Go for the Gold A young marathon runner risks his girlfriend's love when he decides to pursue fame and fortune.
1984 98m/C James Ryan, Cameron Mitchell, Sandra Horne. **VHS, Beta $69.98** *LIV* 𝄞

The Go-Getter Wild slapstick fun in the world of business.
1954 ?m/C Hank McCune, Beverly Garland. **VHS $15.95** *LOO* 𝄞𝄞

Go, Johnny Go! Rock promoter Alan Freed molds a young orphan into rock sensation "Johnny Melody." Musical performances include Ritchie Valens (his only film appearance), Eddie Cochran, Jackie Wilson.
1959 75m/B Alan Freed, Sandy Stewart, Chuck Berry, The Cadillacs, Jimmy Clanton, Eddie Cochran, Jackie Wilson, Ritchie Valens; *D:* Paul Landres. **VHS, Beta, LV $14.95** *QNE, MED, AOV* 𝄞𝄞

Go Kill and Come Back A bounty hunter tracks down a notoriously dangerous train robber.
1968 (PG) 95m/C Gilbert Roland, George Helton, Edd Byrnes; *D:* Enzo G. Castellari. **VHS, Beta $24.95** *MON* 𝄞

The Go-Masters A historic co-production between Japan and China, centering on the ancient strategy board game "Go." A young competitor becomes obsessed with winning at any price. Episodic tale of the relationships between a Japanese and Chinese family spans 30 years and was critically acclaimed in both China and Japan. In Japanese and Chinese with English subtitles.
AKA: Mikan No Taikyoku.
1982 134m/C *JP CH* Rentaro Mikuni, Sun Dao-Lin, Shen Guan-Chu, Misako Honno; *D:* Junya Sato, Duan Jishun. **VHS, Beta $59.95** *SVS, TAM, FCT* 𝄞𝄞𝄞

Go Tell the Spartans In Vietnam, 1964, a hard-boiled major is ordered to establish a garrison at Muc Wa with a platoon of burned out Americans and Vietnamese mercenaries. Blundering but politically interesting war epic pre-dating the flood of 1980s American-Vietnam apologetics. Based on Daniel Ford's novel.
1978 (R) 114m/C Burt Lancaster, Craig Wasson, David Clennon, Marc Singer; *D:* Ted Post. **VHS, Beta, LV $19.98** *VES* 𝄞𝄞𝄞

Go West The brothers Marx help in the making and un-making of the Old West. Weak, late Marx Bros., but always good for a few yucks.
1940 80m/B Groucho Marx, Chico Marx, Harpo Marx, John Carroll, Diana Lewis; *D:* Edward Buzzell. **VHS, Beta, LV $19.95** *MGM, CCB* 𝄞𝄞 ½

The Goalie's Anxiety at the Penalty Kick A chilling landmark film that established Wenders as one of the chief film voices to emerge from post-war Germany. The story deals with a soccer player who wanders around Vienna after being suspended, commits a random murder, and slowly passes over the brink of sanity and morality. A suspenseful, existential adaptation of the Peter Handke novel. In German with English subtitles.
1971 101m/C *GE* Arthur Brauss, Erika Pluhar, Kai Fischer; *D:* Wim Wenders. **VHS, Beta $29.95** *PAV, FCT, GLV* 𝄞𝄞𝄞 ½

God Bless the Child A young single mother loses her home and she and her seven-year-old daughter are forced to live on the streets. Harrowing made for television drama providing no easy answers to the plight of the homeless.
1988 93m/C Mare Winningham, Dorian Harewood, Grace Johnston, Charlaine Woodard; *D:* Larry Elikann; *W:* Dennis Nemec. **VHS $89.95** *WOV* 𝄞𝄞𝄞

God, Man and Devil A wager between God and Satan begins this allegory of money versus the spirit. A poor Torah scribe, Hershele Dubrovner, has a life that glorifies God until Satan, disguised as a business partner, turns him greedy and dishonest. Dubrovner's success destroys both his religion and his community leaving only betrayal and abandonment. In Yiddish with English subtitles.
1949 100m/B Mikhal Mikhalesko, Gustav Berger; *D:* Joseph Seiden. **VHS $54.00** *NCJ* 𝄞𝄞 ½

God Told Me To A religious New York cop is embroiled in occult mysteries while investigating a series of grisly murders. He investigates a religious cult that turns out to be composed of half-human, half-alien beings. A cult-fave Larry Cohen epic. *AKA:* Demon.
1976 (R) 89m/C Tony LoBianco, Deborah Raffin, Sylvia Sidney, Sandy Dennis, Richard Lynch; *W/D:* Larry Cohen. **VHS, Beta, LV $19.98** *NLC* 𝄞𝄞 ½

Godard/Truffaut Shorts A pair of early shorts directed by two French "new wave" masters: Jean-Luc Godard's "All the Boys Are Called Patrick" from 1957 and Francois Truffaut's "Les Mistons" from 1958.
1958 39m/B *FR D:* Francois Truffaut, Jean-Luc Godard. **VHS, Beta $29.95** *DVT, MRV, TAM* 𝄞𝄞 ½

The Goddess Written by Paddy Chayefsky, this is the sordid story of a girl who rises to fame as a celluloid star by making her body available to anyone who can help her career. When the spotlight dims, she keeps going with drugs and alcohol to a bitter end.
1958 105m/B Kim Stanley, Lloyd Bridges, Patty Duke; *D:* John Cromwell; *W:* Paddy Chayefsky. **VHS, Beta, LV $69.95** *RCA* 𝄞𝄞𝄞

The Godfather Coppola's award-winning adaptation of Mario Puzo's novel about a fictional Mafia family in the late 1940s. Revenge, envy, and parent-child conflict mix with the rituals of Italian mob life in America. Minutely detailed, with excellent performances by Pacino, Brando, and Caan as the violence-prone Sonny. The horrific horse scene is an instant chiller. Indisputably an instant piece of American culture. Followed by two sequels.
1972 (R) 171m/C Marlon Brando, Al Pacino, Robert Duvall, James Caan, Diane Keaton, John Cazale, Talia Shire, Richard Conte, Richard Castellano, Abe Vigoda, Alex Rocco, Sterling Hayden, John Marley, Al Lettieri; *W/D:* Francis Ford Coppola. Academy Awards '72: Best Actor (Brando), Best Adapted Screenplay, Best Picture; Nominations: Best Costume Design, Best Director (Coppola), Best Film Editing, Best Sound, Best Supporting Actor (Caan, Duvall, Pacino); Directors Guild of America Awards '72: Best Director (Coppola); Golden Globe Awards '73: Best Actor—Drama (Brando), Best Director (Coppola), Best Film—Drama; National Board of Review Awards '72: 10 Best Films of the Year, Best Supporting Actor (Pacino); National Society of Film Critics Awards '72: Best Actor (Pacino). **VHS, Beta, LV, 8mm $29.95** *PAR, BTV* 𝄞𝄞𝄞𝄞

The Godfather 1902-1959: The Complete Epic Coppola's epic work concerning the lives of a New York crime family. Comprises the first two "Godfather" films, reedited into a chronological framework of the Corleone family history, with much previously discarded footage restored.
1981 386m/C Marlon Brando, Al Pacino, Robert Duvall, James Caan, Richard Castellano, Diane Keaton, Robert De Niro, John Cazale, Lee Strasberg, Talia Shire, Michael Gazzo, Troy Donahue, Joe Spinell, Abe Vigoda, Alex Rocco, Sterling Hayden, John Marley, Richard Conte, G.D. Spradlin, Bruno Kirby, Harry Dean Stanton, Roger Corman, Al Lettieri; *D:* Francis Ford Coppola. **VHS, Beta $99.95** *PAR, FCT* 𝄞𝄞𝄞𝄞

The Godfather, Part 2 A continuation and retracing of the first film, interpolating the maintenance of the Corleone family by the aging Michael, and its founding by the young Vito (De Niro, in a terrific performance) 60 years before in New York City's Little Italy. Often considered the second half of one film, the two films stand as one of American film's greatest efforts, and as a 1970s high-water mark. Combined into one work for television presentation. Followed by a sequel.
1974 (R) 200m/C Al Pacino, Robert De Niro, Diane Keaton, Robert Duvall, James Caan, Danny Aiello, John Cazale, Lee Strasberg, Talia Shire, Michael Gazzo, Troy Donahue, Joe Spinell, Abe Vigoda, Marianna Hill, Fay Spain, G.D. Spradlin, Bruno Kirby, Harry Dean Stanton, Roger Corman, Kathleen Beller; *D:* Francis Ford Coppola; *M:* Nino Rota. Academy Awards '74: Best Adapted Screenplay, Best Art Direction/Set Decoration, Best Director (Coppola), Best Picture, Best Supporting Actor (De Niro), Best Original Score; Nominations: Best Actor (Pacino), Best Costume Design, Best Supporting Actor (Gazzo, Strasberg), Best Supporting Actress (Shire); Directors Guild of America Awards '74: Best Director (Coppola); National Society of Film Critics Awards '74: Best Director (Coppola). **VHS, Beta, LV, 8mm $29.95** *PAR, BTV* 𝄞𝄞𝄞𝄞

The Godfather, Part 3 Don Corleone (Pacino), now aging and guilt-ridden, determines to buy his salvation by investing in the Catholic Church, which he finds to be a more corrupt brotherhood than his own. Meanwhile, back on the homefront, his young daughter discovers her sexuality as she falls in love with her first cousin. While not the best film of the trilogy, it's still a stunning and inevitable conclusion to the story, and Pacino adds some exquisite finishing touches to his trilogy-worn character. Beautifully photographed in Italy by Gordon Willis. Music by Francis' father, Carmine Coppola. Video release contains the final director's cut featuring nine minutes of footage not included in the theatrical release. Also available as part of "The Godfather's Collector's Edition," which contains all three films, along with a 73-minute chronicle of the filming of each movie.
1990 (R) 170m/C Al Pacino, Diane Keaton, Andy Garcia, Joe Mantegna, George Hamilton, Talia Shire, Sofia Coppola, Eli Wallach, Don Novello, Bridget Fonda, John Savage, Al Martino; *W/D:* Francis Ford Coppola. **VHS, Beta, LV, SVS, 8mm $79.98** *PAR, PIA, SUP ⅛⅛⅛*

God's Bloody Acre Three backwoods mountain-dwelling brothers kill construction workers in order to defend their land, and then begin preying on vacationers.
1975 (R) 90m/C Scott Lawrence, Jennifer Gregory, Sam Moree, Shiang Hwa Chyang; *D:* Harry Kerwin. **VHS, Beta $69.95** *TWE Woof!*

God's Country A loner kills a man in self-defense and escapes the pursuing law by disappearing into California Redwood country with his dog.
1946 62m/C Robert Lowery, Helen Gilbert, William Farnum, Buster Keaton; *D:* Robert Tansey. **VHS, Beta, LV** *NO ⅛⅛*

God's Gun Preacher who was once a gunfighter seeks revenge on the men who tried to kill him. *AKA:* A Bullet from God.
1975 (R) 93m/C Richard Boone, Lee Van Cleef, Jack Palance, Sybil Danning; *D:* Frank Kramer. **VHS, Beta $9.99** *CCB, PGN ⅛*

God's Little Acre Delves into the unexpectedly passionate lives of Georgia farmers. One man, convinced there's buried teasure on his land, nearly brings himself and his family to ruin trying to find it. Based on the novel by Erskine Caldwell.
1958 110m/B Robert Ryan, Tina Louise, Michael Landon, Buddy Hackett, Vic Morrow, Jack Lord, Aldo Ray; *D:* Anthony Mann. **VHS, Beta $19.95** *PSM, VEC, WES ⅛⅛⅛*

The Gods Must Be Crazy An innocent and charming film. A peaceful Bushman travels into the civilized world to return a Coke bottle "to the gods." Along the way he meets a transplanted schoolteacher, an oafishly clumsy microbiologist and a gang of fanatical terrorists. A very popular film, disarmingly crammed with slapstick and broad humor of every sort. Followed by a weak sequel.
1984 (PG) 109m/C N!xau, Marius Weyers, Sandra Prinsloo, Louw Verwey, Jamie Uys, Michael Thys, Nic de Jager; *D:* Jamie Uys. **VHS, Beta, LV $19.39** *FOX, FCT, TVC ⅛⅛⅛½*

The Gods Must Be Crazy 2 A slapdash sequel to the original 1981 African chortler, featuring more ridiculous shenanigans in the bush. This time the bushman's children find themselves in civilization and N!xau must use his unique ingenuity to secure their safe return.
1989 (PG) 90m/C N!xau, Lena Farugia, Hans Strydom; *D:* Jamie Uys. **VHS, Beta, LV $19.95** *COL, TTC, FCT ⅛⅛½*

Gods of the Plague Fassbinder goes noir—or grey with lots of sharp lighting—in this gangster-auteur tale of robbery gone awry. The requisite trappings of the crime genre (guys and dolls and cops and robbers) provide a vague backdrop (and a vague plot) for a moody story full of teutonic angst and alienation, and that certain Fassbinder feeling (which, need we say, isn't to everyone's taste). An early effort by the director, who remade the story later the same year as "The American Soldier" (Fassbinder acts in both). In German with (difficult-to-read) English subtitles. *AKA:* Gotter der Pest.
1969 92m/C *GE* Hanna Schygulla, Harry Bear; *D:* Rainer Werner Fassbinder. **VHS $39.99** *TAM ⅛⅛⅛*

The Godsend "Omen" rip-off about a little girl who is thrust upon a couple. After adopting her, they lose their natural family to her evil ways.
1979 (R) 93m/C *CA* Cyd Hayman, Malcolm Stoddard, Angela Pleasence, Patrick Barr; *D:* Gabrielle Beaumont. **VHS, Beta $59.98** *VES ⅛*

Godson Emotionless assassin lives a barren life under the surveillance of Paris police who suspect him in a recent killing. He suddenly discovers that his boss has a contract out on his life. Delon's performance raises this to an average crime drama.
1972 103m/C *FR* Alain Delon, Nathalie Delon, Francois Perier; *D:* Jean-Pierre Melville. **VHS** *PSV ⅛⅛⅛*

Godzilla, King of the Monsters The radioactive monster Godzilla attacks Tokyo and terrifies the world. Burr's scenes are intercut in the American version, where he serves as a narrator telling the monster's tale in flashbacks. *AKA:* Gojira.
1956 80m/B *JP* Raymond Burr, Takashi Shimura; *D:* Terry Morse. **VHS, Beta, LV** *PAR, VES ⅛⅛½*

Godzilla 1985 Moviedom's reptilian superstar sets out to reverse Japan's trade imbalance by destroying Tokyo.
1985 (PG) 91m/C *JP* Raymond Burr, Keiju Kobayashi, Ken Tanaka, Yasuka Sawaguchi; *D:* Kohji Hashimoto, Robert J. Kizer. **VHS, Beta, LV $9.95** *NWV, STE ⅛½*

Godzilla on Monster Island Even Godzilla himself cannot hope to take on both Ghidra and Gigan alone and hope to succeed. Therefore he summons his pal Angillus for help. Together, they offer Earth its only hope of survival. Though the terror may repel you, the movie is a must for Godzilla fans; it's his first speaking part.
1972 89m/C *JP* Hiroshi Ishikawa, Tomoko Umeda, Yuriko Hishimi, Minoru Takashima, Zan Fujita; *D:* Jun Fukuda. **VHS $9.95** *SNC, MRV, NWV ⅛⅛*

Godzilla Raids Again Warner Bros. had a problem securing rights to Godzilla's name. Yearning for a change of pace, the King of Monsters opts to destroy Osaka instead of Tokyo, but the spiny Angorous is out to dethrone our hero. Citizens flee in terror when the battle royale begins. The first Godzilla sequel. *AKA:* Gigantis, the Fire Monster; Godzilla's Counter Attack.
1959 78m/B *JP* Hugo Grimaldi, Makayama, Minoru Chiaki. **VHS $14.99** *VTR ⅛⅛*

Godzilla vs. Biollante Godzilla is back and this time he takes on Biollante, a genetically engineered plant-form, in this super battle of the beasts.
1989 (PG) 104m/C *JP* *W/D:* Kazuki Ohmori. **VHS $69.99** *HBO ⅛⅛*

Godzilla vs. Gigan The Super-Lizard must save a children's amusement park from Gigan and Ghidra, the monsters from outer space. *AKA:* Godzilla on Monster Island.
1972 89m/C *JP* Hiroshi Ishikawa, Minoru Takashima, Tomoko Umeda; *D:* Jun Fukuda. **VHS, Beta, LV $9.95** *NWV, STE, IME ⅛⅛*

Godzilla vs. Megalon Godzilla faces the ultimate challenge of his monstrous career as he is forced to take on Megalon, a giant cockroach, and Gigan, a flying metal creature, simultaneously. Fortunately, his giant robot pal Jet Jaguar is on hand to slug it out side by side with Tokyo's ultimate defender. *AKA:* Gojira Tai Megaro.
1976 (G) 80m/C *JP* Katsuhiko Sasakai, Hiroyuki Kawase, Yutaka Hayashi, Robert Dunham; *D:* Jun Fukuda. **VHS $19.95** *NOS, MRV, NWV ⅛½*

Godzilla vs. Monster Zero Novel Godzilla adventure with the big guy and Rodan in outer space. Suspicious denizens of Planet X require the help of Godzilla and Rodan to rid themselves of the menacing Ghidra, whom they refer to as Monster Zero. Will they, in return, help Earth as promised, or is this just one big, fat double cross? *AKA:* Monster Zero; Battle of the Astros; Invasion of the Astro-Monsters; Invasion of the Astros; Invasion of Planet X; Kaiju Daisenso.
1968 (G) 93m/C *JP* Nick Adams; *D:* Inoshiro Honda. **VHS, Beta $19.95** *PAR, SIM ⅛⅛*

Godzilla vs. Mothra Mighty Mothra is called in to save the populace from Godzilla, who is on a rampage; and he's aided by two junior Mothras who hatch in the nick of time. *AKA:* Godzilla vs. the Thing; Godzilla vs. the Giant Moth; Godzilla Fights the Giant Moth; Mothra vs. Godzilla; Mosura Tai Goira.
1964 88m/C *JP* Akira Takarada, Yuriko Hoshi, Hiroshi Koizumi; *D:* Inoshiro Honda. **VHS, Beta $19.95** *PAR ⅛⅛*

Godzilla vs. the Cosmic Monster Godzilla's worst nightmares become a reality as he is forced to take on the one foe he cannot defeat - a metal clone of himself! To make matters worse, Earth is in dire peril at the hands of cosmic apes. We all need friends, and Godzilla is never more happy to see his buddy King Seeser, who gladly lends a claw. *AKA:* Godzilla Versus the Bionic Monster; Godzilla vs. Mechagodzilla; Gojira Tai Meka-Gojira.
1974 (G) 80m/C *JP* Masaaki Daimon, Kazuya Aoyama, Reiko Tajima, Barbara Lynn, Akihiko Hirata; *D:* Jun Fukuda. **VHS, CV $9.95** *NWV, MRV, VYY ⅛⅛*

Godzilla vs. the Sea Monster The famous giant lizard makes a friend of former enemy Mothra so the two can battle Ebirah, the Sea Monster. *AKA:* Nankai No Kai Ketto; Ebirah, Terror of the Deep; Big Duel in the North.
1966 80m/C *JP* *D:* Jun Fukuda. **VHS, Beta $44.95** *DVT, MRV, HHT Woof!*

Godzilla vs. the Smog Monster The Big G battles a creature born of pollution, a 400-pound sludge blob named Hedora. Great opening song: "Save the Earth." Dubbed in English. *AKA:* Godzilla vs. Hedora; Gojira Tai Hedora; Godzilla vs. Hedora.
1972 (G) 87m/C *JP* Akira Yamauchi, Hiroyuki Kawase, Toshio Shibaki; *D:* Yoshimitu Banno. **VHS, Beta $19.98** *ORI, SIM ⅛*

Godzilla's Revenge A young boy who is having problems dreams of going to Monster Island to learn from Minya, Godzilla's son. Using the lessons in real life, the boy captures some bandits and outwits a bully. Uses footage from "Godzilla vs. the Sea Monster" and "Son of Godzilla" for battle

scenes. One of the silliest Godzilla movies around. **AKA:** Oru Kaiju Daishingeki.
1969 70m/C JP Kenji Sahara, Tomonori Yazaki, Machiko Naka, Sachio Sakai, Chotaro Togin, Yoshibumi Tujima; **D:** Inoshiro Honda. **VHS $9.95** SIM ✍

Goetz von Berlichingen During the reign of Emperor Maximilian, a brave knight fights injustice in the service of the Emperor and becomes a hunted man. In German with English subtitles. **AKA:** Iron Hand.
1980 100m/C GE VHS, Beta $39.95 VCD, GLV ✍✍

Goin' All the Way Seventeen-year-old Monica decides that she has to prove her love to her boyfriend, Artie, by going all the way.
1982 85m/C Deborah Van Rhyn, Dan Waldman, Joshua Cadman, Sherie Miller, Joe Colligan; **D:** Robert Freedman. **VHS, Beta $39.95** MON ✍

Goin' Coconuts Donny and Marie are miscast as Donny and Marie in this smarmy story of crooks and jewels. Seems someone covets the chanteuse's necklace, and only gratuitous crooning can spare the twosome from certain swindling. Big bore on the big island.
1978 (PG) 93m/C Donny Osmond, Marie Osmond, Herb Edelman, Kenneth Mars, Ted Cassidy, Marc Lawrence, Harold Sakata; **D:** Howard Morris. **VHS** NO ✍

Goin' South An outlaw is saved from being hanged by a young woman who agrees to marry him in exchange for his help working a secret gold mine. They try to get the loot before his old gang gets wind of it. A tongue-in-cheek western that served as Nicholson's second directorial effort. Movie debuts of Steenburgen and Belushi.
1978 (PG) 109m/C Jack Nicholson, Mary Steenburgen, John Belushi, Christopher Lloyd, Veronica Cartwright, Richard Bradford, Danny DeVito, Luana Anders, Ed Begley Jr., Anne Ramsey; **D:** Jack Nicholson. **VHS, Beta, LV $19.95** PAR ✍✍✍

Going Ape! Danza inherits a bunch of orangutans. If the apes are treated well, a legacy of $5 million will follow. This is all you need to know.
1981 (PG) 87m/C Tony Danza, Jessica Walter, Danny DeVito, Art Metrano, Rick Hurst; **D:** Jeremy Joe Kronsberg. **VHS, Beta $49.95** PAR ✍✍

Going Back Four friends reunite after college to relive a memorable summer they spent together after graduating from high school.
1983 85m/C Bruce Campbell, Christopher Howe, Perry Mallette, Susan W. Yamasaki; **D:** Ron Teachworth. **VHS, Beta $69.98** LIV, VES ✍½

Going Bananas Wacky adventure about a chimp who is being chased by a sinister circus owner. The monkey runs through Africa dragging along a boy, his caretaker, and a guide. The cast says it all.
1988 (PG) 95m/C Dom DeLuise, Jimmie Walker, David Mendenhall, Herbert Lom; **D:** Boaz Davidson. **VHS, Beta $19.95** MED ✍✍

Going Berserk The members of SCTV's television comedy troupe are featured in this comedy which lampoons everything from religious cults to kung fu movies to "Father Knows Best." Should have been more fun.
1983 (R) 85m/C John Candy, Joe Flaherty, Eugene Levy, Paul Dooley, Pat Hingle, Richard Libertini, Ernie Hudson; **D:** David Steinberg. **VHS, Beta, LV $69.95** MCA ✍½

Going for the Gold: The Bill Johnson Story Biographical tale of the American downhill skier who went from hard-luck punk to Olympic champion in the 1984 games at Sarajevo, Yugoslavia.
1985 100m/C Anthony Edwards, Dennis Weaver, Sarah Jessica Parker, Deborah Van Valkenburgh, Wayne Northrop; **D:** Don Taylor. **VHS $14.95** COL, SVS ✍✍

Going Hollywood Amusing musical/romantic fluff about a French teacher (Davies) who falls in love with a radio crooner (Crosby in his first MGM film). He's got the movie bug and heads for Hollywood, where he becomes an overnight sensation with a sultry costar (D'Orsay). Davies follows and proceeds to get Crosby out of D'Orsay's clutches and winds up replacing her rival in the film, promptly becoming a star herself. The underrated Davies was a fine light comedienne and supplied glamour to the production as well. Kelly, in her film debut, supplied the slapstick. The last Hearst-Cosmopolitan production made with MGM. ♫Temptation; We'll Make Hay While the Sun Shines; Going Hollywood; Our Big Love Scene; After Sundown; Cinderella's Fella; Beautiful Girl; Just an Echo in the Valley.
1933 78m/B Marion Davies, Bing Crosby, Fifi d'Orsay, Stuart Erwin, Patsy Kelly, Ned Sparks; **D:** Walter Walsh; **W:** Donald Ogden Stewart. **VHS $19.98** MGM ✍✍✍

Going Hollywood A documentary that examines the stars and films of the Great Depression of the 1930s.
1983 (G) 75m/C VHS, Beta NO ✍✍✍

Going Home During World War I, Canadian soldiers held in British camps awaiting transport back home stage a riot over the endless delays and intolerable conditions. A fact-based story of the events leading up to this tragedy.
1986 100m/C Nicholas Campbell, Paul Maxwell, Eugene Lipinski. **VHS $79.95** SVS ✍✍½

Going in Style Three elderly gentlemen, tired of doing nothing, decide to liven up their lives by pulling a daylight bank stick-up. They don't care about the consequences because anything is better than sitting on a park bench all day long. The real fun begins when they get away with the robbery. Great cast makes this a winner.
1979 (PG) 91m/C George Burns, Art Carney, Lee Strasberg; **D:** Martin Brest. **VHS, Beta $19.98** WAR ✍✍✍½

Going My Way A musical-comedy about a progressive young priest assigned to a downtrodden parish who works to get the parish out of debt, but clashes with his elderly curate, who's set in his ways. Followed by "The Bells of St. Mary's." Fitzgerald's Oscar-winning Supporting Actor performance was also nominated in the Best Actor category. ♫The Day After Forever; Swingin' On a Star; Too-ra-loo-ra-loo-ra; Going My Way; Silent Night; Habanera; Ave Maria.
1944 126m/B Bing Crosby, Barry Fitzgerald, Rise Stevens, Frank McHugh, Gene Lockhart, Porter Hall; **W/D:** Leo McCarey; **W:** Frank Butler, Frank Cavett. Academy Awards '44: Best Actor (Crosby), Best Director (McCarey), Best Picture, Best Song ("Swinging on a Star"), Best Story & Screenplay, Best Supporting Actor (Fitzgerald); Nominations: Best Actor (Fitzgerald), Best Black and White Cinematography, Best Film Editing; National Board of Review Awards '44: 10 Best Films of the Year; New York Film Critics Awards '44: Best Actor (Fitzgerald), Best Director (McCarey), Best Film. **VHS, Beta, LV $14.95** MCA, IGP, BTV ✍✍✍½

Going Places A cynical, brutal satire about two young thugs traversing the French countryside raping, looting and cavorting as they please. Moreau has a brief role as an ex-con trying to go straight. An amoral, controversial comedy that established both its director and two stars. In French with English subtitles or dubbed. **AKA:** Les Valseuses; Making It.
1974 (R) 122m/C FR Gerard Depardieu, Patrick Dewaere, Miou-Miou, Isabelle Huppert, Jeanne Moreau, Brigitte Fossey; **D:** Bertrand Blier. **VHS, Beta, LV $59.95** COL, INT, TAM ✍✍✍

Going Steady Story of teenage love, set to the beat of fifties rock 'n' roll.
1980 (R) 90m/C VHS, Beta PGN ✍½

Going to Congress/Don't Park There Two typical silent Rogers shorts. With original organ score.
1924 57m/B Will Rogers. **VHS, Beta, 8mm $24.95** VYY ✍✍½

Going to Town Radio team Lum and Abner in one of their last films, as two conmen who scheme to make money from a phony oil well.
1944 77m/B Barbara Hale, Grady Sutton, Florence Lake. **VHS, Beta** GVV ✍

Going Under Subsurface military satire about the U.S.S. Sub Standard, the worst nuclear vessel in the Navy. It's so poorly constructed that the brass would rather sink than inspect it - if only they could. Interesting cast sinks with script headed for dry dock.
1991 (PG) 81m/C Bill Pullman, Wendy Schaal, Ned Beatty, Robert Vaughn, Bud Cort, Michael Winslow. **VHS, Beta $19.98** WAR ✍

Going Undercover A bumbling private investigator is hired to protect a rich, beautiful, and spoiled young woman on her European vacation. Poor excuse for a comedy.
1988 (PG-13) 90m/C Lea Thompson, Jean Simmons, Chris Lemmon; **D:** James Kenelm Clark. **VHS, Beta, LV $29.95** VMK ✍

The Gold & Glory A young underdog runs and wins an iron man triathalon.
1988 (PG-13) 102m/C Colin Friels, Josephine Smulders, Grant Kenny. **VHS, Beta, LV $39.95** LIV ✍

Gold Diggers of 1933 In this famous period musical, showgirls help a songwriter save his Busby Berkeley-choreographed show. Followed by two sequels. ♫We're in the Money; Shadow Waltz; I've Got to Sing a Torch Song; Pettin' in the Park; Remember My Forgotten Man.
1933 96m/B Joan Blondell, Ruby Keeler, Aline MacMahon, Dick Powell, Guy Kibbee, Warren Williams, Ned Sparks, Ginger Rogers; **D:** Mervyn LeRoy. **VHS, Beta, LV $19.98** MGM, FOX, PIA ✍✍✍½

Gold Diggers of 1935 The second Gold Diggers film, having something to do with a New England resort, romance, and a charity show put on at the hotel. Plenty of Berkeleian large-scale drama, especially the bizarre, mock-tragic "Lullaby on Broadway" number, which details the last days of a Broadway baby. ♫I'm Going Shopping With You; The Words Are in My Heart; Lullaby of Broadway.
1935 95m/B Dick Powell, Adolphe Menjou, Gloria Stuart, Alice Brady, Frank McHugh, Glenda Farrell, Grant Mitchell, Hugh Herbert, Wini Shaw; **D:** Busby Berkeley. **VHS, Beta, LV $29.95** MGM, PIA, MLB ✍✍✍

The Gold of Naples A four-part omnibus film about life in Naples, filled with romance and family tragedies, by turns poignant, funny and pensive. Originally six tales;

two were trimmed for U.S. release. In Italian with subtitles. *AKA:* L'Oro Di Napoli.
1954 107m/B *IT* Vittorio De Sica, Eduardo de Filippo, Toto, Sophia Loren, Paolo Stoppa, Silvana Mangano; *D:* Vittorio De Sica. **VHS, Beta** $19.95 *NOS, FCT, APD* 𝄒𝄒𝄒

Gold of the Amazon Women When two explorers set out to find gold, they stumble onto a society of man-hungry women who follow them into the urban jungle of Manhattan. Made for television. There is also a European "R" rated version. *AKA:* Amazon Women.
1979 94m/C Bo Svenson, Anita Ekberg, Bond Gideon, Donald Pleasence; *D:* Mark L. Lester. **VHS, Beta** $59.98 *SUE* 𝄒

Gold Raiders Larry, Moe, and Shemp team up with an insurance agent to take on the bad guys in the wild west. The Stooges are long past their prime.
1951 56m/B George O'Brien, Moe Howard, Moe Howard, Shemp Howard, Larry Fine, Sheila Ryan, Clem Bevans, Lyle Talbot; *D:* Edward L. Bernds. **VHS** *MED* 𝄒

Gold Raiders Team of secret agents are sent to the Jungles of Laos to find a plane carrying $200 million worth of gold, and nothing will get in their way.
1984 106m/C Robert Ginty, Sarah Langenfeld, William Steven. **VHS, Beta** $69.95 *MED* 𝄒½

The Gold Rush Chaplin's most critically acclaimed film. The best definition of his simple approach to film form; adept maneuvering of visual pathos. The "Little Tramp" searches for gold and romance in the Klondike in the mid-1800s. Includes the dance of the rolls, pantomime sequence of eating the shoe, and Chaplin's lovely music.
1925 85m/B Charlie Chaplin, Mack Swain, Tom Murray, Georgina Hale; *D:* Charlie Chaplin. **VHS, Beta, LV, 8mm, 3/4U, Special order formats** $9.95 *NEG, NOS, CAB* 𝄒𝄒𝄒𝄒

Gold Rush/Payday Chaplin drifts along the Arctic tundra, searching for gold and love in "The Gold Rush." In "Payday," he goes out drinking with his buddies.
1925 92m/B Charlie Chaplin, Georgina Hale, Mack Swain. **VHS, Beta** $19.98 *FOX* 𝄒𝄒𝄒

Golden Age of Comedy The great comedians of silent cinema are seen in clips from some of their funniest films.
1958 78m/B Ben Turpin, Harry Langdon, Will Rogers, Jean Harlow, Carole Lombard, Stan Laurel, Oliver Hardy, Keystone Kops. **VHS, Beta, LV** $14.98 *VID, PIA, MLB* 𝄒𝄒𝄒𝄒

Golden Age of Hollywood This episode of "Life Goes to the Movies" examines Hollywood as it quickly became the ultimate dream factory, providing escape from the grimness of the depression.
1977 34m/C Henry Fonda, Shirley MacLaine. **VHS, Beta** *TLF* 𝄒𝄒𝄒𝄒

Golden Boy Holden plays a young and gifted violinist who earns money for his musical education by working as a part-time prizefighter. Fight promoter Menjou has Stanwyck cozy up to the impressionable young man to convince him to make the fight game his prime concern. She's successful but it leads to tragedy. Holden's screen debut, with Cobb as his immigrant father and Stanwyck successfully slinky as the corrupting love interest. Classic pugilistic drama with well-staged fight scenes. Based on Clifford Odet's play with toned down finale.
1939 99m/B William Holden, Adolphe Menjou, Barbara Stanwyck, Lee J. Cobb, Joseph Calleia, Sam Levene, Don Beddoe; *D:* Rouben Mamoulian. **VHS, Beta, LV** $9.95 *GKK* 𝄒𝄒𝄒

The Golden Child When a Tibetan child with magic powers is kidnapped and transported to Los Angeles, Chandler, a professional "finder of lost children" must come to the rescue. The search takes him through Chinatown in a hunt that cliches every Oriental swashbuckler ever made. Good fun.
1986 (PG-13) 94m/C Eddie Murphy, Charlotte Lewis, Charles Dance, Victor Wong, Randall "Tex" Cobb, James Hong; *D:* Michael Ritchie. **VHS, Beta, LV, 8mm** $19.95 *PAR* 𝄒𝄒

The Golden Coach Based on a play by Prosper Merimee, the tale of an 18th century actress in Spanish South America who takes on all comers, including the local viceroy who creates a scandal by presenting her with his official coach. Rare cinematography by Claude Renoir. *AKA:* Le Carrosse D'Or.
1952 101m/C *FR* Anna Magnani, Odoardo Spadaro, Nada Fiorelli, Dante Rino, Duncan Lamont; *D:* Jean Renoir. **VHS, Beta, LV** $29.95 *FCT, CRC* 𝄒𝄒𝄒

Golden Demon An acclaimed Japanese epic, from the novel by Koyo Ozaki, about the destructive powers of wealth on the lives of two star-crossed lovers in medieval Japan. In Japanese with English subtitles. *AKA:* Konjiki Yasha.
1953 95m/C *JP* Jun Negami, Fujiko Yamamoto; *D:* Koji Shima. **VHS, Beta** $29.95 *SUE, NLC, AUD* 𝄒½

Golden Destroyers Hosted by the inimitable Sho Kosugi, this film chronicles the hapless adventures of rampaging golden buddhas.
198? 90m/C **VHS, Beta** $39.95 *TWE* 𝄒

Golden Exterminators Two brothers battle the forces of evil who have killed their martial arts master with the heels of their formidable feet.
197? 86m/C Raymond Chan. **VHS, Beta** $39.95 *UNI* 𝄒

The Golden Honeymoon Ring Lardner's story about an elderly couple who journey to St. Petersburg to celebrate their 50th anniversary. There they encounter the wife's suitor of 50 years past, who is also vacationing with his spouse. Curiosity draws the couples together, and jealousy, doubt and a simmering competitive spirit momentarily jar the marriage. Part of the American Short Story Collection. Made for television.
1980 52m/C James Whitmore, Teresa Wright; *D:* Noel Black. **VHS, Beta** *MON, MTI* 𝄒

Golden Lady Beautiful woman leads her female gang in a deadly game of international intrigue.
1979 90m/C Christina World, Suzanne Danielle, June Chadwick; *D:* Joseph Larraz. **VHS, Beta** *NO* 𝄒½

Golden Ninja Invasion Ninja lords battle in a scheme to conquer the world. Their method? Fighting with sticks, naturally.
198? 85m/C Leonard West, Stephanie Burd. **VHS, Beta** $59.95 *TWE* 𝄒

Golden Ninja Warrior Lady ninjas endeavor to capture a golden statue and gain superiority over chauvinists everywhere.
198? 92m/C **VHS, Beta** $59.95 *TWE* 𝄒

Golden Rendezvous A tale of treachery aboard a "gambler's paradise" luxury liner which is hijacked and held for ransom. Based on Alistair MacLean's novel. *AKA:* Nuclear Terror.
1977 103m/C Richard Harris, David Janssen, John Carradine, Burgess Meredith, Ann Turkel, John Vernon; *D:* Ashley Lazarus. **VHS, Beta** $69.95 *VES* 𝄒𝄒

The Golden Salamander Howard shines in otherwise lackluster adventure about archaeologist searching for ancient ruins in Tunisia who must deal with gun runners and their evil leader, while torridly romancing a beautiful Tunisian girl. Filmed on location in Tunis. Based on the novel by Victor Canning.
1951 96m/B *GB* Trevor Howard, Anouk Aimee, Herbert Lom, Miles Malleson, Walter Rilla, Jacques Sernas, Wilfrid Hyde-White, Peter Copely, Eugene Deckers, Henry Edwards, Marcel Poncin, Percy Walsh, Sybilla Binder, Kathleen Boutall, Valentine Dyall; *D:* Ronald Neame. **VHS** $29.95 *FCT* 𝄒𝄒

The Golden Seal Tale of a small boy's innocence put in direct conflict, because of his love of a rare wild golden seal and her pup, with the failed dreams, pride and ordinary greed of adults.
1983 (PG) 94m/C Steve Railsback, Michael Beck, Penelope Milford, Torquil Campbell; *D:* Frank Zuniga; *M:* John Barry. **VHS, Beta, LV, 8mm** $19.98 *SUE* 𝄒𝄒½

The Golden Stallion Trigger falls in love with a stunning mare. He sees her villainous owners abusing them and kills them. Roy takes the blame for his equine pal, but true love triumphs to save the day.
1949 67m/B Roy Rogers, Dale Evans, Estelita Rodriguez, Pat Brady, Douglas Evans, Frank Fenton, Trigger; *D:* William Witney. **VHS** $12.98 *REP* 𝄒½

Golden Sun Young Kung Fu student decides to investigate the death of his hero, Bruce Lee, and comes up against a sinister conspiracy.
198? 90m/C Lei Hsiao Lung, Chen Pei Ling, Ou-Yang Chung. **VHS, Beta** $29.95 *UNI* 𝄒

Golden Tales and Legends These two volumes of the best-loved fairy tale from the Brothers Grimm and Hans Christian Andersen are sure to captivate every child. Volume one includes "The Frog Prince," "Rapunzel" and "Hansel and Gretel"; the second volume features "The Juggler," "The Golden Apple" and "The Iron Mountain."
1985 60m/C **VHS, Beta** $24.95 *MPI* 𝄒

The Golden Triangle Big battle of the drug pushers set in the mountainous region surrounded by Laos, Thailand, and Burma. Rival gangs fight for control of the world's opium crop.
1980 90m/C Lo Lieh, Sambat Metanen, Tien Ner. **VHS, Beta** $59.98 *OCE* 𝄒½

Golden Voyage of Sinbad In the mysterious ancient land of Lemuria, Sinbad and his crew encounter magical and mystical creatures. A statue of Nirvana comes to life and engages in a sword fight with Sinbad. He later meets up with a one-eyed centaur and a griffin. Ray Harryhausen can once again claim credit for the unusual and wonderful mythical creatures springing to life.
1973 (G) 105m/C John Phillip Law, Caroline Munro, Tom Baker, Douglas Wilmer, Martin Shaw, John Garfield, Gregoire Aslan; *D:* Gordon Hessler; *W:* Brian Clemens. **VHS, Beta, LV** $14.95 *COL, MLB* 𝄒𝄒½

Goldengirl A neo-Nazi doctor tries to make a superwoman of his daughter who has been specially fed, exercised, and emotionally conditioned since childhood to run in the Olympics. Anton's starring debut.
1979 (PG) 107m/C Susan Anton, James Coburn, Curt Jurgens, Robert Culp, Leslie Caron, Harry Guardino, Jessica Walter; *D:* Joseph Sargent. **VHS, Beta** $14.95 *COL, SUE* 𝄒𝄒

Goldenrod A successful rodeo champion is forced to reevaluate his life when he sustains a crippling accident in the ring. Made for television.
1977 100m/C *CA* Tony LoBianco, Gloria Carlin, Donald Pleasence, Donnelly Rhodes; *D:* Harvey Hart. **VHS, Beta $59.95** *PSM* ♫♫½

Goldfinger Ian Fleming's James Bond, Agent 007, attempts to prevent international gold smuggler Goldfinger and his pilot Pussy Galore from robbing Fort Knox. Features villainous assistant Oddjob and his deadly bowler hat. The third in the series is perhaps the most popular. Shirley Bassey sings the theme song. The laserdisc edition includes audio interviews with the director, the writer, the editor, and the production designer; music and sound effects/ dialogue separation; publicity stills, movie posters, trailers, and on-location photos. A treat for Bond fans.
1964 (PG) 117m/C *GB* Sean Connery, Honor Blackman, Gert Frobe, Shirley Eaton, Tania Mallet, Harold Sakata, Cec Linder, Bernard Lee, Lois Maxwell, Desmond Llewelyn, Nadja Regin; *D:* Guy Hamilton; *M:* John Barry. **VHS, Beta, LV $19.98** *MGM, VYG, PIA* ♫♫♫

Goldie Gold & Action Jack Futuristic reporter Goldie Gold and intern Action Jack team up to pursue stories with the help of computerized gadgetry. Animated adventure tale.
1981 40m/C **VHS, Beta $19.95** *WOV, WTA* ♫♫♫

Goldilocks & the Three Bears Entry from "Faerie Tale Theatre" tells the story of Goldilocks, who wanders through the woods and finds the home of three bears—only in this version Goldilocks is a nasty child, and it's the bears who'll get your sympathy.
1983 60m/C Tatum O'Neal, Alex Karras, Brandis Kemp, Donovan Scott, Hoyt Axton, John Lithgow, Carole King; *D:* Gilbert Cates. **VHS, Beta, LV $14.98** *KUI, FOX, FCT* ♫♫½

The Goldwyn Follies Lavish disjointed musical comedy about Hollywood. A movie producer chooses a naive girl to give him advice on his movies. Songs by Ira and George Gershwin, who died an untimely death during the filming. ♫Romeo and Juliet; Water Nymph; Here, Pussy, Pussy; Serenade To a Fish; Love Walked In; Love is Here to Stay; Spring Again; I Was Doing Alright; La Serenata; I Love to Rhyme.
1938 115m/C Adolphe Menjou, Vera Zorina, The Ritz Brothers, Helen Jepson, Phil Baker, Bobby Clark, Ella Logan, Andrea Leeds, Edgar Bergen; *D:* George Marshall; *M:* George Gershwin, Ira Gershwin. **VHS, Beta $19.98** *SUE, HBO* ♫♫

Goldy: The Last of the Golden Bears Orphaned child and a lonely prospector risk their lives to save a Golden Bear from a circus owner. Followed by "Goldy 2: The Saga of the Golden Bear."
1984 91m/C **VHS, Beta $69.98** *LIV, VES* ♫♫½

Goldy 2: The Saga of the Golden Bear Continues the adventures in the High Sierras of an orphan girl and her friend, the Golden Bear.
1985 96m/C **VHS, Beta $69.98** *LIV, VES* ♫

The Golem A huge clay figure is given life by a rabbi in hopes of saving the Jews in the ghetto of medieval Prague. Rarely seen Wegener expressionist myth-opus that heavily influenced the "Frankenstein" films of the sound era.
1920 80m/B *RU* Paul Wegener, Albert Steinruck, Ernst Deutsch, Syda Salmonava; *D:* Paul Wegener. **VHS, Beta, 3/4U $16.95** *SNC, NOS, MRV* ♫♫♫½

Goliath Against the Giants Goliath takes on Bokan, who has stolen his throne. Goliath must fight Amazons, storms, and sea monsters to save the lovely Elea. Goliath conquers all. *AKA:* Goliath Contro I Giganti; Goliat Contra Los Gigantes; Goliath and the Giants.
1963 95m/C *IT SP* Brad Harris, Gloria Milland, Fernando Rey, Barbara Carroll; *D:* Guido Malatesta. **VHS, Beta $19.98** *SNC* ♫♫½

Goliath and the Barbarians Goliath and his men go after the barbarians who are terrorizing and ravaging the Northern Italian countryside during the fall of the Roman Empire. A basic Reeves muscleman epic. *AKA:* Il Terror Dei Baraberi.
1960 86m/C *IT* Steve Reeves, Bruce Cabot; *D:* Carlo Campogalliani. **VHS, Beta $59.95** *MGM* ♫♫

Goliath and the Dragon Even Goliath must have doubts as he is challenged by the evil and powerful King Eurystheus. A must for fans of ridiculous movies with ridiculous monsters. *AKA:* La Vendetta De Ercole.
1961 90m/C *IT FR* Bruce Cabot, Mark Forest, Broderick Crawford, Gaby Andre, Leonora Ruffo; *D:* Vittorio Cottafavi. **VHS, Beta $19.98** *SNC* Woof!

Goliath and the Sins of Babylon Well-sculpted Forest plays yet another mesomorph to the rescue in this poorly dubbed spaghetti legend. Goliath must spare twenty-four virgins whom the evil Crisa would submit as human sacrifice. Forest—who played the mythic Maciste in a number of films—was randomly assigned the identity of Goliath, Hercules or Samson for US viewing; go figure. *AKA:* Maciste, L'Eroe Piu Grande Del Mondo.
1964 80m/C *IT* Mark Forest, Eleanora Bianchi, Jose Greco, Giuliano Gemma, Paul Muller; *D:* Michele Lupo. **VHS $19.98** *SNC* ♫♫

Goliath Awaits Harmon plays an oceanographer who discovers a ship that was sunk by German U-boats during WWI. Nothing much new there, except that the survivors still reside on board the vessel, some 40 years after the oceanliner was torpedoed. And get this: they're living a quasi-Utopian existence. Kind of hard to swallow. Made for TV, it originally aired in two parts.
1981 110m/C Mark Harmon, Robert Forster, Christopher Lee, Eddie Albert, John Carradine, Alex Cord, Emma Samms, Jean Marsh; *D:* Kevin Connor. **VHS, LV** *VMK* ♫♫

Goliathon A ten-story-tall gorilla resides in the jungle and is sought by a group of Hong Kong businessman who want to display the creature. Johnny, the hunter hired to find the beast, discovers both the gorilla and a beautiful jungle goddess. Incredibly campy, with badly dubbed and hilariously awful dialogue. *AKA:* The Mighty Peking Man.
1979 81m/C *HK* Lee Hassen, Evelyn Kraft. **VHS $29.95** *VYY* Woof!

Gone are the Days Shaky adaptation of the play, "Purlie Victorious." A black preacher wants to cause the ruin of a white plantation owner. Alda's screen debut. *AKA:* The Man From C.O.T.T.O.N.; Purlie Victorious.
1963 97m/B Ossie Davis, Ruby Dee, Sorrell Booke, Godfrey Cambridge, Alan Alda, Beah Richards; *D:* Nicholas Webster. **VHS, Beta $69.95** *DIS* ♫♫½

Gone are the Days Government agent (Korman) is assigned to protect a family who witnessed an underworld shooting, but the family would like to get away from both the mob and the police. Made-for-cable Disney comedy is well-acted but done in by cliches.
1984 90m/C Harvey Korman, Susan Anspach, Robert Hogan; *D:* Gabrielle Beaumont. **VHS, Beta $69.95** *DIS* ♫♫

Gone in 60 Seconds Car thief working for an insurance adjustment firm gets double-crossed by his boss and chased by the police. Forty minutes are consumed by a chase scene which destroyed more than 90 vehicles.
1974 105m/C H.B. Halicki, Marion Busia, George Cole, James McIntyre, Jerry Daugirda; *D:* H.B. Halicki. **VHS, Beta $9.95** *MED* ♫♫½

Gone to Ground Mad killer terrorizes a group of vacationers who are trapped in an isolated beach house.
1976 74m/C Charles Tingwell, Elaine Lee, Eric Oldfield, Marion Johns, Robyn Gibbes, Judy Lynne, Dennis Grosvenor, Alan Penney, Marcus Hale. **VHS, Beta** *PGN* ♫

Gone with the West Little Moon and Jud McGraw seek revenge upon the man who stole their cattle.
1972 92m/C James Caan, Stefanie Powers, Sammy Davis Jr., Aldo Ray, Michael Conrad, Michael Walker Jr.; *D:* Bernard Giraudeau. **VHS, Beta $49.95** *UNI* ♫♫½

Gone with the Wind Epic Civil War drama focusing on the life of petulant southern belle Scarlett O'Hara. Starting with her idyllic lifestyle on a sprawling plantation, the film traces her survival through the tragic history of the South during the Civil War and Reconstruction, and her tangled love affairs with Ashley Wilkes and Rhett Butler. Classic Hollywood doesn't get any better than this; one great scene after another, equally effective in its intimate drama and its sweeping spectacle. The train depot scene, one of the more technically adroit shots in movie history, involved hundreds of extras and dummies, and much of the MGM lot was razed to simulate the burning of Atlanta. Beautifully filmed, scored, and acted. Based on Margaret Mitchell's novel. For its 50th anniversary, a 231-minute restored version was released that included the trailer for "The Making of a Legend: GWTW." The laserdisc is available in a limited, numbered edition, fully restored to Technicolor from the original negative, with an enhanced soundtrack and seven minutes of rare footage, including the original trailer.
1939 231m/C Clark Gable, Vivien Leigh, Olivia de Havilland, Leslie Howard, Thomas Mitchell, Hattie McDaniel, Butterfly McQueen, Evelyn Keyes, Harry Davenport, Jane Darwell, Ona Munson, Barbara O'Neil, William Bakewell, Rand Brooks, Ward Bond, Laura Hope Crews, Yakima Canutt, George Reeves, Marjorie Reynolds; *D:* Victor Fleming; *W:* Sidney Howard. Academy Awards '39: Best Actress (Leigh), Best Color Cinematography, Best Director (Fleming), Best Film Editing, Best Interior Decoration, Best Picture, Best Screenplay, Best Supporting Actress (McDaniel); Nominations: Best Actor (Gable), Best Sound, Best Special Effects, Best Supporting Actress (de Havilland), Best Original Score; New York Film Critics Awards '39: Best Actress (Leigh). **VHS, Beta, LV $89.98** *MGM, BTV, RDG* ♫♫♫♫

Gonza the Spearman A gifted samurai lancer is accused of having an affair with the wife of the lord of his province. The lancer must leave to save the woman's honor, because to stay would mean death to them both. In Japanese with English subtitles.
1986 126m/C *JP* Hiromi Goh, Shima Iwashita; *D:* Masahiro Shinoda. **VHS, LV $79.95** *KIV, TAM* ♫♫½

The Good Earth Pearl S. Buck's classic recreation of the story of a simple Chinese farm couple beset by greed and poverty. Outstanding special effects. MGM's last film produced by master Irving Thalberg and dedicated to his memory. Rainer won the second of her back-to-back Best Actress Oscars for her portrayal of the self-sacrificing O-Lan.
1937 138m/B Paul Muni, Luise Rainer, Charley Grapewin, Keye Luke, Walter Connolly; *D:* Sidney Franklin. Academy Awards '37: Best Actress (Rainer), Best Cinematography; Nominations: Best Director (Franklin), Best Film Editing, Best Picture. **VHS, Beta $19.98** MGM, KUI, BTV �️✍✍½

The Good Father An acclaimed British TV movie about a bitter divorced man trying to come to terms with his son, his ex-wife, and his own fury by supporting the courtroom divorce battle of a friend.
1987 (R) 90m/C GB Anthony Hopkins, Jim Broadbent, Harriet Walter, Frances Viner, Joanne Whalley-Kilmer; *D:* Mike Newell. **VHS, Beta $79.95** MED, FOX ✍✍✍

The Good Fight Grace Cragin (Lahti) is a lawyer at a small firm who's asked by her son's best friend to represent him in a tough case against a powerful corporation. The young man is dying of mouth cancer and he wants to sue the tobacco company that makes the chewing tobacco he blames for his illness. Grace is wary of the high-powered litigation necessary but with the increasingly personal aid of her prominent lawyer exhusband (O'Quinn), she is ready to battle the odds. Another fine performance by Lahti in this made for cable television drama.
1992 91m/C Christine Lahti, Terry O'Quinn, Kenneth Welsh, Lawrence Dane, Adam Tresy; *D:* John David Coles; *W:* Beth Gutcheon; *M:* W.G. Snuffy Walden. **VHS, Beta $79.95** PSM ✍✍½

Good Grief, Charlie Brown That lovably misunderstood Charlie Brown is featured again in this Peanuts production.
1983 30m/C *D:* Bill Melendez, Sam Jaimes, Phil Roman. **VHS $14.95** KRT ✍✍½

Good Guys Wear Black A mild-mannered professor keeps his former life as leader of a Vietnam commando unit under wraps until he discovers that he's number one on the CIA hit list. Sequel is "A Force of One."
1978 (PG) 96m/C Chuck Norris, Anne Archer, James Franciscus; *D:* Ted Post. **VHS, Beta, LV $19.98** VES, HBO ✍✍

Good Morning, Babylon The Taviani brothers' first American film. Two young Italian brothers skilled in cathedral restoration come to America and find success building the sets to D.W. Griffith's "Intolerance." Eventually, their fortune is shattered by the onslaught of World War I. *AKA:* Good Morning Babilonia.
1987 (PG-13) 113m/C Vincent Spano, Joaquim de Almeida, Greta Scacchi, Charles Dance, Desiree Becker, Omero Antonutti; *D:* Paolo Taviani, Vittorio Taviani. **VHS, Beta, LV $79.98** LIV, VES ✍✍✍

Good Morning, Vietnam Based on the story of Saigon DJ Adrian Cronauer, although Williams' portrayal is reportedly a bit more extroverted than the personality of Cronauer. Williams spins great comic moments that may have been scripted but likely were not as a man with no history and for whom everything is manic radio material. The character adlibs, swoops and swerves, finally accepting adult responsibility. Engaging all the way with an outstanding period soundtrack.

1987 (R) 121m/C Robin Williams, Forest Whitaker, Bruno Kirby, Robert Edson, Robert Wuhl; *D:* Barry Levinson. Academy Awards '87 Nominations: Best Actor (Williams); Golden Globe Awards '88: Best Actor—Musical/Comedy (Williams). **VHS, Beta, LV, 8mm $29.95** TOU, BVV ✍✍✍

The Good Mother A divorced mother works at creating a fulfilling life for herself and her daughter, with an honest education for her daughter about every subject, including sex. But her ex-husband, unsure of how far this education is being taken, fights her for custody of their 8-year old daughter after allegations of sexual misconduct against the mother's new lover. Based on Sue Miller's bestselling novel. Well acted, weakly edited and scripted.
1988 (R) 104m/C Diane Keaton, Liam Neeson, Jason Robards Jr., Ralph Bellamy, James Naughton, Teresa Wright; *D:* Leonard Nimoy. **VHS, Beta, LV $89.95** TOU ✍✍½

Good Neighbor Sam A married advertising executive (Lemmon) agrees to pose as a friend's husband in order for her to collect a multi-million dollar inheritance. Complications ensue when his biggest client mistakes the friend for his actual wife and decides they're the perfect couple to promote his wholesome product—milk.
1964 130m/C Jack Lemmon, Romy Schneider, Dorothy Provine, Mike Connors, Edward G. Robinson, Joyce Jameson; *D:* David Swift. **VHS, Beta $9.95** GKK ✍✍

Good News A vintage Comden-Green musical about the love problems of a college football star, who will flunk out if he doesn't pass his French exams. Revamping of the 1927 Broadway smash features the unlikely sight of Lawford in a song-and-dance role. ♫Varsity Drag; He's a Lady's Man; Good News; Tait Song; Students Are We; Just Imagine; If You're Not Kissing Me; Football; I Feel Pessimistic; I'd Like to Make You Happy; My Blue Heaven; Pass That Peace Pipe; The French Lesson; Lucky in Love; The Best Things in Life Are Free.
1947 92m/C June Allyson, Peter Lawford, Joan McCracken, Mel Torme; *D:* Charles Walters. **VHS, Beta, LV $19.98** MGM, FCT ✍✍

Good Sam An incurable "Good Samaritan" finds himself in one jam after another as he tries too hard to help people. Lots of missed opportunities for laughs with McCarey's mediocre direction.
1948 116m/B Gary Cooper, Ann Sheridan, Ray Collins, Edmund Lowe, Joan Lorring, Ruth Roman; *D:* Leo McCarey. **VHS $19.98** REP ✍✍

The Good, the Bad, and Huckleberry Hound Journeying out West to begin a ranch, Huckleberry Hound winds up becoming a sheriff in the small town of Two-Bit. Huckleberry stands up against a group of bully brothers who have been terrorizing the town.
1988 94m/C *D:* Ray Patterson; *V:* Daws Butler. **VHS, Beta $29.95** TTC, IME, WTA ✍✍

The Good, the Bad and the Ugly Leone's grandiloquent, shambling tribute to the American Western. Set during the Civil War, it follows the seemingly endless adventures of three dirtbags in search of a cache of Confederate gold buried in a nameless grave. Violent, exaggerated, beautifully crafted, it is the final and finest installment of the "Dollars" trilogy: a spaghetti Western chef d'oeuvre.
1967 161m/C IT Clint Eastwood, Eli Wallach, Lee Van Cleef; *D:* Sergio Leone; *M:* Ennio Morricone. **VHS, Beta, LV $19.98** FOX, MGM, FCT ✍✍✍½

Good Time with a Bad Girl A married millionaire visiting Las Vegas experiments with exotic sexual pleasures when he meets up with Sue, a teenage nymphomaniac. *AKA:* A Good Time, A Bad Girl.
1967 61m/B **VHS, Beta $19.95** VDM ✍

The Good Wife A bored and sexually frustrated wife scandalizes her small Australian town by taking up with the new hotel barman. There's no denying Ward's sexuality, but overall the movie is too predictable. *AKA:* The Umbrella Woman.
1986 (R) 97m/C AU Rachel Ward, Bryan Brown, Sam Neill; *D:* Ken Cameron. **VHS, Beta, LV** KRT, IME ✍✍½

Goodbye Again A romantic drama based on the novel by Francoise Sagan. Bergman is a middle-aged interior decorator whose lover, Montand, has a roaming eye. She finds herself drawn to the son (Perkins) of a client and begins an affair—flattered by the young man's attentions. Montand is outraged and vows to change his ways and marry Bergman if she will give up the young man. A bit soapy, but a must for Bergman fans. *AKA:* Aimez-Vous Brahms.
1961 120m/B Jessie Royce Landis, Ingrid Bergman, Anthony Perkins, Yves Montand, Diahann Carroll; *D:* Anatole Litvak. **VHS** NO ✍✍½

Goodbye Columbus Philip Roth's novel about a young Jewish librarian who has an affair with the spoiled daughter of a nouveau riche family is brought to late-'60s life, and vindicated by superb performances all around. Benjamin and McGraw's first starring roles.
1969 (PG) 105m/C Richard Benjamin, Ali MacGraw, Jack Klugman, Nan Martin, Jaclyn Smith; *D:* Larry Peerce. **VHS, Beta, LV $49.95** PAR ✍✍✍

Goodbye Cruel World Black comedy about a suicidal television anchorman who decides to spend his last day filming the relatives who drove him to the brink.
1982 (R) 90m/C Dick Shawn, Cynthia Sikes, Chuck "Porky" Mitchell; *D:* David Irving. **VHS, Beta $69.98** LIV ✍½

Goodbye Emmanuelle Follows the further adventures of Emmanuelle in her quest for sexual freedom and the excitement of forbidden pleasures. The second sequel to "Emmanuelle."
1979 (R) 92m/C Sylvia Kristel. **VHS, Beta $79.99** HBO ✍½

The Goodbye Girl Neil Simon's story of a former actress, her precocious nine-year-old daughter and the aspiring actor who moves in with them. The daughter serves as catalyst for the other two to fall in love. While Mason's character is fairly unsympathetic, Dreyfuss is great and Simon's dialogue witty.
1977 (PG) 110m/C Richard Dreyfuss, Marsha Mason, Quinn Cummings, Barbara Rhoades, Marilyn Sokol; *D:* Herbert Ross. Academy Awards '77: Best Actor (Dreyfuss); Nominations: Best Picture; Academy Awards '77: Best Actress (Mason), Best Original Screenplay, Best Supporting Actress (Cummings); British Academy Awards '78: Best Actor (Dreyfuss); Golden Globe Awards '78: Best Actor—Musical/Comedy (Dreyfuss), Best Film—Musical/Comedy (Mason), Best Actress—Musical/Comedy (Mason), Best Film—Musical/Comedy; Los Angeles Film Critics Association Awards '77: Best Actor (Dreyfuss). **VHS, Beta, LV $19.98** MGM, BTV ✍✍✍

Goodbye Love Dull comedy about a group of ex-husbands who refuse to pay alimony and end up in jail.

1934 65m/B Charlie Ruggles, Verree Teasdale, Sidney Blackmer, Mayo Methot, Phyllis Barry, Ray Walker, John Kelly, Hale Grace, Luis Alberni; *D:* Herbert Ross. VHS $29.95 *FCT* ♫♫ ½

Goodbye, Mr. Chips An MGM classic, the sentimental rendering of the James Hilton novel about a shy Latin professor in an English school who marries the vivacious Garson only to tragically lose her. He spends the rest of his life devoting himself to his students and becoming a school legend. Multi award-winning soaper featuring Garson's first screen appearance, which was Oscar nominated. Special two-tape letterboxed laserdisc edition includes the original trailer and an extra-special production featurette. Remade in 1969 as a fairly awful musical starring Peter O'Toole.
1939 115m/B Robert Donat, Greer Garson, Paul Henreid, John Mills; *D:* Sam Wood. Academy Awards '39: Best Actor (Donat); Nominations: Best Actress (Garson), Best Director (Wood), Best Film Editing, Best Picture, Best Screenplay, Best Sound; National Board of Review Awards '39: 10 Best Films of the Year. VHS, Beta, LV $24.98 *MGM, BTV, HMV* ♫♫♫ ½

Goodbye, Mr. Chips Ross, whose later achievements include "Steel Magnolias" and "My Blue Heaven" debuted as director with this big-budget but inferior musical re-make of the classic James Hilton novel about a gentle teacher at an English all-boys private school and the woman who helps him demonstrate his compassion and overcome his shyness. O'Toole, although excellent, is categorically a non-singer, while Clark, a popular singer at the time ("Downtown"), musters very little talent in front of the camera. The plot is altered unnecessarily and updated to the WWII era for little reason, and the music is thoroughly forgettable. Nonetheless, the unflappable O'Toole received an Oscar nomination. ♫Fill The World With Love; Where Did My Childhood Go; London is London; And the Sky Smiled; When I Am Older; Walk Through the World; What Shall I Do with Today?; What a Lot of Flowers; Schooldays; Schooldays; When I Was Younger; You and I.
1969 151m/C Peter O'Toole, Petula Clark, Michael Redgrave, George Baker, Sian Phillips, Michael Bryant, Jack Hedley, Herbert Ross; *D:* Herbert Ross; *M:* Leslie Bricusse, John Williams. Academy Awards '69 Nominations: Best Actor (O'Toole), Best Original Score; Golden Globe Awards '70: Best Actor—Musical/Comedy (O'Toole). VHS, Beta, LV $19.98 *MGM, PIA* ♫♫

Goodbye, My Lady Based on the novel by James Street, this is a tear-jerking film about a young Mississippi farmboy who finds and cares for a special dog that he comes to love but eventually must give up.
1956 95m/B Brandon de Wilde, Walter Brennan, Sidney Poitier, Phil Harris, Louise Beavers; *D:* William A. Wellman. VHS, Beta, LV $19.98 *WAR, FCT* ♫♫

Goodbye, New York A New York yuppie on a vacation finds herself penniless and stranded in Israel. She makes the best of the situation by joining a kibbutz and falling for a part-time soldier. Well, of course.
1985 (R) 90m/C *IS* Julie Hagerty, Amos Kollek, Shmuel Shilo; *D:* Amos Kollek. VHS, Beta, LV $79.95 *VES* ♫♫

Goodbye, Norma Jean Detailed and sleazy recreation of Marilyn Monroe's early years in Hollywood. Followed by "Goodnight, Sweet Marilyn."
1975 (R) 95m/C Misty Rowe, Terrence Locke, Patch MacKenzie; *D:* Larry Buchanan. VHS, Beta $19.99 *HBO* ♫

The Goodbye People Balsam is an elderly man who decides to reopen his Coney Island hot dog stand that folded 22 years earlier. Hirsch and Reed help him realize his impossible dream in this sweetly sentimental film.
1983 104m/C Judd Hirsch, Martin Balsam, Pamela Reed, Ron Silver; *W/D:* Herb Gardner. VHS, Beta, LV $14.95 *COL, SUE* ♫♫ ½

Goodbye Pork Pie With the police on their trail, two young men speed on a 1000-mile journey in a small, brand-new, yellow stolen car. Remember: journey of thousand miles always begin in stolen car.
1981 (R) 105m/C *NZ* Tony Barry, Kelly Johnson; *D:* Geoff Murphy. VHS, Beta $69.98 *SUE* ♫ ½

Goodfellas Considered a quintessential picture about "wise guys" and their lives, at turns both violent and funny. A young man grows up in the mob, working hard to advance himself through the ranks, enjoying the life of the rich and violent, and oblivious to the horror of which he is a part. Soon his addiction to cocaine and many wise-guy missteps help unravel his climb to the top. Excellent performances all around (particularly Liotta and Pesci, with De Niro pitching in around the corners), with visionary cinematography and careful pacing. Received Golden Globe nominations for Best Screenplay, Picture, Supporting Actor (Pesci), Supporting Actress (Bracco), and Director. Based on the life of Henry Hill, the ex-mobster now in the Witness Protection Program. Adapted from the book by Nicholas Pileggi.
1990 (R) 146m/C Robert De Niro, Ray Liotta, Joe Pesci, Paul Sorvino, Lorraine Bracco; *D:* Martin Scorsese; *W:* Nicholas Pileggi, Martin Scorsese. Academy Awards '90: Best Supporting Actor (Pesci); Nominations: Best Adapted Screenplay, Best Director (Scorsese), Best Film Editing, Best Picture, Best Supporting Actress (Bracco); British Academy Awards '90: Best Director (Scorsese), Best Film; Los Angeles Film Critics Association Awards '90: Best Director (Scorsese), Best Film, Best Supporting Actor (Pesci), Best Supporting Actress (Bracco); New York Film Critics Awards '90: Best Director (Scorsese), Best Film; National Society of Film Critics Awards '90: Best Director (Scorsese), Best Film. VHS, Beta, LV, 8mm $19.98 *WAR, PIA, FCT* ♫♫♫♫

Goodnight God Bless A depressing movie about a mentally disturbed priest who wanders into an elementary school with murder on his mind. He kills the teacher and all the children—except one. Will he find that one too? It's not worth it to find out.
1987 (R) 90m/C VHS, Beta *NO* ♫

Goodnight, Michelangelo Funny, engaging and somewhat confusing story of the life of an Italian immigrant family as seen through the eyes of its youngest member, eight-year-old Michelangelo. Winner of the 1990 Best Comedy Award at the Greater Fort Lauderdale Film Festival.
1989 (R) 91m/C *IT* Lina Sastri, Kim Cattrall, Giancarlo Giannini, Daniel Desanto; *W/D:* Carlo Liconti. VHS *NO* ♫♫ ½

Goodnight, Sweet Marilyn Supposed "never-before-told" story of Marilyn Monroe's tragic death. According to this, her death was the result of pre-arranged "mercy-killing." Follow-up to director Buchanan's "Goodbye, Norma Jean" (1977) with Lane as the 1960s Marilyn intercut with scenes of Rowe from the first film as young Marilyn. You'd be better off leaving "Sweet Marilyn" to rest in peace.
1989 (R) 100m/C Paula Lane, Jeremy Slate, Misty Rowe; *D:* Larry Buchanan. VHS, Beta *NO* ♫

Goof Balls The tourist denizens of a island golf resort putt and cavort about, and golf isn't all that's on their minds.
1987 (R) 87m/C Ben Gordon, Laura Robinson. VHS, Beta $29.95 *ACA* Woof!

Goon Movie The cast of "The Goon Show," Britain's popular radio comedy series, perform some of their best routines in this, their only film appearance. *AKA:* Stand Easy.
1953 75m/B Peter Sellers, Spike Milligan, Harry Secombe. VHS, Beta $19.95 *VDM* ♫♫

The Goonies Two brothers who are about to lose their house conveniently find a treasure map. They pick up a couple of friends and head for the "X." If they can recover the treasure without getting caught by the bad guys, then all will be saved. Steven Spielberg produced this high-energy action fantasy for kids of all ages. The laserdisc edition comes in a widescreen format.
1985 (PG) 114m/C Sean Astin, Josh Brolin, Jeff B. Cohen, Corey Feldman, Martha Plimpton, John Matuszak, Robert Davi, Anne Ramsey, Mary Ellen Trainor; *D:* Richard Donner. VHS, Beta, LV $19.98 *WAR, PIA* ♫♫ ½

Gor Sword and sorcery: a magic ring sends a meek college professor to "Gor," a faraway world in which survival goes to the fittest and the most brutal. Followed by "Outlaw of Gor."
1988 (PG) 95m/C Urbano Barberini, Rebecca Ferratti, Jack Palance, Paul Smith, Oliver Reed; *D:* Fritz Kiersch. VHS, Beta $19.98 *WAR* ♫ ½

Gorath The world's top scientists are racing to stop a giant meteor from destroying the Earth. *AKA:* Yosei Gorasu.
1964 77m/C *JP* *D:* Inoshiro Honda. VHS, Beta $19.95 *GEM, PSM* ♫♫

Gordon's War When a Vietnam vet returns to his Harlem home, he finds his wife overdosing on the drugs that have infiltrated his neighborhood. He leads a vigilante group in an attempt to clean up the area, which makes for a lot of action; however, there's also an excessive amount of violence.
1973 (R) 89m/C Paul Winfield, Carl Lee, David Downing, Tony King, Grace Jones; *D:* Ossie Davis; *M:* Angelo Badalamenti. VHS, Beta $59.98 *FOX* ♫♫

Gore-Met Zombie Chef From Hell A demon/vampire opens up a seafood restaurant and slaughters his customers. Deliberately campy and extremely graphic.
1987 90m/C Theo Depuay, Kelley Kunicki, C.W. Casey, Alan Marx, Michael O'Neill; *D:* Don Swan. VHS, Beta *NO* Woof!

Gore Vidal's Billy the Kid An unusual treatment of the William Bonney legend in which the Kid is merely a misunderstood teenager caught up in the midst of the brutal range wars. Made for cable television.
1989 100m/C Val Kilmer, Duncan Regehr, Wilford Brimley, Julie Carmen, Michael Parks, Rene Auberjonois, Albert Salmi; *D:* William A. Graham. VHS $9.98 *TTC* ♫♫ ½

The Gorgeous Hussy Crawford stars in this fictionalized biography of Peggy Eaton, Andrew Jackson's notorious belle, who disgraces herself and those around her. A star-studded cast complete with beautiful costumes isn't enough to save this overly long and dull picture.
1936 102m/B Joan Crawford, Robert Taylor, Lionel Barrymore, Melvyn Douglas, James Stewart, Franchot Tone, Louis Calhern; *D:* Clarence Brown. VHS $19.98 *MGM* ♫

Gorgo An undersea explosion off the coast of Ireland brings to the surface a prehistoric sea monster, which is captured and brought to a London circus. Its irate mother appears looking for her baby, creating havoc in her wake.
1961 76m/C *GB* Bill Travers, William Sylvester, Vincent Winter, Bruce Seton, Christopher Rhodes; *D:* Eugene Lourie. VHS, Beta, LV, 3/4U, Special order formats $19.95 *NOS, MRV, UHV* ⅔½

The Gorgon In pre-World War I Germany, the lovely assistant to a mad brain surgeon moonlights as a snake-haired gorgon, turning men to stone. A professor arrives in the village to investigate, only to become another victim.
1964 83m/C *GB* Peter Cushing, Christopher Lee, Richard Pasco, Barbara Shelley, Michael Goodliffe, Patrick Troughton; *D:* Terence Fisher. VHS, Beta, LV $9.95 *GKK, MLB* ⅔⅔

The Gorilla Bumbling Ritzes are hired to protect a country gentleman receiving threats from a killer. Lugosi portrays the menacing butler. Derived from the play by Ralph Spence.
1939 67m/B The Ritz Brothers, Anita Louise, Patsy Kelly, Lionel Atwill, Bela Lugosi; *D:* Allan Dwan. VHS, Beta, LV $19.95 *NOS, SNC, MRV* ⅔⅔

Gorilla A rampaging gorilla is sought by the local game warden and a journalist researching the natives. Filmed on location in the Belgian Congo.
1956 79m/B *SW* Gio Petre, Georges Galley; *D:* Sven Nykvist, Lar Henrik Ottoson. VHS, Beta $19.95 *FCT, VYY* ⅔

Gorillas in the Mist The life of Dian Fossey, animal rights activist and world-renowned expert on the African Gorilla, from her pioneering contact with mountain gorillas to her murder at the hands of poachers. Weaver is totally appropriate as the increasingly obsessed Fossey, but the character moves away from us, just as we need to see and understand more about her. Excellent special effects. Music by Maurice Jarre.
1988 (PG-13) 117m/C Sigourney Weaver, Bryan Brown, Julie Harris, Iain Cuthbertson, John Omirah Miluwi; *D:* Michael Apted. Academy Awards '88 Nominations: Best Actress (Weaver), Best Adapted Screenplay, Best Film Editing, Best Sound, Best Original Score; Golden Globe Awards '88: Best Actress—Drama (Weaver). VHS, Beta, LV $19.95 *MCA, HMV* ⅔⅔⅔

Gorky Park Adaptation of Martin Cruz Smith's bestseller. Three strange, faceless corpses are found in Moscow's Gorky Park. There are no clues for the Russian police captain investigating the incident. He makes the solution to this crime his personal crusade, and finds himself caught in a web of political intrigue. Excellent police procedure yarn.
1983 (R) 127m/C William Hurt, Lee Marvin, Brian Dennehy, Joanna Pacula; *D:* Michael Apted. VHS, Beta, LV $29.98 *VES* ⅔⅔⅔

Gorp Sex, fun, and lewd, sophomoric humor reign at a summer camp. For the bored and witless or those who aspire.
1980 (R) 90m/C Dennis Quaid, Rosanna Arquette, Michael Lembeck, Philip Casnoff, Frank Drescher; *D:* Joseph Ruben. VHS, Beta $79.99 *HBO* Woof!

Gospel According to St. Matthew Perhaps Pasolini's greatest film, retelling the story of Christ in gritty, neorealistic tones and portraying the man less as a divine presence than as a political revolutionary. The yardstick by which all Jesus-films are to be measured. In Italian with English subtitles or dubbed. *AKA:* Il Vangelo

Secondo Matteo; L'Evangile Selon Saint-Matthieu.
1964 136m/B *IT* Enrique Irazoqui, Susanna Pasolini; *D:* Pier Paolo Pasolini. Academy Awards '66 Nominations: Best Art Direction/Set Decoration (B & W), Best Costume Design (B & W), Best Original Score; National Board of Review Awards '66: 5 Best Foreign Films of the Year. VHS, Beta, LV, 8mm $24.95 *NOS, MRV, WBF* ⅔⅔⅔⅔

The Gospel According to Vic A Scottish comedy about a skeptical teacher at a remedial school, who, having survived miraculously from a fall, is taken for proof of the sainthood of the school's patron namesake. *AKA:* Heavenly Pursuits.
1987 (PG-13) 92m/C *GB* Tom Conti, Helen Mirren; *D:* Charles Gormley. VHS, Beta $79.98 *FOX* ⅔⅔

Gotcha! The mock assassination game "Gotcha!" abounds on the college campus and sophomore Edwards is one of the best. What he doesn't know is that his "assassination" skills are about to take on new meaning when he meets up with a female Czech graduate student who is really an international spy.
1985 (PG-13) 97m/C Anthony Edwards, Linda Fiorentino, Alex Rocco, Nick Corri; *D:* Jeff Kanew. VHS, Beta, LV $19.95 *MCA* ⅔⅔½

Gotham A wealthy financier hires private-eye Jones to track down beautiful wife Madsen. It seems that she keeps dunning her husband for money. Sounds easy enough to Jones until he learns that she has been dead for some time. Mystery ventures into the afterlife and back as it twists its way to its surprise ending. Intriguing throwback to '40s detective flicks. Made for television.
1988 100m/C Tommy Lee Jones, Virginia Madsen, Colin Bruce, Kevin Jarre, Denise Stephenson, Frederic Forrest; *D:* Lloyd Fonvielle. VHS, LV $19.98 *CAN* ⅔⅔⅔

Gothic Mary Shelley, Lord Byron, Percy Bysshe Shelley, and John Polidori spend the night in a Swiss villa telling each other ghost stories and experimenting with laudanum and sexual partner combinations. The dreams and realizations of the night will color their lives ever after. Interesting premise, well-carried out, although burdened by director Russell's typical excesses. Soundtrack by Thomas Dolby.
1987 (R) 87m/C Julian Sands, Gabriel Byrne, Timothy Spall, Natasha Richardson; *D:* Ken Russell. VHS, Beta, LV $14.98 *LIV, VES* ⅔⅔⅔

Gotta Dance, Gotta Sing Compilation of memorable dance routines from great Hollywood films.
1984 53m/C Fred Astaire, Ginger Rogers, Shirley Temple, Carmen Miranda, Betty Grable. VHS, Beta $39.95 *RKO* ⅔⅔⅔

Government Agents vs. Phantom Legion Agent Hal Duncan must stop an evil group who is stealing uranium shipments from under the government's nose. Edited from 12 episodes of the original serial on two cassettes.
1951 167m/B Walter Reed, Mary Ellen Kay, Dick Curtis, John Pickard. VHS, Beta $29.98 *REP, MLB* ⅔⅔⅔

Grace Quigley An elderly woman, tired of life, hires a hitman to kill her. Instead they go into business together, bumping off other elderly folk who decide they'd rather be dead. Notoriously inept black comedy noted for being the career embarrassment for both of its stars. *AKA:* The Ultimate Solution of Grace Quigley.

1984 (PG) 102m/C Katharine Hepburn, Nick Nolte, Walter Abel, Chip Zien, Elizabeth Wilson, Kit Le Fever, William Duell, Jill Eikenberry; *D:* Anthony Harvey. VHS, Beta $79.95 *MGM* ⅔½

Grad Night The anticipation for graduation in a small town high school brings surprises no one could have predicted, unless they've seen all the other typical adolescent films.
1981 (R) 85m/C Joey Johnson, Suzanna Fagan, Barry Stolze, Sam Whipple, Caroline Bates; *D:* John Tenorio. VHS, Beta $79.95 *MNC* ⅔

The Graduate The famous, influential slice of comic Americana starring Hoffman as Benjamin Braddock, a shy, aimless college graduate who, without any idea of responsibility or ambition, wanders from a sexual liaison with a married woman (the infamous Mrs. Robinson) to pursuit of her engaged daughter. Benjamin's pursuit of Elaine right to her wedding has become a film classic. Extremely popular and almost solely responsible for establishing both Hoffman and director Nichols. The career advice given to Benjamin, "plastics," became a catchword for the era. Music by Simon & Garfunkel. Based on the novel by Charles Webb. Laserdisc edition includes screen tests, promotional stills, and a look at the creative process involved in making a novel into a movie. A 25th Anniversary Limited Edition is also available, presented in a wide-screen format and including the original movie trailer and interviews with the cast and crew.
1967 106m/C Dustin Hoffman, Anne Bancroft, Katharine Ross, Murray Hamilton, Brian Avery, Marion Lorne, Alice Ghostley, William Daniels, Elizabeth Wilson, Norman Fell, Buck Henry, Richard Dreyfuss, Mike Farrell; *D:* Mike Nichols. Academy Awards '67: Best Director (Nichols); Nominations: Best Adapted Screenplay, Best Cinematography, Best Supporting Actress (Ross); British Academy Awards '68: Best Director (Nichols), Best Film; Directors Guild of America Awards '67: Best Director (Nichols); Golden Globe Awards '68: Best Actress—Musical/Comedy (Bancroft), Best Director (Nichols), Best Film—Musical/Comedy; National Board of Review Awards '67: 10 Best Films of the Year; New York Film Critics Awards '67: Best Director (Nichols). VHS, Beta, LV, 8mm $14.98 *SUE, VYG, CRC* ⅔⅔⅔⅔

Graduation Day Another teen slasher about the systematic murder of members of a high school track team. Notable mainly for brief appearance by Vanna White.
1981 85m/C Christopher George, Patch MacKenzie, E. Danny Murphy, Vanna White; *D:* Herb Freed. VHS, Beta $69.95 *COL* ⅔

Graffiti Bridge Prince preaches love instead of sex and the result is boring. The Lavender One is a Minneapolis nightclub owner who battles with Day over the love of a beautiful woman. Chauvinistic attitudes toward women abound, but the females in the film don't seem to mind. Which must mean they were "acting." Visually interesting, although not as experimental as "Purple Rain." Music made Top Ten.
1990 (PG-13) 90m/C Prince, Morris Day, Jerome Benton, The Time, Jill Jones, Mavis Staples, George Clinton, Ingrid Chavez; *W/D:* Prince. VHS, Beta, LV $19.98 *MVD, WAR* ⅔½

Grain of Sand Based on a true story, an understated French drama about a troubled woman searching her past, and her home town in Corsica, for the man of her dreams. Directorial debut of Meffre. In French with English subtitles.
1984 90m/C *FR* Delphine Seyrig, Genevieve Fontanel, Coralie Seyrig, Michel Aumont; *D:* Pomme Meffre. VHS, Beta $59.95 *FCT* ⅔⅔⅔

Grambling's White Tiger The true story of Jim Gregory, the first white man to play on Grambling College's all-black football team. Jenner's a little too old, but Belafonte, in his TV acting debut, is fine as legendary coach Eddie Robinson. Based on book by Bruce Behrenberg. Made for television.
1981 98m/C Bruce Jenner, Harry Belafonte, LeVar Burton, Ray Vitte, Byron Stewart; **D:** Georg Stanford Brown. **VHS, Beta $39.95** MCA *ℐℐ* ½

Grampa's Monster Movies Grampa (star of "The Munsters" TV show) hosts a tribute to Frankenstein, Dracula, Wolfman and the Mummy, with legends Bela Lugosi, Boris Karloff, Lon Chaney Jr. and Vincent Price.
1990 65m/C VHS, Beta **NO** *ℐℐ* ½

Grampa's Sci-Fi Hits Sequel to Grampa's "Monster Movies," this one carries some of the more fantastic of sci-fi creatures from beyond.
1990 65m/C VHS, Beta **NO** *ℐℐ* ½

Gran Valor en la Facultad de Medicina A Spanish simpleton is mistakenly admitted to medical school.
198? 90m/C *SP* Juan Carlos Calabro, Adriana Aguirre. **VHS, Beta $57.95** UNI *ℐ*

Grand Canyon A group of diverse characters is thrown together through chance encounters while coping with urban chaos in L.A. The main focus is the growing friendship between an immigration lawyer (Kline) and a tow-truck driver (Glover) who meet when Kline's car breaks down in a crime-ridden neighborhood. First-rate performances by the cast make up for numerous moral messages laced throughout the script that are not so subtly thrown at viewers. Sometimes funny, sometimes preachy, this film becomes more relevant in light of the violence that exploded in L.A. during the summer of '92.
1991 (R) 134m/C Danny Glover, Kevin Kline, Steve Martin, Mary McDonnell, Mary Louise Parker, Alfre Woodard, Jeremy Sisto, Tina Lifford, Patrick Malone, Mary Ellen Trainor; **D:** Lawrence Kasdan; **W:** Lawrence Kasdan, Meg Kasdan; **M:** James Newton Howard. Academy Awards '91 Nominations: Best Original Screenplay; National Board of Review Awards '91: 10 Best Films of the Year. **VHS $19.98** FXV *ℐℐℐ*

Grand Canyon Trail Our hero is the owner of a played-out silver mine who is the target of an unscrupulous engineer who thinks there's silver to be found if you know where to look. The first appearance of the Riders of the Purple Sage, who replaced the Sons of the Pioneers.
1948 68m/B Roy Rogers, Andy Devine, Charles Coleman, Jane Frazee, Robert Livingston; **D:** William Witney. **VHS, Beta $9.99** NOS, MED, DVT *ℐ* ½

The Grand Duchess and the Waiter Menjou is a French millionaire who disguises himself as a waiter in order to enter the service of a grand duchess with whom he has fallen in love.
1926 70m/B Adolphe Menjou, Florence Vidor, Lawrence Grant; **D:** Malcolm St. Clair. **VHS, Beta** NO *ℐℐℐ*

The Grand Duel More spaghetti thrills as Lee plays a mysterious gunman who also acts as protector of a young ruffian falsely accused of murder.
1973 ?m/C *IT* Lee Van Cleef, Peter O'Brien, Jess Hahn, Horst Frank. **VHS $16.95** SNC *ℐℐ*

Grand Hotel A star-filled cast is brought together by unusual circumstances at Berlin's Grand Hotel and their lives become hopelessly intertwined over a 24 hour period.

Adapted (and given the red-carpet treatment) from a Vicki Baum novel; notable mostly for Garbo's world-weary ballerina. Time has taken its toll on the concept and treatment, but still an interesting star vehicle.
1932 112m/B Greta Garbo, John Barrymore, Joan Crawford, Lewis Stone, Wallace Beery, Jean Hersholt, Lionel Barrymore; **D:** Edmund Goulding. **VHS, Beta, LV $19.98** MGM, FCT, BTV *ℐℐℐ* ½

Grand Illusion Unshakably classic anti-war film by Renoir, in which French prisoners of war attempt to escape from their German captors during World War I. An indictment of the way Old World, aristocratic nobility was brought to modern bloodshed in the Great War. Renoir's optimism remains relentless, but was easier to believe in before World War II. In French, with English subtitles. The laserdisc version includes an audio essay by Peter Crowe.
1937 111m/B *FR* Jean Gabin, Erich von Stroheim, Pierre Fresnay, Marcel Dalio, Julien Carette, Gaston Modot, Jean Daste, Dita Parlo; **D:** Jean Renoir. Academy Awards '38 Nominations: Best Picture; National Board of Review Awards '38: 5 Best Foreign Films of the Year; New York Film Critics Awards '38: Best Foreign Film. **VHS, Beta, LV, 8mm, 3/4U, Special order formats $29.95** NOS, MRV, FOX *ℐℐℐℐ*

Grand Isle At the turn of the century Grand Isle is the place Louisiana gentry leisurely spend their summers. This is where Edna Pontellier (McGillis), the wife of a rich stockbroker, meets sensitive Creole artist Robert LeBrun (Pasdar). Robert gives Edna all the attention sorely lacking in her marriage and they fall in love. However, Edna's attempts to liberate herself from the strictures of society lead her to tragedy. Based on "The Awakening" by Kate Chopin. Made for cable television.
1992 94m/C Kelly McGillis, Adrian Pasdar, Julian Sands, Jon DeVries, Glenne Headly, Ellen Burstyn; **D:** Mary Lambert; **W:** Hesper Anderson. **VHS, LV $89.98** TTC *ℐℐ* ½

Grand Larceny The daughter of a millionaire/thief has to prove that she can take over the family "business." Lots of action and stunts.
19?? 95m/C Marilu Henner, Omar Sharif, Ian McShane, Louis Jourdan. **VHS $49.95** CAF *ℐℐ*

Grand Master of Shaolin Kung Fu Follow the exploits of Dhama, the very man responsible for the creation of Kung Fu.
19?? 88m/C VHS, Beta **$14.98** NEG *ℐℐ*

Grand Prix A big-budget look at the world of Grand Prix auto racing, as four top competitors circle the world's most famous racing circuits. Strictly for those who like cars racing round and round; nothing much happens off the track. Letterboxed screen is featured in the laserdisc format.
1966 161m/C James Garner, Eva Marie Saint, Yves Montand, Toshiro Mifune, Brian Bedford; **D:** John Frankenheimer. **VHS, Beta, LV $29.99** MGM, FCT *ℐℐ*

Grand Theft Auto In Howard's initial directorial effort, a young couple elopes to Las Vegas in a Rolls Royce owned by the bride's father. The father, totally against the marriage and angered by the stolen Rolls, offers a reward for their safe return and a cross-country race ensues.
1977 (PG) 84m/C Ron Howard, Nancy Morgan, Marion Ross, Barry Cahill, Clint Howard; **D:** Ron Howard. **VHS, Beta $19.98** WAR *ℐℐ*

Grand Tour: Disaster in Time Greenglen is a quiet, small Midwestern town, until it is visited by a sinister group of time traveling aliens. Daniels plays a widowed

innkeeper who must save the town from destruction and save his daughter from being kidnapped by the fiends. Made for cable television.
1992 (PG-13) 98m/C Jeff Daniels, Ariana Richards, Emilia Crow, Jim Haynie, Nicholas Guest, Marilyn Lightstone, George Murdock; **W/ D:** David N. Twohy. **VHS, LV $89.95** ACA *ℐℐ*

Grandes Amigos A young boy finds out the meaning of having a true friend in this comedy-drama In Spanish. **AKA:** Great Friends.
197? 105m/C *SP* Nino Del Arco. **VHS, Beta $49.95** MAD *ℐ*

Grandma's House A brother and sister discover that the house in which they live with their grandmother is chock-full of secrets and strange happenings, including madness, incest, and murder.
1988 (R) 90m/C Eric Foster, Kim Valentine, Brinke Stevens, Ida Lee; **D:** Peter Rader. **VHS, Beta, LV $79.95** ACA *ℐ*

Grandview U.S.A. A low-key look at low-rent middle America, centering on a foxy local speedway owner and the derby-obsessed boys she attracts.
1984 (R) 97m/C Jamie Lee Curtis, Patrick Swayze, C. Thomas Howell, M. Emmet Walsh, Troy Donahue, William Windom, Jennifer Jason Leigh, Ramon Bieri, John Cusack, Joan Cusack, Jason Court; **D:** Randal Kleiser. **VHS, Beta $19.98** FOX *ℐℐ* ½

The Grapes of Wrath John Steinbeck's classic American novel about the Great Depression. We follow the impoverished Joad family as they migrate from the dust bowl of Oklahoma to find work in the orchards of California and as they struggle to maintain at least a little of their dignity and pride. A sentimental but dignified, uncharacteristic Hollywood epic. Written by Nunnally Johnson.
1940 129m/B Henry Fonda, Jane Darwell, John Carradine, Charley Grapewin, Zeffie Tilbury, Dorris Bowdon, Russell Simpson, John Qualen, Eddie Quillan, O.Z. Whitehead, Grant Mitchell; **D:** John Ford. Academy Awards '40: Best Director (Ford), Best Supporting Actress (Darwell); Nominations: Best Actor (Fonda), Best Adapted Screenplay, Best Picture, Best Sound, Best Original Score; New York Film Critics Awards '40: Best Director (Ford), Best Film. **VHS, Beta, LV $19.98** KUI, FOX, BTV *ℐℐℐ* ½

The Grass is Always Greener Over the Septic Tank Based on Erma Bombeck's best-seller. A city family's flight to the supposed peace of the suburbs turns out to be a comic compilation of complications. Made for television.
1978 98m/C Carol Burnett, Charles Grodin, Linda Gray, Alex Rocco, Robert Sampson, Vicki Belmonte, Craig Richard Nelson, Anrae Walterhouse, Eric Stoltz; **D:** Robert Day. **VHS, Beta** NO *ℐℐ*

The Grass is Greener An American millionaire invades part of an impoverished Earl's mansion and falls in love with the lady of the house. The Earl, who wants to keep his wife, enlists the aid of an old girlfriend in a feeble attempt to make her jealous. The two couples pair off properly in the end.
1961 105m/C Cary Grant, Deborah Kerr, Jean Simmons, Robert Mitchum; **D:** Stanley Donen. **VHS, LV $19.98** REP *ℐℐ* ½

Grave of the Fireflies In post-war Japan, in the city of Kobe's train station, a young boy lies dying. A janitor finds a metal canister lying next to the boy and when he opens it ashes fall out. As fireflies gather around, ghostly figures of the boy and his little sister appear, as the story flashes back to the orphaned, homeless Seita and his

sister. The two youngsters struggle in the Japanese countryside but find they cannot escape the hardships of war and have no chance for survival. Stunning animated testimony to the human spirit. Based on the novel by Akiyuki Nosaka. In Japanese with English subtitles.
1988 88m/C *JP W/D:* Isao Takahata. **VHS, LV $39.95** *CPM* ✂✂✂

Grave of the Vampire A vampire rapes and impregnates a modern-day girl. Twenty years later, their son, who grows up to be a bitter bloodsucker, sets out to find his father and kill him. *AKA:* Seed of Terror.
1972 (R) 95m/C William Smith, Michael Pataki, Lyn Peters, Diane Holden, Jay Adler, Kitty Vallacher, Jay Scott, Lieux Dressler; *D:* John Patrick Hayes. **VHS, Beta $49.95** *UNI* ✂

Grave Secrets A professor of psychic phenomena teams up with a medium to find out who—or what—is controlling the life of a young woman.
1989 (R) 90m/C Paul LeMat, Renee Soutendljk, David Warner, Olivia Barash, Lee Ving; *D:* Donald P. Borchers. **VHS, LV $89.98** *SGE* ✂✂½

Grave Secrets: The Legacy of Hilltop Drive The Williams family finds out their dream house is built on the site of an old graveyard. The spirits are not only restless, they're deadly. Based on a true story.
1992 94m/C Jonelle Allen, Patty Duke, David Selby, David Soul, Blake Clark; *D:* John D. Patterson. **VHS $89.95** *WOV, PMS* ✂✂

The Graveyard A mommy spends many years torturing her little boy, David. In one blood-filled day, the fellow seeks his revenge. *AKA:* Persecution; Terror of Sheba; Sheba.
1974 90m/C Lana Turner, Trevor Howard, Ralph Bates, Olga Georges-Picot, Suzan Farmer; *D:* Don Chaffey. **VHS, Beta** *ELV* ✂✂

Graveyard of Horror His wife and baby dead, a man seeking revenge discovers a horrible secret: his brother, a doctor, is stealing the heads from corpses. Dubbed.
1971 105m/C *SP* Bill Curran, Francisco (Frank) Brana, Beatriz Lacy; *D:* Miguel Madrid. **VHS, Beta** *NO* ✂

Graveyard Shift A New York cabby on the night shift is actually a powerful vampire who uses his fares to build an army of vampires. Not to be confused with the 1990 Stephen King scripted film. Followed by "Understudy: Graveyard Shift II."
1987 (R) 89m/C *IT* Silvio Oliviero, Helen Papas, Cliff Stoker; *D:* Gerard Ciccoritti. **VHS, Beta** *NO* ✂½

Graveyard Shift Just because Stephen King wrote the original story doesn't mean its celluloid incarnation is guaranteed to stand your hair on end; unless that's your response to abject boredom. When a man takes over the night shift at a recently reopened textile mill, he starts to find remnants...and they aren't fabric. Seems there's a graveyard in the neighborhood. *AKA:* Stephen King's Graveyard Shift.
1990 (R) 89m/C David Andrews, Kelly Wolf, Stephen Macht, Brad Dourif; *D:* Ralph S. Singleton; *W:* Stephen King, John Esposito. **VHS, Beta, LV $14.95** *PAR, FCT* ✂

Gray Lady Down A nuclear submarine sinks off the coast of Cape Cod and with their oxygen running out, a risky escape in an experimental diving craft seems to be their only hope. Dull, all-semi-star suspenser.
1977 (PG) 111m/C Charlton Heston, David Carradine, Stacy Keach, Ned Beatty, Ronny Cox, Christopher Reeve, Michael O'Keefe, Rosemary Forsyth; *D:* David Greene. **VHS, Beta $59.95** *MCA* ✂✂

Grayeagle When a frontier trapper's daughter is kidnapped by Cheyenne Indians, he launches a search for her recovery. More style than pace in this Western, but worth a look for fans of Johnson.
1977 (PG) 104m/C Ben Johnson, Iron Eyes Cody, Lana Wood, Alex Cord, Jack Elam, Paul Fix, Cindy Butler, Charles B. Pierce; *W/D:* Charles B. Pierce. **VHS, Beta $19.98** *WAR, OM* ✂✂

Grazuole A nine-year-old girl is mockingly made "Beauty Queen" by her malicious playmates.
1969 71m/B *D:* Arunas Zhebrunas. **VHS, Beta** *IHF* ✂✂

Grease Film version of the hit Broadway musical about summer love. Set in the 1950s, this spirited musical follows a group of high-schoolers throughout their senior year. The story offers a responsible moral: act like a tart and you'll get your guy; but, hey, it's all in fun anyway. Followed by a weak sequel. ♫Grease; Summer Nights; Hopelessly Devoted To You; You're the One That I Want; Sandy; Beauty School Dropout; Look at Me, I'm Sandra Dee; Greased Lightnin'; It's Raining on Prom Night; Alone at a Drive-In Movie; Blue Moon; Rock 'n' Roll Is Here To Stay; Those Magic Changes; Hound Dog; Born to Hand-Jive; Tears On My Pillow; Mooning; Freddy My Love; Rock 'n' Roll Party Queen; There Are Worse Things I Could Do; We Go Together; Love is a Many Splendored Thing; Look At Me, I'm Sandra Dee.
1978 (PG) 110m/C John Travolta, Olivia Newton-John, Jeff Conaway, Stockard Channing, Eve Arden, Sha-Na-Na, Frankie Avalon, Sid Caesar; *D:* Randal Kleiser. Academy Awards '78 Nominations: Best Song ("Hopelessly Devoted to You"); People's Choice Awards '79: Best Film. **VHS, Beta, LV $14.95** *PAR, FCT* ✂✂✂

Grease 2 Continuing saga of the T-Birds, the Pink Ladies, and young love at Rydell High. Newton John and Travolta have graduated, leaving Pfeiffer to lead on love-struck book-neb Caulfield. Some okay tunes, though lame story lacks good-humor flair of the original.
1982 (PG) 115m/C Maxwell Caulfield, Michelle Pfeiffer, Adrian Zmed, Lorna Luft, Didi Conn, Eve Arden, Sid Caesar, Tab Hunter; *D:* Patricia Birch. **VHS, Beta, LV $14.95** *PAR* ✂✂

Greased Lightning The story of the first black auto racing champion, Wendell Scott, who had to overcome racial prejudice to achieve his success. Slightly-better-than-average Pryor comedy vehicle.
1977 (PG) 95m/C Richard Pryor, Pam Grier, Beau Bridges, Cleavon Little, Vincent Gardenia; *D:* Michael Schultz. **VHS, Beta $59.95** *WAR* ✂✂½

Greaser's Palace Seaweedhead Greaser, owner of the town's saloon, faces his arch-nemesis in this wide-ranging satiric Christ allegory from the director of "Putney Swope."
1972 91m/C Albert Henderson, Allan Arbus; *D:* Robert Downey; *M:* Jack Nitzsche. **VHS, Beta** *COL, OM* ✂✂½

The Great Adventure Two farm boys capture and attempt to train a wild otter. Unfortunately, the otter longs to once again join his kind despite the boys' efforts. Arne Sucksdorff won an Oscar for his arresting view of animal life. *AKA:* Det Stora Aventyret.
1953 73m/B *SW* Anders Norberg, Kjell Sucksdorff, Arne Sucksdorff; *W/D:* Arne Sucksdorff. **VHS, Beta** *MED* ✂✂✂½

Great Adventure In the severe environment of the gold rush days on the rugged Yukon territory, a touching tale unfolds of a young orphan boy and his eternal bond of friendship with a great northern dog. Based on a Jack London story. Paul Elliots is a pseudonym for Gianfranco Baldanello and Fred Romer is actually Fernando Romero.
1975 (PG) 90m/C *IT SP* Jack Palance, Joan Collins, Fred Romer, Elisabetta Virgili, Remo de Angelis, Manuel de Blas; *D:* Paul Elliotts. **VHS, Beta $19.95** *MED* ✂

The Great Alligator As if you couldn't guess, this one's about a huge alligator who does what other huge alligators do...terrorizes the people at a resort. *AKA:* Il Fiume Del Grande Caimano.
1981 89m/C Barbara Bach, Mel Ferrer, Richard Johnson; *D:* Sergio Martino. **VHS, Beta** *MPI* ✂

The Great American Broadcast Two WWI vets want more than anything to strike it rich. After many failed endeavors, the two try that new-fangled thing called radio. The station takes off, as does the plot. The girlfriend of one vet falls for his partner and numerous other misunderstandings and complications ensue. Charming and crazy musical with an energetic cast. ♫I've Got a Bone To Pick With You; It's All In a Lifetime; I Take to You; Long Ago Last Night; Where You Are; The Great American Broadcast; Albany Bound; Give My Regards to Broadway; If I Didn't Care.
1941 92m/B Alice Faye, John Payne, Jack Oakie, Cesar Romero, The Four Ink Spots, James Newill, Mary Beth Hughes; *D:* Archie Mayo. **VHS** *MLB* ✂✂✂

Great American Cowboy From the stable to the arena, this documentary tells the story of modern rodeo cowboy Larry Mahan.
1973 89m/C *D:* Keith Merrill. **VHS, Beta $69.95** *DIS* ✂✂✂

Great American Traffic Jam A made-for-television farce about the humorous variety of characters interacting on the interstate during a massive California traffic jam. *AKA:* Gridlock.
1980 (PG) 97m/C Ed McMahon, Vic Tayback, Howard Hesseman, Abe Vigoda, Noah Beery Jr., Desi Arnaz Jr., John Beck, Shelley Fabares, James Gregory; *D:* James Frawley. **VHS, Beta $59.98** *FOX* ✂½

The Great Armored Car Swindle An anonymous English businessman becomes involved in international intrigue when he becomes a pawn in a plan to transfer money to a Middle Eastern government under communist rule. But thanks to his wife things don't go off as planned.
1964 58m/B Peter Reynolds, Dermot Walsh, Joanna Dunham, Lisa Gastoni, Brian Cobby; *D:* Lance Comfort. **VHS, Beta $16.95** *SNC* ✂

Great Balls of Fire A florid, comic-book film of the glory days of Jerry Lee Lewis, from his first band to stardom. Most of the drama is derived from his marriage to his 13-year-old cousin. Somewhat overacted but full of energy. The soundtrack features many of the "Killer's" greatest hits re-recorded by Jerry Lee Lewis for the film.
1989 (PG-13) 108m/C Dennis Quaid, Winona Ryder, Alec Baldwin, Trey Wilson, John Doe, Lisa Blount; *D:* Jim McBride. **VHS, Beta, LV $19.98** *ORI* ✂✂½

Great Bank Hoax Three bank managers decide to rob their own bank to cover up the fact that all the assets have been embezzled. *AKA:* The Great Georgia Bank Hoax; Shenanigans.

1978 (PG) 89m/C Richard Basehart, Ned Beatty, Burgess Meredith, Michael Murphy, Paul Sand, Arthur Godfrey; **D:** Joseph Jacoby. **VHS, Beta** $19.98 WAR ♫♫½

The Great Battle Events that led up to the last great WWII North African battle between the Allies and the German Panzers for the Mareth Line. International mishmash. **AKA:** Battleforce; The Greatest Battle. 1979 97m/C GE YU Henry Fonda, Stacy Keach, Samantha Eggar, Helmut Berger, John Huston; **D:** Humphrey Longan. **VHS, Beta** TLF ♫

The Great Caruso The story of opera legend Enrico Caruso's rise to fame, from his childhood in Naples, Italy, to his collapse on the stage of the Metropolitan Opera House. Lanza is superb as the singer, and there are 27 musical numbers to satisfy the opera lover. ♫The Loveliest Night of the Year; Over the Waves; Vesti la Giubba; M'Appari; Celeste Aida; Numi, Pieta; La Fatal Pietra; Sextet from Lucia di Lammermoor; La Donne a Mobile; Che Gelida Manina!; E Lucevan Le Steele; Sweethearts; Because; Ave-Maria; Mattinata; Torna a Surriento; 'Tis the Last Rose of Summer; O Paradiso. 1951 113m/C Mario Lanza, Ann Blyth, Dorothy Kirsten; **D:** Richard Thorpe. Academy Awards '51: Best Sound; Nominations: Best Costume Design (Color), Best Original Score. **VHS, Beta, LV** $19.98 MGM ♫♫½

Great Chase A historical anthology of the funniest and most suspenseful classic movie chases, especially "The General." Also features score by Larry Adler. 1963 79m/B Buster Keaton, Lillian Gish, Pearl White, Noah Beery Jr. **VHS, Beta** $24.98 SUE, NLC ♫♫½

The Great Commandment Young man throws himself into a revolution against the overbearing Roman Empire in 30 A.D. His brother joins him but is killed. The man, who has become influenced by the teachings of Christ, decides to give up his revolution and go off with his brother's widow. (He always loved her anyway.) 1941 78m/B John Beal, Maurice Moscovich, Albert Dekker, Marjorie Cooley, Warren McCullum; **D:** Irving Pichel. **VHS** $29.98 REP ♫

Great Dan Patch The story of the great Dan Patch, the horse that went on to become the highest-earning harness racer in history. 1949 92m/B Dennis O'Keefe, Gail Russell, Ruth Warrick; **D:** Joseph M. Newman. **VHS, Beta** $19.95 WWV, TIM, VEC ♫½

Great Day A soap opera set around the wartime visit of first lady Eleanor Roosevelt to a small British town. It focuses mainly on the wife and daughter of a bitter, alcoholic WWI vet. 1946 62m/B Eric Portman, Flora Robson, Sheila Sim, Isabel Jeans, Walter Fitzgerald, Philip Friend, Marjorie Rhodes, Maire O'Neill, Beatrice Varley; **D:** Lance Comfort. **VHS, Beta** $19.98 TTC ♫½

Great Day in the Morning A rebel sympathizer and a Northern spy are both after Colorado gold to help finance the Civil War. But our Southern gentlemen soon find themselves equally interested in the local ladies. 1956 92m/C Robert Stack, Ruth Roman, Raymond Burr, Virginia Mayo, Alex Nicol, Regis Toomey; **D:** Jacques Tourneur. **VHS, Beta** $15.95 UHV ♫♫½

The Great Dictator Chaplin's first all-dialogue film, a searing satire on Nazism in which he has dual roles as a Jewish barber with amnesia who is mistaken for a Hitlerian dictator, Adenoid Hynkel. A classic scene

involves Hynkel playing with a gigantic balloon of the world. Hitler banned the film's release to the German public due to its highly offensive portrait of him. The film also marked Chaplin's last wearing of the Little Tramp's (and Hitler's equally little) mustache. 1940 126m/B Charlie Chaplin, Paulette Goddard, Jack Oakie, Billy Gilbert, Reginald Gardiner, Henry Daniell; **D:** Charlie Chaplin. Academy Awards '40 Nominations: Best Actor (Chaplin), Best Original Screenplay, Best Picture, Best Supporting Actor (Oakie), Best Original Score; National Board of Review Awards '40: 10 Best Films of the Year; New York Film Critics Awards '40: Best Actor (Chaplin). **VHS, Beta, LV** $19.98 FOX, HMV, GLV ♫♫♫

The Great Escape During WWII, the Nazis gather all of the troublesome allied P.O.W.'s in an escape-proof camp. These prisoners join forces in a single mass break for freedom. A true story based on the novel by Paul Brickhill and scripted by James Clavell and W.R. Burnett. Many of the stunts were performed by McQueen himself, particularly the climatic motorcycle ride, against the wishes of director Sturges. Laserdisc version features an analysis of the true story that inspired the movie, actual photos of the camp, allied prisoners, and German guards, indepth commentaries by director John Sturges, composer Elmer Bernstein, and stuntman Bud Ekins, excerpts from the script by novelist James Clavell, over 250 production photos, and the original movie trailer. 1963 170m/C Steve McQueen, James Garner, Richard Attenborough, Charles Bronson, James Coburn, Donald Pleasence, David McCallum, James Donald, Gordon Jackson; **D:** John Sturges. **VHS, Beta, LV** $29.98 MGM, FOX, VYG ♫♫♫½

The Great Escape 2: The Untold Story This flaccid actioner (you'd think that would be a contradiction of terms) can't decide whether it's a remake of the original or a sequel; it pretends to be a sequel yet spends two-thirds of its reel time retelling—poorly—the first great escape. And once it gets around to the "and then what happened" part, it dispenses with sequel protocol: Pleasance, who played an escapee in the original, is a Nazi bad guy in this go-round. What's more, the casting is screwy: Reeves is unconvincing as a German-speaking British officer who rallies the surviving escapees in revenge against their WWII captors. Made for television and originally shown in two parts, it's been mercifully shortened for video. 1988 93m/C Christopher Reeve, Judd Hirsch, Ian McShane, Donald Pleasence, Anthony John Denison, Judd Taylor, Charles Haid; **D:** Michael Nader, Paul Wendkos. **VHS** $89.95 VMK, TLF ♫♫

Great Expectations Lean's magisterial adaptation of the Dickens tome, in which a young English orphan is graced by a mysterious benefactor and becomes a well-heeled gentleman. Hailed and revered over the years; possibly the best Dickens on film. Well-acted by all, but especially notable is Hunt's slightly mad and pathetic Miss Havisham. Remake of the 1934 film. 1946 118m/B GB John Mills, Valerie Hobson, Anthony Wager, Alec Guinness, Finlay Currie, Jean Simmons, Bernard Miles, Francis L. Sullivan, Martita Hunt; **D:** David Lean. Academy Awards '47: Best Art Direction/Set Decoration (B & W), Best Black and White Cinematography; Nominations: Best Director (Lean), Best Picture, Best Screenplay; National Board of Review Awards '47: 10 Best Films of the Year. **VHS, Beta, LV** $79.98 PAR, LCA, HMV ♫♫♫♫

Great Expectations Animated version of Charles Dickens' classic is about an orphan's rise to gentleman status due to a mysterious benefactor. 1978 72m/C **VHS, Beta** NO ♫♫♫♫

Great Expectations A British television mini-series adaptation of the Dickens epic about Pip and his mysterious benefactor in Victorian London. On two tapes. 1981 300m/C GB Gerry Sundquist, Stratford Johns, Joan Hickson. **VHS, Beta** $29.98 KUI, FOX, SIG ♫♫

Great Expectations Animated story based upon the Dickens classic about a young boy's rise from a humble childhood to find fortune and happiness. 1983 72m/C **D:** Jean Tych. **VHS, Beta** $19.95 VES ♫♫

Great Expectations Dickens classic retold on 3 cassettes. A mysterious benefactor turns a poor orphan boy into a gentleman of means. 1989 325m/C GB Jean Simmons, Anthony Hopkins, John Rhys-Davies; **D:** Kevin Connor. **VHS, Beta** $49.95 DIS ♫♫♫

Great Expectations: The Untold Story Magwitch is an escaped convict, hiding out in the Victorian English countryside, who is aided by the young orphan, Pip. Captured and sent to the penal colonies in Australia, Magwitch serves his time and then discovers a fortune in gold, which he decides to use to make Pip into a gentleman. But Magwitch's enemies would like to get Pip's inheritance for themselves. Based on the Dickens classic, this three-tape miniseries is also available in a 102-minute feature length version. 1987 287m/C John Stanton, Sigrid Thornton, Robert Coleby, Todd Boyce, Anne Louise Lambert, Ron Haddrick, Noel Ferrier; **D:** Tim Burstall. **VHS** $89.95 HMD, FCT ♫♫½

Great Flamarion A woman-hating trickshot artist is nevertheless duped into murdering the husband of his femme fatale assistant after he comes to believe she loves him. He's wrong. 1945 78m/B Dan Duryea, Erich von Stroheim, Mary Beth Hughes; **D:** Anthony Mann. **VHS, Beta** $16.95 SNC, NOS, DVT ♫♫½

The Great Gabbo A ventriloquist can express himself only through his dummy, losing his own identity and going mad at the end. Von Stroheim's first talkie. May quite possibly be the first mentally-twisted-ventriloquist story ever put on film. Von Stroheim hated the movie, believing it to be analogous to his own life. When he tried to buy the rights to the film, presumably to destroy the prints, he found that the property had been already purchased by real-life ventriloquist, Edgar Bergen. Based on a story by Ben Hecht. ♫The New Step; I'm Laughing Ickey; I'm in Love With You; The Ga-Ga Bird; The Web of Love; Every Now and Then. 1929 82m/B Erich von Stroheim, Betty Compson, Don Douglas, Marjorie Kane; **D:** James Cruze. **VHS, Beta, 3/4U, Special order formats** $16.95 SNC, NOS, DVT ♫♫

The Great Gatsby Adaptation of F. Scott Fitzgerald's novel of the idle rich in the 1920s. A mysterious millionaire crashes Long Island society, and finds his heart captured by an impetuous and emotionally impoverished girl. Skillful acting and directing captures the look and feel of this era, but the movie doesn't have the power of the book. Screenplay by Francis Ford Coppola.

1974 (PG) 144m/C Robert Redford, Mia Farrow, Bruce Dern, Karen Black, Patsy Kensit, Howard da Silva, Sam Waterston, Howard da Silva, Edward Herrmann; *D:* Jack Clayton; *M:* Nelson Riddle. VHS, Beta, LV $19.95 *PAR, FCT* ⅛⅛½

The Great Gildersleeve Throckmorton P. Gildersleeve adds another problem to his list; the sister of a local judge wants to marry him. His niece and nephew won't allow it and his attempts to juggle everyone's desires make for fine fun. Peary was also the voice for the popular radio series of the same name.
1943 62m/B Harold Peary, Jane Darwell, Nancy Gates, Charles Arnt, Thurston Hall; *D:* Gordon Douglas. VHS *MED* ⅛½

Great Gold Swindle A dramatization of the 1982 swindling of the Perth Mint in Australia of over $650,000 worth of gold.
1984 101m/C John Hargreaves, Robert C. Hughes, Tony Rickards, Barbara Llewellyn. VHS, Beta $69.98 *LIV* ⅛⅛

The Great Gundown A violent tale set in the Old West. The peace of frontier New Mexico erupts when a half-breed Indian leads a brutal assault on an outlaw stronghold.
1975 98m/C Robert Padilla, Richard Rust, Milila St. Duval; *D:* Paul Hunt. VHS, Beta $29.95 *HHT, VID* ⅛⅛½

Great Guns Stan and Ollie enlist in the army to protect a spoiled millionaire's son but wind up being targets at target practice instead. Not one of their better efforts.
1941 74m/B Stan Laurel, Oliver Hardy, Sheila Ryan, Dick Nelson; *D:* Montague Banks. VHS, Beta $29.98 *FOX, MLB* ⅛⅛

Great Guy One of Cagney's lesser roles as an ex-boxer turned food inspector who wipes out graft in his town. *AKA:* Pluck of the Irish.
1936 50m/B James Cagney, Mae Clarke, Edward Brophy; *D:* John Blystone. VHS, Beta, 3/4U, Special order formats $19.95 *NOS, MRV, PSM* ⅛½

The Great Hunter A village militia captain and his girlfriend seek to destroy the men who killed the girl's father.
1975 91m/C Chia Ling, Wang Yu, Hsu Feng. VHS, Beta $29.95 *UNI* ⅛

The Great Impostor The true story of Ferdinand Waldo Demara, Jr., who during the 1950s, hoodwinked people by impersonating a surgeon, a college professor, a monk, a prison warden and a schoolteacher, with the FBI always one step behind him.
1961 112m/C Tony Curtis, Edmond O'Brien, Arthur O'Connell, Gary Merrill, Raymond Massey, Karl Malden, Mike Kellin, Frank Gorshin; *D:* Robert Mulligan. VHS, Beta $59.95 *MCA* ⅛⅛½

Great Jesse James Raid Jesse James comes out of retirement to carry out a mine theft. Routine.
1949 73m/C Willard Parker, Barbara Payton, Tom Neal, Wallace Ford; *D:* Reginald LeBorg. VHS, Beta *RXM, MRV* ⅛½

Great K & A Train Robbery A railroad detective is hired to find and stop the bandits who have been preying on the K & A Railroad. Silent.
1926 55m/B Tom Mix, Dorothy Dwan, William Walling, Harry Grippe, Carl Miller; *D:* Lewis Seiler. VHS, Beta $52.95 *GPV, GVV* ⅛⅛½

The Great Land of Small Two children enter a fantasy world and try to save it from Evil. For kids.
1986 (G) 94m/C Karen Elkin, Michael Blouin, Michael Anderson Jr., Ken Roberts; *D:* Vojta Jasny. VHS, Beta $19.95 *STE, NWV, HHE* ⅛⅛

Great Leaders of the Bibles The inspiring stories of two Old Testament heroes, Gideon and Samson, are dramatized in this beautifully constructed film.
197? 105m/C Ivo Garrani, Fernando Rey, Giorgio Ceridni. VHS, Beta $49.95 *UHV* ⅛⅛

The Great Lie A great soaper with Davis and Astor as rivals for the affections of Brent, an irresponsible flyer. Astor is the concert pianist who marries Brent and then finds out she's pregnant after he's presumed dead in a crash. The wealthy Davis offers to raise the baby so Astor can continue her career. But when Brent does return, who will it be to? Sparkling, catty fun. Astor's very short, mannish haircut became a popular trend.
1941 107m/B Bette Davis, Mary Astor, George Brent, Lucile Watson, Hattie McDaniel, Grant Mitchell, Jerome Cowan; *D:* Edmund Goulding. VHS, Beta, LV $19.95 *MGM, BTV* ⅛⅛⅛

The Great Locomotive Chase During the Civil War, Parker and his fellow soldiers head into Confederate territory to disrupt railroad supply lines. They take over a locomotive, but are pursued by Confederate Hunter, the conductor of another train; and soon a pursuit is underway. Based on the true story of Andrew's Raiders. *AKA:* Andrews' Raiders.
1956 85m/C Fess Parker, Jeffrey Hunter, Kenneth Tobey; *D:* Francis D. Lyon. VHS, Beta *DIS* ⅛⅛½

The Great Los Angeles Earthquake Made-for-TV disaster movie is the same old story; multiple soap-opera plotlines are spun around terrifying special effects, as L.A. is devastated by three major earth tremors and attendant disasters. Condensed from a two-part miniseries, also known as "The Big One: The Great Los Angeles Earthquake."
1991 106m/C Ed Begley Jr., Joanna Kerns; *D:* Larry Elikann. VHS, Beta $89.98 *VMK* ⅛½

Great Love Experiment Everyone in a high school learns a valuable lesson about beauty and friendship when four popular students try to change the personality of an awkward classmate.
1984 52m/C Tracy Pollan, Esal Morales, Kelly Wolf, Scott Benderer. VHS, Beta *NO* ⅛

The Great Lover Aboard an ocean liner, a bumbler chaperoning school kids gets involved with a gambler, a duchess and a murder. Vintage Bob Hope.
1949 80m/B Bob Hope, Rhonda Fleming, Roland Young, Roland Culver, George Reeves, Jim Backus; *D:* Alexander Hall. VHS, Beta $14.95 *COL, FCT* ⅛½

The Great Madcap A wealthy man believes in lavishly indulging himself which drives his excessively conservative family crazy. Bunuel satirizes behavioral extremes, Christianity, advertising, sex, and a number of other popular absurdities. In Spanish with English subtitles.
1949 90m/B *MX* Fernando Soler, Rosario Granados, Ruben Rogo; *D:* Luis Bunuel. VHS $79.95 *WBF, TAM* ⅛⅛

The Great Man Votes Alcoholic college professor Barrymore falls into a deep depression after his wife's death. His children then plan to create a situation wherein his vote will decide the fate of the new town mayor, thus instilling in him a newly found sense of importance for himself and his children. Satiric and funny.
1938 72m/B John Barrymore, Peter Holden, Virginia Weidler, Katherine Alexander, Donald MacBride, Elisabeth Risdon, Granville Bates, Luis Alberni, J.M. Kerrigan, William Demarest, Roy

Gordon; *D:* Garson Kanin. VHS, Beta $19.98 *TTC* ⅛⅛⅛

Great Massacre Sets the Robin Hood legend against the backdrop of Mainland China.
1969 95m/C VHS, Beta $29.98 *TWE* ⅛

The Great McGinty Sturges' directorial debut, about the rise and fall of a small-time, bribe-happy politician. As written by Sturges, an acerbic, ultra-cynical indictment of modern politics that stands, like much of his other work, as bracingly courageous as anything that's ever snuck past the Hollywood censors. Political party boss Tamiroff chews the scenery wih gusto while Donlevy, in his first starring role, is more than his equal as the not-so-dumb political hack. *AKA:* Down Went McGinty.
1940 82m/B Brian Donlevy, Muriel Angelus, Akim Tamiroff, Louis Jean Heydt, Arthur Hoyt, William Demarest; *W/D:* Preston Sturges. VHS, Beta, LV $14.98 *MCA* ⅛⅛½

Great McGonagall Tale of an unemployed Scot trying to become Britain's poet laureate. Sellers adds a semi-bright spot with his portrayal of Queen Victoria!
1975 95m/C *GB* Peter Sellers, Spike Milligan, Julia Foster; *D:* Joseph McGrath. VHS $49.95 *MOV* ⅛½

The Great Mike Unlikely but moving story of a young boy who convinces track management that his work horse has a chance against the touted thoroughbred. Sentimental, with little innovation, but generally well-acted.
1944 72m/B Stuart Erwin, Robert "Buzzy" Henry, Pierre Watkin, Gwen Kenyon, Carl "Alfalfa" Switzer, Edythe Elliott, Marion Martin; *D:* Wallace Fox. VHS $19.95 *NOS, TIM* ⅛½

Great Missouri Raid Follows the famous adventures of the James/Younger gang and their eventual demise.
1951 81m/C Wendell Corey, MacDonald Carey, Ellen Drew, Ward Bond; *D:* Gordon Douglas. VHS, Beta $19.95 *KRT* ⅛⅛

The Great Moment Story of the Boston dentist who discovered ether's use as an anesthetic in 1845. Confusing at times, changing from comedy to drama and containing flashbacks that add little to the story. Surprisingly bland result from ordinarily solid cast and director.
1944 87m/B Joel McCrea, Betty Field, Harry Carey Sr., William Demarest, Franklin Pangborn, Porter Hall; *D:* Preston Sturges. VHS, Beta $14.98 *MCA* ⅛⅛

The Great Mouse Detective Animated version of the book "Basil of Baker Street" by Eve Titus. Fun adventure about Sherlock-of-the-mouse-world. Not as good as some of the other Disney animated features, but kids will enjoy it nonetheless. In 1992 it was rereleased. *AKA:* The Adventures of the Great Mouse Detective.
1986 (G) 74m/C *D:* John Musker, Ron Clements, Dave Michener, Burny Mattinson; *V:* Vincent Price, Barrie Ingham, Val Bettin, Susanne Pollatschek, Candy Candido, Eve Brenner, Alan Young, Melissa Manchester. VHS, Beta, LV $24.99 *DIS, OM* ⅛⅛⅛

Great Movie Stunts & the Making of Raiders of the Lost Ark Two television specials: "Movie Stunts" demonstrates how major action sequences were designed and executed, and "Making of Raiders" captures the cast and crew as they tackle the many problems created in filming the spectacular scenes.
1981 107m/C Harrison Ford. VHS, Beta, LV $12.95 *PAR* ⅛⅛⅛

The Great Muppet Caper A group of hapless reporters (Kermit, Fozzie Bear, and Gonzo) travel to London to follow up on a major jewel robbery.
1981 (G) 95m/C Jim Henson's Muppets, Charles Grodin, Diana Rigg; *Cameos:* John Cleese, Robert Morley, Peter Ustinov, Peter Falk, Jack Warden; *D:* Jim Henson; *V:* Frank Oz. VHS, Beta, LV $22.99 JHV, FOX 🎬🎬

The Great Northfield Minnesota Raid The Younger/James gang decides to rob the biggest bank west of the Mississippi, but everything goes wrong. Uneven, offbeat western, but Duvall's portrayal of the psychotic Jesse James and Robertson's cunning Cole Younger are notable.
1972 (PG) 91m/C Cliff Robertson, Robert Duvall, Elisha Cook Jr., Luke Askew, R.G. Armstrong, Donald Moffatt, Matt Clark; *W/D:* Philip Kaufman. VHS, Beta $14.98 MCA 🎬🎬½

The Great Outdoors Good cast is mostly wasted in another John Hughes' tale of vacation gone bad. A family's peaceful summer by the lake is disturbed by their uninvited, trouble-making relatives. Aykroyd and Candy are two funny guys done in by a lame script that awkwardly examines friendship and coming of age and throws in a giant bear when things get unbearably slow. May be fun for small fry.
1988 (PG) 91m/C Dan Aykroyd, John Candy, Stephanie Faracy, Annette Bening, Chris Young, Lucy Deakins; *D:* Howard Deutch; *W:* John Hughes. VHS, Beta, LV $14.95 MCA 🎬🎬

Great Race A dastardly villain, a noble hero and a spirited suffragette are among the competitors in an uproarious New York-to-Paris auto race circa 1908, complete with pie fights, saloon brawls, and a confrontation with a feisty polar bear. Overly long and only sporadically funny.
1965 160m/C Jack Lemmon, Tony Curtis, Natalie Wood, Peter Falk, Keenan Wynn, George Macready; *D:* Blake Edwards. Academy Awards '65: Best Sound Effects Editing; Nominations: Best Color Cinematography, Best Film Editing, Best Song ("The Sweetheart Tree"), Best Sound. VHS, Beta, LV $19.98 WAR, PIA, FCT 🎬🎬½

Great Ride State police are after two dirt bikers who are riding through areas where bike riding is illegal.
1978 90m/C Perry Lang, Michael MacRae, Michael Sullivan; *D:* Don Hulette. VHS, Beta NO 🎬

The Great Riviera Bank Robbery A genius executes a bank robbery on the French Riviera netting fifteen million dollars. Based on a true story, the film chronicles the unfolding of the heist.
1979 98m/C Ian McShane, Warren Clarke, Stephen Greif, Christopher Malcolm; *D:* Francis Megahy. VHS, Beta $59.95 MPI 🎬🎬½

The Great Rupert Durante and family are befriended by a helpful squirrel (a puppet) in obtaining a huge fortune. Good fun; Durante shines.
1950 86m/B Jimmy Durante, Terry Moore, Tom Drake, Frank Orth, Sara Haden, Queenie Smith; *D:* Irving Pichel. VHS, Beta $19.98 DVT, HEG 🎬🎬🎬

Great St. Trinian's Train Robbery Train robbers hide their considerable loot in an empty country mansion only to discover, upon returning years later, it has been converted into a girls' boarding school. When they try to recover the money, the thieves run up against a band of pestiferous adolescent girls, with hilarious results. Based on the cartoon by Ronald Searle. Sequel to "The Pure Hell of St. Trinian's."

1966 90m/C *GB* Dora Bryan, Frankie Howerd, Reg Varney, Desmond Walter Ellis; *D:* Sidney Gilliat, Frank Launder. VHS, Beta $59.99 HBO 🎬🎬

The Great Santini Lt. Col. Bull Meechum, the "Great Santini," a Marine pilot now stationed stateside, fights a war involving his frustrated career goals, his repressed emotions, and his family. His family becomes his company of marines, as he abuses them in the name of discipline, because he doesn't allow himself any other way to show his affection. His teen-aged son is forced to face the realities of his father's shortcomings as well as his own, and the racism he witnesses in a small Southern town in the 1960s. With a standout performance by Duvall, the film successfully blends warm humor and tenderness with the harsh cruelties inherent with dysfunctional families and racism. Based on Pat Conroy's autobiographical novel, the movie was virtually undistributed when first released, and then re-released due to critical acclaim. *AKA:* Ace.
1980 (PG) 118m/C Robert Duvall, Blythe Danner, Michael O'Keefe, Julie Ann Haddock, Lisa Jane Persky, David Keith; *D:* Lewis John Carlino. Academy Awards '80 Nominations: Best Actor (Duvall), Best Supporting Actor (O'Keefe); Montreal World Film Festival '80: Best Actor (Duvall); National Board of Review Awards '80: 10 Best Films of the Year. VHS, Beta, 8mm $19.98 WAR 🎬🎬🎬

Great Scout & Cathouse Thursday Marvin and Reed vow to take revenge on their third partner, Culp, who made off with all their profits from a gold mine. The title refers to Marvin's May-December romance with prostitute Lenz. Already forgotten, unfunny, all-star comedy with cutesy title. *AKA:* Wildcat.
1976 (PG) 96m/C Lee Marvin, Oliver Reed, Robert Culp, Elizabeth Ashley, Kay Lenz; *D:* Don Taylor. VHS, Beta $69.98 LIV, VES 🎬½

The Great Skycopter Rescue Ruthless businessmen hire a motorcycle gang to terrorize and scare away the inhabitants of an oil-rich town. A local teenage flying enthusiast organizes his friends into an attack force to fight back.
1982 96m/C William Marshall, Aldo Ray, Russell Johnson, Terry Michos, Terry Taylor; *D:* Lawrence Foldes. VHS, Beta $59.95 MGM 🎬

Great Smokey Roadblock While in the hospital, a sixty-year-old truck driver's rig is repossessed by the finance company. Deciding that it's time to make one last perfect cross country run, he escapes from the hospital, steals his truck, picks up six prostitutes, heads off into the night with the police on his tail, and becomes a folk hero. *AKA:* Last of the Cowboys.
1976 (PG) 84m/C Henry Fonda, Eileen Brennan, Susan Sarandon, John Byner; *D:* John Leone. VHS, Beta $59.95 MED 🎬🎬

The Great Texas Dynamite Chase Two sexy young women drive across Texas with a carload of dynamite. They leave a trail of empty banks with the cops constantly on their trail. *AKA:* Dynamite Women.
1976 (R) 90m/C Claudia Jennings, Jocelyn Jones, Johnny Crawford, Chris Pennock, Tara Strohmeier, Miles Watkins, Bart Braverman; *D:* Michael Pressman. VHS, Beta $39.98 WAR, OM 🎬½

The Great Train Robbery A dapper thief arranges to heist the Folkstone bullion express in 1855, the first moving train robbery. A well-designed, fast-moving costume piece based on Crichton's best-selling novel.

Music by Jerry Goldsmith. *AKA:* The First Great Train Robbery.
1979 (PG) 111m/C *GB* Sean Connery, Donald Sutherland, Lesley-Anne Down, Alan Webb; *D:* Michael Crichton; *M:* Jerry Goldsmith. VHS, Beta, LV $19.98 MGM, FCT, HMV 🎬🎬🎬

The Great Train Robbery: Cinema Begins Three pioneering film shorts: "Billy Whiskers," a collection of Lumiere footage from their most famous films, and the title short.
1903 42m/B Billy Anderson; *D:* Edwin S. Porter, Auguste Lumiere, Hans A. Spanuth. VHS, Beta, 8mm $24.95 VYY 🎬🎬🎬

Great Treasure Hunt Four Western rogues help a blind man steal a wealthy crook's gold.
197? 90m/C Mark Damon, Stan Cooper, Luis Marin; *D:* Tonino Ricci. VHS, Beta $69.95 TWE 🎬

The Great Waldo Pepper Low key and (for Hill) less commercial film about a WWI pilot-turned-barnstormer who gets hired as a stuntman for the movies. Features spectacular World War I vintage aircraft flying sequences.
1975 (PG) 107m/C Robert Redford, Susan Sarandon, Margot Kidder, Bo Svenson, Scott Newman, Geoffrey Lewis, Edward Herrmann; *D:* George Roy Hill. VHS, Beta, LV $19.95 MCA 🎬🎬🎬

A Great Wall A Chinese-American family travels to mainland China to discover the country of their ancestry and to visit relatives. They experience radical culture shock. Wang's first independent feature. In English and Chinese with subtitles. *AKA:* The Great Wall is a Great Wall.
1986 (PG) 103m/C Peter Wang, Sharon Iwai, Kelvin Han Yee, Lin Qinqin; *D:* Peter Wang. VHS, Beta, LV $29.95 PAV, FCT, IME 🎬🎬🎬

The Great Wallendas The true story of the tragedies and triumphs of the Wallendas, a seven-person acrobatic family, who were noted for creating a pyramid on the high wire without nets below them. Made for television.
1978 96m/C Lloyd Bridges, Britt Ekland, Cathy Rigby; *D:* Larry Elikann. VHS, Beta NO 🎬🎬

The Great Waltz The first of two musical biographies on the life of Johann Strauss sees the musician quit his banking job to pursue his dream of becoming a successful composer. A fine, overlooked production rich with wonderful music and romantic comedy. ♫ Tales of Vienna Woods; There'll Come A Time; One Day When We Were Young; Voices of Spring; Du und Du; The Bat; I'm In Love With Vienna; Revolutionary March; There'll Come a Time; An Artist's Life; Only You; The Blue Danube.
1938 102m/B Luise Rainer, Fernand Gravet, Milza Korjus, Hugh Herbert, Lionel Atwill, Curt Bois, Leonid Kinskey, Al Shear, Minna Gombell, George Houston, Bert Roach, Herman Bing, Alma Kruger, Sig Rumann; *D:* Julien Duvivier. VHS $19.98 MGM, FOX, FCT 🎬🎬🎬

The Great War Two Italian soldiers find themselves in the midst of World War I, much against their will. They try a number of schemes to get out of fighting and working, but their circumstance dictates otherwise. Slightly muddled, but generally good acting. *AKA:* La Grande Guerre; La Grande Guerra.
1959 118m/B *FR IT* Vittorio Gassman, Alberto Sordi, Silvana Mangano, Folco Lulli; *D:* Mario Monicelli. VHS $69.95 FCT 🎬🎬

The Great White Hope A semi-fictionalized biography of boxer Jack Johnson, played by Jones, who became the first black heavyweight world champion in 1910. Alex-

ander makes her film debut as the boxer's white lover, as both battle the racism of the times. Two Oscar-nominated performances in what is essentially an ''opened-out'' version of the Broadway play.
1970 (PG) 103m/C James Earl Jones, Jane Alexander, Lou Gilbert, Joel Fluellen, Chester Morris, Robert Webber, Hal Holbrook, R.G. Armstrong, Moses Gunn, Scatman Crothers; **D:** Martin Ritt. **VHS, Beta $39.98** FOX, FCT ♪♪½

The Great Ziegfeld The big, bio-pic of the famous showman; acclaimed in its time as the best musical biography ever done, still considered the textbook for how to make a musical. Look for cameo roles by many famous stars, as well as a walk-on role by future First Lady Pat Nixon. The movie would have stood up as a first-rate biography of Ziegfeld, even without the drop-dead wonderful songs. ♪Won't You Come Play With Me?; It's Delightful to be Married; If You Knew Susie; Shine on Harvest Moon; A Pretty Girl is Like a Melody; You Gotta Pull Strings; She's a Follies Girl; You; You Never Looked So Beautiful; Queen of the Jungle; My Man; A Circus Must Be Different in a Ziegfeld Show; Rhapsody in Blue; On With the Motley; One Fine Day (Une Bel Di); Humoresque Number 7 in G Flat; Yiddle in Your Fiddle; Parade of the Glorified Girls; Look for the Silver Lining; March of the Musketeers; Ol' Man River; Makin' Whoopee; Rio Rita; Tulip Time; Someone Loves You After All.
1936 179m/B William Powell, Luise Rainer, Myrna Loy, Frank Morgan, Reginald Owen, Nat Pendleton, Ray Bolger, Virginia Bruce, Harriet Hocter, Ernest Cossart, Robert Greig, Gilda Gray, Leon Errol, Dennis Morgan, Mickey Daniels, William Demarest; *Cameos:* Fanny Brice; **D:** Robert Z. Leonard; **W:** William Anthony McGuire. Academy Awards '36: Best Actress (Rainer), Best Picture; Nominations: Best Director (Leonard), Best Film Editing, Best Interior Decoration, Best Story; New York Film Critics Awards '36: Best Actress (Rainer). **VHS, Beta, LV $29.98** MGM, BTV ♪♪♪½

The Greatest Autobiography of Cassius Clay, the fighter who could float like a butterfly and sting like a bee. Ali plays himself, and George Benson's hit ''The Greatest Love of All'' is introduced.
1977 (PG) 100m/C Muhammad Ali, Robert Duvall, Ernest Borgnine, James Earl Jones, John Marley, Roger E. Mosley, Dina Merrill, Paul Winfield; **D:** Tom Gries. **VHS, Beta $14.95** COL ♪♪

The Greatest Fights of Martial Arts A compilation of foreign filmdom's best head-kicking matches.
1987 50m/C VHS, Beta $9.95 SAT ♪½

The Greatest Flying Heroes Its up, up, and away with Superman, Flash Gordon, Rocky Jones and others as these flying heroes take to the skies. Also included is a sequence on man's early attempts at flight.
1991 50m/C VHS $14.98 WEM ♪½

The Greatest Show on Earth DeMille is in all his epic glory here in a tale of a traveling circus wrought with glamour, romance, mysterious clowns, a tough ringmaster, and a train wreck.
1952 149m/C Betty Hutton, Cornel Wilde, James Stewart, Charlton Heston, Dorothy Lamour, Lawrence Tierney; **D:** Cecil B. DeMille. Academy Awards '52: Best Picture, Best Story; Nominations: Best Costume Design (Color), Best Director (DeMille), Best Film Editing; Golden Globe Awards '53: Best Director (DeMille), Best Film—Drama. **VHS, Beta, LV $29.95** PAR, BTV ♪♪♪

The Greatest Story Ever Told Christ's journey from Galilee to Golgotha is portrayed here in true international-all-star-epic treatment by director Stevens. A lackluster version of Christ's life, remarkable only for Heston's out-of-control John the Baptist.
1965 196m/C Max von Sydow, Charlton Heston, Sidney Poitier, Claude Rains, Jose Ferrer, Telly Savalas, Angela Lansbury, Dorothy McGuire, John Wayne, Donald Pleasence, Carroll Baker, Van Heflin, Robert Loggia, Shelley Winters, Ed Wynn, Roddy McDowall; **D:** George Stevens. Academy Awards '65 Nominations: Best Art Direction/Set Decoration (Color), Best Color Cinematography, Best Costume Design (Color); National Board of Review Awards '65: 10 Best Films of the Year. **VHS, Beta, LV $29.98** MGM, PIA, RDG ♪♪

Greed A wife's obsession with money drives her husband to murder. Highly acclaimed. Although the original version's length (eight hours) was trimmed to 140 minutes, it remains one of the greatest silent films ever made. Effective use of Death Valley locations. Adapted from the Frank Norris novel, ''McTeague.''
1924 140m/B Dale Fuller, Gibson Gowland, ZaSu Pitts, Jean Hersholt, Chester Conklin; **D:** Erich von Stroheim. **VHS, LV $29.95** MGM ♪♪♪♪

The Greed of William Hart Reworking of the Burke and Hare legend has grave robbers providing Edinburgh medical students with the requisite cadavers. *AKA:* Horror Maniacs.
1948 78m/B *GB* Tod Slaughter, Henry Oscar, Jenny Lynn, Winifred Melville; **D:** Oswald Mitchell. **VHS $19.98** SNC ♪♪

Greedy Terror A cross-country motorcycle trip becomes a real nightmare when two young men realize they're being stalked by a maniac with a thirst for blood.
1978 90m/C Michael MacRae, Perry Lang. **VHS, Beta** NO ♪

Greek Street The owner of small cafe in London discovers a poor girl singing in the street for food. He takes her in and spotlights her songs in his cafe. *AKA:* Latin Love.
1930 51m/B *GB* Sari Maritza, Arthur Ahmbling, Martin Lewis; **D:** Sinclair Hill. **VHS, Beta $19.98** DVT, VYY, HEG ♪♪

The Greek Tycoon Old familiar story about widow of an American president who marries a billionaire shipping magnate and finds that money cannot buy happiness. A transparent depiction of the Onassis/Kennedy marriage, done to a turn.
1978 (R) 106m/C Anthony Quinn, Jacqueline Bisset, James Franciscus, Raf Vallone, Edward Albert; **D:** J. Lee Thompson. **VHS, Beta $59.95** MCA ♪½

Green Archer Fifteen episodes of the famed serial, featuring a spooked castle complete with secret passages and tunnels, trapdoors, and the mysterious masked figure, the Green Archer.
1940 283m/B Victor Jory, Iris Meredith, James Craven, Robert Fiske; **D:** James W. Horne. **VHS, Beta $49.95** NOS, VYY, VCN ♪♪

The Green Berets Cliched wartime heroics co-directed by Wayne and based on Robin Moore's novel. The Duke stars as a Special Forces colonel, leading his troops against the Viet Cong. Painfully insipid pro-war propaganda, notable as the only American film to come out in support of U.S. involvement in Vietnam. Truly embarrassing but did spawn the hit single ''Ballad of the Green Beret'' by Barry Sadler.
1968 (G) 135m/C John Wayne, David Janssen, Jim Hutton, Aldo Ray, George Takei, Raymond St. Jacques; **D:** John Wayne. **VHS, Beta, LV $19.98** WAR, TLF Woof!

Green Card Some marry for love, some for money, others for an apartment in the Big Apple. Refined but socially aware McDowell covets a commodious rent-controlled apartment in Manhattan. The lease stipulates that the apartment be let to a married couple. Enter brusque and burly Depardieu, who covets that elusive green card. To secure said lease and card, they consent to jump the broom. The counterpoint between McDowell, as a stuffy horticulturist, and Depardieu, as a French composer who has none of Cyrano's refinement, works well, and the two adroitly play a couple whose relationship covers the romantic continuum from loveless to love/hate to love less hate. Weir—who earlier directed ''Picnic at Hanging Rock'' and ''Dead Poet's Society,'' among others—is adept at creating an updated screwball-type comedy (he wrote the screenplay as well, with Depardieu in mind). If ''cute story'' and ''happy ending'' are descriptors you look for in a movie, you should find Depardieu's English-language debut entertaining. Nominated for three Golden Globe Awards in Musical/Comedy category: Best Picture, Best Actor (Depardieu) and Best Actress (MacDowell).
1990 (PG-13) 108m/C Gerard Depardieu, Andie MacDowell, Bebe Neuwirth, Gregg Edelman, Robert Prosky, Ann Wedgeworth, Ethan Phillips, Mary Louise Wilson, Lois Smith, Simon Jones; **W/D:** Peter Weir; **M:** Hans Zimmer. Academy Awards '90 Nominations: Best Original Screenplay; Golden Globe Awards '91: Best Actor—Musical/Comedy (Depardieu), Best Film—Musical/Comedy. **VHS, Beta, LV $19.99** TOU ♪♪½

Green Dolphin Street Flimsy romantic epic set in 19th century New Zealand. A young girl marries the beau she and her sister are battling over in this Oscar-winning special effects show which features one big earthquake. Based on the Elizabeth Goudge novel, this was one of MGM's biggest hits in 1947.
1947 161m/B Lana Turner, Van Heflin, Donna Reed, Edmund Gwenn; **D:** Victor Saville. Academy Awards '47: Best Special Effects; Nominations: Best Black and White Cinematography, Best Film Editing, Best Sound. **VHS, Beta $19.98** MGM ♪♪½

Green Dragon Inn When trying to escort an accused murderer to trial, a Ming court emissary finds himself battling against Kung Fu masters.
1982 94m/C Yue Hwa, Lo Lei, Shangkuan Ling-Feng. **VHS, Beta** WVE ♪

Green Eyes Winfield, an ex-GI, returns to post-war Vietnam to search for his illegitimate son who he believes will have green eyes. A highly acclaimed, made-for-television drama featuring moving performances from Winfield and Jonathan Lippe.
1976 100m/C Paul Winfield, Rita Tushingham, Jonathon Lippe, Victoria Racimo, Royce Wallace, Claudia Bryar; **D:** John Erman. **VHS $29.95** LIV ♪♪♪½

Green Fields A quiet romance based on Peretz Hirschbein's legendary tale of a young scholar of the Talmud who leaves the shelter of the synagogue in order to learn about people in the real world. The search takes him to the countryside where he finds himself in the middle of a battle between two families who both want him as a tutor and a suitor for their daughters. In Yiddish with English subtitles. *AKA:* Grine Felder; Gruner Felder.
1937 95m/B Michael Goldstein, Herschel Bernardi, Helen Beverly; **D:** Jacob Ben-Ami. **VHS, Beta $79.95** ERG, NCJ ♪♪½

Green for Danger A detective stages a chilling mock operation to find a mad killer stalking the corridors of a British hospital during World War II. Sim's first great claim to fame (pre-"A Christmas Carol").
1947 91m/B *GB* Trevor Howard, Alastair Sim, Leo Genn; *D:* Sidney Gilliat. **VHS, Beta, LV $59.95** *LCA, RXM* 🐾🐾

The Green Glove A jewel thief steals a beautiful relic from a tiny church. WWII makes it impossible for him to fence it and the church finds a relentless ally to track the thief. Excellent action sequences lift this standard plot slightly above the ordinary.
1952 88m/B Glenn Ford, Geraldine Brooks, Cedric Hardwicke, George Macready, Gaby Andre, Roger Treville, Juliette Greco, Jean Bretonniere; *D:* Rudolph Mate. **VHS $19.95** *NOS, FCT, TIM* 🐾🐾½

Green Grow the Rushes The English government tries to put a stop to brandy smuggling on the coast, but the townspeople drink up the evidence. A young Burton highlights this watered-down comedy. Based on a novel by co-scripter Harold Clewes. *AKA:* Brandy Ashore.
1951 77m/B *GB* Roger Livesey, Honor Blackman, Richard Burton, Frederick Leister; *D:* Derek Twist. **VHS $19.95** *NOS, TIM* 🐾🐾

Green Horizon A bucolic old codger faces a dilemma when he must choose between his granddaughter's future and his disaster-prone natural environment. *AKA:* Afurika Monogatari; A Tale of Africa.
1983 80m/C James Stewart, Philip Sayer, Elenora Vallone. **VHS, Beta $29.95** *FHE* 🐾½

The Green Hornet The feature version of the original serial, in which the Green Hornet and Kato have a series of crime-fighting adventures.
1940 100m/B Gordon Jones, Keye Luke, Anne Nagel, Wade Boteler, Walter McGrail, Douglas Evans, Cy Kendall. **VHS, Beta $49.95** *NOS, GKK, GPV* 🐾🐾🐾

Green Ice An American electronics expert gets involved with a brutal South American government dealing with emeralds and plans a heist with his girlfriend and other cohorts. A little bit of romance, a little bit of action, a lot of nothing much.
1981 109m/C *GB* Ryan O'Neal, Anne Archer, Omar Sharif, John Larroquette; *D:* Ernest Day. **VHS, Beta, LV $19.95** *JTC* 🐾½

Green Inferno A wealthy eccentric who lives deep in the South American jungle incites the natives to rebel. Mercenary agents are then hired to kill him.
198? 90m/C Richard Yesteran, Didi Sherman, Caesar Burner. **VHS, Beta** *NO* 🐾

The Green Man Maurice Allington (Finney), the alcoholic and randy owner of the Green Man Inn in rural England, jokes about the spirits that supposedly haunt the inn. It's not too funny, however, when he discovers the spirits are real and he has to figure out who the spirit of a 17th-century murderer is inhabiting before he kills again. A classy ghost story based on the novel by Kingsley Amis.
1991 150m/C *GB* Albert Finney, Sarah Berger, Linda Marlowe, Michael Hordern, Nickolas Grace; *D:* Elijah Moshinsky; *W:* Malcolm Bradbury. **VHS $89.95** *AAE, TAM, ART* 🐾🐾🐾

Green Pastures An adaptation of Marc Connelly's 1930 Pulitzer Prize-winning play which attempts to retell Biblical stories in Black English Vernacular of the '30s. Southern theater owners boycotted the controversial film which had an all-Black cast.
1936 93m/C Rex Ingram, Oscar Polk, Eddie Anderson, George Reed, Abraham Graves, Myrtle Anderson, Frank Wilson; *D:* William Keighley, Marc Connelly. **VHS, Beta $19.98** *MGM, MOV, FOX* 🐾🐾🐾

The Green Promise A well-meaning but domineering farmer and his four motherless children face disaster as a result of the father's obstinacy. But when he is laid up, the eldest daughter takes over, tries modern methods and equipment, and makes the farm a success. *AKA:* Raging Waters.
1949 90m/B Walter Brennan, Marguerite Chapman, Robert Paige, Natalie Wood; *D:* William D. Russell. **VHS, Beta $24.95** *NOS, DVT, TIM* 🐾🐾

The Green Room Truffaut's haunting tale of a man who, valuing death over life, erects a shrine to all the dead he has known. Offered a chance at love, he cannot overcome his obsessions to take the risk. Based on the Henry James story "Altar of the Dead." In French with subtitles. *AKA:* La Chambre Verte.
1978 (PG) 95m/C *FR* Francois Truffaut, Nathalie Baye, Jean Daste; *D:* Francois Truffaut. **VHS, Beta $19.98** *MGM* 🐾🐾

The Green Slime Danger and romance highlight the journey of a space ship assigned to intercept an oncoming asteroid. Little do the astronauts realize, but they have brought aboard the ship the malevolent alien creatures known as green slime (and we ain't talking jello here). Cheap, U.S./Japanese co-production will leave you feeling lousy in the morning. The title song is legendary among genre aficionados. *AKA:* Gamma Sango Uchu Daisakusen; Battle Beyond the Stars; Death and the Green Slime.
1968 (G) 90m/C *JP* Robert Horton, Richard Jaeckel, Lucianna Paluzzi, Bud Widom, Ted Gunther, Robert Dunham; *D:* Kinji Fukasaku. **VHS, Beta** *MGM Woof!*

The Green Wall A city-dwelling young man attempts to homestead with his family in the Amazon. A lovely and tragic film with stunning photography of the Peruvian forests. First Peruvian feature to be shown in the U.S. In Spanish with English subtitles.
1970 110m/C *SP* Julio Aleman, Sandra Riva; *W/ D:* Armando Robles. **VHS $79.95** *FCT, DVT, HEG* 🐾🐾

Greenstone The green stone is a glowing rock in the forbidden forest that conveys a young boy into an exciting new world.
1985 (G) 48m/C Joseph Corey, John Riley, Kathleen Irvine, Jack Mauck; *D:* Kevin Irvine. **VHS, Beta $19.95** *AHV* 🐾🐾

Greetings De Niro stars in this wild and crazy comedy about a man who tries to help his friend flunk his draft physical. One of DePalma's first films, and a pleasantly anarchic view of the late '60s, wrought with a light, intelligent tone. Followed by the sequel "Hi, Mom."
1968 (R) 88m/C Robert De Niro, Gerrit Graham, Allen Garfield; *D:* Brian DePalma. **VHS, Beta, LV $79.95** *VMK* 🐾🐾🐾

Gregory's Girl The sweet, disarming comedy that established Forsyth. An awkward young Scottish schoolboy falls in love with the female goalie of his soccer team. He turns to his ten-year-old sister for advice, but she's more interested in ice cream than love. His best friend is no help, either, since he has yet to fall in love. A perfect mirror of teenagers and their instantaneous, raw, and all-consuming loves. Very sweet scene with Gregory and his girl lying on their backs in an open space illustrates the simultaneous simplicity and complexity of young love.
1980 91m/C *GB* Gordon John Sinclair, Dee Hepburn, Jake D'Arcy, Chic Murray, Alex Norton, John Bett, Claire Grogan; *D:* Bill Forsyth. **VHS, Beta $69.98** *SUE, TVC* 🐾🐾🐾½

Gremlins Comedy horror with deft satiric edge. Produced by Spielberg. Fumbling gadget salesman Rand Peltzer is looking for something really special to get his son Billy. He finds it in a small store in Chinatown. The wise shopkeeper is reluctant to sell him the adorable "mogwai" but relents after fully warning him "Don't expose him to bright light, don't ever get him wet, and don't ever, ever feed him after midnight." Naturally, this all happens and the result is a gang of nasty gremlins who decide to tear up the town on Christmas Eve. Followed by "Gremlins 2, the New Batch" which is less black comedy, more parody, and perhaps more inventive.
1984 (PG) 106m/C Zach Galligan, Phoebe Cates, Hoyt Axton, Polly Holliday, Frances Lee McCain, Keye Luke, Dick Miller, Corey Feldman, Judge Reinhold; *D:* Joe Dante; *M:* Jerry Goldsmith. **VHS, Beta, LV, 8mm $19.98** *WAR, TLF* 🐾🐾🐾

Gremlins 2: The New Batch The sequel to "Gremlins" is superior to the original, which was quite good. Set in a futuristic skyscraper in the Big Apple, director Dante presents a less violent but far more campy vision, paying myriad surreal tributes to scores of movies, including "The Wizard of Oz" and musical extravaganzas of the past. Also incorporates a Donald Trump parody, takes on television news, and body slams modern urban living. Great fun.
1990 (PG-13) 107m/C Phoebe Cates, Christopher Lee, John Glover, Zach Galligan; *Cameos:* Jerry Goldsmith; *D:* Joe Dante; *M:* Jerry Goldsmith. **VHS, Beta, LV, 8mm $19.95** *WAR, HHE* 🐾🐾🐾½

Grendel, Grendel, Grendel An utterly urbane dragon wants to be friends, but for some reason people are just terrified of Grendel. It's true, he bites a head off once in a while, but nobody's perfect! An ingenious, animated retelling of Beowulf.
1982 90m/C *AU D:* Alexander Stitt; *V:* Peter Ustinov, Arthur Dignam, Julie McKenna, Keith Michell. **VHS, Beta $29.95** *FHE* 🐾🐾

Greta During World War II, a young Polish boy escapes from a detention camp. Now on the run, several bizarre twists of fate place him in the care of Greta, a young girl whose father is an officer in the S.S. In Polish with English subtitles.
1986 60m/C *PL* Janusz Grabowski, Agnieszka Kruszewska, Eva Borowik, Tomasz Grochoczki, Andrzej Precig; *D:* Krzysztof Gruber. **VHS, Beta $39.50** *EVD, TAM* 🐾🐾🐾

The Grey Fox A gentlemanly old stagecoach robber tries to pick up his life after thirty years in prison. Unable to resist another heist, he tries train robbery, and winds up hiding out in British Columbia where he meets an attractive photographer, come to document the changing West. Farnsworth is perfect as the man who suddenly finds himself in the 20th century trying to work at the only craft he knows. Based on the true story of Canada's most colorful and celebrated outlaw, Bill Miner.
1983 (PG) 92m/C *CA* Richard Farnsworth, Jackie Burroughs, Wayne Robson, Timothy Webber, Ken Pogue; *D:* Phillip Borsos. **VHS, Beta, LV $19.95** *MED* 🐾🐾🐾

Grey Gardens For Jackie Kennedy fans, a documentary sure to shock. Filmed in her 79-year-old aunt's rotting Long Island mansion, we're allowed to witness the reclusive Big Edith and her 56-year-old daughter, Little

Edie, singing, dancing, and fighting in this most bizarre of documentaries.
1976 94m/C D: Al Maysles, David Maysles. **VHS $79.95** FCT, KIV ⅛⅛⅛½

Greyfriars Bobby A true story of a Skye terrier named Bobby who, after his master dies, refuses to leave the grave. Even after being coaxed by the local children into town, he still returns to the cemetery each evening. Word of his loyalty spreads, and Bobby becomes the pet of 19th century Edinburgh. Nicely told, with fine location photography and good acting. Great for children and animal lovers.
1961 91m/C Donald Crisp, Laurence Naismith, Kay Walsh; **D:** Don Chaffey. **VHS $69.95** DIS ⅛⅛½

Greystoke: The Legend of Tarzan, Lord of the Apes The seventh Earl of Greystoke becomes a shipwrecked orphan and is raised by apes. Ruling the ape-clan in the vine-swinging persona of Tarzan, he is discovered by an anthropologist and returned to his ancestral home in Scotland, where he is immediately recognized by his grandfather. The contrast between the behavior of man and ape is interesting, and Tarzan's introduction to society is fun, but there's no melodrama or cliffhanging action, as we've come to expect of the Tarzan genre. Due to her heavy southern accent, Andie McDowell (as Jane) had her voice dubbed by Glenn Close.
1984 (PG) 130m/C Christopher Lambert, Ralph Richardson, Ian Holm, James Fox, Andie MacDowell, Ian Charleson, Cheryl Campbell, Nigel Davenport; **D:** Hugh Hudson. **VHS, Beta, LV $19.98** WAR ⅛⅛

Grievous Bodily Harm Morris Martin's wife Claudine is missing. When he finds a videotape of Claudine in very compromising positions, he becomes murderously determined to find out where she has gone.
1989 (R) 136m/C John Waters, Colin Friels, Bruno Lawrence; **D:** Mark Joffe. **VHS, Beta $29.95** FRH ⅛⅛

Griffin and Phoenix: A Love Story A sentimental film about the mortality of two vital people. Falk deserts his family when he learns he has terminal cancer. Clayburgh, also terminally ill, meets him for a short but meaningful affair. Good performances help overcome the tear-jerker aspects of the story. Made for television.
1976 110m/C Peter Falk, Jill Clayburgh, Dorothy Tristan, John Lehne; **D:** Daryl Duke. **VHS $59.98** FOX ⅛⅛½

Griffith Biograph Program Some of the best Biograph shorts are featured: "The Lonely Villa," "The Lonedale Operator," "The New York Hat," "Friends," and "The Unseen Enemy," all produced between 1909 and 1912.
1909 50m/B Mary Pickford, Blanche Sweet, Lillian Gish, Dorothy Gish; **D:** D.W. Griffith. **VHS, Beta, LV** GVV ⅛⅛½

The Grifters Evocative rendering of a terrifying sub-culture. Huston, Cusak, and Bening are con artists, struggling to stay on top in a world where violence, money, and lust are the prizes. Bening and Huston fight for Cusak's soul, while he's determined to decide for himself. Seamless performances and dazzling atmosphere, along with superb pacing, make for a provocative film. Based on a novel by Jim Thompson.
1990 114m/C Anjelica Huston, John Cusack, Annette Bening, Pat Hingle, J.T. Walsh, Charles Napier, Henry Jones, Gailard Sartain; **D:** Stephen Frears; **W:** Donald E. Westlake. Academy Awards '90 Nominations: Best Actress (Huston), Best Adapted Screenplay, Best Director (Frears),

Best Supporting Actress (Bening); Independent Spirit Awards '91: Best Actress (Huston), Best Film; Los Angeles Film Critics Association Awards '90: Best Actress (Huston); National Society of Film Critics Awards '90: Best Actress (Huston), Best Supporting Actress (Bening). **VHS, Beta, LV $19.98** MCA, HBO, PIA ⅛⅛⅛½

Grim Prairie Tales A city slicker and a crazed mountain man meet by a campfire in the high plains one night and pass the time sharing four tales of Western horror. Dourif and Jones are fun, the stories scary, making for an interesting twist on both the horror and the Western genres.
1989 (R) 90m/C Brad Dourif, James Earl Jones, Marc McClure, William Atherton, Scott Paulin; **W/D:** Wayne Coe. **VHS, LV $29.95** ACA, FCT ⅛⅛

The Grim Reaper 22-year-old Bertolucci directed his first feature with this grim and brutal treatment of the investigation of the murder of a prostitute, told via flashbacks and from the disparate perspectives of three people who knew the woman. A commercial bust, the critics were no kinder than the public at the time; not until two years later, with "Before the Revolution," did Bertolucci earn his directorial spurs. The script was written by Pasolini, with whom the erstwhile poet had collaborated on "Accattone" the previous year (as assistant). In Italian with English subtitles. **AKA:** La Commare Secca.
1962 100m/B IT Francesco Rulu, Giancarlo de Rosa; **D:** Bernardo Bertolucci; **W:** Pier Paolo Pasolini. **VHS, LV $29.95** CVC, FCT, TAM ⅛⅛⅛

Grim Reaper Mia Farrow's sister is one of a group of American students vacationing on a Greek island. Farrow learns of the twisted cannibalistic murderer who methodically tries to avenge the tragic deaths of his family.
1981 (R) 81m/C IT Tisa Farrow, George Eastman; **D:** Joe D'Amato. **VHS, Beta $39.95** MON ⅛½

The Grissom Gang Remake of the 1948 British film "No Orchids for Miss Blandish." Darby is a wealthy heiress kidnapped by a family of grotesques, led by a sadistic mother. The ransom gets lost in a series of bizarre events, and the heiress appears to be falling for one of her moronic captors. Director Robert Aldrich skillfully blends extreme violence with dark humor. Superb camera work, editing, and 1920s period sets.
1971 (R) 127m/C Kim Darby, Scott Wilson, Tony Musante, Ralph Waite, Connie Stevens, Robert Lansing, Wesley Addy; **D:** Robert Aldrich. **VHS $29.99** FOX ⅛⅛⅛

Grit of the Girl Telegrapher/In the Switch Tower A pair of silent railroad dramas, which feature thrilling chase sequences, nefarious schemers and virginal heroines. Silent with piano scores by Jon Mirsalis.
1915 47m/B Anna Q. Nilsson, Hal Clements, Walter Edwards, Frank Borzage. **VHS, Beta $19.98** CCB, PEN ⅛⅛⅛

Grizzly Giant, killer grizzly terrorizes a state park in this blatant "Jaws" rip-off. From the same folks who produced "Abby," a blatant "Exorcist" rip-off. Filmed in Georgia. **AKA:** Killer Grizzly.
1976 (PG) 92m/C Christopher George, Richard Jaeckel, Andrew Prine, Victoria (Vicki) Johnson, Charles Kissinger; **D:** William Girdler. **VHS, Beta $9.95** MED ⅛

Grizzly Adams: The Legend Continues A small town is saved from three desperados by Grizzly and his huge grizzly bear pet, Martha.
1990 90m/C Gene Edwards, Link Wyler, Red West, Tony Caruso, Acquanetta, L.Q. Jones; **D:** Ken Kennedy. **VHS** NO ⅛½

Grizzly Golfer When Magoo and his nephew Waldo tee off at the Ozark Hollow Golf Club, a bear becomes involved in the game. Part of the "Mister Magoo" series.
1951 7m/C V: Jim Backus. **VHS, Beta** CHF ⅛½

Grizzly Mountain Man moves to the Sierra Mountains and befriends an Indian.
1980 96m/C VHS, Beta NO ⅛½

The Groove Tube A television series called "The Groove Tube" is the context for these skits that spoof everything on television from commercials to newscasts. Chevy Chase's movie debut.
1972 75m/C Ken Sarasohn, Chevy Chase, Richard Belzer, Marcy Mendham, Bill Kemmill; **D:** Ken Shapiro. **VHS, Beta $19.95** MED ⅛½

Gross Anatomy Light-weight comedy/drama centering on the trials and tribulations of medical students. Modine is the very bright, but somewhat lazy, future doctor determined not to buy into the bitter competition among his fellow students. His lack of desire inflames Lahti, a professor dying of a fatal disease who nevertheless believes in modern medicine. She pushes and inspires him to focus on his potential, and his desire to help people. Worth watching, in spite of cheap laughs. Interesting cast of up-and-comers.
1989 (PG-13) 107m/C Matthew Modine, Daphne Zuniga, Christine Lahti, John Scott Clough, Alice Carter, Robert Desiderio, Zakes Mokae, Todd Field; **D:** Thom Eberhardt. **VHS, Beta, LV $19.99** TOU ⅛⅛½

Gross Jokes The comic producers used Julius Alvin's best-selling book as the inspiration for this joke-fest. Filmed at L.A.'s Improv.
1985 53m/C Tommy Sledge, Barry Diamond, Budd Friedman. **VHS, Beta $29.95** MCA ⅛⅛½

Grotesque After slaughtering a young woman's family as they vacationed in a remote mountain cabin, a gang of bloodthirsty punks are attacked by the family secret, the deformed son. The title says it all.
1987 (R) 79m/C Linda Blair, Tab Hunter, Guy Stockwell, Donna Wilkes, Nels Van Patten; **D:** Joe Tornatore. **VHS, Beta, LV $79.95** MED Woof!

Ground Zero Political thriller, set in the Australian outback in the fifties, in which a man searches for the reasons for his father's murder in the films of the British nuclear tests.
1988 (R) 109m/C AU Colin Friels, Jack Thompson, Donald Pleasence, Natalie Bate, Simon Chilvers, Neil Fitzpatrick, Bob Maza; **D:** Michael Pattinson, Bruce Myles. **VHS, Beta, LV $14.95** LIV ⅛⅛⅛

Ground Zero Ground Zero is the term used to describe the site of a nuclear explosion. San Francisco is threatened with just such a new name in this story of nuclear blackmail. Someone plants an atomic bomb on the Golden Gate Bridge. It must be defused and the culprit caught.
1988 (R) 90m/C Ron Casteel, Melvin Belli, Yvonne D'Angiers; **D:** James T. Flocker. **VHS, Beta $39.95** GHV, VTR ⅛½

Groundhog Day Phil, (Murray) an obnoxious weatherman, is in Punxatawney, PA to cover the annual emergence of the famous rodent from its hole. After he's caught in a blizzard that he didn't predict, he finds himself trapped in a time warp, doomed to relive the same day over and over again until he gets it right. Not surprisingly, he realizes he can be even more obnoxious than usual since tomorrow will never come. He also tries to woo producer MacDowell with new approaches each day. Lighthearted romantic comedy takes a funny premise and manages to carry it through to the end. Murray has fun with the role, although he did get bitten by the groundhog during the scene when they're driving. Elliot, who has been missed since his days as the man under the seats on "Late Night with David Letterman" is perfectly cast as a smart-mouthed cameraman. **1993 (PG) 103m/C** Marita Geraghty, Bill Murray, Andie MacDowell, Chris Elliott, Stephen Tobolowsky, Brian Doyle-Murray, Angela Paton; **D:** Harold Ramis; **W:** Harold Ramis, Daniel F. Rubin; **M:** George Fenton. VHS, LV *NYR ♫♫♫*

The Groundstar Conspiracy Spy thriller brings to life L.P. Davies' novel, "The Alien." After an explosion kills all but one space project scientist, Peppard is sent to investigate suspicions of a cover-up. Meanwhile, the surviving scientist (Sarrazin) suffers from disfigurement and amnesia. He pursues his identity while Peppard accuses him of being a spy. Splendid direction by Lamont Johnson. Sarrazin's best role. **1972 (PG) 96m/C CA** George Peppard, Michael Sarrazin, Christine Belford, Cliff Potts, James Olson, Tim O'Connor, James McEachin, Alan Oppenheimer; **D:** Lamont Johnson. VHS $59.95 *MCA ♫♫♫*

The Group Based upon the novel by Mary McCarthy, the well-acted story deals with a group of graduates from a Vassar-like college as they try to adapt to life during the Great Depression. Has some provocative subject matter, including lesbianism, adultery, and mental breakdowns. Soapy, but a good cast with film debuts of Bergen, Hackett, Pettet, Widdoes, and Holbrook. **1966 150m/C** Candice Bergen, Joanna Pettet, Shirley Knight, Joan Hackett, Elizabeth Hartman, Jessica Walter, Larry Hagman, Kathleen Widdoes, Hal Holbrook, Mary-Robin Redd, Richard Mulligan, James Broderick, Carrie Nye; **D:** Sidney Lumet. VHS, Beta $59.98 *FOX ♫♫½*

Group Marriage Six young professionals fall into a marriage of communal convenience and rapidly discover the many advantages and drawbacks of their thoroughly modern arrangement. **1972 (R) 90m/C** Victoria Vetri, Aimee Eccles, Zack Taylor, Jeff Pomerantz, Claudia Jennings, Jayne Kennedy, Milt Kamen; **D:** Stephanie Rothman. VHS, Beta $39.95 *UHV ♫♫½*

Growing Pains A young couple discover that their newly adopted son possesses extraordinary powers. **1982 60m/C** Gary Bond, Barbara Keilermann, Norman Beaton. VHS, Beta $29.95 *LIV ♫½*

Grown Ups A journalist watches his family slowly disintegrating around him in this adaptation of Jules Feiffer's play. **1986 106m/C** Jean Stapleton, Martin Balsam, Charles Grodin, Marilu Henner, Kerry Segal; **D:** John Madden. VHS, Beta $59.95 *LHV, WAR ♫♫*

Gruesome Twosome Another guts/cannibalism/mutilation fun-fest by Lewis, about someone who's marketing the hair of some very recently deceased college coeds. **1967 75m/C** Elizabeth Davis, Chris Martell; **D:** Herschell Gordon Lewis. VHS, Beta $39.98 *RHI ♫*

Grunt! The Wrestling Movie A spoof of documentaries about the behind-the-scenes world of wrestling. For fans only. **1985 (R) 91m/C** Wally Greene, Steven Cepello, Dick Murdoch, John Tolos; **D:** Allan Holzman. VHS, Beta $19.95 *STE, NWV Woof!*

Gryphon Ricky's new teacher can do all sorts of magical things. Hidden among her tricks are lessons about creativity, beauty, and imagination. Aired on PBS as part of the "Wonderworks" family movie series.

1988 58m/C Amanda Plummer, Sully Diaz, Alexis Cruz; **D:** Mark Cullingham. VHS $29.95 *PME, FCT, HMV Woof!*

Guadalcanal Diary A vintage wartime flag-waver, with a typical crew of Marines battling the "Yellow Menace" over an important base on the famous Pacific atoll. Based on Richard Tregaskis' first-hand account. **1943 93m/B** Preston Foster, Lloyd Nolan, William Bendix, Richard Conte, Anthony Quinn, Richard Jaeckel, Roy Roberts, Minor Watson, Miles Mander, Ralph Byrd, Lionel Stander, Reed Hadley; **D:** Lewis Seiler. VHS, Beta, LV $39.98 *FOX, IME ♫♫½*

The Guardian Residents of a chic New York apartment building hire a security expert/ex-military man to aid them in combatting their crime problem. But one of the liberal tenants thinks their guard's methods may come at too high a cost. Made for cable television. **1984 (R) 102m/C** Martin Sheen, Louis Gossett Jr., Arthur Hill; **D:** David Greene. VHS, Beta, LV $69.98 *LIV, VES ♫½*

The Guardian A young couple unwittingly hires a human sacrificing druid witch as a babysitter for their child. Based on the book "The Nanny" by Dan Greenburg. **1990 (R) 92m/C** Jenny Seagrove, Dwier Brown, Carey Lowell; **D:** William Friedkin. VHS, Beta, LV $19.98 *MCA ♫*

Guardian of the Abyss A young couple who buy an antique mirror get more than they bargained for when they discover that it is the threshold to Hell and the devil wants to come through. **1982 60m/C** Ray Lonnen, Rosalyn Landor, Paul Darrow, Barbara Ewing; **D:** Don Sharp. VHS, Beta $29.95 *LIV ♫*

The Guardsman Broadway's illustrious couple Lunt and Fontanne shine in this adaptation of the clever marital comedy by French playwright Molnar in which they also starred. This sophisticated comedy was their only starring film, although they were offered large sums of money to appear in other movies—they just couldn't tear themselves away from the stage. Remade as "The Chocolate Soldier" and "Lily in Love." **1931 89m/B** Alfred Lunt, Lynn Fontanne, Roland Young, ZaSu Pitts, Maude Eburne, Herman Bing, Ann Dvorak; **D:** Sidney Franklin. VHS $19.98 *MGM ♫♫♫*

Guerilla Brigade A rarely seen Ukrainian epic about Russian/Ukrainian solidarity during the Civil War. In Russian with English subtitles. Also called "Riders." **1939 90m/B** *RU D:* Igor Savchenko. VHS, Beta $59.95 *FCT ♫½*

Guess What We Learned in School Today? Parents in a conservative suburban community protest sex education in the schools. Intended as a satire, but it only reinforces stereotypes. **1970 (R) 85m/C** Richard Carballo, Devin Goldenberg; **D:** John G. Avildsen. VHS, Beta *PGN Woof!*

Guess Who's Coming to Dinner Controversial in its time. A young white woman brings her black fiance home to meet her parents. The situation truly tests their open-mindedness and understanding. Hepburn and Tracy (in his last film appearance) are wonderful and serve as the anchors in what would otherwise have been a rather sugary film (although the screenplay won an Academy Award). Houghton, who portrays the independent daughter, is the real-life niece of Hepburn who garnered an Oscar for her performance.

1967 108m/C Katharine Hepburn, Spencer Tracy, Sidney Poitier, Katherine Houghton, Cecil Kellaway; **D:** Stanley Kramer; **W:** William Rose. Academy Awards '67: Best Actress (Hepburn), Best Original Screenplay; Nominations: Best Actor (Tracy), Best Picture, Best Supporting Actor (Kellaway); British Academy Awards '68: Best Actor (Tracy), Best Actress (Hepburn). VHS, Beta, LV $14.95 *COL, FCT, COL ♫♫♫*

Guest in the House A seemingly friendly young female patient is invited to stay in the family home of her doctor. She skillfully attempts to dissect the family's harmony in the process. **1945 121m/B** Anne Baxter, Ralph Bellamy, Ruth Warrick, Marie McDonald, Margaret Hamilton; **D:** John Brahm. VHS, Beta, 3/4U, Special order formats $19.95 *NOS, CAB, VYY ♫♫½*

Guest Wife Determined to impress his sentimental boss, a quick-thinking bachelor talks his best friend's wife into posing as his own wife, but the hoax gets a bit out of hand and nearly ruins the real couple's marriage. **1945 90m/B** Claudette Colbert, Don Ameche, Dick Foran, Charles Dingle, Wilma Francis; **D:** Sam Wood. VHS *REP ♫♫½*

A Guide for the Married Man One suburban husband instructs another in adultery, with a cast of dozens enacting various slapstick cameos. Based on Frank Tarloff's novel of the same name. Followed by "A Guide for the Married Woman." **1967 91m/C** Walter Matthau, Robert Morse, Inger Stevens, Sue Ann Langdon, Claire Kelly, Elaine Devry; **Cameos:** Lucille Ball, Sid Caesar, Jack Benny, Wally Cox, Jayne Mansfield, Louis Nye, Carl Reiner, Phil Silvers, Terry-Thomas, Sam Jaffe, Jeffrey Hunter, Polly Bergen; **D:** Gene Kelly; **W:** Frank Tarloff; **M:** John Williams. VHS, Beta $59.98 *FOX ♫♫♫*

A Guide for the Married Woman A bored housewife tries to take the romantic advice of a girlfriend to add a little spice to her life. A poor made-for-television follow-up to "A Guide for the Married Man." **1978 96m/C** Cybill Shepherd, Barbara Feldon, Eve Arden, Chuck Woolery, Peter Marshall, Charles Frank; **D:** Hy Averback. VHS, Beta $59.95 *FOX ♫½*

Guilty as Charged A butcher rigs his own private electric chair and captures and executes paroled killers in his personal quest for justice. But when a politician frames an innocent man for murder how far will this vigilante go? **1992 (R) 95m/C** Rod Steiger, Lauren Hutton, Heather Graham, Isaac Hayes; **D:** Sam Irvin. VHS, LV $89.98 *COL ♫♫*

Guilty as Sin Johnson stars as a ruthless Casanova accused of murdering his very wealthy wife. After seeing her win another trial he decides lawyer DeMornay is just the woman to defend him. His persuasive charm does the trick but he's obviously dangerous, she finds out too much, and it may prove fatal. Johnson has fun with this menacing smoothie but De Mornay's supposedly hotshot criminal attorney is just plain dumb. It sounds like "Jagged Edge" but there's no sexual involvement between client and lawyer and no thrill in this thriller. **1993 (R) 104m/C** Don Johnson, Rebecca DeMornay, Jack Warden, Stephen Lang, Dana Ivey, Ron White, Sean McCann, Luis Guzman; **D:** Sidney Lumet; **W:** Larry Cohen. VHS *NYR ♫♫*

Guilty by Suspicion Examination of the 1950's McCarthy investigations by the House Un-American Activities Committee comes off like a bland history lesson. DeNiro plays a director who attended a Communist party meeting in the '30s but who otherwise doesn't have any red connections. He takes the moral high ground and refuses to incrimi-

G

nate his buddy (Wendt) to get off the hook and finds himself blacklisted. Characterized by average performances (excepting Wettig who goes overboard) and a lightweight script. "The Front" (1976) does a better job on this topic. Directorial debut for producer Winkler. Available in widescreen on laserdisc.
1991 (PG-13) 105m/C Robert De Niro, Annette Bening, George Wendt, Patricia Wettig, Sam Wanamaker, Chris Cooper, Ben Piazza, Martin Scorsese, Barry Primus, Gailard Sartain, Stuart Margolin, Barry Tubb, Roxann Biggs, Robin Gammell, Brad Sullivan; **W/D:** Irwin Winkler; **M:** James Newton Howard. **VHS, LV, 8mm $19.98** WAR &&&

Guilty of Innocence A young African-American man finds he's guilty until proven innocent when he runs into the law in Texas. A bold lawyer joins his fight for justice. Based on a true story and made for television.
1987 (PG) 95m/C Dorian Harewood, Dabney Coleman, Hoyt Axton, Paul Winfield, Dennis Lipscomb, Debbi Morgan, Marshall Colt, Victor Love; **D:** Richard T. Heffron. **VHS $89.98** VMK &&

Guilty of Treason A documentary on the life and times of Joszef Cardinal Mindszenty of Hungary, who was imprisoned by the communists as an enemy of the state for speaking out against the totalitarian regime. At the trial, it was revealed that the Cardinal's confession was obtained only by the use of drugs, hypnosis, and torture. A realistic look at the dark side of Communism.
1950 86m/B Charles Bickford, Paul Kelly, Bonita Granville, Richard Derr, Berry Kroeger, Elisabeth Risdon, Roland Winters, John Banner; **D:** Felix Feist. **VHS $24.95** NOS, MRV, TIM &&1/2

Guitarras Lloren Guitarras A popular artist gets frustrated when the girl he loves falls for his brother.
1947 111m/B MX Cuco Sanchez, Lucha Villa, Fernando Soto Mantequilla. **VHS, Beta $54.95** MAD &&1/2

Gulag An American sportscaster is wrongly sentenced to ten years of hard labor in a Soviet prison, and plans his escape from the cruel guards. Good suspense. Made for television.
1985 130m/C GB David Keith, Malcolm McDowell, David Suchet, Warren Clarke; **D:** Roger Young. **VHS, Beta $69.95** PSM &&&1/2

Gulliver A farce about an escaped convict who hides out with a community of dwarves, manipulates them, and eventually impels them to murder.
197? 100m/C Fernando Gomez, Yolanda Farr. **VHS, Beta** NO &1/2

Gulliver's Travels The Fleischer Studio's animated version of Jonathan Swift's classic about the adventures of Gulliver, an English sailor who is washed ashore in the land of Lilliput, where everyone is about two inches tall.
1939 74m/C **D:** Dave Fleischer; **V:** Lanny Ross, Jessica Dragonette. **VHS, LV, 3/4U, Special order formats $8.95** NEG, MRV, NOS &&1/2

Gulliver's Travels In this partially animated adventure the entire land of Lilliput has been constructed in miniature. Cartoon and real life mix in a 3-dimensional story of Dr. Lemuel Gulliver and his discovery of the small people in the East Indies. From the classic by Jonathan Swift.
1977 (G) 80m/C GB Richard Harris, Catherine Schell; **D:** Peter Hunt. **VHS, Beta $19.95** UHV, LME, HHE &&

Gumball Rally An unusual assortment of people converge upon New York for a cross country car race to Long Beach, California where breaking the rules is part of the game.

1976 (PG) 107m/C Michael Sarrazin, Gary Busey, Raul Julia, Nicholas Pryor, Tim McIntire, Susan Flannery; **D:** Chuck Bail. **VHS, Beta $59.95** WAR &&

Gumby and the Moon Boggles Five episodes featuring the notorious claymation character: "Indian Trouble," "Weight and See," "Mystic Magic," "Gabby Auntie" and the title episode.
1956 30m/C **VHS, Beta $14.95** FHE, WTA &&

Gumby's Supporting Cast A series featuring the clay-animated adventures of Gumby's buddies, with six 6-minute episodes per program.
1986 42m/C **VHS, Beta $14.95** FHE, WTA &&

Gumshoe An homage to American hard-boiled detectives. Finney plays a small-time worker in a Liverpool nightclub who decides to become a detective like his movie heroes. He bumbles through a number of interconnecting cases, but finds his way in the end. Good satire of film noir detectives. Music by Andrew Lloyd Webber.
1972 (G) 85m/C Albert Finney, Billie Whitelaw, Frank Finlay, Janice Rule; **D:** Stephen Frears. **VHS, Beta $69.95** RCA &&1/2

The Gumshoe Kid A college-bound kid enters the family detective business to prevent his mother from being evicted. He gets in over his head though, trying to track the fiancee of a wealthy mobster. **AKA:** The Detective Kid.
1989 (R) 98m/C Jay Underwood, Tracy Scoggins, Vince Edwards, Arlene Golonka, Pamela Springsteen; **D:** Joseph Manduke. **VHS, Beta, LV $29.95** ACA &

Gun Cargo Muddled story about a conniving shipowner who fires his crew for demanding shore leave. He replaces them with assorted low-lifes, resulting in the usual hijinks. A terrible performance by an otherwise great cast.
1949 49m/C Rex Lease, Smith Ballow, William Farnum, Gibson Gowland. **VHS, Beta, 8mm $24.95** VYY &

Gun Code The white-hatted cowboy-hero puts a stop to small-town racketeering.
1940 52m/B Tim McCoy, Ina Guest; **D:** Peter Stewart. **VHS, Beta $19.95** VDM &1/2

Gun Crazy Annie Laurie Starr—an ersatz Annie Oakley in a Wild West show—meets gun-coveting Bart Tare, who says a gun makes him feel good inside, "like I'm somebody." Sparks fly, and the two get married and live happily ever after for a couple of nanoseconds until the money starts to run out and fatal femme Laurie's craving for excitement and violence starts to flare up. She convinces Bart to turn to robbery, and the two become lovebirds-on-the-lam (which in turn inspired "Bonnie and Clyde"). Needless to say, they find out in no uncertain terms that crime doesn't pay. But not before Laurie realizes (perhaps) that she really does love Bart. Sleeper's alternate title belies its noir streak. Now a cult fave, it's based on a MacKinlay Kantor story that first appeared in the Saturday Evening Post. Ex-stuntman Russell Harlan's photography is daring, and the realism of the impressive robbery scenes owes in part to the technical consultation of octogenarian former train robber Al Jennings. And watch for a Rusty (Russ) Tamblyn as the 14-year-old Bart. **AKA:** Deadly is the Female.
1949 87m/B Peggy Cummins, John Dall, Berry Kroeger, Morris Carnovsky, Anabel Shaw, Nedrick Young, Trevor Bardette; **D:** Joseph H. Lewis. **VHS $19.98** FOX, FCT &&&

Gun Crazy A gambler becomes enmeshed in an arranged marriage with a cursed Mexican family. Lightweight comedy, good cast. **AKA:** A Talent for Loving.
1969 110m/C Richard Widmark, Chaim Topol, Cesar Romero, Genevieve Page, Judd Hamilton, Caroline Munro; **D:** Richard Quine. **VHS $9.95** SIM &&1/2

Gun Fight at Red Sands Landmark western in the history of Italian cinema. Long before Leone's Eastwood trilogy, this film introduced the theme of an avenging stranger to the genre. Harrison stars as the dark, brooding hero who is out for revenge after learning that his family has been attacked by a gang of bandits. **AKA:** Gringo; Duello Nel Texas.
1963 ?m/C IT Richard Harrison, Giacomo "Jack" Stuart, Sara Lezana; **M:** Ennio Morricone. **VHS $16.95** SNC &&

Gun Fury A panoramic western about a Civil War veteran pursuing the bandits who kidnapped his beautiful bride-to-be. First screened as a 3-D movie.
1953 83m/C Rock Hudson, Donna Reed, Phil Carey, Lee Marvin; **D:** Raoul Walsh. **VHS, Beta, LV $14.95** COL &&1/2

Gun Girls Campy exploitation flick about a gun-toting gang of girls who rob anything or anyone. The guy who fences their goods ends up getting one of them pregnant.
1956 ?m/C Timothy Farrell, Jean Ferguson, Jacquelyn Park, Jean Ann Lewis; **D:** Robert Deltano. **VHS $16.95** SNC &

The Gun in Betty Lou's Handbag Shy, small town librarian with a dull marriage is looking for excitement when she stumbles across a gun used in a murder. She decides excitement will follow her (false) confession to the crime leaving her husband thunderstruck, the police confused, and the gossip line humming. She also intrigues the real bad guy, who comes looking for her. All-round silliness is interspersed with some surprisingly nasty violence given that this is supposed to be a comedy.
1992 (PG-13) 99m/C Penelope Ann Miller, Eric Thal, Alfre Woodard, Cathy Moriarty, William Forsythe, Julianne Moore, Xander Berkeley, Michael O'Neill, Christopher John Fields; **D:** Allan Moyle; **W:** Grace Cary Bickley; **M:** Richard Gibbs. **VHS, Beta, LV $94.95** TOU &

A Gun in the House While being attacked in her own home, a woman shoots one of her assailants. The police find no conclusive evidence of attack and arrest the woman for murder. Exploitive drama on gun control. Made-for-television.
1981 100m/C Sally Struthers, David Ackroyd, Joel Bailey, Jeffrey Tambor; **D:** Ivan Nagy. **VHS, Beta $49.95** VHE, HHE &

Gun Law The hero tackles the Sonora Kid, an outlaw terrorizing Arizona folk. One of the few sound westerns with Hoxie, a silent-era star who hung up his spurs when his voice proved non-photogenic.
1933 59m/B Jack Hoxie, Paul Fix, Mary Carr, Edmund Cobb, Robert Burns; **D:** Lewis Collins. **VHS, Beta** GPV &1/2

Gun Lords of Stirrup Basin A cattleman and the daughter of a homesteader are in love in the Old West, but a seedy lawyer wants to douse their flame. Bullets and fists fly as a result.
1937 55m/B Bob Steele, Louise Stanley, Karl Hackett, Ernie Adams, Frank LaRue, Frank Ball, Steve Clark; **D:** Sam Newfield. **VHS $19.95** NOS, DVT &&

Gun Play Brother and sister venture west to run their father's ranch. Mexican bandits believe the ranch's property houses a revolutionary fortune, and set about recovering it. The brother defends his father's ranch along with a sidekick, who sweeps the sister off her feet. *AKA:* Lucky Boots.
1936 59m/B Guinn Williams, Frank Yaconelli, Marion Shilling, Wally Wales, Charles French; *D:* Albert Herman. **VHS $19.95** *NOS, DVT* ✓✓

The Gun Ranger Our hero plays a Texas Ranger who becomes fed up with soft judges and shady prosecutors and decides to take the law into his own hands.
1934 56m/B Bob Steele, Eleanor Stewart. **VHS, Beta $19.95** *NOS, DVT* ✓✓½

Gun Riders Gunman must seek out and stop a murderer of innocent people. *AKA:* Five Bloody Graves; Five Bloody Days to Tombstone; Lonely Man.
1969 98m/C Scott Brady, Jim Davis, John Carradine; *D:* Al Adamson. **VHS, Beta** *CCB* ✓½

Gun Smugglers/Hot Lead A western double feature: Tim Holt and his sidekick Chito must recover a shipment of stolen guns in "Gun Smugglers," and the duo gallop into action against a gang of train robbers in "Hot Lead."
1951 120m/B Tim Holt, Richard Martin, Martha Hyer. **VHS, Beta $34.95** *RKO, TTC* ✓

Gunblast A convict is released from San Quentin and wastes no time in getting involved with mob-powered drug smuggling.
197? 70m/C Lloyd Allan, Christine Cardan, James Cunningham. **VHS, Beta** *NO* ✓

Guncrazy A girl from the wrong side of the tracks, who has been abused all her life, finds her freedom in a gun. She winds up killing the man who raped her, takes up with an equally lost ex-con, and the two armed misfits go on the run from the law. Barrymore's convincing and the movie is another well-made variation on the lovers-on-the-run theme. Film was inspired by, but is not a remake of the, 1950 movie "Gun Crazy."
1992 (R) 97m/C Drew Barrymore, James LeGros, Billy Drago, Rodney Harvey, Ione Skye, Joe Dallesandro, Michael Ironside; *D:* Tamra Davis; *W:* Matthew Bright. **VHS, Beta, LV $89.95** *ACA, PMS* ✓✓

A Gunfight When Cash is stranded in a small Western town, he meets up with fellow old-time gunfighter Douglas. The two strike up a friendship, but discover the town folk expect a gun battle. Needing money, the two arrange a gunfight for paid admission — winner take all. Cash makes his screen debut.
1971 (PG) 90m/C Kirk Douglas, Johnny Cash, Jane Alexander, Karen Black, Dana Elcar, Keith Carradine, Raf Vallone; *D:* Lamont Johnson. **Beta $59.95** *ALL, MTX* ✓✓

Gunfight at Sandoval A Texas Ranger investigates the headquarters of a criminal gang while hunting for the bandits who killed his partner. Adapted from the "Texas John Slaughter" episodes of the Disney television series.
1959 72m/C Tom Tryon, Beverly Garland, Dan Duryea. **VHS, Beta $69.95** *DIS* ✓½

Gunfight at the O.K. Corral The story of Wyatt Earp and Doc Holliday joining forces in Dodge City to rid the town of the criminal Clanton gang. Filmed in typical Hollywood style, but redeemed by its great stars. Written by Leon Uris.
1957 122m/C Burt Lancaster, Kirk Douglas, Rhonda Fleming, Jo Van Fleet, John Ireland, Kenneth Tobey, Lee Van Cleef, Frank Faylen, DeForest Kelley, Earl Holliman; *D:* John Sturges. **VHS, Beta, LV $14.95** *PAR, FCT* ✓✓✓

Gunfighter A mature, serious, Hollywood-western character study about an aging gunfighter searching for peace and quiet but unable to avoid his reputation and the duel-challenges it invites. One of King's best films.
1950 85m/B Gregory Peck, Helen Westcott, Millard Mitchell, Jean Parker, Karl Malden, Skip Homeier, Mae Marsh; *D:* Henry King. **VHS, Beta, LV $19.98** *FOX* ✓✓✓½

The Gunfighters Lackluster pilot of a proposed Canadian series pits three individualistic relatives against a powerful empire-builder.
1987 100m/C *CA* Art Hindle, Reiner Schoene, Tony Addabbo, George Kennedy, Michael Kane, Lori Hallier; *D:* Clay Borris. **VHS, LV $19.99** *VMK* ✓½

Gunfire A Frank James look-alike cavorts, robs and loots the countryside until the real James decides to set things straight.
1950 59m/B Donald (Don "Red") Barry, Robert Lowery, Pamela Blake, Wally Vernon; *D:* William Berke. **VHS, Beta, LV** *HHE* ✓½

Gunfire A gunfighter is rescued from the hangman's noose by railroad tycoons who want him to kill a farmer. He doesn't kill the man, but runs off with his wife instead, and the incensed railway honchos send assassins after the double-crossing gunman. Peckinpah's part is pretty puny in this leisurely horse opera. *AKA:* China 9, Liberty 37.
1978 94m/C *IT* Fabio Testi, Warren Oates, Jenny Agutter, Sam Peckinpah; *D:* Monte Hellman. **VHS $9.95** *SIM* ✓✓

Gung Ho! Carlson's Raiders are a specially trained group of Marine jungle fighters determined to retake the Pacific island of Makin during World War II.
1943 88m/B Robert Mitchum, Randolph Scott, Noah Beery Jr., Alan Curtis, Grace McDonald; *D:* Ray Enright. **VHS, Beta, 3/4U, Special order formats $9.98** *REP, MRV, NEG* ✓✓

Gung Ho A Japanese firm takes over a small-town U.S. auto factory and causes major cultural collisions. Keaton plays the go-between for employees and management while trying to keep both groups from killing each other. From the director of "Splash" and "Night Shift." Made into a short-lived television series.
1985 (PG-13) 111m/C Michael Keaton, Gedde Watanabe, George Wendt, Mimi Rogers, John Turturro, Clint Howard, Michelle Johnson, So Yamamura, Sab Shimono; *D:* Ron Howard. **VHS, Beta, LV, 8mm $14.95** *PAR* ✓✓½

Gunga Din Based loosely on Rudyard Kipling's famous poem. The prototypical "buddy" film. Three veteran British sergeants in India try to suppress a native uprising, but it's their water boy, the intrepid Gunga Din, who saves the day. Friendship, loyalty, and some of the best action scenes ever filmed. Also available colorized.
1939 117m/B Cary Grant, Victor McLaglen, Douglas Fairbanks Jr., Sam Jaffe, Eduardo Ciannelli, Montagu Love, Joan Fontaine; *D:* George Stevens. **VHS, Beta, LV $14.98** *RKO, TTC, VID* ✓✓✓✓

Gunman from Bodie Second of the Rough Rider series. Jones, McCoy, and Hatton rescue a baby orphaned by rustlers and then go after the bad guys. *AKA:* Gun Man from Bodie.
1941 62m/B Tim McCoy, Buck Jones, Raymond Hatton; *D:* Spencer Gordon Bennet. **VHS, Beta $9.95** *NOS, MRV, VCN* ✓½

Gunners & Guns Vintage western starring King.
1934 51m/B Black King, Edmund Cobb, Edna Asetin, Eddie Davis; *D:* Ray Nazarro. **VHS, Beta $29.95** *VCN* ✓

Gunplay Two cowboys befriend a boy whose father has been killed and search for the murderer.
1951 61m/B Tim Holt, Joan Dixon, Richard Martin. **VHS, Beta** *MED* ✓½

Gunpowder Two Interpol agents endeavor to stop a crime lord from causing the collapse of the world economy.
1984 85m/C David Gilliam, Martin Potter, Gordon Jackson, Anthony Schaeffer. **VHS, Beta $69.98** *LIV, VES* ✓

The Gunrunner Costner plays a Canadian mobster, involved in liquor smuggling, who aids a Chinese rebellion in this 1920s drama. Interesting concept. Received more attention after Costner gained notoriety in later films.
1984 (R) 92m/C *CA* Kevin Costner, Sara Botsford, Paul Soles; *D:* Nardo Castillo. **VHS, LV $19.95** *STE, HHE* ✓½

Guns An international gunrunner puts the moves on buxom women between hair-raising adventures.
1990 (R) 95m/C Erik Estrada, Dona Speir; *W/D:* Andy Sidaris. **VHS, LV $79.95** *COL* ✓✓½

The Guns and the Fury Two American oil riggers in the Middle East, circa 1908, are forced to fight off an attack by a vicious Arab sheik and his tribe.
1983 90m/C Peter Graves, Cameron Mitchell, Michael Ansara, Albert Salmi; *D:* Tony Zarindast. **VHS, Beta $49.95** *WWV* ✓½

Guns at Batasi Attenborough plays a tough British Sergeant Major stationed in Africa during the anti-colonial 1960s. Ultimately the regiment is threatened by rebel Africans. Fine performances make this rather predictable film watchable.
1964 103m/B *GB* Richard Attenborough, Jack Hawkins, Mia Farrow, Flora Robson, John Leyton; *D:* John Guillermin. **VHS** *TCF* ✓✓½

Guns Don't Argue Entertaining schlocker about the rise and fall of famous criminal Dillinger. Non-stop action also features Bonnie and Clyde, Pretty Boy Floyd and Baby Face Nelson.
1957 ?m/C Myron Healey, Jim Davis, Richard Crane. **VHS $16.95** *SNC* ✓✓

Guns for Dollars Mex-Western has four men, including a secret agent and a cossack, tangled up in the Mexican Revolution as they search for a fortune in smuggled jewels. *AKA:* They Call Me Hallelujah.
1973 94m/C *MX* George Hilton, Charles Southwood, Agata Flory, Roberto Camardiel, Paolo Gozlino, Rick Boyd; *D:* Anthony Ascot. **VHS $19.95** *ACA* ✓

Guns in the Dark A cowboy vows never to use a gun again when he believes that he accidentally shot his best friend.
1937 60m/C Johnny Mack Brown, Claire Rochelle; *D:* Sam Newfield. **VHS, Beta $19.95** *NOS, DVT, RXM* ✓

Guns of Diablo Wagon train master Bronson has to fight a gang that controls the supply depot, all the while showing his young helper (beardless boy Russell) the fascinating tricks of the trade.
1964 91m/C Charles Bronson, Kurt Russell, Susan Oliver; *D:* Boris Sagal. **VHS $39.99** *ACE, MTX* ✓✓

Guns of Fury Cisco and Pancho solve the troubles of a small boy in this standard oater.
1945 60m/B Duncan Renaldo. **VHS, Beta $19.95** *NOS, UHV, VCN* ✓½

Guns of Justice Undercover Colorado rangers stop a swindler from forcing homesteaders off their land. *AKA:* Colorado Ranger.

G

1950 60m/B James Ellison, Russell Hayden, Tom Tyler, Raymond Hatton; **D:** Thomas Carr. **VHS, Beta, LV** *NO* 🎬

The Guns of Navarone During World War II, British Intelligence in the Middle East sends six men to the Aegean island of Navarone to destroy guns manned by the Germans. Consistently interesting war epic based on the Alistair MacLean novel, with a vivid cast.
1961 159m/C Gregory Peck, David Niven, Anthony Quinn, Richard Harris, Stanley Baker, Anthony Quayle, James Darren, Irene Papas; **D:** J. Lee Thompson. Academy Awards '61: Best Special Effects; Nominations: Best Adapted Screenplay, Best Director (Thompson); Golden Globe Awards '62: Best Film—Drama. **VHS, Beta, LV** $19.95 *COL* 🎬🎬🎬½

Guns of the Magnificent Seven The third remake of "The Seven Samurai." Action-packed western in which the seven free political prisoners and train them to kill. The war party then heads out to rescue a Mexican revolutionary being held in an impregnable fortress.
1969 (G) 106m/C George Kennedy, Monte Markham, James Whitmore, Reni Santoni, Bernie Casey, Joe Don Baker, Scott Thomas, Michael Ansara, Fernando Rey; **D:** Paul Wendkos. **VHS** $19.98 *MGM* 🎬🎬½

Guns of War This is the true story of how a group of Yugoslavians formed a partisan army to stop the reign of Nazi terror in their native land.
1975 114m/C *YU* **VHS, Beta** *NO* 🎬🎬½

The Gunslinger A woman marshall struggles to keep law and order in a town overrun by outlaws. Unique western with a surprise ending.
1956 83m/C John Ireland, Beverly Garland, Allison Hayes, Jonathan Haze, Dick Miller, Bruno Ve Sota; **D:** Roger Corman; **W:** Charles B. Griffith. **VHS** $19.95 *MLB, TIM, SNC* 🎬½

Gunslinger Armed to the teeth with weaponry, Sartana shows a mining town's heavies how to sling a gun or two.
197? 90m/C John Garko, Tony Vilar; **D:** Anthony Ascot. **VHS, Beta** $19.98 *VDC* 🎬½

Gunsmoke: Return to Dodge The first of the made-for-television movies which reunited most of the cast of the classic television western. Matt Dillon returns to Dodge and Miss Kitty after 12 years only to be trailed by a ruthless adversary.
1987 100m/C James Arness, Amanda Blake, Buck Taylor, Fran Ryan, Earl Holliman, Steve Forrest; **D:** Vincent McEveety. **VHS** *FXV* 🎬🎬½

Gunsmoke Trail Cowpoke Randall saves an heiress from losing her estate to a phony uncle in low-budget Western. Also features the prolific "Fuzzy" St. John in his cowboy's sidekick stage (interestingly, St. John, a nephew of Fatty Arbuckle, later co-starred in the "Lone Rider" series with Randall's brother, Robert Livingston).
1938 59m/C Jack Randall, Al "Fuzzy" St. John. **VHS** $19.99 *NOS, MRV, MOV* 🎬½

Gus A Disney film about the California Atoms, a football team that has the worst record in the league until they begin winning games with the help of their field goal kicking mule of a mascot, Gus. The competition then plots a donkey-napping. Enjoyable comedy for the whole family.
1976 (G) 96m/C Ed Asner, Tim Conway, Dick Van Patten, Ronnie Schell, Bob Crane, Tom Bosley; **D:** Vincent McEveety. **VHS, Beta, LV** *COL, DIS* 🎬½

The Guy from Harlem He's mad, he's from Harlem, and he's not going to take it any more.

1977 86m/C Loye Hawkins, Cathy Davis, Patricia Fulton, Wanda Starr; **D:** Rene Martinez Jr. **VHS** *XVC* 🎬🎬

A Guy Named Joe A sentimental, patriotic Hollywood fantasy about the angel of a dead World War II pilot guiding another young pilot through battle and also helping him to romance his girl, who's still too devoted to his memory. Screenplay by Dalton Trumbo. Remade in 1989 as "Always."
1944 121m/B Spencer Tracy, Irene Dunne, Van Johnson, Ward Bond, James Gleason, Lionel Barrymore, Esther Williams; **D:** Victor Fleming. **VHS, Beta** $19.95 *MGM* 🎬🎬½

The Guyana Tragedy: The Story of Jim Jones Dramatization traces the story of the Reverend Jim Jones and the People's Temple from its beginnings in 1953 to the November 1978 mass suicide of more than 900 people. Boothe is appropriately hypnotic as the Reverend. Made for television.
1980 240m/C Powers Boothe, Ned Beatty, Randy Quaid, Brad Dourif, Brenda Vaccaro, LeVar Burton, Colleen Dewhurst, James Earl Jones; **D:** William A. Graham. **VHS, Beta** $59.95 *VHE, HHE* 🎬🎬

Guys and Dolls New York gambler Sky Masterson takes a bet that he can romance a Salvation Army lady. Great score by Frank Loesser. Based on the stories of Damon Runyon with Blaine, Kaye, Pully, and Silver recreating their roles from the Broadway hit. Brando's not-always-convincing musical debut. 🎵More I Cannot Wish You; My Time of Day; Guys and Dolls; Fugue for Tinhorns; Follow the Fold; Sue Me; Take Back Your Mink; If I Were a Bell; Luck Be a Lady; Pet Me, Poppa; Sit Down, You're Rocking the Boat; I'll Know; A Woman in Love; The Oldest Established; Adelaide's Lament.
1955 150m/C Marlon Brando, Jean Simmons, Frank Sinatra, Vivian Blaine, Stubby Kaye, Sheldon Leonard; **D:** Joseph L. Mankiewicz. Academy Awards '55 Nominations: Best Art Direction/Set Decoration (Color), Best Color Cinematography, Best Costume Design (Color), Best Original Score; Golden Globe Awards '56: Best Actress—Musical/Comedy (Simmons), Best Film—Musical/Comedy. **VHS, Beta, LV** $19.98 *FOX, FCT* 🎬🎬🎬

The Guyver A young college student is transformed into a super-human fighting machine thanks to his discovery of an alien device, "The Guyver." A CIA agent (Hamill) must keep the secret device from falling into the hands of human mutants, the Zoanoids. Based on a Japanese comic book.
1991 92m/C Mark Hamill, Vivian Wu, David Gale, Jeffrey Combs, Michael Berryman; **D:** Steve Wang. **VHS** $89.95 *COL, NLC* 🎬½

Gymkata A gymnast (Olympian Thomas) must use his martial arts skills to conquer and secure a military state in a hostile European country.
1985 (R) 89m/C Kurt Thomas, Tetchie Agbayani, Richard Norton, Conan Lee; **D:** Robert Clouse. **VHS, Beta** $79.95 *MGM* 🎬

Gypsy The life story of America's most famous stripteese queen, Gypsy Rose Lee. Russell gives a memorable performance as the infamous Mama Rose, Gypsy's stage mother. Based on both Gypsy Rose Lee's memoirs and the hit Broadway play by Arthur Laurents. 🎵Small World; All I Need is the Girl; You'll Never Get Away From Me; Let Me Entertain You; Some People; Everything's Coming Up Roses; You Gotta Have a Gimmick; Baby Jane and the Newsboys; Mr. Goldstone, I Love You; Little Lamb; Dainty June and Her Farmboys; Rose's Turn; If Mama Was Married; Broadway, Broadway.

1962 144m/C Rosalind Russell, Natalie Wood, Karl Malden, Ann Jillian, Parley Baer, Paul Wallace, Betty Bruce; **D:** Mervyn LeRoy. Academy Awards '62 Nominations: Best Color Cinematography, Best Costume Design (Color), Best Original Score; Golden Globe Awards '63: Best Actress—Musical/Comedy (Russell). **VHS, Beta, LV** $19.98 *WAR* 🎬🎬🎬

Gypsy A modern day gypsy-blooded Robin Hood cavorts between heists and romantic trysts. Dubbed.
1975 90m/C Alain Delon, Annie Girardot, Paul Meurisse; **D:** Jose Giovanni. **VHS, Beta** $59.95 *FCT* 🎬🎬

Gypsy Blood One of the first screen versions of "Carmen," closer to Prosper Merrimee's story than to the opera, depicting the fated love between a dancing girl and a matador. Lubitsch's first notable film. Silent.
1918 104m/B Pola Negri; **D:** Ernst Lubitsch. **VHS, Beta** $44.95 *FCT, GPV* 🎬🎬

Gypsy Colt Gypsy is the horse beloved by the young Corcoran. But a drought forces her family to sell the animal to a racing stable 500 miles from their home. Gypsy is having none of this, escapes the stables, and returns home to be with Corcoran. Both horse and child actress are naturally appealing.
1954 (G) 72m/C Donna Corcoran, Ward Bond, Frances Dee, Lee Van Cleef, Larry Keating; **D:** Andrew Marton. **VHS** $19.98 *MGM* 🎬🎬½

The Gypsy Warriors Two Army captains during World War II infiltrate Nazi-occupied France in order to prevent the distribution of a deadly toxin and are aided by a band of Gypsies. Made for television.
1978 77m/C Tom Selleck, James Whitmore Jr., Joseph Ruskin, Lina Raymond; **D:** Lou Antonio. **VHS, Beta** $39.95 *MCA* 🎬½

H-Bomb Mitchum stars as a CIA agent who is sent to Bangkok to retrieve two stolen nuclear warheads from a terrorist. It just so happens that his ex-girlfriend's father is the terrorist he must contend with in this stupid movie.
1971 98m/C Olivia Hussey, Chris Mitchum, Krung Savilai; **D:** P. Chalong. **VHS, Beta** *NO* Woof!

H-Man A Japanese sci-fi woofer about a radioactive mass of slime festering under Tokyo. Extremely lame special effects got quite a few unintentional laughs. Dubbed. **AKA:** Bijo to Ekitainigen.
1959 79m/C *JP* Koreya Senda, Kenji Sahara, Yumi Shirakawa, Akihiko Hirata; **D:** Inoshiro Honda. **VHS, Beta** $19.95 *COL* Woof!

Hack O'Lantern Granddad worships Satan, and gets his grandson involved: the result is much bloodshed, violence and evil.
1987 90m/C **D:** Jag Mundhra. **VHS, Beta** *NO* 🎬

Hadley's Rebellion A Georgia farm boy adjusts to relocation at an elitist California boarding school by flaunting his wrestling abilities.
1984 (PG) 96m/C Griffin O'Neal, Charles Durning, William Devane, Adam Baldwin, Dennis Hage, Lisa Lucas; **D:** Fred Walton. **VHS, Beta** $59.98 *FOX* 🎬½

Hail A biting satire of what-might-have-been if certain key cabinet members had their way. **AKA:** Hail to the Chief; Washington, B.C.
1973 (PG) 85m/C Richard B. Shull, Dick O'Neill, Phil Foster, Joseph Sirola, Dan Resin, Willard Waterman, Gary Sandy; **D:** Fred Levinson. **VHS, Beta** *NO* 🎬🎬

Hail, Hero! A dated Vietnam War era drama about a confused hippie rebelling against his parents and the draft. First film for both Douglas and Strauss. Adapted from the novel by John Weston. Includes music by Gordon Lightfoot.

1969 (PG) 97m/C Michael Douglas, Arthur Kennedy, Teresa Wright, John Larch, Charles Drake, Deborah Winters, Peter Strauss; **D:** David Miller. **VHS, Beta** $59.98 FOX ✍½

Hail Mary A modern-day virgin named Mary inexplicably becomes pregnant in this controversial film that discards notions of divinity in favor of the celebration of a lively, intellectual humanism. Godard rejects orthodox narrative structure and bourgeois prejudices. Very controversial, but not up to his breathless beginning work. In French with English subtitles. **AKA:** Je Vous Salue Marie. 1985 (R) 107m/C FR SI GB Myriem Roussel, Thierry Rode, Philippe Lacoste, Manon Anderson; **D:** Jean-Luc Godard. **VHS, Beta, LV** $29.98 LIV, VES, TAM ✍✍½

Hail the Conquering Hero A slight young man is rejected by the Army. Upon returning home, he is surprised to find out they think he's a hero. Biting satire with Demarest's performance stealing the show. 1944 101m/B Eddie Bracken, Ella Raines, William Demarest, Franklin Pangborn, Raymond Walburn; **D:** Preston Sturges, Preston Sturges. **VHS** $14.98 MCA ✍✍✍½

Hair Film version of the explosive 1960s Broadway musical about the carefree life of the flower children and the shadow of the Vietnam War that hangs over them. Great music, as well as wonderful choreography by Twyla Tharp help portray the surprisingly sensitive evocation of the period so long after the fact. Forman has an uncanny knack for understanding the textures of American life. Watch for a thinner Nell Carter. 1979 (PG) 122m/C Treat Williams, John Savage, Beverly D'Angelo, Annie Golden, Nicholas Ray; **D:** Milos Forman. **VHS, Beta, LV** $19.95 MGM ✍✍✍½

The Hairdresser's Husband Antoine (Rochefort) has had an odd obsession since boyhood—hairdressers—and in middle age he finds love with Mathilde (Galiena), a hairdresser he meets and proposes to as she cuts his hair. She accepts, and the two live their quiet lives in her barber shop as she cuts hair and he watches, occasionally breaking out in Arabian dances. A dark and odd yet refreshing film with fine performances by Rochefort and Galiena in this story about fetishism, obsession, and hair. In French with English subtitles. 1992 (R) 84m/C FR Jean Rochefort, Anna Galiena, Roland Bertin, Maurice Chevit, Philippe Clevenot, Jacques Mathou, Claude Aufaure; **W/D:** Patrice Leconte. **VHS** $89.95 PAR, BTV ✍✍

Hairspray Waters' first truly mainstream film, if that's even possible, and his funniest, detailing the struggle in 1962 Baltimore among teenagers for the top spot in a local television dance show. Deals with racism and stereotypes, as well as typical "teen" problems (hair-do's and "hair-don'ts"). Filled with refreshingly tasteful, subtle social satire (although not without its yester-Waters touches; the scene with Debbie Harry, her daughter, and a pimple will please die-hard Waters fans). Ricki Lake is lovable and appealing as Divine's daughter; Divine, in his last film, is likeable as an iron-toting mom. Written and directed by Waters; watch for him in his cameo as the demented shrink. Look also for Divine's appearance as a man. Features some great 60s music, which Waters refers to as "the only known remedy to today's Hit Parade of Hell." Tunes include Gene Pitney's "Town Without Pity" and the Ray Bryant Combo's "Madison Time."

1988 (PG) 94m/C Ricki Lake, Divine, Jerry Stiller, Colleen Fitzpatrick, Sonny Bono, Deborah Harry, Ruth Brown, Pia Zadora; **Cameos:** John Waters; **W/D:** John Waters. **VHS, Beta, LV** $14.95 COL, FCT ✍✍✍

The Hairy Ape Screen adaptation of the Eugene O'Neill play. A beast-like coal stoker becomes obsessed with a cool and distant passenger aboard an ocean liner. 1944 90m/B William Bendix, Susan Hayward, John Loder, Dorothy Comingore, Roman Bohnen, Alan Napier; **D:** Alfred Santell. **VHS** $19.95 NOS, MRV, FCT ✍✍✍

Half a Lifetime The stakes are too high for four friends playing a game of poker. 1986 85m/C Keith Carradine, Gary Busey, Nick Mancuso, Saul Rubinek. **VHS, Beta** $79.95 HBO ✍✍

Half a Loaf of Kung Fu The worthy bodyguards of Sern Chuan are called upon to deliver a valuable jade statue. Thwarted again and again by ruthless robbers, they falter. Only Chan carries on, meeting the enemy alone. Fast action, good story. 1985 98m/C Jackie Chan. **VHS, Beta** NO ✍

Half a Sixpence Former musician Sidney, who earlier directed "Showboat" and "Kiss Me Kate," shows a bit less verve in this production. Based on H.G. Wells' 1905 novel, "Kipps," it sports much of the original cast from its Broadway incarnation. Edwardian orphan Steele, a cloth-dealer-in-training, comes into a large sum of money and proceeds to lose it with great dispatch. Somewhere along the way he loses his girlfriend, too, but she takes him back because musicals end happily. ♫Half a Sixpence; Flash, Bang, Wallop!; All In The Cause Of Economy; I'm Not Talking To You; Money To Burn; The Race Is On; I Don't Believe A Word Of It; A Proper Gentleman; She's Too Far Above Me; This Is My World; If The Rain's Got To Fall; Entr'acte; I Know What I Am. 1967 148m/B Tommy Steele, Julia Foster, Penelope Horner, Cyril Ritchard, Grover Dale; **D:** George Sidney. **VHS** $19.95 PAR, FCT ✍✍

Half a Soldier A spoiled girl gets a big surprise when she steals a car and discovers the body of a gangster in the trunk. 1940 59m/B Heather Angel, John "Dusty" King. **VHS, Beta** $24.95 NOS, DVT, HEG ✍✍

The Half-Breed Routine oater with settlers and Apaches fighting, and the obligatory half-breed stuck in the middle. 1951 81m/B Robert Young, Jack Buetel, Janis Carter, Barton MacLane, Reed Hadley, Porter Hall, Connie Gilchrist; **D:** Stuart Gilmore. **VHS, Beta** $19.98 TTC ✍✍

Half Human Dull Japanese monster movie about an ape-human who terrorizes Northern Japan. When released in the U.S., Carradine and Morris were added. Without subtitles, just Carradine's narration. Director Honda made better movies before and after, with Godzilla and Rodan. 1958 78m/B JP John Carradine, Akira Takarada, Morris Ankrum; **D:** Inoshiro Honda. **VHS** $14.95 RHI, SNC, MLB ✍½

Half Moon Street A brilliant woman scientist supplements her paltry fellowship salary by becoming a hired escort and prostitute, which leads her into various incidents of international intrigue. Adapted from a story by Paul Theroux, "Dr. Slaughter." **AKA:** Escort Girl. 1986 (R) 90m/C Sigourney Weaver, Michael Caine, Keith Buckley, Ian MacInnes; **D:** Bob Swaim. **VHS, Beta, LV, 8mm** $14.98 SUE, NLC ✍✍

Half of Heaven A critically popular film about a young Spanish woman who begins to share certain telepathic powers with her wizened grandmother. In Spanish with English subtitles. **AKA:** La Mitad del Cielo. 1986 95m/C SP Angela Molina, Margarita Lozano; **D:** Manuel Gutierrez Aragon. **VHS, Beta** $29.95 PBS, PAV, FCT ✍✍✍

Half-Shot at Sunrise Madcap vaudeville comedians play AWOL soldiers loose in 1918 Paris. Continuous one-liners, sight gags, and slapstick nonsense. First film appearance of comedy team Wheeler and Woolsey. 1930 78m/B Bert Wheeler, Robert Woolsey, Dorothy Lee, Robert Rutherford, Edna May Oliver; **D:** Paul Sloane. **VHS, Beta, 3/4U, Special order formats** $24.95 VYY, CAB, DVT ✍✍

Half Slave, Half Free The true story of a free black man in the 1840s who is kidnapped and forced into slavery for 12 years. Made for television as part of the "American Playhouse" series on PBS. Followed by "Charlotte Forten's Mission: Experiment in Freedom." **AKA:** Solomon Northrup's Odyssey. 1985 113m/C Avery Brooks, Mason Adams, Petronia Paley, John Saxon, Joe Seneca, Michael Tolan; **D:** Gordon Parks. **VHS, Beta** $59.95 SVS, KAR, KUI ✍✍½

Hallelujah! Haynes plays an innocent young man who turns to religion and becomes a charasmatic preacher after a family tragedy. He retains all his human weaknesses, however, including falling for the lovely but deceitful McKinney. Great music included traditional spirituals and songs by Berlin, such as "At the End of the Road" and "Swanee Shuffle." Shot on location in Tennessee. The first all-black feature film and the first talkie for director Vidor was given the go-ahead by MGM production chief Irving Thalberg, though he knew the film would be both controversial and get minimal release in the deep South. 1929 90m/B Daniel L. Haynes, Nina Mae McKinney, William Fontaine, Harry Gray, Fannie Belle DeKnight, Everett McGarrity; **D:** King Vidor; **M:** Irving Berlin. **VHS** $19.98 MGM, MOV ✍✍✍½

Hallelujah, I'm a Bum A happy-go-lucky hobo reforms and begins a new life for the sake of a woman. Bizarre Depression-era musical with a Rodgers and Hart score and continuously rhyming dialogue. The British version, due to the slang meaning of "bum," was titled "Hallelujah, I'm a Tramp." ♫You Are Too Beautiful; I'll Do It Again; I've Got To Get Back To New York; What Do You Want With Money?; Hallelujah, I'm A Bum; My Pal Bumper; Dear June; Bumper Found A Grand. **AKA:** Hallelujah, I'm a Tramp; The Heart of New York; Happy Go Lucky; Lazy Bones. 1933 83m/B Al Jolson, Madge Evans, Frank Morgan, Chester Conklin; **D:** Lewis Milestone; **W:** Ben Hecht, S.N. Behrman; **M:** Richard Rodgers, Lorenz Hart. **VHS, Beta** LCA, MLB ✍✍½

The Hallelujah Trail A Denver mining town in the late 1800s is about to batten down the hatches for a long winter, and there's not a drop of whiskey to be had. The U.S. Cavalry sends a shipment to the miners, but temperance leader Cora Templeton Massingale (Remick) and her bevy of ladies against liquor—along with a bunch of whiskey-ravening Indians—stand between them and the would-be whistle whetters. A limp Western satire directed by Preston Sturges' brother John, who fared much better when he kept a straight face (he directed "The Great Escape" two years earlier). Based on Bill Gulick's novel, "The Hallelujah Train." Special two-laserdisc set includes additional

footage not seen in over 25 years (though it's already overlong at two and three-quarters hours), the original movie trailer, and a letter-boxed screen.
1965 166m/C Burt Lancaster, Lee Remick, Jim Hutton, Pamela Tiffin, Donald Pleasence, Brian Keith, Martin Landau; **D:** John Sturges. **VHS, LV $29.99** MGM, PIA, FCT ⬭⬭

Halloween John Carpenter's horror classic has been acclaimed "the most successful independent motion picture of all time." A deranged youth returns to his hometown with murderous intent after fifteen years in an asylum. Very, very scary—you feel this movie more than see it.
1978 (R) 90m/C Jamie Lee Curtis, Donald Pleasence, Nancy Loomis, P.J. Soles; **D:** John Carpenter. **VHS, Beta, LV $19.98** MED ⬭⬭⬭½

Halloween 2: The Nightmare Isn't Over! Trying to pick up where "Halloween" left off (minus John Carpenter's direction), the sequel begins with the escape of vicious killer Michael, who continues to murder and terrorize the community of Haddonfield, Illinois. Lacking the innovative intentions of its predecessor, it relies on old-fashioned buckets of blood. No chills, just trauma. Co-scripted by Carpenter.
1981 (R) 92m/C Jamie Lee Curtis, Donald Pleasence, Jeffrey Kramer, Charles Cyphers, Lance Guest; **D:** Rick Rosenthal. **VHS, Beta, LV $19.95** MCA ⬭½

Halloween 3: Season of the Witch Modern druid plans to kill 50 million children with his specially made Halloween masks. Produced by John Carpenter, this second sequel to the 1978 horror classic is not based on the events or characters of its predecessors or successors. Followed by "Halloween 4," and "Halloween 5: The Revenge of Michael Myers" (1989).
1982 (R) 98m/C Tom Atkins, Stacey Nelkin, Dan O'Herlihy, Ralph Strait; **D:** Tommy Lee Wallace. **VHS, Beta, LV $19.95** MCA ⬭⬭

Halloween 4: The Return of Michael Myers The third sequel, wherein the lunatic that won't die returns home to kill his niece.
1988 (R) 88m/C Donald Pleasence, Ellie Cornell, Danielle Harris, Michael Pataki; **D:** Dwight Little. **VHS, Beta, LV $89.98** FOX ⬭

Halloween 5: The Revenge of Michael Myers Fifth in the series, this Halloween is an improvement over 2, 3, and 4, thanks to a few well-directed scare scenes. Unfortunately, the plot remains the same: a psycho behemoth chases down and kills more teens. An open ending promises yet another installment.
1989 (R) 96m/C Donald Pleasence, Ellie Cornell, Danielle Harris, Don Shanks; **D:** Dominique Othenin-Girard. **VHS, Beta, LV $89.98** FOX ⬭½

Halloween Monster Madness A fun-filled giggle-fest ripe with chills featuring all your favorite Hanna-Barbera stars.
1990 ?m/C **VHS $24.95** TTC ⬭½

Halloween Night Ancient evil rises up to destroy the perfect small town.
1990 (R) 90m/C Hy Pyke, Katrina Garner; **D:** Emilio P. Miraglio. **VHS $59.95** ATL ⬭⬭

Halloween with the Addams Family A really pathetic production spawned during the "reunion" craze of the late '70s, sparked only by the lively performance of Coogan's Uncle Fester and the always lovable Lurch. Made for television.
1979 87m/C John Astin, Carolyn Jones, Jackie Coogan, Ted Cassidy. **VHS, Beta** GKK Woof!

The Halls of Montezuma Large, bombastic World War II combat epic. Depicts the Marines fighting the Japanese in the Pacific.
1950 113m/C Richard Widmark, Jack Palance, Reginald Gardiner, Robert Wagner, Karl Malden, Richard Boone, Richard Hylton, Skip Homeier, Jack Webb, Neville Brand, Martin Milner, Bert Freed; **D:** Lewis Milestone. **VHS, Beta $14.98** FOX ⬭⬭½

Hallucination Early flower-power exploiter about expatriate acid heads who murder an antique dealer under the influence of LSD and then attempt to hide at a monastery. Depicts LSD as the catalyst in bringing out the group's criminal behavior. In sepia while everyone's cool, breaking into color during the head trips. **AKA:** Hallucination Generation.
1967 90m/C George Montgomery, Danny Stone; **D:** Edward Mann. **VHS, Beta $19.98** VDC Woof!

Hambone & Hillie An elderly woman makes a 3000-mile trek across the United States to search for the dog she lost in an airport.
1984 (PG) 97m/C Lillian Gish, Timothy Bottoms, Candy Clark, O.J. Simpson, Robert Walker Jr., Jack Carter, Jack Hale Jr., Anne Lockhart; **D:** Roy Watts. **VHS, Beta $19.95** STE, HBO ⬭⬭

Hamburger Hill Popular war epic depicting the famous battle between Americans and Viet Cong over a useless hill in Vietnam. Made in the heyday of 1980s Vietnam backlash, and possibly the most realistic and bloodiest of the lot. Written by Jim Carabatsos.
1987 (R) 104m/C Michael Dolan, Daniel O'Shea, Dylan McDermott, Tommy Swerdlow, Courtney B. Vance, Anthony Barille, Michael Boatman, Don Cheadle; **D:** John Irvin. **VHS, Beta, LV $19.98** LIV, VES, FCT ⬭⬭½

Hamburger...The Motion Picture The life and times of students at Busterburger U., the only college devoted to hamburger franchise management.
1986 (R) 90m/C Leigh McCloskey, Dick Butkus, Randi Brooks, Sandy Hackett; **D:** Mike Marvin. **VHS, Beta, LV $9.95** MED ⬭

Hamlet Splendid adaptation of Shakespeare's dramatic play. Hamlet vows vengeance on the murderer of his father in this tight version of the four hour stage play. Some scenes were cut out, including all of Rosencrantz and Guildenstern. Beautifully photographed in Denmark. An Olivier triumph. Remade several times.
1948 153m/B GB Laurence Olivier, Basil Sydney, Felix Aylmer, Jean Simmons, Stanley Holloway, Peter Cushing, Christopher Lee; **D:** Laurence Olivier; **V:** John Gielgud. Academy Awards '48: Best Actor (Olivier), Best Art Direction/Set Decoration (B & W), Best Costume Design (B & W), Best Picture; Nominations: Best Director (Olivier), Best Supporting Actress (Simmons), Best Original Score; British Academy Awards '48: Best Film; Golden Globe Awards '49: Best Actor—Drama (Olivier). **VHS $19.95** PAR, BTV, HMV ⬭⬭⬭⬭

Hamlet Williamson brings to the screen his stage performance as the classic Shakespeare character. Something is lost in the process, although there are some redeeming moments including those with Faithfull as Ophelia.
1969 (G) 114m/C GB Nicol Williamson, Anthony Hopkins, Marianne Faithfull, Gordon Jackson, Judy Parfitt, Mark Dingham, Anjelica Huston; **D:** Tony Richardson. **VHS, Beta $19.95** COL ⬭⬭½

Hamlet In this tragedy, Shakespeare uses a tense drama of murder, conspiracy, and revenge as a medium for inquiring into the most fundamental problems: justice, guilt, madness, death, and the difficulty of under-

standing oneself and others. Part of the television series "The Shakespeare Plays."
1979 150m/C GB Claire Bloom, Patrick Stewart, Eric Porter, Derek Jacobi. **VHS, Beta $69.95** TLF ⬭⬭⬭

Hamlet Zeffirelli—who has much Shakespeare under his belt, having directed "The Taming of the Shrew," "Romeo and Juliet" and a filmed version of the opera "Otello"—creates a surprisingly energetic and accessible interpretation of the Bard's moody play. Gibson brings charm, humor and a carefully calculated sense of violence, not to mention a good deal of solid flesh, to the eponymous role, and he handles the language skillfully (although if it's a poetic Dane you seek, you'd best stick with Olivier). The cast is uniformly excellent, with exceptional work from Scofield as the ghost of Hamlet's father and Bates as Claudius; Close may seem a tad hysterical at times (not to mention too close to Gibson's age to play his mother), but she brings some insight and nuance to the maternal role. Purists beware: Zeffirelli and co-scriptwriter Christopher DeVore have cut the play to underline the themes of revenge and insanity, and even add a scene at the beginning for the sake of narrative expediency (not that Olivier et al didn't take their liberties). Beautifully costumed and shot on location in Northern Scotland.
1990 (PG) 135m/C Mel Gibson, Glenn Close, Alan Bates, Paul Scofield, Ian Holm, Helena Bonham Carter; **D:** Franco Zeffirelli. **VHS, Beta, LV, 8mm $19.98** WAR, BTV, PIA ⬭⬭⬭½

Hammersmith is Out A violent lunatic cons an orderly into letting him escape. Chases, romance and craziness follow.
1972 (R) 108m/C Richard Burton, Elizabeth Taylor, Peter Ustinov, Beau Bridges; **D:** Peter Ustinov. **VHS, Beta $59.95** PSM ⬭½

Hammett After many directors and script rewrites, Wenders was assigned to this arch neo-noir what-if scenario. Depicts Dashiell Hammett solving a complex crime himself, an experience he uses in his novels. Interesting, but ultimately botched studio exercise, like many from executive producer Francis Coppola, who is said to have reshot much of the film.
1982 (PG) 98m/C Frederic Forrest, Peter Boyle, Sylvia Sidney, Elisha Cook Jr., Marilu Henner; **D:** Wim Wenders; **M:** John Barry. **VHS, Beta $69.95** WAR, TAM ⬭⬭

Hamsin A Jewish landowner and an Arab worker encounter difficulties in their relationship when the government announces plans to confiscate Arab land. In Hebrew with English subtitles.
1983 90m/C Shlomo Tarshish, Yasin Shawap, Hemda Levy, Ruth Geler; **D:** Daniel Wachsmann. **VHS, Beta $79.95** ERG ⬭⬭⬭

The Hand During World War II, three British POWs are tortured by the Japanese. Refusing to give information, two of them have their right hands cut off. The third opts to talk, thereby keeping his hand. After the war, a series of murders occur in London where the victims have their hands amputated. Could there be a connection?
1960 61m/B GB Derek Bond, Ronald Lee Hunt, Reed de Rouen, Ray Cooney, Brian Coleman; **D:** Henry Cass. **VHS, Beta $16.95** SNC ⬭⬭

The Hand A gifted cartoonist's hand is severed in a car accident. Soon, the hand is on the loose with a mind of its own, seeking out victims with an obsessive vengeance. Stone's first film is a unique, surreal psycho-horror pastiche consistently underrated by most critics.

1981 (R) 105m/C *GB* Michael Caine, Andrea Marcovicci, Annie McEnroe, Bruce McGill, Viveca Lindfors; *W/D:* Oliver Stone. **VHS, Beta** $19.98 WAR *ℐℐℐ*

The Hand that Rocks the Cradle DeMornay is frightening as Peyton Flanders, the nanny from hell who charms her way into a suburban Seattle family's life. Sciorra is the pregnant and unbelievably naive Claire Bartel, who unwittingly starts a terrifying chain of events when she brings charges against her new obstetrician who molests her during a check-up. The physician's wife, also pregnant, begins to plot her revenge after she loses her own baby. Peyton literally shows up and gets the nanny job and Claire ignores warnings from her best friend until she notices her husband and daughter are becoming closer to Peyton. The plot is very predictable and preys on the worst fears of viewers: that a nanny or babysitter will betray your trust and harm your child, not to mention that a physician will take advantage of you. Still, the movie is worth it if only to see DeMornay in her fantastic Jeckle and Hyde performance.
1992 (R) 110m/C Annabella Sciorra, Rebecca DeMornay, Matt McCoy, Ernie Hudson, Julianne Moore, Madeline Zima, John de Lancie, Mitchell Laurance; *D:* Curtis Hanson. **VHS, Beta** $94.95 HPH *ℐℐ½*

A Handful of Dust A dry, stately adaptation of the bitter Evelyn Waugh novel about a stuffy young aristocrat's wife's careless infidelity and how it sends her innocent husband to a tragic downfall. A well-meaning version that captures Waugh's cynical satire almost in spite of itself. Set in post-World War I England.
1988 (PG) 114m/C *GB* James Wilby, Kristin Scott Thomas, Rupert Graves, Alec Guinness, Anjelica Huston, Judi Dench; *D:* Charles Sturridge. Academy Awards '88 Nominations: Best Costume Design; British Academy Awards '88: Best Supporting Actress (Dench). **VHS, Beta** $19.95 COL, TVC *ℐℐℐ*

The Handmaid's Tale A cool, shallow but none-the-less chilling nightmare based on Margaret Atwood's bestselling novel, about a woman caught in the machinations of a near-future society so sterile it enslaves the few fertile women and forces them into being child-bearing "handmaids."
1990 (R) 109m/C Natasha Richardson, Robert Duvall, Faye Dunaway, Aidan Quinn, Elizabeth McGovern, Victoria Tennant, Blanche Baker; *D:* Volker Schlondorff; *W:* Harold Pinter. **VHS, Beta, LV** $19.98 HBO, FCT, IME *ℐℐ½*

Hands Across the Border A musical western in which Roy helps a woman find the men who killed her father.
1943 72m/B Roy Rogers, Ruth Terry, Guinn Williams, Onslow Stevens, Mary Treen, Joseph Crehan; *D:* Joseph Kane. **VHS** $19.95 NOS, DVT *ℐ½*

Hands of a Stranger Another undistinguished entry in the long line of remakes of "The Hands of Orlac." A pianist who loses his hands in an accident is given the hands of a murderer, and his new hands want to do more than tickle the ivories. Kellerman has a very small role as does former "Sheena" McCalla.
1962 95m/B Paul Lukather, Joan Harvey, James Stapleton, Sally Kellerman, Irish McCalla; *D:* Newton Arnold. **VHS** $19.98 SNC *ℐℐ*

Hands of a Stranger Policeman's wife is raped during an adulterous tryst. As the painful truth dawns on the cop, he himself dallies with a compassionate lady D.A. while hunting the attacker. About as sordid as a network TV-movie gets without

toppling into sleaze; strong acting and a sober script (by dramatist Arthur Kopit) pull it through. But the plot, from Robert Daly's novel, doesn't justify miniseries treatment; the two-cassette package is excessively long.
1987 179m/C Armand Assante, Beverly D'Angelo, Blair Brown, Michael Lerner, Philip Casnoff, Arliss Howard; *D:* Larry Elikann. **VHS** $89.95 WOV *ℐℐ½*

Hands of Death Thieves use their Ninja skills to stop any one in their path to evil. Action-packed, somewhat contrived.
1988 90m/C Richard Harrison, Mike Abbott; *D:* Geoffrey Ho. **VHS, Beta** IMP *ℐ*

The Hands of Orlac Classic silent film about a pianist whose hands are mutilated in an accident. His hands are replaced by those of a murderer, and his urge to kill becomes overwhelming. Contains restored footage.
1925 ?m/B *AT* Conrad Veidt, Fritz Kortner, Carmen Cartellieri, Paul Adkonas; *D:* Robert Wiene. **VHS** $19.95 LSV *ℐℐ*

The Hands of Orlac Third remake of Maurice Renard's classic tale. When a concert pianist's hands are mutilated in an accident, he receives a graft of a murderer's hands. Obsession sweeps the musician, as he believes his new hands are incapable of music, only violence. Bland adaptation of the original story. *AKA:* Hands of the Strangler.
1960 95m/B *GB FR* Mel Ferrer, Christopher Lee, Felix Aylmer, Basil Sydney, Donald Wolfit, Donald Pleasence; *D:* Edmond T. Greville. **VHS** $16.95 SNC *ℐℐ*

Hands of Steel A ruthless cyborg carries out a mission to find and kill an important scientist. Terrible acting, and lousy writing: an all-around woofer!
1986 (R) 94m/C Daniel Greene, John Saxon, Janet Agren, Claudio Cassinelli, George Eastman; *D:* Martin Dolman. **VHS, Beta** $79.98 LIV Woof!

Hands of the Ripper Jack the Ripper's daughter returns to London where she works as a medium by day and stalks the streets at night. Classy Hammer horror variation on the perennial theme.
1971 (R) 85m/C *GB* Eric Porter, Angharad Rees, Jane Merrow, Keith Bell; *D:* Peter Sasdy. **VHS, Beta** $19.98 VID, MLB *ℐℐ½*

Hands Up Jaunty Confederate spy (played by much-overlooked American comedian Griffith) attempts, amidst much comic nonsense, to thwart Yankee gold mining during the Civil War. Silent.
1926 50m/B Raymond Griffith, Mack Swain, Marion Nixon, Montagu Love; *D:* Clarence Badger. **VHS, Beta** $19.95 GPV *ℐℐ½*

Hands Up Famed Polish film finished in 1967 but not released until 1981 for political reasons (prologue shot in '81 included). Doctors at a medical school reunion reflect upon the effect of Stalinist rule on their education and lives. In Polish with English subtitles and known also as "Rece do Gory."
1981 78m/C *PL* *D:* Jerzy Skolimowski. **VHS, Beta** $49.95 FCT *ℐℐℐ*

Hang 'Em High A cowboy is saved from a lynching and vows to hunt down the gang that nearly killed him in this American-made spaghetti western. Eastwood's first major vehicle made outside of Europe.
1967 114m/C Clint Eastwood, Inger Stevens, Ed Begley Sr., Pat Hingle, James MacArthur; *D:* Ted Post. **VHS, Beta, LV** $19.98 MGM, TLF *ℐℐ½*

Hang Tough A goofy loser of a teenage slob has no luck in life until the older brother of one of his friends shows him the ropes. That's when the laughs begin.

1989 (R) 105m/C Carl Marotte, Lisa Langlois, Charlaine Woodward, Grand Bush, Vincent Bufano; *D:* Daryl Duke. **VHS** $49.95 MNC *ℐℐ½*

Hangar 18 Silly sci-fi drama about two astronauts who collide with a UFO during a shuttle flight. Later they learn that the government is hiding it in a hangar and they try to prove its existence. Shown on TV as "Invasion Force" with an entirely new ending. *AKA:* Invasion Force.
1980 (PG) 97m/C Darren McGavin, Robert Vaughn, Gary Collins, James Hampton, Phillip Abbott, Pamela Bellwood, Tom Hallick, Cliff Osmond, Joseph Campanella; *D:* James L. Conway; *W:* David O'Malley. **VHS, Beta** $19.99 WOV *ℐℐ½*

The Hanged Man Tale of a gunslinger in the Old West who mystically escapes death by hanging. Reborn, he re-evaluates the meaning of justice. Made for television.
1974 78m/C Steve Forrest, Cameron Mitchell, Sharon Acker, Dean Jagger, Will Geer, Barbara Luna, Rafael Campos; *D:* Michael Caffey. **VHS** NO *ℐℐ*

Hangfire When a New Mexican prison is evacuated thanks to a nasty chemical explosion, several prisoners decide it's time for a furlough, and they elect the local sheriff's wife as a traveling companion. Another mediocre actioner from director Maris (scripted by Brian D. Jeffries) it gets an extra bone for stunts kids shouldn't try at home.
1991 (R) 91m/C Brad Davis, Yaphet Kotto, Lee De Broux, Jan-Michael Vincent, George Kennedy, Kim Delaney; *D:* Peter Maris; *W:* Brian D. Jeffries. **VHS, LV** $89.98 COL *ℐℐ*

Hangin' with the Homeboys One night in the lives of four young men. Although the Bronx doesn't offer much for any of them, they have little interest in escaping its confines, and they are more than willing to complain. Characters are insightfully written and well portrayed, with strongest work from Serrano as a Puerto Rican who is trying to pass himself off as Italian. Lack of plot may frustrate some viewers.
1991 (R) 89m/C Mario Joyner, Doug E. Doug, John Leguizamo, Nestor Serrano; *W/D:* Joseph P. Vasquez. **VHS, LV** $19.95 COL, FCT *ℐℐℐ*

Hanging on a Star A small rock band encounters many comic adventures as it climbs its way up the charts. Raffin stars as the band's persistent and competent road agent.
1978 (PG) 92m/C Deborah Raffin, Lane Caudell, Wolfman Jack, Jason Parker, Danil Torppe; *D:* Mike MacFarland. **VHS, Beta** $79.95 MGM *ℐ*

The Hanging Tree Cooper plays a frontier doctor who rescues a thief (Piazza) from a lynch mob and nurses a temporarily blind girl (Schell). Malden is the bad guy who tries to attack Schell and Cooper shoots him. The townspeople take Cooper out to "The Hanging Tree" but this time it's Schell and Piazza who come to his rescue. Slow-paced western with good performances. Scott's screen debut.
1959 108m/B Gary Cooper, Maria Schell, Ben Piazza, Karl Malden, George C. Scott, Karl Swenson, Virginia Gregg, King Donovan; *D:* Delmer Daves; *W:* Wendell Mayes, Halsted Welles; *M:* Max Steiner. **VHS** $29.98 WAR *ℐℐℐ*

The Hanging Woman A man is summoned to the reading of a relative's will, and discovers the corpse of a young woman hanging in a cemetery. As he investigates the mystery, he uncovers a local doctor's plans to zombify the entire world. Not bad at all and quite creepy once the zombies are out in force. Euro-horror star Naschy plays the necrophiliac grave digger, Igor. Also on video

as "Return of the Zombies" and "Beyond the Living Dead."
1972 (R) 91m/C *SP IT* Stan Cooper, Vickie Nesbitt, Marcella Wright, Catherine Gilbert, Gerard Tichy, Paul Naschy; *D:* John Davidson. VHS, Beta $59.95 *WES, UHV, TIM* 🎬🎬½

Hangman's Knot Members of the Confederate Cavalry rob a Union train, not knowing that the war is over. Now facing criminal charges, they are forced to take refuge in a stagecoach stop. Well-done horse opera with a wry sense of humor.
1952 80m/C Randolph Scott, Donna Reed, Claude Jarman Jr., Frank Faylen, Glenn Langan, Richard Denning, Lee Marvin, Jeanette Nolan; *D:* Roy Huggins. VHS, Beta *GKK* 🎬🎬½

Hangmen Ex-CIA agents battle it out on the East side of New York. If you're into very violent, very badly-acted films, then this one's for you.
1987 (R) 88m/C Jake La Motta, Rick Washburne, Doug Thomas; *D:* J. Christian Ingvordsen. VHS, Beta $29.95 *ACA* Woof!

Hanky Panky Insipid comic thriller in which Wilder and Radner become involved in a search for top-secret plans.
1982 (PG) 107m/C Gene Wilder, Gilda Radner, Richard Widmark, Kathleen Quinlan; *D:* Sidney Poitier. VHS, Beta, LV $14.95 *COL* 🎬½

Hanna K. Story of divided passions set in the tumultuous state of Israel. American lawyer Clayburgh tries to settle her personal and political affairs with various Middle-Eastern men. Mediocre Disappointing. Release generated controversy over pro-Palestine stance.
1983 (R) 111m/C *FR* Jill Clayburgh, Gabriel Byrne, Jean Yanne, Muhamad Bakri, David Clannon, Odod Kotler; *D:* Constantin Costa-Gavras. VHS, Beta $59.95 *MCA* 🎬🎬

Hannah and Her Sisters Allen's grand epic about a New York showbiz family, its three adult sisters and their various complex romantic entanglements. Excellent performances by the entire cast, especially Caine and Hershey. Classic Allen themes of life, love, death, and desire are explored in an assured and sensitive manner. Witty, ironic, and heartwarming.
1986 (PG) 103m/C Mia Farrow, Barbara Hershey, Dianne Wiest, Michael Caine, Woody Allen, Maureen O'Sullivan, Lloyd Nolan, Sam Waterston, Carrie Fisher, Max von Sydow, Julie Kavner, Daniel Stern, Tony Roberts, John Turturro; *D:* Woody Allen. Academy Awards '86: Best Original Screenplay, Best Supporting Actor (Caine), Best Supporting Actress (Wiest); Nominations: Best Art Direction/Set Decoration; Academy Awards '86: Best Director (Allen), Best Film Editing, Best Picture; Golden Globe Awards '87: Best Film—Musical/Comedy; New York Film Critics Awards '86: Best Film. VHS, Beta, LV $19.99 *HBO, BTV* 🎬🎬🎬½

Hanna's War A moving film about Hanna Senesh, a young Hungarian Jew living in Palestine, who volunteered for a suicide mission behind Nazi lines during World War II. After her capture by the Germans, she was killed, and is now considered by many to have been a martyr. Detmers is very believable as Hanna and Burstyn puts in a good performance as her mother.
1988 (PG-13) 148m/C Ellen Burstyn, Maruschka Detmers, Anthony Andrews, Donald Pleasence, David Warner, Denholm Elliott, Vincenzo Ricotta, Ingrid Pitt; *D:* Menahem Golan. VHS, Beta, LV $9.99 *CCB, MED, SWC* 🎬🎬½

Hannie Caulder A woman hires a bounty hunter to avenge her husband's murder and her own rape at the hands of three bandits. Excellent casting but uneven direction. Boyd is uncredited as the preacher.

1972 (R) 87m/C Raquel Welch, Robert Culp, Ernest Borgnine, Strother Martin, Jack Elam, Christopher Lee, Diana Dors, Stephen Boyd; *D:* Burt Kennedy. VHS $14.95 *PAR, FCT* 🎬🎬

Hanoi Hilton A brutal drama about the sufferings of American POWs in Vietnamese prison camps. Non-stop torture, filth, and degradation.
1987 (R) 126m/C Michael Moriarty, Paul LeMat, Jeffrey Jones, Lawrence Pressman, Stephen Davies, David Soul, Rick Fitts, Aki Aleong, Gloria Carlin; *D:* Lionel Chetwynd. VHS, Beta, LV $19.98 *WAR* 🎬½

Hanover Street An American bomber pilot and a married British nurse fall in love in war-torn Europe. Eventually the pilot must work with the husband of the woman he loves on a secret mission. A sappy, romantic tearjerker.
1979 (PG) 109m/C Harrison Ford, Lesley-Anne Down, Christopher Plummer, Alec McCowen; *W/ D:* Peter Hyams; *M:* John Barry. VHS, Beta, LV $14.95 *COL* 🎬🎬

Hans Brinker Young Hans Brinker and his sister participate in an ice skating race, hoping to win a pair of silver skates. A musical version of the classic tale.
1969 103m/C Robin Askwith, Eleanor Parker, Richard Basehart, Cyril Ritchard, John Gregson; *D:* Robert Scheerer. VHS, Beta $19.98 *WAR, OM* 🎬🎬½

Hans Christian Andersen Sentimental musical story of Hans Christian Andersen, a young cobbler who has a great gift for storytelling. Frank Loesser's score. Written by Moss Hart. Digitally remastered editions available with stereo sound and original trailer. 🎵The King's New Clothes; I'm Hans Christian Andersen; Wonderful Copenhagen; Thumbelina; The Ugly Duckling; Anywhere I Wander; The Inch Worm; No Two People.
1952 112m/C Danny Kaye, Farley Granger, Zizi Jeanmarie, Joey Walsh; *D:* Charles Vidor. VHS, Beta, LV $14.98 *HBO, SUE, FCT* 🎬🎬

Hansel and Gretel Grimm's fairy tale tells the story of the woodcutter's children who venture into the forest and are caught in the clutches of a wicked old witch. Puppet animation.
1954 82m/C *V:* Anna Russell, Mildred Dunnock. VHS, Beta $19.95 *MED* 🎬½

Hansel and Gretel From Shelly Duvall's "Faerie Tale Theatre" comes the story of two young children who get more than they bargained for when they eat a gingerbread house.
1982 51m/C Rick Schroder, Joan Collins, Paul Dooley, Bridgette Anderson; *D:* James Frawley. VHS, Beta, LV $14.98 *KUI, FOX, FCT* 🎬🎬

Hanussen The third of Szabo and Brandauer's price-of-power trilogy (after "Mephisto" and "Colonel Redl"), in which a talented German magician and clairvoyant (based on a true life figure) collaborates with the Nazis during their rise to power in the 1930s, although he can foresee the outcome of their reign. In German with English subtitles.
1988 (R) 110m/C *GE HU* Klaus Maria Brandauer, Erland Josephson, Walter Schmidinger; *D:* Istvan Szabo. VHS, Beta, LV $79.95 *COL, TAM* 🎬🎬🎬½

The Happiest Millionaire A Disney film about a newly immigrated lad who finds a job as butler in the home of an eccentric millionaire. Based on the book "My Philadelphia Father," by Kyle Chrichton. 🎵What's Wrong With That?; Watch Your Footwork; Valentine Candy; Strengthen the Dwelling; I'll Always Be Irish; Bye-Yum Pum Pum; I Believe in This Country; Detroit; There Are

Those; When A Man Has a Daughter; Let's Have a Drink On It; Are We Dancing?; La Belle Fille D'amour; It Won't Be Long 'til Christmas; Fortuosity.
1967 118m/C Fred MacMurray, Tommy Steele, Greer Garson, Geraldine Page, Lesley Ann Warren, John Davidson; *D:* Norman Tokar. VHS, Beta *DIS, OM* 🎬🎬

Happily Ever After Las Vegas starmaker recruits and manipulates two green performers. Show business life in Vegas is given a truthful treatment in made-for-television drama.
1982 95m/C Suzanne Somers, John Rubinstein, Eric Braeden; *D:* Robert Scheerer. VHS, Beta $69.95 *TLF* 🎬🎬

Happily Ever After A Brazilian housewife meets a bisexual transvestite and has a passionate affair, bringing her into the depths of the criminal underworld. In Portuguese with English subtitles. Contains nudity. *AKA:* Alem Da Paixao.
1986 106m/C *V:* Regina Duarte, Paul Castelli; *D:* Bruno Barreto. VHS, Beta $69.95 *FCT, TAM* 🎬🎬

Happily Ever After Sequel to "Snow White" that begins where the original ends and has no connection whatsoever with Walt Disney. In this one, Snow White and her Prince journey to the Seven Dwarfs' house to invite the guys to their wedding. Meanwhile, the Wicked Queen is found dead in her castle by her brother, Lord Maliss, who vows to get revenge. Lord Maliss turns himself into a flying red dragon and makes off with the Prince. It's now up to Snow White and the Dwarfelles, female cousins of the Seven Dwarfs, to rescue him. In some rather interesting choices made in the casting department, Diller plays Mother Nature and Asner provides the voice of an owl who performs a rap song. Although the animation isn't first-rate, the actors are good and the story is imaginative and easy to follow. Overall, it's decent entertainment for the kiddies.
1993 (G) 80m/C *D:* John Howley; *W:* Martha Moran, Robby London; *V:* Dom DeLuise, Phyllis Diller, Zsa Zsa Gabor, Ed Asner, Sally Kellerman, Irene Cara, Carol Channing, Tracy Ullman. VHS 🎬🎬

Happiness Another zany comedy from the land of the hammer and sickle. Banned in Russia for 40 years, it was deemed to be risque and a bit too biting with the social satire. Silent with orchestral score.
1934 69m/B *RU D:* Alexander Medvedkin. VHS $29.95 *KIV, FCT, TAM* 🎬🎬

Happy Anniversary 007: 25 Years of James Bond Film clip retrospective of the dashing British spy created by Ian Fleming. Hosted by Roger Moore.
1987 59m/C Sean Connery, Roger Moore, George Lazenby, Timothy Dalton; *D:* Mel Stuart. VHS, Beta $14.98 *FOX* 🎬🎬

Happy Birthday, Gemini A coming-of-age comedy about a young man on his 21st birthday worrying about his sexual identity. Based on the play "Gemini" by Albert Innaurato. The closeness of the characters on stage did not translate to the screen.
1980 (R) 107m/C Robert Viharo, Madeline Kahn, Rita Moreno, Alan Rosenberg, Sarah Holcomb, David Marshall Grant, David McIlwraith; *W/D:* Richard Benner. VHS $14.95 *MGM* 🎬½

Happy Birthday to Me Several elite seniors at an exclusive private school are mysteriously killed by a deranged killer who has a fetish for cutlery.
1981 (R) 108m/C *CA* Melissa Sue Anderson, Glenn Ford, Tracy Bregman, Jack Blum, Matt Craven; *D:* J. Lee Thompson. VHS, Beta, LV $69.95 *COL* 🎬½

The Happy Ending Woman struggles with a modern definition of herself and her marriage, causing pain and confusion for her family. Simmons is solid as the wife and mother seeking herself. Michel LeGrand's theme song "What Are You Doing With the Rest of Your Life?" was a big hit.
1969 (PG) 112m/C Jean Simmons, John Forsythe, Lloyd Bridges, Shirley Jones, Teresa Wright, Dick Shawn, Nanette Fabray, Bobby Darin, Tina Louise; **D:** Richard Brooks. **VHS** NO ♫♫½

The Happy Gigolo Soft-core fun about a gigolo in a European hotel making his nightly rounds. Foreign.
197? 73m/C Peter Ham, Margaret Rose Keil, Eva Gross, Rose Gardner, Al Price; **D:** Ilja Nutrof. **VHS, Beta** $29.95 ACA ♫

Happy Go Lovely An unscrupulous theatrical producer casts a chorus girl in a leading role in order to get closer to her boyfriend's fortune. Tired plot, but good performances in this lightweight musical. ♫One-Two-Three; Would You, Could You; London Town.
1951 95m/C Vera-Ellen, David Niven, Cesar Romero, Bobby Howes; **D:** H. Bruce Humberstone. **VHS, Beta** $24.95 NOS, MRV, DVT ♫♫

The Happy Hooker Xaviera Hollander's cheeky (and bestselling) memoir of her transition from office girl to "working girl" has been brought to the screen with a sprightly (though sanitary) air of naughtiness, with Redgrave enjoyable in title role. Followed by "The Happy Hooker Goes to Washington" and "The Happy Hooker Goes Hollywood."
1975 (R) 96m/C Lynn Redgrave, Jean-Pierre Aumont, Nicholas Pryor; **D:** Nicholas Sgarro. **VHS, Beta, LV** $29.95 CAN, VES ♫♫½

The Happy Hooker Goes Hollywood Third film inspired by the title of Xaviera Hollander's memoirs, in which the fun-loving Xaviera comes to Hollywood with the intention of making a movie based on her book, but soon meets up with a series of scheming, would-be producers.
1980 (R) 86m/C Martine Beswick, Chris Lemmon, Adam West, Phil Silvers; **D:** Alan Roberts. **VHS, Beta, LV** $39.98 CAN, MCA ♫

The Happy Hooker Goes to Washington Further adventures of the world's most famous madam. Heatherton (not Redgrave) is Xaviera Hollander this time, testifying before the U.S. Senate in defense of sex. Fairly stupid attempt to milk box office of original. Second in the holy trilogy of Happy Hooker pictures, which also include "The Happy Hooker" and "The Happy Hooker Goes Hollywood."
1977 (R) 89m/C Joey Heatherton, George Hamilton, Ray Walston, Jack Carter; **D:** William A. Levey. **VHS, Beta** $69.95 CAN, VES ♫½

Happy Hour A young brewing scientist discovers a secret formula for beer, and everyone tries to take it from him. Little turns in a good performance as a superspy.
1987 (R) 88m/C Richard Gilliland, Jamie Farr, Tawny Kitaen, Ty Henderson, Rich Little; **D:** John DeBello. **VHS, Beta, LV** $19.95 LIV ♫½

Happy New Year Charming romantic comedy in which two thieves plan a robbery but get sidetracked by the distracting woman who works next door to the jewelry store. Available in both subtitled and dubbed versions. Remade in 1987. **AKA:** The Happy New Year Caper.
1974 114m/C FR IT Francoise Fabian, Lino Ventura, Andre Falcon; **D:** Claude Lelouch. **VHS, Beta** $29.98 SUE ♫♫♫

Happy New Year Two sophisticated thieves plan and execute an elaborate jewel heist that goes completely awry. Remake of the 1974 French film of the same name.
1987 (PG) 86m/C Peter Falk, Wendy Hughes, Tom Courtenay, Charles Durning; **D:** John G. Avildsen. **VHS, Beta** $79.95 COL ♫♫½

Happy New Year, Charlie Brown Strife upsets the Peanuts gang as the New Year's Eve gala becomes a source of tension.
1982 25m/C **D:** Bill Melendez, Sam Jaimes. **VHS, Beta** $9.95 KRT, KAR, WTA ♫♫½

Happy Sex An Italian-made farce about nymphomaniac women in a small Italian village.
1986 60m/C IT Marina Frajese, Guia Lauri. **VHS, Beta** $29.95 MED ♫

Happy Together An eager freshman accidentally gets a beautiful, impulsive girl as his roommate. Together they meet the challenges of secondary education.
1989 (PG-13) 102m/C Helen Slater, Patrick Dempsey, Dan Schneider, Marius Weyers, Barbara Babcock; **D:** Mel Damski. **VHS, Beta, LV** $89.95 LIV ♫

Hard-Boiled Mahoney Slip, Sach, and the rest of the Bowery Boys try to solve a mystery involving mysterious women and missing men. The last film in the series for Bobby Jordan, whose career was ended when he was injured in an accident involving a falling elevator.
1947 64m/B Leo Gorcey, Huntz Hall, Bobby Jordan, Billy Benedict, David Gorcey, Gabriel Dell, Teala Loring, Dan Seymour, Bernard Gorcey, Patti Brill, Betty Compson; **D:** William Beaudine. **VHS** $14.98 WAR ♫♫½

Hard Choices A 15-year-old Tennessee boy is unjustly charged as an accessory to murder, until a female social worker decides to help him. From then on, nothing is predictable. Excellent work by Klenck, McCleery, and Seitz. Don't miss Sayles as an unusual drug dealer. Intelligent, surprising, and powerful. Based on a true story, this is a low profile film that deserves to be discovered.
1984 90m/C Margaret Klenek, Gary McCleery, John Seitz, John Sayles, Liane Curtis, J.T. Walsh, Spalding Gray; **W/D:** Rick King. **VHS, Beta** $79.95 KRT, LHV, WAR ♫♫♫

Hard Country Caught between her best friend's success as a country singer and the old values of a woman's place, a small town girl questions her love and her life style. A warm and intelligent rural drama. Basinger's debut. Music by Michael Martin Murphy.
1981 (PG) 104m/C Jan-Michael Vincent, Kim Basinger, Michael Parks, Gailard Sartain, Tanya Tucker, Ted Neely, Daryl Hannah, Richard Moll; **D:** David Greene. **VHS, LV** NO ♫♫½

Hard Day's Night The Beatles' first film is a joyous romp through an average "day in the life" of the Fab Four, shot in a pseudo-documentary style with great flair by Lester and noted as the first music video. Laser version includes original trailer and an interview with Lester. ♫A Hard Day's Night; Tell Me Why; I Should Have Known Better; She Loves You; I'm Happy Just To Dance With You; If I Fell; And I Love Her; This Boy; Can't Buy Me Love; I Wanna Be Your Man; All My Loving.
1964 90m/B GB John Lennon, Paul McCartney, George Harrison, Ringo Starr; **D:** Richard Lester. **VHS, Beta, LV** $29.95 MVD, MPI, VYG ♫♫♫½

Hard Drivin' Rowdy action featuring Southern stock car drivers with well shot race scenes from the Southern 500.
1960 92m/C Rory Calhoun, John Gentry, Alan Hale Jr.; **D:** Paul Helmick. **VHS, Beta** NO ♫

Hard Frame An ex-con returns home hoping all will turn to sweetness and light when he attempts to make nice-nice with his stepdad, who wouldn't stick by him during his trial. Reynolds' debut into TV moviedom; could be the hirsute actor was thinking of this one when he said his movies were the kind they show in prisons and airplanes because nobody can leave. **AKA:** Hunters Are For Killing.
1970 100m/C Burt Reynolds, Melvyn Douglas, Suzanne Pleshette, Larry Storch, Martin Balsam, Peter Brown, Jill Banner, Donald (Don "Red") Barry, Angus Duncan, Ivor Francis; **D:** Bernard Girard. **VHS** $9.95 SIM ♫½

Hard Hombre Gibson rides and shoots across the screen in one of his best western adventures.
1931 60m/B Hoot Gibson, Lena Basquette, Skeeter Bill Robbins, Jack Byron, Glenn Strange; **D:** Otto Brower. **VHS, Beta** $29.95 GPV, VCN, UHV ♫♫

Hard Hunted Three macho undercover agents try to avoid death at the hands of high-tech guerillas trying to steal nuclear weapons. No-brain actioner, heavy on the display of feminine charms.
1992 (R) 97m/C Dona Speir, Roberta Vasquez, Cynthia Brimhall, Bruce Penhall, R.J. Moore, Tony Peck, Rodrigo Obregon, Al Leong, Michael J. Shane; **W/D:** Andy Sidaris. **VHS** $89.95 COL ♫½

Hard Knocks An ex-con goes from one tragic situation to another, and is eventually stalked by shotgun-wielding rednecks in this grim, powerful drama. Excellent performance by Mann holds this picture together.
1980 85m/C AU Tracey Mann, John Arnold, Bill Hunter, Max Cullen, Tony Barry; **D:** Don McLennan. **Beta** NO ♫♫½

Hard Knocks A young man on the run is tormented by an aging actress and her husband. His attempt to leave a past of violence and pain creates even more havoc.
19?? 90m/C Michael Christian, John Crawford, Donna Wilkes, Keenan Wynn. **VHS, Beta** NO ♫

Hard Knox A hard-nosed Marine pilot is dumped from the service and takes up command at a military school filled with undisciplined punks. A made-for-television movie.
1983 96m/C Robert Conrad, Frank Howard, Alan Ruck, Red West, Bill Erwin, Dean Hill, Joan Sweeney; **D:** Peter Werner. **VHS, Beta** $59.95 KRT, LHV ♫

Hard Part Begins A naive country singer gets sucked into the pratfalls of show business.
198? 87m/C Donnelly Rhodes, Nancy Belle Fuller, Paul Bradley. **VHS, Beta** $49.95 TWE ♫

Hard Promises Average performances and script round out this innocuous domestic comedy-drama about Joey, a man with wandering feet who hasn't been home in so long he doesn't even know his wife has divorced him—until he is accidentally invited to her wedding! Joey hightails it back to discover the intended groom was a hated high-school rival, so he decides to battle to win his ex-wife back. But this time his macho charm may not be enough to smooth out all the marital rough spots.
1992 (PG) 95m/C Sissy Spacek, William L. Petersen, Brian Kerwin, Mare Winningham, Peter MacNicol, Ann Wedgeworth, Amy Wright, Lois Smith, Rip Torn; **D:** Martin Davidson. **VHS, LV, 8mm** COL ♫♫

Hard Rain-The Tet 1968 An American platoon stationed in Saigon must mobilize in the wake of the North Vietnamese Army's Tet offensive. An episode of televi-

sion's "Tour of Duty." Other episodes are also available on tape.
1989 89m/C Terence Knox, Stephen Caffrey; **D:** Bill L. Norton. **VHS $59.95** NWV ⅃

Hard Rock Zombies Four heavy metal band members die horribly on the road and are brought back from the dead as zombies. This horror/heavy metal spoof is somewhat amusing in a goofy way.
1985 (R) 90m/C E.J. Curcio, Sam Mann; **D:** Krishna Shah. **VHS, Beta $69.98** LIV, VES ⅃½

Hard Ticket to Hawaii A shot-on-video spy thriller about an agent trying to rescue a comrade in Hawaii from a smuggling syndicate. Supporting cast includes many Playboy Playmates.
1987 (R) 96m/C Ron Moss, Dona Speir, Hope Marie Carlton, Cynthia Brimhall; **D:** Andy Sidaris. **VHS, Beta $79.95** KRT, LHV, WAR ⅃

Hard Times A Depression-era drifter becomes a bare knuckle street fighter, and a gambler decides to promote him for big stakes. One of grade-B meister Hill's first genre films. A quiet, evocative drama.
1975 (PG) 92m/C Charles Bronson, James Coburn, Jill Ireland, Strother Martin; **D:** Walter Hill. **VHS, Beta, LV $12.95** GKK ⅃⅃⅃

Hard to Hold Rockin' Rick's lukewarm film debut where he falls in love with a children's counselor after an automobile accident. Springfield sings "Love Somebody" with music by Peter Gabriel.
1984 (PG) 93m/C Rick Springfield, Janet Eilber, Patti Hansen, Albert Salmi, Monique Gabrielle; **D:** Larry Peerce. **VHS, Beta, LV $69.95** MCA ⅃½

Hard to Kill Policeman Seagal is shot and left for dead in his bedroom, but survives against the odds, though his wife does not. After seven years, he is well enough to consider evening the score with his assailants. He hides while training in martial arts for the final battle. Strong outing from Seagal, with good supporting cast.
1989 (R) 96m/C Steven Seagal, Kelly Le Brock, Bill Sadler, Frederick Coffin, Bonnie Burroughs, Zachary Rosencrantz, Dean Norris; **D:** Bruce Malmuth. **VHS, Beta, LV, 8mm $19.98** WAR, PIA ⅃⅃

Hard Traveling An unemployed Depression-era farmworker is accused of murder. He must fight a hostile court system to maintain his dignity and salvage the love and respect of his wife. Based on a novel by Alvah Bessie.
1985 (PG) 99m/C J.E. Freeman, Ellen Geer, Barry Corbin, James Gammon, Jim Haynie; **D:** Dan Bessie. **VHS, Beta $19.95** STE, NWV ⅃⅃

Hard Way A world-weary assassin is pressured by his boss to perform one last assignment. A surprise awaits him if he accepts.
1980 88m/C Patrick McGoohan, Lee Van Cleef, Donal McCann, Edna O'Brien; **D:** Mihael Dryhurst. **VHS, Beta $59.95** TWE ⅃⅃

The Hard Way Diminutive Hollywood superstar Fox decides to learn the cop business first hand on the mean streets of New York. Although in pursuit of crazed serial killer Lang, hardened cop Woods is informed by his commanders that he WILL do the necessary training. Nothing special in the way of script or direction, but Woods and Fox bring such intensity and good humor to their roles that the package works. The annoying, self-absorbed actor, Fox has fun poking fun at the L.A. lifestyle, with an entertaining cameo appearance by Marshall as his agent. Woods is on familiar over-the-edge turf as the brittle but dedicated detective who can't believe his bad luck in being chosen as role model for Fox. Though under-

employed, Lang is effectively psychotic. Silly finale almost destroys the film, but other small vignettes—including the bar scene when Fox play-acts as a woman—are terrific.
1991 (R) 91m/C James Woods, Michael J. Fox, Annabella Sciorra, Stephen Lang, L.L. Cool J., John Capodice, Christina Ricci, Karen Gorney; **Cameos:** Penny Marshall; **D:** John Badham; **W:** Daniel Pyne, Lem Dobbs. **VHS, Beta, LV $19.98** MCA, PIA ⅃⅃⅃

Hardbodies Three middle-aged men hit the beaches of Southern California in search of luscious young girls. They find them. Mid-life crisis done stupidly. Followed by a sequel.
1984 (R) 88m/C Grant Cramer, Teal Roberts, Gary Wood, Michael Rapport, Sorrels Pickard, Roberta Collins, Cindy Silver, Courtney Gains, Kristi Somers, Crystal Shaw, Kathleen Kinmont, Joyce Jameson; **D:** Mark Griffiths. **VHS, Beta, LV $79.95** COL ⅃

Hardbodies 2 A sequel to the original comedy hit, dealing with film crew in Greece that is distracted by hordes of nude natives. Sophomoric humor dependent on nudity and profanity for laughs.
1986 (R) 89m/C Brad Zutaut, Brenda Bakke, Fabiana Udenio, James Karen; **D:** Mark Griffiths. **VHS, Beta, LV $9.95** COL Woof!

Hardcase and Fist A framed cop leaves prison with his mind on revenge. The godfather who used him is just his first target.
1989 (R) 92m/C Maureen Lavette, Ted Prior; **D:** Tony Zarindast. **VHS, Beta $79.98** MCG ⅃⅃

Hardcore A Midwestern businessman who is raising a strict Christian family learns of his daughter's disappearance while she is on a church trip. After hiring a streetwise investigator, he learns that his daughter has become an actress in pornographic films out in California. Strong performance by Scott and glimpse into the hardcore pornography industry prove to be convincing points of this film, though it exploits what it condemns. **AKA:** The Hardcore Life.
1979 (R) 106m/C George C. Scott, Season Hubley, Peter Boyle, Dick Sargent; **W/D:** Paul Schrader; **M:** Jack Nitzsche. **VHS, Beta, LV $9.95** COL ⅃⅃½

The Harder They Come A poor Jamaican youth becomes a success with a hit reggae record after he has turned to a life of crime out of desperation. Songs, which are blended nicely into the framework of the film, include "You Can Get It If You Really Want It" and "Sitting In Limbo."
1972 (R) 93m/C Jimmy Cliff, Janet Barkley, Carl Bradshaw; **D:** Perry Henzell. **VHS, Beta, LV $19.95** HBO, CRC, FCT ⅃⅃½

The Harder They Fall A cold-eyed appraisal of the scum-infested boxing world. An unemployed reporter (Bogart in his last role) promotes a fighter for the syndicate, while doing an expose on the fight racket. Bogart became increasingly debilitated during filming and died soon afterward. Based on Budd Schulberg's novel.
1956 109m/B Humphrey Bogart, Rod Steiger, Jan Sterling, Mike Lane, Max Baer; **D:** Mark Robson. **VHS, Beta $19.98** CCB, COL ⅃⅃⅃

Hardhat & Legs Comic complications arise when a New York construction worker falls in love with the woman who's teaching the modern sexuality course in which he's enrolled. Made for television; Ruth Gordon co-scripted this one.
1980 96m/C Sharon Gless, Kevin Dobson, Ray Serra, Elva Josephson, Bobby Short, Jacqueline Brookes, W.T. Martin; **D:** Lee Philips. **VHS, Beta** NO ⅃⅃

Hardly Working A circus clown finds it difficult to adjust to real life as he fumbles about from one job to another. Lewis's last attempt at resuscitating his directorial career. His fans will love it, but others need not bother.
1981 (PG) 90m/C Jerry Lewis, Susan Oliver, Roger C. Carmel, Gary Lewis, Deanna Lund; **D:** Jerry Lewis. **VHS, Beta $59.98** FOX ⅃

Hardware Rag-tag ripoff in which McDermott is a post-apocalyptic garbage picker who gives girlfriend Travis some robot remains he collected (ours is not to ask why), oblivious to the fact that the tidy android was a government-spawned population controller programmed to destroy warm bodies. Seems old habits die hard, and that spells danger, danger, Will Robinson. Much violence excised to avoid x-rating.
1990 (R) 94m/C Dylan McDermott, Stacy Travis, John Lynch, Iggy Pop; **D:** Richard Stanley. **VHS, Beta, LV $19.98** HBO ⅃½

Hardware Wars & Other Film Farces A collection of four award-winning spoofs of big-budget film epics, featuring "Hardware Wars," "Porklips Now," "Bambi Meets Godzilla," and "Closet Cases of the Nerd Kind." Some black-and-white segments.
1981 (G) 48m/C VHS, Beta WAR, OM ⅃½

Harem A beautiful stockbroker gets kidnapped by a wealthy OPEC oil minister and becomes part of his harem. Kingsley stars as the lonely sheik who longs for the love of a modern woman.
1985 107m/C FR Ben Kingsley, Nastassia Kinski; **D:** Alfred Joffe. **VHS, Beta, LV $79.98** LIV, VES ⅃

Harem In the early 1900s, a dastardly Turkish sultan kidnaps an American beauty to add to his harem—mightily displeasingly his jealous first wife. Lots of overwrought romance and drama until she is finally rescued. Made for television.
1986 200m/C Omar Sharif, Nancy Travis, Ava Gardner, Julian Sands, Art Malik, Sarah Miles, Yaphet Kotto, Cherie Lunghi; **D:** Billy Hale. **VHS** STE ⅃⅃

Harlan County, U.S.A. The emotions of 180 coal mining families are seen up close in this classic documentary about their struggle to win a United Mine Workers contract in Kentucky. Award-winning documentary.
1976 (PG) 103m/C D: Barbara Kopple. **VHS, Beta $19.98** COL ⅃⅃

Harlem Nights Two Harlem nightclub owners in the 1930s battle comically against efforts by the Mob and crooked cops to take over their territory. High-grossing, although somewhat disappointing effort from Murphy, who directed, wrote, produced, and starred in this film.
1989 (R) 118m/C Eddie Murphy, Richard Pryor, Redd Foxx, Danny Aiello, Jasmine Guy, Michael Lerner, Arsenio Hall, Della Reese; **D:** Eddie Murphy. **VHS, Beta, LV $14.95** PAR ⅃⅃

Harlem on the Prairie This first-ever western with an all-black cast has Jeffries helping a young lady find hidden gold and foiling a villain. Even though the technical standards and acting are below par, this is worth watching for the singing and a comedy routine done by a well-known contemporary black team. ♫Harlem On The Prairie; Romance In The Rain. **AKA:** Bad Man of Harlem.
1938 54m/B Herbert Jeffries, Mantan Moreland, F.E. Miller, Connie Harris, Maceo B. Sheffield, William Spencer Jr.; **D:** Sam Newfield; **M:** The Four Tunes. **VHS $24.95** NOS ⅃

Harlem Rides the Range Jeffries must outsmart villainous Brooks, who means to swindle a radium mine away from its rightful owner. Early oater of interest only because of its atypical all-black cast and crew.
1939 58m/B Herbert Jeffries, Lucius Brooks, Artie Young, F.E. Miller, Spencer Williams Jr., Clarence Brooks, Tom Southern, Wade Dumas, The Four Tunes, Leonard Christmas; **D:** Richard C. Kahn; **W:** F.E. Miller, Spencer Williams Jr. VHS $24.95 *NOS, MRV, TPV* ⅛½

Harley Diamond is Harley, an L.A. thug-on-a-hog, who's on his way to an extended stay at one of the state's luxury institutions when he's sent to a Texas rehabilitation community. There, he bonds with an ex-biker, and may just find his way back down the straight and narrow. And the local longhorn rednecks applaud his efforts...not.
1990 (PG) 80m/C Lou Diamond Phillips, Eli Cummins, DeWitt Jan, Valentine Kim; **D:** Fred Holmes; **W:** Frank Kuntz, Sandy Kuntz. VHS $89.95 *VMK* ⅛

Harley Davidson and the Marlboro Man An awful rehash of "Butch Cassidy and the Sundance Kid" with blatant vulgarity and pointless sci-fi touches. The title duo are near-future outlaws who rob a bank to save their favorite bar, then find they've stolen mob money. Some action, but it's mostly talk: lewd, meant-to-be-whimsical soul-probing chats between H.D. and M.M. that would bore even the biker crowd—and did.
1991 (R) 98m/C Mickey Rourke, Don Johnson, Chelsea Field, Tom Sizemore, Vanessa Williams, Robert Ginty; **D:** Simon Wincer. VHS, Beta, LV, 8mm $19.98 *MGM, PIA* ⅛

Harlow The more lavish of the two Harlow biographies made in 1965, both with the same title. A sensationalized "scandal sheet" version of Jean Harlow's rise to fame that bears little resemblance to the facts of her life.
1965 125m/C Carroll Baker, Martin Balsam, Red Buttons, Mike Connors, Angela Lansbury, Peter Lawford, Raf Vallone, Leslie Nielsen; **D:** Gordon Douglas. VHS, Beta $14.95 *PAR* ⅛⅛½

Harmagedon When Princess Luna's jetliner explodes she is thrown into a psychic plane where she must battle Genma, an eternal being who has destroyed half the universe. Luna gathers together the heroic Psyonic Warriors and the cyborg Vega to aid in her battle. Animated; in Japanese with English subtitles.
1983 131m/C JP VHS, LV $39.95 *CPM* ⅛⅛

Harmony Lane Highly romanticised rendition of the life of American composer, Stephen Collins Foster (1826-1864). Montgomery, as Foster, manages to lend a hint of credibility to the syrupy, melodramatic script. Very little attention is given to historical fact and almost every scene is orchestrated to showcase the composer's songs. The music steals the show. ♫Beautiful Dreamer; Old Folks at Home; Swanee River; Oh! Susanna; De Camptown Races.
1935 84m/B Douglass Montgomery, Evelyn Venable, Adrienne Ames, Joseph Cawthorn, William Frawley, Florence Roberts, Smiley Burnette, Hattie McDaniel; **D:** Joseph Santley. VHS $24.95 *DVT, NOS, VYY* ⅛

Harmony Trail Maynard stars in another rip-roaring western adventure.
1944 60m/B Ken Maynard. VHS, Beta $19.95 *NOS, VCN, DVT* ⅛½

Harold and Maude A cult classic pairing Bud Cort as a dead-pan disillusioned 20-year-old obsessed with suicide (his staged attempts are a highlight) and a loveable Ruth Gordon as a fun-loving 80-year-old eccentric. They meet at a funeral (a mutual hobby), and develop a taboo romantic relationship, in which they explore the tired theme of the meaning of life with a fresh perspective. Features music by the pre-Islamic Cat Stevens.
1971 (PG) 92m/C Ruth Gordon, Bud Cort, Cyril Cusack, Vivian Pickles, Charles Tyner, Ellen Geer; **D:** Hal Ashby. VHS, Beta, LV, 8mm $14.95 *PAR* ⅛⅛⅛⅛

Harper A tight, fast-moving genre piece about cynical LA private eye Newman investigating the disappearance of Bacall's wealthy husband, adapted by William Golding. Later sequelled in "The Drowning Pool." **AKA:** The Moving Target.
1966 121m/C Paul Newman, Shelley Winters, Lauren Bacall, Julie Harris, Robert Wagner, Janet Leigh, Arthur Hill; **D:** Jack Smight. VHS, Beta, LV $19.98 *WAR, PIA* ⅛⅛⅛

Harper Valley P.T.A. Eden raises hell in Harper Valley after the PTA questions her parental capabilities. Brain candy was adapted from a hit song; TV series followed.
1978 (PG) 93m/C Barbara Eden, Nanette Fabray, Louis Nye, Pat Paulsen, Ronny Cox, Ron Masak, Audrey Christie, John Fiedler, Bob Hastings; **D:** Richard Bennett. VHS, Beta $19.98 *VES* ⅛⅛

Harrad Experiment Adaptation of Robert Rimmer's love-power bestseller in which an experiment-minded college establishes a campus policy of sexual freedom. Famous for the Hedren/Johnson relationship, shortly before Johnson married Hedren's real-life daughter Melanie Griffith. Followed by "The Harrad Experiment."
1973 (R) 98m/C James Whitmore, Tippi Hedren, Don Johnson, Bruno Kirby, Laurie Walters, Victoria Thompson, Elliot Street, Sharon Taggart, Robert Middleton, Billy Sands, Melanie Griffith; **D:** Ted Post. VHS, Beta *UHV, VES* ⅛½

Harrad Summer Sequel to "The Harrad Experiment." College coeds take their sex-education to the bedroom where they can apply their knowledge by more intensive means.
1974 (R) 103m/C Richard Doran, Victoria Thompson, Laurie Walters, Robert Reiser, Bill Dana, Marty Allen; **D:** Steven Hilliard Stern. VHS *UHV* ⅛⅛

Harry & Son A widowed construction worker faces the problems of raising his son. Newman is miscast as the old man and we've all seen Benson play the young role too many times.
1984 (PG) 117m/C Paul Newman, Robby Benson, Ellen Barkin, Wilford Brimley, Judith Ivey, Ossie Davis, Morgan Freeman, Joanne Woodward; **D:** Paul Newman. VHS, Beta, LV $79.98 *VES* ⅛⅛

Harry and the Hendersons An ordinary American family is on vacation in the Northwest when the family car has a collision with Bigfoot. Thinking that the big guy is dead, they throw him on top of the car and head home. Lo and behold, he revives and starts wrecking the furniture and in the process, endears himself to the at-first frightened family. But the arrival of Harry starts the neighbors talking, and the family decides he must return to the wild for his own good. Trouble is, Harry doesn't want to go so he escapes. And the hunt is on. Nice little tale efficiently told, with Lithgow fine as the

frustrated dad trying to hold his Bigfoot-invaded home together.
1987 (PG) 111m/C John Lithgow, Melinda Dillon, Don Ameche, David Suchet; **D:** William Dear. VHS, Beta, LV $19.95 *MCA, APD* ⅛⅛½

Harry and Tonto A gentle comedy about an energetic septuagenarian who takes a cross-country trip with his cat, Tonto. Never in a hurry, still capable of feeling surprise and joy, he makes new friends and visits old lovers. Carney deserved his Oscar. Mazursky has seldom been better.
1974 115m/C Art Carney, Ellen Burstyn, Larry Hagman, Geraldine Fitzgerald, Chief Dan George, Arthur Hunnicutt, Josh Mostel; **D:** Paul Mazursky. Academy Awards '74: Best Actor (Carney); Nominations: Best Original Screenplay; Golden Globe Awards '75: Best Actor—Musical/Comedy (Carney); National Board of Review Awards '74: 10 Best Films of the Year. VHS, Beta $19.98 *FOX, FCT, BTV* ⅛⅛⅛

Harry & Walter Go to New York At the turn of the century, two vaudeville performers are hired by a crooked British entrepreneur for a wild crime scheme. The cast and crew try their hardest, but it's not enough to save this boring comedy. The vaudeville team of Caan and Gould perhaps served as a model for Beatty and Hoffman in "Ishtar."
1976 (PG) 111m/C James Caan, Elliott Gould, Michael Caine, Diane Keaton, Burt Young, Jack Gilford, Charles Durning, Lesley Ann Warren, Carol Kane; **D:** Mark Rydell. VHS, Beta, LV $9.95 *COL* ⅛⅛

Harry Black and the Tiger Jungle adventure involving a one-legged hunter and a man-eating tiger. The hunter initally teams up with the old war buddy who cost him his leg. The motivation grows with each failure to catch the beast and to make matters worse, the friend's wife and son are lost somewhere in the perilous jungle. Filmed in India. **AKA:** Harry Black.
1958 107m/C GB Stewart Granger, Barbara Rush, Anthony Steel; **D:** Hugo Fregonese. VHS *TCF* ⅛⅛

Harry Tracy Whimsical tale of the legendary outlaw whose escapades made him both a wanted criminal and an exalted folk hero. **AKA:** Harry Tracy—Desperado.
1983 (PG) 111m/C CA Bruce Dern, Gordon Lightfoot, Helen Shaver, Michael C. Gwynne; **D:** William A. Graham. VHS, Beta $69.95 *VES* ⅛⅛½

Harry's War A middle-class, middle-aged American declares military war on the IRS in this overdone comedy.
1984 (PG) 98m/C Edward Herrmann, Geraldine Page, Karen Grassle, David Ogden Stiers; **D:** Keith Merrill. VHS, Beta $59.95 *TPI* ⅛⅛

Harum Scarum Elvis tune-fest time! When a movie star (Presley) travels through the Middle East, he becomes involved in an attempted assassination of the king and falls in love with his daughter. He also sings at the drop of a veil: "Shake That Tambourine," "Harem Holiday," and seven others. **AKA:** Harem Holiday.
1965 95m/C Elvis Presley, Mary Ann Mobley, Fran Jeffries, Michael Ansara, Billy Barty, Theo Marcuse, Jay Novello; **D:** Gene Nelson. VHS, Beta $19.95 *MGM* ⅛⅛

Harvest A classically Pagnolian rural pageant-of-life melodrama, wherein a pair of loners link up together in an abandoned French town and completely revitalize it and the land around it. From the novel by Jean Giono. In French with English subtitles. Music by Arthur Honegger.
1937 128m/B FR Fernandel, Gabriel Gabrio, Orane Demazis, Edouard Delmont; **D:** Marcel Pagnol. VHS, Beta $69.95 *INT, MRV, FCT* ⅛⅛⅛⅛

The Harvest Bizarre story sure to ignite small cult following about screenwriter Miguel Ferrer's involvement with the wrong woman at a Mexican hotel. Sultry temptress Leilani Sarelle Ferrer sends Miguel's internal thermometer into convulsions with her preference for ice during lovemaking. However, their tryst turns sour (for him) when L.S. Ferrer takes M. Ferrer to the beach where mystery thugs beat him unconscious. Then they swipe his kidney. Down to a solo kidney but undaunted, he attempts to find the bad guys but soon discovers they're after his remaining internals. One of the few organ abduction films.
1993 (R) 97m/C Miguel Ferrer, Leilani Sarelle Ferrer, Harvey Fierstein, Anthony John Denison, Tim Thomerson, Matt Clark, Henry Silva; **D:** David Marconi; **W:** David Marconi; **M:** Dave Allen, Rick Boston. VHS NYR ♪♪½

Harvest Melody Singing star Gilda Parker travels to farm country for a mere publicity stunt but decides to stay. Corny in more ways than one. ♫You Could Have Knocked Me Over With A Feather; Put It In Reverse; Let's Drive Out To The Drive-In; Tenderly.
1943 70m/B Rosemary Lane, Johnny Downs, Sheldon Leonard, Charlotte Wynters, Luis Alberni, Claire Rochelle, Syd Saylor; **D:** Sam Newfield. VHS $19.95 NOS, LOO ♪♪

Harvey Straightforward version of the Mary Chase play about a friendly drunk with an imaginary 6-foot rabbit friend named Harvey, and a sister who tries to have him committed. A fondly remembered, charming comedy. Hull is a standout, well deserving her Oscar.
1950 104m/B James Stewart, Josephine Hull, Victoria Horne, Peggy Dow, Cecil Kellaway, Charles Drake, Jesse White, Wallace Ford, Nana Bryant; **D:** Henry Koster. Academy Awards '50: Best Supporting Actress (Hull); Nominations: Best Actor (Stewart); Golden Globe Awards '51: Best Supporting Actress (Hull). VHS, Beta, LV $14.95 MCA, BTV, RDG ♪♪♪½

The Harvey Girls Lightweight musical about a restaurant chain that sends its waitresses to work in the Old West. ♫In the Valley Where the Evening Sun Goes Down; Wait and See; On the Atchison, Topeka and the Santa Fe; It's a Great Big World; The Wild Wild West.
1946 102m/C Judy Garland, Ray Bolger, John Hodiak, Preston Foster, Angela Lansbury, Virginia O'Brien, Marjorie Main, Chill Wills, Kenny L. Baker, Selena Royle, Cyd Charisse; **D:** George Sidney; **M:** Harry Warren, Johnny Mercer. Academy Awards '46: Best Song ("On the Atchison, Topeka and Santa Fe"); Nominations: Best Song ("On the Atchison, Topeka and Santa Fe"), Best Original Score. VHS, Beta, LV $19.98 MGM, FCT ♪♪♪

Has Anyone Seen My Pants? A naive farmboy from Texas inherits a hotel in Heidelberg, Germany. Hilarity and sensuality result when he discovers that the hotel is really a brothel.
19?? 86m/C Judith Fritsch, Franz Muxeneder. VHS $39.95 MED ♪

A Hash House Fraud/The Sultan's Wife "A Hash House Fraud" (1915) features a frenetic Keystone chase. "The Sultan's Wife" (1917) concerns a woman who attracts the unwanted attention of a sultan.
1915 33m/B Louise Fazenda, Hugh Fay, Chester Conklin, Gloria Swanson, Bobby Vernon. VHS, Beta $19.98 CCB ♪♪

The Hasty Heart A rowdy, terminally ill Scotsman brings problems and friendships to a makeshift war-time hospital built in the jungles of Burma. Remake of 1949 flick with

Richard Todd and Ronald Reagan in leading roles.
1986 100m/C Gregory Harrison, Cheryl Ladd, Perry King; **D:** Martin Speer. VHS, Beta $59.95 KRT, LHV, WAR ♪♪

Hat Box Mystery A detective's secretary is tricked into shooting a woman and private eye Neal is determined to save her from prison. Although not outstanding, it's worth seeing as perhaps the shortest detective film (a mere 44 min.) to ever make it as a feature.
1947 44m/B Tom Neal, Pamela Blake, Allen Jenkins; **D:** Lambert Hillyer. VHS, Beta, LV $16.95 SNC, WGE, VYY ♪♪

Hatari An adventure-loving team of professional big game hunters ventures to East Africa to round up animals for zoos around the world. Led by Wayne, they get into a couple of scuffs along the way, including one with lady photographer Martinelli who is doing a story on the expedition. Extraordinary footage of Africa and the animals. Fantastic musical score by Henry Mancini.
1962 158m/C John Wayne, Elsa Martinelli, Red Buttons, Hardy Kruger, Gerard Blain, Bruce Cabot; **D:** Howard Hawks; **M:** Henry Mancini. VHS, Beta, LV $49.95 PAR ♪♪♪

Hatchet for the Honeymoon A rather disturbed young man goes around hacking young brides to death as he tries to find out who murdered his wife. Typical sick Bava horror flick; confusing plot, but strong on vivid imagery. **AKA:** Blood Brides; Una Hacka Para la Luna de Miel; Il Roso Segmo Della Pollias.
1970 90m/C SP IT Stephen Forsythe, Dagmar Lassander, Laura Betti, Gerard Tichy; **D:** Mario Bava. VHS, Beta $12.95 MED, TIM, HEG ♪

The Hatfields & the McCoys A made-for-television re-telling of the most famous feud in American history—the legendary mountain war between the Hatfields and the McCoys.
1975 90m/C Jack Palance, Steve Forrest, Richard Hatch, Karen Lamm; **D:** Clyde Ware. VHS, Beta $14.98 WOV ♪♪

Hats Off Clarke and Payne star as opposing press agents in this tedious musical. The only bright spot is the finale, which features white-robed girls on a cloud-covered carousel. ♫Where Have You Been All My Life?; Little Old Rhythm; Twinkle, Twinkle, Little Star; Let's Have Another; Zilch's Hats; Hats Off.
1937 65m/B Mae Clarke, John Payne, Helen Lynd, Luis Alberni, Skeets Gallagher, Franklin Pangborn; **D:** Boris L. Petroff. VHS $19.95 NOS, MLB ♪

The Haunted The ancient curse of an Indian woman haunts a present day family by possessing the body of a beautiful girl. Through the girl, a horrible vengeance is carried out. **AKA:** Haunted.
1979 81m/C Aldo Ray, Virginia Mayo, Anne Michelle, Jim Negele; **D:** Michael de Gaetano. VHS, Beta $9.95 SIM, VHE, HHE ♪

The Haunted Castle One of Murnau's first films, and a vintage, if crusty, example of German expressionism. A nobleman entertains guests at his country mansion when strange things start to occur. Silent, with English titles. **AKA:** Schloss Vogelod.
1921 56m/B Arnold Korff, Lulu Keyser-Korff; **D:** F. W. Murnau. VHS, Beta $16.95 SNC, NOS, VYY ♪♪♪

Haunted Honeymoon Arthritic comedy about a haunted house and a couple trapped there. Sad times for the Mel Brooks alumni participating in this lame horror spoof.

1986 (PG) 82m/C Gene Wilder, Gilda Radner, Dom DeLuise, Jonathan Pryce, Paul Smith, Peter Vaughan, Bryan Pringle, Roger Ashton-Griffiths, Jim Carter; **D:** Gene Wilder. VHS, Beta, LV $34.95 HBO ♪

The Haunted Palace Price plays both a 17th-century warlock burned at the stake and a descendant who returns to the family dungeon and gets possessed by the mutant-breeding forebearer. The movie has its own identity crisis, with title and ambience from Poe but story from H.P. Lovecraft's "The Case of Charles Dexter Ward." Respectable but rootless chills, also available with the quasi-Lovecraft "Curse of the Crimson Altar" on laser disc.
1963 87m/C Vincent Price, Debra Paget, Lon Chaney Jr., Frank Maxwell, Leo Gordon, Elisha Cook, John Dierkes; **D:** Roger Corman. VHS, Beta, LV $59.98 HBO, MLB ♪♪½

Haunted Ranch Reno Red has been murdered and a shipment of gold bullion is missing. A gang on the lookout for the gold tries to convince people that Red's ranch is haunted by his ghost.
1943 56m/B John "Dusty" King, David Sharpe, Max Terhune, Rex Lease, Julie Duncan; **D:** Robert Tansey. VHS, Beta $19.95 NOS, DVT, VYY ♪½

The Haunted Strangler Boris Karloff is a writer investigating a 20-year old murder who begins copying some of the killer's acts. **AKA:** The Grip of the Strangler.
1958 78m/B GB Boris Karloff, Anthony Dawson, Elizabeth Allan; **D:** Robert Day. VHS, Beta $49.95 MED, MPI ♪♪½

Haunted Summer Soft-focus, sex-and-drugs period piece of the bacchanalian summer of 1816 spent by free spirits Lord Byron, Percy Shelley, Mary Shelley, and John Polidori and others that led Mary Shelley to write "Frankenstein." Based on the novel of the same name by Anne Edwards.
1988 (R) 106m/C Alice Krige, Eric Stoltz, Philip Anglim, Laura Dern, Alex Winter; **D:** Ivan Passer. VHS, Beta, LV $79.95 MED ♪♪

Haunted: The Ferryman Adapted by Julian Bond from a Kingsley Amis story, the film deals with a novelist who is mysteriously confronted with various events and macabre set-pieces from his own novel, including a dead ferryman rising from the grave.
1974 50m/C GB Jeremy Brett, Nastasha Parry, Lesley Dunlop; **D:** John Irvin. VHS, Beta $59.95 PSM ♪♪

HauntedWeen All trick, no treat, as a guy nailed by a frat house prank twenty years ago comes back for revenge.
1991 ?m/C Brien Blakely, Blake Pickett, Brad Hanks, Bart White, Leslee Lacey, Ethan Adler; **D:** Doug Robertson. VHS $29.50 CVD ♪½

The Haunting A subtle, bloodless horror film about a weekend spent in a monstrously haunted mansion by a parapsychologist, the mansion's skeptic heir, and two mediums. A chilling adaptation of Shirley Jackson's "The Haunting of Hill House," in which the psychology of the heroine is forever in question.
1963 113m/B Julie Harris, Claire Bloom, Russ Tamblyn, Richard Johnson; **D:** Robert Wise. VHS, Beta, LV $19.98 KUI, MGM ♪♪♪½

Haunting Fear Poe's "The Premature Burial" inspired this pale cheapie about a wife with a fear of early interment. After lengthy nightmares and graphic sex, her greedy husband uses her phobia in a murder plot.
1991 88m/C Jan-Michael Vincent, Karen Black, Brinke Stevens, Michael Berryman; **D:** Fred Olen Ray. VHS $79.95 RHI ♪

The Haunting of Barney Palmer Barney Palmer is sure he has inherited the family magic powers because he is haunted by the ghost of his great uncle. To destroy the curse, he must conquer his fears. Based on the book "The Haunting" by Margaret Mahy. Includes a viewers' guide. Part of the "Wonderworks" series.
199? 55m/C Ned Beatty, Alexis Banas, Eleanor Gibson. **VHS $29.95** PME, HMV, BTV ♫

Haunting of Harrington House A tame teenage haunted house film originally produced for television.
1982 50m/C Dominique Dunne, Roscoe Lee Browne, Edie Adams, Phil Leeds; **D:** Murray Golden. **VHS, Beta $29.95** GEM ♫

The Haunting of Morella Poe-inspired cheapjack exploitation about a an executed witch living again in the nubile body of her teen daughter. Ritual murders result, in between lesbian baths and nude swims. Producer Roger Corman did the same story with more class and less skin in his earlier anthology "Tales of Terror."
1991 (R) 82m/C David McCallum, Nicole Eggert, Maria Ford, Lana Clarkson. **VHS $89.98** NHO ♫

Haunting of Sarah Hardy Ward, as a recently wed heiress, returns to the scene of her unhappy childhood home. In a standard plot, Ward is torn between an apparent haunting and the question of her own sanity. Made for TV film is redeemed by the creditable acting.
1989 92m/C Sela Ward, Michael Woods, Roscoe Born, Polly Bergen, Morgan Fairchild; **D:** Jerry London. **VHS, Beta, LV $59.95** PAR, PIA ♫♫

The Haunting Passion Newlywed Seymour moves into a haunted house only to be seduced by the ghost of the former occupant's dead lover. Effective and erotic presentation. Made for Television.
1983 100m/C Jane Seymour, Gerald McRaney, Millie Perkins, Ruth Nelson, Paul Rossilli, Ivan Bonar; **D:** John Korty. **VHS, Beta $39.95** LIV ♫♫½

Haunts Tormented woman has difficulty distinguishing between fantasy and reality after a series of brutal slayings lead police to the stunning conclusion that dead people have been committing the crimes. **AKA:** The Veil.
1977 (PG) 97m/C Cameron Mitchell, Aldo Ray, May Britt, William Gray Espy, Susan Nohr; **D:** Herb Freed. **VHS, Beta $59.95** MED ♫½

Haunts of the Very Rich A loose remake of "Outward Bound" in which a group of spoiled people on a vacation find themselves spiritually dead. Made for TV.
1972 72m/C Lloyd Bridges, Anne Francis, Donna Mills, Tony Bill, Robert Reed, Moses Gunn, Cloris Leachman, Ed Asner; **D:** Paul Wendkos. **VHS, Beta $59.95** VMK ♫♫½

Havana During the waning days of the Batista regime, a gambler travels to Havana in search of big winnings. Instead, he meets the beautiful wife of a communist revolutionary. Unable to resist their mutual physical attraction, the lovers become drawn into a destiny which is far greater than themselves. Reminiscent of "Casablanca."
1990 (R) 145m/C Robert Redford, Lena Olin, Alan Arkin, Raul Julia, Tomas Milian, Tony Plana, Betsy Brantley, Lise Cutter, Richard Farnsworth, Mark Rydell; **D:** Sydney Pollack; **M:** Dave Grusin. **VHS, Beta, LV $19.98** MCA, FCT, MOV ♫♫½

Having It All A wry television comedy about a love triangle. Dyan Cannon stars as a successful business woman with a husband on each coast, who finds dividing her time is more than she bargained for.

1982 100m/C Dyan Cannon, Barry Newman, Hart Bochner, Melanie Chartoff, Sylvia Sidney; **D:** Edward Zwick. **VHS, Beta, LV $39.95** LIV ♫♫

Having Wonderful Crime Madcap comedy-thriller about a newly married couple who combine sleuthing with a honeymoon. With their criminal lawyer friend along, the trio winds up searching for a magician who has vanished. Fast-paced action and quick dialogue.
1945 70m/B Pat O'Brien, George Murphy, Carole Landis, Lenore Aubert, George Zucco; **D:** Edward Sutherland. **VHS, LV $19.98** TTC, FCT, IME ♫♫½

Having Wonderful Time A young girl tries to find culture and romance on her summer vacation at a resort in the Catskills. Film debut of comic Red Skelton, who wasn't always as old as the hills. Based on a Broadway hit by Arthur Kober.
1938 71m/B Ginger Rogers, Lucille Ball, Eve Arden, Red Skelton, Douglas Fairbanks Jr.; **D:** Alfred Santell. **VHS, Beta $34.95** RKO ♫½

Having Wonderful Time/Carnival Boat A Ginger Rogers double feature: "Having Wonderful Time" (1938)-fun and frolic at an adult summer camp in the Catskills; and "Carnival Boat" (1932)-the lives and loves of rugged loggers in the Pacific Northwest.
1938 134m/B Ginger Rogers, Douglas Fairbanks Jr., Lucille Ball, Ann Miller, Red Skelton, William Boyd. **VHS, Beta $39.95** RKO, TTC ♫♫½

Hawaii James Michener's novel about a New England farm boy who decides in 1820 that the Lord has commanded him to the island of Hawaii for the purpose of "Christianizing" the natives. Filmed on location. Also available in a 181 minute version with restored footage. Available in director's cut version with an additional 20 minutes.
1966 161m/C Max von Sydow, Julie Andrews, Richard Harris, Carroll O'Connor, Bette Midler, Gene Hackman, Jocelyn Lagarde; **D:** George Roy Hill. Academy Awards '66 Nominations: Best Color Cinematography, Best Costume Design (Color), Best Song ("My Wishing Doll"), Best Sound, Best Supporting Actress (Lagarde), Best Original Score; Golden Globe Awards '67: Best Supporting Actress (Lagarde). **VHS, Beta, LV $19.95** FOX ♫♫♫

Hawaii Calls Two young stowaways on a cruise ship are allowed to stay on after one of them (Breen) struts his stuff as a singer. The two then turn sleuth to catch a gang of spies. More ham than a can of Spam, but still enjoyable. ♫That's The Hawaiian In Me; Hawaii Calls; Down Where The Trade Winds Blow; Macushia; Aloha Oe.
1938 72m/B Bobby Breen, Ned Sparks, Irvin S. Cobb, Warren Hull, Gloria Holden, Pua Lani, Raymond Paige, Philip Ahn, Ward Bond; **D:** Eddie Cline. **VHS $19.95** DVT, NOS, HEG ♫♫

Hawaiian Buckaroo A couple of cowboys fight to save their pineapple plantation from a sneaky foreman.
1938 62m/B Smith Ballew, Evelyn Knapp, Benny Burt, Harry Woods, Pat O'Brien; **D:** Ray Taylor. **VHS $19.95** NOS, DVT, GPV ♫

Hawk and Castile Bandits murder, pillage, and terrorize the nobility in Medieval Europe until the Hawk comes onto the scene.
19?? 95m/C Tom Griffith, Jerry Cobb, Nurla Forway, Mari Real. **VHS, Beta** NO ♫

Hawk of the Caribbean Minor Spanish pirate film is presented in an English-dubbed version.
197? 100m/C SP Johnny Desmond, Yvonne Monlaur, Armando Francioli. **VHS, Beta $39.95** VCD ♫

Hawk of the Wilderness A man, shipwrecked as an infant and reared on a remote island by native Indians, battles modern day pirates. Serial in 12 episodes. Also called "Lost Island of Kioga."
1938 195m/B Herman Brix, Mala, William Boyle; **D:** William Witney. **VHS, Beta $29.95** VCN, MLB ♫♫

Hawk the Slayer A comic book fantasy. A good warrior struggles against his villainous brother to possess a magical sword that bestows upon its holder great powers of destruction. Violent battle scenes; Palance makes a great villain.
1981 93m/C Jack Palance, John Terry, Harry Andrews, Roy Kinnear, Ferdinand "Ferdy" Mayne; **D:** Terry Marcel. **VHS, Beta, LV $39.95** LIV ♫♫½

Hawken's Breed Drifter meets American Indian beauty and hears her tale of woe; the two fall for each other and set out together to avenge the murder of the woman's husband and son. Nothing much to crow about.
1987 (R) 93m/C Peter Fonda, Serene Hedin, Jack Elam; **D:** Charles B. Pierce. **VHS, Beta, LV $19.95** STE, VMK, IME ♫♫

Hawkeye After his best friend is murdered by gangsters in a seedy drug deal, Hawkeye, a rough and tumble Texas cop, and his slick new partner hit the streets of Las Vegas with a vengeance.
1988 90m/C Troy Donahue, Chuck Jeffreys, George Chung, Stan Wertlieb; **D:** Leo Fong. **VHS, Beta** NO ♫½

Hawks Somewhere on the road to black-comedy this film gets waylaid by triviality. Two terminally ill men break out of the hospital, determined to make their way to Amsterdam for some last-minute fun. Mediocre at best.
1989 (R) 105m/C GB Anthony Edwards, Timothy Dalton, Janet McTeer, Jill Bennett, Sheila Hancock, Connie Booth, Camille Coduri; **D:** Robert Ellis Miller. **VHS, Beta, LV, 8mm $34.95** PAR ♫½

The Hawks & the Sparrows Shortly after "Mr. Ed" came Pasolini's garrulous crow, which follows a father and son's perambulations through Italy spouting pithy bits of politics. A comic Pasolinian allegory-fest full of then-topical political allusions, the story (written by penman Pier) comes off a bit wooden. Worth watching to see Toto, the Italian comic, in his element. Music by the ever-prolific Ennio Morricone, whose credits include "A Fistful of Dollars," Pasolini's "Decameron," and "Exorcist II." **AKA:** Uccellacci e Uccellini.
1967 91m/B IT Toto, Ninetto Davoli, Femi Benussi; **W/D:** Pier Paolo Pasolini; **M:** Ennio Morricone. **VHS, LV $79.95** WBF, TAM ♫♫

Hawmps! Idiotic comedy about a Civil War lieutenant who trains his men to use camels. When the soldiers and animals begin to grow fond of each other, Congress orders the camels to be set free. Hard to believe this was based on a real life incident.
1976 (G) 98m/C James Hampton, Christopher Connelly, Slim Pickens, Denver Pyle; **D:** Joe Camp. **VHS, Beta $79.95** VES Woof!

Hawthorne of the USA Reid stars as Anthony Hamilton Hawthorne, American extraordinaire. After gambling a fortune away in Monte Carlo, Hawthorne heads to mainland Europe for rest and revelry. Instead, he finds the love of a princess and a Communist coup in the making. Silent with orchestral score.
1919 55m/B Wallace Reid, Harrison Ford, Lila Lee, Tully Marshall; **D:** James Cruze. **VHS, Beta $19.95** GPV ♫♫½

Hay Muertos Que No Hacen Ruido This comedy centers around a plot to pull off a fake murder.
1947 95m/B MX Su Carnal Marcelo, Amanda Del Llano, Tony Diaz. **VHS, Beta** $44.95 MAD ⅋⅋

Hazel's People Bitter and hostile college student attends his friend's funeral in Mennonite country. He discovers not only a way of life he never knew existed, but a personal faith in a living Christ. From the Merle Good novel, "Happy as the Grass Was Green."
1975 (G) 105m/C Geraldine Page, Pat Hingle, Graham Beckel. **VHS, Beta** $29.95 UHV, VGD ⅋½

He is My Brother Two boys survive a shipwreck, landing on an island that houses a leper colony.
1975 (G) 90m/C Keenan Wynn, Bobby Sherman, Robbie Rist; *D:* Edward Dmytryk. **VHS, Beta** NO ⅋½

He Kills Night After Night After Night British police are baffled as they seek the man who has been killing women in the style of Jack the Ripper. And he keeps doing it.
1970 88m/C Jack May, Linda Marlowe, Justine Lord. **VHS, Beta** NO ⅋½

He Knows You're Alone Lame horror flick that focuses on a psychotic killer terrorizing a bride-to-be and her bridal party in his search for a suitable bride of his own.
1980 (R) 94m/C Don Scardino, Elizabeth Kemp, Tom Rolfing, Paul Gleason, Caitlin O'Heaney, Tom Hanks, Patsy Pease; *D:* Armand Mastroianni; *W:* Scott Parker. **VHS, Beta** $59.95 MGM ⅋

He Lives: The Search for the Evil One A man who was imprisoned by Nazis as a child attempts to keep Hitler, now living in Buenos Aires, from starting a 4th Reich.
1988 90m/C Lee Patterson. **VHS, Beta** NO ⅋

He Said, She Said Romance is the topic, but this isn't a typical dating film, instead a couple's relationship unfolds from differing points of view: first, the guy's (by Kwapis) and then the girl's (by Silver). Bacon and Perkins, Baltimore journalists and professional rivals, tell how their romance wound up on the rocks, and why (or so they say). The end result is overlong and lacks the zing of other war between the sexes movies, but real-life couple Silver and Kwapis do humorously highlight the fact that men and women often view the same incidents very differently. Bacon tends to overact, Perkins tends to overreact, and Stone shines as Bacon's ex-girl.
1991 (R) 115m/C Elizabeth Perkins, Kevin Bacon, Sharon Stone, Nathan Lane, Anthony LaPaglia, Stanley Anderson, Charlaine Woodard, Danton Stone, Phil Leeds, Rita Karin; *D:* Marisa Silver, Ken Kwapis; *W:* Brian Hohlfield; *M:* Miles Goodman. **VHS, LV** $14.95 PAR, PIA, CCB ⅋⅋½

He Walked by Night Los Angeles homicide investigators track down a cop killer in this excellent drama. Based on a true story from the files of the Los Angeles police, this first rate production reportedly inspired Webb to create "Dragnet."
1948 80m/B Richard Basehart, Scott Brady, Roy Roberts, Jack Webb, Whit Bissell; *D:* Alfred Werker, Anthony Mann. **VHS, Beta** $16.95 SNC, NOS, KRT ⅋⅋⅋½

He Who Walks Alone Made-for-television film documents the life of Thomas E. Gilmore, who became the South's first elected black sheriff in the 1960s.

1978 74m/C Louis Gossett Jr., Clu Gulager, Mary Alice, James McEachin, Barton Heyman, Barry Brown, Loni Chapman; *D:* Jerrold Freedman. **VHS, Beta** NO ⅋⅋½

The Head A scientist comes up with a serum that can keep the severed head of a dog alive. Before too long, he tries the stuff out on a woman, transferring the head from her own hunchbacked body to that of a beautiful stripper. Weird German epic sports poor special effects and unintentional laughs, but is interesting nonetheless.
1959 92m/B GE Horst Frank, Michel Simon, Paul Dahlke, Karin Kernke, Helmut Schmidt; *W/D:* Victor Trivas. **VHS** $19.98 SNC ⅋⅋

Head Written by Jack Nicholson and Bob Rafelson, this is the infamously plotless musical comedy starring the television fab four of the '60s, the Monkees, in their only film appearance. A number of guest stars appear and a collection of old movie clips are also included. ♫Circle Sky; Can You Dig It; Long Title: Do I Have To Do This All Over Again; Daddy's Song; As We Go Along; The Porpoise Song.
1968 (G) 86m/C Peter Tork, Mickey Dolenz, Davy Jones, Michael Nesmith, Frank Zappa, Annette Funicello, Teri Garr; *D:* Bob Rafelson. **VHS, Beta, LV** $19.95 MVD, COL ⅋⅋⅋

Head of the Family After a woman sacrifices her political ideals and career goals for her role as a family matriarch, she eventually falls apart.
1971 (PG) 105m/C IT FR Nino Manfredi, Leslie Caron, Ugo Tognazzi, Claudine Auger; *W/D:* Nanni Loy. **VHS, Beta** $59.95 GEM ⅋⅋½

Head Office A light comedy revolving around the competition between corporate management and the lower echelon for the available position of chairman.
1986 (PG-13) 90m/C Danny DeVito, Eddie Albert, Judge Reinhold, Rick Moranis, Jane Seymour; *D:* Ken Finkleman. **VHS, Beta** $79.99 HBO ⅋½

Head Over Heels A model married to an older man has an affair with a younger one and cannot decide between them. In French with subtitles.
1967 89m/C FR Brigitte Bardot, Laurent Terzleff, Michael Sarne; *D:* Serge Bourguignon. **VHS, Beta** $19.95 FCT ⅋⅋⅋

Headhunter Voodoo-esque killers are leaving headless bodies all around Miami. Plenty of prosthetic make-up.
1989 92m/C Kay Lenz, Wayne Crawford, John Fatooh, Steve Kanaly, June Chadwick, Sam Williams; *D:* Francis Schaeffer. **VHS, Beta, LV** $29.95 ACA, IME ⅋½

Headin' for the Rio Grande A cowboy and his sheriff brother drive off cattle-rustlers in this Western saga. Ritter's film debut. Songs include "Campfire Love Song," "Jailhouse Lament," and "Night Herding Song."
1936 60m/B Tex Ritter, Eleanor Stewart, Syd Saylor, Warner Richmond, Charles King; *D:* Robert Bradbury. **VHS, Beta** $19.95 NOS, DVT ⅋

Heading for Heaven A mistaken medical report leaves a frazzled realtor believing he has only three months to live, and when he disappears the family suspects the worst. A minor comedy based on a play by Charles Webb.
1947 65m/B Stuart Erwin, Glenda Farrell, Russ Vincent, Irene Ryan, Milburn Stone, George O'Hanlon; *D:* Lewis D. Collins. **VHS** $19.95 NOS, TIM ⅋⅋

Headless Eyes Gory entry into the psycho-artist category. An artist is miffed when mistaken by a woman as a burglar he loses an eye. Not one to forgive and forget,

he becomes quite the eyeball fetishist, culling donations from unsuspecting women. An eye for an eye ad finitum.
1983 78m/C Bo Brundin, Gordon Raman, Mary Jane Early; *D:* Kent Bateman. **VHS** UHV ⅋½

Headline Woman An ongoing feud between a police commissioner and a newspaper's city editor causes a reporter to make a deal with a policeman in exchange for news. A good cast makes this otherwise tired story tolerable.
1935 75m/B Heather Angel, Roger Pryor, Jack LaRue, Ford Sterling, Conway Tearle; *D:* William Nigh. **VHS, Beta** $24.95 NOS, DVT, HEG ⅋⅋

Headwinds Silent romance in which Mr. Right spares helpless girl against her will from marrying Mr. Wrong.
1928 52m/B House Peters, Patsy Ruth Miller. **VHS, Beta** $16.95 GPV ⅋⅋

Healer A doctor forgets his pledge to help the lame and becomes a fashionable physician. A young crippled lad helps him eventually remember his original purpose was to serve others. **AKA:** Little Pal.
1936 80m/B Mickey Rooney, Ralph Bellamy, Karen Morley, Judith Allen, Robert McWade; *D:* Reginald Barker. **VHS, Beta** $19.95 DVT ⅋½

Hear My Song Mickey O'Neill (Dunbar) is an unscrupulous club promoter, who books singers with names like Franc Cinatra, trying to revive his failing nightclub in this charming, hilarious comedy. He books the mysterious Mr. X, who claims he is really the legendary singer Josef Locke who fled England for Ireland because of tax problems, only to find out he is an imposter. To redeem himself with his fiancee and her mother, Locke's former lover, O'Neill goes to Ireland to find the real Locke (Beatty) and bring him to Liverpool to sing. Dunbar is appealing in his role, and Beatty is magnificent as the legendary Locke—so much so that he was nominated for a Golden Globe for Best Supporting Actor.
1991 (R) 104m/C GB Ned Beatty, Adrian Dunbar, Shirley Anne Field, Tara Fitzgerald, William Hootkins, David McCallum; *W/D:* Peter Chelsom. **VHS, Beta** $19.95 PAR ⅋⅋⅋

Hear No Evil Evil Lieut. Philip Brock (Sheen) masterminds the heist of a valuable coin, which he hides in innocent Jillian Shananhan's (Matlin) beeper—thus begins the game of cat-and-mouse between Brock, Shananhan, and her new lover, Ben Kendall (Sweeney). In a twist on "Wait Until Dark" the victim who is stalked here, Shananhan, is not blind but deaf. Despite Matlin's captivating performance, the script is seriously lacking the one element crucial to a mystery-thriller: suspense.
1993 (R) 98m/C Marlee Matlin, D.B. Sweeney, Martin Sheen, John C. McGinley, Christina Carlisi, Greg Elam, Charley Lang; *D:* Robert Greenwald; *W:* R.M. Badat, Kathleen Rowell; *M:* Graeme Revell. **VHS** $94.98 FXV ⅋⅋

The Hearse Incredibly boring horror film in which a young school teacher moves into a mansion left to her by her late aunt and finds her life threatened by a sinister black hearse.
1980 (PG) 97m/C Trish Van Devere, Joseph Cotten; *D:* George Bowers. **VHS, Beta** $54.95 MED Woof!

The Hearst and Davies Affair Married, middle-aged newspaper tycoon William Randolph Hearst falls for teenage Ziegfeld girl Marion Davies and tries to turn her into a Hollywood star. Davies was generally thought to be talented as a comedienne but Hearst insisted on choosing ill-suited dramatic roles for the blond and her career was problematic. Their lavish lifestyle was enhanced when Hearst built San Simeon for Davies and their scandalous affair lasted 35 years. Made for television.

1985 97m/C Robert Mitchum, Virginia Madsen, Fritz Weaver; *D:* David Lowell Rich. **VHS $79.95** ABC, PSM *ℐℐ*½

Heart A down-and-out small-time boxer is given a chance to make a comeback, and makes the Rocky-like most of it.

1987 (R) 93m/C Brad Davis, Jesse Doran, Sam Gray, Steve Buscemi, Frances Fisher; *D:* James Lemmo. **VHS, Beta $19.95** STE, NWV *ℐℐ*½

Heart and Souls Reincarnation comedy casts Downey, Jr. as a mortal whose body is inhabited by four lost souls who died on the night he was born. Now an adult, he must finish what they could not, no matter how outrageous it may be. Talented cast wears plot that's old hat. Downey, Jr. must be looking to do a trilogy of tired reincarnated soul roles—this is his second, "Chances Are" was his first.

1993 ?m/C Robert Downey Jr., Charles Grodin, Tom Sizemore, Alfre Woodard, Kyra Sedgwick, Elisabeth Shue; *D:* Ron Underwood. **VHS** NYR *ℐℐ*½

Heart Beat The fictionalized story of Jack Kerouac (author of "On the Road"), his friend and inspiration Neal Cassady, and the woman they shared, Carolyn Cassady. Based on Carolyn Cassady's memoirs. Strong performances, with Nolte as Cassady and Spacek as his wife, overcome the sometimes shaky narrative.

1980 (R) 105m/C Nick Nolte, John Heard, Sissy Spacek, Ann Dusenberry, Ray Sharkey, Tony Bill, Steve Allen, John Larroquette; *D:* John Byrum; *M:* Jack Nitzsche. **VHS, Beta $59.95** WAR *ℐℐ*½

Heart Condition A deceased black lawyer's heart is donated to a bigoted Los Angeles cop who was stalking the lawyer when he was alive. Soon afterwards the lawyer's ghost returns to haunt the police officer, hoping the officer will help to avenge his murder. Both Hoskins and Washington display fine performances given the unlikely script.

1990 (R) 95m/C Bob Hoskins, Denzel Washington, Chloe Webb, Ray Baker, Ja'net DuBois, Alan Rachins; *D:* James D. Parriott. **VHS, Beta, LV $14.95** COL *ℐℐ*½

The Heart is a Lonely Hunter Set in the South, Carson McCuller's tale of angst and ignorance, loneliness and beauty comes to the screen with the film debuts of Keach and Locke. Arkin gives an instinctive, gentle performance as the deaf mute; Locke's screen debut.

1968 (G) 124m/C Alan Arkin, Cicely Tyson, Sondra Locke, Stacy Keach, Chuck McCann, Laurinda Barrett; *D:* Robert Ellis Miller. Academy Awards '68 Nominations: Best Actor (Arkin), Best Supporting Actor (Locke); New York Film Critics Awards '68: Best Actor (Arkin). **VHS, Beta $19.98** KUI, WAR *ℐℐℐ*

Heart Like a Wheel The story of Shirley Muldowney, who rose from the daughter of a country-western singer to the leading lady in drag racing. The film follows her battles of sexism and choosing whether to have a career or a family. Bedelia's perfomance is outstanding. Fine showings from Bridges and Axton in supporting roles.

1983 (PG) 113m/C Bonnie Bedelia, Beau Bridges, Bill McKinney, Leo Rossi, Hoyt Axton, Dick Miller, Anthony Edwards; *D:* Jonathan Kaplan. **VHS, Beta, LV $59.98** FOX *ℐℐ*½

Heart of a Champion: The Ray Mancini Story Made-for-TV movie based on the life of Ray "Boom Boom" Mancini, former lightweight boxing champi-

on. Inspired by the career his father never had due to WWII, Mancini fought his way to the top. Sylvester Stallone staged the fight sequences.

1985 94m/C Robert (Bobby) Blake, Doug McKeon, Mariclare Costello; *D:* Richard Michaels. **VHS, Beta $59.98** FOX *ℐℐ*

Heart of a Nation Saga of the Montmarte family and their life during three wars, beginning with the Franco-Prussian War and ending with the Nazi occupation in France. Although ordered to be destroyed by the Nazis, this film was saved, along with many others, by the French "Cinema Resistance." In French with English subtitles. *AKA:* Untel Pere et Fils.

1943 111m/B *FR* Louis Jouvet, Raimu, Suzy Prim, Michael Morgan, Renee Devillers; *D:* Paul Graetz. **VHS $24.95** NOS, DVT, HEG *ℐℐℐ*

The Heart of Dixie Three college coeds at a southern university in the 1950s see their lives and values change with the influence of the civil rights movement. College newspaper reporter Sheedy takes up the cause of a black man victimized by racial violence. Lightweight social-conscience fare.

1989 (PG) 96m/C Virginia Madsen, Ally Sheedy, Phoebe Cates, Treat Williams, Kyle Secor, Francesca Roberts, Barbara Babcock, Don Michael Paul, Kurtwood Smith, Richard Bradford; *D:* Martin Davidson. **VHS, Beta, LV $19.98** ORI *ℐℐ*

Heart of Glass A pre-industrial Bavarian village becomes deeply troubled when their glassblower dies without imparting the secret of making his unique Ruby glass. The townspeople go to extremes, from madness to murder to magic, to discover the ingredients. From German director Herzog (who hypnotized his cast daily), this somewhat apocalyptic tale is based on legend. The colors are incredible in their intensity. In German with English subtitles.

1974 93m/C *GE* Josef Bierbichler, Stefan Autter, Scheitz Clemens, Volker Prechtel, Sonia Skiba; *D:* Werner Herzog. **VHS $79.95** NYF, TAM, FCT *ℐℐℐ*

Heart of Humanity An intense drama of love, patriotism, and sacrifice just before the war in a small Canadian village. A traveler who is really a Prussian army lieutenant finds his way to the house of a young man who is about to wed. He ends up falling in love with his fiancee and war is declared just before the wedding. A silent film with music score.

1918 133m/B Dorothy Phillips, Erich von Stroheim; *D:* Allen Holubar. **VHS, Beta, 8mm $49.95** VYY, GPV *ℐℐℐ*

Heart of Midnight An emotionally unstable young woman inherits a seedy massage parlor. She works hard to turn it, and herself, into something better. Nice performance by Leigh.

1989 (R) 93m/C Jennifer Jason Leigh, Brenda Vaccaro, Frank Stallone, Peter Coyote; *D:* Matthew Chapman. **VHS, Beta, LV** NO *ℐℐ*½

Heart of Texas Ryan Flamboyant cowboy star fights with kidnappers and wins in this silent film.

1916 50m/B Tom Mix. **VHS, Beta $19.95** NOS, GPV, DVT *ℐ*½

Heart of the Golden West Roy protects ranchers of Cherokee City from unjust shipping charges.

1942 65m/B Roy Rogers, Smiley Burnette, George "Gabby" Hayes, Bob Nolan, Ruth Terry; *D:* Joseph Kane. **VHS, Beta, 3/4U, Special order formats $19.95** NOS, VYY, VCN *ℐℐ*

Heart of the Rio Grande Spoiled young rich girl tries to trick her father into coming to her "rescue" at a western dude ranch.

1942 70m/B Gene Autry, Smiley Burnette, Fay McKenzie, Edith Fellows, Joseph Stauch Jr.; *D:* William M. Morgan. **VHS, Beta $29.98** CCB, VCN *ℐ*½

Heart of the Rockies The Three Mesquiteers stop a mountain family's rustling and illegal game trappers.

1937 54m/B Bob Livingston, Ray Corrigan, Max Terhune, Lynn (Mary Hart) Roberts, Yakima Canutt, J.P. McGowan; *D:* Joseph Kane. **VHS, Beta $9.95** NOS, VCN, MED *ℐ*½

Heart of the Rockies Roy, along with his trusty horse and dog, takes care of a highway construction project.

1951 67m/B Roy Rogers, Penny Edwards, Gordon Jones, Ralph Morgan, Fred Graham, Mira McKinney; *D:* William Witney. **VHS $19.95** NOS, DVT *ℐ*½

Heart of the Stag On an isolated sheep ranch in the New Zealand outback, a father and daughter suffer the repercussions of an incestuous relationship when she becomes enamored with a hired hand.

1984 (R) 94m/C *NZ* Bruno Lawrence, Mary Regan, Terence Cooper; *D:* Michael Firth. **VHS, Beta, LV $19.95** STE, NWV *ℐℐ*½

Heartaches A reporter tries to track down a murderer who has killed twice.

1947 71m/B Chill Wills, Sheila Ryan, Edward Norris, James Seay. **VHS, Beta $19.95** NOS, DVT, TIM *ℐℐ*

Heartaches A young pregnant woman (Potts) meets up with a crazy girlfriend (Kidder) in this touching film about love and friendship. Although a study in contrasts, the two end up sharing an apartment together in Toronto. Fine performances from Potts and Kidder give life to this romantic comedy.

1982 90m/C *CA* Margot Kidder, Annie Potts, Robert Carradine, Winston Rekert; *D:* Donald Shebib. **VHS, Beta, LV $69.98** LIV, VES *ℐℐℐ*

Heartbeat If you thought pointless Hollywood remakes of French films were a new phenomenon (see "Pure Luck," for example), then note this lighthearted remake of a 1940 Gallic farce. Rogers becomes the best student in a Parisian school for pickpockets, but when she tries out her skills on a dashing diplomat they fall in love instead.

1946 100m/B Ginger Rogers, Jean-Pierre Aumont, Adolphe Menjou, Basil Rathbone, Melville Cooper, Mona Maris, Henry Stephenson, Eduardo Ciannelli; *D:* Sam Wood. **VHS $19.95** NOS, TIM, HEG *ℐℐ*½

Heartbeeps In 1995, two domestic robot servants fall in love and run off together. On a beach they encounter the Energizer Bunny. No, that's not right. Young kids may enjoy the romantic robotic duo of Kaufman and Peters.

1981 (PG) 79m/C Andy Kaufman, Bernadette Peters, Randy Quaid, Kenneth McMillan, Christopher Guest, Melanie Mayron, Jack Carter; *D:* Allan Arkush; *M:* John Williams. **VHS, Beta $39.95** MCA *ℐℐ*

Heartbreak Hotel Johnny Wolfe kidnaps Elvis Presley from his show in Cleveland and drives him home to his mother, a die-hard Elvis fan. Completely unbelievable, utterly ridiculous, and still a lot of fun.

1988 (PG-13) 101m/C David Keith, Tuesday Weld, Charlie Schlatter, Angela Goethals, Jacque Lynn Colton, Chris Mulkey, Karen Landry, Tudor Sherrard, Paul Harkins; *D:* Chris Columbus. **VHS, Beta, LV $89.95** TOU *ℐℐ*½

Heartbreak House A production of George Bernard Shaw's classic play about a captain and his daughter who invite an odd assortment of people into their home for a few days. In the course of their visit, each person shares his ambitions, hopes, and fears. From the "American Playhouse" television series.
1986 118m/C Rex Harrison, Rosemary Harris, Amy Irving; **D:** Anthony Page. **VHS, Beta $59.95** ACA, VTK, PBS ⬟⬟½

The Heartbreak Kid Director May's comic examination of love and hypocrisy. Grodin embroils himself in a triangle with his new bride and a woman he can't have, an absolutely gorgeous and totally unloving woman he shouldn't want. Walks the fence between tragedy and comedy, with an exceptional performance from Berlin. Neil Simon script, based on Bruce Jay Friedman's story.
1972 (PG) 106m/C Charles Grodin, Cybill Shepherd, Eddie Albert, Jeannie Berlin, Audra Lindley, Art Metrano; **D:** Elaine May. **VHS, Beta, LV $19.95** MED ⬟⬟⬟

Heartbreak Ridge An aging Marine recon sergeant is put in command of a young platoon to whip them into shape to prepare for combat in the invasion of Grenada. Eastwood whips this old story into shape too, with a fine performance of a man who's given everything to the Marines. The invasion of Grenada, though, is not epic material. (Also available in English with Spanish subtitles.)
1986 (R) 130m/C Clint Eastwood, Marsha Mason, Everett McGill, Arlen Dean Snyder, Bo Svenson; **D:** Clint Eastwood. **VHS, Beta, LV, 8mm $19.98** WAR TIF ⬟⬟⬟

Heartbreaker Eastern Los Angeles explodes with vicious turf wars when Beto and Hector battle for the affection of Kim, the neighborhood's newest heartbreaker.
1983 (R) 90m/C Fernando Allende, Dawn Dunlap, Michael D. Roberts, Robert Dryer, Apollonia; **D:** Frank Zuniga. **VHS, Beta, LV $49.95** MED ⬟½

Heartbreakers Two male best friends find themselves in the throes of drastic changes in their careers and romantic encounters. On target acting makes this old story new, with a fine performance by Carol Wayne, in her last film before her death. Tangerine Dream performs the musical score.
1984 (R) 98m/C Peter Coyote, Nick Mancuso, Carole Laure, Max Gail, James Laurenson, Carol Wayne, Jamie Rose, Kathryn Harrold; **W/D:** Bobby Roth. **VHS, Beta $79.95** VES ⬟⬟⬟

Heartburn Based on Nora Ephron's own semi-autobiographical novel about her marital travails with writer Carl Bernstein, this is a tepid, bitter modern romance between writers already shell-shocked from previous marriages.
1986 (R) 109m/C Meryl Streep, Jack Nicholson, Steven Hill, Richard Masur, Stockard Channing, Jeff Daniels, Milos Forman, Catherine O'Hara, Maureen Stapleton, Karen Akers, Joanna Gleason, Mercedes Ruehl, Caroline Aaron, Yakov Smirnoff, Wilfrid Hyde-White; **D:** Mike Nichols; **W:** Nora Ephron. **VHS, Beta, LV, 8mm $19.95** PAR ⬟⬟⬟

Heartland Set in 1910, this film chronicles the story of one woman's life on the Wyoming Frontier, the hazards she faces, and her courage and spirit. Stunningly realistic and without cliche. Based on the diaries of Elinore Randall Stewart.
1981 (PG) 95m/C Conchata Ferrell, Rip Torn, Barry Primus, Lilia Skala, Megan Folson; **D:** Richard Pearce. **VHS, Beta $79.99** HBO ⬟⬟⬟½

Hearts & Armour A holy war between Christians and Moors erupts when a Moorish princess is kidnapped. Based on Ludovico Ariosto's "Orlando Furioso."
1983 101m/C IT Tanya Roberts, Leigh McCloskey, Ron Moss, Rick Edwards, Giovanni Visentin; **D:** Giacomo Battiato. **VHS, Beta $19.98** WAR ⬟⬟

Heart's Desire Opera great Richard Tauber stars in this musical of an unknown Viennese singer who falls in love with an English girl.
1937 79m/B GB Richard Tauber, Lenora Corbett, Kathleen Kelly, Paul Graetz; **D:** Paul Stein. **VHS, Beta $29.95** NO ⬟½

Hearts of Darkness: A Filmmaker's Apocalypse This riveting, critically acclaimed documentary about the making of Francis Ford Coppola's masterpiece "Apocalypse Now" is based largely on original footage shot and directed by his wife Eleanor. Also included are recent interviews with cast and crew members including Coppola, Martin Sheen, Robert Duvall, Frederic Forrest and Dennis Hopper.
1991 (R) 96m/C Sam Bottoms, Eleanor Coppola, Francis Ford Coppola, Robert Duvall, Larry Fishburne, Frederic Forrest, Albert Hall, Dennis Hopper, George Lucas, John Milius, Martin Sheen; **W/D:** Fax Bahr, George Hickenlooper. **VHS, Beta $19.95** PAR ⬟⬟⬟⬟

Hearts of Fire A trio of successful rock 'n roll stars work out their confused romantic entanglements. Barely released and then, not even in the U.S. Sad outing for the cast, especially legendary Dylan.
1987 90m/C Bob Dylan, Fionna, Rupert Everett, Julian Glover; **D:** Richard Marquand; **M:** John Barry. **VHS, Beta, LV $19.95** LHV, WAR ⬟

Hearts of Humanity Mawkish melodrama concerning a Jewish antique dealer and his relationship with the son of an Irish cop. An early "Chico and the Man" variant.
1932 56m/B Jean Hersholt, Jackie Searl, J. Farrell MacDonald, Claudia Dell, Charles Delaney, Lucille LaVerne, George Humbert; **D:** Cristy Cabanne. **VHS $19.95** NOS, HEG ⬟⬟

Hearts of the West A fantasy-filled farm boy travels to Hollywood in the 1930s and seeks a writing career. Instead, he finds himself an ill-suited western movie star in this small offbeat comedy-drama that's sure to charm. **AKA:** Hollywood Cowboy.
1975 (PG) 103m/C Jeff Bridges, Andy Griffith, Donald Pleasence, Alan Arkin, Blythe Danner; **D:** Howard Zieff. **VHS, Beta $19.98** MGM ⬟⬟⬟½

Hearts of the World A vintage Griffith epic about a young boy who goes off to World War I and the tribulations endured by both him and his family on the homefront. Overly sentimental but powerfully made melodrama, from Griffith's waning years. Silent with music score.
1918 152m/B Lillian Gish, Robert Harron, Dorothy Gish, Erich von Stroheim, Ben Alexander, Josephine Crowell, Noel Coward, Mary Gish; **D:** D.W. Griffith. **VHS, Beta, LV, 8mm $29.98** VYY, REP, PIA ⬟⬟⬟

Heat Another Andy Warhol-produced journey into drug-addled urban seediness. Features a former child actor/junkie and a has-been movie star barely surviving in a run-down motel. This is one of Warhol's better film productions; even non-fans may enjoy it.
1972 102m/C Joe Dallesandro, Sylvia Miles, Pat Ast; **D:** Paul Morrissey. **VHS, Beta** PAR, FCT ⬟⬟⬟

Heat A Las Vegas bodyguard avenges the beating of an old flame by a mobster's son, and incites mob retaliation. Based on the William Goldman novel.

1987 (R) 103m/C Burt Reynolds, Karen Young, Peter MacNicol, Howard Hesseman; **D:** R.M. Richards. **VHS, Beta, LV $14.95** PAR ⬟½

Heat and Dust A young bride joins her husband at his post in India and is inexorably drawn to the country and its prince of state. Years later her great niece journeys to modern day India in search of the truth about her scandalous and mysterious relative. More than the story of two romances, this is the tale of women rebelling against an unseen caste system which keeps them second-class citizens. Ruth Jhabvala wrote the novel and screenplay.
1982 (R) 130m/C GB Julie Christie, Greta Scacchi, Shashi Kapoor, Christopher Cazenove, Nickolas Grace; **D:** James Ivory. **VHS, Beta $59.95** MCA ⬟⬟⬟

Heat and Sunlight A photographer becomes obsessively jealous of his lover as their relationship comes to an end. Written, directed and starring Nilsson, who used, as with his previous film "Signal 7," a unique improvisational, video-to-film technique.
1987 98m/B Rob Nilsson, Consuelo Faust, Bill Bailey, Don Bajema, Ernie Fosselius; **D:** Rob Nilsson. **VHS, Beta, LV $29.95** CVC ⬟½

Heat of Desire A philosophy professor abandons everything (including his wife) for a woman he barely knows and is conned by her "relatives." With English subtitles. **AKA:** Plein Sud.
1984 (R) 90m/C FR Clio Goldsmith, Patrick Dewaere, Jeanne Moreau, Guy Marchand; **D:** Luc Beraud. **VHS, Beta, LV $59.95** COL ⬟⬟

The Heat of the Day A British officer is accused of treason. As he attempts to find those who framed him, he meets a lovely woman all too willing to help. But whose side is she really on? Set in World War II. Tense and well-acted. Originally made for Masterpiece Theatre.
1991 120m/C Michael York, Patricia Hodge, Peggy Ashcroft, Anna Carteret, Michael Gambon; **W:** Harold Pinter. **VHS $19.95** PBS, PAV ⬟⬟

Heat of the Flame A vicious woodsman captures and rapes a beautiful girl. Psychological games, eroticism and exploitive nudity ensue.
1982 88m/C Tony Ferrandis, Ellie MacLure, Raymond Young, Anthony Mayans. **VHS, Beta $39.95** VCD ⬟

Heat Street Two thugs exact revenge on street gangs for the murders of loved ones. Made for video.
1987 90m/C Quincy Adams, Deborah Gibson, Wendy MacDonald, Del Zamora; **D:** Joseph Merhi. **VHS, Beta $39.95** HHE ⬟

Heat Wave A writer gets involved with a "femme fatale" who kills her wealthy husband for the love of a young pianist.
1954 60m/B GB Alex Nicol, Hillary Brooke, Sidney James, Susan Stephen, Paul Carpenter; **W/D:** Ken Hughes. **VHS, Beta, LV** NO ⬟½

Heat Wave The Watts ghetto uprising of 1965 is a proving ground for a young black journalist. Excellent cast and fine script portrays the anger and frustration of blacks in Los Angeles and the U.S. in the 1960s and the fear of change felt by blacks and whites when civil rights reform began. Strong drama with minimal emotionalism. Made for cable TV.
1990 (R) 92m/C Blair Underwood, Cicely Tyson, James Earl Jones, Sally Kirkland, Margaret Avery; **D:** Kevin Hooks. **VHS, Beta $79.88** TTC ⬟⬟⬟

Heated Vengeance A Vietnam vet returns to the jungle to find the woman he left behind, and runs into some old enemies.

1987 (R) 91m/C Richard Hatch, Michael J. Pollard, Mills Watson, Cameron Dye; **D:** Edward Murphy. **VHS, Beta** $79.95 *MED ♂*

Heathers A clique of stuck-up schoolgirls named Heather rules the social scene until the newest member decides that enough is enough. She and her outlaw boyfriend embark (accidentally on her part, intentionally on his) on a murder spree disguised as a rash of teen suicides. A dense, take-no-prisoners black comedy with buckets of potent slang, satire and unforgiving hostility. Humor this dark is rare; sharply observed and acted, though the end is out of place.
1989 (R) 102m/C Winona Ryder, Christian Slater, Kim Walker, Shannen Doherty, Lisanne Falk, Penelope Milford, Glenn Shadix, Lance Fenton, Patrick Laborteaux; **D:** Michael Lehmann. **VHS, Beta, LV** $19.95 *STE, NWV, FCT ♂♂♂½*

Heatwave Local residents oppose a multi-million dollar residential complex in Australia. Davis portrays a liberal activist, who wages war with the developers, and, in return, becomes involved with a possible murder case.
1983 (R) 92m/C *AU* Judy Davis, Richard Moir, Chris Haywood, Bill Hunter, John Gregg, Anna Jemison; **D:** Phillip Noyce. **VHS, Beta** $59.99 *HBO ♂♂♂*

Heaven An exploration of "heaven" including the idea, the place, and people's views about it. Questions such as "How do you get there?" and "What goes on up there?" are discussed. Offbeat interviews mixed with a collage of celestial images.
1987 (PG-13) 80m/C **D:** Diane Keaton. **VHS, Beta, LV** $14.95 *PAV, FCT ♂♂*

Heaven & Earth A samurai epic covering the battle for the future of Japan between two feuding warlords. The overwhelming battle scenes were actually filmed on location in Canada. In Japanese with English subtitles.
1990 (PG-13) 104m/C *JP* Masahiko Tsugawa, Takaai Enoki; **D:** Haruki Kadowaka. **VHS** $79.98 *LIV, TAM ♂♂½*

Heaven Can Wait Social satire in which a rogue tries to convince the Devil to admit him into Hell by relating the story of his philandering life and discovers that he was a more valuable human being than he thought. A witty Lubitsch treat based on the play "Birthdays."
1943 112m/C Don Ameche, Gene Tierney, Laird Cregar, Charles Coburn, Marjorie Main, Eugene Pallette, Allyn Joslyn, Spring Byington, Signe Hasso, Louis Calhern, Dickie Moore, Florence Bates; **D:** Ernst Lubitsch. **VHS, Beta, LV** $19.98 *FOX, FCT ♂♂♂*

Heaven Can Wait A remake of 1941's "Here Comes Mr. Jordan," about a football player who is mistakenly summoned to heaven before his time. When the mistake is realized, he is returned to Earth in the body of a corrupt executive about to be murdered by his wife. Beatty co-wrote the screenplay with Elaine May. Not to be confused with the 1943 film of the same name.
1978 (PG) 101m/C Warren Beatty, Julie Christie, Charles Grodin, Dyan Cannon, James Mason, Jack Warden; **D:** Warren Beatty, Buck Henry. Academy Awards '78: Best Art Direction/Set Decoration; Nominations: Best Actor (Beatty), Best Adapted Screenplay, Best Director (Beatty, Henry), Best Picture, Best Supporting Actor (Warden), Best Supporting Actress (Cannon), Best Original Score; Golden Globe Awards '79: Best Actor—Musical/Comedy (Beatty), Best Film—Musical/Comedy, Best Supporting Actress (Cannon). **VHS, Beta, LV** $14.95 *PAR, FOX, HMV ♂♂♂*

Heaven Help Us Three mischievous boys find themselves continually in trouble with the priests running their Brooklyn Catholic high school during the mid-1960s. Realistic and humorous look at adolescent life. **AKA:** Catholic Boys.
1985 (R) 102m/C Andrew McCarthy, Mary Stuart Masterson, Kevin Dillon, Malcolm Danare, Jennie Dundas, Kate Reid, Wallace Shawn, Jay Patterson, John Heard, Donald Sutherland, Yeardley Smith, Sherry Steiner, Calvert Deforest; **D:** Michael Dinner. **VHS, Beta, LV** $19.99 *HBO ♂♂½*

Heaven is a Playground On Chicago's South Side an inner city basketball coach and an idealistic young lawyer are determined to change the fate of a group of high school boys. The men use the incentive of athletic scholarships to keep their team in school and away from drugs and gangs.
1991 (R) 104m/C D.B. Sweeney, Michael Warren, Richard Jordan, Victor Love; **W/D:** Randall Fried. **VHS, LV** $19.95 *COL ♂♂½*

Heaven on Earth The story of two orphaned British children who, along with thousands of orphans shipped from England to Canada between 1867 and 1914, try to make new lives in the Canadian wilderness.
1989 101m/C *CA* R.H. Thompson, Sian Leisa Davies, Torguil Campbell, Fiona Reid; **D:** Allen Kroeker; **W:** Margaret Atwood. **VHS, Beta** $79.95 *SVS ♂♂½*

Heavenly Bodies A young woman who dreams of owning a health club will stop at nothing to accomplish her goals. When a rival tries to put her out of business, a "dance-down" takes place in this lame low-budget aerobics musical.
1984 (R) 99m/C *CA* Cynthia Dale, Richard Rebrere, Laura Henry, Stuart Stone, Walter George Alton, Cec Linder; **D:** Lawrence Dane. **VHS, Beta** $19.98 *FOX Woof!*

The Heavenly Kid Leather-jacketed "cool" guy who died in a sixties hot rod crash finally receives an offer to exit limbo and enter heaven. The deal requires that he educate his dull earthly son on more hip and worldly ways. A big problem is that the soundtrack and wardrobe are 1955, whereas the cocky cool greaser supposedly died seventeen years ago in 1968. Mildly entertaining.
1985 (PG-13) 92m/C Lewis Smith, Jane Kaczmarek, Jason Gedrick, Richard Mulligan; **D:** Cary Medoway. **VHS, Beta** $19.99 *HBO ♂♂*

Heavens Above A sharp, biting satire on cleric life in England. Sellers stars as the quiet, down-to-earth reverend who is appointed to a new post in space.
1963 113m/B *GB* Peter Sellers, Cecil Parker, Isabel Jeans, Eric Sykes, Ian Carmichael; **D:** John Boulting, Roy Boulting. **VHS, Beta** $19.98 *HBO, FCT ♂♂♂*

Heaven's Gate The uncut version of Cimino's notorious folly. A fascinating, plotless, and exaggerated account of the Johnson County cattle war of the 1880s. Ravishingly photographed, the film's production almost single-handedly put United Artists out of business.
1981 (R) 220m/C Kris Kristofferson, Christopher Walken, Isabelle Huppert, John Hurt, Richard Masur, Mickey Rourke, Brad Dourif, Joseph Cotten, Jeff Bridges, Sam Waterston, Terry O'Quinn, Geoffrey Lewis; **D:** Michael Cimino. **VHS, Beta, LV** $29.99 *MGM, FCT ♂♂*

Heaven's Heroes Dennis Hill, a dedicated policeman, was killed in the line of duty on August 27, 1977. This film recalls his life and deep faith in Jesus.

1988 72m/C David Ralphe, Heidi Vaughn, James O'Hagen; **D:** Donald W. Thompson. **VHS, Beta** $29.95 *MIV, BPG ♂♂*

Heavy Petting A hilarious compilation of "love scene" footage from feature films of the silent era to the sixties, newsreels, news reports, educational films, old TV shows, and home movies.
1989 75m/C **D:** Obie Benz, Josh Mostel. **VHS, Beta, LV** $29.95 *SUE, ACA ♂♂½*

Heavy Traffic Ralph Bakshi's animated fantasy portrait of the hard-edged underside of city life. A young cartoonist draws the people, places, and paranoia of his environment.
1973 76m/C **D:** Ralph Bakshi. **VHS, Beta** *WAR, OM ♂♂♂*

Hector's Bunyip What's a bunyip? People think it's just Hector's scaly imaginary friend. It therefore comes as quite a surprise when Hector gets kidnapped—by his supposed imaginary friend! Aired on PBS as part of the "Wonderworks" series.
1986 58m/C Scott Bartle, Robert Coleby, Barbara Stephens, Tushka Hose; **D:** Mark Callan. **VHS** $29.95 *PME, FCT, HMV ♂♂♂*

Hedda A dramatization of the Henrik Ibsen play, "Hedda Gabler," about a middle-class pregnant woman. The story finds her frustrated with her life and manipulating those around her with tragic results.
1975 102m/C *GB* Glenda Jackson, Peter Eyre, Timothy West, Jennie Linden, Patrick Stewart; **D:** Trevor Nunn. **VHS, Beta** $59.95 *MED ♂♂½*

Hedda Hopper's Hollywood Newsreel version of the gossip-hound's column, featuring scoops on Ball, Cooper, Minelli and many more.
1942 58m/B Hedda Hopper, Gary Cooper, Lucille Ball, Gloria Swanson, Liza Minnelli. **VHS** $19.95 *REP ♂♂½*

Heidi Johanna Spyri's classic tale puts Shirley Temple in the hands of a mean governess and the loving arms of her Swiss grandfather. Also available colorized. Remade in 1967. Also available with "Poor Little Rich Girl" on Laser Disc.
1937 88m/B Shirley Temple, Jean Hersholt, Helen Westley, Arthur Treacher; **D:** Allan Dwan. **VHS, Beta** $19.95 *FOX, HMV, MLT ♂♂♂*

Heidi The Swiss do their own version of the children's classic by Johanna Spyri. A precocious little girl enjoys life in the Swiss Alps with her grandfather, until her stern aunt takes her away to live in the village in the valley.
1952 98m/B *SI* Elsbeth Sigmund, Heinrich Gretler, Thomas Klameth, Elsie Attenoff; **D:** Luigi Comencini. **VHS** $8.95 *NEG, MRV, KAR ♂♂½*

Heidi The classic story from Johanna Spyri's novel is filmed beautifully in the Swiss Alps in Eastmancolor. Heidi is kidnapped by her mean aunt and forced to work as a slave for a rich family. Her kindly old grandfather comes to her rescue. Family entertainment for all, dubbed in English.
1965 95m/C *AT GE* Eva Maria Singhammer, Gustav Knuth, Lotte Ledl; **D:** Werner Jacobs. **VHS** *NO ♂♂♂*

Heidi The second American adaptation of the classic Johanna Spyri novel tells the story of an orphaned girl who goes to the Swiss Alps to live with her grandfather. Made for television.
1967 100m/C Maximilian Schell, Jennifer Edwards, Michael Redgrave, Jean Simmons; **D:** Delbert Mann; **M:** John Williams. **VHS, Beta** $19.98 *LIV, VES, GLV ♂♂*

Heidi An orphan girl's optimism brings new life to the residents of a village in the Swiss Alps. From the classic children's story by Johanna Spyri.
1979 93m/C VHS, Beta $14.95 PAV ♂♂

The Heiress Based on the Henry James novel "Washington Square," about a wealthy plain Jane, her tyrannical father, and the handsome fortune-seeking scoundrel who seeks to marry her. Musical score by Aaron Copland.
1949 115m/B Olivia de Havilland, Montgomery Clift, Ralph Richardson, Miriam Hopkins; *D:* William Wyler; *M:* Aaron Copland. Academy Awards '49: Best Actress (de Havilland), Best Art Direction/Set Decoration (B & W), Best Costume Design (B & W), Best Original Score; Nominations: Best Black and White Cinematography, Best Director (Wyler), Best Picture, Best Supporting Actor (Richardson); Golden Globe Awards '50: Best Actress—Drama (de Havilland); National Board of Review Awards '49: 10 Best Films of the Year, Best Actor (Richardson). VHS, Beta, LV $14.95 MCA, MLB, BTV ♂♂♂

The Heist An explosive crime thriller...
1988 (R) 93m/C Lee Van Cleef, Karen Black, Edward Albert, Lionel Stander, Robert Alda. VHS NO ♂♂

The Heist A made-for-cable-television film about an ex-con who, upon regaining his freedom, sets out to rip off the crook who framed him. Entertaining enough story with a first-rate cast.
1989 97m/C Pierce Brosnan, Tom Skerritt, Wendy Hughes; *D:* Stuart Orme. VHS, Beta $89.99 HBO, HHE ♂♂

Held for Murder When a vacationing daughter is accused of murder, her mom lovingly takes the blame. Will the daughter come back to clear her mom, or will she let her fry in the electric chair? *AKA:* Her Mad Night.
1932 67m/B Irene Rich, Conway Tearle, Mary Carlisle, Kenneth Thomson, William B. Davidson; *D:* E. Mason Hopper. VHS, Beta $16.95 SNC ♂

Held Hostage The true story of Jerry Levin, a reporter kidnapped by terrorists while on assignment in Beirut, and his wife, Sis, who struggled with the State Department for his release. Made for television.
1991 95m/C Marlo Thomas, David Dukes, G.W. Bailey, Ed Winter, Robert Harper, William Schallert; *D:* Roger Young. VHS CGV ♂♂

Hell Comes to Frogtown In a postnuclear holocaust land run by giant frogs, a renegade who is one of the few non-sterile men left on earth must rescue some fertile women and impregnate them. Sci-fi spoof is extremely low-budget, but fun. Stars "Rowdy" Roddy Piper of wrestling fame.
1988 (R) 88m/C Roddy Piper, Sandahl Bergman, Rory Calhoun, Donald G. Jackson; *D:* Robert J. Kizer. VHS, Beta, LV $19.95 STE, NWV ♂

Hell Commandos Soldiers in World War II struggle to prevent the Nazis from releasing a deadly bacteria that will kill millions. Dubbed.
1969 92m/C IT Guy Madison, Stan Cooper; *D:* J.L. Merino. VHS, Beta NO ♂1/2

Hell Fire Austin Maynard finds himself mixed up with outlaws in the Old West.
1932 60m/B Ken Maynard, Nat Pendleton, Jack Perrin; *D:* Forrest Sheldon. VHS, Beta $19.95 NOS, VCN, DVT ♂1/2

Hell Harbor Caribbean love, murder and greed combine to make this early talkie. Exterior shots were filmed on the west coast of Florida and the beauty of the Tampa area in the 1930s is definitely something to see.
1930 65m/B Lupe Velez, Gibson Gowland, Jean Hersholt, John Holland; *D:* Henry King. VHS, Beta $47.50 GVV ♂♂

Hell High Four high schoolers plan a night of torture and humiliation for an annoying teacher, only to find she has some deadly secrets of her own. Dumber than it sounds.
1986 (R) 84m/C Christopher Stryker, Christopher Cousins, Millie Prezioso, Jason Brill; *D:* Douglas Grossman. VHS, Beta $79.95 PSM ♂

Hell Hounds of Alaska A man goes searching for a kidnapped boy in the gold rush days of Alaska.
197? (G) 90m/C Doug McClure. VHS, Beta $9.95 NO ♂

Hell Hunters Nazi-hunters foil the plot of an old German doctor to poison the population of L.A. Meanwhile, a daughter avenges the death of her mother by blowing up the doctor's jungle compound.
1987 98m/C Stewart Granger, Maud Adams, George Lazenby, Candice Daly, Romulo Arantes, William Berger. VHS, Beta NO ♂

Hell in the Pacific A marvelously photographed (by Conrad Hall) psycho/macho allegory, about an American and a Japanese soldier stranded together on a tiny island and the mini-war they fight all by themselves. Overly obvious anti-war statement done with style.
1969 (PG) 101m/C Lee Marvin, Toshiro Mifune; *D:* John Boorman. VHS, Beta, LV $14.98 FOX ♂♂♂

Hell is for Heroes McQueen stars as the bitter leader of a small infantry squad outmanned by the Germans in this tight World War II drama. A strong cast and riveting climax make this a must for action fans.
1962 90m/B Steve McQueen, Bobby Darin, Fess Parker, Harry Guardino, James Coburn, Mike Kellin, Nick Adams, Bob Newhart; *D:* Don Siegel; *W:* Robert Pirosh, Richard Carr. VHS, Beta, LV $14.95 PAR ♂♂♂1/2

Hell Night Several young people must spend the night in a mysterious mansion as part of their initiation into Alpha Sigma Rho fraternity in this extremely dull low-budget horror flick.
1981 (R) 100m/C Linda Blair, Vincent Van Patten, Kevin Brophy, Peter Barton, Jenny Neumann; *D:* Tom De Simone. VHS, Beta $19.95 MED Woof!

Hell on Frisco Bay An ex-waterfront cop, falsely imprisoned for manslaughter, sets out to clear his name. He soon finds him taking on the Mob, in this thirties-style gangster film. Good performances all around, especially Robinson, who steals every scene he's in.
1955 93m/C Alan Ladd, Edward G. Robinson, Joanne Dru, Fay Wray, William Demarest, Jayne Mansfield; *D:* Frank Tuttle. VHS, Beta $54.95 UHV ♂♂1/2

Hell on the Battleground Group of inexperienced recruits are led into combat by two battle-hardened veterans. Their only hope for survival is a counterattack by U.S. tanks.
1988 (R) 91m/C William Smith, Ted Prior, Fritz Matthews; *D:* David A. Prior. VHS, Beta $9.95 AIP ♂1/2

Hell on Wheels Two successful brothers in the racing industry are torn apart by the same girl. Brotherly love diminishes into a hatred so deep that murder becomes the sole purpose of both.
1967 96m/C Marty Robbins, Jennifer Ashley, John Ashley, Gigi Perreau, Robert Dornan, Connie Smith, Frank Gerstle; *D:* Will Zens. VHS, Beta $39.95 ACA, ACN ♂♂

Hell Raiders A force invades a supposedly defenseless Pacific island, and finds itself fiercely attacked.
1968 90m/C John Agar, Richard Webb, Joan Huntington; *D:* Larry Buchanan. VHS, Beta $79.95 JEF ♂1/2

Hell River In 1941 Yugoslavia, Yugoslav partisans and Nazis battle it out at a place called Hell River.
1975 (PG) 100m/C Rod Taylor, Adam West; *D:* Stole Jankovic. VHS, Beta $69.95 VCD ♂♂

Hell Ship Mutiny Man comes to the aid of a lovely island princess, whose people have been forced to hand over their pearls to a pair of ruthless smugglers. Excellent cast in an unfortunately tepid production.
1957 66m/B Jon Hall, John Carradine, Peter Lorre, Roberta Haynes, Mike Mazurki, Stanley Adams; *D:* Lee Sholem, Elmo Williams. VHS, Beta $16.95 SNC, HEG ♂1/2

Hell Squad Lost in North Africa during WWII, five American GIs wander through the desert. They find numerous pitfalls and unexpected help. Overall, dismal and disappointing.
1958 64m/B Wally Campo, Brandon Carroll; *D:* Burt Topper. VHS $19.95 NOS ♂1/2

Hell Squad Unable to release his son from the Middle Eastern terrorists who kidnapped him, a U.S. ambassador turns to the services of nine Las Vegas showgirls. These gals moonlight as vicious commandos in this low-budget action film with skin.
1985 (R) 88m/C Bainbridge Scott, Glen Hartford, Tina Lee; *W/D:* Kenneth Hartford. VHS, Beta $59.95 MGM, GHV ♂

Hell to Eternity The true story of how World War II hero Guy Gabaldon persuaded 2,000 Japanese soldiers to surrender. Features several spectacular scenes.
1960 132m/B Jeffrey Hunter, Sessue Hayakawa, David Janssen, Vic Damone, Patricia Owens; *D:* Phil Karlson. VHS, Beta $14.98 FOX ♂♂1/2

Hell Up in Harlem A black crime lord recuperates from an assassination attempt and tries to regain his power. Poor sequel to the decent film "Black Caesar."
1973 (R) 98m/C Fred Williamson, Julius W. Harris, Margaret Avery, Gerald Gordon, Gloria Hendry; *D:* Larry Cohen. VHS, Beta $19.98 ORI Woof!

Hellbenders A confederate veteran robs a Union train and must fight through acres of Civil War adversity. Dubbed. Poorly directed and acted. *AKA:* Il Crudeli; Los Despiadados.
1967 (PG) 92m/C IT SP Joseph Cotten, Norman Bengell, Julian Mateos; *D:* Sergio Corbucci; *M:* Ennio Morricone. VHS, Beta $14.95 COL, SUE ♂1/2

Hellbent A crazed musician and a revenge-obssessed housewife embark on an unusual adventure that challenges their very sanity.
1990 90m/C Phil Ward, Lynn Levand, Cheryl Slean, David Marciano; *W/D:* Richard Casey. VHS, Beta NO ♂1/2

Hellbound: Hellraiser 2 In this, the first sequel to Clive Barker's inter-dimensional nightmare, the traumatized daughter from the first film is pulled into the Cenobites' universe. Gore and weird imagery abound. An uncut, unrated version is also available. *AKA:* Hellraiser 2.
1988 (R) 96m/C GB Ashley Laurence, Clare Higgins, Kenneth Cranham, Imogen Boorman, William Hope, Oliver Smith, Sean Chapman, Doug Bradley; *D:* Tony Randel. VHS, Beta, LV $19.95 STE, NWV ♂♂

Hellcats A mob of sleazy, leather-clad female bikers terrorize small Midwestern towns in this violent girl-gang thriller. Even biker movie fans might find this one unworthy.
1968 (R) 90m/C Ross Hagen, Dee Duffy, Sharyn Kinzie, Sonny West, Bob Slatzer; **D:** Bob Slatzer. **VHS, Beta** $19.95 *ACA Woof!*

Hellcats of the Navy Soggy true saga of the WWII mission to sever the vital link between mainland Asia and Japan. The only film that Ronald and Nancy Davis Reagan starred in together and the beginning of their grand romance.
1957 82m/B Ronald Reagan, Nancy Davis, Arthur Franz, Robert Arthur; **D:** Nathan Juran. **VHS, Beta** $9.95 *GKK ♂♂½*

Helldorado A lively western starring the singing cowboy, Roy Rogers. *AKA:* Heldorado.
1946 54m/B Roy Rogers, George "Gabby" Hayes, Dale Evans, Paul Harvey; **D:** William Witney. **VHS, Beta, 3/4U, Special order formats** $19.95 *NOS, VCN, CAB ♂♂*

Heller in Pink Tights The Louis L'Amour story follows the adventures of a colorful theatrical troupe that visits the 1880s West. Performing amid Indians, bill collectors, and thieves, they are often just one step ahead of the law themselves in this offbeat western.
1960 100m/C Sophia Loren, Anthony Quinn, Margaret O'Brien, Steve Forrest, Edmund Lowe; **D:** George Cukor. **VHS, Beta** $14.95 *KRT, PAR, FCT ♂♂*

Hellfighters Texas oil well fire fighters experience trouble between themselves and the women they love.
1968 (G) 121m/C John Wayne, Katharine Ross, Jim Hutton, Vera Miles, Bruce Cabot, Jay C. Flippen; **D:** Andrew V. McLaglen. **VHS, Beta, LV** $14.95 *MCA, PIA ♂♂*

Hellfire A gambler promises to build a church and follow the precepts of the Bible after a minister sacrifices his life for him.
1948 90m/B William Elliott, Marie Windsor, Forrest Tucker, Jim Davis; **D:** R.G. Springsteen. **VHS** $39.98 *REP ♂♂*

The Hellfire Club In 18th century Britain, a young man reaches adulthood and attempts to claim the estate of his father. No ordinary dad, his led the infamous Hellfire Club, an organization specializing in debauchery and depravity. His cousin challenges his claim and kidnaps his fiancee. Historical hokum, complete with swordplay.
1961 88m/C *GB* Keith Michell, Kai Fischer, Adrienne Corri, Peter Arne, David Lodge, Bill Owen, Peter Cushing, Francis Matthews, Desmond Walter Ellis; **D:** Robert S. Baker, Monty Berman. **VHS, Beta** $16.95 *SNC ♂♂*

Hellgate A woman hitchhiking turns out to be one of the living dead. Her benefactor lives to regret picking her up.
1989 (R) 96m/C Abigail Wolcott, Ron Palillo; **D:** William A. Levey. **VHS, LV** $89.95 *VMK Woof!*

Hellhole A young woman who witnesses her mother's murder is sent to a sanitarium where the doctors are perfecting chemical lobotomies. Extremely weak script and poor acting make this a suspenseless thriller.
1985 (R) 93m/C Judy Landers, Ray Sharkey, Mary Woronov, Marjoe Gortner, Edy Williams, Terry Moore, Dyanne Thorne; **D:** Pierre De Moro. **VHS, Beta, LV** $14.95 *COL ♂*

Hellmaster Your basic sicko mad scientist experiments on some unsuspecting college students by injecting them with an addictive drug. The drug also causes some horrifying mutations and makes its victims superhuman (but also super-ugly). Lots of gore. Creative special effects and make-up will appeal to fans of horror.
1992 92m/C John Saxon, David Emge, Amy Raasch; **W/D:** Douglas Schulze. **VHS** $89.95 *AIP ♂*

Hello A small animated fable wherein three extraterrestrial musicians send peace messages to earthlings.
1982 9m/C VHS, Beta, Special order formats $195.00 *PYR ♂*

Hello Again The wife of a successful plastic surgeon chokes to death on a piece of chicken. A year later she returns to life, with comical consequences, but soon discovers that life won't be the same.
1987 (PG) 96m/C Shelley Long, Corbin Bernsen, Judith Ivey, Gabriel Byrne, Sela Ward, Austin Pendleton, Carrie Nye, Robert Lewis, Madeleine Potter; **D:** Frank Perry. **VHS, Beta, LV** $19.99 *TOU ♂♂*

Hello, Dolly! Widow Dolly Levi, while matchmaking for her friends, finds a match for herself. Based on the stage musical adapted from Thornton Wilder's play "Matchmaker." Jerry Herman won an Oscar for his score. Lightweight story needs better actors with stronger characterizations. ♫Hello Dolly; Just Leave Everything to Me; Love is Only Love; Dancing; Walter's Gavotte; It Only Takes a Moment; Ribbons Down My Back; Elegance; It Takes a Woman; Put On Your Sunday Clothes; So Long, Dearie; Before the Parade Passes By; It Takes a Woman.
1969 (G) 146m/C Barbra Streisand, Walter Matthau, Michael Crawford, Louis Armstrong, E.J. Peaker, Marianne McAndrew, Tommy Tune; **D:** Gene Kelly. Academy Awards '69: Best Art Direction/Set Decoration, Best Sound, Best Score; Nominations: Best Cinematography, Best Costume Design, Best Film Editing, Best Picture. **VHS, Beta, LV** $19.98 *FOX, FCT ♂♂*

Hello Mary Lou: Prom Night 2 A sequel to the successful slasher flick, wherein a dead-for-30-years prom queen relegates the current queen to purgatory and comes back to life in order to avenge herself. Wild special effects. *AKA:* The Haunting of Hamilton High; Prom Night 2.
1987 (R) 97m/C Michael Ironside, Wendy Lyon, Justin Louis, Lisa Schrage, Richard Monette; **D:** Bruce Pittman. **VHS, Beta, LV** *NO ♂½*

Hellraiser A graphic, horror fantasy about a woman who is manipulated by the monstrous spirit of her husband's dead brother. In order for the man who was also her lover to be brought back to life, she must lure and kill human prey for his sustenance. Grisly and inventive scenes keep the action fast-paced; not for the faint-hearted. Screenplay written by Barker.
1987 (R) 94m/C *GB* Andrew Robinson, Clare Higgins, Ashley Laurence, Sean Chapman, Oliver Smith; **W/D:** Clive Barker. **Beta, LV, Q** $19.95 *STE, NWV ♂♂½*

Hellraiser 3: Hell on Earth Pinhead is back in this film based on characters created by horrormeister Clive Barker. A strange black box holds the key to sending Pinhead back to Hell and is sought by the heroine, a TV newswoman (Farrell). But Pinhead's human henchman, a nasty nightclub owner, isn't going to make things easy. Imaginative special effects and Bradley's commanding presence as Pinhead aid this shocker, which becomes unfortunately mired in excessive gore. An unrated version at 97 minutes is also available.
1992 (R) 91m/C Doug Bradley, Terry Farrell, Kevin Bernhardt, Paula Marshall, Ken Carpenter, Peter Boynton, Ashley Laurence; **D:** Anthony Hickox; **W:** Peter Atkins. **VHS, LV** *PAR ♂♂*

Hellriders A motorcycle gang rides into a small town and subjects its residents to a reign of terror.
1984 (R) 90m/C Adam West, Tina Louise. **VHS, Beta** $59.95 *TWE Woof!*

Hell's Angels Classic WWI aviation movie created by the fledgling but well-bankrolled studio of Howard Hughes, which had produced "Two Arabian Nights" the year before. Sappy and a bit lumbering, it's still an extravagant spectacle with awesome big air scenes. Hughes fired directors Howard Hawks and Luther Reed, spent a hitherto unprecedented $3.8 million, and was ultimately credited with the film's direction (although James Whale, who wrote the script, spent some time in the director's chair). Three years in the making, the venture cost three pilots their lives and Hughes lost a bundle. Harlow—who replaced Swedish Greta Nissen when Hughes gave the word to let there be sound—was catapulted into blond bombshelldom playing a two-timing dame who dallies with two brothers before they head off to war. And the tinted and two-color scenes—restored in 1989—came well before Ted Turner ever wielded a crayola.
1930 135m/B Jean Harlow, Ben Lyon, James Hall, John Darrow, Lucien Prival; **D:** Howard Hughes. **VHS** $19.98 *MCA, MRV ♂♂♂*

Hell's Angels '69 Figuring on robbing Caesar's Palace for the thrill, two wealthy brothers plot a deadly game by infiltrating the ranks of the Hell's Angels. Upon figuring out that they've been duped, the Angels seek revenge. Average biker epic filmed in Nevada features Hell's Angels Oakland chapter. Co-written by stars Stern (who also produced) and Slate.
1969 (PG) 97m/C Tom Stern, Jeremy Slate, Conny Van Dyke; **D:** Lee Madden. **VHS, Beta** $49.95 *MED ♂♂*

Hell's Angels Forever A revealing ride into the world of honor, violence, and undying passion for motorcycles on the road. Documentary was filmed with cooperation of the Angels. Features appearances by Willie Nelson, Jerry Garcia, Bo Diddley, Kevin Keating and Johnny Paycheck.
1983 (R) 93m/C Willie Nelson, Jerry Garcia, Johnny Paycheck, Bo Diddley; **D:** Richard Chase. **VHS, Beta** $59.95 *MED ♂♂*

Hell's Angels on Wheels Low-budget, two-wheeled Nicholson vehicle that casts him as a gas station attendant who joins up with the Angels for a cross country trip. Laszlo Kovacs is responsible for the photography. One of the better 1960s biker films.
1967 95m/C Jack Nicholson, Adam Roarke, Sabrina Scharf, Jana Taylor, John Garwood; **D:** Richard Rush. **VHS, Beta** $39.95 *VMK ♂♂½*

Hell's Brigade: The Final Assault Low-budget, poorly acted film in which a small band of American commandos is ordered on the most dangerous and important mission of WWII.
1980 (PG) 99m/C Jack Palance, John Douglas, Carlos Estrada; **D:** Henry Mankiewirk. **VHS, Beta** $59.95 *MPI Woof!*

Hell's Harbor In a tiny Caribbean harbor, the owner of a small trading store witnesses a murder committed by a spitfire's father.
1934 64m/B Lupe Velez, Jean Hersholt. **VHS, Beta, LV** *NO ♂*

Hell's Headquarters A startling tale of murder and greed involving a hunt for a fortune in African ivory.
1932 59m/B Jack Mulhall, Barbara Weeks, Frank Mayo; **D:** Andrew L. Stone. **VHS** $16.95 *SNC, NOS, DVT ♂*

Hell's Hinges The next to last Hart western, typifying his good/bad cowboy character. Perhaps Hart's best film.
1916 65m/B William S. Hart, Clara Williams, Jack Standing, Robert McKim; **D:** William S. Hart. **VHS, Beta** $29.95 GPV, VYY *🎬½*

Hell's House After his mother dies, young lad Durkin goes to the city to live with relatives, gets mixed up with moll Davis and her bootlegger boyfriend O'Brien, and is sent to a brutal reform school. Interesting primarily for early appearances by Davis and O'Brien (before he was typecast as the indefatigable good-guy).
1932 80m/B Junior Durkin, Pat O'Brien, Bette Davis, Frank "Junior" Coghlan, Charley Grapewin, Emma Dunn; **D:** Howard Higgin. **VHS, Beta** $19.95 NOS, MRV, NEG *🎬½*

Hell's Wind Staff Two boys uncover a plot to sell their townsmen as slaves to other South East Asian countries.
1982 95m/C Hwang Jang Lee, Mang Yuen Man, Mang Hai. **VHS, Beta** WVE *🎬*

Hellstrom Chronicle A powerful quasi-documentary about insects, their formidable capacity for survival, and the conjectured battle man will have with them in the future.
1971 (G) 90m/C Lawrence Pressman; **D:** Walon Green. **VHS, Beta** COL, OM *🎬🎬🎬*

Helltown A western programmer based on Zane Grey's novel.
1938 60m/B John Wayne; **D:** Charles T. Barton. **VHS, Beta, 3/4U, Special order formats** $19.95 NOS, DVT, VCN *🎬½*

Helltrain Passengers take the ride of their lives on the "Helltrain."
1980 (R) 90m/C **D:** Alain Payet. **VHS** $59.95 UHV Woof!

Help! Ringo's ruby ring is the object of a search by an Arab cult who chase the Fab Four all over the globe in order to acquire the bauble. The laserdisc version includes a wealth of Beatles memorabilia, rare footage behind the scenes and at the film's premiere, and extensive publicity material. ♫Help!; You're Gonna Lose That Girl; You've Got To Hide Your Love Away; The Night Before; Another Girl; Ticket To Ride; I Need You.
1965 (G) 90m/C John Lennon, Paul McCartney, Ringo Starr, George Harrison, Leo McKern, Eleanor Bron; **D:** Richard Lester. **VHS, Beta, LV** $29.95 MVD, MPI, OHO *🎬🎬🎬*

Help Wanted: Male When a magazine publisher discovers that her fiance cannot have children, she looks for someone else who can do the job right. Made for television.
1982 97m/C Suzanne Pleshette, Gil Gerard, Bert Convy, Dana Elcar, Harold Gould, Caren Kaye; **D:** William Wiard. **VHS, Beta** $39.95 WOV *🎬½*

Helter Skelter The harrowing story of the murder of actress Sharon Tate and four others at the hands of Charles Manson and his psychotic "family." Based on the book by prosecutor Vincent Bugliosi, adapted by J.P. Miller. Features an outstanding performance by Railsback as Manson. A TV mini-series.
1976 194m/C Steve Railsback, Nancy Wolfe, George DiCenzo, Marilyn Burns; **D:** Tom Gries. **VHS, Beta** $59.98 FOX *🎬🎬½*

The Henderson Monster Experiments of a genetic scientist are questioned by a community and its mayor. A potentially controversial television drama turns into typical romantic fluff.
1980 105m/C Jason Miller, Christine Lahti, Stephen Collins, David Spielberg, Nehemiah Persoff, Larry Gates; **D:** Waris Hussein. **VHS, Beta** $39.95 LIV *🎬🎬½*

Hennessy An IRA man plots revenge on the Royal family and Parliament after his family is violently killed. Tense political drama, but slightly far-fetched.
1975 (PG) 103m/C GB Rod Steiger, Lee Remick, Richard Johnson, Trevor Howard, Peter Egan, Eric Porter; **D:** Don Sharp. **VHS** $19.99 HBO *🎬🎬½*

Henry IV The adaptation of the Luigi Pirandello farce about a modern-day recluse who shields himself from the horrors of the real world by pretending to be mad and acting out the fantasy of being the medieval German emperor Henry IV. In Italian with English subtitles.
1985 94m/C IT Marcello Mastroianni, Claudia Cardinale, Leopoldo Trieste, Paolo Bonacelli; **D:** Marco Bellochio. **VHS, Beta** $59.95 MED, APD, TAM *🎬🎬½*

Henry IV, Part I Against a background of civil war, Prince Hal, the heir to the throne, appears to waste his youth hanging around taverns in London. The political tensions between the king and the rebels lead to the battle of Shrewsbury, at which time the Prince redeems himself. Part of the television series "The Shakespeare Plays."
1980 147m/C GB Jon Finch, Anthony Quayle, David Gwillim. **VHS, Beta** TLF *🎬🎬🎬*

Henry IV, Part II A colorful panorama of Medieval English life. The young prince is now preparing himself for leadership. The play ends with the death of Henry IV and the coronation of Prince Hal as Henry V. Part of the television series "The Shakespeare Plays."
1980 151m/C GB Jon Finch, Anthony Quayle, David Gwillim. **VHS, Beta** TLF *🎬🎬🎬*

Henry V The classic, epic adaptation of the Shakespeare play, and Olivier's first and most successful directorial effort, dealing with the medieval British monarch that defeated the French at Agincourt. Distinguished by Olivier's brilliant formal experiment of beginning the drama as a 16th Century performance of the play in the Globe Theatre, and having the stage eventually transform into realistic historical settings of storybook color. Music by Sir William Walton. Filmed at the height of World War II suffering in Britain (and meant as a parallel to the British fighting the Nazis), the film was not released in the U.S. until 1946.
1944 136m/C GB Laurence Olivier, Robert Newton, Leslie Banks, Esmond Knight, Renee Asherson, Leo Genn, George Robey, Ernest Thesiger, Felix Aylmer; **D:** Laurence Olivier. Academy Awards '46: Special Prize (Olivier); Nominations: Best Actor (Olivier), Best Interior Decoration, Best Picture, Best Original Score; National Board of Review Awards '46: 10 Best Films of the Year, Best Actor (Olivier). **VHS, Beta** $19.95 PAR, VTK, HMV *🎬🎬🎬🎬*

Henry V England's most admired national hero is shown uniting his people as he embarks on the invasion of France, deals justly with traitors, tirelessly leads his soldiers to victory, and ensures future peace by his marriage to the princess of France. From the "Shakespeare Plays" series.
1980 163m/C GB **VHS, Beta** $19.95 TLF *🎬🎬🎬*

Henry V Stirring, expansive retelling of Shakespeare's drama about the warrior-king of England. Branagh stars as Henry, leading his troops and uniting his kingdom against France. A very impressive production that rivals Olivier's 1945 rendering but differs by stressing the high cost of war—showing the ego-mania, doubts, and subterfuge that underlie the conflict. A marvelous film-directorial debut for Branagh (who also adapted the

screenplay). Wonderful supporting cast includes some of Britain's finest actors.
1989 138m/C GB Kenneth Branagh, Derek Jacobi, Brian Blessed, Alec McCowen, Ian Holm, Richard Briers, Robert Stephens, Robbie Coltrane, Christian Bale, Judi Dench, Paul Scofield, Michael Maloney, Emma Thompson; **W/D:** Kenneth Branagh; **M:** Patrick Doyle. Academy Awards '89: Best Costume Design; Nominations: Best Actor (Branagh), Best Director (Branagh); British Academy Awards '89: Best Director (Branagh). **VHS, LV** $19.98 FOX, SIG, TVC *🎬🎬🎬🎬*

Henry VI, Part 3 The conclusion of the Henry VI chronicles, climaxes with the Duke of Gloucester's plan to murder Henry. Made for television.
1982 120m/C Peter Benson, Julia Foster, Bernard Hill. **VHS, Beta** TLF *🎬🎬½*

Henry VIII Shakespeare's "Henry VIII" spins a web of intrigue and betrayal. Production was shot at one of Henry's favorite visiting spots, Leeds Castle. Part of the television series "The Shakespeare Plays."
1979 165m/C GB Claire Bloom, John Stride, Julian Glover. **VHS, Beta** TLF *🎬🎬½*

Henry & June Based on the diaries of writer Anais Nin, Kaufman's movie focuses on Nin's relationships with author Henry Miller and his wife June. Set in Paris in the early '30s, the setting moves between the impecunious expatriate's cheap room on the Left bank—filled with artists, circus performers, prostitutes and gypsies—to the conservative and well-appointed home of Nin and her banker husband Hugo. June rejoins husband Miller in Paris, finds him engaged in an affair with Nin, and joins them in a triangular relationship, all of which is fastidiously chronicled in Nin's diaries and provides the erotic backdrop to Miller's "Tropic of Capricorn." Scripted by Kaufman and his wife Rose, the movie captures the heady atmosphere of Miller's gay Paris, and no one plays an American better than Ward (who replaced Alec Baldwin in the part and earlier appeared in Kaufman's "The Right Stuff"). The film is noted for having prompted the creation of an NC-17 rating for its adult theme.
1990 (NC-17) 136m/C Fred Ward, Uma Thurman, Maria De Medeiros, Richard E. Grant, Kevin Spacey; **D:** Philip Kaufman. **VHS, LV** $19.98 MCA, FCT *🎬🎬½*

Henry: Portrait of a Serial Killer Based on the horrific life and times of serial killer Henry Lee Lucas, this film has received wide praise for its straight-forward and uncompromising look into the minds of madmen. The film follows Henry and his roommate Otis as they set out on mindless murder sprees (one of which they videotape). Extremely disturbing and graphic film. Unwary viewers should be aware of the grisly scenes and use their own discretion when viewing this otherwise genuinely moving film.
1990 (X) 90m/C Michael Rooker, Tom Towles, Tracy Arnold; **D:** John McNaughton. **VHS, Beta, LV** $79.98 MPI *🎬🎬🎬🎬*

Hepburn & Tracy The finest moments from the legendary film careers of Hepburn and Tracy, as a team and on their own. Some sequences in black and white. A must for fans.
1984 45m/C Katharine Hepburn, Spencer Tracy. **VHS, Beta** $29.95 RKO *🎬🎬🎬🎬*

Her Alibi When successful murder-mystery novelist Phil Blackwood runs out of ideas for good books, he seeks inspiration in the criminal courtroom. There he discovers a beautiful Romanian immigrant named Nina who is accused of murder. He goes to see her in jail and offers to provide her with an

alibi. Narrated by Blackwood in the tone of one of his thriller novels. Uneven comedy, with appealing cast and arbitrary plot.
1988 (PG) 95m/C Tom Selleck, Paulina Porizkova, William Daniels, James Farentino, Hurd Hatfield, Patrick Wayne, Tess Harper, Joan Copeland; **D:** Bruce Beresford. **VHS, Beta, LV, 8mm** $19.98 WAR ⅄⅄

Her Husband's Affairs Tone is an advertising wonder and Ball is his loving wife who always gets credit for his work. Tone does the advertising for an inventor who is searching for the perfect embalming fluid in this rather lifeless comedy.
1947 83m/B Lucille Ball, Franchot Tone, Edward Everett Horton, Gene Lockhart; **D:** Sylvan Simon. **VHS** $9.95 GKK ⅄

Her Life as a Man A female reporter is refused a job as a sportswriter because of her gender. She makes herself up as a man, gets the job, and creates havoc when she has to deal with lustful women on the job. A made-for-television movie.
1983 93m/C Robin Douglas, Joan Collins, Robert Culp, Marc Singer, Laraine Newman; **D:** Robert Ellis Miller. **VHS, Beta** $59.95 LHV ⅄½

Her Silent Sacrifice A silent melodrama about a French girl torn between material wealth and true love.
1918 42m/B Alice Brady, Henry Clive. **VHS, Beta** $24.95 VYY ⅄½

Her Summer Vacation A beautiful teenager spends her summer vacation on a country ranch which belongs to her father. A sensual story about becoming a woman.
19?? 90m/C **D:** Victor Di Mello. **VHS, Beta** $39.98 HHE ⅄½

Herbie Goes Bananas While Herbie the VW is racing in Rio de Janeiro, he is bothered by the syndicate, a pickpocket, and a raging bull. The fourth and final entry in the Disney "Love Bug" movies, but Herbie later made his way to a television series.
1980 (G) 93m/C Cloris Leachman, Charles Martin Smith, Harvey Korman, John Vernon, Alex Rocco, Richard Jaeckel, Fritz Feld; **D:** Vincent McEveety. **VHS, Beta** $69.95 DIS ⅄

Herbie Goes to Monte Carlo While participating in a Paris-to-Monte-Carlo race, Herbie the VW takes a detour and falls in love with a Lancia. Third in the Disney "Love Bug" series.
1977 (G) 104m/C Dean Jones, Don Knotts, Julie Sommars, Roy Kinnear; **D:** Vincent McEveety. **VHS, Beta** $69.95 DIS ⅄⅄

Herbie Rides Again In this "Love Bug" sequel, Herbie comes to the aid of an elderly woman who is trying to stop a ruthless tycoon from raising a skyscraper on her property. Humorous Disney fare. Two other sequels followed.
1974 (G) 88m/C Helen Hayes, Ken Berry, Stefanie Powers, John McIntire, Keenan Wynn; **D:** Robert Stevenson. **VHS, Beta, LV** $19.99 DIS ⅄⅄½

Hercules The one that started it all. Reeves is perfect as the mythical hero Hercules who encounters many dangerous situations while trying to win over his true love. Dubbed in English. Cinematography by Mario Bava. **AKA:** La Tatiche di Ercole.
1958 107m/C IT Steve Reeves, Sylva Koscina, Fabrizio Mioni, Giana Maria Canale, Arturo Dominici; **D:** Pietro Francisci. **VHS, Beta, LV** $14.98 VID, MRV, IME ⅄⅄½

Hercules Lackluster remake of 1957 original finds legendary muscle guy Hercules in the person of Ferrigno's Hulkster fighting against the evil King Minos for his own survival and the love of Cassiopeia, a rival king's daughter.
1983 (PG) 100m/C IT Lou Ferrigno, Sybil Danning, William Berger, Brad Harris, Ingrid Anderson; **D:** Lewis (Luigi Cozzi) Coates. **VHS, Beta, LV** $79.95 MGM, IME ⅄

Hercules 2 The muscle-bound demi-god returns to do battle with more evil foes amidst the same stunningly cheap special effects. **AKA:** The Adventures of Hercules.
1985 (PG) 90m/C IT Lou Ferrigno, Claudio Cassinelli, Milly Carlucci, Sonia Viviani, William Berger, Carlotta Green; **D:** Lewis (Luigi Cozzi) Coates. **VHS** $79.95 MGM ⅄

Hercules Against the Moon Men It's no holds barred for the mighty son of Zeus when evil moon men start killing off humans in a desperate bid to revive their dead queen. **AKA:** Maciste la Regina di Samar.
1964 88m/C IT FR Alan Steel, Jany Clair, Anna Maria Polani; **D:** Giacomo Gentilomo. **VHS, Beta** $16.95 SNC, MRV ⅄

Hercules and the Captive Women Hercules' son is kidnapped by the Queen of Atlantis, and the bare-chested warrior goes on an all-out rampage to save the boy. Directed by sometimes-lauded Cottafavi. **AKA:** Hercules and the Haunted Women; Hercules and the Conquest of Atlantis; Ercole Alla Conquista di Atlantide.
1963 93m/C IT Reg Park, Fay Spain, Ettore Manni; **D:** Vittorio Cottafavi. **VHS, Beta** $9.95 RHI, MRV, TIM ⅄⅄

Hercules and the Princess of Troy Hercules is up to his pecs in trouble as he battles a hungry sea monster in order to save a beautiful maiden. Originally a pilot for a prospective television series, and shot in English, not Italian, with Hercules played by erstwhile Tarzan Scott. Highlights are special effects and color cinematography.
1965 ?m/C IT Gordon Scott, Diana Hyland, Paul Stevens, Everett Sloane. **VHS, Beta** $16.95 SNC, MLB ⅄⅄½

Hercules in New York Motion picture debut of Schwarzenegger as a Herculean mass of muscle sent by dad Zeus to Manhattan, where he behaves likes a geek out of water and eventually becomes a professional wrestling superstar. 250 pounds of stupid, lighthearted fun. Written and produced by Aubrey Wisberg. **AKA:** Hercules: The Movie; Hercules Goes Bananas.
1970 (G) 93m/C Arnold Schwarzenegger, Arnold Stang, Deborah Loomis, James Karen, Ernest Graves; **D:** Arthur Seidelman. **VHS, Beta** $59.98 MPI ⅄½

Hercules in the Haunted World Long before the days of 24-hour pharmacies, Hercules—played yet again by Reeves-clone Park—must journey to the depths of Hell in order to find a plant that will cure a poisoned princess. Better than most muscle operas, thanks to Bava. **AKA:** Ercole al Centro Della Terra.
1964 91m/C IT Reg Park, Leonora Ruffo, Christopher Lee, George Ardisson; **D:** Mario Bava. **VHS, Beta** $9.99 CCB, RHI, MRV ⅄⅄½

Hercules, Prisoner of Evil Spaghetti myth-opera in which Hercules battles a witch who is turning men into werewolves. Made for Italian television by director Dawson (the nom-de-cinema of Antonio Margheriti).
1964 ?m/C IT Reg Park; **D:** Anthony Dawson. **VHS** $19.98 SNC ⅄

Hercules Unchained Sequel to "Hercules" finds superhero Reeves must use all his strength to save the city of Thebes and the woman he loves from the giant Antaeus. **AKA:** Ercole e la Regina di Lidia.

1959 101m/C IT Steve Reeves, Sylva Koscina, Silvia Lopel, Primo Carnera; **D:** Pietro Francisci. **VHS, Beta, LV** $14.95 VDM, SUE, MRV ⅄⅄

Here Come the Girls An unfunny musical-comedy about a chorus boy (Hope) fired for incompetence and then rehired to set a trap when the new singer (Martin) is stalked by a killer. Weak script, weak songs. ♫Girls Are Here To Stay; Never So Beautiful; You Got Class; Desire; When You Love Someone; Ali Baba Be My Baby; Heavenly Days; See the Circus; Peace.
1953 100m/C Bob Hope, Tony Martin, Arlene Dahl, Rosemary Clooney, Millard Mitchell, William Demarest, Fred Clark, Robert Strauss; **D:** Claude Binyon. **VHS** $14.95 PAR ⅄½

Here Come the Littles: The Movie A twelve-year-old boy finds many new adventures when he meets The Littles—tiny folks who reside within the walls of people's houses.
1985 76m/C **D:** Bernard Deyries. **VHS, Beta** $14.98 WTA, FOX ⅄½

Here Come the Marines The Bowery Boys accidentally join the marines and wind up breaking up a gambling ring. **AKA:** Tell It To the Marines.
1952 66m/B Leo Gorcey, Huntz Hall, Tim Ryan; **D:** William Beaudine. **VHS** $19.95 NOS ⅄

Here Comes Droopy The sad-eyed sheriff with the creaky voice saves the day in spite of himself.
1990 (G) 60m/C **VHS** $12.98 MGM, WTA ⅄⅄

Here Comes Garfield Garfield's first step from newspaper to television has Odie getting captured by the dog catcher. After much thought and a lot of lasagna, Garfield decides to rescue him. But a problem ensues when Odie only has until dawn to live.
1990 (G) 24m/C V: Lorenzo Music. **VHS** $12.98 FOX, WTA ⅄⅄

Here Comes Kelly Controlling his temper and hanging on to his job is more than our hero can handle.
1943 63m/C Eddie Quillan, Joan Woodbury, Maxie Rosenbloom; **D:** William Beaudine. **VHS, Beta** GPV ⅄½

Here Comes Mr. Jordan Montgomery is the young prizefighter killed in a plane crash because of a mix-up in heaven. He returns to life in the body of a soon-to-be murdered millionaire. Rains is the indulgent and advising guardian angel. A lovely fantasy/romance remade in 1978 as "Heaven Can Wait." Laserdisc edition includes actress Elizabeth Montgomery talking about her father Robert Montgomery as well as her television show "Bewitched."
1941 94m/B Robert Montgomery, Claude Rains, James Gleason, Evelyn Keyes, Edward Everett Horton; **D:** Alexander Hall; **W:** Sidney Buchman, Seton I. Miller. **VHS, Beta, LV** $19.95 COL, VYG, CRC ⅄⅄⅄⅄

Here Comes Santa Claus A young boy and girl travel to the North Pole to deliver a very special wish to Santa Claus.
1984 78m/C Karen Cheryl, Armand Meffre; **D:** Christian Gion. **VHS, Beta** $14.95 NWV, STE ⅄½

Here Comes the Groom Late, stale Capra-corn, involving a rogue journalist who tries to keep his girlfriend from marrying a millionaire by becoming a charity worker. Includes a number of cameos.
1951 114m/B Bing Crosby, Jane Wyman, Franchot Tone, Alexis Smith, James Barton, Connie Gilchrist, Robert Keith, Anna Maria Alberghetti; **Cameos:** Dorothy Lamour, Phil Harris, Louis Armstrong; **D:** Frank Capra. Academy Awards '51: Best Song ("In the Cool, Cool, Cool of the Evening"); Nominations: Best Story. **VHS, Beta, LV** $14.95 PAR ⅄⅄

Here We Go Again! Fibber McGee and Molly are planning a cross-country trip for their 20th anniversary celebration, but complications abound. Based on the popular NBC radio series.
1942 76m/B Marion Jordan, Jim Jordan, Harold Peary, Gale Gordon, Edgar Bergen, Charlie McCarthy, Mortimer Snerd, Ray Nobel; **D:** Allan Dwan. **VHS, Beta** $9.95 CCB ✠✠

The Hereafter An old church is suddenly overrun by zombies.
1987 92m/C **VHS, Beta** NO ✠

Here's Looking at You, Warner Bros. The 90-year history of Warner Bros. studios is profiled from the silent-era to its current success. Highlights cover the creation of Warners' gangster films, Busby Berkeley musicals, and "Looney Tunes" as well as bloopers and early screen tests by Marlo Brando, Paul Newman, Lana Turner, and Orson Welles. Includes interviews with stars, directors, and producers and numerous film clips.
1993 108m/C **W/D:** Robert Guenette. **VHS, LV** $19.95 WAR ✠

Heritage of the Desert One of the earlier westerns made by the rugged Scott.
1933 62m/B Randolph Scott, Sally Blane, Guinn Williams; **D:** Henry Hathaway. **VHS, Beta** $24.95 DVT, TIM ✠½

The Hero A popular soccer player agrees to throw a game for big cash, and then worries about losing the respect of a young boy who idolizes him. Nothing new in this overly sentimental sports drama. *AKA:* Bloomfield.
1971 (PG) 97m/C Richard Harris, Romy Schneider, Kim Burfield, Maurice Kaufman; **D:** Richard Harris. **VHS, Beta** $59.98 SUE ✠½

Hero Interesting twist on Cinderella fable and modern media satire has television reporter Davis looking for the man who saved her life. It's none other than petty criminal Hoffman, who stumbles upon a plane crash one night, most reluctantly rescues several passengers (including Davis), loses a shoe, and departs unceremoniously before being identified. He later gives his remaining shoe to vagabond Garcia, who then steps up to grab the one million dollars the TV station is offering to the hero of the flight (and possessor of the other shoe). Handsome Garcia delights the media, Davis, and the city at large, while eternally muttering Hoffman stews like an older Ratso Rizzo while doing a term in the clink. Complications ensue. Critically considered disappointing, but wait—Garcia and Hoffman make a great team, and Davis is fetching as the vulnerable media person. Strong language and dark edges may keep away some of the kids, but otherwise this is a fine family fable.
1992 (PG-13) 116m/C Geena Davis, Dustin Hoffman, Andy Garcia, Joan Cusack, Kevin J. O'Connor, Chevy Chase, Maury Chaykin, Stephen Tobolowsky, Christian Clemenson, Tom Arnold, Janis Paige; **D:** Stephen Frears; **W:** David Peoples. **VHS, LV, 8mm** COL ✠✠✠

A Hero Ain't Nothin' But a Sandwich A young urban black teenager gets involved in drugs and is eventually saved from ruin. Slow-moving, over-directed and talky. However, Scott turns in a fine performance. Based on Alice Childress' novel.
1978 (PG) 107m/C Cicely Tyson, Paul Winfield, Larry B. Scott, Helen Martin, Glynn Turman, David Groh; **D:** Ralph Nelson. **VHS, Beta** $14.95 PAR, FCT ✠✠½

Hero and the Terror Perennial karate guy Norris plays a sensitive policeman who conquers his fear of a not-so-sensitive maniac who's trying to kill him. Plenty of action and a cheesy subplot to boot.
1988 (R) 96m/C Chuck Norris, Brynn Thayer, Steve James, Jack O'Halloran, Ron O'Neal, Billy Drago; **D:** William Tannen. **VHS, Beta, LV** $89.95 MED ✠½

Hero at Large An unemployed actor foils a robbery while dressed in a promotional "Captain Avenger" suit, and instant celebrity follows. Lightweight, yet enjoyable.
1980 (PG) 98m/C John Ritter, Anne Archer, Bert Convy, Kevin McCarthy, Kevin Bacon; **D:** Martin Davidson. **VHS, Beta** $59.95 MGM ✠✠½

Hero Bunker Hero bunk about a platoon of heroic Greek soldiers who attempt, at the expense of their personal longevity, to defend an important bunker from enemy invasion.
1971 93m/C John Miller, Maria Xenia; **D:** George Andrews. **VHS, Beta** $39.95 LIV ✠✠

Hero of Rome Rome has many who could be called "hero," but one stands biceps and pecs above the rest.
1963 ?m/C IT Gordon Scott, Gabriella Pallotti. **VHS, Beta** $16.95 SNC ✠✠

Hero of the Year The characters from Falk's "Top Dog" return in this story of a Polish television personality who loses his job and is forced to face unemployment and jobseeking.
1985 115m/C PL **D:** Feliks Falk. **VHS** $49.99 FCT ✠✠

Herod the Great Biblical epic of the downfall of Herod, the ruler of ancient Judea. Scantily clad women abound. Dubbed.
1960 93m/C IT Edmund Purdom, Sandra Milo, Alberto Lupo; **D:** Arnaldo Genoino. **VHS** $16.95 SNC ✠

Heroes An institutionalized Vietnam vet (Winkler) escapes, hoping to establish a worm farm which will support all his crazy buddies. On the way to the home of a friend he hopes will help him, he encounters Field. Funny situations don't always mix with serious underlying themes of mental illness and post-war adjustment.
1977 (PG) 97m/C Henry Winkler, Sally Field, Harrison Ford; **D:** Jeremy Paul Kagan; **M:** Jack Nitzsche. **VHS, Beta** $59.95 MCA ✠✠

Heroes Die Young A cheap independent feature depicting an American commando mission with orders to sabotage German oil fields during World War II.
1960 76m/B Krika Peters, Scott Borland, Robert Getz, James Strother. **VHS, Beta** $19.98 FOX, FCT ✠½

Heroes for Sale Fascinating melodrama about a WWI veteran who returns home and manages to survive one disaster after another. Barthelmess is great in his performance as an American Everyman who must deal with everything from morphine addiction to finding work during the Depression. Fast-paced, patriotic film is helped by ambitious script and the expert direction of Wellman.
1933 72m/B Richard Barthelmess, Loretta Young, Aline MacMahon, Robert Barratt, Grant Mitchell, Douglas Dumbrille, Charley Grapewin, Ward Bond; **D:** William A. Wellman; **W:** Robert Lord, Wilson Mizner. **VHS** MGM ✠✠✠

Heroes in Blue Two brothers join the police force, but one goes astray and hooks up with gangsters. Plenty of action distracts from the cliched story.
1939 60m/B Dick Purcell, Charles Quigley, Bernadene Hayes, Edward Keane; **D:** William Watson. **VHS, Beta** $16.95 SNC ✠✠

Heroes in Hell Two escaped WWII POWs join the Allied underground in an espionage conspiracy against the Third Reich.
1967 90m/C Klaus Kinski, Ettore Manni. **VHS, Beta** NO ✠½

Heroes in the Ming Dynasty Martial arts period exercise set in the Ming Dynasty.
1984 90m/C **VHS, Beta** $39.95 UNI ✠

The Heroes of Desert Storm The human spirit of the people who fought in the high-tech Persian Gulf War is captured in this film that also features real war footage from ABC News.
1991 93m/C Daniel Baldwin, Angela Bassett, Marshall Bell, Michael Alan Brooks, William Bumiller, Michael Champion, Maria Diaz; **D:** Don Ohlmeyer; **W:** Lionel Chetwynd. **VHS, Beta** $79.95 PSM ✠✠

Heroes of the Alamo Remember the Alamo...but forget this movie. Dull, threadbare dramatization of the battle that was scorned even back in '37.
1937 75m/B Rex Lease, Lane Chandler, Roger Williams, Earle Hodgins, Julian Rivero; **D:** Harry Fraser. **VHS, Beta** GPV ✠½

Heroes of the Hills The Three Mesquiteers back up a plan that would allow trusted prisoners to work for neighboring ranchers. Part of "The Three Mesquiteers" series.
1938 54m/B Bob Livingston, Ray Corrigan, Max Terhune. **VHS, Beta** MED ✠½

Heroes of the West Early sound action western serial.
1932 70m/B Noah Beery Jr. **VHS, Beta** $29.95 VCN, MLB ✠½

Heroes Stand Alone When a U.S. spy plane is downed in Central America, a special force is sent in to rescue the crew. Another "Rambo" rip-off.
1989 (R) 90m/C Bradford Dillman, Chad Everett, Wayne Grace, Rick Dean; **D:** Mark Griffiths. **VHS, Beta** $79.99 MGM ✠

Heroes Three When his crewmate is murdered while on leave in in the Far East, a Navy officer enlists the aid of a Chinese detective to track down the killer.
1984 90m/C Rowena Cortes, Mike Kelly, Laurens C. Postma, Lawrence Tan; **D:** S.H. Lau. **VHS, Beta** $99.95 IMP ✠

Hero's Blood A young married couple tries to survive in ancient China despite endless kung-fu marauders attempting to kick the living daylights out of them.
197? 82m/C Cheang Leung, Kan Mei Chai. **VHS, Beta** NO ✠

He's My Girl When a rock singer wins a trip for two to Hollywood, he convinces his agent to dress up as a woman so they can use the free tickets.
1987 (PG-13) 104m/C David Hallyday, T.K. Carter, Misha McK, Jennifer Tilly; **D:** Gabrielle Beaumont. **VHS, Beta** $14.95 LIV ✠½

He's Your Dog, Charlie Brown! An animated Peanuts adventure wherein Charlie Brown decides to send Snoopy back to the Daisy Hill Puppy Farm for obedience lessons.
1968 30m/C **VHS, Beta** $9.98 MED, VTR, WTA ✠½

Hester Street Set at the turn of the century, the film tells the story of a young Jewish immigrant who ventures to New York City to be with her husband. As she reacquaints herself with her husband, she finds that he has abandoned his Old World ideals. The film speaks not only to preserving the

heritage of the Jews, but to cherishing all heritages and cultures. Highly regarded upon release, unfortunately forgotten today.
1975 89m/C Carol Kane, Doris Roberts, Steven Keats, Mel Howard; **D:** Joan Micklin Silver. **VHS, Beta $39.95** *VES, FRV, TAM* ♫♫♫½

Hexed Walter Mitty lives in the person of bellboy Matthew Welsh, who enjoys masquerading as a debonair bon vivant. He finagles his way into the life of Hexina, a beautiful psychotic model who has checked into the hotel where Matthew works in order to murder her blackmailer. She tries to kill Matthew, apparently getting in a little practice, but he'll still follow her anywhere. Inane, charmless comedy that intends to satirize "Fatal Attraction" and similar films.
1993 (R) 93m/C Arye Gross, Claudia Christian, Adrienne Shelly, Lee Ermey, Norman Fell, Michael E. Knight; **W/D:** Alan Spencer. **VHS, LV** *COL* ♫½

Hey Abbott! A compilation of Abbott and Costello routines from their classic television series. Sketches include "Who's On First," "Oyster Stew," "Floogle Street" and "The Birthday Party."
1978 76m/B Bud Abbott, Lou Costello, Phil Silvers, Steve Allen, Joe Besser. **VHS, Beta $14.98** *VID* ♫♫½

Hey, Babu Riba A popular Yugoslavian fit of nostalgia about four men convening at the funeral of a young girl they all loved years before, and their happy, Americana-bathed memories therein. In Serbo-Croatian with English subtitles.
1988 (R) 109m/C *YU* Gala Videnovic, Nebojsa Bakocevic, Dragan Bjelogrlic, Marko Todorovic, Goran Radakovic; **D:** Jovan Acin. **VHS, Beta, LV $19.98** *ORI, TAM* ♫♫½

Hey Good Lookin' Ralph Bakshi's irreverent look at growing up in the 1950s bears the trademark qualities that distinguish his other adult animated features, "Fritz the Cat" and "Heavy Traffic."
1982 87m/C D: Ralph Bakshi. **VHS, Beta $19.98** *WAR, WTA* ♫♫½

Hey There, It's Yogi Bear When Yogi Bear comes out of winter hibernation to search for food, he travels to the Chizzling Brothers Circus. The first feature-length cartoon to come from the H-B Studios, it features the voices of Mel Blanc, J. Pat O'Malley, Julie Bennett and Daws Butler.
1964 98m/C D: William Hanna; **V:** Daws Butler, James Darren, Mel Blanc, H. Pat O'Malley, Julie Bennett. **VHS, Beta, LV $19.95** *WOV, IME, WTA* ♫♫

Hi-De-Ho The great Cab Calloway and his red hot jazz are featured in this film, which has the band caught between rival gangsters. The plot is incidental to the music, anyway. ♫Hi-De-Ho; I Got A Gal Named Nettie; Little Old Lady From Baltimore; A Rainy Sunday.
1935 60m/B Cab Calloway, Ida James, The Peters Sisters; **D:** Josh Binney. **VHS, Beta $19.95** *MVD, NOS, VCN* ♫♫½

Hi-Di-Hi A British television comedy about the shenanigans that inevitably follow when a stuffy Cambridge professor becomes the entertainment manager for a holiday camp.
1988 91m/C *GB* Simon Cadell, Ruth Madoc, Paul Shane, Jeffrey Holland, Leslie Dwyer. **VHS, Beta $39.98** *FOX* ♫♫½

Hi Diddle Diddle Topsy-turvy comedy features young lovers who long for conventional happiness. Instead they are cursed with con-artist parents who delight in crossing that law-abiding line. **AKA:** Diamonds and Crime; Try and Find It.

1943 72m/B Adolphe Menjou, Martha Scott, Dennis O'Keefe, Pola Negri; **D:** Andrew L. Stone. **VHS, Beta $24.95** *NOS, DVT, HEG* ♫½

Hi-Jacked When a parolee trucker's cargo is stolen, he inevitably becomes a suspect and must set out to find the true culprits.
1950 66m/B Jim Davis, Paul Cavanagh, Marsha Jones. **VHS, Beta, LV** *RXM* ♫

Hi, Mom! DePalma's follow-up to "Greetings" finds amateur pornographer/movie maker De Niro being advised by a professional in the field (Garfield) of sleazy filmmaking. De Niro films the residents of his apartment building and eventually marries one of his starlets. One of De Palma's earlier and better efforts with De Niro playing a crazy as only he can. **AKA:** Confessions of A Peeping John; Blue Manhattan.
1970 (R) 87m/C Robert De Niro, Charles Durnham, Allen Garfield, Lara Parker, Jennifer Salt, Gerrit Graham; **W/D:** Brian DePalma. **VHS** *FCT, HHE* ♫♫♫

Hi-Riders A revenge-based tale about large, mag-wheeled trucks and their drivers.
1977 (R) 90m/C Mel Ferrer, Stephen McNally, Neville Brand, Ralph Meeker; **D:** Greydon Clark. **VHS, Beta $49.95** *UHV* ♫

The Hidden A seasoned cop (Nouri) and a benign alien posing as an FBI agent (MacLachlan) team up to track down and destroy a hyper-violent alien who survives by invading the bodies of humans, causing them to go on murderous rampages. Much acclaimed, high velocity action film with state-of-the-art special effects.
1987 (R) 98m/C Kyle MacLachlan, Michael Nouri, Clu Gulager, Ed O'Ross; **D:** Jack Sholder. **VHS, Beta, LV $19.95** *MED, CVS* ♫♫♫

Hidden Agenda A human rights activist and an American lawyer uncover brutality and corruption among the British forces in Northern Ireland. Slow-paced but strong performances. The Northern Irish dialect is sometimes difficult to understand as are the machinations on the British police system. Generally worthwhile.
1990 (R) 108m/C Frances McDormand, Brian Cox, Brad Dourif, Mai Zetterling, John Benfield, Des McAleer, Jim Norton, Maurice Roeves; **D:** Ken Loach. **VHS, LV $19.98** *HBO, PIA, FCT* ♫♫½

Hidden City A film archivist and a statistician become drawn into a conspiracy when a piece of revealing film is spliced onto the end of an innocuous government tape.
1987 112m/C Charles Dance, Cassie Stuart, Alex Norton, Tusse Silberg, Bill Paterson; **D:** Stephen Poliakoff. **VHS, Beta $79.95** *SVS* ♫♫

Hidden Enemy During WWII, a scientist develops a new metal alloy that is stronger than steel yet lighter than aluminum. His nephew must protect his scientist/uncle from spies who would steal the formula to use against the Allies.
1940 63m/B Warren Hull, Kay Linaker, William von Brinken, George Cleveland; **D:** Howard Bretherton. **VHS, Beta $16.95** *SNC, RXM* ♫½

The Hidden Fortress Kurosawa's tale of a warrior who protects a princess from warring feudal lords. An inspiration for George Lucas' "Star Wars" series and deserving of its excellent reputation. In Japanese with English subtitles. The laserdisc edition is letter boxed to retain the film's original integrity. **AKA:** Kakushi Toride No San Akunin; Three Rascals in the Hidden Fortress; Three Bad Men in the Hidden Fortress.
1958 139m/B *JP* Toshiro Mifune, Misa Vehara, Minoru Chiaki; **D:** Akira Kurosawa. **VHS, Beta, LV $29.98** *MED, VYG, FCT* ♫♫♫½

Hidden Gold Routine western for Mix, which has him going undercover to win the confidence of three outlaws and discover where they have hidden their loot.
1933 57m/B Tom Mix. **VHS, Beta $19.95** *DVT, VCN, HEG* ♫½

Hidden Guns Above-average tale of father-and-son lawmen out to reform a town and put the bad guys away. When dad is killed, son goes up against the villain alone. A Greek chorus adds an interesting twist to the action. Erich von Stroheim, Jr. is listed as assistant director.
1956 66m/B Bruce Bennett, Richard Arlen, John Carradine, Faron Young, Angie Dickinson, Guinn Williams; **D:** Albert C. Gannaway. **VHS $19.95** *NOS* ♫♫♫

Hidden Obsession Newscaster Ellen is taking a much needed vacation at an isolated cabin when she learns that a serial killer has escaped from a nearby prison. Luckily, she has a hunky police officer neighbor for protection. But though the escaped killer is captured, the killings go on—with Ellen as the next target.
1992 (R) 92m/C Heather Thomas, Jan-Michael Vincent, Nicholas Celozzi; **D:** John Stewart; **W:** David Reskin. **VHS, LV** *MCA* ♫½

The Hidden Room A doctor finds out about his wife's affair and decides to get revenge on her lover. He kidnaps him, imprisons him in a cellar, and decides to kill him—slowly. Tense melodrama. **AKA:** Obsession.
1949 98m/B *GB* Robert Newton, Sally Gray, Naunton Wayne, Phil Brown, Olga Lindo; **D:** Edward Dmytryk. **VHS, Beta $16.95** *NOS, SNC, RXM* ♫♫♫

Hidden Valley Early Steele western in which everyone is fighting over a map that leads to hidden treasure in the valley.
1932 60m/B Bob Steele, Gertrude Messinger, Francis McDonald; **D:** Robert North Bradbury. **VHS $9.95** *GPV* ♫♫

Hide and Go Shriek Several high school seniors are murdered one by one during a graduation party. Also available in an unrated, gorier version.
1987 (R) 90m/C Annette Sinclair, Brittain Frye, Rebunkah Jones; **D:** Skip Schoolnik. **VHS, Beta, LV** *NO* ♫

Hide and Seek When a high school hacker converts his computer into a nuclear weapon, he finds that it has developed a mind of its own.
1977 60m/C Bob Martin, Ingrid Veninger, David Patrick. **VHS, Beta $59.95** *LHV* ♫

Hide and Seek A study of children living in the land that would soon become Israel. Although they play as normal children, life is particularly difficult. This adversity will lay the foundation for their Israeli citizenry. In Hebrew with English subtitles.
1980 90m/C Gila Almagor, Doron Tavori, Chaim Hadaya; **D:** Dan Wolman. **VHS, Beta $79.95** *ERG, TAM* ♫

Hide in Plain Sight A distraught blue-collar worker searches for his children who disappeared when his ex-wife and her mobster husband are given new identities by federal agents. Caan's fine directorial debut is based on a true story.
1980 (PG) 96m/C James Caan, Jill Eikenberry, Robert Viharo, Kenneth McMillan, Josef Sommer, Danny Aiello; **D:** James Caan. **VHS, Beta $59.95** *MGM* ♫♫♫

Hide-Out A man running from the law winds up at a small farm, falls in love, and becomes reformed by the good family that takes him in. Good supporting cast includes a very young Rooney.

1934 83m/B Robert Montgomery, Maureen O'Sullivan, Edward Arnold, Elizabeth Patterson, Mickey Rooney, Edward Brophy; **D:** Woodbridge S. Van Dyke. **VHS** MGM ♪♪½

The Hideaways A 12-year-old girl and her younger brother run away and hide in the Metropolitan Museum of Art. The girl becomes enamored of a piece of sculpture and sets out to discover its creator. Based on the children's novel by M.E. Kerr. **AKA:** From the Mixed-Up Files of Mrs. Basil E. Frankweiler.
1973 (G) 105m/C Richard Mulligan, George Rose, Ingrid Bergman, Sally Prager, Johnny Doran, Madeline Kahn; **D:** Fielder Cook. **VHS, Beta** $59.95 WAR, VHE, FCT ♪♪½

Hideous Sun Demon A physicist exposed to radiation must stay out of sunlight or he will turn into a scaly, lizard-like creature. Includes previews of coming attractions from classic sci-fi films. **AKA:** Blood On His Lips; Terror From the Sun; The Sun Demon.
1959 75m/B Robert Clarke, Patricia Manning, Nan Peterson; **D:** Robert Clarke. **VHS, Beta** $9.95 NOS, MRV, RHI ♪½

Hider in the House In a peaceful neighborhood a family is about to spend an evening of terror when they discover a psychopath is hiding in the attic of their home.
1990 (R) 109m/C Michael McKean, Gary Busey, Mimi Rogers; **D:** Michael Patrick. **VHS, Beta, LV** $89.98 VES, LIV ♪♪½

Hiding Out A young stockbroker testifies against the Mafia and must find a place to hide in order to avoid being killed. He winds up at his cousin's high school in Delaware, but can he really go through all these teenage troubles once again?
1987 (PG-13) 99m/C Jon Cryer, Keith Coogan, Gretchen Cryer, Annabeth Gish, Tim Quill; **D:** Bob Giraldi. **VHS, Beta** $19.99 HBO ♪♪

The Hiding Place True story of two Dutch Christian sisters sent to a concentration camp for hiding Jews during World War II. Film is uneven but good cast pulls it through. Based on the Corrie Ten Boom book and produced by Billy Graham's Evangelistic Association.
1975 145m/C Julie Harris, Eileen Heckart, Arthur O'Connell, Jeannette Clift; **D:** James F. Collier. **VHS** $49.95 VBL, REP, COV ♪♪

High & Low Fine Japanese film noir about a wealthy businessman who is being blackmailed by kidnappers who claim to have his son. When he discovers that they have mistakenly taken his chauffeur's son he must decide whether to face financial ruin or risk the life of a young boy. Based on an Ed McBain novel. In Japanese with English subtitles. **AKA:** Tengoku To Jigoku.
1962 (R) 143m/B JP Toshiro Mifune, Tatsuya Mihashi, Tatsuya Nakadai; **D:** Akira Kurosawa. **VHS, Beta, LV** $29.95 PAV, IME, TAM ♪♪♪½

High Anxiety Brooks' tries hard to please in this low-brow parody of Hitchcock films employing dozens of references to films like "Psycho," "Spellbound," "The Birds," and "Vertigo." Tells the tale of a height-fearing psychiatrist caught up in a murder mystery. The title song performed a la Sinatra by Brooks is one of the film's high moments. Brooks also has a lot of fun with Hitchcockian camera movements. Uneven (What? Brooks?) but amusing tribute.
1977 (PG) 92m/C Mel Brooks, Madeline Kahn, Cloris Leachman, Harvey Korman, Ron Carey, Howard Morris, Dick Van Patten; **D:** Mel Brooks. **VHS, Beta, LV** $19.98 FOX ♪♪

High Ballin' Truckers Fonda and Reed team up with lady trucker Shaver to take on the gang trying to crush the independent drivers.
1978 (PG) 100m/C CA Peter Fonda, Jerry Reed, Helen Shaver; **D:** Peter Carter. **VHS, Beta** $29.98 LIV, VES ♪

High Command To save his daughter from an ugly scandal, the British general of an isolated Colonial African outpost traps a blackmailer's killer.
1937 84m/B GB Lionel Atwill, Lucie Mannheim, James Mason; **D:** Thorold Dickinson. **VHS, Beta** $19.95 NOS, MRV, VYY ♪♪½

High Country Two misfits, one handicapped, the other an ex-con, on the run from society learn mutual trust as they travel through the Canadian Rockies. **AKA:** The First Hello.
1981 101m/C CA Timothy Bottoms, Linda Purl, George Sims, Jim Lawrence, Bill Berry; **D:** Harvey Hart. **VHS, Beta** $79.95 VES ♪♪½

High Country Calling Wolf pups escape their man-made home and set off a cross-country chase.
1975 (G) 84m/C **VHS, Beta** $29.95 GEM ♪½

High Crime A "French Connection"-style suspense story about the heroin trade. Features high-speed chases and a police commissioner obsessed with capturing the criminals.
1973 91m/C James Whitmore, Franco Nero, Fernando Rey; **D:** Enzo G. Castellari. **VHS, Beta** $49.95 MED ♪♪

High Desert Kill A science-fiction tale will keep you guessing. Aliens landing in the New Mexican desert want something totally unexpected, and a trio of friends will be the first to find out what it is. Written for cable by T. S. Cook ("The China Syndrome").
1990 (PG) 93m/C Chuck Connors, Marc Singer, Anthony Geary, Micah Grant; **D:** Harry Falk. **VHS, Beta** $79.95 MCA ♪♪

High Frequency Two young men monitoring a satellite relay station witness the murder of a woman. Believing they know who the killer's next victim will be, they set out to warn her. Lack of development mars what could have been a tidy little thriller.
1988 105m/C IT Oliver Benny, Vincent Spano, Isabelle Pasco, Anne Canovos; **D:** Faliero Rosati. **VHS, LV** $79.98 MCG ♪♪

High Gear Heartstring-tugger about a race car driver, his girlfriend and the orphan son of a driver killed in a crash. Try to guess the outcome.
1933 65m/B James Murray, Joan Marsh, Jackie Searl, Theodore von Eltz, Lee Moran, Gordon DeMain; **D:** Leigh Jason. **VHS** $19.95 NOS, RXM ♪

High Heels A black comedy about a doctor who believes beauty is only skin deep and marries a plain woman. However, when he meets her beautiful sister, he begins to wonder. In French with English subtitles. **AKA:** Docteur Popaul; Scoundrel in White.
1972 100m/C FR Laura Antonelli, Jean-Paul Belmondo, Mia Farrow, Daniel Ivernel; **D:** Claude Chabrol. **VHS, Beta** $39.95 MON ♪♪

High Heels An outrageous combination murder-melodrama-comedy from Almodovar. Rebecca is a TV anchorwoman in Madrid whose flamboyant singer/actress mother has returned to the city for a concert. Rebecca happens to be married to one of her mother's not-so-ex-flames. When her husband winds up dead, Rebecca confesses to his murder during her newscast—but is she telling the truth or just covering up for mom? Mix in a drag queen/judge, a dancing chorus of wom-

en prison inmates, and a peculiar police detective, and see if the plot convolutions make sense. In Spanish with English subtitles. **AKA:** Tacones Lejanos.
1991 (R) 113m/C SP Victoria Abril, Marisa Paredes, Miguel Bose; **W/D:** Pedro Almodovar. **VHS, Beta** PAR ♪♪♪

High Hopes A moving yet nasty satiric comedy about a pair of ex-hippies maintaining their counter-culture lifestyle in Margaret Thatcher's England, as they watch the signs of conservative "progress" overtake them and their geriatric, embittered Mum. Hilarious and mature.
1989 110m/C GB Philip Davis, Ruth Sheen, Edna Dore; **D:** Mike Leigh. **VHS, Beta** $29.95 ACA ♪♪♪

High Ice Forest ranger and a lieutenant colonel are involved in a clash of wills over a rescue mission high in the snow-capped Washington state peaks.
1980 97m/C David Janssen, Tony Musante; **D:** Eugene S. Jones. **VHS, Beta** $69.95 VES ♪½

High Lonesome Barrymore is a drifter in Big Bend country, suspected in a series of mysterious murders. While he is being held captive, the real killers - thought dead - return to exact revenge on those they hold responsible for the range war in which they were wounded. This was LeMay's only stint as a director.
1950 80m/C John Barrymore Jr., Chill Wills, John Archer, Lois Butler, Kristine Miller, Basil Ruysdael, Jack Elam; **W/D:** Alan LeMay. **VHS** $19.95 NOS ♪♪½

High Noon The award-winning Western about Hadleyville town marshal Will Kane (Cooper) who must face down four professional killers alone, after being abandoned to his fate by the gutless townspeople who professed to admire him. Cooper has just married his young, beautiful Quaker bride (Kelly) when the town learns that a revenge-minded killer will arrive on the noon train to be met by his three cohorts. The sheriff and his bride are urged to leave town, which they do, but Cooper's sense of honor drives him back for the noon showdown. A landmark Western, with Cooper as the ultimate hero figure, his sheer presence overwhelming. Note the continuing use of the ballad written by Dimitri Tamkin, "Do Not Forsake Me, Oh My Darlin'" (sung by Tex Ritter) to heighten the tension and action throughout the film. The laserdisc includes the original theatrical trailer, an appreciative essay by Howard Suber on audio 2, a photo essay of production stills, Carl Foreman's original notes of the film and the complete text of "The Tin Star," the story on which the film is based.
1952 85m/B Gary Cooper, Grace Kelly, Lloyd Bridges, Lon Chaney Jr., Thomas Mitchell, Otto Kruger, Katy Jurado, Lee Van Cleef; **D:** Fred Zinneman; **M:** Dimitri Tiomkin. Academy Awards '52: Best Actor (Cooper), Best Film Editing, Best Song ("High Noon (Do Not Forsake Me, Oh My Darlin')"), Best Score; Nominations: Best Director (Zinneman), Best Picture, Best Screenplay; Golden Globe Awards '53: Best Actor—Drama (Cooper), Best Supporting Actress (Jurado); New York Film Critics Awards '52: Best Director (Zinneman), Best Film. **VHS, LV** $19.98 REP, VYG, TLF ♪♪♪♪

High Noon: Part 2 Majors attempts to fill Gary Cooper's shoes, as Marshal Kane returns a year after the events of the original "High Noon" to remove the corrupt marshal who replaced him. Subtitled "The Return of Will Kane." Made for television.
1980 96m/C Lee Majors, David Carradine, Pernell Roberts, Katherine Cannon; **D:** Jerry Jameson. **VHS, Beta** $14.95 FRH ♪

High Plains Drifter A surreal, violent western focusing on a drifter who defends a town from gunmen intent on meting out death. One of Eastwood's most stylistic directorial efforts, indebted to his "Man with No Name" days with Sergio Leone. Laser format is letterboxed and includes chapter stops and the original theatrical trailer.
1973 (R) 105m/C Clint Eastwood, Verna Bloom, Mitchell Ryan, Marianna Hill; **D:** Clint Eastwood. **VHS, Beta, LV** $19.95 MCA, TLF ✍✍½

High Risk Improbable action-adventure of four unemployed Americans who battle foreign armies, unscrupulous gunrunners, and jungle bandits in a harrowing attempt to steal five million dollars from an expatriate American drug dealer living in the peaceful splendor of his Columbian villa. Interesting in its own run-on way.
1976 (R) 94m/C James Brolin, Anthony Quinn, Lindsay Wagner, James Coburn, Ernest Borgnine, Bruce Davison, Cleavon Little; **D:** Stewart Raffill. **VHS, Beta** $9.98 SUE ✍½

High Road to China A hard-drinking former WWI air ace is recruited by a young heiress who must find her father before his ex-partner takes over his business. Post-"Raiders of the Lost Ark" thrills and romance, but without that tale's panache.
1983 (PG) 105m/C Bess Armstrong, Tom Selleck, Jack Weston, Robert Morley, Wilford Brimley, Brian Blessed; **D:** Brian G. Hutton; **M:** John Barry. **VHS, Beta, LV** $19.98 WAR ✍✍

High Rolling in a Hot Corvette Two carnival workers leave their jobs and hit the road in search of adventure and excitement, eventually turning to crime. *AKA:* High Rolling.
1977 (PG) 82m/C AU Joseph Bottoms, Greg Taylor, Judy Davis, Wendy Hughes; **D:** Igor Auzins. **VHS, Beta** $69.95 VES ✍

High School Caesar A seedy teenage exploitation flick about a rich teenager, with no parental supervision, who starts his own gang to run his high school.
1956 75m/B John Ashley; **D:** O'Dale Ireland. **VHS, Beta** $9.95 RHI, SNC ✍

High School Confidential Teen punk Tamblyn transfers to Santo Bello high school from Chicago and causes havoc among the locals. He soon involves himself in the school drug scene and looks to be the top dog in dealing, but what no one knows is that he's really a narc! A must for midnight movie fans thanks to high camp values, "hep cat" dialogue and the gorgeous Van Doren as Tamblyn's sex-crazed "aunt." *AKA:* Young Hellions.
1958 85m/B Russ Tamblyn, Jan Sterling, John Barrymore Jr., Mamie Van Doren, Diane Jergens, Jerry Lee Lewis, Ray Anthony, Jackie Coogan, Charles Chaplin Jr., Burt Douglas, Michael Landon, Jody Fair, Phillipa Fallon, Robin Raymond, James Todd, Lyle Talbot, William Wellman Jr.; **D:** Jack Arnold. **VHS, Beta** $14.98 REP ✍✍

High School USA A high school class clown confronts the king of the prep-jock-bullies. Antics ensue in this made-for-television sion flick which features many stars from fifties and sixties sitcoms.
1984 96m/C Michael J. Fox, Nancy McKeon, Bob Denver, Angela Cartwright, Elinor Donahue, Dwayne Hickman, Lauri Hendler, Dana Plato, Tony Dow, David Nelson; **D:** Rod Amateau. **VHS, Beta** $59.95 LHV, WAR ✍½

High Season A satire about a beautiful English photographer (Bisset) stranded on an idyllic Greek island with neither money nor inspiration, and the motley assembly of characters who surround her during the tourist season. Written by Clare and Mark Peploe.
1988 (R) 95m/C GB Jacqueline Bisset, James Fox, Irene Papas, Sebastian Shaw, Kenneth Branagh, Robert Stephens; **D:** Clare Peploe. **VHS, Beta, LV, 8mm** $19.98 SUE, FCT, NLC ✍✍½

High Sierra Bogart is Roy "Mad Dog" Earle, an aging gangster whose last job backfires, so he's hiding out from the police in the High Sierras. Screenplay by John Huston and W.R. Burnett, on whose novel it's based. Bogart's first starring role. Remade in 1955 as "I Died A Thousand Times." Also available colorized.
1941 96m/B Humphrey Bogart, Ida Lupino, Arthur Kennedy, Joan Leslie, Cornel Wilde, Henry Travers, Henry Hull; **D:** Raoul Walsh; **W:** John Huston, W.R. Burnett. **VHS, Beta, LV** $19.95 FOX ✍✍✍

High Society A wealthy man attempts to win back his ex-wife who's about to be remarried in this enjoyable remake of "The Philadelphia Story." Cole Porter score. Letterboxed laserdisc format also includes the original movie trailer. ♫High Society Calypso; Little One; Who Wants to Be a Millionaire?; True Love; You're Sensational; I Love You, Samantha; Now You Has Jazz; Well, Did You Evah?; Mind if I Make Love to You?.
1956 107m/C Frank Sinatra, Bing Crosby, Grace Kelly, Louis Armstrong, Celeste Holm, Sidney Blackmer, Louis Calhern; **D:** Charles Walters. **VHS, Beta, LV, 8mm** $19.98 MGM, PIA ✍✍✍

High Spirits An American inherits an Irish castle and a sexy 200-year-old ghost. A painful, clumsy comedy by the fine British director that was apparently butchered by the studio before its release.
1988 (PG-13) 99m/C Daryl Hannah, Peter O'Toole, Steve Guttenberg, Beverly D'Angelo, Liam Neeson, Martin Ferrero, Peter Gallagher, Jennifer Tilly; **D:** Neil Jordan. **VHS, Beta, LV** $19.98 MED ✍✍

High Stakes Kirkland stars as a prostitute who's battling the Mob and falling in love. Limited release in theaters but another fine performance from Kirkland. Also released as "Melanie Rose."
1989 (R) 102m/C Sally Kirkland, Robert LuPone, Richard Lynch, Sarah Gellar, Kathy Bates, W.T. Martin; **D:** Amos Kollek. **VHS, LV** $89.95 VMK ✍✍

High Tide A strong and strange drama once again coupling the star and director of "My Brilliant Career." A small-time rock 'n' roll singer who is stranded in a small, beach town fortuitously meets up with her previously-abandoned teenage daughter. Acclaimed.
1987 (PG-13) 120m/C AU Judy Davis, Jan Adele, Claudia Karvan, Colin Friels; **D:** Gillian Armstrong. **VHS, Beta, LV, 8mm** $19.98 SUE, FCT, NLC ✍✍✍

High Velocity Lame adventure about two mercenaries involved in the challenge of a lifetime—rescuing a kidnapped executive from Asian terrorists. Filmed in Manila.
1976 (PG) 105m/C Ben Gazzara, Paul Winfield, Britt Ekland, Keenan Wynn; **D:** Remi Kramer; **M:** Jerry Goldsmith. **VHS, Beta** $29.95 MED ✍½

High Voltage A fast-moving comedy adventure set in the High Sierras.
1929 62m/B Carole Lombard, William Boyd, Gwen Moore, Billy Bevan; **D:** Howard Higgin. **VHS, Beta** $19.95 NOS, MRV, KRT ✍✍

Higher and Higher Bankrupt aristocrat conspires with servants to regain his fortune, and tries to marry his daughter into money. Sinatra's first big-screen role. ♫You Belong in a Love Song; A Most Important Affair; The Music Stopped; Today I'm A Debutante; A Lovely Way To Spend An Evening; I Couldn't Sleep a Wink Last Night; You're On Your Own; I Saw You First; Disgustingly Rich; Boccherini's Minuet in Boogie.
1944 90m/B Frank Sinatra, Leon Errol, Michele Morgan, Jack Haley, Mary McGuire; **D:** Tim Whelan. **VHS, Beta, LV** $19.98 CCB, IME, TTC ✍✍

Higher Education Andy leaves his small town for a big city college and falls head over heels for a student and a teacher. He didn't know college could be so much fun.
1988 (R) 83m/C Kevin Hicks, Isabelle Mejias, Lori Hallier, Maury Chaykin, Richard Monette; **D:** John Sheppard. **VHS** $9.95 SIM ✍✍

The Highest Honor True story set during World War II of a friendship between an Australian army officer, captured while attempting to infiltrate Singapore, and a Japanese security officer. Too long, but gripping.
1984 (R) 99m/C AU John Howard, Atsuo Nakamura, Stuart Wilson, Michael Aitkens, Steve Bisley; **D:** Peter Maxwell. **VHS, Beta, LV** $19.98 SUE, STE ✍✍½

Highlander A strange tale about an immortal 16th-century Scottish warrior who has had to battle his evil immortal enemy through the centuries. The feud comes to blows in modern-day Manhattan. Connery makes a memorable appearance as the good warrior's mentor. Spectacular battle and death scenes. A cult favorite which spawned a weak sequel and a television series.
1986 (R) 110m/C Christopher Lambert, Sean Connery, Clancy Brown, Roxanne Hart, Beatie Edney, Alan North, Sheila Gish, Jon Polito; **D:** Russell Mulcahy. **VHS, Beta, LV** $19.99 HBO ✍✍✍

Highlander 2: The Quickening The saga of Connor MacLeod and Juan Villa-Lobos continues in this sequel set in the year 2024. An energy shield designed to block out the sun's harmful ultraviolet rays has left planet Earth in perpetual darkness, but there is evidence that the ozone layer has repaired itself. An environmental terrorist and her group begin a sabotage effort and are joined by MacLeod and Villa-Lobos in their quest to save Earth. Stunning visual effects don't make up for the lack of substance.
1991 (R) 90m/C Christopher Lambert, Sean Connery, Virginia Madsen, Michael Ironside, John C. McGinley; **D:** Russell Mulcahy; **W:** Peter Bellwood. **VHS, LV, 8mm** $19.95 COL ✍½

Highpoint When an unemployed man becomes the chauffeur of a wealthy family, he finds himself in the middle of a mysterious murder and part of an international CIA plot. Hard to figure what's happening in this one.
1980 (PG) 91m/C CA Richard Harris, Christopher Plummer, Beverly D'Angelo, Kate Reid, Saul Rubinek; **D:** Peter Carter. **VHS, Beta, LV** $19.95 STE, SUE ✍

Highway 61 Pokey Jones is a shy barber in the small Canadian town of Pickerel Falls who becomes a celebrity when he discovers the frozen corpse of an unknown young man in his backyard. Jackie Bangs is a rock roadie who has stolen her band's stash of drugs and finds herself stranded in the same small town. She quickly proclaims herself the dead man's sister and persuades Pokey to drive her and the corpse to New Orleans for burial, neglecting to mention she has stashed the drugs in the coffin. Amoral Jackie and innocent Pokey begin a wild road trip which also features the sinister Mr. Skin, who says he's the Devil and tries to claim the corpse for himself, and a wasted rock star based on Elvis. Lackluster direction undercuts much of the first-rate acting and amusing story quirks.

1991 (R) 110m/C Valerie Buhagiar, Don McKellar, Earl Pastko, Peter Breck, Art Bergmann; *D:* Bruce McDonald; *W:* Don McKellar. **VHS $89.95** *PAR, FCT* 𝄢𝄢

Highway 13 When a trucker witnesses an "accidental" death at the loading warehouse, he falls under suspicion. He then sets out to clear his name.
1948 60m/B Robert Lowery, Pamela Blake, Lyle Talbot, Michael Whalen, Maris Wrixon, Clem Bevans; *D:* William Berke. **VHS, Beta, LV** *NO* 𝄢½

Highway to Hell Bergen plays the devil in a horror-comedy about going to hell—even if you're not dead yet. Lowe and Swanson are newlyweds on their way to Las Vegas when they're stopped by a "hellcop," who kidnaps the bride and takes her to the netherworld to be the devil's new plaything. Her human hubby doesn't take kindly to this and goes to hell to rescue his bride. Campy flick is played for laughs and has some good special effects.
1992 (R) 93m/C Patrick Bergin, Adam Storke, Chad Lowe, Kristy Swanson, Richard Farnsworth, C.J. Graham, Lita Ford, Kevin Peter Hall, Pamela Gidley, Brian Helgeland; *Cameos:* Gilbert Gottfried; *D:* Ate De Jong. **VHS $89.99** *HBO* 𝄢𝄢

Hijazo de Mi Vidaza The history of a family as told by a mother to her son. In Spanish. *AKA:* Son of My Life.
1977? 90m/C Enrique Cuenca, Eduardo Manzano, Maria Fernanda, Fernando Casanova. **VHS, Beta $49.95** *MAD* 𝄢

Hill Number One A dramatization of the story of Easter, featuring Dean in one of his first major roles as John the Baptist. Made for television.
1951 57m/B James Dean, Michael Ansara, Leif Erickson, Ruth Hussey, Roddy McDowall. **VHS, Beta $19.95** *RHI, FCT, HEG* 𝄢

Hill 24 Doesn't Answer Four Zionist soldiers defend a strategic entrance to Jerusalem. While at their posts, they reflect on their lives and devotion to the cause. Made in Israel, in English. The first Israeli feature film.
1955 101m/B *IS* Edward Mulhare, Haya Harareet, Michael Wager; *D:* Thorold Dickinson. **VHS, Beta $79.95** *ERG, TAM* 𝄢𝄢𝄢

Hillbillies in a Haunted House Two country and western singers en route to the Nashville jamboree encounter a group of foreign spies "haunting" a house. Features Rathbone's last film performance. Sequel to "Las Vegas Hillbillies" (1966). Giant step down for everyone involved.
1967 88m/C Ferlin Husky, Joi Lansing, Don Bowman, John Carradine, Lon Chaney Jr., Basil Rathbone; *D:* Jean Yarborough. **VHS, Beta $29.95** *UHV, AOV* Woof!

Hillbilly Blitzkrieg Two soldiers are sent to the boonies to guard a top-secret missile site from enemy agents. Come-to-life comic strip characters Snuffy Smith, Barney Google and Spark Plug join in the antics. *AKA:* Enemy Round-up.
1942 63m/B Bud Duncan, Cliff Nazarro, Edgar Kennedy, Doris Linden, Lucien Littlefield, Alan Baldwin; *D:* Roy Mack. **VHS $19.95** *NOS, RXM* 𝄢

The Hills Have Eyes Desperate family battles for survival and vengeance against a brutal band of inbred hillbilly cannibals. Craven gore-fest followed by Hills II.
1977 (R) 83m/C Susan Lanier, Robert Houston, Martin Speer, Dee Wallace Stone, Russ Grieve, John Steadman, James Whitworth, Michael Berryman; *D:* Wes Craven. **VHS, Beta $19.95** *STE* Woof!

The Hills Have Eyes, Part 2 Craven reprises Hills with Eyes number one to ill effect. Ignorant teens disregard warnings of a "Hills Have Eyes" refugee, and go stomping into the grim reaper's proving grounds. Predictably bad things happen.
1984 86m/C Michael Berryman, Kevin Blair, John Bloom, Janus Blythe, John Laughlin, Tamara Stafford; *W/D:* Wes Craven. **VHS, Beta $14.99** *HBO* 𝄢

Hills of Utah Autry finds himself in the middle of a feud between the local mine operator and a group of cattlemen, while searching for his father's murderer.
1951 70m/B Gene Autry, Pat Buttram, Denver Pyle; *D:* John English. **VHS, Beta $29.98** *CCB* 𝄢½

The Hillside Strangler Made-for-television, crime-of-the-week drama about the investigation to apprehend the serial killer responsible for 10 deaths in 1977-78. *AKA:* The Case of the Hillside Stranglers.
1989 91m/C Richard Crenna, Dennis Farina, Billy Zane, Tony Plana, James Tolkan, Tasia Valenza; *D:* Steven Gethers. **VHS, Beta $79.95** *FRH* 𝄢½

Himatsuri An acclaimed film detailing the conflicts between man and nature, as a careless lumberjack in a Japanese forest is visited by the ancient gods. In Japanese with English subtitles. *AKA:* Fire Festival.
1985 95m/C *JP* Kinya Kitaoji; *D:* Mitsuo Yanagimachi. **VHS, Beta $29.95** *LHV, WAR, AUD* 𝄢𝄢𝄢

The Hindenburg A dramatization of what might have happened on the fateful night the Hindenburg exploded. Scott plays an investigator who is aware that something is up, and has numerous suspects to interrogate. The laser edition features wide-screen format, digital Stereo Surround, the original trailer and chapter stops.
1975 (PG) 126m/C George C. Scott, Anne Bancroft, William Atherton, Roy Thinnes, Gig Young, Burgess Meredith, Charles Durning, Richard Dysart; *D:* Robert Wise. Academy Awards '75: Best Sound Effects Editing, Best Visual Effects; Nominations: Best Art Direction/Set Decoration, Best Cinematography, Best Sound. **VHS, Beta, LV $19.98** *MCA* 𝄢𝄢

Hips, Hips, Hooray Two supposed "hot shot" salesmen are hired by a cosmetic company to sell flavored lipstick. This lavish musical comedy is one of Wheeler and Woolsey's best vehicles. ♫Tired of It All; Keep Romance Alive; Keep On Doin' What You're Doin'.
1934 68m/B Robert Woolsey, Bert Wheeler, Ruth Etting, Thelma Todd, Dorothy Lee; *D:* Mark Sandrich. **VHS, Beta, LV $19.95** *CCB* 𝄢½

Hired Hand Two drifters settle on a farm belonging to one of their wives, only to leave again seeking to avenge the murder of a friend. TV prints include Larry Hagman in a cameo role.
1971 93m/C Peter Fonda, Warren Oates, Verna Bloom, Severn Darden, Robert Pratt; *Cameos:* Larry Hagman; *D:* Peter Fonda. **VHS, Beta $14.95** *KRT* 𝄢½

Hired to Kill A pair of Mafia hoods plot against each other over a $6 million drug shipment. Previously titled "The Italian Connection."
1973 (R) 90m/C Henry Silva, Woody Strode, Adolfo Celi, Mario Adorf. **Beta** *NO* 𝄢½

Hired to Kill The granite-hewn Thompson plays a male-chauvinist commando grudgingly leading a squad of beautiful mercenary-ettes on an international rescue mission. Not as bad as it sounds (mainly because the ladies aren't complete bimbos), but between senseless plotting, gratuitous

catfights, and a love scene indistinguishable from rape, the Hound found plenty to dislike.
1991 (R) 91m/C Brian Thompson, George Kennedy, Jose Ferrer, Oliver Reed, Penelope Reed, Michelle Moffett, Barbara Lee Alexander, Jordanna Capra; *D:* Peter Rader; *W/D:* Nico Mastorakis. **VHS, Beta** *PAR* 𝄢½

Hiroshima Maiden An American family gains new perspective when they meet a young survivor of the atomic bomb. Based on true stories of Japanese women who stayed with Americans while undergoing surgery to minimize their scars. Originally aired on PBS as part of the "Wonderworks" family movie series.
1988 58m/C Susan Blakely, Richard Masur, Tamlyn Tomita; *D:* Joan Darling. **VHS $29.95** *PME, WNE, HMV* 𝄢½

Hiroshima, Mon Amour A profoundly moving drama exploring the shadow of history over the personal lives of a lonely French actress living in Tokyo and a Japanese architect with whom she's having an affair. Presented in a complex network of flashbacks. Highly influential; adapted by Marguerite Duras from her book. In Japanese with English subtitles.
1959 88m/B *JP FR* Emmanuelle Riva, Eiji Okada, Bernard Fresson; *D:* Alain Resnais. Academy Awards '60 Nominations: Best Story & Screenplay; National Board of Review Awards '60: 5 Best Foreign Films of the Year; New York Film Critics Awards '60: Best Foreign Film. **VHS, Beta, 8mm $29.98** *NOS, MRV, SUE* 𝄢𝄢𝄢𝄢

Hiroshima: Out of the Ashes The terrible aftermath of the bombing of Hiroshima, August, 1945, as seen through the eyes of American and Japanese soldiers, the Japanese people, and a priest. Carefully detailed and realistic, creates an amazing emotional response. Don't miss the scene in which Nelson and his buddy find themselves surrounded by Japanese—the enemy—only to realize that their "captors" have been blinded by the blast. Created as an homage for the 45th anniversary of the bombing.
1990 (PG) 98m/C Max von Sydow, Judd Nelson, Pat Morita; *D:* Peter Werner. **VHS** *VMK* 𝄢𝄢𝄢

His Brother's Ghost When Fuzzy is rubbed out by bandits, Billy Carson (no longer called Billy the Kid thanks to mothers' protestations) convinces his twin brother to impersonate him in order to make the bandits believe they are the victims of hocus pocus from the otherworld. Crabbe—who dressed noir before it was chic—made this during his post sci-fi western period, when he slugged it through some fifty low-rent oaters (usually under the direction of Newfield at PRC studios).
1945 54m/C Buster Crabbe, Al "Fuzzy" St. John, Charles King, Bud Osborne, Karl Hackett, Archie Hall; *D:* Sam Newfield. **VHS $19.99** *NOS, MRV, HEG* 𝄢

His Double Life When a shy gentleman's valet dies, his master assumes the dead man's identity and has a grand time. From the play "Buried Alive" by Arnold Bennett. Remade in 1943 as "Holy Matrimony."
1933 67m/B Roland Young, Lillian Gish, Montagu Love; *D:* Arthur Hopkins. **VHS, Beta $19.95** *NOS, MRV, KRT* 𝄢𝄢½

His Fighting Blood Northwest Mounties in action. Based on a James Oliver Curwood story.
1935 63m/B Kermit Maynard. **VHS, Beta $19.95** *VDM* 𝄢½

His First Command An early talkie wherein a playboy falls in love with the daughter of a cavalry officer, and enlists in order to win her affections.
1929 60m/B William Boyd, Dorothy Sebastian, Gavin Gordon; *D:* Gregory La Cava. **VHS, Beta, 8mm $24.95** VYY 🎭½

His First Flame A classic Langdon silent romantic comedy. Co-written by Frank Capra.
1926 62m/B Harry Langdon, Vernon Dent, Natalie Kingston. **VHS, Beta $19.95** NOS, VYY, GPV 🎭🎭🎭

His Girl Friday The classic, unrelentingly hilarious war-between-the-sexes comedy in which a reporter and her ex-husband editor help a condemned man escape the law while at the same time furthering their own ends as they try to get the big scoop on political corruption in the town. One of Hawks' most furious and inventive screen combats in which women are given uniquely equal (for Hollywood) footing, with staccato dialogue scripted by Charles Lederer and wonderful performances. Based on the Hecht-MacArthur play "The Front Page," which was filmed as the 1931 classic "The Front Page." Remade again in 1974 as "The Front Page" and in 1988 as "Switching Channels." Hawks' masterwork is also available colorized.
1940 92m/B Cary Grant, Rosalind Russell, Ralph Bellamy, Gene Lockhart, John Qualen, Porter Hall, Roscoe Karns, Abner Biberman, Cliff Edwards, Billy Gilbert; *D:* Howard Hawks. **VHS, Beta, 3/4U, Special order formats $9.95** NEG, MRV, NOS 🎭🎭🎭🎭

His Kind of Woman A fall guy, being used to bring a racketeer back to the U.S. from Mexico, discovers the plan and tries to halt it.
1951 120m/B Robert Mitchum, Jane Russell, Vincent Price, Tim Holt, Charles McGraw, Raymond Burr, Jim Backus; *D:* John Farrow. **VHS, Beta** NO 🎭🎭🎭

His Majesty O'Keefe Lancaster stars as a South Seas swashbuckler dealing in the lucrative coconut-oil trade of the mid-1800s. The natives see him as a god and allow him to marry a beautiful maiden. When his reign is threatened by unscrupulous traders, Lancaster springs into action to safeguard his kingdom. Based on a real-life American adventurer, this was the first movie ever filmed in the Fiji Islands.
1953 92m/C Burt Lancaster, Joan Rice, Benson Fong, Philip Ahn, Grant Taylor; *D:* Byron Haskin. **VHS, Beta, LV $59.99** WAR 🎭½

His Majesty, the Scarecrow of Oz/The Magic Cloak of Oz The creator of the Oz stories, L. Frank Baum, wrote, produced and directed these two stories himself, with all the characters from his best-selling children's books.
1914 80m/B *D:* L. Frank Baum. **VHS, Beta $59.95** GVV 🎭🎭½

His Name was King A man goes after the gang who murdered his brother and raped his young wife in the old West.
1985 90m/C IT Richard Harrison, Klaus Kinski, Anne Puskin; *D:* Don Reynolds. **VHS, Beta $14.95** NEG Woof!

His Picture in the Papers An early silent comedy wherein the robust, red-meat-eating son of a health food tycoon must get his father's permission to marry by getting his picture favorably in the paper for advertising's sake. Written by Anita Loos and John Emerson.

1916 68m/B Douglas Fairbanks Sr.; *D:* John Emerson. **VHS, Beta, 8mm $19.95** NOS, VYY, GPV 🎭🎭

His Prehistoric Past/The Bank Two of Chaplin's classic early shorts.
1915 54m/B Charlie Chaplin, Mack Swain, Edna Purviance; *D:* Charlie Chaplin. **VHS, Beta $24.95** VYY 🎭🎭

His Private Secretary Wayne plays the jet-setting son of a wealthy businessman who wants his boy to settle down. And he does - after he meets the minister's beautiful daughter.
1933 60m/B John Wayne, Evelyn Knapp, Alec B. Francis, Reginald Barlow, Natalie Kingston, Arthur Hoyt, Al "Fuzzy" St. John; *D:* Philip H. Whitman. **VHS, Beta $19.98** DVT, HEG 🎭½

His Royal Slyness/Haunted Spooks Two Harold Lloyd shorts. "His Royal Slyness" (1919) offers Harold impersonating the king of a small kingdom, while in "Haunted Spooks" (1920), Harold gets suckered into living in a haunted mansion. Both films include music score.
1920 52m/B Harold Lloyd; *D:* Harold Lloyd. **VHS, Beta $29.95** VYY, CCB 🎭½

His Wife's Lover An actor disguised as an old man wins the heart of a lovely young woman. He decides to test her fidelity by reverting to his handsome young self and attempting to seduce her. An enchanting comedy in Yiddish with English subtitles. *AKA:* Zayn Vaybs Lubovnik.
1931 77m/B Ludwig Satz, Michael Rosenberg, Isadore Cashier, Lucy Levine; *D:* Sidney Goldin. **VHS, Beta $59.95** ERG, FCT, TAM 🎭🎭🎭

Historia de un Gran Amor Two children of rival families fall in love against their parents' wishes. *AKA:* History of a Great Love.
1957 155m/B George Negrete, Sara Garcia, Gloria Marin. **VHS, Beta $64.95** MAD 🎭½

History is Made at Night A wife seeks a divorce from a jealous husband while on an Atlantic cruise; she ends up finding both true love and heartbreak in this story of a love triangle at sea.
1937 98m/B Charles Boyer, Jean Arthur, Leo Carrillo, Colin Clive; *D:* Frank Borzage. **VHS, Beta, LV $19.98** WAR, FCT 🎭🎭🎭

History of the World: Part 1 More misses than hits in this Brooks' parody of historic epics. A bluntly satiric vision of human evolution, from the Dawn of Man to the French Revolution told in an episodic fashion. Good for a few laughs.
1981 (R) 90m/C Mel Brooks, Dom DeLuise, Madeline Kahn, Harvey Korman, Cloris Leachman, Gregory Hines, Pamela Stephenson, Paul Mazursky, Bea Arthur, Fritz Feld, John Hurt, Jack Carter, John Hillerman, John Gavin, Barry Levinson, Ron Carey, Howard Morris, Sid Caesar, Jackie Mason; *D:* Mel Brooks. **VHS, Beta, LV $19.98** FOX 🎭🎭

The History of White People in America A pseudo-documentary look at the complicated life of a white midwestern family. Succeeds in making hilarious fun of many traditional prejudices. Originally made for cable television.
1985 48m/C Martin Mull, Fred Willard, Mary Kay Place, Teri Garr, Bob Eubanks; *D:* Harry Shearer. **VHS, Beta $24.95** MCA 🎭🎭

The History of White People in America: Vol. 2 Mull's television-special comedy satirizing WASP society in America.
1985 40m/C Martin Mull; *D:* Harry Shearer. **VHS, Beta $24.95** MCA 🎭🎭

Hit! When the 15-year-old daughter of a government agent dies of a drug overdose, he deals his revenge to top French heroin traffickers.
1973 (R) 135m/C Billy Dee Williams, Richard Pryor, Gwen Welles, Paul Hampton, Warren Kemmerling, Sid Melton; *D:* Sidney J. Furie; *W:* Alan R. Trustman, David M. Wolf; *M:* Lalo Schifrin. **VHS $14.95** PAR 🎭🎭

The Hit A feisty young hooker gets mixed-up with two strong-armed hired killers as they escort an unusual stool-pigeon from his exile in Spain to their angry mob bosses. Minor cult-noir from the director of "My Beautiful Launderette" and "Dangerous Liaisons."
1985 (R) 105m/C GB Terence Stamp, John Hurt, Laura Del Sol, Tim Roth, Fernando Rey; *D:* Stephen Frears. **VHS, Beta, LV $19.98** SUE, NLC 🎭🎭½

Hit & Run David Marks, a Manhattan cab driver, is haunted by recurring flashbacks of a freak hit-and-run accident in which his wife was struck down on a city street. *AKA:* Revenge Squad.
1982 96m/C Paul Perri, Claudia Cron; *D:* Charles Braverman. **VHS, Beta $59.99** HBO 🎭

Hit Lady An elegant cultured woman becomes a hit lady for the syndicate in this predictable, yet slick gangster movie. Made for television.
1974 74m/C Yvette Mimieux, Dack Rambo, Clu Gulager, Keenan Wynn; *D:* Tracy Keenan Wynn. **VHS, Beta $59.95** PSM 🎭🎭

The Hit List A regular guy fights back brutally when his wife and child are mistakenly kidnapped by the Mafia. Fast-paced action makes up for thin plot.
1988 87m/C Jan-Michael Vincent, Leo Rossi, Lance Henriksen, Charles Napier, Rip Torn; *D:* William Lustig. **VHS, Beta, LV $14.95** COL 🎭🎭

The Hit Man A crime drama that profiles the crisis of a man unfit to commit murder but who does for a price. *AKA:* Il Sicario.
1961 100m/B **VHS, Beta, 3/4U, Special order formats** CIG 🎭

Hit Men Double crosses and gun battles highlight this tale of inner-city crime.
1973 90m/C Henry Silva, Mario Adorf, Woody Strode, Adolfo Celi. **VHS, Beta $19.95** VDC 🎭½

Hit the Deck Second-rate studio musical about sailors on leave and looking for romance. 🎵 Based on the 1927 Broadway musical. 🎵Sometimes I'm Happy; Hallelujah; Why, Oh Why; Keeping Myself For You; More Than You Know; I Know That You Know; Lucky Bird; Leo-Leo; Join the Navy; A Kiss Or Two; The Lady From The Bayou; Ciribiribee.
1955 112m/C Jane Powell, Tony Martin, Debbie Reynolds, Walter Pidgeon, Vic Damone, Gene Raymond, Ann Miller, Russ Tamblyn, J. Carroll Naish, Kay Armen, Richard Anderson; *D:* Roy Rowland; *M:* Vincent Youmans. **VHS, Beta, LV $19.98** MGM 🎭½

Hit the Dutchman Routine gangster flick about Dutch Schultz trying to rise to the top of the New York crime community—with or without the help of underworld pals Legs Diamond and Lucky Luciano. An unrated version is also available.
1992 (R) 116m/C Bruce Nozick, Sally Kirkland, Will Kempe; *D:* Menahem Golan. **VHS $89.95** VMK 🎭

Hit the Ice Newspaper photographers Bud and Lou are mistaken as gangsters in Chicago and the usual complications ensue. Includes an appearance by Johnny Long & His Orchestra. 🎵I'm Like A Fish Out Of Water; Happiness Bound; I'd Like to Set You to Music; Slap Polka.

1943 89m/C Bud Abbott, Lou Costello, Patric Knowles, Elyse Knox, Ginny Simms, Johnny Long & His Orchestra; D: Charles Lamont. VHS, Beta $14.95 MCA ♂♂

Hit the Saddle The Three Mesquiteers track down a gang involved in capturing wild horses although one of three is more interested in the charms of a dance hall girl (played by starlet Rita Cansino who would soon become Rita Hayworth).
1937 54m/B Bob Livingston, Ray Corrigan, Max Terhune, J.P. McGowan, Yakima Canutt, Rita Hayworth; D: Mack V. Wright. VHS, Beta $9.99 NOS, VCN, REP ♂♂

The Hitch-Hiker Two young men off on the vacation of their dreams pick up a psychopathic hitchhiker with a right eye that never closes, even when he sleeps. Taut suspense makes this flick worth seeing.
1953 71m/B Edmond O'Brien, Frank Lovejoy, William Talman, Jose Torvay; D: Ida Lupino. VHS $16.95 SNC ♂♂♂

Hitchcock Classics Collection: Trailers on Tape Collection of 20 previews for such Hitchcock favorites as "Shadow of a Doubt," "Rear Window," "Vertigo," "North by Northwest" and "Psycho." Some trailers are in black and white.
1985 55m/C D: Alfred Hitchcock. VHS, Beta $79.95 SFR ♂♂♂

Hitchcock Collection A collector's set containing three films from the master of suspense. Includes: "The Lady Vanishes," "The 39 Steps," "Vintage Hitchcock"—see him from a set designer to a director. In B/W and color.
1987 200m/C Alfred Hitchcock, Michael Redgrave, Paul Lukas, Robert Donat, Madeleine Carroll; D: Alfred Hitchcock. VHS, Beta $79.95 MPI ♂♂♂

Hitcher A young man picks up a hitchhiker on a deserted stretch of California highway only to be tormented by the man's repeated appearances: is he real or a figment of his imagination? Ferociously funny, sadomasochistic comedy with graphic violence.
1985 (R) 98m/C Rutger Hauer, C. Thomas Howell, Jennifer Jason Leigh; D: Robert Harmon. VHS, Beta, LV $14.98 HBO ♂♂½

The Hitchhiker HBO's chilling horror anthology series contains a trio of terrifying tales. Additional episodes are available. In this first collection, Hamlin stars in "The Curse," about Yuppie occult vengeance; "W.G.O.D." finds Busey and Page caught up in radio religion; and "Hired Help," finds Black with a less than human handyman.
1985 90m/C Harry Hamlin, Gary Busey, Geraldine Page, Karen Black. VHS, Beta, LV $19.98 HBO, WAR, MOV ♂♂½

Hitchhiker 2 Three more episodes from HBO's horror series: "Dead Man's Curve," "Nightshift," and "Last Scene."
1985 90m/C Peter Coyote, Margot Kidder, Darren McGavin, Susan Anspach. VHS, Beta, LV $19.98 HBO, WAR ♂♂½

Hitchhiker 3 Three episodes from the anthology mystery series: "Ghost Writer," "And If We Dream," and "True Believer." Made-for-cable television.
1987 90m/C Ornella Muti, Willem Dafoe, Barry Bostwick, Dayle Haddon, Stephen Collins, Robert Weiss, Tom Skerritt. VHS, Beta, LV $19.98 LHV, WAR ♂♂½

Hitchhiker 4 Three episodes of the cable-television suspense series: "Man's Best Friend," about a lonely man whose pet dog tears his enemies to bits. "Face to Face," about the revenge exacted upon a drug-abusing cosmetic surgeon after he mucks up an operation; and "Videodate," about a guy

being lured into a sinister video performance piece via his use of video dating services.
1987 90m/C Michael O'Keefe, Sybil Danning, Sonja Smits, Robert Vaughn, Shannon Tweed, Greg Henry. VHS, Beta, LV $19.98 LHV, WAR ♂♂½

Hitchhikers Trash film about a bunch of scantily clad female hitchhikers who rob the motorists who stop to pick them up. Keep right on going when you spot this roadkill.
1972 (R) 90m/C Misty Rowe, Norman Klar, Linda Avery; D: Ferd Sebastian. VHS, Beta NO Woof!

The Hitchhiker's Guide to the Galaxy The six episode BBC television adaptation of Douglas Adams' hilarious science-fiction books. Features the intergalatic Ford Prefect, sent to Earth to update its planetary listing in the Hitchhiker's Guide; hapless hero Arthur Dent, a typical Englishman caught up in space mayhem; and an odd assortment of aliens, including Marvin the Paranoid Android. The show's sheer cheesiness is part of the charm. Available in both single-cassette and double-cassette versions, the later includes a copy of the book and a dedication from Adams.
1981 194m/C GB Simon Jones, David Dixon, Sandra Dickinson. VHS, LV $19.98 FOX, MOV Woof!

Hitler The true story of the infamous Nazi dictator's rise to power and his historic downfall. AKA: Women of Nazi Germany.
1962 103m/B Richard Basehart, Maria Emo, Cordula Trantow; D: Stuart Heisler. VHS, Beta $59.98 FOX ♂♂½

Hitler: Dead or Alive Three ex-cons devise a scheme to gain a million-dollar reward for capturing Adolf Hitler in this low-budget production.
1943 64m/B Ward Bond, Dorothy Tree, Bruce Edwards, Warren Hymer, Paul Fix, Russell Hicks, Bob Watson; D: Nick Grinde. VHS, Beta $19.95 NOS, MRV, DVT ♂♂

Hitler: The Last Ten Days Based on an eyewitness account, the story of Hitler's last days in an underground bunker gives insight to his madness.
1973 (PG) 106m/C Alec Guinness, Simon Ward, Adolfo Celi; D: Ennio de Concini. VHS, Beta $49.95 PAR, GLV ♂♂

Hitler's Children Two young people, a German boy and an American girl, are caught in the horror of Nazi Germany. He's attracted to Hitler's rant, she's repelled. Exploitative yet engrossing.
1943 83m/B Tim Holt, Bonita Granville, Otto Kruger, H.B. Warner, Irving Reis, Hans Conried, Lloyd Corrigan; D: Edward Dmytryk. VHS, Beta $19.95 MED, IHF ♂♂♂

Hitler's Daughter Made for TV movie following the trials and tribulations of the illegitimate daughter of Adolf Hitler. She's all grown up now...and wants to rule the United States. She secures a position of power during an election and now Nazi-hunters must figure out her identity before she takes over the world!
1990 (R) 88m/C Kay Lenz, Veronica Cartwright, Melody Anderson, Patrick Cassidy, Carolyn Dunn, Lindsay Merrithew, George R. Robertson; D: James A. Contner. VHS, Beta PAR ♂

The Hitman Norris plays a cop undercover as a syndicate hit man in Seattle, where he cleans up crime by triggering a three-way mob bloodbath between beastly Italian mafiosi, snooty French-Canadian hoods, and fanatical Iranian scum. But he teaches a black kid martial arts, so you know he's politically correct. Action addicts will

give this a passing grade; all others need not apply.
1991 (R) 95m/C Chuck Norris, Michael Parks, Al Waxman, Alberta Watson, Salim Grant, Ken Pogue, Marcel Sabourin, Bruno Gerussi, Frank Ferrucci; D: Aaron Norris. VHS, LV, 8mm $19.98 CAN ♂♂

The Hitter A former prizefighter, his girlfriend, and a washed-up promoter are all on the run in this adventure tale.
1979 (R) 94m/C Ron O'Neal, Adolph Caesar, Sheila Frazier; D: Christopher Leitch. VHS $59.95 SVS ♂♂

Hittin' the Trail The Good Cowboy is mistaken for a murdering varmint, and must prove his innocence.
1937 57m/B Tex Ritter, Charles King, Ray Whitley, The Range Ramblers; D: Robert Bradbury. VHS, Beta $19.95 NOS, VDM ♂

Hitz In a Los Angeles barrio, Musico, a Loco gang member, kills two rival gang members. Arrested and convicted when a young boy named Pepe is coerced into testifying against him, Musico is killed in the courtroom. But the violence doesn't stop. The judge, who wants to reform the juvenile court system, tries to protect Pepe, and both are targeted for death by the Loco gang.
1992 (R) 90m/C Elliott Gould, Emilia Crow, Karen Black, Cuba Gooding Jr. VHS $89.95 VMK ♂♂½

The Hobbit An animated interpretation of J.R.R. Tolkien's novel of the same name. The story follows Bilbo Baggins and his journeys in Middle Earth and encounters with the creatures who inhabit it. He joins comrades to battle against evil beings and creatures. Animator Ralph Bakshi utilizes "live motion" animation to give authentic movement to the characters. Made for television.
1978 76m/C D: Arthur Rankin Jr., Jules Bass; V: Orson Bean, John Huston, Otto Preminger, Richard Boone. VHS, Beta, 8mm $19.95 WAR, SVS, VTK ♂♂♂

Hobgoblins Little creatures escape from a studio vault and wreak havoc.
1987 92m/C Jeffrey Culver, Tom Bartlett; D: Rick Sloane. VHS, Beta $79.95 TWE ♂

The Hoboken Chicken Emergency Arthur's pet chicken weighs 266 pounds, creating a fowl emergency. Originally aired on PBS as part of the "Wonderworks" series.
1984 55m/C Dick Van Patten, Peter Billingsley, Gabe Kaplan, Arlene Golonka; D: Peter Baldwin. VHS $29.95 PME, HMV ♂

Hobo's Christmas A man who left his family to become a hobo comes home for Christmas 25 years later. Hughes turns in a delightful performance as the hobo in this made for television special.
1987 94m/C Barnard Hughes, William Hickey, Gerald McRaney, Wendy Crewson; D: Will MacKenzie. VHS, Beta NO ♂♂

Hobson's Choice A prosperous businessman in the 1890s tries to keep his daughter from marrying, but the strong-willed daughter has other ideas. Remade for television in 1983.
1953 102m/B GB Charles Laughton, John Mills, Brenda de Banzie; D: David Lean. VHS, Beta, LV $19.98 SUE, HBO, NLC ♂♂♂

Hobson's Choice Made-for-television remake of the old family comedy about a crusty, penny-pinching businessman whose headstrong daughter proves to him she'll not become an old maid. Instead she marries one of his employees. Not bad, but not as good as the original.

1983 95m/C Jack Warden, Sharon Gless, Richard Thomas, Lillian Gish; **D:** Gilbert Cates. **VHS, Beta** $59.98 FOX 🎞🎞

Hockey Night A movie for pre- and early teens in which a girl goalie makes the boys' hockey team.
1984 77m/C CA Megan Follows, Rick Moranis, Gail Youngs, Martin Harburg, Henry Ramer; **D:** Paul Shapiro. **VHS, Beta** FHE 🎞🎞½

Hocus Pocus The divine Miss M is back, but this time she's not so sweet. Midler, Najimy, and Parker are 17th century witches accidentally conjured up in the 20th century, appropriately enough on Halloween in Salem, Massachusetts. Seems they were hung 300 years back and they take their revenge in some surprisingly gruesome ways, given the Disney label. They rant, they rave, they sing (only once), they fly. See this one for the three stars who make up for the lack of substance with their comedic talents.
1993 (PG) ?m/C Bette Midler, Kathy Najimy, Sarah Jessica Parker, Thora Birch, Doug Jones, Omri Katz, Vinessa Shaw; *Cameos:* Penny Marshall, Garry Marshall; **D:** Kenny Ortega; **W:** Neil Cuthbert, Mick Garris. **VHS** NYR 🎞🎞

Hoffa The story of union organizer James R. Hoffa who oversaw the rise of the Teamsters, a labor union composed mostly of truck drivers, from its fledgling infancy during the Great Depression to a membership of 2 million by the 1970's. Powerful performances by Nicholson in the title role and De Vito, who plays a union aide, a fictitious composite of several men who actually served Hoffa. This almost affectionate biographical treatment stands out in contrast from a career bristling with tension and violence. Proceeds through a series of flashbacks from the day Hoffa disappeared, July 30, 1975.
1992 (R) 140m/C Jack Nicholson, Danny DeVito, Armand Assante, J.T. Walsh, Frank Whaley, Kevin Anderson, John P. Ryan, Robert Prosky, Natalija Nogulich, Nicholas Pryor; **D:** Danny DeVito. **VHS, LV** $94.98 FXV 🎞🎞🎞

Hog Wild A clique of high school nerds exact revenge on bullies from the local mean motorcycle gang, and a girl is torn between the two factions.
1980 (PG) 97m/C CA Patti D'Arbanville, Tony Rosato, Michael Biehn; **D:** Les Rose. **VHS, Beta** $59.98 NLC 🎞½

The Holcroft Covenant Based upon the complex Robert Ludlum novel. Details the efforts of a man trying to release a secret fund that his Nazi father humanistically set up to relieve the future sufferings of Holocaust survivors. Confusing, and slow, but interesting, nonetheless.
1985 (R) 112m/C GB Michael Caine, Victoria Tennant, Anthony Andrews, Lilli Palmer, Mario Adorf, Michael Lonsdale; **D:** John Frankenheimer. **VHS, Beta, LV** $14.95 MGM, HBO 🎞🎞

Hold 'Em Jail Some good laughs with Wheeler and Woolsey starting a competitive football team at Kennedy's Bidemore Prison.
1932 65m/B Bert Wheeler, Robert Woolsey, Edgar Kennedy, Betty Grable, Edna May Oliver; **D:** Norman Taurog. **VHS, Beta** $34.98 CCB 🎞🎞

Hold That Ghost Abbott and Costello inherit an abandoned roadhouse where the illicit loot of its former owner, a "rubbed out" mobster, is supposedly hidden. *AKA:* Oh, Charlie.
1941 86m/B Bud Abbott, Lou Costello, Joan Davis, Richard Carlson, Mischa Auer, The Andrews Sisters, Ted Lewis & his Band; **D:** Arthur Lubin. **VHS, Beta** $14.95 MCA 🎞🎞

Hold the Dream A made-for-television mini-series sequel to Barbara Taylor Bradford's "A Woman of Substance."

1985 195m/C Jenny Seagrove, Stephen Collins, Deborah Kerr, James Brolin; **D:** Don Sharp. **VHS, Beta** $14.95 ONE 🎞

Hold Your Man Great star vehicle that turns from comedy to drama with Harlow falling for hustler Gable. Harlow and Gable are at their best in this unlikely story of a crooked couple. Direction drags at times, but snappy dialogue and the stars' personalities more than make up for it.
1933 86m/B Jean Harlow, Clark Gable, Stuart Erwin, Dorothy Burgess, Garry Owen, Paul Hurst, Elizabeth Patterson; **D:** Sam Wood; **W:** Anita Loos, Howard Emmett Rogers. **VHS** $19.98 MGM 🎞🎞🎞

A Hole in the Head A comedy-drama about a shiftless but charming lout who tries to raise money to save his hotel from foreclosure and learn to be responsible for his young son. Notable for the introduction of the song "High Hopes."
1959 120m/C Frank Sinatra, Edward G. Robinson, Thelma Ritter, Carolyn Jones, Eleanor Parker, Eddie Hodges, Keenan Wynn, Joi Lansing; **D:** Frank Capra. **VHS, Beta, LV** $14.95 MGM 🎞🎞½

The Holes A Parisian book shop owner's daughter vanishes along with other local citizens and American tourists, and he decides to investigate when the police won't. In French with subtitles. *AKA:* Les Gaspards.
1972 (PG) 92m/C FR Philippe Noiret, Charles Denner, Michael Serraut, Gerard Depardieu. **VHS, Beta** $59.95 FHE, FCT 🎞🎞½

Holiday The classically genteel screwball comedy about a rich girl who steals her sister's fiance. A yardstick in years to come for sophisticated, urbane Hollywood romanticism. Based on the play by Philip Barry who later wrote "The Philadelphia Story." *AKA:* Free to Live; Unconventional Linda.
1938 93m/B Cary Grant, Katharine Hepburn, Doris Nolan, Edward Everett Horton, Ruth Donnelly, Lew Ayres, Binnie Barnes; **D:** George Cukor; **W:** Donald Ogden Stewart, Sidney Buchman. **VHS, Beta, LV** $19.95 RCA, COL 🎞🎞🎞½

Holiday Affair Hollywood yuletide charmer about a pretty widow being courted by two very different men.
1949 86m/B Robert Mitchum, Janet Leigh, Griff Barnett, Wendell Corey, Esther Dale, Henry O'Neill, Henry Morgan, Larry J. Blake; **D:** Don Hartman. **VHS, Beta, LV** RKO, TTC 🎞🎞½

Holiday Hotel A group of wild French vacationers let loose at their favorite little resort hotel along the Brittany coast. Available in French with English subtitles or dubbed into English.
1977 (R) 109m/C FR Sophie Barjae, Daniel Ceccaldi; **D:** Michael Lang. **VHS, Beta** $29.95 SUE 🎞🎞

Holiday in Havana Desi Arnaz is back in Cuba winning hearts and dance contests. Watch only for Desi's presence. 🎵Holiday in Havana; The Arnaz Jam; Straw Hat Song; Rhumba Rumbero; Copacobana; Made For Each Other; I'll Take Romance.
1949 73m/B Desi Arnaz Sr., Lolita Valdez, Mary Hatcher, Ann Doran; **D:** Jean Yarborough. **VHS** GKK 🎞🎞

Holiday in Mexico Pidgeon plays the U.S. ambassador to Mexico whose teenage daughter (Powell) tries to run his life along with her household. He falls for a singer while she develops a crush on an older, respected pianist (Iturbi playing himself). Lots of lively production numbers featuring Xavier Cugat and his orchestra. 🎵I Think Of You; Walter Winchell Rhumba; Yo Te Amo Mucho—And That's That; And Dreams Remain; Holiday in Mexico; Ave Maria; Les Filles de Cadiz;

Italian Street Song; Polonaise in A Flat Major; Goodnight Sweetheart; Three Blind Mice; The Music Goes 'Round and Around; Liebestod; Someone to Love.
1946 127m/C Walter Pidgeon, Jane Powell, Ilona Massey, Jose Iturbi, Roddy McDowall, Xavier Cugat, Hugo Haas; **D:** George Sidney; **W:** Isobel Lennart; **M:** Georgie Stoll. **VHS** $19.98 MGM 🎞🎞½

Holiday Inn Fred Astaire and Bing Crosby are rival song-and-dance men who decide to work together to turn a Connecticut farm into an inn, open only on holidays. Remade in 1954 as "White Christmas." 🎵White Christmas; Be Careful, It's My Heart; Plenty to Be Thankful For; Abraham, Abraham; Let's Say It With Firecrackers; I Gotta Say I Love You Cause I Can't Tell A Lie; Let's Start the New Year Right; Happy Holidays; Song of Freedom; Lazy; Holiday Inn; I'll Capture Your Heart; Easter Parade; Any Bonds Today; You're So Easy To Dance With; I Can't Tell a Lie.
1942 101m/B Bing Crosby, Fred Astaire, Marjorie Reynolds, Walter Abel, Virginia Dale; **D:** Mark Sandrich. Academy Awards '42: Best Song ("White Christmas"); Nominations: Best Story, Best Original Score. **VHS, Beta, LV** $19.95 MCA 🎞🎞🎞

Holiday Rhythm A television promoter is knocked out and dreams of a world-wide trip full of entertainment, comedy, and insanity.
1950 61m/B Mary Beth Hughes, Tex Ritter, David Street, Donald MacBride. **VHS, Beta, LV** NO 🎞½

Hollow Gate Trick or Treat?? Four kids find out when they run into a guy with hungry dogs.
1988 90m/C Addison Randall. **VHS, Beta** NO 🎞½

Hollow Triumph A down-and-out con man assumes the identity of a respected psychiatrist in this film noir. Based on the novel by Murray Forbes. Retitled "The Scar."
1948 83m/B Paul Henreid, Joan Bennett, Eduard Franz, Leslie Brooks; **D:** Steve Sekely. **VHS** $19.98 NOS, MOV, HEG 🎞🎞🎞

Hollywood After Dark McClanahan plays a young starlet trying to make it big in Hollywood. Pure exploitation schlock. Not released theatrically until 1968.
1965 ?m/C Rue McClanahan. **VHS** $16.95 SNC 🎞

Hollywood Bloopers Hilarious outtakes from some of Hollywood's finest movies, featuring stars such as Bette Davis, James Cagney, Humphrey Bogart, Rosalind Russell, Errol Flynn, Kirk Douglas, and many more.
195? 85m/B Lauren Bacall, Ronald Reagan, James Stewart, Joan Blondell, Rosalind Russell, Errol Flynn, Kirk Douglas, Barbara Stanwyck. **VHS, Beta** $19.95 VDM, PPI 🎞🎞½

Hollywood Boulevard Behind-the-scenes glimpse of shoestring-budget movie making offers comical sex, violence, sight gags, one-liners, comedy bits, and mock-documentary footage. Commander Cody and His Lost Planet Airmen are featured.
1976 (R) 93m/C Candice Rialson, Mary Woronov, Rita George, Jonathan Kaplan, Jeffrey Kramer, Dick Miller, Paul Bartel; **D:** Joe Dante, Allan Arkush. **VHS, Beta** $39.98 WAR, OM 🎞🎞½

Hollywood Boulevard 2 A "B" movie studio finds its top actresses being killed off and terror reigns supreme as the mystery grows more intense. Could that psycho-bimbo from outer space have something to do with it?

1989 (R) 82m/C Ginger Lynn Allen, Kelly Monteith, Eddie Deezen, Ken Wright, Steve Vinovich; **D:** Steve Barnett. **VHS, Beta** $79.95 MGM *

Hollywood Canteen A star-studded patriotic extravaganza. Just about every Warner Brothers lot actor turns out for this tribute to love and nationalism. Hutton stars as a lovesick G.I. who has fallen for Joan Leslie. He goes to the Hollywood Canteen hoping to meet her. The workers at the canteen, including Bette Davis, set-up a phony raffle so that he can win a date with Leslie. The sparks fly right away, but then he thinks it's all been just a ruse as he boards his train and Leslie's not there to see him off. But, of course she makes it in the nick of time, declares her love for him, and says she'll wait for him. Kind of a lame story but the talent and musical numbers make this picture fly with charm and style. Before the picture was made there were arguments over actors being labled unpatriotic for not participating in this, and other similar movies being produced at the time. ♫Don't Fence Me In; Sweet Dreams, Sweetheart; You Can Always Tell A Yank; We're Having a Baby; What Are You Doin' the Rest of Your Life; The General Jumped At Dawn; Gettin' Corns For My Country; Voodoo Moon; Tumblin' Tumbleweeds; Ballet in Jive; The Bee; Once to Every Heart.
1944 124m/B Robert Hutton, Dane Clark, Janice Paige, Jonathan Hale, Barbara Brown, James Flavin, Eddie Marr, Ray Teal, Bette Davis, Joan Leslie, Jack Benny, Jimmy Dorsey, Joan Crawford; **W/D:** Delmer Daves. **VHS** $29.98 FOX, FCT ****

Hollywood Chainsaw Hookers A campy, sexy, very bloody parody about attractive prostitutes who dismember their unsuspecting customers.
1988 (R) 90m/C Linnea Quigley, Gunnar Hansen, Jay Richardson, Michelle Bauer; **D:** Fred Olen Ray. **VHS, Beta** NO **

Hollywood Chaos Director Ballantine's stars quit his production before it even starts, so he gets the next best thing - star look-alikes. However, his problems are just beginning. One of his new "stars" is kidnapped, and his reclusive stage manager is hunted as the object of desire for a female motorcycle gang.
1989 90m/C Carl Ballantine, Tricia Leigh Fisher, Kathleen Freeman; **D:** Sean McNamara. **VHS** $79.95 WLA *½

Hollywood Clowns Glenn Ford narrates this tribute to the screen's greatest comedians, with clips from many classic scenes.
1985 60m/C Buster Keaton, W.C. Fields, Charlie Chaplin, Harold Lloyd, Bud Abbott, Lou Costello, Stan Laurel, Oliver Hardy, Groucho Marx, Harpo Marx, Chico Marx, Jerry Lewis, Dean Martin, Red Skelton, Danny Kaye, Betty Hutton, Bob Hope. **VHS, Beta** $29.95 MGM *½

Hollywood Come Home Ray Milland hosts this look at the history of the movie industry from World War II to the early 60's. Also on this tape is "Hollywood Historama," a collection of video biographies of such luminaries as Mae West and John Barrymore.
1962 54m/B Ray Milland. **VHS, Beta, 8mm** $24.99 VYY *½

Hollywood Confidential A beautiful Eastern girl goes to Hollywood and suffers irrevocable corruption.
193? 55m/B VHS, Beta NO *

Hollywood Cop A tough cop in Hollywood goes up against the mob for the sake of a kidnapped boy.

1987 (R) 101m/C Jim Mitchum, David Goss, Cameron Mitchell, Troy Donahue, Aldo Ray; **D:** Amir Shervan. **VHS, Beta** $19.95 CEL *½

Hollywood Crime Wave An examination of crime and criminals as seen in vintage Hollywood gangster films. Features scenes with Humphrey Bogart, James Cagney and Edward G. Robinson.
196? 60m/B VHS, Beta $14.95 MPI *½

The Hollywood Detective An average TV movie that spoofs "Kojak." A TV detective tries it out for real, and gets into troubles for which he can't pause "for a message from our sponsor."
1989 (PG) 88m/C Telly Savalas, Helene Udy, George Coe, Joe Dallesandro, Tom Reese; **D:** Kevin Connor. **VHS, Beta** $79.95 MCA **

Hollywood Erotic Film Festival A package of soft-core shorts, animated as well as live action, from around the world.
1987 75m/C VHS, Beta $59.95 PAR *

The Hollywood Game Head of Hollywood talent agency charms more than the critics with his casting couch-side manner . That is, until his bevy of starlets discover that they are to be the prize behind door number one in his game show/sleaze fest. Not based on a true story.
1989 92m/C Dick Miller, Thelma Houston. **VHS, Beta** $79.95 JEF *½

Hollywood Ghost Stories A view of supernatural activity in Hollywood, on the screen and behind the scenes. Includes interviews with William Peter Blatty, Sir Arthur Conan Doyle, Elke Sommer and others.
1986 75m/C VHS, Beta $29.98 WAR *½

Hollywood Goes to War Five shorts produced for the entertainment of G.I.'s overseas or for home front bond drives: "The All-Star Bond Rally" features Bob Hope, Fibber McGee and Molly, Bing Crosby, Harry James and His Orchestra, Sinatra, Grable, Harpo Marx, and the Talking Pin-Ups; "Hollywood Canteen Overseas Special" features Dinah Shore, Eddie Cantor, Jimmy Durante, and Red Skelton; "Mail Call (Strictly G.I.)" is a filmed "Mail Call" radio program with Don Wilson announcing guests Dorothy Lamour, Cass Daley, and Abbott and Costello doing "Who's on First"; "G.I. Movie Weekly-Sing with the Stars" features Carmen Miranda and her fruit-basket hat, a Portuguese "follow-the-bouncing-ball" sing-along. Richard Lane, and Mel Blanc's voice; and "Invaders in Greasepaint," the story of "Four Jills in a Jeep"-the North African USO tour by Martha Raye, Carol Landis, Mitzi Mayfair, and Kay Francis. Also includes newsreel footage of the girls touring, plus their memorable rendition of the wartime classic tune "Snafu," which was banned from the airwaves for its racy lyrics.
1954 41m/B Bob Hope, Bing Crosby, Frank Sinatra, Betty Grable, Harpo Marx, Jimmy Durante, Eddie Cantor, Red Skelton, Bud Abbott, Lou Costello, Dinah Shore, Dorothy Lamour, Carmen Miranda. **VHS, Beta** $24.95 NO *½

Hollywood Harry A private-eye mystery/parody, about an inept detective who searches for a missing porn actress. **AKA:** Harry's Machine.
1986 (PG-13) 99m/C Robert Forster, Kathrine Forster, Joe Spinell, Shannon Wilcox; **D:** Robert Forster. **VHS, Beta** $79.95 MED *

Hollywood Heartbreak It's heartbreak in tinseltown for a young writer who's trying to pitch his movie script but winds up defending himself from slimy agents and persistent starlets. Another entry for Bartlett's familiar plotlines.

1989 90m/C Mark Moses, Carol Mayo Jenkins, Ron Karabatsos, Richard Romanus, James LeGros; **D:** Lance Dickson. **VHS** NO **

Hollywood High Four attractive teen couples converge on the mansion of an eccentric silent-film star for an unusual vacation experience in this teenage skin flick. Followed by a sequel.
1977 (R) 81m/C Marcy Albrecht, Sherry Hardin, Rae Sperling, Susanne Kevin Mead; **D:** Patrick Wright. **VHS, Beta** $29.98 LIV, VES *

Hollywood High, Part 2 Ignored by their boyfriends for the lure of sun and surf, three comely high school students try their best to regain their interest.
1981 (R) 86m/C April May, Donna Lynn, Camille Warner, Lee Thornburg; **D:** Caruth C. Byrd. **VHS, Beta** $29.98 LIV, VES *

Hollywood Home Movies The home movies of more than 60 celebrities are compiled in this program. Offers a nostalgic look at how the demi-gods of yesteryear lived, worked, played, and relaxed.
1987 (PG) 58m/B Marilyn Monroe, John Wayne, Gregory Peck, Robert Mitchum, Ann-Margret. **VHS, Beta, 3/4U** $19.98 IHF, MPI *

Hollywood Hot Tubs Teen sex romp has adolescent picking up some extra cash and a lot of fun repairing the hot tubs of the rich and famous.
1984 (R) 103m/C Donna McDaniel, Michael Andrew, Katt Shea Ruben, Paul Gunning, Edy Williams, Jewel Shepard; **D:** Chuck Vincent. **VHS, Beta** $79.98 LIV, VES *

Hollywood Hot Tubs 2: Educating Crystal A softcore comedy about a well-tanned ingenue learning about business in Hollywood during numerous hot tub trysts.
1989 103m/C Jewel Shepard, Patrick Day, Remy O'Neill, David Tiefen, Bart Braverman; **D:** Ken Raich. **VHS, Beta, LV** $9.99 CCB, IVE *

Hollywood in Trouble A bumbling middle-aged fool decides to break into the wacky movie-making business.
1987 90m/C Vic Vallard, Jean Levine, Jerry Tiffe, Pamela Dixon, Jerry Cleary. **VHS, Beta** NO *

Hollywood Man A Hollywood actor wants to make his own film but when his financial support comes from the mob there's trouble ahead.
1976 (R) 90m/C William Smith, Don Stroud, Jennifer Billingsley, Mary Woronov, **D:** Jack Starrett. **VHS, Beta** NO *½

Hollywood My Hometown Hollywood host Ken Murray looks at the stars of the glittering movie world.
19?? 60m/B Ken Murray. **VHS, Beta** $19.95 VCN, DVT, HHT *½

Hollywood Mystery A publicity agent stops at nothing to promote his would-be starlet girlfriend. **AKA:** Hollywood Hoodlum.
1934 53m/B June Clyde, Frank Albertson, Joe Crespo; **D:** B. Reeves Eason. **VHS** $19.95 NOS, LOO *½

Hollywood or Bust The zany duo take their act on the road as they head for Tinsel Town in order to meet Lewis' dream girl Ekberg. This was the last film for the Martin & Lewis team and it's not the swan song their fans would have hoped for.
1956 95m/C Dean Martin, Jerry Lewis, Anita Ekberg, Pat Crowley, Maxie Rosenbloom, Willard Waterman; **D:** Frank Tashlin. **VHS** $14.95 PAR, CCB **½

Hollywood Outtakes & Rare Footage A collection of rare and unusual film clips and excerpts that feature dozens of Hollywood stars in screen tests, promotional shorts, home movies, outtakes, television appearances and World War II propaganda shorts. Some segments in black and white. **1983 85m/C** Marilyn Monroe, James Dean, Joan Crawford, Judy Garland, Humphrey Bogart, Ronald Reagan, Bette Davis, Vivien Leigh, Carole Lombard. **VHS, Beta, LV $59.95** *COL, RXM* ✰✰½

Hollywood Party Durante plays a film star who decides to throw a Hollywood bash. Any plot is incidental as it is mainly an excuse to have numerous stars of the day appear in brief comic bits or musical numbers. Mickey Mouse and the Big Bad Wolf of Disney fame also appear in color animated footage combined with live action. Numerous MGM directors worked on parts of the film but Dwan was given the task of trying to pull the various scenes together (he is uncredited onscreen). ♫Hollywood Party; Hello; Reincarnation; I've Had My Moments; Feeling High; Hot Chocolate Soldiers. **1934 72m/B** Jimmy Durante, Stan Laurel, Oliver Hardy, Lupe Velez, Ted Healy, Moe Howard, Curly Howard, Larry Fine, Robert Young, Charles Butterworth, Polly Moran, George Givot, Tom Kennedy; *D:* Allan Dwan; *V:* Walt Disney, Billy Bletcher. **VHS $19.98** *MGM* ✰✰½

Hollywood Scandals and Tragedies A look at the skeletons-in-the-closet surrounding the deaths and private turmoils of James Dean, Rock Hudson, Vivien Leigh, Frances Farmer, Sal Mineo, Sharon Tate, Jayne Mansfield, and others. **1988 90m/C VHS, Beta $79.95** *MPI* ✰✰½

Hollywood Shuffle Townsend's autobiographical comedy about a struggling black actor in Hollywood trying to find work and getting nothing but stereotypical roles. Written, directed, financed by Townsend, who created this often clever and appealing film on a $100,000 budget. **1987 (R) 81m/C** Robert Townsend, Anne-Marie Johnson, Starletta DuPois, Helen Martin, Keenan Ivory Wayans, Damon Wayans; *D:* Robert Townsend; *W:* Robert Townsend, Keenan Ivory Wayans. **VHS, Beta, LV** *NO* ✰✰½

Hollywood Stadium Mystery A boxer turns up dead before a big match and a D.A. investigates. Performances hold this one up, especially by Hamilton who later played Commissioner Gordon on TV's "Batman." **1938 66m/B** Neil Hamilton, Evelyn Venable, Jimmy Wallington, Barbara Pepper, Lucien Littlefield, Lynn (Mary Hart) Roberts, Charles Williams, James Spottswood, Reed Hadley, Smiley Burnette; *D:* David Howard. **VHS, Beta $16.95** *SNC* ✰✰

The Hollywood Strangler Meets the Skid Row Slasher Voiced-over narration, canned music and an unfathomable plot are but a few of this would-be fright fest's finer points. Uninhibited by any narrative connection, two terrors strike fear in the heart of Tinseltown. While a psycho photographer cruises L.A. taking pictures of models he subsequently strangles, a woman working in a bare-bums magazine store takes a stab (with a knife) at lowering the city's derelict population. There's a word for this sort of dribble, and it isn't versimilitude. Steckler used an alias (not surprisingly) for this one—Wolfgang Schmidt. *AKA:* The Model Killer. **1979 (R) 72m/C** Pierre Agostino, Carolyn Brandt, Forrest Duke, Chuck Alford; *D:* Ray Dennis Steckler. **VHS** *NO Woof!*

Hollywood Uncensored A history of Hollywood censorship, including long-suppressed scenes from "King Kong," "The Outlaw," "Carnal Knowledge," "Baby Doll," "Easy Rider," "Woodstock," and more.

1987 75m/C VHS, Beta $9.99 *LIV, FCT Woof!*

Hollywood Varieties A virtually plotless no-star conglomeration of comedy, music, and burlesque. **1950 60m/B** The 3 Rio Brothers, Robert Alda, Glenn Vernon, Eddie Ryan. **VHS, Beta, LV** *NO Woof!*

Hollywood Vice Sqaud Explores the lives of Hollywood police officers and the crimes they investigate. Contains three different story lines involving prostitution, child pornography, and organized crime. The film can't decide to be a comedy send-up of crime stories or a drama and is also crippled by a poor script. Written by the real-life chief of the Hollywood Vice Squad. **1986 (R) 100m/C** Trish Van Devere, Ronny Cox, Frank Gorshin, Leon Isaac Kennedy, Carrie Fisher, Ben Frank, Robin Wright; *D:* Penelope Spheeris. **VHS, LV $79.98** *HHE, MTX* ✰

Hollywood without Makeup Home movie footage taken over the years by Ken Murray includes candid shots of over 100 stars of the film world. **1965 51m/C VHS, Beta, 8mm $24.95** *HHT, MRV, VYY* ✰

Hollywood Zap Two losers, one a Southern orphan, the other a video game nut, hit Hollywood and engage in antics that are meant to be funny, but are actually tasteless. **1986 (R) 85m/C** Ben Frank, Ivan E. Roth, De Waldron, Annie Gaybis, Chuck "Porky" Mitchell; *D:* David Cohen. **VHS, Beta $14.95** *PSM Woof!*

Hollywood's New Blood Young actors making a movie are haunted by a film crew from hell. **1988 90m/C** Bobby Johnson, Francine Lapensee; *D:* James Shyman. **VHS, Beta** *NO* ✰

Holocaust The war years of 1935 to 1945 are relived in this account of the Nazi atrocities, focusing on the Jewish Weiss family, destroyed by the monstrous crimes, and the Dorf family, Germans who thrived under the Nazi regime. Highly acclaimed riveting made-for-television mini-series with an exceptional cast. Won eight Emmys. **1978 475m/C** Michael Moriarty, Fritz Weaver, Meryl Streep, James Woods, Joseph Bottoms, Tovah Feldshuh, David Warner, Ian Holm, Michael Beck, Marius Goring; *D:* Marvin J. Chomsky. **VHS, Beta $69.95** *WOV, SWC* ✰✰✰½

Holocaust Survivors...Remembrance of Love A concentration camp survivor and his daughter attend the 1981 World Gathering of Holocaust Survivors in Tel-Aviv and both find romance. Made for television. *AKA:* Remembrance of Love. **1983 100m/C** Kirk Douglas, Pam Dawber, Chana Eden, Yoram Gal, Robert Clary; *D:* Jack Smight. **VHS, Beta $69.95** *VMK* ✰✰

Holocaust 2000 A nuclear facility in the Sahara Desert becomes plagued with a series of accidents, putting the whole world in jeopardy. *AKA:* The Chosen. **1983 (R) 101m/C** Kirk Douglas, Simon Ward, Virginia McKenna, Anthony Quayle, Alexander Knox; *D:* Alberto De Martino; *M:* Ennio Morricone. **VHS, Beta $69.98** *LIV, VES* ✰½

Holt of the Secret Service Secret service agent runs afoul of saboteurs and fifth-columnists in this 15-episode serial. **1942 225m/B** Jack Holt. **VHS, Beta $49.95** *NOS, MED, DVT* ✰

The Holy Innocents A peasant family is torn asunder by their feudal obligations to their patrons. Set in the 1960s in Franco's Spain. In Spanish with English subtitles. *AKA:* Los Santos Inocentes.

1984 (PG) 108m/C *SP* Alfredo Landa, Francisco Rabal; *D:* Mario Camus. **VHS, Beta $68.00** *LHV, APD, TAM* ✰✰✰

Holy Terror The story of Florence Nightingale, who shocked Victorian society by organizing a nursing staff to aid British soldiers in the Crimean War, is told in this presentation from "George Schaefer's Showcase Theatre." **1965 76m/C** Julie Harris, Denholm Elliott, Torin Thatcher, Kate Reid; *D:* George Schaefer. **VHS, Beta** *FHS* ✰✰

Hombre A white man in the 1880s, raised by a band of Arizona Apaches, is forced into a showdown. In helping a stagecoach full of settlers across treacherous country, he not only faces traditional bad guys, but prejudice as well. Based on a story by Elmore Leonard. **1967 111m/C** Paul Newman, Fredric March, Richard Boone, Diane Cilento, Cameron Mitchell, Barbara Rush, Martin Balsam; *D:* Martin Ritt. **VHS, Beta, LV $19.98** *FOX* ✰✰✰

Home Alone Eight-year-old Kevin is sent to his attic room without supper for misbehaving, and is forgotten the next day when his entire family (including a cousin played by brother Kieran) rushes to catch a plane to France. That's the plausible part. Left alone and besieged by burglars who are plundering the deserted neighborhood, Culkin turns into a pint-sized Rambo defending his suburban castle with the wile and resources of a boy genius with perfect timing and unlimited wherewithal. That's the implausible part. Cute and sentimental, it's chock-full of feel-good sentiment for youngsters and oldsters alike. As the targets of Macauley's preadolescent wrath, house-breakers Pesci and Stern enact painful slapstick with considerable vigor, while Candy has a small but funny part as the leader of a polka band traveling cross-country with mom O'Hara. The highest-grossing picture of 1990, surpassing "Ghost" and "Jaws" in dollars earned. Scripted and produced by the ever hit-seeking Hughes. **1990 (PG) 105m/C** Macaulay Culkin, Catherine O'Hara, Joe Pesci, Daniel Stern, John Heard, Roberts Blossom, John Candy; *D:* John Hughes. **VHS, Beta, LV $24.98** *FXV, IME, RDG* ✰✰✰

Home Alone 2: Lost in New York Kevin McCallister (Culkin) is alone again. The twist is, this time he's wandering about the perilous streets of the Big Apple. In an almost exact duplication of the original blockbuster, Kevin's harebrained family leaves him behind in the shuffle to start their Florida vacation during the Christmas holidays. Boarding the wrong plane, Kevin lands in New York where, wonder of wonders, he once again meets petty crooks Pesci and Stern, prison escapees who somehow survived the torture meted out in the first film. And they want revenge. Plus, he's got prissy hotel manager Curry on his trail. Loaded with cartoon violence and shameless gag replicas from HA1, mega-hit still produces genuine laughs and manages to incorporate fresh material. Culkin is as adorable as ever, with supporting cast all delivering fine performances. Filmed in New York City. **1992 (PG) 120m/C** Macaulay Culkin, Joe Pesci, Daniel Stern, Catherine O'Hara, John Heard, Devin Ratray, Tim Curry, Brenda Fricker, Eddie Bracken, Dana Ivey, Kieran Culkin, Rob Schneider; *Cameos:* Donald Trump; *D:* John Hughes; *M:* John Williams. **VHS, LV $24.98** *FXV, BTV* ✰✰½

The Home and the World Another masterpiece from India's Ray, this film deals with a sheltered Indian woman who falls in love with her husband's friend and becomes

politically committed in the turmoil of 1907-1908. Based on Rabindranath Tagore's novel. In Bengali with English subtitles. *AKA:* Ghare Baire.
1984 130m/C *IN* Victor Banerjee, Soumitra Chatterjee; *D:* Satyajit Ray. **VHS, Beta** $19.95 *COL, TAM, SUE* ♫♫♫ ½

Home at Last An orphan in turn of the century New York finds himself shipped to Nebraska on an orphan train. There he works on the farm of his adopted family, whose own son has died. The boy finds that he must adjust to a new lifestyle as well as strive to be accepted as someone other than a replacement for the couple's son. From the "Wonderworks" series.
1988 55m/C Adrien Brody, Frank Converse, Caroline Lagerfelt, Sascha Radetsky. **VHS** $29.95 *PME, HMV* ♫♫♫ ½

Home Before Midnight A young songwriter falls in love with a 14-year-old, is discovered, and is subsequently charged with statutory rape.
1984 115m/C James Aubrey, Alison Elliot; *D:* Pete Walker. **VHS, Beta** $59.95 *LHV, WAR* ♫ ½

Home Feeling In a black ghetto the residents try to make a viable community.
19?? 60m/C **VHS, Beta** $49.95 *FCT* ♫ ½

Home for Christmas An elderly homeless man, with the love of a young girl, teaches a wealthy family the spirit of Christmas.
1990 96m/C Mickey Rooney; *D:* Peter McCubbin. **VHS** $79.95 *RHI* ♫♫ ½

Home for the Holidays Four daughters are called home on Christmas by their father who is convinced that his second wife is trying to poison him. Made for television. *AKA:* Deadly Desires.
1972 74m/C Eleanor Parker, Walter Brennan, Sally Field, Jessica Walter, Julie Harris; *D:* John Llewellyn Moxey. **VHS, Beta** $24.95 *VMK* ♫♫

Home Free All A Vietnam vet turned revolutionary, turned writer, tries to reacquaint himself with childhood friends only to find one has joined the mob and another is settled in suburbia and none of them are dealing well with adulthood.
1984 92m/C Allan Nicholls, Roland Caccavo, Maura Ellyn, Shelley Wyant, Lucille Rivim; *D:* Stuart Bird. **VHS, Beta** $69.98 *LIV, VES* ♫♫ ½

Home from the Hill A solemn, brooding drama about a southern landowner and his troubled sons, one of whom is illegitimate. This one triumphs because of style. Cinematography by Milton Krasner.
1960 150m/C Robert Mitchum, George Peppard, George Hamilton, Eleanor Parker, Everett Sloane, Luana Parker, Constance Ford; *D:* Vincente Minnelli. **VHS, Beta, LV** $19.98 *MGM* ♫♫♫

Home in Oklahoma A boy will be swindled out of his inheritance and a killer will escape justice until Roy comes to the rescue. Standard series fare.
1947 72m/B Roy Rogers, Dale Evans, Trigger, George "Gabby" Hayes, Carol Hughes; *D:* William Witney. **VHS, Beta, 3/4U, Special order formats** $9.95 *NOS, CAB, DVT* ♫♫

Home is Where the Hart is A rich 103-year-old is kidnapped by a nurse wanting to marry him and become heir to his estate. It's up to his sons, all in their 70s, to rescue him.
1988 (PG-13) 94m/C Martin Mull, Leslie Nielsen, Valri Bromfield, Stephen E. Miller, Eric Christmas, Ted Stidder; *D:* Rex Bromfield. **VHS, Beta, LV** $19.95 *PAR, IME* ♫♫

Home Movies Brian De Palma and his film students at Sarah Lawrence College devised this loose, sloppy comedy which hearkens back to De Palma's early films. Tells the story of a nebbish who seeks therapy to gain control of his absurdly chaotic life.
1979 (PG) 89m/C Kirk Douglas, Nancy Allen, Keith Gordon, Gerrit Graham, Vincent Gardenia, Harry Davenport; *D:* Brian DePalma. **VHS, Beta, LV** $69.98 *LIV, VES, IME* ♫ ½

A Home of Our Own An American priest sets up a home in Mexico for orphan boys and changes their lives for the better. A true story of Father William Wasson.
1975 100m/C Jason Miller. **VHS, Beta** $49.95 *WOV* ♫ ½

Home of the Brave A black soldier is sent on a top secret mission in the South Pacific, but finds that he must battle with his white comrades as he is subjected to subordinate treatment and constant racial slurs. Hollywood's first outstanding statement against racial prejudice.
1949 86m/B Lloyd Bridges, James Edwards, Frank Lovejoy, Jeff Corey; *D:* Mark Robson. **VHS, Beta, LV** $19.98 *REP, FCT* ♫♫♫

Home Remedy An introverted New Jersey bachelor's isolated lifestyle is invaded by a flirtatious housewife and her jealous husband.
1988 92m/C Seth Barrish, Maxine Albert; *D:* Maggie Greenwald. **VHS, Beta** *MNC, TAM* ♫

Home Sweet Home Suggested by the life of John Howard Payne (actor, poet, dramatist, critic, and world-wanderer) who wrote the title song amid the bitterness of his sad life. Silent with musical score.
1914 62m/B Lillian Gish, Dorothy Gish, Henry B. Walthall, Mae Marsh, Blanche Sweet, Donald Crisp, Robert Harron; *D:* D.W. Griffith. **VHS, Beta** $29.95 *VYY, KIV* ♫♫ ½

Home Sweet Home A murdering psychopath escapes from the local asylum, and rampages through a family's Thanksgiving dinner. *AKA:* Slasher in the House.
1980 84m/C Jake Steinfeld, Sallee Elyse, Peter de Paula; *D:* Nettie Pena. **VHS, Beta** $59.95 *MED* ♫ ½

Home to Stay A farmer who has suffered a stroke is fighting off repeated lapses into senility. His son and daughter have conflicting interests as to whether he should be committed to a nursing home. Made for television.
1979 74m/C Henry Fonda, Frances Hyland, Michael McGuire; *D:* Delbert Mann. **VHS, Beta** $59.95 *TLF* ♫♫

Home Town Story A politician is convinced big business is behind his election loss. Fair drama. Watch for Monroe in a bit part.
1951 61m/B Jeffrey Lynn, Donald Crisp, Marjorie Reynolds, Alan Hale Jr., Marilyn Monroe, Barbara Brown, Melinda Plowman; *D:* Arthur Pierson. **VHS** $19.95 *NOS* ♫♫

Homebodies Six senior citizens, disgusted when they learn that they will be callously tossed out of their home, become violent murderers in their shocking attempt to solve their problem. An odd little film made in Cincinnati.
1974 (PG) 96m/C Ruth McDevitt, Linda Marsh, William Hansen, Peter Brocco, Frances Fuller; *D:* Larry Yust. **VHS, Beta** $59.98 *SUE* ♫♫

Homeboy A small-time club boxer who dreams of becoming middleweight champ is offered his big break, but the opportunity is jeopardized by his dishonest manager's dealings. Never released theatrically.

1988 (R) 118m/C Mickey Rourke, Christopher Walken, Debra Feuer, Kevin Conway, Antony Alda, Ruben Blades; *D:* Michael Seresin. **VHS, Beta, LV, CDV** $9.99 *CCB, IVE* ♫♫

Homeboy A Black boxer owes his career to the mob. When he tries to break free is wife is murdered - and he seeks revenge.
198? 93m/C Dabney Coleman, Philip Michael Thomas. **VHS** *SIM* ♫ ½

Homeboys Two East L.A. brothers find themselves on opposite sides of the law in this quickie designed to cash in on gang violence and ghetto dramas.
1992 91m/C Todd Bridges, David Garrison, Ron Odriozola, Ken Michaels; *D:* Lindsay Norgard. **VHS, LV** $89.95 *AIP* ♫

Homecoming Two German prisoners of war escape from a Siberian lead mine. One reaches home first and has an affair with his comrade's wife. Silent.
1928 74m/B *GE* Dita Parlo, Lars Hanson, Gustav Froehlich; *D:* Joe May. **VHS, Beta** $29.95 *FST, GLV* ♫♫♫

Homecoming Average soap opera starring Gable and Turner set amidst the trenches of WW II. Gable plays a selfish doctor who leaves behind his wife and colleague to enlist in the Medical Corps as a major. Turner is the battlefield nurse who forever changes his life. Film is hindered by a story which is far below the talents of the excellent cast. Although voted by the New York Critics as one of the ten worst movies of 1948, the public loved it. Based on the story "The Homecoming of Ulysses" by Sidney Kingsley.
1948 113m/B Clark Gable, Lana Turner, Anne Baxter, John Hodiak, Ray Collins, Gladys Cooper, Cameron Mitchell, Art Baker, Lurene Tuttle; *D:* Mervyn LeRoy; *W:* Paul Osborn, Jan Lustig. **VHS** $19.98 *MGM* ♫♫

Homecoming: A Christmas Story Made-for-television heart-tugger that inspired the television series "The Waltons." A depression-era Virginia mountain family struggles to celebrate Christmas although the whereabouts and safety of their father are unknown. Adapted from the autobiographical novel by Earl Hamner, Jr.
1971 98m/C Richard Thomas, Patricia Neal, Edgar Bergen, Cleavon Little, Ellen Corby; *D:* Fielder Cook. **VHS, Beta** $59.98 *FOX* ♫♫ ½

Homer and Eddie A witless road comedy with Goldberg as a dying sociopath and a mentally retarded Belushi. They take off cross-country to make a little trouble, learn a little about life, and create a less than entertaining movie.
1989 (R) 100m/C Whoopi Goldberg, James Belushi, Karen Black; *D:* Andrei Konchalovsky. **VHS, Beta, LV** $89.95 *HBO* ♫

Homer Comes Home A homely and diligent inventor finds nothing but failure, but sticks it out in hopes of turning his luck around. Silent comedy starring down-home Ray.
1920 55m/B Charles Ray. **VHS, Beta** $16.95 *GPV* ♫♫

Homesteaders of Paradise Valley The Hume brothers oppose Red Ryder and a group of settlers building a dam in Paradise Valley.
1947 54m/B Allan "Rocky" Lane, Robert (Bobby) Blake. **VHS, Beta, 3/4U, Special order formats** $19.95 *NOS, VCN, CAB* ♫ ½

Hometown U.S.A. Set in Los Angeles in the late 50s' this teenage cruising movie is the brainchild of director Baer who is better known as Jethro from that madcap television series "The Beverly Hillbillies."

1979 (R) 97m/C Brian Kerwin, Gary Springer, David Wilson, Cindy Fisher, Sally Kirkland; **D:** Max Baer. **VHS, Beta** $69.98 *LIV, VES Woof!*

Homeward Bound A dying teenager tries to reunite his long-estranged father and grandfather. Made for television.
1980 (G) 96m/C David Soul, Moosie Drier, Barnard Hughes; **D:** Richard Michaels. **VHS, Beta** $59.95 *HMV ⍤*

Homeward Bound: The Incredible Journey Successful remake of the 1963 Disney release "The Incredible Journey." Two dogs and a cat once again try to find their way home after their family relocates, armed with greater depth of character than the original. Hard not to shed a tear for the brave animal trio who develop a trusting bond through assorted misadventures. Based on the novel by Sheila Burnford. Superior family fare.
1993 (G) 85m/C Kevin Timothy Chevalia, Kim Greist, Robert Hays; **D:** Duwayne Dunham; **W:** Linda Woolverton, Carolyn Thompson; **M:** Bruce Broughton; **V:** Don Ameche, Michael J. Fox, Sally Field. **VHS, LV** $22.99 *DIS ⍤⍤⍤*

Homework Young man's after-school lessons with a teacher are definitely not part of the curriculum. Yawning sexploitation.
1982 (R) 90m/C Joan Collins, Michael Morgan, Betty Thomas, Shell Kepler, Wings Hauser, Lee Purcell; **D:** James Beshears. **VHS, Beta, LV** $19.95 *MCA ⍤*

Homewrecker Benson stars as a scientist who invents a computer, with a female voice, as the ultimate domestic worker. Only the computer turns possessive and against Benson's estranged wife.
1992 (PG-13) 88m/C Robby Benson, Sydney Walsh, Sarah Rose Karr; **D:** Fred Walton; **W:** Eric Harlacher; **V:** Kate Jackson. **VHS, Beta** *PAR ⍤⍤*

Homicidal Impulse When Assistant D.A. Tim Casey has an affair with his boss' ambitious niece he doesn't realize the danger he's in. His lover decides to kill her uncle so boyfriend Tim will get his job. Some women will do anything for love. Also available in an unrated version.
1992 (R) 84m/C Scott Valentine, Vanessa Angel. **VHS** $89.98 *LIV ⍤½*

Homicide Terrific police thriller with as much thought as action; a driven detective faces his submerged Jewish identity while probing an anti-Semitic murder and a secret society. Playwright/filmmaker Mamet creates nail-biting suspense and shattering epiphanies without resorting to Hollywood glitz. Rich (often profane) dialogue includes a classic soliloquy mystically comparing a lawman's badge with a Star of David.
1991 (R) 100m/C Joe Mantegna, William H. Macy, Natalija Nogulich, Ving Rhames, Rebecca Pidgeon; **W/D:** David Mamet. **VHS, LV, 8mm** $19.95 *COL, BTV ⍤⍤⍤½*

Homo Eroticus/Man of the Year Handsome servant finds it difficult to satisfy the desires of Bergamo, Italy's socialite.
1971 93m/C *IT* Lando Buzzanca, Rossana Podesta. **VHS, Beta** $59.95 *ONE ⍤*

Honey Attractive writer pays an unusual visit to the home of a distinguished publisher. Brandishing a pistol, she demands that he read aloud from her manuscript. As he reads, a unique fantasy unfolds, a dreamlike erotic tale that may be the writer's own sexual awakening. Or maybe not.
1981 89m/C *IT SP* Clio Goldsmith, Fernando Rey, Catherine Spaak; **D:** Gianfranco Angelucci. **VHS, Beta** $69.95 *VES ⍤½*

Honey, I Blew Up the Kid Screwball suburban inventor Moranis reverses his shrinking process and this time manages to enlarge his two-year-old into a 112-foot giant who gets bigger every time he comes in contact with electricity. Yikes! Loaded with great special effects, this is a charming and funny film that's fit for the whole family. Sequel to "Honey I Shrunk the Kids."
1992 (PG) 89m/C Rick Moranis, Marcia Strassman, Robert Oliveri, Daniel Shalikar, Joshua Shalikar, Lloyd Bridges, John Shea; **D:** Randal Kleiser. **VHS, Beta, LV** $19.99 *DIS ⍤⍤½*

Honey, I Shrunk the Kids The popular Disney fantasy about a suburban inventor. His shrinking device accidentally reduces his kids to 1/4 inch tall, and he subsequently throws them out with the garbage. Now they must journey back to the house through the jungle that was once the back lawn. Accompanied by "Tummy Trouble," the first of a projected series of Roger Rabbit Maroon Cartoons. Followed by "Honey, I Blew Up the Kids."
1989 (G) 101m/C Rick Moranis, Matt Frewer, Marcia Strassman, Kristine Sutherland, Thomas Wilson Brown, Jared Rushton; **D:** Joe Johnston, Rob Minkoff; **V:** Charles Fleischer, Kathleen Turner, Lou Hirsch, April Winchell. **VHS, Beta, LV** $19.99 *DIS, IVE, RDG ⍤⍤½*

The Honey Pot A millionaire feigns death to see the reaction of three of his former lovers. Amusing black comedy with fine performances from all. Based on Moliere's "Volpone." **AKA:** It Comes Up Murder; Anyone for Venice?; Mr. Fox of Venice.
1967 131m/C Rex Harrison, Susan Hayward, Cliff Robertson, Capucine, Edie Adams, Maggie Smith, Adolfo Celi; **W/D:** Joseph L. Mankiewicz. **VHS** $14.95 *MGM ⍤⍤½*

Honeybaby A smooth international soldier of fortune and a bright, sexy American interpreter are entangled in Middle-Eastern turbulence when they must rescue a politician kidnapped by terrorists.
1974 (PG) 94m/C Calvin Lockhart, Diana Sands; **D:** Michael Schultz. **VHS** $19.95 *GEM, MRV ⍤⍤*

Honeyboy Estrada tries to win fame, fortune, and a ticket out of the barrio as an up-and-coming boxer. Outstanding fight scenes, but little else in this made for television drama of the boxing scene.
1982 100m/C Erik Estrada, Morgan Fairchild, James McEachin, Robert Costanzo, Yvonne Wilder; **D:** John Berry. **VHS, Beta** *LIV ⍤½*

Honeymoon A young French woman visiting New York learns she will be deported when her boyfriend is arrested for drug-smuggling. To stay, she is set up in a marriage of convenience and told her new husband will never see or bother her. But hubby has other plans!
1987 96m/C John Shea, Nathalie Baye, Richard Berry, Peter Donat; **D:** Patrick Jamain. **VHS, Beta** $19.98 *LHV, WAR ⍤⍤*

Honeymoon Academy Newly married man has lots to learn in this comic outing. His new wife never told him about her unusual line of business—as an undercover agent! **AKA:** For Better or For Worse.
1990 (PG-13) 94m/C Robert Hays, Kim Cattrall, Leigh Taylor-Young; **D:** Gene Quintano. **VHS, LV** $89.99 *HBO, IME ⍤⍤*

Honeymoon Horror Stranded on an island, three honeymooning couples soon realize their romantic retreat is a nightmare. A crazy man with an axe is tracking them down. Minimally effective.
197? 90m/C Cheryl Black, William F. Pecchi, Bob Wagner. **VHS, Beta** $59.95 *SVS ⍤*

Honeymoon in Vegas Cage is Jack Singer, a momma's boy who is deathly afraid of marrying his girlfriend Betsy (Parker) until finally, she threatens to leave him. They go to Las Vegas for a quickie wedding, but before the couple can say "I do" Jack has lost Betsy in a poker game to professional gambler Tommy Korman (Caan), who thinks Betsy is a dead ringer for his late wife. Korman whisks Betsy off to Hawaii where he tries to woo her with his charm (and money). Meanwhile, Jack desperately searches for Betsy, "aided" by a wacky cab driver and a Hawaiian chief with a penchant for singing Broadway show tunes. Lightweight romantic comedy has its charm, featuring a bevy of Elvis impersonators in every size, shape, and color, including the Flying Elvises, a group of skydivers who wear light-up jumpsuits. Cage is typically maniacal while Caan adds a bit of sinister sophistication. Parker is suitably distraught about the men in her life. Look for former Las Vegas U basketball coach Jerry Tarkanian as one of Caan's gambling buddies.
1992 (PG-13) 95m/C James Caan, Nicolas Cage, Sarah Jessica Parker, Pat Morita, John Capodice, Robert Costanzo, Anne Bancroft, Peter Boyle; **W/D:** Andrew Bergman. **VHS, LV** *COL, NLC, IME ⍤⍤½*

Honeymoon Killers A grim, creepy filmization of a true multiple-murder case wherein an overweight woman and slimy gigolo living on Long Island seduce and murder one lonely woman after another. Independently made and frankly despairing. **AKA:** The Lonely Hearts Killers.
1970 (R) 103m/C Tony LoBianco, Shirley Stoler, Mary Jane Higby, Dortha Duckworth, Doris Roberts, Marilyn Chris, Kip McArdle, Mary Breen, Barbara Cason, Ann Harris, Guy Sorel; **D:** Leonard Kastle. **VHS, Beta, LV** $69.98 *LIV, VES ⍤⍤⍤*

The Honeymoon Machine A lightweight comedy about two American sailors and a computer scam. McQueen and Mullaney hook up with computer expert Hutton to use their ship's computer to beat the gambling odds at an Italian casino. Their commander misinterprets the signals and thinks the ship is being attacked. Fast paced and the computer angle was new territory in '61.
1961 87m/C Steve McQueen, Jack Mullaney, Jim Hutton, Dean Jagger, Paula Prentiss, Brigid Bazlen, Jack Weston; **D:** Richard Thorpe. **VHS** $19.98 *MGM, MOV ⍤⍤½*

The Honeymooners "Classic 39,": TV or Not TV/ Honeymooners Highlights Captain Video and his video rangers are a Kramden household name after Ralph and Ed pool their resources to buy a television. Also includes clips from each of the remaining 38 episodes in "The Honeymooners" series. Video cover illustration by C.F. Payne. This 20 volumes series contains two episodes per tape.
1955 60m/C **VHS** $5.98 *FXV ⍤⍤½*

The Honeymooners Hidden Episodes Three recently-retrieved episodes of the Honeymooners sketches, which were initially aired live as part of the "Jackie Gleason Show." In "Letter to the Boss," Jackie sends some nasty correspondence to his employer when he mistakenly believes that he has been canned. In "Suspense," Ralph fears that Alice is planning his murder when he eavesdrops on her acting practice. In "Dinner Guest," Ralph's plans to suck up to his supervisor meet with hilarious disaster. This "Honeymooners" series contains 28 volumes, which are available separately for

purchase. *AKA:* The Honeymooners: The Lost Episodes.
1953 53m/B Jackie Gleason, Audrey Meadows, Art Carney, Joyce Randolph. **VHS, Beta $29.95** *MPI, FOX, MOV* ⅃⅃½

Honeysuckle Rose A road-touring country-Western singer whose life is a series of one night stands, falls in love with an adoring young guitar player who has just joined his band. This nearly costs him his marriage with this wife, who while waiting patiently for him at home, decides she's had enough. Easygoing performance by Nelson, essentially playing himself. *AKA:* On the Road Again.
1980 (PG) 120m/C Willie Nelson, Dyan Cannon, Amy Irving, Slim Pickens, Joey Floyd, Charles Levin, Priscilla Pointer; *D:* Jerry Schatzberg. **VHS, Beta, LV $19.98** *WAR* ⅃⅃½

Hong Kong Nights Two agents attempt to break up a Chinese smuggling ring run by an unscrupulous madman. Good, action-packed low-budget film.
1935 59m/B Tom Keene, Wera Engels, Warren Hymer, Tetsu Komai, Cornelius Keefe; *D:* E. Mason Hopper. **VHS, Beta $16.95** *SNC* ⅃⅃½

Honky An innocent friendship between a black woman and a white man develops into a passionate romance that has the whole town talking.
1971 (R) 92m/C Brenda Sykes, John Nielson, Maria Donzinger; *D:* William A. Graham. **VHS, Beta $49.95** *UNI* ⅃½

Honky Tonk A western soap opera in which ne'er do well Clark marries Lana and tries to live a respectable life. In this, the first of several MGM teamings between Gable and Turner, the chemistry between the two is evident. So much so in fact that Gable's then wife Carole Lombard let studio head Louis B. Mayer know that she was not at all thrilled. The public was pleased however, and made the film a hit.
1941 106m/B Clark Gable, Lana Turner, Frank Morgan, Claire Trevor, Marjorie Main, Albert Dekker, Chill Wills, Henry O'Neill, John Maxwell, Morgan Wallace, Betty Blythe, Francis X. Bushman; *D:* Jack Conway. **VHS, Beta $19.98** *MGM, CCB* ⅃⅃⅃

Honky Tonk Freeway An odd assortment of people become involved in a small town Mayor's scheme to turn a dying hamlet into a tourist wonderland. You can find better things to do with your evening than watch this accident.
1981 (PG) 107m/C Teri Garr, Howard Hesseman, Beau Bridges, Hume Cronyn, William Devane, Beverly D'Angelo, Geraldine Page; *D:* John Schlesinger. **VHS, Beta $69.99** *HBO* ⅃

Honky Tonk Girl Hilarious exploitation film about a hitch-hiking prostitution ring. Also known as "Highway Hell."
1937 ?m/C Mary Chauning. **VHS, Beta $16.95** *SNC* ⅃

Honkytonk Man Unsuccessful change-of-pace Eastwood vehicle set during the Depression. Aging alcoholic country singer tries one last time to make it to Nashville, hoping to perform at the Grand Ole Opry. This time he takes his nephew (played by Eastwood's real-life son) with him.
1982 (PG) 123m/C Clint Eastwood, Kyle Eastwood, John McIntire, Alexa Kenin, Verna Bloom; *D:* Clint Eastwood. **VHS, Beta, LV $19.98** *WAR* ⅃⅃

Honkytonk Nights A honky-tonkin' romp through an evening in a country/western bar, featuring legendary topless dancer Carol Doda, Georgina ("Devil in Mrs. Jones") Spelvin, and the music of The Hot Licks (minus front man Dan Hicks).

197? (R) 90m/C Carol Doda, Georgina Spelvin, Ramblin' Jack Elliot. **VHS, Beta $59.95** *TPV* ⅃

Honolulu A screwball comedy with Powell providing the musical numbers. Young takes on the dual role of a Hollywood star who meets his exact double, a Hawaii plantation owner. They decide to switch identities to give their lives a little oomph. The star sails to Hawaii, falling for fellow passenger Powell, only to discover he's expected to get married upon his arrival in Honolulu. Anderson and Burns and Allen provide the comic relief. ♫The Leader Doesn't Like Music; This Night Was Made For Dreaming; Honolulu; Hymn To The Sun.
1939 83m/B Robert Young, Eleanor Powell, George Burns, Gracie Allen, Rita Johnson, Eddie Anderson, Clarence Kolb; *D:* Edward Buzzell; *W:* Frank Partos, Herbert Fields; *M:* Franz Waxman. **VHS $19.98** *MGM* ⅃⅃½

Honor Among Thieves Two former mercenaries reteam for a robbery that doesn't come off as planned. Not as fast paced as others in Bronson canon. *AKA:* Farewell, Friend.
1968 (R) 115m/C *FR IT* Charles Bronson, Alain Delon, Brigitte Fossey, Olga Georges-Picot, Bernard Fresson; *D:* Jean Herman. **VHS, Beta $9.99** *CCB, MPI, MON* ⅃½

Honor and Glory Tracy Pride, an FBI agent and martial arts expert, teams up with an Interpol agent, who doubles as a TV anchorwoman, to stop an international banker from getting his greedy hands on the key to a nuclear arsenal. These fighting gals are up against a team of assassins but they can more than handle themselves.
1992 (R) ?m/C Cynthia Rothrock, Donna Jason, Chuck Jeffreys, Gerald Klein, Robin Shou, Richard Yuen; *D:* Godfrey Hall; *W:* Herb Borkland. **VHS $89.95** *IMP* ⅃⅃

Honor of the Range The good sheriff's lady is whisked away by his evil twin brother and the sheriff must go undercover to get her back. Odd plot twists for a seemingly normal western.
1934 60m/B Ken Maynard, Cecilia Parker, Fred Kohler Jr.; *D:* Ken Maynard. **VHS $19.95** *NOS, DVT, HEG* ⅃⅃

Honor Thy Father The everyday life of a real-life Mafia family as seen through the eyes of Bill Bonanno, the son of mob chieftain Joe Bonanno. Adapted from the book by Gay Talese. Made for television.
1973 97m/C Raf Vallone, Richard Castellano, Brenda Vaccaro, Joseph Bologna; *D:* Paul Wendkos. **Beta $14.95** *PSM* ⅃⅃

Hooch Comedy about three members of the New York Mafia who get some unexpected southern hospitality when they try to muscle in on a southern family's moonshine operation.
1976 (PG) 96m/C Gil Gerard, Erika Fox, Melody Rogers, Danny Aiello, Mike Allen, Ray Serra; *D:* Edward Mann. **VHS, Beta $49.95** *PSM* ⅃½

The Hooded Terror A merciless group of murderers take on a G-man.
1938 70m/B Tod Slaughter, Greta Gynt. **VHS $14.99** *NOS, HEG* ⅃½

The Hoodlum A criminal does his best to rehabilitate and, with a little help from his brother, is able to hold a steady job. However the crime bug dies hard and when he spots an armored car, he just can't resist the temptation. Tierney's real brother, Edward, plays his screen brother.
1951 61m/B Lawrence Tierney, Allene Roberts, Marjorie Riordan, Liza Golm, Edward Tierney; *D:* Max Nosseck. **VHS, Beta $16.95** *SNC* ⅃⅃

Hoodlum Empire A senator enlists the aid of a former gangster, now a war hero, in his battle against the syndicate. Loosely based on the Kefauver investigations of 1950-51.
1952 98m/B Brian Donlevy, Claire Trevor, Forrest Tucker, Vera Ralston, Luther Adler, John Russell, Gene Lockhart, Grant Withers, Taylor Holmes, Roy Barcroft, Richard Jaeckel; *D:* Joseph Kane. **VHS $19.98** *REP* ⅃⅃

Hoodoo Ann The story of Hoodoo Ann, from her days in the orphanage to her happy marriage. Silent.
1916 27m/B Mae Marsh, Robert Harron. **VHS, Beta $29.98** *CCB* ⅃⅃

Hook Although he said he was never gonna do it, Peter Pan has grown up. Peter Banning is an uptight, portable phone-toting adult who places work before family and has forgotten all about Neverland and the evil Captain Hook. When Peter and his family visit grandmother Wendy in London, Hook kidnaps the children and takes them to Neverland. With the help of Tinkerbell, his magic pixie dust, and happy thoughts, Peter flies to Neverland to rescue his children and rediscovers his youth while visiting with the Lost Boys. The sets are spectacular; the direction less so. A big budget fantasy with lots of special effects, but lacking the charm it needs to really fly. Still, kids really seem to love this one. P.S.: You'll have to look hard to see Crosby and Close as pirates, but they're there. Futurizes the original concept from the J.M. Barrie classic.
1991 (PG) 142m/C Dustin Hoffman, Robin Williams, Julia Roberts, Bob Hoskins, Maggie Smith, Charlie Korsmo, Caroline Goodall, Amber Scott, Phil Collins, Arthur Malet, Dante Basco; *Cameos:* Glenn Close, David Crosby; *D:* Steven Spielberg; *M:* John Williams. **VHS, Beta, LV, 8mm $24.95** *COL* ⅃⅃

Hook, Line and Sinker A couple of insurance investigators try to help a young woman restore a hotel, and they find romance and run-ins with crooks. Directed by Cline, who later directed W.C. Fields in "The Bank Dick," "My Little Chickadee," and "Never Give a Sucker an Even Break."
1930 75m/B Bert Wheeler, Robert Woolsey, Dorothy Lee, Jobyna Howland, Ralf Harolde, Natalie Moorhead, George F. Marion, Hugh Herbert; *D:* Eddie Cline. **VHS, LV $19.98** *NOS, TTC, FCT* ⅃⅃

The Hooked Generation A group of drug pushers kidnap defenseless victims, rape innocent girls, and even murder their own Cuban drug contacts (and all without the aid of a cohesive plot). Many gory events precede their untimely deaths; few will be entertained.
1969 (R) 92m/C Jeremy Slate, Steve Alaimo. **VHS** *NO* ⅃

Hoomania Award-winning Christian children's film. Hoomania is a board game that fantastically whisks young Kris to a strange world. He meets the most unlikely characters, some of whom aren't too helpful in his journey to Mount Wisdom.
1990 30m/C **VHS, Beta, 3/4U $15.95** *SPW* ⅃

Hooper Lightweight behind-the-scenes satire about the world of movie stuntmen. Reynolds is a top stuntman who becomes involved in a rivalry with an up-and-coming young man out to surpass him. Dated good-ole-boy shenanigans.
1978 (PG) 94m/C Burt Reynolds, Jan-Michael Vincent, Robert Klein, Sally Field, Brian Keith, John Marley, Adam West; *D:* Hal Needham. **VHS, Beta, LV $59.95** *WAR* ⅃⅃½

Hoosiers In Indiana, where basketball is the sport of the gods, a small town high school basketball team gets a new, but surprisingly experienced coach. He makes the team, and each person in it, better than they thought possible. Classic plot rings true because of Hackman's complex and sensitive performance coupled with Hopper's touching portrait of an alcoholic basketball fanatic.
1986 (PG) 115m/C Gene Hackman, Barbara Hershey, Dennis Hopper, David Neidorf; **D:** David Anspaugh; **M:** Jerry Goldsmith. **VHS, Beta, LV** $29.98 *LIV, HBO* √√√

Hootch Country Boys A film packed with moonshine, sheriffs, busty country girls, and chases. **AKA:** Redneck County; The Great Lester Boggs.
1975 (PG) 90m/C Alex Karras, Scott MacKenzie, Dean Jagger, Willie Jones, Bob Ridgely, Susan Denbo, Bob Ginnaven, David Haney; **D:** Harry Z. Thomason. **VHS, Beta** $19.95 *ACA* √

Hopalong Cassidy In this first of a long series of "Hopalong Cassidy" films, Hoppy and his pals intervene in a brewing range war. A gang of rustlers is helped by a two-timing foreman who's playing both sides off each other. After a career in silent films, Boyd was pretty much washed up before taking on the role of Cassidy. He was originally asked to play the villain and declined, but agreed to be the good guy if the character was cleaned up. "Gabby" Hayes' stock character was killed off in this episode, but was brought back for later installments. **AKA:** Hopalong Cassidy Enters.
1935 60m/B William Boyd, James Ellison, Paula Stone, Robert Warwick, Charles Middleton, Frank McGlynn, Kenneth Thomson, George "Gabby" Hayes, James Mason, Franklin Farnum; **D:** Howard Bretherton. **VHS** $19.95 *NOS, MRV* √√√

Hopalong Cassidy: Borrowed Trouble Hoppy must save a righteous teacher from the clutches of kidnappers who plan to place a saloon right next to the school.
1948 61m/B William Boyd, Andy Clyde, Rand Brooks, Elaine Riley, John Kellogg, Helen Chapman; **D:** George Archainbaud. **VHS** *NO* √√½

Hopalong Cassidy: Dangerous Venture "Dangerous Venture" was one of Hoppy's last ventures, produced the final year of the series' 13-year tenure. Hoppy and the gang hunt for Aztec ruins in the great Southwest, and have to deal with renegade Indians and a band of treacherous looters along the way.
1948 55m/B William Boyd, Andy Clyde, Rand Brooks. **VHS, Beta** *NO* √√

Hopalong Cassidy: False Paradise Another late Hopalong has the noir-clad cowboy rushing to the aid of a girl and her dad when control of their ranch is threatened by swindlers with false mining claims.
1948 59m/B William Boyd, Andy Clyde, Rand Brooks; **D:** George Archainbaud. **VHS, Beta** *NO* √√

Hopalong Cassidy: Hoppy's Holiday Boyd—the only celluloid incarnation of Clarence Mulford's pulp hero—plays the Hopster yet again. This time, the non-drinking, non-smoking (what does he do for kicks?) hero and a passel of Bar-20 cowboys visit Mesa City for some well-earned R and R, but find themselves caught in a web of corruption.
1947 60m/B William Boyd, Andy Clyde, Rand Brooks, Jeff Corey; **D:** George Archainbaud. **VHS, Beta** *NO* √√

Hopalong Cassidy: Riders of the Deadline Hoppy turns into a baddie in this episode in order to infiltrate a treacherous gang and apprehend their leader.
1943 70m/B William Boyd, Andy Clyde, Jimmy Rogers, Robert Mitchum; **D:** Lesley Selander. **VHS, Beta** *NO* √√

Hopalong Cassidy: Silent Conflict Lucky is tricked and hypnotized by a traveling medicine man who commands him to rob and kill Hoppy.
1948 61m/B William Boyd, Andy Clyde, Rand Brooks; **D:** George Archainbaud. **VHS, Beta** *NO* √√

Hopalong Cassidy: Sinister Journey Mysterious accidents are plaguing a railroad where an old friend of Hoppy's works, so Hoppy, California, and Lucky take railroad jobs to find out what gives.
1948 58m/B William Boyd, Andy Clyde, Rand Brooks; **D:** George Archainbaud. **VHS, Beta** *NO* √√

Hopalong Cassidy: The Dead Don't Dream Hoppy's sidekick Lucky decides to get married, but happily-ever-afterdom is threatened when the father of Mrs. Lucky-to-be is murdered. When Hoppy sets out to find the killer, he finds himself suspected of the dastardly deed.
1948 55m/B William Boyd, Andy Clyde, Rand Brooks, John Parrish; **D:** George Archainbaud. **VHS, Beta** *NO* √√

Hopalong Cassidy: The Devil's Playground Strange things are afoot in a peaceful valley adjacent to a desolate, forbidding wasteland. When Hoppy and a young woman set out across the wasteland to make a gold delivery, they encounter a band of desperados and begin to unravel the secrets of a dishonest political ring.
1946 65m/B William Boyd, Andy Clyde, Rand Brooks, Elaine Riley; **D:** George Archainbaud. **VHS, Beta** *NO* √√

Hopalong Cassidy: The Marauders After seeking shelter in an abandoned church one rainy night, Hoppy and the boys must defend the kirk when it is threatened by a marauder and his gang.
1947 64m/B William Boyd, Andy Clyde, Rand Brooks; **D:** George Archainbaud. **VHS, Beta** *NO* √√

Hopalong Cassidy: Unexpected Guest When a small fortune is left to a California family, the head count starts to dwindle, and Hoppy aims to find out why.
1947 59m/B William Boyd, Andy Clyde, Rand Brooks, Una O'Connor; **D:** George Archainbaud. **VHS, Beta** *NO* √√½

Hope and Glory Boorman turns his memories of World War II London into a complex and sensitive film. Father volunteered, mother must deal with awakening sexuality of her teen-aged daughter, keep her son in line, balance the ration books and try to make it to the bomb shelter in the middle of the night. Seen through the boy's eyes, war creates a playground of shrapnel to collect and wild imaginings come true.
1987 (PG-13) 97m/C GB Sebastian Rice Edwards, Geraldine Muir, Sarah Miles, Sammi Davis-Voss, David Hayman, Derrick O'Connor, Susan Wooldridge, Jean-Marc Barr, Ian Bannen, Jill Baker, Charley Boorman, Annie Leon, Katrine Boorman, Gerald James; **D:** John Boorman. Academy Awards '87 Nominations: Best Art Direction/Set Decoration, Best Cinematography, Best Director (Boorman), Best Original Screenplay, Best Picture; British Academy Awards '87: Best Film, Best Supporting Actress (Wooldridge); Los Angeles Film Critics Association Awards '87: Best Director (Boorman), Best Film; National Board of Review Awards

'87: 10 Best Films of the Year. **VHS, Beta, LV, 8mm** $14.98 *SUE, FCT, HMV* √√√½

Hoppity Goes to Town Full-length animated feature from the Max Fleischer studios tells the story of the inhabitants of Bugville, who live in a weed patch in New York City. Songs by Frank Loesser and Hoagy Carmichael. **AKA:** Mr. Bug Goes to Town.
1941 77m/C **D:** Dave Fleischer. **VHS, LV** $14.98 *REP, MRV, FCT* √√√½

Hoppy Serves a Writ In this last of the series to be based on the writings of the original author, Texas sheriff Cassidy tries to bring a gang of outlaws to justice. Look for a young Robert Mitchum as one of the villains.
1943 67m/B William Boyd, Andy Clyde, Jay Kirby, Victor Jory, George Reeves, Hal Taliaferro, Robert Mitchum, Byron Foulger, Earle Hodgins, Roy Barcroft; **D:** George Archainbaud. **VHS** $19.95 *NOS, MRV* √√

Hopscotch A C.I.A. agent drops out when his overly zealous chief demotes him to a desk job. When he writes a book designed to expose the dirty deeds of the CIA, he leads his boss and KGB pal on a merry chase. Amiable comedy well-suited for Matthau's rumpled talents.
1980 (R) 107m/C Walter Matthau, Glenda Jackson, Ned Beatty, Sam Waterston, Herbert Lom; **D:** Ronald Neame. **VHS, Beta, LV** $9.95 *COL, SUE* √√√

Horizons West Two brothers go their separate ways after the Civil War. One leads a peaceful life as a rancher but the other, corrupted by the war, engages in a violent campaign to build his own empire. Ryan's outstanding performance eclipses that of the young Hudson.
1952 81m/C Robert Ryan, Julie Adams, Rock Hudson, Raymond Burr, James Arness, John McIntire, Dennis Weaver, Francis Bavier; **D:** Budd Boetticher. **VHS** *MCA* √√½

The Horn Blows at Midnight A band trumpeter falls asleep and dreams he's a bumbling archangel, on Earth to blow the note bringing the end of the world. But a pretty girl distracts him, and...A wild, high-gloss, well-cast fantasy farce, uniquely subversive in its lighthearted approach to biblical Doomsday. Benny made the film notorious by acting ashamed of it in his later broadcast routines.
1945 78m/B Jack Benny, Alexis Smith, Dolores Moran, Allyn Joslyn, Reginald Gardiner, Guy Kibbee, John Alexander, Margaret Dumont; **D:** Raoul Walsh. **VHS** $19.98 *MGM, FCT* √√√

The Horrible Dr. Hichcock A sicko doctor, who accidentally killed his first wife while engaged in sexual antics, remarries to bring the first missus back from the dead using his new wife's blood. Genuinely creepy. Sequelled by "The Ghost." **AKA:** L'Orribile Segreto Del Dr. Hichcock.
1962 76m/C IT Robert Flemyng, Barbara Steele; **D:** Robert Hampton, Riccardo Freda. **VHS** $69.95 *SNC* √√½

Horror Chamber of Dr. Faustus A wickedly intelligent, inventive piece of Grand Guignol about a mad doctor who kills young girls so he may graft their skin onto the face of his accidentally mutilated daughter. In French with English subtitles. **AKA:** Eyes Without a Face; Les Yeux Sans Visage; Occhi Senza Volto.
1959 84m/B FR Alida Valli, Pierre Brasseur, Edith Scob, Francois Guerin; **D:** Georges Franju. **VHS, Beta, LV** $29.95 *SNC* √√√½

Horror Express A creature from prehistoric times, that was removed from its tomb, is transported on the Trans-Siberian railroad. Passengers suddenly discover strange things happening—such as having their souls sucked out of them. *AKA:* Panic on the Trans-Siberian Express; Panico en el Transiberiano.
1972 (R) 88m/C *SP* Christopher Lee, Peter Cushing, Telly Savalas; *D:* Gene Martin. **VHS, Beta $59.95** *SNC, MRV, PSM* 🎬🎬½

Horror Hospital Patients are turned into zombies by a mad doctor in this hospital where no anesthesia is used. Those who try to escape are taken care of by the doctor's guards. *AKA:* Computer Killers.
1973 (R) 91m/C *GB* Michael Gough, Robin Askwith, Vanessa Shaw, Ellen Pollock, Skip Martin, Dennis Price; *D:* Anthony Balch. **VHS, Beta $29.95** *GRG, UHV, MPI* 🎬

Horror Hotel A young witchcraft student visits a small Massachusetts town which has historic ties to witch burnings and discovers a new, and deadly, coven is now active. Well done and atmospheric. *AKA:* The City of the Dead.
1960 76m/B *GB* Christopher Lee, Patricia Jessel, Betta St. John, Dennis Lotis, Venetia Stevenson, Valentine Dyall; *D:* John Llewellyn Moxey. **VHS $19.95** *NOS, MRV, SNC* 🎬🎬½

Horror House on Highway 5 Someone in a Nixon mask kills people in this extremely cheap dud.
1986 90m/C *W/D:* Richard Casey. **VHS, Beta $9.95** *NO Woof!*

The Horror of Dracula The first Hammer Dracula film, in which the infamous vampire is given a new, elegant and ruthless persona, as he battles Prof. Van Helsing after coming to England. Possibly the finest, most inspired version of Bram Stoker's macabre chestnut, and one that single-handedly revived the horror genre. *AKA:* Dracula.
1958 82m/C *GB* Peter Cushing, Christopher Lee, Michael Gough, Melissa Stribling, Carol Marsh, John Van Eyssen, Valerie Gaunt; *D:* Terence Fisher; *W:* Jimmy Sangster. **VHS, Beta, LV $14.95** *WAR, FCT, MLB* 🎬🎬🎬½

The Horror of Frankenstein Spoof of the standard Frankenstein story features philandering ex-med student Baron Frankenstein, whose interest in a weird and esoteric branch of science provides a shocking and up-to-date rendition of the age-old plot. Preceded by "Frankenstein Must Be Destroyed" and followed by "Frankenstein and the Monster from Hell."
1970 93m/C *GB* Ralph Bates, Kate O'Mara, Dennis Price, David Prowse; *D:* Jimmy Sangster. **VHS, Beta $59.99** *HBO, MLB* 🎬🎬

The Horror of It All A multi-faceted look at popular horror stars, including Karloff, Chaney, Lugosi, Price, and others, plus an examination of the dark side of the imaginative minds that produce horror. Also includes a behind-the-scenes peek at the creation of great horror scenes.
1991 58m/C Boris Karloff, Lon Chaney Sr., Bela Lugosi, John Barrymore, Lionel Atwill, John Carradine, Vincent Price. **VHS $24.98** *MPI, FCT* 🎬🎬

Horror of Party Beach Considered to be one of the all-time worst films. Features a mob of radioactive seaweed creatures who eat a slew of nubile, surf-minded teenagers. Featured song: "Zombie Stomp."
1964 71m/C John Scott, Alice Lyon, Allen Laurel; *D:* Del Tenney. **VHS, Beta $39.95** *PSM Woof!*

Horror of the Blood Monsters John Carradine made a career out of being in bad movies, and this one competes as one of the worst. This is an editor's nightmare, made up of black & white film spliced together and colorized. Vampires from outer space threaten to suck all the blood from the people of Earth. *AKA:* Vampire Men of the Lost Planet; Horror Creatures of the Prehistoric Planet; Creatures of the Prehistoric Planet; Creatures of the Red Planet; Flesh Creatures of the Red Planet; The Flesh Creatures; Space Mission of the Lost Planet.
1970 (PG) 85m/C *PH* John Carradine, Robert Dix, Vicki Volante, Jennifer Bishop; *D:* Al Adamson, George Joseph. **VHS, Beta** *VID, REP Woof!*

Horror of the Zombies Bikinied models are pursued by hooded zombies on board a pleasure yacht...the horror. Effete final installment in the "blind dead" trilogy; see also "Tombs of the Blind Dead" and "Return of the Evil Dead." *AKA:* El Buque Maldito.
1974 (R) 90m/C *SP* Maria Perschy, Jack Taylor; *W/D:* Armando de Ossorio. **VHS $59.95** *VID* 🎬

Horror Planet Alien creature needs a chance to breed before moving on to spread its horror. When a group of explorers disturbs it, the years of waiting are over, and the unlucky mother-to-be will never be the same. Graphic and sensationalistic, capitalizing on the popularity of "Aliens." *AKA:* Inseminoid.
1980 (R) 93m/C *GB* Robin Clarke, Jennifer Ashley, Stephanie Beacham, Judy Geeson, Stephen Grives, Victoria Tennant; *D:* Norman J. Warren. **VHS, Beta, LV $9.98** *SUE Woof!*

Horror Rises from the Tomb A 15th century knight and his assistant are beheaded for practicing witchcraft. Five hundred years later, they return to possess a group of vacationers and generally cause havoc.
1972 89m/C *SP* Paul Naschy, Vic Winner, Emma Cohen, Helga Line; *D:* Carlos Aured. **VHS, Beta $59.98** *WES, NLC, LOO* 🎬🎬

The Horror Show Serial killer fries in electric chair, an event that really steams him. So he goes after the cop who brought him in. Standard dead guy who won't die and wants revenge flick. *AKA:* House 3.
1989 (R) 95m/C Brion James, Lance Henriksen, Rita Taggart, Dedee Pfeiffer, Aron Eisenberg, Matt Clark; *D:* James Isaac; *W:* Alan Smithee, Leslie Boehm. **VHS, Beta $19.98** *MGM* 🎬

Horrors of Burke & Hare A gory tale about the exploits of a bunch of 19th-century grave robbers.
1971 94m/C Derren Nesbitt, Harry Andrews, Yootha Joyce; *D:* Vernon Sewell. **VHS, Beta, LV $19.95** *STE, NWV* 🎬

Horrors of the Red Planet Cheapo epic sees astronauts crash on Mars, meet its Wizard, and stumble into a few Oz-like creatures. Technically advised by Forrest J. Ackerman. *AKA:* The Wizard of Mars.
1964 81m/C John Carradine, Roger Gentry, Vic McGee; *D:* David L. Hewitt. **VHS, Beta $19.99** *GHV, MRV, REP* 🎬

The Horse A moving, mature Turkish film about a father and son trying to overcome socioeconomic obstacles and their own frailties in order to make enough money to send the boy to school. In Turkish with English subtitles. *AKA:* Horse, My Horse.
1982 116m/C *TU D:* Ali Ozgenturk. **VHS, Beta $69.95** *KIV, MRV, TAM* 🎬🎬🎬

Horse Feathers Huxley College has to beef up its football team to win the championship game, and the corrupt new college president knows just how to do it. Features some of the brothers' classic routines, and

the songs "Whatever It Is, I'm Against It" and "Everyone Says I Love You."
1932 67m/B Groucho Marx, Chico Marx, Harpo Marx, Zeppo Marx, Thelma Todd, David Landau, Nat Pendleton; *D:* Norman Z. MacLeod. **VHS, Beta, LV $19.95** *MCA* 🎬🎬🎬½

The Horse in the Gray Flannel Suit Disney comedy portrays an advertising executive who links his daughter's devotion to horses with a client's new ad campaign.
1968 (G) 114m/C Dean Jones, Ellen Janov, Fred Clark, Diane Baker, Lloyd Bochner, Kurt Russell; *D:* Norman Tokar. **VHS, Beta** *DIS, OM* 🎬🎬½

The Horse of Pride Chabrol takes a telling look at the everyday life of the peasants of Breton—both their pleasures and their sorrows. In French with English subtitles. French script booklet available. *AKA:* Le Cheval D'Orgueil.
1980 118m/C *FR* Jacques Dufilho, Francois Cluzet; *D:* Claude Chabrol. **VHS, Beta $59.95** *INT, APD, AUD* 🎬🎬½

The Horse Soldiers An 1863 Union cavalry officer is sent 300 miles into Confederate territory to destroy a railroad junction and is accompanied by a fellow officer who is also a pacifist doctor. Based on a true Civil War incident.
1959 114m/C John Wayne, William Holden, Hoot Gibson, Anna Lee, Russell Simpson, Strother Martin; *D:* John Ford. **VHS, Beta $19.98** *MGM, FOX* 🎬🎬½

The Horse Thief Noted as the first movie from the People's Republic of China to be released on video, this epic tells the tale of Norbu, a man who, exiled from his people for horse thievery, is forced to wander the Tibetan countryside with his family in search of work. His son dies while he is in exile, and he, a devout Buddhist, is ultimately forced to accept tribal work in a ritual exorcism, after which he pleads to be accepted back into his clan. Beautiful and image-driven, offering a rare glimpse into the Tibet you won't see in travel brochures. Filmed on location with locals as actors. In Mandarin with English subtitles. *AKA:* Daoma Zei.
1987 88m/C *CH D:* Tian Zhuangzhuang. **VHS $59.95** *KIV, FCT, TAM* 🎬🎬🎬

The Horse Without a Head Stolen loot has been hidden in a discarded toy horse which is now the property of a group of poor children. The thieves, however, have different plans. Good family fare originally shown on the Disney television show.
1963 89m/C Jean-Pierre Aumont, Herbert Lom, Leo McKern, Pamela Franklin, Vincent Winter; *D:* Don Chaffey. **VHS, Beta $69.95** *DIS* 🎬🎬½

Horsemasters A group of young riders enter a special training program in England to achieve the ultimate equestrian title of horsemaster, with Annette having to overcome her fear of jumping. Originally a two-part Disney television show, and released as a feature film in Europe.
1961 85m/C Tommy Kirk, Annette Funicello, Janet Munro, Tony Britton, Donald Pleasence, Jean Marsh, John Fraser, Millicent Martin; *D:* William Fairchild. **VHS, Beta $69.95** *DIS* 🎬🎬

Horsemen An Afghani youth enters the brutal buzkashi horse tournament to please his macho-minded father. Beautifully shot in Afghanistan and Spain by Claude Renoir.
1970 (PG) 109m/C Omar Sharif, Leigh Taylor-Young, Jack Palance, David De, Peter Jeffrey; *D:* John Frankenheimer; *W:* Dalton Trumbo. **VHS, Beta $69.95** *COL* 🎬½

Horseplayer A loner is drawn into a mysterious triangle of decadence and desire in this riveting psychothriller.

1991 (R) ?m/C Brad Dourif, Sammi Davis-Voss, M.K. Harris, Vic Tayback; **D:** Kurt Voss. **VHS, LV** $89.98 *REP ♂ ½*

The Horse's Mouth An obsessive painter discovers that he must rely upon his wits to survive in London. A hilarious adaptation of the Joyce Cary novel. The laserdisc version is accompanied by an episode of the British documentary series "The Art of Film" profiling Guinness and his screen career. *AKA:* The Oracle.
1958 93m/C *GB* Alec Guinness, Kay Walsh, Robert Coote, Renee Houston, Michael Gough; **D:** Ronald Neame. Academy Awards '58 Nominations: Best Adapted Screenplay; National Board of Review Awards '58: 5 Best Foreign Films of the Year, Best Supporting Actress (Walsh). **VHS, Beta, LV** $19.98 *SUE, VYG, HMV ♂♂♂*

The Hospital Cult favorite providing savage, unrelentingly sarcastic look at the workings of a chaotic metropolitan hospital beset by murders, witchdoctors, madness, and plain ineptitude. Scripted by Paddy Chayefsky.
1971 (PG) 101m/C George C. Scott, Diana Rigg, Barnard Hughes, Stockard Channing, Nancy Marchand, Richard Dysart; **D:** Arthur Hiller; **W:** Paddy Chayefsky. Academy Awards '71: Best Story & Screenplay; Nominations: Best Actor (Scott); Berlin International Film Festival '72: Silver Prize. **VHS, Beta** $19.98 *MGM, FOX ♂♂♂½*

Hospital Massacre Psychopathic killer is loose in a hospital. Seems he holds a grudge against the woman who laughed at his valentine when they were children twenty years earlier, and too bad for her that she just checked in as a patient. Former "Playboy" and Hefner playmate Benton frolics in dangerous health care situation presented by the Cannon organization. *AKA:* X-Ray; Ward 13; Be My Valentine, Or Else.
1981 (R) 89m/C Barbi Benton, Jon Van Ness, Chip Lucio; **D:** Boaz Davidson. **VHS, Beta** $59.95 *MGM Woof!*

Hospital of Terror A transmigratory religious fanatic who died on the operating table manages to possess a nurse (Jacobson) before he kicks the bucket, and once in his candystripe incarnation, vents his spleen on the doctors who botched his operation. It's got a little more plasma than Adamson's "AstroZombies," considered by many to be a world-class boner. *AKA:* Nurse Sherri; Terror Hospital; Beyond the Living.
1978 (R) 88m/C Jill Jacobson, Geoffrey Land, Marilyn Joi, Mary Kay Pass, Prentiss Moulden, Clayton Foster; **D:** Al Adamson. **VHS** $19.99 *SSI ♂♂*

The Hostage A young teenager is witness to a gruesome and clandestine burial. The two murderers responsible take it upon themselves to see that their secret is never told.
1967 (PG) 84m/C Don O'Kelly, Harry Dean Stanton, John Carradine, Danny Martins; **D:** Russell S. Doughten Jr. **VHS** $39.95 *ACN ♂♂½*

Hostage Arab terrorists hijack a plane and the passengers start to fight back. Filmed in South Africa.
1987 (R) 94m/C Karen Black, Kevin McCarthy, Wings Hauser; **D:** Hanro Mohr. **VHS, Beta** $79.95 *COL ♂½*

Hostage British Secret Service agent John Rennie is fed up after a difficult mission in Argentina. He thinks he can walk away clean but his superiors beg to differ. He's marked for murder but Rennie has a dangerous plan that could guarantee his safety—only if he returns to Argentina to set things in motion.

Based on the novel "No Place to Hide" by Ted Allbeury.
1992 (R) 100m/C Sam Neill, Talisa Soto, James Fox; **D:** Robert W. Young. **VHS, Beta** *PAR, PMS ♂♂*

The Hostage Tower In France, a group of international crime figures capture the visiting U.S. president's mother, hold her hostage in the Eiffel Tower and demand $30 million in ransom. Made for television.
1980 (PG) 97m/C Peter Fonda, Maud Adams, Britt Ekland, Billy Dee Williams, Keir Dullea, Douglas Fairbanks Jr., Rachel Roberts, Celia Johnson; **D:** Claudio Guzman. **VHS, Beta, LV** $69.98 *SUE ♂♂*

Hostages A gang of criminals kidnap a family on vacation at a Caribbean island.
1979 93m/C Stuart Whitman, Marisa Mell. **VHS, Beta** *NO ♂*

Hostages A harrowing docudrama about the Beirut hostage crisis which combines acutal news footage with scenes of the prisoners and their families. British newsman John McCarthy is kidnapped in 1986 and finds himself held with Irish teacher Brian Keenan, both victims of the Muslim fundamentalist group the Hezbollah. Over the course of years they are held with Americans Terry Anderson, Thomas Sutherland, and Frank Reed and, later, British envoy Terry Waite. Under desperate conditions the men try to hold on to their sanity and humanity as their families struggle for their release against a variety of bureaucratic nightmares and uncertainty. Filmed on location in England, Israel, and Lebanon. Made for cable television.
1993 90m/C Colin Firth, Ciaran Hinds, Jay O. Sanders, Josef Sommer, Harry Dean Stanton, Kathy Bates, Natasha Richardson, Conrad Asquith; **D:** David Wheatley; **W:** Bernard MacLaverty. **VHS** *IMP ♂♂♂*

Hostile Guns A law man discovers a woman he once loved is now an inmate he is transporting across the Texas badlands. Routine with the exception of cameos by veteran actors. Based on a story by Sloan Nibley and James Edward Grant.
1967 91m/C George Montgomery, Yvonne De Carlo, Tab Hunter, John Russell; *Cameos:* Brian Donlevy, Richard Arlen, Fuzzy Knight, Donald (Don "Red") Barry; **D:** R.G. Springsteen; **W:** Steve Fisher, Sloan Nibley. **VHS, LV** $14.95 *PAR ♂♂½*

Hostile Takeover A mild-mannered accountant finally cracks and takes his co-workers hostage. He faces the police in a tense showdown. *AKA:* Office Party.
1988 (R) 93m/C David Warner, Michael Ironside, Kate Vernon, Jayne Eastwood; **D:** George Mihalka. **VHS, Beta, LV** $89.95 *LIV ♂½*

Hot Blood Two bank robbers take an innocent woman hostage and thrust her in the midst of a huge family battle. Another lukewarm entry from the director of "The Arrogant."
1989 89m/C Sylvia Kristel, Alicia Moro, Aldo Sambrel, Gaspar Cano; **D:** Philippe Blot. **VHS, Beta** $79.95 *CAN ♂½*

Hot Box A Filipino-shot, low budget woofer. Prison flick about women who break out and foment a revolution.
1972 (R) 85m/C Andrea Cagan, Margaret Markov, Rickey Richardson, Laurie Rose; **D:** Joe Viola. **VHS, Beta** $24.98 *SUE Woof!*

Hot Bubblegum Three teenagers discover sex, the beach, rock 'n' roll, sex, drag racing, and sex.
1981 (R) 94m/C Jonathan Segall, Zachi Noy, Yiftach Katzur. **VHS, Beta** *PGN ♂*

Hot Child in the City A country girl goes to Los Angeles and searches through the city's fleshpots for her sister's killer. Music by Nick Glider, Lou Reed, Billy Idol, and Fun Boy Three.
1987 85m/C Leah Ayres Hendrix, Shari Shattuck, Geof Pryssir; **D:** John Flores. **VHS, Beta** $14.95 *PSM, PAR ♂*

Hot Chili Four sex-obsessed guys go to Mexico for fun and games, and find just that.
1985 (R) 91m/C Charles Schillaci, Allan J. Kayser, Louisa Moritz; **D:** William Sachs. **VHS, Beta** $79.95 *MGM Woof!*

Hot Chocolate Derek is a sultry Texas tycoon who wants to buy out the French chocolate factory run by Hays. After getting a look at her, work isn't all that's on his mind.
1992 (PG-13) 93m/C Bo Derek, Robert Hays. **VHS, LV** *LIV ♂♂*

Hot Dog...The Movie! There's an intense rivalry going on between an Austrian ski champ and his California challenger during the World Cup Freestyle competition in Squaw Valley. Snow movie strictly for teens or their equivalent.
1983 (R) 96m/C David Naughton, Patrick Houser, Shannon Tweed, Tracy N. Smith; **D:** Peter Markle. **VHS, Beta** $14.95 *MGM, FOX ♂½*

Hot Foot/A Happy Married Couple Two silent comedies: "Hot Foot" (1920), is about Dunn's hobo character in the Chaplin mold; "A Happy Married Couple" (1916), is about a young married couple whose puppy, as described in a letter, is mistaken for a baby by their parents.
1920 51m/B Bobbie Dunn, Neal Burns, Betty Compson. **VHS, Beta, 8mm** $24.95 *VYY ♂½*

Hot Lead & Cold Feet Twin brothers (one a gunfighter, the other meek and mild) compete in a train race where the winner will take ownership of a small western town. Dale not only plays both brothers, but also their tough father. Standard Disney fare.
1978 (G) 89m/C Jim Dale, Don Knotts, Karen Valentine; **D:** Robert Butler; **M:** John Williams. **VHS, Beta** $69.95 *DIS ♂♂*

The Hot Line The world's two superpowers become befuddled when the hot line connecting Washington and Moscow breaks down. Taylor's final film. *AKA:* The Day the Hot Line Got Hot; Le Rouble a Deux Faces; El Rublo de las dos Caras.
1969 87m/C Robert Taylor, Charles Boyer, George Chakiris, Dominique Fabre, Gerard Tichy; **D:** Etienne Perier. **VHS** *REP ♂½*

Hot Money A small-town drama about an ex-con who poses as an assistant sheriff and plots a million-dollar robbery during the town's 4th of July parade. Made shortly before Welles' death, and kept on the shelf for more than five years.
1979 78m/C Orson Welles, Michael Murphy, Bobby Pickett, Michelle Finney. **VHS, Beta** $79.95 *VMK ♂*

Hot Moves Four high school boys make a pact to lose their virginity before the end of the summer.
1984 (R) 89m/C Michael Zorek, Adam Silbar, Jill Schoelen, Debi Richter, Monique Gabrielle, Tami Holbrook, Virgil Frye; **D:** Jim Sotos. **VHS, Beta** $79.98 *VES ♂*

Hot Potato Black Belt Jones rescues a senator's daughter from a megalomaniacal general by using skull-thwacking footwork.
1976 (PG) 87m/C Jim Kelly, George Memmoli, Geoffrey Binney; **D:** Oscar Williams. **VHS, Beta** $59.95 *WAR ♂*

Hot Pursuit A woman who has been framed for murder runs from the law and a relentless hitman.

1984 (PG) 94m/C Mike Preston, Dina Merrill, Kerrie Keane. VHS, Beta $79.95 VMK ♫ ½

Hot Pursuit A prep-school bookworm resorts to Rambo-like tactics in tracking down his girlfriend and her family after being left behind for a trip to the tropics.
1987 (PG-13) 93m/C John Cusack, Robert Loggia, Jerry Stiller, Wendy Gazelle; D: Steven Lisberger. VHS, Beta, LV $79.95 PAR ♫ ½

Hot Resort Young American lads mix work and play when they sign on as summer help at an island resort. Typical teen sex fantasy.
1985 (R) 92m/C Bronson Pinchot, Tom Parsekian, Michael Berz, Linda Kenton, Frank Gorshin; D: John Robins. VHS, Beta $79.95 MGM ♫ ½

The Hot Rock A motley crew of bumbling thieves conspire to steal a huge, priceless diamond; a witty, gritty comedy that makes no moral excuses for its characters and plays like an early-'70s crime thriller gone awry. Written by William Goldman, from a Donald E. Westlake novel. The sequel, 1974's "Bank Shot," stars George C. Scott in the role created by Redford. AKA: How To Steal a Diamond in Four Easy Lessons.
1970 (PG) 97m/C Robert Redford, George Segal, Ron Leibman, Zero Mostel, Moses Gunn, William Redfield, Charlotte Rae, Topo Swope, Paul Sand; D: Peter Yates. VHS, Beta, LV FOX ♫♫♫

Hot Rod A young California hotrodder battles the evil sponsor of a drag race championship. AKA: Rebel of the Road.
1979 97m/C Greg Henry, Robert Culp, Pernell Roberts, Robin Mattson, Grant Goodeve; D: George Armitage. VHS, Beta $59.98 NLC ♫

Hot Rod Girl A concerned police officer (Conners) organizes supervised drag racing after illegal drag racing gets out of hand in his community. AKA: Hot Car Girl.
1956 75m/B Lori Nelson, Chuck Connors, John W. Smith; D: Leslie Martinson. VHS $16.95 SNC, NOS, MHV ♫

Hot Shot An inspirational tale involving a young soccer player who goes to great lengths to take training from a soccer star, played - of course - by Pele.
1986 (PG) 90m/C Pele, Jim Youngs, Billy Warlock, Weyman Thompson, Mario Van Peebles, David Groh; D: Rick King. VHS, Beta $39.98 WAR ♫ ½

Hot Shots! Another entry from "The Naked Gun" team of master movie parodists, this has lots of clever sight gags but the verbal humor often plummets to the ground. Spoofs "Top Gun" and similar gung-ho air corps adventures but doesn't forget other popular films including "Dances with Wolves" and "The Fabulous Baker Boys." Sheen is very funny as ace fighter pilot Sean "Topper" Harley who's to avenge the family honor. Great when you're in the mood for laughs that don't require thought.
1991 (PG-13) 85m/C Charlie Sheen, Cary Elwes, Valeria Golino, Lloyd Bridges, Kevin Dunn, Jon Cryer, William O'Leary, Kristy Swanson, Efrem Zimbalist Jr., Bill Irwin, Heidi Swedberg; Cameos: Charles Barkley, Bill Laimbeer; W/D: Jim Abrahams; M: Sylvester Levay. VHS $19.98 FXV ♫♫♫

Hot Shots! Part Deux Second "Hot Shots" outing isn't as good as the first, but it's not bad either. When Admiral Tug Benson (Bridges) is elected President (yes, of the U.S.), he calls on Sheen's newly pumped-up Topper to take on Saddam Hussein Rambo-style. Topper's love interest Ramada (Golino), returns but this time she's competing with Michelle (Bakke), a sexy CIA agent. Crenna spoofs his own role in the "Rambo"

films as Sheen's mentor. Look for real-life dad Martin in a spoof of "Apocalypse Now." Shtick flies as fast and furious as the bodies, with Bridges even getting a likely last chance to reprise his glory days of "Sea Hunt."
1993 (PG-13) 89m/C Charlie Sheen, Lloyd Bridges, Valeria Golino, Brenda Bakke, Richard Crenna, Miguel Ferrer, Rowan Atkinson, Jerry Haleva, Ryan Stiles, Michael Colyar; Cameos: Martin Sheen, Bob Vila; D: Jim Abrahams; W: Pat Proft, Jim Abrahams; M: Basil Poledouris. VHS NYR ♫♫ ½

Hot Spell In an attempt to repair her marriage and unify her family, a mother plans a reunion-birthday party for her husband. Despair reigns in this sultry, Southern melodrama.
1958 86m/B Shirley Booth, Anthony Quinn, Shirley MacLaine, Earl Holliman, Eileen Heckart; D: Daniel Mann. VHS, Beta $19.95 KRT ♫ ½

The Hot Spot An amoral drifter arrives in a small Texas town and engages in affairs with two women, including his boss's over sexed wife and a young woman with her own secrets. Things begin to heat up when he decides to plot a bank robbery.
1990 (R) 120m/C Don Johnson, Virginia Madsen, Jennifer Connelly, Charles Martin Smith; D: Dennis Hopper; M: Jack Nitzsche. VHS, LV $14.98 ORI, FCT ♫♫ ½

Hot Stuff Officers on a burglary task force decide the best way to obtain convictions is to go into the fencing business themselves.
1980 (PG) 91m/C Dom DeLuise, Jerry Reed, Suzanne Pleshette, Ossie Davis; D: Dom DeLuise. VHS, Beta, LV $14.95 COL ♫

Hot Summer in Barefoot County A state law enforcement officer on the search for illegal moonshiners finds more than he bargained for.
1974 (R) 90m/C Sherry Robinson, Tonia Bryan, Dick Smith; D: Will Zens. VHS, Beta PGN ♫♫

Hot T-Shirts A small town bar owner needs a boost for business, finding the answer in wet T-shirt contests. Softcore trash.
1979 (R) 86m/C Ray Holland, Stephanie Lawlor, Pauline Rose, Corinne Alphen; D: Chuck Vincent. VHS, Beta $39.95 MCA Woof!

Hot Target An ideal mother becomes obsessed with the stranger who seduced her, even after she finds out he's a thief planning to rob her home.
1985 (R) 93m/C NZ Simone Griffeth, Steve Marachuk; D: Denis Lewiston. VHS, Beta, LV $79.98 LIV, VES ♫

The Hot, the Cool, and the Vicious A quiet town turns into a bloody, martial arts playground when three hombres trade blows in a tavern.
1987 ?m/C Wang Tao, Tommy Lee, Sun Chia-Lin. VHS $34.95 OCE ♫

Hot Times Low-budget comedy about a high school boy who, after striking out with the high school girls, decides to go to New York and have the time of his life.
1974 (R) 80m/C Gail Lorber, Amy Farber, Henry Cory; D: Jim McBride. VHS, Beta $39.95 MON ♫

Hot to Trot! A babbling idiot links up with a talking horse in an updated version of the "Francis, the Talking Mule" comedies, by way of Mr. Ed. The equine voice is provided by Candy. Some real funny guys are wasted here.
1988 (PG) 90m/C Bob Goldthwait, Dabney Coleman, Virginia Madsen, Jim Metzler, Cindy Pickett, Tim Kazurinsky, Santos Morales, Barbara Whinnery, Garry Kluger; D: Michael Dinner; V: John Candy. VHS, Beta, LV $19.95 WAR ♫

Hot Touch An art forger with a large heist is besieged by a slashing maniac, and must discover the culprit.
198? 92m/C Wayne Rogers, Samantha Eggar, Marie-France Pisier, Melvyn Douglas. VHS, Beta $69.95 TWE, HHE Woof!

Hot Under the Collar Jerry is a weasel who tries to seduce the luscious Monica by using hypnosis. But his plans backfire and instead Monica enters a convent and takes a vow of chastity. This isn't going to stop Jerry, he tries posing as a priest and even dressing as a nun in order to get her out. Things get even more complicated when a mobster, looking for a fortune in stolen diamonds, sneaks into the convent.
1991 (R) 87m/C Richard Gabai, Angela Visser, Daniel Friedman, Mindy Clarke, Tane McClure; D: Richard Gabai. VHS $89.99 HBO ♫ ½

Hot Water/Safety Last Two classic Harold Lloyd silent comedies, "Hot Water" (1924) and "Safety Last" (1923). "Safety Last" features one of Lloyd's most famous stunt scenes, where he is hanging from the hands of a giant clock on the side of a building, high above the city.
1924 81m/B Harold Lloyd. VHS, Beta TLF ♫ ½

Hot Wire Tired comedy about the unscrupulous side of the car repossession racket.
197? 92m/C George Kennedy, Strother Martin. VHS, Beta PGN ♫ ½

Hotel A pale rehash of the "Grand Hotel" formula about an array of rich characters interacting in a New Orleans hotel. From the Arthur Hailey potboiler; the basis for the television series.
1967 (PG) 125m/C Rod Taylor, Catherine Spaak, Karl Malden, Melvyn Douglas, Merle Oberon, Michael Rennie, Richard Conte, Kevin McCarthy; D: Richard Quine. VHS, Beta $59.95 WAR ♫ ½

Hotel Colonial A young Italian idealist ventures to Columbia to retrieve the body of his brother, who reportedly killed himself. Once there, he finds the dead man is not his brother, and decides to investigate.
1988 (R) 103m/C IT Robert Duvall, John Savage, Rachel Ward, Massimo Troisi; D: Cinzia Torrini. VHS, Beta, LV, 8mm $19.98 SUE, NLC ♫ ½

Hotel du Lac A made-for-British-television adaptation of the Anita Brookner novel about a woman writer languishing at a Swiss lakefront hotel.
1986 75m/C GB Anna Massey, Denholm Elliott, Googie Withers; D: Giles Foster. VHS, Beta $19.95 FOX, TVC ♫♫

Hotel Imperial Set in 1917 Budapest, six Hungarian soldiers ride into a frontier town and find it occupied by Russians. Hall plays Lieutenant Almasy, who takes refuge in the Hotel Imperial. Orchestra scored.
1927 84m/B Pola Negri, James Hall, George Siegmann, Max Davidson; D: Mauritz Stiller. VHS $19.95 GPV ♫♫

The Hotel New Hampshire The witless, amoral adaptation of John Irving's novel about a very strange family's adventures in New Hampshire, Vienna and New York City, which include gang rape, incest, and Kinski in a bear suit.
1984 (R) 110m/C Jodie Foster, Rob Lowe, Beau Bridges, Nastassia Kinski, Wallace Shawn, Wilford Brimley, Amanda Plummer, Anita Morris, Matthew Modine, Lisa Banes; D: Tony Richardson. VHS, Beta, LV $29.98 VES ♫♫

Hotel Reserve A Nazi spy is reportedly afoot in a French resort during World War II, and tension mounts as the guests attempt to flush him out. Critical response to this film is wildly split; some find it obvious, while others

call it well-done and suspenseful. Based on the novel ''Epitaph for a Spy'' by Eric Ambler.
1944 79m/C *GB* James Mason, Lucie Mannheim, Raymond Lovell, Julien Mitchell, Martin Miller, Herbert Lom, Frederick Valk, Valentine Dyall; *D:* Victor Hanbury, Lance Comfort, Max Greene. **VHS, Beta $19.98** *TTC, RXM* 🎬🎬🎬

Hothead A heedless, impulsive soccer player's behavior gets him cut from the team, fired from his mill job, and booted out of his favorite bar. In French with English subtitles or dubbed. *AKA:* Coup de Tete.
1978 98m/C *FR* Patrick Dewaere, Jean Bouise, Michel Aumont, France Dougnac; *D:* Jean-Jacques Annaud. **VHS, Beta $59.95** *COL* 🎬🎬

Hotline After taking a job answering phones at a crisis center, a woman becomes the next target of a psychotic killer. Made for television.
1982 96m/C Lynda Carter, Steve Forrest, Granville Van Dusen, Monte Markham, James Booth; *D:* Jerry Jameson. **VHS** *NO* 🎬🎬

H.O.T.S. A sex-filled fraternity rivalry film, starring a slew of ex-Playboy Playmates in wet shirts. Screenplay co-written by exploitation star Cheri Caffaro. *AKA:* T & A Academy.
1979 (R) 95m/C Susan Kiger, Lisa London, Kimberly Cameron, Danny Bonaduce, Steve Bond; *D:* Gerald Seth Sindell. **VHS, Beta $69.98** *LIV, VES, SIM* 🎬

Houdini Historically inaccurate but entertaining biopic of the infamous magician and escapologist. Chronicles his rise to stardom, his efforts to contact his dearly departed mother through mediums (a prequel to ''Ghost''?), and his heart-stopping logic-defying escapes. First screen teaming of Leigh and Curtis, who had already been married for two years.
1953 107m/C Tony Curtis, Janet Leigh, Torin Thatcher, Angela Clark, Stefan Schnabel, Ian Wolfe, Sig Rumann, Michael Pate, Connie Gilchrist, Mary Murphy, Tor Johnson; *D:* George Marshall. **VHS $14.95** *PAR, FCT* 🎬🎬½

The Hound of the Baskervilles The curse of a demonic hound threatens descendants of an English noble family until Holmes and Watson solve the mystery. Also available with ''Sherlock Holmes Faces Death'' on Laser Disc.
1939 80m/B *GB* Basil Rathbone, Nigel Bruce, Richard Greene, John Carradine, Wendy Barrie, Lionel Atwill, E.E. Clive; *D:* Sidney Lanfield. **VHS, Beta $14.95** *KUI, FOX* 🎬🎬

The Hound of the Baskervilles Cushing's not half bad as Sherlock Holmes as he investigates the mystery of a supernatural hound threatening the life of a Dartmoor baronet. Dark and moody.
1959 86m/C *GB* Peter Cushing, Christopher Lee, Andre Morell; *D:* Terence Fisher. **VHS, Beta, LV $19.98** *MGM, MLB, FOX* 🎬🎬½

The Hound of the Baskervilles Awful spoof of the Sherlock Holmes classic with Cook as Holmes and Moore as Watson (and Holmes' mother). Even the cast can't save it.
1977 84m/C Dudley Moore, Peter Cook, Denholm Elliott, Joan Greenwood, Spike Milligan, Jessie Matthews, Roy Kinnear; *D:* Paul Morrissey. **VHS** *ATV* Woof!

The Hound of the Baskervilles Another remake of the Sherlock Holmes story which finds the great detective investigating the murder of Sir Charles Baskerville and a mysterious haunted moor.
1983 100m/C *GB* Ian Richardson, Donald Churchill, Martin Shaw, Nicholas Clay, Denholm Elliott, Brian Blessed, Ronald Lacey; *D:* Douglas Hickox. **VHS, Beta $59.95** *PAR* 🎬🎬

Hour of Decision When a newspaper columnist turns up dead, a reporter investigates the murder. Things get hairy when he finds the prime suspect is his own wife.
1957 81m/B *GB* Jeff Morrow, Hazel Court, Lionel Jeffries, Anthony Dawson, Mary Laura Wood; *D:* C. Pennington Richards. **VHS, Beta $16.95** *SNC* 🎬½

Hour of the Assassin A mercenary is hired to assassinate a South American ruler, and a CIA operative is sent to stop him. Shot in Peru.
1986 (R) 96m/C Erik Estrada, Robert Vaughn; *D:* Luis Llosa. **VHS, Beta $79.95** *MGM* 🎬½

Hour of the Gun Western saga chronicles what happens after the gunfight at the OK Corral. Garner plays the grim Wyatt Earp on the trail of vengeance after his brothers are killed. Robards is excellent as the crusty Doc Holliday.
1967 100m/C James Garner, Jason Robards Jr., Robert Ryan, Albert Salmi, Charles Aidman, Steve Ihnat, Jon Voight; *D:* John Sturges; *M:* Jerry Goldsmith. **VHS $14.95** *MGM* 🎬🎬

Hour of the Star The poignant, highly acclaimed feature debut by Amaral, about an innocent young woman moving to the city of Sao Paulo from the impoverished countryside of Brazil, and finding happiness despite her socioeconomic failures. Based on Clarice Lispector's novel. In Portuguese with English subtitles. *AKA:* A Hora Da Estrela.
1985 96m/C *BR* Marcelia Cartaxo; *D:* Suzana Amaral. **VHS, Beta $79.95** *KIV, TAM* 🎬🎬🎬½

Hour of the Wolf An acclaimed, surreal view into the tormented inner life of a painter as he and his wife are isolated on a small northern island. Cinematography by Sven Nykvist. In Swedish with English subtitles.
1968 89m/B *SW* Max von Sydow, Liv Ullmann, Ingrid Thulin, Erland Josephson, Gertrud Fridh, Gudrun Brost; *D:* Ingmar Bergman. **VHS, Beta $19.98** *MGM, MRV, FCT* 🎬🎬🎬

House A horror novelist moves into his dead aunt's supposedly haunted house only to find that the monsters don't necessarily stay in the closets. His worst nightmares come to life as he writes about his Vietnam experiences and is forced to relive the tragic events, but these aren't the only visions that start springing to life. It sounds depressing, but is actually a funny, intelligent ''horror'' flick. Followed by several lesser sequels.
1986 (R) 93m/C William Katt, George Wendt, Richard Moll, Kay Lenz; *D:* Steve Miner. **VHS, Beta, LV $19.95** *NWV, STE* 🎬🎬🎬

House 2: The Second Story The flaccid sequel to the haunted-house horror flick concerns two innocent guys who move into the family mansion and discover Aztec ghosts. Has none of the humor which helped the first movie along.
1987 (PG-13) 88m/C John Ratzenberger, Arye Gross, Royal Dano, Bill Maher, Jonathan Stark; *D:* Ethan Wiley. **VHS, Beta, LV $19.95** *NWV, STE* 🎬

House 4: Home Deadly Home Another bad real estate epic on a par with the other unusually inept ''House'' efforts. When her husband (Katt) is killed in an auto accident, a young woman and her daughter move into a mysterious old house. Terror begins to confront them at every turn. We can only hope.
1991 (R) 93m/C Terri Treas, Scott Burkholder, Melissa Clayton, William Katt, Ned Romero; *D:* Lewis Abernathy. **VHS, LV $89.95** *COL, NLC* 🎬½

House Across the Bay Raft, an imprisoned nightclub owner, finds that he is being duped by his attorney who's eager to get his hooks into the lingerie-clad prisoner's wife. But prison isn't going to stop the bitter husband from getting his revenge.
1940 88m/B George Raft, Walter Pidgeon, Joan Bennett, Lloyd Nolan, Gladys George; *D:* Archie Mayo. **VHS, Beta** *NO* 🎬🎬½

The House by the Cemetery When a family moves into a house close to a cemetery, strange things start to happen to them. *AKA:* Quella Villa Accanto Al Cimitero.
1983 (R) 84m/C *IT* Katherine MacColl, Paolo Malco; *D:* Lucio Fulci. **VHS, Beta $69.98** *LIV, VES* 🎬

House Calls A widowed surgeon turns into a swinging bachelor until he meets a witty but staid English divorcee. Wonderful dialogue. Jackson is exceptional. Made into a short-lived TV series.
1978 (PG) 98m/C Walter Matthau, Glenda Jackson, Art Carney, Richard Benjamin, Candice Azzara; *D:* Howard Zieff. **VHS, Beta, LV $69.95** *MCA* 🎬🎬🎬

The House in Marsh Road A faithless husband decides to rid himself of She Who Must Be Obeyed, but his wife's ghost-friend intervenes.
1960 70m/B *GB* Tony Wright, Patricia Dainton, Sandra Dorne, Derek Aylward, Sam Kydd; *D:* Montgomery Tully. **VHS $19.98** *SNC* 🎬🎬

House of Dark Shadows A 150-year-old vampire, accidentally released by a handyman, wreaks havoc on the inhabitants of the Collinswood mansion. Based on the TV daytime soap.
1970 (PG) 97m/C Jonathan Frid, Joan Bennett, Grayson Hall, Kathryn Leigh Scott, Roger Davis, Nancy Barrett, John Carlen, Thayer David; *D:* Dan Curtis. **VHS, Beta $19.98** *MGM* 🎬🎬

House of Death The ex-Playmate of the Year runs in hysterical fear from a knife-wielding lunatic.
1982 (R) 88m/C Susan Kiger, William T. Hicks, Jody Kay, Martin Tucker, Jennifer Chase. **VHS, Beta $59.95** *GEM* 🎬

The House of Dies Drear A modern-day African American family moves into an old house that turns out to be haunted by the ghost of a long dead abolitionist. The family is transported back to the days of slavery as they interact with the ghost. Based on the story by Virginia Hamilton. Aired on PBS as part of the ''Wonderworks'' family movie series.
1988 107m/C Howard E. Rollins Jr., Moses Gunn, Shavar Ross, Gloria Foster, Clarence Williams III; *D:* Allan Goldstein. **VHS $29.95** *HMV, PME* 🎬

House of Errors Two deliverymen pose as reporters to safeguard a prototype machine gun from the bad guys. Contrived plot consisting of outdated comic routines. This was Marsh's last film.
1942 63m/B Harry Langdon, Marian Marsh, Ray Walker, Betty Blythe, John Holland; *D:* Bernard B. Ray. **VHS $19.95** *NOS* 🎬½

House of Evil Karloff operates a torture dungeon and has harmless musical toys turning into mechanical killers. One of his final four films. Like the others, this is a Mexican production but Karloff filmed his scenes in Los Angeles. *AKA:* Dance of Death; Macabre Serenade.
1968 (PG) 75m/C *MX* Boris Karloff, Andres Garcia; *D:* Juan Ibanez. **VHS, Beta $59.95** *SNC, MPI, SVS* Woof!

House of Fear Holmes and Watson investigate the murders of several members of the Good Comrades Club, men who were neither good nor comradely.
1945 69m/B Basil Rathbone, Nigel Bruce, Dennis Hoey, Aubrey Mather, Paul Cavanagh, Gavin Muir; D: Roy William Neill. VHS, Beta $14.98 FOX ♂♂½

House of Frankenstein An evil scientist (Karloff) escapes from prison, and, along with his hunchback manservant, revives Dracula, Frankenstein's monster, and the Wolfman to carry out his dastardly deeds. An allstar cast helps this horror fest along.
1944 71m/B Boris Karloff, J. Carroll Naish, Lon Chaney Jr., John Carradine, Elena Verdugo, Anne Gwynne, Lionel Atwill, Peter Coe, George Zucco, Glenn Strange, Sig Rumann; D: Erle C. Kenton. VHS $14.98 MCA ♂♂½

House of Games The directorial debut of playwright Mamet is a tale about an uptight female psychiatrist who investigates the secret underworld of con-artistry and becomes increasingly involved in an elaborate con game. She's led along her crooked path by smooth-talking con-master Mantegna. A taut, well plotted psychological suspense film with many twists and turns. Stylishly shot, with dialogue which has that marked Mamet cadence. Most of the leads are from Mamet's theater throng (including his wife, Crouse).
1987 (R) 102m/C Joe Mantegna, Lindsay Crouse, Lilia Skala, J.T. Walsh, Meshach Taylor; D: David Mamet. VHS, Beta, LV $19.99 HBO, FCT ♂♂♂

The House of Lurking Death Detectives Tommy and Tuppence find a box of chocolates laced with arsenic at the home of Lois Hargreaves, and the mad old maid is the prime suspect. Based on the Agatha Christie story. Made for British television.
1984 60m/C GB James Warwick, Francesca Annis; W: Agatha Christie. VHS, Beta $14.95 PAV ♂♂½

House of Mystery For a shot at some priceless jewels stolen by the host from a Hindu princess, several guests gather for a weekend in a spine-tingling mansion. A creepy curse keeps them looking over their shoulders.
1934 62m/C Ed Lowry, Verna Hillie, Brandon Hurst, George "Gabby" Hayes; D: William Nigh. VHS $12.95 SNC, DVT, MLB ♂♂

House of Mystery Splendid British remake of 1934 film in which the detective does some true sleuthing to catch the culprits. An old widow is killed for her jewels, but the murderers can't locate the goods. After they try a series of fiendish plans to retrieve them, the detective must work to stop the crooks. AKA: At the Villa Rose.
1941 61m/B GB Kenneth Kent, Judy Kelly, Peter Murray Hill, Walter Rilla, Ruth Maitland; D: Walter Summers. VHS $24.95 NOS, DVT ♂♂½

The House of 1000 Dolls Doleful, not dollful, exploitation thriller as magician Price drugs young girls and sells them to slavery rings. An international production set in Tangiers; dialogue is dubbed. AKA: Haus Der Tausend Freuden.
1967 79m/C GE SP GB Vincent Price, Martha Hyer, George Nader, Ann Smyrner, Maria Rohm; D: Jeremy Summers. VHS, Beta $59.98 HBO ♂

House of Psychotic Women Naschy, Spain's premier horror movie star, plays a studly drifter who winds up in the home of three sisters, one with a horribly scarred arm, one confined to a wheelchair and the other a nymphomaniac. No problemo thinks the hirsute Spaniard, until a series of bizarre murders—in which the victims eyes are ripped out—spoils his fun. Naschy, who usually sprouts fur and fangs, actually doesn't turn into a werewolf. Catchy but inappropriate score. A must for Naschy/bad movie fans. AKA: Los Ojos Azules de la Muneca Rota.
1973 (R) 87m/C SP Paul Naschy, Maria Perscyh, Diana Lorys, Eva Leon, Ines Morales, Tony Pica; D: Carlos Aured; W: Paul Naschy. VHS, Beta $14.98 VID Woof!

The House of Secrets A Yank travels to Britain to collect an inheritance and stays in a dusty old mansion filled with an odd assortment of characters.
1937 70m/B Leslie Fenton, Muriel Evans, Noel Madison, Sidney Blackmer, Morgan Wallace, Holmes Herbert; D: Roland D. Reed. VHS, Beta $16.95 SNC ♂♂

The House of Seven Corpses A crew attempts to film a horror movie in a Victorian manor where seven people died in a variety of gruesome manners. Things take a turn for the ghoulish when a crew member becomes possesed by the house's evil spirits. Good, low budget fun with a competent "B" cast. Filmed in what was the Utah governor's mansion.
1973 (PG) 90m/C John Ireland, Faith Domergue, John Carradine, Carole Wells; D: Paul Harrison. VHS $29.95 GEM, MRV, NEG ♂♂

House of Shadows A 20-year-old murder comes back to haunt the victim's friends in this tale of mystery and terror.
1983 90m/C John Gavin, Yvonne De Carlo, Leonor Manso; D: Richard Wulicher. VHS, Beta $49.95 MED ♂♂½

House of Strangers Conte, in a superb performance, swears vengeance on his brothers, whom he blames for his father's death. Robinson, in a smaller part than you'd expect from his billing, is nevertheless excellent as the ruthless banker father who sadly reaps a reward he didn't count on. Based on Philip Yordan's "I'll Never Go There Again."
1949 101m/B Edward G. Robinson, Susan Hayward, Richard Conte, Luther Adler, Efrem Zimbalist Jr., Debra Paget; D: Joseph L. Mankiewicz. VHS $39.98 FOX, FCT ♂♂♂½

House of Terror A woman and her boyfriend plot to kill her rich boss, while they too are being stalked by some undefined horror.
1987 91m/C Jennifer Bishop, Arell Blanton, Jacquelyn Hyde. VHS, Beta $79.95 TWE ♂

The House of the Arrow Investigating the murder of a French widow, who was killed by a poisoned arrow, a detective must sort through a grab bag of potential suspects. Superior adaptation of the A.E.W. Mason thriller.
1953 73m/B GB Oscar Homolka, Yvonne Furneaux, Robert Urquhart; D: Michael Anderson Sr. VHS, Beta $16.95 NOS, SNC ♂♂

House of the Black Death Horror titans Chaney and Carradine manage to co-star in this as warring warlocks, yet they share no scenes together! Chaney is the evil warlock (the horns are a giveaway) holding people hostage in the title edifice. AKA: Blood of the Man Devil; Night of the Beast.
1965 89m/B Lon Chaney Jr., John Carradine, Katherine Victor, Tom Drake, Andrea King; D: Harold Daniels, Reginald LeBorg. VHS $15.95 NOS, LOO ♂½

House of the Damned A young woman, a mental hospital, a murdered father, a priceless gold statue—mix together and you get a mystery horror movie. A woman tries to solve her father's murder.

19?? 89m/C Donald Pleasence, Michael Dunn. VHS, Beta NO ♂½

House of the Dead Man is trapped inside a haunted house. Scary.
1980 100m/C John Erikson, Charles Aidman, Bernard Fox, Ivor Francis. VHS NO ♂

House of the Living Dead Brattling Manor harbors a murderous and flesh-eating secret ready to lure the unsuspecting. Don't you be one. AKA: Doctor Maniac.
1973 87m/C SA Mark Burns, Shirley Anne Field, David Oxley; D: Ray Austin. VHS, Beta $29.95 UHV, HHE ♂

House of the Long Shadows Comedy mixes with gore, as four of the horror screen's best leading men team up for the first time, although they have only minor roles. Might have been a contender, but Arnaz is miscast as author who stays in spooky house on a bet with Todd. Some wit but not enough. Based on the play "Seven Keys to Baldpate" by George M. Cohan (and novel by Earl Derr Biggers).
1982 (PG) 96m/C Vincent Price, Christopher Lee, Peter Cushing, John Carradine, Desi Arnaz Jr., Sheila Keith, Richard Todd; D: Pete Walker. VHS, Beta $69.95 MGM ♂½

House of the Rising Sun A Los Angeles reporter goes under cover for a story on an exclusive brothel only to discover the owner is a psychopath who has very permanent ways of dealing with troublesome employees. Music by Tina Turner and Bryan Ferry.
1987 86m/C John York, Bud Davis, Deborah Wakeham, Frank Annese; D: Greg Gold. VHS, Beta $79.95 PSM, PAR ♂½

House of the Yellow Carpet A couple try to sell an ancient Persian carpet heirloom, and in doing so transgress some unwritten mystical law. Havoc ensues.
1984 90m/C Roland Josephson, Beatrice Romand; D: Carlo Lizzani. VHS, Beta $69.98 LIV ♂½

The House of Usher Some serious overacting by Reed (as Roderick) and Pleasance (as his balmy brother) almost elevate this Poe retread to "so bad it's good" status, and there are a few admirably grisly moments. But, without other camp virtues, it's merely dreary. Adapted by Michael J. Murray and filmed in South Africa.
1988 (R) 92m/C Oliver Reed, Donald Pleasence, Romy Windsor; D: Alan Birkinshaw; W: Michael J. Murray. VHS, LV $79.95 COL ♂

House of Wax A deranged sculptor (Price, who else?) builds a sinister wax museum that showcases creations that were once alive. A remake of the early horror flick "Mystery of the Wax Museum," and one of the 50s' most popular 3-D films. This one still has the power to give the viewer the creeps, thanks to another chilling performance by Price. Look for a very young Charles Bronson, as well as Carolyn "Morticia Addams" Jones as a victim.
1953 (PG) 88m/C Vincent Price, Frank Lovejoy, Carolyn Jones, Phyllis Kirk, Paul Cavanagh, Charles Bronson; D: Andre de Toth. VHS, Beta, LV $19.98 WAR, MLB ♂♂♂

House of Whipcord Beautiful young women are kidnapped and tortured in this British gore-o-rama. Awful and degrading.
1975 102m/C GB Barbara Markham, Patrick Barr, Ray Brooks, Penny Irving, Anne Michelle; D: Pete Walker. VHS, Beta $39.95 MON, LIV Woof!

The House on Carroll Street New York 1951, the middle of the McCarthy era. A young woman overhears a plot to smuggle Nazi war criminals into the U.S. She's already

lost her job because of accusations of subversion, and it's not easy persuading FBI agent Daniels that she knows what she's talking about. Contrived plot and melodramatic finale help sink this period piece.
1988 (PG) 111m/C Kelly McGillis, Jeff Daniels, Mandy Patinkin, Jessica Tandy; *D:* Peter Yates; *W:* Walter Bernstein. **VHS, Beta, LV $89.99** *HBO ⅄½*

The House on Chelouche Street In Tel-Aviv, during the summer of 1946, 15-year-old Sami, an Egyptian immigrant, tries to help support his mother and family during the upheavals of Palestine under the British mandate. A well thought-out story detailing the struggles of a North African Jewish family before the creation of the country of Israel. In Hebrew with English subtitles.
1973 111m/C *IS* Gila Almagor, Michal Bat-Adam, Shai K. Ophir; *D:* Moshe Mizrahi. **VHS, Beta $29.95** *VYY, NCJ, AUD ⅄⅄½*

The House on Garibaldi Street Spy drama about the capture of Nazi war criminal Adolph Eichmann in Argentina and his extradition to Israel for trial. Based on the book by Isser Harel. Made for television.
1979 96m/C Chaim Topol, Nick Mancuso, Martin Balsam, Janet Suzman, Leo McKern, Charles Gray, Alfred Burke; *D:* Peter Collinson. **VHS, Beta $14.95** *FRH, SWC ⅄⅄½*

House on Haunted Hill A wealthy man throws a haunted house party and offers ten thousand dollars to anyone who can survive the night there. Vintage cheap horror from the master of the macabre Castle. Remembered for Castle's in-theater gimmick of dangling a skeleton over the audiences' heads in the film's initial release. Also available with "Attack of the 50-Foot Woman" on laserdisc.
1958 75m/B Vincent Price, Carol Ohmart, Richard Long, Alan Marshal; *D:* William Castle. **VHS, Beta, LV $14.98** *FOX, SNC, FCT ⅄⅄½*

House on Marsh Road Rare British mystery involving poltergeists and murder in a haunted house. *AKA:* The Invisible Creature.
1960 ?m/C *GB* **VHS $20** *SMW ⅄⅄*

The House on Skull Mountain The four surviving relatives of a deceased voodoo priestess are in for a bumpy night as they gather at the House on Skull Mountain for the reading of her will.
1974 (PG) 85m/C Victor French, Janee Michelle, Mike Evans, Jean Durand; *D:* Ron Honthaner. **VHS, Beta $59.98** *FOX ⅄½*

The House on Sorority Row Less-than-harrowing story of what happens when seven sorority sisters have a last fling and get back at their housemother at the same time. *AKA:* House of Evil; Seven Sisters.
1983 90m/C Eileen Davidson, Kathy McNeil, Robin Meloy; *D:* Mark Rosman. **VHS, Beta, LV $79.95** *VES ⅄½*

The House on Straw Hill A successful novelist is intrigued by an attractive woman who lives in an isolated farmhouse. Her presence inspires gory hallucinations, lust and violence. *AKA:* Expose.
1976 (R) 84m/C Udo Kier, Linda Hayden, Fiona Richmond; *D:* James K. Clarke. **VHS, Beta $19.95** *STE, NWV, MED ⅄½*

House on the Edge of the Park A frustrated would-be womanizer takes revenge on a parade of women during an all-night party. *AKA:* La Casa Nel Parco.
1984 91m/C *IT* David Hess, Annie Belle, Lorraine De Selle; *D:* Ruggero Deodato. **VHS, Beta $69.98** *LIV, VES Woof!*

The House on Tombstone Hill An old, abandoned mansion seems like a good investment to a group of friends. Wrong! The original owner is still around and doesn't like strangers coming to visit.
1992 95m/C Doug Gibson, John Cerna, Sarah Newhouse; *W/D:* J. Riffel. **VHS $89.95** *AIP ⅄½*

House Party A light-hearted, black hip-hop version of a 1950s teen comedy with rap duo Kid 'n' Play. After his father grounds him for fighting, a high-schooler attempts all sorts of wacky schemes to get to his friend's party. Sleeper hit features real-life music rappers and some dynamite dance numbers.
1990 (R) 100m/C Christopher Reid, Christopher Martin, Lawrence Martin, Tisha Campbell, Paul Anthony, Kid 'N' Play, A.J. Johnson, Full Force, Robin Harris; *D:* Reginald Hudlin. **VHS, Beta, LV $14.95** *COL, FCT, NLC ⅄⅄½*

House Party 2: The Pajama Jam Rap stars Kid 'N' Play are back in this hip-hop sequel to the original hit. At Harris Univeristy Kid 'N' Play hustle up overdue tuition by holding a campus "jammie jam jam." A stellar cast shines in this rap-powered pajama bash.
1991 (R) 94m/C Christopher Reid, Christopher Martin, Tisha Campbell, Iman, Queen Latifah, George Stanford Brown, Martin Lawrence; *D:* Doug McHenry, George Jackson. **VHS, LV $19.95** *COL, NLC ⅄⅄½*

The House that Bled to Death Strange things happen to a family when they move into a run-down house where a murder occurred years before.
1981 60m/C Nicholas Ball, Rachel Davies, Brian Croucher, Pat Maynard, Emma Ridley. **VHS, Beta $29.95** *LIV ⅄*

The House that Dripped Blood A Scotland Yard inspector discovers the history of an English country house while investigating an actor's disappearance. Four horror tales written by Robert Bloch comprise the body of this omnibus creeper, following the successful "Tales from the Crypt" mold. Duffell's debut as director.
1971 (PG) 101m/C *GB* Christopher Lee, Peter Cushing, Jon Pertwee, Denholm Elliott, Ingrid Pitt, John Bennett, Tom Adams, Joss Ackland, Chloe Franks; *D:* Peter Duffell; *W:* Robert Bloch. **VHS, Beta $59.95** *PSM ⅄⅄½*

The House that Vanished Semi-exploitative fare about a beautiful young model who witnesses a murder in a house but later can't find the place. Her boyfriend is skeptical. *AKA:* Scream and Die.
1973 (R) 84m/C *GB* Andrea Allan, Karl Lanchbury, Judy Matheson; *D:* Joseph Larraz. **VHS, Beta $14.98** *MED ⅄*

House Where Evil Dwells An American family is subjected to a reign of terror when they move into an old Japanese house possessed by three deadly samurai ghosts. The setting doesn't upgrade the creepiness of the plot.
1982 (R) 88m/C Edward Albert, Susan George, Doug McClure, Amy Barrett; *D:* Kevin Connor. **VHS, Beta $59.95** *MGM ⅄½*

A House without a Christmas Tree A frustrated middle-aged man denies his young daughter her one desire—a Christmas tree. Charming made for cable television holiday fare.
1972 90m/C Jason Robards Jr., Lisa Lucas, Mildred Natwick; *D:* Paul Bogart. **VHS, Beta $14.98** *FXV, FCT ⅄⅄½*

Houseboat Widower Grant with three precocious kids takes up residence on a houseboat with Italian maid Loren who is actually a socialite, incognito. Naturally, they fall in love. Light, fun Hollywood froth.

1958 110m/C Cary Grant, Sophia Loren, Martha Hyer, Eduardo Ciannelli, Murray Hamilton, Harry Guardino; *D:* Melville Shavelson. **Beta, LV, CDV $19.95** *PAR ⅄⅄½*

The Householder An early Merchant-Ivory collaboration featuring a young Indian schoolteacher whose widowed mother arranges his marriage to a woman he doesn't know. The immature couple find their adjustment to marriage fraught with, sometimes amusing, complications. *AKA:* Gharbar.
1963 101m/B *IN* Shashi Kapoor, Leela Naidu, Durga Khote; *D:* James Ivory; *W:* Ruth Prawer Jhabvala. **VHS, LV $79.95** *CVC, TAM ⅄⅄*

The Housekeeper Tushingham's portrayal of a deranged housekeeper brings this movie to life even as she kills off her employers. *AKA:* A Judgement in Stone.
1986 (R) 97m/C *CA* Rita Tushingham, Ross Petty, Jackie Burroughs, Tom Kneebone, Shelly Peterson, Jessica Stern, Jonathan Crombie; *D:* Ousama Rawi. **VHS, Beta, LV $39.95** *WAR ⅄⅄*

Housekeeping A quiet but bizarre comedy by Forsyth (his first American film). A pair of orphaned sisters are cared for by their newly arrived eccentric, free-spirited aunt in a small and small-minded community in Oregon in the 1950s. Conventional townspeople attempt to intervene, but the sisters' relationship with their offbeat aunt has become strong enough to withstand the coercion of the townspeople. May move too slowly for some viewers. Based on novel by Marilynne Robinson.
1987 (PG) 117m/C Christine Lahti, Sarah Walker, Andrea Burchill; *D:* Bill Forsyth. **VHS, Beta $89.95** *COL ⅄⅄⅄*

Housemaster In a British boys' school the housemaster is kind and understanding of his sometimes-unruly charges. The stern new headmaster is not, and the students conspire against him. An okay but dated comedy, featuring characters with names like Bimbo and Button. Based on "Bachelor Born" by Ian Hay, a London stage hit at the time.
1938 95m/B Otto Kruger, Diana Churchill, Phillips Holmes, Rene Ray, Walter Hudd, John Wood, Cecil Parker, Michael Shepley, Jimmy Hanley, Rosamund Barnes; *D:* Herbert Brenon. **VHS $19.95** *NOS, MLB ⅄⅄½*

Housesitter Newton Davis (Martin), an architect/dreamer, builds his high school sweetheart (Delany) a beautiful house and surprises her with a marriage proposal. Delany says no, he has a one-night stand with Gwen (Hawn), and Hawn moves into his empty house and assumes the position of Davis's wife, unbeknownst to him. Gwen spins whoppers of lies and soon has the entire town, including Davis's parents and ex-girlfriend, believing her wacky stories. This romantic screwball comedy is a delight, not only because of Martin and Hawn, but also because of the array of other characters who complicate the stories they spin...and those stories are doozies.
1992 (PG) 102m/C Steve Martin, Goldie Hawn, Dana Delany, Julie Harris, Donald Moffatt, Peter MacNicol, Richard B. Shull, Laurel Cronin, Christopher Durang; *D:* Frank Oz; *W:* Mark Stein, Brian Grazer. **VHS, Beta, LV $19.98** *MCA, PMS, BTV ⅄⅄½*

Housewife A vengeful black man holds an unhappily married Beverly Hills couple hostage in their home.
1972 (R) 96m/C Yaphet Kotto, Andrew Duggan, Joyce Van Patten, Jeannie Berlin; *D:* Larry Cohen. **VHS, Beta $19.95** *STE, NWV ⅄⅄*

How Come Nobody's On Our Side? Two out-of-work stuntmen try astrology to find the best time to make some easy money smuggling marijuana out of Mexico. 1973 (PG) 84m/C Adam Roarke, Larry Bishop, Alexandra Hay, Rob Reiner, Penny Marshall. VHS, Beta $39.95 MON ℐ

How Funny Can Sex Be? Eight risque sketches about love and marriage Italian style. 1976 (R) 97m/C IT Giancarlo Giannini, Laura Antonelli, Dulio Del Prete; D: Dino Risi. VHS, Beta FOX ℐℐ

How Green was My Valley Compelling story of the trials and tribulations of a Welsh mining family, from the youthful perspective of the youngest child (played by a 13-year-old McDowall). Spans 50 years, from the turn of the century, when coal mining was a difficult but fair-paying way of life, and ends, after unionization, strikes, deaths, and child abuse, with the demise of a town and its culture. Considered by many to be director Ford's finest work (and he produced a lot of works over his 40-year tenure in sound films). When WWII prevented shooting on location, producer Zanuck built a facsimile Welsh valley in California (although Ford, born Sean Aloysius O'Fearna, was said to have been thinking of his story as taking place in Ireland rather than Wales). Based on the novel by Richard Llewellyn. 1941 118m/C Walter Pidgeon, Maureen O'Hara, Donald Crisp, Anna Lee, Roddy McDowall, John Loder, Sara Allgood, Barry Fitzgerald, Patric Knowles, Rhys Williams; D: John Ford; W: Philip Dunne. Academy Awards '41: Best Black and White Cinematography, Best Director (Ford), Best Interior Decoration, Best Picture, Best Supporting Actor (Crisp); Nominations: Best Film Editing, Best Screenplay, Best Sound, Best Supporting Actress (Allgood), Best Original Score. VHS, Beta $19.98 FOX ℐℐℐℐ

How I Got into College A slack, uninspired satire about a high school senior who barely manages to get into a local college so he may pursue the girl of his dreams. 1989 (PG-13) 87m/C Corey Parker, Lara Flynn Boyle, Christopher Rydell, Anthony Edwards, Phil Hartman, Brian Doyle-Murray, Nora Dunn, Finn Carter, Charles Rocket; D: Steve Holland. VHS, Beta, LV $89.98 FOX ℐℐ

How I Learned to Love Women A British comedy of errors involving a car-loving youth who learns about women and love. 196? 95m/C GB Anita Ekberg. VHS, Beta NO ℐ

How I Won the War An inept officer must lead his battalion out of England into the Egyptian desert to conquer a cricket field. Indulgent, scarcely amusing Richard Lester comedy; Lennon, in a bit part, provides the brightest moments. 1967 (PG) 111m/C GB John Lennon, Michael Crawford, Michael Hordern; D: Richard Lester. VHS, Beta, LV $59.95 MGM ℐℐ

How Many Miles to Babylon? During WWI, two young men become friends despite their different backgrounds. But one is court-martialed for desertion, and the other is supposed to oversee his execution. Made for British television. 1982 106m/C GB Daniel Day-Lewis, Christopher Fairbank; D: Moira Armstrong. VHS, Beta $19.98 FOX, TVC ℐℐ

How Sweet It Is! Typical American family takes a zany European vacation. Looks like a TV sitcom and is about as entertaining. National Lampoon's version is a lot more fun.

1968 99m/C James Garner, Debbie Reynolds, Maurice Ronet, Paul Lynde, Erin Moran, Marcel Dalio, Terry-Thomas; D: Jerry Paris. VHS $59.95 WAR ℐ

How the Grinch Stole Christmas The classic, made for television Christmas special based upon the Dr. Seuss book about a Christmas-hating gnome who eventually lets the spirit of Christmas in Whoville into his heart. 1965 26m/C V: Boris Karloff. VHS, Beta $14.95 MGM, KUI, WTA ℐℐℐ

How the West was Won A panoramic view of the American West, focusing on the trials, tribulations and travels of three generations of one family, set against the background of wars and historical events. Particularly notable for its impressive cast list and expansive western settings. 1963 (G) 165m/C John Wayne, Carroll Baker, Lee J. Cobb, Spencer Tracy, Gregory Peck, Karl Malden, Robert Preston, Eli Wallach, Henry Fonda, George Peppard, Debbie Reynolds, Carolyn Jones, Richard Widmark, James Stewart, Walter Brennan, Andy Devine, Raymond Massey, Agnes Moorehead, Henry Morgan, Thelma Ritter, Russ Tamblyn; D: John Ford, Henry Hathaway, George Marshall; W: James R. Webb. Academy Awards '63: Best Film Editing, Best Sound, Best Story & Screenplay; Nominations: Best Art Direction/Set Decoration (Color), Best Color Cinematography, Best Costume Design (Color), Best Picture, Best Original Score; National Board of Review Awards '63: 10 Best Films of the Year. VHS, Beta, LV $29.98 MGM ℐℐℐ

How to Be a Perfect Person in Just Three Days Fun comedy for the whole family shows the efforts of a kid striving for perfection before realizing that individuality is more fun. Aired on PBS as part of the "Wonderworks" series. Also available in a 31-minute version. 1984 58m/C Wallace Shawn, Ilan Mitchell-Smith, Hermione Gingold, Joan Micklin Silver. VHS, Beta, 3/4U $29.95 PME, LCA, HMV ℐℐℐ

How to Beat the High Cost of Living Three suburban housewives decide to beat inflation by taking up robbery, and they start by planning a heist at the local shopping mall. Comedic talent can't salvage whipped script and direction. 1980 (PG) 105m/C Jessica Lange, Susan St. James, Jane Curtin, Richard Benjamin, Eddie Albert; D: Dabney Coleman. VHS, Beta $69.98 LIV, VEG ℐ½

How to Break Up a Happy Divorce A divorced woman starts a vigorous campaign to win her ex-husband back by dating another man to make him jealous. Lightweight made-for-television comedy. 1976 74m/C Barbara Eden, Hal Linden, Peter Bonerz, Marcia Rodd, Harold Gould; D: Jerry Paris. VHS, Beta $34.95 WOV ℐℐ

How to Commit Marriage Hope and Wyman have been married for 20 years when they decide to divorce—just when their daughter (Cameron) decides to marry her college boyfriend (Matheson). His father (Gleason) tries to stop the wedding, fails, but sticks around to cause more trouble. Subplots involve the divorced duo's new loves and the fact that they're about to become grandparents but the comedy is completely uninspired. 1969 (PG) 96m/C Bob Hope, Jane Wyman, Jackie Gleason, Joanna Cameron, Tim Matheson, Bea Arthur, Leslie Nielsen, Tina Louise, Paul Stewart, Prof. Irwin Corey; D: Norman Panama; W: Ben Starr, Michael Kanin; M: Joseph J. Lilley. VHS $14.95 COL ℐ½

How to Get Ahead in Advertising A cynical, energetic satire about a manic advertising idea man who becomes so disgusted with trying to sell a pimple cream that he quits the business. Ultimately he grows a pimple of his own that talks and begins to take over his life. Acerbic and hilarious. 1989 (R) 95m/C GB Richard E. Grant, Rachel Ward, Susan Wooldridge, Mick Ford, Richard Wilson; W/D: Bruce Robinson. VHS, Beta, LV NO ℐℐℐ

How to Kill 400 Duponts Bumbling Scotland Yard detective is off to France to stop a master criminal from trying to kill off the rich Dupont family. Why? So he'll be the only one left with any claim to the remaining family fortune. 1965 98m/C Terry-Thomas, Johnny Dorelli, Margaret Lee. VHS, Beta VCD ℐ

How to Make a Monster In-joke from the creators of youth-oriented '50s AIP monster flicks; a mad makeup man's home-brew greasepaint brainwashes the actors. Disguised as famous monsters, they kill horror-hating movie execs. Mild fun if—and only if—you treasure the genre. Conway repeats his role as Teenage Frankenstein, but the studio couldn't get Michael Landon for the Teenage Werewolf. 1958 73m/B Robert Harris, Paul Brinegar, Gary Conway, Gary Clarke, Malcolm Atterbury, Dennis Cross, John Ashley, Morris Ankrum, Walter Reed, Heather Ames; D: Herbert L. Strock. VHS $9.95 COL, MLB ℐ

How to Marry a Millionaire Three models pool their money and rent a lavish apartment in a campaign to trap millionaire husbands. Clever performances by three lead women salvage a vehicle intended primarily to bolster Monroe's career. Filmed just after "Gentlemen Prefer Blonds," it has little to add—except that it is the first movie to be filmed in CinemaScope. Nunnally Johnson wrote the script, based on "The Greeks Had a Word for Them." The opening street scene, with the accompanying theme music by Alfred Newman, were state-of-the-art achievements of screen and sound. 1953 96m/C Lauren Bacall, Marilyn Monroe, Betty Grable, William Powell, David Wayne, Cameron Mitchell; D: Jean Negulesco. VHS, Beta, LV $14.98 FOX ℐℐ½

How to Murder Your Wife While drunk, a cartoonist marries an unknown woman and then frantically tries to think of ways to get rid of her — even contemplating murder. Frantic comedy is tailored for Lemmon. 1964 118m/C Jack Lemmon, Terry-Thomas, Virna Lisi, Eddie Mayehoff, Sidney Blackmer, Claire Trevor, Mary Wickes, Jack Albertson; D: Richard Quine. VHS, Beta $19.95 MGM ℐℐℐ

How to Pick Up Girls Comic tale based on Eric Weber's bestseller follows the exploits of a small-town boy who moves to New York City and finds the secret to picking up women. Made for television. 1978 93m/C Desi Arnaz Jr., Bess Armstrong, Fred McCarren, Polly Bergen, Richard Dawson, Alan King, Abe Vigoda, Deborah Raffin; D: Bill Persky. VHS, Beta $19.98 TWE ℐℐ

How to Seduce a Woman A playboy attempts to bed five supposedly unattainable women. 1974 108m/C Angus Duncan, Marty Ingels, Lillian Randolph. VHS, Beta $39.95 PSM Woof!

How to Stuff a Wild Bikini Last in the too-long tradition of Frankie and Annette do the beach thing movies. This one features a pregnant Funicello (though this is hidden

and not part of the plot). Avalon actually has only a small role as the jealous boyfriend trying to see if Annette will remain faithful while he's away on military duty in Tahiti. Dobie Gillis Hickman is the competition. Keaton is the witch doctor who helps Frankie keep Annette true. "Playboy" playmates wander about in small swimsuits. Garage band extraordinare The Kingsmen play themselves. Brian Wilson of the Beach Boys drops in, sees that the surf's up.
1965 90m/C Frankie Avalon, Annette Funicello, Dwayne Hickman, Beverly Adams, Buster Keaton, Harvey Lembeck, Mickey Rooney, Brian Donlevy; *D:* William Asher. VHS, Beta $19.98 *WAR, OM* ♪♪

How to Succeed in Business without Really Trying Classic musical comedy about a window-washer who charms his way to the top of a major company. Robert Morse repeats his Tony winning Broadway role. Loosely based on a non-fiction book of the same title by Shepherd Mead, whose book Morse purchases on his first day of work. Excellent transfer of stage to film, with choreography by Moreda expanding Bob Fosse's original plan. Dynamite from start to finish. ♪♫I Believe In You; The Company Way; Coffee Break; The Brotherhood of Man; A Secretary Is Not A Toy; Grand Old Ivy; Been A Long Day; Rosemary; Finch's Frolic; Gotta Stop That Man; How To Succeed in Business Without Really Trying.
1967 121m/C Robert Morse, Michele Lee, Rudy Vallee, Anthony Teague, George Fenneman, Maureen Arthur; *W/D:* David Swift; *W:* Abe Burrows; *M:* Frank Loesser. VHS, LV $19.95 *MGM* ♪♪♪½

How U Like Me Now? Comedy set on Chicago's south side focuses on Thomas, an attractive but unmotivated guy with low earning potential, and his girl Valerie, a pretentious overachiever who wants much more than he's able to offer. Robert's second directorial effort offers a fresh look at African Americans on film with plenty of lively supporting characters and witty dialogue. Filmed on a $600,000 budget.
1992 (R) 109m/C Darnell Williams, Salli Richardson, Daniel Gardner, Raymond Whitefield, Debra Crable, Jonelle Kennedy, Byron Stewart, Charnele Brown, Daryl Roberts; *W/D:* Daryl Roberts; *M:* Kahil El Zabar, Chuck Webb. VHS, LV *MCA* ♪♪♪

Howard the Duck A big-budget Lucasfilm adaptation of the short-lived Marvel comic book about an alien, resembling a cigar-chomping duck, who gets sucked into a vortex, lands on Earth and saves it from the Dark Overlords. While he's at it, he befriends a nice young lady in a punk rock band and starts to fall in love. A notorious box-office bomb and one of the '80s worst major films, although it seems to work well with children, given the simple story line and good special effects.
1986 (PG) 111m/C Lea Thompson, Jeffrey Jones, Tim Robbins; *D:* Willard Huyck; *M:* John Barry, Sylvester Levay. VHS, Beta, LV $79.95 *MCA* ♪

Howard's End E.M. Forster's 1910 novel about property, privilege, class differences, and Edwardian society is brought to enchanting life by the Merchant-Ivory team. Margaret and Helen Schlegel live a comfortable, artistic life in London with their younger brother, Tibby. Impulsive and expressive, the sisters take up the causes of two very different families. Helen gets involved with the working-class Leonard Bast, a poor clerk struggling to improve himself, and his somewhat coarse wife. Margaret has rekindled an acquaintance with the wealthy, traditional, Wilcox family and becomes the intimate friend of the dying Mrs. Wilcox, who leaves her country home, Howard's End, to Margaret in a handwritten note. The Wilcox family are appalled and destroy the document but that doesn't end their involvement. When Margaret later marries the widowed Mr. Wilcox all three families are joined together in an ultimately tragic series of events. Visually beautiful with subtle performances where a glance or a gesture says as much as any dialog. Thompson is especially notable as the compassionate Margaret.
1992 (PG) 140m/C *GB* Anthony Hopkins, Emma Thompson, Helena Bonham Carter, Vanessa Redgrave, James Wilby, Sam West, Jemma Redgrave, Nicola Duffett, Prunella Scales, Joseph Bennett; *Cameos:* Simon Callow; *D:* James Ivory; *W:* Ruth Prawer Jhabvala. Academy Awards '92: Best Actress (Thompson), Best Adapted Screenplay, Best Art Direction/Set Decoration; Nominations: Best Cinematography, Best Costume Design, Best Director (Ivory), Best Picture, Best Supporting Actress (Redgrave), Best Original Score; British Academy Awards '93: Best Actress (Thompson); Chicago Film Critics Awards '92: Best Actress (Thompson); Golden Globe Awards '93: Best Actress—Drama (Thompson); Los Angeles Film Critics Association Awards '92: Best Actress (Thompson); National Board of Review Awards '92: 10 Best Films of the Year, Best Actress (Thompson), Best Director (Ivory); National Society of Film Critics Awards '92: Best Actress (Thompson). VHS, LV, 8mm $89.95 *COL, CRC, MOV* ♪♪♪♪

The Howards of Virginia A lavish Hollywood historical epic, detailing the adventures of a backwoodsman and the rich Virginia girl he marries as their families become involved in the Revolutionary War. *AKA:* Tree of Liberty.
1940 117m/B Cary Grant, Martha Scott, Cedric Hardwicke, Alan Marshal, Richard Carlson, Paul Kelly, Irving Bacon, Tom Drake, Anne Revere, Ralph Byrd, Alan Ladd; *D:* Frank Lloyd. VHS, Beta $69.95 *COL* ♪♪½

The Howling A pretty television reporter takes a rest at a clinic and discovers slowly that its denizens are actually werewolves. An in-joke-crammed, highly Dantean horror comedy that pioneered the use of the body-altering prosthetic make-up (by Rob Bottin) now essential for on-screen man-to-wolf transformations. Co-scripted by John Sayles. At last count, followed by five sequels.
1981 (R) 91m/C Dee Wallace Stone, Patrick Macnee, Dennis Dugan, Christopher Stone, Belinda Balaski, Kevin McCarthy, John Carradine, Slim Pickens, Elisabeth Brooks, Robert Picardo, Dick Miller; *D:* Joe Dante; *W:* John Sayles, Terence H. Winkless. VHS, Beta, LV $14.95 *COL, SUE* ♪♪♪

Howling 2: Your Sister is a Werewolf A policeman (the brother of one of the first film's victims) investigates a Transylvanian werewolf-ridden castle and gets mangled for his trouble. Followed by four more sequels.
1985 (R) 91m/C *FR IT* Sybil Danning, Christopher Lee, Annie McEnroe, Marsha Hunt, Reb Brown, Ferdinand "Ferdy" Mayne; *D:* Philippe Mora. VHS, Beta, LV $14.99 *HBO* ♪

Howling 3: The Marsupials Australians discover a pouch-laden form of lycanthrope. Third "Howling" (surprise), second from Mora and better than his first.
1987 (PG-13) 94m/C *AU* Barry Otto, Imogen Annesley, Dasha Blahova, Max Fairchild, Ralph Cotterill, Leigh Biolos, Frank Thring, Michael Pate; *D:* Philippe Mora. VHS, Beta, LV $19.95 *LIV* ♪♪

Howling 4: The Original Nightmare A woman novelist hears the call of the wild while taking a rest cure in the country. This werewolf tale has nothing to do with the other sequels.
1988 (R) 94m/C Romy Windsor, Michael T. Weiss, Anthony Hamilton, Susanne Severeid, Lamya Derval; *D:* John Hough. VHS, Beta, LV $14.95 *LIV* ♪

Howling 5: The Rebirth The fifth in the disconnected horror series, in which a varied group of people stranded in a European castle are individually hunted down by evil.
1989 (R) 99m/C Philip Davis, Victoria Catlin, Elizabeth She, Ben Cole, William Shockley; *D:* Neal Sundstrom. VHS, Beta, LV $14.95 *LIV* ♪

Howling 6: The Freaks Hideous werewolf suffers from multiple sequels, battles with vampire at freak show, and discovers that series won't die. Next up: "Howling 7: The Nightmare that Won't Go Away."
1990 (R) 102m/C Brendan Hughes, Michelle Matheson, Sean Gregory Sullivan, Antonio Fargas, Carol Lynley, Jered Barclay, Bruce Martin Payne; *D:* Hope Perello. VHS, LV $89.95 *LIV, IME* ♪♪½

Huckleberry Finn The musical version of the Mark Twain story about the adventures a young boy and a runaway slave encounter along the Mississippi River.
1974 (G) 114m/C Jeff East, Paul Winfield, Harvey Korman, David Wayne, Arthur O'Connell, Gary Merrill, Natalie Trundy, Lucille Benson, Farrah Fawcett; *D:* J. Lee Thompson. VHS, Beta $14.95 *MGM, FOX* ♪♪

Huckleberry Finn Whitewashed version of the Twain classic features post Opie Howard as the incredible Huck and Dano as the sharp witted short storyist. Stars four members of the Howard clan. Made for TV.
1975 (G) 74m/C Ron Howard, Donny Most, Royal Dano, Antonio Fargas, Jack Elam, Merle Haggard, Rance Howard, Jean Howard, Clint Howard, Shug Fisher, Sarah Selby, Bill Erwin; *D:* Robert Totten. VHS, Beta $14.98 *KUI, FXV, FCT* ♪♪

Huckleberry Finn A version of the classic Mark Twain novel about the adventures a young boy and a runaway slave encounter as they travel down the Mississippi River.
1981 72m/C VHS, Beta $59.98 *LIV, WTA* ♪½

The Hucksters Account of a man looking for honesty and integrity in the radio advertising world and finding little to work with. All performances are excellent; but Greenstreet, as the tyrannical head of a soap company, is a stand out. Deborah Kerr's American debut.
1947 115m/B Clark Gable, Deborah Kerr, Sydney Greenstreet, Adolphe Menjou, Ava Gardner, Keenan Wynn, Edward Arnold; *D:* Jack Conway. VHS, Beta $19.98 *MGM, FCT* ♪♪♪

Hud Newman is a hard-driving, hard-drinking, woman-chasing young man whose life is a revolt against the principles of stern father Douglas. Neal is outstanding as the family housekeeper. Excellent photography.
1963 112m/B Paul Newman, Melvyn Douglas, Patricia Neal, Brandon de Wilde; *D:* Martin Ritt. Academy Awards '63: Best Actress (Neal), Best Black and White Cinematography, Best Supporting Actor (Douglas); Nominations: Best Actor (Newman), Best Adapted Screenplay, Best Art Direction/Set Decoration (B & W), Best Director (Ritt); National Board of Review Awards '63: 10 Best Films of the Year, Best Actress (Neal), Best Supporting Actor (Douglas). VHS, Beta, LV $69.95 *PAR, BTV* ♪♪♪♪

Hudson Hawk A big-budget star vehicle with little else going for it. Willis plays a master burglar released from prison, only to find himself trapped by the CIA into one last theft. Everyone in the cast tries to be extra funny, resulting in a disjointed situation where no one is. Weakly plotted, poorly paced.
1991 (R) 95m/C Bruce Willis, Danny Aiello, Andie MacDowell, James Coburn, Sandra Bernhard, Richard E. Grant, Frank Stallone; *D:* Michael Lehmann. VHS, Beta, LV, 8mm $19.95 COL, PIA *½*

Hue and Cry Nobody believes a young boy when he discovers crooks are sending coded messages in a weekly children's magazine. A detective writer finally believes his story and they set off to capture the crooks.
1947 82m/B *GB* Alastair Sim, Jack Warner, Frederick Piper, Jack Lambert, Joan Dowling; *D:* Charles Crichton. VHS $16.95 SNC, NOS, FCT *½½½*

Hugh Hefner: Once Upon a Time Fascinating look at the "Bunny" king and Playboy Enterprises. His celebrated life of isolation and excess at the Playboy mansions is portrayed as is the founding of "Playboy" magazine in 1953 and the Playboy clubs (with their notorious Bunnies). Includes interviews, home movies, and photographs. Admiring yet not without a few sharp edges.
1992 (R) 91m/C Hugh Hefner; *D:* Robert Heath. VHS, LV $89.95 UND *½½½*

Hughes & Harlow: Angels in Hell The story of the romance that occurred between Howard Hughes and Jean Harlow during the filming of "Hell's Angels" in 1930.
1977 (R) 94m/C Lindsay Bloom, Victor Holchak, David McLean, Royal Dano, Adam Roarke, Linda Cristal; *D:* Larry Buchanan. VHS, Beta NO *½*

Hugo the Hippo Animated musical about a forlorn baby hippo who struggles to survive in the human jungle of old Zanzibar.
1976 (G) 90m/C *V:* Paul Lynde, Burl Ives, Robert Morley, Marie Osmond. VHS, Beta $49.98 FOX *½½*

Hula Unflappable flapper Bow and her gang frolic on a Pacific island without the benefit of sound FX.
1928 64m/B Clara Bow, Clive Brook, Patricia Dupont, Arnold Kent, Agostino Borgato; *D:* Victor Fleming. VHS, Beta $19.95 GPV, FCT *½½*

Hullabaloo Over George & Bonnie's Pictures A light-hearted comedy about valuable paintings in a Rajah's possession and the Englishman who will stop at nothing to get them.
1978 85m/C *GB* Victor Banerjee, Aparna Sen, Larry Pine, Saeed Jaffrey, Peggy Ashcroft; *D:* James Ivory; *W:* Ruth Prawer Jhabvala. VHS, Beta $29.98 SUE, TAM, NLC *½½½*

Human Beasts Jewel robbers face a tribe of hungry cannibals.
1980 90m/C *SP JP* Paul Naschy, Eiko Nagashima; *W/D:* Paul Naschy. VHS, Beta NO *½*

The Human Comedy A small-town boy experiences love and loss and learns the meaning of true faith during WWII. Straight, unapologetically sentimental version of the William Saroyan novel.
1943 117m/B Mickey Rooney, Frank Morgan, James Craig, Fay Bainter, Ray Collins, Donna Reed, Van Johnson, Barry Nelson, Robert Mitchum, Jackie "Butch" Jenkins; *D:* Clarence Brown; *W:* William Saroyan. Academy Awards '43: Best Story; Nominations: Best Actor (Rooney), Best Black and White Cinematography, Best Director (Brown), Best Picture. VHS, Beta, LV $24.98 KUI, MGM *½½½½*

The Human Condition: A Soldier's Prayer A Japanese pacifist escapes from his commanders and allows himself to be captured by Russian troops, hoping for better treatment as a P.O.W. The final part of the trilogy preceded by "The Human Condition: No Greater Love" and "The Human Condition: Road to Eternity." In Japanese with English subtitles.
1961 190m/B *JP* Tatsuya Nakadai, Michiyo Aratama, Yusuke Kawazu, Tamao Nakamura, Chishu Ryu; *D:* Masaki Kobayashi. VHS, Beta $59.95 SVS, TAM *½½½*

The Human Condition: No Greater Love First of a three-part series of films. A pacifist is called into military service and subsequently sent to a run a military mining camp. A gripping look at one man's attempt to retain his humanity in the face of war. Followed by "The Human Condition: Road to Eternity" and "The Human Condition: A Soldier's Prayer." In Japanese with English subtitles.
1958 200m/B *JP* Tatsuya Nakadai, Michiyo Aratama, So Yamamura, Eitaro Ozawa, Akira Ishihama; *D:* Masaki Kobayashi. VHS, Beta $59.95 SVS, TAM *½½½*

The Human Condition: Road to Eternity A Japanese pacifist is on punishment duty in Manchuria where he is beaten by sadistic officers who try to destroy his humanity. The second part of the trilogy, preceded by "The Human Condition: No Greater Love" and followed by "The Human Condition: A Soldier's Prayer." In Japanese with English subtitles. *AKA:* No Greater Love; Ningen No Joken.
1959 180m/B *JP* Tatsuya Nakadai, Michiyo Aratama, Kokinji Katsura, Jun Tatara, Michio Minami, Keiji Sada; *D:* Masaki Kobayashi. VHS, Beta $59.95 SVS, TAM *½½½*

Human Desire Femme fatale Grahame and jealous husband Crawford turn out the lights on Crawford's boss (seems there's some confusion about how Miss Gloria managed to convince the guy to let her hubby have his job back). Ford's wise to them but plays he see no evil because he's gone crackers for Grahame, who by now has decided she'd like a little help to rid herself of an unwanted husband. Bleak, melodramatic, full of big heat, its Lang through and through. Based on the Emile Zola novel "La Bete Humaine," which inspired Renoir's 1938 telling as well.
1954 90m/B Glenn Ford, Gloria Grahame, Broderick Crawford, Edgar Buchanan, Kathleen Case; *D:* Fritz Lang. VHS GKK *½½½*

The Human Duplicators Kiel is an alien who has come to Earth to make androids out of important folk, thus allowing the "galaxy beings" to take over. Cheap stuff, but earnest performances make this more fun than it should be.
1964 82m/C George Nader, Barbara Nichols, George Macready, Dolores Faith, Hugh Beaumont, Richard Kiel, Richard Arlen; *D:* Hugo Grimaldi. VHS, Beta $39.95 LIV *½½*

Human Experiments Psychiatrist in a women's prison conducts a group of experiments in which he destroys the "criminal instinct" in the inmates through brute fear.
1979 (R) 82m/C Linda Haynes, Jackie Coogan, Aldo Ray; *D:* Gregory Goodell. VHS, Beta $39.95 VID *½*

The Human Factor Kennedy stars as a computer expert who tracks down his family's murderers using technology. Bloody and violent.
1975 (R) 96m/C *GB IT* George Kennedy, John Mills, Raf Vallone, Rita Tushingham, Barry Sullivan, Arthur Franz; *D:* Edward Dmytryk; *M:* Ennio Morricone. VHS, Beta $39.95 LIV *½*

Human Gorilla A thriller involving a mad scientist, an insane asylum, a reporter, and various other mysterious trappings. *AKA:* Behind Locked Doors.
1948 58m/B Richard Carlson, Lucille Bremer, Tor Johnson. VHS, Beta $19.95 NO *½*

Human Hearts A creaky old silent starring "Phantom of the Opera" leading lady Philbin. A family is torn apart by a con man and his femme fatale.
1922 99m/B House Peters, Russell Simpson, Mary Philbin. VHS, Beta, 8mm $29.95 VYY *½½*

The Human Monster Scotland Yard inspector investigates five drownings of the blind patients a phony Dr. Orloff (Lugosi) is exploiting for insurance money. Superior Lugosi effort that's modestly violent and tasteless. Based on the Edgar Wallace novel. Written by Patrick Kirwin, Walter Summers, and John Argyle. *AKA:* Dark Eyes of London.
1939 73m/B *GB* Bela Lugosi, Hugh Williams, Greta Gynt; *D:* Walter Summers. VHS, Beta $19.95 NOS, MRV, SNC *½½½*

The Human Shield A man risks his life on a mission to save his brother during the Persian Gulf War.
1992 (R) 88m/C Michael Dudikoff, Tommy Hinkley, Steve Inwood; *D:* Ted Post. VHS, LV $89.99 WAR *½½*

The Human Vapor A normal human being has the ability to vaporize himself at will and use it to terrorize Tokyo. *AKA:* Gasu Ningen Daiichigo.
1968 81m/C *JP* VHS, Beta $19.95 GEM, PSM *½*

Humanoid Defender A made-for-television film about a scientist and an android rebelling against the government that wants to use the android as a warfare prototype.
1985 94m/C Terence Knox, Gary Kasper, Aimee Eccles, William Lucking; *D:* William Lucking. VHS, Beta $39.95 MCA *½½*

Humanoid Woman An animated adventure about a female android battling evil on the planet of Dessa.
1981 100m/C VHS, Beta $39.98 CEL *½½*

Humanoids from the Deep Mutated salmon-like monsters rise from the depths of the ocean and decide to chop on some bikinied babes. Violent and bloody. *AKA:* Monster.
1980 (R) 81m/C Doug McClure, Ann Turkel, Vic Morrow, Cindy Weintraub, Anthony Penya, Denise Balik, D. Barbara Peeters. VHS, Beta WAR, OM *Woof!*

Humongous Brain-dead bevy of teens shipwreck on an island where they encounter a deranged mutant giant who must kill to survive. You'll be rooting for the monster.
1982 (R) 93m/C *CA* Janet Julian, David Wallace, Janet Baldwin; *D:* Paul Lynch. VHS, Beta $14.98 SUE, NLC *Woof!*

Humoresque A talented but struggling young musician finds a patron in the married, wealthy, and older Crawford. His appreciation is not as romantic as she hoped. Stunning performance from Crawford, with excellent supporting cast, including a young Robert Blake. Fine music sequences (Isaac Stern dubbed the violin), and lush production values. Laserdisc version features the original movie trailer.
1946 123m/B Joan Crawford, John Garfield, Oscar Levant, J. Carroll Naish, Joan Chandler, Tom D'Andrea, Peggy Knudsen, Ruth Nelson, Craig Stevens, Paul Cavanagh, Richard Gaines, John Abbott, Robert (Bobby) Blake; *D:* Jean Negulesco. VHS, LV $19.98 MGM, BTV, PIA *½½½½*

The Hunchback of Notre Dame

The first film version of Victor Hugo's novel about the tortured hunchback bellringer of Notre Dame Cathedral, famous for the contortions of Lon Chaney's self-transformations via improvised makeup. Silent.
1923 100m/B Lon Chaney Sr., Patsy Ruth Miller, Norman Kerry, Ernest Torrence; **D:** Wallace Worsley. VHS, LV, 3/4U, **Special order formats $19.98** KIV, MRV, NOS 🐾🐾🐾

The Hunchback of Notre Dame

The best Hollywood version of the Victor Hugo classic, infused with sweep, sadness and an attempt at capturing a degree of spirited, Hugoesque detail. Laughton plays Quasimodo, a deformed Parisian bellringer, who provides sanctuary to a young gypsy woman accused by church officials of being a witch. The final scene of the townspeople storming the cathedral remains a Hollywood classic. Great performances all around; the huge facade of the Notre Dame cathedral was constructed on a Hollywood set for this film. Remake of several earlier films, including 1923's Lon Chaney silent. Remade in 1957 and later for television.
1939 117m/B Charles Laughton, Maureen O'Hara, Edmond O'Brien, Cedric Hardwicke, Thomas Mitchell, George Zucco; **D:** William Dieterle. VHS, Beta, LV, 3/4U, **Special order formats $19.95** RKO, MED, VID 🐾🐾🐾🐾

Hunchback of Notre Dame

It's not often that a classic novel is remade into a classic movie that's remade into a made-for-TV reprise, and survives its multiple renderings. But it's not often a cast so rich in stage trained actors is assembled on the small screen. Hopkins gives a textured, pre-Hannibal Lecter interpretation of Quasimodo, the Hunchback in Hugo's eponymous novel. Impressive model of the cathedral by production designer John Stoll. **AKA:** Hunchback.
1982 (PG) 102m/C Anthony Hopkins, Derek Jacobi, Lesley-Anne Down, John Gielgud, Tim Pigott-Smith, Rosalie Crutchley, Robert Powell; **D:** Michael Tuchner. VHS $89.95 VMK 🐾🐾🐾

Hundra

A warrior queen vows revenge when her all-female tribe is slain by men. Nothing can stop her fierce vendetta—except love.
1985 96m/C IT Laurene Landon, John Gaffari, Ramiro Oliveros, Marissa Casel; **D:** Matt Cimber; **M:** Ennio Morricone. VHS, Beta $59.95 MED 🐾

A Hungarian Fairy Tale

Political satire meets fantasy in a magical tale of a fatherless young boy searching for a surrogate dad. Unusual characters as well as an homage to Mozart's "The Magic Flute." In Hungarian with English subtitles. **AKA:** Hol Volt, Hol Nem Volt.
1987 97m/B HU Arpad Vermes, Maria Varga, Frantisek Husak, Eszter Csakanyi, Szilvia Toth, Judith Pogany, Geza Balkay; **D:** Gyula Gazdag. VHS $59.95 EVD, TAM 🐾🐾🐾

Hungarian Rhapsody

In 1911, a Hungarian nobleman joins the ranks of the rebelling peasants in order to oppose his brother, who represents aristocratic repression. One of Jancso's clearest political films, and one that continues the filmmaker's experiments with long, uncut sequences and dynamic mise-en-scene. In Hungarian with English subtitles.
1978 101m/C HU Gyorgy Cserhalmi, Lajos Balaszovits, Gabor Koncz, Bertalan Solti; **D:** Miklos Jancso. VHS, Beta $59.95 FCT, AUD 🐾🐾🐾

Hunger

In the late 1800's a starving Norwegian writer, unable to sell his work, rejects charity out of pride, and retains his faith in his talent. Based on a novel "Sult" by Knut Hamsun. In Danish with English subtitles.

1966 100m/B DK Per Oscarsson, Gunnel Lindblom. VHS $49.95 FCT, TAM 🐾🐾

The Hunger

A beautiful 2000-year-old vampire needs new blood when she realizes that her current lover, Bowie, is aging fast. Visually sumptuous but sleepwalking modern vampire tale, complete with soft-focus lesbian love scenes between Deneuve and Sarandon. Features a letterboxed screen and original movie trailer on the laserdisc format.
1983 (R) 100m/C Catherine Deneuve, David Bowie, Susan Sarandon, Cliff DeYoung, Ann Magnuson, Dan Hedaya, Willem Dafoe; **D:** Tony Scott. VHS, Beta, LV $79.95 MGM, PIA 🐾🐾

Hunk

A computer nerd sells his soul to the devil for a muscular, beach-blonde physique. Answers the question, "Was it worth it?"
1987 (PG) 102m/C John Allen Nelson, Steve Levitt, Deborah Shelton, Rebecca Bush, James Coco, Avery Schreiber; **D:** Lawrence Bassoff. VHS, Beta, LV $79.95 COL 🐾🐾

The Hunt

A teenage boy accompanies three Spanish Civil War veterans on what is supposed to be a friendly rabbit hunt. Things turn violent, however, when old rivalries and tensions begin to surface. In Spanish with English subtitles. **AKA:** La Caza.
1967 93m/B SP Alfredo Mayo, Ismael Merlo, Jose Maria Prada, Emilio Gutierrez-Caba, Fernando Sanchez Polack; **D:** Carlos Saura. VHS $39.95 TAM 🐾🐾🐾

The Hunt for Red October

Based on Tom Clancy's blockbuster novel, a high-tech Cold War yarn about a Soviet nuclear sub turning rogue and heading straight for U.S. waters, as both the U.S. and the U.S.S.R. try to stop it. Complicated, ill-plotted potboiler that succeeds breathlessly due to the cast and McTiernan's tommy-gun direction. Introduces the character of CIA analyst Jack Ryan who returns in "Patriot Games," though in the guise of Harrison Ford.
1990 (PG) 137m/C Sean Connery, Alec Baldwin, Richard Jordan, Scott Glenn, Joss Ackland, Sam Neill, James Earl Jones, Peter Firth, Tim Curry, Courtney B. Vance, Jeffrey Jones, Fred Dalton Thompson; **D:** John McTiernan. Academy Awards '90: Best Sound Effects Editing; Nominations: Best Film Editing, Best Sound. VHS, Beta, LV, SVS, 8mm $14.95 PAR, SUP 🐾🐾🐾

The Hunt for the Night Stalker

Another one of those True-Detective quickies so beloved by network TV, following two hardworking L.A. cops who tracked down satanic serial killer Richard Ramirez in the mid-1980s. It originally aired (under the title "Manhunt: The Search for the Night Stalker") on the date of the killer's death-sentence verdict; the videotape lacks that particular timely sparkle.
1991 (PG-13) 95m/C Richard Jordan, A. Martinez, Lisa Eilbacher, Julie Carmen, Alan Feinstein; **D:** Bruce Seth Green. VHS, Beta, LV $19.95 ACA 🐾🐾

Hunt the Man Down

An innocent man is charged with murder, and a public defender must find the real killer before time runs out.
1950 68m/B Gig Young, Lynn (Mary Hart) Roberts, Gerald Mohr; **D:** George Archainbaud. VHS, Beta $34.95 RKO 🐾🐾

Hunt the Man Down/Smashing the Rackets

A double feature: In "Hunt the Man Down" (1950) a public defender tries to clear a captured fugitive's name, and in "Smashing the Rackets" (1938) a special prosecutor takes on the gangsters who have corrupted a big city.

1950 137m/B Gig Young, Lynn (Mary Hart) Roberts, Chester Morris, Frances Mercer, Willard Parker, Gerald Mohr, Paul Frees; **D:** George Archainbaud. VHS, Beta $34.95 RKO 🐾🐾½

Hunted!

A young Jewish boy teams up with a resistance fighter to find his mother in Nazi Germany during World War II.
1979 90m/C GE VHS, Beta $29.95 GEM 🐾🐾

Hunted

WWII prisoner attempts to escape from demented officer who seems to enjoy bugging him. Hunted by the MPs, he relies on unorthodox guide to sustain feature length footage.
1988 (PG) 75m/C Andrew Buckland, Richard Carlson, Ron Smerczak, Mercia Van Wyk; **D:** David Lister. VHS $34.95 ACA 🐾🐾

The Hunted Lady

In this television pilot, Mills is an undercover policewoman who is framed by the mob. Tired and predictable.
1977 100m/C Donna Mills, Robert Reed, Lawrence Casey, Andrew Duggan, Will Sampson, Alan Feinstein; **D:** Richard Lang. VHS $39.95 WOV 🐾½

Hunter

Pilot for a television series that never emerged. A government agent uncovers an enemy brainwashing scam.
1973 90m/C John Vernon, Steve Ihnat, Fritz Weaver, Edward Binns, Sabrina Scharf, Barbara Rhoades; **D:** Leonard Horn. VHS LHV 🐾½

Hunter

An attorney is falsely accused of a crime and imprisoned. Released after eight years, he sets out to even the score with the mysterious millionaire who set him up. Made for television.
1977 120m/C James Franciscus, Linda Evans, Broderick Crawford. VHS, Beta $59.95 LHV, WAR 🐾

The Hunter

Action drama based on the real life adventures of Ralph (Papa) Thorson, a modern day bounty hunter who makes his living by finding fugitives who have jumped bail. McQueen's last.
1980 (PG) 97m/C Steve McQueen, Eli Wallach, Kathryn Harrold, LeVar Burton; **D:** Buzz Kulik. VHS, Beta, LV $19.95 PAR 🐾🐾½

Hunter in the Dark

Set in 18th-century Japan, where power, betrayal, and corruption are the dark side of the samurai world. Tanuma is a powerful shogunate minister who becomes involved with Gomyo, the leader of a secret underworld organization of thieves and murderers with a violent honor code. In Japanese with English subtitles.
1980 138m/C JP Tatsuya Nakadai, Tetsuro Tamba, Sonny Chiba; **D:** Hideo Gosha. VHS, LV $79.95 TAM 🐾🐾

The Hunters

A motley crew of pilots learn about each other and themselves in this melodrama set during Korean war. Incredible aerial photography sets this apart from other films of the genre.
1958 108m/C Robert Mitchum, Robert Wagner, Richard Egan, May Britt, Lee Phillips; **D:** Dick Powell. VHS TCF 🐾🐾½

Hunter's Blood

Five urbanites plunge into the Southern wilderness to hunt deer, and are stalked by maniacal hillbillies.
1987 (R) 102m/C Sam Bottoms, Kim Delaney, Clu Gulager, Mayf Nutter; **D:** Robert C. Hughes. VHS, Beta, LV $19.98 SUE, NLC 🐾½

Hunters of the Golden Cobra

Two American soldiers plot to recover the priceless golden cobra from the Japanese general who stole the prized relic during the last days of WWII.
1982 95m/C David Warbeck, Almanta Suska, Alan Collins, John Steiner; **D:** Anthony M. Dawson. VHS, Beta $69.98 LIV, VES 🐾

The Hunting A married woman falls for a ruthless businessman and is drawn into a web of blackmail and murder in this low-budget erotic thriller.
1992 (R) 97m/C John Savage, Kerry Armstrong, Guy Pearce, Rebecca Rigg; *W/D:* Frank Howson. VHS, Beta $19.95 PAR *ℐℐ*

Hurricane A couple on the run from the law are aided by a hurricane and are able to build a new life for themselves on an idyllic island. Filmed two years before the Academy's "special effects" award came into being, but displaying some of the best effects of the decade. Boringly remade in 1979.
1937 102m/B Jon Hall, Dorothy Lamour, Mary Astor, C. Aubrey Smith, Raymond Massey; *D:* John Ford. Academy Awards '37: Best Sound; Nominations: Best Supporting Actor (Mitchell), Best Original Score. VHS, Beta, LV $14.98 SUE *ℐℐℐ*

Hurricane Television's answer to the disaster movie craze of the early 1970s. Realistic hurricane footage and an adequate cast cannot save this catastrophe.
1974 78m/C Larry Hagman, Martin Milner, Jessica Walter, Barry Sullivan, Will Geer, Frank Sutton; *D:* Jerry Jameson. VHS NO *ℐ*

Hurricane And the wind cried, "turkey." Robards is the governor of a tropical island beset with environmental and personal concerns. Virginal daughter Farrow falls for hunky native, standard colonial power/indigenous people complications ensue, vital explanatory footage is cut, and overacting reaches epidemic heights. Then too late the big wind blows in, leveling the place. Expensive (most of the $22 million must have gone to catering) and essentially misdirected remake of the 1937 semi-classic. *AKA:* Forbidden Paradise.
1979 (PG) 120m/C Mia Farrow, Jason Robards Jr., Trevor Howard, Max von Sydow, Timothy Bottoms, James Keach; *D:* Jan Troell. VHS, Beta $14.95 PAR Woof!

Hurricane Express Twelve episodes of the vintage serial, in which the Duke pits his courage against an unknown, powerful individual out to sabotage a railroad.
1932 223m/B John Wayne, Joseph Girard, Conway Tearle, Shirley Grey; *D:* J.P. McGowan, Armand Schaefer. VHS, Beta, 3/4U; Special order formats $16.95 SNC, NOS, RHI *ℐℐ½*

Hurricane Smith Weathers stars as a roughneck Texan who travels to Australia's Gold Coast in search of his missing sister. While in the land of Oz, he gets entangled in a Mafia-style drug and prostitution ring around the "Surfer's Paradise" section of the Gold Coast. Packed with mind-blowing stunts and a good performance from Weathers, this fast-paced action thriller won't disappoint fans of this genre.
1992 (R) 86m/C Carl Weathers, Juergen Prochnow, Tony Bonner, Cassandra Delaney; *D:* Colin Budds. VHS $19.98 WAR *ℐℐ*

Hurricane Sword Thriller sets savage sword play against a background of murder, betrayal, prostitution, and reunion.
197? 86m/C Chen Sau Kei, Li Tai Shing. VHS, Beta NO *ℐ½*

The Hurried Man An international art smuggler like to live life to the extreme. But his obsessions, and a beautiful woman, just may lead to death.
1977 91m/C FR Alain Delon, Christian Barbier, Andre Falcon, Stefano Patrizi. VHS, Beta $59.95 UNI *ℐℐ½*

Hurry, Charlie, Hurry Husband gets in trouble when he bows out of a trip with his social-climber wife when he tells her he must travel to Washington to see the Vice President.
1941 65m/B Leon Errol. VHS, Beta $34.95 RKO, MLB *ℐ*

Hurry Up or I'll Be Thirty A Brooklyn bachelor celebrates his thirtieth birthday by becoming morose, depressed, and enraged. His friends try to help; they fail, but he finds love anyway. For those seeking a better life through celluloid.
1973 87m/C Danny DeVito, John Lefkowitz, Steve Inwood, Linda DeCoff, Ronald Anton, Maureen Byrnes, Francis Gallagher; *D:* Joseph Jacoby. VHS, Beta $69.98 LIV, VES *ℐℐ*

Husband Hunting Working girls hit the beach in search of husbands, and find that love isn't easy to find or hold on to.
196? 90m/C IT Walter Chiari. VHS, Beta NO *ℐ*

Husbands and Lovers Controversial and confusing film focuses on a couple's untraditional marriage. Stephen (Sands) and Alina (Pacula) have agreed to be totally honest with each other and when Alina decides to take a lover, Stephen agrees on the condition that she report back to him every intimate detail of her affair. In the confusion and excitement of this kinky love triangle, everyone starts losing control as sexual boundaries are pushed to the limit. Also available in an unrated version.
1991 (R) 91m/C Julian Sands, Joanna Pacula, Tcheky Karyo; *D:* Mauro Bolognini; *W:* Sergio Bazzini. VHS $89.95 COL *ℐℐ*

Husbands and Wives Art imitates life as Allen-Farrow relationship dissolves on-screen and Woody becomes involved with young student. Mature and penetrating look at modern pair bonding and lonliness, offering more painful honesty and sadness than outright laughs, though still retaining essential Allen charm. Stylistically burdened by experiment with pseudo-documentary telling of tale and spasmodic hand-held cameras that annoy more than entertain. Professor Woody finds his marriage to Mia strained after the couple discover that best friends Davis and Pollack are getting a divorce. Pollack then enjoys late mid-life crisis with a ditsy aerobics instructor while sophisticated and neurotic Davis falls for charming Neeson, whom Mia has secret crush on. Meanwhile, Woody somewhat reluctantly becomes enamoured of writing student Lewis. The usual excellent, intriguing Allen cast with Davis notable as the overwhelming, overbearing wife/friend. Trailers became unintentionally funny in light of highly publicized Farrow/Allen personal problems and the release was bumped up to capitalize on the publicity.
1992 (R) 107m/C Woody Allen, Mia Farrow, Judy Davis, Sydney Pollack, Liam Neeson, Juliette Lewis, Lysette Anthony, Blythe Danner; *W/D:* Woody Allen. Academy Awards '92 Nominations: Best Original Screenplay, Best Supporting Actress (Davis); Chicago Film Critics Awards '93: Best Supporting Actress (Davis); Los Angeles Film Critics Association Awards '92: Best Supporting Actress (Davis); National Board of Review Awards '92: Best Supporting Actress (Davis); National Society of Film Critics Awards '92: Best Supporting Actress (Davis). VHS, LV $89.99 COL, MOV *ℐℐℐ½*

Husbands, Wives, Money, and Murder A couple is pushed over the edge by a nosey census taker and then must dispose of the consequences.
1986 92m/C Garrett Morris, Greg Mullavey, Meredith MacRae, Timothy Bottoms; *D:* Bruce Cook Jr. VHS, Beta $79.95 TWE, HHE *ℐ*

Hush, Hush, Sweet Charlotte A fading southern belle finds out the truth about her fiance's murder when the case is reopened thirty-seven years later by her cousin in an elaborate plot to drive her crazy. Grisly, superbly entertaining Southern Gothic horror tale, with vivid performances from the aging leads.
1965 134m/B Bette Davis, Olivia de Havilland, Joseph Cotten, Agnes Moorehead, Mary Astor, Bruce Dern; *D:* Robert Aldrich. Academy Awards '64 Nominations: Best Art Direction/Set Decoration (B & W), Best Black and White Cinematography, Best Costume Design (B & W), Best Film Editing, Best Song ("Hush, Hush, Sweet Charlotte"), Best Supporting Actress (Moorehead), Best Original Score; Edgar Allan Poe Awards '64: Best Screenplay; Golden Globe Awards '65: Best Supporting Actress (Moorehead). VHS, Beta, LV $19.95 FOX *ℐℐℐ*

Hush Little Baby, Don't You Cry A made-for-television drama about a seemingly normal middle-aged family man who is in actuality a child abuser/murderer.
1986 110m/C Emery L. Kedocia, Gary Glem, Tony Grant, Burt Douglas; *D:* Don Hawks. VHS, Beta $79.95 PSM *ℐ*

Hussy Hooker and her boyfriend find themselves trapped in a web of gangsters and drugs.
1980 (R) 95m/C GB Helen Mirren, John Shea, Jenny Runacre; *D:* Matthew Chapman. VHS, Beta, LV $69.95 VES *ℐ*

Hustle Gritty urban adventure with Reynolds as an L.A. detective investigating a young call girl's death. He becomes romantically entangled with high-priced call girl Deneuve.
1975 (R) 120m/C Burt Reynolds, Catherine Deneuve; *D:* Robert Aldrich. VHS, Beta $24.95 PAR *ℐℐ*

The Hustler The original story of Fast Eddie Felsen and his adventures in the seedy world of professional pool. Newman plays the naive, talented and self-destructive Felsen perfectly, Laurie is oustanding as his lover, and Gleason epitomizes the pool great Minnesota Fats. Rivetingly atmospheric, and exquisitely photographed. Parent to the reprise "The Color of Money," made 25 years later.
1961 134m/B Paul Newman, Jackie Gleason, Piper Laurie, George C. Scott, Myron McCormick; *D:* Robert Rossen. Academy Awards '61: Best Art Direction/Set Decoration (B & W), Best Black and White Cinematography; Nominations: Best Actor (Newman), Best Actress (Laurie), Best Adapted Screenplay, Best Director (Rossen), Best Picture, Best Supporting Actor (Gleason, Scott); British Academy Awards '61: Best Actor (Newman), Best Film; National Board of Review Awards '61: 10 Best Films of the Year, Best Supporting Actor (Gleason). VHS, Beta, LV $19.98 FOX, FCT *ℐℐℐ*

Hustler Squad U.S. Army major and Philippine guerrilla leader stage a major operation to help rid the Philippines of Japanese Occupation forces: they have four combat-trained prostitutes infiltrate a brothel patronized by top Japanese officers. Verrrrery clever.
1976 (R) 98m/C John Ericson, Karen Ericson, Lynda Sinclaire, Nory Wright; *D:* Ted V. Mikels. VHS, Beta $19.95 UHV, MRV *ℐ*

Hustling A reporter writing a series of articles on prostitution in New York City takes an incisive look at their unusual and sometimes brutal world. Notable performance by Remick as the reporter and Clayburgh as a victimized hooker. Made for TV and based on a novel by Gail Sheehy.

1975 96m/C Jill Clayburgh, Lee Remick, Alex Rocco, Monte Markham; *D:* Joseph Sargent. VHS, Beta $49.95 *WOV* ✓✓

Hyena of London A doctor steals the hyena of London's corpse and injects the rabid protoplasm into his own brain with deadly results.
1962 ?m/C Diana Martin, Bernard Price. VHS $15.95 *LOO* ✓✓

Hyper-Sapien: People from Another Star Two cuddly aliens run away from home, are befriended by a lonely farmboy, and are chased all over the wilds of Wyoming.
1986 (PG) 93m/C Sydney Penny, Keenan Wynn, Gail Strickland, Ricky Paull Goldin, Peter Jason, Talia Shire; *D:* Peter Hunt. VHS, Beta, LV $19.98 *WAR* ✓½

The Hypothesis of the Stolen Painting An art collector guides an interviewer around six paintings by Frederic Tonnerre, an academic 19th century painter, in an attempt to solve the mysterious disappearance of a seventh painting. The film presents the paintings as tableaux vivants in which the actors hold poses as they are examined. Based on the novel "Baphomet" by Pierre Klossowski. In French with English subtitles.
1978 78m/B *W/D:* Raul Ruiz. VHS $59.95 *WAC, TAM* ✓✓

Hysteria When an American becomes involved in an accident and has amnesia, a mysterious benefactor pays all his bills and gives the man a house to live in. But a series of murders could mean he's the murderer—or the next victim.
1964 (PG) 85m/B *GB* Robert Webber, Susan Lloyd, Maurice Denham; *D:* Freddie Francis. VHS, Beta $59.95 *MGM, MLB* ✓½

Hysterical Odd little attempt at a horror flick parody features the Hudson Brothers and involves a haunted lighthouse occupied by the vengeful spirit of a spurned woman. Late-night fun.
1983 (PG) 86m/C Brett Hudson, William Hudson, Mark Hudson, Cindy Pickett, Richard Kiel, Julie Newmar, Bud Cort; *D:* Chris Bearde. VHS, Beta, LV $9.98 *SUE* ✓✓

I Accuse My Parents Juvenile delinquent tries to blame a murder and his involvement in a gang of thieves on his mom and dad's failure to raise him properly.
1945 70m/B Mary Beth Hughes, Robert Lowell, John Miljan. VHS, Beta $16.95 *SNC, NOS, DVT* ✓½

I Am a Camera A young English writer develops a relationship with a reckless young English girl in Berlin during the 1930s. Based on the Berlin stories by Christopher Isherwood, later musicalized as "Cabaret."
1955 99m/B *GB* Julie Harris, Shelley Winters, Laurence Harvey, Patrick McGoohan; *D:* Henry Cornelius. VHS, Beta $24.95 *MON* ✓✓✓

I Am a Fugitive from a Chain Gang WWI veteran Muni returns home with dreams of traveling across America. After a brief stint as a clerk, he strikes out on his own. Near penniless, Muni meets up with a tramp who takes him to get a hamburger. He becomes an unwilling accomplice when the bum suddenly robs the place. Convicted and sentenced to a Georgia chain gang, he's brutalized and degraded, though he eventually escapes and lives the life of a criminal on the run. Based on the autobiography by Robert E. Burns. Brutal docu-details combine with powerhouse performances to create a classic. Timeless and thought-provoking.
AKA: I Am a Fugitive From the Chain Gang.

1932 93m/B Paul Muni, Glenda Farrell, Helen Vinson, Preston Foster; *D:* Mervyn LeRoy. Academy Awards '33 Nominations: Best Actor (Muni), Best Picture, Best Sound; National Board of Review Awards '32: 10 Best Films of the Year. VHS, Beta $19.98 *MGM, FOX, CCB* ✓✓✓✓

I Am Curious (Yellow) A woman sociologist is conducting a sexual survey on Swedish society, which leads her to have numerous sexual encounters in all sorts of places. Very controversial upon its U.S. release because of the nudity and sexual content but tame by today's standards. Followed by "I Am Curious (Blue)" which was filmed at the same time. In Swedish with English subtitles.
1967 95m/B *SW* Lena Nyman, Peter Lindgren; *D:* Vilgot Sjoman. VHS $59.95 *HTV* ✓✓½

I Am the Cheese An institutionalized boy undergoes psychiatric treatment; with the aid of his therapist (Wagner) he relives his traumatic childhood and finds out the truth about the death of his parents. A bit muddled, but with its moments. Adapted from a Robert Cormier teen novel.
1983 95m/C Robert MacNaughton, Hope Lange, Don Murray, Robert Wagner, Sudie Bond; *D:* Robert Jiras. VHS, Beta $69.98 *LIV, VES* ✓✓

I Am the Law Robinson is given the task of stopping gangster activity in the city. Although regularly a law professor, he is made special prosecutor and starts canvassing for people to testify. His witnesses become murder victims as an enemy on the inside attempts to thwart the game plan. Robinson is dismissed from the case but continues to pursue justice in streetclothes. Fine performances but somewhat predictable.
1938 83m/B Edward G. Robinson, Otto Kruger, John Beal, Barbara O'Neil, Wendy Barrie, Arthur Loft, Marc Lawrence; *D:* Alexander Hall; *W:* Jo Swerling. VHS, Beta, LV $69.95 *COL, PIA* ✓✓✓

I Beheld His Glory Story based on the experience of Cornelius, the Roman centurion who guarded Christ's tomb.
1953 53m/C George Macready, Robert Wilson, Virginia Wave. VHS $19.95 *REP, MVC* ✓✓✓

I Bury the Living A cemetery manager sticks pins in his map of a graveyard and people mysteriously start to die. Well-done suspense film.
1958 76m/B Richard Boone, Theodore Bikel, Peggy Maurer; *D:* Albert Band. VHS $16.95 *SNC, MRV* ✓✓

I Can't Escape A man attempts to piece his life back together after serving time for a crime he didn't commit. To prove himself to his girlfriend, he tries to break up an illegal stock scam.
1934 60m/B Onslow Stevens, Lila Lee, Russell Gleason, Otis Harlan, Hooper Atchley, Clara Kimball Young; *D:* Otto Brower. VHS, Beta $16.95 *SNC* ✓✓

I, Claudius, Vol. 1: A Touch of Murder/Family Affairs Award-winning Masterpiece Theatre series tells the true story of the Roman Empire and the people determined to rule it. In these first two episodes, Augustus tries to control his conniving second wife, the beautiful Livia, who is determined that her son Tiberius will be the next Roman ruler. Her manipulations lead to bloody mayhem. Brilliant acting. Based on the books by Robert Graves. Also available as a seven-volume set. Made for television.
1991 120m/C *GB* Sian Phillips, Brian Blessed, Derek Jacobi; *D:* Herbert Wise. VHS $24.95 *PBS, PAV, FCT* ✓✓

I, Claudius, Vol. 2: Waiting in the Wings/What Shall We Do With Claudius? Continuation of the Masterpiece Theatre series portraying the true story of the Roman Empire and its rulers. In the third and fourth episodes, Tiberius and his mother Livia attempt to capture the throne with a series of brutal manipulations. Young cousin Claudius, considered an ugly dimwit, watches from afar. Based on the books of Robert Graves. Also available as a seven-volume set. Made for television.
1980 120m/C Derek Jacobi, Sian Phillips, Brian Blessed; *D:* Herbert Wise. VHS $24.95 *PBS, PAV, FCT* ✓✓

I, Claudius, Vol. 3: Poison is Queen/Some Justice Episodes 5 and 6 see Emperor Augustus murdered and Tiberius on the throne he's coveted for so long. But how long can he stay, hiding the treachery that brought him there? Good question. Agrippina, wife of his latest victim, is determined to see him punished, and the Roman masses, not so stupid after all, have begun to see a pattern in the deaths of their best and brightest. Based on the books of Robert Graves. Also available as a seven-volume set. Made for television.
1980 120m/C Derek Jacobi, Sian Phillips, Brian Blessed; *D:* Herbert Wise. VHS $24.95 *PBS, PAV, FCT* ✓✓

I, Claudius, Vol. 4: Queen of Heaven/Reign of Terror In episodes 7 and 8, Caligula begins his evil manipulation of Tiberius, involving him in a wide variety of amoral activities and creating a trail of blood. Based on the books of Robert Graves. Also available as a seven-volume set. Made for television.
1980 120m/C Derek Jacobi, Sian Phillips. VHS $24.95 *PBS, PAV, FCT* ✓✓

I, Claudius, Vol. 5: Zeus, By Jove!/Hail Who? Caligula's schemes result in his rise to the throne after Tiberius. Debauchery rules and murder is a standard procedure that returns to remove the emperor. At last, patient Claudius, the only remaining heir, thought too foolish to be dangerous, ascends the throne. Award-winning Masterpiece Theatre production created by the BBC. Based on the books of Robert Graves. The first episode on this cassette contains the graphic scene of Caligula's evisceration of his sister, as he enacts the life of Zeus in demented belief that he is the god—be forewarned. Also available as a seven-volume set. Made for television.
1980 120m/C Derek Jacobi, John Hurt; *D:* Herbert Wise. VHS $24.95 *PBS, PAV, FCT* ✓✓

I, Claudius, Vol. 6: Fool's Luck/A God in Colchester Episodes 11 and 12 see Emperor Claudius wise in the ways of statesmanship, but foolish in the ways of love. His young wife Messalina creates a furor when her sexual practices become known. In spite of his love, the emperor must punish her. Award-winning BBC production, shown in U.S. on Masterpiece Theatre. Based on the books of Robert Graves. Also available as a seven-volume set.
1980 120m/C Derek Jacobi; *D:* Herbert Wise. VHS $24.95 *PBS, PAV, FCT* ✓✓

I, Claudius, Vol. 7: Old King Log Claudius, aging and sad, resigns himself to his destiny, as his wife makes plans for his death. Claudius wants only the time to complete the journal of his life. Brilliant acting from Jacobi in this BBC production shown in the U.S. on Masterpiece Theatre. Based on

the books of Robert Graves. Also available as a seven-volume set.
1980 60m/C Derek Jacobi; **D:** Herbert Wise. VHS $24.95 *PBS, PAV, FCT* 🎬

I Come in Peace A tough, maverick Texas cop embarks on a one-way ride to Nosebleed City when he attempts to track down a malevolent alien drug czar who kills his victims by sucking their brains. Mindless thrills. **AKA:** Dark Angel.
1990 (R) 92m/C Dolph Lundgren, Brian Benben, Betsy Brantley, Jesse Vint, Michael J. Pollard; **D:** Craig R. Baxley; **M:** Jan Hammer. VHS, Beta, LV $89.95 *MED* 🎬🎬

I Confess When a priest (Clift) hears a murderer's confession, the circumstances seem to point to him as the prime suspect. Tepid, overly serious and occasionally interesting mid-career Hitchcock. Adapted from Paul Anthelme's 1902 play.
1953 95m/B Montgomery Clift, Anne Baxter, Karl Malden, Brian Aherne; **D:** Alfred Hitchcock. VHS, Beta, LV $19.98 *WAR, FCT, MLB* 🎬🎬 ½

I Conquer the Sea Two brothers, who works as whalers, cast their affection on the same woman. Drowns in its own melodrama.
1936 68m/B Steffi Duna, Stanley Morner, Dennis Morgan, Douglas Walton, George Cleveland, Johnny Pirrone; **D:** Victor Halperin. VHS, Beta, 8mm *VYY* 🎬 ½

I Could Go on Singing An aging American songstress, on a tour in Britain, becomes reacquainted with her illegitimate son and his British father, but eventually goes back to the footlights. Garland's last film. Songs include "By Myself" and "It Never Was You." A must for Garland fans. Letterboxed.
1963 99m/C Judy Garland, Dirk Bogarde, Jack Klugman, Aline MacMahon; **D:** Ronald Neame. VHS, Beta, LV $19.98 *MGM* 🎬🎬 ½

I Cover the Waterfront A reporter is assigned to write about a boatman involved in a fishy scheme to smuggle Chinese immigrants into the country wrapped in shark skins. While trying to get the story, the journalist falls in love with the fisherman's daughter. Torrance passed away before its release.
1933 70m/B Claudette Colbert, Ben Lyon, Ernest Torrence, Hobart Cavanaugh; **D:** James Cruze. VHS, Beta $19.95 *NOS, MRV, VYY* 🎬🎬 ½

I Died a Thousand Times Aging gangster Mad Dog Earle (pushup prince Palance) plans one last death-defying heist while hiding from police in the mountains. Meanwhile, the hard boiled gangster softens a bit thanks to surgery-needing girlfriend, but moll Winters doesn't seem to think that three's company. A low rent "High Sierra." From the novel by W.R. Burnett.
1955 109m/C Jack Palance, Shelley Winters, Lori Nelson, Lee Marvin, Earl Holliman, Lon Chaney Jr., Howard St. John; **W:** W.R. Burnett. VHS, LV $59.99 *WAR, PIA, FCT* 🎬🎬

I Dismember Mama Classless story of an asylum inmate who escapes to kill his mother. Although he hates women, his little girls as evidenced by his nine-year-old love interest. Notably lacking in bloody scenes. **AKA:** Poor Albert and Little Annie.
1974 (R) 81m/C Zooey Hall, Joanne Moore Jordan, Greg Mullavey, Marlene Tracy; **D:** Paul Leder. VHS, Beta $24.95 *GEM* Woof!

I Do! I Do! This Los Angeles production of the Broadway musical covers 50 years of a marriage, beginning just before the turn of the century.
1984 116m/C Lee Remick, Hal Linden. VHS, Beta $39.95 *RKO, STS, TTC* Woof!

I Don't Buy Kisses Anymore Heartwarming story starring Alexander and Peeples as two mismatched lovers who end up realizing that they're made for each other. Alexander plays Bernie Fishbine, an overweight Jewish shoe store owner who falls for a psychology graduate student (Peeples). Little does he know, but Peeples is studying him for her term paper, appropriately titled "The Psychological Study of an Obese Male." Alexander gives a great performance, as do Kazan and Jacobi who play Bernie's parents.
1992 (PG) 112m/C Jason Alexander, Nia Peeples, Lainie Kazan, Lou Jacobi, Eileen Brennan, Larry Storch; **D:** Robert Marcarelli. VHS, Beta *PAR* 🎬🎬 ½

I Don't Give a Damn An embittered wounded soldier returns home to his loved ones, rejects them, and becomes more and more uninterested in life itself. Subtitled.
1988 (R) 94m/C *IS* Ika Sohar, Anat Waxman; **D:** Shmuel Imberman. VHS, Beta $59.95 *TWE* 🎬🎬

I Don't Want to Be Born It's got all the right ingredients for overnight camp: a spurned dwarf, a large, howling baby-thing, slice and dice murder and mayhem, and Collins. It could've been so bad. Instead, this "Rosemary's Baby" rehash is just stupid bad. **AKA:** The Devil Within Her.
1975 (R) 90m/C *GB* Joan Collins, Eileen Atkins, Donald Pleasence, Ralph Bates, Caroline Munro; **D:** Peter Sasdy. VHS *NO* 🎬

I Dood It Young tailor's assistant Skelton falls hard for young actress Powell working near his shop. She agrees to date, and eventually marry him, but only to spite her boyfriend who has just run off with another woman. All's well however, when Skelton stumbles across a spy ring, is hailed a hero and heps Powell realize she really loves him. Songs include "Star Eyes," "Hola E Pae," "Swing the Jinx Away," and "Taking a Chance on Love." **AKA:** By Hook or By Crook.
1943 102m/B Red Skelton, Eleanor Powell, Richard Ainley, Patricia Dane, Sam Levene, Thurston Hall, Lena Horne, Butterfly McQueen, Jimmy Dorsey & His Orchestra; **D:** Vincente Minnelli. VHS $19.98 *MGM, CCB* 🎬🎬

I Dream of Jeannie The third and worst bio of Stephen Foster has Foster as a bookkeeper-cum-songwriter alternating between writing tunes and chasing Lawrence. When he dumps her, he goes into a funk. Will he be able to complete the title song? The suspense will kill you. Lots of singing, but not much else.
1952 90m/C Ray Middleton, Bill Shirley, Muriel Lawrence, Lynn Bari, Rex Allen; **D:** Allan Dwan. VHS $19.95 *NOS, VEC* 🎬

I Dream Too Much A musical vehicle for opera star Pons, as a French singer who marries an American composer played by Fonda. Songwriter falls into wife's shadow after pushing her into a singing career; she then raises his spirits a couple of octaves by helping him sell a musical comedy. Went into production after a rival company, Columbia, launched opera singer Grace Moore's acting career. Ball later bought this studio, where she was given her second starring role. ♫ The Jockey on the Carousel; I'm the Echo; I Got Love; I Dream Too Much; Bell Song; Caro Nome.
1935 90m/B Lily Pons, Henry Fonda, Eric Blore, Lucille Ball, Mischa Auer; **D:** John Cromwell. VHS, Beta $19.98 *HHT, TTC* 🎬🎬

I Drink Your Blood Hippie satanists looking for kicks spike an old man's drink with LSD. To get revenge, the old codger's grandson sells the nasty flower children meat

pies injected with the blood of a rabid dog. The hippies then turn into cannibalistic maniacs, infecting anyone they bite. From the man responsible for "I Spit on Your Grave;" originally played on a double bill with "I Eat Your Skin."
1971 (R) 83m/C Bhasker, Jadine Wong, Ronda Fultz, Elizabeth Marner-Brooks, George Patterson, Riley Mills, Iris Brooks, John Damon; **D:** David E. Durston. VHS $18.00 *FRG* 🎬 ½

I Eat Your Skin Cannibalistic zombies terrorize a novelist and his girlfriend on a Caribbean island. Blood and guts, usually shown on a gourmet double bill with "I Drink Your Blood." **AKA:** Zombies; Voodoo Blood Bath; Zombie.
1964 82m/B William Joyce, Heather Hewitt, Betty H. Lindon; **D:** Del Tenney. VHS $9.95 *RHI, SNC, FCT* Woof!

I Give My All Animated Japanese feature for adults. Based on Japanese comic books' "love comedy" genre. A bawdy tale of a rich woman and her daughters' sex adventures. Japanese with English subtitles.
1991 45m/C *JP* VHS $34.95 *CPM* Woof!

I Hate Blondes A group of criminals use a ghostwriter's burglaring stories as instructional manuals. The writer becomes involved with the gang. Relies heavily on visual humor. Notably among the comedy scenes is the author's search for jewels at a get-together. **AKA:** Odio le Bionde.
1983 90m/C *IT* **D:** Giorgio Capitani, Giorgio Capitani. VHS, Beta *PGN* 🎬🎬 ½

I Heard the Owl Call My Name Poignant story of an Anglican priest who is relocated to an Indian fishing village on the ouskirts of Vancouver, British Columbia. Made for television and based on a Margaret Craven book.
1973 74m/C Tom Courtenay, Dean Jagger, Paul Stanley; **D:** Daryl Duke. Beta $14.95 *PSM* 🎬🎬 ½

I Killed Rasputin The "Mad Monk" who rose to power before the Russian Revolution lost his life in a bizarre assassination by Felix Youssoupoff. Film deals with the friendship between the men that ended in betrayal. Well-intentioned, but overwrought. Dubbed.
1967 95m/C *FR IT* Geraldine Chaplin, Gert Frobe, Peter McEnery; **D:** Robert Hossein. VHS, Beta $59.95 *MPI* 🎬 ½

I Killed That Man A prisoner scheduled to die in the electric chair is given an early ticket out when he is found poisoned. Evidence points to an unusual group of suspects. Effective low-budget thriller offers a few unexpected surprises.
1942 72m/B Ricardo Cortez, Joan Woodbury, Iris Adrian, George Pembroke, Herbert Rawlinson, Pat Gleason, Ralf Harolde, Jack Mulhall, Vince Barnett, Gavin Gordon, John Hamilton; **D:** Phil Rosen. VHS, Beta $16.95 *SNC* 🎬🎬 ½

I Know Where I'm Going A young woman (Hiller), who believes that money brings happiness, is on the verge of marrying a rich old man, until she meets a handsome naval officer (Livesey) and finds a happy, simple life. Early on the female lead appears in a dream sequence filmed in the mode of surrealist painter Salvador Deli and avant garde director Luis Bunvelo. Scottish setting and folk songs give a unique flavor. Brown provides a fine performance as a native Scot.
1945 91m/B *GB* Roger Livesey, Wendy Hiller, Finlay Currie, Pamela Brown; **D:** Michael Powell. VHS, Beta $59.95 *LCA, HMV* 🎬🎬

I Know Why the Caged Bird Sings A black writer's memories of growing up in the rural South during the 1930s. Strong performances from Rolle and Good. Made-for-television film is based on the book by Maya Angelou.
1979 100m/C Diahann Carroll, Ruby Dee, Esther Rolle, Roger E. Mosley, Paul Benjamin, Constance Good; **D:** Fielder Cook. **VHS, Beta** $59.95 *KUI* 🎞🎞🎞

I Like Bats Can a psychiatrist help a vampire become a human? Polish dialogue with English subtitles.
1985 90m/C **D:** Grzegorz Warchol. **VHS** $49.95 *FCT* 🎞🎞🎞

I Live in Fear Nakajima, an elderly, wealthy owner of a foundry, becomes increasingly fearful of atomic war and the threats to his family's safety. He tries to persuade them to leave Japan and move with him to Brazil but they fear the family will be ruined financially. Nakajima then burns down his foundry to force his children to move but instead they go to court and have him declared mentally incompetent. He is placed in an institution where he finds peace in the delusion that he has escaped to another planet and that the Earth has indeed suffered a nuclear holocaust. A provocative look at the fear of atomic warfare and radiation. In Japanese with English subtitles. *AKA:* Record of a Living Being; Kimono No Kiroku.
1955 105m/C *JP* Toshiro Mifune, Takashi Shimura, Eiko Miyoshi, Haruko Togo; **D:** Akira Kurosawa. **VHS** $39.95 *FCT* 🎞🎞🎞

I Live in Grosvenor Square An American soldier in Great Britain falls in love with a major's fiancee. Entertaining if a bit drawn out. *AKA:* A Yank In London.
1946 106m/B *GB* Anna Neagle, Rex Harrison, Dean Jagger, Robert Morley, Jane Darwell; **D:** Herbert Wilcox. **VHS** $19.95 *NOS, DVT* 🎞🎞

I Live My Life Stylish glossy flick with Crawford playing a bored New York debutante who travels to Greece and meets a dedicated archaeologist (Aherne). A love/hate relationship ensues in this typical Crawford vehicle where she is witty and parades around in sophisticated fashions, but there is little substance here.
1935 92m/B Joan Crawford, Brian Aherne, Frank Morgan, Aline MacMahon, Eric Blore, Fred Keating, Jessie Ralph, Arthur Treacher, Frank Conroy, Sterling Holloway, Vince Barnett, Hedda Hopper, Lionel Stander; **D:** Woodbridge S. Van Dyke; **W:** Joseph L. Mankiewicz, Gottfried Reinhardt, Ethel B. Borden. **VHS** $19.98 *MGM* 🎞½

I Live with Me Dad A vagrant drunk and his son fight the authorities for the right to be together.
1986 86m/C *AU* Peter Hehir, Haydon Samuels; **D:** Paul Maloney. **VHS, Beta** $79.98 *FOX* 🎞½

I Love All of You Deneuve relives experiences with three former lovers - a composer, a well-intentioned nobody, and a rock star - as she enters into a relationship with a widower.
1983 103m/C *FR* Catherine Deneuve, Jean-Louis Trintignant, Gerard Depardieu, Serge Gainsbourg; **D:** Claude Berri. **VHS, Beta** *NO* 🎞🎞½

I Love Lucy Everyone's favorite redhead in scrape after scrape, along with her Cuban bandleader husband, Ricky Ricardo, and their neighbors Fred and Ethel Mertz. Episodes on this tape include "Lucy Does a TV Commercial" and "Lucy's Italian Movie." Other episodes available.
1952 51m/B Lucille Ball, Desi Arnaz Sr., Vivian Vance, William Frawley. **VHS, LV** $14.98 *FOX, MOV* 🎞🎞½

I Love Melvin Reynolds wants to be a Tinseltown goddess, and O'Connor just wants Reynolds; so he passes himself off as chief lenseman for a famous magazine and promises her a shot at the cover of "Look." Seems he has a little trouble on the follow through. Choreographed by Robert Alton, it's got a best ever football ballet (with Reynolds as pigskin). 🎵A Lady Loves; Saturday Afternoon Before The Game; I Wanna Wander; We Have Never Met As Of Yet; Life Has Its Funny Little Ups And Downs; Where Did You Learn To Dance?; And There You Are.
1953 77m/C Donald O'Connor, Debbie Reynolds, Una Merkel, Richard Anderson, Jim Backus, Allyn Joslyn, Les Tremayne, Noreen Corcoran, Robert Taylor, Howard Keel; **D:** Don Weis. **VHS** $19.98 *MGM, TTC, FCT* 🎞🎞½

I Love My...Wife A medical student plays doctor with hospital nurses when he and his wife stop having sex during her pregnancy. The marriage becomes more strained when their son is born and his mother-in-law moves in. A comedy without the proper dosage of laughs.
1970 (R) 98m/C Elliott Gould, Brenda Vaccaro, Angel Tompkins; **D:** Mel Stuart. **VHS, Beta** $59.95 *MCA* 🎞🎞

I Love N.Y. A young metropolitan couple struggles to find true love amidst disapproving parents and doubting friends. Choppy direction and poor writing contribute to its failure.
1987 100m/C Scott Baio, Kelley Van Der Velden, Christopher Plummer, Jennifer O'Neill, Jerry Orbach, Virna Lisi; **D:** Alan Smithee. **VHS, Beta, LV** *NO* 🎞

I Love You Man down on his luck mistakenly assumes that a woman he meets is a hooker. She plays along, only to find that they are becoming emotionally involved. Pretentious cat-and-mouse game.
1981 (R) 104m/C *BR* Sonia Braga, Paulo Cesar Pereio, Vera Fischer, Tarcisio Meria; **D:** Arnaldo Jabor. **VHS, Beta** $59.95 *MGM* 🎞

I Love You Again A classic screwball comedy with Powell and Loy working together (wonderfully) in something other than their "Thin Man" series. Powell is a gloomy businessman who's about to be divorced by Loy. But after an accident it turns out Powell had been suffering from amnesia and has now regained his memory (which he keeps a secret). It seems Mr. Respectable used to be a con man and he decides to revert to his criminal ways. He also doesn't remember Loy but falls instantly in love with her and must decide what kind of life he wants. Witty dialog, amusing situations, fine direction.
1940 97m/B William Powell, Myrna Loy, Frank McHugh, Edmund Lowe; **D:** Woodbridge S. Van Dyke. **VHS, LV** $19.98 *MGM* 🎞🎞½

I Love You, Alice B. Toklas A straight uptight lawyer decides to join the peace and love generation in this somewhat maniacal satire of the hippie culture. Authored by Paul Mazursky and Larry Tucker. Incidentally, the title's Alice B. Toklas was actually the lifemate of "Lost Generation" author Gertrude Stein. *AKA:* Kiss My Butterfly.
1968 94m/C Peter Sellers, Jo Van Fleet, Leigh Taylor-Young, Joyce Van Patten; **D:** Hy Averback. **VHS, Beta, LV** $19.98 *WAR, FCT* 🎞🎞½

I Love You Rosa Rosa, a young Jewish widow, wrestles big time with old world values. Required by custom to marry her dearly departed's eldest brother, she's not enamored with her newly betrothed. Not that he's not a nice guy; he seems to plan to take his marital duties very seriously. It's just that

he's a tad youthful (eleven years old, to be exact). Much rabbi consulting and soul searching.
1972 90m/C Michal Bat-Adam, Gabi Oterman, Yoseph Shiloah; **W/D:** Moshe Mizrahi. **VHS** $39.95 *FCT, NCJ* 🎞🎞½

I Love You to Death Dry comedy based on a true story, concerns a woman who tries to kill off her cheating husband. Lots of stars, but they never shine. Hurt and Reeves are somewhat amusing as drugged up hit men who struggle with the lyrics to the National Anthem.
1990 (R) 110m/C Kevin Kline, Tracy Ullman, Joan Plowright, River Phoenix, William Hurt, Keanu Reeves, Phoebe Cates; **D:** Lawrence Kasdan. **VHS, Beta, LV** $19.95 *COL* 🎞🎞½

I Love You...Goodbye A frustrated housewife, fed up with the constant role of wife and mother, leaves her family in an effort to find a more challenging and fulfilling life. A good performance by Lange compensates for some of its muddledness.
1973 74m/C Hope Lange, Earl Holliman. **VHS, Beta** *LCA* 🎞🎞

I, Madman A novel-loving horror actress is stalked by the same mutilating madman that appears in the book she's presently reading. We call that bad luck.
1989 (R) 90m/C Jenny Wright, Clayton Rohner, William Cook; **D:** Tibor Takacs. **VHS, Beta, LV** $89.95 *MED* 🎞🎞

I Married a Centerfold Television movie fluff about a young man's amorous pursuit of a model.
1984 100m/C Teri Copley, Timothy Daly, Diane Ladd, Bert Remsen, Anson Williams; **D:** Peter Werner. **VHS, Beta, LV** $79.95 *SVS* 🎞🎞

I Married a Monster from Outer Space The vintage thriller about a race of monster-like aliens from another planet who try to conquer earth. Despite its head-shaking title, an effective '50s sci-fi creeper.
1958 78m/B Tom Tryon, Gloria Talbott, Maxie Rosenbloom, Mary Treen, Ty Hardin; **D:** Gene Fowler. **VHS, Beta** $49.95 *PAR, MLB* 🎞🎞½

I Married a Vampire A country girl in the city is romanced and wed by a dashing vampire. Troma-produced hyper-camp.
1987 85m/C Rachel Gordon, Brendan Hickey; **D:** Jay Raskin. **VHS, Beta** $9.99 *STE, PSM* 🎞🎞

I Married a Witch A witch burned at the stake during the Salem witch trials comes back to haunt the descendants of her accusers and gets romantic with one of them. Wonderfully played fantasy/comedy.
1942 77m/B Veronica Lake, Fredric March, Susan Hayward, Broderick Crawford; **D:** Rene Clair. **VHS, Beta, LV** $59.95 *MLB, WAR* 🎞🎞🎞

I Married a Woman An advertising executive marries a beautiful blonde woman, but finds it very difficult to balance his career and marriage. Low on laughs. Shot in black and white, but includes a fantasy scene in color that features John Wayne. Pay attention to see young Angie Dickinson.
1956 84m/B George Gobel, Diana Dors, Adolphe Menjou, Nita Talbot; **D:** Hal Kanter. **VHS, Beta, LV** $15.95 *UHV* 🎞

I Married an Angel The last MacDonald/Eddy film. A playboy is lured away from his usual interests by a beautiful angel. Adapted from Rodgers and Hart Broadway play. Strange and less than compelling. 🎵I Married An Angel; I'll Tell the Man in the Street; Spring is Here; Tira Lira La; A Twinkle in Your Eye; Aloha Oe; Caprice Viennoise; Chanson Boheme; Anges Purs; Hey Butcher; There Comes a Time; To Count Palaffi; May I

Present the Girl; Now You've Met the Angel; But What of Truth.
1942 84m/C Jeanette MacDonald, Nelson Eddy, Binnie Barnes, Edward Everett Horton, Reginald Owen, Mona Maris, Janis Carter, Inez Cooper, Douglas Dumbrille, Leonid Kinskey, Marion Rosamond, Anne Jeffreys, Marek Windheim; **D:** Woodbridge S. Van Dyke; **W:** Anita Loos; **M:** Richard Rodgers, Lorenz Hart. **VHS, Beta** $19.98 *MGM, MVD* 𝄢𝄢 ½

I Met a Murderer A man kills his nagging wife after a bitter argument and flees from her vengeful brother. Fine fugitive drama with a number of interesting twists.
1939 79m/B James Mason, Pamela Kellino, Sylvia Coleridge; **D:** Roy Kellino. **VHS** $16.95 *SNC, NOS, DVT* 𝄢𝄢 ½

I, Mobster Cochran tells a Senate Sub-Committee of his rise in the ranks of the Underworld—from his humble beginning as a bet collector for a bookie to his position as kingpin of the crime syndicate.
1958 80m/B Steve Cochran, Lita Milan, Robert Strauss, Celia Lovsky; **D:** Roger Corman. **VHS** *NO* 𝄢𝄢 ½

I Never Promised You a Rose Garden A disturbed 16-year-old girl spirals down into madness and despair while a hospital psychiatrist struggles to bring her back to life. Based on the Joanne Greenberg bestseller. Compelling and unyielding exploration of the clinical treatment of schizophrenia.
1977 (R) 90m/C Kathleen Quinlan, Bibi Andersson, Sylvia Sidney, Diane Varsi; **D:** Anthony Page. **VHS, Beta** $59.95 *WAR, OM* 𝄢𝄢𝄢

I Never Sang For My Father A devoted son must choose between caring for his cantankerous but well-meaning father, and moving out West to marry the divorced doctor whom he loves. While his mother wants him to stay near home, his sister, who fell out of her father's favor by marrying out of the family faith, argues that he should do what he wants. An introspective, stirring story based on the Robert Anderson play.
1970 (PG) 90m/C Gene Hackman, Melvyn Douglas, Estelle Parsons, Dorothy Stickney; **D:** Gilbert Cates. Academy Awards '70 Nominations: Best Actor (Douglas), Best Adapted Screenplay, Best Supporting Actor (Hackman); National Board of Review Awards '70: 10 Best Films of the Year. **VHS, Beta, LV** $69.95 *COL* 𝄢𝄢𝄢 ½

I Ought to Be in Pictures After hitch-hiking from New York to Hollywood to break into the movies, a teen-aged actress finds her father, a screenwriter turned alcoholic-gambler. Late, desperately unfunny Neil Simon outing, adapted from a Simon play.
1982 (PG) 107m/C Walter Matthau, Ann-Margret, Dinah Manoff, Lance Guest, Michael Dudikoff; **D:** Herbert Ross. **VHS, Beta** $59.98 *FOX* 𝄢𝄢

I Posed for Playboy Three women—one a college co-ed, one a stockbroker, and one a 37-year-old mother—quench their private passions by posing for Playboy Magazine. Made for television with additional footage added to give it an "R" rating.
1991 (R) 98m/C Lynda Carter, Michelle Greene, Amanda Peterson, Brittany York; **D:** Stephen Stafford. **VHS, LV** $29.98 *REP* 𝄢𝄢

I Remember Mama A true Hollywood heart tugger chronicling the life of a Norwegian immigrant family living in San Francisco during the early 1900s. Dunne plays the mother with a perfect Norwegian accent and provides her family with wisdom and inspiration. A kindly father and four children round out the nuclear family. A host of oddball characters regularly pop in on the household—three high-strung aunts and an eccentric doctor who treats a live-in uncle. Adapted

from John Van Druten's stage play, based on Kathryn Forbes memoirs, "Mama's Bank Account;" a TV series came later. Dunne triumphs in her only character role.
1948 95m/B Irene Dunne, Barbara Bel Geddes, Oscar Homolka, Ellen Corby, Cedric Hardwicke, Edgar Bergen, Rudy Vallee, Barbara O'Neil, Florence Bates; **D:** George Stevens. Academy Awards '48 Nominations: Best Actress (Dunne), Best Black and White Cinematography, Best Supporting Actor (Homolka), Best Supporting Actress (Corby, Bel Geddes); Golden Globe Awards '49: Best Supporting Actress (Corby). **VHS, Beta, LV** $19.98 *CCB, RKO, TTC* 𝄢𝄢𝄢 ½

I See a Dark Stranger Cynical yet whimsical postwar British spy thriller about an angry Irish lass who agrees to steal war plans for the Nazis in order to battle her native enemies, the British—then she falls in love with a British officer. A sharply performed, decidedly jaded view of nationalism and wartime "heroism." **AKA:** The Adventuress; The Adventures.
1946 112m/B *GB* Deborah Kerr, Trevor Howard, Raymond Huntley; **D:** Frank Laudner. **VHS, Beta** $29.95 *VID* 𝄢𝄢𝄢

I Sent a Letter to My Love An aging spinster, faced with the lonely prospect of the death of her paralyzed brother, places a personal ad for a companion in a local newspaper, using a different name. Unknown to her, the brother is the one who answers it, and they begin a romantic correspondence. Well-acted, touching account of relationships that change lives, but it takes its time in telling the story.
1981 102m/C *FR* Simone Signoret, Jean Rochefort, Delphine Seyrig; **D:** Moshe Mizrahi. **VHS, Beta** $59.95 *HBO* 𝄢𝄢𝄢

I Shot Billy the Kid Billy the Kid decides to turn over a new leaf and live a decent life. The cards are stacked against him though: He's killed a man for nearly every year of his life, and old habits are hard to break.
1950 58m/B Donald (Don "Red") Barry, Robert Lowery, Tom Neal, Jack Perrin; **D:** William Berke. **VHS, Beta, LV** *NO* 𝄢 ½

I Shot Jesse James In his first film, director Fuller breathes characteristically feverish, maddened fire into the story of Bob Ford (Ireland) after he killed the notorious outlaw. An essential moment in Fuller's unique, America-as-tabloid-nightmare canon, and one of the best anti-westerns ever made.
1949 83m/B John Ireland, Barbara Britton, Preston Foster, Reed Hadley; **D:** Samuel Fuller. **VHS, Beta** *RXM* 𝄢𝄢𝄢

I Spit on Your Corpse A vicious female hired killer engages in a series of terrorist activities. Stars Spelvin in a non-pornographic role. **AKA:** Girls For Rent.
1974 (R) 90m/C Georgina Spelvin, Susan McIver, Kent Taylor; **D:** Al Adamson. **VHS, Beta** $59.95 *REP* Woof!

I Spit on Your Grave A woman vacationing at an upstate New York lake house is brutally attacked and raped by four men. Left for dead, she recovers and avenges the attack. Violence deserves an "X" rating. Not to be confused with the 1962 film of the same name. Also available in a 102-minute version. **AKA:** Day of the Woman.
1977 (R) 98m/C Camille Keaton, Eron Tabor, Richard Pace, Gunter Kleeman; **W/D:** Mier Zarchi. **VHS, Beta, LV** $39.95 *VES, VID* Woof!

I Stand Condemned A Russian officer is tricked into borrowing money from a spy and is condemned for treason. He's saved when a girl who loves him gives herself to a profiteer. Worth seeing only for young Olivier's performance. **AKA:** Moscow Nights.

1936 90m/B *GB* Laurence Olivier, Penelope Dudley Ward, Robert Cochran; **D:** Anthony Asquith. **VHS, Beta, 8mm, 3/4U, Special order formats** $19.95 *NOS, MRV, VYY* 𝄢𝄢 ½

I Take This Oath A cop is shocked to discover that his uncle is a wanted mobster, responsible for the death of a man. Hackneyed plot.
1940 64m/B Gordon Jones, Joyce Compton, Craig Reynolds, J. Farrell MacDonald, Robert E. Homans; **D:** Sherman Scott. **VHS, Beta** $16.95 *SNC* 𝄢

I, the Jury A remake of the 1953 Mike Hammer mystery in which the famed PI investigates the murder of his best friend. Assante mopes around as Hammer and looks out of place in this slowed-down version.
1982 (R) 111m/C Armand Assante, Barbara Carrera, Laurene Landon, Alan King, Geoffrey Lewis, Paul Sorvino, Jessica James, Leigh Anne Harris, Lynette Harris; **D:** Richard T. Heffron. **VHS, Beta** $19.98 *FOX* 𝄢

I Vitelloni Fellini's semi-autobiographical drama, argued by some to be his finest work. Five young men grow up in a small Italian town. As they mature, four of them remain in Romini and limit their opportunities by roping themselves off from the rest of the world. The characters are multi-dimensional, including a loafer who is supported by his sister and a young stud who impregnates a local woman. The script has some brilliant insights into youth, adulthood and what's in between. **AKA:** The Young and The Passionate; Vitelloni; Spivs.
1953 104m/B *IT* Alberto Sordi, Franco Interlenghi, Franco Fabrizi, Leopoldo Trieste; **D:** Federico Fellini. **VHS, LV** $68.00 *MOV, APD, TAM* 𝄢𝄢𝄢 ½

I Wake Up Screaming An actress' promoter is accused of her murder. Entertaining mystery with a surprise ending. Remade as "Vicki." **AKA:** Hot Spot.
1941 82m/B Betty Grable, Victor Mature, Carole Landis, Laird Cregar, William Gargan, Alan Mowbray, Allyn Joslyn; **D:** H. Bruce Humberstone. **VHS, Beta** $19.98 *FOX* 𝄢𝄢𝄢

I Walked with a Zombie The definitive and eeriest of the famous Val Lewton/Jacques Tourneur horror films. Dee, a young American nurse, comes to Haiti to care for the catatonic matriarch of a troubled family. Local legends bring themselves to bear when the nurse takes the ill woman to a local voodoo ceremony for "healing." Superb, startling images and atmosphere create a unique context for this serious "Jane Eyre"-like story; its reputation has grown through the years.
1943 69m/B Frances Dee, Tom Conway, James Ellison, Christine Gordon, Edith Barrett, Darby Jones, Sir Lancelot; **D:** Jacques Tourneur. **VHS, Beta, LV** $19.98 *MED, FCT, MLB* 𝄢𝄢 ½

I Wanna Be a Beauty Queen Divine hosts the "Alternative Miss World" pageant featuring all sorts of bizarre contestants.
1985 81m/C Divine, Little Nell, Andrew Logan. **VHS, Beta** $19.95 *AHV, FCT* 𝄢𝄢 ½

I Wanna Hold Your Hand Teenagers try to crash the Beatles' appearance on the Ed Sullivan show.
1978 (PG) 104m/C Nancy Allen, Bobby DiCicco, Wendie Jo Sperber, Marc McClure, Susan Kendall Newman, Theresa Saldana, Eddie Deezen, Will Jordan; **D:** Robert Zemeckis. **VHS, Beta, LV** $19.98 *WAR, FCT* 𝄢𝄢 ½

I Want to Live! Based on a scandalous true story, Hayward gives a riveting, Oscar-winning performance as a prostitute framed for the murder of an elderly woman and

sentenced to death in the gas chamber. Producer Walter Wanger's seething indictment of capital punishment. Music by Johnny Mandel.
1958 120m/B Susan Hayward, Simon Oakland, Theodore Bikel, Jill Bennett; **D:** Robert Wise. Academy Awards '58: Best Actress (Hayward); Nominations: Best Adapted Screenplay, Best Black and White Cinematography, Best Director (Wise), Best Sound; Golden Globe Awards '59: Best Actress—Drama (Hayward). **VHS, Beta, LV** $19.98 *MGM, BTV, CCB* ♫♫♫

I Want What I Want A young Englishman wants a sex-change, lives as a woman, falls in love, complications ensue. Not as shocking to watch as it might seem, but more a melodramatic gender-bender.
1972 (R) 91m/C *GB* Anne Heywood, Harry Andrews, Jill Bennett; **D:** John Dexter. **VHS, Beta** $39.95 *PSM* ♫♫

I Was a Teenage TV Terrorist Two teenagers pull on-the-air pranks at the local cable television, blaming it all on an imaginary terrorist group. Cheaply made and pointless, with bad acting and a script by Kevin McDonough. Also released as "Amateur Hour."
1987 85m/C Adam Nathan, Julie Hanlon; **D:** Stanford Singer. **VHS, Beta** $79.98 *LIV* Woof!

I Was a Teenage Werewolf "Rebel Without a Cause" meets "The Curse of the Werewolf" in this drive-in rock'n'roll horror. A troubled young man (pre-Bonanza Landon, in his first feature film appearance) suffers from teen angst and low production values, and falls victim to shrink Bissel. The good doctor turns out to be a bad hypnotist, and Landon's regression therapy takes him beyond childhood into his, gasp, primal past, where he sprouts a premature beard and knuckle hair. Much misconstrued and full of terrible longings, the hirsute highschooler is understood only by girlfriend Lime and misunderstood hair-sprouting teen viewers. Directorial debut of Fowler, who was once Fritz Lang's editor.
1957 70m/B Michael Landon, Yvonne Lime, Whit Bissell, Tony Marshall, Dawn Richard, Barney Phillips, Ken Miller, Cindy Robbins, Michael Rougas, Robert Griffin, Joseph Mell, Malcolm Atterbury, Eddie Marr, Vladimir Sokoloff, Louise Lewis, S. John Launer, Guy Williams, Dorothy Crehan; **D:** Gene Fowler; **W:** Ralph Thornton. **VHS** $9.95 *COL, FCT, MLB* ♫♫½

I Was a Teenage Zombie Spoof of high school horror films features a good zombie against a drug-pushing zombie. Forget the story and listen to the music by Los Lobos, the Fleshtones, the Waitresses, Dream Syndicate and Voilent Femmes.
1987 92m/C Michael Rubin, Steve McCoy, Cassie Madden, Allen Rickman; **D:** John E. Michalakis. **VHS, Beta, LV** $19.98 *NLC* ♫

I Was a Zombie for the FBI Intelligence agency toughens its hiring criteria. Much McCarthyian mirth.
1982 105m/B **D:** Maurice Penczner. **VHS, Beta** *NO* ♫½

I Will Fight No More Forever A vivid recounting of the epic true story of the legendary Chief Joseph who led the Nez Perce tribe on a 1,600-mile trek to Canada in 1877. Disturbing and powerful. Made for television.
1975 100m/C James Whitmore, Ned Romero, Sam Elliott; **D:** Richard T. Heffron. **VHS, Beta** $14.95 *NEG, MRV, GEM* ♫♫

I Will, I Will for Now Tacky sex clinic comedy with Keaton and Gould trying to save their marriage through kinky therapy.

1976 (R) 109m/C Diane Keaton, Elliott Gould, Paul Sorvino, Victoria Principal, Robert Alda, Warren Bellinger; **D:** Norman Panama. **VHS, Beta** $69.95 *MED* ♫♫

I Wonder Who's Killing Her Now? Husband pays to have his wife murdered, then changes his mind. On-again, off-again comedy.
1976 87m/C Bob Dishy, Joanna Barnes, Bill Dana, Vito Scotti; **D:** Steven Hilliard Stern. **VHS** $59.95 ♫♫

Ice Castles A young figure skater's Olympic dreams are dimmed when she is blinded in an accident, but her boyfriend gives her the strength, encouragement, and love necessary to perform a small miracle. Way too schmaltzy.
1979 (PG) 110m/C Robby Benson, Lynn-Holly Johnson, Tom Skerritt, Colleen Dewhurst, Jennifer Warren, David Huffman; **D:** Donald Wrye. **VHS, Beta** $64.95 *COL* ♫♫

The Ice Flood Silent family type comedy of a son who proves to the old man that he wrote the book on life, wagering the successful supervision of dad's lumberjacks.
1926 63m/B Kenneth Harlan, Viola Dana; **D:** George B. Seitz. **VHS, Beta** $9.95 *GPV* ♫♫

Ice House A sophisticated young lady flees Texas for Hollywood, searching for a better life. When her ex-lover shows up and wants her to go back, the lackless turmoil begins. Pairs real-life couple Gilbert and Brinkman.
1989 81m/C Melissa Gilbert, Bo Brinkman, Andreas Manolikakis, Buddy Quaid; **D:** Eagle Pennell. **VHS, Beta** $79.95 *MNC* ♫♫

Ice Palace Two rugged adventurers maintain a lifelong rivalry in the primitive Alaskan wilderness, their relationship dramatizing the development of the 49th state. Silly but entertaining. Based on Edna Ferber's novel; music by Max Steiner.
1960 143m/C Richard Burton, Robert Ryan, Carolyn Jones, Shirley Knight, Martha Hyer, Jim Backus, George Takei; **D:** Vincent Sherman. **VHS, Beta** $59.95 *WAR* ♫♫

Ice Pawn Alex Dalton may finally get to realize his dream of becoming a gold medal ice skater if he can beat Misha, his Russian rival. He soon finds out that Misha isn't his only problem, as he unknowingly becomes a pawn in a game of corruption and greed that could totally ruin his career.
1992 102m/C Paul Cross, Dan Haggerty, Robert Budaska, Chris Thomas; **D:** Barry Samson; **W:** Paul Cross. **VHS** *NO* ♫♫

Ice Pirates Space pirates in the far future steal blocks of ice to fill the needs of a thirsty galaxy. Cool plot has its moments.
1984 (PG) 91m/C Robert Urich, Mary Crosby, Michael D. Roberts, John Matuszak, Anjelica Huston, Ron Perlman, John Carradine, Robert Symonds; **D:** Stewart Raffill. **VHS, Beta, LV** $14.95 *MGM* ♫½

Ice Station Zebra A nuclear submarine races Soviet seamen to find a downed Russian satellite under a polar ice cap. Suspenseful Cold War adventure with music by Michel Legrand. Based on the novel by Alistair MacLean.
1968 (G) 148m/C Rock Hudson, Ernest Borgnine, Patrick McGoohan, Jim Brown, Lloyd Nolan, Tony Bill; **D:** John Sturges. **VHS, Beta, LV** $19.98 *MGM* ♫♫½

Icebox Murders A crazed, motiveless, faceless killer hangs his victims in a walk-in freezer. Store clear of this one.
1987 90m/C Jack Taylor, Mirta Miller. **VHS, Beta** *NO* Woof!

Iced Wild fun turns to horror on a ski trip as a group of college friends are hunted by a maniac on the loose. It's all downhill.
1988 86m/C Debra Deliso, Doug Stevenson, Ron Kologie, Elizabeth Gorcey, Alan Johnson; **D:** Jeff Kwitny. **VHS, Beta** $79.95 *PSM* ♫

Iceman A frozen prehistoric man is brought back to life, after which severe culture shock takes hold. Underwritten but nicely acted, especially by Lone as the primal man.
1984 (PG) 101m/C *CA* Timothy Hutton, Lindsay Crouse, John Lone, David Strathairn, Josef Sommer, Danny Glover; **D:** Fred Schepisi. **VHS, Beta, LV** $69.95 *MCA* ♫♫♫

The Icicle Thief "The Naked Gun" for the art-house crowd. As a stark, black-and-white neo-realist tragedy airs on TV, bright color commercials disrupt the narrative. Soon ads invade the movie itself, and the film's director jumps into his picture to fix the damage. Study up on your postwar Italian cinema and this'll seem hilarious; otherwise the real fun won't kick in until the halfway point. In Italian with English subtitles. *AKA:* Ladri di Saponette.
1989 93m/C *IT* Maurizio Nichetti, Cateria Sylos Labini, Claudio G. Fava; **D:** Maurizio Nichetti. **VHS** $89.95 *FXL, FCT, APD* ♫♫♫

Icy Breasts A French psychiatrist tries to prevent his beautiful but psychotic patient from continuing her murdering spree. Dubbed.
1975 105m/C *FR* Alain Delon, Mireille Darc; **D:** Georges Lautner. **VHS, Beta** $39.95 *FCT* ♫♫♫

I'd Give My Life A gangster's ex-wife is presently married to the governor. He tries to use their honest but framed son to blackmail her.
1936 73m/B Guy Standing, Frances Drake, Tom Brown, Janet Beecher; **D:** Edwin L. Marin. **VHS, Beta** $29.95 *VYY* ♫½

Idaho On a mission to close down houses of ill repute, Rodgers teams up with Autry's old sidekick Burnette.
1943 70m/B Roy Rogers, Harry Shannon, Virginia Grey, Smiley Burnette; **D:** Joseph Kane. **VHS, Beta** $9.95 *NOS, VCN, VDM* ♫½

Idaho Transfer Fonda's second directorial effort; Carradine's first screen appearance. An obnoxious group of teens travel through time to Idaho in the year 2044. Environmental wasteland story is dull and confused. *AKA:* Deranged.
1973 (PG) 90m/C Keith Carradine, Kelley Bohanan; **D:** Peter Fonda. **VHS, Beta** $19.95 *MPI, FCT* Woof!

Identity Crisis Campy fashion maven and flamboyant rapper switch identities causing much tedious overacting. Lifeless murder comedy from the brothers Van Peebles.
1990 (R) 98m/C Mario Van Peebles, Ilan Mitchell-Smith, Nicholas Kepros, Shelly Burch, Richard Clarke; **D:** Melvin Van Peebles. **VHS, LV** $19.95 *ACA* ♫

Identity Unknown Shell-shocked veteran goes AWOL to discover who he is, meeting grieving relatives along the way. Interesting premise is sometimes moving.
1945 70m/B Richard Arlen, Cheryl Walker, Roger Pryor, Bobby Driscoll; **D:** Walter Colmes. **VHS, Beta, 8mm** $29.95 *VYY* ♫♫½

The Idiot Dostoevski's Russian novel is transported by Kurosawa across two centuries to post-war Japan, where the madness and jealousy continue to rage. In Japanese with English subtitles.
1951 166m/B Toshiro Mifune, Masayuki Mori, Setsuko Hara, Yoshiko Kuga; **D:** Akira Kurosawa. **VHS** $79.95 *NYF, TAM* ♫♫♫♫

Idiot's Delight At an Alpine hotel, a song and dance man meets a gorgeous Russian countess who reminds him of a former lover. Incredibly, Gable sings and dances through ''Puttin' on the Ritz,'' the film's big highlight. Based on the Pulitzer Prize-winning play by Robert Sherwood.
1939 107m/B Clark Gable, Norma Shearer, Burgess Meredith, Edward Arnold; **D:** Clarence Brown. **VHS, Beta, LV** $19.98 *CCB, MGM* *♫♫♫*

Idolmaker A conniving agent can make a rock star of anyone. Well-acted fluff with Sharkey taking a strong lead. The first film by hack-meister Hackford and somewhat based on true-life teen fab Fabian.
1980 (PG) 119m/C Ray Sharkey, Tovah Feldshuh, Peter Gallagher, Paul Land, Joe Pantoliano, Maureen McCormick, John Aprea, Richard Bright, Olympia Dukakis, Steven Apostle Peck; **D:** Taylor Hackford. **VHS, Beta, LV** $14.95 *MGM* *♫♫½*

If... Three unruly seniors at a British boarding school refuse to conform. A popular, anarchic indictment of staid British society, using the same milieu as Vigo's ''Zero de Conduite,'' with considerably more violence. The first of Anderson and McDowell's trilogy, culminating with ''O Lucky Man!'' and ''Britannia Hospital.'' In color and black and white.
1969 (R) 111m/C *GB* Malcolm McDowell, David Wood, Christine Noonan, Richard Warwick; **D:** Lindsay Anderson. **VHS, Beta, LV** $49.95 *PAR* *♫♫♫♫*

If Ever I See You Again The creator of ''You Light Up My Life'' stars in the sentimental melodrama. Two adolescent lovers meet again years later and try to rekindle old passions. Done with as much skill as ''Light'' minus a hit song.
1978 (PG) 105m/C Joseph Brooks, Shelley Hack, Jerry Keller; **D:** Joseph Brooks. **VHS, Beta** $69.95 *COL* *♫*

If I Were Rich A playboy on the skids must earn a living for the first time in his life.
AKA: Cash; For Love or Money.
1933 63m/B *GB* Robert Donat, Wendy Barrie, Edmund Gwenn, Clifford Heatherly. **VHS, Beta,** **8mm** $29.95 *VYY, FCT* *♫*

If It's a Man, Hang Up A model is terrified by harrowing telephone calls from a stranger.
1975 71m/C Carol Lynley, Gerald Harper. **VHS, Beta** $29.95 *LIV* *♫½*

If It's Tuesday, This Must Be Belgium A fast-paced, frantic, and funny look at a group of Americans on a whirlwind European tour. The group does a nine-country, 18-day bus tour with clashing, comic personalities and lots of romantic possibilities. Remade as a 1987 television movie.
1969 (G) 99m/C Suzanne Pleshette, Ian McShane, Mildred Natwick, Norman Fell, Michael Constantine, Peggy Cass, Murray Hamilton, Marty Ingels, Sandy Baron, Pamela Britton, Luke Halprin; **D:** Mel Stuart. **VHS, LV** $19.98 *MGM, MOV* *♫♫♫*

If Looks Could Kill Would-be film noir about a man spying on a female embezzler and falling in love.
1986 (R) 90m/C Alan Fisler, Tim Gail, Kim Lambert, Jeanne Marie; **D:** Chuck Vincent. **VHS** $79.95 *REP* *♫♫*

If Looks Could Kill TV stud Grieco makes film debut as a high school class cutup who travels to France with his class to parlez vous for extra credit. Mistaken for a CIA agent, he stumbles into a plot to take over all the money in the whole wide world, and much implausible action and eyelash batting follows. Extra kibbles for supporting characterizations. Oh, and don't be put off by the fact that the Parisian scenes were shot in Montreal.
1991 (PG-13) 89m/C Richard Grieco, Linda Hunt, Roger Rees, Robin Bartlett, Gabrielle Anwar; **D:** William Dear; **W:** Fred Dekker. **VHS, Beta, LV, 8mm** $19.98 *WAR, PIA* *♫♫½*

If Things Were Different Feisty woman struggles to hold her family together after her husband is hospitalized with a nervous breakdown.
1979 96m/C Suzanne Pleshette, Tony Roberts, Arte Johnson, Chuck McCann, Don Murray; **D:** Robert Lewis. **VHS, Beta** $34.98 *WOV* *♫½*

If You Could See What I Hear Irritatingly upbeat true-life story of blind singer-musician, Tom Sullivan. Covers his life from college days to marriage. Sophomoric comedy centers around the hero's irresponsible, and often life-endangering, behavior.
1982 (PG) 103m/C *CA* Marc Singer, R.H. Thompson, Sarah Torgov, Shari Belafonte-Harper; **D:** Eric Till. **VHS, Beta, LV** $79.95 *VES* *♫½*

If You Don't Stop It...You'll Go Blind A series of gauche and tasteless vignettes from various little-known comedians.
1977 (R) 80m/C Pat McCormick, George Spencer, Patrick Wright; **D:** Bob Levy, Keefe Brasselle. **VHS, Beta** $54.95 *MED* *♫½*

If You Knew Susie Two retired vaudeville actors find a letter from George Washington which establishes them as descendants of a colonial patriot and the heirs to a seven billion dollar fortune. ♫If You Knew Susie; My Brooklyn Love Song; What Do I Want With Money?; We're Living the Life We Love, My, How the Time Goes By.
1948 90m/B Eddie Cantor, Joan Davis, Allyn Joslyn, Charles Dingle; **D:** Gordon Douglas. **VHS, Beta** $34.98 *CCB* *♫♫*

Igor & the Lunatics Tasteless tale of a cannibal cult leader released from prison who picks up where he left off.
1985 (R) 79m/C Joseph Eero, Joe Niola, T.J. Michaels; **D:** Billy Parolini. **VHS, Beta** $69.98 *LIV* *♫*

Iguana The videocassette box art makes this look like a horror movie, but it's really a stiff, solemn period drama about a deformed sailor with lizardlike features. After a life of mistreatment he reigns mercilessly over a handful of island castaways. An international coproduction with mostly English dialogue, some Spanish and Portuguese with subtitles.
1989 ?m/C Everett McGill; **D:** Monte Hellman. **VHS** $79.99 *IMP* *♫♫*

Ike Duvall is top brass in this made-for television epic biography tracing Eisenhower's career during World War II. Previously a six-hour mini-series; also titled ''Ike: The War Years.'' **AKA:** Ike: The War Years.
1979 291m/C Robert Duvall, Lee Remick, Darren McGavin, Dana Andrews, Laurence Luckinbill; **D:** Melville Shavelson. **VHS, Beta, LV** $29.95 *STE, VMK* *♫♫½*

Ikiru When a clerk finds out he is dying of cancer, he decides to build a children's playground and give something of himself back to the world. Highly acclaimed, heartbreaking drama from the unusually restrained Kurosawa; possibly his most ''eastern'' film. In Japanese with English subtitles.
1952 134m/B *JP* Takashi Shimura, Kyoko Seki; **D:** Akira Kurosawa. **VHS, Beta, LV** *MED, VYG, CRC* *♫♫♫♫*

Il Sorpasso A braggart, who has failed at everything, spends all his time traveling around Italy in his sportscar. He takes a repressed law student under his wing and decides to teach him how to have fun. In Italian with English subtitles.
1963 116m/B *IT* Vittorio Gassman, Jean-Louis Trintignant; **D:** Dino Risi. **VHS** $59.95 *TAM* *♫♫½*

I'll Cry Tomorrow Hayward brilliantly portrays actress Lillian Roth as she descends into alcoholism and then tries to overcome her addiction. Based on Roth's memoirs. ♫Sing You Sinners; When The Red Red Robin Comes Bob Bob Bobbin' Along; Happiness Is Just A Thing Called Joe; Vagabond King Waltz.
1955 119m/B Susan Hayward, Richard Conte, Eddie Albert, Jo Van Fleet, Margo, Don Taylor, Ray Danton; **D:** Daniel Mann. Academy Awards '55: Best Costume Design (B & W); Nominations: Best Actress (Hayward), Best Art Direction/Set Decoration (B & W), Best Black and White Cinematography; Cannes Film Festival '56: Best Actress (Hayward). **VHS, Beta, LV** $19.98 *MGM* *♫♫♫*

I'll Get You An FBI agent goes to England on the trail of a kidnapping ring. **AKA:** Escape Route.
1953 79m/B George Raft, Sally Gray, Clifford Evans; **D:** Seymour Friedman. **VHS, Beta, LV** *RXM* *♫♫*

I'll Name the Murderer Suspense film in which a gossip columnist starts his own investigation into the murder of a club singer.
1936 ?m/C Ralph Forbes, Marion Shilling; **D:** Raymond K. Johnson. **VHS** $16.95 *SNC* *♫♫*

I'll See You in My Dreams Hokey but fun musical biography of songwriter Gus Kahn (Thomas) and his wife Grace LeBoy (Day). Kahn gets his start in Ziegfeld shows but loses both his career and wife after the 1929 crash. However, she soon returns and everything ends happily ever after. ♫Ain't We Got Fun; Ukelele Lady; The One I Love Belongs To Somebody Else; I'll See You In My Dreams; It Had To Be You; Swingin' Down the Lane; My Buddy; Makin' Whoopee!; Yes Sir, That's My Baby; Carolina In The Morning; Love Me or Leave Me; I Wish I Had A Girl; Nobody's Sweetheart; Pretty Baby; Memories; I Never Knew; Toot, Toot, Tootsie Goodbye; No No Nora; Your Eyes Have Told Me So; San Francisco; The Carioca; I'm Through With Love; Liza; Shine On Harvest Moon.
1951 109m/B Danny Thomas, Doris Day, Frank Lovejoy, Patrice Wymore, James Gleason, Mary Wickes, Jim Backus, Minna Gombell, William Forrest; **D:** Michael Curtiz; **W:** Melville Shavelson, Jack Rose. **VHS** $59.95 *WAR* *♫♫½*

Illegal Crime melodrama stars Robinson as an attorney who risks all to acquit his assistant of murder. Early Mansfield appearance. Remake of ''The Mouthpiece.''
1955 88m/C Edward G. Robinson, Nina Foch, Hugh Marlowe, Jayne Mansfield, Albert Dekker, Ellen Corby, DeForest Kelley, Howard St. John; **D:** Lewis Allen. **VHS** *NO* *♫♫½*

Illegal Entry: Formula for Fear Tracie's scientist father has invented a formula that could change the world. When he's murdered the formula falls into her unsuspecting hands. Tracie might not know what she has but that doesn't stop some very ruthless efforts to get the information others want.
1993 88m/C Sabryn Gene't, Barbara Lee Alexander, Gregory Vignolle, Arthur Roberts, Carol Hoyt; **D:** Henri Charr; **W:** John B. Pfeifer. **VHS** $89.95 *PMH* *♫½*

Illegally Yours Miscast comedy about a college student serving on the jury in trial of old girlfriend. Bring down the gavel on this one.

1987 (PG) 94m/C Rob Lowe, Colleen Camp, Kenneth Mars; **D:** Peter Bogdanovich. VHS, Beta $79.98 FOX ♫

Illicit Behavior A dangerous manipulative woman (Severance) is out to claim a $2 million inheritance in this intricate and seductive police thriller. Included among her victims are her husband; a Hollywood vice cop suspended for use of excessive force; his partner; her husband's internal affairs adversary; and her own psychiatrist.
1991 (R) 101m/C Joan Severance, Robert Davi, James Russo, Jack Scalia, Kent McCord; **D:** Worth Keeter. VHS $79.95 PSM ♫♫½

The Illusion Travels by Streetcar Odd but enchanting story of two men who restore a streetcar, only to find that it will not be used by the city. In a gesture of defiance, they steal the streetcar and take it for one last ride, picking up an interesting assortment of characters along the way. In Spanish with English subtitles. Not released in the U.S. until 1977. **AKA:** La Illusion en Travnia.
1953 90m/B MX Lilia Prado, Carlos Navarro, Domingo Soler, Fernando Soto, Agustin Isunza, Miguel Manzano; **D:** Luis Bunuel. VHS $59.95 CVC, FCT ♫♫♫

Illusions Jan (Locklear) is trying to recover from a nervous breakdown and improve her crumbling marriage when her husband's sexy sister arrives and things start to heat up. Jan thinks her husband and sister-in-law are just a little too close, but when she lets her landlord in on her suspicions, he reacts quite strangely. Will Jan have another nervous breakdown? Mysterious with lots of plot twists. Based on Colley's play "I'll Be Back Before Midnight."
1991 (R) 95m/C Robert Carradine, Heather Locklear, Emma Samms, Ned Beatty; **D:** Victor Kulle; **W:** Peter Colley. VHS, Beta $89.95 PSM ♫♫

The Illustrated Man A young drifter meets a tattooed man. Each tattoo causes a fantastic story to unfold. A strange, interesting, but finally limited attempt at literary sci-fi. Based on the story collection by Ray Bradbury.
1969 (PG) 103m/C Rod Steiger, Claire Bloom, Robert Drivas, Don Dubbins; **D:** Jack Smight; **M:** Jerry Goldsmith. VHS, Beta $19.98 WAR, FCT, MLB ♫♫♫

Ilsa, Harem Keeper of the Oil Sheiks The naughty Ilsa works for an Arab sheik in the slave trade. More graphic violence and nudity. Plot makes an appearance.
1976 (R) 45m/C Dyanne Thorne, Michael Thayer. VHS, LV $59.98 CIC Woof!

Ilsa, She-Wolf of the SS The torture-loving Ilsa runs a medical camp for the Nazis. Plot is incidental to nudity and violence.
1974 (R) 45m/C Dyanne Thorne, Greg Knoph; **D:** Don Edmunds. VHS, LV $59.98 CIC Woof!

Ilsa, the Tigress of Siberia Everyone's favorite torturer has been working her wiles on political prisoners in Russia. After escaping to Canada, her past threatens to catch up with her. As usual, no plot, violence.
1979 85m/C Dyanne Thorne, Michel Morin, Tony Angelo, Terry Coady, Howard Mauer; **D:** Jean LaFleur. VHS NO Woof!

Ilsa, the Wicked Warden Ilsa is now a warden of a woman's prison in South America, behaving just as badly as she always has, until the prisoners stage an uprising. Lots of skin, no violence, no acting. Also: no plot. **AKA:** Ilsa, the Absolute Power; Greta the Mad Butcher.

1978 (R) 90m/C Dyanne Thorne, Lina Romay, Jess (Jesus) Franco; **D:** Jess (Jesus) Franco. VHS, LV $59.98 CIC Woof!

I'm a Fool A two-character romantic study involving an act of insincerity between two race track aficionados. Based on the Sherwood Anderson story. From the American Short Story Collection. Made for television.
1977 38m/C Ron Howard, Amy Irving; **D:** Noel Black. VHS, Beta $24.95 MON, KAR ♫♫½

I'm All Right Jack Sellers plays a pompous communist union leader in this hilarious satire of worker-management relations. Based on Alan Hackney's novel "Private Life."
1959 101m/B Peter Sellers, Ian Carmichael, Terry-Thomas; **D:** John Boulting. VHS, Beta $19.98 HBO, FCT ♫♫♫

I'm Dancing as Fast as I Can A successful television producer hopelessly dependent on tranquilizers tries to stop cold turkey. Good story could be better. Written by David Rabe, based on Barbara Gordon's memoir.
1982 (R) 107m/C Jill Clayburgh, Nicol Williamson, Dianne West, Joe Pesci, Geraldine Page, John Lithgow, Daniel Stern; **D:** Jack Hofsiss. VHS, Beta, LV $69.95 PAR ♫♫

I'm Dangerous Tonight Wallflower Amick (Shelley the Waitress in Twin Peaks) turns into party monster when she dons red dress made from evil ancient Aztec cloak. Many dead soldiers when this girl parties. Based on a Cornell Woolrich short story, it's another in a series of ever more disappointing entries from Hooper, whose cult fave "Texas Chainsaw Massacre" had low as they come production values, but far better scares. Originally cable fare.
1990 (R) 92m/C Madchen Amick, Corey Parker, Lee Ermey, Mary Frann, Dee Wallace Stone, Anthony Perkins; **D:** Tobe Hooper. VHS $79.95 MCA ♫½

I'm from Arkansas The little town of Pitchfork, Arkansas, goes nuts when a pig gives birth to ten piglets.
1944 68m/B El Brendel, Slim Summerville, Iris Adrian, Harry Harvey, Bruce Bennett; **D:** Lew Landers. VHS, Beta $24.95 NOS, MRV, DVT ♫

I'm Gonna Git You Sucka Parody of "blaxploitation" films popular during the '60s and '70s. Funny and laced with out-right bellylaughs. A number of stars who made "blaxploitation" films, including Jim Brown, take part in the gags.
1988 89m/C Keenan Ivory Wayans, Bernie Casey, Steve James, Isaac Hayes, Jim Brown, Ja'net DuBois, Anne-Marie Johnson, Antonio Fargas, Eve Plumb; **D:** Keenan Ivory Wayans. VHS, Beta, LV $19.95 MGM ♫♫

I'm on My Way/The Non-Stop Kid Two classic shorts: "I'm on My Way" (1919), in which Lloyd's dreams of an idyllic marriage are shattered; and "The Non-Stop Kid" (1918), in which Lloyd must contend with a rival for the affection of his beloved.
1918 30m/B Harold Lloyd, Snub Pollard, Bebe Daniels; **D:** Harold Lloyd. VHS, Beta $19.98 CCB ♫♫♫

I'm the Girl He Wants to Kill A woman sees a murder committed, and the murderer sees her. Now he's after her.
1974 71m/C Julie Sommars, Anthony Steel. VHS, Beta NO ♫½

I'm the One You're Looking For A famous model obsessively combs Barcelona for the man who raped her. Suspenseful thriller. In Spanish with English subtitles.

1988 85m/C SP Patricia Adriani, Chus Lampreave, Ricard Borras, Toni Canto, Angel Alcazar, Marta Fedz, Frank Muro, Miriam DeMaeztu; **D:** Jaime Chavarri. VHS, LV $79.95 FXL, FCT, IME ♫♫½

The Image Anchorman Finney, the unscrupulous czar of infotainment, does a little soul delving when a man he wrongly implicated in a savings and loan debacle decides to check into the hereafter ahead of schedule. Seems the newsmonger's cut a few corners en route to the bigtime, and his public is mad as hell and...oops, wrong movie (need we say there are not a few echoes of "Network"?). Finney's great. Made for cable.
1989 91m/C Albert Finney, John Mahoney, Kathy Baker, Swoosie Kurtz, Marsha Mason; **D:** Peter Werner. VHS $89.95 HBO ♫♫½

Image of Bruce Lee Martial arts fight scenes prevail in this story about a jeweler who is swindled out of $1 million worth of diamonds.
197? (G) 88m/C Bruce Li, Chang Wu Lang, Chang Lei, Dana. VHS, Beta $29.95 MED ♫

Image of Death Woman plots to take the life of an old school chum, assume her identity, and then blow up the Capitol.
1977 83m/C Cathy Paine, Cheryl Waters, Tony Banner, Barry Pierce, Sheila Helpmann, Pennie Hackforth-Jones; **D:** Kevin Dobson. VHS, Beta PGN ♫

Image of Passion Weak account of male stripper/lovely advertising executive romance.
1986 90m/C James Horan, Susan Damante Shaw, Edward Bell; **D:** Susan Orlikoff-Simon. Beta $14.95 PSM ♫

Imagemaker Uneven story of a presidential media consultant who bucks the system and exposes corruption.
1986 93m/C Michael Nouri, Jerry Orbach, Jessica Harper, Farley Granger; **D:** Hal Wiener. VHS, Beta, LV $79.98 LIV, VES ♫½

Imitation of Life Remake of the successful 1939 Claudette Colbert outing of the same title, and based on Fanny Hurst's novel, with a few plot changes. Turner is a single mother, more determined to achieve acting fame and fortune than function as a parent. Her black maid, Moore, is devoted to her own daughter (Kohner), but loses her when the girl discovers she can pass for white. When Turner discovers that she and her daughter are in love with the same man, she realizes how little she knows her daughter, and how much the two of them have missed by not having a stronger relationship. Highly successful at the box office.
1959 124m/C Lana Turner, John Gavin, Troy Donahue, Sandra Dee, Juanita Moore, Susan Kohner; **D:** Douglas Sirk. Academy Awards '59 Nominations: Best Supporting Actress (Kohner), Best Supporting Actress (Moore); Golden Globe Awards '60: Best Supporting Actress (Kohner). VHS, Beta $14.95 MCA, FCT ♫♫♫

Immediate Family Childless couple contact a pregnant, unmarried girl and her boyfriend in hopes of adoption. As the pregnancy advances, the mother has doubts about giving up her baby. A bit sugar-coated in an effort to woo family trade.
1989 (PG-13) 112m/C Glenn Close, James Woods, Kevin Dillon, Mary Stuart Masterson; **D:** Jonathan Kaplan; **W:** Barbara Benedek. VHS, Beta, LV $19.95 COL ♫♫½

The Immigrant Chaplin portrays a newly arrived immigrant who falls in love with the first girl he meets. Silent with musical soundtrack added.
1917 20m/B Charlie Chaplin; **D:** Charlie Chaplin. VHS, Beta, 3/4U, Special order formats CAB ♫♫♫½

Immortal Bachelor Good cast can't overcome the silliness of this one. A juror daydreams about the dead husband of a cleaning woman on trial for killing her adulterous spouse. She decides the dead man seems a lot more exciting than her own dull and tiresome husband.
1980 (PG) 94m/C *IT* Giancarlo Giannini, Monica Vitti, Claudia Cardinale, Vittorio Gassman; *D:* Marcello Fondato. **VHS, Beta** $69.95 *VID* �733 ½

Immortal Battalion Entertaining wartime psuedo-documentary follows newly recruited soldiers as they are molded from an ordinary group of carping civilians into a hardened battalion of fighting men by Niven. Uses some actual training and combat footage. Based on idea from Niven and scripted by Ustinov and Eric Ambler. Some prints run to 116 minutes. *AKA:* The Way Ahead.
1944 89m/B David Niven, Stanley Holloway, Reginald Tate, Raymond Huntley, William Hartnell, James Donald, Peter Ustinov; *D:* Carol Reed; *W:* Peter Ustinov, Eric Ambler. **VHS, Beta** $14.95 *NOS, MRV, QNE* �733½

Immortal Sergeant After the battle death of the squad leader, an inexperienced corporal takes command of North African troops during World War II. Fonda gives a strong performance. Based on a novel by John Brody and scripted by Lamar Trotti.
1943 91m/B Henry Fonda, Thomas Mitchell, Maureen O'Hara, Allyn Joslyn, Reginald Gardiner, Melville Cooper, Morton Lowry; *D:* John M. Stahl. **VHS, Beta** $19.98 *FOX* �733½

Immortal Sins Michael and Susan inherited an old Spanish Castle, complete with its own curse, which comes in the form of a seductive women that has haunted families for centuries.
1991 (R) 80m/C Cliff DeYoung, Maryam D'Abo. **VHS** *CGV* �733

The Immortalizer A mad doctor transfers people's brains into young bodies for a price, although it's not as simple as it sounds.
1989 (R) 85m/C Ron Kay, Chris Crone, Melody Patterson, Clarke Lindsley, Clarke Armstrong; *D:* Joel Bender. **VHS, Beta, LV** $79.95 *COL* �733

Impact A woman and her lover plan the murder of her rich industrialist husband, but the plan backfires. More twists and turns than a carnival ride.
1949 83m/B Brian Donlevy, Ella Raines; *D:* Arthur Lubin. **VHS, Beta** $14.95 *NOS, MRV, QNE* �733

The Imperial Japanese Empire Epic of the World War II Pacific seen through Japanese eyes.
1985 130m/C *JP* Tetsuro Tamba, Tomokazu Miura, Teruhiko Saigo, Teruhiko Aoi, Saburo Shinoda, Keiko Sekine, Masako Natsume, Akiko Kana. **VHS, Beta** $69.95 *VCD* �733

Imperial Navy A World War II epic as seen from the Japanese perspective, concentrating on their great navy and its suicide squadrons. Dubbed.
198? 145m/C *JP D:* Paul Aaron. **VHS, Beta** $59.95 *SVS, MOV* �733

Imperial Venus Biography of Napoleon's sister, Paolina Bonaparte—with particular focus on her many loves, lusts and tribulations.
1971 (PG) 121m/C Gina Lollobrigida, Stephen Boyd, Raymond Pellegrin; *D:* Jean Delannoy. **VHS, Beta** $49.95 *UHV* �733

The Importance of Being Donald Three vintage Disney Donald Duck shorts from the early days of World War II: "Donald's Better Self," "Polar Trappers," and "Timber."
1939 25m/C **VHS, Beta** $14.95 *DIS* �733

Importance of Being Earnest Fine production of classic Oscar Wilde comedy-of-manners. Cast couldn't be better or the story funnier.
1952 95m/C Michael Redgrave, Edith Evans, Margaret Rutherford, Michael Denison, Joan Greenwood; *D:* Anthony Asquith. **VHS, Beta** $19.95 *PAR, HMV* �733

The Imported Bridegroom A comedy set at the turn of the century about a man who returns to Poland in order to find his daughter a proper husband.
1989 93m/C Eugene Troobarck, Avi Hoffman, Greta Cowan, Annette Miller; *D:* Pamela Berger. **VHS** $29.95 *ERG, TAM* �733

The Impossible Spy True story of Elie Cohen, an unassuming Israeli who doubled as a top level spy in Syria during the 1960s. Cohen became so close to Syria's president that he was nominated to become the Deputy Minister of Defense before his double life was exposed. Well-acted spy thriller made for cable and is worth a look for espionage fans.
1987 96m/C *GB* John Shea, Eli Wallach; *D:* Jim Goddard. **VHS** $79.99 *HBO, NCJ* �733

The Imposter Improbable tale of a con artist/ex-con who impersonates a high school principal in order to regain his estranged girlfriend, who works as a teacher. Complications ensue when he tackles the school's drug problems. Made for television.
1984 95m/C Anthony Geary, Billy Dee Williams, Lorna Patterson; *D:* Michael Pressman. **VHS, Beta** $79.95 *PSM* �733½

Imposters A comedy centering on the romantic problems between a self-indulgent young man and the woman who cheats on him.
1984 110m/C Ellen McElduff, Charles Ludlum, Lisa Todd, Peter Evans. **VHS, Beta** *NO* �733

Impromptu A smart, sassy, romantic comedy set in 1880s Europe among the era's artistic greats—here depicted as scalawags, parasites and early beatniks. The film's ace is Davis in a lusty, dynamic role as mannish authoress George Sand, obsessively in love with the dismayed composer Chopin. Though he's too pallid a character for her attraction to be credible, a great cast and abundant wit make this a treat.
1990 (PG-13) 108m/C Judy Davis, Hugh Grant, Mandy Patinkin, Bernadette Peters, Julian Sands, Ralph Brown, Georges Corraface, Anton Rodgers, Emma Thompson; *D:* James Lapine. **VHS, LV** $19.95 *HMD, TVC, MOV* �733

Improper Channels Mediocre comedy about a couple trying to recover their daughter after being accused of child abuse.
1982 (PG) 91m/C Monica Parker, Alan Arkin, Mariette Hartley; *D:* Eric Till. **VHS, Beta, LV** $69.95 *VES* �733

Impulse When his wife leaves for a visit with her mother, a young man is thrust into cahoots with gangsters, and wrapped up in an affair with another woman.
1955 81m/B *GB* Arthur Kennedy, Constance Smith, Joy Shelton; *D:* Charles De Latour. **VHS** $29.95 *FCT* �733 ½

Impulse Shatner, a crazed killer, is released from prison and starts to kill again in this low-budget, predictable, critically debased film about child-molesting. *AKA:* Want a Ride, Little Girl?; I Love to Kill.
1974 (PG) 85m/C William Shatner, Ruth Roman, Harold Sakata, Kim Nicholas, Jennifer Bishop, James Dobbs; *D:* William Grefe. **VHS, Beta** $79.95 *LIV, VES* Woof!

Impulse Small town residents can't control their impulses, all because of government toxic waste in their milk. A woman worried about her mother's mental health returns to town with her doctor boyfriend to discover most of the inhabitants are quite mad. Starts strong but...
1984 (R) 95m/C Tim Matheson, Meg Tilly, Hume Cronyn, John Karlen, Bill Paxton, Amy Stryker, Claude Earl Jones, Sherri Stoner; *D:* Graham Baker. **VHS, Beta, LV** $29.98 *VES* �733

Impulse A beautiful undercover vice cop poses as a prostitute, and gives in to base desires. Russell gives a fine performance in this underrated sleeper.
1990 (R) 109m/C Theresa Russell, Nicholas Mele, Eli Danker, Charles McCaughan, Jeff Fahey, George Dzundza; *D:* Sondra Locke. **VHS, Beta, LV** $92.95 *WAR* �733½

Impure Thoughts Four friends meet in the afterlife and discuss their Catholic school days. Odd premise never catches fire.
1986 (PG) 87m/C Brad Dourif, Lane Davies, John Putch, Terry Beaver; *D:* Michael A. Simpson. **VHS, Beta** $19.98 *NLC* �733

In a Cartoon Studio Nine rarely seen cartoon shorts from the Van Beuren Studio, rival to Paul Terry's Aesop Fables Studio in the 1930s: "In a Cartoon Studio (Making 'Em Move)," "Cinderella Blues," "Redskin Blues," "The Ball Game," "Galloping Hoofs (Gallopin' Fanny)," "Gay Gaucho," "Happy Hoboes," "Indian Whoopee," and "Brownie's Victory Garden (How's Crops)."
1934 60m/B **VHS, Beta, 8mm** $24.95 *VYY, WTA* �733

In a Glass Cage A young boy who was tortured and sexually molested by a Nazi official seeks revenge. Years after the war, he shows up at the Nazi's residence in Spain and is immediately befriended by his tormentor's family. Confined to an iron lung, the official is at the mercy of the young man who tortuously acts out the incidents detailed in the Nazi's journal. Suspenseful and extremely graphic, it's well crafted and meaningful but may be just too horrible to watch. Sexual and violent acts place it in the same league as Pasolini's infamous "Salo, or The 120 Days in Sodom." Definitely not for the faint of heart. In Spanish with English subtitles. *AKA:* Tras el Cristal.
1986 110m/C *SP* Gunter Meisner, David Sust, Marisa Paredes, Gisela Echevarria; *D:* Agustin Villaronga. **VHS** $79.95 *CCN, FCT, TAM* �733 ½

In a Lonely Place Hollywood screenwriter has an affair with a starlet while under suspicion of murder. Bogart is outstanding as the hard-drinking brawler. Written by Andrew Solt.
1950 93m/B Humphrey Bogart, Gloria Grahame, Frank Lovejoy, Carl Benton Reid, Art Smith, Jeff Donnell; *D:* Nicholas Ray; *W:* Andrew Solt. **VHS, Beta** $69.95 *COL* �733³½

In a Shallow Grave Shallow treatment of James Purdy's novel about a WWII veteran, badly disfigured in combat at Guadalcanal, who returns to Virginia in an attempt to return to the life he once had with the woman he still loves. Handsome Biehn plays the disfigured vet, Mueller's his ex-fiancee, and Dempsey's the drifter who adds a bisexual hypotenuse to the love triangle. Pokey American Playhouse coproduction.
1988 (R) 92m/C Michael Biehn, Maureen Mueller, Patrick Dempsey, Michael Beach, Thomas Boyd Mason; *D:* Kenneth Bowser. **VHS** *WAR* �733

In a Stranger's Hand Urich stars a respected businessman who happens to find a doll which belongs to a kidnapped young girl. The police have their suspicions but Urich teams up with the child's mother to find the girl and winds up uncovering a child-selling ring. Made for television.
1992 93m/C Robert Urich, Megan Gallagher, Brett Cullen, Vondie Curtis-Hall, Dakin Matthews, Alan Rosenberg, Maria O'Brien; **D:** David Greene. **VHS** $89.98 *TTC* 🎞🎞½

In an Old Manor House Residents of an old house are tormented by the vindictive ghost of a murdered adultress whose husband didn't approve of the, uh, affection she showed his son from a previous marriage. Based on the play by Stanislaw Witkiewicz. In Polish with English subtitles.
1934 90m/C *PL* **D:** Jerzy Kotkowski. **VHS** $49.99 *FCT* 🎞🎞½

In Between When Margo, Jack, and Amy wake up they expect it to be another average day. Instead, these three strangers find themselves together in a peculiar house. An angel informs them that the house is a way station between life and the hereafter. The three must look at their pasts, imagine their futures, and decide whether to return to their old lives or accept death and go on to an afterlife.
1992 (PG-13) 92m/C Wings Hauser, Robin Mattson, Alexandra Paul, Robert Forster. **VHS** $79.95 *MNC* 🎞🎞

In Celebration Three successful brothers return to the old homestead for their parents' 40th wedding celebration. Intense drama but somewhat claustrophobic. Based on a play by David Storey.
1975 (PG) 110m/C *GB CA* Alan Bates, James Bolam, Brian Cox; **D:** Lindsay Anderson. **VHS** *AFF* 🎞🎞🎞

In Cold Blood Truman Capote's supposedly factual novel provided the basis for this hard-hitting docu-drama about two ex-cons who ruthlessly murder a Kansas family in 1959 in order to steal their non-existent stash of money. Blake is riveting as one of the killers.
1967 133m/B Robert (Bobby) Blake, Scott Wilson, John Forsythe; **D:** Richard Brooks. Academy Awards '67 Nominations: Best Adapted Screenplay, Best Cinematography, Best Director (Brooks), Best Original Score; National Board of Review Awards '67: 10 Best Films of the Year, Best Director (Brooks). **VHS, Beta, LV** $19.95 *COL* 🎞🎞🎞½

In Country Based on Bobbie Ann Mason's celebrated novel, the story of a young Kentuckian high schooler (perfectly played by Lloyd) and her search for her father, killed in Vietnam. Willis plays her uncle, a veteran still struggling to accept his own survival, and crippled with memories. Moving scene at the Vietnam Veterans Memorial.
1989 (R) 116m/C Bruce Willis, Emily Lloyd, Joan Allen, Kevin Anderson, Richard Hamilton, Judith Ivey, Peggy Rea, John Terry; **D:** Norman Jewison. **VHS, Beta, LV, 8mm** $19.98 *WAR* 🎞🎞½

The In Crowd A bright high school student gets involved with a local television dance show circa 1965, and must choose between uncertain fame and an Ivy League college. A fair nostalgic look at the period. Leitch is the son of psychedelic folk singer Donovan.
1988 (PG) 96m/C Donovan Leitch, Jennifer Runyon, Scott Plank, Joe Pantoliano; **D:** Mark Rosenthal. **VHS, Beta, LV** $19.98 *ORI* 🎞🎞

In Dangerous Company Beautiful babe balances beaux and battles abound. A brow lowering experience.
1988 (R) 92m/C Tracy Scoggins, Cliff DeYoung, Chris Mulkey, Henry Darrow, Steven Keats, Richard Portnow; **D:** Ruben Preuss. **VHS** *NO* 🎞

In Deadly Heat Crime, revenge, murder, and urban warfare are done once again.
1987 98m/C William Dame, Catherine Dee, M.R. Murphy; **D:** Don Nardo. **VHS, Beta** *JEF* 🎞

In Desert and Wilderness Two kidnapped children escape and are thrust into the wilds of Africa, where they must survive with wits and courage. Based on a novel by Nobel prize-winning author Henyk Sienkiewicz. In Polish with English subtitles.
1973 144m/C *PL* **D:** Wladyslaw Slesicki. **VHS** $49.95 *FCT* 🎞🎞½

In Eagle Shadow Fist Japanese invasion forces meet their match when an unconventional resistance fighter sabotages their advance.
198? 90m/C Jackie Chan. **VHS, Beta** *NO* 🎞

In for Treatment A terminally ill cancer patient, lost in the bureaucracy of the hospital, fights to rediscover the joy of life. Strong and disturbing story. In Dutch with English subtitles.
1982 92m/C *NL* Helmut Woudenberg, Frank Groothof, Hans Man Int Veld; **D:** Eric Van Zuylen, Marja Kok. **VHS, Beta** *NO* 🎞🎞🎞

In Gold We Trust Vincent leads an elite battalion of fighters against a group of rogue American MIAs (!) laying waste to the Vietnemese countryside.
1991 89m/C Jan-Michael Vincent, Sam Jones; **D:** P. Chalong. **VHS** $89.98 *AIP* 🎞🎞

In Harm's Way Overdone story about two naval officers and their response to the Japanese attack at Pearl Harbor. Even the superb cast members (and there are plenty of them) can't overcome the incredible length and overly intricate plot.
1965 165m/B John Wayne, Kirk Douglas, Tom Tryon, Patricia Neal, Paula Prentiss, Brandon de Wilde, Burgess Meredith, Stanley Holloway, Henry Fonda, Dana Andrews, Franchot Tone, Jill Haworth, George Kennedy, Carroll O'Connor, Patrick O'Neal, Slim Pickens, Bruce Cabot, Larry Hagman, Hugh O'Brian, Jim Mitchum, Barbara Bouchet; **D:** Otto Preminger; **M:** Jerry Goldsmith. Academy Awards '65 Nominations: Best Black and White Cinematography; British Academy Awards '65: Best Actress (Neal). **VHS, Beta, LV** $14.95 *PAR* 🎞🎞

In Hot Pursuit Convicted for drug smuggling, two young men stage a daring but not too exciting escape from a southern prison.
1982 90m/C Bob Watson, Don Watson, Debbie Washington. **VHS, Beta** *PGN* 🎞½

The In-Laws A wild comedy with Falk, who claims to be a CIA agent, and Arkin, a dentist whose daughter is marrying Falk's son. The fathers foil a South American dictator's counterfeiting scheme in a delightfully convoluted plot.
1979 (PG) 103m/C Peter Falk, Alan Arkin, Richard Libertini, Nancy Dussault, Penny Peyser, Arlene Golonka, Michael Lembeck, Ed Begley Jr., Rosana De Soto, Art Evans; **D:** Arthur Hiller; **W:** Andrew Bergman; **M:** John Morris. **VHS, Beta, LV** $19.98 *WAR* 🎞🎞🎞

In Like Flint Sequel to "Our Man Flint" sees our dapper spy confronting an organization of women endeavoring to take over the world. Spy spoofery at its low-level best.
1967 107m/C James Coburn, Lee J. Cobb, Anna Lee, Andrew Duggan, Jean Hale; **D:** Gordon Douglas; **M:** Jerry Goldsmith. **VHS, Beta, LV** $19.98 *FOX* 🎞🎞½

In Love and War Woods plays Navy pilot Jim Stockdale, whose plane was grounded over hostile territory and who endured nearly eight years of torture as a POW. Meanwhile, wife Sybil is an organizer of POW wives back in the States. Low octane rendering of the US Navy Commander's true story. Aaron earlier directed "The Miracle Worker," and you may recognize Ngor from "The Killing Fields."
1991 (R) 96m/C James Woods, Jane Alexander, Haing S. Ngor, Concetta Tomei, Richard McKenzie, James Pax; **D:** Paul Aaron; **W:** Carol Schreder. **VHS, LV** $89.95 *VMK* 🎞🎞½

In Love with an Older Woman Ritter takes fewer pratfalls than usual in this film; after all, it's a romantic comedy. Adapted from "Six Months with an Older Woman," the novel by David Kaufelt. Made for television.
1982 100m/C John Ritter, Karen Carlson, Jamie Rose, Robert Mandan, Jeff Altman, George Murdock; **D:** Jack Bender. **VHS, Beta** $14.95 *FRH* 🎞🎞

In Memoriam Tragic and gripping drama about one man's ability, albeit too late, to cope with his unforgettable past. In Spanish with English subtitles.
1976 96m/C *SP* Geraldine Chaplin, Jose Luis Gomez; **D:** Enrique Braso. **VHS** $59.95 *FCT, TAM* 🎞🎞½

In 'n Out An American loser ventures to Mexico to recover a long-lost inheritance, meeting with mildly comic obstacles along the way.
1986 85m/C Sam Bottoms, Pat Hingle. **VHS, Beta** $19.95 *STE, NWV* 🎞½

In Name Only Somber drama about a heartless woman who marries for wealth and prestige and holds her husband to a loveless marriage. Based on "Memory of Love" by Bessie Brewer.
1939 102m/B Carole Lombard, Cary Grant, Kay Francis; **D:** John Cromwell. **VHS, Beta, LV** $19.95 *CCB, RKO, MLB* 🎞🎞½

In Old Caliente Rogers battles the bad guys in the frontier town of Caliente.
1939 60m/B Roy Rogers, Lynn (Mary Hart) Roberts, George "Gabby" Hayes. **VHS, Beta** $9.95 *NOS, VCN, DVT* 🎞½

In Old California Plucky story of a young Boston pharmacist who searches for success in the California gold rush and runs into the local crime boss. Also available colorized.
1942 89m/B John Wayne, Patsy Kelly, Binnie Barnes, Albert Dekker; **D:** William McGann. **VHS** $14.98 *REP* 🎞🎞½

In Old Cheyenne Bank holdups, cattle rustling, fist fights, and even car crashes mix with some good ol' guitar plunking in this western.
1941 60m/B Roy Rogers, George "Gabby" Hayes. **VHS, Beta, 3/4U, Special order formats** $19.95 *NOS, CAB* 🎞½

In Old Colorado Ankrum and his cronies try to stir up trouble over water rights, but Boyd and his pals ride to the rescue.
1941 67m/B William Boyd, Russell Hayden, Andy Clyde, Margaret Hayes, Morris Ankrum, Sarah Padden, Cliff Nazarro, Stanley Andrews, James Seay, Morgan Wallace; **D:** Howard Bretherton. **VHS** $19.95 *NOS* 🎞½

In Old Montana A Cavalry lieutenant tries to settle a cattleman vs. sheep-herding war.
1939 60m/B Fred Scott, Jeanne Carmen, Harry Harvey, John Merton; **D:** Raymond K. Johnson. **VHS, Beta** $19.95 *VDM, GPV* 🎞

In Old New Mexico The Cisco Kid and Pancho reveal the murderer of an old woman—a mysterious doctor who was after an inheritance.
1945 60m/B Duncan Renaldo, Martin Garralaga, Gwen Kenyon, Pedro de Cordoba. **VHS, Beta** $19.95 *NOS, UHV, VYY* ⅓

In Old Santa Fe Cowboy star Maynard's best western, and the first film ever with Autry and Burnette. Maynard is framed for murder and his pals save him.
1934 60m/B Ken Maynard, Gene Autry, Smiley Burnette, Evelyn Knapp, George "Gabby" Hayes, Kenneth Thomson, Wheeler Oakman, George Cheseboro; **D:** David Howard, Joseph Kane. **VHS, Beta** $19.95 *NOS, VCN, DVT* ⅓⅓½

In Person Spry comedy about a movie star who disguises herself to take a vacation incognito and falls in love with a country doctor who is unaware of her identity. ♫Don't Mention Love To Me; Out of Sight, Out of Mind; Got a New Lease on Life.
1935 87m/B Ginger Rogers, George Brent, Alan Mowbray, Grant Mitchell; **D:** William A. Seiter; **M:** Oscar Levant. **VHS, Beta, LV** $19.98 *RKO, TTC* ⅓⅓½

In Praise of Older Women Berenger is just right as a young Hungarian who is corrupted by World War II and a large number of older women. Based on a novel by Stephen Vizinczey.
1978 110m/C *CA* Karen Black, Tom Berenger, Susan Strasberg, Helen Shaver, Alexandra Stewart; **D:** George Kaczender. **VHS, Beta, LV** *FOX, SUE* ⅓⅓

In Search of a Golden Sky Following their mother's death, a motley group of children move in with their secluded cabin-dwelling uncle, much to the righteous chagrin of the welfare department.
1984 (PG) 94m/C Charles Napier, George Flower, Cliff Osmond; **D:** Jefferson Richard. **VHS, Beta** $79.98 *FOX* ⅓⅓

In Search of Anna When a convict is released from jail, he hits the road with a flighty model in search of the girlfriend who corresponded with him in prison. There auto be a law.
1979 90m/C Judy Morris, Richard Moir, Chris Hayward, Bill Hunter; **D:** Esben Storm. **VHS, Beta** $24.95 *AHV* *Woof!*

In Search of Historic Jesus Docudrama of sorts that attempts to pull together a careful tabulation of data about Jesus Christ, who was hardly known to the historians of his time. Low-budget presentation at odds with serious topic. From the makers of the equally suspect "In Search of Noah's Ark."
1979 (PG) 91m/C John Rubinstein, John Anderson; **D:** Henning Schellerup. **VHS, Beta, LV** $79.98 *LIV, UHV, LME* ⅓½

In Search of the Castaways Stirring adventure tale of a teenage girl and her younger brother searching for their father, a ship's captain lost at sea years earlier. Powerful special effects and strong cast make this a winning Disney effort. Based on a story by Jules Verne.
1962 98m/C *GB* Hayley Mills, Maurice Chevalier, George Sanders, Wilfrid Hyde-White, Michael Anderson Jr.; **D:** Robert Stevenson. **VHS, Beta** $19.99 *DIS* ⅓⅓⅓

In the Aftermath Mix of animation and live-action in this post-nuclear wasteland tale never quite works.
1987 85m/C Tony Markes, Rainbow Dolan. **VHS, Beta** $19.95 *STE, NWV* ⅓½

In the Cold of the Night Another drowsy entry into the "to sleep perchance to have a nightmare genre." A photographer with a vivid imagination dreams he murders a woman he doesn't know, and when said dream girl rides into his life on the back of a Harley, Mr. Foto's faced with an etiquette quandary: haven't they met before? Cast includes Hedren (Hitchcock's Marnie and Melanie Griffith's mother).
1989 (R) 112m/C Jeff Lester, Adrienne Sachs, Shannon Tweed, David Soul, John Beck, Tippi Hedren, Marc Singer; **D:** Nico Mastorakis. **VHS, LV** $9.98 *REP* ⅓

In the Custody of Strangers A teenager's parents refuse to help when he is arrested for being drunk and he ends up spending the night in jail. Realistic handling of a serious subject. Sheen and Estevez play the father and son, mimicking their real-life relationship. Made for television.
1982 100m/C Martin Sheen, Jane Alexander, Emilio Estevez, Kenneth McMillan, Ed Lauter, Matt Clark, John Hancock; **D:** Robert Greenwald. **VHS** *MOV* ⅓⅓⅓

In the Days of the Thundering Herd & the Law & the Outlaw In the first feature, a pony express rider sacrifices his job to accompany his sweetheart on a westward trek to meet her father. In the second show, a fugitive falls in love with a rancher's daughter and risks recognition.
1914 76m/B Tom Mix, Myrtle Stedman; **D:** Tom Mix. **VHS, Beta** $24.98 *CCB* ⅓⅓⅓

In the Good Old Summertime This pleasant musical version of "The Shop Around the Corner" tells the story of two bickering co-workers who are also anonymous lovelorn pen pals. Minnelli made her second screen appearance at 18 months in the final scene. ♫I Don't Care; Meet Me Tonight In Dreamland; Play That Barbershop Chord; In the Good Old Summertime; Put Your Arms Around Me Honey; Wait Till the Sun Shines Nellie; Chicago; Merry Christmas.
1949 104m/C Judy Garland, Van Johnson, S.Z. Sakall, Buster Keaton, Spring Byington, Liza Minnelli, Clinton Sundberg; **D:** Robert Z. Leonard. **VHS, Beta, LV** $19.98 *MGM, PIA* ⅓⅓⅓

In the Heat of Passion A low-budget ripoff of "Body Heat" and "Fatal Attraction" starring Kirkland as a married woman who involves a much younger man in a very steamy affair that leads to murder. This movie wants to be a thriller, but is little more than a soft-core sex flick. Also available in an unrated version that contains explicit footage.
1991 (R) 84m/C Sally Kirkland, Nick Corri, Jack Carter, Michael Greene; **W/D:** Rodman Flender. **VHS, LV** $89.95 *COL* ⅓½

In the Heat of the Night A wealthy industrialist in a small Mississippi town is murdered. A black homicide expert is asked to help solve the murder, despite resentment on the part of the town's chief of police. Powerful script with underlying theme of racial prejudice is served well by taut direction and powerhouse performances. Poitier's memorable character Virgil Tibbs appeared in two more pictures, "They Call Me Mister Tibbs" and "The Organization."
1967 109m/C Sidney Poitier, Rod Steiger, Warren Oates, Lee Grant; **D:** Norman Jewison. Academy Awards '67: Best Actor (Steiger), Best Film Editing, Best Picture, Best Sound; Nominations: Best Director (Jewison); British Academy Awards '67: Best Actor (Steiger); Edgar Allan Poe Awards '67: Best Screenplay; Golden Globe Awards '68: Best Actor—Drama (Steiger), Best Film—Drama (Steiger). **VHS, Beta, LV** $19.98 *MGM, FOX, BTV* ⅓⅓⅓½

In the King of Prussia Recreation of the trial of the "Plowshares Eight" radicals who were jailed for sabotaging two nuclear missiles at an electric plant in Pennsylvania.
1983 92m/C Martin Sheen, Rev. Daniel Berrigan. **VHS, Beta** $59.95 *MPI, BUL* ⅓½

In the Land of the Owl Turds The story of a decidely eccentric young man who drives a dada art gallery on wheels while searching for love. Blank's senior thesis film.
1987 30m/C **D:** Harrod Blank. **VHS, Beta** $39.95 *FFM* ⅓½

In the Line of Fire Aging Secret Service agent Frank Horrigan has a dubious reputation as the only active agent to lose a president. Frank's assigned to undercover work until a whacked out lunatic known only as Booth begins calling him, threatening the current president (no, not Bill Clinton) and casting doubt on his honor. So begins an exciting, fast paced cat and mouse game liberally sprinkled with Clint's brand of dry humor. Malkovich's menacing bad guy is spooky in his quest to kill. Eastwood is terrific as the agent who's still trying to reconcile the events from 30 years past, displaying more emotion than previous characters. In one unscripted portion, he cries when remembering that awful day in Dallas. Well-rounded supporting cast includes female agent Russo, who captures Frank's interest, agency Director Mahoney, partner with a heart Mulroney, and pompous White House chief of staff Thompson. Predictable plot (excepting Booth's motives) is clearly meant to pay homage to the agents whose job description might as well read "take the bullet for the president." Eerie special effects include a younger Eastwood superimposed in footage of the Kennedys before the assassination. Filmed with the cooperation of the Secret Service, most scenes are believable, with a few Hollywood-scripted exceptions. Boasts one of the more intriguing trailers in recent history, with the number "6" in "1963" slowly turning to "9" to become "1993" as a clock ticks in the background.
1993 (R) ?m/C Clint Eastwood, John Malkovich, Rene Russo, Dylan McDermott, Gary Cole, Fred Dalton Thompson, John Mahoney, Gregory Alan Williams; **D:** Wolfgang Petersen; **W:** Jeff Maguire; **M:** Ennio Morricone. **VHS** *NYR* ⅓⅓⅓½

In the Money Veteran vaudevillian "Skeets" Gallagher introduces a muddled mass of acts, including a poor imitator of boxing great Gene Tunney, a mad scientist who talks to rabbits and writes rubber checks, and a limp-wristed lisper.
1934 66m/B Lois Wilson, Warren Hymer, Arthur Hoyt, Frank "Junior" Coghlan, Louise Beavers; **D:** Frank Strayer. **VHS** $19.95 *NOS* ⅓

In the Mood Based on fact, this is the story of teenager Sonny Wisecarver, nicknamed "The Woo Woo Kid," who in 1944, seduced two older women and eventually landed in jail after marrying one of them. Look for Wisecarver in a cameo role as a mailman in the film.
1987 (PG-13) 98m/C Patrick Dempsey, Beverly D'Angelo, Talia Balsam, Michael Constantine, Betty Jinnette, Kathleen Freeman, Peter Hobbs, Edith Fellows; **Cameos:** Ellsworth Wisecarver; **W/D:** Phil Alden Robinson. **VHS, Beta, LV** $19.98 *KRT, LHV, WAR* ⅓⅓½

In the Name of the Pope-King An acclaimed historical epic about the politics and warfare raging around the 1867 Italian wars that made the Pope the sole ruler in Rome. In Italian with English subtitles.
1985 115m/C Nino Manfredi; **D:** Luigi Magni. **VHS, Beta** *WBF, FCT* ⅓⅓⅓

In the Navy Abbott and Costello join the Navy in one of four military-service comedies they cranked out in 1941 alone. The token narrative involves about a singing star (Powell) in uniform to escape his female fans, but that's just an excuse for classic A & C routines. With the Andrews Sisters. ♫ Starlight, Starbright; You're Off To See The World; Hula Ba Lua; Gimme Some Skin; A Sailor's Life For Me; We're In The Navy; Anchors Aweigh (instrumental); You're A Lucky Fellow, Mr. Smith (instrumental). **AKA:** Abbott and Costello in the Navy.
1941 85m/B Lou Costello, Bud Abbott, Dick Powell, The Andrews Sisters; **D:** Arthur Lubin. **VHS, LV** $14.95 *MCA ♫♫½*

In the Realm of Passion A wife and her lover murder her husband and dump the body in an abandoned well. Guilt over their actions drive the lovers to return to the scene where they are greeted by the vengeful ghost of the betrayed husband—or is it only their consciences torturing them? In Japanese with English subtitles. **AKA:** Empire of Passion.
1980 108m/C Kazuko Yoshiyuki, Takahiro Tamura, Tatsuya Fuji; **D:** Nagisa Oshima. **VHS** $89.95 *TAM ♫♫*

In the Realm of the Senses Taboo-breaking story of a woman and man who turn their backs on the militaristic rule of Japan in the mid-1930s by plunging into an erotic and sensual world all their own. Striking, graphic work that was seized by U.S. customs when it first entered the country. Violent with explicit sex, and considered by some critics as pretentious, while others call it Oshima's masterpiece.
1976 105m/C *JP FR* Tatsuya Fuji, Eiko Matsuda, Aio Nakajima, Meika Seri; **D:** Nagisa Oshima. **VHS** $89.95 *FXL ♫♫♫*

In the Region of Ice Award-winning short reveals the complexities of the relationship between a nun and a disturbed student.
1976 38m/B Fionnula Flanagan, Peter Lempert; **D:** Peter Werner. **VHS, Beta** *BFA ♫♫♫*

In the Secret State Inspector Strange finds himself faced with the apparent suicide of a colleague on the day of his own retirement from the force. His private investigation into the case finds him mired in murder and espionage.
19?? 107m/C Frank Finlay, Matthew Marsh, Thorley Walters. **VHS** $79.95 *SVS, MOV ♫♫*

In the Shadow of Kilimanjaro A pack of hungry baboons attacks innocent people in the wilderness of Kenya. Based on a true story but the characters are contrived and just plain stupid at times. Quite gory as well. Filmed on location in Kenya.
1986 (R) 105m/C *GB* John Rhys-Davies, Timothy Bottoms, Michele Carey, Irene Miracle, Calvin Jung, Donald Blakely; **D:** Raju Patel. **VHS, Beta** $19.95 *LIV Woof!*

In the Soup Adolpho is a naive New York filmmaker barely scraping by. He decides to sell his script in a classified ad which is answered by the fast-talking Joe, a would-be film producer whose true profession is as a con artist. The two then try numerous (and humorous) ways to raise the money to begin filming. Also available colorized.
1992 (R) 93m/B Steve Buscemi, Seymour Cassel, Jennifer Beals, Will Patton, Pat Moya; **Cameos:** Jim Jarmusch, Carol Kane; **W/D:** Alexandre Rockwell; **W:** Tim Kissell. **VHS, LV** $89.95 *ACA ♫♫½*

In the Spirit New Age couple move from Beverly Hills to New York, where they meet an air-headed mystic and are forced to hide from a murderer. Falk gives solid performance in sometimes rocky production.
1990 94m/C Elaine May, Marlo Thomas, Jeannie Berlin, Peter Falk, Melanie Griffith, Olympia Dukakis, Chad Burton, Thurn Hoffman; **D:** Sandra Seacat. **VHS, Beta** $29.95 *ACA ♫♫½*

In the Steps of a Dead Man A family grieving for a fallen soldier is earmarked for evil by a young man who bears an uncanny resemblance to the dead man. A friend of the family has her suspicions and must find out the truth before something terrible happens.
1974 71m/C Skye Aubrey, John Nolan. **VHS, Beta** *NO ♫½*

In the White City A sailor jumps ship in Lisbon and uses a movie camera to record himself and his search through the twisted streets and alleys of the city for something or someone to connect to. In French, Portuguese, and German with English subtitles. **AKA:** Dans la Ville Blanche.
1983 108m/C *PT SI* Bruno Ganz, Teresa Madruga; **D:** Alain Tanner. **VHS** $79.95 *NYF, TAM ♫♫*

In This House of Brede A sophisticated London widow turns her back on her worldly life to become a cloistered Benedictine nun. Rigg is outstanding as the woman struggling to deal with the discipline of faith. Made for television and based on the novel by Rumer Godden.
1975 105m/C Diana Rigg; **D:** George Schaefer. **VHS, Beta** *LCA, OM ♫♫♫*

In This Our Life Histrionic melodrama handled effectively by Huston about a nutsy woman who steals her sister's husband, rejects him, manipulates her whole family and eventually leads herself to ruin. Vintage star vehicle for Davis, who chews scenery and fellow actors alike. Adapted by Howard Koch from the Ellen Glasgon novel. Score by Max Steiner.
1942 101m/B Bette Davis, Olivia de Havilland, Charles Coburn, Frank Craven, George Brent, Dennis Morgan, Billie Burke, Hattie McDaniel, Lee Patrick, Walter Huston, Ernest Anderson; **D:** John Huston. **VHS, Beta** $19.95 *MGM ♫♫½*

In Too Deep A rock star and a beautiful woman are physically drawn to one another in spite of the fact that any contact between them could have disasterous results.
1990 (R) 106m/C Hugo Race, Santha Press, Rebekah Elmaloglou, John Flaus, Dominic Sweeney; **D:** Colin South. **VHS, Beta** $89.95 *PAR ♫½*

In Trouble Hard-to-follow and frequently aimless story of a pregnant girl who invents a fake rape story that her dull-witted brothers take seriously, embarking on a cross-country search for the culprit.
1967 82m/C *CA* Julie LaChapelle, Katherine Mousseau, Daniel Pilon; **D:** Gilles Carle. **VHS, Beta** $59.95 *NWV Woof!*

In Which We Serve Much stiff upperlipping in this classic that captures the spirit of the British Navy during WWII. The sinking of the destroyer HMS Torrin during the Battle of Crete is told via flashbacks, with an emphasis on realism that was unusual in wartime flag-wavers. Features the film debuts of Johnson and Attenborough, and the first Lean directorial effort. Coward received a special Oscar for his "outstanding production achievement," having scripted, scored, codirected and costarred.

1943 114m/B *GB* Noel Coward, John Mills, Bernard Miles, Celia Johnson, Kay Walsh, James Donald, Richard Attenborough; **D:** Noel Coward, David Lean. Academy Awards '43 Nominations: Best Original Screenplay, Best Picture; National Board of Review Awards '42: 10 Best Films of the Year. **VHS, Beta** $19.95 *NOS, SUE ♫♫♫½*

In Your Face Little known blaxploitation film about a black family harrassed in a white suburb. A black motorcycle gang comes to their rescue. **AKA:** Abar, the First Black Superman.
1977 (R) 90m/C J.Walter Smith, Tobar Mayo, Roxie Young, Tina James; **D:** Frank Packard. **VHS** $59.95 *XVC, HHE ♫½*

Inch High Private Eye Animated yarn about Inch High, the world's smallest private eye, who solves mysteries for the Finkerton Organization.
1973 60m/C VHS, Beta $19.95 *TTC, WTA ♫½*

The Incident A gritty, controversial (at-the-time) drama about two abusive thugs who take over a New York subway car late at night, humiliating and terrorizing each passenger in turn. Film debut for Sheen and Musante as the thugs.
1967 99m/B Martin Sheen, Tony Musante, Beau Bridges, Ruby Dee, Jack Gilford, Thelma Ritter, Brock Peters, Ed McMahon, Gary Merrill, Donna Mills, Jan Sterling, Mike Kellin; **D:** Larry Peerce. **VHS, Beta, LV** $59.98 *FOX ♫♫½*

The Incident Political thriller set during World War II in Lincoln Bluff, Colorado. Matthau is excellent in his TV debut as a small-town lawyer who must defend a German prisoner of war accused of murder at nearby Camp Bremen. An all-star cast lends powerful performances to this riveting made for TV drama.
1989 95m/C Walter Matthau, Susan Blakely, Harry Morgan, Robert Carradine, Barnard Hughes, Peter Firth, William Schallert. **VHS** $79.95 *CAF ♫♫♫*

Incident at Channel Q A heavy-metal rock musical about a suburban neighborhood declaring war on a chain-and-leather deejay.
1986 85m/C Al Corley, Bon Jovi, Deep Purple, Motley Crue, The Scorpions. **VHS, Beta, LV** $19.95 *MVD, BMG, RCA ♫½*

Incident at Map-Grid 36-80 A Soviet-made combination of espionage and sea-battle. Gripping and fascinating look at the U.S. from the pre-Glasnost era.
1983 85m/C *RU VHS TPV, KIV ♫♫*

Incident at Oglala: The Leonard Peltier Story Offers a detailed account of the violent events leading to the murder of two FBI agents in Oglala, South Dakota in 1975. American Indian activist Leonard Peltier was convicted of the murders and is presently serving two consecutive life sentences, but he's cited as a political prisoner by Amnesty International. The documentary examines the highly controversial trial and the tensions between the government and the Oglala Nation stemming back to the Indian occupation of Wounded Knee in 1973. Director Apted is sympathetic to Peltier and offers reasons why he should be allowed a retrial; he examined similar incidents in his film "Thunderheart."
1992 (PG) 90m/C D: Michael Apted; **M:** John Trudell, Jackson Browne. **VHS** $89.98 *LIV, FCT ♫♫♫*

Incoming Freshmen Teen sex-venture about a young innocent girl who discovers sex when she enrolls in a liberal co-ed institution.

1979 (R) 84m/C Ashley Vaughn, Debralee Scott, Leslie Blalock, Richard Harriman, Jim Overbey; **D:** Glenn Morgan, Eric Lewald. **VHS, Beta** $39.95 MCA 🐾½

An Inconvenient Woman When an older married man has an affair with a young seductress, there's suicide, murder, a nasty gossip columnist, a reporter, a knowing society wife, and a lot of cover-ups among the rich and famous. From the novel by Dominick Dunne and based on the Alfred Bloomingdale scandal. Originally a made for television mini-series.
1991 126m/C Rebecca DeMornay, Jason Robards Jr., Jill Eikenberry, Peter Gallagher, Roddy McDowall, Chad Lowe. **VHS, Beta** $79.95 ABC, PSM 🐾🐾

Incredible Detectives A dog, a cat and a crow team up to search for a boy who has been kidnapped by a trio of hoods.
1979 23m/C VHS, Beta $19.95 WOV, WTA 🐾🐾

The Incredible Hulk Bixby is a scientist who achieves superhuman strength after he is exposed to a massive dose of gamma rays. But his personal life suffers, as does his wardrobe. Ferrigno is the Hulkster. The pilot for the television series is based on the Marvel Comics character.
1977 94m/C Bill Bixby, Susan Sullivan, Lou Ferrigno, Jack Colvin; **D:** Kenneth Johnson. **VHS, Beta, LV** $19.95 MCA 🐾🐾½

The Incredible Hulk Returns The beefy green mutant is back and this time he wages war against a Viking named Thor. Very little substance in this made for television flick, so be prepared to park your brain at the door. Followed by "The Trial of the Incredible Hulk."
1988 100m/C Bill Bixby, Lou Ferrigno, Jack Colvin, Lee Purcell, Charles Napier, Steve Levitt; **D:** Nick Corea. **VHS, LV** $19.95 STE, NWV 🐾½

The Incredible Journey A labrador retriever, bull terrier and Siamese cat mistake their caretaker's intentions when he leaves for a hunting trip, believing he will never return. The three set out on a 250 mile adventure-filled trek across Canada's rugged terrain. Entertaining family adventure from Disney taken from Sheila Burnford's book.
1963 80m/C D: Fletcher Markle. **VHS, Beta** $69.95 DIS 🐾🐾½

The Incredible Journey of Dr. Meg Laurel A young doctor returns to her roots to bring modern medicine to the Appalachian mountain people during the 1930's. Made for television featuring Wagner in a strong performance.
1979 143m/C Lindsay Wagner, Jane Wyman, Dorothy McGuire, James Woods, Gary Lockwood; **D:** Guy Green. **VHS, Beta** $59.95 COL 🐾🐾🐾

Incredible Manitoba Animation Prize-winning animated shorts, brought together in honor of the Film Board of Canada's 50th Anniversary. Includes Richard Condie's Oscar-nominated "The Big Snit," and his "Getting Started;" Cordell Barker's "The Cat Came Back" and more fun for the entire family.
1990 51m/C CA VHS, Beta $29.95 WTA, FCT 🐾🐾🐾

Incredible Master Beggars Against all odds, the Beggars challenge the Great Iron Master, using "Tam Leg" tactics versus the "Iron Cloth" fighting style.
1982 (R) 88m/C Tan Tao Liang, Ku Feng, Han Kuo Tsai, Li Tang Ming, Li Hai Sheng, Lui I. Fan, Pan Yao Kun. **VHS, Beta** $59.95 GEM 🐾

Incredible Melting Man Two transformations change an astronaut's life after his return to earth. First, his skin starts to melt, then he displays cannibalistic tendencies. Hard to swallow. Special effects by Rick Baker. Look for director Jonathan Demme in a bit part.
1977 (R) 85m/C Alex Rebar, Burr de Benning, Cheryl "Rainbeaux" Smith; **D:** William Sachs. **VHS, Beta** $69.98 LIV, VES Woof!

The Incredible Mr. Limpet Limp comedy about a nebbish bookkeeper who's transformed into a fish, fulfilling his aquatic dreams. Eventually he falls in love with another fish, and helps the U.S. Navy find Nazi subs during World War II. Partially animated, beloved by some, particularly those under the age of seven. Based on Theodore Pratt's novel.
1964 99m/C Don Knotts, Jack Weston, Carole Cook, Andrew Duggan, Larry Keating, Elizabeth McRae; **D:** Arthur Lubin. **VHS, Beta, LV** $19.98 WAR, WTA 🐾🐾

The Incredible Petrified World Divers are trapped in an underwater cave when volcanic eruptions begin. Suffocating nonsense.
1958 78m/B John Carradine, Allen Windsor, Phyllis Coates, Lloyd Nelson, George Skaff; **D:** Jerry Warren. **VHS** $19.95 NOS, SNC Woof!

The Incredible Rocky Mountain Race The townspeople of St. Joseph, fed up with Mark Twain's destructive feud with a neighbor, devise a shrewd scheme to rid the town of the troublemakers by sending them on a road race through the West. Made for television comedy starring the F-Troop.
1977 97m/C Christopher Connelly, Forrest Tucker, Larry Storch, Mike Mazurki; **D:** James I. Conway. **VHS, Beta** $19.95 STE 🐾🐾

The Incredible Sarah A limp adapted stage biography from "Reader's Digest" of the great actress Sarah Bernhardt. Jackson chews scenery to no avail.
1976 (PG) 105m/C Glenda Jackson, Daniel Massey, Yvonne Mitchell, Douglas Wilmer; **D:** Richard Fleischer. **VHS, Beta, LV** $19.95 STE, IME 🐾🐾

The Incredible Shrinking Man Adapted by Richard Matheson from his own novel, the sci-fi classic is a philosophical thriller about a man who is doused with radioactive mist and begins to slowly shrink. His new size means that everyday objects take on sinister meaning and he must fight for his life in an increasingly hostile, absurd environment. A surreal, suspenseful allegory with impressive special effects. Endowed with the tension usually reserved for Hitchcock films.
1957 81m/B Grant Williams, Randy Stuart, April Kent, Paul Langton, Raymond Bailey; **D:** Jack Arnold. **VHS, Beta, LV** $14.98 MCA, PIA, MLB 🐾🐾🐾½

The Incredible Shrinking Woman "...Shrinking Man" spoof and inoffensive social satire finds household cleaners producing some strange side effects on model homemaker Tomlin, slowly shrinking her to doll-house size. She then encounters everyday happenings as big tasks and not so menial. Her advertising exec husband has a hand in the down-sizing. Sight gags abound but the cuteness wears thin by the end.
1981 (PG) 89m/C Lily Tomlin, Charles Grodin, Ned Beatty, Henry Gibson; **D:** Joel Schumacher. **VHS, Beta, LV** $39.95 MCA 🐾🐾½

The Incredible Two-Headed Transplant Mad scientist Dern has a criminal head transplanted on to the shoulder of big John Bloom and the critter runs amuck. Low-budget special effects guaranteed to give you a headache or two. Watch for onetime Pat "Marilyn Munster" Priest in a bikini.
1971 (PG) 88m/C Bruce Dern, Pat Priest, Casey Kasem, Albert Cole, John Bloom, Berry Kroeger; **D:** Anthony M. Lanza. **VHS** NO Woof!

Incredibly Strange Creatures Who Stopped Living and Became Mixed-Up Zombies The infamous, super-cheap horror spoof that established Steckler (for whom Cash Flagg is a pseudonym), about a carny side show riddled with ghouls and bad rock bands. Assistant cinematographers include the young Laszlo Kovacs and Vilmos Zsigmond. A must-see for connoisseurs of cult and camp. **AKA:** The Teenage Psycho Meets Bloody Mary; The Incredibly Strange Creatures.
1963 90m/C Cash Flagg, Carolyn Brandt, Brett O'Hara, Atlas King, Sharon Walsh; **D:** Ray Dennis Steckler. **VHS, Beta** NO Woof!

Incubus A doctor and his teenaged daughter settle in a quiet New England community, only to encounter the incubus, a terrifying, supernatural demon who enjoys sex murders. Offensive trash.
1982 (R) 90m/C CA John Cassavetes, Kerrie Keane, Helen Hughes, Erin Flannery, John Ireland; **D:** John Hough. **VHS, Beta, LV** $19.98 VES Woof!

Indecency Ellie (Beals) is still recovering from a mental breakdown when she goes to work for Marie (Clarkson) at her ad agency. There Ellie must deal with manipulative associate Nia (Davis) and Marie's charming, estranged husband Mick (Remar), who draws the fragile Ellie into an affair. Then Marie commits suicide—or maybe it was murder.
1992 (PG-13) 88m/C Jennifer Beals, James Remar, Sammi Davis-Voss, Barbara Williams, Christopher John Fields, Ray McKinnon; **D:** Marisa Silver; **W:** Amy Holden Jones, Holly Goldberg Sloan, Alan Ormsby. **VHS, LV** $89.98 MCA 🐾🐾

An Indecent Obsession Colleen McCullough's bestseller about a wartime asylum on the day the Japanese surrendered. Hughes plays the nurse with a heart of gold.
1985 100m/C AU Wendy Hughes, Bill Hunter, Bruno Lawrence; **D:** Lex Marinos. **VHS, Beta** QNE 🐾🐾½

Indecent Proposal High-gloss movie that had couples everywhere discussing the big question: Would you let your wife sleep with a good-looking billionaire in exchange for one million dollars? Of course, proposer Gage is played by the weathered, yet ever gorgeous Redford. Moore and Harrelson make up the happy couple who are financially down on their luck and decide to try Vegas on a last-ditch gambling effort. When Gage offers the couple a million dollars for one night with Moore, it sets the stage for an angst-ridden examination of values by the perfect marrieds. Surreally slick direction from Lyne, but an ultimately empty film. Based on the novel by Jack Engelhard.
1993 (R) 118m/C Robert Redford, Demi Moore, Woody Harrelson, Seymour Cassel, Oliver Platt, Billy Bob Thornton, Rip Taylor, Billy Connolly, Joel Brooks; **Cameos:** Sheena Easton, Herbie Hancock; **D:** Adrian Lyne; **W:** Amy Holden Jones; **M:** John Barry. **VHS** PAR 🐾🐾½

Independence Dramatically recreates the debates, concerns, and events that led up to the U.S. Declaration of Independence in 1776.

1976 30m/C Eli Wallach, Anne Jackson, Pat Hingle, Patrick O'Neal; **D:** John Huston. **VHS, Beta $19.98** *MPI, FHF, KAR* ��½

Independence Day Uneven romantic drama about a small-town photographer, yearning for the big city, who falls in love with a racing car enthusiast, whose sister is a battered wife. Strong cast, particularly Wiest as the abused wife, is left occasionally stranded by a script reaching too hard for social significance. **AKA:** Follow Your Dreams.
1983 (R) 110m/C Kathleen Quinlan, David Keith, Frances Sternhagen, Dianne Wiest, Cliff DeYoung, Richard Farnsworth, Josef Sommer, Cheryl "Rainbeaux" Smith; **D:** Robert Mandel. **VHS, Beta $19.98** *WAR, CCB* ��

The Indestructible Man Chaney, electrocuted for murder and bank robbery, is brought back to life by a scientist. Naturally, he seeks revenge on those who sentenced him to death. Chaney does the best he can with the material.
1956 70m/B Lon Chaney Jr., Marian Carr, Casey Adams; **D:** Jack Pollexfen. **VHS $16.95** *NOS, MRV, SNC* �

The Indian Fighter Exciting actioner has Douglas as a scout hired to lead a wagon train to Oregon in 1870. The train must pass through dangerous Sioux territory and Douglas tries to make peace with the Sioux leader but a secret Indian gold mine and romance cause friction and keep things lively.
1955 88m/C Kirk Douglas, Elsa Martinelli, Walter Abel, Walter Matthau, Diana Douglas, Lon Chaney Jr., Eduard Franz, Alan Hale Jr., Elisha Cook, Harry Landers; **D:** Andre de Toth; **W:** Ben Hecht. **VHS $14.95** *MGM* ���

Indian Paint A pleasant children's film about an Indian boy's love for his horse and his rite of passage. Silverheels was Tonto on television's "The Lone Ranger," while Crawford was the "Rifleman's" son.
1964 90m/C Jay Silverheels, Johnny Crawford, Pat Hogan, Robert Crawford Jr., George Lewis; **D:** Norman Foster. **VHS, Beta $19.95** *UHV* �

The Indian Runner In Penn's debut as a writer-director, he brings us the story of two brothers in Nebraska during the late '60s, who are forced to change their lives with the loss of their family farm. Joe is a good cop and family man who can't deal with the rage of his brother Frank, who has just returned from Vietnam and is turning to a life of crime. Penn does a decent job of representing the struggle between the responsible versus the rebellious side of human nature. Based on the song "Highway Patrolman" by Bruce Springsteen.
1991 (R) 127m/C David Morse, Viggo Mortensen, Sandy Dennis, Charles Bronson, Valeria Golino, Patricia Arquette, Dennis Hopper; **W/D:** Sean Penn. **VHS, LV $19.98** *MGM* ��

The Indian Scarf Heirs to a dead man's fortune are being strangled one by one at the benefactor's country estate. An Edgar Wallace suspense tale.
1963 85m/C **GE** Heinz Drache, Gisela Uhlen, Klaus Kinski; **D:** Alfred Vohrer. **VHS $16.95** *SNC* ��

Indian Summer Yet another addition to the growing 30-something nostalgia genre. Delete the big house, add a crusty camp director (Arkin), change the characters' names (but not necessarily their lives) and you feel like you're experiencing deja vu. This time seven friends and the requisite outsider reconvene at Camp Tamakwa, the real-life summer camp to writer/director Binder. The former campers talk. They yearn. They save Camp Tamakwa and experience personal growth. A must see for those who appreciate

listening to situational jokes that are followed by "I guess you had to be there."
1993 (PG-13) 98m/C Alan Arkin, Matt Craven, Diane Lane, Bill Paxton, Elizabeth Perkins, Kevin Pollak, Sam Raimi, Vincent Spano, Julie Warner, Kimberly Williams, Richard Chevolleau; **D:** Mike Binder; **W:** Mike Binder; **M:** Miles Goodman. **VHS** *NYR* ��

Indian Uprising An army captain tries to keep local settlers from causing trouble with Geronimo and his people when gold is discovered on their territory.
1951 75m/C George Montgomery, Audrey Long, Carl Benton Reid, John Baer, Joe Sawyer; **D:** Ray Nazarro. **VHS, Beta $14.99** *GKK* ��

Indiana Jones and the Last Crusade In this, the third and last Indiana Jones adventure, we find Jones, the fearless archaeologist, once again up against the Nazis in a race to find the Holy Grail. Introduces Connery as Indy's father and explains the origin of the infamous fedora. More adventures, exotic places, dastardly villains, and daring escapes than ever before; a must for Indy fans and a bit tedious for others.
1989 (PG) 126m/C Harrison Ford, Sean Connery, Denholm Elliott, Alison Doody, Julian Glover, John Rhys-Davies, River Phoenix; **D:** Steven Spielberg; **W:** Jeffrey Boam; **M:** John Williams. **VHS, Beta, LV, SVS, 8mm $24.95** *PAR, SUP, TLF* ���

Indiana Jones and the Temple of Doom Daredevil archaeologist Indiana Jones is back and on the trail of the legendary Ankara Stone and a ruthless cult that has enslaved hundreds of children. Enough action for ten movies, special effects galore, and the usual booming John Williams score make it a cinematic roller coaster ride, with less regard for plot and pacing than the original. The scene where a heart is plucked out of a chest is gory, and may be too much for children. Though second of three Indiana Jones movies, it's actually a prequel to "Raiders of the Lost Ark."
1984 (PG) 118m/C Harrison Ford, Kate Capshaw, Ke Huy Quan, Amrish Puri; **D:** Steven Spielberg; **M:** John Williams. Academy Awards '84: Best Visual Effects; Nominations: Best Original Score. **VHS, Beta, LV, 8mm $19.95** *PAR, APD* ���

Indio A Marine-trained half-breed takes it on himself to save the Amazon rain forest. Not a peaceful demonstrator, his tactics are violent ones.
1990 (R) 94m/C Marvin Hagler, Francesco Quinn, Brian Dennehy; **D:** Anthony M. Dawson. **VHS, Beta, LV $89.98** *MED* �

Indio 2: The Revolt Greedy developers are cutting a highway into the Amazon jungle, destroying everything in their path. All is not lost though, because U.S. Marine Sgt. Iron is on top of things, continuing his struggle to unite the Amazon tribes and save the rainforest, no matter what it takes.
1992 (R) 104m/C Marvin Hagler, Charles Napier. **VHS $89.98** *LIV* �

Indiscreet Empty-headed romantic comedy about a fashion designer whose past catches up with her when her ex-lover starts romancing her sister. No relation to the classic 1958 film with Cary Grant and Ingrid Bergman. ♫Come To Me; If You Haven't Got Love.
1931 81m/B Gloria Swanson, Ben Lyon, Barbara Kent; **D:** Leo McCarey. **VHS, Beta $19.95** *NOS, MRV, REP* �½

Indiscreet A charming American diplomat in London falls in love with a stunning actress, but protects himself by saying he is married. Needless to say, she finds out.

Stylish romp with Grant and Bergman at their sophisticated best. Adapted by Norman Krasna from his stage play "Kind Sir."
1958 100m/C Cary Grant, Ingrid Bergman, Phyllis Calvert; **D:** Stanley Donen. **VHS $19.98** *REP, MLB* ���

Indiscreet Indistinctive made for TV rehash of the charming 1958 Grant/Bergman romantic comedy in which a suave American falls for an English actress. Both versions derive from the play "Kind Sir" by Norman Krasna, but this one suffers by comparison.
1988 (PG) 94m/C Robert Wagner, Lesley-Anne Down, Maggie Henderson, Robert McBain, Jeni Barnett; **D:** Richard Michaels. **VHS $79.98** *REP* �½

The Indiscreet Mrs. Jarvis Lansbury stars as Brenda Jarvis, a woman who takes drastic steps to ensure that her checkered past won't come back to haunt her.
19?? 30m/B Angela Lansbury; **D:** Alan Smithee. **VHS $7.95** *RHI* ��

Indiscretion of an American Wife Set almost entirely in Rome's famous Terminal Station, where an ill-fated couple say goodbye endlessly while the woman tries to decide whether to join her husband in the States. Co-written by Truman Capote and trimmed from 87 minutes upon U.S. release. **AKA:** Indiscretion; Terminus Station; Terminal Station Indiscretion.
1954 63m/C **IT** Jennifer Jones, Montgomery Clift, Richard Beymer; **D:** Vittorio De Sica. **VHS, Beta $19.95** *NOS, FOX, HEG* ��

Indomitable Teddy Roosevelt Entertaining mix of newsreel footage and staged scenes traces the career of the feisty president.
1983 93m/C **D:** Harrison Engle. **VHS, Beta** *PSM, CHF* ��½

Infamous Crimes Philo investigates the murders of a playboy and his girlfriends. One of the last of the series whose character was based on the S.S. Van Dine stories. **AKA:** Philo Vance Returns.
1947 64m/B William Wright, Terry Austin, Leon Belasco, Clara Blandick, Iris Adrian, Frank Wilcox; **D:** William Beaudine. **VHS, Beta, 8mm $29.95** *VYY* ��

Infamous Daughter of Fanny Hill Softcore drama about a Victorian floozy who seduces dozens of men.
1987 73m/C Stacy Walker. **VHS, Beta $29.95** *MED* �

Infernal Trio An attorney comes up with a plan involving two sisters (who are his lovers) which will make them both wealthy; but it will also make them both murderers. Sophisticated black comedy based on a true story. In French with English subtitles or dubbed.
1974 100m/C **FR IT** Romy Schneider, Michel Piccoli, Mascha Gonska; **D:** Francis Girod. **VHS $59.95** *CVC, TAM* ��½

Inferno Uneven occult horror tale about a young man who arrives in New York to investigate the mysterious circumstances surrounding his sister's death. Score by Keith Emerson. Dubbed.
1978 (R) 83m/C **IT** Leigh McCloskey, Elenora Giorgi, Irene Miracle, Sacha Pitoeff; **D:** Dario Argento. **VHS, Beta $59.98** *FOX* ��

Inferno in Paradise Mucho macho firefighter and bimbous gal pal photographer get hot while trailing a murderous pyromaniac. More like purgatory in the living room (that is, unless you thought Forsyth's earlier "Chesty Anderson, US Navy" was divine comedy).

1988 115m/C Richard Young, Betty Ann Carr, Jim Davis, Andy Jarrell, Dennis Chun; *D:* Ed Forsyth. **VHS** $19.95 *ACA* ⊘

The Informer Based on Liam O'Flaherty's novel about the Irish Sinn Fein Rebellion of 1922, it tells the story of a hard-drinking Dublin man (Mclaglen) who informs on a friend (a member of the Irish Republican Army) in order to collect a 20-pound reward. When his "friend" is killed during capture, he goes on a drinking spree instead of using the money, as planned, for passage to America. Director Ford allowed McLaglen to improvise his lines during the trial scene in order to enhance the realism, leading to excruciating suspense. Wonderful score by Max Steiner. **1935** 91m/B Victor McLaglen, Heather Angel, Wallace Ford, Margot Grahame, Joseph Sawyer, Preston Foster, Una O'Connor; *D:* John Ford. Academy Awards '35: Best Actor (McLaglen), Best Director (Ford), Best Screenplay, Best Original Score; Nominations: Best Film Editing, Best Picture; National Board of Review Awards '35: 10 Best Films of the Year; New York Film Critics Awards '35: Best Director (Ford), Best Film. **VHS, Beta, LV** $19.98 *VID, MED, BTV* ⊘⊘⊘⊘

Infra-Man If you're looking for a hockey flick that is truly bad, this could be it. Inframan is a superhero who must rescue the galaxy from the clutches of the evil Princess Dragon Mom and her army of prehistoric monsters. Outlandish dialogue (delivered straight) combines with horrible special effects and costumes to create what may well be one of the best camp classics to date. Poorly dubbed in English. *AKA:* The Super Inframan; The Infra Superman. **1976** (PG) 92m/C *HK* Li Hsiu-hsien, Wang Hsieh, Yuan Man-tzu, Terry Liu, Tsen Shu-yi, Huang Chien-lung, Lu Sheng; *D:* Hua-Shan; *W:* Peter Fernandez. **VHS, Beta** $49.95 *PSM Woof!*

Inga Story of a teenage girl becoming a woman. Sensitive and well-acted. **1967** 86m/B *SW* **VHS, Beta** $24.95 *VPL Woof!*

Inherit the Wind Powerful courtroom drama, based on the Broadway play, is actually a fictionalized version of the infamous Scopes "Monkey Trial" of 1925. Tracy is the defense attorney for the schoolteacher on trial for teaching Darwin's Theory of Evolution to a group of students in a small town ruled by religion. March is the prosecutor seeking to put the teacher behind bars and restore religion to the schools. **1960** 128m/B Spencer Tracy, Fredric March, Florence Eldridge, Gene Kelly, Dick York; *D:* Stanley Kramer. Academy Awards '60 Nominations: Best Actor (Tracy), Best Adapted Screenplay, Best Black and White Cinematography, Best Film Editing; Berlin International Film Festival '60: Best Actor (March); National Board of Review Awards '60: 10 Best Films of the Year. **VHS, Beta, LV** $19.98 *FOX, FCT* ⊘⊘⊘½

Inheritance Victorian-era melodrama of a young heiress endangered by her guradian, who plots to murder his charge for her inheritance. Chilling and moody story based on a novel by Sheridan Le Fanu. *AKA:* Uncle Silas. **1947** 103m/B *GB* Jean Simmons, Katina Paxinou, Derrick DeMarney, Derek Bond; *D:* Charles Frank. **VHS, Beta** $29.98 *DVT* ⊘⊘⊘

The Inheritance Wealthy partiarch becomes sexually involved with scheming daughter-in-law. Tawdry tale is nonetheless engaging. *AKA:* L'Eredita Ferramonti. **1976** (R) 121m/C *IT* Anthony Quinn, Fabio Testi, Dominique Sanda; *M:* Mauro Bolognini; *M:* Ennio Morricone. **VHS, Beta** $14.98 *VID* ⊘⊘½

The Inheritor Set in a small New England town, this mystery centers on the death of a young woman and her sister's attempts to uncover the murderer. The local celebrity, a writer, seems to be at the heart of the mystery and the sister finds herself growing interested. Keeps you guessing. **1990** (R) 83m/C Dan Haggerty; *D:* Brian Savegar. **VHS** $79.98 *VID* ⊘⊘

The Inheritors Not-too-subtle tale of a young German boy who becomes involved with a Nazi youth group as his home life deteriorates. Heavy-going anti-fascism creates more message than entertainment. In German with English subtitles or dubbed. **1985** 89m/C *GE* Nikolas Vogel, Roger Schauer, Klaus Novak, Johanna Tomek; *D:* Walter Bannert. **VHS, Beta** $29.98 *SUE, APD, GLV* ⊘½

Inhibition A beautiful heiress has lots of sex with different people in exotic locales. Softcore soap. **1986** 90m/C Claudine Beccaire, Ilona Staller. **VHS, Beta** $29.95 *MED* ⊘

The Initiation Trying to rid herself of a troublesome nightmare, a coed finds herself face-to-face with a psycho. Gory campus slaughterfest. **1984** (R) 97m/C Vera Miles, Clu Gulager, James Read, Daphne Zuniga; *D:* Larry Stewart. **VHS, Beta** $19.95 *STE, HBO* ⊘

Initiation of Sarah College freshman joins a sorority, undergoes abusive initiation, and gains a supernatural revenge. Made-for-television "Carrie" rip-off. **1978** 100m/C Kay Lenz, Shelley Winters, Kathryn Crosby, Morgan Brittany, Tony Bill, Tisa Farrow, Robert Hays, Morgan Fairchild; *D:* Robert Day. **VHS, Beta** $49.95 *WOV* ⊘

Inn of Temptation A bunch of bowling buddies take off for Bangkok on an impulsive weekend, and meet lots of Oriental women. **1986** 72m/C Michael Jacot, Claude Martin. **VHS, Beta** $29.95 *MED* ⊘

Inn of the Damned Detective looks into an inn where no one ever gets charged for an extra day; they simply die. Anderson is watchable. **1974** 92m/C *AU* Alex Cord, Judith Anderson, Tony Bonner, Michael Craig, John Meillon; *D:* Terry Burke. **VHS, Beta** *PGN* ⊘½

The Inn of the Sixth Happiness Inspiring story of Gladys Aylward, an English missionary in 1930s' China, who leads a group of children through war-torn countryside. Donat's last film. **1958** 158m/C Ingrid Bergman, Robert Donat, Curt Jurgens; *D:* Mark Robson. Academy Awards '58 Nominations: Best Director (Robson); National Board of Review Awards '58: Best Actress (Bergman). **VHS, Beta** *FOX* ⊘⊘⊘

Inn on the River Scotland Yard investigates a series of murders taking place on the waterfront by the "Shark's" gang. Remake of "The Return of the Frog." **1962** 95m/C *GE* Klaus Kinski, Joachim Fuchsberger, Brigitte Grothum, Richard Much; *D:* Alfred Vohrer. **VHS** $16.95 *SNC* ⊘⊘½

The Inner Circle A private detective, framed for murder by his secretary, has a limited amount of time to find the real murderer. Confusing. **1946** 57m/B Adele Mara, Warren Douglas, William Frawley, Ricardo Cortez, Virginia Christine; *D:* Philip Ford. **VHS, Beta** $16.95 *SNC* ⊘½

The Inner Circle Ivan Sanshin is a meek, married man working as a movie projectionist for the KGB in 1935 Russia. Sanshin is taken by the KGB to the Kremlin to show movies, primarily Hollywood fea-

tures, to leader Joseph Stalin, a job he cannot discuss with anyone, even his wife. Under the spell of Stalin's personality, Sanshin sees only what he's told and overlooks the oppression and persecution of the times. Based on the life of the projectionist who served from 1935 until Stalin's death in 1953. Filmed on location at the Kremlin. **1991** (PG-13) 122m/C Tom Hulce, Lolita Davidovich, Bob Hoskins, Alexandre Zbruev; *W/ D:* Andrei Konchalovsky. **VHS, LV, 8mm** $19.95 *COL* ⊘⊘⊘

Inner Sanctum Adequate tale of a young girl accosted by a gypsy who claims that tragedy awaits her. Based on a radio show of the same name. **1948** 62m/B Chuck Russell, Mary Beth Hughes, Lee Patrick, Nana Bryant; *D:* Lew Landers. **VHS** $16.95 *SNC* ⊘⊘

Inner Sanctum Cheating husband hires sensuous nurse to tend invalid wife. You can guess the rest; in fact, you have to because the plot ultimately makes no sense. Available in R-rated and sex-drenched unrated editions. **1991** (R) 87m/C Tanya Roberts, Margaux Hemingway, Joseph Bottoms, Valerie Wildman, William Butler, Brett Clark; *D:* Fred Olen Ray. **VHS, LV** $19.95 *COL, PIA Woof!*

Innerspace A space pilot, miniaturized for a journey through a lab rat a la "Fantastic Voyage," is accidentally injected into a nebbish supermarket clerk, and together they nab some bad guys and get the girl. Award-winning special effects support some funny moments between micro Quaid and nerdy Short, with Ryan producing the confused romantic interest. **1987** (PG) 120m/C Dennis Quaid, Martin Short, Meg Ryan, Kevin McCarthy, Fiona Lewis, Henry Gibson, Robert Picardo, John Hora, Wendy Schaal, Orson Bean, Chuck Jones, William Schallert, Dick Miller; *D:* Joe Dante; *M:* Jerry Goldsmith. **VHS, Beta, LV, 8mm** $19.98 *WAR* ⊘⊘½

Innocence Unprotected A film collage that contains footage from the 1942 film "Innocence Unprotected," the story of an acrobat trying to save an orphan from her wicked stepmother, newsreels from Nazi-occupied Yugoslavia, and interviews from 1968 with people who were in the film. Confiscated by the Nazis during final production, "Innocence Unprotected" was discovered by director Makavejev, who worked it into the collage. Filmed in color and black and white; In Serbian with English subtitles. **1968** 78m/C *YU* Dragoljub Aleksic, Ana Milosavljevic, Vera Jovanovic; *D:* Dusan Makavejev. **VHS** $59.95 *FCT* ⊘⊘½

The Innocent The setting: turn of the century Rome, ablaze with atheism and free love. The story: Giannini's a Sicilian aristocrat who ignores wife Antonelli and dallies with scheming mistress O'Neill. Discovering his wife's infidelity, he's profoundly disillusioned, and his manly notion of self disintegrates. Visconti's last film, it was an art house fave and is considered by many to be his best. Lavishly photographed, well set and costumed, and true to the Gabrielle D'Annunzio's novel. *AKA:* L'Innocente. **1976** (R) 125m/C *IT* Laura Antonelli, Jennifer O'Neill, Giancarlo Giannini; *D:* Luchino Visconti. **VHS, Beta** $79.95 *VES, FCT, TAM* ⊘⊘⊘½

Innocent Blood A mediocre modern-day vampire/gangster combo with the beautiful (though red-eyed) Parillaud as the woman with a taste for someone "Italian." Unfortunately, she doesn't finish off her latest meal—mobster Loggia—who finds being

undead very useful to his vicious work. LaPaglia plays the bewildered, love-struck cop involved with the vamp. Parillaud appears nude in several scenes and the gore and violence are stomach-turning.
1992 (R) 112m/C Anne Parillaud, Anthony LaPaglia, Robert Loggia, David Proval, Don Rickles, Rocco Sisto, Kim Coates; **D:** John Landis. **VHS, Beta, LV $94.99** WAR, PMS ✏✏

An Innocent Man Uneven story of Selleck, an ordinary family man and airline mechanic, framed as a drug dealer and sent to prison.
1989 (R) 113m/C Tom Selleck, F. Murray Abraham, Laila Robins, David Rasche; **D:** Peter Yates. **VHS, Beta, LV $19.99** TOU ✏✏½

Innocent Prey When a woman finally summons the courage to bid hasta la vista to her abusive husband, it turns out he's not so quick to say ciao. Definitely not a highlight in Balsam's career.
1988 (R) 88m/C AU P.J. Soles, Martin Balsam, Kit Taylor, Grigor Taylor, John Warnock, Susan Stenmark, Richard Morgan; **D:** Colin Eggleston. **VHS $89.95** SVS ✏✏

Innocent Victim Convoluted tale of revenge and madness. Bacall plays a mad grandmother who kidnaps a boy to take the place of her dead grandson. The kidnapped boy's stepfather then is accused of murdering him, and starts murdering others to get the boy back. **AKA:** The Tree of Hands.
1990 (R) 100m/C Lauren Bacall, Helen Shaver, Paul McGann, Peter Firth; **D:** Giles Foster. **VHS $29.95** ACA ✏

The Innocents Abroad Entertaining adaptation of Mark Twain's novel about a group of naive Americans cruising the Mediterranean. Ensemble cast offers some surprising performances. Originally produced for PBS.
1984 116m/C Craig Wasson, Brooke Adams, David Ogden Stiers. **VHS $19.95** MCA ✏✏½

Innocents in Paris A group of seven Britons visit Paris for the first time. A bit long but enough ooo-la-la to satisfy.
1953 89m/B GB Alastair Sim, Laurence Harvey, Jimmy Edwards, Claire Bloom, Margaret Rutherford; **D:** Gordon Parry. **VHS, Beta** NO ✏✏½

The Inquiry A new twist on the resurrection of Christ. Carradine senses a cover-up when he's sent from Rome to investigate the problem of Christ's missing corpse. He retraces Christ's final days to solve the case in this interesting, offbeat film. Dubbed.
1987 107m/C IT Keith Carradine, Harvey Keitel, Phyllis Logan, Angelo Infanti, Lina Sastri; **D:** Damiano Damiani. **VHS $79.99** HBO ✏✏½

Inquisition Naschy is a 16th century witch hunting judge who finds himself accused of witchcraft.
1976 85m/C SP Paul Naschy, Daniela Giordano, Juan Gallardo; **W/D:** Paul Naschy. **VHS, Beta** VCD ✏½

Insanity A film director becomes violently obsessed with a beautiful actress.
1982 101m/C Terence Stamp, Fernando Rey, Corinne Clery. **VHS, Beta** NO ✏

The Insect Woman Chronicles 45 years in the life of a woman who must work with the diligence of an ant in order to survive. Thoughtfully reflects the exploitation of women and the cruelty of human nature in Japanese society. Beautiful performance from Hidari, who ages from girlhood to middle age. In Japanese with English subtitles. **AKA:** The Insect; Nippon Konchuki.
1963 123m/B JP Sachiko Hidari, Yitsuko Yoshimura, Hiroyuki Nagaes, Sumie Sasaki; **D:** Shohei Imamura. **VHS $29.95** CVC ✏✏✏

Inserts A formerly successful director has been reduced to making porno films in this pretentious, long-winded effort set in a crumbling Hollywood mansion in the 1930s. Affected, windbaggish performances kill it.
1976 (R) 99m/C GB Richard Dreyfuss, Jessica Harper, Veronica Cartwright, Bob Hoskins; **D:** John Byrum. **VHS $59.98** FOX ✏

Inside Daisy Clover Wood is the self-sufficient, junior delinquent waif who becomes a teenage musical star and pays the price for fame in this Hollywood saga set in the 1930s. Discovered by tyrannical studio head Plummer, Daisy is given her big break and taken under his wing for grooming as Swan Studio's newest sensation. She falls for fellow performer, matinee idol Redford, who has some secrets of his own, and eventually has a breakdown from the career pressure. Glossy melodrama is filled with over-the-top performances but its sheer silliness makes it amusing.
1965 128m/C Natalie Wood, Christopher Plummer, Robert Redford, Ruth Gordon, Roddy McDowall, Katharine Bard; **D:** Robert Mulligan. Academy Awards '65 Nominations: Best Art Direction/Set Decoration (Color), Best Costume Design (Color), Best Supporting Actress (Gordon); Golden Globe Awards '66: Best Supporting Actress (Gordon). **VHS, LV** WEA ✏✏½

Inside Information With Tarzan's help, a cop searches out the leader of a ring of jewel thieves.
1934 51m/B Rex Lease, Marion Shilling, Philo McCullough. **VHS, Beta, LV** NO ✏

The Inside Man Double agents struggle to find a submarine-detecting laser device. Based on true incidents in which a soviet sub ran aground in Sweden. Made in Sweden; dubbed.
1984 90m/C SW Dennis Hopper, Hardy Kruger, Gosta Ekman, David Wilson; **D:** Tom Clegg. **VHS, Beta $9.95** SIM, CEL ✏✏½

Inside Moves A look at handicapped citizens trying to make it in everyday life, focusing on the relationship between an insecure, failed suicide and a volatile man who is only a knee operation away from a dreamed-about basketball career.
1980 (PG) 113m/C John Savage, Diana Scarwid, David Morse, Amy Wright; **D:** Richard Donner; **M:** John Barry. **VHS, Beta, LV $19.95** FOX ✏✏½

Inside Out An ex-GI, a jewel thief and a German POW camp commandant band together to find a stolen shipment of Nazi gold behind the Iron Curtain. To find the gold, they help a Nazi prisoner who knows the secret to break out of prison. Good action caper. **AKA:** The Golden Heist; Hitler's Gold.
1975 (PG) 97m/C GB Telly Savalas, Robert Culp, James Mason, Aldo Ray, Doris Kunstmann; **D:** Peter Duffell. **VHS, Beta $59.95** WAR ✏✏½

Inside Out Hiding in his apartment from a world which terrifies him, Jimmy doesn't feel he's missing much—since he has the necessary women and bookies come to him. He soon finds he's not quite as safe as he thought, and the only way out is "out there." Fine performance from Gould, suspenseful pacing.
1991 (R) 87m/C Elliot Gould, Jennifer Tilly, Howard Hesseman, Beah Richards, Timothy Scott, Sandy McPeak, Dana Elcar, Meshach Taylor; **W/D:** Robert Taicher. **VHS $79.95** HMD ✏✏½

Inside the Law A gang of crooks takes over a bank and must stay "inside the law" and resist their natural inclinations. Lots of comic situations.

1942 65m/B Wallace Ford, Frank Sully, Harry Holman, Luana Walters, Lafayette McKee, Danny Duncan, Earle Hodgins; **D:** Hamilton MacFadden. **VHS $19.95** NOS ✏✏

Inside the Lines A World War I tale of espionage and counter-espionage.
1930 73m/B Betty Compson, Montagu Love, Mischa Auer, Ralph Forbes. **VHS, Beta $29.95** VYY ✏✏

Inside the Third Reich A made-for-television mini-series detailing the rise to power within the Third Reich of Albert Speer, top advisor to Hitler. Based on Speer's rather self-serving memoires.
1982 250m/C Derek Jacobi, Rutger Hauer, John Gielgud, Blythe Danner, Maria Schell, Ian Holm, Trevor Howard, Randy Quaid, Viveca Lindfors, Robert Vaughn, Stephen Collins, Elke Sommer, Renee Soutendijk; **D:** Marvin J. Chomsky. **VHS, Beta, LV $34.95** SUE, GLV ✏✏✏

Insignificance A film about an imaginary night spent in a New York hotel by characters who resemble Marilyn Monroe, Albert Einstein, Joe McCarthy, and Joe DiMaggio. Entertaining and often amusing as it follows the characters as they discuss theory and relativity, the Russians, and baseball among other things.
1985 110m/C GB Gary Busey, Tony Curtis, Theresa Russell, Michael Emil, Will Sampson; **D:** Nicolas Roeg. **VHS, Beta, LV $19.98** LHV, WAR ✏✏✏

Inspector Clouseau Cartoon Festival A series of tapes which features five cartoons each from the Pink Panther canon and the diminutive French detective.
1966 32m/C VHS, Beta $14.95 MGM ✏✏✏

The Inspector General Classic Kaye craziness of mistaken identities with the master comic portraying a carnival medicine man who is mistaken by the villagers for their feared Inspector General. If you like Kaye's manic performance, you'll enjoy this one. ♫The Gypsy Drinking Song; Onward Onward; The Medicine Show; The Inspector General; Lonely Heart; Soliloquy For Three Heads; Happy Times; Brodny. **AKA:** Happy Times.
1949 103m/C Danny Kaye, Walter Slezak, Barbara Bates, Elsa Lanchester, Gene Lockhart, Walter Catlett, Alan Hale Jr.; **D:** Henry Koster. **VHS, Beta $19.98** MGM, MRV, NOS ✏✏✏

The Inspector General The filmed performance of Gogol's great play by the Moscow Art Theatre, wherein a provincial town panics when they mistake a wandering moron for the Inspector come to check up on them. In Russian with English subtitles.
1954 128m/B RU D: Vladimir Petrov. **VHS, Beta $44.95** FCT, AUD, TAM ✏½

Inspector Hornleigh A pair of bumbling detectives arrive on the scene when a Chancellor's fortune is stolen. Fine comedy, although the Scottish and British accents can be rather thick now and again.
1939 76m/B GB Gordon Harker, Alastair Sim, Miki Hood, Wally Patch, Steve Geray, Edward Underdown, Hugh Williams, Gibb McLaughlin; **D:** Eugene Forde. **VHS, Beta $16.95** NOS, SNC ✏✏½

Inspector Morse Episodes from the popular British police series about the irascible, romantic (no-known-first-name) Morse and the deadly doings of Oxford, England. Based on the character created by Colin Dexter. Each tape is available individually.
1987? 101m/C GB John Thaw, Kevin Whately, Michael Gough, Clive Swift, Frederick Treves, Amanda Hillwood, Barbara Flynn; **D:** Brian Parker. **VHS $29.95** BFS, TVC, HMV ✏✏½

Inspiration of Mr. Budd A clever barber helps police trap a murderer. Based on a short story by Dorothy L. Sayers. Part of EBE's "Orson Welles' Great Mysteries" series.
1975 25m/C Orson Welles. **VHS, Beta**
BRT ♫♫½

Instant Justice A professional Marine jeopardizes his military career by avenging his sister's murder, vigilante style. Exclusive action. *AKA:* Marine Issue.
1986 (R) 101m/C *GB* Michael Pare, Tawny Kitaen, Charles Napier; *D:* Craig T. Rumar. **VHS, Beta** $79.95 WAR ♫½

Instant Karma Would be comedy depicts young man's far fetched attempts to score babewise. Ask no more what happened to erstwhile teen heart throb Cassidy: he suffers from a major bout of bad karma.
1990 94m/C Craig Sheffer, Chelsea Noble, David Cassidy, Alan Blumenfeld, Glen Hirsch, Marty Ingels, Orson Bean; *D:* Roderick Taylor. **VHS, Beta** $89.98 MGM ♫½

Instant Kung-Fu Man Twin brothers get involved in a case of mistaken identity in this martial arts effort.
1984 104m/C John Liu, Hwang Jang Lee, Yeh Fei Yang. **VHS, Beta** WVE ♫

The Instructor The head of a karate school proves the value of his skill when threatened by the owner of a rival school.
1983 91m/C Don Bendell, Bob Chaney, Bob Saal, Lyndsay Scharnott; *D:* Don Bendell. **Beta** $69.98 LIV, VES ♫

Intent to Kill Lords plays a beautiful Los Angeles vice cop who takes on a gang of drug dealers. Sex and very graphic violence.
1992 (NC-17) 93m/C Traci Lords, Yaphet Kotto, Kevin Benton, Michael Foley; *D:* Charles Kanganis. **VHS, LV** $89.95 PMH ♫½

Interceptor Hijackers attempt to steal a Stealth Bomber in this action-adventure saga which features virtual reality computer-generated imagery in its combat sequences.
1992 (R) 92m/C Juergen Prochnow, Andrew Divoff, Elizabeth Morehead; *D:* Michael Cohn. **VHS, LV** $92.95 VMK ♫♫

Interface A computer game gets out of hand at a university, turning the tunnels beneath the campus into a battleground of good and evil.
1984 88m/C John Davies, Laura Lane, Matthew Sacks. **VHS, Beta** $69.98 LIV, VES ♫½

Interiors Ultra serious, Bergmanesque drama about three neurotic adult sisters, coping with the dissolution of their family. When Father decides to leave mentally unbalanced mother for a divorcee, the daughters are shocked and bewildered. Depressing and humorless, but fine performances all the way around, supported by the elegant camera work of Gordon Willis. Original theatrical trailer available on the laserdisc format.
1978 (R) 95m/C Diane Keaton, Mary Beth Hurt, E.G. Marshall, Geraldine Page, Richard Jordan, Sam Waterston, Kristin Griffith, Maureen Stapleton; *W/D:* Woody Allen. Academy Awards '78 Nominations: Best Actress (Page), Best Director (Allen), Best Original Screenplay, Best Supporting Actress (Stapleton); British Academy Awards '78: Best Supporting Actress (Page). **VHS, Beta, LV** $14.95 MGM ♫♫♫½

Intermezzo Married violinist Ekman meets pianist Bergman and they fall in love. He deserts his family to tour with Bergman, but the feelings for his wife and children become too much. When Bergman sees their love won't last, she leaves him. Shakily, he returns home and as his daughter runs to greet him, she is hit by a truck and he realizes that his family is his true love. One of the great grab-your-hanky melodramas. In Swedish with English subtitles. 1939 English re-make features Bergman's American film debut. *AKA:* Interlude.
1936 88m/B *SW* Gosta Ekman, Inga Tidblad, Ingrid Bergman, Bullen Berglund; *D:* Gustaf Molander. **VHS, LV** $29.95 WAC, LUM, TAM ♫♫♫

Intermezzo Fine, though weepy, love story of a renowned, married violinist who has an affair with his stunningly beautiful protege (Bergman), but while on concert tour realizes that his wife and children hold his heart, and he returns to them. A re-make of the 1936 Swedish film, it's best known as Bergman's American debut. Howard's violin playing was dubbed by Jascha Heifetz. *AKA:* Intermezzo: A Love Story.
1939 70m/B *IT* Ingrid Bergman, Leslie Howard, Edna Best, Ann Todd; *D:* Gregory Ratoff. **VHS, Beta, LV** $59.98 FOX, FCT ♫♫♫

Internal Affairs Wild, sexually charged action piece about an Internal Affairs officer for the L.A.P.D. (Garcia) who becomes obsessed with exposing a sleazy, corrupt street cop (Gere). Drama becomes illogical, but boasts excellent, strung out performances, especially Gere as the creepy degenerate you'd love to bust.
1990 (R) 114m/C Richard Gere, Andy Garcia, Laurie Metcalf, Ron Vawter, Marco Rodriguez, Nancy Travis, William Baldwin, Richard Bradford, William Baldwin, Annabella Sciorra, Michael Beach; *D:* Mike Figgis. **VHS, Beta, LV, 8mm** $14.95 PAR ♫♫½

International Crime Radio hero The Shadow solves a tough crime in this adventure film.
1937 62m/B Rod La Rocque, Astrid Allwyn, William von Brinken; *D:* Charles Lamont. **VHS, Beta** $16.95 SNC, NOS, AOV ♫♫

International House A wacky Dadaesque Hollywood farce about an incredible array of travelers quarantined in a Shanghai hotel where a mad doctor has perfected television. Essentially a burlesque compilation of skits, gags, and routines. Guest stars Rudy Vallee, Baby Rose Marie and Cab Calloway appear on the quaint "television" device, in musical sequences. ♫Tea Cup; Thank Heaven For You; My Bluebirds are Singing the Blues; Reefer Man.
1933 72m/B W.C. Fields, Peggy Hopkins Joyce, Rudy Vallee, George Burns, Cab Calloway, Sari Maritza, Gracie Allen, Bela Lugosi, Sterling Holloway, Baby Rose Marie; *D:* Edward Sutherland. **VHS, Beta, LV** $29.95 MCA, MLB ♫♫½

International Velvet In this long overdue sequel to "National Velvet," adult Velvet, with live-in companion (Plummer), grooms her orphaned niece (O'Neal) to become an Olympic champanion horsewoman. Good photography and performances by Plummer and Hopkins manage to keep the sentiment at a trot.
1978 (PG) 126m/C *GB* Tatum O'Neal, Anthony Hopkins, Christopher Plummer; *D:* Bryan Forbes. **VHS, Beta** $59.95 MGM ♫♫½

Internecine Project Stylistic espionage tale with Coburn's English professor acting as the mastermind behind an unusual series of murders where industrial spies kill each other, so Coburn can garner a top governmet job in D.C. Unexpected ending is worth the viewing. Screenplay by Barry Levinson; based on Mort Elkind's novel.
1973 (PG) 89m/C *GB* James Coburn, Lee Grant, Harry Andrews, Keenan Wynn; *D:* Ken Hughes. **VHS, Beta** $59.98 FOX ♫♫½

The Interns Finessed hospital soaper about interns on the staff of a large city hospital, whose personal lives are fraught with trauma, drugs, birth, death, and abortion. Good performances and direction keep this medical melodrama moving in a gurney-like manner. Followed by the "The New Interns" and the basis for a television series. Adapted from a novel by Richard Frede.
1962 120m/C Cliff Robertson, James MacArthur, Michael Callan, Nick Adams, Stefanie Powers, Suzy Parker, Buddy Ebsen, Telly Savalas, Haya Harareet; *D:* David Swift. **VHS, Beta, LV** $59.95 COL ♫♫½

The Interrogation Grueling depiction of Stalin-era Poland proves that nobody makes anticommunist movies better than those who knew tyranny firsthand. A 1950s cabaret starlet is arrested on false charges and endures years of torment in custody. Banned under Polish martial law in 1982, it circulated illegally in the country until 1989. Janda won an award at Cannes for her transformation from showgirl floozy to defiant heroine. In Polish with English subtitles. *AKA:* Przesluchanie.
1982 118m/C *PL* Krystyna Janda, Janusz Gajos, Adam Ferency, Agnieszka Holland, Anna Romantowska; *D:* Richard Bugajski. **VHS** $79.95 KIV, FCT, TAM ♫♫♫

Interrupted Journey A married man runs away to start a new life with another woman. When she is killed in a train accident, he becomes the prime suspect in her murder. Lots of action and speed, but a disappointing ending.
1949 80m/B *GB* Richard Todd, Valerie Hobson; *D:* Daniel Birt. **VHS** $16.95 NOS, SNC ♫♫½

Interval A middle-aged, globe-trotting woman becomes involved with a young American painter while running from her past. Oberon, 62 at the time, produced and played in this, her last film. Filmed in Mexico.
1973 (PG) 84m/C Merle Oberon, Robert Wolders; *D:* Daniel Mann. **VHS, Beta** $59.95 NLC ♫♫

Intervista A pseudo-documentary look at director Fellini's love of the movies, "Intervista" is a mixture of recollection, parody, memoir, satire, self-examination and fantasy. Fellini himself is the master of ceremonies in this joyous celebration of the studio community that features actors, actresses, bit players, make-up artists, scene painters, publicity agents, technicians, and gate-crashers. The high point of the film arrives with the stars of "La Dolce Vita" re-screening the Fellini masterpiece at Ekberg's country villa. It's a special moment of fantasy vs. reality in this glorious tribute to cinema history. In Italian with English subtitles. *AKA:* Federico Fellini's Intervista.
1987 108m/C *IT* Marcello Mastroianni, Anita Ekberg, Federico Fellini, Sergio Rubini, Lara Wendell; *D:* Federico Fellini. **VHS** $89.95 TRI ♫♫♫

Interzone Humans battle mutants in a post-holocaust world.
1988 97m/C Bruce Abbott. **VHS, Beta** $79.95 MED ♫♫

Intimate Contact Top executive discovers he has AIDS after a business trip fling. Powerful drama as he and his wife try to cope. Excellent, understated performances from Massey and Bloom. Written by Alma Cullen and originally made for cable television.
1987 (PG) 140m/C *GB* Claire Bloom, Daniel Massey, Abigail Cruttenden, Mark Kingston, Sylvia Syms; *D:* Waris Hussein. **VHS, Beta** $79.99 HBO ♫♫♫

Intimate Games Soft-core nonsense about a professor assigning his class to research sexual ethics.
1987? (R) 90m/C VHS, Beta $59.95 *PSM* 🎞

Intimate Moments Madame Claude runs an exclusive call-girl operation catering to the upper echelons of power in France, when she discovers that a newspaper is investigating her business.
1982 (R) 82m/C Alexandra Stewart, Dirke Altevogt. VHS, Beta $69.98 *SUE* 🎞

Intimate Obsession A frustrated wife can't attract her philandering husband. When a handsome bartender takes notice of her, she is drawn into a web of deceit which may ultimately be deadly. An unrated version is also available.
1992 (R) 80m/C VHS $89.98 *WEA* 🎞

Intimate Power True story of French schoolgirl sold into slavery to an Ottoman sultan who becomes the harem queen. She bears an heir and begins to teach her son about his people's rights, in the hope that he will bring about reform in Turkey where he grows up to be a sultan. Good cast supports the exotic storytelling in this made for cable drama.
1989 (R) 104m/C F. Murray Abraham, Maud Adams, Amber O'Shea; *D:* Jack Smight. VHS, Beta, LV $89.99 *HBO* 🎞🎞½

Intimate Story Intimate story of a husband and wife trying unsuccessfully to have a baby, amid the lack of privacy in a Kibbutz. Each blames the other for the problem and tries to escape the problems by focusing on personal fantasies. In Hebrew with English subtitles.
1981 95m/C *IS* Chava Alberstein, Alex Peleg; *D:* Israeli Nadav Levitan. VHS, Beta $79.95 *ERG, TAM* 🎞🎞½

Intimate Stranger Sexy, would-be rock star by day, Harry sets out in search of a steadier source of income. Rather than wait on tables all day, she chooses instead to become a phone-sex girl. This turns out to be an unwise career move, as she promptly finds herself the target of a phone-psycho who just can't take "no" for an answer. Will Debbie be able to shake this loser, or will he put a permanent end to her life-long dreams? Made for television.
1991 (R) 96m/C Deborah Harry, James Russo, Tim Thomerson, Paige French, Grace Zabriskie; *D:* Allan Holzman. VHS, Beta $89.95 *PAR* 🎞½

Intimate Strangers Taut made-for-television expose on battering and its effects on the family. Weaver and Struthers outshine the material, but the finest performance is a cameo by Douglas as Weaver's irascible aged father.
1977 96m/C Dennis Weaver, Sally Struthers, Quinn Cummings, Tyne Daly, Larry Hagman, Rhea Perlman; *Cameos:* Melvyn Douglas; *D:* John Llewellyn Moxey. VHS, Beta $39.95 *WOV* 🎞🎞½

Into the Badlands Mild made for cable TV thriller presents three suspense tales in "Twilight Zone" fashion, linked by the appearance of a mysterious Man in Black. No, it's not Johnny Cash, but Dern as a sinister bounty hunter in the old west, who inspires strange events on the trail.
1992 (R) 89m/C Bruce Dern, Mariel Hemingway, Helen Hunt, Dylan McDermott, Lisa Pelikan, Andrew Robinson; *D:* Sam Pillsbury. VHS $89.95 *MCA* 🎞🎞

Into the Darkness In the world of fashion models, a maniacal, demented killer stalks his prey.
1986 90m/C Donald Pleasence, Ronald Lacey. VHS, Beta $49.95 *WWV* 🎞½

Into the Fire Thriller about a young drifter who, against the backdrop of a Canadian winter, happens upon a roadside lodge and diner, where he gets involved in sex and murder. Title gives a good idea of what to do with this one.
1988 (R) 88m/C *CA* Susan Anspach, Art Hindle, Olivia D'Abo, Lee Montgomery; *D:* Graeme Campbell. VHS, Beta, LV $79.98 *LIV, VES* 🎞

Into the Homeland Seasoned ex-cop (Boothe) infiltrates a white supremacist group which had kidnapped his teenage daughter. Failed "message" about neo-nazi ethics, but good confrontation between Boothe and his son (Howell) make this so-so viewing. Made for cable television.
1987 95m/C Powers Boothe, C. Thomas Howell, Paul LeMat; *D:* Lesli Linka Glatter. VHS, Beta, LV $79.95 *KRT, LHV, WAR* 🎞🎞

Into the Night Campy, off-beat thriller about a middle-aged, jilted deadbeat (Goldblum), who meets a beautiful woman (Pfeiffer) when she suddenly drops onto the hood of his car, with a relentless gang of Arabs pursuing. During their search through L.A. and other parts of California for the one person who can help her out of this mess, a whole crew of Hollywood directors make cameo appearances, making this a delight for film buffs, but occasionally tedious for general audiences. B.B. King sings the title song.
1985 (R) 115m/C Jeff Goldblum, Michelle Pfeiffer, David Bowie, Carl Perkins, Richard Farnsworth, Dan Aykroyd, Paul Mazursky, Roger Vadim, Irene Papas, Bruce McGill, Vera Miles, Clu Gulager, Don Steel, Kathryn Harrold; *Cameos:* Jim Henson, Paul Bartel, David Cronenberg, Jack Arnold, Jonathan Demme, Lawrence Kasdan, Amy Heckerling, Don Siegel, Richard Franklin, Colin Higgins, Andrew Marton; *D:* John Landis; *W:* Ron Koslow. VHS, Beta, LV $19.95 *MCA* 🎞🎞

Into the Sun Hall plays a Hollywood star who encounters real-life danger while hanging out with an Air Force pilot (Pare) to prepare for an upcoming role. Spectacular aerial scenes steal the show, which isn't hard to do in this lackluster movie.
1992 (R) 101m/C Anthony Michael Hall, Michael Pare, Terry Kiser, Deborah Maria Moore; *D:* Fritz Kiersch. VHS, LV *VMK* 🎞½

Into Thin Air A mother searches tirelessly for her college bound son who disappeared on a cross-country drive. Well-done television drama with a good performance from Burstyn. Written by George Rubio.
1985 100m/C Ellen Burstyn, Robert Prosky, Sam Robards, Tate Donovan; *D:* Roger Young. VHS, Beta, LV $79.95 *NBI* 🎞🎞🎞

Intolerance Griffith's largest film in every aspect. An interwoven, four-story epic about human intolerance, with segments set in Babylon, ancient Judea, and Paris. One of the cinema's grandest follies, and greatest achievements. Silent with music score. Laserdisc version contains supplemental material including cuts from other Griffith works. Black and white with some restored color footage.
1916 175m/B Lillian Gish, Mae Marsh, Constance Talmadge, Bessie Love, Elmer Clifton, Erich von Stroheim, Eugene Pallette; *D:* D.W. Griffith. VHS, LV $29.95 *NOS, MRV, KIV* 🎞🎞🎞🎞

Intrigue Former CIA agent (Loggia) defects to the KGB, but wants to return to the US when he realizes he has a progressive illness. Underground agent and old buddy (Glenn) is recruited with orders to smuggle his former colleague out. Tension continues throughout as murder comes along with the

orders. Loads of suspense and twist ending in this made for television nail-biter.
1990 (PG) 96m/C Scott Glenn, Robert Loggia, William Atherton, Martin Shaw; *D:* David Drury. VHS, LV $89.95 *VMK* 🎞🎞½

Intruder A man and his stepson are terrorized by a stranger in a panel truck as they travel from Rome to Paris.
1977 98m/C Jean-Louis Trintignant, Mireille Darc, Adolfo Celi. VHS, Beta $59.95 *VID* 🎞🎞

Intruder A psychotic killer stalks an all-night convenience store shopping for fresh meat (customers beware). Slasher movie fans should get a kick out of the plot twist at the end.
1988 (R) 90m/C Elizabeth Cox, Renee Estevez, Alvy Moore; *D:* Scott Spiegel. VHS, Beta, LV $79.95 *PAR* 🎞🎞

Intruder in the Dust A small southern community develops a lynch mob mentality when a black man is accused of killing a white man. Powerful, but largely ignored portrait of race relations in the South. Solid performances from the whole cast; filmed in Mississippi. Adapted from a novel by William Faulkner.
1949 87m/B David Brian, Claude Jarman Jr., Juano Hernandez, Porter Hall, Elizabeth Patterson; *D:* Clarence Brown. VHS $19.98 *MGM, MOV* 🎞🎞🎞½

Intruder Within Half-baked thriller about crew on an isolated oil rig in Antarctica who, while drilling, unearth a nasty creature that goes around terrorizing the frost-bitten men and occasional stray woman. Made for television.
1981 91m/C Chad Everett, Joseph Bottoms, Jennifer Warren; *D:* Peter Carter. VHS, Beta $69.95 *TWE* 🎞

Intruders Follows the story of three people who have unexplained lapses of time in their lives which they eventually believe are connected to visits by aliens. The three are brought together by a skeptical psychiatrist. The aliens are your typical bugged-eyed, white-faced spooks but part of the film is genuinely unsettling.
1992 162m/C Richard Crenna, Mare Winningham, Susan Blakely, Ben Vereen, Steven Berkoff, Daphne Ashbrook; *D:* Dan Curtis. VHS $89.98 *FXV* 🎞🎞

The Invaders Two Viking brothers battle each other and the Britons. *AKA:* Erik the Conqueror; Gli Invasori; La Ruee Des Vikings; Fury of the Vikings.
1963 88m/C *FR IT* Cameron Mitchell, George Ardisson, Andrea Checchi, Francoise Christophe, Joe Robinson; *D:* Mario Bava. VHS, Beta *NO* 🎞🎞

The Invaders The popular science fiction series created by Larry Cohen stars Thinnes, as David Vincent, who attempts to convince people he has witnessed an alien landing and that they want to take over Earth. "Beach Head" is the pilot episode. Additional episodes available.
1967 53m/C Roy Thinnes, Kent Smith, Diane Baker, J.D. Cannon, James Daly, John Milford, Ellen Corby, Vaughn Taylor; *D:* Joseph Sargent. VHS $14.99 *GKK, MOV* 🎞🎞

Invaders from Mars Young boy cries "martian" in this sci-fi cheapy classic. He can't convince the townspeople of this invasion because they've already been possessed by the alien beings. His parents are zapped by the little green things first, making this perhaps an allegory for the missing Eisenhower/Stepford years. Includes previews of coming attractions from classic science fiction films. Remade in 1986 by Tobe Hooper.

1953 78m/C Helena Carter, Arthur Franz, Jimmy Hunt, Leif Erickson; *D:* William Cameron Menzies. **VHS, Beta** $19.95 *MED, MLB ⅃⅃½*

Invaders from Mars A high-tech re-make of Menzies' 1953 semi-classic about a Martian invasion perceived only by one young boy and a sympathetic (though hysterical) school nurse, played by mother and son Black and Carson. Instant camp.
1986 (PG) 102m/C Hunter Carson, Karen Black, Louise Fletcher, Laraine Newman, Timothy Bottoms, Bud Cort; *D:* Tobe Hooper. **VHS, Beta, LV** $39.95 *MED, IME ⅃½*

Invasion A hospital opens its doors to an accident victim, and his attractive female visitors don't seem sympathetic to the idea of a long hospital stay. Turns out he's an escaped alien prisoner, and the alien babes, intent on intergalactic extradition, place a force field around the hospital and demand his return. Early effort of director Bridges, who later did "The Shooting Party." Interesting, creepy, atmospheric, with very cool camera moves.
1965 82m/B *GB* Edward Judd, Yoko Tani, Valerie Gearon, Lyndon Brook, Tsai Chin, Barrie Ingham; *D:* Alan Bridges. **VHS** $19.98 *MOV ⅃⅃½*

Invasion Earth: The Aliens Are Here! A cheap spoof of monster movies, as an insectoid projectionist takes over the minds of a movie audience. Clips of Godzilla, Mothra and other beasts are interpolated.
1987 84m/C Janice Fabian, Christian Lee; *D:* George Maltland. **VHS, Beta, LV** $19.95 *STE, NWV ⅃*

Invasion Force A terrorist army parachutes into a remote region when a film crew is preparing to set up for an action movie. The moviemakers must scare away the terrorists with their smokepots and blanks. Sounds promising, but proves to be as empty as the movie props used to scare the terrorists.
1990 93m/C Richard Lynch, David Shark, Renee Cline, Douglas Hartier, Graham Times, Angie Synodis; *D:* David A. Prior. **VHS** $79.95 *AIP ⅃*

The Invasion of Carol Enders A woman, almost killed by a prowler, awakens with an expanded consciousness, and tries to convince her near husband that her death wasn't an accident.
1974 72m/C Meredith Baxter Birney, Christopher Connelly, Charles Aidman. **VHS, Beta** $29.95 *LIV ⅃⅃½*

Invasion of Privacy Alex is a psycho prison inmate obsessed with high profile journalist, Hilary. When Hilary interviews Alex for a magazine cover story, his obsession only grows stronger. Then Alex gets paroled and goes to work for Hilary. When he discovers Hilary isn't interested in him, Alex turns his fantasies to her daughter, who has no notion what she's getting into. An unrated version is also available. Made for cable television.
1992 (R) 95m/C Robby Benson, Jennifer O'Neill, Lydie Denier, Ian Ogilvy; *W/D:* Kevin Meyer. **VHS** $89.95 *PSM ⅃⅃*

Invasion of the Animal People Hairy monster from outer space attacks Lapland. Narrated by Carradine, the only American in the cast. Pretty silly. *AKA:* Terror in the Midnight Sun; Space Invasion of Lapland; Horror in the Midnight Sun; Space Invasion from Lapland.
1962 73m/C *SW* Robert Burton, Barbara Wilson, John Carradine; *D:* Virgil W. Vogel, Jerry Warren. **VHS** $19.95 *VMK, SNC, NOS Woof!*

Invasion of the Bee Girls California girls are mysteriously transformed into deadly nymphomaniacs in this delightful campy science fiction romp. Written by Nicholas Meyer who later directed "Star Trek II: The Wrath of Khan" and wrote "The Seven Per Cent Solution." *AKA:* Graveyard Tramps.
1973 85m/C Victoria Vetri, William Smith, Anitra Ford, Cliff Osmond, Wright King, Ben Hammer; *D:* Denis Sanders. **VHS** $69.98 *SUE ⅃⅃⅃*

Invasion of the Blood Farmers In a small New York town, members of an ancient Druidic cult murder young women, taking their blood in the hope of finding the precise, rare blood type to keep their queen alive. A real woofer.
1972 (PG) 86m/C Norman Kelley, Tanna Hunter, Bruce Detrick, Jack Neubeck, Cythia Fleming, Paul Craig Jennings; *D:* Ed Adlum. **VHS, Beta** *NO Woof!*

Invasion of the Body Snatchers The one and only post-McCarthy paranoid sci-fi epic, where a small California town is infiltrated by pods from outer space that replicate and replace humans. A chilling, genuinely frightening exercise in nightmare dislocation. Based upon a novel by Jack Finney; scripted by Sam Peckinpah. Remade in 1978. The laserdisc version contains commentary by Maurice Yacowar, the text of an interview with Siegel, and the original theatrical trailer. The film itself is presented in its original wide-screen format.
1956 80m/B Kevin McCarthy, Dana Wynter, Carolyn Jones, King Donovan, Don Siegel; *D:* Don Siegel. **VHS, LV** $14.98 *REP, VYG, CRC ⅃⅃⅃*

Invasion of the Body Snatchers One of the few instances where a remake is an improvement on the original, which was itself a classic. This time, the "pod people" are infesting San Francisco, with only a small group of people aware of the invasion. A ceaselessly inventive, creepy version of the alien-takeover paradigm, with an intense and winning performance by Sutherland.
1978 (PG) 115m/C Donald Sutherland, Brooke Adams, Veronica Cartwright, Leonard Nimoy, Jeff Goldblum, Kevin McCarthy, Don Siegel, Art Hindle; *D:* Philip Kaufman. **VHS, Beta, LV** $14.95 *MGM ⅃⅃⅃½*

Invasion of the Body Stealers Aliens are thought to be the captors when sky-divers begin vanishing in mid-air. Uneven sci-fi with nothing going for it. *AKA:* Thin Air; The Body Stealers.
1969 91m/C *GB* George Sanders, Maurice Evans, Patrick Allen; *D:* Gerry Levy. **VHS, Beta** $29.95 *LIV Woof!*

Invasion of the Flesh Hunters Group of tortured Vietnam veterans returns home carrying a cannibalistic curse with them. Smorgasbord of gore and sensationalism is not for discriminating tastes. *AKA:* Cannibals in the Streets; Savage Apocalypse; The Slaughterers; Cannibals in the City; Virus.
1982 90m/C *IT* John Saxon, Elizabeth Turner; *W/D:* Anthony Dawson. **VHS, Beta** $69.98 *LIV, VES Woof!*

Invasion of the Girl Snatchers Aliens from another planet, in cahoots with a cult kingpin, subdue young earth girls and force them to undergo bizarre acts that may just rob them of their dignity. Save a bit of your own dignity by staying away. Cheap look, cheap feel, cheap thrills.
1973 90m/C Elizabeth Rush, Ele Grigsby, David Roster; *D:* Lee Jones. **VHS, Beta** $39.95 *UHV Woof!*

Invasion of the Space Preachers Hideous creatures from outer space arrive on Earth with plans for conquest. Led by the seemingly human Reverend Lash, they prey on the innocent and trusting, fleecing God-fearing folk out of their hard earned cash!
1990 100m/C Jim Wolfe, Guy Nelson, Eliska Hahn, Gary Brown, Jesse Johnson, John Riggs; *W/D:* Daniel Boyd. **VHS, Beta** $79.95 *RHI Woof!*

Invasion of the Vampires Burrito bat fest has Count Frankenhausen doing his vampire thing in a small, 16th century village. Atmospheric sets are highlight. Not a good substitute for No Doze. *AKA:* La Invasion de Los Vampiros.
1961 78m/B *MX* Carlos Agosti, Rafael Etienne, Bertha Moss, Tito Junco, Erna Martha Bauman, Fernando Soto, Enrique Garcia Alvarez, David Reynoso; *W/D:* Miguel Morayta. **VHS** $19.98 *SNC ⅃*

Invasion of the Zombies Bare-fisted wrestler Santo faces of brace of zombies in order to prove that men with short necks can hug other men and still be mucho macho.
1961 85m/B *MX* Santo; *D:* Benito Alazraki. **VHS** $19.98 *SNC, HHT ⅃*

Invasion U.S.A. A mercenary defends nothing less than the entire country against Russian terrorists landing in Florida and looking for condos. A record-setting amount of people killed. Count them—it's not like you'll miss anything important. Norris is a bit less animated than a wooden Indian, and the acting is more painful to endure than the violence. Glasnost saved the movie industry from additional paranoia movies of this kind.
1985 (R) 108m/C Chuck Norris, Richard Lynch, Melissa Prophet, Alex Colon, Billy Drago; *D:* Joseph Zito. **VHS, Beta, LV** $14.95 *MGM ⅃*

Investigation A Frenchman plans to murder his wife so he can marry his pregnant mistress, guaranteeing an heir. Subtle study of small town people so concerned with their own welfare that the dirty deeds of the lead character might be overlooked. Fine performances and story development make this worth investigating. In French with English subtitles.
1979 116m/C *FR* Victor Lanoux, Valerie Mairesse; *D:* Etienne Perier. **VHS, Beta** $29.98 *SUE ⅃⅃½*

Invincible Martial arts student must find and correct another student who has turned evil. For Bruce Lee fans, as if they haven't already memorized all the memorable lines—"hiyaah," "ugh," "oof," etc.
1980 (R) 93m/C Bruce Lee, Chen Sing, Ho Chung Dao. **VHS, Beta** *GEM ⅃½*

Invincible Armor Wrong man is accused of murder when an ambitious minister of justice unleashes a sinister plot.
197? 92m/C **VHS, Beta** $39.95 *TWE ⅃*

Invincible Barbarian A young man leads a tribe of amazing Amazon warriors in a sneak attack against the tribe that annihilated his native village. One of those movies that presumes "primitivism" can be recreated through bad acting.
1983 92m/C Diana Roy, David Jenkins. **VHS, Beta** $59.95 *PSM Woof!*

The Invincible Gladiator A gladiator who saves the evil man ruling a land for a boy-king is given command of an army. He eventually leads the army in revolt when the evil man tries to take over the throne. Plodding with stock characters. *AKA:* Il Gladiatore Invincible.
1963 96m/C *IT SP* Richard Harrison, Isabel Corey, Livio Lorenzon; *D:* Frank Gregory. **VHS** $16.95 *SNC ⅃½*

Invincible Gladiators The sons of Hercules labor to aid a prince whose bride had been kidnapped by an evil queen. Laborious to watch.
1964 87m/C Richard Lloyd, Claudia Lange, Tony Freeman; *D:* Robert Mauri. **VHS, Beta** *NO Woof!*

Invincible Mr. Disraeli Presentation from "George Schaefer's Showcase Theatre" deals with the life and career of Benjamin Disraeli, novelist, philosopher, first Earl of Beaconsfield, statesman, and Prime Minister. Basically a tribute. Made for television.
1963 76m/C Trevor Howard, Greer Garson, Hurd Hatfield, Kate Reid; *D:* George Schaefer. **VHS, Beta** *FHS* �✧✧½

Invincible Obsessed Fighter Two heavy-handed warriors (Wong and Chong) battle over a stolen treasure.
198? 92m/C Elton Chong, Michael Wong. **VHS, Beta** *NO* ✧

The Invincible Six An unlikely band of thieves running from the law winds up protecting a small village from marauding bandits. Plenty of action, as you would expect when thieves take on bandits, but with no scene-stealers or sympathetic characters the story lacks interest. Unremarkable choreography by ballet great Rudolf Nureyev. Filmed in Iran.
1968 96m/C Stuart Whitman, Elke Sommer, Curt Jurgens, Jim Mitchum, Ian Ogilvy; *D:* Jean Negulesco. **VHS, Beta** *NO* ✧✧

Invincible Sword A motley band of zany characters use their collective brain power to save their imprisoned chum, amid much chop-suey action.
1978 93m/C Wang Yu; *D:* Hsu Tseng Hung. **VHS** $59.98 *CGH* ✧

Invisible Adversaries A photographer uncovers an extra-terrestrial plot to cause excessive aggression in humans. She and her lover attempt to hold on to their crumbling humanity. Movies like this make you mad enough to tear something up. Enjoyed a meek cult following. In German with English subtitles.
1977 112m/c *GE* Susanne Widl, Peter Weibel; *D:* Valie Export. **VHS, Beta** $59.95 *FCT* ✧✧

The Invisible Avenger Based on the vintage radio character "The Shadow." A detective who can make himself invisible investigates the murder of a New Orleans jazz musician. The mysterious element successful on radio is lost on film, and only the Shadow knows why. *AKA:* Bourbon St. Shadows.
1958 60m/B Richard Derr, Marc Daniels, Helen Westcott, Jeanne Neher; *D:* John Sledge, Ben Parker. **VHS, Beta** $16.95 *SNC, SMW, RXM* ✧✧

The Invisible Dead So many invisible man movies, so little time. A scientist creates an invisible man, imprisons and tortures him. A bit miffed with his host, he who can't be seen escapes, and vents his invisible spleen.
19?? 90m/C *IT* Howard Vernon, Britt Carva; *D:* Jess (Jesus) Franco. **VHS** $59.95 *UHV* ✧

The Invisible Dr. Mabuse Possibly the best of the Dr. Mabuse series sees the mad scientist using an invisibility agent in an attempt to take over the world. Preiss also played the title villian in Fritz Lang's "The Thousand Eyes of Dr. Mabuse." *AKA:* The Invisible Horror; Die Unsichtbaren Krallen des Dr. Mabuse.
1962 89m/B *GE* Lex Barker, Karin Dor, Siegfried Lowitz, Wolfgang Preiss, Rudolf Fernau; *D:* Harald Reinl. **VHS, Beta** $16.95 *SNC* ✧✧✧

The Invisible Ghost A man carries out a series of grisly stranglings while under hypnosis by his insane wife. Typically bad low-budget exploiter about a fun-lovin' crazy couple bringing down property values in the neighborhood.
1941 70m/B Bela Lugosi, Polly Ann Young; *D:* Joseph H. Lewis. **VHS, Beta, 3/4U, Special order formats** $24.95 *NOS, MRV, SNC* ✧½

The Invisible Kid A shy teen manages to make himself invisible, a feat which ironically permits him to get people to notice him. Now he can visit places he's only dreamed of, including the girls' locker room. For those who have dreamed about girls' locker rooms.
1988 95m/C Karen Black, Jay Underwood, Chynna Phillips, Wally Ward, Brother Theodore; *D:* Avery Crounse. **VHS, Beta, LV** *MED* ✧

The Invisible Killer Someone is killing folks by sending poison through telephone lines. A detective and a reporter team up to find the scoundrel by setting up an answering machine that automatically plays back messages to the caller. Bad connection of events leads to a static resolution.
1940 61m/B Grace Bradley, Roland Drew, William Newell; *D:* Sam Newfield. **VHS, Beta** $16.95 *SNC, MLB* ✧½

The Invisible Man The vintage horrorfest based on H. G. Wells' novella about a scientist whose formula for invisibility slowly drives him insane. His mind definitely wandering, he plans plans to use his recipe to rule the world. Rains' first role; though his body doesn't appear until the final scene, his voice characterization is magnificent. The visual detail is excellent, setting standards that are imitated today as they are difficult to surpass; with special effects by John P. Fulton.
1933 71m/B Claude Rains, Gloria Stuart, Dudley Digges, William Harrigan, Una O'Connor; *D:* James Whale. **VHS, Beta, LV** $14.95 *MCA, MLB* ✧✧✧✧

The Invisible Man Returns Price stars as the original invisible man's brother. Using the same invisibility formula, Price tries to clear himself after being charged with murder. He reappears at the worst times, and you gotta love that floating gun. Fun sequel to 1933's classic "The Invisible Man."
1940 81m/B Cedric Hardwicke, Vincent Price, John Sutton, Nan Grey; *D:* Joe May. **VHS** $14.98 *MCA, MLB* ✧✧✧

The Invisible Maniac A crazy voyeur perfects a serum for invisibility and promptly gets a job as a physics teacher in a high school. There he leers at girls taking showers and slaughters students when he is caught. For voyeurs. Get outta here, you maniac.
1990 (R) 87m/C Noel Peters, Shannon Wilsey, Melissa Moore, Robert Ross, Rod Sweitzer, Eric Champnella, Kalei Shellabarger, Gail Lyon, Debra Lamb; *W/D:* Rif Coogan. **VHS** $89.95 *REP Woof!*

The Invisible Monster Special investigators Lane Carlson and Carol Richards battle a mad scientist ready to take over the world with his invisible army. 12 episodes of the original serial edited onto two cassettes. *AKA:* Slaves of the Invisible Monster.
1950 167m/B Richard Webb, Aline Towne, Lane Bradford, Stanley Price, John Crawford, George Meeker; *D:* Fred Brannon **VHS** $29.98 *REP Woof!*

The Invisible Ray For a change, this horror film features Lugosi as the hero, fighting Karloff, a scientist who locates a meteor that contains a powerful substance. Karloff is poisoned and becomes a murdering megalomaniac. Watching Karloff and Lugosi interact, and the great special effects—including a hot scene where a scientist bursts into flames—helps you ignore a generally hokey script.
1936 82m/B Boris Karloff, Bela Lugosi, Frances Drake, Frank Lawton, Beulah Bondi, Walter Kingsford; *D:* Lambert Hillyer. **VHS, Beta, LV** $14.98 *MCA, MLB* ✧✧½

The Invisible Strangler A death-row murderer can make himself invisible and rubs out witnesses who helped put him away; woman risks her life to expose him when the police fail to see the problem. Very violent collection of brutal scenes. Not released theatrically until 1984.
1976 (PG) 85m/C Robert Foxworth, Stefanie Powers, Elke Sommer, Sue Lyon, Leslie Parrish, Marianna Hill; *D:* John Florea. **VHS, Beta** $59.95 *TWE* ✧½

The Invisible Terror A maniac steals a mad scientist's invisibility formula and uses it on a number of innocent victims.
1963 ?m/C Herbert Stass, Ellen Scheirs. **VHS** $16.95 *SNC* ✧✧

Invitation au Voyage Follows the journey of a twin who refuses to accept the death of his sister, a rock singer. The obsession is played fairly well, but it's a no-twin situation, even though the guy can't admit it. Perversity is played to the point of overkill. From the novel "Moi, Ma Soeur Images," by Jean Bany. In French with English subtitles.
1983 (R) 90m/C *FR* Laurent Malet, Nina Scott, Aurore Clement, Mario Adorf; *D:* Peter Del Monte. **VHS, Beta** $59.95 *COL, TAM* ✧✧½

Invitation to a Gunfighter Small town politics change when a paid assassin ambles into town and creates a lot of talk among the neighbors. Like a long joke in which the teller keeps forgetting the important details, the plot grows confusing though it's not complicated. Brynner is interesting as an educated, half-black/half-creole, hired gun.
1964 92m/C Yul Brynner, George Segal, Strother Martin, William Hickey, Janice Rule, Mike Kellin, Pat Hingle; *D:* Richard Wilson. **VHS, Beta** $19.98 *MGM, HHE* ✧✧

Invitation to Hell Tormented maiden has a devil of a time discovering a secret power that can enable her to gracefully decline a satanic summoning. The cliched evil is tormenting.
1984 100m/C Becky Simpson, Joseph Sheahan, Colin Efford, Stephen Longhurst. **VHS, Beta** $79.95 *WVV Woof!*

Invitation to Hell "Faust" meets "All My Children" in celluloid suburbia. Never Emmied Lucci is the devil's dirty worker, persuading upwardly mobile suburbanites to join a really exclusive country club in exchange for a little downward mobility. Urich, a space scientist, and family are new in town, and soul searching Lucci's got her devil vixen sights set on space jock and brood. Bound to disappoint both fans of Craven's early independent work ("Last House on the Left") and his later high gloss ("Nightmare on Elm Street") formulas. Made for the small screen.
1984 100m/C Susan Lucci, Robert Urich, Joanna Cassidy, Kevin McCarthy, Patty McCormack, Joe Regalbuto, Soleil Moon Frye; *D:* Wes Craven. **VHS, Beta** $79.98 *SVS* ✧½

Invitation to the Dance Three classic dance sequences, "Circus," "Ring Around the Rosy," and "Sinbad the Sailor." For dance lovers, featuring excellent performances by Kelly.
1956 93m/C Gene Kelly, Igor Youskevitch, Tamara Toumanova; *D:* Gene Kelly. **VHS, Beta** $19.98 *MGM, CCB* ✧✧½

Invitation to the Wedding When the best friend of a bridegroom falls in love with the bride, he stops at nothing to halt the wedding. Not exactly the Gielgud movie of the year, but there are some excellent scenes between him and Richardson.
1973 (PG) 89m/C John Gielgud, Ralph Richardson, Paul Nicholas, Elizabeth Shepherd; **D:** Joseph Brooks. **VHS, Beta** $69.95 VES 🐾🐾

The Ipcress File The first of the Harry Palmer spy mysteries that made Caine a star. Based upon the bestseller by Len Deighton, it features the flabby, nearsighted spy investigating the kidnapping of notable British scientists. Solid scenes, including a scary brainwashing session, and tongue-firmly-in-British-cheek humor. Lots of camera play to emphasize Caine's myopia. Two sequels: "Funeral in Berlin" and "Billion Dollar Brain."
1965 108m/C GB Michael Caine, Nigel Green, Guy Doleman, Sue Lloyd; **D:** Sidney J. Furie; **M:** John Barry. **VHS, Beta** $29.95 MCA 🐾🐾🐾

Iphigenia Based on the classic Greek tragedy by Euripides, this story concerns the Greek leader Agamemnon, who plans to sacrifice his lovely daughter, Iphigenia, to please the gods. Mere mortals protest and start a save-the-babe movement, but Euripides' moral—you can't please 'em all—is devastatingly realized. Fine adaptation that becomes visually extravagant at times, and an equally fine musical score from Mikos Theodorakis. In Greek with English subtitles.
1977 130m/C GR Irene Papas, Costa Kazakos, Tatiana Papamoskou; **D:** Michael Cacoyannis. **VHS, Beta** $59.95 COL, FHS, TAM 🐾🐾🐾

Iran: Days of Crisis An insightful made-for-cable-TV miniseries recounts America's humiliation at the hands of Iranian radicals in 1979, told from the vantage of a U.S. embassy official married to a Tehran woman. Former Carter administration aides Hamilton Jordan and Gerald Rafshoon devised the docudrama, which spares neither them nor their president in showing how bungled and shortsighted policies led to 52 Americans held hostage for over a year.
1991 185m/C Arliss Howard, Alice Krige, George Grizzard, Tony Goldwyn; **D:** Kevin Connor. **VHS** $89.98 TTC 🐾🐾½

Irezumi A Japanese woman has her body elaborately tattooed to please her lover. Things start off well enough. He's an inept lover, so she has directions tattooed, but then he discovers a "Dear John" letter on her foot just as she gives him the boot. Actually proves an interesting study in obsession and eroticism, with the tattoos drawing the lovers deeper and deeper until they get under each other's skin. In Japanese with English subtitles. AKA: Spirit of Tattoo.
1983 88m/C JP **VHS, Beta, LV** $29.95 PAV, TAM 🐾🐾🐾

Iris Drama follows the passionate and tragic life of New Zealand writer Iris Wilkinson, an international novelist, poet, and journalist. Wilkinson achieved a great deal of acclaim as a writer, but suffered many personal tragedies, and eventually took her own life at age 33. Well intentioned but clunky treatment of powerful subject matter.
1989 90m/C NZ Helen Morse. **VHS, Beta** $160.00 WOM 🐾🐾

Irish Cinderella A silent version of the Cinderella legend set in Ireland, with thematic stress on Irish politics and patriotism.
1922 72m/B Pattie MacNamara. **VHS, Beta, 8mm** $29.95 VYY 🐾🐾

Irish Luck A bellhop turns detective to figure out the mysterious happenings in his hotel. Becomes terminally cute by playing on a luck o' the Irish theme.
1939 58m/B Frankie Darro, Dick Purcell, Sheila Darcy; **D:** Grant Withers, Scott R. Dunlap. **VHS** $24.95 NOS, DVT, HEG 🐾🐾

The Irishman Set in 1920s Australia, the tale of a proud North Queensland family and their struggles to stay together. The Irish immigrant father is a teamster whose horse-drawn wagons are threatened by progress. His fight to preserve old ways is impressive, but gives way to sentimentality.
1978 108m/C AU Lou Brown, Michael Craig, Simon Burke, Robyn Nevin, Bryan Brown; **D:** Donald Crombie. **VHS, Beta** $69.95 VES 🐾🐾½

Irma La Douce A gendarme pulls a one-man raid on a back-street Parisian joint and falls in love with one of the hookers he arrests. Lemmon is great as a well-meaning, incompetent boob, and MacLaine gives her all as the hapless hooker. A plodding pace, however, robs it of the original's zip, though it was a box office smash. Broadway musical is lost without the music.
1963 144m/C Jack Lemmon, Shirley MacLaine, Herschel Bernardi; **D:** Billy Wilder; **M:** Andre Previn. Academy Awards '63: Best Original Score; Nominations: Best Actress (MacLaine), Best Color Cinematography; Golden Globe Awards '64: Best Actress—Musical/Comedy (MacLaine). **VHS, Beta, LV** $19.98 MGM, IME, FOX 🐾🐾½

Iron & Silk A young American searches for himself while he teaches English and learns martial arts in mainland China. Based on the true story of Salzman's travels. His studies of martial arts and Chinese culture provide a model for his students in their studies of American language and culture. Beautiful photography. Fine performances.
1991 (PG) 94m/C Mark Salzman, Pan Qingfu, Jeanette Lin Tsui, Vivian Wu; **D:** Shirley Sun. **VHS, LV** $19.98 LIV, PIA 🐾🐾½

Iron Angel During the Korean War a squadron sets out to silence North Korean guns. They do. Judging by their eternal bickering they must have put the enemy to sleep.
1964 84m/B Jim Davis, Margo Woode, Donald (Don "Red") Barry, L.Q. Jones; **W/D:** Ken Kennedy. **VHS** $15.95 NOS, LOO 🐾½

Iron Cowboy Actor finds romance with film editor while audience stifles yawns. Filmed on the set of "Blue," this pre-"Deliverance" Reynolds comedy never made it to the theaters. (Smithee is actually director Jud Taylor.)
1968 86m/C Burt Reynolds, Barbara Loden, Terence Stamp, Noam Pitlik, Ricardo Montalban, Patricia Casey, Jane Hampton, Joseph Perry; **D:** Alan Smithee. **VHS** $39.98 ACE 🐾🐾

The Iron Crown A 13th-century legend inspired this sometime violent spectacle involving the title totem, a symbol of justice ignored by a powerful king at his peril. There's wonderful pagentry and a notable Tarzan imitator, but the pace is terribly slow. Italian dialogue with English subtitles.
1941 100m/C **D:** Alexandro Blasetti. **VHS** $59.95 FST 🐾🐾

Iron Dragon Strikes Back Man seeks out the men who murdered his martial arts instructor.
1984 90m/C Bruce Li. **VHS, Beta** $39.95 TWE 🐾

The Iron Duke Fair to middlin' historical account of the life of the Duke of Wellington, victor over Napoleon at Waterloo.

1934 88m/B GB George Arliss, Gladys Cooper, A.E. Matthews, Emlyn Williams, Felix Aylmer; **D:** Victor Saville. **VHS, Beta** $19.95 NOS, WFV, KRT 🐾🐾½

Iron Eagle A teenager teams with a renegade fighter pilot to rescue the youth's father from captivity in the Middle East. Predictable but often exciting. Followed by two sequels.
1985 (PG-13) 117m/C Louis Gossett Jr., Jason Gedrick, Tim Thomerson; **D:** Sidney J. Furie. **VHS, Beta, LV** $14.98 FOX 🐾🐾½

Iron Eagle 2 Lower-budget extended adventures of a maverick fighter pilot after he is reinstated in the Air Force. This time he links with an equally rebellious commie fighter and blasts away at nuke-happy Ivan. Yahoo fun for all overt Yankees! Followed by "Aces: Iron Eagle 3." Available in Spanish.
1988 (PG) 102m/C CA IS Louis Gossett Jr., Mark Humphrey, Stuart Margolin, Alan Scarfe, Maury Chaykin, Sharon H. Brandon; **D:** Sidney J. Furie. **VHS, Beta, LV** $14.95 LIV 🐾🐾

Iron Horsemen A motorcycle gang leader has a prophetic vision while tripping on LSD, and returns to his former town to challenge its religious establishment. Also available on video under its original title "J.C." AKA: J.C.
1971 (R) 97m/C William F. McGaha, Hannibal Penny, Joanna Moore, Burr de Benning, Slim Pickens, Pati Delaney; **D:** William F. McGaha. **VHS, Beta** $9.95 SIM, NLC 🐾

The Iron Major Frank Cavanaugh, a famous football coach, becomes a hero in World War I. Standard flag-waving biography to increase morale back home, but fairly well-made.
1943 85m/B Pat O'Brien, Ruth Warrick, Robert Ryan, Leon Ames, Russell Wade, Bruce Edwards; **D:** Ray Enright. **VHS, Beta** $19.98 TTC 🐾🐾½

The Iron Mask Early swashbuckling extravaganza with a master swordsman defending the French king from a scheme involving substitution by a lookalike. Still fairly exciting, thanks largely to director Dwan's flair. Based on Alexandre Dumas' "Three Musketeers" and "The Man in the Iron Mask" with talking sequences.
1929 87m/B Douglas Fairbanks Sr., Nigel de Brulier, Marguerite de la Motte; **D:** Allan Dwan. **VHS, Beta, LV** $9.98 NOS, CCB, DVT 🐾🐾½

Iron Maze A fascinating notion forms the center of this dramatic scrapheap; the classic Japanese "Rashomon" plot shifted to a rusting Pennsylvania steel town. When a Tokyo businessman is found bludgeoned, witnesses and suspects (including his American-born wife) tell contradictory stories. It's too convoluted and contrived to work, with a hollow happy ending tacked on. Oliver Stone helped produce.
1991 (R) 102m/C Jeff Fahey, Bridget Fonda, Hiroaki Murakami, J.T. Walsh, Gabriel Damon, John Randolph, Peter Allas; **D:** Hiroaki Yoshida. **VHS, LV** $89.95 ACA 🐾½

Iron Thunder Liberty is in peril and only much kicking and pec flexing will make the world a kinder gentler place. A thundering bore.
1989 85m/C Iron "Amp" Elmore, George M. Young, Julius Dorsey. **VHS** $79.95 XVC, HHE 🐾½

The Iron Triangle A U.S. officer taken prisoner by the Viet Cong forms a bond with one of his captors. Film lends the viewer an opportunity to see things from the other sides perspective.
1989 (R) 94m/C Beau Bridges, Haing S. Ngor, Liem Whatley; **D:** Eric Weston. **VHS, Beta, LV** $19.95 LIV 🐾🐾

Iron Warrior A barbarian hacks his way through a fantastical world to get to a beautiful princess.
1987 (R) 82m/C Miles O'Keeffe, Savina Gersak, Tim Lane; *D:* Al Bradley. **VHS, Beta** $19.95 MED ♂

Ironclads Memorable dramatization of the five-hour naval battle between the Confederate's Merrimac and the Union's Monitor during the Civil War. The special effects are the only thing worth watching in this overlong tale that includes standard subplots of loyalty, lost loves, and death from war. Made for Television.
1990 94m/C Virginia Madsen, Alex Hyde-White, Reed Edward Diamond, E.G. Marshall, Fritz Weaver; *D:* Delbert Mann. **VHS** $79.98 TTC ♂♂½

Ironheart Slimy Milverstead and his henchman meet lovely young women at dance clubs, drug them, and sell them into slavery. But the trouble really starts when they kill a cop and his former partner, John Keem (Lee), lashes out with his blazing martial arts skill to still the perpetrators.
1992 ?m/C Britton Lee, Bolo Yeung, Richard Norton, Karman Kruschke; *D:* Robert Clouse; *W:* Lawrence Riggins. **VHS** $89.95 IMP ♂½

Ironmaster When a primitive tribesman is exiled from his tribe, he discovers a mysteriously power-filled iron staff on a mountainside.
1983 98m/C George Eastman, Pamela Field. **VHS, Beta** $59.95 PSM ♂

Ironweed Grim and gritty drama about bums living the hard life in Depression-era Albany. Nicholson excels as a former ballplayer turned drunk bothered by visions of the past, and Streep is his equal in the lesser role of a tubercular boozer. Tom Waits also shines. Another grim view from "Pixote" director Babenco. Based on William Kennedy's Pulitzer Prize-winning tragedy, and scripted by Kennedy.
1987 (R) 135m/C Jack Nicholson, Meryl Streep, Tom Waits, Carroll Baker, Michael O'Keefe, Fred Gwynne, Diane Venora, Margaret Whitton; *D:* Hector Babenco; *W:* William Kennedy. **VHS, Beta, LV** $89.98 LIV, VES ♂♂♂

Irreconcilable Differences When her Beverly Hills parents spend more time working and fretting than giving hugs and love, a ten-year-old girl sues them for divorce on the grounds of "irreconcilable differences." The media has a field day when they hear that she would rather go live with the maid. Well cast, with well-developed characterizations. The script, by the creators of "Private Benjamin," is humanely comic rather than uproariously funny.
1984 (PG) 112m/C Ryan O'Neal, Shelley Long, Drew Barrymore, Sam Wanamaker, Allen Garfield, Sharon Stone, Luana Anders; *D:* Charles Shyer. **VHS, Beta, LV** $29.98 LIV, VES ♂♂½

Irving Berlin's America A documentary depicting Berlin's legacy of patriotic pop tunes, shown in a variety of film and performance clips, plus interviews with the stars who sang them.
1986 83m/C Ginger Rogers, Mary Martin, Howard Keel, Kate Smith, Fred Astaire. **Beta** CMR ♂♂½

Is Paris Burning? A spectacularly star-studded but far too sprawling account of the liberation of Paris from Nazi occupation. The script, in which seven writers had a hand, is based on Larrry Collins and Dominique Lapierre's best seller. *AKA:* Paris Brule-T-Il?.

1968 173m/C *FR* Jean-Paul Belmondo, Charles Boyer, Leslie Caron, Jean-Pierre Cassel, George Chakiris, Claude Dauphin, Alain Delon, Kirk Douglas, Glenn Ford, Gert Frobe, Daniel Gelin, E.G. Marshall, Yves Montand, Anthony Perkins, Claude Rich, Simone Signoret, Robert Stack, Jean-Louis Trintignant, Pierre Vaneck, Orson Welles, Bruno Cremer, Suzy Delair, Michael Lonsdale; *D:* Rene Clement; *W:* Gore Vidal, Francis Ford Coppola. **VHS** $29.95 PAR, FCT ♂♂♂

Is There Sex After Death? Often funny satire on the sexual revolution is constructed as a behind-the-scenes view of the porn film world. Odd cast includes Henry and Warhol superstar Woodlawn. Originally rated "X."
1971 (R) 97m/C Buck Henry, Alan Abel, Marshall Efron, Holly Woodlawn, Earl Doud; *D:* Alan Abel, Jeanne Abel. **VHS, Beta** NO ♂♂♂

Is This Goodbye, Charlie Brown? Charlie Brown and the gang struggle to understand their loss when a friend moves away.
1983 25m/C **VHS** $14.95 MED, VTR, WTA ♂♂♂

Isadora A loose, imaginative biography of Isadora Duncan, the cause celebre dancer in the 1920s who became famous for her scandalous performances, outrageous behavior, public love affairs, and bizarre, early death. Redgrave is exceptional in the lead, and Fox provides fine support. Restored from its original 131-minute print length by the director. *AKA:* The Loves of Isadora.
1968 153m/C Vanessa Redgrave, Jason Robards Jr., James Fox, Ivan Tchenko, John Fraser, Bessie Love; *D:* Karel Reisz; *M:* Maurice Jarre. Academy Awards '68 Nominations: Best Actress (Redgrave); Cannes Film Festival '69: Best Actress (Redgrave); National Board of Review Awards '69: 10 Best Films of the Year; National Society of Film Critics Awards '69: Best Actress (Redgrave). **VHS, Beta** $29.95 MCA, HEG ♂♂♂

Ishtar Two astoundingly untalented performers have a gig in a fictional Middle Eastern country and become involved in foreign intrigue. A big-budget box-office bomb produced by Beatty offering few laughs, though it's not as bad as its reputation. Considering the talent involved, though, it's a disappointment, with Beatty and Hoffman laboring to create Hope and Crosby chemistry. Anyone for a slow night?
1987 (PG-13) 107m/C Dustin Hoffman, Warren Beatty, Isabelle Adjani, Charles Grodin; *W/D:* Elaine May. **VHS, Beta, LV** $14.95 COL ♂♂

The Island Poetic examination of a peasant family's daily struggle for existence on a small island. No dialogue in this slow but absorbing work by one of Japan's master directors. *AKA:* Hadaka No Shima; Naked Island.
1961 96m/B *JP* Nobuko Otowa, Taiji Tonoyama, Shinji Tanaka, Masanori Horimoto; *D:* Kaneto Shindo. **VHS, Beta, LV, 8mm** $24.95 IHF, VYY, HHT ♂♂♂½

Island Tautly paced, the story creates an increasingly complex situation, until a World War I army officer is revealed to be the victim of a shocking and ingenious trap.
1977 30m/C John Hurt; *D:* Robert Fuest. **VHS, Beta** LCA ♂♂♂½

The Island New York reporter embarks on a Bermuda triangle investigation, only to meet with the murderous but sterile descendants of seventeenth century pirates on a deserted island. Caine is designated as stud service for the last remaining fertile woman. Almost surreal in its badness. Adapted by Peter Benchley from his novel.

1980 (R) 113m/C Michael Caine, David Warner, Angela Punch McGregor, Frank Middlemass, Don Henderson; *D:* Michael Ritchie; *M:* Ennio Morricone. **VHS, Beta, LV** $19.95 MCA Woof!

The Island at the Top of the World A rich Englishman, in search of his missing son, travels to the Arctic Circle in 1908. The rescue party includes an American archeologist, a French astronaut, and an Eskimo guide. Astonishingly, they discover an unknown, "lost" Viking kingdom. This Jules Verne-style adventure doesn't quite measure up, but kids will like it.
1974 (G) 93m/C David Hartman, Donald Sinden, Jacques Marin, Mako, David Gwillim; *D:* Robert Stevenson. **VHS, Beta** $69.95 DIS ♂♂½

Island Claw A group of marine biologists experimenting on a tropical island discover the "Island Claw," who evolved as the result of toxic waste seeping into the ocean. A festering, oozing woofer. *AKA:* Night of the Claw.
1980 91m/C Barry Nelson, Robert Lansing; *D:* Hernan Cardenas. **VHS, Beta** $69.98 LIV, VES Woof!

Island in the Sun Racial tension pulls apart the lives of the residents of a Caribbean island. Good cast, but a very poor adaptation of Alec Waugh's novel. Marvelous location shots.
1957 119m/C James Mason, Joan Fontaine, Dorothy Dandridge, John Williams, Harry Belafonte; *D:* Robert Rossen. **VHS** TCF ♂♂

Island Monster Also called "Monster of the Island," this film deals with ruthless, kidnapping drug-smugglers led by "monster" Karloff, and the efforts to bring them to justice.
1953 87m/B *IT* Boris Karloff, Renata Vicario, Franco Marzi; *D:* Robert Montero. **VHS, Beta** $29.95 SNC, HHT, LSV ♂½

Island of Adventure Four children explore an island and find a gang of criminals inhabiting it.
1981 85m/C **VHS, Beta** $39.98 SUE ♂½

Island of Blood Buckets of blood abound on a remote island when a film crew's beset by berserk butcher.
1986 84m/C Jim Williams, Dean Richards. **VHS** $59.98 AIP, MOV ♂½

Island of Desire An Army nurse, a doctor, and a young Navy Adonis are trapped on a deserted island. Not surprisingly, a love triangle develops. *AKA:* Saturday Island.
1952 93m/C *GB* Tab Hunter, Linda Darnell, Donald Gray; *D:* Stuart Heisler. **VHS, Beta** $59.95 MLB ♂

Island of Dr. Moreau This remake of the H.G. Wells story "Island of the Lost Souls" (1933) is a bit disappointing but worth watching for Lancaster's solid performance as the scientist who has isolated himself on a Pacific island in order to continue his chromosome research—he can transform animals into near-humans and humans into animals. Neat-looking critters.
1977 (PG) 99m/C Burt Lancaster, Michael York, Nigel Davenport, Barbara Carrera, Richard Basehart; *D:* Don Taylor. **VHS, Beta** $19.98 WAR, OM ♂♂½

Island of Lost Girls Young women are taken to an unknown location in the Far East to be sold as part of a white slave ring.
1973 (R) 85m/C Brad Harris, Tony Kendall, Monica Pardo. **VHS, Beta** $16.95 SNC Woof!

The Island of Nevawuz A beautiful island is in trouble when J.B. Trumphorn decides to make lots of money by building factories and refineries on it. Will the Island of Nevawuz end up a polluted mess?
1980 50m/C VHS, Beta $39.98 *SUE Woof!*

Island of Terror First-rate science fiction chiller about an island overrun by shell-like creatures that suck the bones out of their living prey. Good performances and interesting twists make for prickles up the spine. *AKA:* Night of the Silicates; The Creepers.
1966 90m/C *GB* Peter Cushing, Edward Judd, Carole Gray, Sam Kydd, Niall MacGinnis; *D:* Terence Fisher. **VHS $16.95** *SNC, MLB* 🎞🎞🎞

Island of the Blue Dolphins Based on a popular children's book by Scott O'Dell, this is a true story of a young Native American girl who, with her brother, are stranded on a deserted island when their people accidentally leave them. When the boy is killed, the girl learns to survive by her skills and by befriending the leader of a pack of wild dogs. Good family fare.
1964 99m/C Celia Kaye, Larry Domasin, Ann Daniel, George Kennedy; *D:* James B. Clark. **VHS, Beta $59.95** *MCA* 🎞🎞½

Island of the Burning Doomed A brutal heat wave accompanies invading aliens in this British-made outing. Lee and Cushing carry the picture. *AKA:* Island of the Burning Damned; Night of the Big Heat.
1967 94m/C *GB* Christopher Lee, Peter Cushing, Patrick Allen, Sarah Lawson, Jane Merrow; *D:* Terence Fisher. **VHS** *NO* 🎞🎞½

Island of the Lost An anthropologist's family must fight for survival when they become shipwrecked on a mysterious island.
1968 92m/C Richard Greene, Luke Halpin; *D:* John Florea. **VHS $19.98** *REP, GHV* 🎞½

Island Trader Young lad battles pirates and a crooked tug captain who seek hidden gold that he knows about.
1971 95m/C John Ewart, Ruth Cracknell, Eric Oldfield; *D:* Harold Rubie. **VHS, Beta** *PGN* 🎞

Island Warriors On a remote island, a beautiful Amazon queen rules an army of kung fu masters.
1986 88m/C VHS, Beta $29.99 *BFV* 🎞½

The Islander Sixteen-year-old Inga comes of age among the commercial fishermen of Lake Michigan.
1988 99m/C Kit Wholihan, Jeff Weborg, Celia Klehr, Jacob Mills, Julie Johnson, Mary Ann McHugh, Michael Rock, Sheri Parish; *D:* Phyllis Berg-Pigorsch. **VHS, Beta** *NO* 🎞

Islands A made-for-television drama about a middle-aged ex-hippie and a young rebellious punk who clash during a summer together on a secluded island.
1987 55m/C Louise Fletcher. **VHS, Beta $19.95** *NWV, KIV* 🎞🎞

Islands in the Stream Based on Ernest Hemingway's novel, this film is actually two movies in one. An American painter/sculptor, Thomas Hudson, lives a reclusive life on the island of Bimini shortly before the outbreak of World War II. The first part is a sensitive story of a broken family and the coming of the artist's three sons to live with their father after a four year separation. The second part is a second rate action-adventure.
1977 (PG) 105m/C George C. Scott, David Hemmings, Claire Bloom, Susan Tyrrell, Gilbert Roland; *D:* Franklin J. Schaffner; *M:* Jerry Goldsmith. **VHS, Beta, LV $29.95** *AIM, PAR* 🎞🎞½

Isle of Forgotten Sins Deep sea divers and an evil ship's captain vie for treasure. Good cast and direction but unremarkable material. Also released under the title "Monsoon."
1943 82m/B John Carradine, Gale Sondergaard, Sidney Toler, Frank Fenton; *D:* Edgar G. Ulmer. **VHS, Beta, 8mm $16.95** *SNC, VYY* 🎞🎞

Isle of Secret Passion A romance novel comes to video life as two lovers thrash out their problems on a Greek island.
1985 90m/C Patch MacKenzie, Michael MacRae, Zohra Lampert. **VHS, Beta $14.95** *PSM* 🎞

Isle of the Dead A Greek general is quarantined with seemingly all manner of social vermin on a plague-infested island in the early 1900s. The fear is that vampires walk among them. Characteristically spooky Val Lewton production with some original twists.
1945 72m/B Boris Karloff, Ellen Drew, Marc Cramer; *D:* Mark Robson. **VHS, Beta, LV $19.95** *TTC, MED, FCT* 🎞🎞

Isn't Life Wonderful Outstanding Griffith film depicts the unbearable conditions in post-World War I Germany. Filmed on location.
1924 90m/B Carol Dempster, Neil Hamilton, Lupino Lane, Hans von Schlettow; *W/D:* D.W. Griffith. **VHS, Beta $27.95** *GPV* 🎞🎞🎞🎞

Istanbul An American charms a Belgian student into taking part in a kidnap scheme.
1985 (R) 90m/C *FR* Brad Dourif, Dominique Deruddere, Ingrid De Vos, Francois Beukelaers; *D:* Marc Didden. **VHS, Beta** *NO* 🎞

Istanbul Believing he has stumbled upon the best story of his career, a journalist soon discovers that he has been pulled into a world of guns and violence. *AKA:* Istanbul, Keep Your Eyes Open.
1990 (PG-13) 88m/C *TU SW* Robert Morley, Timothy Bottoms, Twiggy; *D:* Mats Arehn. **VHS, Beta, LV** *IME* 🎞

It A department store clerk with plenty of sex appeal desires her rich boss. Established Bow as a prominent screen siren. Otherwise, it's not particularly interesting. Silent. Adapted by Elinor Glyn from her own story; Glyn also makes an appearance.
1927 71m/B Clara Bow, Gary Cooper, Antonio Moreno; *D:* Clarence Badger. **VHS, Beta, LV $19.95** *GPV, VYG, CRC* 🎞🎞🎞

It Came from Beneath the Sea A giant octopus arises from the depths of the sea to scour San Francisco for human food. Ray Harryhausen effects are special.
1955 80m/B Kenneth Tobey, Faith Domergue, Ian Keith, Donald Curtis; *D:* Robert Gordon. **VHS, Beta, LV $9.95** *GKK, MLB* 🎞🎞🎞

It Came from Hollywood A compilation of scenes from "B" horror and science fiction films of the 1950s, highlighting the funny side of these classic schlock movies. Some sequences in black and white.
1982 (PG) 87m/C *D:* Malcolm Leo. **VHS, Beta, LV $59.95** *PAR* 🎞🎞🎞

It Came From Outer Space Aliens take on the form of local humans to repair their spacecraft in a small Arizona town. Good performances and outstanding direction add up to a fine science fiction film. Based on the story "The Meteor" by Ray Bradbury, who also wrote the script. Originally filmed in 3-D.
1953 81m/B Richard Carlson, Barbara Rush, Charles Drake, Russell Johnson; *D:* Jack Arnold. **VHS** *GKK, MLB* 🎞🎞🎞

It Came Upon a Midnight Clear A heavenly miracle enables a retired (and dead) New York policeman to keep a Christmas promise to his grandson. Made for television.
1984 96m/C Mickey Rooney, Scott Grimes, George Gaynes, Annie Potts, Lloyd Nolan, Barrie Youngfellow; *D:* Peter Hunt. **VHS, Beta $9.95** *GKK* 🎞½

It Conquered the World Vegetable critters from Venus follow a probe satellite back to Earth and drop in on scientist Van Cleef, who'd been their intergalactic pen pal (seems he thought a Venusian invasion would improve the neighborhood). Their travelling companions, little bat creatures, turn earth dwellers into murderous zombies, and it starts to look like the Venusians are trying to make earth their planetary exurbia. Early-vintage zero-budget Corman, for schlock connoisseurs. Remade for television as "Zontar, the Thing from Venus."
1956 68m/B Peter Graves, Beverly Garland, Lee Van Cleef, Sally Fraser, Charles B. Griffith, Russ Bender, Jonathan Haze, Dick Miller, Karen Kadler, Paul Blaisdell; *D:* Roger Corman. **VHS $9.95** *COL, FCT, MLB* 🎞🎞½

It Could Happen to You Stepbrothers raised by a gentle immigrant take different paths in life. When one ends up killing someone during a botched robbery, the other—a lawyer—defends him. Standard '30s morality play.
1937 64m/B Alan Baxter, Andrea Leeds, Owen Davis Jr., Astrid Allwyn, Walter Kingsford, Al Shear; *D:* Phil Rosen. **VHS $19.95** *NOS, KRT* 🎞

It Could Happen to You A drunken advertising executive is charged with murder after a dead nightclub singer is found in his car. His wife sets out to clear him.
1939 64m/C Stuart Erwin, Gloria Stuart, Raymond Walburn, Douglas Fowley, June Gale, Paul Hurst, Richard Lane; *D:* Alfred Werker. **VHS, Beta** *NO* 🎞🎞

It Couldn't Happen Here Fans of the techno-pop duo The Pet Shop Boys can test their loyalty by enduring this feature music-video that actually played a few theaters. The dour pair journey across a surreal England, encountering a sinister blind priest, a philisophical ventriloquist's dummy, and more. Songs, sometimes presented only as muted incidental music, include the title track, "West End Girls," "It's a Sin" and "Always on My Mind."
1988 (PG-13) 87m/C *GB* Neil Tennant, Chris Lowe, Joss Ackland, Neil Dickson, Carmen Du Sautoy, Gareth Hunt; *D:* Jack Bond. **VHS, LV $59.95** *COL, MVD* 🎞

It Happened at Nightmare Inn Average thriller in which Geeson travels to Spanish inn and confronts two mad sisters who run the hotel. Also known as "Nightmare Hotel."
1970 95m/C *SP* Judy Geeson, Aurora Bautista, Esperanza Roy, Victor Alcazar, Lone Fleming; *D:* Eugenio Martin. **VHS $16.95** *SNC* 🎞🎞

It Happened at the World's Fair Fun and light romance comedy has Elvis and a companion (O'Brien) being escorted through the Seattle World's Fair by a fetching Chinese girl. ♫I'm Falling In Love Tonight; They Remind Me Too Much Of You; Take Me To The Fair; Relax; How Would You Like To Be; Beyond the Bend; One Broken Heart For Sale; Cotton Candy Land; A World Of Our Own; Happy Ending.
1963 105m/C Elvis Presley, Joan O'Brien, Gary Lockwood, Kurt Russell, Edith Atwater, Yvonne Craig; *D:* Norman Taurog. **VHS, Beta $19.95** *MGM* 🎞🎞½

It Happened in Brooklyn Former sailor with blue eyes bunks with janitor with big nose in Brooklyn. Sailor and cronies encounter many musical opportunities. Lots of songs and falling in love, little entertainment.
1947 104m/B Frank Sinatra, Kathryn Grayson, Jimmy Durante, Peter Lawford, Gloria Grahame; **D:** Richard Whorf. **VHS** $19.98 *MGM, FCT* 🐾🐾

It Happened in New Orleans A young boy is cared for by a former slave in post-Civil War New Orleans until his Yankee grandmother claims him and takes him to New York. The boy is resented by his family but manages to overcome their hostilities. **AKA:** Rainbow on the River.
1936 86m/B Bobby Breen, May Robson, Alan Mowbray, Benita Hume. **VHS, Beta** $29.95 *VYY* 🐾½

It Happened in the Park A rare film exercise for De Sica, wherein the patrons of the Villa Borghese parks are surveyed for a 24-hour period. In French with English dialogue.
1956 72m/B *FR* **D:** Vittorio De Sica. **VHS, Beta** $24.95 *NOS, FCT, TAM* 🐾🐾½

It Happened One Night Classic Capra comedy about an antagonistic couple determined to teach each other about life. Colbert is an unhappy heiress who runs away from her affluent home in search of contentment. On a bus she meets newspaper reporter Gable, who teaches her how "real" people live. She returns the favor in this first of the 1930s screwball comedies. The plot is a framework for an amusing examination of war between the sexes. Colbert and Gable are superb as affectionate foes. Remade as the musicals "Eve Knew Her Apples" and "You Can't Run Away From It."
1934 105m/B Clark Gable, Claudette Colbert, Roscoe Karns, Walter Connolly, Alan Hale Jr., Ward Bond; **D:** Frank Capra; **W:** Robert Riskin. **VHS, Beta, LV** $19.95 *COL, BTV, HMV* 🐾🐾🐾🐾

It Means That to Me Espionage thriller in which Constantine plays a reporter who's hired by the government to transport top secret micro-film.
1963 ?m/C *FR* Eddie Constantine, Jean-Louis Richard. **VHS** $16.95 *SNC* 🐾🐾

It Rained All Night the Day I Left Two drifters find their fortunes change when they are hired by a wealthy widow. Interesting romance adventure.
1978 (R) 100m/C Louis Gossett Jr., Sally Kellerman, Tony Curtis; **D:** Nicolas Gessner. **VHS, Beta** $29.95 *LIV* 🐾🐾

It Should Happen to You An aspiring model attempts to boost her career by promoting herself on a New York City billboard. The results, however, are continually surprising. Fine comedy teamwork from master thespians Holliday and Lemmon in this, the latter's first film. Written by Ruth Gordon and Garson Kanin.
1954 87m/B Judy Holliday, Jack Lemmon, Peter Lawford; **D:** George Cukor. **VHS, Beta, LV** $9.95 *GKK* 🐾🐾🐾

It Started in Naples Good performances by both Gable and Loren in this comedy-drama about an American lawyer in Italy who, upon preparing his late brother's estate, finds that his brother's nephew is living with a stripper. A custody battle ensues, but love wins out in the end. Loren is incredible in nightclub scenes.
1960 100m/C Clark Gable, Sophia Loren, Marietto, Vittorio De Sica, Paolo Carlini, Claudio Ermelli, Giovanni Filidoro; **D:** Melville Shavelson. **VHS** $14.95 *PAR* 🐾🐾🐾

It Started with a Kiss Reynolds plays a showgirl who impulsively marries an Air Force sargeant (Ford). When he's transfered to Spain they try to make a go of their hasty marriage among numerous comic complications. Flimsy farce with likeable leads.
1959 104m/C Debbie Reynolds, Glenn Ford, Eva Gabor, Gustavo Rojo, Fred Clark, Edgar Buchanan, Robert Warwick, Henry Morgan, Francis Bavier; **D:** George Marshall. **VHS** $19.98 *MGM, MOV* 🐾🐾½

It Takes a Thief Tough cookie Jayne's a buxom gangstress who does the hokey pokey with her criminal minions. A former lover who's been released from the big house seems to think she's been minding the mint for him. Au contraire. **AKA:** The Challenge.
1959 93m/B *GB* Jayne Mansfield, Anthony Quayle, Carl Mohner, Peter Reynolds, John Bennett; **D:** John Gilling. **VHS** *BBF* 🐾🐾

It Takes Two A young man spends his last ten days of bachelorhood cruising down Texas highways with a beautiful car saleswoman. Meanwhile, back at the altar, his bride waits patiently. Upbeat with some genuinely funny moments. From the director of "Pass the Ammo."
1988 (PG-13) 79m/C George Newbern, Leslie Hope, Kimberly Foster, Barry Corbin; **D:** David Beaird. **VHS, Beta** $79.98 *FOX* 🐾🐾

It! The Terror from Beyond Space The sole survivor of a Martian expedition is believed to have murdered his colleagues. He's arrested and brought back to Earth via space ship. En route, a vicious alien, the actual culprit, is discovered on board and begins killing the crew members. A fun science fiction thriller which, 20 years later, would provide Ridley Scott with the plot for "Alien." **AKA:** It! The Vampire From Beyond Space.
1958 68m/B Marshall Thompson, Shawn Smith, Kim Spalding, Ann Doran, Dabbs Greer, Paul Langton, Ray Corrigan; **D:** Edward L. Cahn. **VHS, Beta** *MGM, MLB* 🐾🐾½

It Was a Short Summer, Charlie Brown The Peanuts gang enjoys the summer until it's time to go back to school.
1969 26m/C **D:** Bill Melendez. **VHS** $14.95 *WTA* 🐾🐾½

Italian The story of an Italian immigrant family living in the slums of New York during the turn of the century.
1915 78m/B George Beban, Clara Williams, Leo Wills, J. Frank Burke, Fanny Midgley. **VHS, Beta** $19.95 *GPV, GVV* 🐾🐾½

The Italian Connection A man marked for death by the mob starts his own private war against the organization. Lots of action. **AKA:** Manhunt.
1973 92m/C *IT* Henry Silva, Woody Strode, Mario Adorf, Lucianna Paluzzi; **D:** Fernando Di Leo. **VHS** *AIP* 🐾🐾

The Italian Job Caine and Coward pair up to steal $4 million in gold by causing a major traffic jam in Turin, Italy. During the jam, the pair steals the gold from an armored car. Silliness and chases through the Swiss mountains ensue, culminating in a hilarious ending.
1969 (G) 99m/C *GB* Michael Caine, Noel Coward, Benny Hill, Raf Vallone, Tony Beckley, Rossano Brazzi, Margaret Blye; **D:** Peter Collinson. **VHS** *PAR* 🐾🐾½

The Italian Stallion Stallone plays a man with only one thing on his mind...sex!
1973 90m/C Sylvester Stallone, Henrietta Holm. **VHS, Beta** $79.95 *JEF* 🐾

Italian Straw Hat Classic silent about the chain of errors that ensues when a man's horse eats a woman's hat. His vast, unending struggle to replace the hat is the source of continual comedy. From Eugene Labiche's play. **AKA:** Un Chapeau de Paille d'Italie.
1927 72m/B *FR* Albert Prejean; **D:** Rene Clair. **VHS, Beta** $29.95 *VYY, MRV, INT* 🐾🐾🐾

It's a Bundyful Life The outrageous family from television's "Married with Children" does Christmas in their own inimitable fashion. This parody of "It's a Wonderful Life" features Kinison earning his wings as father Al's guardian angel. See what the family would have been like if Al had never been born...and what Al decides to do about it. Those seeking traditional family fare should look elsewhere.
1992 47m/C Ed O'Neill, Katey Sagal, Christina Applegate, David Faustino, Sam Kinison, Amanda Bearse, Ted McGinley; **D:** Gerry Cohen. **VHS** $14.95 *COL* 🐾🐾

It's a Date A mother and daughter, both actresses, continually get their professional and romantic lives intertwined. It begins when Durbin (the daughter) is offered Kay's (the mother) Broadway role. It continues in Hawaii where the man that Kay is in love with tries to court Durbin. As it's a comedy, of course, all is put right in the end. ♫ Musetta's Waltz; Ave Maria; Loch Lomond; Love Is All; It Happened in Kaloha; Rhythm of the Islands; Hawaiian War Chant.
1940 103m/B Deanna Durbin, Kay Francis, Walter Pidgeon, Samuel S. Hinds, S.Z. Sakall, Henry Stephenson, Charles Lane, Leon Belasco; **D:** William A. Seiter; **W:** Norman Krasna. **VHS** $29.98 *FOX, FCT, MLB* 🐾🐾

It's a Dog's Life The hero and narrator of this story is a wily bull terrier called Wildfire. Wildfire is a tough dog on the mean streets of the Bowery in turn-of-the-century New York. His master has him in dog fights in the local saloon but eventually abandons him. Wildfire is then taken in by the kindly employee of the rich and dog-hating Jagger but naturally manages to win the codger over. Based on the short story "The Bar Sinister" by Richard Harding Davis. **AKA:** The Bar Sinister.
1955 87m/C Jeff Richards, Edmund Gwenn, Dean Jagger; **D:** Hermann Hoffman. **VHS** $19.98 *FCT* 🐾🐾½

It's A Gift A grocery clerk moves his family west to manage orange groves in this classic Fields comedy. Several inspired sequences. The supporting cast shines too. A real find for the discriminating comedy buff. Remake of the silent "It's the Old Army Game."
1934 71m/B W.C. Fields, Baby LeRoy, Kathleen Howard; **D:** Norman Z. MacLeod. **VHS, Beta, LV** $14.95 *MCA, KRT* 🐾🐾🐾½

It's a Great Feeling Another Carson and Day team-up where Carson plays a camera-hogging show-off whom no one wants to direct. He's such an industry piranha that he ends up directing himself! He cons Day, a waitress and would-be actress, by promising her a part in his new film. Some executives hear her sing before she heads back home to Wisconsin, fed up with Hollywood. They make Carson track her down to star in the new picture, but when he arrives she is at the alter with her high school sweetheart. A very funny film just brimming with pure comedy. Many say it's worth it just to see directors Curtiz, Vidor, and Walsh playing around in front of the camera. Appearances by stars Errol Flynn, Joan Crawford, Sydney Greenstreet, Gary Cooper, Danny Kaye, Patricia Neal, Eleanor, Parker,

Edwin G. Robinson, Jane Wyman, and Ronald Reagan.
1949 85m/C Dennis Morgan, Doris Day, Jack Carson, Bill Goodwin, Errol Flynn, Gary Cooper, Joan Crawford, Ronald Reagan, Jane Wyman; **D:** David Butler. **VHS, LV $29.98** *FOX, FCT, MLB* ⅛½

It's a Joke, Son! Follows the fictional politician, Senator Claghorn from the Fred Allen radio show, during his first run for the U.S. Senate.
1947 67m/B Kenny Delmar, Una Merkel; **D:** Ben Stoloff. **VHS $19.95** *NOS, MRV, QNE* ⅛

It's a Mad, Mad, Mad, Mad World Overblown epic comedy with a cast of notables desperately seeking the whereabouts of stolen money. Ultimately exhausting film undone by its length and overbearing performances. Laserdisc contains 20 minutes of supplemental footage, including interviews with some of the surviving cast members.
1963 155m/C Spencer Tracy, Sid Caesar, Milton Berle, Ethel Merman, Jonathan Winters, Jimmy Durante, Buddy Hackett, Mickey Rooney, Phil Silvers, Dick Shawn, Edie Adams, Dorothy Provine, Buster Keaton, Terry-Thomas, Moe Howard, Larry Fine, Joe DeRita, Jim Backus, William Demarest, Peter Falk, Leo Gorcey, Edward Everett Horton, Joe E. Brown, Carl Reiner, ZaSu Pitts, Eddie Anderson, Jack Benny, Jerry Lewis; **D:** Stanley Kramer. Academy Awards '63: Best Sound Effects Editing; Nominations: Best Color Cinematography, Best Song ("It's a Mad, Mad, Mad, Mad World"), Best Sound, Best Original Score. **VHS, Beta, LV $29.99** *FOX, MGM, PIA* ⅛

It's a Mystery, Charlie Brown Peanuts adventure in which Snoopy interrogates everyone on the disappearance of Woodstock's birdhouse.
1987 30m/C D: Phil Roman. **VHS, Beta $14.95** *KRT, WTA* ⅛

It's a Wonderful Life American classic concerns a man saved from suicide by a considerate angel, who then shows the hero how important he's been to the lives of loved ones. Corny but inspirational and heartwarming, with endearing performance by Travers as angel Clarence. Stewart and Reed are typically wholesome. A perfect film for people who want to feel good, joyfully teetering on the border between Hollywood schmaltz and genuine heartbreak. Also available colorized. The laserdisc version includes production and publicity stills, the theatrical trailer, and commentary by film professor Jeanine Basinger. Also available in a 160-minute Collector's Edition with original preview trailer, "The Making of 'It's a Wonderful Life,'" and a new digital transfer from the original negative.
1946 125m/B James Stewart, Donna Reed, Henry Travers, Thomas Mitchell, Lionel Barrymore, Samuel S. Hinds, Frank Faylen, Gloria Grahame, H.B. Warner, Ellen Corby, Sheldon Leonard, Beulah Bondi, Ward Bond; **D:** Frank Capra. Academy Awards '46 Nominations: Best Actor (Stewart), Best Director (Capra), Best Film Editing, Best Picture, Best Sound; Golden Globe Awards '47: Best Director (Capra). **VHS, LV, 3/4U, Special order formats $9.95** *IGP, MRV, NEG* ⅛⅛⅛

It's Alive! Slow-moving dud about a farmer feeding passersby to the area's cave-dwelling lizard man. The ping pong ball-eyed monster puts in a belated appearance that's not worth the wait.
1968 80m/C Tommy Kirk, Shirley Bonne, Bill Thurman; **W/D:** Larry Buchanan. **VHS $15.95** *NOS, LOO* ⅛

It's Alive Cult film about a mutated baby that is born to a normal Los Angeles couple, who escapes and goes on a bloodthirsty, murderous rampage, is a sight to behold. Fantastic score by Bernard Herrmann makes this chilling film a memorable one.
1974 (PG) 91m/C John P. Ryan, Sharon Farrell, Andrew Duggan, Guy Stockwell, James Dixon, Michael Ansara; **D:** Larry Cohen. **VHS, Beta $14.95** *WAR, FCT* ⅛⅛⅛

It's Alive 2: It Lives Again In this sequel to "It's Alive," the original hellspun baby meets up with two more of the same and all three terrorize the city, murdering everyone they can find. Truly horrendous.
1978 (R) 91m/C Frederic Forrest, Kathleen Lloyd, John P. Ryan, Andrew Duggan, John Marley, Eddie Constantine; **D:** Larry Cohen. **VHS, Beta $19.98** *WAR, FCT* Woof!

It's Alive 3: Island of the Alive The second sequel to the tongue-in-cheek horror film, in which the infant mutant of the previous films has been left with other mutations to spawn on a desert island.
1987 (R) 94m/C Michael Moriarty, Karen Black, Laurene Landon, Gerrit Graham, James Dixon, Neal Israel, MacDonald Carey; **D:** Larry Cohen. **VHS, Beta $19.98** *WAR* ⅛

It's Always Fair Weather Three World War II buddies meet again at a 10 year reunion and find that they don't like each other very much. A surprisingly cynical film, written by Betty Comden & Adolph Green, with songs by Comden, Green, and Andre Previn. Director Donen produced "Seven Brides for Seven Brothers" the previous year. ♫Stillman's Gym; March, March; Why Are We Here? (Blue Danube); Music Is Better Than Words; Once Upon A Time; The Time For Parting, I Like Myself; Baby You Knock Me Out; Thanks A Lot But No Thanks; The Binge; Ten Year Montage; Situation Wise.
1955 102m/C Gene Kelly, Cyd Charisse, Dan Dailey, Michael Kidd; **D:** Stanley Donen. **VHS, Beta, LV $19.98** *MGM, FHE* ⅛

It's an Adventure, Charlie Brown! A collection of six vignettes featuring Charlie Brown and the whole Peanuts gang.
1983 50m/C D: Bill Melendez. **VHS, Beta $9.98** *WTA, SHV, VTR* ⅛

It's Arbor Day, Charlie Brown Tribulations aplenty for Charlie Brown as his baseball team turns his field into an Arbor Day garden.
1983 26m/C VHS, Beta $14.95 *KRT, WTA* ⅛

It's Called Murder, Baby The famed porn star gives the viewer a lesson in English vocabulary in this tale of a blackmailed movie queen.
1982 (R) 94m/C John Leslie, Cameron Mitchell, Lisa Trego; **D:** Sam Weston. **VHS, Beta $19.98** *LIV* ⅛

It's Flashbeagle, Charlie Brown/ She's a Good Skate, Charlie Brown A Peanuts double header: In "It's Flashbeagle Charlie Brown," Snoopy infects the Peanuts gang with dance fever, and in "She's a Good Skate Charlie Brown," Snoopy trains Peppermint Patty to become a figure skating champion.
1984 55m/C D: Bill Melendez. **VHS, Beta $29.95** *SHV* ⅛

It's Good to Be Alive The true story of how Brooklyn Dodgers' catcher Roy Campanella learned to face life after an automobile accident left him a quadriplegic. Good performances in this television drama.
1974 100m/C Paul Winfield, Ruby Dee, Louis Gossett Jr.; **D:** Michael Landon. **VHS, Beta $59.95** *PSM* ⅛½

It's in the Bag A shiftless flea circus owner sells chairs he has inherited, not knowing that a fortune is hidden in one of them. **AKA:** The Fifth Chair.
1945 87m/B Fred Allen, Don Ameche, Jack Benny, William Bendix, Binnie Barnes, Robert Benchley; **D:** Richard Wallace. **VHS, LV $19.95** *REP, MED* ⅛½

It's Love Again A streetwise chorus girl poses as a fictional socialite in a light music-hall comedy. ♫It's Love Again; Heaven In Your Arms.
1936 83m/B *GB* Jessie Matthews, Robert Young, Sonnie Hale; **D:** Victor Saville. **VHS, Beta $24.95** *NOS, DVT, HEG* ⅛½

It's Magic, Charlie Brown/ Charlie Brown's All Star In the first of these two stories, Snoopy, "The Great Houndini," makes Charlie Brown disappear. Problems begin when Snoopy finds it difficult conjuring his master back to reality. In the second story, Charlie Brown's baseball team has lost 999 games in a row, and prospects are bleak. New hope arrives when he gets an offer to have the team sponsored in a real league.
1981 55m/C D: Phil Roman. **VHS, Beta $14.95** *SHV, VTR, WTA* ⅛½

It's My Turn A mathematics professor (Clayburgh) struggles in her relationship with live-in lover (Grodin) who sells real-estate in Chicago. She meets retired baseball player (Douglas) and falls in love. "Ho-hum" just about describes the rest.
1980 (R) 91m/C Jill Clayburgh, Michael Douglas, Charles Grodin, Beverly Garland, Steven Hill, Dianne Wiest, Daniel Stern; **D:** Claudia Weill. **VHS, Beta, LV $64.95** *COL* ⅛

It's Not the Size That Counts After the Earth's drinking water is contaminated, Lawson is the only man on Earth not to be struck by impotency. Limp sequel to "Percy," the British comedy about the first man to receive a penis transplant. Promising comedy doesn't deliver. **AKA:** Percy's Progress.
1974 90m/C Leigh Lawson, Elke Sommer, Denholm Elliott, Vincent Price; **D:** Ralph Thomas. **VHS $59.98** *SUE* Woof!

It's the Great Pumpkin, Charlie Brown It's Halloween, and Charlie Brown and his friends are going trick-or-treating, but Linus faithfully awaits the arrival of the Great Pumpkin.
1988 25m/C VHS, Beta $9.98 *MED, VTR, WTA* Woof!

It's the Old Army Game Classic Fields gags in three of his best Ziegfeld Follies sketches: "The Drug Store," "A Peaceful Morning," and "The Family Flivver." The beautiful Brooks serves as his comic foil.
1926 75m/B W.C. Fields, Louise Brooks, Blanche Ring, William Gaxton; **D:** Edward Sutherland. **VHS, Beta $24.95** *GPV* Woof!

It's Three Strikes, Charlie Brown Misfortunes abound in the baseball diamond for the Peanuts gang. Animated.
1986 41m/C D: Bill Melendez, Phil Roman, Robert E. Balzer, Sam Nicholson. **VHS, Beta $14.95** *KRT, WTA* Woof!

It's Your First Kiss, Charlie Brown/Someday You'll Find Her, Charlie Brown In "It's Your First Kiss, Charlie Brown," our hero has to escort the school's homecoming queen to the ball. What's worse, he actually has to kiss her in front of everyone! In "Someday You'll Find Her, Charlie Brown," Charlie Brown sees "the most beautiful girl in the world" on

television and, after recruiting Linus, embarks upon a door-to-door search to find her.
1977 55m/C D: Phil Roman. VHS, Beta $14.95 *SHV, VTR* Woof!

Ivan the Terrible, Part 1 Contemplative epic of Russia's first czar is a classic, innovative film from cinema genius Eisenstein. Visually stunning, with a fine performance by Cherkassov. Ivan's struggles to preserve his country is the main concern of the first half of Eisenstein's masterwork (which he originally planned as a trilogy). In Russian with English subtitles.
1944 96m/B *RU* Nikolai Cherkassov, Ludmila Tselikovskaya, Serafina Birman, Piotr Kadochnikev; *D:* Sergei Eisenstein. VHS, Beta, LV, 8mm, 3/4U $24.95 *NOS, MRV, WST* 𝄃𝄃𝄃𝄃

Ivan the Terrible, Part 2 Landed gentry conspire to dethrone the czar in this continuation of the innovative epic. More stunning imagery from master Eisenstein, who makes no false moves in this one. Slow going, but immensely rewarding. Russian dialogue with English subtitles; contains color sequences.
1946 84m/B *RU* Nikolai Cherkassov, Ludmila Tselikovskaya, Serafina Birman, Piotr Kadochnikev; *D:* Sergei Eisenstein. VHS, Beta, LV, 8mm, 3/4U $24.95 *NOS, MRV, WST* 𝄃𝄃𝄃½

Ivanhoe Knights fight each other and woo maidens in this chivalrous romance derived from the Sir Walter Scott classic. Taylor is suitably noble, while Sanders is familiarly serpentine. Remade in 1982.
1952 107m/C Robert Taylor, Elizabeth Taylor, Joan Fontaine, George Sanders, Finlay Currie, Felix Aylmer; *D:* Richard Thorpe. VHS, Beta $19.98 *MGM* 𝄃𝄃𝄃

Ivanhoe A version of Sir Walter Scott's classic novel of chivalry and knighthood in 12th century England. Made for television. Remake of the 1953 film classic.
1982 142m/C Anthony Andrews, James Mason, Lysette Anthony, Sam Neill, Olivia Hussey, Michael Hordern, Julian Glover, George Innes, Ronald Pickup, John Rhys-Davies, Chloe Franks; *D:* Douglas Camfield. VHS, Beta $19.95 *RCA, TVC, COL* 𝄃𝄃½

I've Always Loved You The drama of love and jealousy explored in an extravagant production filled with classical music. *AKA:* Concerto.
1946 117m/C Philip Dorn, Catherine McLeod; *D:* Frank Borzage. VHS, LV $19.98 *REP, FCT* 𝄃𝄃½

I've Heard the Mermaids Singing Independent Canadian semi-satiric romantic comedy details the misadventures of a klutzy woman who suddenly obtains a desirable job in an art gallery run by a lesbian on whom she develops a crush. Good-natured tone helped considerably by McCarthy's winning performance.
1987 81m/C *CA* Sheila McCarthy, Paule Baillargeon, Ann-Marie MacDonald; *D:* Patricia Rozema. VHS, Beta, LV $19.98 *NLC, FCT* 𝄃𝄃𝄃

Ivory Hunters Conservationists team up to thwart a massacre of elephants by poachers. Predictable made-for-cable entertainment co-produced by the National Audubon Society.
1990 94m/C John Lithgow, Isabella Rossellini, James Earl Jones, Tony Todd, Olek Krupa; *D:* Joseph Sargent; *W:* Richard Guttman, Bill Bozzone. VHS, Beta $79.98 *TTC* 𝄃𝄃½

Izzy & Moe Carney and The Great One are reunited for the last time on screen as former vaudevillians who become federal agents and create havoc amid speak-easies and bathtub gin during Prohibition. A made-for-television movie based on true stories.

1985 92m/C Jackie Gleason, Art Carney, Cynthia Harris; *D:* Jackie Cooper. VHS, Beta, LV $79.95 *VMK* 𝄃𝄃½

J. Edgar Hoover Made for cable adaptation from "My 30 years in Hoover's FBI" by William G. Sullivan and William S. Brown. Biographical drama deals with Hoover's fifty-five year career with the government. Included are his FBI days.
1987 110m/C Treat Williams, Rip Torn, David Ogden Stiers, Andrew Duggan, Art Hindle, Louise Fletcher; *D:* Robert Collins. VHS, Beta, LV $79.98 *MCG* 𝄃𝄃

J-Men Forever! A spoof on early sci-fi/ spy serials in which an alien takeover is attempted via rock-n-roll (your parents warned you). Employs an amusing technique of dubbing footage from dozens of Republic dramas intercut with new film featuring the "Firesign Theater" crew.
1979 (PG) 73m/B Peter Bergman, Phil Proctor; *D:* Richard Patterson. VHS, Beta $59.98 *VES* 𝄃𝄃𝄃

Jabberwalk A "Mondo Cane," American-style. A reckless and funny view of the bizarre in U.S. life.
1979 (R) 110m/C VHS, Beta $59.95 *VCD* 𝄃𝄃

Jabberwocky Pythonesque chaos prevails in the medieval cartoon kingdom of King Bruno the Questionable, who rules with cruelty, stupidity, lust and dust. Jabberwocky is the big dragon mowing everything down in its path until hero Palin decides to take it on. Uneven, but real funny at times.
1977 (PG) 104m/C *GB* Michael Palin, Eric Idle, Max Wall, Deborah Fallender, Terry Jones, John LeMesurier; *D:* Terry Gilliam. VHS, Beta, LV $19.95 *COL* 𝄃𝄃½

Jacare First adventure thriller filmed in the Amazon jungle.
1942 ?m/C Frank Buck. VHS $16.95 *SNC* 𝄃𝄃

J'Accuse A Frenchman creates a device he believes will stop the war but it is confiscated by the government and used as part of the national defense. Subsequently, he goes mad. Gance (known for his 1927 "Napoleon"), remade his 1919 silent film, retelling the powerful anti-war message with great sensitivity. Banned in Nazi Germany. *AKA:* I Accuse; That They May Live.
1937 125m/B *FR* Victor Francen, Jean Max, Deltaire, Renee Devillers; *D:* Abel Gance. VHS $29.95 *CVC, SNC, FCT* 𝄃𝄃𝄃

Jack & the Beanstalk While babysitting, Lou falls asleep and dreams he's Jack in this spoof of the classic fairy tale.
1952 78m/C Bud Abbott, Lou Costello, Buddy Baer; *D:* Jean Yarborough. VHS, Beta $19.95 *NOS, UHV* 𝄃𝄃

Jack & the Beanstalk An animated musical version of the familiar story of Jack, the young boy who climbs a magic beanstalk up into the clouds, where he meets a fearsome giant.
1976 80m/C *W/D:* Peter J. Solmo. VHS, Beta *COL* 𝄃

Jack & the Beanstalk From the "Faerie Tale Theatre" comes this classic tale of Jack, who sells his family's cow for 5 magic beans, climbs the huge beanstalk that sprouts from them, and encounters an unfriendly giant.
1983 60m/C Dennis Christopher, Katherine Helmond, Elliott Gould, Jean Stapleton, Mark Blankfield; *D:* Lamont Johnson. VHS, Beta, LV $14.98 *KUI, FOX, FCT* 𝄃𝄃𝄃

Jack Frost Moving biographical drama that follows a man from the sweat factories of London to his eventual rise to success.

1943 89m/B Michael O'Shea, Susan Hayward. VHS, Beta, 8mm *VYY* 𝄃𝄃½

The Jack Knife Man Sentimental silent treatment of the relationship between a boy and a man. A woman, about to check into the great hereafter, hands over her bundle of joy to a kindly old river man, and the two bond in a familial way despite incessant adversity. Made the year following Vidor's debut as a feature film director (Vidor coproduced and coscripted as well).
1920 70m/B Fred Turner, Todd Harry, Bobby Kelso, Willis Marks, Lillian Leighton, James Corrigan; *D:* King Vidor. VHS, Beta $24.95 *VYY, GPV, FCT* 𝄃𝄃𝄃

Jack London Dramatizes London's most creative years during his careers as oyster pirate, prospector, war correspondent and author. Based on "The Book of Jack London" by Charmian London. *AKA:* The Adventures of Jack London; The Life of Jack London.
1944 94m/B Michael O'Shea, Susan Hayward, Harry Davenport, Virginia Mayo, Frank Craven; *D:* Alfred Santell. VHS, Beta $19.95 *NOS, MRV, DVT* 𝄃½

Jack the Bear Laden with misery, exercise in the maudlin vein centers around one family, a dad and two sons, trying to pick up the pieces after the death of wife and mother Marcovicci. Dad DeVito is the host of a late-night horror show who is as cuddly as a bear—when he's not drinking. That's when eldest son Jack (Steinmiller) takes over as dad to both younger brother and father. While talent and circumstances alone are enough to create what might have been a sensitive study, the emotion is completely overwrought by contrived plot twists, including a kidnapping by the local Nazi (every neighborhood should have one). TV's "thirty-something" director Herskovitz creates an effect somewhat akin to a cement block being dropped on a card house. Point made, and so much for subtlety. Based on a novel by Dan McCall.
1993 (PG-13) 98m/C Danny DeVito, Robert J. Steinmiller Jr., Miko Hughes, Gary Sinise, Art LaFleur, Andrea Marcovicci, Julia Louis-Dreyfus, Reese Witherspoon; *D:* Marshall Herskovitz; *M:* James Horner. VHS *NYR* 𝄃½

Jack the Giant Killer A young farmer joins a medieval princess on a journey to a distant convent. Along the way, they combat an evil wizard, dragons, sea monsters and other mystical creatures, and are assisted by leprechauns, a dog and a chimp. Generally considered a blatant rip-off of "The Seventh Voyage of Sinbad," the film nonetheless delivers plenty of fun and excitement. Jim Danforth of "Gumby" fame provided the stop-motion animation.
1962 (G) 95m/C Kerwin Mathews, Judi Meredith, Torin Thatcher, Walter Burke, Roger Mobley, Barry Kelley, Don Beddoe, Anna Lee, Robert Gist; *D:* Nathan Juran. VHS, Beta, LV $14.95 *MGM, FCT* 𝄃𝄃𝄃

Jack the Ripper An American detective joins Scotland Yard in tracking down the legendary and elusive Jack the Ripper. More gory than most. The last scene is in color.
1960 88m/B *GB* Lee Patterson, Betty McDowall, Barbara Burke, John Le Mesurier, George Rose; *D:* Robert S. Baker, Monty Berman. VHS $16.95 *SNC, PAR* 𝄃𝄃

Jack the Ripper The inimitable Kinski assumes the role of the most heinous criminal of modern history—Jack the Ripper.
1980 (R) 82m/C Klaus Kinski, Josephine Chaplin; *D:* Jess (Jesus) Franco. VHS, Beta $59.95 *VES* 𝄃𝄃

Jack the Ripper Another retelling of the life of the legendary serial killer. Caine is the Scotland Yard inspector who tracks down the murderer. Ending is based on recent evidence found by director/co-writer Wickes. Extremely well done made-for-television film.
1988 200m/C Michael Caine, Armand Assante, Ray McNally, Susan George, Jane Seymour, Lewis Collins; *D:* David Wickes. VHS *VES, LIV* 🎬🎬🎬

Jackie Chan's Police Force Chopsocker Chan's assigned to protect a witness in a drug case. Faced by unsavory thugs, he flies through the air with the greatest of ease. Very cool stunts. *AKA:* The Police Story; Police Force; Jackie Chan's Police Story.
1985 (PG-13) 89m/C *CH* Jackie Chan, Bridget Lin, Maggie Cheung; *D:* Jackie Chan. VHS $79.98 *CGH* 🎬🎬½

The Jackie Robinson Story Chronicles Robinson's rise from UCLA to his breakthrough as the first black man to play baseball in the major league. Robinson plays himself; the film deals honestly with the racial issues of the time.
1950 76m/B Jackie Robinson, Ruby Dee, Minor Watson, Louise Beavers, Richard Lane, Harry Shannon, Joel Fluellen; *D:* Alfred E. Green. VHS $19.95 *NOS, MRV, MOV* 🎬🎬🎬

Jacknife The well-crafted story of a Vietnam veteran who visits his old war buddy and tries to piece together what's happened to their lives since their homecoming. During his visit he encounters anger and hostility from the other veteran, and tenderness from his friend's sister. A masterfully acted, small-scale drama, adapted by Stephen Metcalfe from his play.
1989 (R) 102m/C Robert De Niro, Kathy Baker, Ed Harris, Loudon Wainwright III; *D:* David Jones. VHS, Beta, LV $89.98 *HBO, IME* 🎬🎬🎬

Jacko & Lise A French lad falls in love with a young girl, and abandons his previously decadent lifestyle to win her. Available with English subtitles or dubbed.
1982 (R) 92m/C *FR* Laurent Malet, Annie Girardot; *D:* Walter Bal. VHS, Beta $29.98 *SUE* 🎬🎬

The Jackpot An average Joe wins a bushel of money from a radio quiz show but can't pay the taxes. Maybe that was funny before the age of read-my-lips economics, but the all-star cast doesn't deliver on its promise. Lang, noted for mostly mediocre pictures, went on to direct "The King and I."
1950 87m/C James Stewart, Natalie Wood, Barbara Hale, James Gleason, Fred Clark; *D:* Walter Lang. VHS *NO* 🎬🎬

Jack's Back When a lunatic is killing Los Angeles prostitutes Jack-the-Ripper style, twin brothers get mistakenly involved (Spader in both roles). One of the brothers is accused of the murders and it is up to the other either to clear his name or to provide the final evidence of guilt. A well thought out story with enough twists and turns for any suspense buff.
1987 (R) 97m/C James Spader, Cynthia Gibb, Rod Loomis, Rex Ryon, Robert Picardo, Jim Haynie; *D:* Rowdy Herrington. VHS, Beta, LV $19.95 *PAR* 🎬🎬🎬

Jackson County Jail While driving cross-country, a young woman is robbed, imprisoned, and raped by a deputy, whom she kills. Faced with a murder charge, she flees, with the law in hot pursuit. Also known by its later remade-for-television name, "Outside Chance," this is a minor cult film.
1976 (R) 84m/C Yvette Mimieux, Tommy Lee Jones, Robert Carradine, Severn Darden, Howard Hesseman, Mary Woronov; *D:* Michael Miller. VHS, Beta $39.98 *WAR* 🎬🎬½

The Jacksons: An American Dream Made for television miniseries covering the career of the Jackson 5, the working-class family from Gary, Indiana which became a celebrated show business success. The series begins with the courtship of Joseph and Katherine Jackson and ends with the group's farewell tour in 1984, covering both family and career turmoils. Simplistic, glossy biography.
1992 225m/C Lawrence Hilton-Jacobs, Angela Bassett, Wylie Draper, Angel Vargas, Jacen Wilkerson, Terrence DaShon Howard, Jason Weaver, Jermaine Jackson II, Billy Dee Williams, Vanessa Williams, Holly Robinson; *D:* Karen Arthur. VHS $79.95 *PGV* 🎬🎬½

Jacob Have I Loved Katherine Paterson story about a girl growing up on a Chesapeake island. Part of the "Wonderworks" family movie series from PBS.
1988 57m/C Bridget Fonda, Jenny Robertson, John Kellogg; *D:* Victoria Hochberg. VHS $29.95 *RHU, WNE, PME* 🎬🎬½

Jacob's Ladder A man struggles with events he experienced while serving in Vietnam. Gradually, he becomes unable to separate reality from the strange, psychotic world into which he increasingly lapses. His friends and family try to help him before he's lost forever. Great story potential is flawed by too many flashbacks, leaving the viewer more confused than the characters.
1990 (R) 116m/C Tim Robbins, Elizabeth Pena, Danny Aiello, Matt Craven, Macaulay Culkin; *D:* Adrian Lyne. VHS, Beta, LV $92.95 *LIV, FCT* 🎬🎬½

Jacqueline Bouvier Kennedy A made-for-television biography of the former First Lady, from her childhood to "Camelot," the glorious years with JFK in the White House. Smith bears a physical resemblance to Jackie, but this drama is far too glossy.
1981 150m/C Jaclyn Smith, James Franciscus, Rod Taylor, Donald Moffatt, Dolph Sweet, Stephen Elliott; *D:* Steven Gethers. VHS, Beta $24.95 *VMK* 🎬½

The Jade Mask Chan discovers a murderer and his wife use puppets and masks to make it appear their victims are still alive. Another in the detective series with nothing noteworthy about it. Luke, the brother of actor Keye Luke, takes on the role of Chan's Number Four son.
1945 66m/B Sidney Toler, Mantan Moreland, Edwin Luke, Janet Warren, Hardie Albright, Edith Evanson; *D:* Phil Rosen. VHS $19.98 *MGM* 🎬½

The Jagged Edge The beautiful wife of successful newspaper editor, Jack Forester, is killed and the police want to point the guilty finger at Jack. Attorney Teddy Barnes is brought in to defend him and accidentally falls in love. Taut murder mystery will keep you guessing "whodunit" until the very end.
1985 (R) 108m/C Jeff Bridges, Glenn Close, Robert Loggia, Peter Coyote, John Dehner, Leigh Taylor-Young, Lance Henriksen, James Karen; *D:* Richard Marquand; *M:* John Barry. VHS, Beta, LV, 8mm $14.95 *RCA, COL* 🎬🎬½

Jaguar Three men leave their homes in Niger in order to find jobs in the cities. When they return to their village, they bring back their experiences.
1956 93m/C *D:* Jean Rouch. VHS *INT* 🎬🎬½

Jaguar Lives A high-kicking secret agent tracks down bad boy drug kings around the world.
1979 (PG) 91m/C Joe Lewis, Barbara Bach, Christopher Lee, Woody Strode, Donald Pleasence, Joseph Wiseman, John Huston, Capucine; *D:* Ernie Pintoff. VHS, Beta $79.95 *TWE* 🎬

Jail Bait Early Wood film about a group of small-time crooks who are always in trouble with the law; they blackmail a plastic surgeon into using his talents to help them ditch the cops. Not as "bad" as Wood's "Plan 9 From Outer Space," but still bad enough for camp fans to love (check the cheesy score leftover from an equally cheesy Mexican mad-scientist flick). *AKA:* Hidden Face.
1954 80m/B Timothy Farrell, Clancy Malone, Lyle Talbot, Steve Reeves, Herbert Rawlinson; *D:* Edward D. Wood Jr. VHS, Beta $16.95 *SNC, AOV, LSV* 🎬½

Jailbait: Betrayed By Innocence A man is on trial for statutory rape. Made-for-television.
1986 (R) 90m/C Barry Bostwick, Lee Purcell, Paul Sorvino, Cristen Kauffman, Isaac Hayes; *D:* Elliot Silverstein. VHS, Beta $79.95 *MNC, HHE* 🎬

Jailbird Rock We'd like to tell you that this isn't really a sweet-young-thing-in-prison musical, but it is. When Antin shoots her stepfather (he told her to turn that damn noise down?) she tries to bring down the Big House with song and dance. No kidding.
1988 90m/C Ronald Lacey, Rhonda Aldrich, Robin Antin; *D:* Phillip Schuman. VHS, Beta $79.95 *TWE* 🎬½

Jailbird's Vacation Two ex-cons pose as lumberjacks in order to exact revenge on the bum that put them away. In French with English subtitles.
1965 125m/C *FR* Lino Ventura; *D:* Robert Enrico. VHS, Beta $19.95 *FCT* 🎬🎬

Jailbreakin' A faded country singer and a rebellious youth team up to break out of jail.
1972 90m/C Erik Estrada. VHS, Beta $59.95 *GEM* 🎬

Jailhouse Rock While in jail for manslaughter, a teenager learns to play the guitar. After his release, he slowly develops into a top recording star. Probably the only film that captured the magnetic power of the young Elvis Presley; an absolute must for fans. Also available in a colorized version. 🎵Jailhouse Rock; Treat Me Nice; Baby, I Don't Care; Young and Beautiful; Don't Leave Me Now; I Wanna Be Free; One More Day.
1957 96m/B Elvis Presley, Judy Tyler, Vaughn Taylor, Dean Jones, Mickey Shaughnessy, William Forrest, Glenn Strange; *D:* Richard Thorpe. VHS, Beta, LV $19.95 *MGM* 🎬🎬🎬

Jakarta A love-hardened CIA operative is whisked away to Jakarta for reasons unknown, only to find his thought-to-be-dead lover still alive and caught in a deadly game of espionage.
1988 (R) 94m/C Christopher Noth, Sue Francis Pai, Ronald Hunter; *D:* Charles Kaufman. VHS, Beta, LV *NO* 🎬½

Jake Speed Comic-book mercenary Jake and his loyal associate Remo rescue a beautiful girl from white slave traders. Supposedly a parody of the action adventure genre.
1986 (PG) 93m/C Wayne Crawford, John Hurt, Karen Kopins, Dennis Christopher; *D:* Andrew Lane. VHS, Beta, LV $14.95 *NWV, STE* 🎬½

Jamaica Inn In old Cornwall, an orphan girl becomes involved with smugglers. Remade in 1982; based on the story by Daphne Du Maurier.

1939 98m/B *GB* Charles Laughton, Maureen O'Hara, Leslie Banks, Robert Newton; **D:** Alfred Hitchcock. **VHS, Beta, 3/4U, Special order formats** $16.95 *SNC, NOS, CAB* 𝒜𝒜

Jamaica Inn A made-for-television mini-series based on the old Daphne Du Maurier adventure about highwaymen and moor-lurking thieves in Cornwall. Remake of the 1939 Hitchcock film.
1982 192m/C Patrick McGoohan, Jane Seymour; **D:** Lawrence Gordon Clark. **VHS, Beta** $29.95 *STE, NWV* 𝒜½

James Dean Dean's friend Bast wrote this behind-the-scenes look at the short life of the enigmatic movie star. Made for television. **AKA:** The Legend.
1976 99m/C Stephen McHattie, Michael Brandon, Candy Clark, Amy Irving, Brooke Adams, Dane Clark, Jayne Meadows, Meg Foster; **D:** Robert Butler; **W/D:** William Bast. **VHS, Beta** $19.95 *STE, NWV, SIM* 𝒜𝒜

James Dean Production reflects an exhaustive search through archival film, videotape and photographs, and includes many exclusive interviews with friends of the late actor.
1985 120m/C James Dean; **D:** Claudio Masenza. **VHS, Beta** $69.95 *KRT* 𝒜𝒜

James Dean Story An intimate portrait of James Dean presented by Robert Altman. The program includes never-before-seen outtakes from "East of Eden" and rare footage from the Hollywood premiere of "Giant" and the infamous Highway Public Safety message Dean made for television.
1957 80m/B James Dean; **D:** George W. George. **VHS, Beta, LV** $14.95 *PAV, FCT, PMS* 𝒜𝒜

James Dean: The First American Teenager A look at the life and legend of the charismatic filmstar, with scenes from his films and comments from those who knew him best.
1976 (PG) 83m/C James Dean, Elizabeth Taylor, Sammy Davis Jr., Rock Hudson, Sal Mineo, Natalie Wood, Julie Harris, Jack Larson, Nicholas Ray. **VHS, Beta** $14.98 *VID* 𝒜𝒜

The James Dean 35th Anniversary Collection A must for James Dean fans. This special five-tape collection contains Dean's movies "East of Eden," "Rebel Without a Cause," and "Giant," plus the documentary "Forever James Dean."
19?? ?m/C **VHS, LV** *WAR* 𝒜𝒜

James Joyce: A Portrait of the Artist as a Young Man A moving, lyrical adaptation of the author's autobiography, told through the character of Stephen Dedalus. Joyce's characterizations, words, and scenes are beautifully translated to the medium of film. Excellent casting.
1977 93m/C John Gielgud, T.P. McKenna, Bosco Hogan. **VHS** $29.95 *MFV* 𝒜𝒜

James Joyce's Women Adapted from her one-woman stage show as well as produced by Flanagan, this acclaimed film features enacted portraits of three real-life Joyce associates, including his wife (Nora Barnacle) and three of his famous characters.
1985 (R) 91m/C Fionnula Flanagan, Timothy E. O'Grady, Chris O'Neill; **D:** Michael Pearce. **VHS, Beta** $69.95 *MCA* 𝒜𝒜𝒜

Jane & the Lost City A British farce based on the age-old, barely dressed comic-strip character, Jane, as she stumbles on ancient cities, treasures, villains, and blond/blue-eyed heroes. Low-budget camp fun.

1987 (PG) 94m/C *GB* Kristen Hughes, Maud Adams, Sam Jones; **D:** Terry Marcel. **VHS, Beta** $14.95 *NWV, STE* 𝒜𝒜½

Jane Austen in Manhattan Two rival producers endeavor to stage a long-lost play by Jane Austen. Hodiak is the real-life daughter of Baxter.
1980 108m/C Anne Baxter, Robert Powell, Michael Wager, Sean Young, Kurt Johnson, Katrina Hodiak; **D:** James Ivory. **VHS, Beta** $59.98 *NLC* 𝒜½

Jane Doe Valentine plays a young amnesia victim who is linked to a series of brutal slayings. Quite suspenseful for a television movie.
1983 100m/C Karen Valentine, William Devane, Eva Marie Saint, Stephen E. Miller, Jackson Davies; **D:** Ivan Nagy. **VHS, Beta** $39.95 *LIV* 𝒜𝒜½

Jane Eyre Stiff, early version of Charlotte Bronte's classic gothic romance. English orphan grows up to become the governess of a mysterious manor. Notable as the first talkie version. Remade several times.
1934 67m/B Virginia Bruce, Colin Clive, Beryl Mercer, Jameson Thomas, Aileen Pringle, David Torrence; **D:** Christy Cabanne. **VHS** $16.95 *SNC* 𝒜𝒜

Jane Eyre Excellent adaptation of the Charlotte Bronte novel about the plain governess with the noble heart and her love for the mysterious and tragic Mr. Rochester. Fontaine has the proper backbone and yearning in the title role but to accommodate Welles' emerging popularity the role of Rochester was enlarged. Excellent bleak romantic-Gothic look. Taylor, in her third film role, is seen briefly in the early orphanage scenes.
1944 97m/B Joan Fontaine, Orson Welles, Margaret O'Brien, Peggy Ann Garner, John Sutton, Sara Allgood, Henry Daniell, Agnes Moorehead, Aubrey Mather, Edith Barrett, Barbara Everest, Hillary Brooke, Elizabeth Taylor; **W/D:** Robert Stevenson; **W:** John Houseman, Aldous Huxley; **M:** Bernard Herrmann. **VHS** $19.99 *FXV* 𝒜𝒜𝒜

Jane Eyre A made-for-British-television mini-series based on the famed Charlotte Bronte novel about the maturation of a homeless English waif, her love for the tormented Rochester, and her quest for permanent peace.
1983 239m/C *GB* Timothy Dalton, Zelah Clarke; **D:** Julian Aymes. **VHS, Beta, LV** $29.98 *FOX, SIG, TVC* 𝒜𝒜𝒜

Janis: A Film The famous biographical film about Janis Joplin, from her Texas origins to Woodstock and superstardom, featuring performances with Big Brother and the Holding Company and rare interviews.
1974 (R) 79m/C **D:** Howard Alk. **VHS, Beta** $19.95 *MVD, MCA, FCT* 𝒜𝒜½

The January Man An unorthodox cop, previously exiled by a corrupt local government to the fire department, is brought back to the force in New York City to track down a serial killer. Written by the "Moonstruck" guy, John Patrick Shanley, who apparently peaked with the earlier movie.
1989 (R) 97m/C Kevin Kline, Susan Sarandon, Mary Elizabeth Mastrantonio, Harvey Keitel, Rod Steiger, Alan Rickman, Danny Aiello; **D:** Pat O'Connor; **W:** John Patrick Shanley, Pat O'Connor. **VHS, Beta, LV** $19.98 *FXV* 𝒜𝒜

Japanese Connection Warring crime chiefs fight furiously with deadly kung-fu action until end of movie.
1982 96m/C Li Chao, Yang Wei, Wu Ming-Tsai. **VHS, Beta** $59.95 *GEM* 𝒜

The Jar A recluse discovers a disgusting creature in a jar. He keeps it, only to discover that it is out to kill him.
1984 90m/C Gary Wallace, Karen Sjoberg; **D:** Bruce Toscano. **VHS, Beta** NO 𝒜

Jason and the Argonauts Jason, son of King of Thessaly, sails on the Argo to the land of Colchis, where the Golden Fleece is guarded by a seven-headed hydra. Superb special effects and multitudes of mythological creatures; fun for the whole family.
1963 (G) 104m/C *GB* Todd Armstrong, Nancy Kovack, Gary Raymond, Laurence Naismith, Nigel Green, Michael Gwynn; **D:** Don Chaffey; **W:** Jan Read, Beverly Cross. **VHS, Beta, LV, 8mm** $14.95 *COL, MLB* 𝒜𝒜𝒜

Java Head Young Chinese wife commits suicide so her husband can marry an English girl. Set in mid-1800s England. Based on the novel by Joseph Hergesheimer.
1935 70m/B *GB* Anna May Wong, Elizabeth Allan, John Loder, Edmund Gwenn, Ralph Richardson, George Curzan; **D:** J. Walter Ruben. **VHS, Beta, 8mm** *VYY* 𝒜𝒜𝒜

Jaws Early directorial effort by Spielberg from the Peter Benchley potboiler. A tight, very scary, and sometimes hilarious film about the struggle to kill a giant great white shark that is terrorizing an eastern beach community's waters. The characterizations by Dreyfuss, Scheider, and Shaw are much more endurable than the shock effects. Memorable score by John Williams. Sequelled by "Jaws 2" in 1978, "Jaws 3" 1983, and "Jaws the Revenge" in 1987. Look for Benchley as a TV reporter.
1975 (PG) 124m/C Roy Scheider, Robert Shaw, Richard Dreyfuss, Lorraine Gary, Murray Hamilton, Carl Gottlieb; **Cameos:** Peter Benchley; **D:** Steven Spielberg; **W:** Peter Benchley; **M:** John Williams. Academy Awards '75: Best Film Editing, Best Sound, Best Original Score; Nominations: Best Picture; People's Choice Awards '76: Best Film. **VHS, Beta, LV** $19.95 *MCA* 𝒜𝒜𝒜½

Jaws 2 Unsatisfactory sequel to "Jaws." It's been four years since the man-eating shark feasted on the resort town of Amity; suddenly a second shark stalks the waters and the terror returns. Scheider—who must by now wonder at his tendency to attract large aquatic carnivores with lunch on their minds—battles without his compatriots from the original. And we haven't seen the last of the mechanical dorsal fin yet; two more sequels follow.
1978 (PG) 116m/C Roy Scheider, Lorraine Gary, Murray Hamilton; **D:** Jeannot Szwarc; **M:** John Williams. **VHS, Beta, LV** $19.95 *MCA* 𝒜𝒜½

Jaws 3 Same monster, new setting: in a Sea World-type amusement park, a great white shark escapes from its tank and proceeds to cause terror and chaos. Little connection to the previous "Jaws" sagas. Followed by one more sequel, "Jaws: The Revenge." **AKA:** Jaws 3-D.
1983 (PG) 98m/C Dennis Quaid, Bess Armstrong, Louis Gossett Jr., Simon MacCorkindale, Lea Thompson; **D:** Joe Alves; **M:** John Williams. **VHS, Beta, LV** $19.95 *MCA* 𝒜𝒜

Jaws of Death "Jaws"-like saga of shark terror. Jaeckel illogically strikes out to protect his "friends," the sharks. **AKA:** Mako: The Jaws of Death.
1976 91m/C Richard Jaeckel, Harold Sakata, Jennifer Bishop, John Chandler, Buffy Dee; **D:** William Grefe. **VHS, Beta** *PGN* 𝒜𝒜

Jaws of Justice A Canadian Mountie and his trusty German shepherd track down outlaws in the Canadian Northwest.
1933 55m/B Kazan the Dog, Richard Terry, Lafe McKee. **VHS, Beta, 8mm** $24.95 *VYY* 𝒜½

J

Jaws of Satan Weaver is terrorized by a slimy snake who is, in actuality, the Devil. Not released for 2 years after it was filmed, and generally considered a bomb of the first caliber. Unfortunate work for usually worthwhile Weaver. *AKA:* King Cobra.
1981 (R) 92m/C Fritz Weaver, Gretchen Corbett, Jon Korkes, Norman Lloyd; *D:* Bob Claver. **VHS** *NO Woof!*

Jaws of the Dragon The story of two rival gangs in the Far East.
1976 (R) 96m/C James Nam, Johnny Taylor, Kenny Nam. **VHS, Beta** $24.95 *GEM* ✗

Jaws: The Revenge The third sequel, in which Mrs. Brody is pursued the world over by a seemingly personally motivated Great White Shark. Includes footage not seen in the theatrical release. Each sequel in this series is progressively inferior to the original.
1987 (PG-13) 87m/C Lorraine Gary, Lance Guest, Karen Young, Mario Van Peebles, Michael Caine, Judith Barsi; *D:* Joseph Sargent. **VHS, Beta, LV** $19.95 *MCA* ✗

The Jayhawkers Chandler and Parker battle for power and women in pre-Civil War Kansas.
1959 100m/C Jeff Chandler, Fess Parker, Nicole Maurey, Henry Silva, Herbert Rudley, Frank DeKova, Don Megowan, Leo Gordon; *D:* Melvin Frank. **VHS** $14.95 *PAR, FCT* ✗✗

The Jayne Mansfield Story Television movie recounting the blond bombshell's career from her first career exposure, through her marriage to a bodybuilder, to the famous car crash that beheaded her. *AKA:* Jayne Mansfield: A Symbol of the '50s.
1980 97m/C Loni Anderson, Arnold Schwarzenegger, Raymond Buktencia, Kathleen Lloyd, G.D. Spradlin, Dave Shelley; *D:* Dick Lowry. **VHS, Beta** $39.95 *LIV* ✗

Jazz Singer A Jewish cantor's son breaks with his family to become a singer of popular music. Of historical importance as the first successful part-talkie, with the classic line "You ain't heard nothing yet!" Remade several times. ♫Toot, Toot, Tootsie Goodbye; Blue Skies; My Gal Sal; Waiting for the Robert E. Lee; Dirty Hands, Dirty Face; Mother, I Still Have You; Kol Nidre; Yahrzeit; My Mammy.
1927 89m/B Al Jolson, May McAvoy, Warner Oland, William Demarest, Eugenie Besserer, Myrna Loy; *D:* Alan Crosland. **VHS, Beta, LV** $29.98 *FOX, FCT, MLB* ✗✗½

Jazz Singer Flat and uninteresting (if not unintentionally funny) remake of the 1927 classic about a Jewish boy who rebels against his father and family tradition to become a popular entertainer. Stick with the original, this is little more than a vehicle for Diamond to sing. ♫America; You Baby Baby; Jerusalem; Love on the Rocks; Summer Love; On the Robert E. Lee; Louise; Songs of Life; Hello Again; Amazed and Confused.
1980 (PG) 115m/C Neil Diamond, Laurence Olivier, Lucie Arnaz, Catlin Adams, Franklin Ajaye; *D:* Richard Fleischer. **VHS, Beta, LV, 8mm** $14.95 *PAR Woof!*

Jazzman A comedy set in the late 1920s with a young musician forming a jazz band with two street musicians and a saxophonist who played in the czar's marching band. Their music is condemned as a product of bourgeois society but that doesn't stop them. In Russian with English subtitles.
1984 80m/C *RU* Igor Sklyar, Alexander Chorny; *D:* Karen Chakhnazarov. **VHS** $59.95 *KIV, FCT* ✗✗✗

J.D.'s Revenge Attorney in training Glynn Turman is possessed by the spirit of a gangster who was murdered on Bourbon Street in the early 1940s and grisly blaxploitation results. Ever so slightly better than others of the genre. Shot in New Orleans, with a soundtrack by a then-unknown Prince.
1976 (R) 95m/C Louis Gossett Jr., Glynn Turman; *D:* Arthur Marks; *M:* Prince. **VHS** $59.95 *ORI, FCT* ✗✗½

Je Tu Il Elle A hyperactive young woman desperately seeking the answers to life gradually gains experience and maturity as she travels around France. The directorial debut of Ackerman. In French with English subtitles. *AKA:* I You She He.
1974 90m/B Niels Arestrup, Claire Wauthion, Chantal Akerman; *D:* Chantal Akerman. **VHS** $29.95 *WAC, FCT, TAM* ✗✗½

Jealousy Three dramatic episodes dealing with jealousy. Made for TV.
1984 95m/C Angie Dickinson, Paul Michael Glaser, David Carradine, Bo Svenson; *D:* Jeffrey Bloom. **VHS, Beta** $79.95 *IMP* ✗✗½

Jean de Florette The first of two films (with "Manon of the Spring") based on Marcel Pagnol's novel. A single spring in drought-ridden Provence, France is blocked by two scheming countrymen (Montand and Auteuil). They await the imminent failure of the farm nearby, inherited by a city-born hunchback, whose chances for survival fade without water for his crops. A devastating story with a heartrending performance by Depardieu as the hunchback. Lauded and awarded; in French with English subtitles.
1987 (PG) 122m/C *FR* Gerard Depardieu, Yves Montand, Daniel Auteuil, Elisabeth Depardieu, Ernestine Mazurowna; *D:* Claude Berri. **VHS, Beta, LV** $19.98 *ORI, IME, FCT* ✗✗✗½

Jeeves & Wooster: Jeeves' Arrival Based on P.G. Wodehouse's spoofs of upper-crust British life in the 1920s. The bungling Bertie Wooster, a young man who just can't stay out of trouble, is taken in hand by the unflappable "gentleman's gentleman," Jeeves. Wonderful period detail and fine acting add up to a charming and funny hour. Additional episodes available.
1991 60m/C *GB* Hugh Laurie, Stephen Fry. **VHS** $9.95 *PAV, MOV, TVC* ✗✗✗½

Jekyll & Hyde...Together Again New Wave comic version of the classic story. This time, a serious young surgeon turns into a drug-crazed punk rocker after sniffing a mysterious powder. Mad scientist Blankfield fires and misfires, occasionally eliciting a snort.
1982 (R) 87m/C Mark Blankfield, Bess Armstrong, Krista Errickson, Tim Thomerson; *D:* Jerry Belson. **VHS, Beta** $59.95 *PAR* ✗✗

Jennifer Elaboration of that old "Carrie" theme: a teen-age girl outcast who likes snakes wreaks havoc on her catty classmates in this supernatural thriller. *AKA:* Jennifer (The Snake Goddess).
1978 (PG) 90m/C Lisa Pelikan, Bert Convy, Nina Foch, John Gavin, Wesley Eure; *D:* Brice Mack. **VHS, Beta** $69.98 *LIV, VES* ✗½

Jennifer 8 Mix of familiar genres results in a film about a burned-out cop moving to the suburbs where he finds the eighth victim of a serial killer and falls in love with the chief witness. Garcia is John Berlin, the cop who discovers the hand of the blind female victim, which leads him to her school and Helena Robertson (Thurman), another blind woman who may have the information he needs. Dark and mysterious atmosphere is dramatic, but plot lacks logic and sense of thrill.
1992 (R) 127m/C Andy Garcia, Uma Thurman, Lance Henriksen, Kathy Baker, Graham Beckel, Kevin Conway, John Malkovich; *W/D:* Bruce Robinson. **VHS, Beta, LV** $95.95 *PAR, BTV* ✗✗

Jenny A loveless marriage of convenience between a draft-dodger and a film buff gets turned around as they fall in love despite themselves.
1970 (PG) 90m/C Marlo Thomas, Alan Alda, Marian Hailey, Elizabeth Wilson, Vincent Gardenia, Charlotte Rae; *D:* Edgar J. Scherick. **VHS, Beta** $59.98 *FOX* ✗

Jenny Lamour A dark mystery thriller about a singer accused of murdering a man he thought was stealing his woman. Acclaimed genre piece, dubbed into English. *AKA:* Quai des Orfevres.
1947 95m/B *FR* Louis Jouvet, Suzy Delair, Bernard Blier, Simone Renant; *D:* Henri-Georges Clouzot. **VHS, Beta** $24.95 *NOS, FCT* ✗✗

Jenny's War An unbelievable World War II adventure story of an American teacher (Cannon) who outwits the Gestapo and infiltrates a Nazi POW camp in search of her missing soldier son. Actually based on a true story. From the book by Jack Stoneley. Made for television.
1985 (PG) 192m/C Dyan Cannon, Elke Sommer, Robert Hardy, Nigel Hawthorne, Christopher Cazenove, Patrick Ryecart, Hartmut Becker; *W/D:* Steven Gethers. **VHS** $59.95 *COL* ✗✗½

Jeremiah Johnson The story of a man who turns his back on civilization, circa 1850, and learns a new code of survival in a brutal land of isolated mountains and hostile Indians. In the process, he becomes part of the mountains and their wildlife. A notable and picturesque film.
1972 (PG) 107m/C Robert Redford, Will Geer; *D:* Sydney Pollack. **VHS, Beta, LV** $19.98 *WAR, FCT* ✗✗✗

Jericho Adventures in Africa occur as a court-martialed captain pursues a murderous deserter. *AKA:* Dark Sands.
1938 77m/B *GB* Paul Robeson, Henry Wilcoxon, Wallace Ford; *D:* Thornton Freeland. **VHS, Beta** $44.95 *NOS, HHT, DVT* ✗✗

The Jericho Mile A made-for-television drama about a track-obsessed convicted murderer who is given a chance at the Olympics.
1979 97m/C Peter Strauss, Roger E. Mosley, Brian Dennehy; *D:* Michael Mann. **VHS, Beta** $9.98 *NLC, SUE* ✗✗

The Jerk A jerk tells his rags-to-riches-to-rags story in comedic flashbacks, from "I was born a poor Black child," through his entrepreneurial success in his invention of the "Optigrab," to his inevitable decline. Only film in history with a dog named "Shithead." Martin's first starring role, back in his wild and crazy days; his ridiculous misadventures pay tribute to Jerry Lewis movies of the late sixties. Followed by a TV version released in 1984 as "The Jerk Too," with Mark Blankfield as the Jerk.
1979 (R) 94m/C Steve Martin, Bernadette Peters, Catlin Adams, Bill Macy, Jackie Mason; *D:* Carl Reiner. **VHS, Beta, LV** $14.95 *MCA* ✗✗½

Jesse A heroic nurse ministers to remote Death Valley residents, and state bureaucats hound her for practicing medicine without a license. Although based on a true case and well-acted, this made-for-TV drama just lacks import and impact.
1988 (PG) 94m/C Lee Remick, Scott Wilson, Leon Rippy, Priscilla Lopez, Albert Salmi; *D:* Glenn Jordan. **VHS** $79.98 *REP* ✗✗

Jesse James A Hollywood biography of the famed outlaw. One of director King's best efforts.
1939 105m/C Henry Fonda, Tyrone Power, Randolph Scott, Henry Hull, Jane Darwell, Brian Donlevy; *D:* Henry King. **VHS, Beta, LV** $19.98 *FOX* ✓✓✓

Jesse James at Bay Rodgers is the do-good Jesse who's warring against some crooked railroad execs. Interesting perspective.
1941 54m/B Roy Rogers, George "Gabby" Hayes, Sally Payne; *D:* Joseph Kane. **VHS, Beta, 3/4U, Special order formats** $19.95 *NOS, MRV, VCN* ✓✓

Jesse James Meets Frankenstein's Daughter The gunslinger and Frankenstein's granddaughter, Maria, meet up in the Old West in this wacky combination of western and horror genres.
1965 95m/C John Lupton, Cal Bolder, Narda Onyx, Steve Geray, Estelita, Jim Davis, William Fawcett, Nestor Paiva; *D:* William Beaudine. **VHS, Beta** $19.98 *NOS, SUE* ✓½

Jesse James Rides Again Originally a serial, this feature depicts the further adventures of the West's most notorious outlaw.
1947 181m/B Clayton Moore, Linda Stirling, Roy Barcroft, Tristram Coffin; *D:* Fred Brannon, Thomas Carr. **VHS** $29.98 *REP, MLB* ✓✓

Jesse James Under the Black Flag An interesting western/pseudo biography/flashback in which Coates and James Jr. (the outlaw's son) play themselves. As Coates attempts to gather information from Jesse's decendants, a stranger appears and falls for Jesse's granddaughter, who shuns him. He proceeds to read the Coates biography and the flashback begins, in the Jesse was really a good guy forced off the straight and narrow vein.
1921 59m/B Jesse James Jr., Franklin Coates, Diana Reed, Marguerite Hungerford; *D:* Franklin Coates. **VHS, Beta** $24.95 *GPV, FCT* ✓✓½

The Jesse Owens Story The moving story of the four-time Olympic Gold medal winner's triumphs and misfortunes. A made-for-television movie.
1984 174m/C Dorian Harewood, Debbi Morgan, Georg Stanford Brown, LeVar Burton, George Kennedy, Tom Bosley, Ben Vereen; *D:* Richard Irving. **VHS, Beta** $69.95 *PAR, KUI, FCT* ✓✓

Jessie's Girls In retaliation for the murder of her husband, an angry young woman frees three female prisoners, and they embark on a bloody course of revenge. Together, they track down the killers, and one by one, they fight to even the score. *AKA:* Wanted Women.
1975 (R) 86m/C Sondra Currie, Regina Carrol, Jennifer Bishop; *D:* Al Adamson. **VHS, Beta** $39.95 *MON* ✓½

Jesus A supposedly authenticated life of Christ, using real artifacts.
1979 (G) 118m/C Brian Deacon; *D:* Peter Sykes, John Kirsh. **VHS, Beta** *VBL* ✓✓

Jesus Christ, Superstar A rock opera that portrays, in music, the last seven days in the earthly life of Christ, as reenacted by young tourists in Israel. Outstanding musical score was the key to the success of the film. Based on the stage play by Tim Rice and Andrew Lloyd Weber, film is sometimes stirring while exhibiting the usual heavy-handed Jewison approach. ♫Jesus Christ, Superstar; I Don't Know How To Love Him; What's The Buzz?; Herod's Song; Heaven On Their Minds; Strange Thing, Mystifying; Then We Are Decided; Everything's Alright; This Jesus Must Die; Simon Zealotes; Poor

Jerusalem; Pilate's Dream; The Temple; Dammed For All Time; Could We Start Again, Please?; John 1941; Crucifixion; Judas's Death; The Arrest; Peter's Denial; Pilate and Christ; Blood Money; The Last Supper; Gethsemane; Trial Before Pilate; Hosanna.
1973 (G) 108m/C Ted Neeley, Carl Anderson, Yvonne Elliman, Josh Mostel; *D:* Norman Jewison. **VHS, Beta, LV** $19.98 *MCA* ✓✓✓

Jesus of Montreal A vagrant young actor (stage-trained Canadian star Bluteau) is hired by a Montreal priest to produce a fresh interpretation of an Easter passion play. Taking the good book at its word, he produces a contemporized literal telling that captivates audiences, inflames the men of the cloth, and eventually wins the players' faith. Quebecois director Arcand (keep an eye out for him as the judge) tells a compelling, acerbically satirical and haunting story that never forces its Biblical parallels. In French with English subtitles. *AKA:* Jesus de Montreal.
1989 (R) 119m/C *FR CA* Gilles Pelletier, Lothaire Bluteau, Catherine Wilkening, Robert Lepage, Johanne-Marie Tremblay, Remy Girard, Marie-Christine Barrault; *W/D:* Denys Arcand. Academy Awards '89 Nominations: Best Foreign Language Film; Genie Awards '90: Best Actor (Girard), Best Director (Arcand), Best Film, Best Supporting Actor (Girard). **VHS, LV** $79.95 *ORI, FCT, TAM* ✓✓✓½

Jesus of Nazareth A dramatic recreation of the life of Christ from the Annunciation through the Ascension. The film titles are taken from descriptive biblical passages.
1928 85m/B Philip Van Loan, Anna Lehr, Charles McCaffrey. **VHS, Beta, 8mm** $29.95 *VYY, FCT* ✓✓½

Jesus of Nazareth An all-star cast portrays the life of Christ. A made-for-television mini-series.
1977 371m/C Robert Powell, Anne Bancroft, Ernest Borgnine, Claudia Cardinale, James Mason, Laurence Olivier, Anthony Quinn; *D:* Franco Zeffirelli. **VHS, Beta** $169.95 *CCB, FOX, ECU* ✓✓½

The Jesus Trip Hunted motorcyclists take a young nun hostage in the desert.
1971 86m/C Robert Porter, Tippy Walker; *D:* Russ Mayberry. **VHS, Beta** $57.95 *UNI* ✓½

Jet Attack/Paratroop Command A double feature of "B" war movies. "Jet Attack" is a bad movie about a scientist whose plane gets shot down over Korea. He amazingly survives, only to be taken to a hospital and brainwashed. Enter a squad of soldiers leading a rescue mission who meet up with a beautiful Russian aide and some life-saving guerillas. This movie is so bad it's funny. In "Paratroop Command," a paratrooper accidentally kills a member of his squadron. In order to regain his dignity, the paratrooper sets off land mines in North Africa to prove himself.
1958 139m/B John Agar, Audrey Totter, Gregory Walcott, James Dobson, Richard Bakalayan, Jack Hogan, Jimmy Murphy, Ken Lynch; *D:* Edward L. Cahn, William Witney. **VHS** $14.95 *COL* ✓✓

Jet Benny Show A Buck Rogers/Star Wars-style spoof of Jack Benny's classic TV show.
1986 76m/C Steve Norman, Kevin Dees, Polly MacIntyre, Ted Luedemann; *D:* Roger Evans. **VHS, Beta** $69.95 *NLC* ✓✓

Jet Over the Atlantic Dangerous situation arises as a bomb is discovered aboard a plane en route from Spain to New York. "Airport" rip-off.

1959 92m/B Guy Madison, George Raft, Virginia Mayo, Brett Halsey; *D:* Byron Haskin. **VHS, Beta** *NO* ✓½

Jet Pilot An American Air Force colonel (Wayne) in charge of an Alaskan Air Force base falls in love with a defecting Russian jet pilot (Leigh). They marry, but Wayne suspects Leigh is a spy planted to find out top U.S. secrets. He pretends to defect with her back to Russia to see what he can find out, but they again flee. Ludicrous plot is saved only by spectacular flying scenes, some performed by Chuck Yeager. Although this was filmed in 1950, it took seven more years to be released because producer Hughes couldn't keep his hands off it.
1957 112m/B John Wayne, Janet Leigh, Jay C. Flippen, Paul Fix, Richard Rober, Roland Winters, Hans Conried, Ivan Triesault; *D:* Josef von Sternberg. **VHS, LV** $19.98 *MCA* ✓✓

A Jetson Christmas Carol Even Mr. Spacely gets in the spirit!
1989 30m/C *V:* George O'Hanlon, Penny Singleton, Daws Butler, Mel Blanc. **VHS, Beta, LV** $9.95 *TTC, IME, WTA* ✓✓

The Jetsons Meet the Flintstones Trouble arises when young Elroy Jetson's time machine takes him and his family back to the 25th century B.C. There they meet the Flintstones and the Rubbles, who accidentally get transported into the future. Will either family ever get back home?
1988 100m/C *V:* Mel Blanc, Daws Butler, Jean VanDerPyl, George O'Hanlon, Penny Singleton. **VHS, Beta, LV** $19.95 *TTC, IME, WTA* ✓✓

The Jetsons: Movie The famous outer space family of '60s TV is given a new silver-screened life. George gets a promotion that puts him in charge of an asteroid populated by furry creatures. Ecological concerns are expressed; while this is rare for a cartoon, the story is overall typical.
1990 (G) 82m/C *D:* William Hanna, Joseph Barbera; *V:* George O'Hanlon, Mel Blanc, Penny Singleton, Tiffany, Patric Zimmerman, Don Messick, Jean VanDerPyl, Ronnie Schell, Patti Deutsch, Dana Hill, Russi Taylor, Paul Kreppel, Rick Dees. **VHS, Beta, LV** $14.98 *MCA, APD, WTA* ✓✓

The Jewel in the Crown Epic saga of the last years of British rule in India from 1942-1947 concentrating on an Indian man and the Englishwoman that he loves. Originally shown on British television, it aired in the United States on the PBS series "Masterpiece Theatre." An excellent mini-series that was shown in fourteen segments. Available on five video cassettes.
1984 750m/C *GB* Charles Dance, Susan Wooldridge, Art Malik, Tim Pigott-Smith, Geraldine James, Peggy Ashcroft, Judy Parfitt; *D:* Christopher Morahan, Jim O'Brien. **VHS, Beta** $199.95 *MTI* ✓✓

The Jewel of the Nile Sequel to "Romancing the Stone" with the same cast but new director. Romance novelist Joan thought she found her true love in Jack but finds that life doesn't always end happily ever. After they part ways, Jack realizes that she may be in trouble and endeavors to rescue her from the criminal hands of a charming North African president. Of course, he can always check out this "jewel" at the same time. Chemistry is still there, but the rest of the film isn't quite up to the "Stone's" charm.
1985 (PG) 106m/C Michael Douglas, Kathleen Turner, Danny DeVito, Avner Eisenberg, The Flying Karamazov Brothers, Spiros Focas; *D:* Lewis Teague; *M:* Jack Nitzsche. **VHS, Beta, LV** $19.98 *FOX* ✓✓½

The Jeweller's Shop A highly spiritual tale of two married couples in Poland whose children meet and fall in love much later in Canada. Based on a play by Karol Wojtyla—who later became Pope Jean-Paul II. Adapted under strict Vatican supervision.
1990 90m/C Burt Lancaster, Ben Cross, Olivia Hussey. **VHS $29.95** IGP ♫♫

Jezebel Davis is a willful Southern belle who loses fiance Fonda through her selfish and spiteful ways in this pre-Civil War drama. When he becomes ill, she realizes her cruelty and rushes to nurse him back to health. Davis' role won her an Oscar for Best Actress, and certainly provided Scarlett O'Hara with a rival for most memorable female character of all time.
1938 105m/B Bette Davis, George Brent, Henry Fonda, Margaret Lindsay, Fay Bainter, Donald Crisp, Spring Byington, Eddie Anderson; **D:** William Wyler. Academy Awards '38: Best Actress (Davis), Best Supporting Actress (Bainter); Nominations: Best Cinematography, Best Picture, Best Score. **VHS, Beta, LV $19.98** MGM, FCT, BTV ♫♫♫½

Jezebel's Kiss A sizzling young beauty returns to the town where she grew up and proceeds to destroy any man she pleases.
1990 (R) 96m/C Meg Foster, Malcolm McDowell, Meredith Baxter Birney, Everett McGill, Katherine Barrese; **W/D:** Harvey Keith. **VHS, LV $79.95** COL ♫♫

JFK Costner is former New Orleans district attorney Jim Garrison in this highly controversial examination of President John F. Kennedy's 1963 assassination. Hotly debated because of Stone's theory of a vast conspiracy behind the assassination, "JFK" sparked new calls for Congress to open long-sealed government records from the 1977 House Select Committee on Assassinations investigation. Hailed as one of the year's best films; features outstanding performances from all-star principal and supporting casts, stunning cinematography, and excellent editing. Even Garrison himself shows up as Chief Justice Earl Warren, chairman of the Warren Commission. Considered by many to be a true cinematic masterpiece, Stone's revisionist history still needs to be taken with a grain of salt. Also available in an extended version titled "JFK: The Director's Cut" with 17 minutes of additional footage for $24.98.
1991 (R) 189m/C Kevin Costner, Sissy Spacek, Kevin Bacon, Tommy Lee Jones, Laurie Metcalf, Gary Oldman, Michael Rooker, Jay O. Sanders, Beata Pozniak, Joe Pesci, Donald Sutherland, John Candy, Jack Lemmon, Walter Matthau, Ed Asner, Vincent D'Onofrio, Sally Kirkland, Brian Doyle Murray, Wayne Knight, Tony Plana, Tomas Milian, Sean Stone; **Cameos:** Lolita Davidovich, Frank Whaley, Jim Garrison; **D:** Oliver Stone; **W:** Oliver Stone, Zachary Sklar; **M:** John Williams. Academy Awards '91: Best Cinematography, Best Film Editing; Nominations: Best Adapted Screenplay, Best Director (Stone), Best Picture, Best Sound, Best Supporting Actor (Jones), Best Original Score; Golden Globe Awards '92: Best Director (Stone). **VHS, Beta, LV $24.98** WAR ♫♫♫½

The JFK Conspiracy Did Lee Harvey Oswald act alone? Opinions of government officials, eyewitnesses, and director Oliver Stone, in addition to testimony, photographs, documents, and other evidence, address the perennial American question. Includes footage from the House Select Committee on Assassination. Made for television.
1991 98m/C VHS, LV $24.98 BMG ♫♫♫½

JFK Remembered A look at John F. Kennedy's 1000-day Presidential term, released on the 25th anniversary of his assassination, features interviews, rare film clips, and famous news footage.
1988 54m/C VHS, Beta $29.98 LIV, VES ♫♫♫½

Jigsaw Crime drama with a smattering of cameos by Hollywood favorites. A newspaper reporter is murdered. The dead man's friend, an assistant district attorney, seeks the punks responsible. They send in a seductress to keep the D.A. busy, but she too is murdered. Action and tension in a well-made flick. Based on a story by John Roeburt.
AKA: Gun Moll.
1949 70m/B Franchot Tone, Jean Wallace, Myron McCormick, Marc Lawrence, Winifred Lenihan, Betty Harper, Robert Gist; **Cameos:** Marlene Dietrich, Henry Fonda, Burgess Meredith, John Garfield; **D:** Fletcher Markle. **VHS $16.95** SNC, DVT ♫♫♫

Jigsaw Missing persons lawman is lured into a cover-up more complex than he had bargained for. A tense drama originated as the pilot for a series. **AKA:** Man on the Move.
1971 100m/C James Wainwright, Vera Miles, Richard Kiley, Andrew Duggan, Edmond O'Brien; **D:** William A. Graham. **VHS** LIV ♫♫

Jigsaw A developer is found dead the day after his wedding. His widow and a cop team up to find out who, what, where, and why. Lukewarm Australian mystery export.
1990 85m/C Rebecca Gibney, Dominic Sweeny, Michael Coard. **VHS $59.95** ATL ♫♫

The Jigsaw Man A British-Russian double agent is sent back to England to retrieve a list of Soviet agents which he hid there many years before.
1984 (PG) 90m/C GB Michael Caine, Laurence Olivier, Susan George, Robert Powell, Charles Gray, David Patrick Kelly, Michael Medwin; **D:** Terence Young. **VHS, Beta, LV $79.99** HBO ♫♫

Jigsaw Murders A macho detective is out to solve a grisly murder, but the only available leads are a jigsaw puzzle and the victim's severed, tattooed lower limb.
1989 98m/C Chad Everett, Michelle Johnson, Yaphet Kotto; **D:** Jag Mundhra. **VHS, Beta $79.95** MGM ♫♫

Jim Thorpe: All American The life story of Thorpe, a Native American athlete who gained international recognition for his excellence in many different sports. A must for sports fans. **AKA:** Man of Bronze.
1951 105m/B Burt Lancaster, Phyllis Thaxter, Charles Bickford, Steve Cochran, Dick Wesson; **D:** Michael Curtiz. **VHS, Beta** ISS, WAR ♫♫½

Jimmy the Kid A young boy becomes the unlikely target for an improbable gang of would-be crooks on a crazy, "fool-proof" crime caper. Kiddie comic caper.
1982 (PG) 95m/C Gary Coleman, Cleavon Little, Fay Hauser, Ruth Gordon, Dee Wallace Stone, Paul LeMat, Don Adams; **D:** Gary Nelson. **VHS, Beta $59.99** HBO ♫♫

Jinxed Las Vegas nightclub singer tries to convince a gullible blackjack dealer to murder her crooked boyfriend, but the plan backfires when the gangster electrocutes himself while taking a shower. Offscreen cast disputes were probably much more interesting than onscreen comedy.
1982 (R) 104m/C Bette Midler, Ken Wahl, Rip Torn; **D:** Don Siegel. **VHS, Beta $19.98** MGM ♫♫

The Jitters The murdered dead turn into zombies and seek revenge on their killers.
1988 80m/C Sal Viviano, Marilyn Tokuda, James Hong, Frank Dietz; **D:** John Fasano. **VHS, Beta $79.95** PSM ♫

Jive Junction A group of patriotic teenagers convert a barn into a canteen for servicemen and name it "Jive Junction."
1943 62m/B Dickie Moore, Tina Thayer, Gerra Young, Johnny Michaels, Jack Wagner, Jane Wiley, Beverly Boyd, William Halligan; **D:** Edgar G. Ulmer. **VHS, Beta $24.95** NOS, GVV ♫♫

Jive Turkey Cool dude busts heads.
1976 ?m/C Paul Harris, Frank DeKova, Serena; **D:** Bill Brame. **VHS** MOV ♫½

Jo Jo Dancer, Your Life is Calling Pryor directed and starred in this semi-autobiographical price-of-fame story of a comic, hospitalized for a drug-related accident, who must re-evaluate his life. A serious departure from Pryor's slapstick comedies that doesn't quite make it as a drama; Pryor nevertheless deserves credit for the honesty he demonstrates in dealing with his real-life problems. Music by Herbie Hancock.
1986 (R) 97m/C Richard Pryor, Debbie Allen, Art Evans, Fay Hauser, Barbara Williams, Paula Kelly, Wings Hauser, Carmen McRae, Diahnne Abbott, Scoey Mitchell, Billy Eckstine; **D:** Richard Pryor. **VHS, Beta, LV $14.95** COL ♫♫½

Joan of Arc A touching and devout look at the life of Joan of Arc. Perhaps unfortunately, the film is accurately based on the play by Maxwell Anderson, and adds up to too much talk and too little action.
1948 100m/C Ingrid Bergman, Jose Ferrer, John Ireland, Leif Erickson; **D:** Victor Fleming. Academy Awards '48: Best Color Cinematography, Best Costume Design; Nominations: Best Actress (Bergman), Best Art Direction/Set Decoration (Color), Best Film Editing, Best Supporting Actor (Ferrer), Best Original Score; National Board of Review Awards '48: 10 Best Films of the Year. **VHS, Beta, LV $14.98** VID, IGP, HMV ♫♫½

Joan of Paris A French resistance leader dies so that Allied pilots can escape from the Nazis. A well done, but obviously dated propaganda feature.
1942 91m/B Michele Morgan, Paul Henreid, Thomas Mitchell, Laird Cregar, May Robson, Alexander Granach, Alan Ladd; **D:** Robert Stevenson. **VHS, Beta $19.98** TTC ♫♫♫½

Jock Petersen A light-hearted story about a blonde hunk who enrolls in college, cavorting and seducing his way to questionable fame and fortune. **AKA:** Petersen.
1974 (R) 97m/C Jack Thompson, Wendy Hughes; **D:** Tim Burstall. **VHS, Beta $59.98** NLC ♫

Jocks A whiz-kid tennis team competes in a pro meet in Las Vegas, and paints the town red.
1987 (R) 90m/C Christopher Lee, Perry Lang, Richard Roundtree, Scott Strader; **D:** Steve Carver. **VHS, Beta $79.95** COL ♫½

Joe An odd friendship grows between a businessman and a blue-collar worker as they search together for the executive's runaway daughter. Thrust into the midst of the counter-culture, they react with an orgy of violence.
1970 (R) 107m/C Peter Boyle, Susan Sarandon, Dennis Patrick; **D:** John G. Avildsen. **VHS, Beta, LV $14.95** MGM, VES ♫♫½

Joe Kidd A land war breaks out in New Mexico between Mexican natives and American land barons. Eastwood, once again portraying the "mysterious stranger," must decide with whom he should side, all the while falling in love with Garcia. Lackluster direction results in a surprisingly tedious western, in spite of the cast. One of Eastwood's lowest money grossers. The laserdisc edition is letterboxed and features chapter stops, the original trailer and digital sound.

1972 (PG) 88m/C Clint Eastwood, Robert Duvall, John Saxon, Don Stroud, Stella Garcia, James Wainwright, Paul Koslo, Gregory Walcott, Dick Van Patten, Lynn Marta; D: John Sturges. VHS, Beta, LV $14.95 MCA, PIA 𝒵𝒵½

Joe Louis Story The story of Joe Louis' rise to fame as boxing's Heavyweight Champion of the world.
1953 88m/B Coley Wallace, Paul Stewart, Hilda Simms. VHS, Beta $19.95 NOS, DVT, FCT 𝒵𝒵

Joe Panther Family drama about a young Seminole Indian who stakes his claim in the Anglo world by wrestling alligators. Montalban plays a wise old chieftain who helps the youth handle the conflict between Indian and white societies.
1976 (G) 110m/C Brian Keith, Ricardo Montalban, Alan Feinstein, Cliff Osmond, A. Martinez, Robert Hoffman; D: Paul Krasny. VHS WAR 𝒵𝒵𝒵

Joe Piscopo: New Jersey Special A comedic salute to Piscopo's home state, with guest appearances by Eddie Murphy and Danny DeVito.
1987 60m/C Joe Piscopo, Eddie Murphy, Danny DeVito. VHS, Beta $19.98 LIV, VES 𝒵

Joe Versus the Volcano Expressionistic goofball comedy about a dopey guy who, after finding out he has only months to live, contracts with a millionaire to leap into a volcano alive. Imaginative farce with great "Metropolis"-pastiche visuals that eventually fizzle out. Watch for Ryan in not one, but three roles. Written and directed by the "Moonstruck" Oscar winner.
1990 (PG) 106m/C Tom Hanks, Meg Ryan, Lloyd Bridges, Robert Stack, Amanda Plummer, Abe Vigoda, Dan Hedaya, Barry McGovern, Ossie Davis, Ossie Davis; W/D: John Patrick Shanley; M: Georges Delerue. VHS, Beta, LV, 8mm $19.98 WAR 𝒵

Joe's Bed-Stuy Barbershop: We Cut Heads Lee's first film takes place inside a neighborhood landmark, the corner barbershop. Lee displays the social awareness and urban humor that he honed in his later, bigger films.
1983 60m/C Leon Errol, Morris Carnovsky, Elyse Knox, Billy House, Trudy Marshall; D: Spike Lee. VHS, Beta, 3/4U ICA 𝒵𝒵½

Joey Daddy, a former doo-wopper, looks back on his years of musical success as a waste of time. His son takes to the world of rock guitar with blind fervor. Their argument plays against the backdrop of the "Royal Doo-Wopp Show" at New York City's Radio Music Hall. Features multi-generational rock songs.
1985 (PG) 90m/C Neill Barry, James Quinn. VHS, Beta $69.95 VID 𝒵½

John & Julie Two young people get it together despite many obstacles.
1977 82m/C Colin Gibson, Lesley Dudley. VHS, Beta $29.95 FHE 𝒵½

John and the Missus After the discovery of a copper mine threatens to destroy a nearby town, the Canadian government begins a relocation process. However, one man refuses to give up his generations-old home. Canadian Pinsent's directorial debut, adapting his own 1973 novel.
1987 (PG) 98m/C CA Gordon Pinsent, Jackie Burroughs, Randy Follet, Jessica Steen; D: Gordon Pinsent. VHS, Beta $79.98 CGH 𝒵½

John & Yoko: A Love Story Appalling television movie version of the rock legend's life and marriage. With original Beatles tunes.

1985 146m/C Mark McGann, Kim Mayori, Kenneth Price, Peter Capaldi, Richard Morant, Philip Walsh; D: Sandor Stern. VHS, Beta, LV $79.95 SVS, IME 𝒵

John Cleese on How to Irritate People Cleese, a master at causing irritation, demonstrates how to take care of all those annoying people who irritate you, including job interviewers, bank clerks, waiters, and salesmen. Monty Python alumni Palin and Chapman also join Cleese in the "Airline Pilots" sketch about bored pilots deliberately trying to terrify their passengers.
1968 65m/C John Cleese, Michael Palin, Graham Chapman, Connie Booth. VHS $19.95 WST 𝒵

John F. Kennedy A retrospective of JFK's term in office.
1981 104m/C VHS, Beta, LV $29.95 FOX 𝒵

John Wayne Anthology: Star Packer/Lawless Range In addition to two of Wayne's films, this program captures 40 years of the actor's career.
1934 156m/B John Wayne; D: Robert Bradbury. VHS $9.95 SIM 𝒵

Johnnie Gibson F.B.I. Supposedly based on a true story, the adventures of a beautiful, black FBI agent who falls in love with a man she's investigating. AKA: Johnnie Mae Gibson: FBI.
1987 96m/C Howard E. Rollins Jr., Lynn Whitfield, William Allen Young, Richard Lawson; D: Bill Duke. VHS, Beta $29.95 ACA, PTB 𝒵

Johnny Angel Merchant Marine captain unravels mystery of his father's murder aboard a ship. Tense film noir.
1945 79m/B George Raft, Claire Trevor, Signe Hasso, Lowell Gilmore, Hoagy Carmichael; D: Edwin L. Marin. VHS, Beta, LV $19.98 RKO, CCB, TTC 𝒵𝒵𝒵

Johnny Apollo Upright college student Power keeps his nose clean until Dad's sent to jail for playing with numbers. Scheming to free his old man (Arnold) from the big house, he decides crime will pay for the stiff price tag of freedom. Predictable and melodramatic, but well directed.
1940 93m/B Tyrone Power, Dorothy Lamour, Lloyd Nolan, Edward Arnold, Charley Grapewin, Lionel Atwill; D: Yves Allegret. VHS, Beta $14.98 FOX, FCT 𝒵𝒵½

Johnny Appleseed True story of the legendary American who spent his life planting apple trees across the country. Comedy the entire family will enjoy from Shelly Duvall's "Tall Tales and Legends" series. Originally broadcast on cable television.
1986 60m/C Martin Short, Rob Reiner, Molly Ringwald. VHS $19.98 FOX 𝒵½

Johnny Barrows, El Malo An ex-Vietnam vet battles crime on urban streets. In Spanish.
197? 90m/C SP Fred Williamson. VHS, Beta $57.95 UNI 𝒵½

Johnny Be Good A too-talented high school quarterback is torn between loyalty to his best friend and to his girlfriend amid bribery and schemings by colleges eager to sign him up.
1988 (R) 91m/C Anthony Michael Hall, Robert Downey Jr., Paul Gleason, Uma Thurman, John Pankow, Steve James, Seymour Cassel, Michael Greene, Marshall Bell, Deborah May; D: Bud Smith. VHS, Beta, LV $19.98 ORI 𝒵

Johnny Belinda A compassionate physician cares for a young deaf mute woman and her illegitimate child. Tension builds as the baby's father returns to claim the boy.

1948 103m/B Jane Wyman, Lew Ayres, Charles Bickford, Agnes Moorehead; D: Jean Negulesco. Academy Awards '48: Best Actress (Wyman); Nominations: Best Actor (Ayres), Best Art Direction/Set Decoration (B & W), Best Black and White Cinematography, Best Director (Negulesco), Best Film Editing, Best Picture, Best Screenplay, Best Sound, Best Supporting Actor (Bickford), Best Supporting Actress (Moorehead), Best Original Score; Golden Globe Awards '49: Best Actress—Drama (Wyman), Best Film—Drama. VHS, Beta $19.98 MGM, BTV, CCB 𝒵𝒵𝒵

Johnny Belinda A television movie adaptation of the Elmer Harris weepie about a small town doctor who befriends an abused deaf girl. Remake of the 1948 film.
1982 95m/C Richard Thomas, Rosanna Arquette, Dennis Quaid, Candy Clark, Roberts Blossom, Fran Ryan; D: Anthony Page. VHS, Beta $59.95 LIV 𝒵𝒵

Johnny Come Lately An elderly editor helps out an ex-newspaperman with a police charge. The two then team up to expose political corruption despite threats from a rival newspaperman. AKA: Johnny Vagabond.
1943 97m/B James Cagney, Grace George, Marjorie Main, Marjorie Lord, Hattie McDaniel, Ed McNamara; D: William K. Howard. VHS, LV $19.98 REP, PIA 𝒵𝒵½

Johnny Dangerously A gangster spoof about Johnny Dangerously, who turned to crime in order to pay his mother's medical bills. Now, Dangerously wants to go straight, but competitive crooks would rather see him dead than law-abiding and his mother requires more and more expensive operations. Crime pays in comic ways.
1984 (PG-13) 90m/C Michael Keaton, Joe Piscopo, Danny DeVito, Maureen Stapleton, Marilu Henner, Peter Boyle, Griffin Dunne, Glynnis O'Connor, Dom DeLuise, Richard Dimitri, Ray Walston, Dick Butkus, Alan Hale Jr., Bob Eubanks; D: Amy Heckerling. VHS, Beta $79.98 FOX 𝒵𝒵

Johnny Eager Glossy crime melodrama starring Taylor as an unscrupulous racketeer and Turner as the daughter of D.A. Arnold who falls for him and ends up becoming a pawn in his schemes. Heflin won an Oscar for his outstanding performance as Taylor's alcoholic confidant. Excellent direction by LeRoy makes this a top-rate gangster film. Based on a story by James Edward Grant.
1942 107m/B Robert Taylor, Lana Turner, Edward Arnold, Van Heflin, Robert Sterling, Patricia Dane, Glenda Farrell, Barry Nelson, Henry O'Neil, Charles Dingle, Cy Kendall; D: Mervyn LeRoy; W: James Edward Grant, John Lee Mahin. VHS $19.98 MGM 𝒵𝒵𝒵

Johnny Firecloud A modern Indian goes on the warpath when the persecution of his people reawakens his sense of identity.
1975 94m/C Victor Mohica, Ralph Meeker, Frank De Kova, Sacheen Little Feather, David Canary, Christina Hart; D: William Allen Castleman. VHS, Beta $49.95 PSM 𝒵

Johnny Frenchman Rival fishing groups battle it out, complicated by a romance across the water. Featured in the cast are real fishermen and villagers from Cornwall, as well as authentic Free French Resistance fighters from WWII.
1946 104m/B GB Francoise Rosay, Tom Walls, Patricia Roc, Ralph Michael, Frederick Piper, Pierre Richard, Carroll O'Connor; D: Charles Frend. VHS $19.95 NOS 𝒵𝒵

Johnny Got His Gun Dalton Trumbo's story of a young war veteran who realizes that his arms and legs have been amputated.

1971 (R) 111m/C Timothy Bottoms, Jason Robards Jr., Donald Sutherland, Diane Varsi, Kathy Field; *D:* Dalton Trumbo. **VHS, Beta, LV** $59.95 *MED ✔✔*

Johnny Guitar Women strap on six-guns in Nicholas Ray's unintentionally hilarious, gender-bending western. A guitar-playing loner wanders into a small town feud between lovelorn saloon owner Crawford and McCambridge, the town's resident lynchmob-leading harpy. This fascinating cult-favorite has had film theorists arguing for decades: is it a parody, a political McCarthy-era allegory, or Freudian exercise? The off-screen battles of the two female stars are equally legendary. Stick around for the end credits to hear Peggy Lee sing the title song. **1953** 110m/C Joan Crawford, Ernest Borgnine, Sterling Hayden, Mercedes McCambridge, Scott Brady, Ward Bond, Royal Dano, John Carradine; *D:* Nicholas Ray. **VHS, Beta, LV** $14.98 *REP ✔✔✔ ½*

Johnny Handsome An ugly, deformed hood, after he's been double-crossed and sent to prison, volunteers for a reconstructive surgery experiment and is released with a new face, determined to hunt down the scum that set him up. A terrific modern B-picture based on John Godey's "The Three Worlds of Johnny Handsome." **1989** (R) 96m/C Mickey Rourke, Ellen Barkin, Lance Henriksen, Elizabeth McGovern, Morgan Freeman, Forest Whitaker, Scott Wilson; *D:* Walter Hill. **VHS, Beta, LV** $19.95 *LIV ✔✔✔*

Johnny Nobody A mysterious stranger murders a writer who has been taunting the residents of a quaint Irish town. A sleeper of a thriller, especially in the treatment of the town's reaction to this murder. **1961** 88m/B *GB* William Bendix, Aldo Ray, Nigel Patrick, Yvonne Mitchell, Cyril Cusack; *D:* Nigel Patrick. **VHS, Beta** *NO ✔✔ ½*

Johnny Reno Laughable western that has U.S. Marshal Andrews trying to save an accused killer from lynching. Of interest for star-watching only. Based on a story by Steve Fisher, A.C. Lyles, and Andrew Craddock. **1966** 83m/C Dana Andrews, Jane Russell, Lon Chaney Jr., John Agar, Lyle Bettger, Tom Drake, Richard Arlen, Robert Lowery; *D:* R.G. Springsteen; *W:* Steve Fisher. **VHS** $14.95 *PAR ✔ ½*

Johnny Shiloh An underage youth becomes a heroic drummer during the Civil War. Originally a two-part Disney television show. **1963** 90m/C Kevin Corcoran, Brian Keith, Darryl Hickman, Skip Homeier; *D:* James Neilson. **VHS, Beta** $69.95 *DIS ✔✔*

Johnny Suede Hip kid with big hair wanders the city seeking an identity via a pair of retro black suede elevator shoes. Sleepy surreal comedy walks Pitt through two romantic entanglements and a rendezvous with his own rock idol in his quest for musical talent and pop singer nirvana (not necessarily in that order). Candidate for induction into the David Lynch Movie Musuem of the Weird. **1992** (R) 97m/C Brad Pitt, Calvin Levels, Nick Cave, Wilfredo Giovanni Clark, Alison Moir, Peter McRobbie, Tina Louise, Michael Mulheren, Catherine Keener; *W/D:* Tom DiCillo. **VHS** *PAR ✔✔ ½*

Johnny Tiger A teacher has his hands full when he arrives at the Seminole Reservation in Florida to instruct the Indian children. **1966** 100m/C Robert Taylor, Geraldine Brooks, Chad Everett, Brenda Scott; *D:* Paul Wendkos. **VHS, Beta** *REP ✔✔ ½*

Johnny Tremain & the Sons of Liberty The story of the gallant American patriots who participated in the Boston Tea Party. **1958** 85m/C Sebastian Cabot, Hal Stalmaster, Luanna Patten, Richard Beymer; *D:* Robert Stevenson. **VHS, Beta** $69.95 *DIS ✔✔*

Johnny We Hardly Knew Ye Well-made biographical drama recounts John F. Kennedy's first political campaign for local office in Boston in 1946. Made for television. **1977** 90m/C Paul Rudd, Kevin Conway, William Prince, Burgess Meredith, Tom Berenger, Brian Dennehy, Kenneth McMillan; *D:* Gilbert Gates. **VHS, Beta** *TLF ✔✔ ½*

A Joke of Destiny, Lying in Wait Around the Corner Like a Bandit A irreverent satire about a Minister of the Interior (Tognazzi, of "La Cage aux Folles" fame) who becomes trapped in his high-tech limousine before a vital press conference. An exaggerated vision of Italian bureaucracy. With English subtitles. *AKA:* A Joke of Destiny. **1984** (PG) 105m/C *IT* Ugo Tognazzi, Piera Degli Esposti, Gastone Moschin, Renzo Montagnani, Valeria Golino; *D:* Lina Wertmuller. **VHS, Beta** $59.95 *LHV, APD ✔✔*

Jokes My Folks Never Told Me Series of blackouts and sketches featuring a bevy of beautiful women. **1977** 82m/C Sandy Johnson, Mariwin Roberts; *D:* Gerry Woolery. **VHS, Beta** $59.98 *SUE ✔*

The Jolly Paupers A pre-war comedy made in Warsaw about two small-town Jews who try to achieve fame and fortune in the face of setbacks, community quarrels, and insanity. In Yiddish with English subtitles. *AKA:* Freylekhe Kabtsonim. **1938** 62m/B Shimon Dzigan, Yisroel Shumacher, Max Bozyk, Menasha Oppenheim; *D:* Zygmund Turkow. **VHS** $89.95 *ALD ✔✔ ½*

Jolson Sings Again This sequel to "The Jolson Story" brings back Larry Parks as the ebullient entertainer, with Jolson himself dubbing Parks's voice for the songs. Picking up where the other film ended, the movie chronicles Jolson's comeback in the 1940s and his tireless work with the USO overseas during World War II and the Korean War. ♫After You've Gone; Chinatown, My Chinatown; Give My Regards to Broadway; I Only Have Eyes For You; I'm Just Wild About Harry; You Made Me Love You; I'm Looking Over a Four-Leaf Clover; Is It True What They Say About Dixie?; Ma Blushin' Rose; Let Me Sing and I'm Happy; Baby Face; Sonny Boy; About a Quarter to Nine; Anniversary Song; For Me and My Gal; California Here I Come; Rockabye Your Baby; Carolina in the Morning; Toot, Toot, Tootsie Goodbye; April Showers; Swanee; My Mammy; I'll Take Romance; It's A Blue World; Learn to Croon; Back In Your Own Backyard; When the Red Red Robin Comes Bob Bob Bobbin' Along. **1949** 96m/C Larry Parks, William Demarest, Barbara Hale, Bill Goodwin; *D:* Henry Levin. **VHS, Beta, LV** $19.95 *COL ✔✔*

The Jolson Story A smash Hollywood bio of Jolson, from his childhood to superstardom. Features dozens of vintage songs from Jolson's parade of hits. Jolson himself dubbed the vocals for Parks, rejuvenating his own career in the process. ♫Swanee; You Made Me Love You; By the Light of the Silvery Moon; I'm Sitting On Top of the World; There's a Rainbow Round My Shoulder; My Mammy; Rock-A-Bye Your Baby With a Dixie Melody; Liza; Waiting for the Robert E. Lee; April Showers; About A Quarter To Nine; I Want A Girl Just Like the

Girl That Married Dear Old Dad; The Anniversary Song; The Spaniard Who Blighted My Life; Let Me Sing and I'm Happy; When You Were Sweet Sixteen; Toot Toot Tootsie Goodbye; Eli Eli; On the Banks of the Wabash; Ma Blushin' Rose; Ave Maria; After the Ball; Blue Bell; Every Little Movement Has a Meaning Of Its Own; Avalon; California, Here I Come. **1946** 128m/C Larry Parks, Evelyn Keyes, William Demarest, Bill Goodwin, Tamara Shayne, John Alexander, Jimmy Lloyd, Ludwig Donath; *D:* Alfred E. Green; *M:* Morris Stoloff. Academy Awards '46: Best Sound, Best Score; Nominations: Best Actor (Parks), Best Color Cinematography, Best Film Editing, Best Supporting Actor (Demarest). **VHS, Beta, LV** $19.95 *COL ✔✔✔*

Jonah Who Will Be 25 in the Year 2000 A group of eight friends, former 60s radicals, try to adjust to growing older and coping with life in the 70s. The eccentric octet include a disillusioned journalist turned gambler, an unorthodox teacher, and a grocery store cashier who gives away food to the elderly. Wonderful performances highlight this social comedy. In French with English subtitles. *AKA:* Jonas—Qui Aura 25 Ans en l'an 2000. **1976** 110m/C *SI* Jean-Luc Bideau, Myriam Meziere, Miou-Miou, Jacques Denis, Rufus, Dominique Labourier, Roger Jendly, Miriam Boyer, Raymond Bussieres, Jonah; *W/D:* Alain Tanner. **VHS** $79.95 *NYF ✔✔✔ ½*

Jonathan Livingston Seagull Based on the best-selling novella by Richard Bach, this film quietly envisions a world of love, understanding, achievement, hope and individuality. **1973** (G) 99m/C James Franciscus, Juliet Mills; *D:* Hall Bartlett; *M:* Neil Diamond. **VHS, Beta** $29.95 *PAR ✔✔ ½*

Joni An inspirational story based on the real life of Tada (playing herself) who was seriously injured in a diving accident, and her conquering the odds. A born-again feature film based on the book by Tada. **1979** (G) 75m/C Joni Eareckson Tada, Bert Remsen, Katherine De Hetre, Cooper Huckabee; *D:* James F. Collier. **VHS, Beta** $59.95 *LIV ✔✔*

Jornada de Muerte An ex-cop is hired to bring an important anti-Mob witness to trial via transcontinental train, and must fend off Mob attack squads in the process. In Spanish. **1987** 90m/C *SP* Fred Williamson, Bernie Kuby, Heidi Dobbs. **VHS, Beta** $49.95 *UNI ✔*

Jory A young man's father is killed in a saloon fight, and he must grow up quickly to survive. **1972** (PG) 96m/C Robby Benson, B.J. Thomas, John Marley; *D:* Jorge Fons. **VHS, Beta** $9.95 *COL, XVC ✔*

Joseph & His Brethren A full-length dramatization of the Old Testament story. *AKA:* The Story of Joseph and His Brethren; Joseph Sold to His Brothers. **1960** 103m/C Geoffrey Horne, Robert Morley; *D:* Irving Rapper. **VHS, Beta** $49.95 *UHV, VGD ✔*

Joseph Andrews This adaptation of a 1742 Henry Fielding novel chronicles the rise of Joseph Andrews from servant to personal footman (and fancy) of Lady Booby. **1977** (R) 99m/C *GB* Ann-Margret, Peter Firth, Jim Dale, Michael Hordern, Beryl Reid; *D:* Tony Richardson. **VHS, Beta** $49.95 *PAR ✔✔*

Josepha A husband and wife, both actors, are forced to re-examine their relationship when the wife finds a new love while on a film location. In French with English subtitles.

1982 (R) 114m/C **FR** Miou-Miou, Claude Brasseur, Bruno Cremer; **D:** Christopher Frank. **VHS, Beta** $59.95 *COL, TAM* ♫♫♫

The Josephine Baker Story Made-for-cable bio of exotic entertainer/activist Josephine Baker, a black woman who found superstardom in pre-WWII Europe, but repeated rejection in her native US. At times trite treatment turns her eventful life into a standard rise-and-fall showbiz tale, but a great cast and lavish scope pull it through. Whitfield recreates Baker's (sometimes topless) dance routines; Carol Dennis dubs her singing.
1990 (R) 129m/C Lynn Whitfield, Ruben Blades, David Dukes, Craig T. Nelson, Louis Gossett Jr., Kene Holliday, Vivian Bonnell; **D:** Brian Gibson. **VHS** $19.98 *HBO, FCT* ♫♫♫

Josh and S.A.M. Road movie for youngsters with a twist: the driver can barely see over the dashboard. Josh and Sam are brothers whose parents are splitting. They cope by taking off on their own. Sam, meanwhile has been convinced by Josh that he's not a real boy at all, but rather a S.A.M.: Strategically Altered Mutant. Weber's directorial debut will appeal to young kids, but adults will see over the dashboard and through the transparent plot.
1993 (PG-13) ?m/C Martha Plimpton, Christopher Penn, Stephen Tobolowsky, Joan Allen, Noah Fleiss, Jacob Tierney, Ronald Guttman; **D:** Billy Weber; **W:** Frank Deese. **VHS** *NYR* ♫♫

Joshua Western drama about a vigilante who tracks down the group of outlaws that killed his mother. *AKA:* Black Rider.
1976 (R) 75m/C Fred Williamson, Isela Vega; **D:** Larry Spangler. **VHS** *NO* ♫

Joshua Then and Now When a Jewish-Canadian novelist (Woods) is threatened by the breakup of his marriage to his WASPy wife, compounded by a gay scandal, he re-examines his picaresque history, including his life with his gangster father (Arkin). A stirring story that is enhanced by a strong performance by Woods, as well as a picturesque Canadian backdrop. Adapted by Mordecai Richler from his own novel.
1985 (R) 102m/C James Woods, Gabrielle Lazure, Alan Arkin, Michael Sarrazin, Chuck Shamata; **D:** Ted Kotcheff. **VHS, Beta** $79.98 *FOX* ♫♫♫

Jour de Fete Tati's first film, dealing with a French postman's accelerated efforts at efficiency after viewing a motivational film of the American post service. Wonderful slapstick moments. In French with English subtitles. *AKA:* The Big Day; Holiday.
1948 79m/B **FR** Jacques Tati, Guy Decomble, Paul Fankeur; **D:** Jacques Tati. **VHS, Beta, LV** $19.95 *VDM, SUE, VYG* ♫♫♫½

Journey Violent story of a girl who is rescued from the Sagueney River and falls in love with her rescuer. Choosing to remain in the remote pioneer community of this "hero," she brings everyone bad luck and misery.
1977 (PG) 87m/C **CA** Genevieve Bujold, John Vernon; **D:** Paul Almond. **VHS, Beta** $54.95 *UHV* ♫

Journey Back to Oz Animated special features Dorothy and Toto returning to visit their friends in the magical land of Oz.
1971 90m/C **V:** Liza Minnelli, Ethel Merman, Paul Lynde, Milton Berle, Mickey Rooney, Danny Thomas. **VHS, Beta** $14.95 *FHE, KAR, HHE* ♫

Journey Beneath the Desert Three engineers discover the lost-but-always-found-in-the-movies kingdom of Atlantis when their helicopter's forced down in the

sunny Sahara. A poor hostess with a rotten disposition, the mean sub-saharan queen doesn't roll out the welcome mat for her grounded guests, so a beautiful slave babe helps them make a hasty exit. Dawdling Euro production with adequate visuals. *AKA:* Antinea, l'Amante Della Citta Sepolta.
1961 105m/C **FR IT** Haya Harareet, Jean-Louis Trintignant, Brad Fulton, Amadeo Nazzari, George Riviere, Giulia Rubini, Gabriele Tinti, Gian Maria Volonte; **D:** Edgar G. Ulmer, Giuseppe Masini, Frank Borzage. **VHS, Beta** $16.95 *SNC* ♫♫

Journey for Margaret Young and Day star as an expectant American couple living in London during WWII so Young can cover the war for a newspaper back home. After she loses her baby during an air raid, Day heads back to the States. Young stays in London where he meets two young orphans and takes them under his wing. He decides to take them back to the United States and adopt them, but problems arise. A real tearjerker and a good story that shows the war through the eyes of children. O'Brien's first film. Based on the book by William L. White.
1942 81m/B Robert Young, Laraine Day, Fay Bainter, Signe Hasso, Margaret O'Brien, Nigel Bruce, G.P. Huntley Jr., William Severn, Doris Lloyd, Halliwell Hobbes, Jill Esmond; **D:** Woodbridge S. Van Dyke. **VHS** $19.98 *MGM, FCT* ♫♫♫

Journey into Fear During World War II, an American armaments expert is smuggled out of Istanbul, but Axis agents are close behind. From the novel by Eric Ambler; remade for television in 1974.
1942 71m/B Joseph Cotten, Dolores Del Rio, Orson Welles, Agnes Moorehead, Norman Foster; **D:** Norman Foster. **VHS, Beta, LV** $19.95 *RKO, MED, RXM* ♫♫♫

Journey into Fear A remake of the 1942 Orson Welles classic about a geologist ensnared in Turkish intrigue and murder. *AKA:* Burn Out.
1974 96m/C **CA** Sam Waterston, Vincent Price, Shelley Winters, Donald Pleasence, Zero Mostel, Yvette Mimieux, Ian McShane; **D:** Daniel Mann. **VHS, Beta** $59.98 *LIV* ♫½

Journey into the Beyond A brain-incinerating look at the inexplicable world of the supernatural. Includes examinations of voodoo, bare-handed surgery and psychic sex that are guaranteed to fry your soul.
1976 (R) 83m/C **VHS, Beta** *FHE* ♫½

Journey of Honor During a civil war in 17th century Japan, a nearly defeated Shogun sends his son, Lord Mayeda, to Spain to buy guns from King Phillip III. Along the way he must fight shipboard spies and fierce storms, and once Mayeda arrives in Spain, he is confronted by the evil Duke Don Pedro. In defeating Don Pedro, Mayeda saves King Phillip, gets his guns, and wins the love of Lady Cecilia. To get revenge, Don Pedro plots to capture the Japanese ship and enslave everyone on board. Lots of action and fine acting. Based on a story by martial artist Sho Kosugi.
1991 (PG-13) 107m/C Sho Kosugi, David Essex, Kane Kosugi, Christopher Lee, Norman Lloyd, Ronald Pickup, John Rhys-Davies, Dylan Kussman, Toshiro Mifune; **D:** Gordon Hessler. **VHS, Beta, LV** *MCA* ♫♫½

Journey of Hope Powerful drama about Kurdish family that sells its material possessions in hopes of emigrating legally to Switzerland, where life will surely be better. During the perilous journey, smugglers take their money and the family must attempt crossing the formidable slopes of the Swiss

Mountains on foot. Based on a true story. In Turkish with English subtitles.
1990 (PG) 111m/C **SI** Necmettin Cobanoglu, Nur Surer, Emin Sivas, Yaman Okay, Mathias Gnaedinger, Dietmar Schoenherr; **W/D:** Xavier Koller. **VHS, LV** $92.99 *HBO, TAM* ♫♫♫½

The Journey of Natty Gann With the help of a wolf (brilliantly portrayed by a dog) and a drifter, a 14-year-old girl travels across the country in search of her father in this warm and touching film. Excellent Disney representation of life during the Great Depression.
1985 (PG) 101m/C Meredith Salenger, John Cusack, Ray Wise, Scatman Crothers, Lainie Kazan, Verna Bloom; **D:** Jeremy Paul Kagan. **VHS, Beta, LV** $29.95 *DIS* ♫♫♫½

Journey Through Rosebud A re-enactment of the 1970s protest at Wounded Knee by Native Americans.
1972 93m/C Robert Forster, Eddie Little Sky; **D:** Tom Giles. **VHS, Beta** $59.98 *NLC* ♫♫♫½

Journey to Spirit Island A young Native American girl dreams of her ancestors who are buried on Spirit Island, an ancient burial ground. However, the island is now scheduled to be developed into a resort. With the help of three friends the girl tries to protect the land. Filmed in the Pacific Northwest.
1992 (PG) 93m/C Brandon Douglas, Gabriel Damon, Tony Acierto, Nick Ramus, Marie Antoinette Rodgers, Tarek McCarthy; **D:** Laszlo Pal. **VHS** $89.95 *ACA* ♫♫½

Journey to the Center of the Earth A scientist and student undergo a hazardous journey to find the center of the earth and along the way they find the lost city of Atlantis. Based upon the Jules Verne novel.
1959 132m/C James Mason, Pat Boone, Arlene Dahl, Diane Baker, Thayer David; **D:** Henry Levin. **VHS, Beta, LV** $19.98 *FOX, FCT* ♫♫♫

Journey to the Center of the Earth An animated version of the Jules Verne classic adventure about a scientist's quest to reach the earth's core.
1976 50m/C **VHS, Beta** $19.95 *MGM, WTA* ♫♫♫

Journey to the Center of the Earth A young nanny and two teenage boys discover Atlantis while exploring a volcano.
1988 (PG) 83m/C Nicola Cowper, Paul Carafotes, Ilan Mitchell-Smith; **D:** Rusty Lemorande. **VHS, Beta, LV** $79.95 *CAN* ♫♫♫

Journey to the Center of Time A scientist and his crew are hurled into a time trap when a giant reactor explodes.
1967 83m/C Lyle Waggoner, Scott Brady, Gigi Perreau, Anthony Eisley; **D:** David L. Hewitt. **VHS, Beta** $19.95 *ACA, GHV* ♫½

Journey to the Far Side of the Sun Chaos erupts in the Earth's scientific community when it is discovered that a second, identical Earth is on the other side of the Sun. Both planets end up sending out identical exploratory missions. The denouement is worth the journey. *AKA:* Doppelganger.
1969 (G) 92m/C **GB** Roy Thinnes, Ian Hendry, Lynn Loring, Patrick Wymark, Loni von Friedl, Herbert Lom, Ed Bishop; **D:** Robert Parrish. **VHS, Beta** $29.95 *MCA* ♫♫♫

Journey to the Lost City Architect living in India happens upon a lost city, the rulership of which is being contested by two brothers. In the midst of fighting snakes and tigers, he falls in love with Paget, a beautiful dancer. This feature is actually a poorly edited hybrid of two Lang German adven-

tures, "Der Tiger von Eschnapur" and "Das Indische Grabmal" merged for U.S. release. *AKA:* Tiger of Bengal.
1958 95m/C *GE FR IT* Debra Paget, Paul Christian, Walter Reyer, Claus Holm, Sabine Bethmann, Valeri Inkizhinov, Rene Deltgen, Lucianna Paluzzi; *D:* Fritz Lang. **VHS, Beta** $16.95 *SNC* ♫♫½

Journeys from Berlin/1971 This is the true story about a woman who tries to find a solution to her own problems in life.
1984 125m/C VHS, Beta NO ♫♫½

Joy House An American woman be-friends a handsome French playboy when her husband sends gangsters to kill him. *AKA:* The Love Cage; Les Felins.
1964 98m/B Jane Fonda, Alain Delon, Lola Albright; *D:* Rene Clement. **VHS, Beta** $39.95 *MON* ♫♫

The Joy of Knowledge Godard's experimental use of language and image in a plotless narrative. Berto and Leaud sit to-gether on a bare sound stage and are exposed to popular culture through images, word association, and conversation. In French with English subtitles. Also known as "Le Gai Savoir."
1965 96m/C *FR* Juliet Berto, Jean-Pierre Leaud; *W/D:* Jean-Luc Godard. **VHS** $39.95 *FCT* ♫½

Joy of Living Vintage screwball farce about a randy playboy trying to win over a pragmatic songstress. With music by Jerome Kern. ♫You Couldn't Be Cuter; A Heavenly Party; What's Good About Goodnight; Just Let Me Look At You.
1938 90m/B Irene Dunne, Douglas Fairbanks Jr., Allie Brady, Guy Kibbee, Jean Dixon, Eric Blore, Lucille Ball, Warren Hymer, Billy Gilbert, Frank Milan; *D:* Tay Garnett; *M:* Jerome Kern, Dorothy Fields. **VHS, Beta, LV** $19.98 *RKO, TTC* ♫♫♫

Joy of Sex An undercover narcotics agent is sent to Southern California's Richard M. Nixon High School to investigate the school's extracurricular activities. Typical teen sex flick; no relation to the book.
1984 (R) 93m/C Cameron Dye, Michelle Meyrink, Colleen Camp, Christopher Lloyd, Ernie Hudson, Lisa Langlois; *D:* Martha Coolidge. **VHS, Beta** $79.95 *PAR* ♫

Joy Ride to Nowhere Two young women steal a Cadillac with two million dollars in the trunk and ride away with the owner hot on their tail.
1978 (PG) 86m/C Leslie Ackerman, Sandy Serrano, Len Lesser, Mel Welles, Ron Ross, Speed Stearns. **VHS, Beta** $19.95 *NEG* ♫

Joy Sticks Joy sticks in question are down at the arcade. Businessman wants to shut down local video game palace. Inhabi-tants just say no.
1983 (R) 88m/C Joe Don Baker, Leif Green, Jim Greenleaf, Scott McGinnis, Jonathan Gries; *D:* Greydon Clark. **VHS, Beta, LV** $79.95 *VES* Woof!

Joyful Laughter The dreary life of an Italian movie bit player draws strength from Magnani's powerful emotions as she repeat-edly comes near to success only to find disappointment. Set in Rome. With English subtitles.
1954 106m/C *IT D:* Mario Monicelli. **VHS** $59.95 *FST* ♫♫

Joyless Street Silent film focuses on the dismal life of the middle class in Austria during an economic crisis. Lovely piano score accompanies the film.
1925 96m/B *GE* Greta Garbo, Werner Krauss, Asta Nielsen; *D:* G.W. Pabst. **VHS, Beta, LV** $29.95 *VYY, MRV, FST* ♫♫♫½

Joyride Mistreated by a union official, three friends steal a car for a joy ride and plummet into a life of crime.
1977 (R) 91m/C Desi Arnaz Jr., Robert Carradine, Melanie Griffith, Anne Lockhart; *D:* Joseph Ruben. **VHS, Beta** $29.98 *LIV, VES* ♫½

Ju Dou Breath-taking story of an aging factory owner in search of an heir. He takes a third wife, but she finds caring in the arms of another man, when her husband's brutality proves too much. Beautiful color cinematog-raphy, excellent acting and epic story. Oscar nominee for Best Foreign Film. In Chinese with English subtitles.
1990 (PG-13) 98m/C *CH* Gong Li, Li Baotian, Li Wei, Zhang Yi, Zheng Jian; *D:* Zhang Yimou. **VHS, LV** $19.98 *LIV, PIA, TAM* ♫♫♫♫

Juarez A revolutionary leader overthrows the Mexican government and then becomes President of the country. Based on the true story of Benito Pablo Juarez.
1939 132m/B Paul Muni, John Garfield, Bette Davis, Claude Rains, Gale Sondergaard; *D:* William Dieterle. **VHS, Beta** $19.95 *MGM, FCT* ♫♫

Jubal A rancher (Borgnine) seeks advice from a cowhand (Ford) about pleasing his wife, but another cowhand (Steiger) implies that Ford is "advising" Borgnine's wife, as well. A western take on "Othello."
1956 101m/C Glenn Ford, Rod Steiger, Ernest Borgnine, Felicia Farr, Charles Bronson, Valerie French, Noah Beery Jr.; *D:* Delmer Daves. **VHS, Beta, LV** $9.95 *RCA, IME* ♫♫

Jubilee Adam Ant stars as a punk who takes over Buckingham Palace and turns it into a recording studio. Music by Eno, Adam and the Ants, and Siouxsie and the Ban-shees.
1978 103m/C *GB* Jordan, Toyah Wilcox, Jenny Runacre, Little Nell; *M:* Siouxsie & the Banshees, Wayne County. **VHS, Beta** $29.95 *MVD, MFV, TAM* ♫♫

Jubilee Trail Wagon trail western follows the lives of a group of pioneers from New Orleans to California. A woman goes through a marriage, a baby, and her husband's death. Ralston has some good tunes in this lush picture.
1954 103m/C Vera Ralston, Joan Leslie, Forrest Tucker, John Russell, Ray Middleton, Pat O'Brien; *D:* Joseph Kane. **VHS** $14.95 *REP* ♫♫½

Jud Society's refusal to understand a young soldier returning from the Vietnam conflict leads him to violence and tragedy. Jonnings first film; music by Stu Phillips of Creedence Clearwater Revival.
1971 (PG) 80m/C Joseph Kaufmann, Robert Deman, Alix Wyeth, Norman Burton, Claudia Jennings, Maurice Sherbanee, Vic Dunlop, Bonnie Bittner; *D:* Gunther Collins. **VHS, Beta** $49.95 *PSM* ♫½

Jud Suess Classic, scandalous Nazi anti-Semitic tract about a Jew who rises to power under the duchy of Wuerttemberg by step-ping on, abusing, and raping Aryans. A film that caused riots at its screenings and trage-dy for its cast and crew, and the Third Reich's most notorious fictional expression of policy. In German with English subtitles.
1940 100m/B *GE* Ferdinand Marian, Werner Krauss, Heinrich George, Kristina Soderbaum, Eugene Klopfer; *D:* Veit Harlan. **VHS, Beta, 3/4U** $24.95 *NOS, VCD, IHF* ♫♫♫

Judex Judex, a sensitive cloaked hero-avenger, fights master criminal gangs. In French with English subtitles. Remake of the silent French serial.
1964 103m/B *FR IT* Channing Pollock, Francine Berge, Jacques Jouanneau; *D:* Georges Franju. **VHS, Beta** $24.95 *NOS, SNC, HHT* ♫♫½

The Judge A courtroom crime-drama about the consequences of infidelity. A law-yer sends an acquitted hit man to kill his wife and her lover. Things go amiss and the lawyer winds up dead.
1949 69m/B Milburn Stone, Katherine DeMille, Paul Guilfoyle, Jonathan Hale; *D:* Elmer Clifton. **VHS** $16.95 *SNC* ♫½

The Judge and the Assassin In-triguing courtroom drama. A prejudiced judge has his values challenged when he must decide if a child-killer is insane or not. The relationship that develops between the judge and the killer is the film's focus. Excellent direction by Tavernier. In French with English subtitles. *AKA:* Le Juge et L'assassin.
1975 130m/C *FR* Philippe Noiret, Michel Galabru, Isabelle Huppert, Jean-Claude Brialy; *D:* Bertrand Tavernier. **VHS, Beta, LV** $79.95 *CVC, IME, TAM* ♫♫♫½

Judge Horton and the Scottsboro Boys A courtroom drama focusing on a famous 1931 trial. A coura-geous judge must battle the South in the case of nine black men charged with gang-raping two white women. Made for televi-sion.
1976 100m/C Arthur Hill, Vera Miles, Ken Kercheval, Suzanne Lederer, Tom Ligon; *D:* Fielder Cook. **VHS** $59.95 *LIV* ♫♫½

Judge Priest Small-town judge in the old South stirs up the place with stinging humor and common-sense observances as he tan-gles with prejudices and civil injustices. Fun-ny, warm slice-of-life is occasionally defeated by racist characterizations. Ford remade it later as "The Sun Shines Bright." Taken from the Irvin S. Cobb stories.
1934 80m/B Will Rogers, Stepin Fetchit, Anita Louise, Henry B. Walthall; *D:* John Ford. **VHS, Beta, 3/4U, Special order formats** $19.95 *NOS, MRV, PSM* ♫♫♫

Judge Roy Bean This western series set in Langtry, Texas in 1870 starred Bu-chanan as the self-appointed "Law West of the Pecos," trying to maintain order in a lawless territory. Two episodes per tape.
1955 55m/B Edgar Buchanan, Jack Beutel, Jackie Loughery; *D:* Jack Beutel, Jackie Loughery. **VHS, Beta** $19.99 *MOV, MVC* ♫♫♫

The Judge Steps Out Pleasant, light comedy about a hen-pecked, Bostonian judge who decides he's had enough and heads for balmy California. There he finds a job in a restaurant and, more importantly, a sympathetic friend in its female owner. He soon finds himself falling for the woman, and realizes he faces an important decision.
1949 91m/B Alexander Knox, Ann Sothern, George Tobias, Sharyn Moffett, Florence Bates, Frieda Inescort, Myrna Dell, Ian Wolfe, H.B. Warner; *D:* Boris Ingster. **VHS** $19.95 *TTC* ♫♫½

Judgment A devout Catholic couple are shocked to learn that their young son has been molested by the popular priest of their small Louisiana parish. When they find out their son is not the first victim, and other families have been coerced into silence, they vow to fight back. Tasteful treatment of a real court case. Made for cable.
1990 (PG-13) 89m/C Keith Carradine, Blythe Danner, Jack Warden, David Strathairn; *W/D:* Tom Topor. **VHS** $89.98 *HBO* ♫♫♫

Judgment at Nuremberg It's 1948 and a group of high-level Nazis are on trial for war crimes. Chief Justice Tracy must resist political pressures as he presides over the trials. Excellent performances throughout, especially by Dietrich and Garland. Considers to what extent an individual may be held

J

accountable for actions committed under orders of a superior officer. Consuming account of the Holocaust and World War II; deeply moving and powerful. Based on a "Playhouse 90" television program. **1961 178m/B** Spencer Tracy, Burt Lancaster, Richard Widmark, Montgomery Clift, Maximilian Schell, Judy Garland, Marlene Dietrich, William Shatner; **D:** Stanley Kramer. Academy Awards '61: Best Actor (Schell), Best Adapted Screenplay; Nominations: Best Actor (Tracy), Best Art Direction/Set Decoration (B & W), Best Black and White Cinematography, Best Costume Design (B & W), Best Director (Kramer), Best Film Editing, Best Picture, Best Supporting Actor (Clift), Best Supporting Actress (Garland); Golden Globe Awards '62: Best Actor—Drama (Schell), Best Director (Kramer); New York Film Critics Awards '61: Best Actor (Schell). **VHS, Beta, LV $29.98** MGM, FOX, BTV 🎬🎬🎬🎬

Judgment Day Four college buddies pick the wrong New England town for their vacation. It seems that the town made a deal with the Devil in 1689 to save themselves from the plague, and now the Dark Master is here to collect. **1988 (PG-13) 93m/C** Kenneth McLeod, David Anthony Smith, Monte Markham, Gloria Hayes, Peter Mark Richman, Cesar Romero; **D:** Ferde Grofe Jr. **VHS, Beta** NO 🎬

Judgment in Berlin East German family hijacks a U.S. airliner into West Germany, and then must stand trial in Berlin before a troubled American judge. Based on a true 1978 incident and the book by Herbert J. Stern. **AKA:** Escape to Freedom. **1988 (PG) 92m/C** Martin Sheen, Sam Wanamaker, Max Gail, Sean Penn, Heinz Hoenig, Carl Lumbly, Max Volkert Martens, Harris Yulin, Joshua Sinclair, Jutta Speidel; **D:** Leo Penn. **VHS, Beta, LV $29.95** COL 🎬🎬½

Judith of Bethulia A young widow uses her charm and wits to save her city from attack by the Assyrians. Based on the Apocrypha, this is the last film Griffith directed for Biograph. It was re-released as "Her Condoned Sin" in 1971, including two reels of Griffith's outtakes. **1914 65m/B** Blanche Sweet, Henry B. Walthall, Mae Marsh, Robert Harron, Lillian Gish, Dorothy Gish, Kate Bruce, Harry Carey Sr.; **W/D:** D.W. Griffith. **VHS, LV $19.95** NOS, GPV, VYY 🎬🎬🎬

Juggernaut Not the classic disaster film of the '70s. A young woman hires a sinister doctor (Karloff) to murder her wealthy husband. The doctor, who happens to be insane, does away with the husband and then goes on a poisoning spree. Seems to drag on forever. **1937 64m/B** Boris Karloff, Mona Goya, Arthur Margetson. **VHS, Beta $19.95** NOS, SNC. VYY 🎬½

Juggernaut Well-done drama about a doomed luxury liner. A madman plants bombs aboard a cruise ship and mocks the crew about his plan over the wireless. The countdown ensues, while the bomb experts struggle to find the explosives. Suspenseful with good direction. **1974 (PG-13) 109m/C** GB Richard Harris, Omar Sharif, David Hemmings, Anthony Hopkins, Shirley Knight, Ian Holm, Roy Kinnear, Freddie Jones; **D:** Richard Lester. **VHS $14.95** MGM, FOX 🎬🎬🎬

The Juggler of Notre Dame A hobo and a street juggler embark on an unusual journey that will change the lives of the people they meet. Based on a medieval folktale about the special gift given to the Virgin Mary on Christmas morning. **1984 110m/C** Carl Carlson, Patrick Collins, Melinda Dillon, Merlin Olsen, Gene Roche. **VHS, Beta** PAU 🎬🎬½

Juice Day-to-day street life of four Harlem youths as they try to earn respect ("juice") in their neighborhood. Q, an aspiring deejay, is talked into a robbery by his friends but everything takes a turn for the worse when one of the others, Bishop, gets hold of a gun. The gritty look and feel of the drama comes naturally to Dickerson in his directorial debut. Prior to his first film, Dickerson served as cinematographer for Spike Lee's "Do the Right Thing" and "Jungle Fever." **1992 (R) 95m/C** Omar Epps, Jermaine Hopkins, Tupac Shakur, Khalil Kain, Cindy Herron, Vincent Laresca, Samuel L. Jackson; **W/D:** Ernest R. Dickerson. **VHS $19.95** PAR 🎬🎬½

Juke Joint "Amos 'n Andy" star Spencer Williams acted in and directed this tale of two men who arrive in Hollywood with only 25 cents between them. Features an all-black cast and musical numbers. **1947 60m/B** Spencer Williams Jr., Judy Jones, Mantan Moreland; **D:** Spencer Williams Jr. **VHS, Beta $39.95** NOS, VCN, DVT 🎬½

Jules and Jim A beautiful film with perfect casting, particularly of Moreau. Set from 1912 to 1932, it is the story of a friendship between two men and their twenty-year love for the same woman. Werner is the shy German Jew and Serre the fun-loving Frenchman, who meet as students. The two men discover and woo the bohemian, destructive Moreau, although it is Werner she marries. After World War I, the friends are reunited but the marriage of Moreau and Werner is in trouble and she has an affair with Serre, which leads to tragedy for all three. Adapted from the novel by Henri-Pierre Roche. In French with English subtitles. **AKA:** Jules et Jim. **1962 104m/B** FR Jeanne Moreau, Oskar Werner, Henri Serre, Marie DuBois, Vanna Urbino; **D:** Francois Truffaut. **VHS, Beta, LV $59.98** FOX, APD, HMV 🎬🎬🎬🎬

Julia A woman tries to lose her virginity while vacationing in the Swiss Alps. **1974 (R) 83m/C** Sylvia Kristel, Jean-Claude Bouillon, Terry Torday. **VHS, Beta $59.95** GEM Woof!

Julia The story recounted in Lillian Hellman's fictional memoir "Pentimento." Fonda plays Hellman as she risks her life smuggling money into Germany during World War II for the sake of Julia, her beloved childhood friend (Redgrave), who is working in the Resistance. All cast members shine in their performances; watch for Streep in her screen debut. **1977 (PG) 118m/C** Jane Fonda, Jason Robards Jr., Vanessa Redgrave, Maximilian Schell, Hal Holbrook, Rosemary Murphy, Meryl Streep, Lisa Pelikan; **D:** Fred Zinneman; **W:** Alvin Sargent. Academy Awards '77: Best Adapted Screenplay, Best Supporting Actor (Robards), Best Supporting Actress (Redgrave); Nominations: Best Actress (Fonda), Best Cinematography, Best Costume Design, Best Director (Zinneman), Best Film Editing, Best Picture, Best Supporting Actor (Schell), Best Original Score; Golden Globe Awards '78: Best Actress—Drama (Fonda), Best Supporting Actress (Redgrave); New York Film Critics Awards '77: Best Supporting Actor (Schell). **VHS, Beta, LV $19.98** FOX, BTV 🎬🎬🎬½

Julia and Julia A beautiful American woman in Trieste is tossed between two seemingly parallel dimensions, one in which her husband died six years earlier in a car crash, and the other in which he didn't. A purposefully obscure Italian-made psychological thriller, filmed in high-definition video and then transferred to film stock, it has a very different look and feel from other films of the genre. Intriguing and engaging most of the time, slow moving and confusing some of

the time, it ultimately challenges but fails adequately to reward the viewer. **1987 (R) 98m/C** Kathleen Turner, Sting, Gabriel Byrne, Gabriel Ferzetti, Angela Goodwin; **D:** Peter Del Monte. **VHS, Beta, LV $19.98** FOX 🎬🎬½

Julia has Two Lovers Minimalist comedy-drama about a woman torn between two men—her dull fiance and a mysterious phone caller. Mostly a long phone conversation; don't expect blistering action. **1991 (R) 87m/C** Daphna Kastner, David Duchovny, David Charles; **D:** Bashar Shbib. **VHS $89.98** NO 🎬

Julia Misbehaves Charming comedy that has Garson returning to ex-husband Pidgeon and daughter Taylor after an 18-year absence. Taylor is about to be married at a chateau in France and wants Garson to be there. While traveling to France from England, Garson encounters a bunch of colorful circus characters who are taking their act to Paris. Wonderful slapstick scenes give the stars a chance to have some real fun. Based on the novel "The Nutmeg Tree" by Margery Sharp. **1948 99m/B** Greer Garson, Walter Pidgeon, Peter Lawford, Cesar Romero, Elizabeth Taylor, Lucile Watson, Nigel Bruce, Mary Boland, Reginald Owen; **D:** Jack Conway. **VHS $19.98** MGM 🎬🎬🎬

Juliet of the Spirits Fellini uses the sparse story of a woman (Fellini's real-life wife) deliberating over her husband's possible infidelity to create a wild, often senseless surrealistic film. With a highly symbolic internal logic and complex imagery, Fellini's fantasy ostensibly elucidates the inner life of a modern woman. In Italian with English subtitles. **AKA:** Giulietta Degli Spiriti. **1965 142m/C** IT Giulietta Masina, Valentina Cortese, Sylva Koscina, Mario Pisu; **D:** Federico Fellini. Academy Awards '66 Nominations: Best Art Direction/Set Decoration (Color), Best Costume Design (Color); National Board of Review Awards '65: 5 Best Foreign Films of the Year; New York Film Critics Awards '65: Best Foreign Film. **VHS, Beta, LV $69.95** CVC, MRV, VDM 🎬🎬🎬

Julius Caesar All-star version of the Shakespearean tragedy, heavily acclaimed and deservedly so. Working directly from the original Shakespeare, director Mankiewicz produced a lifelike, yet poetic production. **1953 121m/B** James Mason, Marlon Brando, John Gielgud, Greer Garson, Deborah Kerr, Louis Calhern, Edmond O'Brien, George Macready, John Hoyt, Michael Pate; **W/D:** Joseph L. Mankiewicz. Academy Awards '53: Best Art Direction/Set Decoration (B & W); Nominations: Best Actor (Brando), Best Black and White Cinematography, Best Picture, Best Original Score; British Academy Awards '53: Best Actor (Brando), Best Actor (Gielgud). **VHS, Beta $19.98** MGM 🎬🎬🎬½

Julius Caesar Subpar adaptation of the Shakespeare play about political greed and corruption within the Roman Empire. **1970 116m/C** GB Charlton Heston, John Gielgud, Jason Robards Jr., Richard Chamberlain, Robert Vaughn, Diana Rigg; **D:** Stuart Burge. **VHS, Beta $19.98** NOS, REP, APD 🎬🎬

Julius Caesar A drama of power, assassination, and revenge set in ancient Rome as complicated human beings are shown in conflict with one another and themselves. Part of the television series "The Shakespeare Plays." **1979 161m/C** Richard Pasco, Keith Mitchell, Charles Gray. **VHS, Beta, LV $49.95** TLF 🎬🎬🎬

July Group A Quaker family's peaceful existence is threatened when kidnappers invade their home and hold them for ransom.
197? 75m/C Nicholas Campbell, Calvin Butler, Maury Chaykin. **VHS, Beta** $59.95 TWE ✍✍½

The Jumper An abstract, theatrical narrative about a cast of tragi-comic characters floundering through their meaningless lives. In German with English subtitles. *AKA:* Der Toderspringer.
1985 90m/C GE D: Benno Trachtmann. **VHS, Beta** $39.95 FCT ✍✍½

Jumpin' at the Boneyard Gritty family drama about the trials of two dispossessed brothers, set on the streets of New York. Deeply depressed, out-of-work, divorced Manny hates his recently deceased father, adores his mother, and is estranged from his younger brother, Danny. Danny is a scared crack addict who's supported by a hooker/girlfriend. The two brothers reunite for a trip into their scarred past when Danny tries to rob his brother's apartment to get dope money. Manny starts to believe that the only way to redeem his own life is to get his brother into a rehab program. Good acting helps to overcome some script weaknesses but this is one depressing movie.
1992 (R) 107m/C Tim Roth, Alexis Arquette, Danitra Vance, Samuel L. Jackson, Kathleen Chalfant, Luis Guzman; *W/D:* Jeff Stanzler. **VHS, LV** $94.98 FXV ✍✍

Jumpin' Jack Flash A bank worker is humorously embroiled in international espionage when her computer terminal picks up distress signals from a British agent in Russia. Marshall's directing debut. Good performances from a fun cast and a particularly energetic effort by Goldberg are held back by an average and predictable script.
1986 (R) 98m/C Whoopi Goldberg, Stephen Collins, Carol Kane, Annie Potts, Jonathan Pryce, James Belushi, Jon Lovitz; *Cameos:* Michael McKean, Tracy Ullman, Roscoe Lee Browne, Sara Botsford, Jeroen Krabbe, Phil Hartman, Tracy Reiner, Paxton Whitehead, Jamey Sheridan, Garry Marshall, Peter Michael Goetz; *D:* Penny Marshall. **VHS, Beta, LV** $19.98 FOX ✍✍½

Jumping Jacks Martin and Lewis are a couple of nightclub performers who wind up in the paratroop corps instead of performing their act for the soldiers. Martin gets to sing and Lewis gets to parachute into enemy territory and capture a general.
1952 96m/B Dean Martin, Jerry Lewis, Mona Freeman, Don DeFore, Robert Strauss, Ray Teal; *D:* Norman Taurog. **VHS** $19.95 PAR ✍✍

Junction 88 Early all-black musical chock full of great dancing and hot music.
1940 60m/B Noble Sissle, Bob Howard. **VHS, Beta** $24.95 NOS, DVT ✍

June Bride Fast-paced and entertaining comedy in which Davis and Montgomery are teamed up as magazine writers. A hilarious battle of the sexes erupts as they're sent to Indiana to do a feature story on June brides. Look for Debbie Reynolds in her film debut.
1948 97m/B Bette Davis, Robert Montgomery, Fay Bainter, Betty Lynn, Tom Tully, Barbara Bates, Jerome Cowan, Mary Wickes; *D:* Bretaigne Windust; *W:* Ranald MacDougall. **VHS** $19.98 MGM ✍✍✍

June Night A woman who was victimized by a shooting incident cannot escape the public eye due to her former promiscuous behavior. In Swedish with English subtitles.
1940 90m/C SW Ingrid Bergman, Marianne Lofgren, Gunnar Sjoberg, Olaf Widgren; *D:* Per Lindberg. **VHS, Beta, LV** $29.95 WAC, LUM, TAM ✍✍

Jungle A princess and an American adventurer lead an expedition into the Indian wilds to discover the source of recent elephant attacks.
1952 74m/B Rod Cameron, Cesar Romero, Marie Windsor; *D:* William Berke. **VHS, Beta, LV** NO ✍

Jungle Assault Two Vietnam vets with nothing left to lose are called back into the bloodiest action of their lives. Their assignment is to locate and destroy a terrorist base and bring back an American general's brainwashed daughter.
1989 86m/C William Smith, Ted Prior, William Zipp; *D:* David A. Prior. **VHS, Beta** AIP ✍

Jungle Book A lavish version of Rudyard Kipling's stories about Mowgli, the boy raised by wolves in the jungles of India. Musical score by Miklos Rosza. *AKA:* Rudyard Kipling's Jungle Book.
1942 109m/C Sabu, Joseph Calleia, Rosemary DeCamp, Ralph Byrd, John Qualen; *D:* Zoltan Korda. **VHS, LV, 3/4U, Special order formats** $9.95 NEG, MRV, REP ✍✍

The Jungle Book Based on Kipling's classic, a young boy raised by wolves must choose between his jungle friends and human "civilization." Along the way he meets a variety of jungle characters including zany King Louie, kind-hearted Baloo, wise Bagherra and the evil Shere Khan. Great, classic songs including "Trust in Me," "I Wanna Be Like You," and Oscar-nominated "Bare Necessities." Last Disney feature overseen by Uncle Walt himself and a must for kids of all ages.
1967 78m/C D: Wolfgang Reitherman; *V:* Phil Harris, Sebastian Cabot, Louis Prima, George Sanders, Sterling Holloway, J. Pat O'Malley, Verna Felton, Darlene Carr. **VHS, Beta, LV** $24.99 DIS, BVV, FCT ✍✍✍

Jungle Bride Three people are shipwrecked and one of them is a suspected murderer.
1933 66m/B Anita Page, Charles Starrett. **VHS, Beta, LV** $16.95 SNC, NOS, WGE ✍✍½

Jungle Drums of Africa Jungle adventures abound as Moore and Coates encounter lions, wind tunnels, voodoo and enemy agents in deepest Africa. A 12-episode serial re-edited onto two cassettes. *AKA:* U-238 and the Witch Doctor.
1953 167m/B Clayton Moore, Phyllis Coates, Roy Glenn, John Cason; *D:* Fred Brannon. **VHS** REP, MLB ✍½

Jungle Fever A married black architect's affair with his white secretary provides the backdrop for a cold look at an interracial love affair. Lee focuses more on the discomfort of the friends and families involved than with the intense world created by the lovers for themselves. The movie provides the quota of humor and fresh insight we expect from Lee, but none of the joyous sexuality experienced by the black lovers in "She's Gotta Have It." In fact, Lee tells us that interracial love is unnatural, never more than skin deep. His lovers have "Jungle Fever," a blind obsession with the allure of the opposite race. A very fine cast but if you don't agree with Lee's viewpoint, a real disappointment as well.
1991 (R) 131m/C Wesley Snipes, Annabella Sciorra, John Turturro, Samuel L. Jackson, Ossie Davis, Ruby Dee, Lonette McKee, Anthony Quinn; *W/D:* Spike Lee. **VHS, Beta, LV** $19.98 MCA, CCB, FCT ✍✍✍

Jungle Goddess Two mercenaries set out for the reward offered for finding a wealthy heiress last seen in the jungles of Africa.

1949 61m/B George Reeves, Wanda McKay, Ralph Byrd, Armida; *D:* Lewis D. Collins. **VHS, Beta, LV** NO ✍½

Jungle Heat While searching for a pygmy tribe, an anthropologist and her pilot run into a pack of anthropoid mutants. *AKA:* Dance of the Dwarfs.
1984 (PG) 93m/C Peter Fonda, Deborah Raffin; *D:* Gus Trikonis. **VHS, Beta** $59.95 TWE ✍½

Jungle Hell Sabu comes to the rescue of an Indian tribe being harassed by flying saucers, death rays and radioactive debris.
1955 ?m/B Sabu, David Bruce, George E. Stone, K.T. Stevens; *D:* Norman A. Cerf. **VHS, Beta** $16.95 SNC ✍✍

Jungle Holocaust One member of a scientific team survives an attack by a cannibal tribe and in an effort of self-preservation becomes one of them.
1985 90m/C **VHS, Beta** $59.95 VCD ✍

Jungle Inferno Nature boy, a fugitive from the government, fights lions, tigers and pursuing feds in this story of escape and survival.
197? 90m/C Brad Harris. **VHS, Beta** WWV ✍

Jungle Master Noble British types hunt for Karzan, the jungle's number one guy, with the aid of a tribal priestess and a lovely photo-journalist. Must see for trash movie fans.
1956 90m/C John Kitzmiller, Simone Blondell, Edward Mann; *D:* Miles Deem. **VHS, Beta** NO ✍

Jungle Patrol In 1943 New Guinea, a squadron of entrapped fliers are confronted with a beautiful USO entertainer. Romance and show tunes follow.
1948 72m/B Kristine Miller, Arthur Franz, Richard Jaeckel, Ross Ford, Tommy Noonan, Gene Reynolds; *D:* Joseph M. Newman. **VHS, Beta** $39.95 SVS ✍½

Jungle Raiders An Indiana Jones-esque mercenary searches the steamy jungles of Malaysia for a valuable jewel, the Ruby of Gloom. *AKA:* Legenda Del Rubio Malese; Captain Yankee.
1985 (PG-13) 102m/C Lee Van Cleef, Christopher Connelly, Marina Costa; *D:* Anthony M. Dawson. **VHS, Beta** $79.95 MGM ✍½

Jungle Siren Nazis in Africa try to foment rebellion amongst the black natives against the white residents. Crabbe and a white woman raised in the jungle set things right.
1942 68m/B Ann Corio, Buster Crabbe, Evelyn Wahl, Milton Kibbee; *D:* Sam Newfield. **VHS, Beta** $16.95 SNC, MLB ✍✍

The Jungle Trap Steve Davis thought he could escape his past living in Africa. However, when the judge who wrongly sentenced his brother to death arrives, he plots revenge.
19?? 30m/B Ronald Reagan. **VHS** $7.95 RHI ✍✍

Jungle Warriors Seven fashion models are abducted by a Peruvian cocaine dealer. To escape him, they must become Jungle Warriors.
1984 (R) 96m/C GE MX Sybil Danning, Marjoe Gortner, Nina Van Pallandt, Paul Smith, John Vernon, Alex Cord, Woody Strode, Kai Wulff; *D:* Ernst R. von Theumer. **VHS, Beta** $59.95 MED ✍½

Junior A raving, drooling lunatic cuts up girls with a chainsaw.
1986 80m/C Suzanne DeLaurentis, Linda Singer, Jeremy Ruthford, Michael McKeever. **VHS, Beta** $9.99 STE, PSM Woof!

Junior Bonner A rowdy modern-day western about a young drifting rodeo star who decides to raise money for his father's new ranch by challenging a formidable bull.
1972 (PG) 100m/C Steve McQueen, Robert Preston, Ida Lupino, Ben Johnson, Joe Don Baker, Barbara Leigh; **D:** Sam Peckinpah. **VHS, Beta $19.98** FOX �22�$

Junior G-Men The Dead End Kids fight Fifth Columnists who are trying to sabotage America's war effort. Twelve episodes.
1940 237m/B Billy Halop, Huntz Hall. **VHS, Beta $49.95** NOS, VCN, VYY �22�$

Junior G-Men of the Air The Dead End Kids become teen-age flyboys in this twelve-episode serial adventure.
1942 215m/B Billy Halop, Huntz Hall. **VHS, Beta $26.95** SNC, NOS, MED �22½

Junior High School A comically, on target film detailing the romantic yearnings, petty cruelties, and claustrophobia of 8th grade existence.
1978 60m/C Paula Abdul. **VHS, Beta** PIC �22½

The Junkman Movie maker whose new film is about to be premiered is being chased by a mysterious killer. Promoted as "the ultimate car chase film" since the production used and destroyed over 150 automobiles. From the makers of "Gone in 60 Seconds."
1982 (R) 97m/C H.B. Halicki, Christopher Stone, Susan Shaw, Hoyt Axton, Lynda Day George, Freddy Cannon & the Belmonts; **D:** H.B. Halicki. **VHS, Beta $18.95** TWE �22½

Juno and the Paycock Perhaps if Hitchcock hadn't been so faithful to O'Casey this early effort would have been less stagey and more entertaining. In Dublin during the civil uprising, a poor family is torn apart when they receive news of an imminent fortune. Hitchcock's reported to have said that "drama is life with the dull bits left out," though here too many dull bits remain.
1930 96m/B Sara Allgood, Edward Chapman, John Longden, John Laurie, Maire O'Neill; **D:** Alfred Hitchcock. **VHS $19.98** NOS, VEC, HHT �22½

Jupiter Menace An examination of speculative theories dealing with the inevitable end of the world. Kennedy predicts a continuing cycle of unnatural occurrences and disasters which will culminate with the tilting of the earth's axis in the year 2000.
1982 84m/C George Kennedy, Greg Michaels; **D:** Lee Auerbach, Peter Matulavich. **VHS, Beta $69.99** HBO �22½

Jupiter's Darling This spoof of Hannibal (Keel) and Amytis (Williams) gravely misses the mark in making funny the world of the Roman Empire. Amytis has the job of distracting Hannibal from attacking the Eternal City, and does so through musical interludes and unfunny jokes. ♫I Have A Dream; If This Be Slav'ry; I Never Trust A Woman; Hannibal's Victory March; Don't Let This Night Get Away; The Life Of An Elephant; Horatio's Narration.
1955 96m/C Esther Williams, Howard Keel, George Sanders, Gower Champion, Marge Champion, Norma Varden, Richard Haydn, William Demarest, Douglas Dumbrille, Michael Ansara, Martha Wentworth, Chris Alcaide, William Tannen; **D:** George Sidney. **LV $19.98** MGM �22

Jupiter's Thigh A madcap married pair of treasure-hunters honeymoon in Greece in search of an ancient statue's lost thigh. Available in French with English subtitles, or dubbed into English.
1981 96m/C FR Annie Girardot, Philippe Noiret; **D:** Phillipe DeBroca. **VHS, Beta $29.98** SUE, FCT �22½

Jurassic Park Michael Crichton's spine-tingling thriller translates well (although not faithfully) to the big screen due to its main attraction—realistic, rampaging dinosaurs. Eccentric millionaire Dr. John Hammond (Attenborough) genetically clones dinosaurs from prehistoric DNA (don't worry, "Mr. D.N.A." will explain the basics), builds a secret theme park on an isolated island, and plans on cashing in just as soon as he can get insurance and other minor matters out of the way. A disgruntled employee tries to smuggle some embryos off the island, turns off the electric barrier preventing the beasts from escaping, and the ride begins when the dinos turn out to be smarter and less controllable than anyone expected. Paleontologist couple Drs. Grant (Neill) and Sattler (Dern) are brought to the island to verify authenticity while Goldblum is a smart-mouthed mathematician. Also present are Hammond's two young granchildren. Plot is driven by contrivance and the characters, with Goldblum's cynic the notable exception, are thin. But it doesn't matter—the dinos are the true stars, thrilling and chilling the audience. Created from a combination of models and computer animation, Spielberg again sets a new standard for special effects. Violent and suspenseful, with realistic attack scenes reminiscent of "Jaws," this one definitely isn't for the 10 and under set, even though most of the advertising is aimed at them.
1993 (PG-13) 126m/C Sam Neill, Laura Dern, Jeff Goldblum, Richard Attenborough, Bob Peck, Martin Ferrero, Joseph Mazzello, Ariana Richards, Samuel L. Jackson, Wayne Knight; **D:** Steven Spielberg; **W:** David Koepp, Michael Crichton, Malia Scotch Marmo; **M:** John Williams; **V:** Richard Kiley. **VHS** NYR �22�2½

Just a Gigolo Bowie stars in this unusual melodrama about a Prussian war vet turned male prostitute. He spends most of his time working for the sexiest of women. Splendid cast, but a bit incoherent.
1979 (R) 105m/C GE David Bowie, Sydne Rome, Kim Novak, David Hemmings, Maria Schell, Curt Jurgens, Marlene Dietrich; **D:** David Hemmings. **VHS, LV $59.95** TAM, MOV, LUM �22½

Just Another Girl on the I.R.T. Double debut from two African American women, writer/director Harris, and actress Johnson, captures the sass and wit of a girl from the projects who has a plan for her life. Seventeen-year-old Chantal challenges the authority around her with assurance, arguing with her history teacher, for example, that the mortality rate among African American infants and teenage males is more relevant to her life than a lesson on the Holocaust (although interesting parallels could be drawn). Chantal's life takes an unexpected turn, however, when she gets pregnant and chooses to spend her intended abortion money on a shopping spree. What starts as a strong statement becomes weak and cloudy as Chantal loses her focus, and writer Harris is unable to offer any answers to or even insight on the plight of being a poor single mother. This observation, however, is not to dismiss the realism and raw talent portrayed in a picture filmed in a remarkable seventeen days for $130,000. Winner of a special jury prize at the Sundance Film Festival.
1993 (R) 96m/C Ariyan Johnson, Kevin Thigpen, Ebony Jerido, Jerard Washington, Chequita Jackson, William Badget; **D:** Leslie Harris; **W:** Leslie Harris. **VHS** NYR �22½

Just Another Pretty Face An aging detective catches a gang of jewel smugglers, and gets involved with their young moll. In French with English subtitles. **AKA:** Be Beautiful but Shup Up.
1958 110m/B FR Henri Vidal, Mylene Demongeot, Isabelle Miranda; **D:** Henri Verneuil. **VHS, Beta $19.95** FCT, TAM �22½

Just Around the Corner Temple helps her Depression-poor father get a job after she befriends a cantankerous millionaire. ♫This Is A Happy Little Ditty; I'm Not Myself Today; I'll Be Lucky With You; Just Around the Corner; I Love To Walk in the Rain; Brass Buttons and Epaulets.
1938 70m/B Shirley Temple, Charles Farrell, Bert Lahr, Joan Davis, Bill Robinson, Cora Witherspoon, Franklin Pangborn; **D:** Irving Cummings. **VHS, Beta $19.98** FOX �22½

Just Before Dawn Another murderers stalk campers story; humans resort to their animal instincts in their struggle for survival. Not to be confused with the William Castle film (1946) from the "Crime Doctor" series.
1980 (R) 90m/C Chris Lemmon, Deborah Benson, Greg Henry, George Kennedy; **D:** Jeff Lieberman. **VHS, Beta** PGN �22

Just Between Friends Two women become friends, not knowing that one is having an affair with the husband of the other. Allan Burns directorial debut.
1986 (PG-13) 110m/C Mary Tyler Moore, Christine Lahti, Sam Waterston, Ted Danson, Jim Mackrell, Jane Greer; **D:** Allan Burns. **VHS, Beta $79.99** HBO �22

Just for the Hell of It A quartet of teenage punks ruthlessly terrorize their suburban Miami 'hood while an innocent kid gets blamed. More exploitation from schlock king Lewis, who also wrote the theme song, "Destruction Inc" (pic's alternate title). Essentially the same cast as the director's "She Devils on Wheels," filmed simultaneously. **AKA:** Destruction, Inc.
1968 85m/C Rodney Bedell, Ray Sager, Nancy Lee Noble, Agi Gyenes, Steve White; **D:** Herschell Gordon Lewis. **VHS $20.00** SMW Woof!

Just Like Weather Contemporary Hong Kong and the city's looming return to control by mainland China provide the backdrop for the troubled marriage of a young couple. Couple endure abortion, arrest, and veterinarian episodes before departing for on U.S. trip with high hopes.
1986 98m/C HK Christine Lee, Lee Chi-Keung, Allen Fong; **D:** Allen Fong. **VHS $39.95** FCT �22�2

Just Me & You An "It Happened One Night" made-for-television tale of an unlikely couple who fall in love with each other when chance brings them together on a cross-country drive. Written by Lasser.
1978 100m/C Louise Lasser, Charles Grodin; **D:** Charles Erman. **VHS, Beta** NO �22½

Just One of the Guys When the school newspaper refuses to accept the work of an attractive young girl, she goes undercover as a boy to prove that her work is good. She goes on to befriend the school's nerd, and even helps him grow out of his awkward stage, falling for him in the process. Very cute, but predictable.
1985 (PG-13) 100m/C Joyce Hyser, Clayton Rohner, Billy Jacoby, Toni Hudson, Leigh McCloskey, Sherilyn Fenn; **D:** Lisa Gottlieb. **VHS, Beta, LV $79.95** COL �22

Just Plain Daffy A compilation of pre-1948 Daffy Duck cartoon favorites.
1948 60m/C Bob Clampett, Robert McKimson, Friz Freleng, Frank Tashlin. **VHS, Beta $14.95** MGM, WTA �22�2½

Just Suppose Prince in waiting decides he'd prefer the simple life, travels to the land of the free in search of honest work and is felled by cupid's arrow. All's well 'til duty calls, and his princely presence is expected back in the royal fold. Features beautiful boy Barthelmess, whom Lillian Gish described as having "the most beautiful face of any man who ever went before a camera." Silent.
1926 90m/B Richard Barthelmess, Lois Moran, Geoffrey Kerr, Henry Vibart, George Spelvin; *D:* Kenneth Webb. **VHS, Beta** $19.95 *GPV* 🎬🎬½

Just Tell Me What You Want A wealthy, self-made married man finally drives his longtime mistress away when he refuses to let her take over the operation of a failing movie studio he has acquired. After she falls for another man, the tycoon does everything he can to win her back. The department store battle between MacGraw and King is priceless.
1980 (R) 112m/C Alan King, Ali MacGraw, Myrna Loy, Keenan Wynn, Tony Roberts; *D:* Sidney Lumet. **VHS, Beta** $19.98 *WAR* 🎬🎬½

Just Tell Me You Love Me Three budding con artists plot to make easy money in this Hawaiian romp.
1980 (PG) 90m/C Robert Hegyes, Debralee Scott, Lisa Hartman, Ricci Martin, June Lockhart; *D:* Tony Mordente. **VHS, Beta** $69.98 *LIV, VES* 🎬

Just the Way You Are An attractive musician struggles to overcome a physical handicap and winds up falling in love while on vacation in the French Alps.
1984 (PG) 96m/C Kristy McNichol, Robert Carradine, Kaki Hunter, Michael Ontkean, Alexandra Paul, Lance Guest, Timothy Daly, Patrick Cassidy; *D:* Edouard Molinaro. **VHS, Beta** $14.95 *MGM* 🎬

Just William's Luck A precocious English brat sneaks into an old mansion, which just happens to be the headquarters for a gang of thieves. Based on British series of children's books.
1947 87m/B *GB* William A. Graham, Garry Marsh; *D:* Val Guest. **VHS, Beta** $29.95 *VYY* 🎬🎬

Justice A crusading attorney tries to keep a waterfront kangaroo court from applying its harsh justice to an admitted killer. A television crime-drama also titled "Flight from Fear."
1955 26m/B William Prince, Jack Klugman, Biff McGuire, Jack Warden. **VHS, Beta** $19.95 *VYY* 🎬🎬

Justice of the West The Lone Ranger and his sidekick, Tonto, perform good deeds in the Old West, including helping to retrieve stolen gold, helping to build an Indian school, and giving a blind man a fresh perspective on life.
1961 71m/C Clayton Moore, Jay Silverheels; *D:* Earl Bellamy. **VHS, Beta** $29.95 *MGM* 🎬

Justice Rides Again Mix tries to uphold law and order, but he's up against some very tough outlaws.
193? 55m/B Tom Mix. **VHS, Beta** $29.95 *VCN* 🎬½

Justicia para los Mexicanos A gang of outlaws make a big mistake when they try to blame Mexican citizens for their crimes. The righteous folks show they're not pushovers.
19?? ?m/C *MX* Tony Kendall. **VHS, Beta** *MAD* 🎬

Justin Morgan Had a Horse The true story of a colonial school teacher in post-Revolutionary War Vermont who first bred the Morgan horse, the first and most versatile American breed.

1981 91m/C Don Murray, Lana Wood, Gary Crosby; *D:* Hollingsworth Morse. **VHS, Beta** $69.95 *DIS* 🎬🎬

Justine In the 1930s, a prostitute who marries an Egyptian banker becomes involved with a variety of men and a plot to arm Palestinian Jews in their revolt against English rule. A condensed film version of Lawrence Durrell's "The Alexandria Quartet."
1969 115m/C *IS* Anouk Aimee, Michael York, Dirk Bogarde, Philippe Noiret, Michael Constantine, John Vernon, Jack Albertson; *D:* George Cukor; *M:* Jerry Goldsmith. **VHS, Beta** $59.98 *FOX, HHE* 🎬🎬

K-9 After having his car destroyed by a drug dealer, "I work alone" Belushi is forced to take on a partner—a German Shepherd. Together they work to round up the bad guys and maybe chew on their shoes a little. Sometimes amusing one-joke comedy done in by a paper-thin script. Both the dog and Belushi are good, however.
1989 (PG-13) 111m/C James Belushi, Mel Harris, Kevin Tighe, Ed O'Neill, Cotter Smith; *D:* Rod Daniel. **VHS, Beta, LV** $19.95 *MCA* 🎬🎬½

K-9000 The Hound salutes the idea behind this standard sci-fi crime-fighter; a cyberdog fights the forces of evil with the aid of a cop, a lady reporter, and the usual cliches. Made For television.
1989 96m/C Chris Mulkey, Catherine Oxenberg; *D:* Kim Manners; *M:* Jan Hammer. **VHS** $64.95 *FRH* 🎬🎬

Kafka Disappointing and gloomy Soderbergh film that serves no purpose whatsoever. Irons plays Kafka, an insurance workers by day and a writer by night. The movie exists largely without interest until Kafka uncovers an office conspiracy and makes his way to the enemy's castle headquarters. From then on, "Kafka" is nothing but a conventional horror film. Irons is wasted in a role that requires nothing but an impeccable British accent. On the plus side, the film is exquisitely shot in black and white until the castle scenes, when the cinematography is switched to color.
1991 (PG-13) 100m/C Jeremy Irons; *D:* Steven Soderbergh. **VHS, Beta, LV** $89.00 *PAR, TAM, PMS* 🎬½

Kagemusha A thief is rescued from the gallows because of his striking resemblance to a warlord in 16th Century Japan. When the ambitious warlord is fatally wounded, the thief is required to pose as the warlord. In Japanese with English subtitles. *AKA:* The Shadow Warrior; The Double.
1980 (PG) 160m/C *JP* Tatsuya Nakadai, Tsutomu Yamazaki, Kenichi Hagiwara; *D:* Akira Kurosawa. Academy Awards '80 Nominations: Best Art Direction/Set Decoration, Best Foreign Language Film; British Academy Awards '80: Best Director (Kurosawa); Cannes Film Festival '80: Best Film; Cesar Awards '81: Best Foreign Film; National Board of Review Awards '80: 5 Best Foreign Films of the Year. **VHS, Beta** $19.98 *FOX, APD, TAM* 🎬🎬🎬½

Kalifornia "Badlands" meets the '90s in road trip with the hitchhikers from hell. Early Grayce (Pitt) is your average slimeball who murders his landlord and hops a ride with his girlfriend Adele (Lewis) from Kentucky to California with two grad students who are touring serial murder landmarks. The real ride begins when serial killer expert Brian (Duchovny) begins to suspect Grayce's sociopathic tendencies. Pitt and Lewis were still an item when they made this. Pitt reportedly wanted to play against type, and as pretty boy gone homicidal, he succeeds.

1993 (NC-17) ?m/C Juliette Lewis, Brad Pitt, David Duchovny, Michele Forbes, Sierra Pecheur, Lois Hall, Gregory Mars Martin; *D:* Dominic Sena; *W:* Tim Metcalfe. **VHS** *NYR* 🎬🎬½

Kameradschaft A great, early German sound film about Germans struggling to free themselves and French miners trapped underground on the countries' border. In German and French with English subtitles.
1931 80m/B *GE* Ernst Busch, Alexander Granach, Fritz Kampers; *D:* G.W. Pabst. **VHS, Beta, 3/4U** $29.98 *SUE, MRV, IHF* 🎬🎬🎬½

Kamikaze A Japanese World War II action drama about suicide pilots.
1945 100m/B *JP* **VHS, Beta** $14.99 *VCD, RXM* 🎬

Kamikaze '89 German director Fassbinder has the lead acting role (his last) in this offbeat story of a police lieutenant in Berlin, circa 1989, who investigates a puzzling series of bombings. Music by Tangerine Dream. In German with English subtitles.
1983 90m/C *GE* Rainer Werner Fassbinder, Gunther Kaufman, Boy Gobert; *D:* Wolf Gromm. **VHS, Beta** $59.95 *MGM, FCT, GLV* 🎬🎬🎬

Kanal Wajda's first major success, a grueling account of Warsaw patriots, upon the onset of the Nazis toward the end of the war, fleeing through the ruined city's sewers. Highly acclaimed. In Polish with English subtitles or dubbed. *AKA:* They Loved Life.
1956 96m/B *PL* Teresa Izewska, Tadeusz Janczar; *D:* Andrzej Wajda. **VHS, Beta** $29.98 *SUE, TAM, NLC* 🎬🎬🎬½

Kandyland An over-the-hill stripper takes a young innocent stripper under her wing.
1987 (R) 94m/C Sandahl Bergman, Kimberly Evenson, Charles Laulette, Bruce Baum; *D:* Robert Allen Schnitzer. **VHS, Beta, LV** $19.95 *STE, NWV* 🎬

Kangaroo An Australian adaptation of the semi-autobiographical D.H. Lawrence novel. A controversial English novelist and his wife move to the Outback in 1922, and are confronted with all manner of prejudice and temptation.
1986 (R) 115m/C *AU* Judy Davis, Colin Friels; *D:* Tim Burstall. **VHS, Beta** $79.95 *MCA* 🎬🎬🎬

The Kansan The marshal in a Kansas town won't rest until he's stamped out all traces of corruption.
1943 79m/B Richard Dix, Victor Jory, Albert Dekker; *D:* George Archainbaud. **VHS, Beta** $19.95 *NOS, MRV, HEG* 🎬🎬

Kansas Two young men, one a lawless rebel, the other a rational loner, stage a bank heist, and then go on the lam. Lame plot and very weak acting combine to make this film a dud.
1988 (R) 111m/C Matt Dillon, Andrew McCarthy, Leslie Hope, Kyra Sedgwick; *D:* David Stevens. **VHS, Beta, LV** $19.95 *MED* 🎬

Kansas City Confidential An ex-cop on the wrong side of the law launches a sophisticated armored car heist. A disgruntled ex-con gets arrested for the crime on circumstantial evidence. When released, he scours the underworld for the real thieves.
1952 98m/B John Payne, Coleen Gray, Preston Foster, Neville Brand, Lee Van Cleef, Jack Elam; *D:* Phil Karlson. **VHS** $16.95 *NOS, MGM, RXM* 🎬🎬🎬

Kansas City Massacre A made-for-television film chronicling the efforts of Melvin Purvis, as he tracked down Depression-era hoods. First called "Melvin Purvis, G-Man."
1975 99m/C Dale Robertson, Sally Kirkland, Bo Hopkins, Scott Brady, Lynn Loring, Matt Clark, Mills Watson, Robert Walden; *D:* Dan Curtis. **VHS, Beta** $59.95 *VMK* 🎬½

Kansas Pacific A group of Confederate sympathizers try to stop the Kansas Pacific Railroad from reaching the West Coast in the 1860s.
1953 73m/C Sterling Hayden, Eve Miller, Barton MacLane, Reed Hadley, Douglas Hadley; *D:* Ray Nazarro. VHS, Beta $14.95 *NOS, MRV, QNE* 🎞

The Kansas Terrors The "Three Mesquiteers" head for the Caribbean to deliver a herd of horses and wind up in a battle against local despot.
1939 57m/B Bob Livingston, Raymond Hatton, Duncan Renaldo, Jacqueline Wells, Yakima Canutt, Richard Alexander, Maureen McCormack; *D:* George Sherman. VHS $19.95 *NOS* 🎞

Kaos The Taviani brothers adaptation of four stories by Luigi Pirandello ("The Other Son," "Moonstruck," "The Jar," and "Requiem"), which look at peasant life in Sicily, ranging from the comic to the tragic. A fictional epilog, "Conversing with Mother," has Pirandello talking with the spirit of his dead mother. As with any anthology some stories are stronger than others but all possess the Taviani's great visual style and some fine acting. In Italian with English subtitles. *AKA:* Chaos-Kaos.
1985 (R) 188m/C *IT* Margarita Lozano, Claudio Bigagli, Massimo Bonetti, Omero Antonutti, Enrica Maria Modugno, Ciccio Ingrassia, Franco Franchi, Biagio Barone, Salvatore Rossi, Franco Scaldati, Pasquale Spadola, Regina Bianchi; *D:* Paolo Taviani, Vittorio Taviani. VHS $29.98 *MGM* 🎞🎞🎞

Kapo A 14-year-old Jewish girl and her family are imprisoned by the Nazis in a concentration camp. There, the girl changes identities with the help of the camp doctor, and rises to the position of camp guard. She proceeds to become taken with her power until a friend commits suicide and jolts the girl back into harsh reality. An Academy Award nominee for Best Foreign Film (lost to "The Virgin Spring"). Primarily English dialogue, with subtitles for foreign language.
1959 116m/B *IT FR YU* Susan Strasberg, Laurent Terzieff, Emmanuelle Riva, Gianno Garko; *W/D:* Gillo Pontecorvo. VHS *DVT, HEG* 🎞🎞🎞

The Karate Kid A teen-age boy finds out that Karate involves using more than your fists when a handyman agrees to teach him martial arts. The friendship that they develop is deep and sincere; the Karate is only an afterthought. From the director of the original "Rocky," this movie is easy to like.
1984 (PG) 126m/C Ralph Macchio, Pat Morita, Elisabeth Shue, Randee Heller, Martin Kove, Chad McQueen; *D:* John G. Avildsen; *W:* Robert Mark Kamen. VHS, Beta, LV, 8mm $19.95 *COL* 🎞🎞🎞½

The Karate Kid: Part 2 Sequel to the first film wherein our high-kicking hero tests his mettle in real-life karate exchanges in Okinawa, and settles a long-standing score. Followed by a second sequel.
1986 (PG) 95m/C Ralph Macchio, Pat Morita, Danny Kamekona, Martin Kove, Tamlyn Tomita; *D:* John G. Avildsen; *W:* Robert Mark Kamen. VHS, Beta, LV, 8mm $19.95 *RCA, COL* 🎞🎞½

The Karate Kid: Part 3 The second sequel, wherein the high-kicking young guy again battles an evil nemesis and learns about himself.
1989 (PG) 105m/C Ralph Macchio, Pat Morita; *D:* John G. Avildsen; *W:* Robert Mark Kamen. VHS, Beta, LV, 8mm $19.95 *COL* 🎞🎞

Karate Killer Kung Fu master seeks revenge on a brutal and vicious gang.
1973 (R) 95m/C VHS, Beta $54.95 *HHT* 🎞

Karate Polish Style Polish painter duo paint, plaster and draw blood. A sort of "Dances with Poles" in Warsaw's Mazurian Lake District. In Polish with English subtitles. Not a Polish joke.
1982 91m/C *PL* D: Jerzy Wojcik. VHS $49.95 *FCT* 🎞

Karate Warrior Young martial artist is beaten and left for dead by Filipino crime syndicate. Bones mended, he prescribes a dose of their medicine. Plenty of rest and retaliation.
19?? 90m/C Jared Martin, Ken Watanabe. VHS, Beta $79.98 *IMP* 🎞½

Karate Warriors Chiba takes his battle against crime to the streets.
197? 90m/C Sonny Chiba. VHS, Beta *NO* 🎞

Kashmiri Run Action adventure about trio on the lam from Chinese communists chasing them through Tibet.
1969 (R) 101m/C *SP* Pernell Roberts, Alexandra Bastedo, Julian Mateos, Gloria Gamata; *D:* John Peyser. VHS $29.95 *LIV* 🎞

Katherine A young heiress rejects her pampered lifestyle and becomes a violent revolutionary, rebelling against social injustices and the system that spawned them. Made for television. Also released on video as "The Radical."
1975 98m/C Sissy Spacek, Art Carney, Jane Wyatt, Henry Winkler, Julie Kavner; *D:* Jeremy Paul Kagan. VHS, Beta, LV $19.95 *STE, NWV, IME* 🎞

Katie's Passion In 19th century Holland, a young girl acquires fame, money, power and love through her wiles. In Dutch with English subtitles. *AKA:* Cathy Tippel; Keetje Tippel; Hot Sweat.
1975 (R) 104m/C *NL* Rutger Hauer, Monique Van De Ven, Eddie Brugman, Hannah De Leeuwe, Andrea Domburg; *D:* Paul Verhoeven. VHS, Beta $29.95 *CVC* 🎞

Kavik the Wolf Dog Heartwarming story of a courageous dog's love and suffering for the boy he loves. Made for television. *AKA:* The Courage of Kavik, the Wolf Dog.
1984 99m/C Ronny Cox, Linda Sorensen, Andrew Ian McMillian, Chris Wiggins, John Ireland; *D:* Peter Carter. VHS, Beta $19.95 *MED* 🎞½

Keaton's Cop Another cheap cop comedy involving the mistaken identity of an important mob witness.
1990 (R) 95m/C Lee Majors, Abe Vigoda, Don Rickles; *D:* Bob Burge. VHS, Beta, LV $14.95 *MGM, OM* 🎞

The Keep At the height of the Nazi onslaught, several German soldiers unleash an unknown power from a medieval stone fortress. Technically impressive but lacking in all other aspects.
1983 (R) 96m/C Scott Glenn, Alberta Watson, Juergen Prochnow, Robert Prosky, Gabriel Byrne; *D:* Michael Mann. VHS, Beta $79.95 *PAR* 🎞🎞

Keep 'Em Flying Bud and Lou star in the this wartime morale-booster that hasn't aged well. The duo follow their barnstorming friend into flight academy; a not-too-taxing plot includes five musical numbers and two Martha Rayes (she plays twins). ♫ Pig Foot Pete; Together; I'm Looking for the Boy with the Wistful Eyes; Let's Keep 'Em Flying; I'm Getting Sentimental Over You.
1941 86m/B Bud Abbott, Lou Costello, Martha Raye; *D:* Arthur Lubin. VHS, LV $14.95 *MCA* 🎞🎞

Keep It Up, Jack! A good for nothing, out-of-work actor winds up with a bordello on his hands. Lucky for him it comes with a bunch of blonde beauties to keep him company.
1975 90m/C Mark Jones, Sue Longhurst, Maggie Burton, Steve Viedor; *D:* Tom Parker. VHS *NO* 🎞

Keep My Grave Open A woman lives in an isolated house where a series of strange murders take place. She attributes them to her brother, but does he really exist? Made cheaply, but not without style; filmed in Harrison County, Texas. *AKA:* The House Where Hell Froze Over.
1980 (R) 85m/C Camilla Carr, Gene Ross, Stephen Tobolowsky, Ann Stafford, Sharon Bunn, Chelcie Ross; *D:* S.F. Brownrigg. VHS, Beta $9.95 *UNI* 🎞🎞

Keep Punching A gambler/boxer is almost destroyed by life in the fast lane, as well as by a seductive woman.
1939 80m/C Henry Armstrong, Mae Johnson; *Cameos:* Canada Lee; *D:* John Clein. VHS $34.95 *FCT* 🎞🎞

Keep the Change Joe Starling is an artist with painter's block, living in California with his girlfriend Astrid. He decides to revisit the family ranch in Deadrock, Montana, and his crackpot Uncle Smitty and saintly Aunt Lureen. The family ranch is coveted by the evil Overstreet (typecasting for Palance), whose daughter was once loved by Joe but is now married to his ex-best friend. Character more than plot rules this moody, low-key story based on a novel by Thomas McGuane. Made for cable television.
1992 (PG-13) 95m/C William L. Petersen, Lolita Davidovich, Rachel Ticotin, Buck Henry, Jack Palance, Fred Dalton Thompson, Jeff Kober, Lois Smith; *D:* Andy Tennant. VHS, LV $89.98 *TTC* 🎞🎞

Keeper Wealthy patients at Underwood Asylum suffer unspeakable horrors while under the care of Lee. Detective Dick Driver investigates. Obscure horror spoof.
1984 96m/C *CA* Christopher Lee, Tell Schreiber, Sally Gray; *W/D:* Tom Drake. VHS, Beta $49.95 *TWE, HHE* 🎞🎞

Keeper of the City Gossett stars as a tough detective out to get a vigilante (LaPaglia) who is roaming the streets of Chicago. LaPaglia turns in a good performance as the son of a Mafia operative who wants to rid himself of the Mafia ties that have controlled him. As he pursues his deadly course of action, a newspaper journalist tags him "The Gangster Killer" who is always interfering in Gossett's business. Good performances and an intriguing story line combine to make this action-packed thriller worthwhile, although the script isn't as good as Di Pega's novel, which he adapted himself.
1992 (R) 95m/C Louis Gossett Jr., Peter Coyote, Anthony LaPaglia, Renee Soutendijk, Aeryk Egan, Tony Todd; *D:* Bobby Roth; *W:* Gerald Di Pega. VHS, Beta, LV $89.98 *FXV* 🎞🎞½

Keeping On Television movie with a pro-union stance. A preacher, who is also a millworker, teams up with an organizer to try to unionize the mill. Originally produced for the PBS "American Playhouse" series.
1981 75m/C Dick Anthony Williams, Carol Kane, James Broderick, Marcia Rodd, Rosalind Cash, Carl Lee, Danny Glover, Guy Boyd; *D:* Barbara Kopple. VHS $59.95 *TWE* 🎞🎞½

Keeping Track Two tourists witness a murder and robbery and find the stolen $5 million on a New York-bound train. The two are relentlessly pursued by everyone, including the CIA and Russian spies.
1986 (R) 102m/C Michael Sarrazin, Margot Kidder, Alan Scarfe, Ken Pogue, Vlasta Vrana, Donald Pilon; **D:** Robin Spry. **VHS, Beta, LV** $19.98 *NLC* 🐾

Keetje Tippei In 1881 Amsterdam, a young Dutch prostitute works her way out of poverty and enters a world of education and wealth. A Victorian tale of exploitation with a tough and intelligent Cinderella heroine. In Dutch with English subtitles.
1975 104m/C *NL* Monique Van De Ven, Rutger Hauer; **D:** Paul Verhoeven. **VHS, Beta, LV** $79.95 *CVC, IME, TAM* 🐾🐾

Kelly's Heroes A misfit band of crooks are led by Eastwood on a daring mission: to steal a fortune in gold from behind enemy lines. In the process, they almost win World War II. Sutherland is superb, as is McLeod, in his pre-Love Boat days.
1970 (R) 145m/C Clint Eastwood, Donald Sutherland, Telly Savalas, Gavin McLeod, Don Rickles, Carroll O'Connor, Stuart Margolin, Harry Dean Stanton; **D:** Brian G. Hutton. **VHS, Beta, LV** $19.98 *MGM, TLF* 🐾🐾🐾

Kemek An eccentric chemical company owner has his mistress push a new mind-control drug on an American writer, and has them killed after discovering their subsequent affair. Unfortunately, he didn't count on the woman's ex-husband seeking revenge.
1988 (R) 82m/C David Hedison, Helmut Snider, Mary Woronov, Alexandra Stewart, Cal Haynes. **VHS, Data** 🐾🐾

Kennedy The long television mini-series biography of JFK from his inauguration to assassination.
1983 278m/C Martin Sheen, Blair Brown, Vincent Gardenia, Geraldine Fitzgerald, E.G. Marshall, John Shea; **D:** Richard Hartley. **VHS, Beta** $14.99 *STE, PSM* 🐾🐾

The Kennedys Don't Cry A sensitive and detailed look at the triumphs and tragedies of the Kennedy clan. Rare footage and interviews trace the growth of Joseph P. Kennedy's children and their influence on American history. Some segments are in black and white.
1983 100m/C VHS, Beta $59.95 *MPI* 🐾🐾

The Kennel Murder Case Debonair detective Philo Vance suspects that a clear-cut case of suicide is actually murder. Fourth Vance mystery starring Powell. Remade as "Calling Philo Vance" in 1940.
1933 73m/B William Powell, Mary Astor, Jack LaRue, Ralph Morgan, Eugene Pallette; **D:** Michael Curtiz. **VHS, Beta, 3/4U, Special order formats** $16.95 *SNC, NOS, HHT* 🐾🐾🐾

Kenny Rogers as the Gambler Rogers stars as Brady Hawkes, debonair gambler searching for a son he never knew he had. Based on the Rogers song of the same name. One of the highest rated TV movies ever. Followed by three sequels.
1980 94m/C Kenny Rogers, Christine Belford, Bruce Boxleitner, Harold Gould, Clu Gulager, Lance LeGault, Lee Purcell, Noble Willingham; **D:** Dick Lowry. **VHS** *WKV* 🐾🐾½

Kenny Rogers as the Gambler, Part 2: The Adventure Continues The surprise success of the made-for-TV western based on the popular Kenny Rogers' song spawned this equally popular sequel. Rogers returns as Brady Hawkes, this time searching for his kidnapped son. Followed by two more sequels.

1983 195m/C Kenny Rogers, Bruce Boxleitner, Linda Evans, Harold Gould, David Hedison, Clu Gulager, Johnny Crawford; **D:** Dick Lowry. **VHS, Beta, 8mm** $24.95 *WKV* 🐾🐾½

Kenny Rogers as the Gambler, Part 3: The Legend Continues Roger's third attempt at humanizing the gambler from his hit '70s song. This time, the Gambler gives a hand with the mediating between the warring U.S. government and the Sioux nation. Sitting Bull and Buffalo Bill add credibility to this average undertaking. Made for TV.
1987 190m/C Kenny Rogers, Bruce Boxleitner, Linda Gray, Melanie Chartoff, Matt Clark, George Kennedy, Dean Stockwell, Charles Durning, Jeffrey Jones, George American Horse; **D:** Dick Lowry. **VHS, Beta** *WKV* 🐾

Kent State Made-for-television drama recounts the tragic events that took place at Kent State University in 1970, when student demonstrators faced National Guardsmen. Goldstone won an Emmy for Outstanding Direction.
1981 120m/C Talia Balsam, Ellen Barkin, Jane Fleiss, John Getz, Keith Gordon; **D:** James Goldstone. **VHS, Beta** $39.95 *MCA* 🐾🐾

Kentuckian Burt Lancaster stars as a rugged frontiersman who leaves with his son to go to Texas. On their journey the two are harassed by fighting mountaineers.
1955 104m/C Burt Lancaster, Walter Matthau, Diana Lynn, John McIntire, Dianne Foster, Una Merkel, John Carradine; **D:** Burt Lancaster. **VHS, Beta** $19.98 *FOX* 🐾🐾½

Kentucky Blue Streak Young jockey is framed for murder while riding at an "illegal" racetrack. Later, almost eligible for parole, he escapes from jail to ride "Blue Streak" in the Kentucky Derby.
1935 61m/B Eddie Nugent, Frank "Junior" Coghlan, Patricia Scott, Ben Carter. **VHS, Beta** $24.95 *VYY* 🐾½

Kentucky Fried Movie A zany potpourri of satire about movies, television, commercials, and contemporary society. Written by Abrahams and the Zuckers, who were later known for "Airplane!"
1977 (R) 85m/C Bill Bixby, Jerry Zucker, Jim Abrahams, David Zucker, Donald Sutherland, Henry Gibson, George Lazenby; **D:** John Landis. **VHS, Beta, LV** $59.95 *MED* 🐾🐾🐾

Kentucky Jubilee At the jubiloo, a movie director is kidnapped and the master of ceremonies, among others, decides to find him.
1951 67m/B Jerry Colonna, Jean Porter, James Ellison, Raymond Hatton, Fritz Feld. **VHS, Beta, LV** *RXM* 🐾½

Kentucky Kernels A pair of down and out magicians (thirties comic duo Wheeler and Woolsey) happen upon a young boy (Little Rascal Spanky) who happens to be heir to a fortune. The three head for the rascal's Kentucky home, where they're welcomed with southern inhospitality. Much feuding and slapsticking. **AKA:** Triple Trouble.
1934 75m/B Bert Wheeler, Robert Woolsey, Mary Carlisle, George "Spanky" McFarland, Noah Beery Sr., Lucille LaVerne, Willie Best; **D:** George Stevens. **VHS, LV** $19.98 *TTC, FCT* 🐾🐾

Kentucky Rifle A Comanche Indian tribe will let a group of stranded pioneers through their territory only if they agree to sell the Kentucky rifles aboard their wagon.
1955 80m/C Chill Wills, Lance Fuller, Cathy Downs, Jess Barker, Sterling Holloway, Jeanne Cagney; **D:** Carl K. Hittleman. **VHS, Beta** $29.95 *MON, HHE* 🐾½

Kept Husbands A factory worker saves two lives in an industrial accident, and the boss invites him home to dinner. When he meets the boss' daughter, romance blooms. But their different backgrounds cause difficulties. A bit dull, and dated by its chauvinism.
1931 76m/B Dorothy Mackaill, Joel McCrea, Robert McWade, Florence Roberts, Clara Kimball Young, Mary Carr, Ned Sparks, Bryant Washburn; **D:** Lloyd Bacon. **VHS** $19.95 *NOS, HEG* 🐾🐾

Kerouac Documentary frames the life of the beat poet Jack Kerouac with excerpts from his appearance on the Steve Allen Show in 1959. The film includes interviews with many of Kerouac's contemporaries. **AKA:** Jack Kerouac's America.
1984 90m/C Lawrence Ferlinghetti, Allen Ginsberg, William S. Burroughs, Steve Allen, Jack Kerouac. **VHS, Beta** $39.95 *AHV* 🐾🐾

The Key A long, slow World War II drama about the key to an Italian girl's apartment that gets passed from tugboat skipper to tugboat skipper before dangerous missions. Ultimately she finds true love, or does she? Based on the novel "Stella" by Jan de Hartog.
1958 134m/B *GB* William Holden, Sophia Loren, Trevor Howard, Oscar Homolka, Kieron Moore; **D:** Carol Reed; **W:** Carl Foreman. **VHS, Beta, LV** $69.95 *COL* 🐾🐾

Key Exchange Kevin Scott and Paul Kurta based this contemporary look at love and commitments on Kevin Wade's popular play. Two New York City "yuppies" have reached a point in their relationship where an exchange of apartment keys commonly occurs—but they are hesitant.
1985 (R) 96m/C Brooke Adams, Ben Masters, Daniel Stern, Tony Roberts, Danny Aiello, Annie Golden; **D:** Barnet Kellman. **VHS, Beta** $79.98 *FOX* 🐾🐾½

Key Largo A gangster melodrama set in Key West, Florida, where hoods take over a hotel in the midst of a hurricane. Based on a play by Maxwell Anderson.
1948 101m/B Humphrey Bogart, Lauren Bacall, Claire Trevor, Edward G. Robinson, Lionel Barrymore; **D:** John Huston; **W:** Richard Brooks, John Huston. **VHS, Beta, LV** $19.98 *MGM, FOX, PIA* 🐾🐾🐾

The Key Man A radio show host manages to get mixed up with gangsters after recreating a crime on the air. He uses his knowledge of crime to thwart the crooks. **AKA:** Life at Stake.
1957 63m/B *GB* Lee Patterson, Hy Hazell, Colin Gordon, Philip Leaver, Paula Byrne; **D:** Montgomery Tully. **VHS, Beta** $16.95 *NOS, SNC* 🐾½

The Key to Rebecca The Nazis and the British go head-to-head in war torn North Africa. As the Germans push their way across Egypt, they find an unexpected ally in a half-German/half-Arab killer behind the British lines. Tense, well made thriller, originally a mini-series. On two cassettes. Made for television.
1985 190m/C David Soul, Cliff Robertson, Robert Culp, Season Hubley, Lina Raymond, Anthony Quayle, David Hemmings; **D:** David Hemmings. **VHS** $89.95 *WOV* 🐾🐾½

Key to Vengeance Lone wolf battles bad guy with wealth of weapons. Vengeance is mine saith the guy with the most toys.
197? 90m/C Patrick L'Argent, Laura Yang. **VHS** *NO* 🐾½

The Keys of the Kingdom An earnest adaptation of A.J. Cronin's novel about a young Scottish missionary spreading God's word in 19th Century China.
1944 137m/B Gregory Peck, Thomas Mitchell, Edmund Gwenn, Vincent Price, Roddy McDowall, Cedric Hardwicke, Peggy Ann Garner, James Gleason, Anne Revere, Rose Stradner, Sara Allgood, Abner Biberman, Arthur Shields; **D:** John M. Stahl; **W:** Joseph L. Mankiewicz, Nunnally Johnson. **VHS, Beta, LV $19.98** FOX, IGP *ἀἀἀ*

The KGB: The Secret War Reheated Cold War fare. **AKA:** Lethal.
1986 (PG-13) 90m/C Sally Kellerman, Michael Ansara, Michael Billington. **VHS, LV** HHE *ἀ½*

Khartoum A sweeping but talky adventure epic detailing the last days of General "Chinese" Gordon as the title city is besieged by Arab tribes in 1884.
1966 134m/C Charlton Heston, Laurence Olivier, Ralph Richardson, Richard Jordan, Alexander Knox, Hugh Williams, Nigel Green, Michael Hordern, Johnny Sekka; **D:** Basil Dearden. **VHS, Beta, LV $19.98** MGM, PIA, CCB *ἀἀ½*

The Kick Fighter Would you believe the hero has to kickbox to finance his kid sister's operation? Grungy, Bangkok-set chopsocky cheapie leaves no cliche untouched, but fights are well-staged. A strange end credit lauds real-life champ Urquidez, here a bad guy.
1991 92m/C Richard Norton, Benny "The Jet" Urquidez, Glen Ruehland, Franco Guerrero, Erica Van Wagener, Steve Rackman; **D:** Anthony Maharaj. **VHS $79.95** AIP *ἀ*

Kick of Death: The Prodigal Boxer A young boxer is accused of a murder he didn't commit, and fights a battle to the death to prove it.
198? (R) 90m/C Mang Sei, Suma Wah Lung, Pa Hung; **D:** Chai Yang Min. **VHS, Beta $19.95** GEM *ἀ*

Kickboxer The brother of a permanently crippled kickboxing champ trains for a revenge match.
1989 (R) 97m/C Jean-Claude Van Damme, Rochelle Ashana, Dennis Chan, Dennis Alexio; **D:** David Worth, Mark DiSalle. **VHS, Beta, LV $19.98** HBO *ἀ½*

Kickboxer 2: The Road Back Mitchell takes over for Van Damme in this action sequel which finds our athletic hero seeking revenge on the kickboxer who murdered his brother.
1990 (R) 90m/C Sasha Mitchell, Peter Boyle, John Diehl; **D:** Albert Pyun. **VHS, LV $19.98** HBO, MOV *ἀ½*

Kickboxer 3: The Art of War Mitchell returns in this second sequel. This time the American kickboxing champ flies to Rio for a big match which turns out to be fixed by a local mobster. For a little more fun our hero saves a kidnapped girl and fights a hired killer.
1992 (R) 92m/C Sasha Mitchell, Dennis Chan, Richard Comar, Noah Verduzco, Althea Miranda, Ian Jacklin; **D:** Rick King. **VHS, LV $89.98** LIV *ἀ½*

Kickboxer the Champion The opium trade is in for a kick to the stomach when Archer challenges the big man in charge to a deathly duel.
1991 ?m/C Don Murray, Wayne Archer; **D:** Alton Cheung. **VHS $79.95** WLA *ἀ*

Kicks Two well-off San Francisco professionals play high-risk games with each other, culminating in a life-or-death hunt. Made for television.

1985 97m/C Anthony Geary, Shelley Hack, Tom Mason, Ian Abercrombie, James Avery; **D:** William Wiard. **VHS, Beta $79.95** WWV *ἀ½*

The Kid Sensitive and sassy film about a tramp who takes home an orphan. Chaplin's first feature. Also launched Coogan as the first child superstar.
1921 60m/B Charlie Chaplin, Jackie Coogan, Edna Purviance; **D:** Charlie Chaplin. **VHS $29.98** FCT, MLB *ἀἀἀ*

Kid Young guy carries grudge for the murder of his parents and seeks pound of flesh. Enter mysterious beautiful woman and copious complications. Good sound FX.
1990 (R) 94m/C C. Thomas Howell, Lee Ermey, Brian Austin Green, Sarah Trigger; **D:** John Mark Robinson. **VHS, Beta, LV $89.95** LIV, IME *ἀἀ½*

Kid and the Killers Young orphan and a hardened criminal band together to pursue a villain.
198? (PG) 90m/C Jon Cypher. **VHS, Beta** NO *ἀ*

The Kid Brother The shy, weak son of a tough sheriff, Harold fantasizes about being a hero like his father and big brothers, falls in love with a carnival lady, and somehow saves the day. Classic silent comedy.
1927 84m/B Harold Lloyd, Walter James, Jobyna Ralston; **D:** Ted Wilde. **VHS, Beta** TLF *ἀἀἀ½*

Kid Colter Enjoyable family film about a city kid who goes to visit his dad in a remote wilderness area of the Pacific Northwest. While there he is abducted by two grizzly mountain men and left for dead, but survives and pursues his abductors relentlessly. Received the Film Advisory Board Award of Excellence and the Award of Merit from the Academy of Family Films.
1985 101m/C Jim Stafford, Jeremy Shamos, Hal Terrance, Greg Ward, Jim Turner; **W/D:** David O'Malley. **VHS, Beta $79.98** FOX *ἀἀ½*

Kid Courageous An athlete goes west, tracks ore mine thieves and prevents a hot-blooded spitfire from marrying the wrong man.
1935 53m/B Bob Steele. **VHS, Beta $19.95** NOS *ἀ*

Kid Dynamite A Bowery Boys series episode. Gorcey is a boxer who is kidnapped to prevent his participation in a major fight. The real fighting occurs when his brother is substituted, and Gorcey is smitten. **AKA:** Queen of Broadway.
1943 73m/B Leo Gorcey, Huntz Hall, Bobby Jordan, Gabriel Dell, Pamela Blake; **D:** Wallace Fox. **VHS $19.95** NOS, HEG *ἀ*

A Kid for Two Farthings An episodic, sentimental portrait of the Jewish quarter in London's East End, centered on a boy with a malformed goat he thinks is a magic unicorn capable of granting wishes and bringing happiness to his impoverished 'hood. Acclaimed adaptation of a novel by screenwriter Wolf Mankowitz, also on tape in a shorter rehash as "The Unicorn."
1955 96m/C Jonathan Ashmore. **VHS $39.95** HMV, FCT *ἀἀ½*

Kid from Brooklyn A shy, musically inclined milkman becomes a middleweight boxer by knocking out the champ in a street brawl. Remake of "The Milky Way" by Harold Lloyd. Available with digitally remastered stereo and original movie trailer. ♫Sunflower Song; Hey, What's Your Name; You're the Cause Of It All; Welcome, Burleigh; I Love An Old-Fashioned Song; Josie.
1946 113m/C Danny Kaye, Virginia Mayo, Eve Arden, Fay Bainter, Walter Abel; **D:** Norman Z. MacLeod. **VHS, Beta, LV $19.98** HBO, SUE *ἀἀ*

Kid from Gower Gulch A singing, non-horse-riding cowboy enters a rodeo through a clever ruse.
1947 56m/B Spade Cooley. **VHS, Beta, LV $19.95** NOS *ἀ*

The Kid from Left Field Bat boy for the San Diego Padres transforms the team from losers to champions when he passes on the advice of his father, a "has-been" ballplayer, to the team members. A made-for-television remake of the 1953 classic.
1979 80m/C Gary Coleman, Robert Guillaume, Ed McMahon, Tab Hunter; **D:** Adell Aldrich. **VHS, Beta $69.95** VES *ἀἀ*

Kid from Not-So-Big A family film that tells the story of Jenny, a young girl left to carry on her grandfather's frontier-town newspaper. When two con-men come to town, Jenny sets out to expose them.
1978 87m/C Jennifer McAllister, Veronica Cartwright, Robert Viharo, Paul Tulley; **D:** Bill Crain. **VHS, Beta $39.98** WAR, OM *ἀ*

Kid Galahad Well acted boxing drama with Robinson playing an honest promoter who wants to make Morris into a prize fighter. Davis plays the girl they both want. Remade as "The Wagons Roll at Night" and then made again as an Elvis Presley vehicle. Shown on television. **AKA:** The Battling Bellhop.
1937 101m/B Edward G. Robinson, Bette Davis, Humphrey Bogart, Wayne Morris, Jane Bryan, Harry Carey Sr.; **D:** Michael Curtiz; **W:** Seton I. Miller. **VHS $19.98** MGM *ἀἀἀ*

Kid Galahad The King plays a young boxer who weathers the fight game, singing seven songs along the way. ♫King of the Whole Wide World; This Is Living; I Got Lucky; A Whistling Tune; Home Is Where The Heart Is; Riding the Rainbow; Love Is For Loves.
1962 95m/C Elvis Presley, Lola Albright, Charles Bronson, Ned Glass, Joan Blackman, Ed Asner, Gig Young; **D:** Phil Karlson. **VHS, Beta $19.95** MGM *ἀἀ*

The Kid/Idle Class The Little Tramp adopts a homeless orphan in "The Kid," Chaplin's first feature-length film. This tape also includes "The Idle Class," a rare Chaplin short.
1921 85m/B Charlie Chaplin, Jackie Coogan, Edna Purviance, Chuck Reisner, Lita Grey; **D:** Charlie Chaplin. **VHS, Beta $19.98** FOX *ἀἀἀ*

Kid Millions Vintage musical comedy in which a dull-witted Brooklyn boy must travel to exotic Egypt to collect an inherited fortune. The finale is filmed in early three-strip Technicolor. Lucille Ball appears as a Goldwyn Girl. ♫Your Head on My Shoulder; Ice Cream Fantasy; An Earful of Music; When My Ship Comes In; Okay Toots; I Want to be a Minstrel Man; Mandy.
1934 90m/B Eddie Cantor, Ethel Merman, Ann Sothern, George Murphy; **D:** Roy Del Ruth. **VHS, Beta $19.98** SUE, HBO *ἀἀ½*

Kid 'n' Hollywood and Polly Tix in Washington These two "Baby Burlesks" shorts star a cast of toddlers, featuring the most famous moppet of all time, Shirley Temple, in her earliest screen appearances.
1933 20m/B Shirley Temple. **VHS, Beta $19.98** CCB *ἀἀ½*

Kid Ranger A ranger shoots an innocent man, but later sets things straight by bringing the real culprit to justice.
1936 57m/B Bob Steele, William Farnum; **D:** Robert North Bradbury. **VHS, Beta $24.98** WGE, VYY *ἀ*

Kid Sister A young girl is determined to grab her sister's boyfriend for herself, and enlists the aid of a burglar to do it.
1945 56m/B Roger Pryor, Judy Clark, Frank Jenks, Constance Worth. **VHS, Beta** $24.95 VYY 🎬½

Kid Vengeance After witnessing the brutal slaying of his family, a boy carries out a personal vendetta against the outlaws.
1975 (R) 90m/C Leif Garrett, Jim Brown, Lee Van Cleef, John Marley, Glynnis O'Connor; *D:* Joseph Manduke. **VHS, Beta** $59.95 PGN 🎬½

The Kid Who Loved Christmas After his adoptive mother is killed in a car accident, a young boy is taken from his adoptive father. The boy, upset about being removed from his new family, writes to Santa Claus for help. A touching yuletide drama. This was Sammy Davis, Jr.'s last film. Made for television.
1990 118m/C Cicely Tyson, Michael Warren, Sammy Davis Jr., Gilbert Lewis, Ken Page, Della Reese, Esther Rolle, Ben Vereen, Vanessa Williams, John Beal, Trent Cameron, Arthur Seidelman. **VHS** PAR 🎬🎬

The Kid with the Broken Halo Coleman and Guillaume are paired again in this unsuccessful pilot for a TV series. A young angel, out to earn his wings, must try to help three desperate families, with the help of an experienced angel.
1982 100m/C Gary Coleman, Robert Guillaume, June Allyson, Mason Adams, Ray Walston, John Pleshette, Kim Fields, Georg Stanford Brown, Telma Hopkins; *D:* Leslie Martinson. **VHS** NO 🎬🎬

The Kid with the 200 I.Q. When an earnest boy genius enters college at age 13, predictable comic situations arise that involve his attempts at impressing his idolized astronomy professor (Guillaume), as well as an equally unrequited bout of first love. Harmless comedy, one of a series of squeaky-clean made-for-TV family fare starring Coleman.
1983 96m/C Gary Coleman, Robert Guillaume, Harriet Hilliard Nelson, Dean Butler, Karli Michaelson, Christina Murrull, Mel Stewart; *D:* Leslie Martinson. **VHS, Beta** $49.95 LIV 🎬🎬

Kidco The true story of a money-making corporation headed and run by a group of children ranging in age from nine to sixteen.
1983 (PG) 104m/C Scott Schwartz, Elizabeth Gorcey, Cinnamon Idles, Tristine Skyler; *D:* Ronald F. Maxwell. **VHS, Beta** $59.98 FOX 🎬🎬

Kidnap Syndicate Kidnappers swipe two boys, releasing one—the son of a wealthy industrialist who meets their ransom demands. When they kill the other boy, a mechanic's son, the father goes on a revengeful killing spree.
1976 (R) 105m/C IT James Mason, Valentina Cortese; *D:* Fernando Di Leo. **VHS, Beta** $29.95 VID 🎬½

Kidnapped A young boy is sold by his wicked uncle as a slave, and is helped by an outlaw. A Disney film based on the Robert Louis Stevenson classic.
1960 94m/C Peter Finch, James MacArthur, Peter O'Toole; *D:* Robert Stevenson. **VHS, Beta** $19.99 DIS 🎬🎬½

Kidnapped When a teenage girl is kidnapped by pornographers, her sister seeks help from a tough cop and together they go undercover to find her. Plot is flimsy cover for what is actually an exploitative piece.
1987 (R) 100m/C David Naughton, Barbara Crampton, Lance LeGault, Chick Vennera, Charles Napier; *D:* Howard Avedis. **VHS, Beta, LV** NO Woof!

Kidnapping of Baby John Doe Tragedy strikes a family's newborn, and they must make the terrifying decision between life and death. A doctor and nurse, however, take matters into their own hands to save the baby.
1988 90m/C Helen Hughes, Jayne Eastwood, Janet-Laine Green, Geoffery Boues, Peter Gerretsen. **VHS, Beta** NO Woof!

The Kidnapping of the President The U.S. president is taken hostage by Third World terrorists. The Secret Service is on the ball trying to recover the nation's leader. Well-integrated subplot involves the vice president in a scandal. Engrossing political thriller. Based on novel by Charles Templeton.
1980 (R) 113m/C CA William Shatner, Hal Holbrook, Van Johnson, Ava Gardner, Miguel Fernandez; *D:* George Mendeluk. **VHS, Beta** NO 🎬🎬½

Kid's Auto Race/Mabel's Married Life "Kid's Auto Race" (1914) concerns a kiddie-car contest; "Mabel's Married Life" (1915) is about flirtations in the park between married sweethearts. Piano and organ scores. *AKA:* Kid Auto Races at Venice.
1915 21m/B Charlie Chaplin, Mabel Normand, Mack Swain; *D:* Mack Sennett. **VHS, Beta** $19.98 CCB 🎬½

Kid's Last Ride Three tough guys come into town to settle a feud.
1941 55m/B Ray Corrigan, John "Dusty" King, Max Terhune, Luana Walters, Edwin Brian; *D:* S. Roy Luby. **VHS** $19.95 NOS, DVT 🎬

The Kill A rough, cynical, hard-boiled, womanizing detective tracks down stolen cash in downtown Macao.
1973 81m/C Richard Jaeckel, Henry Duval, Judy Washington. **VHS, Beta** $19.95 STE, NWV 🎬🎬½

Kill Alex Kill A Vietnam POW returns to find his family murdered, and uses the crime underworld to take revenge.
1983 88m/C Tony Zarindast, Tina Bowmann, Chris Ponti. **VHS, Beta** $59.95 GEM Woof!

Kill and Go Hide A young girl visits her mother's grave nightly to communicate with and command the ghoul-like creatures that haunt the surrounding woods. *AKA:* The Child.
1976 95m/C **VHS, Beta** NO 🎬

Kill and Kill Again A martial arts champion attempts to rescue a kidnapped Nobel Prize-winning chemist who has developed a high-yield synthetic fuel. Colorful, tongue-in-cheek, and fun even for those unfamiliar with the genre.
1981 (PG) 100m/C James Ryan, Anneline Kriel, Stan Schmidt, Bill Flynn, Norman Robinson, Ken Gampu, John Ramsbottom; *D:* Ivan Hall. **VHS, Beta** $19.95 MED 🎬🎬½

Kill, Baby, Kill A small Transylvania town is haunted by the ghost of a seven-year-old witchcraft victim, and the town's suicide victims all seem to have hearts of gold (coins, that is). Lots of style and atmosphere in this Transylvanian tale from horror tongue in cheekster Bava. Considered by many genre connoisseurs to be the B man's finest, except that it bears early symptoms of the director's late onset infatuation with the zoom shot. *AKA:* Curse of the Living Dead; Operacione Paura.
1966 83m/C IT Erika Blanc, Giacomo "Jack" Stuart, Fabienne Dali, Giana Vivaldi; *D:* Mario Bava. **VHS** $19.98 SNC, FRG 🎬🎬🎬

Kill Castro Ever hear the one about the exploding cigar? Key West boat skipper is forced to carry a CIA agent to Cuba on a mission to assassinate Castro. Low-budget adventure that's deadly dull.
1980 (R) 90m/C Sybil Danning, Albert Salmi, Michael Gazzo, Raymond St. Jacques, Woody Strode, Stuart Whitman, Robert Vaughn, Caren Kaye; *D:* Chuck Workman. **VHS, Beta** NO 🎬

Kill Cruise The depressed and alcoholic skipper of the yacht Bella Donna gives up sailing until he meets two beautiful young women who want to sail to Bermuda for a taste of the good life. The calm of the Atlantic is disturbed when they are plagued by bad weather and fierce storms, and tensions rise as the two women's jealousies erupt. Will it set the climate for murder?
1990 (R) 99m/C Juergen Prochnow, Patsy Kensit, Elizabeth Hurley; *W/D:* Peter Keglevic. **VHS, Beta, LV** MCA 🎬🎬

Kill Factor A spy thriller with a dash of martial arts. *AKA:* Death Dimension.
19?? 91m/C Jim Kelly, George Lazenby, Aldo Ray, Harold Sakata, Terry Moore. **VHS, Beta** $19.95 ACA 🎬

Kill Line Kim stars as Joe, a street fighter who seeks to clear his name after serving a 10-year prison sentence for a crime he didn't commit. When he finds his brother's family has been murdered by criminals looking for the millions he supposedly stole, Joe wages a one-man martial arts war against a corrupt police force and the gang of thugs who are looking for the money.
1991 (R) 93m/C Bobby Kim, Michael Parker, Marlene Zimmerman, H. Wayne Lowery, C.R. Valdez, Mark Williams, Ben Pfeifer; *W/D:* Richard H. Kim. **VHS** $89.95 HMD 🎬🎬

Kill Me Again A woman hires a private detective to fake her death, which only gets him targeted by her boyfriend, the Mob, and the cops.
1989 (R) 93m/C Val Kilmer, Joanne Whalley-Kilmer, Michael Madsen, Jonathan Gries, Bibi Besch; *D:* John Dahl **VHS, Beta** $89.95 MGM 🎬½

Kill My Wife...Please! Comic adventure of a despicable husband trying to bump off his wife in order to cash in on her insurance policy.
19?? 90m/C Bob Dishy, Joanna Barnes, Bill Dana; *D:* Steven Hilliard Stern. **VHS** $19.95 HHE 🎬🎬

Kill or Be Killed Martial arts champion is lured to a phony martial arts contest by a madman bent on revenge.
1980 (PG) 90m/C James Ryan, Charlotte Michelle, Norman Combes; *D:* Ivan Hall. **VHS, Beta** $54.95 MED 🎬

The Kill Reflex A tough black cop and his beautiful rookie partner battle the mob and corruption.
1989 (R) 90m/C Maud Adams, Fred Williamson, Bo Svenson, Phyllis Hyman; *D:* Fred Williamson. **VHS, Beta, LV** $79.95 COL 🎬

Kill Slade When a United Nations food-aid diversion conspiracy is uncovered by a beautiful journalist, a plan to kidnap her is put into action. Romance follows.
1989 (PG-13) 90m/C SA Patrick Dollaghan, Lisa Brady, Anthony Fridjhon, Danny Keogh, Alfred Nowke; *D:* Bruce McFarlane. **VHS, Beta, LV** $19.98 SUE, NLC 🎬

Kill Squad Squad of martial arts masters follow a trail of violence and bloodshed to a vengeful, deadly battle of skills.
1981 (R) 85m/C Jean Claude, Jeff Risk, Jerry Johnson, Bill Cambra, Cameron Mitchell. **VHS, Beta** NO 🎬

Kill the Golden Goose Two martial arts masters work on opposite sides of a government corruption and corporate influence peddling case.
1979 (R) 91m/C Brad von Beltz, Ed Parker, Master Bong Soo Han; *D:* Elliot Hong. **VHS, Beta $59.95** *GEM* ✍

Killcrazy On the way to a weekend camping trip, five Vietnam vets released from a mental hospital are slowly massacred by a group of dangerous killers until one of the vets decides to fight back.
1989 94m/C David Heavener, Danielle Brisebois, Burt Ward, Lawrence Hilton-Jacobs, Bruce Glover, Gary Owens, Rachelle Carson; *W/ D:* David Heavener. **VHS, LV $89.98** *MED, IME* ✍

Killer An ex-convict sets up an ingenious bank robbery, and gets double-crossed himself.
197? 87m/C Henry Silva. **VHS, Beta** *NO* ✍

The Killer Jeffrey Chow is a gangster gunman who wants out. He's hired by his best friend to perform one last killing, but it doesn't go as smoothly as he wanted. He's almost caught by "Eagle" Lee, a detective who vows to hunt him down using Jennie, a singer blinded by Chow in crossfire. Lots of action and gunfights, but also pretty corny and sentimental. Very similar to American action movies, but using Chinese and Asian cultural conventions. A good introduction to the Chinese gangster-flick genre. Available with subtitles or dubbed in English. *AKA:* Die Xue Shuang Xiong.
1990 (R) 110m/C *HK* Chow Yun-fatt, Sally Yeh, Danny Lee, Kenneth Tsang, Chu Kong; *W/D:* John Woo. **VHS $89.95** *FXL, ART, BTV* ✍✍✍ ½

Killer Bait Muddled drama about an innocent couple who find a large sum of money accidentally dropped into their car by mobsters. Possession of the money leads the greedy wife to ruin when she gets involved with gangsters, blackmail, and murder. Also known as "Killer Bait."
1949 99m/C Lizabeth Scott, Don DeFore, Dan Duryea, Arthur Kennedy, Kristine Miller, Barry Kelley; *D:* Byron Haskin. **VHS $16.95** *SNC* ✍✍ ½

Killer Commandos Mercenaries go to the rescue of an oppressed African nation to overthrow the sinister white supremacy dictator.
19?? 87m/C Cameron Mitchell, Anthony Eisley. **VHS** *NO* ✍

Killer Dill Also killer dull. A meek salesman is misidentified as a death-dealing gangster, and the comic mixups begin.
1947 71m/B Stuart Erwin, Anne Gwynne, Frank Albertson, Mike Mazurki, Milburn Stone, Dorothy Granger; *D:* Lewis D. Collins. **VHS $19.95** *NOS* ✍ ½

Killer Diller All-black musical revue featuring Nat King Cole and his Trio.
1948 70m/B Dusty Fletcher, Nat King Cole, Butterfly McQueen, Moms Mabley, George Wiltshire; *D:* Joe Binney. **VHS, Beta $19.95** *MVD, NOS, DVT* ✍ ½

Killer Elephants A Thai man struggles to save his plantation, his wife, and his baby from the terrorists hired by a land baron to drive him away from his property.
1976 83m/C Sung Pa, Alan Yen, Nai Yen Ne, Yu Chien. **VHS, Beta $29.95** *UNI* ✍✍

The Killer Elite Straight-ahead Peckinpah fare examining friendship and betrayal. Two professional assassins begin as friends but end up stalking each other when they are double-crossed. This minor Peckinpah effort is murky and doesn't have a clear resolution, but is plenty bloody. Lots of Dobermans roam through this picture too.

1975 (PG) 120m/C James Caan, Robert Duvall, Arthur Hill, Gig Young, Burt Young, Mako, Bo Hopkins; *D:* Sam Peckinpah. **VHS, Beta, LV $14.95** *MGM* ✍✍ ½

Killer Fish A scheme to steal and then hide a fortune in emeralds at the bottom of a tank full of piranhas backfires as the criminals find it impossible to retrieve them...as if that took a lot of foresight. Director Dawson is AKA Antonio Margheriti. Filmed in Brazil. *AKA:* Deadly Treasure of the Piranha.
1979 (PG) 101m/C *BR GB* Lee Majors, James Franciscus, Margaux Hemingway, Karen Black, Roy Brocksmith, Marisa Berenson; *D:* Anthony M. Dawson. **VHS, Beta $59.98** *FOX* ✍

Killer Force Predictable adventure involving international diamond smuggling.
1975 (R) 100m/C Telly Savalas, Peter Fonda, Maud Adams; *D:* Val Guest. **VHS, Beta $69.98** *LIV, VES* ✍✍ ½

Killer Image A photographer unwittingly sees more than he should and becomes involved in a lethal political coverup. At the same time a wealthy senator targets him and he must fight for his life. Viewers might feel they have to fight their boredom.
1992 (R) 97m/C John Pyper-Ferguson, Michael Ironside, M. Emmet Walsh, Krista Errickson; *D:* David Winning. **VHS, Beta** *PAR* ✍

A Killer in Every Corner Three psychology students visit a loony professor and succumb to his hair-raising shenanigans.
1974 80m/C Joanna Pettet, Patrick Magee, Max Wall, Eric Flynn. **VHS, Beta $29.95** *LIV* ✍

Killer Inside Me The inhabitants of a small Western town are unaware that their mild-mannered deputy sheriff is actually becoming a crazed psychotic murderer. From the novel by Jim Thompson.
1976 (R) 99m/C Stacy Keach, Susan Tyrrell, Tisha Sterling, Keenan Wynn, John Dehner, John Carradine, Don Stroud; *D:* Burt Kennedy. **VHS, Beta $59.95** *WAR, OM* ✍✍

Killer Klowns from Outer Space Bozo-like aliens resembling demented clowns land on earth and set up circus tents to lure Earthlings in. Visually striking, campy but slick horror flick that'll make you think twice about your next visit to the big top. Mood is heightened by a cool title tune by the Dickies. Definitely has cult potential!
1988 (PG-13) 90m/C Grant Cramer, Suzanne Snyder, John Allen Nelson, Royal Dano, John Vernon; *D:* Stephen Chiodo. **VHS, Beta, LV $19.95** *MED, CVS* ✍✍ ½

Killer Likes Candy An assassin stalks the King of Kafiristan, and a CIA operative tries to stop him.
1978 86m/C Kerwin Mathews, Marilu Tolo; *D:* Richard Owens. **VHS, Beta $59.95** *GEM, MRV* ✍

Killer on Board Folks spending their holiday on a cruise ship are afflicted by a fatal virus and subsequently quarantined. Typical made-for-TV disaster flick.
1977 100m/C Claude Akins, Beatrice Straight, George Hamilton, Patty Duke, Frank Converse, Jane Seymour, William Daniels; *D:* Philip Leacock. **VHS, Beta $49.95** *LIV* ✍✍

Killer Party Three coeds pledge a sorority and are subjected to a hazing that involves a haunted fraternity house. Standard horror plot; Paul Bartel ("Eating Raoul"; "Lust in the Dust") is the only significant element.
1986 (R) 91m/C Elaine Wilkes, Sherry Willis-Burch, Joanna Johnson, Paul Bartel, Martin Hewitt, Ralph Seymour; *D:* William Fruet. **VHS, Beta $79.98** *FOX* **Woof!**

The Killer Shrews Lumet (Sidney's father) creates a serum that causes the humble shrew to take on killer proportions. The creatures are actually dogs in makeup. Goude was 1957's Miss Universe.
1959 70m/B James Best, Ingrid Goude, Baruch Lumet, Ken Curtis; *D:* Ray Kellogg. **VHS $19.98** *SNC, MRV, HHT* ✍✍

Killer Tomatoes Eat France Professor Gangrene takes his tomato fetish to France, where the giant vegetables try to take over the streets. The fourth in the killer-vegetable series.
1991 94m/C John Astin, Marc Price, Steve Lundquist; *D:* John DeBello. **VHS, LV $92.98** *FXV* ✍ ½

Killer Tomatoes Strike Back The third "Killer Tomatoes" movie isn't in the league of "The Naked Gun" satires, but it's still bright parody for the Mad Magazine crowd, as tomato-mad scientist Astin harnesses the powers of trash-TV in a planned vegetable invasion. Perhaps due to a 'Killer Tomatoes' cartoon series at the time, this isn't as saucy as its predecessors and is acceptable for family audiences.
1990 87m/C John Astin, Rick Rockwell, Crystal Carson, Steve Lundquist, John Witherspoon; *D:* John DeBello. **VHS $39.98** *FXV, IME* ✍

Killer with Two Faces A woman is terrorized by the evil twin of her boyfriend. Made for television.
1974 70m/C Donna Mills, Ian Hendry, David Lodge, Roddy McMillian. **VHS, Beta $12.95** *LIV* ✍

Killer Workout A murderer stalks the clients of a sweat/sex/muscle-filled gym. *AKA:* Aerobicide.
1986 (R) 89m/C **VHS, Beta $29.95** *ACA* ✍

The Killers After two hired assassins kill a teacher, they look into his past and try to find leads to a $1,000,000 robbery. Reagan's last film. Remake of 1946 film of the same name, which was loosely based on a short story by Ernest Hemingway. Originally intended for television, but released to theaters instead due to its violence. *AKA:* Ernest Hemingway's The Killers.
1964 95m/C Lee Marvin, Angie Dickinson, John Cassavetes, Ronald Reagan, Clu Gulager, Claude Akins, Norman Fell; *D:* Don Siegel; *M:* John Williams. **VHS, Beta $39.95** *MCA* ✍✍

Killers Remote jungles of southern Africa are the scene of a military coup.
1988 83m/C Cameron Mitchell, Alicia Hammond, Randy Dix; *D:* Ewing Miles Brown. **VHS, Beta $39.95** *GHV* ✍

The Killer's Edge Cop is caught between rock and hard place in L.A. when he's forced to confront criminal who once saved his life in 'Nam. Plenty of gut busting and soul wrenching.
1990 (R) 90m/C Wings Hauser, Robert Z'Dar, Karen Black. **VHS, LV $79.95** *PMH* ✍✍ ½

Killers from Space Cheap sci-fi flick in which big-eyed men from beyond Earth bring scientist Graves back to life to assist them with their evil plan for world domination.
1954 80m/B Peter Graves, Barbara Bestar, James Scay; *D:* W. Lee Wilder. **VHS, Beta $9.95** *NOS, MRV, RHI* **Woof!**

Killer's Kiss A boxer and a dancer set out to start a new life together when he saves the woman from an attempted rape. Gritty, second feature from Kubrick was financed by friends and family and shows signs of his budding talent.
1955 67m/C Frank Silvera, Jamie Smith, Irene Kane, Jerry Jarret; *W/D:* Stanley Kubrick. **VHS** *FCT* ✍✍ ½

Killer's Moon Four sadistic psychopaths escape from a prison hospital and unleash their murderous rage on anyone who crosses their path.
1984 90m/C VHS, Beta *NO* ⅃

The Killing The dirty, harsh, street-level big heist epic that established Kubrick and presented its genre with a new and vivid existentialist aura, as an ex-con engineers the rip-off of a racetrack with disastrous results. Displays characteristic nonsentimental sharp-edged Kubrick vision. Cinematography by Lucien Ballard. Based on the novel "Clean Break" by Lionel White.
1956 83m/B Sterling Hayden, Marie Windsor, Elisha Cook Jr., Jay C. Flippen, Vince Edwards, Timothy Carey, Coleen Gray, Joe Sawyer, Ted de Corsia; *D:* Stanley Kubrick. **VHS, Beta, LV $19.95** *MGM, VYG* ⅃⅃⅃

A Killing Affair Set in West Virginia, 1943, this is the story of a widow who takes in a drifter who she believes is the man who killed her husband. She begins to fall for him, but cannot be sure if she should trust him. Vague and melodramatic. From the novel "Monday, Tuesday, Wednesday" by Robert Houston. Saperstein's directorial debut.
1985 (R) 100m/C Peter Weller, Kathy Baker, John Glover, Bill Smitrovich; *D:* David Saperstein; *M:* John Barry. **VHS, Beta, LV $9.99** *STE, PSM* ⅃

Killing at Hell's Gate A made-for-television movie about a group of whitewater rafters being picked off by snipers as they travel down river.
1981 96m/C Robert Urich, Deborah Raffin, Lee Purcell; *D:* Jerry Jameson. **VHS, Beta $59.98** *FOX* ⅃ ½

Killing Cars A German car designer's pet project, a car that runs without gas, is halted by the influence of an Arab conglomerate. He nevertheless tries to complete it, and is hunted down.
1985 (R) 104m/C Juergen Prochnow, Senta Berger, William Conrad, Agnes Soral; *D:* Michael Verhoeven. **VHS, Beta $79.95** *VMK, HHE, STE* ⅃ ½

The Killing Edge In post-nuclear holocaust Earth, a lone warrior seeks justice, and his family, in a lawless land.
1986 85m/C Bill French, Marv Spencer; *D:* Lindsay Shonteff. **VHS $39.98** *VCD, HHE* ⅃ ½

Killing 'em Softly Segal portrays a down-on-his-luck musician who accidentally murders a music manager during an argument. Cara's boyfriend is accused and to clear his name, the singer moonlights as a detective. She and Segal end up falling in love. Disappointing.
1985 90m/C *CA* George Segal, Irene Cara; *D:* Max Fischer. **VHS, Beta $79.95** *PSM, HHE* ⅃

The Killing Fields Based on the New York Times' Sydney Schanberg's own account of his friendship with Cambodian interpreter Dith Pran. They separated during the fall of Saigon, when the Western journalists fled leaving behind countless assistants, secretaries, and interpreters who were later accused of collusion with the enemy by the vicious Khmer Rouge and killed or sent to re-education camps during the bloodbath known as "Year Zero." Schanberg continued to search for Pran through the Red Cross and U.S. government, while Pran struggled to survive, secretly drinking ox blood to supplement his meager food supply until he was able to escape, walking miles to the Thailand border. Ngor's own experiences echoed much of the film's. Debut of Malkovich is intense. Joffe's directorial debut

shows a generally sure hand, with only a bit of melodrama at the end.
1984 (R) 142m/C *GB* Sam Waterston, Haing S. Ngor, John Malkovich, Athol Fugard, Craig T. Nelson, Julian Sands, Spalding Gray, Bill Paterson; *D:* Roland Joffe. Academy Awards '84: Best Cinematography, Best Film Editing, Best Supporting Actor (Ngor); Nominations: Best Actor (Waterston), Best Adapted Screenplay, Best Director (Joffe), Best Picture; Golden Globe Awards '85: Best Supporting Actor (Ngor). **VHS, Beta, LV $19.98** *WAR, PIA, BTV* ⅃⅃⅃ ½

Killing Floor A black sharecropper during World War I travels to Chicago to get work in the stockyards and becomes a voice in the growing labor movement. Made for television.
1985 (PG) 118m/C Damien Leake, Alfre Woodard, Moses Gunn, Clarence Felder, Bill Duke; *D:* William Duke. **VHS, Beta, LV $14.95** *COL, SUE, FCT* ⅃⅃

The Killing Game A husband-wife cartoonist team link up with an unhinged playboy and act out a murder mystery comic they produce together. In French with subtitles. *AKA:* All Weekend Lovers; Jeu de Massacre.
1967 90m/C *FR* Jean-Pierre Cassel, Claudine Auger, Michael Duchaussoy, Anna Gaylor; *D:* Alain Jessua. **VHS, Beta $39.95** *FCT* ⅃⅃ ½

The Killing Game A slew of Californians kill and betray each other for lustful reasons.
1987 90m/C Chad Hayward, Cynthia Killion, Geoffrey Sadwith; *D:* Joseph Merhi. **VHS, Beta** *NO* ⅃

Killing Heat An independent career woman living in South Africa decides to abandon her career to marry a struggling jungle farmer. Based on Doris Lessing's novel "The Grass is Singing." *AKA:* The Grass is Singing.
1984 (R) 104m/C *GB SW* Karen Black, John Thaw, John Kani, John Moulder-Brown; *D:* Michael Raeburn. **VHS, Beta $59.98** *FOX* ⅃ ½

Killing Hour A psychic painter finds that the visions she paints come true in a string of grisly murders. Her ability interests a television reporter and a homicide detective. *AKA:* The Clairvoyant.
1984 (R) 97m/C Elizabeth Kemp, Perry King, Norman Parker, Kenneth McMillan; *D:* Armand Mastroianni. **VHS, Beta $79.98** *FOX* ⅃⅃

Killing in a Small Town Candy Morrison seems like the perfect member of her small Texas community—she's married, has children, and even teaches Bible school. But Candy needs a little excitement in her life, which she gets by initiating a brief affair with fellow church-goer Stan. However, when Stan's wife Peggy finds out she confronts Candy—with an axe. Candy defends herself and winds up killing Peggy, by striking her with the axe 41 times (shades of Lizzie Borden)! But was Candy only defending herself? Or did she seek to get her own sort of revenge? Good performances by Hershey as the frustrated Candy and Dennehy as her skeptical lawyer. Based on a true story; originally a television miniseries.
1990 (R) 95m/C Barbara Hershey, Brian Dennehy, Hal Holbrook, Richard Gilliland, John Terry; *D:* Stephen Gyllenhaal. **VHS, LV $89.95** *VMK* ⅃⅃ ½

Killing in the Sun Gripping struggle for prosperous smuggling in the Mediterranean consume mobsters from three countries.
19?? (R) 90m/C Henry Silva, Michael Constantine. **VHS** *NO* ⅃

The Killing Kind Man released from prison is obsessed with wreaking vengeance on his daft lawyer and his accuser. His vendetta eventually draws his mother into

the fray as well. Fine performance by Savage.
1973 95m/C Ann Sothern, John Savage, Ruth Roman, Luana Anders, Cindy Williams; *D:* Curtis Harrington. **VHS $14.99** *PGN* ⅃ ½

The Killing Machine A Japanese World War II army veteran uses his martial arts skills to subdue local black market gangs.
1976 89m/C Sonny Chiba. **VHS, Beta $9.99** *STE, PSM* ⅃

The Killing Mind A young girl witnesses a grisly murder that is never solved. Twenty years later she (Zimbalist) becomes a cop who specializes in trapping psychos. Haunted by her memories, she and a reporter (Bill) team up to find the killer, never suspecting that she is his next victim. Originally made-for-cable-television.
1990 96m/C Stephanie Zimbalist, Tony Bill, Daniel Roebuck; *D:* Michael Ray Rhodes. **VHS $89.98** *WOV* ⅃

The Killing of a Chinese Bookie Gazzara runs a Sunset Strip nightclub and is in hock to loan sharks. When he can't come up with the cash, he's offered a deal—get rid of a troublesome Chinese bookie and all debts will be forgiven. But it turns out the bookie is highly connected in the Asian mob and nothing goes as planned. Cassavette's improv technique makes for a self-indulgent and endless film.
1976 (R) 109m/C Ben Gazzara, Jean-Pierre Cassel, Zizi Johari, Soto Joe Hugh, Robert Phillips, Timothy Carey, Morgan Woodward; *W/D:* John Cassavetes. **VHS $89.95** *TOU* ⅃⅃

Killing of Angel Street A courageous young woman unwittingly becomes the central character in an escalating nightmare about saving a community from corrupt politicians and organized crime.
1981 (PG) 101m/C *AU* Liz Alexander, John Hargreaves; *D:* Donald Crombie. **VHS, Beta $14.98** *VID, FCT* ⅃⅃

Killing of Randy Webster A father attempts to prove that his son did not die as a criminal when Texas policemen shot him after transporting a stolen van across state lines.
1981 90m/C Hal Holbrook, Dixie Carter, Sean Penn, Jennifer Jason Leigh; *D:* Sam Wanamaker. **VHS, Beta** *NO* ⅃ ½

The Killing of Sister George Racy, sensationalized film based on the Frank Marcus black comedy/melodrama about a lesbian love triangle between a television executive and two soap opera stars. Things get a little uncomfortable when they learn one of their characters is to be written out of the show. Shot in England.
1969 (R) 138m/C Beryl Reid, Susannah York, Coral Browne, Ronald Fraser, Patricia Medina, Hugh Paddick, Cyril Elaine Church, Brandan Dillon; *D:* Robert Aldrich. **VHS, Beta $79.98** *FOX* ⅃⅃

Killing Stone A freelance writer uncovers a small town sheriff's plot to cover up a scandalous homicide. Made for television and written by Landon.
1978 120m/C Gil Gerard, J.D. Cannon, Jim Davis, Nehemiah Persoff; *D:* Michael Landon. **VHS, Beta $49.95** *PSM* ⅃⅃

Killing Streets A commando learns that his twin brother is being held hostage in Lebanon and plans a rescue mission. A standard farfetched actioner; noteworthy for a real sense of despair over the endless carnage in the Mideast. Some dialogue in Arabic with subtitles.
1991 109m/C Michael Pare, Lorenzo Lamas; *D:* Stephen Cornwell. **VHS $89.98** *VES, LIV* ⅃⅃

The Killing Time A minor, effective murder thriller about a quiet small resort town suddenly beset by a web of murder, double-crossings, blackmail, and infidelity. They seem to coincide with the appearance of a mysterious stranger posing as the town's deputy sheriff just as the new sheriff is about to take up the badge.
1987 (R) 94m/C Kiefer Sutherland, Beau Bridges, Joe Don Baker, Wayne Rogers; **D:** Rick King. **VHS, Beta, LV $19.95** *NWV, STE* 🎞🎞

The Killing Zone Convict nephew of onetime Drug Enforcement agent rewrites zoning ordinances to hunt for Mexican drug lord south of the border.
1990 90m/C Daron McBee, James Dalesandro, Melissa Moore, Armando Silvestre, Augustine Beral, Sydne Squire, Deborah Dare; **D:** Addison Randall. **VHS $29.95** *PMH* 🎞½

Killings at Outpost Zeta Earthmen investigate a barren planet where previous expeditions have disappeared, and find hordes of aliens.
1980 92m/C Gordon Devol, Jackie Ray, James A. Watson Jr. **VHS, Beta $69.95** *UHV* 🎞

Killjoy A sleazy surgeon's daughter is the prey in this television thriller. The plot twists are led by the array of people who become involved. A clever suspense mystery. Made for television. **AKA:** Who Murdered Joy Morgan?.
1981 100m/C Kim Basinger, Robert Culp, Stephen Macht, Nancy Marchand, John Rubinstein, Ann Dusenberry, Ann Wedgeworth; **D:** John Llewellyn Moxey. **VHS, Beta $49.95** *LIV* 🎞🎞½

Killpoint Special task force is assembled to catch the criminals who robbed a National Guard armory for its weapons.
1984 (R) 89m/C Leo Fong, Richard Roundtree, Cameron Mitchell; **D:** Frank Harris. **VHS, Beta, LV $79.98** *LIV, VES* 🎞½

Killzone A brainwashed Vietnam vet breaks down during a training exercise and embarks on a psychotic killing spree.
1985 86m/C Ted Prior, David James Campbell, Richard Massery; **D:** David A. Prior. **VHS, Beta $69.98** *VES* 🎞

Kilma, Queen of the Amazons A shipwrecked sailor finds himself on an island populated by man-hating Amazons. When a shipload of lusty sailors arrive to rescue him, carnage ensues.
1986 90m/C **VHS, Beta** *NO Woof!*

Kim A colorful Hollywood adaptation of the Rudyard Kipling classic about an English boy disguised as a native in 19th Century India, and his various adventures.
1950 113m/C Errol Flynn, Dean Stockwell, Paul Lukas, Cecil Kellaway; **D:** Victor Saville. **VHS, Beta $19.98** *MGM* 🎞🎞🎞

Kind Hearts and Coronets Black comedy in which an ambitious young man sets out to bump off eight relatives in an effort to claim a family title. Guinness is wonderful in his role as all eight of the fated relations. Based on Roy Horiman's novel.
1949 104m/B Alec Guinness, Dennis Price, Valerie Hobson, Joan Greenwood; **D:** Robert Hamer. **VHS, Beta, LV $19.98** *HBO, FCT, HMV* 🎞🎞🎞½

A Kind of Loving Two North English young people marry rashly as a result of pregnancy, find they really didn't like each other all that much, but manage to adjust.
1962 107m/B *GB* Alan Bates, Thora Hird, June Ritchie; **D:** John Schlesinger. **VHS, Beta $59.99** *HBO* 🎞🎞🎞

Kindergarten Endearing tale based on a true story of a young Russian street violinist. During World War II, the boy meets a variety of interesting people as he travels throughout the Soviet Union. In Russian with English subtitles.
1984 143m/C *RU* Klaus Maria Brandauer; **D:** Yevgeny Yevtushenko. **VHS $59.99** *KIV* 🎞🎞🎞

Kindergarten Cop Pectoral perfect cop Kimble (Schwarzenegger) stalks mama's boy/criminal Crisp (Tyson) by locating the drug lord's ex and his six-year-old son. When the pec man's female partner succumbs to a nasty bout of food poisoning, he's forced to take her place as an undercover kindergarten teacher in the drowsy Pacific northwest community where mother and son reside incognito. A cover all the bases Christmas release, it's got romance, action, comedy and cute. And box office earnings to match Arnie's chest measurements. A bit violent for the milk and cookie set.
1990 (PG-13) 111m/C Arnold Schwarzenegger, Penelope Ann Miller, Pamela Reed, Linda Hunt, Richard Tyson, Carroll Baker, Cathy Moriarty, Park Overall, Richard Portnow, Jayne Brook; **D:** Ivan Reitman; **W:** Murray Salem, Herschel Weingrod, Timothy Harris; **M:** Randy Edelman. **VHS, Beta, LV $19.95** *MCA, CCB* 🎞🎞½

The Kindred A young student discovers that his mother the biologist has created a hybrid creature using his body tissue. Naturally, he is horrified and begins to search for his test-tube brother; the problem is, this brother likes eating people. Not too bad; boasts some good acting.
1987 (R) 92m/C Rod Steiger, Kim Hunter, David Allan Brooks, Timothy Gibbs, Amanda Pays, Talia Balsam; **D:** Stephen Carpenter. **VHS, Beta, LV $14.98** *LIV, VES* 🎞🎞½

King Docudrama with terrific cast follows the life and career of one of the greatest nonviolent civil rights leaders of all time, Martin Luther King. Made for television.
1978 272m/C Paul Winfield, Cicely Tyson, Roscoe Lee Browne, Ossie Davis, Art Evans, Ernie Banks, Howard E. Rollins Jr., William Jordan, Cliff DeYoung; **W/D:** Abby Mann. **VHS, Beta $69.99** *HBO* 🎞🎞🎞

The King and Four Queens Gable, on the run from the law, happens upon a deserted town, deserted, that is, except for a woman and her three daughters. Clark soon discovers that the women are looking for $100,000 in gold that one of their missing husbands had stolen. True to form, conniving Clark wastes no time putting the moves on each of them to find the whereabouts of the loot.
1956 86m/C Clark Gable, Eleanor Parker, Jo Van Fleet, Jean Wiles, Barbara Nichols, Sara Shane, Roy Roberts, Arthur Shields, Jay C. Flippen; **D:** Raoul Walsh. **VHS, Beta $19.98** *MGM, CCB* 🎞🎞½

The King and I Adaptation of Rogers and Hammerstein's Broadway play based on the novel "Anna and the King of Siam" by Margaret Landon. An English governess is hired to teach the King of Siam's many children and bring them into the 20th century. She has more of a job than she realizes, for this is a king, a country, and a people who value tradition above all else. Her intelligence and good humor eventually begin to convince the King that she'll not destroy the world he loves, and they discover characteristics in each other. Features one of Rodgers and Hammerstein's best-loved scores. Brynner made this role his and his alone, playing it over 4,000 times on stage and screen before his death. Kerr's voice was dubbed when she sang; the voice you hear is Marni Nixon, who also dubbed the star's singing voices in "West Side Story" and "My Fair Lady." A wonderful film with important messages. 🎵Shall We Dance?; Getting To Know You; Hello, Young Lovers; We Kiss in a Shadow; I Whistle a Happy Tune; March of the Siamese Children; I Have Dreamed; A Puzzlement; Something Wonderful; Song of the King; The Small House of Uncle Thomas.
1956 133m/C Deborah Kerr, Yul Brynner, Rita Moreno, Martin Benson, Terry Saunders, Rex Thompson, Alan Mowbray, Carlos Rivas; **D:** Walter Lang; **W:** Ernest Lehman; **M:** Richard Rodgers, Oscar Hammerstein. Academy Awards '56: Best Actor (Brynner), Best Art Direction/Set Decoration (Color), Best Costume Design (Color), Best Sound, Best Score; Nominations: Best Actress (Kerr), Best Color Cinematography, Best Director (Lang), Best Picture; Golden Globe Awards '57: Best Actress—Musical/Comedy (Kerr), Best Film—Musical/Comedy. **VHS, Beta, LV $19.98** *FOX, BTV, RDG* 🎞🎞🎞🎞

King Arthur, the Young Warlord The struggle that was the other side of Camelot—the campaign against the Saxon hordes. The early, somewhat violent years of King Art.
1975 (PG) 90m/C Oliver Tobias, Michael Gothard, Jack Watson, Brian Blessed, Peter Firth; **D:** Sidney Hayers, Pat Jackson, Peter Sasdy. **VHS, Beta $29.95** *GEM* 🎞🎞

King Boxer A famous martial arts school is taken over by a menacing gang. When a student-to-be finds this out, he enlists himself to take on the best individual of the gang in a deadly match.
1990 106m/C Lo Lieh, Wang Ping. **VHS $69.95** *NO* 🎞

King Boxers Kurate stars in this tale of elephant hunts, warding off Triad Society gangs, and personal combat. Nainam is a former Thailand fists and kick boxing champion.
1980 (R) 90m/C Yasuka Kurata, Johnny Nainam. **VHS, Beta $59.95** *GEM* 🎞🎞

King Creole The King goes film noir as a teenager with a criminal record who becomes a successful pop singer in New Orleans but is threatened by his ties to crime, represented by Walter Matthau. One of the better Elvis films, based on Harold Robbins' "A Stone for Danny Fisher." Features Elvis' last film appearance before his service in the Army. 🎵King Creole; Banana; New Orleans; Turtles, Berries and Gumbo; Crawfish; Don't Ask Me Why; As Long As I Have You; Trouble; Hard-Headed Woman; Lover Doll; Dixieland Rock; Young Dreams; Steadfast, Loyal and True.
1958 115m/B Elvis Presley, Carolyn Jones, Walter Matthau, Dean Jagger, Dolores Hart, Vic Morrow, Paul Stewart; **D:** Michael Curtiz. **VHS, Beta, LV $19.95** *MVD, FOX* 🎞🎞½

King David The story of David, the legendary Biblical hero whose acts of bravery paved the way for him to become king of Israel.
1985 (PG-13) 114m/C Richard Gere, Alice Krige, Cherie Lunghi, Hurd Hatfield, Edward Woodward; **D:** Bruce Beresford. **VHS, Beta, LV $79.95** *PAR* 🎞½

King Dinosaur A new planet arrives in the solar system, and a scientific team checks out its giant iguana-ridden terrain.
1955 63m/B Bill Bryant, Wanda Curtis, Patti Gallagher, Douglas Henderson. **VHS, Beta, LV** *MLB* 🎞½

A King in New York Chaplin plays the deposed king of a European mini-monarchy who comes to the United States in hope of making a new life. Looks critically at 1950s-

era America, including Cold War paranoia and over reliance on technology. Containing Chaplin's last starring performance, this film wasn't released in the U.S. until 1973. Uneven but interesting.
1957 105m/B *GB* Charlie Chaplin, Dawn Addams, Michael Chaplin, Oliver Johnston, Maxine Audley, Harry Green; *D:* Charlie Chaplin. VHS, Beta $19.98 *FOX* ♫♫

King Kelly of the U.S.A. Robertson carries on a forgettable romance with a princess aboard a trans-Atlantic line.
1934 64m/B Guy Robertson, Irene Ware, Edgar Kennedy, Franklin Pangborn, Joyce Compton, Ferdinand Gottschalk, William von Brinken, Otis Harlan; *D:* Leonard Fields. VHS $19.95 *NOS* ♫

King Kong The original beauty and the beast film classic tells the story of Kong, a giant ape captured in Africa and brought to New York as a sideshow attraction. Kong falls for Wray, escapes from his captors and rampages through the city, ending up on top of the newly built Empire State Building. Moody Max Steiner score adds color. Willis O'Brien's stop-motion animation still holds up well. Remade numerous times with various theme derivations. Available in a colorized version. The laserdisc, produced from a superior negative, features extensive liner notes and running commentary by film historian Ronald Haver.
1933 105m/B Fay Wray, Bruce Cabot, Robert Armstrong, Frank Reicher, Noble Johnson; *D:* Ernest B. Schoedsack. VHS, Beta, LV, 8mm $19.98 *TTC, RKO, MED* ♫♫♫♫

King Kong An oil company official travels to a remote island to discover it inhabited by a huge gorilla. The transplanted beast suffers unrequited love in classic fashion: monkey meets girl, monkey gets girl and brandishes her while atop the World Trade Center. An updated remake of the 1933 movie classic that also marks the screen debut of Lange. Impressive sets and a believable King Kong romp around New York City in this film.
1976 (PG) 135m/C Jeff Bridges, Charles Grodin, Jessica Lange, Rene Auberjonois, John Randolph, Ed Lauter, Jack O'Halloran; *D:* John Guillermin; *M:* John Barry. Academy Awards '76: Best Visual Effects; Nominations: Best Cinematography, Best Sound. VHS, Beta, LV, 8mm $24.95 *PAR, HMV* ♫♫

King Kong Lives Unnecessary sequel to the 1976 remake of "King Kong," in which two scientists get the big ape, now restored after his asphalt-upsetting fall, together with a lady ape his size and type.
1986 (PG-13) 105m/C Brian Kerwin, Linda Hamilton, John Ashton, Peter Michael Goetz; *D:* John Guillermin. VHS, Beta, LV $14.95 *MED, WAR* ♫

King Kong Versus Godzilla The planet issues a collective shudder as the two mightiest monsters slug it out for reasons known only to themselves. Humankind can only stand by and watch in impotent horror as the tide of the battle sways to and fro, until one monster stands alone and victorious. *AKA:* King Kong Tai Godzilla.
1963 105m/C *JP* Inoshiro Honda, Michael Keith, Tadao Takashima; *D:* Thomas Montgomery. VHS $9.95 *GKK* ♫♫½

King Kung Fu A karate master raises a gorilla, and sends it from Asia to the U.S. There, two out-of-work reporters decide to release it from captivity and then recapture it so they can get the story and some needed recognition. The background they don't have on the gorilla is that its master taught it kung fu.

1987 (G) 90m/C John Balee, Tom Leahy, Maxine Gray, Bill Schwartz; *D:* Bill Hayes. VHS *NO* ♫

King Lear Brook's version of Shakespeare tragedy. The king drives away the only decent daughter he has, and when he realizes this, it is too late. Powerful performances and interesting effort at updating the bard.
1971 137m/B *GB* Paul Scofield, Irene Worth, Jack MacGowran, Alan Webb, Cyril Cusack, Patrick Magee; *D:* Peter Brook. VHS $29.95 *NOS, DVT* ♫♫♫½

King Lear Loosely adapted from Shakespeare's tragedy of a king who loses everything. A fragmented French existential reading with gangster undercurrent. This updated version is dark, ominous, wandering, and strange. Scripted by Norman Mailer and not like the other 1984 remake. Or any other remake, for that matter.
1987 91m/C *SI* Peter Sellars, Burgess Meredith, Molly Ringwald, Jean-Luc Godard, Woody Allen; *D:* Jean-Luc Godard; *W:* Norman Mailer. VHS $59.95 *TAM, CAN* ♫½

King of America A Greek sailor and a local labor agent battle over who will become King of America.
1980 90m/C *D:* Dezso Magyar. VHS, Beta *NO* ♫

King of Comedy An unhinged would-be comedian haunts and eventually kidnaps a massively popular Johnny Carson-type television personality. A cold, cynical farce devised by Scorsese seemingly in reaction to John Hinckley's obsession with his film "Taxi Driver." Controlled, hard-hitting performances, especially by De Niro and Lewis.
1982 (PG) 101m/C Robert De Niro, Jerry Lewis, Sandra Bernhard, Tony Randall, Diahnne Abbott, Shelley Hack, Liza Minnelli; *D:* Martin Scorsese. VHS, Beta, LV $19.95 *COL, FCT* ♫♫♫

The King of Hearts In World War I, a Scottish soldier finds a battle-torn French town evacuated of all occupants except a colorful collection of escaped lunatics from a nearby asylum. The lunatics want to make him their king, which is not a bad alternative to the insanity of war. Bujold is cute as ballerina wannabe; look for Serrault ("La Cage aux Folles") as, not surprisingly, a would-be effeminate hairdresser. Light-hearted comedy with a serious message; definitely worthwhile. *AKA:* Le Roi de Coeur.
1966 101m/C *FR GB* Alan Bates, Genevieve Bujold, Adolfo Celi, Francoise Christophe, Micheline Presle; *D:* Phillipe DeBroca. VHS, Beta, LV $19.95 *MGM, TAM, TVC* ♫♫♫

King of Jazz A lavish revue built around the Paul Whiteman Orchestra with comedy sketches and songs by the stars on Universal Pictures' talent roster. (Though billed as the King of Jazz, Whiteman was never as good as jazz's real royalty.) Filmed in two-color Technicolor with a cartoon segment by Walter Lantz. ♫Rhapsody in Blue; So the Bluebirds and the Blackbirds Got Together; Mississippi Mud; It Happened in Monterey; Ragamuffin Romeo; Happy Feet; Song of the Dawn; A Bench in the Park.
1930 93m/C Paul Whiteman, John Boles, Jeanette Loff, Bing Crosby; *D:* John Murray Anderson. VHS, Beta $19.98 *MCA, MLB, RXM* ♫♫½

King of Kings DeMille depicts the life of Jesus Christ in this highly regarded silent epic. The resurrection scene appears in color. Remade by Nicholas Ray in 1961.
1927 115m/B H.B. Warner, Dorothy Cumming, Ernest Torrence, Joseph Schildkraut, Jacqueline Logan, Victor Varconi, William Boyd; *D:* Cecil B. DeMille. VHS, Beta $69.95 *MSP* ♫♫½

The King of Kings The life of Christ is intelligently told, with an attractive visual sense and a memorable score by Miklos Rosza. Narrated by Orson Welles. Remake of Cecil B. DeMille's silent film, released in 1927. Laserdisc format features a special letterboxed edition of this film.
1961 170m/C Jeffrey Hunter, Siobhan McKenna, Hurd Hatfield, Robert Ryan, Rita Gam, Viveca Lindfors, Rip Torn; *D:* Nicholas Ray. VHS, Beta, LV $29.98 *MGM, PIA, IGP* ♫♫♫

King of Kong Island Intent on world domination, a group of mad scientists implant receptors in the brains of gorillas on Kong Island, and the monster apes run amok.
1978 92m/C *SP* Brad Harris, Marc Lawrence; *D:* Robert Morris. VHS, Beta $54.95 *UHV* Woof!

King of Kung-Fu Martial arts adventure featuring plenty of kung-fu kicks.
198? 90m/C Bobby Baker, Nam Chun Pan, Lam Chun Chi. VHS, Beta *NO* ♫

The King of Marvin Gardens Nicholson stars as a Midwest radio jock who prefers to reminisce about his life and family back in Atlantic City, New Jersey to playing records. When Nicholson returns for a visit he finds brother Dern, king of the get-rich-quick schemers, working for a black crime syndicate. Dern is involved in another scheme which means embezzling money from his boss—not a smart idea although Nicholson can't dissuade him. Talky drama also features Burstyn as Dern's neglected girlfriend.
1972 (R) 104m/C Jack Nicholson, Bruce Dern, Ellen Burstyn, Scatman Crothers, Julia Anne Robinson, Charles Lavine, Arnold Williams, Josh Mostel; *D:* Bob Rafelson; *W:* Jacob Brackman. VHS $59.95 *COL, BTV* ♫♫½

King of New York Drug czar Frank White (Walken), recently returned from a prison sabbatical, regains control of his New York drug empire with the aid of a loyal network of black dealers. How? Call it dangerous charisma, an inexplicable sympatico. Headquartered in Manhattan's chic Plaza hotel, he ruthlessly orchestrates the drug machine, while funneling the profits into a Bronx hospital for the poor. The motive? As inscrutable as White himself, who's smooth, calculating, driven by some unfathomable vision. Walken, the master of the inscrutable, makes White's power tangible, believable, yet never fathomable. Scripted by Nicholas St. John, directed by crime stylist/ cult director Ferrara ("China Girl," "Crime Story").
1990 (R) 106m/C Christopher Walken, Larry Fishburne, David Caruso, Victor Argo, Wesley Snipes, Janet Julian, Joey Chin, Giancarlo Esposito; *D:* Abel Ferrara. VHS, LV $89.95 *LIV* ♫♫♫

King of the Bullwhip Two undercover U.S. Marshals are sent to Tioga City to stop the killing and looting of a masked bandit, whose whip is as dangerous as his gun.
1951 59m/B Lash LaRue, Al "Fuzzy" St. John, Anne Gwynne, Tom Neal, Jack Holt, Dennis Moore, Michael Whalen, George Lewis; *D:* Ron Ormond. VHS, Beta $19.95 *NOS, VCN, DVT* ♫½

King of the Congo Crabbe, in his last serial, as a pilot who is frantically searching for an important piece of film. In 15 parts.
1952 ?m/B Buster Crabbe, Gloria Dee; *D:* Spencer Gordon Bennet, Wallace Grissell. VHS *MLB* ♫½

King of the Cowboys Roy fights a gang of saboteurs and saves a defense installation.
1943 54m/B Roy Rogers, Smiley Burnette, James Bush. VHS $9.99 *NOS, VCN, DVT* ♫

King of the Damned On an island prison Veidt leads a convict's revolt against the cruel administrator (Hallard), who gets killed. Before he dies, Hallard alerts a convenient warship, which begins shelling the island. Hallard's daughter, who has fallen for Veidt, pleads for the men and everyone is given a fair trial. Miscast and ineptly performed, although Veidt retains some dignity. **1936 81m/B** *GB* Conrad Veidt, Helen Vinson, C.M. Hallard, Noah Beery Sr., Percy Walsh, Raymond Lovell, Cecil Ramage, Peter Croft; *D:* Walter Forde. **VHS** *HCV ℐℐ*

King of the Forest Rangers Ranger Steve King must stop an evil archaeologist from finding a treasure whose secret lies within an ancient Indian rug pattern. Edited from an original, 12 episode serial on two cassettes. **1946 167m/B** Larry Thompson, Helen Talbot, Stuart Hamblen, Anthony Warde. **VHS, Beta** $29.98 *REP, MLB ℐ*

King of the Grizzlies The mystical relationship between a Cree Indian and a grizzly cub is put to the acid test when the full grown bear attacks a ranch at which the Indian is foreman. **1969 (G) 93m/C** Chris Wiggins, John Yesno; *D:* Ron Kelly. **VHS, Beta** $69.95 *DIS ℐℐ½*

King of the Gypsies Interesting drama. A young man, scornful of his gypsy heritage, runs away from the tribe and tries to make a life of his own. He is summoned home to his grandfather's deathbed where he is proclaimed the new king of the gypsies, thus incurring the wrath of his scorned father. From Peter Maas's best-selling novel. **1978 (R) 112m/C** Sterling Hayden, Eric Roberts, Susan Sarandon, Brooke Shields, Shelley Winters, Annie Potts, Annette O'Toole, Judd Hirsch, Michael Gazzo, Roy Brocksmith; *D:* Frank Pierson. **VHS, Beta, LV** $14.95 *PAR, CCB ℐℐ½*

King of the Hill Quiet depression-era drama focuses on Aaron, a 12-year-old who lives in a seedy hotel in St. Louis. The family is barely scraping by: his mother is in a tuberculosis sanitarium, his younger brother has been sent away to live with relatives, and Aaron must fend for himself when his father gets work as a traveling salesman. Aaron excels at school and his efforts there, as well as his hotel friends, manage to provide him with some semblance of a regular life. Soderbergh's third directorial effort is unsentimental but admiring of his character's resourcefulness and imagination during difficult times. Based on the book by A.E. Hochner which describes his own childhood. **1993 (PG-13) 102m/C** Jesse Bradford, Jeroen Krabbe, Lisa Eichhorn, Karen Allen, Spalding Gray, Elizabeth McGovern, Joseph Chrest, Adrien Brody, Cameron Boyd, Chris Samples, Katherine Heigl, Amber Benson, John McConnell, Ron Vawter, John Durbin, Lauryn Hill, David Jensen; *D:* Steven Soderbergh; *W:* Steven Soderbergh; *M:* Cliff Martinez. **VHS** *NYR ℐℐℐ*

The King of the Kickboxers The villains make kung-fu snuff movies with unwitting actors killed on camera. Otherwise, same old junk about a karate cop back in Bangkok to get the dude who squashed his brother. Pretty racist at times. **1991 (R) 90m/C** Loren Avedon, Richard Jaeckel, Billy Blanks, Don Stroud, Keith Cooke; *D:* Lucas Lowe. **VHS** $89.95 *IMP Woof!*

King of the Kongo A handsome young man is sent by the government to Nuhalla, deep in the jungle, to break up a gang of ivory thieves. Serial made in silent and sound versions.

1929 213m/B Jacqueline Logan, Boris Karloff, Richard Tucker; *D:* Richard Thorpe. **VHS, Beta** $49.95 *NOS, VYY, MLB ℐℐ*

King of the Mountain The "Old King" and the "New King" must square off in this tale of daredevil road racers who zoom through the streets of Hollywood. Interesting cast trapped by tired script. **1981 (PG) 92m/C** Richard Cox, Harry Hamlin, Dennis Hopper, Joseph Bottoms, Deborah Van Valkenburgh, Dan Haggerty; *D:* Noel Nosseck. **VHS, Beta** $24.98 *SUE ℐℐ½*

King of the Pecos A young lawyer (who's also adept at the shootin' iron) exacts revenge on his parents' killers in the courtroom. Well made early Wayne outing, with good character development, taut pacing and beautiful photography. **1936 54m/B** John Wayne, Muriel Evans, Cy Kendall, Jack Clifford, John Beck, Yakima Canutt; *D:* Joseph Kane. **VHS** $9.98 *REP, MLB ℐℐ½*

The King of the Roaring '20s: The Story of Arnold Rothstein "True" story of infamous gangster, Arnold Rothstein, a brilliant and ruthless gambler who practically ran New York in the twenties. This version of his life focuses on his rise to power, the dealings with his enemies, and his crumbling personal life. Superficial due mostly to the weak screenplay. Adapted from the book "The Big Bankroll" by Leo Katcher. *AKA:* The Big Bankroll. **1961 106m/B** David Janssen, Dianne Foster, Mickey Rooney, Jack Carson, Diana Dors, Dan O'Herlihy, Mickey Shaughnessy, Keenan Wynn; *D:* Joseph M. Newman. **VHS, Beta** $19.98 *FOX, FCT ℐℐ½*

King of the Rocketmen Jeff King thwarts an attempt by traitors to steal government scientific secrets. Serial in twelve episodes. Later released as a feature titled "Lost Planet Airmen." **1949 156m/B** Tristram Coffin, Mae Clarke, I. Stanford Jolley; *D:* Fred Brannon. **VHS, LV** $29.98 *MED, VCN, REP ℐ½*

King of the Rodeo Cowpolk Hoot wins a rodeo and catches a thief in the Windy City. Hoot's final silent ride into the sunset. **1928 54m/B** Hoot Gibson, Katherine Crawford, Slim Summerville, Charles French, Monte Montague, Joseph Girard; *D:* Henry MacRae. **VHS, Beta** $14.95 *GPV ℐℐ*

King of the Stallions A dangerous stallion is a menacing threat to the herd and the cowboys and Indians and other scattered wildlife. Chief Thundercloud is the only one capable of tackling the matter. Largely Indian cast, including Iron Eyes Cody, famed for the anti-litter campaign. **1942 63m/B** Chief Thundercloud, Princess Bluebird, Chief Yowlachie, Rick Vallin, Dave O'Brien, Barbara Felker, Iron Eyes Cody; *D:* Edward Finney. **VHS** $19.95 *NOS, DVT ℐ½*

King of the Texas Rangers Tom King, Texas Ranger, finds that his father's killers are a group of saboteurs who have destroyed American oil fields. This twelve episode serial comes on two tapes. **1941 195m/B** Sammy Baugh, Neil Hamilton; *D:* William Witney, John English. **VHS** $59.95 *REP, MRV, MLB ℐ½*

King of the Wild Horses Engaging children's story about a wild stallion that comes to the rescue. Terrific action photography of Rex going through his paces. Look for Chase in a rare dramatic role. Silent. **1924 50m/B** Rex, Edna Murphy, Leon Barry, Pat Hartigan, Frank Butler, Charley Chase; *D:* Fred Jackman. **VHS, Beta** *NO ℐℐℐ*

King of the Zombies Mad scientist creates his own zombies without souls, to be used as the evil tools of a foreign government. Zombie nonsense. **1941 67m/B** John Archer, Dick Purcell, Mantan Moreland, Henry Victor, Joan Woodbury; *D:* Jean Yarborough. **VHS, Beta** $24.95 *NOS, MRV, SNC Woof!*

The King on Main Street A king on vacation in America finds romance. **1925 ?m/C** Adolphe Menjou, Bessie Love. **VHS, Beta** *NO ℐℐ½*

King, Queen, Knave Sexy black comedy about a shy, awkward 19-year-old boy, keenly aware that his interest in girls is not reciprocated. He has to go live with his prosperous uncle and his much younger wife when his parents are killed. Based on the Vladimir Nabokov novel. *AKA:* Herzbube. **1974 94m/C** *GE* Gina Lollobrigida, David Niven, John Moulder-Brown; *D:* Jerzy Skolimowski. **VHS, Beta** $69.98 *SUE ℐℐℐ*

King Ralph When the rest of the royal family passes away in a freak accident, lounge lizard Ralph finds himself the only heir to the throne. O'Toole is the long-suffering valet who tries to train him for the job. Funny in spots and Goodman is the quintessential good sport, making the whole outing pleasant. Sometimes too forced. **1991 (PG) 96m/C** John Goodman, Peter O'Toole, Camille Coduri, Joely Richardson, John Hurt; *D:* David S. Ward. **VHS, Beta, LV** $19.95 *MCA, CCB ℐℐ*

King Rat Drama set in a World War II Japanese prisoner-of-war camp. Focuses on the effect of captivity on the English, Australian, and American prisoners. An American officer bribes his Japanese captors to live more comfortably than the rest. Based on James Clavell's novel. **1965 134m/B** George Segal, Tom Courtenay, James Fox, James Donald, Denholm Elliott, Patrick O'Neal, John Mills; *D:* Bryan Forbes; *M:* John Barry. **VHS, Beta** $59.95 *COL ℐℐℐ*

King Solomon's Mines The search for King Solomon's Mines leads a safari through the treacherous terrain of the desert, fending off sandstorms, Zulus, and a volcanic eruption. Adapted from the novel by H. Rider Haggard and remade twice. **1937 80m/B** Cedric Hardwicke, Paul Robeson, Roland Young, John Loder, Anna Lee; *D:* Robert Stevenson. **VHS, Beta** $16.95 *SNC, NOS, HMV ℐℐℐ*

King Solomon's Mines A lavish version of the classic H. Rider Haggard adventures about African explorers searching out a fabled diamond mine. Remake of the 1937 classic; remade again in 1985. **1950 102m/C** Stewart Granger, Deborah Kerr, Richard Carlson, Hugo Haas, Lowell Gilmore; *D:* Compton Bennett. Academy Awards '50: Best Color Cinematography, Best Film Editing; Nominations: Best Picture. **VHS, Beta** $14.98 *MGM ℐℐℐ*

King Solomon's Mines The third remake of the classic H. Rider Haggard novel about a safari deep into Africa in search of an explorer who disappeared while searching for the legendary diamond mines of King Solomon. Updated but lacking the style of the previous two films. Somewhat imperialistic, racist point of view. **1985 (PG-13) 101m/C** Richard Chamberlain, John Rhys-Davies, Sharon Stone, Herbert Lom; *D:* J. Lee Thompson; *M:* Jerry Goldsmith. **VHS, Beta** $14.98 *MGM ℐ½*

King Solomon's Mines This cartoon version of the H. Rider Haggard novel chronicles the adventures of big game hunter Alan Quartermain as he searches for a missing man and a fantastic lost treasure.
1986 60m/C *V:* Tom Burlinson, Arthur Dignam. VHS, Beta NO ♫½

King Solomon's Treasure The great white adventurer takes on the African jungle, hunting for hidden treasure in the Forbidden City. Ekland stars as a Phoenician Queen—need we say more??
1976 90m/C *CA GB* David McCallum, Britt Ekland, Patrick Macnee, Wilfrid Hyde-White; *D:* Alvin Rakoff. VHS, Beta $59.95 *UHV* ♫

Kingdom of the Spiders A desert town is invaded by swarms of killer tarantulas, which begin to consume townspeople.
1977 (PG) 90m/C William Shatner, Tiffany Bolling, Woody Strode; *D:* John Cardos. VHS, Beta $19.95 *UHV, FCT* ♫♫½

Kingfisher Caper A power struggle between a businessman, his brother, and a divorced sister is threatening to rip a family-owned diamond empire apart.
1976 (PG) 90m/C Hayley Mills, David McCallum; *D:* Dirk DeVilliers. VHS, Beta $9.95 *MED* ♫♫

Kingfisher the Killer Charles, the Raging Titan of Ninja skill, stalks the bad gang that killed his mother and hits them with nunchakos.
198? 90m/C Sho Kosugi. VHS, Beta $39.95 *TWE* ♫

Kings and Desperate Men Apprentice terrorists plea their case at a public forum when they take a rakish talk show host hostage.
1983 118m/C *GB* Patrick McGoohan, Alexis Kanner, Andrea Marcovicci, Robin Spry, Frank Moore; *D:* Alexis Kanner. VHS NO ♫♫½

Kings Go Forth Hormones and war rage in this love triangle set against the backdrop of WWII France. Sinatra loves Wood who loves Curtis. When Sinatra asks for her hand in marriage she refuses because she's mixed—half black, half white. He says it doesn't matter, but she still declines because she's in love with Curtis. When Sinatra tells Curtis that Wood is mixed, Curtis says that it doesn't matter to him either because he'd never planned on marrying her. Meanwhile, the war continues. Not particularly satisfying on either the war or race front. Based on a novel by Joe David Brown.
1958 109m/B Frank Sinatra, Tony Curtis, Natalie Wood, Leora Dana; *D:* Delmer Daves. VHS, Beta $19.98 *MGM* ♫♫½

Kings of the Road—In the Course of Time A writer and a film projectionist travel by truck across Germany. The film stands out for its simple and expressive direction, and truly captures the sense of physical and ideological freedom of being on the road. A landmark Wenders epic. In German with English subtitles.
1976 176m/B *GE* Ruediger Vogler, Hanns Zischler, Lisa Kreuzer; *D:* Wim Wenders. VHS, Beta $29.95 *PAV, FCT, GLV* ♫♫♫½

Kings, Queens, Jokers Package includes a foolish lover and ghosts in "Haunted Spooks," an escaped convict in "Dangerous Females," and a search for lost jewels in "Stolen Jools."
193? 60m/B Harold Lloyd, Marie Dressler, Polly Moran, Edward G. Robinson, Gary Cooper, Joan Crawford. VHS, Beta *CCB* ♫♫♫½

King's Ransom When the Japanese Emperor's Pearl is stolen, the underworld is abuzz with excitement. But only the wealthiest individuals are invited to bid for the jewel

at Cameron King's secret casino. There, untold pleasures, and dangers, await them.
1991 ?m/C Miles O'Keeffe, Dedee Pfeiffer, Christopher Atkins; *D:* Hugh Parks. VHS NO Woof!

The King's Rhapsody Flynn is an heir who abdicates his throne in order to be with the woman he loves. But when the king dies, Flynn sacrifices love for honor and goes back to marry a princess. Very dated and Flynn is long past his swashbuckling-romantic days.
1955 93m/C *GB* Errol Flynn, Anna Neagle, Patrice Wymore, Martita Hunt, Finlay Currie, Frank Wolff, Joan Benham, Reginald Tate, Miles Malleson; *D:* Herbert Wilcox. VHS $29.95 *FCT* ♫♫

Kings Row The Harry Bellamann best-selling Middle American potboiler comes to life. Childhood friends grow up with varying degrees of success, in a decidedly macabre town. All are continually dependent on and inspired by Parris (Cummings) a psychiatric doctor and genuine gentleman. Many cast members worked against type with unusual success. Warner held the film for a year after its completion, in concern for its dark subject matter, but it received wide acclaim. Shot completely within studio settings—excellent scenic design by William Cameron Menzies, and wonderful score by Erich W. Korngold.
1941 127m/B Ann Sheridan, Robert Cummings, Ronald Reagan, Betty Field, Charles Coburn, Claude Rains, Judith Anderson, Nancy Coleman, Karen Verne, Maria Ouspenskaya, Harry Davenport, Ernest Cossart, Pat Moriarity; *D:* Sam Wood. VHS, Beta $19.98 *MGM, FOX, CCB* ♫♫♫

The King's Whore Dalton stars as a 17th-century king who falls obsessively in love with the wife of one of his courtiers. His passions lead him to make a decision between the woman and the throne. Good-looking costume epic with obligatory sword fights.
1990 (R) 111m/C Timothy Dalton, Valeria Golino, Feodor Chaliapin, Margaret Tyzack. VHS, LV $92.95 *VMK* ♫♫

Kinjite: Forbidden Subjects A cop takes on a sleazy pimp whose specialty is recruiting teenage girls, including the daughter of a Japanese business man. Slimy, standard Bronson fare.
1989 (R) 97m/C Charles Bronson, Juan Fernandez, Peggy Lipton; *D:* Lee Thompson. VHS, Beta, LV $14.95 *MGM, CAN* ♫♫

A Kink in the Picasso MTV personality Daddo joins a cast of criminals who chase after a Picasso artwork and a counterfeit. Artless Australian production.
1990 84m/C Peter O'Brien, Jon Finlayson, Jane Clifton, Andrew Daddo; *D:* Marc Gracie. VHS $79.95 *ATL* ♫

Kino Pravda/Enthusiasm Two famous documentaries by Vertov, the first a prime example of his pioneering avant-garde newsreels that helped establish Soviet montage aesthetic, and the second the famous portrait of Don Basin coal miners, augmented by the famous use of sound editing/montage. In Russian with English titles.
1931 120m/B *RU D:* Dziga Vertov. VHS, Beta $69.95 *FCT, FST* ♫♫

Kipling's Women Supposedly based on Rudyard Kipling's "The Ladies," only with much more sexual content.
1963 50m/C Margie Sutton, Lisa Gordon, Felix de Cola. VHS, Beta $19.95 *VDM* ♫

Kipperbang During the summer of 1948, a 13-year-old boy wishes he could kiss the girl of his dreams. He finally gets the chance in a school play. Not unsatisfying, but falls

short of being the bittersweet coming-of-age drama it could have been. *AKA:* Ptang, Yang, Kipperbang.
1982 (PG) 85m/C *GB* John Albasiny, Abigail Cruttenden, Alison Steadman; *D:* Michael Apted. VHS, Beta $59.95 *NO*

Kipps Based on H.G. Wells' satirical novel. A young British shopkeeper inherits a fortune and tries to join high society while neglecting his working-class girlfriend. Set the stage for the musical "Half a Sixpence." *AKA:* The Remarkable Mr. Kipps.
1941 95m/B *GB* Michael Redgrave, Phyllis Calvert, Michael Wilding; *D:* Carol Reed. VHS, Beta, 3/4U, Special order formats $19.95 *NOS, HHT, CAB* ♫♫

The Kirlian Witness A woman uses the power of telepathic communication with house plants to solve her sister's murder. *AKA:* The Plants Are Watching.
1978 (PG) 88m/C Nancy Snyder, Joel Colodner, Ted Leplat; *D:* Jonathan Sarno. VHS, Beta NO ♫

Kismet Original screen version of the much filmed lavish Arabian Nights saga (remade in '30, '44 and '55). A beggar is drawn into deception and intrigue among Bagdad upper-crusters. Glorious sets and costumes; silent with original organ score.
1920 98m/B Otis Skinner, Elinor Fair, Herschel Mayall; *D:* Louis Gasnier. VHS $29.95 *VYY* ♫♫♫

Kismet A big budget Arabian Nights musical drama of a Baghdad street poet who manages to infiltrate himself into the Wazir's harem. The music was adapted from Borodin by Robert Wright and George Forrest. Original trailer and letterboxed screen available in special laserdisc edition. ♫Fate; Not Since Ninevah; Baubles, Bangles, and Beads; Stranger in Paradise; Bored; Night of My Nights; The Olive Tree; And This Is My Beloved; Sands of Time.
1955 113m/C Howard Keel, Ann Blyth, Dolores Gray, Vic Damone; *D:* Vincente Minnelli. VHS, Beta, LV $19.98 *MGM, PIA, FCT* ♫♫

The Kiss Garbo, the married object of earnest young Ayres' lovelorn affection, innocently kisses him nighty night since a kiss is just a kiss. Or so she thought. Utterly misconstrued, the platonic peck sets the stage for disaster, and murder and courtroom anguish follow. French Feyder's direction is stylized and artsy. Garbo's last silent and Ayres' first film.
1929 89m/B Greta Garbo, Conrad Nagel, Holmes Herbert, Lew Ayres, Anders Randolf; *D:* Jacques Feyder. VHS $29.98 *MGM, FCT* ♫♫♫

The Kiss A kind of "Auntie Mame from Hell" story in which a mysterious aunt visits her teen-age niece in New York, and tries to apprentice her to the family business of sorcery, demon possession, and murder. Aunt Felicity's kiss will make you appreciate the harmless cheek-pinching of your own aunt; your evening would be better spent with her, rather than this movie.
1988 (R) 98m/C Pamela Collyer, Peter Dvorsky, Joanna Pacula, Meredith Salenger, Mimi Kuzyk, Nicholas Kilbertus, Jan Rubes; *D:* Pen Densham. VHS, Beta, LV $19.95 *COL, IME* ♫

Kiss and Be Killed Crazy guy with knife cuts short couple's wedding night. Shortchanged widow is mighty miffed. Will she have to return the wedding gifts?
1991 (R) 89m/C Caroline Ludvik, Crystal Carson, Tom Reilly, Chip Hall, Ken Norton, Jimmy Baio; *D:* Tom Milo. VHS, Beta, 8mm $79.95 *MNC* ♫½

Kiss and Kill Lee returns in his fourth outing as Fu Manchu. This time the evil one has injected beautiful girls with a deadly poison that reacts upon kissing. They are then sent out to seduce world leaders. Not on par with the previous movies, but still enjoyable. Sequel to ''Castle of Fu Manchu.'' *AKA:* Blood of Fu Manchu; Against All Odds. 1968 (R) 91m/C Christopher Lee, Richard Greene, Shirley Eaton, Tsai Chin, Maria Rohm, H. Marion Crawford; *D:* Jess (Jesus) Franco. VHS $14.99 *MRV* 🐾🐾

A Kiss Before Dying Botched adaptation of Ira Levin's cunning thriller novel (filmed before in 1956). This flick serves up an exploded head in the first few minutes. So much for subtlety. The highlight is Dillon's chilly role as a murderous opportunist bent on marrying into a wealthy family. Young plays two roles (not very well) as lookalike sisters on his agenda. The ending was hastily reshot and it shows. 1991 (R) 93m/C Matt Dillon, Sean Young, Max von Sydow, Diane Ladd, James Russo, Martha Gehman, Ben Browder, Joy Lee, Adam Horovitz; *D:* James Dearden. VHS, Beta, LV $19.98 *MCA, PIA* 🐾🐾

Kiss Daddy Goodbye A widower keeps his two children isolated in order to protect their secret telekinetic powers. When he is killed by bikers, the kids attempt to raise him from the dead. Also on video as ''Revenge of the Zombie'' and ''The Vengeful Dead.'' 1981 (R) 81m/C Fabian, Marilyn Burns, Jon Cedar, Marvin Miller; *D:* Patrick Regan. VHS, Beta $59.95 *MRV, IVE, GHV* 🐾½

Kiss Daddy Goodnight A Danish-made thriller about a beautiful young girl who seduces men, drugs them and takes their money. One man turns the tables on her, however, and decides that she will only belong to him. 1987 (R) 89m/C *DK* Uma Thurman, Paul Dillon, Paul Richards, David Brisbin; *D:* P.I. Huemer. VHS, Beta $29.95 *ACA* 🐾

A Kiss for Mary Pickford A rare, hilarious cinematic oddity, a film formulated from Kuleshov montage techniques from footage of the famous American couple's visit to Russia in 1926, wherein a regular guy tries to win a girl through friendship with the stars. Fairbanks and Pickford didn't know of their role in this film, being spliced in later according to montage theory. 1927 70m/B Mary Pickford, Douglas Fairbanks Sr., Igor Ilinsky; *D:* Sergei Komarov. VHS, Beta $49.95 *FCT* 🐾🐾½

Kiss Me a Killer The ancient thriller plot about a young wife and her lover who scheme to kill her middle-aged husband. It's set in L.A.'s Latino community, but extensive shots of salsa music and ethnic cooking hardly raise this above the mediocre. 1991 (R) 91m/C Julie Carmen, Robert Beltran, Guy Boyd, Ramon Franco, Charles Boswell; *D:* Marcus De Leon. *COL* 🐾🐾

Kiss Me Deadly Aldrich's adaptation of Mickey Spillane's private eye tale has been called the meeting of ''art'' and pulp literature. At the least, its the meeting of high concept and low brow. Meeker, as Mike Hammer, is a self interested rough and tumble all American dick (detective, that is). When a woman to whom he happened to give a ride is found murdered, he follows the mystery (because he sniffs a golden goose) straight into a nuclear conspiracy. A pretty standard spy story, that. Aldrich, with tongue deftly in cheek, styles a message through the medium. His pugilistic editorial style (one scene cuts to the next with Hammer falling unconscious and waking), topsy turvy camerawork and rat-a-tat-tat pacing tell volumes about Hammer, the world he orbits, and that special fifties kind of paranoia. Now a cult fave, not always critic raved, it's considered

to be the American grandaddy to the French New Wave. Cinematography by Ernest Laszlo. 1955 105m/B Ralph Meeker, Albert Dekker, Paul Stewart, Wesley Addy, Cloris Leachman, Strother Martin, Marjorie Bennett; *D:* Robert Aldrich. VHS, Beta, LV $19.98 *MGM, FCT* 🐾🐾½

Kiss Me Goodbye Young widow Fields can't shake the memory of her first husband, a charismatic but philandering Broadway choreographer, who's the antithesis of her boring but devoted professor fiance. She struggles with the charming ghost of her first husband, as well as her domineering mother, attempting to understand her own true feelings. Harmless but two-dimensional remake of ''Dona Flor and Her Two Husbands.'' 1982 (PG) 101m/C Sally Field, James Caan, Jeff Bridges, Paul Dooley, Mildred Natwick, Claire Trevor; *D:* Robert Mulligan. VHS, Beta $59.98 *FOX* 🐾🐾

Kiss Me Kate A married couple can't separate their real lives from their stage roles in this musical-comedy screen adaptation of Shakespeare's ''Taming of the Shrew,'' based on Cole Porter's Broadway show. Bob Fosse bursts from the screen—particularly if you see the 3-D version—when he does his dance number. 🎵 Out of This World; From This Moment On; Wunderbar; So In Love; I Hate Men; Were Thine That Special Face; I've Come To Wive It Wealthily In Padua; Where Is The Life That Late I Led?; Always True To You Darling In My Fashion; Why Can't You Behave; Kiss Me Kate; Tom, Dick, or Harry; We Open in Venice; Too Darn Hot; I Hate Men; Brush Up Your Shakespeare. 1953 110m/C Kathryn Grayson, Howard Keel, Ann Miller, Tommy Rall, Bob Fosse, Bobby Van, Keenan Wynn, James Whitmore; *D:* George Sidney. VHS, Beta, LV $19.98 *MGM, PIA, FCT* 🐾🐾🐾

Kiss Me, Kill Me Confused woman is on the run after she may have murdered someone. 1969 (R) 91m/C Carroll Baker, George Eastman, Isabelle DeFunes, Ely Gallo. VHS, Beta *PGN* 🐾½

Kiss Me, Stupid! Once condemned as smut, this lesser Billy Wilder effort now seems no worse than an average TV sitcom. Martin basically plays himself as a horny Vegas crooner stranded in the boondocks. A local songwriter wants Dino to hear his tunes but knows the cad will seduce his pretty wife, so he hires a floozy to pose as the tempting spouse. It gets better as it goes along, but the whole thing suffers from staginess, being an adaptation of an Italian play ''L'Ora Della Fantasia'' by Anna Bonacci. 1964 (PG) 126m/B Dean Martin, Kim Novak, Ray Walston, Felicia Farr, Cliff Osmond, Barbara Pepper, Doro Merande, Howard McNear, Henry Gibson, John Fiedler, Mel Blanc; *D:* Billy Wilder. VHS, Beta, LV $19.98 *MGM* 🐾🐾

KISS Meets the Phantom of the Park The popular '70s rock band is featured in this Dr. Jekyll-esque Halloween horror tale, interspersed with musical numbers. *AKA:* Attack of the Phantoms. 1978 96m/C Gene Simmons, Paul Stanley, Peter Criss, Ace Frehley, Anthony Zerbe, Deborah Ryan, John Dennis Johnston; *D:* Gordon Hessler. VHS, Beta $10.98 *MVD, WOV* 🐾½

Kiss My Grits A good ole boy hightails it to Mexico with his girlfriend and son, chased by mobsters and the law. 1982 (PG) 101m/C Bruce Davison, Anthony (Tony) Franciosa, Susan George, Bruno Kirby; *D:* Jack Starrett. VHS, Beta $49.95 *MED* 🐾

Kiss of Death Paroled when he turns state's evidence, Mature must now watch his back constantly. Widmark, in his film debut, seeks to destroy him. Police chief Donlevy tries to help. Filmed on location in New York, this gripping and gritty film is a vision of the most terrifying sort of existence, one where nothing is certain, and everything is dangerous. Excellent. 1947 98m/B Victor Mature, Richard Widmark, Anne Grey, Brian Donlevy, Karl Malden, Coleen Gray; *D:* Henry Hathaway. VHS $39.98 *FOX, FCT* 🐾🐾🐾

Kiss of the Spider Woman From the novel by Manuel Puig, an acclaimed drama concerning two cell mates in a South American prison, one a revolutionary, the other a homosexual. Literate, haunting, powerful. 1985 (R) 119m/C *BR* William Hurt, Raul Julia, Sonia Braga, Jose Lewgoy; *D:* Hector Babenco. Academy Awards '85: Best Actor (Hurt); Nominations: Best Adapted Screenplay, Best Director (Babenco), Best Picture; British Academy Awards '85: Best Actor (Hurt); Cannes Film Festival '85: Best Actor (Hurt); Independent Spirit Awards '86: Best Foreign Film. VHS, Beta, LV, 8mm $19.95 *COL, BTV, NLC* 🐾🐾🐾

Kiss of the Tarantula Teen girl who lives with her family in a mortuary battles inner torment and vents anxiety by releasing her deadly pet spiders on those whom she despises. Eight-legged ''Carrie'' rip-off written by Warren Hamilton. 1975 (PG) 85m/C Eric Mason; *D:* Chris Munger. VHS, Beta $19.95 *MPI, FCT* 🐾

Kiss Shot Goldberg is a struggling single mother who loses her job but still must make the mortgage payments. She takes a job as a waitress but realizes it isn't going to pay the bills so she tries her hand as a pool hustler. Frantz is the promoter who finances her bets and Harewood, the pool-shooting playboy whose romantic advances are destroying her concentration. 1989 88m/C Whoopi Goldberg, Dennis Franz, Dorian Harewood, David Marciano, Teddy Wilson; *D:* Jerry London. VHS, Beta $89.95 *ACA, MOV* 🐾

Kiss the Night An unfortunate hooker falls head over heels for a man she had the pleasure of doing business with. To her chagrin, it is much harder to leave the street than she thought. A dramatic and timely presentation. 1987 (R) 99m/C Patsy Stephens, Warwick Moss, Gary Aron Cook; *D:* James Ricketson. VHS $79.95 *MCG* 🐾🐾

Kiss Tomorrow Goodbye A brutal, murderous escaped convict rises to crime-lord status before his inevitable downfall. Based on a novel by Horace McCoy. 1950 102m/B James Cagney, Barbara Payton, Ward Bond, Luther Adler, Helena Carter, Steve Brodie, Rhys Williams; *D:* Gordon Douglas. VHS, LV $19.98 *REP* 🐾🐾

Kisses Lauren Bacall hosts an entertaining look at screen kisses from yesterday and today. 1991 47m/C VHS, Beta $14.98 *TTC* 🐾🐾

Kisses for My President Silly comedy about the first woman elected President and her trials and tribulations. MacMurray is the husband who has to adjust to the protocol of being ''First Man.'' Bergen is miscast, but the other performers are just fine. 1964 113m/C Fred MacMurray, Polly Bergen, Arlene Dahl, Edward Andrews, Eli Wallach, Donald May; *D:* Curtis Bernhardt. VHS *WAR* 🐾🐾½

Kissin' Cousins Air Force officer on a secluded base in the South discovers a local hillbilly is his double. Presley quickie that includes country tunes such as "Smokey Mountain Boy" and "Barefoot Ballad" as well as the title song.
1964 96m/C Elvis Presley, Arthur O'Connell, Jack Albertson, Glenda Farrell, Pam Austin, Yvonne Craig, Cynthia Pepper, Donald Woods, Tommy Farrell, Beverly Powers; **D:** Gene Nelson. **VHS, Beta $19.95** MGM *2 ½*

The Kissing Place A woman who abducted her "son" years ago tracks the boy to New York City to prevent him from finding his biological family.
1990 90m/C Meredith Baxter Birney, David Ogden Stiers; **D:** Tony Wharmby. **VHS, Beta $29.95** PAR *2 ½*

Kit Carson Frontiersman Kit Carson leads a wagon train to California, fighting off marauding Indians all the way.
1940 97m/B Jon Hall, Dana Andrews, Ward Bond, Lynn Bari; **D:** George B. Seitz. **VHS, Beta $14.95** MED *2*

The Kitchen Toto Set in 1950 Kenya as British rule was being threatened by Mau Mau terrorists. A young black boy is torn between the British for whom he works and the terrorists who want him to join them. Complex and powerful story of the Kenyan freedom crusade.
1987 (PG-13) 96m/C GB Bob Peck, Phyllis Logan, Robert Urquhart, Edward Judd; **D:** Harry Hook. **VHS, Beta, LV $79.95** WAR *222*

Kitty and the Bagman A comedy about two rival madames who ruled Australia in the 1920s.
1982 (R) 95m/C AU Liddy Clark; **D:** Donald Crombie. **VHS, Beta $59.98** SUE *2*

Kitty Foyle From the novel by Christopher Morley, Rogers portrays the white-collar working girl whose involvement with a married man presents her with both romantic and social conflicts.
1940 108m/B Ginger Rogers, Dennis Morgan, James Craig, Gladys Cooper, Ernest Cossart, Eduardo Ciannelli; **D:** Sam Wood. Academy Awards '40: Best Actress (Rogers); Nominations: Best Adapted Screenplay, Best Director (Wood), Best Picture, Best Sound. **VHS, Beta $19.98** VID, MED, CCB *222*

The Klansman Race relations come out on the short end in this film about a sheriff trying to keep the lid on racial tensions in a southern town. Even the big-name cast can't save what comes off as a nighttime soaper rather than a serious drama. **AKA:** Burning Cross; KKK.
1974 (R) 112m/C Lee Marvin, Richard Burton, Cameron Mitchell, Lola Falana, Lucianna Paluzzi, Linda Evans, O.J. Simpson; **D:** Terence Young. **VHS $14.95** PAR, FCT *2*

Klondike Fever Join the young Jack London as he travels from San Francisco to the Klondike fields during the Great Gold Rush of 1898. **AKA:** Jack London's Klondike Fever.
1979 (PG) 118m/C Rod Steiger, Angie Dickinson, Lorne Greene; **D:** Peter Carter. **VHS, Beta** NO *2 ½*

Klute A small-town policeman (Sutherland) comes to New York in search of a missing friend and gets involved with a prostitute/would-be actress (Fonda) being stalked by a killer. Intelligent, gripping drama.
1971 (R) 114m/C Jane Fonda, Donald Sutherland, Charles Cioffi, Roy Scheider, Rita Gam, Jean Stapleton; **D:** Alan J. Pakula. Academy Awards '71: Best Actress (Fonda); Nominations: Best Story & Screenplay; Golden Globe Awards '72: Best Actress—Drama (Fonda); New York Film Critics Awards '71: Best

Actress (Fonda); National Society of Film Critics Awards '71: Best Actress (Fonda). **VHS, Beta, LV $19.98** WAR, BTV *222 ½*

The Klutz A bumbling fool, on the way to visit his girlfriend, becomes accidentally embroiled in a bank robbery and other ridiculous mishaps. Light French comedy; dubbed.
1973 87m/C FR Claude Michaud, Louise Portal, Guy Provost; **D:** Pierre Rose. **VHS, Beta $19.95** STE, NWV *22*

Knife in the Water A journalist, his wife and a hitchhiker spend a day aboard a sailboat. Sex and violence can't be far off. Tense psychological drama. Served as director Polanski's debut. In Polish with English subtitles. **AKA:** Noz w Wodzie.
1962 94m/B PL Leon Niemczyk, Jolanta Umecka, Zygmunt Malandowicz; **D:** Roman Polanski. Academy Awards '63 Nominations: Best Foreign Language Film; Venice Film Festival '62: International Critics Award. **VHS, Beta, LV $39.95** HMV, FOX, VYY *2222*

Knight Moves Suspenseful thriller about a series of murders which take place at an international resort where a championship chess match is underway. The prime suspect is a chess master who has an unlikely affair with a beautiful police psychologist called in to decipher the mind of the murderer. Filmed in the Pacific Northwest.
1993 (R) 105m/C Christopher Lambert, Diane Lane, Tom Skerritt, Daniel Baldwin; **D:** Carl Schenkel; **W:** Brad Mirman; **M:** Anne Dudley. **VHS, LV $92.98** REP *22*

Knight Without Armour A journalist opposed to the Russian monarchy falls in love with the daughter of a czarist minister in this classic romantic drama.
1937 107m/B GB Marlene Dietrich, Robert Donat; **D:** Jacques Feyder. **VHS, Beta $14.98** SUE *222*

Knightriders The story of a troupe of motorcyclists who are members of a traveling Renaissance Fair.
1981 (R) 145m/C Ed Harris, Gary Lahti, Tom Savini, Amy Ingersoll; **D:** George A. Romero. **VHS, Beta $54.95** MED *22 ½*

Knights & Emeralds Cross-cultural rivalries and romances develop between members of two high school marching bands in a British factory town as the national band championships draw near.
1987 (PG) 90m/C GB Christopher Wild, Beverly Hills, Warren Mitchell; **D:** Ian Emes. **VHS, Beta $19.95** WAR *2 ½*

Knights of the City Miami street gangs fight each other over their "turf." One leader decides to opt out, using music. ♫Let the Music Play; Cry of the City; Jailhouse Rap; T.K. and Jessie Rap; Kurtis Blow Rap; Bounce; My Part of Town; Can You Feel It; Love Goes Up and Down; Flying; Fire; Bed of Ashes; Dance Teach/Down Street Rap; You Can Do It; I Won't Give It Away; You're Not the Only One; Contagious.
1985 (R) 87m/C Nicholas Campbell, John Mengatti, Wendy Barry, Stoney Jackson, Fat Boys, Michael Ansara, Janine Turner; **D:** Dominic Orlando; **W/D:** Leon Isaac Kennedy. **VHS, Beta $14.95** NWV, STE *2*

Knights of the Range Vintage western.
1940 66m/B Russell Hayden, Victor Jory; **D:** Lesley Selander. **VHS, Beta $29.95** VCN, MLB *2 ½*

Knights of the Round Table The story of the romantic triangle between King Arthur, Sir Lancelot and Guinevere during the civil wars of sixth century England.

1953 106m/C Robert Taylor, Ava Gardner, Mel Ferrer, Anne Crawford, Felix Aylmer, Stanley Baker; **D:** Richard Thorpe. **VHS, Beta, LV $19.95** MGM *22 ½*

Knock on Any Door A young hoodlum from the slums is tried for murdering a cop. He is defended by a prominent attorney who has known him from childhood.
1949 100m/B Humphrey Bogart, John Derek, George Macready; **D:** Nicholas Ray. **VHS, Beta, LV $9.95** COL *22*

Knock Outs Samantha not only loses her shirt at a sorority strip poker marathon but she loses her tuition money to a gang of biker chicks. Then Samantha and a bevy of bikini-clad friends decide to pose for a swimsuit calendar to earn some cash but are secretly videotaped in the nude by some local sleaze promoters. Tired of being taken advantage of these lovelies take up martial arts and challenge their nefarious girl biker rivals to a winner-take-all wrestling match, not forgetting about the purveyors of the not-so-secret videotape.
1992 90m/C Chona Jackson, Sindi Rome, Brad Zutaut; **D:** John Bowen. **VHS $79.95** HMD *2*

The Knockout/Dough and Dynamite Two Chaplin shorts: "The Knockout" (1914), in which Charlie referees a big fight; "Dough and Dynamite" (1914), in which a labor dispute at a bake shop leaves Charlie in charge when the regular baker walks out.
1914 54m/B Charlie Chaplin, Fatty Arbuckle, Mabel Normand, The Keystone Cops; **D:** Charlie Chaplin, Sydney Chaplin. **VHS, Beta $29.95** VYY *222*

Knute Rockne: All American Life story of Notre Dame football coach Knute Rockne, who inspired many victories with his powerful speeches. Reagan, as the dying George Gipp, utters that now-famous line, "Tell the boys to win one for the Gipper." **AKA:** A Modern Hero.
1940 96m/B Ronald Reagan, Pat O'Brien, Gale Page, Donald Crisp, John Qualen; **D:** Lloyd Bacon. **VHS, Beta $19.98** MGM, FHE *222*

Kohlberg Powerful epic about a Prussian town's rebellion against Napoleon's occupation forces. Classic German film produced during the final years of WW II.
1945 ?m/C GE **VHS $44.95** AUD *22*

Kojak: The Belarus File The bald-headed detective of prime-time television fame searches for a neo-Nazi who is killing Holocaust survivors in New York. Made for television.
1985 95m/C Telly Savalas, Suzanne Pleshette, Max von Sydow, George Savalas; **D:** Robert Markowitz. **VHS, Beta $39.95** MCA *22*

Kojiro A sprawling epic by prolific Japanese director Inagaki about a dashing rogue's bid for power in feudal times. With English subtitles.
1967 152m/C JP Kikunosuke Onoe, Tatsuya Nakadai; **D:** Hiroshi Inagaki. **VHS, Beta** VDA *222*

Koko Cartoons: No. 1 A collection of Koko's best cartoons, including "Flies," "Koko's Cartoon Factory," "Koko's Thanksgiving," "Sweet Adeline," and "The Fortune Teller."
1927 50m/C **D:** Max Fleischer. **VHS, Beta** GVV *222*

Kolberg The true story of a Prussian town heroically withstanding Napoleon. Produced by Joseph Goebbels in the last days of the Third Reich, it is best remembered as the film whose expensive production and momentous use of real German soldiers, supplies, and ammunition eventually helped to fell the

Axis war machine. In German with English subtitles. *AKA:* Burning Hearts.
1945 118m/C *GE* Kristina Soderbaum, Heinrich George, Horst Caspar, Paul Wegener; *D:* Veit Harlan. **VHS, Beta, 3/4U $39.95** *FCT, IHF, GLV*

Konrad Konrad, an "instant" child made in a factory, is accidentally delivered to an eccentric woman. The factory wants him back when the mistake is discovered, but Konrad stands up against it. Includes a viewers' guide. Part of the "Wonderworks" series.
199? 110m/C Ned Beatty, Polly Holliday, Max Wright, Huckleberry Fox. **VHS $29.95** *PME, HMV, BTV*

Koroshi Secret Agent John Drake is dispatched to Hong Kong to disband a secret society who is killing off international political figures.
1967 100m/C Patrick McGoohan, Kenneth Griffith, Yoko Tani; *D:* Michael Truman, Peter Yates. **VHS, Beta $59.95** *MPI* ♫½

Kostas A migrant Greek taxi driver romantically pursues a wealthy Australian divorcee in England.
1979 (R) 88m/C Takis Emmanuel, Wendy Hughes; *D:* Paul Cox. **VHS, Beta $69.98** *LIV, VES* ♫♫

Kotch An elderly man resists his children's attempts to retire him. Warm detailing of old age with a splendid performance by Matthau. Lemmon's directorial debut.
1971 (PG) 113m/C Walter Matthau, Deborah Winters, Felicia Farr; *D:* Jack Lemmon. **VHS $59.98** *FOX* ♫♫♫

Kowloon Assignment Comic book superhero Golgo 13 comes to life in this action film dealing with a drug war in the Hong Kong underground.
1977 93m/C Sonny Chiba. **VHS, Beta** *NO* ♫

Koyaanisqatsi A mesmerizing film that takes an intense look at modern life (the movie's title is the Hopi word for "life out of balance"). Without dialogue or narration, it brings traditional background elements, landscapes and cityscapes, up front to produce a unique view of the structure and mechanics of our daily lives. Riveting and immensely powerful. A critically acclaimed score by Philip Glass, and Reggio's cinematography prove to be the perfect match to this brilliant film. Followed by "Powaqqatsi."
1983 87m/C *D:* Godfrey Reggio; *M:* Philip Glass. **VHS, Beta, LV $14.95** *MVD, PAV, FCT* ♫♫♫♫

Kramer vs. Kramer Highly acclaimed family drama about an advertising executive husband and child left behind when their wife and mother leaves on a quest to find herself, and the subsequent courtroom battle for custody when she returns. Hoffman and Streep give exacting performances as does young Henry. Successfully moves you from tears to laughter and back again. Based on the novel by Avery Corman.
1979 (PG) 105m/C Dustin Hoffman, Meryl Streep, Jane Alexander, Justin Henry, Howard Duff, JoBeth Williams; *D:* Robert Benton. Academy Awards '79: Best Actor (Hoffman), Best Adapted Screenplay, Best Director (Benton), Best Picture, Best Supporting Actress (Streep); Nominations: Best Cinematography, Best Film Editing, Best Supporting Actor (Henry); Golden Globe Awards '80: Best Actor—Drama (Hoffman), Best Film—Drama, Best Supporting Actress (Streep); National Board of Review Awards '79: 10 Best Films of the Year, Best Supporting Actress (Streep); National Society of Film Critics Awards '79: Best Actor (Hoffman), Best Director (Benton), Best Supporting Actress (Streep). **VHS, Beta, LV $19.95** *COL, PIA, BTV* ♫♫♫½

The Krays An account of British gangsters Reggie and Ronnie Kray, the brothers who ruled London's East End with brutality and violence, making them bizarre celebrities of the sixties. The leads are portrayed by Gary and Martin Kemp, founders of the British pop group Spandau Ballet.
1990 (R) 119m/C *GB* Gary Kemp, Martin Kemp, Billie Whitelaw, Steven Berkoff, Susan Fleetwood, Charlotte Cornwell; *D:* Peter Medak. **VHS, LV, 8mm $19.95** *COL, FCT* ♫♫♫½

Kriemhilde's Revenge The second film, following "Siegfried," of Lang's "Die Nibelungen," a lavish silent version of the Teutonic legends Wagner's "Ring of the Nibelungen" was based upon. In this episode, Kriemhilde avenges Siegfried's death by her marriage to the Kings of the Huns, thus fulfilling a prophecy of destruction.
1924 95m/B *GE* Paul Richter, Margareta Schoen; *D:* Fritz Lang. **VHS, LV $19.95** *CCB, IHF, REP* ♫♫♫♫

Kronos A giant robot from space drains the Earth of all its energy resources. A good example of this genre from the 50s. Includes previews of coming attractions from classic science fiction films.
1957 78m/B Jeff Morrow, Barbara Lawrence, John Emery; *D:* Kurt Neumann. **VHS, Beta, LV $19.95** *MED, MLB* ♫♫½

Krull Likeable fantasy adventure set in a world peopled by creatures of myth and magic. A prince embarks on a quest to find the Glaive (a magical weapon) and then rescues his young bride, taken by the Beast of the Black Fortress.
1983 (PG) 121m/C *GB* Ken Marshall, Lysette Anthony, Freddie Jones, Francesca Annis, Liam Neeson; *D:* Peter Yates. **VHS, Beta, LV $14.95** *GKK* ♫♫

Krush Groove The world of rap music is highlighted in this movie, the first all-rap musical. ♫King of Rock; Don't You Dog Me; A Love Bizarre; Pick Up the Pace; If I Ruled the World; Holly Rock; It's Like That; Feel the Spin; I Can't Live Without My Radio; Please Don't Go; My Secret; She's On It; Pump It Up/Let's Get Funky; All You Can Eat; I Want You to Be My Girl; Fat Boys; Can You Rock It Like This; Tender Love; Love Triangle; You're Blind; Kold Krush; Krush Groovin'; Can't Stop the Street.
1985 (R) 95m/C Blair Underwood, Eron Tabor, Kurtis Blow, Fat Boys, Sheila E; *D:* Michael Schultz. **VHS, Beta, LV $79.95** *WAR* ♫

K2: The Ultimate High Two men, one a skirt-chasing lawyer, the other a happily married physicist, tackle the world's second largest mountain—the K-2 in Kashmir, northern Pakistan. They encounter a number of dangers, including an ascent of sheer rock face, an avalanche, and a fall down perpendicular mountain ice, but even the exciting mountain-climbing scenes can't hold up this watered down movie. The film was actually shot on Canada's Mount Waddington. Based on the play by Patrick Meyers.
1992 (R) 104m/C Michael Biehn, Matt Craven, Raymond J. Barry, Luca Bercovici, Patricia Charbonneau, Julia Nickson-Soul, Hiroshi Fujioka, Jamal Shah; *D:* Franc Roddam; *W:* Patrick Meyers, Scott Roberts. **VHS, Beta** *PAR* ♫♫

Kuffs Slater stars as George Kuffs, a young guy who reluctantly joins his brother's highly respected private security team in this original action comedy. After his brother is gunned down in the line of duty, George finds himself the new owner of the business. Out to avenge his brother, George pursues a crooked art dealer as he battles crime on the streets of San Francisco. Worthwhile premise is hampered by a predictable plot and mediocre acting.
1992 (PG-13) 102m/C Christian Slater, Tony Goldwyn, Milla Jovovich, Bruce Boxleitner, Troy Evans, George De La Pena, Leon Rippy; *W/D:* Bruce A. Evans; *W:* Raynold Gideon; *M:* Harold Faltermeyer. **VHS, Beta, LV $19.98** *MCA* ♫♫

Kung Fu A fugitive Buddhist quasi-Asian martial arts master accused of murder in his native land, roams across the Old West fighting injustice. Served as a pilot for the successful television series and was reincarnated 14 years later in the sequel, "Kung Fu: The Movie."
1972 75m/C Keith Carradine, David Carradine, Barry Sullivan, Keye Luke; *D:* Jerry Thorpe. **VHS, Beta $24.98** *WAR* ♫♫½

Kung Fu Avengers On his way to a karate show at Madison Square Garden, our hero Li confronts the abominable Mr. Chin and his deadly henchman. Another footstomper.
1985 90m/C Bruce Li, Carl Scott, Jim James, Ku Feng. **VHS, Beta $59.95** *PSM* ♫

Kung Fu Commandos Five martial arts masters must face an evil warlord's army to rescue a captured agent.
1980 (R) 90m/C John Liu, Shangkuan Ling-Feng. **VHS, Beta $59.95** *PSM, GEM* ♫

Kung Fu for Sale Young kung fu enthusiast, along with his mentor, fight for the respect of his family.
1981 95m/C Chong Hua. **VHS, Beta** *NO* ♫

Kung Fu from Beyond the Grave The ultimate warrior/zombies are summoned from the cold earth for evil purposes. Not for the brain-active.
19?? 90m/C Billy Chong, Sung Kam Shing, Lo Lieh, Hui Piu Wan. **VHS, Beta $29.95** *OCE* ♫

Kung Fu Genius Nasty assassin-types are trying to annex his home town and that is making the kung fu genius angry.
1969 88m/C **VHS, Beta $39.95** *TWE* ♫

Kung Fu Hero Martial arts heroes try to help overthrow the "Evil Empire," by infiltrating the Forbidden City.
1989 96m/C **VHS, Beta** *NO* ♫

Kung Fu Hero 2 Chinese martial artists risk it all to take on the forces of evil.
1990 96m/C Wang Fu; *D:* Yu Lianqi. **VHS, Beta** *NO* ♫

The Kung Fu Kid Thanks to his martial arts mastery, a young man is able to rise above his poor upbringing and become an undercover cop.
19?? 90m/C Weiman Chan, Nora Miao. **VHS, Beta $49.95** *OCE* ♫

The Kung Fu Kid from Peking In 1940s Shanghai, martial artists slug it out for the skull of the Peking man in order to prove the theory of evolution.
19?? 90m/C **VHS, Beta $29.95** *OCE* ♫

Kung Fu Kids A group of abandoned orphans become kung fu street performers to earn money.
1984 85m/C **VHS, Beta $39.95** *OCE, TWE* ♫

Kung Fu Massacre Farmers hire hard-handed mercenaries to fight evil war lords.
1982 (R) 90m/C Yangzi, Pi Li Lee. **VHS, Beta $12.95** *LIV* ♫

Kung Fu of Eight Drunkards Ching dynasty warriors battle it out using a karate technique that gives them the appearance of being drunk.
19?? 188m/C **VHS, Beta** *BFV* ♫

Kung Fu Powerhouse No one dares to get in the way of a powerful kung fu drug lord. If they do, they die!

19?? 90m/C Kam Kong, Yasuka Kurata, Lee Ka Ting. VHS, Beta $49.95 *OCE* 🐾

Kung Fu Rebels Rebels are fearsome enough, but when they're kung fu masters, the establishment has real trouble on its hands.
1980 90m/C Wang Chung, Wen Ching Lung, Chang Mei. VHS, Beta *NO* 🐾½

Kung Fu Shadow The forces of good and evil are at odds once again in this dubbed kung fu epic.
1985 90m/C Tien Pang, Chia Ling. VHS, Beta $14.95 *SVS* 🐾

Kung Fu Strongman A peace-loving blacksmith is forced to crush, kill, and destroy when he is framed for a robbery.
19?? 90m/C Lei Chen, Lung Fei, Kam Kong. VHS, Beta $49.95 *OCE* 🐾

Kung Fu Terminator A lady terminator proves that her fists are just as quick and deadly as any man's.
19?? 90m/C Wang Kuang Hsiung, Liu Hao Yi. VHS, Beta $49.95 *OCE* 🐾

Kung Fu: The Movie Carradine reprises his role as Kwai Chang Caine from the television show of the '70s. In this made-for-television fare he's hunted by evil warlord Mako, who's involved in the California opium trade. Mako sends assassin Lee (son of martial-arts star Bruce) after Caine. Luke appears in flashbacks as the young Grasshopper's blind mentor, Master Po.
1986 93m/C David Carradine, Mako, Brandon Lee, Keye Luke, Kerrie Keane, Martin Landau, William Lucking, Luke Askew, Benson Fong; D: Richard Lang. VHS, Beta $59.99 *WAR* 🐾🐾½

Kung Fu Vampire Buster Two Taoist kung fu priests take on coffins, cemeteries, and vampires. Good luck! The ultimate (tasteless) cross-genre flick.
19?? 90m/C Lu Fang, Wang Hsiao Feng, Chien Hsiao Hou. VHS, Beta $49.95 *OCE* Woof!

The Kung Fu Warrior A vacationing young Kung fu enthusiast gets caught up in a bizarre chain of events that force him to fight for his life.
1987 91m/C Chang Lei, Kuan Hai Shan. VHS, Beta $39.95 *TWE* 🐾

Kung Fu Zombie A member of the undead rises and seeks vengeance on those responsible for his plight.
1982 (R) 90m/C Billy Chong, Chinag Tao. VHS, SVS *OCE* 🐾½

Kung Fu's Hero A detective must resort to killing with Kung Fu to stop a slave/drug ring.
19?? 90m/C VHS, Beta $49.95 *OCE* 🐾

Kurt Vonnegut's Monkey House Dramatization of four short stories from Vonnegut's "Welcome to the Monkey House" collection, including a twist on the familiar Frankenstein tale. Made for cable television.
199? 100m/C Frank Langella. VHS $79.95 *PAV* 🐾🐾

Kwaidan A haunting, stylized quartet of supernatural stories, each with a surprise ending. Adapted from the stories of Lafcadio Hearn, an American author who lived in Japan just before the turn of the century. The visual effects are splendid. In Japanese with English subtitles.
1964 164m/C JP Michiyo Aratama, Rentaro Mikuni, Katsuo Makamura; D: Masaki Kobayashi. VHS, Beta, LV $24.95 *NOS, HMV, SNC* 🐾🐾🐾🐾

L.A. Bad A Puerto Rican street thug learns he has cancer, and must come to terms with his own impending death.

1985 (R) 101m/C Esai Morales, Janice Rule, John Phillip Law, Chuck Bail, Carrie Snodgress. VHS, Beta $9.99 *STE, PSM* 🐾

La Balance An underworld stool-pigeon is recruited by the Parisian police to blow the whistle on a murderous mob. Baye, as a prostitute in love with the pimp-stoolie, is a standout. Critically acclaimed in France; won many Caesar awards, including for Best Picture. In French with English subtitles.
1982 (R) 103m/C FR Philippe Leotard, Nathalie Baye, Bob Swaim; D: Reymond LePlont. VHS, Beta $79.95 *TAM, FOX* 🐾🐾🐾

La Bamba A romantic biography of the late 1950s pop idol Ritchie Valens, concentrating on his stormy relationship with his half-brother, his love for his WASP girlfriend, and his tragic, sudden death in the famed plane crash that also took the lives of Buddy Holly and the Big Bopper. Soundtrack features Setzer, Huntsberry, Crenshaw, and Los Lobos as, respectively, Eddie Cochran, the Big Bopper, Buddy Holly, and a Mexican bordello band.
1987 (PG-13) 99m/C Lou Diamond Phillips, Esai Morales, Danielle von Zernaeck, Joe Pantoliano, Brian Setzer, Marshall Crenshaw, Howard Huntsberry, Rosana De Soto, Elizabeth Pena; D: Luis Valdez. VHS, Beta, LV, 8mm $14.95 *COL* 🐾🐾🐾

La Bella Lola A poor singer falls in love with a rich politician in nineteenth century society.
1987 113m/C MX Sara Montiel, Antonio Charriello, Frank Villard, Luisa Mattiol. VHS, Beta $53.95 *MAD* 🐾🐾

La Bete Humaine A dark, psychological melodrama about human passion and duplicity, as an unhinged trainman plots with a married woman to kill her husband. Wonderful performances and stunning photography. Based on the Emile Zola novel. In French with English subtitles. 1954 Hollywood remake, "Human Desire," was directed by Fritz Lang. *AKA:* The Human Beast.
1938 90m/B FR Jean Gabin, Simone Simon, Julien Carette, Fernand Ledoux; D: Jean Renoir. VHS, Beta, 8mm, 3/4U, Special order formats $24.95 *NOS, HHT, CAB* 🐾🐾🐾½

La Boca del Lobo Peru's civil strife inspired this sluggish drama about government troops occupying a jungle village. Tormented by unseen communist guerillas, the stressed-out soldiers reach the breaking point. *AKA:* The Lion's Den.
1989 111m/C AR D: Francisco J. Lombardi. VHS $68.00 *CCN, APD* 🐾🐾

La Boum A teenager's adjustment to the changes brought about by a move to Paris is compounded by her parents' marital problems. Followed by "La Boum 2."
1981 90m/C FR Sophie Marceau, Claude Brasseur, Brigitte Fossey, Denise Grey, Bernard Giraudeau; D: Claude Pinoteau. VHS, Beta $59.95 *COL* 🐾🐾½

L.A. Bounty A beautiful cop and a bounty hunter go after the same murderer. Hauser steals the show as a psychopath who has completely blown a gasket.
1989 (R) 85m/C Sybil Danning, Wings Hauser, Henry Darrow, Lenore Kasdorf, Robert Hanley; D: Worth Keeter. VHS, Beta, LV $9.99 *CCB, IVE* 🐾🐾

La Cage aux Folles Adaption of the popular French play. A gay nightclub owner and his transvestite lover play it straight when Tognazzi's son from a long-ago liaison brings his fiancee and her conservative parents home for dinner. Charming music and lots of fun. So successful, it was followed by two sequels, "La Cage Aux Folles II & III"

and also a Broadway musical. In French with English subtitles.
1978 (R) 91m/C FR Ugo Tognazzi, Michel Serrault, Michel Galabru, Claire Maurier, Remy Laurent, Benny Luke; D: Edouard Molinaro; M: Ennio Morricone. Academy Awards '79 Nominations: Best Adapted Screenplay, Best Costume Design, Best Director (Molinaro); Cesar Awards '79: Best Actor (Serrault); Golden Globe Awards '80: Best Foreign Film. VHS, Beta, LV $19.98 *MGM, FOX, VYG* 🐾🐾🐾½

La Cage aux Folles 2 Albin sets out to prove to his companion that he still has sex appeal, and gets mixed up in some espionage antics. This sequel to the highly successful "La Cage aux Folles" loses some steam, but is still worth seeing. Followed by "La Cage Aux Folles III: The Wedding."
1981 (R) 101m/C FR Ugo Tognazzi, Michel Serrault, Marcel Bozzuffi, Michel Galabru, Benny Luke; D: Edouard Molinaro; M: Ennio Morricone. VHS, Beta, LV $19.98 *MGM, FCT, FOX* 🐾🐾½

La Cage aux Folles 3: The Wedding The flamboyant drag queen Albin must feign normalcy by marrying and fathering a child in order to collect a weighty inheritance. Final segment of the trilogy; inferior to the previous films. In French with English subtitles.
1986 (PG-13) 88m/C FR Michel Serrault, Ugo Tognazzi, Michel Galabru, Benny Luke, Stephane Audran; D: Georges Lautner; M: Ennio Morricone. VHS, Beta, LV $29.95 *RCA, TAM, COL* 🐾½

La Carcel de Laredo Two young lovers find they have made the biggest mistake of their lives when they have a baby out of wedlock.
1984 ?m/C MX Rodolfo de Anda, Eleazar Garcia Chelelo; D: Rodolfo de Anda. VHS, Beta *NO* 🐾🐾

La Casa de Madame Lulu A man who falls in love with a prostitute disrupts life in a brothel in this satire on the balance of power between men and women.
1965 90m/C MX Libertad Leblanc, Enzo Viena, Elena Lucena, Juan C. Altavista VHS, Beta $39.95 *MAD* 🐾🐾

La Casa del Amor A woman doctor visits a brothel in order to solve some of the sexual problems of her patients.
1987 90m/C MX Zulma Faiad, Elena Lucena, Enrique Liporace, Jorge Porcel. VHS, Beta $54.95 *MAD* 🐾🐾

La Chamuscada A group of Mexican rebels fight against the army so they can live their lives freely.
1987 97m/C MX VHS, Beta $58.95 *MAD* 🐾

La Chevre A screwball French comedy about two policemen (Richard and Depardieu—picture Nick Nolte and Gene Wilder with accents) stumbling along the path of a missing heiress who suffers from chronic bad luck. Contains a hilarious scene with chairs used to test the luck of the investigative team; based on one partner's ability to sit on the only broken chair in a rather large collection, he is judged to be sufficiently jinxed to allow them to recreate the same outrageous misfortunes that befell the heiress in her plight. In French with English subtitles. *AKA:* The Goat.
1981 91m/C Gerard Depardieu, Pierre Richard, Corynne Charbit, Michel Robin, Pedro Armendariz Jr.; D: Francis Veber. VHS, Beta $69.95 *FCT, TAM* 🐾🐾🐾½

La Chienne This dark French film is a troubling tale of a bedraggled husband whose only excitement is his painting hobby until he becomes consumed by the ever-tempting prostitute Lulu. Director Renoir broke ground with his use of direct sound

and Paris shooting locations, and the experiment was a hit. Film portrays marriage with acidity; Renoir's own marriage broke up as a result of this film's casting. Based on the novel by Georges de la Fouchardiere. Although produced in 1931, this film didn't reach American theaters until 1975. In French with English subtitles. Remade by Fritz Lang in 1945 as "Scarlet Street." *AKA:* Isn't Life A Bitch?; The Bitch.
1931 93m/B *FR* Michel Simon, Janie Mareze, Georges Flament; *D:* Jean Renoir. VHS, Beta, LV $59.95 *INT, TAM* ✗✗✗✗

La Choca A gang of smugglers deep in the jungle turn on a member and slaughter him. The victim's wife and child must struggle to survive and avenge their loved one's fate.
1973 94m/C *MX* Pilar Pellicer, Gregorio Casal, Armando Silvestre; *D:* Emilio Fernandez. VHS, Beta *NO* ✗

La Chute de la Maison Usher An expressionistic, abstracted adaptation of the Poe story "The Fall of the House of Usher" about an evil mansion and its ruined denizens. Less plot than the successful rendering of the story's mood through acclaimed director Luis Bunuel's cinematic experiments. Silent. *AKA:* The Fall of the House of Usher.
1928 48m/B *FR* Marguerite Gance, Jean Debucourt, Charles Lamy; *D:* Jean Epstein. VHS, Beta $59.95 *FCT, GVV* ✗✗✗½

La Cicada The sparks fly when a woman and her seventeen-year-old daughter become rivals for the affections of the same man. *AKA:* The Cricket.
1983 90m/C *IT* Clio Goldsmith, Virna Lisi, Anthony (Tony) Franciosa, Renato Salvatori; *D:* Alberto Lattuada. VHS, Beta $29.98 *SUE* ✗½

La Corona de un Campeon A boxer and a wrestler attempt to beat each others brains in.
1987 90m/C *MX* Andres Garcia, Rogelio Guerra, Norma Lazarendo, Crox Alvarado. VHS, Beta $53.95 *MAD* ✗✗

L.A. Crackdown A ruthless yet compassionate policewoman goes after crack dealers and pimps who are exploiting women. Pretty trashy fare; followed by "L.A. Crackdown." Made for video.
1987 90m/C Pamela Dixon, Tricia Parks, Kita Harrison, Jeffrey Olson, Michael Coon; *D:* Joseph Merhi. VHS, Beta *NO* ✗

L.A. Crackdown 2 A woman cop goes undercover as a dancer in a dance hall to try to catch a psychotic killer who stalks hookers in this silly sequel to "L.A. Crackdown."
1988 90m/C Pamela Dixon, Anthony Gates, Joe Vance, Cynthia Miguel, Lisa Anderson, Bo Sabato; *D:* Joseph Merhi. VHS, Beta $79.95 *HHE* ✗

La Cucaracha A lavish production filled with Mexican songs and dances. The first three-strip, live-action Technicolor film ever made. Historically interesting.
1934 21m/C Steffi Duna. VHS, Beta $19.95 *VYY* ✗✗✗

La Diosa Arrodillada A marriage ends in divorce because the husband is in love with another woman. *AKA:* The Kneeling Goddess.
1947 89m/B *MX* Maria Felix, Arturo de Cordova, Rosario Granados; *D:* Roberto Gavaldon. VHS, Beta $39.95 *MAD* ✗

La Dolce Vita In this influential and popular work a successful, sensationalistic Italian journalist covers the show-biz life in Rome, and alternately covets and disdains its glitzy shallowness. The film follows his dealings with the "sweet life" over a pivotal week. A surreal, comic tableaux with award-

winning costuming; one of Fellini's most acclaimed films. Music by Nino Rota. In Italian, subtitled in English.
1960 174m/B *IT* Marcello Mastroianni, Anita Ekberg, Anouk Aimee, Alain Cuny, Lex Barker, Yvonne Furneaux, Barbara Steele, Nadia Gray, Magali Noel, Walter Santesso, Jacques Sernas; *D:* Federico Fellini. Academy Awards '61: Best Costume Design (B & W); Nominations: Best Art Direction/Set Decoration (B & W), Best Director (Fellini), Best Story & Screenplay; Cannes Film Festival '60: Best Film; National Board of Review Awards '63: 5 Best Foreign Films of the Year; New York Film Critics Awards '63: Best Foreign Film. VHS, LV $24.98 *TAM, REP, APD* ✗✗✗✗

La Femme Nikita Besson—who directed "Subway" and "Le Dernier Combat"—wrote and directed this stylish French noir version of Pygmalion. Having killed a cop during a drugstore theft gone awry, young French sociopath Nikita (Parillaud) is reprieved from a death sentence in order to enroll in a government finishing school, of sorts. Trained in etiquette and assasination, she's released after three years, and starts a new life with a new beau, all the while carrying out agency-mandated assassinations. Parillaud is excellent as the once-amoral street urchin transformed into a woman of depth and sensitivity—a bitterly ironic moral evolution for a contract killer. Remade as "Point of No Return."
1991 (R) 117m/C *FR* Anne Parillaud, Jean-Hughes Anglade, Tcheky Karyo, Jeanne Moreau; *W/D:* Luc Besson. VHS $19.95 *VMK, FCT, BTV* ✗✗✗

La Fuerza Inutil A college professor tries to join the radical actions of his students.
1987 103m/C *MX* Rafael Baledon, Veronica Castro, Roberto Jordan, Silvia Mariscal. VHS, Beta $58.95 *MAD* ✗✗

La Fuga del Rojo An inmate is aided in his escape attempt so he can smuggle arms across the border.
1987 120m/C *MX* Mario Almada, Patricia Rivera, Carmen Del Valle, Noe Murayama. VHS, Beta $59.95 *MAD* ✗

L.A. Gangs Rising The streets of Los Angeles run red with blood as a gang war explodes into bloody fury.
1989 87m/C David Kyle, Steve Bond, John Ashton; *D:* John Bushelman. VHS, Beta $9.95 *SIM* ✗✗

La Generala A woman seeks vengeance for her brother's death after the Mexican Revolution.
1987 90m/C *MX* Maria Felix. VHS, Beta $59.95 *MAD* ✗✗

L.A. Goddess A hard-living, and drinking, movie star and her beautiful stunt double both fall for a studio head. Both of these women know what they want and the man in the middle hasn't got a clue. Also available in an unrated version.
1992 (R) 92m/C Kathy Shower, Jeff Conaway, David Heavener, Wendy McDonald, Joe Estevez, James Hong; *D:* Jag Mundhra; *W:* Jerry Davis. VHS $79.95 *PSM* ✗½

La Grande Bourgeoise Historical romance about the clash of aristocratic society and the new bourgeoisie in 1897 Italy. Great cast tries to save the true tale of murder and political intrigue from film's slow pacing, but in the end it's the movie's visual polish that shines forth. In Italian with subtitles. *AKA:* The Murri Affair.
1974 115m/C *IT* Catherine Deneuve, Giancarlo Giannini, Fernando Rey, Tina Aumont; *D:* Mauro Bolognini; *M:* Ennio Morricone. VHS, Beta $69.95 *FCT* ✗✗½

L.A. Heat When a vice cop's partner is killed, he seeks revenge on the murderers, only to find that his own department may have been involved. Followed by "L.A. Vice."
1988 90m/C Jim Brown, Lawrence Hilton-Jacobs; *D:* Joseph Merhi. VHS, Beta $19.95 *PAR, HHE* ✗½

La Hifa Sin Padre A country girl gains fame as a folk singer in Mexico City.
1987 90m/C *MX* Jaime Moreno, Mercedes Castro, Roberto "Flaco" Guzman, Dacia Gonzales. VHS, Beta $79.95 *MAD* ✗✗½

La Hija del General Moving story of a young girl becoming a woman in revolutionary Spain. She loses her mother and friends to the brutal government which her father heads.
1984 101m/C *SP* Jorge Russek, Juan Ferrara, Rocio Brambilia, Patricia Aspillaga. VHS, Beta $69.95 *MED* ✗

La Hora 24 A beggar with the power of premonition foresees dire consequences in the next 24 hours.
1987 102m/C *SP* Julio Aleman, Diana Ferreti, Jose Natera, Carlos Rotzinger; *D:* Fernando Duran. VHS, Beta $74.95 *CCV* ✗

La Isla Encantada The new adventures of Robinson Crusoe and Man Friday, as they pursue wild beasts and cannibals and fight off pirates. *AKA:* The Enchanted Island.
1984 90m/C VHS, Beta $57.95 *UNI* ✗½

La Jetee/An Occurrence at Owl Creek Bridge Two of the greatest film shorts: first, a landmark sci-fi film, told almost completely through still photographs, about a time traveler from a post-World War III future who re-experiences a pivotal moment in his life as a child; second, adapted from the Ambrose Bierce story, about a soldier lynched during the civil war who appears to escape at the last moment. In French with English subtitles.
1964 60m/B *FR D:* Chris Marker, Chris Marker, Robert Enrico. VHS, Beta $34.95 *FCT* ✗½

La Justicia Tiene Doce Anos A twelve-year-old girl decides to rid the world of evil.
1987 88m/C *MX* Joaquin Cordero, Iran Eroy, Jorge Mistral, Sergio Guzik. VHS, Beta $57.95 *MAD* ✗✗

L.A. Law The pilot episode of the acclaimed dramatic series, in which the staff of a Los Angeles law firm tries a variety of cases.
1986 97m/C Michael Tucker, Jill Eikenberry, Harry Hamlin, Richard Dysart, Jimmy Smits, Alan Rachins, Susan Ruttan, Susan Dey, Corbin Bernsen; *D:* Gregory Holbit. VHS, Beta $79.98 *FOX* ✗✗✗

La Lectrice Artesian landscapes, Beethoven sonatas, and a Raymond Jean novel titled "La Lectrice" provide the backdrop for Constance (Miou-Miou) to read aloud to her boyfriend in bed, and from there she imagines herself the novel's heroine, who hires out her services as a reader to various odd characters. She reads from "L'Amant," "Alice," "War and Peace," and "Les Fleurs du Mal." Richly textured and not overly intellectual. In French with English subtitles. *AKA:* The Reader.
1988 (R) 98m/C *FR* Miou-Miou, Maria Casares, Patrick Chesnais, Christian Ruche; *D:* Michel DeVille. VHS, Beta, LV $79.98 *ORI, TAM* ✗✗½

La Ley del Revolver This is an Old West adventure where the law of the gun speaks for and against justice. In Spanish. *AKA:* The Law of the Gun.
1978 90m/C *SP* Michael Rivers, Angel Del Pozo, Lucia Gil Fernandez. VHS, Beta *HHT* ✗

La Mansion de la Locura A journalist goes into a horrifying castle owned by a madman.
1987 83m/C *MX* Claudio Brook, Arthur Dansel, Ellen Sherman, Martin La Salle. **VHS, Beta** $75.95 *MAD* 🐾🐾½

La Marchanta A poor woman comes to Mexico City and becomes a street merchant.
1973 100m/C *MX* Lucha Villa, Adalberto "Resortes" Martinez, Antonio "Clavillazo" Espino; **D:** Arturo Martinez. **VHS, Beta** $59.95 *MAD* 🐾🐾

La Marseillaise Sweeping epic by Renoir made before he hit his stride with "Grand Illusion." It details the events of the French Revolution in the summer of 1789 using a cast of thousands. The opulent lifestyle of the French nobility is starkly contrasted with the peasant lifestyle of poverty and despair. The focus is on two new recruits who have joined the Marseilles division of the revolutionary army as they begin their long march to Paris, the heart of France. As they travel, they adopt a stirring and passionate song that embodies the spirit and ideals of the revolution known as "La Marseillaise," now France's national anthem. In French with English subtitles.
1937 130m/B *FR* Pierre Renoir, Lisa Delamare, Louis Jouvet, Aime Clarimond, Andrex Andrisson, Paul Dullac; **W/D:** Jean Renoir. **VHS, Beta** $24.95 *NOS, INT, HHT* 🐾🐾🐾½

La Mentira A man falls in love with a woman he had previously wanted to kill. Based on the novel by Caridad Bravo Adams.
1987 107m/C *MX* Enrique Lizalde, Julissa, Bianca Sanchez, David Estuardo. **VHS, Beta** $73.95 *MAD* 🐾🐾½

La Montana del Diablo Two men escape from slavery and then ask the superhero El Payo for help. *AKA:* The Devil's Mountain.
1987 89m/C *MX* Jorge Rivero, Ernesto Yanez, Carmen Vicarte, Miguel Garza. **VHS, Beta** $75.95 *MAD* 🐾🐾½

La Notte Brava Italian drama focusing on the life of Rome's aimless youth in the late fifties. *AKA:* Lusty Night in Rome.
1959 96m/B *IT* **VHS, Beta, 3/4U, Special order formats** *CIG* 🐾🐾

La Nueva Cigarra A brothel is quarantined with the bubonic plague, and the customers are caught with their proverbial pants down. In Spanish.
1986 90m/C *SP* Toco Gomez, Haydee Balsa, Gogo Andreu, Olga Zubarry. **VHS, Beta** $57.95 *UNI* 🐾🐾

La Nuit de Varennes This semi-historical romp is based on an actual chapter in French history when King Louis XVI and Marie Antoinette fled from revolutionary Paris to Varennes in 1791. On the way they meet an unlikely group of characters, including Cassanova and Thomas Paine. At times witty and charming, the melange of history and fiction is full of talk, sometimes profane, punctuated by sex and nudity. Director Scola's imagination stretches to light up this night. In French with English subtitles.
1982 (R) 133m/C *FR IT* Marcello Mastroianni, Harvey Keitel, Jean-Louis Barrault, Hanna Schygulla, Jean-Claude Brialy; **D:** Ettore Scola. **VHS, Beta, LV** $59.95 *COL, IME, APD* 🐾🐾🐾

La Pachange The tenants of a Mexican apartment enjoy wild nights of drinking and sex. *AKA:* The Big Party.
1987 85m/C *MX* Julissa, Claudia Islas, Gregorio Casal, Sergio Jimenez. **VHS, Beta** $58.95 *MAD* 🐾

La Passante An otherwise peace-loving man murders the Paraguayan ambassador to France. In somewhat clumsy flashback style the murderer's orphaned childhood and other memories provide motives for the murder. Though posed more slowly than typical intrigue plots, the movie blends love and the legacy of Nazism, passion and politics in an engaging way, spiced with nudity and some violence. In her last screen appearance Schneider movingly portrays dual roles. In French with English subtitles. *AKA:* La Passante du Sans Souci; The Passerby.
1983 106m/C *FR GE* Romy Schneider, Michel Piccoli, Helmut Griem, Gerard Klein, Matthieu Carriere, Maria Schell; **D:** Jacques Rouffio. **VHS, Beta, LV** $29.95 *PAV, TAM* 🐾🐾🐾

La Pastorela An adaptation of the traditional Spanish Christmas play about the shepherds' journey to Bethlehem. Told through the eyes of a young Hispanic girl, using contemporary references to make this a modern-day story. Available in English and Spanish versions.
1992 80m/C Linda Ronstadt, Cheech Marin, Paul Rodriguez, Karla Montana, Don Novello, Robert Beltran, Freddy Fender, Falco Jimenez; **W/D:** Luis Valdez; **M:** Los Lobos. **VHS** $19.98 *BMG, MVD* 🐾🐾🐾

La Petite Bande Seven British schoolchildren run away from home and wind up in the French countryside, being chased by police and causing havoc wherever they go. Based on a true story.
1984 (PG) 91m/C **D:** Michel DeVille. **VHS, Beta** $59.95 *COL, TAM* 🐾🐾½

La Petite Sirene A young girl obsessed with the story of the Little Mermaid ingratiates herself to a 40-year-old garage mechanic. Seeing him as her prince charming, she persists in trying to make him a part of her life, in spite of his resistance. In French with English subtitles.
1980 104m/C *FR* Laura Alexis, Philippe Leotard, Evelyne Dress, Marie DuBois; **W/D:** Roger Andrieux. **VHS** $59.95 *WAC, FCT, TAM* 🐾🐾

La Puritaine Before his planned reconciliation with his daughter, the artistic manager of a theater has young actresses portray different sides of the daughter's personality. In French with English subtitles.
1986 90m/C Michel Piccoli, Sandrine Bonnaire; **D:** Lou Doillon. **VHS** $49.95 *FCT* 🐾🐾½

La Red del Egano Police search for the mastermind behind a series of jewel robberies. Dubbed into Spanish. *AKA:* The Web of Deception.
1971 90m/C *SP* Thomas Hunter, Marilia Branco, Gabriele Tinti. **VHS, Beta** *NO* 🐾

La Ronde A classic comedy of manners and sharply witty tour-de-farce in which a group of people in 1900 Vienna keep changing romantic partners until things wind up where they started. Ophuls' swirling direction creates a fast-paced farce of desire and regret with wicked yet subtle style. Based on Arthur Schnitzler's play and remade as "Circle of Love." In French with English subtitles.
1951 97m/B *FR* Simone Signoret, Anton Walbrook, Simone Simon, Serge Reggiani, Daniel Gelin, Danielle Darrieux, Jean-Louis Barrault, Fernand Gravet, Odette Joyeux, Isa Miranda, Gerard Philippe; **D:** Max Ophuls. Academy Awards '51 Nominations: Best Art Direction/Set Decoration (B & W), Best Screenplay; British Academy Awards '51: Best Film. **VHS, Beta** $29.98 *SUE, APD, TAM* 🐾🐾🐾½

La Signora di Tutti An early Italian biography of Gaby Doriot, a movie star whose professional success is paired by personal misery. Prestigious director Ophuls, working in exile from his native Germany, was unable to complete many projects in the years leading up to and during WWII. This is one of the few. Watch for innovative camera work intended to underscore the film's mood. In Italian with English subtitles.
1934 92m/B *IT* Isa Miranda; **D:** Max Ophuls. **VHS, Beta** $59.95 *CVC, FCT, TAM* 🐾🐾🐾

L.A. Story Livin' ain't easy in the city of angels. Harris K. Telemacher (Martin), a weatherman in a city where the weather never changes, wrestles with the meaning of life and love while consorting with beautiful people, distancing from significant other Henner, cavorting with valley girl Parker, and falling for newswoman Tennant (Martin's real life wife). Written by the comedian, the story's much more than a Martin vehicle, full of keen insights into the everyday problems and ironies of living in the Big Tangerine. (It's no wonder the script's full of so much thoughtful detail: Martin is said to have worked on it intermittently for seven years.) A charming, fault forgiving but not fault ignoring portrait that'll make you gush with the thought that life isn't half bad feeling.
1991 (PG-13) 98m/C Steve Martin, Victoria Tennant, Richard E. Grant, Marilu Henner, Sarah Jessica Parker, Sam McMurray, Patrick Stewart, Iman, Kevin Pollack; **D:** Mick Jackson; **W:** Steve Martin. **VHS, Beta, LV** $92.95 *LIV, WAR* 🐾🐾🐾

La Strada A simple-minded girl, played by Fellini's wife, Marsha, is sold to a brutal, coarse circus strong-man and she falls in love with him despite his abuse. They tour the countryside and eventually meet up with a gentle acrobat, played by Basehart, who alters their fate. This Fellini masterwork was the director's first internationally acclaimed film, and is, by turns, somber and amusing as it demonstrates the filmmaker's sensitivity to the underprivileged of the world and his belief in spiritual redemption. Features a haunting score by Nino Rota. Academy Award winner for Best Foreign Film. Subtitled in English. *AKA:* The Road.
1954 107m/B *IT* Giulietta Masina, Anthony Quinn, Richard Basehart, Aldo Silvani; **D:** Federico Fellini. Academy Awards '56: Best Foreign Language Film; Nominations: Best Original Screenplay; National Board of Review Awards '56: 5 Best Foreign Films of the Year; New York Film Critics Awards '56: Best Foreign Film. **VHS, Beta, LV** $29.98 *SUE, IME, APD* 🐾🐾🐾🐾

La Symphonie Pastorale A Swiss pastor takes in an orphan blind girl who grows up to be beautiful. The pastor then competes for her affections with his son. Quiet drama based on the Andre Gide novel, with breathtaking mountain scenery as the backdrop for this tragedy rife with symbolism.
1946 105m/B *FR* Pierre Blanchar, Michele Morgan, Jean Desailly, Line Noro, Andree Clement; **D:** Jean Delannoy. **VHS** *FLI* 🐾🐾🐾½

La Terra Trema The classic example of Italian neo-realism, about a poor Sicilian fisherman, his family and their village. A spare, slow-moving, profound and ultimately lyrical tragedy, this semi-documentary explores the economic exploitation of Sicily's fishermen. Filmed on location with the villagers playing themselves; highly acclaimed though not commercially successful. In Sicilian with English subtitles. Some radically cut versions may be available, but are to be avoided. Franco Zefferelli was one of the assistant directors. *AKA:* Episoda Del Mare; The Earth Will Tremble.
1948 161m/B *IT* Antonio Pietrangeli; **D:** Luchino Visconti. **VHS, Beta** $89.95 *FCT, TAM* 🐾🐾🐾½

La Trinchera A Spanish western centering around the Mexican Revolution.

1987 91m/C *MX* David Reynoso, Ignacio Lopez Tarso, Julio Aleman, Pilar Pellicer. **VHS, Beta** $59.95 *MAD* ♂

La Truite A young woman leaves her family's rural trout farm and a loveless marriage to seek her fortune in high finance and corporate mayhem. The complicated plot, full of intrigue and sexual encounters, sometimes lacks focus. Slickly filmed. **AKA:** The Trout.
1983 (R) 80m/C *FR* Isabelle Huppert, Jean-Pierre Cassel, Daniel Olbrychski, Jeanne Moreau, Jacques Spiesser, Ruggero Raimondi, Alexis Smith, Craig Stevens; **D:** Joseph Losey. **VHS, Beta** $59.95 *COL* ♂♂♂

La Venganza del Kung Fu A woman becomes a kung fu champ to avenge the death of her family.
1987 105m/C *MX* Charlie C.C. Lau, Wong Dong, Mao Ying, Ting Shan Si. **VHS, Beta** $34.80 *MAD* ♂♂

La Venganza del Rojo A doctor helps the rebels in a revolution.
1987 90m/C *MX* Mario Almada, Ferdinando Almada, Carmen Del Valle, Noe Murayama, Jorge Patino. **VHS, Beta** $59.95 *MAD* ♂♂

La Vengeance d'une Femme Refined Cecile and sultry Suzy are two sides of a love triangle whose third member, Cecile's husband, has just died. Cecile decides to get to know his mistress better, which naturally has Suzy worried. Is Cecile out for revenge or does she sincerely want to befriend the "other woman." Based on Dostoyevski's "The Eternal Husband." In French with English subtitles.
1989 133m/C *FR* Isabelle Huppert, Beatrice Dalle; **W/D:** Jacques Doillon; **W:** Jean-Francois Goyet. **VHS** $79.95 *TAM* ♂♂

L.A. Vice A detective is transferred to the vice squad, where he must investigate a series of murders. Sequel to "L.A. Heat."
1989 90m/C Jim Brown, Lawrence Hilton-Jacobs, William Smith; **D:** Joseph Merhi. **VHS, Beta** *PAR* ♂♂

La Vie Continue A middle-aged woman suddenly finds herself widowed after 20 years of marriage and tries to build a new life for herself and her children. Girardot's performance can't quite dispel melodramatic suds. Loosely and more effectively remade as "Men Don't Leave." In French with English subtitles or dubbed.
1982 93m/C *IT* Annie Girardot, Jean-Pierre Cassel, Michel Aumont, Pierre Dux, Guilia Salvatori, Emmanuel Goyet, Rivera Andres; **D:** Moshe Mizrahi. **VHS, Beta** $59.95 *COL, TAM* ♂♂½

La Violetera A poor flower vendor falls in love with a rich diplomat despite their opposite positions in society. **AKA:** The Violet.
1971 90m/C Sara Montiel, Raf Vallone, Frank Villard. **VHS, Beta** $39.95 *MAD* ♂

La Virgen de Guadalupe A miracle occurs amidst fighting between the Aztecs and the Spaniards.
1987 82m/C *SP* Fernando Allende, Valentin Trujillo, Angelica Chain. **VHS, Beta** $75.95 *MAD* ♂♂½

Laboratory Things go awry when the earthling subjects of an alien experiment revolt against their captors.
1980 93m/C Camille Mitchell, Corinne Michaels, Garnett Smith. **VHS, Beta** $49.95 *UHV* ♂

Labyrinth Fascinating adventure directed by Henson and written by Monty Python's Terry Jones. While baby-sitting her baby brother Toby, Connelly is so frustrated she asks the goblins to take him away. When the Goblin King, played by Bowie, comes to answer her idle wish, she must try to rescue

Toby by solving the fantastic labyrinth. If she does not find him in time, Toby will become one of the goblins forever. During her journey, Connelly is befriended by all sorts of odd creatures created by Henson, and she grows up a little along the way. A wonderful movie for the whole family. Produced by George Lucas; songs written and sung by David Bowie.
1986 (PG) 90m/C David Bowie, Jennifer Connelly, Toby Froud; **D:** Jim Henson. **VHS, Beta, LV, 8mm** $14.98 *SUE, NLC* ♂♂♂

Labyrinth of Passion A screwball farce, directed by Almodavar, featuring a host of strange characters running around Madrid in search of sex and laughter. They find plenty of both. An early film by an influential director. In Spanish with English subtitles. **AKA:** Laberinto de Pasiones.
1982 100m/C *SP* Antonio Banderas, Imanol Arias, Celia Roth; **W/D:** Pedro Almodovar. **VHS, Beta, LV** $79.95 *CCN, IME, TAM* ♂♂½

The Lacemaker Huppert's first shot at stardom, on videodisc with digital sound and a letterboxed print. A young beautician and a university student fall in love on vacation but soon begin to realize the differences in their lives. Adapted from the novel by Pascal Laine. In French with English subtitles. **AKA:** La Dentiellere.
1977 107m/C *FR SI GE* Isabelle Huppert, Yves Beneyton, Florence Giorgetti, Anna Marie Duringer; **D:** Claude Goretta. **LV** $79.95 *HMV, CRC, VYG* ♂♂♂½

L'Addition A prison drama about the struggle between a soon-to-be-released prisoner and a sadistic guard.
1985 (R) 85m/C *FR* Richard Berry, Richard Bohringer, Victoria Abril; **D:** Denis Amar. **VHS, Beta** $69.95 *MOR* ♂♂½

Ladies Club A group of rape victims get together and begin to victimize rapists.
1986 (R) 86m/C Bruce Davison, Karen Austin, Diana Scarwid, Shera Danese, Beverly Todd; **D:** A.K. Allen. **VHS, Beta** $79.95 *MED* ♂½

The Ladies' Man Piecemeal Lewis farce, with Jerry playing a clutzy handyman working at a girls' boarding house. Some riotous routines balanced by slow pacing.
1961 106m/C Jerry Lewis, Helen Traubel, Jack Kruschen, Doodles Weaver, Gloria Jean; **D:** Jerry Lewis. **VHS, Beta, LV** $14.95 *PAR* ♂♂

Ladies Man Spy adventure with Constantine playing super sleuth/agent, Lemmy Caution, on the French Riviera.
1962 ?m/C Eddie Constantine. **VHS** $16.95 *SNC* ♂♂

Ladies of the Chorus Monroe stars as a burlesque chorus girl who shares the stage with her mom (Jergens) and a handful of other beauties. She meets and falls in love with a wealthy socialite (Brooks), but her mother completely disapproves of the relationship. Monroe later learns that her mother was in love with the same man several years before. Although only her second film appearance, Monroe's talents are already quite apparent in this low-budget musical romance. ♫Every Baby Nees a Da Da Daddy; Anyone Can Tell I Love You; Crazy For You; You're Never Too Old; Ladies of the Chorus.
1949 61m/B Adele Jergens, Marilyn Monroe, Rand Brooks, Nana Bryant, Steve Geray, Bill Edwards; **D:** Phil Karlson. **VHS** $19.95 *COL* ♂♂

Ladies of the Lotus Bloodthirsty Vancouver gangsters raid Lotus, Inc., a modeling agency, and sell beautiful young women into slavery. As bad as it sounds.
1987 120m/C *CA* Richard Dale, Angela Read, Patrick Bermel, Darcia Carnie; **D:** Lloyd A. Simandl, Douglas C. Nicolle. **VHS, Beta** *NO* ♂

Ladies on the Rocks Aspiring comediennes Micha and Laura pack up their van and take their bizarre cabaret act on the road through rural Denmark. They find their private lives disintegrating but turn each disaster into new material for their act. In Danish with English subtitles. **AKA:** Koks I Kulissen.
1983 100m/C *DK* Helle Ryslinge, Anne Marie Helger, Flemming Quist Moller; **D:** Christian Braad Thomsen. **VHS** $79.95 *NYF, TAM* ♂♂½

Ladies They Talk About Stanwyck stars as a tough-talking gun moll who belongs to a gang of bank robbers. They get caught and Stanwyck is sent to the female division of San Quentin. The acting is great in this pre-Code prison movie, but the film gets a bit punchy at times. Based on the true-life experiences of actress Dorothy Mackaye, who went to jail after her husband was killed in a fight with actor Paul Kelley, who was also sent to prison. Adapted from the play "Women in Prison" by Dorothy Mackaye and Carlton Miles. **AKA:** Women in Prison.
1933 69m/B Barbara Stanwyck, Preston Foster, Lyle Talbot, Dorothy Burgess, Lillian Roth, Maude Eburne, Harold Huber, Ruth Donnelly; **D:** Howard Bretherton, William Keighley. **VHS** $19.98 *MGM* ♂♂½

Lady and the Tramp The animated Disney classic about two dogs which fall in love. Tramp is wild and carefree; Lady is a spoiled house pet who runs away from home after her owners have a baby. They don't make dog romances like this anymore. ♫He's a Tramp; La La Lu; Siamese Cat Song; Peace on Earth; Bella Notte.
1955 (G) 76m/C **D:** Hamilton Luske; **V:** Larry Roberts, Peggy Lee, Barbara Luddy, Stan Freberg, Alan Reed. **VHS, Beta, LV** $29.95 *DIS, APD* ♂♂♂♂

Lady Avenger A woman is bent on getting revenge on her brother's killers.
1989 (R) 90m/C Peggie Sanders. **VHS, Beta** $79.95 *NO* ♂

Lady Be Good Adapted from the 1924 Gershwin Broadway hit, the plot's been revamped, much to the critics' distaste ("Variety" called it "molasses paced"). Sothern and Young play a tunesmith duo who excel at musical harmony and marital strife. Applauded for its music (the critics loved Hammerstein's and the Gershwins' tunes), the show's Academy Award winning song was, ironically, written by Jerome Kern. And if that's not enough, levity man Skelton and hoofer Powell are thrown in for good measure. ♫The Last Time I Saw Paris; So Am I; Oh Lady Be Good; Fascinating Rhythm; Hang On To Me; You'll Never Know; You're Words, My Music; Saudades.
1941 111m/B Eleanor Powell, Ann Sothern, Robert Young, Lionel Barrymore, John Carroll, Red Skelton, Dan Dailey, Virginia O'Brien, Tom Conway, Phil Silvers, Doris Day; **D:** Norman Z. McLeod; **M:** Oscar Hammerstein, George Gershwin, Ira Gershwin. **VHS** $19.98 *MGM, TTC, FCT* ♂♂½

Lady Beware A psychotic doctor becomes obsessed with a beautiful store-window dresser who specializes in steamy, erotic fantasies. When he wages a campaign of terror against her, she realizes that she must stop him before he kills her.
1987 (R) 108m/C Diane Lane, Michael Woods, Cotter Smith, Viveca Lindfors, Tyra Ferrell, Peter Nevargic, Edward Penn; **D:** Karen Arthur. **VHS, Beta, LV** $14.95 *LIV* ♂♂

Lady by Choice Lombard stars as a beautiful young fan dancer who is arrested for a lewd public performance. Taking the advice of her press agent, she hires an old bag lady to pose as her mother on Mother's

L

Day. Robson portrays her ''mother'' and comes to think of Lombard as her own daughter. Robson encourages Lombard to give up fan dancing and to strive for greater things in life. She also pushes her into romance with a wealthy young man (Pryor). Robson is excellent in her role as ''mother'' and Lombard shows great comic talent in this charming film.
1934 78m/C Carole Lombard, May Robson, Roger Pryor, Walter Connolly, Raymond Walburn, James Burke; **D:** David Burton; **W:** Jo Swerling. **VHS** $19.95 COL ⅍½

Lady Caroline Lamb Lady Caroline is a passionate young lady in 19th-century England, who, although the wife of a member of Parliament, has an affair with Lord Byron and brings about her own downfall. Costume drama that never quite goes anywhere.
1973 123m/C GB IT Sarah Miles, Richard Chamberlain, Jon Finch, Laurence Olivier, John Mills, Ralph Richardson; **D:** Robert Bolt. **Beta** $14.95 PSM ⅍

Lady Chatterley's Lover English-woman has bad luck to have husband shot up during WWI and sent home paralyzed. In her quest for sexual fulfillment, she takes a new lover, the estate's earthy gamekeeper. Limp adaptation of D.H. Lawrence's novel. In French with English subtitles. AKA: L'Amant de Lady Chatterley.
1955 102m/B FR Danielle Darrieux, Erno Crisa, Leo Genn; **D:** Marc Allegret. **VHS, Beta, LV** $24.95 NOS, MRV, HHT ⅍½

Lady Chatterley's Lover Remake of the 1955 film version of D.H. Lawrence's classic novel of an English lady who has an affair with the gamekeeper of her husband's estate. Basically soft-focus soft porn.
1981 (R) 107m/C GB FR Sylvia Kristel, Nicholas Clay, Shane Briant; **D:** Just Jaeckin. **VHS, Beta, LV** $79.95 MGM ⅍½

Lady Cocoa Routine story of a young woman who gets released from jail for 24 hours and sets out for Las Vegas to find the man who framed her.
1975 (R) 93m/C Lola Falana, Joe ''Mean Joe'' Greene, Gene Washington, Alex Dreier; **D:** Matt Cimber. **VHS, Beta** $49.95 UNI ⅍

The Lady Confesses Average mystery that involves Hughes trying to clear her boyfriend of murder. Independently produced. ''Leave it to Beaver'' fans will want to watch for ''Ward Cleaver'' Beaumont.
1945 66m/B Mary Beth Hughes, Hugh Beaumont, Edmund MacDonald, Claudia Drake, Emmett Vogan; **D:** Sam Newfield. **VHS** $16.95 NOS, SNC ⅍

Lady Dragon A woman and her husband are viciously attacked and only she survives. Found by an old man, she learns a number of martial arts tricks and goes out to get her revenge.
1992 (R) 89m/C Cynthia Rothrock, Richard Norton, Robert Ginty, Bella Esperance, Hengko Tornando; **W/D:** David Worth. **VHS** $89.95 IMP ⅍

The Lady Eve Two con artists, out to trip up wealthy beer tycoon Fonda, instead find themselves tripped up when one falls in love with the prey. Ridiculous situations, but Sturges manages to keep them believable and funny. With a train scene that's every man's nightmare. Perhaps the best Sturges ever. Later remade as ''The Birds and the Bees.''
1941 93m/B Barbara Stanwyck, Henry Fonda, Charles Coburn, Eugene Pallette, William Demarest, Eric Blore, Melville Cooper; **D:** Preston Sturges. Academy Awards '41 Nominations: Best Story; National Board of Review Awards '41: 10

Best Films of the Year. **VHS, Beta, LV** $14.98 MCA, RKO ⅍⅍⅍⅍

Lady for a Day Delightful telling of the Damon Runyon story, ''Madame La Gimp,'' about an apple peddler (Robson) down on her luck, who is transformed into a lady by a criminal with a heart. ''Lady By Choice'' is the sequel.
1933 96m/B May Robson, Warren William, Guy Kibbee, Glenda Farrell, Ned Sparks, Jean Parker, Walter Connolly; **D:** Frank Capra. **VHS, Beta, LV** $29.95 CVC, VYG, CRC ⅍⅍⅍½

Lady for a Night The female owner of a gambling riverboat does her best to break into high society, when murder threatens to spoil her plans. Cast and costumes burdened by pacing.
1942 88m/B John Wayne, Joan Blondell, Ray Middleton, Philip Merivale, Blanche Yurka, Edith Barrett, Leonid Kinskey, Montagu Love; **D:** Leigh Jason. **VHS** $14.98 REP ⅍

Lady Frankenstein Frankenstein's lovely daughter graduates from medical school and returns home. When she sees what her father's been up to, she gets some ideas of her own. Good fun for fans of the genre. AKA: La Figlia di Frankenstein; The Daughter of Frankenstein; Madame Frankenstein.
1972 (R) 84m/C IT Joseph Cotten, Sara (Rosalba Neri) Bay, Mickey Hargitay, Paul Muller; **D:** Mel Welles. **VHS, Beta** $9.98 SNC, SUE, HEG ⅍½

Lady from Louisiana A lawyer in old New Orleans out to rid the city of corruption falls in love with the daughter of a big-time gambler. Great storm scene.
1942 84m/B John Wayne, Ona Munson, Dorothy Dandridge, Ray Middleton, Henry Stephenson, Helen Westley, Jack Pennick; **D:** Bernard Vorhaus. **VHS** $14.98 REP ⅍

Lady from Nowhere A woman is the only witness to a gangland rub-out and is subsequently pursued by both the mob and the police. Unfortunately for her, the gangsters catch up with her first.
1936 60m/B Mary Astor, Charles Quigley, Thurston Hall, Victor Kilian, Spencer Charters; **D:** Gordon Wiles. **VHS, Beta** $16.95 SNC ⅍

The Lady from Shanghai An unsuspecting seaman becomes involved in a web of intrigue when a woman hires him to work on her husband's yacht. Hayworth (a one-time Mrs. Orson Welles), in her only role as a villainess, plays a manipulative, sensual schemer. Wonderful and innovative cinematic techniques from Welles, as usual, including a tense scene in a hall of mirrors. Filmed on a yacht belonging to Errol Flynn.
1948 87m/B Orson Welles, Rita Hayworth, Everett Sloane, Glenn Anders, Ted de Corsia, Erskine Sanford, Gus Schilling; **W/D:** Orson Welles. **VHS, Beta, LV** $19.95 COL, MLB ⅍⅍⅍½

Lady from Yesterday An American couple's life is shattered by the appearance of the husband's Vietnamese mistress and her 10-year-old son. Made for television.
1985 87m/C Wayne Rogers, Bonnie Bedelia, Pat Hingle, Barrie Youngfellow, Blue Deacort, Tina Chen; **D:** Robert Day. **VHS, Beta** NO ⅍

Lady Godiva Rides A bad, campy version of the story of Lady Godiva. Godiva comes to the United States with a bevy of scantily clad maidens and winds up in the Old West. When the town villain threatens to compromise her, Tom Jones comes to the rescue. The film (of course) features Godiva's naked ride on horseback through the town.
1968 88m/C Marsha Jordan, Forman Shane; **D:** A.C. Stephen. **VHS** $19.95 VDM ⅍

Lady Grey A poor farmer's daughter rises to the top of the country music charts, but at a price.
1982 111m/C Ginger Alden, David Allen Coe; **D:** Worth Keeter. **VHS, Beta** $59.99 HBO ⅍

Lady Ice Sutherland, as an insurance investigator on the trail of jewel thieves, follows them to Miami Beach and the Bahamas. After stealing a diamond he enters into partnership with a crook's daughter. Worth seeing for the cast.
1973 (PG) 93m/C Donald Sutherland, Jennifer O'Neill, Robert Duvall, Eric Braeden; **D:** Tom Gries. **VHS, Beta** WWV ⅍

Lady in a Cage A wealthy widow is trapped in her home elevator during a power failure and becomes desperate when hoodlums break in. Shocking violence ahead of its time probably plays better than when first released. Young Caan is a standout among the star-studded cast.
1964 95m/B Olivia de Havilland, Ann Sothern, James Caan, Jennifer Billingsley, Jeff Corey, Scatman Crothers, Rafael Campos; **D:** Walter Grauman. **VHS, Beta** $49.95 PAR ⅍⅍⅍

Lady in Cement The second Tony Rome mystery, in which the seedy Miami dick finds a corpse with cement shoes while swimming.
1968 (R) 93m/C Frank Sinatra, Raquel Welch, Richard Conte, Martin Gabel, Lainie Kazan, Pat Henry, Steve Peck, Joe E. Lewis, Dan Blocker; **D:** Gordon Douglas. **VHS, Beta** $59.98 FOX ⅍½

Lady in Distress A British drama about an unhappily married man who witnesses an apparent murder. He discovers, however, it was actually the prank of an illusionist and his flirtatious wife. He soon finds himself becoming increasingly involved with their lives. AKA: A Window in London.
1939 59m/B GB Michael Redgrave, Paul Lukas, Sally Gray; **D:** Herbert Mason. **VHS, Beta** $16.95 SNC, VYY, MLB ⅍½

The Lady in Question A Parisian shopkeeper, played by Aherne, sits on a jury that acquits Hayworth of murder. His interest doesn't end with the trial, however, and matters heat up when his son also becomes involved. Remake of a melodramatic French release. AKA: It Happened in Paris.
1940 81m/B Rita Hayworth, Glenn Ford, Brian Aherne, Irene Rich, Lloyd Corrigan, George Coulouris, Evelyn Keyes, Curt Bois, Edward Norris; **D:** Charles Vidor. **VHS, Beta, LV** $19.95 COL, CCB ⅍½

Lady in Red A story of America in the '30s, and the progress through the underworld of the woman who was Dillinger's last lover. AKA: Guns, Sin and Bathtub Gin.
1979 90m/C Pamela Sue Martin, Louise Fletcher, Robert Conrad, Christopher Lloyd; **D:** Lewis Teague; **W:** Tom Sayles. **VHS, Beta** $69.98 LIV, VES ⅍

Lady in the Death House A framed woman is set to walk the last mile, as a scientist struggles to find the real killer in time.
1944 57m/B Jean Parker, Lionel Atwill, Marcia Mae Jones. **VHS, Beta** $24.95 VYY ⅍

Lady in the Lake Why is it everyone wants to get artsy with pulp fiction? Actor Montgomery directs himself in this Philip Marlowe go-round, using a subjective camera style to imitate Chandler's first person narrative (that means the only time we get to see Marlowe/Montgomery's mug is in a mirror. That pretty well says it all). Having decided to give up eyeing privately, Marlowe turns to the pen to tell the tangled tale of the lady in the lake: once upon a time, a detective was hired to find the wicked wife of a paying client...Some find the direction clever. Others consider MGM chief Louis B. Mayer, who made sure this was Montgomery's last project with MGM, to be a wise man. **1946 103m/B** Robert Montgomery, Lloyd Nolan, Audrey Totter, Tom Tully, Leon Ames, Jayne Meadows; **D:** Robert Montgomery. **VHS, Beta** $19.98 *MGM, FCT* 🎬🎬½

The Lady in White Small-town ghost story about murder and revenge. Young Haas is accidentally locked in school one night and is visited by the ghost of a little girl; he is determined to find her murderer. Well-developed characters, interesting style, and suspenseful plot make for a sometimes slow but overall exceptional film. **1988 (PG-13) 92m/C** Lukas Haas, Len Cariou, Alex Rocco, Katherine Helmond, Jason Presson, Renato Vanni, Angelo Bertolini, Jared Rushton; **D:** Frank Laloggia. **VHS, Beta, LV** *NO* 🎬🎬🎬

Lady Jane An accurate account of the life of 15-year-old Lady Jane Grey, who secured the throne of England for 9 days in 1553 as a result of political maneuvering by noblemen and the Church-of-England. A wonderful film even for non-history buffs. Carter's first film. **1985 (PG-13) 140m/C** *GB* Helena Bonham Carter, Cary Elwes, Sara Kestelman, Michael Hordern, Joss Ackland, Richard Johnson, Patrick Stewart; **D:** Trevor Nunn. **VHS, Beta, LV** $79.95 *PAR, TVC* 🎬🎬🎬½

Lady Killer Racy, pre-Code comedy with mobster Cagney hiding out in Hollywood. He gets discovered and becomes a big star, but his old gang turns up to blackmail him. Lots of movie "in" jokes and Clarke (of "Public Enemy" fame) is great as a wisecracking moll. Based on the story "The Finger Man" by Rosalind Keating Shaffer. **1933 74m/B** James Cagney, Mae Clarke, Leslie Fenton, Margaret Lindsay, Henry O'Neill, Raymond Hatton, George Chandler; **D:** Roy Del Ruth; **W:** Ben Markson, Lillie Hayward. **VHS** $19.98 *MGM* 🎬🎬🎬

Lady Mobster When her parents are murdered a young girl is taken in by a Mafia family. She grows up to be a shrewd lawyer but winds up working in her adoptive family's crime syndicate in order to take revenge on her parents' murderers. Exaggerated and silly but watchable for its so-bad-it's-good qualities. Made for television. **1988 (PG-13) 94m/C** Susan Lucci, Michael Nader, Roscoe Born, Joseph Wiseman; **D:** John Llewellyn Moxey. **VHS, Beta, LV** $89.98 *TTC* 🎬

Lady of Burlesque Burlesque dancer is found dead, strangled with her own G-string. Clever and amusing film based on "The G-String Murders" by Gypsy Rose Lee. **AKA:** Striptease Lady. **1943 91m/B** Barbara Stanwyck, Michael O'Shea, Janis Carter, Pinky Lee; **D:** William A. Wellman. **VHS, Beta, 3/4U, Special order formats** $9.95 *NEG, MRV, NOS* 🎬🎬½

The Lady of the Camellias Neumeier brings to film the ballet he created out of Dumas' "The Lady of the Camelias" and Abbe Prevost's "Manon Lescaut," set to the music of Chopin. **AKA:** Die Kameliendame. **1987 125m/C** Marcia Haydee, Ivan Liska, Francois Klaus, Colleen Scott, Vladimir Klos, Lynne Charles, Jeffrey Kirk, Gigi Hyatt, Beatrice Cordua, Victor Hughes, William Parton, Richard Hoynes, John Neumeier; **D:** John Neumeier. **VHS, Beta** $39.95 *MVD, KUL* 🎬🎬

Lady of the Evening A prostitute and a crook team up to seek revenge against the mob. **1979 (PG) 110m/C** *IT* Sophia Loren, Marcello Mastroianni. **VHS, Beta** *NO* 🎬🎬

Lady of the House A true story about a madame who rose from operator of a brothel to become a political force in San Francisco. **1978 100m/C** Dyan Cannon, Susan Tyrrell, Colleen Camp, Armand Assante; **D:** Ralph Nelson. **VHS, Beta** $49.95 *PSM* 🎬🎬

Lady of the Lake Rare silent adventure film in which an exiled girl saves the king from outlaws in Scotland. Orchestra score. **1928 47m/B** *GB* Percy Marmont, Benita Hume, Huddon Mason, Lawson Butt; **D:** James A. Fitzpatrick. **VHS** $14.95 *GPV* 🎬🎬

Lady of the Rising Sun A female doctor in the Orient makes house calls at a brothel and finds reason to stay. **198? 91m/C** Chai Lee, Ilona Staller. **VHS, Beta** $29.95 *MED Woof!*

Lady on the Bus Sexually frustrated newlywed bride rides the city buses looking for men to satisfy her. This bothers her husband. Shot in Rio de Janeiro. In Portuguese with English subtitles. **1978 (R) 102m/C** *BR* Sonia Braga; **D:** Neville D'Almeida. **VHS, Beta, LV** $69.98 *LIV, VES* 🎬🎬

The Lady Refuses A stuffy Victorian father is disappointed in his wastrel son and decides a poor but honest young woman could be the making of him. Problems arise when the girl falls for the father instead. **1931 70m/B** Betty Compson, John Darrow, Margaret Livingston, Gilbert Emery; **D:** George Archainbaud. **VHS, Beta** $24.95 *DVT* 🎬🎬

The Lady Says No A photographer must photograph an attractive author who has written a book uncomplimentary toward the male sex. **1951 80m/B** Joan Caulfield, David Niven, James Robertson Justice, Francis Bavier, Henry Jones, Jeff York, Robert Williams; **D:** Frank Ross. **VHS** $29.95 *FCT* 🎬🎬

Lady Scarface Murderous mobster queen breaks the law, bats men around, and takes the cops on a merry chase. Cheap, fast-paced action. **1941 66m/B** Mildred Coles, Dennis O'Keefe, Frances Neal, Judith Anderson, Eric Blore; **D:** Frank Woodruff. **VHS, Beta** $34.95 *RKO* 🎬🎬

Lady Scarface/The Threat A crime double feature: "Lady Scarface" (1941), a clever cop is on the trail of a dangerous gunwoman; and "The Threat" (1949), a ruthless killer escapes from prison intent on murdering those who convicted him. **1949 132m/B** Dennis O'Keefe, Judith Anderson, Robert Knapp, Eric Blore, Charles McGraw, Michael O'Shea, Virginia Grey; **D:** Frank Woodruff. **VHS, Beta** $34.95 *RKO, TTC* 🎬🎬

Lady Sings the Blues Jazz artist Billie Holiday's life becomes a musical drama depicting her struggle against racism and drug addiction in her pursuit of fame and romance. What could be a typical price-of-fame story is saved by Ross' inspired performance as the tragic singer. 🎵My Man; Strange Fruit; God Bless the Child; Don't Explain; T'Ain't Nobody's Business If I Do; Lady Sings the Blues; All Of Me; The Man I Love; Our Love Is Here To Stay; I Cried For You; Mean To Me; Them There Eyes; What A Little Moonlight Can Do; Lover Man (Oh Where Can You Be?); You've Changed; Good Morning Heartache; Gimme a Pigfoot and a Bottle of Beer. **1972 (R) 144m/C** Diana Ross, Billy Dee Williams, Richard Pryor; **D:** Sidney J. Furie. **VHS, Beta, LV** $29.95 *PAR, FCT* 🎬🎬½

Lady Stay Dead A gory Australian shocker about another faceless, knife-wielding psychotic chasing a girl. **1983 100m/C** *AU* **VHS, Beta** $59.95 *VCD* 🎬½

Lady Street Fighter A well-armed female combat fighter battles an organization of assassins to avenge her sister's murder. **1986 73m/C** Renee Harmon, Joel McCrea Jr. **VHS, Beta** $59.95 *UNI* 🎬

Lady Takes a Chance A romantic comedy about a New York working girl with matrimonial ideas and a rope-shy rodeo rider who yearns for the wide open spaces. Fine fun on the range. **1943 86m/B** John Wayne, Jean Arthur, Phil Silvers, Charles Winninger; **D:** William A. Seiter. **VHS, Beta** $29.95 *VID* 🎬🎬

Lady Terminator A student on an anthropology expedition digs up more than she bargained for when she is possessed by an evil spirit and goes on a rampage. **1989 (R) 83m/C** Barbara Constable, Christopher Hart, Joseph McGlynn, Claudia Rademaker; **D:** Jalil Jackson. **VHS, Beta** *NO* 🎬½

The Lady Vanishes When a kindly old lady disappears from a fast-moving train, her young friend finds an imposter in her place and a spiraling mystery to solve. Hitchcock's first real winner, a smarmy, wit-drenched British mystery that precipitated his move to Hollywood. Along with "39 Steps," considered an early Hitchcock classic. From the novel "The Wheel Spins," by Ethel Lina White. Special edition contains short subject on Hitchcock's cameos in his films. Remade in 1979. **1938 99m/B** *GB* Margaret Lockwood, Paul Lukas, Michael Redgrave, May Whitty, Googie Withers, Basil Radford, Naunton Wayne, Cecil Parker; **Cameos:** Alfred Hitchcock; **D:** Alfred Hitchcock. **VHS, Beta, LV, 3/4U, Special order formats** $16.95 *SNC, NOS, SUE* 🎬🎬🎬🎬

Lady Vanishes In this reworking of the '38 Alfred Hitchcock film, a woman on a Swiss bound train awakens from a nap to find that the elderly woman seated next to her was kidnapped. Falls short of the original movie due to the "screwball" nature of the main characters, Gould and Shepherd. George Axelrod wrote the script which is based on Ethel Lina White's novel "The Wheel Spins." **1979 95m/C** *GB* Elliott Gould, Cybill Shepherd, Angela Lansbury, Herbert Lom; **D:** Anthony Page. **VHS, Beta, LV** $9.95 *MED, MRV* 🎬½

Lady Windermere's Fan The silent, Lubitsch adaptation of the Oscar Wilde tale concerning an upper-class couple's marriage being almost destroyed by suspected adultery. **1926 66m/B** Ronald Colman, May McAvoy, Bert Lytell; **D:** Ernst Lubitsch. **VHS, Beta, 8mm** $29.95 *VYY, GPV* 🎬🎬½

The Lady with the Dog A bittersweet love story based on the Anton Chekhov story, about two married Russians who meet by chance in a park, fall in love, and realize they are fated to a haphazard, clandestine affair. In Russian with English titles. **1959 86m/B** *RU* Iya Savvina, Alexei Batalov, Ala Chostakova, N. Alisova; **D:** Yosif Heifitz. **VHS, Beta** $29.95 *WST, FCT, TAM* 🎬🎬🎬

The Lady Without Camelias A young woman is discovered by a film producer who casts her in a successful movie and eventually marries her. Convinced that she can sustain a career as a serious actress, the producer is dismayed by the job offers that come her way, usually of a sexually exploitive nature. What follows is a tragic decline in her career. **1953 106m/C** *IT* **VHS, Beta, 3/4U, Special order formats** *CIG* 🎬🎬

Ladybugs Hangdog salesman Dangerfield would like to move up his company's corporate ladder. But that's only going to be possible if the Ladybugs, a girls' soccer team sponsored by the company, turns into a group of winners. Dangerfield knows nothing about soccer and the girls are lousy but Dangerfield manages to persuade his secretary to serve as assistant coach and his fiancee's athletic son to masquerade as a girl and lead the team to victory. Obvious fluff may appeal to Dangerfield fans.
1992 (PG-13) 91m/C Rodney Dangerfield, Jackee, Jonathan Brandis, Ilene Graff, Vinessa Shaw, Tom Parks, Jeanetta Arnetta, Nancy Parsons, Blake Clark, Tommy Lasorda; *D:* Sidney J. Furie. **VHS, Beta** $19.95 *PAR* ♂♂½

Ladyhawke In medieval times, a youthful pickpocket befriends a strange knight who is on a mysterious quest. This unlikely duo, accompanied by a watchful hawk, are enveloped in a magical adventure.
1985 (PG-13) 121m/C Matthew Broderick, Rutger Hauer, Michelle Pfeiffer, John Wood, Leo McKern; *D:* Richard Donner. **VHS, Beta, LV** $19.98 *WAR* ♂♂♂

Ladykiller Rogers stars as a burned-out cop who goes to a dating service to find a man who'll give her the attention she craves. When she meets wealthy professional Shea she thinks he's the one but her cop's curiosity about her lover's past may cost her her life.
1992 (R) 92m/C Mimi Rogers, John Shea, Alice Krige, Tom Irwin; *D:* Michael Scott; *W:* Shelley Evans. **VHS, LV** $89.98 *MCA* ♂♂

Ladykillers A gang of bumbling bank robbers is foiled by a little old lady. Hilarious antics follow, especially on the part of Guinness, who plays the slightly demented-looking leader of the gang. Script by William Rose. *AKA:* The Lady Killers.
1955 87m/C *GB* Alec Guinness, Cecil Parker, Katie Johnson, Herbert Lom, Peter Sellers; *D:* Alexander MacKendrick. **VHS, Beta** $19.98 *HBO, FCT, HMV* ♂♂♂½

Ladykillers At the glitzy L.A. club Ladykillers, men strip as the women cheer. At the climax of the performance, one of the dancers is brutally murdered, live on stage. In this decadent world of glitter and sex, the women are the hunters and the men are the reward.
1988 97m/C Marilu Henner, Susan Blakely, Lesley-Anne Down, Thomas Calabro; *D:* Robert Lewis; *W:* Greg Dinallo. **VHS, Beta** $79.95 *PSM* ♂♂

The Lady's Maid's Bell Based upon the story by Edith Wharton, this ghost story deals with the new maid in a family estate who discovers the ghost of another past maid.
1985 60m/C **VHS, Beta** $59.95 *PSM* ♂♂

Lafayette Escadrille Action and romance in World War I via the famed flying unit manned by American volunteers. Hunter is banal in the lead role as is his romance with a reformed prostitute (Choreau). Director Wellman actually was a member of the squadron and his son plays him in the film but the director regarded the film as a failure because of studio interference. *AKA:* Hell Bent for Glory.
1958 92m/B Tab Hunter, Etchika Choreau, William Wellman Jr., Joel McCrea, Dennis Devine, Marcel Dalio, David Janssen, Paul Fix, Will Hutchins, Clint Eastwood; *D:* William A. Wellman; *W:* A.S. Fleischman; *M:* Leonard Rosenman. **VHS** $19.98 *WAR* ♂♂½

L'Age D'Or Bunuel's first full-length film and his masterpiece of sex, repression, and, of course, death. A hapless man is prevented from reaching his beloved by middle-class morality, forces of the establishment, the Church, government and every bastion of modern values. Banned for years because of its anti-religious stance. Co-scripted by Dali. A mercilessly savage, surreal satire, the purest expression of Bunuel's wry misanthropy. In French with English subtitles. *AKA:* Age of Gold.
1930 62m/B *FR* Gaston Modot, Lya Lys, Max Ernst, Pierre Prevert, Marie Berthe Ernst, Paul Eluard; *W/D:* Luis Bunuel; *W:* Salvador Dali. **VHS, Beta, LV** $59.95 *FCT, IME, GVV* ♂♂♂♂

Lagrimas de Amor A bank cashier, a night club singer, and her lover form an unusual love triangle.
1987 94m/C *MX* Ana Louisa Peluffo, Carlos Lopez Moctezuma, Sergio Bustamante. **VHS, Beta** $24.95 *MAD* ♂♂½

Laguna Heat A tired LA cop investigates a series of murders that are related to an old friend of his father's. Based on a novel by T. Jefferson Parker. Made for television.
1987 110m/C Harry Hamlin, Jason Robards Jr., Catherine Hicks, Rip Torn, Anne Francis; *D:* Simon Langton. **VHS, Beta, LV** $79.95 *LHV, WAR* ♂½

Lai Shi: China's Last Eunuch A starving Chinese child becomes a eunuch in order to garner wealth in the Emperor's palace. But he is castrated at a historically inopportune moment (as if there's a good time for such modification), just prior to the turbulent 1920s. In Cantonese with English subtitles.
1988 100m/C *CH D:* Chan Tsi-liang. **VHS** $39.95 *FCT* ♂½

The Lair of the White Worm Scottish archaeologist uncovers a strange skull, and then a bizarre religion to go with it, and then a very big worm. An unusual look at the effects of Christianity and paganism on each other, colored with sexual innuendo and, of course, giant worms. A cross between a morality play and a horror film. Adapted from Bram Stoker's last writings, written while he was going mad from Bright's disease. Everything you'd expect from Russell.
1988 (R) 93m/C *GB* Amanda Donohoe, Sammi Davis-Voss, Catherine Oxenberg, Hugh Grant, Peter Capaldi, Stratford Johns, Paul Brooke; *D:* Ken Russell. **VHS, Beta, LV** $14.98 *VES, LIV* ♂♂♂

Lake Consequence Severance plays a suburban housewife, with a scandalous past, who accidentally gets locked in her camper. Next thing she knows the camper is stolen by a handsome man and his lovely partner-in-crime. The trio wind up at a distant lake, where Severance doesn't know whether to escape or to give in to her growing sexual attraction to her captors. An unrated version at 90 minutes is also available.
1992 (R) 85m/C Joan Severance, Billy Zane, May Karasun; *D:* Rafael Eisenman; *W:* Zalman King, Melanie Finn, Henry Cobbold; *M:* George Clinton. **VHS, LV** $89.98 *REP* ♂♂

The Lamb Intent on proving to his sweetheart that he's not the coward people say he is, a guy heads west to engage in various manly activities, including fisticuffs, karate and Indian kidnapping. Fairbanks' debut on film (he was already an established Broadway star) set the mold for the American leading man: moral, cheerful, physical, and not hard to look at. A popular guy with the public, Fairbanks formed his own film company the following year. Story's based on D.W. Griffith's book, "The Man and the Test."
1915 60m/B Douglas Fairbanks Sr., Seena Owen, Lillian Langdon, Monroe Salisbury, Kate Toncray, Alfred Paget, William E. Lowery; *D:* Christy Cabanne. **VHS, Beta** $24.95 *GPV, FCT* ♂♂½

Lambada By day, he's a high school teacher in Beverly Hills; by night, a Latin dirty dancer cum tutor of ghetto teens. The very first of several films based on the short-lived dance craze.
1989 (PG) 104m/C J. Eddie Peck, Melora Hardin, Adolfo "Shabba Doo" Quinones, Ricky Paull Goldin, Dennis Burkley; *D:* Joel Silberg. **VHS, Beta, LV** $89.95 *WAR, OM* ♂

Lamp at Midnight Presentation from "George Schaefer's Showcase Theatre" deals with three critical periods in the life of Italian astronomer Galileo Galilei, from his invention of the telescope, through his appearance at the Holy Office of the Inquisition, to the publication of his "Dialogue on the Two Systems of the World." For those in a planetary state of mind.
1966 76m/C Melvyn Douglas, David Wayne, Michael Hordern, Hurd Hatfield, Kim Hunter; *D:* George Schaefer. **VHS, Beta** *FHS* ♂♂½

Lana in Love A lonely woman places an ad in the personal section in hopes of finding her Mr. Right.
1992 90m/C Daphna Kastner, Clark Gregg. **VHS, Beta** *NO* ♂♂

The Land Before Time Lushly animated children's film about five orphaned baby dinosaurs who band together and try to find the Great Valley, a paradise where they might live safely. Works same parental separation theme as Bluth's "American Tail." Charming, coy, and shamelessly tearjerking; producers included Steven Spielberg and George Lucas.
1988 (G) 70m/C *D:* Don Bluth; *M:* James Horner; *V:* Pat Hingle, Helen Shaver, Gabriel Damon, Candice Houston, Burke Barnes, Judith Barsi, Will Ryan. **VHS, Beta, LV** $19.95 *MCA, FCT, APD* ♂♂♂

Land of Doom An amazon and a warrior struggle for survival in a post-holocaust fantasy setting.
1984 87m/C Deborah Rennard, Garrick Dowhen; *D:* Peter Maris. **VHS, Beta** $19.98 *LIV* ♂

The Land of Faraway A Swedish boy is whisked off to a magical land where he does battle with evil knights and flies on winged horses. Dubbed; based on a novel by Astrid Lindgren.
1987 (G) 95m/C Timothy Bottoms, Christian Bale, Susannah York, Christopher Lee, Nicholas Pickard; *D:* Vladimir Grammatikov. **VHS, Beta** $9.99 *STE, PSM* ♂♂

Land of Fury British naval officer Hawkins steps on New Zealand's shore and into trouble when he accidently walks on sacred Maori burial ground. Very British, very dated colonial saga, based on the novel "The Seekers" by John Guthrie. *AKA:* The Seekers.
1955 90m/C *GB* Jack Hawkins, Glynis Johns, Noel Purcell, Ian Fleming; *D:* Ken Annakin. **VHS** $19.95 *NOS* ♂♂

Land of Hunted Men The Range Busters are on the case as they track down the hideout of terrorizing gunmen.
1943 58m/B Ray Corrigan, Dennis Moore, Max Terhune. **VHS, Beta** $19.95 *NOS, DVT* ♂

Land of the Lawless A group of outlaws rule over a barren wasteland. What's the point?
1947 54m/B Rachel Brown, Raymond Hatton, Christine McIntyre, Tristram Coffin; *D:* Lambert Hillyer. **VHS** $19.95 *NOS, DVT* ♂

Land of the Minotaur Small village is the setting for horrifying ritual murders, demons, and disappearances of young terrorists. Score by Brian Eno. Fans of Pleasence and Cushing won't want to miss this. *AKA:* The Devil's Men.
1977 (PG) 88m/C *GB* Donald Pleasence, Peter Cushing, Luan Peters; *D:* Costa Carayiannis. VHS, Beta $29.95 *UHV, MRV* ✡✡

Land of the Pharaohs An epic about the building of Egypt's Great Pyramid. Hawkins is the extremely talkative pharoah and Collins plays his sugary-sweet yet villainous wife. Sort of campy, but worth watching for the great surprise ending.
1955 106m/C Jack Hawkins, Joan Collins, James Robertson Justice, Dewey Martin, Alexis Minotis, Sydney Chaplin; *D:* Howard Hawks. VHS, LV *WAR* ✡✡½

Land Raiders Savalas plays a man who hates Apaches and wants their land, but is distracted when his brother arrives on the scene, igniting an old feud.
1969 101m/C Telly Savalas, George Maharis, Arlene Dahl, Janet Landgard; *D:* Nathan Juran. VHS, Beta *GKK* ✡✡

Land That Time Forgot A World War I veteran, a beautiful woman, and their German enemies are stranded in a land outside time filled with prehistoric creatures. Based on the 1918 novel by Edgar Rice Burroughs. Followed in 1977 by "The People that Time Forgot."
1975 (PG) 90m/C *GB* Doug McClure, John McEnery, Susan Penhaligon; *D:* Kevin Connor. VHS, Beta $59.98 *LIV, VES* ✡✡

Landlord Blues A trashy slumlord without morals or a conscience goes one step too far, and a tenant retaliates with munitions.
1987 96m/C Mark Boone, Raye Dowell, Richard Litt, Bill Rice, Mary Schultz, Gigi Williams; *D:* Jacob Burckhardt. VHS, Beta $79.95 *MNC* ✡✡

Landslide As a geologist, suffering from memory loss, comes closer to discovering his identity his life is endangered by a sinister plot.
1992 (PG-13) 95m/C Anthony Edwards, Tom Burlinson, Joanna Cassidy, Melody Anderson, Ronald Lacey, Ken James, Lloyd Bochner; *D:* Jean-Claude Lord. VHS, LV $89.98 *REP* ✡✡½

L'Annee des Meduses Bare-chested French nymphettes cavort and scheme against each other and a slimy gigolo on the Mediterranean beaches. Dubbed.
1986 (R) 110m/C Valerie Kaprisky, Barnard Giradeau. VHS, Beta $69.95 *FCT* ✡½

Lantern Hill During the Depression, a 12-year-old girl attempts to fan the embers between her estranged parents. Made for cable Wonderworks production, filmed partly on Canada's Prince Edward Island. Based on a story by Lucy Maud Montgomery, whose "Anne of Green Gables" is also part of the Wonderworks series.
1990 (G) 112m/C *CA* Sam Waterston, Colleen Dewhurst, Sarah Polley, Marion Bennett; *D:* Kevin Sullivan. VHS, LV $29.95 *BVV, FCT* ✡✡½

Laramie Kid A vintage Tyler sagebrush saga.
1935 60m/B Tom Tyler, Alberta Vaughn, Al Ferguson, Murdock McQuarrie, George Cheseboro; *D:* Harry S. Webb. VHS, Beta $19.95 *NOS, DVT, RXM* ✡

Larks on a String Banned for 23 years, this wonderful film is Menzel's masterpiece, even better than his Oscar winning "Closely Watched Trains." Portrays the story of life in labor camps where men and women are re-educated at the whim of the government. No matter what the hardships, these people find humor, hope and love. Their individuality will not be lost, nor their humanity dissolved. Excellent performances, tellingly directed with a beautiful sense of composition and tone. Screenplay written by Menzel and Bohumil Hrabil, author of the short story on which it is based. In Czech with English subtitles.
1968 96m/C *CZ* Vaclav Neckar, Jitka Zelenohorska, Jaroslav Satoransky, Rudolf Hrusinsky; *D:* Jiri Menzel. VHS $79.95 *FXL, TAM* ✡✡✡½

Larry Based on the Nevada State Hospital case history of a 26-year-old man, institutionalized since infancy, who is discovered to be of normal intelligence and must learn to live the life he has always been capable of living. Made for television.
1974 80m/C Frederic Forrest, Tyne Daly, Katherine Helmond, Michael McGuire, Robert Walden; *D:* William A. Graham. VHS, Beta *LCA* ✡✡

Las Doce Patadas Mortales del Kung Fu Kung Fu masters square off in this martial arts epic.
1987 95m/C *MX* Liang Hsian Lung, Ku Feng, Han Kuo Tsai. VHS, Beta $34.80 *MAD* ✡✡

Las Vegas Hillbillys A pair of country-singing hillbillies inherit a saloon in Las Vegas and enjoy wine, moonshine, and song. These two make the Clampetts look like high society. Followed, believe it or not, by "Hillbillys in a Haunted House." ♫Money Greases the Wheel. *AKA:* Country Music.
1966 85m/C Mamie Van Doren, Jayne Mansfield, Ferlin Husky, Sonny James; *D:* Arthur C. Pierce. VHS, Beta $29.95 *NLC* ✡

Las Vegas Lady Three shrewd casino hostesses plot a multi-million dollar heist in the nation's gambling capital. Non-captivating caper.
1976 (PG) 90m/C Stella Stevens, Stuart Whitman, George de Cecenzo, Andrew Stevens; *D:* Noel Nosseck. VHS, Beta $49.95 *PSM* ✡

Las Vegas Serial Killer A serial killer, let out of prison on a technicality, starts killing again. Made for video by Camp.
1986 90m/C Pierre Agostino, Ron Jason, Tara MacGowan, Kathryn Downey. VHS, Beta *NO Woof!*

The Las Vegas Story Gambling, colorful sights, and a murder provide the framework for this non-compelling fictional guided-tour of the city. Save your money for the slots.
1952 88m/B Victor Mature, Jane Russell, Vincent Price, Hoagy Carmichael, Brad Dexter; *D:* Robert Stevenson. VHS, Beta *NO Woof!*

Las Vegas Strip War A Vegas hotel owner angers his rivals by building up a floundering casino. Hudson's last TV movie. *AKA:* The Vegas Strip Wars.
1984 96m/C Rock Hudson, Sharon Stone, James Earl Jones, Pat Morita; *D:* George Englund. VHS, Beta $69.98 *LIV* ✡½

Las Vegas Weekend A computer nerd goes to Las Vegas and discovers fun.
1985 83m/C Barry Hickey, Macka Foley, Ray Dennis Steckler; *W/D:* Dale Trevillion. VHS, Beta $19.95 *STE, NWV* ✡

Laser Mission When it is discovered that the Soviets have laser weapon capabilities, an agent is given the task of destroying the weapon and kidnapping the scientist who developed it.
1990 83m/C Brandon Lee. VHS, LV $79.98 *TTC* ✡½

Laser Moon A serial killer uses a surgical laser beam to kill his beautiful victims, and he strikes at every full moon. When he announces his next attack on a late-night radio talk show the police call in a beautiful rookie cop (Lords) to use as bait.
1992 90m/C Traci Lords, Crystal Shaw, Harrison Leduke, Bruce Carter; *D:* Bruce Carter. VHS $89.95 *HMD* ✡✡

Laserblast Standard wimp-gets-revenge story in which a frustrated young man finds a powerful and deadly laser which was left near his home by aliens; upon learning of its devastating capabilities, his personality changes and he seeks revenge against all who have taken advantage of him.
1978 (PG) 87m/C Kim Milford, Cheryl "Rainbeaux" Smith, Keenan Wynn, Roddy McDowall; *D:* Michael Raye. VHS, Beta, LV $29.95 *MED* Woof!

The Laserman Exotic black comedy about a Chinese-American scientist who, when not fending off his overbearing Jewish mother or having telepathic orgasms, is contending with a band of political terrorists.
1990 92m/C Marc Hayashi, Peter Wang, Tony Leung, Sally Yeh, Maryann Urbano, Joan Copeland; *W/D:* Peter Wang. VHS $79.95 *HTV* ✡✡

The Lash of the Penitents An explosive documentary about Southern fundamentalist cults.
1939 70m/B VHS, Beta $16.95 *SNC, NOS, DVT* ✡

Lassie: Adventures of Neeka America's best friend joins her Native American buddy, Neeka, for a journey through a forest in the Pacific Northwest. They camp out in a deserted settlement, pull an elderly gentleman out of a frigid pond, and risk their lives to release horses from a stable during a raging wildfire.
1968 75m/B Jed Allan, Mark Miranda, Robert Rockwell, Lassie; *D:* Richard Moder, Jack B. Hively. VHS, Beta *NO* ✡

Lassie, Come Home In first of the Lassie series, the famed collie is reluctantly sold and makes a treacherous cross-country journey back to her original family.
1943 90m/C Roddy McDowall, Elizabeth Taylor, Donald Crisp, Edmund Gwenn, May Whitty, Nigel Bruce, Elsa Lanchester, J. Pat O'Malley, Lassie; *D:* Fred M. Wilcox. Academy Awards '43 Nominations: Best Color Cinematography; National Board of Review Awards '43: 10 Best Films of the Year. VHS, Beta, LV $19.98 *MGM* ✡✡½

Lassie from Lancashire Not the famous Collie—but here, a Colleen. A pair of struggling lovebirds try to make it in show biz against all odds, including the girl's lunatic aunt, who locks her away before an audition.
1938 67m/B Marjorie Brown, Hal Thompson, Marjorie Sandford, Lassie, Mark Daly. VHS, Beta $29.95 *VYY* ✡✡

Lassie: The Miracle A TV-movie featuring the faithful collie saving new-born pups and befriending a mute boy.
1975 90m/C Lassie. VHS, Beta $29.95 *MGM* ✡

Lassie: Well of Love Various installments of the classic television series featuring the heroic collie are combined to create a movie-length presentation for home video. Lassie takes two young pups under her paw and, in the process, loses her way. As she tries to get home, she brings joy back into the lives of two despondent children. Finally, the old girl faces death when she tumbles into an abandoned well and must depend on humans for rescue.

L

1990 76m/C Lassie, Mary Gregory, Robert Donner. **VHS, Beta** NO ⚹

Lassie's Great Adventure Lassie and her master Timmy are swept away from home by a runaway balloon. After they land in the Canadian wilderness, they learn to rely on each other through peril and adventure. Made for television.
1962 104m/C June Lockhart, Jon Provost, Hugh Reilly, Lassie; **D:** William Beaudine. **VHS, Beta** $29.99 MGM ⚹⚹½

Lassiter Selleck plays a jewel thief who is asked to steal diamonds from the Nazis for the FBI. Supporting cast adds value to what is otherwise a fairly ordinary adventure drama.
1984 (R) 100m/C Tom Selleck, Jane Seymour, Lauren Hutton, Bob Hoskins, Joe Regalbuto, Ed Lauter, Warren Clarke; **D:** Roger Young. **VHS, Beta, LV** $19.98 WAR ⚹⚹½

Last Action Hero Rumored to have cost $80 million, action-spoof of movies within a movie was critically maimed and disappointing at box office. And Ah-nold thought he was concocting a marketing buzz-saw with family appeal. Danny (O'Brien, in his screen debut), a movie-mad, fatherless preteen gets sucked into a film starring his action-hero idol Jack Slater (guess who). Slater is the kind of guy who never loses a fight and is impervious to gunfire and explosions (and he has a really cool car and a really big gun). When a passel of bad guys escapes from the movie, Slater and Danny head back into the real world where Jack discovers punches hurt and bullets kill and encounters the real Arnold. Lots of big name stars in small roles and cameos round out the cast. The concept isn't new and has been done better before, though Arnold possesses his usual self-mocking charm, which is more than can be said for the movie as a whole. Cluttered with inside Hollywood gags, script was shared by four writers, with an uncredited assist from William Goldman.
1993 (PG-13) 130m/C Arnold Schwarzenegger, Austin O'Brien, Mercedes Ruehl, F. Murray Abraham, Charles Dance, Anthony Quinn, Robert Prosky, Tommy Noonan, Frank McRae, Art Carney, Brigitte Wilson; *Cameos:* Sharon Stone, M.C. Hammer, Chevy Chase, Jean-Claude Van Damme, Tori Spelling, Joan Plowright, Adam Ant, James Belushi, James Cameron, Tony Curtis, Timothy Dalton, Tony Danza, Edward Furlong, Little Richard, Damon Wayans, Robert Patrick; **D:** John McTiernan; **M:** Michael Kamen. **VHS** NYR ⚹⚹

The Last American Hero The true story of how former moonshine runner Junior Johnson became one of the fastest race car drivers in the history of the sport. Entertaining slice of life chronicling whiskey running and stock car racing, with Bridges superb in the lead. Based on articles, written by Tom Wolfe. *AKA:* Hard Driver.
1973 (PG) 95m/C Jeff Bridges, Valerie Perrine, Gary Busey, Art Lund, Geraldine Fitzgerald, Ned Beatty; **D:** Lamont Johnson. **VHS, Beta** $59.98 FOX ⚹⚹⚹

Last American Virgin Usual brainless teen sex comedy about three school buddies who must deal with a plethora of problems in their search for girls who are willing. Music by Blondie, The Cars, The Police, The Waitresses, Devo, U2, Human League, and Quincy Jones.
1982 (R) 92m/C Lawrence Monoson, Diane Franklin, Steve Antin, Louisa Moritz; **D:** Boaz Davidson. **VHS, Beta** $79.95 MGM ⚹⚹

The Last Angry Man An old, idealistic Brooklyn doctor attracts a television producer wanting to make a documentary about his life and career, and the two conflict. Muni was Oscar-nominated for this, his last film.
1959 100m/B Paul Muni, David Wayne, Betsy Palmer, Luther Adler, Dan Tobin; **D:** Daniel Mann. **VHS, Beta** $69.95 COL ⚹⚹⚹½

The Last Bastion A World War II drama emphasizing the political struggle between Churchill, MacArthur, Roosevelt, and Australia's John Curtin.
1984 160m/C AU Robert Vaughn, Timothy West. **VHS, Beta** $19.95 ACA ⚹⚹

The Last Boy Scout This formula thriller stars Willis as a private eye and Wayans as an ex-quarterback teaming up against a pro-football team owner who will stop at nothing to get political backing for a bill promoting legalized gambling on sports. Another variation of the violent buddy-picture by "Lethal Weapon" screenwriter Black.
1991 (R) 105m/C Bruce Willis, Damon Wayans, Halle Berry, Chelsea Field, Noble Willingham, Taylor Negron, Danielle Harris, Bruce McGill; **D:** Tony Scott; **W:** Shane Black. **VHS, LV** $19.98 WAR ⚹⚹

Last Bullet A young westerner chases after a band of outlaws to avenge the cold-blooded murder of his parents.
1950 55m/B James Ellison, Russell Hayden, John Cason. **VHS, Beta, LV** NO ⚹⚹

Last Call Clearly, Joe Sixpack won't rent this bimbo fest for its subtle plot. Katt, a mafiosi cheated real estate guy, decides to even the score with the assistance of gal pal/playmate of the year Tweed, who's more than willing to compromise her position. A direct to video release, it also features the talents of playboy emerita Stevens.
1990 (R) 90m/C William Katt, Shannon Tweed, Joseph Campanella, Stella Stevens, Matt Roe; **D:** Jag Mundhra. **VHS, Beta** $89.95 PAR ⚹

Last Challenge of the Dragon A son brings death to his family by humiliating the underworld martial arts king of the city.
1980 (R) 90m/C Bruce Lee. **VHS, Beta** $59.95 GEM ⚹

The Last Chance A realistic look at the efforts of three WWII Allied officers to help a group of refugees escape across the Alps from Italy to Switzerland. The officers are played by former pilots who were shot down over Switzerland. In spite of this—or perhaps because of it—the acting is superb. Watch for inspirational scene of refugees singing.
1945 105m/B E.G. Morrison, John Hoy, Ray Reagan, Odeardo Mosini, Sigfrit Steiner, Emil Gerber; **D:** Leopold Lindtberg. **VHS** $19.95 NOS ⚹⚹⚹

Last Chase Famed race car driver becomes a vocal dissenter against the sterile society that has emerged, in this drama set in the near future. Made for television.
1981 (PG) 106m/C CA Lee Majors, Burgess Meredith, Chris Makepeace, Alexandra Stewart; **D:** Martyn Burke. **VHS, Beta** $69.95 VES ⚹½

Last Command Famous powerful silent film by Sternberg about a expatriate Czarist general forging out a pitiful living as a silent Hollywood extra, where he is hired by his former adversary to reenact the revolution he just left. Next to "The Last Laugh," this is considered Jannings' most acclaimed performance. Deeply ironic, visually compelling film with a new score by Gaylord Carter.

1928 88m/B Emil Jannings, William Powell, Evelyn Brent; **D:** Josef von Sternberg. Academy Awards '28: Best Actor (Jannings); Nominations: Best Original Screenplay, Best Picture. **VHS, Beta** $14.95 PAR, FCT, BTV ⚹⚹⚹⚹

The Last Command Jim Bowie and his followers sacrifice their lives in defending the Alamo. A good cast holds its own against a mediocre script; battle scenes are terrific.
1955 110m/C Sterling Hayden, Richard Carlson, Ernest Borgnine, J. Carroll Naish, Virginia Grey; **D:** Frank Lloyd. **VHS** $14.95 REP, PAR ⚹⚹½

The Last Contract An artist who pays his bills by working as a hitman, kills the wrong man. As a result, he must fear for his life since a counterhit is inevitable.
1986 (R) 85m/C Jack Palance, Rod Steiger, Bo Svenson, Richard Roundtree, Ann Turkel; **D:** Allan A. Buckhantz. **VHS** $19.95 ACA ⚹⚹

Last Cry for Help A psychiatrist helps a seventeen-year-old high school coed who, fearing she has disappointed her parents, attempts suicide. Typical made-for-television melodrama that attempts to make a statement, but falls short. Definitely not the "Partridge Family."
1979 98m/C Linda Purl, Shirley Jones, Tony LoBianco, Murray Hamilton, Grant Goodeve; **D:** Hal Sitowitz. **VHS, Beta** $29.95 UNI ⚹½

Last Dance Five scantily-clad exotic dancers are ready to compete for the title of Miss Dance-TV, but trouble ensues when the dancers start turning up dead.
1991 86m/C Cynthia Bassinet, Elaine Hendrix, Kurt T. Williams, Allison Rhea, Erica Ringston; **D:** Anthony Markes. **VHS, Beta, LV** $79.95 PSM ⚹½

Last Day of the War A German scientist is chased by Americans and Germans as WWII winds to its conclusion. Filmed in Spain.
1969 (PG) 96m/C SP George Maharis, Maria Perschy, James Philbrook, Gerard Herter; **D:** Juan Antonio Bardem. **VHS, Beta** $39.95 LIV ⚹½

The Last Days of Chez Nous Armstrong's dramatic comedy about a family falling apart has Ganz as a homesick Frenchman married to controlling, successful Australian writer Harrow. Trouble starts when his wayward sister-in-law Fox returns home to live with them and his wife decides to take an extended holiday with her father. Ganz suddenly finds himself only too involved in Fox's complicated life. Self-involved characters with messy emotional lives leave viewers feeling rather distant, though cast, and particularly Ganz, strive for intimacy.
1992 (R) 96m/C AU Bruno Ganz, Lisa Harrow, Kerry Fox, Kiri Paramore, Bill Hunter; **D:** Gillian Armstrong; **W:** Helen Garner; **M:** Paul Grabowsky. **VHS** NYR ⚹⚹½

The Last Days of Dolwyn A man banned for thievery from his Welsh village returns bent upon revenge. He plans to buy the entire district when it is designated part of a water reservoir project, but finds plans thwarted by a dowager and her stepson. Burton's first film was based on a true story. *AKA:* Woman of Dolwyn; Dolwyn.
1949 95m/B GB Edith Evans, Emlyn Williams, Richard Burton, Anthony James, Barbara Couper, Alan Aynesworth, Hugh Griffith, Roddy Hughes, Tom Jones; **W/D:** Emlyn Williams. **VHS** $29.95 FCT ⚹⚹½

Last Days of Frank & Jesse James A tired television-movie rehash of the well-known western legend in which the famous brothers try to be like others after their personal war against society ends.

1986 100m/C Johnny Cash, Kris Kristofferson, June Carter Cash, Willie Nelson, Margaret Gibson, Gail Youngs; *D:* William A. Graham. **VHS, Beta** $19.95 *STE, VMK* 🎬 ½

The Last Days of Patton A made-for-television movie depicting the aging general's autumn years as a controversial ex-Nazi defender and desk-bound World War II historian. Scott reprises his feature-film role.
1986 146m/C George C. Scott, Ed Lauter, Eva Marie Saint, Richard Dysart, Murray Hamilton, Kathryn Leigh Scott; *D:* Delbert Mann. **VHS, Beta** $89.98 *FOX* 🎬 ½

Last Days of Pompeii Vintage DeMille-style epic based on Lord Lytton's book, where the eruption of Vesuvius threatens noblemen and slaves alike. State-of-the-art special effects still look fantastic today. Remade in 1960; available colorized.
1935 96m/B Preston Foster, Alan Hale Jr., Basil Rathbone, John Wood, Louis Calhern, David Holt, Dorothy Wilson, Wryley Birch, Gloria Shea; *D:* Ernest B. Schoedsack. **VHS, Beta** *TTC* 🎬🎬 ½

The Last Days of Pompeii Superman Reeves plays a gladiator trying to clean up the doomed town of Pompeii in this remake of the 1935 classic. Some spectacular scenes, including the explosive climax when the mountain blows its top. *AKA:* Ultimi Giorni di Pompeii.
1960 105m/C *IT* Steve Reeves, Christine Kaufmann, Barbara Carroll, Anne Marie Baumann, Mimmo Palmara; *D:* Mario Bonnard; *W:* Sergio Leone. **VHS** $9.95 *GKK* 🎬🎬

The Last Detail Two hard-boiled career petty officers (Nicholson and Young) are commissioned to transfer a young sailor facing an eight-year sentence for petty theft from one brig to another. In an act of compassion, they attempt to show the prisoner a final good time. Nicholson shines in both the complexity and completeness of his character. Adapted from a Daryl Ponicsan novel.
1973 (R) 104m/C Jack Nicholson, Otis Young, Randy Quaid, Clifton James, Michael Moriarty, Carol Kane, Nancy Allen; *Cameos:* Gilda Radner; *D:* Hal Ashby; *W:* Robert Towne. Academy Awards '73 Nominations: Best Actor (Nicholson), Best Adapted Screenplay, Best Supporting Actor (Quaid); British Academy Awards '74: Best Actor (Nicholson); Cannes Film Festival '74: Best Actor (Nicholson); National Board of Review Awards '74: 10 Best Films of the Year; New York Film Critics Awards '74: Best Actor (Nicholson); National Society of Film Critics Awards '74: Best Actor (Nicholson). **VHS, Beta, LV** $14.95 *COL, WME* 🎬🎬🎬🎬

The Last Dragon It's time for a Motown kung fu showdown on the streets of Harlem, for there is scarcely enough room for even one dragon. *AKA:* Berry Gordy's The Last Dragon.
1985 (PG-13) 108m/C Taimak, Vanity, Christopher Murney, Julius J. Carry III, Faith Prince; *D:* Michael Schultz. **VHS, Beta** $29.95 *FOX* 🎬 ½

The Last Embrace A feverish thriller in the Hitchcock style dealing with an ex-secret serviceman who is convinced someone is trying to kill him.
1979 (R) 102m/C Roy Scheider, Janet Margolin, Christopher Walken, John Glover, Charles Napier, Mandy Patinkin; *D:* Jonathan Demme. **VHS, Beta** $14.95 *MGM, FOX* 🎬🎬🎬

The Last Emperor Deeply ironic epic detailing life of Pu Yi, crowned at the age of three as the last emperor of China before the onset of communism. Follows Pu Yi from childhood to manhood (sequestered away in the Forbidden City) to fugitive to puppet-ruler to party proletariat. O'Toole portrays the sympathetic Scot tutor who educates the adult Pu Yi (Lone) in the ways of the western world after Pu Yi abdicates power in 1912. Shot on location inside the People's Republic of China with a cast of thousands; authentic costumes. Rich, visually stunning movie. Music by David Byrne, Ryuichi Sakamoto, and Cong Su; cinematography by Vittorio Storaro.
1987 (PG-13) 140m/C *IT* John Lone, Peter O'Toole, Joan Chen, Victor Wong, Ryuichi Sakamoto, Dennis Dun, Maggie Han; *D:* Bernardo Bertolucci. **VHS, Beta, LV, SVS, 8mm** $19.98 *COL, FCT, BTV* 🎬🎬🎬🎬

Last Exit to Brooklyn Hubert Selby, Jr.'s shocking book comes to the screen in a vivid film. Leigh gives a stunning performance as a young Brooklyn girl caught between the Mafia, union men, and friends struggling for something better. Set in the 1950s. Fine supporting cast; excellent pacing.
1990 (R) 102m/C Jennifer Jason Leigh, Burt Young, Stephen Lang, Ricki Lake, Jerry Orbach, Maia Danzinger; *D:* Uli Edel. **VHS, LV** $89.95 *COL, FCT* 🎬🎬🎬 ½

Last Fight Boxer risks his life and his girlfriend for a shot at the championship title. Watch and see if he could've been a contender.
1982 (R) 85m/C Fred Williamson, Willie Colon, Ruben Blades, Joe Spinell, Darlanne Fluegel; *D:* Fred Williamson. **VHS, Beta** $69.99 *HBO* 🎬 ½

The Last Five Days Based on the true story of a girl and her brother who, in 1943 Munich, were arrested for distributing anti-Nazi propaganda. The film covers the five days between their capture and execution. In German with English subtitles.
1982 112m/C *GE* Lena Stolze, Irm Hermann; *D:* Percy Adlon. **VHS** $79.95 *CVC, TAM* 🎬🎬

The Last Flight of Noah's Ark Disney adventure concerns a high-living pilot, a prim missionary, and two stowaway orphans who must plot their way off a deserted island following the crash landing of their broken-down plane.
1980 (G) 97m/C Elliott Gould, Genevieve Bujold, Rick Schroder, Vincent Gardenia, Tammy Lauren; *D:* Charles Jarrott. **VHS, Beta** $69.95 *DIS* 🎬🎬 ½

Last Flight Out: A True Story Hours before Saigon fell to the Vietcong in 1975, Vietnamese and Americans rushed to board the last commercial flight out of Vietnam. Lukewarm account of a true story.
1990 99m/C James Earl Jones, Richard Crenna, Haing S. Ngor, Eric Bogosian. **VHS, 8mm** $39.95 *MNC* 🎬🎬

Last Flight to Hell When a drug lord is kidnapped, Brown is sent to South America to rescue the slimeball. His interest in the job picks up when the drug lord's 11-on-a-scale-of-ten daughter joins him for the chase.
19?? 94m/C Reb Brown, Chuck Connors. **VHS** $79.98 *AIP* 🎬🎬

The Last Fling When Selleca has her mind set on a romantic fling, Ritter is headed for trouble. She wants love for one night, he wants it forever. Will they solve this difference of opinion? Will true love prevail? Will Ritter consent to being used as a one-night stand? Weakly plotted and poorly acted comedy. Made for television.
1986 95m/C John Ritter, Connie Sellecca, Scott Bakula, Shannon Tweed, Paul Sand, John Bennett Perry; *D:* Corey Allen. **VHS, LV** $29.95 *ACA* 🎬 ½

Last Four Days A chronicle of the final days of Benito Mussolini.
1977 (PG) 91m/C Rod Steiger, Henry Fonda, Franco Nero; *D:* Carlo Lizzani. **VHS, Beta** $69.98 *LIV* 🎬🎬

Last Frontier Serial of 12 chapters contains shades of spectacular figures in Western history: Custer, Hickok, and others in a background of grazing buffalo, boom towns, and covered wagon trails.
1932 216m/B Lon Chaney Jr., Yakima Canutt, Francis X. Bushman; *D:* Spencer Gordon Bennet, Thomas L. Story. **VHS, Beta** $14.95 *VCN, VYY, DVT* 🎬🎬 ½

Last Game A college student is torn between his devotion to his blind father and going out for the college's football team.
1980 107m/C Howard Segal, Ed L. Grady, Terry Alden; *D:* Martin Beck. **VHS, Beta** $59.99 *HBO* 🎬🎬

Last Gun A legendary gunman on the verge of retirement has to save his town from a reign of terror before turning his gun in.
1964 98m/C Cameron Mitchell. **VHS, Beta** *NO* 🎬🎬

Last Holiday A man who is told he has a few weeks to live decides to spend them in a posh resort where people assume he is important. Script by J. B. Priestley.
1950 89m/B *GB* Alec Guinness, Kay Walsh, Beatrice Campbell, Wilfrid Hyde-White, Bernard Lee; *D:* Henry Cass. **VHS, Beta** $39.95 *TVC, RXM, LCA* 🎬🎬🎬

The Last Horror Film Beautiful queen of horror films is followed to the Cannes Film Festival by her number one fan who, unbeknownst to her, is slowly murdering members of her entourage in a deluded and vain attempt to capture her attentions. Title refers to lack of plans for a sequel. *AKA:* The Fanatic.
1982 (R) 87m/C Caroline Munro, Joe Spinell, Judd Hamilton; *D:* David Winters. **VHS, Beta** $59.95 *MED Woof!*

The Last Hour A Wall Street crook crosses a Mafia punk, so the latter holds the former's wife hostage in an unfinished skyscraper. Fortunately the lady's first husband is a gung-ho cop eager to commence the DIE HARD-esque action. Undistinguished fare that gives away the climax in an opening flash-forward.
1991 (R) 85m/C Michael Pare, Shannon Tweed, Bobby DiCicco, Robert Pucci; *D:* William Sachs. **VHS, Beta, LV** $19.95 *ACA* 🎬

Last House on Dead End Street Gore galore as actors die for their art in this splatter flick about snuff films. *AKA:* The Fun House.
1977 (R) 90m/C Steven Morrison, Dennis Crawford, Lawrence Bornman, Janet Sorley; *D:* Victor Janos. **VHS** $54.95 *SUN Woof!*

Last House on the Left Two girls are kidnapped from a rock concert by a gang of escaped convicts; the girls' parents exact bloody revenge when the guilty parties pay an intended housecall. Controversial and grim low-budget shocker; loosely based on Bergman's "The Virgin Spring."
1972 (R) 83m/C David Hess, Lucy Grantham, Sandra Cassel, Mark Sheffler, Fred J. Lincoln; *D:* Wes Craven. **VHS, Beta, LV** $19.98 *LIV, VES, HHE Woof!*

The Last Hunter A soldier fights for his life behind enemy lines during the Vietnam War. *AKA:* Hunter of the Apocalypse.
1980 (R) 97m/C *IT* Tisa Farrow, David Warbeck, Tony King, Bobby Rhodes, Margit Evelyn Newton, John Steiner, Alan Collins; *D:* Anthony M. Dawson. **VHS, Beta** $69.98 *LIV, VES* 🎬

Last Hurrah An aging Irish-American mayor battles corruption and political backbiting in his effort to get re-elected for the last time. Semi-acclaimed heart warmer, based on the novel by Edwin O'Connor.

1958 121m/B Spencer Tracy, Basil Rathbone, John Carradine, Jeffrey Hunter, Dianne Foster, Pat O'Brien, Edward Brophy, James Gleason, Donald Crisp, Ricardo Cortez, Wallace Ford, Frank McHugh, Jane Darwell; **D:** John Ford. **VHS, Beta, LV $19.95** COL ⅋⅋½

Last Innocent Man An attorney who quit law due to a guilty conscience is lured into defending a suspected murderer. Things become even more complicated when he begins having an affair with his client's seductive wife. A well-acted and suspense-filled flick. Made for cable television.
1987 113m/C Ed Harris, Roxanne Hart, Bruce McGill, Clarence Williams III, Rose Gregorio; **D:** Roger Spottiswoode. **VHS, Beta $79.95** LHV, WAR ⅋⅋½

The Last Laugh An elderly man, who as the doorman of a great hotel was looked upon as a symbol of "upper class," is demoted to washroom attendant due to his age. Important due to camera technique and consuming performance by Jannings. Silent with music score. **AKA:** Der Letzte Mann.
1924 77m/B GE Emil Jannings, Maly Delshaft, Max Hiller; **D:** F. W. Murnau. **VHS, Beta, 3/4U, Special order formats $19.95** NOS, MRV, IHF ⅋⅋⅋½

The Last Man on Earth Price is the sole survivor of a plague which has turned the rest of the world into zombies, who constantly harass him. Uneven U.S./Italian production manages to convey a creepy atmosphere of dismay. **AKA:** L'Ultimo Uomo Della Terra.
1964 86m/B IT Vincent Price, Franca Bettoya, Giacomo Rossi-Stuart, Emma Danieli; **D:** Ubaldo Ragona, Sidney Salkow. **VHS $16.95** SNC, MRV ⅋⅋

Last Man Standing A cheap, gritty drama about bare-knuckle fist fighting. Wells stars as a down-on-his-luck prizefighter trying to find work that doesn't involve pugilism.
1987 (R) 89m/C William Sanderson, Vernon Wells, Franco Columbo; **D:** Damian Lee. **VHS, Beta $29.95** ACA ⅋

The Last Married Couple in America A couple fight to stay happily married amidst the rampant divorce epidemic engulfing their friends.
1980 (R) 103m/C George Segal, Natalie Wood, Richard Benjamin, Valerie Harper, Dom DeLuise, Priscilla Barnes; **D:** Gilbert Cates. **VHS, Beta $69.95** MCA ⅋⅋

Last Mercenary An angry ex-soldier kills everyone who makes him mad.
1984 90m/C Tony Marsina, Malcolm Duff, Kitty Nichols, Louis Walser. **VHS, Beta** NO Woof!

The Last Metro Truffaut's alternately gripping and touching drama about a theater company in Nazi-occupied Paris. In 1942, Lucas Steiner (Bennent) is a successful Jewish theater director who is forced into hiding. He turns the running of the theater over to his wife, Marion (the always exquisite Deneuve), who must contend with a pro-Nazi theater critic (Richard) and her growing attraction to the company's leading man (Depardieu), who is secretly working with the Resistance. In French with English subtitles. **AKA:** Le Dernier Metro.
1980 135m/C FR Catherine Deneuve, Gerard Depardieu, Heinz Bennent, Jean-Louis Richard, Jean Poiret, Andrea Ferreol, Paulette Dubost, Sabine Haudepin; **D:** Francois Truffaut. Academy Awards '80 Nominations: Best Foreign Language Film; Cesar Awards '81: Best Actor (Depardieu), Best Actress (Deneuve), Best Director (Truffaut), Best Film. **VHS, Beta, LV $39.95** HMV, FOX, APD ⅋⅋⅋

The Last Mile The staff of a prison prepares for the execution of a celebrated murderer.
1932 70m/B Preston Foster, Howard Phillips, George E. Stone; **D:** Sam Bischoff. **VHS, Beta $19.95** NOS, MRV, KRT ⅋⅋

The Last Movie A movie stunt man stays in a small Peruvian town after his filming stint is over. Hopper's confused, pretentious follow-up to "Easy Rider," has a multitude of cameos but little else. Given an award by the Italians; nobody else understood it. Kristofferson's film debut; he also wrote the music. Based on a story by Hopper and Stern. **AKA:** Chinchero.
1971 (R) 108m/C Dennis Hopper, Julie Adams, Peter Fonda, Kris Kristofferson, Sylvia Miles, John Phillip Law, Russ Tamblyn, Rod Cameron; **D:** Dennis Hopper; **W:** Stewart Stern. **VHS $79.95** UHV ⅋⅋

Last Night at the Alamo Patrons fight to stop the destruction of their Houston bar, the Alamo, which is about to be razed to make room for a modern skyscraper. Insightful comedy written by the author of "The Texas Chainsaw Massacre."
1983 80m/B Sonny Davis, Lou Perry, Steve Matilla, Tina Hubbard, Doris Hargrave; **D:** Eagle Pennell; **W:** Kim Henkel. **VHS** NO ⅋⅋⅋

The Last of England A furious non-narrative film by avant-garde filmmaker Jarman, depicting the modern British landscape as a funereal, waste-filled rubble-heap—as depleted morally as it is environmentally.
1987 87m/C GB Tilda Swinton, Spencer Leigh; **D:** Derek Jarman. **VHS, Beta, LV $29.95** MFV, TAM ⅋⅋⅋½

The Last of His Tribe In 1911 an anthropologist befriends an Indian and discovers that Ishi is the last surviving member of California's Yahi tribe. Ishi then becomes a media and scientific society darling, spending the remainder of his remaining life in captivity to academia. A good portrayal of the Native American plight. Based on a true story; made for cable television.
1992 (PG-13) 90m/C Jon Voight, Graham Greene, David Ogden Stiers, Jack Blessing, Anne Archer, Daniel Benzali; **D:** Harry Hook. **VHS, LV $89.99** WAR ⅋⅋

The Last of Mrs. Cheyney Remake of Norma Shearer's 1929 hit, based on the play by Frederick Lonsdale, about a sophisticated jewel thief in England. Crawford stars as the jewel thief who poses as a wealthy woman to get into parties hosted by London bluebloods. Dripping with charm, she works her way into Lord Drilling's mansion where she plans a huge heist. The film is handled well, and the cast gives solid performances throughout. This chic comedy of high society proved to be one of Crawford's most popular films of the '30s.
1937 98m/B Joan Crawford, Robert Montgomery, William Powell, Frank Morgan, Nigel Bruce, Jessie Ralph; **D:** Richard Boleslawski, George Fitzmaurice. **VHS $19.98** MGM ⅋⅋⅋

The Last of Mrs. Lincoln Intimate made for TV portrayal of the famous first lady. Film focuses on Mary Todd Lincoln's life from the assassination of her husband, through her autumn years, and her untimely downfall.
1976 118m/C Julie Harris, Robby Benson, Patrick Duffy. **VHS, Beta** NO ⅋⅋½

The Last of Philip Banter An alcoholic writer is terrified to learn events in his life exactly match a mysterious manuscript.
1987 (R) 105m/C Tony Curtis, Greg Henry, Irene Miracle, Scott Paulin, Kate Vernon; **D:** Herve Hachuel. **VHS $79.95** REP ⅋½

The Last of Sheila A movie producer invites six big-star friends for a cruise aboard his yacht the "Sheila." He then stages an elaborate "Whodunnit" parlor game to discover which one of them murdered his wife. Scripted by Stephen Sondheim and Anthony Perkins.
1973 (PG) 119m/C Richard Benjamin, James Coburn, James Mason, Dyan Cannon, Joan Hackett, Raquel Welch, Ian McShane; **D:** Herbert Ross; **W:** Anthony Perkins, Shel Silverstein. **VHS, Beta $64.95** WAR ⅋⅋½

Last of the Clintons A range detective tracks an outlaw gang amid spur jinglin', sharp shootin' and cow punchin'.
1935 64m/B Harry Carey Sr. **VHS, Beta, LV $19.95** NOS ⅋½

Last of the Comanches Cavalry and Indians fight for water when both are dying of thirst in the desert. **AKA:** The Sabre and the Arrow.
1952 85m/C Broderick Crawford, Barbara Hale, John Stewart, Lloyd Bridges, Mickey Shaughnessy, George Mathews; **D:** Andre de Toth. **VHS, Beta $14.99** GKK ⅋⅋

The Last of the Finest Overzealous anti-drug task force cops break the rules in trying to put dealer-drug lords in prison; ostensibly a parallel on the Iran-Contra affair. **AKA:** Street Legal; Blue Heat.
1990 (R) 106m/C Brian Dennehy, Joe Pantoliano, Jeff Fahey, Bill Paxton, Deborra-Lee Furness, Guy Boyd, Henry Darrow, Lisa Jane Persky, Michael C. Gwynne; **D:** John MacKenzie; **M:** Jack Nitzsche. **VHS, Beta, LV $14.98** ORI ⅋½

The Last of the Mohicans Serial based on James Fenimore Cooper's novel of the life-and-death struggle of the Mohican Indians during the French and Indian War. Twelve chapters, 13 minutes each. Remade as a movie in 1936 and 1992 and as a television movie in 1977.
1932 230m/B Edwina Booth, Harry Carey Sr., Hobart Bosworth, Frank "Junior" Coghlan; **D:** Ford Beebe, B. Reeves Eason. **VHS, Beta $49.95** NOS, VCN, VYY ⅋⅋

The Last of the Mohicans James Fenimore Cooper's classic about the French and Indian War in colonial America is brought to the screen. Remake of the 1932 serial was remade itself in 1977 for television.
1936 91m/B Randolph Scott, Binnie Barnes, Bruce Cabot, Henry Wilcoxon, Heather Angel, Hugh Buckler; **D:** George B. Seitz. **VHS, Beta $12.95** LIV, MED, CCB ⅋⅋½

The Last of the Mohicans The classic novel by James Fenimore Cooper about the scout Hawkeye and his Mohican companions, Chingachgook and Uncas during the French and Indian war, comes to life in this made-for-television film. Remake of a 1932 serial and a 1936 film.
1985 (R) 97m/C Steve Forrest, Ned Romero, Andrew Prine, Don Shanks, Robert Tessier, Jane Actman; **D:** James L. Conway. **VHS, Beta $19.95** STE, UHV ⅋⅋

The Last of the Mohicans It's 1757 at the height of the French and English territorial war in the American colonies, with various Native American tribes allied to either side. Into this battle runs (there's a lot of running in this film) Hawkeye (Day-Lewis), a white frontiersman raised by the Mohicans, who wants nothing to do with either "civilized" side. That is, until he rescues the beautiful Cora (Stowe), daughter of an English officer. A revenge-minded Huron Indian named Magua (the menacing Studi) causes trouble for all concerned and there are a number of smoke-filled battle scenes and some graphic Indian attacks to contend with.

Dialog and character development are minimal—the real pleasure in this film adaptation, which draws from both the James Fenimore Cooper novel and the 1936 film version, is in its lush look and its attractive stars. Director Mann ("Miami Vice") has an eye-catching way with visuals and both Day-Lewis and Stowe are physically graceful and romantic in their roles. Means shines in his film debut as Hawkeye's foster-father, "The Last of the Mohicans." Released on video in a letterbox format.
1992 (R) 110m/C Daniel Day-Lewis, Madeleine Stowe, Wes Studi, Russell Means, Eric Schweig, Jodhi May, Steven Waddington, Maurice Roeves; W/D: Michael Mann; W: Christopher Crowe; M: Trevor Jones, Randy Edelman. VHS, LV $94.98 FXV ✍✍✍

Last of the Pony Riders When the telegraph lines linking the East and West Coasts are completed, Gene and the other Pony Express riders find themselves out of a job. Autry's final feature film.
1953 59m/B Gene Autry, Smiley Burnette, Kathleen Case; D: George Archainbaud. VHS, Beta $37.50 CCB ✍½

Last of the Red Hot Lovers Not so funny adaptation of Neil Simon's Broadway hit. Middle-aged man decides to have a fling and uses his mother's apartment to seduce three very strange women.
1972 (PG) 98m/C Alan Arkin, Paula Prentiss, Sally Kellerman, Renee Taylor; D: Gene Saks; W: Neil Simon. VHS, Beta, LV $14.95 PAR ✍½

Last of the Redmen An adaptation of James Fenimore Cooper's "The Last of the Mohicans" geared toward youngsters. Hall must lead three children of a British general through dangerous Indian territory. They have a number of adventures including meeting up with Uncas, the last of the Mohicans, who's a villain in this mangled version.
1947 79m/C Jon Hall, Michael O'Shea, Evelyn Ankers, Julie Bishop, Buster Crabbe, Rick Vallin, Frederick Worlock, Guy Hedlund; D: George Sherman; W: Herbert Dalmas. VHS $19.95 COL ✍½

Last of the Warrens A cowboy returns home after World War I to discover that an unscrupulous storekeeper has stolen his property.
1936 56m/C Bob Steele, Charles King. VHS, Beta $19.95 NOS, DVT ✍

Last of the Wild Horses Range war almost starts when ranch owner is accused of trying to force the small ranchers out of business.
1949 86m/B Mary Beth Hughes, James Ellison, Jane Frazee. VHS, Beta NO ✍½

The Last Outlaw Action-packed western with Cooper following his success of "Wings" with Paramount. Most excellent equine stunts.
1927 61m/B Gary Cooper, Jack Luden, Betty Jewel; D: Arthur Rosson. VHS, Beta $19.95 GPV, FCT ✍✍

Last Outlaw The last of the famous badmen of the old West is released from jail and returns home to find that times have changed. The action climaxes in an old-time blazing shoot-out.
1936 79m/B Harry Carey Sr., Hoot Gibson, Henry B. Walthall, Tom Tyler, Russell Hopton, Alan Curtis, Harry Woods, Barbara Pepper; D: Christy Cabanne. VHS, Beta $29.95 VCN ✍✍

The Last Picture Show Working with Larry McMurtry's novel, McMurtry and Bogdanovich scripted this slice of life/nostalgic farewell to an innocent age. Soap opera with heart and soul, breathing life into both the time and place. That place is Archer City, a

backwater Texas town, and the time is the early fifties, when football jock buddies Bridges and Bottoms first cut their teeth in the Real World. Most of the story is played out at the local hangout run by Sam the Lion, an ex-cowboy both boys look up to. Bridges is hooked up with spoiled pretty girl Sheperd, while Bottoms, a sensitive guy, is having an affair with the coach's neglected wife (Leachman). Loss of innocence, disillusionment and confusion are played out against the backdrop of a town about to close its cinema. Shepherd's and Bottoms' film debut. Stunningly photographed in black and white (Bogdanovich claimed he didn't want to "prettify" the picture by shooting in color) by Robert Surtees. Available in a laserdisc special edition with 17 minutes restored. Followed by a weak sequel, "Texasville." A boxed set featuring both films is also available.
1971 (R) 118m/B Jeff Bridges, Timothy Bottoms, Ben Johnson, Cloris Leachman, Cybill Shepherd, Ellen Burstyn, Eileen Brennan, Clu Gulager, Sharon Taggart, Randy Quaid; D: Peter Bogdanovich. Academy Awards '71: Best Supporting Actor (Johnson), Best Supporting Actress (Leachman); Nominations: Best Adapted Screenplay, Best Cinematography, Best Director (Bogdanovich), Best Picture, Best Supporting Actor (Bridges), Best Supporting Actress (Burstyn); Golden Globe Awards '72: Best Supporting Actor (Johnson). VHS, LV, 8mm $19.95 COL, VYG, CRC ✍✍✍✍

Last Plane Out A Texas journalist sent out on assignment to Nicaragua falls in love with a Sandanista rebel. Based on producer Jack Cox's real-life experiences as a journalist during the last days of the Samosa regime. Low-budget propaganda.
1983 (R) 90m/C Jan-Michael Vincent, Lloyd Batista, Julie Carmen, Mary Crosby, David Huffman, William Windom; D: David Nelson. VHS, Beta $19.95 STE, FOX ✍½

The Last Polka SCTV vets Candy and Levy are Yosh and Stan Schmenge, polka kings interviewed for a "documentary" on their years in the spotlight and on the road. Hilarious spoof on Martin Scorsese's "The Last Waltz," about The Band's last concert. Several fellow Second City-ers keep the laughs coming. If you liked SCTV or "This is Spinal Tap," you'll like this. Made for cable (HBO).
1984 54m/C John Candy, Eugene Levy, Rick Moranis, Robin Duke, Catherine O'Hara; D: John Blanchard. VHS, Beta $19.98 LIV, VES ✍✍✍

The Last Porno Flick A pornographic movie script winds up in the hands of a couple of goofy cab drivers. The twosome sneak the movie's genre past the producers, families, and police.
1974 (PG) 90m/C Michael Pataki, Marianna Hill, Carmen Zapata, Mike Kellin, Colleen Camp, Tom Signorelli, Antony Carbone; D: Ray Marsh. VHS NO ✍

The Last Prostitute Two teenage boys search for a legendary prostitute to initiate them into manhood, only to discover that she has retired. They hire on as laborers on her horse farm, and one of them discovers the meaning of love. Made for cable TV.
1991 (PG-13) 93m/C Sonia Braga, Wil Wheaton, David Kaufman, Woody Watson, Dennis Letts, Cotter Smith; D: Lou Antonio. VHS $89.95 MCA ✍✍

The Last Radio Station A mini-musical with a largely Motown soundtrack about a failing radio station supported by old rock songs: "Reflections," "Nowhere to Run," "Dancing in the Street" and others.
1986 60m/C VHS, Beta, LV $19.95 MCA, MVD ✍✍

The Last Remake of Beau Geste A slapstick parody of the familiar Foreign Legion story from the Mel Brooks-ish school of loud genre farce. Gary Cooper makes an appearance by way of inserted footage from the 1939 straight version.
1977 (PG) 85m/C Marty Feldman, Ann-Margret, Michael York, Peter Ustinov, James Earl Jones; D: Marty Feldman. VHS, Beta $14.95 MCA ✍✍

Last Resort A married furniture executive unknowingly takes his family on vacation to a sex-saturated, Club Med-type holiday spot, and gets more than he anticipated. *AKA:* She Knew No Other Way.
1986 (R) 80m/C Charles Grodin, Jon Lovitz; D: Zane Buzby. VHS, Beta, LV $79.98 LIV, VES ✍✍

Last Reunion Rare British ghost story starring Gough.
1955 ?m/C GB Michael Gough. VHS $20 SMW ✍✍

The Last Reunion The only witness to a brutal killing of a Japanese official and his wife during WWII seeks revenge on the guilty American platoon, thirty-three years later. Violent.
1980 98m/C Cameron Mitchell, Leo Fong, Chanda Romero, Vic Silayan, Hal Bokar, Philip Baker Hall; D: Jay Wertz. VHS $16.95 SNC ✍½

The Last Ride Another movie probing the dark side of hitchhiking. This time our hero thumbs a ride with a truck driver who plans to bypass the next city...for hell.
1991 84m/C Dan Ranger, Michael Hilow. VHS $79.98 AIP ✍

The Last Ride of the Dalton Gang A long-winded retelling of the wild adventures that made the Dalton gang legendary among outlaws.
1979 146m/C Larry Wilcox, Jack Palance, Randy Quaid, Cliff Potts, Dale Robertson, Don Collier; D: Dan Curtis. VHS, Beta $19.98 WAR, OM ✍✍

The Last Riders Motorcycle centaur Estrada revs a few motors fleeing from cycle club cronies and crooked cops. Full throttle foolishness.
1990 (R) 90m/C Erik Estrada, William Smith, Armando Silvestre, Kathrin Lautner; D: Joseph Merhi. VHS, LV $19.95 PMH, HHE ✍

Last Rites A priest at St. Patrick's Cathedral in New York allows a young Mexican woman to seek sanctuary from the Mob, who soon come after both of them.
1988 (R) 103m/C Tom Berenger, Daphne Zuniga, Chick Vennera, Dane Clark, Carlo Pacchi, Anne Twomey, Paul Dooley, Vassili Lambrinos; D: Donald P. Bellisario. VHS, Beta, LV $19.98 FOX ✍✍

The Last Safari A young man on safari in Africa befriends a bitter professional guide in a drama hampered by a poor script. Granger and Garas set out to hunt the rampaging elephant which killed Granger's friend. Granger thinks killing the beast will restore his courage and help him overcome the guilt he feels. Based on the novel "Gilligan's Last Elephant" by Gerald Hanley.
1967 111m/C Stewart Granger, Kaz Garas, Gabriella Licudi, Johnny Sekka, Liam Redmond; D: Henry Hathaway. VHS $14.95 PAR ✍✍½

The Last Season Shoot 'em up involving a bunch of hunters. Their aimless destruction provokes the good guy to save the forest they are demolishing. A battle ensues.
1987 90m/C Christopher Gosch, Louise Dorsey, David Cox; D: Raja Zahr. VHS TPV Woof!

The Last Slumber Party A slumber party is beset by a homicidal maniac. Heavy metal soundtrack.
1987 89m/C Jan Jensen, Nancy Meyer. VHS, Beta $19.95 UHV Woof!

L

Last Song A singer's husband discovers a plot to cover up a fatal toxic-waste accident, and is killed because of it. It's up to her to warn the authorities before becoming the next victim.
1980 (PG) 96m/C Lynda Carter, Ronny Cox, Nicholas Pryor, Paul Rudd, Jenny O'Hara; *D:* Alan J. Levi. VHS, Beta $59.98 FOX ⅋½

The Last Starfighter A young man who becomes an expert at a video game is recruited to fight in an inter-galactic war. Listless adventure which explains where all those video games come from. Watch for O'Herlihy disguised as a lizard.
1984 (PG) 100m/C Lance Guest, Robert Preston, Barbara Bosson, Dan O'Herlihy, Catherine Mary Stewart, Cameron Dye, Kimberly Ross, Wil Wheaton; *D:* Nick Castle. VHS, Beta, LV $19.95 MCA ⅋⅋

Last Summer Three teenagers discover love, sex, and friendship on the white sands of Fire Island, N.Y. The summer vacation fantasy world they create shatters when a sweet but homely female teenager joins their group. Based on a novel by Evan Hunter.
1969 (R) 97m/C Barbara Hershey, Richard Thomas, Bruce Davison, Cathy Burns; *D:* Frank Perry. VHS, Beta $59.98 FOX ⅋⅋½

The Last Supper A repentant Cuban slave-owner in the 18th-century decides to cleanse his soul and convert his slaves to Christianity by having twelve of them reenact the Last Supper. Based on a true story. In Spanish with English subtitles.
1976 110m/C SP Nelson Villagra, Silvano Rey, Lamberto Garcia, Jose Antonio Rodriguez, Samuel Claxton, Mario Balmasada, Thomas Gutierrez Alea. VHS, Beta $69.95 NYF, FCT, TAM ⅋⅋⅋

Last Tango in Paris Rated "X" upon release. Brando plays a middle-aged American who meets a French girl and tries to forget his wife's suicide with a short, extremely steamy affair. Bertolucci proves to be a master; Brando gives one of his best performances. Very controversial when made, still quite explicit. Visually stunning.
1973 (R) 129m/C IT FR Marlon Brando, Maria Schneider, Jean-Pierre Leaud; *D:* Bernardo Bertolucci. Academy Awards '73 Nominations: Best Actor (Brando), Best Director (Bertolucci); New York Film Critics Awards '73: Best Actor (Brando); National Society of Film Critics Awards '73: Best Actor (Brando). VHS, Beta, LV $19.98 MGM, FOX, VYG ⅋⅋⅋½

The Last Temptation of Christ Scorcese's controversial adaptation of the Nikos Kazantzakis novel, portraying Christ in his last year as an ordinary Israelite tormented by divine doubt, human desires and the voice of God. The controversy engulfing the film, as it was heavily protested and widely banned, tended to divert attention from what is an exceptional statement of religious and artistic vision. Excellent score by Peter Gabriel.
1988 (R) 164m/C Willem Dafoe, Harvey Keitel, Barbara Hershey, Harry Dean Stanton, Andre Gregory, David Bowie, Verna Bloom, Juliette Caton, John Lurie, Roberts Blossom, Irvin Kershner, Barry Miller, Tomas Arana, Nehemiah Persoff, Paul Herman; *D:* Martin Scorsese; *W:* Paul Schrader. VHS, Beta, LV $19.95 MCA ⅋⅋½

The Last Time I Saw Paris A successful writer reminisces about his love affair with a wealthy American girl in post-World War II Paris.
1954 116m/C Elizabeth Taylor, Van Johnson, Walter Pidgeon, Roger Moore, Donna Reed, Eva Gabor; *D:* Richard Brooks. VHS, Beta, LV $19.98 MGM, MRV, NOS ⅋⅋½

The Last Tomahawk Colorful and action packed reworking of Cooper's "Last of the Mohicans."
1965 ?m/C GE IT Anthony Steffen, Karin Dor, Dan Martin, Joachim Fuchsberger. VHS $16.95 SNC ⅋⅋

The Last Train Romance most hopeless in the heart of France during zee beeg war. French, very French.
1974 ?m/C Romy Schneider, Jean-Louis Trintignant. VHS, Beta $59.99 WWV ⅋⅋

Last Train from Gun Hill An all-star cast highlights this suspenseful story of a U.S. marshall determined to catch the man who raped and murdered his wife. Excellent action packed western.
1959 94m/C Kirk Douglas, Anthony Quinn, Carolyn Jones, Earl Holliman, Brad Dexter, Brian Hutton, Ziva Rodann; *D:* John Sturges. VHS $19.95 STE ⅋⅋⅋

The Last Tycoon An adaptation of the unfinished F. Scott Fitzgerald novel about the life and times of a Hollywood movie executive of the 1920s. Confusing and slow moving despite a blockbuster conglomeration of talent. Joan Collins introduces the film.
1976 (PG) 123m/C Robert De Niro, Tony Curtis, Ingrid Boulting, Jack Nicholson, Jeanne Moreau, Peter Strauss, Robert Mitchum, Theresa Russell, Donald Pleasence, Ray Milland, Dana Andrews, John Carradine, Anjelica Huston; *D:* Elia Kazan; *W:* Harold Pinter. Academy Awards '76 Nominations: Best Art Direction/Set Decoration; National Board of Review Awards '76: 10 Best Films of the Year. VHS, Beta, LV $19.95 PAR, PIA, FCT ⅋⅋⅋

The Last Unicorn Peter Beagle's popular tale of a beautiful unicorn who goes in search of her lost, mythical "family." Music by Jimmy Webb.
1982 (G) 95m/C *D:* Jules Bass; *V:* Alan Arkin, Jeff Bridges, Tammy Grimes, Angela Lansbury, Mia Farrow, Robert Klein, Christopher Lee, Keenan Wynn. VHS, Beta, LV $19.95 JTC, FOX, KAH ⅋⅋½

The Last Valley A scholar tries to protect a pristine 17th century Swiss valley, untouched by the Thirty Years War, from marauding soldiers. Historical action with an intellectual twist.
1971 (PG) 128m/C Michael Caine, Omar Sharif, Florinda Bolkan, Nigel Davenport, Per Oscarsson, Arthur O'Connell; *D:* James Clavell; *M:* John Barry. VHS ABC ⅋

The Last Voyage Suspenseful disaster film in which Stack and Malone play a married couple in jeopardy while on an ocean cruise. To make the film more realistic, the French liner Ile de France was actually used in the sinking scenes. Although a bit far-fetched, film is made watchable because of fine performances and excellent camerawork.
1960 91m/C Robert Stack, Dorothy Malone, George Sanders, Edmond O'Brien, Woody Strode, Jack Kruschen; *W/D:* Andrew L. Stone. VHS $19.98 MGM ⅋⅋½

The Last Waltz Martin Scorsese filmed this rock documentary featuring the farewell performance of The Band, joined by a host of musical guests that they have been associated with over the years. Songs include: "Up On Cripple Creek," "Don't Do It," "The Night They Drove Old Dixie Down," "Stage Fright" (The Band), "Helpless" (Young), "Coyote" (Mitchell), "Caravan" (Morrison), "Further On Up the Road" (Clapton), "Who Do You Love" (Hawkins), "Mannish Boy" (Waters), "Evangeline" (Harris), "Baby, Let Me Follow You Down" (Dylan).

1978 (PG) 117m/C The Band, Bob Dylan, Neil Young, Joni Mitchell, Van Morrison, Eric Clapton, Neil Diamond, Emmylou Harris, Muddy Waters, Ronnie Hawkins; *D:* Martin Scorsese. VHS, Beta, LV $19.95 MVD, MGM ⅋⅋½

Last War A nuclear war between the United States and Russia triggers Armageddon.
1968 79m/C Frankie Sakai, Nobuko Otowa, Akira Takarada, Yuriko Hoshi; *D:* Shue Matsubayashi. VHS, Beta $19.95 GEM ⅋

The Last Warrior A good-looking but exploitive "Hell in the Pacific" rip-off, as an American and a Japanese soldier battle it out alone on a remote island during World War II. *AKA:* Coastwatcher.
1989 (R) 94m/C Gary Graham, Cary-Hiroyuki Tagawa, Maria Holvoe; *D:* Martin Wragge. VHS, Beta, LV $14.95 SVS, COL ⅋½

The Last Wave An Australian attorney takes on a murder case involving an aborigine and he finds himself becoming distracted by apocalyptic visions concerning tidal waves and drownings that seem to foretell the future. Weir's masterful creation and communication of time and place are marred by a somewhat pat ending.
1977 (PG) 109m/C AU Richard Chamberlain, Olivia Hamnett, David Gulpilil, Frederick Parslow; *D:* Peter Weir. VHS, Beta FCT, RHI ⅋⅋⅋

The Last Winter An American woman fights to find her Israeli husband who has disappeared in the 1973 Yom Kippur War. Trouble is, an Israeli woman thinks the man she's looking for is really her husband too.
1984 (R) 92m/C IS Kathleen Quinlan, Yona Ellan, Zipora Peled, Michael Schnider; *D:* Riki Shelach. VHS, Beta $79.95 COL ⅋⅋

The Last Winters From Jean Charles Tacchella, writer-producer-director of "Cousin Cousine," comes his first short film about an old couple's bittersweet romance. In French with English subtitles.
1971 23m/C FR *D:* Jean-Charles Tacchella. VHS, Beta $79.98 INT, MTI ⅋⅋½

Last Witness A man on the run from the government claims that he is innocent and was unjustly persecuted, but the government sees him as a dangerous threat. Nothing will stop the hunt for the escaped man, no matter what it costs.
1988 85m/C Jeff Henderson. VHS, Beta $79.95 TWE ⅋

The Last Woman on Earth Two men vie for the affections of the sole surviving woman after a vague and unexplained disaster of vast proportions. Robert Towne, who appears herein under the pseudonym Edward Wain, wrote the script (his first screenwriting effort). You might want to watch this if it were the last movie on earth, although Corman fans will probably love it.
1961 71m/C Antony Carbone, Edward Wain, Betsy Jones-Moreland; *D:* Roger Corman; *W:* Robert Towne. VHS $16.95 NOS, MRV, SNC Woof!

The Last Word Comedy drama about struggling inventor Harris fighting to protect his home, family, and neighbors from a corrupt real estate deal involving shady politicians, angry policemen, and a beautiful television reporter. *AKA:* Danny Travis.
1980 (PG) 103m/C Richard Harris, Karen Black, Martin Landau, Dennis Christopher, Bill McGuire, Christopher Guest, Penelope Milford, Michael Pataki. VHS, Beta $69.98 SUE ⅋⅋

Last Year at Marienbad A young man tries to lure a mysterious woman to run away with him from a hotel in France. Once a hit on the artsy circuit, it's most interesting for its beautiful photography. In French with

English subtitles. *AKA:* L'Anee Derniere a Marienbad.

1961 93m/B *FR IT* Delphine Seyrig, Giorgia Albertazzi, Sacha Pitoeff, Luce Garcia-Ville; *D:* Alain Resnais. **VHS, Beta, 8mm, 3/4U, Special order formats** $29.95 *NOS, MRV, VYY* 🎦🎦🎦

L'Atalante Vigo's great masterpiece, a slight story about a husband and wife quarreling, splitting, and reuniting around which has been fashioned one of the cinema's greatest poetic films. In French with English subtitles.

1934 82m/B *FR* Dita Parlo, Jean Daste, Michel Simon; *D:* Jean Vigo. **VHS, Beta** $24.95 *NOS, HHT, PMS* 🎦🎦🎦½

Late Chrysanthemums A middle-aged geisha has settled into comfortable retirement as a money lender. When she hears a former lover wants to visit her, she tries to recapture her old glamour only to be disillusioned. Based on a short story by Fumiko Hayashi. In Japanese with English subtitles.

1954 101m/B *JP* Haruko Sugimura, Chikako Hosokawa, Sadako Sawahura; *D:* Mikio Naruse. **VHS** $79.95 *WAC, TAM* 🎦🎦

Late Extra A novice reporter attempts to track down a notorious bank robber and gets some help from a savvy female journalist. Mason's first role of substance.

1935 69m/B *GB* Virginia Cherrill, James Mason, Alastair Sim, Ian Colin, Clifford McLaglen, Cyril Cusack, David Horne, Antoinette Cellier, Donald Wolfit, Michael Wilding; *D:* Albert Parker. **VHS, Beta** $16.95 *SNC* 🎦🎦

Late for Dinner In 1962 Willie, a young, married man, and his best friend Frank are framed by a sleazy land developer. On the run, the two decide to become guinea pigs in a cryonics experiment and wind up frozen for 29 years. It's now 1991 and Willie wants to find his family—only his wife is middle-aged and his daughter is all grown-up. Can he make a life with them again or has time indeed passed him by?

1991 (PG) 93m/C Brian Wimmer, Peter Berg, Marcia Gay Harden, Peter Gallagher; *D:* W.D. Richter. **VHS, LV** $19.95 *COL, NLC* 🎦🎦

The Late Show A veteran private detective finds his world turned upside down when his ex-partner comes to visit and winds up dead, and a flaky woman whose cat is missing decides to become his sidekick. Carney and Tomlin are fun to watch in this sleeper, a tribute to the classic detective film noirs.

1977 (PG) 93m/C Art Carney, Lily Tomlin, Bill Macy, Eugene Roche, Joanna Cassidy, John Considine; *D:* Robert Benton. Academy Awards '77 Nominations: Best Original Screenplay; Edgar Allan Poe Awards '77: Best Screenplay; National Board of Review Awards '77: 10 Best Films of the Year. **VHS, Beta, LV** $64.95 *WAR* 🎦🎦🎦

Late Spring An exquisite Ozu masterpiece. A young woman lives with her widowed father for years. He decides to remarry so that she can begin life for herself. Highly acclaimed, in Japanese with English subtitles. Reworked in 1960 as "Late Autumn."

1949 107m/B *JP* Setsuko Hara, Chishu Ryu, Jun Usami, Haruko Sugimura; *D:* Yasujiro Ozu. **VHS, Beta** $49.95 *FCT* 🎦🎦🎦🎦

Late Summer Blues Experience the life and death decisions of seven teenagers who have finished their finals and face now a more difficult test: serving in the Israeli Armed Forces in the Suez Canal. In Hebrew with English subtitles. *AKA:* Blues La-Chofesh Ha-Godol.

1987 101m/C *IS* Dor Zweigenbom, Shahar Segal, Yoav Zafir; *D:* Renen Schorr. **VHS** $79.95 *HMV, AUD* 🎦🎦

Lathe of Heaven In a late twentieth century world suffocating from pollution, a young man visits a dream specialist. He then dreams of a world free from war, pestilence, and overpopulation. At times, these dreams have disastrous side effects. Based on futuristic novel by Ursula K. LeGuin; produced for PBS.

1980 120m/C Bruce Davison, Kevin Conway, Margaret Avery; *D:* David Loxton. **VHS, Beta** *WNE* 🎦🎦½

Latin Lovers Turner plays a wealthy heiress who can't decide if men love her for herself or her money in this festive Brazilian romp. Lund and Montalban portray the suitors vying for her affection. Although not one of MGM's best musicals, the music is good because of the Brodszky-Robin tunes. ♫Night and You; Carlotta, You Gotta Be Mine; A Little More of Your Armor; Come To My Arms; I Had To Kiss You.

1953 104m/C Lana Turner, Ricardo Montalban, John Lund, Louis Calhern, Jean Hagen, Eduard Franz, Beulah Bondi; *D:* Mervyn LeRoy; *W:* Isobel Lennart. **VHS** $19.98 *MGM* 🎦🎦½

Latino The self-tortured adventures of a Chicano Green Beret who, while fighting a covert U.S. military action in war-torn Nicaragua, begins to rebel against the senselessness of the war.

1985 108m/C Robert Beltran, Annette Cardona, Tony Plana; *D:* Haskell Wexler. **VHS, Beta, LV** $79.98 *FOX, TAM* 🎦🎦½

Lauderdale Two college schmoes hit the beach looking for beer and babes. Few laughs for the sober and mature. Surf's down in this woofer.

1989 (R) 91m/C Darrel Gilbeau, Michelle Kemp, Jeff Greenman, Lara Belmonte; *D:* Bill Milling. **VHS, Beta, LV** $59.99 *PAR* Woof!

Laugh with Linder! Compilation of Linder shorts, including "Max Learns to Skate" and "Max and His Dog."

1913 70m/B Max Linder. **VHS, Beta** $47.50 *GVV* Woof!

Laughfest Five classic slapstick shorts: "It's a Gift" (1923), with Snub Pollard, "Barney Oldfield's Race for a Life" (1913), "Kid Auto Races" and "Busy Day" (1914), both with Charlie Chaplin, and "Daredevil" (1923), starring Ben Turpin.

191? 59m/B Ben Turpin, Barney Oldfield, Mabel Normand, Charlie Chaplin, Snub Pollard. **VHS, Beta** $19.98 *CCB* Woof!

Laughing at Life A mercenary leaves his family to fight in South America. Years later, when he is the leader of said country, he meets a man who turns out to be his son. Rehashed plot has been done better.

1933 72m/B Victor McLaglen, William Boyd, Lois Wilson, Henry B. Walthall, Regis Toomey; *D:* Ford Beebe. **VHS** $24.95 *NOS, DVT, HEG* 🎦½

Laughing Policeman Two antagonistic cops embark on a vengeful hunt for a mass murderer through the seamy underbelly of San Francisco. Adapted from the Swedish novel by Per Wahloo and Maj Sjowallo. *AKA:* An Investigation of Murder.

1974 (R) 111m/C Walter Matthau, Bruce Dern, Louis Gossett Jr.; *D:* Stuart Rosenberg. **VHS, Beta** $59.98 *FOX* 🎦🎦½

Laughing Sinners Society girl Crawford attempts suicide after Hamilton dumps her and is rescued by Gable—a Salvation Army worker! Predictable drama with some unintentionally funny moments. Gable and Crawford were having an off-screen romance at the time which accounts for the sparks generated on-screen. Based on the play "Torch Song" by Kenyon Nicholson.

1931 71m/B Joan Crawford, Neil Hamilton, Clark Gable, Marjorie Rambeau, Guy Kibbee, Cliff Edwards, Roscoe Karns; *D:* Harry Beaumont. **VHS** $19.98 *MGM* 🎦🎦

Laura A detective assigned to the murder investigation of the late Laura Hunt finds himself falling in love with her painted portrait. Superb collaboration by excellent cast and fine director. Superior suspense yarn, enhanced by a love story. Based on the novel by Vera Caspary. Rouben Mamoulian was the original director, then Preminger finished the film. Score by David Raskin.

1944 85m/B Gene Tierney, Dana Andrews, Clifton Webb, Lane Chandler, Vincent Price, Judith Anderson, Grant Mitchell, Dorothy Adams; *D:* Otto Preminger. Academy Awards '44: Best Black and White Cinematography; Nominations: Best Director (Preminger), Best Interior Decoration, Best Screenplay, Best Supporting Actor (Webb). **VHS, Beta, LV** $19.98 *FXV, PMS* 🎦🎦🎦🎦

Laurel & Hardy and the Family Four zany comedies seeing the boys in all kinds of trouble involving homelife. Includes "Brats," "Perfect Day," "Their First Mistake" and "Twice Two."

1933 85m/B Stan Laurel, Oliver Hardy. **VHS** $14.98 *VTR, FCT* 🎦🎦🎦🎦

Laurel & Hardy: Another Fine Mess The boys find themselves the owners of a magnificent Beverly Hills mansion. Yeah right. Lots of physical comedy and hilarious dialogue with a "special appearance" by Laurel in drag as a maid. Based on a sketch written by Laurel's father. Colorized.

1930 37m/C Stan Laurel, Oliver Hardy. **VHS** $9.95 *CAF* 🎦🎦🎦🎦

Laurel & Hardy: At Work Three short films collected here. Includes "Towed in a Hole," "Busy Bodies," and "The Music Box."

1932 70m/B Oliver Hardy, Stan Laurel. **VHS** $14.98 *VTR, FCT* 🎦🎦🎦🎦

Laurel & Hardy: Be Big Stan and Ollie ditch their wives to go to a swinging stag party at their club. Of course everything goes wrong in their quest for lascivious fun. Filled with tons of sight gags. Colorized.

1931 25m/C Stan Laurel, Oliver Hardy. **VHS** $9.95 *CAF, MOV* 🎦🎦🎦🎦

Laurel & Hardy: Below Zero It's the Great Depression of 1929, and Laurel and Hardy are about as depressed as you can get, working for pennies as street musicians. Their luck changes when they find a full wallet lying in the snow. But, as the saying goes, a fool and his money are soon parted. Colorized.

1930 25m/C Stan Laurel, Oliver Hardy. **VHS** $9.95 *CAF, MOV* 🎦🎦🎦🎦

Laurel & Hardy: Berth Marks Laurel & Hardy take a hilarious train trip to Pottsville for a vaudeville performance. Colorized.

1929 25m/C Stan Laurel, Oliver Hardy. **VHS** $9.95 *CAF* 🎦🎦🎦🎦

Laurel & Hardy: Blotto Laurel and Hardy want to get drunk, but they can't get any alcohol and their wives won't let them get away. When they finally do escape, they wind up at the swanky Rainbow Club, where they're drastically out of their element. Colorized.

1930 25m/C Stan Laurel, Oliver Hardy. **VHS** $9.95 *CAF* 🎦🎦🎦🎦

Laurel & Hardy: Brats Stan and Ollie play not only themselves but also their children when their wives go away and they have to babysit. The children, of course, wreak havoc wherever they go, playing on

the hilariously oversized props and sets. One of the few films in which only Laurel and Hardy appear. Colorized.
1930 25m/C Stan Laurel, Oliver Hardy. **VHS $9.95** *CAF, MOV* 🐾🐾🐾🐾

Laurel & Hardy: Chickens Come Home Ollie is running for mayor, but things go crazy when an ex-girlfriend shows up and blackmails him with a compromising photo. Stan, acting as Ollie's campaign manager, tries to help, but things just get worse. A remake of their own film "Love 'Em and Weep." Colorized.
1931 25m/C Stan Laurel, Oliver Hardy, James Finlayson. **VHS $9.95** *CAF, MOV* 🐾🐾🐾🐾

Laurel & Hardy Comedy Classics, Vol. 1 A collection of four classic comedy shorts starring Laurel and Hardy: "The Music Box," which won an Academy Award for Best Short Subject, "Country Hospital," "The Live Ghost," and "Twice Two," all from 1932-33.
1933 84m/B Stan Laurel, Oliver Hardy, Mae Busch, May Wallace, Charlie Hall, Billy Gilbert. **VHS, Beta $9.95** *MED* 🐾🐾🐾🐾

Laurel & Hardy Comedy Classics, Vol. 2 A collection of four Laurel and Hardy shorts from 1930 including "Blotto," "Towed in a Hole," "Brats," and "Hog Wild."
1930 75m/B Stan Laurel, Oliver Hardy, Billy Gilbert, Tiny Sandford, Anita Garvin. **VHS, Beta $9.95** *MED* 🐾🐾🐾🐾

Laurel & Hardy Comedy Classics, Vol. 3 Laurel and Hardy star in four separate comedy shorts, including "Oliver the 8th," "Busy Bodies," "Their First Mistake," and "Dirty Work," all from 1933-34.
1934 75m/B Stan Laurel, Oliver Hardy, Billy Gilbert, Mae Busch, Tiny Sandford. **VHS, Beta $9.95** *MED* 🐾🐾🐾🐾

Laurel & Hardy Comedy Classics, Vol. 4 Laurel and Hardy star in four of their comedy shorts from 1931-32. Included are "Another Fine Mess," "Come Clean," "Laughing Gravy," and "Any Old Part."
1932 75m/B Stan Laurel, Oliver Hardy, Jacqueline Wells, James Finlayson, Thelma Todd. **VHS, Beta $9.95** *MED* 🐾🐾🐾🐾

Laurel & Hardy Comedy Classics, Vol. 5 Four classic comedy shorts starring Laurel and Hardy. Included are "Be Big," "The Perfect Day," "Night Owls," and "Help Mates," from 1929-31.
1931 84m/B Stan Laurel, Oliver Hardy, Edgar Kennedy, James Finlayson, Blanche Payson. **VHS, Beta $19.95** *MED* 🐾🐾🐾🐾

Laurel & Hardy Comedy Classics, Vol. 6 Laurel and Hardy comedy shorts are presented in this package: "Our Wife," "The Fixer Uppers," "Them Thar Hills," and "Tit for Tat," from 1932-35.
1935 75m/B Stan Laurel, Oliver Hardy, Charlie Hall, Billy Gilbert, Ben Turpin, Mae Busch, James Finlayson. **VHS, Beta $19.95** *MED* 🐾🐾🐾🐾

Laurel & Hardy Comedy Classics, Vol. 7 Four Laurel and Hardy two-reelers are combined on this tape: "Me and My Pal" (1933), "The Midnight Patrol" (1933), "Thicker than Water" (1935), and the classic "Below Zero" (1930).
1937 90m/B Stan Laurel, Oliver Hardy, Mae Busch, Daphne Pollard, James Finlayson. **VHS, Beta $19.95** *MED* 🐾🐾🐾🐾

Laurel & Hardy Comedy Classics, Vol. 8 Compilation of Laurel and Hardy shorts includes: "Men O' War" (1929), "Scram" (1932), "Laurel and Hardy Murder Case" (1930) and "One Good Turn" (1931).
193? 90m/B Stan Laurel, Oliver Hardy, Lewis R. Foster, James W. Horne, James Parrott. **VHS, Beta $19.95** *MED* 🐾🐾🐾🐾

Laurel & Hardy Comedy Classics, Vol. 9 Includes the shorts: "Beau Hunks" (1931), "Chickens Come Home" (1931), "Going Bye-Bye" (1934), and "Berth Marks" (1929).
193? 100m/B Stan Laurel, Oliver Hardy. **VHS, Beta $19.95** *MED* 🐾🐾🐾🐾

Laurel & Hardy: Hog Wild Hilarity ensues when Laurel and Hardy try to fix the radio antenna on Hardy's roof. It may sound easy, but come on, this is Laurel and Hardy. Colorized.
1930 25m/C Stan Laurel, Oliver Hardy. **VHS $9.95** *CAF, MOV* 🐾🐾🐾🐾

Laurel & Hardy: Laughing Gravy The boys' pet dog, oddly named Laughing Gravy, gets them into trouble with their landlord who keeps trying to evict them. So funny even the mashed potatos will laugh. Colorized.
1931 25m/C Stan Laurel, Oliver Hardy. **VHS $9.95** *CAF, MOV* 🐾🐾🐾🐾

Laurel & Hardy: Men O'War Laurel & Hardy star as two sailors on shore leave trying to impress the ladies. Things go from bad to worse when they take two ladies out on a date. Features the memorable soda fountain and canoe scenes. Colorized.
1929 25m/C Stan Laurel, Oliver Hardy, Gloria Greer, Anne Cornwall. **VHS $9.95** *CAF* 🐾🐾🐾🐾

Laurel & Hardy: Night Owls When a cop needs to capture some crooks to save his job, he sets up a fake break-in and catches two bungling burglars—Laurel and Hardy. Lots of sight gags and slapstick. Colorized.
1930 25m/C Stan Laurel, Oliver Hardy, Edgar Kennedy. **VHS $9.95** *CAF, MOV* 🐾🐾🐾🐾

Laurel & Hardy On the Lam Four Laurel & Hardy classics are collected, including "Scram," "Another Fine Mess," "One Good Turn," and "Going Bye-Bye."
1930 90m/B Oliver Hardy, Stan Laurel. **VHS $14.98** *VTR, FCT* 🐾🐾🐾🐾

Laurel & Hardy: Perfect Day Laurel & Hardy plan a quiet picnic with their wives, but car trouble turns their day into a disaster. Colorized.
1929 25m/C Stan Laurel, Oliver Hardy, Edgar Kennedy. **VHS $9.95** *CAF* 🐾🐾🐾🐾

Laurel & Hardy Special A unique program of Laurel and Hardy films including the first film they appeared in together—"Lucky Dog" (1918), "The Soilers," a wild Laurel spoof of The Spoilers, "Kill or Cure," "Near Dublin," "The Sleuths," "Laurel and Hardy's Trip to Britain," and "Stan Visits Ollie," a color home movie of their last visit together.
19?? 60m/B Stan Laurel, Oliver Hardy. **VHS, Beta $57.95** *GVV* 🐾🐾½

Laurel & Hardy Spooktacular Stan and Ollie scream through four spooky comedies, including "The Live Ghost," "The Laurel-Hardy Murder Case," "Oliver the Eighth" and "Dirty Work."
1934 95m/B **VHS $14.98** *VTR, FCT* 🐾🐾½

Laurel & Hardy: Stan "Helps" Ollie Four Stan and Ollie classics including "County Hospital," "Me and My Pal," "Hog Wild" and "Helpmates."
1933 85m/B Stan Laurel, Oliver Hardy. **VHS $14.98** *VTR, FCT* 🐾🐾½

Laurel & Hardy: The Hoose-Gow Laurel and Hardy are mistakenly picked up by the police and sent to prison to do hard labor. Hilarity ensues when they try to convince the warden that they're innocent. Colorized.
1929 25m/C VHS $9.95 *CAF, MOV* 🐾🐾½

Laurel & Hardy, Vol. 1 Animated adventures of Laurel and Hardy.
196? 59m/C VHS, Beta *NO* 🐾🐾½

Laurel & Hardy, Vol. 2 Animated short cartoons starring Laurel and Hardy.
196? 59m/C VHS, Beta *NO* 🐾🐾½

Laurel & Hardy, Vol. 3 More animated adventures of Laurel and Hardy.
196? 59m/C VHS, Beta *NO* 🐾🐾½

Laurel & Hardy, Vol. 4 Animated shorts starring cartoon characters of Laurel and Hardy.
196? 59m/C VHS, Beta *NO* 🐾🐾½

The Lavender Hill Mob A prim and prissy bank clerk schemes to melt the bank's gold down and re-mold it into miniature Eiffel Tower paper-weights for later resale. The foolproof plan appears to succeed, but then develops a snag. An excellent comedy that is still a delight to watch. Also available with "The Man in the White Suit" on laserdisc.
1951 78m/B *GB* Alec Guinness, Stanley Holloway, Sidney James, Alfie Bass, Marjorie Fielding, John Gregson, *Cameos:* Audrey Hepburn; *D:* Charles Crichton; *W:* T.E.B. Clarke. Academy Awards '52: Best Story & Screenplay; Nominations: Best Actor (Guinness); British Academy Awards '51: Best Film. **VHS, Beta, LV $19.98** *HBO, FCT, HMV* 🐾🐾🐾½

L'Avventura A stark, dry and minimalist exercise in narrative by Antonioni, dealing with the search for a girl on an Italian island by her lethargic socialite friends who eventually forget her in favor of their own preoccupations. A highly acclaimed, innovative film, somewhat less effective now, in the wake of many film treatments of angst and amorality. Subtitled in English. Laser edition features the original trailer, commentary and a collection of still photographs from Antonioni's work. *AKA:* The Adventure.
1960 145m/C *IT* Monica Vitti, Gabriele Ferzetti, Lea Massari, Dominique Blanchar, James Addams; *D:* Michelangelo Antonioni. **VHS, Beta, LV $29.95** *CVC, VDM, VYG* 🐾🐾½

Law and Disorder Two average Joes, fed up with the rate of rising crime, start their own auxiliary police group. Alternately funny and serious with good performances from the leads.
1974 (R) 103m/C Carroll O'Connor, Ernest Borgnine, Ann Wedgeworth, Anita Dangler, Leslie Ackerman, Karen Black, Jack Kehoe; *D:* Ivan Passer; *M:* Angelo Badalamenti. **VHS** *COL* 🐾🐾🐾

The Law and Jake Wade Gripping western starring Taylor as a former bank robber turned marshal. His old partner (Widmark) turns up and forces Taylor to lead him to buried loot.
1958 86m/C Robert Taylor, Richard Widmark, Patricia Owens, Robert Middleton, Henry Silva, DeForest Kelley, Burt Douglas, Eddie Firestone; *D:* John Sturges. **VHS $19.98** *MGM* 🐾🐾½

Law and Lawless A roving cowboy brings justice to a gang of cattle thieves in this film.

1933 58m/B Jack Hoxie. **VHS, Beta** $19.95 NOS, DVT 🎬

Law and Order Billy the Kid impersonates a Cavalry lieutenant in order to swindle his aunt out of her money. Also called ''Billy the Kid's Law and Order.''
1942 58m/B Buster Crabbe, Al ''Fuzzy'' St. John. **VHS, Beta** $9.95 VDM, MRV 🎬🎬

Law of Desire A wicked, Almodovarian attack-on-decency farce about a love-obsessed gay Madridian and his transsexual brother-sister, among others, getting hopelessly entangled in cross-gender relationships. Unlike the work of any other director; in Spanish with English subtitles. **AKA:** La Ley del Deseo.
1986 100m/C SP Carmen Maura, Eusebio Poncela, Antonio Banderas, Bibi Andersson; **D:** Pedro Almodovar. **VHS, Beta, LV** $79.95 CCN, TAM 🎬🎬🎬 ½

Law of the Jungle A lady scientist and a fugitive team up to uncover a secret Nazi radio base in the jungle.
1942 61m/B Arline Judge, John ''Dusty'' King, Mantan Moreland, Martin Wilkins, Arthur O'Connell; **D:** Jean Yarborough. **VHS, Beta** $16.95 SNC 🎬 ½

Law of the Land A made-for-television sagebrush epic with the author/artist of ''Garfield'' portraying an accused but innocent man searching for a murderer.
1976 100m/C Jim Davis, Don Johnson, Barbara Parkins, Charles Martin Smith. **VHS, Beta** $14.98 WOV 🎬

Law of the Lash Cowboys and rustlers battle it out.
1947 54m/B Lash LaRue, Al ''Fuzzy'' St. John. **VHS, Beta** $9.99 NOS, MRV, VCN 🎬

Law of the Pampas Boyd and Hayden ride off to South America to deliver some cattle, but the bad guys intervene. This is Toler's first outing as Hoppy's sidekick, briefly replacing ''Gabby'' Hayes.
1939 72m/B William Boyd, Russell Hayden, Steffi Duna, Sidney Toler, Sidney Blackmer, Pedro de Cordoba, Eddie Dean, Glenn Strange; **D:** Nate Watt. **VHS** $19.95 NOS 🎬

Law of the Saddle The Lone Rider pits himself against a gang of outlaws.
1945 60m/B Bob Livingston. **VHS, Beta** $29.95 VCN, MLB 🎬 ½

Law of the Sea A family on a sinking ship is rescued by a lecherous sea captain who makes advances on the wife and blinds the husband in a fight. Twenty years later, the husband meets him again, recognizes his laugh and exacts revenge.
1938 63m/B Priscilla Dean, Sally Blane, Ralph Ince, Rex Bell, William Farnum. **VHS, Beta, LV** $24.95 VYY 🎬

Law of the Underworld An innocent couple is framed for the robbery of a jewelry store which resulted in the death of a clerk. When they are arrested, their fate lies in the hands of the gangster responsible for the crime. Will he let them fry in the electric chair, or will his conscience get the better of him?
1938 58m/B Chester Morris, Anne Shirley, Eduardo Ciannelli, Walter Abel, Richard Bond, Lee Patrick, Paul Guilfoyle, Frank M. Thomas, Eddie Acuff, Jack Arnold; **D:** Lew Landers. **VHS, Beta** $16.95 SNC 🎬 ½

Law of the Wild The search for a magnificent stallion that was hijacked by race racketeers before a big sweepstakes race is shown in this 12 chapter serial.
1934 156m/B Rex, Rin Tin Tin Jr, Bob Custer. **VHS, Beta** $26.95 SNC, NOS, VCN 🎬 ½

The Law Rides Rush of gold claims causes an outbreak of murder and robbery.

1936 57m/B Bob Steele. **VHS, Beta** $29.95 DVT 🎬

The Law Rides Again Prairie lawmen bring a cheating Indian agent to justice.
1943 56m/B Ken Maynard, Hoot Gibson, Betty Miles, Jack LaRue; **D:** William Castle. **VHS** $19.95 NOS, MRV, DVT 🎬

Law West of Tombstone A former outlaw moves to a dangerous frontier town in order to restore the peace.
1938 73m/B Tim Holt, Harry Carey Sr., Evelyn Brent; **D:** Glenn Tryon. **VHS, Beta** MED 🎬🎬 ½

Lawless Frontier In the early West, the Duke fights for law and order.
1935 53m/B John Wayne, George ''Gabby'' Hayes, Sheila Terry, Earl Dwire; **D:** Robert North Bradbury. **VHS, Beta, 3/4U, Special order formats** $9.98 REP, NOS, VYY 🎬 ½

The Lawless Land Post-holocaust America is ruled by a tyrant. Two young lovers who can't take it anymore go on the lam to escape the despotic rule.
1988 (R) 81m/C Leon Berkeley, Xander Berkeley, Nick Corri, Amanda Peterson; **D:** Jon Hess. **VHS, Beta** $79.95 MGM 🎬

The Lawless Nineties Wayne plays a government agent sent to guarantee honest elections in the Wyoming territory. Hayes is exceptional as the newspaper editor who backs him up. Re-made in 1940 as ''The Dark Command.''
1936 55m/B John Wayne, Ann Rutherford, Lane Chandler, Harry Woods, George ''Gabby'' Hayes, Charles King, Sam Flint; **D:** Joseph Kane. **VHS** $12.98 REP 🎬🎬

Lawless Range Wayne and the marshal's posse save the ranchers from trouble.
1935 56m/B John Wayne, Sheila Manners, Jack Curtis, Earl Dwire; **D:** Robert Bradbury. **VHS** $9.98 REP, NOS, MRV 🎬 ½

A Lawless Street Scott portrays a sheriff who rides the Colorado Territory cleaning up lawless towns. His dedication to duty has caused his wife to leave him and she won't come back until he lays downs his guns forever, which may come sooner than they think after he rides into the corrupt town of Medicine Bend. Based on the novel ''Marshal of Medicine Bend'' by Brad Ward.
1955 78m/B Randolph Scott, Angela Lansbury, Warner Anderson, Jean Parker, Wallace Ford, John Emery, James Bell, Ruth Donnelly, Michael Pate, Don Megowan, Jeanette Nolan; **D:** Joseph H. Lewis; **W:** Kenneth Gamet. **VHS** $19.95 COL 🎬🎬 ½

Lawman Brutal western about a fanatical U.S. marshal (Lancaster) who rides into town after Cobb and his six ranch hands. The cowboys have accidentally killed a man and Lancaster is determined to bring them to justice no matter what the cost. Though the entire town is against him that doesn't stop his mission. Brooding and relentless with fine performances, particularly by Ryan as the local marshall living on past glories.
1971 (PG) 95m/C Burt Lancaster, Robert Ryan, Lee J. Cobb, Sheree North, Joseph Wiseman, Robert Duvall, Albert Salmi, J.D. Cannon, John McGiver, Richard Jordan, John Beck, Ralph Waite, John Hillerman, Richard Bull; **D:** Michael Winner; **W:** Gerald Wilson. **VHS** $19.98 MGM 🎬🎬🎬

A Lawman is Born A tough-as-nails marshal goes gunning for a pack of no-good, land-stealing varmits in this installment of the Johnny Mack Brown movie serials. Be sure to count the number of bullets each cowboy can fire from a six-shooter before being forced to reload; you may be surprised.

1937 58m/B Johnny Mack Brown, Iris Meredith, Warner Richmond, Mary MacLaren, Dick Curtis, Earle Hodgins, Charles King, Frank LaRue; **D:** Sam Newfield. **VHS, Beta** $19.99 NOS, MOV, MRV 🎬🎬🎬

Lawmen Government agents fight to enforce the law in the badlands.
1944 55m/B Johnny Mack Brown, Raymond Hatton. **VHS, Beta** $19.95 NOS, DVT 🎬 ½

The Lawnmower Man Brosnan is a scientist who uses Fahey, a dim-witted gardener, as a guinea pig to test his experiments in ''virtual reality,'' an artificial computer environment. With the use of drugs and high-tech equipment, Brosnan is able to increase Fahey's mental powers—but not necessarily for the better. Fantastic special effects and a memorable ''virtual reality'' sex scene. Based on a short story by Stephen King. Available in an unrated version which contains 32 more minutes of footage.
1992 (R) 108m/C Jeff Fahey, Pierce Brosnan, Jenny Wright, Mark Bringleson, Geoffrey Lewis, Jeremy Slate, Dean Norris; **D:** Brett Leonard; **W:** Brett Leonard, Gimel Everett. **VHS, LV** $94.95 COL, FCT, MOV 🎬🎬

Lawrence of Arabia Exceptional biography of T.E. Lawrence, a British military ''observer'' who strategically aids the Bedouins battle the Turks during World War I. Lawrence, played masterfully by O'Toole in his first major film, is a hero consumed more by a need to reject British tradition than to save the Arab population. He takes on Arab costume and a larger-than-life persona. Stunning photography of the desert in all its harsh reality. Laser edition contains 20 minutes of restored footage and a short documentary about the making of the film. Available in letterboxed format.
1962 (PG) 221m/C GB Peter O'Toole, Omar Sharif, Anthony Quinn, Alec Guinness, Jack Hawkins, Claude Rains, Anthony Quayle, Arthur Kennedy, Jose Ferrer; **D:** David Lean; **W:** Robert Bolt; **M:** Maurice Jarre. Academy Awards '62: Best Art Direction/Set Decoration (Color), Best Color Cinematography, Best Director (Lean), Best Film Editing, Best Picture, Best Sound, Best Original Score; Nominations: Best Actor (O'Toole), Best Adapted Screenplay, Best Supporting Actor (Sharif); British Academy Awards '62: Best Actor (O'Toole), Best Film; Directors Guild of America Awards '62: Best Director (Lean); Golden Globe Awards '63: Best Director (Lean), Best Film—Drama, Best Supporting Actor (Sharif). **VHS, Beta, LV** $34.95 COL, VYG, CRC 🎬🎬🎬🎬

The Lawrenceville Stories Chronicles the life and times of a group of young men at the prestigious Lawrenceville prep school in 1905. Galligan plays William Hicks, alias ''The Prodigious Hickey,'' the ringleader of their obnoxious stunts. Based on the stories of Owen Johnson, which originally ran in the Saturday Evening Post. Shown on ''American Playhouse'' and The Disney Channel. Tapes are available separately or as a set.
1987? 180m/C Zach Galligan, Edward Herrmann, Nicholas Rowe, Allan Goldstein, Robert Joy, Stephen Baldwin; **D:** Robert Iscove. **VHS** $69.95 MON 🎬🎬 ½

Laws of Gravity Critically acclaimed debut film from 29-year-old writer/director Gomez is a three day slice of life set in Brooklyn. Hotheaded Jon (Trese) and married friend Jimmy (Greene) channel violent energy into their relationships and illegal activities. Camera follows ''cinema verite'' style and captures urban tension as it trails them through a gun heist and subsequent arrest.

1992 (R) 100m/C Peter Greene, Edie Falco, Adam Trese, Arabella Field; **W/D:** Nick Gomez. VHS $89.95 TRI ✻✻✻

The Lazarus Syndrome Astute doctor teams up with an ex-patient of the chief of surgery in an effort to expose the chief's unethical surgical procedures. 1979 90m/C Louis Gossett Jr., E.G. Marshall. VHS, Beta NO ✻

LBJ: A Biography Produced for the PBS series "The American Experience," this four-hour revisionist look at LBJ is one of the most critically acclaimed political documentaries of our time. Divided into four segments. "Beautiful Texas" chronicles Johnson's rise to power. "My Fellow Americans" focuses on his years as an unelected president. The Great Society and and the escalation of war in Vietnam are covered in "We Shall Overcome." "The Last Believer" highlights events leading to Johnson's withdrawal from politics. 1991 240m/C **W/D:** David Grubin. VHS $39.95 PAV, PBS, SIG ✻✻✻

LBJ: The Early Years The early years of President Lyndon Balnes Johnson's political career are dramatized in this made-for-television movie. Winning performances hoist this above other biographies. 1988 144m/C Randy Quaid, Patti LuPone, Morgan Brittany, Pat Hingle, Kevin McCarthy, Barry Corbin, Charles Frank; **D:** Peter Werner. VHS, Beta $29.95 FRH ✻✻✻

Le Bal You won't find many films with the music of Paul McCartney and Chopin in the credits, and even fewer without dialogue. With only music and dancing the film uses a French dance hall to illustrate the changes in French society over a fifty-year period. Based on a French play. ♫La Vie en Rose; In the Mood; Michelle; Top Hat White Tie and Tails; Let's Face the Music and Dance; Harlem Nocturne; Shuffle Blues; Tutti Frutti; Only You; Fleur de Paris; La Marseillaise. 1982 112m/C IT FR **D:** Ettore Scola; **M:** Irving Berlin, Paul McCartney, John Lennon, Frederick Chopin. Academy Awards '83 Nominations: Best Foreign Language Film; Cesar Awards '84: Best Director (Scola), Best Film. VHS $79.99 WAR, FCT, TAM ✻✻✻

Le Beau Mariage An award-winning comedy from the great French director about a zealous woman trying to find a husband and the unsuspecting man she chooses to marry. In French with English subtitles **AKA:** A Good Marriage; The Well-Made Marriage. 1982 (R) 97m/C FR Beatrice Romand, Arielle Dombasle, Andre Dussollier; **D:** Eric Rohmer. VHS, Beta $59.95 TAM ✻✻✻

Le Beau Serge A convalescing Frenchman returns to his home village and tries to help an old friend, who's become a hopeless drunkard, change his life. Chabrol's first film, and a major forerunner of the nouvelle vague. In French with English subtitles. **AKA:** Handsome Serge. 1958 97m/B FR Gerard Blain, Jean-Claude Brialy, Michele Meritz, Bernadette LaFont; **D:** Claude Chabrol. VHS, Beta $79.95 FCT ✻✻✻

Le Bonheur A seemingly happily married carpenter (Drouot) takes a vacation with his wife and children where he meets the local postal clerk and the two begin a passionate affair. Unwilling to leave his family, Drouot believes the two women can share him but when his wife discovers his infidelity she kills herself. His grief does not cause Drouot to stop the affair, instead he moves in with his mistress. An uninvolving, unbelievable tale with a lovely Mozart score. In French with English subtitles. **AKA:** Happiness.

1965 87m/C FR Jean-Claude Drouot, Claire Drouot, Marie-France Boyer; **W/D:** Agnes Varda. VHS $29.95 FCT ✻✻½

Le Boucher In a provincial French town a sophisticated schoolmistress is courted by the shy local butcher—who turns out to be a sex murderer. A well-played thriller that looks at sexual frustration. In French with English subtitles. **AKA:** The Butcher. 1969 94m/C FR Stephane Audran, Jean Yanne, Antonio Passalia; **D:** Claude Chabrol. VHS, LV $79.95 CVC, TAM ✻✻✻

Le Bourgeois Gentilhomme Translated "The Would-Be Gentleman." A comedy-ballet in five acts in prose, performed by the Comedie Francaise. Subtitled in English. 1958 97m/C **D:** Comedie Francaise. VHS, Beta $24.95 VYY, APD, TAM ✻✻✻

Le Cas du Dr. Laurent A country doctor in a small French town tries to introduce methods of natural childbirth to the native women, but meets opposition from the superstitious villagers. Fine performance by Gabin. 1957 88m/B FR Jean Gabin, Nicole Courcel; **D:** Jean-Paul LeChanois. VHS, Beta $29.95 NOS, VYY, DVT ✻✻✻

Le Cavaleur A light hearted comedy about a philandering concert pianist. **AKA:** Practice Makes Perfect. 1978 90m/C FR Jean Rochefort, Lila Kedrova, Nicole Garcia, Annie Girardot, Danielle Darrieux; **D:** Philippe de Broca. VHS, Beta NO ✻✻

Le Chat A middle-aged couple's marriage dissolves into a hate-filled battle of wits, centering around the husband's love for their cat. In French with English subtitles. **AKA:** The Cat. 1975 88m/C FR Jean Gabin, Simone Signoret, Annie Cordy, Jacques Rispal; **D:** Pierre Granier-Deferre. VHS, Beta, LV $59.95 FCT, LUM, PIA ✻✻✻½

Le Complot When de Gaulle announces his intention to abandon Algeria, several army officers, feeling that their service has been in vain, stage a coup. There's suspense aplenty as the Gaulists, the leftists, and the police spy and are spied upon. In French with English subtitles. **AKA:** The Conspiracy. 1973 120m/C FR Michel Bouquet, Jean Rochefort; **D:** Rene Gainville. VHS, LV $79.95 CVC, FCT, TAM ✻✻✻

Le Corbeau A great, notorious drama about a small French village whose everyday serenity is ruptured by a series of poison pen letters that lead to suicide and despair. The film was made within Nazi-occupied France, sponsored by the Nazis, and has been subjected to much misdirected malice because of it. In French with English subtitles. **AKA:** The Raven. 1943 92m/B FR Pierre Fresnay, Noel Roquevort, Ginette LeClerc, Pierre Larquey, Antoine Belpetre; **D:** Henri-Georges Clouzot. VHS, Beta $24.95 NOS, HHT, TAM ✻✻✻

Le Crabe Tambour Rochefort plays a dying naval captain remembering his relationship with his first officer. Revealed via flashbacks, the recollections concern the adventures which transpired on a North Atlantic supply ship. Great performances from all and award-winning cinematography by Raoul Coutard. Winner of several French Cesars. A French script booklet is available. 1977 120m/C FR Jean Rochefort, Claude Rich, Jacques Dufilho, Jacques Perrin, Odile Versuis, Aurore Clement; **D:** Pierre Schoendoerffer. VHS, LV $59.95 INT, IME, APD ✻✻✻

Le Dernier Combat A stark film about life after a devastating nuclear war marks the directorial debut of Besson. The characters fight to survive in a now speechless world by staking territorial claims and forming new relationships with other survivors. An original and expressive film made without dialogue. **AKA:** The Last Battle. 1984 (R) 93m/B FR Pierre Jolivet, Fritz Wepper, Jean Reno, Jean Bouise, Christiane Kruger; **D:** Luc Besson. VHS, Beta COL, OM ✻✻✻

Le Doulos Compelling story of an ex-convict and his buddy, a man who may be a police informant. Chronicles the efforts of the snitch (the "doulos" of the title) to bring the criminal element before the law. Melville blends in several plot twists and breathes a new-French life into the cliche-ridden genre. 1961 108m/B FR Serge Reggiani, Jean-Paul Belmondo, Michel Piccoli; **D:** Jean-Pierre Melville. VHS, Beta $59.95 INT, TAM ✻✻✻

Le Gentleman D'Epsom A French comedy about a breezy con man who scams everyone around him in order to keep up his upwardly mobile appearance and to put his bets down at the racetrack. Subtitled in English. 1962 83m/B FR Jean Gabin, Paul Frankeur. VHS, Beta $19.95 TAM, KRT ✻✻

Le Grand Chemin A sweet, slice-of-life French film about a young boy's idyllic summer on a family friend's farm while his mother is having a baby. Hubert's son plays the boy Louis in this retelling of the director's own childhood. In French with English subtitles. Remade with an American setting in 1991 as "Paradise." **AKA:** The Grand Highway. 1987 107m/C FR Anemone, Richard Bohringer, Antoine Hubert, Vanessa Guedj, Christine Pascal, Raoul Billerey, Pascale Roberts; **D:** Jean-Loup Hubert. VHS, Beta, LV $29.95 PAV, FCT, TAM ✻✻✻

Le Joli Mai A famous documentary that established Marker, depicting the everyday life of Paris denizens on the occasion of the end of the Algerian War, May 1962, when France was at peace for the first time since 1939. In French with English subtitles. 1962 180m/B FR **D:** Chris Marker. VHS, Beta $29.95 FCT ✻✻✻

Le Jour Se Leve The dark, expressionist film about a sordid and destined murder/love triangle that starts with a police standoff and evolves into a series of flashbacks. The film that put Carne and Gabin on the cinematic map. Highly acclaimed. French with English subtitles. Remade in 1947 as "The Long Night." **AKA:** Daybreak. 1939 85m/B FR Jean Gabin, Jules Berry, Arletty, Jacqueline Laurent; **D:** Marcel Carne. VHS, Beta $29.95 HHT, VYY, APD ✻✻✻½

Le Magnifique Belmondo is a master spy and novelist who mixes fantasy with reality when he chases women and solves cases. 1976 84m/C FR Jean-Paul Belmondo, Jacqueline Bisset. VHS, Beta $59.95 PSM ✻✻

Le Mans The famous 24-hour Grand Prix race sets the stage for this tale of love and speed. McQueen (who did his own driving) is the leading race driver, a man who battles competition, fear of death by accident, and emotional involvement. Excellent documentary-style race footage almost makes up for weak plot and minimal acting. 1971 (G) 106m/C Steve McQueen, Elga Andersen, Ronald Leigh-Hunt, Luc Merenda; **D:** Lee H. Katzin. VHS, LV $39.98 FOX, FCT ✻✻✻

L

Le Million A comedy/musical masterpiece of the early sound era which centers on an artist's adventures in searching for a winning lottery ticket throughout Paris. Highly acclaimed member of the Clair school of subtle French farce. In French with English subtitles.
1931 89m/B *FR* Annabella, Rene Lefevre, Paul Olivier, Louis Allibert; *D:* Rene Clair. **VHS, Beta** $29.95 *NOS, VYY, DVT ♫♫♫½*

Le Petit Amour A popular French comedy about the fateful romance between a 40-year-old divorced woman and a 15-year-old boy obsessed with a kung fu video game. In French with English subtitles. *AKA:* Kung Fu Master.
1987 (R) 80m/C *FR* Jane Birkin, Mathieu Demy, Charlotte Gainsbourg, Lou Doillon; *D:* Agnes Varda. **VHS, Beta** $79.95 *PSM ♫♫♫*

Le Plaisir An anthology of three Guy de Maupassant stories, "Le Masque," "Le Modele," and "La Maison Teillier," about the search for pleasure. In French with English subtitles. *AKA:* House of Pleasure.
1952 97m/B *FR* Claude Dauphin, Simone Simon, Jean Gabin, Danielle Darrieux; *D:* Max Ophuls. **VHS, Beta** $24.95 *NOS, DVT, TAM ♫♫½*

Le Repos du Guerrier Star vehicle for Bardot in which she plays a respectable woman who abandons societal norms to pursue an unbalanced lover. In French with English subtitles. *AKA:* Warrior's Rest.
1962 100m/C *FR* Brigitte Bardot, Robert Hossein, James Robertson Justice, Jean-Mark Bory; *D:* Roger Vadim. **VHS, Beta** $19.95 *KRT, TAM ♫♫*

Le Secret This classic French thriller with a shocking ending finds an escaped convict seeking shelter with a reclusive couple in the mountains. His tales of abuse and torture create tension for the pair as one believes the woeful story and the other doesn't. Dubbed in English.
1974 103m/C *FR* Jean-Louis Trintignant, Philippe Noiret, Jean-Francois Adam; *D:* Robert Enrico; *M:* Ennio Morricone. **VHS, Beta** *NO ♫♫♫*

Le Sex Shop A man turns his little book store into a porn equipment palace, to make ends meet. When his relationship with his wife gets boring, they begin to use their erotic merchandise and adopt a swinging lifestyle.
1973 (R) 92m/C *FR* Claude Berri, Juliet Berto, Daniel Auteuil, Nathalie Delon; *D:* Claude Berri. **VHS, Beta** *COL ♫♫♫*

Leader of the Band An out-of-work musician tries to train the world's worst high school band. Music by Dick Hyman. Landesberg helps this attempted comedy along.
1987 (PG) 90m/C Steve Landesberg, Gailard Sartain, Mercedes Ruehl, James Martinez, Calvert Deforest; *D:* Nessa Hyams. **VHS, Beta, LV** $14.95 *LIV ♫♫*

League of Gentlemen An ex-Army officer plots a daring bank robbery using specially skilled military personnel and irreproachable panache. Hilarious British humor fills the screen.
1960 115m/B *GB* Jack Hawkins, Nigel Patrick, Richard Attenborough, Roger Livesey, Bryan Forbes; *D:* Basil Dearden. **VHS, Beta** $39.95 *FCT ♫♫♫½*

A League of Their Own During World War II, a women's baseball league was formed. Playing under professional rules, the women's league drew over a million fans a year. This film explores the league, its ten teams, and the athletes who helped change America's attitude towards women in sports.
1987 27m/C VHS, 3/4U *FLL ♫♫♫½*

A League of Their Own Charming look at sports history follows the Rockford Peaches, one of the teams in the real-life All American Girls Professional Baseball League that was formed in the 1940s when the men were off at war. Main focus is on the sibling rivalry between Davis, the beautiful, crackerjack catcher, and Petty, the younger, insecure pitcher as they leave their Oregon farm for life in the big leagues. Hanks is wonderful as the boozy coach who reluctantly leads the team to the World Series. A great cast of characters rounds out the film, including the sarcastic talent scout (Lovitz), the opinionated, sleazy former taxi dancer (Madonna), the loud-mouthed bouncer from the Bronx (O'Donnell), and the shy, homely girl who gradually breaks out of her shell (Cavanagh). Features many hilarious comedy sequences, including the "There's no crying in baseball" scene. Lots of baseball for the sports fan.
1992 (PG) 124m/C Tom Hanks, Geena Davis, Madonna, Lori Petty, Jon Lovitz, David Strathairn, Garry Marshall, Bill Pullman, Rosie O'Donnell, Megan Cavanagh, Tracy Reiner, Bitty Schram, Ann Cusack, Anne Elizabeth Ramsay, Freddie Simpson, Renee Coleman; *D:* Penny Marshall; *W:* Lowell Ganz, Babaloo Mandel. **VHS, Beta, LV, 8mm** *COL ♫♫♫*

Lean on Me The romanticized version of the career of Joe Clark, a tough New Jersey teacher who became the principal of the state's toughest, worst school and, through controversial hard-line tactics, turned it around.
1989 (PG-13) 109m/C Morgan Freeman, Robert Guillaume, Beverly Todd, Alan North, Lynne Thigpen; *D:* John G. Avildsen. **VHS, Beta, LV, 8mm** $19.98 *WAR, FCT ♫♫♫*

Leap of Faith Jonas Nightengale (Martin) is a traveling evangelist/scam artist whose tour bus is stranded in an impoverished farm town. Nevertheless he sets up his show and goes to work, aided by the technology utilized by accomplice Winger. Both Martin and Winger begin to have a change of heart after experiencing love—Winger with local sheriff Neeson and Martin after befriending a waitress (Davidovich) and her crippled brother (Haas). Martin is in his element as the slick revivalist with the hidden heart but the film is soft-headed as well as soft-hearted.
1992 (PG-13) 110m/C Steve Martin, Debra Winger, Lolita Davidovich, Liam Neeson, Lukas Haas, Meatloaf, Philip S. Hoffman; *D:* Richard Pearce; *W:* Janus Cercone; *M:* Cliff Eidelman. **VHS, Beta, LV** $95.95 *PAR, BTV ♫♫½*

Leap Year Made at the apex of the 300 pound comedian's career, "Leap Year" wasn't released in the States until the sixties. Tried for manslaughter in 1921 (with two hung juries), Fatty was forced off camera and his films were taken out of circulation (although he did return to cinema behind the camera using the pseudonym William Goodrich).
1921 60m/B Fatty Arbuckle. **VHS, Beta** $24.95 *GPV, FCT ♫♫½*

The Learning Tree A beautifully photographed adaptation of Parks' biographical novel about a fourteen-year-old black boy in the 1920s South, living on the verge of manhood, maturity, love, and wisdom.
1969 (PG) 107m/C Kyle Johnson, Alex Clarke, Estelle Evans, Dana Elcar; *D:* Gordon Parks. **VHS, Beta** $19.98 *WAR, FCT, AFR ♫♫*

Leather Boys A teen-aged girl marries a mechanic and then begins to look beyond the boundaries of marriage. Considered very controversial in the 60s, but less so now.
1963 103m/C *GB* Rita Tushingham, Dudley Sutton, Colin Campbell; *D:* Sidney J. Furie. **VHS, Beta** $59.95 *VID ♫♫*

Leather Burners Hoppy goes under cover to get the goods on a suspected rustler. When his cover is blown, the bad guys frame him for murder. Look for Robert Mitchum in his third bit part in this series.
1943 66m/B William Boyd, Andy Clyde, Jay Kirby, Victor Jory, George Givot, Bobby Larson, George Reeves, Hal Taliaferro, Forbes Murray, Robert Mitchum; *D:* Joseph Henabery. **VHS** $19.95 *NOS, MRV ♫*

Leather Jackets Sweeney plays a nice guy who lets involvement with a childhood pal destroy his life. Elwes is the friend, now gang member, in trouble with both the cops and members of a rival gang, who needs Sweeney's help to escape. Fonda plays Sweeney's girlfriend caught between the two men. Essentially a routine fugitive pic with an attractive cast.
1990 (R) 90m/C D.B. Sweeney, Bridget Fonda, Cary Elwes, Christopher Penn, Marshall Bell, James LeGros, Jon Polito, Craig Ng, Ginger Lynn Allen; *W/D:* Lee Drysdale. **VHS, LV** *COL ♫♫*

Leatherface: The Texas Chainsaw Massacre 3 The human-skin-wearing cannibal is at it again in this, the second sequel to the Tobe Hooper proto-mess. This one sports a bit more humor and is worth seeing for that reason.
1989 (R) 81m/C Kate Hodge, William Butler, Ken Foree, Tom Hudson, R.A. Mihailoff; *D:* Jeff Burr. **VHS, Beta, LV** $19.95 *COL ♫*

The Leatherneck Love unrequited in a faraway place starring soon to be cowboy (Hopalong Cassidy) matinee idol Boyd and Hale, the real life dad of Gilligan Island's skipper.
1928 65m/B William Boyd, Alan Hale Jr., Diane Ellis. **VHS, Beta** $24.95 *GPV, FCT ♫♫*

Leave 'Em Laughing Rooney plays Chicago clown Jack Thum in this based-on-real-life TV movie. Thum takes in orphans even though he cannot find steady work, and then discovers he has cancer.
1981 103m/C Mickey Rooney, Anne Jackson, Allen Goorwitz, Elisha Cook Jr., William Windom, Red Buttons, Michael Le Clair; *D:* Jackie Cooper. **VHS, Beta** $14.95 *FRH ♫♫*

Leave It to the Marines A jerky guy wanders into a recruiting office instead of a marriage license bureau and unwittingly signs on for military service.
1951 66m/B Sid Melton, Mara Lynn. **VHS, Beta, LV** *NO ♫½*

Leaves from Satan's Book Impressionistic episodes of Satan's fiddling with man through the ages, from Christ to the Russian Revolution. An early cinematic film by Dreyer, with ample indications of his later brilliance. Silent.
1919 165m/B *DK* Helge Milsen, Halvart Hoft, Jacob Texiere; *D:* Carl Theodor Dreyer. **VHS, Beta** $39.95 *FCT, GPV, GVV ♫♫½*

Leaving Normal Darly, a fed-up waitress, and Marianne, an abused housewife, meet at a bus stop in Normal, Wyoming and decide to blow town. Together they travel across the American West, through Canada, and up to Alaska, where Lahti's ex-boyfriend has left her a house. Because both women have made bad choices all their lives, they decide to leave their futures to chance, and they end up finding their nirvana. Plot is similar to "Thelma & Louise," but "Leaving Normal" doesn't come close to the innovativeness of the former. Sappy and sentimental to the point of annoyance at times.

1992 (R) 110m/C Christine Lahti, Meg Tilly, Lenny Von Dohlen, Maury Chaykin, James Gammon, Patrika Darbo, Eve Gordon, James Eckhouse, Brett Cullen, Rutanya Alda; D: Edward Zwick; W: Edward Solomon. VHS, LV $19.98 MCA 🎞️½

L'Ecole Buisoniere In a provincial French school a teacher with modern ideas inspires his students with a passion for learning until the suspicious parents are aroused. In French with English subtitles. 1951 108m/C FR D: Jean-Paul Le Chanois. VHS $29.95 FCT, TAM 🎞️🎞️½

Left for Dead A millionaire is accused of brutally killing his wife, and discovers in his search for an alibi that he is the victim of a conspiracy. 1978 82m/C Elke Sommer, Donald Pilon; D: Murray Markowitz. VHS, Beta $69.98 LIV, VES 🎞️½

The Left Hand of God After an American pilot escapes from a Chinese warlord in post-World War II, he disguises himself as a Catholic priest and takes refuge in a missionary hospital. Bogie is great as the flyboy/cleric. 1955 87m/C Humphrey Bogart, E.G. Marshall, Lee J. Cobb, Agnes Moorehead, Gene Tierney; D: Edward Dmytryk. VHS, Beta $19.98 FOX 🎞️🎞️🎞️

The Left-Handed Gun An offbeat version of the exploits of Billy the Kid, which portrays him as a 19th-century Wild West juvenile delinquent. Newman's role, which he method-acted, was originally intended for James Dean. Based on a 1955 Philco teleplay by Gore Vidal. 1958 102m/B Paul Newman, Lita Milan, John Dehner; D: Arthur Penn. VHS, Beta $19.98 WAR, TLF 🎞️🎞️🎞️

The Legacy An American couple become privy to the dark secrets of an English family gathering in a creepy mansion to inherit an eccentric millionaire's fortune. Death and demons abound. AKA: The Legacy of Maggie Walsh. 1979 (R) 100m/C GB Katharine Ross, Sam Elliott, John Standing, Roger Daltrey, Ian Hogg; D: Richard Marquand. VHS, Beta $19.95 MCA 🎞️½

A Legacy for Leonette A girl is led into a web of murder and love in this torrid romance novel brought to video. 1985 90m/C Loyita Chapel, Michael Anderson Jr., Dinah Anne Rogers. Beta $14.95 PSM Woof!

Legacy of Horror A weekend at the family's island mansion with two unfriendly siblings sounds bad enough, but when terror, death, and a few family skeletons pop out of the closets, things go from bad to weird. All-round poor effort with substantial gore. A remake of the director's own "The Ghastly Ones." 1978 (R) 83m/C Elaine Boies, Chris Broderick, Marilee Troncone, Jeannie Cusik; D: Andy Milligan. VHS, Beta $59.95 MPI Woof!

Legacy of Lies Zack Resnick is a serious, honest Chicago cop assigned to a murder investigation. He first discovers the killers got the wrong man and then finds out a lot of family secrets he wishes he didn't know. His cop-father is on the take to the Mob, which is really no surprise since Zack's grandfather turns out to be a retired gangland boss, all of which leaves Zack wondering where his loyalties lie. Too intricate plot hampers the story's flow but the cast performances are well worth watching. Made for cable television.

1992 (R) 94m/C Michael Ontkean, Martin Landau, Eli Wallach, Joe Morton, Patricia Clarkson, Gerry Becker, Chelcie Ross, Ron Dean; D: Jason Meshover-Iorg; W: David Black. VHS, LV $89.98 MCA 🎞️🎞️½

Legal Eagles An assistant D.A. faces murder, mayhem, and romance while prosecuting a girl accused of stealing a portrait painted by her father. Redford sparkles in this otherwise convoluted tale from Reitman, while Hannah lacks depth as the daffy thief. 1986 (PG) 116m/C Robert Redford, Debra Winger, Daryl Hannah, Brian Dennehy, Terence Stamp, Steven Hill, David Clennon, Roscoe Lee Browne, Ivan Reitman; D: Ivan Reitman. VHS, Beta, LV $14.95 MCA 🎞️🎞️½

Legal Tender Rude talk-show host Downey as a corrupt S & L chief? Big, menacing Davi as a romantic hero? Give this ofteninept thriller credit for creative casting, if little else. Roberts adds steamy sex appeal as a lovely saloon-keeper imperiled by deadly bank fraud. 1990 (R) 93m/C Robert Davi, Tanya Roberts, Morton Downey Jr.; D: Jag Mundhra. VHS, Beta $89.95 PSM 🎞️½

Legend A colorful, unabashedly Tolkienesque fantasy about the struggle to save an innocent waif from the Prince of Darkness. Set in a land packed with unicorns, magic swamps, bumbling dwarves and rainbows. Produced in Great Britain. 1986 (PG) 89m/C GB Tom Cruise, Mia Sara, Tim Curry, David Bennett, Billy Barty, Alice Playten; D: Ridley Scott; M: Jerry Goldsmith. VHS, Beta, LV $14.95 MCA 🎞️🎞️

Legend of Alfred Packer The true story of how a guide taking five men searching for gold in Colorado managed to be the sole survivor of a blizzard. 1980 87m/C Patrick Dray, Ron Haines, Bob Damon, Dave Ellingson; D: Jim Roberson. VHS, Beta NO 🎞️½

Legend of Big Foot Facing a spree of killings, a local town mobilizes to stop the legendary beast. 1982 92m/C Stafford Morgan, Katherine Hopkins. VHS, Beta NO 🎞️

Legend of Billie Jean Billie Jean believed in justice for all. When the law and its bureaucracy landed hard on her, she took her cause to the masses and inspired a generation. 1985 (PG-13) 92m/C Helen Slater, Peter Coyote, Keith Gordon, Christian Slater, Richard Bradford, Yeardley Smith, Dean Stockwell; D: Matthew Robbins. VHS, Beta $79.98 FOX 🎞️🎞️

The Legend of Black Thunder Mountain A children's adventure in the mold of "Grizzly Adams" and "The Wilderness Family." 1979 (G) 90m/C Holly Beeman, Steve Beeman, Ron Brown, F.A. Milovich; D: Tom Beeman. VHS, Beta NO 🎞️½

The Legend of Blood Castle Another version of the Countess of Bathory legend, in which an evil woman bathes in the blood of virgins in an attempt to keep the wrinkles away. Released hot on the heels of Hammer's "Countess Dracula." AKA: The Female Butcher; Blood Ceremony; Ceremonia Sangrienta. 1972 (R) 87m/C IT SP Lucia Bose, Ewa Aulin; D: Jorge Grau. VHS, Beta $9.95 NO 🎞️

Legend of Boggy Creek A dramatized version of various Arkansas Bigfoot sightings. 1975 (G) 87m/C Willie E. Smith, John P. Nixon, John W. Gates, Jeff Crabtree, Buddy Crabtree; D: Charles B. Pierce. VHS, Beta $59.98 LIV, MRV 🎞️½

Legend of Earl Durand In Wyoming 1939, a man spends his life searching for justice and freedom. His Robin Hood actions cause a manhunt of massive proportions. 1974 90m/C Martin Sheen, Peter Haskell, Keenan Wynn, Slim Pickens, Anthony Caruso; D: John D. Patterson. VHS NO 🎞️½

Legend of Eight Samurai An ancient Japanese princess hires a group of eight samurai to destroy the witch who reigns over her clan. 1984 130m/C VHS, Beta $9.99 STE, PSM 🎞️

The Legend of Frank Woods Gunslinger returns to the land of the free after an extended holiday south of the border. Mistaken for an expected preacher in a small town, he poses as the padre and signs on the dotted line to take out a new lease on life. 1977 88m/C Troy Donahue, Brad Steward, Kitty Vallacher, Michael Christian; D: Deno Paoli. VHS $9.95 SIM 🎞️🎞️

Legend of Frenchie King When prospectors discover oil on disputed land, two families feud over their conflicting claims to the property. Adult western still working out the kinks has Bardot heading a band of female outlaws. AKA: Petroleum Girls. 1971 96m/C Brigitte Bardot, Claudia Cardinale, Michael J. Pollard, Micheline Presle; D: Christian Jaque. VHS, Beta PGN 🎞️½

The Legend of Hell House A multimillionaire hires a team of scientists and mediums to investigate his newly acquired haunted mansion. It seems that the creepy house has been the site of a number of deaths and may hold clues to the afterlife. A suspenseful, scary screamfest. Matheson wrote the screenplay from his novel "Hell House." 1973 (PG) 94m/C Roddy McDowall, Pamela Franklin, Clive Revill, Gayle Hunnicutt, Clive Revill; D: John Hough; W: Richard Matheson. VHS, Beta, LV $19.98 FOX 🎞️🎞️🎞️

The Legend of Hillbilly John Hillbilly John holds off the devil with a strum of his six-string. While demons plague the residents of rural America, the hayseed messiah wanders about saving the day. AKA: Who Fears the Devil; My Name is John. 1973 (G) 86m/C Severn Darden, Denver Pyle, Susan Strasberg, Hedge Capers; D: John Newland. VHS, Beta, LV $19.95 STE, NWV 🎞️

The Legend of Jedediah Carver A rancher battles desert elements and hostile Indians in a desperate bid for survival. 197? 90m/C DeWitt Lee, Joshua Hoffman, Val Chapman, Richard Montgomery, David Terril; D: DeWitt Lee. VHS $39.95 XVC 🎞️

Legend of Lobo The story of Lobo, a crafty wolf who seeks to free his mate from the clutches of greedy hunters. A Disney wildlife adventure. 1962 67m/C VHS, Beta $69.95 DIS 🎞️½

The Legend of Robin Hood Robin Hood of Sherwood Forest returns in this animated version of his adventures. 1951 47m/C VHS, Beta $19.95 MGM, WTA 🎞️🎞️½

The Legend of Sea Wolf A sadistic sea captain forcefully rules his crew in this weak version of Jack London's novel. Also known as "Wolf Larsen." 1975 (PG) 90m/C Chuck Connors, Barbara Bach, Joseph Palmer. VHS, Beta $9.95 NO 🎞️🎞️

The Legend of Sleepy Hollow The story of Ichabod Crane and the legendary ride of the headless horseman by Washington Irving; narrated by Crosby. Also includes two classic short cartoons, "Lonesome Ghosts" (1932) with Mickey Mouse and "Trick or Treat" (1952) with Donald Duck.

1949 45m/C **D:** Jack Kinney, Clyde Geronomi, James Algar. **VHS, Beta** $12.99 *DIS, WTA* ⅃⅃

The Legend of Sleepy Hollow
Washington Irving's classic tale of the Headless Horseman of Sleepy Hollow is brought to life on the screen. Made for television.
1979 (G) 100m/C Jeff Goldblum, Dick Butkus, Paul Sand, Meg Foster, James Griffith, John S. White. **VHS, Beta, LV** $19.95 *STE, UHV, LME* ⅃⅃½

The Legend of Sleepy Hollow
Classic Washington Irving tale is given the Shelly Duvall treatment in her "Tall Tales and Legends" series. When a snooty teacher goes too far, the town blacksmith decides to play the ultimate Halloween trick on him. Made for cable television.
1986 51m/C Ed Begley Jr., Beverly D'Angelo, Charles Durning, Tim Thomerson. **VHS** $19.98 *FOX* ⅃⅃½

The Legend of Suram Fortress
Based on a Georgian folktale about a medieval fortress that collapses as soon as it is built. The village soothsayer tells a young man he must sacrifice himself, by bricking himself up alive within the fortress walls, if the building is every to stand. In Russian with English subtitles. **AKA:** Legenda Suramskoi Kreposti.
1985 89m/C *RU* Levan Outchanechvili, Zourab Kipchidze; **D:** Sergei Paradjanov. **VHS** $59.95 *KIV* ⅃

Legend of the Dinosaurs Slavering, teeth-gnashing dinosaurs are discovered on Mt. Fuji.
1983 92m/C **VHS, Beta** $39.95 *CEL* Woof!

Legend of the Lone Ranger The fabled Lone Ranger (whose voice is dubbed throughout the entire movie) and the story of his first meeting with his Indian companion, Tonto, are brought to life in this weak and vapid version of the famous legend. The narration by Merle Haggard leaves something to be desired as do most of the performances.
1981 (PG) 98m/C Klinton Spilsbury, Michael Horse, Jason Robards Jr., Richard Farnsworth, Christopher Lloyd, Matt Clark; **D:** William A. Fraker; **M:** John Barry. **VHS, Beta** $29.98 *FOX* ⅃½

Legend of the Lost Two men vie for desert treasure and desert women. Interesting only because of Wayne, but certainly not one of his more memorable films.
1957 109m/C John Wayne, Sophia Loren, Rossano Brazzi, Kurt Kasznar, Sonia Moser; **D:** Henry Hathaway. **VHS** $19.98 *MGM* ⅃

Legend of the Northwest The loyalty of a dog is evidenced in the fierce revenge he has for the drunken hunter who shot and killed his master.
1978 (G) 83m/C Denver Pyle. **VHS, Beta** $19.95 *STE, GEM, HHE* ⅃⅃

The Legend of the Sea Wolf Adaptation of Jack London's dramatic adventure novel, "The Sea Wolf." A slave driving ship captain rescues a shipwreck victim and sets to abusing him along with the rest of his crew. A rebellion ensues. Superb musical score benefits the strong acting and good pace. **AKA:** Wolf Larsen; Larsen, Wolf of the Seven Seas.
1958 83m/B Barry Sullivan, Peter Graves, Gita Hall, Thayer David; **D:** Harmon Jones. **VHS** *NO* ⅃⅃½

Legend of the Werewolf A child who once ran with the wolves has forgotten his past, except when the moon is full.
1975 (R) 90m/C *GB* Peter Cushing, Hugh Griffith, Ron Moody, David Rintoul, Lynn Dalby; **D:** Freddie Francis. **VHS, Beta** *MRV* ⅃⅃

The Legend of the Wolf Woman
The beautiful Daniella assumes the personality of the legendary wolfwoman, leaving a trail of gruesome killings across the countryside. Genre fans will find this one surprisingly entertaining. Also on video as "Werewolf Woman."
1977 (R) 84m/C *IT* Anne Borel, Fred Stafford, Tino Carey, Elliot Zamuto, Ollie Reynolds, Andrea Scotti, Karen Carter; **D:** Raphael D. Silver. **VHS, Beta** $19.95 *VIP, UHV* ⅃⅃½

Legend of Valentino Made-for-television docudrama traces the legendary exploits of one of the silver screen's greatest lovers, Rudolph Valentino. Typical TV-movie fare that lacks the power of the legend's life.
1975 96m/C Franco Nero, Suzanne Pleshette, Lesley Ann Warren, Yvette Mimieux, Judd Hirsch, Milton Berle, Harold J. Stone; **D:** Melville Shavelson. **VHS, Beta** $49.95 *PSM, MRV, NLC* ⅃⅃½

The Legend of Valentino A biographical documentary of perhaps the world's greatest lover, beginning with his immigration to America and ending at his unexpected, sudden death.
1983 71m/B **VHS, Beta** $24.98 *SUE* ⅃⅃½

Legend of Walks Far Woman A made for television film about a proud Sioux woman fighting for survival and her tribe during the American-Indian Wars. Welch is miscast. From Colin Stuart's novel.
1982 120m/C Raquel Welch, Nick Mancuso, Bradford Dillman; **D:** Mel Damski. **VHS, Beta** *NO* ⅃

The Legend of Wolf Mountain
Three children are held hostage by two prison escapees in the Utah mountains. They are aided in their escape by a Native American "wolf spirit." With the criminals on their trail will the three be able to survive in the wilderness until a search party can find them?
1992 (PG) 91m/C Mickey Rooney, Bo Hopkins, Don Shanks, Vivian Schilling, Robert Z'Dar, David Shark, Nicole Lund, Natalie Lund, Matthew Lewis, Jonathan Best; **D:** Craig Clyde. **VHS, LV** $89.95 *HMD* ⅃⅃½

Legion of Iron Adventures in a computer-run, neo-Roman civilization where men and women battle for supremacy.
1990 (R) 85m/C Kevin T. Walsh, Erica Nann, Regie De Morton, Camille Carrigan; **D:** Yakov Bentsvi. **VHS, Beta, LV** $79.95 *COL* ⅃

Legion of Missing Men Professional soldiers of fortune, the French Foreign Legion, fight the evil sheik Ahmed in the Sahara.
1937 62m/B Ralph Forbes, Ben Alexander, Hala Linda. **VHS, Beta** $29.95 *VYY* ⅃½

Legion of the Lawless Group of outlaws band together in order to spread terror and confusion among the populace.
1940 59m/B George O'Brien, Virginia Vale. **VHS, Beta** *MED* ⅃½

Legs Backstage story of three girls who are competing for a job with Radio City Music Hall's Rockettes. Made for television.
1983 91m/C Gwen Verdon, John Heard, Sheree North, Shanna Reed, Maureen Teefy; **D:** Jerrold Freedman. **VHS, Beta** $59.95 *PSM* ⅃⅃

The Lemon Drop Kid Second version of the Damon Runyon chestnut about a racetrack bookie who must recover the gangster's money he lost on a bet. As the fast-talking bookie, Hope sparkles. ♫Silver Bells; It Doesn't Cost a Dime to Dream; They Obviously Want Me to Sing.

1951 91m/B Bob Hope, Lloyd Nolan, Fred Clark, Marilyn Maxwell, Jane Darwell, Andrea King, William Frawley, Jay C. Flippen, Harry Bellaver; **D:** Sidney Lanfield; **W:** Frank Tashlin, Edmund Hartman, Robert O'Brien. **VHS, Beta, LV** $14.95 *COL* ⅃⅃½

The Lemon Sisters Three women, friends and performance partners since childhood, struggle to buy their own club. They juggle the men in their lives with less success. Great actresses like these should have done more with this interesting premise, and the excellent male cast has much more potential.
1990 (PG-13) 93m/C Diane Keaton, Carol Kane, Kathryn Grody, Elliott Gould, Ruben Blades, Aidan Quinn; **D:** Joyce Chopra. **VHS, LV** $19.98 *HBO, FCT* ⅃⅃

Lemora, Lady Dracula A pretty young church singer is drawn into the lair of the evil Lady Dracula, whose desires include her body as well as her blood. Horror fans will enjoy some excellent atmosphere, particularly in a scence where the girl's church bus is attacked by zombie-like creatures; Smith remains a '70s "B" movie favorite. Perhaps a double feature with "Lady Frankenstein...?" **AKA:** The Lady Dracula; The Legendary Curse of Lemora.
1973 (PG) 80m/C Leslie Gilb, Cheryl "Rainbeaux" Smith, William Whitton, Steve Johnson, Monty Pyke, Maxine Ballantyne, Parker West, Richard Blackburn; **D:** Richard Blackburn. **VHS** $18.00 *FRG* ⅃

Lena's Holiday Fluffy comedy about a winsome East German girl visiting L.A. for the first time, and the culture-shock that ensues. Sharp script and performances.
1991 (PG-13) 97m/C Felicity Waterman, Chris Lemmon, Pat Morita, Susan Anton, Michael Sarrazin, Nick Mancuso, Bill Dana, Liz Torres; **D:** Michael Keusch. **VHS, Beta, LV** $89.95 *PSM* ⅃⅃

Leningrad Cowboys Go America
An outlandish Finnish band, the Leningrad Cowboys, pack up their electric accordians and their one dead member and go on tour in America. With matching front-swept pompadours and pointy shoes, the group's appearance is the picture's best joke—and one of its only jokes, as the road trip plods in deadpan fashion that may bore viewers. It's best appreciated by fans of comic minimalist Jim Jarmusch (who has a guest role). In Finnish with English subtitles.
1989 (PG-13) 78m/C *FI* Jim Jarmusch, Matti Pellonpaa, Kari Vaananen, Nicky Tesco; **D:** Aki Kaurismaki. **VHS, LV** $79.98 *ORI, FCT, TAM* ⅃⅃½

Lenny Smokey nightclubs, drug abuse and obscenities abound in Hoffman's portrayal of the controversial comedian Lenny Bruce, whose use of street language led to his eventual blacklisting. Perrine is a gem as his stripper wife. Adapted from the Julian Barry play, this is a visually compelling piece that sharply divided critics upon release.
1974 (R) 111m/B Dustin Hoffman, Valerie Perrine, Jan Miner, Stanley Beck; **D:** Bob Fosse. Academy Awards '74 Nominations: Best Actor (Hoffman), Best Actress (Perrine), Best Adapted Screenplay, Best Cinematography, Best Director (Fosse), Best Picture; Cannes Film Festival '75: Best Actress (Perrine); National Board of Review Awards '74: 10 Best Films of the Year, Best Supporting Actress (Perrine). **VHS, Beta, LV** $19.98 *MGM, FOX* ⅃⅃⅃

Lenny Bruce Performance Film A videotape of one of Lenny Bruce's last nightclub appearances at Basin Street West in San Francisco. Also included is "Thank You Masked Man," a color cartoon parody of the Lone Ranger legend, with Lenny Bruce providing all the character voices.

1968 72m/B Lenny Bruce. **VHS, Beta** $59.95 *VES, RHI, MVD* ♫♫♫

Leon Morin, Priest A young priest and a widow, who happens to be a Communist, fall in love during the WWII German occupation of France. Based on the novel by Beatrix Beck. In French with English subtitles.
1961 118m/B *IT FR* Jean-Paul Belmondo, Emmanuelle Riva; *D:* Jean-Pierre Melville. **VHS** $59.95 *INT, TAM, FCT* ♫♫½

Leonard Part 6 A former secret agent comes out of retirement to save the world from a crime queen using animals to kill agents. In the meantime, he tries to patch up his collapsing personal life. Wooden and disappointing; produced and co-written by Cosby, who himself panned the film.
1987 (PG) 83m/C Bill Cosby, Gloria Foster, Tom Courtenay, Joe Don Baker; *D:* Paul Weiland. **VHS, Beta, LV** $89.95 *COL* ♫

Leonor Idiotic medieval drivel with Ullmann rising from the dead after husband Piccoli seals her in a tomb. Directed by the son of Luis Bunuel.
1975 90m/C *FR SP IT* Liv Ullmann, Michel Piccoli, Ornella Muti; *D:* Juan Bunuel; *M:* Ennio Morricone. **VHS, Beta** *FOX* ♫

Leopard Fist Ninja A masked ninja whacks away at American hoodlums in a fit of Maoist, anti-capitalistic fury. Dubbed.
198? 88m/C Willie Freeman, Jack Lam, Chuck Horry. **VHS, Beta** *NO* ♫

Leopard in the Snow The romance between a race car driver allegedly killed in a crash and a young woman is the premise of this film.
1978 (PG) 89m/C Keir Dullea, Susan Penhaligon, Kenneth More, Billie Whitelaw; *D:* Gerry O'Hara. **VHS, Beta** $59.98 *SUE* ♫♫

The Leopard Man An escaped leopard terrorizes a small town in New Mexico. After a search, the big cat is found dead, but the killings continue. Minor but effective Jacques Tourneur creepie. Based on Cornell Woolrich's novel "Black Alibi." Another Val Lewton Horror production.
1943 66m/B Jean Brooks, Isabel Jewell, James Bell, Margaret Landry, Dennis O'Keefe, Margo, Rita Corday; *D:* Jacques Tourneur. **VHS, Beta, LV** $19.95 *MED* ♫♫½

The Leopard Woman Long before the cat lady cut her first claws, there was the leopard woman. Vamp Glaum finds much trouble to meow about on the Equator.
1920 66m/B Louise Glaum. **VHS, Beta** $19.95 *GPV, FCT* ♫♫

Leper A melodrama of forbidden love between a wealthy nobleman and a beautiful high school teacher. The townspeople try to destroy the love between the two because of their different social classes. In Polish with English subtitles. Also known as "Tredowata."
1976 100m/C *PL* Elzbieta Starostecka, Leszek Teleszynski; *D:* Jerzy Hoffman. **VHS** $49.95 *FCT* ♫♫

Lepke The life and fast times of Louis "Lepke" Buchalter from his days in reform school to his days as head of Murder, Inc. and his execution in 1944.
1975 (R) 110m/C Tony Curtis, Milton Berle, Gianni Russo, Vic Tayback, Michael Callan; *D:* Menahem Golan. **VHS, Beta** $59.95 *WAR* ♫♫½

Leprechaun A sadistic 600-year-old leprechaun winds up wreaking havoc in North Dakota. If this makes no particular sense, neither does the film which is basic horror story excess. A man goes to Ireland for his mother's funeral, steals the gold belonging to the leprechaun, locks the creature up, and

winds up accidentally taking the evil imp back to the States with him. When the leprechaun gets free, he wants a bloodthirsty revenge—and shoes. One of the so-called humorous bits is the leprechaun's shoe fetish. Irish eyes will not be smiling watching this mess.
1993 (R) 92m/C Warwick Davis, Jennifer Aniston, Ken Olandt, Mark Holton, John Sanderford, Robert Gorman; *W/D:* Mark Jones. **VHS, LV** $94.95 *VMK* Woof!

Les Assassins de L'Ordre A righteous French judge faces the case of an innocent man killed by police brutality. Subtitled in English. *AKA:* Law Breakers.
1971 100m/C *FR* Jacques Brel, Catherine Rouvel, Michael Lonsdale, Charles Denner; *D:* Marcel Came. **VHS, Beta** $29.95 *TAM* ♫♫

Les Biches An exquisite film that became a landmark in film history with its theme of bisexuality and upper class decadence. A rich socialite picks up a young artist drawing on the streets of Paris, seduces her, and then takes her to St. Tropez. Conflict arises when a suave architect shows up and threatens to come between the two lovers. In French with English subtitles. *AKA:* The Heterosexuals.
1968 95m/C *FR* Stephane Audran, Jean-Louis Trintignant, Jacqueline Sassard; *D:* Claude Chabrol. **VHS, LV** $79.95 *CVC, TAM, LUM* ♫♫♫½

Les Bons Debarras In French with English subtitles, this Canadian film follows a lonely 13-year-old's effort to win her mother's exclusive love.
1981 114m/C *CA* Marie Tifo, Charlotte Laurier, German Houde; *D:* Francis Mankiewicz. **VHS, Beta** *NO* ♫♫½

Les Carabiniers A cynical, grim anti-war tract, detailing the pathetic adventures of two young bums lured into enlisting with promises of rape, looting, torture and battle without justification. Controversial in its day, and typically elliptical and non-narrative. In French with English subtitles. *AKA:* The Soldiers.
1963 80m/B *GB IT FR* Anna Karina, Genevieva Galea, Marino Mase; *D:* Jean-Luc Godard. **VHS, Beta** $29.95 *FCT* ♫♫♫

Les Comperes A woman suckers two former lovers into finding her wayward son by secretly telling each ex he is the natural father of the punk. Depardieu is a streetwise journalist who teams up with a suicidal hypochondriac/wimp (Richard) to find the little brat. Humorous story full of bumbling misadventures. In French with English subtitles.
1983 92m/C *FR* Pierre Richard, Gerard Depardieu, Anny Duperey, Michel Aumont; *W/D:* Francis Veber. **VHS, Beta, LV** $59.99 *MED, FCT, TAM* ♫♫♫

Les Enfants Terrible The classic, lyrical treatment of adolescent deviance adapted by Cocteau from his own play, wherein a brother and sister born into extreme wealth eventually enter into casual crime, self-destruction, and incest. In French with English subtitles. *AKA:* The Strange Ones.
1950 105m/B *FR* Edouard Dermithe, Nicole Stephane, Jean Cocteau; *D:* Jean-Pierre Melville. **VHS, Beta** $59.98 *FCT, TAM* ♫♫♫

Les Girls When one member of a performing troupe writes her memoirs, the other girls sue for libel. Told through a series of flashbacks, this story traces the girls' recollections of their relationships to American dancer Kelly. Cole Porter wrote the score for this enjoyable "Rashomon"-styled musical. Laserdisc features include the original trailer and letterboxed screen. ♫Les Girls; Flower Song; You're Just Too, Too; Ca C'est

L'Amour; Ladies In Waiting; La Habanera; Why Am I So Gone (About That Gal?).
1957 114m/C Gene Kelly, Mitzi Gaynor, Kay Kendall, Taina Elg, Jacques Bergerac, Henry Daniell, Patrick Macnee; *D:* George Cukor. Academy Awards '57: Best Costume Design; Nominations: Best Art Direction/Set Decoration, Best Sound; Golden Globe Awards '58: Best Actress—Musical/Comedy (Kendall), Best Film—Musical/Comedy. **VHS, Beta, LV** $19.98 *MGM* ♫♫½

Les Grandes Gueules From the director of the classic "An Occurrence at Owl Creek Bridge," comes this comedy-drama about a sawmill owner dealing with two ex-convicts hired as lumberjacks. In French with English subtitles. *AKA:* Jailbirds' Vacation.
1965 125m/C *FR* Lino Ventura, Bourvil, Marie DuBois; *D:* Robert Enrico. **VHS, Beta** $19.95 *KRT, TAM* ♫♫½

Les Miserables Victor Hugo's classic novel about small-time criminal Jean Valjean and 18th-century France. After facing poverty and prison, escape and torture, Valjean is redeemed by the kindness of a bishop. As he tries to mend his ways, he is continually hounded by the policeman Javert, who is determined to lock him away. The final act is set during a student uprising in the 1730s. This version is the best of many, finely detailed and well-paced with excellent cinematography by Gregg Toland.
1935 108m/B Fredric March, Charles Laughton, Cedric Hardwicke, Rochelle Hudson, John Beal, Frances Drake, Florence Eldridge, John Carradine; *D:* Richard Boleslawski. Academy Awards '35 Nominations: Best Cinematography, Best Picture; Academy Awards '36: Best Film Editing; National Board of Review Awards '35: 10 Best Films of the Year. **VHS, Beta, LV** $59.98 *FOX, APD* ♫♫♫♫

Les Miserables Hugo's classic novel done up Italian style with lavish sets and spectacle. Dubbed in English.
1952 119m/B *IT* Gino Cervi, Valentina Cortese; *D:* Riccardo Freda. **VHS** $29.95 *FCT, VYY* ♫♫½

Les Miserables An epic French adaptation of the Victor Hugo standard about Valjean, Javert, and injustice. Although this doesn't reach the level of the 1935 classic, it is still worth watching. Dubbed in English.
1957 210m/C *FR GE* Jean Gabin, Daniele Delorme, Bernard Blier, Bourvil, Gianni Esposito, Serge Reggiani; *D:* Jean-Paul LeChanois. **VHS, Beta** $29.95 *FCT, VEC* ♫♫♫

Les Miserables An excellent made-for-television version of the Victor Hugo classic about the criminal Valjean and the policeman Javert playing cat-and-mouse in 18th-century France. Dauphin's last film role.
1978 150m/C Richard Jordan, Anthony Perkins, John Gielgud, Cyril Cusack, Flora Robson, Celia Johnson, Claude Dauphin; *D:* Glenn Jordan. **VHS, Beta, LV** $59.98 *FOX* ♫♫♫½

Les Miserables Victor Hugo's classic novel comes to life in this beautifully animated family feature.
1979 70m/C **VHS, Beta** $29.95 *FHE, APD, WTA* ♫♫

Les Mistons This study of male adolescence finds five teen-age boys worshiping a beautiful girl from afar, following her everywhere, spoiling her dates, and finally reaching maturity in light of their mistakes.
1957 18m/C *FR* *D:* Francois Truffaut. **VHS, Beta** *FLI* ♫♫♫

Les Patterson Saves the World An obnoxious ambassador to an anonymous Middle Eastern country teams up with the singularly distastefully named Dr. Herpes to stop a new killer disease about to engulf the world.

1990 (R) 105m/C Barry Humphries, Pamela Stephenson, Thaao Penghlis, Andrew Clarke, Joan Rivers; *D:* George Miller. VHS $14.95 HMD *Il* ½

Les Rendez-vous D'Anna An independent woman travels through Europe and comes face to face with its post-war modernism. In French with English subtitles. *AKA:* The Meetings of Anna.
1978 120m/C *FR BE GE* Aurore Clement, Helmut Griem, Magali Noel, Hanns Zischler, Lea Massari, Jean-Pierre Cassel; *W/D:* Chantal Akerman. VHS $29.95 WAC, TAM *Il Il*

Les Violons du Bal Follows the story of a young Jewish boy and his family's attempted escape from Nazi-occupied France during World War II. The boy grows up to be a filmmaker obsessed with making a movie about his childhood experiences. In French with English subtitles.
1974 110m/C *FR* Marie-Jose Nat, Jean-Louis Trintignant; *D:* Michael Drach. VHS $79.95 CVC, TAM, PMS *Il Il*

Les Visiteurs du Soir A beautiful, charming fairy tale about the devil's intrepid interference with a particular love affair in 15th-century France, which he cannot squelch. Purportedly a parable about Hitler's invasion of France. Interestingly, this was released after the Nazi occupation of France, so one assumes that the Germans didn't make the connection. In French with English subtitles. *AKA:* The Devil's Envoys.
1942 110m/B *FR* Arletty, Jules Berry, Marie Dea, Alain Cuny, Fernand Ledoux, Marcel Herrand; *D:* Marcel Carne; *W:* Jacques Prevert, Pierre Laroche. VHS, Beta $59.95 FCT, TAM *Il Il Il* ½

Less Than Zero An adaptation of Bret Easton Ellis' popular, controversial novel about a group of affluent, drug-abusing youth in Los Angeles. McCarthy and Gertz play friends of Downey who try to get him off his self-destructive path—to no avail. Although it tries, the film fails to inspire any sort of sympathy for this self-absorbed and hedonistic group. Mirrors the shallowness of the characters although Downey manages to rise above this somewhat. Music by the Bangles, David Lee Roth, Poison, Roy Orbison, Aerosmith and more.
1987 (R) 98m/C Andrew McCarthy, Jami Gertz, Robert Downey Jr., James Spader; *D:* Marek Kanievska. VHS, Beta, LV $19.98 FOX *Il*

Lesson in Love A gynecologist's philandering is discovered by his wife, who then starts an affair of her own. Change of pace for Bergman as he does this modest comedy. In Swedish with English subtitles. *AKA:* En Lekiton i Karlek.
1954 95m/B *SW* Gunnar Bjornstrand, Eva Dahlbeck, Harriet Andersson; *D:* Ingmar Bergman. VHS, Beta $29.98 SUE, TAM, NLC *Il Il* ½

Let 'Em Have It Exciting action saga loosely based on the newly formed FBI and its bouts with John Dillinger. Car chases and tommy guns abound in this fairly ordinary film. *AKA:* False Faces.
1935 90m/B Richard Arlen, Virginia Bruce, Bruce Cabot, Harvey Stephens, Eric Linden, Joyce Compton, Gordon Jones; *D:* Sam Wood. VHS $19.95 NOS, IVE, MGM *Il Il* ½

Let 'er Go Gallegher A youngster sees a murder, tells his newspaper buddy about it, and the guy writes an article about the crime. It's a big hit, the guy's ego starts to overinflate, and his life starts to head downwind until he decides its time for him and the little guy to rope themselves a miscreant.

1928 57m/B Frank "Junior" Coghlan, Elinor Fair, Wade Boteler; *D:* Elmer Clifton. VHS, Beta $19.95 GPV, FCT *Il Il*

Let Him Have It A controversial film about youth in postwar England and a miscarriage of British justice. On November 2, 1952 two Londoners, Christopher Craig, 16, and Derek Bentley, 19, climbed onto the roof of a candy warehouse in an apparent burglary attempt. When police arrived Bentley was captured. Craig, who had a gun, shot and wounded one policeman and killed another. According to testimony Bentley shouted to his friend "Let him have it" but did he mean shoot or give the officer the gun? With those words the epileptic Bentley, whose IQ was 66, was sentenced to death by the British courts. The uproar over the sentence at the time was reignited by the film and has led to a request for a reexamination of evidence and sentencing by the British Home Office.
1991 (R) 115m/C *GB* Christopher Eccleston, Paul Reynolds, Tom Bell, Eileen Atkins, Clare Holman, Michael Elphick, Mark McGann, Tom Courtenay; *D:* Peter Medak. VHS, LV $89.95 COL, NLC *Il Il Il*

Let It Be Documentary look at a Beatles recording session, giving glimpses of the conflicts which led to their breakup. Features appearances by Yoko Ono and Billy Preston.
1970 80m/C John Lennon, Paul McCartney, George Harrison, Ringo Starr, Billy Preston, Yoko Ono; *D:* Michael Lindsay-Hogg; *M:* The Beatles. VHS, Beta, LV FOX *Il Il*

Let It Ride Dreyfuss is a small-time gambler who finally hits it big at the track. Some funny moments but generally a lame script cripples the cast, although the horses seem unaffected. Garr is okay as his wife who slips further into alcoholism with each race.
1989 (PG-13) 91m/C Richard Dreyfuss, Teri Garr, David Johansen, Jennifer Tilly, Allen Garfield, Ed Walsh, Michelle Phillips, Mary Woronov, Robbie Coltrane, Richard Edson, Cynthia Nixon; *D:* Joe Pytka. VHS, Beta, LV, 8mm $14.95 PAR *Il Il*

Let It Rock A maniacal promoter makes superstars out of his new band by staging publicity stunts. Not one of Hopper's better efforts. Filmed in Germany, but Roger Corman bought the U.S. rights and added clips from other movies before it was released here.
1986 75m/C *GE* Dennis Hopper, David Hess; *D:* Roland Klick. VHS, Beta $79.95 MED *Il*

L'Etat Sauvage This French political thriller finds its heart in the middle of racism. The story unfolds around a newly independent African republic and a love affair between a black cabinet minister and a white Frenchwoman. Corruption abounds in this film based on George Conchon's award-winning novel. In French with English subtitles. *AKA:* The Savage State.
1978 111m/C *FR* Marie-Christine Barrault, Claude Brasseur, Jacques Dutronc, Doura Mane, Michel Piccoli; *D:* Francis Girod. VHS, Beta, LV $59.95 INT, TAM *Il Il Il* ½

Lethal Games Stallone and Vaccaro lead a small community against a blood-thirsty band of criminals.
1990 83m/C Frank Stallone, Brenda Vaccaro, Dave Adams, Christopher Whalley, Heidi Paine, Karen Russell; *D:* John Bowen. VHS $79.95 AIP *Il Il*

Lethal Lolita—Amy Fisher: My Story The only made-for-television Amy Fisher story out of three whose cast members even remotely resemble the real people—except of course actress Parker is actually pretty. Minor details aside, this ac-

count is Amy's story, purchased by NBC for an undisclosed amount, portraying her as an incest victim who gets involved with an opportunistic married jerk who drags her into prostitution, leading her to take out her frustration on his wife. If this is true, the obvious question is "why?"...to which she answers, "He loves me. We have great sex. And he fixes my car." Oh.
1992 93m/C Noelle Parker, Ed Marinaro, Kathleen Lasky, Boyd Kestner, Marianna Pascal, Lawrence Dane, Kate Lynch. VHS $89.98 TTC *Il Il*

Lethal Obsession Two cops battle street crime and a powerful drug ring. Music by Tony Carey. Filmed in Germany. *AKA:* Der Joker.
1987 (R) 100m/C *GE* Michael York, Elliott Gould, Tahnee Welch, Peter Maffay, Armin Mueller-Stahl; *D:* Peter Patzak. VHS, Beta $29.95 VMK *Il* ½

Lethal Pursuit A popular singer who returns to the town where she grew up is tormented by her ex-boyfriend, a criminal.
1988 90m/C Mitzi Donahue, Blake Gahner, John Wildman; *D:* Donald M. Jones. VHS, Beta $79.95 NO *Il*

Lethal Weapon In Los Angeles, a cop nearing retirement (Glover) unwillingly begins work with a new partner (Gibson), a suicidal, semi-crazed risk-taker who seems determined to get the duo killed. Both Vietnam vets, the pair uncover a vicious heroin smuggling ring run by ruthless ex-Special Forces personnel. Packed with plenty of action, violence, and humorous undertones. Clapton's contributions to the musical score are an added bonus. Gibson and Glover work well together and give this movie extra punch. Followed by (so far) two sequels.
1987 (R) 110m/C Mel Gibson, Danny Glover, Gary Busey, Mitchell Ryan, Tom Atkins, Darlene Love, Traci Wolfe, Steve Kahan; *D:* Richard Donner; *W:* Shane Black; *M:* Michael Kamen, Eric Clapton. VHS, Beta, LV, 8mm $19.98 WAR *Il Il Il*

Lethal Weapon 2 This sequel to the popular cop adventure finds Gibson and Glover taking on a variety of blond South African "diplomats" who try to use their diplomatic immunity status to thwart the duo's efforts to crack their smuggling ring. Gibson finally finds romance, and viewers learn the truth about his late wife's accident. Also features the introduction of obnoxious, fast-talking con artist Leo ("OK, OK") Getz, adeptly played by Pesci, who becomes a third wheel to the crime-fighting team. Followed by a second sequel.
1989 (R) 114m/C Mel Gibson, Danny Glover, Joe Pesci, Joss Ackland, Derrick O'Connor, Patsy Kensit, Darlene Love, Traci Wolfe, Steve Kahan, Mary Ellen Trainor; *D:* Richard Donner; *W:* Jeffrey Boam; *M:* Michael Kamen, Eric Clapton, David Sanborn. VHS, Beta, LV, 8mm $19.98 WAR *Il Il Il*

Lethal Weapon 3 Murtaugh and Riggs return for more action in another slam-bang adventure. Murtaugh hopes his last week before retirement will be a peaceful one—but partner Riggs isn't about to let him go quietly. An attempted armed robbery's trail leads them to a brutal ex-cop who is stealing and reselling police-confiscated weapons and ammo. Aiding them is a female Internal Affairs cop who proves to be more than a match for Riggs and the annoyingly helpful Leo Getz. The film starts with an entire building exploding and doesn't let up from there. Glover and Gibson maintain a continuing appeal as the bickering buddies and Pesci adds comic relief.

1992 (R) 118m/C Mel Gibson, Danny Glover, Joe Pesci, Rene Russo, Stuart Wilson, Steve Kahan, Darlene Love, Traci Wolfe, Gregory Millar, Jason Meshover-Iorg, Delores Hall; **D:** Richard Donner; **W:** Jeffrey Boam, Robert Mark Kamen; **M:** Michael Kamen, Eric Clapton, David Sanborn. VHS, LV, 8mm $99.99 WAR, PMS ⊿⊿½

Lethal Woman A group of beautiful women, all once victimized by rapes, is recruited to an island by the "Lethal Woman," who plots revenge on any man who dares to vacation on the island.
1988 96m/C Shannon Tweed, Merete Van Kamp. VHS, Beta, LV $29.98 VID ⊿½

Let's Dance A young widow tries to protect her son from his wealthy, paternal grandmother; while Fred dances his way into her heart. More obscure Astaire vehicle, but as charming as the rest. Needless to say, great dancing. ♫Tunnel of Love; The Hyacinth; Piano Dance; Jack and the Beanstalk; Can't Stop Talking; Oh, Them Dudes; Why Fight the Feeling?.
1950 112m/C Betty Hutton, Fred Astaire, Roland Young, Ruth Warrick, Sheppard Strudwick, Lucile Watson, Barton MacLane, Gregory Moffett, Melville Cooper; **D:** Norman Z. McLeod. VHS, Beta, LV $14.95 PAR ⊿⊿½

Let's Do It! Soft-core sex antics abound, with a special appearance by Playmate Amanda Cleveland.
1984 (R) 60m/C Greg Bradford, Brit Helfer, Amanda Cleveland. VHS, Beta $39.95 AHV ⊿

Let's Do It Again Atlanta milkman and his pal, a factory worker, milk two big-time gamblers out of a large sum of money in order to build a meeting hall for their fraternal lodge. Lesser sequel to "Uptown Saturday Night."
1975 (PG) 113m/C Sidney Poitier, Bill Cosby, John Amos, Jimmie Walker, Ossie Davis, Denise Nicholas, Calvin Lockhart; **D:** Sidney Poitier. VHS, Beta $19.98 WAR ⊿½

Let's Get Harry Americans led by mercenaries mix it up with a Columbian cocaine franchise in an attempt to rescue their friend, Harry. Never released theatrically, for good reason. **AKA:** The Rescue.
1987 (R) 107m/C Robert Duvall, Gary Busey, Michael Schoeffling, Tom Wilson, Glenn Frey, Rick Rossovich, Ben Johnson, Matt Clark, Mark Harmon, Gregory Sierra, Elpidia Carrillo; **D:** Alan Smithee. VHS, Beta, LV $14.99 HBO ⊿½

Let's Get Lost Absorbing documentary of Chet Baker, the prominent '50s "cool" jazz trumpeter (and occasional vocalist) who succumbed, like many of his peers, to drug addiction. Weber's black-and-white, fashion photography style well suits his subject. Downbeat, but rarely less than worthy.
1988 125m/B Chet Baker; **D:** Bruce Weber. VHS $89.95 MVD, COL ⊿½

Let's Get Married A young doctor's weakness under pressure brings him to the brink of babbling idiocy when his wife goes into early labor.
1963 90m/B Anthony Newley, Ann Aubrey. VHS, Beta NO ⊿

Let's Get Tough The East Side Kids, unable to enlist because of their age, harass local Oriental shopkeepers and eventually get involved with a murder.
1942 52m/B Leo Gorcey, Bobby Jordan, Huntz Hall, Gabriel Dell, Sammy Morrison; **D:** Wallace Fox. VHS, Beta, 8mm $24.95 NOS, VYY, RXM ⊿

Let's Go! The son of a cement company president sets out to prove his worth to the firm by landing a contract with the town of Hillsboro. For some unknown reason, he sets off on an amazing set of stunts. Silent with original organ music.

1923 79m/B Richard Talmadge, Hal Clements, Eileen Percy, Tully Marshall; **D:** W.K. Howard. VHS, Beta, 8mm $29.99 VYY, GPV ⊿½

Let's Go Collegiate Two college rowers promise their girlfriends that they'll win the big race, but their plans are almost frustrated when their best oarsman is drafted. Their only hope lies in replacing him with a truck driver. ♫Look What You've Done To Me; Sweet 16; Let's Do A Little Dreaming.
1941 62m/B Frankie Darro, Marcia Mae Jones, Jackie Moran, Keye Luke, Mantan Moreland, Gale Storm; **D:** Jean Yarborough. VHS $19.95 NOS ⊿½

Let's Kill All the Lawyers Low-budget satirical spoof about one man's angst over whether to become a lawyer is witty, entertaining, and not just for legal eagles. Law-firm intern, Foster Merkul (Frederick), ends up apprenticed to a sleazeball named Junior Rawley (Vezina), who teaches him that money—not justice is the name of the game in the law biz. Growing increasingly disillusioned, Foster sets up to reform the system with the help of Satori, a beautiful and mysterious creature of his imagination. Shot at sites in and around Detroit, this independent production features lots of cameos by local media celebrities.
1993 ?m/C Rick Frederick, James Vezina, Michelle De Vuono, Maggie Patton, Marty Smith; **D:** Ron Senkowski; **W:** Ron Senkowski. VHS NYR ⊿⊿½

Let's Make it Legal Amusing comedy of a married couple who decide to get a divorce after 20 years of marriage. Colbert stars as the woman who decides to leave her husband, Carey, because he's a chronic gambler. They part as friends, but soon Colbert's old flame, Scott, is back in town and things get rather complicated. A solid cast serves as the main strength in this film.
1951 77m/B Claudette Colbert, MacDonald Carey, Zachary Scott, Barbara Bates, Robert Wagner, Marilyn Monroe; **D:** Richard Sale; **W:** Hugh Herbert. VHS $14.98 FXV ⊿⊿½

Let's Make Love An urbane millionaire discovers he is to be parodied in an off-Broadway play, and vows to stop it—until he falls in love with the star of the show. He then ends up acting in the play. ♫My Heart Belongs to Daddy; Let's Make Love; Specialization; Incurably Romantic; Sing Me a Song That Sells; You With the Crazy Eyes; Give Me the Simple Life.
1960 118m/C Yves Montand, Marilyn Monroe, Tony Randall, Frankie Vaughan, Bing Crosby, Gene Kelly, Milton Berle; **D:** George Cukor. VHS, Beta $14.98 FOX ⊿⊿½

Let's Make Up When it comes to giving her heart, Neagle can't decide between two dashing men. **AKA:** Lilacs in the Spring.
1955 94m/C GB Errol Flynn, Anna Neagle, David Farrar, Kathleen Harrison, Peter Graves; **D:** Herbert Wilcox. VHS GKK, MLB, MRV ⊿⊿

Let's Scare Jessica to Death A young woman who was recently released from a mental hospital is subjected to unspeakable happenings at a country home with her friends. She encounters murder, vampires, and corpses coming out of nowhere. A supernatural thriller with quite a few genuine scares.
1971 (PG) 89m/C Zohra Lampert, Barton Heyman, Kevin J. O'Connor, Gretchen Corbett, Alan Manson; **D:** John Hancock. VHS, Beta $49.95 PAR ⊿½

Let's Sing Again Eight-year-old singing sensation Bobby Breen made his debut in this dusty musical vehicle, as a runaway orphan who becomes the pal of a washed-up opera star in a traveling show. ♫Let's Sing

Again; Lullaby; Farmer in the Dell; La Donna e Mobile.
1936 70m/B Bobby Breen, Henry Armetta, George Houston, Vivienne Osborne, Grant Withers, Inez Courtney, Lucien Littlefield; **D:** Kurt Neumann. VHS $15.95 NOS, LOO, DVT ⊿⊿

The Letter When a man is shot and killed on a Malaysian plantation, the woman who committed the murder pleads self-defense. Her husband and his lawyer attempt to free her, but find more than they expected in this tightly-paced film noir. Based on the novel by W. Somerset Maugham. Davis emulated the originator of her role, Jeanne Eagels, in her mannerisms and line readings, although Eagels later went mad from drug abuse and overwork.
1940 96m/B Bette Davis, Herbert Marshall, James Stephenson, Gale Sondergaard, Bruce Lester, Cecil Kellaway, Victor Sen Yung; **D:** William Wyler. VHS, Beta, LV $19.95 FOX, MGM ⊿⊿⊿⊿

Letter from an Unknown Woman A woman falls in love with a concert pianist on the eve of his departure. He promises to return but never does. The story is told in flashbacks as the pianist reads a letter from the woman. A great romantic melodrama.
1948 90m/B Joan Fontaine, Louis Jourdan, Mady Christians, Marcel Journet, Art Smith; **D:** Max Ophuls. VHS $14.98 REP ⊿⊿⊿

Letter of Introduction A struggling young actress learns that her father is really a well known screen star and agrees not to reveal the news to the public.
1938 104m/B Adolphe Menjou, Edgar Bergen, George Murphy, Eve Arden, Ann Sheridan; **D:** John M. Stahl. VHS, Beta $19.95 NOS, MRV, HHT ⊿⊿½

Letter to Brezhnev Acclaimed independent film about two working-class Liverpool girls who fall in love with two furloughed Russian sailors. When the men eventually return to the USSR, one of the girls contacts the Russian Secretary General in an effort to rejoin her lover. Amusing tale of different relationships.
1986 (R) 94m/C GB Margi Clarke, Alexandra Pigg, Peter Firth, Ken Campbell, Tracy Lea; **D:** Chris Bernard. VHS, Beta, LV $19.98 LHV, IME, WAR ⊿⊿⊿

A Letter to Three Wives Crain, Darnell, and Sothern star as three friends who, shortly before embarking on a Hudson River boat trip, each receive a letter from Holm (who's never shown), the fourth member in their set. The letter tells them that she has run off with one of their husbands but does not specify his identity. The women spend the rest of the trip reviewing their sometimes shaky unions which provides some of the funniest and most caustic scenes, including Douglas (as Sothern's husband) ranting against the advertising business which supports his wife's radio soap opera. Sharp dialogue, moving performances. Remade for television in 1985.
1949 103m/B Jeanne Crain, Linda Darnell, Ann Sothern, Kirk Douglas, Paul Douglas, Jeffrey Lynn, Thelma Ritter; **W/D:** Joseph L. Mankiewicz; **V:** Celeste Holm. Academy Awards '49: Best Director (Mankiewicz), Best Screenplay; Nominations: Best Picture; Directors Guild of America Awards '48: Best Director (Mankiewicz). VHS, Beta, LV $19.98 FXV ⊿⊿⊿⊿

Letters from My Windmill A series of three short stories: "The Three Low Masses," "The Elixir of Father Gaucher," and "The Secret of Master Cornille" from respected director Pagnol. The unique format only enhances this film. In French with English subtitles.

1954 116m/B FR Henri Velbert, Yvonne Gamy, Robert Vattier, Roger Crouzet; D: Marcel Pagnol. VHS $29.95 NOS, DVT, APD 𝄞𝄞𝄞½

Letters from the Park In Cuba, 1913, two taciturn would be lovers hire a poet, Victor La Place, to write love letters to each other. Normal proboscis aside, the poet follows the fate of Cyrano, and finds himself the unhappy hypotenuse in a triangular romance. Made for Spanish television. In Spanish with English subtitles.
1988 85m/C SP Victor Laplace, Ivonne Lopez, Miguel Paneque; D: Thomas Gutierrez Alea; W: Gabriel Garcia Marquez, Thomas Gutierrez Alea. VHS $79.95 FXL, FCT, APD 𝄞𝄞𝄞

Letters to an Unknown Lover During World War II, a man and woman engage in sexual and emotional combat. AKA: Les Louves.
1984 101m/C GB FR Cherie Lunghi, Mathilda May, Yves Beneyton, Ralph Bates; D: Peter Duffell. VHS, Beta $29.95 ACA 𝄞𝄞½

Letting Go Made for television comedy-drama about a broken-hearted career woman and a young widower who fall in love.
1985 (PG) 94m/C John Ritter, Sharon Gless, Joe Cortese; D: Jack Bender. VHS, Beta $79.95 AIP 𝄞𝄞

Letting the Birds Go Free When a stranger is caught stealing from a farmer's barn, the farmer and his son decide to let the villain work off his crime. Some very interesting relationships develop from this arrangement.
1986 60m/C Lionel Jeffries. VHS $11.95 PSM 𝄞𝄞

Leviathan A motley crew of ocean-floor miners are trapped when they are accidentally exposed to a failed Soviet experiment that turns humans into insatiable, regenerating fish-creatures.
1989 (R) 98m/C Peter Weller, Ernie Hudson, Hector Elizondo, Amanda Pays, Richard Crenna, Daniel Stern, Lisa Eilbacher, Michael Carmine, Meg Foster; D: George P. Cosmatos; M: Jerry Goldsmith. VHS, Beta, LV $19.98 MGM 𝄞𝄞

L'Homme Blesse A serious erotic film about an 18-year-old boy, cloistered by an overbearing family, and his sudden awakening to his own homosexuality. In French with English subtitles. AKA: The Wounded Man.
1983 90m/C FR Jean-Hughes Anglade, Roland Bertin, Vittorio Mezzogiorno; D: Patrice Chereau. VHS, Beta $79.95 TAM, CCN 𝄞𝄞𝄞

Liana, Jungle Goddess A variation on the Greystoke legend featuring a beautiful (and topless) jungle goddess who is discovered living in the wilds of Africa. Thinking that she may be the lost granddaughter of a wealthy English nobleman, she's brought back to London for a reunion. Will civilization prove to be as dangerous as the jungle?
1956 ?m/C Marion Michael, Hardy Kruger. VHS $16.95 SNC 𝄞𝄞

Lianna Acclaimed screenwriter/director John Sayles wrote and directed this story of a woman's romantic involvement with another woman. Chronicles an unhappy homemaker's awakening to the feelings of love that she develops for a female professor. Sayles makes an appearance as a family friend.
1983 (R) 110m/C Jon DeVries, Linda Griffiths, Jane Hallaren, Jo Henderson, Jessica Wright MacDonald; Cameos: John Sayles; D: John Sayles. VHS, Beta $69.95 VES 𝄞𝄞

The Liars Mystery in which a Frenchman strikes it rich in Africa, then returns home to Paris in search of a mate, but is set up by con artists instead. In French with English subtitles.

1964 92m/C Dawn Addams, Jean Servais; D: Edmond T. Greville. VHS $29.95 FCT, TAM 𝄞𝄞

Liar's Edge Tweed portrays a single mother whose teenaged son, Mark, is plagued by violent fantasies. When she remarries and her new husband and sleazy brother-in-law move in, Mark's hallucinations become stronger until he believes he's witnessed a murder. The murder turns out to be a fact and his new stepfather is involved but can Mark prove it. Filmed on location in Niagra Falls.
1992 (R) 97m/C Shannon Tweed, Nicholas Shields, David Keith, Joseph Bottoms, Christopher Plummer; W/D: Ron Oliver. VHS, LV $89.95 NLC, IME 𝄞𝄞

Liar's Moon A local boy woos and weds the town's wealthiest young lady, only to be trapped in family intrigue.
1982 (PG) 106m/C Cindy Fisher, Matt Dillon, Christopher Connelly, Susan Tyrrell; D: David Fisher. VHS, Beta $29.98 VES 𝄞𝄞

Libeled Lady A fast, complicated screwball masterwork, dealing with a newspaper editor's efforts to get something on a bratty heiress with the help of his own fiancee and a reporter he recently fired. One of the era's funniest Hollywood films. Remade in 1946 as "Easy to Wed."
1936 98m/B Myrna Loy, Spencer Tracy, Jean Harlow, William Powell, Walter Connolly, Charley Grapewin, Cora Witherspoon, E.E. Clive, Charles Trowbridge, Dennis O'Keefe, Hattie McDaniel; D: Jack Conway. VHS, Beta, LV $29.95 MGM 𝄞𝄞𝄞½

Liberation of L.B. Jones A wealthy black undertaker wants a divorce from his wife, who is having an affair with a white policeman. Wyler's final film.
1970 (R) 101m/C Lee J. Cobb, Lola Falana, Barbara Hershey, Anthony Zerbe, Roscoe Lee Browne; D: William Wyler. VHS, Beta $59.95 COL, FCT

Liberators Kinski stars as a criminal soldier battling with the American authorities, German troops, and his fugitive partner.
1977 91m/C Klaus Kinski. VHS, Beta $9.95 UNI 𝄞

Liberty & Bash Two boyhood friends who served together in Vietnam reunite to rid their neighborhood of drug pushers and save the life of a friend.
1990 (R) 92m/C Miles O'Keeffe, Lou Ferrigno, Mitzi Kapture, Richard Eden, Cheryl Paris, Gary Conway; D: Myrl A. Schreibman. VHS, Beta $89.95 FRH 𝄞

License to Drive When teen Haim fails the road test for his all-important driver's license, he steals the family car for a hot date with the girl of his dreams. The evening starts out quietly enough, but things soon go awry. If Haim survives the weekend, he'll definitely be able to pass his driving test on Monday morning. Semi-funny in a demolition derby sort of way.
1988 (PG-13) 90m/C Corey Feldman, Corey Haim, Carol Kane, Richard Masur; D: Greg Beeman. VHS, Beta, LV $19.98 FOX 𝄞𝄞

License to Kill Constantine stars as Agent Nick Carter involved with Oriental spies and a new secret weapon.
1964 100m/C FR Eddie Constantine, Yvonne Monlaur, Paul Frankeur; D: Henri Decoin. VHS $16.95 SNC 𝄞𝄞

License to Kill A young girl is killed by a drunk driver, devastating both families. A made-for-television movie with a strong message against drinking and driving.

1984 96m/C James Farentino, Don Murray, Penny Fuller, Millie Perkins, Donald Moffatt, Denzel Washington, Ari Meyers; D: Judd Taylor. VHS, Beta, LV $59.95 GEM 𝄞𝄞

License to Kill The 18th Bond film, and Dalton's second, in which drug lords try to kill 007's best friend and former CIA agent. Disobeying orders for the first time and operating without his infamous "license to kill," Bond goes after the fiends. Fine outing for Dalton (and Bond, too).
1989 (PG-13) 133m/C GB Timothy Dalton, Carey Lowell, Robert Davi, Frank McRae, Talisa Soto, David Hedison, Anthony Zerbe, Everett McGill, Wayne Newton, Benicoi Del Toro, Desmond Llewelyn, Priscilla Barnes; D: John Glen. VHS, Beta, LV $19.98 FOX 𝄞𝄞𝄞

The Lickerish Quartet It's hilarious, realistic family fun as a couple watches a porno flick with their young son, and then act out their own zany sexual fantasies!!!
1970 (R) 90m/C Silvana Venturelli, Frank Wolff; D: Radley Metzger. VHS, Beta NO 𝄞½

The Lie An womanizing Italian journalist jumps from sack to sack in this nonsensical bed-hopping drama.
1984 97m/C IT Ben Cross, Stefania Sandrelli, Amanda Sandrelli, Leslie Lyon, Claudia Cavalcanti; D: Giovanni Soldati. VHS, Beta, LV $79.98 VES, IME 𝄞𝄞

Liebestraum An architectural expert, his old college friend and the friend's wife form a dangerous triangle of passion and lust that strangely duplicates a situation that led to a double murder forty years earlier.
1991 (R) 109m/C Kevin Anderson, Bill Pullman, Pamela Gidley, Kim Novak; W/D: Mike Figgis. VHS, LV $19.98 MGM 𝄞𝄞

Lies Complicated mystery about a murder/thriller movie plot becoming reality as it is being filmed, revolving around a scam to collect an inheritance from a rich guy in a mental hospital.
1983 (PG) 93m/C GB Ann Dusenberry, Gail Strickland, Bruce Davison, Clu Gulager, Bert Remsen, Dick Miller; D: Ken Wheat, Jim Wheat. VHS, Beta $79.98 FOX 𝄞𝄞½

Lies Before Kisses A woman finds out her loving husband has been spending time with a beautiful call girl. When the call girl is murdered the husband is accused. His wife decides to help him clear his name but she just may have her own type of revenge in mind.
1992 (PG-13) 93m/C Jaclyn Smith, Ben Gazzara, Nick Mancuso, Greg Evigan, Penny Fuller, James Karen; D: Lou Antonio; W: Ellen Weston. VHS, Beta $89.98 TTC, PMS 𝄞𝄞

Lies My Father Told Me Simple drama about growing up in the 1920s in a Jewish ghetto. The story revolves around a young boy's relationship with his immigrant grandfather. Quiet and moving.
1975 (PG) 102m/C CA Yossi Yadin, Len Birman, Marilyn Lightstone, Jeffery Lynas; D: Jan Kadar. Academy Awards '75 Nominations: Best Original Screenplay; Golden Globe Awards '76: Best Foreign Film. VHS COL 𝄞𝄞𝄞

Lies of the Twins A beautiful model becomes involved with her therapist and his identical, and irresponsible, twin brother.
1991 93m/C Isabella Rossellini, Aidan Quinn, Iman, John Pleshette; D: Tim Hunter. VHS $79.95 MCA 𝄞𝄞

Lt. Robin Crusoe, U.S.N. A light-earted navy pilot crash lands amusingly on a tropical island, falls hard for an island babe and schemes intensely against the local evil ruler. Lackluster Disney debacle.
1966 (G) 113m/C Dick Van Dyke, Nancy Kwan, Akim Tamiroff; D: Byron Paul. VHS, Beta DIS, OM 𝄞

The Life and Adventures of Santa Claus Animated story of how Santa became the symbol of Christmas. Based on the novel by L. Frank Baum.
1985 49m/C **W:** L. Frank Baum; **V:** Alfred Drake, Earle Hyman. **VHS, Beta $12.95** *WAR, WTA* ♂

The Life and Assassination of the Kingfish Recommended by the NEA, this story of Louisiana politician Huey Long is riveting. Asner gives a profound performance.
1976 96m/C Ed Asner, Nicholas Pryor, Diane Kagan; **D:** Robert Collins. **VHS, Beta** *NO* ♂

The Life and Death of Colonel Blimp Chronicles the life of a British soldier who survives three wars (Boer, World War I, and World War II), falls in love with three women (all portrayed by Kerr), and dances a fine waltz. Fine direction and performance abound. *AKA:* Colonel Blimp.
1943 115m/C *GB* Roger Livesey, Deborah Kerr, Anton Walbrook, Ursula Jeans, Albert Lieven; **D:** Michael Powell, Emeric Pressburger. **VHS, Beta, LV $19.98** *VID, VYG* ♂♂♂♂

The Life & Loves of a Male Stripper A shot-on-video feature about a male stripper who aspires to be a songwriter. Produced by Chippendales alumni.
1987 82m/C Rafael, Carl Fuerst, Dennis Landry, Jeffrey Allen, Troy. **Beta** *NO Woof!*

The Life and Loves of Mozart Despite the title, this is really about the great composer's later life at the time of the premiere of "Die Zauberfloete" ("The Magic Flute"). This is only partly saved by a stellar performance from Werner, as well as the music. Other than that, it gets bogged down in titillation about W.A.M.'s romantic life. In German with English subtitles.
1959 87m/C Oskar Werner, Johanna Matz, Angelika Hauff; **D:** Karl Hartl; **M:** The Vienna State Opera, The Vienna Philharmonic Orchestra; **V:** Anton Dermota. **VHS $24.95** *NOS, VEC* ♂♂½

Life and Nothing But Two young women search for their lovers at the end of World War I. They're helped by a French officer brutalized by the war and driven to find all of France's casualties. Romantic, evocative, and saddening. In French with English subtitles. *AKA:* La Vie est Rien d'Autre.
1989 (PG) 135m/C *FR* Philippe Noiret, Sabine Azema, Francoise Perrot; **W/D:** Bertrand Tavernier. **VHS, Beta $79.98** *ORI, FCT, TAM* ♂♂♂½

Life & Times of Captain Lou Albano The long and illustrious career of wrestling's most notorious manager.
1985 97m/C Captain Lou Albano, Mr. Fuji, Mr. Saito. **VHS, Beta $59.95** *CSM* ♂♂♂½

Life & Times of Grizzly Adams Lightweight family adventure film based on the rugged life of legendary frontiersman, Grizzly Adams, that served as the launching pad for the TV series. Grizzly is mistakenly chased for a crime he didn't commit and along the way befriends a big bear.
1974 (G) 93m/C Dan Haggerty, Denver Pyle, Lisa Jones, Marjorie Harper, Don Shanks; **D:** Richard Friedenberg. **VHS, Beta $19.95** *UHV* ♂♂

Life & Times of Judge Roy Bean Based on the life of the famed Texas "hanging judge," the film features Newman as the legendary Bean who dispenses frontier justice in the days of the Wild West. Filled with gallows humor. Gardner sparkles as actress Lily Langtry.
1972 (PG) 124m/C Paul Newman, Stacy Keach, Ava Gardner, Jacqueline Bisset, Anthony Perkins, Roddy McDowall, Victoria Principal; **D:** John Huston. **VHS, Beta, LV $19.98** *WAR* ♂♂½

The Life & Times of the Chocolate Killer Police turn against the hand that's helped them save property and lives, by framing a good samaritan with deeds done by the "Chocolate Killer."
1988 75m/C Michael Adrian, Rod Browning, Tabi Cooper. **VHS $79.95** *VMK* ♂

Life Begins for Andy Hardy Andy gets a job in New York before entering college and finds the working world to be a sobering experience. Surprisingly downbeat and hard-hitting for an Andy Hardy film. Garland's last appearance in the series.
1941 100m/B Mickey Rooney, Judy Garland, Lewis Stone, Ann Rutherford, Fay Holden, Gene Reynolds, Ralph Byrd; **D:** George B. Seitz. **VHS, Beta $19.95** *MGM* ♂♂♂

Life is a Circus, Charlie Brown/You're the Greatest, Charlie Brown Two Peanuts favorites appear on this tape. In the Emmy award-winning "Life Is a Circus, Charlie Brown," Snoopy falls in love with Fifi, a French poodle circus performer, and winds up as a member of the traveling circus. In "You're the Greatest, Charlie Brown," our hero has a chance to win a decathlon in the Junior Olympics. With Peppermint Patty coaching, anything can happen!
1980 60m/C **D:** Phil Roman. **VHS, Beta $14.95** *SHV, VTR, WTA* ♂♂♂

Life is Beautiful A politically neutral man is arrested and tortured in pre-revolutionary Lisbon, and forced to make, and act on, a political commitment. Dubbed.
1979 102m/C *PT* Giancarlo Giannini, Ornella Muti; **D:** Grigorij Ciukhrai. **VHS, Beta $19.95** *STE, NWV* ♂♂½

Life is Sweet The consuming passions of food and drink focus the lives of an oddball English working-class family beset by hopeless dreams and passions. Mother is always fixing family meals—in between helping her friend open a gourmet restaurant which features such revolting dishes as pork cyst and prune quiche. Dad is a chef who buys a snack truck and dreams of life on the road. Natalie and Nicola, the grown twins, eat their meals in front of the television but Nicola is also a bulemic who binges and purges on choclate bars behind her bedroom door. An affectionate, if sometimes unattractive, look at a chaotic family.
1991 (R) 103m/C *GB* Alison Steadman, Jane Horrocks, Jim Broadbent, Claire Skinner, Timothy Spall, Stephen Rea; **W/D:** Mike Leigh. **VHS, LV $14.98** *REP, BTV* ♂♂♂½

The Life of Emile Zola Writer Emile Zola intervenes in the case of Alfred Dreyfus who was sent to Devil's Island for a crime he did not commit. Well-crafted production featuring a handsome performance from Muni.
1937 117m/B Paul Muni, Gale Sondergaard, Gloria Holden, Joseph Schildkraut; **D:** William Dieterle. Academy Awards '37: Best Picture, Best Screenplay, Best Supporting Actor (Schildkraut); Nominations: Best Actor (Muni), Best Director (Dieterle), Best Interior Decoration, Best Sound, Best Story, Best Original Score. **VHS, Beta $19.98** *MGM, BTV* ♂♂♂½

A Life of Her Own Turner stars as a farm girl who takes her dream of becoming a top model to the Big Apple. She signs with an agency and is befriended by Dvorak, an aging model, who acts as her mentor. Turner finds success and is soon the toast of the town until she gets involved with a married

man (Milland) and her life starts to crumble. Average soap opera with flimsy script. Turner is good, but Dvorak steals the show in her role as an over-the-hill fashion plate.
1950 108m/B Lana Turner, Ray Milland, Tom Ewell, Louis Calhern, Ann Dvorak, Barry Sullivan, Jean Hagen, Phyllis Kirk, Sara Haden; **D:** George Cukor; **W:** Isobel Lennart. **VHS $19.98** *MGM* ♂♂½

Life of Oharu A near masterpiece rivaled only by "Ugetsu" in the Mizoguchi canon, this film details the slow and agonizing moral decline of a woman in feudal Japan, from wife to concubine to prostitute. A scathing portrait of social pre-destination based on a novel by Ibara Saikaku. In Japanese with English subtitles. *AKA:* Diary of Oharu; Saikaku Ichidai Onna.
1952 136m/B *JP* Kinuyo Tanaka, Toshiro Mifune; **D:** Kenji Mizoguchi. **VHS, Beta $39.95** *VYY, APD, TAM* ♂♂♂½

A Life of Sin Scandalous drama about an impoverished Caribbean girl who rises to wealth and power as a world-famous madame. Colon stars as the beautiful Isabel, who is betrayed by her childhood friend Paulo (Julia) and rejected by the Catholic bishop (Ferrer) in this tragic story of passion and greed.
1992 (R) 112m/C Raul Julia, Miriam Colon, Jose Ferrer; **D:** Efrain Lopez Neris; **W:** Emilio Diaz Valcarcel. **VHS $89.95** *COL, PMS* ♂♂

Life of Verdi Epic mini-series biography of the famous composer, with many excerpts of his music sung by Luciano Pavarotti, Renata Telbaldi, and Maria Callas. Made for television.
1984 600m/B *IT* Ronald Pickup, Carla Fracci. **VHS, Beta $124.95** *IIMV, KUL, MVD* ♂♂

Life on a String Set in the distant past, this is a lyrical story of a young boy searching for a cure for his blindness. His possible cure involves a myth which requires him to devote his life to music and the breaking of 1000 strings on a banjo. Adapted from a story by Shi Tiesheng. In Chinese with English subtitles.
1990 110m/C *CH* **D:** Chen Kaige. **VHS $79.95** *FCT, KIV* ♂♂

Life Stinks So does the film. A grasping tycoon bets he can spend a month living on the street without money, resulting in cheap laughs, heavy-handed sentiment and one musical number. Those expecting the innovative, hilarious Brooks of "Young Frankenstein" or "Blazing Saddles" will be very disappointed—these jokes are stale and the timing is tedious. Those looking for a Chaplinesque tale for modern times should stick with Chaplin.
1991 (PG) 93m/C Mel Brooks, Jeffrey Tambor, Lesley Ann Warren, Stuart Pankin, Howard Morris, Teddy Wilson, Michael Ensign, Billy Barty, Carmine Caridi, Rudy DeLuca; **W/D:** Mel Brooks; **W:** Rudy DeLuca. **VHS, Beta, LV $92.99** *MGM* ♂

Life with Father Based on the writings of the late Clarence Day, Jr., this is the story of his childhood in New York City during the 1880s. A delightful saga about a stern but loving father and his relationship with his knowing wife and four red-headed sons.
1947 118m/C William Powell, Irene Dunne, Elizabeth Taylor, Edmund Gwenn, ZaSu Pitts, Jimmy Lydon, Martin Milner; **D:** Michael Curtiz. Academy Awards '47 Nominations: Best Actor (Powell), Best Art Direction/Set Decoration (Color), Best Color Cinematography; New York Film Critics Awards '47: Best Actor (Powell). **VHS, Beta $9.95** *NEG, MRV, NOS* ♂♂♂½

Life With Mikey Typical Fox effort is a light, sweet comedy. Michael "Mikey" Chapman (Fox) is a washed-up former child star who now half-heartedly runs a minor talent agency for other pint-sized would-be thespians. Ever mindful of his previous glory, he believes he is doomed to obscurity when a 10-year-old Brooklyn pickpocket reanimates his taste for life. Streetwise Angela (Vidal) may have the talent to take them both into the big time. Her home life, however, would keep a whole staff of social workers busy. When she shows up at Chapman's door with suitcase in hand, he finds out what growing up really means.
1993 (PG) ?m/C Michael J. Fox, Cyndi Lauper, Nathan Lane, Christina Vidal, David Huddleston, Victor Garber, David Krumholtz; *D:* James Lapine; *W:* Marc Lawrence; *M:* Alan Menken. **VHS** *NYR ♫♫½*

Lifeboat When a German U-boat sinks a freighter during World War II, the eight survivors seek refuge in a tiny lifeboat. Tension peaks after the drifting passengers take in a stranded Nazi. Hitchcock saw a great challenge in having the entire story take place in a lifeboat and pulled it off with his usual flourish. In 1989, the film "Dead Calm" replicated the technique. From a story by John Steinbeck. Bankhead shines.
1944 96m/B Tallulah Bankhead, John Hodiak, William Bendix, Canada Lee, Walter Slezak, Hume Cronyn, Henry Hull, Mary Anderson; *D:* Alfred Hitchcock. Academy Awards '44 Nominations: Best Director (Hitchcock); National Board of Review Awards '44: 10 Best Films of the Year; New York Film Critics Awards '44: Best Actress (Bankhead). **VHS, Beta, LV** $19.98 *HMV, FOX ♫♫♫½*

Lifeforce A beautiful female vampire from outer space drains Londoners and before long the city is filled with disintegrating zombies in this hi-tech thriller. Sex was never stranger.
1985 (R) 100m/C Steve Railsback, Peter Firth, Frank Finlay, Patrick Stewart, Michael Gothard, Nicholas Ball, Aubrey Morris, Nancy Paul, Mathilda May; *D:* Tobe Hooper. **VHS, Beta, LV** $9.99 *FHE, LIV, VES ♫♫½*

Lifeguard The lifeguard lives by the credo that work is for people who cannot surf. Aging, he questions whether he should give up the beach life and start selling Porsches. Made for television.
1975 (PG) 96m/C Sam Elliott, Anne Archer, Stephen Young, Parker Stevenson, Kathleen Quinlan; *D:* Daniel Petrie. **VHS, Beta** $14.95 *PAR ♫♫*

Lifepod A group of intergalactic travelers is forced to evacuate a luxury space liner when a mad computer sabotages the ship.
1980 94m/C Joe Penny, Jordan Michaels, Kristine DeBell. **VHS, Beta** $49.95 *UHV ♫*

Lifespan A young American scientist visiting Amsterdam discovers experiments involving a drug that halts aging.
1975 85m/C Klaus Kinski, Hiram Keller, Tina Aumont; *D:* Alexander Whitelaw. **VHS, Beta** $69.95 *VES ♫*

The Lifetaker A woman lures an unsuspecting young man into her home where she seduces him. Violence and sex ensue.
1989 97m/C Lea Dregorn, Peter Duncan, Terence Morgan; *D:* Michael Papas. **VHS** $79.98 *SVS Woof!*

The Lift Unsuspecting passengers meet an unfortunate fate when they take a ride in a demonic elevator in a highrise. In this film the last stop isn't ladies' lingerie, but death. In Dutch with English subtitles.
1985 (R) 95m/C *NL* Huub Stapel, Willeke Van Ammelrooy; *D:* Dick Maas. **VHS, Beta, LV** $59.95 *MED, TAM ♫♫*

The Light Ahead Lovers Fishke and Hodel dream of escaping the poverty and prejudices of their shtetl for the possibilities of big city life in Odessa. They're aided in their quest by enlightened bookseller Mendele who turns the town's superstitions to their advantage. Based on the stories of social satirist Mendele Mokher Seforim. In Yiddish with English subtitles.
1939 94m/B David Opatoshu, Isadore Cashier, Helen Beverly; *D:* Edgar G. Ulmer. **VHS** $72.00 *NCJ ♫♫½*

Light at the Edge of the World A band of pirates torments a lighthouse keeper near Cape Horn after he sees a shipwreck they caused.
1971 (PG) 126m/C Kirk Douglas, Yul Brynner, Samantha Eggar; *D:* Kevin Billington. **VHS, Beta** $69.95 *MED ♫♫*

The Light in the Forest Disney adaptation of the classic Conrad Richter novel about a young man, kidnapped by Indians when he was young, who is forcibly returned to his white family.
1958 92m/C James MacArthur, Fess Parker, Carol Lynley, Wendell Corey, Joanne Dru, Jessica Tandy, Joseph Calleia, John McIntire; *D:* Herschel Daugherty. **VHS, Beta** $69.95 *DIS ♫♫½*

The Light in the Jungle The biography of Nobel Peace Prize winner Dr. Albert Schweitzer. He established a hospital in Africa and had to overcome many obstacles, including tribal superstitions and European bureaucracy to make it successful and bring health care to the area.
1991 (PG) 91m/C Malcolm McDowell, Susan Strasberg, Andrew Davis; *D:* Gray Hof-meyr. **VHS, LV** $89.98 *LIV ♫♫½*

Light of Day A rock 'n roll semi-musical about a working class brother and sister who escape from their parents and aimless lives through their bar band. Script tends to fall flat although both Fox and Jett are believable. Title song written by Bruce Springsteen.
1987 (PG-13) 90m/C Michael J. Fox, Joan Jett, Gena Rowlands, Jason Miller, Michael McKean; *D:* Paul Schrader. **VHS, Beta, LV** $29.98 *LIV, VES ♫♫*

The Light of Faith A sick young woman is cured when she touches the Holy Grail, which a man stole from her former lover in order to help her. Silent.
1922 33m/C Lon Chaney Sr., Hope Hampton; *D:* Clarence Brown. **VHS, Beta, 3/4U** $16.95 *SNC, BFA, CNM ♫♫*

The Light of Western Stars Brian plays a young woman from the east who comes to claim her late brother's ranch. She meets her murdered brother's best friend (Arlen) who is a drunken cowboy, and he falls madly in love with her. Wanting to impress her, he quickly sobers up and prevents a gang from taking over the ranch. This was Paramount's first talking adaptation of a Grey novel and the third version of this particular Grey novel; silent versions were made in 1918 and 1925.
1930 70m/B Richard Arlen, Mary Brian, Regis Toomey, Harry Green, Syd Saylor, George Chandler; *D:* Otto Brower, Edwin H. Knopf. **VHS** $9.95 *GPV ♫♫½*

The Light of Western Stars A proper Eastern woman goes West and falls in love with a drunken lout.
1940 67m/B Victor Jory, Jo Ann Sayers, Russell Hayden, Morris Ankrum; *D:* Lesley Selander. **VHS** $19.95 *NOS, DVT ♫*

Light Sleeper Schrader's moody look at upscale drug dealers in New York. Dafoe is John LaTour, a 40 year-old drug courier to the club scene. Since his boss (Sarandon) is giving up the drug business for the safer world of natural cosmetics, John must look to his own future. His life becomes even more complicated when he runs into a bitter ex-flame (Delany) and finds the attraction is still overpowering. Cynical, contemplative, and menacing.
1992 (R) 103m/C Willem Dafoe, Susan Sarandon, Dana Delany, David Clennon, Mary Beth Hurt; *W/D:* Paul Schrader. **VHS, LV** $92.98 *LIV ♫♫*

Light Years Garish animated fantasy epic about an idyllic land suddenly beset by evil mutations and death rays. Re-edited and dubbed from the original French version created by Rene Laloux and written by Raphael Cruzel; script by Isaac Asimov.
1988 (PG) 83m/C *FR D:* Harvey Weinstein, Harvey Weinstein; *V:* Glenn Close, Jennifer Grey, Christopher Plummer, Penn Jillette, John Shea, David Johansen, Bridget Fonda, Paul Schaffer. **VHS, Beta, LV** $29.95 *VMK, WTA ♫♫*

Lightblast A San Francisco policeman tries to stop a deadly explosive-wielding mad scientist from blowing the city to kingdom come.
1985 89m/C Erik Estrada, Michael Pritchard; *D:* Enzo G. Castellari. **VHS, Beta** $69.98 *LIV ♫*

The Lighthorseman A compelling World War I drama following several battle-hardened men of the Australian Light-Horse mounted infantry stationed in the Middle Eastern desert and the new recruit who joins their ranks and craves acceptance. Superbly filmed, particularly the final battle scene which pits the Aussies against the Turks for control of the wells at the Beersheba. Fine performance by Andrews in this epic which contains the essential elements of a good war movie—horses, guns, and more horses. Originally filmed at 140 minutes.
1987 (PG-13) 110m/C *AU* Jon Blake, Peter Phelps, Tony Bonner, Bill Kerr, Nick Wateres, John Walton, Tim McKenzie, Sigrid Thornton, Anthony Andrews; *D:* Simon Wincer. **VHS, Beta** $79.95 *WAR ♫♫♫*

Lightnin' Carson Rides Again A tough frontier lawman tracks down his payroll-carrying nephew who's been accused of murder and thievery.
1938 58m/B Colonel Tim McCoy, Joan Barclay, Ted Adams, Forrest Taylor; *D:* Sam Newfield. **VHS, Beta, 8mm** $19.95 *NOS, VYY ♫½*

Lightning Bill Bill champions good in battling rustlers.
1935 46m/B Buffalo Bill Jr. **VHS, Beta, LV** *NO ♫*

Lightning Bill Crandall Gunman heads south for the quiet life. Unfortunately, Arizona proves the scene of a fierce battle between various factions of cattlemen. The gunman aids the good guys, and tries to win the daughter's heart.
1937 60m/B Bob Steele, Lois January, Charles King, Frank LaRue, Ernie Adams, Earl Dwire, Dave O'Brien; *D:* Sam Newfield. **VHS** $19.95 *NOS, DVT ♫½*

Lightning Bolt Someone is stealing moon rockets from Cape Kennedy, and secret agent Harry Sennet must find out who is doing this devilish deed. It leads him to an evil madman who plots to destroy the world from his underwater hideout. Cheap and unintentionally funny. *AKA:* Operazione Goldman.
1967 96m/C *IT SP* Anthony Eisley, Wandisa Leigh, Folco Lulli, Diana Lorys, Ursula Parker; *D:* Anthony Dawson. **VHS** $16.95 *SNC ♫*

L

The Lightning Incident McKeon plays a young Santa Fe sculptor whose worst nightmares come true when her baby is kidnapped by a devil-worshipping cult. Discovering she has a powerful psychic gift, she pursues the kidnappers across the country in a race to save her baby. Almost as bad as it sounds.
1991 (R) 90m/C Nancy McKeon, Polly Bergen, Tantoo Cardinal, Elpidia Carrillo, Tim Ryan; **D:** Michael Switzer; **W:** Michael J. Murray. **VHS, Beta** *PAR* 🐾

Lightning Kung Fu Three brothers senselessly battle entire armies with their feet.
197? 94m/C John Li, Hung Kam-Bo, Cheung Ying. **VHS, Beta** *NO* 🐾

Lightning Over Water An odd, touching documentary co-arranged by Ray and Wenders, all about Ray's last months dying of cancer in his New York loft, his editing of his final film "We Can't Go Home Again," his film corpus and career in general.
1980 91m/C Nicholas Ray, Wim Wenders, Ronee Blakley, Tom Farrel, Gerry Bamman; **D:** Wim Wenders. **VHS, Beta, LV** $59.95 *PAV, IME, TAM* 🐾

Lightning Raiders When a stage coach filled with mail gets robbed, Billy Carson (Crabbe) and Fuzzy (St. John) set off to avenge the postal system. One of the last Crabbe/St. John efforts; perhaps they should have called it quits a few films earlier.
1945 61m/C Buster Crabbe, Al "Fuzzy" St. John, Mady Lawrence, Henry Hall, Steve Darrell, I. Stanford Jolley, Karl Hackett, Roy Brent, Marin Sais, Al Ferguson; **D:** Sam Newfield; **W:** Elmer Clifton. **VHS** *HEG* 🐾

Lightning Range Roosevelt stars as a U.S. Deputy Marshal who continually foils the nefarious plots of a gang of outlaws.
1933 50m/B Buddy Roosevelt, Lafe McKee. **VHS, Beta** $19.95 *NOS* 🐾

Lightning Strikes West U.S. Marshal trails an escaped convict, eventually catches him, and brings him in to finish paying his debt to society.
1940 57m/B Ken Maynard. **VHS, Beta** $19.95 *VCN, UHV* 🐾½

Lightning: The White Stallion An old gambler and his two young friends enter a horse race in order to win their beloved white stallion back from thieves.
1986 (PG) 93m/C Mickey Rooney, Susan George, Isabel Lorca; **D:** William A. Levey. **VHS, Beta** $19.98 *MED* 🐾½

Lightning Warrior Western suspense about pioneer life and the unraveling of a baffling mystery. Twelve chapters, 13 minutes each.
1931 156m/B George Brent, Frankie Darro, Rin Tin Tin Jr; **D:** Armand Schaefer, Ben Kline. **VHS, Beta** $27.95 *VCN* 🐾½

Lights, Camera, Action, Love A romance novel on tape, in which a young actress finds the path to stardom littered with pain, pornography, and seediness.
1985 90m/C **VHS, Beta** $14.95 *PSM* 🐾

Lights! Camera! Murder! When a twelve-year-old boy witnesses a filmed murder, he becomes the next target.
1989 89m/C John Barrett; **D:** Frans Nel. **VHS** $79.95 *ATL* 🐾🐾

Lights of Old Santa Fe A cowboy rescues a beautiful rodeo owner from bankruptcy. The original, unedited version of the film.
1947 78m/B Roy Rogers, Dale Evans, George "Gabby" Hayes, Bob Nolan, The Pioneers. **VHS, Beta** $19.95 *NOS, DVT* 🐾½

The Lightship On a stationary lightship off the Carolina coast, the crew rescues three men from a disabled boat, only to find they are murderous criminals. Duvall as a flamboyant homosexual psychopath is memorable, but the tale is pretentious, overdone, and hackneyed. Based on Siegfried Lenz's story.
1986 (PG-13) 87m/C Robert Duvall, Klaus Maria Brandauer, Tom Bower, William Forsythe, Arliss Howard; **D:** Jerzy Skolimowski. **VHS, Beta** $79.95 *FOX* 🐾🐾

Like Father, Like Son First and worst of a barrage of interchangeable switcheroo movies that came out in '87-'88. Moore is in top form, but the plot is contrived.
1987 (PG-13) 101m/C Dudley Moore, Kirk Cameron, Catherine Hicks, Margaret Colin, Sean Astin; **D:** Rod Daniel. **VHS, Beta, LV** $19.95 *COL* 🐾

Like Water for Chocolate Magical Mexican fairytale set in the early 1900s about family, love, and the power of food. Formidable Mama Elena is left a widow with three daughters. The youngest, Tita, grows up in the kitchen surrounded by all the magic Nacha, the housekeeper, can impart to her about food. Tita falls in love with the handsome Pedro but Mama insists that Tita follow family tradition, remaining unmarried and caring for her mother until the day she dies. Pedro decides if he can't marry Tita at least he can remain near her by marrying her elder sister Rosaura. The heartbroken Tita cooks to release her sorrows and longings, all of which so permeates the food that every emotion Tita feels infect all who eat her cooking (for better or worse). Wonderfully sensuous and slyly exaggerated. Based on the novel by Esquivel who also wrote the screenplay and whose husband, Arau, directed. In Spanish with English subtitles. *AKA:* Como Agua para Chocolate.
1993 (R) 113m/C *MX* Lumi Cavazos, Marco Leonardi, Regina Torne, Mario Ivan Martinez, Ada Carrasco, Yareli Arizmendi, Claudette Maille, Pilar Aranda; **D:** Alfonso Arau; **W:** Laura Esquivel; **M:** Leo Brower. **VHS** *NYR* 🐾🐾🐾½

Li'l Abner Al Capp's famed comic strip comes somewhat to life in this low-budget comedy featuring all of the Dogpatch favorites. *AKA:* Trouble Chaser.
1940 78m/C Granville Owen, Martha Driscoll, Buster Keaton; **D:** Albert Rogell. **VHS, Beta** $24.95 *NOS, MRV, DVT* 🐾½

Li'l Abner High color Dogpatch drama adapted from the Broadway play (with most of the original cast) based on the Al Capp comic strip. When Abner's berg is considered as a site for atomic bomb testing, the natives have to come up with a reason why they should be allowed to exist. A Jean De Paul-Johnny Mercer musical; choreography by Michael Kidd and Dee Dee Wood. 🎵Jubilation T. Cornpone; Don't Take That Rag Off'n the Bush; A Typical Day; If I Had My Druthers; Room Enuff for Us; Namely You; The Country's in the Very Best of Hands; Unnecessary Town; I'm Past My Prime; I Wish It Could Be Otherwise; Put 'Em Back the Way They Wuz; Matrimonial Stomp.
1959 114m/C Peter Palmer, Leslie Parrish, Stubby Kaye, Julie Newmar, Howard St. John, Stella Stevens, Billie Hayes, Joe E. Marks; **D:** Melvin Frank. **VHS, Beta** $14.95 *PAR, FCT* 🐾🐾½

Lili Delightful musical romance about a 16-year-old orphan who joins a traveling carnival and falls in love with a crippled, embittered puppeteer. Heartwarming and charming, if occasionally cloying. Leslie Caron sings the films's song hit, "Hi-Lili, Hi-Lo."
1953 81m/C Leslie Caron, Jean-Pierre Aumont, Mel Ferrer, Kurt Kasznar, Zsa Zsa Gabor; **D:** Charles Walters; **M:** Bronislau Kaper. Academy Awards '53: Best Score; Nominations: Best Actress (Caron), Best Art Direction/Set Decoration (Color), Best Color Cinematography, Best Director (Walters), Best Screenplay; British Academy Awards '53: Best Actress (Caron); National Board of Review Awards '53: 10 Best Films of the Year. **VHS, Beta** $19.98 *MGM* 🐾🐾🐾

Lilies of the Field Five East German nuns enlist the aid of a free-spirited U.S. Army veteran. They persuade him to build a chapel for them and teach them English. Poitier is excellent as the itinerant laborer, holding the saccharine to an acceptable level, bringing honesty and strength to his role. Actress Skala had been struggling to make ends meet in a variety of day jobs until this opportunity. Poitier was the first African-American man to win an Oscar, and the first African-American nominated since Hattie MacDaniel in 1939. Followed by "Christmas Lilies of the Field," (1979).
1963 94m/B Sidney Poitier, Lilia Skala, Lisa Mann, Isa Crino, Stanley Adams; **D:** Ralph Nelson; **M:** Jerry Goldsmith. Academy Awards '63: Best Actor (Poitier); Nominations: Best Adapted Screenplay, Best Black and White Cinematography, Best Picture, Best Supporting Actress (Skala); Berlin International Film Festival '63: Best Actor (Poitier); Golden Globe Awards '64: Best Actor—Drama (Poitier); National Board of Review Awards '63: 10 Best Films of the Year. **VHS, Beta** $19.98 *MGM, FOX, BTV* 🐾🐾🐾

Liliom Boyer goes to heaven and is put on trial to see if he is deserving of his wings. Lang's first film after leaving Nazi Germany is filled with wonderful ethereal imagery, surprising coming from the man responsible for such grim visions as "Metropolis." In French only.
1935 85m/B *FR* Charles Boyer, Madeleine Ozeray, Florelle, Roland Toutain; **D:** Fritz Lang. **VHS, Beta** $16.95 *SNC, DVT, HEG* 🐾🐾🐾

Lilith Therapist-in-training Beatty falls in love with beautiful mental patient Seberg and approaches madness himself. A look at the doctor-patient relationship among the mentally ill and at the nature of madness and love. Doesn't always satisfy, but intrigues. Rossen's swan song.
1964 114m/B Warren Beatty, Jean Seberg, Peter Fonda, Gene Hackman, Kim Hunter; **D:** Robert Rossen. **VHS, Beta** $59.95 *COL, MLB* 🐾🐾🐾

Lillie The life of Edwardian beauty Lillie Langtry, known as "The Jersey Lily," is portrayed in this British made-for-television drama. Defying the morals of the times, Lillie was the first publicly acknowledged mistress of the Prince of Wales, only one of her numerous lovers. On seven cassettes. Shown on "Masterpiece Theatre" on PBS.
1979 690m/C *GB* Francesca Annis, Cheryl Campbell, John Castle, Dennis Lili, Peter Egan, Anton Rodgers, Ann Firbank. **VHS** $149.95 *SIG, TVC, HMV* 🐾🐾🐾

Lily in Love An aging stage star disguises himself as a suave Italian to star in his playwright wife's new play, and woos her to test her fidelity. Charming, warm, and sophisticated. Loosely based on Molnar's "The Guardsman." Made for television. *AKA:* Playing for Keeps; Jatszani Kell.
1985 (PG-13) 100m/C *HU* Maggie Smith, Christopher Plummer, Elke Sommer, Adolph Green; **D:** Karoly Makk. **VHS, Beta, LV** $79.98 *LIV, VES* 🐾🐾½

Lily of Killarney A musical comedy romance about a British lord who arranges to pay his debts via horse-races, arranged marriages and inheritances. *AKA:* The Bride of the Lake.
1934 82m/B *GB* Gina Malo, John Garrick, Stanley Holloway; *D:* Maurice Elvey. **VHS, Beta, 8mm** $29.95 *VYY* ✰✰

Lily was Here After her fiancee is senselessly murdered, a young woman named Lily is forced to turn to a life of crime in order to survive. A series of petty thefts evolves into a huge crime wave and Lily soon finds herself the object of a massive manhunt. Lily must make the ultimate choice between freedom and motherhood in this shocking thriller. Soundtrack by Dave Stewart features hit instrumental theme ''Lily was Here'' by saxophonist Candy Dulfur.
1989 (R) 110m/C Marion Van Thijn, Thom Hoffman, Adrian Brine, Dennis Rudge; *W/D:* Ben Verbong; *W:* Sytze Van Der Laan, Willem Jan Otten. **VHS** *TAM* ✰✰½

Limelight A nearly washed-up music hall comedian is stimulated by a young ballerina to a final hour of glory. A subtle if self-indulgent portrait of Chaplin's own life, featuring an historic pairing of Chaplin and Keaton.
1952 120m/B Charlie Chaplin, Claire Bloom, Buster Keaton, Nigel Bruce; *D:* Charlie Chaplin. **VHS, Beta, LV** $19.98 *FOX* ✰✰✰

Limit Up An ambitious Chicago Trade Exchange employee makes a deal with the devil to corner the market in soybeans. Turgid attempt at supernatural comedy, featuring Charles as God. Catch Sally Kellerman in a cameo as a nightclub singer.
1989 (PG-13) 88m/C Nancy Allen, Dean Stockwell, Brad Hall, Danitra Vance, Ray Charles, Luana Anders; *Cameos:* Sally Kellerman; *D:* Richard Martini. **VHS, Beta, LV** *NO* ✰✰

The Limping Man Bridges returns to post-World War II London to renew a wartime romance. On the way, he gets caught up in solving a murder. Unexceptional of-its-era thriller.
1953 76m/B *GB* Lloyd Bridges, Moira Lister, Leslie Phillips, Helene Cordet, Alan Wheatley; *D:* Charles De Latour. **VHS, Beta** $16.95 *SNC, RXM* ✰✰

Linchamiento Cattle ranchers and farmers battle it out again. Dubbed into Spanish. *AKA:* Lynching.
1968 90m/C *IT* Glen Saxson, Gordon Mitchell, Christine Schmidt, King MacQueen. **VHS, Beta** *NO* ✰

Lincoln County Incident A satiric western starring secondary-school children.
1980 47m/C VHS, Beta $14.98 *VID* ✰½

The Lindbergh Kidnapping Case The famous Lindbergh baby kidnapping in 1932 and the trial and execution of Bruno Hauptmann, convincingly portrayed by Hopkins. DeYoung as Lindbergh is blah, but the script is quite good. Made for TV.
1976 150m/C Anthony Hopkins, Joseph Cotten, Cliff DeYoung, Walter Pidgeon, Dean Jagger, Martin Balsam, Laurence Luckinbill, Tony Roberts; *D:* Buzz Kulik. **VHS, Beta** $69.95 *COL* ✰✰✰

The Line Not-so-hot anti-war drama about a sit-down strike at a military installation by Vietnam veteran prison inmates. Leans heavily on recycled footage from director Siegel's own ''Parade'' (1971).
1980 (R) 94m/C Russ Thacker, David Doyle, Erik Estrada; *D:* Robert Siegel. **VHS, Beta** *NO* ✰✰½

The Linguini Incident An inept escape artist, a pathological liar, a lingerie designer, a deaf restaurant hostess who throws out one-liners in sign language, and two sinister, yet chic, restaurant owners get together in this marginal comedy about magic and adventure.
1992 (R) 99m/C Rosanna Arquette, David Bowie, Eszter Balint, Andre Gregory, Buck Henry, Viveca Lindfors, Marlee Matlin, Lewis Arquette; *Cameos:* Julian Lennon, Iman; *W/D:* Richard Shepard; *W:* Tamar Brott. **VHS, LV** $89.95 *IME* ✰✰

Link A primatologist and his nubile assistant find their experiment has gone—you guessed it—awry, and their hairy charges are running—yep, that's right—amok. Run for your life!
1986 (R) 103m/C *GB* Elisabeth Shue, Terence Stamp; *D:* Richard Franklin; *M:* Jerry Goldsmith. **VHS, Beta** $19.99 *HBO* Woof!

The Lion Has Wings The story of how Britain's Air Defense was set up to meet the challenge of Hitler's Luftwaffe during their ''finest hour.'' Dated, now-quaint but stirring wartime period piece. ''Docudrama'' style was original at the time.
1940 75m/B Merle Oberon, Ralph Richardson, Flora Robson, June Duprez; *D:* Michael Powell, Brian Desmond Hurst. **VHS, Beta, LV** *SUE, RXM* ✰✰½

The Lion in Winter Medieval monarch Henry II and his wife, Eleanor of Aquitane, match wits over the succession to the English throne and much else in this fast-paced film version of James Goldman's play. The family, including three grown sons, and visiting royalty are united for the Christmas holidays fraught with tension, rapidly shifting allegiances, and layers of psychological manipulation. Superb dialogue and perfectly realized characterizations. O'Toole and Hepburn are triumphant. Shot on location, this literate costume drama surprised the experts with its box-office success.
1968 (PG) 134m/C Peter O'Toole, Katharine Hepburn, Jane Merrow, Nigel Terry, Timothy Dalton, Anthony Hopkins, John Castle; *D:* Anthony Harvey; *W:* James Goldman; *M:* John Barry. Academy Awards '68: Best Actress (Hepburn), Best Adapted Screenplay, Best Score; Nominations: Best Actor (O'Toole), Best Costume Design, Best Director (Harvey), Best Picture; Directors Guild of America Awards '68: Best Director (Harvey); Golden Globe Awards '69: Best Actor—Drama (O'Toole), Best Film—Drama; National Board of Review Awards '68: 10 Best Films of the Year; New York Film Critics Awards '68: Best Film. **VHS, Beta, LV, Special order formats** $14.95 *COL, BTV, TVC* ✰✰✰✰

A Lion is in the Streets Cagney stars as a backwoods politician in a southern state who fights on the side of the sharecroppers and wins their support when he exposes the corrupt practices of a powerful businessman. On his way up the political ladder, however, Cagney betrays and exploits the very people who support him. Although this is a familiar storyline, Cagney is riveting as the corrupt politician, and Hale is wonderful as his patient wife.
1953 88m/C James Cagney, Barbara Hale, Anne Francis, Warner Anderson, John McIntire, Jeanne Cagney, Lon Chaney Jr., Frank McHugh, Larry Keating, Onslow Stevens; *D:* Raoul Walsh. **VHS** *WAR* ✰✰✰

The Lion Man Arabian tale of a boy raised by lions.
1936 ?m/B Jon Hall, Ted Adams. **VHS** $15.95 *LOO* ✰✰

Lion Man Raised by wild animals, the son of King Solomon returns to his father's kingdom and roars his way to the throne.
1979 91m/C Steve Arkin. **VHS, Beta** $19.99 *BFV* ✰

Lion of Africa A down-to-earth woman doctor and an abrasive diamond dealer share a truck ride across Kenya. Filmed on location in East Africa. Fine lead performances in otherwise nothing-special made-for-cable adventure.
1987 115m/C Brian Dennehy, Brooke Adams, Joseph Shiloal; *D:* Kevin Connor. **VHS, Beta** $79.95 *LHV, WAR* ✰✰

Lion of the Desert Bedouin horse militias face-off against Mussolini's armored terror in this epic historical drama. Omar Muktar (Quinn as the ''Desert Lion'') and his Libyan guerrilla patriots kept the Italian troops of Mussolini (Steiger) at bay for 20 years. Outstanding performances enhanced by the desert backdrop. A British-Libyan co-production. *AKA:* Omar Mukhtar.
1981 (PG) 162m/C *GB* Anthony Quinn, Oliver Reed, Irene Papas, Rod Steiger, Raf Vallone, John Gielgud; *D:* Moustapha Akkad. **VHS, Beta** *NO* ✰✰✰

The Lion of Thebes A muscleman unhesitatingly jumps into the thick of things when Helen of Troy is kidnapped. A superior sword and sandal entry.
1964 ?m/C *IT* Mark Forest, Yvonne Furneaux. **VHS, Beta** $16.95 *SNC* ✰✰✰

The Lion of Venice A kid and an old Venetian gondolier see a stone lion move and uncover a legend of secret treasure.
1982 73m/C VHS, Beta $29.95 *GEM* ✰

Lionheart A romantic portrayal of the famous English King Richard the Lionheart's early years. Meant for kids, but no Ninja turtles herein—and this is just as silly, and slow to boot.
1987 (PG) 105m/C Eric Stoltz, Talia Shire, Nicola Cowper, Dexter Fletcher, Nicholas Clay, Deborah Barrymore, Gabriel Byrne; *D:* Franklin J. Schaffner; *M:* Jerry Goldsmith. **VHS, Beta, LV** $19.98 *WAR* ✰½

Lionheart Van Damme deserts the foreign legion and hits the streets when he learns his brother has been hassled. Many fights ensue, until you fall asleep. *AKA:* A.W.O.L.; Wrong Bet.
1990 (R) 105m/C Jean-Claude Van Damme, Harrison Page, Deborah Rennard, Lisa Pelikan, Brian Thompson; *D:* Sheldon Lettich. **VHS, Beta, LV** $19.98 *MCA, PIA* ✰½

Lion's Den A night club performer and a detective head west to fight crime in this film.
1936 59m/B Tim McCoy, Dave O'Brien. **VHS, Beta** $19.95 *NOS, DVT* ✰½

The Lion's Share A gang of bank robbers have their loot stolen and go after the guy who ripped them off.
1979 105m/C *SP* Julio de Grazia, Luisina Brando, Fernanda Mistral, Ulises Dumont, Julio Chavez. **VHS, Beta** *NO* ✰

Lip Service Satirical comedy-drama about the TV news industry. An ambitious young newscaster befriends a veteran reporter. He then manipulates his way to replace him on the reporter's morning program. Dooley as the veteran and Dunne as the upstart are fun to watch in this well-done cable rip-off of ''Broadcast News.''
1988 67m/C Griffin Dunne, Paul Dooley; *D:* William H. Macy. **VHS, Beta** $79.95 *PSM* ✰✰✰

Lipstick Fashion model Margaux seeks revenge on the man who brutally attacked and raped her, after he preys on her kid sister (real-life sis Mariel, in her debut).

Exquisitely exploitative excuse for entertainment.
1976 (R) 90m/C Margaux Hemingway, Anne Bancroft, Perry King, Chris Sarandon, Mariel Hemingway; **D:** Lamont Johnson. **VHS, Beta, LV $59.95** PAR Woof!

Liquid Dreams In this fast-paced, futuristic thriller, Daly goes undercover as an erotic dancer in a glitzy strip joint to try and solve her sister's murder. She finds that the owner and clientele deal not only in sexual thrills, but also in a strange brain-sucking ritual that provides the ultimate rush. Also available in an unrated version.
1992 (R) 92m/C Richard Steinmetz, Candice Daly, Barry Dennen, Juan Fernandez, Tracy Walter, Frankie Thorn, Paul Bartel, Mink Stole; **D:** Mark Manos. **VHS, Beta $89.95** ACA ✍✍

Liquid Sky An androgynous bisexual model living in Manhattan is the primary attraction for a UFO, which lands atop her penthouse in search of the chemical nourishment that her sexual encounters provide. Low-budget, highly creative film may not be for everyone, but the audience for which it was made will love it. Look for Carlisle also playing a gay male.
1983 (R) 112m/C Anne Carlisle, Paula Sheppard, Bob Brady; **D:** Slava Tsukerman. **VHS, Beta, LV $59.95** MED ✍✍✍

Lisa A young girl develops a crush on the new guy in town and arranges a meeting with him in which she pretends to be her mother. Little does she realize he's a psychotic serial killer. Lock your doors! Don't let anyone in if they have this video!
1990 (PG-13) 95m/C Staci Keanan, Cheryl Ladd, D.W. Moffett, Tanya Fenmore, Jeffrey Tambor, Julie Cobb; **D:** Gary Sherman. **VHS $19.98** FOX ✍

Lisa and the Devil An unfortunate outing for Savalas and Sommer, about devil worship. Poor writing and directing leave little room for redemption. Just like on the telly, Telly's sucking on a sucker. **AKA:** The House of Exorcism; La Casa Dell' Exorcismo.
1975 (R) 93m/C IT Telly Savalas, Elke Sommer, Sylva Koscina, Robert Alda; **D:** Mario Bava. **VHS $19.95** VDM, MPI Woof!

Lisbon First film directed by Milland, shot in Portugal, details the adventures of a sea captain entangled in international espionage and crime while attempting to rescue damsel O'Hara's husband from communist doings. A familiar plot told with less-than-average panache.
1956 90m/C Ray Milland, Claude Rains, Maureen O'Hara, Francis Lederer, Percy Marmont; **D:** Ray Milland. **VHS, Beta $59.98** NO ✍✍

The List of Adrian Messenger A crafty murderer resorts to a variety of disguises to eliminate potential heirs to a family fortune. Solid Huston-directed thriller with a twist: you won't recognize any of the name stars.
1963 98m/B Kirk Douglas, George C. Scott, Robert Mitchum, Dana Wynter, Burt Lancaster, Frank Sinatra; **D:** John Huston; **M:** Jerry Goldsmith. **VHS, Beta $59.95** MCA ✍✍✍

Listen, Darling Garland is appealing in her first big screen role as Pinky Wingate, who decides to find the perfect husband for her widowed mother (Astor). Pinky and her friend Buzz (Bartholomew) manage to find Pidgeon and have him become the engaging objection of everyone's affections. ♫Zing! Went the Strings of My Heart; Ten Pins in the Sky; On the Bumpy Road to Love.
1938 70m/C Judy Garland, Freddie Bartholomew, Mary Astor, Walter Pidgeon, Alan Hale Sr.; **D:** Edwin L. Marin. **VHS $19.98** MGM, FCT ✍✍½

Listen to Me A small-town college debate team heads for the big time when they go to a national debate tournament. The usual mutual-distaste-turns-to-romance thing. Cheesy-as-all-get-out climactic abortion debate, in front of supposed real-life Supreme Court justices—yeah, right. And Kirk Cameron: get an accent, will ya?
1989 (PG-13) 109m/C Kirk Cameron, Jami Gertz, Roy Scheider, Amanda Peterson, Tim Quill, Christopher Atkins; **D:** Douglas Day Stewart; **M:** David Foster. **VHS, Beta, LV $19.95** COL ✍½

Listen to Your Heart Office romance in the '80s! Sounds like a mediocre, forgettable made-for-TV comedy-drama—which is exactly what it is. If Jackson was the brainy one on "Charlie's Angels," why wasn't she smart enough to avoid this one?
1983 90m/C Tim Matheson, Kate Jackson; **D:** Don Taylor. **VHS, Beta $59.98** FOX ✍½

Lisztomania Russell's excessive vision of what it must have been like to be classical composer/musician Franz Liszt, who is depicted as the first pop star. Rock opera in the tradition of "Tommy" with none of the sense or music.
1975 (R) 106m/C GB Roger Daltrey, Sara Kestelman, Paul Nicholas, Fiona Lewis, Ringo Starr; **D:** Ken Russell. **VHS, Beta, LV $19.98** WAR Woof!

The Little American World War I drama sees a young woman sending her lover off to war. Silent.
1917 80m/B Mary Pickford, Jack Holt, Raymond Hatton, Walter Long. **VHS, Beta $32.95** GPV ✍✍½

Little Annie Rooney A policeman's tomboy daughter spends her time mothering her father and brother while getting into mischief with street punks. Minor melodrama. Silent.
1925 60m/B Mary Pickford, William Haines, Walter James, Gordon Griffith, Vola Vale; **D:** William Beaudine. **VHS, Beta, LV $19.95** NOS, CCB, IME ✍✍

Little Ballerina A young dancer struggles against misfortune and jealousy to succeed in the world of ballet, under the auspices of Fonteyn.
1947 62m/B Margot Fonteyn, Anthony Newley, Martita Hunt, Yvonne Marsh. **VHS, Beta $19.95** VYY ✍✍

Little Big Horn Low-budget depiction of Custer et al. at Little Big Horn actually has its gripping moments; solid acting all around helps. **AKA:** The Fighting Seventh.
1951 88m/B Marie Windsor, John Ireland, Lloyd Bridges, Reed Hadley, Hugh O'Brian, Jim Davis; **D:** Charles Marquis Warren. **VHS, Beta** MRV ✍✍½

Little Big Man Based on Thomas Berger's picaresque novel, this is the story of 121-year-old Jack Crabb and his quixotic life as gunslinger, charlatan, Indian, ally to George Custer, and the only white survivor of Little Big Horn. Told mainly through flashbacks. Hoffman provides a classic portrayal of Crabb, as fact and myth are jumbled and reshaped.
1970 (PG) 135m/C Dustin Hoffman, Faye Dunaway, Chief Dan George, Richard Mulligan, Martin Balsam, Jeff Corey, Aimee Eccles; **D:** Arthur Penn. **VHS, Beta, LV $19.98** FOX, HMV ✍✍✍

Little Big Master A crafty knight-errant who heads a gang of beggars finds it difficult adjusting to military life.
1977? 90m/C Huang I Lung, Man Li Peng. **VHS, Beta $39.95** UNI ✍

Little Boy Lost The true story of the disappearance of a young boy in Australia.
1978 (G) 92m/C John Hargreaves, Tony Barry, Lorna Lesley; **D:** Alan Spires. **VHS, Beta** NO ✍✍

Little Caesar A small-time hood rises to become a gangland czar, but his downfall is as rapid as his rise. Still thrilling. The role of Rico made Robinson a star and typecast him as a crook for all time.
1930 80m/B Edward G. Robinson, Glenda Farrell, Sidney Blackmer, Douglas Fairbanks Jr.; **D:** Mervyn LeRoy. **VHS, Beta $19.95** FOX, FCT ✍✍✍

Little Church Around the Corner Silent small town melodrama about a preacher who falls in love with a mine owner's daughter, but finds he isn't dad's favorite fella when he confronts him about poor mining conditions. When the mine caves in, the preacher man's caught between a rock and hard place when his sweetie's family needs protection from an angry mob.
1923 70m/B Kenneth Harlan, Hobart Bosworth, Walter Long, Pauline Starke, Alec B. Francis, Margaret Seddon, George Cooper; **D:** William A. Seiter. **VHS, Beta $19.95** GPV ✍✍½

The Little Colonel After the Civil War, an embittered Southern patriarch turns his back on his family, until his dimple-cheeked granddaughter softens his heart. Hokey and heartwarming. Shirley's first teaming with Bill "Bojangles" Robinson features the famous dance scene. Adapted by William Conselman from the Annie Fellows Johnston best-seller.
1935 80m/B Shirley Temple, Lionel Barrymore, Evelyn Venable, John Lodge, Hattie McDaniel, Bill Robinson, Sidney Blackmer; **D:** David Butler. **VHS, Beta $19.98** FOX ✍✍✍

Little Darlings Distasteful promise has summer campers Kristy and Tatum in a race to lose their virginity. Kristy is better (at acting, that is); but who cares? And just who is meant to be the market for this movie, anyway?
1980 (R) 95m/C Tatum O'Neal, Kristy McNichol, Matt Dillon, Armand Assante, Margaret Blye; **D:** Ronald F. Maxwell. **VHS, Beta, LV $14.95** PAR Woof!

Little Dorrit, Film 1: Nobody's Fault The mammoth version of the Dickens tome, about a father and daughter trapped interminably in the dreaded Marshalsea debtors' prison, and the good samaritan who works to free them. Told in two parts (on four tapes), "Nobody's Fault," and "Little Dorrit's Story."
1988 369m/C GB Alec Guinness, Derek Jacobi, Cyril Cusack, Sarah Pickering, Joan Greenwood, Max Wall, Amelda Brown, Daniel Chatto, Miriam Margolyes, Bill Fraser, Roshan Seth, Michael Elphick; **D:** Christine Edzard. Academy Awards '88 Nominations: Best Adapted Screenplay, Best Supporting Actor (Guinness); Los Angeles Film Critics Association Awards '88: Best Film, Best Supporting Actor (Guinness). **VHS, Beta, LV $89.95** WAR, SIG, TVC ✍✍✍

Little Dorrit, Film 2: Little Dorrit's Story The second half of the monumental adaptation of Dicken's most popular novel during his lifetime tells of Amy Dorrit's rise from debtor's prison to happiness.
1988 369m/C GB Alec Guinness, Derek Jacobi, Cyril Cusack, Sarah Pickering, Joan Greenwood, Max Wall, Amelda Brown, Daniel Chatto, Miriam Margolyes, Bill Fraser, Roshan Seth, Michael Elphick; **D:** Christine Edzard. **VHS, Beta, LV $89.95** WAR, SIG, TVC ✍✍✍

Little Dragons A grandfather and two young karate students rescue a family held captive by a backwoods gang.

1980 90m/C Ann Sothern, Joe Spinell, Charles Lane, Chris Petersen, Pat Petersen, Sally Boyden, Rick Lenz, Sharon Weber, Tony Bill; **D:** Curtis Hanson. **VHS, Beta $19.95** AHV 𝕀

The Little Drummer Boy The classic story of "The Little Drummer Boy" is brought to life with colorful animation in this delightful film.
1968 30m/C D: Takeya Nakamura; **V:** Teddy Eccles, Jose Ferrer, Paul Frees. **VHS, Beta $14.95** FHE, WTA 𝕀

The Little Drummer Girl An Israeli counterintelligence agent recruits an actress sympathetic to the Palestinian cause to trap a fanatical terrorist leader. Solid performances from Keaton as the actress and Kinski as the Israli counterintelligence office sustain interest through a puzzling, somethimes boring and frustrating, cinematic maze of espionage. Keaton is at or near her very best. Based on the bestselling novel by John Le Carre.
1984 (R) 130m/C Diane Keaton, Klaus Kinski, Yorgo Voyagis, Sami Frey, Michael Cristofer, Anna Massey, Thorley Walters; **D:** George Roy Hill. **VHS, Beta, LV $19.98** WAR 𝕀𝕀𝕀

The Little Foxes A vicious southern woman will destroy everyone around her to satisfy her desire for wealth and power. Filled with corrupt characters who commit numerous revolting deeds. The vicious matriarch is a part made to fit for Davis, and she makes the most of it. Script by Lillian Hellman from her own play.
1941 116m/B Bette Davis, Herbert Marshall, Dan Duryea, Teresa Wright, Charles Dingle, Richard Carlson; **D:** William Wyler. **VHS, Beta, LV $14.98** SUE 𝕀𝕀𝕀½

The Little Girl Who Lives Down the Lane Engrossing, offbeat thriller about a strange 13-year-old girl whose father is never home, and who hides something - we won't say what - in her basement. Very young Foster is excellent, as are her supporters. Then there's a child molester who knows what she's hiding. . .
1976 (PG) 90m/C Jodie Foster, Martin Sheen, Alexis Smith, Scott Jacoby; **D:** Nicolas Gessner. **VHS, Beta, LV $29.98** LIV, VES 𝕀𝕀½

Little Girl...Big Tease Teen society girl is kidnapped and exploited (along with the viewer) by a group which includes her teacher.
1975 (R) 86m/C Jody Ray, Rebecca Brooke; **D:** Roberto Mitrotti. **VHS, Beta** PGN 𝕀

Little Gloria...Happy at Last Mini series based on the best-selling book about the custody battle over child heiress Gloria Vanderbilt, and her tumultuous youth. Lansberry leads a fine cast as the poor little rich girl's aunt Gertrude, the matriarchal family power broker. Made for television.
1984 180m/C Bette Davis, Angela Lansbury, Christopher Plummer, Maureen Stapleton, Martin Balsam, Barnard Hughes, John Hillerman; **D:** Waris Hussein. **VHS, Beta $79.95** PSM, PAR 𝕀𝕀½

Little Heroes An impoverished little girl gets through hard times with the aid of her loyal dog (the Hound can relate). A low-budget family tearjerker that nonetheless works, it claims to be based on a true story.
1991 78m/C Raeanin Simpson, Katherine Willis, Keith Christensen, Hoover the Dog; **W/D:** Craig Clyde. **VHS $79.95** HMD 𝕀𝕀½

Little Heroes of Shaolin Temple The "Prince of Blood" attacks the Shaolin temple, but the Master's Ninjas await him.
1972 90m/C Cheng Tain Syh, Hw-Luen, Li Shuen Hwa, Tang Chen Da. **VHS, Beta $29.95** TWE 𝕀

Little House on the Prairie, Vol. 1 The pilot for the television series based on the life of Laura Ingalls Wilder and her family's struggles on the American plains in the 1860s. Other episodes are also available on tape, including one in which Patricia Neal guest stars as a terminally ill widow seeking a home for her children. Neal's performance earned her a best actress Emmy in 1975.
1974 98m/C Michael Landon, Karen Grassle, Victor French, Melissa Gilbert, Melissa Sue Anderson; **D:** Michael Landon. **VHS, Beta $19.98** WAR, OM 𝕀𝕀

Little Johnny Jones George M. Cohan's classic musical is featured in a 1980 revival. Songs include "Yankee Doodle Dandy" and "Give My Regards to Broadway."
1980 93m/C VHS, Beta $59.95 WAR, OM 𝕀𝕀𝕀

Little Ladies of the Night Former pimp tries to save Purl and other teenagers from the world of prostitution. Exploitation posing as "significant drama." **AKA:** Diamond Alley.
1977 96m/C Linda Purl, David Soul, Clifton Davis, Carolyn Jones, Louis Gossett Jr.; **D:** Marvin J. Chomsky. **VHS, Beta $49.95** PSM 𝕀

Little Laura & Big John The true-life exploits of the small-time Ashley Gang in the Florida everglades around the turn of the century. Fabian's comeback vehicle, for what it's worth.
1973 82m/C Fabian, Karen Black; **D:** Luke Moberly. **VHS, Beta $14.98** VID 𝕀𝕀

Little Lips A young French girl is awakened sexually.
197? 77m/C Katya Berger. **VHS, Beta $49.95** TWE 𝕀

Little Lord Fauntleroy The vintage Hollywood version of the Frances Hodgson Burnett story of a fatherless American boy who discovers he's heir to a British dukedom. Also available in computer-colorized version. Well cast, charming, remade for TV in 1980. Smith is loveable as the noble tyke's crusty old guardian.
1936 102m/B Freddie Bartholomew, C. Aubrey Smith, Mickey Rooney, Dolores Costello, Jessie Ralph, Guy Kibbee; **D:** John Cromwell. **VHS, Beta, 3/4U, Special order formats $19.95** NOS, MRV, VEC 𝕀𝕀½

Little Lord Fauntleroy A poor boy in New York suddenly finds himself the heir to his grandfather's estate in England. Lavish remake of the 1936 classic, adapted from Frances Hodgson Burnett's novel. Well-deserved Emmy winner for photography; Guinness is his usual old-pro self. Made for TV.
1980 98m/C Rick Schroder, Alec Guinness, Victoria Tennant, Eric Porter, Colin Blakely, Connie Booth, Rachel Kempson; **D:** Jack Gold. **VHS, Beta $14.95** FHE, STE 𝕀𝕀½

Little Man Tate A seven-year-old genius is the prize in a tug of war between his mother, who wants him to lead a normal life, and a domineering school director who loves him for his intellect. An acclaimed directorial debut for Foster, with overtones of her own extraordinary life as a child prodigy.
1991 (PG) 99m/C Jodie Foster, Dianne Wiest, Harry Connick Jr., Adam Hann-Byrd; **D:** Jodie Foster. **VHS $19.98** ORI, CCB 𝕀𝕀𝕀

Little Marines Three young boys journey into the wilderness for three days of fun and instead embark on an incredible adventure.
1990 90m/C Stephen Baker, Steve Landers Jr., Noah Williams; **D:** A.J. Hixon. **VHS** MHF 𝕀𝕀𝕀

The Little Match Girl A musical version of the Hans Christian Andersen classic about a girl whose dying grandmother tells her of the magic in the matches she sells.
1984 54m/C Monica McSwain, Nancy Duncan, Matt McKim, Don Hays; **D:** Mark Hoeger. **VHS, Beta $14.98** SUE 𝕀

The Little Match Girl The Hans Christian Andersen Yuletide classic about an orphan selling magical matches this time set in the 1920's, with the littlest "Cosby" kid in the title role. Ain't she cute?
1987 90m/C GB John Rhys-Davies, Rue McClanahan, Roger Daltrey, Twiggy, Natalie Morse; **D:** Michael Lindsay-Hogg. **VHS, Beta $19.95** ACA 𝕀𝕀

Little Men A modern version of the classic juvenile story by Louisa May Alcott is too cute for words.
1940 86m/B Jack Oakie, Jimmy Lydon, Kay Francis, George Bancroft; **D:** Norman Z. McLeod. **VHS, Beta $19.95** NOS, MRV, QNE 𝕀½

The Little Mermaid An animated version of Hans Christian Andersen's tale about a little mermaid who rescues a prince whose boat has capsized. She immediately falls in love and wishes that she could become a human girl. Not to be confused with the 1989 Disney version.
1978 (G) 71m/C D: Tim Reid. **VHS, Beta $19.95** STE, GEM 𝕀𝕀½

The Little Mermaid From "Faerie Tale Theatre" comes an adaptation of the Hans Christian Andersen tale of a little mermaid who makes a big sacrifice to win the prince she loves.
1984 60m/C Karen Black, Brian Dennehy, Helen Mirren, Pam Dawber, Treat Williams; **D:** Robert Iscove. **VHS, Beta $14.98** KUI, FOX, FCT 𝕀𝕀½

The Little Mermaid A headstrong teenage mermaid falls in love with a human prince and longs to be human too. She makes a pact with the evil Sea Witch to trade her voice for a pair of legs; based on the famous Hans Christian Andersen tale. Charming family musical, which harks back to the classic days of Disney animation. Songs include "Under the Sea" and "Kiss the Girl."
1989 (G) 82m/C D: John Musker, Ron Clements; **M:** Alan Menken; **V:** Jodi Benson, Christopher Daniel Barnes, Pat Carroll, Rene Auberjonois, Samuel E. Wright, Buddy Hackett, Jason Marin, Edie McClurg, Kenneth Mars, Nancy Cartwright. Academy Awards '89: Best Song ("Under the Sea"), Best Original Score; Nominations: Best Song ("Kiss the Girl"). **VHS, Beta, LV, 8mm $14.98** DIS, BVV, APD 𝕀𝕀𝕀

Little Minister An adaptation of the James Barrie novel about a prissy Scottish pastor who falls in love with a free-spirited gypsy...he thinks she is, in fact, the local earl's daughter, played to perfection by the young Hepburn.
1934 101m/B Katharine Hepburn, John Beal, Alan Hale Jr., Donald Crisp; **D:** Richard Wallace. **VHS, Beta $19.98** RKO, TTC 𝕀𝕀𝕀

Little Miss Broadway Orphan Temple brings the residents of a theatrical boarding house together in hopes of getting them into show business. She and Durante give worthwhile performances. Also available in computer-colorized version. ♫Be Optimistic; How Can I Thank You; I'll Build a Broadway For You; If All the World Were Paper; Thank You For the Use of the Hall; We Should Be Together; Swing Me an Old-Fashioned Song; When You Were Sweet 16; Happy Birthday to You; Auld Lang Syne.

1938 70m/B Shirley Temple, George Murphy, Jimmy Durante, Phyllis Brooks, Edna May Oliver, George Barbier, Donald Meek, Jane Darwell; **D:** Irving Cummings. VHS, Beta $19.98 FOX 🐾🐾

Little Miss Innocence Recording executive tries to survive the amorous advances of the two attractive female hitchhikers that he drove home.
1973 79m/C John Alderman, Sandra Dempsey, Judy Medford; **D:** Chris Warfield. VHS, Beta $24.95 AHV 🐾

Little Miss Marker Heartwarming story starring Temple, who is the IOU for a gambling debt and steals her way into everyone's heart. Remade three times as "Sorrowful Jones," as "40 Pounds of Trouble," and in 1980 with the original title. *AKA:* Girl in Pawn.
1934 88m/B Adolphe Menjou, Shirley Temple, Dorothy Dell, Charles Bickford, Lynne Overman; **D:** Alexander Hall. VHS $49.95 MCA 🐾🐾🐾

Little Miss Marker Mediocre remake of the often retold story of a bookie who accepts a little girl as a security marker for a $10 bet. Disappointing performance from Curtis adds to an already dull film.
1980 (PG) 103m/C Walter Matthau, Julie Andrews, Tony Curtis, Bob Newhart, Lee Grant, Sara Stimson, Brian Dennehy; **D:** Walter Bernstein. VHS, Beta $49.95 MCA 🐾½

Little Monsters A young boy (Savage) discovers a monster (Mandel) under his bed and eventually befriends it. The pair embark on adventures that land them in trouble. Hardworking, talented cast hurdles the weak script, but can't save the film.
1989 (PG) 100m/C Fred Savage, Howie Mandel, Margaret Whitton, Ben Savage, Daniel Stern, Rick Ducommun; **D:** Richard Alan Greenberg. VHS, Beta $14.95 MGM 🐾🐾

Little Moon & Jud McGraw A wronged Indian woman and a framed cowpoke take their revenge on a small, corrupt town, razing it overnight. Already-weak plot is disabled by too many flashbacks.
1978 92m/C James Caan, Sammy Davis Jr., Stefanie Powers, Aldo Ray; **D:** Bernard Girard. VHS, Beta $59.95 PSM 🐾½

Little Murders Black comedy set in New York City. A woman convinces a passive photographer to marry her. Gardenia gives an excellent performance as the woman's father. A shadow of crime, depression, and strife seem to hangs over the funny parts of this film; more often depressing than anything else. Adapted by Jules Feiffer from his own play.
1971 (PG) 108m/C Elliott Gould, Marcia Rodd, Vincent Gardenia, Elizabeth Wilson, Jon Korkes, Donald Sutherland, Alan Arkin, Lou Jacobi; **D:** Alan Arkin; **W:** Jules Feiffer. VHS, Beta $59.98 FOX 🐾🐾🐾

Little Nellie Kelly Garland plays both mother and daughter in a film based on a musical comedy by George M. Cohan. Garland is married to Irish cop Murphy but dies in childbirth. The film then advances twenty years to daughter Garland who is trying to make good on the stage and have a romance with a young man her father disapproves of. ♫Nellie Kelly I Love You; Nellie is a Darling; It's a Great Day For the Irish; A Pretty Girl Milking Her Cow; Danny Boy; Singing in the Rain.
1940 100m/B Judy Garland, George Murphy, Charles Winninger, Douglas McPhail; **D:** Norman Taurog. VHS $19.98 MGM, FCT 🐾🐾½

Little Nemo: Adventures in Slumberland A bland animated tale of a young boy whose dreams take him to Slumberland. There, Nemo unwittingly unleashes

a monster from Nightmare Land who kidnaps Slumberland's king. Nemo must then rescue the king—aided by the king's daughter, a comic squirrel sidekick, and a mischievous con-frog. Based on Winsor McCay's 1900 comic strip. Has some cute comic moments for the kiddies and, while the animation is better than Saturday-morning cartoon quality, it's not Disney.
1992 (G) 85m/C **D:** Masami Hata, William T. Hurtz; **V:** Gabriel Damon, Mickey Rooney, Rene Auberjonois, Daniel Mann, Laura Mooney, Bernard Erhard, William E. Martin. VHS, LV $24.95 HMD, WTA 🐾🐾½

A Little Night Music Features four interwoven, contemporary love stories adapted from the Broadway play, and based loosely on Bergman's "Smiles of a Summer Night." Taylor's pathetic rendition of "Send in the Clowns" should be banned. Filmed on location in Austria.
1977 (PG) 110m/C Elizabeth Taylor, Diana Rigg, Hermione Gingold, Len Cariou, Lesley-Anne Down; **D:** Harold Prince. Academy Awards '77: Best Adapted Score; Nominations: Best Costume Design. VHS, Beta, LV $9.98 SUE 🐾½

Little Nikita A California boy (Phoenix) discovers that his parents are actually Soviet spies planted as American citizens for eventual call to duty. Poitier's performance as the FBI agent tracking the spies is about the only spark in this somewhat incoherent thriller.
1988 (PG) 98m/C River Phoenix, Sidney Poitier, Richard Bradford, Richard Lynch, Caroline Kava, Lucy Deakins; **D:** Richard Benjamin. VHS, Beta, LV $14.95 COL 🐾🐾

Little Noises Glover stars as an artist who seeks not only fame and fortune, but also the love of his best friend (O'Neal). He finally creates a piece that his agent loves, but problems arise.
1991 91m/C Crispin Glover, Tatum O'Neal, Rik Mayall, Tate Donovan, John C. McGinley; **W/D:** Jane Spencer. VHS, Beta $89.95 PSM 🐾🐾

Little Orphan Annie The unjustly forgotten first sound adaptation of the comic strip. Max Steiner's fun score adds a lot, as does the good cast.
1932 60m/B May Robson, Buster Phelps, Mitzie Green, Edgar Kennedy; **D:** John S. Robertson. VHS, Beta $29.98 CCB 🐾🐾½

The Little Prince Disappointing adaptation of the classic children's story by Antoine de Saint-Exupery, about a little boy from asteroid B-612. Lousy Lerner and Loewe score underscores a general lack of magic or spontaneity. ♫It's a Hat; I Need Air; I'm On Your Side; Be Happy; You're a Child; I Never Met a Rose; Why Is the Desert (Lovely to See)?; Closer and Closer and Closer; Little Prince (From Who Knows Where).
1974 (G) 88m/C **GB** Richard Kiley, Bob Fosse, Steven Warner, Gene Wilder; **D:** Stanley Donen; **M:** John Barry. VHS, Beta, LV $14.95 PAR 🐾🐾

The Little Princess Based on the Frances Hodgson Burnett children's classic; perhaps the best of the moppet's films. Shirley is a young schoolgirl in Victorian London sent to a harsh boarding school when her Army officer father is posted abroad. When her father is declared missing, the penniless girl must work as a servant at the school to pay her keep, all the while haunting the hospitals, never believing her father has died. A classic tearjerker.
1939 91m/B Shirley Temple, Richard Greene, Anita Louise, Ian Hunter, Cesar Romero, Arthur Treacher, Sybil Jason, Miles Mander, Marcia Mae Jones, E.E. Clive; **D:** Walter Lang. VHS, Beta, LV $9.95 NEG, MRV, NOS 🐾🐾🐾½

A Little Princess A three-cassette adaptation of Frances Hodgson Burnett's book. In Victorian England, kind-hearted Sara is forced into poverty when her father suddenly dies. Can his longtime friend find her and restore her happiness? Originally aired on PBS as part of the "Wonderworks" family movie series.
1987 180m/C **GB** Amelia Shankley, Nigel Havers, Maureen Lipman; **D:** Carol Wiseman. VHS $29.99 WNE, PME, SIG 🐾🐾🐾½

Little Rascals A collection of early silent escapades of the Little Rascals circa 1924.
1924 60m/B Farina Hoskins, Joe Cobb. VHS, Beta $14.98 VDM 🐾🐾🐾½

Little Rascals, Book 1 Three "Our Gang" shorts: "Railroadin'" (1929), in which the gang takes off on a runaway train; "A Lad and a Lamp" (1932), wherein they find an Aladdin's lamp; and "Beginner's Luck" (1935), in which Spanky wins a dress for a young actress.
193? 59m/B Farina Hoskins, Joe Cobb, Matthew "Stymie" Beard, George "Spanky" McFarland, Carl "Alfalfa" Switzer, Mary Ann Jackson. VHS, Beta $29.98 CCB 🐾🐾🐾½

Little Rascals, Book 2 A second package of "Our Gang" two-reelers: "Bear Shooters" (1930), in which the Gang goes hunting but runs into some bootleggers; "Forgotten Babies" (1933), has Spanky baby-sitting for the gang's brothers and sisters; and "Teacher's Beau" (1935), where the gang cooks up a scheme to chase their teacher's fiance away.
193? 56m/B Matthew "Stymie" Beard, Wheezer Hutchins, George "Spanky" McFarland, Carl "Alfalfa" Switzer VHS, Beta $29.98 CCB 🐾🐾🐾½

Little Rascals, Book 3 Three more "Our Gang" installments are packaged on this tape: "Dogs Is Dogs"(1931), "Anniversary Trouble" (1935) and "Three Men in a Tub" (1938).
1938 54m/B Wheezer Hutchins, Dorothy DeBorba, Matthew "Stymie" Beard, George "Spanky" McFarland, Carl "Alfalfa" Switzer, Darla Hood. VHS, Beta $29.98 CCB 🐾🐾🐾½

Little Rascals, Book 4 Another package of Our Gang favorites, including "Helping Grandma" (1931), "Little Papa" (1935) and "Bear Facts" (1938).
193? 52m/B Matthew "Stymie" Beard, George "Spanky" McFarland, Carl "Alfalfa" Switzer, Darla Hood. VHS, Beta $29.98 CCB 🐾🐾🐾½

Little Rascals, Book 5 The comic adventures of the Little Rascals continue in this package of three original shorts: "Readin' and Writin'," (1932), "Sprucin' Up" (1935) and "Reunion in Rhythm" (1937).
193? 49m/B Breezy Brisbane, Matthew "Stymie" Beard, George "Spanky" McFarland, Carl "Alfalfa" Switzer, Darla Hood. VHS, Beta $29.98 CCB 🐾🐾🐾½

Little Rascals, Book 6 Three more classic "Our Gang" comedy shorts are packaged on this tape: "Free Eats" (1932), "Arbor Day" (1936) and "Mail and Female" (1937).
193? 48m/B Matthew "Stymie" Beard, Breezy Brisbane, George "Spanky" McFarland, Carl "Alfalfa" Switzer, Darla Hood, Dorothy DeBorba, Billy Gilbert. VHS, Beta $29.98 CCB 🐾🐾🐾½

Little Rascals, Book 7 The "Our Gang" kids serve up another portion of comedy in these three shorts: "Hook and Ladder" (1932), "The Lucky Corner" (1936) and "Feed 'Em and Weep" (1938).

193? 47m/B George "Spanky" McFarland, Breezy Brisbane, Dickie Moore, Matthew "Stymie" Beard, Scotty Beckett, Carl "Alfalfa" Switzer, Darla Hood. **VHS, Beta** $29.98 CCB *ᛦᛦ* ½

Little Rascals, Book 8 More fun and nuttiness with "Our Gang" in three original short comedies, "Bouncing Babies" (1929), "Two Too Young" (1936), and "The Awful Tooth" (1938).
193? 42m/B Mary Ann Jackson, Darla Hood, George "Spanky" McFarland, Carl "Alfalfa" Switzer. **VHS, Beta** $29.98 CCB *ᛦᛦ* ½

Little Rascals, Book 9 The Little Rascals scamper into more mischief in these three original shorts: "Little Daddy" (1931), "Spooky Hooky" (1936), and "Hide and Shriek" (1938).
193? 48m/B Darla Hood, George "Spanky" McFarland, Carl "Alfalfa" Switzer, Matthew "Stymie" Cooper. **VHS, Beta** $29.98 CCB *ᛦᛦ* ½

Little Rascals, Book 10 The tenth compilation of original "Our Gang" comedies includes "The First Seven Years" (1929), "Bored of Education" (1936), and "Rushin' Ballet" (1937).
193? 41m/B Jackie Cooper, Mary Ann Jackson, George "Spanky" McFarland, Carl "Alfalfa" Switzer, Darla Hood. **VHS, Beta** $29.98 CCB *ᛦᛦ* ½

Little Rascals, Book 11 The Little Rascals go dramatic in these three shorts, all with a "putting-on-a-show" theme: "Pay As You Exit" (1936), "Three Smart Boys" (1937) and "Our Gang Follies of 1938."
1938 42m/B George "Spanky" McFarland, Carl "Alfalfa" Switzer, Darla Hood. **VHS, Beta** $29.98 CCB *ᛦᛦ* ½

Little Rascals, Book 12 The Little Rascals explore a haunted house, take a train ride and play football in these three original shorts: "Moan and Groan, Inc." (1929), "Choo-Choo!" (1932) and "The Pigskin Palooka" (1937).
1937 53m/B Jackie Cooper, Farina Hoskins, Mary Ann Jackson, George "Spanky" McFarland, Carl "Alfalfa" Switzer, Darla Hood. **VHS, Beta** $29.98 CCB *ᛦᛦ* ½

Little Rascals, Book 13 The Our Gang kids return in three more original shorts: "Shivering Shakespeare" (1930), "The First Round-Up" (1934) and "Fishy Tales" (1937).
1937 48m/B Jackie Cooper, George "Spanky" McFarland, Edgar Kennedy, Carl "Alfalfa" Switzer. **VHS, Beta** $29.98 CCB *ᛦᛦ* ½

Little Rascals, Book 14 Package of shorts leads off with Our Gang's first talkie, "Small Talk" (1929), a three-reeler. The other two entries are "Little Sinner" (1935) and "Hearts Are Thumps" (1937).
193? 52m/B Darla Hood, Mary Ann Jackson, George "Spanky" McFarland, Carl "Alfalfa" Switzer. **VHS, Beta** $29.98 CCB *ᛦᛦ* ½

Little Rascals, Book 15 Those rascally imps return once again in three more original shorts: "When the Wind Blows" (1930), "For Pete's Sake" (1934) and "Glove Taps" (1937).
193? 50m/B Edgar Kennedy, Tommy "Butch" Bond, George "Spanky" McFarland, Wheezer Hutchins. **VHS, Beta** $29.98 CCB *ᛦᛦ* ½

Little Rascals, Book 16 Three more charming episodes featuring the original brat pack. The urchins of yesteryear star in "Love Business," "Hi Neighbor," and "Came the Brawn."

193? 30m/B Matthew "Stymie" Beard, Carl "Alfalfa" Switzer, George "Spanky" McFarland, Darla Hood; *D:* Fred Wolf. **VHS, Beta** $19.95 REP, CCB *ᛦᛦ* ½

Little Rascals, Book 17 Three classic shorts, "Boxing Gloves," "The Kid from Borneo," and "Roamin' Holiday."
1931 46m/B Jean Darling, George "Spanky" McFarland, Darla Hood. **VHS, Beta** $29.98 CCB *ᛦᛦ* ½

Little Rascals, Book 18 Here are two early "Our Gang" comedies from the silent era: "Saturday's Lesson" (1929) and "Wiggle Your Ears" (1929).
1929 41m/B Farina Hoskins, Wheezer Hutchins, Mary Ann Jackson, Joe Cobb. **VHS, Beta** $29.98 CCB *ᛦᛦ* ½

Little Rascals: Choo Choo/Fishy Tales Spanky, Darla, Buckwheat, Stymie, and Alfalfa in two uncut installments of the groundbreaking children's comedy.
1932 30m/B George "Spanky" McFarland, Darla Hood, Carl "Alfalfa" Switzer, Matthew "Stymie" Beard. **VHS** $9.98 REP, CCB *ᛦᛦ* ½

Little Rascals Christmas Special Spanky and the Little Rascals attempt to raise enough money to buy a winter coat for Spanky's mom and learn the true meaning of Christmas along the way.
1979 60m/C Darla Hood, Matthew "Stymie" Beard; *D:* Fred Wolf, Charles Swenson. **VHS, Beta** $29.95 FHE *ᛦᛦ* ½

Little Rascals Collector's Edition, Vol. 1-6 A collection put together by Spotlight containing six individual two-reelers. Twelve episodes total featuring the rambunctious bunch of child stars.
19?? 180m/B George "Spanky" McFarland, Darla Hood, Carl "Alfalfa" Switzer, Matthew "Stymie" Beard. **VHS, Beta** $89.95 REP *ᛦᛦ* ½

Little Rascals Comedy Classics, Vol. 1 Vivacious collection of six of the gang's original episodes. This presentation contains "Railroadin'," "A Lad and a Lamp," "Beginner's Luck," "Bear Shooters," "Forgotten Babies," and "Teacher's Beau."
19?? 112m/B George "Spanky" McFarland, Darla Hood, Carl "Alfalfa" Switzer, Matthew "Stymie" Beard. **VHS, Beta** $19.95 REP, CCB *ᛦᛦ* ½

Little Rascals Comedy Classics, Vol. 2 Second volume of the mischievous gang's uncut, original shorts. The six episodes on this installment are "Pay as You Exit," "Three Smart Boys," "Our Gang Follies of 1938," "The First Round-Up," "Shivering Shakespeare," and "Fishy Tales."
19?? 90m/B George "Spanky" McFarland, Darla Hood, Carl "Alfalfa" Switzer, Matthew "Stymie" Beard. **VHS** $19.95 REP, CCB *ᛦᛦ* ½

Little Rascals: Fish Hooky/Spooky Hooky Two uncut classics featuring those mischievous little pranksters.
1933 30m/B Carl "Alfalfa" Switzer, Darla Hood, George "Spanky" McFarland, Matthew "Stymie" Beard. **VHS** $9.98 REP, CCB *ᛦᛦ* ½

Little Rascals: Honkey Donkey/Sprucin' Up The gang's comic capers continue in "Honky Donkey" and "Sprucin' Up."
1934 30m/B George "Spanky" McFarland, Darla Hood, Carl "Alfalfa" Switzer, Matthew "Stymie" Beard. **VHS** $9.95 REP *ᛦᛦ* ½

Little Rascals: Little Sinner/Two Too Young The gang stars in "Little Sinner" and "Two Too Young."
1935 30m/B George "Spanky" McFarland, Darla Hood, Carl "Alfalfa" Switzer, Matthew "Stymie" Beard. **VHS** $9.98 REP, CCB *ᛦᛦ* ½

Little Rascals: Mush and Milk/Three Men in a Tub Two uncensored features starring those lovable urchins.
1933 30m/B George "Spanky" McFarland, Carl "Alfalfa" Switzer, Darla Hood, Matthew "Stymie" Beard. **VHS** $9.98 REP, CCB *ᛦᛦ* ½

Little Rascals on Parade A collection of six vintage "Our Gang" shorts from the '30s: "Free Eats," "Arbor Day," "Mail and Female," "Hook and Ladder," "The Lucky Corner" and "Feed 'Em and Weep."
1937 60m/B George "Spanky" McFarland, Carl "Alfalfa" Switzer, Darla Hood. **VHS** $19.95 REP, CCB *ᛦᛦ* ½

Little Rascals: Pups is Pups/Three Smart Boys Two of the most hilarious features from the Little Rascals.
1930 30m/B George "Spanky" McFarland, Carl "Alfalfa" Switzer, Darla Hood, Matthew "Stymie" Beard. **VHS** $9.98 REP, CCB *ᛦᛦ* ½

Little Rascals: Readin' and Writin'/Mail and Female Two uncut features starring those delightful rapscallions.
1931 30m/B George "Spanky" McFarland, Carl "Alfalfa" Switzer, Darla Hood, Matthew "Stymie" Beard. **VHS** $9.98 REP, CCB *ᛦᛦ* ½

Little Rascals: Reunion in Rhythm/Mike Fright Join the gang in the outrageous episodes "Reunion in Rhythm" and "Mike Fright."
1937 30m/B George "Spanky" McFarland, Darla Hood, Carl "Alfalfa" Switzer, Matthew "Stymie" Beard. **VHS** $9.98 REP, CCB *ᛦᛦ* ½

Little Rascals: Spanky/Feed 'Em and Weep Two hilarious features with the antics of those crazy kids.
1932 30m/B George "Spanky" McFarland, Carl "Alfalfa" Switzer, Darla Hood, Matthew "Stymie" Beard. **VHS** $9.98 REP, CCB *ᛦᛦ* ½

Little Rascals: The Pinch Singer/Framing Youth Mischievous youngsters run amok in "The Pinch Singer" and "Framing Youth."
1936 30m/B George "Spanky" McFarland, Darla Hood, Carl "Alfalfa" Switzer, Matthew "Stymie" Beard. **VHS** $9.98 REP, CCB *ᛦᛦ* ½

Little Rascals Two Reelers, Vol. 1 Wacky youngsters two reeler containing "Lazy Days," and "Spooky Hooky."
1929 30m/B George "Spanky" McFarland, Carl "Alfalfa" Switzer, Darla Hood, Matthew "Stymie" Beard. **VHS** $14.95 REP *ᛦᛦ* ½

Little Rascals Two Reelers, Vol. 2 Comic two-reeler from those mischievous youngsters containing "Bedtime Worries," and "Glove Taps."
1933 30m/B George "Spanky" McFarland, Darla Hood, Carl "Alfalfa" Switzer, Matthew "Stymie" Beard. **VHS** $14.95 REP *ᛦᛦ* ½

Little Rascals Two Reelers, Vol. 3 Those troublesome youngsters are back in a two-reeler containing "Second Childhood" and "Hide and Shriek."
1936 30m/B George "Spanky" McFarland, Darla Hood, Carl "Alfalfa" Switzer, Matthew "Stymie" Beard. **VHS** $14.95 REP *ᛦᛦ* ½

Little Rascals Two Reelers, Vol. 4 Two reeler containing "When the Wind Blows," and "Hearts are Thumps."
1930 30m/B George "Spanky" McFarland, Darla Hood, Carl "Alfalfa" Switzer, Matthew "Stymie" Beard. **VHS** $14.95 REP *ᛦᛦ* ½

Little Rascals Two Reelers, Vol. 5 These two episodes of the gang feature "Hi Neighbor," and "Came the Brawn."
1934 30m/B George "Spanky" McFarland, Darla Hood, Carl "Alfalfa" Switzer, Matthew "Stymie" Beard. **VHS** $14.95 REP *ᛦᛦ* ½

Little Rascals Two Reelers, Vol. 6 The gang frolics in this two-reeler containing "Love Business," and "Pigskin Palooka."
1936 30m/B George "Spanky" McFarland, Darla Hood, Carl "Alfalfa" Switzer, Matthew "Stymie" Beard. VHS $14.95 REP *ℐℐℐ½*

Little Rascals, Vol. 1 Here is a collection of three uncut "Little Rascals" short subjects. In "Boxing Gloves" (1929), Chubby and Joe decide two settle their differences over who should have Jean Darling's love by staging a winner-take-all boxing match. In "The Kid from Borneo" (1933), Spanky thinks he's met a crazy relative when he confuses an untamed human from Borneo for his uncle from the circus. In "Roamin' Holiday" (1936), Alfalfa and Spanky lead the gang on a journey fit for a hobo.
1929 50m/B Darla Hood, George "Spanky" McFarland, Carl "Alfalfa" Switzer, Matthew "Stymie" Beard. VHS $14.95 REP, CCB *ℐℐℐ½*

Little Rascals, Vol. 2 Another uncut compilation of three classic episodes featuring the goofy gang. In "The First Seven Years" (1930), Speck and Jackie battle for the attention of a beautiful Mary Ann. In the award-winning "Bored of Education" (1936), Spanky and Alfalfa devise a plan to play hooky from school by developing very acute tooth problems. In "Rushin' Ballet" (1937), Alfalfa and Spanky establish the Secret Revengers Club and liberate Buckwheat and Porky from the bonds of tyranny.
1930 50m/B George "Spanky" McFarland, Carl "Alfalfa" Switzer. VHS $9.95 REP, CCB *ℐℐℐ½*

Little Red Riding Hood From "Faerie Tale Theatre" comes the retelling of the story about a girl (Mary Steenburgen) off to give her grandmother a picnic basket, only to get stopped by a wicked wolf McDowell. Not particularly faithful, but fun and scary.
1983 60m/C Mary Steenburgen, Malcolm McDowell; D: Graeme Clifford. VHS, Beta, LV $14.98 FOX, FCT *ℐℐℐ*

Little Red Schoolhouse A hardnosed schoolteacher hunts for a truant lad and both of them land in jail.
1936 64m/C Frank "Junior" Coghlan, Dickie Moore, Ann Doran. VHS, Beta $19.95 NOS, KRT, FCT *ℐℐ*

A Little Romance An American girl living in Paris falls in love with a French boy; eventually they run away, to seal their love with a kiss beneath a bridge. Olivier gives a wonderful, if not hammy, performance as the old pickpocket who encourages her. Gentle, agile comedy based on the novel by Patrick Cauvin.
1979 (PG) 110m/C Laurence Olivier, Diane Lane, Thelonious Bernard, Sally Kellerman, Broderick Crawford; D: George Roy Hill; M: Georges Delerue. Academy Awards '79: Best Original Score; Nominations: Best Adapted Screenplay. VHS, Beta, LV $19.98 WAR, PIA, TAM *ℐℐℐ*

A Little Sex Capshaw, in her screen debut, finds herself the wife of womanizer Matheson. Harmless, but pointless, with a TV-style plot.
1982 (R) 94m/C Tim Matheson, Kate Capshaw, Edward Herrmann, Wallace Shawn, John Glover; D: Bruce Paltrow. VHS, Beta $59.95 MCA *ℐℐ*

Little Shop of Horrors The landmark cheapie classic, which Roger Corman reputedly filmed in three days, about a nebbish working in a city florist shop who unknowingly cultivates an intelligent plant that demands human meat for sustenance. Notable for then-unknown Nicholson's appearance as a masochistic dental patient. Hilarious, unpretentious farce—if you liked this one, check out Corman's "Bucket of Blood" for more of the same. Inspired a musical of the same name, remade as a movie again in 1986. Available colorized.
1960 70m/B Jackie Joseph, Jonathan Haze, Mel Welles, Jack Nicholson, Dick Miller; D: Roger Corman. VHS, Beta, LV $19.98 NEG, MRV, NOS *ℐℐℐ½*

Little Shop of Horrors During a solar eclipse, Seymour buys an unusual plant and takes it back to the flower shop where he works. The plant, Audrey 2, becomes a town attraction as it grows at an unusual rate, but Seymour learns that he must feed Audrey fresh human blood to keep her growing. Soon, Audrey is giving the orders ("Feed me") and timid Seymour must find "deserving" victims. Martin's performance as the masochistic dentist is alone worth the price. Song, dance, gore, and more prevail in this outrageous musical comedy. Four Top Levi Stubbs is the commending voice of Audrey 2. Based on the off-broadway play, which was based on Roger Corman's 1960 horror spoof. ♫Mean Green Mother From Outer Space; Some Fun Now; Your Day Begins Tonight.
1986 (PG-13) 94m/C Rick Moranis, Ellen Greene, Vincent Gardenia, Steve Martin, James Belushi, Christopher Guest, Bill Murray, John Candy; D: Frank Oz; M: Alan Menken, Howard Ashman. VHS, Beta, LV $19.98 WAR, HMV *ℐℐℐ*

Little Sister Prankster Silverman, on a dare, dresses up as a girl and joins a sorority. Problems arise when he falls in love with his "big sister" (Milano) in the sorority. What will happen when she finds out the truth? Will we care?
1992 (PG-13) 94m/C Jonathan Silverman, Alyssa Milano. VHS $89.98 LIV *ℐ½*

Little Sweetheart A reworking of "The Bad Seed," with a nine-year-old girl engaging in murder, burglary, and blackmail, ruining the adults around her. Based on "The Naughty Girls" by Arthur Wise.
1990 (R) 93m/C John Hurt, Karen Young, Barbara Bosson, John McMartin, Cassie Barasch; D: Anthony Simmons. VHS, Beta, LV, 8mm $79.95 SUE *ℐ½*

The Little Theatre of Jean Renoir A farewell by director Jean Renoir featuring three short films. In the first, Renoir's humanist beliefs are apparent in "The Last Christmas Dinner," a Hans Christian Andersen-inspired story. Next, "The Electric Floor Waxer" is a comic opera. The third piece is called "A Tribute to Tolerance." Slight but important late statement by a great director. In French with English subtitles.
1971 100m/C Jean Renoir, Fernand Sardou, Jean Carmet, Francoise Arnoul, Jeanne Moreau; W/D: Jean Renoir. VHS, Beta, LV $49.95 INT, FLI, IME *ℐℐ*

The Little Thief Touted as Francois Truffaut's final legacy, this trite mini-drama is actually based on a story he co-wrote with Claude de Givray about a post-World War II adolescent girl who reacts to the world around her by stealing and petty crime. In French with English subtitles. Truffaut's hand is markedly absent, but this film is a testament to his abruptly and sadly truncated career. Director Miller was Truffaut's long-time assistant.
1989 (PG-13) 108m/C FR Charlotte Gainsbourg, Simon de la Brosse, Didier Bezace, Raoul Billerey, Nathalie Cardone; D: Claude Miller. VHS, Beta, LV $89.99 HBO, TAM *ℐℐℐ*

Little Tough Guys The Little Tough Guys (a.k.a. Dead End Kids) come to the rescue of Halop, a young tough guy gone bad to avenge his father's unjust imprisonment. First of the "Little Tough Guys" series for the former Dead End Kids, who later became the East Side Kids before eventually evolving into the Bowery Boys.
1938 84m/B Helen Parrish, Billy Halop, Leo Gorcey, Marjorie Main, Gabriel Dell, Huntz Hall; D: Harold Young. VHS, Beta, 3/4U, Special order formats $19.95 NOS, MRV, VYY *ℐℐ*

Little Treasure A stripper heads for Mexico to search for her long-lost father, and ends up looking for treasure with an American guy. Disappointing effort of director Sharp.
1985 (R) 95m/C Burt Lancaster, Margot Kidder, Ted Danson, Joseph Hacker, Malena Doria; W/D: Alan Sharp. VHS, Beta, LV $79.95 COL *ℐ½*

The Little Valentino One day in the aimless life of a young punk who gets by on his wits and petty theft. Jeles' directorial debut. In Hungarian with English subtitles.
1979 102m/B HU D: Andras Jeles. VHS $59.95 FCT, AUD *ℐℐ*

Little Vegas Looks like easy street for a young man who inherits a bundle from his girlfriend, but he's forced to wake up and smell the cappucino when her family and the other residents of the tiny desert berg think there's a gigolo in the woodpile. Much strife with siblings as he wages a battle for the bucks with the son while wooing the woman's daughter, with a measure of mob inflicted plot twists. Mildly amusing, cut from vein of you can't get rich quick and get away with it.
1990 (R) 90m/C Michael Nouri, Jerry Stiller, John Sayles, Anthony John Denison, Catherine O'Hara, Bruce McGill, Anne Francis, Bob Goldthwait; W/D: Perry Lang. VHS, LV $89.95 COL *ℐℐ½*

Little Vera Extremely well-done Soviet film chronicles the life of a young working-class woman who loves rock music and who has been profoundly affected by Western Civilization. Post-glasnost Soviet production gives Westerners a glimpse into the Russian way of life. A box-office bonanza back home. In Russian with English subtitles. AKA: Malenkaya Vera.
1988 130m/C RU Natalia Negoda, Andrei Sokolov, Yuri Nazarov, Ludmila Zaisova, Alexander Niegreva; D: Vassili Pitchul. VHS, Beta, LV $34.95 FCT, LUM, WBF *ℐℐℐ*

Little White Lies Jillian and Matheson meet and fall in love in an exotic vacation. But both are traveling under assumed identities—she's a policewoman tracking a jewel thief and he's an incognito doctor. When they reunite stateside they try to stick to their ruses in humdrum comedic fashion. Made for network TV.
1989 88m/C Ann Jillian, Tim Matheson; D: Anson Williams. VHS $79.95 RHI *ℐℐ*

Little Women Louisa May Alcott's Civil War story of the four March sisters—Jo, Beth, Amy, and Meg—who share their loves, their joys, and their sorrows. Everything about this classic film is wonderful, from the lavish period costumes to the excellent script by Victor Heerman and Sarah Mason, and particularly the captivating performances by the cast. A must-see for fans of Alcott and Hepburn, and others will find it enjoyable. Remade in 1949 and again in 1978 for television.
1933 107m/B Katharine Hepburn, Joan Bennett, Paul Lukas, Edna May Oliver, Frances Dee, Spring Byington; D: George Cukor. Academy Awards '33: Best Adapted Screenplay; Nominations: Best Director (Cukor), Best Picture; Venice Film Festival '34: Best Actress (Hepburn). VHS, Beta, 8mm $19.98 MGM, KUI, IGP *ℐℐℐℐ*

Little Women Stylized color remake of the George Cukor 1933 classic. Top-notch if too obvious cast portrays Louisa May Alcott's story of teenage girls growing up against the backdrop of the Civil War. Remade again, for television in 1978.
1949 121m/C June Allyson, Peter Lawford, Margaret O'Brien, Elizabeth Taylor, Janet Leigh, Mary Astor; **D:** Mervyn LeRoy. Academy Awards '49: Best Art Direction/Set Decoration (Color); Nominations: Best Color Cinematography. **VHS** $19.98 MGM ♫♫♫

Little Women The third screen version of Louisa May Alcott's classic story. Lackluster compared to the previous attempts, particularly the sterling 1933 film, but still worthwhile. During the Civil War, four sisters share their lives as they grow up and find romance. Garson's television debut. Followed by a television series.
1978 200m/C Meredith Baxter Birney, Susan Dey, Ann Dusenberry, Eve Plumb, Dorothy McGuire, Robert Young, Greer Garson, Cliff Potts, William Shatner; **D:** David Lowell Rich. **VHS** NO ♫♫

Little World of Don Camillo A French-made farce based on the beloved novels of Giovanni Guareschi. Earthy priest Don Camillo clashes repeatedly with his friendly enemy, the communist mayor of a tiny Italian village. The hero talks directly to God, whose voice is provided by Orson Welles, also narrator of the English version. Charming, good-natured approach. **AKA:** Le Petit Monde de Don Camillo.
1951 106m/B FR IT Fernandel, Gino Cervi, Sylvia, Vera Talqui; **D:** Julien Duvivier. **VHS, Beta, 8mm** $29.95 VYY, FCT ♫♫♫

The Littlest Angel Musical about a shepherd boy who dies falling off a cliff and wants to become an angel. He learns a valuable lesson in the spirit of giving. Made for TV.
1969 77m/C Johnny Whitaker, Fred Gwynne, E.G. Marshall, Cab Calloway, Connie Stevens, Tony Randall. **VHS, Beta** $14.98 SUE, NEG, KAR ♫♫

The Littlest Horse Thieves Good Disney film about three children and their efforts to save some ponies who work in mines. The children take it upon themselves to see that the animals escape the abuse and neglect they are put through. Filmed on location in England with excellent photography. **AKA:** Escape from the Dark.
1976 (G) 109m/C Alastair Sim, Peter Barkworth; **D:** Charles Jarrott. **VHS, Beta** $69.95 DIS ♫♫½

The Littlest Outlaw A Mexican peasant boy steals a beautiful stallion to save it from being destroyed. Together, they ride off on a series of adventures. Disney movie filmed on location in Mexico.
1954 73m/C Pedro Armendariz Sr., Joseph Calleia, Andres Velasquez; **D:** Roberto Gavaldon. **VHS, Beta** $69.95 DIS ♫♫½

The Littlest Rebel Temple stars in this well-done piece set during the Civil War in the Old South. She befriends a Union officer while protecting her father at the same time. She even goes to Washington to talk with President Lincoln. Nice dance sequences by Temple and Robinson. Available in computer-colored version.
1935 70m/B Shirley Temple, John Boles, Jack Holt, Bill Robinson, Karen Morley, Willie Best; **D:** David Butler. **VHS, Beta** $19.98 FOX ♫♫½

Littlest Warrior Zooshio, the littlest warrior, is forced to leave his beloved forest and experiences many adventures before he is reunited with his family. Animated.
1975 70m/C **VHS, Beta** $24.95 FHE ♫♫½

Live a Little, Love a Little Itinerant photographer Elvis juggles two different jobs by running around a lot. Sexually more frank than earlier King vehicles. ♫Almost in Love; A Little Less Conversation; Edge of Reality; Wonderful World.
1968 90m/C Elvis Presley, Michele Carey, Rudy Vallee, Don Porter, Dick Sargent, Sterling Holloway, Eddie Hodges; **D:** Norman Taurog. **VHS, Beta** $19.95 MGM ♫♫

Live a Little, Steal a Lot Surprisingly well-done film of two Florida beach bums who engineer the heist of the Star of India. Nice chase scenes add to an already fine action film. **AKA:** Murph the Surf; You Can't Steal Love.
1975 (PG) 101m/C Robert Conrad, Don Stroud, Donna Mills, Robyn Millan, Burt Young; **D:** Marvin J. Chomsky. **VHS** $19.98 WAR, OM ♫♫½

Live and Let Die Agent 007 is out to thwart the villainous Dr. Kananga, a black mastermind who plans to control western powers with voodoo and hard drugs. Moore's first appearance as Bond. Can't we have the real Bond back? Title song by Paul McCartney.
1973 (PG) 131m/C GB Roger Moore, Jane Seymour, Yaphet Kotto, Clifton James, Julius W. Harris, Geoffrey Holder, David Hedison, Gloria Hendry, Bernard Lee, Lois Maxwell, Madeleine Smith, Roy Stewart; **D:** Guy Hamilton; **M:** George Martin. **VHS, Beta, LV** $19.98 MGM, FOX, TLF ♫♫

Live! From Death Row Cassidy plays a tabloid TV host who'll do anything to get ratings. She's set to do a live interview with a condemned serial killer (Davison) shortly before his execution. But Davison and his fellow death-row inmates take Cassidy and her crew hostage as he decides to use the show for his own media message.
1992 94m/C Joanna Cassidy, Bruce Davison, Art LaFleur, Calvin Levels, Michael D. Roberts; **W/D:** Patrick Duncan. **VHS** $79.95 ABC, PSM ♫♫

The Live Wire Stunt-ridden action fare featuring Talmadge at his most daring. This adventure is complete with desert island, lost treasure, stowaways, evil-doers, and a race against the clock.
1934 57m/B Richard Talmadge, George Walsh, Charles French, Alberta Vaughn; **D:** Harry S. Webb. **VHS, Beta** $24.95 NOS, DVT, GPV ♫

Live Wire Brosnan is an FBI bomb expert who needs a new line of work. He's up against a terrorist psychopath who has his greedy hands on a new type of explosive. It's liquid, undetectable, looks as innocent as a glass of water, and is capable of blowing up Washington, D.C. Made for cable television. Also available in an unrated version.
1992 (R) 85m/C Pierce Brosnan, Ben Cross, Ron Silver, Lisa Eilbacher; **D:** Christian Duguay. **VHS** $89.95 COL, NLC ♫♫½

The Lives of a Bengal Lancer One of Hollywood's greatest rousing adventures. Three British Lancers, of varying experience, encounter a vicious revolution against colonial rule. Rivaled only by "Gunga Din" as the ultimate 1930s swashbuckler. Swell plot; lotsa action; great comraderie. Based on the novel by Major Francis Yeats-Brown.
1935 110m/B Gary Cooper, Franchot Tone, Richard Cromwell, Guy Standing; **D:** Henry Hathaway. Academy Awards '35 Nominations: Best Adapted Screenplay, Best Director (Hathaway), Best Film Editing, Best Interior Decoration, Best Picture, Best Sound; National Board of Review Awards '35: 10 Best Films of the Year. **VHS, Beta** $14.98 MCA ♫♫♫♫

Livin' Large An African-American delivery boy gets the break of his life when a nearby newscaster is shot dead. Grabbing the microphone and continuing the story, he soon finds himself hired by an Atlanta news station as an anchorman, fulfilling a life-long dream. But problems arise when he finds himself losing touch with his friends, his old neighborhood and his roots. Comedy "deals" with the compelling issue of blacks finding success in a white world by trivializing the issue at every turn and resorting to racial stereotypes.
1991 (R) 96m/C Terrence "T.C." Carson, Lisa Arrindell, Blanche Baker, Nathaniel "Afrika" Hall, Julia Campbell; **D:** Michael Schultz; **M:** Herbie Hancock. **VHS** $92.99 HBO ♫♫

Livin' the Life A young Englishman entertains a series of troublesome Mitty-esque fantasies.
1984 83m/C Rupert Everett, Christina Raines, Catherine Rabett; **D:** Francis Megahy. **VHS, Beta** $69.98 LIV, VES ♫½

The Living Coffin Woman has alarm rigged on her coffin in case she's buried alive. And they called her paranoid. Loosely based on Poe's "Premature Burial." **AKA:** El Grito de la Muerte.
1958 72m/C MX Gaston Santos, Maria Duval, Pedro de Aguillon; **D:** Fernando Mendez. **VHS** $19.98 SNC ♫½

The Living Daylights The 17th Bond film. After being used as a pawn in a fake Russian defector plot, our intrepid spy tracks down an international arms and opium smuggling ring. Fine debut by Dalton as 007 in a rousing, refreshing cosmopolitan shoot-em-up. Let's be frank: we were all getting a little fatigued of Roger Moore.
1987 (PG) 130m/C Timothy Dalton, Maryam D'Abo, Jeroen Krabbe, John Rhys-Davies, Robert Brown, Joe Don Baker, Desmond Llewelyn; **D:** John Glen; **M:** John Barry. **VHS, Beta, LV** $19.98 MGM, TLF, FOX ♫♫♫

The Living Dead An English film about a mad, re-animating scientist. **AKA:** The Scotland Yard Mystery.
1936 76m/B GB Gerald du Maurier, George Curzan. **VHS, Beta** $24.95 NOS, SNC, DVT ♫♫

Living Free Sequel to "Born Free," based on the nonfictional books by Joy Adamson. Recounts the travails of Elsa the lioness, who is now dying, with three young cubs that need care. Nice and pleasant, but could you pick up the pace?
1972 (G) 91m/C Susan Hampshire, Nigel Davenport; **D:** Jack Couffer. **VHS, Beta, LV** $9.95 COL, GKK ♫♫½

The Living Head Archaeologists discover the ancient sepulcher of the great Aztec warrior, Acatl. Ignoring a curse, they steal his severed head and incur the fury of Xitsliapoli. They should have known better. Dubbed in English. **AKA:** La Cabeza Viviente.
1959 75m/B MX Mauricio Garces, Ana Louisa Peluffo, German Robles, Abel Salazar; **D:** Chano Urueto. **VHS, Beta** $29.95 SNC, VYY ♫½

Living on Tokyo Time Interesting but often dull, low budget independent comedy about a young Japanese woman who hitches up with a boorish Japanese-American man in order to stay in the United States. An Asian view of Asian-America, filmed on location in San Francisco.
1987 83m/C Minako Ohashi, Ken Nakagawa, Kate Connell; **D:** Steven Okazaki. **VHS, Beta** $19.98 NLC, TAM ♫♫½

Living to Die Vegas gumshoe is assigned to investigate a blackmailed official, and discovers a woman believed to be dead is alive and beautiful and living incognito. This mystifies him.
1991 (R) 84m/C Wings Hauser, Darcy Demoss, Asher Brauner, Arnold Vosloo, Jim Williams; *D:* Wings Hauser. VHS $19.95 *PMH, HHE* ⅐½

The Lizzies of Mack Sennett Three quick-paced, hilarious Sennett "Tin Lizzie" comedies: "Lizzies of the Field," "Leading Lizzie Astray" and "Love, Speed and Thrills." Plenty of signature slapstick from the master.
1915 51m/C Billy Bevan, Fatty Arbuckle, Mack Swain, Chester Conklin; *D:* Mack Sennett. VHS, Beta $24.95 *VYY* ⅐½

Loaded Guns Airline stewardess-cum-double agent must totally immobilize a top drug trafficking ring. Pathetic spy tale with plenty of unintended laughs
1975 90m/C Ursula Andress, Woody Strode; *D:* Fernando Di Leo. VHS, Beta $59.95 *LIV, MON* Woof!

Loaded Pistols Story set in the old West starring Gene Autry.
1948 80m/B Gene Autry; *D:* John English. VHS, Beta $19.95 *NOS, VCN, DVT* ⅐

Loan Shark An ex-convict gets a job at a tire company, working undercover to expose a loan shark ring. Hackneyed plot moves quickly.
1952 79m/B George Raft, John Hoyt; *D:* Seymour Friedman. VHS, Beta, LV *NO* ⅐⅐

Lobster for Breakfast An Italian gag-fest about a toilet salesman infiltrating his friend's confused marital existence just to make a sale. With English subtitles; also available in a dubbed version.
1982 (R) 96m/C *IT* Enrico Montesano, Claude Brasseur, Claudine Auger; *D:* Giorgio Capitani. VHS, Beta $39.98 *SUE* ⅐⅐½

Lobster Man from Mars When rich movie producer (Curtis) learns from his accountant that he must produce a flop or be taken to the cleaners by the IRS, he buys a homemade horror movie from a young filmmaker. The film is an ultra-low budget production featuring a kooky lobster man and a screaming damsel. The premise peters out about halfway through, but there are enough yuks to keep you going.
1989 (PG) 84m/C Tony Curtis, Deborah Foreman, Patrick Macnee. VHS, Beta, LV $14.95 *LIV* ⅐⅐

Local Badman A dim-witted cowhand saves the day in this rip-roaring tale of the old west.
1932 60m/B Hoot Gibson. VHS, Beta $19.95 *NOS, UHV, RXM* ⅐

Local Hero Riegert is a yuppie representative of a huge oil company who endeavors to buy a sleepy Scottish fishing village for excavation, and finds himself hypnotized by the place and its crusty denizens. Back in Texas at company headquarters, tycoon Lancaster deals with a psycho therapist and gazes at the stars looking for clues. A low-key, charmingly offbeat Scottish comedy with its own sense of logic and quiet humor, poetic landscapes, and unique characters, epitomizing Forsyth's original style.
1983 (PG) 112m/C *GB* Peter Riegert, Denis Lawson, Burt Lancaster, Fulton Mackay, Jenny Seagrove, Peter Capaldi; *D:* Bill Forsyth. VHS, Beta, LV $19.98 *WAR* ⅐⅐⅐⅐

The Loch Ness Horror The famed monster surfaces and chomps on the local poachers—and with good reason. Would that it had munched this movie's producer in, say, 1981.
1982 93m/C Barry Buchanan, Miki McKenzie, Sandy Kenyon; *D:* Larry Buchanan. VHS, Beta $39.95 *MON* Woof!

Lock and Load Why are all the soldiers in the 82nd Airborne stealing vast sums, then committing suicide? One of the guys involved wants to know.
1990 (R) ?m/C Jack Vogel; *D:* David A. Prior. VHS $79.95 *AIP* ⅐⅐

Lock Up Peaceful con Stallone, with only six months to go, is harassed and tortured by vicious prison warden Sutherland in retribution for an unexplained past conflict. Lackluster and moronic; semi-color; surely Sutherland can find better roles.
1989 (R) 115m/C Sylvester Stallone, Donald Sutherland, Sonny Landham, John Amos, Darlanne Fluegel, Frank McRae; *D:* John Flynn. VHS, Beta $14.95 *LIV* ⅐½

Lockdown Charged with his partner's murder, a detective is forced to ponder the perennial puzzle of life. Not a pretty sight.
1990 90m/C Joe Estevez, Mike Farrell, Richard Lynch. VHS $89.95 *VMK* ⅐½

The Lodger A mysterious lodger is thought to be a rampaging mass murderer of young women. First Hitchcock film to explore the themes and ideas that would become his trademarks. Silent. Climactic chase is memorable. Remade three times. Look closely for the Master in his first cameo. *AKA:* The Case of Jonathan Drew; The Lodger: A Case of London Fog.
1926 91m/B Ivor Novello, Marie Ault, Arthur Chesney, Malcolm Keen; *Cameos:* Alfred Hitchcock; *D:* Alfred Hitchcock. VHS, Beta $19.95 *NOS, GPV, VYY* ⅐⅐⅐

The Lodger Based on the true story of the murderer (Jack the Ripper) who stalked the gloomy streets of Whitechapel in 1889, slashing the throats of prostitutes. Cregar has been called the most haunting of the screen Rippers. He lurkingly plays the house-guest who bewilders his hosts, the Burtons, with his bizarre ways. As the film proceeds, they truly become unhinged by the similarities between "Slade" and the killer. Considered by fans to be the classic of the Ripper genre. Adapted from the book of the same name by Marie Belloc Lowndes.
1944 84m/B Merle Oberon, George Sanders, Laird Cregar, Cedric Hardwicke, Sara Allgood, Aubrey Mather, Queenie Leonard; *D:* John Brahm. VHS ⅐⅐⅐

Logan's Run In the 23rd century, a hedonistic society exists in a huge bubble and people are only allowed to live to the age of 30. Intriguing concepts and great futuristic sets prevail here. Based on the novel by William Nolan and George Clayton.
1976 120m/C Michael York, Jenny Agutter, Richard Jordan, Roscoe Lee Browne, Farrah Fawcett, Peter Ustinov, Camilla Carr, Ann Ford; *D:* Michael Anderson Sr.; *M:* Jerry Goldsmith. Academy Awards '76: Best Visual Effects; Nominations: Best Art Direction/Set Decoration, Best Cinematography. VHS, Beta, LV $59.95 *MGM* ⅐⅐½

Lois Gibbs and the Love Canal Mason's television movie debut as Lois Gibbs, a housewife turned activist, fighting the authorities over chemical-dumping in the Love Canal area of Niagara Falls, New York. The script doesn't convey the seriousness of developments in that region.
1982 100m/C Marsha Mason, Robert Gunton, Penny Fuller, Roberta Maxwell, Jeremy Licht, Louise Latham; *D:* Glenn Jordan. VHS *NO* ⅐⅐

Lola A wonderful tale of a nightclub dancer and her amorous adventures. Innovative film that marked the beginning of French New Wave. In French with English subtitles.
1961 90m/B *FR* Anouk Aimee, Marc Michel, Elina Labourdette, Jacques Harden; *D:* Jacques Demy. VHS $59.95 *INT, TAM* ⅐⅐⅐

Lola A teenaged girl links up romantically with a considerably older writer of pornographic books. One would expect more from such a good cast, but the film never follows through. British release was originally 98 minutes. *AKA:* The Statutory Affair; Twinky.
1969 (PG) 88m/C *GB IT* Charles Bronson, Susan George, Trevor Howard, Michael Craig, Honor Blackman, Lionel Jeffries, Robert Morley, Jack Hawkins, Orson Bean, Kay Medford, Paul Ford; *D:* Richard Donner. VHS $59.95 *FCT, MRV* ⅐½

Lola Montes Ophuls' final masterpiece recounts the life and sins of the famous courtesan, mistress of Franz Liszt and the King of Bavaria. Ignored upon release, but hailed later by the French as a cinematic landmark. Presented in its original wide-screen format; in French with English subtitles. Also available in a 110 minute version. Adapted from an unpublished novel by Cecil Saint-Laurent.
1955 140m/C *FR* Martine Carol, Peter Ustinov, Anton Walbrook, Ivan Desny, Oskar Werner; *D:* Max Ophuls. Beta, LV $69.95 *CRC, TAM, NLC* ⅐⅐⅐⅐

Lolita A middle-aged professor is consumed by his lust for a teenage nymphet in this strange film considered daring in its time. Based on Vladimir Nabokov's novel. Watch for Winters' terrific portrayal as Lolita's sex-starved mother.
1962 152m/B *GB* James Mason, Shelley Winters, Peter Sellers, Sue Lyon; *D:* Stanley Kubrick. VHS, Beta, LV $19.98 *MGM, PIA, CRC* ⅐⅐⅐

London Kills Me A slice-of-life story London-style. Set at the end of the Thatcher era, Clint is a homeless drifter dealing drugs to get by. He's trying to get enough money for a new pair of shoes which will enable him to get a job in a fancy restaurant and away from his aimless life. His friend Muffdiver leads the group of drug pushers and is obsessed with money and power. Sylvie is the sultry junkie who drifts between Clint, Muffdiver, and her drug needs. The directorial debut of Kureishi is more a collection of characters and situations than a complete film but there are moments of disturbing intensity and odd sweetness.
1991 (R) 105m/C *GB* Justin Chadwick, Steven Mackintosh, Emer McCourt, Roshan Seth, Fiona Shaw, Brad Dourif; *W/D:* Hanif Kureishi. VHS, LV $89.98 *LIV, PMS* ⅐⅐

London Melody Neagle is a spirited Cockney busker who meets a kindly Italian diplomat who decides to finance her musical education. He promptly also falls in love with her. *AKA:* Girl in the Street.
1937 71m/B *GB* Anna Neagle, Tullio Carminati, Robert Douglas, Horace Hodgers; *D:* Herbert Wilcox. VHS, Beta, 8mm $29.95 *VYY* ⅐½

The Lone Avenger Average oater centers around a bank panic, with two-gun Maynard clearing up the trouble.
1933 60m/B Ken Maynard, Muriel Gordon, James Marcus. VHS, Beta, 3/4U, Special order formats $19.95 *NOS, VCN, CAB* ⅐⅐

Lone Bandit Vintage western starring Chandler.

1933 57m/B Lane Chandler, Doris Brook, Wally Wales; *D:* J.P. McGowan. **VHS, Beta $27.95** *VCN* ♫ ½

The Lone Defender A dozen episodes of the western serial starring the canine crusader, Rin Tin Tin.
1932 235m/B Rin Tin Tin, Walter Miller, June Marlowe, Buzz Barton, Josef Swickard, Frank Lanning, Bob Kortman; *D:* Richard Thorpe. **VHS, Beta $19.95** *VDM, GPV, MLB* ♫ ½

The Lone Ranger Western serial about the masked man and his faithful Indian sidekick. From a long-sought print found in Mexico, this program is burdened by a noisy sound track, two completely missing chapters, an abridged episode #15, and Spanish subtitles.
1938 234m/B Lee Powell; *D:* William Witney, John English. **VHS, Beta $49.95** *NOS, VYY, VCN* ♫ ½

Lone Ranger Tonto and that strange masked man must prevent a war between ranchers and Indians in the first of the "Lone Ranger" series. "Hi-ho Silver!"
1956 87m/C Clayton Moore, Jay Silverheels, Lyle Bettger, Bonita Granville; *D:* Stuart Heisler. **VHS, Beta $29.95** *MGM* ♫ ½

The Lone Ranger Two volumes of three cartoons each depict the adventures of the famous lawman.
1980 60m/C **VHS, Beta $29.95** *FHE* ♫ ½

Lone Ranger and the Lost City of Gold Three Indian men are found dead, and the Lone Ranger and Tonto set out to discover the killers.
1958 80m/C Clayton Moore, Jay Silverheels, Douglas Kennedy; *D:* Lesley Selander. **VHS** *NO* ♫♫

The Lone Rider in Cheyenne One of the last in the "Lone Rider" series. The Lone Rider is out to clear the name of an innocent man accused of murder.
1942 59m/B George Houston, Al "Fuzzy" St. John; *D:* Sigmund Neufeld. **VHS $19.95** *NOS, DVT, HEG* ♫ ½

The Lone Rider in Ghost Town Outlaws "haunt" a ghost town to protect their hidden mine and the Lone Rider and his pal, Fuzzy, are out to solve the mystery. Installment in the short-lived "Lone Rider" series.
1941 64m/B George Houston, Al "Fuzzy" St. John, Budd Buster; *D:* Sigmund Neufeld. **VHS $19.95** *NOS, DVT, HEG* ♫ ½

The Lone Runner An adventurer rescues a beautiful heiress from Arab kidnappers in this dud.
1988 (PG) 90m/C Miles O'Keeffe, Ronald Lacey, Michael J. Aronin, John Steiner, Al Yamanouchi; *D:* Ruggero Deodato. **VHS, Beta, LV $79.95** *MED* Woof!

Lone Star Law Men A U.S. marshal has his hands full in a border town overrun with bandits. Keene stars as the deputy marshall who goes undercover and joins the gang in an attempt to foil their crooked plans.
1942 58m/B Tom Keene, Frank Yaconelli, Sugar Dawn, Betty Miles; *D:* Robert Tansey. **VHS $19.95** *NOS, DVT* ♫

The Lone Star Ranger Former outlaw O'Brien is trying to go straight by helping to bring a gang of rustlers to justice. Interesting plot twist in the link between his girlfriend and the head of the gang.
1939 64m/B George O'Brien, Sue Carol, Walter McGrail, Warren Hymer, Russell Simpson; *D:* A.E. Erickson. **VHS $19.95** *DVT, HEG* ♫ ½

Lone Wolf A werewolf terrorizes a high school, and a few computerniks track it down.

1988 97m/C Dyann Brown, Kevin Hart, Jamie Newcomb, Ann Douglas; *D:* John Callas. **VHS, Beta $79.95** *PSM* ♫

Lone Wolf McQuade Martial arts action abounds in this modern-day Western which pits unorthodox Texas Ranger Norris against a band of gun-running mercenaries led by Carradine. Oh, and there's a conflict-ridden love interest as well. Violent (and not particularly literary) but worthy entry in chop-socky genre.
1983 107m/C Chuck Norris, Leon Isaac Kennedy, David Carradine, L.Q. Jones, Barbara Carrera; *D:* Steve Carver. **VHS, Beta, LV $19.98** *VES* ♫♫ ½

The Loneliest Runner Based on the true story of an Olympic track star who, as a teenager, suffered humiliation as a bed-wetter. The real-life experiences of producer-director Landon are presented in a touching and sensitive manner. Made for television.
1976 74m/C Michael Landon, Lance Kerwin, DeAnn Mears, Brian Keith, Melissa Sue Anderson; *D:* Michael Landon. **VHS, Beta $19.98** *WAR, OM* ♫♫

The Loneliness of the Long Distance Runner Courtenay, in his award winning film debut, turns in a powerful performance as an angry young man infected by the poverty and hopelessness of the British slums. His first attempt at crime is a bust and lands him in a boys reformatory where he is recruited by the headmaster, for the running team. While training for the big event with a rival school, Redgrave's obsession with winning the race and Courtenay's continued indifference to the outcome lock the two in an intriguing, seemingly one-sided power struggle. Though widely overlooked when first released, it has since been praised as one of the finest teenage angst films of the '60s. A riveting depiction on a boy's rite of passage into manhood. *AKA:* Rebel with a Cause.
1962 104m/B *GB* Tom Courtenay, Michael Redgrave, Avis Bunnage, Peter Madden, James Bolam, Julia Foster, Topsy Jane, Frank Finlay; *D:* Tony Richardson. **VHS, Beta $19.98** *WAR, SNC* ♫♫♫

Lonely are the Brave A free-spirited cowboy out of sync with the modern age tries to rescue a buddy from a local jail, and in his eventual escape is tracked relentlessly by modern law enforcement. A compelling, sorrowful essay on civilized progress and exploitation of nature. Adapted from the novel "Brave Cowboy" by Edward Abbey.
1962 107m/B Kirk Douglas, Walter Matthau, Gena Rowlands, Carroll O'Connor, George Kennedy; *D:* David Miller; *M:* Jerry Goldsmith. **VHS, Beta $19.95** *MCA* ♫♫♫

The Lonely Guy Romantic comedy with Martin as a jilted writer who writes a best-selling book about being a lonely guy and finds stardom does have its rewards. Based on "The Lonely Guy's Book of Life" by Bruce Jay Friedman.
1984 (R) 91m/C Steve Martin, Charles Grodin, Judith Ivey, Steve Lawrence, Robyn Douglass, Merv Griffin, Dr. Joyce Brothers; *D:* Arthur Hiller; *M:* Jerry Goldsmith. **VHS, Beta, LV $19.95** *MCA* ♫♫ ½

Lonely Hearts An endearing Australian romantic comedy about a piano tuner, who at 50 finds himself alone after years of caring for his mother, and a sexually insecure spinster, whom he meets through a dating service. Wonderful performances and a good script make this a delightful film that touches the human heart.

1982 (R) 95m/C *AU* Wendy Hughes, Norman Kaye, Jon Finlayson, Julia Blake, Jonathon Hardy; *W/D:* Paul Cox. **VHS, Beta $24.98** *SUE* ♫♫♫

Lonely Hearts A handsome con man works his wiles on a lonely woman in this erotic thriller. Standard plot wastes a good cast.
1991 (R) 109m/C Eric Roberts, Beverly D'Angelo, Joanna Cassidy. **VHS $89.98** *LIV* ♫ ½

Lonely in America Charming romantic comedy of a newcomer in New York City. Arun (Chowdhry) has just arrived from India and has quite a few things to learn about life in the Big Apple.
1990 96m/C Ranjit Chowdhry, Adelaide Miller, Robert Kessler, Melissa Christopher, David Toney, Tirlok Malik; *W/D:* Barry Brown; *W:* Satyajit Joy Palit. **VHS $89.95** *ACA* ♫♫ ½

The Lonely Lady Young writer comes to Hollywood with dreams of success, gets involved with the seamy side of movie-making, and is driven to a nervous breakdown. Pia needs acting lessons, yet it probably wouldn't have helped this trash. Adapted from the novel by Harold Robbins.
1983 (R) 92m/C Pia Zadora, Lloyd Bochner, Bibi Besch, Joseph Cali, Ray Liotta; *D:* Peter Sasdy. **VHS, Beta, LV $59.95** *MCA* Woof!

Lonely Man A gunfighter tries to end his career, but is urged into one last battle. Strong performances and tight direction make up for weak plot.
1957 87m/B Jack Palance, Anthony Perkins, Neville Brand, Elaine Aiken; *D:* Henry Levin. **VHS, Beta $14.95** *PAR, KRT* ♫♫ ½

The Lonely Passion of Judith Hearne A self-effacing Dublin spinster meets a man who gives her his attention, but she must overcome her own self-doubt and crisis of faith. Adapted from Brian Moore's 1955 novel. Excellent performances from both Hoskins and Smith.
1987 (R) 116m/C Maggie Smith, Bob Hoskins, Wendy Hiller, Marie Kean, Ian McNeice, Alan Devlin, Rudi Davies, Prunella Scales; *D:* Jack Clayton; *W:* Peter Nelson. **VHS $79.98** *CAN* ♫♫♫

The Lonely Sex Creepy and bizarre film in which a maniac kidnaps a young girl and is then harassed by her psychotic housemate.
1959 ?m/C Jean Evans, Karl Light, Mary Gonzales. **VHS $16.95** *SNC* ♫ ½

Lonely Trail/Three Texas Steers Double your pleasure with two early Duke operas. In "Lonely Trail," Wayne dukes it out with dastardly carpetbaggers after the Civil War, while "Three Texas Steers," part of the "Three Mesquiteers" series, has Wayne and company spare a gal rancher/major babe from certain peril.
1939 112m/B John Wayne, George "Gabby" Hayes, Ray Corrigan, Raymond Hatton; *D:* George Sherman. **VHS $14.98** *REP* ♫ ½

Lonely Wives A lawyer hires an entertainer to serve as his double because of his marital problems.
1931 86m/B Edward Everett Horton, Patsy Ruth Miller, Laura La Plante, Esther Ralston; *D:* Russell Mack. **VHS, Beta $19.95** *NOS, VYY* ♫♫

Lonelyhearts Clift plays a reporter who is assigned the lovelorn column of his paper and gets too immersed in the problems of his readers. Given the superior cast and excellent material, this is a somewhat disappointing adaptation of the brilliant Nathanael West novel "Miss Lonelyhearts." Film debuts of both Stapleton and director Donehue.

1958 101m/B Montgomery Clift, Robert Ryan, Myrna Loy, Dolores Hart, Maureen Stapleton, Frank Maxwell, Jackie Coogan, Mike Kellin; **D:** Vincent J. Donehue. **VHS** $19.98 *MGM, SUE* 🦴🦴½

Loners Three teenagers run from the Southwest police after they are accused of murdering a highway patrolman.
1972 (R) 80m/C Dean Stockwell, Gloria Grahame, Scott Brady, Alex Dreier, Pat Stich; **D:** Sutton Roley. **VHS, Beta** $69.95 *VID* 🦴🦴

Lonesome Dove A classic western saga with Duvall and Jones outstanding as the two aging ex-Texas Rangers who decide to leave their quiet lives for a last adventure—a cattle drive from Texas to Montana. Along the way they encounter a new love (Lane), a lost love (Huston), and a savage renegade Indian (well-played by Forrest). Based on Larry McMurtry's Pulitzer Prize winning novel, this handsome television miniseries is a finely detailed evocation of the Old West, with a wonderful cast and an equally fine production. Available in a four volume boxed set.
1989 480m/C Robert Duvall, Tommy Lee Jones, Anjelica Huston, Danny Glover, Diane Lane, Rick Schroder, D.B. Sweeney; **D:** Simon Windsor. **VHS** $99.95 *CAF, TVC* 🦴🦴🦴½

Lonesome Trail Routine Western that differs from the average oater by having the good guys use bows and arrows to fight their battles.
1955 73m/B Jimmy Wakely, Lee White, Lorraine Miller, John James; **D:** Richard Bartlett. **VHS, Beta** *NO* 🦴½

Long Ago Tomorrow A paralyzed athlete enters a church-run home for the disabled rather than return to his family as the object of their pity. A love affair with a woman, who shares the same disability, helps the athlete to adapt. *AKA:* The Raging Moon.
1971 (PG) 90m/C *GB* Malcolm McDowell, Nanette Newman, Bernard Lee, Georgia Brown, Gerald Sim; **D:** Bryan Forbes. **VHS, Beta** $59.95 *COL* 🦴🦴

The Long Dark Hall Courtroom drama in which an innocent man is brought to trial when his showgirl mistress is found dead.
1951 86m/B *GB* Rex Harrison, Lilli Palmer, Denis O'Dea, Raymond Huntley, Patricia Wayne, Anthony Dawson; **D:** Anthony Bushell, Reginald Beck. **VHS, Beta** $16.95 *SNC* 🦴🦴½

Long Day's Journey into Night A brooding, devastating film based on Eugene O'Neill's most powerful and autobiographical play. Depicts a day in the life of a family deteriorating under drug addiction, alcoholism, and imminent death. Hepburn's performance is outstanding. Music by Andre Previn. In 1988, the Broadway version was taped and released on video.
1962 174m/B Ralph Richardson, Katharine Hepburn, Dean Stockwell, Jeanne Barr, Jason Robards Jr.; **D:** Sidney Lumet. Academy Awards '62 Nominations: Best Actress (Hepburn); Cannes Film Festival '62: Best Actress (Hepburn); National Board of Review Awards '62: 10 Best Films of the Year, Best Supporting Actor (Robards). **VHS, LV** $39.98 *REP* 🦴🦴🦴🦴

Long Day's Journey into Night A taped version of the Broadway production of the epic Eugene O'Neill play about a Southern family deteriorating under the weight of terminal illness, alcoholism and drug abuse. In 1962 a movie adaptation of the play was released with outstanding performances from its cast.

1988 169m/C Jack Lemmon, Bethel Leslie, Peter Gallagher, Kevin Spacey, Jodie Lynne McLintock; **D:** Jonathan Miller. **VHS, Beta** $59.98 *LIV, VES* 🦴½

The Long Days of Summer Set in pre-World War II America, this film portrays a Jewish attorney's struggle against the prejudices of the New England town where he lives. Sequel to "When Every Day Is the Fourth of July." Made for television.
1980 105m/C Dean Jones, Joan Hackett, Louanne, Donald Moffatt, Andrew Duggan, Michael McGuire; **D:** Dan Curtis. **VHS** $49.95 *LIV* 🦴🦴

Long Gone In the fifties, an over-the-hill minor-league player/manager is given a last lease on life and the pennant with two talented rookies and a sexy baseball groupie. Made for cable television.
1987 113m/C William L. Petersen, Henry Gibson, Katy Boyer, Virginia Madsen; **D:** Martin Davidson. **VHS, Beta, LV** $19.98 *LHV, WAR* 🦴🦴½

The Long Good Friday Set in London's dockland, this is a violent story of a crime boss who meets his match. Hoskin's world crumbles over an Easter weekend when his buildings are bombed and his men murdered. He thinks its the work of rival gangsters only to discover an even deadlier threat is behind his troubles. One of the best of the crime genre, with an exquisitely charismatic performance by Hoskins.
1979 109m/C Bob Hoskins, Helen Mirren, Dave King, Bryan Marshall, George Coulouris, Pierce Brosnan, Derek Thompson, Eddie Constantine; **D:** John MacKenzie. **VHS, Beta** $19.99 *HBO* 🦴🦴🦴½

The Long Goodbye Raymond Chandler's penultimate novel's got that certain Altman feeling. Which is to say that some of the changes to the pulp auteur's story have pushed purist noses out of joint: Gould is cast as an insouciant anti-Marlowe, the film noir atmosphere has been transmuted into a Hollywoodesque film neon, genre jibing abounds, and the ending has been rewritten. But the updating, tongue in cheeking and revamping all serve a purpose, which is to make Marlowe a viable character in a contemporary world. Adapted by Leigh Brackett (who co-scripted Hawks' "Big Sleep") and handsomely photographed by Vilmos Zsigmond, with a clever score by John Williams. And don't miss bulky boy Arnold in cameo (his second film appearance).
1973 (R) 112m/C Elliott Gould, Helen Mirren, Eddie Constantine, Dave King, Mark Rydell, Henry Gibson, Sterling Hayden; *Cameos:* Arnold Schwarzenegger, David Carradine; **D:** Robert Altman; **W:** Leigh Brackett; **M:** John Williams. **VHS, Beta, LV** $19.98 *MGM, FCT* 🦴🦴🦴

The Long Gray Line Power gives an outstanding performance as Marty Maher, a humble Irish immigrant who became an institution at West Point. This is the inspiring story of his rise from an unruly cadet to one of the academy's most beloved instructors. O'Hara does a fine job of playing his wife, who like her husband, adopts the young cadets as her own. Director Ford gracefully captures the spirit and honor associated with West Point in this affectionate drama.
1955 138m/C Tyrone Power, Maureen O'Hara, Robert Francis, Donald Crisp, Ward Bond, Betsy Palmer, Phil Carey, John Ford. **VHS** $19.95 *COL* 🦴🦴🦴

The Long Haul A truck driver becomes involved with crooks as his marriage sours.
1957 88m/C Victor Mature, Diana Dors, Patrick Allen, G.M. Anderson; **D:** Ken Hughes. **VHS** *GKK* 🦴🦴

The Long, Hot Summer A tense, well-played adaptation of the William Faulkner story about a wanderer latching himself onto a tyrannical Mississippi family. The first on-screen pairing of Newman and Woodward, and one of the best; music by Alex North. Remade for television in 1986.
1958 117m/C Paul Newman, Orson Welles, Joanne Woodward, Lee Remick, Anthony (Tony) Franciosa, Angela Lansbury, Richard Anderson; **D:** Martin Ritt. **VHS, Beta** $19.98 *FOX* 🦴🦴🦴½

The Long, Hot Summer A made-for-television version of the William Faulkner story, "The Hamlet," about a drifter taken under a Southern patriarch's wing. He's bribed into courting the man's unmarried daughter. Wonderful performances from the entire cast, especially Ivey and surprisingly, Johnson. Remake of the 1958 film with Paul Newman and Joanne Woodward that is on par with the original.
1986 172m/C Don Johnson, Cybill Shepherd, Judith Ivey, Jason Robards Jr., Ava Gardner, William Russ, Wings Hauser, William Forsythe, Albert Hall; **D:** Stuart Cooper. **VHS, Beta** $59.98 *FOX* 🦴🦴🦴

The Long Island Four Four Nazi saboteurs are smitten by the decadent nightlife of the Big Apple in 1942. The late Grafstrom's Super-8 film, based on a true story, was an underground hit.
1980 100m/C **D:** Anders Grafstrom. **VHS** $59.95 *MWF* 🦴🦴

Long John Silver Famed pirate John Silver plans a return trip to Treasure Island to search for the elusive treasure; unofficial sequel to "Treasure Island" by Disney. *AKA:* Long John Silver Returns to Treasure Island.
1953 106m/C *AU* Robert Newton, Connie Gilchrist, Kit Taylor, Grant Taylor, Rod Taylor; **D:** Byron Haskin. **VHS, Beta, 3/4U, Special order formats** $29.95 *GEM, MRV, CAB* 🦴½

Long Journey Back The biographical story of a young woman's rehabilitation after her injury in a school bus accident. Produced for television.
1978 100m/C Mike Connors, Cloris Leachman, Stephanie Zimbalist, Katy Kurtzman; **D:** Mel Damski. **VHS** $39.95 *LIV* 🦴🦴

The Long, Long Trailer A couple on their honeymoon find that trailer life is more than they bargained for. Lots of fun with charming direction from Minelli, and Ball's incredible slapstick style.
1954 97m/C Desi Arnaz Sr., Lucille Ball, Marjorie Main, Keenan Wynn; **D:** Vincente Minnelli. **VHS, LV** $19.98 *BTV, MGM, FCT* 🦴🦴½

The Long Riders Excellent mythic western in which the Jesse James and Cole Younger gangs raid banks, trains, and stagecoaches in post-Civil War Missouri. Stylish, meticulous and a violent look back, with one of the better slow-motion shootouts in Hollywood history. Notable for the portrayal of four sets of brothers by four Hollywood brother sets. Complimented by excellent Ry Cooder score.
1980 (R) 100m/C Stacy Keach, James Keach, Randy Quaid, Dennis Quaid, David Carradine, Keith Carradine, Robert Carradine, Christopher Guest, Nicholas Guest, Pamela Reed, Savannah Smith, James Whitmore Jr., Harry Carey Jr.; **D:** Walter Hill; **M:** Ry Cooder. **VHS, Beta, LV** $19.95 *MGM* 🦴🦴🦴

Long Shadows An analysis of how the resonating effects of the Civil War can still be felt on society, via interviews with a number of noted writers, historians, civil rights activists and politicians.
1986 88m/C Robert Penn Warren, Studs Terkel, Jimmy Carter, Robert Coles, Tom Wicker. **VHS, Beta, 3/4U** *JAF* 🦴½

Long Shot Two foosball enthusiasts work their way through local tournaments to make enough money to make it to the World Championships in Tahoe.
1981 100m/C Ian Giatti. VHS, Beta $19.99 HBO ♫½

Long Time Gone An over-the-hill detective tries to solve a murder while dealing with his bratty, alienated 11-year-old son. Made for television.
1986 97m/C Paul LeMat, Wil Wheaton, Ann Dusenberry, Barbara Stock; D: Robert Butler. VHS, Beta $79.95 WWV ♫

The Long Voyage Home A talented cast performs this must-see screen adaptation of Eugene O'Neill's play about crew members aboard a merchant steamer in 1939. Wayne plays a young lad from Sweden who is trying to get home and stay out of trouble as he and the other seaman get shore leave.
1940 105m/B John Wayne, Thomas Mitchell, Ian Hunter, Barry Fitzgerald, Mildred Natwick, John Qualen; D: John Ford. Academy Awards '40 Nominations: Best Black and White Cinematography, Best Film Editing, Best Picture, Best Screenplay, Best Original Score; National Board of Review Awards '40: 10 Best Films of the Year; New York Film Critics Awards '40: Best Director (Ford). VHS, Beta, LV $19.98 WAR ♫♫♫½

The Long Walk Home In Montgomery Alabama, in the mid 1950s, sometime after Rosa Parks refused to sit in the black-designated back of the bus, Martin Luther King Jr. led a bus boycott. Spacek is the affluent white wife of a narrow-minded businessman while Goldberg is their struggling black maid. When Spacek discovers that Goldberg is supporting the boycott by walking the nine-mile trek to work, she sympathizes with the woman's familial responsibilities and tries to help. Hubby becomes unhappy camper when given the news and the plot marches inevitably toward a white-on-white showdown on racism while more quietly exploring gender equality between the women. Outstanding performances by Spacek and Goldberg, and a great fifties feel.
1989 (PG) 95m/C Sissy Spacek, Whoopi Goldberg, Dwight Schultz, Ving Rhames, Dylan Baker; D: Richard Pearce. VHS, LV $14.98 LIV, IME, FCT ♫♫♫

A Long Way Home A television movie about a grown man searching for his long-lost siblings, after the three of them were given up for adoption after birth.
1981 97m/C Timothy Hutton, Brenda Vaccaro, Rosanna Arquette, Paul Regina, George Dzundza, John Lehne, Bonnie Bartlett; D: Robert Markowitz. VHS, Beta $59.95 LIV ♫

The Long Weekend When a vacationing couple goes camping and carelessly destroys a forest, Mother Nature turns her powers of retribution on them.
1986 95m/C VHS, Beta $59.95 TWE ♫

The Longest Day The complete story of the D-Day landings at Normandy on June 6, 1944, as seen through the eyes of American, French, British, and German participants. Exhaustively accurate details and extremely talented cast make this one of the all-time great Hollywood epic productions. The first of the big budget, all-star war productions; based on the book by Cornelius Ryan. Three directors share credit.
1962 179m/C John Wayne, Richard Burton, Red Buttons, Robert Mitchum, Henry Fonda, Robert Ryan, Paul Anka, Mel Ferrer, Edmond O'Brien, Fabian, Sean Connery, Roddy McDowall, Arletty, Curt Jurgens, Rod Steiger, Jean-Louis Barrault, Peter Lawford, Robert Wagner, Sal Mineo, Leo Genn, Richard Beymer, Jeffrey Hunter, Stuart

Whitman, Eddie Albert, Tom Tryon, Alexander Knox, Ray Danton, Kenneth More, Richard Todd, Gert Frobe, Christopher Lee; D: Ken Annakin; W: Bernhard Wicki. Academy Awards '62: Best Black and White Cinematography, Best Special Effects; Nominations: Best Art Direction/Set Decoration (B & W), Best Film Editing, Best Picture; National Board of Review Awards '62: 10 Best Films of the Year. VHS, Beta, LV $29.97 FOX, TLF, HMV ♫♫♫½

The Longest Drive Two brothers comb the wildest parts of the West for their sister, whom they believe is living with Indians. A made for television movie originally titled "The Quest," which became a brief television series. Highlights include colorful performances from the veteran actors and a unique horse/camel race. A continuation of the series is available on video as "The Captive: The Longest Drive 2." *AKA:* The Quest.
1976 92m/C Kurt Russell, Tim Matheson, Brian Keith, Keenan Wynn, Neville Brand, Cameron Mitchell, Morgan Woodward, Iron Eyes Cody, Luke Askew; D: Lee H. Katzin. VHS, LV $89.95 VMK ♫♫

The Longest Yard A one-time pro football quarterback, now an inmate, organizes his fellow convicts into a football team to play against the prison guards. Filmed on location at Georgia State Prison.
1974 (R) 121m/C Burt Reynolds, Eddie Albert, Bernadette Peters, Ed Lauter, Richard Kiel; D: Robert Aldrich. Academy Awards '74 Nominations: Best Film Editing; Golden Globe Awards '75: Best Film—Musical/Comedy. VHS, Beta, LV $14.95 PAR ♫♫½

The Longshot Four bumblers try to raise cash to put on a sure-bet racetrack tip in this sorry comedy. Mike Nichols is the executive producer.
1986 (PG-13) 89m/C Tim Conway, Harvey Korman, Jack Weston, Ted Wass, Jonathan Winters, Stella Stevens, Anne Meara; D: Paul Bartel. VHS, Beta $59.95 HBO Woof!

Longtime Companion Critically acclaimed film follows a group of gay men and their friends during the 1980s. The closely knit group monitors the progression of the AIDS virus from early news reports until it finally hits home and begins to take the lives of their loved ones. One of the first films to look at the situation in an intelligent and touching manner. Produced by the PBS "American Playhouse" company.
1990 (R) 100m/C Stephen Caffrey, Patrick Cassidy, Brian Cousins, Bruce Davison, John Dossett, Mark Lamos, Dermot Mulroney, Mary Louise Parker, Michael Schoeffling, Campbell Scott, Robert Joy; D: Norman Rene. Academy Awards '90 Nominations: Best Supporting Actor (Davison); Golden Globe Awards '91: Best Supporting Actor (Davison); Independent Spirit Awards '91: Best Supporting Actor (Davison); New York Film Critics Awards '90: Best Supporting Actor (Davison); National Society of Film Critics Awards '90: Best Supporting Actor (Davison). VHS $19.95 VMK, FCT, BTV ♫♫♫½

Look Back in Anger Based on John Osbourne's famous play, the first British "angry young man" film, in which a squalor-living lad takes out his anger on the world by seducing his friend's wife.
1958 99m/B GB Richard Burton, Claire Bloom, Mary Ure, Edith Evans, Gary Raymond; D: Tony Richardson. VHS, Beta, LV $24.98 SUE ♫♫♫½

Look Back in Anger A working class man angered by society's hypocrisy lashes out at this upper class wife, his mistress, and the world. Inferior remake of 1958 film version starring Richard Burton, based on '50s stage hit.

1980 100m/C Malcolm McDowell, Lisa Banes, Fran Brill, Raymond Hardie, Lindsay Anderson. VHS, Beta $19.98 WAR, OM ♫♫

Look Back in Anger There's something about John Osborne's play that brings out the angry young man in British leads. Richard Burton played Osborne's irascible guy in 1958, Malcom McDowell looked back angrily in '80, and now Branagh convincingly vents his spleen on wife and mistress in this made for British TV production. Director Jones earlier filmed "84 Charing Cross Road" and "Jacknife."
1989 114m/C GB Kenneth Branagh, Emma Thompson, Gerard Horan, Siobhan Redmond; D: David Jones. VHS $29.99 HBO ♫♫♫

Look Out Sister Jordan and an all-black cast star in this musical satire of westerns. "Two Gun" Jordan saves a dude ranch from foreclosure and wins the girl. Lots of black culture, slang and music from the '40s. Broad but enjoyable humor. ♫Caledonia; Don't Burn the Candle at Both Ends.
1948 64m/B Louis Jordan, Suzette Harbin, Monte Hawley, Maceo B. Sheffield; D: Bud Pollard. VHS $24.95 NOS ♫♫♫

Look Who's Laughing Bergen's plane lands in a town conveniently populated by radio stars. Not much plot here, but it might be worth a look to fans of the stars including Jim and Marion Jordan, better known as Fibber McGee and Molly.
1941 79m/B Edgar Bergen, Jim Jordan, Marion Jordan, Lucille Ball, Harold Peary, Lee Bonnell; D: Allan Dwan. VHS, Beta $19.98 TTC, MLB ♫♫

Look Who's Talking When Alley bears the child of a married, and quite fickle man, she sets her sights elsewhere in search of the perfect father; Travolta is the cabbie with more on his mind than driving Alley around and babysitting. All the while, the baby gives us his views via the voice of Bruce Willis. A very light comedy with laughs for the whole family.
1989 (PG-13) 90m/C John Travolta, Kirstie Alley, Olympia Dukakis, George Segal, Abe Vigoda, Bruce Willis; D: Amy Heckerling. VHS, Beta, LV $19.95 COL, RDG ♫♫♫

Look Who's Talking, Too If Academy Awards for Stupidest Sequel and Lamest Dialogue existed, this diaper drama would have cleaned up. The second go-round throws the now married accountant-cabbie duo into a marital tailspin when Alley's babysitting brother moves in and the Saturday Night dancer moves out. Meanwhile, Willis cum baby smartasses incessantly. A once-clever gimmick now unencumbered by plot; not advised for linear thinkers. The voice of Arnold, though, is a guarantee you'll get one laugh for your rental.
1990 (PG-13) ?m/C Kirstie Alley, John Travolta, Olympia Dukakis, Elias Koteas; D: Amy Heckerling; V: Bruce Willis, Mel Brooks, Damon Wayans, Roseanne (Barr) Arnold. VHS, LV, 8mm $19.95 COL, PIA ♫

The Lookalike A made for cable adaptation of Kate Wilhelm's novel. Bereaved mother Gilbert questions her sanity when she thinks she sees her daughter after she was killed in an automobile accident. Could this girl provide answers to questions about her past?
1990 (PG-13) 88m/C Melissa Gilbert, Diane Ladd, Frances Lee McCain, Jason Scott Lee, Thaao Penghlis; D: Gary Nelson. VHS $79.98 MCA ♫♫

Looker Stunning models are made even more beautiful by a plastic surgeon, but one by one they begin to die. Finney plays the Beverly Hills surgeon who decides to investigate when he starts losing all his clients.
1981 (PG) 94m/C Albert Finney, James Coburn, Susan Dey, Leigh Taylor-Young; **D:** Michael Crichton. **VHS, Beta, LV** $64.95 *WAR* ✂✂½

Lookin' to Get Out Comedy about two gamblers running from their debts. They wind up at the MGM Grand in Las Vegas trying to get out of a mess.
1982 (R) 70m/C Ann-Margret, Jon Voight, Burt Young; **D:** Hal Ashby. **VHS, Beta** $59.98 *FOX* ✂✂½

Looking for Miracles Two brothers, separated during the Depression because of poverty, get a chance to cultivate brotherly love when they're reunited in 1935. A Wonderworks production based on the A.E. Hochner novel.
1990 (G) 104m/C Zachary Bennett, Greg Spottiswood, Joe Flaherty. **VHS, LV** $29.95 *BVV, DIS, FCT* ✂✂½

Looking for Mr. Goodbar Young teacher Keaton seeks companionship and love by frequenting single's bars and furthers her self-destruction by her aimless intake of drugs and alcohol. In need of a father figure, she makes herself available to numerous men and eventually regrets her hedonistic behavior. Unpleasant, aimless characters do little for this dreary film, whose sexual theme sparked a bit of public conversation when first released. Based on the bestselling novel by Judith Rossner. Oscar nominations for supporting actress Weld, and cinematography.
1977 (R) 136m/C Diane Keaton, Tuesday Weld, Richard Gere, Tom Berenger, William Atherton, Richard Kiley; **D:** Richard Brooks. **VHS, Beta, LV** $39.95 *PAR* ✂✂

The Looking Glass War Polish defector is sent behind the Iron Curtain on a final mission to photograph a rocket in East Berlin. He's guided by frustrated British security officers Rogers and Richardson, who both offer sly turns. An otherwise slow-moving adaptation of John Le Carre's best-selling spy novel.
1969 (PG) 108m/C *GB* Christopher Jones, Ralph Richardson, Pia Degermark, Anthony Hopkins, Susan George; **D:** Frank Pierson. **VHS, Beta** $59.95 *COL, MLB* ✂✂

Looney Looney Looney Bugs Bunny Movie A feature-length compilation of classic Warner Brothers cartoons tied together with new animation. Cartoon stars featured include Bugs Bunny, Elmer Fudd, Porky Pig, Yosemite Sam, Duffy Duck and Foghorn Leghorn. **AKA:** Friz Freleng's Looney Looney Looney Bugs Bunny Movie.
1981 (G) 80m/C **D:** Friz Freleng, Friz Freleng, Chuck Jones, Bob Clampett; **V:** Mel Blanc, June Foray. **VHS, Beta** $19.98 *WAR, FCT, WTA* ✂✂✂

Looney Tunes Video Show, Vol. 1 Seven Warner Brothers cartoon classics of the 1940s and 50s: Bugs Bunny and the Tasmanian Devil in "Devil May Hare," Sylvester in "Birds of a Father," Daffy Duck and Porky Pig in "The Ducksters," the Road Runner and Wile E. Coyote in "Zipping Along," Sylvester and Tweety in "Room and Bird," Elmer Fudd in "Ant Pasted," and Speedy Gonzales in "Mexican Schmoes."
19?? 49m/C **D:** Chuck Jones, Bob Clampett, Friz Freleng. **VHS, Beta** $12.95 *WAR, WTA* ✂✂✂

Looney Tunes Video Show, Vol. 2 More Warner Brothers cartoon favorites: Daffy Duck in "Quackodile Tears," Porky Pig in "An Egg Scramble," Sylvester and Speedy Gonzales in "Cats and Bruises," Foghorn Leghorn in "All Fowled Up," Bugs Bunny and Yosemite Sam in "14 Carrot Rabbit," Professor Calvin Q. Calculus in "The Hole Idea," and Pepe Le Pew in "Two Scents Worth."
19?? 48m/C **D:** Chuck Jones, Friz Freleng, Bob Clampett. **VHS, Beta** $12.95 *WAR, WTA* ✂✂✂

Looney Tunes Video Show, Vol. 3 Seven more Warner Brothers cartoon shorts: Daffy Duck and Speedy Gonzales in "The Quacker Tracker," the Wolf and Sheepdog in "Double or Mutton," Claude Cat and Bulldog in "Feline Frameup," Bugs Bunny in "Eight Ball Bunny," Foghorn Leghorn in "A Featured Leghorn," Porky Pig and Sylvester in "Scaredy Cat" and Pepe Le Pew in "Louvre, Come Back to Me."
19?? 48m/C **D:** Chuck Jones, Bob Clampett, Friz Freleng. **VHS, Beta** $12.95 *WAR, WTA* ✂✂✂

Looney Tunes Video Show, Vol. 4 Another Warner Brothers cartoon assortment: Sylvester and Tweety in "Ain't She Tweet," Daffy Duck and Speedy Gonzales in "Astroduck," Bugs Bunny in "Backwoods Bunny," Pepe Le Pew in "Heaven Scent," Elmer Fudd in "Pests for Guests," Sylvester in "Lighthouse Mouse" and the Wolf and Sheepdog in "Don't Give Up the Sheep."
19?? 47m/C **D:** Chuck Jones, Bob Clampett, Friz Freleng. **VHS, Beta** $12.95 *WAR, OM* ✂✂✂

Looney Tunes Video Show, Vol. 5 An additional package of Warner Brothers cartoons: Sylvester and Tweety in "Tugboat Granny," Daffy Duck in "Stork Naked," the Road Runner and Wile E. Coyote in "Fastest with the Mostest," Bugs Bunny in "Forward March Hare," Foghorn Leghorn in "Feather Dusted," Daffy Duck and Porky Pig in "China Jones" and Pepe Le Pew in "Odor of the Day."
19?? 51m/C **D:** Chuck Jones, Bob Clampett, Friz Freleng. **VHS, Beta** $12.95 *WAR, OM* ✂✂✂

Looney Tunes Video Show, Vol. 6 More classic Warner Brothers cartoons: Foghorn Leghorn in "Feather Bluster," the Road Runner and Wile E. Coyote in "Lickety Splat," Bugs Bunny in "Bowery Bugs," Daffy Duck and Speedy Gonzales in "Daffy Rents," Porky Pig in "Dough for the Dodo," Sylvester and Elmer Fudd in "Heir Conditioned" and Pepe Le Pew in "Scent of the Matterhorn."
19?? 49m/C **D:** Chuck Jones, Friz Freleng, Bob Clampett. **VHS, Beta** $12.95 *WAR, OM* ✂✂✂

Looney Tunes Video Show, Vol. 7 Seven additional Warner Brothers cartoon classics: Bugs Bunny in "A-Lad-In His Lamp," the Road Runner and Wile E. Coyote in "Beep Beep," Yosemite Sam in "Honey's Money," Foghorn Leghorn in "Weasel Stop," Daffy Duck and Elmer Fudd in "Don't Ax Me," Sylvester and Tweety in "Muzzle Tough" and Foghorn Leghorn in "The Egg-Cited Rooster."
19?? 48m/C **D:** Chuck Jones, Friz Freleng, Bob Clampett. **VHS, Beta** $12.95 *WAR, OM* ✂✂✂

Loophole An out-of-work architect, hard pressed for money, joins forces with an elite team of expert criminals, in a scheme to make off with millions from the most established holding bank's vault. **AKA:** Break In.
1983 105m/C *GB* Albert Finney, Martin Sheen, Susannah York, Robert Morley, Colin Blakely, Jonathan Pryce; **D:** John Quested. **VHS, Beta** $59.95 *MED, HHE, MTX* ✂✂

Loose Cannons Yet another mismatched-cop-partner comedy, wherein a mystery is ostensibly solved by a veteran cop and a schizophrenic detective.

1990 (R) 95m/C Gene Hackman, Dan Aykroyd, Dom DeLuise, Ronny Cox, Nancy Travis, David Alan Grier; **D:** Bob Clark. **VHS, Beta, LV** $14.95 *COL* ✂

Loose Connections A feminist driving to a convention in Europe advertises for a travelmate, and gets a hopeless chauvinist who is masquerading as a gay man in this offbeat cult comedy.
1987 90m/C *GB* Lindsay Duncan, Stephen Rea, Robbie Coltrane; **D:** Richard Eyre. **VHS, Beta** $79.95 *PAV* ✂✂

Loose in New York Much to her surprise, a cynical socialite begins to fall for her computer-arranged mate.
198? 91m/C Rita Tushingham, Aldo Maccione; **D:** Gian Polidoro. **VHS, Beta** *WWV* ✂✂

Loose Screws Four perverted teenagers are sent to a restrictive academy where they continue their lewd ways in this stupid sequel to "Screwballs."
1985 (R) 75m/C *CA* Bryan Genesse, Karen Wood, Alan Deveau, Jason Warren; **D:** Rafal Zeilinski. **VHS, Beta** $79.98 *LIV* ✂

Loose Shoes A collection of vignettes that satirize movie trailers, teasers and special announcements. Murray's film debut. **AKA:** Coming Attractions.
1980 (R) 84m/C Bill Murray, Howard Hesseman, Jaye P. Morgan, Buddy Hackett, Misty Rowe, Susan Tyrrell; **D:** Ira Miller. **VHS, Beta** $39.98 *FOX* ✂✂

Loot...Give Me Money, Honey! Black comedy about a motley crew of greed-driven golddiggers who chase after a heisted fortune in jewels, which is hidden in a coffin belonging to one of the thieves' mother. From Joe Orton's play.
1970 101m/C *GB* Richard Attenborough, Lee Remick, Hywel Bennett, Milo O'Shea, Roy Holder; **D:** Silvio Narizzano. **VHS, Beta** $59.95 *WWV* ✂✂½

Lord Jim A ship officer (O'Toole) commits an act of cowardice that results in his dismissal and disgrace, which leads him to the Far East in search of self-respect. Excellent supporting cast. Based on Joseph Conrad's novel.
1965 154m/C Peter O'Toole, James Mason, Curt Jurgens, Eli Wallach, Jack Hawkins, Paul Lukas, Akim Tamiroff, Daliah Lavi, Andrew Keir, Jack MacGowran, Walter Gotell; **W/D:** Richard Brooks. **VHS, Beta** $19.95 *COL, TVC* ✂✂✂

Lord of the Flies Proper English schoolboys stranded on a desert island during a nuclear war are transformed into savages. A study in greed, power, and the innate animalistic/survivalistic instincts of human nature. Based on William Golding's novel, which he described as a journey to the darkness of the human heart.
1963 91m/B *GB* James Aubrey, Tom Chapin, Hugh Edwards, Roger Elwin, Tom Gamen; **D:** Peter Brook. **VHS, Beta, LV** *NO* ✂✂✂½

Lord of the Flies Inferior second filming of the famed William Golding novel about schoolboys marooned on a desert island who gradually degenerate into savages. Lushly photographed, yet redundant and poorly acted.
1990 (R) 90m/C Balthazar Getty, Danuel Pipoly, Chris Furrh, Badgett Dale, Edward Taft, Andrew Taft; **D:** Harry Hook. **VHS, Beta, LV, 8mm** $19.95 *COL, SUE, TVC* ✂✂

The Lord of the Rings An animated interpretation of Tolkien's classic tale of the hobbits, wizards, elves, and dwarfs who inhabit Middle Earth. Animator Ralph Bakshi used live motion animation to give his characters more life-like and human motion. Features the voice of Christopher Guard. Well

done in spite of the difficulty of adapting from Tolkien's highly detailed and lengthy works.
1978 (PG) 128m/C *D:* Ralph Bakshi; *V:* Christopher Guard, John Hurt. **VHS, Beta $19.98** *HBO, FCT, WTA* 🐾🐾

The Lords of Discipline A military academy cadet is given the unenviable task of protecting a black freshman from racist factions at a southern school circa 1964. Based on Pat Conroy's autobiographical novel.
1983 (R) 103m/C David Keith, Robert Prosky, Barbara Babcock, Judge Reinhold, G.D. Spradlin, Rick Rossovich, Michael Biehn; *D:* Franc Roddam. **VHS, Beta, LV $39.95** *PAR* 🐾🐾½

The Lords of Flatbush Four street toughs battle against their own maturation and responsibilities in 1950s Brooklyn. Winkler introduces the leather-clad hood he's made a career of and Stallone introduces a character not unlike Rocky. Interesting slice of life.
1974 (PG) 88m/C Sylvester Stallone, Perry King, Henry Winkler, Susan Blakely, Armand Assante, Paul Mace; *D:* Stephen Verona, Martin Davidson. **VHS, Beta, LV $14.95** *COL* 🐾🐾½

Lords of Magick Two warriors chase an evil sorcerer and the princess he's kidnapped across time to the 20th century.
1988 (PG-13) 98m/C Jarrett Parker, Matt Gauthier, Brendan Dillon Jr.; *D:* David Marsh. **VHS, Beta $79.95** *PSM* 🐾

Lords of the Deep A Roger Corman cheapie about underwater technicians trapped on the ocean floor with a race of aliens. A film rushed out to capitalize on the undersea sci-fi subgenre highlighted by "The Abyss."
1989 (PG-13) 95m/C Bradford Dillman, Priscilla Barnes, Melody Ryane, Eb Lottimer, Daryl Haney; *D:* Mary Ann Fisher. **VHS, Beta $79.95** *MGM* Woof!

Lorenzo's Oil Based on the true story of Augusto and Michaela Odone's efforts to find a cure for their 5-year-old son, Lorenzo, diagnosed with the rare and incurable disease ALD (Adrenoleukodystrophy). Confronted by a medical community which is slow-moving and clinically cold in character, the Odones embark on their own quest for a cure. Sarandon delivers an outstanding and emotionally charged performance as Lorenzo's determined mother. Nolte is his equally devoted Italian father, complete with black hair and hand gestures. Together they are a powerful presence in a film which could have easily degenerated into a made-for-TV movie, but is instead a tribute to what love and hope can accomplish.
1992 (PG-13) 135m/C Nick Nolte, Susan Sarandon, Zach O'Malley-Greenberg, Peter Ustinov, Kathleen Wilhoite; *W/D:* George Miller; *W:* Nick Enright. **VHS, Beta, LV $89.99** *MCA, MOV, BTV* 🐾🐾🐾

Los Amores de Marieta Love and jealousy abound amidst the Mexican Revolution.
1987 100m/C *MX* Elvira Quintana, Joaquin Cordero, Gina Romand. **VHS, Beta $59.95** *MAD* 🐾🐾

Los Apuros de Dos Gallos Four Mexican singing aces spend some time at a ranch serenading the ranch hands. *AKA:* The Troubles of Two Roosters.
1969 102m/C *MX* Miguel Aceves Mejia, Marco Antonio Muniz, Lilian de Celis. **VHS, Beta $69.95** *MAD* 🐾

Los Asesinos Two rival bandits arrive in a lawless town and fight for control. Dialogue in Spanish.

1968 95m/C *MX* Nick Adams, Regina Torne, Pedro Armendariz Jr., Elsa Cardenas. **VHS, Beta $29.95** *UNI* 🐾

Los Caciques A comic-book hero comes alive and stops an evil empire of crime.
1987 96m/C *MX* Jorge Rivero, Pedro Armendariz Sr., Carmen Vicarte, Mario Alberto Rodriquez. **VHS, Beta $79.95** *MAD* 🐾🐾½

Los Cacos A group of eleven friends try to steal a large sum of money but they run into problems.
1987 80m/C *MX* Silvia Pinal, Milton Rodriguez. **VHS, Beta $59.95** *MAD* 🐾

Los Caifanes A group of men live life on the edge, challenging death at every minute.
1987 95m/C *MX* Julissa, Enrique Alvarez Felix, Sergio Jimenez, Oscar Chavez. **VHS, Beta $55.95** *MAD* 🐾🐾

Los Dos Hermanos A woman causes two brothers to hate each other.
1987 92m/C *MX* Jorge Rivero, Gregorio Casal, Nadia Milton, Sergio Jimenez. **VHS, Beta $75.95** *MAD* 🐾🐾½

Los Hermanos Centella Two brothers from Northern Mexico change from bandits to people who protect the oppressed.
1965 105m/C *MX* Dacia Gonzales, Jaime Fernandez, Dagoberto Rodriguez, Guillermo Rivas. **VHS, Beta $39.95** *MAD* 🐾🐾

Los Hermanos Diablo Jose, Julio, and Juan are the Diablo brothers, and they are determined to keep outlaws and Indians off their ranch.
1965 90m/B *MX* Mauricio Garces, Abel Salazar, Rafael Baledon. **VHS, Beta $39.95** *MAD* 🐾🐾

Los Hombres Piensan Solo en Solo Two ne'er-do-wells get the experience of their lives when they babysit a "little sister."
1976 90m/C *SP* Alberto Olmedo, Susana Gimenez, Jorge Porcel. **VHS, Beta $49.95** *MED* 🐾½

Los Jinetes de la Bruja A witch and her horsemen avenge the death of innocent puppeteers on a Frenchman's ranch. *AKA:* The Witch's Horsemen.
1976 93m/C Blanca Sanchez, Kitty De Hoyos, Ferdinando Almada, Mario Almada. **VHS, Beta $69.95** *MAD* 🐾

Los Olvidados From surrealist Bunuel, a powerful story of the poverty and violence of young people's lives in Mexico's slums. In Spanish with English subtitles. *AKA:* The Young and the Damned.
1950 81m/B *MX* Alfonso Mejias, Roberto Cobo; *D:* Luis Bunuel. **VHS, Beta, 8mm $68.00** *NOS, HHT, DVT* 🐾🐾½

Los Sheriffs de la Frontera Two lawmen have to rid a town of mean bad guys.
1947 90m/B *MX* Fernando Casanova, Juan Gallardo. **VHS, Beta $39.95** *MAD* 🐾🐾

Los Tres Amores de Losa A girl becomes friends with a famous actress in Madrid and then falls in love with her cousin.
1947 90m/B *MX* Lola Flores, Agustin Lara, Luis Aguilar, Abel Salazar. **VHS, Beta $39.95** *MAD* 🐾🐾

Los Tres Calaveras The story of the Skeleton trio from its beginnings to the top of the international music charts. *AKA:* The Three Skeletons.
1964 105m/B *MX* Javier Solis, Lucha Villa, Joaquin Cordero, Manuel Lopez Ochoa, Ruben Zepeda Novelo; *D:* Fernando Cortes. **VHS, Beta $44.95** *MAD* 🐾🐾

Los Vampiros de Coyacan Two wrestlers are summoned to help a girl who has fallen under the spell of a vampire.

1987 87m/C *MX* German Robles, Mil Mascaras, Superzan, Sasha Montenegro. **VHS, Beta $69.95** *MAD* 🐾

The Losers Four motorcyclists are hired by the U.S. Army to rescue a presidential advisor who is being held captive by Asian bad guys.
1970 (R) 96m/C William Smith, Bernie Hamilton, Adam Roarke, Houston Savage, Brad Johnson, Vernon Wells; *D:* Jack Starrett. **VHS, Beta $29.95** *ACA* 🐾½

Losin' It Four teens travel across the Mexican border to Tijuana on a journey to lose their virginity. Cruise meets a married woman who says she is in town for a divorce, while the others become caught up in frenzied undertakings of their own.
1982 (R) 104m/C Tom Cruise, John Stockwell, Shelley Long, Jackie Earle Haley; *D:* Curtis Hanson. **VHS, Beta, LV $9.98** *SUE, NLC* 🐾🐾

Lost A young girl runs away into the wilderness because of the resentment she feels toward her new stepfather.
1983 92m/C Sandra Dee, Don Stewart, Ken Curtis, Jack Elam, Sheila Newhouse. **VHS, Beta $49.95** *PSM* 🐾½

Lost When their boat capsizes in the Pacific, three sailors desperately cling to life, drifting aimlessly for 74 days. Based on a true story, this film is adult-fare.
1986 93m/C *CA* Michael Hogan, Helen Shaver, Kenneth Welsh; *D:* Peter Rowe. **VHS, Beta $79.98** *CGH, HHE, BMV* 🐾🐾

Lost and Found An American professor of English and an English film production secretary fall in love on a skiing vacation. Good cast but Segal and Jackson did romance better in "A Touch of Class."
1979 (PG) 104m/C George Segal, Glenda Jackson, Maureen Stapleton, Hollis McLaren, John Cunningham, Paul Sorvino, John Candy, Martin Short; *D:* Melvin Frank. **VHS, Beta $9.95** *GKK* 🐾🐾½

Lost Angels A glossy "Rebel Without a Cause" '80s reprise providing a no-holds-barred portrait of life in the fast lane. A wealthy, disaffected San Fernando Valley youth immerses himself in sex, drugs and rock 'n' roll. Ultimately he is arrested and sent by his parents to a youth home, where a dedicated therapist assists his tortuous road back to reality.
1989 (R) 116m/C Donald Sutherland, Adam Horovitz, Amy Locane, Kevin Tighe, John C. McGinley; *D:* Hugh Hudson. **VHS, Beta, LV $19.98** *ORI* 🐾🐾½

The Lost Boys Santa Cruz seems like a dull town when Michael, his younger brother, and their divorced mom move into their eccentric grandfather's home. But when Michael falls for a pretty girl with some hard-living friends he takes on more than he imagines—these partying teens are actually a group of vampires. Some humor, some bloodletting violence, and an attractive cast help out this updated vampire tale. Rock-filled soundtrack.
1987 (R) 97m/C Jason Patric, Kiefer Sutherland, Corey Haim, Jami Gertz, Dianne Wiest, Corey Feldman, Barnard Hughes, Edward Herrmann; *D:* Joel Schumacher. **VHS, Beta, LV, 8mm $14.95** *WAR* 🐾🐾

Lost Canyon Hoppy tries to help a fugitive who's been framed for bank robbery. This is the second installment distributed by United Artists. The song "Jingle, Jangle, Jingle" is sung by the Sportsman Quartet.
1943 61m/B William Boyd, Jay Kirby, Andy Clyde, Lola Lane, Douglas Fowley, Herbert Rawlinson; *D:* Lesley Selander. **VHS $19.95** *NOS* 🐾🐾

L

The Lost Capone Made for cable TV version of the story of Al Capone's youngest brother, a clean living small town sheriff who struggles with his sibling's reputation at every turn.
1990 (PG-13) 93m/C Ally Sheedy, Eric Roberts, Adrian Pasdar; *W/D:* John Gray. VHS, Beta $79.95 *TTC* �᧿�᧿✂

The Lost City A feature version of the rollicking vintage movie serial about a lost jungle city, adventurers and mad scientists.
1934 74m/B William Boyd, Kane Richmond, George ''Gabby'' Hayes, Claudia Dell; *D:* Harry Revier. VHS, Beta $19.95 *NOS, SNC, DVT* ✂✂

Lost City of the Jungle 13-chapter serial focusing on a crazed Atwill, in his last screen role, believing that he can rule the world from the heart of a deep, dark jungle by utilizing a special mineral. The final Universal serial.
1945 169m/B Russell Hayden, Lionel Atwill, Jane Adams; *D:* Ray Taylor, Lewis D. Collins. VHS, Beta $49.95 *NOS, GPV, DVT* ✂✂

The Lost Command A French colonel, relieved of his command, endeavors to regain power by battling a powerful Arab terrorist with his own specially trained platoon of soldiers. Crisp adventure set in post-WWII North Africa. Based on ''The Centurions'' by Jean Larteguy.
1966 129m/C Anthony Quinn, Michele Morgan, George Segal, Alain Delon, Maurice Ronet, Claudia Cardinale; *D:* Mark Robson. Beta $69.95 *COL* ✂✂½

The Lost Continent An expedition searching for a lost rocket on a jungle island discovers dinosaurs and other extinct creatures.
1951 82m/B Cesar Romero, Hillary Brooke, Chick Chandler, John Hoyt, Acquanetta, Sid Melton, Whit Bissell, Hugh Beaumont; *D:* Sam Newfield. VHS, Beta, LV $19.98 *MRV, MLB* ✂½

Lost Diamond Bumbling spies search for a smuggled gem.
1974 83m/C Juan Ramon, Sonia Rivas, Ricardo Bauleo. VHS, Beta $39.95 *MED* ✂

The Lost Empire Three bountiful and powerful women team up to battle the evil Dr. Syn Do.
1983 (R) 86m/C Melanie Vincz, Raven De La Croix, Angela Aames, Paul Coufos, Robert Tessier, Angus Scrimm, Angelique Pettyjohn, Kenneth Tobey; *D:* Jim Wynorski. VHS, Beta $69.98 *LIV* ✂

Lost Honeymoon Monkeyshines abound as a soldier marries a girl while in a state of amnesia, and then wakes up to find twin daughters.
1947 70m/B Franchot Tone, Ann Richards; *D:* Leigh Jason. VHS, Beta $24.95 *NOS, DVT, HEG* ✂✂

The Lost Honor of Katharina Blum A woman becomes involved with a man who's under police surveillance and finds her life open to public scrutiny and abuse from the media and the government. Based on Heinrich Boll's Nobel Prize-winning novel. In German with English subtitles. Remade for television as ''The Lost Honor of Kathryn Beck.'' *AKA:* Die Verlorene Ehre Der Katharina Blum.
1975 (R) 97m/C *GE* Angela Winkler, Mario Adorf, Dieter Laser, Juergen Prochnow; *D:* Volker Schlondorff, Margarethe von Trotta. VHS, Beta $29.98 *SUE, APD, GLV* ✂✂

Lost Horizon A group of strangers fleeing revolution in China are lost in the Tibetan Himalayas and stumble across the valley of Shangri La. The inhabitants of this Utopian community have lived for hundreds of years in kindness and peace — but what will the intrusion of these strangers bring? The classic romantic role for Colman. Capra's directorial style meshed perfectly with the pacifist theme of James Hilton's classic novel, resulting in one of the most memorable films of the 1930s. This version restores more than 20 minutes of footage which had been cut from the movie through the years. Music score by Dimitri Tiomkin. ♫Lost Horizon; Share the Joy; The Dance of the Fathers; Living Together, Growing Together; I Might Frighten Her Away; The Things I Will Not Miss; If I Could Go Back; Where Knowledge Ends (Faith Begins); Question Me an Answer; I Come to You; Reflections.
1937 132m/B Ronald Colman, Jane Wyatt, H.B. Warner, Sam Jaffe, Thomas Mitchell, Edward Everett Horton, Isabel Jewell, John Howard, Margo; *D:* Frank Capra. Academy Awards '37: Best Film Editing, Best Interior Decoration; Nominations: Best Picture, Best Sound, Best Supporting Actor (Warner), Best Original Score. VHS, Beta, LV $19.95 *COL, PIA, RDG* ✂✂✂✂

The Lost Idol/Shock Troop In ''The Lost Idol,'' a lone soldier raids a sacred temple in order to retrieve a golden idol. ''Shock Troop'' tells of top secret mission to destroy a powerful computer that lies behind enemy lines.
198? 219m/C Danny Aiello, Lyle Alzado, Erik Estrada. VHS *NO* ✂✂✂

Lost in a Harem Abbott & Costello play magicians in a theatrical troupe stranded in a desert kingdom ruled by an evil sheik. The sheik's nephew (and rightful heir) hires the two to steal some magic rings and the pretty Maxwell to play footsie with his susceptible uncle in an attempt to regain his kingdom. Average comedy with musical numbers by Jimmy Dorsey and His Orchestra.
1944 89m/B Bud Abbott, Lou Costello, Marilyn Maxwell, John Conte, Douglas Dumbrille, Lottie Harrison; *D:* Charles Riesner. VHS $19.98 *MGM* ✂✂½

Lost in America After deciding that he can't ''find himself'' at his current job, advertising executive David Howard and his wife sell everything they own and buy a Winnebago to travel across the country. This Albert Brooks comedy is a must-see for everyone who thinks that there is more in life than pushing papers at your desk and sitting on ''Mercedes leather.'' Available in widescreen on laserdisc.
1985 (R) 91m/C Albert Brooks, Julie Hagerty, Michael Greene, Tom Tarpey, Garry Marshall; *D:* Albert Brooks. VHS, Beta, LV $19.98 *WAR* ✂✂✂

Lost in the Barrens Two young boys, one a Canadian Indian and the other a rich white boy, get lost in the wilderness of the Canadian north. Out of necessity and common need they become close and form a lifelong friendship. Based on the book by Farley Mowat.
1991 95m/C *CA* Graham Greene, Nicholas Shields. VHS *CGV* ✂✂

Lost in Yonkers Arty and Jay are two teenage brothers who, while their widowed father looks for work, are sent to live with their stern grandmother, small-time gangster uncle, and childlike aunt in 1942 New York. Ruehl reprises her Tony award-winning performance as Aunt Bella, who loses herself in the movies while trying to find a love of her own, out from under the oppressive thumb of her domineering mother (Worth). Performances by the adults are more theatrical than necessary but the teenagers do well in their observer roles. Based on the play by Neil Simon, which again chronicles his boyhood. *AKA:* Neil Simon's Lost in Yonkers.
1993 (PG) 112m/C Mercedes Ruehl, Irene Worth, Richard Dreyfuss, Brad Stoll, Mike Damus, David Strathairn, Robert Miranda, Jack Laufer, Susan Merson; *D:* Martha Coolidge; *W:* Neil Simon; *M:* Elmer Bernstein. VHS *NYR* ✂✂½

The Lost Jungle Circus legend Beatty searches for his girl and her dad in the jungle. Animal stunts keep it interesting. Serial in 12 chapters, 13 minutes each.
1934 156m/B Clyde Beatty, Cecilia Parker. VHS, Beta $19.95 *NOS, VCN, VDM* ✂✂

The Lost Language of Cranes David Leavitt's novel is transported from New York to present-day London but the wrenching emotional drama remains the same. A family is in crisis as long-hidden secrets concerning homosexuality and infidelity are finally revealed. The title refers to one character's social worker's thesis on a young boy from a dysfunctional family who imitates the movements of the building cranes he sees. Fine performances by all. Adult sexual situations.
1992 90m/C *GB* Brian Cox, Eileen Atkins, Angus MacFadyen, Corey Parker, Cathy Tyson; *Cameos:* John Schlesinger, Rene Auberjonois. VHS $89.98 *FOX, BTV* ✂✂✂

Lost Legacy: A Girl Called Hatter Fox Tradition and technology are at odds in the life of a young Indian girl. Strong cast makes this work. Made for television and better than average.
1977 100m/C Ronny Cox, Joanelle Romero, Conchata Ferrell; *D:* George Schaefer. VHS $59.95 *GEM* ✂✂½

The Lost Missile A lost, alien missile circles the Earth, causing overheating and destruction on the planet's surface. A scientist works to find a way to save the planet before it explodes into a gigantic fireball. Director Burke's last film.
1958 70m/B Robert Loggia, Ellen Parker, Larry Kerr, Phillip Pine, Marilee Earle; *D:* William Berke. VHS $18.00 *FRG* ✂✂

Lost Moment A publisher travels to Italy to search for a valuable collection of a celebrated author's love letters, but finds a neurotic woman in his way. Based on Henry James' ''Aspern Papers.''
1947 89m/B Robert Cummings, Agnes Moorehead, Susan Hayward; *D:* Martin Gabel. VHS $14.98 *REP* ✂✂

The Lost One A German scientist's lover is suspected of selling his findings to England during World War II. Based on a true story; Lorre's only directorial outing. *AKA:* Der Verlone.
1951 97m/B *GE* Peter Lorre, Karl John, Renate Mannhardt; *D:* Peter Lorre. VHS *NO* ✂✂

The Lost Patrol WWI British soldiers lost in the desert are shot down one by one by Arab marauders as Karloff portrays a religious soldier convinced he's going to die. The usual spiffy Ford exteriors peopled by great characters with a stirring score by Max Steiner. Based on the story, ''Patrol'' by Philip MacDonald.
1934 66m/B Victor McLaglen, Boris Karloff, Reginald Denny, Wallace Ford, Alan Hale Jr.; *D:* John Ford. Academy Awards '34 Nominations: Best Score; National Board of Review Awards '34: 10 Best Films of the Year. VHS, Beta, LV $14.98 *CCB, MED, RXM* ✂✂✂½

Lost Planet Airmen A feature-length condensation of the 12-part sci-fi serial ''King of the Rocket Men.'' Rocket Man is pitted against the sinister Dr. Vulcan in this intergalactic battle of good and evil.
1949 65m/B Tristram Coffin, Mae Clarke, Dale Van Sickel; *D:* Fred Brannon. VHS, Beta *AOV, DVT, RXM* ✂½

The Lost Platoon A troop of soldiers are transformed into vampires.
1989 (R) 120m/C David Parry, William Knight, Sean Heyman; **D:** David A. Prior. **VHS, Beta** $79.95 AIP ♫ ½

The Lost Samurai Sword A group of characters searches for the legendary sword, which bestows awesome powers on the person who possesses it.
1987 90m/C **VHS, Beta** $49.95 OCE ♫ ½

Lost Squadron A look at the dangers stuntmen go through in movie-making.
1932 79m/B Richard Dix, Erich von Stroheim; **D:** George Archainbaud. **VHS, Beta, LV** RXM ♫♫ ½

The Lost Stooges From the trio's one year at MGM, rare clips of them performing their famous slapstick gags. In black and white and color.
1933 68m/B Moe Howard, Curly Howard, Larry Fine, Clark Gable, Joan Crawford, Jimmy Durante, Robert Montgomery. **VHS, Beta** $14.98 TTC ♫♫ ½

The Lost Tribe A man takes his wife on a trek through the jungle to find his lost brother.
1989 96m/C John Bach, Darien Teakle; **D:** John Laing. **VHS, Beta** MED ♫

The Lost Weekend The heartrending Hollywood masterpiece about alcoholism, depicting a single weekend in the life of a writer, who cannot believe he's addicted. Except for its pat ending, it is an uncompromising, startlingly harsh treatment, with Milland giving one of the industry's bravest lead performances ever. Acclaimed then and now.
1945 100m/B Ray Milland, Jane Wyman, Phillip Terry, Howard da Silva, Doris Dowling, Frank Faylen; **D:** Billy Wilder. Academy Awards '45: Best Actor (Milland), Best Director (Wilder), Best Picture, Best Screenplay; Nominations: Best Black and White Cinematography, Best Film Editing, Best Original Score; Cannes Film Festival '46: Best Film (Milland), Best Film; Golden Globe Awards '46: Best Actor—Drama (Milland), Best Director (Wilder), Best Film—Drama; National Board of Review Awards '45: 10 Best Films of the Year, Best Actor (Milland). **VHS, Beta, LV** $14.95 MCA, PAR, BTV ♫♫♫♫

The Lost World A zoology professor leads a group on a South American expedition in search of the "lost world," where dinosaurs roam in this silent film. Based on a story by A. Conan Doyle.
1925 62m/B Wallace Beery, Lewis Stone, Bessie Love, Lloyd Hughes; **D:** Harry Hoyt. **VHS, Beta, LV** $19.95 NOS, MRV, VYY ♫♫ ½

Lost Zeppelin A dirigible becomes lost in the wastes of Antarctica, forcing its passengers to combat the elements. Impressive special effects and miniatures for its time.
1929 73m/B Conway Tearle, Virginia Valli, Ricardo Cortez, Duke Martin, Kathryn McGuire; **D:** Edward Sloman. **VHS, Beta** $16.95 SNC ♫♫

Lots of Luck A knee-slapping comedy about a family that wins the million-dollar lottery and sees that money doesn't solve all problems. Disney made for cable.
1985 88m/C Martin Mull, Annette Funicello, Fred Willard, Polly Holliday; **D:** Peter Baldwin. **VHS, Beta** $69.95 DIS ♫♫

Lottery Bride In this charming musical, Jeanette MacDonald is the lottery bride who is won by the brother of the man she really loves. A fine outing for all involved, particularly the supporting cast. ♫You're an Angel; My Northern Lights; Come Drink to the Girl That You Love; Yubla; Round She Whirls; Shoulder to Shoulder; High and Low; Napoli; Two Strong Men; I'll Follow the Trail.
1930 85m/B Jeanette MacDonald, Joe E. Brown, ZaSu Pitts, John Garrick, Carroll Nye; **D:** Paul Stein. **VHS, Beta** $34.98 CCB ♫♫ ½

Louis Armstrong: Chicago Style How Louis Armstrong managed to survive the mob's death threats in the early 1930s and become a great jazz trumpeter-vocalist is the incident portrayed in this television movie.
1975 74m/C Ben Vereen, Red Buttons, Janet MacLachlan, Margaret Avery; **D:** Lee Philips. **VHS, Beta** $19.95 WOV ♫♫ ½

Louisiana A belle of the Old South tries to get back the family plantation by romancing the new owner, even though she loves someone else. Oh, and then the Civil War breaks out. Made for television.
1987 130m/C Ian Charleson, Margot Kidder, Victor Lanoux, Len Cariou, Lloyd Bochner; **D:** Phillipe DeBroca. **VHS, Beta** $9.99 STE, PSM ♫

Louisiana Purchase Successful screen adaptation of the Broadway musical features several performers from the original cast, lavish costumes, and great musical numbers. As usual, Hope's comedy is extremely funny, especially his famous filibuster scene in Congress. Based on the stage musical by Morrie Ryskind and B. G. DeSylva.
1941 95m/C Bob Hope, Vera Zorina, Victor Moore, Dona Drake, Irene Bordoni, Raymond Walburn, Maxie Rosenbloom, Frank Albertson; **D:** Irving Cummings. **VHS** $14.98 MCA ♫♫ ½

Louisiana Story The final effort by the master filmmaker, depicting the effects of oil industrialization on the southern Bayou country as seen through the eyes of a young boy. One of Flaherty's greatest, widely considered a premiere achievement. Music is provided by composer Virgil Thomson.
1948 77m/B **D:** Robert Flaherty; **M:** Virgil Thompson. Academy Awards '48 Nominations: Best Story; National Board of Review Awards '48: 10 Best Films of the Year. **VHS, Beta** $29.95 HMV, VYY, DVT ♫♫♫

Loulou A woman leaves her middle-class husband for a leather-clad, uneducated jock who is more attentive. Romantic and erotic. In French with English subtitles.
1980 (R) 110m/C FR Isabelle Huppert, Gerard Depardieu, Guy Marchand; **D:** Maurice Pialat. **VHS, Beta** $79.95 NYF, TAM ♫♫♫ ½

The Lovable Cheat Pretty lame adaptation of Balzac's play "Mercadet Le Falseur," about a father who cons money from his friends in order to line up a marriage suitable for his daughter.
1949 75m/B Charlie Ruggles, Peggy Ann Garner, Richard Ney, Alan Mowbray, Iris Adrian, Ludwig Donath, Fritz Feld; **D:** Richard Oswald. **VHS** FCT ♫♫

Love Torocsik, touted as Hungary's leading actress in the '70s, plays a young woman whose husband has been imprisoned for political crimes. Living in a cramped apartment with her mother-in-law, she keeps the news from the aged and dying woman (Darvas) by reading letters she's fabricated to keep alive the woman's belief that her son is a successful movie director in America. Set in their shabby apartment, the story is punctuated by the older woman's dreamy remembrances of things past. Exceptional performances by both women, it was Darvas' final film. Based on two novellas by Tibor Dery, it won a special jury prize at the 1973 Cannes film festival and was listed among the year's best films by "Time" and "The New York Times." In Hungarian with English subtitles.
1972 100m/C HU Lili Darvas, Mari Torocsik, Ivan Darvas; **D:** Karoly Makk. **VHS, LV** $59.95 CVC, IME, TAM ♫♫♫ ½

Love Affair An excellent comedy about a shipboard romance which gets side-tracked by events back on shore. McCarey remade his own film in 1957 with Cary Grant and Deborah Kerr as "An Affair to Remember."
1939 87m/B Irene Dunne, Charles Boyer, Maria Ouspenskaya, Lee Bowman, Astrid Allwyn; **D:** Leo McCarey. **VHS** $19.95 NOS, MRV, TTC ♫♫♫ ½

The Love Affair, or The Case of the Missing Switchboard Operator Makavejev's second film, a dissertation on the relationship between sex and politics, involving an affair between a switchboard operator and a middle-aged ex-revolutionary, is told in the director's unique, farcically disjointed manner. In Serbian with English subtitles. **AKA:** Switchboard Operator; Case of the Missing Switchboard Operator; Ljubarni Slucaj; An Affair of the Heart.
1967 73m/B YU Eva Ras, Slobodan Aligrudic, Ruzica Sokic; **D:** Dusan Makavejev. **VHS, Beta** $59.95 FCT ♫♫♫

Love Affair: The Eleanor & Lou Gehrig Story The true story, told from Mrs. Gehrig's point of view, of the love affair between baseball great Lou Gehrig and his wife Eleanor from his glory days as a New York Yankee, to his battle with an incurable disease. A television drama that is supported by Herrmann and Danner's convincing portrayals.
1977 96m/C Blythe Danner, Edward Herrmann, Patricia Neal, Ramon Bieri, Lainie Kazan; **D:** Fielder Cook. **VHS, Beta** $7.50 WOV ♫♫♫

Love Among the Ruins A made-for-television romance about an aging, wealthy widow who, after being scandalously sued for breach of promise by her very young lover, turns for aid to an old lawyer friend who has loved her silently for more than forty years.
1975 100m/C Laurence Olivier, Katharine Hepburn, Leigh Lawson, Colin Blakely; **D:** George Cukor; **M:** John Barry. **VHS, Beta, LV** $59.98 FOX ♫♫♫

Love and Anarchy An oppressed peasant vows to assassinate Mussolini after a close friend is murdered. Powerful drama about the rise of Italian fascism. In Italian with English subtitles. **AKA:** Film d'Amore et d'Anarchia.
1973 108m/C IT Giancarlo Giannini, Mariangela Melato; **D:** Lina Wertmuller. **VHS, Beta** $59.95 COL, APD ♫♫♫

Love and Bullets An Arizona homicide detective is sent on a special assignment to Switzerland to bring a mobster's girlfriend back to the United States to testify against him in court.
1979 (PG) 95m/C GB Charles Bronson, Jill Ireland, Rod Steiger, Strother Martin, Bradford Dillman, Henry Silva, Michael Gazzo; **D:** Stuart Rosenberg. **VHS, Beta** $19.98 FOX ♫ ½

Love and Death In 1812 Russia, a condemned man reviews the follies of his life. Woody Allen's satire on "War and Peace," and every other major Russian novel.
1975 (PG) 89m/C Woody Allen, Diane Keaton, Georges Adel, Despo Diamantidou, Frank Adu, Harold Gould; **D:** Woody Allen. **VHS, Beta, LV** $19.98 FOX ♫♫♫

Love and Faith Two lovers are torn between their love for each other and their faiths during sixteenth-century Japan. English subtitles.
1978 154m/C JP Toshiro Mifune, Takashi Shimura, Yoshiko Nakana; **D:** Kei Kumai. **VHS, Beta** VDA ♫♫♫

Love and Hate Marital hell/murder mystery based on a true Canadian case. Joanne (Nelligan), the wife of wealthy rancher-politico Colin (Walsh), leaves her publicly charismatic and privately abusive husband with two thirds of their brood. A bitter battle for custody is waged, and Joanne is soon found savagely slain. The number one suspect: philandering ex-spouse Colin. Based on Maggie Siggins' "A Canadian Tragedy," the faux biography originally aired in two parts on Canadian TV as "Love and Hate: The Story of Colin and Joanne Thatcher."
1990 156m/C Kate Nelligan, Ken Walsh, Leon Pownall, John Colicos, Noam Zylberman, Victoria Snow, Cedric Smith; **D:** Francis Mankiewicz; **W:** Suzette Couture. **VHS, Beta, LV** $99.95 PAR *ZZ*½

Love & Murder Poorly developed tale of a photographer and his bevy of with beautiful models involved with murder and love, not necessarily in that order.
1991 (R) 87m/C Todd Waring, Kathleen Lasky, Ron White, Wayne Robeson; **D:** Steven Hilliard Stern. **VHS** $89.95 HMD *Z*½

Love and the Frenchwoman A French tale tracing the nature of love through stages. Deals with a story about where babies come from, puppy love, saving sex for marriage, and the way some men treat women. **AKA:** La Francaise et L'Amour.
1960 135m/B *FR* Jean-Paul Belmondo, Pierre-Jean Vaillard, Marie-Jose Nat, Annie Girardot; **D:** Jean Delannoy. **VHS, Beta** $29.95 DVT, MRV, HEG *ZZZ*

Love Angels Italian prostitutes are stalked by a killer. Soft-core nudity; dubbed.
1987 80m/C *IT* Maria Fiore, Krista Nell, Andrea Scotti. **VHS, Beta** $29.95 MLD Woof!

Love at First Bite Intentionally campy spoof of the vampire film. Dracula is forced to leave his Transylvanian home as the Rumanian government has designated his castle a training center for young gymnasts. Once in New York, the Count takes in the night life and falls in love with a woman whose boyfriend embarks on a campaign to warn the city of Dracula's presence. Hamilton of the never-fading tan is appropriately tongue-in-cheek in a role which resurrected his career.
1979 (PG) 93m/C George Hamilton, Susan St. James, Richard Benjamin, Dick Shawn, Arte Johnson, Sherman Hemsley, Isabel Sanford; **D:** Stan Dragoti. **VHS, Beta, LV** $9.98 ORI, WAR *ZZ*½

Love at First Sight A pre-"Saturday Night Live" hack job for Aykroyd, playing a blind man who falls in love with a girl he bumps into. ♫ Love at First Sight. **AKA:** Love is Blind; At First Sight.
1976 86m/C Dan Aykroyd, Mary Ann McDonald, George Murray, Barry Morse; **D:** Rex Bromfield. **VHS, Beta** NO *Z*

Love at Large Hired by a beautiful woman, a private detective accidentally follows the wrong man and winds up being followed with her. He vies with a female detective in solving this case of mistaken identity.
1989 (R) 90m/C Tom Berenger, Elizabeth Perkins, Anne Archer, Ann Magnuson, Annette O'Toole, Kate Capshaw, Ted Levine, Kevin J. O'Connor, Ruby Dee, Neil Young; **D:** Alan Rudolph. **VHS, Beta, LV** $89.98 ORI, FCT *ZZZ*

Love at Stake It's condo owners versus the witches in this charming parody that features a hilarious cameo by Dr. Joyce Brothers and a very sexy performance from Carrera.
1987 (R) 83m/C Patrick Cassidy, Kelly Preston, Bud Cort, Barbara Carrera, Stuart Pankin, Dave Thomas, Georgia Brown, Annie Golden; **Cameos:** Dr. Joyce Brothers; **D:** John Moffitt. **VHS, LV** $19.98 SUE, NLC *ZZ*½

Love at the Top Ladies' foundation designer falls in love with her boss's son-in-law, jeopardizing her career.
1986 90m/C Janis Paige, Richard Young, Jim McKrell; **D:** John Bowab. **Beta** $14.95 PSM *ZZ*½

The Love Boat All aboard! Love's waiting for you in this special movie presentation of the immensely popular television series. Captain Stuebing, Julie, Gopher, Isaac (your bartender) and a whole host of celebrities at the end of their careers, fall in and out of love as they sail back and forth between expensive resorts.
197? ?m/C Gavin MacLeod, Bernie Kopell, Ted Lange, Lauren Tewes. **VHS** GKK *ZZ*½

The Love Bug A race car driver (Jones) is followed home by Herbie, a white Volkswagen with a mind of its own. Eventually, Jones follows the "Love Bug" to a life of madcap fun. Followed by several sequels.
1968 (G) 110m/C Dean Jones, Michele Lee, Hope Lange, Robert Reed, Bert Convy; **D:** Robert Stevenson. **VHS, Beta, LV** $19.99 DIS *ZZ*½

Love Butcher A crippled old gardener kills his female employers with his garden tools and cleans up neatly afterward.
1982 (R) 84m/C Erik Stern, Kay Neer, Robin Sherwood; **D:** Mikel Angel, Don Jones. **VHS, Beta** $39.95 MON *ZZ*½

Love by Appointment An unlikely romantic comedy with a very unlikely cast has two businessmen meeting up with European prostitutes. Made for television.
1976 96m/C Ernest Borgnine, Robert Alda, Francoise Fabian, Corinne Clery. **VHS, Beta** $59.98 NLC *Z*

Love Camp A woman is invited to a swinger's holiday camp, frolics for a while, then is told she can never leave. Suspenseful hijinks ensue.
1976 100m/C Laura Gemser, Christian Anders, Gabriele Tinti. **VHS, Beta** $29.95 AHV *Z*

Love Child The story of a young woman in prison who becomes pregnant by a guard and fights to have and keep her baby.
1982 (R) 97m/C Amy Madigan, Beau Bridges, MacKenzie Phillips, Albert Salmi; **D:** Larry Peerce. **VHS, Beta** $49.95 WAR *ZZ*

Love Circles Soft-core fluff about a pack of cigarettes that perpetually exchanges hands (revealing a handful of smutty encounters), and evidently goes unsmoked.
1985 (R) 84m/C John Sibbit, Marie France, Josephine Jacqueline Jones, Pierre Burton. **VHS, Beta** $79.95 MGM Woof!

Love Crazy Powell and Loy team once again for a non-"Thin Man" romp through a married-people farce. Via a nosy mother-in-law and a series of misunderstandings, Powell and Loy squabble almost to the point of divorce. Not the wry wit the team was known for, but zany, high-action comedy at its best.
1941 99m/B William Powell, Myrna Loy, Gail Patrick, Jack Carson, Florence Bates, Sidney Blackmer, Sig Rumann; **D:** Jack Conway. **VHS** $19.98 MGM *ZZZ*½

Love Crimes A con man (Bergin) poses as a photographer who sexually intimidates women while playing on their erotic fantasies. Young is the Atlanta district attorney who sets out to nail him when none of his victims will testify against him, only she may be enjoying her undercover work more than she realizes. Implausible and sleazy. Also available in an unrated version.
1992 (R) 84m/C Sean Young, Patrick Bergin, Arnetia Walker, James Read; **D:** Lizzie Borden. **VHS, LV** $92.99 HBO *Z*

Love Desperados Cowboys and ranchers' wives mix it up in a lot of softcore hay.
1986 99m/C Virginia Gordon, James Arena. **VHS, Beta** $29.95 MED *Z*

Love 'Em and Leave 'Em A tale of life and love in the dizzying, roaring '20s starring the sexy and capricious Louise Brooks. Silent with orchestral score.
1927 70m/B Louise Brooks, Evelyn Brent, Lawrence Gray; **D:** Frank Tuttle. **VHS, Beta** $24.95 GPV *ZZZ*

The Love Factor A secret agent tries to foil the plans of a race of topless female aliens in this sleazy softcore sci-fi film. Also known as "Zeta One."
1969 ?m/C *GB* Robin Hawdon, James Robertson Justice, Yutte Stensgaard. **VHS** $16.95 3NC *Z*

Love Field Pfeiffer is a Jackie Kennedy-obsessed hairdresser who decides to travel by bus to D.C. when she hears about President Kennedy's assassination. Along the way she gets involved in an interracial friendship with the secretive Haysbert, who's traveling with his young daughter. Pfeiffer's Lurene is basically a sweet dim bulb and Haysbert has an unfortunately written one-note character (mainly exasperation). The 6-year-old McFadden (in her debut) makes the most impact.
1991 (PG-13) 104m/C Michelle Pfeiffer, Dennis Haysbert, Stephanie McFadden, Brian Kerwin, Louise Latham, Peggy Rea, Beth Grant; **D:** Jonathan Kaplan; **W:** Don Roos; **M:** Jerry Goldsmith. **VHS, LV** $89.99 ORI, MOV *ZZ*½

Love Film A train trip from Budapest, Hungary to Lyon, France leads a young man to recall his past as he journeys to visit a childhood sweetheart. Jancsi and Kata's friendship has been disrupted by the 1956 uprising and Jancsi wonders if the love once developing between them has been broken by distance and time. In Hungarian with English subtitles.
1970 130m/C *HU* Andras Balint, Judit Halasz; **D:** Istvan Szabo. **VHS** $39.95 TAM *ZZ*

Love Finds Andy Hardy Young Andy Hardy finds himself torn between three girls before returning to the girl next door. Garland's first appearance in the acclaimed Andy Hardy series features her singing "In Between" and "Meet the Best of my Heart." Also available with "Andy Hardy Meets Debutante" on Laser Disc.
1938 90m/B Mickey Rooney, Judy Garland, Lana Turner, Ann Rutherford, Fay Holden, Lewis Stone, Marie Blake, Cecilia Parker, Gene Reynolds; **D:** George B. Seitz. **VHS, Beta, LV** $19.95 MGM *ZZZ*

The Love Flower A man kills his second wife's lover and escapes with his daughter to a tropical island, pursued by a detective and a young adventurer. Interesting ending wraps things up nicely. Silent.
1920 70m/B Carol Dempster, Richard Barthelmess, George MacQuarrie, Anders Randolf, Florence Short; **W/D:** D.W. Griffith. **VHS, Beta** NO *ZZ*½

Love for Lydia Made for British television miniseries following wayward beauty Lydia, orphaned heiress to a manufacturing fortune, through the high-spirited 1920s. Set in the industrial Midlands and farming communities of England, Lydia dazzles every man she meets, often to an unhappy end.

L

Based on the novel by H.E. Bates. Available as a seven cassette boxed set.
1979 657m/C *GB* Mel Martin, Christopher Blake, Peter Davison, Jeremy Irons, Michael Aldridge, Rachel Kempson, Beatrix Lehmmann. **VHS** $199.95 *FCT, SIG* 🐾🐾

Love from a Stranger Thriller about a working woman who wins a lottery. Soon she is charmed by and marries a man whom she later suspects may be trying to kill her. Remade in 1947.
1937 90m/B *GB* Ann Harding, Basil Rathbone, Binnie Hale, Bruce Seton, Bryan Powley, Jean Cadell; *D:* Rowland V. Lee. **VHS** $19.95 *NOS, SNC, NWV* 🐾🐾

Love from a Stranger In this remake of the 1937 film, a young newlywed bride fears that the honeymoon is over when she suspects that her husband is a notorious killer and that she will be his next victim. *AKA:* A Stranger Walked In.
1947 81m/B Sylvia Sidney, John Hodiak, John Howard, Ann Richards, Isobel Elsom, Ernest Cossart; *D:* Richard Whorf. **VHS, Beta, LV** $19.95 *STE, NWV* 🐾🐾½

The Love Goddesses A sixty-year examination of some of the most beautiful women on the silver screen, reflecting with extraordinary accuracy the customs, manners and mores of the times. Released theatrically in 1972.
1965 83m/B Marlene Dietrich, Greta Garbo, Jean Harlow, Gloria Swanson, Mae West, Betty Grable, Rita Hayworth, Elizabeth Taylor, Marilyn Monroe, Theda Bara, Claudette Colbert, Dorothy Lamour; *D:* Saul J. Turell. **VHS, Beta, LV** $14.95 *COL, SUE, VYG* 🐾🐾½

Love Happy A group of impoverished actors accidentally gain possession of valuable diamonds. Unfortunately for them, detective Groucho is assigned to recover them!
1950 85m/B Groucho Marx, Harpo Marx, Chico Marx, Vera-Ellen, Ilona Massey, Marion Hutton, Raymond Burr, Marilyn Monroe; *D:* David Miller. **VHS, LV** $19.98 *REP* 🐾🐾½

Love has Many Faces Judith Crist was too kind when she said this was for connoisseurs of truly awful movies. Playgal Turner marries beachboy Robertson and many faces come between them. Much melodrama. Filmed on location.
1965 104m/C Lana Turner, Cliff Robertson, Hugh O'Brian, Ruth Roman, Stefanie Powers, Virginia Grey, Ron Husmann; *D:* Alexander Singer. **VHS, Beta** $9.95 *GKK* 🐾½

Love Hurts A guy looking for romance finds his hands full with a number of beautiful women. Will he find the love he craves, or will the pain be too much to bear?
1991 (R) 110m/C Jeff Daniels, Judith Ivey, John Mahoney, Cynthia Sikes, Amy Wright; *D:* Bud Yorkin. **VHS** $14.98 *LIV, VES* 🐾🐾

A Love in Germany A tragic love affair develops between a German shopkeeper's wife and a Polish prisoner-of-war in a small German village during World War II. In German with English subtitles. *AKA:* Un Amour En Allemagne; Eine Liebe in Deutschland.
1984 (R) 110m/C *FR GE* Hanna Schygulla, Piotr Lysak, Elisabeth Trissenaar, Armin Mueller-Stahl; *D:* Andrzej Wajda. **VHS, Beta** $59.95 *COL, APD, GLV* 🐾🐾½

Love in the Afternoon A Parisian private eye's daughter (Hepburn) decides to investigate a philandering American millionaire (Cooper) and winds up falling in love with him. Cooper's a little old for the Casanova role but Hepburn is always enchanting.
1957 126m/B Gary Cooper, Audrey Hepburn, John McGiver, Maurice Chevalier; *D:* Billy Wilder. **VHS, Beta** $49.98 *FOX, IME* 🐾🐾½

Love in the City Five stories of life, love and tears in Rome. In Italian with English subtitles and narration.
1953 90m/B *IT* Ugo Tognazzi, Maresa Gallo, Caterina Rigoglioso, Silvia Lillo; *D:* Michelangelo Antonioni, Federico Fellini, Dino Risi, Carlo Lizzani, Alberto Lattuada, Francesco Maselli, Cesare Zavattini. **VHS, Beta** $24.95 *NOS, FCT, APD* 🐾🐾🐾

Love in the Present Tense A woman's romantic novel on video, dealing with an affair that reawakens the torpid, tragic life of a beautiful ex-model.
1985 90m/C **VHS, Beta** $14.95 *PSM* 🐾

Love is a Many-Splendored Thing A married American war correspondent and a beautiful Eurasian doctor fall in love in post-World War II Hong Kong. They struggle with racism and unhappiness, until he's sent to Korea to observe the Army's activities there. Based on the novel by Han Suyin. The extensive LA Asian acting community got some work out of this film, although the leads are played by Caucasians. Oscar winning song was a very big popular hit.
1955 102m/C William Holden, Jennifer Jones, Torin Thatcher, Isobel Elsom, Jorja Curtright, Virginia Gregg, Richard Loo; *D:* Henry King; *M:* Alfred Newman. Academy Awards '55: Best Costume Design (Color), Best Song ("Love Is a Many-Splendored Thing"), Best Score; Nominations: Best Actress (Jones), Best Art Direction/Set Decoration (Color), Best Color Cinematography, Best Picture, Best Sound. **VHS, Beta, LV** $19.98 *FXV* 🐾🐾

Love is Better Than Ever Lightweight romantic-comedy casts Taylor as a dancing instructor who travels to the Big Apple for a convention. Once there, she meets and falls for talent agent Parks. Carefree, bachelor Parks is too busy to be bothered by small town Taylor, but Liz is determined to land her man. Release of this picture was held back because of Parks' blacklisting by the McCarthy committee. *AKA:* The Light Fantastic.
1952 81m/B Larry Parks, Elizabeth Taylor, Josephine Hutchinson, Tom Tully, Ann Doran, Elinor Donahue, Kathleen Freeman; *Cameos:* Gene Kelly; *D:* Stanley Donen; *W:* Ruth Brooks Flippen. **VHS** $19.98 *MGM* 🐾🐾½

Love Kills Is the man a beautiful heiress falls in love with actually an assassin hired by her husband to kill her? Find out in this steamy suspenser.
1991 (PG-13) 92m/C Virginia Madsen, Lenny Von Dohlen, Erich Anderson, Kate Hodge, Jim Metzler; *D:* Brian Grant. **VHS, Beta** *PAR* 🐾🐾

Love Laughs at Andy Hardy Andy Hardy, college boy, is in love and in trouble. Financial and romantic problems come to a head when Andy is paired with a six-foot tall blind date. One in the series.
1946 93m/B Mickey Rooney, Lewis Stone, Sara Haden, Lina Romay, Bonita Granville, Fay Holden; *D:* Willis Goldbeck. **VHS, Beta** $19.95 *NOS, MRV, QNE* 🐾🐾

Love Leads the Way The true story of how Morris Frank established the seeing-eye dog system in the 1930s.
1984 99m/C Timothy Bottoms, Eva Marie Saint, Arthur Hill, Susan Dey, Ralph Bellamy, Ernest Borgnine, Patricia Neal; *D:* Delbert Mann. **VHS, Beta** $69.95 *DIS* 🐾🐾

Love Lessons An Italian-made softcore film about a millionaire who hires a sultry art teacher to instruct his virginal son. Dubbed.
1985 80m/C *IT* Maria Louise Zetha, Yara Dawe, Ben Carra. **VHS, Beta** $29.95 *MED* 🐾🐾

Love Letters A young disc jockey falls under the spell of a box of love letters that her mother left behind which detailed her double life. She, in turn, begins an affair with a married man. Thoughtful treatment of the psychology of infidelity. *AKA:* Passion Play; My Love Letters.
1983 (R) 102m/C Jamie Lee Curtis, Amy Madigan, Bud Cort, Matt Clark, Bonnie Bartlett, Sally Kirkland, James Keach; *D:* Amy Jones. **VHS, Beta, LV** $79.98 *LIV, VES, IME* 🐾🐾🐾

Love, Lies and Murder Shocking psychological thriller in which a businessman convinces his daughter and sister-in-law to murder his wife and then sends his daughter to prison for the crime. The "perfect murder" is not so perfect, however, when the daughter learns that her father has remarried and is now living an insurance-rich lifestyle. She decides to fight back in this true made-for-television story of bizarre murder and deception.
1991 (PG-13) 190m/C Clancy Brown, John Ashton, Sheryl Lee, Moira Kelly, Ramon Bieri, Ken Walsh, Tom Bower, John M. Jackson; *D:* Robert Markowitz. **VHS, LV** $89.98 *REP* 🐾🐾½

The Love Machine A power-hungry newscaster climbs the corporate ladder by sleeping with many, including the president's wife. An adaptation of Jacqueline Susann's novel.
1971 (R) 108m/C John Phillip Law, Dyan Cannon, Robert Ryan, Jackie Cooper, David Hemmings, Jodi Wexler, William Roerick, Maureen Arthur, Shecky Greene, Clinton Greyn, Sharon Farrell, Alexandra Hay, Eve Bruce, Greg Mullavey, Edith Atwater, Gene Baylos, Claudia Jennings, Mary Collinson, Madeleine Collinson, Ann Ford, Gayle Hunnicutt; *D:* Jack Haley Jr. **VHS, Beta** $69.95 *COL, MLB* 🐾½

Love Me Deadly A young woman tries to get her husband interested in her new hobby-necrophilia.
1976 (R) 95m/C Mary Wilcox, Lyle Waggoner, Christopher Stone, Timothy Scott. **VHS, Beta** $24.95 *GEM* 🐾

Love Me or Leave Me A hard-hitting biography of '20s torch singer Ruth Etting and her rise and fall at the hand of her abusive, gangster husband, a part just made for Cagney. Day emotes and sings expressively in one of the best performances of her career. ♫I'll Never Stop Loving You; Never Look Back; Shaking the Blues Away; Mean to Me; Love Me or Leave Me; Sam, the Old Accordian Man; At Sundown; Everybody Loves My Baby; Five Foot Two; I'm Sitting on Top of the World; Stay on the Right Side, Sister; It All Depends on You; Ten Cents a Dance; My Blue Heaven; You Made Me Love You.
1955 122m/C Doris Day, James Cagney, Cameron Mitchell, Robert Keith, Tom Tully; *D:* Charles Vidor. Academy Awards '55: Best Story; Nominations: Best Actor (Cagney), Best Screenplay, Best Song ("I'll Never Stop Loving You"), Best Sound, Best Original Score. **VHS, Beta, LV** $19.98 *MGM* 🐾🐾🐾

Love Me Tender A Civil War-torn family is divided by in-fighting between two brothers who both seek the affections of the same woman. Presley's first film. Songs include "Poor Boy," "We're Gonna Move," and the title tune.
1956 89m/B Elvis Presley, Richard Egan, Debra Paget, Neville Brand, Mildred Dunnock, James Drury, Barry Coe; *D:* Robert D. Webb. **VHS, Beta** $19.95 *MVD, FOX* 🐾🐾

Love Meetings Pasolini acts as director and interviewer to query a wide-range of individuals on their experiences at love, including homosexuality, prostitution, marital

L

and non-marital interludes. In Italian with English subtitles. *AKA:* Comizi d'Amore.
1964 90m/B *IT D:* Pier Paolo Pasolini. VHS, LV $79.99 *WBF, TAM* �️✓½

Love Nest Lundigan stars as Jim Scott, the landlord of an apartment building brimming with wacky tenants, including Monroe, Paar, and Fay. He dreams of becoming a famous writer, but his time is always filled with fixing up the building and trying to pay the mortgage. When one of the tenants ends up in jail because he was living off wealthy widows, Scott's luck changes. This moderately funny film is a good look at the early careers of Monroe and Paar.
1951 84m/B William Lundigan, June Haver, Frank Fay, Marilyn Monroe, Jack Paar; *D:* Joseph M. Newman. VHS $14.98 *FXV* ✓✓

Love Notes Three short vignettes of soft core fantasy, in the life of an ordinary guy.
1988 60m/C Jeff Daniels, Christine Veronica. VHS, Beta $29.95 *AHV* ✓✓

The Love of Three Queens The loves, on and off stage, of a beautiful actress in a European traveling theatre group.
1954 80m/C Gerard Oury, Massimo Serato, Robert Beatty, Cathy O'Donnell, Terence Morgan, Hedy Lamarr; *D:* Marc Allegret. VHS, Beta $29.95 *PGN, FCT, VDM* ✓

Love on the Dole In a gloomy industrial section of England during the early '30s a family struggles to survive and maintain dignity. Grim Depression drama salvaged by great acting.
1941 89m/B *GB* Deborah Kerr, Clifford Evans, George Carney; *D:* John Baxter. VHS, Beta $19.95 *NOS, VYY* ✓✓

Love on the Run Enjoyable romantic comedy starring Crawford as a rich American heiress and Gable and Tone (Crawford's real husband at the time) as journalists stationed in Europe. Gable and Tone are assigned to cover an international aviator, who turns out to be an evil spy, as well as the upcoming wedding of flighty Crawford. When Crawford asks for help in getting out of her marriage, Gable and Tone steal a plane and the trio is chased across Europe by spies. Wild and farfetched plot, but the stars make it worthwhile. Based on the story "Beauty and the Beast" by Alan Green and Julian Brodie.
1936 80m/B Joan Crawford, Clark Gable, Franchot Tone, Reginald Owen, Mona Maris, Ivan Lebedeff, Charles Judels, William Demarest; *D:* Woodbridge S. Van Dyke; *W:* John Lee Mahin, Manuel Seff, Gladys Hurlbut. VHS $19.98 *MGM* ✓✓½

Love on the Run The further amorous adventures of Antoine Doinel, hero of "The 400 Blows," "Stolen Kisses," and "Bed and Board." Doinel is now in his thirties and newly divorced. He renews affairs with several women from his past but, after his mother's death, must contend with his emotional immaturity and his inability to sustain a relationship. In French with English subtitles. *AKA:* L'Amour en Fuite.
1978 95m/C *FR* Jean-Pierre Leaud, Marie-France Pisier, Claude Jade; *D:* Francois Truffaut. VHS, Beta $39.95 *HMV, WAR* ✓✓✓

Love on the Run A beautiful lawyer helps a wrongly-accused convict escape from prison, then they both evade the law. Made for television.
1985 102m/C Stephanie Zimbalist, Adam Baldwin, Constance McCashin, Howard Duff; *D:* Gus Trikonis. VHS, Beta $69.95 *COL* ✓½

Love or Money? A small comedy about a yuppie who must choose between a woman and a real estate deal.

1988 (PG-13) 90m/C Timothy Daly, Haviland Morris, Kevin McCarthy, Shelley Fabares, David Doyle, Allen Havey; *D:* Todd Hallowell. VHS, Beta, LV $29.95 *HMD, HBO* ✓½

The Love Pill Mankind takes giant step forward when medical profession develops pill to create insatiable appetite for sex in women. Best taken with No Doze.
1971 82m/C Henry Woolf, Toni Sinclair, David Pugh, Melinda Schurcher; *D:* Kenneth Turner. VHS $29.95 *ACA* ✓½

Love Potion #9 Two nerdy biochemists procure a love potion that they test on animals. Meeting with success they agree to test it on themselves. Predictably, the scientists are transformed and fall in love with each other. Features a talented young cast, with an amusing cameo by Anne Bancroft, but the script from Launer is a real disappointment because of its shallow characters and lame gags. Inspired by the song by Jerry Leiber and Mike Stoller.
1992 (PG-13) 96m/C Tate Donovan, Sandra Bullock, Mary Mara, Dale Midkiff, Hillary Bailey Smith, Dylan Baker; *Cameos:* Anne Bancroft; *W/D:* Dale Launer. VHS, LV *FXV* ✓½

Love Scenes A director casts his wife in a sexy movie role, and finds she's getting along famously with her co-star.
1984 (R) 83m/C Tiffany Bolling, Britt Ekland. VHS, Beta $59.95 *MGM* ✓

Love Songs A mother of two is confronted with her husband's abandonment and a subsequent romance with a younger man. In French with English subtitles or dubbed. ♫Leave It to Me; Psychic Flash; I Am With You Now; Human Race; We Can Dance; One More Moment; From the Heart; This Must Be Heaven.
1985 (R) 107m/C *FR CA* Catherine Deneuve, Christopher Lambert; *D:* Elie Chouraqui. VHS, Beta $79.98 *LIV, VES, TAM* ✓✓

Love Story The famous line providing an out for every apologetic partner fed the enormous popular appeal of this melodrama. O'Neal is the son of Boston's upper crust at Harvard; McGraw's the daughter of a poor Italian on scholarship to study music at Radcliffe. They find happiness, but only for a brief period. Timeless story, simply told, with artful direction from Hiller pulling exceptional performances from the young duo (who have never done as well since). The end result is perhaps better than Segal's simplistic novel, which was produced after he sold the screenplay and became a best-seller before the picture's release—great publicity for any film.
1970 (PG) 100m/C Ryan O'Neal, Ali MacGraw, Ray Milland, John Marley, Tommy Lee Jones; *D:* Arthur Hiller. Academy Awards '70: Best Original Score; Nominations: Best Actor (O'Neal), Best Actress (MacGraw), Best Director (Hiller), Best Picture, Best Story & Screenplay, Best Supporting Actor (Marley); Golden Globe Awards '71: Best Actress—Drama (MacGraw), Best Director (Hiller), Best Film—Drama; National Board of Review Awards '70: 10 Best Films of the Year. VHS, Beta, LV $19.95 *PAR* ✓✓✓

Love Strange Love A young boy develops a bizarre relationship with his mother who works in a luxurious bordello. Also available in an unedited 120-minute version.
1982 97m/C Vera Fischer, Mauro Mendonca. VHS, Beta $79.98 *LIV, VES* ✓½

Love Streams A quirky character drama about a writer and his sister who struggle to find love despite their personal problems.
1984 (PG-13) 122m/C Gena Rowlands, John Cassavetes, Diahnne Abbott, Seymour Cassel; *D:* John Cassavetes. VHS, Beta $79.95 *MGM* ✓✓½

Love That Bob This popular comedy sitcom starred Cummings as Bob Collins, a girl-crazy photographer, DeCamp as his widowed sister, and Davis as Schultzy, his gal Friday. The series ran from 1955-1959. Two episodes per tape.
1955 50m/B Bob Cummings, Ann B. Davis, Rosemary DeCamp. VHS $19.99 *MOV, SHO* ✓✓½

Love Thrill Murders A film about a Mansonesque lunatic who is worshipped and obeyed by a mob of runaways and dropouts.
1971 (R) 89m/C Troy Donahue. VHS, Beta $69.98 *LIV, VES Woof!*

Love Under Pressure Man and woman's marriage starts to evaporate when they realize their son is seriously disturbed.
198? 92m/C Karen Black, Keir Dullea. VHS $19.99 *ACA* ✓✓

Love with a Perfect Stranger This Harlequin Romance takes place in Italy where a young widow meets a dashing Englishman. He changes her life forever.
1986 102m/C Marilu Henner, Daniel Massey. VHS, Beta $19.95 *PAR* ✓✓

Love with the Proper Stranger A quiet, gritty romance about an itinerant musician and a young working girl in Manhattan awkwardly living through the consequences of their one night stand. Moved Wood well into the realm of adult roles, after years playing teen-agers and innocents. Although the story is about an Italian neighborhood and family, an exceptional number of the cast members were Jewish, as was the screenwriter. Story does not conclude strongly, although this did not hamper the box office returns.
1963 102m/B Natalie Wood, Steve McQueen, Edie Adams, Herschel Bernardi, Tom Bosley, Harvey Lembeck, Penny Santon, Virginia Vincent, Nick Alexander, Augusta Ciolli; *D:* Robert Mulligan. VHS, Beta, LV $19.95 *PAR* ✓✓✓

Love Without Fear A dramatic, heart-rendering look at children with AIDS. Story focuses on the lives of three women from completely different backgrounds who adopt babies with AIDS and develop a special love for these children. Also shows their confrontations with a society which fears the disease and the women's strength to reach out and make a difference.
1990 ?m/C VHS *NO* ✓✓✓

Love Without Pity Rochant's theatrical debut is a modern romance, with more distance and alienation than joy. A lovely, successful grad student loses her heart to a jobless, unambitious layabout who wants total commitment from her. Untypical, sardonic love story may be too cynical for sentimental types. In French with English subtitles.
1991 95m/C *FR* Hippolyte Girardot, Mireille Perrier, Jean Marie Rollin; *W/D:* Eric Rochant. VHS $79.98 *TAM, ORI* ✓✓½

Love Your Mama An urban black drama about the strong Dorothy whose faith helps her cope with her many family complications, including her drunken husband, car thief son, and pregnant teenage daughter. Believable role models and good performances help out this amateur filmmaking effort.
1993 (PG-13) 93m/C Audrey Morgan, Carol E. Hall, Andre Robinson, Ernest Rayford; *W/D:* Ruby L. Oliver. VHS $89.95 *HMD, BTV* ✓✓½

The Loved One A famously outlandish, death-mocking farce based on Evelyn Waugh's satire about a particularly horrendous California funeral parlor/cemetery and

how its denizens do business. A shrill, protracted spearing of American capitalism.
1965 118m/B Robert Morse, John Gielgud, Rod Steiger, Liberace, Anjanette Comer, Jonathan Winters, James Coburn, Dana Andrews, Milton Berle, Tab Hunter, Robert Morley, Lionel Stander, Margaret Leighton, Roddy McDowall, Bernie Kopell, Alan Napier; *D:* Tony Richardson; *W:* Terry Southern, Christopher Isherwood. **VHS, Beta, LV $19.95** *MGM ♂♂♂*

Loveless A menacing glance into the exploits of an outcast motorcycle gang. In the 50s, a group of bikers on their way to the Florida Cycle Races stop for lunch in a small-town diner. While repairs are being made on their motorcycles, they decide to take full advantage of their situation.
1983 (R) 85m/C Robert Gordon, Willem Dafoe, J. Don Ferguson; *D:* Kathryn Bigelow. **VHS, Beta $59.95** *MED ♂♂*

Lovelines Two rock singers from rival high schools meet and fall in love during a panty raid. Laughs uncounted ensue.
1984 (R) 93m/C Greg Bradford, Michael Winslow, Mary Beth Evans, Don Michael Paul, Tammy Taylor, Stacey Toten, Miguel Ferrer, Shecky Greene, Aimee Eccles, Sherri Stoner; *D:* Rod Amateau. **VHS, Beta $79.98** *FOX ♂*

Lovely to Look At Three wanna-be Broadway producers (Skelton, Keel, Champion) go to gay Paree to peddle Skelton's half interest in Madame Roberta's, a chi chi dress shop. There, they meet the shop's other half interest, two sisters (Champion and Miller), and together they stage a fashion show to finance the floundering hospice of haute couture. Lavish production, light plot. Filmed in Technicolor based on Kern's 1933 Broadway hit (inspired by Alice Duer Miller's "Gowns by Roberta"). Vincent Minelli staged the fashion show, with gowns by Adrian (watch for cop-beater Zsa Zsa as a model). Laserdisc format features the original motion picture trailer. ♫Opening Night; Smoke Gets in Your Eyes; Lovely to Look At; The Touch of Your Hand; Yesterdays; I Won't Dance; You're Devastating; The Most Exciting Night; I'll Be Hard to Handle.
1952 105m/C Kathryn Grayson, Red Skelton, Howard Keel, Gower Champion, Marge Champion, Ann Miller, Zsa Zsa Gabor, Kurt Kasznar, Marcel Dalio, Diane Cassidy; *D:* Mervyn LeRoy; *M:* Jerome Kern. **VHS, LV $19.98** *MGM, TTC, PIA ♂♂♂*

Lovely...But Deadly Young girl wages a war against the drug dealers in her school after her brother dies of an overdose.
1982 (R) 95m/C Lucinda Dooling, John Randolph, Richard Herd, Susan Mechsner, Mel Novak; *D:* David Sheldon. **VHS, Beta $69.98** *LIV, VES ♂½*

The Lover Portrays the sexual awakening of a teenaged French girl and her older Chinese lover in Indochina in 1929. The characters, who remain nameless, meet on a ferry where the man is instantly smitten by the girl's beauty. Detached, determined, and unromantic (the opposite of her indolent lover), she allows herself to be seduced for the experience, and money, he offers. The film is equally detached, including the beautifully photographed but uninvolving sex scenes. Moreau narrates as the adult now looking back on her life. Film debut of March. Filmed on location in Vietnam. Based on the semi-autobiographical novel by Marguerite Duras who reputiated director Annuad's film when it was released in France. Duras even wrote a sequel "L'Amant de la Chine du Nord" ("The Lover from North China"), which is basically her own film scenario. Also available in an unrated, letterbox version at 115 minutes.

1992 (R) 103m/C *FR* Jane March, Tony Leung, Frederique Meininger, Arnaud Giovanietti, Melvil Poupaud, Lisa Faulkner, Xiem Mang; *W/D:* Jean-Jacques Annaud; *W:* Gerard Brach. **VHS, Beta, LV $94.95** *MGM, BTV ♂♂*

Lover Come Back More Day-Hudson antics in which an advertising executive falls in love with his competitor but that doesn't stop him from stealing her clients. Is there no shame?
1961 107m/C Rock Hudson, Doris Day, Tony Randall, Edie Adams, Joe Flynn, Ann B. Davis, Jack Oakie, Jack Albertson, Jack Kruschen, Howard St. John; *D:* Delbert Mann. **VHS, Beta $14.95** *KRT, MOV ♂♂½*

Loverboy A college schnook takes a summer job as a Beverly Hills pizza delivery boy and is preyed upon by many rich and sex-hungry housewives.
1989 (PG-13) 105m/C Patrick Dempsey, Kate Jackson, Barbara Carrera, Kirstie Alley, Carrie Fisher, Robert Ginty; *D:* Joan Micklin Silver. **VHS, Beta, LV $19.95** *COL ♂*

The Lovers Chic tale of French adultery with Moreau starring as a provincial wife whose shallow life changes overnight when she meets a young man. Had a controversial American debut because of the film's tender eroticism and innocent view of adultery. In French with English subtitles.
1959 90m/B *FR* Jeanne Moreau, Alain Cuny, Jose-Luis De Villalonga, Jean-Mark Bory; *W/D:* Louis Malle. **VHS $69.95** *NYF, FCT, ART ♂♂♂*

Lovers: A True Story An erotic love triangle taking place in 1950s Madrid, while Spain is under the suffocating dictatorship of Franco. Paco is a naive young man with a virginal, hardworking fiancee named Trini. Things would seem to be headed for an average, productive life until Paco rents a room from young widow Luisa who makes her living as a con artist. Luisa and Paco are soon embarked on a sexual affair bordering on obsession. When Trini discovers what's going on she turns out to have a more passionate, and violent, nature than even Paco could imagine. Steamy and highly dramatic with excellent performances. Based on a true story. In Spanish with English subtitles. An unrated version is also available.
1990 (R) 105m/C *SP* Victoria Abril, Jorge Sanz, Maribel Verdu; *D:* Vicente Aranda. **VHS $89.95** *WOV, TAM ♂♂♂*

Lovers and Liars A romantic adventure in Rome turns into a symphony of zany mishaps when the man forgets to tell the woman that he is married!! *AKA:* Travels with Anita; A Trip with Anita.
1981 (R) 93m/C *IT* Goldie Hawn, Giancarlo Giannini, Laura Betti; *M:* Ennio Morricone. **VHS, Beta $24.98** *SUE ♂*

Lovers and Other Strangers Two young people decide to marry after living together for a year and a half. Various tensions surface between them and among their families as the wedding day approaches. Good comedy features some charming performances. Keaton's first film.
1970 (R) 106m/C Gig Young, Bea Arthur, Bonnie Bedelia, Anne Jackson, Harry Guardino, Michael Brandon, Richard Castellano, Bob Dishy, Marian Hailey, Cloris Leachman, Anne Meara, Diane Keaton; *D:* Cy Howard. Academy Awards '70: Best Song ("For All We Know"); Nominations: Best Adapted Screenplay, Best Supporting Actor (Castellano). **VHS** *FOX ♂♂♂*

Lovers Like Us Two people each leave their spouses, meet one another, and fall in love. *AKA:* Le Sauvage; The Savage.

1975 103m/C *FR* Catherine Deneuve, Yves Montand, Luigi Vannucchi, Tony Roberts, Dana Wynter; *D:* Jean-Paul Rappeneau. **VHS, Beta** *NO ♂♂½*

Lovers of Their Time A romantic novel on tape, about forbidden love and other problems.
1985 60m/C Edward Petherbridge, Cheryl Prime, Lynn Farleigh; *D:* Robert Knights. **Beta $11.95** *PSM ♂*

Loves & Times of Scaramouche Eighteenth-century rogue becomes involved in a plot to assassinate Napoleon and winds up seducing Josephine in the process. Dubbed. *AKA:* Scaramouche.
1976 92m/C *IT* Michael Sarrazin, Ursula Andress, Aldo Maccione; *D:* Enzo G. Castellari. **VHS, Beta $19.95** *SUE, COL ♂½*

Loves of a Blonde A shy girl falls in love with a visiting pianist when the reservist army comes to her small town. Touching look at the complications of love and our expectations. In Czechoslovakian with English subtitles. *AKA:* A Blonde in Love; Lasky Jedne Plavovlasky.
1965 88m/B *CZ* Jana Brejchova, Josef Sebanek, Vladimir Pucholt; *D:* Milos Forman. **VHS, Beta $59.95** *COL, TAM ♂♂♂½*

The Loves of Carmen Film version of the classic Prosper Merrimee novel about a tempestuous Spanish gypsy and the soldier who loves her. Hayworth is great to look at and the film's main selling point.
1948 98m/C Rita Hayworth, Glenn Ford, Ron Randell, Victor Jory, Arnold Moss, Luther Adler, Joseph Buloff; *D:* Charles Vidor. **VHS, Beta $19.95** *COL ♂♂½*

The Loves of Edgar Allen Poe A bland biographical drama about young Poe's adoption, his treatment at the hands of his foster father, his rejection by a woman for a more well-off man, his marriage to his first cousin, and his early death from alcoholism.
1942 67m/B Linda Darnell, Sheppard Strudwick, Virginia Gilmore, Jane Darwell, Mary Howard; *D:* Harry Lachman. **VHS** *TCF ♂*

The Loves of Hercules The mythic mesomorph finds a mate with equiponderant chest measurements, and must save her from an evil queen. Somehow it eludes him that both queen and maiden are Miss Jayne in red and black wigs. Kudos for worst dubbing and special effects; a must see for connoisseurs of kitsch. *AKA:* Hercules and the Hydra.
1960 94m/C *IT FR* Jayne Mansfield, Mickey Hargitay; *D:* Carlo L. Bragaglia. **VHS $19.98** *SNC, VDM Woof!*

The Loves of Irina Franco's dreamy, sanguine, produced-on-a-dime tale of a vampiress. She cruises the Riviera, seducing and nibbling on a variety of men and women. Spanish release known as "Erotikill," not for most tastes.
1987 95m/C Lina Romay, Monica Swin, Jack Taylor, Alice Arno; *D:* Jess (Jesus) Franco. **VHS, Beta $29.95** *MED ♂*

Love's Savage Fury Two escapees from a Union prison camp seek out a hidden treasure that could determine the outcome of the Civil War. A bad made-for-television "Gone With the Wind" rip-off.
1979 100m/C Jennifer O'Neill, Perry King, Robert Reed, Raymond Burr, Connie Stevens, Ed Lauter; *D:* Joseph Hardy. **VHS, Beta $49.95** *PSM Woof!*

Lovesick A very-married New York psychiatrist goes against his own best judgment when he falls in love with one of his patients.

L

1983 (PG) 98m/C Dudley Moore, Elizabeth McGovern, Alec Guinness, John Huston, Ron Silver; *D:* Marshall Brickman. **VHS, Beta, LV $19.98** *WAR, PIA* 🎬🎬

Lovespell A retelling of the legend of Isolde and Tristan. Stilted direction and writing, but another chance to reminisce on Richard Burton. *AKA:* Tristan and Isolde.
1979 91m/C Richard Burton, Kate Mulgrew, Nicholas Clay, Cyril Cusack, Geraldine Fitzgerald, Niall Toibin, Diana Van Der Vlis, Niall O'Brien; *D:* Tom Donovan. **VHS** *NO* 🎬

Lovey: A Circle of Children 2 Teacher for special children takes in a terrified girl diagnosed as brain damaged or schizophrenic, and discovers love and intelligence in the girl as well as finding some important insights into her own life.
1982 120m/C Jane Alexander, Kris McKeon; *D:* Judd Taylor. **VHS, Beta** *TLF* 🎬🎬

Loving The full-length, shot-on-video pilot for the daytime television soap opera, with various guest stars. Exteriors shot at C.W. Post Center on Long Island.
1984 120m/C Lloyd Bridges, Geraldine Page. **VHS, Beta $69.95** *SVS* 🎬🎬½

Loving Couples Two happily married couples meet at a weekend resort...and switch partners. Tired and predictable but it has its moments.
1980 (PG) 120m/C Shirley MacLaine, James Coburn, Susan Sarandon, Stephen Collins, Sally Kellerman; *D:* Jack Smight. **VHS, Beta $29.98** *VES* 🎬🎬

Loving You A small town boy with a musical style all his own becomes a big success thanks to the help of a female press agent. Features many early Elvis hits. ♫Loving You; Teddy Bear; Lonesome Cowboy; Got a Lot of Livin' To Do; Party; Mean Woman Blues; Hot Dog.
1957 101m/C Elvis Presley, Wendell Corey, Lizabeth Scott, Dolores Hart, James Gleason; *D:* Hal Kanter. **VHS, Beta, LV $19.98** *WAR, OM* 🎬🎬

Low Blow A kung fu expert tracks down a mind-bending cult.
1985 90m/C Cameron Mitchell, Leo Fong; *D:* Frank Harris. **VHS, Beta $69.98** *LIV, VES* 🎬

The Lower Depths Renoir's adaptation of the Maxim Gorky play about a thief and a financially ruined baron learning about life from one another. In French with English subtitles. *AKA:* Les Bas Fonds; Underground.
1936 92m/B *FR* Jean Gabin, Louis Jouvet, Vladimir Sokoloff, Robert Le Vigan, Suzy Prim; *D:* Jean Renoir. **VHS, Beta $39.95** *FCT, DVT, GVV* 🎬🎬½

The Lower Depths Kurosawa sets the Maxim Gorky play in Edo during the final Tokugawa period, using Noh theatre elements in depicting the lowly denizens of a low-rent hovel. In Japanese with English subtitles.
1957 125m/B *JP* Toshiro Mifune, Isuzu Yamada, Ganjiro Nakamura, Kyoko Kagawa, Bokuzen Hidari; *D:* Akira Kurosawa. **VHS, Beta $24.95** *SVS, FCT, TAM* 🎬🎬🎬½

Lower Level While working late, an attractive business woman becomes trapped in an office building by her psychotic secret admirer.
1991 (R) 88m/C David Bradley, Elizabeth Gracen, Jeff Yagher; *D:* Kristine Peterson. **VHS, LV $9.98** *REP* 🎬

Loyalties A strong treatment of the issue of sexual abuse of girls by men, and of an upper-class woman's willingness to establish a true friendship with a woman of a so-called lower economic class.
1986 (R) 98m/C *CA* Kenneth Welsh, Tantoo Cardinal, Susan Wooldridge, Vera Martin, Christopher Barrington-Leigh; *D:* Anne Wheeler. **VHS $9.95** *SIM* 🎬🎬½

Loyola, the Soldier Saint A biography of the founder of the Jesuits from his years as a page in the Spanish court to his daring exploits on the battle field and, finally, his spiritual awakening at the University of Paris. Narrated by Father Alfred J. Barrett.
1952 93m/B Rafael Duran, Maria Rosa Jiminez; *D:* Jose Diaz Morales. **VHS** *IVY, KEP* 🎬🎬½

Lucas A high school brain falls in love with the new girl in town, and tries to win her by trying out for the football team. Genuine film about the perils of coming of age. Thoughtful, non-condescending, and humorous.
1986 (PG-13) 100m/C Corey Haim, Kerri Green, Charlie Sheen, Winona Ryder, Courtney Thorne-Smith, Thomas E. Hodges; *D:* David Seltzer. **VHS, Beta $14.98** *FXV, FOX* 🎬🎬🎬

The Lucifer Complex Nazi doctors are cloning exact duplicates of such world leaders as the Pope and the President of the United States on a remote South American island in the year 1996.
1978 91m/C Robert Vaughn, Merrie Lynn Ross, Keenan Wynn, Aldo Ray; *D:* David L. Hewitt, Kenneth Hartford. **VHS, Beta $59.95** *UHV* 🎬

Lucky Devil Lucky devil wins car and motors around the country to the tune of organ music.
1925 63m/B Richard Dix, Esther Ralston, Edna May Oliver, Tom Findley; *D:* Frank Tuttle. **VHS, Beta $19.95** *GPV, FCT* 🎬½

Lucky Jim A junior lecturer in history at a small university tries to get himself in good graces with the head of his department, but is doomed from the start by doing the wrong things at the worst possible times. Minus the social satire of the Kingsley Amis novel on which it was based; what's left is a cheerful comedy.
1958 91m/B *GB* Ian Carmichael, Terry-Thomas, Hugh Griffith; *D:* John Boulting. **VHS, Beta $59.99** *HBO* 🎬🎬½

Lucky Luciano A violent depiction of the final years of Lucky Luciano, gangster kingpin. *AKA:* A Proposito Luciano; RE: Lucky Luciano.
1974 (R) 108m/C *IT FR* Edmond O'Brien, Rod Steiger, Vincent Gardenia, Gian Marie Volonte; *D:* Francesco Rosi. **VHS, Beta $9.95** *NLC* 🎬🎬

Lucky Luke: Daisy Town A full-length animated feature starring Lucky Luke, the all-American cowboy who saves the little community of Daisy Town from the hot-headed Dalton Brothers gang. A wacky western spoof.
1971 75m/C **VHS, Beta, LV $49.95** *DIS, WTA* 🎬🎬

Lucky Luke: The Ballad of the Daltons Easygoing cowboy hero Lucky Luke gets involved in a wild feud with the bumbling Dalton Brothers gang in this animated feature.
1978 82m/C **VHS, Beta, LV $49.95** *DIS, WTA* 🎬🎬

Lucky Me A group of theater entertainers are stranded in Miami and are forced to work in a hotel kitchen. They soon acquire the support of a wealthy oilman (Goodwin) who invests in their show, but not before his spoiled daughter tries to thwart all plans. ♫Lucky Me; Superstition Song; I Speak to the Stars; Take a Memo to the Moon; Love You Dearly; Bluebells of Broadway; Parisian Pretties; Wanna Sing Like an Angel; High Hopes; Men.
1954 100m/C Doris Day, Robert Cummings, Phil Silvers, Eddie Foy Jr., Nancy Walker, Martha Hyer, Bill Goodwin, Marcel Dalio, James Burke, Jack Shea, William Bakewell, Charles Cane, Ray

Teal, Tom Powers, Angie Dickinson, Dolores Dorn; *D:* Jack Donohue. **VHS, LV $19.98** *WAR, CCB* 🎬🎬

Lucky Partners When an artist and an errand girl share a winning lottery ticket, funny complications arise as they embark on a fantasy honeymoon. Although Rogers' innocence and Coleman's savoir faire provide an interesting contrast, the script isn't equal to the status of its stars.
1940 101m/B Ronald Colman, Ginger Rogers, Jack Carson, Spring Byington, Harry Davenport; *D:* Lewis Milestone. **VHS, Beta $19.98** *RKO, TTC* 🎬🎬

Lucky Stiff A fat, unpopular dweeb has the shock of his life when a radiant woman falls in love with him, the strangeness of which becomes evident when he meets her very weird family.
1988 (PG) 93m/C Donna Dixon, Joe Alaskey; *D:* Anthony Perkins. **VHS, Beta, LV $89.95** *COL* 🎬🎬

Lucky Terror Routine Hoot cowboy drama.
1936 60m/B Hoot Gibson, Kone Andre, Charles King; *D:* Alan James. **VHS, Beta $19.95** *NOS, GPV, VCN* 🎬

Lucky Texan Wayne plays a tough easterner who goes West and finds himself involved in a range war.
1934 61m/B John Wayne, George "Gabby" Hayes, Yakima Canutt; *D:* Robert North Bradbury. **VHS, Beta, 3/4U, Special order formats $9.98** *REP, COL, MRV* 🎬½

Lucy and Desi: Before the Laughter The meeting and early married life of actress/comedian Lucille Ball and Cuban bandleader Desi Arnaz is depicted in this routine biopic. Film depicts Desi's womanizing, their struggles with fame, and their efforts to get their television show on the air. Fisher does well as television's favorite redhead but this made-for-television effort is melodramatic. Daughter Lucy Arnaz vehemently opposed this depiction of her parents' life.
1991 (PG-13) 95m/C Frances Fisher, Maurice Benard, John Wheeler, Robin Pearson Rose; *D:* Charles Jarrott; *W:* William Luce. **VHS, LV $89.98** *REP, PMS* 🎬🎬½

Luggage of the Gods A lost tribe of cave people are confronted with civilization when suitcases fall from an airplane. Low-budget comedy reminiscent of "The Gods Must Be Crazy."
1987 (G) 78m/C Mark Stolzenberg, Gabriel Barre, Gwen Ellison; *D:* David Kendall. **VHS, Beta $29.95** *ACA* 🎬🎬

Lullaby of Broadway Many songs highlight this flimsy musical about a girl (Day) who ventures from England to the Big Apple in search of an acting career. She soon discovers that her mom has become a has-been actress now performing in a Greenwich Village dive. Day struggles to gain her own success while coping with her mother's downfall. ♫Lullaby of Broadway; You're Getting to Be a Habit With Me; Just One of Those Things; Somebody Loves Me; I Love the Way You Say Goodnight; Fine and Dandy; Please Don't Talk About Me When I'm Gone; A Shanty in Old Shanty Town; We'd Like to Go On A Trip; Zing! Went the Strings Of My Heart; You're Dependable.
1951 93m/C Doris Day, Gene Nelson, S.Z. Sakall, Billy DeWolfe, Gladys George, Florence Bates; *D:* David Butler. **VHS $19.98** *WAR, CCB* 🎬🎬½

Lumiere An acclaimed drama about four actresses who, during the course of one night together, make pivotal decisions about their lives and relationships. Moreau's first directorial effort; dubbed.
1976 (R) 101m/C FR Jeanne Moreau, Lucia Bose, Francine Racette, Caroline Cartier, Keith Carradine; D: Jeanne Moreau. VHS, Beta $29.98 SUE *½*

The Lunatic A robust, oversexed, and scheming German tourist travels to Jamaica where she meets the village idiot, a man who regularly holds conversations with the local plants. The two hook up with a butcher, and the three live happily in the hills, that is until the money is gone. The Jamaican scenery, a few bawdy laughs, and a great reggae soundtrack make this one worthwhile.
1992 (R) 93m/C GB Julie T. Wallace, Paul Campbell, Reggie Carter, Carl Bradshaw; D: Lol Creme. VHS, Beta $89.95 ACA *½*

Lunatics: A Love Story Hank (Raimi) is an ex-mental patient poet suffering from hallucinations and afraid to leave his Los Angeles apartment. For companionship he dials a party-line until, one day, he misdials and insteads gets the number of a local pay telephone, which is answered by a naive woman dumped by her boyfriend. When Nancy (Foreman) decides to visit Hank you learn she's as crazy as he is—so it only makes sense they would fall in love. A well-acted fable of how love fragilely connects even the most unlikely of people.
1992 (PG-13) 87m/C Theodore Raimi, Deborah Foreman, Bruce Campbell, Brian McCree, Eddie Rosmaya, Michele Stacey; W/D: Josh Beck. VHS, LV NO *½½½*

Lunatics & Lovers Musician meets a bizarre nobleman who is in love with an imaginary woman.
1976 (PG) 92m/C IT Marcello Mastroianni, Lino Toffalo; D: Flavio Mogherini. VHS, Beta $59.98 FOX *½*

Lunch Wagon Two co-eds are given a restaurant to manage during summer vacation and wind up involved in a hilarious diamond chase and sex romp. AKA: Come 'n' Get It; Lunch Wagon Girls.
1981 (R) 88m/C Rick Podell, Candy Moore, Pamela Bryant, Rosanne Katon; D: Ernie Pintoff. VHS, Beta $19.95 MED *½½*

Lupo When threatened with the loss of his home and the separation of his family, an exuberant Greek man challenges the modern world.
1970 (G) 99m/C Yuda Barkan, Gabi Armoni, Esther Greenberg; D: Menahem Golan. VHS, Beta $59.95 MGM *½½*

Lure of the Islands Federal agents track wanted criminals to an island retreat in this highly predictable low-budget thriller.
1942 61m/B Margie Hart, Robert Lowery, Guinn Williams, Warren Hymer, Gale Storm; D: Jean Yarborough. VHS, Beta $16.95 NOS, SNC *½*

Lure of the Sila Italian melodrama about a young peasant girl infiltrating a landowner's home in order to avenge the death of her brother and mother. Dubbed and more interesting than it sounds.
1949 72m/B IT Silvana Mangano, Amadeo Nazzari, Vittorio Gassman; D: Duilio Coletti. VHS, Beta, 8mm $29.95 VYY *½½*

Lurkers An unappealing metaphysical morass about a woman who has been haunted throughout her life by...something.
1988 (R) 90m/C Christine Moore, Gary Warner, Marina Taylor, Carissa Channing, Tom Billett; D: Roberta Findlay. VHS $79.95 MED Woof!

Lust for a Vampire The sanguine tale of a deadly vampire who indiscriminately preys on pupils and teachers when she enrolls at a British finishing school. Moody and erotically charged, with an impressive ending. Quasi-sequel to "The Vampire Lovers." AKA: To Love a Vampire.
1971 (R) 95m/C GB Ralph Bates, Barbara Jefford, Suzanna Leigh, Michael Johnson, Yutte Stensgaard, Pippa Steele; D: Jimmy Sangster. VHS, Beta, LV $59.99 HBO, MLB *½½*

Lust for Freedom An undercover cop decides to hit the road after she sees her partner gunned down. She winds up near the California-Mexico border, where she is wrongly imprisoned with a number of other young women in a white slavery business. This low-budget film includes lots of steamy women-behind-bars sex scenes.
1987 92m/C Melanie Coll, William J. Kulzer; D: Eric Louzil. VHS $89.95 AIP, MOV *½*

Lust for Gold Ford battles against greedy former lover Lupino and her husband for control of the Lost Dutchman gold mine.
1949 90m/B Ida Lupino, Glenn Ford, Gig Young, William Prince, Edgar Buchanan, Will Geer, Paul Ford, Jay Silverheels; D: Sylvan Simon. VHS, Beta GKK *½½*

Lust for Life Absorbing, serious biography of Vincent Van Gogh, from his first paintings to his death. Remarkable for Douglas' furiously convincing portrayal. Featuring dozens of actual Van Gogh works from private collections. Music by Miklos Rozsa; based on an Irving Stone novel, produced by John Houseman.
1956 122m/C Kirk Douglas, Anthony Quinn, James Donald, Pamela Brown, Everett Sloane, Henry Daniell, Niall MacGinnis, Noel Purcell, Lionel Jeffries, Jill Bennett; D: Vincente Minnelli. Academy Awards '56: Best Supporting Actor (Quinn); Nominations: Best Actor (Douglas), Best Adapted Screenplay, Best Art Direction/Set Decoration (Color); Golden Globe Awards '57: Best Actor—Drama (Douglas); National Board of Review Awards '56: 10 Best Films of the Year; New York Film Critics Awards '56: Best Actor (Douglas). VHS, Beta, LV $39.95 MGM, BTV *½½½*

Lust in the Dust When part of a treasure map is found on the derriere of none other than Divine, the hunt is on for the other half. This comedy western travels to a sleepy town called Chile Verde (green chili for those who don't speak Spanish) and the utterly ridiculous turns comically corrupt. Deliciously distasteful fun. Features Divine singing a bawdy love song in his/her break from John Waters.
1985 (R) 85m/C Tab Hunter, Divine, Lainie Kazan, Geoffrey Lewis, Henry Silva, Cesar Romero, Gina Gallego, Courtney Gains, Woody Strode; D: Paul Bartel. VHS, Beta, LV $14.95 NWV, STE, HHE *½½½*

The Lusty Men Two rival rodeo champions, both in love with the same woman, work the rodeo circuit until a tragic accident occurs. Mitchum turns in a fine performance as the has-been rodeo star trying to make it big again.
1952 113m/B Robert Mitchum, Susan Hayward, Arthur Kennedy, Arthur Hunnicutt; D: Nicholas Ray. VHS, Beta, LV $15.95 UHV *½½½*

Luther A well-acted characterization of Martin Luther's development from a young seminarian to his leadership of the Reformation Movement.
1974 (G) 112m/C Stacy Keach, Patrick Magee, Hugh Griffith, Robert Stephens, Alan Badel; D: Guy Green. VHS $39.95 MGS *½½½*

Luther the Geek Little Luther's visit to the circus is dramatically changed when he sees the geek, a sideshow freak. Since then Luther has taken to biting off chicken's heads and drinking their blood in his small Illinois town; the town will never be the same. (And neither will you if you watch this stupid film.)
1990 90m/C Edward Terry, Joan Roth, J. Jerome Clarke, Tom Mills; D: Carlton J. Albright. VHS NO Woof!

Luv Although good cast tries hard, they can't do much with this comic farce. Three intellectuals, including one that's suicidal, discuss the trials and tribulations of their middle-class New York existence.
1967 (PG) 95m/C Jack Lemmon, Peter Falk, Elaine May; D: Clive Donner. VHS, Beta, LV $9.95 GKK *½*

Luzia Ohana stars as a tough and sexy Brazilian cowgirl who is caught in the middle of a class struggle where the personal is definitely political. Her horseriding skills and beauty give her options in both lifestyles. Will she choose to side with the squatters or the wealthy landowners? In Portuguese with English subtitles.
1988 112m/C BR Claudia Ohana, Thales Pan Chacon, Jose de Abreu, Luiza Falcao; D: Fabio Barreto. VHS $79.95 FXL, TAM *½½½*

Lydia Sentimental drama in which an elderly lady (Oberon) gets to relive her romantic past when she has a reunion with four of her lost loves. Well acted and directed, Oberon gives one of her best performances ever. Adapted from the highly regarded French film "Un Carnet de Bal."
1941 98m/B Merle Oberon, Joseph Cotten, Alan Marshal, George Reeves; D: Julien Duvivier. VHS, Beta, LV SUE *½½½*

Lying Lips All-black detective mystery about a young nightclub singer framed for murder. Her boyfriend then turns detective to clear her name.
1939 60m/B Edna Mae Harris, Carmen Newsome, Earl Jones, Amanda Randolph; D: Oscar Micheaux. VHS, Beta $24.95 FCT, VCN, DVT *½½*

M The great Lang dissection of criminal deviance, following the tortured last days of a child murderer, and the efforts of both the police and the underground to bring him to justice. Poetic, compassionate, and chilling. Inspired by real-life serial killer known as "Vampire of Dusseldorf," Lang also borrowed story elements from Jack the Ripper's killing spree. Lorre's screen debut. Lang's personal favorite among his own films. In German with English subtitles. Remade in 1951.
1931 99m/B GE Peter Lorre, Ellen Widmann, Inge Landgut, Gustav Grundgens; D: Fritz Lang. VHS, Beta, LV, 8mm, 3/4U $16.95 SNC, NOS, HHT *½½½½*

Ma Barker's Killer Brood Biography of the infamous American criminal and her four sons, edited together from a television serial. The shoot-em-up scenes and Tuttle's performance keep the pace from slackening.
1960 82m/B Lurene Tuttle, Tristram Coffin, Paul Dubov, Nelson Leigh, Myrna Dell, Vic Lundin, Donald Spruance; D: Bill Karn. VHS, Beta $16.95 SNC, DVT, HEG *½*

Mabel & Fatty Three silent shorts featuring the two stars, made with Mack Sennett: "He Did and He Didn't," "Mabel and Fatty Viewing The World's Fair at San Francisco" (with scenes of the actual 1914 World's Fair) and "Mabel's Blunder."
1916 61m/B Mabel Normand, Fatty Arbuckle, Al "Fuzzy" St. John. VHS, Beta, 8mm $24.95 VYY *½½*

Mac Immigrant carpenter's funeral is the starting point for the story of his three sons, construction workers who live in Queens, New York in the 1950s. The story follows the lives of the brothers as they gain perspective on their lives. The eldest is Mac (Turturro), a meticulous perfectionist who quits a job because his boss cuts too many corners. He and Vico (Badalucco) and Bruno (Capotorto) are swept up in the booming economic prosperity of post-war America. Turturro's directorial debut is a labor of love and a tribute to a standard of achievement that the little man once fought to uphold in this country. Fine performances from newcomers Badalucco and Capotorto are complemented by smaller roles from Amos, Barkin, and Turturro's real-life wife Borowitz.
1993 (R) 118m/C John Turturro, Carl Capotorto, Michael Badalucco, Katherine Borowitz, John Amos, Olek Krupa, Ellen Barkin, John Turturro, Joe Paparone; **D:** John Turturro; **W:** John Turturro, Brandon Cole; **M:** Richard Termini, Vin Tese. VHS *NYR* ✂✂✂

Mac and Me Lost E.T.-like alien stranded on Earth befriends a wheelchair-bound boy. Aimed at young kids, it's full of continual product plugs, most notably for McDonald's. Make the kids happy and stick to the real thing.
1988 (PG) 94m/C Christine Ebersole, Jonathan Ward, Katrina Caspary, Lauren Stanley, Jade Calegory; **D:** Stewart Raffill. VHS, Beta, LV $19.98 *ORI* ✂

Macabre A beautiful woman, lustful and precocious, kills her husband and his twin brother.
1977 89m/C Larry Ward, Teresa Gimpera, Giacomo "Jack" Stuart. VHS, Beta *NO* ✂✂

Macao On the lam for a crime he didn't commit, an adventurer sails to the exotic Far East, meets a buxom cafe singer, and helps Interpol catch a notorious crime boss. A strong film noir entry. Russell sneers, Mitchum wise cracks. Director von Sternberg's last film for RKO.
1952 81m/B Robert Mitchum, Jane Russell, William Bendix, Gloria Grahame; **D:** Josef von Sternberg. VHS, Beta, LV $19.95 *MED* ✂✂✂

Macario Traditional Mexican fable about a desperate farmer who makes a deal with the Devil for healing powers. His gift only leads to greater misfortunes, of course. In Spanish with English subtitles.
1958 91m/B *MX* Ignacio Lopez Tarso, Pina Pellicer, Enrique Lucero; **D:** Roberto Gavaldon. VHS, Beta, LV $59.95 *CVC, MAD, TAM* ✂

Macaroni An uptight American businessman returns to Naples forty years after being stationed there in World War II. Comedic situations abound when he is reunited with his Italian war buddy, brother of his lover. Pleasant acting can't save irritating script. *AKA:* Maccheroni.
1985 (PG) 104m/C *IT* Jack Lemmon, Marcello Mastroianni, Daria Nicolodi, Isa Danieli; **D:** Ettore Scola. VHS, Beta, LV $79.95 *PAR, TAM* ✂✂

MacArthur General Douglas MacArthur's life from Corregidor in 1942 to his dismissal a decade later in the midst of the Korean conflict. Episodic sage with forceful Peck but weak supporting characters. Fourteen minutes were cut from the original version; intended to be Peck's "Patton," it falls short of the mark.
1977 (PG) 130m/C Gregory Peck, Ivan Bonar, Ward Costello, Nicholas Coster, Dan O'Herlihy; **D:** Joseph Sargent; **M:** Jerry Goldsmith. VHS, Beta, LV $19.95 *MCA, TLF* ✂✂✂

MacArthur's Children A poignant evocation of life in a Japanese fishing village as it faces the end of World War II and American occupation. Not as good as some of the other Japanese films, but it is an interesting look at the changes in culture caused by their defeat in the war. In Japanese with English subtitles.
1985 115m/C *JP* Masako Natsume, Shima Iwashita, Hiromi Go, Takaya Yamamauchi, Shiori Sakura, Ken Watanabe, Juzo Itami, Yoshiyuka Omori; **D:** Masahiro Shinoda. VHS, Beta, LV $29.95 *PAV, FCT, TAM* ✂✂✂

Macbeth Shakespeare's classic tragedy is performed in this film with a celebrated lead performance by Welles, who plays the tragic king as a demonic leader of a barbaric society. A low budget adaptation with cheap sets, a 3-week shooting schedule, lots of mood, and an attempt at Scottish accents. After making this film, Welles took a ten-year break from Hollywood.
1948 111m/B Orson Welles, Jeanette Nolan, Dan O'Herlihy, Roddy McDowall, Robert Coote; **D:** Orson Welles. VHS, LV $19.98 *REP, TVC* ✂✂✂½

Macbeth Polanski's notorious adaptation of the Shakespearean classic, marked by realistic design, unflinching violence, and fatalistic atmosphere. Contains stunning fight scenes and fine acting. Polanski's first film following the grisly murder of his pregnant wife, actress Sharon Tate, was torn apart by critics. It is in fact a worthy continuation of his work in the horror genre. Very well made. First film made by Playboy Enterprises. Originally rated X.
1971 (R) 139m/C Jon Finch, Nicholas Selby, Martin Shaw, Francesca Annis, Terence Baylor; **D:** Roman Polanski. VHS, Beta, LV $19.95 *COL, HMV* ✂✂✂

Macbeth An extraordinary version of Shakespeare's "Macbeth" in which all the fire, ambition and doom of his text come brilliantly to life.
1976 137m/C Eric Porter, Janet Suzman. 3/4U, **Special order formats** $19.95 *TLF* ✂✂✂

Macbeth Another production of the classic tragedy by Shakespeare. Produced as part of HBO's Thames Collection.
1990 110m/C Michael Jayston, Leigh Hunt. VHS, Beta $39.99 *HBO* ✂

Machine Gun Kelly Corman found Euro appeal with this thirties style gangster bio. Bronson, who was just gaining a reputation as an action lead, stars as criminal Kelly, who's convinced by his moll to give up bank robbery for kidnapping. Amsterdam, the wisecracking writer from "The Dick Van Dyke Show," is the fink who turns him in. Scripted by R. Wright Campbell.
1958 80m/B Charles Bronson, Susan Cabot, Morey Amsterdam, Barboura Morris, Frank De Kova, Jack Lambert, Wally Campo; **D:** Roger Corman. VHS $9.95 *COL, FCT* ✂✂½

Macho Callahan A Civil War convict escapes from a frontier jail bent on tracking down the man who imprisoned him. (The escaped prisoner bit is a recurring theme in Janssen's oeuvre.) Confused script even has a one-armed Carradine!
1970 (R) 99m/C David Janssen, Jean Seberg, David Carradine, Lee J. Cobb; **D:** Bernard L. Kowalski. VHS, Beta $9.95 *COL, NLC* ✂✂

Macho Dancer A seamy look at Manila's gay underworld. A rural lad comes to city looking for work to support his family and winds up as a male prostitute. Features nudity and explicit sexual situations. In Tagalog with English subtitles.
1988 136m/C *PH* **D:** Lino Brocka. VHS $79.95 *FCT* ✂✂

Macho y Hembra Three young people explore their sexuality away from the confines of society. Venezuelan version of "Jules et Jim."
1985 90m/C Orlando Ordaneta, Elva Escobar, Irene Arcila; **D:** Mauricio Walerstein. VHS, Beta *MAD* ✂✂✂

Machoman The matchless, peerless, Machoman knows all the best killing methods including: Lizard Fists, Crane Kung Fu, and the Drunken Fist.
197? 94m/C Araujo, Enyaw Liew, Jerry Rages. VHS, Beta *NO* ✂

Maciste in Hell Inexplicably living in 17th century Scotland, Italian hero Maciste pursues witch into the depths of Hell. *AKA:* Witch's Curse.
1960 78m/C *IT* Kirk Morris, Helene Chanel, Vira Silenti, Andrea Bosic, Angelo Zanolli, John Karlsen; **D:** Riccardo Freda. VHS $19.98 *UNI, SNC* ✂½

Mack The Mack is a pimp who comes out of retirement to reclaim a piece of the action in Oakland, California. Violent blaxploitation flick was a box office dynamite at time of release. Early Pryor appearance.
1973 (R) 110m/C Max Julien, Richard Pryor, Don Gordon, Roger E. Mosley, Carol Speed; **D:** Michael Campus. VHS, Beta $9.98 *NLC* ✂½

Mack & Carole Lombard began her screen career, in earnest, as a Mack Sennett comedienne. These three shorts represent her earliest screen work.
1928 60m/B Carole Lombard. VHS, Beta $49.50 *GVV* ✂½

Mack Sennett Comedies: Vol. 1 Four Sennett films are included: "The Eyes Have It," "The Cannon Ball," "The Desperate Scoundrel," and "Pride of Pikeville." Ben Turpin and the Keystone Cops at their manic best.
1921 85m/B Ben Turpin, Chester Conklin, Ford Sterling, Minta Durfee; **D:** Mack Sennett. VHS $29.98 *REP* ✂½

Mack Sennett Comedies: Vol. 2 Four more Sennett shorts are featured: "Mabel and Fatty Adrift," "Mabel, Fatty, and the Law," "Fatty's Tin-Type Tangle," and "Our Congressman." The last film features Will Rogers in a lampoon of Capitol Hill.
1916 84m/B Fatty Arbuckle, Mabel Normand, Will Rogers, Madge Hunt; **D:** Mack Sennett. VHS $29.98 *HEP* ✂½

Mack the Knife Terrible adaptation of Brecht and Weill's "Threepenny Opera," detailing the adventures of a master thief in love with an innocent girl. Too much music, too much dancing, too much emoting. *AKA:* The Threepenny Opera.
1989 (PG-13) 121m/C Raul Julia, Roger Daltrey, Richard Harris, Julie Walters, Clive Revill, Erin Donovan, Rachel Robertson, Julia Migenes-Johnson; **D:** Menahem Golan. VHS, Beta, LV $89.95 *COL* Woof!

MacKenna's Gold Grim desperados trek through Apache territory to uncover legendary cache of gold in this somewhat inflated epic. Subdued stars Peck and Shariff vie for attention here with such overactors as Cobb, Meredith, and Wallach. Meanwhile, Newmar (Catwoman of TV's Batman) swims nude. A must for all earthquake buffs.
1969 (PG) 128m/C Gregory Peck, Omar Sharif, Telly Savalas, Julie Newmar, Edward G. Robinson, Keenan Wynn, Ted Cassidy, Eduardo Ciannelli, Eli Wallach, Raymond Massey, Lee J. Cobb, Burgess Meredith, Anthony Quayle; **D:** J. Lee Thompson. VHS, Beta, LV $12.95 *GKK* ✂✂½

Mackintosh Man An intelligence agent must undo a communist who has infiltrated the free world's network in this solid but somewhat subdued thriller. Good cast keeps narrative rolling, but don't look here for nudity-profanity-violence fix.
1973 (PG) 100m/C Paul Newman, Dominique Sanda, James Mason, Ian Bannen, Nigel Patrick, Harry Andrews, Leo Genn, Peter Vaughan, Michael Hordern; *D:* John Huston; *W:* Walter Hill. VHS, Beta $19.98 WAR *ZZ* ½

Macon County Line A series of deadly mistakes and misfortunes lead to a sudden turn-around in the lives of three young people when they enter a small Georgia town and find themselves accused of brutally slaying the sheriff's wife. Sequelled by "Return to Macon County" in 1975, starring Don Johnson and Nick Nolte.
1974 (R) 89m/C Alan Vint, Jesse Vint, Cheryl Waters, Geoffrey Lewis, Joan Blackman, Max Baer; *D:* Richard Compton. VHS, Beta $9.98 SUE *ZZ* ½

Macumba Love An author journeys to Brazil to prove a connection between mysterious murders and voodoo. A tedious suspense exploitation travelogue with generous servings of cheesecake and calypso music.
1960 86m/C Walter Reed, Ziva Rodann, William Wellman Jr., June Wilkinson, Ruth de Souza; *D:* Douglas Fowley. VHS NO *Z*

Mad About Money An early sound comedy about a bespectacled mild-mannered fellow who runs up against a Mexican spitfire. ♫Oh So Beautiful; Perpetual Motion; Little Lost Tune; Dustin' The Stars. *AKA:* He Loved an Actress; Stardust.
1930 80m/B Lupe Velez, Wallace Ford, Ben Lyon, Harry Langdon, Jean Colin; *D:* Melville Brown. VHS, Beta $24.95 NOS, DVT, HEG *ZZ*

Mad About You Millionaire helps his daughter measure prospective suitors. Adam West is not the fourth man in the Montgomery Clift-James Dean-Marlon Brando chain of American acting greats.
1990 (PG) 92m/C Claudia Christian, Joseph Gian, Adam West, Shari Shattuck; *D:* Lorenzo Doumani. VHS, Beta, LV $29.95 ACA Woof!

Mad at the Moon Western thriller in which a young bride (Masterson) discovers that the man she married is less than human with the rising of the full moon. The only one who can protect her is her husband's half-brother played by Bochner. Masterson gives a great performance as a woman torn apart by a terrifying family secret out on the American plains.
1992 (R) 98m/C Mary Stuart Masterson, Hart Bochner, Fionnula Flanagan, Cec Verrell; *W/D:* Martin Donovan; *W:* Richard Pelusi. VHS, LV $89.98 REP *ZZ*

The Mad Bomber Grim lawman Edwards tracks deranged bomber Connors, who is determined to blow up anyone who ever offended him. A must for all connoisseurs of acting that is simultaneously overblown and flat. *AKA:* Police Connection; Detective Geronimo.
1972 80m/C Vince Edwards, Chuck Connors, Neville Brand; *D:* Bert I. Gordon. VHS, Beta $24.95 MRV, WWV Woof!

Mad Bull Sensitive wrestler finds meaning in life when he falls in love. If you ever cared about Karras, then you probably already saw this. If you never cared about Karras, then you probably never heard of this. If you ever cared about Anspach, rent "Five Easy Pieces" instead.
1977 96m/C Alex Karras, Susan Anspach, Nicholas Colasanto, Tracy Walter; *D:* Walter Doniger. VHS, Beta $59.99 HBO *Z*

The Mad Butcher Typically unhinged mental patient seeks teenage flesh for his various instruments of torture and death. Buono has never been more imposing.
1972 (R) 90m/C IT Victor Buono, Karin Field, Brad Harris, John Ireland; *D:* John Zuru. VHS, Beta GHV, MRV *Z*

Mad Death The British Isles take extreme steps to quarantine themselves against rabies from the European continent. This condensed TV miniseries preys on fears of the worst, as an outbreak of the virus spreads from dogs and other pets to humans, and special commandoes are mobilized.
1985 120m/C GB VHS $49.95 FCT *ZZ*

Mad Doctor of Blood Island Dull band of travelers arrive on mysterious tropical island and encounter bloodthirsty creature. Warning: This film is not recognized for outstanding achievements in acting, dialogue, or cinematography. *AKA:* Tomb of the Living Dead; Blood Doctor.
1969 110m/C John Ashley; *D:* Gerardo (Gerry) De Leon. VHS, Beta NO Woof!

Mad Dog An escaped convict seeks revenge on the cop responsible for his imprisonment.
1984 90m/C Helmut Berger, Marisa Mell; *D:* Sergio Grieco. VHS, Beta $24.95 VDC Woof!

Mad Dog and Glory Cast against type, Murray and De Niro play each other's straight man in this dark romantic comedy produced by Martin Scorsese and written by Price. Meek "Mad Dog" (De Niro) is an off-duty police photographer who happens upon a convenience store robbery and manages to save the life of Frank (Murray), gangster by day, stand-up comic by night. To settle up, Frank offers him Glory (Thurman), who's working off her brother's debt to Frank, to use however Mad Dog wants for a week. Turns out what Mad Dog wants is to keep her, and she wants to keep him, but Frank doesn't want to lose his money-maker. Directed by McNaughton, who established himself with "Henry: Portrait of a Serial Killer." No knee-slappers here, often confused and uneven, but redeemed by something of an original take on the situation.
1993 (R) 97m/C Robert De Niro, Uma Thurman, Bill Murray, David Caruso, Mike Starr, Tom Towles, Kathy Baker, Derek Anunciation; *D:* John McNaughton; *W:* Richard Price. VHS, LV MCA *ZZ* ½

Mad Dog Morgan Hopper delivers as engaging outlaw roaming outlands of nineteenth-century Australia. Quirky and violent G'day man. Based on a true story. *AKA:* Mad Dog.
1976 (R) 93m/C AU Dennis Hopper, David Gulpilil; *D:* Philippe Mora. VHS, Beta $59.99 HBO, SIM *ZZ* ½

The Mad Executioners Scotland Yard inspector searches for a sex maniac who decapitates women. In the meantime, a group of vigilantes capture criminals and sentence them without a trial. Confusing film with a predictable ending. Based on the book "White Carpet" by Bryan Edgar Wallace. *AKA:* Der Henker Von London.
1965 92m/B GE Hansjorg Felmy, Maria Perschy, Dieter Borsche, Rudolph Forster, Chris Howland, Wolfgang Preiss; *D:* Edwin Zbonek. VHS $16.95 SNC *ZZ*

Mad Love A brilliant surgeon (Lorre) falls madly in love with an actress, but she rebuffs him. When her pianist husband's hands are cut off in a train accident, Lorre agrees to attach new hands, using those of a recently executed murderer. Lorre then kills the man's stepfather, and to drive him crazy uses psychological terror to make the pianist think he killed him. There's also an appearance by the supposedly executed murderer who shows up to reclaim his hands. A real chiller about obsessive love and psychological fear. The only downfall to this one is the unnecessary comic relief by Healy. Lorre's first American film. *AKA:* The Hands of Orlac.
1935 83m/B Peter Lorre, Colin Clive, Frances Drake, Ted Healy, Edward Brophy, Sara Haden, Henry Kolker; *D:* Karl Freund. VHS $19.98 MGM *ZZZ*

Mad Max Set on the stark highways of the post-nuclear future, an ex-cop seeks personal revenge against a rovin' band of vicious outlaw bikers who killed his wife and child. Futuristic scenery and excellent stunt work make for an exceptionally entertaining action-packed adventure. Followed by "The Road Warrior" (also known as "Mad Max 2") in 1981 and "Mad Max Beyond Thunderdome" in 1985.
1980 (R) 93m/C Mel Gibson, Joanne Samuel, Hugh Keays-Byrne, Steve Bisley, Tim Burns, Roger Ward; *D:* George Miller. VHS, Beta, LV $29.98 LIV, VES *ZZZ* ½

Mad Max Beyond Thunderdome Max drifts into evil town ruled by Turner and becomes gladiator, then gets dumped in desert and is rescued by band of feral orphans. Third in a bleak, extremely violent, often exhilirating series.
1985 (PG-13) 107m/C AU Mel Gibson, Tina Turner, Helen Buday, Frank Thring, Bruce Spence, Robert Grubb, Angelo Rossitto, Angry Anderson, George Spartels, Rod Zuanic; *D:* George Miller, George Ogilvie. VHS, Beta, LV, 8mm $19.98 WAR *ZZ* ½

Mad Miss Manton A socialite turns detective to solve murder. Pleasant comedy-mystery provides occasional laughs and suspense.
1938 80m/B Barbara Stanwyck, Henry Fonda, Hattie McDaniel, Sam Levene, Miles Mander; *D:* Leigh Jason. VHS, Beta, LV $39.95 RKO, TTC *ZZ*

Mad Mission 3 Chinese man vacationing in Paris becomes involved in plot to recover precious jewels stolen from England's royal crown. Has there already been "Mad Mission" and "Mad Mission 2"?
1984 81m/C Richard Kiel, Sam Kui, Karl Muka, Sylvia Chang, Tsuneharu Sugiyama; *D:* (blank). VHS, Beta $59.99 HBO *Z* ½

The Mad Monster This "Wolf Man"-inspired cheapie looks like a misty relic today. A mad scientist furthers the war effort by injecting wolf's blood into a handyman, who becomes hairy and anti-social.
1942 77m/B Johnny Downs, George Zucco, Anne Nagel, Sarah Padden, Glenn Strange, Gordon DeMain, Mae Busch; *D:* Sam Newfield. VHS $15.95 NOS, LOO, VCN *Z* ½

Mad Monster Party Frankenstein is getting older and wants to retire from the responsibilities of being senior monster, so he calls a convention of creepy creatures to decide who should take his place—The Wolfman, Dracula, the Mummy, the Creature, It, the Invisible Man, or Dr. Jekyll and Mr. Hyde. Animated using the process of "Animagic."
1968 94m/C *D:* Jules Bass; *V:* Boris Karloff, Ethel Ennis, Phyllis Diller. VHS, Beta $14.95 COL, SUE *ZZ* ½

Mad Wax: The Surf Movie A flimsy plot about a window-cleaner who discovers a magical surfing wax serves as a framework for lots and lots of scenes of surfin' dudes.

1990 45m/C Richard Cram, Marvin Foster, Aaron Napolean, Tom Carroll, Bryce Andrews, Ross Clarke-Jones; *D:* Michael Hohensee. **VHS, Beta** $14.95 *PAV, FCT* ✂️

The Mad Whirl The Roarin' Twenties are a mad mad whirl in this silent silent piece of period period.
1925 80m/B Myrtle Stedman, Barbara Bedford, Alec B. Francis, George Fawcett, Joseph Singleton. **VHS, Beta** $24.95 *GPV, FCT* ✂️½

Mad Youth A teenage girl falls in love with a man whom her slutty, alcoholic mother had been chasing. Bottom of the barrel production provides many unintentional laughs. Extraneous South American dance sequences included as character development.
1940 61m/B Mary Ainslee, Betty Atkinson, Willy Castello, Betty Compson, Tommy Wonder; *W/D:* Willis Kent. **VHS, Beta** $16.95 *SNC* Woof!

Madam Satan Extremely bizarre DeMille film highlighted by lavish musical numbers and outrageous costumes. A wealthy socialite realizes she's losing her husband to a young showgirl, so she turns herself into a sultry French tramp, wearing makeup and a costume that disguises her appearance. She entices her husband at a masquerade party aboard a zeppelin—surely one of the wildest party scenes ever captured on film. Chorus girls perform several exotic dance numbers inside the airship that are nothing short of fantastic. However, a storm breaks out and the floating dirigible is struck by lightning. Will the mad party-goers make it to safety or will they crash and burn? (like this pic did at the box office).
1930 115m/B Kay Johnson, Reginald Denny, Lillian Roth, Roland Young, Boyd Irwin, Elsa Peterson; *D:* Cecil B. DeMille. **VHS** $19.98 *MGM* ✂️½

Madame Bovary A young adultress with delusions of romantic love finds only despair in this offbeat adaptation of Flaubert's masterpiece. In French with English subtitles.
1934 102m/B *FR* Pierre Renoir, Valentine Tessier, Max Dearly; *D:* Jean Renoir. **VHS, Beta** $59.95 *HTV, TAM* ✂️✂️✂️

Madame Bovary Young adultress with delusions of romantic love finds only despair, even in this Hollywood version of Flaubert's classic. Mason/Flaubert is put on trial for indecency following publication of the novel, with the story told from the witness stand. While this device occasionally slows the narrative, astute direction helps the plot along. Minnelli's handling of the celebrated ball sequence is superb.
1949 115m/B Jennifer Jones, Van Heflin, Louis Jourdan, James Mason, Gene Lockhart, Gladys Cooper, George Zucco; *D:* Vincente Minnelli. **VHS, Beta** $19.98 *MGM, CCB* ✂️✂️✂️

Madame Bovary Provincial 19th century France is the setting for the tragedy of a romantic woman. Emma Bovary is bored by her marriage to an unsuccessful country doctor and longs for passion and excitement. She allows herself to be seduced (and abandoned) by a local aristocrat and herself seduces a young banker. Emma also finds herself under an increasing burden of debt as she struggles to pay for all the finery bought in her quest for luxury. Unwilling to have her husband discover the extent of her deceit, and realizing she will never find the passion she desires, Emma takes drastic, and tragic, measures. A sumptuous-looking film, with an extraordinary performance by Huppert. In French with English subtitles. Based on the novel by Gustave Flaubert.

1991 (PG-13) 130m/C *FR* Isabelle Huppert, Jean-Francois Balmer, Christophe MaLavoy, Jean Yanne; *D:* Claude Chabrol. **VHS, LV** $14.98 *REP, TAM, BTV* ✂️✂️½

Madame Curie The film biography of Madame Marie Curie, the woman who discovered Radium. A deft portrayal by Garson, who is reteamed with her "Mrs. Miniver" co-star, Pidgeon. Certainly better than most biographies from this time period and more truthful as well.
1943 124m/B Greer Garson, Walter Pidgeon, Robert Walker, May Whitty, Henry Travers, C. Aubrey Smith, Albert Basserman, Victor Francen, Reginald Owen, Van Johnson; *D:* Mervyn LeRoy. **VHS, LV** $19.98 *MGM, CCB* ✂️✂️✂️

Madame Rosa An aging Jewish prostitute tends prostitutes' offspring in this warmhearted work. A survivor of the Holocaust, the old woman finds her spirit revived by one of her charges—an abandoned Arab boy. In French with English subtitles. *AKA:* La Vie Devant Sol.
1977 (PG) 105m/C *FR IS* Simone Signoret, Claude Dauphin; *D:* Moshe Mizrahi. **VHS, Beta** $59.95 *HTV, VES* ✂️✂️✂️

Madame Sin Aspiring world dominator enlists former CIA agent in scheme to obtain nuclear submarine. Davis is appealing as evil personified, in her first television movie.
1971 91m/C Bette Davis, Robert Wagner; *D:* David Greene. **VHS, Beta** $9.99 *CCB, FOX* ✂️✂️½

Madame Sousatzka Eccentric, extroverted piano teacher helps students develop spiritually as well as musically. When she engages a teenage Indian student, however, she finds herself considerably challenged. MacLaine is perfectly cast in this powerful, winning film.
1988 (PG-13) 113m/C Shirley MacLaine, Peggy Ashcroft, Shabana Azmi, Twiggy, Leigh Lawson, Geoffrey Bayldon; *D:* John Schlesinger; *W:* John Schlesinger, Ruth Prawer Jhabvala. **VHS, Beta, LV** $19.95 *MCA* ✂️✂️✂️

Madame X Turner is perfectly cast in this oft-filmed melodrama about a social outcast who is tried for murder and defended by her unknowing son, who believes her long dead. Bennett's last film. *AKA:* Absinthe.
1966 100m/C Lana Turner, John Forsythe, Ricardo Montalban, Burgess Meredith, Virginia Grey, Constance Bennett, Keir Dullea; *D:* David Lowell Rich. **VHS, Beta** $14.95 *MCA* ✂️✂️

M.A.D.D.: Mothers Against Drunk Driving Emotionally gripping television movie recounts the story of Candy Lightner, who, after her daughter was killed in a drunk driving accident, founded M.A.D.D. and built it into a nationwide organization. Similar to "License to Kill," which dramatized the effect that a drunk driving accident can have on the families of those involved.
1983 97m/C Mariette Hartley, Paula Prentiss, Bert Remsen; *D:* William A. Graham. **VHS, Beta** $39.95 *MCA* ✂️✂️½

Made for Each Other Newlyweds must overcome meddlesome in-laws, poverty, and even serious illness in this classic melodrama. Dated but appealing.
1939 85m/B James Stewart, Carole Lombard, Charles Coburn, Lucile Watson; *D:* John Cromwell. **VHS, Beta, 3/4U, Special order formats** $9.95 *NEG, MRV, NOS* ✂️✂️✂️

Made for Love Couple journeys romantically in Egypt until disaster strikes: they fall into a tomb and can't get out.
1926 65m/B Leatrice Joy, Edmund Burns, Ethel Wales, Brandon Hurst, Frank Butler; *D:* Paul Sloane. **VHS, Beta** $19.95 *GPV, FCT* ✂️½

Made in America High-energy, lightweight comedy starring Whoopi as a single mom whose daughter Long discovers that she was artificially inseminated at a sperm bank. Much to everyone's surprise, she learns that dear old dad is white, obnoxious, country-western car dealer Danson. Overwrought with obvious gags, it's basically a one-joke movie. Nonetheless, Goldberg and Danson chemically connect onscreen (and offscreen as well, reportedly bonding decisively during production), while supporting actor Smith grabs comedic attention as Teacake, Long's best friend. Both Goldberg and Danson deserve better material, which may occur with their next pairing, "Pink Vodka Blues."
1993 (PG-13) 109m/C Whoopi Goldberg, Ted Danson, Will Smith, Nia Long, Paul Rodriguez, Jennifer Tilly, Peggy Rea, Clyde Kusatsu; *D:* Richard Benjamin; *W:* Holly Goldberg Sloan; *M:* Mark Isham. **VHS** *NYR* ✂️✂️

Made in Argentina An Argentinean couple living in New York decide to return for a visit. Having left for political reasons, they still harbor bitterness.
1986 90m/C *AR* Luis Brandoni, Marta Bianchi, Leonor Manso; *D:* Juan Jose Jusid. **VHS, Beta** $69.98 *VES* ✂️✂️

Made in Heaven Arid comedy in which British newlyweds try to sustain honeymoon for entire year. The bride, however, eventually suspects her husband of shenanigans with the maid. If this sounds good, then you may like it.
1952 90m/C *GB* Petula Clark, David Tomlinson, Sonja Ziemann, A.E. Matthews; *D:* John Paddy Carstairs. **VHS, Beta** $29.98 *VID, HMV* ✂️✂️

Made in Heaven Two souls in heaven fall in love and must find each other after being reborn on Earth if they are to remain eternal lovers. Contains ethereal interpretations of heaven and several cameo appearances by famous actors and musicians.
1987 (PG) 102m/C Timothy Hutton, Kelly McGillis, Maureen Stapleton, Mare Winningham, Ann Wedgeworth, Don Murray, Amanda Plummer, Timothy Daly; *Cameos:* Ellen Barkin, Neil Young, Tom Petty, Ric Ocasek, Tom Robbins, Debra Winger, Gary Larsen, David Rasche; *D:* Alan Rudolph. **VHS, Beta, LV** $19.98 *LHV, WAR* ✂️✂️½

Made in USA Wayward dudes engage vixen while cruising Midwest. Trouble, however, awaits. Note: This is not Godard's mid-sixties classic.
1988 (R) 82m/C Adrian Pasdar, Lori Singer, Christopher Penn; *D:* Ken Friedman. **VHS, Beta, LV** $19.98 *SUE, NLC* ✂️½

Madeleine Courtroom drama of woman charged with poisoning her French lover in 1850s Scotland. Directed by the same David Lean who made "Bridge on the River Kwai" and "Lawrence of Arabia". Here, though, he was merely trying to provide a vehicle for his wife, actress Todd. Intrigued? *AKA:* The Strange Case of Madeleine.
1950 114m/B Ann Todd, Leslie Banks, Ivan Desny; *D:* David Lean. **VHS, Beta** $14.95 *LCA* ✂️✂️½

Mademoiselle Fifi Simon stars as a French laundress in 1870 France who refuses to give in to her small town's Prussian oppressors. The film title is the nickname of the most brutal of the Prussian officers, played by Kreuger. An unsuccessful attempt at political allegory for the devastation of World War II.
1944 69m/B Simone Simon, John Emery, Kurt Kreuger, Alan Napier, Jason Robards Sr.; *D:* Robert Wise. **VHS, LV** $19.98 *FCT* ✂️½

Mademoiselle Striptease Bardot stars as a young woman who finds a valuable stolen book. Her attempts to disassociate herself from the actual theft are supposed to be funny. Bardot is characteristically appealing. *AKA:* Please! Mr. Balzac; While Plucking the Daisy; En Effeuillant la Marguerite.
1957 100m/B Brigitte Bardot, Robert Hirsch, Daniel Gelin; *D:* Marc Allegret. **VHS, Beta $29.95** *STV, MRV* 𝄢𝄢½

Madhouse A troubled horror film star tries to bring his "Dr. Death" character to television, but during production people begin dying in ways remarkably similar to the script. A strong genre cast should hold the fans' attention during this mild adaptation of Angus Hall's novel "Devilday."
1974 92m/C *GB* Vincent Price, Peter Cushing, Robert Quarry, Adrienne Corri, Natasha Pyne, Linda Hayden, Michael Parkinson; *D:* Jim Clark. **VHS, Beta** *HBO* 𝄢𝄢

Madhouse A woman has bizarre recollections of her twin sister whom she finally meets when she escapes from a mental hospital. Lots of violence and gore, has definite cult potential.
1987 90m/C Trish Everly, Michael MacRae, Dennis Robertson, Morgan Hart; *D:* Ovidio G. Assonitis. **VHS, Beta** *NO* 𝄢𝄢

Madhouse New homeowners find themselves unable to expel loathsome, boorish guests. Presumably, a comedy cashing in on two of sitcom's brightest talents.
1990 (PG-13) 90m/C John Larroquette, Kirstie Alley, Alison La Placa, John Diehl, Jessica Lundy, Bradley Gregg, Dennis Miller, Robert Ginty; *D:* Tom Ropelewski. **VHS, Beta, LV $14.98** *ORI* 𝄢𝄢

Madhouse Mansion A horror actor revives his career and becomes embroiled in murder. Plenty of in-jokes and clips from older movies. *AKA:* Ghost Story.
1974 (PG) 86m/C *GB* Marianne Faithfull, Leigh Lawson, Anthony Bate, Larry Dann, Sally Grace, Penelope Keith, Vivian Mackerell, Murray Melvin, Barbara Shelley; *D:* Stephen Weeks. **VHS** *NO* 𝄢𝄢½

Madigan Realistic and exciting and among the best of the behind-the-scenes urban police thrillers. Hardened NYC detectives (Widmark and Guardino) lose their guns to a sadistic killer and are given 72 hours to track him down. Fonda is the police chief none too pleased with their performance. Adapted by Howard Rodman, Abraham Polonsky, and Harry Kleiner from Richard Dougherty's "The Commissioner."
1968 101m/C Richard Widmark, Henry Fonda, Inger Stevens, Harry Guardino, James Whitmore, Susan Clark, Michael Dunn, Don Stroud; *D:* Don Siegel. **VHS, Beta $59.95** *MCA* 𝄢𝄢𝄢

Madigan's Millions Incompetent Treasury agent treks to Italy to recover funds swiped from deceased gangster. This is Hoffman's first film, and is to his career what "The Last Chalice" was to Paul Newman's and "Studs and Kitty" was to Sylvester Stallone. Recommended only to the terminally foolhardy.
1967 (G) 89m/C Dustin Hoffman, Elsa Martinelli, Cesar Romero; *D:* Stanley Prager. **VHS, Beta $59.95** *WWV* Woof!

Madman Deranged Soviet Jew joins Israeli army to more effectively fulfill his desire to kill loathsome Soviets. Good date movie for those nights when you're home alone. Weaver's first starring role.
1979 (R) 95m/C *IS* Sigourney Weaver, Michael Beck, F. Murray Abraham; *D:* Dan Cohen. **VHS, Beta $19.95** *NEG* 𝄢

Madman Camp leader prompts terror when he revives legend regarding ax murderer. Seems that when you call his name, he appears. Buffoon does not believe story and calls out madman's name. Madman hears the call and emerges from forest, says hi, and hacks everyone to death. Lesson learned, case closed. Filmed on Long Island.
1982 (R) 89m/C Alexis Dubin, Tony Fish. **VHS, Beta $69.99** *HBO, HHE* 𝄢

Mado A middle-aged businessman's life is undone when he falls for a mysterious woman. Piccoli and Schneider are, as usual, convincing. Another of underrated director Sautet's effective, low-key works. In French with subtitles.
1976 130m/C Romy Schneider, Michel Piccoli, Charles Denner; *D:* Claude Sautet. **VHS, Beta $59.95** *FCT* 𝄢𝄢𝄢

Madox-01 Animated feature aimed at mature audiences. When a bungling tank operator gets trapped in the army's newest tank, two rivals join forces to free him. In Japanese with English subtitles.
1991 50m/C *JP* **VHS, LV $34.95** *CPM, WTA, TAM* 𝄢𝄢½

Madron Road western filmed in the Israel desert, complete with menacing Apaches, wagon train massacre, a nun and a gunslinger.
1970 (PG) 93m/C Richard Boone, Leslie Caron, Paul Smith; *D:* Jerry Hopper. **VHS, Beta $59.95** *UHV* 𝄢½

The Madwoman of Chaillot Four men conspire to drill for oil which they believe lurks under Paris. Hepburn finds out about their plot and tells each man that oil is bubbling up through her basement. Before the men can arrive at her house to confirm this, she and her three cronies hold a mock trial and sentence the men to death. Features a stellar cast, but this modern-day adaptation of Jean Giraudoux's play "La Folle de Chaillot" falls flat.
1969 (G) 142m/C Katharine Hepburn, Charles Boyer, Claude Dauphin, Edith Evans, John Gavin, Paul Henreid, Oscar Homolka, Margaret Leighton, Giulietta Masina, Nanette Newman, Richard Chamberlain, Yul Brynner, Donald Pleasence, Danny Kaye, Fernand Gravet; *D:* Bryan Forbes; *W:* Edward Anhalt. **VHS, LV** *WAR* 𝄢½

Mae West This made-for-television film details West's life from her humble beginnings to her racy film stardom. Jillian does a good job bringing the buxom legend back to life.
1984 97m/C Ann Jillian, James Brolin, Piper Laurie, Roddy McDowall; *D:* Lee Philips. **VHS, Beta $59.95** *LHV* 𝄢𝄢½

Maedchen in Uniform A scandalous early German talkie about a rebellious schoolgirl who falls in love with a female teacher and commits suicide when the teacher is punished for the relationship. A controversial criticism of lesbianism and militarism that impelled the Nazis, rising to power two years later, to exile its director. It was also banned in the United States. In German with English subtitles. Remade in 1965. *AKA:* Girls in Uniform.
1931 90m/B *GE* Dorothea Wieck, Ellen Schwannecke, Hertha Thiele; *D:* Leontine Sagan. **VHS, Beta $29.98** *SUE, MRV, TAM* 𝄢𝄢𝄢½

Mafia la Ley Que Non Perdona A Mafia kingpin struggles to maintain his power through violence. Dubbed into Spanish.
1979 90m/C Gordon Mitchell, Antonella Lualdi. **VHS, Beta** *NO* 𝄢½

Mafia Princess The daughter of a Mafia boss tries to discover her own identity despite her father's involvement in crime. Based on a best-selling autobiography by a real-life member of a Mob family, Antoinette Giancana. Made for television.
1986 100m/C Tony Curtis, Susan Lucci, Kathleen Widdoes, Chuck Shamata, Louie Dibianco; *D:* Robert Collins. **VHS** *NO* 𝄢𝄢

Mafia vs. Ninja The mob wants to control the city, but the Ninja has other ideas.
1984 90m/C Alexander Lou, Silvio Azzolini, Wang Hsia, Charlema Hsu, Eugene Trammel. **VHS, Beta $59.95** *WWV* 𝄢½

Magdalene Somewhere in medieval Europe, a violent Baron seeks revenge on a beautiful whore that spurned him. Small-budget costumer.
1988 (PG) 89m/C Steve Bond, Nastassia Kinski, David Warner, Gunter Meisner, Ferdinand "Ferdy" Mayne, Anthony Quayle, Franco Nero, Janet Agren; *D:* Monica Teuber. **VHS, Beta, LV $89.99** *PAR, FCT* 𝄢½

Magee and the Lady The crusty captain of a rusty ship must warm up to a spoiled debutante or lose his ship to a foreclosure firm. Could be better. Made for TV. *AKA:* She'll Be Sweet.
1978 (PG) 92m/C *AU* Tony LoBianco, Sally Kellerman; *D:* Gene Levitt. **VHS, Beta $19.95** *ACA* 𝄢𝄢

Magic Ventriloquist Hopkins and his dummy, an all-too-human counterpart, get involved with a beautiful but impressionable woman lost between reality and the irresistible world of illusion. Spine-chilling psychodrama with a less-than-believable premise. Screenplay by William Goldman ("the Princess Bride"), from his novel.
1978 (R) 106m/C Anthony Hopkins, Ann-Margret, Burgess Meredith, Ed Lauter; *D:* Richard Attenborough; *M:* Jerry Goldsmith. **VHS, Beta, LV $14.98** *SUE, NLC* 𝄢𝄢½

Magic Adventure Animated adventure about a brother and his sister who are in for the time of their lives when they meet the Wind Wizard who sends them on an unexpected journey.
1987? 82m/C **VHS, Beta** *NO* 𝄢𝄢½

The Magic Christian A series of related skits about a rich man (Sellers) and his son (Starr) who try to prove that anyone can be bought. Raucous, now somewhat dated comedy; music by Badfinger, including Paul McCartney's "Come and Get It."
1969 (PG) 101m/C *GB* Peter Sellers, Ringo Starr, Isabel Jeans, Wilfrid Hyde-White, Graham Chapman, John Cleese, Peter Graves, John Lennon, Yoko Ono, Richard Attenborough, Leonard Frey, Laurence Harvey, Christopher Lee, Spike Milligan, Yul Brynner, Roman Polanski, Raquel Welch; *D:* Joseph McGrath. **VHS, Beta, LV $59.98** *REP, MRV, PIA* 𝄢𝄢𝄢

The Magic Flute Bergman's acclaimed version of Mozart's famous comic opera, universally considered one of the greatest adaptations of opera to film ever made. Staged before a live audience for Swedish television. In Swedish with English subtitles.
1973 (G) 134m/C *SW* Josef Kostlinger, Irma Urrila, Hakan Hagegard, Elisabeth Erikson; *D:* Ingmar Bergman. **VHS, Beta, LV $29.95** *HMV, PAR, VTK* 𝄢𝄢𝄢½

The Magic Fountain Three princes search for a magic fountain whose waters will cure their ailing father. Two of them, however, take the evil course and are turned into ravens by a wicked dwarf. Based on the fairy tale "Das Wasser des Lebens" by the Brothers Grimm.

1961 82m/C Peter Nestler, Helmo Kinderman, Josef Marz, Catherine Hansen, Cedric Hardwicke; D: Allan David. VHS $16.95 SNC ♂♂

The Magic Legend of the Golden Goose A retelling of the familiar brothers Grimm chestnut.
1965 72m/C VHS, Beta UHV ♂

Magic of Lassie Stewart is engaging as the nice grandpa who refuses to sell his land to mean rich guy Roberts. Innocuous, pleasant remake of "Lassie Come Home." Stewart sings, as do Pat Boone and daughter Debby.
1978 (G) 100m/C James Stewart, Mickey Rooney, Stephanie Zimbalist, Alice Faye, Pernell Roberts, Lassie; D: Don Chaffey. VHS, Beta $19.95 MGM ♂♂

Magic on Love Island Romantic misadventures ensue when eight ladies go on vacation to Love Island, a tropical paradise.
1980 96m/C Adrienne Barbeau, Bill Daily, Howard Duff, Dody Goodman, Dominique Dunne, Lisa Hartman, Janice Paige; D: Earl Bellamy. VHS, Beta NO ♂

Magic Serpent Fantasy set in medieval Japan features a grand duel in magic between a good hero and evil sorcerer who transform into a giant dragon and a giant frog to do battle.
1966 ?m/C VHS $20 SMW ♂

The Magic Sword A family-oriented adventure film about a young knight who sets out to rescue a beautiful princess who is being held captive by an evil sorcerer and his dragon.
1962 80m/C Basil Rathbone, Estelle Winwood, Gary Lockwood; D: Bert I. Gordon. VHS, Beta $14.95 MGM, MRV, VYY ♂♂

Magic Town An opinion pollster investigates a small town which exactly reflects the views of the entire nation, making his job a cinch. The publicity causes much ado in the town with ensuing laughs. Uneven but entertaining.
1947 103m/B Jane Wyman, James Stewart, Kent Smith, Regis Toomey, Donald Meek; D: William A. Wellman. VHS $19.98 REP ♂♂½

The Magic Voyage of Sinbad Sinbad embarks on a fantastic journey after promising the people of his Covasian home that he will find the elusive Phoenix, the bird of happiness. Unreleased in the U.S. until 1962; rewritten for the American screen by a young Coppola. AKA: Sadko.
1952 79m/C RU Sergey Stolyarov, Alla Larionova, Mark Troyanovsky; D: Alexander Ptushko; W: Francis Ford Coppola. VHS, Beta $16.95 SNC ♂♂

Magical Mystery Tour On the road with an oddball assortment of people, the Beatles experience a number of strange incidents around the English countryside. Originally made for British television. Songs include: "The Fool on the Hill," "Blue Jay Way," "Your Mother Should Know," and the title tune.
1967 55m/C GB John Lennon, George Harrison, Ringo Starr, Paul McCartney, Victor Spinetti. VHS, Beta, LV $29.95 MVD, MED, WFV ♂

Magical Wonderland Join a handsome prince and his fair young maiden as they venture through such fairy tale classics as "Beauty and the Beast" and "Sleeping Beauty."
1985 90m/C VHS, Beta $39.95 UHV ♂♂

The Magician A master magician in 19th century Sweden (von Sydow) wreaks ill in this darkly comical, supernatural parable. Dark, well photographed early Bergman effort. In Swedish with English subtitles.

1958 101m/B SW Max von Sydow, Ingrid Thulin, Gunnar Bjornstrand, Bibi Andersson, Naima Wifstrand; D: Ingmar Bergman. VHS, Beta, LV $29.95 SUE, MRV, HHT ♂♂♂

The Magician of Lublin Based on an unusual story by Issac Bashevis Singer. Follows the exploits of a magician/con man in turn-of-the-century Poland whose personal flaws kill his career, until a chance emerges for one last trick. A good example of movie not as good as book; this rendering is superficial, badly acted and unsatisfying. Made soon after Singer won the Nobel Prize for literature in 1978.
1979 (R) 105m/C Alan Arkin, Valerie Perrine, Louise Fletcher, Lou Jacobi, Shelley Winters; D: Menahem Golan. VHS, Beta $79.99 HBO ♂½

The Magnificent When the government is overthrown by a band of mercenaries led by Lord Lu, the deposed emperor disappears. Lots of head kicking and action shots.
197? 80m/C Chen Sing, Bruce Lai, Col Len Rei Lee, Jane Jennings. VHS, Beta $59.95 SVS ♂

Magnificent Adventurer Ostensibly a biography of Benvenuto Cellini, the Florentine sculptor, with a concentration on his love life and swordplay.
1976 94m/C Brett Halsey. VHS, Beta $59.95 UNI ♂

The Magnificent Ambersons Welles' second film. A fascinating, inventive translation of the Booth Tarkington novel about a wealthy turn of the century family collapsing under the changing currents of progress. Pure Welles, except the glaringly bad tacked-on ending that the studio shot (under the direction of the great Robert Wise and Fred Fleck), after taking the film from him. It seems they wanted the proverbial happy ending. Also available on laserdisc, with interviews and the original story boards.
1942 88m/B Joseph Cotten, Anne Baxter, Tim Holt, Richard Bennett, Dolores Costello, Erskine Sanford, Ray Collins, Agnes Moorehead; D: Orson Welles. Academy Awards '42 Nominations: Best Black and White Cinematography, Best Interior Decoration, Best Picture, Best Supporting Actress (Moorehead); New York Film Critics Awards '42: Best Actress (Moorehead). VHS, Beta, LV $19.95 RKO, VID, VYG ♂♂♂

The Magnificent Dope Fonda is likeable, as usual, as the hapless yokel in the big city. A trip to New York to take a course on being successful is his prize for winning a "laziest man" contest. He falls for his teacher; she uses his crush to motivate him. Funny and entertaining.
1942 83m/B Henry Fonda, Lynn Bari, Don Ameche, Edward Everett Horton, Hobart Cavanaugh, Pierre Watkin; D: Walter Lang. VHS TCF ♂♂½

Magnificent Duo Chop-socky headkicking between two hard-footed veterans.
197? 84m/C Britton Lee, Chris Kim. VHS, Beta $39.95 UNI ♂

The Magnificent Kick The story of a master Wong-Fai-Hung, inventor of the "Kick without Shadow," which was practiced by the late Bruce Lee.
1980 90m/C VHS, Beta NO ♂

The Magnificent Matador The story of an aging matador who faces death in the bullring to win the love of a woman. Quinn is the bullfighter on the horns of a dilemma. Lots of bull in script carried by harried bull in ring. AKA: The Brave and the Beautiful.
1955 94m/C Anthony Quinn, Maureen O'Hara, Thomas Gomez; D: Budd Boetticher. VHS, Beta $29.95 VHE ♂♂½

Magnificent Obsession A drunken playboy (Hudson) kills a man and blinds his wife in an automobile accident. Plagued by guilt, he devotes his life to studying medicine in order to restore the widow's sight. Well-acted melodrama lifted Hudson to stardom. Faithful to the 1935 original, based on a novel by Lloyd C. Douglas.
1954 108m/C Jane Wyman, Rock Hudson, Barbara Rush, Agnes Moorehead; D: Douglas Sirk. VHS, Beta $14.95 MCA ♂♂½

Magnificent Seven Western remake of Akira Kurosawa's classic "The Seven Samurai." Mexican villagers hire gunmen to protect them from the bandits who are destroying their town. Most of the actors were relative unknowns, though not for long. Sequelled by "Return of the Seven" in 1966, "Guns of the Magnificent Seven" in 1969, and "The Magnificent Seven Ride" in 1972. Excellent score.
1960 126m/C Yul Brynner, Steve McQueen, Robert Vaughn, James Coburn, Charles Bronson, Horst Buchholz, Eli Wallach, Brad Dexter; D: John Sturges. VHS, Beta, LV $19.98 MGM, FOX, TLF ♂♂♂♂

Magnum Force Eastwood's second "Dirty Harry" movie. Harry finds a trail leading from a series of gangland killings straight back to the P.D. Less gripping than "Dirty Harry" (1971); followed by "The Enforcer" (1976), "Sudden Impact" (1983), and "The Dead Pool" (1988). Holbrook is cast intriguingly against type, and the premise is good, but little else recommends this too-violent installment.
1973 (R) 124m/C Clint Eastwood, Hal Holbrook, Mitchell Ryan, David Soul, Robert Urich, Tim Matheson, Kip Niven; D: Ted Post. VHS, Beta, LV $19.98 WAR, TLF ♂♂

Magnum Killers A young man becomes involved in a web of deadly intrigue when he sets out to find who cheated him out of a small fortune during a card game.
1976 92m/C Sombat Methance, Prichela Lee. VHS, Beta $29.95 UNI ♂

Magoo's Puddle Jumper Magoo backs off a pier in his "new" used car and points out all the underwater sights to his nephew Waldo. Part of the "Mister Magoo" series.
1956 7m/C V: Jim Backus. VHS, Beta CHF ♂

The Mahabharata Adapted from the myths and folklore of ancient India, the screen version of the original 9 hour stage play is the story of a devastating war between two powerful clans. Initially broadcast on public television, the 6 hour movie is divided into three 2 hour tapes, "The Game of Dice," "Exile in the Forest," and "The War."
1989 318m/C GB FR Robert Langton-Lloyd, Antonin Stahly-Vishwanadan, Bruce Myers; D: Peter Brook; W: Jean-Claude Carriere; M: Toshi Tsuchitori. VHS, LV $99.95 BOK, BTV, FCT ♂

Mahler Strange Russell effort on the life of the great composer Gustav Mahler. Imperfect script is rescued by fine acting.
1974 (PG) 110m/C Robert Powell, Georgina Hale, Richard Morant, Lee Montague, Terry O'Quinn; D: Ken Russell. VHS, Beta HBO, OM ♂♂♂

Mahogany Poor girl becomes world-famous high fashion model and designer, ditches boyfriend in the old neighborhood, gets a career boost when she daringly appears in a dress of her own creation at a Roman fashion show, and still yearns for the boy back home. Motown attempt to make mainstream hit that's glossy and predictable.

1975 (PG) 109m/C Diana Ross, Billy Dee Williams, Jean-Pierre Aumont, Anthony Perkins, Nina Foch; D: Berry Gordy. VHS, Beta, LV $14.95 PAR, CCB, FCT &1/2

The Maid An offbeat comedy romance with Sheen as the house husband to Bisset's female executive character. Nice acting; charming, if unoriginal, premise.
1990 (PG) 91m/C Martin Sheen, Jacqueline Bisset, Jean-Pierre Cassel, James Faulkner; D: Ian Toynton. VHS, Beta, LV $89.98 MED &&1/2

Maid in Sweden Naive country girl visits Stockholm for the first time and has some bizarre encounters with men.
1983 90m/C SW Kristina Lindberg, Monika Ekman; D: Floch Johnson. VHS, Beta $42.95 PGN &1/2

Maid to Order Rich girl Sheedy's fairy godmother puts her in her place by turning her into a maid for a snooty Malibu couple. Good-natured and well-acted if rather mindless Cinderella story.
1987 (PG) 92m/C Ally Sheedy, Beverly D'Angelo, Michael Ontkean, Dick Shawn, Tom Skerritt, Valerie Perrine; D: Amy Jones. VHS, Beta, LV $14.95 LIV &1/2

Maid's Night Out Pleasant, simple-minded mistaken-identity comedy. Fontaine is an heiress; rich-guy posing-as-milkman Lane thinks she is a maid. They fall in love, of course.
1938 64m/B Joan Fontaine, Allan "Rocky" Lane, Hedda Hopper, George Irving, William Brisbane, Billy Gilbert, Cecil Kellaway; D: Ben Holmes. VHS RKO, MLB &

The Main Event Streisand plays a wacky—and bankrupt—cosmetic executive who must depend on the career of washed-up boxer O'Neal to rebuild her fortune. Desperate (and more than a little smitten), she badgers and bullies him back into the ring. Lame, derivative screwball comedy desperate to suggest chemistry of Streisand and O'Neal's "What's Up, Doc?" (1972). Streisand sings the title song.
1979 (PG) 105m/C Barbra Streisand, Ryan O'Neal; D: Howard Zieff. VHS, Beta $19.98 WAR &&

Main Street to Broadway Superficial story of a struggling playwright. Interesting mainly for abundant big-name cameos. Based on a story by Robert E. Sherwood.
1953 102m/B Tom Morton, Mary Murphy, Agnes Moorehead, Herb Shriner, Rosemary DeCamp, Clinton Sundberg; Cameos: Lionel Barrymore, Ethel Barrymore, James Barrymore, Shirley Booth, Cornel Wilde, Rex Harrison, Joshua Logan, Helen Hayes, Mary Martin; D: Tay Garnett. VHS, Beta $59.95 MPI, MLB &&

Maitresse An examination of the sexual underworld in the same vein as "Blue Velvet" and "Crimes of Passion." Director Schroeder also created "Reversal of Fortune." In French with English subtitles.
1976 112m/C Gerard Depardieu; D: Barbet Schroeder. VHS $59.99 WAR, BTV, FCT &&

Major Barbara A wealthy, idealistic girl joins the Salvation Army against her father's wishes. Based on the play by George Bernard Shaw. The excellent adaptation of the original and the cast make this film a winner. Deborah Kerr's film debut.
1941 90m/B GB Wendy Hiller, Rex Harrison, Robert Morley, Sybil Thorndike, Deborah Kerr; D: Gabriel Pascal. VHS, Beta $39.95 LCA, FCT, HMV &&&1/2

Major Dundee A Union army officer (Heston) chases Apaches into Mexico with a motley collection of prisoner volunteers. Too long and flawed; would have been better had

Peckinpah been allowed to finish the project. Excellent cast.
1965 124m/C Charlton Heston, Richard Harris, James Coburn, Jim Hutton, Ben Johnson, Slim Pickens; D: Sam Peckinpah. VHS, Beta $12.95 GKK &&1/2

Major League Comedy about a pathetic major league baseball team whose new owner schemes to lose the season and relocate the team to Miami. Predictable sports spoof scripted by David Ward ("The Sting"). Sheen is okay as the pitcher with control problems (both on and off the field), while Bernsen seems to be gazing affectionately at "L.A. Law" from a distance. Good for a few laughs, particularly those scenes involving Dennis Haysbert as a slugger with voodoo on his mind (and in his locker) and Snipes as a base stealer whose only problem is getting on base.
1989 (R) 107m/C Tom Berenger, Charlie Sheen, Corbin Bernsen, James Gammon, Margaret Whitton, Bob Uecker, Rene Russo, Wesley Snipes, Dennis Haysbert; D: David S. Ward. VHS, Beta, LV, 8mm $14.95 PAR &&&

The Majorettes Eek! Someone is lurking around a high school murdering the majorettes with their own batons. A bare-bones plot lurks within this otherwise worthless pic.
1987 (R) 93m/C Kevin Kindlan, Terrie Godfrey, Mark V. Jevicky; D: John Russo. VHS, Beta $69.98 LIV, VES &

Make a Million The Depression is played (successfully) for yuks in this tale of an economics professor fired from his post for advocating radical income redistribution. He doesn't get mad, he gets even: he makes a million by advertising for money.
1935 66m/B Charles Starrett, Pauline Brooks. VHS, Beta $29.95 VYY &&

Make a Wish A noted composer goes stale in this colorful musical about backstage life. The comic relief provides the films best moments. Music by Oscar Strauss. ♫Music In My Heart; My Campfire Dreams; Make a Wish; Old Man Rip.
1937 80m/B Basil Rathbone, Leon Errol, Bobby Breen, Ralph Forbes; D: Kurt Neumann. VHS, Beta $29.95 VYY &&

Make Haste to Live Good, scary thriller. A woman survives attempted murder by her husband; moves far away to raise their infant daughter. He does time, then returns for revenge. McGuire is good as the terrorized wife.
1954 90m/B Dorothy McGuire, Stephen McNally, Edgar Buchanan, John Howard; D: William A. Seiter. VHS $19.98 REP &&1/2

Make Me an Offer Somewhat slow-moving comedy centering on an antique dealer who attempts to buy an expensive vase from an old man. From the novel by Wolf Mankowitz.
1955 88m/C GB Peter Finch, Adrienne Corri, Rosalie Crutchley, Finlay Currie; D: Cyril Frankel. VHS $59.98 SUE &

Make Me an Offer Made-for-TV movie about selling real estate in Hollywood. Better than similar efforts.
1980 97m/C Susan Blakely, Stella Stevens, Patrick O'Neal; D: Jerry Paris. VHS, Beta $59.98 NLC &1/2

Make Mine Mink Oft-hilarious British comedy about guests at an elegant but run-down mansion who become unlikely thieves, stealing furs for charity. Good cast headed by Terry-Thomas.
1960 100m/C GB Terry-Thomas, Billie Whitelaw, Hattie Jacques; D: Robert Asher. VHS, Beta $19.98 VID &&&

Make Room for Tomorrow Subtle, somewhat funny French comedy about generations in a family. A man in mid-life crisis has to cope with his father, son, and grandfather on the grandfather's 90th birthday.
1981 (R) 106m/C FR Victor Lanoux, Jane Birkin, George Wilson; D: Peter Kassovitz. VHS, Beta $29.95 SUE &&

Make-Up A doctor turned circus clown uses his medical skills when an elephant renders a society girl unconscious. After she awakens the two become involved. The clown's daughter objects, but is soon caught up in an accusation that she murdered the lion tamer. Her father the clown tries to save the day. Predictable doctor/clown relationship.
1937 72m/B Nils Asther, June Clyde, Judy Kelly, Kenne Duncan, John Turnbull; D: Alfred Zeisler. VHS $24.95 NOS, DVT &

Makin' It Three trampy barmaids rise to the top of the music business due to every talent except singing. AKA: Running Hot.
19?? 92m/C Rory Calhoun, Darrow Igus, Gwen Owens. VHS, Beta $19.95 ACA &

Making Contact A small boy's telekinetic powers enable him to bring to life his favorite toys. The ridicule he suffers because of this leads him to set off on terrifying adventures with only his toys and a friend for company.
1986 (PG) 83m/C Joshua Morrell, Eve Kryll; D: Roland Emmerich. VHS, Beta $14.95 NWV, STE &1/2

Making Love A closet homosexual risks his 8-year marriage by getting involved with a carefree writer. What could be a powerful subject gets only bland treatment.
1982 (R) 112m/C Kate Jackson, Harry Hamlin, Michael Ontkean, Wendy Hiller, Arthur Hill, Nancy Olson, Terry Kiser, Camilla Carr, Michael Dudikoff; D: Arthur Hiller. VHS, Beta $69.98 FOX &&

Making Mr. Right Under-rated satire about a high-powered marketing and image consultant who falls in love with the android that she's supposed to be promoting. Unbelievable comedy is shaky at times, but Magnuson and Malkovich create some magic.
1986 (PG-13) 95m/C John Malkovich, Ann Magnuson, Glenne Headly, Ben Masters, Laurie Metcalf, Polly Bergen; D: Susan Seidelman. VHS, Beta, LV $19.99 HBO &&

The Making of "A Brief History of Time" A behind-the-scenes look at Morris' film, based on the best-seller by physicist Stephen Hawking. Includes interviews with the director and producers.
1992 30m/C D: Errol Morris. VHS PAR &&1/2

The Making of a Legend: "Gone With the Wind" An exhaustive tribute to the American classic on its 50th anniversary, featuring miles of film clips, wardrobe tests, interviews with surviving cast and crew members, and scads of production trivia.
1989 130m/C Clark Gable, Vivien Leigh, Carole Lombard, Laurence Olivier, David O. Selznick, Margaret Mitchell, Ann Rutherford, Butterfly McQueen, Evelyn Keyes, Leslie Howard, Olivia de Havilland, Thomas Mitchell, Ona Munson, Ward Bond, Hattie McDaniel, Victor Fleming, Sam Wood, George Cukor, Paulette Goddard, Lana Turner, Jean Arthur, Joan Bennett, Tallulah Bankhead, Melvyn Douglas, George Reeves, Fred Crane. VHS, Beta, LV $29.95 MGM &&1/2

Making the Grade Jersey tough kid owes the mob; attends prep school in place of a rich kid who can't be bothered. Better than similar '80s teen flicks, but not by much. AKA: Preppies.

1984 (PG) 105m/C Judd Nelson, Joanna Lee, Dana Olsen, Ronald Lacey, Scott McGinnis, Gordon Jump, Carey Scott, Andrew Dice Clay; **D:** Dorian Walker. VHS, Beta $79.95 MGM *√√*

The Makioka Sisters Much praised drama centering around the lives of four Japanese sisters who are heiresses to the family fortune and, hence, must be found proper husbands. The efforts of the older sisters to "match" their younger siblings are entwined with a gradual realization on the part of the elders that the quiet way of life representative of their own formative years is passing away with the advent of World War II. The movie is as visually stunning as it is poignant. In Japanese with English subtitles.
1983 140m/C JP Keiko Kishi, Yoshiko Sakuma, Sayuri Yoshinaga; **D:** Kon Ichikawa. VHS $59.99 FCT, TAM *√√√*

Malarek Tough Montreal journalist Victor Malarek exposed abuse in that city's teen detention center in his book "Hey, Malarek." Compelling lead performance from Koteas in decent though not great screen adaptation.
1989 (R) 95m/C Michael Sarrazin, Elias Koteas, Al Waxman, Kerrie Keane; **D:** Roger Cardinal. VHS, Beta, LV $14.95 SVS, COL *√√*

Malcolm An offbeat comedy about a slightly retarded young man who is mechanically inclined and his unusual entry into a life of crime. Directorial debut for actress Tass, whose husband David Parker wrote the screenplay (and designed the Tinkertoys). Music score performed by The Penguin Cafe Orchestra.
1986 (PG-13) 86m/C AU Colin Friels, John Hargreaves, Lindy Davies; **D:** Nadia Tass. VHS, Beta, LV $79.98 LIV, VES *√√½*

Malcolm X Lee's biography of the controversial black activist is a stirring tribute to a martyr in the struggle for black liberation. Malcolm X (Washington) is a sort of spiritual rags-to-riches story about a man who went from street hustler to religious/political leader. Hitting bottom during his imprisonment in the 1950's, Malcolm becomes a Black Muslim and then a leader in the Nation of Islam. His eventual break with the group and assassination in 1965 left a legacy of black nationalism, self-determination, and racial pride. Though all the performances are fine (notably Freeman Jr. as Elijah Muhammad) it is Washington's convincing performance in the title role that keeps the film (and the man) alive. Based on "The Autobiography of Malcolm X" written by Malcolm X and Alex Haley.
1992 (PG-13) 201m/C Denzel Washington, Angela Bassett, Al Freeman Jr., Delroy Lindo, Albert Hall, Kate Vernon, Lonette McKee, Ernest Thompson, Theresa Randle, Tommy Randle, James McDaniel, Joan LaMarre, Spike Lee; **Cameos:** Christopher Plummer, Karen Allen, Peter Boyle, William Kunstler, Bobby Seale, Al Sharpton; **W/D:** Spike Lee; **W:** Arnold Perl. Academy Awards '92 Nominations: Best Actor (Washington), Best Costume Design; Chicago Film Critics Awards '93: Best Actor (Washington), Best Film; MTV Movie Awards '93: Best Actor (Washington); New York Film Critics Awards '93: Best Actor (Washington). VHS, Beta, LV, 8mm $94.99 WAR, MOV, BTV *√√√*

Male and Female A group of British aristocrats is shipwrecked on an island and must allow their efficient butler (Meighan) to take command for their survival. Swanson is the spoiled rich girl who falls for his social inferior. Their rescue provides a return to the rigid British class system. Based on the play "The Admirable Crichton" by James M. Barrie.
1919 ?m/B Gloria Swanson, Thomas Meighan, Lila Lee, Raymond Hatton, Bebe Daniels; **D:** Cecil B. DeMille. VHS, Beta NO *√√√*

Malibu Beach The California beach scene is the setting for this movie filled with bikini clad girls, tanned young men, and instant romances. For connoisseurs of the empty-headed teen beach movie.
1978 (R) 93m/C Kim Lankford, James Daughton; **D:** Robert J. Rosenthal. VHS, Beta $9.99 STE, PSM, UHV *√½*

The Malibu Beach Vampires Three unscrupulous yuppies, Congressman Teri Upstart, Col. Ollie West and Rev. Timmy Fakker, keep beautiful mistresses in their Malibu beach house. What they don't know is, the girls are all really vampires who have injected them with a serum that compels them to tell the truth! Will our "heroes" continue to dupe the American Public, or will the sexy blood suckers cause their downfall?
1991 (R) 90m/C Angelyne, Becky Le Beau, Joan Rudelstein, Marcus A. Frishman, Rod Sweitzer, Francis Creighton, Anet Anatelle, Yvette Buchanan, Cherie Romaors, Kelly Galindo; **D:** Francis Creighton. VHS NO *√½*

Malibu Bikini Shop Two brothers manage a beachfront bikini shop in Malibu, and spend their time ogling the customers and arguing about running the "business." Just another excuse for parading babes in bathing suits across the naked screen.
1986 (R) 90m/C Michael David Wright, Bruce Greenwood, Barbara Horan, Debra Blee, Jay Robinson, Galyn Gorg, Ami Julius, Frank Nelson, Kathleen Freeman, Rita Jenrette; **W/D:** David Wechter. VHS, Beta $19.98 FOX *√*

Malibu Express Mystery/adventure plot about a P.I. is the excuse; babes in swimsuits is the reason for this waste of time.
1985 (R) 101m/C Darby Hinton, Sybil Danning, Art Metrano, Shelley Taylor Morgan, Niki Dantine, Barbara Edwards; **D:** Andy Sidaris. VHS, Beta $14.95 MCA *√*

Malibu High The accidental death of a young prostitute's client leads her to a new series of illegal activities of the "sex and hit" variety. Dark, sleazy, and antisocial; belies Beach Boys-esque title.
1979 (R) 92m/C Jill Lansing, Stuart Taylor; **D:** Irvin Berwick. VHS, Beta $19.95 UHV *√*

Malibu Hot Summer Three aspiring young women combine their talents in acting, music, and athletics to find their careers as they spend a fun-filled summer in Malibu.
1981 89m/C Terry Congie, Leslie Brander, Roselyn Royce. VHS, Beta $49.95 VHE *√*

Malicious A housekeeper hired for a widower and his three sons becomes the object of lusty affection of all four men. As Papa makes plans to court and marry her, his fourteen-year-old son plots to have her as a companion on his road to sensual maturity. Dubbed in English. **AKA:** Malizia.
1974 (R) 98m/C IT Laura Antonelli, Turi Ferro, Alessandro Momo, Tina Aumont; **D:** Salvatore Samperi. VHS, Beta $49.95 PAR *√√*

Malone A burnt-out secret agent stumbles into a real-estate swindle/murder plot in Oregon and sets out to stop it. Film tries hard but doesn't succeed in being believable.
1987 (R) 92m/C Burt Reynolds, Lauren Hutton, Cliff Robertson, Kenneth McMillan, Scott Wilson, Cynthia Gibb; **D:** Harley Cokliss. VHS, Beta, LV $19.98 ORI *√½*

Malou A young French woman tries to uncover the truth about her late mother's life, sifting through wildly contradictory evidence in the desire to discover her own identity and avoid her mother's mistakes. A feminist story. In German with English subtitles.
1983 (R) 95m/C Grischa Huber, Ingrid Caven, Helmut Griem; **D:** Jeanine Meerapfel. VHS, Beta $34.95 SUE, GLV *√√*

Malta Story A British World War II flier becomes involved with the defense of Malta.
1953 103m/B Alec Guinness, Jack Hawkins, Anthony Steel, Flora Robson, Muriel Pavlow; **D:** Brian Desmond Hurst. VHS, Beta $14.95 SUE *√√½*

The Maltese Falcon A good first screen version of the Dashiell Hammett story about private detective Sam Spade's search for the elusive Black Bird. Remade five years later as "Satan Met a Lady" with Bette Davis. Its most famous remake, however, occurred in 1941 with Humphrey Bogart in the lead. **AKA:** Dangerous Female.
1931 80m/B Bebe Daniels, Ricardo Cortez, Dudley Digges, Thelma Todd, Una Merkel, Dwight Frye, Robert Elliott; **D:** Roy Del Ruth. VHS, Beta GPV *√√*

The Maltese Falcon After the death of his partner, detective Sam Spade finds himself enmeshed in a complicated, intriguing search for a priceless statuette. "It's the stuff dreams are made of," says Bogart of the Falcon. Excellent, fast-paced film noir with outstanding performances, great dialogue, and concentrated attention to details. Director Huston's first film and Greenstreet's talky debut. First of several films by Bogart and Astor. Based on the novel by Dashiell Hammett. Also available colorized.
1941 101m/B Humphrey Bogart, Mary Astor, Peter Lorre, Sydney Greenstreet, Ward Bond, Barton MacLane, Gladys George, Lee Patrick, Elisha Cook Jr.; **D:** Walter Huston; **D:** John Huston. VHS, Beta, LV $19.98 MGM, FOX, TLF *√√√√*

Mama Dracula Fletcher stars in this poor satire of the horror genre. She's a vampire who needs the blood of virgins to stay young. Her son helps out—what good son wouldn't?
1980 90m/C FR Louise Fletcher, Bonnie Schneider, Maria Schneider, Marc-Henri Wajnberg, Alexander Wajnberg, Jess Hahn; **D:** Boris Szulzinger. VHS $79.95 TWE Woof!

Mama, There's a Man In Your Bed When a powerful executive is framed for insider trading, the only witness to the crime and his only hope is an earthy cleaning woman named Juliette. Together they plot revenge and takeovers in her tiny apartment, filled with children. Soon, he regains his former position of power but realizes his life isn't complete without his co-conspirator. In French with English subtitles. **AKA:** Romuald et Juliet.
1989 (PG) 111m/C FR Daniel Auteuil, Firmine Richard, Pierre Vernier, Maxime LeRoux, Gilles Privat, Muriel Combeau, Catherine Salviat, Sambou Tati; **W/D:** Coline Serreau. VHS, Beta, LV $89.99 HBO, FCT, TAM *√√√*

Mama Turns a Hundred A baronial family (a bizarre set of characters) is celebrating their mother's 100th birthday at her estate. One of the daughter's seduces her brother-in-law, another has a uniform fetish, a religious zealot is desperate to hang-glide, and several of them are trying to kill poor Mama. But of course she prevails, although sick and ailing. Slow-paced yet uproarious film full of inept characters who bumble along. In Spanish with English subtitles.
1979 (R) 100m/C SP Geraldine Chaplin, Fernando Gomez, Amparo Munoz; **D:** Carlos Savrat. VHS, Beta $59.95 INT, AUD, TAM *√√√*

Mama's Dirty Girls A gangster mom's daughters take over where their mother left off and have the time of their lives.
1974 (R) 82m/C Gloria Grahame, Paul Lambert, Sondra Currie, Candice Rialson, Mary Stoddard; **D:** John Hayes. VHS, Beta $69.95 TWE *√√√*

Mambo A poor young dancer inspires patronage and lust by dancing the Mambo. Although attracted to Gassman, she marries Rennie for his money. Technically weak but artistically interesting, though Rennie and Mangano have done their roles somewhat better elsewhere.
1955 94m/B Silvana Mangano, Michael Rennie, Vittorio Gassman, Shelley Winters, Katherine Dunham, Mary Clare, Eduardo Ciannelli; **D:** Robert Rossen. **VHS $19.95** NOS, HTV, TAM ♂♂½

The Mambo Kings Armand and Banderas (in his first English speaking role) play Cesar and Nestor Castillo, two brothers who flee Cuba and go to New York to hit it big playing mambo music. Just as their star begins to rise, their dreams are crushed when the quick-tempered Cesar (Assante) angers a mob boss. Soon, however, Desi Arnaz Sr., played by his son Desi Arnaz Jr., sees the brothers and asks them to appear on the "I Love Lucy" show. This funny and technical scene leads to the climactic confrontation between the brothers. Good cast and great music make this one worthwhile. Based on the Pulitzer prizewinning novel "The Mambo Kings Play Songs of Love" by Oscar Hijuelos.
1992 (R) 100m/C Armand Assante, Antonio Banderas, Cathy Moriarty, Maruschka Detmers, Desi Arnaz Jr., Celia Cruz, Roscoe Lee Browne, Vondie Curtis-Hall, Tito Puente, Talisa Soto; **D:** Arne Glimcher. **VHS, LV, 8mm $19.98** WAR, FCT ♂♂♂

Mame In an adaptation of the Broadway musical "Auntie Mame" by Jerry Herman, Ball plays a dynamic woman who takes it upon herself to teach a group of eccentrics how to live life to the fullest. Arthur plays Mame's friend just as splendidly as she did in the Broadway version, but Ball in her last feature film is a lame Mame. Overly ambitious production avoids reaching goal. ♫Mame; We Need a Little Christmas; If He Walked Into My Life; Bosom Buddies; It's Today; Loving You; My Best Girl; What Do I Do Now? (Gooch's Sont); Open a New Window; The Man in the Moon; St. Bridget; The Letter.
1974 (PG) 132m/C Lucille Ball, Bea Arthur, Robert Preston, Joyce Van Patten, Bruce Davison; **D:** Gene Saks. **VHS, Beta, LV $19.98** WAR, PIA ♂♂

Mamele Picon prematurely becomes the "mother" of her seven siblings when their mother dies. Quintessential Yiddish musical with the usual shimmering performance from Picon. In Yiddish with English subtitles. **AKA:** Little Mother.
1938 95m/B PL Molly Picon, Max Bozyk, Edmund Zayenda; **D:** Joseph Green. **VHS, Beta $79.95** ERG, TAM ♂♂

A Man, a Woman, and a Bank Two con-men plan to rob a bank by posing as workers during the bank's construction. An advertising agency woman snaps their picture for a billboard to show how nice the builders have been, then becomes romantically involved with one of the would-be thieves. Nice performances, but wacky touches aren't plentiful enough or well-timed to sustain comedy. Also called "A Very Big Weekend."
1979 (PG) 100m/C CA Donald Sutherland, Brooke Adams, Paul Mazursky; **D:** Noel Black. **VHS, Beta $9.98** SUE, NLC ♂♂½

A Man, a Woman and a Killer Unusual film within a film shows the actual making of a movie while unfolding a story of a hired killer. A joint project from the direc-

tors of the well-received "Emerald Cities" and "Chan is Missing."
19?? 75m/C **D:** Rick Schmidt, Wayne Wang. **VHS $59.95** FCT ♂♂½

A Man About the House Two unmarried English sisters move into the Italian villa they have inherited. There, one marries the caretaker, who secretly plans to regain the property that once belonged to his family. When the newly married sister is found dead, her sibling sets out to solve the murder.
1947 83m/B GB Kieron Moore, Margaret Johnston, Dulcie Gray, Guy Middleton, Felix Aylmer; **D:** Leslie Arliss. **VHS $16.95** NOS, SNC ♂♂½

A Man Alone Man falsely accused of robbing a stagecoach hides not alone but with comely sheriff's daughter. Milland's debut behind the camera.
1955 96m/C Ray Milland, Ward Bond, Mary Murphy, Raymond Burr, Lee Van Cleef; **D:** Ray Milland. **VHS $14.95** REP ♂♂

A Man and a Woman When a man and a woman, both widowed, meet and become interested in one another but experience difficulties in putting their past loves behind them. Intelligently handled emotional conflicts within a well-acted romantic drama, acclaimed for excellent visual detail. Remade in 1977 as "Another Man, Another Chance." Followed in 1986 with "A Man and A Woman: 20 Years Later." Dubbed. **AKA:** Un Homme et Un Femme.
1966 102m/C FR Anouk Aimee, Jean-Louis Trintignant, Pierre Barouh, Valerie Lagrange; **W/D:** Claude Lelouch. Academy Awards '66: Best Foreign Language Film, Best Original Screenplay; Nominations: Best Actress (Aimee), Best Director (Lelouch); British Academy Awards '67: Best Actress (Aimee); Cannes Film Festival '66: Best Film; Golden Globe Awards '67: Best Actress—Drama (Aimee), Best Foreign Film. **VHS, Beta $19.98** WAR, APD, TAM ♂♂♂

A Man and a Woman: 20 Years Later Slouchy sequel to the highly praised "A Man and a Woman" that catches up with a couple after a long separation. The sad romantic complications of the original are more mundane in this sequel, which is burdened by a film-within-a-film script as well as shots from the original. In French with English subtitles. **AKA:** Un Homme Et Une Femme: Vingt Ans Deja.
1986 (PG) 112m/C FR Jean-Louis Trintignant, Anouk Aimee, Richard Berry; **D:** Claude Lelouch. **VHS, Beta $19.98** WAR, TAM ♂½

Man & Boy A black Civil War veteran, played by Bill Cosby, encounters bigotry and prejudice when he tries to set up a homestead in Arizona. An acceptable family film, some might be disappointed that Cosby is not playing this one for laughs. **AKA:** Ride a Dark Horse.
1971 (G) 98m/C Bill Cosby, Gloria Foster, George Spell, Henry Silva, Yaphet Kotto; **D:** E.W. Swackhamer. **VHS, Beta $59.95** COL ♂♂

The Man and the Monster When a concert pianist sells his soul to the devil, he fails to realize that part of the deal has him turning into a hideous beast every time he hears a certain piece of music. Maybe it was "Stairway to Heaven."
1965 78m/B MX Enrique Rambal, Abel Salazar, Martha Roth; **D:** Rafael Baledon. **VHS $19.98** SNC ♂½

Man Bait A complex web of intrigue and mystery surrounds a blackmailed book dealer when he allows a blonde woman to catch his eye. A competently made film. **AKA:** The Last Page.

1952 78m/B GB George Brent, Marguerite Chapman, Diana Dors; **D:** Terence Fisher. **VHS, Beta, LV** MLB ♂♂½

Man Beast The abominable snowman is sought and found in this grade-Z '50s monster movie.
1955 65m/B Rock Madison, Virginia Maynor, George Skaff, Lloyd Nelson, Tom Maruzzi; **D:** Jerry Warren. **VHS, Beta $19.95** NOS, MRV, RHI ♂

Man Bites Dog A pseudo-documentary about a serial killer, filled with ever-mounting violence. Ben is the killer being followed by a two-man camera/sound crew (which he's hired), who record his casual carnage without lifting a finger to stop him. Indeed his continued killing and robbing is to pay for financing the documentary about himself. This satire on film violence, as well as reality-based television shows, is both appalling and humorous in a sick way. In French with English subtitles.
1992 (NC-17) 95m/B BE Benoit Poelvoorde, Remy Belvaux, Andre Bonzel; **W/D:** Benoit Poelvoorde, Remy Belvaux, Andre Bonzel; **W:** Vincent Tavier. **VHS** FXL ♂♂

A Man Called Adam A jazz musician is tortured by prejudice and the guilt created by his having accidentally killed his wife and baby years before. Davis is appropriately haunted, but the film is poorly produced.
1966 103m/B Sammy Davis Jr., Louis Armstrong, Ossie Davis, Cicely Tyson, Frank Sinatra Jr., Lola Falana, Mel Torme, Peter Lawford; **D:** Leo Penn. **VHS, Beta $14.95** COL, NLC ♂½

A Man Called Horse After a wealthy Britisher is captured and tortured by the Sioux Indians in the Dakotas, he abandons his formal ways and discovers his own strength. As he passes their torture tests, he is embraced by the tribe. In this very realistic and gripping portrayal of American Indian life, Harris provides a strong performance. Sequelled by "Return of a Man Called Horse" (1976) and "Triumphs of a Man Called Horse" (1983).
1970 (PG) 114m/C Richard Harris, Judith Anderson, Jean Gascon, Stanford Howard, Manu Tupou, Dub Taylor; **D:** Elliot Silverstein. **VHS, Beta $59.98** FOX ♂♂♂

A Man Called Peter A biographical epic about Peter Marshall, a Scottish chaplain who served the U.S. Senate. Todd does his subject justice by sensitively showing all that was human in Marshall, and a talented supporting cast makes for a thoroughly watchable film.
1955 119m/C Richard Todd, Jean Peters, Marjorie Rambeau, Jill Esmond, Les Tremayne, Robert Burton; **D:** Henry Koster. **VHS, Beta $19.98** FOX ♂♂♂

A Man Called Rage Rage is the only man capable of safely escorting a group of pioneers through a nuclear wasteland infested with mutants and cannibals.
1984 90m/C IT Stelio Candelli, Conrad Nichols; **D:** Anthony Richmond. **VHS, Beta $39.95** LIV Woof!

A Man Called Sarge Sophomoric comedy about a daffy WWII sergeant leading his squad against the Germans at Tobruk.
1990 (PG-13) 88m/C Gary Kroeger, Marc Singer, Gretchen German, Jennifer Runyon; **D:** Stuart Gillard. **VHS, Beta, LV $79.95** WAR, OM ♂½

A Man Called Sledge Garner fans might be surprised to see the star play a villain in this violent story of a gang of outlaws who wind up fighting each over a cache of gold. This is mainstream Western entertainment.

1971 93m/C James Garner, Dennis Weaver, Claude Akins, John Marley, Laura Antonelli; *D:* Vic Morrow. **VHS, Beta** *GKK* ☆☆

Man Called Tiger A Chinese martial arts expert infiltrates a ruthless Japanese gang in order to find the man who murdered his father.
1981 (R) 97m/C **VHS, Beta** $9.98 *SUE* ☆

A Man Escaped There's an excruciating realism about Bresson's account of a WWII Resistance fighter's escape from a Nazi prison just before he was to be executed by the Gestapo. It's the sounds and lingering camera shots, not the wham bam variety of action, that create and sustain the film's suspense. Bresson, who had been a Nazi prisoner, solicited the supervision of Andre Devigny, whose true story the film tells. Contributing to the realistic feel was the use of non professional actors. An award-winning film that fellow director Truffaut lauded as the most crucial French film of the previous ten years. In French with English subtitles. *AKA:* Un Condamne a Mort s'est Echappe; The Wind Bloweth Where it Listeth.
1957 102m/B Francois Leterrier; *D:* Robert Bresson. **VHS** $59.95 *TAM, FST* ☆☆☆½

Man Facing Southeast The acclaimed Argentinean film about the sudden appearance of a strange man in an asylum who claims to be an extraterrestrial, and a psychologist's attempts to discover his true identity. The sense of mystery intensifies when the new patient indeed seems to have some remarkable powers. Although the pace at times lags, the story intriguingly keeps one guessing about the stranger right to the end. In Spanish, with English subtitles. *AKA:* Hombre Mirando Al Sudeste; Man Looking Southeast.
1986 (R) 105m/C *AR* Lorenzo Quinteros, Hugo Soto, Ines Vernengo; *D:* Eliseo Subiela. **VHS, Beta, LV** $19.95 *ETE, NWV, IME* ☆☆☆½

A Man for All Seasons Sterling, heavily Oscar-honored biographical drama concerning the life and subsequent martyrdom of 16th-century Chancellor of England, Sir Thomas More (Scofield). Story revolves around his personal conflict when King Henry VIII (Shaw) seeks a divorce from his wife, Catherine of Aragon, so he can wed his mistress, Anne Boleyn—events that ultimately lead the King to bolt from the Pope and declare himself head of the Church of England. Remade for television in 1988 with Charlton Heston in the lead role.
1966 (G) 120m/C *GB* Paul Scofield, Robert Shaw, Orson Welles, Wendy Hiller, Susannah York; *D:* Fred Zinneman; *W:* Robert Bolt. Academy Awards '66: Best Actor (Scofield), Best Adapted Screenplay, Best Color Cinematography, Best Costume Design (Color), Best Director (Zinneman), Best Picture; Nominations: Best Supporting Actor (Shaw), Best Supporting Actress (Hiller); British Academy Awards '67: Best Actor (Scofield), Best Film; Directors Guild of America Awards '66: Best Director (Zinneman); Golden Globe Awards '67: Best Actor—Drama (Scofield), Best Director (Zinneman), Best Film—Drama; National Board of Review Awards '66: 10 Best Films of the Year, Best Actor (Scofield), Best Director (Zinneman), Best Supporting Actor (Shaw). **VHS, Beta, LV** $19.95 *COL, BTV, TVC* ☆☆☆☆

A Man for All Seasons Fresh from the London stage, Heston directs and stars in this version of Robert Bolt's play depicting the conflict between Henry VIII and his chief advisor, Sir Thomas More. Strong supporting cast. Made for cable TV.

1988 150m/C Charlton Heston, Vanessa Redgrave, John Gielgud, Richard Johnson, Roy Kinnear, Martin Chamberlain; *D:* Charlton Heston. **VHS, LV** $79.98 *TTC* ☆☆☆

Man Friday Stranded on a deserted island, a man forces a native from a neighboring island to be his slave. Based on the classic story "Robinson Crusoe" by Daniel Defoe, this adaptation charts the often-brutal treatment the native receives as his captor tries to civilize him. Through his intelligence, the enslaved man regains his freedom and returns home with his former captor, who then seeks acceptance from the native's tribe. A sometimes confusing story line and excessive blood and guts detract from this message-laden story.
1976 (PG) 115m/C *GB* Peter O'Toole, Richard Roundtree, Peter Cellier, Christopher Cabot, Joel Fluellen; *D:* Jack Gold. **VHS** *FOX* ☆☆

The Man from Atlantis Patrick Duffy stars as the water-breathing alien who emerges from his undersea home, the Lost City of Atlantis. The made-for-TV movie led to a brief television series.
1977 60m/C Patrick Duffy, Belinda J. Montgomery, Victor Buono; *D:* Lee H. Katzin. **VHS, Beta** $19.95 *WOV* ☆☆

The Man from Beyond Frozen alive, a man returns 100 years later to try and find his lost love. Silent.
1922 50m/B Harry Houdini, Arthur Maude; *D:* Burton King. **VHS, Beta** $16.95 *SNC, VYY, DVT* ☆☆½

Man from Button Willow Classic animated adventure is the story of Justin Eagle, a man who leads a double life. He is a respected rancher and a shrewd secret agent for the government, but in 1869 he suddenly finds himself the guardian of a four-year-old Oriental girl, leading him into a whole new series of adventures. Strictly for younger audiences.
1965 (G) 79m/C *V:* Dale Robertson, Edgar Buchanan, Barbara Jean Wong, Howard Keel. **VHS, Beta** $42.95 *PGN* ☆☆

Man from Cairo An American in Algiers is mistaken for a detective in search of gold lost during World War II and decides to play along.
1954 82m/B *IT* George Raft, Giana Maria Canale; *D:* Ray Enright. **VHS, Beta, LV** *NO* ☆☆

Man from Cheyenne Cowboy comes home to find his town under a siege of terror from a lawless gang of cattle rustlers. He gets mad and seeks some frontier justice.
1942 54m/B Roy Rogers, Gale Storm, George "Gabby" Hayes, Sally Payne. **VHS, Beta** $19.95 *NOS, DVT, RXM* ☆

Man from Clover Grove Hilarity takes over a town when a nutty boy inventor puts the sheriff in a spin.
1978 (G) 96m/C Ron Masak, Cheryl Miller, Jed Allan, Rose Marie. **VHS, Beta** $19.95 *MED* ☆½

Man from Colorado An odd Technicolor western about two Civil War vets at odds, one an honest marshall, the other a sadistic judge. Solid Western fare with a quirky performance by Ford.
1949 99m/C William Holden, Glenn Ford, Ellen Drew, Ray Collins, Edgar Buchanan, Jerome Courtland, James Millican, Jim Bannon; *D:* Henry Levin. **VHS, Beta** $14.95 *COL* ☆☆½

Man from Deep River A photographer is captured by a savage tribe in Thailand and forced to undergo a series of grueling initiation rites. Full of very violent and sickening tortures inflicted on both human and animal victims.
1977 (R) 90m/C *IT* Ivan Rassimov; *D:* Umberto Lenzi. **VHS, Beta** $59.98 *PSM* Woof!

The Man from Gun Town McCoy comes to the rescue of a woman who has been framed by an evil gang for the murder of her brother.
1936 58m/B Tim McCoy, Billie Seward, Rex Lease, Jack Clifford, Wheeler Oakman, Bob McKenzie; *D:* Ford Beebe. **VHS** $19.95 *NOS, DVT* ☆½

Man from Headquarters Good silent mystery in which a U.S. agent takes on a gang of foreign operatives.
1928 ?m/B Cornelius Keefe, Edith Roberts. **VHS** $16.95 *SNC* ☆☆

The Man from Hell Sheriff Russell goes undercover to expose the head of a gang of outlaws. Low-budget fare.
1934 55m/B Reb Russell, Fred Kohler Jr., Ann Darcy, George "Gabby" Hayes, Jack Rockwell, Charles French, Charles "Slim" Whitaker, Yakima Canutt; *D:* Lewis Collins. **VHS** $19.95 *DVT, HEG, GPV* ☆

Man from Hell's Edges An innocent cowpoke escapes from jail and brings the real baddy to justice.
1932 63m/B Bob Steele, Nancy Drexel, Julian Rivero, Robert E. Homans, George "Gabby" Hayes; *D:* Robert North Bradbury. **VHS, Beta** $19.95 *NOS, DVT* ☆½

Man from Laramie A ranch baron who is going blind worries about which of his two sons he will leave the ranch to. Into this tension-filled familial atmosphere rides Stewart, a cow-herder obsessed with hunting down the men who sold guns to the Indians that killed his brother. Needless to say, the tension increases. Tough, surprisingly brutal western, the best of the classic Stewart-Mann films.
1955 104m/C James Stewart, Arthur Kennedy, Donald Crisp, Alex Nicol, Cathy O'Donnell, Aline MacMahon, Wallace Ford, Jack Elam; *D:* Anthony Mann. **VHS, Beta** $14.95 *COL* ☆☆☆½

The Man from Music Mountain Worthless mining stock is sold in a desert mining town, but Gene and Smiley clear that up, with a little singing as well.
1938 54m/B Gene Autry, Smiley Burnette, Carol Hughes, Polly Jenkins. **VHS, Beta** $19.95 *NOS, VDM, HHT* ☆☆

Man from Nowhere A henpecked man gets the break of his life when his domineering wife and mother-in-law believe he's dead. Based on the novel by Luigi Pirandello. In French with English subtitles.
1937 98m/B *FR* Pierre Blanchar, Ginette LeClerc; *D:* Pierre Chenal. **VHS** $59.95 *FCT, AUD* ☆☆½

The Man from Painted Post Fairbanks plays a Cattlemen's Association detective who comes to the range to stop the cattle rustlers as well as to find the man who murdered his sister.
1917 ?m/B Douglas Fairbanks Sr., Eileen Percy, Frank Campeau, Monte Blue; *D:* Joseph Henabery. **VHS** *GVV* ☆

The Man from Snowy River Stunning cinematography highlights this otherwise fairly ordinary adventure story set in 1880's Australia. A young man comes of age in the outback while taming a herd of wild horses. In a dual role, Douglas portrays battling brothers, one a rich landowner and the other a one-legged prospector. Based on the epic poem by A.B. "Banjo" Paterson and followed by "Return to Snowy River Part II." A big hit in Australia and not directed by "Mad Max's" Miller, but another Miller named George.

1982 (PG) 104m/C Kirk Douglas, Tom Burlinson, Sigrid Thornton, Terence Donovan, Tommy Dysart, Jack Thompson, Bruce Kerr; *D:* George Miller. **VHS, Beta, LV** $14.98 *FOX, TVC, HMV* ♂♂½

Man from Texas Singing and gun-slinging Tex defends a kid accused of horse thieving until the kid turns bad and Tex must bring him in.
1939 55m/B Tex Ritter, Hal Price, Charles B. Wood, Vic Demourelle Sr.; *D:* Al Herman. **VHS, Beta** $19.95 *NOS, VDM* ♂♂

Man from the Alamo A soldier sent from the Alamo during its last hours to get help is branded as a deserter, and struggles to clear his name. Well acted, this film will satisfy those with a taste for action.
1953 79m/C Glenn Ford, Julie Adams, Chill Wills, Victor Jory; *D:* Budd Boetticher. **VHS, Beta** $14.95 *KRT* ♂♂♂

Man from Thunder River A group of cowboys uncover a plot to steal gold ore and wind up saving a young girl's life in the process. Standard western with lots of action.
1943 55m/B Bill Elliott, George "Gabby" Hayes, Anne Jeffreys, Ian Keith, John James; *D:* John English. **VHS, Beta** $29.95 *DVT* ♂♂

The Man from U.N.C.L.E. Vaughn and McCallum star as Napoleon Solo and Illya Kuryakin, two super-cool super-agents battling the evil forces of THRUSH. The series ran from 1964-1968. Two epsiodes per tape; additional episodes available. On this tape: "The Project Strigas Affair" has Solo and Illya against a Balkan intelligence agent. In "The Never Never Affair" an innocent translator is captured by a ruthless THRUSH operator who's after some valuable microfilm.
1964 110m/B Robert Vaughn, David McCallum, Leo G. Carroll, Leonard Nimoy, William Shatner, Barbara Feldon, Cesar Romero. **VHS, Beta** $14.95 *MGM, MOV* ♂♂

Man from Utah The Duke tangles with the crooked sponsor of some rodeo events who has killed several of the participants. Also available with "Blue Steel" on Laser Disc.
1934 55m/B John Wayne, George "Gabby" Hayes, Polly Ann Young; *D:* Robert Bradbury. **VHS, Beta, LV** $8.95 *NEG, NOS, MRV* ♂½

The Man in Grey In a story of romantic intrigue set in nineteenth-century England, a Marquis's wife is betrayed by her vile husband and the schoolmate she once befriended who has an affair with him. Stunning costumes and fine performances compensate for the overly extravagant production values in a work that helped bring stardom to Mason.
1945 116m/B *GB* James Mason, Margaret Lockwood, Stewart Granger, Phyllis Calvert; *D:* Leslie Arliss. **VHS, Beta** $29.95 *VID* ♂♂♂

A Man in Love An international romantic melodrama set during the Italian filming of a biography of suicidal author Cesar Pavese. The self-important lead actor and a beautiful supporting actress (Coyote and Scacchi) become immersed in the roles and fall madly in love, oblivious to the fact that Coyote is married and Scacchi's engaged. The two make a steamy pair, to the detriment of friends, family, and the movie they're making. Kurys' first English-language film is visually appealing with a lush, romantic score, seamlessly weaving the story lines among vivid characters. *AKA:* Un Homme Amoureux.

1987 (R) 110m/C *FR* Peter Coyote, Greta Scacchi, Jamie Lee Curtis, Peter Riegert, Jean Pigozzi, John Berry, Claudia Cardinale, Vincent Lindon; *D:* Diane Kurys. **VHS, Beta, LV** $14.95 *COL, SUE* ♂♂♂

The Man in the Gray Flannel Suit A very long and serious adaptation of the Sloan Wilson novel about a Madison Avenue advertising exec trying to balance his life between work and family. The Hollywood treatment falls short of the adaptation potential of the original story.
1956 152m/C Gregory Peck, Fredric March, Jennifer Jones, Ann Harding, Arthur O'Connell, Henry Daniell, Lee J. Cobb, Marisa Pavan, Gene Lockhart, Keenan Wynn, Gigi Perreau, Joseph Sweeney, Kenneth Tobey, DeForest Kelley; *D:* Nunnally Johnson. **VHS, Beta, LV** $39.98 *FOX* ♂♂½

The Man in the Iron Mask Swashbuckling tale about twin brothers separated at birth. One turns out to be King Louis XIV of France, and the other a carefree wanderer and friend of the Three Musketeers. Their eventual clash leads to action-packed adventure and royal revenge. Remake of the "The Iron Mask" (1929) with Douglas Fairbanks. Remade for television in 1977 with Richard Chamberlain.
1939 110m/B Louis Hayward, Alan Hale Jr., Joan Bennett, Warren Williams, Joseph Schildkraut, Walter Kingsford, Marion Martin; *D:* James Whale. **VHS, Beta** $9.99 *CCB, MED* ♂♂♂

The Man in the Iron Mask A tyrannical French king kidnaps his twin brother and imprisons him on a remote island. Chamberlain, the king of the miniseries, is excellent in a dual role in this big production swashbuckler. Adapted from the Dumas classic. Made for television.
1977 105m/C Richard Chamberlain, Patrick McGoohan, Louis Jourdan, Jenny Agutter, Ian Holm, Ralph Richardson; *D:* Mike Newell. **VHS, Beta** $19.98 *LIV, FOX, FCT* ♂♂♂

The Man in the Mist Private investigators Tommy and Tuppence Beresford find themselves trying to solve a murder while on vacation in a provincial hotel. Made for British television and based upon the Agatha Christie story.
1983 51m/C *GB* Francesca Annis, James Warwick; *W:* Agatha Christie. **VHS, Beta** $14.95 *PAV* ♂♂♂

The Man in the Moon Beautifully rendered coming-of-age tale. On a farm outside a small Louisiana town in the 1950s, 14 year-old Dani wonders if she will ever be as pretty and popular as her 17 year-old sister Maureen. This becomes especially important as Dani is beginning to notice boys, particularly Court, the 17 year-old young man she meets when swimming. Although Dani and Maureen have always been especially close a rift develops between the sisters after Court meets Maureen. Intelligently written, excellent direction, lovely cinematography, and exceptional acting make this a particularly worthwhile and entertaining film.
1991 (PG-13) 100m/C Reese Witherspoon, Emily Warfield, Jason London, Tess Harper, Sam Waterston, Gail Strickland; *D:* Robert Mulligan. **VHS** $19.98 *MGM* ♂♂♂½

The Man in the Raincoat French film about a bumbling clarinet player who is erroneously tracked down as a murderer. Strenuous efforts to evoke laughter usually fail. Dubbed.
1957 97m/B *FR* Fernandel, John McGiver, Bernard Blier; *D:* Julien Duvivier. **VHS, Beta, 8mm** $29.95 *VYY* ♂♂

The Man in the Santa Claus Suit A costume shop owner has an effect on three people who rent Santa Claus costumes from him. Astaire plays seven different roles in this made for television film. Average holiday feel-good movie.
1979 96m/C Fred Astaire, Gary Burghoff, John Byner, Nanette Fabray, Bert Convy; *D:* Corey Allen. **VHS, Beta** $69.95 *MED* ♂♂

Man in the Silk Hat A collection of the nearly-forgotten French comic's early silent comedy shorts, made in France before his resettlement in America.
1915 96m/B *FR* Max Linder; *D:* Maud Linder. **VHS, Beta** $59.95 *TAM* ♂♂

Man in the Silk Hat Gabriel-Maximilien Leuvielle, known in films as Max Linder, is now credited with developing the style of silent-movie slapstick comedy that Mack Sennett, Charlie Chaplin, and others became more famous for in their time. Here, Linder's daughter has done a fine job writing and directing a film full of historic footage of her father's work.
1983 99m/B Mack Sennett, Buster Keaton, Charlie Chaplin, Max Linder. **VHS, Beta** $24.95 *XVC, MED* ♂♂♂

Man in the White Suit A humble laboratory assistant in a textile mill invents a white cloth that won't stain, tear, or wear out, and can't be dyed. The panicked garment industry sets out to destroy him and the fabric, resulting in some sublimely comic situations and a variety of inventive chases. Also available with "Lavender Hill Mob" on Laser Disc.
1951 82m/B *GB* Alec Guinness, Joan Greenwood; *D:* Alexander MacKendrick. Academy Awards '52 Nominations: Best Screenplay; National Board of Review Awards '52: 10 Best Films of the Year. **VHS, Beta** $19.98 *HBO, HMV* ♂♂♂½

Man in the Wilderness Harris is part of an expedition traveling through the Northwest Territory. He's mauled by a grizzly and left for dead by leader Huston. While Harris fights for survival, he also plots revenge. Blood and violence is somewhat offset by good lead performances.
1971 (PG) 108m/C Richard Harris, John Huston, Henry Wilcoxon, Percy Herbert, Dennis Waterman, Prunella Ransome, Norman Rossington, James Doohan; *D:* Richard Sarafian; *W:* Jack DeWitt; *M:* Johnny Harris. **VHS** $29.98 *WAR* ♂♂½

The Man Inside Undercover agent infiltrates a powerful underworld narcotics ring and finds his honesty tested when $2 million is at stake.
1976 96m/C *CA* James Franciscus, Stefanie Powers, Jacques Godin; *D:* Gerald Mayer. **VHS, Beta** $49.95 *TWE* ♂½

The Man Inside Lukewarm Cold War saga based on the true story of Gunther Wallraff, a West German journalist who risked all to expose the corruption behind a large European newspaper.
1990 (PG) 93m/C *NL GE* Juergen Prochnow, Peter Coyote, Nathalie Baye, Dieter Laser, Monique Van De Ven, Sylvie Granotier; *W/D:* Bobby Roth. **VHS, LV** $89.95 *COL, PIA* ♂♂

Man is Not a Bird Follows the destructive love of a factory engineer and a hairdresser in a small Yugoslavian mining town. In Serbian with English subtitles.
1965 80m/B *YU* Eva Ras, Milena Dravic, Janez Urhovec; *D:* Dusan Makavejev. **VHS, Beta** $59.95 *FCT* ♂♂½

A Man Like Eva A weird, morbid homage to and portrait of Rainer Werner Fassbinder after his inevitable death, detailing his work-obsessed self-destruction. Mattes, one of Fassbinder's favorite actresses, plays him in drag, in an eerie gender-crossing transformation. In German with English subtitles. *AKA:* Ein Mann wie Eva.
1983 92m/C *GE* Eva Mattes, Lisa Kreuzer, Charles Regnier, Werner Stocker; *D:* Radu Gabrea. **VHS, Beta $79.95** *FCT, APD, GLV* 𝄢𝄢𝄢

Man of a Thousand Faces A tasteful and touching portrayal of Lon Chaney, from his childhood with his deaf and mute parents to his success as a screen star. Recreates some of Chaney's most famous roles, including the Phantom of the Opera and Quasimodo in "Notre Dame." Cagney is magnificent as the long-suffering film star who was a genius with makeup and mime.
1957 122m/B James Cagney, Dorothy Malone, Jane Greer, Marjorie Rambeau, Jim Backus, Roger Smith, Robert Evans; *D:* Joseph Pevney. **VHS $14.98** *MCA* 𝄢𝄢𝄢½

Man of Aran Celebrated account of a fisherman's struggle for survival on a barren island near the west coast of Ireland, featuring amateur actors. Three years in the making, it's the last word in man against nature cinema, and a visual marvel. A former explorer, Flaherty became an influential documentarian. Having first gained fame with "Nanook of the North," he compiled an opus of documentaries made for commercial release.
1934 132m/B *D:* Robert Flaherty. **VHS $29.95** *HMV, GVV* 𝄢𝄢𝄢

Man of Destiny Bonaparte (Keach) and a mysterious woman battle good-humoredly over a collection of love letters. From a Bernard Shaw story. Charming and well-acted.
1973 60m/C Stacy Keach, Samantha Eggar. **VHS, Beta** *NO* 𝄢𝄢½

Man of Evil The hard times of the illegitimate daughter of a member of the British Parliament in the early 1900s, told with an astonishing number of plot twists and a plodding melodramtic style. Based on the novel "Fanny by Gaslight." *AKA:* Fanny by Gaslight.
1948 108m/B *GB* Phyllis Calvert, James Mason, Wilfred Lawson, Stewart Granger, Margaretta Scott, Jean Kent, John Laurie, Stuart Lindsell, Nora Swinburne, Amy Veness, Ann Wilton, Helen Haye, Cathleen Nesbitt, Guy le Feuvre, John Turnbull, Peter Jones; *D:* Anthony Asquith. **VHS $29.95** *FCT* 𝄢𝄢

Man of Flowers Because of his puritan upbringing, a reclusive art collector has trouble coping with his feelings of sexuality. He pays a woman to disrobe in front of him, but is never able to bring himself to see her naked. A moody piece with overtones of black humor, this work has limited audience appeal.
1984 91m/C *AU* Norman Kaye, Alyson Best, Chris Haywood, Sarah Walker, Julia Blake, Bob Ellis, Werner Herzog; *D:* Paul Cox. **VHS, Beta, LV $69.98** *LIV, VES* 𝄢𝄢½

Man of La Mancha Arrested by the Inquisition and thrown into prison, Miguel de Cervantes relates the story of Don Quixote. Not nearly as good as the Broadway musical it is based on. ♫It's All the Same; The Impossible Dream; Barber's Song; Man of La Mancha; Dulcinea; I'm Only Thinking of Him; Little Bird, Little Bird; Life as It Really Is; The Dubbing; A Little Gossip; Aldonza; Golden Helmet of Mambrino; The Psalm.

1972 (PG) 129m/C Peter O'Toole, Sophia Loren, James Coco, Harry Andrews, John Castle, Brian Blessed; *D:* Arthur Hiller. Academy Awards '72 Nominations: Best Original Score; National Board of Review Awards '72: 10 Best Films of the Year, Best Actor (O'Toole). **VHS, Beta, LV $19.99** *FOX, FCT* 𝄢½

Man of Legend An adventure-romance filmed in Morocco; a WWI German soldier flees to the Foreign Legion and fights with nomadic rebels, ultimately falling in love with their chief's beautiful daughter. An unoriginal desert saga.
1971 (PG) 95m/C *IT SP* Peter Strauss, Tina Aumont, Pier Paola Capponi; *D:* Sergio Grieco. **VHS, Beta $59.95** *UHV* 𝄢𝄢

Man of Marble A satire on life in post-WWII Poland. A young filmmaker sets out to tell the story of a bricklayer who, because of his exceptional skill, once gained popularity with other workers. He became a champion for worker rights, only to then find himself being persecuted by the government. The conclusion was censored by the Polish government. Highly acclaimed and followed by "Man of Iron" in 1981. In Polish with English subtitles.
1976 160m/C *PL* Krystyna Janda, Jerzy Radziwilowicz, Tadeusz Lomnicki, Jacek Lomnicki, Krystyna Zachwatowicz; *D:* Andrzej Wajda. **VHS $79.95** *NYF, FCT, TAM* 𝄢𝄢𝄢

A Man of Passion Quinn plays an aging artist living pleasurably on a Mediterranean isle. His summer guest is his uptight grandson, a classical pianist. Naturally, Gramps is about to teach the kid to loosen up, including appreciating one of his lovely artist's models. Another variation for Quinn on his "Zorba" personality but it works.
199? (R) 90m/C Anthony Quinn, Ramon Sheen, Maud Adams, Elizabeth Ashley, R.J. Williams, Ray Walston, Victoria Vera; *W/D:* J. Anthony Loma. **VHS $89.95** *ATV* 𝄢𝄢

Man of the Forest A cowboy goes to the aid of a damsel in distress and he winds up being framed for murder for his efforts. Based on Zane Grey's novel.
1933 59m/B *GB* Randolph Scott, Verna Hillie, Harry Carey Sr., Noah Beery Sr., Barton MacLane; *D:* Henry Hathaway. **VHS $19.95** *NOS, DVT, MLB* 𝄢𝄢

Man of the Frontier A vital irrigation project is being sabotaged, but Autry exposes the culprits. *AKA:* Red River Valley.
1936 60m/B Gene Autry, Smiley Burnette, Frances Grant; *D:* B. Reeves Eason. **VHS, Beta $19.95** *NOS, VDM, VCN* 𝄢𝄢

Man of the West Bad guy turned good guy Cooper is asked by his neighborhood town fathers to take a tidy hunk of moolah to another city to recruit a school marm. Ambushed en route by his former partners in crime (who are led by his wacko uncle) he's forced to revert to his wanton ways in order to survive and to save innocent hostages. There's a raging debate among Cooper-philes whether this late effort has been unduly overlooked or duly ignored. A number of things conspire to give it a bad rap: Cooper does little but look mournful until the very end; there's no hiding the fact that he's older than Cobb, who plays his uncle; and the acting is in general more befitting of a B-grade slice and dicer. You be the judge. Scripted by Reginald Rose.
1958 100m/C Gary Cooper, Julie London, Lee J. Cobb, Arthur O'Connell, Jack Lord, John Dehner, Royal Dano, Guy Wilkerson, Emory Parnell; *D:* Anthony Mann. **VHS, Beta $19.98** *MGM, FCT* 𝄢𝄢½

Man of Violence A vulgar, tasteless man spends the worthless hours of his wasted life lurking about the more wretched entrance-ways of his native land. *AKA:* The Sex Racketeers.
1971 107m/C Michael Latimer, Luan Peters; *D:* Pete Walker. **VHS, Beta $39.95** *MON* 𝄢

Man on a String In order to bring down a Mob boss the feds first frame cop Peter King and send him to the pen. When he gets out, King uses his prison contacts to get in with the Mob and winds up pitting two rival gangs against each other in order to destroy them both. Made for television.
1971 (PG) 73m/C Christopher George, Jack Warden, Keith Carradine, Joel Grey, William Schallert, Kitty Winn; *D:* Joseph Sargent. **VHS** *COL* 𝄢𝄢½

Man on Fire Told via flashback, a cynical ex-CIA man is hired as a bodyguard for the daughter of a wealthy Italian couple, who is soon thereafter kidnapped by terrorists. He goes to her rescue with all the subtlety of a wrecking ball. Decent cast goes down the tubes in this botched thriller.
1987 (R) 92m/C *FR* Scott Glenn, Brooke Adams, Danny Aiello, Joe Pesci, Paul Shenar, Jonathan Pryce, Jade Malle; *D:* Elie Chouraqui. **VHS, Beta, LV $89.98** *LIV, VES* 𝄢

Man on the Eiffel Tower Laughton plays Inspector Maigret, the detective created by novelist Georges Simenon, in a highly suspenseful and cerebral mystery about a crazed killer who defies the police to discover his identity. This is the first film Meredith directed.
1948 82m/C Charles Laughton, Burgess Meredith, Franchot Tone, Patricia Roc; *D:* Burgess Meredith. **VHS, Beta $19.95** *NOS, MRV, GEM* 𝄢𝄢𝄢

Man on the Run A robbery takes place in the store where an Army deserter is trying to sell his gun, and he ends up taking the rap. It's up to a lovely lady lawyer to prove his innocence. Efficiently told "B" crime drama.
1949 82m/B *GB* Derek Farr, Joan Hopkins, Edward Chapman, Laurence Harvey, H. Marion Crawford, Alfie Bass, John Bailey, John Stuart, Edward Underdown, Leslie Perrins, Kenneth More, Martin Miller, Eleanor Summerfield; *W/D:* Lawrence Huntington. **VHS, Beta $16.95** *SNC* 𝄢𝄢

Man on the Run After an unwitting involvement with a small robbery, a teenager finds himself the object of a police manhunt for a murder suspect.
1974 (R) 90m/C Kyle Johnson, James B. Sikking, Terry Carter; *D:* Herbert L. Strock. **VHS, Beta $59.95** *PSM* 𝄢½

The Man Outside After a CIA agent is fired for allegedly assisting another agent in defecting to the East, he becomes involved in further intrigue. A Russian spy is looking to defect. In the process, the ex-agent is framed for murder. Straightforward espionage tale taken from Gene Stackleborg's novel "Double Agent."
1968 (R) 98m/C *GB* Van Heflin, Heidelinde Weis, Pinkas Braun, Peter Vaughan, Charles Gray, Ronnie Barker; *D:* Samuel Gallu. **VHS $19.95** *VIR* 𝄢𝄢

Man Outside Logan is an ex-lawyer who takes to the Arkansas outback after his wife dies. Anthropologist/teacher Quinlan takes a shine to him. He seems like an okay guy, but bad guy Dillman has made it look like he's a child snatcher. Slick on the outside but empty inside independent effort. Look for former members of The Band in supporting roles.
1988 (PG-13) 109m/C Robert F. Logan, Kathleen Quinlan, Bradford Dillman, Rick Danko, Levon Helm; *D:* Mark Stouffer. **VHS, LV** *NO* 𝄢

The Man That Corrupted Hadleyburg
Entertaining adaptation of a Mark Twain short story about a stranger's plot of revenge against the hypocritical residents of a small town. Originally made for television.
1980 40m/C Robert Preston, Fred Gwynne, Frances Sternhagen; **D:** Ralph Rosenblum. **VHS, Beta $24.95** *MON, KAR* *♫*

The Man They Could Not Hang
A good doctor tinkering with artificial hearts is caught by police while experimenting on a willing student. When the doctor is convicted and hanged for a murder, his assistant uses the heart to bring him back to life. No longer a nice guy, he vows revenge against the jurors that sentenced him. Karloff repeated the same story line in several films, and this one is representative of the type.
1939 70m/B Boris Karloff, Lorna Gray, Roger Pryor, Robert Wilcox; **D:** Nick Grinde. **VHS, Beta $9.95** *GKK* *♫♫½*

Man Trouble
A divorcing opera singer (Barkin) seeks the help of a sleazy attack-dog trainer (Nicholson) when she becomes the victim of a stalker. Nicholson hits on her, first because that's one of his habits, and then because he is being paid to by a billionaire who wants him to steal the manuscript of a tell-all book about him written by Barkin's sister. Although both Nicholson and Barkin are excellent actors, they lack the electricity to make the romance credible, and the jokes are weak. Supporting cast, including D'Angelo, Stanton, and McKean, provide the funny parts in this otherwise dull film.
1992 (PG-13) 100m/C Jack Nicholson, Ellen Barkin, Harry Dean Stanton, Beverly D'Angelo, Michael McKean, Saul Rubinek, Viveka Davis, Veronica Cartwright, David Clennon, John Kapelos, Paul Mazursky; **D:** Bob Rafelson; **W:** Carole Eastman. **VHS, LV $94.98** *FXV* *♫♫*

The Man Who Broke 1,000 Chains
A made-for-television movie about a man who is committed to a chain gang after World War II for a petty crime, and his efforts, after escaping, in making a new life for himself. An unimaginative plot is occasionally highlighted by a good scene or two.
1987 113m/C Val Kilmer, Charles Durning, Sonia Braga; **D:** Daniel Mann. **VHS, Beta $79.95** *LHV, WAR* *♫♫*

The Man Who Came to Dinner
Based on the Moss Hart-George S. Kaufman play, this comedy is about a bitter radio celebrity (Woolley) on a lecture tour (a character based on Alexander Woolcott). He breaks his hip and must stay in a quiet suburban home for the winter. While there, he occupies his time by barking orders, being obnoxious and generally just driving the other residents nuts. Woolley reprises his Broadway role in this film that succeeds at every turn, loaded with plenty of satiric jabs at the Algonquin Hotel Roundtable regulars.
1941 112m/B Monty Woolley, Bette Davis, Ann Sheridan, Jimmy Durante, Reginald Gardiner, Richard Travis, Billie Burke, Grant Mitchell, Mary Wickes, George Barbier, Ruth Vivian, Elisabeth Fraser; **D:** William Keighley. **VHS, Beta, LV $19.95** *MGM* *♫♫♫½*

The Man Who Could Work Miracles
A mild-mannered draper's assistant becomes suddenly endowed with supernatural powers to perform any feat he wishes. Great special effects (for an early film) and fine performances result in a classic piece of science fiction.
1937 82m/B Ralph Richardson, Joan Gardner, Roland Young; **D:** Lothar Mendes. **VHS, Beta, LV $14.98** *SUE* *♫♫♫½*

The Man Who Envied Women
The non-narrative feminist story of a smug womanizer: the man "who knows almost too much about women."
1985 125m/C Bill Raymond, Larry Loonin, Trisha Brown; **W/D:** Yvonne Rainer. **VHS, Beta, 3/4U** *NO* *♫½*

The Man Who Fell to Earth
Entertaining and technically adept cult classic about a man from another planet (Bowie, in a bit of typecasting) who ventures to earth in hopes of finding water to save his family and drought-stricken planet. Instead he becomes a successful inventor and businessman, along the way discovering the human vices of booze, sex, and television. Also available in a restored version at 138 minutes. Remade for television in 1987 and based on Walter Tevis' novel.
1976 (R) 118m/C GB David Bowie, Candy Clark, Rip Torn, Buck Henry, Bernie Casey; **D:** Nicolas Roeg. **VHS, Beta, LV $19.95** *COL* *♫♫♫½*

The Man Who Guards the Greenhouse
Tracy must come to terms with her attraction for Jeff as well as once again trying to write a meaningful novel.
1988 150m/C Christopher Cazenove, Rebecca Dewey. **VHS $79.95** *LHV* *♫♫♫½*

Man Who Had Power Over Women
Disappointing sex farce about the exploits of a carnally insatiable (and married) talent executive (Taylor) who has an affair with every woman he meets and creates problems aplenty. Adapted from a novel by Gordon Williams.
1970 (R) 89m/C GB Rod Taylor, James Booth, Carol White, Penelope Horner, Clive Francis; **D:** John Krish. **VHS, Beta $59.98** *SUE* *♫♫*

The Man Who Haunted Himself
While a man lies in critical condition on the operating table after a car accident, his alter-ego emerges and turns his ideal life into a nightmare until the man recovers and moves toward a fateful encounter. An expanded version of an episode of the television series "Alfred Hitchcock Presents," this was Moore's first movie after having starred in the TV series "The Saint," and it was Dearden's last film; he died in a car accident the following year. Appeals primarily to those fascinated by "Hitchcock" or "The Twilight Zone"—where mystery matters most. Filmed in London.
1970 94m/C GB Roger Moore, Hildegarde Neil, Olga Georges-Picot; **D:** Basil Dearden. **VHS, Beta $59.99** *HBO* *♫♫*

The Man Who Knew Too Much
Hitchcock's first international success. A British family man on vacation in Switzerland is told of an assassination plot by a dying agent. His daughter is kidnapped to force his silence. In typical Hitchcock fashion, the innocent person becomes caught in a web of intrigue; the sticky situation culminates with surprising events during the famous shootout in the final scenes. Remade by Hitchcock in 1956.
1934 75m/B GB Leslie Banks, Edna Best, Peter Lorre, Nova Pilbeam, Pierre Fresnay; **D:** Alfred Hitchcock. **VHS, Beta, 3/4U, Special order formats $16.95** *SNC, MRV, NOS* *♫♫♫*

The Man Who Knew Too Much
Hitchcock's remake of his 1934 film, this time about an American doctor and his family vacationing in Marrakech. They become involved in a complicated international plot involving kidnapping and murder. While Doris tries to save the day by singing "Que Sera, Sera," Stewart tries to locate his abducted son. More lavish settings and forms of intrigue make this a less focused and, to some, inferior version.
1956 (PG) 120m/C James Stewart, Doris Day, Brenda de Banzie, Bernard Miles, Ralph Truman, Daniel Gelin, Alan Mowbray, Carolyn Jones, Hillary Brooke; **D:** Alfred Hitchcock. **VHS, Beta, LV $19.95** *MCA, HHE* *♫♫½*

The Man Who Laughs
Veidt's sensitive performance highlights this silent classic. He plays a young man whose features are surgically altered into a permanent smile because his family are political enemies of the current ruler. The man is befriended by the owner of a sideshow who first exhibits him as a freak but later finds Veidt gaining fame as a clown. A beautiful blind girl in the show loves Veidt for who he is and the two find happiness.
1927 110m/B Conrad Veidt, Mary Philbin, Olga Baclanova, Josephine Crowell, George Siegmann, Brandon Hurst; **D:** Paul Leni. **VHS** *GPV* *♫♫♫½*

The Man Who Lived Again
Boris strives to be a brain-switcher, and suspense builds around the question of whether or not he will change his mind. Shot in England with fine sets and a definite Anglo feel to the proceedings, with Karloff doing one of his better mad scientist routines. **AKA:** The Man Who Changed His Mind; The Brainsnatchers; Dr. Maniac.
1936 61m/B GB Boris Karloff, Anna Lee, John Loder, Frank Cellier, Lyn Harding, Cecil Parker; **D:** Robert Stevenson. **VHS, Beta, 8mm $14.95** *SNC, VYY, MLB* *♫♫½*

Man Who Loved Cat Dancing
Reynolds is an outlaw on the run after avenging his wife's murder and robbing a safe with pals Hopkins and Warden, and Miles has recently escaped from her abusive husband. It's love on the run as Burt and Sarah are pursued by bounty hunters and their tragic pasts—coming close to making us care, but doesn't mean as much in movies as it does in dancing. Based on Marilyn Durham's novel.
1973 (PG) 114m/C Burt Reynolds, Sarah Miles, Jack Warden, Lee J. Cobb, Jay Silverheels, Robert Donner; **D:** Richard Sarafian; **M:** John Williams. **VHS, Beta $19.98** *MGM, FCT* *♫♫*

The Man Who Loved Women
An intelligent, sensitive bachelor writes his memoirs and recalls the many, many, many women he has loved. Truffaut couples sophistication and lightheartedness, the thrill of the chase and, when it leads to an accidental death, the wondering what-it's-all-about in the mourning after. In French with English subtitles. Remade in 1983. **AKA:** L'Homme Qui Aimait les Femmes.
1977 119m/C FR Charles Denner, Brigitte Fossey, Leslie Caron; **D:** Francois Truffaut. **VHS, Beta, LV $19.98** *MGM, TAM* *♫♫♫*

The Man Who Loved Women
A remake of the 1977 French film, this is slower, tries to be funnier, and is less subtle than the original. Reynolds is a Los Angeles sculptor whose reputation as a playboy leads him to a psychoanalyst's couch, where a lot of talk slows the action—though Burt & Julie (the shrink) do share the couch.
1983 (R) 110m/C Burt Reynolds, Julie Andrews, Kim Basinger, Marilu Henner, Cynthia Sikes, Jennifer Edwards; **D:** Blake Edwards. **VHS, Beta $79.95** *COL* *♫♫*

The Man Who Never Was
Tense true story (with melodramatic embroidery) from WWII shows in step-by-step detail how Britain duped the Axis by letting them find an Allied corpse bearing phony invasion plans. Based on the book by the scheme's mastermind Ewen Montagu, played by Webb; Peter

Sellers provides the voice of an offscreen Winston Churchill.
1955 102m/C *GB* Clifton Webb, Gloria Grahame, Robert Flemyng, Josephine Griffin, Stephen Boyd, Andre Morell, Laurence Naismith, Geoffrey Keen, Michael Hordern; *D:* Ronald Neame. **VHS, Beta** $19.98 *FOX, FCT* 🐾🐾

The Man Who Shot Liberty Valance
Tough cowboy Wayne and idealistic lawyer Stewart join forces against dreaded gunfighter Liberty Valance, played leatherly by Marvin. While Stewart rides to Senatorial success on his reputation as the man who shot the villain, he suffers moral crises about the act, but is toughened up by Wayne. Wayne's use of the word "pilgrim" became a standard for his impersonators. Strong character acting, great Western scenes, and value judgements to ponder over make this last of Ford's black and white westerns among his best.
1962 119m/B James Stewart, John Wayne, Vera Miles, Lee Marvin, Edmond O'Brien, Andy Devine, Woody Strode; *D:* John Ford. **VHS, Beta, LV** $14.95 *PAR, HMV* 🐾🐾🐾½

The Man Who Skied Down Everest
Documentary about a Japanese athlete who undertakes a demanding downhill run, and the cost (human and financial) of getting there.
1975 (G) 86m/C **VHS** *NO* 🐾🐾½

The Man Who Wagged His Tail
A mean slumlord is turned into a dog as the result of a curse cast upon him. In order to return to his human form, he must be loved by someone. Despite his attempts to be loved, the dog alienates his only friend and must try to redeem himself. Played for fun, this is a mildly amusing fantasy filmed in Spain and Brooklyn. Not released in the U. S. until 1961. *AKA:* An Angel Passed Over Brooklyn; Un Angelo e Sceso a Brooklyn.
1957 91m/B *IT SP* Peter Ustinov, Pablito Calvo, Aroldo Tieri, Silvia Marco; *D:* Ladislao Vajda. **VHS** $16.95 *SNC* 🐾🐾½

The Man Who Wasn't There
A member of the State department receives a formula from a dying spy that can render him invisible, see? He has to use the formula to protect himself from the police and other spies, becoming a comic "Invisible Man," see? Generally chaotic tale that's bad, but not so bad that it's worth seeing, though you might want to see what invisibility looks like in 3-D.
1983 (R) 111m/C Steve Guttenberg, Jeffrey Tambor, Art Hindle, Lisa Langlois; *D:* Bruce Malmuth. **VHS, Beta** $59.95 *PAR* 🐾

The Man Who Would Be King
A grand, old-fashioned adventure based on the classic story by Rudyard Kipling about two mercenary soldiers who travel from India to Kafiristan in order to conquer it and set themselves up as kings. Splendid characterizations by Connery and Caine, and Huston's royal directorial treatment provides it with adventure, majestic sweep, and well-developed characters.
1975 (PG) 129m/C Sean Connery, Michael Caine, Christopher Plummer, Saeed Jaffrey; *D:* John Huston. **VHS, Beta, LV** $19.98 *FOX* 🐾🐾🐾🐾

The Man Who Would Not Die
During his investigation of several deaths, a man discovers that all of the deceased were actually the same man. It seems the deaths were part of a intricate scheme to cover up a million dollar heist. Two of the top three actors are killed early on; it's not very suspenseful. It's more like the mystery that would not die. From Charles Williams' novel

"The Sailcloth Shroud." *AKA:* Target in the Sun.
1975 (PG) 83m/C Dorothy Malone, Keenan Wynn, Aldo Ray; *D:* Robert Arkless. **VHS, Beta** $59.95 *WAR, OM* 🐾🐾

Man with a Cross
Archaeologists of the cinema may want to unearth this early Rossellini, made by the future father of neo-realist cinema as a propaganda piece for the fascist war effort. A heroic Italian chaplain on the Russian front ministers to foe and friend alike, and even converts a few commies to Christ. Not as awful as it sounds—but never forget where this came from.
1943 88m/B *IT D:* Roberto Rossellini. **VHS** $59.95 *FST* 🐾🐾

A Man with a Maid
A bizarre British exploitation pic mixes spookhouse cliches and sex, as a young man finds his new bachelor pad haunted by Jack the Ripper. Originally shot in 3-D and known variously as "The Groove Room" and "What the Swedish Butler Saw." It didn't help.
1973 83m/C Sue Longhurst, Martin Long, Diana Dors; *D:* Vernon Becker. **VHS** $19.95 *VDM* 🐾

The Man with a Movie Camera
A plotless, experimental view of Moscow through the creative eye of the cameraman Dziga Vertov, founder of the Kino Eye. The editing methods and camera techniques used in this silent film were very influential and still stand up to scrutiny today.
1929 69m/B *RU D:* Dziga Vertov. **VHS, Beta, 3/4U** $35.95 *IHF, MRV, DVT* 🐾🐾🐾½

The Man with Bogart's Face
Sacchi is no Bogart, but he does imitate him well. Bogart fans will enjoy this fond tribute to the late great actor, but the story uncertainly wavers between genuine detective story and detective spoof. *AKA:* Sam Marlowe, Private Eye.
1980 (PG) 106m/C Robert Sacchi, Misty Rowe, Sybil Danning, Franco Nero, Herbert Lom, Victor Buono, Olivia Hussey; *D:* Robert Day. **VHS, Beta** $59.98 *FOX* 🐾

The Man with One Red Shoe
Hanks is a lovable clod of a violinist who ensnares himself in a web of intrigue when CIA agents, both good and evil, mistake him for a contact by his wearing one red shoe. Sporadically funny remake of the French "The Tall Blond Man with One Black Shoe."
1985 (PG) 92m/C Tom Hanks, Dabney Coleman, Lori Singer, Carrie Fisher, James Belushi, Charles Durning, Edward Herrmann, Tommy Noonan, Gerrit Graham, David Lander, David Ogden Stiers; *D:* Stan Dragoti. **VHS, Beta** $14.98 *FXV, FOX* 🐾🐾

The Man with the Golden Arm
A gripping film version of the Nelson Algren junkie melodrama, about an ex-addict who returns to town only to get mixed up with drugs again. Considered controversial in its depiction of addiction when released, with Sinatra's performance as Frankie Machine a stand-out.
1955 119m/B Frank Sinatra, Kim Novak, Eleanor Parker, Arnold Stang, Darren McGavin, Robert Strauss, George Mathews, John Conte, Doro Merande; *D:* Otto Preminger. **VHS, Beta** $9.95 *NOS, MRV, NEG* 🐾🐾

The Man with the Golden Gun
Roger Moore is the debonair secret agent 007 in this ninth James Bond flick. Assigned to recover a small piece of equipment which can be utilized to harness the sun's energy, Bond engages the usual bevy of villains and beauties.
1974 (PG) 134m/C *GB* Roger Moore, Christopher Lee, Britt Ekland, Maud Adams, Herve Villechaize, Clifton James, Soon-Teck Oh, Richard Loo, Marc Lawrence, Bernard Lee, Lois

Maxwell, Desmond Llewelyn; *D:* Guy Hamilton; *M:* John Barry. **VHS, Beta, LV** $19.98 *MGM, FOX* 🐾🐾½

The Man with Two Brains
Did you hear the one about the brilliant neuro-surgeon who falls in love with a woman in his laboratory? He only has two problems: dealing with his covetous wife and finding a body for his cerebral lover. Plenty of laughs in this spoof of mad scientist movies that is redeemed from potential idiocy by the cast's titillating performances. Listen closely and you'll recognize the voice of Spacek as the brain-in-the-jar of Martin's dreams.
1983 (R) 91m/C Steve Martin, Kathleen Turner, David Warner, Sissy Spacek; *W/D:* Carl Reiner; *W:* Steve Martin, George Gipp. **VHS, Beta, LV** $34.98 *WAR* 🐾🐾🐾

Man with Two Heads
Doctor Jekyll gets in touch with his innermost feelings when his muffed experiments turn him into, gasp, Mr. Blood. Another forlorn addition to the Dr. Jekyll retread collection.
1972 (R) 80m/C *W/D:* Andy Milligan. **VHS** *NO* 🐾

The Man with Two Lives
Well done horror thriller about a wealthy young man who's killed in a car accident, then brought back to life by a mad scientist. At precisely the moment his life is restored, a murderous gangster is executed and his soul enters the young man's body.
1942 ?m/C Edward Norris, Addison Richards, Marlo Dwyer. **VHS** $16.95 *SNC* 🐾🐾½

The Man Without a Face
Gibson plays a badly scarred man in Maine who must help a lonely boy who has no father. Makeup on Gibson was said to have made everyone on the set uncomfortable during filming. First foray for Gibson into the director's chair. Adapted from a novel by Isabelle Holland.
1993 ?m/C Mel Gibson, Margaret Whitton, Fay Masterson, Richard Masur, Gaby Hoffman, Geoffrey Lewis, Nick Stahl, Geoffrey Lewis, Jack DeMave; *D:* Mel Gibson; *W:* Malcolm MacRury. **VHS** *NYR* 🐾🐾½

Man Without a Star
A cowboy helps ranchers stop a ruthless cattle owner from taking over their land. The conflict between freedom in the wild west and the need for order and settlements is powerfully internalized in Douglas, whose fight for justice will tame the cowboy code he lives by. You'll shed a tear for the fading frontier.
1955 89m/B Kirk Douglas, Jeanne Crain, Claire Trevor, William Campbell; *D:* King Vidor. **VHS, Beta** $19.95 *MCA* 🐾🐾½

Man, Woman & Child
A close, upscale California family is shocked when a child from the husband's long-ago affair with a Frenchwoman appears at their door. Pure sentimentalism, as the family confronts this unexpected development. Two hankies—one each for fine performances by Sheen and Danner. Based on a sentimental novel by Erich Segal of "Love Story" fame, who co-wrote the script.
1983 (PG) 99m/C Martin Sheen, Blythe Danner, Craig T. Nelson, David Hemmings; *D:* Dick Richards. **VHS, Beta** $59.95 *PAR* 🐾🐾

Manchurian Avenger
Desperados have wrested control of a Colorado gold rush town from Joe Kim's family, but he'll put an end to that, chop chop.
1984 (R) 87m/C Bobby Kim, Bill Wallace; *D:* Ed Warnick. **VHS, Beta** $69.99 *HBO* 🐾

The Manchurian Candidate
Political thriller about an American Korean War vet who suspects that he and his platoon may have been brainwashed during the war, with his highly decorated, heroic friend pro-

grammed by commies to be an operational assassin. Loaded with shocks, conspiracy, inventive visual imagery, and bitter political satire of naivete and machinations of the left and right. Excellent performances by an all-star cast, with McGiver and Lansbury particularly frightening. Based on the Richard Condon novel. Featuring a special interview with Sinatra and Frankenheimer in which Sinatra is deified.
1962 ·126m/B Frank Sinatra, Laurence Harvey, Angela Lansbury, Janet Leigh, James Gregory, Leslie Parrish, John McGiver, Henry Silva; *D:* John Frankenheimer. Academy Awards '62 Nominations: Best Film Editing, Best Supporting Actress (Lansbury); Golden Globe Awards '63: Best Supporting Actress (Lansbury); National Board of Review Awards '62: Best Supporting Actress (Lansbury). **VHS, Beta, LV $19.95** *MGM* 🎬🎬🎬

The Mandarin Mystery In the process of trying to retrieve a stolen Mandarin stamp, detective Ellery Queen uncovers a counterfeiting ring. Some fine performances, but a muddled script creates a mystery as to whether or not the action is played for laughs.
1937 65m/B Eddie Quillan, Charlotte Henry, Rita La Roy, Wade Boteler, Franklin Pangborn, George Irving, Kay Hughes, William Newell; *D:* Ralph Staub. **VHS, Beta $16.95** *NOS, SNC* 🎬½

Mandela A gripping, powerful drama about human rights and dignity, tracing the real-life trials of Nelson and Winnie Mandela. The story focuses on the couple's early opposition to South African apartheid, as well as the events leading up to Nelson's life-imprisonment sentencing in 1964. Excellent, restrained performances from Glover and Woodard. Made for cable television.
1987 135m/C Danny Glover, Alfre Woodard, John Matshikiza, Warren Clarke, Allan Cordunner, Julian Glover; *D:* Philip Saville. **VHS, Beta $79.99** *HBO, KUI, FCT* 🎬🎬🎬

Mandinga A plantation owner develops an obsession for one of his female slaves. Made to cash in on the already exploitive "Mandingo"; two wrongs don't make a right.
1977 100m/C Anthony Gismond; *D:* Mario Pinzauti. **VHS, Beta $59.95** *PAR* 🎬

Mandingo Overheated Southern-fried tale of slavery in the Deep South, circa 1840, dealing with the tangled loves and hates of a family and their slaves. Heavyweight boxer Norton made his screen debut in the title role as the slave who makes his master money with his boxing prowess. King is the wastrel son who makes Norton's wife, another slave, his mistress. Followed by 1975's "Drum." Based on the novel by Kyle Onstott.
1975 (R) 127m/C James Mason, Susan George, Perry King, Richard Ward, Ken Norton, Ben Masters, Brenda Sykes, Paul Benedict, Ji Tu Cambuka; *D:* Richard Fleischer. **VHS, Beta, LV $59.95** *PAR* 🎬🎬

Mandroid Two scientists design a high-tech robot, Mandroid, to handle a powerful new element they've discovered. Dr. Zimmer and daughter Zanna want to use their creation to help mankind while mad scientist Dr. Drago wants the power Mandroid can give him. When a laboratory accident leaves Drago horribly disfigured it also gives him the chance to steal Mandroid and put his evil plan into action. Filmed on location in Romania.
1993 (R) 81m/C Brian Cousins, Jane Caldwell, Michael DellaFemina, Curt Lowens, Patrick Ersgard, Robert Symonds; *D:* Joakim Ersgard; *W:* Jackson Barr, Earl Kenton. **VHS, Beta** *PAR* 🎬½

Mandy Poignant drama of a deaf child and the family who must come to terms with her deafness. Well-developed plot and well performed; an intelligent treatment in all. *AKA:* Crash of Silence.
1953 93m/B *GB* Phyllis Calvert, Jack Hawkins, Mandy Miller; *D:* Alexander MacKendrick. **VHS, Beta** *LCA* 🎬🎬🎬

Manfish Two men venture out in a boat, the Manfish, to hunt for sunken treasure in the Caribbean. Only one survives the trip, as his greed destroys the other. The scenes off the Jamaican coast are lovely, but the story fails to take hold. Though there is a star aboard in Chaney, you'll look astern and bow out with a sinking feeling. Derived from two Edgar Allan Poe stories, "The Gold Bug" and "The Tell-Tale Heart."
1956 76m/C John Bromfield, Lon Chaney Jr., Victor Jory, Barbara Nichols; *D:* W. Lee Wilder. **VHS $16.95** *NOS, SNC* 🎬½

The Mango Tree A young man comes of age in a small Australian town during the 1920s. Everything is well done, if not dramatic or fascinating.
1977 93m/C *AU* Geraldine Fitzgerald, Robert Helpmann, Diane Craig, Gerald Kennedy, Christopher Pate; *D:* Kevin Dobson. **VHS, Beta $69.95** *VID* 🎬🎬½

The Manhandlers After the uncle of a young woman is killed by the mob, she goes after them for revenge. For your entertainment pleasure, best stick with the soup commercial of the same name.
1973 (R) 87m/C Cara Burgess, Judy Brown, Vince Cannon, Rosalind Miles; *D:* Lee Madden. **VHS, Beta $69.95** *TWE* 🎬

Manhattan Allen plays a successful television writer yearning to be a serious writer. He struggles through a series of ill-fated romances, including one with a high school senior Hemingway, who is about a quarter century younger, and another with Keaton, who's also having an on-again, off-again affair with Murphy, Allen's best friend. A scathingly serious and comic view of modern relationships in urban America and of the modern intellectual neuroses. Shot in black-and-white to capture the mood of Manhattan and mated with an excellent Gershwin soundtrack, the video version preserves the widescreen effect that adds yet another impressive element to the overall production.
1979 (R) 96m/B Woody Allen, Diane Keaton, Meryl Streep, Mariel Hemingway, Michael Murphy, Wallace Shawn, Anne Byrne, Karen Allen; *W/D:* Woody Allen; *W:* Marshall Brickman. Academy Awards '79 Nominations: Best Original Screenplay, Best Supporting Actress (Hemingway); British Academy Awards '79: Best Film; Cesar Awards '80: Best Foreign Film; National Board of Review Awards '79: 10 Best Films of the Year; New York Film Critics Awards '79: Best Director (Allen); National Society of Film Critics Awards '79: Best Actress (Keaton), Best Director (Allen). **VHS, Beta, LV $19.98** *MGM, PIA* 🎬🎬🎬🎬

Manhattan Baby Unscary horror film about an archaeologist who digs up a relic that draws evil into the world and infects an American girl with powers that lead to many deaths. Advice to you that might have saved the archaeologist: don't dig this.
1982 90m/C *IT* Christopher Connelly, Martha Taylor; *D:* Lucio Fulci. **VHS, Beta $69.98** *LIV* 🎬

Manhattan Melodrama Powell and Gable are best friends from childhood, growing up together in an orphanage. Their adult lives take different paths, however, as Powell becomes a respected prosecuting attorney while Gable becomes a notorious gambler/racketeer. Lovely Loy is Gable's girl who

comes between the two. Eventually, Powell must prosecute his life-long friend for murder in order to win the governorship. One of Gable's toughest roles; Powell's character, however, is a bit unbelievable as his ethics seem to extend beyond love and friendship. This is the first film to team Powell and Loy, who would go on to make 13 more films together, including the "Thin Man" series.
1934 93m/B Clark Gable, William Powell, Myrna Loy, Leo Carrillo, Nat Pendleton, George Sidney, Isabel Jewell, Muriel Evans, Claudelle Kaye, Frank Conroy, Jimmy Butler, Mickey Rooney, Edward Van Sloan; *D:* Woodbridge S. Van Dyke. **VHS, Beta, LV $19.98** *MGM, CCB* 🎬🎬🎬½

Manhattan Merry-Go-Round One of the movies where a corrupt boss—in this case a record producer—threatens a bunch of good people as a pretense for a plot when the movie simply serves as a showcase for stars. Features many singing stars of the thirties ("where have you gone Cab Calloway?") plus Joltin' Joe, who ended up having a hit-streak in another genre. 🎵Mama I Wanna Make Rhythm; Manhattan Merry-Go-Round; Heaven?; I Owe You; It's Round Up Time in Reno.
1937 89m/B Cab Calloway, Louis Prima, Ted Lewis, Ann Dvorak, Phil Regan, Kay Thompson, Gene Autry, Joe DiMaggio; *D:* Charles Riesner. **VHS, Beta $19.95** *NOS, VCN, HHT* 🎬🎬

Manhattan Murder Mystery Keaton and Allen are two New Yorkers who get involved in a mystery when their neighbor dies under mysterious circumstances.
1993 m/C Woody Allen, Diane Keaton, Anjelica Huston, Alan Alda; *W/D:* Woody Allen. **VHS** 🎬🎬

The Manhattan Project An exceptionally bright teenager decides to build a nuclear bomb for his project at the New York City science fair. He's out to prove how dangerously easy it is to build big bombs. When he steals plutonium from a local government installation, the feds attempt to nab the precocious youngster. Light moral overtones abound. Director Brickman co-wrote similarly titled "Manhattan." *AKA:* Manhattan Project: The Deadly Game.
1986 (PG-13) 117m/C John Lithgow, Christopher Collet, Cynthia Nixon, Jill Eikenberry, John Mahoney, Sully Boyer, Richard Council, Robert Schenkkan, Paul Austin; *D:* Marshall Brickman. **VHS, Beta, LV $19.99** *HBO* 🎬🎬

Manhunt A man marked for execution by the mob launches his own assault on the organization's headquarters. Action and Italian food, but not much else. Dubbed. *AKA:* The Italian Connection; La Mala Ordina.
1973 (R) 93m/C *IT* Henry Silva, Mario Adorf, Woody Strode. **VHS, Beta $59.95** *MED* 🎬🎬

The Manhunt A framed cowhand escapes from prison to prove his innocence. Made-for-TV movie.
1986 89m/C Ernest Borgnine, Bo Svenson, John Ethan Wayne; *D:* Larry Ludman. **VHS, Beta $59.95** *MED* 🎬

Manhunt for Claude Dallas Mountain man uses game wardens for firing practice, ticks off local sheriff Torn, is tossed behind bars, checks out ahead of schedule and becomes a legend in his own time. Mediocre made-for-TV macho man melodrama. From the novel "Outlaw" by Jeff Long.
1986 93m/C Matt Salinger, Rip Torn, Claude Akins, Pat Hingle, Lois Nettleton, Beau Starr, Frederick Coffin; *D:* Jerry London; *W:* John Gay. **VHS, Beta $79.95** *PSM* 🎬🎬

Manhunt in the African Jungle An American undercover agent battles Nazi forces in Africa. A serial in fifteen episodes.

1954 240m/B Rod Cameron, Joan Marsh, Duncan Renaldo. **VHS, LV $29.98** *VCN, REP, MLB* ♂♂

Manhunt of Mystery Island Serial about the super-powered Captain Mephisto. *AKA:* Captain Mephisto and the Transformation Machine.
1945 100m/C Linda Stirling, Roy Barcroft, Richard Bailey, Kenne Duncan; *D:* Spencer Gordon Bennet. **VHS, Beta, LV** *MED, MLB* ♂♂

Manhunter A made-for-television escapade about a World War I Marine who returns home from China in 1933 to track down a bunch of gangsters headed by his sister.
1974 78m/C Ken Howard, Stefanie Powers, Gary Lockwood, Tim O'Connor, L.Q. Jones; *D:* Walter Grauman. **VHS, Beta, LV $19.98** *WAR, TWE, PIA* ♂

Manhunter A mercenary sets out to disengage organized crime from high-level politics. Produced by Owensby.
1983 92m/C Earl Owensby, Johnny Popwell, Doug Hale, Elizabeth Upton; *D:* Earl Owensby. **VHS, Beta $49.95** *MED* ♂♂½

Manhunter An FBI forensic specialist—who retired after a harrowing pursuit of a serial killer—is called back to duty to find a psychotic family killer. His technique: to match the thought processes of serial killers and thus anticipate their moves. Intense thriller, based on the Thomas Harris novel "Red Dragon." Harris also wrote "The Silence of the Lambs," which won several Academy Awards in 1992. The "Lambs" character, Hannibal ("The Cannibal") Lecter, appears in this movie as well. Director Mann applies the slick techniques he introduced in the popular television series "Miami Vice," creating a quiet, moody intensity broken by sudden onslaughts of violence. Available in widescreen on laserdisc. *AKA:* Red Dragon.
1986 (R) 100m/C William L. Petersen, Kim Greist, Joan Allen, Brian Cox, Dennis Farina, Stephen Lang, Tommy Noonan; *D:* Michael Mann. **VHS, Beta, LV $49.95** *WAR* ♂♂

Mania Fine adaptation of the Burke and Hare grave robbing legend. Cushing is the doctor who needs corpses and Pleasence and Rose provide them by any means. Highly atmospheric representation of dismal, 19th century Edinburgh. Very graphic for its time. *AKA:* The Flesh and the Fiends; Fiendish Ghouls; Psycho Killers.
1960 87m/B *GB* Peter Cushing, June Laverick, Donald Pleasence, George Rose, Dermot Walsh, Renee Houston, Billie Whitelaw, John Cairney, Michael Balfour; *D:* John Gilling. **VHS $16.95** *SNC, DVT, MLB* ♂♂½

Mania Four suspense/murder stories set in a sleazy urban milieu.
198? 120m/C Deborah Grover, Stephen Hunter, Lenore Zann, Wayne Robson. **Beta** *NO* ♂♂

Maniac A scientist has designs on raising the dead and searches for victims on which to experiment. Bizarre "adults only" exploitation feature was considered very risque for its time, and includes eaten eyeballs, a cat fight with syringes and a rapist who thinks he's an orangutan. A must for genre aficionados.
1934 67m/B Bill Woods, Horace Carpenter, Ted Edwards, Phyllis Diller, Thea Ramsey, Jennie Dark, Marcel Andre, Celia McGann; *D:* Dwain Esper. **VHS, Beta $14.95** *VDM, SNC, MRV* Woof!

Maniac An American artist living in France becomes involved with the daughter of a cafe owner, not suspecting that murder will follow. Seems that her old man is locked up in an insane asylum for torching the daughter's rapist several years earlier.

1963 86m/B *GB* Kerwin Mathews, Nadia Gray, Donald Houston, Liliane Brousse; *D:* Michael Carreras. **VHS, Beta $49.95** *COL, MLB* ♂♂

Maniac A New York cop hunts down an arrow-shooting and obviously crazed Vietnam veteran who endeavors to hold an entire Arizona town for ransom. Which is entirely appropriate, since the cast is in it only for the money. *AKA:* Ransom; Assault on Paradise; The Town That Cried Terror.
1978 (PG) 87m/C Oliver Reed, Deborah Raffin, Stuart Whitman, Jim Mitchum, Edward Brett; *D:* Richard Compton. **VHS, Beta $24.98** *SUE* ♂

Maniac A psycho murderer slaughters and scalps his victims, adding the "trophies" to his collection. Carries a self-imposed equivalent "X" rating due to its highly graphic gore quotient. For extremely strong stomachs only.
1980 91m/C Joe Spinell, Caroline Munro, Gail Lawrence, Kelly Piper, Tom Savini; *D:* William Lustig; *W/D:* William Lustig **VHS, Beta $54.95** *MED* Woof!

Maniac Cop In New York city, a cop goes beyond the realm of sanity and turns vigilante. Low-budget slasher/thriller that too often sags.
1988 (R) 92m/C Tom Atkins, Bruce Campbell, Laurene Landon, Richard Roundtree, William Smith, Robert Z'Dar, Sheree North; *D:* William Lustig; *W:* Larry Cohen. **VHS, Beta $19.98** *TWE, HHE* ♂

Maniac Cop 2 Recently released from prison, a grossly disfigured policeman forms a one-man vigilante squad, seeking revenge for his unjust incarceration. Blood and guts fly as any plot shortcomings are cleverly disguised by an array of violent video deaths. Sequel to "Maniac Cop."
1990 (R) 90m/C Robert Davi, Claudia Christian, Michael Lerner, Bruce Campbell, Laurene Landon, Robert Z'Dar, Clarence Williams III, Leo Rossi; *D:* William Lustig; *W:* Larry Cohen. **VHS, LV $89.95** *LIV* ♂

Maniac Cop 3 The grossly disfigured policeman returns yet again to exact gory vengeance as the good guys try to get rid of him once and for all.
1993 (R) 85m/C Robert Z'Dar, Robert Davi, Gretchen Becker, Paul Gleason, Doug Savant, Caitlin Dulany; *D:* William Lustig, Joel Soisson; *W:* Larry Cohen; *M:* Jerry Goldsmith. **VHS $89.95** *ACA* ♂

Maniac Warriors A nuclear apocalypse has caused some strange changes in the population—and not for the better. Blood-crazed mutants attack the heavily armed inhabitants of New State Idaho and there's lots of mayhem in store.
199? 91m/C Tom Schioler, Frank Wilson, Melanie Kilgour. **VHS $89.95** *AIP, MOV* ♂

The Manions of America The long and sometimes interesting rags-to-riches tale of Rory O'Manion, a feisty Irish patriot who leaves his native land during the potato famine of 1845 to settle in America. Originally a television miniseries.
1981 290m/C Pierce Brosnan, Kate Mulgrew, Linda Purl, David Soul, Kathleen Beller, Simon MacCorkindale; *D:* Joseph Sargent, Charles S. Dubin. **VHS, Beta $69.95** *PSM, PAR* ♂♂½

Manipulator A deranged ex-movie make-up man (Rooney, playing to type) kidnaps a young actress and holds her prisoner in a deserted Hollywood sound stage.
1971 (R) 91m/C Mickey Rooney, Luana Anders, Keenan Wynn; *D:* Yabo Yablonsky. **VHS, Beta $69.98** *LIV, VES* ♂

The Manitou A San Francisco woman suffers from a rapidly growing neck tumor which eventually grows into a 400-year-old Indian witch doctor. (I hate when that happens.) Redeemed only by good special effects, especially those that kept Curtis, Strasberg, and Meredith from laughing.
1978 (PG) 104m/C Susan Strasberg, Tony Curtis, Stella Stevens, Ann Sothern, Burgess Meredith, Michael Ansara; *D:* William Girdler. **VHS, Beta, LV $9.95** *COL, NLC* ♂♂

Mankillers A group of tough female convicts are enlisted to hunt down and rub out a psycho drug dealer, all the while displaying their feminine charms.
1987 90m/C Edd Byrnes, Gail Fisher, Edy Williams, Lynda Aldon, William Zipp, Christopher Lunde, Susanne Tegman, Marilyn Stafford, Paul Bruno, Byron Clark; *D:* David A. Prior. **VHS, Beta $14.95** *SVS, COL* ♂

Mannequin Tracy and Crawford star in this romantic story of a poor girl who finds temporary happiness by marrying a wealthy man after ditching her con-artist husband. Somewhat predictable, the movie reads like a "People" magazine story on The Donald and Ivana. Written by Joseph L. Mankiewicz, the story is kept afloat by Tracy and Crawford (in their only film together) with an able assist from Curtis.
1937 95m/B Joan Crawford, Spencer Tracy, Alan Curtis, Ralph Morgan, Leo Gorcey, Elisabeth Risdon, Paul Fix; *D:* Frank Borzage. **VHS $19.98** *MGM, MED* ♂♂½

Mannequin A young artist creates a store window display using various mannequins, one of which contains the spirit of an ancient Egyptian woman. She comes to life when he is around, and naturally none of his co-workers believe him. Very light comedy, featuring two pretty stars and music by Jefferson Starship.
1987 (PG) 90m/C Andrew McCarthy, Kim Cattrall, Estelle Getty, James Spader, Meshach Taylor, Carole Davis, G.W. Bailey; *D:* Michael Gottlieb. **VHS, Beta, LV $9.99** *OCD, MED* ♂♂

Mannequin 2: On the Move Less of a sequel, more of a lame rehash proving that the first "Mannequin" could have been even dumber. At this rate part three will be off the scale. Now it's a lovesick Teutonic princess frozen for 1,000 years who revives in a department store. Taylor reprises his grotesque gay role.
1991 (PG) 95m/C Kristy Swanson, William Ragsdale, Meshach Taylor, Terry Kiser, Stuart Pankin; *D:* Stewart Raffill. **VHS, LV $92.98** *LIV, PIA* Woof!

Mannikin A chilling supernatural short by Robert Bloch about a young singer who is possessed by a demon.
1977 28m/C Ronee Blakley, Keir Dullea; *D:* Donald W. Thompson. **VHS, Beta** *LCA* Woof!

Manny's Orphans An out-of-work teacher takes on a lovable home for orphaned boys. Dull remake of "Bad News Bears." *AKA:* Here Come the Tigers.
1978 (PG) 92m/C Richard Lincoln, Malachy McCourt, Sel Skolnick; *D:* Sean S. Cunningham. **VHS, Beta $69.98** *LIV, VES* ♂

Manon Tragic tale of a French woman condemned for her affair with a Resistance fighter. They flee to Paris, where her brother forces her into prostitution. Based on the novel "Manon Lescaut" by Abbe Antoine-Francois Prevost. In French, with English subtitles.
1950 91m/B Cecile Aubry, Michel Auclair, Serge Reggiani, Henri Vilbert, Daniel Ivernel; *D:* Henri-Georges Clouzot. **VHS $24.95** *NOS* ♂♂

Manon of the Spring In this excellent sequel to "Jean de Florette," the adult daughter of the dead hunchback, Jean, discovers who blocked up the spring on her father's land. She plots her revenge, which proves greater than she could ever imagine. Montand is astonishing. Based on a Marcel Pagnol novel. In French with English subtitles. *AKA:* Manon des Sources; Jean de Florette 2.
1987 (PG) 113m/C *FR* Yves Montand, Daniel Auteuil, Emmanuelle Beart, Hippolyte Girardot; *D:* Claude Berri. **VHS, Beta, LV $19.98** *ORI, APD, TAM* 🎜🎜🎜½

Manos, the Hands of Fate Family vacations in the lone star state and find themselves deep in the heart of a Satanic cult. More low concept fodder from erstwhile El Paso fertilizer salesman Warren.
1966 74m/C Tom Nayman, Diane Mahree, Hal P. Warren, John Reynolds; *W/D:* Hal P. Warren. **VHS $19.98** *SNC* 🎜

Manos Torpes A man who is left to die in the desert is rescued by someone who teaches him how to avenge his would-be killers.
1965 93m/C *MX* Peter Lee Lawrence, Alberto De Mendoza, Pilar Velasquez. **VHS, Beta $45.95** *MAD* 🎜🎜

Man's Best Friend Here is a collection of nine cartoons, featuring such lovable canines as Cuddles, Snoozer, Duffy Dog and Dizzy.
1964 51m/C VHS, Beta $14.95 *MCA, WTA* 🎜🎜

Man's Country A rip-roarin' western saga filled with the usual action and danger, as ranger Randall leads the fight against a band of nasties headed by Long, in a dual role as twin brothers.
1938 55m/B Jack Randall, Ralph Peters, Marjorie Reynolds, Walter Long; *D:* Robert Hill. **VHS, Beta $19.95** *NOS, DVT* 🎜🎜

Man's Favorite Sport? A slapstick comedy about a renowned fishing expert author who actually hates fishing, but is forced to compete in a major tournament by a romantically inclined publicity agent. Very funny in spots. Music by Henry Mancini.
1963 121m/C Rock Hudson, Paula Prentiss, Charlene Holt, Maria Perschy, John McGiver; *D:* Howard Hawks. **VHS, Beta $14.95** *MCA, CCB* 🎜🎜½

Man's Land A ranch needs savin', and Hoot's the guy to do it in this formulaic Gibson epic.
1932 65m/B Hoot Gibson, Marion Shilling, Skeeter Bill Robbins, Alan Bridge; *D:* Phil Rosen. **VHS, Beta** *UHV* 🎜½

Mansfield Park Fanny is an impoverished young woman, snubbed by society, who earns the respect and love of her cousin in a BBC mini-series adaptation of the Jane Austen classic set in 19th century England.
1985 261m/C *GB* Sylvestria Le Touzel, Bernard Hepton, Anna Massey, Donald Pleasence; *D:* David Giles. **VHS, Beta $29.98** *FOX, TVC, HMV* 🎜🎜½

The Manster Another masterpiece from the director who brought us "Monster from Green Hell." Womanizing, whiskey swilling American journalist receives mysterious injection from crazed scientist and sprouts unsightly hair and extra head. Although shot in the land of the rising sun, lips move in sync with dialogue. *AKA:* The Manster—Half Man, Half Monster; The Split.
1959 72m/B *JP* Peter Dyneley, Jane Hylton, Satoshi Nakamura, Terri Zimmern; *D:* Kenneth Crane. **VHS $19.98** *SNC, MRV* 🎜

Mantis in Lace A go-go dancer slaughters men while tripping on LSD. Cinematography by pre-"Easy Rider" Laslo Kovacs. Watch it for the "hep" dialogue. *AKA:* Lila.
1968 (R) 68m/C Susan Stewart, Steve Vincent, M.K. Evans, Vic Lance, Pat Barrington, Janu Wine, Stuart Lancaster, John Carrol, Judith Crane, Cheryl Trepton; *D:* William Rotsler. **VHS** *NO* 🎜½

Mantrap Early silent success by Fleming, who later directed "Gone with the Wind" and "The Wizard of Oz." Fabled flapper Bow tempts a lawyer on retreat in the woods.
1926 66m/B Clara Bow, Ernest Torrence, Percy Marmont, Eugene Pallette, Tom Kennedy; *D:* Victor Fleming. **VHS, Beta $19.95** *GPV, FCT* 🎜🎜

The Manxman Hitchcock's last silent film, a romantic melodrama about ambition and infidelity on the Isle of Man.
1929 129m/B *GB* Carl Brisson, Anny Ondra; *D:* Alfred Hitchcock. **VHS, Beta $49.95** *VYY, MRV, MLB* 🎜🎜½

Many Faces of Sherlock Holmes A documentary look at the various incarnations of the famous sleuth from A. Conan Doyle's stories to various film portrayals.
1986 58m/C Christopher Plummer, Basil Rathbone, Christopher Lee. **VHS, Beta $79.95** *PSM* 🎜🎜½

Many Wonder A wealthy woman is pursued by three men...at the same time! Will one of them turn out to be Mr. Right?
1989 40m/C *D:* Craig Lowy. **VHS $59.95** *CIG* 🎜½

Map of the Human Heart Thirty-year saga told in flashback. Young Eskimo Avik (Lee) and his Metis love interest Albertine (Parillaud) struggle with racism in a white world. They meet and become friends as children in a Montreal hospital where both are being treated. Their cross-cultural relationship is not approved of and, consequently, they are separated, leaving Avik only a chest X-ray with which to remember Albertine. Years later, the pair meet up in Dresden where Avik finds that his love is engaged to his once close friend, denying her heritage and living in the white world that he has for so long been fighting. Mediocre movie with extraordinary Arctic scenery.
1993 (R) 109m/C Jason Scott Lee, Anne Parillaud, Patrick Bergin, Robert Joamie, Annie Galipeau, John Cusack, Jeanne Moreau; *D:* Vincent Ward; *W:* Vincent Ward, Louis Nowra. **VHS** *HBO* 🎜🎜

Marat/Sade A theatrical production presented by patients at a mental institution is directed by the Marquis de Sade. Well directed and visually effective, featuring Jackson's first film performance. Based on a play by Peter Weiss. Some theaters were forced to add extensions to the marquee when the film was first released. *AKA:* Persecution and Assassination of Jean-Paul Marat as Performed by the Inmates of the Asylum of Charenton Under the Direction of the Marquis De Sade.
1966 (R) 115m/C *GB* Patrick Magee, Clifford Rose, Glenda Jackson, Ian Richardson, Brenda Kempner, Ruth Baker, Michael Williams; *D:* Peter Brook. **VHS, LV $34.95** *WBF, MGM, LUM* 🎜🎜🎜

Marathon When a middle-aged jogger's ego gets a boost through the attention of a beautiful young woman, he takes up marathon running. Light comedy. Made for television.
1980 100m/C Bob Newhart, Leigh Taylor-Young, Herb Edelman, Dick Gautier, Anita Gillette, John Hillerman; *D:* Jackie Cooper. **VHS $59.95** *LIV* 🎜🎜

Marathon Man Nightmarish chase-thriller in which a graduate student becomes entangled in a plot involving a murderous Nazi fugitive. As student Hoffman is preparing for the Olympic marathon, he is reunited with his secret-agent brother, setting the intricate plot in motion. Courtesy of his brother, Hoffman becomes involved with Olivier, an old crazed Nazi seeking jewels taken from concentration camp victims. Nonstop action throughout, including a torture scene sure to set your teeth on edge. William Goldman adapted the screenplay from his novel.
1976 (R) 125m/C Dustin Hoffman, Laurence Olivier, Marthe Keller, Roy Scheider, William Devane, Fritz Weaver; *D:* John Schlesinger. Academy Awards '76 Nominations: Best Supporting Actor (Olivier); Golden Globe Awards '77: Best Supporting Actor (Olivier). **VHS, Beta, LV $24.95** *PAR* 🎜🎜🎜

Marauder The prince of Venice leads a sea-faring onslaught against ransacking pirates and enemy fleets.
1965 90m/C *IT* Gordon Scott, Maria Canale, Franca Bettoya; *D:* Luigi Capuano. **VHS, Beta** *NO* 🎜🎜

Marbella A luxury resort in Spain is the setting for a big caper heist of three million dollars from a monarchical tycoon.
1985 96m/C Rod Taylor, Britt Ekland; *D:* Miguel Hermoso. **VHS, Beta $29.98** *LIV* 🎜½

Marcados por el Destino Three Mexicans come into America looking for a better life, but they don't find it.
1987 95m/C *MX* Julio Aleman, Roberto "Flaco" Guzman, Alma Murillo. **VHS, Beta $77.95** *MAD* 🎜🎜½

March of the Wooden Soldiers The classic Mother Goose tale about the secret life of Christmas toys, with Laurel and Hardy as Santa's helpers who must save Toyland from the wicked Barnaby. A Yuletide "must see." Also available in a colorized version. *AKA:* Babes in Toyland.
1934 73m/B Stan Laurel, Oliver Hardy, Charlotte Henry, Henry Kleinbach (Brandon), Felix Knight, Jean Darling, Johnny Downs, Marie Wilson; *D:* Charles "Buddy" Rogers, Gus Meins. **VHS, LV $29.95** *NOS, GKK, IME* 🎜🎜🎜

March or Die Great potential, unrealized. An American joins the French Foreign Legion during World War I after his dismissal from West Point. Following the brutality of training, he is assigned to guard an archeological expedition in Morocco, where he pulls together a rag-tag outfit for the mission. Hackman proves once again the wide range of his acting abilities, surmounting the cliched and fairly sadistic plot. Shot on location in the Sahara Desert.
1977 (PG) 104m/C *GB* Gene Hackman, Terence Hill, Max von Sydow, Catherine Deneuve, Ian Holm; *D:* Dick Richards. **VHS** *FOX* 🎜🎜½

Marciano A made-for-television version of the great boxer's life. Average fight movie.
1979 97m/C Tony LoBianco, Vincent Gardenia; *D:* Bernard L. Kowalski. **VHS, Beta $9.98** *SUE, NLC* 🎜🎜

Marco Entertaining musical adventure of Marco Polo's life casts Arnaz as Marco Polo and Mostel as Kublai Khan. A couple of cutups, right? One of the first films to combine animation with live action. Shot partially on location in the Orient. 🎜By Damn; Walls; A Family Man; Spaghetti.
1973 109m/C Desi Arnaz Jr., Zero Mostel, Jack Weston, Cie Cie Win; *D:* Seymour Robbie. **VHS, Beta $49.95** *PSM* 🎜🎜

Marco Polo, Jr. Marco Polo, Jr., the daring descendant of the legendary explorer, travels the world in search of his destiny in this song-filled, feature-length, but poorly animated, fantasy.
1972 82m/C **D:** Eric Porter; **V:** Bobby Rydell. VHS, Beta $24.95 *FHE, WTA* ♂

Mardi Gras for the Devil Black magic and the occult combine as a New Orleans cop tries to catch a killer who strikes only at Mardi Gras. The cop's got his work cut out for him since the killer is no mere mortal but a demon who believes in human sacrifice.
1993 (R) 95m/C Robert Davi, Michael Ironside, Lesley-Anne Down, Lydie Denier, Mike Starr, Margaret Avery, John Amos; **W/D:** David A. Prior. VHS, Beta $89.95 *PSM* ♂♂

Mardi Gras Massacre Aztec priest arrives in New Orleans during Mardi Gras to revive the blood ritual of human sacrifice to an Aztec god. A police detective relentlessly pursues him. Much gore and gut-slicing, with no redeeming social value. **AKA:** Crypt of Dark Secrets.
1978 92m/C Curt Dawson, Gwen Arment, Wayne Mack, Laura Misch; **D:** Jack Weis. VHS, Beta $49.95 *VHE* Woof!

Margin for Murder Mike Hammer investigates a mysterious accident that killed his best friend. Made for television. **AKA:** Mickey Spillane's Margin for Murder.
1981 98m/C Kevin Dobson, Cindy Pickett, Donna Dixon, Charles Hallahan; **D:** Daniel Haller. VHS, Beta $59.95 *PSM* ♂♂

Maria A young man returns to his hometown to rekindle a romance with his childhood sweetheart. **AKA:** Marie.
1971 102m/C *MX* Fernando Allende, Taryn Power, Alicia Caro, Jose Suarez; **D:** Tito Davison. VHS, Beta $67.45 *MAD* ♂♂

Maria and Mirabella Two little girls rescue their friend KiKi the Frog in this action adventure. Combines animation with live action techniques.
1990 60m/C VHS $9.95 *AIP* ♂♂

Maria Candelaria Society rejects a woman because people don't like her mother. (She posed nude for an artist, and the town responds by stoning her to death, proving that going against small-town morals can be lethal). Eventually, time and circumstance push daughter onto mother's path in this tragic soaper. Del Rio portrays the scorned young woman, although she was 40 years old. **AKA:** Portrait of Maria; Xochimilco.
1946 96m/B *MX* Dolores Del Rio, Pedro Armendariz Jr., Margarita Cortes; **D:** Emilio Fernandez. VHS, Beta $44.95 *MAD, AUD* ♂♂

Maria Chapdelaine An early film from the renowned French director, in which a brutish trapper and a sophisticated battle for the love of a girl in the Canadian wilderness. English subtitles. Remade in 1984.
1934 75m/B *FR* Jean Gabin, Jean-Pierre Aumont, Madeleine Renaud; **D:** Julien Duvivier. VHS, Beta $44.95 *HHT* ♂♂♂

Maria Chapdelaine Around the turn of the century, a young girl in the Northern Canadian wilderness endures a year of passion, doomed love, and tragedy. In French with subtitles. Remake of a 1935 French film.
1984 108m/C *FR CA* Nick Mancuso, Carole Laure, Claude Rich, Pierre Curzi; **D:** Gilles Carle. VHS, Beta $59.95 *MED* ♂♂½

Mariachis Mexican folklore and music are included in this Western.

1949 90m/B *MX* Antonio Badu, Isobel Del Puerto, Fernando Casanova, Beatriz Aguirre, Jose Angel ''Ferrusquilla'' Espinosa; **D:** Adolfo Fernandez Bustamante. VHS, Beta $54.95 *MAD* ♂♂

Marianela A disfigured peasant girl cares for a blind man, and the two fall in love. She doesn't tell him about her appearance until the day comes that he regains his sight. In Spanish.
1972 113m/C *SP* Pierre Orcel, Rocio Durcal; **D:** Angelino Fons. VHS, Beta *MED* ♂♂½

Maria's Child Light comedy about a dancer who becomes pregnant and must decide whether or not to keep the baby. When her live-in boyfriend (not the father) admits he cheated on her, she kicks him out. Unable to make up her mind, she imagines a dialogue with the fetus. Second of a trilogy by British television screenwriter Malcolm McKay on the subject of forgiveness.
1993 97m/C *GB* Yolanda Vasquez, David O'Hara, Fiona Shaw, Alec McCowen, Sophie Okenado, Linda Davidson, Rudi Davies, Nicholas Woodeson, Anita Zagaria; **D:** Malcolm McKay; **W:** Malcolm McKay; **M:** Philip Appleby. VHS *NYR* ♂♂½

Maria's Day Chronicles the plague-riddled downfall of a formerly aristocratic and wealthy Hungarian family in the years following the failed 1849 Revolution. In Hungarian with English subtitles.
1984 113m/C **D:** Judit Elek. VHS, Beta $59.95 *FCT, AUD* ♂♂♂

Maria's Lovers The wife (Kinski) of an impotent WWII veteran (Savage) succumbs to the charms of a rakish lady-killer (Spano). Savage turns to the charms of an older woman, finds love again with Kinski, but is still impotent; she gets pregnant by a wandering minstrel (Carradine) and on we go to film climax. Offbeat and uneven, representing Russian director Konchalovsky's first American film and one of Kinski's better roles.
1984 (R) 103m/C Nastassia Kinski, John Savage, Robert Mitchum, Keith Carradine, Anita Morris, Bud Cort, Karen Young, Tracy Nelson, John Goodman, Vincent Spano; **D:** Andrei Konchalovsky. VHS, Beta $14.95 *MGM* ♂♂½

Maricela Young Maricela Flores and her mother have come to the U.S. from El Salvador to escape the fighting. Living with a Southern Californian family, Maricela has a hard time adjusting to American life and, in particular, dealing with prejudice. An entry in the PBS ''Wonderworks'' series.
1988 55m/C Linda Lavin, Carlina Cruz. VHS $29.95 *PME, HMV, BTV* ♂♂½

Marie In this true story, a divorced (and battered) mother works her way through school and the system to become the first woman to head the Parole Board in Tennessee. Finding rampant corruption, she blows the whistle on her bosses, who put her life in jeopardy. Spacek gives a powerful performance, as does first-time actor Thompson, portraying himself as the abused woman's attorney. Based on the book by Peter Maas.
1985 (PG-13) 113m/C Sissy Spacek, Jeff Daniels, Keith Szarabajka, John Cullum, Morgan Freeman, Fred Dalton Thompson, Don Hood; **D:** Roger Donaldson. VHS, Beta $79.95 *MGM* ♂♂♂

Marie Antoinette An elephantine costume drama chronicling the French queen's life from princesshood to her final days before the Revolution. A Shearer festival all the way, and a late example of MGM's overstuffed period style and star-power. Overlong, but engrossing for the wrong reasons. Morley, in his first film, plays Louis XVI. Power's only MGM loan-out casts him as a

Swedish count and Marie's romantic dalliance. Based on a book by Stephan Zweig, with script assistance from (among others) F. Scott Fitzgerald.
1938 160m/B Norma Shearer, Tyrone Power, John Barrymore, Robert Morley, Gladys George, Anita Louise, Joseph Schildkraut, Henry Stephenson, Reginald Gardiner, Peter Bull, Albert Dekker, Joseph Calleia, George Zucco, Cora Witherspoon, Barry Fitzgerald, Mae Busch, Harry Davenport; **D:** Woodbridge S. Van Dyke. VHS, Beta, LV $19.98 *MGM, PIA* ♂♂½

Marie Galante Fine spy drama has Tracy running into Gallien in Panama (years earlier she had been left there after a kidnapping). He finds her most helpful in his attempt to thwart the bombing of the Panama Canal. It's the performances that raise this otherwise standard thriller up a few notches.
1934 88m/B Spencer Tracy, Katie Galian, Ned Sparks, Helen Morgan, Sig Rumann, Leslie Fenton, Jay C. Flippen; **D:** Henry King. VHS, Beta $16.95 *NOS, SNC, HEG* ♂♂♂

Marihuana An unintentionally hilarious, ''Reefer Madness''-type cautionary film about the exaggerated evils of pot smoking. A real dopey film favored by right-winger zealots. **AKA:** Marijuana: The Devil's Weed.
1936 57m/B Harley Wood, Hugh McArthur, Pat Carlyle; **D:** Dwain Esper. VHS, Beta $16.95 *SNC, VYY, HEG* ♂

Marilyn Rock Hudson narrates this documentary on the life of Marilyn Monroe.
1963 83m/B VHS, EJ *NO* ♂

Marilyn: The Untold Story Nominated for an Emmy, Hicks elevates what could easily have been a dull made-for-TV movie with her remarkable performance as Marilyn Monroe. Based on the book by Norman Mailor.
1980 156m/C Catherine Hicks, Richard Basehart, Frank Converse, John Ireland, Sheree North, Anne Ramsey, Viveca Lindfors, Jason Miller, Bill Vint; **D:** Jack Arnold, John Flynn, Lawrence Schiller. VHS *ABC* ♂♂♂

Marine Raiders Marines train and then fight at Guadalcanal. A typical flag-waver, watchable but not particularly engaging.
1943 90m/B Pat O'Brien, Robert Ryan, Ruth Hussey, Frank McHugh, Barton MacLane; **D:** Harold Schuster. VHS, Beta $19.98 *TTC* ♂♂

Marius This is the first of Marcel Pagnol's trilogy (''Fanny'' and ''Cesar'' followed), about the lives and adventures of the people of Provence, France. Marius is a young man who dreams of going away to sea. When he acts on those dreams, he leaves behind his girlfriend, Fanny. Realistic dialogue and vivid characterizations. Adapted by Pagnol from his play. The musical play and film ''Fanny'' (1961) were adapted from this trilogy.
1931 125m/B *FR* Raimu, Pierre Fresnay, Charpin, Orane Demazis; **D:** Alexander Korda. VHS, Beta, LV $24.95 *NOS, MRV, INT* ♂♂♂♂

Marjoe Documentary follows the career of rock-style evangelist Marjoe Gortner, who spent 25 years of his life touring the country as a professional preacher. Marjoe later went on to become an actor and professional fundraiser.
1972 (PG) 88m/C Marjoe Gortner; **D:** Howard Smith, Sarah Kernochan. VHS, Beta $59.95 *COL* ♂♂♂♂

Marjorie Morningstar A temperate Hollywood adaptation of the Herman Wouk story of a young actress who fails to achieve stardom and settles on being a housewife. Wood slipped a bit on this story.
1958 123m/C Natalie Wood, Gene Kelly, Martin Balsam, Claire Trevor, Ed Wynn, Everett Sloane, Carolyn Jones; **D:** Irving Rapper. VHS $14.98 *REP* ♂♂

The Mark Story of a convicted child molester who cannot escape his past upon his release from prison. Whitman gives a riveting performance as the convict.
1961 127m/B *GB* Stuart Whitman, Maria Schell, Rod Steiger, Brenda de Banzie, Maurice Denham, Donald Wolfit, Paul Rogers, Donald Houston; *D:* Guy Green. **VHS, Beta** *VTR* ♂♂♂½

Mark of Cain Twin brothers, one normal, the other a raving lunatic with murderous tendencies, confuse the authorities who imprison the nice guy, allowing the nutcase to chase after his beautiful sister-in-law.
1984 90m/C Robin Ward, Wendy Crewson, August Schellenberg; *D:* Bruce Pittman. **VHS, Beta** $69.98 *LIV, VES* ♂♂½

Mark of the Beast Two students inadvertently videotape an assassination, and are then relentlessly pursued by the killer.
19?? 90m/C James Gordon, Carolyn Guillet, David Smulker; *D:* Robert Stewart. **VHS** *NO* ♂

Mark of the Devil Witchcraft and romance don't mix, as a Medieval witch hunter and a sexy girl accused of witchery discover. Notoriously graphic torture scenes add to the mayhem but the weird part is that this is based on true stories. *AKA:* Burn, Witch, Burn; Brenn; Hexe, Brenn.
1969 (R) 96m/C *GB GE* Herbert Lom, Olivera Vuco, Udo Kier, Reggie Nalder, Herbert Fux, Michael Maien, Ingeborg Schoener, Johannes Buzalski, Gaby Fuchs; *D:* Michael Armstrong. **VHS, Beta** $69.98 *VES, LIV, VDM* ♂

Mark of the Devil 2 Sadistic witch-hunters torture satan's servants and torch sisters of mercy, whilst trying to horn in on a nobleman's fortune. It's just not as gross without the vomit bags.
1972 (R) 90m/C *GB GE* Erika Blanc, Anton Diffring, Reggie Nalder; *D:* Adrian Hoven. **VHS** $29.98 *VDM* ♂

The Mark of the Hawk A uniquely told story of African nations struggling to achieve racial equality after gaining independence. Songs include "This Man Is Mine," sung by Kitt. *AKA:* The Accused.
1957 83m/C *GB* Sidney Poitier, Eartha Kitt, Juano Hernandez, John McIntire; *D:* Michael Audley. **VHS, Special order formats** *MRV* ♂♂♂

Mark of the Scorpion A gang member is placed in peril when he pilfers a ruby ring from a perished princess.
1990 90m/C Mahamed Attifi. **VHS, Beta** *IMP* ♂

Mark of the Spur A cowboy must find out who left a mysterious spur mark on his horse.
1932 60m/B Bob Custer, Lillian Rich, Franklin Farnum, Bud Osborne; *D:* J.P. McGowan. **VHS, Beta** $19.95 *NOS, DVT* ♂½

Mark of the Vampire A murder in a small town is solved through the use of vaudeville actors who pose as vampires. Great cast, surprise ending.
1935 61m/B Lionel Barrymore, Bela Lugosi, Elizabeth Allan; *D:* Tod Browning. **VHS, Beta** $19.95 *MGM, MLB* ♂♂♂

Mark of Zorro Fairbanks plays a dual role as the hapless Don Diego and his dashing counterpart, Zorro, the hero of the oppressed. Silent film.
1920 80m/B Douglas Fairbanks Sr., Marguerite de la Motte, Noah Beery Sr.; *D:* Fred Niblo. **VHS, LV, 3/4U, Special order formats** $19.95 *REP, MRV, GPV* ♂♂♂

The Mark of Zorro The dashing Power swashbuckles his way through this wonderfully acted and directed romp. He plays the foppish son of a 19th-century California aristocrat who is secretly the masked aven-ger of the oppressed peons. Bromberg plays the wicked governor, with the beautiful niece (Darnell) beloved by Power, and Rathbone is supremely evil as his cruel minion. Lots of swordplay with a particularly exciting duel to the death between Rathbone and Power. Based on the novel "The Curse of Capistra-no" by Johnston McCulley. Remake of the 1921 silent film and followed by a number of other Zorro incarnations.
1940 93m/B Tyrone Power, Linda Darnell, Basil Rathbone, Gale Sondergaard, Eugene Pallette, J. Edward Bromberg, Montagu Love, Janet Beecher; *D:* Rouben Mamoulian; *W:* John Taintor Foote; *M:* Alfred Newman. **VHS** $19.98 *FXV* ♂♂♂½

Mark Twain and Me Robards portrays the aging and irascible Mark Twain, attended by a neglected but devoted daughter, and befriended by a young girl, as they travel on the same ship. Based on a true story.
1991 93m/C Jason Robards Jr., Talia Shire, Amy Stewart. **VHS** $19.99 *DIS, BTV* ♂♂½

Mark Twain's A Connecticut Yankee in King Arthur's Court A man from Connecticut falls asleep and finds himself in King Arthur's Court.
1978 60m/C Richard Basehart, Roscoe Lee Browne, Paul Rudd. **VHS, Beta, LV** $64.95 *MAS* ♂♂½

Marked for Death Having killed a prostitute, DEA agent Seagal decides it's time to roll out the white picket fence in the 'burbs with the little woman and brood. Trouble is, a bunch of guys with dreadlocks don't approve of his early retirement, and the Jamaican gangsters plan to send him and his family to the great Rasta playground in the sky. Whereupon the Stevester kicks and punches and wags his ponytail. Much blood flows, mon. Tunes by Jimmy Cliff. *AKA:* Screwface.
1990 (R) 93m/C Steven Seagal, Joanna Pacula, Basil Wallace, Keith David, Tom Wright, Danielle Harris, Arlen Dean Snyder, Teri Weigel; *D:* Dwight Little. **VHS, LV** $14.98 *FXV, CCB* ♂½

Marked for Murder Another in the Texas Ranger series. In this entry, the Rangers come to the rescue when a rancher war appears inevitable.
1945 58m/B Tex Ritter, Dave O'Brien, Guy Wilkerson; *W/D:* Elmer Clifton. **VHS, LV** $79.95 *VMK* ♂½

Marked for Murder Two TV station employees are framed for murder after being sent out to find a missing videocassette. Renee Estevez is part of the Sheen/Estevez dynasty.
1989 (R) 88m/C Renee Estevez, Wings Hauser, Jim Mitchum, Ross Hagen, Ken Abraham; *D:* Rick Sloane. **VHS, Beta** $79.95 *VMK* ♂½

Marked Money Amiable captain takes in boy who'll soon roll in the dough and swindlers show up on the scene. The captain's courageous girl and her pilot beau step in to right the rookery.
1928 61m/B Frank "Junior" Coghlan, George Duryea, Tom Kennedy, Bert Woodruff, Virginia Bradford, Maurice Black, Jack Richardson; *D:* Spencer Gordon Bennet. **VHS, Beta** $19.95 *GPV, FCT* ♂♂

Marked Trails One clue stamps out the guilty parties in this wild west saga.
1944 59m/B Hoot Gibson, Bob Steele. **VHS, Beta** $19.95 *NOS, DVT* ♂

Marked Woman Gangster drama about crusading District Attorney who persuades a group of clipjoint hostesses to testify against their gangster boss. A gritty studio melodrama loosely based on a true story.
1937 97m/B Bette Davis, Humphrey Bogart, Eduardo Ciannelli, Isabel Jewell, Jane Bryan, Mayo Methot, Allen Jenkins, Lola Lane; *D:* Lloyd Bacon. **VHS, Beta, LV** $19.95 *MGM* ♂♂♂

Marlon Brando Documentary recounting the life and career of Hollywood's most rebellious superstar.
1985 120m/C Marlon Brando; *D:* Claudio Masenza. **VHS, Beta** *KRT* ♂♂♂

Marlowe Updated telling by Stirling Silliphant of Chandler's "The Little Sister" sports retro guy Garner as Philip Marlowe, gumshoe. Hired by a mystery blonde to find her misplaced brother, rumpled sleuth Marlowe encounters kicking Bruce Lee in his first film. Slick looking, but the story's a bit slippery.
1969 (PG) 95m/C James Garner, Gayle Hunnicutt, Carroll O'Connor, Rita Moreno, Sharon Farrell, William Daniels, Bruce Lee; *D:* Paul Bogart. **VHS, Beta** $19.98 *MGM, FCT* ♂♂½

Marnie A lovely blonde with a mysterious past robs her employers and then changes her identity. When her current boss catches her in the act and forces her to marry him, he soon learns the puzzling aspects of Marnie's background. Criticized at the time of its release, the movie has since been accepted as a Hitchcock classic.
1964 130m/C Tippi Hedren, Sean Connery, Diane Baker, Bruce Dern; *D:* Alfred Hitchcock; *W:* Jay Presson Allen. **VHS, Beta, LV** $19.95 *MCA* ♂♂½

Maroc 7 Slow story of a secret agent after a thief suffering from a split personality.
1967 92m/C Gene Barry, Elsa Martinelli, Cyd Charisse, Leslie Phillips; *D:* Gerry O'Hara. **VHS** *PAR* ♂

Marooned Tense thriller casts Crenna, Hackman, and Franciscus as astronauts stranded in space after a retro-rocket misfires and their craft is unable to return to earth.
1969 (G) 134m/C Gregory Peck, David Janssen, Richard Crenna, James Franciscus, Gene Hackman, Lee Grant; *D:* John Sturges. Academy Awards '69: Best Visual Effects; Nominations: Best Cinematography, Best Sound. **VHS, Beta, LV** $9.95 *GKK* ♂♂

Marquis A bizarre satire combining sex, lust, and the French Revolution, based on the writings of the Marquis de Sade. Amusing, decadent, and not for the prudish. In French with English subtitles.
1990 88m/C *FR D:* Henri Xhonneux. **VHS** $59.95 *TAM* ♂

The Marquis de Sade's Justine Two sisters who have been abused in a convent are turned out. They each adapt to worldly life in different ways in this classic tale stretching the boundaries of human depravity.
19?? 90m/C Koo Stark, Martin Potter. **VHS, Beta** $79.95 *JEF* ♂♂

The Marriage Circle A pivotal silent comedy depicting the infidelity of several married couples in Vienna. Director Lubitsch's first American comedy. Remade as a musical, "One Hour With You," in 1932. Silent.
1924 90m/B Florence Vidor, Monte Blue, Marie Prevost, Creighton Hale, Adolphe Menjou, Harry Myers, Dale Fuller; *D:* Ernst Lubitsch. **VHS** $19.95 *NOS, MOV, VYY* ♂♂♂

Marriage is Alive and Well A wedding photographer reflects on the institution of marriage from his unique perspective. Made for television.

1980 100m/C Joe Namath, Jack Albertson, Melinda Dillon, Judd Hirsch, Susan Sullivan, Fred McCarren, Swoosie Kurtz; **D:** Russ Mayberry. **VHS** $59.95 *LIV* ⅋

Marriage Italian Style When an engaged man hears that his mistress is on her death bed, he goes to her side and, in an emotional gesture, promises to marry her if she survives. She does, and holds him to his promise. After they're married, however, she gives him a big surprise—three grown sons. A silly film, but DeSica's direction keeps it from being too fluffy. Lots of fun. Based on the play "Filumena Marturano" by Eduardo De Filippo.
1964 102m/C *IT* Sophia Loren, Marcello Mastroianni, Aldo Puglisi, Tecla Scarano, Marilu Tolo; **D:** Vittorio De Sica. Academy Awards '64 Nominations: Best Actress (Loren), Best Foreign Language Film; Golden Globe Awards '65: Best Foreign Film. **VHS** *STE* ⅋⅋⅋

The Marriage of Maria Braun In post-WWII Germany, a young woman uses guile and sexuality to survive as the nation rebuilds itself into an industrial power. The first movie in Fassbinder's trilogy about German women in Germany during the post war years, it is considered one of the director's finest films, and an indispensable example of the New German Cinema. In German with English subtitles. *AKA:* Die Ehe Der Maria Braun.
1979 (R) 120m/C *GE* Hanna Schygulla, Klaus Lowitsch, Ivan Desny; **D:** Rainer Werner Fassbinder. **VHS, Beta** $79.95 *NYF, COL, GLV* ⅋⅋⅋⅋

Married? Couple endures 365 days of marital bliss in order to inherit big bucks. Some do it for less.
1926 65m/B Owen Moore, Constance Bennett; **D:** George Terwilliger. **VHS, Beta** $24.95 *GPV, FCT* ⅋½

A Married Man Story focusing on a bored British lawyer who begins cheating on his wife. Amid the affair, someone gets murdered. Made for television.
1984 200m/C *GB* Anthony Hopkins, Ciaran Madden, Lise Hilboldt, Yvonne Coulette, John LeMocurier, Sophie Ashton; **D:** John Davies. **VHS, Beta** $69.95 *LIV* ⅋⅋

Married to It Three vastly different couples work together to plan a pageant at a private school. Struggling hippie leftovers Bridges and Channing quietly hope the rest of the world will just join hands and live in peace. '80s-era corporate cutthroats Shepherd and Silver shamelessly meddle with their troubled daughter's education. Starry-eyed newlyweds Masterson and Leonard grope for acceptance in the big city after being handicapped by a Norman Rockwell upbringing in Iowa. Contrived plot offers few humourous moments, with the main focus revolving around coping rather than comedy. And the coping is slow business, done by characters you don't care about with problems that don't matter.
1993 (R) 112m/C Beau Bridges, Stockard Channing, Robert Sean Leonard, Mary Stuart Masterson, Cybill Shepherd, Ron Silver; **D:** Arthur Hiller; **W:** Janet Kovalcik; **M:** Henry Mancini. **VHS** *NYR* ⅋⅋

Married to the Mob After the murder of her husband, an attractive Mafia widow tries to escape "mob" life, but ends up fighting off amorous advances from the current mob boss. A snappy script and a spry performance by Pfeiffer pepper this easily-watched film. Continued Demme's streak of great films that included "Silence of the Lambs."
1988 (R) 102m/C Michelle Pfeiffer, Dean Stockwell, Alec Baldwin, Matthew Modine, Mercedes Ruehl, Anthony J. Nici, Joan Cusack, Ellen Foley, Chris Isaak, Jonathan Demme; **D:** Jonathan Demme. **VHS, Beta, LV** $19.98 *ORI* ⅋⅋⅋

Married Too Young High school honeys elope, despite disapproval from the parental units. When the boy groom trades his med school plans for a monkey wrench in order to support the little missus, he finds much trouble with the hot rod heavies. *AKA:* I Married Too Young.
1962 76m/B Harold Lloyd Jr., Jana Lund, Anthony Dexter, Marianna Hill, Trudy Marshall, Brian O'Hara, Nita Loveless; **D:** George Moskov. **VHS** $59.98 *HHT, SNC* ⅋⅋

A Married Woman Dramatizes a day in the life of a woman who has both a husband and a lover. One of Godard's more mainstream efforts. *AKA:* La Femme Mariee.
1965 94m/B *FR* Macha Meril, Phillippe LeRoy, Bernard Noel; **D:** Jean-Luc Godard. **VHS, Beta, 8mm** $29.95 *NOS, MRV, DVT* ⅋⅋⅋

Marry Me, Marry Me While in Paris, a Jewish encyclopedia salesman falls in love with a pregnant Belgian woman. A sensitive story about European Jewish families. Berri wrote, produced, directed, and starred in this romantic comedy. *AKA:* Mazel Tov Ou le Mariage.
1969 (R) 87m/C *FR* Elisabeth Wiener, Regine, Claude Berri, Louisa Colpeyn; **D:** Claude Berri. **VHS** *LHV* ⅋⅋⅋

The Marrying Man Young man meets his match when his buddies take him to Las Vegas for his bachelor party. He falls like a ton of bricks for the singer, not knowing she belongs to the local crime lord, who catches them together and forces them to marry. They immediately get a divorce, but can't forget each other. They eventually re-marry, again and again and again. Silly story supposedly based on the story of Harry Karl (eventual husband of Debbie Reynolds) and Marie MacDonald. Although the off-stage romance between Basinger and Baldwin created quite a stir, none of the chemistry is captured here. Ineffective, not funny, poorly paced, not well acted. A good example of what happens when egotistical stars get their way.
1991 (R) 116m/C Alec Baldwin, Kim Basinger, Robert Loggia, Armand Assante, Elisabeth Shue, Paul Reiser, Fisher Stevens, Peter Dobson, Gretchen Wyler; **D:** Jerry Rees; **W:** Neil Simon. **VHS, LV** $19.99 *HPH* ⅋½

Mars Needs Women When the Martian singles scene starts to drag, Mars boys cross the galaxy in search of fertile earth babes to help them repopulate the planet. Seems Batgirl Craig, the go-go dancing lady scientist, is at the top of their dance cards.
1966 80m/C Tommy Kirk, Yvonne Craig; **W/D:** Larry Buchanan. **VHS** $19.98 *SNC* ⅋

Marshal of Cedar Rock Marshal Rocky Lane sets a prisoner free, thinking the guy will lead him to a stash of stolen bank funds. Seems he miscalculates, but by way of consolation, he routs a rotten railroad agent who's rooking innocent people. Features the equine talent of Black Star.
1953 54m/B Allan "Rocky" Lane, Phyllis Coates, Roy Barcroft, William Henry, Robert Shayne, Eddy Waller; **D:** Harry Keller. **VHS** $19.99 *HEG, DVT, NOS* ⅋⅋

Marshal of Heldorado An outlaw-infested town needs an injection of law and order.
1950 53m/B James Ellison, Russell Hayden, Raymond Hatton, Fuzzy Knight; **D:** Thomas Carr. **VHS** $19.95 *NOS, DVT* ⅋

The Marshal's Daughter A father and daughter team up to outwit an outlaw. Features many cowboy songs, including the title track by Tex Ritter.
1953 71m/B Tex Ritter, Ken Murray, Laurie Anders, Preston Foster, Hoot Gibson; **D:** William Berke. **VHS** $19.95 *NOS, MOV, HEG* ⅋½

Martial Law A film solely for martial arts fans. Two cops use their hands, feet, and other body parts to fight crime.
1990 90m/C Chad McQueen, Cynthia Rothrock, David Carradine, Andy McCutcheon; **D:** S.E. Cohen. **VHS** $89.98 *MED, FOX* ⅋½

Martial Law 2: Undercover Two cops, martial arts experts and part of an elite police force called Martial Law, go undercover to investigate the murder of a colleague. They uncover a fast-growing crime ring headed by a bad cop and a nightclub owner. The nightclub is host to the city's rich and powerful, who are treated to a bevy of beautiful women, protected by martial arts experts, and entertained by martial arts fights to the death. Lots of high-kicking action.
1991 (R) 92m/C Jeff Wincott, Cynthia Rothrock, Paul Johansson, Evan Lurie, L. Charles Taylor, Sherrie Rose, Billy Drago; **D:** Kurt Anderson; **W:** Richard Brando, Jiles Fitzgerald. **VHS, LV** $19.98 *MCA* ⅋½

Martial Monks of Shaolin Temple/Dragon Against Vampire Two full-length martial arts thrillers.
1983 171m/C **VHS, Beta** $7.00 *VTR* ⅋½

The Martian Chronicles: Part 1 Series episode "The Explorers." Adapted from Ray Bradbury's critically acclaimed novel. Futuristic explorations of the planet Mars. Strange fates of the discovery teams make everything more curious. Made for television.
1979 120m/C Rock Hudson, Bernie Casey, Nicholas Hammond, Darren McGavin; **D:** Michael Anderson Sr. **VHS, Beta** $14.95 *FRH* ⅋½

The Martian Chronicles: Part 2 Episode following the television movie. This part is called "The Settlers." The planet Mars meets with its first colonization and the settlers watch the Earth explode.
1979 97m/C Rock Hudson, Fritz Weaver, Roddy McDowall, Bernie Casey, Darren McGavin, Gayle Hunnicutt, Barry Morse, Bernadette Peters; **D:** Michael Anderson Sr. **VHS, Beta** $14.95 *FRH* ⅋½

The Martian Chronicles: Part 3 In the final chapter of this space saga, the Martian's secrets become known and will forever change man's destiny. Adapted from Ray Bradbury's classic novel; made-for-television.
1979 97m/C Rock Hudson, Bernadette Peters, Christopher Connelly, Fritz Weaver, Roddy McDowall, Bernie Casey, Nicholas Hammond, Darren McGavin, Gayle Hunnicutt, Barry Morse; **D:** Michael Anderson Sr. **VHS, Beta** $14.95 *FRH* ⅋⅋½

Martians Go Home! Joke-loving Martians come to earth and pester a nerdy composer.
1990 (PG-13) 89m/C Randy Quaid, Margaret Colin, Anita Morris, John Philbin, Ronny Cox, Gerrit Graham, Barry Sobel, Vic Dunlop; **D:** David Odell. **VHS, Beta, LV** $9.99 *CCB, IVE* ⅋½

Martin Martin is a charming young man, though slightly mad. He freely admits of the need to drink blood. Contemporary vampire has found a new abhorrent means of killing his victims.
1977 (R) 96m/C John Amplas, Lincoln Maazel; **D:** George A. Romero. **VHS, Beta, LV** $19.99 *HBO* ⅋⅋⅋

Martin Luther French-made biography of the 16th century reformer who began the Protestant Reformation.
1953 105m/B **FR** Niall MacGinnis, John Ruddock, Pierre Leeavre, Guy Verney. **VHS, Beta** $19.95 *NOS, UHV, VGD* 🎞️🎞️½

Martin's Day An unusual friendship develops between an escaped convict and the young boy he kidnaps.
1985 (PG) 99m/C **CA** Richard Harris, Lindsay Wagner, James Coburn, Justin Henry, Karen Black, John Ireland; **D:** Alan Gibson. **VHS, Beta** $14.95 *MGM, FOX* 🎞️🎞️

Marty The empty life of a Bronx butcher is forever altered when he meets an equally lonely young woman. The original television version of the famous story, later filmed in 1955, starring Ernest Borgnine. Written by Paddy Chayefsky.
1953 58m/B Rod Steiger, Nancy Marchand; **D:** Delbert Mann; **W:** Paddy Chayefsky. **VHS, Beta** *NO* 🎞️🎞️

Marty Marty is a painfully shy bachelor who feels trapped in a pointless life of family squabbles. When he finds love, he also finds the strength to break out of what he feels is a meaningless existence. A sensitive and poignant film; written by Paddy Chayefsky, who went on to script new territory in "Altered States." Remake of a television version that originally aired in 1953. Notable for Borgnine's sensitive portrayal, one of his last quality jobs before sinking into the B-Movie sludge Pit.
1955 91m/B Ernest Borgnine, Betsy Blair, Joe De Santis, Ester Minciotti, Jerry Paris, Karen Steele; **D:** Delbert Mann; **W:** Paddy Chayefsky. Academy Awards '55: Best Actor (Borgnine), Best Director (Mann), Best Picture, Best Screenplay; Nominations: Best Art Direction/Set Decoration (B & W), Best Black and White Cinematography, Best Supporting Actor (Mantell), Best Supporting Actress (Blair); British Academy Awards '55: Best Actor (Borgnine), Best Actress (Blair); Golden Globe Awards '56: Best Actor—Drama (Borgnine); National Board of Review Awards '55: 10 Best Films of the Year, Best Actor (Borgnine). **VHS, Beta, LV** $19.98 *MGM, FOX, BTV* 🎞️🎞️🎞️

Marvelous Stunts of Kung Fu Beautiful woman, fortune teller, and martial arts hero team up to seek vengeance against the evil empire.
1983 86m/C Ling Yun, Wei Ping Line, Lung Fei. **VHS, Beta** $39.95 *TWE* 🎞️

Marvin & Tige A deep friendship develops between an aging alcoholic and a streetwise 11-year-old boy after they meet one night in an Atlanta park.
1984 (PG) 104m/C John Cassavetes, Gibran Brown, Billy Dee Williams, Fay Hauser, Denise Nicholas-Hill; **D:** Eric Weston. **VHS, Beta** $24.98 *SUE* 🎞️🎞️½

The Marx Brothers in a Nutshell A tribute to the Marx Brothers, narrated by Gene Kelly. Contains clips from "Duck Soup," "Horse Feathers," "Animal Crackers," "Cocoanuts," and "Room Service." Also contains rare outakes and interviews with the brothers, plus guest appearances by Dick Cavett, Robert Klein, David Steinberg, and others. Indispensible.
1990 100m/B Groucho Marx, Chico Marx, Harpo Marx, Zeppo Marx, Robert Klein, David Steinberg, George Fenneman, Dick Cavett. **VHS, LV** $19.98 *FCT* 🎞️🎞️🎞️

Mary and Joseph: A Story of Faith A speculative look at the experiences and courtship of Mary and Joseph before the birth of Jesus. Made for television.
1979 100m/C Blanche Baker, Jeff East, Colleen Dewhurst, Stephen McHattie, Lloyd Bochner, Paul Hecht; **D:** Eric Till. **VHS, Beta** $59.95 *LIV* 🎞️

Mary, Mary, Bloody Mary Young beautiful artist ravages Mexico with her penchant for drinking blood. Turns out she's a bisexual vampire. When even her friends become victims, her father steps in to end the bloodbath.
1976 (R) 85m/C Christina Ferrare, David Young, Helena Rojo, John Carradine; **D:** Carlos Lopez Moctezuma. **VHS, Beta** *NO* 🎞️

Mary of Scotland The historical tragedy of Mary, Queen of Scots and her cousin, Queen Elizabeth I of England is enacted in this classic film. Traces Mary's claims to the throne of England which ultimately led to her execution. Based on the Maxwell Anderson play.
1936 123m/B Katharine Hepburn, Fredric March, Florence Eldridge, Douglas Walton, John Carradine, Robert Barratt, Gavin Muir, Ian Keith, Moroni Olsen, William Stack, Alan Mowbray; **D:** John Ford. **VHS, Beta, LV** *RKO, TTC* 🎞️🎞️🎞️

Mary Poppins A magical English nanny arrives one day on the East Wind and takes over the household of a very proper London banker. She introduces her two charges to her friends and family, including Bert, the chimney sweep (Van Dyke), and eccentric Uncle Albert (Wynn). She also changes the lives of everyone in the family. From her they learn that life can always be happy and joyous if you take the proper perspective. Film debut of Andrews. Based on the books by P.L. Travers. A Disney classic that hasn't lost any of its magic. 🎵Chim Chim Cheree; A Spoonful of Sugar; The Perfect Nanny; Sister Suffragette; The Life I Lead; Stay Awake; Feed the Birds; Fidelity Feduciary Bank; Let's Go Fly a Kite; Jolly Holliday; I Love to Laugh; Step in Time; A Man Has Dreams; Supercalifragilisticexpialidocious.
1964 139m/C Ed Wynn, Hermione Baddeley, Julie Andrews, Dick Van Dyke, David Tomlinson, Glynis Johns; **D:** Robert Stevenson. Academy Awards '64: Best Actress (Andrews), Best Film Editing, Best Song ("Chim Chim Cher-ee"), Best Visual Effects, Best Score; Nominations: Best Adapted Screenplay, Best Art Direction/Set Decoration (Color), Best Color Cinematography, Best Costume Design (Color), Best Director (Stevenson), Best Picture, Best Sound, Best Original Score; Golden Globe Awards '65: Best Actress—Musical/Comedy (Andrews). **VHS, Beta, LV** $24.99 *DIS, APD, BTV* 🎞️🎞️½

Mary White The true story of Mary White, the sixteen-year-old daughter of a newspaper editor who rejects her life of wealth and sets out to find her own identity.
1977 102m/C Ed Flanders, Kathleen Beller, Tim Matheson, Donald Moffatt, Fionnula Flanagan; **D:** Judd Taylor. **VHS, Beta** $29.95 *PAR* 🎞️🎞️

Masada Based on Ernest K. Gann's novel "The Antagonists," this dramatization recreates the first-century A.D. Roman siege of the fortress Masada, headquarters for a group of Jewish freedom fighters. Abridged from the original television presentation.
1981 131m/C Peter O'Toole, Peter Strauss, Barbara Carrera, Anthony Quayle, Giulia Pagano, David Warner; **D:** Boris Sagal; **M:** Jerry Goldsmith. **VHS, Beta** $59.95 *MCA* 🎞️🎞️🎞️

Mascara A group inspecting a transvestite's death are led into the seedy underground world of Belgian nightlife.
1987 (R) 99m/C **BE** Derek De Lint, Charlotte Rampling, Michael Sarrazin; **D:** Patrick Conrad. **VHS, Beta** $79.95 *WAR* 🎞️🎞️

Masculine Feminine A young Parisian just out of the Army engages in some anarchistic activities when he has an affair with a radical woman singer. Hailed as one of the best French New Wave films. In French with English subtitles. **AKA:** Masculin Feminin.
1966 103m/B **FR** Jean-Pierre Leaud, Chantal Goya, Marlene Jobert; **D:** Jean-Luc Godard. **VHS, Beta** $69.95 *NYF, DVT, VDM* 🎞️🎞️🎞️½

M*A*S*H Hilarious, irreverent, and well-cast black comedy about a group of surgeons and nurses at a Mobile Army Surgical Hospital in Korea. The horror of war is set in counterpoint to their need to create havoc with episodic late-night parties, practical jokes, and sexual antics. An all-out anti-war festival, highlighted by scenes that starkly uncover the chaos and irony of war. Altman establishes his influential style here, using the deliberate fragmentation of images and overlapping of sound and dialogue. Ring Lardner, Jr., won an Oscar for his screenplay, loosely adapted from the novel by the pseudonymous Richard Hooker. Subsequent hit TV series moved even further from the source novel.
1970 (R) 116m/C Donald Sutherland, Elliott Gould, Tom Skerritt, Sally Kellerman, JoAnn Pflug, Robert Duvall, Rene Auberjonois, Roger Bowen, Gary Burghoff, Fred Williamson, John Schuck, Bud Cort, G. Wood; **D:** Robert Altman; **W:** Ring Lardner Jr. Academy Awards '70: Best Adapted Screenplay; Nominations: Best Director (Altman), Best Film Editing, Best Picture, Best Supporting Actress (Kellerman); Cannes Film Festival '70: Best Film; Golden Globe Awards '71: Best Film—Musical/Comedy. **VHS, Beta, LV** $19.98 *FOX* 🎞️🎞️🎞️🎞️

M*A*S*H: Goodbye, Farewell & Amen The final two-hour special episode of the television series "M*A*S*H" follows Hawkeye, B.J., Colonel Potter, Charles, Margaret, Klinger, Father Mulcahy, and the rest of the men and women of the 4077th through the last days of the Korean War, the declaration of peace, the dismantling of the camp, and the fond and tearful farewells.
1983 120m/C Alan Alda, Mike Farrell, Harry Morgan, David Ogden Stiers, Loretta Swit, Jamie Farr, William Christopher. **VHS, Beta, LV** *FOX, OM* 🎞️🎞️🎞️½

The Mask A deservedly obscure gory horror film about a masked killer, filmed mostly in 3-D. With special 3-D packaging and limited edition 3-D glasses. **AKA:** Eyes of Hell; The Spooky Movie Show.
1961 85m/B **CA** Paul Stevens, Claudette Nevins, Bill Walker, Anne Collings, Martin Lavut; **D:** Julian Roffman. **VHS, Beta, LV** $12.95 *RHI, MLB* 🎞️🎞️

Mask A dramatization of the true story of a young boy afflicted with craniodiaphyseal dysplasia (Elephantitis). The boy overcomes his appearance and revels in the joys of life in the California bikers' community. Well acted, particularly the performances of Stoltz and Cher. A touching film, well-directed by Bogdanovich, that only occasionally slips into maudlin territory.
1985 (PG-13) 120m/C Cher, Sam Elliott, Eric Stoltz, Estelle Getty, Richard Dysart, Laura Dern, Harry Carey Jr., Lawrence Monoson, Marsha Warfield, Barry Tubb, Andrew Robinson; **D:** Peter Bogdanovich. **VHS, Beta, LV** $19.95 *MCA* 🎞️🎞️🎞️

The Mask of Dijon A mad magician suspects that his wife is cheating on him and tries to hypnotize her into killing her supposed paramour. The plan goes awry when the wife uses a gun loaded with blanks. Von Stroheim's performance makes it worthwhile.
1946 73m/B Erich von Stroheim, Jeanne Bates, Willaim Wright, Edward Van Sloan, Denise Vernac; **D:** Lew Landers. **VHS** $19.95 *NOS* 🎞️🎞️½

The Mask of Fu Manchu The evil Dr. Fu Manchu and his equally evil daughter set out to capture the scimitar and golden mask of Genghis Khan. With them, they will be able to destroy all white men and rule the world. Although a detective from Scotland Yard tries to stop them, the pair obtain the treasures and begin sadistically torturing their victims to death. Can they be stopped before they destroy the earth? One of the creepiest entries in the Fu Manchu series, and Loy's last oriental role. Based on the novel by Sam Rohmer.
1932 72m/B Boris Karloff, Lewis Stone, Karen Morley, Charles Starrett, Myrna Loy, Jean Hersholt, Lawrence Grant, David Torrence; **D:** Charles Brabin. **VHS** $19.98 *MGM* ⫞½

Mask of the Dragon A soldier's friend and girlfriend track down his killer after he delivers a golden curio to a shop in Los Angeles.
1951 54m/B Richard Travis, Sheila Ryan, Richard Emory, Jack Reitzen. **VHS, Beta, LV** *NO* ⫞

The Masked Marvel The Masked Marvel saves America's war industries from sabotage. Serial in twelve episodes. *AKA:* Sakima and the Masked Marvel.
1943 195m/B William Forrest, Louise Currie, Johnny Arthur; **D:** Spencer Gordon Bennet. **VHS** $29.98 *VCN, REP, MLB* ⫞½

Masks of Death New adventure for Sherlock Holmes, as he is pulled from retirement to find the murderer of three unidentified corpses found in London's East End.
1986 80m/C Peter Cushing, John Mills, Anne Baxter, Ray Milland; **D:** Roy Ward Baker. **VHS, Beta, LV** $19.98 *LHV, IME, WAR* ⫞⫞

Mason of the Mounted Harmless enough western in which a Canadian Mountie tracks down a murderer in the U.S.
1932 58m/B Bill Cody, Nancy Drexel, Art Smith; **D:** Trem Carr. **VHS** $19.95 *NOS, DVT, HEG* ⫞⫞

Masque of the Red Death An integral selection in the famous Edgar Allan Poe/Roger Corman canon, it deals with an evil prince who traffics with the devil and playfully murders any of his subjects not already dead of the plague. Photographed by Nicholas Roeg. Remade in 1989 with Corman as producer.
1965 88m/C *GB* Vincent Price, Hazel Court, Jane Asher, Patrick Magee; **D:** Roger Corman. **VHS, Beta** $59.98 *LIV, MLB* ⫞⫞⫞

Masque of the Red Death Roger Corman's second attempt at Edgar Allan Poe's horror tale pales compared to his Vincent Price version made 25 years earlier. Under-aged cast adds youth appeal but subtracts credibility from the fable of a sadistic prince and his sycophants trying to ignore the plague outside castle walls. Only late in the plot does veteran actor Macnee add proper note of doom.
1989 (R) 90m/C Patrick Macnee, Jeffery Osterhage, Adrian Paul, Tracy Reiner, Maria Ford; **D:** Larry Brand. **VHS, Beta, LV** $79.95 *MGM, IME* ⫞⫞

Masque of the Red Death Unrecognizable Poe mutation has guests invited to the mansion of a dying millionaire, only to be murdered by an unknown stalker. One scene features a pendulum, and that's it for literary faithfulness.
1990 (R) 94m/C Frank Stallone, Brenda Vaccaro, Herbert Lom, Michelle McBride, Christine Lunde; **D:** Alan Birkinshaw. **VHS, LV** *COL, PIA* ⫞½

Masque of the Red Death/Premature Burial Double feature of horror classics adapted from Edgar Allan Poe's work. Price stars in "Masque of the Red Death" as a satan worshiper. Millard plays a man obsessed with the fear of catastrophe in "Premature Burial."
1965 175m/C Vincent Price, Hazel Court, Jane Asher, Patrick Magee, Nigel Green, Ray Milland; **D:** Roger Corman. **VHS, LV** $44.95 *IME* ⫞½

Masquerade A lonely young heiress meets a handsome "nobody" with a mysterious background and it is love at first sight. The romance distresses everyone in the circle of the elite because they assume that he is after her money and not her love. At first it seems decidedly so, then definitely not, and then nothing is certain. A real romantic thriller, with wonderful scenes of the Hamptons.
1988 (R) 91m/C Rob Lowe, Meg Tilly, John Glover, Kim Cattrall, Doug Savant, Dana Delany; **D:** Bob Swaim; **M:** John Barry. **VHS, Beta, LV** $19.98 *FOX* ⫞⫞⫞

Mass Appeal An adaptation of the Bill C. Davis play about the Ideological debate between a young seminarian and a complacent but successful parish pastor. Lemmon has had better roles and done better acting.
1984 (PG) 99m/C Jack Lemmon, Zeljko Ivanek, Charles Durning, Louise Latham, James Ray, Sharee Gregory, Talia Balsam; **D:** Glenn Jordan. **VHS, Beta, LV** $19.95 *MCA* ⫞⫞

Massacre at Central High A new student takes matters into his own hands when gang members harass other students at a local high school. Other than some silly dialogue, this low-budget production is above average.
1976 (R) 85m/C Derrel Maury, Andrew Stevens, Kimberly Beck, Robert Carradine, Roy Underwood, Steve Bond; **W/D:** Renee Daalder. **VHS** $79.95 *MPI* ⫞⫞½

Massacre in Dinosaur Valley A dashing young paleontologist and his fellow explorers go on a perilous journey down the Amazon in search of the Valley of the Dinosaur.
1985 98m/C Michael Sopkiw, Suzanne Carvall. **VHS, Beta** $69.98 *LIV* ⫞½

Massacre in Rome A priest opposes a Nazi colonel's plan to execute Italian civilians in retaliation for the deaths of 33 German soldiers. Strong drama based on a real event.
1973 (PG) 110m/C Richard Burton, Marcello Mastroianni, Leo McKern, John Steiner, Anthony Steel; **D:** George P. Cosmatos; **M:** Ennio Morricone. **VHS, Beta** $29.99 *HBO* ⫞⫞½

Massive Retaliation Hordes of pesky villagers seek refuge within the secluded safety of a family's country house as World War III approaches.
1985 90m/C Tom Bower, Peter Donat, Karlene Crockett, Jason Gedrick, Michael Pritchard; **D:** Thomas A. Cohen. **VHS, Beta, LV** $19.98 *LIV, VES* ⫞

Master Blaster Friendly game of survival with paintball guns goes awry when one of the contestants exchanges the play guns for deadly weapons.
1985 (R) 94m/C Jeff Moldovan, Donna Rosae, Joe Hess, Peter Lunblad; **D:** Glenn Wilder. **VHS** *PSM* ⫞½

Master Harold and the Boys Stagey cable presentation of South African Athol Fugard's play about relationship between white man and two black servants. Occasionally provocative.
1984 90m/C Matthew Broderick; **D:** Michael Lindsay-Hogg. **VHS, Beta** $19.98 *LHV, WAR* ⫞⫞⫞

Master Key Features 13 complete chapters of this action-adventure serial.
1944 169m/B Jane Wiley, Milburn Stone, Lash LaRue, Dennis Moore. **VHS, Beta** $49.95 *NOS, DVT, MLB* ⫞½

Master Killer (The Thirty-Sixth Chamber) Master Killers are made, not born. Liu trains as he readies himself for an attack on the brutal Manchu assassins. *AKA:* The Thirty-Sixth Chamber.
1984 (R) 109m/C Liu Chia Hui; **D:** Liu Chia Liang. **VHS, Beta** $9.98 *SUE* ⫞

The Master Killers Two brothers who hate each other's guts try to kill each other for their dead father's money.
1973 95m/C Donald O'Brien; **D:** George Bonge. **VHS, Beta** *NO* ⫞

Master Mind A renowned Japanese super sleuth attempts to solve the theft of a sophisticated midget android.
1973 86m/C Zero Mostel, Keiko Kishi, Bradford Dillman, Herbert Berghof, Frankie Sakai; **D:** Alex March. **VHS, Beta** $9.95 *UNI* ⫞⫞

Master Ninja First in the continuing adventures of the Master and Max (Van Cleef and Van Patten) follow the pair across the US in their search for the Master's long-lost daughter. They're pursued by Kosugi. Originally filmed for television; each tape includes two programs. *AKA:* The Master.
1978 93m/C Lee Van Cleef, Sho Kosugi, Timothy Van Patten. **VHS, Beta** $9.99 *QVD, TWE* ⫞½

Master Ninja 2 The Master and his assistant Max travel across the United States to search for his long lost daughter in these two episodes from the television series.
1983 92m/C Sho Kosugi, Lee Van Cleef, Timothy Van Patten, David McCallum, Cotter Smith. **VHS, Beta** $39.95 *TWE* ⫞½

Master Ninja 3 The Master and Max are back again in two new adventures originally aired as part of a television series. In "Fat Tuesday," the duo chop-sock a gun-running operation in New Orleans. In "Joggernaut," they help a mother and daughter get their produce to market.
1983 93m/C Sho Kosugi, Lee Van Cleef, Timothy Van Patten, Diana Muldaur, Mabel King. **VHS, Beta** $39.98 *TWE* ⫞½

Master Ninja 4 The Master and Max travel to New York and Las Vegas seeking his long lost daughter in this collection of two episodes from "The Master" television series.
1983 93m/C Lee Van Cleef, Timothy Van Patten, Sho Kosugi, George Maharis. **VHS, Beta** $39.95 *TWE* ⫞½

Master Ninja 5 Two more episodes from the television series: In "Kunoichi," a female martial arts assassin stalks the Master; "The Java Tiger" features a deadly race to find buried treasure.
1983 92m/C Sho Kosugi, Lee Van Cleef, Timothy Van Patten. **VHS, Beta** $39.95 *TWE* ⫞½

The Master of Ballantrae Flynn plays James Durrisdear, the heir to a Scottish title, who gets involved in a rebellion with Bonnie Prince Charlie against the English crown. When the rebellion fails, Flynn heads for the West Indies where he and his partner amass quite a fortune through piracy. Flynn eventually returns to Scotland where he finds that his brother has taken over his title as well as his longtime love. Based on the novel by Robert Louis Stevenson. Flynn's riotous life had put him long past his peak swashbuckling days, as this film unfortunately demonstrates.

1953 89m/C Errol Flynn, Roger Livesey, Anthony Steel, Beatrice Campbell, Yvonne Furneaux, Jacques Berthier, Felix Aylmer, Mervyn Johns; *D:* William Keighley. **VHS, Beta, LV** $59.99 *WAR* ♫♫

Master of Death A young man trains for 18 years in the martial arts to avenge his parents' murder.
19?? 90m/C **VHS, Beta** $29.95 *OCE* ♫

Master of Dragonard Hill A low-rent swashbuckling romance-novel pastiche.
1989 92m/C Oliver Reed, Eartha Kitt. **VHS, Beta** $79.95 *MED* ♫

Master of Kung Fu A Kung Fu instructor calls upon his former teacher to help him fend off loan sharks who want to take over his school.
1977 88m/C Yu Chan Yuan, Chi Hsiao Fu. **VHS, Beta** $59.98 *FOX* ♫

Master of the House Story of a spoiled husband, a type extinct in this country but still in existence abroad. Silent with titles in English. *AKA:* Thou Shalt Honour Thy Wife.
1925 118m/B *D:* Carl Theodor Dreyer. **VHS, Beta** $49.95 *FCT, TAM, VYY* ♫♫♫

Master of the World Visionary tale of a fanatical 19th century inventor who uses his wonderous flying fortress as an antiwar weapon. Adapted from "Robur, the Conqueror" and "Master of the World," both by Jules Verne.
1961 95m/C Vincent Price, Charles Bronson, Henry Hull; *D:* William Witney. **VHS, Beta** $19.98 *WAR, OM* ♫♫½

Master of the World Animated version of the famed Jules Verne classic about a mad scientist who endeavors to take over the world. In HiFi.
1976 50m/C **VHS, Beta** $19.95 *MGM* ♫♫½

Master Race Absorbing cautionary tale of a German officer who escapes retribution when the Nazis collapse, continuing to hold control over the inhabitants of a small town through intimidation.
1944 98m/B George Coulouris, Lloyd Bridges, Osa Massen, Nancy Gates, Stanley Ridges; *D:* Herbert Biberman. **VHS, Beta** $29.95 *RKO, TTC* ♫♫½

Master Touch When a legendary safe-cracker is released from prison, he attempts one last heist at a Hamburg insurance company. *AKA:* Hearts and Minds; Un Uomo da Rispettare.
1974 (PG) 96m/C *GE IT* Kirk Douglas, Florinda Bolkan, Giuliano Gemma; *D:* Michele Lupo; *M:* Ennio Morricone. **VHS, Beta** $59.95 *PSM* ♫½

The Masters of Menace The men in blue are mighty miffed when a bunch of bikers break parole to pay their last respects to a comrade in leather. Comic bits by Candy, Belushi, Aykroyd and Wendt provide little relief.
1990 (PG-13) 97m/C David Rasche, Catherine Bach, Dan Aykroyd, James Belushi, John Candy, George Wendt, Tino Insana; *D:* Daniel Raskov; *W:* Tino Insana. **VHS, LV** $89.95 *COL* ♫½

Masters of the Universe A big-budget live-action version of the cartoon character's adventures, with He-Man battling Skeletor for the sake of the universe.
1987 (PG) 109m/C Dolph Lundgren, Frank Langella, Billy Barty, Courteney Cox, Meg Foster; *D:* Gary Goddard. **VHS, Beta, LV** $19.98 *WAR* ♫♫

Masters of Venus Eight-part serial about spaceships, space maidens and the like.
1959 121m/B Ferdinand "Ferdy" Mayne. **VHS, Beta** $24.95 *SNC, VDM* ♫½

Master's Revenge When a girl is kidnapped by a violent motorcycle gang, martial artists are called in to rescue her. Originally released as, "Devil Rider."
1971 78m/C Sharon Mahon, Ridgely Abele, Johnny Pachivas. **VHS** $19.95 *ACA* ♫½

Mata Hari During World War I, a lovely German spy steals secrets from the French through her involvement with two military officers. Lavish production and exquisite direction truly make this one of Garbo's best. Watch for her exotic pseudo-strip tease.
1932 90m/B Greta Garbo, Ramon Novarro, Lionel Barrymore, Lewis Stone, C. Henry Gordon, Karen Morley, Alec B. Francis; *D:* George Fitzmaurice. **VHS, Beta** $19.98 *MGM, FCT* ♫♫♫

Mata Hari Racy, adventure-prone story of WWI's most notorious spy, Mata Hari, who uses her seductive beauty to seduce the leaders of Europe. Stars "Emmanuelle" Kristel.
1985 (R) 105m/C Sylvia Kristel, Christopher Cazenove, Oliver Tobias, Gaye Brown, Gottfried John; *D:* Curtis Cunningham. **VHS, Beta** $79.95 *MGM* ♫♫

Matador Bizarre, entertaining black comedy about a retired matador who satiates his desire to kill by appearing in snuff films. He meets his match in an equally deadly woman and the two are drawn closer together by a young bullfighting student who confesses to a series of murders. Not for all tastes, but fine for those who like the outrageous. In Spanish with English subtitles.
1986 90m/C *SP* Assumpta Serna, Antonio Banderas, Nacho Martinez, Eva Cobo, Carmen Maura, Julieta Serrano, Chus Lampreave; *D:* Pedro Almodovar. **VHS, Beta, LV** $79.95 *CCN, TAM, TAM* ♫♫½

The Match Factory Girl In the final segment of his "working class" trilogy producer/director/writer Kaurismaki brings us Iris, a plain, shy outsider who subsists by sharing a drab dwelling with her one-dimensional mother and stepfather, working in a match factory, and hoping desperately for romantic love. Her gray world is transformed when the extraordinary occurs—she spots a brightly colored party dress in a shop window, buys it, wears it to a bar, and meets the Scandinavian creep who will soon get her pregnant and dump her. Angry at the world, Iris seeks revenge, and in so doing the audience learns that Iris has become very real and very human. In a short 70 minutes, Kaurismaki makes his point that beauty can exist in ugly places. Finnish with English subtitles. *AKA:* Tulitkkutehtaan Tytto.
1991 70m/C *SW FI* Kati Outinen, Elina Salo, Esko Nikkari, Vesa Vierikko; *D:* Aki Kaurismaki; *W:* Aki Kaurismaki. **VHS** *NYR* ♫♫½

The Matchmaker An adaptation of the Thornton Wilder play concerning two young men in search of romance in 1884 New York. Later adapted as "Hello Dolly." An amusing diversion.
1958 101m/B Shirley Booth, Anthony Perkins, Shirley MacLaine, Paul Ford, Robert Morse, Perry Wilson, Wallace Ford, Russell Collins, Rex Evans, Gavin Gordon, Torben Meyer; *D:* Joseph Anthony. **VHS, Beta, LV** $19.95 *PAR, PIA, FCT* ♫♫♫

Matewan An acclaimed dramatization of the famous Matewan massacre in the 1920s, in which coal miners in West Virginia, reluctantly influenced by a young union organizer, rebelled against terrible working conditions. Complex and imbued with myth, the film is a gritty, moving, powerful drama with typically superb Sayles dialogue and Haskell Wexler's beautiful and poetic cinematography. Jones delivers an economical yet intense portrayal of the black leader of the miners. The director makes his usual on-screen appearance, this time as an establishment-backed reactionary minister. Partially based on the Sayles novel "Union Dues."
1987 (PG-13) 130m/C Chris Cooper, James Earl Jones, Mary McDonnell, William Oldham, Kevin Tighe, David Strathairn; *D:* John Sayles. Academy Awards '87 Nominations: Best Cinematography; Independent Spirit Awards '88: Best Cinematography. **VHS, Beta, LV** $79.95 *LHV, WAR* ♫♫♫½

Matilda Family fare about a entrepreneur who decides to manage a boxing kangaroo, which nearly succeeds in defeating the world heavyweight champion. Uneven and occasionally engaging. Based on Paul Gallico's novel.
1978 (PG) 103m/C Elliott Gould, Robert Mitchum, Harry Guardino, Clive Revill; *D:* Daniel Mann. **VHS, Beta** $69.98 *LIV, VES* ♫♫

Matinee '60s-style shocking schlock screams "MANT: Half-man, Half-ant, All Terror!" from the movie marquee after Lawrence Woolsey (Goodman), promoter extraordinare, and Ruth Corday (Moriarty), his leading lady on-screen and off, roll into Key West circa 1962. Meanwhile, adolescent Gene Loomis (Fenton) listens to his health teacher push the benefits of red meat and his girlfriend question life and the air raid drills, while worrying about his dad, a Navy man stationed in Cuba. What better diversion for a Cold War kid than to do some odd jobs for a movie maven who specializes in unreality? Director Dante builds sly parallels between real life and movie horror by juxtaposing Woolsey (modeled after B-movie king William Castle) hyping his flick, shown in "Atomo-Vision," against JFK solemnly announcing the Russian's approach.
1992 (PG) 98m/C John Goodman, Cathy Moriarty, Simon Fenton, Omri Katz, Lisa Jakub, Kellie Martin, Jesse Lee, Lucinda Jenney, James Villemaire, Robert Picardo, Dick Miller, John Sayles, Mark McCracken; *D:* Joe Dante; *M:* Jerry Goldsmith. **VHS, Beta, LV** $95.98 *MCA, BTV* ♫♫½

Matinee at the Bijou, Vol. 1 This volume in a series of eight contains the cartoon "Little Red Hen," the shorts "Candy For Your Health," and "Fox Movietone Newsreel," and the feature film "Fatal Glass of Beer."
19?? 90m/B **VHS** $14.99 *NO* ♫♫½

Matinee at the Bijou, Vol. 2 This volume in a series of eight contains the cartoon "A Waif's Welcome," the short "Dangerous Females," and the feature "Little Men."
19?? 90m/B **VHS** $14.99 *NO* ♫♫

Matinee at the Bijou, Vol. 3 This volume in a series of eight has the cartoon "Magic Mummy," short "Desert Demons," and feature "One Frightened Night."
19?? 90m/B **VHS** $14.99 *NO* ♫♫

Matinee at the Bijou, Vol. 4 This volume in a series of eight contains the cartoon "The Pincushion Man," the short "Famous People at Play," and the feature "Ladies Crave Excitement."
19?? 90m/B **VHS** $14.99 *NO* ♫♫

Matinee at the Bijou, Vol. 5 This volume in a series of eight contains the cartoon "A Little Bird Told Me," short "Star Reporter," and feature "I'd Give My Life."
19?? 90m/B **VHS** $14.99 *NO* ♫♫

Matinee at the Bijou, Vol. 6 This volume in a series of eight contains the cartoon ''Song a Day,'' the short ''Musical Charmers,'' and the feature ''Sing While You're Able.''
19?? 90m/B VHS $14.99 NO 🎞🎞½

Matinee at the Bijou, Vol. 7 This volume in a series of eight contains the cartoon ''Cobweb Hotel,'' the short ''Hotel Anchovy,'' and the feature ''Young Dynamite.''
19?? 90m/B VHS $14.99 NO 🎞🎞½

Matinee at the Bijou, Vol. 8 This volume in a series of eight contains the cartoon ''On with the New,'' the short ''The Truth about Taxes,'' and the feature ''Remedy for Riches.''
19?? 90m/B VHS $14.99 NO 🎞🎞½

The Mating Game A fast-paced comedy about a tax collector, a beautiful girl, and a wily farm couple. Randall is the straitlaced IRS agent who finds out that the farming Larkins have never paid taxes and use a complicated barter system to get along. Randall falls for farm daughter Reynolds, gets drunk with her Pa, and decides to help the family out of their government dilemma—to the dismay of his superiors. Randall has a terrific drunk scene among his many comedic capers and Reynolds is a highlight.
1959 96m/C Tony Randall, Debbie Reynolds, Paul Douglas, Una Merkel, Fred Clark, Philip Ober, Charles Lane; **D:** George Marshall. **VHS $19.98** MGM 🎞🎞🎞

Mating Season Successful female attorney Arnaz meets good-natured laundromat owner Luckinbill at a bird-watching retreat. Romance ensues. Made for television.
1981 96m/C Lucie Arnaz, Laurence Luckinbill; **D:** John Llewellyn Moxey. **VHS, Beta $14.95** LCA 🎞🎞½

Matrimaniac A man goes to great lengths to marry a woman against her father's wishes. Silent with music score.
1916 48m/B Douglas Fairbanks Sr., Constance Talmadge. **VHS, Beta $29.95** VYY, GPV 🎞🎞

A Matter of Degrees Weeks before his graduation, a beatnik-type college senior finally acquires a goal: romancing a mystery girl...or maybe saving the student radio station...or not. The hero's aimlessness permeates the script, which never goes anywhere in its exploration of campus ennui. Good photography and a great stratum of alternative music groups on the soundtrack: Dream Syndicate, Pere Ubu, Schooly D, Pixies, Poi Dog Pondering, Minutemen, and Throwing Muses.
1990 (R) 89m/C Arye Gross, Judith Hoag, Tom Sizemore, John Doe; **Cameos:** John F. Kennedy Jr., Fred Schneider, Kate Pierson; **D:** W.T. Morgan. **VHS, Beta $89.95** PSM 🎞🎞

A Matter of Dignity Young girl, forced into marriage with millionaire, eventually brings ruin to the entire family. Why? In Greek with English subtitles.
1957 104m/B GR Georges Pappas, Ellie Lambetti, Athena Michaelidou, Eleni Zafirou; **D:** Michael Cacoyannis. **VHS, Beta $59.95** FCT 🎞🎞

A Matter of Life and Death True story follows the real-life experiences of nurse Joy Ufema who has devoted her life to helping terminally ill patients. Exceptional work from Lavin. Made for television.
1981 98m/C Linda Lavin, Salome Jens, Gail Strickland, Gerald S. O'Loughlin, Ramon Bieri, Tyne Daly, Larry Breeding, John Bennett Perry; **D:** Russ Mayberry. **VHS** NO 🎞🎞

A Matter of Love Two couples indulge in spouse swapping while vacationing at the beach.
1978 (R) 89m/C Michelle Harris, Mark Anderson, Christy Neal, Jeff Alin; **D:** Chuck Vincent. **VHS, Beta $69.98** LIV, VES 🎞

A Matter of Principle The perennial Christmas special about a Scrooge-like character's yuletide change of heart. He decides it's time to shape up when he realizes he may lose his family permanently.
1983 60m/C Alan Arkin, Barbara Dana, Tony Arkin; **D:** Gwen Arner. **VHS, Beta $19.95** ACA 🎞

A Matter of Time Maid is taught to enjoy life by an eccentric, flamboyant contessa, then finds the determination to become an aspiring actress. Often depressing and uneven, arguably Minnelli's worst directing job and his last film. Also Boyer's last appearance and first bit for Bergman's daughter Rosellini, in a small part as a nun.
1976 (PG) 97m/C Liza Minnelli, Ingrid Bergman, Charles Boyer, Tina Aumont, Spiros Andros, Anna Proclemer; **D:** Vincente Minnelli. **VHS, Beta $69.95** VES Woof!

A Matter of WHO A detective for the World Health Organization, or WHO, investigates the disease related deaths of several oil men. Travelling to the Middle East, he uncovers a plot by an unscrupulous businessman to control the oil industry by killing off its most powerful members. Although intended as a comedy, the subject matter is too grim to be taken lightly.
1962 92m/B GB Terry-Thomas, Alex Nicol, Sonja Ziemann, Richard Briers, Clive Morton, Vincent Ball, Honor Blackman, Carol White, Martin Benson, Geoffrey Keen; **D:** Don Chaffey. **VHS, Beta $16.95** SNC 🎞🎞

Matters of the Heart Young pianist searches for an opportunity to display his talents, much to the disapproval of his veteran father. He meets a successful but embittered musician who takes him under her wing and passion between the two soon flares. Made for cable TV and based on ''The Country of the Heart'' by Barbara Wershba.
1990 94m/C Jane Seymour, Christopher Gartin, James Stacy, Geoffrey Lewis, Nan Martin, Allen Rich, Clifford David, Katherine Cannon; **D:** Michael Rhodes. **VHS $89.95** MCA 🎞🎞

Maurice Based on E.M. Forster's novel about a pair of Edwardian-era Cambridge undergraduates who fall in love, but must deny their attraction and abide by British society's strict norms regarding homosexuality. Maurice finds, however, that he cannot deny his nature, and must come to a decision regarding family, friends, and social structures. A beautiful and stately film of struggle and courage.
1987 (R) 139m/C GB James Wilby, Hugh Grant, Rupert Graves, Mark Tandy, Ben Kingsley, Denholm Elliott, Simon Callow, Judy Parfitt, Helena Bonham Carter; **D:** James Ivory. **VHS, Beta, LV $79.95** LHV, IME, WAR 🎞🎞🎞

Mausoleum Only one man can save a woman from eternal damnation.
1983 (R) 96m/C Marjoe Gortner, Bobbie Bresee, Norman Burton, LaWanda Page, Shari Mann; **D:** Michael Dugan. **VHS, Beta, LV $14.98** SUE 🎞🎞

Maverick Queen Barbara Stanwyck, owner of a gambling casino and a member of the ''Wild Bunch'' outlaw gang, is torn between going straight for the love of a lawman or sticking with the criminals. Stanwyck is perfectly cast in this interesting Western.
1955 90m/C Barbara Stanwyck, Barry Sullivan, Wallace Ford, Scott Brady, Jim Davis, Mary Murphy; **D:** Joseph Kane. **VHS $14.95** REP 🎞🎞½

Maverick: The Collector's Edition Offbeat television western starring Garner as conniving gambler Bret Maverick. The premiere show, ''War of the Silver Kings,'' finds Maverick falling out with the richest man in town over a card game. ''Point Blank'' features Connors as a conniving bank clerk. Additional episodes are available.
195? 100m/B James Garner, Mike Connors. **VHS $19.98** WAR, MOV 🎞🎞½

Max Compilation of hilarious Linder shorts plus two features, ''Seven Years Bad Luck'' and ''The Three Must-Get-Theres''
1922 90m/B Max Linder. **VHS, Beta $49.50** GVV 🎞🎞½

Max A night watchman watches an aspiring actress who is working on her performance in a Broadway play. He tells her she would be better off marrying a doctor.
1979 20m/C Jack Gilford, Lynn Lipton; **D:** Joseph Gilford, Jennifer Lax. **VHS, Beta** CFV 🎞🎞

Max and Helen Uneven, but sensitive and at times highly moving made for TV story of two lovers who are victims of the holocaust. Max (Williams) survives both Nazi and Stalinist camps out of both love for his fiancee and guilt for having lived while she did not.
1990 94m/C GB Treat Williams, Alice Krige, Martin Landau, Jodhi May, John Phillips; **D:** Philip Saville. **VHS, Beta $9.98** TTC 🎞🎞½

Max Dugan Returns A Simon comedy about an ex-con trying to make up with his daughter by showering her with presents bought with stolen money. Sweet and light, with a good cast.
1983 (PG) 98m/C Jason Robards Jr., Marsha Mason, Donald Sutherland, Matthew Broderick, Kiefer Sutherland; **D:** Herbert Ross; **W:** Neil Simon. **VHS, Beta, LV $59.98** FOX 🎞🎞

Max Fleischer's Documentary Features Two scientific films, ''Evolution'' and ''Einstein's Theory of Relativity,'' from Fleischer's early studio were made to finance their cartoons. Features animated sequences.
1923 60m/B **D:** Max Fleischer. **VHS, Beta** GVV 🎞🎞

Max Fleischer's Popeye Cartoons Compilation of three classic color Popeye two-reelers from the late 30's, wherein Popeye meets Ali Baba, Aladdin and Sindbad the Sailor.
1939 56m/C **D:** Max Fleischer. **VHS, Beta, LV $14.95** HEP 🎞🎞

Max Headroom, the Original Story The computer-generated, British Channel-4 comedy personality stars in his first film, actually a shot-on-video feature about an innocent reporter who is transformed by an evil futuristic TV station into Headroom, the perfect (read: artificial) talk show host.
1986 60m/C GB Matt Frewer, Nickolas Grace, Hilary Tindall, Amanda Pays, Rocky Morton, Annabel Jankel. **VHS, Beta, LV $29.95** LHV, WAR 🎞🎞½

Max Maven's Mindgames Magician Max Maven performs mindgames with the use of playing cards, signs and symbols, and magic with money in such settings as Las Vegas, a tropical jungle, the moon and an operating room.
1984 56m/C VHS, Beta $29.95 MCA 🎞🎞

Maxie Highly predictable, and forgettable, comedy where a ghost of a flamboyant flapper inhabits the body of a modern-day secretary, and her husband is both delighted and befuddled with the transformations in his spouse. Close is okay, but the film is pretty flaky.

1985 (PG) 98m/C Glenn Close, Ruth Gordon, Mandy Patinkin, Barnard Hughes, Valerie Curtin, Harry Hamlin; **D:** Paul Aaron. **VHS, Beta, LV $19.99** *HBO* ⅛⅛

Maxim Xul A professor of the occult is forced to tangle with a beast from Hell that possesses enormous strength and an insatiable appetite for human blood.

1991 90m/C Adam West, Jefferson Leinberger, Hal Strieb, Mary Schaeffer; **D:** Arthur Egeli. **VHS** *NO* ⅛

Maximum Breakout A beautiful and wealthy girl is kidnapped, her boyfriend left for dead. But he recovers and leads a posse of mercenaries to the rescue.

1991 93m/C Sydney Coale Phillips; **D:** Tracy Lynch Britton. **VHS $56.96** *AIP* ⅛½

Maximum Force Three renegade cops join together to infiltrate the underworld and bring to justice both the city's leading crime king and their own corrupt chief of police.

1992 (R) 90m/C Sam Jones, Sherrie Rose, Jason Lively, John Saxon, Richard Lynch, Mickey Rooney, Jeff Langton; **D:** Joseph Merhi. **VHS, LV $89.95** *PMH* ⅛

Maximum Overdrive Based upon King's story "Trucks," recounts what happens when a meteor hits Earth and machines run by themselves, wanting only to kill people. Score by AC/DC.

1986 (R) 97m/C Emilio Estevez, Pat Hingle, Laura Harrington, Christopher Murvey, Yeardley Smith; **D:** Stephen King. **VHS, Beta, LV $19.98** *LHV, WAR* ⅛

Maximum Security A small-budget prison film detailing the tribulations of a model prisoner struggling to resist mental collapse.

1987 113m/C Geoffrey Lewis, Jean Smart, Robert Desiderio; **D:** Bill Duke. **VHS, LV $19.95** *STE, NWV* ⅛

Maximum Thrust A few white men confront a deadly Caribbean voodoo tribe.

1987 80m/C Rick Gianasi, Joe Derrig, Jennifer Kanter, Mizan Nunes. **Beta** *NO Woof!*

May Fools Malle portrays individuals collectively experiencing personal upheaval against the backdrop of unrelated social upheaval. An upper crusty family gathers at a country estate for the funeral of the clan's matriarch, while the May of '68 Parisian riots unfold. Few among the family members mourn the woman's passing, save her son Milou (Piccoli) who leads a pastoral existence tending grapes on the estate. Milou's daughter (Miou-Miou), like the others, is more concerned with her personal gain, suggesting, to her father's horror, that they divide the estate in three. Touching, slow, keenly observed. Malle cowrote with Jean Claude Carriere; music by Stephane Grappelli. In French with English subtitles. *AKA:* Milou en Mai; Milou in May.

1990 (R) 105m/C *FR* Michel Piccoli, Miou-Miou, Michael Duchaussoy, Dominique Blanc, Harriet Walter, Francois Berleand, Paulette Dubost; **D:** Louis Malle. **VHS, LV $79.95** *ORI, FXL, FCT* ⅛⅛

May Wine A sexy, romantic comedy starring "Twin Peaks" alumna, Boyle.

1990 (R) 85m/C Guy Marchand, Lara Flynn Boyle, Joanna Cassidy. **VHS, LV $89.98** *MED* ⅛

Maya After the death of his mother, young Terry (North) goes to join his big-game hunting father in India. After a quarrel Terry runs off and meets an Indian boy who has promised his dying father he will deliver a sacred white elephant to a jungle temple. The two lads join forces for the trek and have all

sorts of adventures along the way. Basis for a short-lived television series.

1966 91m/C Jay North, Clint Walker, Sajid Kahn, I.S. Johar; **D:** John Berry; **W:** John Fante. **VHS $14.95** *MGM* ⅛½

Maya A teacher of fashion in a high school becomes the object of a student's devotion and another teacher's insane jealousy.

1982 114m/C Berta Dominguez, Joseph D. Rosevich; **D:** Agust Agustsson. **VHS, Beta** *NO Woof!*

Mayalunta A young artist is emotionally tortured by a dying older couple.

1986 90m/C *SP* Federico Luppi, Miguel Angel Sola, Barbara Mujica. **VHS $59.98** *VES Woof!*

Maybe I'll Be Home in the Spring Denise (Field) is estranged from her family and decides to leave home for life on a commune where she becomes involved with drugs. When she decides to return home everyone finds it hard to adjust. Made for television. *AKA:* Deadly Desire.

1970 (PG) 90m/C Sally Field, Jackie Cooper, Eleanor Parker, David Carradine, Lane Bradbury; **D:** Joseph Sargent. **VHS $9.99** *VTR* ⅛

Mayerling Considered one of the greatest films about doomed love. Story of the tragic and hopeless affair between Crown Prince Rudolf of Hapsburg and young Baroness Marie Vetsera. Heart wrenching and beautiful, with stupendous acting. Remade in 1968. In French with English subtitles.

1936 95m/B Charles Boyer, Danielle Darrieux; **D:** Anatole Litvak. **VHS, Beta $29.95** *NOS, MRV, FCT* ⅛⅛⅛½

Mayflower Madam Fairly unsexy and uninteresting made-for-TV movie recounting the business dealings and court battles of the real-life Sydney Biddle Barrows. Barrows/Bergen is a prominent New York socialite and madam of an exclusive escort service whose clientele includes businessmen and dignitaries.

1987 (R) 93m/C Candice Bergen, Chris Sarandon, Chita Rivera; **D:** Lou Antonio. **VHS, Beta $19.95** *STE, VMK* ⅛⅛

Mayhem Two loners in Hollywood confront all types of urban low-life murderers, drug pushers, and child molesters.

1987 90m/C Raymond Martino, Pamela Dixon, Robert Gallo, Wendy MacDonald. **VHS, Beta** *NO* ⅛

Maytime Lovely story of an opera star (MacDonald) and penniless singer (Eddy) who fall in love in Paris, but her husband/teacher (Barrymore) interferes. One of the best films the singing duo ever made. ♫Maytime Finale; Virginia Ham and Eggs; Vive l'Opera; Student Drinking Song; Carry Me Back to Old Virginny; Reverie; Jump Jim Crow; Road to Paradise; Page's Aria; Les Filles de Cadiz; Street Singer; Now is the Month of Maying; Chi Mi Frena; William Tell Overture; Soldier's Chorus; Anvil Chorus; Miserer; Largo Al Factotum; Caro Nome; La Donna E Mobile; O, Du Mein Holder Abendstern; Liebestod; Sempre Libera; Summer Is Icumen In; Mazurka; Napoleonic Waltz; Plantons La Vigne; The Last Rose of Summer; I Dreamt I Dwelt in Marble Halls; Santa Lucia; Nobles Seigneurs; Une Dame Noble Et Sage; Road to Paradise; Sidewalks of New York; Columbia, The Gem of the Ocean; Will You Remember?.

1937 132m/B Jeanette MacDonald, Nelson Eddy, John Barrymore, Herman Bing, Tom Brown, Lynne Carver; **D:** Robert Z. Leonard; **W:** Noel Langley. **VHS, LV $19.98** *MGM* ⅛⅛⅛

Maytime in Mayfair A dress shop owner's rival is getting all the goodies first, for which he takes the heat from his partner. When he finds out how the rival is doing it, the partners up and head for a vacation in the south of France. Overly simplistic but charming kitsch, helped along by Technicolor shots of the fashions and sets.

1952 94m/C Anna Neagle, Michael Wilding, Peter Graves, Nicholas Phipps, Tom Walls, Tom Walls Jr.; **D:** Herbert Wilcox. **VHS $19.95** *NOS* ⅛⅛

The Maze Made-for-British-television mystery about a young girl who meets the ghost of her mother's first love in her garden estate.

1985 60m/C *GB* Francesca Annis, James Bolam, Sky McCatskill. **VHS, Beta $59.95** *PSM* ⅛⅛⅛

Mazes and Monsters A group of university students becomes obsessed with playing a real life version of the fantasy role-playing game, Dungeons and Dragons. Adapted for television from the book by Rona Jaffe. *AKA:* Rona Jaffe's Mazes and Monsters.

1982 100m/C *CA* Tom Hanks, Wendy Crewson, David Wallace, Chris Makepeace, Lloyd Bochner, Peter Donat, Murray Hamilton, Vera Miles, Louise Sorel, Susan Strasberg, Steven Hilliard Stern, Anne Francis; **D:** Steven Hilliard Stern. **VHS $19.98** *LHV, HHE* ⅛⅛½

Mazurka English-dubbed Danish sex farce about a parochial school's teacher and his efforts to lose his virginity at the school dance.

1970 91m/C *DK* **VHS, Beta $29.95** *FCT, VYY* ⅛⅛½

McBain In this exciting fast-paced action-thriller, POW Robert McBain (Walken) leads a group of veterans into battle against the Columbian drug cartel. Stunning cinematography and superb performances combine to make this a riveting action film you won't soon forget.

1991 104m/C Christopher Walken, Maria Conchita Alonso, Michael Ironside, Steve James, Jay Patterson, Thomas G. Waites; **W/D:** James Glickenhaus. **VHS $19.98** *MCA* ⅛⅛½

McCabe & Mrs. Miller Altman's characteristically quirky take on the Western casts Beatty as a self-inflated entrepreneur who opens a brothel in the Great North. Christie is the madame who helps stabilize the haphazard operation. Unfortunately, success comes at a high price, and when gunmen arrive to enforce a business proposition, Beatty must become the man he has, presumably, merely pretended to be. A poetic, moving work, and a likely classic of the genre. Music by Leonard Cohen. Based on the novel by Edmund Naughton.

1971 (R) 121m/C Warren Beatty, Julie Christie, William Devane, Keith Carradine, John Schuck, Rene Auberjonois, Shelley Duvall; **D:** Robert Altman. **VHS, Beta, LV $19.98** *WAR, PIA* ⅛⅛⅛⅛

The McConnell Story True story of ace flyer McConnell, his heroism during WWII and the Korean conflict, and his postwar aviation pioneer efforts. Fine acting from Allyson and Ladd, with good support from Whitmore and Faylen. *AKA:* Tiger in the Sky.

1955 107m/C Alan Ladd, June Allyson, James Whitmore, Frank Faylen; **D:** Gordon Douglas; **M:** Max Steiner. **VHS, Beta $19.98** *WAR, FCT* ⅛⅛½

The McGuffin A film critic's inquisitiveness about the activities of his neighbors gets him caught up in murder and a host of other problems. A takeoff of Alfred Hitchcock's 1954 classic "Rear Window."

1985 95m/C *GB* Charles Dance, Ritza Brown, Francis Matthews, Brian Glover, Phyllis Logan, Jerry Stiller, Anna Massey; *D:* Colin Bucksey. **VHS** $79.95 *SVS* 🎞️🎞️

McLintock! Rowdy western starring Wayne as a tough cattle baron whose refined wife (O'Hara) returns from the east after a two-year separation. She wants a divorce and custody of their 17-year-old daughter (Powers), who's been away at school. In the meantime, he's hired a housekeeper (De Carlo), whose teenage son (real-life son Patrick) promptly falls for Powers. It's a battle royal between the feisty wife and cantankerous husband but no one out-dukes the Duke. Other Wayne family members involved in the production include daughter Aissa (as the housekeeper's daughter) and son Michael who produced the film.
1963 127m/C John Wayne, Maureen O'Hara, Yvonne De Carlo, Patrick Wayne, Stefanie Powers, Jack Kruschen, Chill Wills, Jerry Van Dyke, Edgar Buchanan, Bruce Cabot, Perry Lopez, Michael Pate, Strother Martin, Gordon Jones; *D:* Andrew V. McLaglen; *W:* James Edward Grant. **VHS, LV** $14.99 *MPI, GKK, ING* 🎞️🎞️🎞️

The McMasters Set shortly after the Civil War, the film tells the story of the prejudice faced by a black soldier who returns to the southern ranch on which he was raised. Once there, the rancher gives him half of the property, but the ex-soldier has difficulty finding men who will work for him. When a group of Native Americans assist him, a band of bigoted men do their best to stop it. The movie was released in two versions with different endings. In one, prejudice prevails; in the other, bigotry is defeated. *AKA:* The Blood Crowd; The McMasters...Tougher Than the West Itself.
1970 (PG) 89m/C Burl Ives, Brock Peters, David Carradine, Nancy Kwan, Jack Palance, Dane Clark, L.Q. Jones, Alan Vint, John Carradine; *D:* Alf Kjellin. **VHS** $19.95 *STE, XVC* 🎞️🎞️

McQ After several big dope dealers kill two police officers, a lieutenant resigns to track them down. Dirty Harry done with an aging Big Duke.
1974 (PG) 116m/C John Wayne, Eddie Albert, Diana Muldaur, Clu Gulager, Colleen Dewhurst, Al Lettieri, Julie Adams, David Huddleston; *D:* John Sturges. **VHS, Beta, LV** $19.98 *WAR, PIA* 🎞️🎞️½

McVicar A brutish and realistic depiction of crime and punishment based on the life of John McVicar, who plotted to escape from prison. From the book by McVicar.
1980 (R) 90m/C *GB* Roger Daltrey, Adam Faith, Cheryl Campbell; *D:* Tom Clegg. **VHS, Beta, LV** $29.98 *VES* 🎞️🎞️½

Me and Him An unsuspecting New Yorker finds himself jockeying for position with his own instincts when his libido decides it wants a life of its own. *AKA:* Ich und Er.
1989 (R) 94m/C *GE* Griffin Dunne, Carey Lowell, Ellen Greene, Craig T. Nelson; *D:* Doris Dorrie; *V:* Mark Linn-Baker. **VHS, LV** $79.95 *COL* 🎞️½

The Meal During a dinner party held by a wealthy woman, the rich and powerful guests divulge each others' secrets with reckless disregard for the consequences. *AKA:* Deadly Encounter.
1975 (R) 90m/C Dina Merrill, Carl Betz, Leon Ames, Susan Logan, Vicki Powers, Steve Potter; *D:* R. John Hugh. **VHS** $19.95 *UHV, MOV* 🎞️🎞️

Mean Dog Blues A musician is convicted of hit-and-run driving after hitching a ride with an inebriated politician.

1978 (PG) 108m/C George Kennedy, Kay Lenz, Scatman Crothers, Greg Henry, Gregory Sierra, Tina Louise, William Windom; *D:* Mel Stuart. **VHS, Beta** $69.98 *LIV, VES* 🎞️🎞️½

Mean Frank and Crazy Tony A mobster and the man who idolizes him attempt a prison breakout in this fun, action-packed production.
1975 (R) 92m/C *IT* Lee Van Cleef, Tony LoBianco, Jean Rochefort, Jess Hahn; *D:* Michele Lupo. **VHS, Beta** $39.95 *LIV* 🎞️🎞️

Mean Johnny Barrows When Johnny Barrows returns to his home town after being dishonorably discharged from the Army he is offered a job as a gang hitman.
1975 83m/C Fred Williamson, Roddy McDowall, Stuart Whitman, Luther Adler, Jenny Sherman, Elliott Gould; *D:* Fred Williamson. **VHS, Beta** $49.95 *UNI* 🎞️½

Mean Machine A man and his beautiful cohort plot revenge on organized crime for the murder of his father.
1973 (R) 89m/C Chris Mitchum, Barbara Bouchet, Arthur Kennedy. **VHS, Beta** *MON* 🎞️🎞️

Mean Season A vicious mass murderer makes a Miami crime reporter his confidante in his quest for publicity during his killing spree. In time, the madman's intentions become clear as the tensions and headlines grow with each gruesome slaying. Then the reporter must come to terms with the idea that he is letting himself be used due to the success that the association is bringing him. Suspenseful story with a tense ending. Good performance from Russell as the reporter.
1985 (R) 106m/C Kurt Russell, Mariel Hemingway, Richard Jordan, Richard Masur, Andy Garcia, Joe Pantoliano, Richard Bradford, William Smith; *D:* Phillip Borsos. **VHS, Beta, LV** $14.99 *HBO* 🎞️🎞️

Mean Streets A grimy slice of street life in Little Italy among lower echelon Mafiosos, unbalanced punks, and petty criminals. A riveting, free-form feature film, marking the formal debut by Scorsese (five years earlier he had completed a student film, "Who's That Knocking At My Door?"). Unorthodox camera movement and gritty performances by De Niro and Keitel, with underlying Catholic guilt providing the moral conflict. Excellent early '60s soundtrack.
1973 (R) 112m/C Harvey Keitel, Robert De Niro, David Proval, Amy Robinson, Richard Romanus, David Carradine, Robert Carradine, Cesare Danova; *D:* Martin Scorsese. **VHS, Beta, LV** $19.98 *WAR, PIA* 🎞️🎞️🎞️🎞️

Mean Streets of Kung Fu Ugliness of the nastiest kind brings battle and bloodshed to the dirty boulevards of China.
1983 84m/C Barry Chan. **VHS, Beta** $59.95 *WWV* 🎞️½

The Meanest Men in the West Two criminal half-brothers battle frontier law and each other.
1976 (PG) 92m/C Charles Bronson, Lee Marvin, Lee J. Cobb, James Drury, Albert Salmi, Charles Grodin; *D:* Samuel Fuller; *W:* Charles S. Dubin. **VHS, Beta** $19.95 *MCA* 🎞️

Measure for Measure "Measure for Measure" is one of Shakespeare's most controversial comedies. It deals with the law of Vienna—a law where a sexual relationship between unmarried people is punishable by death. Part of the television series "The Shakespeare Plays."
1979 145m/C *GB* Kate Nelligan, Tim Pigott-Smith, Christopher Strauli. **VHS, Beta** *TLF* 🎞️🎞️½

Meatballs The Activities Director at a summer camp who is supposed to organize fun for everyone prefers his own style of "fun." If you enjoy watching Murray blow

through a movie, you'll like this one even as it lapses into box office sentimentality.
1979 (PG) 92m/C *CA* Bill Murray, Harvey Atkin, Kate Lynch; *D:* Ivan Reitman. **VHS, Beta, LV** $24.95 *PAR* 🎞️🎞️

Meatballs 2 The future of Camp Sasquatch is in danger unless the camp's best fighter can beat Camp Patton's champ in a boxing match. The saving grace of Bill Murray is absent in this one.
1984 (PG) 87m/C Archie Hahn, John Mengatti, Tammy Taylor, Kim Richards, Ralph Seymour, Richard Mulligan, Hamilton Camp, John Larroquette, Pee-Wee Herman, Misty Rowe, Elayne Boosler; *D:* Ken Wiederhorn. **VHS, Beta, LV, 8mm** $79.95 *COL* 🎞️½

Meatballs 3 Second sequel to the teenage sex/summer camp comedy. Enough is enough!
1987 (R) 95m/C Sally Kellerman, Shannon Tweed, George Buza, Isabelle Mejias, Al Waxman, Patrick Dempsey; *D:* George Mendeluk. **VHS, Beta** $19.95 *LIV* Woof!

Meatballs 4 Feldman stars as a water skier hired to serve as recreation director of Lakeside Water Ski Camp. His enemy is Monica (Douglas) of a nearby rival camp who wants to buy out Lakeside's owner and use the land for real estate development. Lame plot only serves to showcase some good water skiing stunts.
1992 (R) 87m/C Corey Feldman, Jack Nance, Sarah Douglas, Bojesse Christopher; *D:* Bob Logan. **VHS** $89.90 *HBO* 🎞️½

The Meateater Disgusting horror flick of a disfigured hermit who inhabits a closed-up movie house. When it is reopened he turns into a stereotypical slasher. Vegetarians beware: references throughout about eating meat.
1979 84m/C Arch Jaboulian, Diane Davis, Emily Spendler; *D:* Derek Savage. **VHS, Beta** *NO* Woof!

The Mechanic Bronson stars as Arthur Bishop, a wealthy professional killer for a powerful organization. He has innumerable ways to kill. *AKA:* Killer of Killers.
1972 (R) 100m/C Charles Bronson, Jan-Michael Vincent, Keenan Wynn, Jill Ireland, Linda Ridgeway; *D:* Michael Winner. **VHS, Beta, LV** $14.95 *MGM, FOX* 🎞️🎞️

Mechanical Crabs A scientist develops the ultimate war weapon: giant mechanical crabs, strong enough to crush anything in their path and devour metal, grow, and multiply. They eventually turn on the scientist and eliminate him.
1977 10m/C **VHS, Beta** *BFA* Woof!

The Medal of Honor Features 17 segments which highlight amazing and daring aerial feats, in tribute to the flying Medal of Honor recipients.
1985 100m/B **VHS, Beta** $29.95 *BVG, FGF, AVL* Woof!

Medea Medea, who betrayed her homeland for Jason, is becoming wary of his boredom with her. The classic story of love and revenge ensues thereafter in unbridled fury and passion.
1959 107m/B Colleen Dewhurst, Zoe Caldwell, Judith Anderson; *D:* Jose Quintero. **VHS** *IVY, FHS* Woof!

Medea Cinema poet Pasolini directs opera diva Callas in this straightforward adaptation of Euripides's classic about a sorceress whose escapades range from assisting in the theft of the Golden Fleece to murdering her own children. Not Pasolini at his best, but still better than most if what you're looking for is something arty. In Italian with English subtitles.

1970 118m/C *IT* Maria Callas, Guiseppi Gentile, Laurent Terzieff; *D:* Pier Paolo Pasolini. VHS, Beta $49.95 *HMV, VAI, APD* *Woof!*

Medic Boone stars as Dr. Konrad Stuner, the protagonist in this controversial series, ranked as television's first realistic medical show and based on real-life incidents. Featured are two episodes "My Brother Joe" and "Flash of Darkness." Additional episodes available.
1954 55m/B Richard Boone. VHS, Beta $19.95 *HEG, MOV* *Woof!*

Medicine Man Benny stars as a con-man who fronts a medicine show in this early talkie comedy.
1930 57m/B Jack Benny, Betty Bronson, E. Allen Warren, George E. Stone, Tom Dugan; *D:* Scott Pembroke; *M:* Jerry Goldsmith. VHS, Beta $19.95 *NOS, DVT, VYY* 🎬½

Medicine Man Connery's usual commanding presence and the beautiful scenery are the only things to recommend in this lame effort. Dr. Robert Campbell (Connery) is a biochemist working in the Amazon rain forest on a cancer cure. Bracco plays Dr. Rae Crane, a fellow researcher sent by the institute sponsoring Campbell to see how things are going. Although Crane is uptight and Campbell is gruff, they fall in love (supposedly), but they're sorely lacking in chemistry. Oh, Campbell's cancer cure is made from a rare flower being eradicated by the destruction of the rain forest. This politically correct cause meets romance falls short of ever being truly entertaining.
1992 (PG-13) 105m/C Sean Connery, Lorraine Bracco, Jose Wilker, Rodolfo de Alexandra, Francisco Tsirene Tsere Rereme, Elias Monteiro da Silva; *D:* John McTiernan. VHS, Beta $94.95 *HPH* 🎬

The Mediterranean in Flames In Nazi-occupied Greece, a small but brave resistance is formed to fight its captors. One of the women within the group is forced to seduce a Nazi officer in an attempt to learn enemy secrets.
1972 85m/C *GR* Costas Karras, Costas Precas; *D:* Dimis Dadiras. VHS, Beta *NO* 🎬½

Mediterraneo A languid, charming comedy based on the premise that love does make the world go 'round—especially in wartime. In 1941, eight misfit Italian soldiers are sent to a tiny Greek island in the Aegean for four months of lookout duty. When their radio is broken and their relief ship is torpedoed, the men appear to be stranded on a deserted island. Only then do the islanders appear, a group of women, children, and old men, the able-bodied men having been taken by the previous German occupiers. Seemingly forgotten by their commanders, the soldiers are soon absorbed into the life of the island, finding love and liberty in this idyllic setting. In Italian with English subtitles.
1992 (R) 90m/C *IT* Diego Abatantuono, Giuseppe Cederna, Claudio Bigagli, Vanna Barba, Claudio Bisio, Luigi Alberti, Ugo Conti, Memo Dini, Vasco Mirandola, Luigi Montini, Irene Grazioli, Antonio Catania; *D:* Gabriele Salvatores. VHS, Beta, LV $94.95 *TOU, IME* 🎬🎬🎬

The Medium A phony medium is done in by her own trickery in this filmed version of the Menotti opera.
1951 80m/B Marie Powers, Anna Maria Alberghetti, Leo Coleman; *W/D:* Gian-Carlo Menotti. VHS, Beta $49.95 *MVD, VAI* 🎬🎬🎬

Medium Cool Commentary on life in the '60s focuses on a television news cameraman and his growing apathy with the events around him. Shot during the riots of 1968. A frightening depiction of detachment in modern society.

1969 111m/C Robert Forster, Verna Bloom, Peter Bonerz, Marianna Hill; *D:* Haskell Wexler. VHS, Beta *PAR, OM* 🎬🎬🎬½

Medusa A bizarre series of events occur when an abandoned yacht containing two lifeless bodies is found on the Aegean Sea. Also released on video as "Twisted."
1974 103m/C George Hamilton, Cameron Mitchell, Lucianna Paluzzi, Theodore Roubanis; *D:* Gordon Hessler. VHS, Beta $16.95 *SNC, PSM, SIM* 🎬

Medusa Against the Son of Hercules This time the strongman takes on the evil Medusa and her deadly army of rock men. *AKA:* Perseus the Invincible.
1962 ?m/C *IT* Richard Harrison. VHS, Beta $16.95 *SNC* 🎬

The Medusa Touch A man is struck over the head and is admitted to a hospital. Meanwhile, strange disasters befall the surrounding city. It seems that despite his unconscious state, the man is using his telekinetic powers to will things to happen....
1978 (R) 110m/C *GB* Richard Burton, Lino Ventura, Lee Remick, Harry Andrews, Alan Badel, Marie-Christine Barrault, Michael Hordern, Derek Jacobi, Jeremy Brett; *D:* Jack Gold. VHS *FOX* 🎬

Meet Dr. Christian The good old doctor settles some problems. Part of a series.
1939 72m/B Jean Hersholt, Robert Baldwin, Paul Harvey; *D:* Bernard Vorhaus. VHS, Beta $19.95 *NOS, DVT, VYY* 🎬½

Meet John Doe A social commentary about an unemployed, down-and-out man selected to be the face of a political goodwill campaign. Honest and trusting, he eventually realizes that he is being used to further the careers of corrupt politicians. Available in colorized version.
1941 123m/B Gary Cooper, Barbara Stanwyck, Edward Arnold, James Gleason, Walter Brennan, Spring Byington, Gene Lockhart, Regis Toomey, Ann Doran; *D:* Frank Capra. VHS, LV, 3/4U, Special order formats $14.95 *NOS, MRV, PSM* 🎬🎬🎬

Meet Me in Las Vegas Compulsive gambler/cowboy Dailey betters his luck when he hooks up with hoofer girlfriend Charisse. Much frolicking and dancing and cameo appearances by a truckload of stars. A little more entertaining than a game of solitaire. 🎵The Girl With the Yaller Shoes; If You Can Dream; Hell Hath No Fury; Lucky Charm; I Refuse to Rock 'n Roll; Rehearsal Ballet; Sleeping Beauty Ballet; Frankie and Johnny.
1956 112m/C Dan Dailey, Cyd Charisse, Agnes Moorehead, Lili Darvas, Jim Backus, Cara Williams, Betty Lynn, Oscar Karlweis, Liliane Montevecchi, Jerry Colonna, Frankie Laine; *Cameos:* Debbie Reynolds, Frank Sinatra, Peter Lorre, Vic Damone, Tony Martin, Elaine Stewart; *D:* Roy Rowland; *W:* Isobel Lennart. VHS, LV $19.98 *MGM, TTC, FCT* 🎬🎬

Meet Me in St. Louis Wonderful music in this charming tale of a St. Louis family during the 1903 World's Fair. One of Garland's better musical performances. 🎵You and I; Skip to My Lou; Over the Bannister; Meet Me In St. Louis; Brighten the Corner; Summer In St. Louis; All Hallow's Eve; Ah, Love; The Horrible One; Goodbye My Lady Love; Under the Anheuser Bush; Little Brown Jug; The Fair; Trolley Song; Have Yourself a Merry Little Christmas; I Was Drunk Last Night; The Boy Next Door; Under the Bamboo Tree.
1944 113m/C Judy Garland, Margaret O'Brien, Mary Astor, Lucille Bremer, Tom Drake, June Lockhart, Harry Davenport; *D:* Vincente Minnelli. Academy Awards '44 Nominations: Best Color Cinematography, Best Screenplay, Best Song ("The Trolley Song"), Best Original Score;

National Board of Review Awards '44: 10 Best Films of the Year. VHS, Beta, LV, 8mm $19.98 *MGM, TLF, HMV* 🎬🎬🎬½

Meet Sexton Blake A detective is hired to find a ring and some secret papers that were stolen from the corpse of a man killed in an air raid. He discovers that the papers contained the plans for a new metal alloy to be used in planes. Entertaining for its melodramatic elements.
1944 80m/B *GB* David Farrar, John Varley, Magda Kun, Gordon McLeod, Manning Whiley; *W/D:* John Harlow. VHS, Beta $16.95 *SNC* 🎬

Meet the Hollowheads Family situation comedy set in a futuristic society.
1989 (PG-13) 89m/C John Glover, Nancy Mette, Richard Portnow, Matt Shakman, Juliette Lewis, Anne Ramsey; *D:* Tom Burman. VHS, LV $39.95 *MED, IME* 🎬½

Meet the Mob A country spinster visits her son in the big city and is mistaken for a notorious murderess. Complications arise when she tries to keep the boy honest. Could have worked better.
1942 62m/B ZaSu Pitts, Roger Pryor, Warren Hymer, Gwen Kenyon, Douglas Fowley, Elizabeth Russell, Tristram Coffin, Lester Dorr, Wheeler Oakman, Bud McTaggart; *D:* Jean Yarborough. VHS $19.95 *NOS* 🎬

Meet the Navy Post-war musical revue about a pianist and a dancer.
1946 81m/B Joan Pratt, Margaret Hurst, Lionel Murton. VHS, Beta $29.95 *NO* 🎬

Meet the Parents A young man visits his fiance's parents and every nightmare, every tragedy that can possibly happen, does. From the minds of "National Lampoon," with an appearance by beyond-bizarre comedian Emo Phillips.
1991 ?m/C Greg Glionna, Jacqueline Cahill, Dick Galloway, Carol Wheeler, Mary Ruth Clarke, Emo Phillips; *D:* Greg Glionna. VHS *NO* 🎬

Meeting at Midnight Charlie Chan is invited to a seance to solve a perplexing mystery. Chan discovers that they use mechanical figures and from there on solving the murder is easy.
1944 67m/B Sidney Toler, Joseph Crehan, Mantan Moreland, Frances Chan, Ralph Peters, Helen Beverly; *D:* Phil Rosen. VHS, Beta $19.98 *MGM, VCN, MRV* 🎬

The Meeting: Eddie Finds a Home Ben Davidson finds an orphan pup rummaging through the trash and cautiously begins a relationship of trust.
1990 ?m/C VHS $14.95 *SPW* 🎬

Meeting Venus Backstage drama featuring Close as Karin Anderson, a world-famous Swedish opera diva. An international cast of characters adds to this sophisticated film of romance, rivalry and political confrontation set amidst a newly unified Europe.
1991 (PG-13) 121m/C Glenn Close, Niels Arestrup, Erland Josephson, Johanna Ter Steege, Maria De Medeiros; *D:* Istvan Szabo; *V:* Kiri Te Kanawa. VHS, Beta, LV $92.99 *WAR* 🎬🎬½

Meetings with Remarkable Men An acclaimed, visually awesome film version of the memoir by Gurdjieff, about his wanderings through Asia and the Middle East searching for answers and developing his own spiritual code. Mildly entertaining but only of true interest to those familiar with the subject.
1979 108m/C Terence Stamp, Dragan Maksimovic, Mikica Dmitrijevic; *D:* Peter Brook. VHS, Beta $69.95 *TAM* 🎬🎬½

Megaforce Futuristic thriller directed by stuntman Needham follows the adventures of the military task force, Megaforce, on its mission to save a small democratic nation from attack. Bostwick leads the attack. 'Nuff said.
1982 (PG) 99m/C Barry Bostwick, Persis Khambatta, Edward Mulhare, Henry Silva, Michael Beck, Ralph Wilcox; **D:** Hal Needham. **VHS, Beta $19.98** FOX *Woof!*

Megaville Set in the not too distant future, corrupt politician Travanti struggles to corner the market on the evil technology "Dream-a-Life," which aims to control the rebellious "riff-raff" of Megaville. He does all of his dealings while up against a hitman who has a defective memory chip in his brain.
1991 (R) 96m/C Billy Zane, Daniel J. Travanti, J.C. Quinn, Grace Zabriskie; **W/D:** Peter Lehner. **VHS $89.98** LIV *&&*

Mein Kampf The rise and fall of German fascism and its impact upon the world is examined in this documentary.
1960 120m/C **D:** Erwin Leiser. **VHS, Beta, LV $39.95** SUE, MRV, FCT *&&*

Melanie Drama tells the tale of one poor woman's courage, determination, and optimism, as she tries to regain her child from her ex-husband. She befriends musician Cummings (a founding member of "Guess Who" rock band) who helps. Usual cliches balanced by good performances.
1982 (PG) 109m/C CA Glynnis O'Connor, Paul Sorvino, Don Johnson, Burton Cummings; **D:** Rex Bromfield. **VHS, Beta $69.95** VES *&&½*

Melodie en Sous-Sol Two ex-convicts, one old and one young, risk their lives and freedom for one last major heist: a gambling casino. In French with English subtitles. **AKA:** Any Number Can Win.
1963 118m/B FR Jean Gabin, Alain Delon, Viviane Romance; **D:** Henri Verneuil. **VHS, Beta $19.95** KRT, TAM *&&*

Melody Sensitive but slow study of a special friendship which enables two pre-teens to survive in a regimented and impersonal world. Features music by the Bee Gees.
1971 (G) 106m/C GB Jack Wild, Mark Lester, Colin Barrie, Roy Kinnear; **D:** Waris Hussein. **VHS, Beta $69.98** SUE *&&*

Melody Cruise Boring musical romantic comedy that can't stay with any one of those three things for more than a minute without careening into one of the other two. ♫I Met Her at a Party; He's Not the Marrying Kind; Isn't This a Night For Love; This is the Hour.
1932 75m/B Phil Harris, Charlie Ruggles, Greta Nissen, Helen Mack, Chick Chandler; **D:** Mark Sandrich. **VHS, Beta $19.98** TTC *&&*

Melody for Three In the tradition of matchmaker, Doctor Christian aids in the reuniting of music-teacher mother and great-conductor father, who have been divorced for years, in order to help the couple's son, a violin prodigy.
1941 69m/B Jean Hersholt, Fay Wray; **D:** Erle C. Kenton. **VHS, Beta, 8mm $19.95** NOS, VYY, DVT *&&*

Melody in Love A young girl visits her cousin and her swinging friends on a tropical island. Dubbed.
1978 90m/C Melody O'Bryan, Sasha Hehn; **D:** Hubert Frank. **VHS, Beta $59.98** FOX *&*

Melody Master Romanticized biography of composer Franz Schubert, chronicling his personal life and loves, along with performances of his compositions. If you just have to know what drove the composer of "Ave Maria" it may hold your interest, but otherwise not very compelling. **AKA:** New Wine.
1941 80m/B Alan Curtis, Ilona Massey, Binnie Barnes, Albert Basserman, Billy Gilbert, Sterling Holloway. **VHS, Beta $19.95** NOS, VYY, DVT *&&*

Melody Ranch Gene returns to his home town as an honored guest and appointed sheriff. But gangster MacLane is determined to drive him out of town. ♫Melody Ranch; Call of the Canyon; We Never Dream the Same Dream Twice; Vote for Autry; My Gal Sal; Torpedo Joe; What Are Cowboys Made Of?; Rodeo Rose; Back in the Saddle Again; Go Back to the City Again.
1940 84m/C Gene Autry, Jimmy Durante, George "Gabby" Hayes, George "Gabby" Hayes, Ann Miller, Barton MacLane, Joe Sawyer, Horace McMahon; **D:** Joseph Santley. **VHS, Beta $19.95** CCB, VCN *&&½*

Melody Trail Autry wins $1000 in a rodeo, loses the money to a gypsy, gets a job, falls for his employer's daughter...and in the end captures a kidnapper and cattle rustlers. ♫Hold On, Little Doggie, Hold On; On the Prairie; Lookin for the Lost Chord; The Hurdy Gurdy Man; My Prayer For Tonight; End of the Trail; I'd Love a Home in the Mountains.
1935 60m/B Gene Autry, Smiley Burnette, Ann Rutherford; **D:** Joseph Kane. **VHS, Beta $37.95** CCB, VCN *&*

Melvin and Howard Story of Melvin Dummar, who once gave Howard Hughes a ride. Dummar later claimed a share of Hughes's will. Significant for Demme's direction and fine acting from Steenburgen/Le-Mat, and Robards in a small role as Hughes. Offbeat and very funny.
1980 (R) 95m/C Paul LeMat, Jason Robards Jr., Mary Steenburgen, Michael J. Pollard, Dabney Coleman, Elizabeth Cheshire, Pamela Reed, Cheryl "Rainbeaux" Smith; **D:** Jonathan Demme. Academy Awards '80: Best Original Screenplay, Best Supporting Actress (Steenburgen); Nominations: Best Supporting Actor (Robards); Los Angeles Film Critics Association Awards '80: Best Supporting Actress (Steenburgen); National Board of Review Awards '80: 10 Best Films of the Year; New York Film Critics Awards '80: Best Director (Demme), Best Supporting Actress (Steenburgen). **VHS, Beta, LV $14.95** MCA, BTV *&&&½*

Melvin Purvis: G-Man Mediocre action film has dedicated federal agent tracking killer Machine Gun Kelly across American Midwest during Depression. Made for television. **AKA:** The Legend of Machine Gun Kelly.
1974 78m/C Dale Robertson, Harris Yulin, Margaret Blye, Matt Clark, Elliot Street, Dick Sargent, John Karlen, David Canary; **D:** Dan Curtis. **VHS $69.95** HBO *&&*

The Member of the Wedding While struggling through her adolescence, a twelve-year-old girl growing up in 1945 Georgia seeks solace from her family's cook. Based on Carson McCullers's play, this story of family, belonging, and growth is well acted and touching.
1952 90m/C Ethel Waters, Julie Harris, Brandon de Wilde, Arthur Franz; **D:** Fred Zinneman. **VHS, Beta** NO *&&&*

The Member of the Wedding TV rehash of Carson McCuller's play about a young girl who finds she's got some growing up to do when big brother marries. No match for Zinnemann's '52 version, or for Mann's earlier "All Quiet on the Western Front" and "Marty."
1983 90m/C Dana Hill, Pearl Bailey, Howard E. Rollins Jr.; **D:** Delbert Mann. **VHS $49.95** VHE *&&*

Memoirs of an Invisible Man Nick Halloway, a slick and shallow stock analyst, is rendered invisible by a freak accident. When he is pursued by a CIA agent-hit man who wants to exploit him, Nick turns for help to Alice, a documentary filmmaker he has just met. Naturally, they fall in love along the way. Effective sight gags, hardworking cast can't overcome pitfalls in script, which indecisively meanders between comedy and thrills.
1992 (PG-13) 99m/C Chevy Chase, Daryl Hannah, Sam Neill, Michael McKean, Stephen Tobolowsky, Jim Norton, Patricia Heaton, Rosalind Chao; **D:** John Carpenter. **VHS, LV $19.98** WAR *&½*

Memorial Day Good cast highlights this made-for-television outing covering a Vietnam veterans reunion. With the old memories come new problems for the men and their families.
1983 120m/C Mike Farrell, Shelley Fabares, Keith Mitchell, Bonnie Bedelia, Robert Walden, Edward Herrmann, Danny Glover; **D:** Joseph Sargent. **VHS** NO *&&*

Memorial Valley Massacre When campers settle for a weekend in a new, unfinished campground, they're slaughtered in turn by a nutty hermit.
1988 (R) 93m/C Cameron Mitchell, William Smith, John Kerry, Mark Mears, Lesa Lee, John Caso; **D:** Robert C. Hughes. **VHS, Beta, LV $19.98** SUE, NLC *&*

Memories of a Marriage A nostalgic look at a couple's many years of marriage, from the husband's point of view, as they face their most trying times. Touchingly reminiscent as it spans the youthful years of new love and marriage to the more quiet, solid years of matured love. In Danish with English subtitles.
1990 90m/C DK Ghita Norby, Frits Helmuth, Rikke Bendsen, Henning Moritzen; **D:** Kaspar Rostrup. **VHS $79.95** FXL, TAM *&&&*

Memories of Hell Examines the special bonds of friendship that have been maintained among the New Mexicans who survived one of World War II's most brutal battles and subsequent prisoner experiences.
1987 57m/C **VHS, Beta, 3/4U** CEN *&&&*

Memories of Me A distraught doctor travels to L.A. to see his ailing father and make up for lost time. Both the doctor and his father learn about themselves and each other. Story of child/parent relationships attempts to pull at the heartstrings but only gets as far as the liver. Co-written and co-produced by Crystal, this film never quite reaches the potential of its cast.
1988 (PG-13) 103m/C Billy Crystal, Alan King, JoBeth Williams, David Ackroyd, Sean Connery, Janet Carroll; **D:** Henry Winkler. **VHS, Beta, LV $19.98** FOX *&&*

Memories of Murder A woman suffering from amnesia is stalked by a merciless killer, apparently seeking revenge. Can she regain her memory and understand why she is being hunted, before it's too late?
1990 104m/C Vanity, Nancy Allen, Robin Thomas; **D:** Robert Lewis. **VHS, Beta $79.98** PSM *&&*

Memories of Underdevelopment Set in the early 1960s. An antirevolutionary, Europeanized intellectual takes a stand against the new government in Cuba. In Spanish with English subtitles.
1968 97m/B Sergio Corrieri, Daisy Granados; **W/D:** Thomas Gutierrez Alea. **VHS $69.95** NYF, FCT, TAM *&&½*

Memory of Us Still-relevant story of a married, middle-aged woman who starts to question her happiness as a wife and mother. Written by its star Geer, whose father, Will, plays a bit part.
1974 (PG) 93m/C Ellen Geer, Jon Cypher, Barbara Colby, Peter Brown, Robert Hogan, Rose Marie, Will Geer; *D:* H. Kaye Dyal. VHS $19.95 ACA *ℐℐ*

Memphis In 1957 three white drifters (two men and a woman) decide to secure some easy money by kidnapping the young grandson of the richest black businessman in Memphis. They think it's an easy job since, given the prejudice of the times, the police will do little or nothing but they reckon without the resources of the black community itself. Based on the novel "September, September" by Shelby Foote. Originally made for cable.
1991 (PG-13) 92m/C Cybill Shepherd, John Laughlin, J.E. Freeman, Richard Brooks, Moses Gunn. VHS, Beta, LV $89.98 TTC *ℐℐ½*

Memphis Belle Satisfying Hollywood version of the documentary of the same name captures the true story of the final mission of a WWII bomber crew stationed in England. The boys of the Memphis Belle were the first group of B-17 crewmen to complete a 25 mission tour—no small feat in an air war that claimed many lives. Up and coming young actors work well as an ensemble cast; Lithgow has a nice turn as an army PR guy determined to exploit their boyish good looks to the people back home. Caton-Jones effectively uses 1940s film techniques and thrilling flight footage, making up for a script which might be considered hokey by today's standards. Film debut of singer Connick. Produced by Catherine Wyler, whose father William made the original.
1990 (PG-13) 107m/C Matthew Modine, John Lithgow, Eric Stoltz, Sean Astin, Harry Connick Jr., Reed Edward Diamond, Tate Donovan, D.B. Sweeney, Billy Zane, David Strathairn, Jane Horrocks; *D:* Michael Caton-Jones; *W:* Monte Merrick; *M:* George Fenton. VHS, Beta, LV, 8mm $19.95 WAR, FCT, HHE *ℐℐℐ*

Memphis Belle: A Story of a Flying Fortress The entire final mission of the B-25 bomber "Memphis Belle" and its daring daylight attack on the submarine pens at Wilhelmshaven, Germany is captured through newsreel footage. The crew was the first to complete a 25 run mission. A film version of the story was released in 1990 as "Memphis Belle." Produced by William Wyler.
1944 43m/C VHS, Beta, 3/4U $24.95 TPV, NOS, HHT *ℐℐℐ*

The Men A paraplegic World War II veteran sinks into depression until his former girlfriend manages to bring him out of it. Marlon Brando's first film. A thoughtful story that relies on subtle acting and direction. *AKA:* Battle Stripe.
1950 85m/B Marlon Brando, Teresa Wright, Everett Sloane, Jack Webb; *D:* Fred Zinneman. Academy Awards '50 Nominations: Best Story & Screenplay; National Board of Review Awards '50: 10 Best Films of the Year. VHS $19.98 REP *ℐℐℐ½*

Men... A funny and insightful satire about a man who discovers his loving wife has been having an affair with a young artist. In a unique course of revenge, the husband ingratiates himself with the artist and gradually turns him into a carbon copy of himself. In German; dubbed in English.
1985 99m/C GE Heiner Lauterbach, Uwe Ochsenknecht, Ulrike Kriener, Janna Marangosoff; *D:* Doris Dorrie. VHS, Beta NO *ℐℐℐ½*

Men are not Gods Verbose film (precursor to "A Double Life") about an actor playing Othello who nearly kills his wife during Desdemona's death scene.
1937 90m/B GB Rex Harrison, Miriam Hopkins, Gertrude Lawrence; *D:* Walter Reisch. VHS, Beta, LV SUE *ℐℐ½*

Men at Work Garbage collectors Sheen and Estevez may not love their work, but at least it's consistent from day to day. That is, until they get wrapped up in a very dirty politically-motivated murder. And who will clean up the mess when the politicians are through trashing each other? A semi-thrilling semi-comedy that may leave you semi-satisfied.
1990 (PG-13) 98m/C Charlie Sheen, Emilio Estevez, Leslie Hope, Keith David; *W/D:* Emilio Estevez. VHS, Beta, LV $19.95 COL, FOX *ℐℐ*

Men Don't Leave A recent widow tries to raise her kids single-handedly, suffers big city life and regains her love life. Good performances by all, especially Cusack. By the director of "Risky Business."
1989 (PG-13) 115m/C Jessica Lange, Arliss Howard, Joan Cusack, Kathy Bates, Charlie Korsmo, Corey Carrier, Chris O'Donnell; *D:* Paul Brickman; *W:* Barbara Benedek, Paul Brickman. VHS, Beta, LV, 8mm $19.98 WAR *ℐℐ½*

Men in Love A young San Franciscan travels to Hawaii with the cremated remains of his lover, who has succumbed to AIDS. There he encounters a supportive group of men who nurse him back to sexual and spiritual wholeness.
1990 87m/C Doug Self, Joe Tolbe, Emerald Starr, Kutira Decosterd; *D:* Mark Huestis; *W:* Starr Emerald Catamas Scott. VHS $59.95 WBF, FCT, TAM *ℐℐ*

Men in War Korean War drama about a small platoon trying to take an enemy hill by themselves. A worthwhile effort with some good action sequences.
1957 100m/B Robert Ryan, Robert Keith, Aldo Ray, Vic Morrow; *D:* Anthony Mann. VHS, Beta $19.95 FGF, MRV, WWV *ℐℐ½*

Men of Boys Town Sequel to 1938's "Boys Town" has the same sentimentality, even more if that's possible. Father Flanagan's reformatory faces closure, while the kids reach out to an embittered new inmate. Worth seeing for the ace cast reprising their roles.
1941 106m/B Spencer Tracy, Mickey Rooney, Darryl Hickman, Henry O'Neill, Lee J. Cobb, Sidney Miller; *D:* Norman Taurog. VHS $19.98 MGM, FCT *ℐℐ½*

Men of Ireland A Dublin medical student cavorts with islanders off the Irish coast. Uninspired programmer with authentic native folk of the Blasket Islands, plus their songs and dances.
1938 62m/B IR Cecil Ford, Eileen Curran, Brian O'Sullivan, Gabriel Fallon; *D:* Dick Bird. VHS, Beta, 8mm $24.95 VYY *ℐ*

Men of Respect Shakespeare meets the mafia in this misbegotten gangster yarn. Turturro, a gangster MacBeth, is prodded by wife and psychic to butcher his way to the top o' the mob. Well acted but ill conceived, causing Bard's partial roll over in grave.
1991 (R) 113m/C John Turturro, Katherine Borowitz, Peter Boyle, Dennis Farina, Chris Stein, Steven Wright, Stanley Tucci; *W/D:* William Reilly. VHS, LV, 8mm $19.95 COL, PIA *ℐℐ*

Men of Sherwood Forest Robin Hood and his band take it to the sheriff et al in this colorful Hammer version of the timeless legend.
1957 77m/C GB Don Taylor, Reginald Beckwith, Eileen Moore, Davis King-Wood, Patrick Holt, John Van Eyssen, Douglas Wilmer; *D:* Val Guest. VHS $16.95 NOS, SNC, DVT *ℐℐ½*

Men of Steel Two Canadian military officers, one French and one English, must struggle to survive when their plane crashes in the wilderness. Besides contending with the surroundings, they must deal with one another's instilled bitterness and underlying prejudices.
1988 91m/C Allan Royal, Robert Lalonde, David Ferry, Mavor Moore, Yvan Ponton; *D:* Donald Shebib. VHS, Beta TWE *ℐ*

Men of the Fighting Lady An action-adventure with plenty of exciting battle footage. Features the stories of selected pilots stationed on a U.S. aircraft carrier in the Pacific during the Korean War. The stories, told to Calhern as writer James A. Michener, center around the lead pilot Johnson. Dramatic airflights include a scene in which Johnson helps a blinded Martin land his plane safely on the carrier deck. Ruggerio's editing of the war footage was so expertly done that he was questioned by the Pentagon when they had a hard time believing the scenes were achieved by skillful editing and painted backdrops. Look for Jerry "Beaver" Mathers as one of Keenan Wynn's sons.
1954 81m/C Van Johnson, Walter Pidgeon, Louis Calhern, Dewey Martin, Keenan Wynn, Frank Lovejoy, Robert Horton, Bert Freed, Jerry Mathers; *D:* Andrew Marton. VHS, Beta $19.98 MGM *ℐℐℐ½*

Men of Two Worlds Classical musician raised in Africa is the toast of Europe until he finds out he's got a voodoo curse, and suddenly he's got the heebie jeebies too bad to play chopsticks. *AKA:* Witch Doctor; Kisenga, Man of Africa.
1946 90m/C GB Robert Adams, Eric Portman, Orlando Martins, Phyllis Calvert, Arnold Marle, Cathleen Nesbitt, David Horne, Cyril Raymond; *D:* Thorold Dickinson. VHS, Beta $16.95 SNC *ℐℐ*

The Men Who Tread on the Tiger's Tail Twelfth-century Japan is the setting for this struggle of power between two brothers, one a reigning shogun, the other on the run. English subtitles.
1945 60m/B JP *D:* Akira Kurosawa. VHS, Beta, 3/4U $29.95 IHF *ℐℐ½*

Menace on the Mountain Family-oriented drama about a father and son who battle carpetbagging Confederate deserters during the Civil War.
1970 (G) 89m/C Patricia Crowley, Albert Salmi, Charles Aidman. VHS, Beta $69.95 DIS *ℐℐ*

Menage Depardieu is the homosexual crook who breaks into the home of an impoverished couple—the dominating Miou-Miou and her submissive husband, Blanc. An unrepentant thief, he begins to take over their lives, introducing them to the wonderful world of crime, among other, more kinky, pastimes. Gender-bending farce that doesn't hold up to the end but is worth watching for sheer outrageousness. In French with English subtitles. *AKA:* Tenue de Soiree.
1986 84m/C FR Gerard Depardieu, Michel Blanc, Miou-Miou; *D:* Bertrand Blier. VHS $89.95 TRI, TAM, FCT *ℐℐ*

The Men's Club Seven middle-aged buddies get together for a single night, and bare their respective souls and personal traumas, talking about women and eating

and drinking. Banal. Based on novel by Leonard Michael.
1986 (R) 100m/C Harvey Keitel, Roy Scheider, Craig Wasson, Frank Langella, David Dukes, Richard Jordan, Treat Williams, Stockard Channing, Jennifer Jason Leigh, Ann Dusenberry, Cindy Pickett, Gwen Welles; **D:** Peter Medak. **VHS, Beta, LV $19.95** PAR ♪♪½

Menschenfrauen A philandering journalist is put in his place by the four women with whom he is simultaneously having relationships. In German with English subtitles.
1980 100m/C GE **D:** Valie Export. **VHS, Beta $59.95** FCT ♪♪½

Mephisto An egomaniacal actor, compellingly played by Brandauer, sides with the Nazis to further his career, with disastrous results. The first of three brilliant films by Szabo and Brandauer exploring the price of power and personal sublimation in German history. Critically hailed. In German with English subtitles. From the novel by Klaus Mann. Followed by ''Colonel Redl'' and ''Hanussen.''
1981 144m/C HU Klaus Maria Brandauer, Krystyna Janda, Ildiko Bansagi, Karin Boyd, Rolf Hoppe, Christine Harbort, Gyorgy Cserhalmi, Christiane Graskoff, Peter Andorai, Ildiko Kishonti; **D:** Istvan Szabo. **VHS, Beta $69.95** HBO, GLV, TAM ♪♪♪½

The Mephisto Waltz A journalist gets more than a story when he is granted an interview with a dying pianist. It turns out that he is a satanist and the cult he is a part of wants the journalist. A chilling adaptation of the Fred Mustard Stewart novel that also features a haunting musical score by Jerry Goldsmith.
1971 (R) 108m/C Alan Alda, Jacqueline Bisset, Barbara Parkins, Curt Jurgens, Bradford Dillman, William Windom, Kathleen Widdoes; **D:** Paul Wendkos; **M:** Jerry Goldsmith. **VHS $59.98** FOX ♪♪♪

The Mercenaries Romantic warrior fights to save the lives and honor of his people who are under attack from mercenaries murdering and raping their way across Europe.
1965 98m/C Debra Paget. **Beta $39.95** AIP ♪½

The Mercenaries A tough guy given the assignment to kill Fidel Castro, encounters all sorts of adversity along the way. Also called ''Cuba Crossing,'' ''Kill Castro,'' ''Assignment: Kill Castro,'' ''Key West Crossing,'' ''Sweet Dirty Tony.''
1980 92m/C Stuart Whitman, Robert Vaughn, Caren Kaye, Raymond St. Jacques, Woody Strode, Sybil Danning, Albert Salmi, Michael Gazzo; **D:** Chuck Workman. **VHS, Beta $59.95** ACA ♪

Mercenary Fighters An American soldier-of-fortune fights for both sides of an African revolution. Shot in South Africa.
1988 (R) 90m/C Peter Fonda, Reb Brown, Ron O'Neal, Jim Mitchum; **D:** Riki Shelach. **VHS, Beta, LV $79.95** MED ♪½

The Merchant of Four Seasons Story focuses on the depression and unfulfilled dreams of an average street merchant. Direction from Fassbinder is slow, deliberate, and mesmerizing. In German with English subtitles.
1971 88m/C Hans Hirschmuller, Irm Hermann, Hanna Schygulla, Andrea Schober, Gusti Kreissl; **W/D:** Rainer Werner Fassbinder. **VHS, Beta $79.95** NYF, TAM ♪♪♪

Merchants of War Sent out by the CIA on a mission, two best friends are soon the target of one of the most dangerous terrorists in the world. The fanatical Islamic terrorist soon casts his wrath upon the two men.

1990 (R) 100m/C Asher Brauner, Jesse Vint, Bonnie Beck; **D:** Peter M. MacKenzie. **VHS $89.95** VMK ♪

Mere Jeevan Saathi A bizarre, unclassifiable Indian film with music, fantasy, special effects, violence, and flamboyant mise-en-scene. In Hindi with English subtitles. English title: ''My Life Partner.''
1965 126m/C IN Lata Mangeskar. **VHS, Beta $29.95** VYY, AUD ♪♪½

Meridian: Kiss of the Beast A beautiful heiress is courted, kidnapped and loved by a demonic man-beast.
1990 90m/C Sherilyn Fenn, Malcom Jamieson, Hilary Mason, Alex Daniels, Phil Fondacaro; **D:** Charles Band; **W:** Dennis Paoli. **VHS, Beta, LV $19.95** PAR ♪♪

Merlin and the Sword Poor use of a good cast in this treatment of the legend of Merlin, Arthur and Excalibur. **AKA:** Arthur the King.
1985 94m/C Malcolm McDowell, Edward Woodward, Candice Bergen, Dyan Cannon; **D:** Clive Donner. **VHS, Beta $69.98** LIV, VES ♪

Mermaids It's the halcyon Kennedy days, when fun foods were a major food group. Mrs. Flax (Cher) is the flamboyant mother of two who hightails out of town every time a relationship threatens to turn serious. Having moved some eighteen times, her daughters, Charlotte, 15, and Kate, 8, are a little the worse for wear, psychologically speaking. One aspires to join the sisterly persuasion though not Catholic, and the other holds her breath under water. Now residing in Massachusetts after her latest fiasco de coeur, Mrs. Flax starts having those I got you babe feelings for Hoskins, a shoe store owning kinda guy. Amusing, well-acted multi-generational coming of ager based on a novel by Patty Dann.
1990 (PG-13) 110m/C Cher, Winona Ryder, Bob Hoskins, Christina Ricci, Michael Schoeffling, Caroline McWilliams, Jan Miner; **D:** Richard Benjamin; **W:** June Roberts; **M:** Jack Nitzsche. **VHS, Beta, LV $14.98** ORI ♪♪♪

The Mermaids of Tiburon A marine biologist and a criminal travel to a remote island off Mexico in search of elusive, expensive ''fire pearls.'' There they encounter a kingdom of lovely mermaids who promptly liven things up. Filmed in ''Aquascope'' for your viewing pleasure. **AKA:** The Aqua Sex.
1962 77m/C Diane Webber, George Rowe, Timothy Carey, Jose Gonzalez-Gonzalez, John Mylong, Gil Baretto, Vicki Kantenwine, Nani Morrissey, Judy Edwards, Jean Carroll, Diana Cook, Karen Goodman, Nancy Burns; **W/D:** John Lamb. **VHS $18.00** FRG ♪

Merrill's Marauders Chandler is the commander of a battle-hardened regiment fighting in the jungles of Burma in 1944. The exhausted unit gains their latest objective and expects to be relieved, only to be continuously pushed into more fighting down the line. Director Fuller excels at showing the confusion of battle; Chandler's last film role (he died before the film was released).
1962 98m/C Jeff Chandler, Ty Hardin, Peter Brown, Andrew Duggan, Will Hutchins, Claude Akins; **W/D:** Samuel Fuller; **W:** Milton Sperling; **M:** Howard Jackson. **VHS $19.98** WAR ♪♪½

Merry Christmas, Mr. Lawrence An often overlooked drama about a World War II Japanese POW camp. The film is a taut psychological drama about clashing cultures and physical and emotional survival. Focusing on the tensions between Bowie as a British POW and camp commander Sakamoto, who also composed the outstanding score. A haunting and intense film about the horrors of war.

1983 (R) 124m/C GB JP David Bowie, Tom Conti, Ryuichi Sakamoto, Takeshi, Jack Thompson; **D:** Nagisa Oshima. **VHS, Beta $59.95** MCA ♪♪♪

Merry Christmas to You A collection of cartoons, singalongs, and Lone Ranger and Lassie adventures that all carry a Christmas theme are featured on this tape.
1980 80m/C **VHS, Beta** MED ♪♪♪

Merry-Go-Round A handsome Austrian count is engaged to a woman of his class when he meets the beautiful Agnes, who works as an organ grinder for the local merry-go-round. He disguises himself to woo her but finally decides to marry his fiance, although Agnes continues to love him. But the story doesn't end for the two lovers who are destined to be together. Producer Thalberg and director von Stroheim battled over the expense and length of the film until Thalberg had the director replaced. However, much of the film still shows the von Stroheim brilliance and attention to lavish detail.
1923 110m/B Norman Kerry, Mary Philbin, Cesare Gravina, Edith Yorke, George Hackathorne; **D:** Rupert Julian, Erich von Stroheim. **VHS $29.95** FCT, HEG ♪♪♪

The Merry Widow The first sound version of the famous Franz Lehar operetta, dealing with a playboy from a bankrupt kingdom who must woo and marry the land's wealthy widow or be tried for treason. A delightful musical comedy, with a sterling cast and patented Lubitschian gaiety. Made as a silent in 1912 and 1925; remade in color in 1952. ♪Girls, Girls, Girls; Vilia; Tonight Will Teach Me to Forget; Melody of Laughter; Maxim's; The Girls at Maxim's; The Merry Widow Waltz; If Widows are Rich; Russian Dance. **AKA:** The Lady Dances.
1934 99m/B Maurice Chevalier, Jeanette MacDonald, Edward Everett Horton, Una Merkel, George Barbier, Minna Gombell, Ruth Channing, Sterling Holloway, Henry Armetta, Barbara Leanard, Donald Meek, Akim Tamiroff, Herman Bing; **D:** Ernst Lubitsch; **M:** Franz Lehar, Lorenz Hart. **VHS, Beta, LV $19.98** MGM ♪♪♪½

The Merry Widow Turner is a rich widow who goes to her husband's homeland of Marshovia to dedicate a statue to his memory. The country is deeply in debt and the king would like the widow to marry a local count and remain (along with her fortune). Lamas is charming as the intended bridegroom but Turner, though lovely looking, is miscast as the widow and her singing was dubbed by Erwin. Songs include ''The Merry Widow Waltz,'' ''Can-Can,'' ''Girls, Girls, Girls,'' and ''I'm Going to Maxim's.'' Uninspired remake of the 1934 film, which only benefits from being shot in color and the lavish production values. Based on the operetta by Lehar.
1952 105m/C Lana Turner, Fernando Lamas, Una Merkel, Richard Haydn, Thomas Gomez, John Abbott, Marcel Dalio, King Donovan, Robert Coote; **Cameos:** Gwen Verdon; **D:** Curtis Bernhardt; **W:** Sonya Levien, William Ludwig; **M:** Franz Lehar; **V:** Trudy Erwin. **VHS $19.98** MGM ♪♪½

Mesa of Lost Women Mad scientist creates brave new race of vicious women with long fingernails. So bad it's a wanna-B. Addams Family buffs will spot the Fester in Coogan. **AKA:** Lost Women; Lost Women of Zarpa.
1952 70m/B Jackie Coogan, Richard Travis, Allan Nixon, Mary Hill, Robert Knapp, Tandra Quinn, Lyle Talbot, Katherine Victor, Angelo Rossitto, Herbert Tevos; **D:** Ron Ormond. **VHS $16.95** NOS, MRV, SNC **Woof!**

Mesmerized Based on the work by Jerzy Skolimowski, the film is a dramatization of the Victoria Thompson murder case in 1880's New Zealand. A teenaged orphaned girl marries an older man and decides after years of abuse to kill him through hypnosis. An unengaging drama, though the lovely New Zealand landscape serves as a fitting contrast to the film's ominous tone. *AKA:* Shocked.
1984 90m/C *GB NZ AU* John Lithgow, Jodie Foster, Michael Murphy, Dan Shor, Harry Andrews; *D:* Michael Laughlin. **VHS, Beta $89.98** LIV, VES *🎬🎬*

Mesquite Buckaroo Two cowboys bet over who is the better bronco buster, but one of them gets kidnapped.
1939 59m/B Bob Steele, Carolyn Curtis, Frank LaRue, Juanita Fletcher, Charles King; *D:* Harry S. Webb. **VHS, Beta $19.95** NOS, DVT *🎬*

Messalina, Empress of Rome Ancient Rome is torn to bits in the zaniest manner possible in this Italian-French coproduction.
1980 100m/C VHS, Beta VCD *🎬*

Messalina vs. the Son of Hercules A Roman slave leads a rebellion against the emperor Messalina. Italian; dubbed into English.
1964 105m/C *IT* Richard Harrison, Marilu Tolo, Lisa Gastoni; *D:* Umberto Lenzi. **VHS, Beta $16.95** SNC, NLC *🎬*

The Messenger A man right out of prison sets out to avenge his wife's murder by an Italian drug syndicate.
1987 (R) 95m/C Fred Williamson, Sandy Cummings, Christopher Connelly, Cameron Mitchell. **VHS, Beta** NO *🎬*

Messenger of Death A tough detective investigates the slaughter of a Mormon family, and uncovers a conspiracy centering around oil-rich real estate.
1988 (R) 90m/C Charles Bronson, Trish Van Devere, Laurence Luckinbill, Daniel Benzali, Marilyn Hassett, Jeff Corey, John Ireland, Penny Peyser, Gene Davis; *D:* J. Lee Thompson. **VHS, Beta, LV $89.95** MED *🎬🎬½*

The Messiah Rossellini's final film, a rarely-seen version of the life of Christ, completely passed over any notions of divinity to portray Him as a morally perfect man. In Italian with subtitles.
1975 145m/C *IT* *D:* Roberto Rossellini. **VHS, Beta $39.95** FCT, MVD *🎬🎬🎬½*

Messiah of Evil California coastal town is invaded by zombies. Confusing low-rent production from the writers of "American Graffiti." *AKA:* Dead People; Return of the Living Dead; Revenge of the Screaming Dead; The Second Coming.
1974 (R) 90m/C Marianna Hill, Joy Bang, Royal Dano, Elisha Cook Jr., Michael Greer; *W/D:* Gloria Katz, Willard Huyck. **VHS, Beta $24.95** GEM, MRV *🎬*

Metallica Alien warmongers endeavor to conquer Earth and scientists try to stop them.
1985 90m/C Anthony Newcastle, Sharon Baker; *D:* Al Bradley. **VHS, Beta** NO *🎬*

Metalstorm It's the science fiction battle of the ages with giant cyclops and intergalactic magicians on the desert planet of Lemuria.
1983 (PG) 84m/C Jeffrey Byron, Mike Preston, Tim Thomerson, Kelly Preston, Richard Moll; *D:* Charles Band. **VHS, Beta, LV $59.95** MCA *🎬*

Metamorphosis Novice scientist foolishly uses himself as the guinea pig for his anti-aging experiments. He quickly loses control of the project.

1990 (R) 90m/C Gene Le Brock, Catherine Baranov, Stephen Brown, Harry Cason, Jason Arnold; *D:* G.L. Eastman. **VHS, Beta $89.95** IMP *🎬*

Meteor American and Soviet scientists attempt to save the Earth from a fast-approaching barrage of meteors from space in this disaster dud. Destruction ravages parts of Hong Kong and the Big Apple.
1979 (PG) 107m/C Sean Connery, Natalie Wood, Karl Malden, Brian Keith, Martin Landau, Trevor Howard, Henry Fonda, Joseph Campanella, Richard Dysart; *D:* Ronald Neame. **VHS, Beta $19.98** WAR, OM *Woof!*

The Meteor Man Townsend plays a school teacher who reluctantly becomes a hero when he acquires semi-super powers after being hit by a meteor. In this satirical role, Meteor Man flies only four feet off the ground and wears costumes fashioned by his mother. He decides to use his newfound abilities to help clean up his urban community where drugs and crime have become a way of life. Includes interesting cameos by Cosby, Sinbad, Vandross, and Page.
1993 (PG-13) m/C Robert Townsend, Robert Guillaume, Marla Gibbs, James Earl Jones, Frank Gorshin, Sinbad, Luther Vandross, LaWanda Page; *Cameos:* Bill Cosby; *D:* Robert Townsend; *W:* Robert Townsend. **VHS** NYR *🎬🎬½*

Meteor Monster A young boy is hit by a meteor and is somehow transformed into a raving, slime-covered maniac. *AKA:* Teenage Monster.
1957 73m/C Anne Gwynne, Stuart Wade, Gloria Castillo, Charles Courtney; *D:* Jacques Marquette. **VHS, Beta $39.95** SNC *Woof!*

Metropolis Now a classic meditation on futurist technology and mass mentality, this fantasy concerns mechanized society. Original set design and special effects made this an innovative and influential film in its day. Is now considered one of the hippest films of the sci-fi genre. Silent, with musical score. The 1984 re-release features some color tinting, reconstruction, and a digital score with songs by Pat Benatar, Bonnie Tyler, and Queen.
1926 115m/B *GE* Brigitte Helm, Alfred Abel, Gustav Froehlich, Rudolf Klein-Rogge; *D:* Fritz Lang. **VHS, Beta, LV, 3/4U, Special order formats $16.95** SNC, NOS, MRV *🎬🎬🎬🎬*

Metropolitan The Izod set comes of age on Park Avenue during Christmas break. Tom Townsend (Clements), a member of the (gasp) middle class, finds himself drawn into a circle of self proclaimed urban haute bourgeoisie types. It seems they're embarrassingly short on male escorts, and, even without the compulsory navy overcoat, he's an adequate stand-in at the group's many deb party/group dates. Much juvenescent philosophizing and hormone quelling. Intelligently written and carefully made, it transcends the flirting with adulthood genre. Festival praised.
1990 (PG-13) 98m/C Carolyn Farina, Edward Clements, Taylor Nichols, Christopher Eigeman, Taylor Nichols, Allison Rutledge-Parisi, Dylan Hundley, Isabel Gillies, Bryan Leder, Will Kempe, Elizabeth Thompson; *W/D:* Whit Stillman; *M:* Mark Suozzi. Academy Awards '90 Nominations: Best Original Screenplay; Independent Spirit Awards '91: Best First Feature; New York Film Critics Awards '90: Best Director (Stillman). **VHS, LV $19.95** COL, PIA, FCT *🎬🎬🎬*

Mexican Bus Ride A good-natured Bunuel effort about a newlywed peasant who travels to the big city to attend to his mother's will. While en route, he encounters a diversity of people on the bus and some temptation. In Spanish with English subtitles.

1951 85m/B *MX* Lilia Prado, Esteban Marquez, Carmelita Gonzalez; *D:* Luis Bunuel. **VHS, Beta $39.95** FCT, APD, AUD *🎬🎬½*

Mexican Hayride Bud heads a gang of swindlers and Lou is the fall guy. When things up north get too hot, the boys head south of the border to cool off and start a mining scam. Watch for the hilarious bull-fighting scene. Believe it or not, this is based on a Cole Porter musical—minus the music.
1948 77m/B Bud Abbott, Lou Costello, Virginia Grey, Luba Malina, John Hubbard, Pedro de Cordoba, Fritz Feld, Tom Powers, Pat Costello, Frank Fenton; *D:* Charles T. Barton. **VHS $14.98** MCA *🎬🎬*

Mexican Spitfire at Sea The feisty wife from South of the Border heads for Hawaii to close a deal for her husband. He goes along to help her, impersonating nobility. The thin story line keeps it from being quite as good as the first "Mexican Spitfire" film. Most of the action takes place aboard ship.
1942 73m/B Lupe Velez, Leon Errol, Charles "Buddy" Rogers, ZaSu Pitts, Elisabeth Risdon, Florence Bates, Marion Martin, Eddie Dunn, Harry Holman; *D:* Leslie Goodwins. **VHS $19.95** NOS *🎬🎬*

Mexican Spitfire/Smartest Girl in Town A comedy double feature: In "Mexican Spitfire," a man impersonates an English lord in order to save a contract for the spitfire's husband. In "The Smartest Girl in Town," a photographer's model mistakes a millionaire for a fellow magazine model.
1940 125m/B Lupe Velez, Leon Errol, Donald Woods, Ann Sothern, Gene Raymond. **VHS, Beta $34.95** RKO, TTC *🎬🎬*

MGM: When the Lion Roars Three-part documentary covering the history and films of the Metro-Goldwyn-Mayer (MGM) studio from its beginnings in 1924 with the release of the studio's first film ("He Who Gets Slapped"), through its glory years, to the studio's gradual decline and ever-changing leadership. MGM brought out such films as "The Wizard of Oz," "Gone With the Wind," the Andy Hardy series, and the Thin Man films. Features clips of films and stars as well as footage of studio executives, including Louis B. Mayer and legendary studio chief and producer Irving Thalberg. Tapes are available individually or as a three-tape set. Originally made for cable television.
1992 360m/C VHS, LV MGM *🎬½*

MGM's The Big Parade of Comedy An anthology of more than 50 of MGM's stars and comedians in some of their funniest screen moments. Looks at Laurel & Hardy, the Marx Brothers, W.C. Fields, Clark Gable, Jean Harlow, Greta Garbo, and others.
1992 100m/C VHS $19.98 MGM *🎬½*

Miami Blues Cold-blooded killer plays cat-and-mouse with bleary cop while diddling unflappable prostitute. Violent and cynical, with appropriate performances from three leads.
1990 (R) 97m/C Fred Ward, Alec Baldwin, Jennifer Jason Leigh, Nora Dunn, Charles Napier, Jose Perez, Paul Gleason; *D:* George Armitage. **VHS, Beta, LV $14.98** ORI, IME *🎬🎬½*

Miami Cops When a cop's father is killed by a drug smuggler, he and his partner pursue the murderer over two continents. Italian-made adventure is a bit drawn-out.
1989 103m/C *IT* Richard Roundtree, Harrison Muller, Dawn Baker, Michael J. Aronin; *D:* Al Bradley. **VHS, Beta $79.95** CAN *🎬*

Miami Horror A Florida scientist is experimenting with bacteria from space, trying to recreate a human only to have his efforts stolen by a crook. His intentions for the use of the experiment are not exactly for the furtherance of science.
1987 85m/C *IT* David Warbeck, Laura Trotter, Lawrence Loddi, John Ireland; *D:* Martin Herbert. VHS, Beta *NO* *II*

Miami Supercops Two goofy policemen strike out against such threats as a gang that hassles buses, the attempted kidnapping of an Orange Bowl quarterback, and a multi-million-dollar robbery.
1985 97m/C Terence Hill, Bud Spencer, Jackie Castellano, C.V. Wood Jr.; *D:* Bruno Corbucci. VHS, Beta **$19.98** *WAR* *II* ½

Miami Vendetta L.A. vice cop risks it all to avenge his friend's death at the hands of Cuban drug smugglers.
1987 90m/C Sandy Brooke, Frank Gargani, Maarten Goslins, Barbara Pilavin; *D:* Steven Seemayer. VHS, Beta *NO* *II*

Miami Vice Pilot for the popular television series paired Crockett and Tubbs for the first time on the trail of a killer in Miami's sleazy underground. Music by Jan Hammer and other pop notables.
1984 99m/C Don Johnson, Philip Michael Thomas, Saundra Santiago, Michael Talbott, John Diehl, Gregory Sierra; *D:* Thomas Carter. VHS, Beta, LV **$14.95** *MCA* *III* ½

Miami Vice 2: The Prodigal Son The second full-length television movie spawned by the popular series, following the laconic Floridians to the gritty streets of New York.
1985 99m/C Don Johnson, Philip Michael Thomas, Edward James Olmos, Penn Jillette. VHS, Beta, LV **$14.95** *MCA* *II*

The Michigan Kid Two boys fight for the same girl in this silent love triangle set in Alaska. Film's most notable scene is of a raging forest fire, considered a classic even today.
1928 62m/B Conrad Nagel, Renee Adoree, Fred Esmelton, Virginia Grey, Adolph Milar, Lloyd Whitlock; *D:* Irwin Willat. VHS, Beta *GPV* *II*

Mickey Spoof on high society as a penniless young woman moves in with relatives and works as the family's maid. Silent film.
1917 105m/B Mabel Normand, Lew Cody, Minta Durfee; *D:* Mack Sennett. VHS, Beta **$19.95** *NO3, VYY, DVT* *II*

Mickey A tomboy becomes a woman even as she plays matchmaker for her own father and sings a few songs. Not too exciting; you may fall asleep if you're slipped this "Mickey." Based on the novel "Clementine," by Peggy Goodin.
1948 87m/C Lois Butler, Bill Goodwin, Irene Hervey, John Sutton, Hattie McDaniel; *D:* Ralph Murphy. VHS **$19.95** *NOS* *II*

Mickey Rooney in the Classic Mickey McGuire Silly Comedies The classic boyhood series starring Rooney is also hosted by the actor. Three volumes available.
19?? 40m/C VHS **$9.99** *SUM* *II*

Mickey the Great Stitched together from several late 20's Mickey McGuire shorts, starring 10-year-old Rooney.
1939 70m/B Billy Barty, Mickey Rooney. VHS, Beta **$24.95** *NOS, DVT, VYY* *II*

Mickey's Christmas Carol Mickey Mouse returns along with all the other Disney characters in this adaptation of the Charles Dickens classic. Included in this video cassette is a documentary on how the featurette was made.
1983 (G) 25m/C VHS, Beta, LV, 3/4U, EJ, **Special order formats $12.99** *DIS, MTI, DSN* *III*

Micki & Maude When a man longs for a baby, he finds that his wife, Micki, is too busy for motherhood. Out of frustration, he has an affair with Maude that leads to her pregnancy. Still shocked by the news of his upcoming fatherhood, the man learns that his wife is also expecting.
1984 (PG-13) 117m/C Dudley Moore, Amy Irving, Ann Reinking, Richard Mulligan, Wallace Shawn, George Gaynes, Andre the Giant; *D:* Blake Edwards. VHS, Beta, LV **$79.95** *COL* *III*

Microwave Massacre Killer kitchen appliances strike again as late lounge comic Vernon murders nagging wife and 'waves her. Overcome by that Betty Crocker feeling, he goes on a microwave murdering/feeding spree of the local ladies. Lots of Roger Corman copying.
1983 (R) 80m/C Jackie Vernon, Loren Schein, Al Troupe; *D:* Wayne Berwick. VHS **$59.95** *RHI, FCT* *II*

Mid-Channel Young stars as a neglected married woman.
1920 70m/B Clara Kimball Young. VHS, Beta **$16.95** *NOS, MRV, GPV* *II*

Mid Knight Rider Penniless actor becomes a male prostitute at the service of bored, rich women. At an all-night orgy, he suddenly goes on a rampage, nearly killing one of his customers.
1984 76m/C Michael Christian, Keenan Wynn. VHS, Beta **$49.95** *TWE* *II*

The Midas Touch A flea market merchant in 1956 Budapest has the ability to turn items into gold. In Hungarian with English subtitles.
1989 100m/C *HU W/D:* Geza Beremenyi. VHS, Beta **$79.95** *EVD, FCT, TAM* *II*

Middle Age Crazy Story of a Texas building contractor who takes life pretty lightly until his own father dies. Then he becomes immersed in a mid-life crisis and has an affair with a Dallas Cowboys' cheerleader. Ann-Margret plays the victim wife of the middle aged swingin' guy.
1980 (R) 95m/C *CA* Bruce Dern, Ann-Margret, Graham Jarvis, Eric Christmas, Deborah Wakeham; *D:* John Trent. VHS **$59.98** *FOX* *II* ½

Midnight A jury foreman's daughter is romantically involved with a gangster who is interested in a particular case before it appears in court. The foreman, who sentenced a girl to death, faces a dilemma when his own daughter is arrested for the same crime. An early Bogart appearance in a supporting role led to a rerelease of the film as "Call it Murder" after Bogart made it big. Weak melodrama. *AKA:* Call it Murder.
1934 74m/B Humphrey Bogart, Sidney Fox, O.P. Heggie, Henry Hull, Richard Whorf, Margaret Wycherly, Lynne Overman; *D:* Chester Erskine. VHS, Beta **$34.98** *CCB, DVT, KRT* *II* ½

Midnight Russo, who cowrote the original "Night of the Living Dead," wrote and directed this film about a runaway girl who is driven out of her home by a lecherous stepfather and meets two young thieves and then a family of cultists. Russo adapted his own novel. He also attains some of "Night of the Living Dead's" low-budget ambience. *AKA:* Backwoods Massacre.
1981 (R) 88m/C Lawrence Tierney, Melanie Verliin, John Hall, John Amplas; *D:* John Russo. VHS, Beta **$79.95** *VMK* *II*

Midnight Murder-thriller involving the vampirish hostess of a television horror movie showcase and a fanatical fan.
1989 (R) 90m/C Lynn Redgrave, Tony Curtis, Steve Parrish, Rita Gam, Gustav Vintas, Karen Witter, Frank Gorshin, Wolfman Jack; *D:* Norman Thaddeus Vane. VHS, Beta, LV **$89.85** *SVS* *II*

Midnight at the Wax Museum A man attempts to spend an evening in a wax museum's chamber of horrors, only to find that he is the target of a murder plot. *AKA:* Midnight at Madame Tussaud's.
1936 66m/B Lucille Lisle, James Carew, Charles Oliver, Kim Peacock; *D:* George Pearson. VHS **$24.95** *NOS, DVT, SNC* *II*

Midnight Auto Supply Dealers in hot car parts, working out of the garage behind the local brothel, become persuaded to donate some of their profits to the cause of Mexican farm workers. Also called "Love and the Midnight Auto Supply."
1978 91m/C Michael Parks, Rory Calhoun, Scott Jacoby, Rod Cameron, Colleen Camp, Linda Cristal, John Ireland; *D:* James Polakof. VHS **$79.95** *MNC* *II* ½

Midnight Cabaret A New York nightclub-based Satanic cult selects a child actress to bear Satan's child.
1990 (R) 94m/C VHS, Beta, LV **$19.98** *WAR* Woof!

A Midnight Clear Sensitive war drama that takes place in the Ardennes Forest, near the French-German border in December 1944. It's Christmastime and six of the remaining members of a 12-member squad are sent on a dangerous mission to an abandoned house to locate the enemy. Filmed in a dreamy surreal style, the setting is somewhat reminiscent of a fairytale, although a sense of anguish filtrates throughout the picture. A solid script, excellent direction, and a good cast make this a worthwhile film that pits the message of peace against the stupidity of war. Adapted from the novel by William Wharton.
1992 (PG) 107m/C Peter Berg, Kevin Dillon, Arye Gross, Ethan Hawke, Gary Sinise, Frank Whaley, John C. McGinley, Larry Joshua, Curt Lowens; *W/D:* Keith Gordon. VHS, LV *COL, PMS* *III*

Midnight Cop A young woman gets tangled up in a web of murder, intrigue, prostitution and drugs, and she enlists the aid of a cop to help get her out of it.
1988 (R) 100m/C Michael York, Morgan Fairchild, Frank Stallone, Armin Mueller-Stahl; *D:* Peter Patzak. VHS, Beta, LV **$29.95** *VMK, HHE* *II*

Midnight Cowboy Drama about the relationship between a naive Texan hustler and a seedy derelict, set in the underbelly of New York City. Graphic and emotional character study is brilliantly acted and engaging. Shocking and considered quite risque at the time of its release, this film now carries an "R" rating. It is the only film carrying an "X" rating ever to win the Best Picture Oscar. From James Leo Herlihy's novel. Laserdisc version features: audio commentary by director John Schlesinger and producer Jereome Hellman, behind the scenes production photos, and original movie trailer.
1969 (R) 113m/C Dustin Hoffman, Jon Voight, Sylvia Miles, Brenda Vaccaro, John McGiver, Bob Balaban, Barnard Hughes; *D:* John Schlesinger; *W:* Waldo Salt; *M:* John Barry. Academy Awards '69: Best Adapted Screenplay, Best Director (Schlesinger), Best Picture; Nominations: Best Actor (Hoffman), Best Actor (Voight), Best Film Editing, Best Supporting Actress (Miles); British Academy Awards '69: Best Actor (Hoffman), Best Director (Schlesinger), Best Film; Directors Guild of America Awards '69: Best Director (Schlesinger); New York Film Critics Awards '69: Best Actor (Voight); National Society of Film Critics Awards '69: Best Actor

(Voight), Best Film. **VHS, Beta, LV** $19.98 *MGM, VYG, CRC* ♫♫♫ ½

Midnight Crossing Two married couples are subjected to jealousy, betrayal and uncloseted-skeletons as their pleasure cruise on a yacht turns into a ruthless search for sunken treasure.
1987 (R) 96m/C Faye Dunaway, Daniel J. Travanti, Kim Cattrall, John Laughlin, Ned Beatty; *D:* Roger Holzberg. **VHS, Beta, LV** $89.98 *LIV, VES* ♫♫

Midnight Dancer A young ballerina is forced to work as an erotic dancer.
1987 97m/C *AU* Deanne Jeffs, Mary Regan; *D:* Pamela Gibbons. **VHS, Beta** $29.95 *ACA* ♫♫

Midnight Express A gripping and powerful film based on the true story of Billy Hayes. Davis plays Hayes as a young American in Turkey who is busted trying to smuggle hashish. He is sentenced to a brutal and nightmarish prison for life. After enduring tremendous mental and physical torture, he seeks escape along the "Midnight Express." Not always easy to watch, but the overall effect is riveting and unforgettable.
1978 (R) 120m/C *TU* John Hurt, Randy Quaid, Brad Davis, Paul Smith, Bo Hopkins, Oliver Stone; *D:* Alan Parker; *M:* Giorgio Moroder. Academy Awards '78: Best Adapted Screenplay, Best Score; Nominations: Best Director (Parker), Best Film Editing, Best Picture, Best Supporting Actor (Hurt); British Academy Awards '78: Best Director (Parker), Best Supporting Actor (Hurt); National Board of Review Awards '78: 10 Best Films of the Year. **VHS, Beta, LV, 8mm** $14.95 *COL* ♫♫♫

Midnight Faces Mysterious doings abound in a house in the Florida bayous, recently inherited by Bushman. Silent, with original organ music.
1926 72m/B Francis X. Bushman, Rocky Aoki, Jack Perrin, Kathryn McGuire. **VHS, Beta, 8mm** $16.95 *SNC, VYY, LSV* ♫♫

Midnight Fear When a sexually demented killer skins a woman alive, Sheriff Hanley sets out to find whodunit. He suspects two weird brothers, who turn out to be holding a woman hostage, but the situation may not be so simple. Carradine plays the good-guy sheriff in this creeper.
1990 90m/C David Carradine, Craig Wasson; *D:* Bill Crain. **VHS** $79.95 *RHI* ♫ ½

Midnight Girl A fading opera impresario plots to steal a family's fortune. Lugosi before he became Dracula. Silent.
1925 84m/B Bela Lugosi, Lila Lee. **VHS, Beta, 8mm** $19.95 *NOS, VYY, DVT* ♫ ½

The Midnight Hour A group of high schoolers stumbles upon a vintage curse that wakes up the dead. Made for television. More humor than horror.
1986 97m/C Shari Belafonte-Harper, LeVar Burton, Lee Montgomery, Dick Van Patten, Kevin McCarthy, Jonelle Allen, Peter DeLuise, Dedee Pfeiffer, Mark Blankfield; *D:* Jack Bender. **VHS** $89.95 *VMK* ♫ ½

Midnight Lace Acceptable thriller about a woman in London who is being harassed by a telephone creep. Day is at her frantic best, and Harrrison is suitably charming. Handsome Gavin later became American ambassador to Mexico. Adapted from the play "Matilda Shouted Fire."
1960 108m/C Doris Day, Rex Harrison, John Gavin, Myrna Loy, Roddy McDowall; *D:* David Miller. **VHS, Beta** $59.95 *MCA* ♫♫ ½

Midnight Limited A detective sets out to thwart the criminals who would rob the "Midnight Limited" train on its route from New York to Montreal.

1940 61m/B John "Dusty" King, Marjorie Reynolds, George Cleveland, Edward Keane, Pat Flaherty, Monty Collins, I. Stanford Jolley; *D:* Howard Bretherton. **VHS, Beta** $16.95 *SNC* ♫♫

Midnight Madness Five teams of college students search the city of Los Angeles for clues leading to hundreds and thousands of dollars in buried treasure.
1980 (PG) 110m/C David Naughton, Stephen Furst, Debra Clinger, Eddie Deezen, Michael J. Fox, Maggie Roswell; *D:* David Wechter. **VHS, Beta** *BVV, OM* ♫

Midnight Movie Massacre Retro splatterama has really gross alien land outside a movie theater in 1956, and the really weird movie patrons try to terminate it.
1988 86m/C Robert Clarke, Ann Robinson; *D:* Mark Stock. **VHS** $19.95 *UHV* ♫♫ ½

The Midnight Phantom Incredibly rare horror film featuring a bizarre murder at a midnight lecture.
1935 ?m/B Reginald Denny. **VHS** $12.95 *SNC* ♫♫

Midnight Run An ex-cop, bounty hunter must bring in an ex-mob accountant who has embezzled big bucks from his former boss. After he catches up with the thief, the hunter finds that bringing his prisoner from New York to Los Angeles will be very trying, especially when it is apparent that the Mafia and FBI are out to stop them. The friction between the two leads—De Niro and Grodin—is fun to watch, while the action and comic moments are enjoyable.
1988 (R) 125m/C Robert De Niro, Charles Grodin, Yaphet Kotto, John Ashton, Dennis Farina, Joe Pantoliano; *D:* Martin Brest; *W:* George Gallo. **VHS, Beta, LV** $19.95 *MCA* ♫♫♫

Midnight Warning A woman thinks she's going off the deep-end when her brother and all records of his existence disappear. Based on an urban legend that appeared somewhere around the time of the 1893 World's Fair. Remade in 1952 as "So Long at the Fair."
1932 63m/B William Boyd, Claudia Dell, Henry Hall, John Harron, Hooper Atchley; *D:* Spencer Gordon Bennet. **VHS** $12.95 *SNC, NOS, DVT* ♫♫ ½

Midnight Warrior A reporter strikes it big when he investigates the underside of L.A. nightlife, but things go terribly wrong when he becomes wrapped up in the sleaze.
1989 90m/C Bernie Angel, Michelle Berger, Kevin Bernhardt, Lilly Melgar; *D:* Joseph Merhi. **VHS, Beta** $29.95 *PAR* ♫

Midnite Spares A young man's search for the men who kidnapped his father leads him into the world of car thieves and chop-shops.
1985 90m/C Bruce Spence, Gia Carides, James Laurie. **VHS, Beta** *NO* ♫♫

A Midsummer Night's Dream Famed Reinhardt version of the Shakespeare classic, featuring nearly every star on the Warner Brothers lot. The plot revolves around the amorous battle between the king and queen of a fairy kingdom, and the humans who are drawn into their sport. Features de Havilland's first film role. Classic credit line: Dialogue by William Shakespeare.
1935 117m/B James Cagney, Dick Powell, Joe E. Brown, Hugh Herbert, Olivia de Havilland, Ian Hunter, Mickey Rooney, Victor Jory, Arthur Treacher, Billy Barty; *D:* Max Reinhardt, William Dieterle. Academy Awards '35: Best Cinematography, Best Film Editing; Nominations: Best Picture. **VHS, Beta** $19.98 *MGM, FOX* ♫♫♫

A Midsummer Night's Dream Fine acting from the Royal Shakespeare Company cast in this filmed version of the play. Makes very little use of the Athens, Greece scenery.
1968 124m/C Derek Godfrey, Barbara Jefford, Hugh Sullivan, Nicholas Selby, David Warner, Michael Jayston, Diana Rigg, Helen Mirren, Ian Richardson, Judi Dench, Ian Holm, Paul Rogers, Sebastian Shaw, Bill Travers; *D:* Peter Hall. **VHS** *WAR* ♫♫♫

A Midsummer Night's Dream Shakespeare has created some of his most fanciful and unforgettable characters in this tale of devilish fairies, bewitched lovers and stolid workingmen-cum-actors.
1982 120m/C Helen Mirren, Peter McEnery, Brian Clover. **VHS, Beta** $19.98 *FOX, TLF* ♫♫ ½

A Midsummer Night's Sex Comedy Allen's homage to Shakespeare, Renoir, Chekhov, Bergman, and who knows who else is an engaging ensemble piece about hijinks among friends and acquaintances gathered at a country house at the turn of the century. Standouts include Ferrer as pompous professor and Steenburgen as Allen's sexually repressed wife. Mia's first for the Woodman.
1982 (PG) 88m/C Woody Allen, Mia Farrow, Mary Steenburgen, Tony Roberts, Julie Hagerty, Jose Ferrer; *W/D:* Woody Allen. **VHS, Beta** $19.98 *WAR* ♫♫ ½

Midway The epic World War II battle of Midway, the turning point in the war, is retold through Allied and Japanese viewpoints by a big all-star cast saddled with dumpy dialogue and enough weaponry to seize Hollywood on any given Wednesday.
1976 (PG) 132m/C Charlton Heston, Henry Fonda, James Coburn, Glenn Ford, Hal Holbrook, Robert Mitchum, Cliff Robertson, Robert Wagner, Kevin Dobson, Christopher George, Toshiro Mifune, Tom Selleck; *D:* Jack Smight; *M:* John Williams. **VHS, Beta, LV** $19.95 *MCA, TLF* ♫♫

The Mighty Ducks Bad News Bears on skates. Selfish yuppie lawyer is arrested for drunk driving and as part of his community service sentence, he is forced to coach an inner-city hockey team full of the usual misfits and underachievers. Although sarcastic and skeptical, Coach Gordon Bombay (Estevez) eventually bonds with the Ducks and learns to treat them with respect. Dual themes of teamwork and redemption are repeated constantly, and it gets a bit hokey at times, but the kids won't mind with this fun Disney film, while adults will appreciate the sarcasm.
1992 (PG) 114m/C Emilio Estevez, Joss Ackland, Lane Smith, Heidi Kling, Josef Sommer; *D:* Stephen Herek; *W:* Steven Brill. **VHS, Beta, LV** $94.95 *TOU* ♫♫ ½

Mighty Joe Young Tongue-in-cheek King Kong variation features giant ape brought to civilization and exploited in a nightclub act, whereupon things get darned ugly. Bullied and given the key to the liquor cabinet, mild-mannered Joe goes on a drunken rampage, but eventually redeems himself by rescuing orphans from a fire. Special effects (courtesy of Willis O'Brien and the great Ray Harryhausen) probably film's greatest asset. Also available colorized.
1949 94m/B Terry Moore, Ben Johnson, Robert Armstrong, Frank McHugh; *D:* Ernest B. Schoedsack. **VHS, Beta, LV** $19.95 *TTC, VID* ♫♫ ½

Mighty Jungle Lost in the Amazon jungle, a hunter must fight off killer iguanas, man-eating crocodiles and bloodthirsty natives who perform human sacrifices.

1964 90m/C Marshall Thompson, David Dalie. VHS, Beta *PGN* 🐾🐾

The Mighty Pawns Inner-city kids turn to chess when their teacher inspires them to stay off the streets. Originally aired on PBS as part of the "Wonderworks" family movie series.
1987 58m/C Paul Winfield, Alfonso Ribeiro, Terence Knox, Rosalind Cash, Teddy Wilson; *D:* Eric Laneuville. VHS $29.95 *PME, HMV* 🐾🐾

The Mighty Quinn While investigating the local murder of a rich white guy the black Jamaican head of police becomes convinced that the prime suspect, a childhood friend, is innocent. As the police chief, Denzel is good in this off-beat comedy mystery.
1989 (R) 98m/C Denzel Washington, Robert Townsend, James Fox, Mimi Rogers, M. Emmet Walsh, Sheryl Lee Ralph, Esther Rolle; *D:* Carl Schenkel. VHS, Beta, LV $19.98 *FOX* 🐾🐾½

Mike's Murder Disjointed drama about a shy bank teller who falls for a slick tennis player. When he is murdered, she investigates the circumstances, placing herself in dangerously close contact with his seedy, drug-involved buddies. The twists and confused plot leave the viewer bewildered.
1984 (R) 109m/C Debra Winger, Mark Keyloun, Paul Winfield, Darrell Larson, Dan Shor, William Ostrander; *D:* James Bridges; *M:* John Barry. VHS, Beta $79.95 *WAR* 🐾½

Mikey Mikey seems like such a sweet little boy—but these awful things keep happening all around him. At every foster home and every school people have such dreadful, and deadly, accidents. But innocent Mikey couldn't be to blame—or could he.
1992 (R) 92m/C Ashley Laurence, John Diehl, Lyman Ward, Josie Bisset; *D:* Dennis Dimster. VHS $89.95 *IMP* 🐾½

Mikey & Nicky Quirky, uneven film about longtime friends dodging a hit man during one long night. Bears little evidence of time and money invested. Cassavetes and Falk, however, provide some salvation.
1976 (R) 105m/C John Cassavetes, Peter Falk, Ned Beatty, Oliver Clark, William Hickey; *W/D:* Elaine May. VHS, Beta $69.95 *WAR, OM* 🐾🐾½

The Milagro Beanfield War Redford's endearing adaptation of John Nichols's novel about New Mexican townfolk opposing development. Seemingly simple tale provides plenty of insight into human spirit. Fine cast, with especially stellar turns from Blades, Braga, and Vennera. Oscar-winning score by Dave Grusin.
1988 (R) 118m/C Chick Vennera, John Heard, Ruben Blades, Sonia Braga, Daniel Stern, Julie Carmen, Christopher Walken, Richard Bradford, Carlos Riquelme, James Gammon, Melanie Griffith, Freddy Fender, M. Emmet Walsh; *D:* Robert Redford. VHS, Beta, LV $14.98 *MCA* 🐾🐾½

Mildred Pierce Gripping melodrama features Crawford as hard-working divorcee rivaling daughter for man's love. Things, one might say, eventually get ugly. Adaptation of James M. Cain novel is classic of its kind.
1945 113m/B Joan Crawford, Jack Carson, Zachary Scott, Eve Arden, Ann Blyth, Bruce Bennett; *D:* Michael Curtiz. Academy Awards '45: Best Actress (Crawford); Nominations: Best Black and White Cinematography, Best Picture, Best Screenplay, Best Supporting Actress (Arden, Blyth). VHS, Beta, LV $19.98 *MGM, FOX, BTV* 🐾🐾🐾½

Miles from Home Times are tough for farmers Frank and Terry Roberts. The brothers are about to have another bad harvest and the bank is threatening to foreclose. In a symbolic last ditch effort to save their pride, they decide to burn the farm and leave. On

their journey, they meet strangers who recognize the pair and help them escape the police. A melodrama with many members of Chicago's Steppenwolf Theater. *AKA:* Farm of the Year.
1988 (R) 113m/C Richard Gere, Kevin Anderson, John Malkovich, Brian Dennehy, Judith Ivey, Penelope Ann Miller, Laurie Metcalf, Laura San Giacomo, Daniel Roebuck, Helen Hunt; *D:* Gary Sinise. VHS, Beta, LV $19.98 *WAR* 🐾🐾

Miles to Go A successful businesswoman tries to enjoy her last days after learning she has terminal cancer.
1986 88m/C Mimi Kuzyk, Tom Skerritt, Jill Clayburgh; *D:* David Greene. VHS, Beta *NO* 🐾½

Miles to Go Before I Sleep A retired, lonely man and a delinquent girl distrust each other but eventually reach out in mutual need.
1974 78m/C Martin Balsam, MacKenzie Phillips, Kitty Winn, Elizabeth Wilson; *D:* Fielder Cook. VHS, Beta *LCA* 🐾🐾½

Militant Eagle Usual good vs. evil, complete with nobles, warriors, and villains who fight to the death.
19?? 90m/C Choi Yue, Lu Ping, Pai Ying. VHS, Beta *NO* 🐾

Milky Way Loopy comedy about milkman who finds unhappiness after accidentally knocking out champion boxer. Adequate, but not equal to Lloyd's fine silent productions.
1936 89m/B Harold Lloyd, Adolphe Menjou, Verree Teasdale, Helen Mack, William Gargan; *D:* Leo McCarey. VHS, Beta, LV $29.95 *NOS, MRV, VYY* 🐾🐾½

The Milky Way Wicked anti-clerical farce. Two bums team on religious pilgrimage and encounter seemingly all manner of strangeness and sacrilege in this typically peculiar Bunuel work. Perhaps the only film in which Jesus is encouraged to shave. In French with English subtitles.
1968 102m/C *FR* Laurent Terzieff, Paul Frankeur, Delphine Seyrig, Alain Cuny, Bernard Verley, Michel Piccoli, Edith Scob; *D:* Luis Bunuel; *W:* Jean-Claude Carriere. VHS, Beta, LV $24.95 *XVC, MED, FCT* 🐾🐾🐾

Mill of the Stone Women Sculpture-studying art student encounters strange carousel with beautiful babes rather than horsies, and soon finds out that the statues contain shocking secrets. Filmed in Holland, it's offbeat and creepy. *AKA:* Il Mulino Delle Donne di Pietra; Horror of the Stone Women; The Horrible Mill Women.
1960 94m/C *FR IT* Pierre Brice, Scilla Gabel, Danny Carrel, Wolfgang Preiss, Herbert Boenne, Liana Orfei; *D:* Giorgio Ferroni. VHS $16.95 *SNC, PGN* 🐾½

The Mill on the Floss Based on George Eliot's classic novel, this film follows the course of an ill-fated romance and family hatred in rural England. Underwhelming, considering the source.
1937 77m/B *GB* James Mason, Geraldine Fitzgerald, Frank Lawton, Victoria Hopper, Fay Compton, Griffith Jones, Mary Clare; *D:* Tim Whelan. VHS, Beta $19.95 *NOS, MRV, KRT* 🐾🐾

Millenium The Earth of the future is running out of time. The people are sterile and the air is terrible. To keep the planet viable, Ladd and company must go back in time and yank people off planes that are doomed to crash. Great special effects and well-thought out script make this a ball of fun.
1989 (PG-13) 108m/C Kris Kristofferson, Cheryl Ladd, Daniel J. Travanti, Lloyd Bochner, Robert Joy, Brent Carver, Maury Chaykin, David McIlwraith, Al Waxman; *D:* Michael Anderson Sr. VHS, Beta, LV $9.99 *IVE, CCB* 🐾🐾½

Miller's Crossing From the Coen brothers (makers of "Blood Simple" and "Raising Arizona") comes this extremely dark entry in the gangster movie sweepstakes of 1990. Jewish, Italian, and Irish mobsters spin webs of deceit, protection, and revenge over themselves and their families. Byrne is the protagonist, but no hero, being as deeply flawed as the men he battles. Harden stuns as the woman who sleeps with Byrne and his boss, Finney, in hopes of a better life and protection for her small-time crook brother. Visually exhilarating, excellently acted and perfectly paced.
1990 (R) 115m/C Albert Finney, Gabriel Byrne, Marcia Gay Harden, John Turturro, Jon Polito, J.E. Freeman; *W/D:* Joel Coen; *W:* Ethan Coen. VHS, Beta, LV $14.98 *FXV, FCT* 🐾🐾🐾½

Millie Creaky melodrama about a divorcee who wants every man but one. He pursues her teenage daughter instead, leading to tragedy and courtroom hand-wringing. Twelvetrees still stands out in this hokum, based on a Donald Henderson novel considered daring in its day.
1931 85m/B Helen Twelvetrees, Robert Ames, Lilyan Tashman, Joan Blondell, Peter Halliday, James Hall, Anita Louise, Frank McHugh; *D:* John Francis Dillon. VHS $19.95 *NOS* 🐾½

Million Dollar Duck A family duck is doused with radiation and begins to lay gold eggs. Okay Disney family fare, especially for youngsters.
1971 (G) 92m/C Dean Jones, Sandy Duncan, Joe Flynn, Tony Roberts; *D:* Vincent McEveety. VHS, Beta *DIS, OM* 🐾½

Million Dollar Haul Tarzan sniffs out a ring of warehouse thieves.
1935 60m/B Reed Howes, Janet Chandler, William Farnum. VHS, Beta, LV *NO* 🐾

Million Dollar Kid When a group of thugs wreak havoc in the neighborhood, the East Side Kids try to help a wealthy man put a stop to it. They face an even greater dilemma when they discover that the man's son is part of the gang. Part of the "Bowery Boys" series.
1944 65m/B Leo Gorcey, Huntz Hall, Gabriel Dell, Louise Currie, Noah Beery Jr., Iris Adrian, Mary Gordon; *D:* Wallace Fox. VHS $24.95 *NOS, DVT, VYY* 🐾🐾

Million Dollar Mermaid The prototypical Williams aquashow, with the requisite awesome Berkeley dance numbers. As a biography of swimmer Annette Kellorman it isn't much, but as an MGM extravaganza, it fits the bill.
1952 115m/C Esther Williams, Victor Mature, Walter Pidgeon, Jesse White, David Brian, Maria Tallchief, Howard Freeman, Busby Berkeley; *D:* Mervyn LeRoy. VHS, Beta $19.98 *MGM* 🐾🐾

Million Dollar Mystery Silent suspense film involving an old house, a secret society, and a million dollars in missing money.
1927 ?m/B VHS $16.95 *SNC* 🐾🐾

Million Dollar Mystery A dying man's last words indicate that several million dollars have been stashed near a diner. Chaos breaks out as nearly everyone in town tries to dig up the loot.
1987 (PG) 95m/C Eddie Deezen, Penny Baker, Tom Bosley, Rich Hall, Wendy Sherman, Rick Overton, Mona Lyden; *D:* Richard Fleischer. VHS, LV $79.95 *HBO* 🐾½

A Million to One An athlete trains for the Olympic decathlon, and catches the eye of an upper-class woman in the process. The lead actor was actually a shot-putter in the 1932 Olympic Games.

1937 60m/B Herman Brix, Joan Fontaine, Monte Blue, Kenneth Harlan, Reed Howes; *D:* Lynn Shores. **VHS** $24.95 *VYY* 🎬🎬½

Millions To a family of millionaires, money is everything, and the heir to the family fortune is willing to do anything to get his hands on all that money. Even if it means sleeping with his sister-in-law and cousin! Lucky for him they happen to be beautiful models. **1990** (R) 118m/C *IT* Billy Zane, Lauren Hutton, Carol Alt, Alexandra Paul, Catherine Hickland, Donald Pleasence; *D:* Carlo Vanzina. **VHS, Beta** $89.95 *PSM* 🎬½

Milo & Otis Charming tale of a kitten named Milo and his best friend, a puppy named Otis. The two live on a farm and, when exploring the countryside, Milo is swept down a rushing river. Otis goes after to rescue his friend and the two begin a series of adventures as they try to return home. **19??** (G) 76m/C **VHS** $19.95 *COL* 🎬🎬½

Milo Milo Comedy about some very silly French people who propose to steal the Venus de Milo from the Louvre. **196?** 110m/C Antonio Fargas, Joe Higgins. **VHS, Beta** $39.95 *VCD* 🎬🎬

The Milpitas Monster Creature spawned in a Milpitas, California, waste dump terrorizes the town residents. **1975** (PG) 80m/C Doug Hagdahl, Scott A. Henderson, Scott Parker; *D:* Robert L. Burrill. **VHS, Beta** $19.98 *UHV* 🎬

Mimi Melodrama with a down-on-his-luck playwright falling for a poor lass who provides him with the needed inspiration to be a winner. The question is, will she die before he hits the big time? Loosely based on "La Vie de Boheme" by Henri Murger. **1935** 98m/B *GB* Douglas Fairbanks Jr., Gertrude Lawrence, Diana Napier, Harold Warrender, Carol Goodner, Richard Bird, Austin Trevor, Lawrence Hanray, Paul Graetz, Martin Walker; *D:* Paul Stein. **VHS** $29.95 *FCT, VYY* 🎬🎬

Min & Bill Patchy early talkie about two houseboat dwellers fighting to preserve their waterfront lifestyle and keep their daughter from being taken to a "proper" home. **1930** 66m/B Marie Dressler, Wallace Beery, Marjorie Rambeau, Dorothy Jordan; *D:* George Roy Hill. **VHS, Beta** $19.98 *MGM, BTV, FHE* 🎬🎬

Mind, Body & Soul When a woman witnesses a human sacrifice performed by her boyfriend's satanic cult, she goes to the police. The cops, however, believe she is part of the cult, so she is forced to rely on the public defender to protect her from angry cult members. Pretty dull, but Hauser and Allen add some spice to this hokey thriller. **1992** (R) 93m/C Wings Hauser, Ginger Lynn Allen, Jay Richardson, Ken Hill, Jesse Kaye, Tami Bakke; *D:* Rick Sloane. **VHS** $89.95 *AIP* 🎬🎬

Mind Games A young couple and their ten-year-old son pick up a hitcher in their mobile home, never suspecting that he's a deranged psychology student ready to pit the family against each other as an experiment. **1989** (R) 93m/C Edward Albert, Shawn Weatherly, Matt Norero, Maxwell Caulfield; *D:* Bob Yari. **VHS** $79.98 *FOX, HHE* 🎬½

Mind Snatchers An American G.I. becomes involved in U.S. Army experimental psychological brain operations when he is brought into a western European hospital for treatment. Also know as "The Happiness Cage."

1972 (PG) 94m/C Christopher Walken, Ronny Cox, Ralph Meeker, Joss Ackland; *D:* Bernard Girard. **VHS, Beta** $59.95 *PSM* 🎬🎬½

Mind Trap A beautiful movie star's family is killed due to her father's involvement with naval research. The government wants no part of her troubles so she is forced to take the law into her own hands. **1991** 90m/C Dan Haggerty, Lyle Waggoner, Martha Kincare, Thomas Elliot, Samuel Steven; *D:* Eames Demetrios. **VHS** *NO* 🎬🎬½

Mind Warp A future society exercises mental control and torture over its citizens. *AKA:* Grey Matter; The Brain Machine. **1972** (R) 92m/C James Best, Barbara Burgess, Gil Peterson, Gerald McRaney, Marcus J. Grapes, Doug Collins; *D:* Joy Houck Jr. **VHS, Beta** $19.95 *ACA* 🎬½

Mindfield An innocent man gets trapped by the CIA and is used by them in mind control experiments. **1989** (R) 91m/C *CA* Michael Ironside, Lisa Langlois, Christopher Plummer, Stefan Wodoslowsky, Sean McCann; *D:* Jean-Claude Lord. **VHS, Beta, LV** *NO* 🎬½

Mindkiller A tongue-in-cheek gore-fest about a shy young guy who develops his brain in an effort to be socially accepted. Unfortunately, he overdoes it and his brain mutates, bursts from his head and runs around on its own. An aspiring cult classic. **1987** 84m/C Joe McDonald, Christopher Wade, Shirley Ross, Kevin Hart; *D:* Michael Krueger. **VHS, Beta** $79.95 *PSM* 🎬½

Mindwalk A feature-length intellectual workout; a physicist, poet and politician stroll the ancient grounds of Mont St. Michel monastery in France and discuss the need to change mankind's view of the universe. Uncinematic? Perhaps, but it entertainingly conveys the epochal ideas of scientist/author Fritjof Capra (whose book was adapted for the screen by younger brother Bernt). **1991** (PG) 111m/C Liv Ullmann, Sam Waterston, John Heard, Ione Skye; *D:* Bernt Capra; *W:* Fritjof Capra. **VHS, Beta** *PAR* 🎬🎬🎬

Mindwarp Because of ecological disaster, future residents of Earth live in a sterile place called "Inworld" and program their dreams through a computer system that hooks to the base of the skull. Judy (Alicia) seeks answers about her missing father by hooking into her mother's brain, accidentally killing her. Judy is cast out of "Inworld" to Earth's wasteland where she is captured by "Crawlers" but soon rescued by human survivor, Stover (Campbell). Together they fight the horrid environment, but soon they are both captured by the "Crawlers." Judy discovers the awful truth about her father in the "Crawlers" landfill world, and the truth may kill her. **1991** (R) 91m/C Marta Alicia, Bruce Campbell, Angus Scrimm, Elizabeth Kent, Mary Becker; *D:* Steve Barnett; *W:* Henry Dominick. **VHS, LV** *COL* 🎬🎬

Mine Own Executioner Determined but unstable psychologist in postwar London struggles to treat schizophrenic who suffered torture by Japanese while wartime prisoner. Strong, visually engrossing fare. **1947** 102m/B *GB* Burgess Meredith, Kieron Moore, Dulcie Gray, Christine Norden, Barbara White, John Laurie, Michael Shepley; *D:* Anthony Kimmins. **VHS, Beta** $19.95 *NOS, DVT, HHT* 🎬🎬🎬

Mines of Kilimanjaro An archaeology student heads for Africa to investigate his professor's murder and comes up with a heap of trouble. **1987** (PG-13) 88m/C Christopher Connelly, Tobias Hoels, Gordon Mitchell, Elena Pompei; *D:* Mino Guerrini. **VHS, Beta** $79.95 *IMP* 🎬½

Ministry of Vengeance A psychotic murderer who hates grapes of any kind finds the woman of his dreams - she's a psychotic murderer who hates grapes! Together they find bliss - until the plumber discovers their secret! **1989** (R) 90m/C John Schneider, Ned Beatty, George Kennedy, Yaphet Kotto, James Tolkan, Apollonia. **VHS, Beta, LV** $89.95 *LIV* 🎬

The Miniver Story Weepy sequel to "Mrs. Miniver" reunites the family in post-WWII England, but clearly lacks the inspiration of the original. Garson is again Mrs. Miniver and she's secretly suffering from a never-named fatal disease. She decides to straighten out the family troubles before her time is up, including her daughter's love life and her husband's plan to move to Brazil. Depressing and glum. **1950** 104m/B *GB* Greer Garson, Walter Pidgeon, John Hodiak, Leo Genn, Cathy O'Donnell, Reginald Owen, Anthony Bushell; *D:* H.C. Potter; *W:* Ronald Millar, George Froeschel. **VHS** $19.98 *MGM* 🎬🎬

Minnesota Clay A blind gunman, who aims by sound and smell, is marked by two rival gangs and a tempestuous tramp. *AKA:* L'Homme du Minnesota. **1965** 89m/C *FR IT* Cameron Mitchell, Diana Martin; *D:* Sergio Corbucci. **VHS, Beta, LV** *NO* 🎬½

A Minor Miracle Tender family fare about a group of orphaned children who band together under the loving guidance of their guardian (Huston) to save St. Francis School for boys from the town planners. Warms the cockles. **1983** (G) 100m/C John Huston, Pele, Peter Fox. **VHS, Beta, LV** $9.95 *COL, SUE* 🎬🎬

Minsky's Follies Recreation of an old time burlesque revue complete with strippers. **1983** 60m/C Phyllis Diller, Rip Taylor, Stubby Kaye. **VHS, Beta** $39.95 *RKO* 🎬

A Minute to Pray, A Second to Die A notorious, wanted-dead-or-alive gunman retreats to the amnesty of the New Mexico Territory, but finds he cannot shake his past. *AKA:* Un Minuto Per Pregare, Un Istante Per Morire; Dead or Alive; Outlaw Gun. **1967** 100m/C *IT* Robert Ryan, Arthur Kennedy, Alex Cord; *D:* Franco Giraldi. **VHS, Beta** $19.98 *FOX, TPV* 🎬🎬

The Miracle An innocent peasant woman is seduced by a shepherd and becomes convinced that her pregnancy will produce a second Christ. Controversial, compelling film derived from a story by Federico Fellini. In Italian with English subtitles. *AKA:* Ways of Love. **1948** 43m/B *IT* Anna Magnani, Federico Fellini; *D:* Roberto Rossellini. **VHS, Beta** $24.95 *NOS, FCT, APD* 🎬🎬🎬

The Miracle Irish teens, whose strong friendship is based upon their equally unhappy home lives, find both tested when a secretive American woman turns up in town. Excellent debuts from Byrne and Pilkington but tedious pacing in a dreamy script that tells too much too soon. Worth watching just for D'Angelo's smouldering rendition of "Stardust." **1991** (PG) 97m/C *GB* Beverly D'Angelo, Donal McCann, Niall Byrne, Lorraine Pilkington; *W/D:* Neil Jordan. **VHS, LV** $89.98 *LIV* 🎬🎬½

Miracle at Moreaux Three Jewish children fleeing from Nazis find sanctuary with a nun and her wards. Based on Clare Huchet Bishop's book "Twenty and Ten."

Originally aired on PBS as part of the "Wonderworks" family movie series.
1986 58m/C Loretta Swit, Marsha Moreau, Robert Joy, Ken Pogue, Robert Kosoy, Talya Rubin; **D:** Paul Shapiro. VHS $29.95 PME, HMV, IGP ♂♂½

Miracle Beach Scotty McKay has lost his job, his apartment, and his girl. Then he gets rejected by Dana, the super model he's secretly adored. Can things get any worse? Scotty decides to take a walk along the beach and sort things out when he stumbles across a girl genie, named Jeanie, who has been sent to Earth on a good will mission. Scotty gets Jeanie to grant his every material wish in order to dazzle model Dana. But when Jeanie falls in love with Scotty can she get him to recognize the difference between true love and fantasy?
1992 (PG-13) 88m/C Dean Cameron, Felicity Waterman, Ami Dolenz, Alexis Arquette, Martin Mull, Pat Morita, Vincent Schiavelli; **D:** Skott Snider. VHS, LV $89.95 COL ♂½

Miracle Down Under A family endures arduous times in 1890s Australia before a Christmas miracle changes their fortunes. Inoffensive Disney-produced drama. Australia has two directors named George Miller—one directs Mad Max movies, the other directs family fare such as "The Man from Snowy River." This Miller is the latter.
1987 101m/C AU Dee Wallace Stone, John Waters, Charles Tingwell, Bill Kerr, Andrew Ferguson; **D:** George Miller. VHS, Beta $29.95 BVV, IGP ♂♂½

Miracle in Harlem A gang tries to take over a candy shop and when the gang leader is killed, the evidence points to the foster daughter of the shop owner. The script suffers from cliched dialog and less-than-believable situations, but the all-black cast turns in good performances.
1948 69m/B Sheila Guyse, Stepin Fetchit, Hilda Offley, Lawrence Criner, Monte Hawley; **D:** Jack Kemp. VHS $24.95 NOS ♂♂

Miracle in Milan An innocent, child-like fantasy about heavenly intervention driving capitalists out of a Milanese ghetto and helping the poor to fly to a new Utopia. Happy mixture of whimsicality and neo-realism, co-written with Cesare Zavattini. In Italian with English subtitles. **AKA:** Miracolo a Milano.
1951 95m/B IT Francesco Golisano, Brunella Bova, Emma Gramatica, Paolo Stoppa; **D:** Vittorio De Sica. VHS, Beta, LV $79.95 HMV, FCT, VYG ♂♂♂

Miracle in Rome Man digs up dead daughter and finds her body in perfect condition despite 12-year interment. Attempting to convince the local clergy that she's miracle material, he finds them less than eager to elect her to sainthood. Made for Spanish TV. In Spanish with English subtitles. **AKA:** Milagro en Roma.
1988 76m/C SP Frank Ramirez, Gerardo Arellano, Amalia Duque Garcia, Lisandro Duque, Daniel Priolett; **D:** Lisandro Duque Naranjo; **W:** Lisandro Duque Naranjo, Gabriel Garcia Marquez. VHS, LV $79.95 FXL, FCT, APD ♂♂½

Miracle in the Wilderness A Christmas western based on Paul Gallico's novella, "The Snow Goose." Kristofferson stars as Jericho Adams, a former Indian fighter, who turns to farming to support his wife and child. When they are captured by a raiding party of Blackfeet, Adams discovers they have never heard the story of the Nativity.
1991 88m/C Kris Kristofferson, Kim Cattrall; **D:** Kevin Dobson. VHS, LV $89.98 FCT ♂♂½

Miracle Kid Standard story of a young boxer who'd rather be something else. His romance is interrupted when he becomes successful in the ring.
1942 66m/B Tom Neal, Carol Hughes, Betty Blythe, Minta Durfee, Gertrude Messinger; **D:** William Beaudine. VHS $19.95 NOS ♂♂

Miracle Mile A riveting, apocalyptic thriller about a mild-mannered misfit who, while inadvertently standing on a street corner at 2 a.m., answers a ringing pay phone. The caller is a panicked missile-silo worker who announces that the bombs have been launched for an all-out nuclear war. With about an hour left before the end, he decides to head into the city and rendezvous with his new girlfriend. A surreal, wicked farce sadly overlooked in theatrical release. Music by Tangerine Dream.
1989 (R) 87m/C Anthony Edwards, Mare Winningham, John Agar, Denise Crosby, Lou Hancock; **W/D:** Steve DeJarnatt. VHS, Beta, LV $89.99 HBO ♂♂♂

Miracle of Morgan's Creek The breakneck comedy that stands as Sturges' premier achievement. Details the misadventures of a wartime floozy who gets drunk, thinks she marries a soldier on leave, gets pregnant by him, forgets the whole thing, and then tries to evade scandal by getting a local schnook to marry her again. And she's expecting sextuplets. Hilarious, out-to-make-trouble farce that shouldn't have, by all rights, made it past the censors of the time. Sturges' most scathing assault on American values earned him an Oscar nomination for writing. Remade as "Rock-A-Bye Baby" in 1958.
1944 98m/B Eddie Bracken, Betty Hutton, Diana Lynn, Brian Donlevy, Akim Tamiroff, Porter Hall, Emory Parnell, Alan Bridge, Julius Tannen, Victor Potel, Almira Sessions, Chester Conklin, William Demarest; **W/D:** Preston Sturges VHS, Beta $14.95 PAR, CCB ♂♂♂♂

Miracle of Our Lady of Fatima Slick cold-war version of the supposedly true events surrounding the sighting of a holy vision by three children in Portugal during World War I. **AKA:** The Miracle of Fatima.
1952 102m/C Gilbert Roland, Susan Whitney, Sherry Jackson, Sammy Ogg, Angela Clark, Frank Silvera, Jay Novello; **D:** John Brahm. VHS, Beta, LV $19.98 WAR, IGP ♂♂

The Miracle of the Bells A miracle occurs after a dead movie star is buried in the cemetary of her modest hometown. Given the premise, the casting is all the more peculiar. Adapted by Ben Hecht from Russell Janney's novel.
1948 120m/B Fred MacMurray, Alida Valli, Frank Sinatra, Lee J. Cobb; **D:** Irving Pichel. VHS, Beta $19.98 REP, IGP ♂♂

Miracle of the Heart: A Boys Town Story A television movie based on the story of Boys Town, and an old priest who sticks up for Boys Town's principles in the face of a younger priest with rigid ideas.
1986 100m/C Art Carney, Casey Siemaszko, Jack Bannon; **D:** Georg Stanford Brown. VHS, Beta $69.95 COL ♂♂

The Miracle of the White Stallions A disappointing Disney adventure about the director of a Viennese riding academy who guides his prized Lipizzan stallions to safety when the Nazis occupy Austria in World War II. **AKA:** The Flight of the White Stallions.
1963 92m/C Robert Taylor, Lilli Palmer, Eddie Albert, Curt Jurgens; **D:** Arthur Hiller. VHS, Beta $69.95 DIS ♂½

Miracle on Ice Occasionally stirring television film recounts the surprise triumph of the American hockey team over the touted Soviet squad during the 1980 Winter Olympics at Lake Placid.
1981 150m/C Karl Malden, Steve Guttenberg, Andrew Stevens, Lucinda Dooling, Jessica Walter; **D:** David Hillard Stern. VHS, Beta NO ♂♂½

Miracle on 34th Street The actual Kris Kringle is hired as Santa Claus for the Macy's Thanksgiving parade but finds difficulty in proving himself to the cynical parade sponsor. When the boss's daughter also refuses to acknowledge Kringle, he goes to extraordinary lengths to convince her. Holiday classic equal to "It's a Wonderful Life," with Gwenn and Wood particularly engaging. Also available colorized. **AKA:** The Big Heart.
1947 97m/B Maureen O'Hara, John Payne, Edmund Gwenn, Natalie Wood, William Frawley, Porter Hall, Gene Lockhart, Thelma Ritter, Jack Albertson; **W/D:** George Seaton. Academy Awards '47: Best Story & Screenplay, Best Supporting Actor (Gwenn); Nominations: Best Picture. VHS, Beta, LV $14.98 CCB, FOX, HMV ♂♂♂♂

Miracle Rider: Vol. 1 Old West guns-and-hero tale. In fifteen chapters.
1935 195m/B Tom Mix, Joan Gale, Charles Middleton; **D:** Armand Schaefer. VHS, Beta, 3/4U, Special order formats $49.95 NOS, MRV, VCN ♂♂♂♂

Miracle Rider: Vol. 2 Serial covers excitement in the Old West.
1935 135m/C Tom Mix, Joan Gale, Charles Middleton; **D:** Armand Schaefer. VHS, Beta, 3/4U, Special order formats $69.95 VCN, MRV, VYY ♂½

The Miracle Worker Depicts the unconventional methods that teacher Anne Sullivan used to help the deaf and blind Helen Keller adjust to the world around her and shows the relationship that built between the two courageous women. An intense, moving experience. William Gibson adapted his own play for the screen.
1962 107m/B Anne Bancroft, Patty Duke, Victor Jory, Inga Swenson, Andrew Prine, Beah Richards; **D:** Arthur Penn. Academy Awards '62: Best Actress (Bancroft), Best Supporting Actress (Duke); Nominations: Best Adapted Screenplay, Best Costume Design (B & W), Best Director (Penn); National Board of Review Awards '62: 10 Best Films of the Year, Best Actress (Bancroft). VHS, Beta $19.98 MGM, BTV, CCB ♂♂♂½

The Miracle Worker Remade for television story of blind, deaf and mute Helen Keller and her teacher, Annie Sullivan, whose patience and perseverance finally enable Helen to learn to communicate with the world. Duke was Keller in the 1962 original, but plays the teacher in this version.
1979 98m/C Patty Duke, Melissa Gilbert; **D:** Paul Aaron. VHS, Beta $59.95 WAR, OM ♂♂♂

Miracles Comedic misfire pairs a recently divorced couple as reluctant adventurers dodging jewel thieves and peculiar tribes in South America. In a desperate move to create a plot, Mexican jewel thieves, strange tribal rites, and some outrageously unlikely coincidences reunite the family. If this sounds good, see "Romancing the Stone" instead.
1986 (PG) 90m/C Tom Conti, Teri Garr, Paul Rodriguez, Christopher Lloyd, Jorge Russek, Charles Rocket, Bob Nelson; **D:** Jim Kouf. VHS, Beta, LV $79.99 HBO, IME ♂½

Mirage An amnesiac finds himself the target of a dangerous manhunt in New York City in this offbeat thriller. Peck is particularly sympathetic in the lead, and McCarthy, Matthau, and Kennedy all shine in supporting

roles. Worth it just to hear thug Kennedy grunt, "I owe this man some pain!" Music score by Quincy Jones.
1966 108m/B Gregory Peck, Diane Baker, Walter Matthau, Jack Weston, Kevin McCarthy, Walter Abel, George Kennedy; **D:** Edward Dmytryk. VHS, Beta $14.95 KRT, MLB &&&

Mirele Efros A widowed but successful businesswoman finds herself at odds with her daughter-in-law in this film set in the turn of the century. In Yiddish with English subtitles.
1938 80m/B Berta Gersten, Michael Rosenberg, Ruth Elbaum, Albert Lipton, Sarah Krohner, Moishe Feder; **D:** Joseph Berne. VHS, Beta $79.95 ERG, TAM && ½

The Mirror Wonderful child's view of life in Russia during WWII. Black and white flashbacks of important events in the country's history are interspersed with scenes of day-to-day family life. In Russian with English subtitles. **AKA:** Zerkalo; A White White Boy.
1975 106m/C RU Margarita Terekhova, Philip Yankovsky, Ignat Daniltsev, Oleg Yankovsky; **D:** Andrei Tarkovsky. VHS $39.95 TAM, TPV, KIV &&&

The Mirror Crack'd While filming a movie in the English countryside, an American actress is murdered and Miss Marple must discover who the killer is. Based on the substantially better Agatha Christie novel.
1980 (PG) 105m/C GB Elizabeth Taylor, Rock Hudson, Kim Novak, Tony Curtis, Edward Fox, Geraldine Chaplin, Charles Gray, Pierce Brosnan; **D:** Guy Hamilton; **W:** Agatha Christie. VHS, Beta, LV $19.99 HBO &&

Mirror Images Although sexy twins Kaitlin and Shauna may look alike, they couldn't have more diverse personalities. Yet the gorgeous twins find their lives thrown together in a mad tornado of passion and danger when they each encounter a handsome, mysterious stranger. Could it be that this guy has something more on his mind than love, something like... murder? Also available in an even steamier unrated version.
1991 (R) 94m/C Delia Sheppard, Jeff Conaway, Richard Arbolino, John O'Hurley, Korey Mall, Julie Strain, Nels Van Patten; **D:** Alexander Gregory Hippolyte. VHS $89.95 ACA & ½

Mirror, Mirror The prolific Ms. Black turns on the ol' black magic when her daughter's classmates decide it's open season for taunting shrinking violets. Thanks to a magical mirror on the wall, the cheerleading classmates are willed to the great pep rally in the sky.
1990 (R) 105m/C Karen Black, Rainbow Harvest, Kristin Datillo, Ricky Paull Goldin, Yvonne De Carlo, William Sanderson; **D:** Marina Sargenti. VHS, LV $19.95 ACA & ½

Mirror of Death A woman subject to physical abuse gets more than she bargains for when she seeks revenge by unleashing the gruesome Queen of Hell. Watch this if you dare!
1987 85m/C Julie Merrill, Kuri Browne, John Reno, Deryn Warren. VHS, Beta $14.95 SVS &

Mirrors Woman finds that her dreams lead to death and destruction in New Orleans.
1978 83m/C Kitty Winn, Peter Donat, William Swetland, Mary-Robin Redd, William Burns; **D:** Noel Black. VHS, Beta NO &

Mirrors A Detroit-born ballerina goes to the Big Apple in search of fame and glory, leaving behind her journalist boyfriend. This upbeat love story features some spectacular dance routines and a behind-the-scenes look at a Broadway dancer's lifestyle. Originally made for television.

1985 99m/C Timothy Daly, Marguerite Hickey, Antony Hamilton; **D:** Harry Winer. VHS $89.95 VMK && ½

The Misadventures of Merlin Jones A pair of college sweethearts become embroiled in a rollicking chimp-napping scandal. Disney pap done appropriately. A sequel, "The Monkey's Uncle," followed.
1963 (G) 90m/C Tommy Kirk, Annette Funicello, Leon Ames, Stuart Erwin, Connie Gilchrist; **D:** Robert Stevenson. VHS, Beta $69.95 DIS & ½

The Misadventures of Mr. Wilt Bumbling college lecturer has to convince inept inspector that he murdered a blowup doll, not his mean missing wife. Based on Tom Sharpe's bestseller. **AKA:** Wilt.
1990 84m/C GB Griff Rhys Jones, Mel Smith, Alison Steadman, Diana Quick; **D:** Michael Tuchner. VHS VMK &&

Mischief Alienated youths form a friendship during James Dean's heydey. Warning: this film offers a fairly convincing recreation of the 1950s.
1985 (R) 97m/C Doug McKeon, Catherine Mary Stewart, Kelly Preston, Chris Nash, D.W. Brown, Jami Gertz, Margaret Blye, Graham Jarvis, Terry O'Quinn; **D:** Mel Damski. VHS, Beta, LV $79.98 FOX &&

Misery Caan plays an author who decides to chuck his lucrative but unfulfilling pulp novels and get serious with his work by finishing off his most popular character, Misery Chastain, in the final installment of a tired romance series. But on his way to the city in a heavy snowstorm, he crashes on a remote highway and is seriously hurt. Fate seems to intervene when Bates, his biggest fan ever, saves his life with rudimentary medical care. Trouble is, she's a Stephen King kinda gal, and she forces him to resurrect Misery from dead letterdom. Glib, brutal, and ever so balmy, Bates garnered an Oscar for her role. Screenplay adapted from the King story by William Goldman.
1990 (R) 107m/C James Caan, Kathy Bates, Lauren Bacall, Richard Farnsworth, Frances Sternhagen, Graham Jarvis; **D:** Rob Reiner. VHS, Beta, LV, SVS $19.95 COL, NLC, BTV &&&

The Misfit Brigade Variation on the "Dirty Dozen" finds German misfits recruited for warfare by desperate Nazis during WWII. **AKA:** Wheels of Terror.
1987 (R) 99m/C Bruce Davison, Oliver Reed, David Carradine, David Patrick Kelly, D.W. Moffett, Keith Szarabajka; **D:** Gordon Hessler. VHS, Beta $19.98 TWE &&

The Misfits A cynical floozy befriends grim cowboys in this downbeat drama. Compelling performances from leads Clift, Monroe (screenwriter Miller's wife), and Gable. Last film for the latter two performers, and nearly the end for Clift.
1961 124m/B Clark Gable, Marilyn Monroe, Montgomery Clift, Thelma Ritter, Eli Wallach, James Barton, Estelle Winwood; **D:** John Huston. VHS, Beta, LV $19.98 FOX, FCT &&&

Misfits of Science Pilot for a failed television series about a group of teens with special powers who fight to save the world.
1985 96m/C Dean Paul Martin, Kevin Peter Hall, Mark Thomas Miller, Kenneth Mars, Courteney Cox; **D:** Philip DeGuere. VHS, Beta $39.95 MCA &

Mishima: A Life in Four Chapters Somewhat detached account and indulgent portrayal of the narcissistic Japanese author (and actor, filmmaker, and militarist) alternates between stylized interpretations of his books and a straightforward account of his life. Culminates in a pseudo-military operation that, in turn, resulted in

Mishima's ritualistic suicide. A U.S./Japanese production. Innovative design by Eiko Ishioka. In Japanese with English subtitles.
1985 (R) 121m/C Ken Ogata, Kenji Sawada, Yasosuke Bando; **W/D:** Paul Schrader; **W:** Leonard Schrader; **M:** Philip Glass. VHS, Beta $79.95 WAR, TAM &&&

Mision Suicida Santo joins forces with a beautiful Interpol agent in his quest to break a spy ring.
1987 90m/C MX Santo, Lorena Velasquez, Elsa Cardenas, Dagoberto Rodriguez. VHS, Beta $49.95 MAD &&

Miss A & Miss M A young girl is shocked when she realizes that two teachers she has befriended also live together.
1986 60m/C Kika Markham, Jennifer Hilary. VHS $11.95 PSM &&

Miss All-American Beauty A behind-the-scenes look at a smalltime Texas beauty pageant. Lane stars as a contestant who comes to realize her self-respect is more important than winning an award. Meadow's mean pageant director adds an ironic edge that the movie as a whole lacks. Made for television.
1982 96m/C Diane Lane, Cloris Leachman, David Dukes, Jayne Meadows, Alice Hirson, Brian Kerwin; **D:** Gus Trikonis. VHS, Beta $39.95 LIV & ½

Miss Annie Rooney Intended to bill the child star in a more mature role, Temple receives her first screen kiss in this story about a poor Irish girl who falls in love with a wealthy young man. The well-worn plot is weighed down by lifeless dialogue.
1942 (G) 86m/B Shirley Temple, Dickie Moore, William Gargan, Guy Kibbee, Peggy Ryan, June Lockhart; **D:** Edwin L. Marin. VHS, Beta $12.95 LIV, MED &

Miss Firecracker Hunter, longing for love and self-respect, decides to change her promiscuous image by entering the local beauty pageant in her conservative southern hometown. The somewhat drippy premise is transformed by a super script and cast into an engaging and upbeat film. Henley's script was adapted from her own Off-Broadway play where Hunter created the role. Actress Lahti, wife of director Schlamme, makes a brief appearance.
1989 (PG) 102m/C Holly Hunter, Scott Glenn, Mary Steenburgen, Tim Robbins, Alfre Woodard, Trey Wilson, Bert Remsen, Ann Wedgeworth, Christine Lahti, Amy Wright; **D:** Thomas Schlamme; **W:** Beth Henley. VHS, Beta, LV $89.99 HBO &&&

Miss Grant Takes Richmond Zipperhead secretary finds herself in hot water a la Lucy when she finds out the company she's been working for is really the front for a gambling getup. Only Lucy fans need apply. **AKA:** Innocence is Bliss.
1949 87m/B Lucille Ball, William Holden, Janis Carter, James Gleason, Gloria Henry, Frank McHugh, George Cleveland, Arthur Space, Willaim Wright, Jimmy Lloyd; **D:** Lloyd Bacon. VHS $19.95 COL, FCT &&

Miss Julie Melodramatic stew adapted from from the August Strindberg play about a confused noblewoman who disgraces herself when she allows a servant to seduce her. In Swedish with English subtitles.
1950 90m/B SW Anita Bjork, Ulf Palme, Anders Henrikson; **D:** Alf Sjoberg. VHS, Beta $19.95 COL, SUE, TAM &&

Miss Mary A compassionate English governess in Buenos Aires conflicts with the honor-obsessed family she works for and Argentina's tumultuous history. Christie gives a wonderful performance. Some profanity and nudity.

1986 (R) 100m/C *AR* Julie Christie, Donald McIntire, Sofia Viruboff; *D:* Maria-Luisa Bemberg. VHS, Beta $9.99 *STE, NWV* 𝍅𝍅½

Miss Melody Jones A beautiful young black woman's dreams of stardom unravel as she is forced to pander to prurient men by disrobing publicly for financial recompense. **1973** 86m/C Philomena Nowlin, Ronald Warren, Jacqueline Dalya, Peter Jacob; *W/D:* Bill Brame. VHS $39.95 *XVC* 𝍅

Miss Right A young man determines to find the ideal woman for himself and casts aside his other romantic interests. Sputtering lightweight comedy. **1981** (R) 98m/C William Tepper, Karen Black, Virna Lisi, Margot Kidder, Marie-France Pisier; *D:* Paul Williams. VHS, LV $14.95 *SVS, IME* 𝍅

Miss Rose White Sedgwick is a young career woman in post-WWII New York, whose family secrets are about to come out. Assimilated Rose White was born Rayzel Weiss, a Polish Jew, and sent to the U.S. as a young girl before World War II devastated her family. Long after the war is over she receives word that the older sister she thought was dead has survived the camps and is coming to America. The haunted Luisa causes Rose, who thought she put her past behind her, to question her values and the secrets shared between Luisa and their stern father. Based on the play "A Shayna Maidel" by Barbara Lebow. A Hallmark Hall of Fame presentation. **1992** (PG) 95m/C Kyra Sedgwick, Amanda Plummer, Maximilian Schell, D.B. Sweeney, Penny Fuller, Milton Selzer, Maureen Stapleton; *D:* Joseph Sargent; *W:* Anna Sandor. VHS $89.98 *REP, BTV* 𝍅𝍅𝍅

Miss Sadie Thompson Based on the novel "Rain" by W. Somerset Maugham. Promiscuous tart Hayworth arrives on a Pacific island occupied by a unit of Marines and a sanctimonious preacher played by Ferrer (father of Miguel Ferrer of TV's "Twin Peaks" and "On the Air"). While Hayworth parties with the Marines and becomes involved with Ray's Sgt. O'Hara, Ferrer moralizes and insists she return to the mainland to face moral charges. The quasi-musical, with a scattering of dubbed songs by Hayworth, includes a memorable erotic dance scene complete with a tight dress and dripping sweat. Hayworth's strong performance carries the picture with Ferrer and Ray turning in cardboard versions of their Maugham characters. Originally filmed in 3-D. **1953** 91m/C Rita Hayworth, Jose Ferrer, Aldo Ray, Charles Bronson; *D:* Curtis Bernhardt. VHS, Beta, LV $19.95 *COL* 𝍅𝍅𝍅

Missile to the Moon First expedition to the moon encounters not acres of dead rock but a race of gorgeous women in lingerie and high heels. A bad but entertaining remake of "Cat Women of the Moon," featuring a bevy of beauty contest winners from New Hampshire to Yugoslavia. Who says truth is stranger than fiction. **1959** 78m/B Gary Clarke, Cathy Downs, K.T. Stevens, Laurie Mitchell, Michael Whalen, Nina Bara, Richard Travis, Tommy Cook, Marjorie Hellen; *D:* Richard Cunha. VHS, Beta $9.95 *RHI, SNC, CNM* 𝍅½

Missiles of October Telling the story of the October 1962 Cuban Missile crisis, this made-for-TV drama keeps you on the edge of your seat while unfolding the sequence of events within the U.S. Government. Well written, with a strong cast including Devane, who turns in a convincing performance—guess who—J.F.K.

1974 155m/C William Devane, Ralph Bellamy, Martin Sheen, Howard da Silva; *D:* Anthony Page. VHS, Beta $59.95 *MPI, LCA* 𝍅𝍅𝍅

Missing At the height of a military coup in Chile (never named in the movie), a young American writer (Shea) disappears. Lemon, as Shea's father, is a right-wing Christian Scientist who has flown into the country to get to the bottom of his son's disappearance. Shea's wife, played by Spacek, has been living a bohemian lifestyle with her husband in Chile and is the political opposite of her father-in-law. While chafing and bickering, they search for information about the missing Shea, encountering obnoxious American diplomats and scary Chilean officials. Outstanding performances by Spacek and Lemon along with excellent writing and direction result in a gripping and thought-provoking thriller. Based on the book by Thomas Hauser from the true story of Charles Horman. **1982** (PG) 122m/C Jack Lemmon, Sissy Spacek, John Shea, Melanie Mayron, David Clennon, Charles Cioffi, Joe Regalbuto, Richard Venturo, Janice Rule; *D:* Constantin Costa-Gavras. Academy Awards '82: Best Adapted Screenplay; Nominations: Best Actor (Lemmon), Best Actress (Spacek), Best Picture; Cannes Film Festival '82: Best Actor (Lemmon), Best Film. VHS, Beta, LV $19.95 *MCA* 𝍅𝍅𝍅½

The Missing Corpse When a newspaper publisher's worst rival is murdered, he fears that he will be implicated. He decides the only thing to do is hide the body to prevent its being discovered. Enjoyable, light comedy/mystery. **1945** 62m/B J. Edward Bromberg, Eric Sinclair, Frank Jenks, Isabelle Randolph, Paul Guilfoyle, John Shay, Lorell Sheldon; *D:* Albert Herman. VHS $16.95 *NOS, MRV, SNC* 𝍅𝍅

Missing in Action An army colonel returns to the Vietnam jungle to settle some old scores and rescue some POWs while on an MIA fact-finding mission. Box office smash. **1984** (R) 101m/C Chuck Norris, M. Emmet Walsh; *D:* Joseph Zito. VHS, Beta, LV $14.95 *MGM, TLF, PIA* 𝍅½

Missing in Action 2: The Beginning Set in Vietnam, this prequel to the original "Missing in Action" provides some interesting background on Norris's rocky relationship with communism. Packed with violence, bloodshed and torture. **1985** (R) 96m/C Chuck Norris, Soon-Teck Oh, Cosie Costa, Steven Williams; *D:* Lance Hool. VHS, Beta, LV $14.95 *MGM* 𝍅

Missing Link A strange, meditative quasi-documentary depicting the singular adventures of a humanoid silently transversing the African wilderness and confronting various natural phenomena. Beautifully photographed. Make-up by Rick Baker. **1988** (PG) 92m/C Peter Elliott, Michael Gambon; *D:* David Hughes. VHS, Beta $89.95 *MCA* 𝍅𝍅½

Missing Pieces A woman takes a job as a private investigator in order to find her journalist husband's killer. Effective made-for-television mystery taken from the novel "A Private Investigation" by Karl Alexander. **1983** 96m/C Elizabeth Montgomery, Louanne, John Reilly, Ron Karabatsos, Robin Gammell, Julius W. Harris; *D:* Mike Hodges. VHS *LIV* 𝍅𝍅½

The Mission Sweeping, cinematically beautiful historical drama about an 18th-century Jesuit mission in the Brazilian jungle. The missionaries struggle against the legalized slave trade of Portugal and political factions within the church. Written by Robert Bolt of "A Man for All Seasons" fame, its visual intensity is marred by length and so much overt symbolism that an emotional

coolness surfaces when the action slows. Nonetheless, epic in ambition and nearly in quality. Ennio Morricone's musical score is magnificent. **1986** (PG) 125m/C Robert De Niro, Jeremy Irons, Ray McAnally, Philip Bosco, Aidan Quinn, Liam Neeson, Cherie Lunghi, Rev. Daniel Berrigan; *D:* Roland Joffe; *M:* Ennio Morricone. Academy Awards '86: Best Cinematography; Nominations: Best Art Direction/Set Decoration, Best Costume Design, Best Director (Joffe), Best Film Editing, Best Picture, Best Original Score; British Academy Awards '86: Best Supporting Actor (McAnally); Cannes Film Festival '86: Best Film. VHS, Beta, LV, 8mm $19.98 *WAR, PIA* 𝍅𝍅𝍅

Mission Batangas Unremarkable adventure-war-heist movie tells the story of a shallow American WWII pilot (Weaver) and a missionary nurse (Miles), who team up to steal the Philippine government's entire stock of gold bullion from the Japanese who captured it. Beautiful scenery, shot in the Philippines, adds something to an otherwise vacant effort. **1969** 100m/C Dennis Weaver, Vera Miles, Keith Larsen; *D:* Keith Larsen. VHS, Beta, LV $19.95 *STE, NWV* 𝍅½

Mission Corbari One heavily armed and ill-tempered hombre takes on the Nazis, with indifferent results. **197?** 88m/C VHS, Beta *WWV* 𝍅

Mission Galactica: The Cylon Attack Spaceship Battlestar Galactica is stranded in space without fuel and open to attack from the chrome-plated Cylons. Adama (Greene) is forced to stop Commander Cain's (Bridges) efforts to launch an attack against the Cylons, while countering the attacks of the Cylon leader. Warmed over made-for-television sci-fi. **1979** 108m/C Lorne Greene, Lloyd Bridges, Richard Hatch, Dirk Benedict. VHS, Beta, LV $19.95 *MCA* 𝍅𝍅

Mission in Morocco When an oilman scouting for oil fields in the Sahara is killed, his partner, Barker, hops a jet to Morocco to find the whereabouts of a microfilm that gives the location of a valuable oil deposit. The search for the secret microfilm is complicated by competing parties also interested in the black gold. Ho-hum action adventure. **1959** 79m/C Lex Barker, Juli Reding. VHS $19.98 *REP* 𝍅

Mission Inferno The ups and downs of a hot-blooded Korean War commando taking revenge, escaping prison, fighting and just plain making war. **1984** 90m/C VHS, Beta $39.95 *VCD* 𝍅

Mission Kiss and Kill Enchanting title. A movie filled with martial arts, beautiful girls, and exotic settings that takes place in the early days of the Chinese Republic. **19??** 90m/C *CH* Lung Fei, Lu I Lung, Yuan Lung. VHS, Beta $29.95 *OCE* 𝍅

Mission Manila An ex-CIA operative and Manila-based drug addict is called by his ex-lover to return to Manila to help his brother, who has gotten in much the same trouble he had. **1987** (R) 98m/C Larry Wilcox. VHS, Beta, LV *NO* 𝍅

Mission Mars American astronauts McGavin and Adams, on a mission to the red planet, discover the bodies of two cosmonauts floating in space. After landing on the planet's surface, they find a third cosmonaut, this one in a state of suspended animation. While putting the viewer to sleep, they proceed to revive the third cosmonaut and have

at it with the sinister alien force responsible for all the trouble.
1967 87m/C Darren McGavin, Nick Adams, George DeVries; **D:** Nicholas Webster. **VHS, Beta $29.95** UNI *I*

Mission: Monte Carlo An episode from the television series "The Persuaders," wherein our two vacationing adventurers discover a girl's drowned body and try to solve the case.
1975 102m/C Roger Moore, Tony Curtis, Susan George, Annette Andre, Alfred Marks, Laurence Naismith; **D:** Basil Dearden, Roy Ward Baker. **VHS, Beta $59.98** FOX *II*

Mission of Justice Revel in non-stop martial arts action with this tale of a cop who goes undercover to get the goods on a corrupt female politico, who also happens to run her own ruthless private army.
1992 (R) ?m/C Jeff Wincott, Brigitte Nielsen, Matthias Hues, Luca Bercovici, Cyndi Pass, Billy "Sly" Williams, Tony Burton; **D:** Steve Barnett. **VHS, LV $89.98** REP *I*

Mission of the Shark A top secret naval mission leads to a scandal-ridden court martial in this true WWII saga, based on the worst sea disaster in naval history. The U.S.S. Indianapolis has just completed a secret mission when it is torpedoed by enemy subs. The survivors spend five days in shark-infested waters awaiting rescue and, when the Navy points fingers, the ship's highly decorated and well-respected Captain McVay accepts responsibility for the good of the service. Contains some harrowing scenes of sailors versus sharks. Made for television.
1991 92m/C Stacy Keach, Richard Thomas, Steve Landesburg, Carrie Snodgress; **D:** Robert Iscove. **VHS $89.95** TRI *III*

Mission Phantom A group of spies on a mission in Russia plans to steal some diamonds and help a woman get to the United States.
1979 90m/C Andrew Ray, Ingrid Sholder, Peter Martell; **D:** James Reed. **VHS, Beta $59.95** UHV *I*

Mission Stardust An internationally produced but thoroughly unambitious adaptation of the once-popular Perry Rhodan sci-fi serial, in which Rhodan and his team bring ill aliens back to Earth and defend them against evil spies. Dubbed. **AKA:** 4...3...2...1...Morte.
1968 90m/C GE IT SP Essy Persson, Gianni Rizzo, Lang Jeffries, Pinkas Braun; **D:** Primo Zeglio. **VHS, Beta $9.95** RHI *I*½

Mission to Death An adventure extravaganza in which a group of friends must risk their very lives.
1966 76m/C Jim Brewer, James E. McLarty, Jim Westerbrook, Robert Stolper, Dudley Hafner, Jerry Lasater. **VHS** LBD *I*½

Mission to Glory This dozer tells the story of Father Francisco "Kino" Kin, a tough, seventeenth-century priest in California who took on the Apaches and murderous Conquistadors in defense of his people. **AKA:** The Father Kino Story.
1980 (PG) 100m/C Richard Egan, John Ireland, Cesar Romero, Ricardo Montalban, Rory Calhoun, Michael Ansara, Keenan Wynn, Aldo Ray; **D:** Ken Kennedy. **VHS, Beta $29.95** WES, IGP *II*

Mission to Kill An American demolitions expert, Ginty, joins a Latin American guerrilla force in battling tyrannical junta forces. This action-packed, fast-paced thriller is big on revenge and violence but not much else.
1985 (R) 97m/C Robert Ginty, Olivia D'Abo, Cameron Mitchell; **D:** David Winters. **VHS, Beta $79.95** MED *I*½

Mission to Venice Flynn plays a sleuth attempting to find a missing husband when he accidentally stumbles upon a ring of spies.
1963 ?m/C Sean Flynn, Madeleine Robinson. **VHS $16.95** SNC *II*

The Missionary A mild-mannered English missionary returns to London from his work in Africa and is recruited into saving the souls of a group of prostitutes. Aspiring to gentle comedy status, it's often formulaic and flat, with Palin and Smith fighting gamely to stay above script level. Still, good for some laughs, particularly during the near classic walking butler sequence.
1982 (R) 86m/C GB Michael Palin, Maggie Smith, Trevor Howard, Denholm Elliott, Michael Hordern; **D:** Richard Loncraine. **VHS, Beta $19.95** PAR, TVC, FCT *II*½

Mississippi Burning Hard-edged social drama centers around the civil rights movement in Mississippi in 1964. When three activists turn up missing, FBI agents Hackman and Dafoe are sent to head up the investigation. Unfortunately, this is another example of a "serious" film about racial conflict in which white characters predominate and blacks provide background.
1988 (R) 101m/C Gene Hackman, Willem Dafoe, Frances McDormand, Brad Dourif, Lee Ermey, Gailard Sartain, Stephen Tobolowsky, Michael Rooker, Pruitt Taylor Vince, Badja Djola, Kevin Dunn, Frankie Faison, Tom Mason; **D:** Alan Parker. Academy Awards '88: Best Cinematography; Nominations: Best Actor (Hackman), Best Director (Parker), Best Film Editing, Best Picture, Best Sound, Best Supporting Actress (McDormand); Berlin International Film Festival '88: Best Actor (Hackman); National Board of Review Awards '88: 10 Best Films of the Year, Best Actor (Hackman), Best Director (Parker), Best Supporting Actress (McDormand). **VHS, Beta, LV $19.98** ORI *III*

Mississippi Masala "Masala" is an Indian seasoning made of different-colored spices blended together, as this film is a blend of romance, comedy, and social conscience. An interracial romance sets off a cultural collision in a small Southern town. Mina is a young Indian woman whose family were exiled from Uganda in a purge of Asians by Idi Amin. They've settled, somewhat unwillingly, into running a motel in Greenwood, Mississippi. Demetrius is an ambitious black man with his own carpet-cleaning business. When Mina and Demetrius fall in love both families disapprove and it appears the lovers will be parted by the racial tensions. Washington and Choudhury are engaging as the lovers with Seth, as Mina's unhappy father, especially watchable.
1992 (R) 118m/C Denzel Washington, Sarita Choudhury, Roshan Seth, Sharmila Tagore, Charles S. Dutton, Joe Seneca, Ranjit Chowdhry; **Cameos:** Mira Nair; **D:** Mira Nair. **VHS, LV $92.95** COL, FCT *III*

Mississippi Mermaid Truffaut generally succeeds in merging his own directorial style with Hitchcockian suspense, but this is not considered one of his best. Millionaire tobacco planter Belmondo looks for a bride in the personals and finds Deneuve. Belmondo feels lucky landing this beauty until she leaves him and takes his money with her. A lookalike, also played by Deneuve, takes over his wife's role and attempts to poison Belmondo. Look for numerous references to the movies, including Bogart, Balzac and Cocteau. In French and English subtitles.
1969 (PG) 110m/C FR IT Jean-Paul Belmondo, Catherine Deneuve, Michel Bouquet, Nelly Borgeaud, Marcel Berbert, Martine Ferriere; **W/D:** Francois Truffaut. **VHS $19.99** MGM, FCT, TAM *III*

Missouri Breaks Thomas McGuane wrote the screenplay for this offbeat tale of Montana ranchers and rustlers fighting over land and livestock in the 1880s. Promising combination of script, cast and director unfortunately yields rather disappointing results, though both Brando and Nicholson chew up scenery to their hearts' content.
1976 (PG) 126m/C Jack Nicholson, Marlon Brando, Randy Quaid, Kathleen Lloyd, Frederic Forrest, Harry Dean Stanton; **D:** Arthur Penn; **M:** John Williams. **VHS, Beta $19.98** FOX *II*

Missouri Traveler An orphan boy struggles to get his own farm in Missouri. Family fare based on John Buress' novel.
1958 103m/C Lee Marvin, Gary Merrill, Brandon de Wilde, Paul Ford. **VHS, Beta** MRV *III*

Missourians Small-town sheriff Hale helps a Polish rancher overcome ethnic prejudice among the townspeople. The situation worsens with the arrival in town of the rancher's outlaw brother. Strong direction and engaging storyline.
1950 60m/B Monte Hale, Paul Hurst. **VHS, Beta $29.95** DVT *II*½

Mrs. Amworth E.F. Benson's classic tale of the occult, in which a mysterious and deadly epidemic attacking a quiet English village is diagnosed to be the work of a vampire.
1977 29m/C Glynis Johns; **D:** Alvin Rakoff. **VHS, Beta $14.95** LCA *II*½

Mrs. Brown, You've Got a Lovely Daughter The Herman's Hermits gang inherits a greyhound and attempts to make a racer out of him while singing their songs. For the Brit group's diehard fans only. ♫It's Nice To Be Out in the Morning; Ooh, She's Done It Again; Lemon and Lime; The World is for the Young; Holiday Inn; The Most Beautiful Thing in My Life; Daisy Chain; Mrs. Brown, You've Got a Lovely Daughter; There's a King of Hush.
1968 (G) 95m/C Peter Noone, Stanley Holloway, Mona Washbourne; **D:** Saul Swimmer. **VHS, Beta $59.95** MGM *I*½

Mrs. Miniver A moving tale of a courageous, gentle middle-class British family and its struggle to survive during World War II. A classic that garnered six Academy Awards, it's recognized for contributions to the Allied effort. Contains one of the most powerful orations in the film history, delivered by Wilcoxon, who portrayed the vicar. Followed by "The Miniver Story." Adapted from Jan Struther's book.
1942 134m/B Greer Garson, Walter Pidgeon, Teresa Wright, May Whitty, Richard Ney, Henry Travers, Reginald Owen, Henry Wilcoxon, Helmut Dantine, Aubrey Mather, Rhys Williams, Tom Conway, Peter Lawford; **D:** William Wyler. Academy Awards '42: Best Actress (Garson), Best Black and White Cinematography, Best Director (Wyler), Best Picture, Best Screenplay, Best Supporting Actress (Wright); Nominations: Best Actor (Pidgeon), Best Film Editing, Best Sound, Best Supporting Actor (Travers), Best Supporting Actress (Whitty). **VHS, Beta, LV $19.98** MGM, PIA, BTV *IIII*

Mrs. Parkington Overblown epic drama spanning six decades tells the story of the rise and fall of an American dynasty made on easy money. Garson plays the woman who goes from working as a maid in a boarding house to living a life of luxury when she marries a multimillionaire. This was the fifth pairing of Garson and Pidgeon and although it's not one of their best, it proved to be a big hit with audiences. Lavish costumes and good performances by Garson and Moorehead. Based on the novel by Louis Bromfield.

1944 124m/B Greer Garson, Walter Pidgeon, Edward Arnold, Frances Rafferty, Agnes Moorehead, Selena Royle, Gladys Cooper, Lee Patrick; **D:** Tay Garnett; **W:** Robert Thoeren, Polly James. Academy Awards '44 Nominations: Best Actress (Garson), Best Supporting Actress (Moorehead); Golden Globe Awards '45: Best Supporting Actress (Moorehead). VHS $19.98 MGM 𝖏𝖏½

Mrs. R's Daughter An outraged mother fights the judicial systems in order to bring her daughter's rapist to trial. Based on a true story and made for television.
1979 97m/C Cloris Leachman, Season Hubley, Donald Moffatt, John McIntire, Stephen Elliott, Ron Rifkin; **D:** Dan Curtis. VHS, Beta $19.98 WAR, OM 𝖏𝖏

Mrs. Silly Romance novel on tape, following the exploits of an aging woman who in losing material wealth, gains contentment.
1985 60m/C Maggie Smith, James Villers, Cyril Luckham. Beta $11.95 PSM 𝖏

Mrs. Soffel Falling in love with a convicted murderer and helping him flee confinement occupies the time of the prison warden's wife. Effectively captures the 1901 setting, yet a dark pall fairly strangles any emotion. Based on a true story.
1985 (PG-13) 110m/C Diane Keaton, Mel Gibson, Matthew Modine, Edward Herrmann, Trini Alvarado, Terry O'Quinn; **D:** Gillian Armstrong. VHS, Beta, LV $14.95 MGM 𝖏𝖏½

Mrs. Wiggs of the Cabbage Patch A warm, funny, and altogether overdone story of a mother whose husband abandons her, leaving the woman to raise their four children alone. It's Thanksgiving, so the rich visit the poor household to deliver a turkey dinner, and in the end all live happily ever after. Not one of Fields' larger roles; he doesn't even make an appearance until midway through the schmaltz.
1934 80m/B Pauline Lord, ZaSu Pitts, W.C. Fields, Evelyn Venable, Donald Meek; **D:** Norman Taurog. VHS $9.95 GKK 𝖏𝖏½

Mistaken Identity A swank hotel is the setting for this so-so comedy about three con men who wind up conning each other as much as their supposed victims. A couple of light romances are also thrown in for good measure.
1936 75m/B Chick Chandler, Evelyn Knapp, Berton Churchill, Patricia Farr, Richard Carle, Bradley Page, Lew Kelly; **D:** Phil Rosen. VHS $29.95 VYY 𝖏½

Mistaken Identity All-black mystery set against the background of a nightclub, and featuring a production number, "I'm a Bangi from Ubangi."
1941 60m/B Nellie Hill, George Oliver. VHS, Beta $29.95 VCN, DVT, RXM 𝖏½

Mr. Ace A congresswoman decides to run for governor without the approval of the loyal political kingpin, Mr. Ace.
1946 85m/B George Raft, Sylvia Sidney, Sara Haden, Stanley Ridges; **D:** Edwin L. Marin. VHS, Beta, LV $14.95 SVS, COL 𝖏½

Mr. & Mrs. Bridge Set in the thirties and forties in Kansas City, Ivory's adaptation of Evan S. Connell's novels painstakingly portrays an upper middle-class family struggling to survive within an emotional vacuum. Newman and Woodward, together for the first time in many years as Walter and Ivory Bridge, bring a wealth of experience and insight to their characterizations. Many consider this to be Newman's best, most subtle and nuanced performance.
1991 (PG-13) 127m/C Joanne Woodward, Paul Newman, Kyra Sedgwick, Blythe Danner, Simon Callow, Diane Kagan, Robert Sean Leonard, Saundra McClain, Margaret Welsh, Austin

Pendleton, Gale Garnett, Remak Ramsay; **D:** James Ivory; **W:** Ruth Prawer Jhabvala. VHS, LV $92.99 HBO, PIA, FCT 𝖏𝖏𝖏𝖏

Mr. & Mrs. Smith Hitchcock's only screwball comedy, an underrated, endearing farce about a bickering but happy modern couple who discover their marriage isn't legitimate and go through courtship all over again. Vintage of its kind, with inspired performances. Smartly written by Norman Krasna, with crackling dialogue.
1941 95m/B Carole Lombard, Robert Montgomery, Gene Raymond, Jack Carson, Lucile Watson; **D:** Alfred Hitchcock. VHS, Beta, LV $19.95 MED, TTC 𝖏𝖏𝖏½

Mr. Arkadin Screenwriter, director, star Welles, adapting from his own novel, gave this plot a dry run on radio during early 1950s. Welles examines the life of yet another ruthless millionaire, but this one can't seem to remember the sordid source of all that cash. Investigator Arden follows the intriguing and descending trail to a surprise ending. As in "Citizen Kane," oblique camera angles and layered dialogue prevail, but this time only serve to confuse the story. Shot over two years around Europe, required seven years of post production before finding distribution in 1962. **AKA:** Confidential Report.
1955 99m/B GB Orson Welles, Akim Tamiroff, Michael Redgrave, Patricia Medina, Mischa Auer; **D:** Orson Welles. VHS, Beta, LV $24.95 VDM, HTV 𝖏𝖏𝖏

Mr. Baseball Washed-up American baseball player tries to revive his career by playing in Japan and experiences cultures clashing under the ballpark lights. Semi-charmer swings and misses often enough to warrant return to minors. Film drew controversy during production when Universal was bought by the Japanese Matsushita organization and claims of both Japan- and America-bashing were thrown about.
1992 (PG-13) 109m/C Tom Selleck, Ken Takakura, Toshi Shioya, Dennis Haysbert, Aya Takanashi; **D:** Fred Schepisi; **W:** Gary Ross, Kevin Wade, Monte Merrick. VHS, Beta, LV MCA 𝖏𝖏

Mr. Bill Looks Back Featuring Sluggo's Greatest Hits Mr. Bill (of "Saturday Night Live" fame) creator Walter Williams supplies new material as well as previously filmed footage of the luckless little clay guy.
1983 31m/C VHS, Beta $39.95 PAV 𝖏𝖏½

Mr. Billion Engaging chase adventure comedy about an Italian mechanic who stands to inherit a billion dollar fortune if he can travel from Italy to San Francisco in twenty days. Of course, things get in his way. Hill made his American debut in this film.
1977 (PG) 89m/C Jackie Gleason, Terence Hill, Valerie Perrine, Slim Pickens, Chill Wills; **D:** Jonathan Kaplan. VHS, Beta $59.98 FOX 𝖏𝖏

Mr. Bill's Real Life Adventures A made-for-television live-action adventure for the "Saturday Night Live" clay star, portrayed by Scolari, who is victimized as usual by his nemesis, Mr. Sluggo.
1986 43m/C Peter Scolari, Valerie Mahaffey, Lenore Kasdorf, Michael McManus; **D:** Jim Drake. VHS, Beta $29.95 PAR 𝖏

Mr. Blandings Builds His Dream House Classic comedy features Grant as an adman who tires of city life and moves his family to the country, where his troubles really begin. Grant is at his funniest. Loy and Douglas provide strong backup. A must for all homeowners.

1948 93m/B Cary Grant, Myrna Loy, Melvyn Douglas, Reginald Denny, Louise Beavers; **D:** H.C. Potter. VHS, Beta, LV $19.95 TTC, MED, MLB 𝖏𝖏𝖏½

Mr. Boggs Steps Out A pencil-pusher wins a bundle and invests it in a barrel factory. Trouble arises when a slickster tries to close it down. Even with the usual romantic entanglements, the film has trouble staying interesting.
1938 68m/B Stuart Erwin, Helen Chandler, Toby Wing, Tully Marshall, Spencer Charters, Otis Harlan, Walter Byron, Milburn Stone; **D:** Gordon Wiles. VHS $19.95 NOS 𝖏½

Mr. Corbett's Ghost A young man, displeased with his boss's managerial finesse, cuts a deal with a soul collector who pink slips the guy to the great unemployment line in the sky. Once a boss always a boss, and the guy's ghost stops in to say boo, while the soul collector is hot to get his hands on his part of the bargain. Huston's final film appearance. Made for television.
1990 60m/C John Huston, Paul Scofield, Burgess Meredith. VHS $24.95 MON, KAR 𝖏𝖏

Mr. Deeds Goes to Town Typical Capra fare offers Cooper as philanthropic fellow who inherits $20 million and promptly donates it to the needy. He also manages to find time to fall in love with a beautiful reporter. Arthur is the hard-edged reporter determined to fathom the good guy's motivation. Superior entertainment. Based on Clarence Budington Kelland's play "Opera Hut."
1936 118m/B Gary Cooper, Jean Arthur, Raymond Walburn, Walter Catlett, Lionel Stander, George Bancroft, H.B. Warner, Ruth Donnelly, Douglas Dumbrille, Margaret Seddon, Margaret McWade; **D:** Frank Capra; **W:** Robert Riskin. Academy Awards '36: Best Director (Capra); Nominations: Best Actor (Cooper), Best Picture, Best Screenplay, Best Sound; National Board of Review Awards '36: 10 Best Films of the Year; New York Film Critics Awards '36: Best Film. VHS, Beta, LV $19.95 COL, PIA, BTV 𝖏𝖏𝖏½

Mr. Destiny Mid-level businessman Belushi has a mid-life crisis of sorts when his car dies. Wandering into an empty bar, he encounters bartender Caine who serves cocktails and acts omniscient before taking him on the ten-cent tour of life as it would've been if he hadn't struck out in a high school baseball game. Less than wonderful rehash of "It's a Wonderful Life."
1990 (PG-13) 110m/C James Belushi, Michael Caine, Linda Hamilton, Jon Lovitz, Bill McCutcheon, Hart Bochner, Rene Russo, Jay O. Sanders, Maury Chaykin, Pat Corley, Douglas Seale, Courteney Cox, Kathy Ireland; **D:** James Orr. VHS, Beta, LV $19.99 TOU, FCT 𝖏𝖏

Mr. Emmanuel An elderly Jewish widower leaves his English home in 1935 in quest of the mother of a German refugee boy, and is subjected to shocking treatment in Germany.
1944 97m/B Felix Aylmer, Greta Gynt, Walter Rilla, Jean Simmons. VHS, Beta LCA 𝖏𝖏½

Mr. Frost Goldblum feigns fascination in this lackluster tale of the devil incarnate, who is imprisoned after owning up to a series of grisly murders, and who hides his true identity after approached by a woman psychiatrist.
1989 (R) 92m/C Jeff Goldblum, Kathy Baker, Alan Bates, Roland Giraud, Jean-Pierre Cassel; **D:** Phillip Setbon; **W:** Phillip Setbon, Brad Lynch. VHS $39.95 SVS, FCT, IME 𝖏

Mister Halpren & Mister Johnson Gleason attends the funeral of a longtime friend and one time flame, and becomes acquainted with the woman's hus-

band (Olivier). Heavyweight cast wasted on flimsy script...and away we go!
1983 57m/C Laurence Olivier, Jackie Gleason; *D:* Alvin Rakoff. **VHS, Beta** NO 🐾🐾

Mr. Hobbs Takes a Vacation Good-natured comedy in which beleaguered parents try to resolve family squabbles while the entire brood is on a seaside vacation. Stewart and O'Hara are especially fine and funny as the well-meaning parents.
1962 116m/C James Stewart, Maureen O'Hara, Fabian, John Saxon, Marie Wilson, John McGiver, Reginald Gardiner; *D:* Henry Koster. **VHS, Beta** $19.98 FOX, HMV 🐾🐾🐾

Mr. Horn Based on the William Goldman western novel, this slow-paced film about folk-hero Tom Horn capturing the famous Apache warrior, Geronimo, is average at best.
1979 200m/C David Carradine, Richard Widmark, Karen Black, Jeremy Slate, Enrique Lucero, Jack Starrett; *D:* Jack Starrett. **VHS** $59.95 LIV 🐾🐾

Mr. Hulot's Holiday Superior slapstick details the misadventures of a dullard's seaside holiday. Inventive French comedian Tati at his best. Light-hearted and natural, with magical mime sequences. Followed by "Mon Oncle." *AKA:* Les Vacances de Monsieur Hulot; Monsieur Hulot's Holiday.
1953 86m/B FR Jacques Tati, Natalie Pascaud, Michelle Rolia; *D:* Jacques Tati. Academy Awards '55 Nominations: Best Story & Screenplay; National Board of Review Awards '54: 5 Best Foreign Films of the Year. **VHS, Beta, LV, 8mm** $29.98 NOS, MRV, VYY 🐾🐾🐾½

Mr. Inside, Mr. Outside A television movie about two New York City cops, one undercover, one not, trying to infiltrate a tough diamond-smuggling ring.
1974 74m/C Tony LoBianco, Hal Linden; *D:* William A. Graham. **VHS, Beta** $59.95 VMK 🐾½

Mister Johnson In 1923 Africa, an educated black man working for the British magistrate constantly finds himself in trouble, thanks to backfiring schemes. This highly enjoyable film from the director of "Driving Miss Daisy" suffers only from the underdevelopment of the intriguing lead character. Based on the novel by Joyce Cary.
1991 (PG-13) 105m/C Pierce Brosnan, Edward Woodward, Maynard Eziashi, Beatie Edney, Denis Quilley, Nick Reding; *D:* Bruce Beresford. **VHS** $89.98 VES, LIV 🐾🐾🐾

Mr. Kingstreet's War An idealistic game warden and his wife defend the wildlife of Africa against the fighting Italian and British armies at the dawn of World War II. *AKA:* Heroes Die Hard.
1971 92m/C John Saxon, Tippi Hedren, Rossano Brazzi, Brian O'Shaughnessy; *D:* Percival Rubens. **VHS, Beta** UHV, SIM 🐾🐾½

Mr. Klein Cleverly plotted script and fine direction in this dark and intense film about a French-Catholic merchant who buys valuables from Jews trying to escape Nazi occupied France in 1942, paying far less than what the treasures are worth. Ironically, he is later mistaken for a Jew by the same name who has been using this man's reputation as a cover.
1975 (PG) 122m/C Alain Delon, Jeanne Moreau; *D:* Joseph Losey. **VHS, Beta** $59.95 COL, SWC 🐾🐾🐾

Mr. Love A meek gardener is perceived by neighbors as a fool until he dies and numerous women arrive for his funeral. Is it his cologne? The radishes?
1986 (PG-13) 91m/C GB Barry Jackson, Maurice Denham, Margaret Tyzack; *D:* Roy Battersby. **VHS, Beta** $19.98 WAR 🐾🐾½

Mr. Lucky Likeable wartime drama about a gambler who hopes to swindle a philanthropic organization, but then falls in love and determines to help the group in a fundraising effort. Grant is, no surprise, excellent as the seemingly cynical con artist who actually has a heart of gold. Cliched, but nonetheless worthwhile. Later developed into a television series.
1943 99m/B Cary Grant, Laraine Day, Charles Bickford, Gladys Cooper, Paul Stewart, Henry Stephenson, Florence Bates; *D:* H.C. Potter. **VHS, Beta, LV** $19.98 MED, RXM, TTC 🐾🐾🐾

Mr. Magoo in Sherwood Forest As Friar Tuck, the nearsighted Mr. Magoo involves Robin Hood and his Merry Men in a series of zany adventures.
1964 83m/C *V:* Jim Backus. **VHS, Beta, LV** $12.95 PAR, WTA 🐾🐾🐾

Mr. Magoo in the King's Service Mr. Magoo is off on the King's business in this wacky full-length cartoon adventure.
1966 92m/C *V:* Jim Backus. **VHS, Beta** $24.95 PAR, WTA 🐾🐾

Mr. Magoo: Man of Mystery In this episode, Mr. Magoo plays four legendary literary and comic strip heroes: Dr. Watson, Dr. Frankenstein, the Count of Monte Cristo and Dick Tracy.
1964 96m/C *V:* Jim Backus. **VHS, Beta** $24.95 PAR, WTA 🐾🐾

Mr. Magoo's Christmas Carol Nearsighted Mr. Magoo, as Ebeneezer Scrooge, receives Christmas visits from three ghosts in this entertaining version of Dickens' classic tale.
1962 52m/C *V:* Jim Backus. **VHS, Beta, LV** $12.95 PAR, WTA 🐾🐾

Mr. Magoo's Storybook Mr. Magoo acts out all the parts in versions of three famous tales of literature: "Snow White and the Seven Dwarfs," "Don Quixote," and "A Midsummer Night's Dream."
1964 113m/C *V:* Jim Backus. **VHS, Beta** $14.95 PAR, WTA 🐾🐾

Mr. Majestyk When a Vietnam veteran's attempt to start an honest business is thwarted by Mafia hitmen and the police, he goes after them with a vengeance.
1974 (PG) 103m/C Charles Bronson, Al Lettieri, Linda Cristal, Lee Purcell; *D:* Richard Fleischer. **VHS, Beta** $14.95 MGM 🐾🐾½

Mister Mean A man who once worked for a mafia don is now given the task of rubbing him out. For Cosa Nostra diehards and gluttons for Roman scenery.
1977 98m/C IT Fred Williamson; *D:* Fred Williamson. **VHS, Beta** NO 🐾

Mr. Mike's Mondo Video A bizarre, outrageous comedy special declared too wild for television conceived by the "Saturday Night Live" alumnus Mr. Mike.
1979 (R) 75m/C Michael O'Donoghue, Dan Aykroyd, Jane Curtin, Carrie Fisher, Teri Garr, Joan Haskett, Deborah Harry, Margot Kidder, Bill Murray, Laraine Newman, Gilda Radner, Julius LaRosa, Paul Schaffer, Sid Vicious. **VHS, Beta** $59.95 PAV 🐾

Mr. Mom A tireless auto exec loses his job and stays home with the kids while his wife becomes the breadwinner. He's forced to cope with the rigors of housework and child care, resorting to drugs, alcohol and soap operas. Keaton's funny as homebound Dad chased by killer appliances and poker buddy to the ladies in the neighborhood. Written by John Hughes and produced by Aaron Spelling.

1983 (PG) 92m/C Michael Keaton, Teri Garr, Christopher Lloyd, Martin Mull, Ann Jillian, Jeffrey Tambor, Edie McClurg, Valri Bromfield; *D:* Stan Dragoti. **VHS, Beta, LV** $29.98 LIV, VES 🐾🐾

Mr. Moto's Last Warning One of the better in the series of Mr. Moto, the wily detective! Lorre is convincing in the title role and gets good support from character villains Carradine and Sanders in this story of saboteurs converging on the Suez Canal plotting to blow up the French Fleet.
1939 71m/B Peter Lorre, George Sanders, Ricardo Cortez, John Carradine, Virginia Field, Robert Coote; *D:* Norman Foster. **VHS, Beta, 3/4U, Special order formats** $16.95 SNC, NOS, CAB 🐾🐾🐾

Mr. Moto's Last Warning/ Meeting at Midnight The first film finds Moto at the Suez Canal trying to save France's flotilla from a deadly conspiracy. The second feature is classic Charlie Chan fare. This time his driver, Birmingham, gets Chan caught in the midst of the occult.
1944 130m/B Sidney Toler, Peter Lorre, Mantan Moreland. **VHS, Beta** AOV 🐾🐾🐾

Mr. Music Crosby is a successful songwriter who would rather enjoy life on the golf course than pen any more tunes. He's persuaded by his secretary to help out an old-time producer who's fallen on hard times by writing a new Broadway show. Light-hearted fluff. Based on the play "Accent on Youth" by Samson Raphaelson which had been filmed in 1935. ♫Life is So Precious; Accidents Will Happen; High on the List; Wouldn't It Be Funny; Wasn't I There?; Mr. Music; Once More the Blue and White; Milady; Then You'll Be Home.
1950 113m/B Bing Crosby, Nancy Olson, Charles Coburn, Robert Stack, Tom Ewell, Ruth Hussey, Charles Kemper, Donald Woods, Gower Champion, Marge Champion; *Cameos:* Groucho Marx, Peggy Lee; *D:* Richard Haydn. **VHS** $14.95 PAR 🐾🐾½

Mr. Nanny For those who fear change, this predictable plot should serve as comforting assurance that Hollywood will still sacrifice substance for the quick buck. Basic story line has the child-hating Hulkster playing nanny/bodyguard to a couple of bratty kids. Meanwhile, his arch rival (Johansen) hatches a scheme to gain world dominance by kidnapping the kids for the ransom of their father's top secret computer chip. Never fear—in this world, the good guys kick butt, naturally, and everyone learns a lesson.
1993 (PG) 85m/C Hulk Hogan, Sherman Hemsley, Austin Pendleton, Robert Gorman, Madeline Zima, Mother Love, David Johansen; *D:* Michael Gottlieb; *W:* Ed Rugoff, Michael Gottlieb; *M:* David Johansen, Brian Koonin. **VHS** NYR 🐾🐾

Mr. Nice Guy In the near future, a hired gun strives for national recognition as the best of his now legitimate profession. Comedy with few laughs.
1986 (PG-13) 92m/C Michael MacDonald, Jan Smithers, Joe Silver. **VHS, Beta** $19.95 STE, NWV 🐾

Mr. North Capra-corn fable about a charming, bright Yale graduate who encounters admiration and disdain from upper-crust Rhode Island residents when news of his miraculous "cures" spreads. Marks the directorial debut of Danny Huston, son of John Huston, who co-wrote the script and served as executive producer before dying several weeks into shooting. Set in the 1920s and adapted from Thornton Wilder's "Theophilus North."

1988 (PG) 90m/C Anthony Edwards, Robert Mitchum, Lauren Bacall, Harry Dean Stanton, Anjelica Huston, Mary Stuart Masterson, Virginia Madsen, Tammy Grimes, David Warner, Hunter Carson; **D:** Danny Huston; **W:** John Huston, Janet Roach. VHS, Beta, LV *NO ℤℤ½*

Mr. Peabody & the Mermaid Lightweight fish story about a middle-aged married man who hooks a beautiful mermaid while fishing in the Caribbean and eventually falls in love with her. Powell is smooth as always, though hampered by the unrestrained absurdity of it all. Scripted by Nunnally Johnson from the novel by Guy and Constance Jones. Also available colorized. **1948** 89m/B William Powell, Ann Blyth; **D:** Irving Pichel. VHS *$14.98 REP ℤℤ½*

Mr. Peek-A-Boo A French clerk discovers he has the ability to walk through walls. Although friends try to coax him into a life of crime, he instead comes to the aid of an English girl who is being blackmailed. Goodnatured French comedy was shot with English dialogue for the American market. *AKA:* Garou Garou le Passe Muraille. **1950** 74m/B *FR* Joan Greenwood, Bourvil, Marcel Arnold, Roger Treville; **D:** Jean Boyer. VHS, Beta *$16.95 SNC ℤℤ½*

Mr. Reeder in Room 13 Based on the mystery stories created by Edgar Wallace, Mr. Reeder (a cultured English gentleman who fights crime) enlists the aid of a young man to get evidence on a gang of counterfeiters. **1938** 66m/B Gibb McLaughlin. VHS, Beta *$29.95 VYY ℤℤ*

Mister Roberts The crew of a Navy cargo freighter in the South Pacific during World War II relieves the boredom of duty with a series of elaborate practical jokes, mostly at the expense of their long-suffering and slightly crazy captain, who then determines that he will get even. The ship's cargo officer, Mr. Roberts, longs to be transferred to a fighting vessel and see some action. Originally a hit Broadway play (based on the novel by Thomas Heggen) which also featured Fonda in the title role. Great performance from Lemmon as Ensign Pulver. Powell's last film. Sequelled in 1964 by "Ensign Pulver," and later a short-lived television series as well as a live television special. Newly transferred in 1988 from a pristine stereo print. **1955** 120m/C Henry Fonda, James Cagney, Jack Lemmon, William Powell, Betsy Palmer, Ward Bond, Harry Carey Jr.; **D:** John Ford, Mervyn LeRoy; **W:** Frank Nugent, Joshua Logan. Academy Awards '55: Best Supporting Actor (Lemmon); Nominations: Best Picture; Academy Awards '55: Best Sound; National Board of Review Awards '55: 10 Best Films of the Year. VHS, Beta *$19.98 WAR, BTV ℤℤℤℤ*

Mr. Robinson Crusoe Rollicking adventure in the South Seas as Fairbanks makes a bet that he can live on a desert island for a year without being left any refinements of civilization. Of course, a woman arrives. Written by Fairbanks, with a score by Alfred Newman. **1932** 76m/B Douglas Fairbanks Sr., William Farnum, Maria Alba, Earle Brown; **D:** Edward Sutherland. VHS, Beta, LV *$19.95 NOS, GPV, CCB ℤℤ½*

Mr. Rossi's Dreams Mr. Rossi gets to act out his fantasies of being Tarzan, Sherlock Holmes, and a famous movie star in this film. **1983** 80m/C **D:** Bruno Bozzetto. VHS, Beta *$39.95 FHE, WTA ℤℤ½*

Mr. Rossi's Vacation Mr. Rossi and his dog Harold go off in search of quiet on a let's get away-from-it-all vacation. **1983** 82m/C *IT* **D:** Bruno Bozzetto. VHS, Beta *$39.95 FHE, WTA ℤℤ½*

Mr. Saturday Night Crystal, in his directorial debut, stars as Buddy Young, Jr., a self-destructive comedian whose career spans five decades. His nasty one-liners and witty jokes combine with poignancy in this satisfying comedy/drama. Paymer is excellent as Young's long-suffering, faithful brother and manager. Watch for Lewis in a cameo role. Expectations were very high and the box office results were disappointing, but fans of Crystal shouldn't miss this one. The video also includes additional footage and outtakes selected and hosted by Crystal. **1992** (R) 118m/C Billy Crystal, David Paymer, Julie Warner, Helen Hunt, Mary Mara, Jerry Orbach, Ron Silver; *Cameos:* Jerry Lewis; **W/D:** Billy Crystal; **W:** Babaloo Mandel, Lowell Ganz; **M:** Marc Shaiman. VHS, LV *$89.99 NLC, IME, MOV ℤℤ½*

Mr. Scarface A young man searches for the man who murdered his father years earlier in a dark alley. **1977** (R) 85m/C Jack Palance, Edmund Purdom, Al Cliver, Harry Baer, Gisela Hahn; **D:** Fernando Di Leo. VHS, Beta *$19.95 WWV ℤ½*

Mr. Skeffington A super-grade soap opera spanning 26 years in the life of a ravishing, spoiled New York socialite. The beauty with a fondness for bedrooms marries for convenience, abuses her husband, then enjoys a highly equitable divorce settlement. Years later when diphtheria leaves her totally deformed and no man will have her, she is saved by her former husband. Based on the novel by "Elizabeth" (Mary Annette Beauchamp Russell) and adapted by "Casablanca's" Julius and Philip Epstein. **1944** 147m/B Bette Davis, Claude Rains, Walter Abel, Richard Waring, George Coulouris, John Alexander; **D:** Vincent Sherman. VHS, Beta, LV *$19.95 MGM ℤℤℤ*

Mr. Skitch Weak Rogers offering. Couple loses their farm and begins cross country jaunt with mishaps at every turn. All ends well when their daughter meets an Army cadet, but few laughs and lots of loose ends. **1933** 70m/B Will Rogers, ZaSu Pitts, Rochelle Hudson, Charles Starrett; **D:** James Cruze. VHS *$19.98 FOX, FCT ℤℤ*

Mr. Smith Goes to Washington In another classic from Hollywood's golden year of 1939, Jimmy Stewart plays an idealistic and naive young man who is selected to fill in for an ailing Senator. Upon his arrival in the Capitol, he is inundated by a multitude of corrupt politicians. He takes a stand for his beliefs and tries to denounce many of those he feels are unfit for their positions, meeting with opposition from all sides. Great cast is highlighted by Stewart in one of his most endearing performances. A quintessential Capra tale sharply written by Sidney Buchman from Lewis Foster's story. Outstanding in every regard. **1939** 130m/B James Stewart, Jean Arthur, Edward Arnold, Claude Rains, Thomas Mitchell, Beulah Bondi, Eugene Pallette, Guy Kibbee, Harry Carey Sr., H.B. Warner, Porter Hall, Jack Carson; **D:** Frank Capra. Academy Awards '39: Best Story; Nominations: Best Actor (Stewart), Best Director (Capra), Best Interior Decoration, Best Picture, Best Screenplay, Best Sound, Best Supporting Actor (Rains, Carey), Best Score; National Board of Review Awards '39: 10 Best Films of the Year; New York Film Critics Awards '39: Best Actor (Stewart). VHS, Beta, LV *$19.95 COL, PIA, HMV ℤℤℤℤ*

Mr. Superinvisible Searching to cure the common cold, a bumbling scientist invents a bizarre virus, then strives with his loyal (of course) sheepdog to keep it from falling into the wrong hands. The Disney-like plot, featuring enemy agents and invisibilty may appeal to youngsters. *AKA:* Mr. Invisible; L'Inafferrabile Invincible. **1973** (G) 90m/C *IT GE SP* Dean Jones, Ingeborg Schoener, Gastone Moschin; **D:** Anthony M. Dawson. VHS, Beta *$9.95 NO ℤℤ*

Mr. Sycamore A sappy mail carrier escapes his badgering wife by sprouting into a tree. A potentially whimsical piece that wilts. **1974** 90m/C Jason Robards Jr., Jean Simmons, Sandy Dennis; **D:** Pancho Kohner. VHS, Beta *$39.95 WOV ℤ½*

Mr. Walkie Talkie Tired of a sargeant's jabber-jaws, a soldier requests to be relocated to the front lines, only to find his catty comrade has followed. Set during the Korean War and featuring some truly amusing escapades set between the lulls in the war. **1952** 65m/B William Tracy, Joe Sawyer; **D:** Frod Guiol. VHS, Beta, LV *NO ℤℤ*

Mr. Winkle Goes to War A weak, nerdy former banker is drafted for service during World War II and proves himself a hero by bulldozing a Japanese foxhole. Bits of genuine war footage add a measure of realism to an otherwise banal flag-waving comedy that is based on a novel by Theodore Pratt. **1944** 80m/B Edward G. Robinson, Ruth Warrick, Richard Lane, Robert Armstrong; **D:** Alfred E. Green. VHS, Beta *$59.95 COL ℤℤ*

Mr. Wise Guy The East Side Kids break out of reform school to clear one of the Kids' brother of a murder charge. Typical pre-Bowery Boys vehicle. **1942** 70m/B Leo Gorcey, Huntz Hall, Billy Gilbert, Guinn Williams, Benny Rubin, Douglas Fowley, Ann Doran, Jack Mulhall, Warren Hymer, David Gorcey; **D:** William Nigh. VHS, Beta *$19.95 NOS, QNE, DVT ℤℤ*

Mr. Wong, Detective The first in the Mr. Wong series, the cunning detective traps a killer who feigns guilt to throw suspicion away from himself. The plot is loaded with the usual twists and villains. However, Karloff is a standout. **1938** 69m/B Boris Karloff, Grant Withers; **D:** William Nigh. VHS, Beta *$19.95 NOS, MRV, HHT ℤℤ*

Mr. Wong in Chinatown Third of the Mr. Wong series finds James Lee Wong investigating the murder of a wealthy Chinese woman. She had been helping to fund the purchase of airplanes to equip China in its 1930s' struggle with Japan. **1939** 70m/B Boris Karloff, Grant Withers, William Royle, Marjorie Reynolds, Peter George Lynn, Lotus Long, Richard Loo; **D:** William Nigh. VHS *$16.95 NOS, MRV, SNC ℤ½*

Misterios de Ultratumba All the horrors that go on inside an insane asylum occur in this film, some unintentionally. **1947** 90m/B *MX* Gaston Santos, Rafael Bertrand, Mapita Cortes; **D:** Fernando Mendez. VHS, Beta *$39.95 MAD ℤℤ*

Mistral's Daughter Frothy miniseries, based on the Judith Krantz novel, about a French artist and his relationship with three beautiful women. Formulaic TV melodrama offers sexual scenes and revealing glimpses. Produced, like other Krantz miniseries, by author's hubby, Steve. **1984** 390m/C Stefanie Powers, Lee Remick, Stacy Keach, Robert Urich, Timothy Dalton; **D:** Douglas Hickox. VHS, Beta *$79.95 LIV ℤ½*

Mistress A classic Japanese period piece about an innocent woman who believes she's married to a ruthless industrialist, only to find he is already married and she is but his mistress. Her love for a medical student unleashes tragedy. Subtly moving in a low-key way; starkly beautiful in black and white. In Japanese, with English subtitles. *AKA:* Wild Geese.
1953 106m/B *JP* Hideko Takamine, Hiroshi Akutagawa; *D:* Shiro Toyoda. **VHS, Beta** $79.95 *SUE, TAM* ⅃⅃⅃

Mistress Weepy made-for-television melodrama about a woman who makes a living as a mistress. When her lover dies, she must learn to stand on her own two feet.
1987 96m/C Victoria Principal, Alan Rachins, Don Murray; *D:* Michael Tuchner. **VHS** $79.98 *REP* ⅃½

Mistress A weak script does in a formidable cast in a behind-the-scenes look at movie making. Wuhl plays Marvin Landisman, a failed director/screenwriter, who's approached by has-been producer Jack Roth (Landau) who says he's found a backer to finance a movie from one of Marvin's old scripts. It turns out Roth has three men (De Niro, Aiello, and Wallach) ready to finance the film as long as each of their mistresses, who all have acting ambitions, gets the starring role. Double-dealing at a bargain basement level sets up the rest of this lifeless comedy.
1991 (R) 100m/C Robert Wuhl, Martin Landau, Robert De Niro, Eli Wallach, Danny Aiello, Sheryl Lee Ralph, Jean Smart, Tuesday Weld, Jace Alexander, Laurie Metcalf; *Cameos:* Christopher Walken, Ernest Borgnine; *W/D:* Barry Primus; *W:* J.F. Lawton. **VHS, LV** $92.98 *LIV, PMS* ⅃⅃

Mistress of the Apes A woman searches for her missing husband in Africa with a group of scientists and discovers a tribe of near-men, who may be the missing link in evolution (or perhaps, a professional football team). Into their little group she is accepted, becoming their queen. Buchanan earned his reputation as a maker of horrible films honestly. Includes the songs "Mistress of the Apes" and "Ape Lady."
1979 (R) 88m/C Jenny Neumann, Barbara Leigh, Garth Pillsbury, Walt Robin, Stuart Lancaster, Suzy Mandel; *W/D:* Larry Buchanan. **VHS, Beta** $39.95 *MON Woof!*

Mistress of the World A scientist, aided by Swedish Intelligence agent Ventura, works to protect his gravity-altering invention from Chinese agents. Partly based on a German serial from the silent film era, but not up to director Dieterle's usual fare. A must-see for Ventura fans and Mabuse mavens.
1959 107m/C Martha Hyer, Micheline Presle, Gino Cervi, Lino Ventura, Sabu, Wolfgang Preiss; *D:* William Dieterle. **VHS, Beta** *VMK* ⅃⅃

Mistress Pamela When young Pamela goes to work in the household of handsome Lord Devonish, he sets about in wild pursuit of her virginity. Loosely based on the 1740 work "Pamela" by Samuel Richardson, considered the first modern English novel. Read the book unless you only have 95 minutes to spend finding out who gets what.
1974 (R) 95m/C Anne Michelle, Julian Barnes, Anna Quayle, Rosemary Dunham; *D:* Jim O'Connor. **VHS, Beta** *NO* ⅃½

Misty Ladd and Smith are two kids who capture a wild pony and teach it to run around in circles and step over things. Based on Marguerite Henry's bestselling "Misty of Chincoteague," and filmed on an island off the coast of Virginia.
1961 92m/C David Ladd, Arthur O'Connell, Pam Smith; *D:* James B. Clark. **VHS** $14.95 *PAR, WAX, FCT* ⅃⅃½

Misunderstood A former black market merchant has to learn how to relate to his sons after his wife dies. The father, now a legitimate businessman, is more concerned with running his shipping business than growing closer to his boys. Fine acting can't overcome a transparent plot.
1984 (PG) 92m/C Gene Hackman, Susan Anspach, Henry Thomas, Rip Torn, Huckleberry Fox; *D:* Jerry Schatzberg. **VHS, Beta** $79.95 *MGM* ⅃⅃½

Misunderstood A father learns his lonely son is full of love and sensitivity when a tragedy reveals that it is this son who takes the blame for all the wrongs his brother commits.
1987 101m/C Anthony Quayle, Stefano Colagrande, Simone Gianozzi, John Sharp; *D:* Luigi Comencini. **VHS, Beta** $59.95 *IMP* ⅃⅃½

Mitchell Tough cop battles drug traffic and insipid script. Big screen release with that certain TV look.
1975 (R) 90m/C Joe Don Baker, Linda Evans, Martin Balsam, John Saxon, Merlin Olsen, Harold J. Stone; *D:* Andrew V. McLaglen. **VHS** $9.95 *SIM* ⅃

Mixed Blood From the renowned underground film-maker, a dark comedy that examines the seedy drug subculture in New York. Violent, fast, and funny.
1984 (R) 98m/C Marilia Pera, Richard Vlacia, Linda Kerridge, Geraldine Smith, Angel David; *D:* Paul Morrissey. **VHS, Beta** $59.95 *MED* ⅃⅃½

M'Lady's Court A lawyer searching for an heiress in a convent of lusty maidens has loads of fun. None too captivating.
198? 92m/C Sonia Jeanine, Maja Hoppe. **VHS, Beta** $29.95 *MED* ⅃

Mo' Better Blues Not one of his more cohesive or compelling works, Lee's fourth feature is on the surface a backstage jazz biopic. But there hasn't been a Lee feature that wasn't vitally concerned with complicated racial issues and though subtle and indirect, this is no exception. Bleek Gilliam is a handsome, accomplished jazz trumpeter who divides his limited extra-curricular time between Clarke (newcomer Williams), an aspiring jazz vocalist, and Indigo (junior Lee sibling Joie), a down-to-earth school teacher. What's interesting is not so much the story of self-interested musician and ladies' man Gilliam, but the subtle racial issues his life draws into focus. The Branford Marsalis Quartet provides the music for Bleek's group, scored by Lee's dad Bill (on whose life the script is loosely based).
1990 (R) 129m/C Denzel Washington, Spike Lee, Joie Lee, Wesley Snipes, Cynda Williams, Giancarlo Esposito, Robin Harris, Bill Nunn, John Turturro, Dick Anthony Williams, Ruben Blades; *W/D:* Spike Lee. **VHS, Beta, LV** $19.95 *MCA, FCT* ⅃⅃½

Mo' Money Damon Wayans is a small-time con-artist who is inspired to go straight by a beautiful woman (Dash). He lands a job at the credit card company she works for, but temptation overcomes him, he swipes some plastic, and the scamming begins anew. With the help of his younger brother (played by real-life younger brother Marlon), they get involved in an even bigger, more dangerous scam being operated by the credit card company's head of security. Crude formula comedy driven by energetic, inventive performances by the brothers Wayans. Needless to say, will be especially enjoyed by fans of TV's "In Living Color."
1992 (R) 97m/C Damon Wayans, Marlon Wayans, Stacey Dash, Joe Santos, John Diehl, Harry J. Lennix, Mark Beltzman, Quincy Wong, Larry Brandenburg; *D:* Peter Macdonald; *W:*

Damon Wayans. **VHS, Beta, LV, 8mm** *COL* ⅃⅃½

Moana, a Romance of the Golden Age An early look through American eyes at the society of the people of Samoa, in the Pacific Islands. Picturesque successor to Flaherty's "Nanook of the North."
1926 76m/B Ta'avale, Fa'amgase, Moana; *D:* Robert Flaherty. **VHS** $29.95 *GPV, FCT* ⅃⅃⅃½

Mob Boss Gangster films spoof starring Hickey as the head of a successful California crime ring. When his beautiful wife conspires to have him killed, he is left just breaths away from his demise. He calls his nerdy son to his bedside to ask him to take over the family business. But this kid thinks that money laundering requires detergent! Take this one down for a walk by the river in its new cement shoes.
1990 (R) 93m/C Eddie Dezen, Morgan Fairchild, William Hickey, Stuart Whitman; *D:* Fred Olen Ray. **VHS** $89.95 *VMK* ⅃

Mob Story Vernon stars as a big-wig mob boss on the run from the government and a few of his "closest" friends. He plans to disappear into Canada, but if his girl (Kidder) and best friend (Waxman) find him first he'll be traveling in a body-bag. Very silly, but fun.
1990 (R) 98m/C John Vernon, Margot Kidder, Al Waxman, Kate Vernon; *D:* Gabriel Markiw, Jancarlo Markiw. **VHS, Beta, LV** *IME* ⅃½

Mob War A bloody Mafia adventure in which a sausage factory plays a large role.
1978 102m/C **VHS, Beta, LV** $79.98 *VCD Woof!*

Mob War A war breaks out between the head of New York's underworld and a media genius. After deciding to become partners, the "family" tries to take over. For fun, count how many times the word "respect" pops up in the script. Tries hard but fails.
1988 (R) 96m/C John Christian, David Henry Keller, Jake La Motta, Johnny Stumper; *D:* J. Christian Ingvordsen. **VHS, Beta** $79.98 *MCG* ⅃½

Mobsters It sounded like a great idea, casting the hottest young actors of the '90s as youthful racketeers "Lucky" Luciano, Meyer Lansky, Bugsy Siegel, and Frank Costello. But it would take an FBI probe to straighten out the blood-choked plot, as the pals' loyalties get tested the hard way in a dismembered narrative. Sicker than the violence is a seeming endorsement of the glamorous hoods.
1991 (R) 104m/C Christian Slater, Patrick Dempsey, Richard Grieco, Costas Mandylor, Anthony Quinn, F. Murray Abraham, Lara Flynn Boyle, Michael Gambon, Christopher Penn; *D:* Michael Karbelnikoff. **VHS, Beta, LV** $19.98 *MCA, CCB* ⅃½

Moby Dick Ray Bradbury and Huston co-wrote the screenplay adapted from Herman Melville's high seas saga. Peck as Captain Ahab, obsessed with desire for revenge upon the great white whale, Moby Dick, isn't always believable. Those moments when it clicks, however, make the film more than worthwhile.
1956 116m/C Gregory Peck, Richard Basehart, Orson Welles, Leo Genn, Harry Andrews, Friedrich Ledebur; *D:* John Huston. **VHS, Beta, LV** $19.95 *FOX, BMV, HMV* ⅃⅃⅃

Moby Dick An animated version of the Herman Melville classic.
1977 52m/C **VHS, Beta, LV** $19.95 *MGM* ⅃⅃⅃

Moby Dick & the Mighty Mightor A collection of six animated adventures featuring Moby Dick, a super whale who uses his incredible speed to fight crime, and The Mighty Mightor, a young man who uses

his unlimited physical powers to protect his Stone Age village.
1967 49m/C **VHS, Beta** $19.95 *TTC, WTA ℤℤ*

Mockery Chaney plays a peasant working for a Russian countess. He becomes involved in a peasant revolution against the rich and threatens the countess but eventually saves her from the mob.
1927 75m/B Lon Chaney Sr., Barbara Bedford, Ricardo Cortez, Emily Fitzroy; *D:* Benjamin Christiansen. **VHS** $29.95 *FCT ℤℤ ½*

The Mod Squad The ultimate sixties series features a trio of young misfits who are recruited by a gruff police captain in Southern California. Their undercover assignments take them into the counter-culture. The series was created by former L.A. police officer Bud Ruskin, and was based on his own experiences. Two episodes per tape: "Teeth of the Barracuda" explains the formation of the Mod Squad, while "Mother of Sorrow" finds a generation gap leading to murder. Additional episodes are available.
1968 60m/C Michael Cole, Clarence Williams III, Peggy Lipton, Tige Andrews, Lee Grant, Richard Dreyfuss. **VHS** $19.99 *MOV ℤℤ ½*

Model Behavior Fresh from college, an aspiring photographer pines for a glamorous model.
1982 86m/C Richard Bekins, Bruce Lyons, Cindy Harrel; *D:* Bud Gardner. **VHS, Beta** $79.98 *LIV ℤ ½*

Modern Girls Teen comedy about three bubble-headed LA rock groupies and their various wild adventures during a single night on the town. Surprising in that the three lead actresses waste their talents in this lesson in exploitation. Bruce Springsteen's younger sister portrays a drug user.
1986 (PG-13) 82m/C Cynthia Gibb, Daphne Zuniga, Virginia Madsen; *D:* Jerry Kramer. **VHS, Beta, LV** $19.95 *PAR ℤ ½*

Modern Love An average slob realizes that marriage, fatherhood and in-law-ship isn't quite what he expected. Benson stars, directs and produces as well as co-starring with real-life wife DeVito. A plotless hodge-podge of bits that were more successful in "Look Who's Talking" and "Parenthood."
1990 (R) 89m/C Robby Benson, Karla DeVito, Rue McClanahan, Kaye Ballard, Frankie Valli, Cliff Bemis, Louise Lasser, Burt Reynolds, Lyric Benson; *D:* Robby Benson. **VHS, Beta** $79.95 *SVS ℤ*

Modern Problems A man involved in a nuclear accident discovers he has acquired telekinetic powers, which he uses to turn the tables on his professional and romantic rivals. A fine cast but an unsuccessful fission trip.
1981 (PG) 93m/C Chevy Chase, Patti D'Arbanville, Mary Kay Place, Brian Doyle-Murray, Nell Carter, Dabney Coleman; *D:* Ken Shapiro. **VHS, Beta** $14.98 *FOX ℤℤ*

Modern Romance The romantic misadventures of a neurotic film editor who is hopelessly in love with his girlfriend but can't seem to maintain a normal relationship with her. Smart and hilarious at times and always simmering with anxiety. Offers an honest look at relationships as well as an accurate portrait of filmmaking.
1981 (R) 102m/C Albert Brooks, Kathryn Harrold, Bruno Kirby, George Kennedy, James L. Brooks, Bob Einstein; *D:* Albert Brooks. **VHS, Beta, LV** $14.95 *COL ℤℤℤ*

Modern Times This "mostly" silent film finds Chaplin playing a factory worker who goes crazy from his repetitious job on an assembly line and his boss' demands for greater speed and efficiency. Ultimately en-

compassing the tyranny of machine over man, this cinematic masterpiece has more relevance today than ever. Chaplin wrote the musical score which incorporates the tune "Smile."
1936 87m/B Charlie Chaplin, Paulette Goddard, Henry Bergman, Stanley Sandford, Gloria de Haven, Chester Conklin; *D:* Charlie Chaplin. **VHS, Beta, LV** $19.98 *FOX, HMV ℤℤℤℤ*

The Moderns One of the quirkier directors around, this time Rudolph tries a comedic period piece about the avant-garde art society of 1920s Paris. Fleshed out with some familiar characters (Ernest Hemingway, Gertrude Stein) and some strange art-world types. The tone is not consistently funny but, instead, romantic as the main characters clash over art and love.
1988 (R) 126m/C Keith Carradine, Linda Fiorentino, John Lone, Genevieve Bujold, Geraldine Chaplin, Wallace Shawn, Kevin J. O'Connor; *D:* Alan Rudolph. **VHS, Beta, LV, 8mm** $14.98 *SUE, NLC ℤℤℤ*

Mogambo Remake of "Red Dust," this is the steamy story of a love triangle between an African game hunter, a proper British lady, and an American showgirl in the jungles of Kenya.
1953 115m/C Clark Gable, Ava Gardner, Grace Kelly; *D:* John Ford. Academy Awards '53 Nominations: Best Actress (Gardner), Best Supporting Actress (Kelly); Golden Globe Awards '54: Best Supporting Actress (Kelly); National Board of Review Awards '53: 10 Best Films of the Year. **VHS, Beta** $19.98 *MGM, FCT, CCB ℤℤℤ*

Mohammed: Messenger of God Sprawling saga of the genesis of the religion of Islam, with Quinn portraying Mohammed's uncle, Hamza, an honored warrior. The story behind the movie might prove much more successful as a sequel than did the movie itself. The filming itself created a religious controversy. *AKA:* The Message; Al-Ris-Alah.
1977 (PG) 180m/C *GB* Damien Thomas, Anthony Quinn, Irene Papas, Michael Ansara, Johnny Sekka, Michael Forest, Neville Jason; *D:* Moustapha Akkad. **VHS** *NO ℤℤ*

Mohawk A cowboy and his Indian maiden try to stop a war between Indian tribes and fanatical landowners.
1956 80m/C Rita Gam, Neville Brand, Scott Brady, Lori Nelson; *D:* Kurt Neumann. **VHS, Beta** $19.95 *NOS, MRV, GEM ℤ ½*

Mole Men Against the Son of Hercules Italian muscleman Maciste battles the pale-skinned denizens of an underground city.
1961 ?m/C *IT* Mark Forest. **VHS, Beta** $16.95 *SNC ℤ ½*

The Mole People A really bad fifties creature feature which finds two archeologists accidentally discovering an underground civilization of albinos who shun all forms of light. They've also enslaved the local populace of half-human, half-mole creatures who decide to help the good guys escape by rising up in a revolt against their evil masters. When the weapon of choice is a flashlight you know not to expect much.
1956 78m/B John Agar, Cynthia Patrick, Hugh Beaumont, Alan Napier, Nestor Paiva, Phil Chambers; *D:* Virgil W. Vogel; *W:* Laszlo Gorog. **VHS** $14.98 *MCA ℤ*

Moliere An adaptation of Mikhail Bulgakov's comedy/drama of the life of the great French playwright performed by members of the Royal Shakespeare Company.
1984 112m/C Anthony Sher; *D:* Bill Alexander. **VHS, Beta, LV** $39.98 *TTC, TAM ℤℤℤ*

Molly & Lawless John Average western, with Miles the wife of a sadistic sheriff who helps a prisoner escape the gallows so they can run away together. Enough cliches for the whole family to enjoy.
1972 90m/C Sam Elliott, Vera Miles; *D:* Gary Nelson. **VHS, Beta** *PGN ℤℤ*

Molly Maguires Dramatization based on a true story, concerns a group of miners called the Molly Maguires who resort to using terrorist tactics in their fight for better working conditions during the Pennsylvania Irish coal mining rebellion in the 1870s. During their reign of terror, the Mollies are infiltrated by a Pinkerton detective who they mistakenly believe is a new recruit. It has its moments but never fully succeeds. Returned less than fifteen percent of its initial eleven million dollar investment.
1970 (PG) 123m/C Sean Connery, Richard Harris, Samantha Eggar, Frank Finlay; *D:* Martin Ritt. **VHS, Beta** $14.95 *PAR, CCB ℤℤ ½*

Mom When his mother is bitten by a flesh-eater, Clay Dwyer is at a loss as to what to do. How do you tell your own mother that she must be destroyed, lest she continue to devour human flesh? A campy horror/comedy.
1989 (R) 95m/C Mark Thomas Miller, Art Evans, Mary McDonough, Jeanne Bates, Brion James, Stella Stevens, Claudia Christian; *D:* Patrick Rand. **VHS, LV** $79.95 *COL, PIA ℤℤ*

Mom & Dad An innocent young girl's one night of passion leads to an unwanted pregnancy. Stock footage of childbirth and a lecture on the evils of syphilis concludes this campy schlock that features the national anthem. Banned or denied release for years, this movie is now a cult favorite for its time-capsule glimpse at conventional 1940s sexual attitudes.
1947 97m/B Hardie Albright, Sarah Blake, George Eldridge, June Carlson, Jimmy Clark, Bob Lowell; *D:* William Beaudine. **VHS, Beta** $19.95 *VDM ℤℤ*

Mom and Dad Save the World A suburban housewife (Garr) is transported along with her husband in the family station wagon to the planet Spengo, ruled by King Tod Spengo (Lovitz), who has fallen in love with her and wants to save her from his plans to blow up Earth. While trying to prevent the king from marrying her and killing her, Garr and Jones wind up in many goofy situations and wind up saving the Earth from its imminent doom. Uninspired comedy just isn't funny, and the excellent cast is misused, especially Idle and Shawn. Save this one for the kiddies.
1992 (PG) 87m/C Teri Garr, Jeffrey Jones, Jon Lovitz, Eric Idle, Wallace Shawn, Dwier Brown, Kathy Ireland, Thalmus Rasulala; *D:* Greg Beeman. **VHS, LV** $92.99 *HBO ℤ ½*

Mom, the Wolfman and Me An 11-year-old girl arranges and manages the love affair of her mother, an ultra-liberated photographer, and an unemployed teacher, who is also the owner of an Irish wolfhound. Charming adaptation of a novel by Norma Klein.
1980 100m/C Patty Duke, David Birney, Danielle Brisebois, Keenan Wynn, Viveca Lindfors, John Lithgow; *D:* Edmond Levy. **VHS, Beta** *TLF ℤℤ ½*

Moment in Time A romantic novel on tape, about a guy, a girl, and their various troubles.
1984 60m/C Jean Simmons. **Beta** $11.95 *PSM ℤ*

Mommie Dearest Film based on Christina Crawford's memoirs of her incredibly abusive and violent childhood at the hands of her adoptive mother, actress Joan Crawford.

The story is controversial and sometimes trashy, but fairly well done nevertheless. **1981 (PG) 129m/C** Faye Dunaway, Diana Scarwid, Steve Forrest, Mara Hobel, Rutanya Alda, Harry Goz, Howard da Silva; *D:* Frank Perry. VHS, Beta, LV $59.95 *PAR* 🐾🐾

Mon Oncle Tati's celebrated comedy contrasts the simple life of Monsieur Hulot with the technologically complicated life of his family when he aids his nephew in war against his parents' ultramodern, push-button home. An easygoing, delightful comedy, this is the director's first piece in color. Sequel to ''Mr. Hulot's Holiday,'' followed by ''Playtime.'' In French with English subtitles. *AKA:* My Uncle; My Uncle, Mr. Hulot. **1958 110m/C** *FR* Jacques Tati, Jean-Pierre Zola, Adrienne Serrantie, Alain Bacourt; *D:* Jacques Tati. VHS, Beta, LV, 8mm $24.95 *NOS, MRV, SUE* 🐾🐾🐾🐾

Mon Oncle Antoine A splendid tale of young Benoit, who learns about life from a surprisingly compassionate uncle, who works as everything from undertaker to grocer in the depressed area where they live. **1971 104m/C** *CA* Jean Duceppe, Olivette Thibault; *D:* Claude Jutra. VHS $79.95 *HMV, FLI, APD* 🐾🐾🐾½

Mon Oncle D'Amerique Three French characters are followed as they try to find success of varying kinds in Paris, interspersed with ironic lectures by Prof. Henri Laborit about the biology that impels human behavior. Their disappointments lead them to dream of a legendary American uncle, who could make their desires come true. An acclaimed, witty comedy by former Nouvelle Vague filmmaker, dubbed into English. *AKA:* Les Somnambules. **1980 (PG) 123m/C** *FR* Gerard Depardieu, Nicole Garcia, Roger-Pierre, Marie DuBois; *D:* Alain Resnais. Academy Awards '80 Nominations: Best Original Screenplay; New York Film Critics Awards '80: Best Foreign Film. VHS, Beta $79.95 *NYF, BTV* 🐾🐾🐾½

Mona Lisa Jordan's wonderful, sad, sensitive story of a romantic, small-time hood who gets personally involved with the welfare and bad company of the high-priced whore he's been hired to chauffeur. Hoskins is especially touching and Caine is chilling as a suave gangster. Fine film debut for Tyson. Brilliantly filmed and critically lauded. **1986 (R) 104m/C** *GB* Bob Hoskins, Cathy Tyson, Michael Caine, Clarke Peters, Kate Hardie, Robbie Coltrane, Zoe Nathenson, Sammi Davis-Voss, Rod Bedall, Joe Brown, Pauline Melville; *D:* Neil Jordan. Academy Awards '86 Nominations: Best Actor (Hoskins); British Academy Awards '86: Best Actor (Hoskins); Cannes Film Festival '86: Best Actor (Hoskins); Golden Globe Awards '87: Best Actor—Drama (Hoskins); Los Angeles Film Critics Association Awards '86: Best Actor (Hoskins); New York Film Critics Awards '86: Best Actor (Hoskins); National Society of Film Critics Awards '86: Best Actor (Hoskins). VHS, Beta, LV *NO* 🐾🐾🐾½

Mona's Place Some really tired (and probably dirty) miners take a weekend off to go to the local brothel. Unfortunately, a rival gang decides to attack. **1989 (R) 80m/C** James Whitworth, Shawn Devereaux, Sebastian Gregory, Donna Stanley, Paul Harper; *W/D:* John Hayes. VHS *NO* 🐾

Mondo Cane A documentary showcasing the eccentricities of human behavior around the world, including cannibalism, pig killing and more. Dubbed in English. Inspired a rash of ''shockumentaries'' over the next several years. The song ''More'' made its debut in this film. **1963 (R) 105m/C** *IT D:* Gualtiero Jacopetti. VHS, Beta $16.95 *SNC, VDC, VDM* 🐾🐾

Mondo Cane 2 More documentary-like views of the oddities of mankind and ethnic rituals around the world. Enough, already. *AKA:* Mondo Pazzo. **1964 (R) 94m/C** *IT D:* Gualtiero Jacopetti. VHS, Beta $19.95 *VDC, HHE* 🐾

Mondo Magic A compilation of tribal rituals offering viewers a look on the darker side of matters magical. **1976 100m/C** *D:* Melvin Ashford. VHS, Beta *NO* 🐾½

Mondo Trasho A major trasho film of the last day in the life of a most unfortunate woman, complete with sex and violence. First full length effort from cult filmmaker Waters, who was also writer, producer, and editor. **1970 95m/B** Divine, Mary Vivian Pearce, John Leisenring, Mink Stole, David Lochary, Chris Atkinson; *D:* John Waters. VHS, Beta $39.98 *FLL* Woof!

The Money The quest for money drives a young man to kidnap the child that his girlfriend is baby-sitting. Average but Workman's direction is right on the money. **1975 (R) 88m/C** Laurence Luckinbill, Elizabeth Richards, Danny DeVito, Graham Beckel; *D:* Carl Workman. VHS $59.95 *GHV* 🐾🐾

Money Madness Beaumont (Ward Cleaver) plays a taxi driver turned thief in this curiosity. **1947 ?m/C** Hugh Beaumont, Frances Rafferty. VHS $16.95 *SNC* 🐾

Money Movers Aussie thieves plan megabuck bank robbery but heist and plot go sour. An oft told tale based on a true story. Features early appearance from burly boy Brown. **1978 94m/C** *AU* Terence Donovan, Ed Devereaux, Tony Bonner, Lucky Grills, Charles Tingwell, Candy Raymond, Bryan Brown, Alan Cassell; *W/D:* Bruce Beresford. VHS $79.95 *IMP* 🐾🐾

The Money Pit A young yuppie couple encounter sundry problems when they attempt to renovate their newly purchased, seemingly self-destructive, Long Island home. However, the collapse of their home leads directly to the collapse of their relationship as well. Somewhat modeled after ''Mr. Blandings Builds His Dream House.'' Hanks and Long fail to jell as partners and the many sight gags are on the predictable side. A Spielberg production. **1986 (PG) 91m/C** Tom Hanks, Shelley Long, Alexander Godunov, Maureen Stapleton, Philip Bosco, Joe Mantegna, Josh Mostel; *D:* Richard Benjamin. VHS, Beta, LV $14.95 *MCA* 🐾🐾

Money to Burn Aging high school counselor and two senior citizens develop a plan to steal $50 million dollars from the Federal Reserve Bank. Harmless bit of fun. **1983 90m/C** Jack Kruschen, Meegan King, David Wallace, Phillip Pine; *D:* Virginia Stone. VHS, Beta $42.95 *PGN* 🐾🐾

The Mongols Splashy Italian production has Genghis Khan's son repelling invading hordes while courting buxom princess. Pairing of Palance and Ekberg makes this one worthy of consideration. *AKA:* Les Mongols. **1960 105m/C** *IT FR* Jack Palance, Anita Ekberg, Antonella Lualdi, Franco Silva, Gianni Garko, Roldano Lupi, Gabriella Pallotti; *D:* Andre de Toth, Leopoldo Savona, Riccardo Freda. VHS $16.95 *SNC* 🐾🐾½

Mongrel El-cheapo kennel horror about a man who dreams he's a wild murderous mutt. His relief upon waking up is short-lived, however, when he discovers the people he killed in his dreams are actually dead. Flick will make you want to gnaw on a bone.

1983 90m/C Aldo Ray, Terry Evans; *D:* Robert Burns. VHS, Beta *PGN* Woof!

Monika Two teenagers who run away together for the summer find the winter brings more responsibility than they can handle when the girl becomes pregnant and gives birth. Lesser, early Bergman, sensitively directed, but dull. Adapted by Bergman from a Per Anders Fogelstrom novel. In Swedish with English subtitles. *AKA:* Summer with Monika. **1952 96m/B** *SW* Harriet Andersson, Lars Ekborg, John Harryson, Georg Skarstedt, Dagmar Ebbesen, Ake Gronberg; *W/D:* Ingmar Bergman. VHS $29.95 *CVC* 🐾🐾½

Monique A sophisticated career woman is about to unleash a terrifying secret on her new husband. **1983 96m/C** Florence Giorgetti, John Ferris. VHS, Beta *NO* 🐾

Monkey Boy Decent sci-fi horror from Britain, about a cunning human-ape hybrid that escapes from a genetics lab after massacring the staff. Not excessively gruesome or vulgar, and some sympathy is aroused for the killer mutant. Based on the novel ''Chimera'' by scriptwriter Stephen Gallagher. **1990 104m/C** John Lynch, Christine Kavanagh, Kenneth Cranham; *D:* Lawrence Gordon Clark. VHS, Beta $79.95 *PSM* 🐾🐾½

Monkey Business Marx Brothers run amok as stowaways on ocean liner. Fast-paced comedy provides seemingly endless amount of gags, quips, and pratfalls, including the fab four imitating Maurice Chevalier at Immigration. This film, incidentally, was the group's first to be written—by noted humorist S.J. Perelman—directly for the screen. **1931 77m/B** Groucho Marx, Harpo Marx, Chico Marx, Zeppo Marx, Thelma Todd, Ruth Hall, Harry Woods; *D:* Norman Z. McLeod. VHS, Beta, LV $19.95 *MCA* 🐾🐾🐾½

Monkey Business A scientist invents a fountain-of-youth potion, a lab chimpanzee mistakenly dumps it into a water cooler, and then grown-ups start turning into adolescents. Top-flight crew occasionally labors in this screwball comedy, though comic moments shine. Monroe is the secretary sans skills, while absent-minded Grant and sexy wife Rogers race hormonally as teens. Written by Ben Hecht, I.A.L. Diamond, and Charles Lederer. **1952 97m/B** Cary Grant, Ginger Rogers, Charles Coburn, Marilyn Monroe, Hugh Marlowe, Larry Keating, George Winslow; *D:* Howard Hawks, Howard Hawks; *W/D:* Charles Lederer; *W:* Ben Hecht, Charles Lederer, I.A.L. Diamond. VHS, Beta, LV $14.98 *FOX* 🐾🐾🐾

Monkey Grip An unmarried woman copes with parenthood and a drug-addicted boyfriend while working on the fringe of Australia's music business. Grim but provocative, based on Helen Graham's novel (and adapted by Graham and Cameron). **1982 101m/C** *AU* Noni Hazlehurst, Colin Friels, Alice Garner, Harold Hopkins, Candy Raymond; *D:* Ken Cameron. VHS $24.98 *SUE* 🐾🐾🐾

Monkey Hustle Vintage blaxploitation has trouble hustling laffs. The Man plans a super freeway through the ghetto, and law abiding do gooders join forces with territorial lords of vice to fight the project. Shot in the Windy City. **1977 (PG) 90m/C** Yaphet Kotto, Rudy Ray Moore, Rosalind Cash, Debbi Morgan, Thomas Carter; *D:* Arthur Marks. VHS $59.95 *ORI, FCT* 🐾

Monkey in the Master's Eye A martial arts adventure spiced with low comedy, in the story of a buffoonish slave rising to martial arts infamy.

M

1972 92m/C VHS, Beta $39.95 UNI 🎞

Monkey Kung Fu A young man learns kung fu from a master and, amidst kicking enemies in the head, cavorts and bumbles comically. Dubbed.
198? 96m/C Chen Mu-Chuan, Sun Jung-Chi. VHS, Beta NO 🎞

Monkey Shines Based on the novel by Michael Stuart, this is a sick, scary yarn about a quadriplegic who is given a specially trained capuchin monkey as a helpmate. However, he soon finds that the beast is assuming and acting on his subconscious rages. *AKA:* Monkey Shines: An Experiment in Fear.
1988 (R) 108m/C Jason Beghe, John Pankow, Melanie Parker, Christine Forrest, Stephen Root, Kate McNeil, Joyce Van Patten; *D:* George A. Romero. VHS, Beta, LV $19.98 ORI 🎞🎞

Monkeys, Go Home! Dumb Disney yarn about young American who inherits a badly neglected French olive farm. When he brings in four chimpanzees to pick the olives, the local townspeople go on strike. People can be so sensitive. Based on "The Monkeys" by G. K. Wilkinson. Chevalier's last film appearance.
1966 89m/C Dean Jones, Yvette Mimieux, Maurice Chevalier, Clement Harari, Yvonne Constant; *D:* Andrew V. McLaglen. VHS, Beta $69.95 DIS 🎞🎞

Monkey's Uncle A sequel to Disney's "The Misadventures of Merlin Jones" and featuring more bizarre antics and scientific hoopla, including chimps and a flying machine.
1965 90m/C Tommy Kirk, Annette Funicello, Leon Ames, Arthur O'Connell; *D:* Robert Stevenson. VHS, Beta $69.95 DIS 🎞½

The Monocle Steele plays a seductive villainess in this rare, spy/comedy thriller.
1964 ?m/C FR Paul Meurisse, Barbara Steele, Marcel Dallo. VHS $16.95 SNC 🎞🎞

The Monolith Monsters A geologist investigates a meteor shower in Arizona and discovers strange crystals. The crystals attack humans and absorb their silicone, causing them to grow into monsters. Good "B" movie fun.
1957 76m/B Grant Williams, Lola Albright, Les Tremayne, Trevor Bardette; *D:* John Sherwood. VHS $18.00 FRG, MLB 🎞🎞

Monsieur Beaucaire The Duke of Chartres ditches France posing as a barber, and once in Britain, becomes a lawman. Not a classic Valentino vehicle.
1924 100m/B Rudolph Valentino, Bebe Daniels, Lois Wilson, Doris Kenyon, Lowell Sherman, John Davidson; *D:* Sidney Olcott. VHS, Beta $19.95 GPV 🎞½

Monsieur Beaucaire Entertaining Hope vehicle that casts him as a barber impersonating a French nobleman in the court of Louis XV. He's set to wed a Spanish princess in order to prevent a full-scale war from taking place. However, he really wants to marry social-climber chambermaid Caulfield. Director Marshall was at his best here. Based on the novel by Booth Tarkington.
1946 93m/B Bob Hope, Joan Caulfield, Patric Knowles, Marjorie Reynolds, Cecil Kellaway, Joseph Schildkraut, Reginald Owen, Constance Collier; *D:* George Marshall; *W:* Melvin Frank, Norman Panama. VHS $14.98 MCA 🎞🎞🎞

Monsieur Hire The usual tale of sexual obsession and suspense. Mr. Hire spends much of his time trying to spy on his beautiful young neighbor woman, alternately alienated and engaged by her love affairs. The voyeur soon finds his secret affairs have entangled him in a vicious intrigue. Political rally set-

piece is brilliant. Excellent acting, intense pace, elegant photography. Based on "Les Fiancailles de M. Hire" by Georges Simenone and adapted by Leconte and Patrick Dewolf. In French with English subtitles. *AKA:* M. Hire.
1989 (PG-13) 81m/C FR Michel Blanc, Sandrine Bonnaire, Luc Thuillier, Eric Berenger, Andre Wilms; *D:* Patrice Leconte; *W:* Patrice Leconte. VHS, LV $39.95 FXL, FCT, IME 🎞🎞🎞½

Monsieur Verdoux A thorough Chaplin effort, as he produced, directed, wrote, scored and starred. A prim and proper bank cashier in Paris marries and murders rich women in order to support his real wife and family. A mild scandal in its day, though second-thought pacifism and stale humor date it. A bomb upon release (leading Chaplin to shelve it for 17 years) and a cult item today, admired for both its flaws and complexity. Raye fearlessly chews scenery and croissants. Initially based upon a suggestion from Orson Welles.
1947 123m/B Charlie Chaplin, Martha Raye, Isobel Elsom, Mady Correll, Marilyn Nash, Irving Bacon, William Frawley, Allison Roddan, Robert Lewis; *W/D:* Charlie Chaplin. Academy Awards '47 Nominations: Best Original Screenplay; National Board of Review Awards '47: 10 Best Films of the Year. VHS, Beta, LV $19.98 FOX 🎞🎞🎞

Monsieur Vincent True story of 17th century figure St. Vincent de Paul, who forsakes worldly possessions and devotes himself to tending the less fortunate. Inspirational. In French with English subtitles.
1947 111m/B FR Pierre Fresnay, Lisa Delamare, Aime Clairmond; *D:* Maurice Cloche. VHS, Beta $29.95 NOS, MRV, DVT 🎞🎞🎞

Monsignor Callow, ambitious priest befriends mobsters and even seduces a nun while managing Vatican's business affairs. No sparks generated by Reeve and Bujold (who appears nude in one scene), and no real conviction related by most other performers. Absurd, ludicrous melodrama best enjoyed as unintentional comedy. Based on Jack Alain Leger's book.
1982 (R) 121m/C Christopher Reeve, Fernando Rey, Genevieve Bujold, Jason Miller; *D:* Frank Perry; *M:* John Williams. VHS, Beta $59.98 FOX Woof!

Monsignor Quixote A small town priest takes on the persona of his ancestor, Don Quixote, and prepares to battle the evil he sees around him. Based on the novel by Graham Greene.
1991 118m/C Alec Guinness. VHS $59.99 FCT, TAM 🎞🎞½

The Monster This silent horror film has all the elements that would become genre standards. A mad scientist (Chaney), working in an asylum filled with lunatics, abducts strangers to use in his fiendish experiments to bring the dead back to life. There's the obligatory dungeon and even a lovely heroine that needs rescuing. Great atmosphere and Chaney's usual spine-tingling performance.
1925 86m/B Lon Chaney Sr., Gertrude Olmsted, Johnny Arthur, Charles Sellon; *D:* Roland West. VHS $29.95 FCT 🎞🎞🎞

Monster Boodthirsty alien indiscriminately preys on gaggle of teens in wilds of civilization. Performers struggle with dialogue and their own self-esteem.
1978 (R) 98m/C Jim Mitchum, Diane McBain, Roger Clark, John Carradine, Phil Carey, Anthony Eisley, Keenan Wynn; *D:* Herbert L. Strock. VHS, Beta $24.95 GHV, MRV 🎞

Monster a Go-Go! Team of go-go dancers battle a ten-foot monster from outerspace whose mass is due to a radiation mishap. He can't dance, either.
1965 70m/B Phil Morton, June Travis, Bill Rebane, Sheldon Seymour; *D:* Herschell Gordon Lewis. VHS, Beta $39.95 UHV Woof!

The Monster and the Stripper A bayou creature is pursued by a gangster who foolishly hopes to realize considerable profits from the venture.
1973 (R) 90m/C VHS, Beta $59.95 NO 🎞

The Monster Club Price and Carradine star in this music-horror compilation, featuring songs by Night, B.A. Robertson, The Pretty Things and The Viewers. Soundtrack music by John Williams, UB 40 and The Expressos.
1985 104m/C GB Vincent Price, Donald Pleasence, John Carradine, Stuart Whitman, Britt Ekland, Simon Ward, Patrick Magee; *D:* Roy Ward Baker. VHS, Beta, LV $39.95 LIV 🎞🎞

The Monster Demolisher Nostradamus' descendent shares the family penchant for sanguine cocktails, and threatens a professor who protects himself with an electronic wonder of modern technology. Edited from a sombrero serial; if you make it through this one, look up its Mexican siblings, "Curse of Nostradamus" and "Genie of Darkness."
1960 ?m/B MX German Robles; *D:* Frederick Curiel. VHS $19.98 NOS, LOO 🎞🎞

Monster Dog A rock band is mauled, threatened, and drooled upon by an untrainable mutant canine. Rock star Cooper plays the leader of the band. No plot, but the German shepherd is worth watching.
1982 88m/C Alice Cooper, Victoria Vera; *D:* Clyde Anderson. VHS, Beta $69.95 TWE Woof!

Monster from Green Hell An experimental rocket containing radiation-contaminated wasps crashes in Africa, making giant killer wasps that run amok. Stinging big bug horror.
1958 71m/B Jim Davis, Robert Griffin, Barbara Turner, Eduardo Ciannelli; *D:* Kenneth Crane. VHS, Beta $14.95 NOS, MRV, SNC 🎞

Monster from the Ocean Floor An oceanographer in a deep-sea diving bell is threatened by a multi-tentacled creature. Roger Corman's first production. *AKA:* It Stalked the Ocean Floor; Monster Maker.
1954 66m/C Anne Kimball, Stuart Wade; *D:* Wyott Ordung. VHS, Beta $29.98 VMK 🎞

Monster High Bloodthirsty alien indiscriminately preys on gaggle of teens in wilds of civilization. Even the people who made this one may not have seen it all the way through.
1989 (R) 89m/C David Marriott, Dean Iandoli, Diana Frank, D.J. Kerzner; *D:* Rudiger Poe. VHS, Beta, LV $89.95 COL 🎞

Monster in a Box Master storyteller Gray spins a wonderful tale about his life, including stories about his adventures at a Moscow film festival, a trip to Nicaragua, and his first experience with California earthquakes. Filled with wit, satire, and hilarity. Filmed before an audience, this is based on Gray's Broadway show of the same title. By the way, the monster in the box is a 1,900-page manuscript of his autobiography and the box in which he lugs it around.
1992 (PG-13) 88m/C Spalding Gray; *D:* Nick Broomfield; *W:* Spalding Gray; *M:* Laurie Anderson. VHS, LV $89.95 NLC, COL 🎞🎞🎞

Monster in the Closet A gory horror spoof all about a rash of San Francisco murders that all take place inside closets. A news reporter and his scientist friend decide they will be the ones to protect California from the

evil but shy creatures. From the makers of "The Toxic Avenger."
1986 (PG) 87m/C Donald Grant, Claude Akins, Denise DuBarry, Stella Stevens, Howard Duff, Henry Gibson, Jesse White, John Carradine; **D:** Bob Dahlin. **VHS, Beta $19.98** *LHV, WAR ⅛⅛*

The Monster Maker Low-budget gland fest in which deranged scientist develops serum that inflates heads, feet, and hands. He recklessly inflicts others with this potion, then must contend with deformed victims while courting a comely gal.
1944 65m/B J. Carroll Naish, Ralph Morgan, Wanda McKay, Terry Frost; **D:** Sam Newfield. **VHS, Beta, 3/4U, Special order formats $19.95** *NOS, MRV, SNC ⅛⅛*

The Monster of London City During a stage play about Jack the Ripper, murders occur paralleling those in the production. The lead actor finds himself to be the prime suspect. Lightweight horror from Germany. *AKA:* Das Ungeheuer von London City.
1964 87m/B GE Hansjörg Felmy, Marianne Koch, Dietmar Schoenherr, Hans Nielsen; **D:** Edwin Zbonek. **VHS, Beta $16.95** *SNC ⅛½*

The Monster of Piedras Blancas During a seaside festival, two fisherman are killed by a bloodthirsty oceanic critter with no respect for holidays. The fishing village is determined to find it and kill it. Low-budget, with amateurish effects and poor acting.
1957 72m/B Les Tremayne, Jeanne Carmen, Forrest Lewis; **D:** Irvin Berwick. **VHS $14.98** *VDM, MRV, REP Woof!*

The Monster Squad Youthful monster enthusiasts find their community inundated by Dracula, Frankenstein creature, Wolf Man, Mummy, and Gill Man(!?!), who are all searching for a life-sustaining amulet. Somewhat different, but still somewhat mediocre.
1987 (PG-13) 82m/C Andre Gower, Stephen Macht, Tommy Noonan, Duncan Regehr; **D:** Fred Dekker. **VHS, Beta, LV $19.98** *LIV, VES ⅛½*

The Monster that Challenged the World Huge, ancient eggs are discovered in the Salton Sea and eventually hatch into killer, crustaceous caterpillars. Superior monster action.
1957 83m/B Tim Holt, Audrey Dalton, Hans Conried, Harlen Ward, Casey Adams, Mimi Gibson, Gordon Jones; **D:** Arnold Laven. **VHS $18.00** *FRG, MLB ⅛⅛½*

The Monster Walks A whodunit thriller, complete with stormy nights, suspicious cripples, weird servants, a screaming gorilla, and a spooky house. Not unique but entertaining. *AKA:* The Monster Walked.
1932 60m/B Rex Lease, Vera Reynolds, Mischa Auer, Willie Best; **D:** Frank Strayer. **VHS, Beta $12.95** *SNC, NOS, CCB ⅛⅛*

Monsters Crash the Pajama Party Mad scientist is discovered conducting weird experiments by a group of teens who enter a supposedly haunted house. This one was much better in the theater, because "monsters" would run through the audience and select a victim. Then the monsters and the victim would magically appear on the screen. Weird.
1965 ?m/C Don Brandon. **VHS $16.95** *SNC ⅛⅛*

The Monster's Demolisher More terror about the cravings of the blood starved vampire, Nostradamus.
1960 ?m/C German Robles. **VHS $16.95** *SNC ⅛⅛*

Montana Hoyce and Bess Guthrie are long-married and strong-willed ranchers who are at odds over the family ranch in Montana. He wants to sell the land to a power compa-

ny for oil drilling but she wants to keep the land in the family. Made for cable television.
1990 (PG) 91m/C Gena Rowlands, Richard Crenna, Lea Thompson, Justin Deas, Elizabeth Berridge, Scott Coffey; **D:** William A. Graham; **W:** Larry McMurtry. **VHS, Beta $89.95** *TTC, FCT ⅛⅛½*

Montana Belle A buxom bandit teams with the notorious Dalton Brothers before embarking on a life of reform. In the cardgame of life, Russell is always holding a pair.
1952 81m/C Jane Russell, George Brent, Scott Brady, Forrest Tucker, Andy Devine, Jack Lambert, John Litel, Ray Teal; **D:** Allan Dwan. **VHS, Beta $19.98** *TTC ⅛⅛*

Monte Carlo A sexy Russian woman aids the Allies by relaying important messages during World War II. Fun, made for television production featuring Collins at her seductive best.
1986 200m/C Joan Collins, George Hamilton, Lisa Eilbacher, Lauren Hutton, Robert Carradine, Malcolm McDowell; **D:** Anthony Page. **VHS, Beta $29.95** *STE, NWV ⅛⅛*

Monte Carlo Nights Wrongly convicted murderer determines to prove his innocence even as he is tracked by police.
1934 60m/B Mary Brian, John Darrow, Kate Campbell, Robert Frazer, Astrid Allwyn, George "Gabby" Hayes, George Cleveland; **D:** William Nigh. **VHS, Beta $16.95** *SNC ⅛½*

Monte Walsh Aging cowboy sees declining of Old West, embarks on mission to avenge best friend's death. Subdued, moving western worthy of genre greats Marvin and Palance. Cinematographer Fraker proves himself a proficient director in this, his first venture. Based on Jack Schaefer's novel.
1970 (PG) 100m/C Lee Marvin, Jack Palance, Jeanne Moreau, Jim Davis, Mitchell Ryan; **D:** William A. Fraker; **M:** John Barry. **VHS, Beta $59.98** *FOX ⅛⅛⅛*

Montenegro Offbeat, bawdy comedy details experiences of bored, possibly mad housewife who lands in a coarse, uninhibited ethnic community. To its credit, this film remains unpredictable to the end. And Anspach, an intriguing, resourceful—and attractive—actress, delivers what is perhaps her greatest performance. *AKA:* Montenegro—Or Pigs and Pearls.
1981 97m/C SW Susan Anspach, Erland Josephson; **W/D:** Dusan Makavejev. **VHS, Beta $69.99** *HBO ⅛⅛⅛½*

Monterey Pop This pre-Woodstock rock 'n roll festival in Monterey, California features landmark performances by some of the most popular sixties rockers. Compelling for the performances, and historically important as the first significant rock concert film. Appearances by Jefferson Airplane, Janis Joplin, Jimi Hendrix, Simon and Garfunkel, The Who, and Otis Redding.
1968 72m/C The Jefferson Airplane, Janis Joplin, Jimi Hendrix, Art Garfunkel, Paul Simon, Pete Townsend, Roger Daltrey, Keith Moon, John Entwhistle; **D:** James Desmond. **VHS, Beta, LV, 8mm $29.95** *SVS, VTK, VYG ⅛⅛⅛½*

A Month in the Country The reverently quiet story of two British WWI veterans, one an archeologist and the other a church painting restorer, who are working in a tiny village while trying to heal their emotional wounds. Based on the novel by J.L. Carr with a screenplay by Simon Frag.
1987 92m/C GB Colin Firth, Natasha Richardson, Kenneth Branagh, Patrick Malahide; **D:** Pat O'Connor. **VHS, Beta, LV $79.95** *LHV, WAR ⅛⅛⅛*

Monty Python and the Holy Grail Britain's famed comedy band assaults the Arthurian legend in a cult classic replete with a Trojan rabbit and an utterly dismembered, but inevitably pugnacious, knight. Fans of manic comedy—and graphic violence—should get more than their fill here.
1975 (PG) 90m/C GB Graham Chapman, John Cleese, Terry Gilliam, Eric Idle, Terry Jones, Michael Palin, Carol Cleveland, Connie Booth, Neil Innes, Patsy Kensit; **D:** Terry Gilliam, Terry Jones. **VHS, Beta, LV, 8mm $19.95** *COL, SIG, TVC ⅛⅛⅛½*

Monty Python Live at the Hollywood Bowl The revered comedy group perform many of their most celebrated routines in this uproarious performance documentary. A must-see for all Python aficionados.
1982 78m/C GB Eric Idle, Michael Palin, John Cleese, Terry Gilliam, Terry Jones, Graham Chapman; **D:** Terry Hughes. **VHS, Beta, LV $69.95** *HBO, PAR ⅛⅛⅛*

Monty Python Meets Beyond the Fringe More fine British humor is featured in this compendium of skits, sketches, routines, and sequences. Those who know, will know. Those who don't probably won't enjoy it anyway.
19?? 85m/C GB Graham Chapman, John Cleese, Terry Gilliam, Eric Idle, Terry Jones, Michael Palin. **VHS** *UHV ⅛⅛*

Monty Python's Flying Circus The original classic irreverant BBC comedy series that introduced the gang of six comics to the world. Two episodes per tape. Four skits: "The Architect's Sketch," "The Naughty Chemist," "Ministry of Silly Walks," and "The Piranha Brothers."
1971 60m/C GB Michael Palin, Graham Chapman, Eric Idle, John Cleese, Terry Jones, Terry Gilliam, Carol Cleveland, Connie Booth, Neil Innes; **D:** Ian MacNaughton. **VHS, Beta, LV $19.99** *MOV, PAR ⅛⅛⅛*

Monty Python's Life of Brian Often riotous spoof of Christianity tracks hapless peasant mistaken for the messiah in 32 A.D. Film reels from routine to routine, and only the most pious will remain unmoved by a chorus of crucifixion victims. Probably the group's most daring, controversial venture. *AKA:* Life of Brian.
1979 (R) 94m/C GB Graham Chapman, John Cleese, Terry Gilliam, Eric Idle, Terry Jones, Michael Palin, George Harrison; **D:** Terry Jones. **VHS, Beta, LV $19.98** *PAR, PIA, SIG ⅛⅛⅛½*

Monty Python's Parrot Sketch Not Included To celebrate their 20th anniversary, the crazy guys of Monty Python put together this collection of some of their funniest sketches. The parrot was pretty disappointed that he wasn't included.
1990 75m/C Graham Chapman, John Cleese, Terry Gilliam, Eric Idle, Terry Jones, Michael Palin. **VHS $19.95** *PAR, SIG, TVC ⅛⅛⅛½*

Monty Python's The Meaning of Life Funny, technically impressive film conducts various inquiries into the most profound questions confronting humanity. Notable among the sketches here are a live sex enactment performed before bored schoolboys, a student-faculty rugby game that turns quite violent, and an encounter between a physician and a reluctant, untimely organ donor. Another sketch provides a memorable portrait of a glutton prone to nausea. And at film's end, the meaning of life is actually revealed.
1983 (R) 107m/C GB Graham Chapman, John Cleese, Terry Gilliam, Eric Idle, Terry Jones, Michael Palin, Carol Cleveland; **D:** Terry Jones. **VHS, Beta, LV $14.95** *MCA, CCB, SIG ⅛⅛⅛*

The Moon and Sixpence Stockbroker turns ambitious painter in this adaptation of W. Somerset Maugham's novel that was, in turn, inspired by the life of artist Paul Gaugin. Fine performance from Sanders. Filmed mainly in black and white, but uses color sparingly to great advantage. Compare this one to "Wolf at the Door," in which Gaugin is played by Donald Sutherland.
1943 89m/B George Sanders, Herbert Marshall, Steve Geray, Doris Dudley, Eric Blore, Elena Verdugo, Florence Bates, Albert Basserman, Heather Thatcher; **D:** Albert Lewin. **VHS** *MGM, IVY* ⍟⍟⍟

Moon 44 A space prison is overrun by thugs who terrorize their fellow inmates. Fine cast, taut pacing. Filmed in Germany.
1990 (R) 102m/C *GE* Malcolm McDowell, Lisa Eichhorn, Michael Pare, Stephen Geoffreys, Roscoe Lee Browne; **D:** Roland Emmerich. **VHS, LV $89.95** *LIV, IME, BTV* ⍟⍟½

Moon in Scorpio Three Vietnam-vet buddies go sailing and are attacked by the back-from-the-dead victims of a bloody war crime.
1986 90m/C John Phillip Law, Britt Ekland, William Smith; **D:** Gary Graver. **VHS, Beta $79.95** *TWE* ⍟½

Moon in the Gutter In a ramshackle harbor town, a man searches despondently for the person who killed his sister years before. Various sexual liaisons and stevedore fights intermittently spice up the action. Nasty story that doesn't make much sense on film. In French with English subtitles. *AKA:* La Lune Dans le Caniveau.
1984 (R) 109m/C *FR IT* Gerard Depardieu, Nastassia Kinski, Victoria Abril, Vittorio Mezzogiorno, Dominique Pinon; **D:** Jean-Jacques Beineix. **VHS, Beta $59.95** *COL* ⍟½

Moon is Blue A young woman flaunts her virginity in this stilted adaptation of F. Hugh Herbert's play. Hard to believe that this film was once considered risque. Good performances, though, from Holden and Niven.
1953 100m/B William Holden, David Niven, Maggie McNamara; **D:** Otto Preminger. Academy Awards '53 Nominations: Best Actress (McNamara), Best Film Editing, Best Song ("The Moon is Blue"); Golden Globe Awards '54: Best Actor—Musical/Comedy (Niven). **Beta, LV $29.98** *FOX* ⍟⍟½

Moon Madness An astronomer takes a trip to the moon to find the Selenites, proprietors of the fountain of youth.
1983 82m/C VHS, Beta $69.95 *VES* ⍟⍟½

Moon of the Wolf A small town in bayou country is terrorized by a modern-day werewolf that rips its victims to shreds. Made-for-television.
1972 74m/C David Janssen, Barbara Rush, Bradford Dillman, John Beradino; **D:** Daniel Petrie. **VHS, Beta $49.95** *WOV, GKK* ⍟

Moon Over Harlem A musical melodrama about a widow who unwittingly marries a fast-talking gangster involved in the numbers racket. The film features 20 chorus girls, a choir, and a 60-piece orchestra.
1939 67m/B Bud Harris, Cora Green, Alec Lovejoy, Sidney Bechet; **D:** Edgar G. Ulmer. **VHS, Beta $24.95** *FCT, DVT, NOS* ⍟½

Moon Over Miami Manhunting trio meet their match in this engaging musical. A remake of 1938's "Three Blind Mice," this was later remade in 1946 as "Three Little Girls in Blue." ♫Moon Over Miami; I've Got You All To Myself; What Can I Do For You?; Kindergarten Congo; You Started Something; Oh Me Oh Mi-Am-Mi; Solitary Seminole; Is That Good?; Loveliness and Love.

1941 91m/C Don Ameche, Betty Grable, Robert Cummings, Carole Landis, Charlotte Greenwood, Jack Haley; **D:** Walter Lang. **VHS, Beta $19.95** *FOX* ⍟⍟½

Moon Over Parador An uneven comedy about a reluctant American actor who gets the role of his life when he gets the chance to pass himself off as the recently deceased dictator of a Latin American country. A political strongman wants to continue the charade until he can take over, but the actor begins to enjoy the benefits of dictatorship.
1988 (PG-13) 103m/C Richard Dreyfuss, Sonia Braga, Raul Julia, Jonathan Winters, Fernando Rey, Ed Asner, Dick Cavett, Michael Greene, Sammy Davis Jr., Polly Holliday, Charo, Marianne Sagebrecht, Dana Delany; **D:** Paul Mazursky. **VHS, Beta, LV $19.95** *MCA* ⍟⍟½

Moon Pilot An astronaut on his way to the moon encounters a mysterious alien woman who claims to know his future.
1962 98m/C Tom Tryon, Brian Keith, Edmond O'Brien, Dany Saval, Tommy Kirk; **D:** James Neilson. **VHS, Beta $69.95** *DIS* ⍟⍟

Moon-Spinners Lightweight Disney drama featuring Mills as a young tourist traveling through Crete who meets up with a young man, accused of being a jewel thief, and the two work together to find the real jewel thieves. Watch for silent film star Pola Negri.
1964 (PG) 118m/C Hayley Mills, Peter McEnery, Eli Wallach, Pola Negri; **D:** James Neilson. **VHS, Beta** *DIS, OM* ⍟⍟

The Moon Stallion A charming tale of mystery and fantasy for children and adults. Professor Purwell is researching King Arthur. His blind daughter soon becomes involved with supernatural events and a white horse that appears to lead her into adventures not of this age.
197? 95m/C *GB* **VHS $29.95** *DTG, HMV* ⍟⍟½

Mooncussers A children's film detailing the exploits of a precocious 12-year-old determined to exact revenge upon a band of ruthless pirates.
1962 85m/C Kevin Corcoran, Rian Garrick, Oscar Homolka; **D:** James Neilson. **VHS, Beta $69.95** *DIS* ⍟½

Moonfleet Follows the adventures of an 18th century buccaneer who tries to swindle a young lad in his charge of a valuable diamond. From J. Meade Falkner's novel.
1955 89m/C Stewart Granger, Jon Whiteley, George Sanders, Viveca Lindfors, Joan Greenwood, Ian Wolfe; **D:** Fritz Lang. **VHS, LV $34.98** *MGM* ⍟⍟½

Moonlight Sonata Professional concert pianist Paderewski performs his way through a confusing soap-opera of a film. Includes performances of Franz Liszt's "Second Hungarian Rhapsody" and Frederic Chopin's "Polonaise."
1938 80m/B *GB* Ignace Jan Paderewski, Charles Farrell, Marie Tempest, Barbara Greene, Eric Portman; **D:** Lothar Mendes. **VHS $19.95** *NOS, DVT* ⍟⍟½

Moonlight Sword & Jade Lion Kung fu action takes place in ancient China.
197? 94m/B Mao Yin, Wong Do, So Chan Ping. **VHS, Beta $29.95** *OCE* ⍟

Moonlighting Compelling drama about Polish laborers illegally hired to renovate London flat. When their country falls under martial law, the foreman conceals the event and pushes workers to complete project. Unlikely casting of Irons as foreman is utterly successful.

1982 (PG) 97m/C *PL GB* Jeremy Irons, Eugene Lipinski, Jiri Stanislav, Eugeniusz Haczkiewicz; **D:** Jerzy Skolimowski. **VHS, Beta, LV $49.95** *MCA* ⍟⍟½

Moonlighting The television-pilot for the popular detective show, where Maddie and David, the daffy pair of impetuous private eyes, meet for the first time and solve an irrationally complex case.
1985 93m/C Cybill Shepherd, Bruce Willis, Allyce Beasley; **D:** Robert Butler. **VHS, Beta $19.95** *WAR, OM* ⍟⍟½

The Moonraker Compelling action scenes highlight this tale set at the end of the English Civil War, as the Royalists attempt to sneak the king out of England and into France.
1958 82m/C *GB* George Baker, Sylvia Syms, Peter Arne, Marius Goring, Clive Morton, Gary Raymond, Richard Leech, Patrick Troughton; **D:** David MacDonald. **VHS $19.95** *NOS* ⍟⍟½

Moonraker Uninspired Bond fare has 007 unraveling intergalactic hijinks. Bond is aided by a female CIA agent, assaulted by a giant with jaws of steel, and captured by Amazons when he sets out to protect the human race. Moore, Chiles, and Lonsdale all seem to be going through the motions only.
1979 (PG) 136m/C *GB* Roger Moore, Lois Chiles, Richard Kiel, Michael Lonsdale, Corinne Clery, Geoffrey Keen, Emily Bolton, Walter Gotell, Bernard Lee, Lois Maxwell, Desmond Llewelyn; **D:** Lewis Gilbert; **M:** John Barry. **VHS, Beta, LV $19.98** *MGM, TLF* ⍟⍟

Moonrise A melodramatic tale about the son of an executed murderer who becomes the object of derision in the small town where he lives. One tormentor finally attacks him, and the young man must make a split-second decision that may affect his own mortality.
1948 90m/B Dane Clark, Gail Russell, Ethel Barrymore, Allyn Joslyn, Harry Morgan, Lloyd Bridges, Selena Royle, Rex Ingram, Harry Carey Jr.; **D:** Frank Borzage. **VHS, LV $19.98** *REP* ⍟⍟

Moon's Our Home A fast-paced, breezy, screwball comedy about an actress and adventurer impulsively marrying and then bickering through the honeymoon. Silliness at its height. Fonda and Sullavan were both married and then divorced before filming this movie.
1936 80m/B Margaret Sullavan, Henry Fonda, Beulah Bondi, Charles Butterworth, Margaret Hamilton, Walter Brennan; **D:** William A. Seiter. **VHS, Beta $14.95** *KRT* ⍟⍟½

Moonshine County Express Three sexy daughters of a hillbilly moonshiner set out to run the still and avenge their father's murder.
1977 (PG) 97m/C John Saxon, Susan Howard, William Conrad, Morgan Woodward, Claudia Jennings, Jeff Corey, Dub Taylor, Maureen McCormick, Albert Salmi, Candice Rialson; **D:** Gus Trikonis. **VHS, Beta $39.98** *WAR* ⍟½

Moonshine Mountain A country-western star travels with his girlfriend to the singer's home in backwoods Carolina. When the girl is killed by a lusting resident, all hell breaks loose. One of gore-meister Lewis' excursions into the dramatic. *AKA:* White Trash on Moonshine Mountain.
1964 90m/C Chuck Scott, Adam Sorg, Jeffrey Allen, Bonnie Hinson, Carmen Sotir, Ben Moore, Pat Patterson, Mark Douglas; **D:** Herschell Gordon Lewis. **VHS, Beta $16.95** *SNC* Woof!

Moonstruck Winning romantic comedy about widow engaged to one man but falling in love with his younger brother in Little Italy. Excellent performances all around, with Cher particularly fetching as attractive, hapless widow. Unlikely casting of usually dominating

Aiello, as unassuming mama's boy also works well, and Cage is at his best as a tormented one-handed opera lover/baker. **1987 (PG-13) 103m/C** Cher, Nicolas Cage, Olympia Dukakis, Danny Aiello, Vincent Gardenia, Julie Bovasso, Louis Guss, Anita Gillette, Feodor Chaliapin, John Mahoney; **D:** Norman Jewison; **W:** John Patrick Shanley. Academy Awards '87: Best Actress (Cher), Best Original Screenplay, Best Supporting Actress (Dukakis); Nominations: Best Director (Jewison), Best Picture, Best Supporting Actor (Gardenia); Golden Globe Awards '88: Best Actress—Musical/Comedy (Cher), Best Supporting Actress (Dukakis). **VHS, Beta, LV $19.98** *MGM, BTV, HMV* 🎬🎬🎬 ½

Moontrap An astronaut discovers an alien frozen in space and returns to Earth with it. Once thawed, the creature reveals its horrible secret. **1989 92m/C** Walter Koenig, Bruce Campbell, Leigh Lombardi; **D:** Robert Dyke. **VHS, LV** *IME* 🎬🎬

Morals for Women This soap-opera's so old it almost predates soap. A secretary becomes the Kept Woman of her boss in the Big Bad City. She escapes, but not for long. **1931 65m/B** Bessie Love, Conway Tearle, John Holland, Natalie Moorhead, Emma Dunn, June Clyde; **D:** Mort Blumenstock. **VHS $15.95** *NOS, LOO* 🎬 ½

Moran of the Lady Letty Seaweed saga of Ramon Laredo (Valentino), a high society guy who's kidnapped aboard a pirate barge. When the salty dogs rescue/capture Moran (a theme ahead of its time?) from a ship fuming with burning coal, Ramon is smitten in a big way with the boyish girl and battles contagiously to prevent the pirates from selling her as a slave. Excellent fight scenes with much hotstepping over gangplanks and swinging from masts, with a 60-foot death dive from above. Little known Dalton was a celluloid fave in the 'teens and twenties, and Valentino is atypically cast as a man's man. The sheik himself is said not to have like this one because it undermined his image as a ladies' man. **1922 71m/B** Dorothy Dalton, Rudolph Valentino, Charles Brinley, Walter Long, Emil Jorgenson; **D:** George Melford. **VHS, Beta $32.95** *GPV, FCT* 🎬🎬 ½

More Smells like teen angst in the sixties when a German college grad falls for an American in Paris, to the tune of sex, drugs, and Pink Floyd. Schroeder's first effort as director, it's definitely a sixties pic. In French with English subtitles. **1969 110m/C** Mimsy Farmer, Klaus Grunberg, Heinz Engelmann, Michel Chanderli; **D:** Barbet Schroeder. **VHS, Beta $59.99** *WAR, BTV,* *FCT* 🎬🎬 ½

More American Graffiti Sequel to 1973's acclaimed '50s homage "American Graffiti" charts various characters' experiences in the more radical '60s. George Lucas didn't direct, Richard Dreyfuss didn't reprise. Ron Howard doesn't direct, he acts. B.W.L. Norton doesn't direct either, though he's credited. Pass on this one and have that root canal done instead. **1979 (PG) 111m/C** Candy Clark, Bo Hopkins, Ron Howard, Paul LeMat, MacKenzie Phillips, Charles Martin Smith, Anna Bjorn, Richard Bradford, Cindy Williams, Scott Glenn; **D:** B.W.L. Norton. **VHS, LV $14.98** *MCA* 🎬 ½

More! Police Squad More episodes from the seminal spoof of television cop shows, episodes entitled "Revenge and Remorse," "The Butler Did It" and "Testimony of Evil." **1982 75m/C** Leslie Nielsen, Alan North, Rex Hamilton, Peter Lupus. **VHS, Beta, LV $19.95** *PAR* 🎬 ½

The More the Merrier Likeable romantic comedy in which working girl must share apartment with two bachelors in Washington, D.C., during WWII. Arthur is especially endearing as a young woman in male company. **1943 104m/B** Joel McCrea, Jean Arthur, Charles Coburn, Richard Gaines, Bruce Bennett, Ann Savage, Ann Doran, Frank Tully, Grady Sutton; **D:** George Stevens. Academy Awards '43: Best Supporting Actor (Coburn); Nominations: Best Actress (Arthur), Best Director (Stevens), Best Picture, Best Story; New York Film Critics Awards '43: Best Director (Stevens). **VHS, Beta, LV $19.95** *COL, BTV* 🎬🎬🎬

More Wild, Wild West Another feature-length continuation of the satirical television series, with Winters taking on Conrad and Martin. Made for television. **1980 94m/C** Robert Conrad, Ross Martin, Jonathan Winters, Victor Buono; **D:** Burt Kennedy. **VHS, Beta $59.98** *FOX* 🎬🎬

Morgan! Offbeat comedy in which deranged artist copes with divorce by donning ape suit. Some laughs ensue. Based on David Mercer's play. **AKA:** Morgan: A Suitable Case for Treatment; A Suitable Case for Treatment. **1966 93m/B** *GB* Vanessa Redgrave, David Warner, Robert Stephens, Irene Handl; **D:** Karel Reisz. Academy Awards '66 Nominations: Best Actress (Redgrave), Best Costume Design (B & W); Cannes Film Festival '66: Best Actress (Redgrave). **VHS, Beta, LV** *HBO* 🎬🎬 ½

Morgan Stewart's Coming Home When Dad needs a good family image in his political race, he brings Morgan home from boarding school. Fortunately, Morgan can see how his parents are using him and he doesn't approve at all. He decides to turn his family's life upside down while pursuing the love of his life. **AKA:** Home Front. **1987 (PG-13) 96m/C** Jon Cryer, Lynn Redgrave, Nicholas Pryor, Viveka Davis, Paul Gleason, Andrew Duncan, Savely Kramarov, John Cullum, Robert Sedgwick, Waweru Njenga, Sudhir Rad; **D:** Alan Smithee. **VHS, Beta, LV $34.95** *HBO* 🎬

Morgan the Pirate Steve Reeves is at his finest as Morgan, an escaped slave who becomes a notorious pirate in the Caribbean and is wrongly condemned to death in this brisk, sea-going adventure. **AKA:** Capitaine Morgan; Morgan il Pirata. **1960 93m/C** *FR IT* Steve Reeves, Valerie Lagrange; **D:** Andre de Toth. **VHS, Beta, LV $39.98** *SUE* 🎬🎬

Morituri Gripping wartime drama in which an Allied spy tries to persuade German gunboat captain to surrender his vessel. Brando is—no surprise—excellent. **AKA:** Saboteur: Code Name Morituri; The Saboteur. **1965 123m/C** Marlon Brando, Yul Brynner, Trevor Howard, Janet Margolin, Wally Cox, William Redfield; **D:** Bernhard Wicki; **M:** Jerry Goldsmith. **VHS, Beta $19.98** *FOX* 🎬🎬🎬

A Mormon Maid Young woman and her family, after being saved from an Indian attack by a Mormon group, come to live among them without converting to their beliefs. Considered a shocking expose of controversial Mormon practices, including polygamy. **1917 78m/B** Mae Murray, Frank Borzage, Hobart Bosworth, Noah Beery Sr.; **D:** Robert Z. Leonard. **VHS, Beta $52.95** *GVV, VYY* 🎬 ½

Morning After A predictable suspense-thriller about an alcoholic actress who wakes up one morning with a corpse in bed next to her, but cannot remember anything about the night before. She evades the police, accidentally meets up with an ex-cop, and works

with him to unravel an increasingly complicated mystery. **1986 (R) 103m/C** Jane Fonda, Jeff Bridges, Raul Julia, Diane Salinger, Richard Foronjy, Geoffrey Scott, Kathleen Wilhoite, Frances Bergen, Rick Rossovich, Kathy Bates; **D:** Sidney Lumet. **VHS, Beta, LV $19.98** *LHV, WAR* 🎬🎬

Morning Glory Small-town girl finds love and fame in the big city. Predictable fare nonetheless boasts fine performances from Hepburn and Fairbanks. Adapted from Zoe Atkins' stage play. **1933 74m/B** Katharine Hepburn, Douglas Fairbanks Jr., Adolphe Menjou, Mary Duncan; **D:** Lowell Sherman. **VHS, Beta, LV $19.98** *RKO, CCB, MED* 🎬🎬 ½

Morocco A foreign legion soldier falls for a world-weary chanteuse along the desert sands. Cooper has never been more earnest, and Dietrich has never been more blase and exotic. In her American film debut, Dietrich sings "What am I Bid?" A must for anyone drawn to improbable, gloriously well-done kitsch. Based on Benno Vigny's novel, "Amy Jolly." **1930 97m/B** Marlene Dietrich, Gary Cooper, Adolphe Menjou, Ullrich Haupt, Francis McDonald, Eve Southern, Paul Porcasi; **D:** Josef von Sternberg. **VHS, Beta, LV $14.95** *MCA* 🎬🎬🎬 ½

Morons from Outer Space Slow-witted aliens from elsewhere in the universe crash onto Earth, but unlike other sci-fis, these morons become internationally famous, despite them acting like intergalactic stooges. Plenty of sight gags. **1985 (PG) 87m/C** *GB* Griff Rhys Jones, Mel Smith, James B. Sikking, Dinsdale Landen, Jimmy Nail, Joanne Pearce, Paul Brown; **D:** Mike Hodges. **VHS $14.95** *MGM, HBO* 🎬🎬

Mortal Passions Another "Double Indemnity" rip-off, with a scheming tramp manipulating everyone around her with betrayal, sex, and murder. Her dead husband's brother eventually ignites old flames to steer her away from his money. **1990 (R) 96m/C** Zach Galligan, Krista Errickson, Michael Bowen, Luca Bercovici, Sheila Kelley, David Warner; **D:** Andrew Lane. **VHS, Beta $89.98** *FOX* 🎬 ½

Mortal Sins A TV evangelist finds more than salvation at the altar, when bodies begin to turn up. The detective has his eyes close-mouthed, but more than a little interested in the preacher's daughter. A tense psychosexual thriller. **1990 (R) 85m/C** Brian Benben, Anthony LaPaglia, Debrah Farentino; **D:** Yuri Sivo. **VHS $29.95** *ACA, FXV* 🎬

Mortal Sins Reeve stars as parish priest Thomas Cusack, who hears the confession of a serial killer. What's worse is that the killer is preying on the women of Cusack's parish. Since he can't break the seal of the confessional, the good Father tries to stop the killer himself before another murder takes place. **1992 (PG-13) 93m/C** Christopher Reeve; **D:** Bradford May. **VHS, LV $89.98** *FXV* 🎬🎬

Mortal Thoughts Best friends find their relationship tested when the brutal husband of one of them is murdered. Moore and Headly are exceptional, capturing the perfect inflections and attitudes of the hard-working New Jersey beauticians sure of their friendship. Excellent pacing, fine supporting cast, with Keitel and Willis stand-outs. **1991 (R) 104m/C** Demi Moore, Bruce Willis, Glenne Headly, Harvey Keitel, John Pankow, Billie Neal; **D:** Alan Rudolph. **VHS, Beta, LV, 8mm $19.95** *COL* 🎬🎬 ½

Mortuary Young woman's nightmares come startlingly close to reality.
1981 (R) 91m/C Christopher George, Lynda Day George, Paul Smith; *D:* Howard Avedis. **VHS, Beta** $79.98 *LIV, VES* ✗

Mortuary Academy To win an inheritance two brothers must attend the family mortician school, a situation paving the way for aggressively tasteless jokes on necrophilia. An attempt to recapture the successful black humor of the earlier Bartel/Woronov teaming ''Eating Raoul,'' this one's dead on arrival.
1991 (R) 86m/C Christopher Atkins, Perry Lang, Paul Bartel, Mary Woronov, Tracy Walter, Lynn Danielson, Cesar Romero, Wolfman Jack; *D:* Michael Schroeder. **VHS, LV** $79.95 *COL* ✗

Mosby's Marauders A young boy joins a Confederate raiding company during the Civil War and learns about bravery, war, and love.
1966 79m/C Kurt Russell, James MacArthur, Jack Ging, Peggy Lipton, Nick Adams; *D:* Michael O'Herlihy. **VHS, Beta** $69.95 *DIS* ✗✗

Moscow Does Not Believe in Tears Three Soviet women realize very different fates when they pursue their dreams in 1950's Moscow. Bittersweet, moving fare that seems a somewhat surprising production from pre-Glasnost USSR. Brief nudity and violence. In Russian with English subtitles. *AKA:* Moscow Distrusts Tears; Moskwa Sljesam Nje Jerit.
1980 115m/C *RU* Vera Alentova, Irina Muravyova, Raisa Ryazanova, Natalie Vavilova, Alexei Batalov; *D:* Vladimir Menshov. **VHS, Beta, LV** $59.95 *COL, IME, TAM* ✗✗✗

Moscow on the Hudson Good-natured comedy has Williams as Soviet defector trying to cope with new life of freedom in fast-paced, freewheeling melting pot of New York City. Williams is particularly winning as naive jazzman, though Alonso also scores as his Hispanic love interest. Be warned though, it's not just played for laughs.
1984 (R) 115m/C Robin Williams, Maria Conchita Alonso, Cleavant Derricks, Alejandro Rey, Elya Baskin; *D:* Paul Mazursky **VHS, Beta, LV, 8mm** $14.95 *COL* ✗✗✗

Moses Lancaster goes biblical as Moses, the man with the tablets. Edited from the 360-minute British television series, with no improvement obvious from the economy, except that the bad parts are shorter. Poor chatter and scattered bouts of acting are surpassed in inadequacy only by special effects. Screenplay by Anthony Burgess and Vittorio Bonicelli.
1976 (PG) 141m/C Burt Lancaster, Anthony Quayle, Ingrid Thulin, Irene Papas, William Lancaster; *D:* Gianfranco DeBosio; *M:* Ennio Morricone. **VHS, Beta** $19.98 *FOX* Woof!

The Mosquito Coast Ambitious adaptation of Paul Theroux's novel about an asocial inventor who transplants his family to a rainforest to realize his utopian dream. A nightmare ensues. Ford tries hard, but supporters Mirren and Phoenix are main appeal of only intermittently successful drama. Written by Paul Schrader.
1986 (PG) 119m/C Harrison Ford, Helen Mirren, River Phoenix, Andre Gregory, Martha Plimpton, Conrad Roberts, Butterfly McQueen, Adrian Steele, Hilary Gordon, Rebecca Gordon, Dick O'Neill; *D:* Peter Weir. **VHS, Beta, LV** $19.98 *WAR* ✗✗½

The Most Dangerous Game Shipwrecked McRae washed ashore on the island of Banks's Count Zaroff, a deranged sportsman with a flair for tracking humans. Guess who becomes the mad count's next target. Oft-told tale is compellingly related in

this, the first of many using Richard Connell's famous short story. If deja vu sets in, don't worry. This production uses most of the scenery, staff, and cast from its studio cousin, ''King Kong.'' Remade in 1945 as ''A Game of Death'' and in 1956 as ''Run for the Sun.'' *AKA:* The Hounds of Zaroff.
1932 78m/B Joel McCrea, Fay Wray, Leslie Banks, Robert Armstrong; *D:* Ernest B. Schoedsack, Irving Pichel. **VHS, Beta, 3/4U, Special order formats** $16.95 *SNC, NOS, MED* ✗✗✗

Most Wanted A psychopath with a penchant for raping nuns and collecting crucifixes is tracked down by a special police unit in this made-for-television film. Became a TV series.
1976 78m/C Robert Stack, Shelly Novack, Leslie Charleson, Tom Selleck, Sheree North; *D:* Walter Grauman. **VHS, Beta** $49.95 *WOV* ✗½

Motel Hell A completely tongue-in-cheek gore-fest about a farmer who kidnaps tourists, buries them in his garden, and reaps a human harvest to grind into his distinctive brand of smoked, preservative-free sausage.
1980 (R) 102m/C Rory Calhoun, Nancy Parsons, Paul Linke, Nina Axelrod, Wolfman Jack, Elaine Joyce, Dick Curtis; *D:* Kevin Connor. **VHS, Beta, LV** $19.98 *MGM* ✗½

Mother Pudovkin's innovative classic about a Russian family shattered by the uprising in 1905. A masterpiece of Russian cinema that established Pudovkin, and rivaled only Eisenstein for supremacy in montage, poetic imagery, and propagandistic ideals. Based on Maxim Gorky's great novel, it's one of cinematic history's seminal works. Striking cinematography, stunning use of montage make this one important. Silent with English subtitles.
1926 70m/B *RU* Vera Baranovskaya, Nikolai Batalov; *D:* Vsevolod Pudovkin. **VHS, Beta, 3/4U** $24.95 *NOS, IHF, DVT* ✗✗✗½

Mother A Japanese family is undone after the devastation of WWII. An uncharacteristically dramatic, and thus more accessible, film from one of the Japanese cinema's greatest masters. In Japanese with English subtitles. *AKA:* Okasan.
1952 98m/B *JP* Kinuyo Tanaka, Kyoko Kagawa, Eiji Okada, Akihiko Katayama; *D:* Mikio Naruse. **VHS, Beta, LV** $49.00 *SVS, FCT, IME* ✗✗✗½

Mother & Daughter: A Loving War A made-for-television film about three women experiencing motherhood. Special appearance by Harry Chapin as himself.
1980 96m/C Tuesday Weld, Frances Sternhagen, Kathleen Beller, Jeanne Lang, Ed Winter; *D:* Burt Brinckerhoff. **VHS, Beta** $59.98 *NLC* ✗½

Mother Doesn't Always Know Best A strange relationship between a young count and his widowed mother initiates a strange series of events.
1967 95m/C Senta Berger; *D:* Alfredo Gianelli. **VHS, Beta** *NO* ✗½

Mother Goose Rock 'n' Rhyme Duvall follows the success of her ''Faerie Tale Theatre'' series with a new comedic fable, starring some of Hollywood's top names. Great fun for the whole family.
1990 96m/C Shelley Duvall, Teri Garr, Howie Mandel, Jean Stapleton, Ben Vereen, Bobby Brown, Art Garfunkel, Dan Gilroy, Deborah Harry, Cyndi Lauper, Little Richard, Paul Simon, Stray Cats, ZZ Top, Harry Anderson, Elayne Boosler, Woody Harrelson, Cheech Marin, Garry Shandling. **VHS, Beta** $79.98 *MED* ✗½

Mother, Jugs and Speed Black comedy about the day-to-day tragedies encountered by a group of ambulance drivers. Interesting mix of stars.

1976 (PG) 95m/C Bill Cosby, Raquel Welch, Harvey Keitel, Allen Garfield, Larry Hagman, Bruce Davison, Dick Butkus, L.Q. Jones, Toni Basil; *D:* Peter Yates. **VHS** $79.98 *FOX* ✗✗½

Mother Kusters Goes to Heaven Mrs. Kusters's husband is a frustrated factory worker who goes over the edge and kills the factory owner's son and himself. Left alone, she learns that everyone is using her husband's death to further their own needs, including her daughter, who uses the publicity to enhance her singing career. A statement that you should trust no one, not even your family and friends. This film was banned from the Berlin Film Festival because of its political overtones. In German with English subtitles. *AKA:* Mutter Kusters Fahrt Zum Himmel.
1976 108m/C *GE* Brigitte Mira, Ingrid Caven, Armin Meier, Irm Hermann, Gottfried John, Margit Carstensen; *W/D:* Rainer Werner Fassbinder. **VHS** $79.95 *NYF* ✗✗✗

Mother Lode The violent conflict between twin brothers (played by Heston) is intensified by greed, near madness, and the all-consuming lust for gold in this action-adventure. Heston's son, Fraser Clarke Heston, wrote as well as produced the film. *AKA:* Search for the Mother Lode; The Last Great Treasure.
1982 (PG) 101m/C Charlton Heston, Nick Mancuso; *D:* Charlton Heston. **VHS, Beta** $79.95 *VES* ✗½

Mother of Kings Livin' ain't easy for a widowed charwoman thanks to WWII and Stalinism. Innovative use of newsreel scenes. In Polish with English subtitles.
1982 126m/C *PL* Magda Teresa Wojcik. **VHS** $49.99 *FCT* ✗✗

Mother's Day Three women who were former college roommates plan a reunion together in the wilderness. All goes well until they are dragged into an isolated house by two insane boys who constantly watch television, ardently consume the products advertised, and then terrorize and torture people to please their mom. Sanitized gore with black satiric intentions. Co-written by Warren D. Leight.
1980 98m/C Tiana Pierce, Nancy Hendrickson, Deborah Luee, Holden McGuire, Billy Ray McQuade, Rose Ross; *W/D:* Charles Kaufman. **VHS, Beta** $49.95 *MED* ✗½

Mothra Classic Japanese monster shenanigans about an enraged giant caterpillar that invades Tokyo while searching for the Alilenas, a set of very tiny, twin princesses who've been kidnapped by an evil nightclub owner in the pursuit of big profits. After tiring of crushing buildings and wreaking incidental havoc, the enormous crawly thing zips up into a cocoon and emerges as Mothra, a moth distinguished by both its size and bad attitude. Mothra and the wee babes make appearances in later Godzilla epics.
1962 101m/C *JP* Yumi Ito, Frankie Sakai, Lee Kresel, Emi Ito; *D:* Inoshiro Honda. **VHS, Beta** $9.95 *GKK* ✗✗✗

Motor Patrol A cop poses as a racketeer to infiltrate a car-stealing ring.
1950 66m/B Don Castle, Jane Nigh, Charles Victor. **VHS, Beta, LV** *NO* ✗½

Motor Psycho When a motorcycle gang rapes a woman, she and her husband pursue them into the desert to seek their brutal revenge.
1965 73m/B Haji, Alex Rocco, Stephen Oliver, Holle K. Winters, Joseph Cellini, Thomas Scott, Coleman Francis, Sharon Lee; *D:* Russ Meyer. **VHS** *RMF* ✗½

Motorama A 10-year-old juvenile delinquent becomes obsessed with winning a gas station contest which involves collecting game cards. So he steals a car and hits the road where he gets his first tattoo and encounters a beautiful "older" woman (Barrymore) and lots of trouble.
1991 (R) 89m/C Jordan Christopher Michael, Martha Quinn, Flea, Michael J. Pollard, Meatloaf, Drew Barrymore, Garrett Morris, Robin Duke, Sandy Baron, Mary Woronov, Susan Tyrrell, John Laughlin, John Diehl, Robert Picardo, Jack Nance, Vince Edwards, Dick Miller, Allyce Beasley; **D:** Barry Shils; **W:** Joe Minion; **M:** Andy Summers. **VHS $89.95** COL, BTV ✗✗

Motorcycle Gang It's the summer of '57, and Randy plans to bring home the title at the Pacific Motorcycle Championships for his club, the "Skyriders." But first his old rival Nick, who's just out of jail, turns up and challenges Randy to an illegal street race. Will Randy succumb to peer pressure and race? Lame plot + lame acting = lame movie.
1957 78m/B Steven Terrell, John Ashley, Anne Neyland, Carl "Alfalfa" Switzer, Raymond Hatton; **D:** Edward L. Cahn; **W:** Lou Rusoff. **VHS $9.95** COL ✗

Motorcycle Squad A policeman is dishonorably discharged so he can get the "inside" dope on a gang of crooks in this 'B' thriller.
1937 ?m/C Kane Richmond, Wynne Gibson. **VHS $16.95** SNC ✗½

Motown's Mustang Eleven old Motown hits are used as the framework for this new musical drama featuring cameos by various artists, about a '64 Mustang passing through various owners' hands and cultural changes.
1986 43m/C Clyde Jones, Christi Shay, Louis Carr Jr., Billy Preston, The Temptations. **VHS, Beta, LV $19.95** MCA ✗½

Mouchette A lonely 14-year-old French girl, daughter of a drunk father and dying mother, eventually finds spiritual release by committing suicide. Typically somber, spiritual fare from unique master filmmaker Bresson. Perhaps the most complete expression of Bresson's austere, Catholic vision. In French with English subtitles.
1960 80m/B FR Nadine Nortier, Maria Cardinal, Paul Hebert; **D:** Robert Bresson. **VHS, Beta $59.95** FCT, TAM ✗✗✗½

Moulin Rouge Colorful, entertaining portrait of acclaimed Impressionist painter Toulouse-Lautrec, more famous for its production stories than on-screen drama, Ferrer delivers one of his most impressive performances as the physically stunted, cynical artist who basked in the seamy Montmartre nightlife.
1952 119m/C Jose Ferrer, Zsa Zsa Gabor, Christopher Lee, Peter Cushing, Colette Marchand, Katherine Kath, Michael Balfour, Eric Pohlmann; **D:** John Huston. Academy Awards '52: Best Art Direction/Set Decoration (Color), Best Costume Design (Color); Nominations: Best Actor (Ferrer), Best Director (Huston), Best Film Editing, Best Picture, Best Supporting Actress (Marchand); National Board of Review Awards '53: 5 Best Foreign Films of the Year. **VHS, Beta, LV $19.95** MGM ✗✗✗½

The Mountain A man and his shady younger brother set out to inspect a Paris-routed plane that crashed in the French Alps. After some harrowing experiences in climbing the peak, it becomes evident that one brother has designs to save whatever he can, while the other intends to loot it. Many real, as well as staged, climbing scenes. Based on Henri Troyat's novel.

1956 105m/C Spencer Tracy, Robert Wagner, Claire Trevor, William Demarest, Richard Arlen, E.G. Marshall; **D:** Edward Dmytryk. **VHS, Beta $19.95** PAR ✗✗

Mountain Charlie Mountain girl's life is destroyed by three drifters.
1980 96m/C Denise Neilson, Dick Robinson, Rick Guinn, Lynn Seus; **D:** George Stapleford. **VHS, Beta** NO ✗½

Mountain Family Robinson An urban family, seeking escape from the hassles of city life, moves to the Rockies, determined to get back to nature. They soon find that nature may be more harsh than rush-hour traffic and nasty bosses when a bear comes calling. More "Wilderness Family"-type adventures.
1979 (G) 102m/C Robert F. Logan, Susan Damante Shaw, Heather Rattray, Ham Larsen, William Bryant, George Flower; **D:** John Cotter. **VHS, Beta $9.98** MED ✗✗

Mountain Fury A spoof based on the novel by Alexandre Dumas wherein two brothers separated at birth are reunited and battle against an evil French baron.
1990 (R) 90m/C VHS NO ✗✗

Mountain Man Historically accurate drama about Galen Clark's successful fight in the 1860s to save the magnificent wilderness area that is now Yosemite National Park. Together with naturalist John Muir, he fought a battle against the lumber companies who wanted the timber and won President Lincoln's support for his cause. **AKA:** Guardian of the Wilderness.
1977 96m/C Denver Pyle, John Dehner, Ken Berry, Cheryl Miller, Don Shanks, Cliff Osmond, Jack Kruschen, Ford Rainey; **W/D:** David O'Malley. **VHS, Beta** LME ✗✗½

The Mountain Men Dull adventure drama set in the American West of the 1880s. Two trappers argue about life and have trouble with Indians.
1980 (R) 102m/C Charlton Heston, Brian Keith, John Glover, Seymour Cassel, Victor Jory; **D:** Richard Lang. **VHS, Beta, LV $9.95** COL ✗½

The Mountain Road Listless drama of an American squadron stationed in China during the last days of WWII. Only Stewart makes this drab film worthwhile.
1960 102m/B James Stewart, Harry Morgan, Glenn Corbett, Mike Kellin; **D:** Daniel Mann. **VHS $14.99** COL ✗½

Mountains of the Moon Sprawling adventure detailing the obsessive search for the source of the Nile conducted by famed Victorian rogue/explorer Sir Richard Burton and cohort John Hanning Speke in the late 1800s. Spectacular scenery and images. Director Rafelson, better known for overtly personal films such as "Five Easy Pieces" and "The King of Marvin Gardens," shows considerable skill with this epic. Cinematography by Roger Deakins. From William Harrison's novel "Burton and Speke."
1990 (R) 140m/C Patrick Bergin, Iain Glen, Fiona Shaw, Richard E. Grant, Peter Vaughan, Roger Rees, Bernard Hill, Anna Massey, Leslie Phillips; **D:** Bob Rafelson. **VHS, Beta, LV $89.95** LIV ✗✗✗½

Mountaintop Motel Massacre A resort motel's hostess is a raving lunatic who regularly slaughters her guests.
1986 (R) 95m/C Bill Thurman, Anna Chappell, Will Mitchell; **D:** Jim McCullough. **VHS, Beta $19.95** STE, NWV Woof!

Mouse and His Child A gentle animated fantasy adventure about a toy wind-up mouse and his child who fall into the clutches of a villainous rat when they venture into the outside world.

1977 83m/C **D:** Fred Wolf; **V:** Peter Ustinov, Cloris Leachman, Andy Devine. **VHS, Beta $19.95** COL, WTA ✗✗

The Mouse That Roared With its wine export business going down the drain, a tiny, desperate country decides to declare war on the United States in hopes that the U.S., after its inevitable triumph, will revive the conquered nation. So off to New York go 20 chain-mail clad warriors armed with bow and arrow. Featured in three roles, Sellers is great as the duchess, less effective (though still funny) as the prime minister, and a military leader. A must for Sellers' fans; maintains a sharp satiric edge throughout. Based on the novel by Leonard Wibberley.
1959 83m/C GB Peter Sellers, Jean Seberg, Leo McKern; **D:** Jack Arnold. **VHS, Beta $19.95** COL ✗✗✗

Movers and Shakers An irreverent spoof of Hollywood depicting a filmmaker's attempt to render a best-selling sex manual into a blockbuster film. Written and co-produced by Charles Grodin, the film fails to live up to its potential and wastes a star-studded cast.
1985 (PG) 100m/C Walter Matthau, Charles Grodin, Gilda Radner, Vincent Gardenia, Bill Macy, Tyne Daly, Steve Martin, Penny Marshall, Luana Anders; **D:** William Asher; **W:** Charles Grodin. **VHS, Beta $79.95** MGM ✗½

The Movie House Massacre A psychopath runs rampant in a theatre killing and maiming moviegoers. No refunds are given.
1978 80m/C Mary Woronov. **VHS, Beta $24.95** AHV, MRV ✗

Movie Maker A young filmmaker ineptly raises money for his next film. **AKA:** Smart Alec.
1986 87m/C Zsa Zsa Gabor, Antony Alda, Orson Bean, Bill Henderson; **D:** Jim Wilson. **VHS, Beta $79.98** LIV ✗

Movie, Movie Acceptable spoof of 1930s films features Scott in twin-bill of black and white "Dynamite Hands," which lampoons boxing dramas, and "Baxter's Beauties," a color send-up of Busby Berkeley musicals. There's even a parody of coming attractions. Wholesome, mildly entertaining.
1978 (PG) 107m/B Stanley Donen, George C. Scott, Trish Van Devere, Eli Wallach, Red Buttons, Barbara Harris, Barry Bostwick, Harry Hamlin, Art Carney; **D:** Stanley Donen. **VHS** FOX ✗✗½

A Movie Star's Daughter The daughter of a famous movie star moves to a new town and school. She is afraid her popularity is due to her famous father. She must make choices and learn the real meaning of friendship. Also available in a 33-minute edited version.
1979 46m/C Frank Converse, Trini Alvarado; **D:** Robert Fuest. **VHS, Beta, 3/4U $14.95** LCA ✗✗½

Movie Struck Originally released as "Pick a Star," this Hollywood behind-the-scenes story of a girl waiting for her big break features guest appearances by Laurel and Hardy.
1937 70m/B Stan Laurel, Oliver Hardy, Jack Haley, Patsy Kelly, Rosina Lawrence; **D:** Edward Sedgwick. **VHS, Beta, 3/4U, Special order formats $19.95** NOS, CAB, VYY ✗½

Movie Stuntmen A retired Hollywood stunt man takes a job for a dead friend so that the friend's widow can receive the fee. Good stunt work taken mostly from old Richard Taldmadge movies almost makes up for poor production. **AKA:** Hollywood Thrillmakers; Hollywood Stunt Man.

1953 56m/B James Gleason, William Henry; **D:** Bernard B. Ray. VHS $19.95 NOS *�*

Movie...In Your Face Japanese mobsters want to take over a movie studio. This supposed comedy comes with a "PU-13" rating—"Stinks to anyone with an I.Q. over 13," make of that what you will and be forewarned that it's also deliberatley sophomoric and tasteless.
1990 85m/C Tommy Sledge. VHS $89.95 HTV *�I*

Moving An engineer must relocate his family from New Jersey to Idaho in order to get his dream job. Predictable calamities ensue. Not apt to move you.
1988 (R) 89m/C Richard Pryor, Randy Quaid, Dana Thomas, Dave Thomas, Rodney Dangerfield, Stacey Dash; **D:** Alan Metter. VHS, Beta, LV, 8mm $19.98 WAR *�I*

Moving Out Adolescent migrant Italian boy finds it difficult to adjust to his new surroundings in Melbourne, Australia.
1983 91m/C Vince Colosimo, Sally Cooper, Maurice Devincentis, Tibor Gyapjas; **D:** Michael Pattinson. VHS, Beta $69.95 VID *�II*

Moving Target A young woman witnesses the brutal murder of her boyfriend by mobsters and flees to Florida. Unbeknownst to her, the thugs are still after her. Although top-billed, Blair's role is actually a supporting one.
1989 (R) 85m/C *IT* Linda Blair, Ernest Borgnine, Stuart Whitman, Charles Pitt, Jainine Linde, Kurt Woodruff; **D:** Marius Mattei. VHS, Beta $14.95 HMD *�II½*

Moving Targets A young girl and her mother find themselves tracked by a homicidal maniac.
1987 95m/C *AU* Michael Aitkens, Carmen Duncan, Annie Jones, Shane Briant; **D:** Chris Langman. VHS, Beta $29.95 ACA *�II*

Moving Violation Crooked cops chase two young drifters who have witnessed the local sheriff commit a murder. Corman car chase epic.
1976 (PG) 91m/C Eddie Albert, Kay Lenz, Stephen McHattie, Will Geer, Loni Chapman; **D:** Charles S. Dubin. VHS, Beta, LV $59.98 FOX *�II*

Moving Violations This could be entitled "Adventures in Traffic Violations School." A wise-cracking tree planter is sent to traffic school after accumulating several moving violations issued to him by a morose traffic cop. Bill Murray's little brother in feature role.
1985 (PG-13) 90m/C John Murray, Jennifer Tilly, James Keach, Brian Backer, Sally Kellerman, Fred Willard, Clara Peller, Wendie Jo Sperber; **D:** Neal Israel. VHS, Beta, LV $79.98 FOX *�I*

Mozart: A Childhood Chronicle An experimental, semi-narrative portrait of the immortal composer, from the ages of seven to twenty, filmed on authentic locations and with the original instruments of the era. Entire soundtrack is composed of Mozart's music. In German with English subtitles.
1976 224m/B *GE* **D:** Klaus Kirschner. VHS, Beta, LV $99.95 KIV, IME, GLV *�III*

The Mozart Brothers An angst-ridden Swedish opera director decides to break all the rules while doing an innovative production of Mozart's "Don Giovanni." At first he horrifies his conservative opera company but as his vision is gradually realized their resistance breaks down. A wonderful look at behind-the-scenes chaos and not just for opera aficionados. In Swedish with English subtitles.

1986 111m/C *SW* Etienne Glaser, Philip Zanden, Henry Bronett; **D:** Suzanne Osten. VHS TAM *�III*

The Mozart Story After Mozart's death, music minister to the Emperor, Antonio Salieri, reflects on how his jealousy and hatred of the musical genius held the great composer back and contributed to his death. Originally filmed in Austria in 1937, scenes were added for the U.S. release in 1948.
1948 91m/B Hans Holt, Winnie Markus, Irene von Meyendorf, Rene Deltgen, Edward Vedder, Wilton Graff, Walther Jansson, Curt Jurgens, Paul Hoerbiger; **D:** Karl Hartl. VHS, Beta $24.95 VYY, GLV *�II*

Ms. 45 Rough, bristling cult favorite about a mute girl who, in response to being raped and beaten twice in one night, goes on a man-killing murder spree. Wild ending. *AKA:* Angel of Vengeance.
1981 (R) 84m/C Zoe Tamerlis, Steve Singer, Jack Thibeau, Peter Yellen, Darlene Stuto, Editta Sherman, Albert Sinkys, Jimmy Laine; **D:** Abel Ferrara. VHS, Beta, LV $49.95 LIV *�III*

Much Ado About Nothing Shakespeare for the masses details romance between two sets of would-be lovers—the battling Beatrice and Benedick (Thompson and Branagh) and the ingenuous Hero and Claudio (Beckinsdale and Leonard). Washington is the noble warrior leader, Reeves his evil half-dressed half-brother, and Keaton serves comic relief as the officious, bumbling Dogberry. Enthusiastic and invigorating action and acting by all the principles with Reeves cutting the proper menacing figure with a minimal amount of dialogue. Sunlit, lusty, and revealing about all the vagaries of love, with Branagh bringing passion to his quest of making Shakespeare more approachable. "Much Ado," like his earlier "Henry V," breaks tradition and succeeds by bringing the characters to life as real people rather than stiff and stuffy characters. Filmed on location in Tuscany, Italy.
1993 (PG-13) 110m/C *GB* Kenneth Branagh, Emma Thompson, Robert Sean Leonard, Kate Beckinsale, Denzel Washington, Keanu Reeves, Michael Keaton, Brian Blessed, Phyllida Law, Imelda Staunton, Gerard Horan, Jimmy Yuill, Richard Clifford, Ben Elton; **D:** Kenneth Branagh; **M:** Patrick Doyle. VHS NYR *�III½*

Mugsy's Girls A messy comedy about six sorority women, educated in the refined skills of bar mud wrestling, who wallow in a Las Vegas championship tournament. Features pop singer Laura Branigan. *AKA:* Delta Pi.
1985 (R) 87m/C Ruth Gordon, Laura Branigan, Eddie Deezen; **D:** Kevin Brodie. VHS, Beta $79.98 LIV, VES *�I*

Multiple Maniacs Waters at his most perverse. Divine's travelling freak show, filled with disgusting side-show sex acts, is the vehicle used for robbing and killing hapless spectators. One of the best scenes of a sordid lot is Divine being raped by Lobstora, a 15-foot broiled lobster.
1970 90m/B Divine, David Lochary, Mary Vivian Pearce, Edith Massey, Mink Stole; **D:** John Waters. VHS $39.98 CGH *�I*

The Mummy Eerie chills mark this classic horror tale of an Egyptian priest, buried alive nearly 4000 years earlier, who comes back to life after a 1921 archeological dig. Eight hours of extraordinary makeup transformed Karloff into the macabre mummy, who believes the soul of the long-deceased (and probably long-decayed) lover resides in the body of a young woman. Marked the directing debut of famed German cinematographer Freund.

1932 72m/B Boris Karloff, Zita Johann, David Manners, Edward Van Sloan; **D:** Karl Freund. VHS, Beta, LV $14.95 MCA, TLF *�III½*

The Mummy A group of British archaeologists discover they have made a grave mistake when a mummy kills off those who have violated his princess' tomb. A summation of all the previous "mummy" films, this one has a more frightening mummy (6'4" Lee) who is on screen much of the time. Additionally, there is pathos in this monster, not merely murder and revenge. An effective remake of the 1932 classic.
1959 88m/C *GB* Peter Cushing, Christopher Lee, Felix Aylmer, Yvonne Furneaux; **D:** Terence Fisher. VHS, Beta, LV $14.95 WAR, MLB *�III*

Mummy & Curse of the Jackal Upon opening the tomb of female mummy, a man is cursed to roam the streets of Las Vegas as a werejackal. Impossibly inept.
1967 86m/C Anthony Eisley, Martina Pons, John Carradine, Saul Goldsmith; **D:** Oliver Drake. VHS $19.95 ACA *Woof!*

The Mummy's Hand Two archaeologists (Foran and Ford) searching for the tomb of ancient Egyptian Princess Ananka discover more than they bargained for when they find that an evil and deadly mummy is the tomb's guardian. From there the plot unravels, but the good cast and a mix of scares and comedy make this worth watching.
1940 70m/B Dick Foran, Wallace Ford, Peggy Moran, Cecil Kellaway, George Zucco, Tom Tyler, Eduardo Ciannelli, Charles Trowbridge; **D:** Christy Cabanne. VHS $14.98 MCA *�II½*

The Mummy's Revenge A fanatic revives a mummy with virgin blood. The first mummy movie to feature open gore.
1973 91m/C *SP* Paul Naschy, Jack Taylor, Maria Silva, Helga Line; **D:** Carlos Aured; **W:** Paul Naschy. VHS, Beta $49.95 UNI *�I*

Munchie A forgotten alien critter is discovered in a mine shaft by young Gage. Munchie turns out to be a good friend, protecting Gage from bullies and granting other wishes. Frequent sight gags help keep the film moving but it's still awfully slow. Sequel to "Munchies" (1987).
1992 (PG) 80m/C Loni Anderson, Andrew Stevens, Arte Johnson, Jamie McEnnan; **D:** Jim Wynorski; **V:** Dom DeLuise. VHS $89.98 NHO *�I½*

Munchies "Gremlins" rip-off about tiny aliens who love beer and fast food, and invade a small town. Lewd and ribald.
1987 (PG) 83m/C Harvey Korman, Charles Stratton, Nadine Van Der Velde; **D:** Bettina Hirsch. VHS, Beta $14.98 MGM *�I*

Munster's Revenge Television movie based on the continuing adventures of the 1960s comedy series characters. Herman, Lily, and Grandpa have to contend with robot replicas of themselves that were created by a flaky scientist.
1981 96m/C Fred Gwynne, Yvonne De Carlo, Al Lewis, Jo McDonnel, Sid Caesar, Ezra Stone, Howard Morris, Bob Hastings, K.C. Martel; **D:** Don Weis. VHS, Beta $14.98 MCA *�II*

The Muppet Christmas Carol Christmas classic features all the muppet favorites together and in Victorian garb. Gonzo the Great as Dickens narrates the tale as Scrooge (Caine) takes his legendary Christmas Eve journey escorted by three (flannel) spirits. Directed by Brian Henson, Jim's son, the film is as heartwarming as the Cratchit's crackling fire, but doesn't quite achieve the former muppet magic. Also features some sappy songs by Williams.

1992 (G) 120m/C Michael Caine; *D:* Brian Henson; *M:* Paul Williams; *V:* Dave Goelz, Steve Whitmire, Jerry Nelson, Frank Oz. VHS, LV $22.99 DIS ♪♪♪

The Muppet Movie Seeking fame and footlights, Kermit the Frog and his pal Fozzie Bear travel to Hollywood, and along the way are joined by sundry human and muppet characters, including the lovely Miss Piggy. A delightful cult favorite filled with entertaining cameos, memorable (though somewhat pedestrian) songs and crafty special effects—Kermit rides a bike and rows a boat! A success for the late Jim Henson. ♫The Rainbow Connection; Frog's Legs So Fine; Movin Right Along; Can You Picture That?; Never Before; Something Better; This Looks Familiar; I'm Going Back There Someday.
1979 (G) 94m/C *GB* Jim Henson's Muppets; *Cameos:* Edgar Bergen, Milton Berle, Mel Brooks, Madeline Kahn, Steve Martin, Carol Kane, Paul Williams, Charles Durning, Bob Hope, James Coburn, Dom DeLuise, Elliott Gould, Cloris Leachman, Telly Savalas, Orson Welles; *D:* James Frawley; *V:* Jim Henson, Frank Oz. VHS, Beta, LV $22.99 JHV, FOX ♪♪♪½

Muppets Take Manhattan Following a smashing success with a college musical, the Muppets take their show and talents to Broadway, only to face misfortune in the form of an unscrupulous producer. A less imaginative script than the first two Muppet movies, yet an enjoyable experience with numerous major stars making cameo appearances.
1984 (G) 94m/C Jim Henson's Muppets; *Cameos:* Dabney Coleman, James Coco, Art Carney, Joan Rivers, Gregory Hines, Linda Lavin, Liza Minnelli, Brooke Shields, John Landis; *D:* Frank Oz; *V:* Jim Henson, Frank Oz. VHS, Beta, LV $14.98 FOX, HMV ♪♪♪

Murder Believing in a young woman's innocence, one jurist begins to organize the pieces of the crime in order to save her. Fine early effort by Hitchcock based on play "Enter Sir John," by Clemense Dane and Helen Simpson.
1930 92m/B *GB* Herbert Marshall, Nora Baring, Phyllis Konstam, Miles Mander; *D:* Alfred Hitchcock. VHS, Beta, 3/4U, Special order formats $16.95 SNC, NOS, HHT ♪♪♪

Murder Ahoy Miss Marple looks perplexed when dead bodies surface on a naval cadet training ship. Dame Marge is the dottie detective in the final, and least appealing, of her four Agatha Christie films of the sixties (although it was released in the States prior to "Murder Most Foul").
1964 74m/B Margaret Rutherford, Lionel Jeffries, Charles Tingwell, William Mervyn, Francis Matthews; *D:* George Pollock; *W:* Agatha Christie. VHS, Beta $19.98 MGM, FCT ♪♪½

Murder at 45 R.P.M. A singer and her lover suspect each other of her husband's murder. Things become sticky when she receives a recorded message from her dead husband. Average. *AKA:* Meurtre en 45 Tours.
1965 98m/C *FR* Danielle Darrieux, Michel Auclair, Jean Servais, Henri Guisol; *D:* Etienne Perier. VHS $16.95 SNC ♪♪

Murder at Midnight The killings begin with a game of charades in which the gun wasn't supposed to be loaded, and continue as members of English high society die one by one. "Blondie" director Strayer still working on his change of pace.
1931 69m/B Alice White, Leslie Fenton, Aileen Pringle, Hale Hamilton, Robert Elliott, Clara Blandick, Brandon Hurst; *D:* Frank Strayer. VHS, Beta, 8mm $12.95 SNC, NOS, DVT ♪♪

Murder at the Baskervilles Sherlock Holmes is invited to visit Sir Henry Baskerville at his estate, but then finds that Baskerville's daughter's fiance is accused of stealing a race horse and murdering its keeper. Based on Sir Arthur Conan Doyle's story "Silver Blaze." *AKA:* Silver Blaze.
1937 67m/B *GB* Arthur Wontner, Ian Fleming, Lyn Harding; *D:* Thomas Bentley. VHS, Beta $16.95 SNC, CCB, REP ♪♪

Murder at the Gallop Snooping Miss Marple doesn't believe a filthy rich oldtimer died of natural causes, despite the dissenting police point of view. Wheedling her way into the police investigation, she discovers the secret of the Gallop club, a place where people bounce up and down on top of horses. Much mugging between Dame Margaret and Morley. Marple's assistant, Mr. Stringer, is the real life Mr. Dame Margaret. Based on Christy's Poirot mystery "After the Funeral."
1963 81m/B Margaret Rutherford, Robert Morley, Flora Robson, Charles Tingwell, Duncan Lamont; *D:* George Pollock; *W:* Agatha Christie. VHS, Beta $19.98 MGM, FCT ♪♪♪½

Murder at the Vanities Vintage murder mystery set against a musical revue format, in which a tough detective must find a killer before the Earl Carroll-based cabaret ends and he or she will escape with the exiting crowd. Also featured is a mind-boggling production number based on the song "Marijuana." ♫Marijuana; Lovely One; Where Do They Come From Now; Live and Love Tonight; Cocktails for Two; Ebony Rhapsody.
1934 91m/B Victor McLaglen, Kitty Carlisle, Jack Oakie, Duke Ellington, Carl Brisson; *D:* Mitchell Leisen. VHS, Beta $59.95 MCA ♪♪½

Murder by Death Capote is an eccentric millionaire who invites the world's greatest detectives to dinner, offering one million dollars to the one who can solve the evening's murder. Entertaining and hammy spoof of Agatha Christie's "And Then There Were None" and the earlier "Ten Little Indians."
1976 (PG) 95m/C Peter Falk, Alec Guinness, David Niven, Maggie Smith, Peter Sellers, Eileen Brennan, Elsa Lanchester, Nancy Walker, Estelle Winwood, Truman Capote, James Coco; *D:* Robert Moore; *W:* Neil Simon. VHS, Beta, LV $19.95 COL, TVC ♪♪½

Murder by Decree Realistic and convincing version of the Jack the Ripper story. Sherlock Holmes and Dr. Watson find a vast web of conspiracy when they investigate the murders of Whitechapel prostitutes. Based partially on facts, it's a highly detailed suspenser with interesting camera work and fine performances.
1979 (PG) 120m/C *CA* Christopher Plummer, James Mason, Donald Sutherland, Genevieve Bujold, Susan Clark, David Hemmings, Frank Finlay, John Gielgud, Anthony Quayle; *D:* Bob Clark. VHS, Beta $19.98 SUE, NLC ♪♪♪

Murder by Moonlight Rival agents investigate a mysterious murder in a prosperous mining colony on the moon. Not only do they discover a dastardly trail that leads all the way back to Earth, but a strange romantic attraction for each other. Originally broadcast on British TV.
1991 (PG-13) 94m/C *GB* Julian Sands, Brigitte Nielsen, Gerald McRaney, Jane Laputaine, Brian Cox; *D:* Michael Lindsay-Hogg. VHS $89.95 VMK ♪♪

Murder by Natural Causes A made-for-TV brain teaser in which a woman and her lover plot to kill her mind-reader husband. Lots of twists make this fun for viewers who enjoy a challenge.
1979 96m/C Hal Holbrook, Barry Bostwick, Katharine Ross, Richard Anderson; *D:* Robert Day. VHS, Beta NO ♪♪♪

Murder by Night Amnesia victim Urich is found next to a dead body, the result of a gruesome murder. Urich is the only witness and thinks he may be the next victim. Others think he's the killer. Made for cable mystery with enough twists to make it worthwhile.
1989 (PG-13) 95m/C Robert Urich, Kay Lenz, Jim Metzler, Richard Monette, Michael Ironside; *D:* Paul Lynch. VHS, Beta $79.95 MCA ♪♪½

Murder by Numbers Murder in the art world stumps a detective. What might have been a good suspense story is ruined by bad editing and a lack of continuity, resulting in confusion rather than suspense.
1989 (PG-13) 91m/C Sam Behrens, Shari Belafonte-Harper, Ronee Blakley, Stanley Kamel, Jayne Meadows, Debra Sandlund, Dick Sargent, Cleavon Little; *W/D:* Paul Leder. VHS, Beta, LV NO ♪½

Murder by Phone A deranged technician has turned his phone into an instrument of electronic death. Chamberlain is the visiting professor trying to discover who's permanently disconnecting the numbers of his students. Good cast decides to test schlock meter. *AKA:* Bells; The Calling.
1982 (R) 79m/C *CA* Richard Chamberlain, John Houseman, Sara Botsford; *D:* Michael Anderson Sr.; *M:* John Barry. VHS, Beta $19.98 WAR ♪♪

Murder by Television Low-budget murder mystery with Lugosi in a dual role as twins—one good, one not so. When a professor and the evil twin are murdered, the instrument of death suspected is...television. Still an exotic and misunderstood invention when this was made, TV sometimes invoked fear and suspicion in the general public. Historically interesting and Lugosi fans will appreciate seeing him in a non-vampiric role. *AKA:* The Houghland Murder Case.
1935 55m/B Bela Lugosi, George Meeker; *D:* Clifford Sandforth. VHS, Beta $24.95 NOS, SNC, VYY ♪½

Murder by the Book A mystery writer finds that his fictional character, a hard-boiled private eye, has taken control of his life. With his new macho persona the writer solves a crime and saves the obligatory dame. Based on the novel "Alter Ego" by Mel Arrighi. Made for television. *AKA:* Alter Ego.
1987 100m/C Robert Hays, Catherine Mary Stewart, Celeste Holm, Fred Gwynne, Christopher Murney; *D:* Mel Damski. VHS, Beta NO ♪♪½

Murder Elite A murdering maniac terrorizes the rural English countryside, where MacGraw has returned after losing all her money in America. Poor acting and direction make this one a dust-gatherer.
1986 98m/C Ali MacGraw, Billie Whitelaw, Hywel Bennett; *D:* Claude Whatham. VHS, Beta $69.98 LIV, VES ♪½

Murder for Sale Secret Agent 117 stages an elaborate scam in order to infiltrate a ring of terrorists and criminals. Ask for Bond next time.
1970 90m/C John Gavin, Margaret Lee, Curt Jurgens. VHS, Beta $59.95 MED ♪

Murder in Coweta County Griffith and Cash are strong in this true-crime drama based on the book by Margaret Anne Barnes. Griffith is a Georgia businessman

who thinks he's gotten away with murder; Cash is the lawman who tenaciously pursues him. Based on an actual 1948 case. Made for television.
1983 100m/C Johnny Cash, Andy Griffith, Earl Hindman, June Carter Cash, Cindi Knight, Ed Van Nuys; **D:** Gary Nelson. **VHS, Beta $39.95** LIV ✍✍½

Murder-in-Law Graphic slasher flick about a mother-in-law from hell who escapes from an insane asylum and terrorizes her son-in-law (Estevez) and his family in a series of gruesome killings.
1992 (R) 97m/C Marilyn Adams, Joe Estevez, Sandy Snyder, Darrel Guilbeau; **D:** Tony Jiti Gill. **VHS** MNC ✍

Murder in New Hampshire: The Pamela Smart Story A sleazy true story about a young high school teacher who seduces an impressionable student into murdering her husband. Hunt's fine as the seductress but this made-for-television fare is just average.
1991 (PG-13) 93m/C Helen Hunt, Chad Allen, Larry Drake, Howard Hesseman, Ken Howard, Michael Learned; **D:** Joyce Chopra. **VHS, Beta $89.98** TTC, PMS ✍✍½

Murder in Space Nine multinational astronauts are stranded aboard a space station when they discover one of them is a murderer. This creates anxiety, particularly since the killer's identity is unknown. Oatmeal salesman Brimley is the earth-bound mission control chief trying desperately to finger a spaceman while the bodies pile up. Made for television.
1985 95m/C Wilford Brimley, Martin Balsam, Michael Ironside; **D:** Steven Hilliard Stern. **VHS, Beta $79.95** VMK ✍✍

Murder in Texas Made for television docudrama looks at the strange but true events surrounding the death of society woman Joan Robinson Hill, first wife of prominent plastic surgeon, Dr. John Hill, and daughter of wealthy oilman Ash Robinson. Well-crafted script and effective performances keep your interest. Griffith was Emmy nominated. From the book "Prescription Murder," written by the doctor's second wife.
1981 200m/C Farrah Fawcett, Katharine Ross, Andy Griffith, Sam Elliott, Craig T. Nelson, Barbara Sammeth; **D:** William Hale. **VHS, Beta $59.95** VHE, HHE ✍✍✍

Murder in the Doll House Private detective must find out who is systematically killing off the family of a Japanese toy executive. With English subtitles.
1979 92m/C JP Yusaku Matsuda, Hiroko Shino, Yoko Nosaki. **VHS, Beta $59.95** VDA, AUD ✍½

Murder in the Footlights Murder drama involving a socialite and a vaudeville team.
1951 ?m/C GB Lesley Brook, David Hutcheson. **VHS $16.95** SNC ✍✍

Murder in the Old Red Barn Based on the real murder of an unassuming girl by a randy squire. Stiff, melodramatic performances are bad enough, but the playstyle production, unfamiliar to modern viewers, is the last nail in this one's coffin. **AKA:** Maria Marten.
1936 67m/B GB Tod Slaughter, Sophie Stewart, D.J. Williams, Eric Portman; **D:** Milton Rosmer. **VHS, Beta $16.95** NOS, MRV, SNC ✍

A Murder is Announced From the critically acclaimed BBC television series. While on holiday, super-sleuth Marple encounters a murder that was advertised in the local newspaper one week prior to its occurrence. Based on the 1952 Agatha Christie

novel, Hickson shines once again as Christie's detective extraordinaire.
1987 155m/C GB Joan Hickson; **D:** David Giles; **W:** Agatha Christie. **VHS, Beta $29.98** FOX, HMV ✍✍

Murder Mansion Some decent scares ensue when a group of travelers is stranded in an old haunted mansion.
1970 84m/C SP Evelyn Stewart, Analia Gade; **D:** Francisco Lara Polop. **VHS, Beta $59.98** UNI, SNC ✍½

Murder Masters of Kung Fu An evil student kills his kind master and then tries to seduce his beautiful, grieving daughter. But she's no sap and gives him more than he bargained for, including a healthy dose of vengeance.
1985 93m/C Yim Nam Hei, Tien Pang. **VHS, Beta $39.95** WWV ✍

Murder Most Foul Erstwhile school marm Dame Margaret is excellent as the only jury member to believe in the accused's innocence. Posing as a wealthy actress to insinuate herself into the local acting troupe, she sniffs out the true culprit. Based on the Poirot mystery "Mr. McGinty's Dead."
1965 90m/B Margaret Rutherford, Ron Moody, Charles Tingwell, Megs Jenkins, Dennis Price, Ralph Michael; **D:** George Pollock; **W:** Agatha Christie. **VHS, Beta $19.98** MGM, FCT ✍✍✍

Murder Motel Inept made-for-television spine-tingler about a motel keeper who makes a practice of killing his customers. There's always a vacancy at the Murder Motel, at least until the fiancee of one of his victims decides to look into the matter.
1974 80m/C Robyn Millan, Derek Francis, Ralph Bates, Edward Judd. **VHS, Beta $29.95** LIV ✍

Murder, My Sweet Down on his luck private detective Philip Marlowe (Powell) searches for an ex-convict's missing girl-friend through a dark world of murder, mayhem and ever-twisting directions. Classic film noir screen version of Raymond Chandler's tense novel "Farewell, My Lovely," which employs flashback fashion using that crisp Chandler narrative. A breakthrough dramatically for singer Powell; Chandler's favorite version. Remade using the novel's title in 1975. **AKA:** Farewell, My Love.
1944 95m/B Dick Powell, Claire Trevor, Mike Mazurki, Anne Shirley, Miles Mander; **D:** Edward Dmytryk. **VHS, Beta, LV $19.95** MED, CCB ✍✍✍½

Murder of a Moderate Man An Interpol agent sets out for the Alps to apprehend an assassin gunning down political leaders. A British-made effort based on a novel by John Howlett.
197? 165m/C GB Denis Quilley, Susan Fleetwood. **VHS $49.95** FCT, MOV ✍½

The Murder of Mary Phagan Lemmon stars as John Slaton, governor of Georgia during one of America's most notorious miscarriages of justice. In 1913, timid, Jewish factory manager Leo Frank is accused of the brutal murder of a female worker. Prejudice and a power hungry prosecuting attorney conspire to seal the man's fate at the end of the hangman's noose. Sensing the injustice, Slaton re-opens the case, causing riots in Atlanta. Top notch television drama, featuring a superb recreation of turn of the century atmosphere and a compelling, true story which was not finally resolved until the 1970s.
1987 (PG) 251m/C Jack Lemmon, Peter Gallagher, Richard Jordan, Robert Prosky, Paul Dooley, Rebecca Miller, Kathryn Walker, Charles S. Dutton, Kevin Spacey, Wendy J. Cooke; **D:** Billy Hale. **VHS $79.98** ORI ✍✍✍½

Murder on Approval Conway is a carbon-copy Sherlock Holmes, called in to verify the authenticity of a stamp and getting involved in murder. Slow-paced, weak and transparent. **AKA:** Barbados Quest.
1956 70m/B Tom Conway, Delphi Lawrence, Brian Worth, Michael Balfour, John Colicos; **D:** Bernard Knowles. **VHS $19.95** NOS ✍

Murder on Flight 502 A crisis arises on a 747 flight from New York to London when a terrorist runs amuck. Big cast of TV stars and Stack as the pilot keep this stale murder flick from getting lost in the ozone.
1975 97m/C Farrah Fawcett, Sonny Bono, Ralph Bellamy, Theodore Bikel, Dane Clark, Polly Bergen, Laraine Day, Fernando Lamas, George Maharis, Hugh O'Brian, Molly Picon, Walter Pidgeon, Robert Stack; **D:** George McCowan. **VHS, Beta $49.95** PSM ✍✍

Murder on Line One A London murderer films his crimes for his later viewing pleasure. The police arrest a suspect, but the killings continue. Both the police and viewer are soon aware that they've made a mistake.
1990 103m/C Emma Jacobs, Peter Blake, Simon Shepherd, Allan Surtees, Andrew Wilde, Dirkan Tulane, Neil Duncan, Brett Forrest; **D:** Anders Palm. **VHS, Beta $29.95** ACA, TTC ✍✍

Murder on the Bayou Down on the L'siana bayou, a white guy who thinks civil rights are color coded is murdered, and an elderly black man is accused of the crime. Made for TV, well performed, engaging. From the novel by Ernest J. Gaines. **AKA:** A Gathering of Old Men.
1991 (PG) 91m/C Louis Gossett Jr., Richard Widmark, Holly Hunter. **VHS, LV $89.95** VMK ✍✍✍

Murder on the Campus A reporter investigates the apparent suicide of his brother at Cambridge University. He discovers that a number of other mysterious deaths have occurred as well. Interesting characterizations hampered by predictability. **AKA:** Out of the Shadow.
1952 61m/B GB Terence Longden, Donald Gray, Diane Clare, Robertson Hare, Dermot Walsh; **W/D:** Michael Winner. **VHS, Beta $16.95** NOS, MRV, SNC ✍✍

Murder on the High Seas Infidelity and murder aboard a cruise ship.
1932 ?m/C Natalie Moorhead, Jack Mulhall. **VHS $16.95** SNC ✍✍

Murder on the Midnight Express Made-for-television mystery about spies, thieves, honeymooners and a corpse aboard an all-night train. All aboard.
1974 70m/C Judy Geeson, James Smilie, Charles Gray. **VHS, Beta $12.95** LIV ✍½

Murder on the Orient Express An Agatha Christie mystery lavishly produced with an all-star cast. In 1934, a trainful of suspects and one murder victim make the trip from Istanbul to Calais especially interesting. Super-sleuth Hercule Poirot sets out to solve the mystery. An entertaining whodunit, ably supported by the remarkable cast. Followed by "Death on the Nile."
1974 (PG) 128m/C GB Albert Finney, Martin Balsam, Ingrid Bergman, Lauren Bacall, Sean Connery, Richard Widmark, Anthony Perkins, John Gielgud, Jacqueline Bisset, Jean-Pierre Cassel, Wendy Hiller, Rachel Roberts, Vanessa Redgrave, Michael York, Colin Blakely, George Coulouris; **D:** Sidney Lumet; **W:** Agatha Christie. Academy Awards '74: Best Supporting Actress (Bergman); Nominations: Best Actor (Finney), Best Adapted Screenplay, Best Cinematography, Best Costume Design, Best Original Score; British Academy Awards '74: Best Supporting Actor (Gielgud), Best Supporting Actress (Bergman). **VHS, Beta, LV $69.95** PAR, BTV ✍✍✍

Murder on the Yukon An installment in the "Renfrew of the Royal Mounted" series. Newill and O'Brien's vacation plans are ruined when they find a corpse in a canoe and must investigate. Lots of action, but a somewhat threadbare production. Based on "Renfrew Rides North" by Lauri York Erskine.
1940 57m/B James Newill, Dave O'Brien, Polly Ann Young; **D:** Louis Grasnier. **VHS, Beta** $12.95 *VDM* ✂️½

Murder Once Removed A private eye discovers that a respectable doctor has a bedside manner that women are dying for. Made for television.
1971 74m/C John Forsythe, Richard Kiley, Barbara Bain, Joseph Campanella; **D:** Charles S. Dubin. **VHS, Beta** $59.95 *LHV* ✂️½

Murder One Two half-brothers escape from a Maryland prison and go on a killing spree, dragging their younger brother with them. Low-budget and it shows. Based on a true story.
1988 (R) 83m/C Henry Thomas, James Wilder, Stephen Shellan, Errol Slue; **D:** Graeme Campbell. **VHS, Beta, LV** $19.98 *SUE, NLC* ✂️

Murder 101 Brosnan plays Charles Lattimore, an author and English professor who specializes in murder mysteries. He gives his students a rather unique assignment of planning the perfect murder. When a student is killed right before his eyes and a fellow teacher turns up dead, Lattimore realizes he's being framed for murder. Surprising twists abound in this stylish thriller.
1991 (PG-13) 93m/C Pierce Brosnan, Dey Young, Raphael Sbarge, Kim Thomson; **D:** Bill Condon. **VHS** $89.98 *MCA* ✂️✂️

Murder or Mercy Still timely story of a famous doctor accused of killing his terminally ill wife. Focuses on the morality of mercy killing. Made for television.
1974 78m/C Melvyn Douglas, Bradford Dillman, David Birney, Denver Pyle, Mildred Dunnock; **D:** Harvey Hart. **VHS** $49.95 *WOV* ✂️✂️½

Murder Ordained Yet another true-crime network miniseries, this time about a Kansas minister and her lover plotting the demise of their spouses. Good acting for this sort of thing. In two-cassette package.
1987 183m/C Keith Carradine, JoBeth Williams, Terry Kinney, Guy Boyd, Terence Knox, Darrell Larson, M. Emmet Walsh, Kathy Bates; **D:** Mike Robe. **VHS** $79.95 *FRH* ✂️✂️½

Murder Over New York Episode in the Charlie Chan mystery series. Chan visits New York City and becomes involved in an investigation at the airport. With the aid of his klutzy son, he sleuths his way through a slew of suspects until the mystery is solved. Standard fare for the Chan fan.
1940 65m/B Sidney Toler, Marjorie Weaver, Robert Lowery, Ricardo Cortez, Donald MacBride, Melville Cooper, Sen Yung; **D:** Harry Lachman. **VHS, Beta** $19.98 *FOX* ✂️✂️

Murder Rap An aspiring musician/sound technologist becomes involved with a mysterious woman and her plot to kill her husband. Complications galore, especially for the viewer.
1987 90m/C John Hawkes, Seita Kathleen Feigny; **D:** Kliff Keuhl. **VHS, Beta** $79.95 *UHV* ✂️

Murder She Said Dame Margaret, playing the benign Miss M for the first time, witnesses a murder on board a train, but the authorities don't seem inclined to believe her. Posing as a maid at an estate near where she thought the body was dropped, she solves the murder and lands three more Miss Marple movies. Based on Christy's "4:50 From Paddington," it features Marple-to-be

Hickson as the cook. *AKA:* Meet Miss Marple.
1962 87m/B Margaret Rutherford, Arthur Kennedy, Nadia Pavlova, James Robertson Justice, Thorley Walters, Charles Tingwell, Conrad Phillips; **D:** George Pollock; **W:** Agatha Christie. **VHS, Beta** $19.98 *MGM, FCT* ✂️✂️½

Murder Story An aspiring mystery writer finds himself mixed up in a real murder and winds up involving his mentor as well. An overdone story, but a reasonably enjoyable film.
1989 (PG) 90m/C Christopher Lee, Bruce Boa; **D:** Eddie Arno, Markus Innocenti. **VHS, Beta, LV** $29.95 *FHS, ACA* ✂️✂️½

Murder: Ultimate Grounds for Divorce A quiet weekend of camping turns into a night of horror for two couples when one of them plans an elaborate murder scheme.
1985 90m/C Roger Daltrey, Toyah Wilcox, Leslie Ash, Terry Raven. **VHS, Beta** $59.95 *LHV, WAR* ✂️

Murder Weapon One by one, a group of men learn just how dangerous women can be. Sex is just the first on their list of weapons! Epic trash nonsense.
1990 (R) 90m/C Linnea Quigley. **VHS, LV** $79.95 *CGH* ✂️

Murder with Music A musical drama featuring an all-black cast.
1945 60m/B Bob Howard, Noble Sissle, Nellie Hill; **D:** George P. Quigley. **VHS, Beta** $29.95 *NOS, DVT, VDM* ✂️✂️

Murderer in the Hotel An inspector is lead to a remote hotel run by a peculiar couple while investigating the murder of a wealthy woman. In Spanish.
1983 99m/C *MX* Jose Alonso, Blanca Guerra; **D:** Luis Mandoki. **VHS, Beta** *NO* ✂️✂️

Murderers Among Us: The Simon Wiesenthal Story Powerful re-enactment of concentration camp survivor Simon Wiesenthal's search for war criminals. Kingsley's gripping performance drives this made-for-cable film. Be prepared for disturbing death camp scenes.
1989 157m/C Ben Kingsley, Renee Soutendijk, Craig T. Nelson, Paul Freeman; **D:** Brian Gibson. **VHS** $89.99 *HBO, FCT* ✂️✂️✂️

Murderer's Keep Secret ingredients used in the Central Meat Market's hamburger are discovered by a young, deaf girl. Beware of filler, she learns, particularly if it's someone you know.
1988 89m/C Vic Tayback, Talia Shire, Robert Walden; **D:** Paulmichel Miekhe. **VHS, Beta** $24.95 *GHV* Woof!

Murderers' Row Daredevil bachelor and former counter-espionage agent Matt Helm is summoned from his life of leisure to ensure the safety of an important scientist. Martin's attempt as a super-spy doesn't wash, and Margret is implausible as the kidnapped scientist's daughter. Unless you want to hear Martin sing "I'm Not the Marrying Kind," don't bother. Second in the "Matt Helm" series.
1966 108m/C Dean Martin, Ann-Margret, Karl Malden, Beverly Adams, James Gregory; **D:** Henry Levin. **VHS, Beta** $14.95 *COL* ✂️½

Murderer's Wife A teacher at a private school seeks to prevent one of her students from making the same mistakes she did in her youth. An episode from the 1950's television drama series, "Fireside Theatre."
19?? 24m/B Audrey Totter, John Howard, June Kenney, Michael Chapin. **VHS, Beta** $19.98 *CCB* ✂️½

Murderlust Employers in search of a security guard make a poor choice in offering the position to a sexually frustrated man whose hobbies include strangling prostitutes. Poor hiring decisions come into play later when he secures a job at an adolescent crisis center.
1986 90m/C Eli Rich, Rochelle Taylor, Dennis Gannon, Bonnie Schneider, Lisa Nichols; **D:** Donald M. Jones. **VHS, Beta** $79.95 *PSM* Woof!

Murderous Vision Television fixture Boxleitner is a bored detective in this outing. But one day, while tracking a young mother in the missing persons bureau, he stumbles upon the trail of a serial killer. Enter a beautiful psychic who wants to help, add a race to catch the murderer, and Bruce suddenly has his hands full. Made for television.
1991 (R) 93m/C Bruce Boxleitner, Laura Johnson, Robert Culp; **D:** Gary Sherman. **VHS** *PAR* ✂️✂️

Murders at Lynch Cross Made-for-British-television mystery about a weird, isolated hotel on the Yorkshire moors.
1985 60m/C *GB* Jill Bennett, Joanna David, Barbara Jefford, Sylvia Syms. **VHS, Beta** $59.95 *PSM* ✂️✂️

Murders in the Rue Morgue Lugosi stars as a deranged scientist (what a stretch) who wants to find a female companion for his pet gorilla. He kidnaps a beautiful woman and prepares to make her the gorilla's bride. Very loosely based on the story by Edgar Allan Poe, which has been remade several times.
1932 61m/B Bela Lugosi, Sidney Fox, Leon Ames, Brandon Hurst, Arlene Francis; **D:** Robert Florey. **VHS** $14.98 *MCA* ✂️✂️½

Murders in the Rue Morgue A young woman has frightening dreams inspired by a play that her father is producing in Paris at the turn of the century. After many people associated with the production become murder victims, the girl becomes involved with one of her father's former associates, a man who killed her mother years ago and then faked his own suicide. The fourth film based on Edgar Allan Poe's classic horror story.
1971 (PG) 87m/C Jason Robards Jr., Lilli Palmer, Herbert Lom, Michael Dunn, Christine Kaufmann, Adolfo Celi; **D:** Gordon Hessler. **VHS, Beta** *NO* ✂️✂️½

The Murders in the Rue Morgue The fifth filmed version of the Edgar Allan Poe story. Set in 19th-century Paris; actors in a mystery play find their roles coming to life. Scott is terrific, with good supporting help. Made for television.
1986 (PG) 92m/C George C. Scott, Rebecca DeMornay, Val Kilmer, Ian McShane, Neil Dickson; **D:** Jeannot Szwarc. **VHS** $89.95 *VMK* ✂️✂️✂️

Muriel A complex, mosaic drama about a middle-aged woman who meets an old lover at Boulogne, and her stepson who cannot forget the needless suffering he caused a young woman named Muriel while he was a soldier at war. Throughout, director Alain Resnais plumbs the essential meanings of memory, age, and the anxieties created from the tension between personal and public actions. Acclaimed; in French with subtitles. *AKA:* Muriel, Ou le Temps d'Un Retour; The Time of Return; Muriel, Or the Time of Return.
1963 115m/C *FR IT* Delphine Seyrig, Jean-Pierre Kerien, Nita Klein, Jean-Baptiste Thierree; **D:** Alain Resnais. **VHS, Beta** $79.95 *FCT* ✂️✂️✂️½

Murmur of the Heart Honest treatment of a fourteen-year-old's coming of age. After his older brothers take him to a prostitute for his first sexual experience, he comes down with scarlet fever. He then travels to a health spa with his mom to recover. There they find that their mother-son bond is stronger than most. Music by Charlie Parker is featured in the score. In French with English subtitles.
1971 (R) 118m/C FR Benoit Ferreux, Daniel Gelin, Lea Massari, Corinne Kersten, Jacqueline Chauveau, Marc Wincourt, Michael Lonsdale; *D:* Louis Malle. **VHS, Beta, LV $79.98** ORI, TAM 𝄞𝄞𝄞½

Murph the Surf Fact-based, engrossing story of two beach bums turned burglars who grow bored with small-time robbery and plan a trip to New York City to steal the Star of Africa sapphire. Notable among the many action scenes is a boat chase through the inland waterways of Miami, Florida. *AKA:* Live a Little, Steal a Lot; You Can't Steal Love.
1975 (PG) 102m/C Robert Conrad, Don Stroud, Donna Mills, Luther Adler, Robyn Millan, Paul Stewart; *D:* Marvin J. Chomsky. **VHS, Beta $19.98** WAR, OM 𝄞𝄞½

Murphy's Fault Dark comedy about a night watchman/writer plagued by a series of bad luck incidents.
1988 (PG-13) 94m/C Patrick Dollaghan, Anne Curry, Stack Pierce; *D:* Robert J. Smawley. **VHS, Beta, LV $89.95** VMK 𝄞𝄞

Murphy's Law A hard-headed cop gets framed for his ex-wife's murder and embarks on a mission to find the actual killer. He is slowed down by a smart-mouthed prostitute who is handcuffed to him during his search. Casting a female in the role of a psycho-killer is unique to the genre.
1986 (R) 101m/C Charles Bronson, Carrie Snodgress, Kathleen Wilhoite, Robert F. Lyons, Richard Romanus, Angel Tompkins, Bill Henderson, James Luisi, Janet MacLachlan, Lawrence Tierney; *D:* J. Lee Thompson. **VHS, Beta, LV $19.95** MED 𝄞

Murphy's Romance A young divorced mother with an urge to train horses pulls up the stakes and heads for Arizona with her son. There she meets a pharmacist who may be just what the doctor ordered to help her build a new life.
1985 (PG-13) 107m/C James Garner, Sally Field, Brian Kerwin, Corey Haim; *D:* Martin Ritt. **VHS, Beta, LV $14.95** COL, HMV 𝄞𝄞𝄞

Murphy's War In World War II, the Germans sink an English ship and gun down most of its crew. An Irishman, however, survives and returns to health with the help of a nurse. He then seeks revenge on those who killed his crewmates, even after he learns the war has ended. O'Toole is interesting as the revenge-minded seaman though saddled with a mediocre script.
1971 (PG) 106m/C GB Peter O'Toole, Sian Phillips, Philippe Noiret; *D:* Peter Yates; *M:* John Barry. **VHS, Beta $9.99** CCB, PAR 𝄞𝄞

Murrow A cable television biography of the renowed chain-smoking journalist who changed broadcasting history by fearlessly voicing his liberal ideas on the air waves. His life was more interesting though Travanti does his best to breathe some life into the script.
1985 114m/C Daniel J. Travanti, Dabney Coleman, Edward Herrmann; *D:* Jack Gold. **VHS, Beta $9.98** FCT, LIV 𝄞𝄞½

Muscle Beach Party Frankie and Annette team up for another romp in the sand. Trouble begins when a new gym opens up on beachfront property and hardbodies muscle in on surfer turf. Renowned actor Lorre breaks up a fight between the two groups in a cameo role, his last screen appearance before he died. Watch for "Little" Stevie Wonder before he became big. ♫Muscle Beach Party; Runnin' Wild; Muscle Bustle; My First Love; Surfin' Woodie; Surfer's Holiday; Happy Street; A Girl Needs a Boy.
1964 94m/C Frankie Avalon, Annette Funicello, Buddy Hackett, Lucianna Paluzzi, Don Rickles, John Ashley, Jody McCrea, Morey Amsterdam, Peter Lupus, Candy Johnson, Dan Haggerty; *Cameos:* Peter Lorre; *D:* William Asher. **VHS, Beta, LV $29.95** VTR 𝄞𝄞½

Muse Concert: No Nukes Concert film of performances held at New York's Madison Square Garden for the benefit of the anti-nuclear power movement. Features Jackson Browne, Crosby, Stills and Nash, James Taylor, Bruce Springsteen, the Doobie Brothers, Bonnie Raitt, Carly Simon, and John Hall. Excellent editing keeps the joint hopping, while Bruce steals the show.
1980 (PG) 103m/C Jackson Browne, David Crosby, Stephen Stills, Graham Nash, James Taylor, Bruce Springsteen, The Doobie Brothers, Bonnie Raitt, Carly Simon, John Hall; *D:* Julian Schlossberg. **VHS, Beta** FOX 𝄞𝄞𝄞

Music Box An attorney defends her father against accusations that he has committed inhumane Nazi war crimes. If she loses, her father faces deportation. As the case progresses, she must struggle to remain objective in the courtroom and come to terms with the possibility that her father is guilty. Lange's portrayal of an ethnic character is highly convincing.
1989 (R) 126m/C Jessica Lange, Frederic Forrest, Lukas Haas, Armin Mueller-Stahl, Michael Rooker, Donald Moffatt, Cheryl Lynn Bruce; *D:* Constantin Costa-Gavras; *W:* Joe Eszterhas. **VHS, Beta, LV $19.95** IVF, JCF 𝄞𝄞½

Music Box/Helpmates These two classic, award-winning comedy shorts by the dynamic duo have been color-enhanced by Colorization.
1932 50m/B Stan Laurel, Oliver Hardy. **VHS, Beta $19.95** QNE 𝄞𝄞½

Music in My Heart Two taxi cabs crash and spur the love of Martin and Hayworth. She proceeds to break off her engagement to save Martin from deportation. Hayworth's last low-budget film before becoming a Hollywood goddess.
1940 69m/B Rita Hayworth, Tony Martin, Edith Fellows, Alan Mowbray, Eric Blore, George Tobias, Joseph Crehan, George Humbert, Phil Tead; *D:* Joseph Santley; *M:* Andre Kostelanetz. **VHS $19.95** COL, CCB 𝄞½

The Music Lovers Russell's version of Tchaikovsky's tormented life and glorious achievements is a shocker, a movie that infuriates professed music lovers but, nonetheless, has introduced many a neophyte to the world of classical music via its sensationalism. Homosexual Tchaikovsky marries an admirer to appease the Russian government and his financial benefactor. Stunned when he discovers his wife is a nymphomaniac, he banishes her to a netherworld of prostitution and eventual insanity which Russell mercilessly explores. Tchaikovsky's own squalid life is hardly better, though he does enjoy success before the bottom falls out.
1971 (R) 122m/C GB Richard Chamberlain, Glenda Jackson, Max Adrian, Christopher Gable, Kenneth Colley, Izabella Telezynska, Maureen Pryor; *D:* Ken Russell. **VHS, LV $19.99** MGM, MLB, FCT 𝄞𝄞½

The Music Man A con man in the guise of a traveling salesman gets off the train in River City, Iowa. After hearing about plans to build a pool hall, he argues that such an establishment would be the gateway to hell for the young, impressionable males of the town. He then convinces the River Cityians to look toward the future of the community and finance a wholesome children's marching band. Although the huckster plans to take their money and run before band instruments arrive, his feelings for the town librarian cause him to think twice about fleeing the Heartland. This isn't just a slice of Americana; it's a whole pie. The acting and singing are terrific "with a capital 'T' and that rhymes with 'P' and that stands for" Preston, who epitomizes the charismatic pitchman. ♫Seventy-six Trombones; Trouble; If You Don't Mind; Till There Way You; The Wells Fargo Wagon; Being in Love; Goodnight, My Someone; Rock Island; Iowa Stubborn; Sincere; The Sadder But Wiser Girl; Gary, Indiana; Marian, the Librarian; Lida Rose/Will I Ever Tell You?; Shipoopi; Pick a Little, Goodnight Ladies; It's You; My White Knight; The Piano Lesson.
1962 151m/C Robert Preston, Shirley Jones, Buddy Hackett, Hermione Gingold, Paul Ford, Pert Kelton, Ron Howard; *D:* Morton DaCosta. Academy Awards '62: Best Adapted Score; Nominations: Best Art Direction/Set Decoration (Color), Best Costume Design (Color), Best Film Editing, Best Picture, Best Sound; Golden Globe Awards '63: Best Film—Musical/Comedy. **VHS, Beta, LV $19.98** WAR, TLF 𝄞𝄞𝄞𝄞

Music Shoppe Four teenagers form a rock band with the assistance of the local music store proprietor. Interesting cast.
1982 (G) 93m/C Gary Crosby, Nia Peeples, Danny Medina, Stephen Schwartz, David Jackson, Jesse White, Doug Kershaw, Giselle MacKenzie. **VHS, Beta** GEM 𝄞𝄞

The Music Teacher A Belgian costume drama dealing with a famed singer who retires to devote himself to teaching two students exclusively. In time, he sees his prized pupils lured into an international competition by an old rival of his. Although the singing is sharp, the story is flat. In French with yellow English subtitles. *AKA:* Le Maitre de Musique.
1988 (PG) 95m/C BE Patrick Bauchau, Sylvie Fennec, Phillipe Volter, Jose Van Dam, Johan Leysen, Anne Roussel; *D:* Gerard Corbiau. **VHS, Beta, LV $79.98** ORI, TAM 𝄞𝄞½

Musica Proibita A serious opera-spiced drama about a young romance crushed by adultery in the teenage couple's ancestry. In Italian with English subtitles.
1943 93m/B Tito Gobbi, Maria Mercader. **VHS, Beta $29.98** VYY, APD, TAM 𝄞𝄞½

Musico, Poeta y Loco Wild and crazy antics abound in this film.
1947 90m/B MX Tin Tan. **VHS, Beta $48.95** MAD 𝄞𝄞

Mussolini & I Docudramatization of the struggle for power between Italy's Benito Mussolini and his son-in-law, Galeazzo Ciano. Narrated by Sarandon in the role of Il Duce's daughter. Made for cable television. *AKA:* Mussolini: The Decline and Fall of Il Duce.
1985 130m/C Bob Hoskins, Anthony Hopkins, Susan Sarandon, Annie Girardot; *D:* Alberto Negrin. **VHS, Beta $19.95** NLC 𝄞𝄞½

Mutant Another argument for the proper disposal of toxic waste. Hazardous materials transform the people of a southern town into monsters. *AKA:* Night Shadows.

1983 (R) 100m/C Wings Hauser, Bo Hopkins, Jennifer Warren, Lee Montgomery; **D:** John Cardos. **VHS, Beta, LV** $19.95 *LIV, VES ♫½*

Mutant Hunt Made for video movie about a battle between robots gone haywire and an all-American hero. The detective cyborgs are set free while high on a sexual stimulant called Euphoron to wreak their technological havoc on a rampage in Manhattan. *AKA:* Matt Riker.
1987 90m/C Rick Gianasi, Mary-Anne Fahey; **D:** Tim Kincaid. **VHS, Beta** $69.95 *UHV Woof!*

Mutant on the Bounty A musician, lost in space as a beam of light for 23 years, is transported aboard a spaceship. Once he materializes, it becomes apparent that he has undergone some incredible physical changes. As if that's not enough, the crew then must flee from a couple of thugs who are trying to steal a vial of serum they have on board. A space spoof that never gets into orbit.
1989 93m/C John Roarke, Deborah Benson, John Furey, Victoria Catlin, John Fleck, Kyle T. Heffner; **D:** Robert Torrance. **VHS** $14.95 *HMD ♫½*

Mutant Video Six comedic, award-winning short-subject films from Jim Belushi and Rob Riley. Outrageous humor.
1976 60m/B James Belushi, Rob Riley. **VHS, Beta** $19.95 *LIV ♫½*

Mutants In Paradise Comedy about a human guinea-pig who always gets involved in some sort of mishap.
1988 78m/C Brad Greenquist, Robert Ingham, Anna Nicholas, Edith Massey. **VHS, Beta** $59.95 *TWE Woof!*

Mutator A corporation makes a tiny genetic mistake and winds up creating a new life form...a demonic pussycat who preys on humans.
1990 (R) 91m/C Brion James, Carolyn Ann Clark, Milton Raphiel Murrill; **D:** John R. Bowey; **W:** Lynn Rose Higgins. **VHS, Beta** $89.98 *PSM ♫♫*

The Muthers Women prisoners escape from their confinement in a South American jungle.
1976 (R) 101m/C Jeanne Bell, Rosanne Katon, Jayne Kennedy, Trina Parks; **D:** Cirio H. Santiago. **VHS, Beta** *NO ♫♫*

The Mutilator After accidentally bumping off his mother, a young man stalks five high school students wanting to cut them up into tiny bits. An unedited version is also available. Bloody boredom. *AKA:* Fall Break.
1985 (R) 85m/C Jack Chatham, Trace Cooper, Frances Raines, Bill Hitchcock; **D:** Buddy Cooper. **VHS, Beta, LV** $79.98 *LIV, VES Woof!*

Mutiny In the War of 1812, the crew of an American ship carrying $10 million in gold fight among themselves for a part of France's donation to the war effort. The beautiful photography doesn't make up for the predictability of the storyline.
1952 76m/C Mark Stevens, Gene Evans, Angela Lansbury, Patric Knowles; **D:** Edward Dmytryk. **VHS, Beta** $19.95 *NOS, UHV ♫♫*

Mutiny in the Big House A man is sent to prison for writing a bad ten dollar check and must choose between seeking salvation with the prison chaplain or toughing it out with a hardened convict. Surprisingly good low-budget programmer, produced by former actor Grant Withers.
1939 83m/B Charles Bickford, Barton MacLane, Pat Moriarity, Dennis Moore, William Royle, Charles Foy, George Cleveland; **D:** William Nigh. **VHS, Beta** $16.95 *SNC ♫♫½*

The Mutiny of the Elsinore A writer on board an old sailing ship fights mutineers and wins back both the helm and the captain's daughter. Tedious British flotsam that made hash of an oft-filmed Jack London tale, and made news even in 1939 for its use of modern-day slang and clothing in the period setting.
1939 74m/B Paul Lukas, Lyn Harding, Kathleen Kelly, Clifford Evans, Ben Soutten, Jiro Soneya; **D:** Roy Lockwood. **VHS** $19.95 *NOS ♫*

Mutiny on the Bounty Compelling adaptation of the true story of sadistic Captain Bligh, Fletcher Christian and their turbulent journey aboard the HMS Bounty. No gray here: Laughton's Bligh is truly a despicable character and extremely memorable in this MGM extravaganza. Remade twice, in 1962 and again in 1984 as "The Bounty." Much, much better than the 1962 remake.
1935 132m/B Clark Gable, Franchot Tone, Charles Laughton, Donald Crisp, Dudley Digges, Spring Byington, Henry Stephenson, Eddie Quillan; **D:** Frank Lloyd. Academy Awards '35: Best Picture; Nominations: Best Actor (Gable), Best Actor (Tone, Laughton), Best Adapted Screenplay, Best Director (Lloyd), Best Film Editing, Best Score; National Board of Review Awards '35: 10 Best Films of the Year; New York Film Critics Awards '35: Best Actor (Laughton). **VHS, Beta, LV, 8mm** $19.98 *MGM, BMV, BTV ♫♫♫♫*

Mutiny on the Bounty Based on the novel by Charles Nordhoff and James Norman Hall, this account of the 1789 mutiny led by Fletcher Christian against Captain Bligh of the Bounty is highlighted by lavish photography. Can't navigate the same perfect course set by the 1935 classic. Marlon Brando seems miscast, giving a choppy performance as the mutiny leader.
1962 177m/C Marlon Brando, Trevor Howard, Richard Harris, Hugh Griffith; **D:** Lewis Milestone. **VHS, Beta, LV** $29.98 *MGM ♫♫*

Mutual Respect A dying wealthy man sets out to find the son he never knew.
1977 (PG) 88m/C Lloyd Bridges, Beau Bridges. **VHS, Beta** $9.95 *ACA ♫½*

My African Adventure Silly tale of an ambassador's son discovering a talking monkey in Africa and meeting a slew of opportunistic misfits in his travels. A comedy unfortunately short on laughs. Based on Tamar Burnstein's book.
1987 93m/C Dom DeLuise, Jimmie Walker; **D:** Sam Firstenberg. **VHS, Beta** *MED Woof!*

My American Cousin Award-winning Canadian coming-of-age comedy about a 12-year-old girl who falls for her rebellious, fun-loving 17-year-old American cousin over summer vacation. Followed by "American Boyfriends."
1985 (PG) 94m/C *CA* Margaret Langrick, John Wildman, Richard Donat, Jane Mortifee; **W/D:** Sandy Wilson. **VHS, Beta, LV** $19.95 *MED ♫♫♫*

My Apprenticeship The second film of Donskoi's trilogy on Maxim Gorky has the writer earning his living, at the age of eight, as an apprentice to a bourgeois family. Although they promise him an education, Gorky is forced to learn to read on his own and eventually sets off on a series of land and sea voyages. He recognizes that the poverty and abuse he has suffered is typical of the lives of most Russians and he encounters the beginnings of revolution. In Russian with English subtitles. Preceded by "My Childhood" and followed by "My Universities."
1939 100m/C *RU* **D:** Mark Donskoi. **VHS** $39.95 *FCT ♫♫♫*

My Beautiful Laundrette Omar (Warnecke), the nephew of a Pakistani businessman, is given the opportunity to better himself by turning his uncle's run-down laundry into a profitable business. He reunites with Johnny (Day Lewis), a childhood friend and a working-class street punk, and they go into the business together. They find themselves battling the prejudice of each other's families and friends in order to succeed. An intelligent look at the sexuality, race relations and economic problems of Thatcher's London. Great performances by a relatively unknown cast (for contrast, note Day Lewis' performance in "Room with a View," released in the same year).
1986 (R) 93m/C Gordon Warnecke, Daniel Day-Lewis, Saeed Jaffrey, Roshan Seth; **D:** Stephen Frears; **W:** Hanif Kureishi. **VHS, Beta, LV** $79.95 *LHV, WAR ♫♫♫*

My Best Friend Is a Vampire Another teenage vampire story, about trying to cope with certain changes that adolescence and bloodsucking bring. Good supporting cast.
1988 (PG) 90m/C Robert Sean Leonard, Evan Mirand, Cheryl Pollak, Rene Auberjonois, Cecilia Peck, Fannie Flagg, Kenneth Kimmins, David Warner, Paul Wilson; **D:** Jimmy Huston. **VHS** $14.99 *HBO ♫♫*

My Best Friend's Girl Coy, sardonic French romance about a woman who slaloms between two buddies working at a ski resort. Fine performances from all. Never makes it to the top of the hill. In French with English subtitles. *AKA:* La Femme De Mon Pote.
1984 99m/C *FR* Isabelle Huppert, Thierry Lhermitte, Coluche, Francoise Perrot; **D:** Bertrand Blier. **VHS, Beta** $19.95 *COL, TAM, SUE ♫♫½*

My Best Girl Mary attempts to bring her new sweetheart home for dinner, with disastrous results. A gentle satire on middle-American life in the 1920s. Organ score by Gaylord Carter.
1927 78m/B Mary Pickford, Charles "Buddy" Rogers; **D:** Sam Taylor. **VHS, Beta, LV** $19.95 *CCB ♫♫*

My Bloody Valentine Psychotic coal miner visits the peaceful little town of Valentine Bluffs on the night of the yearly Valentine Ball. Many of the townspeople have their hearts removed with a pick axe and sent to the sheriff in candy boxes. The bloodiest scenes were cut out to avoid an X-rating.
1981 (R) 91m/C *CA* Paul Kelman, Lori Hallier; **D:** George Mihalka. **VHS, Beta, LV** $19.95 *PAR ♫♫*

My Blue Heaven After agreeing to rat on the Mafia, Martin is dropped into suburbia as part of the witness protection program. Moranis plays the FBI agent assigned to help the former mobster become an upstanding citizen. Adjusting to life in the slow lane isn't easy for an ex con who has grown accustomed to the big time. Not the typical role for Martin, who plays a brunette with a New York accent and is handcuffed by bad writing.
1990 (PG-13) 96m/C Steve Martin, Rick Moranis, Joan Cusack, Melanie Mayron, Carol Kane, Bill Irwin, William Hickey, Daniel Stern; **D:** Herbert Ross. **VHS, Beta, LV** $92.95 *WAR, BTV ♫♫*

My Bodyguard An undersized high school student fends off attacking bullies by hiring a king-sized, withdrawn lad as his bodyguard. Their "business" relationship, however, develops into true friendship. An adolescent coming of age with more intelligence and sensitivity than most of its ilk, and

a pack of up and coming stars as well as old stand-bys Houseman and Gordon.
1980 (PG) 96m/C Chris Makepeace, Adam Baldwin, Martin Mull, Ruth Gordon, Matt Dillon, John Houseman, Joan Cusack, Craig Richard Nelson; *D:* Tony Bill. VHS, Beta $14.98 FOX *♫♫♫*

My Boys are Good Boys A young foursome steal from an armored car and have to face the consequences. Quirky with an implausible storyline.
1978 (PG) 90m/C Ralph Meeker, Ida Lupino, Lloyd Nolan, David Doyle; *D:* Bethel Buckalew. VHS, Beta NO *♫*

My Breakfast with Blassie Kaufman and professional wrestler Blassie meet for breakfast and carry on a comical dialogue.
1983 60m/C Andy Kaufman, Freddie Blassie; *D:* Johnny Legend, Linda Lautrec. VHS, Beta $39.95 RHI *♫*

My Brilliant Career A headstrong young woman spurns the social expectations of turn-of-the-century Australia and pursues opportunities to broaden her intellect and preserve her independence. Davis is wonderful as the energetic and charismatic community trendsetter. Based on an autobiographical novel by Miles Franklin which has been marvelously transferred to the screen. Armstrong deserves credit for her fine direction.
1979 (G) 101m/C Judy Davis, Sam Neill, Wendy Hughes; *D:* Gillian Armstrong. Academy Awards '80 Nominations: Best Costume Design; Australian Film Institute '79: Best Film; British Academy Awards '80: Best Actress (Davis). VHS, Beta $69.95 VES *♫♫♫ ½*

My Brother has Bad Dreams Young man with sibling tosses and turns in bed.
1988 97m/C Nick Kleinholz, Marlena Lustic. VHS $29.98 UHV *♫*

My Champion Chance meeting propels Mike Gorman and Miki Tsuwa into a relationship based on the strong bonds of love and athletic competition.
1984 101m/C Yoko Shimada, Chris Mitchum. VHS, Beta $59.95 MED *♫*

My Chauffeur When a wise-cracking female is hired on as a chauffeur at an all-male chauffeur service, sparks fly. And when the owner takes a definite liking to her work, things take a turn for the worse. As these sort of sexploitation flicks go, this is one of the better ones.
1986 (R) 94m/C Deborah Foreman, Sam Jones, Howard Hesseman, E.G. Marshall; *D:* David Beaird. VHS, Beta, LV $79.98 LIV, VES *♫♫ ½*

My Childhood The first of director Donskoi's trilogy on the life of Maxim Gorky, based on Gorky's autobiographical stories. In this first film, Donskoi depicts Gorky's childhood of abuse and poverty with his grandparents in the 1870s. Eventually, Gorky is forced into the streets and he becomes a wandering beggar. In Russian with English subtitles. Followed by ''My Apprenticeship'' and ''My Universities.''
1938 100m/C RU *D:* Mark Donskoi. VHS $39.95 FCT *♫♫♫*

My Cousin Vinny Vinny Gambini (Pesci), a lawyer who took the bar exam six times before passing, goes to Wahzoo City, Alabama to get his cousin and a friend off the hook when they're accused of killing a store clerk. Leather jackets, gold chains, Brooklyn accents, and his fiancee Tomei's penchant for big hair and bold clothing don't go over well with conservative judge Gwynne, causing plenty of misunderstandings. Surprising hit with simplistic story reaches popular

heights via entertaining performances by the entire cast. Tomei in particular steals every scene she's in and has an Oscar to prove it.
1992 (R) 120m/C Joe Pesci, Ralph Macchio, Marisa Tomei, Mitchell Whitfield, Fred Gwynne, Lane Smith, Austin Pendleton, Bruce McGill; *D:* Jonathan Lynn. VHS $94.98 FXV, MOV, PMS *♫♫♫*

My Darlin' Clementine Shelly Duvall gives the famous song about a miner who bemoans the loss of his daughter and her size nine shoes her own touch in this entry from the ''Tall Tales and Legends'' series. Made for cable television.
1986 49m/C Shelley Duvall, Ed Asner, David Dukes, John Matuszak. VHS $19.98 FOX *♫♫♫*

My Darling Clementine One of the best Hollywood westerns ever made, this recounts the precise events leading up to and including the gunfight at the O.K. Corral. Ford allegedly knew Wyatt Earp and used his stories to recount the details vividly, though not always accurately. Remake of 1939's ''Frontier Marshal.''
1946 97m/B Henry Fonda, Victor Mature, Walter Brennan, Linda Darnell, Tim Holt, Ward Bond, John Ireland; *D:* John Ford. VHS, Beta, LV $19.98 FOX, TLF *♫♫♫ ½*

My Dear Secretary After she marries her boss, a woman grows jealous of the secretary that replaces her. Comedic dialogue and antics result.
1949 94m/C Kirk Douglas, Laraine Day, Keenan Wynn, Rudy Vallee, Florence Bates, Alan Mowbray; *D:* Charles Martin; *W/D:* Charles Martin. VHS, Beta $19.95 NOS, MRV, KRT *♫♫ ½*

My Demon Lover This sex comedy is complicated by the hero's transformation into a demon whenever he is aroused. Saved from complete mediocrity by Family Ties's Valentine in a likable performance.
1987 (PG-13) 90m/C Scott Valentine, Michelle Little, Arnold Johnson; *D:* Charles Loventhal. VHS, Beta, LV $14.95 COL *♫♫*

My Dinner with Andre Two friends talk about their lives and philosophies for two hours over dinner one night. A wonderful exploration into storytelling, the conversation juxtaposes the experiences and philosophies of nerdish, bumbling Shawn and the globe-trotting spiritual pilgrimage of Gregory, in this sometimes poignant, sometimes comic little movie that starts you thinking.
1981 110m/C Andre Gregory, Wallace Shawn; *D:* Louis Malle. VHS, Beta, LV $19.95 PAV, TAM, HMV *♫♫♫ ½*

My Dog Shep An orphan and his dog run away and are pursued diligently when it is discovered that he is a wealthy heir.
1946 71m/B Tom Neal, William Farnum, Lannie Rees, Flame; *D:* Ford Beebe. VHS, Beta, LV $19.95 NOS, VYY *♫ ½*

My Dog, the Thief A helicopter weatherman is unaware that the lovable St. Bernard he has adopted is a kleptomaniac. When the dog steals a valuable necklace from a team of professional jewel thieves, the fun begins.
1969 88m/C Joe Flynn, Elsa Lanchester, Roger C. Carmel, Mickey Shaughnessy, Dwayne Hickman, Mary Ann Mobley; *D:* Robert Stevenson. VHS, Beta $69.95 DVT *♫*

My Dream is Yours Day plays an up and coming radio star in this Warner Brothers musical comedy with a cameo from Bugs Bunny in a dream sequence. This fresh, fun remake of ''Twenty Million Sweethearts'' is often underrated, but is well worth a look. *♫*My Dream is Yours; Some Like You; Tic, Tic, Tic; Love Finds a Way; I'll String Along with You; Canadian Capers; Freddie Get Ready; You Must Have Been a Beautiful

Baby; Jeepers, Creepers; Nagasaki; With Plenty of Money and You.
1949 101m/C Jack Carson, Doris Day, Lee Bowman, Adolphe Menjou, Eve Arden, S.Z. Sakall, Selena Royle, Edgar Kennedy; *Cameos:* Bugs Bunny; *D:* Michael Curtiz. VHS $29.95 FOX, FCT, MLB *♫♫ ½*

My Fair Lady Colorful production of Lerner and Loewe's musical version of ''Pygmalion,'' about an ill-mannered cockney girl who is plucked from her job as a flower girl by Professor Henry Higgins. Higgins makes a bet with a colleague that he can turn this rough diamond into a ''lady.'' Winner of eight Academy Awards. Hepburn's singing voice is dubbed by Marni Nixon, who was also responsible for the singing in ''The King and I'' and ''West Side Story;'' the dubbing may have undermined her chance at an Oscar nomination. Typecasting role for Harrison as the crusty, egocentric Higgins. A timeless classic. *♫*Why Can't the English?; Wouldn't It Be Lovely?; I'm an Ordinary Man; With a Little Bit of Luck; Just You Wait, 'Enry 'Iggins; The Servant's Chorus; The Rain in Spain; I Could Have Danced all Night; Ascot Gavotte; On the Street Where You Live; The Embassy Waltz; You Did It; Show Me; The Flower Market; Get Me To the Church on Time; A Hymn to Him; Without You; I've Grown Accustomed to Her Face.
1964 (G) 170m/C Audrey Hepburn, Rex Harrison, Stanley Holloway, Wilfrid Hyde-White, Theodore Bikel, Mona Washbourne, Jeremy Brett, Robert Coote, Gladys Cooper; *D:* George Cukor; *M:* Frederick Loewe, Alan Jay Lerner. Academy Awards '64: Best Actor (Harrison), Best Adapted Score, Best Art Direction/Set Decoration (Color), Best Color Cinematography, Best Costume Design (Color), Best Director (Cukor), Best Picture, Best Sound; Nominations: Best Adapted Screenplay, Best Film Editing, Best Supporting Actor (Holloway), Best Supporting Actress (Cooper); British Academy Awards '65: Best Film; Directors Guild of America Awards '64: Best Director (Cukor); Golden Globe Awards '65: Best Actor—Musical/Comedy (Harrison), Best Director (Cukor), Best Film—Musical/Comedy; National Board of Review Awards '64: 10 Best Films of the Year; New York Film Critics Awards '64: Best Actor (Harrison), Best Film. VHS, Beta, LV $19.98 FOX, FCT, BTV *♫♫♫ ½*

My Father is Coming German immigrant, Vicky, is trying to get an acting career off the ground in New York. She shares her apartment with Ben, a gay man, and generally does more work as a waitress than actress. Vicky's alarmed when her father, Hans, arrives for a visit. She's told him she's married (Vicky's also gay), so Ben agrees to pose as her husband. The rest of the film details Vicky's complicated love life, unsuccessful career tryouts, and her father's increasing bewilderment. It's meant as a sort of reverse, and perverse, innocents abroad, with the two Germans adrift in zany New York but this only works fitfully.
1991 82m/C GE Shelley Kastner, Alfred Edel, David Bronstein, Mary Lou Graulau, Michael Massee, Annie Sprinkle, Bruce Benderson; *W/D:* Monika Treut. VHS $59.95 *♫♫*

My Father, My Rival A high school student's crush on his teacher leads to emotional complications when his widowed father becomes romantically involved with her.
1985 60m/C Lance Guest. VHS, Beta NO *♫*

My Father's Glory Based on Marcel Pagnol's tales of his childhood, this is a sweet, beautiful memory of a young boy's favorite summer in the French countryside of the early 1900s. Not much happens, yet the film is such a perfect evocation of the milieu that one is carried swiftly into the dreams and thoughts of all the characters. One half of a duo, followed by "My Mother's Castle." In French with English subtitles. *AKA:* La Gloire de Mon Pere.

1991 (G) 110m/C *FR* Julien Ciamaca, Philippe Caubere, Nathalie Roussel, Therese Liotard, Didier Pain; *D:* Yves Robert. **VHS $79.98** *TAM, ORI* ⅃⅃⅃

My Father's House Magazine editor recounts his youth while recovering from a heart attack. He measures his own quality of life against the life that his father led and begins to question his own choices with regard to his family.

1975 96m/C Cliff Robertson, Robert Preston, Eileen Brennan, Rosemary Forsyth. **VHS, Beta $49.95** *WOV* ⅃⅃

My Father's Nurse While father convalesces upstairs, the family frolics about the house and plots his dispatch. When his new nurse secretly cures him, he takes to a wheelchair and mounts a comedic covert counter offensive.

1985 97m/C VHS, Beta $39.95 *VCD, MOV* ⅃

My Father's Wife A bored wife gets sexual attention from her maturing stepson. Soft-core.

198? 80m/C Carroll Baker. **VHS, Beta $29.95** *MED* ⅃

My Favorite Blonde Beautiful British spy Carroll convinces Hope to aid her in carrying out a secret mission. Lots of fun as Hope and his trained penguin, along with Carroll, embark on a cross-country chase to elude the Nazis. Hope's behavior is hilarious and the pacing of the film is excellent. Based on a story by Melvin Frank and Norman Panama.

1942 78m/B Bob Hope, Madeleine Carroll, Gale Sondergaard, George Zucco, Lionel Royce, Walter Kingsford, Victor Varconi; *Cameos:* Bing Crosby; *D:* Sidney Lanfield; *W:* Frank Butler, Don Hartman. **VHS $14.98** *MCA* ⅃⅃

My Favorite Brunette Detective parody starring Hope as a photographer turned grumbling private eye. He becomes involved with a murder, a spy caper, and a dangerous brunette (Lamour).

1947 85m/B Bob Hope, Dorothy Lamour, Peter Lorre, Lon Chaney Jr., Reginald Denny, Bing Crosby; *D:* Elliott Nugent. **VHS, Beta, LV, 3/4U, Special order formats $9.95** *NEG, MRV, NOS* ⅃⅃½

My Favorite Wife A handsome widower remarries only to discover that his first wife, who was shipwrecked seven years prior and presumed dead, has reappeared. Eventually, a judge must decide what to do in this most unusual situation, completely lacking precedent. A farcical and hilarious story filled with a clever cast. The 1963 remake "Move Over Darling" lacks the style and wit of this presentation. Also available colorized.

1940 88m/B Irene Dunne, Cary Grant, Randolph Scott, Gail Patrick; *D:* Garson Kanin; *W:* Samuel Spewack, Bella Spewack, Leo McCarey. **VHS, Beta, LV $19.98** *MED, MLB, TTC* ⅃⅃

My Favorite Year A young writer on a popular live television show in the 1950s is asked to keep a watchful eye on the week's guest star—his favorite swashbuckling movie hero. Through a series of misadventures, he discovers his matinee idol is actually a drunkard and womanizer who has trouble living up to his cinematic standards. Sterling performance from O'Toole, with memorable portrayal from Bologna as the show's host, King Kaiser (a take-off of Sid Caesar from "Your Show of Shows"). *AKA:* My Favourite Year.

1982 (PG) 92m/C Peter O'Toole, Mark Linn-Baker, Joseph Bologna, Jessica Harper, Lainie Kazan, Bill Macy, Anne De Salvo, Lou Jacobi, Adolph Green, Cameron Mitchell, Gloria Stuart; *D:* Richard Benjamin. **VHS, Beta, LV $19.95** *MGM* ⅃⅃⅃

My First Wife Strong drama about a self-indulgent man's devastation when his wife abruptly leaves him after ten years of marriage. Realistic and well-acted.

1984 (PG) 95m/C *AU* John Hargreaves, Wendy Hughes, Lucy Angwin, Anna Jemison, David Cameron; *D:* Paul Cox. **VHS** *NO* ⅃⅃½

My Forbidden Past Melodrama set in 1890 New Orleans centers on a young woman (Gardner) with an unsavory past who unexpectedly inherits a fortune and vows to break up the marriage of the man (Mitchum) she loves. His wife is murdered and he is charged with doing the deed until Gardner, exposing her past, wins his love and helps to extricate him.

1951 81m/B Ava Gardner, Melvyn Douglas, Robert Mitchum; *D:* Robert Stevenson. **VHS, Beta $19.95** *MED* ⅃⅃

My Friend Flicka Boy makes friends with four-legged beast. Dad thinks the horse is full of wild oats, but young Roddie trains it to be the best gosh darned horse in pre-Disney family faredom. Based on Mary O'Hara book, followed by "Thunderhead, Son of Flicka," and TV series.

1943 89m/C Roddy McDowall, Preston Foster, Rita Johnson, James Bell, Jeff Corey; *D:* Harold Schuster. **VHS, Beta $14.98** *FXV, FCT, HMV* ⅃⅃⅃

My Friend Irma An adaptation of the radio series, featuring Wilson as the dumb blonde with boyfriend trouble and Lynn as her sensible pal. The film debut of Martin (singing) and Lewis (mugging) as juice-bar operators. Followed by a sequel, "My Friend Irma Goes West," and later by a television series.

1949 103m/B Marie Wilson, Diana Lynn, John Lund, Don DeFore, Dean Martin, Jerry Lewis, Hans Conried; *D:* George Marshall. **VHS $19.95** *PAR* ⅃½

My Geisha MacLaine and husband experience bad karma because she wants to be in his new film. In pancake makeup and funny shoes, she poses as a geisha girl and is cast as Madame Butterfly. Her husband, however, is one sharp cookie. Filmed in Japan.

1962 120m/C Shirley MacLaine, Yves Montand, Edward G. Robinson, Robert Cummings; *D:* Jack Cardiff. **VHS $14.95** *PAR, WAX, FCT* ⅃⅃½

My Girl Chlumsky is delightful in her film debut as an 11-year old tomboy who must come to grips with the realities of life. Culkin plays her best friend Thomas, who understands her better than anyone else, including her father, a mortician, and his girlfriend, the makeup artist at the funeral parlor. Some reviewers questioned whether young children would be able to deal with some unhappy occurrences in the film, but most seemed to classify it as a movie the whole family would enjoy.

1991 (PG) 102m/C Dan Aykroyd, Jamie Lee Curtis, Macaulay Culkin, Anna Chlumsky, Griffin Dunne; *D:* Howard Zieff; *W:* Laurice Elehwany. **VHS, LV, 8mm $19.95** *COL* ⅃⅃½

My Girl Tisa Chronicles the experiences of a young immigrant woman who struggles to survive in the U.S. at the turn of the century and hopes to bring her father over from their home country. Based on a play by Lucille S. Prumbs and Sara B. Smith.

1948 95m/B Lilli Palmer, Sam Wanamaker, Akim Tamiroff, Alan Hale Jr., Hugo Haas, Gale Robbins, Stella Adler; *D:* Elliott Nugent. **VHS $19.98** *REP* ⅃⅃½

My Grandpa is a Vampire When 12 year-old Lonny and his pal visit Grandpa Cooger in New Zealand Lonny discovers a long-hidden family secret—Grandpa's a vampire! This doesn't stop either boy from joining with Grandpa in lots of scary adventures.

1992 (PG) 90m/C Al Lewis, Justin Gocke, Milan Borich, Noel Appleby; *D:* David Blyth. **VHS $89.98** *REP* ⅃½

My Heroes Have Always Been Cowboys An aging rodeo rider returns to his hometown to recuperate and finds himself forced to confront his past. His ex-girlfriend, his dad and his sister all expect something from him. He learns how to give it, and gains the strength of purpose to get back on the bull that stomped him. Excellent rodeo footage, solid performances, but the story has been around the barn too many times to hold much interest.

1991 (PG) 106m/C Scott Glenn, Kate Capshaw, Ben Johnson, Balthazar Getty, Mickey Rooney, Gary Busey, Tess Harper; *D:* Stuart Rosenberg. **VHS, Beta, LV $9.99** *VTR, FXV, COL* ⅃⅃½

My Lady of Whims Clara Bow's dad disapproves of debutante daughter's desire to hang out with the girls who just want to have fun.

1925 42m/B Clara Bow, Betty Baker, Carmelita Geraghty, Donald Keith, Lee Moran. **VHS, Beta $19.95** *GPV, FCT* ⅃

My Left Foot A gritty, unsentimental drama based on the life and autobiography of cerebral-palsy victim Christy Brown. Considered an imbecile by everyone but his mother (Fricker, in a stunning award-winning performance) until he teaches himself to write. He survives his impoverished Irish roots to become a painter and writer using his left foot, the only appendage over which he has control. He also falls in love and finds some heartaches along the way. Day-Lewis is astounding; the supporting cast, especially Shaw and Cusack, match him measure for measure.

1989 (R) 103m/C *IR* Daniel Day-Lewis, Brenda Fricker, Ray McAnally, Cyril Cusack, Fiona Shaw, Hugh O'Conor, Adrian Dunbar, Ruth McCabe, Alison Whelan; *D:* Jim Sheridan; *W:* Shane Connaughton. Academy Awards '89: Best Actor (Day-Lewis), Best Supporting Actress (Fricker); Nominations: Best Adapted Screenplay, Best Director (Sheridan), Best Picture; Independent Spirit Awards '90: Best Foreign Film; Los Angeles Film Critics Association Awards '89: Best Actor (Day-Lewis), Best Supporting Actress (Fricker); New York Film Critics Awards '89: Best Actor (Day-Lewis); National Society of Film Critics Awards '89: Best Actor (Day-Lewis). **VHS, Beta, LV $89.99** *HBO, BTV, HMV* ⅃⅃⅃⅃

My Life as a Dog A troublesome boy is separated from his brother and is sent to live with relatives in the country when his mother is taken ill. Unhappy and confused, he struggles to understand sexuality and love and tries to find security and acceptance. Remarkable Swedish film available with English subtitles or dubbed. *AKA:* Mitt Liv Som Hund.

1985 101m/C *SW* Anton Glanzelius, Tomas Van Bromssen, Anki Liden; *D:* Lasse Hallstrom. Academy Awards '87 Nominations: Best Adapted Screenplay, Best Director (Hallstrom); Golden Globe Awards '88: Best Foreign Film; Independent Spirit Awards '88: Best Foreign Film. **VHS, Beta, LV $79.95** *PAR, TAM, HMV* ⅃⅃⅃⅃

My Life to Live A woman turns to prostitution in this probing examination of sexual, and social, relations. Idiosyncratic Godard has never been more starstruck than

in this vehicle for the endearing Karina, his wife at the time. A classic. In French with English subtitles. *AKA:* Vivre Savie; It's My Life.
1962 85m/B FR Anna Karina, Sady Rebbot, Andre S. Labarthe, Guylaine Schlumberger; *W/D:* Jean-Luc Godard. **VHS, Beta $24.95** *NOS, NYF, DVT* 🐾🐾🐾🐾

My Little Chickadee Classic comedy about a gambler and a fallen woman who marry for convenience so they can respectably enter an unsuspecting town. Sparks fly in their adventures together. Fields and West are both at their best playing their larger-than-life selves.
1940 91m/B W.C. Fields, Mae West, Joseph Calleia, Dick Foran, Margaret Hamilton, Donald Meek; *D:* Eddie Cline. **VHS, Beta, LV $14.98** *MCA, MLB* 🐾🐾🐾

My Little Girl A rich Philadelphia girl idealistically volunteers her time to help local institutionalized orphans, but meets with opposition.
1987 (R) 118m/C Mary Stuart Masterson, James Earl Jones, Geraldine Page, Anne Meara, Peter Gallagher; *D:* Connie Kaiserman. **VHS, Beta, LV $9.99** *STE, PSM* 🐾🐾

My Little Pony: The Movie Animated tale about the siege of Ponyland by malevolent witches.
1986 87m/C *D:* Michael Joens; *V:* Danny DeVito, Cloris Leachman, Tony Randall, Madeline Kahn. **VHS, Beta $9.99** *VTR, WTA* 🐾🐾

My Love For Yours The romantic tale of a young man hoping to win the love of a beautiful but icy girl. A tad silly in parts, but the clever dialogue moves the story along. *AKA:* Honeymoon in Bali.
1939 99m/B Fred MacMurray, Madeleine Carroll, *D:* Edward H. Griffith. **VHS, Beta, 3/4U, Special order formats $19.95** *NOS, CAB* 🐾🐾 ½

My Lucky Stars A cop goes undercover and unfortunately for the criminals he happens to be a skull-fracturing martial arts expert!!
198? 90m/C Jackie Chan, Richard Ng, Samo Hung. **VHS, Beta** *NO* 🐾🐾 ½

My Man Adam A dreamy, Mitty-esque high schooler falls in love with a girl (Daryl's auburn-haired sister, Page Hannah), and becomes ensnared in a real life crime, leaving his friend to bail him out. Typical boy-meets-girl, boy-gets-in-trouble yarn.
1986 (R) 84m/C Raphael Sbarge, Veronica Cartwright, Page Hannah, Larry B. Scott, Charlie Barnett, Arthur Pendleton, Dave Thomas; *D:* Roger L. Simon. **VHS, Beta $79.98** *FOX* 🐾🐾

My Man Godfrey A spoiled rich girl picks up someone she assumes is a bum as part of a scavenger hunt and decides to keep him on as her butler. In the process, he teaches her about life, money, and happiness. Top-notch screwball comedy defines the genre. Lombard is a stunner alongside the equally charming Powell. Remade in 1957 with June Allyson and David Niven. From the novel by Eric Hatch.
1936 95m/B William Powell, Carole Lombard, Gail Patrick, Alice Brady, Mischa Auer, Eugene Pallette; *D:* Gregory La Cava. **VHS, Beta, 3/4U, Special order formats $9.95** *NEG, MRV, NOS* 🐾🐾🐾🐾

My Michael Sensitive adaptation of Amos Oz's novel set in Jerusalem in the late 1950s. A young woman is stifled by marriage and the conventions of her bourgeois life and her fantasies begin to take over. In Hebrew with English subtitles.
1975 90m/C *IS* Efrat Lavie, Oded Kotler; *D:* Dan Wolman. **VHS, Beta $79.95** *ERG, FCT, TAM* 🐾🐾🐾

My Mom's a Werewolf An average suburban mother gets involved with a dashing stranger and soon, to her terror, begins to turn into a werewolf. Her daughter and companion must come up with a plan to regain dear, sweet mom.
1989 (PG) 90m/C Susan Blakely, John Saxon, John Schuck, Katrina Caspary, Ruth Buzzi, Marilyn McCoo, Marcia Wallace, Diana Barrows; *D:* Michael Fischa. **VHS, Beta, LV $79.95** *PSM* 🐾 ½

My Mother's Castle The second half of the two part film series based on the autobiography of Marcel Pagnol. Picking up where "My Father's Glory" left off, the family begins a series of vacations in a beautiful country home. Dynamically acted and tenderly directed, charming and suitable for the entire family. In French with English subtitles. *AKA:* Le Chateau de Ma Mere.
1991 (PG) 98m/C *FR* Philippe Caubere, Nathalie Roussel, Didier Pain, Therese Liotard, Julien Ciamaca, Victorien Delmare; *D:* Yves Robert. **VHS $79.98** *TAM, ORI* 🐾🐾🐾 ½

My Mother's Secret Life Dull drama focusing on a long-forgotten daughter who suddenly appears on her mother's doorstep and discovers that mom makes a living as a high-priced hooker.
1984 100m/C Loni Anderson, Paul Sorvino, Amanda Wyss, James Sutorius, Sandy McPeak; *D:* Robert Markowitz. **VHS, Beta $79.95** *PSM* 🐾 ½

My Name Called Bruce When the unstoppable "Bruce" is teamed with a sexy secret agent, the criminals of Hong Kong issue a collective shudder.
198? 90m/C Bruce Le. **VHS, Beta $19.99** *BFV* 🐾 ½

My Name is Ivan Tarkovsky's first feature film is a vivid, wrenching portrait of a young Soviet boy surviving as a spy behind enemy lines during WWII. Technically stunning, heralding the coming of modern cinema's greatest formalist. In Russian with English subtitles. *AKA:* Ivan's Childhood; The Youngest Spy.
1962 84m/B *RU* Kolya Burlyayev, Valentin Zubkov, Ye Zharikov, S. Krylov; *D:* Andrei Tarkovsky. **VHS, Beta, LV $79.95** *FXL, FCT, TAM* 🐾🐾🐾 ½

My Name is Nobody Fast-paced spaghetti-western wherein a cocky, soft-hearted gunfighter is sent to kill the famous, retired outlaw he reveres, but instead they band together. *AKA:* Il Mio Nome e Nessuno.
1974 (PG) 115m/C Henry Fonda, Terence Hill, R.G. Armstrong; *D:* Tonino Valerii; *M:* Ennio Morricone. **VHS, Beta $14.95** *KRT, HHE* 🐾🐾 ½

My Neighborhood A debonair bar-owner leads a double life as a knife wielding psychopath.
1984 35m/C VHS, Beta *NO* 🐾🐾 ½

My New Partner Amiable French comedy in which cynical veteran cop is saddled with straight arrow rookie partner. French Cesars for best film and best director, but remember: They like Jerry Lewis too. In French with English subtitles. *AKA:* Les Ripoux.
1984 (PG) 106m/C *FR* Philippe Noiret, Thierry Lhermitte, Regine, Grace de Capitani, Claude Brosset, Julien Guiomar; *W/D:* Claude Zidi. **VHS, Beta, LV $29.95** *MED, IME* 🐾🐾 ½

My Night at Maud's Typically subtle Rohmer entry concerns quandary of upright fellow who finds himself drawn to comparatively carefree woman. Talky, somewhat arid film is one of director's Six Moral Tales. You'll either find it fascinating or wish you were watching "Rocky XXIV" instead. Cine-

matography by Nestor Almendros; in French with English subtitles. *AKA:* My Night with Maud; Ma Nuit Chez Maud.
1969 111m/B *FR* Jean-Louis Trintignant, Francoise Fabian, Marie-Christine Barrault, Antoine Vitez; *D:* Eric Rohmer. **VHS, Beta, LV $29.98** *MED, TAM, APD* 🐾🐾🐾

My Nights With Susan, Sandra, Olga, and Julie A few extremely strange young women open their farm to a weary adventurer on his way to France.
19?? 78m/C *NL* Willeke Van Ammelrooy; *D:* Pin de La Parra. **VHS, Beta** *MED* 🐾

My Old Man Plucky teen and her seedy horsetrainer father come together over important horse race. Oates makes this one worth watching on a slow evening. A Hemingway story made for television.
1979 102m/C Kristy McNichol, Warren Oates, Eileen Brennan; *D:* John Erman. **VHS, Beta $9.95** *CAF* 🐾🐾 ½

My Old Man's Place A veteran, with two war buddies and a girl, returns to his father's run-down farm, hoping to fix it up. Sexual tensions arise and violence erupts.
1971 (R) 93m/C Arthur Kennedy, Michael Moriarty, Mitchell Ryan, William Devane, Topo Swope; *D:* Edwin Sherin. **VHS, Beta $79.95** *PSM* 🐾 ½

My Other Husband A woman has two husbands and families, one in Paris and one in Trouville, who eventually meet each other. Seems silly but grows into a sensitive and sad portrait of married life. In French with English subtitles. *AKA:* Attention! Une Femme Peut en Cacher une Autre.
1985 (PG-13) 110m/C *FR* Miou-Miou, Rachid Ferrache, Roger Hanin; *D:* Georges Lautner. **VHS, Beta $59.95** *COL, TAM* 🐾🐾 ½

My Outlaw Brother A man travelling West to visit his brother in Mexico meets a Texas Ranger on the train. The man discovers that his brother is an outlaw, and teams up with the Ranger to capture him. *AKA:* My Brother, the Outlaw.
1951 82m/B Mickey Rooney, Wanda Hendrix, Robert Preston, Robert Stack, Jose Torvay; *D:* Elliott Nugent. **VHS $19.98** *MOV, MRV* 🐾🐾

My Own Private Idaho Director Van Sant of "Drugstore Cowboy" returns to the underworld to examine another group of outsiders, this time young, homosexual hustlers. On the streets of Seattle, narcoleptic hustler Mike meets slumming rich boy, Scott and together they begin a search for Mike's lost mother, which leads them back to Mike's home in Idaho and on a journey to Italy. Stunning visuals and an elliptical plot, as well as a terrific performance by Phoenix, highlight this search for love, the meaning of life, and power. Van Sant couples these activities with scenes from Shakespeare's "Henry IV" for a sometimes inscrutable, but always memorable film. Look for director Richert's Falstaff role as an aging chickenhawk.
1991 (R) 105m/C River Phoenix, Keanu Reeves, James Russo, William Richert, Rodney Harvey, Michael Parker, Flea, Chiara Caselli, Udo Kier; *D:* Gus Van Sant. **VHS, LV $19.95** *COL, NLC* 🐾🐾🐾

My Pal Trigger Roy is unjustly imprisoned in this high adventure on the plains. Better than usual script and direction makes this is one of the more entertaining of the singing cowboy's films.
1946 79m/B Roy Rogers, George "Gabby" Hayes, Dale Evans; *D:* Frank McDonald. **VHS, Beta $19.95** *NOS, MRV, HHT* 🐾🐾

My Pleasure Is My Business Cinematic autobiography of Xaviera Hollander, the world's most renowned prostitute of the seventies, and the zany occurrences which abound in her profession.
1974 (R) 85m/C *CA* Xaviera Hollander, Henry Ramer, Colin Fox, Ken Lynch, Jayne Eastwood; *D:* Al Waxman. VHS *NO* ♫♫

My Samurai When young Peter McCrea witnesses a gang murder he turns to his martial-arts expert friend Young Park to help him. On the run from both the gang and the police Peter learns self-defense and the courage to face his fears.
1992 (R) 87m/C Julian Lee, Mako, Terry O'Quinn, Bubba Smith, Jim Turner, Carlos Palomino, John Kallo; *D:* Fred Dresch. VHS $89.95 *IMP* ♫½

My Science Project Teenager Stockwell stumbles across a crystal sphere with a funky light. Unaware that it is an alien time-travel device, he takes it to school to use as a science project in a last-ditch effort to avoid failing his class. Chaos follows and Stockwell and his chums find themselves battling gladiators, mutants, and dinosaurs. Plenty of special effects and a likeable enough, dumb teenage flick.
1985 (PG) 94m/C John Stockwell, Danielle von Zernaeck, Fisher Stevens, Raphael Sbarge, Richard Masur, Barry Corbin, Ann Wedgeworth, Dennis Hopper, Candace Silvers, Beau Dremann, Pat Simmons, Pamela Springsteen; *D:* Jonathan Betuel. VHS, Beta, LV $79.95 *TOU* ♫½

My Side of the Mountain A thirteen-year-old boy decides to emulate his idol, Henry David Thoreau, and gives up his home and his family to live in the Canadian mountains.
1969 (G) 100m/C *CA* Teddy Eccles, Theodore Bikel; *D:* James B. Clark. VHS, Beta $29.95 *KUI*, *PAR* ♫♫½

My Sister Eileen Ruth and Eileen are two small-town Ohio sisters who move to Manhattan seeking excitement. They live in a basement apartment in Greenwich Village with an assortment of oddball tenants as they pursue success and romance. Everyone is daffy and charming, as is the film. The songs are fun but unmemorable, however the choreography is by Bob Fosse, who also dances and acts as one sister's suitor. This film has a prolific history—the original 1942 film was based on a Broadway play, which was based on a series of autobiographical stories published in the New Yorker. The play was later turned into a Broadway musical known as "Wonderful Town," which has nothing to do with this film musical version of the original stories. ♫Give Me a Band and My Baby; It's Bigger Than You and Me; There's Nothing Like Love; As Soon As They See Eileen; I'm Great; Conga; Atmosphere.
1955 108m/C Janet Leigh, Betty Garrett, Jack Lemmon, Bob Fosse, Kurt Kasznar, Dick York, Lucy Marlow, Tommy Rall, Barbara Brown, Horace McMahon; *W/D:* Richard Quine; *W:* Blake Edwards; *M:* Jules Styne. VHS $19.95 *COL*, *MOV* ♫♫♫

My Sister, My Love Odd tale of two sisters' incestuous relationship and what happens when one of them takes another lover. The cage of the alternate titles refers to the place where their pet apes are kept and seems to symbolize the confining nature of their life together. *AKA:* The Cage; The Mafu Cage.
1978 (R) 102m/C Lee Grant, Carol Kane, Will Geer, James Olson; *D:* Karen Arthur. VHS $59.95 *UHV* ♫½

My Son, the Vampire Last of Britain's Old Mother Riley series in which Lucan plays the Irish housekeeper in drag. Lugosi is a crazed scientist who thinks he's a vampire and wants to take over the world with his giant robot. Mother Riley interferes. Theme song by Alan Sherman. *AKA:* Old Mother Riley Meets the Vampire; The Vampire and the Robot; Vampire Over London; Mother Riley Meets the Vampire.
1952 72m/B *GB* Bela Lugosi, Arthur Lucan, Dora Bryan, Richard Wattis; *D:* John Gilling. VHS $19.98 *NOS*, *SNC* ♫♫

My Song Goes Round the World Chronicles the romantic foibles of a singing trio and the one girl they decide they all love.
1934 68m/B Joseph Schmidt, John Loder, Charlotte Ander; *D:* Richard Oswald. VHS $29.95 *NOS*, *DVT* ♫½

My Stepmother Is an Alien When eccentric physicist Aykroyd sends a message beam to another galaxy on a stormy night, the last thing he expects is a visit from beautiful alien Basinger. Unfortunately, he does not realize that this gorgeous blonde is an alien and he continues to court her despite her rather odd habits. Only the daughter seems to notice the strange goings on, and her dad ignores her warnings, enabling Basinger's evil sidekick to continue in its plot to take over the Earth.
1988 (PG-13) 108m/C Dan Aykroyd, Kim Basinger, Jon Lovitz, Alyson Hannigan, Joseph Maher, Seth Green, Wesley Mann, Adrian Sparks, Juliette Lewis, Tanya Fenmore; *D:* Richard Benjamin. VHS, Beta, LV $14.95 *COL* ♫♫

My Sweet Charlie Unwed, pregnant white woman hides out with black lawyer in backwater Texas. Better than it sounds, with nice performances by Duke and Freeman. Made for television.
1970 97m/C Patty Duke, Al Freeman Jr., Ford Rainey, William Hardy, Chris Wilson, Archie Moore, Noble Willingham; *D:* Lamont Johnson. VHS, Beta $39.95 *MCA* ♫♫½

My Sweet Victim A young couple who recently moved to the United States from Poland try to make a go of their own business. The business fails, and so does their marriage. Will it end in murder?
1985 92m/C Candice Bergen, Juergen Prochnow. VHS $9.99 *QVD* ♫♫

My Therapist A sex therapist's boyfriend cannot bear the thought of her having intercourse with other men as part of her work. Soft core.
1984 81m/C Marilyn Chambers; *D:* Gary Legon. VHS, Beta *NO* Woof!

My Tutor When a high school student is in danger of flunking French, his parents hire a private tutor to help him learn the lessons. It becomes clear that his studies will involve many more subjects, however. Standard teen sex comedy.
1982 (R) 97m/C Caren Kaye, Matt Lattanzi, Kevin McCarthy, Clark Brandon, Bruce Bauer, Arlene Golonka, Crispin Glover, Shelley Taylor Morgan, Francesca "Kitten" Natavidad, Jewel Shepard, Marilyn Tokuda; *D:* George Bowers. VHS, Beta, LV $14.95 *MCA* ♫½

My Twentieth Century This quirky gem of a movie is a charming, sentimental journey through the early 1900s. Twins Dora and Lili are separated in early childhood. They reunite as grown, very different women on the Orient Express after they both (unknowingly) have sex with the same man. Dora is a sex kitten, while Lili is a radical equipped with explosives. When the two sisters come together, they both lose their destructive, dependent selves (Dora on men,

Lili on politics) and become independent women. Lots of sidelights and subplots that are sure to amuse the viewer. In Hungarian with English subtitles. *AKA:* Az en XX. Szazadom.
1990 104m/B *HU CA* Dortha Segda, Oleg Jankowski, Peter Andorai, Gabor Mate; *W/D:* Ildiko Enyedi. VHS $89.95 *FXL*, *TAM* ♫♫♫

My Universities In the final part of Donskoi's trilogy on Maxim Gorky, Gorky is a young man at university who is introduced to radical politics by several liberal intellectuals. He makes his first attempts at writing and joins the revolution as he leaves his painful past behind. In Russian with English subtitles. Preceded by "My Childhood" and "My Apprenticeship."
1940 100m/C *RU D:* Mark Donskoi. VHS $39.95 *FCT* ♫♫♫

My Wicked, Wicked Ways Cleverly cast, low-budget television drama based on the autobiography of Errol Flynn.
1984 95m/C Duncan Regehr, Barbara Hershey, Hal Linden, Darren McGavin; *D:* Don Taylor. VHS, Beta $59.98 *FOX* ♫♫½

My Wonderful Life Softcore gristle about a beautiful tramp climbing the social ladder via the boudoir.
1990 (R) 107m/C Pierre Cosso, Jean Rochefort, Massimo Venturiello, Carol Alt, Elliott Gould; *D:* Carlo Vanzina. VHS, Beta, LV $79.95 *COL* ♫

Myra Breckinridge A tasteless version of the Gore Vidal novel. An alleged satire of a film critic who undergoes a sex change operation and then plots the destruction of the American male movie star stereotype. Should have more laughs, especially with West in the title role. Created an outcry from all sides, and hung out to dry by studio where it's reportedly still blowing in the wind.
1970 (R) 94m/C Mae West, John Huston, Raquel Welch, Rex Reed, Farrah Fawcett, Jim Backus, John Carradine, Andy Devine, Tom Selleck; *D:* Michael Sarne. VHS, Beta *FOX*, *MLB* Woof!

The Mysterians A race of gigantic scientific intellects from a doomed planet attempts to conquer Earth. They want to rebuild their race by reproducing with earth women. Earth fights back. From the director of "Godzilla." Dubbed in English from Japanese. *AKA:* Earth Defense Forces; Chikyu Boelgun.
1958 85m/C *JP* Kenji Sahara, Yumi Shirakawa, Takashi Shimura; *D:* Inoshiro Honda. VHS, Beta $29.95 *UHV*, *MLB* ♫♫½

Mysteries A rich tourist becomes obsessed by a beautiful local girl. As his obsession grows, his behavior becomes stranger. Interesting and well-acted. The film is an adaptation of the famous love story by Nobel-laureate Knut Hamsun. Suffers from poor dubbing.
1984 100m/C Rutger Hauer, Sylvia Kristel, David Rappaport, Rita Tushingham; *D:* Paul de Lussanet. VHS, Beta $69.95 *WWV* ♫½

Mysteries From Beyond Earth The bizarre world of psychic phenomena and the paranormal is explored in this compelling film. Among the many areas of investigation are UFO's, Kirlian Photography, psychic healing, and witchcraft.
1976 95m/C VHS, Beta $29.95 *UHV* ♫♫

Mysterious Desperado Young man, about to inherit a large estate, is framed on a murder charge by land grabbers.
1949 61m/B Tim Holt, Richard Martin. VHS, Beta $39.95 *RKO* ♫½

Mysterious Desperado/Rider From Tucson A western double feature. In "Mysterious Desperado," a young man is framed for a crime he did not commit. In "Rider From Tucson," evil claim jumpers will resort to murder to gain control of a gold mine.
1949 121m/B Tim Holt, Richard Martin. **VHS, Beta $39.95** *RKO, TTC* 𝄞𝄞 ½

Mysterious Doctor Satan A mad satanic scientist builds an army of mechanical robots to rob and terrorize the nation. In 15 episodes.
1940 250m/B Eduardo Ciannelli, Robert Wilcox, Ella Neal; *D:* William Witney. **VHS $29.95** *REP, VCN, MLB* 𝄞𝄞

Mysterious Island Exhilirating sci-fi classic adapted from Jules Verne's novel about escaping Civil War soldiers who go up in Verne balloon and come down on a Pacific island populated by giant animals. They also encounter two shipwrecked English ladies, pirates, and Captain Nemo (and his sub). Top-rate special effects by master Ray Harryhausen and music by Bernard Herrmann.
1961 101m/C *GB* Michael Craig, Joan Greenwood, Michael Callan, Gary Merrill, Herbert Lom, Beth Rogan, Percy Herbert, Dan Jackson, Nigel Green; *D:* Cy Endfield. **VHS, Beta, LV $19.95** *COL, MLB* 𝄞𝄞𝄞 ½

Mysterious Island of Beautiful Women A male sextet is stranded on a South Sea island, where they must endure the trials of an angry tribe of conveniently bikini-clad women.
1979 100m/C Jamie Lyn Bauer, Jayne Kennedy, Kathryn Davis, Deborah Shelton, Susie Coelho, Peter Lawford, Steven Keats, Clint Walker; *D:* Joseph Pevney. **VHS $39.95** *LIV* 𝄞

Mysterious Jane Amid soft-focus nudity, a husband and his lover conspire to institutionalize his wife.
198? 90m/C Amber Lee, Sandy Carey. **VHS, Beta $29.95** *MED* 𝄞

The Mysterious Lady Pre-Ninotchka Garbo plays Russian spy who betrays her mother country because she does not want to be alone.
1928 99m/B Greta Garbo, Conrad Nagel, Gustav von Seyffertitz, Richard Alexander, Albert Pollet, Edward Connelly. **VHS $29.99** *MGM, FCT* 𝄞𝄞 ½

The Mysterious Magician Entertaining suspense story of the mad murderer known as "The Wizard," who was thought by Scotland Yard to be dead, but the current murderwave in London suggests otherwise. Based on an Edgar Wallace story.
1965 95m/C *GE* Joachim Fuchsberger, Eddi Arent, Sophie Hardy, Karl John, Heinz Drache; *D:* Alfred Vohrer. **VHS $16.95** *SNC* 𝄞𝄞 ½

Mysterious Mr. Wong The Thirteen Coins of Confucius put San Francisco's Chinatown in a state of terror until Mr. Wong arrives.
1935 56m/B Arline Judge, Wallace Ford; *D:* William Nigh. **VHS, Beta, 3/4U, Special order formats $24.95** *NOS, MRV, SNC* 𝄞 ½

Mysterious Planet Humans fight off alien hordes in this space flick.
1984 90m/C **VHS, Beta $59.95** *VCD* 𝄞

The Mysterious Rider A cowboy tries to prevent unscrupulous homesteaders from cheating farmers out of their land. *AKA:* The Fighting Phantom.
1933 59m/B Kent Taylor, Lona Andre, Gail Patrick, Warren Hymer, Berton Churchill; *D:* Fred Allen. **VHS $12.95** *SNC, DVT* 𝄞𝄞 ½

The Mysterious Rider A man framed for murder must help innocent homesteaders from being cheated out of their land. *AKA:* Mark of the Avenger.
1938 75m/B Douglas Dumbrille, Sidney Toler, Russell Hayden, Charlotte Field; *D:* Lesley Selander. **VHS $19.95** *NOS, DVT* 𝄞 ½

The Mysterious Rider Routine oater has Crabbe and St. John helping a couple of kids protect their inheritance.
1942 56m/B Buster Crabbe, Al "Fuzzy" St. John, Caroline Burke, John Merton, Kermit Maynard, Jack Ingram, Charles "Slim" Whitaker; *D:* Sherman Scott. **VHS $19.95** *DVT, HEG* 𝄞𝄞

The Mysterious Stranger Printer's apprentice is given to bouts of daydreaming about a magic castle in Austria. Based on Twain tale.
1982 89m/C Chris Makepeace, Lance Kerwin, Fred Gwynne; *D:* Peter Hunt. **VHS $19.95** *MCA* 𝄞𝄞

Mysterious Two Two aliens visit the Earth in an effort to enlist converts to travel the universe with them.
1982 100m/C Jan Forsythe, Priscilla Pointer, Noah Beery Jr., Vic Tayback, James Stephens, Karen Werner, Robert Englund, Robert Pine; *D:* Gary Sherman. **VHS, Beta $59.95** *LIV* 𝄞𝄞 ½

Mystery at Castle House Three precocious children stumble onto a mystery when their friends disappear at a neighborhood castle.
1982 80m/C **VHS, Beta $14.98** *VID* 𝄞𝄞 ½

Mystery at Fire Island A clever young girl and her cousin encounter some strange people as they try to find out why their fisherman friend mysteriously vanished.
1981 62m/C Frank Converse, Barbara Byrne, Beth Ehlers, Eric Gurry. **VHS, Beta** *NO* 𝄞

Mystery Date A sort of teen version of "After Hours," in which a shy college guy gets a date with the girl of his dreams, only to be mistaken for a master criminal and pursued by gangsters, police and a crazed florist. Not terrible, but if you're old enough to drive you're probably too old to watch with amusement.
1991 (PG-13) 98m/C Ethan Hawke, Teri Polo, Brian McNamara, Fisher Stevens, D.D. Wong; *D:* Jonathan Wacks. **VHS $92.98** *ORI* 𝄞𝄞

Mystery in Swing An all-black mystery with music, about a trumpet player who has snake venom put on his mouthpiece.
1940 66m/B F.E. Miller, Monte Hawley, Marguerite Whitten, Tom Moore, Ceepee Johnson; *D:* Arthur Dreifuss. **VHS, Beta $29.95** *VYY* 𝄞𝄞

Mystery Island Beautifully filmed underwater scenes in this children's film about four youths who discover a deserted island which they name Mystery Island, and a retired pirate who lives there. When the children find counterfeit money and the bad guys return for it, the old pirate's clever plans keep the kids safe.
1981 75m/C **VHS, Beta $14.98** *VID* 𝄞𝄞 ½

Mystery Liner Dead bodies are found aboard ocean liner and passengers are concerned about it. Slow-moving sea cruise. *AKA:* The Ghost of John Holling.
1934 62m/B Noah Beery Sr., Astrid Allwyn, Cornelius Keefe, Gustav von Seyffertitz, Edwin Maxwell, Booth Howard, George "Gabby" Hayes; *D:* William Nigh. **VHS, Beta $16.95** *NOS, SNC* 𝄞𝄞 ½

The Mystery Man A Chicago reporter goes on a drinking binge and ends up in St. Louis. There he stumbles upon a mystery which may involve the paper for which he

works. He teams up with a beautiful woman to try to crack the case.
1935 65m/B Robert Armstrong, Maxine Doyle, Henry Kolker, Leroy Mason, James Burke; *D:* Ray McCarey. **VHS, Beta $16.95** *SNC* 𝄞𝄞 ½

Mystery Man Below-average episode has rancher Hoppy being bothered by rustlers. Boyd solves things in the usual way, while Clyde provides the laughs.
1944 58m/B William Boyd, Andy Clyde, Jimmy Rogers, Don Costello, Francis McDonald, Forrest Taylor, Eleanor Stewart; *D:* George Archainbaud. **VHS $19.95** *NOS* 𝄞 ½

Mystery Mansion Fortune in gold and a hundred-year-old mystery lead three children into an exciting treasure hunt. Family fare.
1983 (PG) 95m/C Dallas McKennon, Greg Wynne, Jane Ferguson. **VHS, Beta $19.95** *MED* 𝄞𝄞

Mystery Mountain Twelve episodes depict the villain known as the "Rattler" attempting to stop the construction of a railroad over Mystery Mountain.
1934 156m/B Ken Maynard, Gene Autry, Smiley Burnette; *D:* Otto Brower, B. Reeves Eason. **VHS, Beta, 3/4U, Special order formats $49.95** *NOS, VCN, CAB* 𝄞𝄞

The Mystery of Alexina True story of Herculine Adelaide Barbin, a 19th-century French hermaphrodite, who, after growing up a woman, fell in love with another woman and was actually revealed to be a man. Subtitled. Written by Jean Gruault. *AKA:* Mystere Alexina.
1986 86m/C *FR* Vuillemin, Valeri Stroh; *D:* Rene Feret. **VHS, Beta $29.98** *SUE, NLC* 𝄞𝄞 ½

Mystery of Mr. Wong The largest star sapphire in the world, the "Eye of the Daughter of the Moon," is stolen from a museum in its home country of China. Mr. Wong becomes involved in trying to trace its trail and the perpetrator of the murders that follow in its wake. One in the series of detective films.
1939 67m/B Boris Karloff, Grant Withers, Dorothy Tree, Lotus Long; *D:* William Nigh. **VHS $19.98** *MOV, MRV, DVT* 𝄞 ½

Mystery of the Hooded Horseman Tex finds himself pitted against a very strange adversary.
1937 61m/B Tex Ritter, Iris Meredith, Charles King, Joseph Girard, Lafe McKee; *D:* Ray Taylor. **VHS, Beta $19.95** *NOS, VDM, DVT* 𝄞𝄞

Mystery of the Leaping Fish/ Chess Fever Two silent shorts. One, filmed in 1916, is a surreal comedy-mystery, written by Todd Browning, about a doped-up detective named Coke Ennyday and his hallucinatory, sped-up adventures. The second, made in 1925 during the Moscow Chess Tournament, is a parody of professional chess playing and the fever with which it grips a country. Pudovkin's second directorial credit.
1925 64m/B Douglas Fairbanks Sr., Bessie Love, Alma Rubens; *D:* John Emerson, Vsevolod Pudovkin; *W:* Tod Browning. **VHS, Beta, 8mm $29.95** *VYY, MRV* 𝄞𝄞 ½

The Mystery of the Mary Celeste Tale of terror based on the bizarre case of the "Marie Celeste," an American ship found adrift and derelict on the Atlantic Ocean on December 5, 1872. *AKA:* The Phantom Ship; The Mystery of the Marie Celeste.
1937 64m/B Bela Lugosi, Shirley Grey, Edmund Willard. **VHS, Beta, 3/4U, Special order formats $24.95** *CCB, MRV, VYY* 𝄞𝄞

Mystery of the Million Dollar Hockey Puck Sinister diamond smugglers learn a lesson on ice from a pair of orphan lads. Features the National Hockey League's Montreal Canadians in one of their few film appearances.
1987 88m/C Michael MacDonald, Angele Knight, The Montreal Canadians; *D:* Jean LaFleur, Peter Svatek. **VHS, Beta** NO *🎬* ½

Mystery of the Riverboat Louisiana and the Mississippi River are the background for these 13 episodes of mystery and murder.
1944 90m/B Robert Lowery, Eddie Quillan; *D:* Henry MacRae. **VHS, Beta $29.95** UHV, MLB *🎬🎬* ½

Mystery of the Wax Museum Rarely seen, vintage horror classic about a wax-dummy maker who, after a disfiguring fire, resorts to murder and installs the wax-covered bodies of his victims in his museum. Famous for its pioneering use of two-strip Technicolor. Remade in 1953 in 3-D as "House of Wax."
1933 77m/C Lionel Atwill, Fay Wray, Glenda Farrell; *D:* Michael Curtiz. **VHS, Beta, LV $19.98** MGM, MLB *🎬🎬🎬*

Mystery Plane An inventor devises a new bomb-dropping mechanism, and must evade secret agents on his way to deliver it to the government.
1939 60m/B John Trent, Marjorie Reynolds, Milburn Stone, Peter George Lynn, Polly Ann Young; *D:* George Waggner. **VHS, Beta $19.95** NOS, DVT, HEG *🎬* ½

Mystery Ranch A cowboy finds himself in strange predicaments out on the range.
1934 52m/B George O'Brien, Charles Middleton, Cecilia Parker; *D:* David Howard. **VHS, Beta $19.95** NOS, DVT *🎬* ½

Mystery Squadron Twelve chapters, 13 minutes each. Daredevil air action in flight against the masked pilots of the Black Ace.
1933 240m/B Bob Steele, Guinn Williams, Lucille Browne, Jack Mulhall, J. Carroll Naish, Jack Mower; *D:* Colbert Clark. **VHS, Beta, 3/4U, Special order formats $49.95** NOS, VCN, DVT *🎬* ½

Mystery Train A run down hotel in Memphis is the scene for three vignettes concerning the visit of foreigners to the U.S. Themes of mythic Americana, Elvis, and life on the fringe pervade this hip and quirky film. The three vignettes all tie together in clever and funny overlaps. Waits fans should listen for his performance as a DJ.
1989 (R) 110m/C Masatoshi Nagase, Youki Kudoh, Jay Hawkins, Cinque Lee, Joe Strummer; *D:* Jim Jarmusch; *V:* Tom Waits. **VHS, LV $79.98** ORI *🎬🎬🎬*

Mystery Trooper Adventures in the great wilderness full of prospecting, greed, and Indians all being observed by the Royal Mounties. Ten chapters of the serial at 20 minutes each.
1932 200m/B Robert Frazer, Buzz Barton. **VHS, Beta, 3/4U, Special order formats $24.95** GPV, NOS, CAB *🎬🎬*

Mystic Circle Murder Reporter sets out to uncover phony mediums, particularly the Great La Gagge, whose fake apparitions are so convincing that it caused one of his clients to have a heart attack. Cheaply made, and it's obvious. Watch for a cameo by Harry Houdini's wife, who talks about life after death. Also known as "Religious Racketeers." Based on a story by director O'Connor.
1939 69m/B Betty Compson, Robert Fiske, Helene Le Berthon, Arthur Gardner; *D:* Frank O'Connor. **VHS $16.95** SNC *🎬*

Mystic Pizza Two sisters and their best friend, work at the Mystic Pizza Parlor in the seaside town of Mystic, Connecticut. One is uncertain about marriage and leaves her fiance at the altar, another falls for a rich preppie, and the third, the smart girl with college plans, falls for a married man. Throughout several months, they struggle with their hopes, their loves, the caste system which keeps townies and tourists separate, and their family rivalries. Charming performances featuring the screen debut of Roberts.
1988 (R) 101m/C Annabeth Gish, Julia Roberts, Lili Taylor, Vincent D'Onofrio, William R. Moses, Adam Storke; *D:* Daniel Petrie. **VHS, Beta, LV** NO *🎬🎬🎬*

Nabonga The daughter of an embezzler, whose plane crashes in the jungle, befriends a gorilla who protects her. Soon a young man comes looking for the embezzler's cash, meets the woman and the ape, and together they go on a wonderful journey. *AKA:* Gorilla; Jungle Woman.
1944 72m/B Buster Crabbe, Fifi d'Orsay, Barton MacLane, Julie London, Herbert Rawlinson; *D:* Sam Newfield. **VHS $16.95** SNC, NOS, MOV *🎬🎬*

Nadia Entertaining account of the life of Nadia Comaneci, the Romanian gymnast who earned six perfect tens with her stunning performance at the 1976 Olympic Games. Made for television.
1984 100m/C Talia Balsam, Jonathan Banks, Simone Blue, Johann Carlo, Carrie Snodgress; *D:* Alan Cooke. **VHS, Beta $19.95** FHE, STP *🎬🎬* ½

Nadine In Austin circa 1954, an almost divorced beautician witnesses a murder and goes undercover with her estranged husband to track down the murderer, before he finds her. Plenty of low-key humor. Well-paced fun; Basinger is terrific.
1987 (PG) 83m/C Jeff Bridges, Kim Basinger, Rip Torn, Gwen Verdon, Glenne Headly, Jerry Stiller; *D:* Robert Benton. **VHS, Beta, LV $19.98** FOX *🎬🎬* ½

Nail Gun Massacre A crazed killer with a penchant for nailing bodies to just about anything goes on a hammering spree. In horrific, vivid color.
1986 90m/C Rocky Patterson, Ron Queen, Beau Leland, Michelle Meyer; *D:* Bill Lesley. **VHS, Beta** NO Woof!

Nails Harry "Nails" Niles (Hopper) is a tough, experienced cop whose partner has been killed by drug dealers. Harry doesn't take this well and decides to go on a violent search for revenge. Archer is wasted as Harry's estranged wife and Hopper can sleepwalk through this type of cliched wild-man role. Made for cable television.
1992 (R) 96m/C Dennis Hopper, Anne Archer, Tomas Milian, Cliff DeYoung; *D:* John Flynn. **VHS, Beta, LV $89.98** FXV *🎬* ½

Nairobi Affair Savage and Heston fight poachers and each other in Kenya, when the father has an affair with his son's ex-wife. Mediocre, derivative script, but beautiful scenery. Made for television.
1988 (PG) 95m/C Charlton Heston, John Savage, Maud Adams, John Rhys-Davies, Connie Booth; *D:* Marvin J. Chomsky. **VHS, Beta $79.95** VMK *🎬🎬*

Nais Vintage Pagnolian peasant drama. A hunchback sacrifices himself for the girl he loves. She escapes to another man's arms. Adapted from the Emile Zola novel "Nais Micoulin." In French with English subtitles.
1945 105m/B *FR* Fernandel; *D:* Fernand Lauterier; *W:* Marcel Pagnol. **VHS, Beta, 8mm $29.95** VYY, FCT, DVT *🎬🎬🎬*

The Naked and the Dead Sanitized adaptation of Norman Mailer's bestselling novel about army life in the Pacific during World War II. Resentment between officers and enlisted men proves to be almost as dangerous as the Japanese. Uneven acting and cliched characterizations make this an average outing. Don't expect to hear the profane language that sensationalized the book, because most of it was edited out of the screenplay.
1958 131m/C Aldo Ray, Cliff Robertson, Joey Bishop, Raymond Massey, Lili St. Cyr, James Best; *D:* Raoul Walsh. **VHS, Beta $15.95** UHV *🎬🎬* ½

The Naked Angels Rape, mayhem, beatings, and road-hogging streetbikes highlight this biker film, acted, in part, by actual bikers, and in part by others who were actually (almost) actors. The gang war rages from Los Angeles to Las Vegas. Roger Corman was the executive producer.
1969 (R) 83m/C Michael Greene, Richard Rust, Felicia Guy; *W/D:* Bruce Clark. **VHS, Beta $39.95** CRV *🎬*

Naked Cage Brutal women's prison film that is borderline soft-core, about an innocent country woman, a horseriding fanatic, who is framed for a robbery and sent to the slammer. There, she contends with lesbian wardens and inmates. Disgusting.
1986 (R) 97m/C Shari Shattuck, Angel Tompkins, Lucinda Crosby, Christina Whitaker; *D:* Paul Nicholas. **VHS, Beta $19.95** COL Woof!

The Naked City A film noir classic which makes spectacular use of its New York City locations. In this documentary-style drama, a beautiful playgirl is murdered and police detectives Fitzgerald and Taylor are left without clues. The film is spent running down weak leads and interviewing various suspects and witnesses. When they finally get a break, it leads to playboy Duff, who hired a goon to actually commit the murder. A spectacular ending takes place on the Brooklyn Bridge between cops and killer. Producer Hellinger also provided the hard-boiled narration, patterned after the tabloid newspaper stories he once wrote. The film served as the impetus for the television show of the same name. Hellinger's film postscript also became the television show's noted tagline: "There are eight million stories in the naked city, this has been one of them."
1948 96m/B Barry Fitzgerald, Don Taylor, Howard Duff, Ted de Corsia, Dorothy Hart; *D:* Jules Dassin. Academy Awards '48: Best Black and White Cinematography, Best Film Editing; Nominations: Best Story. **VHS $69.95** IVY *🎬🎬🎬* ½

The Naked Civil Servant Remarkable film, based on the life of flamboyant homosexual Quentin Crisp, who came out of the closet in his native England, long before his lifestyle would be tolerated by Britains. For mature audiences.
1975 80m/C John Hurt; *D:* Jack Gold. **VHS, Beta $19.99** HBO *🎬🎬🎬* ½

The Naked Edge Cooper stars as a middle-aged businessman whose wife suspects him of murder after she begins snooping into his business affairs. Cooper's last film and far from his best. Poor direction and holes in the screenplay divert from what could have been a tight thriller.
1961 99m/C *GB* Gary Cooper, Deborah Kerr, Eric Portman, Diane Cilento, Hermione Gingold, Peter Cushing, Michael Wilding, Ronald Howard; *D:* Michael Anderson Sr.; *W:* Joseph Stefano. **VHS $19.98** MGM, MOV *🎬🎬*

The Naked Face A psychiatrist tries to find out why his patients are being killed. He gets no help from police, who suspect he is the murderer. A dull affair featuring unusual casting of Moore, while Steiger's suspicious police captain character provides spark. From the novel by Sidney Sheldon.
1984 (R) 105m/C Roger Moore, Rod Steiger, Elliott Gould, Art Carney, Anne Archer, David Hedison; *D:* Bryan Forbes. VHS, Beta $79.95 MGM 🎬🎬

The Naked Flame O'Keefe plays an investigator in a strange town inhabited by weird, religious fanatics. After he arrives, the womenfolk shed their clothes in this pitiful, pathetic hilarity.
1968 (R) ?m/C Dennis O'Keefe, Linda Bennett, Kasey Rogers. VHS $16.95 SNC Woof!

The Naked Gun: From the Files of Police Squad More hysterical satire from the creators of "Airplane!" The short-lived television cop spoof "Police Squad" moves to the big screen and has Lt. Drebin uncover a plot to assassinate Queen Elizabeth while she is visiting Los Angeles. Nearly nonstop gags and pratfalls provide lots of laughs. Nielsen is perfect as Drebin and the supporting cast is strong; cameos abound.
1988 (PG-13) 85m/C Leslie Nielsen, Ricardo Montalban, Priscilla Presley, George Kennedy, O.J. Simpson, Nancy Marchand, John Houseman; *Cameos:* Weird Al Yankovic, Reggie Jackson, Dr. Joyce Brothers; *D:* David Zucker; *W:* Jerry Zucker, Jim Abrahams, David Zucker, Pat Proft. VHS, Beta, LV, 8mm $14.95 PAR 🎬🎬🎬

Naked Gun 2 1/2: The Smell of Fear Lt. Drebin returns to rescue the world from a faulty energy policy devised by the White House and oil-lords. A notch down from the previous entry but still hilarious cop parody. Nielsen has this character down to a tee, and there's a laugh every minute. Laserdisc version is letterboxed and features dolby surround sound.
1991 (PG-13) 85m/C Leslie Nielsen, Priscilla Presley, George Kennedy, O.J. Simpson, Robert Goulet, Richard Griffiths, Jacqueline Brookes, Lloyd Bochner, Tim O'Connor, Peter Mark Richman; *Cameos:* Mel Torme, Eva Gabor, Weird Al Yankovic; *W/D:* David Zucker; *W:* Pat Proft; *M:* Ira Newborn. VHS, Beta, LV, 8mm $19.95 PAR, PIA 🎬🎬½

Naked Hills Meandering tale about a man (Wayne) who, suffering from gold fever, searches for 40 years in 19th Century California and ends up out of luck, losing his wife and family.
1956 72m/C David Wayne, Keenan Wynn, James Barton, Marcia Henderson, Jim Backus, Denver Pyle, Myrna Dell, Frank Fenton, Fuzzy Knight; *W/D:* Josef Shaftel. VHS NO 🎬½

Naked in the Night Cheap German exploitation film about the dangers of promiscuous women. Dubbed in English.
1958 ?m/C GE Eva Bartok, Alexander Kerst. VHS $16.95 SNC 🎬

Naked in the Sun The true story of events leading to the war between the Osceola and Seminole Indians and a slave trader. Somewhat slow.
1957 95m/C James Craig, Lita Milan, Barton MacLane, Tony Hunter; *D:* R. John Hugh. VHS $19.98 REP 🎬

Naked Is Better A couple of buffoons pose as hospital workers so they can play doctor with a hospitalized actress.
1973 93m/C Alberto Olmedo, Jorge Porcel, Jorge Barreiro, Maria Casan. VHS, Beta $39.95 MED 🎬

Naked Jungle Suspenseful, well-done jungle adventure of a plantation owner (Heston) in South America and his North American mail-order bride (Parker), who do battle with a deadly, miles-long siege of red army ants. Realistic and worth watching. Produced by George Pal, shot by Ernest Laszlo and based on the story "Leiningen vs. the Ants" by Carl Stephenson.
1954 95m/C Charlton Heston, Eleanor Parker, Abraham Sofaer, William Conrad; *D:* Byron Haskin. VHS, Beta, LV $19.95 PAR 🎬🎬🎬

Naked Kiss Fuller's most savage, hysterical film noir. A brutalized prostitute escapes her pimp and tries to enter respectable small-town society. She finds even more perversion and sickness there. *AKA:* The Iron Kiss.
1964 92m/B Constance Towers, Anthony Eisley, Michael Dante, Virginia Grey, Patsy Kelly, Betty Bronson; *D:* Samuel Fuller. LV $79.95 HMV, VYG 🎬🎬½

Naked Lie A District Attorney and a judge engage in an ultra-steamy affair and inevitably clash when she is assigned as a prosecutor on the politically explosive case over which he is presiding.
1989 89m/C Victoria Principal, James Farentino, Glenn Withrow, William Lucking, Dakin Matthews; *D:* Richard A. Colla. VHS $79.95 ING 🎬🎬

Naked Lunch Whacked-out movie based on William S. Burroughs's autobiographical account of drug abuse, homosexuality, violence, and weirdness set in the drug-inspired land called Interzone. Hallucinogenic images are carried to the extreme: typewriters metamorphose into beetles, bloblike creatures with sex organs scurry about, and characters mainline insecticide. Some of the characters are clearly based on writers of the Beat generation, including Jane and Paul Bowles, Allen Ginsberg, and Jack Kerouac.
1991 (R) 117m/C Peter Weller, Judy Davis, Ian Holm, Julian Sands, Roy Scheider; *W/D:* David Cronenberg. VHS $94.98 TCF, TAM 🎬🎬🎬

Naked Massacre A maniac kills nurses, leaving no clues for the police to follow.
198? 90m/C Matthieu Carriere, Carol Laurie; *D:* Denis Heroux. VHS, Beta $19.98 VDC 🎬

Naked Obsession A city councilman running for mayor is mugged in one of the seedier parts of the city. He's found by a homeless man who takes him to a kinky nightclub where the councilman is promptly seduced by a topless bar hostess with secrets of her own. Also available in an unrated version.
1991 (R) 93m/C William Katt, Maria Ford, Rick Dean; *D:* Dan Golden. VHS $89.98 VES, MOV 🎬½

Naked Paradise A young woman moves in with her mother and step-sister and finds difficulty in adjusting.
1978 (R) 86m/C Laura Gemser, Annie Belle. VHS, Beta UHV 🎬½

The Naked Prey Unnerving African adventure which contains some unforgettably brutal scenes. A safari guide (Wilde), leading a hunting party, must watch as an indigenous tribe murders all his companions, and according to their customs, allows him to be set free, sans clothes or weapons, to be hunted by the best of the tribe.
1966 96m/C Cornel Wilde, Gertrude Van Der Berger, Ken Gampu; *D:* Cornel Wilde. VHS, Beta, LV $19.95 PAR 🎬🎬🎬

The Naked Spur A compulsive bounty hunter tracks down a vicious outlaw and his beautiful girlfriend. An exciting film from the Mann-Stewart team and considered one of their best, infusing the traditional western

with psychological confusion. Wonderful use of Rockies locations.
1953 93m/C James Stewart, Robert Ryan, Janet Leigh, Millard Mitchell; *D:* Anthony Mann. VHS, Beta $19.98 MGM, TLF 🎬🎬🎬½

Naked Sun Beguiling mystery set during the Carnival at Rio chock full of suspense, romance, and just a touch of the supernatural.
197? 90m/C VHS NO 🎬🎬

The Naked Sword of Zorro Deadly Don Luis taxes the town by day and violates the women by night, but Zorro takes a stand and saves the town. When he's not dressed as Zorro, he is Don Diego, an inept fool, but when he puts that suit on, look out. The ladies can't keep their hands off of him. There are more lusty females than villains, but there's still lots of swordplay and action.
1969 94m/C VHS $19.95 VDM 🎬

The Naked Truth A greedy publisher tries to get rich quick by publishing a scandal magazine about the "lurid" lives of prominent citizens. Well-drawn characters in an appealing offbeat comedy. *AKA:* Your Past is Showing.
1958 92m/C GB Peter Sellers, Terry-Thomas, Shirley Eaton, Dennis Price; *D:* Mario Zampi. VHS, Beta $59.95 SUE 🎬🎬½

Naked Vengeance A woman's husband is murdered, she is beaten and raped, and she becomes a vengeful, vicious killing machine. Gratuitous violence, distasteful to the max. *AKA:* Satin Vengeance.
1985 (R) 97m/C Deborah Tranelli, Kaz Garas, Bill McLaughlin; *D:* Cirio H. Santiago. VHS, Beta $79.98 LIV Woof!

Naked Venus Ulmer's last film is a slow-paced tale about an American artist, married to a model who poses in the nude and belongs to a nudist camp, whose wealthy mother tries to tear the marriage apart. Discrimination and intolerance of nudist camps is explored.
1958 80m/B Patricia Conelle; *D:* Edgar G. Ulmer. VHS, Beta $19.95 VDM 🎬½

Naked Warriors Ancient Romans capture beautiful women from around the world and force them to compete in gladiatorial games. New World exploitation gem featuring mostly Italian cast, including Bay, who starred in the previous year's "Lady Frankenstein." *AKA:* The Arena.
1973 (R) 75m/C Margaret Markov, Pam Grier, Lucretia Love, Paul Muller, Daniel Vargas, Marie Louise, Mary Count, Sara (Rosalba Neri) Bay, Vic Karis, Sid Lawrence, Peter Cester, Anna Melita; *D:* Steve Carver. VHS, Beta $79.95 MGM 🎬🎬

The Naked Witch College student researching witchcraft digs up the grave of a long-dead witch. She comes back to life and takes revenge on the village that killed her years earlier. The nude shots feature someone's finger over the camera lens to cover the witch's vital organs. *AKA:* The Naked Temptress.
1964 60m/C Beth Porter, Robert Burgos, Bryarly Lee, Lee Forbes; *D:* Andy Milligan. VHS $16.95 SNC 🎬

Naked Youth Seedy drive-in cheapie about two punks breaking out of juvenile prison and heading south of the border on a trail filled with crime, drugs, and loose women. *AKA:* Wild Youth.
1959 80m/B Robert Hutton, John Goddard, Carol Ohmart, Jan Brooks, Robert Arthur, Steve Rowland, Clancy Cooper; *D:* John F. Schreyer. VHS, Beta $9.95 RHI, SNC Woof!

Nam Angels Hell's Angels enter Southeast Asia and rescue POWs.

1988 (R) 91m/C Brad Johnson, Vernon Wells, Kevin Duffis. **VHS, Beta** $79.95 *MED ♂*

A Name for Evil Having grown tired of city living, a couple moves to an old family estate out in the country near the Great Lakes. Strange sounds in the night are the first signs of the terror to come.
1970 (R) 74m/C Robert Culp, Samantha Eggar, Sheila Sullivan, Mike Lane; *D:* Bernard Girard. **VHS, Beta** *PGN ♪♪*

The Name of the Rose An exhaustive, off-center adaptation of the bestselling Umberto Eco novel about violent murders in a 14th-century Italian abbey. An English monk struggles against religious fervor in his quest to uncover the truth.
1986 (R) 128m/C Sean Connery, F. Murray Abraham, Christian Slater, Ron Perlman, William Hickey, Feodor Chaliapin, Elya Baskin, Michael Lonsdale; *D:* Jean-Jacques Annaud. **VHS, Beta, LV** $14.95 *NLC ♪♪½*

Namu, the Killer Whale Based on the true story of a marine biologist (Lansing) who gets the perfect opportunity to study killer whales when one is confined to a small cove. The local fisherman want to kill the creature because it feeds on the salmon they catch but they are persuaded against their baser instincts. Filmed on location in the San Juan Islands of Puget Sound. The real Namu lived at the Seattle Public Aquarium.
1966 89m/C Robert Lansing, John Anderson, Robin Mattson, Richard Erdman, Lee Meriwether, Joe Higgins; *D:* Laslo Benedek. **VHS** $14.95 *MGM ♪♪½*

Nana French version of Emile Zola's novel about an actress-prostitute who seduces the high society of Paris in the late 1880s, and suffers a heart-breaking downfall and death. Film has three remakes of the original 1926 version.
1955 118m/C *FR* Charles Boyer, Martine Carol. **VHS, Beta** $24.95 *NOS, DVT, HEG ♪♪♪*

Nana A lavishly photographed, graphic adaptation of the Emile Zola novel about a Parisian whore who acquires power by seducing the richest and politically formidable men. Dubbed.
1982 92m/C *IT* Katya Berger, Jean-Pierre Aumont; *M:* Dan Wolman; *M:* Ennio Morricone. **VHS, Beta** $79.95 *FCT, MGM ♪♪½*

Nanami, First Love A controversial Japanese film about a man madly in love with a beautiful prostitute he cannot satisfy sexually. Explicit; in Japanese with English subtitles.
1968 104m/B *JP D:* Susumu Hani. **VHS, Beta, 8mm** $29.95 *VYY, FCT, TAM ♪♪♪*

Nancy Astor A portrait of the beautiful, spirited Virginian who became a member of the British Parliament.
1982 55m/C *GB* Lisa Harrow, James Fox, Dan O'Herlihy, Sylvia Syms. **VHS, Beta** *TLF ♪♪*

Nancy Drew, Reporter The young sleuth gets to play reporter after winning a newspaper contest. In no time at all, she's involved in a murder mystery.
1939 68m/B Bonita Granville, John Litel, Frank Thomas Jr., Mary Lee, Sheila Bromley, Betty Amann, Dick Jones, Olin Howland; *D:* William Clemens. **VHS** $19.95 *HTV, NOS ♪♪*

Nancy Goes to Rio Actresses Powell and Sothern compete for the same part in a play and for the same man. Catch is, they're mother and daughter. Zany consequences ensue. Sothern's last film for MGM. ♫Time and Time Again; Shine On Harvest Moon; Cha Bomm Pa Pa; Yipsee-I-O; Magic is the Moonlight; Musetta's Waltz; Love is Like This; Nancy Goes to Rio.

1950 99m/C Ann Sothern, Jane Powell, Barry Sullivan, Carmen Miranda, Louis Calhern, Scotty Beckett, Hans Conried, Glenn Anders; *D:* Robert Z. Leonard. **VHS** $19.98 *MGM, MLB, CCB ♪♪½*

Napoleon A vivid, near-complete restoration of Gance's epic silent masterpiece about the famed conqueror's early years, from his youth through the Italian Campaign. An innovative, spectacular achievement with its use of multiple split screens, montage, color, and triptychs. Produced by Kevin Brownlow with a score by Carmine Coppola and given a gala theatrical re-release in 1981. Remade in 1955.
1927 235m/C *FR* Albert Dieudonne, Antonin Artaud, Pierre Batcheff, Gina Manes, Armand Bernard, Harry Krimer, Albert Bras, Abel Gance, Georges Cahuzac; *D:* Abel Gance. **VHS, Beta, LV** $29.95 *MCA, TAM ♪♪♪♪*

Napoleon Depicts life story of Napoleon from his days as a soldier in the French army to his exile on the Island of Elba. Falls short of the fantastic 1927 silent classic as it attempts to delve into Napoleon the man, as opposed to his conquests. Some might find it too slow for their tastes.
1955 123m/C *FR* Raymond Pellegrin, Orson Welles, Maria Schell, Yves Montand, Erich von Stroheim, Jean Gabin, Jean-Pierre Aumont; *D:* Sacha Guitry. **VHS, Beta, LV** $19.95 *NOS, MRV, MPI ♪♪*

Napoleon and Samantha Disney adventure about Napoleon, an orphan (Whitaker), who is befriended by Danny, a college student (Douglas). After the death of his grandfather, Napoleon decides to take Major, his elderly pet lion, and follow Danny, who is herding goats for the summer, across the American northwest mountains and they are joined by Samantha (Foster in her film debut). Worth watching.
1972 91m/C Jodie Foster, Johnny Whitaker, Michael Douglas, Will Geer, Henry Jones; *D:* Bernard McEveety. **VHS, Beta** $69.95 *DIS ♪♪♪*

The Narcotics Story Bad film on the same vein as "Reefer Madness." Originally intended as a police training film, this shows the evils and destruction of heroin addiction. Portrayals of drug addicts are hilarious. *AKA:* The Dreaded Persuasion.
1958 75m/C Sharon Strand, Darlene Hendricks, Herbert Crisp, Fred Marratto; *D:* Robert W. Larsen. **VHS** $16.95 *SNC Woof!*

Narda or The Summer Two young men decide they will share a girlfriend during a summer romance, only Narda has other plans. She decides that both men will belong to her rather than the other way around. In Spanish with English subtitles.
1976 96m/C *MX* Hector Bonilla, Enrique Alvarez Felix; *D:* Juan Guerrero. **VHS** $24.98 *TAM ♪♪*

The Narrow Margin Well-made, harrowing adventure about a cop who is in charge of transporting a gangster's widow to a trial where she is to testify. On the train he must try to keep her safe from the hit-men who would murder her. A real cat and mouse game—one of the best suspense movies of the '50s.
1952 71m/B Charles McGraw, Marie Windsor, Jacqueline White, Queenie Leonard, Gordon Gebert, Don Beddoe, Harry Harvey; *D:* Alfred E. Green. **VHS** $19.98 *TTC, MLB, TTC ♪♪♪*

Narrow Margin Archer reluctantly agrees to testify against the mob after witnessing a murder, and Los Angeles D.A. Hackman is assigned to protect her on the train through the Rockies back to L.A. Bad idea, she finds out. No match for its '52 predecessor.

1990 (R) 99m/C Gene Hackman, Anne Archer, James B. Sikking, J.T. Walsh, M. Emmet Walsh; *D:* Peter Hyams. **VHS, LV** $19.95 *LIV ♪♪*

Narrow Trail A silent classic that still stands as one of the best Westerns ever made. A tough cowboy with a troubled past hopes a good woman can save him. But she's seen trouble, too. They meet up again in San Francisco's Barbary Coast. A horse race might hold the answer.
1917 56m/B William S. Hart, Sylvia Bremer, Milton Ross; *D:* William S. Hart. **VHS, Beta** $15.95 *NOS, GPV, CCB ♪♪♪½*

Nashville Altman's stunning, brilliant film tapestry that follows the lives of 24 people during a political campaign/music festival in Nashville. Seemingly extemporaneous vignettes, actors playing themselves (Elliott Gould and Julie Christie), funny, touching, poignant character studies concerning affairs of the heart and despairs of the mind. Repeatedly blurs reality and fantasy. ♫I'm Easy; Two Hundred Years; Keep A'Goin'; One, I Love You; Let Me Be the One; The Day I Looked Jesus in the Eye; For the Sake of the Children; I Never Get Enough; It Don't Worry Me; Honey; Down to the River; Tapedeck in His Tractor (The Cowboy Song); Bluebird; My Idaho Home; Dues; Sing a Song; The Heart of a Gentle Woman; Rose's Cafe; Old Man Mississippi; Since You've Gone; Trouble in the U.S.A.; My Baby's Cookin' in Another Man's Pan; Swing Low, Sweet Chariot; Yes, I Do; Memphis; I Don't Know If I Found It in You; Rolling Stone.
1975 (R) 159m/C Keith Carradine, Lily Tomlin, Henry Gibson, Ronee Blakley, Keenan Wynn, David Arkin, Geraldine Chaplin, Lauren Hutton, Shelley Duvall, Barbara Harris, Allen Garfield, Karen Black, Christina Raines; *D:* Robert Altman; *W:* Joan Tewkesbury. Academy Awards '75: Best Song ("I'm Easy"); Nominations: Best Director (Altman), Best Picture, Best Supporting Actress (Blakley, Tomlin); National Board of Review Awards '75: 10 Best Films of the Year, Best Director (Altman), Best Supporting Actress (Blakley); National Society of Film Critics Awards '75: Best Director (Altman), Best Film, Best Supporting Actor (Gibson), Best Supporting Actress (Tomlin). **VHS, Beta, LV** $79.95 *PAR ♪♪♪♪*

Nashville Beat Gang targets the citizens of Nashville, Tennessee, until two tough cops stomp the gang's delusion that Southern folk are easy marks.
1989 110m/C Kent McCord, Martin Milner; *D:* Bernard L. Kowalski. **VHS** *NO ♪♪*

Nashville Girl Innocent country girl who wants to make good in the country music scene, rises to the top of the Nashville success ladder, by compromising everything and hanging out with stereotyped no-goods in the show biz world. It's as good as a yawn. *AKA:* Country Music Daughter; New Girl in Town.
1976 (R) 90m/C Monica Gayle, Johnny Rodriguez; *D:* Gus Trikonis. **VHS, Beta** $59.98 *NLC ♂*

The Nasty Girl A bright young German model plans to enter a national essay contest on the topic of her hometown's history during the Third Reich. While researching the paper, she's harassed and even brutalized, but refuses to cease her sleuthing. Excellent performances, tight direction, with comedic touches that charmingly imparts an important message. Based on a true story. In German with English subtitles.
1990 (PG-13) 93m/C *GE* Lena Stolze, Monika Baumgartner, Michael Gahr; *W/D:* Michael Verhoeven. **VHS** $89.99 *TAM, HBO ♪♪♪½*

Nasty Habits Broad farce depicting a corrupt Philadelphia convent as a satiric parallel to Watergate, with nuns modeled on Nixon, Dean and Mitchell. Includes cameo appearances by various media personalities. Based on the British novel "The Abbess of Crewe" by Muriel Spark.
1977 (PG) 92m/C *GB* Glenda Jackson, Geraldine Page, Anne Jackson, Melina Mercouri, Sandy Dennis, Susan Penhaligon, Anne Meara, Edith Evans, Rip Torn, Eli Wallach, Jerry Stiller; *Cameos:* Mike Douglas, Bill Jorgensen, Jessica Savitch, Howard K. Smith; *D:* Michael Lindsay-Hogg. VHS, Beta $69.95 *MED* ⅃⅃

Nasty Hero Hard-boiled ex-con comes to Miami to avenge the car thieves who framed him and got him sent to the slammer. This is car-chase scene heaven—little plot or drama.
1989 (PG-13) 79m/C Robert Sedgwick, Carlos Palomino, Scott Feraco, Mike Starr, Rosanna DaVon; *D:* Nick Barwood. VHS, Beta, LV $79.95 *COL* ⅃½

Nasty Rabbit Ridiculous spoof about Soviet spies intent on releasing a rabbit with a hideous Communist disease into the U.S. Everyone gets in on the chase: Nazi forces, cowboys and indians, sideshow freaks, banditos—what is the point? *AKA:* Spies-A-Go-Go.
1964 88m/C Arch Hall Jr., Micha Terr, Melissa Morgan, John Akana; *D:* James Landis. VHS, Beta $59.95 *RHI* ⅃

Natas...The Reflection A reporter persists in validating an Indian demon myth.
1983 (PG) 90m/C Randy Mulkey, Pat Bolt, Craig Hensley, Kelli Kuhn. VHS, Beta $29.95 *LIV* ⅃

Nate and Hayes Set during the mid-1800s in the South Pacific, the notorious real-life swashbuckler Captain "Bully" Hayes ("good pirate") helps young missionary Nate recapture his fiancee from a cutthroat gang of evil slave traders. Entertaining "jolly rogers" film.
1983 (PG) 100m/C *NZ* Tommy Lee Jones, Michael O'Keefe, Max Phipps, Jenny Seagrove; *D:* Ferdinand Fairfax. VHS, Beta, LV $14.95 *PAR* ⅃⅃½

Nathalie Comes of Age Soft-core Italian flick in which a young girl is lured into making a dirty movie by a lustful entrepreneur. Dubbed.
1986 93m/C *IT* Marcella Petri, Grazia de Giorgi. VHS, Beta $29.95 *MED* Woof!

A Nation Aflame Anti-Klan film is based on a story by Thomas L. Dixon, the author of "The Clansman," from which D.W. Griffith made "The Birth of a Nation." In this story, a con man gains control of the state's government through an ultra-nationalistic secret society, and eventually pays for his corruption.
1937 70m/B Lila Lee, Noel Madison, Snub Pollard; *D:* Norma Trelvar. VHS, Beta $16.95 *SNC, NOS, GVV* ⅃½

National Adultery The eternal triangle is sketched in this comedy for adults only, starring 1981 Miss Spain.
19?? 90m/C *IT* VHS, Beta *VCD* ⅃½

National Lampoon Goes to the Movies Parodies of popular Hollywood genres, including cop thrillers, melodramas, and inspirational biographies, done in goofy "Lampoon" style.
1981 89m/C Robby Benson, Candy Clark, Diane Lane, Christopher Lloyd, Peter Riegert, Richard Widmark, Henny Youngman. VHS $14.99 *MOV* ⅃⅃

National Lampoon's Animal House Classic Belushi vehicle running amuck. Set in 1962 and responsible for launching Otis Day and the Knights and defining cinematic food fights. Every college tradition from fraternity rush week to the homecoming pageant is irreverently and relentlessly mocked in this wild comedy about Delta House, a fraternity on the edge. Climaxes with the homecoming parade from hell. Sophomoric, but very funny, with a host of young stars who went on to more serious work. Remember: "Knowledge is good." *AKA:* Animal House.
1978 (R) 109m/C John Belushi, Tim Matheson, John Vernon, Donald Sutherland, Peter Riegert, Stephen Furst, Bruce McGill, Mark Metcalf, Verna Bloom, Karen Allen, Tom Hulce, Mary Louise Weller, Kevin Bacon; *D:* John Landis. VHS, Beta, LV $14.95 *MCA* ⅃⅃⅃½

National Lampoon's Christmas Vacation The third vacation for the Griswold family finds them hosting repulsive relatives for Yuletide. The sight gags, although predictable, are sometimes on the mark. Quaid is a standout as the slovenly cousin. *AKA:* Christmas Vacation.
1989 (PG-13) 93m/C Chevy Chase, Beverly D'Angelo, Randy Quaid, Diane Ladd, John Randolph, E.G. Marshall, Doris Roberts, Julia Louis-Dreyfus, Mae Questel, William Hickey, Brian Doyle-Murray, Juliette Lewis, Johnny Galecki, Nicholas Guest, Miriam Flynn; *D:* Jeremiah S. Chechik; *W:* John Hughes; *M:* Angelo Badalamenti. VHS, Beta, LV, 8mm $19.98 *WAR* ⅃⅃½

National Lampoon's Class of '86 This is a live stage comedy show written and sponsored by the infamous adult humor magazine, featuring a new cast of comics. *AKA:* Class of '86.
1986 86m/C Rodger Bumpass, Veanne Cox, Annie Golden, John Michael Higgins, Tommy Koenig. VHS, Beta $29.95 *PAR* ⅃⅃½

National Lampoon's Class Reunion Class reunion with some very wacky guests and a decided lack of plot or purpose. Things go from bad to worse when a crazed killer decides to join in on the festivities. Disappointing with very few laughs. *AKA:* Class Reunion.
1982 (R) 85m/C Shelley Smith, Gerrit Graham, Michael Lerner; *D:* Michael Miller. VHS, Beta, LV $29.98 *LIV, VES* Woof!

National Lampoon's European Vacation Sappy sequel to "Vacation" that has witless Chase and his family bumbling around in the land "across the pond." The Griswolds nearly redefine the term "ugly American." Stonehenge will never be the same. *AKA:* European Vacation.
1985 (PG-13) 94m/C Chevy Chase, Beverly D'Angelo, Dana Hill, Jason Lively, Victor Lanoux, John Astin; *D:* Amy Heckerling; *W:* John Hughes, Robert Klane, Eric Idle. VHS, Beta, LV, 8mm $19.98 *WAR* ⅃½

National Lampoon's Loaded Weapon 1 Cop Jack Colt (Estevez) and partner Wes Luger (Jackson) attempt to recover a microfilm which contains a formula for turning cocaine into cookies. Essentially a sendup of the popular "Lethal Weapon" series, although other movies and themes make an appearance, well sort of. Short on plot and long on slapstick, but that's the whole point. Tired formula creates nostalgia for the grandaddy of them all, "Airplane." Lots of cameos, including one from sibling spoof star Sheen. The magazine folded while the movie was in production, an ominous sign. *AKA:* Loaded Weapon 1.

1993 (PG-13) 83m/C Emilio Estevez, Samuel L. Jackson, Jon Lovitz, Tim Curry, Kathy Ireland, William Shatner; *Cameos:* Dr. Joyce Brothers, James Doohan, Richard Moll, F. Murray Abraham, Dennis Leary, Corey Feldman, Phil Hartman, J.T. Walsh, Erik Estrada, Larry Wilcox, Allyce Beasley, Charlie Sheen; *D:* Gene Quintano; *W:* Gene Quintano, Don Holley. VHS *NLC* ⅃½

National Lampoon's Vacation The Clark Griswold (Chase) family of suburban Chicago embarks on a westward cross-country vacation via car to the renowned "Wally World." Ridiculous and hysterical misadventures, including a falling asleep at the wheel sequence and the untimely death of Aunt Edna. *AKA:* Vacation.
1983 (R) 98m/C Chevy Chase, Beverly D'Angelo, Imogene Coca, Randy Quaid, Christie Brinkley, James Keach, Anthony Michael Hall, John Candy, Eddie Bracken, Brian Doyle-Murray, Eugene Levy; *D:* Harold Ramis; *W:* John Hughes. VHS, Beta, LV $19.98 *WAR* ⅃⅃⅃

National Velvet A young English girl wins a horse in a raffle and is determined to train it to compete in the famed Grand National race. Taylor, only 12 at the time, is superb in her first starring role. Rooney also gives a fine performance. Filmed with a loving eye on lushly decorated sets, this is a masterpiece version of the story of affection between a girl and her pet. Based on the novel by Enid Bagnold and followed by "International Velvet" in 1978.
1944 124m/C Elizabeth Taylor, Mickey Rooney, Arthur Treacher, Donald Crisp, Anne Revere, Angela Lansbury, Reginald Owen; *D:* Clarence Brown. Academy Awards '45: Best Film Editing, Best Supporting Actress (Revere); Nominations: Best Color Cinematography, Best Director (Brown). VHS, Beta, LV, 8mm $19.98 *MGM, KUI, TLF* ⅃⅃⅃⅃

Native Son A young black man from the ghettos of Chicago is hired as a chauffeur by an affluent white family. His job is to drive their head-strong daughter anywhere she wants to go. Unintentionally, he kills her, tries to hide, and is ultimately found guilty. Based on the classic novel by Richard Wright, who also stars. Remade in 1986. Unprofessional direction and low budget work against the strong story.
1951 91m/B Richard Wright, Jean Wallace, Nicholas Joy, Gloria Madison, Charles Cane; *D:* Pierre Chenal. VHS $24.95 *NOS, FCT* ⅃⅃½

Native Son This second film adaptation of the classic Richard Wright novel is chock full of stars and tells the story of a poor black man who accidentally kills a white woman and then hides the body. Changes in the script soft-soap some of the novel's disturbing truths and themes—so-so drama for those who have not read the book.
1986 (R) 111m/C Geraldine Page, Oprah Winfrey, Matt Dillon, John Karlen, Elizabeth McGovern, Akosua Busia, Carroll Baker, Victor Love; *D:* Jerrold Freedman. VHS, Beta, LV $14.98 *LIV, KUI, FCT* ⅃⅃½

Nativity Unmemorable, made-for-TV portrayal of the romance between Mary and Joseph (of the Bible story), Joseph's response to Mary's pregnancy, and the birthing of Jesus. Not exactly a Bible epic, the direction and acting are uninspired.
1978 97m/C John Shea, Madeleine Stowe, Jane Wyatt, John Rhys-Davies, Kate O'Mara; *D:* Bernard L. Kowalski. VHS, Beta $59.98 *FOX* ⅃⅃

The Natural A beautifully filmed movie about baseball as myth. A young man, whose gift for baseball sets him apart, finds that trouble dogs him, particularly with a woman. In time, as an aging rookie, he must fight against his past to lead his team to the

World Series, and win the woman who is meant for him. From the Bernard Malamud story with a musical score by Randy Newman.
1984 (PG) 134m/C Robert Redford, Glenn Close, Robert Duvall, Kim Basinger, Wilford Brimley, Barbara Hershey, Richard Farnsworth, Robert Prosky, Darren McGavin, Joe Don Baker, Michael Madsen; **D:** Barry Levinson. **VHS, Beta, LV** $14.95 COL, PIA 𝄢𝄢𝄢

Natural Enemies A successful publisher begins to consider suicide and murder as the cure for his family's increasing alienation and despair. A dark and depressing drama written by Kanew.
1979 (R) 100m/C Hal Holbrook, Louise Fletcher, Jose Ferrer, Viveca Lindfors; **D:** Jeff Kanew; **W/ D:** Jeff Kanew. **VHS, Beta** $59.95 COL 𝄢𝄢½

Nature's Playmates A beautiful private eye tours Florida nudist camps in search of a missing man with a distinctive tattoo on his posterior. One of H.G. Lewis' obscure "nudie" flicks, sexually tame by modern standards, awful by any standards.
1962 56m/B Vicki Miles, Scott Osborne; **D:** Herschell Gordon Lewis. **VHS** $19.95 VDM 𝄢

Naughty Co-Eds College girls tell each other their own first love experiences. Lowbrow fun.
198? (R) 90m/C VHS, Beta $39.95 WWV Woof!

Naughty Knights Soft-core romp in a medieval setting. Toss it in the moat. **AKA:** Up the Chastity Belt.
1971 (PG) 94m/C Frankie Howerd, Graham Crowden, Bill Fraser, Roy Hudd, Hugh Paddick, Anna Quayle, Eartha Kitt, Dave King, Fred Emney; **D:** Bob Kellett. **VHS, Beta** $19.95 ACA 𝄢

Naughty Marietta A French princess switches identities with a mail-order bride to escape from her arranged marriage, and is captured by pirates. When she's saved by a dashing Indian scout, it's love at first sight. The first MacDonald-Eddy match-up and very popular in its day. 🎵Italian Street Song; Chansonette; Antoinette and Anatole; Prayer; Tramp, Tramp, Tramp; The Owl and the Bobcat; 'Neath the Southern Moon; Mon Ami Pierrot; Ship Ahoy; I'm Falling in Love with Someone; Ah, Sweet Mystery of Life.
1935 106m/B Jeanette MacDonald, Nelson Eddy, Frank Morgan, Elsa Lanchester, Douglas Dumbrille, Cecilia Parker; **D:** Woodbridge S. Van Dyke. Academy Awards '35: Best Sound; Nominations: Best Picture. **VHS, Beta, LV** $19.95 MGM 𝄢𝄢½

The Naughty Nineties Bud and Lou help a showboat owner fend off crooks in the 1890s. Usual slapstick shenanigans, but highlighted by verbal banter. Includes the first on-screen rendition of the classic "Who's on First?" routine. 🎵Rolling Down the River; Uncle Tom's Cabin; I Can't Get You Out of My Mind; On A Sunday Afternoon; I'd Leave My Happy Home for You; Nora Malone; Ma Blushin' Rosie; The Showboat's Comin' to Town; A Blarney from Killarney; Rosie, My Little Posie; I Give My Heart to You, Oo-ooh.
1945 72m/B Bud Abbott, Lou Costello, Henry Travers, Alan Curtis, Joe Sawyer, Rita Johnson, Joe Kirk, Lois Collier; **D:** Jean Yarborough. **VHS, Beta** $14.95 MCA, MLB 𝄢𝄢

Naughty Roommates A pair of seductive women share everything from clothing, to housework, to boyfriends and dates.
19?? 90m/C VHS NO 𝄢𝄢

Navajo Joe The sole survivor of a massacre single-handedly kills each person involved in the atrocity, and aids a terrorized, though unappreciative, town in the process. Low-budget Spanish-Italian western only

worth watching because of Reynolds. Filmed in Spain.
1967 89m/C IT SP Burt Reynolds, Aldo Sambrel, Tanya Lopert, Fernando Rey; **D:** Sergio Corbucci; **M:** Ennio Morricone. **VHS** $14.95 MGM 𝄢½

The Navigator Ever the quick thinker, Keaton actually bought a steamer headed for the scrap heap and used it to film an almost endless string of sight gags. Rejected by a socialite, millionaire Keaton finds himself alone with her on the abandoned boat. As he saves her from various and sundry perils, the gags and thrills abound—including one stunt that was inspired by a near-accident on the set. Too bad they don't make 'em like this anymore. Silent.
1924 60m/B Buster Keaton, Kathryn McGuire, Frederick Vroom, Noble Johnson, Clarence Burton, H. M. Clugston; **D:** Buster Keaton, Donald Crisp. **VHS** NO 𝄢𝄢𝄢

The Navigator A creative time-travel story of a 14th-century boy with visionary powers who leads the residents of his medieval English village away from a plague by burrowing through the earth's core and into late 20th-Century New Zealand. Quite original and refreshing.
1988 (PG) 92m/C NZ Hamish McFarlane, Bruce Lyons, Chris Haywood, Marshall Napier, Noel Appleby; **D:** Vincent Ward. **VHS** NO 𝄢𝄢𝄢

The Navy Comes Through Salty sailors aboard a mangy freighter beat the odds and sink Nazi warships and subs with the greatest of ease. Boy meets girl subplot is added for good measure. Morale booster includes newsreel footage.
1942 81m/B Pat O'Brien, George Murphy, Jane Wyatt, Jackie Cooper, Carl Esmond, Max Baer, Desi Arnaz Sr., Ray Collins, Lee Bonnell, Frank Jenks; **D:** Edward Sutherland. **VHS** $19.98 TTC 𝄢𝄢

Navy SEALS A group of macho Navy commandos, whose regular work is to rescue hostages from Middle Eastern underground organizations, finds a stash of deadly weapons. They spend the balance of the movie attempting to destroy the arsenal. Sheen chews the scenery as a crazy member of the commando team. Lots of action and violence, but simplistic good guys - bad guys philosophy and plot weaknesses keep this from being more than below average.
1990 (R) 113m/C Charlie Sheen, Michael Biehn, Joanne Whalley-Kilmer, Rick Rossovich, Cyril O'Reilly, Bill Paxton, Dennis Haysbert, Paul Sanchez, Ron Joseph, Nicholas Kadi; **D:** Lewis Teague. **VHS, Beta, LV** $14.98 ORI 𝄢½

Navy vs. the Night Monsters When horrifying, acid-secreting plant monsters try to take over the world, Van Doren and the Navy must come to the rescue, with the action taking place in a tropical South Pole setting. Amazing deployment of talents.
1966 87m/C Mamie Van Doren, Anthony Eisley, Pamela Mason, Bobby Van, Russ Bender; **W/D:** Michael Hoey. **VHS, Beta** $42.95 PGN Woof!

Navy Way Hurriedly produced war propaganda film in which a boxer gets inducted into the Navy just before his title shot.
1944 74m/B Robert Lowery, Jean Parker; **D:** William H. Pine, William C. Thomas. **VHS** $24.95 NOS, DVT, HEG 𝄢

Nazarin Bunuel's scathing indictment of Christianity finds its perfect vehicle in the adventures of a defrocked priest attempting to relive Christ's life. Gathering a group of disciples, he wanders into the Mexican desert as a cross between Christ and Don Quixote. Filmed in Mexico, this is Bunuel at his grimmest. In Spanish with English subtitles.

1958 92m/B MX Francisco Rabal, Rita Macedo, Margo Lopez, Rita McLedo, Ignacio Tarso, Jesus Fernandez; **D:** Luis Bunuel. **VHS, Beta, LV** $69.95 MAD, TAM 𝄢𝄢𝄢

Nea Comic drama about a young girl from a privileged home who writes a best selling pornographic novel anonymously. When her book writing talents are made public through betrayal, she gets even in a most unique way. Subtitled "A Young Emmanuelle." Kaplan also performs. Appealing and sophisticated.
1978 (R) 101m/C Sami Frey, Ann Zacharias, Heinz Bennent; **D:** Nelly Kaplan. **VHS, Beta** $59.95 COL 𝄢𝄢½

Near Dark A farm boy falls in unwillingly with a family of thirsty, outlaw-fringe vampires who roam the West in a van. The first mainstream effort by Bigelow, and a rollicking, blood-saturated, slaughterhouse of a movie, with enough laughs and stunning imagery to revive the genre. Music by Tangerine Dream.
1987 (R) 95m/C Adrian Pasdar, Jenny Wright, Bill Paxton, Jenette Goldstein, Lance Henriksen, Tim Thomerson, Joshua Miller; **D:** Kathryn Bigelow. **VHS, Beta, LV** $19.99 HBO, IME 𝄢𝄢𝄢

Near Misses Missable farce with Reinhold as a bigamist in the foreign service. To make time for a mistress he swaps identities with a young Marine in Paris, but then the KGB kidnaps the imposter. Doors slam in hallways all over the place as the performers crank up the mixups to maximum frenzy, but with little effect since you really don't care much about these fools.
1991 93m/C Judge Reinhold, Casey Siemaszko; **D:** Baz Taylor. **VHS, Beta, LV** $89.98 FXV 𝄢½

'Neath Brooklyn Bridge The Boys from the Bowery get tangled up in crime when they try to help a young girl whose guardian was murdered.
1942 61m/B Leo Gorcey, Huntz Hall, Bobby Jordan, Sammy Morrison, Anne Gillis, Noah Beery Jr., Marc Lawrence, Gabriel Dell; **D:** Wallace Fox. **VHS** $19.95 NOS, MRV, PME 𝄢

'Neath Canadian Skies Mounted lawman who says "eh" a lot tracks murdering gang of mine looters.
1946 41m/B CA Russell Hayden, Inez Cooper, Cliff Nazarro, Kermit Maynard, Jack Mulhall. **VHS, Beta, LV, 8mm** $24.95 VYY 𝄢

'Neath the Arizona Skies Low budget oater epic about a cowhand who finds all the action he and his friends can handle as they try to rescue a young Indian girl (and oil heiress) who has been kidnapped. 'Nuff said.
1934 54m/B John Wayne, George "Gabby" Hayes, Sheila Terry; **D:** Harry Fraser. **VHS** $9.98 REP, NOS, SVS 𝄢𝄢

Necessary Parties Based on Barbara Dana's book that has a 15-year-old boy filing a lawsuit to stop his parents' divorce. Originally aired on PBS as part of the "Wonderworks" family movie series.
1988 120m/C Alan Arkin, Mark Paul Gosselaar, Barbara Dana, Adam Arkin, Donald Moffatt, Julie Hagerty, Geoffrey Pierson, Taylor Fry; **D:** Gwen Arner. **VHS** $29.95 PME, WNE, HMV 𝄢𝄢

Necessary Roughness After losing their NCAA standing, the Texas Southern University (passing for the real Texas State) Armadillos football team looks like it's headed for disaster. The once proud football factory is now composed of assorted goofballs instead of stud players. But hope arrives in the form of a 34-year-old farmer with a golden arm, ready to recapture some lost dreams as quarterback. Can this unlikey team rise above itself and win a game, or will their hopes be squashed all over the field?

1991 (PG-13) 108m/C Scott Bakula, Robert Loggia, Harley Jane Kozak, Sinbad, Hector Elizondo, Kathy Ireland; **D:** Stan Dragoti. **VHS, Beta, LV** $19.95 PAR *ℐℐ*

Necromancer: Satan's Servant After a woman is brutally raped, she contacts a sorceress and makes a pact with the devil to ensure her successful revenge. Plenty of graphic violence and nudity.
1988 (R) 90m/C Elizabeth Cayton, Russ Tamblyn, Rhonda Dorton; **D:** Dusty Nelson. **VHS, Beta, LV** $79.98 MCG, IME *ℐℐ*

Necropolis A witch burned at the stake 300 years ago is brought back to life as a motorcycle punkette in New York searching for a sacrificial virgin (in New York?). New wave horror should have been watchable.
1987 (R) 77m/C Leeanne Baker, Michael Conte, Jacquie Fritz, William Reed, Paul Ruben; **D:** Bruce Hickey. **VHS, Beta** $79.98 LIV, VES *ℐ*

Ned Kelly Dramatizes the life of Australia's most notorious outlaw. Kelly (Jagger) and his family start off as horse thieves and proceed from there. A manhunt results in death and the eventual capture and execution of Kelly. The very contemporary British Jagger was miscast as a period Australian and British director Richardson seems to have lacked an empathy for the material, given his lethargic direction. **AKA:** Ned Kelly, Outlaw.
1970 (PG) 100m/C GB Mick Jagger, Allen Bickford, Geoff Gilmour, Mark McManus, Serge Lazareff, Peter Sumner, Ken Shorter, James Elliott, Diane Craig, Susan Lloyd, Clarissa Kaye; **W/D:** Tony Richardson; **W:** Ian Jones; **M:** Shel Silverstein. **VHS** $14.95 MGM *ℐℐ ½*

Needful Things Stephen King film adaptations are becoming as prolific as his novels, though few seem to improve the transition from page to screen. This time a scheming Maine shopkeeper sells unsuspecting small towners peculiar items that, not surprisingly, begin to cause horror and mayhem. Directorial debut for Heston (yes, Charlton's son).
1993 ?m/C Ed Harris, Bonnie Bedelia, Max von Sydow, Amanda Plummer; **D:** Fraser Heston. **VHS** NYR *ℐℐ ½*

Nefertiti, Queen of the Nile Woman, married against her will, turns into Nefertiti. For fans of Italo-Biblical epics only.
1964 97m/C IT Jeanne Crain, Vincent Price, Edmund Purdom, Amadeo Nazzari, Liana Orfei; **D:** Fernando Cerchio. **VHS** NO *ℐℐ*

Negatives A couple indulge in sexual fantasies to dangerous extremes, with the man first impersonating Dr. Crippen, the early 1900s murderer, and later a World War I flying ace. When a photographer friend joins the fun, the action careens off the deep end.
1968 90m/C GB Peter McEnery, Diane Cilento, Glenda Jackson, Maurice Denham, Norman Rossington; **D:** Peter Medak. **VHS** NO *ℐℐ*

The Neighborhood Thief Two thieves team up for the heist of their lives, but can they trust each other?
1983 84m/C MX Alfonso Zayas, Alberto Rojas, Angelica Chain. **VHS, Beta** $74.95 VVC *ℐℐ*

Neighbors The Keeses (Belushi and Walker) live in a quiet, middle-class suburban neighborhood where life is calm and sweet. But their new neighbors, Ramona and Vic (Aykroyd and Moriarty), prove to be loud, obnoxious, crazy, and freeloading. Will Earl and Enid Keese mind their manners as their neighborhood disintegrates? Some funny moments, but as the script fades, so do the laughs. Belushi's last waltz is based on Thomas Berger's novel.
1981 (R) 90m/C John Belushi, Dan Aykroyd, Kathryn Walker, Cathy Moriarty; **D:** John G. Avildsen. **VHS, Beta, LV** $14.95 GKK *ℐℐ*

Nelvanamation Four cosmic fantasies are featured in this program, including "Please Don't Eat the Planet," "A Cosmic Christmas," "The Devil and Daniel Mouse," and "Romie-O and Julie-8." The latter two are also available individually.
1980 100m/C **VHS, Beta** WAR, OM *ℐℐ*

Nelvanamation II This is a second anthology of fantasy cartoons for children of all ages, featuring "Take Me Out to the Ball Game," with music by Rick Danko, and "The Jack Rabbit Story" with music by John Sebastian.
1981 50m/C **V:** Phil Silvers, Garrett Morris. **VHS, Beta** WAR, OM *ℐℐ*

Nemesis Futuristic thriller that combines cybernetics and cyborgs in post-nuclear Los Angeles. Gruner plays a human (although he's mostly composed of mechanical replacement parts) in a world overwrought with system cowboys, information terrorists, bio-enhanced gangsters, and cyborg outlaws. Film's biggest flaw is the extremely confusing script that makes no attempt at logic whatsoever. Special visual effects are good despite the obviously low f/x budget.
1993 (R) 95m/C Olivier Gruner, Tim Thomerson, Cary-Hiroyuki Tagawa, Merele Kennedy, Yuji Okumoto, Marjorie Monaghan, Nicholas Guest, Vincent Klyn; **D:** Albert Pyun; **W:** Rebecca Charles; **M:** Michael Rubini. **VHS, LV** $94.95 IMP, UND *ℐ ½*

Neon City Title refers to a rumored city of refuge in the year 2053, where eight misfit adventurers in an armored transport seek safety from the Earth's toxic environment and "Mad Max" cliches.
1991 (R) 99m/C Michael Ironside, Vanity, Lyle Alzado, Valerie Wildman, Nick Klar, Juliet Landau, Arsenio "Sonny" Trinidad, Richard Sanders; **D:** Monte Markham. **VHS** $89.95 VMK *ℐℐ*

The Neon Empire Tepid tale of two gangsters battling inner mob opposition and backstabbing to build Las Vegas. Ostensibly based on the story of Bugsy Siegel and Meyer Lansky. Written by Pete Hamill. Made for cable.
1989 (R) 120m/C Martin Landau, Ray Sharkey, Gary Busey, Harry Guardino, Julie Carmen, Linda Fiorentino, Dylan McDermott; **D:** Larry Peerce. **VHS, Beta, LV** $39.95 FRH *ℐ ½*

Neon Maniacs An even half-dozen fetish-ridden zombies stalk the streets at night, tearing their victims into teensy weensy bits. Brave teenagers try to stop the killing. Brave viewers will stop the tape.
1986 (R) 90m/C Allan Hayes, Lelani Sarelle, Bo Sabato, Donna Locke, Victor Elliot Brandt; **D:** Joseph Mangine. **VHS, Beta** $79.98 LIV, VES Woof!

Neptune Factor Scientists board a special new deep-sea sub to search for their colleagues lost in an undersea earthquake. Diving ever deeper into the abyss that swallowed their friend's Ocean Lab II, they end up trapped themselves. The plot's many holes sink it. **AKA:** The Neptune Disaster; An Underwater Odyssey.
1973 (G) 94m/C Ben Gazzara, Yvette Mimieux, Walter Pidgeon, Ernest Borgnine; **D:** Daniel Petrie. **VHS, Beta** $59.98 FOX *ℐ*

Neptune's Daughter A swim-happy bathing suit designer finds romance and deep pools of studio water to dive into. Typically lavish and ridiculous Williams aquaparade. ♫Baby, It's Cold Outside; I Love Those Men; My Heart Beats Faster.

1949 92m/C Esther Williams, Red Skelton, Ricardo Montalban, Betty Garrett, Keenan Wynn, Xavier Cugat, Ted de Corsia, Mike Mazurki, Mel Blanc, Juan Duvall, George Mann; **D:** Edward Buzzell. **VHS, Beta, LV** $19.98 MGM *ℐℐ*

The Nervous Wreck Harrison Ford (not the one from "Indiana Jones") heads West, seeking a cure for what he believes is a terminal illness. Once there, he becomes romantically entangled with the sheriff's fiancee, uses a wrench to hold up a gas station, and gets involved in other shenanigans. And then he discovers he's going to live after all.
1926 70m/B Harrison Ford, Phyllis Haver, Chester Conklin, Mack Swain, Hobart Bosworth, Charles Gerrard; **D:** Scott Sidney. **VHS, Beta** NO *ℐℐℐ*

The Nest Tragic romance of an elderly man and a 13-year-old girl is helped along by superior script and directing.
1980 109m/C SP Ana Torrent, Hector Alterio, Patricia Adriani; **D:** Jaime de Arminan. **VHS, Beta** $68.00 SUE, APD *ℐℐ ½*

The Nest A small island is overcome by giant cockroaches created by, you guessed it, a scientific experiment gone wrong. Special effects make it watchable.
1988 (R) 89m/C Robert Lansing, Lisa Langlois, Franc Luz, Terri Treas, Stephen Davies, Diana Bellamy, Nancy Morgan; **D:** Terence H. Winkless. **VHS, Beta** $79.95 MGM *ℐℐ ½*

The Nesting Too-long tale of a neurotic author who rents a haunted Victorian manor and finds herself a pawn in a ghostly plan for revenge. Features Grahame's last performance.
1980 (R) 104m/C Robin Groves, John Carradine, Gloria Grahame, Christopher Loomis, Michael Lally; **D:** Armand Weston. **VHS, Beta** $59.95 WAR *ℐ ½*

Netherworld A young man investigating his mysterious, dead father travels to his ancestral plantation in the bayou. To his horror, he discovers that his father was involved in the black arts. Now two beautiful young witches are after him. Can he possibly survive this madness?
1991 (R) 87m/C Michael C. Bendetti, Denise Gentile, Anjanette Comer, Holly Floria, Robert Burr; **D:** David Schmoeller; **M:** Edgar Winter. **VHS, LV** PAR *ℐ ½*

Network As timely now as it was then; a scathing indictment of the television industry and its propensity towards self-prostitution. A television newscaster's mental breakdown turns him into a celebrity when the network tries to profit from his illness. The individual characters are startlingly realistic and the acting is excellent. Written by Paddy Chayefsky.
1976 (R) 121m/C Faye Dunaway, Peter Finch, William Holden, Robert Duvall, Wesley Addy, Ned Beatty, Beatrice Straight; **D:** Sidney Lumet; **W:** Paddy Chayefsky. Academy Awards '76: Best Actor (Finch), Best Actress (Dunaway), Best Original Screenplay, Best Supporting Actress (Straight); Nominations: Best Actor (Holden), Best Cinematography, Best Director (Lumet), Best Film Editing, Best Picture, Best Supporting Actor (Beatty); Golden Globe Awards '77: Best Actor—Drama (Finch), Best Actress—Drama (Dunaway), Best Director (Lumet); National Board of Review Awards '76: 10 Best Films of the Year. **VHS, Beta, LV** $19.98 MGM, BTV *ℐℐℐ ½*

Neurotic Cabaret Would-be actress dances exotically and finds more exotic ways to roll in dough.
1990 90m/C Edwin Neal, Tammy Stone. **VHS** $79.95 AIP *ℐ ½*

Neutron and the Black Mask Man wears mask with lightning bolts and gains comic book style powers to do deathly battle with a scientist with a neutron bomb up his sleeve. First Neutron feature.
1961 80m/B *MX* Wolf Ruvinskis, Julio Aleman, Armando Silvestre, Rosita Arenas, Claudio Brook; **D:** Frederick Curiel. **VHS $19.98** *SNC* ✂️

Neutron vs. the Amazing Dr. Caronte Dr. Caronte from "Neutron and the Black Mask" just won't give up that neutron bomb and let the series die.
1961 80m/B *MX* Wolf Ruvinskis, Julio Aleman, Armando Silvestre, Rosita Arenas, Rodolfo Landa; **D:** Frederick Curiel. **VHS $19.98** *SNC* ✂️

Neutron vs. the Death Robots Guy with a mask takes on army of killer robots and neutron bomb to protect the world from future sequels.
1962 80m/B *MX* Wolf Ruvinskis, Julio Aleman, Armando Silvestre, Rosita Arenas; **D:** Frederick Curiel. **VHS $19.98** *SNC* ✂️

Neutron vs. the Maniac Man in mask hunts guys who kill people.
1962 80m/B *MX* Wolf Ruvinskis. **VHS $19.98** *SNC* ✂️

Nevada City Roy outwits a financier who is trying to monopolize transportation in California.
1941 54m/B Roy Rogers, Trigger. **VHS, Beta $27.95** *VCN* ✂️½

Nevada Smith The half-breed Nevada Smith (previously introduced in Harold Robbins' story "The Carpetbaggers" and film of same name) seeks the outlaws who killed his parents. Standard western plot, characters. Later remade as a TV movie.
1966 135m/C Steve McQueen, Karl Malden, Brian Keith, Arthur Kennedy, Raf Vallone, Suzanne Pleshette; **D:** Henry Hathaway. **VHS, Beta, LV $14.95** *PAR* ✂️✂️

The Nevadan A marshal goes in search of an outlaw's gold cache, only to be opposed by a crooked rancher. Good scenery and action, but not one of Scott's best. *AKA:* The Man From Nevada.
1950 81m/C Randolph Scott, Dorothy Malone, Forrest Tucker, Frank Faylen, George Macready, Charles Kemper, Jeff Corey, Tom Powers, Jock Mahoney; **D:** Gordon Douglas. **VHS, Beta** *GKK* ✂️½

Never a Dull Moment New York songwriter falls for rodeo Romeo, moves out West, and finds welcome wagon deficient. Mediocre songs; many dull moments. ♫Once You Find Your Guy; Sagebrush Lullaby; The Man With the Big Felt Hat.
1950 89m/B Irene Dunne, Fred MacMurray, William Demarest, Andy Devine, Gigi Perreau, Natalie Wood, Philip Ober, Jack Kirkwood, Ann Doran, Margaret Gibson; **D:** George Marshall. **VHS $19.98** *TTC, FCT* ✂️✂️

Never a Dull Moment Mobsters mistake an actor for an assassin in this gag-filled adventure. They threaten the thespian into thievery, before the trouble really starts when Ace, the actual assassin, arrives.
1968 (G) 90m/C Dick Van Dyke, Edward G. Robinson, Dorothy Provine, Henry Silva, Joanna Moore, Tony Bill, Slim Pickens, Jack Elam; **D:** Jerry Paris. **VHS, Beta, LV $39.95** *DIS* ✂️✂️

Never Cry Wolf A young biologist is sent to the Arctic to study the behavior and habitation of wolves, then becomes deeply involved with their sub-society. Based on Farley Mowat's book. Beautifully photographed.
1983 (PG) 105m/C Charles Martin Smith, Brian Dennehy, Samson Jorah; **D:** Carroll Ballard. **VHS, Beta, LV $19.99** *DIS* ✂️✂️✂️½

Never Forget Made-for-cable-TV true story of California resident Mel Mermelstein (played by Nimoy), a survivor of Hitler's death camps who accepted a pro-Nazi group's challenge to prove in court that the Holocaust of six million Jews really happened. A sincere, well-meaning courtroom drama that just can't surmount the uncinematic nature of the source material.
1991 94m/C Leonard Nimoy, Blythe Danner, Dabney Coleman; **D:** Joseph Sargent; **M:** Henry Mancini. **VHS, Beta $89.98** *TTC* ✂️

Never Give a Sucker an Even Break An almost plotless comedy, based on an idea reputedly written on a napkin by Fields (he took screenplay credit as Otis Criblecoblis), and features Fields at his most unleashed. It's something of a cult favorite, but not for all tastes. Classic chase scene ends it. Fields' last role in a feature-length film. *AKA:* What a Man.
1941 71m/B W.C. Fields, Gloria Jean, Franklin Pangborn, Leon Errol, Margaret Dumont; **D:** Eddie Cline. **VHS, Beta, LV $14.95** *MCA, KRT* ✂️✂️✂️½

Never Let Go A man unwittingly tracks down the mastermind of a gang of racketeers. Sellers sheds his comedic image to play the ruthless and brutal gang boss, something he shouldn't have done.
1960 91m/C *GB* Peter Sellers, Richard Todd, Elizabeth Sellars, Carol White; **D:** John Guillermin; **M:** John Barry. **VHS, Beta** *SUE* ✂️✂️

Never Love a Stranger A young man becomes a numbers runner for a mobster and ultimately winds up heading his own racket. Later he finds himself in conflict with his old boss and the district attorney. No surprises here. Based on the Harold Robbins' novel.
1958 93m/B John Barrymore Jr., Steve McQueen, Lita Milan, Robert Bray; **D:** Robert Stevens. **VHS $19.98** *REP* ✂️

Never on Sunday An American intellectual tries to turn a Greek prostitute into a refined woman. Fine performances and exhilarating Greek photography. Fun all around.
1960 91m/B *GR* Melina Mercouri, Tito Vandis, Jules Dassin, Mitsos Liguisos; **D:** Jules Dassin. Academy Awards '60: Best Song ("Never on Sunday"); Nominations: Best Actress (Mercouri), Best Costume Design (B & W), Best Director (Dassin), Best Story & Screenplay; Cannes Film Festival '60: Best Actress (Mercouri). **VHS, Beta $19.98** *MGM, HMV* ✂️✂️✂️

Never on Tuesday Two jerks from Ohio head to California and find themselves stuck midway in the desert with a beautiful girl, who has plans of her own.
1988 (R) 90m/C Claudia Christian, Andrew Lauer, Peter Berg; **Cameos:** Charlie Sheen, Emilio Estevez; **D:** Adam Rifkin. **VHS, Beta, LV $14.95** *PAR* ✂️½

Never Pick Up a Stranger When a local hooker is murdered, her cop boyfriend, who never gives up on a case, hunts her killer with a vengeance. Extremely graphic. Also on video as "Bloodrage."
1979 82m/C Ian Scott, Judith-Marie Bergan, James Johnston, Lawrence Tierney; **D:** Joseph Bigwood. **VHS, Beta $49.95** *LIV, BFV* ✂️½

Never Say Die Two innocents are thrown into a web of international intrigue and acquit themselves rather well. Lots of explosions and car crashes for a film shot in New Zealand.
1990 98m/C *NZ* George Wendt, Lisa Eilbacher; **D:** Geoff Murphy. **VHS, Beta $29.95** *HBO, JTC* ✂️½

Never Say Never Again James Bond matches wits with a charming but sinister tycoon who is holding the world nuclear hostage as part of a diabolical plot by SPECTRE. Connery's return to the world of Bond after 12 years is smooth in this remake of "Thunderball" hampered by an atrocious musical score. Carrera is stunning as Fatima Blush.
1983 (PG) 134m/C Sean Connery, Klaus Maria Brandauer, Max von Sydow, Barbara Carrera, Kim Basinger, Edward Fox, Bernie Casey, Pamela Salem, Rowan Atkinson, Valerie Leon, Prunella Gee, Saskia Cohen Tanugi; **D:** Irvin Kershner. **VHS, Beta, LV $19.98** *WAR, TLF* ✂️✂️½

Never So Few A military commander and his outnumbered troops overcome incredible odds against the Japanese. There is a lot of focus on romance, but the script and acting make a strong impression nonetheless. Based on the novel by Tom T. Chamales.
1959 124m/C Frank Sinatra, Gina Lollobrigida, Peter Lawford, Steve McQueen, Richard Johnson, Paul Henreid, Charles Bronson; **D:** John Sturges. **VHS, LV $29.95** *MGM* ✂️✂️½

Never Steal Anything Small A tough union boss pushes everyone as he battles the mob for control of the waterfront. A strange musical-drama combination that will be of interest only to the most ardent Cagney and Jones fans. Based on the Maxwell Anderson/Rouben Mamoulian play "The Devil's Hornpipe." Largely forgettable songs. ♫I'm Sorry, I Want a Ferrari; I Haven't Got a Thing to Wear; It Takes Love to Make a Home; Never Steal Anything Small; Helping Out Friends.
1959 94m/C James Cagney, Shirley Jones, Cara Williams; **D:** Charles Lederer. **VHS, Beta $59.95** *MCA* ✂️½

Never Too Late to Mend Victorian British play about the abuses of the penal system which had, upon its initial London West End run, caused Queen Victoria to institute a sweeping program of prison reform. The movie caused considerably less stir.
1937 67m/B Tod Slaughter, Marjorie Taylor, Jack Livesey, Ian Colin; **D:** David MacDonald. **VHS, Beta, 8mm $29.95** *SNC, MRV, VYY* ✂️✂️

Never Too Young to Die A young man is drawn into a provocative espionage adventure by his late father's spy associates. Together they try to discover who killed the young man's father. High point may be Simmons as a crazed hermaphrodite plotting to poison L.A.
1986 (R) 97m/C John Stamos, Vanity, Gene Simmons, George Lazenby; **D:** Gil Bettman. **VHS, Beta, LV $14.95** *COL, NLC* ✂️

Never Wave at a WAC A Washington socialite joins the Women's Army Corps hoping for a commission that never comes. She has to tough it out as an ordinary private. A reasonably fun ancestor of "Private Benjamin," with a cameo by Gen. Omar Bradley as himself. *AKA:* The Private Wore Skirts.
1952 87m/B Rosalind Russell, Paul Douglas, Marie Wilson, William Ching, Arleen Whelan, Leif Erickson, Hillary Brooke, Regis Toomey; **Cameos:** Omar Bradley; **D:** Norman Z. McLeod. **VHS $19.95** *NOS, DVT, HEG* ✂️✂️½

Never Weaken/Why Worry? Silent comedy shorts from Harold. In "Never Weaken" (1921), Lloyd hustles customers. In "Why Worry?" (1923), he plays a wealthy young man who journeys to South America for his health and gets caught in the middle of a revolution.
1923 78m/B Harold Lloyd. **VHS, Beta** *TLF* ✂️✂️✂️

The NeverEnding Story A lonely young boy helps a warrior save the fantasy world in his book from destruction by the Nothing. A wonderful, intelligent family movie about imagination, with swell effects and a sweet but not overly sentimental script. The music was composed by Klaus Doldinger and Giorgio Moroder. Petersen's first English-language film, based on the novel by Michael Ende.
1984 (PG) 94m/C Barret Oliver, Noah Hathaway, Gerald McRaney, Moses Gunn, Tami Stronach, Patricia Hayes, Sydney Bromley; *D:* Wolfgang Petersen. VHS, Beta, LV, 8mm $19.98 WAR, PIA, GLV ♫♫♫ ½

The NeverEnding Story 2: Next Chapter Disappointing sequel to the first story that didn't end. Boy Oliver staves off life of couch potatodom reading books and escaping into fantasy land. Even the kids may wander away. But wait: contains the first Bugs Bunny theatrical cartoon in 26 years, "Box Office Bunny."
1991 (PG) 90m/C Jonathan Brandis, Kenny Morrison, Clarissa Burt, John Wesley Shipp, Martin Umbach; *D:* George Miller. VHS, LV, 8mm $19.95 WAR, PIA, APD ♫♫

Nevil Shute's The Far Country Made-for-television adaptation of a typical gothic romance by the author of "On the Beach."
1985 115m/C Michael York, Sigrid Thornton. VHS, Beta QNE ♫ ½

The New Adventures of Pippi Longstocking Decent cast is trapped in another musical rehashing of the Astrid Lindgren children's books about a precocious red-headed girl and her fantastic adventures with horses, criminals, and pirates.
1988 (G) 100m/C Tami Erin, Eileen Brennan, Dennis Dugan, Dianne Hull, George DiCenzo, John Schuck, Dick Van Patten; *D:* Ken Annakin. VHS, Beta, LV $19.95 COL, TVC ♫ ½

The New Adventures of Tarzan: Vol. 1 Twelve episodes, each 22 minutes long, depict the adventures of Edgar Rice Burrough's tree-swinging character—Tarzan. Also known as "Tarzan and the Green Goddess."
1935 260m/B Herman Brix, Ula Holt, Frank Baker, Dale Walsh, Lewis Sargent; *D:* Edward Kull. VHS, Beta $26.95 SNC, NOS, VCN ♫ ½

The New Adventures of Tarzan: Vol. 2 Tarzan goes nuts in this spectacular adventure.
1935 25m/B Bruce Bennett, Ula Holt; *D:* Edward Kull. VHS, Beta RXM ♫ ½

The New Adventures of Tarzan: Vol. 3 More adventure with the vine swinger.
1935 25m/B Bruce Bennett, Ula Holt; *D:* Edward Kull. VHS, Beta RXM ♫ ½

The New Adventures of Tarzan: Vol. 4 The jungle man swings into action in this incredible adventure.
1935 25m/B Bruce Bennett, Ula Holt; *D:* Edward Kull. VHS, Beta RXM ♫ ½

The New Centurions Rookies training for the Los Angeles Police Department get the inside info from retiring cops. Gritty and realistic drama based on the novel by former cop Joseph Wambaugh. Tends to be disjointed at times, but overall is a good adaptation of the bestseller. Scott, excellent as the retiring beat-walker, is supported well by the other performers.
1972 (R) 103m/C George C. Scott, Stacy Keach, Jane Alexander, Scott Wilson, Erik Estrada; *D:* Richard Fleischer. VHS, Beta, LV $14.95 COL, FCT ♫♫ ½

New Faces of 1952 Based on the hit Broadway revue. The plot revolves around a Broadway show that is about to be closed down, and the performers who fight to keep it open. Lots of hit songs. Mel Brooks is credited as a writer, under the name Melvin Brooks. ♫C'est Si Bon; Santa Baby; Uskadara; Monotonous; Bal Petit Bal; Boston Beguine; I'm in Love with Miss Logan; Penny Candy; Time for Tea.
1954 98m/C Ronny Graham, Eartha Kitt, Robert Clary, Alice Ghostley, June Carroll, Carol Lawrence, Paul Lynde; *D:* Harry Horner. VHS, Beta $29.95 FCT, NOS, VAI ♫♫ ½

New Fist of Fury During World War II, a former pickpocket becomes a martial arts whiz with the assistance of his fiancee, and fights the entire Imperial Army.
1985 120m/C Jackie Chan; *D:* Jackie Chang. VHS, Beta NO ♫

The New Frontier Wayne is a small-town sheriff whose predecessor, his father, was murdered. The local saloon-keeper and his gang do everything they can to prevent Wayne from bringing the culprit to justice. *AKA:* Frontier Horizon.
1935 59m/B John Wayne, Muriel Evans, Murdock McQuarrie, Mary MacLaren, Warner Richmond; *D:* Carl Pierson. VHS $19.95 NOS, MLB ♫ ½

The New Gladiators In the future, criminals try to kill each other on television for public entertainment. Two such gladiators discover that the network's computer is using the games in order to take over mankind, and they attempt to stop it. Even if the special effects were any good, they couldn't save this one.
1987 90m/C *IT* Jared Martin, Fred Williamson, Eleanor Gold, Howard Ross, Claudio Cassinelli; *D:* Lucio Fulci. VHS, Beta $79.95 MED Woof!

The New Invisible Man A so-so Mexican adaptation of the popular H.G. Wells novel has a prisoner receiving a vanishing drug from his brother, who created it—perhaps to aid an escape attempt. Also called "H.G. Wells' New Invisible Man."
1958 95m/B MX Arturo de Cordova, Ana Louisa Peluffo, Jorge Mondragon; *D:* Alfredo B. Crevenna. VHS $16.95 SNC ♫♫

New Jack City Just say no ghetto-melodrama. Powerful performance by Snipes as wealthy Harlem drug lord sought by rebel cops Ice-T and Nelson. Music by Johnny Gill, 2 Live Crew, Ice-T and others. Available with Spanish subtitles.
1991 (R) 101m/C Wesley Snipes, Ice-T, Mario Van Peebles, Chris Rock, Judd Nelson, Tracy C. Johns, Allen Payne, Kim Park; *D:* Mario Van Peebles. VHS, LV $19.98 WAR, PIA, CCB ♫♫ ½

The New Kids An orphaned brother and sister find out the limitations of the good neighbor policy. A sadistic gang terrorizes them after their move to a relatives' home in Florida. They go after expected revenge.
1985 (R) 90m/C Shannon Presby, Lori Loughlin, James Spader, Eric Stoltz; *D:* Sean S. Cunningham. VHS, Beta, LV $79.95 COL ♫♫

A New Kind of Love Romantic fluff starring real-life couple Newman and Woodward who meet en route to Paris and end up falling in love. Newman plays a reporter and Woodward is a fashion designer in this light comedy set amidst the sights of Paris.
1963 110m/C Paul Newman, Joanne Woodward, Thelma Ritter, Eva Gabor, Maurice Chevalier, George Tobias; *W/D:* Melville Shavelson. VHS, Beta $14.95 PAR ♫♫ ½

A New Leaf A playboy who has depleted his financial resources tries to win the hand of a clumsy heiress. May was the first woman to write, direct and star in a movie. She was unhappy with the cuts that were made by the studio, but that didn't seem to affect its impact with the public. Even with the cuts, the film is still funny and May's performance is worth watching.
1971 (G) 102m/C Walter Matthau, Elaine May, Jack Weston, George Rose, William Redfield, James Coco; *W/D:* Elaine May. VHS $14.95 PAR, CCB ♫♫ ½

A New Life An uptight stockbroker is abandoned by his wife. The New York singles scene beckons both of them to a new chance at life. Appealing performances cannot completely mask the old story line, but it's definitely worth a look.
1988 (PG-13) 104m/C Alan Alda, Ann-Margret, Hal Linden, Veronica Hamel, John Shea, Mary Kay Place; *W/D:* Alan Alda. VHS, Beta, LV $89.95 PAR ♫♫ ½

New Mafia Boss Italian-made plodder has Savalas taking over a huge Mafia family and all hell breaking loose. *AKA:* Crime Boss.
1972 (PG) 90m/C *IT* Telly Savalas, Lee Van Cleef, Antonio Sabato, Paolo Tedesco; *D:* Alberto De Martino. VHS, Beta $59.95 VCD ♫ ½

New Moon An adaptation of the operetta by Sigmund Romberg and Oscar Hammerstein II. A French heiress traveling on a boat that is captured by pirates falls in love with their leader. Remake of the 1930 film. Includes the 1935 Robert Benchley MGM short "How to Sleep." ♫Dance Your Cares Away; Stranger in Paris; The Way They Do It in Paris; Lover Come Back; Shoes; Softly as in a Morning Sunrise; One Kiss; Troubles of the World; No More Weeping; Wailing; Wanting You; Stout Hearted Men; Ombre Ma Full; Marianne; The Marseillaise; Bayou Trouble Tree.
1940 106m/B Jeanette MacDonald, Nelson Eddy, Buster Keaton, Joe Yule, Jack Perrin, Mary Boland; *D:* Robert Z. Leonard. VHS, Beta $19.95 MGM ♫♫ ½

New Orleans After Dark A pair of New Orleans detectives tour the city, crime-buster style, and bag a dope ring. Average crime tale, shot on location in the Big Easy.
1958 69m/B Stacy Harris, Louis Sirgo, Ellen Moore; *D:* John Sledge. VHS $15.95 NOS, LOO ♫♫

New Pastures Three ex-convicts run into some humorous situations when they go back to their small hometown. A semi-acclaimed Czech comedy, with subtitles.
1962 92m/B CZ *D:* Vladimir Cech. VHS, Beta, 3/4U $39.95 IHF ♫♫ ½

New Year's Day Jaglom continues his look at modern relationships in this story of a man reclaiming his house from three female tenants. Introspective character study lightened by humor and insight.
1989 (R) 90m/C Maggie Jakobson, Gwen Welles, Melanie Winter, Milos Forman, Michael Emil, Henry Jaglom; *W/D:* Henry Jaglom. VHS, Beta $79.98 PAR, BTV, FCT ♫♫♫

New Year's Evil Every hour during a New Year's Eve concert, a madman kills an unsuspecting victim. After each killing, the murderer informs a local disc jockey of his deed. Little does the disc jockey know that she will soon be next on his list. No suspense, bad music makes this one a holiday wrecker. Slash and crash written by Leonard Neubauer.
1978 (R) 88m/C Roz Kelly, Kip Niven, Chris Wallace, Louisa Moritz, Grant Kramer, Jed Mills; *D:* Emmett Alston. VHS, Beta $19.98 PGN, CAN Woof!

New York, New York A tragic romance evolves between a saxophonist and an aspiring singer/actress in this salute to the big-band era. A love of music isn't enough to hold them together through career rivalries and life on the road. Fine performances by De Niro and Minnelli and the supporting cast. Re-released in 1981 with the "Happy Endings" number, which was cut from the original. Look for "Big Man" Clarence Clemons on sax. ♫New York, New York; There Goes the Ball Game; Happy Endings; But the World Goes 'Round; Night in Tunisia; Opus One; Avalon; You Brought a New Kind of Love to Me; I'm Getting Sentimental Over You; Song of India; Blue Moon; Don't Blame Me; Once In a While; Don't Get Around Much Anymore; Do Nothing Till You Hear from Me; You Are My Lucky Star; It's a Wonderful World; Hold Tight; Bugle Call Rag; Don't Be That Way; For All We Know; South America, Take It Away; Taking a Chance on Love; The Man I Love; Just You, Just Me; Honeysuckle Rose; Flip the Dip; Game Over; V-J Stomp; Hazoy; Once Again Right Away; Bobby's Dream.
1977 (PG) 163m/C Robert De Niro, Liza Minnelli, Lionel Stander, Barry Primus, Mary Kay Place, Dick Miller, Diahnne Abbott; *D:* Martin Scorsese. **VHS, Beta, LV $29.98** *FOX* 🎬🎬🎬

New York Nights The lives of nine New Yorkers intertwine in a treacherous game of passion and seduction. Liberal borrowing from plot of "La Ronde."
1984 (R) 104m/C Corinne Alphen, George Auyer, Bobbi Burns, Peter Matthey, Cynthia Lee, Willem Dafoe; *D:* Simon Nuchtern. **VHS, Beta $79.98** *LIV* 🎬

New York Ripper A New York cop tracks down a rampaging murderer in this dull, mindless slasher flick.
1982 88m/C *IT* Fred Williamson; *D:* Lucio Fulci. **VHS, Beta $49.95** *VMK* Woof!

New York Stories Entertaining anthology of three separate short films by three esteemed directors, all set in New York. In "Life Lessons" by Scorsese, an impulsive artist tries to prevent his live-in girlfriend from leaving him. "Life Without Zoe" by Coppola involves a youngster's fantasy about a wealthy 12-year-old who lives mostly without her parents. Allen's "Oedipus Wrecks," generally considered the best short, is about a 50-year-old man who is tormented by the specter of his mother.
1989 (PG) 124m/C Nick Nolte, Rosanna Arquette, Woody Allen, Mia Farrow, Mae Questel, Julie Kavner, Talia Shire, Giancarlo Giannini, Don Novello, Patrick O'Neal, Peter Gabriel, Paul Herman, Deborah Harry; *D:* Woody Allen, Martin Scorsese, Francis Ford Coppola. **VHS, Beta, LV $19.99** *TOU* 🎬🎬🎬

New York's Finest Three prostitutes are determined to leave their calling and marry very eligible millionaires. But becoming society ladies is more difficult than they thought. Would-be sophisticated comedy misfires.
1987 (R) 80m/C Ruth Collins, Jennifer Delora, Scott Thompson Baker, Heidi Paine, Jane Hamilton, Alan Naggar, John Altamura, Alan Fisler, Josey Duval; *D:* Chuck Vincent. **VHS, Beta $29.95** *ACA* 🎬

The Newlydeads An uptight, conservative, honeymoon resort owner murders one of his guests and finds out that "she" is really a he. Fifteen years later, on his wedding night, all of his guests are violently murdered by the transvestite's vengeful ghost. Oddball twist to the usual slasher nonsense.

1987 84m/C Scott Kaske, Jim Williams, Jean Levine, Jay Richardson; *D:* Joseph Merhi. **VHS, Beta** NO 🎬½

Newman's Law A city detective is implicated in a corruption investigation. While on suspension, he continues with his own investigation of a large drug ring and finds corruption is closer than he thought. Director Heffron's first feature film.
1974 (PG) 98m/C George Peppard, Roger Robinson, Eugene Roche, Gordon Pinsent, Louis Zorich, Abe Vigoda; *D:* Richard T. Heffron. **VHS, Beta $59.95** *MCA* 🎬🎬

News at Eleven A fading news anchorman is pressured by his ambitious young boss to expose a touchy local sex scandal, forcing him to consider the public's right to know versus the rights of the individual. About average for made-for-television drama.
1986 95m/C Martin Sheen, Peter Riegert, Barbara Babcock, Sheree J. Wilson, Sydney Penny, David S. Sheiner, Christopher Allport; *D:* Mike Robe. **VHS, Beta, LV $9.98** *TTC* 🎬🎬

News from Home A plotless look at life and survival in New York City, with narration from a young girl's mother.
1976 90m/C *W/D:* Chantal Akerman. **VHS $79.95** *WAC, FCT* 🎬🎬

Newsfront A story about two brothers, both newsreel filmmakers, and their differing approaches to life and their craft in the 1940s and '50s. Tribute to the days of newsreel film combines real stories and fictionalized accounts with color and black and white photography. Noyce's feature film debut.
1978 110m/C *AU* Bill Hunter, Gerard Kennedy, Angela Punch McGregor, Wendy Hughes, Chris Haywood, John Ewart, Bryan Brown; *D:* Phillip Noyce. **VHS, LV $59.98** *SUE* 🎬🎬🎬

Newsies An unfortunate attempt at an old-fashioned musical with a lot of cute kids and cardboard characters and settings. The plot, such as it is, concerns the 1899 New York newsboys strike against penny-pinching publisher Joseph Pulitzer. Bale plays the newsboy's leader and at least shows some charisma in a strictly cartoon setting. The songs are mediocre but the dancing is lively. However, none of it moves the story along. Strictly for the kids. Choreographer Ortega's feature-film directorial debut.
1992 (PG) 121m/C Christian Bale, Bill Pullman, Robert Duvall, Ann-Margret, Michael Lerner, Kevin Tighe, Charles Cioffi, Luke Edwards, Max Casella, David Moscow; *D:* Kenny Ortega; *M:* Alan Menken, Jack Feldman. **VHS, Beta $19.99** *DIS* 🎬½

Next of Kin A daughter moves into her dead mother's retirement home and discovers an unspeakable evil that lurks there. Typical horror stuff has some very creepy moments; filmed in New Zealand.
1982 90m/C *AU* Jackie Kerin, John Jarratt, Gerida Nicholson, Alex Scott; *D:* Tony Williams. **VHS, Beta, LV, 8mm** NO 🎬

Next of Kin A young man experiencing familial difficulties undergoes experimental video therapy when he views a videotape of an Armenian family who gave their son up for adoption. When he discovers the actual family he insinuates himself into their life, determined to be their long-lost son.
1984 72m/C *CA* Patrick Tierney; *W/D:* Atom Egoyan. **VHS $29.95** *CVC, FCT, TAM* 🎬🎬

Next of Kin A Chicago cop returns to his Kentucky home to avenge his brother's brutal murder. Swayze's return to action films after his success in "Dirty Dancing" is unimpressive.

1989 (R) 108m/C Patrick Swayze, Adam Baldwin, Bill Paxton, Helen Hunt, Andreas Katsulas, Ben Stiller, Michael J. Pollard, Liam Neeson; *D:* John Irvin; *M:* Jack Nitzsche. **VHS, Beta, LV, 8mm $19.98** *WAR* 🎬🎬

Next One Mysterious visitor from another time winds up on an isolated Greek island as the result of a magnetic storm. The local inhabitants are amazed when the visitor displays some Christ-like characteristics.
1984 105m/C Keir Dullea, Adrienne Barbeau, Jeremy Licht, Peter Hobbs; *D:* Nico Mastorakis. **VHS, Beta $69.95** *VES* 🎬½

Next Stop, Greenwich Village An affectionate, autobiographical look by Mazursky at a Brooklyn boy with acting aspirations, who moves to Greenwich Village in 1953. Good performances, especially by Winters as the overbearing mother.
1976 (R) 109m/C Lenny Baker, Christopher Walken, Ellen Greene, Shelley Winters, Lou Jacobi, Mike Kellin; *W/D:* Paul Mazursky. **VHS $59.98** *FXV* 🎬🎬🎬

Next Summer A large, character-studded French family pursues power, love and beauty. Excellent performances. In French with English subtitles. *AKA:* L'Ete Prochain.
1984 120m/C *FR* Jean-Louis Trintignant, Claudia Cardinale, Fanny Ardant, Philippe Noiret, Marie Trintignant; *D:* Nadine Trintignant. **VHS, Beta** *FCT, TAM* 🎬🎬🎬

Next Time I Marry Lucy fraternizes with ditch digger Ellison because she needs to hitch a Yankee in order to inherit $20 mill. Seems she really loves a foreigner, though. Not much to bobaloo about. Director Kanin's second effort.
1938 65m/B Lucille Ball, James Ellison, Lee Bowman, Granville Bates, Mantan Moreland, Florence Lake; *D:* Garson Kanin. **VHS $19.98** *TTC, FCT, MLB* 🎬½

Next Victim The unfaithful wife of an Austrian diplomat attempts to find out who has been slicing up beautiful jet-setters. Tepid mystery. *AKA:* Lo Strano Vizio Della Signora Wardh; The Next Victim.
1971 (PG) 87m/C George Hilton, Edwige French, Christina Airoldi, Ivan Rassimov; *D:* Sergio Martino. **VHS, Beta $19.95** *GEM, NEG* 🎬

Next Victim A beautiful woman confined to a wheelchair is stalked by a lunatic killer. You've seen it before, and done better.
1974 80m/C *GB* Carroll Baker, T.P. McKenna, Ronald Lacey, Maurice Kaufman; *D:* James Ormerod. **VHS, Beta $29.95** *LIV* 🎬

The Next Voice You Hear Lives are changed forever when a group of people hear the voice of God on the radio. Interesting premise presented seriously.
1950 84m/B James Whitmore, Nancy Davis, Gary Gray, Lillian Bronson, Art Smith, Tom D'Andrea, Jeff Corey, George Chandler; *D:* William A. Wellman. **VHS, Beta $19.98** *MGM* 🎬🎬½

Next Year If All Goes Well Two young lovers struggle to overcome insecurities while establishing a relationship. Dubbed.
1983 95m/C *FR* Isabelle Adjani, Thierry Lhermitte, Mariann Chazel; *D:* Jean-Loup Hubert. **VHS, Beta $19.95** *STE, HBO* 🎬🎬½

Ni Chana Ni Juana A girl gets herself into lots of wacky situations on her trip to the capitol in search of her lover.
1987 102m/C *MX* Maria Elena Velasco, Armando Calvo, Carmen Montejo. **VHS, Beta $79.95** *MAD* 🎬🎬½

Niagara During their honeymoon in Niagara Falls, a scheming wife (Monroe) plans to kill her crazed war-vet husband (Cotten). Little does she know that he is plotting to

double-cross her. Steamy, quasi-Hitchcockian mystery ably directed, with interesting performances. Monroes sings "Kiss."
1952 89m/B Joseph Cotten, Jean Peters, Marilyn Monroe, Casey Adams, Don "The Dragon" Wilson; *D:* Henry Hathaway. **VHS, Beta, LV $14.98** *FOX* 🎬🎬½

Nice Girl Like Me An orphaned young girl roams Europe, getting pregnant twice by two different men. She eventually finds love in the form of a kind caretaker. Harmless fluff. Based on Anne Piper's novel "Marry At Leisure."
1969 (PG) 91m/C *GB* Harry Andrews, Barbara Ferris, Gladys Cooper, Bill Hinnant, James Villers; *D:* Desmond Davis. **VHS, Beta $59.98** *NLC* 🎬🎬

Nice Girls Don't Explode A girl telekinetically starts fires when sexually aroused. This puts a bit of a damper on her relationship with O'Leary, much to her mother's delight. Matchless entertainment.
1987 (PG) 92m/C Barbara Harris, Wallace Shawn, Michelle Meyrink, William O'Leary; *D:* Chuck Martinez. **VHS, Beta $19.95** *STE, NWV* 🎬🎬

Nice Neighbor An acclaimed film about an outwardly self-sacrificing neighbor who cold-bloodedly manipulates his fellow rooming house tenants for his own ends. In Hungarian with English subtitles.
1979 90m/C *HU* Laszlo Szabo, Margit Dayka, Agi Margittay; *D:* Zsolt Kedzi-Kovacs. **VHS, Beta $59.95** *FCT* 🎬🎬

Nicholas and Alexandra Epic chronicling the final years of Tsar Nicholas II, Empress Alexandra and their children. Their lavish royal lifestyle gives way to imprisonment and eventual execution under the new Lenin government. Beautiful, but overlong costume epic that loses steam in the second half. Based on the biography by Robert Massie. Available in widescreen format on laserdisc.
1971 (PG) 183m/C Michael Jayston, Janet Suzman, Tom Baker, Laurence Olivier, Michael Redgrave, Harry Andrews, Jack Hawkins, Alexander Knox, Curt Jurgens; *D:* Franklin J. Schaffner. Academy Awards '71: Best Art Direction/Set Decoration, Best Costume Design; Nominations: Best Actress (Suzman), Best Cinematography, Best Picture, Best Original Score; National Board of Review Awards '71: 10 Best Films of the Year. **VHS, Beta, LV $29.95** *COL, TVC* 🎬🎬½

Nicholas Nickleby An ensemble cast works hard to bring to life Charles Dickens' novel about an impoverished family dependent on their wealthy but villainous uncle. Young Nicholas is an apprentice at a school for boys, and he and a student run away to a series of exciting adventures. An enjoyable film, though it is hard to tell the entire story in such a small amount of time. *AKA:* The Life and Adventures of Nicholas Nickleby.
1946 108m/B *GB* Cedric Hardwicke, Stanley Holloway, Derek Bond, Alfred Drayton, Sybil Thorndike, Sally Ann Howes, Bernard Miles, Mary Merrall, Cathleen Nesbitt; *D:* Alberto Cavalcanti. **VHS, Beta $19.98** *HBO, MRV, PSM* 🎬🎬🎬

Nicholas Nickleby An animated version of the classic Charles Dickens novel.
1987 72m/C VHS, Beta $19.98 *LIV* 🎬🎬🎬

Nick Knight An L.A. cop on the night beat is really a good-guy vampire, who quaffs cattle blood as he tracks down another killer who's draining humans of their plasma. A gimmicky pilot for a would-be TV series that never bit.
198? 92m/C Rick Springfield, Michael Nader, Laura Johnson. **VHS $19.95** *STE* 🎬🎬

Nickel & Dime A con artist's luck turns bad when the IRS catches up with him, impounds all his worldly goods, and sticks him with an officious auditor. But if Jack can find the heiress to a fortune, within 48 hours, he can claim a hefty finder's fee and his money worries will be a thing of the past.
1992 (PG) 96m/C C. Thomas Howell, Wallace Shawn, Lise Cutter, Lynn Danielson, Roy Brocksmith; *W/D:* Ben Moses; *W:* Seth Front, Eddy Polon. **VHS $89.95** *COL* 🎬🎬

Nickel Mountain Heartwarming story of a suicidal 40-year-old man who finds a new reason to live when he falls in love with a pregnant 16-year-old girl who works at his diner. Langenkamp particularly appealing. Based on a John Gardner novel.
1985 88m/C Michael Cole, Heather Langenkamp, Ed Lauter, Brian Kerwin, Patrick Cassidy, Grace Zabriskie, Don Beddoe; *D:* Drew Denbaum. **VHS, Beta $59.95** *LHV* 🎬🎬½

Nicole The downfall of a wealthy woman who is able to buy everything she wants except love.
1972 (R) 91m/C Leslie Caron, Catherine Bach, Ramon Bieri; *D:* Itsvan Ventilla. **VHS, Beta** *GHV* 🎬

Nido de Aguilas Two brothers stripped of their ranch search for the band of thieves who killed their parents. *AKA:* Eagle's Nest.
1976 93m/C *MX* Mario Almada, Martha Elena Cervantes. **VHS, Beta $55.95** *MAD* 🎬

The Night After Halloween A young woman gets the shock of her life when she discovers that her boyfriend is a crazed killer.
1983 (R) 90m/C *IT* Chantal Contouri, Robert Bruning, Sigrid Thornton. **VHS, Beta** *NO* 🎬

Night After Night After Night A killer prowls the streets of London for beautiful female throats to slash. The police are baffled, as usual, and the citizens are terrified. A Jack the Ripper rip-off.
1970 98m/C Jack May, Linda Marlowe; *D:* Lewis J. Force. **VHS, Beta** *MED* 🎬

Night Ambush A Nazi general is kidnapped on Crete by British agents, who embark on a dangerous trip to the coast where a ship awaits to take them to Cairo. The general tries to thwart their plans, but they outwit him at every turn. Based on a novel by W. Stanley Moss that details a similar real-life event. *AKA:* Ill Met By Moonlight.
1957 100m/B *GB* Dirk Bogarde, Marius Goring, David Oxley, Cyril Cusack, Christopher Lee; *D:* Michael Powell, Emeric Pressburger. **VHS $29.95** *VID* 🎬🎬½

Night and Day Sentimental musical about the life of bon-vivant composer-extraordinaire Cole Porter. His intensity and the motivations for his music are dramatized, but this film succeeds best as a fabulous showcase for Porter's songs. ♫Begin the Beguine; My Heart Belongs to Daddy; You're the Top; I've Got You Under My Skin; Just One of Those Things; I Get a Kick Out of You; Night and Day; What Is This Thing Called Love; Do I Love You; An Old-Fashioned Garden; Miss Otis Regrets; Love For Sale; In the Still of the Night; Bullfrog; You Do Something to Me; Easy to Love; Let's Do It; I'm Unlucky at Gambling; Rosalie; You've Got That Thing; Don't Fence Me In; I'm in Love Again; Anything Goes; I Wonder What's Become of Sally; You Do Something to Me; It Was Just One of Those Things.

1946 128m/C Cary Grant, Alexis Smith, Jane Wyman, Eve Arden, Mary Martin, Alan Hale Jr., Monty Woolley, Ginny Simms, Dorothy Malone; *D:* Michael Curtiz. **VHS, Beta $29.98** *FOX, FCT* 🎬🎬½

Night and the City A film noir classic about a hustler's money-making schemes. Widmark is Harry Fabian, a small-time promoter working for slimy nightclub owner Sullivan, whose job is to hustle the marks into the club where his girlfriend Tierney is the singer. Widmark also happens to be romancing Sullivan's wife, Withers, and wants her to back his latest con. But his schemes go awry and Fabian's on the run for his life. Widmark gives a riveting performance of a lowlife whose brains don't match his ambitions. Filmed in London with appropriate brooding tawdriness. Adapted from the novel by Gerald Kersh; remade in 1992.
1950 95m/B *GB* Richard Widmark, Gene Tierney, Googie Withers, Francis L. Sullivan, Hugh Marlowe, Herbert Lom, Mike Mazurki, Charles Farrell; *D:* Jules Dassin; *W:* Joe Eisinger; *M:* Franz Waxman. **VHS $19.99** *FXV, MOV* 🎬🎬🎬½

Night and the City Harry Fabian (De Niro), a con-artist/ambulance-chaser, concocts a scheme to make it big, and approaches an old boxing great (Warden) to come out of retirement and revive a local boxing night. Problem is, although Harry has energy and ambition, he also has a talent for making enemies out of the wrong people, like the boxer's brother (King), a neighborhood mobster. Helen Nassaros (Lange) is a bar-owner's wife and Harry's lover, who has ambitions of her own. Filled with details more interesting than the plot, "Night and the City" is about fast-living, fast-talking New Yorkers, a vehicle which showcases De Niro's talent. Winkler's remake of the 1950 Jules Dassin film.
1992 (R) 98m/C Robert De Niro, Jessica Lange, Cliff Gorman, Alan King, Jack Warden, Eli Wallach, Barry Primus, Pedro Sanchez; *Cameos:* Regis Philbin, Joy Philbin, Richard Price; *D:* Irwin Winkler; *W:* Richard Price. **VHS, LV $94.98** *FXV* 🎬🎬🎬

Night Angel A beautiful seductress lures men into a deadly trap from which only true love can free them.
1990 (R) 90m/C Isa Anderson, Linda Ashby, Debra Feuer, Helen Martin, Karen Black; *D:* Dominique Othenin-Girard. **VHS, Beta, LV $89.95** *FRH* 🎬🎬🎬

A Night at the Opera The Marx Brothers get mixed up with grand opera in this, their first MGM-produced epic. Jones, as an opera singer on the rise, sings "Alone" and "Cosi Cosa." Written by George S. Kaufman and Mollie Ryskind, it's blessed with a big budget that the brothers use to reach epic anarchic heights. One of the best Marx Brothers' films, it features scenes which were perfected and tested on live audiences before their inclusion, including the Groucho-Chico paper-tearing contract negotiation and the celebrated stateroom scene, in which the Marxists are joined in a small shipboard closet by two maids, the ship's engineer, his assistant, a manicurist, a young woman, a cleaning lady, and four food-laden waiters. The first effort without Zeppo. Also available on laserdisc with letterboxing, digital sound, original trailers, production photos, memorabilia, and soundtrack commentary by film critic Leonard Maltin.
1935 92m/B Groucho Marx, Chico Marx, Harpo Marx, Allan Jones, Kitty Carlisle, Sig Rumann, Margaret Dumont, Walter Woolf King; *D:* Sam Wood. **VHS, Beta, LV $19.95** *MGM, VYG, CRC* 🎬🎬🎬🎬

Night Beast Alien creature lands his spaceship near a small town and begins a bloody killing spree. Recycled plot.
1983 90m/C Tom Griffith, Dick Dyszel, Jaimie Zemarel. VHS, Beta $42.95 *PGN* ✗

Night Beat A labored crime drama from postwar Britain. Two army pals pursue diverging careers. One becomes a cop, the other a crook. Want to bet that they meet again?
1948 95m/B *GB* Anne Crawford, Maxwell Reed, Ronald Howard, Christine Norden; *D:* Harold Huth. VHS $15.95 *LOO* ✗✗½

The Night Before Snobby high school beauty Loughlin loses a bet and has to go to the prom with the school geek Reeves. On the way, they get lost on the wrong side of the tracks, and become involved with pimps, crime and the police. A drunken Reeves loses Loughlin as well as his father's car. Typical teen farce.
1988 (PG-13) 90m/C Keanu Reeves, Lori Loughlin, Trinidad Silva, Michael Greene, Theresa Saldana, Suzanne Snyder; *D:* Thom Eberhardt. VHS, Beta $79.99 *HBO* ✗½

Night Breed A teenager flees a chaotic past to slowly become a member of a bizarre race of demons that live in a huge, abandoned Canadian graveyard, a place where every sin is forgiven. Based on Barker's novel "Cabal," and appropriately gross, nonsensical and strange. Good special effects almost save this one.
1990 (R) 102m/C *CA* Craig Sheffer, Anne Bobby, David Cronenberg, Charles Haid; *D:* Clive Barker. VHS, Beta, LV $89.98 *MED* ✗½

The Night Brings Charlie A disfigured tree surgeon is the prime suspect in some grisly murders committed with a tree trimming saw. Obviously, everyone in the town fears him as a result. Not a sequel to "Roots."
1990 90m/C Kerry Knight, Joe Fishback, Aimee Tenalia, Monica Simmons; *D:* Tom Logan. VHS *NO* ✗½

Night Call Nurses Three gorgeous nurses find danger and intrigue on the night shift at a psychiatric hospital. Third in the "nurse" quintet is back on target, shrugging off the previous film's attempts at "serious" social commentary. Miller provides comic relief. Preceded by "The Student Nurses" and "Private Duty Nurses" and followed by "The Young Nurses," and "Candy Stripe Nurses." Also on video as "Young L.A. Nurses 2."
1972 (R) 85m/C Patricia T. Byrne, Alana Collins, Mittie Lawrence, Dennis Young, Felton Perry, Stack Pierce, Richard Young, Dennis Dugan, Dick Miller; *D:* Jonathan Kaplan. VHS, Beta $59.98 *NLC* ✗✗

Night Caller from Outer Space When a woman-hunting alien arrives in London, women begin to disappear. At first, incredibly, no one makes the connection, but then the horrible truth comes to light. *AKA:* Blood Beast from Outer Space; The Night Caller.
1966 84m/B *GB* John Saxon, Maurice Denham, Patricia Haines, Alfred Burke, Jack Watson, Aubrey Morris; *D:* John Gilling. VHS, Beta, LV $14.95 *SVS, COL* ✗½

Night Children Tough L.A. cop teams with a parole officer to battle a nasty gang leader. The battle is quite violent and senseless.
1989 (R) 90m/C David Carradine, Nancy Kwan, Griffin O'Neal, Tawny Fere; *D:* Norbert Meisel. VHS, Beta $79.95 *VMK* ✗

The Night Club Swinging single stands to gain fortune if he weds a certain girl, and, as luck would have it, he falls for her. When the usual hearts and roses don't convince her he's earnest, he tries to prove his love is true by attempting suicide and hiring a hit man.
1925 62m/B Raymond Griffith, Vera Reynolds, Wallace Beery, Louise Fazenda; *D:* Frank Urson. VHS, Beta $19.95 *GPV* ✗✗½

Night Creature A tough, Hemingway-type writer is determined to destroy the man-eating black leopard which nearly killed him once before. Filmed in Thailand. *AKA:* Out of the Darkness; Fear.
1979 (PG) 83m/C Donald Pleasence, Nancy Kwan, Ross Hagen; *D:* Lee Madden. VHS, Beta $19.95 *UHV* ✗

Night Cries After a woman's baby dies at birth, she has persistent dreams that he is alive and in trouble. No one will believe her when she tells them that something is wrong. Made for television.
1978 100m/C Susan St. James, Michael Parks, William Conrad; *D:* Richard Lang. VHS, Beta *WOV* ✗✗½

Night Crossing The fact-based story of two East German families who launch a daring escape to the West in a homemade hot air balloon. Exciting action for the whole family, or even parts of it.
1981 (PG) 106m/C John Hurt, Jane Alexander, Glynnis O'Connor, Doug McKeon, Beau Bridges; *D:* Delbert Mann; *M:* Jerry Goldsmith. VHS, Beta $69.95 *DIS* ✗✗½

The Night Cry Silent canine melodrama has sheep-murdering dog sentenced to death row until he saves little girl from unbelievably big bird.
1926 65m/B Rin Tin Tin, John Harron, June Marlowe, Mary Louise Miller; *D:* Herman C. Raymaker. VHS, Beta *GPV, GVV* ✗✗

The Night Evelyn Came Out of the Grave A wealthy Italian playboy, obsessed with his dead, flame-haired wife, lures living redheads into his castle, where he tortures and kills them. Standard '70s Euro/horror/sex stuff enlivened by the presence of the incredible Erika Bianc as a stripper who works out of a coffin. *AKA:* La Notte Che Evelyn Usca Dalla Tomba.
1971 (R) 99m/C *IT* Anthony Steffen, Marina Malfatti, Rod Murdock, Erika Blanc, Giacomo Rossi-Stuart, Umberto Raho; *D:* Emilio P. Miraglio. VHS $18.00 *FRG* ✗½

Night Eyes Surveillance can be a dangerous profession, especially when your boss happens to be the jealous husband of a very sexy woman. Watching turns to yearning for this professional peeper, but he may just get more than he bargained for. Roberts is worth watching. *AKA:* Hidden Vision.
1990 (R) 95m/C Andrew Stevens, Tanya Roberts, Warwick Sims, Cooper Huckabee; *D:* Emilio P. Miraglio. VHS, Beta, LV $89.99 *PAR* ✗

Night Eyes 2 A security expert assigned to protect the sultry wife of a foreign diplomat finds himself spending a little too much time eyeing her through his hidden cameras. Soon he can no longer control his desire and he makes a move on her that may have international implications. Also available in an unrated version.
1991 (R) 97m/C Andrew Stevens, Shannon Tweed, Tim Russ, Richard Chaves, Geno Silva; *D:* Rodney McDonald. VHS, Beta $89.95 *PSM* ✗½

Night Flight from Moscow A Soviet spy defects with a fistful of secret documents that implicate every free government. Then the CIA must decide if he's telling the

truth. Complex espionage thriller. *AKA:* The Serpent.
1973 (PG) 113m/C *FR IT GE* Yul Brynner, Henry Fonda, Dirk Bogarde, Virna Lisi, Philippe Noiret, Farley Granger, Robert Alda, Marie DuBois, Elga Andersen; *D:* Henri Verneuil; *M:* Ennio Morricone. VHS, Beta $59.98 *NLC* ✗✗½

A Night for Crime A movie star disappears during the filming of a movie. When she turns up dead, a bumbling cop suspects everyone on the set.
1942 75m/B Glenda Farrell, Lyle Talbot, Lena Basquette, Donald Kirke, Ralph Sanford; *D:* Alexis Thurn-Taxis. VHS $24.95 *NOS, DVT* ✗✗

Night Friend A priest sets out to help a young woman caught up in a world of drug abuse and prostitution. Exploitation morality flick.
1987 (R) 94m/C Art Carney, Chuck Shamata, Jayne Eastwood, Heather Kjollesdal; *D:* Peter Gerretsen. VHS, Beta $79.95 *PSM* ✗

A Night Full of Rain Italian communist tries unsuccessfully to seduce vacationing American feminist. They meet again in San Francisco and wedding bells chime. They argue. They argue more. They put all but rabid Wertmuller fans to sleep. The director's first English-language film. *AKA:* End of the World (in Our Usual Bed in a Night Full of Rain).
1978 (R) 104m/C *IT* Giancarlo Giannini, Candice Bergen, Anne Byrne, Flora Carabella; *W/D:* Lina Wertmuller. VHS $59.98 *WAR, FCT* ✗½

Night Gallery Rod Serling is the tour guide through an unusual art gallery consisting of portraits that reflect people's greed, desire and guilt. Made for television pilot for the series, which ran from 1969 to 1973. Three stories, including "Eyes," which saw novice Spielberg directing veteran Crawford.
1969 95m/C Joan Crawford, Roddy McDowall, Tom Bosley, Barry Sullivan, Ossie Davis, Sam Jaffe, Kate Greenfield; *D:* Steven Spielberg, Boris Sagal. VHS, Beta $59.95 *MCA* ✗½

Night Game A cop links a string of serial killings to the night games won by the Houston Astros. Brave cast tries hard, but is retired without a hit.
1989 95m/C Roy Scheider, Karen Young, Paul Gleason, Lane Smith, Carlin Glynn; *D:* Peter Masterson. VHS, Beta, LV $89.99 *HBO* ✗½

Night Games Raped as a child, California girl Pickett has trouble relating to her husband. To overcome her sexual anxieties, she engages in a number of bizarre fantasies.
1980 (R) 100m/C Cindy Pickett, Joanna Cassidy, Barry Primus, Gene Davis; *D:* Roger Vadim; *M:* John Barry. VHS, Beta, LV $69.98 *SUE* ✗

The Night God Screamed A fanatical cult leader is convicted of murder and the cult goes wild. *AKA:* Scream.
198? (PG) 85m/C Michael Sugich, Jeanne Crain, James B. Sikking; *D:* Lee Madden. VHS, Beta $19.98 *TWE* Woof!

The Night Has Eyes Tense melodrama concerns a young teacher who disappears on the Yorkshire moors at the same spot where her girlfriend had vanished the previous year. Early film appearance for Mason. *AKA:* Terror House.
1942 79m/B *GB* James Mason, Joyce Howard, Wilfred Lawson, Mary Clare; *D:* Leslie Arliss. VHS, Beta $19.95 *NOS, NWV, FCT* ✗✗

A Night in Casablanca Groucho, Harpo and Chico find themselves in the luxurious Hotel Casablanca, going after some leftover Nazis searching for treasure. One of the later Marx Brothers' films, but still loaded with the familiar wisecracks and mayhem.

1946 85m/B Groucho Marx, Harpo Marx, Chico Marx, Charles Drake, Dan Seymour, Sig Rumann; **D**: Archie Mayo. VHS, Beta *NO* 𝔊𝔊𝔊

A Night in Heaven A college teacher gets involved with one of her students, who moonlights as a male stripper. Will he earn that extra credit he needs to pass? Uninspired, overly explicit. Look for Denny Terrio of "Dance Fever" fame.
1983 (R) 85m/C Christopher Atkins, Lesley Ann Warren, Carrie Snodgress, Andy Garcia; **D**: John G. Avildsen. VHS, Beta $59.98 *FOX Woof!*

A Night in the Life of Jimmy Reardon A high school Casanova watches his friends leave for expensive schools while he contemplates a trip to Hawaii with his rich girlfriend, a ruse to avoid the dull business school his father has picked out. Well photographed, but acting leaves something to be desired. Based on Richert's novel "Aren't You Even Going to Kiss Me Good-bye?"
1988 (R) 95m/C River Phoenix, Meredith Salenger, Matthew L. Perry, Louanne, Ione Skye, Ann Magnuson, Paul Koslo, Jane Hallaren, Jason Court; **D**: William Richert. VHS, Beta, LV $19.98 *FOX* 𝔊𝔊1/2

Night Is My Future A young musician, blinded in an accident, meets a girl who tries to bring him happiness. Usual somber Bergman, but unimportant story. In Swedish with English subtitles. **AKA**: Music in Darkness.
1947 89m/B SW Mai Zetterling, Birger Malmsten, Naima Wifstrand, Olof Winnerstrand, Hilda Borgstrom; **D**: Ingmar Bergman. VHS, Beta $29.95 *TAM, VYY, DVT* 𝔊𝔊1/2

Night Life A teenager gets the all-out, high-stakes ride of his life when four cadavers are re-animated in his uncle's mortuary.
1990 (R) 92m/C Scott Grimes, John Astin, Cheryl Pollak, Alan Blumenfeld; **D**: David Acomba; **W**: Keith Critchlow. VHS, LV $79.95 *COL* 𝔊𝔊

Night Life in Reno When a man leaves his wife, she sets out for Reno and falls in love with a married man. When her new love is killed by his jealous wife, the woman returns to her husband and they begin their marriage anew. Watchable melodrama.
1931 58m/B Jameson Thomas, Dorothy Christy, Virginia Valli, Carmelita Geraghty. VHS, Beta, LV *NO* 𝔊𝔊

Night Master A handful of karate students practice their homework with much higher stakes away from the classroom. For them, deadly Ninja games are the only way to study.
1987 87m/C Tom Jennings, Nicole Kidman, Vince Martin; **D**: Mark Joffe. VHS, Beta $79.95 *ACA* 𝔊

'night, Mother A depressed woman, living with her mother, announces one evening that she is going to kill herself. Her mother spends the evening reliving their lives and trying to talk her out of it, but the outcome seems inevitable. Well acted, though depressing. Based on Marsha Norman's Pulitzer Prize-winning novel.
1986 (PG-13) 97m/C Sissy Spacek, Anne Bancroft; **D**: Thomas Moore. VHS, Beta, LV $79.95 *MCA* 𝔊𝔊1/2

Night Moves While tracking down a missing teenager, a Hollywood detective uncovers a bizarre smuggling ring in the Florida Keys. Hackman is realistic as the detective whose own life is unraveling and in one of her early roles, Griffith plays the teenager. The dense, disjointed plot reaches a shocking end. Underrated when released and worth a view.

1975 (R) 100m/C Gene Hackman, Susan Clark, Jennifer Warren, Melanie Griffith, Harris Yulin, Edward Binns, Kenneth Mars, James Woods, Dennis Dugan, Max Gail; **D**: Arthur Penn. VHS, Beta $19.98 *WAR* 𝔊𝔊𝔊1/2

Night Nurse Stanwyck is a nurse who uncovers a sordid plot involving the murder of two young children for an inheritance. An entertaining, overlooked crime-drama, initially notorious for Stanwyck and roommate Blondell's continual onscreen dressings and undressings. Gable is compelling in an early, villainous role.
1931 72m/B Barbara Stanwyck, Ben Lyon, Joan Blondell, Charles Winninger, Charlotte Merriam, Eddie Nugent, Blanche Frederici, Allan "Rocky" Lane, Walter McGrail, Ralf Harolde, Clark Gable; **D**: William A. Wellman. VHS, LV *MGM* 𝔊𝔊𝔊

Night Nurse Young nurse signs on to care for an aging, wheelchair-ridden opera star, only to find that the house is haunted.
1977 80m/C Davina Whitehouse, Kay Taylor, Gary Day, Kate Fitzpatrick; **D**: Igor Auzins. VHS, Beta $42.95 *PGN* 𝔊

Night of a Thousand Cats A reclusive playboy cruises Mexico City in his helicopter, searching for beautiful women. It seems he needs their bodies for his cats who, for some reason, eat only human flesh. He keeps the heads, for some reason, for his private collection. A really odd '70s cannibal cat entry, but it moves along nicely and features some truly groovy fashions (floppy hats, translucent blouses, etc.). Not to be confused with the 1963 film of the same name. From the director of "Night of the Bloody Apes" and "Survive!" **AKA**: La Noche de Los Mil Gatos; Blood Feast.
1972 (R) 83m/C MX Anjanette Comer, Zulma Faiad, Hugo Stiglitz, Christa Linder, Teresa Velasquez, Barbara Ange; **D**: Rene Cardona Jr. VHS, Beta $19.95 *PGN, ACA, JEF* 𝔊𝔊

Night of Bloody Horror Tale of a former mental patient who is believed to be responsible for the brutal murders of his ex-girlfriends. A night of bloody horror indeed, as the gore is liberally spread.
1976 (R) 89m/C Gaye Yellen, Evelyn Hendricks, Gerald McRaney. VHS, Beta *PGN* 𝔊1/2

Night of Dark Shadows An abominable film which even fans of the TV show have a hard time liking. The last of the Collins family and his new bride are sent 150 years into the past. Sequel to "House of Dark Shadows." **AKA**: Curse of Dark Shadows.
1971 (PG) 97m/C David Selby, Lara Parker, Kate Jackson, Grayson Hall, John Karlen, Nancy Barrett, James Storm; **D**: Dan Curtis. VHS, Beta $19.98 *MGM Woof!*

Night of Evil Girl is released from reform school and promptly wins a beauty contest. Her bid to win the Miss America title is blown to smithereens however, when it is discovered that she has been secretly married all along. From there she resorts to working in strip joints and attempts to pull off an armed robbery. As exploitation fare goes, a winner. Written by Lewis Perino.
1962 88m/B Lisa Gaye, William Campbell; **D**: Richard Galbreath. VHS, Beta $16.95 *SNC* 𝔊1/2

Night of Horror Zombies attack four young people stranded in the wilderness.
198? (R) 76m/C Steve Sandkuhler, Gae Schmitt, Rebecca Bach, Jeff Canfield. VHS, Beta *GHV, MRV* 𝔊1/2

Night of Terror A bizarre family conducts brain experiments on themselves and then begins to kill each other. Bloodshed for the whole family.
1987 105m/C Renee Harmon, Henry Lewis. VHS $49.95 *IME* 𝔊1/2

Night of the Assassin Priest leaves his pulpit to become a terrorist. He plans a surprise for a U.N. secretary visiting Greece that would put the U.S. and Greek governments in the palm of his hand. Hard to believe.
1977 98m/C Klaus Kinski, Michael Craig, Eva Renzi; **D**: Robert McMahon. VHS, Beta $69.98 *LIV* 𝔊

Night of the Blood Beast An astronaut comes back from space with an alien growing inside his body. The low budget defeats a valiant attempt at a story. Alternative title: "Creature from Galaxy 27."
1958 65m/B Michael Emmet, Angela Greene, John Baer, Ed Nelson; **D**: Bernard L. Kowalski. VHS $16.95 *SNC, MRV* 𝔊1/2

Night of the Bloody Apes When a doctor transplants an ape's heart into his dying son's body, the son goes berserk. Gory Mexican-made horror at its finest. **AKA**: Gomar the Human Gorilla; La Horriplante Bestia Humana.
1968 (R) 84m/C MX Jose Elias Moreno, Carlos Lopez Moctezuma, Armando Silvestre, Norma Lazarendo, Augustin Martinez Solares, Gina Moret, Noelia Noel, Gerard Zepeda; **D**: Rene Cardona Jr. VHS, Beta $59.95 *MPI Woof!*

Night of the Bloody Transplant A lunatic scientist switches hearts from one person to another in this bloody gorefest. Footage of real surgery adds authenticity, but not believeability.
1986 (R) 90m/C Dick Grimm; **D**: David W. Hanson. VHS, Beta $24.95 *UHV Woof!*

Night of the Cobra Woman A woman who can turn herself into a cobra needs constant sex and snake venom to keep her eternally young. Shot on location in the Philippines. One-time underground filmmaker Meyer co-wrote the script, for the Corman factory.
1972 (R) 85m/C PH Joy Bang, Marlene Clark, Roger Garrett, Slash Marks, Vic Diaz; **D**: Andrew Meyer. VHS, Beta *NO* 𝔊

Night of the Comet After surviving the explosion of a deadly comet, two California girls discover that they are the last people on Earth. When zombies begin to chase them, things begin to lose their charm. Cute and funny, but the script runs out before the movie does.
1984 (PG-13) 90m/C Catherine Mary Stewart, Kelli Maroney, Robert Beltran, Geoffrey Lewis, Mary Woronov, Sharon Farrell, Michael Bowen; **W/D**: Thom Eberhardt. VHS, Beta $19.98 *FOX* 𝔊𝔊1/2

Night of the Creeps In 1958 an alien organism lands on earth and infects a person who is then frozen. Thirty years later he is accidentally unfrozen and starts spreading the infection throughout a college town. B-movie homage contains every horror cliche there is. Director Dekker's first film.
1986 (R) 89m/C Jason Lively, Jill Whitlow, Tom Atkins, Dick Miller, Steve Marshall; **D**: Fred Dekker. VHS, Beta, LV $14.99 *HBO* 𝔊𝔊1/2

Night of the Cyclone A complex but not overly interesting thriller about a big city cop who goes to an island paradise in search of his missing daughter and finds murder.
1990 (R) 90m/C Kris Kristofferson, Jeffrey Meek, Marisa Berenson, Winston Ntshona, Gerrit Graham; **D**: David Irving. VHS, LV $89.98 *REP* 𝔊𝔊

Night of the Death Cult After moving to a quiet seaside community, a young couple is plagued by cult practising human sacrifice in order to appease the Templars, a zombie-like pack of ancient clergymen who rise from the dead and torture the living. Last

in a four film series about the Templars. *AKA:* Night of the Seagulls.
1975 90m/C *SP* Victor Petit, Julie James, Maria Kosti, Sandra Mozarowsky; *D:* Armando de Ossorio. **VHS, Beta $69.95** *SVS* ✍✍

Night of the Demon Anthropology students are attacked by the legendary Bigfoot. Later they discover that he has raped and impregnated a young woman. Gore and sex prevail.
1980 97m/C Jay Allen, Michael J. Cutt, Bob Collins, Jodi Lazarus; *D:* James C. Watson. **VHS, Beta $49.95** *VHE Woof!*

Night of the Demons A gory, special-effects-laden horror farce about teenagers calling up demons in a haunted mortuary. On Halloween, of course.
1988 (R) 92m/C Linnea Quigley, Cathy Podewell, Alvin Alexis, William Gallo, Mimi Kinkade, Lance Fenton; *D:* Kevin S. Tenney. **VHS, LV $89.98** *REP* ✍✍

Night of the Fox An American officer with top secret knowledge is captured by Germans on the brink of D-day. His home team plans to kill him if he cannot be rescued before spilling the beans. On-location filming adds much. Made for cable.
1990 (R) 95m/C Michael York, Deborah Raffin, George Peppard; *D:* Charles Jarrott. **VHS, LV $89.95** *VMK* ✍✍

Night of the Generals A Nazi intelligence officer is pursuing three Nazi generals who may be involved in the brutal murder of a Warsaw prostitute. Dark and sinister, may be too slow for some tastes. Based on Hans Helmut Kirst's novel. *AKA:* La Nuit de Generaux.
1967 (R) 148m/C Peter O'Toole, Omar Sharif, Tom Courtenay, Joanna Pettet, Donald Pleasence, Christopher Plummer, Philippe Noiret, John Gregson; *D:* Anatole Litvak. **VHS, Beta, LV $9.95** *COL* ✍✍✍

Night of the Ghouls Second to last in Wood's celebrated series of inept horror films that began with "Bride of the Monster" and "Plan 9 from Outer Space." This one tells of a phony spiritualist who swindles the grieving by pretending to raise the dead. To his great surprise he actually does enliven some cadavers, who then go after him. Unreleased for over 20 years because Wood couldn't pay the film lab. Not quite as classically bad as his other films, but still a laugh riot. Wood's last directorial effort was "Sinister Urge." *AKA:* Revenge of the Dead.
1959 69m/B Paul Marco, Tor Johnson, Duke Moore, Kenne Duncan, John Carpenter, Criswell; *D:* Edward D. Wood Jr. **VHS, Beta $9.95** *RHI, SNC, MED Woof!*

Night of the Grizzly An ex-lawman's peaceful life as a rancher is threatened when a killer grizzly bear goes on a murderous rampage terrorizing the residents of the Wyoming countryside.
1966 99m/C Clint Walker, Martha Hyer; *D:* Joseph Pevney. **VHS, Beta $29.95** *PAR* ✍✍

Night of the Howling Beast The selling point of this one is an epic, first-time battle between a werewolf and a Yeti. Unfortunately it lasts about fifteen seconds. Naschy's eighth stint as the wolfman. *AKA:* The Werewolf and the Yeti.
1975 (R) 87m/C *SP* Paul Naschy, Grace Mills, Castillo Escalona, Silvia Solar, Gil Vidal; *D:* Miguel Iglesias Bonns. **VHS, Beta** *REP* ✍

The Night of the Hunter The nightmarish story of a psychotic preacher who marries a lonely widow with two children in the hopes of finding the cache of money her thieving husband had stashed. A dark, terrifying tale, completely unique in Hollywood's

history. Mitchum is terrific. Written by James Agee, from novel by Davis Grubb and, sadly, Laughton's only directorial effort.
1955 93m/B Robert Mitchum, Shelley Winters, Lillian Gish, Don Beddoe, Evelyn Varden, Peter Graves, James Gleason, Billy Chapin; *D:* Charles Laughton. **VHS, Beta, LV $19.98** *MGM, VYG* ✍✍✍

The Night of the Iguana An alcoholic ex-minister acts as a tour guide in Mexico, becoming involved with a spinster and a hotel owner. Based on Tennessee Williams' play. Excellent performances from Burton and Gardner.
1964 125m/B Richard Burton, Deborah Kerr, Ava Gardner, Grayson Hall, Sue Lyon; *D:* John Huston. Academy Awards '64: Best Costume Design (B & W); Nominations: Best Art Direction/Set Decoration (B & W), Best Black and White Cinematography, Best Supporting Actress (Hall). **VHS, Beta $19.98** *MGM* ✍✍✍

Night of the Juggler An ex-cop encounters countless obstacles in trying to track down his daughter's kidnapper in New York City. Just a tad too complicated for some tastes.
1980 (R) 101m/C James Brolin, Cliff Gorman, Richard Castellano, Mandy Patinkin, Julie Carmen; *D:* Robert Butler. **VHS, Beta $49.95** *MED* ✍✍½

Night of the Kickfighters A mighty band of martial artists takes on a terrorist group that has in their possession a secret weapon that could destroy the world.
1991 87m/C Andy Bauman, Adam West, Marcia Karr; *D:* Buddy Reyes. **VHS $89.98** *AIP* ✍

Night of the Laughing Dead Veteran British comedy cast perform unthinkable spoof. Man stands to inherit lotsa money as his family members kick the bucket one by one. *AKA:* Crazy House; House in Nightmare Park.
1975 90m/C *GB* Ray Milland, Frankie Howerd, Rosalie Crutchley, Kenneth Griffith; *D:* Peter Sykes. **VHS, LV** *MGM* ✍½

Night of the Living Babes Two yuppie men go looking for fun at a brothel. They get their just deserts in the form of sex-seeking female zombies.
1987 60m/C Michelle McClellan, Connie Woods, Andrew Nichols, Louie Bonanno; *D:* Jon Valentine. **VHS** *NO Woof!*

Night of the Living Dead Cult favorite is low budget but powerfully frightening. Space experiments set off a high level of radiation that makes the newly dead return to life, with a taste for human flesh. Handful of holdouts find shelter in a farmhouse. Claustrophobic, terrifying, gruesome, extreme, and yes, humorous. Followed by "Dawn of the Dead" (1979) and "Day of the Dead" (1985). Romero's directorial debut. Available in a colorized version. *AKA:* Night of the Flesh Eaters.
1968 90m/B Judith O'Dea, Duane Jones, Russell Streiner, Karl Hardman; *D:* George A. Romero. **VHS, LV, 3/4U, Special order formats $19.95** *REP, MRV, NOS* ✍✍✍

Night of the Living Dead A bunch of people are trapped in a farmhouse and attacked by ghouls with eating disorders. Remake of the '68 classic substitutes high tech blood 'n' guts for bona fide frights.
1990 (R) 92m/C Tony Todd, Patricia Tallman, Tom Towles; *D:* Tom Savini; *W:* George A. Romero. **VHS, LV $19.95** *COL* ✍✍

Night of the Ninja Hop 'n' kick mystery about the search for a missing diamond. Investigator is led down a deadly trail as he tracks Ninja assassins who know where the gem is hidden.
19?? ?m/C **VHS $59.99** *IMP* ✍½

Night of the Sharks Mercenaries in a downed plane go after a jewel-ridden shipwreck despite a plethora of sharks.
1989 87m/C Treat Williams, Christopher Connelly, Antonio Fargas, Janet Agren; *D:* Anthony Richmond. **VHS, Beta, LV $79.95** *LIV Woof!*

Night of the Shooting Stars Set in an Italian village during the last days of World War II, this film highlights the schism in the village between those who support the fascists and those who sympathize with the Allies. This division comes to a head in the stunning final scene. A poignant, deeply moving film. *AKA:* The Night of San Lorenzo.
1982 (R) 106m/C *IT* Omero Antonutti, Margarita Lozano; *D:* Paolo Taviani, Vittorio Taviani. **VHS, Beta $29.95** *MGM, APD, AUD* ✍✍✍

Night of the Sorcerers An expedition to the Congo uncovers a bizarre tribe of vampire leopard women who lure young girls to their deaths.
1970 85m/C Jack Taylor, Simon Andrew, Kali Hansa; *D:* Armando de Ossorio. **VHS, Beta $49.95** *UNI Woof!*

Night of the Strangler A love affair between a white society girl and a young black man causes a chain of events that end with brutal murders in New Orleans.
1973 (R) 88m/C Mickey Dolenz, James Ralston, Susan McCullough; *D:* Joy Houck Jr. **VHS, Beta $42.95** *PGN* ✍✍

Night of the Warrior Music videos and martial arts don't mix...not here, anyway. A hunky exotic-dance-club owner pays his disco bills by fighting in illegal, underground blood matches, but not enough to make it exciting. Lamas stars with real life wife Kinmont and mom Dahl.
1991 (R) 96m/C Lorenzo Lamas, Anthony Geary, Kathleen Kinmont, Arlene Dahl. **VHS, LV $89.95** *VMK* ✍

Night of the Wilding Very, very loosely based on the story of the female jogger who was gang-raped and left for dead in New York's Central Park. Made for television, soon after the actual incident occurred.
1990 90m/C Erik Estrada, Kathrin Lautner; *D:* Joseph Merhi. **VHS, Beta, LV** *NO* ✍

Night of the Zombies WWII soldiers with eating disorders shuffle through 88 minutes of gratuitous gore, while pursued by porn star cum intelligence agent. From the director of "Bloodsucking Freaks." *AKA:* Gamma 693; Night of the Wehrmacht Zombies.
1981 (R) 88m/C James Gillis, Ryan Hilliard, Samantha Grey, Joel M. Reed; *W/D:* Joel M. Reed. **VHS $49.99** *PSM* ✍

Night of the Zombies Staff of a scientific research center are killed and then resurrected as cannibals who prey on the living. The living will suffer again if trapped into watching. Mattel is pseudonym for director Vincent Dawn. Cheap, dubbed, and possessing minimal coherence. *AKA:* Apocalipsis Canibal; Hell of the Living Dead; Zombie Creeping Flesh.
1983 101m/C *IT SP* Margit Evelyn Newton, Frank Garfield, Selan Karay; *D:* Bruno Mattei. **VHS, Beta $49.95** *VES, PSM Woof!*

Night on Earth Jarmusch's "road" movie comprises five different stories taking place on the same night in five different cities—Los Angeles, New York, Paris, Rome, and Helsinki—between cabbies and their passengers. In Los Angeles a high-powered casting agent takes a liking to her young cabbie and thinks she found her next star. The New York setting features a cabbie who is an East German refugee and really

can't drive and his eager passenger who needs to get to Brooklyn. Paris has an African immigrant fascinated by his beautiful, blind, and supremely independent fare. In Rome an appalled priest is the reluctant confessor to an exuberant Italian's recital of his sexual sins. Finally, in Helsinki, it's 4 A.M. and three drunken revelers join their driver in a litany of personal complaints. As with any anthology some stories work better than others but all have their moments in this ambitious film with its outstanding international cast. Subtitled in English for the three foreign segments.
1991 (R) 125m/C Winona Ryder, Gena Rowlands, Giancarlo Esposito, Armin Mueller-Stahl, Rosie Perez, Beatrice Dalle, Roberto Benigni, Paolo Bonacelli, Matti Pellonpaa, Kari Vaananen, Sakari Kuosmanen, Tomi Salmela; **W/D:** Jim Jarmusch; **M:** Tom Waits. **VHS, LV** $92.95 NLC, TAM, FFF *ⅠⅠⅠ*

Night Partners Bored housewives assist the police to patrol the streets after the kids have gone to bed. Originally made for television with the intention of turning it into a series, but the script doesn't hold water.
1983 100m/C Yvette Mimieux, Diana Canova, Arlen Dean Snyder, M. Emmet Walsh, Patricia Davis, Larry Linville; **D:** Noel Nosseck. **VHS, Beta** $39.95 NWV *ⅠⅠ½*

Night Patrol The streets of Hollywood will never be the same after the night patrol runs amuck in the town. Crude imitation of "Police Academy."
1985 (R) 87m/C Linda Blair, Pat Paulsen, Jaye P. Morgan, Jack Riley, Murray Langston, Billy Barty, Pat Morita, Sydney Lassick, Andrew Dice Clay; **D:** Jackie Kong. **VHS, Beta, LV** $9.95 NWV, STE Woof!

The Night Porter Max, an ex-SS concentration camp officer, unexpectedly meets his former lover-victim at the Viennese hotel where he works as the night porter. After they get reacquainted, the couple must hide from the porter's ex-Nazi friends who want the women dead because they fear she will disclose their past. A sado-masochistic voyage not for the faint-hearted. **AKA:** Il Portiere de Notte.
1974 (R) 115m/C IT Dirk Bogarde, Charlotte Rampling, Phillippe LeRoy, Gabriel Ferzetti, Isa Miranda; **D:** Liliana Cavani. **VHS, Beta, LV** $19.98 SUE, GLV, TAM *ⅠⅠ*

Night Rhythms Nick West is a radio talk show host with a sexy voice that causes his women listeners to reveal their most intimate fantasies and problems to him on the air. When one listener goes too far, it's murder, and Nick must work to prove his innocence in the crime if he intends to save his career—and his life. Also available in an unrated version.
1992 (R) ?m/C Martin Hewitt, Delia Sheppard, David Carradine, Terry Tweed, Sam Jones, Deborah Driggs, Julie Strain; **D:** Alexander Gregory Hippolyte. **VHS** $89.95 IMP, MOV *ⅠⅠ½*

Night Rider A cowboy posing as a gunman ends a trail of murder and violence in a small western town.
1932 54m/B Harry Carey Sr., George "Gabby" Hayes. **VHS, Beta** $19.95 NOS, DVT *Ⅰ*

Night Riders of Montana A state ranger helps a group of ranchers to fight off a band of rustlers.
1950 60m/B Allan "Rocky" Lane. **VHS, Beta** $24.95 DVT *Ⅰ*

Night Ripper A psychopathic killer stalks high fashion models and kills them by carving them up. Lots of violence.
1986 88m/C James Hansen, April Anne, Larry Thomas; **D:** Jeff Hathcock. **VHS, Beta** NO *Ⅰ*

Night School A police detective must find out who has been decapitating the women attending night school at Wendell College. Ward's first film. **AKA:** Terror Eyes.
1981 (R) 89m/C Edward Albert, Rachel Ward, Leonard Mann, Drew Snyder, Joseph R. Sicari; **D:** Ken Hughes. **VHS, Beta** $19.98 FOX *Ⅰ*

Night Screams Violent scare-monger about two escaped convicts who crash a high school house party. Kids and convicts start getting killed, one by one.
1987 85m/C Joe Manno, Ron Thomas, Randy Lundsford, Megan Wyss; **D:** Allen Plone. **VHS, Beta** $79.95 PSM *Ⅰ*

Night Shadow A woman, returning home after being away for years, picks up a hitchhiker. Soon after her arrival, terrible serial killings begin, and only she has the nerve to track down the killer.
1990 (R) 90m/C Brenda Vance, Dana Chan, Tom Boylan; **W/D:** Randolph Cohlan. **VHS** NO *Ⅰ*

Night Shift Two morgue attendants, dull Winkler and manic Keaton, decide to spice up their latenight shift by running a call-girl service on the side. Keaton turns in a fine performance in his film debut, and Howard's sure-handed direction almost overcome the silly premise.
1982 (R) 106m/C Henry Winkler, Michael Keaton, Shelley Long, Kevin Costner, Pat Corley, Bobby DiCicco, Nita Talbot, Richard Belzer, Shannen Doherty; **D:** Ron Howard. **VHS, Beta, LV** $19.98 WAR *ⅠⅠ*

Night Slasher A madman enjoys spilling the innards of London prostitutes with his dagger.
1984 87m/C Jack May, Linda Marlowe. **VHS, Beta** $49.95 UNI *Ⅰ*

Night Stage to Galveston Autry leads his Texas Rangers on a mission to uncover corruption in the Texas State Police during the turbulent post-Civil War era.
1952 61m/B Gene Autry, Pat Buttram, Virginia Huston, Thurston Hall; **D:** George Archainbaud. **VHS, Beta** $29.98 CCB *ⅠⅠ½*

Night Stalker A horror film about two 12,000-year-old cannibals who terrorize the citizens of Los Angeles in their search for immortality. Lots of violence and sex.
1979 90m/C Aldo Ray. **VHS, Beta** $29.98 FOX, HHE *ⅠⅠ½*

Night Stalker A bloodthirsty serial killer is tracked by a detective through the streets in New York. The usual rigamarole of fisti-cuffs, gunplay, and car chases ensure. Impressive acting from Napier raises the film from the run-of-the-mill.
1987 (R) 91m/C Charles Napier, John Goff, Robert Viharo, Robert Z'Dar, Joseph Gian, Gary Crosby, Joan Chen, Michelle Reese; **D:** Max Cleven. **VHS, Beta** $79.98 VES *ⅠⅠ*

The Night Stalker: Two Tales of Terror Two episodes from the television series "Kolchak: The Night Stalker" in which McGavin plays a nosy newspaper reporter who constantly stumbles upon occult phenomenon. Episodes are "Jack the Ripper" and "The Vampire."
1974 98m/C Darren McGavin, Simon Oakland. **VHS, Beta** MCA *Ⅰ*

Night Terror Everyone's after a hausfrau who saw a highway patrolman murdered on an expressway...including the psychotic murderer. Pretty standard fare. Made for television.
1976 73m/C Valerie Harper, Richard Romanus, Michael Tolan, Beatrice Manley, John Quade, Quinn Cummings, Nicholas Pryor; **D:** E.W. Swackhamer. **VHS, Beta** $59.95 WOV *Ⅰ*

Night Terror A man wakes up from a nightmare only to find that his terrors are still present.
1989 90m/C Lloyd B. Mote, Jeff Keel, Guy Ecker, Jon Hoffman, Michael Coopet; **D:** Michael Weaver, Paul Howard. **VHS, Beta** NO *ⅠⅠ*

The Night the City Screamed It's the hottest day of the year, the city experiences a massive blackout, and nighttime brings out less-than-noble emotions amongst the citizenry. Made for television.
1980 (PG) 96m/C Raymond Burr, Georg Stanford Brown, Linda Purl, Robert Culp, Clifton Davis, David Cassidy, George DiCenzo, Gary Frank, Don Meredith, Shelley Smith, Vic Tayback, Dick Anthony Williams; **D:** Harry Falk; **W:** Larry Brody. **VHS** $59.95 COL *ⅠⅠ½*

The Night the Lights Went Out in Georgia Loosely based on the popular hit song, the film follows a brother and sister as they try to cash in on the country music scene in Nashville. McNichol is engaging.
1981 (PG) 112m/C Kristy McNichol, Dennis Quaid, Mark Hamill, Don Stroud; **D:** Ronald F. Maxwell. **VHS, Beta** $69.95 SUE, TWE *ⅠⅠ*

The Night They Raided Minsky's Chaotic but interesting period comedy about a young Amish girl who leaves her tyrannical father to come to New York City in the 1920s. She winds up at Minsky's Burlesque and accidentally invents the striptease. Lahr's last performance—he died during filming. Cowritten by Norman Lear. ♫The Night They Raided Minsky's; Take Ten Terrific Girls But Only 9 Costumes; How I Love Her; Perfect Gentleman; You Rat, You; Penny Arcade; Wait For Me. **AKA:** The Night They Invented Striptease.
1969 (PG) 97m/C Jason Robards Jr., Britt Ekland, Elliott Gould, Bert Lahr, Norman Wisdom, Denholm Elliott; **D:** William Friedkin. **VHS, Beta** $19.98 FOX *ⅠⅠⅠ*

The Night They Robbed Big Bertha's Bungling burglar attempts to knock off Big Bertha's massage parlor.
1983 83m/C Robert Nichols. **VHS, Beta** $42.95 PGN *Ⅰ*

The Night They Saved Christmas A Christmas special in which Santa's North Pole headquarters are endangered by the progress of an expanding oil company. Will the attempts of three children be enough to save the day?
1987 94m/C Art Carney, Jaclyn Smith, Paul Williams, Paul LeMat; **D:** Jackie Cooper. **VHS, Beta** $9.95 CAF, STE, PSM *ⅠⅠ½*

Night Tide Hopper in another off the wall character study, this time as a lonely sailor. He falls for a mermaid (Lawson) who works at the dock. She may be a descendent of the man-killing Sirens. Interesting and different little love story, sometimes advertised as horror, which it is not.
1963 84m/B Dennis Hopper, Gavin Muir, Luana Anders, Marjorie Eaton, Tom Dillon; **D:** Curtis Harrington. **VHS** $16.95 SNC, FRG *ⅠⅠ½*

Night Time in Nevada Young woman heads West to claim $50,000 trust left by dear old dad, but his crooked lawyer and associate have their hands in the pot. Cowboy Roy rides horse and flexes dimples while helping helpless girl.
1948 67m/B Roy Rogers, Adele Mara, Andy Devine, Grant Withers, Joseph Crehan; **D:** William Witney. **VHS, Beta, 8mm** $19.95 NOS, HEG, VYY *ⅠⅠ½*

A Night to Remember A murder-mystery writer's wife convinces him to move to a new apartment because she thinks the change might help him finish a novel he started long ago. When they find a dead

body behind their new building, they try their hands at sleuthing. A clever and witty mystery, indeed, supported by likeable performances.
1942 91m/B Loretta Young, Brian Aherne, Sidney Toler, Gale Sondergaard, Willairn Wright, Donald MacBride, Blanche Yurka; **D:** Richard Wallace. **VHS $69.95** COL ♪♪♪

A Night to Remember Gripping tale of the voyage of the Titanic with an interesting account of action in the face of danger and courage amid despair. Large cast is effectively used. Adapted by Eric Ambler from the book by Walter Lord.
1958 119m/B Kenneth More, David McCallum, Anthony Bushell, Honor Blackman, Michael Goodliffe, George Rose, Laurence Naismith, Frank Lawton, Alec McCowen; **D:** Roy Ward Baker; **W:** Eric Ambler. **VHS, Beta, LV $19.95** PAR, HMV ♪♪♪

The Night Train to Kathmandu A young girl accompanies her parents on a research expedition to Nepal, where her head is turned by an exotically handsome young Sherpa. Old story without much help from actors or director. Made for cable.
1988 102m/C Milla Jovovich, Pernell Roberts, Eddie Castrodad; **D:** Robert Wiemer. **VHS, Beta, LV $14.95** PAR ♪♪

Night Train to Munich There's Nazi intrigue galore aboard a big train when a scientist's daughter joins allied intelligence agents in retrieving some secret documents. From the book "Report on a Fugitive" by Gordon Wellesley. **AKA:** Night Train; Gestapo.
1940 93m/B GB Margaret Lockwood, Rex Harrison, Paul Henreid; **D:** Carol Reed. **VHS, Beta $24.95** NOS, DVT, HEG ♪♪♪

Night Train to Terror Strange things start happening on the train where a rock band makes its last appearance. Clips from other horror flicks were pieced together to make this film that's so bad it's almost good.
1984 (R) 98m/C John Phillip Law, Cameron Mitchell, Marc Lawrence, Charles Moll, Ferdinand "Ferdy" Mayne; **D:** Jay Schlossberg-Cohen. **VHS, Beta $79.95** PSM Woof!

Night Vision A young writer in the big city is given a video monitor by a street thief which is equipped with some remarkable features, including the ability to present scenes of future murders and demon worship.
1987 102m/C Ellie Martins, Stacy Carson, Shirley Ross, Tony Carpenter; **D:** Michael Krueger. **VHS, Beta $79.95** PSM ♪

The Night Visitor A man in a prison for the criminally insane seeks violent vengeance on those he believes have set him up. Heavily detailed, slow moving. Ullman and von Sydow can do better.
1970 (PG) 106m/C GB DK Max von Sydow, Liv Ullmann, Trevor Howard, Per Oscarsson, Andrew Keir; **D:** Laslo Benedek. **VHS, Beta $59.95** UHV ♪♪½

Night Visitor A retired police detective teams up with a teenage peeping tom to disclose the identity of a satanic serial killer. The killer, of course, is one of the youth's teachers. **AKA:** Never Cry Devil.
1989 (R) 95m/C Derek Rydell, Shannon Tweed, Elliott Gould, Allen Garfield, Michael J. Pollard, Richard Roundtree, Henry Gibson; **D:** Rupert Hitzig. **VHS, Beta $79.95** MGM ♪

The Night Walker Stanwyck is always worth watching and she has the best moments in this psycho-thriller which suffers from a low-budget and confused script. The basic story has Stanwyck as a rich widow with a recurring nightmare featuring a faceless lover. There's also a too-helpful law-

yer (Taylor), a suspicious private detective (Bochner)—and maybe her husband isn't so dead after all. Taylor and Stanwyck, who had once been married, worked together for the first time in 27 years.
1964 86m/B Barbara Stanwyck, Robert Taylor, Lloyd Bochner, Hayden Rorke, Judith Meredith, Rochelle Hudson; **D:** William Castle; **W:** Robert Bloch. **VHS $14.98** MCA ♪♪½

Night Warning A slasher gorefest redeemed by Tyrrell's go-for-broke performance. She plays a sexually repressed aunt who makes up for her problems by going on murderous rampages. Hide the kitchen knives! **AKA:** Nightmare Maker; Butcher Baker (Nightmare Maker).
1982 (R) 96m/C Bo Svenson, Jimmy McNichol, Susan Tyrrell, Julia Duffy; **D:** William Asher. **VHS, Beta $19.99** HBO ♪♪

Night Wars Two ex-POWs who are plagued by their memories turn to dream therapy to relive their escape. Eventually, they rescue a buddy they left behind.
1988 90m/C Dan Haggerty, Brian O'Connor, Cameron Smith; **D:** David A. Prior. **VHS, Beta $14.95** SVS, COL ♪½

Night Watch A woman recovering from a nervous breakdown witnesses a murder, but no one will believe her. **AKA:** Le Trou; Il Buco.
1972 100m/C GB Elizabeth Taylor, Laurence Harvey, Billie Whitelaw; **D:** Brian G. Hutton. **VHS, Beta $9.95** MED ♪½

The Night We Never Met Three yuppies bring different visions of romance to a time-share apartment in New York's Greenwich Village. Sam (Broderick) needs a quiet space to get over being dumped by a flaky performance artist (Tripplehorn). Ellen (Sciorra) is looking for space to paint away from the confines of her thick-headed spouse (Mantell). Brian, the organizer of the living arrangement, wants a space where he can be one of the boys and escape from his cloying fiancee (Bateman). Things go awry when Ellen mistakes clod Brian for sensitive Sam and throws herself into the arms of the wrong man.
1993 (R) 99m/C Matthew Broderick, Jeanne Tripplehorn, Kevin Anderson, Justine Bateman, Annabella Sciorra, Christine Baranski, Doris Roberts, Dominic Chianese, Michael Mantell, Tim Guinee, Greg Germann, Dana Wheeler-Nicholson, Louise Lasser, Bill Campbell, Ranjit Chowdhry, Garry Shandling, Katherine Houghton, Brooke Smith; **D:** Warren Leight; **W:** Warren Leight; **M:** Evan Lurie. **VHS** NYR ♪♪

Night Zoo A confusing story about a father/son reconciliation and the lurid underworld of drugs and sex in Montreal. The graphic sex and violence undermines the sensitive aspects of the film. **AKA:** Un Zoo, La Nuit.
1987 115m/C CA Gilles Maheu, Roger Le Bel, Lynne Adams, German Houde; **D:** Jean-Claude Lauzon. **VHS, Beta, LV $9.99** STE, NWV, IME ♪♪

Nightbreaker Revelation of the U.S. government's deliberate exposure of servicemen to atomic bomb tests and the resulting radiation, in order to observe the effects on humans. Sheen and his son, Estevez, portray a U.S. doctor in the 1980s and the 1950s, respectively.
1989 100m/C Martin Sheen, Emilio Estevez, Lea Thompson, Melinda Dillon, Nicholas Pryor; **D:** Peter Markle. **VHS $9.98** TTC ♪♪♪

The Nightcomers A pretend "prequel" to Henry James's "The Turn of the Screw," wherein an Irish gardener trysts with the nanny of two watchful children who believe that lovers unite in death. Don't be fooled: stick to the original.

1972 (R) 96m/C GB Marlon Brando, Stephanie Beacham, Thora Hird; **D:** Michael Winner. **VHS, Beta, LV, CDV $14.95** COL, NLC ♪

Nightfall Ray, accused of a crime he didn't commit, is forced to flee from both the law and the underworld. Classic example of film noir, brilliantly filmed by Tourneur.
1956 78m/B Aldo Ray, Brian Keith, Anne Bancroft, Jocelyn Brando, James Gregory, Frank Albertson; **D:** Jacques Tourneur. **VHS** GKK ♪♪♪

Nightfall Television adaptation of the classic Isaac Asimov short story. A planet that has two suns (and therefore no night) experiences an eclipse and its inhabitants go mad.
1988 (PG-13) 87m/C David Birney, Sarah Douglas, Alexis Kanner, Andra Millian; **D:** Paul Mayersberg. **VHS, Beta $79.95** MGM ♪♪

Nightflyers Aboard a weathered space freighter, the crew experience a series of deadly accidents caused by an unknown evil presence. From a novella by George R.R. Martin; T.C. Blake is better known as Robert Collector.
1987 (R) 88m/C Michael Praed, Michael Des Barres, Catherine Mary Stewart, John Standing, Lisa Blount; **D:** T.C. Blake. **VHS, Beta, LV, Special order formats $9.99** CCB, IVE ♪½

Nightforce Five buddies plunge into Central American jungles to rescue a young girl held by terrorists.
1986 (R) 87m/C Linda Blair, James Van Patten, Chad McQueen, Richard Lynch, Cameron Mitchell; **D:** Lawrence Foldes. **VHS, Beta** NO ♪

Nighthawks New York City cops scour Manhattan to hunt down an international terrorist on the loose. They race from disco to subway to an airborne tramway. Exciting and well paced. Hauer's American film debut.
1981 (R) 100m/C Sylvester Stallone, Billy Dee Williams, Rutger Hauer, Lindsay Wagner, Nigel Davenport, Persis Khambatta, Catherine Mary Stewart, Joe Spinell; **D:** Bruce Malmuth. **VHS, Beta, LV $19.98** MCA ♪♪½

The Nightingale From "Faerie Tale Theatre" comes the story of an Emperor who discovers the value of true friendship and loyalty from his palace kitchen maid who gives him a nightingale.
1983 60m/C Mick Jagger, Barbara Hershey, Bud Cort, Mako; **D:** Ivan Passer. **VHS, Beta, LV $14.98** KUI, FOX, FCT ♪♪½

Nightkill Simple love affair turns into a deadly game of cat and mouse when a bored wife plots to do away with her wealthy, powerful husband with the aid of her attractive lover. Mitchum is the reluctant investigator pulled into the game.
1980 (R) 104m/C Jaclyn Smith, Mike Connors, James Franciscus, Robert Mitchum, Sybil Danning; **D:** Ted Post. **VHS, Beta $24.98** SUE, NLC ♪♪½

Nightlife A vampiress, who rises from the dead after a hundred years, spends her time looking for blood to drink. Made for cable.
1990 93m/C Ben Cross, Maryam D'Abo, Keith Szarabajka; **D:** Daniel Taplitz. **VHS, Beta, LV $79.95** MCA ♪♪½

Nightmare Boring splatterthon has a young boy hacking his father and his aggressive mistress to pieces when he discovers them in bed. He grows up to be a psycho who continues along the same lines. Humorless and dreadful, the original ads claimed Tom Savini did the special effects. He had nothing to do with it. **AKA:** Blood Splash.
1982 97m/C Baird Stafford, Sharon Smith, C.J. Cooke, Mik Cribben, Kathleen Ferguson, Danny Ronan; **W/D:** Romano Scavolini. **VHS, Beta** NO Woof!

Nightmare at Bittercreek Four babes and a tour guide are pursued by psycho gang in the Sierra mountains. Made for television nightmare in your living room.
1991 (PG-13) 92m/C Tom Skerritt, Joanna Cassidy, Lindsay Wagner, Constance McCashin, Janne Mortil; *D:* Tim Burstall. VHS $89.95 *VMK* ✍✍

Nightmare at 43 Hillcrest A family's life becomes a living hell when the police mistakenly raid their house. Based on a true story.
1974 72m/C Jim Hutton, Mariette Hartley. VHS, Beta *NO* ✍✍

Nightmare at Noon Watered-down thriller about a small desert town beset by violent terrorists (who are really locals gone mad from a chemical experiment dumped into the water system). Only the sheriff's small staff is there to stop them.
1987 (R) 96m/C Wings Hauser, George Kennedy, Bo Hopkins, Brion James, Kimberly Beck, Kimberly Ross; *D:* Nico Mastorakis. VHS $79.98 *REP* ✍

Nightmare Castle Jealous mad scientist murders his wife and her lover. Then he conducts a bizarre experiment, using the dead couple's blood to rejuvenate an old servant. Not quite satisfied with his revenge, he then seeks to marry his late wife's sister after realizing that she has been left the inheritance. In time, the perturbed ghosts of the late lovers appear and seek revenge. A real nightmare. *AKA:* Amanti d'Oltretomba; Night of the Doomed; The Faceless Monsters; Lovers From Beyond the Tomb.
1965 90m/B *IT* Barbara Steele, Paul Muller, Helga Line; *D:* Allan Grunewald; *M:* Ennio Morricone. VHS, Beta $11.95 *SNC, HHT* ✍✍

Nightmare in Badham County Two girls get arrested on trumped-up charges in a small backwoods town. They soon discover that the prison farm is a front for a slavery ring. Made for television. *AKA:* Nightmare.
1976 100m/C Deborah Raffin, Lynne Moody, Chuck Connors, Della Reese, Robert Reed, Ralph Bellamy, Tina Louise; *D:* John Llewellyn Moxey. VHS, Beta $19.95 *VMK* ✍

Nightmare in Blood Vampires lurk in San Francisco and wreak havoc on the night life. *AKA:* Horror Convention.
1975 90m/C Kerwin Mathews, Jerry Walter, Barrie Youngfellow; *D:* John Stanley. VHS, Beta $59.95 *VCD* ✍½

Nightmare in Red China A campy film examining life in communist China with an all-Indian cast.
1955 67m/B VHS, Beta *NO* Woof!

Nightmare in Wax After suffering disfigurement in a fight with a studio boss, a former make-up man starts a wax museum. For fun, he injects movie stars with a formula that turns them into statues. *AKA:* Crimes in the Wax Museum.
1969 91m/C Cameron Mitchell, Anne Helm; *D:* Bud Townsend. VHS, Beta $29.95 *UHV, MRV* ✍½

A Nightmare on Elm Street A feverish and genuinely frightening horror film about Freddy Krueger (Englund), a scarred maniac in a fedora and razor-fingered gloves who kills neighborhood teens in their dreams and, subsequently, in reality. Of the children-fight-back genre, in which the lead victim (Langenkamp) goes to great lengths of ingenuity to destroy Freddy. In the tradition of "Friday the 13th" and "Halloween," this movie spawned a "Freddy" phenomenon: four sequels (to date); a TV series ("Freddy's Nightmares," a horror anthology show host-

ed by Englund that had little to do with the plot of the original movie but capitalized on his character); and an army of razor-clawed trick or treaters at Halloween. Englund went on to direct a horror movie of his own ("976-EVIL").
1984 (R) 92m/C John Saxon, Heather Langenkamp, Ronee Blakley, Robert Englund, Amanda Wyss, Nick Corri, Johnny Depp, Charles Fleischer; *W/D:* Wes Craven. VHS, Beta, LV $24.95 *MED, CVS, IME* ✍✍½

A Nightmare on Elm Street 2: Freddy's Revenge Mediocre sequel to the popular horror film. Freddy, the dream-haunting psychopath with the ginsu knife hands, returns to possess a teenager's body in order to kill again. Nothing new here, however praise is due for the stunning high-tech dream sequence.
1985 (R) 87m/C Mark Patton, Hope Lange, Clu Gulager, Robert Englund, Kim Myers; *D:* Jack Sholder. VHS, Beta, LV $34.95 *MED, CVS, IME* ✍½

A Nightmare on Elm Street 3: Dream Warriors Chapter three in this slice and dice series. Freddy Krueger is at it again, haunting the dreams of unsuspecting suburban teens. Langenkamp, the nightmare-freaked heroine from the first film, returns to counsel the latest victims of Freddy-infested dreams. Noted for the special effects wizardry but little else, Part Three was produced on a $4.5 million shoe string and took in more than $40 million, making it one of the most successful independently produced films in Hollywood. Followed by "Nightmare on Elmstreet 4: Dream Master."
1987 (R) 96m/C Patricia Arquette, Robert Englund, John Saxon, Craig Wasson, Heather Langenkamp, Dick Cavett, Priscilla Pointer, Larry Fishburne; *D:* Chuck Russell; *M:* Angelo Badalamenti. VHS, Beta, LV $36.95 *MED, CVS, IME* ✍✍

A Nightmare on Elm Street 4: Dream Master Freddy Krueger is still preying on people in their dreams, but he may have met his match as he battles for supremacy with a telepathically talented girl. What Part 4 lacks in substance, it makes up for in visual verve, including scenes of a kid drowning in his waterbed, and a pizza covered with pepperoni-like faces of Freddy's previous victims. This box office bonanza set a new record as the most successful opening weekend of any independently released film. Followed by "A Nightmare on Elm Street: A Dream Child."
1988 (R) 99m/C Robert Englund, Rodney Eastman, Danny Hassel, Andras Jones, Tuesday Knight, Lisa Wilcox, Ken Sagoes; *D:* Renny Harlin. VHS, Beta, LV $36.95 *MED, CVS, IME* ✍✍½

A Nightmare on Elm Street 5: Dream Child The fifth installment of Freddy Krueger's never-ending adventures. Here, America's favorite knife-wielding burn victim, unable to best the Dream Master from the previous film, haunts the dreams of her unborn fetus. Gore fans may be disappointed to discover that much of the blood and guts ended up on the cutting room floor.
1989 (R) 90m/C Robert Englund, Lisa Wilcox, Kelly Jo Minter, Danny Hassel; *D:* Stephen Hopkins. VHS, Beta, LV, Special order formats $89.95 *IME, MED* ✍✍

Nightmare on the 13th Floor A travel writer at an old hotel glimpses murder on a supposedly non-existent floor. Nasty devil-worshippers are afoot, but the chills in this mild made-for-cable throwaway seldom dip below room temperature.

1990 (PG-13) 85m/C Michael Greene, John Karlen, Louise Fletcher, Alan Fudge, James Brolin; *D:* Walter Grauman. VHS, Beta *PAR* ✍

Nightmare Sisters Three sorority sisters become possessed by a demon and then sexually ravage a nearby fraternity.
1987 (R) 83m/C Brinke Stevens, Michelle McClellan, Linnea Quigley; *D:* David DeCoteau. VHS, Beta $79.95 *TWE* Woof!

Nightmare Weekend A professor's evil assistant lures three young women into his lab and performs cruel and vicious experiments that transform the girls and their dates into crazed zombies.
1986 (R) 86m/C Dale Midkiff, Debbie Laster, Debra Hunter, Lori Lewis; *D:* Henry Sala. VHS, Beta $79.98 *LIV* ✍

The Nightmare Years An American reporter in Nazi Germany dares to report the truth to an unbelieving world. Based on a true story. Two cassettes.
1989 237m/C Sam Waterston, Marthe Keller, Kurtwood Smith; *D:* Anthony Page. VHS, Beta $89.98 *TTC* ✍

Nightmares A less-than-thrilling horror anthology featuring four tales in which common, everyday occurrences take on the ingredients of a nightmare. In the same vein as "Twilight Zone" and "Creepshow."
1983 (PG) 99m/C Christina Raines, Emilio Estevez, Moon Zappa, Lance Henriksen, Richard Masur, Veronica Cartwright; *D:* Joseph Sargent. VHS, Beta $59.95 *MCA* ✍

Nights and Days Adaptation of writer Maria Dabrowska's tale about a Polish family chronicles the persecution, expulsions, and land grabbing that occurred after the unsuccessful Uprising of 1864. In Polish with English subtitles.
1976 255m/C *PL* Jadwiga Baranska, Jerzy Binczycki; *D:* Jerzy Antczak. VHS $69.95 *FCT* ✍½

Nights in White Satin A made-for-video Cinderella story about the growing love between a fashion photographer and a young model whose boyfriend has just been murdered.
1987 96m/C Kenneth Gilman, Priscilla Harris; *D:* Michael Bernard. VHS, Beta $79.95 *PSM, PAR* ✍½

Nights of Cabiria Fellini classic which details the personal decline of a naive prostitute who thinks she's found true love. In Italian with English subtitles or dubbed. Basis for the musical "Sweet Charity." *AKA:* Le Nottie de Cabiria; Cabiria.
1957 111m/B *IT* Giulietta Masina, Amadeo Nazzari; *D:* Federico Fellini. VHS, Beta $29.95 *NOS, VYY, APD* ✍✍✍½

Nightstalker A brother and sister who were condemned to eternal death 12,000 years ago must eat virgins to keep their bodies from rotting. Trouble is, while they search for dinner, the movie decomposes. For mature audiences with no fantasies of celluloid nirvana.
1979 90m/C Aldo Ray. VHS, Beta $39.95 *LIV* Woof!

Nightstick New York vigilante cop fights nasties who threaten to blow the lid off the city. Worse, they kidnap super cop's girl forcing him to save her along with the city. Lots of violence, predictable plot, and mediocre acting leave this one without much bang. *AKA:* Calhoun.
1987 (R) 90m/C Bruce Fairbairn, Kerrie Keane, John Vernon, Robert Vaughn, Isaac Hayes, Leslie Nielsen; *D:* Joseph L. Scanlan. VHS, Beta $79.95 *COL* ✍½

Nightwing Suspense drama about three people who risk their lives to exterminate a colony of plague-carrying vampire bats in New Mexican Indian community. From the novel by Martin Cruz Smith and adapted by Smith, Steve Shagan, and Bud Shrake. OK viewing for the undiscriminating palate.
1979 (PG) 103m/C Nick Mancuso, David Warner, Kathryn Harrold, Strother Martin; *D:* Arthur Hiller. **VHS, Beta, LV $39.95** COL ♫♫½

Nightwish Students do more than homework when a professor leads them into their own horrifying dreams. Soon it becomes impossible to distinguish dreams from reality.
1989 (R) 96m/C Jack Starrett, Robert Tessier; *D:* Bruce Cook Jr. **VHS, LV $89.95** VES ♫♫½

Nijinsky An opulent biography of the famous ballet dancer. His exciting and innovative choreography gets little attention. The film concentrates on his infamous homosexual lifestyle and his relationship with impresario Sergei Diaghilev (Bates, in a tour-de-force performance). Lovely to look at, but slow and unconvincing.
1980 (R) 125m/C Alan Bates, George De La Pena, Leslie Browne, Alan Badel, Carla Fracci, Colin Blakely, Ronald Pickup, Ronald Lacey, Vernon Dobtcheff, Jeremy Irons, Frederick Jaeger, Janet Suzman, Sian Phillips; *D:* Herbert Ross. **VHS, Beta $29.95** PAR ♫♫

Nikki, the Wild Dog of the North When a Malemute pup is separated from his Canadian trapper master, he teams up with a bear cub for a series of adventures. Later the pup is reunited with his former master for still more adventures. Adapted from a novel by James Oliver Curwood for Disney.
1961 (G) 73m/C *CA* Jean Coutu; *D:* Jack Couffer, Don Haldane. **VHS, Beta $69.95** DIS ♫½

Nine Ages of Nakedness The story of a man whose ancestors have been plagued by a strange problem: beautiful, naked women who create carnal chaos.
1969 88m/C Harrison Marks. **VHS, Beta $19.95** VDM, MED, MRV ♫

9 1/2 Ninjas A cautious and disciplined martial artist trains a young and flirtatious woman in the ways of the ninja. His life becomes exciting in more ways than one, when he realizes she's being followed by ninjas with more on their minds than her training—they want to assassinate her! Crazy mixture of sex, kung fu and humor make this film one surprise after another.
1990 (R) 88m/C Michael Phenicie, Andee Gray, Tiny Lister; *D:* Aaron Worth. **VHS, Beta, LV $9.98** REP ♫♫½

9 1/2 Weeks A chance meeting between a Wall Street executive and an art gallery employee evolves into an experimental sexual relationship that borders on sado-masochism. The video version is more explicit than the one viewed in theaters, but by much. Strong characterizations by both actors prevent this from being strictly pornographic. Well written, with strength of male and female personalities nicely balanced. Not for all tastes, and definitely not for children.
1986 (R) 114m/C Mickey Rourke, Kim Basinger, Margaret Whitton, Karen Young, David Margulies; *D:* Adrian Lyne; *M:* Jack Nitzsche. **VHS, Beta, LV $19.95** MGM ♫♫

Nine Days a Queen An historical drama based on the life of Lady Jane Grey, proclaimed Queen of England after the death of Henry VIII of England and summarily executed for treason by Mary Tudor after a nine-day reign. An obscure tragedy with good performances and absorbing storyline.

Remade as "Lady Jane" (1985). *AKA:* Lady Jane Grey; Tudor Rose.
1934 80m/B *GB* John Mills, Cedric Hardwicke, Nova Pilbeam, Sybil Thorndike, Leslie Perrins, Felix Aylmer, Miles Malleson; *D:* Robert Stevenson. **VHS, Beta $44.95** HHT, DVT ♫♫♫

Nine Deaths of the Ninja Faceless ninja warrior Kosugi leads a team of commandos on a mission to rescue a group of political prisoners held captive in the Philippine jungles. Features Ozone-depleted plot, incongruous performances, and inane dialogue, not to mention two main villains—a neurotic Nazi in a wheelchair and a black lesbian amazon—who chew jungle and bring bad art to a new level of appreciation. Amazing in its total badness. Produced by Cannon.
1985 (R) 93m/C Sho Kosugi, Brent Huff, Emelia Lesniak, Regina Richardson; *W/D:* Emmett Alston. **VHS, Beta $69.95** MED Woof!

984: Prisoner of the Future A shocking, futuristic tale of human self-destruction.
1984 70m/C Don Francks, Stephen Markle. **VHS, Beta** NO Woof!

The Nine Lives of Elfego Baca Venerable Western hero Loggia faces a veritable army of gunfighters and bandits. Action-packed but not too violent; family fun.
1958 78m/C Robert Loggia, Robert Simon, Lisa Montell, Nestor Paiva; *D:* Norman Foster. **VHS, Beta $69.95** DIS ♫♫

Nine Lives of Fritz the Cat Fritz feels that life's too square in the 70's, so he takes off into some of his other lives for more adventure. Cleaner but still naughty sequel to the X-rated *Fritz the Cat*, featuring neither the original's writer/director Ralph Bakshi nor cartoonist Robert Crumb. Tame and lame. Animated.
1974 77m/C *D:* Robert Taylor. **VHS, LV $19.98** VES ♫♫

9 to 5 In this caricature of large corporations and women in the working world, Coleman plays the male chauvinist boss who calls the shots and keeps his employees, all female, under his thumb. Three of the office secretaries daydream of Coleman's disposal and rashly kidnap him after a silly set of occurrences threaten their jobs. While they have him under lock and key, the trio take office matters into their own hands and take a stab at running things their own way, with amusing results. The basis for a television series.
1980 (PG) 111m/C Jane Fonda, Lily Tomlin, Dolly Parton, Dabney Coleman, Sterling Hayden; *D:* Colin Higgins. **VHS, Beta, LV $19.98** FOX ♫♫½

976-EVIL Englund (the infamous Freddy from the Nightmare on Elm Street epics) directs this horror movie where a lonely teenager dials direct to demons from hell.
1988 (R) 102m/C Stephen Geoffreys, Jim Metzler, Maria Rubell, Sandy Dennis, Robert Picardo, Leslie Deane, Pat O'Bryan; *D:* Robert Englund. **VHS, Beta, LV $14.95** COL ♫½

976-EVIL 2: The Astral Factor Satan returns the call in this supernatural thriller that sequels the original film.
1991 (R) 93m/C Patrick O'Bryan, Rene Assa, Debbie James; *D:* Jim Wynorski. **VHS $89.98** LIV, VES ♫½

1900 Bertolucci's impassioned epic about two Italian families, one land-owning, the other, peasant. Shows the sweeping changes of the 20th century begun by the trauma of WWI and the onslaught of Italian socialism. Edited down from its original 360-minute length and dubbed in English from

three other languages, the film suffers somewhat from editing and from its nebulous lack of commitment to any genre. Elegantly photographed by Vittorio Storaro. Also titled "Novecento."
1976 (R) 255m/C *FR IT GE* Robert De Niro, Gerard Depardieu, Burt Lancaster, Donald Sutherland, Dominique Sanda, Sterling Hayden, Laura Betti, Francesca Bertini, Werner Bruhns, Stefania Sandrelli, Anna Henkel, Alida Valli, Stefania Sandrelli; *D:* Bernardo Bertolucci. **VHS, Beta, LV $29.95** PAR, TAM ♫♫♫

1918 An adaptation of the Horton Foote play about the effects of World War I and an influenza epidemic on a small Texas town. Slow-moving but satisfying. Score by Willie Nelson. Originally produced for PBS's "American Playhouse." Prequeled by "On Valentine's Day."
1985 89m/C Matthew Broderick, Hallie Foote, William Converse Roberts, Rochelle Oliver, Michael Higgins, Horton Foote Jr.; *D:* Ken Harrison. **VHS, Beta $79.98** FOX ♫♫½

1931: Once Upon a Time in New York Prohibition-era gangsters war, beat each other up, make headlines, and drink bathtub gin.
1972 90m/C Richard Conte, Adolfo Celi, Lionel Stander, Irene Papas. **VHS, Beta $59.95** VCD ♫♫

1939, The Movies' Vintage Year: Trailers on Tape A compilation of coming attractions from such classics as "Gunga Din," "Idiot's Delight," "Juarez," "Dark Victory" and "Gone With The Wind." Some segments are in color.
1939 60m/B Cary Grant, Clark Gable, Vivien Leigh. **VHS, Beta $34.95** SFR ♫♫

1941 Proved to be the most expensive comedy of all time with a budget exceeding $35 million. The depiction of Los Angeles in the chaotic days after the bombing of Pearl Harbor combines elements of fantasy and black humor.
1979 (PG) 120m/C John Belushi, Dan Aykroyd, Patti LuPone, Ned Beatty, Slim Pickens, Murray Hamilton, Christopher Lee, Tim Matheson, Toshiro Mifune, Warren Oates, Robert Stack, Nancy Allen, Elisha Cook Jr., Lorraine Gary, Treat Williams, Mickey Rourke; *D:* Steven Spielberg; *W:* Robert Zemeckis, Bob Gale; *M:* John Williams. **VHS, Beta, LV $14.95** MCA, PIA, CCB ♫♫½

1969 Three teenage friends during the 1960s become radicalized by the return of one of their friends from Vietnam in a coffin. Critically lambasted directorial debut for "On Golden Pond" author Ernest Thompson.
1989 (R) 96m/C Kiefer Sutherland, Robert Downey Jr., Winona Ryder, Bruce Dern, Joanna Cassidy, Mariette Hartley; *D:* Ernest Thompson. **VHS, Beta, LV $19.98** MED ♫♫♫½

1984 A very fine adaptation of George Orwell's infamous novel, this version differs from the overly simplistic and cautionary 1954 film because of fine casting and production design. The illegal love affair of a government official becomes his attempt to defy the crushing inhumanity and lack of simple pleasures of an omniscient government. Filmed in London, it skillfully visualizes our time's most central prophetic nightmare.
1984 (R) 117m/C *GB* John Hurt, Richard Burton, Suzanna Hamilton, Cyril Cusack, Gregory Fisher, Andrew Wilde, Rupert Baderman; *D:* Michael Radford. **VHS, Beta, LV $19.95** LIV ♫♫♫½

1990: The Bronx Warriors Good street gang members combat evil corporate powers in a semi-futuristic South Bronx. Lame copy of "Escape from New York." *AKA:* 1990 I Guerrieri del Bronx; Bronx Warriors.

1983 (R) 86m/C *IT* Vic Morrow, Christopher Connelly, Fred Williamson; *D:* Enzo G. Castellari. **VHS, Beta** $59.95 *MED* Woof!

90 Days Charming independently made Canadian comedy about two young men handling their respective romantic dilemmas—one awaiting an oriental fiancee he's never met, the other who is being kicked out of his house by his wife.
1986 99m/C *CA* Stefan Wodoslowsky, Sam Grana, Christine Pak; *D:* Giles Walker. **VHS, Beta** $79.98 *FOX* 🎞🎞🎞

92 in the Shade Based upon McGuane's novel, the film deals with a bored, wealthy rogue who becomes a fishing guide in the Florida Keys, and battles against the competition of two crusty, half-mad codgers. Sloppy, irreverent comedy as only a first-time writer-turned-director can fashion.
1976 (R) 91m/C Peter Fonda, Warren Oates, Margot Kidder, Burgess Meredith, Harry Dean Stanton; *D:* Thomas McGuane. **VHS, Beta** $59.98 *FOX* 🎞🎞🎞

99 & 44/100 Dead Frankenheimer falters with this silly gangster flick. Harris is hired to kill Dillman, by local godfather O'Brien. Originally written as a satirical look at gangster movies, but it doesn't stick to satire, and as a result is disappointing. *AKA:* Call Harry Crown.
1974 (PG) 98m/C Richard Harris, Chuck Connors, Edmond O'Brien, Bradford Dillman, Ann Turkel; *D:* John Frankenheimer. VHS *FOX* 🎞

99 Women Sympathetic prison warden attempts to investigate conditions at a women's prison camp. Thin and exploitative view of lesbianism behind bars that sensationalizes the subject. *AKA:* Isle of Lost Women.
1969 (R) 90m/C *GB SP GE IT* Maria Schell, Herbert Lom, Mercedes McCambridge, Lucianna Paluzzi; *D:* Jess (Jesus) Franco. **VHS, Beta** $39.98 *NO* 🎞½

Ninja 3: The Domination Ninja master must remove the spirit of a deadly ninja assassin from a young woman intent on wreaking havoc among the Phoenix police department. Extremely silly super ninja epic utterly uninhibited by the usual plot conventions. Produced by Cannon and written by James R. Silke.
1984 (R) 92m/C Lucinda Dickey, Sho Kosugi; *D:* Sam Firstenberg. **VHS, Beta** $14.95 *MGM* 🎞🎞

Ninja Academy Seven wimps, losers, and spoiled brats come to the Ninja Academy to learn the art. Will they make it?
1990 (R) 93m/C Will Egan, Kelly Randall, Gerald Okomura, Michael David, Robert Factor, Jeff Robinson; *D:* Nico Mastorakis. VHS *NO* 🎞½

Ninja: American Warrior An evil ninja takes on the U.S. Drug Enforcement Agency when the authorities threaten to shut him down.
1990 90m/C Joff Houston, John Wilford; *D:* Tommy Cheng. **VHS, Beta** $59.95 *IMP* 🎞½

Ninja Avengers A man seeks revenge on the ninja priest who imprisoned him.
1988 90m/C **VHS, Beta** $59.95 *IMP* 🎞

Ninja Blacklist The Iron Hand leads an unchallenged reign of terror—until two warriors vow to take him down!
1990 90m/C Sonny Qui. **VHS, Beta** $19.99 *BFV* 🎞½

Ninja Brothers of Blood A guy falls for a rival gang member's girl. Neither the gang nor the guy's former girlfriend take kindly to this!
1989 90m/C Marcus Gibson, Fonda Lynn, Brian McClave, Jonathan Soper; *D:* Raymond Woo. **VHS, Beta** $59.95 *IMP* 🎞

Ninja Champion White-clad and masked ninja heros come to the aid of some Interpol agents tracking down a sleazy diamond smuggler. Invisible storyline features very little actual ninja. Extremely unconvincing and poorly dubbed.
1987? 90m/C *HK* Bruce Baron, Richard Harrison; *W/D:* Godfrey Ho. **VHS, Beta** $39.95 *TWE* Woof!

Ninja Checkmate An evil ninja seems indestructible, but finally he meets his match.
1990 90m/C Simon Lee, Jack Long, Jeanie Chang. **VHS, Beta** $49.95 *OCE* 🎞

Ninja Commandments Everything is at stake when an evil warrior takes on the greatest fighter in the land: the winner will rule the empire!
1987 90m/C Richard Harrison, Dave Wheeler; *D:* Joseph Lai. **VHS, Beta** $59.95 *IMP* 🎞

Ninja Condors A young man grows up to avenge the murder of his father.
1987 85m/C Alexander Lou, Stuart Hugh; *D:* James Wu. **VHS, Beta** $59.95 *TWE* 🎞

Ninja Connection Ninja terrorism is employed as a scare tactic to deter a group who wants to break up an international drug ring.
1990 90m/C Patricia Greenford, Jane Kingsly, Joe Nelson, Louis Roth, Henry Steele, Stuart Steen; *D:* York Lam. **VHS, Beta** $59.95 *IMP* 🎞

Ninja Death Squad A team specializing in political assassinations is hunted down by a special agent.
1987 89m/C Glen Carson, Patricia Goodman, Joff Houston, Billy Jones, Wallace Jones, John Wilford; *D:* Tommy Cheng. **VHS, Beta** $59.95 *IMP* 🎞

Ninja Demon's Massacre Ninja named Willie responds to federal investigations into his spying business by wearing a black robe and slashing feds with long swords.
1987? 89m/C Ted Brooke, James Lear. **VHS, Beta** $59.95 *TWE* 🎞

Ninja Destroyer Ninja warriors battle over an emerald mine.
197? (R) 92m/C *HK* Bruce Baron, Stuart Smith; *W/D:* Godfrey Ho. **VHS, Beta** $19.98 *TWE* 🎞

Ninja Dragon Two Ninjas are hired in a gang war and dazzle all those who watch by kicking their enemies to death.
198? 92m/C Richard Harrison. **VHS, Beta** $59.95 *TWE* 🎞

Ninja Dragons Two teenagers are sent to visit their shady Uncle Bob in L.A. The boy wants to meet his martial arts movie idol and his sister her favorite soap opera hunk. But they wind up being chased by the mobsters Uncle Bob owes money to.
1992 (PG) ?m/C Stephen Furst, Joseph Campanella, Don "The Dragon" Wilson, Lauren Tewes, Sondra Kerns, Billy Hufsey, Irwin Keyes, Chris Mitchum; *D:* Joseph Merhi; *W:* Stephen Smoke. VHS *PMH* 🎞

The Ninja Empire The feds fail to find the killer of young prostitutes and as a last result they call on the one group they know they can trust—Ninjas.
1990 90m/C **VHS, Beta** $59.95 *IMP* 🎞

Ninja Enforcer A ninja warrior destroys all his foes.
197? ?m/C Lin Chang, Kim Bhang, Cze Young. VHS *NO* 🎞

Ninja Exterminators Low-grade kung-fu antics mascarading as ninja rib-kicking bonanza. Dubbed.
1981 85m/C *HK* Jacky Cheng, Ko Shou Liang, Tai Chen. **VHS, Beta** $59.95 *WWV* Woof!

Ninja Fantasy Ninja drug smugglers and government officials battle over a large drug shipment. Everybody go chop socky. Not much in way of ninja fantasy. Dubbed.
1986 95m/C *HK* Adam Nell, Ian Frank, Jordan Heller, Ken Ashley, Jenny Mills, Jack Rodman; *D:* Bruce Lambert; *W:* Anthony Green. VHS, Beta $59.95 *TWE* Woof!

Ninja Force of Assassins Two espionage buddies part ways in Southeast Asia over a Ninja crimelord war, and engage in much head-kicking.
1977? 79m/C Jim Davis, Louis Hill; *D:* Victor Sears. **VHS, Beta** $59.95 *TWE* 🎞

Ninja Holocaust A running argument about a secret Swiss bank account gives license for rampant head-kicking and rib-cracking.
198? ?m/C Bruce Chen, Jim Brooks, Martin Lee, Joe Resinick. **VHS, Beta** *NO* 🎞

Ninja Hunt This time, ninjas kick international terrorists in the head while searching for secret formula. Poorly dubbed pseudo ninja developed by Godfrey Ho.
198? 92m/C *HK* Bruce Baron, Stuart Smith; *D:* Joseph Lai; *W:* Stephen Saul. **VHS, Beta** $59.95 *TWE* Woof!

The Ninja Hunter When a Shaolin temple is destroyed, an angry abbot swears vengeance on the perpetrators. He immediately makes good on his threat.
1990 90m/C **VHS, Beta** $34.95 *OCE* 🎞

Ninja in Action American woman, abetted by her head-kicking lover, hits Hong Kong to find her father's killer and locate a fortune in diamonds. More kung-fu than ninja action but does feature gratuitous sex while following the international ninja standard for poor dubbing.
198? 90m/C *HK* Stuart Steen, Christine O'Hara; *D:* Tommy Cheung; *W:* Brent Hays. **VHS, Beta** $59.95 *TWE* 🎞½

Ninja in the Claws of the C.I.A. KGB ninjas from the Soviet Union take on ninjas from the CIA in an all-out, high-stakes battle of immense proportions.
1983 102m/C John Liu. **VHS, Beta** *NO* 🎞

Ninja in the Deadly Trap Chinese general Chieh Chikuang uses his martial arts skills to defeat the Japanese forces that loot and plunder China's coastal provinces.
1985 90m/C **VHS, Beta** $49.95 *WES, OCE* 🎞

Ninja in the U.S.A. Drug lords hire men who kick and make funny noises to protect them.
1988 ?m/C Alexander Lou, Yau Jin Tomas. VHS $29.95 *OCE* 🎞

Ninja Kill Assassinations and national coups are the aim of the Purple Ninjas. Master Gordon must stop them all with some inspired heel-to-skull fighting.
1987 92m/C Richard Harrison, Stuart Smith. **VHS, Beta** $59.95 *TWE* 🎞

Ninja Knight Heaven's Hell This time the ninja is given all he can handle in the way of bone-bruising kicks and chops.
19?? ?m/C **VHS** $59.95 *IMP* 🎞

Ninja Massacre Gangsters covet a secret manual of kung fu techniques. Heel-splintering battles break out as a result.
1984 87m/C Lo Lieh, Pai Ying, Lung Jun Ehr, Tiki Shirtee. **VHS, Beta** $59.95 *GEM, MRV* 🎞

Ninja Masters of Death Terrorists reign supreme until the white ninja saves the city.
1985 90m/C Mick Jones, Chris Peterson, Daniel Wells, Richard Young; *D:* Bruce Lambert. **VHS, Beta** $59.95 *IMP* 🎞

Ninja Mission First Scandinavian ninja epic follows CIA agent and his group of ninja fighters as they embark on a hazardous mission to rescue two people from a Soviet prison. They use their fighting skills (Swedish ninjas favor guns more than ninjutsu) against Russian soldiers. Dubbed.
1984 (R) 95m/C *SW* Christopher Kohlberg, Curt Brober, Hanna Pola; *D:* Mats Helge. **VHS, Beta** $59.95 *MED* 🎗½

Ninja Nightmare A man seeks revenge for his family's death.
1988 (R) 98m/C Leo Fong. **VHS, Beta** $9.99 *STE, PSM* 🎗

Ninja of the Magnificence When the ninja master is killed, factions within his group battle for control.
1989 90m/C Sam Baker, Patrick Frbezar, Clive Hadwen, Tim Michael, Renato Sala; *D:* Charles Lee. **VHS, Beta** $59.95 *IMP* 🎗½

Ninja Operation: Licensed to Terminate Two warriors risk broken noses and twisted limbs to take on the Black Ninja Empire.
1987 89m/C Richard Harrison, Paul Marshall, Jack McPeat, Grant Temple; *D:* Joseph Lai. **VHS, Beta** $59.95 *IMP* 🎗

Ninja Phantom Heroes Two Vietnam vets are imprisoned for war crimes. One escapes and forms his own secret ninja society.
1987 90m/C Glen Carson, George Dickson, Allen Leung, Christine Wells; *D:* Bruce Lambert. **VHS, Beta** $59.95 *TWE* 🎗

The Ninja Pirates In the Sung Dynasty, a group of bloodthirsty pirates are hunted down after stealing a golden treasure.
1990 90m/C Chi Lan, Lo Lieh, Carter Wong, Nancy Yan. **VHS, Beta** $49.95 *OCE* 🎗½

Ninja Powerforce Two childhood friends end up as members of rival ninja gangs in the midst of a bloody war. Usual assortment of ninja-inflicted injuries result.
1990 90m/C Jonathan Bould, Richard Harrison; *D:* Joseph Lai. **VHS, Beta** $59.95 *IMP* 🎗½

Ninja Showdown A warrior must take on a number of vicious bandits in order to defend his small town. He vows revenge on anyone who threatens his people.
1990 92m/C Richard Harrison; *D:* Joseph Lai. **VHS, Beta** $59.95 *TWE* 🎗

Ninja: Silent Assassin An agent working for Interpol goes after a drug ring on a personal vendetta, avenging the brutal murder of his wife.
1990 90m/C **VHS, Beta** $59.95 *IMP* 🎗½

Ninja Squad Empires, families, and honor are at stake in a fierce battle of heel-to-head action.
198? 92m/C Dave Wheeler, Richard Harrison, Timalden. **VHS, Beta** $59.95 *TWE* 🎗

Ninja Strike Force The Black Ninjas steal the powerful "spirit sword," and go on a bloody rampage.
1988 89m/C Richard Harrison, Gary Carter; *D:* Joseph Lai. **VHS, Beta** $59.95 *IMP* 🎗½

Ninja Supremo A rebellious teenager studies Kung-fu, and then returns to his village a hero after he gains expertise in his chosen field.
1990 100m/C David Tao, Yueh Wah, Sun Yueh. **VHS, Beta** $49.95 *OCE* 🎗½

Ninja Swords of Death A noble warrior challenges a vicious assassin who uses a spur-sword. He is nearly decapitated in the process.
1990 90m/C Chang Ying Chun, Chia Ling, Tien Pang, Kong Pun. **VHS, Beta** $29.95 *OCE* 🎗½

Ninja Terminator Possession of all three pieces of the Golden Warrior turns the holder into the magically super-powered "Ninja Terminator." Three students battle for that honor. Very bad indeed.
1969 92m/C **VHS** $59.95 *TWE* Woof!

Ninja the Battalion Agents from America, the Soviet Union, and China try to recover germ warfare secrets stolen by the Japanese secret service.
1990 90m/C Roger Crawford, Sam Huxley, Alexander Lou, Dickson Warn; *D:* Victor Sears. **VHS, Beta** $59.95 *TWE* 🎗

Ninja the Protector A ninja tracks down and kicks the ninja head of a counterfeiting ring.
198? 92m/C Richard Harrison. **VHS, Beta** $19.98 *TWE* 🎗

Ninja, the Violent Sorcerer Murderer, with the help of Chinese vampires, does battle with the ghost of a dead gambling lord's wife and the gambling lord's living brother. Often tedious even with above average production and incredible plot.
1986 90m/C *W:* Daniel Clough. **VHS, Beta** $59.95 *TWE* 🎗½

Ninja the Wonder Boy The story of a young boy's magical and humorous journey toward becoming a master ninja.
1985 89m/C **VHS, Beta** $24.95 *PAR, WTA* 🎗½

Ninja Thunderbolt A sleazy woman lusts after power and money and somehow becomes involved with ninjas.
1985 92m/C Jackie Chan, Richard Harrison, Wang Tao; *D:* Godfrey Ho. **VHS, Beta** $59.95 *TWE* 🎗½

Ninja Turf Teenage kick artists rip off a Hollywood drug dealer and are pursued by a swarm of ninja hitmen. *AKA:* L.A. Streetfighters.
1986 (R) 83m/C Jun Chong, Bill Wallace, Rosanna King, James Lew, Phillip Rhee. **VHS, Beta, LV** $79.95 *COL* 🎗

Ninja USA A Vietnam vet hires Ninjas to help him smuggle drugs, and they have a hard time adjusting to American ways, eventually turning on each other.
198? 80m/C **VHS, Beta** $59.95 *TWE* 🎗

Ninja Vengeance The corrupt sheriff of a small Texas town, who also leads the KKK, is terrorizing a young African-American local. Then our lone hero rides into town on his trusty motorcycle to save the day. Only this time instead of your average gunman, he's a ninja.
1993 (R) 87m/C Stephen K. Hayes, Janet K. Pawlak, Craig Boyett, David Paul Lord; *W/D:* Karl Armstrong; *W:* Carrie Armstrong. **VHS** $89.95 *COL* 🎗½

Ninja vs. Bruce Lee Lee investigates a secret ninja sect involved in smuggling.
1990 90m/C Bruce Lee. **VHS, Beta** $49.95 *OCE* 🎗

Ninja vs. Ninja A scientist has found a cure for heroin addiction, but ninja drug lords won't let his discovery see the light of day!
1990 90m/C Hui Hsiao Chiang, Callan Leong. **VHS, Beta** $49.95 *OCE* 🎗½

Ninja vs. the Shaolin Savage fighting between priests and ninjas results in one of the bloodiest pages in history.
1984 90m/C Alexander Lou, John Wu; *D:* Jacky Hwong. **VHS, Beta** *OCE* 🎗½

Ninja Warriors An evil warrior plans to take over the world with the help of his brainwashed Ninja zombies.
1985 90m/C Ron Marchini, Paul Vance. **VHS, Beta** $9.99 *CCB, IVE* 🎗½

Ninja Wars One ninja takes on five ninja assassins who, along with an evil ninja sorcerer, have kidnapped his ninja girlfriend. Medieval ninja nonsense that's essentially incoherent. In Japanese with English dubbing.
1984 95m/C **VHS, Beta** $79.95 *PSM* Woof!

The Ninja Wolves During the Ming Dynasty, Japanese ninjas stage a bloody invasion of China.
1990 90m/C Yue Hwa. **VHS, Beta** $49.95 *OCE* 🎗½

Ninja's Extreme Weapons Blue Ninja takes it to the streets when his brother is killed by the underworld.
1990 90m/C James Gray, Donald Muir; *D:* Victor Sears. **VHS, Beta** $59.95 *TWE, HHE* 🎗½

Ninotchka Delightful romantic comedy. Garbo is a cold Russian agent sent to Paris to check up on her comrades, who are being seduced by capitalism. She inadvertently falls in love with a playboy, who melts her communist heart. Garbo talks and laughs. Satirical, energetic, and witty. Later a Broadway musical called "Silk Stockings."
1939 (R) 110m/B Greta Garbo, Melvyn Douglas, Ina Claire, Sig Rumann, Felix Bressart, Bela Lugosi; *D:* Ernst Lubitsch. Academy Awards '39 Nominations: Best Actress (Garbo), Best Picture, Best Screenplay, Best Story; National Board of Review Awards '39: 10 Best Films of the Year. **VHS, Beta, LV, 8mm** $24.95 *MGM* 🎗🎗🎗½

The Ninth Configuration Based on Blatty's novel "Twinkle, Twinkle, Killer Kane" (also the film's alternate title), this is a weird and surreal tale of a mock rebellion of high-ranking military men held in a secret base hospital for the mentally ill. Keach is good as the commander who is just as insane as the patients. Available in many different lengths, this is generally considered to be the best. *AKA:* Twinkle, Twinkle, Killer Kane.
1979 (R) 115m/C Stacy Keach, Scott Wilson, Jason Miller, Ed Flanders, Neville Brand, Alejandro Rey, Robert Loggia; *D:* William Peter Blatty. **VHS, Beta, LV** $19.95 *STE, NWV* 🎗🎗🎗

Nitti: The Enforcer Made-for-TV saga about Al Capone's brutal enforcer and right hand man, Frank Nitti. Diversified cast, (Moriarty in particular) do their best to keep things moving along, and the atmosphere is consistently and appropriately violent. Made to capitalize on the success of 1987's "The Untouchables."
1988 (PG-13) 94m/C Anthony LaPaglia, Vincent Guastaferro, Trini Alvarado, Michael Moriarty, Michael Russo, Louis Guss, Bruno Kirby; *D:* Michael Switzer. **VHS** $89.95 *ACA* 🎗🎗

No Big Deal Dillon is a streetwise teenager who makes friends at his new school. Blah promise; bad acting makes this no big deal.
1983 (PG-13) 86m/C Kevin Dillon, Sylvia Miles, Tammy Grimes, Jane Krakowski, Christopher Gartin, Mary Joan Negro; *D:* Robert Charlton. **VHS** $79.95 *BTV* 🎗½

No Comebacks Two British mysteries, made for television from stories by Frederick Forsyth: "A Careful Man," about a dying millionaire who cheats his heirs, and "Privilege," about a clever stamp dealer who exacts revenge upon a libelous gossip columnist.
1985 60m/C *GB* Milo O'Shea, Cyril Cusack, Dan O'Herlihy, Gayle Hunnicutt. **VHS, Beta** $59.95 *PSM* 🎗½

No Dead Heroes Green Beret Vietnam war hero succumbs to Soviet scheming when they plant a computer chip in his brain. Unoriginal and unworthy.

1987 86m/C Max Thayer, John Dresden, Toni Nero; **D:** J.C. Miller. **VHS, Beta** $69.95 SVS 🎬

No Deposit, No Return Tedious, silly, pointless Disney action comedy. Rich brats persuade bumbling crooks to kidnap them, offer them for ransom to millionaire grandfather. **AKA:** Double Trouble.
1976 (G) 115m/C David Niven, Don Knotts, Darren McGavin, Barbara Feldon, Charles Martin Smith; **D:** Norman Tokar; **M:** John Williams. **VHS, Beta** $69.95 DIS 🎬

No Drums, No Bugles A West Virginia farmer and conscientious objector leaves his family to live alone in a cave for three years during the Civil War. Bad direction spoils Sheen's good performance.
1971 (G) 85m/C Martin Sheen, Davey Davidson, Denine Terry, Rod McCary; **D:** Clyde Ware. **VHS, Beta** $39.95 NEG 🎬½

No Greater Love Capraesque Soviet war movie. A peasant woman mobilizes her village against the Nazis to avenge her family's death. Dubbed into English by the Soviets for Western circulation during World War II.
1943 74m/B RU Vera Maretskaya; **D:** Frederic Ermler. **VHS, Beta, 3/4U** $35.95 FCT, IHF 🎬🎬½

No Grumps Allowed! A package of episodes of the children's fantasy series.
1969 90m/C **VHS, Beta** $19.98 SUE 🎬🎬½

No Holds Barred Cheesy, campy remake of cheesy, campy 1952 wrestling movie. Hulk Hogan on the big screen, at last.
1989 (PG-13) 98m/C Hulk Hogan, Kurt Fuller, Joan Severance, Tiny Lister; **D:** Thomas J. Wright. **VHS, Beta, LV** $19.95 COL 🎬½

No Love for Johnnie Well acted if unoriginal political drama. Finch is a British M.P. who fails in both public and private life. Based on the novel by Wilfred Fienburgh.
1960 105m/B GB Peter Finch, Stanley Holloway, Donald Pleasence, Mary Peach, Mervyn Johns, Dennis Price, Oliver Reed, Billie Whitelaw; **D:** Ralph Thomas. **VHS, Beta** NO 🎬

No Man of Her Own Gable and Lombard in their only screen pairing. A gambler marries a local girl on a bet and attempts to hide his secret life from her. Neither star's best film.
1932 81m/B Carole Lombard, Clark Gable, Grant Mitchell, Elizabeth Patterson; **D:** Wesley Ruggles. **VHS, Beta, LV** $14.95 MCA, KRT 🎬🎬½

No Man's Land Undercover cop Sweeney tails playboy Sheen but is seduced by wealth and glamour. Flashy surfaces, shiny cars, little substance.
1987 (R) 107m/C Charlie Sheen, D.B. Sweeney, Lara Harris, Randy Quaid; **D:** Peter Werner. **VHS, Beta, LV** $19.98 ORI 🎬🎬

No Man's Law Hardy plays the depraved villian desperate to get the goldmine owned by an old prospector and his beautiful daughter. But the mine is protected by Rex the Wonder Horse!
1921 ?m/B Oliver Hardy, Barbara Kent, James Finlayson, Theodore von Eltz; **D:** Fred Jackman. **VHS** NO 🎬🎬½

No Man's Range Unremarkable, typical, predictable Western: good guys, bad guys, guns, bullets, horses. **AKA:** No Man's Land.
1935 56m/B Bob Steele. **VHS, Beta** NO 🎬

No Mercy A Chicago cop (Gere) plunges into the Cajun bayou in order to avenge the murder of his partner. He falls for a beautiful girl enslaved by the killer, but that doesn't stop him from using her to flush out the powerful swamp-inhabiting crime lord. Absurd story without much plot.

1986 (R) 108m/C Richard Gere, Kim Basinger, Jeroen Krabbe, George Dzundza, William Atherton, Ray Sharkey, Bruce McGill; **D:** Richard Pearce. **VHS, Beta, LV** $19.95 COL 🎬🎬

No, No Nanette Lackluster filming of the Broadway production which fared better on the stage. Stock story of a young woman (Neagle) who rescues her uncle from financial ruin and finds romance in the process.
1940 96m/B Anna Neagle, Richard Carlson, Victor Mature, Roland Young, ZaSu Pitts, Eve Arden, Billy Gilbert, Keye Luke; **D:** Herbert Wilcox. **VHS** $19.95 NOS 🎬½

No One Cries Forever When a prostitute breaks away from a gangster-madam after finding love, she is tracked down and disfigured. Swedish; dubbed.
1985 96m/C Elke Sommer, Howard Carpendale, Zoli Marks; **D:** Jans Rautenbach. **Beta** NO Woof!

No Place to Hide A girl's father drowns and she blames herself. Her mother and psychologist try to convince the girl that her father's spirit isn't stalking her. She doesn't believe them. Made for television.
1981 120m/C Keir Dullea, Mariette Hartley, Kathleen Beller, Arlen Dean Snyder, Gary Graham, John Llewellyn Moxey; **D:** John Llewellyn Moxey. **VHS, Beta** $59.95 PSM 🎬½

No Place to Run An elderly man fights for custody of his grandson, then kidnaps him and flees with him to Canada. Made for TV.
1972 78m/C Herschel Bernardi, Larry Hagman, Stefanie Powers, Neville Brand; **D:** Delbert Mann. **VHS, Beta** $59.95 VMK 🎬🎬

No Prince for My Cinderella A schizophrenic girl who has turned to prostitution is sought desperately by her social worker.
1978 100m/C Robert Reed. **VHS, Beta** $49.95 WOV 🎬🎬

No Problem A man is pursued, shot, and drops dead in the apartment of an unsuspecting man who doesn't know what to do with the body. Dubbed in English.
197? 94m/C FR Miou-Miou. **VHS, Beta** NO 🎬🎬

No Regrets for Our Youth A feminist saga depicting the spiritual growth of a foolish Japanese girl during the tumultous years of World War II. In Japanese with English subtitles.
1946 110m/B JP Setsuko Hara; **D:** Akira Kurosawa. **VHS** $29.95 CVC, TAM 🎬🎬🎬

No Retreat, No Surrender A young American kick-boxer battles a formidable Russian opponent and wins, quite improbably, after having been tutored by the ghost of Bruce Lee in an abandoned house. Notable as Van Damme's debut, but little else recommends this silly "Rocky" rehash. Followed by "No Retreat, No Surrender II."
1986 (PG) 85m/C Kurt McKinney, J.W. Fails, Jean-Claude Van Damme; **D:** Corey Yuen. **VHS, Beta, LV** $14.95 NWV, STE 🎬

No Retreat, No Surrender 2 With help from two karate experts, a man sets out to find his girlfriend who has been kidnapped by Soviets. Has little or nothing to do with the movie to which it is ostensibly a sequel. High level kick-boxing action sequences.
1989 (R) 92m/C Loren Avedon, Max Thayer, Cynthia Rothrock; **D:** Corey Yuen. **VHS, Beta** $79.98 MCG 🎬

No Retreat, No Surrender 3: Blood Brothers Sibling martial arts rivals decide to bond in a manly way when CIA agent dad is most heinously slain by terrorists. Answers the burning question: "Whatever became of Joseph Campanella?"

1991 (R) 97m/C Keith Vitali, Loren Avedon, Joseph Campanella. **VHS** $89.95 IMP 🎬

No Room to Run Concert promoter's life turns into a nightmare of deadly corporate intrigue when he arrives in Australia. Luckily, he finds time to fall in love. Made for television hokum.
1978 101m/C AU Richard Benjamin, Paula Prentiss, Barry Sullivan; **D:** Robert Lewis. **VHS, Beta** $9.95 ACA 🎬

No Safe Haven A government agent seeks revenge for his family's death.
1987 (R) 92m/C Wings Hauser, Marina Rice, Robert Tessier; **D:** Ronnie Rondell. **VHS, Beta** $79.98 MCG 🎬

No Secrets A young man on the run seeks refuge with three girls in an isolated house. His dread secret isn't so dread, leaving this mild teen-oriented thriller starved for lack of menace.
1991 (R) 92m/C Adam Coleman Howard, Amy Locane, Heather Fairfield, Traci Lin; **D:** Dezso Magyar. **VHS, LV** $89.98 COL, PIA 🎬½

No Small Affair A 16-year-old aspiring photographer becomes romantically involved with a sultry 22-year-old rock star. Musical score by Rupert Holmes.
1984 (R) 102m/C Jon Cryer, Demi Moore, George Wendt, Peter Frechette, Elizabeth Daily, Tim Robbins, Jennifer Tilly, Rick Ducommun, Ann Wedgeworth; **D:** Jerry Schatzberg. **VHS, Beta, LV** $19.95 COL 🎬🎬

No Surrender An unpredictable, darkly charming comedy about a Liverpool nightclub newly managed by Angelis. On New Year's Eve, a small drunken war is triggered when two groups of irate senior citizens are booked into the club and clash over their beliefs. The group is made up of Protestants and Catholics and the fight resembles the ongoing conflicts in modern-day Northern Ireland, although most of the action takes place in the loo. Watch for Costello as an inept magician.
1986 (R) 100m/C GB Ray McAnally, Michael Angelis, Avis Bunnage, James Ellis, Tom Georgeson, Mark Mulholland, Joanne Whalley-Kilmer, Elvis Costello; **D:** Peter Smith. **VHS, Beta** $79.95 PSM 🎬🎬🎬

No Survivors, Please Aliens from Orion take over politicians in order to rule the Earth. Bizarre, obscure, based on true story. **AKA:** Der Chef Wuenscht Keine Zeugen; The Chief Wants No Survivors.
1963 92m/B GE Maria Perschy, Uwe Friedrichsen, Robert Cunningham, Karen Blanguernon, Gustavo Rojo; **D:** Hans Albin, Peter Berneis. **VHS** $19.98 MOV 🎬🎬

No Time for Romance A sprightly musical with an all-black cast. First such film to be shot in color.
1948 ?m/C Bill Walker. **VHS** $39.95 FCT 🎬🎬

No Time for Sergeants Hilarious film version of the Broadway play by Ira Levin. Young Andy Griffith is excellent as the Georgia farm boy who gets drafted into the service and creates mayhem among his superiors and colleagues. Story also told on an earlier television special and later in a series. Note Don Knotts and Benny Baker in small roles along with Jameel Farah who went on to star in TV's M*A*S*H after changing his name to Jamie Farr.
1958 119m/B Andy Griffith, Nick Adams, Murray Hamilton, Don Knotts, Jamie Farr, Myron McCormick; **D:** Mervyn LeRoy. **VHS, Beta, LV** $19.98 WAR 🎬🎬🎬

No Time to Die In Indonesia, two corporate pawns and a beautiful reporter battle for the possession of a new laser cannon.

1978 87m/C Chris Mitchum, John Phillip Law, Grazyna Dylong. **VHS, Beta** $59.95 TWE *⅞*

No Trace A writer who broadcasts his crime stories as part of a radio show is the victim of blackmail. It seems a former associate is aware that the stories are all based in fact. A Scotland Yard detective investigates when murder rears its ugly head. 1950 76m/B *GB* Hugh Sinclair, Dinah Sheridan, John Laurie, Barry Morse, Michael Brennan, Dora Bryan; *D:* John Gilling. **VHS, Beta** $16.95 SNC *⅞⅞*

No Way Back Way. Writer, director, and producer Williamson portrays Jess Crowder, a man-for-hire who is an expert with guns, fists, and martial arts. An angry look at the white establishment. 1974 (R) 92m/C Fred Williamson, Charles Woolf, Tracy Reed, Virginia Gregg, Don Cornelius; *D:* Fred Williamson. **VHS, Beta** $49.95 UNI *⅞⅞*

No Way Out Career Navy man Costner is involved with a beautiful, sexy woman who is murdered. Turns out she was also the mistress of the Secretary of Defense, Costner's boss. Assigned to investigate the murder, he suddenly finds himself the chief suspect. A tight thriller based on 1948's ''The Big Clock,'' with a new surprise ending. 1987 (R) 114m/C Kevin Costner, Sean Young, Gene Hackman, Will Patton, Howard Duff, George Dzundza, Iman, Chris D, Marshall Bell; *D:* Roger Donaldson. **VHS, Beta, LV** $14.95 HBO *⅞⅞⅞*

No Way to Treat a Lady Steiger is a psychotic master of disguise who stalks and kills various women in this suspenseful cat-and-mouse game. Segal, as the detective assigned to the case, uncovers clues, falls in love, and discovers that his new girl may be the killer's next victim. 1968 108m/C Rod Steiger, Lee Remick, George Segal, Eileen Heckart, Murray Hamilton; *D:* Jack Smight. **VHS, Beta** $49.95 PAR *⅞⅞⅞*

Noa at Seventeen The political/social turmoil of Israel in 1951 is allegorically depicted by the school vs. kibbutz debate within a young girl's middle-class family. In Hebrew with English subtitles. 1982 86m/C *IS* Dalia Shimko, Idit Zur, Shmuel Shilo, Moshe Havazelet; *D:* Isaac Yeshurun. **VHS, Beta** $79.95 ERG, FCT, TAM *⅞⅞⅞*

The Noble Ninja In a fantastic prehistoric world, a ninja does battle with foes both real and supernatural. 1990 90m/C Tsui Fung, Lo Lieh. **VHS, Beta** OCE *⅞⅞*

Nobody's Daughter The tragedy of an eight-year-old orphan shuttled from one family to another, all of whom are only interested in the money the government will pay for her care. In Hungarian with English subtitles. 1976 90m/C *HU* Zsuzsi Czinkoczi; *D:* Lazlo Ranody. **VHS** $59.95 EVD, TAM *⅞⅞½*

Nobody's Fool Another entry in the genre of quirky Americana, this romantic comedy concerns a hapless Midwestern waitress suffering from low-self esteem who falls in love with a traveling stage-hand. Written by Beth Henley. 1986 (PG-13) 107m/C Rosanna Arquette, Eric Roberts, Mare Winningham, Louise Fletcher, Jim Youngs; *D:* Evelyn Purcell. **VHS, Beta, LV** $19.98 LHV, WAR *⅞⅞*

Nobody's Perfect Where ''Tootsie'' and ''Some Like it Hot'' collide (or more likely crash and burn). A lovesick teenager masquerades as a girl and joins the tennis team to be near his dream girl. Takes its title from Joe E. Brown's famous last line in ''Some Like it Hot.''

1990 (PG-13) 90m/C Chad Lowe, Gail O'Grady, Patrick Breen, Kim Flowers, Robert Vaughn; *D:* Robert Kaylor. **VHS, Beta, LV** $89.98 MED *⅞*

Nobody's Perfekt Supposed comedy about three psychiatric patients who decide to extort $650,000 from the city of Miami when their car is wrecked. Lacks laughs and generally considered a turkey. 1979 (PG) 95m/C Gabe Kaplan, Robert Klein, Alex Karras, Susan Clark; *D:* Peter Bonerz. **VHS, Beta** $69.95 COL *Woof!*

Nocturna Hard times have fallen upon the house of Dracula. To help pay the taxes on the castle, the owners have converted it to the Hotel Transylvania. In order to increase business and the blood supply at the hotel, Nocturna books a disco group to entertain the guests. Hard times fell on this script, too. It's no wonder that director Tampa hid behind the alias Harry Hurwitz. *AKA:* Nocturna, Granddaughter of Dracula. 1979 (R) 82m/C Yvonne De Carlo, John Carradine, Tony Hamilton, Nai Bonet; *D:* Harry Tampa. **VHS, Beta, LV** $44.95 MED *Woof!*

Nocturne A police lieutenant investigates the supposed suicide of a famous composer and uncovers dark secrets that suggest murder is afoot. An overlooked RKO production shines thanks to Raft's inimitable tough guy performance and some offbeat direction. For film noir completists. 1946 88m/B George Raft, Lynn Bari, Virginia Huston, Joseph Pevney, Myrna Dell, Edward Ashley, Walter Sande, Mabel Paige; *D:* Edwin L. Marin. **VHS, Beta, LV** $19.98 TTC *⅞⅞½*

Noel's Fantastic Trip Noel and his dog travel through outer space in a single prop airplane seeking adventure. 1984 69m/C **VHS, Beta** $19.95 COL, WTA *⅞⅞½*

Noises Off An Americanization of a British farce about a group of second-rate actors touring in a sex comedy and their convoluted private lives. Wretched rehearsals and equally disastrous preformances, backstage sniping, lovers' quarrels, and a beleaguered director all bumble along together. It worked better on stage, where it was a Broadway hit, but the actors at least have some fun with the material. Based on the play by Michael Frayn. 1992 (PG-13) 101m/C Michael Caine, Carol Burnett, Denholm Elliott, Julie Hagerty, Marilu Henner, Mark Linn-Baker, Christopher Reeve, John Ritter, Nicolette Sheridan; *D:* Peter Bogdanovich. **VHS, Beta, LV** $19.99 TOU, PMS *⅞⅞½*

Nomad Riders A la ''Mad Max,'' (though with an even smaller budget and a decided lack of originality) one rugged man goes after the bikers who killed his wife and daughter. 1981 82m/C Wayne Chema, Richard Cluck, Ron Gregg; *D:* Frank Roach. **VHS, Beta** $69.98 LIV, VES *⅞*

Nomads A supernatural thriller set in Los Angeles about a French anthropologist who is mysteriously killed, and the woman doctor who investigates and becomes the next target of a band of strange street people with nomadic spirits. Nomad notables include pop stars Adam Ant and Josie Cotton. 1986 (R) 91m/C Pierce Brosnan, Lesley-Anne Down, Adam Ant, Anna Maria Monticelli; *D:* John McTiernan. **VHS, Beta, LV** $29.95 IME, PAR *⅞⅞½*

Nomads of the North Vintage silent melodrama set in the North Woods with the requisite young girl beset by evil villians, a climactic forest fire, and a dashing Mountie who allows a man wrongly sought by the law to be reunited with the woman he secretly loves.

1920 109m/B Lon Chaney Sr., Lewis Stone, Betty Blythe. **VHS, Beta, 8mm** $16.95 SNC, GPV, VYY *⅞*

Nomugi Pass A young woman working in a Japanese silk mill in the early 1900s must endure hardship and abuse. English subtitles. 1979 154m/C *JP* Shinobu Otake, Meiko Harada, Rentaro Mikuni, Takeo Jii. **VHS, Beta** VDA *⅞⅞½*

Non-Stop New York Mystery tale with interesting twist. A wealthy woman can give an alibi for a murder suspect, but no one will listen, and she is subsequently framed. Pays homage to Hitchcock with its photography and humor. Quick and charming. 1937 71m/B Anna Lee, John Loder, Francis L. Sullivan, Frank Cellier; *D:* Robert Stevenson. **VHS** $16.95 NOS, SNC *⅞⅞½*

None But the Brave During World War II, an American bomber plane crash-lands on an island already inhabited by stranded Japanese forces. After a skirmish, the two groups initiate a fragile truce, with the understanding that fighting will resume if one or the other sends for help. The Americans repair their radio unit and must decide on their next actions. Sinatra's directorial debut is a poor effort. 1965 105m/C Frank Sinatra, Clint Walker, Tommy Sands, Brad Dexter, Tony Bill, Tatsuya Mihashi, Takeshi Kato, Sammy Jackson; *D:* Frank Sinatra; *M:* John Williams. **VHS, Beta, LV** $59.95 WAR, FCT *⅞⅞*

None But the Lonely Heart In the days before World War II, a Cockney drifter (Grant) wanders the East End of London. When his get-rich-quick schemes fail, his dying shopkeeper-mother tries to help and lands in prison. Interesting characterization of life in the slums. Odets not only directed, but wrote the screenplay. 1944 113m/B Cary Grant, Ethel Barrymore, Barry Fitzgerald, Jane Wyatt, Dan Duryea, George Coulouris, June Duprez; *D:* Clifford Odets. Academy Awards '44: Best Supporting Actress (Barrymore); Nominations: Best Actor (Grant), Best Film Editing, Best Original Score; National Board of Review Awards '44: 10 Best Films of the Year. **VHS, Beta** $19.95 MED, BTV *⅞⅞⅞*

Noon Sunday A cold war situation in the Pacific islands explodes into an orgy of death. 1971 (PG) 104m/C Mark Lenard, John Russell, Linda Avery, Keye Luke. **VHS, Beta** $19.95 ACA *⅞*

Noon Wine Dramatization of Katherine Anne Porter's classic story about a Swedish worker on a Texas farm who becomes the center of a family battle. Made for PBS' American Playhouse. 1984 60m/C Fred Ward, Lise Hilboldt, Stellan Skarsgard, Jon Cryer; *D:* Michael Fields. **VHS, Beta** $24.95 MON, FCT, KAR *⅞⅞⅞*

The Noose Hangs High This broad comedy has our heroes as window washers mistaken for gamblers and getting involved with a bunch of gangsters. Much physical and verbal shenanigans as only these two can do it. The bits may be a bit old, but they're done with a fresh twist. Some good word play with the phrase ''You can't be here'' runs in the same vein as their classic ''Who's on first?'' routine. Genuinely funny. 1948 77m/B Bud Abbott, Lou Costello, Cathy Downs, Joseph Calleia, Leon Errol, Mike Mazurki, Jack Overman, Fritz Feld, Vera Martin, Joe Kirk, Matt Willis, Benny Rubin; *D:* Charles T. Barton. **VHS** $19.98 MGM, NOS *⅞⅞⅞*

Norma After a young woman's husband is killed at war, she starts sleeping with every man she can find. After a year of this, she decides maybe she has a problem and enlists the aid of a psychotherapist. Through hypnosis he finally unlocks her terrible sexual secret. Truly awful.
1989 (R) 80m/C Art Metrano, Mady Maguire, Chris Warfield, William Rotsler, George Flower; **D:** William Rotsler. **VHS $29.95** HHE *

Norma Rae A poor, uneducated textile worker joins forces with a New York labor organizer to unionize the reluctant workers at a Southern mill. Field was a surprise with her fully developed character's strength, beauty, and humor; her Oscar was well-deserved. Ritt's direction is top-notch. Jennifer Warnes sings the theme song, "It Goes Like It Goes," which also won an Oscar.
1979 (PG) 114m/C Sally Field, Ron Leibman, Beau Bridges, Pat Hingle; **D:** Martin Ritt. Academy Awards '79: Best Actress (Field), Best Song ("It Goes Like It Goes"); Nominations: Best Adapted Screenplay, Best Picture; Golden Globe Awards '80: Best Actress—Drama (Field); Los Angeles Film Critics Association Awards '79: Best Actress (Field); National Board of Review Awards '79: Best Actress (Field); New York Film Critics Awards '79: Best Actress (Field). **VHS, Beta, LV $19.98** FOX, BTV *♪♪♪*

Norman Conquest Conway finds himself drugged and framed for murder in this bargain-basement thriller. Bartok is the leader of a diamond-smuggling operation who may be involved. **AKA:** Park Plaza.
1953 75m/B GB Tom Conway, Eva Bartok, Joy Shelton, Sidney James, Richard Wattis, Robert Adair, Ian Fleming; **W/D:** Bernard Knowles. VHS **$19.95** NOS, SNG *♪*

The Norman Conquests, Part 1: Table Manners Part one of playwright Alan Ayckbourn's comic trilogy of love unfulfilled, as the charmingly unreliable Norman (Conti) works his amorous wiles on three women.
1980 108m/C GB Tom Conti, Richard Briers, Penelope Keith. **VHS, Beta $59.99** HBO, TVC *♪♪♪*

The Norman Conquests, Part 2: Living Together Part two concerns the happenings in the living room during Norman's disastrous weekend of unsuccessful seduction.
1980 93m/C GB Tom Conti, Penelope Keith, Richard Briers. **VHS, Beta $59.99** HBO, TVC *♪♪♪*

The Norman Conquests, Part 3: Round and Round the Garden Part three concerns Norman's furtive appearance in the garden, which suggests that the weekend is going to misfire.
1980 106m/C GB Tom Conti, Penelope Keith, Richard Briers. **VHS, Beta $59.99** HBO, TVC *♪♪♪*

Norman Loves Rose A precocious 13-year-old and his married sister-in-law join forces in this substandard comedy. When Rose tries to help Norman by teaching him about sex, she learns a little too—she's pregnant.
1982 (R) 95m/C AU Carol Kane, Tony Owen, Warren Mitchell, Myra de Groot; **D:** Henri Safran. **VHS, Beta $69.98** LIV, VES *♪1/2*

Norman's Awesome Experience Three adolescents are transported back in time to the Roman Empire. Bill and Ted, anyone?
1988 (PG-13) 90m/C Tom McCamus, Laurie Paton, Jaques Lussier; **D:** Paul Donovan. **VHS, Beta $14.95** NO Woof!

Norseman Leader of a band of Norsemen sets sail for the New World in search of his missing royal father. Low-budget Viking adventure.
1978 (PG) 90m/C Lee Majors, Cornel Wilde, Mel Ferrer, Christopher Connelly; **D:** Charles B. Pierce. **VHS, Beta $69.98** LIV, VES *♪1/2*

North and South Lavish spectacular about a friendship tested by the turbulent times leading up to Civil War. Orry Main (Swayze) is a South Carolina plantation owner while his best friend George Hazard (Read) comes from a Pennsylvania industrial family. Swayze is also involved in a doomed romance with the beautiful Madeline (Down), who's forced to marry the odious Justin LaMotte (Carradine). Lots of intrigue and excitement. Based on the novel by John Jakes. Filmed on location in Charleston, South Carolina. Originally broadcast as a 12-hour television miniseries, which was followed by a sequel dealing with the years of the Civil War. Available on six cassettes.
1985 561m/C Patrick Swayze, James Read, Lesley-Anne Down, David Carradine, Kirstie Alley, Philip Casnoff, Jean Simmons, Inga Swenson, Jonathon Frakes, Genie Francis, Terri Garber, Georg Stanford Brown, Olivia Cole, David Ogden Stiers, Robert Guillaume, Hal Holbrook, Gene Kelly, Robert Mitchum, Johnny Cash, Elizabeth Taylor. **VHS, Beta $199.98** WAR *♪♪♪*

The North Avenue Irregulars A slapstick Disney comedy along the same lines as some of their earlier laugh-fests. A priest and three members of the local ladies' club try to bust a crime syndicate. Though the premise is silly, there are still lots of laughs in this family film.
1979 (G) 99m/C Edward Herrmann, Barbara Harris, Susan Clark, Karen Valentine, Michael Constantine, Cloris Leachman, Melora Hardin, Alan Hale Jr., Ruth Buzzi, Patsy Kelly, Virginia Capers; **D:** Bruce Bilson. **VHS $69.95** DIS *♪♪1/2*

North by Northwest Grant is a self-assured Madison Avenue ad executive who inadvertently gets involved with international spies when they believe him to be someone else. His problems are compounded when he is framed for murder. The movie that has Grant and Saint dangling from the faces of Mount Rushmore and also contains the segment where a plane chases Grant through farm fields. Performances by the cast are exceptional, particularly Grant's. As with other Hitchcock productions, plenty of plot twists are mixed with tongue-in-cheek humor. Considered by many to be one of Hitchcock's greatest films. Also available on videodisc with letter boxing, digital soundtrack, special interview with Hitchcock, production and publicity photos, storyboards, and original movie trailer.
1959 136m/C Cary Grant, Eva Marie Saint, James Mason, Leo G. Carroll, Martin Landau, Jessie Royce Landis; **D:** Alfred Hitchcock. Academy Awards '59 Nominations: Best Art Direction/Set Decoration (Color), Best Film Editing, Best Story & Screenplay; Edgar Allan Poe Awards '59: Best Screenplay. **VHS, Beta, LV $19.95** MGM, PIA, VYG *♪♪♪♪*

North Dallas Forty Based on the novel by former Dallas Cowboy Peter Gent, the film focuses on the labor abuses in pro-football. One of the best football movies ever made, it contains searing commentary and very good acting, although the plot is sometimes dropped behind the line of scrimmage.
1979 (R) 119m/C Nick Nolte, Mac Davis, Charles Durning, Bo Svenson, Brian Dennehy, John Matuszak, Dayle Haddon, Steve Forrest, Dabney Coleman, G.D. Spradlin; **D:** Ted Kotcheff. **VHS, Beta, LV $14.95** PAR *♪♪♪1/2*

North of the Border A cowboy in Canada gets involved with back-stabbing and treachery in and around Alberta.
1946 40m/B CA Russell Hayden, Lyle Talbot, Inez Cooper, Douglas Fowley, Jack Mulhall; **D:** B. Reeves Eason. **VHS, Beta, LV $24.95** VYY, WGE *♪1/2*

North of the Great Divide Standard Rogers programmer, with Roy as a half-breed mediator between salmon fisherman and Indians.
1950 67m/C Roy Rogers, Penny Edwards, Gordon Jones, Roy Barcroft, Jack Lambert, Douglas Evans, Noble Johnson; **D:** William Witney. **VHS $12.98** REP *♪1/2*

North Shore A young surfer from Arizona hits the beaches of Hawaii and discovers love, sex, and adventure. Only redeeming quality is surfing footage.
1987 (PG) 96m/C Matt Adler, Nia Peeples, John Philbin, Gregory Harrison, Christina Raines; **D:** Will Phelps. **VHS, Beta $79.95** MCA *♪1/2*

The North Star Gripping war tale of Nazis over-running an eastern Russian city, with courageous villagers fighting back. Colorized version available. **AKA:** Armored Attack.
1943 108m/B Dana Andrews, Walter Huston, Anne Baxter, Farley Granger, Walter Brennan, Erich von Stroheim, Jack Perrin, Dean Jagger; **D:** Lewis Milestone. **VHS, Beta, 3/4U, Special order formats $19.95** NOS, MRV, VYY *♪♪♪*

North to Alaska A gold prospector encounters many problems when he agrees to pick up his partner's fiancee in Seattle to bring her home to Nome, Alaska, in the 1890s. Overly slapstick at times, but great fun nonetheless. Loosely based on Laszlo Fodor's play "The Birthday Gift."
1960 120m/C John Wayne, Stewart Granger, Ernie Kovacs, Fabian, Capucine; **D:** Henry Hathaway. **VHS, Beta, LV $19.98** FOX *♪♪♪*

Northanger Abbey Catherine is a young woman whose head is turned by her romance readings of dark secrets, sinister castles, dashing heroes, and helpless women. When the handsome Henry Tilney invites her to visit his ancestral home, Northanger Abbey, it seems all her fancies have come to life. A somewhat tepid adaptation of Jane Austen's parody of the popular Gothic romances of her day.
198? 90m/C GB Peter Firth. **VHS $29.95** TVC *♪♪1/2*

Northeast of Seoul Three people will stop at nothing to steal a legendary jewel-encrusted sword out of Korea.
1972 (PG) 84m/C Anita Ekberg, John Ireland, Victor Buono; **D:** David Lowell Rich. **VHS, Beta $59.95** MGM *♪*

Northern Lights A small, black-and-white independent drama depicting the struggle of a lowly farmer combating governmental forces in the 1915 heartland. Subtitled.
1979 85m/B Robert Behling, Susan Lynch, Joe Spano, Rob Nilsson, Henry Martinson, Marianne Astrom-DeFina, Ray Ness, Helen Ness; **D:** Rob Nilsson, John Hanson. **VHS, Beta $19.95** STE, NWV *♪♪♪*

Northern Pursuit A Canadian Mountie disguises himself to infiltrate a Nazi spy ring in this exciting adventure film. Based on Leslie White's "Five Thousand Trojan Horses."
1943 94m/B Errol Flynn, Helmut Dantine, Julie Bishop, Gene Lockhart, Tom Tully; **D:** Raoul Walsh. **VHS, Beta $19.98** MLB *♪♪1/2*

Northville Cemetery Massacre Gang of bikers comes to town and all hell breaks loose. The result is a horribly bloody war between the townsfolk and the gang.

Yup, it was a massacre. *AKA:* The Northfield Cemetery Massacre.

1976 (R) 81m/C David Hyry, Craig Collicott, Jan Sisk. **VHS, Beta** *PGN* ⬤

Northwest Outpost Eddy is a California cavalry officer in this lightweight operetta. He helps a young woman who is trying to free her husband from jail, and after his death they are able to pursue their relationship. Eddy's last film. ♫Weary; Raindrops on a Drum; Tell Me With Your Eyes; One More Mile to Go; Russian Easter Hymn; Love is the Time; Nearer and Dearer. *AKA:* End of the Rainbow.

1947 91m/B Nelson Eddy, Ilona Massey, Hugo Haas, Elsa Lanchester, Lenore Ulric; *D:* Allan Dwan. **VHS $19.98** *REP* ⬤⬤½

Northwest Passage The lavish first half of a projected two-film package based on Kenneth Roberts' popular novel, depicting the troop of Rogers' Rangers fighting the wilderness and hostile Indians. Beautifully produced; the second half was never made and the passage itself is never seen.

1940 126m/C Spencer Tracy, Robert Young, Ruth Hussey, Walter Brennan, Nat Pendleton, Robert Barratt, Lumsden Hare; *D:* King Vidor. **VHS, Beta $19.98** *MGM* ⬤⬤⬤

Northwest Trail Royal Canadian Mountie Steele's assignment is to escort Woodbury across the wilderness. She's carrying a large sum of money to save her uncle's business. Problem is, killers are on their trail.

1946 75m/C Bob Steele, Joan Woodbury, John Litel, Raymond Hatton, Madge Bellamy, Charles Middleton; *D:* Derwin Abrahams. **VHS, Beta $19.95** *NOS, WGE, HHT* ⬤

A Nos Amours Craving the attention she is denied at home, a young French girl searches for love and affection from numerous boyfriends in hopes of eradicating her unhappy home. Occasional lapses in quality and slow pacing hamper an otherwise excellent effort. The characterization of the girl Suzanne is especially memorable. In French with English subtitles.

1984 (R) 99m/C *FR* Sandrine Bonnaire, Dominique Besnehard, Maurice Pialat, Evelyne Ker; *D:* Maurice Pialat. **VHS, Beta, LV $59.95** *COL, TAM* ⬤⬤⬤

Nosferatu The first film adaptation of Bram Stoker's "Dracula" remains one of the creepiest and most atmospheric versions. Murnau knew how to add just the right touches to make this one of the best vampire films ever made. All it lacks is the name of Dracula, which was changed due to copyright problems with Stoker's widow. Filmed in Bavaria. Silent with music and English titles. Remade by Werner Herzog in 1979. *AKA:* Nosferatu, Eine Symphonie des Grauens; Nosferatu, A Symphony of Terror; Nosferatu, A Symphony of Horror; Nosferatu, The Vampire.

1922 63m/B *GE* Max Schreck, Alexander Granach, Gustav von Wagenheim, Greta Schroeder; *D:* F. W. Murnau. **VHS, Beta, LV $29.95** *KIV, MRV, NOS* ⬤⬤⬤⬤

Nosotros A thief tries to straighten up his life so he can win the love of a pretty girl. *AKA:* We.

1944 87m/B *MX* Ricardo Montalban, Emilia Guiu, Esther Luquin, Carlos M. Baena; *D:* Fernando A. Rivero. **VHS, Beta $34.95** *MAD* ⬤

Not as a Stranger Glossy film about the medical profession and the varying degrees of dedication shown by doctors. Mitchum stars as an medical student who can't afford to pay his tuition, so he marries nurse de Havilland and continues going to school on her money, although their relationship is far from being a loving one. Producer Kramer's directorial debut. Based on the book by Morton Thompson.

1955 135m/B Olivia de Havilland, Robert Mitchum, Frank Sinatra, Gloria Grahame, Broderick Crawford, Charles Bickford, Myron McCormick, Lon Chaney Jr.; *D:* Stanley Kramer. **VHS $19.98** *MGM* ⬤⬤½

Not for Publication A woman working as both a tabloid reporter and a mayoral campaign worker uncovers governmental corruption with the help of a shy photographer and a midget. Meant to be on par with older screwball comedies but lacking the wit and subtlety.

1984 (R) 87m/C Nancy Allen, David Naughton, Richard Paul, Alice Ghostley, Laurence Luckinbill; *D:* Paul Bartel. **VHS, Beta $69.99** *HBO* ⬤⬤

Not My Kid The 15-year-old daughter of a surgeon brings turmoil to her family when she becomes heavily involved in drugs. Producer Polson, along with Dr. Miller Newton, wrote the original book for this emotional story that is one of the better treatments of this important subject. Made for television.

1985 120m/C George Segal, Stockard Channing, Viveka Davis; *D:* Michael Tuchner. **VHS, Beta $79.95** *SVS* ⬤⬤½

Not of This Earth In a remake of the 1957 Roger Corman quickie, an alien wearing sunglasses makes an unfriendly trip to Earth. In order to save his dying planet he needs major blood donations from unsuspecting Earthlings. Not a match for the original version, some may nevertheless want to see ex-porn star Lords in her role as the nurse.

1988 (R) 92m/C Traci Lords, Arthur Roberts, Lenny Juliano, Rebecca Perle; *D:* Jim Wynorski. **VHS, Beta $14.98** *MGM* ⬤½

Not Quite Love Pre-pubescent ghetto waif and a self-appointed prophet seek love in uncaring city. Much music, singing and foot-stomping.

1988 30m/C *D:* David Scmidlapp. **VHS $29.95** *FCT, MWF* ⬤⬤

Not Quite Paradise A young American medical student falls in love with a young Israeli girl on an Israeli kibbutz. Also called "Not Quite Jerusalem."

1986 (R) 106m/C Sam Robards, Joanna Pacula; *D:* Lewis Gilbert. **VHS, Beta $19.95** *STE, NWV* ⬤

Not Tonight Darling A bored suburban housewife becomes involved with a fast-talking businessman who leads her into a web of deceit and blackmail.

1972 (R) 70m/C Luan Peters, Vincent Ball, Jason Twelvetrees. **VHS, Beta $59.95** *GEM* ⬤

Not Without My Daughter Overwrought drama shot in Israel about American Field, who travels with her Arab husband and their daughter to his native Iran, where (he must have forgotten to tell her) she has no rights. He decides the family will stay, using beatings and confinement to persuade his uncooperative wife, but she risks all to escape with daughter. Based on the true story of Betty Mahmoody.

1990 (PG-13) 107m/C Sally Field, Alfred Molina; *D:* Brian Gilbert. **VHS, Beta, LV, 8mm $92.99** *MGM, PIA, FCT* ⬤⬤½

Notes for an African Orestes Director Pasolini's insight into how a filmmaker works and what motivates him, as the camera reveals his plans to film a modern day version of Aeschylus' "Orestes" in Africa.

1970 75m/B *D:* Pier Paolo Pasolini; *M:* Gato Garbieri. **VHS, 3/4U, Special order formats $29.95** *MFV, CIG, TAM* ⬤⬤

Nothing But the Night Lee's company produced this convoluted story of orphans who are victims of a cult that uses them in their quest for immortality. *AKA:* The Devil's Undead; The Resurrection Syndicate.

1972 (PG) 90m/C *GB* Christopher Lee, Peter Cushing, Diana Dors, Georgia Brown, Keith Barron, Fulton Mackay, Gwyneth Strong; *D:* Peter Sasdy. **VHS** *SNC* ⬤

Nothing But Trouble Laurel & Hardy's last film for MGM is a complicated tale of two servants who wind up protecting an exiled boy king from the machinations of his power-mad uncle.

1944 70m/B Stan Laurel, Oliver Hardy, Henry O'Neill, Mary Boland, David Leland, John Warburton, Connie Gilchrist, Philip Merivale; *D:* Sam Taylor. **VHS $19.98** *MGM* ⬤⬤½

Nothing But Trouble Yuppie couple out for weekend drive find themselves smoldering in small town hell thanks to a traffic ticket. Horror and humor mix like oil and water in Aykroyd's debut as director.

1991 (PG-13) 93m/C Dan Aykroyd, Demi Moore, Chevy Chase, John Candy, Taylor Negron, Bertila Demas, Valri Bromfield; *D:* Dan Aykroyd. **VHS, Beta, LV, 8mm $92.99** *WAR, PIA* ⬤

Nothing in Common In his last film, Gleason plays the abrasive, diabetic father of immature advertising agency worker Hanks. After his parents separate, Hanks learns to be more responsible and loving in caring for his father. Comedy and drama are blended well here with the help of satirical pokes at the ad business and Hanks turns in a fine performance, but the unorganized, lengthy plot may lose some viewers.

1986 (PG) 119m/C Tom Hanks, Jackie Gleason, Eva Marie Saint, Bess Armstrong, Hector Elizondo; *D:* Garry Marshall. **VHS, Beta, LV $19.98** *WAR, HBO* ⬤⬤

Nothing Personal Confused mix of romantic comedy and environmental themes. Lawyer (?) Somers attempts to help college professor Sutherland prevent the slaughter of seals. Enter romance (hey, but what about the baby seals?). Enlivened by appearances of Canadian SCTV vets and Somers's first starring theatrical role.

1980 (PG) 96m/C Donald Sutherland, Suzanne Somers, Dabney Coleman, John Dehner, Roscoe Lee Browne, Catherine O'Hara; *D:* George Bloomfield. **VHS, Beta, LV $69.98** *LIV, VES* ⬤½

Nothing Sacred A slick, overzealous reporter takes advantage of a small-town girl's situation. As a publicity stunt, his newspaper brings her to the Big Apple to distract her from her supposedly imminent death in order to manipulate the public's sentiment as a means to sell more copy. Innocent young Lombard, however, is far from death's door, and deftly exploits her exploitation. Scripted by Ben Hecht, it is a scathing indictment of the mass media and the bovine mentality of the masses. The diametric opposite of Frank Capra's optimism, it is both hysterically funny and bitterly cynical, and boasts Lombard's finest performance as the small-town rube who orchestrates the ruse. Remade in 1954 as "Living It Up." Musical score by Oscar Levant.

1937 75m/C Fredric March, Carole Lombard, Walter Connolly, Sig Rumann, Charles Winninger, Margaret Hamilton; *D:* William A. Wellman. **VHS, Beta, LV, 3/4U, Special order formats $19.95** *NOS, MRV, VYY* ⬤⬤⬤½

Nothing Underneath An American guy goes to Rome to search for his model twin sister, who may be one of the victims of a series of scissor killings.

1985 95m/C Tom Schanley, Renee Simonsen, Nicola Perring, Donald Pleasence; **D:** Carlo Vanzina. **VHS, Beta $79.95** SVS 🐾🐾½

Notorious Post-World War II story of a beautiful playgirl sent by the US government to marry a suspected spy living in Brazil. Grant is the agent assigned to watch her. Duplicity and guilt are important factors in this brooding, romantic spy thriller. Suspenseful throughout, with a surprise ending. The acting is excellent all around and Hitchcock makes certain that suspense is maintained throughout this classy and complex thriller. Laser edition contains original trailer, publicity photos, and additional footage. 1946 101m/B Cary Grant, Ingrid Bergman, Claude Rains, Louis Calhern, Madame Konstantin; **D:** Alfred Hitchcock. **VHS, Beta, LV $19.98** FOX, VYG, CRC 🐾🐾🐾🐾

A Nous la Liberte Two tramps encounter industrialization and automation, making one into a wealthy leader, the other a nature-loving iconoclast. A poignant, fantastical masterpiece by Clair, made before he migrated to Hollywood. Though the view of automation may be dated, it influenced such films as Chaplin's "Modern Times." In French with English subtitles. 1931 87m/B FR Henri Marchand, Raymond Cordy, Rolla France, Paul Olivier; **W/D:** Rene Clair. Academy Awards '32 Nominations: Best Interior Decoration; National Board of Review Awards '32: 5 Best Foreign Films of the Year. **VHS, Beta, 8mm $49.95** TAM, NOS, MRV 🐾🐾🐾🐾

Nous N'Irons Plus au Bois On the outskirts of a forest held by the Germans, a small group of French resistance fighters capture a German soldier during World War II. He actually wants to join forces with them, however, after falling in love with a lovely young French girl. In French; subtitled in English. 1969 98m/C FR Marie-France Pisier, Siegfried Rauch, Richard Leduc; **D:** Georges Dumoulin. **VHS, Beta** NO 🐾🐾

Nouvelle Vague Delon and Giordano are an attractive, powerful, and very wealthy couple involved in Godard's usual sexual and political themes, which has society geared toward support of the rich. In French with English subtitles. 1990 89m/C SI FR Alain Delon, Domiziana Giordano, Roland Amstutz, Laurence Cote, Christophe Odent; **W/D:** Jean-Luc Godard. **VHS $79.95** TAM 🐾🐾½

Novel Desires Brian Freedman is a bestselling author who teams up with his writing rival, Vicky Chance. But it isn't just their imaginations they give free reign to, it's all their desires as well. 1992 (R) 80m/C Tyler Gains, Caroline Monteith, Mitchell Clark, Lisa Hayland; **D:** Lawrence Unger. **VHS $79.95** CEL 🐾½

Now and Forever Young wife's life is shattered when her unfaithful husband is wrongly accused and convicted of rape. After he is sent to prison, she begins drinking and taking drugs. From the novel by Danielle Steel, it will appeal most to those who like their romances a la Harlequin. 1982 (R) 93m/C AU Cheryl Ladd, Robert Coleby, Carmen Duncan, Christine Amor, Aileen Britton; **D:** Adrian Carr. **VHS, Beta, LV $59.95** MCA 🐾½

Now, Voyager Davis plays a lonely spinster who is transformed into a vibrant young woman by therapy. She comes out of her shell to have a romantic affair with a suave European (who turns out to be married) but still utters the famous phrase "Oh, Jerry, we have the stars. Let's not ask for the moon." Definitely melodramatic, but an involving sto-

ry nonetheless. Based on a novel by Olive Higgins Prouty. 1942 117m/B Bette Davis, Gladys Cooper, Claude Rains, Paul Henreid, Bonita Granville; **D:** Irving Rapper; **M:** Max Steiner. Academy Awards '42: Best Score; Nominations: Best Actress (Davis), Best Supporting Actress (Cooper). **VHS, Beta, LV $19.95** MGM 🐾🐾🐾½

Now You See Him, Now You Don't Light Disney comedy involving a gang of crooks who want to use a college student's invisibility formula to rob a local bank. Sequel to Disney's "The Computer Wore Tennis Shoes." 1972 (G) 85m/C Kurt Russell, Joe Flynn, Cesar Romero, Jim Backus; **D:** Robert Butler. **VHS, Beta $69.95** DIS 🐾🐾

Nowhere to Hide A widow whose Marine officer husband has been assassinated is chased by some bad guys who are after a helicopter part (say what?) and she must fight for survival for herself and her 6 year-old son. 1987 (R) 91m/C Amy Madigan, Daniel Hugh-Kelly, Michael Ironside; **D:** Mario Azzopardi. **VHS, Beta $79.95** LHV, HHE, WAR 🐾🐾

Nowhere to Hide A hitman is hired to kill a young boy who witnesses a brutal murder. The hitman, however, decides he's already killed too many people and wants to get out of the business. Will he become the next murder target? 19?? 80m/C Paul Winfield, Rod Taylor. **VHS $9.99** QVD 🐾🐾

Nowhere to Run Slipshod version of a true story about a series of murders in Caddo, Texas in 1960. Carradine, paroled from prison, murders for revenge while six high school seniors get involved in the chase and in the seedy side of politics, police, and their own puberty. 1988 (R) 87m/C David Carradine, Jason Priestly, Kieran Mulroney, Henry Jones; **D:** Carl Franklin. **VHS, Beta $79.95** MGM 🐾

Nowhere to Run Kickboxer with heart seeks cross-over movie to establish real acting career. Unfortunately, even if such a movie existed, Van Damme wouldn't know what to do with it. Arquette plays the damsel in distress, facing eviction from the family farm with her two small children. Fortunately for Van Damme's escaped convict character, she is also a very lonely widow (nudge, nudge). He saves the day by abusing the daylights out of the big bad bankers, yet also finds time to play surrogate dad. Whatta guy. 1993 (R) 95m/C Jean-Claude Van Damme, Rosanna Arquette, Kieran Culkin, Tiffany Taubman, Joss Ackland, Ted Levine; **D:** Robert Harmon; **W:** Joe Eszterhas, Leslie Boehm, Randy Feldman; **M:** Mark Isham. **VHS, LV, 8mm** COL 🐾½

Nuclear Conspiracy A reporter disappears while investigating a huge nuclear waste shipment, and his wife searches for him. 1985 115m/C Birgit Doll, Albert Fortell. **VHS, Beta $69.95** VMK 🐾½

The Nude Bomb Maxwell Smart (would you believe?) tries to save the world from a bomb that only destroys clothing and would leave everyone in the buff. Old hat lines. Followed by the television movie "Get Smart, Again!" **AKA:** The Return of Maxwell Smart. 1980 (PG) 94m/C Don Adams, Dana Elcar, Pamela Hensley, Sylvia Kristel, Norman Lloyd, Rhonda Fleming, Joey Forman; **D:** Clive Donner. **VHS, LV $79.95** MCA, PIA 🐾🐾½

Nude on the Moon Lunar expedition discovers moon inhabited by people who bare skin as hobby. Groovy theme song, "I'm Mooning Over You, My Little Moon Doll." Part of Joe Bob Brigg's "Sleaziest Movies in the History of the World" series. 1961 83m/C **D:** Doris Wishman. **VHS $19.98** SVI Woof!

Nudity Required Two pals use the casting couch, pretending to be Hollywood producers, to seduce young women. Silly comedy with gratuitous nudity (Ms. Newmar included). Hardly a laugh to be found. 1990 90m/C Julie Newmar, Troy Donahue, Brad Zutaut, Billy Frank, Ty Randolph, Alvin Silver, Eli Rich, Phil Hock; **D:** John Bown. **VHS** NO 🐾

Nudo di Donna A witty comedy about a Venetian bookseller who is becoming tired of marital struggles with his sexy wife of 16 years. He wanders into a fashion photography shop, sees a backside nude photo of a model who looks like his wife, and he takes off in fiery pursuit to find the subject of the photo. Venetian location photography is quite nice. In Italian with English subtitles. **AKA:** Portrait of a Woman, Nude. 1983 112m/C IT Nino Manfredi, Jean-Pierre Cassel, George Wilson, Elenora Giorgi; **D:** Nino Manfredi. **VHS, Beta, LV $29.95** PAV, APD 🐾🐾🐾

Number 1 of the Secret Service A handsome secret agent must foil the plans of a millionaire industrialist to destroy the economy. Spy spoof that's marginally interesting. 1977 (PG) 87m/C GB Nicky Henson, Geoffrey Keen, Sue Lloyd, Aimi MacDonald, Richard Todd; **D:** Lindsay Shonteff. **VHS, Beta $79.95** MGM 🐾🐾

Number One with a Bullet Two unorthodox "odd couple" detectives are demoted after losing a key witness, but still set out on their own to unearth a drug czar. Carradine and Williams are better than this standard action material. 1987 (R) 103m/C Robert Carradine, Billy Dee Williams, Peter Graves, Valerie Bertinelli; **D:** Jack Smight. **VHS, Beta $14.95** MGM 🐾🐾

Number Seventeen A humorous early thriller by the Master Hitchcock, before the likes of "The 39 Steps." An unsuspecting hobo accidentally discovers a jewel thief's cache. The chase is on—superb final chase sequence involving a bus and a train. Based on the play by J. Jefferson Farjeon. 1932 64m/B Leon M. Lion, Anne Grey, John Stuart, Donald Calthrop; **D:** Alfred Hitchcock. **VHS, Beta, 8mm, 3/4U, Special order formats $16.95** SNC, NOS, HHT 🐾🐾🐾

The Nun A young woman, unable to meet financial obligations, is forced into a convent. Victimized by the mother superior and betrayed by a clergyman who befriends her, she escapes from the convent and eventually ends up in a bordello, despairing and suicidal. Not a cheery story. Banned in France for two years. In French with English subtitles. 1966 155m/C FR Anna Karina, Lilo (Liselotte) Pulver, Micheline Presle, Christine Lenier, Francine Berge, Francisco Rabal, Wolfgang Reichmann, Catherine Diamant, Yori Bertin; **D:** Jacques Rivette. **VHS $59.95** INT, FCT, TAM 🐾🐾½

Nuns on the Run Idle and Coltrane are two nonviolent members of a robbery gang who double-cross their boss during a hold-up and disguise themselves as nuns while on the run from both the Mob and the police. Catholic humor, slapstick, and much fun with habits dominate. Idle and Coltrane do their best to keep the so-so script moving with its one-joke premise.

1990 (PG-13) 95m/C Eric Idle, Robbie Coltrane, Janet Suzman, Camille Coduri, Robert Patterson, Tom Hickey, Doris Hare, Lila Kaye; *D:* Jonathan Lynn. VHS, Beta, LV $89.98 FOX *ℐℐ*

The Nun's Story The melancholy tale of a young nun working in the Congo and Belgium during World War II, and struggling to reconcile her free spirit with the rigors of the order. Highly acclaimed; from the Kathryn Hulme novel.
1959 152m/C Audrey Hepburn, Peter Finch, Edith Evans, Peggy Ashcroft, Mildred Dunnock, Dean Jagger, Beatrice Straight, Colleen Dewhurst; *D:* Fred Zinneman. Academy Awards '59 Nominations: Best Actress (Hepburn), Best Adapted Screenplay, Best Color Cinematography, Best Director (Zinneman), Best Film Editing, Best Picture, Best Sound, Best Original Score; British Academy Awards '59: Best Actress (Hepburn); National Board of Review Awards '59: 10 Best Films of the Year, Best Director (Zinneman), Best Supporting Actress (Evans). VHS, Beta, LV $19.98 WAR *ℐℐℐ½*

Nurse A recently widowed woman resumes her career as a nurse in a large urban hospital, after her son leaves for college. Based on Peggy Anderson's book. Made for television; became a weekly series.
1980 105m/C Michael Learned, Robert Reed, Antonio Fargas; *D:* David Lowell Rich. VHS, Beta $59.95 LIV *ℐℐ½*

Nurse Edith Cavell Fine performances in this true story of Britain's famous nurse who aided the Belgian underground during World War I, transporting wounded soldiers out of the German-occupied country. Decidedly opposes war and, ironically, was released just as World War II began to heat up in 1939.
1939 95m/B George Sanders, Edna May Oliver, ZaSu Pitts, Robert Coote, May Robson, Anna Neagle; *D:* Herbert Wilcox. VHS, Beta, 3/4U, Special order formats $19.95 NOS, CAB, KRT *ℐℐℐ*

Nurse on Call A bevy of trampy nurses cavort throughout a big city hospital. Softcore.
1988 80m/C Anne Tilson, Jennie Martinez, Christopher Floyd. VHS, Beta $29.95 MED *ℐ*

Nutcase A trio of young children in New Zealand attempt to thwart a group of terrorists who threaten to reactivate a large city's volcanoes unless they are given a large sum of money. Novel twist there.
1983 49m/C NZ Nevan Rowe, Ian Watkin, Michael Wilson; *D:* Roger Donaldson. VHS, Beta $14.98 VID *ℐ*

Nutcracker, A Fantasy on Ice An ice-skating version of the famed story and Tchaikovsky ballet aired as a television special in 1983.
1983 85m/C Dorothy Hamill. VHS, Beta $19.95 VMK *ℐ*

The Nutcracker Prince The classic children's Christmas tale comes alive in this feature-length animated special.
1991 75m/C CA *D:* Paul Schibli; *V:* Kiefer Sutherland, Megan Follows, Michael MacDonald, Phyllis Diller, Peter O'Toole. VHS, LV, 8mm $19.98 WAR, WTA *ℐℐ*

Nutcracker Sweet Ridiculous drama about a beautiful and powerful socialite (Collins) who runs a renowned ballet company with an iron fist. A Russian ballerina defects and infiltrates Collins's company to try out her own treacherous motives.
1984 101m/C Joan Collins, Finola Hughes, Paul Nicholas; *D:* Anwar Kawadri. VHS, Beta $69.98 LIV, VES *ℐ*

Nutcracker: The Motion Picture A lavish, stage-bound filmization of the Tchaikovsky ballet, designed by Maurice Sendak.

1986 82m/C Pacific Northwest Ballet; *D:* Carroll Ballard. VHS, Beta $14.95 PAR, KRT, KAR *ℐ*

Nuts A high-priced prostitute attempts to prove her sanity when she's accused of manslaughter. Ashamed of her lifestyle, and afraid of her reasons for it, her parents attempt to institutionalize her. A filmed version of Tom Topor's play that manages to retain its mesmerizing qualities. Fine performances, although the funnygirl goes over the top on several occasions. Score by Streisand.
1987 (R) 116m/C Barbra Streisand, Richard Dreyfuss, Maureen Stapleton, Karl Malden, James Whitmore, Robert Webber, Eli Wallach, Leslie Nielsen; *D:* Martin Ritt. VHS, Beta, LV, 8mm $19.98 WAR *ℐℐ*

Nuts in May Two smug, middle-aged, middle-class vegetarians go on a camping trip and totally alienate their cynical, working-class fellow campers.
1976 84m/C GB Alison Steadman; *D:* Mike Leigh. VHS $79.95 WBF, BTV *ℐℐ*

The Nutty Professor A mild-mannered chemistry professor creates a potion that turns him into a suave, debonair, playboy type with an irresistible attraction to women. Lewis has repeatedly denied the slick character is a Dean Martin parody, but the evidence is quite strong. Easily Lewis's best film.
1963 107m/C Jerry Lewis, Stella Stevens, Howard Morris, Kathleen Freeman; *D:* Jerry Lewis. VHS, Beta, LV $14.95 PAR *ℐℐℐ*

Nyoka and the Tigermen The adventures of the jungle queen Nyoka and her rival Vultura in their search for the lost tablets of Hippocrates. In 15 episodes. *AKA:* Nyoka and the Lost Secrets of Hippocrates; Perils of Nyoka.
1942 250m/B Kay Aldridge, Clayton Moore; *D:* William Witney. VHS, LV $29.98 VCN, REP, MLB *ℐℐℐ*

O Lucky Man Surreal, black comedy following the rise and fall and eventual rebirth of a modern British coffee salesman. Several actors play multiple roles with outstanding performances throughout. Price's excellent score combines with the hilarity for an extraordinary experience.
1973 (R) 178m/C GB Malcolm McDowell, Ralph Richardson, Rachel Roberts, Arthur Lowe, Alan Price, Helen Mirren, Mona Washbourne; *D:* Lindsay Anderson. VHS, Beta $29.95 WAR *ℐℐℐℐ*

O Pioneers! Lange plays Alexandra Bergson, an unmarried woman at the turn of the century, who inherits her family's Nebraska homestead because her father knows how much she loves the land. Although the family has prospered through Alexandra's smart investments, her brothers come to resent her influence. When her first love returns after fifteen years and the romance is rekindled, family resentments surface once again. Based on the novel by Willa Cather. A Hallmark Hall of Fame presentation.
1991 (PG) 99m/C Jessica Lange, David Strathairn, Tom Aldredge, Reed Edward Diamond, Anne Heche, Heather Graham, Josh Hamilton, Leigh Lawson; *W/D:* Glenn Jordan. VHS, LV $14.98 REP, FCT *ℐℐ½*

O Youth and Beauty Film dealing with one of author Cheever's favorite themes, the American male's fear of losing his identity. Frustrated by the onset of age, a man tries to recapture his college years and athletic ability by hurdling furniture. From the "Cheever Short Stories" series.
1979 60m/C Michael Murphy, Kathryn Walker. VHS, Beta FLI *ℐℐ*

Oasis of the Zombies European students set out to find buried treasure in Saharan oasis but instead find bevy of hungry Nazis with eating disorders.
1982 75m/C SP FR Manuel Gelin, France Jordan, Jeff Montgomery, Miriam Landson, Eric Saint-Just, Caroline Audret, Henry Lambert; *D:* A.M. Frank. VHS, Beta $59.95 UHV *ℐ*

Oath of Vengeance Billy the Kid rides the West once more.
1944 50m/B Buster Crabbe, Al "Fuzzy" St. John, Jack Ingram, Charles King; *D:* Sam Newfield. VHS, Beta $27.95 VCN *ℐ½*

The Object of Beauty Two Americans, trapped in Europe by their love of pleasure and their lack of money, bicker over whether to sell their one object of value - a tiny Henry Moore sculpture. When it disappears, their relationship is challenged. Excellent acting and telling direction. Forces an examination of one's own value placement.
1991 (R) 105m/C Andie MacDowell, John Malkovich, Joss Ackland, Lolita Davidovich, Peter Riegert, Bill Paterson, Rudi Davies; *D:* Michael Lindsay-Hogg. VHS, LV $89.95 LIV *ℐℐℐ*

Objective, Burma! Deemed by many to be the greatest and most moving World War II production released during the war. American paratroopers are dropped over Burma where their mission is to destroy a Japanese radar station. The Americans led by Flynn are successful in wiping out the station, but they are spotted and descended upon by Japanese forces. Impeded from returning to Allied lines, the American soldiers must try to survive enemy encounters, exhaustion, starvation, and the elements until they are rescued. Splendid performance by Flynn and exceptional direction from Walsh; these excellent performances are enhanced by Waxman's energetic score.
1945 142m/B Errol Flynn, James Brown, William Prince, George Tobias, Henry Hull, Warner Anderson, Richard Erdman, Mark Stevens, Anthony Caruso, Hugh Beaumont; *D:* Raoul Walsh; *W:* Ranald MacDougall, Lester Cole; *M:* Franz Waxman. VHS, Beta $19.98 MGM *ℐℐℐℐ*

Oblomov A production of the classic Goncharov novel about a symbolically inert Russian aristocrat whose childhood friend helps him find a reason for action. Well made, with fine performances. In Russian with English subtitles. *AKA:* A Few Days in the Life of I.I. Oblomov; Neskolko Dnei iz Zhizni I.I. Oblomov.
1981 145m/C RU Oleg Tabakov, Elena Solovei; *D:* Nikita Mikhalkov. VHS, Beta $59.95 TPV, KIV, AUD *ℐℐℐ*

The Oblong Box Coffins, blood, and live corpses fill drawn-out and lifeless adaptation of Edgar Allan Poe story. English aristocrat Price attempts to hide his disfigured brother in an old tower. Brother predictably escapes and rampages through town before being killed. *AKA:* Edgar Allen Poe's The Oblong Box.
1969 (PG) 91m/C GB Vincent Price, Christopher Lee, Alastair Williamson, Hilary Dwyer, Peter Arne, Harry Baird, Carl Rigg, Sally Geeson, Maxwell Shaw; *D:* Gordon Hessler. VHS, Beta $69.99 HBO *ℐℐ*

The Obsessed Uninspiring story with Farrar suspected of murdering his wife. Competent performances, but this mystery isn't developed with any sense of style and the killer's real identity will be obvious to anyone watching. Cliches and stereotyped situations don't add anything. *AKA:* The Late Edwina Black.

N

1951 77m/B *GB* David Farrar, Geraldine Fitzgerald, Roland Culver, Jean Cadell, Mary Merrall; *D:* Maurice Elvey. VHS, LV $16.95 *SNC, NOS, MOV* ✂✂

Obsessed Semi-realistic tale of a woman's exhausting desire for revenge against hit-and-run driver who killed her son. Cast acceptable but lack of psychological foundation weakens plot.
1988 (PG-13) 100m/C Kerrie Keane, Alan Thicke, Colleen Dewhurst, Saul Rubinek, Daniel Pilon, Lynne Griffin; *D:* Robin Spry. VHS, Beta, LV *NO* ✂½

Obsession A rich, lonely businessman meets a mysterious young girl in Italy, the mirror image of his late wife who was killed by kidnappers. Intriguing suspense film that's not quite up to comparisons with Hitchcock thrillers. Music by Hitchcock-collaborator Bernard Herrmann.
1976 (PG) 98m/C Cliff Robertson, Genevieve Bujold, John Lithgow; *D:* Brian DePalma. Academy Awards '76 Nominations: Best Original Score; National Board of Review Awards '76: 10 Best Films of the Year. VHS, Beta, LV $12.95 *COL, PIA, HHE* ✂✂½

Obsession: A Taste for Fear Diane's high fashion models are being killed and although there are plenty of suspects, she can't find the killer.
1989 (R) 90m/C Virginia Hey, Gerard Darmon, Carlo Mucari; *D:* Piccio Raffanini. VHS, Beta $89.95 *IMP* ✂½

Obsessive Love A lonely, mentally unstable typist (Mimieux) becomes obsessed with her soap opera hero and decides to go to Hollywood to seduce him. She transforms herself into a sleek and stunning Hollywood temptress to woo him, and at first he goes along with her—until he realizes that she is insane. An average made-for-TV movie of the older woman/younger man genre.
1984 97m/C Yvette Mimieux, Simon MacCorkindale, Kin Shriner, Constance McCashin, Allan Miller, Lainie Kazan; *D:* Steven Hilliard Stern. VHS $59.98 *LIV* ✂✂½

O.C. and Stiggs Two teens spend a summer harassing a neighbor and his family. Flimsy attempts at comedy fall flat. A failed adaptation of a National Lampoon short story, it was held for three years before release.
1987 (R) 109m/C Daniel H. Jenkins, Neill Barry, Jane Curtin, Tina Louise, Jon Cryer, Dennis Hopper, Paul Dooley, Ray Walston, Louis Nye, Martin Mull, Melvin Van Peebles; *D:* Robert Altman. VHS, Beta $79.98 *FOX* ✂½

The Occult Experience An engrossing study into the world of devil-worshippers, shamans, and the like. This documentary actually records exorcisms and other rituals. Not for the faint hearted.
1984 87m/C VHS, LV $14.95 *COL, SVS* ✂½

The Occultist Satan worshippers do the dance of death as they skin men alive for their evil purposes.
1989 82m/C Rick Gianasi. VHS, Beta $79.95 *UNI* Woof!

An Occurrence at Owl Creek Bridge A man is about to be hanged when the rope snaps, and he is able to swim to safety. He entertains thoughts of his family while making his way home. Suddenly, his new-found sweetness of life comes to a halt. Based on a short story by Ambrose Bierce. Telecast on "The Twilight Zone" in 1963.
1962 27m/B *FR D:* Robert Enrico. VHS, Beta $19.95 *FST, VYY, HEG* ✂✂✂½

An Occurrence at Owl Creek Bridge/Coup de Grace "Occurrence at Owl Creek Bridge" (1962), from a story by Ambrose Bierce documents the last moments of a man about to be hanged for sabotage. "Coup de Grace" (1978) tells the story of a group of friends who are caught up amongst the turmoil of the Bolshevik revolution.
1962 123m/B Margarethe von Trotta, Matthias Habich, Rudiger Kirschstein, Matthieu Carriere, Valeska Gert; *D:* Volker Schlondorff, Robert Enrico. VHS, Beta *HEG* ✂✂✂½

Ocean Drive Weekend Several college students congregate at "Ocean Drive" for a weekend of beer, sex, and dancing. Stereotypical characters, lack of plot, and poor versions of 1960 classics combine for boring and inane comedy.
1985 (PG-13) 98m/C Robert Peacock, Charles Redmond, Tony Freeman; *D:* Bryan Jones. VHS, Beta $69.98 *LIV, VES* Woof!

Ocean's 11 A gang of friends plans to rob five Las Vegas casinos simultaneously. Part of the "A Night at the Movies" series, this tape simulates a 1960 movie evening, with Bugs Bunny cartoon, "Person to Bunny;" a newsreel; and coming attractions for "The Sundowners" and "Sunrise at Campobello."
1960 148m/C Frank Sinatra, Dean Martin, Sammy Davis Jr., Angie Dickinson, Peter Lawford; *D:* Lewis Milestone. VHS, Beta, LV $19.98 *WAR* ✂½

Oceans of Fire Average rehash of the tension-filled world of oil riggers. Lives of two ex-cons are threatened when they hire on as divers for world's deepest undersea oil rig.
1986 (PG) 100m/C Gregory Harrison, Billy Dee Williams, Cynthia Sikes, Lyle Alzado, Tony Burton, Ray "Boom Boom" Mancini, David Carradine, Ken Norton; *D:* Steve Carver. VHS, Beta, LV $79.95 *VMK* ✂

Octagon Norris protects a woman from threatening Ninja warriors in average kung-fu adventure. Enough action and violence for fans of the genre.
1980 (R) 103m/C Chuck Norris, Karen Carlson, Lee Van Cleef, Kim Lankford, Art Hindle, Jack Carter; *D:* Eric Karson. VHS, Beta, LV $19.95 *MED* ✂✂

Octaman Comical thriller featuring non-threatening octopus-man discovered by scientists in Mexico. Rip-off of director Essex's own "Creature from the Black Lagoon." Not without its curiosity factor: young Rick Baker designed the octopus man, while actress Angeli died of a drug overdose during filming.
1971 79m/C Kerwin Mathews, Pier Angeli, Harry Guardino, David Essex, Jeff Morrow, Norman Fields; *D:* Harry Essex. VHS, Beta $19.95 *GEM, WWV, PSM* ✂½

Octavia A contemporary fable about a blind girl who befriends a convict and learns about life and love.
1982 (R) 93m/C Susan Curtis; *D:* David Beaird. VHS, Beta $59.98 *NLC* ✂

October Silent masterpiece based on John Reed's "Ten Days That Shook The World." Eisenstein, commissioned by the Soviet government, spared no expense to chronicle the Bolshevik Revolution of 1917 (in a flattering Communist light, of course). He was later forced to cut his portrayal of Leon Trotsky, who was then an enemy of the state. Includes rare footage of the Czar's Winter Palace in Leningrad. Haunting score by Shostakovich. *AKA:* Ten Days That Shook The World.
1927 103m/B *RU* VHS, LV $29.95 *WST, VYY, IHF* ✂✂✂½

October Man When a model is found murdered, a stranger with mental problems must prove his innocence to others and himself. Strong characters make good, suspensful mystery reminiscent of Hitchcock.
1948 95m/B John Mills, Joan Greenwood, Edward Chapman, Joyce Carey, Kay Walsh, Felix Aylmer, Juliet Mills; *D:* Roy Ward Baker. VHS, Beta *LCA* ✂✂✂

Octopussy The Bond saga continues as Agent 007 is on a mission to prevent a crazed Russian general from launching a nuclear attack against the NATO forces in Europe. Lots of special effects and gadgets keep weak plot moving.
1983 (PG) 140m/C *GB* Roger Moore, Maud Adams, Louis Jourdan, Kristina Wayborn, Kabir Bedi; *D:* John Glen; *M:* John Barry. VHS, Beta, LV $19.98 *MGM, FOX, TLF* ✂✂

The Odd Angry Shot Australian soldiers fighting in Vietnam discover the conflict is not what they expected. Ironic perspective of men struggling with their feelings about the war. More of an unremarkable drama with comic overtones than a combat film, it will appeal to those who prefer good direction to bloodshed.
1979 90m/C *AU D:* Tom Jeffrey. VHS, Beta $69.98 *LIV, VES* ✂✂½

The Odd Couple Two divorced men with completely opposite personalities move in together. Lemmon's obsession with neatness drives slob Matthau up the wall, and their inability to see eye-to-eye results in many hysterical escapades. A Hollywood rarity, it is actually better in some ways than Neil Simon's original Broadway version. Basis for the hit television series.
1968 (G) 106m/C Jack Lemmon, Walter Matthau; *D:* Gene Saks. VHS, Beta, LV $14.95 *PAR* ✂✂✂½

The Odd Job Insurance salesman Chapman, depressed after his wife leaves him, hires a hit man to kill himself. Chapman then has a hard time shaking his stalker after deciding he wants to live. Monty Python fans will enjoy seeing ex-troupe member Chapman again, but the comic's heart isn't in this unoriginal story.
1978 100m/C *GB* Graham Chapman; *D:* Peter Medak. VHS, Beta $69.95 *VES* ✂✂

Odd Jobs When five college friends look for jobs during summer break, they wind up running their own moving business with the help of the mob. Good comic talent, but a silly slapstick script results in only a passable diversion.
1985 (PG-13) 89m/C Paul Reiser, Scott McGinnis, Rick Overton, Robert Townsend; *D:* Mark Story. VHS, Beta $79.95 *HBO* ✂✂

Odd Man Out An Irish revolutionary is injured during a robbery attempt. Suffering from gunshot wounds and closely pursued by the police, he must rely on the help of others who could betray him at any moment. A gripping tale of suspense and intrigue that will keep the proverbial seat's edge warm until the final credits. Adapted from F.L. Green's novel, previously filmed as "The Last Man." *AKA:* Gang War.
1947 111m/B *GB* James Mason, Robert Newton, Dan O'Herlihy, Kathleen Ryan, Cyril Cusack; *D:* Carol Reed. Academy Awards '47 Nominations: Best Film Editing; British Academy Awards '47: Best Film; National Board of Review Awards '47: 10 Best Films of the Year. VHS, Beta, LV $19.95 *PAR* ✂✂✂

Odd Obsession One of Ichikawa's first films, about an elderly Japanese gentleman with a young wife whose feelings of jealousy and impotence eventually wreak havoc on

the marriage. In Japanese with English subtitles. *AKA:* The Key.
1960 96m/C *JP* Machiko Kyo, Ganjiro Nakamura; *D:* Kon Ichikawa. **VHS, Beta $19.95** COL, SUE, TAM *♫♫* ½

The Odd Squad Five GIs in World War II defend a bridge from the enemy, and manage in doing so to have loads of laughs.
1986 (R) 82m/C Johnny Dorelli, Vincent Gardenia; *D:* D.E.P. Clucher. **VHS, Beta $9.99** STE, PSM *♫*

Oddball Hall Two aging jewel thieves hide out in the African wilds, masquerading as powerful "wizards." When they head back to civilization, an African tribe beseeches the phony sorcerers to cure their long drought.
1991 (PG) 87m/C Don Ameche, Burgess Meredith. **VHS $89.98** WAR *♫♫*

Oddballs In another attempt to capitalize on the success of Bill Murray's "Meatballs," this summer camp story follows three campers and their pathetic attempts to lose their virginity. Brooks has his moments, but there is little else to recommend here.
1984 (PG-13) 92m/C Foster Brooks, Jason Sorokin, Wally Wodchis, Konnie Krome; *D:* Miklos Lente. **VHS, Beta $79.98** LIV Woof!

Odds and Evens Italian supercops pretend they don't have badges in order to clean up illegal betting and gambling rings in sunny Miami. Odds are this spaghetti cop-o-rama won't keep Morpheus at bay.
1978 (PG) 109m/C *IT* Terence Hill, Bud Spencer; *D:* Sergio Corbucci. **VHS, Beta $79.95** WAR *♫* ½

Ode to Billy Joe The 1967 Bobby Gentry hit song of the same title is expanded to tell why a young man jumped to his death off the Tallahatchie Bridge. The problems of growing up in the rural South and teenage romance do not match the appeal of the theme song. Benson and O'Connor, however, work well together.
1976 (PG) 106m/C Robby Benson, Glynnis O'Connor, Joan Hotchkis, Sandy McPeak, James Best; *D:* Max Baer. **VHS, Beta $19.98** CCB, WAR *♫♫*

The Odessa File During 1963, a German journalist attempts to track down some SS war criminals who have formed a secret organization called ODESSA. The story, from Frederick Forsyth's novel, drags in some places, but the scene where bad guy Schell and reporter Voight finally confront each other is a high point. Musical score by Andrew Lloyd Webber.
1974 (PG) 128m/C *GB* Jon Voight, Mary Tamm, Maximilian Schell, Maria Schell, Derek Jacobi; *D:* Ronald Neame. **VHS, Beta, LV $9.95** GKK *♫♫* ½

L'Odeur des Fauves One of a cynical reporter's scandalous stories gets an innocent man killed, compelling the reporter somehow to make restitution. Subtitled in English.
1966 86m/C *FR* Maurice Ronet, Josephine Chaplin, Vittorio De Sica; *D:* Richard Balducci. **VHS, Beta** KRT *♫*

The Odyssey of the Pacific Three young Cambodian refugees encounter retired train engineer Rooney living in the woods where a railway station once thrived. Together they work to restore an old locomotive. The ordinary, inoffensive script will not endanger quality family time. *AKA:* The Emperor of Peru.
1982 82m/C *CA* Mickey Rooney, Monique Mercure; *D:* Fernando Arrabal. **VHS, Beta $39.95** MCA *♫♫* ½

Oedipus Rex Contained, and highly structured rendering of Sophocles' Greek tragedy, by the Stratford (Ontario) Festival Players; this production belongs on the stage, not the screen. Rain went on to be the voice of the Hal 9000 computer in Stanley Kubrick's "2001: A Space Odyssey." *AKA:* King Oedipus.
1957 87m/C *CA* Douglas Campbell, Douglas Rain, Eric House, Eleanor Stuart; *D:* Tyrone Guthrie. **VHS** HMV, WBF *♫♫* ½

Oedipus Rex A new twist on the famous tragedy as Pasolini gives the story a modern prologue and epilogue. The classic plot has Oedipus spiraling downward into moral horror as he tries to avoid fulfilling the prophecy that he will murder his father and sleep with his mother. Cross-cultural curiosities include Japanese music and Lenin-inspired songs, some written by Pasolini who also stars as the high priest. In Italian with English subtitles. *AKA:* Edipo Re.
1967 110m/C *IT* Franco Citti, Silvana Mangano, Alida Valli, Julian Beck, Pier Paolo Pasolini; *D:* Pier Paolo Pasolini. **VHS $59.95** FST, TAM, FCT *♫♫♫*

Of Cooks and Kung-Fu A martial arts culinary adventure.
198? 90m/C Jacky Cheng, Chia Kai, Lee Kuen. **VHS, Beta $57.95** OCE *♫♫*

Of Human Bondage The first movie version of W. Somerset Maugham's classic novel in which a young, handicapped medical student falls in love with a crude cockney waitress, in a mutually destructive affair. Established Davis's role as the tough, domineering woman. Remade in 1946 and 1964.
1934 84m/B Bette Davis, Leslie Howard, Frances Dee, Reginald Owen, Reginald Denny, Alan Hale Jr.; *D:* John Cromwell. **VHS, Beta, LV, 3/4U, Special order formats $9.95** NEG, MRV, NOS *♫♫♫*

Of Human Bondage An essentially decent man falls fatally in love with an alluring but heartless waitress, who subtly destroys him. Based on the W. Somerset Maugham novel. Miscast and least interesting of the three film versions, although Novak gives a good performance.
1964 100m/B *GB* Kim Novak, Laurence Harvey, Robert Morley, Roger Livesey, Siobhan McKenna; *D:* Henry Hathaway, Ken Hughes; *W:* Bryan Forbes. **VHS, Beta $24.95** MGM *♫♫*

Of Mice and Men A powerful adaptation of the classic Steinbeck tragedy about the friendship between two itinerant Southern ranch hands during the Great Depression. Chaney is wonderful as the gentle giant and mentally retarded Lenny, cared for by migrant worker Meredith. They both get into an irreversible situation when a woman is accidentally killed. Music by Aaron Copland.
1939 107m/C Lon Chaney Jr., Burgess Meredith, Betty Field, Bob Steele, Noah Beery Jr., Charles Bickford; *D:* Lewis Milestone. **VHS, Beta $59.95** NO *♫♫♫♫*

Of Mice and Men Made-for-television remake of the classic Steinbeck tale, casting TV's Baretta (Blake) as George and Quaid as Lenny. Worth watching.
1981 150m/C Robert (Bobby) Blake, Randy Quaid, Lew Ayres, Mitchell Ryan, Ted Neely, Cassie Yates, Pat Hingle, Whitman Mayo, Dennis Fimple, Pat Corley; *D:* Reza Badiyi. **VHS, Beta $14.99** STE, PSM, KUI *♫♫♫*

Of Mice and Men Set on the migratory farms of California, John Steinbeck's novel covers the friendship of the simple-minded Lennie, his protector George, and a flirtatious farm wife who doesn't know Lennie's strength. Director Sinise got permission from

Steinbeck's widow to film the novel (actually the third adaptation).
1992 (PG-13) 110m/C John Malkovich, Sherilyn Fenn, Casey Siemaszko, Joe Morton, Ray Walston, Gary Sinise, John Terry, Richard Riehle; *D:* Gary Sinise; *W:* Horton Foote. **VHS, LV $94.99** MGM, PMS *♫♫♫* ½

Of Unknown Origin Weller encounters a mutated rampaging rat in his New York townhouse while his family is away on vacation. His house becomes the battleground in a terror-tinged duel of survival. A well-done rat thriller not for those with a delicate stomach.
1983 (R) 88m/C *CA* Peter Weller, Jennifer Dale, Lawrence Dane, Kenneth Welsh, Louis Del Grande, Shannon Tweed; *D:* George P. Cosmatos. **VHS, Beta $19.98** WAR *♫♫* ½

Off Beat A shy librarian unluckily wins a spot in a police benefit dance troupe, and then falls in love with a tough police woman. With a screenplay by playwright Mark Medoff, and a good supporting cast, it still manages to miss the mark.
1986 (PG) 92m/C Judge Reinhold, Meg Tilly, Cleavant Derricks, Fred Gwynne, John Turturro, Jacques D'Amboise, James Tolkan, Joe Mantegna, Harvey Keitel, Amy Wright; *D:* Michael Dinner. **VHS, Beta, LV $79.95** TOU *♫* ½

Off Limits When a boxing manager is drafted into the Army, he freely breaks regulations in order to train a fighter as he sees fit. Hope and Rooney, while not in peak form, make a snappy duo in this amusing romp.
1953 89m/B Bob Hope, Mickey Rooney, Marilyn Maxwell, Marvin Miller; *D:* George Marshall. **VHS, Beta, LV $19.98** KRT *♫♫* ½

Off Limits A spree of murders involving Vietnamese hookers draws two cops from the Army's Criminal Investigation Department into the sleazy backstreets of 1968 Saigon. There is little mystery as to who the killer is in this tale that seems written more for the sake of foul language and gratuitous gunfights than actual plot.
1987 (R) 102m/C Willem Dafoe, Gregory Hines, Fred Ward, Scott Glenn, Amanda Pays, Keith David, David Alan Grier; *D:* Christopher Crowe. **VHS, Beta, LV $14.98** FOX *♫* ½

Off on a Comet An animated adaptation of the Jules Verne story about a group of people carried through the cosmos on a comet. In HiFi.
1979 52m/C VHS, Beta $19.95 MGM *♫* ½

Off the Mark Neely is a young athlete suffering from a childhood affliction that causes spasms in his legs. Facing the ultimate challenge, he must overcome his handicap and defeat a talented woman athlete and a Russian student in a triathlon competition. An unremarkable effort, it had a limited one-week run in theaters.
1987 (R) 89m/C Mark Neely, Terry Farrell, Jon Cypher, Clarence Gilyard Jr.; *D:* Bill Berry. **VHS, Beta** FRH *♫♫*

Off the Wall Two hitchhikers wind up in a southern maximum security prison after being accused of a crime they did not commit. What follows is a series of shenanigans as they try to escape. This supposed comedy falls flat in every way with the possible exception of Arquette's portrayal of the governor's daughter.
1982 (R) 86m/C Paul Sorvino, Rosanna Arquette, Patrick Cassidy, Billy Hufsey, Monte Markham, Mickey Gilley; *D:* Rick Friedberg. **VHS, Beta $29.98** LIV, VES *♫*

Off Your Rocker Representatives of a corporate conglomerate find that the residents of Flo Adler's Mapleview Nursing Home can still muster stiff resistance to a threatened takeover.
1980 99m/C Milton Berle, Red Buttons, Lou Jacobi, Dorothy Malone, Helen Shaver, Sharon Acker, Helen Hughes; **D:** Morley Markson, Larry Pall. **VHS, Beta $59.95** *ONE* ✂✂½

The Offence Connery plays a London detective who beats a suspected child molester to death during a police interrogation. Turns out he's reacting to a long-buried molestation incident from his own childhood. A chilling psycho-drama highlighted by a strong lead performance by Connery. **AKA:** Something Like the Truth.
1973 (R) 108m/C *GB* Sean Connery, Trevor Howard, Vivien Merchant, Ian Bannen, Derek Newark, John Hallam, Peter Bowles; **D:** Sidney Lumet. **VHS $14.95** *MGM* ✂✂✂

Offerings After a boy is tormented by a gang of children who cause him to fall down a well, his resulting brain injuries turn him into a psychopathic killer. Seeking revenge ten years later, he systematically murders his oppressors, offering bits of their anatomy to the one girl who treated him kindly. A typical slasher movie, the plot is only slightly better than the worst examples of the genre.
1989 (R) 96m/C G. Michael Smith, Loretta L. Bowman; **D:** Christopher Reynolds. **VHS, Beta $89.95** *SGE* ✂

Office Romances A woman who has moved to London from the country is seduced by her employer. Because of her plain appearance, she is flattered by his attention even though he is married and has no real feelings for her. Competently made, nonetheless hard to watch because of the slow pace.
1986 60m/C *GB* Judy Parfitt, Ray Brooks, Suzanne Burden. **VHS, Beta $11.95** *PSM* ✂✂

An Officer and a Gentleman Young drifter Gere, who enters Navy Officer Candidate School because he doesn't know what else to do with his life, becomes a better person almost despite himself. Winger is the love interest who sets her sights on marrying Gere, and Gossett is the sergeant who whips him into shape. Strong performances by the whole cast made this a must-see in 1982 that is still appealing, despite the standard Hollywood premise.
1982 (R) 126m/C Richard Gere, Louis Gossett Jr., David Keith, Lisa Eilbacher, Debra Winger, Robert Loggia, Lisa Blount; **D:** Taylor Hackford; **M:** Jack Nitzsche. Academy Awards '82: Best Song ("Up Where We Belong"), Best Supporting Actor (Gossett); Nominations: Best Actress (Winger), Best Film Editing, Best Original Screenplay, Best Original Score. **VHS, Beta, LV, 8mm $14.95** *PAR, FCT, BTV* ✂✂✂

The Official Story A devastating drama about an Argentinian woman who realizes her young adopted daughter may be a child stolen from one of the thousands of citizens victimized by the country's repressive government. A powerful, important film. In Spanish with English subtitles or dubbed. **AKA:** La Historia Oficial; The Official History; The Official Version.
1985 (R) 112m/C *AR* Norma Aleandro, Hector Alterio, Chunchuna Villafane, Patricio Contreras; **D:** Luis Puenzo. Academy Awards '85: Best Foreign Language Film; Nominations: Best Original Screenplay; Cannes Film Festival '85: Best Actress (Aleandro); Golden Globe Awards '86: Best Foreign Film. **VHS, Beta, LV $19.95** *PAV, APD, AUD* ✂✂✂½

Offnight When a man is put on the day shift for the first time in fifteen years, his turns to chaos.
1984 47m/C VHS, Beta *NO* ✂½

The Offspring In four stories of past evils Price reveals his hometown can force folks to kill. Not the usual Price material: dismemberment, cannibalism, and necrophilia clash with his presence. Strong yuk factor. **AKA:** From a Whisper to a Scream.
1987 (R) 99m/C Vincent Price, Cameron Mitchell, Clu Gulager, Terry Kiser, Susan Tyrrell, Harry Caesar, Rosalind Cash, Martine Beswick, Angelo Rossitto, Lawrence Tierney; **D:** Jeff Burr. **VHS, Beta, LV $14.95** *LIV* ✂✂

Oh, Alfie In every man's life, there comes a time to settle down... but never when you're having as much fun as Alfie! Inadequate sequel to "Alfie." **AKA:** Alfie Darling.
1975 (R) 99m/C *GB* Joan Collins, Alan Price, Jill Townsend; **D:** Ken Hughes. **VHS, Beta $59.95** *MON, HHE* ✂✂

Oh, Bloody Life! Young actress faces deportation during the Stalin era in Hungary because of her aristocratic family ties. In Hungarian with English subtitles.
1988 115m/C *HU* Udvaros Dorottya, Szacsvay Laszlo, Kern Andras, Bezeredi Zoltan, Oze Lajos, Lukacs Margit; **W/D:** Peter Bacso. **VHS $49.95** *EVD, TAM* ✂✂½

Oh! Calcutta! Film version of the first nude musical to play on Broadway, which caused a sensation in the late 1960s. It's really a collection of skits, some of which were written by such notables as John Lennon, Sam Shepard, and Jules Feiffer. And it's not that funny or erotic.
1972 105m/C Bill Macy, Mark Dempsey, Raina Barrett, Samantha Harper, Patricia Hawkins, Mitchell McGuire; **D:** Guillaume Martin Aucion. **VHS, Beta $29.95** *VID* ✂½

Oh Dad, Poor Dad (Momma's Hung You In the Closet & I'm Feeling So Sad) Cult fave black comedy about a bizarre family on a vacation in Jamaica. The domineering mother travels with a coffin containing the stuffed body of her late husband. Additional corpses abound. Based on the play by Arthur L. Kopit.
1967 86m/C Rosalind Russell, Robert Morse, Barbara Harris, Hugh Griffith, Lionel Jeffries, Jonathan Winters; **D:** Richard Quine. **VHS, Beta $49.95** *PAR* ✂✂

Oh, God! God, in the person of Burns, recruits Denver as his herald in his plan to save the world. Despite initial skepticism, Denver, in his film debut, keeps faith and is rewarded. Sincere performances and optimistic end make for satisfying story. Followed by "Oh God! Book 2" and "Oh God! You Devil."
1977 (PG) 104m/C George Burns, John Denver, Paul Sorvino, Ralph Bellamy, Teri Garr, William Daniels, Donald Pleasence, Barnard Hughes, Barry Sullivan, Dinah Shore, Jeff Corey, David Ogden Stiers; **D:** Carl Reiner. **VHS, Beta, LV $19.98** *WAR* ✂✂½

Oh, God! Book 2 Burns returns as the "Almighty One" in strained sequel to "Oh God!" This time he enlists the help of a young girl to remind others of his existence. The slogan she concocts saves God's image, but not the movie. Followed by "Oh, God! You Devil."
1980 (PG) 94m/C George Burns, Suzanne Pleshette, David Birney, Louanne, Conrad Janis, Wilfrid Hyde-White, Hans Conried, Howard Duff; **D:** Gilbert Cates. **VHS, Beta $19.98** *WAR* ✂

Oh, God! You Devil During his third trip to earth, Burns plays both the Devil and God as he first takes a struggling musician's soul, then gives it back. A few zingers and light atmosphere save unoriginal plot. The second sequel to "Oh, God!"
1984 (PG) 96m/C George Burns, Ted Wass, Roxanne Hart, Ron Silver, Eugene Roche, Robert Desiderio; **D:** Paul Bogart. **VHS, Beta, LV $19.98** *WAR* ✂✂

Oh, Heavenly Dog! A private eye returns from the dead as a dog to solve his own murder. Man's best friend and intelligent to boot. The famous dog Benji's third film, and his acting improves with each one. Adults may find this movie slow, but kids will probably love it.
1980 (PG) 104m/C Chevy Chase, Jane Seymour, Omar Sharif, Robert Morley; **D:** Joe Camp. **VHS, Beta $19.98** *FOX* ✂✂

Oh, Mr. Porter Billeted at an obscure railway post, the stationmaster hero renovates the place and hires a special train to transport the area soccer team. Trouble arises when the train is hijacked by gun smugglers.
1937 85m/B *GB* Will Hay, Moore Marriot, Graham Moffatt, Frederick Piper; **D:** Marcel Varnel. **VHS $19.95** *NOS* ✂½

Oh Susannah Robbed and thrown from a train, Autry and the two drifters who rescue him follow the thieves to Mineral Springs. Their journey is plagued by too many songs and the bad guys are predictably punished in the end.
1938 59m/B Gene Autry, Booth Howard, Smiley Burnette, Frances Grant, Donald Kirke, Clara Kimball Young; **D:** Joseph Cane. **VHS, Beta $19.95** *NOS, VDM, HHT* ✂½

Oh, What a Night Bittersweet coming of age tale about a lonely 17-year-old (Haim) who has moved with his father and step-mother to a chicken farm in 1955 Ontario. After struggling with the untimely death of his mother, Haim falls in love with an older woman who has a husband and two kids. Features a great fifties soundtrack and beautiful scenes of the Canadian countryside.
1992 (PG-13) 93m/C *CA* Corey Haim, Barbara Williams, Keir Dullea, Genevieve Bujold, Robbie Coltrane; **D:** Eric Till. **VHS, LV $89.95** *COL, NLC* ✂✂

O'Hara's Wife Loving wife Harley continues to care for her family even after her untimely death. Only husband Asner, however, can see her ghost. Lightweight, made-for-television drama traps good cast.
1982 87m/C Ed Asner, Mariette Hartley, Jodie Foster, Tom Bosley, Perry Lang, Ray Walston; **D:** William S. Bartman. **VHS, Beta $69.95** *VES* ✂½

O.H.M.S. Convoluted story about a New York hood (Ford) who flees to England where he joins the British Army by posing as a Canadian. He buddies up with Mills and they both fall for Lee. His regiment is sent to China, via ship, and Lee just happens to be a stowaway. In China, Ford manages to prove his worth by saving Lee from bandits. Maybe it's not supposed to make sense.
1937 71m/B *GB* Wallace Ford, John Mills, Anna Lee, Frank Cellier, Frederick Leister, Peter Croft; **D:** Raoul Walsh. **VHS** *HCV* ✂½

Oil Seven men fight a raging oil fire that threatens to destroy an entire country. Unfortunately, the movie is unable to ignite any interest at all.
1978 (PG) 95m/C Ray Milland, Woody Strode, Stuart Whitman, Tony Kendall, William Berger; **D:** Mircea Dragan. **VHS, Beta $19.95** *UHV* ✂

Oklahoma! Jones's film debut; a must-see for musical fans. A cowboy and country girl fall in love, but she is tormented by another unwelcomed suitor. At over two hours, cuteness wears thin for some. Actually filmed in Arizona. Adapted from Rodgers and Hammerstein's broadway hit with origi-

nal score; choreography by Agnes de Mille. ♫Oh, What a Beautiful Morning; Surrey with the Fringe on Top; I Cain't Say No; Many a New Day; People Will Say We're in Love; Poor Jud Is Dead; All 'Er Nuthin'; Everything's Up to Date in Kansas City; The Farmer and the Cowman; Out of My Dreams; Oklahoma; Kansas City; Pore Jud.
1955 145m/C Gordon MacRae, Shirley Jones, Rod Steiger, Gloria Grahame, Eddie Albert, Charlotte Greenwood, James Whitmore, Gene Nelson, Barbara Lawrence, Jay C. Flippen; **D:** Fred Zinneman; **W:** Sonya Levien, William Ludwig; **M:** Richard Rodgers, Oscar Hammerstein. Academy Awards '55: Best Sound, Best Score; Nominations: Best Color Cinematography, Best Film Editing. **VHS, Beta, LV $19.98** *FOX, RDG, HMV* 🎞🎞🎞½

Oklahoma Annie Storekeeper Canova joins the new sheriff in booting undesirables out of town, and tries to sing her way into his heart. Amazingly, it works—not for delicate ears.
1951 90m/C Judy Canova, Fuzzy Knight, Grant Withers, John Russell, Denver Pyle, Allen Jenkins, Almira Sessions; **D:** R.G. Springsteen. **VHS, Beta** *MLB* 🎞

Oklahoma Badlands Lane and his horse outsmart a corrupt newspaper publisher trying to steal land from a female rancher. An early directorial work for veteran stuntman Canutt.
1948 59m/B Allan "Rocky" Lane, Mildred Coles; **D:** Yakima Canutt. **VHS, Beta $29.95** *DVT* 🎞½

Oklahoma Bound A feisty farmer tries to save his failing farm through a series of ostensibly comedic, unsuccessful schemes.
1981 92m/C F.E. Bowling, Dan Jones; **D:** Patrick C. Poole. **VHS, Beta $19.95** *UHV* 🎞

Oklahoma Crude Sadistic oil trust rep Palence battles man-hating Dunaway for her well. Drifter Scott helps her resist on the promise of shared profits. In this 1913 setting, Dunaway tells Scott she wishes she could avoid men altogether, but later settles for him.
1973 (PG) 108m/C George C. Scott, Faye Dunaway, John Mills, Jack Palance, Harvey Jason, Woodrow Parfrey; **D:** Stanley Kramer. **VHS** *FOX* 🎞🎞½

Oklahoma Cyclone A group of bronco busters find action and adventure on the prairie. Second of eight talkies in Steele series, includes his first of few singing roles.
1930 64m/B Bob Steele, Al "Fuzzy" St. John, Nita Ray, Charles King; **D:** John P. McCarthy. **VHS $19.95** *NOS, GPV, DVT* 🎞½

Oklahoma Kid Offbeat, hilarious western with Bogie as the villain and gunfighter Cagney seeking revenge for his father's wrongful death. Highlight is Cagney's rendition of "I Don't Want To Play In Your Yard," complete with six-shooter accompaniment.
1939 82m/B James Cagney, Humphrey Bogart, Rosemary Lane, Ward Bond, Donald Crisp, Charles Middleton, Harvey Stephens; **D:** Lloyd Bacon. **VHS, Beta $19.98** *MGM* 🎞🎞🎞

The Oklahoman A routine western with some trivia value. Town doc McCrea helps Indian Pate keep his land. Talbott plays Indian maiden in same year as her title role in Daughter of Jekyll. Continuity buffs will note Hale wears the same outfit in m ost scenes.
1956 80m/C Joel McCrea, Barbara Hale, Brad Dexter, Gloria Talbott, Verna Felton, Douglas Dick, Michael Pate; **D:** Francis D. Lyon. **VHS, Beta $19.98** *FOX* 🎞🎞

Old Barn Dance Autry and his singing cowboys are selling horses until a crooked tractor company puts them out of business. They join a radio program, discovers that it is owned by the same company that put them

out of the horse-selling business, and runs the crooks out of town.
1938 54m/B Gene Autry, Smiley Burnette, Roy Rogers; **D:** Joseph Kane. **VHS, Beta $19.95** *NOS, VCN, DVT* 🎞½

Old Boyfriends Shire is weak as a psychologist searching for old boyfriends in order to analyze her past. Strange combination of Carradine and Belushi may draw curious fans. Screenplay by Leonard and Paul Schrader.
1979 (R) 103m/C Talia Shire, Richard Jordan, John Belushi, Keith Carradine, John Houseman, Buck Henry; **D:** Joan Tewkesbury; **W:** Leonard Schrader, Paul Schrader. **VHS, Beta, LV $9.95** *NLC* 🎞🎞

Old Corral Sheriff Autry protets his love interest, a girl fleeing the Mob. *AKA:* Texas Serenade.
1936 54m/B Gene Autry, Roy Rogers, Smiley Burnette; **D:** Joseph Kane. **VHS, Beta $19.95** *NOS, MRV, DVT* 🎞🎞

The Old Curiosity Shop Webster and Benson are an old gambler and his daughter in this well-made film adaptation of the Dickens tale. Their miserly landlord tries to ruin their lives by evicting them and forcing them into a life of poverty. Remade as "Mr. Quilp" in 1957.
1935 90m/B Ben Webster, Elaine Benson, Hay Petrie, Beatrix Thompson, Gibb McLaughlin, Reginald Purdell; **D:** Thomas Bentley. **VHS $19.95** *NOS* 🎞🎞½

The Old Curiosity Shop Flat musical version of the Charles Dickens story about an evil man who wants to take over a small antique shop run by an elderly man and his granddaughter. ♫When a Felon Needs a Friend; Somewhere; Love Has the Longest Memory; Happiness Pie; The Sport of Kings; What Shouldn't Happen to a Dog; Quilp. *AKA:* Mr. Quilp.
1975 (G) 118m/C *GB* Anthony Newley, David Hemmings, David Warner, Jill Bennett, Peter Duncan, Michael Hordern; **D:** Michael Tuchner. **VHS, Beta $39.98** *SUE* 🎞🎞

The Old Curiosity Shop An animated adaptation of the classic Dickens story about a young girl and her grandfather who are evicted from their curiosity shop by an evil man.
1984 (G) 72m/C **VHS, Beta $19.98** *LIV* 🎞🎞

The Old Dark House An atmospheric horror film, with more than a touch of comedy, well-directed by Whale. In an old haunted house live the bizarre Femm family: the 102 year-old patriarch, an atheist son, a religious fanatic daughter, and a crazed pyromanic son, all watched over by the mute, scarred, and psychotic butler (Karloff's first starring role). Into this strange group wander five unsuspecting, stranded travelers who set all sorts of dastardly plots in motion. Based on the novel "Benighted" by J.B. Priestley.
1932 71m/B Boris Karloff, Melvyn Douglas, Charles Laughton, Gloria Stuart, Ernest Thesiger, Raymond Massey, Lillian Bond, Eva Moore, Brember Wills, John Dudgeon; **D:** James Whale. **VHS $29.95** *FCT* 🎞🎞🎞

Old Enough Slow-moving coming-of-age comedy on the rich kid-poor kid friendship theme. Silver's directing debut; she's also responsible for the screenplay.
1984 (PG) 91m/C Sarah Boyd, Rainbow Harvest, Neill Barry, Danny Aiello, Susan Kingsley, Roxanne Hart, Alyssa Milano, Fran Brill, Anne Pitoniak; **D:** Marisa Silver. **VHS, Beta $59.95** *MED* 🎞🎞

Old Explorers Two old friends refuse to let old age lessen their want for excitement, so they get together on a regular basis to set out on dangerous, imaginary adventures. They search for Atlantis, explore the Himalayan Mountains, and visit the Bermuda Triangle. After one of the men survives a stroke, the two set out on a real-life adventure on a tugboat cruising down the Mississippi River. Although the leads put in strong performances, they can't hide the slow-moving plot or the thin action sequences. Based on the play by James Cada and Mark Keller.
1990 (PG) 91m/C Jose Ferrer, James Whitmore, Jeffrey Gadbois, Caroline Kaiser, William Warfield, Christopher Pohlad, Storm Richardson, William M. Pohlad. **VHS, LV $89.95** *ACA* 🎞🎞½

Old Gringo Adapted from Carlos Fuentes' novelization of writer Ambrose Bierce's mysterious disappearance in Mexico during the revolution of 1913. Features Fonda in the unlikely role of a virgin schoolteacher, Smits as her revolutionary lover, and Peck as her hero. Soggy acting by all but Peck, whose presence is wasted in a sketchy character. Technical problems and cheesy sets and costumes—look for the dusk backdrop in the dance scene and Smits' silly moustache. Better to read the book.
1989 (R) 119m/C Jane Fonda, Gregory Peck, Jimmy Smits, Patricio Contreras, Jenny Gago, Gabriela Roel, Sergio Calderon, Guillermo Rios, Anne Pitoniak, Pedro Armendariz Jr.; **D:** Luis Puenzo. **VHS, Beta, LV, 8mm $14.95** *COL* 🎞🎞½

Old Gun A grief-plagued doctor finds he must seek out and kill each Nazi involved in the slaughter of his wife and child to ease his pain. Excellent directing and a fully formed main character.
1976 141m/C Philippe Noiret, Romy Schneider, Jean Bouise; **D:** Robert Enrico. **VHS, Beta $49.95** *MED* 🎞🎞

Old Ironsides Silent, black-and-white version of the big budget/important director and stars action-adventure. Merchant marines aboard the famous Old Ironsides battle 19th century Barbary pirates in rousing action scenes. Home video version features an engaging organ score by Gaylord Carter. Based on the poem "Constitution" by Oliver Wendell Holmes.
1926 111m/B Esther Ralston, Wallace Beery, Boris Karloff, Charles Farrell, George Bancroft; **D:** James Cruze. **VHS, Beta $29.95** *PAR* 🎞🎞🎞

The Old Maid After her beau is killed in the Civil War, a woman allows her cousin to raise her illegitimate daughter, and therein begins a years-long struggle over the girl's affections. High grade soaper based on Zoe Adkin's stage adaptation of Edith Wharton's novel.
1939 96m/B Bette Davis, Miriam Hopkins, George Brent, Donald Crisp, Jane Bryan, Louise Fazenda, Henry Stephenson; **D:** Edmund Goulding. **VHS, Beta $19.95** *MGM* 🎞🎞🎞

Old Mother Riley's Ghosts A group of spies "haunt" Mother Riley's castle home in a futile attempt to scare her out; she turns the tables. Some good scares and laughs. Part of the Old Mother Riley series. Look for similarities to later Monty Python films.
1941 82m/B *GB* Arthur Lucan, Kitty McShane, John Stuart; **D:** John Baxter. **VHS, Beta $16.95** *NOS, SNC* 🎞🎞

Old Spanish Custom Only a Keaton fan could love this comedy, set in Spain and filmed in England. One of his rarest—and poorest—sound films. He plays a bumbling rich yachtsman smitten with Tovar, a Spanish maiden who uses him to make her lover jealous. *AKA:* The Invader.

1936 58m/B *GB* Buster Keaton, Lupita Tova, Lyn Harding, Esme Percy; **D:** Adrian Brunel. **VHS, Beta** $19.95 *GPV, VDM, VYY* 🐾

Old Swimmin' Hole Small-town friends Moran and Jones try to bring their single parents together; his mother can't afford to finance his dream to be a doctor. Dull, melodramatic ode to heartland America, reminiscent of "Our Town." *AKA:* When Youth Conspires.
1940 78m/B Marcia Mae Jones, Jackie Moran, Leatrice Joy, Charles D. Brown; **D:** Robert McGowan. **VHS, Beta** $29.95 *VYY* 🐾🐾

Old Yeller Disney Studios' first and best boy-and-his-dog film. Fifteen-year-old Kirk is left in charge of the family farm while Parker is away. When his younger brother brings home a stray dog, Kirk is displeased but lets him stay. Yeller saves Kirk's life, but contracts rabies in the process. Kirk is forced to kill him. Keep tissue handy, especially for the kids. Stong acting, effective scenery—all good stuff. Based on the novel by Fred Gipson. Sequel "Savage Sam" released in 1963.
1957 (G) 84m/C Dorothy McGuire, Fess Parker, Tommy Kirk, Kevin Corcoran, Jeff York, Beverly Washburn, Chuck Connors; **D:** Robert Stevenson. **VHS, Beta, LV** $19.99 *DIS* 🐾🐾🐾½

Oldest Living Graduate Fonda is memorable in his last stage role as the oldest graduate of a Texas military academy. He and his son clash when Fonda refuses to give up his land. Teleplay features strong performances from Leachman and other big-name cast members.
1982 75m/C Cloris Leachman, Henry Fonda, John Lithgow, Timothy Hutton, Harry Dean Stanton, David Ogden Stiers, George Grizzard, Penelope Milford. **VHS, Beta** $49.95 *VHE* 🐾🐾🐾½

Oldest Profession A study of prostitution from prehistoric times to the future. Generally unexciting and unfunny. In six segments meant as vehicles for their directors. *AKA:* Le Plus Vieux Metier du Monde.
1967 97m/C *FR GE IT* Raquel Welch, Jeanne Moreau, Elsa Martinelli, Michele Mercier; **D:** Jean-Luc Godard, Philippe de Broca, Claude Autant-Lara, Franco Indovina, Mauro Bolognini, Michael Pfleghar. **VHS, Beta, LV** $19.95 *STE, NWV, IME* 🐾

Oliver! Splendid big-budget musical adaptation of Dickens' "Oliver Twist." An innocent orphan is dragged into a life of crime when he is befriended by a gang of pickpockets. 🎵Food, Glorious Food; Oliver; Boy For Sale; Where Is Love?; Consider Yourself; Pick a Pocket or Two; I'd Do Anything; Be Back Soon; As Long As He Needs Me; Who Will Buy?; It's a Fine Life; Reviewing the Situation; Oom-Pah-Pah.
1968 (G) 145m/C *GB* Mark Lester, Jack Wild, Ron Moody, Shani Wallis, Oliver Reed, Hugh Griffith; **D:** Carol Reed. Academy Awards '68: Best Art Direction/Set Decoration, Best Director (Reed), Best Picture, Best Sound, Best Score; Nominations: Best Actor (Moody), Best Adapted Screenplay, Best Cinematography, Best Costume Design, Best Film Editing, Best Supporting Actor (Wild); Golden Globe Awards '69: Best Actor—Musical/Comedy (Moody), Best Film—Musical/Comedy; National Board of Review Awards '68: 10 Best Films of the Year. **VHS, Beta, LV** $19.95 *COL, BTV, HMV* 🐾🐾🐾½

Oliver Twist Silent version of the Dickens classic is a vehicle for young Jackie Coogan. As orphan Oliver Twist, he is subjected to many frightening incidents before finding love and someone to care for him. Remade numerous times, most notably in 1933 and 1948 and as the musical "Oliver!" in 1968.

1922 77m/B Jackie Coogan, Lon Chaney Sr., Gladys Brockwell, George Siegmann, Esther Ralston; **D:** Frank Lloyd. **VHS, Beta** $19.95 *NOS, CCB* 🐾🐾🐾

Oliver Twist The first talking version of Dickens' classic about an ill-treated London orphan involved with youthful gang of pickpockets. Moore was too young—at five—to be very credible in the lead role. The 1948 version is much more believable.
1933 70m/B Dickie Moore, Irving Pichel, William Boyd, Barbara Kent; **D:** William J. Cowan. **VHS, Beta** $19.95 *NOS, MRV, HHT* 🐾🐾

Oliver Twist Charles Dickens' immortal story of a workhouse orphan who is forced into a life of crime with a gang of pickpockets. The best of many film adaptations, with excellent portrayals by the cast.
1948 116m/C *GB* Robert Newton, John Howard Davies, Alec Guinness, Francis L. Sullivan, Anthony Newley, Kay Walsh, Diana Dors, Henry Stephenson; **D:** David Lean. **VHS, Beta, LV** $19.95 *PAR, DVT, FHS* 🐾🐾🐾🐾

Oliver Twist Good made-for-television version of the classic Dicken's tale of a boy's rescue from a life of crime. Scott's Fagin is a treat, and period details are on the mark. Scripted by James Goldman.
1982 72m/C George C. Scott, Tim Curry, Michael Hordern, Timothy West, Lysette Anthony, Eileen Atkins, Cherie Lunghi; **D:** Clive Donner. **VHS, Beta** $19.98 *VES* 🐾🐾🐾

Oliver Twist A British television miniseries adaptation of the Charles Dickens classic about an orphan boy plunging into the underworld of 19th-century London. On two tapes.
1985 333m/C *GB* Ben Rodska, Eric Porter, Frank Middlemass, Gillian Martell. **VHS, Beta** $29.98 *FOX, SIG, HMV* 🐾🐾🐾

Oliver's Story A "not so equal" sequel to "Love Story," where widower O'Neal wallows in grief untils rich heiress Bergen comes along. He falls in love again, this time with money.
1978 (PG) 90m/C Ryan O'Neal, Candice Bergen, Ray Milland, Edward Binns, Nicola Pagetti, Charles Haid; **D:** John Korty. **VHS, Beta** $19.95 *PAR* 🐾

Olivia Abused housewife moonlights as a prostitute and begins killing her customers. She falls in love with an American businessman and flees to America when her husband finds out about the affair. Revenge and murder are the result.
1983 90m/C Suzanna Love, Robert Walker Jr., Jeff Winchester; **D:** Ulli Lommel. **VHS, Beta** $49.95 *VHE* 🐾½

Olivier, Olivier Holland's directorial follow-up to "Europa, Europa" is based on a 1984 French newspaper story and evokes "The Return of Martin Guerre" and its update, "Sommersby." Much beloved nine-year-old boy disappears from his home in a small French town and his dysfunctional family unit falls apart. Mom obsesses and falls into trances, dad escapes to North Africa, and sister Nadine develops telekinetic powers in order to cope. Six years later a detective brings an amnesiac teenager, who has been working as a hustler in Paris, to the boy's family. Is it the missing Olivier? Dad returns from North Africa, Olivier's mother embraces him wholeheartedly, and skeptical Nadine goes to bed with him. All the family members, in some fashion, need to believe in the truth of Olivier's reappearance. Spooky, provocative, and emotionally resonate. In French with English subtitles.
1992 (R) 110m/C *FR* Francois Cluzet, Brigitte Rouan, Gregoire Colin, Marina Golovine, Jean-Francois Stevenin, Frederic Quiring; **D:** Agnieszka Holland; **W:** Agnieszka Holland. **VHS** *NYR* 🐾🐾🐾

Olly Olly Oxen Free Junkyard owner Hepburn helps two boys fix up and fly a hot-air balloon, once piloted by McKenzie's grandfather, as a surprise for the man's birthday. Beautiful airborne scenes over California and a dramatic landing to the tune of the "1812 Overture," but not enough to make the whole film interesting. *AKA:* The Great Balloon Adventure.
1978 89m/C Katharine Hepburn, Kevin McKenzie, Dennis Dimster, Peter Kilman; **D:** Richard A. Colla. **VHS, Beta** *TLF* 🐾🐾

Olongape: The American Dream A young woman works in a cheap bar while waiting for the chance to come to America.
1989 97m/C Jacklyn Jose, Susan Africa, Chanda Romero, Joel Torre, Marilou Sadiua; **D:** Chito Rono. **VHS, Beta** $59.95 *TWE* 🐾½

Omar Khayyam In medieval Persia, Omar (Wilde) becomes involved in a romance with the Shah of Persia's fiancee, while trying to fight off a faction of assassins trying to overthrow the Shah. Although this film has a great cast, the script is silly and juvenile, defeating the cast's fine efforts.
1957 101m/C Cornel Wilde, Michael Rennie, Debra Paget, Raymond Massey, John Derek, Yma Sumac, Margaret Hayes, Joan Taylor, Sebastian Cabot; **D:** William Dieterle. **VHS** *PAR* 🐾🐾

Omega Cop In a post-apocalyptic future, there's only one cop left. He uses his martial arts skills and tons of guns attempting to rescue three women, but the violence doesn't cover the poor acting and shoddy production. Fans of TV's Batman might enjoy this for West's presence.
1990 (R) 89m/C Ron Marchini, Adam West, Stuart Whitman, Troy Donahue, Meg Thayer, Jennifer Jostyn, Chrysti Jimenez, D.W. Landingham, Chuck Katzakian; **D:** Paul Kyriazi. **VHS** $14.95 *HMD* 🐾

Omega Man In post-holocaust Los Angeles, Heston is immune to the nuclear effects and battles those who aren't—an army of vampires bent on destroying what's left of the world. Strong suspense with considerable violence, despite the PG rating. Based on the science fiction thriller "I Am Legend," by Richard Matheson.
1971 (PG) 98m/C Charlton Heston, Anthony Zerbe, Rosalind Cash, Paul Koslo; **D:** Boris Sagal. **VHS, Beta** $14.95 *WAR* 🐾🐾½

Omega Syndrome Neo-Nazis kidnap Wahl's daughter. He and Vietnam buddy DiCenzo get her back. Ho hum. DiCenzo's is the best performance. Tolerable for vigilante film fans.
1987 (R) 90m/C Ken Wahl, Ron Kuhlman, George DiCenzo, Doug McClure; **D:** Joseph Manduke. **VHS, Beta** $14.95 *NWV, STE* 🐾½

The Omen A young boy who has been adopted into an American diplomat's family is later realized to be the son of Satan. Bizarre and inexplicable deaths seem to happen when he is around. The shock and gore that was prevalent in "The Exorcist" is replaced in this film with more suspense and believable effects. Well-done horror film that doesn't insult the viewer's intelligence. Followed by two sequels: "Damien—Omen II" and "The Final Conflict." *AKA:* Birthmark.
1976 (R) 111m/C Gregory Peck, Lee Remick, Billie Whitelaw, David Warner, Holly Palance, Richard Donner; **D:** Richard Donner; **M:** Jerry Goldsmith. Academy Awards '76: Best Original Score; Nominations: Best Song ("Ave Satani"). **VHS, Beta, LV** $19.98 *FOX* 🐾🐾½

Omen IV: The Awakening It turns out Damien of Omens past had a daughter, Delia, who takes up where dear old devilish Dad left off. Delia is adopted by your basic

clueless couple and proceeds to wreak havoc wherever she goes, including getting rid of several interfering adults. She also plans to make her adoptive father, a U.S. senator, President, so that his delightful child anti-Christ can have him carry out all her evil plans.
1991 97m/C Faye Grant, Michael Woods, Michael Lerner, Asia Vieira; *D:* Jorge Montesi, Dominique Othenin-Girard. VHS $89.98 FXV *᪄᪄*

Omoo Omoo, the Shark God A sea captain is cursed when he removes the black pearls from a stone shark god in this extremely cheap adventure.
1949 58m/B Ron Randell, Devera Burton, Trevor Bardette, Pedro de Cordoba, Richard Benedict, Rudy Robles, Michael Whalen, George Meeker; *D:* Leo Leonard. VHS $16.95 SNC *᪄*

On a Clear Day You Can See Forever A psychiatric hypnotist helps a girl stop smoking and finds that in trances she remembers previous incarnations. He falls in love with one of the women she used to be. Alan Jay Lerner of ''My Fair Lady'' and ''Camelot'' wrote the lyrics and the book. Based on a musical by Lerner and Burton Lane. ♫On a Clear Day, You Can See Forever; Come Back to Me; What Did I Have That I Don't Have?; He Isn't You; Hurry, It's Lovely Up Here; Go To Sleep; Love with All the Trimmings; Melinda.
1970 (G) 129m/C Barbra Streisand, Yves Montand, Bob Newhart, Jack Nicholson, Simon Oakland; *D:* Vincente Minnelli. VHS, Beta, LV $14.95 PAR *᪄᪄*

On an Island with You Williams plays a movie star who finds romance on location in Hawaii in this musical extravaganza. Contains many of Williams' famous water ballet scenes and a bevy of bathing beauties. ♫On an Island with You; If I Were You; Taking Miss Mary to the Ball; Dog Song; Buenas Noches, Buenos Aires; Wedding Samba; I Can Do Without Broadway, But Can Broadway Do Without Me?.
1948 107m/C Esther Williams, Peter Lawford, Ricardo Montalban, Jimmy Durante, Cyd Charisse, Leon Ames; *D:* Richard Thorpe. VHS $19.98 MGM *᪄᪄½*

On Approval Hilarious British farce in which two women trade boyfriends. Lillie's performance provides plenty of laughs. Brook runs the show as leading man, co-author, director, and co-producer. Based on the play by Frederick Lonsdale.
1944 80m/B *GB* Clive Brook, Beatrice Lillie, Googie Withers, Roland Culver; *D:* Clive Brook. VHS, Beta $19.95 NOS, MRV, HHT *᪄᪄᪄*

On Borrowed Time Engrossing tale of Death (Hardwicke) coming for an old man (Barrymore) who isn't ready to die so he traps him in his backyard apple tree. Performances are first rate in this good adaptation of the stage success (originally by Eugene O'Neill). Hardwicke is especially a standout; he gave up theatre for Hollywood after making this film.
1939 99m/B Lionel Barrymore, Cedric Hardwicke, Beulah Bondi, Una Merkel, Bob Watson, Henry Travers; *D:* Harold Bucquet. VHS $19.98 MGM *᪄᪄᪄*

On Dangerous Ground A world-weary detective is sent to the countryside to investigate a murder. He encounters the victim's revenge-hungry father and the blind sister of the murderer. In the hateful father the detective sees a reflection of the person he has become. In the blind woman, he learns the redeeming qualities of humanity and compassion. A well-acted example of film noir that features the composer Bernard Herrman's favorite score.

1951 82m/B Robert Ryan, Ida Lupino, Ward Bond, Ed Begley Sr., Cleo Moore, Charles Kemper; *D:* Nicholas Ray. VHS, Beta, LV $39.95 TTC *᪄᪄᪄*

On Golden Pond Henry Fonda won his first, and long overdue, Oscar for his role as the curmudgeonly patriarch of the Thayer family. He and his wife have grudgingly agreed to look after a young boy while at their summer home in Maine. Through his gradually affectionate relationship with the boy, Fonda learns to allay his fears of mortality. He also gains an understanding of his semi-estranged daughter. Jane Fonda plays his daughter and Hepburn is his loving wife in this often funny adaptation of Ernest Thompson's 1978 play. Predictable but deeply moving. Henry Fonda's final screen appearance.
1981 (PG) 109m/C Henry Fonda, Jane Fonda, Katharine Hepburn, Dabney Coleman, Doug McKeon, William Lanteau; *D:* Mark Rydell; *W:* Ernest Thompson. Academy Awards '81: Best Actor (Fonda), Best Actress (Hepburn); Nominations: Best Actor (Fonda), Best Cinematography, Best Director (Rydell), Best Film Editing, Best Sound, Best Supporting Actress (Fonda), Best Original Score; British Academy Awards '82: Best Actress (Hepburn); Golden Globe Awards '82: Best Actor—Drama (Fonda), Best Film—Drama. VHS, Beta, LV, SVS $14.95 FHE, SUP, KAR *᪄᪄᪄½*

On Her Majesty's Secret Service In the sixth 007 adventure, Bond again confronts the infamous Blofeld, who is planning a germ-warfare assault on the entire world. Australian Lazenby took a crack at playing the super spy, with mixed results. Many feel this is the best-written of the Bond films and might have been the most famous, had Sean Connery continued with the series. Includes the song ''We Have All the Time In the World,'' sung by Louis Armstrong.
1969 (PG) 144m/C *GB* George Lazenby, Diana Rigg, Telly Savalas, Gabriel Ferzetti, Ilse Steppat, Bernard Lee, Lois Maxwell, Desmond Llewelyn, Catherine Schell, Julie Ege, Joanna Lumley, Mona Chong, Anouska Hempel, Jenny Hanley; *D:* Peter Hunt; *W:* John Barry. VHS, Beta, LV $19.98 MGM, FOX, TLF *᪄᪄᪄*

On Moonlight Bay Set in small-town Indiana in 1917 with Day as the tomboyish Marjorie who falls for college man MacRae. Her father (Ames) doesn't approve but the trouble really begins when Marjorie's younger brother gets into trouble at school. The incorrigible Wesley (Gray) blames everything on dear old dad and MacRae feels he must come to Marjorie's rescue! Gray steals the movie as the bratty brother—otherwise its business as usual. Based on Booth Tarkington's ''Penrod'' stories and followed by ''By the Light of the Silvery Moon.'' ♫Love Ya; On Moonlight Bay; Till We Meet Again; Pack Up Your Troubles In Your Old Kit Bag; I'm Forever Blowing Bubbles; Christmas Story; Tell Me Why Nights Are Lonely; Cuddle Up a Little Closer; Every Little Movement Has a Meaning All Its Own.
1951 95m/C Doris Day, Gordon MacRae, Leon Ames, Billy Gray, Rosemary DeCamp, Mary Wickes, Ellen Corby, Esther Dale; *D:* Roy Del Ruth; *W:* Melville Shavelson, Jack Rose; *M:* Max Steiner. VHS, LV $59.95 WAR *᪄᪄½*

On the Air Live with Captain Midnight Socially challenged teen finds hipness as a rebel DJ operating an illegal radio station from his van. Leading actor is the son of the director/writer/producer but nepotism does not a good film make. *AKA:* Captain Midnight.
1979 90m/C Tracy Sebastian; *D:* Ferd Sebastian. VHS, Beta NO *᪄½*

On the Beach A group of survivors attempt to live normal lives in post-apocalyptic Australia, waiting for the inevitable arrival of killer radiation. Astaire is strong in his first dramatic role. Though scientifically implausible, still a good anti-war vehicle. Based on the best-selling novel by Nevil Shute.
1959 135m/B Gregory Peck, Anthony Perkins, Donna Anderson, Ava Gardner, Fred Astaire; *D:* Stanley Kramer. Academy Awards '59 Nominations: Best Film Editing, Best Original Score; National Board of Review Awards '59: 10 Best Films of the Year. VHS, Beta, LV $19.98 FOX, FCT *᪄᪄᪄½*

On the Block Beautiful babe has trouble walking street in Baltimore.
1991 (R) 96m/C Howard E. Rollins Jr., Marilyn Jones, Blaze Starr. VHS $89.95 VMK *᪄½*

On the Comet Zeman's fourth fantasy based on Jules Verne stories, about a chunk of the Earth's crust suddenly becoming a comet and giving its passengers a ride through the galaxy. Complete with Zeman's signature animation fantasias. In English. *AKA:* Na Komete; Hector Servadac's Ark.
1968 76m/C *CZ* Emil Horvath Jr., Magda Vasarykova, Frantisek Filipovsky; *D:* Karel Zeman. VHS, Beta $19.99 FCT, MRV *᪄᪄᪄*

On the Edge A narcotics agent tracks down a wealthy Brazilian drug kingpin.
1982 82m/C Anthony Steffen. VHS, Beta NO *᪄*

On the Edge A drama about the inevitable Rocky-esque triumph of Dern as an aging marathon runner. Simultaneous to his running endeavor, Dern is trying to make up for lost time with his father. Available in two versions, one rated, the other unrated with a racy appearance by Pam Grier as the runner's interracial lover.
1986 (PG-13) 86m/C Bruce Dern, John Marley, Bill Bailey, Jim Haynie, Pam Grier; *D:* Rob Nilsson. VHS, Beta NO *᪄᪄½*

On the Edge: The Survival of Dana Another entry from the world of low-quality made-for-TV films. A young girl moves with her family to a new town. When she falls in with the ''bad'' crowd, her ethical standards are challenged. A stinker that may appeal to those with campy tastes. Not for the discriminating palate.
1979 92m/C Melissa Sue Anderson, Robert Carradine, Marion Ross, Talia Balsam, Michael Pataki, Kevin Breslin, Judge Reinhold, Barbara Babcock; *D:* Jack Starrett. VHS, Beta GEM *Woof!*

On the Line Two Mexico-US border guards, one hard-bitten, the other sympathetic to the illegal immigrants' plight, battle it out over a beautiful Mexican whore. Disjointed and confusing.
1983 95m/C *SP* David Carradine, Victoria Abril, Scott Wilson, Sam Jaffe, Jesse Vint; *D:* Jose Luis Borau. VHS, Beta $19.98 SUE, NLC *᪄½*

On the Nickel An ex-alcoholic returns to Fifth Street in Los Angeles to save his friend from a life of despair. Tom Waits' musical score enhances this sentimental skid row drama. Scripted, directed and produced by ''The Waltons''' Waite.
1980 (R) 96m/C Ralph Waite, Donald Moffatt, Hal Williams, Jack Kehoe; *D:* Ralph Waite. VHS, Beta $69.95 VES *᪄᪄*

On the Night Stage Gruff bandit (legendary Hart) loses his girl-of-questionable-values to town preacher. One of the first feature length westerns.
1915 83m/B William S. Hart, Robert Edeson, Rhea Mitchell, Shorty Hamilton; *D:* Reginald Barker. VHS, Beta, 8mm $29.95 GPV, VYY *᪄᪄*

On the Old Spanish Trail Rogers becomes a singing cowboy with a traveling tent show in order to pay off a note signed by the Sons of the Pioneers.
1947 56m/B Roy Rogers, Jane Frazee, Andy Devine, Tito Guizar; **D:** William Witney. **VHS, Beta $9.95** NOS, MRV, VCN �🐾½

On the Right Track Young orphan living in Chicago's Union Station has the gift of being able to pick winning race horses. May be appealing to fans of Coleman and "Different Strokes" television show, but lacks the momentum to keep most viewers from switching tracks.
1981 (PG) 98m/C Gary Coleman, Lisa Eilbacher, Michael Lembeck, Norman Fell, Maureen Stapleton, Herb Edelman; **D:** Lee Philips. **VHS, Beta $59.95** FOX �🐾

On the Run An ex-con and his gal cut a law-defying swath through the Bayou.
1985 (R) 96m/C Jack Conrad, Rita George, Dub Taylor, David Huddleston. **VHS, Beta $59.95** GEM �🐾

On the Third Day A headmaster finds a mysterious stranger in his house who turns out to be his long-lost illegitimate son.
1983 101m/C Richard Marant, Catherine Schell, Paul Williamson. **VHS, Beta $59.95** LHV �🐾

On the Town Kelly's directorial debut features three sailors on a one day leave search for romance in the Big Apple. Filmed on location in New York City, with uncompromisingly authentic flavor. Based on the successful Broadway musical, with a score composed by Leonard Bernstein, Betty Comden, and Adolph Green. Additional songs by Roger Edens. ♫New York, New York; I Feel Like I'm Not Out of Bed Yet; Come Up to My Place; Miss Turnstiles Ballet; Main Street; You're Awful; On the Town; You Can Count on Me; Pearl of the Persian Sea; Pre-Historic Man; That's All There Is, Folks; A Day in New York.
1949 98m/C Gene Kelly, Frank Sinatra, Vera-Ellen, Ann Miller, Betty Garrett; **D:** Gene Kelly, Stanley Donen. **VHS, Beta, LV $19.98** MGM �🐾🐾🐾

On the Waterfront A trend-setting, gritty portrait of New York dock workers embroiled in union violence. Cobb is the gangster union boss, Steiger his crooked lawyer, and Brando, Steiger's ex-fighter brother who "could've been a contender!" Intense performances and excellent direction stand up well today. The picture was a huge financial success.
1954 108m/B Marlon Brando, Rod Steiger, Eva Marie Saint, Lee J. Cobb, Karl Malden; **D:** Elia Kazan; **W:** Budd Schulberg. Academy Awards '54: Best Actor (Brando), Best Art Direction/Set Decoration (B & W), Best Black and White Cinematography, Best Director (Kazan), Best Film Editing, Best Picture, Best Story & Screenplay, Best Supporting Actress (Saint); Nominations: Best Supporting Actor (Cobb), Best Supporting Actor (Malden, Steiger), Best Original Score; Directors Guild of America Awards '54: Best Director (Kazan); Golden Globe Awards '55: Best Actor—Drama (Brando), Best Director (Kazan), Best Film—Drama; National Board of Review Awards '54: 10 Best Films of the Year; New York Film Critics Awards '54: Best Actor (Brando), Best Director (Kazan), Best Film. **VHS, Beta, LV $19.95** COL, PIA, BTV �🐾🐾🐾🐾

On the Yard An attempt to realistically portray prison life. Focuses on a murderer who runs afoul of the leader of the prisoners and the system. A fairly typical prison drama with above average performances from Heard and Kellin.
1979 (R) 102m/C John Heard, Thomas G. Waites, Mike Kellin, Joe Grifasi; **D:** Raphael D. Silver. **VHS, Beta $69.95** MED �🐾🐾

On Top of Old Smoky Autry and the Cass County Boys are mistaken for Texas Rangers by a gang of land poachers.
1953 59m/B Gene Autry, Smiley Burnette, Gail Davis, Sheila Ryan; **D:** George Archainbaud. **VHS, Beta $29.98** CCB �🐾½

On Top of the Whale Two scholars move onto the estate of strange but wealthy benefactor to conduct research on the few survivors of a disappearing clan of Indians. Two tribesmen speak bizarre dialect which utilizes only one word while others confound the researchers with stories of ghosts and graveyards. Dutch comedy subtitled in English.
1982 93m/C NL **D:** Raul Ruiz. **VHS $59.95** KIV, FCT, TAM �🐾🐾

On Valentine's Day Author Horton Foote based this story loosely on his parents' lives. A wealthy young Southern girl marries a poor but decent young man and finds herself ostracized from her family. A prequel to the same author's "1918." Produced with PBS for "American Playhouse." **AKA:** Story of a Marriage.
1986 (PG) 106m/C Hallie Foote, Matthew Broderick, Michael Higgins, Steven Hill, William Converse-Roberts; **D:** Ken Harrison. **VHS, Beta $19.98** LHV �🐾🐾½

On Wings of Eagles During the 1979 Iranian revolution two American executives are imprisoned by Islamic radicals. Help arrives in the form of covert agents of their boss—Texas tycoon H. Ross Perot (played by Crenna). Don't expect strict historical veracity or insight from this network miniseries (based on the "nonfiction novel" by Ken Follett), an okay but lengthy "mission impossible." It came out in a two-cassette set, just in time for Perot's 1992 presidential campaign.
1986 221m/C Burt Lancaster, Richard Crenna, Paul LeMat, Esai Morales, Constance Towers, Jim Metzler, James Sutorius, Lawrence Pressman, Karen Carlson, Cyril O'Reilly; **D:** Andrew V. McLaglen. **VHS $89.95** WOV �🐾🐾

Onassis Romanticized biography of Greek shipping magnate Aristotle Onassis, from the poverty of his youth to his later wealth and family and romantic liaisons and tragedies. Julia is adequate as the title character but English actress Annis is badly miscast as Jackie Kennedy Onassis. However, Seymour is terrific as Onassis' lover, opera star Maria Callas. Quinn, who played Onassis in "The Greek Tycoon," plays Onassis' father in this one. Based on the novel by Peter Evans. Originally a made for television miniseries known as "The Richest Man in the World: The Story of Aristotle Onassis."
1988 120m/C Raul Julia, Jane Seymour, Francesca Annis, Anthony Quinn, Anthony Zerbe, Lorenzo Quinn; **D:** Waris Hussein. **VHS, LV $89.98** TTC �🐾½

Once a Hero The dregs of society, the Cicero Gang, have taken Captain Justice's number one fan and his mother hostage. Is it really curtains for rosy cheeks, bubble gum, and apple pie? But wait, it's Captain Justice, the man, the myth, to the rescue!
1988 74m/C Jeff Lester, Robert Forster, Milo O'Shea; **D:** Claudia Weill. **VHS $9.99** NWV, STE �🐾🐾

Once Around Renata Bella (Hunter) is 30ish, lonely, and after a breakup with her longtime boyfriend, forced to move back home. At loose ends, she accepts a job selling vacation timeshares and meets a boisterous, self-assured (read utterly obnoxious) Lithuanian salesman, Sam Sharpe (Dreyfuss). Sam sweeps her off her feet and showers her with affection and gifts and then tries hard—too hard—to please her close-knit Italian family. Renata is torn between her love for her family and her love and loyalty to Sam. Casting doesn't get much better than the group assembled here and Hallstrom steers everyone to wonderful performances in his American directorial debut. One flaw is the script, a light romantic comedy that swerves into heavy drama at times: bring kleenex.
1991 (R) 115m/C Richard Dreyfuss, Holly Hunter, Danny Aiello, Gena Rowlands, Laura San Giacomo, Roxanne Hart, Danton Stone, Tim Guinee, Greg Germann; **D:** Lasse Hallstrom; **W:** Malia Scotch Marmo; **M:** James Horner. **VHS, Beta, LV $19.98** MCA, PIA, FCT �🐾🐾½

Once Before I Die Army soldiers caught in the Philippines during World War II struggle to survive and elude the Japanese. A single woman traveling with them becomes the object of their spare time considerations. A brutal, odd, and gritty war drama. Director/actor Derek was Andress' husband at the time.
1965 97m/C PH Ursula Andress, John Derek, Richard Jaeckel, Rod Lauren, Ron Ely; **D:** John Derek. **VHS** MOV �🐾🐾½

Once Bitten A centuries-old though still remarkably youthful vampiress comes to Los Angeles to stalk male virgins. That may be the wrong city, but she needs their blood to retain her youthful countenance. Vampire comedy theme was more effectively explored in 1979s Love at First Bite. Once Bitten is notable, however for the screen debut of comic Carrey who would later gain fame on the TV show In Living Color.
1985 (PG-13) 94m/C Lauren Hutton, Jim Carrey, Cleavon Little, Karen Kopins, Thomas Balltore, Skip Lackey; **D:** Howard Storm. **VHS, Beta, LV $79.98** LIV, VES �🐾

Once in Paris... A bittersweet romance about a scriptwriter working in Paris, the chauffeur who befriends him, and the aristocratic British woman with whom the writer falls in love. Beautiful French scenery and the engaging performance of Lenoir as the chauffeur make this film a diverting piece of entertainment.
1979 (PG) 100m/C Wayne Rogers, Gayle Hunnicutt, Jack Lenoir; **D:** Frank D. Gilroy. **VHS, Beta $9.95** SUE, MED �🐾🐾½

Once is Not Enough Limp trash-drama concerning the young daughter of a has-been movie producer who has a tempestuous affair with a writer who reminds her of her father. Based on the novel by Jacqueline Susann. **AKA:** Jacqueline Susann's Once is Not Enough.
1975 (R) 121m/C Kirk Douglas, Deborah Raffin, David Janssen, George Hamilton, Brenda Vaccaro, Alexis Smith, Melina Mercouri; **D:** Guy Green. Academy Awards '75 Nominations: Best Supporting Actress (Vaccaro); Golden Globe Awards '76: Best Supporting Actress (Vaccaro). **VHS, Beta $59.95** PAR �🐾½

Once Upon a Brothers Grimm An original musical fantasy in which the Brothers Grimm meet a succession of their most famous storybook characters including Hansel and Gretel, the Gingerbread Lady, Little Red Riding Hood, and Rumpelstiltskin.
1977 102m/C Dean Jones, Paul Sand, Cleavon Little, Ruth Buzzi, Chita Rivera, Teri Garr. **VHS, Beta $39.95** UHV �🐾

Once Upon a Crime Extremely disappointing comedy featuring a high profile cast set in Europe. The plot centers around Young and Lewis finding a dachshund and travelling from Rome to Monte Carlo to return the stray and collect a $5,000 reward. Upon arrival in Monte Carlo, they find the dog's owner dead and they end up getting implicated for the murder. Other prime suspects include Belushi, Candy, Hamilton, and Shepherd. Weak script is made bearable only by the comic genius of Candy.

1992 (PG) 94m/C John Candy, James Belushi, Cybill Shepherd, Sean Young, Richard Lewis, Ornella Muti, Giancarlo Giannini, George Hamilton, Joss Ackland, Elsa Martinelli; **D:** Eugene Levy. VHS $19.98 MGM 🐾½

Once Upon a Forest Socially concerned animated tale of three woodland creatures who get involved in a daring race against time when the life of their young friend is at stake. A tanker ruptures while rolling through their idyllic glen, spilling toxic gas and endangering the lives of the animals. Michelle the wee badger becomes ill, and her three "furling" friends set off in search of a herbal medicine to cure her. Ecologically correct story by "American Tail" creator David Kirschner is light on humor and heavier on the gloom, as the little animals encounter oppressive human society and their big, bad machines. Animation is serviceable, though not up to Don Bluth standards (and a long, long way from Disney). Crawford, the voice of Michelle's wise old uncle, has a song, while Vereen as a marsh bird with a yen for preaching breaks into a fervent gospel number written by Andrae Crouch. Produced by Hanna-Barbera. For an evening of anti-pollution, treat the earth kindly animation, see it with "Ferngully."

1993 m/C D: Charles Grosvenor; **W:** Mark Young, Kelly Ward; **V:** Michael Crawford, Ben Vereen. VHS 🐾🐾

Once Upon a Honeymoon Set in 1938, Grant is an American radio broadcaster reporting on the oncoming war. Rogers is the ex-showgirl who unknowingly marries a Nazi. In this strange, uneven comedy, Grant tries to get the goods on him and also rescue Rogers. The plot is basic and uneven with Grant attempting to expose the Nazi and save Rogers. However, the slower moments are offset by some fairly surreal pieces of comedy.

1942 116m/B Ginger Rogers, Cary Grant, Walter Slezak, Albert Dekker; **D:** Leo McCarey. VHS, Beta, LV $19.98 CCB, TTC, FCT 🐾🐾

Once Upon a Midnight Scary Price narrates a collection of three tales of terror, "The Ghost Belonged to Me," "The Legend of Sleepy Hollow," and "The House with a Clock in Its Walls." Aimed at the kiddies.

1990 50m/C Rene Auberjonois, Severn Darden; **D:** Neil Cox. VHS GEM, MRV 🐾🐾

Once Upon a Scoundrel A ruthless Mexican land baron arranges to have a young woman's fiancee thrown in jail so he can have her all to himself.

1973 (G) 90m/C Zero Mostel, Katy Jurado, Tito Vandis, Priscilla Garcia, A. Martinez; **D:** George Schaefer. VHS, Beta $9.99 STE, PSM 🐾🐾½

Once Upon a Time A pretty girl, her puppy, a charming prince, and a grinch combine for a magical, wondrous animated fantasy.

1976 (G) 83m/C VHS, Beta $29.95 GEM 🐾🐾½

Once Upon a Time Two rival tribes spoil the love of a prince and princess in ancient times. Animated.

1987 92m/C VHS, Beta $39.95 MED 🐾🐾½

Once Upon a Time in America The uncut original version of director Leone's saga of five young men growing up in Brooklyn during the '20s who become powerful mob figures. Also available in a 143-minute version. Told from the perspective of

De Niro's Noodles as an old man looking back at 50 years of crime, love, and death, told with a sweeping and violent elegance.

1984 (R) 225m/C Robert De Niro, James Woods, Elizabeth McGovern, Treat Williams, Tuesday Weld, Burt Young, Joe Pesci, Danny Aiello, Darlanne Fluegel, Jennifer Connelly; **D:** Sergio Leone; **M:** Ennio Morricone. VHS, Beta, LV $29.98 WAR 🐾🐾🐾½

Once Upon a Time in the West The uncut version of Leone's sprawling epic about a band of ruthless gunmen who set out to murder a mysterious woman waiting for the railroad to come through. Filmed in John Ford's Monument Valley, it's a revisionist western with some of the longest opening credits in the history of the cinema. Fonda is cast against type as an extremely cold-blooded villain. Script was coauthored by Leone, Bernardo Bertolucci, and Dario Argento and the brilliant score contributed by Ennio Morricone.

1968 (PG) 165m/C *IT* Henry Fonda, Jason Robards Jr., Charles Bronson, Claudia Cardinale, Keenan Wynn, Lionel Stander, Woody Strode, Jack Elam; **D:** Sergio Leone; **M:** Ennio Morricone. VHS, Beta, LV $24.95 PAR 🐾🐾🐾½

Once Upon a Time in Vietnam This politically irksome drama about Vietnam was filmed in Georgia. *AKA:* How Sleep the Brave.

198? 90m/C VHS, Beta VCD 🐾

One Against the Wind A true story of one woman's courage against great odds. British Mary Liddell and her children are living in Paris during the WWII Nazi occupation. Mary's secret agenda is to smuggle downed Allied pilots out of the country to safety without arousing Nazi suspicions. Great performances by Davis as the resourceful Mary and Neill as one of the pilots she rescues. A Hallmark Hall of Fame presentation.

1991 (PG) 96m/C Judy Davis, Sam Neill, Denholm Elliott, Anthony Higgins, Christien Anholt, Kate Beckinsale, Frank Middlemass; **D:** Larry Elikann. VHS $89.98 REP 🐾🐾🐾

One A.M. Charlie is a drunk who must first battle a flight of stairs in order to get to bed. Silent with music track.

1916 20m/B Charlie Chaplin. VHS, Beta, 3/4U, Special order formats CAB 🐾🐾🐾

The One and Only An egotistical young man is determined to make it in show business. Instead, he finds himself in the world of professional wrestling. Most of the humor comes from the wrestling scenes, with Winkler and Darby's love story only serving to dilute the film.

1978 (PG) 98m/C Henry Winkler, Kim Darby, Gene Saks, William Daniels, Harold Gould, Herve Villechaize; **D:** Carl Reiner. VHS, Beta $69.95 PAR 🐾🐾½

The One and Only, Genuine, Original Family Band A harmonious musical family becomes divided when various members take sides in the presidential battle between Benjamin Harrison and Grover Cleveland, a political era that has been since overlooked.

1968 (G) 110m/C Walter Brennan, Buddy Ebsen, Lesley Ann Warren, Kurt Russell, Goldie Hawn, Wally Cox, Richard Deacon, Janet Blair; **D:** Michael O'Herlihy. VHS, Beta, LV $9.99 DIS 🐾🐾🐾

One Arabian Night When an exotic dancer in a traveling carnival troupe is kidnapped into a harem, a dwarf acts on his unrequited love and avenges her death by murdering the sheik who killed her. Secured a place in American filmmaking for director Lubitsch. *AKA:* Sumurun.

1921 85m/B *GE* Pola Negri, Ernst Lubitsch, Paul Wegener; **D:** Ernst Lubitsch. VHS, Beta $29.95 FCT, GPV, GLV 🐾

The One Arm Swordsmen Many one-armed men are persecuted for the murder committed by one fugitive one-armed man, and they decide to group together to track him down themselves.

1972 109m/C VHS, Beta $39.95 UNI 🐾

One Armed Executioner An Interpol agent seeks revenge on his wife's murderers.

1980 (R) 90m/C Franco Guerrero, Jody Kay; **D:** Bobby A. Auarez. VHS, Beta PGN 🐾🐾

One Away Gypsy escapes from a South African prison and the police are in hot pursuit.

1980 (PG) 83m/C Elke Sommer, Bradford Dillman, Dean Stockwell. VHS, Beta $39.95 MON 🐾

One Body Too Many A mystery spoof about a wacky insurance salesman who's mistaken for a detective. The usual comedy of errors ensues. A contrived mish-mash—but it does have Lugosi going for it.

1944 75m/B Jack Haley, Jean Parker, Bela Lugosi, Lyle Talbot; **D:** Frank McDonald. VHS, Beta, 3/4U, Special order formats $19.95 NOS, SNC, HHT 🐾🐾

One Brief Summer Love triangles and intrigues abound on a spectacular country manor. An aging woman is mortified by her father's interest in a young seductress, who finds herself attracted to the old man, but not only him.

1970 (R) 86m/C Clifford Evans, Felicity Gibson, Jennifer Hilary, Jan Holden, Peter Egan; **D:** John MacKenzie. VHS $14.95 LPC Woof!

One Cooks, the Other Doesn't A most unlikely story of a man's ex-wife and his son moving back into his house, where he's now living with his new wife. Made for television.

1983 96m/C Suzanne Pleshette, Joseph Bologna, Rosanna Arquette, Oliver Clark; **D:** Richard Michaels. VHS, Beta $39.95 LIV 🐾🐾

One Crazy Summer A group of wacky teens spend a fun-filled summer on Nantucket Island in New England. This follow-up to "Better Off Dead" is offbeat and fairly charming, led by Cusack's perplexed cartoonist and with comic moments delivered by Goldthwait.

1986 (PG) 94m/C John Cusack, Demi Moore, William Hickey, Curtis Armstrong, Bob Goldthwait, Mark Metcalf; **D:** Steve Holland. VHS, Beta, LV $19.98 WAR 🐾🐾½

One Dark Night Two high school girls plan an initiation rite for one of their friends who is determined to shed her "goody-goody" image. West is the caped crusader of TV series "Batman" fame. *AKA:* Mausoleum.

1982 (R) 94m/C Meg Tilly, Adam West, David Mason Daniels, Robin Evans; **D:** Tom McLoughlin. VHS, Beta $69.95 HBO 🐾🐾½

One Day in the Life of Ivan Denisovich The film version of Nobel Prize-winner Alexander Solzhenitsyn's novel about a prisoner's experiences in a Soviet labor camp. A testament to human endurance. Photography be Sven Nykvist.

1971 105m/C *NO GB* Tom Courtenay, Alfred Burke, Espen Skjonberg, James Maxwell, Eric Thompson; **D:** Caspar Wrede. VHS, LV $79.95 SVS, TAM 🐾🐾

One Deadly Owner A made-for-television film about a possessed Rolls-Royce torturing its new owner. Quite a vehicle for the usually respectable set of wheels.

1974 80m/C Donna Mills, Jeremy Brett, Robert Morris, Laurence Payne. **VHS, Beta** $29.95 LIV ✗

One Deadly Summer Revenge drama about a young girl who returns to her mother's home village to ruin three men who had assaulted her mother years before. Very well acted. From the novel by Sebastien Japrisot. In French with English subtitles. **AKA:** L'Ete Meurtrier.
1983 (R) 134m/C FR Isabelle Adjani, Alain Souchon, Suzanne Flon; **D:** Jean Becker. **VHS, Beta** $59.95 MCA, TAM ✗✗✗

One Down, Two to Go! When the mob is discovered to be rigging a championship karate bout, two dynamic expert fighters join in a climactic battle against the hoods. Example of really bad "blaxploitation" that wastes talent, film, and the audience's time.
1982 (R) 84m/C Jim Brown, Fred Williamson, Jim Kelly, Richard Roundtree; **D:** Fred Williamson. **VHS, Beta** $59.95 MED, HHE Woof!

One-Eyed Jacks An often engaging, but lengthy, psychological western about an outlaw who seeks to settle the score with a former partner who became a sheriff. Great acting by all, particularly Brando, who triumphed both as star and director. Stanley Kubrick was the original director, but Brando took over mid-way through the filming. The photography is wonderful and reflects the effort that went into it.
1961 141m/C Marlon Brando, Karl Malden, Katy Jurado, Elisha Cook Jr., Slim Pickens, Ben Johnson, Pina Pellicer, Timothy Carey; **D:** Marlon Brando. **VHS, Beta, LV** $79.95 PAR ✗✗✗½

One-Eyed Soldiers Young woman, criminal, and dwarf follow trail to mysterious key to unlock $15 million treasure. Much cheesy intrigue.
1967 83m/C GB YU Dale Robertson, Lucianna Paluzzi; **D:** Jean Christopher. **VHS** NO ✗

One-Eyed Swordsman A handicapped samurai battles shogun warriors. With English subtitles.
1963 95m/C JP Tetsuro Tamba, Haruko Wanibuchi; **D:** Seiichiro Uchikawa. **VHS, Beta** VDA ✗

One False Move Black psycho Pluto, his white-trash partner Ray, and Ray's biracial lover Fantasia are three low-level drug dealers on the streets of Los Angeles who get involved in murder. Fleeing the city for Fantasia's small hometown in Arkansas, they come up against the local sheriff and two L.A. cops sent to bring them back. Not a typical crime thriller, first-time feature director Franklin is more interested in a psychological character study of racism and smalltown mores than in your average shoot 'em up action picture. Good performances, especially by Williams as the deceptive bad girl.
1991 (R) 105m/C Bill Paxton, Cynda Williams, Michael Beach, Jim Metzler, Earl Billings, Billy Bob Thornton; **D:** Carl Franklin; **W:** Billy Bob Thornton, Tom Epperson. **VHS, LV** $89.95 COL, FCT ✗✗✗

One Flew Over the Cuckoo's Nest Sweeping all major Academy Awards, this film is a touching, hilarious, dramatic, and completely effective adaptation of Ken Kesey's novel. Nicholson plays a two-bit crook, who, facing a jail sentence, feigns insanity to be sentenced to a cushy mental hospital. The hospital is anything but cushy, with a tyrannical head nurse out to squash any vestige of the patients' independence. Nicholson proves to be a crazed messiah and catalyst for these mentally troubled patients and a worthy adversary for the head nurse. A

classic that performs superbly on numerous levels.
1975 (R) 129m/C Jack Nicholson, Brad Dourif, Louise Fletcher, Will Sampson, William Redfield, Danny DeVito, Christopher Lloyd, Scatman Crothers; **D:** Vincent Schiavelli, Milos Forman; **W:** Ken Kesey; **M:** Jack Nitzsche. Academy Awards '75: Best Actor (Nicholson), Best Actress (Fletcher), Best Adapted Screenplay, Best Director (Forman), Best Picture; Nominations: Best Cinematography, Best Film Editing, Best Supporting Actor (Dourif), Best Original Score; British Academy Awards '76: Best Actor (Nicholson), Best Actress (Fletcher), Best Director (Forman), Best Film, Best Supporting Actor (Dourif); Golden Globe Awards '76: Best Actor—Drama (Nicholson), Best Actress—Drama (Fletcher), Best Director (Forman), Best Film—Drama; National Board of Review Awards '75: 10 Best Films of the Year, Best Actor (Nicholson); National Society of Film Critics Awards '75: Best Actor (Nicholson); People's Choice Awards '77: Best Film. **VHS, Beta, LV** $19.99 HBO, BTV ✗✗✗✗

One Frightened Night An eccentric millionaire informs his family members that he is leaving each of them one million dollars...as long as his long-lost granddaughter doesn't reappear. Guess who comes to dinner.
1935 69m/B Mary Carlisle, Wallace Ford, Hedda Hopper, Charley Grapewin; **D:** Christy Cabanne. **VHS, Beta** $19.95 NOS, KRT, VYY ✗✗½

One from the Heart The film more notable for sinking Coppola's Zoetrope studios than for its cinematic context. Garr and Forrest are a jaded couple who seek romantic excitement with other people. An extravagant (thus Coppola's finance problems) fantasy Las Vegas set, pretty to look at but does little to enhance the weak plot. Score by Waits, a much-needed plus.
1982 (R) 100m/C Teri Garr, Frederic Forrest, Nastassia Kinski, Raul Julia, Lainie Kazan, Rebecca DeMornay, Harry Dean Stanton; **D:** Francis Ford Coppola. **VHS, Beta, LV** $79.95 COL ✗✗

One Good Cop A noble, inconsistent attempt to do a police thriller with a human face, as a young officer and his wife adopt the three little daughters of his slain partner from the force. But it reverts to a routine action wrapup, with 'Batman' Keaton even donning a masked-avenger getup to get revenge.
1991 (R) 105m/C Michael Keaton, Rene Russo, Anthony LaPaglia, Kevin Conway, Rachel Ticotin, Grace Johnston, Blair Swanson, Rhea Silver-Smith, Tony Plana, Benjamin Bratt, Charlaine Woodard; **W/D:** Heywood Gould. **VHS, Beta, LV** $19.99 HPH ✗✗½

100 Rifles Native American bank robber and Black American lawman join up with a female Mexican revolutionary to help save the Mexican Indians from annihilation by a despotic military governor. What it lacks in political correctness it makes up for in fits of action. Although quite racy in its day for its interracial sex sizzle of Brown and Rachel, it's tame and overblown by today's standards.
1969 (R) 110m/C Jim Brown, Raquel Welch, Burt Reynolds, Fernando Lamas; **D:** Tom Gries; **M:** Jerry Goldsmith. **VHS, Beta** $19.98 FOX, FXV ✗✗

101 Dalmations Disney classic and one of the highest-grossing animated films in the history of Hollywood centers around two dogowners, Roger and Anita, and their respective spotted pets, Pongo and Perdita. When Pongo and Perdita's puppies are kidnapped by Cruella de Vil, villainess extraordinaire, to make a simply fabulous spotted coat, the parents enlist the aid of various

animals, including a dog named Colonel, a horse, a cat, and a goose to rescue the doomed pups. Imagine their surprise when they find not only their own puppies, but 84 more as well. You can expect a happy ending and lots of spots—6,469,952 to be exact. Songs include "Remember When," "Cruella de Vil," "Dalmatian Plantation," and "Kanine Krunchies Kommercial." Based on the children's book by Dodie Smith. Technically notable for the first time use of the Xerox process to transfer the animator's drawings onto celluloid, which made the film's opening sequence of dots evolving into 101 barking dogs possible.
1961 (G) 79m/C **D:** Wolfgang Reitherman, Hamilton Luske; **V:** Rod Taylor, Betty Lou Gerson, Lisa Davis, Ben Wright, Frederick Worlock, J. Pat O'Malley. **VHS, Beta** $24.99 DIS, OM ✗✗✗½

125 Rooms of Comfort A mental patient has bizarre fantasies that create havoc among those who stand in his way.
1983 82m/C **VHS, Beta** TWE ✗✗

One in a Million: The Ron LaFlore Story The true story of Detroit Tigers' star Ron LeFlore, who rose from the Detroit ghetto to the major leagues. Adaptation of LeFlore's autobiography, "Breakout." A well-acted and compelling drama with Burton in a standout performance.
1978 90m/C LeVar Burton, Madge Sinclair, Billy Martin, James Luisi; **D:** William A. Graham. **VHS, Beta** NO ✗✗½

One Last Run It's drama on the slopes as a variety of individuals confront their pasts/fears/personal demons via extreme skiing. Features the performances of champion skiers Franz Weber and Scot Schmidt.
1989 82m/C Russell Todd, Ashley Laurence, Craig Branham, Jimmy Aleck, Tracy Scoggins, Nels Van Patten, Chuck Connors; **W/D:** Peter Winograd, Glenn Gebhard. **VHS, Beta** $79.95 PSM ✗½

One Little Indian An AWOL cavalry man and his Indian ward team up with a widow and her daughter in an attempt to cross the New Mexican desert. A tepid presentation from the usually high quality Disney studio.
1973 90m/C James Garner, Vera Miles, Jodie Foster, Clay O'Brien, Andrew Prine, Bernard McEveety; **D:** Bernard McEveety; **M:** Jerry Goldsmith. **VHS, Beta** $69.95 DIS ✗✗

One Magic Christmas Disney feel-good film about a disillusioned working woman whose faith in Christmas is restored when her guardian angel descends to Earth and performs various miracles. Somewhat cliched and tiresome, but partially redeemed by Stanton and Steenburgen's presence.
1985 (G) 88m/C Mary Steenburgen, Harry Dean Stanton, Gary Basaraba, Michelle Meyrink, Arthur Hill; **D:** Phillip Borsos. **VHS, Beta, LV** $19.99 DIS ✗✗½

One Man Force L.A. narcotics cop Jake Swan goes on a vigilante spree. Huge in body and vengeful in spirit, he makes his partner's murderers pay!
1989 (R) 92m/C John Matuszak, Ronny Cox, Charles Napier, Sharon Farrell, Sam Jones, Chance Boyer, Richard Lynch, Stacey Q; **D:** Dale Trevillion. **VHS, Beta, LV** $29.95 ACA ✗✗

One Man Jury LAPD lieutenant, wearied by an ineffective justice system, becomes a one-man vigilante avenger. Pale Dirty Harry rip-off with over acting and an overdose of violence.
1978 (R) 95m/C Jack Palance, Chris Mitchum, Joe Spinell, Pamela Shoop; **D:** Charles Martin. **VHS, Beta** $19.95 UHV ✗

One Man Out An ex-CIA agent diverts his psychological problems into his new job: assassin for a South American despot. His jaded view of life changes when he meets and falls in love with an American journalist. Trouble in paradise when he is ordered to kill her. One man out was not enough, they should have done away with the entire crew of this stinker.
1989 (R) 90m/C Stephen McHattie, Deborah Van Valkenburgh, Aharon Ipale, Ismael Carlo, Michael Champion, Dennis A. Pratt; **D:** Michael Kennedy. **VHS, Beta, LV** $14.95 *SVS, COL* ◻️

One Man's War A human-rights crusader in repressive Paraguay won't be silenced, even after government thugs torture and murder his son. He fights obsessively to bring the killers to justice. The true story of the Joel Filartiga family is heartfelt but ultimately a dramatic letdown; an epilogue proves that full story hasn't been told.
1990 (PG-13) 91m/C Anthony Hopkins, Norma Aleandro, Fernanda Torres, Ruben Blades; **D:** Sergio Toledo. **VHS** $89.99 *HBO* ◻️◻️½

One Million B.C. The strange saga of the struggle of primitive cavemen and their battle against dinosaurs and other monsters. Curiously told in flashbacks, this film provided stock footage for countless dinosaur movies that followed. Portions of film rumored to be directed by cinematic pioneer D. W. Griffith. **AKA:** The Cave Dwellers; Cave Man; Man and His Mate.
1940 80m/B Victor Mature, Carole Landis, Lon Chaney Jr.; **D:** Hal Roach, Hal Roach Jr. **VHS, Beta** $9.95 *MED, RXM* ◻️◻️½

One Minute Before Death A woman is buried in a catatonic state, and returns from the grave to exact retribution. Supposedly based loosely on Poe.
1988 87m/C Giselle MacKenzie. **VHS, Beta** *NO* ◻️

One Minute to Zero Korean War action film divides its time between an army romance and war action. The lukewarm melodrama features Mitchum as a colonel in charge of evacuating American civilians but who ends up bombing refugees.
1952 105m/B Robert Mitchum, Ann Blyth, William Talman, Charles McGraw, Margaret Sheridan, Richard Egan, Eduard Franz, Robert Osterloh, Robert Gist; **D:** Tay Garnett. **VHS, Beta** *RKO, TTC* ◻️◻️

One More Chance While he was in jail, an ex-con's family moves away without leaving a forwarding address. When he's released he strikes up a friendship with a woman from the neighborhood who knows where they've gone.
1990 102m/C Kirstie Alley, John Lamotta, Logan Clarke, Michael Pataki, Hector Maisonette; **D:** Sam Firstenberg. **VHS, Beta** $59.95 *WAR, OM* ◻️½

One More Saturday Night Franken and Davis, "Saturday Night Live" alumni, wrote this film about a small town going wild on the weekend. Dry, taxing, and unfunny. Averages about 1 laugh per 1/2 hour—at 1 1/2 hours, it's way too long.
1986 (R) 96m/C Al Franken, Tom Davis, Nan Woods, Dave Reynolds; **D:** Dennis Klein. **VHS, Beta, LV** $9.95 *RCA* ◻️

One Night of Love Moore's best quasi-operetta, about a young American diva rebelling in response to her demanding Italian teacher. "Pygmallion"-like story has her falling in love with her maestro. Despite being nearly 60 years old, this film is still enchanting and fresh. ♫One Night of Love; Ciri-Biri-Bin; Sempre Libera; Sextet; Ciribiribin; Tis the Last Rose of Summer; Habanera; Un bel

di; None But the Lonely Heart; Indian Love Call.
1934 95m/B Grace Moore, Tullio Carminati, Lyle Talbot, Jane Darwell, Nydia Westman, Mona Barrie, Jessie Ralph, Luis Alberni; **D:** Victor Schertzinger. Academy Awards '34: Best Sound, Best Score; Nominations: Best Actress (Moore), Best Director (Schertzinger), Best Film Editing, Best Picture. **VHS, Beta, LV** $19.95 *COL* ◻️◻️◻️½

One Night Only A gorgeous law student decides to make big money by hiring herself and her friends out as hookers to the school football team.
1984 87m/C Lenore Zann, Jeff Braunstein, Grant Alianak; **D:** Timothy Bond. **VHS, Beta** $59.98 *FOX* ◻️◻️◻️½

One Night Stand Woman's chance encounter with a man in a singles bar leads to an evening of unexpected terror. Adapted from a play for Canadian television. Billed as a horror flick, it is really more of a drama.
1977 90m/C *CA* Chapelle Jaffe, Brent Carver. **VHS, Beta** $49.95 *TWE* ◻️◻️

One Night Stand Four young people attempt to amuse themselves at the empty Sydney Opera House on the New Year's Eve, that night World War III begins. An odd commentary on nuclear war that sees the bomb as the ultimate bad joke. Features an appearance by alternative rock group Midnight Oil.
1984 94m/C Tyler Coppin, Cassandra Delaney, Jay Hackett, Saskia Post; **D:** John Duigan. **VHS, Beta** $59.98 *SUE* ◻️◻️◻️

One of My Wives Is Missing An ex-New York cop tries to solve the mysterious disappearance of a newlywed socialite. Things become strange when she reappears but is discovered as an imposter. Above average acting in a film adapted from the play, "The Trap for a Lonely Man."
1976 97m/C Jack Klugman, Elizabeth Ashley, James Franciscus; **D:** Glenn Jordan. **VHS, Beta** $59.95 *LHV* ◻️◻️½

One of Our Aircraft Is Missing The crew of an R.A.F. bomber downed in the Netherlands, struggle to escape Nazi capture. A thoughtful study of wars and the men who fight them, with an entertaining melodramatic plot. Look for the British version, which runs 106 minutes. Some of the American prints only run 82 minutes.
1941 103m/B *GB* Godfrey Tearle, Eric Portman, Hugh Williams, Pamela Brown, Googie Withers, Peter Ustinov; **D:** Emeric Pressburger, Michael Powell. Academy Awards '42 Nominations: Best Original Screenplay; National Board of Review Awards '42: 10 Best Films of the Year. **VHS** $19.95 *NOS, MRV, REP* ◻️◻️◻️½

One of Our Dinosaurs Is Missing An English nanny and her cohorts help British Intelligence retrieve a microfilm—concealing dinosaur fossil from the bad guys that have stolen it. Disney film was shot on location in England.
1975 (G) 101m/C Peter Ustinov, Helen Hayes, Derek Nimmo, Clive Revill, Robert Stevenson, Joan Sims; **D:** Robert Stevenson. **VHS, Beta** $69.95 *DIS* ◻️◻️

One on One A Rocky-esque story about a high school basketball star from the country who accepts an athletic scholarship to a big city university. He encounters a demanding coach and intense competition. Light weight drama that is economically entertaining.
1977 (PG) 100m/C Robby Benson, Annette O'Toole, G.D. Spradlin, Gail Strickland, Melanie Griffith; **D:** Lamont Johnson. **VHS, Beta** $39.98 *WAR* ◻️◻️½

One Plus One A dramatization, believe it or not, of the Kinsey sex survey of the 1950s. Participants in a sex lecture talk about and demonstrate various "risque" practices, such as premarital sex and extramarital affairs. Despite this film, the sexual revolution went on as planned. **AKA:** Exploring the Kinsey Report.
1961 114m/B *CA* Leo G. Carroll, Hilda Brawner, William Traylor, Kate Reid, Ernest Graves; **W/D:** Arch Oboler. **VHS, Beta** $16.95 *SNC* ◻️

One-Punch O'Day Boxing boy tries to buy back hometown's oil livelihood by winning prizefight. Much patient waiting for his honey.
1926 60m/B Billy Sullivan, Jack Herrick, Charlotte Merriam; **D:** Harry J. Brown. **VHS, Beta** $19.95 *GPV, FCT* ◻️

One Rainy Afternoon A bit-player kisses the wrong girl in a Paris theater causing a massive uproar that brands him as a notorious romantic "monster." Patterned after a German film, the story lacks depth and zest.
1936 80m/B Francis Lederer, Ida Lupino, Hugh Herbert, Roland Young, Donald Meek; **D:** Rowland V. Lee. **VHS, Beta** $19.95 *NOS, MRV, VYY* ◻️◻️

One Russian Summer During the Russian Revolution, a cripple seeks revenge on the corrupt land baron who murdered his parents. An unfortunate attempt to dramatize a novel by M. Lermontov.
1973 (R) 112m/C Oliver Reed, Claudia Cardinale, John McEnery, Carole Andre, Ray Lovelock; **D:** Antonio Calenda. **VHS, Beta** $59.95 *UHV* Woof!

One Shoe Makes It Murder A shady casino owner hires ex-cop Mitchum to investigate the disappearance of his unfaithful wife. Adapted from Eric Bercovici's novel, the story does little to enhance Mitchum's TV debut.
1982 100m/C Robert Mitchum, Angie Dickinson, Mel Ferrer, Howard Hesseman, Jose Perez; **D:** William Hale. **VHS, Beta** $89.95 *LIV* ◻️◻️

One Sings, the Other Doesn't Seeking contentment, a conservative widow and a liberal extrovert help each other cope in a man's world. Endearing characters, but a superficial treatment of dated feminist issues. In French with English subtitles. **AKA:** L'Une Chante L'Autre Pas.
1977 105m/C *FR BE* Valerie Mairesse, Therese Liotard; **D:** Agnes Varda. **VHS, Beta** $59.95 *COL, TAM* ◻️◻️½

One Step Beyond This creepy anthology series featured stories of the occult and supernatural which were supposedly based on true incidents. Two episodes per tape. Includes "Message from Clara" starring Barbara Baxley and Robert Ellenstein and "The Sorcerer" with Christopher Lee and Martin Benson.
1959 60m/B **D:** John Newland. **VHS** $19.99 *MOV, HEG* ◻️◻️½

One Step to Hell Good cop rescues gold-miner's widow from three escaped convicts. Beautiful African scenery helps save an otherwise mediocre film. **AKA:** Caccia Ai Violenti; King of Africa.
1968 90m/C Ty Hardin, Rossano Brazzi, Pier Angeli, George Sanders, Tab Hunter, Sandy Howard. **VHS, Beta** $39.95 *NO* ◻️½

One Summer Love Man checks out from loony bin, searches for family ties and befriends beautiful woman who works in a moviehouse. **AKA:** Dragonfly.

1976 95m/C Beau Bridges, Susan Sarandon, Mildred Dunnock, Ann Wedgeworth, Michael B. Miller, Linda Miller, James Noble, Frederick Coffin; *D:* Gilbert Cates; *W:* N. Richard Nash. **VHS** $79.99 *HBO* 🎞🎞½

One That Got Away A loyal German Luftwaffe pilot captured by the British becomes obsessed with escape. Fast paced and exciting. Based on a true story. **1957** 111m/B Hardy Kruger, Colin Gordon, Alec Gordon; *D:* Roy Ward Baker. **VHS, Beta** *NO* 🎞🎞🎞

One Third of a Nation Depression era film contrasts the conditions of slum life with those in high society. A young entrepreneur inherits a city block in ruins, only to fall in love with a young woman who lives there and help her crippled brother. Timely social criticism. **1939** 79m/B Sylvia Sidney, Leif Erickson, Myron McCormick, Sidney Lumet; *D:* Dudley Murphy. **VHS** $19.95 *NOS, PAR, MLB* 🎞🎞½

1001 Arabian Nights In this Arabian nightmare, the nearsighted Mr. Magoo is known as "Azziz" Magoo, lamp dealer and uncle of Aladdin. **1959** 76m/C *D:* Jack Kinney; *V:* Jim Backus, Kathryn Grant, Hans Conried, Herschel Bernardi. **VHS, Beta** $19.95 *COL* 🎞🎞½

One Too Many Exploitation film depicting the evils of alcoholism. Campy, but slick. *AKA:* The Important Story of Alcoholism; Killer With a Label. **1951** ?m/C Ruth Warrick, Richard Travis, Victor Kilian, Onslow Stevens, Lyle Talbot. **VHS** $16.95 *SNC* 🎞

One Touch of Venus Love fills a department store when a window dresser kisses a statue of the goddess Venus—and she comes to life. Appealing adaptation of the Broadway musical, with songs by Kurt Weill and Ogden Nash. 🎵Speak Low; The Trouble with Women; That's Him; Don't Look Now But My Heart Is Showing; My Week. **1948** 82m/B Ava Gardner, Robert Walker, Eve Arden, Dick Haymes, Olga San Juan, Tom Conway; *D:* William A. Seiter. **VHS** $14.98 *REP, MLB* 🎞🎞½

One Trick Pony Once-popular rock singer/songwriter struggles to keep his head above water in a turbulent marriage and in the changing currents of popular taste. Simon wrote the autobiographical screenplay and score, but let's hope he is more sincere in real life. A good story. **1980** (R) 100m/C Paul Simon, Blair Brown, Rip Torn, Joan Hackett, Mare Winningham, Lou Reed, Harry Shearer, Allen Goorwitz, Daniel Stern; *D:* Robert M. Young. **VHS, Beta** $24.98 *WAR* 🎞🎞½

One, Two, Three Cagney, an American Coca-Cola exec in Germany, zealously pursues any opportunity to run Coke's European operations. He does the job too well and loses his job to a Communist hippy turned slick capitalist. Fast-paced laughs, wonderful cinematography, and a fine score. **1961** 110m/B James Cagney, Horst Buchholz, Arlene Francis; *D:* Billy Wilder. Academy Awards '61 Nominations: Best Black and White Cinematography; National Board of Review Awards '61: 10 Best Films of the Year. **VHS, Beta, LV** $19.98 *MGM* 🎞🎞🎞½

One Wild Moment Comic complications arise when a divorced man is seduced by his best friend's daughter while vacationing. Warm and charming. Later re-made as "Blame It on Rio." In French with English subtitles.

1978 (R) 88m/C *FR* Jean-Pierre Marielle, Victor Lanoux, Agnes Soral, Christine Dejoux, Martine Sarcey; *D:* Claude Berri. **VHS, Beta** $59.95 *COL, TAM* 🎞🎞½

One Wish Too Many A young boy finds a marble that grants wishes. He has the time of his life with his teachers and the school bullies, but runs into trouble when he creates a giant steam roller which overruns London. Winner of Best Children's Film, 1956 Venice Film Festival, but it is hard to say why. **1955** 55m/B *GB* Anthony Richmond, Rosalind Gourgey, John Pike; *D:* John Durst. **VHS, Beta** $16.95 *SNC* 🎞🎞½

One Woman or Two Paleontologist Depardieu is duped by beautiful ad-exec who plans to use his findings to push perfume. Remake of "Bringing Up Baby," this screwball comedy has a few screws loose. Dubbed. *AKA:* Une Femme ou Deux. **1985** (PG-13) 100m/C *FR* Gerard Depardieu, Sigourney Weaver, Dr. Ruth Westheimer; *D:* Daniel Vigne. **VHS, Beta** $19.98 *LIV, VES, TAM* 🎞🎞½

Onibaba A brutal parable about a mother and her daughter-in-law in war-ravaged medieval Japan who subsist by murdering stray soldiers and selling their armor. One soldier beds the daughter, setting the mother-in-law on a vengeful tirade. Review of the film varied widely, hailed by some as a masterpiece and by others as below average; in Japanese with subtitles. *AKA:* The Demon; The Devil Woman. **1964** 103m/B *JP* Nobuko Otowa, Yitsuko Yoshimura, Kei Sato; *D:* Kaneto Shindo. **VHS, Beta** $29.95 *CVC, TAM* 🎞🎞🎞

The Onion Field True story about the mental breakdown of an ex-cop who witnessed his partner's murder. Haunted by the slow process of justice and his own feelings of insecurity, he is unable to get his life together. Based on the novel by Joseph Wambaugh, who also wrote the screenplay. Compelling script and excellent acting. **1979** (R) 126m/C John Savage, James Woods, Ronny Cox, Franklyn Seales, Ted Danson; *D:* Harold Becker. **VHS, Beta, LV** $14.98 *SUE, NLC* 🎞🎞🎞½

Only Angels Have Wings Melodramatic adventure about a broken-down Peruvian air mail service. Large cast adds to the love tension between Grant, a pilot, and Arthur, a showgirl at the saloon. **1939** 121m/B Cary Grant, Thomas Mitchell, Richard Barthelmess, Jean Arthur, Noah Beery Jr., Rita Hayworth, Sig Rumann, John Carroll; *D:* Howard Hawks. **VHS, Beta** $19.95 *COL* 🎞🎞🎞🎞

Only Once in a Lifetime A love story about an Hispanic immigrant painter looking for success in America. **1983** 90m/C Miguel Robelo, Estrellita Lopez, Sheree North. **VHS, Beta** $49.95 *VHE, MOV* 🎞

Only One Night Upon finding out that he's the illegitimate son of an aristocrat, a circus attendant joins high society and is promptly matched with a beautiful woman. In Swedish with English subtitles. *AKA:* En Enda Natt. **1942** 87m/B *SW* Ingrid Bergman, Edvin Adolphson, Aino Taube, Olof Sandborg, Erik Berglund, Marianne Lofgren, Magnus Kesster; *D:* Gustaf Molander. **VHS, Beta, LV** $29.95 *WAC, LUM, TAM* 🎞🎞

Only the Lonely Middle-aged cop, Candy, falls in love with a shy undertaker's assistant, Sheedy, and is torn between love and dear old Mom, O'Hara, in her first role in years. Candy is an unlikely leading man and even the jokes are forced. But the restaurant

scene makes the whole thing well worth seeing. **1991** (PG) 104m/C John Candy, Ally Sheedy, Maureen O'Hara, Anthony Quinn, Kevin Dunn, James Belushi, Milo O'Shea, Bert Remsen, Macaulay Culkin; *W/D:* Chris Columbus. **VHS, Beta, LV** $19.98 *FXV* 🎞🎞½

Only the Valiant Action-packed story of a cavalry officer who struggles to win his troops respect while warding off angry Apaches. Fast-paced Western fun requires little thought. **1950** 105m/B Gregory Peck, Ward Bond, Gig Young, Lon Chaney Jr., Barbara Payton, Neville Brand; *D:* Gordon Douglas. **VHS, LV** $14.95 *REP* 🎞🎞

Only Two Can Play Sellers is a hilarious Casanova librarian who puts the moves on a society lady to get a promotion. Funny, of course, and based on Kingsley Amis' novel "That Uncertain Feeling." **1962** 106m/C *GB* Peter Sellers, Virginia Maskell, Mai Zetterling, Richard Attenborough; *D:* Sidney Gilliat. **VHS, Beta** $69.95 *COL* 🎞🎞🎞

Only Way A semi-documentary account of the plight of the Jews in Denmark during the Nazi occupation. Despite German insistence, the Danes succeeded in saving most of their Jewish population from the concentration camps. **1970** (G) 86m/C Jane Seymour, Martin Potter, Benjamin Christiansen. **VHS, Beta** $19.95 *UHV* 🎞🎞½

The Only Way Home Two bikers end up in big trouble when one of them kills a wealthy man, and they kidnap his wife. Filmed entirely in Oklahoma. **1972** (PG) 86m/C Bo Hopkins, Beth Brickell, Steve Sandor, G.D. Spradlin; *D:* G.D. Spradlin. **VHS, Beta** $39.95 *WWV* 🎞🎞

Only When I Laugh Neil Simon reworked his Broadway flop "The Gingerbread Lady" to produce this poignant comedy about the relationship between an aging alcoholic actress and her teenage daughters. *AKA:* It Hurts Only When I Laugh. **1981** (R) 120m/C Marsha Mason, Kristy McNichol, James Coco, Joan Hackett, David Dukes, Kevin Bacon, John Bennett Perry; *D:* Glenn Jordan. Academy Awards '81 Nominations: Best Actress (Mason), Best Supporting Actor (Coco), Best Supporting Actress (Hackett); Golden Globe Awards '82: Best Supporting Actress (Hackett). **VHS, Beta, LV** $19.95 *COL* 🎞🎞🎞

Only with Married Men Carne's hassle-free dating routine is disrupted when a sly bachelor pretends that he's married to get a date. A middle-aged persons answer to a teenage sex comedy. Pretty bad. **1974** 74m/C David Birney, Judy Carne, Gavin McLeod, John Astin; *D:* Jerry Paris. **VHS, Beta** $59.95 *LHV* 🎞

Only You A shy guy has always searched for true romance. But his cup runneth over when he meets, and must choose between, two beautiful women—your basic beach babe and a sensible beauty. What's a guy to do? **1992** (PG-13) 85m/C Andrew McCarthy, Kelly Preston, Helen Hunt. **VHS** $89.98 *LIV* 🎞½

Open All Hours A British television comedy about a small corner shop and its viciously greedy, opportunistic owner. **1983** 85m/C *GB* Ronnie Barker, Lynda Baron, David Jason, Stephenie Cole. **VHS, Beta** $14.98 *FOX* 🎞

Open City A leader in the Italian underground resists Nazi control of the city. A stunning film, making Rossellini's realistic style famous. Co-scripted by Fellini. In Italian

with English subtitles. *AKA:* Roma, Citta Aperta; Rome, Open City.
1945 103m/B *IT* Anna Magnani, Aldo Fabrizi; *D:* Roberto Rossellini. Academy Awards '46 Nominations: Best Screenplay; National Board of Review Awards '46: 5 Best Foreign Films of the Year; New York Film Critics Awards '46: Best Foreign Film. **VHS, Beta, 8mm** $59.95 *CVC, MRV, NOS* ✗✗✗✗

Open Doors Bitter review of Fascist rule and justice. The Fascist regime promises security, safety, and tranquility. So, on the morning that a white collar criminal murders his former boss, murders the man who got his job, and then rapes and murders his wife, tensions rise and the societal structures are tested. The people rally for his death. A judge and a juror struggle to uphold justice rather than serve popular passions. Winner of 4 Donatello Awards, Italian Golden Globes for Best Film, Best Actor, and Best Screenplay, and many international film awards. In Italian with English subtitles. *AKA:* Porte Aperte.
1989 (R) 109m/C *IT* Gian Marie Volonte, Ennio Fantastichini, Lidia Alfonsi; *D:* Gianni Amelio. **VHS** $79.98 *ORI, FCT, TAM* ✗✗✗½

Open House Radio psychologist and beautiful real estate agent search for the killer of real estate agents and their clients. A mystery-thriller for the very patient.
1986 95m/C Joseph Bottoms, Adrienne Barbeau, Mary Stavin, Rudy Ramos; *D:* Jag Mundhra. **VHS, Beta** $79.95 *PSM* ✗

Open Secret Jewish residents are plagued by a gang of anti-semitic thugs. Violence and destruction escalate until a fed up police lieutenant, tenaciously played by Ireland, and a victimized shop owner (Tyne) join forces to just say no more. When the gang learns the shopkeeper has caught their dastardly deeds on camera, the battle begins in earnest. Fast-paced and intriguing suspense.
1948 70m/B John Ireland, Jane Randolph, Roman Bohnen, Sheldon Leonard, George Tyne, Morgan Farley, Ellen Lowe, Anne O'Neal, Arthur O'Connell; *D:* John Reinhardt. **VHS, Beta** $16.95 *SNC* ✗✗

Opening Night Very long study about an actress (Rowlands) and the play she's about to open in on Broadway. Backstage turmoil increases her own insecurities and the bad luck persists when an adoring fan dies in an accident on opening night. Performances carry this neurotic epic along, including Cassavettes as Rowland's co-star and Blondell as the playwright.
1977 (PG-13) 144m/C Gena Rowlands, John Cassavetes, Joan Blondell, Ben Gazzara, Paul Stewart, Zohra Lampert, Laura Johnson; *W/D:* John Cassavetes. **VHS, Beta** $89.95 *TOU, BTV* ✗✗½

Opera do Malandro A lavish Brazilian take off of "The Threepenny Opera." Married hustler falls for a beautiful entrepreneur longing to get rich off of American goods. Based on Chico Buarque's musical play. In Portuguese, with subtitles.
1987 106m/C *BR* Edson Celulari, Claudia Ohana, Elba Ramalho, Ney Latorraca; *D:* Ruy Guerra. **VHS, Beta, LV** *NO* ✗✗½

Operation Amsterdam Four agents have fourteen hours to snare $10 million in diamonds from under the noses of local Nazis. Based on a true story. Full of 1940s wartime action and suspense.
1960 103m/B Peter Finch, Eva Bartok, Tony Britton, Alexander Knox; *D:* Michael McCarthy. **VHS, Beta** $59.95 *SUE* ✗✗

Operation C.I.A. A plot to assassinate the U.S. ambassador in Saigon inspires brave CIA agent Reynolds to wipe out the bad guys. Action-packed and somewhat exciting. *AKA:* Last Message From Saigon.
1965 90m/C Burt Reynolds, John Hayt, Kieu Chinh, Danielle Aubry; *D:* Christian Nyby. **VHS, Beta** $59.98 *FOX, DVT, HEG* ✗✗

Operation Cross Eagles Routine WWII military thriller with Conte and Calhoun on a mission to rescue an American general in exchange for their German prisoner. Their mission is complicated by a traitor in the group. Conte's only directorship. *AKA:* Unakrsna Vatra.
1969 90m/C *YU* Richard Conte, Rory Calhoun, Aili King, Phil Brown; *D:* Richard Conte. **VHS** $79.95 *SVS* ✗✗

Operation Crossbow Action-packed espionage tale in which a trio of agents are assigned to destroy a Nazi munitions installation. Exciting ending and sensational pyrotechnics. *AKA:* The Great Spy Mission; Code Name: Operation Crossbow.
1965 116m/C Sophia Loren, George Peppard, Trevor Howard, John Mills, Richard Johnson, Tom Courtenay, Jeremy Kemp, Anthony Quayle; *D:* Michael Anderson Sr. **VHS** $19.98 *MGM* ✗✗✗

Operation Dames A squadron of soldiers must go behind Korean enemy lines to locate a missing U.S.O. troupe and bring them to safety. Low budget and not very funny for a supposed comedy.
1959 73m/B Eve Meyer, Chuck Henderson, Don Devlin, Ed Craig, Cindy Girard; *D:* Louis Clyde Stouman. **VHS** $9.95 *COL* ✗✗½

Operation Haylift The true story of the U.S. Air Force's efforts to rescue starving cattle and sheep herds during Nevada's blizzards of 1949. The Air Force provided realism for the film with planes, equipment, and servicemen.
1950 73m/B Bill Williams, Tom Brown, Ann Rutherford, Jane Nigh; *D:* William Berke. **VHS, Beta, LV** *NO* ✗✗

Operation Inchon A foreign film depicting the battle in Devil Ridge during the Korean War.
1981 90m/C **VHS, Beta** $39.95 *VCD* ✗

Operation Julie A detective searches out a huge drug ring that manufactures LSD.
1985 100m/C Colin Blakely, Lesley Nightingale, Clare Powney; *D:* Bob Mahoney. **VHS, Beta** $59.98 *LIV* ✗½

Operation 'Nam A group of bored Vietnam vets return to 'Nam to rescue their leader from a POW camp. Nothing special, but features John Wayne's son.
1985 85m/C Oliver Tobias, Christopher Connelly, Manfred Lehman, John Steiner, Ethan Wayne, Donald Pleasence; *D:* Larry Ludman. **VHS** $79.95 *IMP* ✗✗

Operation Orient A statue laden with drugs is stolen when an international drug smuggler tries to bring it to the U.S.
19?? 94m/C Gianni Gori, Gordon Mitchell; *D:* Elia Milonakos. **VHS, Beta** *MED* ✗✗

Operation Petticoat Submarine captain Grant teams with wheeler-dealer Curtis to make his sub seaworthy. They're joined by a group of Navy women, and the gags begin. Great teamwork from Grant and Curtis keeps things rolling. Jokes may be considered sexist these days. Later remake and TV series couldn't hold a candle to the original.
1959 120m/C Cary Grant, Tony Curtis, Joan O'Brien, Dina Merrill, Gene Evans, Arthur O'Connell, Virginia Gregg; *D:* Blake Edwards. **VHS, LV** $19.98 *REP* ✗✗✗½

Operation Thunderbolt Israeli-produced depiction of Israel's July 14, 1976 commando raid on Entebbe, Uganda to rescue the passengers of a hijacked plane. Better than the American versions "Raid on Entebbe" and "Victory at Entebbe" in its performances as well as the information provided, much of it unavailable to the American filmmakers. *AKA:* Entebbe: Operation Thunderbolt.
1977 120m/C Yehoram Gaon, Assaf Dayan, Ori Levy, Klaus Kinski; *D:* Menahem Golan. **VHS, Beta** $59.95 *MGM* ✗✗½

Operation War Zone A platoon of soldiers uncovers a plot by corrupt officers to continue the Vietnam war and sell weapons.
1989 86m/C Joe Spinell. **VHS, Beta** *AIP* ✗

The Oppermann Family On two tapes, the long epic made for German television about a family trying to survive in Berlin during the rise of Hitler. In German with subtitles.
1982 238m/C *GE D:* Egon Monk. **VHS, Beta** $99.95 *FCT, APD* ✗✗½

The Opponent A young boxer saves a young woman's life, not realizing that she has mob connections, thus embroiling him in a world of crime.
1989 (R) 102m/C *IT* Daniel Greene, Ernest Borgnine, Julian Gemma, Mary Stavin, Kelly Shaye Smith; *D:* Sergio Martino. **VHS, LV** $89.95 *VMK* ✗✗

Opportunity Knocks Carvey's first feature film has him impersonating a friend of a rich suburbanite's family while hiding from a vengeful gangster. They buy it, and give him a job and the daughter. Not hilarious, but not a dud either.
1990 (PG-13) 105m/C Dana Carvey, Robert Loggia, Todd Graff, Milo O'Shea, Julia Campbell, James Tolkan; *D:* Donald Petrie. **VHS, Beta, LV** $19.95 *MCA* ✗✗½

Opposing Force The commander of an Air Force camp simulates prisoner-of-war conditions for realistic training, but he goes too far, creating all too real torture situations. He preys on the only female in the experiment, raping her as part of the training. A decent thriller. *AKA:* Hellcamp.
1987 (R) 97m/C Tom Skerritt, Lisa Eichhorn, Anthony Zerbe, Richard Roundtree, Robert Wightman, John Considine, George Kee Chueng, Paul Joynt, Jay Louden, Ken Wright, Dan Hamilton; *D:* Eric Karson. **VHS, Beta** $19.99 *HBO* ✗✗

The Opposite Sex Bevy of women battle mediocre script in adaptation of 1939's "The Women." Laserdisc includes original trailer and letterboxed screen. ♫The Opposite Sex; Dere's Yellow Gold on de Trees (De Banana); A Perfect Love; Rock and Roll Tumbleweed; Now! Baby, Now; Jungle Red; Young Man with a Horn.
1956 115m/C June Allyson, Joan Collins, Dolores Gray, Ann Sheridan, Ann Miller, Leslie Nielsen, Agnes Moorehead, Joan Blondell; *D:* David Miller. **VHS, LV** $19.98 *MGM, PIA, FCT* ✗✗

The Opposite Sex and How to Live With Them Yuppies (Gross and Cox) from different backgrounds (he's Jewish, she's a WASP) meet, fall in love, fight, break up, and reunite, inspiring yawning disinterest. All this while their two best buddies (Pollack and Brown) offer what is meant to be "candid insights" delivered directly to the camera. Flat and formulaic romantic comedy wants to sparkle, but script lacks both purpose and point, and worse, takes way too much time not getting there. Winner of the annual Grammar Police award

for the worst example of a semantically incorrect title in recent years.
1993 (R) 86m/C Arye Gross, Courteney Cox, Kevin Pollack, Julie Brown, Mitch Ryan, Philip Bruns, Mitzi McCall, B.J. Ward; **D:** Matthew Meshekoff; **W:** Noah Stern; **M:** Ira Newborn. **VHS** *NYR Woof!*

Options Nerdy Hollywood agent Salinger treks to Africa to ''option'' a princess's life story—hence the title. He gets mixed up with her kidnapping and with her. Misplaced cameos by Roberts and Anton drag down the overall comedy content, which isn't to high to begin with.
1988 (PG) 105m/C Matt Salinger, Joanna Pacula, John Kani, James Keach; **Cameos:** Susan Anton, Eric Roberts; **D:** Camilo Vila. **VHS, LV** $89.98 *LIV, VES* ♂♂

The Oracle A woman takes a new apartment only to find that the previous occupant's spirit is still a resident. The spirit tries to force her to take revenge on his murderers. Not bad for a low-budget thriller, but bad editing is a distraction.
1985 94m/C Caroline Capers Powers, Roger Neil; **D:** Roberta Findlay. **VHS, Beta** $59.95 *LIV* ♂

Orca Ridiculous premise has a killer whale chasing bounty hunter Harris to avenge the murder of its pregnant mate. Great for gore lovers, especially when the whale chomps Derek's leg off. **AKA:** Orca—Killer Whale.
1977 (PG) 92m/C Richard Harris, Charlotte Rampling, Bo Derek, Keenan Wynn, Will Sampson; **D:** Michael Anderson Sr.; **M:** Ennio Morricone. **VHS, Beta, LV** $19.95 *PAR Woof!*

Orchestra Wives A drama bursting with wonderful Glenn Miller music. A woman marries a musician and goes on the road with the band and the other wives. Trouble springs up with the sultry singer who desperately wants the woman's new husband. The commotion spreads throughout the group. ♫People Like You and Me; At Last; Serenade in Blue; I've Got a Gal in Kalamazoo.
1942 98m/B George Montgomery, Glenn Miller, Lynn Bari, Carole Landis, Jackie Gleason, Cesar Romero, Ann Rutherford, Virginia Gilmore, Mary Beth Hughes, Harry Morgan; **D:** Archie Mayo. **VHS, Beta, LV** $19.98 *FXV, FCT* ♂♂♂

Ordeal by Innocence Sutherland is an amateur sleuth in 1950s England convinced he has proof that a convicted murderer is innocent, but no one wishes to reopen the case. Big-name cast is essentially wasted. Based on an Agatha Christie story.
1984 (PG-13) 91m/C Donald Sutherland, Christopher Plummer, Faye Dunaway, Sarah Miles, Ian McShane, Diana Quick, Annette Crosbie, Michael Elphick; **D:** Desmond Davis; **W:** Agatha Christie. **VHS, Beta, LV** $79.95 *MGM* ♂½

The Ordeal of Dr. Mudd His name was Mudd—a fitting moniker after he unwittingly aided President Lincoln's assassin. Dr. Mudd set John Wilkes Boothe's leg, broken during the assassination, and was jailed for conspiracy. He became a hero in prison for his aid during yellow fever epidemics and was eventually released. A strong and intricate performance by Weaver keeps this made-for-television drama interesting. Mudd's descendants are still trying to completely clear his name of any wrongdoing in the Lincoln assassination.
1980 143m/C Dennis Weaver, Susan Sullivan, Richard Dysart, Michael McGuire, Nigel Davenport, Arthur Hill; **D:** Paul Wendkos. **VHS, Beta** $39.95 *LIV* ♂♂♂

Order of the Black Eagle A Bondish spy and his sidekick, Typhoon the Baboon, battle neo-Nazis planning to bring Hitler back to life in this silly tongue-in-cheek thriller.
1987 (R) 93m/C *GB* Ian Hunter, Charles K. Bibby, William T. Hicks, Jill Donnellan; **D:** Worth Keeter. **VHS, Beta** $19.95 *CEL* ♂½

Order of the Eagle An innocent scouting trip turns into a non-stop nightmare when an Eagle Scout uncovers some dangerous information.
1989 88m/C Frank Stallone. **VHS, Beta** *AIP* ♂½

Order to Kill A gambling boss puts out a contract on a hit man.
1973 110m/C Jose Ferrer, Helmut Berger, Sydne Rome, Kevin McCarthy; **D:** Jose Maesso. **VHS, Beta** *NO* ♂♂½

Ordet A man who believes he is Jesus Christ is ridiculed until he begins performing miracles, which result in the rebuilding of a broken family. A statement on the nature of religious faith vs. fanaticism by the profoundly religious Dreyer, and based on the play by Kaj Munk. In Danish with English subtitles. **AKA:** The Word.
1955 126m/B *DK* Henrik Malberg; **D:** Carl Theodor Dreyer. **VHS, Beta** $24.95 *NOS, WFV, TAM* ♂♂♂½

Ordinary Heroes The story is familiar but the leads make it worthwhile. Anderson is strong as a blinded Vietnam vet readjusting to life at home. Bertinelli's portrayal of his former girlfriend is eloquent. Nice work on an overdone story.
1985 105m/C Richard Dean Anderson, Doris Roberts, Valerie Bertinelli; **D:** Peter H. Cooper. **VHS** $79.99 *HRO* ♂♂½

Ordinary People Powerful, well-acted story of a family's struggle to deal with one son's accidental death and the other's subsequent guilt-ridden suicide attempt. Features strong performances by all, but Moore is especially believable as the cold and rigid mother. McGovern's film debut as well as Redford's directorial debut. Based on the novel by Judith Guest.
1980 (R) 124m/C Mary Tyler Moore, Donald Sutherland, Timothy Hutton, Judd Hirsch, M. Emmet Walsh, Elizabeth McGovern, Adam Baldwin, Dinah Manoff, James B. Sikking; **D:** Robert Redford; **W:** Alvin Sargent. Academy Awards '80: Best Adapted Screenplay, Best Director (Redford), Best Picture, Best Supporting Actor (Hutton); Nominations: Best Actress (Moore), Best Supporting Actor (Hirsch); Golden Globe Awards '81: Best Actress—Drama (Moore), Best Director (Redford), Best Film—Drama, Best Supporting Actor (Hutton); National Board of Review Awards '80: 10 Best Films of the Year, Best Director (Redford). **VHS, Beta, LV** $14.95 *PAR, BTV* ♂♂♂½

Oregon Trail A western serial in 15 chapters, each 13 minutes long.
1939 195m/B Johnny Mack Brown, Fuzzy Knight; **D:** Ford Beebe. **VHS, Beta** $29.95 *VCN, DVT, MLB* ♂♂♂½

The Organization Poitier's third and final portrayal of Detective Virgil Tibbs, first seen in ''In the Heat of the Night.'' This time around he battles a drug smuggling ring with a vigilante group. Good action scenes and a realistic ending.
1971 (PG) 108m/C Sidney Poitier, Barbara McNair, Sheree North, Raul Julia; **D:** Don Medford. **VHS, Beta** $14.95 *MGM, FOX* ♂♂♂

Orgy of the Dead Classic anti-canon film scripted by Ed Wood, Jr. from his own novel. Two innocent travelers are forced to watch an even dozen nude spirits dance in a cardboard graveyard. Hilariously bad.

1965 90m/C Criswell, Fawn Silver, William Bates, Pat Barringer; **D:** A.C. Stephen; **W:** Edward D. Wood Jr. **VHS, Beta** $19.95 *RHI Woof!*

Orgy of the Vampires Tourists wander into village during cocktail hour. **AKA:** Vampire's Night Orgy.
1973 (R) 86m/C *SP IT* Jack Taylor, Charo Soriano, Dianik Zurakowska, John Richard; **D:** Leon Klimovsky. **VHS** $19.99 *SNC* ♂

Oriane A troubled Venezuelan woman must leave France for her native soil when her aunt dies. Once there, in the place where she spent youthful summers, she begins to recall her incestuous past.
1985 88m/C Daniela Sliverio, Doris Wells, Philippe Rouleau, David Crotto; **D:** Fina Torres. **VHS** *NO* ♂

The Original Adventures of Betty Boop Three Boop classics: ''Betty and Henry,'' ''Betty and the Little King,'' and ''Betty in Blunderland.''
1934 38m/B **VHS, Beta** $29.95 *JEF* ♂

The Original Fabulous Adventures of Baron Munchausen An adventure fantasy that takes the hero all over, from the belly of a whale, eventually landing him on the surface of the moon. **AKA:** The Fabulous Baron Munchausen.
1961 84m/C *CZ* Milos Kopecky, Jana Brejchova, Rudolph Jelinek, Jan Werich; **D:** Karel Zeman. **VHS, LV** *NO* ♂♂½

The Original Flash Gordon Collection Four vintage Flash Gordon serials from the 1930s were recently re-edited into feature length films and released as this collection. Great stuff, including ''Spaceship to the Unknown,'' ''Deadly Ray From Mars,'' ''Peril From Planet Mongo,'' and ''Purple Death From Outer Space.''
1901 366m/B Buster Crabbe. **VHS** $79.95 *QHV, FCT* ♂♂½

Original Intent A successful lawyer, facing a mid-life crisis, jeopardizes both his family and career when he decides to defend a homeless shelter from eviction proceedings. What might have been a powerful drama about one man's crusade to help the homeless instead merely melodramtic. Actor/activist Sheen appears briefly as a homeless man.
1991 (PG) 97m/C Jay Richardson, Candy Clark, Kris Kristofferson, Vince Edwards, Cindy Pickett, Robert DoQui, Joe Campanella; **Cameos:** Martin Sheen; **W/D:** Robert Marcarelli. **VHS, Beta** *PAR* ♂♂

Orion's Belt Three Norwegian adventurers must flee through the wilderness when they discover a secret Soviet base on the Europe/Russia/Greenland border.
1985 (PG) 87m/C **VHS, Beta** $19.95 *STE, NWV* ♂♂

Orlak, the Hell of Frankenstein The monster of Frankenstein is revived for the purposes of revenge. The monster is forced to wear a helmet, as his face melted during the obligatory electrification. In Spanish only, no English subtitles. **AKA:** Orlak, El Infierno de Frankenstein.
1960 103m/B *MX* Joaquin Cordero, Andres Soler, Rosa de Castilla, Irma Dorante, Armando Calvo, Pedro de Aguillon, David Reynoso; **D:** Rafael Baledon. **VHS, Beta** $16.95 *SNC* ♂

The Orphan A young orphaned boy seeks revenge against his cruel aunt who is harassing him with sadistic discipline.
1979 80m/C Mark Evans, Joanna Miles, Peggy Feury; **D:** John Ballard. **VHS, Beta** $49.95 *PSM, RHI* ♂½

An Orphan Boy of Vienna A homeless street urchin with a beautiful singing voice is accepted into the wonderful world of the Choir, but is later unjustly accused of stealing. Performances by the Vienna Boys' Choir redeem the melodramatic plot. In German with English subtitles.
1937 87m/B *GE* The Vienna Boys Choir; *D:* Max Neufeld. **VHS, Beta, 3/4U $29.95** *VYY, IHF, GLV* ♫♫½

Orphan Train A woman realizes her New York soup kitchen can't do enough to help the neighborhood orphans, so she takes a group of children out West in hopes of finding families to adopt them. Their journey is chronicled by a newspaper photographer and a social worker. Based on the actual "orphan trains" of the mid- to late 1800s. From the novel by Dorothea G. Petrie. Made for television.
1979 150m/C Jill Eikenberry, Kevin Dobson, Glenn Close, Linda Manz; *D:* William A. Graham. **VHS $14.95** *PSM, KAR, HHE* ♫♫

Orphans A sensitive edge-of-glasnost portrait of a young boy's discovery of love, friendship, and literature. In Russian with English subtitles.
1983 97m/C *D:* Nikolai Gubenko. **VHS, Beta $79.95** *FCT* ♫♫♫

Orphans A gangster on the run is kidnapped by a tough New York orphan but soon takes control by befriending his abductor's maladjusted brother. Eventually each brother realizes his need for the older man, who has become a father figure to them. This very quirky film is salvaged by good performances. Based on the play by Lyle Kessler.
1987 (R) 116m/C Albert Finney, Matthew Modine, Kevin Anderson; *D:* Alan J. Pakula. **VHS, Beta, LV $19.95** *LHV, WAR* ♫♫♫

Orphans of the North The story of Bedrock Brown's search for gold and his lost partner. Filmed on location in Alaska with non-professional actors. Impressive footage of America's "last frontier," including the flora and fauna.
1940 56m/C *W/D:* Norman Dawn. **VHS, Beta, 8mm $24.95** *VYY* ♫

Orphans of the Storm Two sisters are separated and raised in opposite worlds—one by thieves, the other by aristocrats. Gish's poignant search for her sister is hampered by the turbulent maelstrom preceding the French Revolution. Silent. Based on the French play "The Two Orphans."
1921 190m/B Lillian Gish, Dorothy Gish, Monte Blue, Joseph Schildkraut; *D:* D.W. Griffith. **VHS, LV $19.98** *NOS, MRV, CCB* ♫♫♫½

Orpheus Cocteau's fascinating, innovative retelling of the Orpheus legend in a modern, though slightly askew, Parisian setting. Classic visual effects and poetic imagery. In French with English subtitles. *AKA:* Orphee.
1949 95m/B Jean Marais, Francois Perier, Maria Casares; *D:* Jean Cocteau. **VHS, Beta, 8mm $16.95** *SNC, NOS, SUE* ♫♫½

Orpheus Descending Lust and hatred in small Southern town. Confusing, poorly paced, but interesting for Anderson as Elvis-style drifter and Redgrave as woman addicted to love. Made-for-cable version of the 1989 Broadway revival of Tennessee Williams play.
1991 117m/C Vanessa Redgrave, Kevin Anderson, Anne Twomey, Miriam Margolyes, Brad Sullivan; *D:* Peter Hall; *W:* Tennessee Williams, Peter Hall. **VHS $79.95** *TTC, FCT* ♫♫½

Osa Yet another post-nuke flick with the usual devastated landscape, leather-clad survivors, and hokey dialog. It's sometimes funny, despite everyone's effort to make it dramatic. The supposed plot centers on one woman's efforts to break up a man's monopoly on clean water.
1985 94m/C Kelly Lynch, Daniel Grimm, Phillip Vincent, Etienne Chicot, John Forristal, Pete Walker, David Hausman, Bill Moseley; *D:* Oleg Egorov. **VHS** *NEG* ♫½

Osaka Elegy A study of Japanese cultural rules when society condemns a woman for behavior that is acceptable for a man. In Japanese with English subtitles. *AKA:* Woman of Osaka.
1936 71m/B *JP* Isuzu Yamada; *D:* Kenji Mizoguchi. **VHS $59.95** *SVS, TAM* ♫♫½

The Oscar Unless you enjoy razzing bad acting, this is not for you. Meant as a comeuppance for Hollywood, by Hollywood, this story of a star climbing the ladder of success and squashing fingers on every rung is too schlocky to succeed. The climax, when the scumbag star thinks he's won an Oscar and stands up, only to find it's for someone else, was based on Frank Capra's embarrassing experience with the same situation.
1966 (R) 119m/C Stephen Boyd, Elke Sommer, Jill St. John, Tony Bennett, Milton Berle, Eleanor Parker, Joseph Cotten, Edie Adams, Ernest Borgnine, Ed Begley Sr., Walter Brennan, Broderick Crawford, James Dunn, Peter Lawford, Merle Oberon, Bob Hope, Frank Sinatra; *D:* Russel Rouse. **VHS, Beta $19.95** *SUE* ♫½

Oscar The improbable casting of Stallone in a 1930s style crime farce (an attempt to change his image) is hard to imagine, and harder to believe. Stallone has little to do as he plays the straight man in this often ridiculous story of a crime boss who swears he'll go straight. Cameos aplenty, with Curry's the most notable. Based on a French play by Claude Magnier.
1991 (PG) 109m/C Sylvester Stallone, Ornella Muti, Peter Riegert; *Cameos:* Tim Curry, Chazz Palminteri; *D:* John Landis. **VHS, LV $19.99** *COL, IME, TOU* ♫♫

Oscar's Greatest Moments: 1971-1991 Collection of highlights from the Oscar ceremonies, featuring footage from the past 21 years. Proceeds from video sales benefit the Center for Motion Picture Study.
1992 110m/C *D:* Jeff Margolis. **VHS, LV, 8mm $19.95** *COL, BTV* ♫♫

Ossessione An adaptation of "The Postman Always Rings Twice," transferred to Fascist Italy, where a drifter and an innkeeper's wife murder her husband. Visconti's first feature, which initiated Italian neo-realism, was not released in the U.S. until 1975 due to a copyright dispute. In Italian with English subtitles.
1942 135m/B *IT* Massimo Girotti, Clara Calamai, Juan deLanda, Elio Marcuzzo; *D:* Luchino Visconti. **VHS, Beta $79.95** *FCT, TAM* ♫♫♫½

The Osterman Weekend Peckinpah was said to have disliked the story and the script in this, his last film, which could account for the convoluted and confusing end result. Adding to the problem is the traditional difficulty of adapting Robert Ludlum's complex psychological thrillers for the screen. The result: cast members seem to not quite "get it" as they portray a group of friends, one of whom has been convinced by the CIA that the others are all Soviet spies.
1983 (R) 102m/C Burt Lancaster, Rutger Hauer, Craig T. Nelson, Dennis Hopper, John Hurt, Chris Sarandon, Meg Foster, Helen Shaver; *D:* Sam Peckinpah. **VHS, Beta, LV $79.99** *HBO* ♫♫

Otello A performance of the Verdi opera taped at the Arena di Verona in Rome.
1982 135m/C Kiri Te Kanawa, Vladimir Atlantov, Piero Cappucilli. **VHS, Beta, LV $39.95** *HMV, HBO, PIA* ♫♫♫

Otello An uncommon film treat for opera fans, with a stellar performance by Domingo as the trouble Moor who murders his wife in a fit of jealous rage and later finds she was never unfaithful. Be prepared, however, for changes from the Shakespeare and Verdi stories, necessitated by the film adaptation. Highly acclaimed and awarded; in Italian with English subtitles.
1986 123m/C *IT* Placido Domingo, Katia Ricciarelli, Justino Diaz; *D:* Franco Zeffirelli. **VHS, Beta $79.95** *HMV, MED, MVD* ♫♫♫½

Othello A silent version of Shakespeare's tragedy, featuring Jannings as the tragic Moor. Titles are in English; with musical score.
1922 81m/B *GE* Emil Jannings, Lya de Putti, Werner Krauss; *D:* Dimitri Buchowetzki. **VHS, Beta $29.95** *NOS, VYY, DVT* ♫♫½

Othello Welles' striking adaptation of the Shakespeare tragedy casts him as the self-deluding Moor, with MacLiammoir as the despicable Iago and Cloutier as innocent victim, Desdemona. Welles filmed his epic over a four-year period due to budget difficulties, which also resulted in his filming in a number of different countries and settings. The film underwent a $1 million restoration, supervised by Welles' daughter, prior to its limited theatrical re-release in 1992.
1952 90m/B Orson Welles, Michael MacLiammoir, Suzanne Cloutier, Robert Coote, Hilton Edwards, Michael Lawrence, Nicholas Bruce, Fay Compton, Doris Dowling, Jean Davis, Joseph Cotten, Joan Fontaine; *D:* Orson Welles. **VHS $89.95** *ACA* ♫♫♫

Othello Shakespeare's keen understanding of jealousy in love results in perhaps his greatest triumph as a stage play and his prime example of the tragic hero, Othello. Made for television.
1982 120m/C *GB* Anthony Hopkins, Bob Hoskins, Penelope Wilton. **VHS, Beta, LV** *TLF* ♫♫

The Other Eerie, effective thriller adapted by Tyron from his supernatural novel. Twin brothers represent good and evil in a 1930s Connecticut farm town beset with gruesome murders and accidents. A good scare, with music by Jerry Goldsmith.
1972 (PG) 100m/C Martin Udvarnoky, Chris Udvarnoky, Uta Hagen, Diana Muldaur, Christopher Connelly, Victor French, John Ritter; *D:* Robert Mulligan; *M:* Jerry Goldsmith. **VHS, Beta $59.98** *FOX* ♫♫♫

Other Hell Schlocky Italian-made chiller has the devil inhabiting a convent where he does his damnest to upset the nuns. Gross, but not scary—lots of cliche dark-hallway scenes and fright music.
1985 (R) 88m/C *IT* Carlo De Meyo, Francesca Carmeno; *D:* Stefan Oblowsky. **VHS, Beta $69.98** *LIV, VES* ♫

Other People's Money DeVito is "Larry the Liquidator," a corporate raider with a heart of stone and a penchant for doughnuts. When he sets his sights on a post-smokestack era, family-owned cable company, he gets a taste of love for the first time in his life. He and Miller, the daughter of the company president and also its legal advisor, court one another while sparring over the fate of the company. Unbelievably clipped ending mars otherwise enterprising comedy about the triumph of greed in corporate America. Based on the off-Broadway play by Jerry Sterner.

1991 (R) 101m/C Danny DeVito, Penelope Ann Miller, Dean Jones, Gregory Peck, Piper Laurie; **D:** Norman Jewison. **VHS, LV, 8mm $19.98** WAR, CCB ⅃⅃½

The Other Side of Midnight The dreary, depressingly shallow life story of a poor French girl, dumped by an American GI, who sleeps her way to acting stardom and a profitable marriage, then seeks revenge for the jilt. Based on Sidney Sheldon's novel, it's not even titillating—just a real downer.
1977 (R) 160m/C Susan Sarandon, Marie-France Pisier, John Beck, Raf Vallone, Clu Gulager, Sorrell Booke; **D:** Charles Jarrott. **VHS, Beta, LV $59.98** FOX Woof!

The Other Side of the Mountain Tear-jerking true story of Olympic hopeful skier Jill Kinmont, paralyzed in a fall. Bridges helps her pull her life together. A sequel followed two years later. Based on the book "A Long Way Up" by E. G. Valens. **AKA:** A Window to the Sky.
1975 (PG) 102m/C Marilyn Hassett, Beau Bridges, Dabney Coleman, John Garfield, Griffin Dunne; **D:** Larry Peerce. **VHS, Beta $59.95** MCA ⅃⅃

The Other Side of the Mountain, Part 2 Quadriplegic Jill Kinmont, paralyzed in a skiing accident that killed her hopes for the Olympics, overcomes depression and the death of the man who helped her to recover. In this chapter, she falls in love again and finds happiness. More tears are jerked.
1978 (PG) 99m/C Marilyn Hassett, Timothy Bottoms; **D:** Larry Peerce. **VHS, Beta $59.95** MCA ⅃⅃

Oubliette A peripheral version of Francois Villon, in what is a recently discovered and restored film, the earliest extant Chaney film.
1914 35m/B Lon Chaney Sr. **VHS, Beta $39.50** GVV, LSV ⅃⅃

Our Daily Bread Vidor's sequel to the 1928 "The Crowd." A young couple inherit a farm during the Depression and succeed in managing the land. A near-classic, with several sequences highly influenced by directors Alexander Dovshenko and Sergei Eisenstein. Director Vidor also co-scripted this film, risking bankruptcy to finance it. **AKA:** Miracle of Life.
1934 80m/B Karen Morley, Tom Keene, John Qualen, Barbara Pepper, Addison Richards; **D:** King Vidor. **VHS, Beta, LV $19.95** NOS, SUE, KRT ⅃⅃⅃

Our Dancing Daughters Flapper (Crawford on the brink of stardom) falls hard for millionaire who's forced into arranged marriage, but obliging little missus kicks bucket so Crawford can step in.
1928 98m/B Joan Crawford, Johnny Mack Brown, Nils Asther, Dorothy Sebastian, Anita Page; **D:** Harry Beaumont. **VHS, Beta $19.98** MGM, FCT ⅃⅃½

Our Family Business Made for television and meant as a series pilot, this generally plodding "Godfather"-type story is saved by good performances by Wanamaker and Milland.
1981 74m/C Sam Wanamaker, Vera Miles, Ray Milland, Ted Danson, Chip Mayer; **D:** Robert Collins. **VHS $59.95** LIV ⅃⅃

Our Gang Two silent "Our Gang" comedies, including "Thundering Fleas" and "Shivering Spooks."
1926 57m/B Joe Cobb, Farina Hoskins, Mary Kornman, Mickey Daniels, Scooter Lowry. **VHS, Beta, 8mm $24.95** VYY ⅃⅃

Our Gang Comedies The five shorts on this cassette show the gang at their comedic best. They include "The Big Premiere," "Bubbling Troubles," "Clown Princes," "Don't Lie" and "Farm Hands."
194? 53m/B Robert (Bobby) Blake, Billie "Buckwheat" Thomas, George "Spanky" McFarland, Darla Hood, Carl "Alfalfa" Switzer, Tommy "Butch" Bond, Eugene "Porky" Lee, Shirley "Muggsy" Coates, Joe "Corky" Geil, Billy "Froggy" Lauglin. **VHS, Beta $29.95** MGM ⅃⅃

Our Gang Comedy Festival A 20-year span of comedy from the Little Rascals, including rare silent features.
1988 45m/B Joe Cobb, Farina Hoskins, Mary Kornman, Mickey Daniels, Scooter Lowry. **VHS** GKK ⅃⅃

Our Gang Comedy Festival 2 More riotous good times with The Little Rascals, including silent footage.
1989 45m/B Joe Cobb, Farina Hoskins, Mary Kornman, Mickey Daniels, Scooter Lowry. **VHS** GKK ⅃⅃

Our Hospitality One of Keaton's finest silent films, with all the elements in place. William McKay (Keaton) travels to the American South on a quaint train (a near-exact replica of the Stephenson Rocket), to claim an inheritance as the last survivor of his family. En route, a young woman traveler informs him that her family has had a long, deadly feud with his, and that they intend to kill him. McKay resolves to get the inheritance, depending on the Southern rule of hospitality to guests to save his life until he can make his escape. Watch for the river scene where, during filming, Keaton's own life was really in danger.
1923 74m/B Buster Keaton, Natalie Talmadge, Joe Keaton, Buster Keaton Jr., Kitty Bradbury, Joe Roberts; **D:** Buster Keaton. **VHS, LV $49.95** HBO ⅃⅃⅃⅃

Our Little Girl A precocious little tyke tries to reunite her estranged parents by running away to their favorite vacation spot. Sure to please Shirley Temple fans, despite a lackluster script.
1935 63m/B Shirley Temple, Joel McCrea, Rosemary Ames, Lyle Talbot, Erin O'Brien Moore; **D:** John S. Robertson. **VHS, Beta $19.98** FOX ⅃⅃

Our Man Flint James Bond clone Derek Flint uses gadgets and his ingenuity to save the world from an evil organization, GALAXY, that seeks world domination through control of the weather. The plot moves quickly around many bikini-clad women, but still strains for effect. Spawned one sequel: "In Like Flint."
1966 107m/C James Coburn, Lee J. Cobb, Gila Golan, Edward Mulhare, Benson Fong, Shelby Grant, Sigrid Valdis, Gianna Serra, James Brolin, Helen Funai, Michael St. Clair; **D:** Daniel Mann; **M:** Jerry Goldsmith. **VHS, Beta, LV $19.98** FOX ⅃⅃

Our Miss Brooks Quietly pleasing version of the television series. Miss Brooks pursues the "mother's boy" biology professor. The father of the child she begins tutoring appears taken with her. The professor takes notice.
1956 85m/B Eve Arden, Gale Gordon, Nick Adams, Richard Crenna, Don Porter; **D:** Al Lewis. **VHS** WAR ⅃⅃½

Our Modern Maidens Scandalous jazz-age drama in which Crawford and Fairbanks both fall in love with other people before their wedding is to take place. This sequel to "Our Dancing Daughters" features beautiful gowns and lush, opulent Art Deco

interiors. Based on a story by Josephine Lovett.
1929 75m/B Joan Crawford, Rod LaRocque, Douglas Fairbanks Jr., Anita Page, Josephine Dunn; **D:** Jack Conway; **W:** Josephine Lovett. **VHS $19.98** MGM ⅃⅃½

Our Relations Confusion reigns when Stan and Ollie meet the twin brothers they never knew they had, a pair of happy-go-lucky sailors. Laurel directs the pair through madcap encounters with their twins' wives and the local underworld. One of the pair's best efforts, though not well-remembered. Based on a story by W.W. Jacobs.
1936 94m/B Stan Laurel, Oliver Hardy, Alan Hale Jr., Sidney Toler, James Finlayson, Daphne Pollard; **D:** Harry Lachman. **VHS, Beta $19.95** MED, CCB, MLB ⅃⅃⅃½

Our Town Small-town New England life in Grover's Corners in the early 1900s is celebrated in this well-performed and directed adaptation of the Pulitzer Prize-winning play by Thornton Wilder. Film debut of Scott.
1940 90m/B Martha Scott, William Holden, Thomas Mitchell, Fay Bainter, Guy Kibbee, Beulah Bondi, Frank Craven; **D:** Sam Wood. Academy Awards '40 Nominations: Best Actress (Scott), Best Interior Decoration, Best Picture, Best Sound, Best Original Score; National Board of Review Awards '40: 10 Best Films of the Year. **VHS, Beta, 3/4U, Special order formats $9.95** NEG, MRV, NOS ⅃⅃⅃

Our Town Television version of Thornton Wilder's classic play about everyday life in Grovers Corners, a small New England town at the turn of the century. It hews more closely to the style of the stage version than the earlier film version.
1977 120m/C Ned Beatty, Sada Thompson, Ronny Cox, Glynnis O'Connor, Robby Benson, Hal Holbrook, John Houseman; **D:** Franklin Schaffer. **VHS, Beta, LV $74.95** VTK, MAS ⅃⅃⅃

Our Vines Have Tender Grapes A change of pace role for the volatile Robinson who plays a kind Norwegian widower, living in Wisconsin with his daughter, the spunky O'Brien. The film is made-up of small-town moments as O'Brien learns a few of life's lessons, eased by the thoughtful compassion of Robinson. Based on the novel "For Our Vines Have Tender Grapes" by George Victor Martin.
1945 105m/B Edward G. Robinson, Margaret O'Brien, James Craig, Agnes Moorehead, Jackie "Butch" Jenkins, Morris Carnovsky, Frances Gifford, Sara Haden, Louis Jean Heydt; **D:** Roy Rowland; **W:** Dalton Trumbo. **VHS $19.98** MGM, MOV ⅃⅃⅃½

Out A drifter's travels throughout the U.S. from the sixties to the eighties. Successfully manages to satirize just about every conceivable situation but keeps from posturing by not taking itself too seriously. Adapted from an experimental novel by Ronald Sukenick.
1988 88m/C Peter Coyote, Danny Glover, O-Lan Shepard, Jim Haynie, Scott Beach, Semu Haute; **D:** Eli Hollander. **VHS** NO ⅃⅃½

Out Cold Black comedy follows the misadventures of a butcher who believes he has accidentally frozen his business partner; the iced man's girlfriend, who really killed him; and the detective who tries to solve the crime. Too many poor frozen body jokes may leave the viewer cold.
1989 (R) 91m/C John Lithgow, Teri Garr, Randy Quaid, Bruce McGill; **D:** Malcolm Mowbray. **VHS, Beta, LV $89.98** HBO ⅃½

Out for Justice A psycho Brooklyn hood goes on a murder spree, and homeboy turned lone-wolf cop Seagal races other police and the mob to get at him. Bloodthirsty and profane, it does try to depict N.Y.C.'s

Italian-American community—but 90 percent of them are dead by the end so what's the point? Better yet, why does it open with a quote from Arthur Miller? Better still, what's Daffy Duck doing on this tape peddling Warner Brothers T-shirts to kid viewers?! **1991 (R) 91m/C** Steven Seagal, William Forsythe, Jerry Orbach. **VHS, Beta, LV, 8mm** $19.98 *WAR, PIA ☆☆½*

Out of Africa An epic film of the years spent by Danish authoress Isak Dinesen (her true name is Karen Blixen) on a Kenya coffee plantation. She moved to Africa to marry, and later fell in love with Denys Finch-Hatten, a British adventurer. Based on several books, including biographies of the two lovers. Some critics loved the scenery and music; others despised the acting and the script. A definite "no" for those who love action. **1985 (PG) 161m/C** Meryl Streep, Robert Redford, Klaus Maria Brandauer, Michael Kitchen, Malick Bowens, Michael Gough, Suzanna Hamilton; *D:* Sydney Pollack; *W:* Kurt Luedtke; *M:* John Barry. Academy Awards '85: Best Adapted Screenplay, Best Art Direction/Set Decoration, Best Cinematography, Best Director (Pollack), Best Picture, Best Sound, Best Original Score; Nominations: Best Actress (Streep), Best Costume Design, Best Supporting Actor (Brandauer); Golden Globe Awards '86: Best Film—Drama, Best Supporting Actor (Brandauer). **VHS, Beta, LV** $19.98 *MCA, BTV ☆☆☆*

Out of Bounds An Iowa farmboy picks up the wrong bag at the Los Angeles airport, and is plunged into a world of crime, drugs, and murder. Plenty of action, but the fast pace can't hide huge holes in the script or the silliness of Hall playing a tough kid on the run from the law. **1986 (R) 93m/C** Anthony Michael Hall, Jenny Wright, Jeff Kober; *D:* Richard Tuggle. **VHS, Beta, LV** $79.95 *COL ☆½*

Out of Control A plane full of rich teenagers crash on a secluded island and must battle a gang of vicious smugglers to survive. A teen sex theme keeps working its way in, leaving the viewer as confused as the actors and actresses appear to be. **1985 (R) 78m/C** Betsy Russell, Martin Hewitt, Claudia Udy, Andrew J. Lederer; *D:* Allan Holzman. **VHS, Beta, LV** $9.95 *NWV, STE ☆*

Out of Order A German-made film about people stuck in an office building's malevolent, free-thinking elevator. Dubbed. **1984 87m/C** *GE* Renee Soutendijk, Goetz George, Wolfgang Kieling, Hannes Jaenicke; *D:* Carl Schenkel. **VHS, Beta** $69.98 *LIV, VES ☆½*

Out of Season Mother and teenage daughter compete for the attentions of the mother's mysterious ex-lover. We never know who wins the man in this enigmatic drama set in an English village, and hints of incest make the story even murkier. Had only a short run in the U.S. *AKA:* Winter Rates. **1975 (R) 90m/C** *GB* Cliff Robertson, Vanessa Redgrave, Susan George; *D:* Alan Bridges. **VHS, Beta** $19.95 *UHV ☆☆*

Out of Sight, Out of Her Mind After witnessing her daughter burned alive, Alice is released from a mental institution. She tries to start a new life, but her daughter won't let her—she keeps appearing, crying out for help. **1989 (R) 94m/C** Susan Blakely, Eddie Albert, Wings Hauser. **VHS, Beta, LV** *PSM, PAR ☆☆*

Out of the Blue There's trouble in paradise for a married man when a shady lady passes out in his apartment. Thinking she is dead, he tries to get rid of the body. The antics with his neighbor and wife provide plenty of laughs.

1947 86m/B George Brent, Virginia Mayo, Carole Landis, Turhan Bey, Ann Dvorak; *D:* Leigh Jason. **VHS, Beta, LV** $19.95 *STE, NWV ☆☆½*

Out of the Blue A harsh, violent portrait of a shattered family. When an imprisoned father's return fails to reunite this Woodstock-generation family, the troubled teenage daughter takes matters into her own hands. "Easy Rider" star Hopper seems to have reconsidered the effects of the 1960s. **1982 (R) 94m/C** Dennis Hopper, Linda Manz, Raymond Burr; *D:* Dennis Hopper. **VHS, Beta** $59.95 *MED ☆☆☆*

Out of the Body A man is possessed by a spirit that likes to kill young, beautiful women. This makes him (and the viewer) uncomfortable. **1988 (R) 91m/C** Mark Hembrow, Tessa Humphries; *D:* Brian Trenchard-Smith. **VHS, LV** $79.95 *SVS ☆*

Out of the Dark The female employees of a telephone-sex service are stalked by a killer wearing a clown mask in this tongue-in-cheek thriller. A few laughs amid the slaughter. Look for Divine. **1988 (R) 98m/C** Cameron Dye, Divine, Karen Black, Bud Cort, Lynn Danielson, Geoffrey Lewis, Paul Bartel, Tracy Walter, Silvania Gallardo, Starr Andreeff, Lainie Kazan, Tab Hunter; *D:* Michael Schroeder. **VHS, Beta, LV** $89.95 *COL ☆½*

Out of the Darkness A television movie about the personal life of the New York detective who hunted and arrested sexual killer Son of Sam. Sheen shines in a tight suspenser. **1985 (R) 96m/C** Martin Sheen, Hector Elizondo, Matt Clark; *D:* Judd Taylor. **VHS, Beta, LV** $19.95 *STE, VMK ☆☆☆*

Out of the Past A private detective gets caught in a complex web of love, murder, and money in this film noir classic. The plot is torturous but clear thanks to fine directing. Mitchum became an overnight star after this film, which was overlooked but now considered one of the best in its genre. Remade in 1984 as "Against All Odds." *AKA:* Build My Gallows High. **1947 97m/B** Robert Mitchum, Kirk Douglas, Jane Greer, Rhonda Fleming, Steve Brodie, Dickie Moore; *D:* Jacques Tourneur. **VHS, Beta, LV** $19.98 *MED, TTC ☆☆☆½*

Out of the Rain A small town becomes a hotbed of deceit and lies due to the influence of drugs. A man and and a woman engage in a passionate struggle to free themselves from the town's grip. **1990 (R) 91m/C** Bridget Fonda, Michael O'Keefe, John E. O'Keefe, John Seitz, Georgine Hall, Al Shannon; *D:* Gary Winick; *W:* Shem Bitterman. **VHS, Beta, LV** $9.99 *CCB, LIV ☆☆½*

The Out-of-Towners A pair of Ohio rubes travels to New York City and along the way everything that could go wrong does. Lemmon's performance is excellent and Neil Simon's script is, as usual, both wholesome and funny. **1970 (G) 98m/C** Jack Lemmon, Sandy Dennis, Anne Meara, Sandy Baron, Billy Dee Williams; *D:* Arthur Hiller; *W:* Neil Simon. **VHS, Beta, LV** $14.95 *PAR ☆☆☆*

Out on a Limb MacLaine plays herself in this made-for-television miniseries based on her best-selling book by the same name. In the midst of love affairs with an unnamed British politician and a mysterious teacher, she learns about her past, present, and future through meditation and her beliefs in reincarnation. Features footage of psychics performing spiritual channeling. Beautiful scenery filmed on location in California, Hong

Kong, London, Hawaii, Sweden, and Peru, but the acting is just average, and the movie is slow in some parts. A 234-minute special collector's edition is also available. **1987 160m/C** Shirley MacLaine, Charles Dance, John Heard, Anne Jackson, Jerry Orbach; *D:* Robert Butler. **VHS, Beta** $89.95 *PSM ☆☆*

Out on a Limb Lame comedy follows the misadventures of financial whiz Bill Campbell (Broderick). His young sister is convinced their stepfather is a criminal and persuades her brother to return home. On his way, Bill is robbed and abandoned by a woman hitchhiker, then found by two moronic brothers. It also turns out his stepfather has a twin brother who wants revenge for past crimes. Frantic chase scenes and lots of noise do not a comedy make. Broderick and Jones also appeared together in "Ferris Bueller's Day Off." **1992 (PG) 82m/C** Matthew Broderick, Jeffrey Jones, Heidi Kling, John Reilly, Marian Mercer, Larry Hankin, David Margulies; *D:* Francis Veber. **VHS, Beta, LV** $19.95 *MGM ☆*

Out on Bail A law-abiding citizen witnesses a murder, only to discover the crooked town council is behind the slaying. **1989 (R) 102m/C** Robert Ginty, Kathy Shower, Tom Badal, Sydney Lassick; *D:* Gordon Hessler. **VHS, Beta** $89.95 *TWE ☆½*

Outcast A young tough heads west to seize the family ranch wrongfully held by a conniving uncle. Of course he finds love as well, and enjoys gun and fistfights in this exciting though unspectacular western. **1954 90m/C** John Derek, Jim Davis, Joan Davis; *D:* William Witney. **VHS** $19.98 *REP ☆☆*

The Outcast Story of three brothers who live by the ax, love from the heart, hate with passion, and die violently. Trouble is they have to recite from a script written in crayon. **1984 86m/C** Ben Dekker, Sandra Prinsloo. **VHS** $19.95 *REP ☆½*

The Outcasts A Taiwanese film about young gay boys in an urban jungle who are given shelter and protection by an aging photographer. In Chinese with English subtitles. **1986 102m/C** *TW D:* Yu Kan-Ping. **VHS, Beta** $79.95 *FCT ☆☆☆*

Outcasts of the City The sort of negligible film filler that TV killed off. An American officer in post-WWII Germany romances a German girl, then gets blamed for the death of her Boche beau. **1958 61m/B** Osa Massen, Robert Hutton, Maria Palmer, Nestor Paiva, John Hamilton, George Neise, Norbert Schiller, George Sanders; *D:* Boris L. Petroff. **VHS** $19.95 *NOS ☆☆*

The Outer Limits: Galaxy Being "There is nothing wrong with your TV set..." in this sci-fi series which ran from 1963-1965. In the show's pilot episode an obsessed scientist transmits a pure-energy being from Andromeda into our universe, and chaos ensues. Additional episodes are available. **1963 53m/B** Cliff Robertson, Jacqueline Scott, Lee Phillips, William O. Douglas Jr.; *D:* Leslie Stevens. **VHS, Beta** $12.98 *MGM, MOV ☆☆*

The Outing A group of high school kids sneaks into a museum at night to party, and get hunted down by a 3,000-year-old genie-in-a-lamp. The genie idea is original enough to make things interesting. Mediocre special effects and run-of-the-mill acting. *AKA:* The Lamp. **1987 (R) 87m/C** Deborah Winters, James Huston; *D:* Tom Daley. **VHS, Beta** $14.95 *LIV ☆☆*

Outland On a volcanic moon of Jupiter, miners begin suffering from spells of insanity. A single federal marshal begins an investigation that threatens the colony's survival. No more or less than a western in space, and the science is rather poor. Might make an interesting double feature with "High Noon," though.
1981 (R) 109m/C Sean Connery, Peter Boyle, Frances Sternhagen, James B. Sikking; *D:* Peter Hyams; *M:* Jerry Goldsmith. VHS, Beta, LV $19.98 WAR, PIA ⅔⅔

The Outlaw Hughes's variation on the saga of Billy the Kid, which spends more time on Billy's relationship with girlfriend Rio than the climactic showdown with Pat Garrett. The famous Russell vehicle isn't as steamy as it must have seemed to viewers of the day, but the brouhaha around it served to keep it on the shelf for six years. Also available colorized.
1943 123m/B Jane Russell, Jack Beutel, Walter Huston, Thomas Mitchell; *D:* Howard Hughes. VHS, Beta, LV, 3/4U, Special order formats $8.95 NEG, MRV, NOS ⅔⅔

The Outlaw and His Wife An early silent film about a farmer, accused of a petty crime, who flees with his wife into the mountains to escape the police. This powerful drama was a breakthrough film for the early Swedish movie industry.
1917 73m/B *SW* Victor Sjostrom, Edith Erastoff; *D:* Victor Sjostrom. VHS, Beta, LV $29.95 KIV, FCT, TAM ⅔⅔½

The Outlaw Bikers—Gang Wars The original road warriors take it to the streets as rival biker gangs square off.
1970 90m/C Clancy Syrko, Des Roberts, King John III, Jack Jackson; *D:* Lawrence Merrick. VHS, Beta $60.05 NCM ⅔⅔½

Outlaw Blues An ex-convict becomes a national folk hero when he sets out to reclaim his stolen hit song about prison life. St. James is charming in her first major movie role. A grab bag of action, drama, and tongue-in-cheek humor.
1977 (PG) 101m/C Peter Fonda, Susan St. James, Johnny Crawford, Michael Lerner, James Callahan; *D:* Richard T. Heffron. VHS, Beta $59.95 WAR ⅔⅔

Outlaw Express After the annexing of California, a U.S. marshall is sent to stop a gang of outlaws who have been raiding Spanish landowners.
1938 57m/B Bob Baker, Cecilia Callejo, Leroy Mason, Don Barclay, Carleton Young; *D:* George Waggner. VHS, Beta $24.95 DVT ⅔½

Outlaw Force A Vietnam veteran country singer tracks down the vicious rednecks that kidnapped his daughter and raped and killed his wife. Heavener did all the work in this low-budget, low-quality take-off on "Death Wish."
1987 (R) 95m/C David Heavener, Frank Stallone, Paul Smith, Robert Bjorklund, Devin Dunsworth; *D:* David Heavener. VHS, Beta $19.98 TWE ⅔

Outlaw Fury Another Shamrock Ellison epic, this time dealing with a coward proving himself by killing the bad guys.
1950 55m/B James Ellison, Russell Hayden. VHS, Beta, LV NO ⅔½

Outlaw Gang A marshal investigates a rash of rancher killings, leading to a conflict between Indians and local land and water companies.
1949 59m/B Donald (Don "Red") Barry, Robert Lowery, Betty Adams. VHS, Beta, LV NO ⅔½

The Outlaw Josey Wales Eastwood plays a farmer with a motive for revenge—his family was killed and for years he was betrayed and hunted. His desire to play the lone killer is, however, tempered by his need for family and friends. He kills plenty, but in the end finds happiness. Considered one of the last great Westerns, with many superb performances. Eastwood took over directorial chores during filming from Philip Kaufman, who co-scripted. Adapted from "Gone To Texas" by Forest Carter.
1976 (PG) 135m/C Clint Eastwood, Chief Dan George, Sondra Locke, Matt Clark, John Vernon, Bill McKinney, Sam Bottoms; *D:* Clint Eastwood, Philip Kaufman. VHS, Beta, LV $19.98 WAR, TLF ⅔⅔⅔½

Outlaw Justice Worn oater plot has our hero infiltrating a gang of outlaws to bring them to justice and save the heroine.
1932 56m/C Jack Hoxie, Dorothy Gulliver, Donald Keith, Kermit Maynard, Charles King, Tom London; *D:* Armand Schaefer. VHS, Beta GPV ⅔⅔

Outlaw of Gor Once again, the mild professor is transported to Gor, where he has new, improved, bloody adventures. Lots of sword-play, but no magic. Sequel to "Gor." From the novel by John Norman.
1987 (PG) 89m/C Rebecca Ferratti, Urbano Barberini, Jack Palance, Donna Denton; *D:* John Cardos. VHS, Beta $19.98 WAR ⅔½

Outlaw of the Plains Another of Crabbe's cowboy pictures in which he played hero Billy Carson, now bailing his trouble-prone sidekick out of a land swindle. Very plain indeed.
1946 56m/B Buster Crabbe, Al "Fuzzy" St. John, Patti McCarty, Charles King, Karl Hackett, John Cason, Bud Osborne, Budd Buster, Charles "Slim" Whitaker; *D:* Sam Newfield. VHS $19.95 NOS ⅔

Outlaw Riders Three outlaw bikers take it on the lam after committing a series of disastrous bank robberies.
1972 (PG) 84m/C Sonny West, Darlene Duralia, Bambi Allen, Bill Bonner; *D:* Tony Houston. VHS, Beta $59.95 WWV ⅔

Outlaw Roundup The Texas Rangers battle an outlaw gang. Guess who wins.
1944 51m/B Tex O'Brien, Jim Newill, Guy Wilkerson, Helen Chapman, Jack Ingram, I. Stanford Jolley; *D:* Harry Fraser. VHS, Beta $19.95 NOS, MRV, VDM ⅔

Outlaw Rule Standard action-packed western adventure pitting outlaws against the law of the West.
1936 61m/B Reb Russell, Betty Mack, Yakima Canutt, Jack Rockwell, John McGuire, Alan Bridge; *D:* S. Roy Luby. VHS, Beta $19.95 NOS, VCN, HEG ⅔½

The Outlaw Tamer Western adventure starring Chandler.
1933 56m/B Lane Chandler, J.P. McGowan, Janet Morgan, George "Gabby" Hayes; *D:* J.P. McGowan. VHS, Beta VCN ⅔

Outlaw Trail The Trail Blazers put an end to a counterfeiter's evil ways.
1944 53m/B Hoot Gibson, Bob Steele, Chief Thundercloud, Jennifer Holt, Cy Kendall; *D:* Robert Tansey. VHS, Beta $19.95 NOS, DVT ⅔½

Outlaw Women A western town is run by a woman who won't let male outlaws in—until one wins her heart.
1952 76m/C Marie Windsor, Jackie Coogan, Carla Balenda; *D:* Sam Newfield. VHS, Beta $59.95 MON ⅔

Outlaws of Sonora A man transports money to a neighboring town while his outlaw double tries to steal it from him.
1938 58m/B Bob Livingston, Ray Corrigan, Max Terhune, Jack Mulhall, Otis Harlan; *D:* George Sherman. VHS $19.95 NOS, DVT ⅔½

Outlaws of the Desert Having run out of bad guys in the Old West, Hoppy and his pals head to Arabia to buy some horses. Once there, they get involved in a kidnapping. Russell Hayden is replaced as Hoppy's sidekick by Brad King. Duncan ("The Cisco Kid") Renaldo plays the sheik.
1941 66m/B William Boyd, Brad King, Andy Clyde, Forrest Stanley, Jean Phillips, Duncan Renaldo, George Lewis; *D:* Howard Bretherton. VHS $19.95 NOS ⅔½

Outlaws of the Range Action western featuring outlaws who terrorize the countryside.
1936 60m/B Bill Cody, Catherine Cotter, William McCall, Gordon Griffith; *D:* Al Herman. VHS, Beta VCN ⅔½

Outlaw's Paradise Cowboy hero McCoy plays not only a lawman out to catch mail thieves, but also the chief outlaw he's hunting! That's one way to keep the budget low.
1939 62m/B Tim McCoy, Benny Corbett, Joan Barclay, Ted Adams, Forrest Taylor, Bob Terry; *D:* Sam Newfield. VHS $15.95 NOS, LOO, RXM ⅔

Outpost in Morocco A desert soldier is sent to quiet the restless natives and falls for the rebel leader's daughter. The good guys win, but the love interest is sacrificed. Glory before love boys, and damn the story.
1949 92m/B George Raft, Marie Windsor, Akim Tamiroff, John Litel, Eduard Franz; *D:* Robert Florey. VHS $19.95 NOS, MRV, MGM ⅔½

Outrage! An upstanding citizen guns down his daughter's killer and turns himself in to police. His ambitious lawyer fights an open-and-shut homicide case with both fair and foul means. Not a shootout like the cassette box suggests, but an okay courtroom drama attacking excesses of the legal system. From a novel by Henry Denker, made for TV by producer Irwin Allen.
1986 96m/C Robert Preston, Beau Bridges, Anthony Newley, Mel Ferrer, Burgess Meredith, Linda Purl, William Allen Young; *D:* Walter Grauman. VHS $89.95 VMK ⅔⅔½

Outrageous! An offbeat, low-budget comedy about the strange relationship between a gay female impersonator and his pregnant schizophrenic friend. The pair end up in New York, where they feel right at home. Russell's impersonations of female film stars earned him the best actor prize at the Berlin Film Festival.
1977 (R) 100m/C *CA* Craig Russell, Hollis McLaren, Richard Easley, Allan Moyle, Helen Shaver; *D:* Richard Benner. VHS, Beta $64.95 COL ⅔⅔⅔

Outrageous Fortune Two would-be actresses - one prim and innocent and one wildly trampy - chase after the same two-timing boyfriend and get involved in a dangerous CIA plot surrounding a deadly bacteria. Tired plot. Mediocre acting and formula jokes, but somehow still funny. Disney's first foray into comedy for grown-ups.
1987 (R) 112m/C Shelley Long, Bette Midler, George Carlin, Peter Coyote; *D:* Arthur Hiller. VHS, Beta, LV $19.95 TOU ⅔⅔

Outside Chance A soapy, sanitized remake of Mimieux's film, "Jackson County Jail," wherein an innocent woman is persecuted in a small Southern jail. Made for television.
1978 92m/C Yvette Mimieux, Royce D. Applegate; *D:* Michael Miller. VHS, Beta $59.98 NLC ⅔

Outside Chance of Maximillian Glick A sentimental Canadian comedy about a boy's dreams and his tradition-bound Jewish family.
1988 (G) 94m/C *CA* Noam Zylberman, Fairuza Balk, Saul Rubinek; *D:* Allan Goldstein. **VHS, Beta** $14.95 *HMD* 🎬🎬

The Outside Man A French hit man is called to Los Angeles to knock off a crime boss, which he does. But then an American hit man is hired to do in the Frenchman. The climatic showdown is set around the crime boss' body, which happens to be embalmed in a sitting position. Decidedly offbeat. *AKA:* Un Homme Est Mort.
1973 (PG) 104m/C *FR* Jean-Louis Trintignant, Roy Scheider, Ann-Margret, Angie Dickinson, Georgia Engel, Carlo De Meyo, Umberto Orsini, Ted DeCorsia, Felice Orlandi, John Hillerman; *D:* Jacques Deray. **VHS** $14.95 *MGM* 🎬🎬

Outside the Law Lon Chaney plays dual roles of the underworld hood in "Black Mike Sylva," and a Chinese servant in "Ah Wing." Silent.
1921 77m/B Lon Chaney Sr., Priscilla Dean, Ralph Lewis, Wheeler Oakman; *D:* Tod Browning. **VHS, Beta** $16.95 *SNC, CCB, VYY* 🎬🎬

The Outsiders Based on the popular S.E. Hinton book, the story of a teen gang from the wrong side of the tracks and their conflicts with society and each other. Melodramatic and over-done, but teen-agers still love the story. Good soundtrack and cast ripples with up and coming stars. Followed by a television series. Coppola adapted another Hinton novel the same year, "Rumble Fish."
1983 (PG) 91m/C C. Thomas Howell, Matt Dillon, Ralph Macchio, Patrick Swayze, Diane Lane, Tom Cruise, Emilio Estevez, Rob Lowe, Tom Waits, Leif Garrett; *D:* Francis Ford Coppola. **VHS, Beta, LV** $19.98 *WAR* 🎬🎬½

Outtakes A piecemeal compilation of comedy skits, concentrating on sex and genre parody.
1985 (R) 85m/C Forrest Tucker, Bobbi Wexler, Joleen Lutz; *D:* Jack M. Sell. **VHS, Beta** $79.95 *SVS* 🎬½

The Oval Portrait An adaptation of the Edgar Allan Poe suspense tale about a Civil War-era maiden, her illicit love for a Confederate soldier and her eventual death.
1988 89m/C Giselle MacKenzie, Barry Coe; *D:* Regelio A. Gonzalez Jr. **VHS, Beta** *NO* 🎬½

Over Her Dead Body A bumbling cop and a dizzy girl end up hauling around a woman's corpse after a hilarious mishap. *AKA:* Enid is Sleeping.
1991 (R) 105m/C Judge Reinhold, Elizabeth Perkins, Rhea Perlman. **VHS** $89.98 *LIV, VES* 🎬🎬

Over Indulgence A young woman witnesses a murder in an affluent society in British East Africa.
1987 (R) 95m/C Denholm Elliott, Holly Aird, Michael Byrne, Kathryn Pogson; *D:* Ross Devenish. **VHS, Beta** $79.98 *MCG* 🎬🎬

Over the Brooklyn Bridge A young Jewish man (Gould) must give up his Catholic girlfriend (Hemingway) in order to get his uncle (Caesar) to lend him the money he needs to buy a restaurant in Manhattan. Nowhere near as funny as it should be, and potentially offensive to boot. *AKA:* My Darling Shiksa.
1983 (R) 100m/C Elliott Gould, Sid Caesar, Shelley Winters, Margaux Hemingway, Carol Kane, Burt Young; *D:* Menahem Golan. **VHS, Beta** $79.95 *MGM* 🎬🎬

Over the Edge The music of Cheap Trick, The Cars, and The Ramones highlights this realistic tale of alienated suburban youth on the rampage. Dillon makes his screen debut in this updated, well-done "Rebel Without a Cause." Shelved for several years, the movie was finally released after Dillon made it big. Sleeper with excellent direction and dialogue.
1979 (PG) 91m/C Michael Kramer, Matt Dillon, Pamela Ludwig, Vincent Spano; *D:* Jonathan Kaplan. **VHS, Beta** $19.98 *WAR* 🎬🎬½

Over the Hill Dukakis stars as Alma, an eccentric widow who decides to leave her well-meaning son's restrictive home in Maine to visit her estranged daughter Elizabeth in Sydney, Australia. Embarassed by her peculiarities Elizabeth arranges a holiday away but Mom has her own plans. She wants to "loop the loop," and make a complete circuit around the Australian continent. Soon Alma is on the road, meeting fellow eccentrics and experiencing a variety of adventures.
1993 (PG) 102m/C Olympia Dukakis, Sigrid Thornton, Derek Fowlds, Pippa Grandison; *D:* George Miller. **VHS, LV** *NLC, COL, IME* 🎬🎬½

Over the Summer Strong drama about a troubled teen who escapes the city for a summer with her grandparents. No cliches here—the grandfather lusts after the granddaughter and eventually kills himself, and problems remain at the end. Intelligent and entertaining, though marred by needless nude scenes.
1985 97m/C Laura Hunt, Johnson West, Catherine Williams, David Romero; *D:* Teresa Sparks. **VHS, Beta** $69.98 *LIV, VES* 🎬🎬½

Over the Top The film that started a nationwide arm-wrestling craze. A slow-witted trucker decides the only way he can retain custody of his estranged son, as well as win the boy's respect, is by winning a big arm-wrestling competition. Stallone is an expert at grinding these movies out by now, and the kid (General Hospital's Mikey) is all right, but the end result is boredom, as it should be with an arm-wrestling epic.
1986 (PG) 94m/C Sylvester Stallone, Susan Blakely, Robert Loggia, David Mendenhall; *D:* Menahem Golan. **VHS, Beta, LV** $19.98 *WAR* 🎬½

Overboard A wealthy, spoiled woman falls off of her yacht and into the arms of a low-class carpenter who picks her up and convinces her she is in fact his wife, and mother to his four brats. Just when she learns to like her life, the tables are turned again. Even though it's all been done before, you can't help but laugh at the screwy gags.
1987 (PG) 112m/C Goldie Hawn, Kurt Russell, Katherine Helmond, Roddy McDowall, Edward Herrmann; *D:* Garry Marshall. **VHS, Beta, LV** $19.98 *FOX, HMV* 🎬🎬

The Overcoat An adaptation of Nikolai Gogol's classic story about the dehumanizing life endured in 20th-century bureaucracy. All a menial civil servant wants is a new overcoat. When he finally gets one, this treasured article not only keeps him warm but makes him feel self-satisfied as well. In Russian with English subtitles.
1959 93m/B *RU* Rolan Bykov; *D:* Alexei Batalov. **VHS, Beta** $59.95 *HTV, TAM* 🎬🎬🎬½

Overdrawn at the Memory Bank In a futuristic tyranny, a romantic rebel becomes somehow fused with the spirit of Humphrey Bogart in the milieu of "Casablanca," and lives out a cliched version of the film character's adventures.
1983 84m/C Raul Julia, Linda Griffiths; *D:* Douglas Williams. **VHS, Beta** $19.95 *STE, NWV* 🎬🎬

Overexposed All the wackos love the sultry soap star Oxenburg; one is a killer. Eighty minutes and a bunch of bodies later the killer is unmasked. Plenty of suspense and some original gore. Based on the true stories of fans who stalk celebrities.
1990 (R) 80m/C Catherine Oxenberg, David Naughton, Jennifer Edwards, Karen Black; *D:* Larry Brand. **VHS** $79.98 *MGM* 🎬🎬

Overkill A detective and the vengeance-minded brother of a dead Japanese-American fight back against the controlling Yakuza in Little Tokyo.
1986 (R) 81m/C Steve Rally, John Nishio, Laura Burkett, Roy Summerset; *D:* Ulli Lommel. **Beta** *NO* 🎬

Overland Mail Fifteen episodes of the vintage serial filled with western action.
1941 225m/B Lon Chaney Jr., Helen Parrish. **VHS, Beta** $49.95 *NOS, VCN, MLB* 🎬

Overland Stage Raiders The "Three Mesquiteers" ride again, this time to guard a Greyhound bus! The trio must protect a shipment of gold from hijackers. This is the last film for Brooks, who had starred in the German masterpiece "Pandora's Box" in 1929.
1938 55m/B John Wayne, Ray Corrigan, Max Terhune, Louise Brooks, John Archer, Frank LaRue, Yakima Canutt; *D:* George Sherman. **VHS** $9.95 *REP, NOS* 🎬🎬🎬

Overlanders The Japanese may invade, but rather than kill 1,000 head of cattle, these Aussies drive the huge herd across the continent, facing danger along the way. Beautifully photographed, featuring the "Australian Gary Cooper" and a stampede scene to challenge "Dances with Wolves."
1946 91m/B *AU* Chips Rafferty, Daphne Campbell, Jean Blue, John Nugent Hayward; *D:* Harry Watt. **VHS, Beta** $19.95 *NOS, DVT, HEG* 🎬🎬🎬

The Overlanders A group of nine men, two women and a boy challenge the forbidding Canadian Northwest circa 1862.
1979 76m/C **VHS, Beta** $59.95 *TWE* 🎬🎬

Overnight Sensation A modern adaptation of the W. Somerset Maugham story about a traditional marriage being tested by the wife's sudden literary success.
1983 30m/C Louise Fletcher, Robert Loggia, Shari Belafonte-Harper. **VHS, Beta, Special order formats** $225.00 *PYR* 🎬🎬

Overseas: Three Women with Man Trouble Three beautiful sisters in French colonial Algeria surround themselves in a life of luxury to avoid the incredible social changes going on around them. Each sister has a different perspective on her life, and the perspectives are graphically revealed. Lush photography set in the Mediterranean. In French with English subtitles.
1990 96m/C *FR* Nicole Garcia, Marianne Basler, Philippe Galland, Pierre Doris, Brigitte Rouan; *D:* Brigitte Rouan; *W:* Brigitte Rouan. **VHS** $89.95 *FXL, ART, BTV* 🎬🎬🎬

Overthrow American sportswriter finds himself caught up in violence and intrigue in Buenos Aires.
1982 (R) 90m/C John Phillip Law, Lewis Van Bergen, Roger Wilson; *D:* Larry Ludman. **VHS, Beta** $79.95 *IMP, HHE, VTR* 🎬½

Overture An episode of "The Persuaders." Brett and Danny are tricked into helping a retired judge. This adventure leads them to the Mediterranean and a gorgeous gal.
1975 52m/C *GB* Roger Moore, Tony Curtis. **VHS** $39.95 *SVS* 🎬½

Overture to Glory A Jewish cantor longs for the world of opera. He leaves his wife and son to fulfill his passion, but eventually he loses his voice and humbly returns home on Yom Kippur, the Jewish Day of Atonement. He learns that his son has passed away. Grief-stricken, he goes to the synagogue. There, the cantor regains his voice as he performs Kol Nidre in a passionate and melodious rendering. In Yiddish with English subtitles. *AKA:* Der Vilner Shtot Khazn.
1940 85m/B Helen Beverly, Florence Weiss. VHS, Beta $79.95 ERG, TAM &&½

The Owl and the Pussycat Nerdy author gets the neighborhood hooker evicted from her apartment. She returns the favor, and the pair hit the street—and the sack—in Buck Henry's hilarious adaptation of the Broadway play. Streisand's first non-singing role.
1970 (PG) 96m/C Barbra Streisand, George Segal, Robert Klein, Allen Garfield; *D:* Herbert Ross. VHS, Beta, LV $9.95 GKK &&&

The Ox Slow-moving, simple tale, set in rural Sweden in the 1860's during a famine. Desperate to feed his family a tenant farmer kills his employer's ox. Consumed by guilt, the man is quickly found out and sentenced to life imprisonment. Pardoned after six years, the farmer returns to his family, to find out his wife has survived by doing things he finds difficult to forgive. Based on a true story. Directorial debut of Nykvist, the long-time cinematographer for Ingmar Bergman, well displays his familiarity with composition and lighting to heighten mood. In Swedish with English subtitles.
1991 91m/C SW Stellan Skarsgard, Ewa Froling, Lennart Hjulstrom, Max von Sydow, Liv Ullmann, Bjorn Granath, Erland Josephson; *W/D:* Sven Nykvist; *W:* Lasse Summanen. VHS, Special order formats $490.00 ICA &&½

The Ox-Bow Incident A popular rancher is murdered, and a mob of angry townspeople can't wait for the sheriff to find the killers. They hang the young man, despite the protests of Fonda, a cowboy with a conscience. Excellent study of mob mentality with strong individual characterizations. A brilliant western based on a true story by Walter Van Tilburg Clark. Also see "Twelve Angry Men"—less tragic but just as moving. *AKA:* Strange Incident.
1943 75m/B Henry Fonda, Harry Morgan, Dana Andrews, Anthony Quinn, Frank Conroy, Harry Davenport, Jane Darwell, William Eythe, Mary Beth Hughes; *D:* William A. Wellman. Academy Awards '43 Nominations: Best Picture; National Board of Review Awards '43: 10 Best Films of the Year, Best Director (Wellman). VHS, Beta, LV $19.98 FOX &&&&

The Ox-Bow Incident Usually called "Lynch Mob," this is a television play based upon the famous book and 1943 film about mob ethics.
1955 45m/B Cameron Mitchell, Robert Wagner, Raymond Burr. VHS, Beta $19.98 NOS, DVT &&&

Oxford Blues An American finagles his way into England's Oxford University and onto the rowing team in pursuit of the girl of his dreams. Beautiful scenery, but the plot is wafer-thin. Remake of "Yank at Oxford."
1984 (PG-13) 98m/C Rob Lowe, Ally Sheedy, Amanda Pays, Julian Sands, Michael Gough, Gail Strickland; *D:* Robert Boris. VHS, Beta, LV $19.98 FOX &&

Ozzie & Harriet Meet television's Nelson family in this 7-volume series, which contains two episodes of the sitcom per tape. In "The Pancake Mix," Ricky wants to get a refund from the baking company. In "The New Chairs," the department store sends the Nelsons more chairs than they had bargained for.
196? 55m/B Ozzie Nelson, Harriet Hilliard Nelson, David Nelson, Ricky Nelson. VHS $19.99 NOS, MOV &&

Pace That Kills An anti-drug cautionary drama from the Roaring '20s, one of many now marketed on cassette as campy fun. Beware, though, a little bit of this stuff goes a long way. A young man goes to the big city to find his missing sister and winds up hooked on heroin.
1928 87m/B Owen Gorin, Virginia Roye, Florence Turner. VHS, Beta, 8mm $29.95 VYY &

Pacific Heights Young San Francisco couple takes on mammoth mortgage assuming tenants will write their ticket to the American dream, but psychopathic tenant Keaton moves in downstairs and redecorates. He won't pay the rent and he won't leave. Creepy psycho-thriller has lapses but builds to effective climax.
1990 (R) 103m/C Melanie Griffith, Matthew Modine, Michael Keaton, Mako, Nobu McCarthy, Laurie Metcalf, Carl Lumbly, Dorian Harewood, Luca Bercovici, Tippi Hedren, Sheila McCarthy, Dan Hedaya, Beverly D'Angelo, Nicholas Pryor, Miriam Margolyes; *D:* John Schlesinger. VHS, LV $19.98 FOX &&&

Pacific Inferno During World War II, American POWs endeavor to break out of a Japanese prison camp in the Philippines. Their goal is to prevent their captors from retrieving millions of dollars worth of sunken U.S. gold. Made for cable television.
1985 90m/C Jim Brown, Richard Jaeckel, Tim Brown; *D:* Rolf Bayer. VHS, Beta NO &&

The Pack A group of dogs become wild when left on a resort island. A marine biologist leads the humans who fight to keep the dogs from using vacationers as chew toys. Fine production values keep it from going to the dogs. Made with the approval of the American Humane Society who helped with the treatment of stage hands. *AKA:* The Long, Dark Night.
1977 (R) 99m/C Joe Don Baker, Hope Alexander-Willis, R.G. Armstrong, Richard B. Shull; *D:* Robert Clouse. VHS, Beta $19.98 WAR &&½

Pack Up Your Troubles Laurel and Hardy make good on a promise to help find the grandfather of a girl whose father was killed in WWI. All they know is the grandfather's last name though—Smith. Wholesome R and R. *AKA:* We're In the Army Now.
1932 68m/B Stan Laurel, Oliver Hardy, James Finlayson, Jacquie Lyn; *D:* George Marshall. VHS, Beta $14.98 MED, FCT, MLB &&½

The Package An espionage thriller about an army sergeant who loses the prisoner he escorts into the U.S. When he tries to track him down, he uncovers a military plot to start World War III. Hackman is believable in his role as the sergeant.
1989 (R) 108m/C Gene Hackman, Tommy Lee Jones, Joanna Cassidy, Dennis Franz, Pam Grier, John Heard, Reni Santoni, Thalmus Rasulala; *D:* Andrew Davis. VHS, Beta, LV $19.98 ORI &&½

Packin' It In A Los Angeles family is in for a rude awakening when they leave the city for a quieter life in the Oregon woods. There they encounter a band of survivalists with semi-comedic results.
1983 92m/C Richard Benjamin, Paula Prentiss, Molly Ringwald, Tony Roberts, Andrea Marcovicci; *D:* Judd Taylor. VHS, Beta NO &&

Paco A young, South American boy heads for the city, where he meets his uncle. He discovers his uncle is the leader of a gang of youthful thieves. Predictable and sluggish.
1975 (G) 89m/C Jose Ferrer, Panchito Gomez, Allen Garfield, Pernell Roberts, Andre Marquis; *D:* Robert Vincent O'Neil. VHS, Beta PGN, GHV &½

Paddy A young Irish lad realizes his sexual potential by seducing every woman he can find. Freudians will have a field day. *AKA:* Goodbye to the Hill.
1970 (PG) 97m/C IR Des Cave, Milo O'Shea, Darbnia Molloy, Peggy Cass; *D:* Daniel Haller. VHS, Beta $59.98 NO &

Padre Padrone The much acclaimed adaptation of the Gavino Ledda autobiography about his youth in agrarian Sardinia with a brutal, tyrannical father. Eventually he overcomes his handicaps, breaks the destructive emotional ties to his father and successfully attends college. Highly regarded although low budget; in an Italian dialect (Sardinian) with English subtitles. *AKA:* Father Master; My Father, My Master.
1977 113m/C IT Omero Antonutti, Saverio Marconi, Marcella Michelangeli, Fabrizio Forte, Salverio Marioni; *D:* Paolo Taviani, Vittorio Taviani. VHS, Beta $59.95 COL, TAM &&&½

Pagan Love Song A dull musical which finds Keel in Tahiti taking over his uncle's coconut plantation and falling in love with Williams. Surprise! Williams performs one of her famous water ballets, which is the only saving grace in this lifeless movie. ♫The House of Singing Bamboo; Singing in the Sun; Etiquette; Why Is Love So Crazy; Tahiti; The Sea of the Moon; Pagan Love Song; Coconut Milk.
1950 76m/C Esther Williams, Howard Keel, Minna Gombell, Rita Moreno; *D:* Robert Alton. VHS $19.98 MGM &&

Paid to Kill A failing businessman hires a thug to kill him in order to leave his family insurance money, but when the business picks up, he can't contact the thug to cancel the contract. The actors' lack of talent is matched only by the characters' lack of motivation. *AKA:* Five Days.
1954 71m/B GB Dane Clark, Paul Carpenter, Thea Gregory; *D:* Montgomery Tully. VHS, Beta, LV NO &

Pain in the A— A hit man helps a suicidal shirt salesman solve his marital problems in this black comedy that was later Americanized as "Buddy, Buddy." Not for all tastes, but has acquired a reputation for its dark wit. In French with English subtitles.
1977 (R) 90m/C FR IT Lino Ventura, Jacques Brel, Caroline Cellier; *D:* Edouard Molinaro. VHS, Beta $59.95 COL, TAM &&&

Paint It Black A violent/steamy mystery and action flick from the director of "River's Edge," in which a young man from the silverspoon set develops a fascination for an artist.
1989 (R) 101m/C Sally Kirkland, Rick Rossovich, Martin Landau, Doug Savant, Peter Frechette, Julie Carmen, Jason Bernhard, Monique Van De Ven; *D:* Tim Hunter. VHS, Beta, LV $89.98 LIV, VES &&½

Paint Your Wagon A big-budget western musical-comedy about a gold mining boom town, and two prospectors sharing the same Mormon wife complete with a classic Lerner and Lowe score. Marvin chews up the sagebrush and Eastwood attempts to sing, although Seberg was mercifully dubbed. Overlong, with patches of interest, pretty songs, and plenty of panoramic scenery. Adapted by Paddy Chayevsky from L&L

play. ♫I Talk To the Trees; I Still See Elisa; I'm On My Way; Hand Me Down That Can O' Beans; Whoop-Ti-Ay; They Call the Wind Maria; There's a Coach Comin' In; Wandrin' Star; Best Things; The Gospel of No Name City; A Million Miles Away Behind the Door; The First Thing You Know; Gold Fever. **1969 (PG) 164m/C** Lee Marvin, Clint Eastwood, Jean Seberg, Harve Presnell; *D:* Joshua Logan; *M:* Frederick Loewe, Andre Previn, Alan Jay Lerner. **VHS, Beta, LV $29.95** PAR ⅋⅋½

Painted Desert Gable's first film role of any consequence came in this early sound western. Gable plays a villain opposite "good guy" William Boyd.
1931 80m/B William Boyd, Helen Twelvetrees, George O'Brien, Clark Gable, William Farnum; *D:* Howard Higgin. **VHS, Beta, 3/4U, Special order formats $19.95** NOS, MRV, HHT ⅋⅋

The Painted Hills Lassie outsmarts crooked miners and rescues her friends. Surprise, Surprise! Overly sentimental, but action packed and beautifully shot. Lassie's last outing with MGM.
1966 90m/C Paul Kelly, Bruce Cowling, Gary Gray, Art Smith, Ann Doran, Lassie; *D:* Harold F. Kress. **VHS, Beta $9.95** BPG, MRV ⅋⅋½

The Painted Stallion This 12-chapter serial features a mysterious figure on a painted stallion who attempts to maintain peace between Mexicans and Indians.
1937 212m/B Ray Corrigan, Hoot Gibson, Duncan Renaldo, Leroy Mason, Yakima Canutt; *D:* William Witney, Ray Taylor. **VHS, LV $29.98** NOS, VDM, REP ⅋⅋½

The Painted Veil Adaptation of a W. Somerset Maugham story. Garbo, once again the disillusioned wife turning to the affections of another man, is magnificent, almost eclipsing the weak script. Lost money at the box office, but for Garbo fans, an absolute must.
1934 83m/B Greta Garbo, Herbert Marshall, George Brent, Warner Oland, Jean Hersholt; *D:* Richard Boleslawski. **VHS, Beta $19.98** MGM, FCT ⅋⅋½

Paisan Six episodic tales of life in Italy, several featuring Allied soldiers and nurses during World War II. One of the stories tells of a man who tries to develop a relationship without being able to speak Italian. Another focuses on a young street robber who is confronted by one of his victims. Strong stories that covers a wide range of emotions. In Italian with English subtitles.
1946 90m/B *IT* Maria Michi, Carmela Sazio, Gar Moore, William Tubbs, Harriet White, Robert Van Loon, Dale Edmonds, Carla Pisacane, Dots Johnson; *W/D:* Roberto Rossellini; *W:* Federico Fellini. Academy Awards '49 Nominations: Best Story & Screenplay; National Board of Review Awards '48: 5 Best Foreign Films of the Year, Best Director (Fellini); Venice Film Festival '46: Special Prize. **VHS, Beta, 8mm, 3/4U, Special order formats $24.95** NOS, HHT, CAB ⅋⅋⅋

Pajama Game A spritely musical about the striking workers of a pajama factory and their plucky negotiator, who falls in love with the boss. Based on the hit Broadway musical, which was based on Richard Bissell's book "Seven and a Half Cents" and adapted for the screen by Bisell and George Abbott. Bob Fosse choreographed the dance numbers. ♫I'm Not at All in Love; Small Talk; There Once Was a Man; Steam Heat; Hernando's Highway; Hey There; Once-a Year-Day; Seven and a Half Cents; I'll Never Be Jealous Again; Racing with the Clock; The Pajama Game; Her Is.
1957 101m/C Doris Day, John Raitt, Eddie Foy Jr., Reta Shaw, Carol Haney; *D:* Stanley Donen, George Abbott. **VHS, Beta, LV $19.98** WAR ⅋⅋⅋½

Pajama Party Beach blanket bingo lost in space. Martian Kirk comes to Earth, scouting for a possible invasion. He falls into the lap of Annette and decides instead to save the planet. All the usual beach movie faces are present, including cameos by Avalon, Rickles, and Keaton. ♫It's That Kind of Day; There Has to Be a Reason; Where Did I Go Wrong?; Pajama Party; Beach Ball; Among the Young; Stuffed Animal.
1964 82m/C Tommy Kirk, Annette Funicello, Elsa Lanchester, Harvey Lembeck, Jesse White, Jody McCrea, Donna Loren, Susan Hart, Bobbi Shaw, Cheryl Sweeten, Luree Holmes, Candy Johnson, Dorothy Lamour, Toni Basil; *Cameos:* Buster Keaton, Frankie Avalon, Don Rickles; *D:* Don Weis. **VHS, LV** NO ⅋⅋

Pajama Tops A stage production of the classic French bedroom farce, taped live at the Music Hall Theatre in Toronto, Canada. Includes all the trials of marriage including adultery and deceit.
1983 105m/C Robert Klein, Susan George, Pia Zadora. **VHS** NO ⅋⅋½

Pal Joey Musical comedy about an opportunistic singer who courts a wealthy socialite in hopes that she will finance his nightclub. His play results in comedic complications. Stellar choreography, fine direction, and beautiful costumes complement performances headed by Hayworth and Sinatra. Oscar overlooked his pal Joey when awards were handed out. Songs include some of Rodgers and Hart's best. Based on John O'Hara's book and play. ♫Zip; Bewitched, Bothered and Bewildered; I Could Write a Book; That Terrific Rainbow; Whad Do I Care for a Dame?; Happy Hunting Horn; Plant You Now, Dig You Later; Do It the Hard Way; Take Him; There's a Small Hotel; I Didn't Know What Time It Was; My Funny Valentine; In Our Little Den of Iniquity; Great Big Town; The Lady Is a Tramp.
1957 109m/C Frank Sinatra, Rita Hayworth, Kim Novak; *D:* George Sidney; *M:* Richard Rodgers, Lorenz Hart. Academy Awards '57 Nominations: Best Art Direction/Set Decoration, Best Costume Design, Best Film Editing, Best Sound; Golden Globe Awards '58: Best Actor—Musical/Comedy (Sinatra). **VHS, Beta, LV $19.95** COL, PIA ⅋⅋⅋

Palais Royale Craven plays an ad exec who gets involved in the world of gangsters in the late 50s.
1988 100m/C *CA* Matt Craven, Kim Cattrall, Dean Stockwell; *D:* Martin Lavut. **VHS** REP ⅋½

Pale Blood A serial killer in Los Angeles is leaving his victims drained of blood. Could it be that a vampire is stalking the modern American metropolis, or is this merely the workings of a bloodthirsty psychopath?
1991 (R) 93m/C George Chakiris, Wings Hauser, Pamela Ludwig, Diana Frank, Darcy Demoss; *D:* VV Dachin Hsu. **VHS, LV $79.95** SVS ⅋½

Pale Rider A mysterious nameless stranger rides into a small California gold rush town to find himself in the middle of a feud between a mining syndicate and a group of independent prospectors. Christlike Eastwood evokes comparisons to "Shane." A classical western theme treated well complemented by excellent photography and a rock-solid cast.
1985 (R) 116m/C Clint Eastwood, Michael Moriarty, Carrie Snodgress, Sydney Penny, Richard Dysart, Richard Kiel, Christopher Penn, John Russell, Charles Hallahan; *D:* Clint Eastwood. **VHS, Beta, LV, 8mm $19.98** WAR, TLF ⅋⅋⅋

The Paleface A cowardly dentist becomes a gunslinging hero when Calamity Jane starts aiming for him. A rip-roarin' good time as the comventions of the Old West are

turned upside down. Includes the Oscar-winning song "Buttons and Bows." The 1952 sequel is "Son of Paleface." Remade in 1968 as "The Shakiest Gun in the West."
1948 91m/C Jane Russell, Bob Hope, Robert Armstrong, Iris Adrian, Robert Watson; *D:* Norman Z. MacLeod. **VHS, Beta, LV $14.95** MCA ⅋⅋⅋

The Palermo Connection Not the action-thriller the cassette box claims, but a cynical study of a crusading N.Y.C. mayoral candidate who honeymoons in Mafia-haunted Sicily and learns that the War On Crime has already been lost. Gore Vidal helped script this remote adaptation of "To Forget Palermo" by Edmonde Charles-Roux.
1991 (R) 100m/C James Belushi, Mimi Rogers, Joss Ackland, Philippe Noiret, Vittorio Gassman, Caroline Rosi; *D:* Francesco Rosi. **VHS, LV $89.95** LIV ⅋⅋

Palm Beach The lives of two petty thieves, a runaway, and a private detective intertwine at Palm Beach Down Under. Best appreciated by fans of things Aussie.
1979 90m/C *AU* Bryan Brown, Nat Young, Ken Brown, Amanda Berry; *D:* Albie Thomas. **VHS, Beta $19.95** AHV ⅋⅋

The Palm Beach Story Colbert and McCrea play a married couple who have everything—except money. The wife decides to divorce her current husband, marry a rich man, and finance her former husband's ambitions. She decides the best place to husband-hunt is Palm Beach. A Sturges classic screwball comedy.
1942 88m/B Claudette Colbert, Joel McCrea, Mary Astor, Rudy Vallee, William Demarest, Franklin Pangborn; *D:* Preston Sturges. **VHS, Beta, LV $14.98** MCA ⅋⅋⅋

Palm Springs Weekend A busload of love-hungry kids head south and get involved in routine hijinks. Actually shot in Palm Springs with adove average performances by a handful of stars.
1963 100m/C Troy Donahue, Ty Hardin, Connie Stevens, Stefanie Powers, Robert Conrad, Jack Weston, Andrew Duggan; *D:* Norman Taurog. **VHS, Beta, LV $19.98** WAR ⅋⅋½

Palooka Based on the comic strip, this film portrays a fast-talking boxing manager and his goofy, lovable protege. The young scrapper fights James Cagney's little brother. Durante sings his classic tune, "Inka-Dinka-Doo," and packs a punch in the lead. A two-fisted comedy with a witty dialogue and fine direction. Not a part of the Palooka series of the 1940s. *AKA:* Joe Palooka; The Great Schnozzle.
1934 (G) 86m/B Jimmy Durante, Stuart Erwin, Lupe Velez, Robert Armstrong, Thelma Todd, William Cagney; *D:* Ben Stoloff. **VHS, Beta, 3/4U, Special order formats $19.95** NOS, QNE, VYY ⅋⅋½

Pals Old friends stumble across $3 million in cash and learn the predictable lesson that money can't buy happiness. A terribly trite TV-movie with an exceptional cast.
1987 90m/C Don Ameche, George C. Scott, Sylvia Sidney, Susan Rinell, James Greene; *D:* Lou Antonio. **VHS $89.95** VMK ⅋⅋

Pals of the Range A framed ranch owner breaks out of jail in order to catch the real cattle thieves. Ho hum in the Old West.
1935 55m/B Rex Lease. **VHS, Beta $19.95** NOS ⅋

Pals of the Saddle The intrepid trio go after enemy agents who are trying to smuggle chemicals for poisonous gas into Mexico. This is the first of the series in which the Duke played the part of Stony Brooke.

Somewhat convoluted plot, but nevertheless enjoyable.
1938 55m/B John Wayne, Ray Corrigan, Max Terhune, Doreen McKay, Josef Forte, Ted Adams, Curly Dresden; **D:** George Sherman. **VHS** $19.95 NOS ♪♪½

The Pamela Principle A bored, middle-aged man thinks his prayers are answered when he meets a sexy 20-year-old model and begins a sordid affair with her. Soon, however, he finds himself in a tense situation when he must choose between his family or his fantasy. Also available in an unrated version.
1991 (R) ?m/C J.K. Dumont, Veronica Cash, Shelby Lane, Troy Donahue, Frank Pesce; **D:** Toby Phillips. **VHS** $89.95 IMP ♪♪

Panama Hattie Screen adaptation of Cole Porter's delightful Broadway musical. Unfortunately, something (like a plot) was lost in transition. Southern runs a saloon for our boys down in Panama. Among the musical numbers and vaudevillian acts some spies show up. Several screenwriters and directors, including Vincente Minnelli, worked uncredited on this picture, to no avail. Horne's second screen appearance. ♪It Was Just One of Those Things; Fresh as a Daisy; I've Still Got My Health; Let's Be Buddies; Make It Another Old Fashioned; Hattie from Panama; Good Neighbors; I'll Do Anything for You; The Son of a Gun Who Pick on Uncle Sam; Did I Get Stinkin' at the Savoy?; The Sping; La Bumba Rhumba; Berry Me Not; Hail, Hail, the Gang's All Here.
1942 79m/B Ann Sothern, Dan Dailey, Red Skelton, Virginia O'Brien, Rags Ragland, Alan Mowbray, Ben Blue, Carl Esmond, Lena Horne, Roger Moore; **D:** Norman Z. McLeod; **M:** Cole Porter. **VHS** $19.98 MGM, CCB ♪♪

Panama Lady Ball stars as the sexy, sultry "Panama Lady" in this old-fashioned romance. She gets involved in some shady business south of the border. A lackluster remake of "Panama Flo."
1939 65m/B Lucille Ball, Evelyn Brent. **VHS, Beta** $19.95 VID ♪½

Panama Menace An agent heads to Panama to thwart spies who are after a special paint that makes things invisible. Poor effort all around, in spite of Beaumont's presence. **AKA:** South of Panama.
1941 68m/B Roger Pryor, Virginia Vale, Lionel Royce, Lucien Prival, Duncan Renaldo, Lester Dorr, Hugh Beaumont; **D:** Jean Yarborough. **VHS, Beta** $16.95 SNC ♪

Panama Patrol Just as they are about to be married, two Army officers are called to duty in Panama. It seems that the Chinese have infiltrated the area with spies and something's got to be done. Too much attention to minor parts of the plot slows the story occasionally, but performances and photography compensate for some of the sluggishness.
1939 67m/B Leon Ames, Charlotte Wynters, Weldon Heyburn, Adrienne Ames, Abner Biberman, Hugh McArthur, Donald (Don "Red") Barry; **D:** Charles Lamont. **VHS, Beta** $16.95 SNC ♪♪½

Panamint's Bad Man Ballaw is a poor man's Gary Cooper fighting for justice against stagecoach robbers. Almost as much flavor as tumbleweed.
1938 59m/B Smith Ballew, Evelyn Daw, Noah Beery Sr.; **D:** Ray Taylor. **VHS, Beta** $19.95 NOS, VDM, DVT ♪

Pancho Barnes Routine biography of one of the first female pilots of the 1920s. Barnes is a bored debutante who finds her challenge in life when she learns to fly, becoming a barnstormer and movie stunt pilot. Her ambitions naturally get in the way of her romantic life. Good flying scenes. Made for television.
1988 (PG) 150m/C Valerie Bertinelli, Ted Wass, Sam Robards, James Stephens, Cynthia Harris, Geoffrey Lewis; **D:** Richard T. Heffron; **W:** John Hayes. **VHS** ORI ♪♪½

Pancho Villa Savalas has the lead in this fictional account of the famous Mexican, He leads his men in a raid on an American fort after being hoodwinked in an arms deal. Connors tries to hold the fort against him. The finale, in which two trains crash head on, is the most exciting event in the whole darn movie.
1972 (PG) 92m/C SP Telly Savalas, Clint Walker, Anne Francis, Chuck Connors, Angel Del Pozo, Luis Davila; **D:** Eugenio Martin. **VHS** $42.95 PGN ♪½

Pancho Villa Returns It's 1913, and noble Mexican General Pancho Villa leads his merry men against the assassins of President Madera. This Mexican production (filmed in English) paints a partisan portrait of title character as a good-hearted revolutionary folk hero, not the roving bandit later notorious north of the border.
1950 95m/B MX Leo Carrillo, Esther Fernandez, Jeanette Comber, Rodolfa Acosta; **W/D:** Miguel Contreras Torres. **VHS** $15.95 NOS, LOO ♪

Pandemonium A spoof of teen slasher films involving murder at Bambi's Cheerleading School. Seems that nationwide, cheerleaders have been brutally eliminated from their squads, leaving Bambi's as the last resort for the terminally perky. Smothers is interesting and more intelligent than his TV persona (although not by much) as the Mountie hero, assisted by Paul Reubens in a pre-Pee-Wee role. Kane steals the show as Candy, a pleasant lass with hyperkinetic powers. **AKA:** Thursday the 12th.
1982 (PG) 82m/C CA Tom Smothers, Carol Kane, Miles Chapin, Paul Reubens, Judge Reinhold, Tab Hunter, Marc McClure, Donald O'Connor, Eve Arden, Eileen Brennan, Edie McClurg; **D:** Alfred Sole. **VHS, Beta** $79.95 MGM ♪♪½

Pandora's Box This silent classic marked the end of the German Expressionist era and established Brooks as a major screen presence. She plays the tempestuous Lulu, who destroys everyone she comes in contact with, eventually sinking to prostitution and a fateful meeting with Jack the Ripper. Silent with orchestral score. **AKA:** Die Buechse Der Pandora.
1928 110m/B GE Louise Brooks, Fritz Kortner, Francis Lederer; **D:** G.W. Pabst. **VHS, Beta** $29.98 SUE, MRV, VDM ♪♪♪♪

Panic A scientist terrorizes a small town when he becomes hideously deformed by one of his bacteria experiments. He should have known better.
1983 90m/C David Warbeck, Janet Agren. **VHS, Beta** $59.95 MPI ♪½

Panic Button Mel Brooks took the plot from this film and made "The Producers," which was much better. Italian gangsters produce a television show and stack the deck so that it will fail. Unbeknownst to them, the star has figured out what they are doing and works to make it a success. Shot in Italy, mainly in Venice and Rome.
1962 90m/B IT Maurice Chevalier, Eleanor Parker, Jayne Mansfield, Mike Connors, Akim Tamiroff; **D:** George Sherman. **VHS** $29.95 NO ♪½

Panic in Echo Park A doctor races against time to find the cause of an epidemic that is threatening the health of a city. Good performances compensate for a predictable plot. Made for television.
1977 78m/C Dorian Harewood, Robin Gammell, Catlin Adams, Ramon Bieri, Movita; **D:** John Llewellyn Moxey. **VHS** NO ♪♪

Panic in Needle Park Drugs become an obsession for a young girl who goes to New York for an abortion. Her new boyfriend is imprisoned for robbery in order to support both their habits. She resorts to prostitution to continue her drug habit, and trouble occurs when her boyfriend realizes she was instrumental in his being sent to jail. Strikes a vein in presenting an uncompromising look at drug use. May be too much of a depressant for some. Pacino's first starring role.
1975 (R) 90m/C Al Pacino, Kitty Winn, Alan Vint, Richard Bright, Kiel Martin, Warren Finnerty, Raul Julia, Paul Sorvino; **D:** Jerry Schatzberg. **VHS, LV** FOX ♪♪♪

Panic in the Streets The Black Death threatens New Orleans in this intense tale. When a body is found on the water front, a doctor (Widmark) is called upon for a diagnosis. The carrier proves to be deadly in more ways than one. Fine performances, taut direction (this was one of Kazan's favorite movies). Filmed on location in New Orleans.
1950 96m/B Richard Widmark, Jack Palance, Barbara Bel Geddes, Paul Douglas, Zero Mostel; **D:** Elia Kazan. **VHS, LV** $39.98 FOX, FCT ♪♪♪

Panic in the Year Zero! Milland and family leave Los Angeles for a fishing trip just as the city is hit by a nuclear bomb. Continuing out into the wilderness for safety, the family now must try to survive as their world crumbles around them. Generally considered the best of Milland's five directorial efforts. **AKA:** End of the World.
1962 92m/B Ray Milland, Jean Hagen, Frankie Avalon, Mary Mitchell, Joan Freeman, Richard Garland, Rex Holman; **D:** Ray Milland. **VHS** $18.00 FRG ♪♪½

Panic on the 5:22 Wealthy commuters are kidnapped and held hostage by terrorist hoodlums in a suburban train club car. Standard made for television vehicle.
1974 78m/C Lynda Day George, Laurence Luckinbill, Ina Balin, Bernie Casey; **D:** Harvey Hart. **VHS, Beta** $14.95 WOV ♪♪

Panic Station Two guys get lonely at remote satellite relay station. **AKA:** The Plains of Heaven.
1982 90m/C AU Richard Moir, Reg Evans, Gerard Kennedy; **D:** Ian Pringle. **VHS** $19.95 ACA ♪♪

Panique A study of mob psychology in slums of post-World War II Paris. Two lovers frame a stranger for murder. Dark and tautly paced thriller taken from the novel by Georges Simenon. In French with English subtitles. **AKA:** Panic.
1947 87m/B FR Michel Simon, Viviane Romance; **D:** Julien Duvivier. **VHS, Beta, 3/4U, Special order formats** $24.95 NOS, HHT, CAB ♪♪♪

Pantaloons A man who fancies himself to be irresistible chases women for sport. A quaint and lively period film.
1957 93m/C FR Fernandel, Carmen Sevilla, Fernando Rey; **D:** John Berry. **VHS** YYY ♪♪

Panther Squad Litter of sex kittens led by Danning get into major scraps to save world.
1984 77m/C Sybil Danning. **VHS** NO ♪

P

The Panther's Claw Murder befalls an opera troupe, but a sleuth with the memorable name of Thatcher Colt is on the case. A quick-moving mystery quickie that delivers on its own modest terms.
1942 72m/B Sidney Blackmer, Byron Foulger, Rick Vallin, Herbert Rawlinson; **D:** William Beaudine. **VHS** $15.95 NOS, LOO *∄*

Papa's Delicate Condition Based on the autobiographical writings of silent screen star Corinne Griffith. Gleason is Papa whose "delicate condition" is a result of his drinking. His antics provide a constant headache to his family. A paean to turn-of-the-century family life. No I.D.s required as the performances are enjoyable for the whole family. Features the Academy Award-winning song "Call Me Irresponsible."
1963 98m/C Jackie Gleason, Glynis Johns, Charlie Ruggles, Laurel Goodwin, Elisha Cook Jr., Murray Hamilton. **VHS, Beta** $14.95 KRT *∄∄∄*

The Paper Chase Students at Harvard Law School suffer and struggle through their first year. A realistic, sometimes acidly humorous look at Ivy League ambitions, with Houseman stealing the show as the tough professor. Wonderful adaptation of the John Jay Osborn novel which later became the basis for the acclaimed television series.
1973 (PG) 111m/C Timothy Bottoms, Lindsay Wagner, John Houseman, Graham Beckel, Edward Herrmann, James Naughton, Craig Richard Nelson, Bob Lydiard; **D:** James Bridges; **M:** John Williams. Academy Awards '73: Best Supporting Actor (Houseman); Nominations: Best Adapted Screenplay, Best Sound; Golden Globe Awards '74: Best Supporting Actor (Houseman); National Board of Review Awards '73: Best Supporting Actor (Houseman). **VHS, Beta, LV** $19.98 FOX, BTV *∄∄∄*

Paper Lion A comedy "documentary" about bestselling writer George Plimpton's tryout game as quarterback with the Detroit Lions. Film debut of Alan Alda. Helped Karras make the transition from the gridiron to the silver screen. Moves into field goal range but doesn't quite score.
1968 107m/C Alan Alda, Lauren Hutton, Alex Karras, Ann Turkel, John Gordy, Roger Brown, "Sugar Ray" Robinson, Roy Scheider, David Doyle; **D:** Alex March. **VHS, Beta** NO *∄∄½*

Paper Man A group of college students create a fictitious person in a computer for a credit card scam. The scheme snowballs, resulting in murder and hints of possible artificial intelligence. But it's just standard network TV fare, with a creepy performance by Stockwell as a computer whiz.
1971 90m/C Dean Stockwell, Stefanie Powers, James Stacy, Elliot Street, Tina Chen, James Olson, Ross Elliott; **D:** Walter Grauman. **VHS** $39.95 XVC *∄∄*

Paper Marriage In Canada, a less than successful Chinese boxer agrees to marry a Hong Kong girl for a promise of payment in order that she may become a citizen. The money never comes, but the nearly betrothed pair discover that they love each other, after all. In Cantonese with English subtitles.
1988 102m/C CH Samo Hung, Maggie Cheung; **D:** Alfred Cheung. **VHS** $39.95 FCT, MOV, ACA *∄*½

Paper Marriage Yet another variation on the marriage in order to gain citizenship but yes we're going to fall in love films. A young Polish woman has fallen for an uppercrust English doctor she's met in Warsaw. When Alicja arrives in England, she's promptly dumped by the cad. She's ambitious and wants to stay in England so Alicja arranges a marriage of convenience with small-time crook Aiden, who finds his new bride is more than he bargained for.
1993 88m/C GB PL Gary Kemp, Joanna Trepechinska, Rita Tushingham, Richard Hawley, David Horovitch, William Ilkley, Mark McKellen, Ann Mitchell, Sadie Frost; **W/D:** Krzysztof Lang; **W:** Marek Kreutz. **VHS** $89.95 ACA *∄∄*½

Paper Mask When a promising young doctor is killed in an auto accident, an unscrupulous, psychotic porter assumes his identity. He uses said identity to, among other things, initiate an affair with a sultry co-worker. How long will this madman play his unholy game, and at what cost?
1991 (R) 105m/C GB Paul McGann, Amanda Donohoe, Frederick Treves, Barbara Leigh-Hunt, Jimmy Yuill; **D:** Christopher Morahan. **VHS** $89.95 ACA *∄∄*½

Paper Moon Award-winning story set in depression-era Kansas with Ryan O'Neal as a Bible-wielding con who meets up with a nine-year-old orphan. During their travels together, he discovers that the orphan (his daughter, Tatum) is better at "his" game than he is. Irresistible chemistry between the O'Neals, leading to Tatum's Oscar win (she is the youngest actor ever to take home a statue). Cinematically picturesque and cynical enough to keep overt sentimentalism at bay. Based on Joe David Brown's novel, "Addie Pray."
1973 (PG) 102m/B Ryan O'Neal, Tatum O'Neal, Madeline Kahn, John Hillerman, Randy Quaid; **D:** Peter Bogdanovich. Academy Awards '73: Best Supporting Actress (O'Neal); Nominations: Best Adapted Screenplay, Best Sound, Best Supporting Actress (Kahn); National Board of Review Awards '73: 10 Best Films of the Year. **VHS, Beta, LV** $49.95 PAR, BTV *∄∄*½

Paper Tiger Niven plays an imaginative English tutor who fabricates fantastic yarns fictionalizing his past in order to impress his student, the son of the Japanese ambassador to a Southeast Asian country. Poorly executed karate, misdirection, and a simplistic storyline work against it.
1974 104m/C GB David Niven, Toshiro Mifune, Eiko Ando, Hardy Kruger; **D:** Ken Annakin. **VHS, Beta** SUE, OM *∄∄*

A Paper Wedding A middle-aged literature professor with a dead-end career and equally dead-end romance with a married man is persuaded by her lawyer sister to marry a Chilean political refugee to avoid his deportation. Of course, they must fool an immigration official and their fake marriage does turn into romance, but this is no light-hearted "Green Card." Bujold shines. In French and Spanish with English subtitles. **AKA:** Les Noces de Papier.
1989 90m/C CA Genevieve Bujold, Manuel Aranguiz, Dorothee Berryman; **D:** Michel Brault. **VHS, LV** $79.95 CTL, TAM, LUM *∄∄*

Paperback Hero A hot-shot hockey player turns to crime when his team loses its financial backing. Choopy storyline could use a Zamboni, while Dullea should be penalized for occasionally losing his rustic accent. Still the supporting actors skate through their roles and, for periods, it works. A slapshot that ultimately clangs off the goal post.
1973 94m/C CA Keir Dullea, Elizabeth Ashley, John Beck, Dayle Haddon; **D:** Peter Pearson. **VHS** $79.95 CGH *∄∄*

Paperhouse An odd fantasy about a young girl plagued by recurring dreams that begin to influence real life. Very obtuse, British-minded film with "Twilight Zone" feel that manages to capture genuine dreamness. Not for all audiences, but intriguing nonetheless.

1989 92m/C GB Glenne Headly, Ben Cross, Charlotte Burke, Elliott Spiers; **D:** Bernard Rose. **VHS, Beta, LV** $89.98 LIV, VES *∄∄∄*

Papillon McQueen is a criminal sent to Devil's Island in the 1930s determined to escape from the Lemote prison. Hoffman is the swindler he befriends. A series of escapes and recaptures follow. Box-office winner based on the autobiographical writings of French thief Henri Charriere. Excellent portrayal of prison life and fine performances from the prisoners. Certain segments would have been better left on the cutting room floor. The film's title refers to the lead's butterfly tattoo.
1973 (PG) 150m/C Steve McQueen, Dustin Hoffman, Victor Jory, George Coulouris, Anthony Zerbe; **D:** Franklin J. Schaffner; **M:** Jerry Goldsmith. **VHS, Beta, LV** $19.98 FOX, WAR *∄∄∄*

Para Servir a Usted A waiter gets mixed in with the high society crowd that he works for.
1987 95m/C MX Enrique Rambal, Claudia Islas, Norma Lazarendo, Ofelia Guillman. **VHS, Beta** $55.95 MAD *∄∄*

Parade A series of vignettes in a circus, "Parade" is actually a play within a play, meshing the action with events offstage. The laser disc edition includes Rene Clement's 1936 "Soigne Ton Gauche," Tati's inspiration.
1974 85m/C FR Jacques Tati; **W/D:** Jacques Tati. **VHS, LV** $59.95 HMV, VYG, CRC *∄∄∄*

The Paradine Case A passable Hitchcock romancer about a young lawyer who falls in love with the woman he's defending for murder, not knowing whether she's innocent or guilty. Script could be tighter and more cohesive. Seventy thousand dollars of the three million budget were spent recreating the original Bailey courtroom. Based on the novel by Robert Hichens.
1947 125m/B Gregory Peck, Alida Valli, Ann Todd, Louis Jourdan, Charles Laughton, Charles Coburn, Ethel Barrymore, Leo G. Carroll; **D:** Alfred Hitchcock. **VHS, Beta, LV** $19.98 FOX *∄∄*½

Paradise Young American boy and beautiful English girl on a 19th-century jaunt through the Middle East are the sole survivors when their caravan is massacred. Left to their own devices, they discover a magnificent oasis and the joys of frolicking naked and experience (surprise) their sexual awakening. Do a double-take: it's the "Blue Lagoon" all over, with a bit more nudity and a lot more sand.
1982 (R) 100m/C Phoebe Cates, Willie Aames, Richard Curnock, Tuvio Tavi; **D:** Stuart Gillard. **VHS, Beta, LV** $24.98 SUE, NLC *∄∄*

Paradise A young boy is sent to the country to live with his pregnant mother's married friends (real life husband and wife Johnson and Griffith). From the outset it is clear that the couple are experiencing marital troubles, making the boy's assimilation all the more difficult. Help arrives in the form of a sprightly ten-year-old girl, with whom he forms a charming relationship. Largely predictable, this remake of the French film "Le Grand Chemin" works thanks to the surprisingly good work of its ensemble cast, and the gorgeous scenery of South Carolina, where the movie was filmed.
1991 (PG-13) 112m/C Melanie Griffith, Don Johnson, Elijah Wood, Thora Birch, Sheila McCarthy, Eve Gordon, Louise Latham, Greg Travis, Sarah Trigger; **D:** Mary Agnes Donoghue; **W:** Mary Agnes Donoghue. **VHS, Beta** $92.95 TOU *∄∄∄*

Paradise Alley Rocky tires of boxing, decides to join the WWF. Three brothers brave the world of professional wrestling in an effort to strike it rich and move out of the seedy Hell's Kitchen neighborhood of New York, circa 1946. Stallone wrote, stars in, and makes his directorial debut in addition to singing the title song. He makes a few good moves as director, but is ultimately pinned to the canvas.
1978 (PG) 109m/C Sylvester Stallone, Anne Archer, Armand Assante, Lee Canalito, Kevin Conway; *D:* Sylvester Stallone; *W/D:* Sylvester Stallone. VHS, Beta, LV $19.98 MCA ℤℤ

Paradise Canyon Early Wayne "B" thriller, in which he plays an undercover government agent sent to track down a group of counterfeiters.
1935 59m/B John Wayne, Yakima Canutt, Marion Burns. VHS $9.98 REP, NOS, SVS ℤ 1/2

Paradise, Hawaiian Style Out-of-work pilot returns to Hawaii, where he and a buddy start a charter service with two helicopters. Plenty of gals are wooed by "the Pelvis." Filmed four years after Elvis's first Pacific piece, "Blue Hawaii." Presley, showing the first signs of slow-down, displays no surprises here. ♫Paradise, Hawaiian Style; Scratch My Back (Then I'll Scratch Yours); Stop Where You Are; This Is My Heaven; House of Sand; Queenie Wahine's Papaya; Datin'; Drums of the Islands; A Dog's Life; Sand Castles; Bill Bailey, Won't You Please Come Home?.
1966 91m/C Elvis Presley, Suzanna Leigh, James Shigeta, Donna Butterworth, Irene Tsu, Julie Parrish, Philip Ahn, Mary Treen, Marianna Hill, John Doucette, Grady Sutton; *D:* Michael Moore. VHS, Beta $14.98 FOX, MVD ℤ 1/2

Paradise in Harlem All-black musical in which a cabaret performer witnesses a gangland murder, sees his sick wife die, and is pressured into leaving town by the mob. Have a nice day.
1940 83m/B Frank Wilson, Mamie Smith, Edna Mae Harris, Juanita Hall; *D:* Joseph Seiden. VHS, Beta $39.95 NOS, FCT, VCN ℤ 1/2

Paradise Island Down-scale musical romance about an ingenue on her way to join her fiance in the South Seas, only to find that he has gambled away his money. The opportunistic saloon owner tries to put the moves on her. Will the two lovers be reunited? ♫I've Got a Girl In Every Port; Drinking Song; Lazy Breezes; Just Another Dream.
1930 68m/B Kenneth Harlan, Marceline Day, Thomas Santschi, Paul Hurst, Victor Potel, Gladden James, Will Stanton; *D:* Bert Glennon. VHS $19.95 NOS ℤ

Paradise Motel Teen exploitation film centered around a motel predominantly used for one-night rendezvous. High school heroes and jocks battle for the affections of a beautiful classmate.
1984 (R) 87m/C Bob Basso, Gary Hershberger, Jonna Leigh Stack, Robert Krantz; *D:* Cary Medoway. VHS, Beta $19.98 FOX ℤ

Paradisio Dying inventor wills Oxford professor an authentic pair of X-ray specs. Spies come gunning for the professor, chasing him through Europe. Doc keeps forgetting he's being chased while using the special specs to see (sometimes in 3-D) through the clothing of young women. Meager plot does not get in way of 3-D nudie exploitation.
1961 (R) 82m/C Arthur Howard, Eva Waegner. VHS, Beta $19.95 STE, NWV, VDM ℤ 1/2

Parallax View A reporter tries to disprove a report which states that a presidential candidate's assassination was not a conspiracy. As he digs deeper and deeper, he uncovers more than he bargained for and becomes a pawn in the conspirators' further plans. Beatty is excellent and the conspiracy is never less than believable. A lesser-known, compelling political thriller that deserves to be more widely seen.
1974 (R) 102m/C Warren Beatty, Hume Cronyn, William Daniels, Paula Prentiss, Kenneth Mars, Bill McKinney, Anthony Zerbe, Walter McGinn; *D:* Alan J. Pakula. VHS, Beta $14.95 PAR ℤℤℤ 1/2

Parallel Corpse A mortuary attendant finds a murder victim hidden in a coffin and blackmails the remorseless killer.
1983 89m/C Buster Larsen, Jorgen Kiil, Agneta Ekmanner, Masja Dessau. VHS, Beta $49.95 MED ℤ

Paralyzed An unconscious journalist, mistaken for dead in a hospital emergency room, flashes back to the investigation that embroiled him in his predicament.
197? 90m/C Ingrid Thulin, Jean Sorel, Mario Adorf; *W/D:* Aldo Lado. VHS, Beta $59.95 MPI ℤℤ

Paramedics A motley crew of cavorting paramedics battle their evil captain. Another parody of people in uniform. A comedy with little flair.
1988 (PG-13) 91m/C George Newbern, Christopher McDonald, John P. Ryan, Ray Walston, Lawrence Hilton-Jacobs; *D:* Stuart Margolin. VHS, Beta, LV $79.98 LIV, VES ℤ 1/2

Paranoia Beautiful jet-set widow is trapped in her own Italian villa by a young couple who drug her to get her to perform in various sex orgies, which are probably the most interesting part of this muddled affair. *AKA:* Orgasmo; A Beautiful Place to Kill; A Quiet Place to Kill.
1969 94m/C IT Carroll Baker, Lou Castel, Colette Descombes; *D:* Umberto Lenzi. VHS, Beta REP ℤ

Parasite A small town is beset by giant parasites. An "Alien" ripoff originally filmed in 3-D, during that technique's brief return in the early '80s. Bad films like this killed it both the first and second times. An unpardonable mess that comes off as a stinky sixth-grade film project.
1981 (R) 90m/C Demi Moore, Gale Robbins, Luca Bercovici, James Davidson, Al Fann, Cherie Currie, Cheryl "Rainbeaux" Smith, Vivian Blaine; *D:* Charles Band. VHS, Beta, LV $89.95 PAR Woof!

Pardon Mon Affaire When a middle-aged civil servant gets a look at a model in a parking garage, he decides it's time to cheat on his wife. Enjoyable French farce. Re-made in the United States as "The Woman in Red" and followed by "Pardon Mon Affair, Too!" Subtitled. *AKA:* Un Elephant a Trompe Enormement.
1976 (PG) 107m/C FR Jean Rochefort, Claude Brasseur, Guy Bedos, Victor Lanoux, Daniele Delorme, Martine Sarcey, Anny Duperey; *D:* Yves Robert. VHS, Beta, LV $29.98 SUE ℤℤℤ

Pardon Mon Affaire, Too! Pale sequel to the first popular French comedy, "Pardon Mon Affair." This time the four fantasy-minded buddies withstand the trials of marriage and middle-class life. With English subtitles or dubbed. *AKA:* We Will All Meet in Paradise.
1977 105m/C FR Jean Rochefort, Claude Brasseur, Guy Bedos; *D:* Yves Robert. VHS, Beta $29.98 SUE ℤℤℤ

Pardon My Sarong Bud and Lou star as Chicago bus drivers who end up shipwrecked on a South Pacific island when they get involved with notorious jewel thieves. The island natives think Lou is a god! Standard Abbott & Costello fare.
1942 83m/B Bud Abbott, Lou Costello, Virginia Bruce, Robert Paige, Lionel Atwill, Leif Erickson, William Demarest, Samuel S. Hinds; *D:* Erle C. Kenton. VHS $14.98 MCA ℤℤ 1/2

Pardon My Trunk Struggling against poverty on his teacher's salary, a man and his family receive a gift from a Hindu prince—an elephant. De Sica carries this silly premise beyond mere slapstick. Dubbed. *AKA:* Hello Elephant; Bvongiorno, Elefante.
1952 85m/B IT Sabu, Vittorio De Sica; *D:* Gianni Franciolini. VHS, Beta $29.95 VYY ℤℤ

Pardon Us Laurel and Hardy are thrown into prison for bootlegging. Plot meanders along aimlessly, but the duo have some inspired moments. The first Laurel and Hardy feature. *AKA:* Jail Birds.
1931 78m/B Stan Laurel, Oliver Hardy, June Marlowe, James Finlayson; *D:* James Parrott. VHS, Beta $19.95 MED, CCB, MLB ℤℤ 1/2

The Parent Trap Mills plays a dual role in this heartwarming comedy as twin sisters who conspire to bring their divorced parents together again. Well known Disney fluff. Followed by several made-for-television sequels featuring the now grown-up twins.
1961 127m/C Hayley Mills, Maureen O'Hara, Brian Keith, Charlie Ruggles, Una Merkel, Leo G. Carroll; *D:* David Swift. VHS, Beta, LV $19.99 DIS ℤℤ 1/2

Parenthood Four grown siblings and their parents struggle with various levels of parenthood. From the college drop-out, to the nervous single mother, to the yuppie couple raising an overachiever, every possibility is explored, including the perspective from the older generation, portrayed by Robards. Genuinely funny with dramatic moments that work most of the time, with an affecting performance from Martin and Wiest. Director Howard has four kids and was inspired to make this film when on a European jaunt with them.
1989 (PG-13) 124m/C Steve Martin, Mary Steenburgen, Dianne Wiest, Martha Plimpton, Keanu Reeves, Tom Hulce, Jason Robards Jr., Rick Moranis, Harley Jane Kozak, Leaf Phoenix; *D:* Ron Howard. VHS, Beta, LV $19.95 MCA ℤℤℤ

Parents Dark satire of middle class suburban life in the 50s, centering on a young boy who discovers that his parents aren't getting their meat from the local butcher. Gives new meaning to leftovers and boasts a very disturbing barbecue scene. Balaban's debut is a strikingly visual and creative gorefest with definite cult potential. The eerie score is by Angelo Badalamenti, who also composed the music for "Blue Velvet," "Wild at Heart," and the television series "Twin Peaks."
1989 (R) 81m/C Randy Quaid, Mary Beth Hurt, Sandy Dennis; *D:* Bob Balaban; *M:* Angelo Badalamenti. VHS, Beta, LV $14.98 LIV, VES, HHE ℤℤℤ

Paris Belongs to Us An early entry in the French "new wave" of naturalistic cinema, this psychological mystery drama has a woman investigating a suicide linked to a possible worldwide conspiracy. Interesting, if somewhat dated by Cold War elements. *AKA:* Paris Nous Appartient; Paris is Ours.
1960 120m/B FR Jean-Claude Brialy, Betty Schneider, Gianni Esposito, Francoise Prevost; *W/D:* Jacques Rivette; *W:* Jean Gruault. VHS $29.95 VDM ℤℤ 1/2

Paris Blues Two jazz musicians, one white, one black, strive for success in Paris and become involved with American tourists who want to take them back to the States. Score by Duke Ellington and an appearance by Armstrong make it a must-see for jazz fans.

1961 100m/B Paul Newman, Sidney Poitier, Joanne Woodward, Diahann Carroll, Louis Armstrong, Barbara Lange; *D:* Martin Ritt. **VHS, Beta** $19.98 *FOX* ♫♫½

Paris Express When a man steals money from his employer, he boards the Paris Express to escape from the police. A bit convoluted, but well acted. Based on the George Simenon story. *AKA:* The Man Who Watched Trains Go By.
1953 82m/C Claude Rains, Herbert Lom, Felix Aylmer, Marius Goring, Anouk Aimee, Marta Toren; *D:* Harold French. **VHS, Beta** $16.95 *SNC, NOS, MRV* ♫♫½

Paris Holiday An actor heading for Paris to buy a noted author's latest screenplay finds mystery and romance. Entertaining chase scenes as the characters try to find the elusive script.
1957 100m/C Bob Hope, Fernandel, Anita Ekberg, Martha Hyer, Preston Sturges; *D:* Gerd Oswald. **VHS, Beta** $9.95 *UNI* ♫♫½

Paris is Burning Livingston's documentary portrayal of New York City's transvestite balls where men dress up, dance, and compete in various categories. Filmed between 1985 and 1989, this is a compelling look at a subculture of primarily black and Hispanic men and the one place they can truly be themselves. Madonna noted this look and attitude (much watered down) in her song "Vogue."
1991 (R) 71m/C Dorian Corey, Pepper Labeija, Venus Xtravaganza, Octavia St. Laurant, Willi Ninja, Anji Xtravaganza, Freddie Pendavis, Junior Labeija; *D:* Jennie Livingston. **VHS** $89.95 *ACA, FCT* ♫♫♫

Paris, Texas After four years a drifter returns to find his son is being raised by his brother because the boy's mother has also disappeared. He tries to reconnect with the boy. Written by Sam Shepard in his usual introspective style. Acclaimed by many film critics, but others found it to be too slow. Music by Ry Cooder.
1983 (PG) 145m/C *FR GE* Harry Dean Stanton, Nastassia Kinski, Dean Stockwell, Hunter Carson, Aurore Clement; *D:* Wim Wenders. **VHS, Beta, LV** $19.98 *FOX* ♫♫♫½

Paris Trout Believing himself above the law, southern Trout (Hopper) shoots the mother and sister of a young black man who reneged on his IOU. Lawyer Harris is forced to defend a man he knows deserves to be punished, and wife Hershey suffers long. Adapted by Pete Dexter from his National Book Award-winning novel. Made for cable.
1991 (R) 98m/C Dennis Hopper, Barbara Hershey, Ed Harris; *D:* Stephen Gyllenhaal; *W:* Pete Dexter. **VHS, Beta, LV** $89.98 *MED, FXV, FCT* ♫♫½

Paris When It Sizzles A screenwriter and his secretary fall in love while working on a film in Paris, confusing themselves with the script's characters. Star-studded cast deserves better than this lame script. Shot on location in Paris. Holden's drinking—he ran into a brick wall while under the influence—and some unresolved romantic tension between him and Hepburn affected shooting. Deitrich, Sinatra, Astaire, Ferrer, and Curtis show up for a party on the set.
1964 110m/C William Holden, Audrey Hepburn, Gregoire Aslan, Raymond Bussieres, Tony Curtis, Fred Astaire, Frank Sinatra, Noel Coward, Marlene Dietrich, Mel Ferrer; *D:* Richard Quine. **VHS, Beta** $29.95 *PAR* ♫♫

The Park is Mine A deranged and desperate Vietnam vet takes hostages in Central Park. Semi-infamous film, notable for being the first movie made for HBO on cable and for being filmed in Toronto, before the

inexpensive practice of filming in Canada became widespread.
1985 102m/C Tommy Lee Jones, Yaphet Kotto, Helen Shaver; *D:* Steven Hilliard Stern. **VHS, Beta** $59.98 *FOX* ♫♫

Parker An executive is kidnapped, then released, but does not know why. Unable to live with the mystery, he tracks his kidnappers down into a world of blackmail, drugs, and intrigue.
1984 100m/C Bryan Brown, Kurt Raab. **VHS, Beta** $59.95 *LHV* ♫♫

Parlor, Bedroom and Bath A family tries to keep a young woman from seeing that her love interest is flirting with other prospects. Doesn't live up to the standard Keaton set in his silent films. Keaton spoke French and German for foreign versions. *AKA:* Romeo in Pyjamas.
1931 75m/B Buster Keaton, Charlotte Greenwood, Cliff Edwards, Reginald Denny; *D:* Edward Sedgwick. **VHS, Beta** $19.95 *NOS, VYY, VDM* ♫♫

Parole, Inc. FBI takes on the underground in this early crime film. Criminals on parole have not served their sentences, and the mob is responsible. A meagerly financed yawner.
1949 71m/B Michael O'Shea, Evelyn Ankers, Turhan Bey, Lyle Talbot; *D:* Alfred Zeisler. **VHS** $16.95 *NOS, SNC* ♫♫

Paroled to Die A man frames a young rancher for a bank robbery and a murder he committed in this wild west saga. Predictable and bland.
1937 66m/B Bob Steele, Kathleen Elliott. **VHS, Beta** $19.95 *NOS, DVT* ♫½

Parting Glances Low-budget but acclaimed film shows the relationship between two gay men and how they deal with a close friend's discovery of his exposure to the AIDS virus. Touching and realistic portrayals make this a must see. In 1990 Sherwood died of AIDS without completing any other films.
1986 (R) 90m/C John Bolger, Richard Ganoung, Steve Buscemi; *D:* Bill Sherwood. **VHS, Beta** $79.98 *FOX, TAM* ♫♫♫

Partner An extremely shy young man invents a strong alter ego to cope with the world but this second personality comes to dominate—with tragic results. In Italian with English subtitles.
1968 110m/C *IT* Pierre Clementi, Stefania Sandrelli, Tina Aumont; *D:* Bernardo Bertolucci; *M:* Ennio Morricone. **VHS** $39.95 *TAM* ♫♫♫

Partners A straight, macho cop must pose as the lover of a gay cop to investigate the murder of a gay man in Los Angeles' homosexual community. Sets out to parody "Cruising"; unfortunately, the only source of humor the makers could find was in ridiculous homosexual stereotypes that are somewhat offensive and often unfunny. Written by "La Cage aux Folles'" Francis Veber.
1982 (R) 93m/C Ryan O'Neal, John Hurt, Kenneth McMillan, Robyn Douglass, Jay Robinson, Rick Jason; *D:* James Burrows. **VHS, Beta** $79.95 *PAR* ♫♫

The Party Disaster-prone Indian actor wreaks considerable havoc at a posh Hollywood gathering. Laughs come quickly in this quirky Sellers vehicle.
1968 99m/C Peter Sellers, Claudine Longet, Marge Champion, Sharron Kimberly, Denny Miller, Gavin MacLeod, Carol Wayne; *D:* Blake Edwards. **VHS** $19.95 *MGM, TVC* ♫♫♫

Party Animal A college stud teaches a shy farm boy a thing or two about the carnal aspects of campus life.

1983 (R) 78m/C Timothy Carhart, Matthew Causey, Robin Harlan; *D:* David Beaird. **VHS, Beta** $79.98 *LIV* ♫

Party Camp A rowdy summer camp counselor endeavors to turn a tame backwoods camp into a non-stop party. Late entry in the "Meatballs"-spawned genre fails to do anything of even minor interest.
1987 96m/C Andrew Ross, Billy Jacoby, April Wayne, Kirk Cribb; *D:* Gary Graver. **VHS, Beta** $79.98 *LIV* ♫

Party Favors Erotic dancing, strip tease acts, and general hilarity are featured in this party tape.
1989 (R) 83m/C Jeannie Winters, Marjorie Miller, Gail Thackray; *D:* Ed Hansen. **VHS, Beta** $79.98 *LIV, VES* Woof!

Party Girl A crime drama involving an attorney representing a 1920s crime boss and his henchmen when they run afoul of the law. The lawyer falls in love with a nightclub dancer who successfully encourages him to leave the mob, but not before he is wounded in a gang war attack, arrested, and forced to testify against the mob as a material witness. The mob then takes his girlfriend hostage to prevent his testifying, leading to an exciting climax. Must-see viewing for Charisse's steamy dance numbers.
1958 99m/C Robert Taylor, Cyd Charisse, Lee J. Cobb, John Ireland, Kent Smith, Claire Kelly, Corey Allen; *D:* Nicholas Ray. **VHS, Beta, LV** $19.98 *MGM* ♫♫♫½

Party Girls Escort service girls run afoul of the law in this hokey melodrama.
1929 67m/B Douglas Fairbanks Jr., Jeanette Loff, Judith Barrie, Marie Prevost, John St. Polis, Lucien Prival; *D:* Victor Halperin. **VHS, Beta** $16.95 *NOS, LOO, SNC* ♫½

Party Girls for Sale Mystery thriller in which a young girl's body is found on the beach in Rio de Janeiro. Also known as "Violated."
1954 ?m/C Raymond Burr, Scott Brady, Johanna Matz. **VHS** $16.95 *SNC* ♫♫

Party Incorporated Marilyn Chambers (of "Behind the Green Door" fame) stars as a young widow with a huge tax load who gives parties to pay it off. Also known as "Party Girls." *AKA:* Party Girls.
1989 (R) 80m/C Marilyn Chambers, Kurt Woodruff, Christine Veronica, Kimberly Taylor; *D:* Chuck Vincent. **VHS, LV** $19.95 *STE, NWV, IME* ♫♫

Party Line A veteran police captain and a district attorney team up to track down a pair of killers who find their victims through party lines.
1988 (R) 90m/C Richard Hatch, Shawn Weatherly, Richard Roundtree, Leif Garrett, Greta Blackburn; *D:* William Webb. **VHS, Beta** $14.95 *SVS* ♫♫

Party! Party! A bunch of kids go nuts and have a party when their parents leave.
1983 100m/C *GB M:* Sting, David Bowie, The Clash, Joe Jackson, Elvis Costello. **VHS** $29.95 *ACA* ♫♫

Party Plane Softcore fun-fest about a plane full of oversexed stewardesses.
1990 81m/C Kent Stoddard, Karen Annarino, John Goff, Jill Johnson; *D:* Ed Hansen. **VHS, Beta, LV** $79.98 *VES* ♫

Pascali's Island A Turkish spy becomes involved with an adventurer's plot to steal rare artifacts, then finds himself ensnared in political and personal intrigue. Superior tragedy features excellent performances from Kingsley, Dance, and Mirren.

1988 (PG-13) 106m/C *GB* Ben Kingsley, Helen Mirren, Charles Dance, Sheila Allen, Vernon Dobtcheff; *D:* James Dearden. **VHS, Beta, LV $14.95** LIV ♫♫♫½

Pass the Ammo Entertaining comedy about a young couple who attempt to steal back $50,000 of inheritance money that a televangelist swindled from the family. One of the more creative satires on this religious TV phenomenon.
1988 (R) 93m/C Bill Paxton, Tim Curry, Linda Kozlowski, Annie Potts, Anthony Geary, Dennis Burkley, Glenn Withrow; *D:* David Beaird. **VHS, Beta, LV $89.95** LIV ♫♫½

Passage of the Dragon A village is caught in the middle of a martial arts war.
19?? 86m/C **VHS $14.98** NEG ♫♫½

A Passage to India An ambitious adaptation of E.M. Forster's complex novel about relations between Brits and Indians in the 1920s. Drama centers on a young British woman's accusations that an Indian doctor raped her while serving as a guide in some rather ominous caves. Film occasionally flags, but is usually compelling. Features particularly strong performances from Bannerjee, Fox, and Davis.
1984 (PG) 163m/C *GB* Peggy Ashcroft, Alec Guinness, James Fox, Judy Davis, Victor Banerjee, Nigel Havers; *D:* David Lean; *M:* Maurice Jarre. Academy Awards '84: Best Supporting Actress (Ashcroft), Best Original Score; Nominations: Best Adapted Screenplay, Best Art Direction/Set Decoration, Best Director (Lean), Best Film Editing, Best Cinematography, Best Costume Design, Best Sound; Academy Awards '87: Best Actress (Davis); British Academy Awards '85: Best Actress (Ashcroft); Golden Globe Awards '85: Best Foreign Film, Best Supporting Actress (Ashcroft). **VHS, Beta, LV $19.95** COL, BTV, HMV ♫♫♫

Passage to Marseilles Hollywood propaganda in which convicts escape from Devil's Island and help French freedom fighters combat Nazis. Routine but entertaining. What else could it be with Bogart, Raines, Greenstreet, and Lorre, who later made a pretty good film set in Casablanca?
1944 110m/B Humphrey Bogart, Claude Rains, Sydney Greenstreet, Peter Lorre, Helmut Dantine, George Tobias, John Loder, Eduardo Ciannelli, Michele Morgan; *D:* Michael Curtiz. **VHS, Beta** FOX ♫♫♫

Passed Away When family patriarch Jack Scanlan dies, his entire family gets together for the funeral and a big Irish wake. The family, of course, is made up of a weird group of characters, including a good, steadfast son (Hoskins), a dim-witted but good-looking son (Petersen), a rebellious daughter (Reed), and a left-wing nun who works in Central America and is accompanied by an illegal alien (McDormand). Throw in a mysterious female mourner and a pregnant granddaughter who goes into labor at the graveside and you come up with a movie that exploits death and uses every comic death cliche ever imagined. Talented cast is wasted in a movie that should have passed away.
1992 (PG-13) 96m/C Bob Hoskins, Jack Warden, William L. Petersen, Helen Lloyd Breed, Maureen Stapleton, Pamela Reed, Tim Curry, Peter Riegert, Blair Brown, Patrick Breen, Nancy Travis, Teri Polo, Frances McDormand; *W/D:* Charlie Peters. **VHS, Beta $19.99** HPH ♫½

The Passenger A dissatisfied television reporter changes identities with a dead man while on assignment in Africa, then learns that he is posing as a gunrunner. Mysterious, elliptical production from Italian master Antonioni, who co-wrote. Nicholson is fine in the low-key role, and Schneider is surprisingly winning as the woman drawn to him. The object of much debate, hailed by some as quintessential cinema and by others as slow and unrewarding. *AKA:* Profession: Reporter.
1975 (PG) 119m/C *IT* Jack Nicholson, Maria Schneider, Ian Hendry, Jenny Runacre, Steven Berkoff; *D:* Michelangelo Antonioni. **VHS, Beta $19.98** WAR ♫♫♫½

Passenger 57 Classic movie-of-the-week fare. Anti-terrorist specialist John Cutter (Snipes) leaves his profession because of his wife's murder, and coincidentally boards the same plane as Charles Rane (Payne), an apprehended evil terrorist headed to trial in L.A. Somehow, Rane's thugs have also sneaked aboard with plans to hijack the plane, and it's up to Cutter to use his skills and save the day. Athletic Snipes is convincing in his role but can't make up for the plot's lack of premise.
1992 (R) 84m/C Wesley Snipes, Bruce Payne, Tom Sizemore, Alex Datcher, Bruce Greenwood, Robert Hooks, Elizabeth Hurley, Michael Horse; *D:* Kevin Hooks; *W:* David Loughery, Dan Gordon; *M:* Stanley Clarke. **VHS, LV $94.99** WAR ♫

The Passing Two men find themselves trapped in the darker vicissitudes of life. The two lead almost parallel lives until an extraordinary event unites them.
1988 96m/C James Plaster, Welton Benjamin Johnson, Lynn Dunn, Albert B. Smith; *D:* John Huckert. **VHS** NO ♫♫½

The Passing of Evil Bisset is a star-struck Canadian undone by the bright lights and big cities of America. By age 22, she's a burnt-out prostitute in Las Vegas. Cheerless but compelling. *AKA:* The Grasshopper; Passione.
1970 (R) 96m/C Jacqueline Bisset, Jim Brown, Joseph Cotten, Corbett Monica, Ramon Bieri, Christopher Stone, Roger Garrett, Stanley Adams, Dick Richards, Tim O'Kelly, Ed Flanders; *D:* Jerry Paris. **VHS $29.98** WAR ♫♫½

The Passing of the Third Floor Back Boarding house tenants improve their lives after being inspired by a mysterious stranger. They revert, though, when he leaves. Now you know. Based on a Victorian morality play.
1936 80m/B *GB* Conrad Veidt, Rene Ray, Frank Cellier, Anna Lee, John Turnbull, Cathleen Nesbitt; *D:* Berthold Viertel. **VHS, Beta $16.95** SNC ♫♫

Passion Paris, and the decadent Louis XV falls for the lovely Jeanne, making her his mistress, much to the scandal of the nation. Respectable silent version of "Madame DuBarry" is a relatively realistic costume drama, but it doesn't rate with the best German films of this period.
1919 135m/B *GE* Pola Negri, Emil Jannings, Harry Liedtke; *D:* Ernst Lubitsch. **VHS, Beta $44.99** VYY, GLV ♫♫½

Passion When a rancher's young family falls victim to rampaging desperadoes, he enlists an outlaw's aid to avenge the murders of his loved ones.
1954 84m/C Raymond Burr, Cornel Wilde, Yvonne De Carlo, Lon Chaney Jr., John Qualen; *D:* Allan Dwan. **VHS, Beta** NO ♫♫

Passion Fish McDonnell plays May-Alice, a soap opera actress who is paralyzed after a taxi accident in New York. Confined to a wheelchair, the bitter woman moves back to her Louisiana home and alienates a number of live-in nurses until Chantelle (Woodard), who has her own problems, comes along. Blunt writing and directing by Sayles overcome the story's inherent sentimentality as do the spirited performances of the leads, including Curtis-Hall as the rogue romancing Chantelle and Strathairn as the Cajun bad boy McDonnell once loved. The laserdisc is available in letterbox format.
1992 (R) 136m/C Mary McDonnell, Alfre Woodard, David Strathairn, Vondie Curtis-Hall, Nora Dunn, Sheila Kelley, Angela Bassett, Leo Burmester; *W/D:* John Sayles. Academy Awards '92 Nominations: Best Actress (McDonnell), Best Original Screenplay; Independent Spirit Awards '93: Best Supporting Actress (Woodard). **VHS, LV $89.99** COL, MOV, BTV ♫♫♫

Passion Flower A tropical romantic melodrama made for network TV and set in Singapore, where an ambitious banker falls in love with the daughter of island's wealthiest smuggler. The mixture of high finance, low-dealing and lust only proves moderately passionate.
1986 (PG-13) 95m/C Bruce Boxleitner, Barbara Hershey, Nicol Williamson; *D:* Joseph Sargent. **VHS $89.95** VMK ♫♫

Passion for Life A new teacher uses revolutionary methods to engage students, but draws ire from staid parents in rural France. Worthwhile drama. In French with English subtitles. *AKA:* L'Ecole Buissonniere; I Have a New Master.
1948 89m/B Bernard Blier, Julliette Faber, Edouard Delmont; *D:* Jean-Paul LeChanois. **VHS, Beta $59.95** FCT ♫♫½

Passion for Power Two men involved in a drug-smuggling syndicate attempt to take over the business. Complications arise when they both fall for a beautiful, deceitful woman who turns them against one another.
1985 94m/C *SP* Hector Suarez, Sasha Montenegro, Manuel Capetillo, Alejandra Peniche. **VHS** NO ♫♫½

The Passion of Anna A complicated psychological drama about four people on an isolated island. Von Sydow is an ex-con living a hermit's existence when he becomes involved with a crippled widow (Ullmann) and her two friends—all of whom have secrets in their pasts. Brutal and disturbing. Wonderful cinematography by Sven Nykvist. Filmed on the island of Faro. In Swedish with English subtitles.
1970 (R) 101m/C *SW* Max von Sydow, Liv Ullmann, Bibi Andersson, Erland Josephson, Erik Hell; *W/D:* Ingmar Bergman. **VHS $19.98** MGM ♫♫♫

The Passion of Evelyn An Italian soft-core adventure about a seductive count and a group of willing women. Dubbed and retitled.
198? 80m/C *IT* Femi Benussi, Krista Nell. **VHS, Beta $29.95** MED ♫

The Passion of Joan of Arc Masterful silent film relates the events of St. Joan's trial and subsequent martyrdom. Moving, eloquent work features legendary performace by Falconetti. Also rates among master Dreyer's finest efforts. A classic. Silent with music.
1928 114m/B *FR* Maria Falconetti, Eugena Sylvaw, Maurice Schultz, Antonin Artaud; *D:* Carl Theodor Dreyer. **VHS, Beta $29.95** NOS, MRV, VYY ♫♫♫♫

Passion of Love Military captain becomes the obsession of his commander's mysterious cousin when he reports to an outpost far from home. Daring and fascinating. An unrelentingly passionate historical romance guaranteed to heat up the VCR. Dubbed. Received a special award at the Cannes Film Festival. *AKA:* Passione d'Amore.

P

1982 117m/C *IT FR* Laura Antonelli, Bernard Giraudeau, Valeria D'Obici, Jean-Louis Trintignant; *D:* Ettore Scola. **VHS, Beta $69.95** *VES, TAM* 🐾🐾🐾

Passionate Thief Two pickpockets and a bumbling actress plan to rip off the guests at a posh New Year's Eve party with slightly comic results. Not much to recommend in this slow moving flick. *AKA:* Risate de Gioia. **1960** 100m/C *IT* Anna Magnani, Ben Gazzara, Toto, Fred Clark; *D:* Mario Monicelli. **VHS, Beta $19.95** *NLC* 🐾🐾½

Passione d'Amore A foolhardy cavalry officer already has buxom Antonelli for a lover, but he nonetheless falls in love with a mysterious but homely recluse. Intriguing, often moving. Costume drama set in 19th-century Italy. **1982** 117m/C *IT FR D:* Ettore Scola. **Beta, 3/4U, Special order formats** *CIG* 🐾🐾🐾

The Passover Plot A controversial look at the crucifixion of Christ which depicts him as a Zealot leader who, aided by his followers, faked his death and then "rose" to win new converts. **1975** (PG) 105m/C Harry Andrews, Hugh Griffith, Zalman King, Donald Pleasence, Scott Wilson; *D:* Michael Campus. **VHS, Beta $59.95** *CAN* 🐾🐾

Passport to Pimlico Farce about a London neighborhood's residents who discover an ancient charter proclaiming their right to form their own country within city limits. Passable comedy. **1949** 81m/B *GB* Stanley Holloway, Margaret Rutherford, Hermione Baddeley, Naunton Wayne, Basil Radford; *D:* Henry Cornelius. **VHS, Beta $19.95** *NOS, HBO, PSM* 🐾🐾½

Past Midnight Richardson plays a social worker who believes recently paroled killer Hauer was wrongly convicted. She attempts to prove his innocence while also falling in love—a dangerous combination. Richardson's beautiful and Hauer's making a successful career out of playing handsome psychos. **1992** (R) 100m/C Natasha Richardson, Rutger Hauer, Clancy Brown, Guy Boyd; *D:* Jan Eliasberg; *W:* Frank Norwood. **VHS, LV** *COL* 🐾🐾

Pastime A bittersweet baseball elegy set in the minor leagues in 1957. A boyish 41-year-old pitcher can't face his impending retirement and pals around with the team pariah, a 17-year-old black rookie. Splendidly written and acted, it's a melancholy treat whether you're a fan of the game or not, and safe for family attendance. The only drawback is a grungy, low-budget look. *AKA:* One Cup of Coffee. **1991** (PG) 94m/C William Russ, Scott Plank, Glenn Plummer, Noble Willingham, Jeffrey Tambor, Deidre O'Connell; *D:* Robin B. Armstrong. **VHS, LV $19.95** *COL* 🐾🐾🐾

Pat and Mike War of the sexes rages in this comedy about a leathery sports promoter who futilely attempts to train a woman for athletic competition. Tracy and Hepburn have fine chemistry, but supporting players contribute too. Watch for the first on-screen appearance of Bronson (then Charles Buchinski) as a crook. **1952** 95m/B Spencer Tracy, Katharine Hepburn, Aldo Ray, Jim Backus, William Ching, Sammy White, Phyllis Povah, Charles Bronson, Chuck Connors, Mae Clarke, Carl "Alfalfa" Switzer; *D:* George Cukor; *W:* Ruth Gordon, Garson Kanin. **VHS, Beta, LV $29.95** *MGM* 🐾🐾🐾

Pat Garrett & Billy the Kid Coburn is Garrett, one-time partner of Billy the Kid (Kristofferson), turned sheriff. He tracks down and eventually kills the outlaw. The uncut director's version which was released on video is a vast improvement over the theatrically released and television versions. Dylan's soundtrack includes the now famous "Knockin' on Heaven's Door." **1973** 106m/C Kris Kristofferson, James Coburn, Bob Dylan, Richard Jaeckel, Katy Jurado, Chill Wills, Charles Martin Smith, Slim Pickens, Harry Dean Stanton; *D:* Sam Peckinpah; *W:* Rudy Wurlitzer. **VHS, Beta, LV $19.95** *MGM, PIA* 🐾🐾🐾

A Patch of Blue A kind-hearted blind girl falls in love with a black man without acknowledging racial differences. Good performances from Hartman and Poitier are film's strongest assets. **1965** 108m/C Sidney Poitier, Elizabeth Hartman, Shelley Winters, Wallace Ford, Ivan Dixon, John Qualen, Elisabeth Fraser, Kelly Flynn; *D:* Guy Green; *M:* Jerry Goldsmith. Academy Awards '65: Best Supporting Actress (Winters); Nominations: Best Actress (Hartman), Best Art Direction/Set Decoration (B & W), Best Black and White Cinematography. **VHS, Beta $19.98** *MGM, BTV* 🐾🐾½

Patchwork Girl of Oz A very early silent film production by Baum that brought his own Oz books to the screen. **1914** 80m/B *D:* L. Frank Baum. **VHS, Beta $19.95** *NOS, DVT, VYY* 🐾🐾

Paternity Routine comedy about middle-aged manager of Madison Square Gardens (Reynolds) who sets out to find a woman to bear his child, no strings attached. The predictability of the happy ending makes this a yawner. Steinberg's directorial debut. **1981** (PG) 94m/C Burt Reynolds, Beverly D'Angelo, Lauren Hutton, Norman Fell, Paul Dooley, Elizabeth Ashley; *D:* David Steinberg. **VHS, Beta, LV $39.95** *PAR* 🐾🐾

Pather Panchali Somber, moving story of a young Bengali boy growing up in impoverished India. Stunning debut from India's master filmmaker Ray, who continued the story in "Aparajito" and "World of Apu." A truly great work. In Bengali with English subtitles. *AKA:* The Song of the Road; The Saga of the Road; The Lament of the Path. **1954** 112m/B *IN* Kanu Banerjee, Karuna Banerjee, Uma Das Gupta, Subir Banerji; *D:* Satyajit Ray. **VHS, Beta $24.95** *NOS, FCT, MRV* 🐾🐾🐾🐾

Pathfinder A young boy in Lapland of 1,000 years ago comes of age prematurely after he falls in with cutthroat nomads who already slaughtered his family and now want to wipe out the rest of the village. Gripping adventure in the ice and snow features stunning scenery. In Lappish with English subtitles and based on an old Lapp fable. **1987** 88m/C *NO* Mikkel Gaup, Nils Utsi, Svein Scharffenberg, Helgi Skulason, Sara Marit Gaup, Sverre Porsanger; *W/D:* Nils Gaup. **VHS $79.95** *FXL, FCT, TAM* 🐾🐾🐾½

Paths of Glory Classic anti-war drama set in WWI France. A vain, ambitious officer imposes unlikely battle strategy on his hapless troops, and when it fails, he demands that three soldiers be selected for execution as cowards. Menjou is excellent as the bloodiest French officer, with Douglas properly heroic as the French officer who knows about the whole disgraceful enterprise. Fabulous, wrenching fare from filmmaking great Kubrick, who co-wrote. Based on a true story from Humphrey Cobb's novel of the same name. **1957** 86m/B Kirk Douglas, Adolphe Menjou, George Macready, Ralph Meeker, Richard Anderson, Wayne Morris, Timothy Carey, Susanne Christian; *D:* Stanley Kubrick. **VHS, Beta, LV $19.98** *MGM, FOX* 🐾🐾🐾🐾

Paths to Paradise Compson and Griffith share criminal past, reunite at gala event to snatch priceless necklace and head south of the border. World-class chase scene. **1925** 78m/B Raymond Griffith, Betty Compson, Thomas Santschi, Bert Woodruff, Fred Kelsey; *D:* Clarence Badger. **VHS, Beta $19.95** *GPV* 🐾🐾🐾

Patrick Coma patient suddenly develops strange powers and has a weird effect on the people he comes in contact with. **1978** (PG) 115m/C *AU* Robert Helpmann, Susan Penhaligon, Rod Mullinar; *D:* Richard Franklin. **VHS, Beta** *NO* 🐾½

Patriot An action film about an ex-Navy commando who battles a band of nuclear-arms smuggling terrorists. Edited via George Lucas' electronic editor, Edit Droid. **1986** (R) 88m/C Jeff Conaway, Michael J. Pollard, Leslie Nielsen, Greg Henry, Simone Griffeth; *D:* Frank Harris. **VHS, Beta, LV $79.98** *LIV, VES* 🐾½

Patriot Games Jack Ryan, retired CIA analyst, takes his wife and daughter to England on a holiday and ends up saving a member of the Royal Family from assassination by IRA extremists. Ryan, who has killed one of the terrorists, then becomes the target of revenge by the dead man's brother. Seeking additional protection for his family, Ryan rejoins the CIA and begins a deadly game of hide and seek. Good action sequences; Ford and Archer are fine as the Ryans. Adapted from the novel by Tom Clancy. Companion to "The Hunt for Red October," with Ford taking over the role of Ryan from Alec Baldwin. Since this movie did well, we can expect two more from Ford, who's becoming the king of trilogies. **1992** (R) 117m/C Harrison Ford, Anne Archer, Patrick Bergin, Thora Birch, Sean Bean, Richard Harris, James Earl Jones, James Fox, Samuel L. Jackson, Polly Walker; *D:* Phillip Noyce. **VHS, Beta** *PAR* 🐾🐾🐾

The Patriots A German prisoner works as a shoemaker in a small village during WWI. A lyrical drama in German and Russian with English titles. **1933** 82m/B *RU D:* Boris Barnett. **VHS, Beta, 3/4U $29.95** *FCT, IHF* 🐾🐾🐾

The Patsy Shady producers attempt to transform a lowly bellboy into a comedy superstar. Not one of Lewis's better efforts; Lorre's last film. **1964** 101m/C Jerry Lewis, Ina Balin, Everett Sloane, Phil Harris, Keenan Wynn, Peter Lorre, John Carradine, Hans Conried, Richard Deacon, Scatman Crothers, Del Moore, Neil Hamilton, Buddy Lester, Nancy Kulp, Norman Alden, Jack Albertson; *D:* Jerry Lewis. **VHS, Beta $59.95** *IME* 🐾🐾

Patsy, Mi Amor A modern woman eventually chooses to give herself to an older man, and finds life with him powerful and adventurous. **1987** 94m/C *MX* Julio Aleman, Ofelia Medina, Joaquin Cordero, Leticia Robles, Carlos Cortes, Julian Pastor. **VHS, Beta $55.95** *MAD* 🐾🐾

Patterns Realistic depiction of big business. Heflin starts work at a huge New York office that is under the ruthless supervision of Sloane. Serling's astute screenplay (adapted from his TV play) is adept at portraying ruthless, power-struggling executives and the sundry workings of a large corporation. Film has aged slightly, but it still has some edge to it. Originally intended for television. *AKA:* Patterns of Power. **1956** 83m/B Van Heflin, Everett Sloane, Ed Begley Sr., Beatrice Straight, Elizabeth Wilson; *D:* Fielder Cook; *W:* Rod Serling. **VHS $19.95** *NOS, MGM, MRV* 🐾🐾🐾

Pattes Blanches A reclusive aristocrat always wears white spats, causing ridicule in the small fishing village where he lives. Trouble comes when a local saloon-keeper becomes resentful of the rich man's advances on his girlfriend. Moody, sensual French melodrama exploring class, money and sex. Adaptation of a play by Jean Anouilh. In French with English subtitles. *AKA:* White Paws.
1949 92m/B *FR* Suzy Delair, Fernand Ledoux, Paul Bernard, Michel Bouquet; *D:* Jean Gremillon. **VHS** *INT, FCT* 𝟚𝟚½

Patti Rocks Offbeat, realistic independent effort concerns a foul chauvinist who enlists a friend to accompany him on a visit to a pregnant girlfriend who turns out to be less than the bimbo she's portrayed as en route. Mulkey shines as the sexist. Written by Mulkey, Morris, Landry, and Jenkins. Same characters featured earlier in "Loose Ends."
1988 (R) 86m/C Chris Mulkey, John Jenkins, Karen Landry, David L. Turk, Stephen Yoakam; *D:* David Burton Morris. **VHS, Beta, LV** *NO* 𝟚𝟚𝟚

Patton Lengthy but stellar bio of the vain, temperamental American general who masterminded significant combat triumphs during WWII. "Old Blood and Guts," who considered himself an 18th-century commander living in the wrong era, produced victory after victory in North Africa and Europe, but not without a decided impact upon his troops. Scott is truly magnificent in the title role, and Malden shines in the supporting role of General Omar Bradley. Not a subtle film, but neither is its subject. Interesting match-up with the 1986 made for TV movie "The Last Days of Patton," also starring Scott. *AKA:* Patton—Lust for Glory; Patton: A Salute to a Rebel.
1970 (PG) 171m/C George C. Scott, Karl Malden, Stephen Young, Michael Strong, Frank Latimore, James Edwards, Lawrence Dobkin, Michael Bates, Tim Considine; *D:* Franklin J. Schaffner; *W:* Francis Ford Coppola, Edmund H. North; *M:* Jerry Goldsmith. Academy Awards '70: Best Actor (Scott), Best Art Direction/Set Decoration, Best Director (Schaffner), Best Film Editing, Best Picture, Best Sound, Best Story & Screenplay; Nominations: Best Original Score; Directors Guild of America Awards '70: Best Director (Schaffner); Golden Globe Awards '71: Best Actor—Drama (Scott); National Board of Review Awards '70: 10 Best Films of the Year, Best Actor (Scott); National Society of Film Critics Awards '70: Best Actor (Scott). **VHS, Beta, LV** $29.98 *FOX, TLF, BTV* 𝟚𝟚𝟚½

Patty Hearst Less than fascinating, expressionistic portrait of Hearst from her kidnapping through her brainwashing and eventual criminal participation with the SLA. An enigmatic film that seems to only make Hearst's transformation into a Marxist terrorist all the more mysterious. Based on Hearst's book, "Every Secret Thing."
1988 (R) 108m/C Natasha Richardson, William Forsythe, Ving Rhames, Frances Fisher, Jodi Long, Dana Delany; *D:* Paul Schrader. **VHS, Beta, LV** $19.98 *MED* 𝟚½

Paul and Michelle The equally dull sequel to "Friends" finds the two lovers a little older but no wiser. Paul has graduated from his British school and returns to France to seek out Michelle and their child. They try to rekindle their romance but the stresses of everyday life cause them problems.
1974 (R) 102m/C *GB FR* Sean Bury, Anicee Alvina, Keir Dullea, Ronald Lewis, Catherine Allegret, Georges Beller; *D:* Lewis Gilbert. **VHS** $14.95 *PAR* 𝟚

Paul Bartel's The Secret Cinema A woman cannot determine whether her life is real or a film by a maniacal director. Offbeat, creative, and a little disturbing. Followed by Bartel's short "Naughty Nurse."
1969 37m/B *D:* Paul Bartel. **VHS, Beta** $29.95 *RHI* 𝟚𝟚½

Paul Robeson Major events in the life of the popular actor are recounted in this one-man performance. Originally staged by Charles Nelson Reilly.
197? 118m/C James Earl Jones; *D:* Lloyd Richards. **VHS, Beta** $39.95 *KAR* 𝟚𝟚

Pauline at the Beach A young woman accompanies her more experienced cousin to the French coast for a summer of sexual hijinks. Contemplative, not coarse, though the leads look great in—and out—of their swimsuits. Breezy, typically talky fare from small-film master Rohmer. Cinematography by Nester Almendro. In French with English subtitles. *AKA:* Pauline a la Plage.
1983 (R) 95m/C *FR* Amanda Langlet, Arielle Dombasle, Pascal Greggory, Rosette; *W/D:* Eric Rohmer. **VHS, Beta, LV** $24.95 *XVC, MED, TAM* 𝟚𝟚𝟚½

Paul's Case In turn-of-the-century Pittsburgh, an ambitious young man enters the upper crust of New York society through deceiving pretenses. Based on a story by Willa Cather. Made for television.
1980 52m/C Eric Roberts, Michael Higgins, Lindsay Crouse; *D:* Lamont Johnson. **VHS, Beta** $24.95 *MON, MTI, KAR* 𝟚½

Pawnbroker A Jewish pawnbroker in Harlem is haunted by his grueling experiences in a Nazi camp during the Holocaust. Powerful and well done. Probably Steiger's best performance. Adapted from a novel by Edward Lewis Wallant.
1965 120m/B Rod Steiger, Brock Peters, Geraldine Fitzgerald, Jaime Sanchez, Thelma Oliver; *D:* Sidney Lumet. Academy Awards '65 Nominations: Best Actor (Steiger); Berlin International Film Festival '65: Best Actor (Steiger); British Academy Awards '66: Best Actor (Steiger). **VHS, LV** $19.98 *REP* 𝟚𝟚𝟚½

Pawnshop Charlie is employed as a pawnbroker's assistant. Silent with music track.
1916 20m/B Charlie Chaplin. **VHS, Beta, 3/4U**, Special order formats *CAB, FST* 𝟚𝟚𝟚½

Pay Off A lunatic psychiatrist seeks murderous revenge on his ex-patient/girlfriend and her family.
1989 87m/C Michael Fitzpatrick, Veronika Mattson, Margareta Krook; *D:* George Tirl. **VHS, Beta** $59.95 *TWE* 𝟚

Pay or Die A crime boss' men turn on him and kidnap his daughter.
1983 (R) 92m/C Dick Adair, Johnny Wilson; *D:* Bobby Suarez. **VHS, Beta** $29.95 *LIV* 𝟚

Payback A brawny young man uses firepower to avenge those who have wronged him.
1989 90m/C Jean Carol. **VHS, Beta** *NO* 𝟚

Payback A convict sets out to avenge his brother's death, and creates all sorts of mayhem in the process. Produced by Bob "Newlywed Game" Eubanks and scored by Daryl "Captain and Tenille" Dragon.
1990 (R) 94m/C Corey Michael Eubanks, Michael Ironside, Teresa Blake, Bert Remsen, Vincent Van Patten, Don Swayze; *D:* Russell Solberg. **VHS** $89.98 *REP* 𝟚

Payday Rip Torn stars as a declining country music star on tour in this portrayal of the seamy side of show business, from groupies to grimy motels. Don Carpenter's script and fine performances make this an engaging, if rather draining, drama not easily found on the big screen.
1972 98m/C Rip Torn, Anna Capri, Michael C. Gwynne, Jeff Morris; *D:* Daryl Duke. **VHS, Beta** $59.99 *HBO* 𝟚𝟚½

The Payoff The old-fashioned newspaper-reporter-as-crime-fighter routine. When the city's special prosecutor is murdered a daring newshawk investigates and tracks the bad guys. But will he spell their names right?
1943 74m/B Lee Tracy, Tom Brown, Tina Thayer, Evelyn Brent, Jack La Rue, Ian Keith, John Maxwell; *D:* Arthur Dreifuss. **VHS** $19.95 *NOS, LOO* 𝟚𝟚

Payoff An ex-cop discovers the identity of gangsters who killed his parents. He traces them to a Lake Tahoe resort and plots revenge. Familiar crime story with a good cast.
1991 (R) 111m/C Keith Carradine, Kim Greist, Harry Dean Stanton, John Saxon, Jeff Corey; *D:* Stuart Cooper. **VHS, Beta, LV** $89.98 *FXV* 𝟚𝟚

Peacekillers A mean bunch of bikers visit a commune to kidnap a young woman. The gang has a big surprise in store for them when the girl escapes.
1971 86m/C Michael Ontkean, Clint Ritchie, Paul Krokop; *D:* Douglas Schwartz. **VHS, Beta** $19.95 *NWV, STE* 𝟚½

Peacemaker Two aliens masquerading as human cops stalk each other through a major city.
1990 (R) 90m/C Robert Forster, Lance Edwards, Hilary Shepard, Bert Remsen, Robert Davi; *D:* Kevin S. Tenney. **VHS, Beta, LV** $89.95 *FRH* 𝟚

The Peacock Fan The Peacock Fan is protected by a deadly curse, with certain death to anyone who possesses it.
1929 50m/B Lucien Preval. **VHS, Beta** $10.95 *SNC, VYY* 𝟚½

The Peanut Butter Solution An imaginative 11-year-old boy investigates a strange old house which is haunted by friendly ghosts who are in possession of a magic potion.
1985 (PG) 96m/C *D:* Michael Rubbo. **VHS, Beta** $14.95 *NWV, STE, HHE* 𝟚𝟚½

The Pearl Based on a John Steinbeck story, a Mexican fisherman, living in poverty, finds a magnificent pearl and he thinks it will improve the lives of his family. He is bewildered by what this pearl really brings—liars and thieves. Simple, yet larger-than-life film, beautifully photographed; a timeless picture capturing human nature.
1948 77m/B *MX* Pedro Armendariz Sr., Maria Elena Marques, Fernando Wagner, Charles Rooner; *D:* Emilio Fernandez. **VHS** $69.95 *FCT, MAS* 𝟚𝟚𝟚

The Pearl of Death Holmes and Watson investigate the theft of a precious pearl.
1944 69m/B Basil Rathbone, Nigel Bruce, Dennis Hoey, Miles Mander, Rondo Hatton, Evelyn Ankers; *D:* Roy William Neill. **VHS, Beta** $14.98 *FOX* 𝟚𝟚½

Pearl of the South Pacific A trio of adventurers destroy a quiet and peaceful island when they ransack it for pearl treasures. *AKA:* South Sea Woman.
1955 85m/C Dennis Morgan, Virginia Mayo, David Farrar; *D:* Allan Dwan. **VHS, Beta** *NO* 𝟚𝟚

The Peasants Poignant rural Polish saga pits father against son due to the passion they share for one woman. In two tapes, based on Wladyslaw Reymont's Nobel prize-winning novel. In Polish with English subtitles.
19?? 184m/C *PL* **VHS** $69.99 *FCT* 𝟚𝟚½

Peck's Bad Boy Impudent, precocious brat causes his parents considerable grief. Someone should lock this kid in a room with W.C. Fields or the Alien. Silent film based on the stories by George Wilbur Peck.
1921 51m/B Jackie Coogan, Thomas Meighan, Raymond Hatton, Wheeler Oakman, Lillian Leighton; D: Sam Wood. **VHS, Beta, LV** $19.95 NOS, MRV, CCB ♪♪

Peck's Bad Boy A wedge is driven between a young boy and his adoptive father when the man's sister and her son move in. The aunt wants her son to be number one, causing much discord. Cooper is excellent in his role as the adopted son.
1934 70m/B Thomas Meighan, Jackie Cooper, Dorothy Peterson, Jackie Searl, O.P. Heggie, Harvey Clark, Lloyd Ingraham; D: Eddie Cline. **VHS** $19.95 NOS, MLB ♪♪½

Peck's Bad Boy with the Circus The circus will never be the same after the mischievous youngster and his buddies get done with it. Gilbert and Kennedy provide the high points.
1938 67m/B Tommy Kelly, Anne Gillis, George "Spanky" McFarland, Edgar Kennedy, Billy Gilbert; D: Eddie Cline. **VHS, Beta** $19.95 NOS, VYY, DVT ♪♪

Pecos Bill Meet the man who used the Grand Canyon for a swimmin' hole, dug the Rio Grande and used the Texas panhandle for a fryin' pan. From Shelly Duvall's "Tall Tales and Legends" series. Originally made for cable television.
1986 50m/C Steve Guttenberg, Martin Mull, Claude Akins, Rebecca DeMornay. **VHS** $19.98 FOX, COL ♪♪

Pecos Kid A child has his parents killed, and grows up embittered, vengeful and thirsty for blood.
1935 56m/B Fred Kohler Jr. **VHS, Beta, LV** $19.95 NOS ♪

Peddlin' in Society A fruit vendor makes it big on the black market and lives the good life, until poor investments force her back to her old means. Strong perfomances by Magnani and De Sica. In Italian with English subtitles. AKA: Da Bancarella a Bancarotta.
1947 85m/B IT Anna Magnani, Vittorio De Sica, Virgilio Riento, Laura Gore; D: Gennaro Righelli. **VHS** DVT, HEG ♪♪

The Pedestrian A prominent German industrialist is exposed as a Nazi officer who supervised the wholesale devastation of a Greek village during WWII. Impressive debut for director Schell, who also appears in a supporting role. AKA: Der Fussgaenger.
1973 (PG) 97m/C GE SI Maximilian Schell, Peggy Ashcroft, Lil Dagover, Francoise Rosay, Elisabeth Bergner; D: Maximilian Schell. Academy Awards '73 Nominations: Best Foreign Language Film; Golden Globe Awards '74: Best Foreign Film; National Board of Review Awards '74: 5 Best Foreign Films of the Year. **VHS, Beta** $69.98 SUE, GLV, SWC ♪♪♪½

The Pee-Wee Herman Show The original HBO special which introduced Pee-Wee to the world. Hilarious stuff, with help from Captain Carl (Hartman), Miss Yvonne, and other assorted pals. Warning: Not to be confused with Pee Wee's children's show.
1982 60m/C Pee-Wee Herman, Phil Hartman, John Paragon. **VHS** $29.95 HBO ♪♪♪½

Pee-Wee's Big Adventure Zany, endearing comedy about an adult nerd's many adventures while attempting to recover his stolen bicycle. Chock full of classic sequences, including a barroom encounter between Pee-Wee and several ornery bikers. A

colorful, exhilerating experience written by Reubens, Phil Hartman, and Michael Varhol.
1985 (PG) 92m/C Pee-Wee Herman, Elizabeth Daily, Mark Holton, Diane Salinger, Judd Omen; D: Tim Burton. **VHS, Beta, LV** $19.98 WAR ♪♪♪½

Pee-Wee's Playhouse Christmas Special Pee Wee does an extended Playhouse episode for Christmas, with a load of guest stars.
1988 49m/C Pee-Wee Herman, Whoopi Goldberg, Zsa Zsa Gabor, Grace Jones, Dinah Shore, Frankie Avalon, Annette Funicello, Joan Rivers, Oprah Winfrey, Charo, Earle Johnson, k.d. lang, Kareem Abdul-Jabbar, Del Rubio Triplets, Little Richard. **VHS, Beta, LV** $9.99 VTR ♪♪♪

Pee-Wee's Playhouse Festival of Fun Five fun-filled episodes of the playhouse!
1988 123m/C Pee-Wee Herman. **VHS, Beta** $79.95 MED ♪♪♪½

Peeping Tom Controversial, unsettling thriller in which a psychopath lures women before his film camera, then records their deaths at his hand. Unnerving subject matter is rendered impressively by British master Powell. A classic of its kind, but definitely not for everyone. This is the original uncut version of the film, released in the U.S. in 1979 with the assistance of Martin Scorsese.
1963 88m/C Karl-Heinz Boehm, Moira Shearer, Anna Massey, Maxine Audley, Esmond Knight, Shirley Anne Field, Brenda Bruce, Pamela Green, Jack Watson, Nigel Davenport, Susan Travers, Veronica Hurst; D: Michael Powell. **VHS, Beta, LV** $39.95 AOV ♪♪♪½

Peg O' My Heart Taylor portrays the motherless Irish charmer sent to live with her mother's English relatives during the Irish rebellion. Of course, she must overcome their upper-class English snobbery to become a part of the family.
1922 85m/B Laurette Taylor, Mahlon Hamilton, Russell Simpson, Ethel Grey; D: King Vidor. **VHS** GPV ♪♪

Peggy Sue Got Married Uneven but entertaining comedy about an unhappily married woman seemingly unable to relive her life when she falls unconscious at a high school reunion and awakens to find herself back in school. Turner shines, but the film flags often, and Cage isn't around enough to elevate entire work. O'Connor scores, though, as the sensitive biker. Look for musician Marshall Crenshaw as part of the reunion band.
1986 (PG-13) 103m/C Kathleen Turner, Nicolas Cage, Catherine Hicks, Maureen O'Sullivan, John Carradine, Helen Hunt, Lisa Jane Persky, Barbara Harris, Joan Allen, Kevin J. O'Connor, Barry Miller; D: Francis Ford Coppola; M: John Barry. **VHS, Beta, LV** $19.98 FOX ♪♪½

The Peking Blond French-fried spyfilm boasts lousy acting unencumbered by plot. Amnesiac may or may not hold secrets coveted by Americans, Russians and Chinese. AKA: The Blonde From Peking; Le Blonde de Pekin.
1968 80m/C FR Mireille Darc, Claudio Brook, Edward G. Robinson, Pascale Roberts; D: Nicolas Gessner. **VHS** $29.99 MRV ♪½

Pelle the Conqueror Overpowering tale of a Swedish boy and his widower father who serve landowners in late 19th-century Denmark. Compassionate saga of human spirit contains numerous memorable sequences. Hvenegaard is wonderful as young Pelle, but von Sydow delivers what is probably his finest performance as a sympathetic weakling. American distributors foolishly trimmed the film by some 20 minutes (140

minute version). From the novel by Martin Anderson Nexo. In Swedish with English subtitles.
1988 160m/C SW DK Max von Sydow, Pelle Hvenegaard, Erik Paaske, Bjorn Granath, Axel Strobye, Astrid Villaume, Troels Asmussen, John Wittig, Anne Lise Hirsch Bjerrum; D: Bille August. Academy Awards '88: Best Foreign Language Film; Nominations: Best Actor (von Sydow); Cannes Film Festival '88: Best Film; Golden Globe Awards '89: Best Foreign Film. **VHS, Beta, LV** $19.98 HBO, TAM ♪♪♪

Penalty Phase An up-for-election judge must decide a murder case in which his future, as well as the defendant's, is in question. Made for television.
1986 94m/C Peter Strauss, Melissa Gilbert, Jonelle Allen; D: Tony Richardson. **VHS, Beta** $19.95 STE, NWV ♪♪

Pendulum A police captain struggles to prove himself innocent of his wife's—and his wife's lover's—murders. Wow.
1969 (PG) 106m/C George Peppard, Jean Seberg, Richard Kiley, Madeline Sherwood, Charles McGraw, Marj Dusay; D: George Schaefer. **VHS, Beta, LV** $59.95 COL ♪♪

The Penitent A remote village's annual reenactment of the crucifixion of Christ serves as the backdrop for Assante's affair with his friend's (Julia) wife. Quirky little tale that focuses a shade too much on the romantic problems of the trio rather than the intriguing religious practices going on around them.
1988 (PG-13) 94m/C Raul Julia, Armand Assante, Rona Freed, Julie Carmen; D: Cliff Osmond. **VHS, Beta** $29.95 LIV ♪♪

Penitentiary A realistic story of a black fighter who survives his prison incarceration by winning bouts against the other prisoners. Well-made and executed, followed by two progressively worse sequels.
1979 (R) 99m/C Leon Isaac Kennedy, Jamaa Fanaka; D: Jamaa Fanaka. **VHS, Beta** $59.95 UNI, FCT ♪♪½

Penitentiary 2 A welterweight fighter is after the man who murdered his girlfriend, who, luckily, is incarcerated in the same prison as Our Hero. Sometimes things just work out right.
1982 108m/C Leon Isaac Kennedy, Mr. T, Leif Erickson, Ernie Hudson, Glynn Turman; D: Jamaa Fanaka. **VHS, Beta** $14.95 MGM, HHE ♪

Penitentiary 3 Once again, Kennedy as the inmate boxer extraordinaire punches his way out of various prison battles. Another punch-drunk sequel.
1987 (R) 91m/C Leon Isaac Kennedy, Anthony Geary, Steve Antin, Ric Mancini, Kessler Raymond, Jim Bailey; D: Jamaa Fanaka. **VHS, Beta** $19.98 WAR ♪½

Penn and Teller Get Killed The comedy team with a cult following are pursued by an assassin through dozens of pratfalls in this dark comedy.
1990 (R) 91m/C Penn Jillette, Jilette Teller, Caitlin Clarke, Leonardo Cimino, David Patrick Kelly; D: Arthur Penn. **VHS, Beta, LV** $89.95 WAR ♪♪♪

Pennies From Heaven Underrated, one-of-a-kind musical about a horny sheet-music salesman in Chicago and his escapades during the Depression. Extraordinary musical sequences have stars lip-synching to great effect. Martin is only somewhat acceptable as the hapless salesman, but Peters and Harper deliver powerful performances as the women whose lives he ruins. Walken brings down the house in a stunning song-and-dance sequence. Adapted by Dennis Potter from his British television series. ♫The Clouds Will Soon Roll By; Did You Ever See

A Dream Walking?; Yes, Yes; Pennies From Heaven; Love Is Good for Anything That Ails You; I Want to Be Bad; Let's Misbehave; Life Is Just a Bowl of Cherries; Let's Face the Music and Dance.
1981 (R) 107m/C Steve Martin, Bernadette Peters, Christopher Walken, Jessica Harper, Vernel Bagneris; **D:** Herbert Ross; **W:** Dennis Potter. Academy Awards '81 Nominations: Best Adapted Screenplay, Best Costume Design, Best Sound; Golden Globe Awards '82: Best Actress—Musical/Comedy (Peters). **VHS, Beta, LV $19.99** *MGM, FCT* �)✓✓✓½

Penny Serenade Newlyweds adopt a child, but tragedy awaits. Simplistic story nonetheless proves to be a moving experience. They don't make 'em like this anymore, and no one plays Grant better than Grant. Dunne is adequate. Also available colorized.
1941 120m/B Cary Grant, Irene Dunne, Beulah Bondi, Edgar Buchanan; **D:** George Stevens. **VHS, LV, 3/4U, Special order formats $9.95** *NEG, NOS, PSM* ✓✓✓

Penthouse Baxter is a corporation lawyer who, for a change of pace, defends a gangland boss (Pendleton). His success loses him his high-society clientele but wins him Pendleton's respect and protection. But Baxter then gets involved in a further series of gang-related crimes, which nearly cost him his life. Also aiding Baxter is Loy, playing a smart-cookie gun moll, who would take her wisecracks to "The Thin Man" the following year. Good combo of melodrama, suspense, and humor. **AKA:** Crooks in Clover.
1933 90m/B Warner Baxter, Myrna Loy, Nat Pendleton, C. Henry Gordon, Mae Clarke, Charles Butterworth, Phillips Holmes; **D:** Woodbridge S. Van Dyke. **LV** *MGM* ✓✓✓

The Penthouse Givens stars as a wealthy young woman stalked by an old boyfriend who just happens to have escaped from a mental institution. When he traps her in her home, she has two choices—love him or die. Based on the novel by Elleston Trevor.
1992 93m/C Robin Givens, David Hewlett, Cedric Smith, Donnelly Rhodes, Robert Guillaume; **D:** David Greene. **VHS $89.98** *TTC* ✓✓

The People A young teacher takes a job in a small town and finds out that her students have telepathic powers and other strange qualities. Adapted from a novel by Zenna Henderson. Good atmosphere, especially for a TV movie.
1971 74m/C Kim Darby, Dan O'Herlihy, Diane Varsi, William Shatner; **D:** John Korty. **VHS, Beta $59.95** *PSM* ✓✓½

People Are Funny Battling radio producers vie to land the big sponsor with an original radio idea. Comedy ensues when one of them comes up with a great idea—stolen from a local station.
1946 94m/B Jack Haley, Rudy Vallee, Ozzie Nelson, Art Linkletter, Helen Walker; **D:** Sam White. **VHS, Beta $29.95** *NO* ✓✓

The People Next Door Seventies attempt at exposing the drug problems of suburban youth. Typical middle-class parents Wallach and Harris are horrified to discover that daughter Winters is strung out on LSD. They fight to expose the neighborhood pusher while struggling to understand their now-alien daughter. Based on J.P. Miller's television play.
1970 93m/C Deborah Winters, Eli Wallach, Julie Harris, Stephen McHattie, Hal Holbrook, Cloris Leachman, Nehemiah Persoff; **D:** David Greene. **VHS** *NO* ✓✓

The People That Time Forgot Sequel to "The Land That Time Forgot," based on the Edgar Rice Burroughs novel. A rescue team returns to a world of prehistoric monsters to rescue a man left there after the first film.
1977 (PG) 90m/C *GB* Doug McClure, Patrick Wayne, Sarah Douglas, Dana Gillespie, Thorley Walters, Shane Rimmer; **D:** Kevin Connor. **VHS, Beta $9.98** *SUE* ✓✓½

The People Under the Stairs Adams is part of a scheme to rob a house in the slums owned by a mysterious couple (Robie and McGill, both of "Twin Peaks" fame). After his friends are killed off in a gruesome fashion, he discovers that the couple aren't the house's only strange inhabitants—homicidal creatures also lurk within.
1991 (R) 102m/C Everett McGill, Wendy Robie; **W/D:** Wes Craven. **VHS, Beta, LV $19.98** *MCA* ✓✓½

The People vs. Jean Harris Follows the trial of Jean Harris. Shortly before this film was released, she had been convicted of murder in the death of Dr. Herman Tarnower, the author of "The Scarsdale Diet." Harris was a head mistress in a private school all the while. Made for television. Burstyn was nominated for an Emmy Award for best actress.
1981 147m/C Ellen Burstyn, Martin Balsam, Richard Dysart, Peter Coyote, Priscilla Morrill, Sarah Marshall, Millie Slavin; **D:** George Schaefer. **VHS, Beta** *NO* ✓✓✓

People Who Own the Dark A small farming community becomes possessed by a supernatural light during an explosion. The people, who have all been blinded, discover that the world is ending.
1975 (R) 87m/C Paul Naschy, Tony Kendall, Maria Perschy, Terry Kemper, Tom Weyland, Anita Brock, Paul Mackey; **W/D:** Armando de Ossorio. **VHS $19.95** *SUN, MRV* ✓✓

People's Choice A small town boy suffers laryngitis, becomes a radio personality via his new huskiness, and claims he's a notorious criminal.
1946 68m/B Drew Kennedy, Louise Arthur, George Meeker, Rex Lease, Fred Kelsey. **VHS, Beta, LV** *NO* ✓✓

Pepe Le Moko An influential French film about a notorious gangster holed up in the Casbah, emerging at his own peril out of love for a beautiful woman. Stirring film established Gabin as a matinee idol. Cinematography is particularly fine too. Based upon the D'Ashelbe novel. The basis for both "Algiers," the popular Boyer-Lamarr melodrama, and the musical "The Casbah." In French with English subtitles.
1937 87m/B *FR* Jean Gabin, Mireille Balin, Gabriel Gabrio, Lucas Gridoux; **D:** Julien Duvivier. **VHS, Beta, 8mm, 3/4U, Special order formats $29.95** *NOS, VYY, HHT* ✓✓✓

Pepe Le Pew's Skunk Tales Eight Le Pew shorts, including "Who Scent You?," "The Cat's Bah" and "Scent-imental Romeo," most by Academy Award-winning director Chuck Jones.
1953 56m/C **D:** Chuck Jones, Robert McKimson, Bob Clampett. **VHS, Beta $12.95** *WAR, WTA* ✓✓✓

Pepi, Luci, Bom and Other Girls on the Heap Almodovar's low-budget directorial debut will be of interest primarily to the director's aficionados. Pepi (Maura's debut role) is a Madrid heiress who gets in trouble when her neighbor, a policeman, notices her marijuana plants. She offers sexual favors in return for silence but is raped instead. Pepi later decides on revenge by seducing Luci, the policeman's wife, aided

by her girlfriend, Bom. There's lots of partying, drugs, promiscuity, and violence, none of it very involving. In Spanish with English subtitles. **AKA:** Pepi, Luci, Bom y Otras Chicas del Monton.
1980 80m/C *SP* Carmen Maura, Eva Siva, Olivido Gara, Felix Rotaeta; **W/D:** Pedro Almodovar. **VHS $79.95** *FCT, TAM, CCN* ✓✓½

Pepper International intrigue and super spying abound in fast-paced, sexy, and not altogether intelligent adventure featuring Pepper, a female secret agent in the James Bond tradition.
1982 88m/C **VHS, Beta $69.95** *VES* ✓½

Pepper and His Wacky Taxi Father of four buys a '59 Cadillac and starts a cab company. Time-capsule fun.
1972 (G) 79m/C John Astin, Frank Sinatra Jr., Jackie Gayle, Alan Sherman; **D:** Alex Grasshof. **VHS, Beta $19.95** *UNI* ✓½

Perfect A "Rolling Stone" reporter goes after the shallowness of the Los Angeles health club scene, and falls in love with the aerobics instructor he's going to write about. "Rolling Stone" publisher Wenner plays himself. As bad as it sounds.
1985 (R) 120m/C John Travolta, Jamie Lee Curtis, Carly Simon, Marilu Henner, Laraine Newman, Jann Wenner, Anne De Salvo; **D:** James Bridges. **VHS, Beta, LV $14.95** *COL* ✓½

The Perfect Bride A pretty young nursing prepares to marry her fiance, but his sister thinks she is hiding a secret. Could the bride-to-be have murder on her mind? Is it possible she lures men to the altar in order to avenge a past so hideous only a scriptwriter could have dreamed it up? Made for cable.
1991 (R) 95m/C Sammi Davis-Voss, Kelly Preston, Linden Ashby, Marilyn Rockafellow, Ashley Tillman; **D:** Terrence O'Hara. **VHS, Beta, LV $89.98** *FXV* ✓½

Perfect Crime A Scotland Yard inspector must find out who has been killing off executives of a powerful world trust.
1978 90m/C Joseph Cotten, Anthony Steel, Janet Agren. **VHS, Beta $29.95** *VID* ✓✓

Perfect Family Standard woman-and-kids-in-peril-from-psycho tale. Maggie is a recent widow with two young daughters who's looking for a nanny and a handyman. She hires brother and sister combo Janice and Alan, who, of course, are too good to be true. One is a sociopath who has murdered a family once before. Guess along with Maggie who the nut might be.
1992 (R) 92m/C Jennifer O'Neill, Bruce Boxleitner, Joanna Cassidy, Juliana Hansen, Shiri Appleby; **D:** E.W. Swackhamer; **W:** Christian Stoianovich, Phoebe Dorin; **M:** Nicholas Pike. **VHS, Beta** *PAR* ✓✓

Perfect Furlough A corporal wins a week in Paris with a movie star, accompanied by a female Army psychologist. Pretty bizarre, but it works. **AKA:** Strictly for Pleasure.
1959 93m/C Tony Curtis, Janet Leigh, Keenan Wynn, Linda Cristal, Elaine Stritch; **D:** Blake Edwards. **VHS, Beta $14.95** *KRT, MLB* ✓✓½

Perfect Killer Van Cleef stars as a world weary Mafia hit-man who is double-crossed by his girl, set up by his best friend, and hunted by another hired assassin. Also on video as "Satanic Mechanic."
1977 (R) 85m/C Lee Van Cleef, Tita Barker, John Ireland, Robert Widmark; **D:** Marlon Sirko. **VHS, Beta $49.95** *PSM, SIM* ✓✓½

Perfect Match A timid young woman and an unambitious young man meet each other through the personal ads and then lie to each other about who they are and what they do for a living.

1988 (PG) 93m/C Marc McClure, Jennifer Edwards, Diane Stilwell, Rob Paulsen, Karen Witter; **D:** Mark Deimel. **VHS, Beta** $79.98 MCG 🐾🐾

Perfect Strangers Thriller develops around a murder and the child who witnesses it. The killer attempts to kidnap the young boy, but problems arise when he falls in love with the lad's mother. **AKA:** Blind Alley.
1984 (R) 90m/C Anne Carlisle, Brad Rijn, John Woehrle, Matthew Stockley, Ann Magnuson, Stephen Lack; **D:** Larry Cohen. **VHS, Beta** $24.98 SUE, NLC 🐾🐾

Perfect Timing Soft-core film about a fledgling photographer who can't turn his orgy-like photo sessions into anything profitable.
1984 87m/C Stephen Markle, Michelle Scarabelli; **D:** Rene Bonniere. **VHS, Beta** $69.98 LIV Woof!

Perfect Victims Beautiful models are being hunted by a killer, and a police officer wants to catch the psychopath before he strikes again.
1987 (R) 100m/C Deborah Shelton, Clarence Williams III, Lyman Ward, Tom Dugan; **D:** Shuki Levy. **VHS, Beta, LV** $29.95 ACA 🐾

The Perfect Weapon Kenpo karate master Speakman severs family ties and wears funny belt in order to avenge underworld murder of his teacher.
1991 (R) 85m/C Jeff Sanders, Jeff Speakman; **D:** Mark DiSalle; **W:** David Wilson. **VHS, Beta, LV** $14.95 PAR, PIA 🐾🐾

Perfect Witness A restaurant owner witnesses a mob slaying and resists testifying against the culprit to save his family and himself. Made for cable television. Filmed in New York City.
1989 104m/C Brian Dennehy, Aidan Quinn, Stockard Channing; **D:** Robert Mandel. **VHS, Beta, LV** $89.99 HBO 🐾🐾½

Perfectly Normal Two friends end up in hilarious situations when one opens an eccentric restaurant with a mysterious, newly found fortune.
1991 106m/C Michael Riley, Robbie Coltrane, Kenneth Welsh, Eugene Lipinski; **D:** Yves Simoneau; **W:** Eugene Lipinski, Paul Quarrington. **VHS, Beta, LV** $19.95 ACA 🐾🐾

Performance Grim and unsettling psychological account of a criminal who hides out in a bizarre house occupied by a peculiar rock star and his two female companions. Entire cast scores high marks, with Pallenberg especially compelling as a somewhat mysterious and attractive housemate to mincing Jagger. A cult favorite, with music by Jack Nitzsche under the direction of Randy Newman.
1970 (R) 104m/C GB James Fox, Mick Jagger, Anita Pallenberg; **D:** Donald Cammell, Nicolas Roeg; **M:** Jack Nitzsche. **VHS, Beta, LV** $19.98 WAR 🐾🐾🐾½

Perfume Five beautiful, black childhood friends join together to conquer the cosmetics industry with their new perfume, Sassy. But can they resist all the temptations success brings and keep both their company and their friendship?
1991 98m/C Cheryl Francis Harrington, Kathleen Bradley Overton, Shy Jefferson, Lynn Marlin, Eugina Wright, Ted Lange; **D:** Roland S. Jefferson. **VHS** $89.95 XVC 🐾🐾

Perfumed Nightmare Unique, appealing fable about a Filipino youth who discovers the drawbacks of social and cultural progress when he moves to Paris. Director Tahimik also plays the lead role. Imaginative, yet remarkably economical, this film was produced for $10,000 and received the Inter-

national Critics Award at the Berlin Film Festival. In Tagalog with English dialogue and subtitles.
1989 93m/C PH Kidlat Tahimik, Dolores Santamaria, Georgette Baudry, Katrin Muller, Harmut Lerch; **D:** Kidlat Tahimik. **VHS** $17.00 UWA 🐾🐾🐾

Peril From the novel "Sur La Terre Comme Au Ciel" by Rene Belletto. Deals with a music teacher's infiltration into a wealthy family and the sexually motivated, back-stabbing murder plots that ensue. DeVille does poorly with avant-garde technique. In French with English subtitles. **AKA:** Peril en la Demeure.
1985 (R) 100m/C FR Michel Piccoli, Christophe MaLavoy, Richard Bohringer, Nicole Garcia, Anais Jeanneret; **D:** Michel DeVille. **VHS, Beta** $59.95 RCA, TAM 🐾🐾½

The Perils of Gwendoline A young woman leaves a convent to search for her long-lost father, in this adaptation of a much funnier French comic strip of the same name. What ends up on the screen is merely a very silly rip-off of the successful "Raiders of the Lost Ark," and of primary interest for its numerous scenes of amply endowed Kitaen in the buff. **AKA:** Gwendoline; The Perils of Gwendoline in the Land of the Yik-Yak.
1984 (R) 88m/C FR Tawny Kitaen, Brent Huff, Zabou, Bernadette LaFont, Jean Rougerie; **D:** Just Jaeckin. **VHS, Beta, LV** $79.98 LIV, VES 🐾🐾½

The Perils of Pauline All twelve episodes of this classic melodrama/adventure serial in one package, featuring dastardly villains, cliff-hanging predicaments, worldwide chases, and that remarkable character, Pearl White.
1934 238m/B Evelyn Knapp, Robert Allen, James Durkin, Sonny Ray, Pat O'Malley; **D:** Ray Taylor. **VHS, Beta** $29.95 NOS, VYY, MLB 🐾🐾

The Perils of Pauline A musical biography of Pearl White, the reigning belle of silent movie serials. Songs by Frank Loesser include "I Wish I Didn't Love You So," an Academy Award nominee. Look for lots of silent film stars.
1947 96m/C Betty Hutton, John Lund, Constance Collier, William Demarest, Billy DeWolfe; **D:** George Marshall. **VHS, Beta, 3/4U, Special order formats** $19.95 NEG, NOS, PSM 🐾🐾

Perils of the Darkest Jungle Tiger Woman battles money-mad oil profiteers to protect her tribe. This twelve episode serial comes on two tapes. **AKA:** The Tiger Woman; Jungle Gold.
1944 180m/B Linda Stirling, Allan "Rocky" Lane, Duncan Renaldo, George Lewis; **D:** Spencer Gordon Bennet. **VHS, LV** $29.95 REP, MLB 🐾🐾½

Period of Adjustment Heartwarming comedy about young newlyweds adjusting to the pressures of domestic life and trying to help the troubled marriage of an older couple. Based on the play by Tennessee Williams.
1962 112m/B Anthony (Tony) Franciosa, Jane Fonda, Jim Hutton, Lois Nettleton, John McGiver, Jack Albertson; **D:** George Roy Hill; **W:** Isobel Lennart. **VHS** $19.98 MGM 🐾🐾🐾

Periphery Shot in Berlin, this fictional narrative tells the story of a group of refugees from World War II who build their own society in which they communicate telepathically. They are hunted down by the press and the police. The film raises questions about the inability of society to deal with alternative lifestyles.
1986 29m/C VHS, 3/4U NO 🐾🐾½

Permanent Record A hyper-sincere drama about a popular high schooler's suicide and the emotional reactions of those he has left behind. Reeves gives a great performance. Cinematography by Frederick Elmes.
1988 (PG-13) 92m/C Alan Boyce, Keanu Reeves, Michelle Meyrink, Jennifer Rubin, Pamela Gidley, Kathy Baker; **D:** Marisa Silver. **VHS, Beta, LV** $89.95 PAR 🐾🐾½

Permanent Vacation A young man disenchanted with New York City decides to escape to Europe to forget about his problems.
1984 80m/C John Lurie, Chris Parker. **VHS, Beta** NO 🐾🐾½

Permission To Kill Grim spy drama features Bogard as an agent determined to prevent the return of a third-world radical to a totalitarian state.
1975 (PG) 96m/C GB Dirk Bogarde, Ava Gardner, Timothy Dalton, Frederic Forrest; **D:** Cyril Frankel. **VHS, Beta** $39.98 SUE 🐾🐾½

Perry Mason Returns Perry Mason returns to solve another baffling mystery. This time he must help his longtime assistant, Della Street, when she is accused of killing her new employer.
1985 95m/C Raymond Burr, Barbara Hale, William Katt, Patrick O'Neal, Richard Anderson, Cassie Yates, Al Freeman Jr.; **D:** Ron Satlof. **VHS, Beta** $29.98 MCG 🐾🐾🐾

Perry Mason: The Case of the Lost Love Super-lawyer Mason defends the husband of a former lover he hadn't seen in 30 years. The solution to the mystery may catch viewer off guard.
1987 98m/C Raymond Burr, Barbara Hale, William Katt, Jean Simmons, Gene Barry, Robert Walden, Stephen Elliott, Robert Mandan, David Ogden Stiers; **D:** Ron Satlof. **VHS** $19.95 STE 🐾🐾½

Persona A famous actress turns mute and is treated by a talkative nurse at a secluded cottage. As their relationship turns increasingly tense, the women's personalities begin to merge. Memorable, unnerving—and atypically avant garde—fare from cinema giant Bergman. First of several collaborations between the director and leading lady Ullman. In Swedish with English subtitles.
1966 100m/C SW Bibi Andersson, Liv Ullmann, Gunnar Bjornstrand; **D:** Ingmar Bergman. **VHS, Beta, 8mm** $19.98 MGM, VYY, VDM 🐾🐾🐾🐾

Personal Best Lesbian lovers compete while training for the 1990 Olympics. Provocative fare often goes where few films have gone before, but overly stylized direction occasionally overwhelms characterizations. It gleefully exploits locker-room nudity, with Hemingway in her pre-implant days. Still, an ambitious, often accomplished production. Towne's directorial debut. Music by Jack Nitzsche.
1982 (R) 126m/C Mariel Hemingway, Scott Glenn, Patrice Donnelly; **D:** Robert Towne. **VHS, Beta** $69.95 WAR 🐾🐾🐾

Personal Exemptions In this stock comedy a frenzied IRS auditor learns that her daughter is smuggling aliens into the country, her son is brokering with some businessmen she's targeted for tax fraud, and her husband is having an affair with a high-school girl.
1988 (PG) 100m/C Nanette Fabray, John Cotton; **D:** Peter Rowe. **VHS, Beta** $14.95 HMD 🐾½

Personal Property Taylor tries every trick in the book to win Harlow over in this MGM romantic fluff. Not that big on laughs, but plenty of good shots of Harlow and a beefcake scene of Taylor in a bathtub, who was the darling of the MGM lot and worked with every leading lady. This was the only film Harlow and Taylor made together. Remake of the 1931 film "The Man in Possession." *AKA:* Personal Property.

1937 84m/B Robert Taylor, Jean Harlow, Reginald Owen, Una O'Connor, E.E. Clive, Henrietta Crosman, Cora Witherspoon; *D:* Woodbridge S. Van Dyke; *W:* Hugh Mills. VHS $19.98 *MGM* 🎞🎞½

Personal Services A bawdy satire loosely based on the life and times of Britain's modern-day madam, Cynthia Payne, and her rise to fame in the world of prostitution. Written by David Leland. Payne's earlier years were featured in the film "Wish You Were Here."

1987 (R) 104m/C *GB* Julie Walters, Alec McCowen, Shirley Stelfox; *D:* Terry Jones. VHS, Beta, LV $29.98 *LIV, VES* 🎞🎞½

The Personals A recently divorced young man takes out a personal ad in a newspaper to find the woman of his dreams. But it isn't quite that simple in this independent comedy shot entirely in Minneapolis.

1983 (PG) 90m/C Bill Schoppert, Karen Landry, Paul Eiding, Michael Laskin, Vickie Dakil; *D:* Peter Markle. VHS, Beta $29.98 *SUE* 🎞🎞½

Personals Chilling drama that casts O'Neill as an unnoticed librarian, until she begins to meet (and kill) the men who answer her ads. Zimbalist is a widow who is determined to learn the truth. Made for television.

1990 93m/C Stephanie Zimbalist, Jennifer O'Neill, Robin Thomas, Clark Johnson, Gina Gallego, Rosemary Dunsmore, Colm Feore; *D:* Steven Hilliard Stern. VHS, Beta, LV $79.95 *PAR, PIA* 🎞🎞

The Persuaders The first two episodes of Moore and Curtis as international playboy crime fighters.

1971 52m/C *GB* Roger Moore, Tony Curtis, Alex Scott, Joan Collins, Robert Hutton; *D:* Basil Dearden. VHS, Beta $39.95 *SVS* 🎞🎞

Pet Sematary A quirky adaptation of Stephen King's bestseller about a certain patch of woods in the Maine wilderness that rejuvenates the dead, and how a newly located college MD eventually uses it to restore his dead son. Mildly creepy.

1989 (R) 103m/C Dale Midkiff, Fred Gwynne, Denise Crosby, Stephen King; *D:* Mary Lambert. VHS, Beta, LV, 8mm $14.95 *PAR* 🎞🎞

Pet Sematary 2 Lame sequel to original Stephen King flick. After seeing his mother electrocuted, a teen and his veterinarian father move to the Maine town where the legendary Pet Sematary is located. Horror begins when the boy's friend's dog is shot by his stepfather, and the boys bury the dog in the "sematary." King wasn't involved with this film, so the story isn't very coherent, but shock value and special effects are great. Not recommended for those with a weak stomach.

1992 (R) 102m/C Anthony Edwards, Edward Furlong, Clancy Brown, Jared Rushton, Darlanne Fluegel, Lisa Waltz, Jason McGuire, Sarah Trigger; *D:* Mary Lambert; *W:* Richard Outten. VHS, Beta, LV *PAR* 🎞½

Pete Kelly's Blues A jazz musician in a Kansas City speakeasy is forced to stand up against a brutal racketeer. The melodramatic plot is brightened by a nonstop flow of jazz tunes sung by Lee and Fitzgerald and played by an all-star lineup that includes Dick Cathcart, Matty Matlock, Eddie Miller and George Van Eps. ♫Sugar; Somebody Loves Me; Bye Bye Blackbird; What Can I Say After I Say I'm Sorry?; He Needs Me; Sing a Rainbow; Pete Kelly's Blues.

1955 96m/C Jack Webb, Janet Leigh, Edmond O'Brien, Lee Marvin, Martin Milner, Peggy Lee, Ella Fitzgerald, Jayne Mansfield; *D:* Jack Webb. VHS, Beta, LV $19.98 *WAR, PIA* 🎞🎞

Pete 'n' Tillie Amiable comedy turns to less appealing melodrama as couple meets, marries, and endures tragedy. Film contributes little to director Ritt's hit-and-miss reputation, but Matthau and Burnett shine in leads. Adapted by Julius J. Epstein from a Peter de Vries' story.

1972 (PG) 100m/C Walter Matthau, Carol Burnett, Geraldine Page, Barry Nelson, Rene Auberjonois, Lee Montgomery, Henry Jones, Kent Smith; *D:* Martin Ritt; *W:* Julius J. Epstein; *M:* John Williams. Academy Awards '72 Nominations: Best Adapted Screenplay, Best Supporting Actress (Page); British Academy Awards '73: Best Actor (Matthau). VHS, Beta $79.95 *MCA* 🎞🎞½

Pete Townsend: White City The Who guitarist portrays a musician who helps bring a close friend and his estranged wife back together. This semi-autobiographical film includes music from Townsend.

1985 60m/C Pete Townsend, Andrew Wilde, Frances Barber; *D:* Richard Lowenstein. VHS, Beta, LV $19.95 *MVD, VES* 🎞🎞½

Peter and the Wolf and Other Tales A collection of live-action stories using dance, music and poetry in "Jabberwocky," "The Ugly Duckling" and the title story.

1984 82m/C VHS, Beta *NO* 🎞🎞½

Peter Gunn Detective Peter Gunn returns, only to find himself being hunted by both the mob and the Feds. A TV movie reprise of the vintage series that has none of the original cast members.

1989 97m/C Peter Strauss, Barbara Williams, Jennifer Edwards, Charles Cioffi, Pearl Bailey, Peter Jurasik, David Rappaport; *D:* Blake Edwards. VHS $19.95 *STE* 🎞🎞

Peter Lundy and the Medicine Hat Stallion A teenaged Pony Express rider must outrun the Indians and battle the elements in order to carry mail from the Nebraska Territory to the West Coast in this made-for-television film. Good family entertainment. *AKA:* The Medicine Hat Stallion; Pony Express.

1977 85m/C Leif Garrett, Mitchell Ryan, Bibi Besch, John Quade, Milo O'Shea; *D:* Michael O'Herlihy. VHS, Beta $69.98 *LIV, VES* 🎞🎞½

Peter Pan Disney classic about a boy who never wants to grow up. Based on J.M. Barrie's book and play. Still stands head and shoulders above any recent competition in providing fun family entertainment. Terrific animation and lovely hummable music.

1953 (G) 76m/C *D:* Hamilton Luske; *V:* Bobby Driscoll, Kathryn Beaumont, Hans Conried, Heather Angel, Candy Candido. VHS, Beta, LV $24.99 *DIS, APD, HMV* 🎞🎞🎞

Peter Pan A TV classic, this videotape of a performance of the 1954 Broadway musical adapted from the J.M. Barrie classic features Mary Martin in one of her most famous incarnations, as the adolescent Peter Pan. Songs include "I'm Flying," "Neverland," and "I Won't Grow Up."

1960 100m/C Mary Martin, Cyril Ritchard, Sondra Lee, Heather Halliday, Luke Halprin; *D:* Vincent J. Donehue. VHS, Beta, LV $24.99 *GKK, COL, MLT* 🎞🎞🎞½

Peter the First: Part 1 The first half of Petrov's Soviet epic about the early years of Tsar Peter I's reign. Lavish, in Russian with English subtitles.

1937 95m/B *RU D:* Vladimir Petrov. VHS, Beta $29.95 *FCT, TAM* 🎞🎞

Peter the First: Part 2 The second half of Petrov's epic, also titled "The Conquests of Peter the Great," covering the triumphs and final years of the famous Tsar. In Russian with English subtitles.

1938 104m/B *RU D:* Vladimir Petrov. VHS, Beta $29.95 *FCT, TAM* 🎞🎞

Peter the Great Dry but eye-pleasing TV mini-series follows the life of Russia's colorful, very tall ruler from childhood on. Much of the interesting cast is wasted in tiny roles.

1986 371m/C Maximilian Schell, Laurence Olivier, Omar Sharif, Vanessa Redgrave, Ursula Andress. VHS $29.95 *STE, AUD* 🎞🎞🎞

Peter's Friends Peter (Fry) has recently inherited a grand manor house located outside London and invites some chums to celebrate a New Year's Eve weekend, ten years after they've been at university together. They include Maggie, a mousy, lonely editor (Thompson) worried about her biological clock; Roger and Mary (Laurie and Staunton), who are trying to hold together after the death of their son; Sarah (Emmanuel) and her latest unsuitable lover (Slattery); and once-promising writer Andrew (Branagh), who has found success in Hollywood working on a sitcom starring his appalling, neurotic wife (Rudner). The ensemble cast and post-college reunion themes have lead to "Big Chill" comparisons although this film has a more lightweight charm and sly wit.

1992 (R) 102m/C *GB* Kenneth Branagh, Rita Rudner, Emma Thompson, Stephen Fry, Hugh Laurie, Imelda Staunton, Alphonsia Emmanuel, Tony Slattery, Alex Lowe, Alex Scott, Phyllida Law; *D:* Kenneth Branagh; *W:* Rita Rudner, Martin Bergman. VHS, LV $92.99 *HBO, DTV* 🎞🎞½

Pete's Dragon Elliot, an enormous, bumbling dragon with a penchant for clumsy heroics, becomes friends with poor orphan Pete. Combines brilliant animation with the talents of live actors for an interesting effect.

1977 (G) 128m/C Helen Reddy, Shelley Winters, Mickey Rooney, Jim Dale, Red Buttons, Sean Marshall, Jim Backus, Jeff Conaway; *D:* Don Chaffey; *V:* Charlie Callas. VHS, Beta, LV $24.99 *DIS, FCT, WTA* 🎞🎞½

Petit Con A live-action version of the popular French comic strip wherein a young rebel drops out of society to live with aging hippies. With English subtitles.

1984 (R) 90m/C *FR* Guy Marchand, Michel Choupon, Caroline Cellier, Bernard Brieux, Soudad Amidou; *D:* Gerard Lauzier. VHS, Beta $59.95 *LHV* 🎞🎞½

Petrified Forest Patrons and employees are held captive by a runaway gangster's band in a desert diner. Often gripping, with memorable performances from Davis, Howard, and Bogart. Based on the play by Robert Sherwood with Howard and Bogart recreating their stage roles.

1936 83m/B Bette Davis, Leslie Howard, Humphrey Bogart, Dick Foran, Charley Grapewin, Porter Hall; *D:* Archie Mayo. VHS, Beta $19.95 *FOX, MGM* 🎞🎞🎞

Petulia Overlooked, offbeat drama about a flighty woman who spites her husband by dallying with a sensitive, recently divorced surgeon. Classic '60s document and cult favorite offers great performance from the appealing Christie, with Scott fine as the vulnerable surgeon. On-screen performances by the Grateful Dead and Big Brother. Among idiosyncratic director Lester's best. Photographed by Nicholas Roeg. From the novel "Me and the Arch Kook Petulia" by John Haase.

1968 (R) 105m/C George C. Scott, Richard Chamberlain, Julie Christie, Shirley Knight, Arthur Hill, Joseph Cotten, Pippa Scott, Richard Dysart; *D:* Richard Lester; *M:* John Barry. **VHS, Beta $19.98** WAR ✗✗✗

Peyton Place Passion, scandal, and deception in a small New England town set the standard for passion, scandal, and deception in soap operadom. Shot on location in Camden, Maine. Performances and themes now seem dated, but box office blockbuster. Written by John Michael Hayes from Grace Metalious' popular novel and followed by "Return to Peyton Place."
1957 157m/C Lana Turner, Hope Lange, Lee Phillips, Lloyd Nolan, Diane Varsi, Lorne Greene, Russ Tamblyn, Arthur Kennedy, Terry Moore, Barry Coe, David Nelson, Betty Field, Mildred Dunnock, Leon Ames; *D:* Mark Robson. **VHS, LV $39.98** FOX, FCT ✗✗✗

Phantasm A small-budgeted, hallucinatory horror fantasy about two parentless brothers who discover weird goings-on at the local funeral parlor, including the infamous airborne, brain-chewing chrome ball. Creepy, unpredictable nightmare fashioned on a shoestring by young independent producer Coscarelli. Scenes were cut out of the original film to avoid "X" rating. Followed by "Phantasm II."
1979 (R) 90m/C Michael Baldwin, Bill Thornbury, Reggie Bannister, Kathy Lester, Terrie Kalbus, Ken Jones, Susan Harper, Lynn Eastman, David Arntzen, Angus Scrimm, Bill Cone; *D:* Don A. Coscarelli. **VHS, Beta, LV $14.95** COL, SUE ✗✗ ½

Phantasm II Teen psychic keeps flashing on villainous Tall Man. A rehash sequel to the original, cultishly idiosyncratic fantasy, wherein more victims are fed into the interdimensional abyss and Mike discovers that the horror is not all in his head. Occasional inspired gore; bloodier than its predecessor. More yuck for the buck.
1988 (R) 97m/C James Le Gros, Reggie Bannister, Angus Scrimm; *D:* Don A. Coscarelli. **VHS, Beta, LV $14.98** MCA ✗✗

The Phantom Rare cheapie of a hooded killer terrorizing a group of people in a haunted house.
1931 ?m/C Guinn Williams, Wilfrid Lucas. **VHS $12.95** SNC ✗✗

The Phantom Broadcast A popular radio crooner is murdered. The main suspect is his hunchbacked accompanist and manager, who had all along secretly pre-recorded his own velvet voice for the crooner to lip-sync along with. A tightly plotted minor thriller that holds up surprisingly well. *AKA:* Phantom of the Air.
1933 63m/B Ralph Forbes, Gail Patrick, Vivienne Osborne, Guinn Williams, George "Gabby" Hayes; *D:* Phil Rosen. **VHS, Beta, 8mm $29.95** NOS, VYY, FCT ✗✗ ½

Phantom Brother A semi-spoof about a teenager left orphaned by a car crash that wiped out his entire family, and who is subsequently haunted by his dead brother. Even thinner than it sounds.
1988 92m/C Jon Hammer, Patrick Molloy, John Gigante, Mary Beth Pelshaw; *D:* William Szarka. **VHS, Beta $69.95** NO ✗ ½

The Phantom Bullet Hoot wants to holler at his father's murderers.
1926 60m/B Hoot Gibson. **VHS, Beta $16.95** GPV ✗ ½

The Phantom Chariot A fantasy depicting the Swedish myth about how Death's coach must be driven by the last man to die each year. Silent.
1920 89m/B SW *D:* Victor Sjostrom. **VHS, Beta $16.95** SNC, FCT, GVV ✗✗ ½

The Phantom Creeps Evil Dr. Zorka, armed with a meteorite chunk which can bring an army to a standstill, not to mention build a robot and a giant spider, provides the impetus for this enjoyable serial in 12 episodes.
1939 75m/B Bela Lugosi, Dorothy Arnold, Robert Kent, Regis Toomey. **VHS, Beta, 3/4U, Special order formats $19.95** NOS, SNC, VCN ✗✗ ½

The Phantom Empire Autry faces the futuristic "Thunder Riders" from the subterranean city of Murania, located 20,000 feet beneath his ranch. A complete serial in twelve episodes. If you only see one science fiction western in your life, this is the one.
1935 245m/B Gene Autry, Frankie Darro, Betsy King Ross, Smiley Burnette. **VHS, Beta $24.95** NOS, SNC, VYY ✗✗

Phantom Empire A woman who rules over a lost city takes a bunch of scientists prisoner and forces them to be slaves.
1987 (R) 85m/C Ross Hagen, Jeffrey Combs, Dawn Wildsmith, Robert Quarry, Susan Stokey, Michelle Bauer, Russ Tamblyn, Sybil Danning; *D:* Fred Olen Ray. **VHS, Beta $79.95** PSM ✗✗

Phantom Express Experienced old engineer is dismissed from his job because no one believes his explanation that a mysterious train caused the wreck of his own train. He aims to find justice.
1932 65m/B J. Farrell MacDonald, Sally Blane, William Collier Jr., Hobart Bosworth; *D:* Emory Johnson. **VHS, Beta $12.95** SNC, NOS, IUF ✗✗

Phantom Fiend A gentle musician becomes a suspect when a series of Jack-the-Ripper type murders terrorize London. Is he the nice guy known by his girlfriend and the people in his lodging house, or is the musician really JTR? Based on the novel "The Lodger" by Marie Belloc-Lowndes.
1935 70m/B GB Ivor Novello, Elizabeth Allan, A.W. Baskcomb, Jack Hawkins, Barbara Everest, Peter Gawthorne, P. Kynaston Reeves; *D:* Maurice Elvey. **VHS $29.95** FCT ✗ ½

The Phantom Flyer Stunt pilot helps out a cattle-owning frontier family bedeviled by rustlers. Silent.
1928 54m/B Al Wilson. **VHS, Beta, 8mm $24.95** VYY, GPV, RXM ✗ ½

Phantom from Space An invisible alien lands on Earth, begins killing people, and is pursued by a pair of scientists.
1953 72m/B Ted Cooper, Rudolph Anders, Noreen Nash, James Seay, Harry Landers; *D:* W. Lee Wilder. **VHS, Beta $16.95** NOS, SNC ✗ ½

The Phantom from 10,000 Leagues Slimy sea monster attacks swimmers and fishermen; investigating oceanographer pretends not to notice monster is hand puppet. Early AIP release, when still named American Releasing Company.
1956 80m/B Kent Taylor, Cathy Downs, Michael Whalen, Helene Stanton, Phillip Pine; *D:* Dan Milner. **VHS $19.98** NOS, SNC, MLB ✗

The Phantom in the House A woman commits a murder and has her inventor husband take the rap. While he's in prison, she gets rich off of his work. Things get hairy when he is released fifteen years later and is introduced to his daughter as a friend of the family. Melodramatic film was originally made with and without sound.
1929 64m/B Ricardo Cortez, Nancy Welford, Henry B. Walthall, Grace Valentine; *D:* Phil Rosen. **VHS, Beta $16.95** SNC ✗✗

Phantom Killer A district attorney tries to hang a murder rap on a most improbable suspect. When the man is acquitted, the DA quits his job to find the truth, which takes a

disturbing twist. The plot is a thinly veiled rehash of "The Sphinx" (1933).
1942 61m/B Dick Purcell, Joan Woodbury, John Hamilton, Warren Hymer, Kenneth Harlan, J. Farrell MacDonald, Mantan Moreland; *D:* William Beaudine. **VHS $19.95** NOS ✗✗

The Phantom Light A lighthouse keeper is murdered under strange circumstances and a mysterious light keeps appearing at the scene. Detective Hale joins up with a navy man and another lighthouse keeper to solve the crime. A low-budget mystery with good atmosphere and some humor.
1935 75m/B GB Binnie Hale, Gordon Harker, Ian Hunter, Donald Calthrop; *D:* Michael Powell. **VHS** HCV ✗✗ ½

Phantom of Chinatown Mr. Wong is called in to solve another murder in the final entry in the series. The first to have an Asian actor portray the lead, as Luke replaced Boris Karloff.
1940 61m/B Keye Luke, Lotus Long, Grant Withers, Paul McVey, Charles Miller; *D:* Phil Rosen. **VHS $16.95** NOS, SNC, HEG ✗

Phantom of Death A brilliant pianist, stricken by a fatal disease that causes rapid aging, goes on a murderous rampage.
1987 (R) 95m/C IT Michael York, Donald Pleasence, Edwige Fenech; *D:* Ruggero Deodato. **VHS, Beta $79.95** VMK ✗ ½

The Phantom of 42nd Street An actor and a cop team up to find the killer of a wealthy uncle.
1945 58m/B Dave O'Brien, Kay Aldridge, Alan Mowbray, Frank Jenks; *D:* Martin Mooney. **VHS $16.95** SNC, NOS, MRV ✗✗

Phantom of Liberty Master surrealist Bunuel's episodic film wanders from character to character and from event to event. Animals wander through a man's bedroom, soldiers conduct military exercises in an inhabited area, a missing girl stands before her parents even as they futilely attempt to determine her whereabouts, and an assassin is found guilty, then applauded and led to freedom. They don't get much more surreal than this. If you think you may like it, you'll probably love it. Bunuel, by the way, is among the firing squad vicitms in the film's opening enactment of Goya's May 3, 1808. In French with English subtitles. *AKA:* Le Fantome de la Liberte; The Specter of Freedom.
1968 104m/C FR Adrianna Asti, Jean-Claude Brialy, Michel Piccoli, Adolfo Celi, Monica Vitti; *D:* Luis Bunuel. **VHS, Beta, LV $24.95** XVC, TAM, APD ✗✗ ½

The Phantom of Soho A Scotland Yard detective investigates the murders of several prominent businessmen and is assisted by a beautiful mystery writer. *AKA:* Das Phantom von Soho.
1964 92m/B GE Dieter Borsche, Barbara Rutting, Hans Sohnker, Peter Vogel, Helga Sommerfeld, Werner Peters; *D:* Franz Gottlieb. **VHS, Beta $16.95** SNC ✗✗

Phantom of the Air Twelve chapters of high-flying adventure with Tom Tyler!
1933 230m/B Tom Tyler, Gloria Shea, William Desmond, Leroy Mason, Walter Brennan; *D:* Ray Taylor. **VHS $29.95** GPV, UHV, MLB ✗✗

Phantom of the Mall: Eric's Revenge A murderous spirit haunts the local mall. Gore flows like water.
1989 91m/C Morgan Fairchild, Kari Whitman, Jonathan Goldsmith, Derek Rydell; *D:* Richard S. Friedman. **VHS, Beta, LV $19.95** FRH ✗

Phantom of the Opera Deranged, disfigured music lover haunts the sewers of a Parisian opera house and kills to further the career of an unsuspecting young soprano.

P

First of many film versions still packs a wollop, with fine playing from Chaney, Sr. Silent with two-color Technicolor "Bal Masque" sequence.
1925 79m/B Lon Chaney Sr., Norman Kerry, Mary Philbin, Gibson Gowland; D: Rupert Julian. VHS, Beta, LV, 8mm, 3/4U, Special order formats $9.95 NEG, NOS, CCB ♪♪♪

Phantom of the Opera Second Hollywood version—the first with legacy—of Gastron Leroux novel about a madman who promotes fear and mayhem at a Paris opera house. Raines is good in lead; Eddy warbles away.
1943 92m/C Claude Rains, Nelson Eddy, Susanna Foster, Edgar Barrier, Leo Carrillo, Hume Cronyn, J. Edward Bromberg; D: Arthur Lubin. Academy Awards '43: Best Color Cinematography, Best Interior Decoration; Nominations: Best Sound. VHS, Beta, LV $14.95 MCA ♪♪♪

The Phantom of the Opera A gory, "Elm Street"-ish version of the Gaston Leroux classic, attempting to cash in on the success of the Broadway musical.
1989 (R) 93m/C Robert Englund, Jill Schoelen, Alex Hyde-White, Bill Nighy, Terence Harvey, Stephanie Lawrence; D: Dwight Little. VHS, Beta, LV $14.95 COL ♪½

Phantom of the Paradise A rock 'n roll parody of "Phantom of the Opera." Splashy, only occasionally horrific spoof in which cruel music executive Williams, much to his everlasting regret, swindles a songwriter. Violence ensues. Not for most, or even many, tastes. Graham steals the film as rocker Beef. A failure at the box office, and now a cult item (small enthusiastic cult with few outside interests) for its oddball humor and outrageous rock star parodies. Williams also wrote the turgid score. ♪Goodbye, Eddie, Goodbye; Faust; Upholstery; Special to Me; Old Souls; Somebody Super Like You; Life At Last; The Hell of It; The Phantom's Theme (Beauty and the Beast).
1974 (PG) 92m/C Paul Williams, William Finley, Jessica Harper, Gerrit Graham; D: Brian DePalma. VHS, Beta, LV $19.98 FOX ♪♪

Phantom of the Ritz Bizarre accidents begin to take place when Ed Blake and his girlfriend start renovating the old Ritz Theater. It seems the theater is inhabited by a rather angry ghost and somebody's got to deal with it before the Ritz can rock and roll. Featuring the fabulous sounds of the Fifties.
1988 (R) 89m/C Peter Bergman, Deborah Van Valkenburgh, The Coasters; D: Allen Plone. VHS, Beta $79.95 PSM ♪♪

Phantom of the West Ten-episode serial about a rancher who becomes "The Phantom of the West" in order to smoke out his father's killer.
1931 166m/B William Desmond, Thomas Santschi, Tom Tyler; D: Ross Lederman. VHS, Beta $49.95 NOS, VYY, VCN ♪♪

Phantom Patrol A mystery writer is kidnapped and someone impersonates him. Mountie Maynard must come to the rescue.
1936 60m/B Kermit Maynard, Joan Barclay, Paul Fix, Julian Rivero, Eddie Phillips, Roger Williams; D: Charles Hutchinson. VHS, Beta $24.95 DVT, NOS ♪½

The Phantom Planet An astronaut crash-lands on an asteroid and discovers a race of tiny people living there. Having breathed the atmosphere, he shrinks to their dimunitive size and aids them in their war against brutal invaders. Infamously peculiar.
1961 82m/B Dean Fredericks, Coleen Gray, Tony Dexter, Dolores Faith, Francis X. Bushman, Richard Kiel; D: William Marshall. VHS, Beta $16.95 NOS, SNC ♪½

Phantom Rancher Roaring melodrama finds Maynard donning a mask to find the real Phantom, who is causing havoc.
1939 61m/B Ken Maynard. VHS, Beta UHV, VCN ♪½

Phantom Ranger A federal agent masquerades as a crook to catch a band of counterfeiters.
1938 54m/B Tim McCoy, Suzanne Kaaren, Karl Hackett, John St. Polis, John Merton, Harry Strang; D: Sam Newfield. VHS $19.95 NOS, DVT ♪½

The Phantom Rider Mystery fills the old West in this serial composed of fifteen chapters.
1937 152m/B Buck Jones, Maria Shelton. VHS, Beta $29.98 REP, MLB, VCN ♪½

The Phantom Ship The true story of the "Marie Celeste," a ship found in 1872 off the coast of England with her sails set but minus any of her crew. Also known as "The Mystery of the Marie Celeste."
1937 61m/B Bela Lugosi, Shirley Grey, Arthur Margetson. VHS, Beta $19.95 NOS, SNC, MRV ♪♪

Phantom Thunderbolt A man who has falsely spread the rumor that he's a gunfighter is hired to chase away some good-for-nothings.
1933 62m/B Ken Maynard, Frances Lee, Frank Rice, William Gould, Bob Kortman; D: Alan James. VHS, Beta $19.95 NOS, DVT, MTX ♪½

Phantom Tollbooth A young boy drives his car into an animated world, where the numbers are at war with the letters and he has been chosen to save Rhyme and Reason, to bring stability back to the Land of Wisdom. Completely unique and typically Jonesian in its intellectual level and interests. Bright children will be interested, but this is really for adults who will understand the allegory. Based on Norman Justers' metaphorical novel.
1969 (G) 89m/C D: Chuck Jones; V: Mel Blanc, Hans Conried. VHS, Beta $19.95 MGM, WTA ♪♪♪

The Phantom Treehouse This is an animated children's tale of two kids plunging into a fantasy world through a mysterious swamp-based treehouse.
1984 76m/C VHS, Beta $14.98 VID, WTA ♪½

Phar Lap Saga of a legendary Australian racehorse who rose from obscurity to win nearly 40 races in just three years before mysteriously dying in 1932. American version runs 10 minutes shorter than the Aussie one. AKA: Phar Lap: Heart of a Nation.
1984 (PG) 107m/C AU Ron Leibman, Tom Burlinson, Judy Morris, Celia de Burgh; D: Simon Wincer. VHS, Beta $14.98 FOX ♪♪½

Pharaoh An expensive Polish epic about the power plays of royalty in ancient Egypt. Dubbed.
1966 125m/B PL Jerzy Zelnick; D: Jerzy Kawalerowicz. VHS, Beta FCT ♪♪

Pharmacist A day in the life of a hapless druggist undone by disgruntled customers and robbers. Typical Fields effort.
1932 19m/B Elise Cavanna, Babe Kane, W.C. Fields, Grady Sutton. VHS, Beta $24.98 CCB ♪♪½

Phase 4 A tale of killer ants retaliating against the humans attempting to exterminate them.
1974 (PG) 84m/C Nigel Davenport, Michael Murphy, Lynne Frederick; D: Saul Bass. VHS, Beta, LV $39.95 PAR ♪♪

Phedre Jean Racine's adaptation of the Greek legend involving Phedre, Theseus, and Hippolyte. Bell is the only one worth watching in this weak and stagy picture. In French with English subtitles.
1968 93m/C Marie Bell; D: Pierre Jourdan. VHS, Beta $29.95 VYY, APD, TAM ♪½

Phenomenal and the Treasure of Tutankamen Fiendish criminal genius steals priceless golden mask of King Tut. Superhero Phenomenal is less than dry spaghetti sci-fi.
197? (R) 90m/C IT Mauro Parenti, Lucretia Love. VHS $29.99 UHV ♪♪

Phffft! Holliday and Lemmmon are a bored couple who decide to divorce, date others, and take mambo lessons. By no stretch of plausibility, they constantly run into each other and compete in the same mambo contest.
1954 91m/B Judy Holliday, Jack Lemmon, Jack Carson, Kim Novak, Luella Gear, Merry Anders; D: Mark Robson. VHS GKK ♪♪½

The Philadelphia Experiment A WWII sailor falls through a hole in time and lands in the mid-1980s, whereupon he woos a gorgeous woman. Sufficient chemistry between Pare and Allen, but PG rating is an indication of the film's less-than-graphic love scenes.
1984 (PG) 101m/C Michael Pare, Nancy Allen, Eric Christmas, Bobby DiCicco; D: Stewart Raffill. VHS, Beta, LV $19.99 HBO, STE ♪½

The Philadelphia Story A woman's plans to marry again go awry when her dashing ex-husband arrives on the scene. Matters are further complicated when a loopy reporter—assigned to spy on the nuptials—falls in love with the blushing bride. Classic comedy, with trio of Hepburn, Grant, and Stewart all serving aces. Based on the hit Broadway play by Philip Barry, and remade as the musical "High Society" in 1956 (stick to the original). Also available colorized.
1940 112m/B Katharine Hepburn, Cary Grant, James Stewart, Ruth Hussey, Roland Young; D: George Cukor; W: Donald Ogden Stewart. Academy Awards '40: Best Actor (Stewart), Best Screenplay; Nominations: Best Actress (Hepburn), Best Director (Cukor), Best Picture, Best Supporting Actress (Hussey). VHS, Beta, LV $19.98 MGM, BTV, HMV ♪♪♪

Philby, Burgess and MacLean: Spy Scandal of the Century The true story of the three infamous British officials who defected to the Soviet Union in 1951, after stealing some vital British secrets for the KGB.
1984 83m/C GB Derek Jacobi, Anthony Bate, Michael Culver; D: Gordon Flemyng. VHS, Beta $59.95 MTI ♪♪½

Phobia Patients at a hospital are mysteriously being murdered. Stupid and unpleasant story that lasts too long and probably should never have started.
1980 (R) 91m/C CA Paul Michael Glaser, Susan Hogan; D: John Huston. VHS, Beta $69.95 PAR Woof!

Phoenix Aging queen summons her marksman to find the Phoenix, a mythical bird that she believes will bring her eternal life. With English subtitles.
1978 137m/C JP Tatsuya Nakadai, Tomisaburo Wakayama, Raoru Yumi, Reiko Ohara. VHS, Beta $29.95 VDA ♪½

Phoenix Team Two agents discover their mutual attraction can be deadly in the spy business.
1980 90m/C Don Francks, Elizabeth Shepherd. VHS, Beta $49.95 TWE ♪

P

Phoenix the Ninja A young girl grows up to be a ninja warrior and battles everyone who would deign to impede her.
198? 92m/C Sho Kosugi. **VHS, Beta** $59.95 TWE 🐾

Phoenix the Warrior Sometime in the future, female savages battle each other for control of the now ravaged earth. A newcomer seeks the tribe most worthy of receiving the last man on the planet, thereby continuing the human race.
1988 90m/C Persis Khambatta, James H. Emery, Peggy Sands, Kathleen Kinmont; **D:** Robert Hayes. **VHS** $79.95 SVS 🐾

The Phone Call 900-number morality tale about high-powered executive who calls phone sex line and is connected with escaped homicidal maniac who takes a toll on him and his family.
1989 (R) 95m/C Michael Sarrazin, Linda Smith, Ron Lea, Lisa Jakub; **D:** Allan Goldstein. **VHS** $79.95 MNC 🐾🐾

Phone Call from a Stranger After a plane crash, a survivor visits the families of three of the victims whom he met during the flight. Written by Nunnally Johnson.
1952 96m/B Bette Davis, Gary Merrill, Michael Rennie, Shelley Winters, Hugh Beaumont, Keenan Wynn, Eve Arden, Craig Stevens; **D:** Jean Negulesco. **VHS, Beta** $19.98 FOX 🐾🐾½

Photographer A photographer turns into a murderer, showing the negative side of his personality.
1975 (PG) 94m/C Michael Callan; **D:** William B. Hillman. **VHS, Beta** $59.98 NLC 🐾

Physical Evidence A lawyer finds herself falling for an ex-cop turned murder suspect while she tries to defend him for a crime he doesn't remember committing.
1989 (R) 99m/C Burt Reynolds, Theresa Russell, Ned Beatty, Kay Lenz, Ted McGinley; **D:** Michael Crichton. **VHS, Beta, LV** $89.98 LIV, VES, HHE 🐾🐾

P.I. Private Investigations Corrupt, drug-dealing cops stalk another cop who can finger them.
1987 (R) 91m/C Martin Balsam. **VHS, Beta** FOX 🐾

Piaf Musical drama chronicles the life of Edith Piaf, France's legendary singer of the Roaring '20s. Her rise from the streets, bout with temporary blindness, and many self-destructive attempts at experiencing life are retold in music.
1981 (PG) 114m/C Jane Lapotaire. **VHS, Beta** FOX 🐾

A Piano for Mrs. Cimino Declared senile and incompetent, a widowed woman fights for control of her own life. Good script helps this made for TV soaper.
1982 100m/C Bette Davis, Keenan Wynn, Alexa Kenin, Penny Fuller, Christopher Guest, George Hearn; **D:** George Schaefer. **VHS, Beta** $59.95 GEM 🐾🐾🐾

Picasso Trigger An American spy tries to catch an elusive murderer. The sequel to "Hard Ticket to Hawaii" and "Malibu Express."
1989 (R) 99m/C Steve Bond, Dona Speir, John Aprea, Hope Marie Carlton, Guich Koock; **D:** Andy Sidaris. **VHS** $19.98 WAR 🐾🐾

Pick a Star Lawrence is a small-town girl who wins a contest and is off to Hollywood. Only no one pays any attention to her except for publicity man Haley, who arranges her screen test. Naturally, she knocks the studio bosses for a loop and becomes a star. Laurel & Hardy are featured in a couple of comedy segments showing the newcomer some backstage silliness and movie business on the set of a Western they're filming (with Finlayson, better known as a director, cast as the duo's director). **AKA:** Movie Struck.
1937 70m/B Rosina Lawrence, Jack Haley, Patsy Kelly, Mischa Auer, Stan Laurel, Oliver Hardy, Charles Halton, Tom Dugan, Russell Hicks, James Finlayson; **D:** Edward Sedgwick. **VHS** $19.98 MGM 🐾🐾

The Pick-Up Artist The adventures of a compulsive Don Juan who finds he genuinely loves the daughter of an alcoholic who's in debt to the mob. Standard story with no surprises.
1987 (PG-13) 81m/C Robert Downey Jr., Molly Ringwald, Dennis Hopper, Harvey Keitel, Danny Aiello, Vanessa Williams, Robert Towne, Mildred Dunnock, Lorraine Bracco, Joe Spinell; **D:** James Toback. **VHS, Beta, LV** $19.98 FOX 🐾🐾

Pick-Up Summer Two suburban boys cruise their town after school lets out, chasing a pair of voluptuous sisters. **AKA:** Pinball Summer; Pinball Pick-Up.
1979 (R) 99m/C CA Michael Zelniker, Carl Marotte; **D:** George Mihalka. **VHS, Beta** $59.95 NWV 🐾

Pickpocket Slow moving, documentary-like account of a petty thief's existence is a moral tragedy inspired by "Crime and Punishment." Ending is particularly moving. Classic filmmaking from Bresson, France's master of austerity. In French with English subtitles.
1959 75m/B FR Martin LaSalle, Marika Green, Pierre Leymarie; **D:** Robert Bresson. **VHS, Beta** $59.95 FCT, INT, TAM 🐾🐾🐾½

Pickup on South Street Petty thief Widmark lifts woman's wallet only to find it contains top secret Communist micro-film for which pinko agents will stop at nothing to get back. Intriguing look at the politics of the day. The creme of "B" movies.
1953 80m/B Richard Widmark, Jean Peters, Thelma Ritter, Murvyn Vye, Richard Kiley, Milburn Stone; **W/D:** Samuel Fuller. **VHS, Beta** $19.98 FOX, FCT 🐾🐾🐾

The Pickwick Papers Comedy based on the Dickens classic wherein Mrs. Bardell sues the Pickwick Club for breach of promise.
1954 109m/B GB James Hayter, James Donald, Nigel Patrick, Hermione Gingold, Hermione Baddeley, Kathleen Harrison; **D:** Noel Langley. **VHS, Beta** $19.98 UHV 🐾🐾½

Picnic A wanderer arrives in a small town and immediately wins the love a his friend's girl. The other women in town seem interested too. Strong, romantic work, with Holden excelling in the lead. Novak provides a couple pointers too. Lavish Hollywood adaptation of the William Inge play, with music score by George Duning, including the popular "Moonglow/Theme from Picnic."
1955 113m/C William Holden, Kim Novak, Rosalind Russell, Susan Strasberg, Arthur O'Connell, Cliff Robertson, Betty Field, Verna Felton, Reta Shaw, Nick Adams, Phyllis Newman, Raymond Bailey; **D:** Joshua Logan. Academy Awards '55: Best Art Direction/Set Decoration (Color), Best Film Editing; Nominations: Best Picture, Best Supporting Actor (O'Connell); Golden Globe Awards '56: Best Director (Logan); National Board of Review Awards '55: 10 Best Films of the Year. **VHS, Beta, LV** $19.95 COL, PIA 🐾🐾🐾½

Picnic at Hanging Rock School outing in 1900 into a mountainous region ends tragically when three girls disappear. Eerie film is strong on atmosphere, as befits mood master Weir. Lambert is extremely photogenic—and suitable subdued—as one of the girls to disappear. Otherwise beautifully photographed on location. From the novel by Joan Lindsey.
1975 (PG) 110m/C AU Margaret Nelson, Rachel Roberts, Dominic Guard, Helen Morse, Jacki Weaver; **D:** Peter Weir. **VHS, Beta** VES, OM 🐾🐾🐾

Picnic on the Grass A strange, whimsical fantasy heavily evocative of the director's Impressionist roots; a science-minded candidate for the president of Europe throws a picnic as public example of his earthiness, and falls in love with a peasant girl. In French with English subtitles. **AKA:** Le Dejeuner Sur l'Herbe; Lunch on the Grass.
1959 92m/C FR Paul Meurisse, Catherine Rouvel, Fernand Sardou, Jacqueline Morane, Jean-Pierre Granval; **D:** Jean Renoir. **VHS, Beta** $49.95 FCT, INT, TAM 🐾🐾

Picture Mommy Dead Well acted melodrama involving a scheming shrew who struggles to drive her mentally disturbed stepdaughter insane for the sake of cold, hard cash.
1966 85m/C Don Ameche, Zsa Zsa Gabor, Martha Hyer, Susan Gordon; **D:** Bert I. Gordon. **VHS, Beta** $9.98 NLC 🐾

Picture of Dorian Gray Hatfield plays the rake who stays young while his portrait ages in this adaptation of Oscar Wilde's classic novel. Lansbury steals this one.
1945 110m/B Hurd Hatfield, George Sanders, Donna Reed, Angela Lansbury, Peter Lawford, Lowell Gilmore; **D:** Albert Lewin. Academy Awards '45: Best Black and White Cinematography; Nominations: Best Interior Decoration, Best Supporting Actress (Lansbury); Golden Globe Awards '46: Best Supporting Actress (Lansbury). **VHS, Beta, LV** $19.98 MGM, FHE, TVC 🐾🐾🐾

Picture of Dorian Gray Another version of Wilde's renowned novel about a man who retains his youthful visage while his portrait shows the physical ravages of aging. Davenport is particularly appealing in the lead. Made for television.
1974 130m/C Shane Briant, Nigel Davenport, Charles Aidman, Fionnula Flanagan, Linda Kelsey, Vanessa Howard; **D:** Glenn Jordan. **VHS, Beta** $29.95 LIV 🐾🐾

A Piece of Pleasure Marriage declines due to a domineering husband in this familiar domestic study from French master Chabrol. Good, but not among the director's best efforts. In French with English subtitles.
1970 100m/C **D:** Claude Chabrol. **VHS, Beta** FCT 🐾🐾🐾

Piece of the Action An ex-cop beats two con men at their own game when he convinces them to work for a Chicago community center. Music by Curtis Mayfield.
1977 (PG) 135m/C Sidney Poitier, Bill Cosby, James Earl Jones, Denise Nicholas, Hope Clarke, Tracy Reed, Tito Vandis, Ja'net DuBois; **D:** Sidney Poitier. **VHS, Beta** $19.98 WAR 🐾🐾½

Pieces Chain-saw wielding madman roams a college campus in search of human parts for a ghastly jigsaw puzzle. Gory and loathsome.
1983 (R) 90m/C IT SP Christopher George, Lynda Day George, Paul Smith; **D:** J.P. Simon. **VHS, Beta** $79.98 VES Woof!

Pied Piper of Hamelin The evergreen classic of the magical piper who rids a village of rats and then disappears with the village children into a mountain when the townspeople fail to keep a promise.
1957 90m/C Van Johnson, Claude Rains, Jim Backus, Kay Starr, Lori Nelson; **D:** Bretaigne Windust. **VHS, Beta** $14.95 KAR, NOS, MED 🐾🐾

The Pied Piper of Hamelin From Shelley Duvall's "Faerie Tale Theatre" comes the story of how a man with a magic flute charmed the rats out of Hamelin.

1984 60m/C Eric Idle; **D:** Nicholas Meyer. **VHS, Beta** $14.98 FOX, FCT ♫♫

Pier 23 A private eye is hired to bring a lawless ex-convict to a priest's custody, but gets an imposter instead. A web of intrigue follows.
1951 57m/B Hugh Beaumont, Ann Savage, David Bruce, Raymond Greenleaf. **VHS, Beta, LV** NO ♫♫

Pierrot le Fou A woman fleeing a gangster joins a man leaving his wife in this stunning, occasionally confusing classic from iconoclast Godard. A hallmark in 1960s improvisational filmmaking, with rugged Belmondo and always-photogenic Karina effortlessly excelling in leads. In French with English subtitles.
1965 110m/C FR IT Samuel Fuller, Jean-Pierre Leaud, Jean-Paul Belmondo, Anna Karina, Dirk Sanders; **D:** Jean-Luc Godard. **VHS, LV** $59.95 INT, FCT, IME ♫♫♫½

Pigeon Feathers A young man realizes a greater understanding of life in this adaptation of a John Updike tale.
1988 45m/C Christopher Collet, Caroline McWilliams; **W:** John Updike. **VHS** $24.95 MON, KAR ♫♫½

Pigs Young woman who has escaped from a mental hospital teams up with an evil old man to go on a murdering spree. They complement each other beautifully. She kills them and he disposes of the bodies by making pig slop out of them. **AKA:** Daddy's Deadly Darling; The Killers.
1973 90m/C Toni Lawrence, Marc Lawrence, Jesse Vint, Katharine Ross; **W/D:** Marc Lawrence. **VHS, Beta** $9.95 PGN, MRV ♫½

Pilgrim, Farewell Dramatic story about a dying woman who needs to tie up loose ends before her death and goes looking for her estranged teenage daughter. Made for television for PBS' "American Playhouse."
1982 110m/C Elizabeth Huddle, Christopher Lloyd, Laurie Pranage, Lesley Paxton, Shelley Wyant, Robert Brown; **D:** Michael Roemer. **VHS, Beta** FLI ♫♫

Pillow Talk Sex comedy in which a man woos a woman who loathes him. By the way, they share the same telephone party line. Narrative provides minimal indication of the film's strengths, which are many. Classic '50's comedy with masters Day and Hudson exhibiting considerable rapport, even when fighting. Lighthearted, constantly funny.
1959 102m/C Rock Hudson, Doris Day, Tony Randall, Thelma Ritter, Nick Adams, Lee Patrick; **D:** Michael Gordon. Academy Awards '59: Best Story & Screenplay; Nominations: Best Actress (Day), Best Art Direction/Set Decoration (Color), Best Supporting Actress (Ritter). **VHS, Beta, LV** $14.95 MCA, CCB ♫♫♫½

The Pilot This film examines the value of honesty with one's friends.
1982 (PG) 98m/C Cliff Robertson, Diane Baker, Frank Converse, Dana Andrews, Amber O'Shea, Edward Binns, Gordon MacRae; **D:** Cliff Robertson. **VHS, Beta** $42.95 PGN, HHE ♫♫

Pilot Young girl discovers the debilitating effects of dishonesty when she becomes a break-dancing champion.
1984 27m/C Kelly Jo Minter, Adolph "Oz" Alvarez, Katie Rich. **VHS, Beta** PAU ♫½

Pimpernel Smith Seemingly scatter-brained archaeology professor is actually a dashing agent rescuing refugees from evil Nazis in WWII France. Howard is well cast, but the film is somewhat predictable, and it's too long. Wonderful scene, though, in which a Nazi officer champions Shakespeare as Aryan. **AKA:** Mister V.

1942 121m/B GB Leslie Howard, Mary Morris, Francis L. Sullivan, David Tomlinson; **D:** Leslie Howard. **VHS, Beta** $29.95 VYY ♫♫

Pin A boy's imaginary friend assists in the slaying of various enemies. Horror effort could be worse.
1988 (R) 103m/C Cyndy Preston, David Hewlett, Terry O'Quinn; **D:** Sandor Stern. **VHS, Beta, LV** $19.95 STE, NWV, IME ♫♫½

Pin Down Girls Great schlock about girl wrestlers. Also known as "Racket Girls."
1951 ?m/C Clara Mortensen, Rita Martinez. **VHS** $16.95 SNC ♫

Pin-Up Girl Grable plays a secretary who becomes an overnight sensation during World War II. Loosely based on her famous pinup poster that was so popular at the time, the movie didn't even come close to being as successful. The songs aren't particularly memorable, although Charlie Spivak and his Orchestra perform. ♫Once Too Often; Yankee Doodle Dandy; I'll Be Marching to a Love Song; You're My Little Pin Up Girl; Story of the Very Merry Widow; Time Alone Will Tell; Don't Carry Tales Out of School; Red Robins, Bob Whites and Blue Birds.
1944 83m/C Betty Grable, Martha Raye, Jon Harvey, Joe E. Brown, Eugene Pallette, Mantan Moreland; **D:** H. Bruce Humberstone. **VHS, LV** $19.98 FOX, FXV ♫♫

The Pinchcliffe Grand Prix Master inventor designs the ultimate race car.
1981 (G) 88m/C **VHS, Beta** $19.95 STE, GEM ♫

Ping Pong A Chinese patriarch drops dead in London's Chinatown, leaving a young law student to disentangle his will, and get mixed up with his cross-cultured family.
1987 (PG) 100m/C David Yip, Lucy Sheen, Robert Lee, Lam Fung, Victor Kan, Ric Young; **D:** Po Chich Leong. **VHS, Beta, LV** NO ♫♫½

The Pink Angels Transvestite bikers wheel their way to Los Angeles, turning many heads as they go.
1971 (R) 88m/C John Alderman, Tom Basham, Henry Olek, Dan Haggerty, Michael Pataki; **D:** Lawrence Brown. **VHS, Beta** $49.95 PSM ♫½

Pink at First Sight The Pink Panther returns in a new animated collection of his funniest adventures.
1984 49m/C **VHS, Beta** $12.95 MGM, WTA ♫½

Pink Cadillac A grizzled, middle-aged bondsman is on the road, tracking down bail-jumping crooks. He helps the wife and baby of his latest target escape from her husband's more evil associates. Eastwood's performance is good and fun to watch, in this otherwise lightweight film.
1989 (PG-13) 121m/C Clint Eastwood, Bernadette Peters, Timothy Carhart, Michael Des Barres, William Hickey; **D:** Buddy Van Horn. **VHS, Beta, LV** $19.98 WAR ♫♫½

The Pink Chiquitas Sci-fi spoof about a detective battling a mob of meteorite-traveling Amazons.
1986 (PG-13) 86m/C Frank Stallone, Eartha Kitt, Bruce Pirrie, McKinlay Robinson, Elizabeth Edwards, Claudia Udy; **D:** Anthony Currie. **VHS, Beta** $9.99 STE, PSM ♫

Pink Flamingos Divine, the dainty 300-pound transvestite, faces the biggest challenge of his/her career when he/she competes for the title of World's Filthiest Person. Tasteless, crude, and hysterical film; this one earned Waters his title as "Prince of Puke." If there are any doubts about this honor—or Divine's rep—watch through to the end to catch Divine chewing real dog excrement, all the time wearing a you-know-what grin.

1973 (R) 95m/C Divine, David Lochary, Mary Vivian Pearce, Danny Mills, Mink Stole, Edith Massey; **D:** John Waters. **VHS, Beta, LV** NO ♫♫

Pink Floyd: The Wall Film version of Pink Floyd's 1979 LP, "The Wall." A surreal, impressionistic tour-de-force about a boy who grows up numb from society's pressures. The concept is bombastic and overwrought, but Geldof manages to remain somewhat likeable as the cynical rock star and the Gerald Scarfe animation perfectly complements the film. Laserdisc edition includes the original theatrical trailer and the letterboxed format of the film.
1982 (R) 95m/C GB Bob Geldof, Christine Hargreaves, Bob Hoskins; **D:** Alan Parker. **VHS, Beta, LV** $19.95 MVD, MGM, PIA ♫♫½

Pink Motel Several people spend a night meant to be romantic at a pink stucco motel which caters to couples. Comic stiff with Diller and Pickens as the owners of said pink motel. **AKA:** Motel.
1982 (R) 90m/C Phyllis Diller, Slim Pickens, Terri Berland, Squire Fridell; **D:** Mike MacFarland. **VHS, Beta** $19.99 HBO Woof!

Pink Nights A high school nebbish is suddenly pursued by three beautiful girls, and his life gets turned upside-down.
1987 (PG) 87m/C Shaun Allen, Kevin Anderson, Larry King, Johnathan Jamcovic Michaels; **D:** Philip Koch. **VHS, Beta, LV** $19.95 STE, NWV ♫

The Pink Panther A bumbling, disaster-prone inspector invades a Swiss ski resort and becomes obsessed with capturing a jewel thief hoping to lift the legendary "Pink Panther" diamond. Said thief is also the inspector's wife's lover, though the inspector doesn't know it. Slick slapstick succeeds on strength of Sellers' classic portrayal of Clouseau, who accidentally destroys everything in his path while speaking in a funny French accent. Written by Edwards and Maurice Richlin. Followed by "A Shot In the Dark," "Inspector Clouseau" (without Sellers), "The Return of the Pink Panther," "The Pink Panther Strikes Again," "Revenge of the Pink Panther," "Trail of the Pink Panther," and "Curse of the Pink Panther." Memorable Pink Panther theme supplied by Henry Mancini.
1964 113m/C Peter Sellers, David Niven, Robert Wagner, Claudia Cardinale, Capucine, Brenda de Banzie; **D:** Blake Edwards. **VHS, Beta, LV** $19.98 MGM, FOX, TVC ♫♫♫

The Pink Panther Strikes Again Strong series entry has the incompetent inspector tracking his former boss, who has gone insane and has become preoccupied with destroying the entire world. A must for Sellers buffs and anyone who appreciates slapstick. Fifth Panther film, once again scored by Mancini and written by Edwards and Frank Waldman.
1976 (PG) 103m/C GB Peter Sellers, Herbert Lom, Lesley-Anne Down, Colin Blakely, Leonard Rossiter, Burt Kwuok; **D:** Blake Edwards. **VHS, Beta, LV** $19.95 FOX, TVC ♫♫♫

Pink Strings and Sealing Wax A brutish pub owner in Victorian England is poisoned by his abused wife. She tries to involve the son of a chemist with the idea of blackmailing the father. Fine period flavor.
1945 75m/B GB Mervyn Johns, Mary Merrall, Gordon Jackson, Googie Withers, Sally Ann Howes, Catherine Lacey, Garry Marsh; **D:** Robert Hamer. **VHS, Beta** $16.95 SNC ♫♫

Pinocchio Second Disney animated film featuring Pinocchio, a little wooden puppet, made with love by the old woodcarver Geppetto, and brought to life by a good fairy. Except Pinocchio isn't content to be just a

puppet—he wants to become a real boy. Lured off by a sly fox, Pinocchio undergoes a number of adventures as he tries to return safely home. Has some scary scenes, including Geppetto, Pinocchio, and their friend Jiminy Cricket getting swallowed by a whale, and Pleasure Island, where naughty boys are turned into donkeys. An example of animation at its best and a Disney classic that has held up over time. ♫When You Wish Upon a Star; Give a Little Whistle; Turn on the Old Music Box; Hi-Diddle-Dee-Dee (An Actor's Life For Me); I've Got No Strings.
1940 (G) 87m/C *D:* Ben Sharpsteen; *V:* Dick Jones, Cliff Edwards, Evelyn Venable, Walter Catlett, Frankie Darro, Charles Judels, Don Brodie, Christian Rub. **VHS, Beta, LV $24.99** *DIS, WTA* ⅔⅔⅔⅔

Pinocchio Classic Pinocchio story in musical form.
1976 76m/C Danny Kaye, Sandy Duncan. **VHS, Beta $14.98** *UHV* ⅔⅔

Pinocchio Pee Wee Herman is the puppet who wants to be a real little boy in this "Faerie Tale Theatre" adaptation of this children's classic.
1983 60m/C Pee-Wee Herman, James Coburn, Carl Reiner, Lainie Kazan; *D:* Peter Medak. **VHS, Beta $14.98** *FOX, FCT* ⅔⅔

Pinocchio's Storybook Adventures Pinocchio takes over for an ailing puppet master and puts on a show for a group of children.
1979 80m/C *D:* Ron Merk. **VHS, Beta $9.99** *VTR* ⅔ ½

Pinto Canyon An honest sheriff does away with a band of cattle rustlers.
1940 55m/B Bob Steele, Louise Stanley, Kenne Duncan, Ted Adams, Steve Clark, Budd Buster; *D:* Raymond K. Johnson. **VHS $19.95** *NOS, DVT* ⅔ ½

Pinto Rustlers A cowboy left orphaned by a gang of rustlers seeks revenge.
1936 52m/C Tom Tyler, Catherine Cotter. **VHS, Beta $19.95** *NOS, DVT* ⅔ ½

Pioneer Marshal Lawman Hale disguises himself as a criminal to track down an embezzler.
1949 60m/B Monte Hale, Paul Hurst. **VHS, Beta $29.95** *DVT* ⅔

Pioneer Woman A family encounters hostility when they set up a frontier homestead in Nebraska in 1867. Told from the feminine perspective, the tale is strewn with hurdles, both personal and natural. *AKA:* Pioneers.
1973 74m/C Joanna Pettet, William Shatner, David Janssen; *D:* Buzz Kulik. **VHS, Beta $14.98** *WOV, SIM* ⅔

The Pioneers Ritter sets out to protect a wagon train.
1941 59m/B Tex Ritter. **VHS, Beta** *VCN* ⅔ ½

Pipe Dreams A couple tries to repair their broken marriage against the backdrop of the Alaskan pipeline's construction.
1976 (PG) 89m/C Gladys Knight, Barry Hankerson, Bruce French, Sally Kirkland, Sherry Bain; *D:* Stephen Verona. **VHS, Beta $14.95** *COL, SUE* ⅔⅔

Pippi Goes on Board The fourth and last film in the Swedish series finds Pippi's father arriving one day to take her sailing to Taka-Kuka, his island kingdom. She can't bear to leave her friends and jumps off the ship to return home. The series is poorly dubbed and technically flawed, which the kids probably won't notice. Based on the books by Astrid Lindgren. Preceded by "Pippi Longstocking," "Pippi in the South Seas," and "Pippi on the Run."

1975 (G) 83m/C *SW* Inger Nilsson; *D:* Olle Hellbron. **VHS, Beta $19.95** *GEM, MOV* ⅔⅔ ½

Pippi in the South Seas Pippi, a fun-loving, independent, red haired little girl, and her two friends decide to rescue her father, who is being held captive by a band of pirates on a South Sea island. Naturally, clever Pippi saves the day. Poorly dubbed and edited. Based on the children's book by Astrid Lindgren. Follows "Pippi Longstocking" and precedes "Pippi on the Run" and "Pippi Goes on Board." *AKA:* Pippi Langstrump Pa de Sju Haven.
1974 (G) 99m/C *SW* Inger Nilsson; *D:* Olle Hellbron. **VHS, Beta $19.95** *GEM, MOV* ⅔⅔ ½

Pippi Longstocking This little red-headed, pigtailed terror is left alone by her sailor father as he heads out to sea. Not that Pippi minds, since it gives her the chance to create havoc in her town through the antics of her pets, a monkey and a horse. Pippi's antics may amuse the kiddies but adults will find her obnoxious. Poorly dubbed and technically somewhat shaky. Based on the children's book by Astrid Lindgren. Followed by "Pippi in the South Seas," "Pippi on the Run," and "Pippi Goes on Board."
1973 (G) 99m/C *SW* Inger Nilsson; *D:* Olle Hellbron. **VHS, Beta $19.95** *GEM, MOV* ⅔⅔ ½

Pippi on the Run The third film in the series finds Pippi on the trail of two friends who have run away from home. The three have many adventures before deciding home is best. Preceded by "Pippi Longstocking" and "Pippi in the South Seas," followed by "Pippi Goes on Board." Film lacks technical and dubbing skills. Based on the children's book by Astrid Lindgren.
1974 (G) 99m/C *SW* **VHS, Beta $19.99** *GEM, MOV* ⅔⅔ ½

Pippin Video version of the stage musical about the adolescent son of Charlemagne finding true love. Adequate record of Bob Fosse's Broadway smash. Features Vereen recreating his original Tony Award-winning role.
1981 120m/C Ben Vereen, William Katt, Martha Raye, Chita Rivera. **VHS, Beta, LV $29.95** *UHV, FHE, PIA* ⅔⅔⅔

Piranha A rural Texas resort area is plagued by attacks from ferocious man-eating fish which a scientist created to be used as a secret weapon in the Vietnam War. Spoofy horror film features the now-obligatory Dante film in-jokes in the background.
1978 (R) 90m/C Bradford Dillman, Heather Menzies, Kevin McCarthy, Keenan Wynn, Barbara Steele, Dick Miller, Paul Bartel; *D:* Joe Dante. **VHS, Beta $39.98** *WAR, OM* ⅔⅔ ½

Piranha 2: The Spawning Diving instructor and a biochemist seek to destroy piranha mutations that are murdering tourists at a club. Early Cameron exercise in gore tech that's a step down from original "Piranha." *AKA:* Piranha 2: Flying Killers.
1982 (R) 88m/C Steve Marachuk, Lance Henriksen, Ricky Paul; *D:* James Cameron. **VHS, Beta, LV $29.98** *SUE, NLC* ⅔ ½

The Pirate A traveling actor poses as a legendary pilot to woo a lonely woman on a remote Caribbean island. Minnelli always scores with this type of fare, and both Garland and Kelly make the most of the Cole Porter score. ♫Be a Clown; Nina; Mack the Black; You Can Do No Wrong; Sweet Ices, Papayas, Berry Man; Sea Wall; Serafin; The Ring; Judy Awakens; Not Again!; The Tight Rope; The Mast; Love of My Life; You Can Do No Wrong.

1948 102m/C Judy Garland, Gene Kelly, Walter Slezak, Gladys Cooper, George Zucco, Reginald Owen, Nicholas Brothers; *D:* Vincente Minnelli. **VHS, Beta, LV $19.98** *MGM* ⅔⅔⅔

Pirate Movie Gilbert and Sullivan's "The Pirates of Penzance" is combined with new pop songs in this tale of fantasy and romance. Feeble attempt to update a musical that was fine the way it was.
1982 (PG) 98m/C Kristy McNichol, Christopher Atkins, Ted Hamilton, Bill Kerr, Garry McDonald; *D:* Ken Annakin. **VHS, Beta $59.95** *FOX* ⅔⅔ ½

Pirate Warrior Grade-B pirate flick about slavery and the evil Tortuga.
1964 86m/C Ricardo Montalban, Vincent Price, Liana Orfei; *D:* Mary Costa. **VHS, Beta** *NO* ⅔⅔

Pirates Blustery, confused effort at a big-budgeted retro-adventure, about a highly regarded pirate and his gains and losses on the high seas. Broad comedy, no story to speak of.
1986 (PG-13) 124m/C Walter Matthau, Cris Campion, Damien Thomas, Richard Pearson, Charlotte Lewis, Olu Jacobs, David Patrick Kelly, Roy Kinnear, Bill Fraser, Jose Santamaria; *D:* Roman Polanski. **VHS, Beta** *LIV* ⅔ ½

The Pirates of Penzance Gilbert and Sullivan's comic operetta is the story of a band of fun-loving pirates, their reluctant young apprentice, the "very model of a modern major general," and his lovely daughters. An adaptation of Joseph Papp's award-winning Broadway play.
1983 112m/C Kevin Kline, Angela Lansbury, Linda Ronstadt, Rex Smith, George Rose; *D:* Wilford Leach. **VHS, Beta, LV $29.95** *MCA, FOX* ⅔⅔

Pirates of the Coast A Spanish naval commander teams up with a group of pirates to even the score with an evil governor during the 1500s.
1961 102m/C Lex Barker, Estella Blain, Livio Lorenzon, Liana Orfei; *D:* Domenico Paolella. **VHS, Beta $29.95** *UNI* ⅔ ½

Pirates of the High Seas Crabbe helps a friend save his shipping line from sabotage. A serial in fifteen chapters.
1950 ?m/C Buster Crabbe, Lois Hall, Tommy Farrell, Gene Roth, Tristram Coffin; *D:* Spencer Gordon Bennet, Thomas Carr. **VHS** *MLB* ⅔ ½

Pirates of the Seven Seas In the further tales of "Sandokan the Great," the pirate hero helps save the heroine's father from an evil English Imperialist.
1962 90m/C Steve Reeves, Jacqueline Sassard, Andrea Bosic; *D:* Umberto Lenzi. **VHS, Beta** *NO* ⅔⅔

Pistol: The Birth of a Legend Biography of "Pistol" Pete Maravich, the basketball star who defied age limitations in the 1960s to play on his varsity team.
1990 (G) 104m/C Adam Guier, Nick Benedict, Boots Garland, Millie Perkins; *D:* Frank C. Schroeder. **VHS, Beta $19.95** *COL, SVS* ⅔⅔ ½

The Pit Autistic boy gets his chance for revenge. The townspeople who humiliate him are in for a surprise after he stumbles across a huge hole in the forest, at the bottom of which are strange and deadly creatures.
1981 (R) 96m/C Sammy Snyders, Sonja Smits, Jeannie Elias, Laura Hollingsworth; *D:* Lew Lehman. **VHS, Beta $19.95** *STE, SUE* ⅔ ½

The Pit and the Pendulum A woman and her lover plan to drive her brother mad, and he responds by locking them in his torture chamber, which was built by his loony dad, whom he now thinks he is. Standard Corman production only remotely derived from the classic Poe tale, with the cast chewing on Richard Matheson's loopy script. A landmark in Gothic horror.

1961 80m/C Vincent Price, John Kerr, Barbara Steele, Luana Anders; **D:** Roger Corman. **VHS, Beta $19.98** *WAR, OM* ♫♫♫

The Pit & the Pendulum
Retelling of the classic Poe short story, mixed with his "A Cask of Amantillado" and set during the Spanish Inquisition. Great special effects and professional scary guy, Lance Henriksen.
1991 (R) 97m/C Lance Henriksen, Rona De Ricci, Jonathan Fuller, Jeffrey Combs, Tom Towles, Stephen Lee, Francis Bay, Oliver Reed; **D:** Stuart Gordon. **VHS, LV $19.95** *PAR* ♫♫½

Pitfall
Gritty tale in which an insurance salesman, bored with his routine suburban life and family, follows his less noble instincts—and finds himself up to his ears in stolen goods, adultery and murder.
1948 85m/B Dick Powell, Jane Wyatt, Lizabeth Scott, Raymond Burr, John Litel, Byron Barr, Ann Doran; **D:** Andre de Toth. **VHS, LV $19.98** *REP, FCT* ♫♫♫

Pixote
Wrenching, documentary-like account of an orphan-boy's life on the streets in a Brazil metropolis. Graphic and depressing, it's not for all tastes but nonetheless masterfully done. In Portuguese with English subtitles.
1981 127m/C *BR* Fernando Ramos Da Silva, Marilia Pera, Jorge Juliao; **D:** Hector Babenco. **VHS, Beta $59.95** *COL* ♫♫♫

P.K. and the Kid
A runaway kid meets up with a factory worker on his way to an arm wrestling competition and they become friends.
1985 90m/C Molly Ringwald, Paul LeMat, Alex Rocco, John Madden, Esther Rolle; **D:** Lou Lombardo. **VHS, Beta, LV $79.95** *LHV, WAR* ♫♫

A Place Called Glory
Barker comes to the aid of the local townsfolk in Glory city who have their hands full with a gang of bloodthirsty outlaws. *AKA:* Die Holle von Manitoba.
1966 92m/C Lex Barker, Pierre Brice, Marianne Koch. **VHS $16.95** *SNC* ♫♫

A Place Called Today
Sordid tale of big city politics where violence and fear in the streets is at the heart of the campaign. Also called "City in Fear."
1972 105m/C Cheri Caffaro, J. Herbert Kerr Jr., Lana Wood, Richard Smedley, Tim Brown; **D:** Don Schain. **VHS, Beta $39.95** *MON* ♫

Place in Hell
The Japanese armed forces camouflage a Pacific island beach which they are holding and invite the American forces to invade it during World War II.
1965 106m/C Guy Madison, Helene Chanel, Monty Greenwood. **VHS, Beta $49.95** *UNI* ♫½

A Place in the Sun
Melodramatic adaptation of "An American Tragedy," Theodore Dreiser's realist classic about an ambitious laborer whose aspirations to the high life with a gorgeous debutante are threatened by his lower-class lover's pregnancy. Clift is magnificent in the lead, and Taylor and Winters also shine in support. Burr, however, grossly overdoes his role of the vehement prosecutor. Still, not a bad effort from somewhat undisciplined director Stevens.
1951 120m/B Montgomery Clift, Elizabeth Taylor, Shelley Winters, Raymond Burr, Anne Revere; **D:** George Stevens; **M:** Franz Waxman. Academy Awards '51: Best Black and White Cinematography, Best Costume Design (B & W), Best Director (Stevens), Best Film Editing, Best Screenplay, Best Score; Nominations: Best Actor (Clift), Best Actress (Winters), Best Picture; Directors Guild of America Awards '51: Best Director (Stevens); Golden Globe Awards '52: Best Film—Drama; National Board of Review Awards '51: 10 Best Films of the Year. **VHS, Beta, LV $19.95** *PAR, PIA, BTV* ♫♫♫

Place of Weeping
Early entry in the anti-apartheid sweepstakes (made in South Africa, no less). A South African woman opposes her nation's racist policies. A reporter supports her.
1986 (PG) 88m/C *SA* James Whylie, Geini Mhlophe; **D:** Darrell Roodt. **VHS, Beta $19.95** *STE, NWV, FCT* ♫♫½

Places in the Heart
A young widow determines to make the best of a bad situation on a small farm in Depression-era Texas, fighting poverty, racism, and sexism while enduring back-breaking labor. Support group includes a blind veteran and a black drifter. Hokey but nonetheless moving film is improved significantly by strong performances by virtually everyone in the cast. In his debut, Malkovich shines through this stellar group. Effective dust-bowl photography by Nestor Almendros.
1984 (PG) 113m/C Sally Field, John Malkovich, Danny Glover, Ed Harris, Lindsay Crouse, Amy Madigan, Terry O'Quinn; **W/D:** Robert Benton. Academy Awards '84: Best Actress (Field), Best Original Screenplay; Nominations: Best Costume Design, Best Director (Benton), Best Picture, Best Supporting Actor (Malkovich), Best Supporting Actress (Crouse); Golden Globe Awards '85: Best Actress—Drama (Field). **VHS, Beta, LV $19.98** *FOX, BTV, HMV* ♫♫♫

The Plague Dogs
Two dogs carrying a plague escape from a research center and are tracked down in this unlikely animated film. A bit ponderous. And yes, that is Hurt's voice. Written by Rosen from the novel by Richard Adams, author of "Watership Down."
1982 99m/C **W/D:** Martin Rosen; **V:** John Hurt, Christopher Benjamin, Judy Geeson, Barbara Leigh-Hunt, Patrick Stewart. **VHS, Beta $9.98** *NLC* ♫♫½

Plain Clothes
An undercover cop masquerades as a high school student to solve the murder of a teacher. He endures all the trials that made him hate high school the first time around.
1988 (PG) 98m/C Arliss Howard, George Wendt, Suzy Amis, Diane Ladd, Abe Vigoda, Robert Stack; **D:** Martha Coolidge. **VHS, Beta $14.95** *PAR* ♫♫½

The Plainsman
Western legends Wild Bill Hickock, Buffalo Bill, and Calamity Jane team up for adventure in this big, empty venture. Just about what you'd expect from splashy director DeMille.
1937 113m/B Gary Cooper, Jean Arthur, Charles Bickford, Anthony Quinn, George "Gabby" Hayes, Porter Hall; **D:** Cecil B. DeMille; **M:** John Williams. **VHS, Beta, LV $14.98** *MCA, MLB* ♫♫½

Plan 9 from Outer Space
Two or three aliens in silk pajamas conspire to resurrect several slow-moving zombies from a cardboard graveyard in order to conquer the Earth. Spaceships that look suspiciously like paper plates blaze across the sky. Pitiful, inadvertently hilarious fright worth a look if you're desperate to kill time since it's in the running for the "dumbest movie ever made" award. Lugosi's actual screen time is under two minutes, since he had the good sense to die before the film was complete. Enjoy the taller and younger replacement (the chiropractor of Wood's wife) they found for Lugosi, who remains hooded to protect his identity. *AKA:* Grave Robbers from Outer Space.
1956 78m/B Bela Lugosi, Tor Johnson, Lyle Talbot, Vampira, Gregory Walcott; **D:** Edward D. Wood Jr. **VHS, Beta, LV $19.95** *NOS, SNC, MED* Woof!

Planes, Trains & Automobiles
A one-joke Hughes comedy saved by Martin and Candy. A straight-laced businessman (played straight by Martin) on the way home for Thanksgiving meets up with a oafish, bad-luck-ridden boor who turns his efforts to get home upside down. Martin and Candy both turn in fine performances, and effectively straddle a thin line between true pathos and hilarious buffoonery. Bacon and McClurg, both Hughes alumni, have small but funny roles.
1987 (R) 93m/C Steve Martin, John Candy, Edie McClurg, Kevin Bacon, Michael McKean, William Windom, Laila Robins, Martin Ferrero, Charles Tyner; **D:** John Hughes. **VHS, Beta, LV, 8mm $19.95** *PAR* ♫♫½

Planet Burg
A classic Soviet sci-fi flick about a space exploration team landing on Venus. Their job becomes a rescue mission when one of the crew is stranded. Although there are some silly moments, some good plot twists and acting make up for them. In Russian with English subtitles.
1962 90m/C *RU* Vladimir Temelianov, Gennadi Vernov, Kyunna Ignatova; **D:** Pavel Klushantsev. **VHS, Beta $16.95** *SNC* ♫♫½

Planet Earth
In the year 2133, a man who has been in suspended animation for 154 years is revived to lead the troops against a violent group of women (and mutants, too!).
1974 78m/C John Saxon, Janet Margolin, Ted Cassidy, Diana Muldaur, Johana DeWinter, Christopher Gary; **D:** Marc Daniels. **VHS $59.95** *UNI* ♫♫½

Planet of Blood
Space opera about an alien vampire discovered on Mars by a rescue team. If you've ever seen the Soviet film "Niobo Zowiot," don't be surprised if some scenes look familiar; the script was written around segments cut from that film. *AKA:* Queen of Blood.
1966 81m/C John Saxon, Basil Rathbone, Judi Meredith, Dennis Hopper, Florence Marly; **D:** Curtis Harrington. **VHS $16.95** *SNC, NOS, MRV* ♫♫

Planet of the Apes
Astronauts crash land on a planet where apes are masters and humans are merely brute animals. Superior science fiction with sociological implications marred only by unnecessary humor. Heston delivers one of his more plausible performances. Superb ape makeup creates realistic pseudo-simians of McDowall, Hunter, Evans, Whitmore, and Daly. Adapted by Rod Serling and Michael Wilson from Pierre Boulle's novel, "Monkey Planet." Musical score by Jerry Goldsmith. Followed by four sequels and two television series.
1968 (G) 112m/C Charlton Heston, Roddy McDowall, Kim Hunter, Maurice Evans, Linda Harrison, James Whitmore, James Daly; **D:** Franklin J. Schaffner; **M:** Jerry Goldsmith. Academy Awards '68 Nominations: Best Costume Design, Best Original Score; National Board of Review Awards '68: 10 Best Films of the Year. **VHS, Beta, LV $19.98** *FOX* ♫♫♫½

Planet of the Dinosaurs
Survivors from a ruined spaceship combat huge savage dinosaurs on a swampy uncharted planet.
1980 (PG) 85m/C James Whitworth; **D:** James K. Shea. **VHS, Beta $39.95** *AHV* ♫½

Planet of the Vampires
Astronauts search for missing comrades on a planet dominated by mind-bending forces. Acceptable atmospheric filmmaking from genre master Bava, but it's not among his more compelling ventures. *AKA:* Terror in Space; Terreur dans l'Espace; Space Mutants; The Demon Planet.

1965 86m/C *IT* Barry Sullivan, Norman Bengell, Angel Aranda, Evi Marandi; *D:* Mario Bava. **VHS, Beta** $9.98 *ORI, HBO* ♂♂½

Planet on the Prowl A fiery planet causes earthly disasters, so a troop of wily astronauts try to destroy it with the latest technology. They fail, leading one sacrificial soul to do it himself. *AKA:* War Between the Planets.
1965 80m/C *IT* Giacomo ''Jack'' Stuart, Amber Collins, Peter Martell, John Bartha, Halina Zalewska, James Weaver; *D:* Anthony M. Dawson. **VHS, Beta** *NO* ♂

Planets Against Us Science fiction tale of escaped alien humanoid robots who take refuge on Earth, but whose touch is fatal. Good special effects. *AKA:* I Pianeti Contro di Noi; The Man with the Yellow Eyes; Hands of a Killer; The Monster with Green Eyes.
1961 85m/B *IT FR* Michel Lemoine, Maria Pia Luzi, Jany Clair; *D:* Romano Ferrara. **VHS** $16.95 *SNC* ♂½

Platinum Blonde Screwball comedy in which a newspaper journalist (Williams) marries a wealthy girl (Harlow) but finds that he doesn't like the restrictions and confinement of high society. Yearning for a creative outlet, he decides to write a play and hires a reporter (Young) to collaborate with him. The results are funny and surprising when Young shows up at the mansion flanked by a group of hard-drinking, fun-loving reporters.
1931 86m/B Loretta Young, Robert Williams, Jean Harlow, Louise Closser Hale; *D:* Frank Capra; *W:* Jo Swerling, Dorothy Howell. **VHS** $19.95 *COL* ♂♂♂

Platinum High School Divorced father Rooney is appalled when his son is ''accidentally'' killed while off at an exclusive military academy. His suspicions are aroused by the prevaricating school commander and he discovers some horrible truths about his son's death and life at the school. *AKA:* Trouble at 16; Rich, Young, and Deadly.
1960 91m/B Mickey Rooney, Terry Moore, Dan Duryea, Conway Twitty, Warren Berlinger, Yvette Mimieux, Jimmy Boyd, Richard Jaeckel, Harold Lloyd Jr., Elisha Cook Jr., Jimmy Murphy; *D:* Charles Haas; *W:* Robert Smith. **VHS** $9.98 *REP* ♂½

Platoon A grunt's view of the Vietnam War is provided in all its horrific, inexplicable detail. Sheen is wooden in the lead, but both Dafoe and Berenger are resplendent as, respectively, good and bad soldiers. Strong, visceral filmmaking from fearless director Stone, who based the film on his own GI experiences. Highly acclaimed; considered by many to be the most realistic portrayal of the war on film.
1986 (R) 113m/C Charlie Sheen, Willem Dafoe, Tom Berenger, Francesco Quinn, Forest Whitaker, John C. McGinley, Kevin Dillon, Richard Edson, Reggie Johnson, Keith David, Johnny Depp; *W/D:* Oliver Stone. Academy Awards '86: Best Director (Stone), Best Film Editing, Best Picture, Best Sound; Nominations: Best Cinematography, Best Original Screenplay, Best Supporting Actor (Berenger, Dafoe); British Academy Awards '87: Best Director (Stone); Directors Guild of America Awards '86: Best Director (Stone); Golden Globe Awards '87: Best Director (Stone), Best Film—Drama, Best Supporting Actor (Berenger); National Board of Review Awards '86: 10 Best Films of the Year. **VHS, Beta, LV** $19.98 *LIV, HBO, BTV* ♂♂♂½

Platoon Leader A battle-drenched portrait of a West Point lieutenant in Vietnam. When he first arrives, he must win the trust of his men, who have been on their tours for a much longer time. As time goes on, he slowly becomes hardened to the realities of the brutal life in the field. Made on the heels of the widely acclaimed ''Platoon,'' but it doesn't have the same power. Norris is martial arts king Chuck Norris' brother.
1987 (R) 97m/C Michael Dudikoff, Brian Libby, Robert F. Lyons, Rick Fitts, Jesse Dabson, William Smith, Michael De Lorenzo; *D:* Aaron Norris. **VHS, Beta, LV** $19.98 *MED* ♂♂

Platoon the Warriors The underworld rages with violence when two kingpins, Rex and Bill, become bitter and declare war over a botched drug deal.
1988 90m/C David Coley, Dick Crown, James Miller, Don Richard, Alex Sylvian; *D:* Philip Ko. **VHS, Beta** *NO* ♂

Platypus Cove An adopted boy tracks down the culprits responsible for the sabotage of his family's boat, a crime for which he was suspected. Australian.
1986 72m/C Paul Smith; *D:* Peter Maxwell. **VHS, Beta** $59.98 *EMB, SUE* ♂

Play Dead Poor Yvonne De Carlo plays a psychotic woman who trains a dog to rip people to shreds. *AKA:* Satan's Dog.
1981 89m/C Yvonne De Carlo, Stephanie Dunham, David Culliname, Glenn Kezer, Ron Jackson, Carolyn Greenwood; *D:* Peter Wittman. **VHS** $19.95 *ACA* ♂

Play It Again, Charlie Brown The Peanuts gang goes bananas when Lucy enlists Schroeder to play rock music at a PTA meeting.
1970 25m/C Charles M. Schulz. **VHS, Beta** $14.95 *SHV, VTR, WTA* ♂

Play It Again, Sam Allen is—no surprise—a nerd, and this time he's in love with his best friend's wife. Modest storyline provides a framework of endless gags, with Allen borrowing heavily from ''Casablanca.'' Bogey even appears periodically to counsel Allen on the ways of wooing women. Superior comedy isn't hurt by Ross directing instead of Allen, who adapted the script from his own play.
1972 (PG) 85m/C Woody Allen, Diane Keaton, Tony Roberts, Susan Anspach, Jerry Lacy, Jennifer Salt, Joy Bang, Viva, Herbert Ross; *D:* Herbert Ross. **VHS, Beta, LV, 8mm** $19.95 *PAR* ♂♂♂½

Play Misty for Me A radio deejay obliges a psychotic woman's song request and suddenly finds himself the target of her obsessive behavior, which rapidly turns from seductive to murderous. Auspicious directorial debut for Eastwood, borrowing from the Siegel playbook (look for the director's cameo as a barkeep). Based on a story by Heims.
1971 (R) 102m/C Clint Eastwood, Jessica Walter, Donna Mills, John Larch, Irene Hervey, Jack Ging; *Cameos:* Don Siegel; *D:* Clint Eastwood; *W:* Jo Heims, Dean Reisner. **VHS, Beta, LV** $19.95 *MCA, TLF* ♂♂♂

Play Murder for Me Saxophonist performing in a seedy Buenos Aires nightclub has his world turned upside down when a former lover suddenly re-enters his life. She still has her eye on him, but she's now the woman of a notorious mobster. Soon the musician finds himself drawn into the usual deadly world of crime, deceit, and unharnessed passion.
1991 (R) 80m/C Jack Wagner, Tracy Scoggins; *D:* Hector Olivera. **VHS** $89.98 *NHO* ♂♂

Play Nice A detective hunts down a murderous psychopath but is shocked when he discovers his suspect is a woman—and someone he knows. Also available in an unrated version.
1992 (R) 90m/C Ed O'Ross. **VHS** $89.95 *VMK* ♂½

Playboy of the Western World An innkeeper's daughter is infatuated with a young man who says he murdered his father. Adapted from the classic play by John Millington Synge.
1962 96m/C *IR* Siobhan McKenna, Gary Raymond; *D:* Brian Desmond Hurst. **VHS, Beta** $59.99 *HBO* ♂♂½

The Playboys In 1957, in a tiny Irish village, Tara Maguire causes a scandal by having a baby out of wedlock. Tara's beauty attracts lots of men—there's a former beau who kills himself (Tara blames it on bad luck and bad land), the obsessive, middle-aged Sergeant Hegarty, and the newest arrival, Tom Castle, an actor with a rag-tag theatrical troupe called ''The Playboys.'' A slow-moving and simple story with particularly good performances by Wright as the strong-willed Tara and Finney as Hegarty, clinging to a last chance at love and family. The Playboys' hysterically hammy version of ''Gone With the Wind'' is a gem. Directorial debut of Mackinnon. Filmed in the village of Redhills, Ireland, the hometown of co-writer Connaughton.
1992 (PG-13) 114m/C Albert Finney, Aidan Quinn, Robin Wright, Milo O'Shea, Alan Devlin, Niamh Cusack, Ian McElhinney, Niall Buggy, Adrian Dunbar; *D:* Gilles Mackinnon; *W:* Shane Connaughton, Kerry Crabbe. **VHS** $92.99 *HBO, FCT* ♂♂♂

The Player Altman's biting satire about disposable Hollywood is a clever and entertaining look at the movie industry and the greed that controls it. Robbins is dead-on as Griffin Mill, a young studio executive harrassed by a disgruntled writer who sends him cryptic postcards. When a screenwriter turns up dead following a meeting with Mill, the hotshot production chief becomes a prime suspect. Besides having to worry about the murder rap, Mill must also deal with the young new genius (Gallagher), who is out to replace him. Interwoven throughout is the multi-level satirizing of Hollywood's ethics (or lack thereof) by a man who obviously knows. Led by Robbins, the entire main cast turns in strong performances. Robbins contributes a masterful, complicated performance as Mill, both cold and vulnerable, and forever searching for the right buttons to push and the proper back to stab. Stockwell and Grant are also good for a few laughs as a neurotic agent and a British author who manage to survive in the cynical world of Hollywood. Part of the fun is spotting one of the 65 cameos of stars playing themselves. The laserdisc version also includes a commentary by director Altman, interviews with 20 screenwriters, and deleted celebrity cameos.
1992 (R) 123m/C Tim Robbins, Greta Scacchi, Fred Ward, Whoopi Goldberg, Peter Gallagher, Brion James, Cynthia Stevenson, Vincent D'Onofrio, Dean Stockwell, Richard E. Grant, Dina Merrill, Sydney Pollack, Lyle Lovett, Randall Batinkoff, Gina Gershon; *Cameos:* Burt Reynolds, Cher, Nick Nolte, Jack Lemmon, Lily Tomlin, Marlee Matlin, Julia Roberts, Bruce Willis, Anjelica Huston, Elliott Gould, Sally Kellerman, Steve Allen, Richard Anderson, Harry Belafonte, Shari Belafonte-Harper, Karen Black, Gary Busey, Robert Carradine, James Coburn, Cathy Lee Crosby, John Cusack, Brad Davis, Peter Falk, Teri Garr, Leeza Gibbons, Scott Glenn, Jeff Goldblum, Joel Grey, Buck Henry, Kathy Ireland, Sally Kirkland, Andie MacDowell, Martin Mull, Mimi Rogers, Jill St. John, Susan Sarandon, Rod Steiger, Joan Tewkesbury, Robert Wagner, Michael Tolkin; *D:* Robert Altman; *W:* Michael Tolkin; *M:* Thomas Newman. Academy Awards '92 Nominations: Best Adapted Screenplay, Best Director (Altman), Best Film Editing; Cannes Film Festival '92: Best Actor (Robbins), Best Director (Altman); Golden Globe

Awards '93: Best Actor—Musical/Comedy (Robbins), Best Film—Musical/Comedy; Independent Spirit Awards '93: Best Film; New York Film Critics Awards '93: Best Director (Altman), Best Film. **VHS, LV** $89.99 *NLC, CRC, MOV* 𝄞𝄞𝄞𝄞

Players Young tennis hustler touring Mexico hooks up with beautiful and mysterious older woman. They seem to be from different worlds yet their love grows. She inspires him enough to enter Wimbledon. Several tennis pros appear, including Guillermo Vilas, John McEnroe, and Ilie Nastase. Almost as boring as watching a real tennis game.
1979 (PG) 120m/C Ali MacGraw, Dean Paul Martin, Maximilian Schell, Pancho Gonzales; *D:* Anthony Harvey; *M:* Jerry Goldsmith. **VHS, Beta** $49.95 *PAR* 𝄞

Playgirl Killer After impulsively murdering a restless model, an artist continues to kill indiscriminately, keeping his spoils on ice. Sedaka croons between kills and luxuriates poolside—seemingly oblivious to the plot of the film—while a female decoy is sent to bait the killer for the police. For adult viewers. *AKA:* Decoy for Terror.
1966 86m/C *CA* William Kerwin, Jean Christopher, Andree Champagne, Neil Sedaka; *D:* Erick Santamaria. **VHS, Beta** $19.95 *STE, NWV* 𝄞

Playing Away A team of Caribbean cricket players meet a team of stuffy Brits on the field in a clash of the cultures.
1987 100m/C *GB* Norman Beaton, Robert Urquhart; *D:* Horace Love. **VHS, Beta, LV** $19.98 *NLC* 𝄞

Playing for Keeps Three high school grads turn a dilapidating hotel into a rock 'n roll resort. Music by Pete Townshend, Peter Frampton, Phil Collins, and others.
1986 (PG-13) 103m/C Daniel Jordano, Matthew Penn, Leon Grant, Harold Gould, Jimmy Baio; *D:* Bob Weinstein. **VHS, Beta, LV** $79.95 *MCA* 𝄞

Playing for Time Compelling, award-winning television drama based on actual experiences of a Holocaust prisoner who survives by leading an inmate orchestra. Strong playing from Redgrave and Mayron. Pro-Palestinian Redgrave's political beliefs made her a controversial candidate for the role of Jewish Fania Fenelon, but her stunning performance is on the mark.
1980 148m/C Vanessa Redgrave, Jane Alexander, Maud Adams, Verna Bloom, Melanie Mayron; *D:* Daniel Mann. **VHS, Beta** *NO* 𝄞𝄞𝄞

Playing the Field Romantic entanglements involving a soccer referee. Stupid badly-dubbed sex farce.
1974 (R) 90m/C *IT* Joan Collins, Lando Buzzanca; *D:* Louis D'Amico. **VHS** *NO* Woof!

Playing with Fire A young girl gets caught up in drugs, casual sex, and murder.
197? 87m/C Karen Tungay, Danny Keogh, Sam Marais; *D:* Alan Nathanson. **VHS, Beta** $19.95 *WWV* 𝄞

Playmates Barrymore is practically wasted in his last film as a down-on-his-luck actor who agrees to turn bandleader Kyser into a Shakespearean actor. Bizarre comedy is funny at times, but leaves the audience wondering what Barrymore thought he was doing. ♫Humpty Dumpty Heart; How Long Did I Dream?; Que Chica?; Romeo Smith and Juliet Jones; Thank Your Lucky Stars and Stripes.
1941 96m/B Kay Kyser, John Barrymore, Ginny Simms, Lupe Velez, May Robson, Patsy Kelly, Peter Lind Hayes, George Cleveland; *D:* David Butler. **VHS, Beta** $19.98 *TTC* 𝄞

Playmates Two divorced buddies fall in love with each other's ex-wives in this made for television flick. Typical Alda vehicle isn't bad.
1972 78m/C Doug McClure, Alan Alda, Connie Stevens, Barbara Feldon, Eileen Brennan, Tiger Williams, Severn Darden; *D:* Theodore J. Flicker. **VHS, Beta** $19.98 *VMK* 𝄞𝄞½

Playroom Archaeologist McDonald is completing his father's search for the tomb of a medieval boy-prince. But someone, or something, has been waiting for him for a long, long time. When he finally reaches the long-sought-after tomb, he discovers that it is a torture chamber where his worst nightmares become realities. The demonic prince who was buried in the tomb has picked Chris as his playmate, and the rest of the staff as his personal toys.
1990 (R) 87m/C Lisa Aliff, Aron Eisenberg, Christopher McDonald, James Purcell, Jamie Rose, Vincent Schiavelli; *D:* Manny Coto. **VHS, LV** $89.98 *REP* 𝄞𝄞

Playtime Occasionally enterprising comedy in which the bemused Frenchman Hulot tries in vain to maintain an appointment in an urban landscape of glass and steel. The theme of cold, unfeeling civilization is hardly unique, but the film is nonetheless enjoyable. The third in the Hulot trilogy, preceded by "Mr. Hulot's Holiday" and "Mon Oncle." In French with English subtitles.
1967 108m/C *FR* Jacques Tati, Barbara Dennek, Jacqueline Lecomte, Jack Gautier; *D:* Jacques Tati. **VHS, Beta** $29.98 *SUE, TAM, NLC* 𝄞𝄞𝄞

Plaza Suite Three alternating skits from Neil Simon's play about different couples staying at the New York hotel. Matthau shines in all three vignettes. Some of Simon's funnier stuff, with the first sketch being the best: Matthau and Stapleton are a couple celebrating their 24th anniversary. She's sentimental, while he's yearning for his mistress. Number two has producer Matthau putting the make on old flame Harris, while the finale has father Matthau coaxing his anxious daughter out of the bathroom on her wedding day.
1971 (PG) 114m/C Walter Matthau, Maureen Stapleton, Barbara Harris, Lee Grant, Louise Sorel; *D:* Arthur Hiller. **VHS, Beta, LV** $14.95 *PAR* 𝄞𝄞𝄞

Please Don't Eat My Mother A softcore remake of "Little Shop of Horrors" in which a lonely voyeur plays host to a human-eating plant. *AKA:* Hungry Pets; Glump.
1972 95m/C Buck Kartalian, Renee Bond; *D:* Carl Monson. **VHS** $19.98 *MOV, VDM* Woof!

Please Don't Eat the Daisies City couple and kids leave the Big Apple for the country and are traumatized by flora and fauna. Goofy sixties fluff taken from Jean Kerr's book and the basis for the eventual TV series.
1960 111m/C Doris Day, David Niven, Janice Paige, Spring Byington, Richard Haydn, Patsy Kelly, Jack Weston, Margaret Lindsay; *D:* Charles Walters. **VHS, Beta, LV** $19.98 *MGM, FCT* 𝄞𝄞½

Pleasure A saga of love, treachery, and melodrama in English society where self-indulgence held priority and good manners were the rule.
1931 53m/B Conway Tearle, Roscoe Karns, Carmel Myers, Lena Basquette. **VHS, Beta, LV** $19.95 *NOS* 𝄞𝄞

A Pleasure Doing Business Three high school buddies, now in their 40s, are reunited at a stag party, where they decide to go into business as managers in "the oldest profession."
1979 (R) 86m/C Conrad Bain, John Byner, Alan Oppenheimer, Misty Rowe, Phyllis Diller, Tom Smothers; *D:* Steve Vagnino. **VHS, Beta** $49.95 *VHE* 𝄞

Pleasure in Paradise Two beautiful sisters inherit a bar from their uncle who just may have been murdered. Their suspicions (and other things) are aroused by a handsome mystery man who wants to buy the bar from them.
1992 (R) 85m/C **VHS** $79.95 *CEL* 𝄞𝄞

Pleasure Palace A gambling lady's-man (Sharif) meets his match when he helps a woman casino owner (Lange). Made for television.
1980 96m/C Omar Sharif, Victoria Principal, J.D. Cannon, Gerald S. O'Loughlin, Jose Ferrer, Hope Lange, Alan King; *D:* Walter Grauman. **VHS, Beta** $29.95 *LIV* 𝄞𝄞

Pleasure Resort Trashy resort where sexually inhibited people come to work it all out. Staffed by professional, skilled technicians ready to help their guests any way they know how.
1990 (R) 80m/C Annette Haven, Kay Parker. **VHS** *NO* 𝄞

Pleasure Unlimited A housewife experiments with bisexuality, group sex, and more in this softcore release.
1986 (X) 85m/C Angela Carnon, Terry Johnson, Harvey Shane. **VHS, Beta** $29.95 *MED* 𝄞

Pledge Night Tale of horror and revenge. Killed years before in a fraternity hazing, Sid returns for the brothers who did him in. Gory and violent.
1990 (R) 90m/C Will Kempe, Shannon McMahon, Todd Eastland, Paul Ziller; *M:* Anthrax. **VHS** $89.95 *IMP* 𝄞𝄞

Plenty Difficult but worthwhile film with Streep in top form as a former member of the French Resistance, who upon returning to England finds life at home increasingly tedious and banal and begins to fear her finest hours may be behind her. Gielgud is flawless as the aging career diplomat. Adapted by David Hare from his play, an allegory to British decline.
1985 (R) 119m/C Meryl Streep, Tracy Ullman, Sting, John Gielgud, Charles Dance, Ian McKellan, Sam Neill; *D:* Fred Schepisi. **VHS, Beta, LV** $19.99 *HBO* 𝄞𝄞½

The Plot Against Harry Jewish racketeer Harry Plotnik checks out of prison, and finds the outside world ain't what it used to be. Attempting to lead an honest life only makes matters worse. Completely overlooked when first released in 1969 (and quickly shelved) because it was considered to have no commercial potential, Roemer's crime comedy found an enthusiastic audience when it was rediscovered twenty years later.
1969 81m/B Martin Priest, Ben Lang, Maxine Woods, Henry Nemo; *W/D:* Michael Roemer. **VHS** $79.95 *NYF, FCT* 𝄞𝄞𝄞

The Ploughman's Lunch A BBC news reporter claws and lies his way to the top. He then discovers that he is the victim of a far more devious plan. Engrossing and well made, although some of the political views are simplistic.
1983 107m/C Jonathan Pryce, Charlie Dore, Tim Curry, Rosemary Harris, Frank Finlay, Bill Paterson; *D:* Richard Eyre. **VHS, Beta** $59.98 *SUE* 𝄞𝄞𝄞

Plumber A plumber who makes a house call extends his stay to psychologically torture the woman of the house. Originally made for Australian television.
1979 76m/C *AU* Judy Morris, Ivar Kants, Robert Coleby; *D:* Peter Weir. **VHS, Beta** $59.95 *MED* ♫♫½

Plunder Road A pair of crooks cook up a plan to rob a train bound for the San Francisco Mint that's carrying a fortune in gold bullion. Top notch B-film noir.
1957 76m/B Gene Raymond, Jeanne Cooper, Wayne Morris, Elisha Cook Jr.; *D:* Hubert Cornfield. **VHS** $19.98 *REP* ♫♫½

Plunge Into Darkness Quiet weekend in the mountains turns into a nightmare for an ex-Olympic runner and his family.
1977 77m/C Bruce Barry, Olivia Hamnett, Ashley Greenville, Wallace Eaton, Tom Richards; *D:* Peter Maxwell. **VHS, Beta** *PGN* ♫ ½

Plutonium Baby A mutated kid, whose mother was killed by the same radiation exposure that infected him, tracks down the guilty party in New York in this comic-book style film.
1987 85m/C Patrick Molloy, Danny Guerra; *D:* Ray Hirschman. **VHS, Beta** $79.95 *TWE* ♫

Plutonium Incident A female technician at a nuclear power plant suspects the facility to be less safe than it appears, and faces a diabolical plan of harassment when she attempts to bring attention to the hazards.
1982 90m/C Janet Margolin, Powers Boothe, Bo Hopkins, Joseph Campanella; *D:* Richard Michaels. **VHS, Beta** *TLF* ♫♫

Pocatello Kid Maynard stretches in a dual role as the wrongly convicted Kid and the Kid's no-good sheriff brother.
1931 60m/B Ken Maynard. **VHS, Beta** $19.95 *NOS, VCN, VDM* ♫ ½

Pocket Money Down-on-their-luck cowpokes foolishly do business with crooked rancher in attempt to make comeback in faltering acting careers. Star-powered, moderately entertaining modern western-comedy based on the novel ''Jim Kane'' by J.K.S. Brown.
1972 (PG) 100m/C Paul Newman, Lee Marvin, Strother Martin, Christine Belford, Wayne Rogers, Hector Elizondo, Gregory Sierra; *D:* Stuart Rosenberg. **VHS, Beta** $59.95 *WAR, FCT* ♫♫

Pocketful of Miracles Capra's final film, a remake of his 1933 ''Lady for a Day,'' is just as corny and sentimental but doesn't work quite as well. Davis is delightful as Apple Annie, a down-on-her-luck street vendor who will go to any extreme to hide her poverty from the well-married daughter she adores. Ford is terrific as the man who transforms Annie into a lady in time for her daughter's visit. Touching. Maybe too touching. Also marks Ann-Margret's film debut.
1961 136m/C Bette Davis, Glenn Ford, Peter Falk, Hope Lange, Arthur O'Connell, Ann-Margret, Thomas Mitchell, Jack Elam, Edward Everett Horton, David Brian, Mickey Shaughnessy; *D:* Frank Capra. Academy Awards '61 Nominations: Best Costume Design (Color), Best Song (''Pocketful of Miracles''), Best Supporting Actor (Falk); Golden Globe Awards '62: Best Actor—Musical/Comedy (Ford). **VHS, Beta, LV** $19.98 *MGM, FOX, CCB* ♫♫½

A Pocketful of Rye Based on Agatha Christie's novel featuring the sleuthing Miss Marple. She faces another murderous puzzle, this one based on an old nursery rhyme. Made for British television.
1987 101m/C *GB* Joan Hickson; *D:* Guy Slater; *W:* Agatha Christie. **VHS, Beta** $29.98 *FOX, HMV* ♫♫

Poco The story of Poco, a shaggy little dog who travels across the country to search for the young girl who owns him.
1977 88m/C Chill Wills, Michelle Ashburn, John Steadman. **VHS, Beta** $69.98 *LIV, VES* ♫

Poetic Justice Justice (Jackson in her big screen debut, for better or worse) gives up plans for college to follow a career in cosmetology when her boyfriend is brutally murdered. She copes with her loss by dedicating herself to poetry writing (provided by no less than poet Maya Angelou) and meets postal worker Shakur. Singleton's second directorial effort is about the girlz n the hood and boasts a lighter script (well, it is about a hairdresser) focusing less on the Boyz-style morality and more on the trials and tribulations of Jackson's Justice. Production stopped on the South Central L.A. set during the '92 riots, but the aftermath provided poignant pictures for later scenes.
1993 (R) ?m/C Janet Jackson, Tupac Shakur, Tyra Ferrell, Regina King, Joe Torry; *D:* John Singleton; *W:* John Singleton; *M:* Stanley Clarke. **VHS** *NYR* ♫♫½

Pogo for President: "I Go Pogo" Animated adventure with Walt Kelly's Pogo Possum becoming an unlikely presidential candidate when Howland Owl proclaims him the winner of a election.
1984 (PG) 120m/C *V:* Jonathan Winters, Vincent Price, Ruth Buzzi, Stan Freberg, Jimmy Breslin. **VHS, Beta** $49.95 *DIS, WTA* ♫♫½

Poil de Carotte A semi-famous French melodrama about a young boy harassed by his overbearing mother to the point of disaster, redeemed finally by the love of his father. In French with English subtitles. *AKA:* The Red Head.
1931 90m/B *FR* Harry Baur, Robert Lynen, Catherine Fontenoy; *D:* Julien Duvivier. **VHS, Beta** $24.95 *NOS, FCT, MRV* ♫♫

The Point Charming and sincere made-for-television animated feature about the rejection and isolation of a round-headed child in a world of pointy-headed people. Excellent score written and performed by Harry Nilsson.
1971 74m/C *D:* Fred Wolf. **VHS, Beta, LV** $14.98 *FHE, VES, WTA* ♫♫½

Point Blank Adapted from Stark's ''The Hunter.'' The film's techniques are sometimes compared to those of Resnais and Godard. Double-crossed and believed dead, gangster Marvin returns to claim his share of the loot from the Organization. Hard-nosed examination of the depersonalization of a mechanized urban world.
1967 92m/C Lee Marvin, Angie Dickinson, Keenan Wynn, Carroll O'Connor, Lloyd Bochner, Michael Strong; *D:* John Boorman. **VHS, Beta** $79.95 *MGM* ♫♫½

Point Break If you can suspend your disbelief—and you'd need a crane—then this crime adventure is just dandy. Reeves plays a young undercover FBI kid sent to infiltrate a gang of bank-robbing surfer dudes. Swayze is the leader of the beach subculture, a thrillseeker who plays cat-and-mouse with the feds in a series of excellent action scenes.
1991 (R) 117m/C Patrick Swayze, Keanu Reeves, Gary Busey, Lori Petty, John C. McGinley, Chris Pederson, Bojesse Christopher, Julian Reyes, Daniel Beer; *D:* Kathryn Bigelow. **VHS, LV** $19.98 *FXV* ♫♫½

Point of No Return Fonda plays Maggie, a drugged-out loser condemned to death for her part in a murder spree. She's given a reprieve if she agrees to work as a government assassin. Her supervisor Bob (Byrne) takes a personal interest in her training which Maggie successfully completes. Relocated to Venice, California, she lets herself care for a scruffy photographer (Mulroney) and after several assignments, Maggie decides she wants out. But when a killing goes awry Victor the Cleaner (the creepy Keitel) is sent to take care of things, including Maggie—permanently. Fonda displays a certain perkiness as the assassin and Is better in her early surly scenes. Flashy, exacting, but ultimately innocuous remake of the 1990 French thriller ''La Femme Nikita.''
1993 (R) 108m/C Bridget Fonda, Gabriel Byrne, Dermot Mulroney, Miguel Ferrer, Anne Bancroft, Olivia D'Abo, Harvey Keitel; *D:* John Badham; *W:* Robert Getchell, Alexandra Seros; *M:* Hans Zimmer. **VHS** *NYR* ♫♫½

Point of Terror A handsome rock singer seduces a record company executive's wife in order to further his career.
1971 (R) 88m/C Peter Carpenter, Dyanne Thorne, Lory Hansen, Leslie Simms; *D:* Alex Nicol. **VHS, Beta** $39.95 *UHV* ♫

The Pointsman A quirky, small film based on the novel by Jean Paul Franssens. A beautiful Scandinavian woman accidentally gets off a train in Northern Scotland, where the only shelter is a small railway outpost, and the only company is a mysterious pointsman who lives by the comings and goings of the trains. The couple's increasing isolation as winter falls and their lack of a common language persists is portrayed with both humor and poignancy. *AKA:* De Wisselwachter.
1986 (R) 95m/C *NL* Jim Van Der Woude, Stephane Excoffier, John Kraaykamp, Josse De Pauw, Ton Van Dort; *D:* Jos Stelling. **VHS, Beta, LV** $79.98 *LIV, VES* ♫♫½

Poison A controversial, compelling drama weaving the story of a seven year-old boy's murder of his father with two other tales of obsessive, fringe behavior. From the director of the underground hit ''Superstar: The Karen Carpenter Story,'' which was shot using only a cast of ''Barbie'' dolls.
1991 (R) 85m/C Edith Meeks, Larry Maxwell, Susan Norman, Scott Renderer, James Lyons; *D:* Todd Haynes. **VHS** $89.95 *FXL, TAM* ♫♫♫

Poison Ivy A routine, made for television comedy about a chaotic and lusty summer camp.
1985 97m/C Michael J. Fox, Nancy McKeon, Robert Klein, Caren Kaye; *D:* Larry Elikann. **VHS, Beta** $69.95 *RCA* ♫♫

Poison Ivy Barrymore is right on target as a junior femme fatale in this trashy tale of a wayward teenager and her takeover of her best friend's family. Ivy has no discernable family life and quickly attaches herself to the lonely, neglected Cooper (Gilbert). Cooper's father (Skerritt) is a preoccupied television executive and her mother (Ladd) is bedridden and dying of emphysema. Cooper lets Ivy move into her home and watches as she systematically seduces both her mother (emotionally) and her father (physically). But when Ivy's homewrecking turns lethal, Cooper must fight her ''friend'' to save herself. Glossy, over-done pulp. An unrated version is also available.
1992 (R) 91m/C Drew Barrymore, Sara Gilbert, Tom Skerritt, Cheryl Ladd; *W/D:* Katt Shea Ruben; *W:* Andy Ruben. **VHS** *COL, NLC, PMS* ♫♫

Poker Alice A lively Western starring Elizabeth Taylor as a sometime gambler who wins a brothel in a poker game.

1987 100m/C Elizabeth Taylor, George Hamilton, Tom Skerritt, Richard Mulligan, David Wayne, Susan Tyrrell, Pat Corley; **D:** Arthur Seidelman; **W:** James Lee Barrett. VHS, Beta $19.95 STE, NWV ✓✓

Police French police drama with the intense Depardieu as a cop hunting an Algerian drug boss. Matters grow complicated when he falls for the elusive crook's girlfriend. Sometimes gripping, but uneven; the actors were encouraged to improvise. Inspired by the novel ''Bodies Are Dust'' by P.J. Wolfson. In French with English subtitles.
1985 113m/C **FR** Gerard Depardieu, Sophie Marceau, Sandrine Bonnaire; **D:** Maurice Pialat; **W:** Catherine Breillat. VHS $79.95 NYF, FCT, TAM ✓✓½

Police Academy In an attempt to recruit more cops, a big-city police department does away with all its job standards. The producers probably didn't know that they were introducing bad comedy's answer to the ''Friday the 13th'' series, but it's hard to avoid heaping the sins of its successors on this film. Besides, it's just plain dumb.
1984 (R) 96m/C Steve Guttenberg, Kim Cattrall, Bubba Smith, George Gaynes, Michael Winslow, Leslie Easterbrook, Georgina Spelvin, Debralee Scott; **D:** Hugh Wilson. VHS, Beta, LV, 8mm $19.98 WAR ✓½

Police Academy 2: Their First Assignment More predictable idiocy from the cop shop. This time they're determined to rid the precinct of some troublesome punks. No real story to speak of, just more high jinks in this mindless sequel.
1985 (PG-13) 87m/C Steve Guttenberg, Bubba Smith, Michael Winslow, Art Metrano, Colleen Camp, Howard Hesseman, David Graf, George Gaynes; **D:** Jerry Paris. VHS, Beta, LV $19.98 WAR ✓

Police Academy 3: Back in Training In yet another sequel, the bumbling cops find their alma mater is threatened by a budget crunch and they must compete with a rival academy to see which school survives. The ''return to school'' plot allowed the filmmakers to add new characters to replace those who had some scruples about picking up yet another ''Police Lobotomy'' check. Followed by three more sequels.
1986 (PG) 84m/C Steve Guttenberg, Bubba Smith, David Graf, Michael Winslow, Marion Ramsey, Art Metrano, Bob Goldthwait, Leslie Easterbrook, Tim Kazurinsky, George Gaynes, Shawn Weatherly; **D:** Jerry Paris. VHS, Beta, LV $19.98 WAR ✓

Police Academy 4: Citizens on Patrol The comic cop cutups from the first three films aid a citizen's patrol group in their unnamed, but still wacky, hometown. Moronic high jinks ensue. Fourth in the series of five (or is it six?) that began with ''Police Academy''.
1987 (PG) 88m/C Steve Guttenberg, Bubba Smith, Michael Winslow, David Graf, Tim Kazurinsky, George Gaynes, Colleen Camp, Bob Goldthwait, Sharon Stone; **D:** Jim Drake. VHS, Beta, LV $19.98 WAR ✓

Police Academy 5: Assignment Miami Beach The fourth sequel, wherein the misfits-with-badges go to Miami and bumble about in the usual manner. It's about time these cops were retired from the force.
1988 (PG) 89m/C Bubba Smith, David Graf, Michael Winslow, Leslie Easterbrook, Rene Auberjonois, Marion Ramsey, Janet Jones, George Gaynes, Matt McCoy; **D:** Alan Myerson. VHS, Beta, LV $19.98 WAR Woof!

Police Academy 6: City Under Siege In what is hoped to be the last in a series of bad comedies, the distinguished graduates pursue three goofballs responsible for a crime wave.
1989 (PG) 85m/C Bubba Smith, David Graf, Michael Winslow, Leslie Easterbrook, Marion Ramsey, Matt McCoy, Bruce Mahler, G.W. Bailey, George Gaynes; **D:** Peter Bonerz. VHS, LV $89.95 WAR ✓

Police Court The son of a faded, alcoholic screen star tries to bring the old fellow back to prominence.
1937 62m/B Nat Barry, Henry B. Walthall, Leon Janney. VHS, Beta, LV NO ✓✓

Police Squad! Help Wanted! Three episodes from the brilliant, short-lived television spoof, with the patented pun-a-second style of humor typical of the makers of ''Airplane!'' and ''The Naked Gun,'' which was based on this show. Episodes included: ''A Substantial Gift,'' ''Ring of Fear,'' and ''Rendezvous at Big Gulch.'' See also ''More! Police Squad.''
1982 75m/C Leslie Nielsen, Alan North, Ed Williams, William Duell; **W/D:** Jerry Zucker, David Zucker, Jim Abrahams. VHS, Beta, LV $19.95 PAR ✓✓

Policewoman Centerfold Exploitative rendering based on the true story of a cop who posed for a pornographic magazine. Anderson is appealing in the lead.
1983 100m/C Melody Anderson, Ed Marinaro, Donna Pescow, Bert Remsen, David Spielberg; **D:** Reza Badiyi. VHS, Beta $39.95 IVE ✓

Policewomen Female undercover agent must stop a ring of gold smugglers.
1973 (R) 99m/C Sondra Currie, Tony Young, Phil Hoover, Elizabeth Stuart, Jeanne Bell; **D:** Lee Frost. VHS, Beta $59.95 VID ✓½

A Polish Vampire in Burbank A shy vampire in Burbank tries again and again to find blood and love. Wacky.
1980 84m/C Mark Pirro, Lori Sutton, Eddie Deezen; **D:** Mark Pirro. VHS, Beta $9.95 NO ✓✓

Pollyanna A young orphan girl is adopted by her cold, embittered aunt and does her best to bring joy and gladness to all the new people she meets. Silent with music score.
1920 60m/B Mary Pickford. VHS, Beta, LV $19.95 CCB ✓✓½

Pollyanna Based on the Eleanor Porter story about an enchanting young girl whose contagious enthusiasm and zest for life touches the hearts of all she meets. Mills is perfect in the title role and was awarded a special Oscar for outstanding juvenile performance. A distinguished supporting cast is the icing on the cake in this delightful Disney confection. Original version was filmed in 1920 with Mary Pickford.
1960 134m/C Hayley Mills, Jane Wyman, Richard Egan, Karl Malden, Nancy Olson, Adolphe Menjou, Donald Crisp, Agnes Moorehead, Kevin Corcoran; **D:** David Swift. VHS, Beta, LV $19.99 DIS ✓✓✓½

Poltergeist He's listed only as co-writer and co-producer, but this production has Stephen Spielberg written all over it. A young family's home becomes a house of horrors when they are terrorized by menacing spirits who abduct their five-year-old daughter...through the TV screen! Roller-coaster thrills and chills, dazzling special effects, and perfectly timed humor highlight this stupendously scary ghost story.
1982 (PG) 114m/C JoBeth Williams, Craig T. Nelson, Beatrice Straight, Heather O'Rourke, Zelda Rubinstein, Dominique Dunne, Oliver Robbins, Richard Lawson, James Karen; **D:**

Tobe Hooper; **M:** Jerry Goldsmith. VHS, Beta, LV $19.95 MGM ✓✓✓✓

Poltergeist 2: The Other Side Adequate sequel to the Spielburg-produced venture into the supernatural, where demons follow the Freeling family in their efforts to recapture the clairvoyant young daughter Carol Anne. The film includes sojourns into Indian lore and a four-foot high agave worm designed by H.R. Giger. The movie was followed by ''Poltergeist 3'' in 1988.
1986 (PG-13) 92m/C Craig T. Nelson, JoBeth Williams, Heather O'Rourke, Will Sampson, Julian Beck, Geraldine Fitzgerald, Oliver Robbins, Zelda Rubenstein; **D:** Brian Gibson; **M:** Jerry Goldsmith. VHS, Beta, LV $19.95 MGM, PIA ✓✓½

Poltergeist 3 Wrestling with the supernatural has finally unnerved Carol Ann and she's sent to stay with her aunt and uncle in Chicago where she attends a school for gifted children with emotional disorders. Guess who follows her? Uninspired acting, threadbare premise, and one ghastly encounter too many. Oddly, O'Rourke died suddenly four months before the film's release.
1988 (PG-13) 97m/C Tom Skerritt, Nancy Allen, Heather O'Rourke, Lara Flynn Boyle, Zelda Rubinstein; **D:** Gary Sherman. VHS, Beta, LV $19.95 MGM, PIA ✓½

Polyester Amusing satire on middle-class life, described by John Waters as '''Father Knows Best' gone berserk.'' A forlorn housewife (Divine) pines away for the man of her dreams while the rest of her life is falling apart at the seams. Written, produced, and directed by Waters, the movie was filmed in ''Odorama,'' a hilarious gimmick in which theatre goers were provided with scratch-n-sniff cards, containing specific scents corresponding to key scenes. Video watchers will have to use their imagination in experiencing smells ranging from air-freshener to intestinal gas. The first of John Waters' more mainstream films. Features songs by Bill Murray and Debbie Harry.
1981 (R) 86m/C Divine, Tab Hunter, Edith Massey, Mink Stole, Stiv Bators, David Samson, Mary Garlington, Kenneth King, Joni-Ruth White; **D:** John Waters. VHS, Beta $19.95 COL, HBO ✓✓½

Pom Pom Girls High school seniors, intent on having one last fling before graduating, get involved in crazy antics, clumsy romances, and football rivalries.
1976 (R) 90m/C Robert Carradine, Jennifer Ashley, Michael Mullins, Cheryl ''Rainbeaux'' Smith, Dianne Lee Hart, Lisa Reeves, Bill Adler; **D:** Joseph Ruben. VHS, Beta $9.99 STE, UHV ✓

Pony Express Buffalo Bill Cody and Wild Bill Hickok join forces to extend the Pony Express mail route west to California through rain and sleet, snow and hail. Far from a factual account but good for extending the myth of the Old West.
1953 101m/C Charlton Heston, Rhonda Fleming, Jan Sterling, Forrest Tucker; **D:** Jerry Hopper. VHS, Beta $14.95 PAR, KRT, HHE ✓✓✓

Pony Express Rider Young man with a mission joins up with the Pony Express hoping to bag the male responsible for killing his pa. The well-produced script boasts a bevy of veteran western character actors, all lending, solid, rugged performances.
1976 (G) 100m/C Stewart Peterson, Henry Wilcoxon, Buck Taylor, Maureen McCormick, Joan Caulfield, Ken Curtis, Slim Pickens, Dub Taylor, Jack Elam; **D:** Robert Totten. VHS TPI ✓✓✓

Pool Hustlers A romantic comedy about an amateur billiards whiz who finds love and successfully defeats the national champ. In Italian with English subtitles.
1983 101m/C IT Francesco Nuti, Guiliana de Sio, Marcello Loti; *D:* Maurizio Ponzi. VHS, Beta $24.95 *XVC, MED, TAM* ✍½

Pool Sharks W.C. Fields' first film features the comedian's antics while playing a pool game to win the love of a woman. Silent.
1915 10m/B W.C. Fields. VHS, Beta *FLI* ✍✍½

Poor Girl, A Ghost Story A young girl takes a job as a governess at an English mansion and is besieged by all manner of strange goings-on.
1974 52m/C AU Lynn Miller, Angela Thorne; *D:* Michael Apted. VHS, Beta $59.95 *PSM* ✍

A Poor Little Rich Girl Mary Pickford received raves in this film, in which she portrayed Gwendolyn, with everything money could buy, except the attention of her family. Gwendolyn has a bizarre dream in which she sees a number of horrors and is tempted by death. Elaborate sets and special effects, as well as Pickford's delicate performance, madke this one special. Organ score.
1917 64m/B Mary Pickford, Madeline Traverse, Charles Wellesley, Gladys Fairbanks; *D:* Maurice Tourneur. VHS, Beta $19.98 *CCB, VYY* ✍✍✍

The Poor Little Rich Girl A motherless rich girl wanders away from home and is "adopted" by a pair of struggling vaudevillians. With her help, they rise to the big time. Also available with "Heidi" on laserdisc. ♫Oh My Goodness; Buy a Bar of Barry's; Wash Your Neck With a Cake of Peck's; Military Man; When I'm with You; But Definitely; You've Gotta Eat Your Spinach, Baby.
1936 79m/B Shirley Temple, Jack Haley, Alice Faye, Gloria Stuart, Michael Whalen, Sara Haden, Jane Darwell; *D:* Irving Cummings. VHS, Beta $19.95 *FOX* ✍✍½

Poor Little Rich Girl: The Barbara Hutton Story Bio-drama of the one-time richest woman in America, Woolworth heiress Hutton (Fawcett), and her extravagant lifestyle. She married seven times (including actor Cary Grant) until falling into self-destructive alcohol and drug addictions. Lavishly presented but superficial. Based on the book by C. David Heymann. Originally a two-part television movie.
1987 98m/C Farrah Fawcett, Bruce Davison, Kevin McCarthy, Burl Ives, James Read, Stephane Audran, Anne Francis, David Ackroyd, Tony Peck, Zoe Wanamaker; *D:* Charles Jarrott; *W:* Dennis Turner; *M:* Richard Rodney Bennett. VHS $59.98 *LIV* ✍✍½

Poor Pretty Eddie A young black singer gets waylaid and taken in by a twisted white Southern clan. An incredibly sleazy movie which boasts Shelly Winters performing a strip act. Also on video as "Black Vengeance," "Redneck County," and "Heartbreak Motel."
1973 (R) 90m/C Leslie Uggams, Shelley Winters, Michael Christian, Ted Cassidy, Slim Pickens, Dub Taylor; *D:* Richard Robinson. Beta *VID, MRV* ✍½

Poor White Trash An architect arrives in bayou country with plans to design a new building. He meets with resistance from the locals but falls for the sensual daughter of one of his staunchest detractors. *AKA:* Bayou.
1957 83m/B Peter Graves, Lita Milan, Douglas Fowley, Timothy Carey, Jonathan Haze; *D:* Harold Daniels. VHS, Beta *NO* ✍½

Poor White Trash 2 A young couple, vacationing in Louisiana's bayou country, are introduced to an unusual brand of southern hospitality by the eponymous group of locals. *AKA:* Scum of the Earth.
1975 (R) 90m/C Gene Ross, Ann Stafford, Norma Moore, Camilla Carr; *D:* S.F. Brownrigg. VHS, Beta *NO* ✍

Pop Always Pays A father gets in a jam when he has to make good on a bet with his daughter's boyfriend.
1940 67m/B Walter Catlett, Dennis O'Keefe, Leon Errol, Adele Pearce; *D:* Leslie Goodwins. VHS, Beta *RKO, MLB* ✍✍

Pop Goes the Cork Three films by the man Chaplin referred to as his "professor," Max Linder: "Be My Wife," "Seven Years Bad Luck," and "The Three Must-Get-Theres." Linder was the foremost film comedian in early twentieth-century France, and made these three films during a stay in America.
1922 87m/B Max Linder. VHS, Beta *CCB* ✍✍

Popcorn A killer stalks a movie audience who is unaware that his crimes are paralleling those in the very film they are watching.
1989 (R) 93m/C Jill Schoelen, Tom Villard, Dee Wallace Stone, Derek Rydell, Elliott Hurst, Kelly Jo Minter, Malcolm Danare, Ray Walston, Tony Roberts; *D:* Mark Herrier. VHS, LV, 8mm $89.95 *COL* ✍✍

Pope John Paul II A made-for-television biography of the Pontiff, from childhood to world eminence.
1984 150m/C Albert Finney, Michael Crompton, Nigel Hawthorne, John McEnery, Brian Cox; *D:* Herbert Wise. VHS, Beta $19.98 *PSM, IGP* ✍✍

The Pope Must Diet Coltrane stars as a misfit who accidentally becomes Pope Dave I. Living up to the benevolence suggested by his title, Pope Dave proposes to use Vatican money to create a children's fund. But there are those in the organization who have different, less noble plans for the cash, and soon Dave finds himself the target of a mob hit. Frantic comedy caused a stir with its original title "The Pope Must Die," with many newspapers refusing to run ads for the film. This, coupled with lukewarm critical reviews, led to a very brief stint at the box office. *AKA:* The Pope Must Die.
1991 (R) 87m/C GB Robbie Coltrane, Alex Rocco, Beverly D'Angelo, Herbert Lom, Paul Bartel, Salvatore Cascio, Balthazar Getty; *D:* Peter Richardson. VHS, Beta, LV $92.98 *MED* ✍½

The Pope of Greenwich Village A film about two Italian-American cousins who struggle to escape the trap of poverty in New York's Greenwich Village. When a small crime goes wrong in a big way, the two must learn about deception and loyalty. Mostly character study; Page is exceptional. Inferior re-run of the "Mean Streets" idea.
1984 (R) 122m/C Eric Roberts, Mickey Rourke, Daryl Hannah, Geraldine Page, Tony Musante, M. Emmet Walsh, Kenneth McMillan, Burt Young; *D:* Stuart Rosenberg. VHS, Beta, LV $19.98 *CCB, MGM* ✍✍½

Popeye The cartoon sailor brought to life is on a search to find his long-lost father. Along the way, he meets Olive Oyl and adopts little Sweet Pea. Script by Jules Feiffer, music by Harry Nilsson. Williams accomplishes the near-impossible feat of physically resembling the title character, and the whole movie does accomplish the maker's stated goal of "looking like a comic strip," but it isn't anywhere near as funny as it should be.
1980 (PG) 114m/C Robin Williams, Shelley Duvall, Ray Walston, Paul Dooley, Bill Irwin, Paul Smith, Linda Hunt, Richard Libertini; *D:* Robert Altman. VHS, Beta, LV $14.95 *PAR* ✍✍

Popeye and Friends in Outer Space Popeye and Olive Oyl take their act into the ozone and beyond. As always, they get into big trouble with their arch enemy, Bluto. Luckily for Popeye and all concerned, cans of spinach are not as rare in outer space as Halley's Comet.
19?? 60m/C VHS, Beta $9.95 *MED* ✍✍

Popeye and Friends in the South Seas Join Popeye, Olive Oyl, Wimpy and Sweet Pea as they embark on a series of comedic adventures.
1961 59m/C V: Jack Mercer, Jackson Beck, Mae Questel, Arnold Stang. VHS, Beta $29.95 *MED* ✍✍

Popeye and Friends in the Wild West The famous spinach eating sailor is back in ten gallon hat and spurs for uproarious western adventures. Also included in this cartoon collection are Krazy Kat, Beetle Bailey and Snuffy Smith.
1984 60m/C VHS, Beta $29.95 *MED* ✍✍

Popeye Assorted Cartoons Cartoon antics featuring Popeye the spinach-loving sailor man.
1989 30m/C VHS *NO* ✍✍

Popeye Cartoons Spinach-gobbling sailor is back in three favorite adventures: "Popeye the Sailor Meets Sinbad the Sailor," "Aladdin and His Wonderful Lamp," and "Popeye the Sailor Meets Ali Baba's Forty Thieves."
1936 56m/C VHS, LV $29.99 *REP* ✍✍

Popeye Color Festival Popeye meets up with Sinbad the Sailor, Ali Baba, and Aladdin in this collection of vintage cartoons from the '30s.
193? 56m/C VHS, Beta $19.95 *NO* ✍✍

Popeye Parade Contains three early episodes of the Popeye animated series including "Popeye Meets Sinbad," "Popeye Meets Aladdin" and "Popeye Meets Ali Baba."
1935 60m/C Popeye. VHS, Beta $19.95 *MVC* ✍✍

Popeye the Sailor Cartoon package includes "Popeye Meets Aladdin and His Wonderful Lamp," "Popeye Meets Ali Baba and His 40 Thieves," and "Popeye the Sailor Meets Sinbad the Sailor."
193? 54m/C VHS, Beta, 8mm *VYY, WFV, BTV* ✍✍

Popeye: Travelin' on About Travel Popeye and Olive Oyl visit foreign and exotic lands in this hilarious program.
1984 60m/C VHS, Beta $29.95 *MED* ✍✍

Popi Arkin is the heart and soul of this poignant charmer in his role as a Puerto Rican immigrant hell-bent on securing a better life outside the ghetto for his two sons. His zany efforts culminate in one outrageous scheme to set them adrift off the Florida coast in hopes they will be rescued and raised by a wealthy family. Far fetched, but ultimately heartwarming.
1969 (G) 115m/C Alan Arkin, Rita Moreno, Miguel Alejandro, Ruben Figueroa; *D:* Arthur Hiller. VHS, Beta *NO* ✍✍✍

The Poppy is also a Flower A star-laden, antidrug drama produced by the United Nations. Filmed on location in Iran, Monaco, and Italy. Based on a drug trade thriller by Ian Fleming that explains how poppies, converted into heroin, are brought into the United States. Made for television.

AKA: Poppies Are Also Flowers; Opium Connection.
1966 (PG) 100m/C E.G. Marshall, Trevor Howard, Gilbert Roland, Eli Wallach, Marcello Mastroianni, Angie Dickinson, Rita Hayworth, Yul Brynner, Trini Lopez, Bessie Love; **D:** Terence Young. **VHS, Beta** $9.95 *SIM ℐℐ½*

Pork Chop Hill A powerful, hard-hitting account of the last hours of the Korean War. Peck is totally believable as the man ordered to hold his ground against the hopeless onslaught of Chinese Communist hordes. A chilling, stark look in the face of a no-win situation. Top notch cast and masterful directing.
1959 97m/B Gregory Peck, Harry Guardino, Rip Torn, George Peppard, James Edwards, Bob Steele, Woody Strode, Robert (Bobby) Blake, Martin Landau, Norman Fell, Bert Remsen; **D:** Lewis Milestone. **VHS, Beta, LV** $59.95 *MGM ℐℐℐ*

Porky Pig and Company Seven vintage 'toons featuring Porky, Daffy and Hubie & Bertie: ''Old Glory,'' ''Tom Turk and Daffy,'' ''House Menace,'' ''The Aristo Cat,'' ''Wagon Wheels'' and ''Roughly Speaking.''
1948 60m/C D: Friz Freleng, Friz Freleng, Chuck Jones, Robert McKimson. **VHS, Beta** $14.95 *MGM, WTA ℐℐℐ*

Porky Pig and Daffy Duck Cartoon Festival Eight classic Daffy and Porky shorts, including ''Tick Tock Tuckered,'' ''Duck Soup to Nuts,'' and ''Baby Bottleneck.''
1944 57m/C D: Chuck Jones, Bob Clampett, Robert McKimson. **VHS, Beta** $19.95 *MGM ℐℐℐ*

Porky Pig Cartoon Festival Porky is highlighted in this retrospective of his early career.
1945 36m/C D: Robert McKimson, Friz Freleng. **VHS, Beta** $14.95 *MGM ℐℐℐ*

Porky Pig Cartoon Festival: Tom Turk and Daffy Duck Five vintage Porky shorts, including ''Old Glory,'' ''My Favorite Duck'' and the title cartoon are featured.
1944 38m/C D: Robert McKimson, Friz Freleng. **VHS, Beta** $14.95 *MGM ℐℐℐ*

Porky Pig Tales Six fabulous cartoons featuring that bumbling yet charming porker. You'll l-l-l-love it!
1989 45m/C V: Mel Blanc. **VHS** $14.95 *WAR, WTA ℐℐℐ*

Porky Pig's Screwball Comedies This compilation of Porky Pig's classic cartoons includes ''You Ought to Be in Pictures,'' ''Boobs in the Woods,'' and ''Wearing of the Grim.''
1952 59m/C D: Chuck Jones, Robert McKimson, Friz Freleng. **VHS, Beta** $12.95 *WAR, WTA ℐℐℐ*

Porky's Investigation of teen horniness set in South Florida during the fab '50s. Irreverent comedy follows the misadventures of six youths imprisoned in Angel Beach High School who share a common interest: girls. Their main barrier to sexual success: the no-touch babes they lust after and the incredibly stupid adults who run the world. Fairly dumb and tasteless with occasional big laughs that earned mega bucks at the drive-in and created perceived popular outcry for more porky: ''Porky's II: The Next Day'' (1983) and ''Porky's Revenge'' (1985).
1982 (R) 94m/C CA Dan Monahan, Wyatt Knight, Scott Colomby, Tony Ganios, Mark Herrier, Cyril O'Reilly, Roger Wilson, Bob Clark, Kim Cattrall, Kaki Hunter; **D:** Bob Clark. **VHS, Beta, LV** $14.98 *FXV, FOX ℐℐ½*

Porky's 2: The Next Day More tame tomfoolery about teenage sex drives, Shakespeare, fat high school teachers, the Ku Klux Klan, and streaking in the Florida high school where it all began. Outright caricature shares the stage with juvenile humor, some of which may induce laughter.
1983 (R) 100m/C CA Bill Wiley, Dan Monahan, Wyatt Knight, Cyril O'Reilly, Roger Wilson, Tony Ganios, Mark Herrier, Scott Colomby. **VHS, Beta, LV** $29.95 *FOX ℐℐ*

Porky's Revenge The Angel Beach High School students are out to get revenge against Porky who orders the school basketball coach to throw the championship game. The second of the ''Porky's'' sequels.
1985 (R) 95m/C CA Dan Monahan, Wyatt Knight, Tony Ganios, Nancy Parsons, Chuck ''Porky'' Mitchell, Kaki Hunter, Kimberly Evenson, Scott Colomby; **D:** James Komack. **VHS, Beta, LV** $29.98 *FOX ℐ*

The Pornographers Bizzare, black comedy focuses on a part-time porno filmmaker lusting after the daughter of the widow he lives with and trying to cope with his family, the world, and himself. A perversely fascinating exploration of contemporary Japenses society and the many facets of sexual emotion. In Japanese with English subtitles.
1966 128m/B JP Shoichi Ozawa, Massaomi Konda, Sumiko Sakamota, Haruo Tanaka, Keiko Sagowa; **D:** Shohei Imamura. **VHS** $29.95 *CVC, TAM ℐℐℐ*

Porridge A British comedy inspired by the popular BBC situation comedy of the title, about a habitual criminal and convict who makes the most of his time in prison. **AKA:** Doing Time.
1991 105m/C GB Ronnie Barker, Fulton Mackay, Peter Vaughan, Julian Holloway, Geoffrey Bayldon; **D:** Dick Clement. **VHS** $29.95 *BFS ℐℐ*

Port Arthur A sweeping Japanese film describing the Russo-Japanese Wars in the early 1900's.
1983 140m/C JP **VHS, Beta** $69.95 *VCD ℐℐ½*

Port of Call Early Bergman drama about a seaman on the docks who falls for a troubled woman whose wild, unhappy past has earned her an unsavory reputation. The hopeful, upbeat tone seems incongruous with the grim harbor/slum setting. It's minor Bergman but the seeds of his trademark themes can be seen taking shape, making it a must-see for avid fans. In Swedish with English subtitles.
1948 100m/B SW Ivine-Christine Jonsson, Bengt Eklund, Erik Hell, Berta Hall, Mimi Nelson; **D:** Ingmar Bergman. **VHS, Beta** $29.98 *SUE, TAM, NLC ℐℐℐ*

The Port of Missing Girls A young woman implicated in a murder stows away on a freighter. There she becomes caught up in a waterfront world of pirates, smugglers and other assorted undesirables.
1938 56m/B Harry Carey Sr., Judith Allen, Milburn Stone, Betty Compson; **D:** Karl Brown. **VHS, Beta, 8mm** $24.95 *VYY ℐ*

Port of New York A narcotics gang is smuggling large quantities of drugs into New York. A government agent poses as a gang member in order to infiltrate the mob and get the goods on them. Brynner's film debut.
1949 82m/B Scott Brady, Yul Brynner, K.T. Stevens; **D:** Laslo Benedek. **VHS, Beta** $19.95 *NOS, VYY, DVT ℐℐ*

Portfolio Real-life models star in this gritty drama about rising to the top of the fashion heap. Music by Eurythmics, Fun Boy Three and others.

1988 (R) 83m/C Paulina Porizkova, Julie Wolfe, Carol Alt, Kelly Emberg. **VHS, LV** $79.95 *SVS ℐℐ*

Portnoy's Complaint Limp screen adaptation of Philip Roth's novel follows the frustrating experiences of a sexually obsessed young man as he relates them to his psychiatrist.
1972 (R) 101m/C Richard Benjamin, Karen Black, Lee Grant, Jeannie Berlin, Jill Clayburgh; **D:** Ernest Lehman. **VHS, Beta** $19.98 *WAR ℐ½*

The Portrait Longtime real-life friends Bacall and Peck on-screen together for the first time in 37 years prove they are still shining stars as they play aging parents to Peck's real-life daughter, Cecilia Peck. The younger Peck is an artist preparing for a exhibition and asks her parents to sit for a portrait. This is the pole around which their relationships and reconciliations swing in this emotional made-for-cable-tv drama based loosely on Tina Howe's 1983 off-Broadway play, ''Painting Churches.''
1993 89m/C Lauren Bacall, Gregory Peck, Cecilia Peck, Paul McCrane, Joyce O'Connor, Donna Mitchell, Mitchell Laurance, William Prince, Augusta Dabney; **D:** Arthur Penn; **W:** Lynn Roth. **VHS, LV** $89.98 *TTC, BTV ℐℐℐ*

Portrait in Terror A master thief and a deranged artist plan a heist of a Titian painting in an oddball suspense piece. Not a great success, but atmospheric and weird.
1966 81m/B Patrick Magee, William Campbell, Anna Pavane; **D:** Jack Hill. **VHS** $20.00 *SMW ℐ½*

Portrait of a Hitman Aspiring painter leads a double life as a professional hitman. Ragged feature feels more abandoned than finished, as if most of the movie had been shot and then the money ran out. All leads turn in paycheck performances, no more. **AKA:** Jim Buck.
1977 85m/C Jack Palance, Rod Steiger, Richard Roundtree, Bo Svenson, Ann Turkel; **D:** Allan A. Buckhantz. **VHS, Beta** $49.95 *WWV ℐ*

Portrait of a Lady A spirited young American woman is taken to England and insists on complete freedom to choose her own future and make her own choices. Based on the 1881 novel by Henry James.
1967 240m/C GB Richard Chamberlain, Suzanne Neve, Edward Fox. **VHS** $59.95 *BFS, TVC ℐ*

Portrait of a Rebel: Margaret Sanger TV docudrama about the struggle of Margaret Sanger to repeal the Comstock Act of 1912, which prohibited the distribution of birth control information.
1982 96m/C Bonnie Franklin, David Dukes, Milo O'Shea; **D:** Virgil W. Vogel. **VHS, Beta** *TLF ℐℐ½*

Portrait of a Showgirl Inexperienced showgirl learns the ropes of Las Vegas life from a veteran of the Vegas stages. Made for television.
1982 100m/C Lesley Ann Warren, Rita Moreno, Tony Curtis, Dianne Kay, Howard Morris; **D:** Steven Hilliard Stern. **VHS, Beta** $59.95 *PSM ℐℐ*

Portrait of a Stripper A widowed mother works part-time as a stripper to support her son. Trouble arises when her father-in-law attempts to prove that she is an unfit mother.
1979 100m/C Lesley Ann Warren, Edward Herrmann, Vic Tayback, Sheree North; **D:** John Alonzo. **VHS, Beta** $69.95 *VES ℐ*

Portrait of a White Marriage An extended made-for-cable comedy special revamping certain old ''Mary Hartman, Mary Hartman'' and ''Fernwood 2-Night'' conventions; a moronic talk show host moves his cheap show to his hometown of Hawkins Falls in order to boost the ratings.

1988 81m/C Martin Mull, Mary Kay Place, Fred Willard, Michael McKean, Harry Shearer, Jack Riley, Conchata Ferrell; **D:** Harry Shearer. **VHS, Beta** $39.95 MCA ⚔️⚔️½

Portrait of Grandpa Doc
As a young artist prepares for his first one-man show, he struggles to complete a painting which he especially wants to have ready for the show—a portrait of his grandfather, who died seven years earlier. Well, okay.
1977 28m/C Melvyn Douglas, Bruce Davison, Barbara Rush, Anne Seymour, Keith Blanchard. **VHS, Beta** BFA, ECU ⚔️½

Portrait of Jennie
In this haunting, romantic fable, a struggling artist is inspired by and smitten with a strange and beautiful girl who also suspects may be the spirit of a dead woman. A fine cast works wonders with what could have been a forgettable story. The last reel was tinted green in the original release with the last scene shot in technicolor. Oscar-winning special effects. **AKA:** Jennie; Tidal Wave.
1948 86m/B Joseph Cotten, Jennifer Jones, Cecil Kellaway, Ethel Barrymore, David Wayne, Lillian Gish, Henry Hull, Florence Bates, Felix Bressart, Anne Francis; **D:** William Dieterle. Academy Awards '48: Best Special Effects; Nominations: Best Black and White Cinematography; Venice Film Festival '49: Best Actor (Cotten). **VHS, Beta, LV** $39.98 FOX ⚔️⚔️⚔️½

Portrait of Teresa
Havana housewife has to balance motherhood, textile job, and cultural group activities without the cooperation of her husband. Vega skillfully portrays the lingering archaic attitudes and insulting assumptions that still confront post-revolution women. A fine eye for the revealing moments and movements of everyday life. In Spanish with English subtitles.
1979 115m/C Daisy Granados, Aldolfo Llaurado, Alina Sanchez, Alberto Molina; **D:** Pastor Vega. **VHS** $69.95 NYF, FCT, TAM ⚔️⚔️⚔️

Portrait of the Artist as a Young Man
Based on Joyce's autobiographical novel. Dramatizes the childhood, school days, adolescence, and early manhood of Stephen Dedalus. Filmed in Ireland.
1978 93m/C IR T.P. McKenna, John Gielgud. **VHS, Beta** $29.95 MFV, FLI ⚔️⚔️½

Posed For Murder
A young centerfold is stalked by a psycho who wants her all for himself.
1989 (R) 90m/C Charlotte J. Helmkamp, Carl Fury, Rick Gianasi, Michael Merrins; **D:** Brian Thomas Jones. **VHS, Beta** $79.95 ACA ⚔️⚔️

The Poseidon Adventure
The cruise ship Poseidon is on its last voyage from New York to Athens on New Year's Eve when it is capsized by a tidal wave. The ten survivors struggle to escape the water-logged tomb. Oscar-winning special effects, such as Shelley Winters floating in a boiler room. Created an entirely new genre of film making—the big cast disaster flick.
1972 (PG) 117m/C Gene Hackman, Ernest Borgnine, Shelley Winters, Red Buttons, Jack Albertson, Carol Lynley; **D:** Ronald Neame; **M:** John Williams. Academy Awards '72: Best Song ("The Morning After"), Best Visual Effects; Nominations: Best Art Direction/Set Decoration, Best Cinematography, Best Costume Design, Best Film Editing, Best Sound, Best Supporting Actress (Winters), Best Original Score; Golden Globe Awards '73: Best Supporting Actress (Winters). **VHS, Beta, LV** $19.98 FOX ⚔️⚔️½

Positive I.D.
A troubled housewife learns that the man who raped her years before is getting released on parole. She devises a second persona for herself with which to entrap him and get her revenge.

1987 (R) 96m/C Stephanie Rascoe, John Davies, Steve Fromholz; **D:** Andy Anderson. **VHS, Beta** $79.95 MCA ⚔️⚔️

The Positively True Adventures of the Alleged Texas Cheerleader-Murdering Mom
Satirical melodrama about Texas housewife Wanda Holloway (Hunter), who was accused of hiring a hitman to murder the mother of her daughter's chief cheerleading rival. Ruthless and hilarious, this fact-based TV movie goes way over the top in satirizing suburban lifestyle excess and media overkill. Hunter, complete with whiney Texas twang, is perfect in her role as self-absorbed Wanda and Bridges is great as her loopy ex-brother-in-law and partner in planned homicide. "Cheerleader-Murdering Mom" is a riot compared to the usual dramatic movies served up by the networks.
1993 (R) 99m/C Holly Hunter, Beau Bridges, Swoosie Kurtz; **D:** Michael Ritchie. **VHS** HBO ⚔️⚔️⚔️

Posse
There's a hidden agenda, fueled by political ambition, in a lawman's (Douglas) dauntless pursuit of an escaped bandit (Dern). An interesting contrast between the evil of corrupt politics and the honesty of traditional lawlessness. Well performed, well photographed, and almost insightful.
1975 (PG) 94m/C Kirk Douglas, Bruce Dern, James Stacy, Bo Hopkins, Luke Askew, David Canary, Alfonso Arau, Kate Woodville, Mark Roberts; **D:** Kirk Douglas. **VHS, Beta, LV** $14.95 PAR ⚔️⚔️⚔️

Posse
Big, brawny western shot with MTV in mind that tells the tale of how blacks helped to tame the American frontier. Or, as the advertising put it, "The untold story of the wild West." Or, spaghetti western meets blaxploitation meets the magnificent seven. However categorized, intent is to show a side of Americana seldom seen, a goal realized. The five principal characters (misfits, in the usual "Dirty Dozen" tradition) are brought together during the Spanish-American War, at which time they're betrayed by a cruel and vicious cavalry officer (Zane). Led by Mario Van Peebles, the newly formed posse desert their posts as infantrymen and take off with a cache of gold to the black utopia of Freemansville, as Van Peebles looks to settle old scores. While awaiting Zane and crew, the wild bunch clash with goons intent on taking the town, since it lies on a railroad route. Woody Strode, perhaps the greatest black Western star, appears at both the beginning and ending, while several other veteran black performers appear in cameos.
1993 (R) 109m/C Mario Van Peebles, Stephen Baldwin, Charles Lane, Tiny Lister, Big Daddy Kane, Billy Zane, Blair Underwood, Melvin Van Peebles, Salli Richardson, Tone Loc, Pam Grier, Isaac Hayes; **D:** Mario Van Peebles; **W:** Sy Richardson, Dario Scardapane; **M:** Michel Colombier. **VHS** NYR ⚔️⚔️⚔️

Possessed
A poor factory girl becomes a wealthy Park Avenue sophisticate when she falls in love with a rich lawyer who wants to be governor. Not to be confused with Crawford's 1947 movie of the same name, but worth a look. Gable and Crawford make a great couple!
1931 77m/B Joan Crawford, Clark Gable, Wallace Ford, Skeets Gallagher, John Miljan; **D:** Clarence Brown. **VHS, Beta** $19.98 MGM ⚔️⚔️½

The Possessed
Crawford is at her melodramatic best as a crazed gal who can't find happiness with either hunk Heflin or bland Massey. First film for Brooks. From the story "One Man's Secret" by Rita Weiman.

1947 109m/B Joan Crawford, Van Heflin, Raymond Massey, Geraldine Brooks, Stanley Ridges, John Ridgely, Nana Bryant, Moroni Olsen; **D:** Curtis Bernhardt. **VHS, LV** $19.98 MGM ⚔️⚔️⚔️

The Possessed
Farentino is a priest who loses his faith, but regains it after an apparently fatal auto accident. Hackett is the headmistress of a private girls' school which is in need of an exorcist, since one of her student's appears to be possessed, and Farentino seems just the man for the job. Fairly tame, since originally made for TV.
1977 (PG-13) 75m/C James Farentino, Joan Hackett, Diana Scarwid, Claudette Nevins, Eugene Roche, Ann Dusenberry, Dinah Manoff, P.J. Soles; **D:** Jerry Thorpe. **VHS, Beta** $59.95 UNI ⚔️½

Possession
Returned from a long mission, a secret agent notices that his wife is acting very strangely. She's about to give birth to a manifestation of the evil within her! Gory, hysterical, over-intellectual and often unintelligible. Originally shown in a longer version in Europe.
1981 (R) 97m/C FR GE Isabelle Adjani, Sam Neill, Heinz Bennent, Margit Carstensen, Shaun Lawtor; **D:** Andrzej Zulawski. **VHS, Beta** $69.98 LIV, VES ⚔️

The Possession of Joel Delaney
Blend of occult horror and commentary on social mores works for the most part, but some viewers may be put off by the low production values and spottiness of the script. MacLaine is a wealthy divorcee who must deal with the mysterious transformations affecting her brother. Skeptical at first, she begins to suspect he is the victim of Caribbean voodoo.
1972 (R) 105m/C Shirley MacLaine, Perry King, Michael Hordern, David Elliott, Robert Burr; **D:** Waris Hussein. **VHS** $19.95 PAR ⚔️⚔️½

Possession: Until Death Do You Part
When one man's attraction for a beautiful young woman becomes an obsession, a bizarre series of inexplicable events unravels a terrifying account of passion and revenge.
1990 93m/C Monica Marko, John R. Johnston, Sharlene Martin, Cat Williamson; **D:** Michael Mazo, Lloyd A. Simandl. **VHS** $79.98 CGH ⚔️

Postal Inspector
An extraordinary tale of a postal inspector's life. Crime, romance, and natural disaster all overtake this civil servant. Catch the song "Let's Have Bluebirds On All Our Wallpaper."
1936 58m/B Carlos Cortez, Patricia Ellis, Michael Loring, Bela Lugosi, David Oliver, Wallis Clark; **D:** Otto Brower. **VHS** $16.95 SNC, LSV ⚔️⚔️

Postcards from the Edge
Fisher's best-selling novel, tamed and tempered for the big screen in a tour-de-force of talent. Streep very fine as a delightfully harried actress struggling with her career, her drug dependence, and her competitive, overwhelming show-biz mother. The script, also written by Fisher, is bitingly clever and filled with refreshingly witty dialogue. Lots of cameos by Hollywood's hippest.
1990 (R) 101m/C Meryl Streep, Shirley MacLaine, Dennis Quaid, Gene Hackman, Richard Dreyfuss, Rob Reiner, Mary Wickes, Conrad Bain, Annette Bening, Michael Ontkean, Dana Ivey; **Cameos:** Robin Bartlett, Anthony Heald, Oliver Platt, CCH Pounder; **D:** Mike Nichols; **W:** Carrie Fisher. **VHS, Beta, LV, 8mm** $19.95 COL, FCT ⚔️⚔️⚔️½

The Postman Always Rings Twice
Even without the brutal sexuality of the James M. Cain novel, Garfield and Turner sizzle as the lust-laden lovers in this lurid tale of fatal attraction. Garfield steals the show as

the streetwise drifter who blows into town and lights a fire in Turner. As their affair steams up the two conspire to do away with her husband and circumstances begin to spin out of control. Tense and compelling. A classic.
1946 113m/B Lana Turner, John Garfield, Cecil Kellaway, Hume Cronyn, Leon Ames, Audrey Totter, Alan Reed; *D:* Tay Garnett. **VHS, Beta, LV** $19.98 *MGM ♂♂♂½*

The Postman Always Rings Twice It must be true because he's ringing again in Mamet's version of James M. Cain's depression-era novel. This time Nicholson plays the drifter and Lange the amoral wife with an aged husband. Truer to the original story than the 1946 movie in its use of brutal sex scenes, it nevertheless lacks the power of the original. Nicholson works well in this time era and Lange adds depth and realism to the character of Cora. But in the end it remains dreary and easily forgettable.
1981 (R) 123m/C Jack Nicholson, Jessica Lange, John Colicos, Anjelica Huston, Michael Lerner, John P. Ryan, Christopher Lloyd; *D:* Bob Rafelson; *W:* David Mamet. **VHS, Beta, LV** $19.98 *FOX, PIA, WAR ♂♂*

Postmark for Danger Detectives do their best to smash a diamond smuggling ring that operates between Britain and the U.S. Along the way a number of people are killed. *AKA:* Portrait of Alison.
1956 84m/B *GB* Terry Moore, Robert Beatty, William Sylvester, Josephine Griffin, Geoffrey Keen, Henry Oscar; *D:* Guy Green. **VHS, Beta** $16.95 *SNC ♂♂½*

Postmark for Danger/Quicksand A "film noire" double feature. In "Postmark for Danger," a young actress returns from the dead to find a criminal, while in "Quicksand," a mechanic becomes indebted to the mob when he borrows extra money for a date.
1956 155m/B *GB* Terry Moore, Robert Beatty, Mickey Rooney, Jeanne Cagney, Peter Lorre; *D:* Guy Green. **VHS, Beta** *SNC ♂♂*

Pot O' Gold Stewart plays a wealthy young man who signs on with a struggling band. He convinces his uncle, who has a radio program, to let the band perform during a radio giveaway show he has concocted. Slight comedy, Stewart notwithstanding. *AKA:* The Golden Hour.
1941 87m/B Paulette Goddard, James Stewart, Art Carney, Horace Heidt Band; *D:* George Marshall. **VHS, Beta, 3/4U, Special order formats** $19.95 *NOS, CCB, VYY ♂♂*

Pound Puppies and the Legend of Big Paw The Pound Puppies, known for breaking dogs out of pounds and delivering them to safe and secure homes, are featured in their first full-length musical (and merchandising effort). Fifties music.
1988 76m/C *D:* Pierre de Celles; *V:* Nancy Cartwright, George Rose, B.J. Ward, Ruth Buzzi, Brennan Howard. **VHS** $19.95 *FHE, WTA ♂♂*

Pouvoir Intime What happens when robbers of an armored car lock the guard in the vehicle, and he decides to fight back? This film offers one possible scenario. Available in dubbed or subtitled versions.
1987 (PG-13) 86m/C *FR* Marie Tifo, Pierre Curzi, Yvan Ponton, Jaques Lussier; *D:* Yves Simoneau. **VHS** *NO ♂♂½*

P.O.W. Deathcamp A combat unit is captured and tortured by the Vietcong in this typical Vietnam story.
1989 92m/C Charles Black, Bill Balbridge, Rey Malonzo; *D:* Jett C. Espirtu. **VHS** $79.95 *ATL ♂♂*

The P.O.W. Escape The adventures of a surly American commander captured as a POW during the final days of the Vietnam War. *AKA:* Behind Enemy Lines.
1986 (R) 90m/C David Carradine, Mako, Charles R. Floyd, Steve James; *D:* Gideon Amir. **VHS, Beta, LV** $19.95 *RCA ♂½*

Powaqqatsi: Life in Transformation Director Reggio's follow-up to "Koyaanisqatsi" doesn't pack the wallop of its predecessor. Still, the cinematography is magnificent and the music of Philip Glass is exquisitely hypnotic as we are taken on a spellbinding video collage of various third world countries and see the price they've paid in the name of progress. Part 2 of a planned trilogy.
1988 (G) 95m/C *D:* Godfrey Reggio; *M:* Philip Glass. **VHS, Beta** $89.95 *CAN ♂♂♂½*

Powder Keg Railroad company hires a rowdy team of investigators to retrieve a hijacked train. Action never quits. The idea for the television pilot "The Bearcats" came from this movie.
1970 93m/C Rod Taylor, Dennis Cole, Michael Ansara, Fernando Lamas, Tisha Sterling; *D:* Douglas Heyes. **VHS, Beta** $7.95 *SIM, WOV ♂♂*

Powdersmoke Range Crooked frontier politician plots to steal valuable ranch property. The new owners, however, have other ideas. First in "The Three Mesquiteer" series.
1935 71m/B Harry Carey Sr., Hoot Gibson, Tom Tyler, Guinn Williams, Bob Steele, Sam Hardy, Patricia "Boots" Mallory, Franklin Farnum, William Desmond, William Farnum, Buzz Barton, Wally Wales, Art Mix, Buffalo Bill Jr., Buddy Roosevelt; *D:* Wallace Fox. **VHS, Beta** *MED, RXM ♂½*

Power Two dam-building construction workers vie with each other for the local girls. Silent.
1928 60m/B William Boyd, Alan Hale Jr., Carole Lombard, Joan Bennett; *D:* Howard Hughes. **VHS, Beta** $24.95 *FCT, GPV, GVV ♂♂½*

Power A Jewish ghetto inhabitant in 18th-century Wurtemburg works his way out of the gutter and into some authority by pleasing the whims of an evil duke. Based on the novel by Leon Fuechtwangler. *AKA:* Jew Suss.
1934 105m/B *GB* Conrad Veidt, Benita Hume, Frank Vosper, Cedric Hardwicke, Gerald du Maurier, Pamela Ostrer, Joan Maude, Paul Graetz, Mary Clare, Percy Parsons, Dennis Hoey, Gibb McLaughlin, Francis L. Sullivan; *D:* Lothar Mendes. **VHS** *DVT, HEG ♂♂½*

The Power An ancient clay idol that was created by the Aztecs and possesses incredible destructive power is unleashed on modern man.
1980 (R) 87m/C Warren Lincoln, Susan Stokey, Lisa Erickson, Jeffrey Obrow; *D:* Stephen Carpenter. **VHS** $69.98 *LIV, VES ♂½*

Power A study of corporate manipulations. Gere plays a ruthless media consultant working for politicians. Fine cast can't find the energy needed to make this great, but it is still interesting. Lumet did better with same material in "Network."
1986 (R) 111m/C Richard Gere, Julie Christie, E.G. Marshall, Gene Hackman, Beatrice Straight, Kate Capshaw, Denzel Washington, Fritz Weaver, Michael Learned, E. Katherine Kerr, Polly Rowles, Matt Salinger, J.T. Walsh; *D:* Sidney Lumet. **VHS, Beta, LV** $19.98 *LHV, WAR ♂♂♂*

The Power of One A good cast is generally wasted in another liberal, white look at apartheid. Set in South Africa during the 1940s, P.K. is a white orphan of British descent who is sent to a boarding school run by Afrikaaners (South Africans of German descent). Humiliated and bullied, particularly when England and Germany go to war, P.K. is befriended by a German pianist and a black boxing coach who teach him to box and stand up for his rights. P.K. does exactly that as he grows up to be a first-rate boxer and teacher. Preachy and filled with stereotypes. Based on the novel by Bryce Courtenay.
1992 (PG-13) 126m/C Stephen Dorff, Armin Mueller-Stahl, Morgan Freeman, John Gielgud, Fay Masterson, Marius Weyers, Tracy Brooks Swope, John Osborne, Daniel Craig, Dominic Walker, Alois Mayo, Ian Roberts, Maria Marais; *D:* John G. Avildsen; *W:* Robert Mark Kamen. **VHS, LV** $19.98 *WAR ♂♂*

The Power of the Ninjitsu A young man inherits the leadership of a martial arts crime gang, the Scorpions, but the elder members muscle him out of his place. He returns for revenge and has the old ones running scared. Power to the Ninjitsu!
1988 90m/C Britton Lee, Adam Frank, Peter Ujaer; *D:* Joseph Lai. **VHS, Beta** $59.95 *IME ♂*

Power, Passion & Murder A young, glamorous movie star has an affair with a married man that begins the end of her career in 1930s Hollywood.
1983 104m/C Michelle Pfeiffer, Darren McGavin, Stella Stevens; *D:* Paul Bogart, Leon Ichaso. **VHS, Beta, LV** $79.95 *VMK, IME, HHE ♂½*

Power Play Young army colonel from a small European country joins forces with rebels to overthrow the government. After the coup, the group discovers that in their midst is a traitor. So who is it? Suspense never builds adequately. *AKA:* Operation Overthrow.
1981 95m/C *CA GB* Peter O'Toole, David Hemmings, Donald Pleasence, Barry Morse; *D:* Martyn Burke. **VHS, Beta** $49.95 *MED, SIM ♂½*

The Power Within An electrified stuntman finds he can send electrical shocks from his hands and becomes the victim of a kidnapping plot.
1979 90m/C Eric Braeden, David Hedison, Susan Howard, Art Hindle; *D:* John Llewellyn Moxey. **VHS, Beta** $59.95 *PSM ♂½*

Powerforce CIA agent must use martial arts in order to save the free world.
1983 (R) 98m/C Bruce Lee, Bruce Baron. **VHS, Beta** *NO ♂*

Powwow Highway Remarkably fine performances in this unusual, thought-provoking, poorly-titled foray into the plight of Native Americans. Farmer shines as the unassuming, amiable Cheyenne traveling to New Mexico in a beat-up Chevy with his Indian activist buddy, passionately portrayed by Martinez. On the journey they are constantly confronted with the tragedy of life on a reservation. A sobering look at government injustice and the lingering spirit of a people lost inside their homeland.
1989 (R) 105m/C Gary Farmer, A. Martinez, Amanda Wyss, Rene Handren-Seals, Graham Greene; *D:* Joanelle Romero, Jonathan Wacks. **VHS, Beta** $89.95 *WAR, OM ♂♂♂½*

The Practice of Love A woman journalist's investigation of a murder casts suspicion on her two male lovers. The film raises the question of whether love is even possible in a world dominated by men's struggles for power. In German with English subtitles.
1984 90m/C *GE D:* Valie Export. **VHS** $59.95 *FCT, MOV ♂♂*

Prairie Badmen Outlaws are after a treasure map in the possession of the owner of a medicine show. It's up to our hero to stop them. One of the "Billy Carson" western series.
1946 55m/B Buster Crabbe. **VHS, Beta** *VCN* 🎬½

The Prairie King Will grants three people the same gold mine but stipulates only one may own it. Silent quandary.
1927 58m/B Hoot Gibson, Barbara Worth, Charles Sellon, Albert Priscoe. **VHS, Beta** $19.95 *GPV* 🎬½

Prairie Moon Autry becomes the guardian of three tough kids from Chicago after they inherit a ranch. The kids help Autry round up a gang of rustlers.
1938 58m/B Gene Autry, Smiley Burnette. **VHS, Beta** *CCB, VCN, DVT* 🎬½

Prairie Pals Deputies go undercover to rescue a kidnapped scientist.
1942 60m/B William Boyd, Lee Powell. **VHS, Beta** *VCN* 🎬½

Prancer An eight-year-old girl whose mother has recently died thinks an injured reindeer she has found belongs to Santa. She lovingly nurses him back to health. Harmless family entertainment.
1989 (G) 102m/C Sam Elliott, Rebecca Harrell, Cloris Leachman, Rutanya Alda, John Joseph Duda, Abe Vigoda, Michael Constantine, Ariana Richards; **D:** John Hancock. **VHS, Beta, LV, 8mm** $19.95 *COL, ORI, FCT* 🎬½

Pray for Death When a mild-mannered Japanese family is victimized by a crime syndicate in L.A., a master ninja comes to the rescue. Higher quality production than most ninja adventures.
1985 (R) 93m/C James Booth, Robert Ito, Sho Kosugi, Shane Kosugi, Kane Kosugi, Donna Kei Benz; **D:** Gordon Hessler; **W:** James Booth. **VHS, Beta** *NO* 🎬🎬

Pray for the Wildcats Three advertising executives' promotional trip from (or to?) Hell. Anything to please a client.
1974 96m/C Andy Griffith, William Shatner, Angie Dickinson, Janet Margolin, Marjoe Gortner, Lorraine Gary; **D:** Robert Lewis. **VHS, Beta** $69.95 *REP* 🎬½

Pray TV A sly con man turns a failing television station into a profitable one when the station starts to broadcast around-the-clock religious programming. Made for television. *AKA:* KGOD.
1980 (PG) 92m/C Dabney Coleman, Archie Hahn, Joyce Jameson, Nancy Morgan, Roger E. Mosley, Marcia Wallace; **D:** Rick Friedberg. **VHS, Beta, LV** $69.95 *VES* 🎬🎬

Pray TV A television movie expose of broadcast religion in which a young preacher chooses between orthodox religion and lots of money. Not as cutting an indictment as it could have been.
1982 100m/C John Ritter, Ned Beatty, Madolyn Smith, Richard Kiley, Louise Latham, Jonathan Prince, Michael Currie, Lois Areno; **D:** Robert Markowitz. **VHS, Beta** $9.98 *SUE* 🎬🎬

A Prayer for Katarina Horovitzova Stunning tale of a Polish singer who struggles to find the meaning and beauty of life while working to trade Nazi prisoners in U.S. jails for Jews hoping to emigrate. Based on the Arnost Lustig novel. Confiscated by the Czech Communist government and kept from the screen for 21 years. In Czechoslovakian with English subtitles.
1969 60m/C CZ Jiri Adamira, Lenka Fiserova, Cestmir Randa. **VHS** $59.95 *FCT* 🎬🎬🎬½

Prayer for the Dying An IRA hitman longs to quit, but he has to complete one last assignment. The hit is witnessed by a priest who becomes an unwitting associate when the hitman hides out at the church. Fine performances from Bates and Rourke, though Hodges and Rourke were not satisfied with finished film.
1987 104m/C Mickey Rourke, Alan Bates, Bob Hoskins, Sammi Davis-Voss, Liam Neeson; **D:** Mike Hodges. **VHS, Beta, LV** *NO* 🎬🎬½

Prayer of the Rollerboys Violent, futuristic, funky action as Haim infiltrates a criminal gang of syncopated roller-blading neo-nazi youth with plans for nationwide domination. Though routinely plotted and predictable, it's got great skating stunts and a wry vision of tomorrow's shattered USA—broke, drug-soaked, homeless, foreign-owned; even sharper when you realize this is a Japanese-American co-production.
1991 (R) 94m/C Corey Haim, Patricia Arquette, Christopher Collet, Julius W. Harris, J.C. Quinn, Jake Dengel; **D:** Rick King. **VHS, LV** $19.95 *ACA* 🎬🎬½

Praying Mantis The professor's scheming nurse murdered his family and plans to marry him for his money. She enlists the aid of the professor's assistant in her evil plot.
1983 119m/C Jonathan Pryce, Cherie Lunghi, Ann Cropper, Carmen Du Sautoy, Pinkas Braun; **D:** Jack Gold. **VHS, Beta** $59.95 *QNE* 🎬🎬

Preacherman Phony preacher travels through the South, fleecing gullible congregations wherever he goes.
1983 (R) 90m/C Amos Huxley, Marian Brown, Adam Hesse. **VHS, Beta** *PGN* 🎬½

Predator Schwarzenegger leads a team of CIA-hired mercenaries into the Central American jungles to rescue hostages. They encounter an alien force that begins to attack them one by one. Soon it's just Arnold and the Beast in this attention-grabbing, but sometimes silly, suspense film.
1987 (R) 107m/C Arnold Schwarzenegger, Jesse Ventura, Sonny Landham, Bill Duke, Elpidia Carrillo, Carl Weathers, R.G. Armstrong; **D:** John McTiernan. **VHS, Beta, LV** $14.98 *FXV* 🎬🎬½

Predator 2 Tough cop takes time away from battling drug dealers to deal with malicious extraterrestrial who exterminated Arnold's band of commandos in "Predator." Miss-billed as sequel, its only resemblance to the original is that the predator has inexplicably returned (this time to the thick of L.A.). Gorey action aplenty, little logic. Fine cast dominated by minority performers can't save this one.
1990 (R) 105m/C Danny Glover, Gary Busey, Ruben Blades, Maria Conchita Alonso, Bill Paxton, Robert Davi, Adam Baldwin, Kent McCord, Morton Downey Jr., Calvin Lockhart, Teri Weigel; **D:** Stephen Hopkins. **VHS, Beta, LV** $14.98 *FXV, CCB* 🎬🎬

Prehistoric Women A tribe of prehistoric women look for husbands the old-fashioned way—they drag them back to their caves from the jungle. So bad it's almost good. *AKA:* Slave Girls.
1950 74m/C Laurette Luez, Allan Nixon, Mara Lynn, Joan Shawlee, Judy Landon; **D:** Greg Tallas. **VHS, Beta** $9.99 *FHE, NOS, RHI* Woof!

Prehysteria Fantasy/adventure about a widower, his 11-year-old son and teenage daughter, and what happens when some mysterious eggs from South America accidentally wind up at their farm. Imagine their surprise when the eggs hatch and out pop a brood of pygmy dinosaurs. The dinosaurs are cute (as is the family), the villain is dumb, and the violence minimal.
1993 (PG) 86m/C Brett Cullen, Austin O'Brien, Samantha Mills, Colleen Morris, Tony Longo, Stuart Fratkin, Stephen Lee; **D:** Albert Band, Charles Band; **W:** Greg Suddeth, Mark Goldstein. **VHS, Beta** *PAR* 🎬🎬½

Prelude to a Kiss Disappointing screen adaptation of Craig Lucas' hit play features Baldwin and Ryan as young lovers in this romantic fantasy. Ryan is Rita, a free-spirited bartender and Baldwin is Peter, a conservative writer, who decide to marry after a whirlwind courtship. At their wedding reception, Rita obligingly kisses one of their guests, an old man (Walker). Then, on their honeymoon, Peter begins to notice a number of changes to Rita's character and comes to realize this is truly not the girl he married. The delicate fantasy which worked on stage struggles to survive the "opening up" of the screen adaptation though Baldwin (who reprises his stage role) and Ryan are appealing.
1992 (PG-13) 106m/C Alec Baldwin, Meg Ryan, Sydney Walker, Ned Beatty, Patty Duke, Kathy Bates, Stanley Tucci; **D:** Norman Rene. **VHS, LV** $19.98 *FXV, PMS* 🎬🎬

Prelude to War A compact look at the events of 1931-39; includes a series of contrasts between free societies and totalitarian governments. From the "Why We Fight" series.
1942 53m/B **D:** Frank Capra. **VHS, Beta** $19.95 *REP, MPI, HHT* 🎬🎬

Premature Burial A cataleptic Englishman's worst fears come true when he is buried alive. He escapes and seeks revenge on his doctor and his greedy wife. Based upon the story by Edgar Allen Poe.
1962 81m/C Ray Milland, Richard Ney, Hazel Court, Heather Angel; **D:** Roger Corman. **VHS, Beta** $69.98 *LIV, VES, MLB* 🎬🎬

Premonition Three drug-riddled '60s college students experience similar premonitions of death, and subsequently either die or become tormented.
1971 (PG) 83m/C Carl Crow, Tim Ray, Winfrey Hester Hill, Victor Izay; **D:** Alan Rudolph. **VHS, Beta** *NO* 🎬½

The Premonition Parapsychologist searching for a missing child is drawn into a frightening maze of dream therapy and communication with the dead. Well-done paranorm tale written by Anthony Mahon and filmed on location in Mississippi.
1975 (PG) 94m/C Richard Lynch, Sharon Farrell, Jeff Corey, Ellen Barber, Edward Bell, Danielle Brisebois; **D:** Robert Allen Schnitzer. **VHS, Beta** $24.98 *SUE* 🎬🎬½

Prep School A very proper New England prep school is turned topsy-turvy by two rambunctious co-eds. They're determined to break every one of the school's cardinal rules.
1981 (PG-13) 97m/C Leslie Hope, Andrew Sabiston; **D:** Paul Almond. **VHS, Beta** $79.95 *PSM* 🎬

Preppies Yet another teen sex comedy, but this time Ivy Leaguer Drake must pass his exams to receive his $50 million inheritance. Lots of skirt chasing as his conniving cousin leads him astray.
1982 (R) 83m/C Dennis Drake, Peter Brady Reardon, Steven Holt, Nitchie Barrett, Cindy Manion, Katt Shea Ruben, Lynda Wiesmeier; **D:** Chuck Vincent. **VHS, Beta** $29.98 *LIV, VES* 🎬½

Presenting Lily Mars A small-town girl comes to New York to make it on Broadway. Based on the Booth Tarkington novel. ♫When I Look at You; Three O'Clock in the Morning; Kulebiaka; Is It Love? (Or The Gypsy in Me); Broadway Rhythm; Sweethearts of America; Where There's Music;

Every Little Movement Has a Meaning All Its Own; Tom, Tom the Piper's Son.
1943 105m/B Judy Garland, Van Heflin, Fay Bainter, Richard Carlson, Tommy Dorsey, Bob Crosby & His Orchestra; **D:** Norman Taurog. **VHS, Beta** $19.98 *MGM* 🐾🐾

The President's Analyst A superbly written, brilliantly executed satire from the mind of Theodore J. Flicker, who wrote as well as directed. Coburn steals the show as a psychiatrist who has the dubious honor of being appointed "secret shrink" to the President of the U.S. Pressures of the job steadily increase his paranoia until he suspects he is being pursued by agents and counter agents alike. Is he losing his sanity or...? Vastly entertaining.
1967 104m/C James Coburn, Godfrey Cambridge, Severn Darden, Joan Delaney, Pat Harrington, Will Geer, William Daniels; **W/D:** Theodore J. Flicker. **VHS** $14.95 *PAR* 🐾🐾🐾½

President's Mistress A security agent searches for his sister's murderer, while trying to obscure the fact that she was having an affair with the President.
1978 97m/C Beau Bridges, Susan Blanchard, Larry Hagman, Joel Fabiani, Karen Grassle; **D:** John Llewellyn Moxey. **VHS, Beta** *NO* 🐾½

The President's Mystery A lawyer decides to turn his back on society by giving up his practice and his marriage. Eventually he meets and falls in love with another woman. The most interesting aspect of the film is that it is based on a story by Franklin D. Roosevelt, which was published in "Liberty" magazine. The story was supposedly better than its screen adaptation. **AKA:** One For All.
1936 80m/B Henry Wilcoxon, Betty Furness, Sidney Blackmer, Evelyn Brent; **D:** Phil Rosen. **VHS, Beta** $16.95 *SNC* 🐾½

The President's Plane is Missing When Air Force One disappears, the less than trustworthy Vice President takes control. Could there be a dire plot in the making? Based on a novel by Rod Serling's brother Robert J. Serling.
1971 100m/C Buddy Ebsen, Peter Graves, Arthur Kennedy, Rip Torn, Louise Sorel, Raymond Massey, James Wainwright, Mercedes McCambridge, Dabney Coleman, Joseph Campanella; **D:** Daryl Duke. **VHS** $69.98 *REP* 🐾🐾

The Presidio An easy going police detective must investigate a murder on a military base where he and the base commander have sparred before. The commander becomes downright nasty when his daughter shows an interest in the detective. Good action scenes in San Francisco almost covers up script weaknesses, but not quite.
1988 (R) 97m/C Sean Connery, Mark Harmon, Meg Ryan, Jack Warden, Mark Blum, Jenette Goldstein; **D:** Peter Hyams. **VHS, Beta, LV, 8mm** $89.95 *PAR* 🐾🐾

Pressure Point Poitier stars as a prison psychiatrist treating an inmate who is a racist and a member of the Nazi party. Darin gives an excellent performance as the Nazi patient in this intelligent drama based on a true case.
1962 87m/B Sidney Poitier, Bobby Darin, Peter Falk, Carl Benton Reid, Barry Gordon, Howard Caine, Mary Munday; **D:** Hubert Cornfield. **VHS** $19.98 *MGM* 🐾🐾🐾

Presumed Guilty An innocent man is released from prison only to find he is once again a wanted man! So he gets his gal, who happens to be the sheriff's daughter, is beaten up and in the end winds up living happily ever after.

1991 91m/C Jack Vogel, Holly Floria, Sean Holton, Wayne Zanelotti, Bradley Rockwell, Sharon Young, Al Schuerman; **W/D:** Lawrence L. Simeone. **VHS** $79.98 *AIP* 🐾

Presumed Innocent Assistant district attorney is the prime suspect when a former lover turns up brutally murdered. Cover-ups surround him, the political climate changes, and friends and enemies switch sides. Slow-paced courtroom drama with excellent performances from Ford, Julia, and Bedelia. Skillfully adapted by Pakula and Pierson from the best-seller by Chicago attorney Scott Turow.
1990 (R) 127m/C Harrison Ford, Brian Dennehy, Bonnie Bedelia, Greta Scacchi, Raul Julia, Paul Winfield, John Spencer, Joe Grifasi, Anna Maria Horsford, Sab Shimono, Christine Estabrook, Michael Tolan; **W/D:** Alan J. Pakula; **W:** Frank Pierson; **M:** John Williams. **VHS, Beta, LV, 8mm** $19.98 *WAR, FCT* 🐾🐾🐾

Pretty Baby Shield's launching pad and Malle's first American film is a masterpiece of cinematography and style, nearly upstaged by the plodding storyline. Carradine manages to be effective but never succeeds at looking comfortable as the New Orleans photographer besotted with, and subsequently married to, an 11-year old prostitute (Shields). Low key, disturbingly intriguing story, beautifully photographed by Sven Nykist.
1978 (R) 109m/C Brooke Shields, Keith Carradine, Susan Sarandon, Barbara Steele, Diana Scarwid, Antonio Fargas; **D:** Louis Malle. Academy Awards '78 Nominations: Best Original Score; National Board of Review Awards '78: 10 Best Films of the Year. **VHS, Beta, LV** $69.95 *PAR* 🐾🐾🐾

Pretty in Pink More teenage angst from the pen of John Hughes. Poor girl falls for a rich guy. Their families fret, their friends are distressed, and fate conspires against them. The pair plans to go to prom together, but peer pressure creates difficulties. If you can suspend your disbelief that a teenaged girl with her own car and answering machine is financially inferior, then you may very well be able to accept the entire premise. Slickly done and adequately, if not enthusiastically, acted. In 1987, Hughes remade this film and put himself in the director's chair with much of the same result. "Some Kind of Wonderful" is the same story with the rich/pauper characters reversed by gender.
1986 (PG-13) 96m/C Molly Ringwald, Andrew McCarthy, Jon Cryer, Harry Dean Stanton, James Spader, Annie Potts, Andrew Dice Clay, Margaret Colin, Alexa Kenin, Gina Gershon, Dweezil Zappa; **D:** Howard Deutch. **VHS, Beta, LV, 8mm** $14.95 *PAR* 🐾🐾½

Pretty Poison You won't need an antidote for this one. Original, absorbing screenplay, top-notch acting, and on target direction combine to raise this low-budget, black comedy above the crowd. Perkins at his eerie best as a burned-out arsonist who cooks up a crazy scheme and enlists the aid of a hot-to-trot high schooler, only to discover too late she has some burning desires of her own. Weld is riveting as the turbulent teen.
1968 89m/C Anthony Perkins, Tuesday Weld, Beverly Garland, John Randolph, Dick O'Neill; **D:** Noel Black. **VHS** *ING, MLB* 🐾🐾🐾½

Pretty Smart Two diametrically opposed sisters at a European finishing school team up against a drug-dealing, voyeuristic teacher. Pretty lame.
1987 (R) 84m/C Tricia Leigh Fisher, Patricia Arquette, Dennis Cole, Lisa Lorient; **D:** Dimitri Logothetis. **VHS, Beta** $19.95 *STE, NWV* Woof!

Pretty Woman An old story takes a fresh approach as a successful but stuffy business man hires a fun-loving, energetic young hooker to be his companion for a week. The film caused some controversy over its upbeat portrayal of prostitution, but its popularity at the box office catapulted Roberts to stardom.
1990 (R) 117m/C Richard Gere, Julia Roberts, Ralph Bellamy, Jason Alexander, Laura San Giacomo, Hector Elizondo; **D:** Garry Marshall. Academy Awards '90 Nominations: Best Actress (Roberts); Golden Globe Awards '91: Best Actress—Musical/Comedy (Roberts); People's Choice Awards '91: Best Film, Best Film—Musical/Comedy. **VHS, Beta, LV** $19.99 *TOU* 🐾🐾🐾

Prettykill A confusing storyline with numerous subplots involves detective with a paramour/prostitute (Hubley) attempting to stalk a mad killer while contending with her split personality.
1987 (R) 95m/C David Birney, Susannah York, Season Hubley, Yaphet Kotto, Suzanne Snyder, Germane Honde; **D:** George Kaczender. **VHS, Beta, LV** $19.98 *WAR* Woof!

The Prey Poorly done horror show about a predator who is looking for a mate in the Colorado Rockies and kills five campers in the process.
1980 (R) 80m/C Debbie Thureson, Steve Bond, Lori Lethin, Jackie Coogan; **D:** Edwin Scott Brown. **VHS, Beta** $19.99 *HBO, STE* 🐾

Prey for the Hunter Four businessmen on a big-game hunt decide they're bored with their usual prey. They persuade a photojournalist to join them in a game with paint pellet guns except they decide to use real bullets and the journalist becomes their new target. An old and tired plot with nothing new to distinguish it.
1992 (R) 90m/C Todd Jensen, Andre Jacobs, Michelle Bestbior, Evan J Klisser, David Butler, Allan Granville; **D:** John H. Parr. **VHS** $89.95 *COL* 🐾

Prey of the Chameleon A female serial killer escapes from her asylum, ready to rip more men to shreds. However a tough lady cop has other ideas and goes all out to put an end to the madwoman's doings. Can she stop this fiend before the man she loves becomes the next victim?
1991 (R) 91m/C Daphne Zuniga, James Wilder, Alexandra Paul, Don Harvey; **D:** Fleming Fuller. **VHS, Beta** $89.95 *PCM* 🐾

Priceless Beauty Musician Lambert was only looking when he spotted the bottle which changed his life. Beautiful genie (Lane) lives inside, and is waiting just for him! Fun premise, good score, nice chemistry between the actors.
1990 (R) 94m/C Christopher Lambert, Diane Lane, Francesco Quinn; **D:** Charles Finch. **VHS, LV** $89.98 *REP* 🐾🐾½

Prick Up Your Ears Film biography of popular subversive playwright Joe Orton depicts his rise to fame and his eventual murder at the hands of his homosexual lover in 1967. Acclaimed for its realistic and sometimes humorous portrayal of the relationship between two men in a society that regarded homosexuality as a crime, the film unfortunately pays scant attention to Orton's theatrical success. The occasional sluggishness of Alan Bennett's script detracts a bit from the three leads' outstanding performances.
1987 (R) 110m/C *GB* Gary Oldman, Alfred Molina, Vanessa Redgrave, Julie Walters, Lindsay Duncan, Wallace Shawn, James Grant, Frances Barber, Janet Dale, David Atkins; **D:** Stephen Frears. **VHS, Beta, LV** *NO* 🐾🐾🐾

Pride and Prejudice Classic adaptation of Austen's classic novel of manners as a young marriageable woman spurns the suitor her parents choose for her. Excellent cast vividly recreates 19th century England, aided by the inspired set design that won the film an Oscar.
1940 114m/B Greer Garson, Laurence Olivier, Edmund Gwenn, Edna May Oliver, Mary Boland, Maureen O'Sullivan, Ann Rutherford, Frieda Inescort; *D:* Robert Z. Leonard. **VHS, Beta, LV $24.95** MGM &&&½

Pride and Prejudice BBC mini-series adaptation of Jane Austen's novel about 19th century British mores and the attempts of five sisters to get married.
1985 226m/C *GB* Elizabeth Garvie, David Rintoul; *D:* Cyril Coke. **VHS, Beta, LV $29.98** KUI, FOX, SIG && ½

The Pride and the Passion A small group of resistance fighters battling for Spanish independence in 1810 must smuggle a 6-ton cannon across the rugged terrain of Spain. Miscasting, especially of Sinatra as a Spanish peasant, hurts this film.
1957 132m/C Cary Grant, Frank Sinatra, Sophia Loren; *D:* Stanley Kramer. **VHS, Beta $19.98** FOX &&

Pride of Jesse Hallum A made-for-television film about an illiterate man, played by country singer Cash, who learns, after much trial and tribulation, to read.
1981 105m/C Johnny Cash, Brenda Vaccaro, Eli Wallach; *D:* Gary Nelson. **VHS, Beta $59.98** FOX && ½

Pride of St. Louis A romanticized and humorous portrait of famed baseball player-turned-commentator Dizzy Dean.
1952 93m/B Dan Dailey, Joanne Dru, Richard Crenna, Richard Hayden, Hugh Sanders; *D:* Harmon Jones; *W:* Herman J. Mankiewicz. **VHS, Beta $19.98** FOX &&

Pride of the Bowery The Dead End Kids versus a boxing hopeful in training camp. *AKA:* Here We Go Again.
1941 60m/B Leo Gorcey, David Grocey, Huntz Hall, Gabriel Dell, Billy Halop, Bobby Jordan; *D:* Joseph H. Lewis. **VHS, Beta, 3/4U, Special order formats $19.95** NOS, CAB, DVT &

Pride of the Clan Silent drama with Pickford and Moore as Scottish sweethearts battling a bit of adversity. When Pickford's father is lost at sea, she moves onto his fishing boat. She meets Moore, a fishing boy, and falls in love. But, he inherits a fortune and his parents forbid him to see Pickford. He goes off to live the good life but comes back to dramatically rescue Pickford.
1918 80m/B Mary Pickford, Matt Moore; *D:* Maurice Tourneur. **VHS, Beta $19.95** GPV &&½

The Pride of the Yankees Excellent portrait of baseball great Lou Gehrig. Beginning as he joined the Yankees in 1923, the film follows this great American through to his moving farewell speech as his career was tragically cut short by the disease that bears his name. Cooper is inspiring in the title role.
1942 128m/B Gary Cooper, Teresa Wright, Babe Ruth, Walter Brennan, Dan Duryea; *D:* Sam Wood. Academy Awards '42: Best Film Editing; Nominations: Best Actress (Wright); Academy Awards '42: Best Actor (Cooper), Best Black and White Cinematography, Best Interior Decoration, Best Picture, Best Sound, Best Story, Best Original Score. **VHS, Beta, LV $19.98** FOX &&&½

Priest of Love Arty account of the final years of the life of then-controversial author D.H. Lawrence, during which time he published "Lady Chatterly's Lover." A slow-moving but interesting portrayal of this complex man and his wife as they grapple with his imminent death from tuberculosis.
1981 (R) 125m/C *GB* Ian McKellan, Janet Suzman, John Gielgud, Helen Mirren, Jorge Rivero; *D:* Christopher Miles. **VHS, Beta $79.99** HBO && ½

Primal Impulse An astronaut, stranded on the moon because of a sinister experimental double-cross, unleashes a mental scream which possesses a young woman's mind back on earth.
1974 90m/C Klaus Kinski. **VHS, Beta** NO && ½

Primal Rage A student is bitten by an experimental monkey, and begins to manifest his primal urges physically. Special effects by Carlo Rimbaldi.
1990 92m/C Bo Svenson, Patrick Lowe, Mitch Watson, Cheryl Arutt, Sarah Buxton; *D:* Vittoria Rambaldi. **VHS, Beta $19.98** WAR &

Primal Scream The Year is 1993. Earth's fuel sources are rapidly decaying and the top secret project to mine a revolutionary new energy source is underway—independently managed by a corrupt corporation.
1987 (R) 95m/C Kenneth John McGregor, Sharon Mason, Julie Miller, Jon Maurice, Mickey Shaughnessy; *D:* William Murray. **VHS** NO && ½

Primary Motive Taut political thriller with Nelson as Andy Blumenthal, a press secretary who finds that an opposing candidate's campaign is covered by a web of lies. Blumenthal exposes the lies, but the candidate denies them and pulls further ahead in the polls. When the candidate's wife gives Blumenthal an extremely damaging piece of information, will the polls finally turn against him?
1992 (R) 93m/C Judd Nelson, Richard Jordan, Sally Kirkland, Justine Bateman, John Savage; *W/D:* Daniel Adams; *W:* William Snowden III. **VHS, Beta, LV $89.95** FXV &&

Primary Target A mercenary reunites his 'Nam guerilla unit to rescue a diplomat's wife kidnapped by a Laotian jungle lord.
1989 (R) 85m/C John Calvin, Miki Kim, Joey Aresco, Chip Lucio, John Ericson, Colleen Casey; *D:* Clark Henderson. **VHS, Beta $79.98** MGM &

Prime Cut Veritable orgy of drug trafficking, prostitution, extortion, loan sharking, fisticuffs and gangsters getting ground into mincemeat. Sleazy but well-made crime melodrama has its followers, but is best known as Spacek's film debut.
1972 86m/C Lee Marvin, Gene Hackman, Sissy Spacek, Angel Tompkins, Gregory Walcott; *D:* Michael Ritchie. **VHS, Beta $59.98** FOX &&½

Prime Evil A brave and determined nun infiltrates a sect of devil worshipping monks in an attempt to end their demonic sacrifices. The question is, will this sister slide beneath Satan's cleaver?
1988 (R) 87m/C William Beckwith, Christine Moore; *D:* Roberta Findlay. **VHS, LV $19.95** STE &&

The Prime of Miss Jean Brodie Oscar-winning performance by Smith as a forward-thinking teacher in a Scottish Girls' school during the 1920s. She captivates her impressionable young students with her fascist ideals and free-thinking attitudes in this adaptation of the play taken from Muriel Spark's novel.
1969 (PG) 116m/C *GB* Maggie Smith, Pamela Franklin, Robert Stephens, Celia Johnson, Gordon Jackson, Jane Carr; *D:* Ronald Neame; *W:* Jay Presson Allen. Academy Awards '69: Best Actress (Smith); Nominations: Best Song ("Jean"); British Academy Awards '69: Best Actress (Smith), Best Supporting Actress (Johnson). **VHS, Beta $79.98** FOX, BTV &&&

Prime Risk A young engineer who discovers an electronic method to break into automated teller machines finds that it leads to more trouble when she discovers that foreign agents are hot on her trail.
1984 (PG-13) 98m/C Toni Hudson, Lee Montgomery, Sam Bottoms; *D:* W. Farkas. **VHS, Beta $79.98** LIV & ½

Prime Suspect An honest citizen becomes the prime suspect after the coverage of a murder by an over-ambitious television reporter.
1982 100m/C Mike Farrell, Teri Garr, Veronica Cartwright, Lane Smith, Barry Corbin, James Sloyan, Charles Aidman; *D:* Noel Black. **VHS, Beta** NO &&

Prime Suspect A young man escapes from a mental institution to clear his name after being wrongfully accused of murdering his girlfriend.
1988 89m/C Susan Strasberg, Frank Stallone, Billy Drago, Doug McClure; *D:* Mark Rutland. **VHS $79.95** SVS &&

Prime Target Small-town cop John Bloodstone (Heavener) is recruited by the FBI to transfer a mafia boss (Curtis) from a safehouse to the courthouse. He has to keep the former mobster alive long enough to testify against the "family." Their cross-country adventure is heightened by a murderous confrontation with evil forces that want them both dead.
1991 (R) 87m/C David Heavener, Tony Curtis, Isaac Hayes, Jenilee Harrison, Robert Reed, Andrew Robinson, Don Stroud; *W/D:* David Heavener. **VHS $59.95** HMD &&

The Prime Time Horrid film about a teen girl who leaves home and gets involved with a teen gang and a slimy detective. She's also kidnapped by a weird beatnik artist who forces her to pose nude. Black's film debut. Also known as "Hellkitten."
1960 76m/B JoAnn LeCompte, Frank Roche, James Brooks, Ray Gronwold, Maria Pavelle, Robert Major, Karen Black; *D:* Herschell Gordon Lewis. **VHS $16.95** SNC Woof!

Prime Time Forgotten satirical comedy about what would happen if the censors took a day off from American television.
1980 (R) 73m/C Warren Oates, David Spielberg. **VHS, Beta** PGN & ½

The Primitive Lover Early silent comedy about young wife who decides she deserves more than her marriage is giving her.
1916 67m/B Constance Talmadge, Kenneth Harlan, Harrison Ford; *D:* Sidney Franklin. **VHS, Beta $19.95** GPV &&

Primo Baby A troublesome 15-year-old girl learns responsibility when she must care for a crippled racehorse. They both have a chance at success when she enters the thoroughbred in a race.
1988 97m/C **VHS $89.95** WOV &&½

Primrose Path Melodramatic soaper with comedic touches about a wrong-side-of-the-tracks girl falling for and then losing an ambitious young go-getter running a hamburger stand.
1940 93m/B Ginger Rogers, Joel McCrea, Marjorie Rambeau, Henry Travers, Miles Mander, Queenie Vasser, Joan Carroll, Vivienne Osborne; *D:* Gregory La Cava. **VHS, Beta $19.98** RKO, TTC &&½

Prince and the Great Race Three Australian children search the outback to find their kidnapped horse who is scheduled to run in the big New Year's Day Race.
1983 91m/C *AU* John Ewart, John Howard, Nicole Kidman. **VHS, Beta $14.98** LIV &&

The Prince and the Pauper Satisfying adaptation of the classic Mark Twain story of a young street urchin who trades places with the young king of England. Wonderful musical score by noted composer Erich Wolfgang Korngold who provided the music for many of Flynn's adventure films. Also available in a computer-colorized version.
1937 118m/B Errol Flynn, Claude Rains, Alan Hale Jr., Billy Mauch, Montagu Love, Henry Stephenson, Barton MacLane; **D:** William Keighley. **VHS, Beta, LV $19.95** FOX, MLB, CCB ✓✓✓

The Prince and the Pauper A prince and a poor young boy swap their clothes and identities, thus causing a lot of confusion for their families. Based on the story by Mark Twain.
1962 93m/C Guy Williams, Laurence Naismith, Donald Houston, Jane Asher, Walter Hudd. **VHS, Beta $12.99** DIS ✓✓

The Prince and the Pauper An animated version of the famous Mark Twain tale about a prince in medieval England who changes places with a pauper to see how the other half lives and finds out more than he expected.
1971 47m/C **VHS, Beta $19.98** MGM, KUI, MRV ✓✓

The Prince and the Pauper Remake of the 1937 Errol Flynn film employing lavish sets and a tongue-in-cheek attitude among the all-star cast, who occasionally wander adrift when the director stops for tea. When an English prince and a pauper discover that they have identical appearances, they decide to trade places with each other. From Mark Twain's classic. *AKA:* Crossed Swords.
1978 (PG) 113m/C GB Oliver Reed, Raquel Welch, Mark Lester, Ernest Borgnine, George C. Scott, Rex Harrison, Charlton Heston, Sybil Danning; **D:** Richard Fleischer. **VHS, Beta $19.98** MED ✓✓½

The Prince and the Showgirl An American showgirl in 1910 London is wooed by the Prince of Carpathia. Part of the "A Night at the Movies" series, this tape simulates a 1957 movie evening, with a Sylvester the Cat cartoon, "Greedy for Tweety," a newsreel and coming attractions for "Spirit of St. Louis."
1957 127m/C Laurence Olivier, Marilyn Monroe, Sybil Thorndike; **D:** Laurence Olivier. **VHS, Beta, LV $19.98** WAR ✓✓½

Prince Jack Profiles the turbulent political career of President John F. Kennedy.
1983 100m/C Lloyd Nolan, Dana Andrews, Robert Guillaume, Cameron Mitchell; **D:** Bert Lovitt. **VHS, Beta $69.98** LIV ✓✓

Prince of Bel Air A pool-cleaning playboy who makes a habit of one night stands meets a woman and starts falling in love with her. Originally a made-for-television movie.
1987 (R) 95m/C Mark Harmon, Kirstie Alley, Robert Vaughn, Patrick Laborteaux, Deborah Harmon; **D:** Charles Braverman. **VHS, Beta, LV $89.95** ACA ✓½

The Prince of Central Park Two young orphans are forced by circumstance to live in a tree in New York's Central Park until they are befriended by a lonely old woman. An above-average made for television adaptation of the novel by Evan H. Rhodes, the story was later used for a Broadway play.
1977 76m/C Ruth Gordon, T.J. Hargrave, Lisa Richards, Brooke Shields, Marc Vahanian, Dan Hedaya; **D:** Harvey Hart. **VHS, Beta $59.95** LIV ✓✓✓

Prince of Darkness University students release Satan, in the form of a mysterious chemical, unwittingly on the world. Written by Martin Quatermass (a pseudonym of Carpenter). Strong personnel does not save this dreary and slow-moving cliche plot.
1987 (R) 102m/C Donald Pleasence, Lisa Blount, Victor Wong, Jameson Parker, Dennis Dun; **D:** John Carpenter. **VHS, Beta, LV $14.98** MCA ✓½

Prince of Pennsylvania A mild comedy about a spaced-out youth who kidnaps his own father in hopes of nabbing a family inheritance.
1988 (R) 113m/C Keanu Reeves, Fred Ward, Amy Madigan, Bonnie Bedelia, Jeff Hayenga; **D:** Ron Nyswaner. **VHS, Beta, LV $29.95** COL ✓½

Prince of the City Docu-drama of a police officer who becomes an informant in an effort to end corruption within his narcotics unit, but finds he must pay a heavy price. Based on a true story, the powerful script by Sidney Lumet and Jay Preston (from Robert Daley's book) carries the tension through what would otherwise be an overly long film. Excellent performances make this a riveting character study.
1981 (R) 167m/C Treat Williams, Jerry Orbach, Richard Foronjy, Don Billett, Kenny Marino, Lindsay Crouse, Lance Henriksen; **D:** Sidney Lumet. **VHS, Beta, LV $19.98** WAR ✓✓✓

The Prince of Thieves Robin Hood helps Lady Marian extricate herself from a forced marriage in this adventure made with younger audiences in mind.
1948 72m/C Jon Hall, Patricia Morison, Adele Jergens, Alan Mowbray, Michael Duane; **D:** Howard Bretherton. **VHS** COL ✓✓

The Prince of Tides Conroy's sprawling southern-fried saga is neatly pared down to essentials in this tale of the dysfunctional Wingo family. Tom Wingo (a bravura performance by Nolte), a failed teacher with a shaky marriage, leaves his home in South Carolina for New York, in order to aid his fragile twin sister Savannah who has attempted suicide. Susan Lowenstein (Streisand), Savannah's psychiatrist, asks Tom's help in discovering his sister's problems, rooted in their gothic family past. There is Lila, the self-possessed mother aiming for a better life; Henry, the brutal shrimper father; and Luke, the older brother who died violently. Dark family tragedies are gradually revealed as Tom, who has also blocked out the memories, comes to grips with his own demons under Lowenstein's ministering aid. Streisand is restrained in both her own performance and in her direction although a subplot dealing with Lowenstein's bad marriage and rebellious son is a predictable distraction. The South Carolina low country, and even New York City, never looked better. Conroy adapted the screenplay from his novel of the same name with Johnston's help.
1991 (R) 132m/C Nick Nolte, Barbra Streisand, Blythe Danner, Kate Nelligan, Jeroen Krabbe, Melinda Dillon, George Carlin, Jason Gould, Brad Sullivan; **D:** Barbra Streisand; **W:** Pat Conroy, Becky Johnston; **M:** James Newton Howard. Academy Awards '91 Nominations: Best Actor (Nolte), Best Adapted Screenplay, Best Art Direction/Set Decoration, Best Cinematography, Best Picture, Best Supporting Actress (Nelligan), Best Original Score; Golden Globe Awards '92: Best Actor—Drama (Nolte); Los Angeles Film Critics Association Awards '91: Best Actor (Nolte). **VHS, Beta, LV, 8mm $19.95** COL ✓✓✓

Prince Valiant When his royal dad is exiled by an evil tyrant, brave young Wagner brushes aside bangs and journeys to Camelot to seek the help of King Arthur. Based on Harold Foster's classic comic strip.

1954 100m/C James Mason, Janet Leigh, Robert Wagner, Debra Paget, Sterling Hayden, Victor McLaglen, Donald Crisp, Brian Aherne, Barry Jones, Mary Philips; **D:** Henry Hathaway; **W:** Dudley Nichols. **VHS, Beta $14.98** FXV, FCT ✓✓½

Princess Academy A self-respecting young debutante battles the ways of her elitist finishing school.
1987 (R) 90m/C FR Eva Gabor, Lu Leonard, Richard Paul, Lar Park Lincoln, Carole Davis; **D:** Bruce Block. **VHS, Beta $79.98** LIV ✓

The Princess & the Call Girl A call girl asks her look-alike roommate to take her place in Monaco for a lavishly erotic weekend.
1984 90m/C Carol Levy, Shannah Hall, Victor Bevine; **D:** Radley Metzger. **VHS, Beta $59.95** MON ✓✓

The Princess and the Pea From "Faerie Tale Theatre" comes the story of a princess who tries to prove that she's a blueblood by feeling the bump of a tiny pea under the thickness of twenty mattresses.
1983 60m/C Liza Minnelli, Tom Conti, Tim Kazurinsky, Pat McCormick, Beatrice Straight; **D:** Tony Bill. **VHS, Beta, LV $14.98** KUI, FOX, FCT ✓✓✓

The Princess and the Pirate Hope at his craziest as a vaudvillian who falls for a beautiful princess while on the run from buccaneers on the Spanish Main. Look for Crosby in a closing cameo performance. Available in digitally remastered stereo with original movie trailer.
1944 94m/C Bob Hope, Walter Slezak, Walter Brennan, Virginia Mayo, Victor McLaglen; *Cameos:* Bing Crosby; **D:** David Butler. **VHS, Beta, LV $19.98** HBO, SUE ✓✓✓

The Princess and the Swineherd A German adaptation of the Brothers Grimm fairy tale about a young suitor who tries to please a materialistic princess.
1960 82m/B GE **VHS, Beta $29.95** VYY ✓½

The Princess Bride A modern update of the basic fairy tale crammed with all the cliches, this adventurously irreverent love story centers around a beautiful maiden and her young swain as they battle the evils of the mythical kingdom of Florin to be reunited with one another. Great dueling scenes and offbeat satire of the genre make this fun for adults as well as children. Based on William Goldman's cult novel, with music by Mark Knopfler (vocal by Willy DeVille).
1987 (PG) 98m/C Cary Elwes, Mandy Patinkin, Robin Wright, Wallace Shawn, Peter Falk, Andre the Giant, Chris Sarandon, Christopher Guest, Billy Crystal, Carol Kane, Fred Savage, Peter Cook, Mel Smith; **D:** Rob Reiner. **VHS, Beta, LV, SVS, 8mm $19.95** COL, SUE, SUP ✓✓✓½

Princess Cinderella A live-action dramatization of the famous fantasy. Dubbed in English.
193? 75m/B SP Silvana Jachino, Roberto Villa. **VHS, Beta $59.95** JEF ✓✓

Princess Daisy Made for television movie about a beautiful model who claws her way to the top of her profession while trying to find true love and avoid the clutches of her rotten half-brother. Adapted from Judith Krantz's glitzy best-selling novel.
1983 200m/C Merete Van Kamp, Lindsay Wagner, Claudia Cardinale, Stacy Keach, Ringo Starr, Barbara Bach; **D:** Waris Hussein. **VHS, Beta $14.95** STE, FOX, MOV ✓

Princess in Exile Young people struggle with their life-threatening illnesses at a special summer camp. They find that love and friendship hold the key to dreams about the future. Excellent cast of newcomers.

Based on a novel of the same name by Mark Schreiber.

1990 (PG-13) 103m/C *CA* Zachary Ansley, Nicholas Shields, Stacy Mistysyn, Alexander Chapman, Chuck Shamata; *D:* Giles Walker. **VHS, Beta, LV $89.95** *FRH, FCT* 🎬🎬½

Princess Tam Tam Pleasing French adaptation of Shaw's "Pygmalion," as a beautiful native African woman is "westernized" by a handsome writer and then introduced to high society as an exotic princess. A musical notable for its spectacular choreography and on-location Tunisian scenery. Story by Pepito Abatino, who was then Baker's husband. In French with English subtitles.

1935 77m/B *FR* Josephine Baker, Albert Prejean, Germaine Aussey, Viviane Romance; *D:* Edmond T. Greville. **VHS, Beta, LV $29.95** *MVD, KIV, APD* 🎬🎬🎬

The Princess Who Never Laughed A stern king holds a laugh-off contest to make his morose daughter happy in this adaptation of the Brothers Grimm story from the "Faerie Tale Theatre" series.

1984 60m/C Ellen Barkin, Howard Hesseman, Howie Mandel, Mary Woronov. **VHS, Beta $14.98** *KUI, FOX, FCT* 🎬🎬🎬

Princess Yang Kwei Fei Set in 8th-century China and based on the life of the last T'ang emperor and the beautiful servant girl he loves and makes his bride. She falls victim to court jealousies and he to his greedy family, though even death cannot end their love. Beautifully filmed and acted romantic tragedy. In Japanese with English subtitles. *AKA:* Yokihi; The Empress Yang Kwei Fei.

1955 91m/C *JP* Machiko Kyo, Masayuki Mori, Sakae Ozawa, So Yamamura; *D:* Kenji Mizoguchi. **VHS $79.95** *NYF* 🎬🎬🎬

The Principal A tough, down-on-his-luck high school teacher is hired as the principal of a relentlessly violent, uncontrollable high school. Naturally he whips it into shape.

1987 (R) 109m/C James Belushi, Louis Gossett Jr., Rae Dawn Chong; *D:* Christopher Cain. **VHS, Beta, LV $14.95** *COL* 🎬🎬½

Prison The zombified body of an unjustly executed inmate haunts Creedmore Prison, stalking the guard that killed him. His search is aided by the terrified inmates.

1988 (R) 102m/C Lane Smith, Chelsea Field, Viggo Mortensen, Lincoln Kilpatrick, Tom Everett, Tiny Lister; *D:* Renny Harlin. **VHS, Beta, LV $19.95** *STE, NWV* 🎬½

Prison Break A convict plans a daring prison escape in order to clear his name for a murder he did not commit.

1938 72m/B Barton MacLane, Glenda Farrell, Ward Bond. **VHS, Beta $16.95** *SNC, NOS, MRV* 🎬🎬

Prison Planet In the year 2200 Earth is under the dictatorship of an evil king, with only a band of intrepid rebels to oppose him. Blaine, one of the rebels, gets himself arrested and sent to prison in search of the true ruler, the king's brother. But the prison is protected by a brutal warlord and his equally sadistic warriors, whom Blaine must battle if he ever hopes to find truth and justice.

1992 (R) 90m/C James Phillips, Jack Willcox, Michael Foley, Deborah Thompson-Carlin; *W/D:* Armand Gazarian. **VHS** *COL* 🎬½

Prison Stories: Women on the Inside Three short dramatizations of stories depicting the life of women inside prison walls. The first, "New Chicks," directed by Spheeris, tells the story of two lifelong friends and partners in crime. When one woman (Chong) becomes pregnant, she

goes to the leader of the toughest prison gang for protection, risking her only true friendship. "Esperanza," directed by Deitch, tells the story of a woman on the inside trying to prevent her family from following the same destructive path. Finally, Silver's "Parole Board" features Davidovich as a murderess up for parole but reluctant to leave the security of the prison. A blunt and gritty portrayal of prison gangs, the lifestyle of female inmates, and their fears of returning to life on the outside. Originally produced for cable.

1991 94m/C Rae Dawn Chong, Annabella Sciorra, Lolita Davidovich, Talisa Soto, Rachel Ticotin, Grace Zabriskie; *D:* Penelope Spheeris, Donna Deitch, Joan Micklin Silver. **VHS, Beta** *PSM* 🎬🎬🎬

Prison Train Travelogue of a convicted murderer's cross-country journey to begin his prison sentence at Alcatraz. *AKA:* People's Enemy.

1938 84m/B Fred Keating, Linda (Dorothy Comingore) Winters, Clarence Muse, Faith Bacon, Alexander Leftwich, Nestor Paiva, Franklin Farnum; *D:* Gordon Wiles. **VHS $29.95** *VYY, MOV* 🎬🎬½

The Prisoner Gritty drama about a Cardinal imprisoned in a Soviet bloc country as his captors attempt to break his determination not to be used as a propaganda tool. Interactions between the prisoner and his interrogator are riveting. Based on the real-life experiences of Cardinal Mindszenty, a Hungarian activist during and after WWII.

1955 91m/B *GB* Alec Guinness, Jack Hawkins, Raymond Huntley, Wilfred Lawson; *D:* Peter Glenville. **VHS $69.95** *COL* 🎬🎬🎬

The Prisoner: Arrival Introductory episode of the cult television series. McGoohan stars as a former British spy abducted and held captive in a mysterious village where everyone is assigned a number. As Number 6 he tries to figure out what's going on and how he can get out. Additional episodes available.

1968 52m/C *GB* Patrick McGoohan, Virginia Maskell, Guy Doleman, Paul Eddington, George Baker, Angelo Muscat, Barbara Yu Ling, Stephanie Randall; *D:* Don Chaffey. **VHS, Beta, LV $29.95** *VTK, MPI, MOV* 🎬🎬🎬

Prisoner Cell Block H Popular Australian television soap opera set in Wentworth Detention Center, a women's prison. Primary characters include Franky, a violent lesbian biker in for armed robbery; Karen, who murdered her husband and is the object of Franky's affection; and naive Lynn, accused of kidnapping and attempted murder. Two episodes per cassette.

1980 95m/C *AU* Carol Burns, Kerry Armstrong, Patsy King, Gerard Maguire, Barry Quin, Mary Ward, Monica Maughan, Fiona Spence, Val Lehman, Pieta Tommano. **VHS $19.98** *MPI* 🎬🎬

Prisoner in the Middle Janssen is the only man who can stop a nuclear warhead from falling into the hands of rival Middle East factions. Originally released as "Warhead."

1974 (PG) 87m/C David Janssen, Karin Dor, Christopher Stone, Turia Tan, David Semadar, Art Metrano; *D:* John O'Conner. **VHS, Beta, LV, 8mm $69.95** *ACA, MTX, QVD* 🎬🎬

Prisoner of Honor A made-for-cable-TV retelling of notorious Dreyfus Affair, in which a Jewish officer in the 19th-century French military was accused of treason based on little evidence and lots of bigotry. George Piquart (Dreyfuss), the anti-semitic counterintelligence head, grows to realize Dreyfuss' innocence and fights zealously for the truth. Russell's flamboyant direction

takes the heroic tale into the realm of the surreal; this may not be a thoroughly accurate account, but it's one of the more eye-filling.

1991 (PG) 90m/C Richard Dreyfuss, Oliver Reed, Peter Firth, Jeremy Kemp, Brian Blessed; *D:* Ken Russell. **VHS $89.99** *HBO* 🎬🎬🎬

Prisoner of Rio The made-for-cable-TV satire about scruple-less television evangelists and their nefarious schemes at acquiring their audience's money.

1989 90m/C Steven Berkoff, Paul Freeman; *D:* Lech Majewski. **VHS, Beta $89.95** *MOV* 🎬🎬

Prisoner of Second Avenue A New Yorker in his late forties faces the future, without a job or any confidence in his ability, with the help of his understanding wife. Based on the Broadway play by Neil Simon.

1974 (PG) 98m/C Jack Lemmon, Anne Bancroft, Gene Saks, Elizabeth Wilson, Sylvester Stallone, F. Murray Abraham; *D:* Melvin Frank. **VHS, Beta, LV $19.98** *WAR* 🎬🎬½

Prisoner of Zenda An excellent cast and splendid photography make this the definitive film adaptation of Anthony Hope's swashbuckling novel. A British commoner is forced to pose as his cousin, the kidnapped king of a small European country, to save the throne. Complications of the romantic sort ensue when he falls in love with the queen. Excellent acting, robust sword play, and beautifully designed costumes make this an enjoyable spectacle.

1937 101m/B Ronald Colman, Douglas Fairbanks Jr., Madeleine Carroll, David Niven, Raymond Massey, Mary Astor, C. Aubrey Smith, Montagu Love, Byron Foulger, Alexander D'Arcy; *D:* John Cromwell; *W:* Donald Ogden Stewart, John Balderston, Wills Root. **VHS, Beta, LV $19.98** *MGM* 🎬🎬🎬½

Prisoner of Zenda Less-inspired remake of the 1937 version of Anthony Hope's novel, of a man resembling the monarch of a small country who is forced to pose as King during the coronation ceremony, becomes enamored with the queen, and finds himself embroiled in a murder plot. Worth watching for the luxurious costumes and lavish sets. Cast as a Cardinal here, Stone starred in the 1922 version.

1952 101m/C Stewart Granger, Deborah Kerr, Louis Calhern, James Mason, Jane Greer, Lewis Stone; *D:* Richard Thorpe. **VHS, Beta, LV $19.98** *MGM* 🎬🎬½

Prisoner of Zenda Flat comedic interpretation of Anthony Hope's swashbuckling tale of two identical men who switch places, only to find things complicated by a murder. Sellers stars in the double role of Prince Rudolph of Ruritania and Syd, the cockney cab driver who doubles for Rudolph when the Prince is imprisoned by his jealous brother Michael.

1979 (PG) 108m/C Peter Sellers, Jeremy Kemp, Lynne Frederick, Lionel Jeffries, Elke Sommer; *D:* Richard Quine. **VHS, Beta $39.95** *MCA* 🎬

Prisoners of Inertia Two newlyweds travel to New York city and find themselves caught up in a whirlwind adventure in this well-acted but lazily scripted comedy drama.

1989 (R) 92m/C Amanda Plummer, Christopher Rich, John C. McGinley; *D:* Jay Noyles Seles. **VHS $79.95** *BTV* 🎬🎬½

Prisoners of the Lost Universe Talk-show hostess and her buddy are transported to a hostile universe by a renegade scientist. The two terrified humans search desperately for the dimensional door that is their only hope of escape. Made for television.

1984 94m/C Richard Hatch, Kay Lenz, John Saxon; *D:* Terry Marcel. **VHS, Beta** *NO* 🎬½

Prisoners of the Sun Right after WWII an Australian captain fights to convict Japanese officers for atrocities against Allied POWs, but he's stonewalled by both the U.S. military and still-defiant enemy prisoners. This fiery drama from Down Under packs a punch as it questions whether wartime justice even exists; similar in that way to Brown's earlier "Breaker Morant." Takei (Sulu of the original "Star Trek") makes an imposing Japanese admiral. *AKA:* Blood Oath.
1991 (R) 109m/C *AU* Bryan Brown, George Takei, Terry Quinn, John Back, Toshi Shioya, Deborah Unger; *D:* Stephen Wallace. **VHS, Beta** $92.98 *PAR* ♫♫♫

Private Affairs The mistress of a well-known surgeon becomes jealous when the doctor decides to have a fling with a gorgeous young swim instructor. Italian-made cheapie.
1989 83m/C *IT* Guiliana de Sio, Kate Capshaw, David Naughton, Luca Barbareschi, Michele Placido; *D:* Francesco Massaro. **VHS, Beta** $29.95 *ACA* ♫

The Private Affairs of Bel Ami "This is the story of a scoundrel," proclaims the opening. Sanders is ideally cast as a suave cad who rises in 1880s Parisian society, largely through stategic seduction of prominent women. Moralistically minded Old Hollywood toned down the talky adaptation of the Guy de Maupassant novel, but it's still drama of a high order.
1947 112m/B George Sanders, Angela Lansbury, Ann Dvorak, Frances Dee, John Carradine, Susan Douglas, Hugo Haas, Marie Wilson, Albert Basserman, Warren William, Katherine Emery, Richard Fraser; *W/D:* Albert Lewin. **VHS** $19.98 *REP, FCT* ♫♫♫

Private Benjamin Lighthearted fare about a pampered New York Jewish princess who impulsively enlists in the U.S. Army after her husband dies on their wedding night. Hawn, who also produced, creates a character loveable even at her worst moments and brings a surprising amount of depth to this otherwise frivolous look at high society attitudes. The basis for the television series.
1980 (R) 110m/C Goldie Hawn, Eileen Brennan, Albert Brooks, Robert Webber, Armand Assante, Barbara Barrie, Mary Kay Place, Sally Kirkland, Craig T. Nelson, Harry Dean Stanton, Sam Wanamaker; *D:* Howard Zieff. **VHS, Beta, LV** $19.98 *WAR* ♫♫½

Private Buckaroo War time entertainment in which Harry James and his orchestra get drafted. They decide to put on a show for the soldiers and get help from the Andrews Sisters. ♫Don't Sit Under the Apple Tree with Anyone Else But Me; Three Little Sisters; Private Buckaroo; Johnny Get Your Gun Again; We've Got a Job to Do; You Made Me Love You; Six Jerks in a Jeep; That's the Moon My Son; I Love the South; Nobody Knows the Trouble I've Seen; Ma, I Miss Your Apple Pie.
1942 70m/B The Andrews Sisters, Harry James, Joe E. Lewis, Dick Foran, Shemp Howard, Mary Wickes, Donald O'Connor; *D:* Eddie Cline. **VHS, Beta, 3/4U, Special order formats** $19.95 *NOS, HEG, CAB* ♫½

Private Contentment This is a drama about a young soldier's experiences before he goes off to war in 1945.
1983 90m/C Trini Alvarado, Peter Gallagher, John McMartin, Kathryn Walker; *D:* Vivian Matalon. **VHS, Beta** *FLI* ♫♫

Private Duty Nurses Three nurses take on racism, war wounds, and a menage-a-trois (between one nurse, a doctor, and a drug addict). Second in Roger Corman's "nurse" quintet takes itself too seriously to be entertaining, but the gals make good use of those exciting new inventions, waterbeds. Preceded by "The Student Nurses" and followed by "Night Call Nurses," "The Young Nurses," and "Candy Stripe Nurses." Also on video as "Young L.A. Nurses 1."
1971 (R) 80m/C Katherine Cannon, Joyce Williams, Pegi Boucher, Joseph Kaufmann, Dennis Redfield, Herbert Jefferson Jr., Paul Hampton, Paul Gleason; *W/D:* George Armitage. **VHS, Beta** $59.98 *NLC, SUE* ♫½

The Private Eyes Light and uneven comedic romp with Knotts and Conway as bungling sleuths engaged to investigate two deaths. They're led on a merry chase through secret passages to a meeting with a ghostly adversary.
1980 (PG) 91m/C Don Knotts, Tim Conway, Trisha Noble, Bernard Fox; *D:* Lang Elliott. **VHS, Beta, LV** $29.98 *VES* ♫½

The Private Files of J. Edgar Hoover Scandal-mongering "biography" of J. Edgar Hoover's private, sex-filled life.
1977 (PG) 112m/C Broderick Crawford, Dan Dailey, Jose Ferrer, Rip Torn, Michael Parks, Raymond St. Jacques, Ronee Blakley; *D:* Larry Cohen. **VHS** $69.99 *HBO* ♫♫½

A Private Function A ribald gag-fest dealing with Palin as a Yorkshireman who steals and fattens a wily contraband pig against the backdrop of post-World War II rationing. The satire ranges from biting to downright nasty, but Palin is always likeable in the center of it all.
1984 (PG) 96m/C *GB* Michael Palin, Maggie Smith, Denholm Elliott, Bill Paterson, Liz Smith; *D:* Malcolm Mowbray. **VHS, Beta** $19.95 *PAR, HBO, TVC* ♫♫½

Private Hell 36 Two detectives become guilt-ridden after keeping part of some stolen money recovered after a robbery. Co-produced and co-written by Lupino, who also sings.
1954 81m/B Ida Lupino, Howard Duff, Steve Cochran; *D:* Don Siegel. **VHS, LV** $19.95 *REP* ♫♫

The Private History of a Campaign That Failed Adaptation of the Mark Twain story about a cowardly troop of Confederate soldiers.
1987 89m/C Pat Hingle, Edward Herrmann. **VHS, Beta** $19.95 *MCA* ♫½

Private Investigations A made-for-video thriller about a nosey reporter who gets himself and his adult son in trouble while investigating drug-pushing cops.
1987 (R) 91m/C Ray Sharkey, Clayton Rohner, Talia Balsam, Anthony Zerbe, Paul LeMat; *D:* Nigel Dick. **VHS, Beta** $14.95 *MGM, FOX* ♫½

Private Lessons Teenage boy is left alone for the summer in the care of an alluring maid and a scheming chauffeur.
1981 (R) 83m/C Eric Brown, Sylvia Kristel, Howard Hesseman; *D:* Alan Myerson. **VHS, Beta, LV** $24.95 *MCA* ♫

Private Lessons A boy can't concentrate on his piano lessons when he gets a beautiful new teacher. You won't be able to concentrate on anything but comedy.
19?? 90m/C Carroll Baker. **VHS, Beta** $79.95 *JEF* ♫♫

Private Life Suddenly with time on his hands, a Soviet official scrutinizes his relationships. After a number of revelations, he is forced to make new choices based on what he has learned. Oscar nominee in 1983. In Russian with English subtitles. *AKA:* Chastnaya Zhizn.
1982 103m/C *RU* Mikhail Ulyanov, Ita Sanvina, Irina Gubanova; *D:* Edgar Ryazanov. **VHS** $59.95 *KIV, FCT* ♫♫½

Private Life of Don Juan Appropriately slow-moving British costume drama set in 17th-century Spain finds an aging Don Juan struggling to maintain his usual antics in the pursuit of beautiful women. Furthermore, his reputation is being upstaged by a young imposter. Notable only as the last film appearance by Douglas Fairbanks Sr., and based on the play by Henri Bataille. *AKA:* Don Juan.
1934 87m/B *GB* Douglas Fairbanks Sr., Merle Oberon, Binnie Barnes, Melville Cooper, Joan Gardner, Benita Hume, Athene Seyler; *D:* Alexander Korda. **VHS, Beta, 3/4U, Special order formats** $9.95 *NEG, NOS, GPV* ♫♫

The Private Life of Henry VIII Lavish historical spectacle lustily portraying the life and lovers of notorious British Monarch, King Henry VIII. A tour de force for Laughton as the robust 16th-century king, with outstanding performances by the entire cast.
1933 97m/B *GB* Charles Laughton, Binnie Barnes, Elsa Lanchester, Robert Donat, Merle Oberon; *D:* Alexander Korda. Academy Awards '33: Best Actor (Laughton); Nominations: Best Picture. **VHS, Beta, LV, 3/4U, Special order formats** $19.98 *HBO, NOS, PSM* ♫♫♫♫

The Private Life of Sherlock Holmes A unique perspective on the life of the famous detective reveals a complex character. Beautifully photographed, with fine performances by the supporting cast, the film boasts a haunting musical score but received suprisingly little recognition despite the high caliber direction by Wilder, who co-wrote with I.A.L. Diamond.
1970 (PG) 125m/C *GB* Robert Stephens, Colin Blakely, Genevieve Page, Irene Handl, Stanley Holloway, Christopher Lee, Clive Revill; *D:* Billy Wilder. **VHS** $59.98 *FOX* ♫♫♫½

Private Lives Stylish adaptation of Noel Coward play starring Shearer and Montgomery as a couple with a tempestuous relationship. Although once married, they have since divorced and married other mates. While honeymooning at the same french hotel (Quelle coincidence!), they have trouble showing affection to their new spouses and realize they still feel passionately about one another. Excellent acting combined with Coward's witty dialogue makes this film a treat.
1931 92m/B Norma Shearer, Robert Montgomery, Reginald Denny, Una Merkel, Jean Hersholt; *D:* Sidney Franklin. **VHS** $19.98 *MGM* ♫♫♫½

The Private Lives of Elizabeth & Essex Cast reads like a Who's Who in Hollywood in this lavishly costumed dramatization of the love affair between Queen Elizabeth I and the Second Earl of Essex. Forced to choose between her Kingdom and her lover, Davis' monarch is the epitome of a regal women. Fobray made her first film appearance as an adult in the adaptation of Maxwell Anderson's "Elizabeth the Queen."
1939 106m/C Bette Davis, Errol Flynn, Vincent Price, Nanette Fabray, Olivia de Havilland, Alan Hale Jr., Donald Crisp, Leo G. Carroll; *D:* Michael Curtiz. **VHS, Beta** $19.98 *FOX* ♫♫♫

Private Manoeuvres A comely Swiss military adviser gives her all to uplift the morale of the men at Camp Samantha.
1983 79m/C Zachi Noy, Yoseph Shiloah, Dvora Bekon. **VHS, Beta** $59.95 *MGM* Woof!

A Private Matter Based on the true story of Sherri Finkbine (hostess of TV's "Romper Room") and the controversy surrounding her decision to terminate her pregnancy in 1962. Pregnant with her fifth child, she discovered her sleeping medication contained thalidomide, known to cause severe birth defects. Although technically illegal, her doctor agreed to quietly perform an abortion. Sherri warned a local newspaper reporter about the drug's dangers and her identity was mistakenly revealed. A storm of adverse publicity forced her to Sweden for the abortion. Great performances highlight this complex and traumatic issue. Made for cable television.
1992 (PG-13) 89m/C Sissy Spacek, Aidan Quinn, Estelle Parsons; *W:* William Nicholson. **VHS, LV $89.99** *HBO* ♪♪♪

Private Parts A bizarre first attempt at feature length for Bartel. Black comedy featuring a runaway, a voyeuristic photographer and a hotel full of strange people who participate in murder and a variety of freakish sexual acts.
1972 (R) 87m/C Ayn Ruymen, Lucille Benson, John Ventantonio, Laurie Main, Stanley Livingston, Charles Woolf; *D:* Paul Bartel. **VHS $18.00** *FRG* ♪

Private Passions A sultry woman gives her teenaged cousin a lesson in love during his European vacation.
1985 86m/C Sybil Danning. **VHS, Beta $59.95** *PSM* ♪

Private Popsicle Sex comedy starring Europe's popular Popsicle team. Dubbed in English.
1982 (R) 111m/C Zachi Noy, Jonathan Segall, Yftach Katzur. **VHS, Beta $59.95** *MGM, GLV* ♪

Private Resort Curious house detective and a bumbling thief interrupt the highjinks of two girl-crazy teens on a quest for fun at an expensive Miami hotel. Occasionally funny plodder.
1984 (R) 82m/C Johnny Depp, Rob Morrow, Karyn O'Bryan, Emily Longstreth, Tony Azito, Hector Elizondo, Dody Goodman, Leslie Easterbrook, Andrew Dice Clay; *D:* George Bowers. **VHS, Beta, LV $14.95** *COL* ♪♪

Private Road: No Trespassing A stock car racer and a top engineer compete over a military project, cars and a rich heiress.
1987 (R) 90m/C George Kennedy, Greg Evigan, Mitzi Kapture; *D:* Raphael Nussbaum. **VHS, Beta $79.95** *TWE* ♪♪

Private School Two high school girls from the exclusive Cherryvale Academy for Women compete for the affections of a young man from nearby Freemount Academy for Men, while Cherryvale's headmistress is trying to raise funds to build a new wing. Banal teen sexploitation comedy with better-than-average cast.
1983 (R) 89m/C Phoebe Cates, Betsy Russell, Kathleen Wilhoite, Sylvia Kristel, Ray Walston, Matthew Modine, Michael Zorek, Fran Ryan, Jonathan Prince, Kari Lizer, Richard Stahl; *D:* Noel Black. **VHS, Beta, LV $14.95** *MCA* ♪½

The Private Secretary Horton is a mild-mannered clergyman who finds out his identity has been usurped by a young man with a great many angry creditors. Horton has some amusing comic bits but the film, based on a popular Victorian farce "Der Bibliotheker" by Van Moser, did not translate well to the screen.
1935 70m/B *GB* Edward Everett Horton, Barry Mackay, Oscar Asche, Judy Gunn, Michael Shepley, Alastair Sim; *D:* Henry Edwards. **VHS** *HCV* ♪½

Private War Training for an elite force turns deadly when the commanding officer makes the rules. Now it's a private war between two brutal fighting machines. Screenplay by De Palma, from a Jan Guillou story.
1990 (R) 95m/C Martin Hewitt, Joe Dallesandro, Kimberly Beck; *D:* Frank De Palma. **VHS $89.98** *REP* ♪½

Privates on Parade Film centering around the comic antics of an Army song-and-dance unit entertaining the troops in the Malayan jungle during the late '40s. Occasionally-inspired horseplay based on Peter Nichols play.
1984 (R) 107m/C *GB* John Cleese, Denis Quilley, Simon Jones, Joe Melia, Nicola Pagetti, Julian Sands; *D:* Michael Blakemore. **VHS, Beta $19.95** *PAR, HBO, TVC* ♪♪½

Prix de Beaute A woman's boyfriend does not know that she has won a beauty contest. Brooks' last starring role and the only film she did in France. In French with English subtitles. *AKA:* Miss Europe.
1930 93m/B *FR* Louise Brooks, Jean Bradin, George Charlia, Gaston Jacquet; *D:* Augusto Genina. **VHS, Beta $59.95** *INT, TAM* ♪½

The Prize Gripping spy story laced with laughs based on a novel by Irving Wallace (as adapted by Ernest Lehman). In Stockholm, writer accepts the Nobel prize for dubious reasons and then finds himself in the midst of political intrigue. Newman and Sommer turn in great performances in this action drama.
1963 136m/C Paul Newman, Edward G. Robinson, Elke Sommer, Leo G. Carroll, Diane Baker, Micheline Presle, Gerard Oury, Sergio Fantoni; *D:* Mark Robson; *M:* Jerry Goldsmith. **VHS $19.98** *MGM, REP, MLB* ♪♪♪

Prize Fighter Comedy team of Knotts and Conway take on Depression-era boxing. Fight manager Knotts and his pugilistic protege Conway unknowingly get involved with a powerful gangster, who convinces them to fight in a fixed championship match. Written by Conway and most enjoyable if intelligence is suspended at onset.
1979 (PG) 99m/C Tim Conway, Don Knotts; *D:* Michael Preece. **VHS, Beta $9.95** *MED* ♪♪

Prize of Peril A French television game show rewards it winners with wealth and its losers with execution. Not always the best policy to learn what's behind Door #1.
1984 95m/C *FR* Michel Piccoli, Marie-France Pisier; *D:* Yves Boisset. **VHS, Beta $79.98** *LIV* ♪♪

The Prize Pulitzer Watered-down, made-for-television account of the scandalous divorce between publishing heir Herbert "Pete" Pulitzer and his young wife Roxanne. Based on the book "The Prize Pulitzer" by Roxanne Pulitzer. Also known as "Roxanne: The Prize Pulitzer."
1989 95m/C Perry King, Chynna Phillips, Courteney Cox, Betsy Russell, Sondra Blake, Caitlin Brown; *D:* Richard A. Colla. **VHS** *CAF* ♪♪

The Prizefighter and the Lady In his first film role boxer Baer (who won the heavyweight boxing crown in 1934) is a natural as a fighter who falls for a beautiful nightclub singer (Loy). Baer and Loy get, but don't stay, together but she does turn out to be his lucky charm in the big fight finale. Fellow professional boxer Carnera, Baer's opponent in the climatic fight scene, refused to lose as the script indicated and the film ending was eventually rewritten. The likeable Baer later earned his living as an actor. *AKA:* Every Woman's Man.

1933 102m/B Max Baer, Myrna Loy, Otto Kruger, Primo Carnera, Walter Huston, Vince Barnett, Muriel Evans; *D:* Woodbridge S. Van Dyke. **LV** *MGM* ♪♪♪

Prizzi's Honor Highly stylized, sometimes leaden black comedy about an aging and none-to-bright hit man from a New York mob family who breaks with family loyalties when he falls for an upwardly mobile tax consultant who's also a hired killer. Skirting caricature in every frame, Nicholson is excellent in his portrayal of the thick-skulled mobster, as are Angelica Huston as the hot-to-trot Mafia daughter and Hickey as the Don. Adapted by Richard Condon and Janet Roach from Condon's novel.
1985 (R) 130m/C Jack Nicholson, Kathleen Turner, Robert Loggia, John Randolph, Anjelica Huston, Lawrence Tierney, William Hickey, Lee Richardson; *D:* John Huston. Academy Awards '85: Best Supporting Actress (Huston); Nominations: Best Actor (Nicholson); Best Adapted Screenplay, Best Costume Design, Best Director (Huston), Best Film Editing, Best Picture, Best Supporting Actor (Hickey); Golden Globe Awards '86: Best Actor—Musical/Comedy (Nicholson), Best Actress—Musical/Comedy (Turner), Best Director (Huston), Best Film—Musical/Comedy; New York Film Critics Awards '85: Best Film. **VHS, Beta, LV $29.98** *LIV, VES, BTV* ♪♪♪

Probation A dashing young man in trouble with the law receives an unusual sentence; he must become a chauffeur for a spoiled society girl. Grable's first film role is a small one. *AKA:* Second Chances.
1932 60m/B Sally Blane, J. Farrell MacDonald, Eddie Phillips, Clara Kimball Young, Betty Grable; *D:* Richard Thorpe. **VHS, Beta $16.95** *NOS, SNC* ♪♪

Probe A detective uses computer-age technology to apprehend criminals. Pilot for the television series "Search."
1972 95m/C Hugh O'Brian, Elke Sommer, John Gielgud, Burgess Meredith, Angel Tompkins, Lilia Skala, Kent Smith, Alfred Ryder, Jaclyn Smith; *D:* Russ Mayberry; *W:* Leslie Stevens. **VHS $59.95** *UNI* ♪♪½

Problem Child Ritter decides to adopt Oliver out of the goodness of his heart, but it seems young Oliver's already got a father figure named Beelzebub. Potential for laughs is unmet.
1990 (PG) 81m/C John Ritter, Michael Oliver, Jack Warden, Amy Yasbeck, Gilbert Gottfried, Michael Richards, Peter Jurasik; *D:* Dennis Dugan. **VHS, LV $19.95** *MCA* ♪½

Problem Child 2 Ritter and his nasty adopted son are back, but this time there's an equally malevolent little girl. They team up to prevent Ritter's upcoming marriage to a socialite. Low slapstick junk.
1991 (PG-13) 91m/C John Ritter, Michael Oliver, Laraine Newman, Amy Yasbeck, Jack Warden, Ivyann Schwan, Gilbert Gottfried, James Tolkan, Charlene Tilton, Alan Blumenfeld; *D:* Brian Levant. **VHS, Beta, LV $19.98** *MCA, PIA* ♪

The Prodigal Luke's New Testament Bible story of the son seduced by greed slickly transfered to the silver screen by MGM. A colorful cast is the main attraction.
1955 113m/C Lana Turner, Edmund Purdom, Louis Calhern, Audrey Dalton, Neville Brand, Walter Hampden, Taina Elg, Francis L. Sullivan, Joseph Wiseman, Sandy Descher, John Dehner, Cecil Kellaway, Henry Daniell, Paul Cavanagh, Tracey Roberts, Jay Novello, Dorothy Adams, Richard Devon; *D:* Richard Thorpe. **LV $19.98** *MGM* ♪♪

The Prodigal A born-again family drama in which a sundered family is brought together by the return of a once-estranged son.

1983 (PG) 109m/C John Hammond, Hope Lange, John Cullum, Morgan Brittany, Ian Bannen, Arliss Howard, Joey Travolta, Billy Graham. VHS, Beta, LV $59.95 LIV �䄴

Prodigal Boxer: The Kick of Death A son must avenge his father's death by facing two kung fu masters.
1973 (R) 90m/C Meng Fei, Pa Hung, Suma Wah Lung. VHS, Beta, LV $19.95 GEM, MRV ✄

The Prodigal Planet Small group of believers continue their struggle against the world government UNTIE by disrupting their communication network. Sequel to "Thief in the Night," "A Distant Thunder," and "Image of the Beast."
1988 67m/C William Wellman Jr., Linda Beatie, Cathy Wellman, Thom Rachford; D: Donald W. Thompson. VHS, Beta MIV, HHE ✄

The Producers Considered one of Brooks' best films, this hilarious farce follows an attempted swindle by a con artist and his accountant who attempt to stage a Broadway flop only to have it backfire. Achieving cult status, the film is known for musical interlude "Springtime for Hitler." The phony play was later actually produced by Alan Johnson.
1968 90m/C Zero Mostel, Gene Wilder, Dick Shawn, Kenneth Mars, Estelle Winwood; W/D: Mel Brooks. Academy Awards '68: Best Story & Screenplay; Nominations: Best Supporting Actor (Wilder). VHS, Beta, LV, 8mm $14.95 COL, VYG, CRC ✄✄✄½

Professional Killers 1 Trio of hired assassins wanders about the countryside killing people during Japan's Feudal Era.
1973 87m/C Jiro Tamiya, Koji Takahashi. VHS, Beta NO ✄

The Professionals Action and adventure count for more than a storyline in this exciting western about four mercenaries hired by a wealthy cattle baron to rescue his young wife from Mexican kidnappers. Breathtaking photography recreates turn-of-the-century Mexico in this adaptation of the Frank O'Rourke novel.
1966 (PG) 117m/C Burt Lancaster, Lee Marvin, Claudia Cardinale, Jack Palance, Robert Ryan, Woody Strode, Ralph Bellamy; D: Richard Brooks. VHS, Beta, LV $69.95 COL, PIA ✄✄✄½

Professionals When the daily rigors of cocaine smuggling begin to dampen their spirits, the "Professionals" plan an exciting plutonium heist. From the British Action Show.
1976 104m/C Gordon Jackson, Martin Shaw, Lewis Collins. VHS, Beta, LV $59.95 TWE ✄✄

The Professor Rare sci-fi thriller featuring a werewolf, an eccentric scientist and a communist plot. Also includes several 'werewolf' oriented movie trailers.
1958 30m/C Doug Hobart, John Copeland, Irene Barr. VHS $16.95 SNC ✄✄

Profile A newsman gets an editorial job for a magazine called "Profile," and promptly falls in love with the boss's daughter. Complications arise when the boss's wife puts the moves on him. As if that isn't trouble enough, he finds himself accused of embezzlement. Average entertainment with some notable performances and an interesting chase scene.
1954 65m/B John Bentley, Kathleen Byron, Thea Gregory, Stuart Lindsell; D: Francis Searle. VHS, Beta $16.95 SNC ✄✄½

Programmed to Kill A beautiful terrorist is captured by the CIA and transformed into a buxom bionic assassin. AKA: Retaliator.

1986 (R) 91m/C Robert Ginty, Sandahl Bergman, James Booth, Louise Caire Clark; D: Allan Holzman. VHS, Beta $79.95 MED ✄✄

Project A-ko Set in the near future, this Japanese animated feature, which is intended for adults, concerns teenagers with strange powers, an alien spaceship, and lots of action. Seventeen year-old A-ko possesses superhuman strength and a ditzy sidekick, C-ko. B-ko, the spoiled and rich daughter of a business tycoon, decides to fight A-ko for C-ko's companionship. Meanwhile, an alien spaceship is headed toward Earth with unknown intentions. Somehow, everything ties together—watch and see how. In Japanese with English subtitles.
1986 86m/C VHS, LV $39.95 CPM, TAM, WTA ✄✄

Project: Alien Science fiction fans in search of a good extraterrestrial flick should avoid this teaser, for it has nothing to do with aliens. As the film begins, Earth is allegedly being attacked by beings from space, and a vast array of scientists, militia and journalists track the aliens. What's actually happening revolves around the testing of deadly biological weapons. Shot in Yugoslavia.
1989 92m/C Michael Nouri, Darlanne Fluegel, Maxwell Caulfield, Charles Durning; D: Frank Shields; W: Anthony Able. VHS, LV $89.95 VMK ✄

Project: Eliminator A group of terrorists kidnap a designer of "smart" weapons, and it's up to a hard-hitting special forces unit to get him back. Filmed in New Mexico.
1991 (R) 89m/C David Carradine, Frank Zagarino, Drew Snyder, Hilary English, Vivian Schilling; W/D: H. Kaye Dyal. VHS $89.98 NO ✄½

Project: Kill! Head of a murder-for-hire squad suddenly disappears and his former assistant is hired to track him down dead or alive.
1977 94m/C Leslie Nielsen, Gary Lockwood, Nancy Kwan. VHS, Beta PGN, QVD ✄

Project Moon Base Espionage runs rampant on a spaceship headed by a female officer. Eventually the ship is stranded on the moon. Actually filmed for a television series "Ring Around the Moon." A cold-war sexist relic.
1953 64m/B Donna Martell, Hayden Rourke; D: Richard Talmadge. VHS, Beta VMK ✄½

Project: Nightmare Seems not all dreams are wish fulfillment, when these nightmares start coming true.
19?? 75m/C Charles Miller, Elly Koslo, Lance Dickson; D: Don Jones. VHS $19.99 ACA, MOV ✄½

Project: Shadowchaser Action-packed would-be thriller about a billion dollar android who escapes from a top secret government laboratory. Programmed with superhuman strength and no human emotions the android and five terrorists take over a hospital (located in a skyscraper no less). Their hostages include the President's daughter and the terrorists demand a 50 million dollar ransom. With a four-hour deadline the FBI calls in the hospital architect to advise them—only they've got the wrong man—and the android's creator, who wants his creation back—no matter what the cost. A low budget Terminator clone.
1992 (R) 97m/C Martin Kove, Meg Foster, Frank Zagarino, Paul Koslo, Joss Ackland; D: John Eyres. VHS $89.95 PSM ✄½

Project X A bemused Air Force pilot is assigned to a special project involving chimpanzees. He must decide where his duty lies when he realizes the semi-intelligent chimps are slated to die.

1987 (PG) 107m/C Matthew Broderick, Helen Hunt; D: Jonathan Kaplan. VHS, Beta, LV $19.98 FOX ✄✄½

The Projectionist A must-see for movie buffs, Dangerfield made his screen debut in this story about a projectionist in a seedy movie house whose real-life existence begins to blur into the films he continuously watches. Made on a limited budget, this creative effort by Hurwitz was the first film to utilize the technique of superimposition.
1971 (PG) 84m/C Rodney Dangerfield, Chuck McCann, Ina Balin; D: Harry Hurwitz. VHS, Beta $69.98 LIV, VES ✄✄✄

Prom Night A masked killer stalks four high school girls during their senior prom as revenge for a murder which occurred six years prior. Sequelled by "Hello Mary Lou: Prom Night II" and "Prom Night III: The Last Kiss."
1980 (R) 91m/C CA Jamie Lee Curtis, Leslie Nielsen; D: Paul Lynch. VHS, Beta, LV $19.95 NLC ✄✄

Prom Night 3: The Last Kiss The second sequel, in which the reappearing high school ghoul beguiles a lucky teenager.
1989 (R) 97m/C Tim Conlon, Cyndy Preston, Courtney Taylor; D: Ron Oliver, Peter Simpson. VHS, Beta, LV $14.95 LIV ✄

Prom Night 4: Deliver Us From Evil Yet another gory entry in the Prom series (one would hope it will be the last). Another group of naive teens decide that they can have more fun at a private party than at the prom. They host the party in a summer home that was once a monastery, but the festive affair soon turns into a night of terror when an uninvited guest crashes the party. For true fans of slasher flicks.
1991 (R) 95m/C Nikki DeBoer, Alden Kane, Joy Tanner, Alle Ghadban; D: Clay Borris. VHS $89.98 LIV ✄

The Promise Weepie outdated story about star-crossed lovers Michael (Collins) and Nancy (Quinlan). A car accident leaves Michael comatose and Nancy badly disfigured. Michael's mother (Straight), who loathes Nancy, sees her chance to finally break them up. She offers to pay for Nancy's plastic surgery if she'll leave Michael forever, then Mom tells her son his girlfriend's dead. A year later Nancy, with her new face and new identity, and Michael meet. From the novel by Danielle Steele. AKA: Face of a Stranger.
1978 (PG) 97m/C Stephen Collins, Kathleen Quinlan, Beatrice Straight, Laurence Luckinbill, William Prince, Michael O'Hare; D: Gilbert Cates; W: Garry Michael White. VHS $89.98 MCA ✄✄

Promise Her Anything A widow (Caron) with a baby decides to make her boss (Cummings), a child psychologist who hates kids, her new husband. So she stashes the kid with her upstairs neighbor (Beatty), a would-be filmmaker who earns his living making blue movies. But the filmmaker has romantic designs on the widow and decides the baby may be his way to make a good impression. Beatty isn't very believable in this type of light-romantic comedy and the farcical situations are forced.
1966 98m/C GB Warren Beatty, Leslie Caron, Robert Cummings, Hermione Gingold, Lionel Stander, Keenan Wynn, Cathleen Nesbitt; D: Arthur Hiller; W: William Peter Blatty. VHS $14.95 PAR ✄✄

Promise to Murder An early murder-drama episode from the "Climax" television series.
1956 60m/B Peter Lorre, Louis Hayward, Ann Harding. VHS, Beta $24.95 NOS, DVT ✄½

P

Promised a Miracle Based on the true story of a religious couple who sought help for their diabetic son through prayer rather than conventional medical means. Following the boy's death in 1974 the couple were charged with manslaughter. From the non-fiction account "We Let Our Son Die" by Larry Parker. Made for television.
1988 (PG) 94m/C Rosanna Arquette, Judge Reinhold, Tom Bower, Gary Bayer, Maria O'Brien; **D:** Stephen Gyllenhaal; **W:** David Hill. **VHS, LV** $89.98 *REP* ♂♂½

Promised Land Two high school friends from the rural northwestern U.S. come together several years after graduation under tragic circumstances. Writer Hoffman's semi-autobiographical, disillusioned look at the American Dream was re-discovered by movie goers due to its excellent dramatic performances, notable also as the first film produced by Robert Redford's Sundance Institute. *AKA:* Young Hearts.
1988 (R) 110m/C Kiefer Sutherland, Meg Ryan, Tracy Pollan, Jason Gedrick, Googy Gress, Deborah Richter, Sandra Seacat, Jay Underwood; **D:** Michael Hoffman. **VHS, Beta, LV** $29.98 *LIV, VES* ♂♂♂

Promises in the Dark Drama focusing on the complex relationship between a woman doctor and her 17-year-old female patient who is terminally ill with cancer. Hellman's directorial debut.
1979 (PG) 118m/C Marsha Mason, Ned Beatty, Kathleen Beller, Susan Clark, Paul Clemens, Donald Moffatt, Michael Brandon; **D:** Gerome Hellman. **VHS, Beta** $59.95 *WAR* ♂♂½

Promises! Promises! Having difficulty getting pregnant, a woman goes on a cruise with her husband. While on board, they meet another couple, all get drunk, and change partners. Of course, both women find themselves pregnant, leaving the paternity in doubt. Famous primarily as the movie Mansfield told "Playboy" magazine she appeared "completely nude" in. *AKA:* Promise Her Anything.
1963 90m/B Jayne Mansfield, Marie McDonald, Tommy Noonan, Fritz Feld, Claude Stroud. **VHS, Beta** $24.95 *SIM* ♂½

The Promoter Horatio Alger comedy stars Guinness as an impoverished student who gives himself a surreptitious leg up in life by altering his school entrance exam scores. Outstanding performances enliven this subtle British comedy of morals. *AKA:* The Card.
1952 87m/B *GB* Alec Guinness, Glynis Johns, Petula Clark, Valerie Hobson, Michael Hordern; **D:** Ronald Neame. **VHS, Beta** *NO* ♂♂♂

Proof Directorial debut of Moorhouse tells a tale of manipulation, friendship, and obsessive love between a blind photographer, Martin, his housekeeper, and the young man he befriends. Martin, mistrustful of the world around him, takes photographs as "proof" of the reality of his life. A chance meeting with Andy provides Martin with his "eyes" and the opportunity to expand his world and emotions—something his housekeeper, Celia, would be only too happy to help him with. Unhealthy triangle leads all three to a re-evaluation of their lives. Propelled by terrific performances and enough humor to balance its emotional content.
1991 (R) 90m/C *AU* Hugo Weaving, Genevieve Picot, Russell Crowe, Heather Mitchell, Jeffrey Walker; **W/D:** Jocelyn Moorhouse. **VHS, LV** $89.95 *NLC, COL, TAM* ♂♂♂

Proof of the Man A Japanese co-production about a murder in Tokyo that takes on international importance.
1984 100m/C *JP* George Kennedy, Broderick Crawford, Toshiro Mifune. **VHS, Beta** $69.95 *VCD* ♂

Property A comedy about a group of leftover '60s radicals adjusting to 1970s corporate America.
1978 92m/C VHS, 3/4U *NO* ♂½

Prophecy A doctor and his wife travel to Maine to research the effects of pollution caused by the lumber industry. They encounter several terrifying freaks of nature and a series of bizarre human deaths. Laughable horror film.
1979 (PG) 102m/C Talia Shire, Robert Foxworth, Armand Assante, Victoria Racimo, Richard Dysart; **D:** John Frankenheimer. **VHS, Beta** $19.95 *PAR* ♂½

A Propos de Nice First film by French director Vigo, the silent film parodies French travelogues in a manner that indicates the director's later brilliance.
1929 25m/B *FR* **D:** Jean Vigo. **VHS, Beta** *FST, MRV* ♂♂♂

Prospero's Books Greenaway's free-ranging adaptation of Shakespeare's "The Tempest" has all his usual hallmarks of the bizarre. Gielgud is the aged Prospero, exiled to a magical island with his innocent daughter Miranda, and 24 beloved books containing the magician's recipe for life, each of which becomes a separate chapter in the film. Greenaway mixes film and high-definition video to create, with cinematographer Sacha Vierny, dazzling visuals that threaten to overwhelm but don't quite, thanks to both Greenaway's skill and the astonishing performance of the then 87 year-old Gielgud.
1991 (R) 129m/C John Gielgud, Michel Blanc, Erland Josephson, Isabelle Pasco, Tom Bell, Kenneth Cranham, Michael Clark; **W/D:** Peter Greenaway. **VHS, Beta, LV** $89.98 *FXV, FCT* ♂♂♂

Protect Your Daughters Hilarious schlock featuring good girls getting involved with sex and alcohol. Also known as "Reckless Decision."
1932 ?m/B VHS $16.95 *SNC* ♂

Protector A semi-martial arts cops 'n' robbers epic about the cracking of a Hong Kong-New York heroin route.
1985 (R) 94m/C Jackie Chan, Danny Aiello; **D:** James Glickenhaus. **VHS, Beta, LV** $79.95 *WAR* ♂

Protocol A series of comic accidents lead a Washington cocktail waitress into the U.S. State Department's employ as a protocol official. Once there she is used as a pawn to make an arms deal with a Middle Eastern country. Typical Hawn comedy with an enjoyable ending.
1984 (PG) 100m/C Goldie Hawn, Chris Sarandon, Andre Gregory, Cliff DeYoung, Ed Begley Jr., Gail Strickland, Richard Romanus, Keith Szarabajka, James Staley, Kenneth Mars, Kenneth McMillan, Archie Hahn, Amanda Bearse; **D:** Herbert Ross. **VHS, Beta, LV** $19.98 *WAR* ♂♂

Prototype Made-for-television revision of the Frankenstein legend has award-winning scientist Plummer as the creator of the first android. Fearful of the use the military branch of government has in mind for his creation, he attempts to steal back his discovery, in this suspenseful adventure.
1983 100m/C Christopher Plummer, David Morse, Frances Sternhagen, James Sutorius; **D:** David Greene. **VHS, LV** $14.95 *LIV* ♂♂♂

Prototype X29A The year is 2057 in a desolate, lawless Los Angeles. A research scientist is conducting experiments on a crippled ex-soldier named Hawkins when they suddenly go awry, turning him into a half-man, half-machine robot. Known as Prototype, the creature goes on a hunting and killing spree. Lame "Terminator" & "Robocop" takeoff.
1992 (R) 98m/C Brenda Swanson. **VHS, LV** $89.95 *VMK* ♂½

The Proud and the Damned Five Civil-War-veteran mercenaries wander into a Latin American war and get manipulated by both sides. *AKA:* Proud, Damned, and Dead.
1972 (PG) 95m/C Chuck Connors, Aron Kincaid, Cesar Romero; **D:** Ferde Grofe Jr. **VHS, Beta** $19.95 *NOS, UHV, MRV* ♂

Proud Men A cattle rancher and his expatriate son are separated by bitterness toward each other. Good acting from Heston and Strauss, plus good action sequences, but totally ordinary script.
1987 95m/C Charlton Heston, Peter Strauss, Nan Martin, Alan Autry, Belinda Balaski, Red West; **D:** William A. Graham. **VHS** $89.98 *TTC* ♂♂

Proud Rebel A character study of a stubborn widower who searches for a doctor to aid him in dealing with the problems of his mute son, and of the woman who helps to tame the boy. Ladd's real-life son makes his acting debut.
1958 99m/C Alan Ladd, Olivia de Havilland, Dean Jagger, Harry Dean Stanton; **D:** Michael Curtiz. **VHS, Beta** $69.98 *SUE* ♂♂♂

Providence An interesting score highlights this British fantasy drama of a dying writer envisioning his final novel as a fusion of the people from his past with the circumstances he encounters on a daily basis. The first English-language effort by French director Resnais. Score by Miklos Rozsa.
1977 (R) 104m/C *GB* John Gielgud, Dirk Bogarde, Ellen Burstyn, David Warner, Elaine Stritch; **D:** Alain Resnais. **VHS, Beta** $59.95 *COL* ♂♂♂

Provoked What would you do if your husband were being held hostage by a gang of ruthless, but stupid, escaped cons? Well, Maranne actually wants her husband back (maybe 'cause they're newlyweds) and no by-the-book police chief (Jones) is gonna stop her. This bride gets her hands on some automatic weaponry and look out! Shot in eight days with a $130,000 budget.
1989 90m/C Cindy Maranne, McKeiver Jones III, Harold W. Jones, Sharon Blair, Bob Fall, Joe Sprosty, Phyllis Durant, Tara Untiedt; **D:** Rick Pamplin; **W:** Tara Untiedt, Steve Pake. **VHS, Beta** $69.95 *RAE, HHE* ♂♂½

Prowler Heflin is a cop who responds to a prowler scare and finds the beautiful married Keyes worried about an intruder. He learns she will inherit a lot of money if anything happens to her husband so he seduces her and then "accidentally" kills her husband, supposedly mistaking him for a prowler. Keyes then marries Heflin but when she learns the truth her own life is in danger. Tidy thriller with Heflin doing a good job as the unpredictable villain.
1951 92m/B Van Heflin, Evelyn Keyes, Katherine Warren, John Maxwell; **D:** Joseph Zito. **VHS, Beta** *NO* ♂♂½

The Prowler A soldier returns from duty during World War II, only to find his girl in bed with another guy. He kills them, and for unclear reasons, returns to the same town 35 years later to kill more people. An effectsfest for Tom Savini. *AKA:* Rosemary's Killer.
1981 (R) 87m/C Vicky Dawson, Christopher Goutman, Cindy Weintraub, Farley Granger, John Seitz, Lawrence Tierney; **D:** Joseph Zito. **VHS** $49.95 *VHE* ♂

Prudential Family Playhouse Presentation of Sinclair Lewis' "Dodsworth." Tells the story of a wealthy American couple who travel from their small town to Europe.
1950 53m/B Ruth Chatterton, Walter Abel, Cliff Hall, Eva Marie Saint. **VHS, Beta** $24.95 *VYY ♫*

Prurient Interest A video play revolving around a movie producer's battle with the Board of Censors for approval of his feature "Eat Me in St. Louis."
1974 20m/B VHS, Beta *EAI ♫*

PSI Factor A civilian researcher working at the NASA space track station observes and records signals coming from planet Serius B.
1980 91m/C Peter Mark Richman, Gretchen Corbett, Tom Martin; **D:** Quentin Masters. **VHS** $79.95 *MNC ♫♫½*

Psych-Out A deaf girl searches Haight-Ashbury for her runaway brother. She meets hippies and flower children during the Summer of Love. Psychedelic score with Strawberry Alarm Clock and The Seeds. Somewhere in the picture, Nicholson whangs on lead guitar.
1968 95m/C Jack Nicholson, Bruce Dern, Susan Strasberg, Dean Stockwell, Henry Jaglom; **D:** Richard Rush. **VHS, Beta, LV** $19.99 *HBO ♫♫½*

Psychedelic Fever A swinging look at the free-love decade of the 1960s.
1990 (R) 80m/C D: William Rostler. **VHS** *NO ♫*

The Psychic An ad executive gains psychic powers after he falls off a ladder and tries to conquer the world. A later effort by gore-king Lewis, notable only for sex scenes inserted by Lewis to make the movie salable.
1968 90m/C Dick Genola, Robin Guest, Bobbi Spencer; **D:** Herschell Gordon Lewis. **VHS, Beta** *NO Woof!*

The Psychic A psychic envisions her own death and attempts to alter the prediction.
1978 (R) 90m/C Jennifer O'Neill, Marc Porel, Evelyn Stewart, Gabriel Forzetti, Gianno Garko; **D:** Lucio Fulci. **VHS, Beta** *NO ♫*

Psychic A college student with psychic powers believes he knows who the next victim of a demented serial killer will be. The problem is: no one will believe him. And the victim is the woman he loves.
1991 (R) 92m/C Michael Nouri, Catherine Mary Stewart, Zach Galligan. **VHS** $89.95 *VMK ♫½*

Psychic Killer A wrongfully committed asylum inmate acquires psychic powers and decides to use them in a deadly revenge. Good cast in cheapie horror flick.
1975 (PG) 89m/C Jim Hutton, Paul Burke, Julie Adams, Neville Brand, Aldo Ray, Rod Cameron, Della Reese; **D:** Ray Danton. **VHS, Beta** $14.98 *SUE ♫½*

Psycho Hitchcock counted on his directorial stature and broke all the rules in this story of violent murder, transvestism, and insanity. Based on Robert Bloch's novelization of an actual murder, Leigh plays a fleeing thief who stops at the secluded Bates Motel where she meets her death in Hitchcock's classic "shower scene." Shot on a limited budget in little more than a month, "Psycho" changed the Hollywood horror film forever. Music by Bernard Herrman. Followed by "Psycho II" (1983), "Psycho III" (1986), and a made-for-television movie.
1960 109m/B Anthony Perkins, Janet Leigh, Vera Miles, John Gavin, John McIntire, Martin Balsam, Simon Oakland, Ted Knight; **D:** Alfred Hitchcock. *Academy Awards '60 Nominations: Best Art Direction/Set Decoration (B & W), Best Black and White Cinematography, Best Director (Hitchcock), Best Supporting Actress (Leigh); Edgar Allan Poe Awards '60: Best Screenplay;*

Golden Globe Awards '61: Best Supporting Actress (Leigh). **VHS, Beta, LV** $19.95 *MCA, TLF ♫♫♫♫*

Psycho 2 This sequel to the Hitchcock classic finds Norman Bates returning home after 22 years in an asylum to find himself haunted by "mother" and caught up in a series of murders. In a surprisingly good horror film, Perkins and Miles reprise their roles from the original "Psycho." Perkins went on to direct yet another sequel, "Psycho 3."
1983 (R) 113m/C Anthony Perkins, Vera Miles, Meg Tilly, Robert Loggia, Dennis Franz; **D:** Richard Franklin; **M:** Jerry Goldsmith. **VHS, Beta, LV** $19.95 *MCA ♫♫*

Psycho 3 The second sequel to Hitchcock's "Psycho" finds Norman Bates drawn into his past by "mother" and the appearance of a woman who reminds him of this original victim. Perkins made his directorial debut in this film that stretches the plausibility of the storyline to its limits, but the element of parody throughout makes this an entertaining film for "Psycho" fans.
1986 (R) 93m/C Anthony Perkins, Diana Scarwid, Jeff Fahey, Roberta Maxwell, Robert Alan Browne; **D:** Anthony Perkins. **VHS, Beta, LV** $19.95 *MCA ♫♫*

Psycho 4: The Beginning Prequels "Psycho" when, at the behest of a radio talk show host, Norman Bates recounts his childhood and reveals the circumstances that aided in the development of his peculiar neuroses. Stefano wrote the original screenplay and the original score is used, but this doesn't even come close to the original.
1990 (R) 96m/C Anthony Perkins, Henry Thomas, Olivia Hussey, CCH Pounder, Warren Frost, Donna Mitchell; **D:** Mick Garris; **W:** Joseph Stefano; **M:** Bernard Herrmann. **VHS, Beta** $79.95 *MCA, PIA ♫♫*

Psycho Cop Six college undergrads on a weekend retreat are menaced and picked off one at a time by a crazed local cop.
1988 89m/C Bobby Ray Shafer; **D:** Wallace Potts. **VHS, Beta** $89.95 *NO ♫½*

Psycho from Texas Quiet Southern town is disrupted by the kidnapping of a wealthy oil man, followed by a string of meaningless murders. **AKA:** The Butcher.
1983 (R) 85m/C King John III, Candy Dee, Janel King. **VHS, Beta** *PGN ♫*

Psycho Girls Very low budget horror flick redeemed by spurts of weird black humor. Crazed woman is released from institution to seek out sister who should have been put away in the first place. She crashes anniversary celebration and, well, let's just say she's not the life of the party. Never released theatrically.
1986 (R) 87m/C *CA* John Haslett Cuff, Darlene Mignacco, Agi Gallus, Rose Graham, Silvio Oliviero, Michael Hoole, Pier Giorgia DiCicco, Fernne Kane; **W/D:** Gerard Ciccoritti; **W:** Michael Boekner. **VHS, Beta** $79.95 *MGM ♫*

Psychomania Semi-limpid mystery thriller about a former war hero and painter who is suspected of being the demented killer stalking girls on campus. To prove his innocence, he tracks the killer himself. **AKA:** Violent Midnight.
1963 95m/C Lee Phillips, Sheppard Strudwick, Jean Hale, Dick Van Patten, Sylvia Miles, James Farentino; **D:** Richard Hilliard. **VHS, Beta** $24.95 *SNC, HHT ♫½*

Psychomania A drama of the supernatural, the occult, and the violence which lies just beyond the conventions of society for a group of dead motorcyclists, the Living Dead, who all came back to life after commit-

ting suicide with the help of the devil. **AKA:** The Death Wheelers.
1973 (R) 89m/C *GB* George Sanders, Beryl Reid, Nicky Henson, Mary Laroche, Patrick Holt; **D:** Don Sharp. **VHS, Beta** $29.95 *MED, WWV, MRV ♫♫*

Psychopath A film about a modern-day, slightly unhinged, Robin Hood and his escapades, stealing from other thieves and giving to the victimized.
1968 90m/C *GB* Klaus Kinski, George Martin, Ingrid Schoeller; **D:** Guido Zurli. **VHS, Beta** $59.95 *LTG ♫½*

Psychopath A nutso children's television personality begins to murder abusive parents. Fairly gory, and definitely not for family viewing. **AKA:** An Eye for an Eye.
1973 (PG) 85m/C Tom Basham, Gene Carlson, Gretchen Kanne; **D:** Larry G. Brown; **M:** John Williams. **VHS, Beta** $69.95 *MED ♫*

Psychos in Love A psychotic murderer who hates grapes of any kind finds the woman of his dreams—she's a psychotic murderer who hates grapes! Together they find bliss—until the plumber discovers their secret!
1987 90m/C Carmine Capobianco, Debi Thibeault, Frank Stewart; **D:** Gorman Bechard. **VHS, Beta** $69.95 *UHV ♫*

The Psychotronic Man An innocent man suddenly finds he possesses amazing and dangerous powers, enabling him to control outside events with a thought.
1991 88m/C Peter Spelson, Christopher Carbis, Curt Colbert, Robin Newton, Paul Marvel; **D:** Jack M. Sell. **VHS** *UNI ♫½*

PT 109 The World War II exploits of Lieutenant (j.g.) John F. Kennedy in the South Pacific. Part of the "A Night at the Movies" series, this tape simulates a 1963 movie evening, with a Foghorn Leghorn cartoon ("Banty Raids"), a newsreel on the JFK assassination, and coming attractions for "Critic's Choice" and "Four for Texas."
1963 159m/C Cliff Robertson, Ty Hardin, Ty Hardin, Robert (Bobby) Blake, Robert Culp, James Gregory; **D:** Leslie Martinson. **VHS, Beta, LV** $19.98 *WAR, PIA ♫♫*

Puberty Blues Two Australian girls become part of the local surfing scene in order to be accepted by the "in crowd" at their high school.
1981 (R) 86m/C *AU* Neil Schofield, Jad Capelja; **D:** Bruce Beresford. **VHS, Beta** $59.95 *MCA ♫♫½*

A Public Affair Exposes the evils and abuses of collection agencies without even a shred of humor. Certainly gets its point across, but will bore any audience to tears or spontaneous naps.
1962 71m/B Myron McCormick, Edward Binns, Harry Carey Jr., Rocky Aoki. **VHS, Beta** $29.99 *VYY ♫½*

Public Cowboy No. 1 Cattle thieves use a radio, airplanes, and refrigerator trucks in their updated rustling schemes.
1937 54m/B Gene Autry, William Farnum. **VHS, Beta** $19.95 *NOS, VCN, DVT ♫½*

Public Enemy Cagney's acting career was launched by this story of two Irish boys growing up in a Chicago shantytown to become hoodlums during the prohibition era. Cagney and Woods hook up with molls Clarke and Blondell on their rise to the top. Considered the most realistic "gangster" film, Wellman's movie is also the most grimly brutal due to its release prior to Hollywood censorship. The scene where Cagney smashes a grapefruit in Clarke's face was credited with starting a trend in abusing film heroines. **AKA:** Enemies of the Public.

1931 85m/B James Cagney, Edward Woods, Leslie Fenton, Joan Blondell, Mae Clarke, Jean Harlow; *D:* William A. Wellman. VHS, Beta, LV $19.95 MGM, FOX 𝕚𝕚𝕚½

The Public Eye
Underappreciated film noir homage depicts Pesci as a crime photographer with an unsuspected romantic streak. It's 1942 in New York City and Leon "Bernzy" Bernstein is a cynical freelancer always looking for the perfect shot. Hershey's the recent widow who learns that her nightclub-owner husband had been indebted to the mob. Hershey would like to sever the ties and decides Pesci would be a likely patsy for helping her out. Hershey seems decorative and the romantic angle between her and Pesci never quite develops, but Pesci delivers a rich, low-key performance as the visionary, hard-boiled artist. Climatic mob shootout is cinematic bullet ballet. Based loosely on the career of '40s photog Weegee, who defined New York and its times in his work.
1992 (R) 98m/C Joe Pesci, Barbara Hershey, Stanley Tucci, Richard Foronjy, Richard Riehle, Jared Harris, Jerry Adler, Dominic Chianese, Gerry Becker; *W/D:* Howard Franklin; *M:* John Barry. VHS, Beta, LV MCA 𝕚𝕚𝕚

Pucker Up and Bark Like a Dog
A young artist and his inspirationally lovely actress girl-friend find themselves in strange and crazy situations. Good cast gives this potential.
1989 (R) 94m/C Lisa Zane, Jonathan Gries, Paul Bartel, Robert Culp; *D:* Paul S. Parco. VHS $79.95 FRH, BTV 𝕚

Pudd'nhead Wilson
An adaptation of a Mark Twain story about a small-town lawyer who discovers the illicit exchange of a white infant for a light-skinned negro infant by a slave woman. Made for television as an "American Playhouse" presentation on PBS.
1987 87m/C Ken Howard; *D:* Alan Bridges. VHS, Beta $19.95 MCA 𝕚½

Pueblo Affair
A dramatization of the capture of the American spy ship "Pueblo" by the North Koreans, during which time the crew was tortured, imprisoned, and all intelligence documents were confiscated.
1973 99m/C Hal Holbrook, Andrew Duggan, Richard Mulligan, George Grizzard, Gary Merrill, Mary Fickett; *D:* Anthony Page. VHS, Beta LME 𝕚𝕚𝕚

Pulp
Caine, playing a mystery writer, becomes a target for murder when he ghostwrites the memoirs of a movie gangster from the 1930s. Directed deftly by Rooney.
1972 (PG) 95m/C GB Michael Caine, Mickey Rooney, Lionel Stander, Lizabeth Scott, Nadia Cassini, Dennis Price, Al Lettieri; *D:* Mike Hodges. VHS, Beta NO 𝕚𝕚½

Pulse
Electricity goes awry in this science-fiction thriller about appliances and other household devices that become supercharged and destroy property and their owners.
1988 (PG-13) 90m/C Cliff DeYoung, Roxanne Hart, Joey Lawrence, Charles Tyner, Dennis Redfield, Robert Romanus, Myron Healey; *D:* Paul Golding. VHS, Beta, LV $19.95 COL 𝕚𝕚

Pulsebeat
Flick about warring health club owners. As boring as it sounds unless you're in the mood for lots of on-screen aerobics. If so, rent Jane Fonda instead. Dubbed.
1985 92m/C SP Daniel Greene, Lee Taylor Allen, Bob Small, Alice Moore, Helga Line, Alex Intriago, Peter Lupus; *D:* Marice Tobias. VHS, Beta $69.98 LIV Woof!

The Puma Man
Puma Man is a super hero who must stop the evil Dr. Kobras from using an ancient mask in his attempt to become ruler of the world. Unreleased theatrically in the U.S., this low budget Sci fi/horror mix is so bad one wonders why an actor like Pleasence would sign on. Special effects these days are so extraordinary that the ones employed here are laughable.
1980 80m/C IT Donald Pleasence, Walter George Alton, Sydne Rome, Miguel Angel Fuentes; *D:* Alvin J. Neitz, Alberto De Martino. VHS, Beta $59.95 PSM Woof!

Pump Up the Volume
High school newcomer leads double life as Hard Harry, sarcastic host of an illegal radio broadcast and Jack Nicholson soundalike. Anonymously popular with his peers, he invites the wrath of the school principal due to his less than flattering comments about the school administration. Slater seems to enjoy himself as defiant deejay while youthful cast effectively supports.
1990 (R) 105m/C Christian Slater, Scott Paulin, Ellen Greene, Samantha Mathis, Cheryl Pollak, Annie Ross; *W/D:* Allan Moyle. VHS, LV, 8mm $14.95 COL, FCT, MVD 𝕚𝕚½

Pumping Iron
A widely acclaimed documentary look at the sport of bodybuilding, following the behind-the-scenes action surrounding the competition for the Mr. Olympia title. The grueling training ritual and the constant striving for perfection are all explored.
1976 (PG) 90m/C Arnold Schwarzenegger, Mike Katz, Franco Columbo, Lou Ferrigno; *D:* George Butler. VHS, Beta, LV $24.95 COL, SCH, RHI 𝕚𝕚½

Pumping Iron 2: The Women
This sequel to "Pumping Iron" takes an in-depth look at the world of female body building. The documentary also follows the ladies to a competition held at Caesar's Palace in Las Vegas.
1985 107m/C Lori Bowen, Bev Francis, Rachel McLish, Carla Dunlap, Lydia Cheng; *D:* George Butler. VHS, Beta, LV $79.95 VES 𝕚𝕚½

Pumpkinhead
A farmer evokes a demon from the earth to avenge his son's death. When it continues on its murdering rampage, the farmer finds he no longer has any control over the vicious killer.
1988 (R) 89m/C Lance Henriksen, John DiAquino, Kerry Remsen, Matthew Hurley, Jeff East, Kimberly Ross; *D:* Stan Winston. VHS, Beta, LV $19.95 MGM 𝕚𝕚½

Punch the Clock
Attractive female thief finds her bail bondsman very exciting; he's ready to help her any way he can.
1990 (R) 88m/C Michael Rogan, Chris Moore, James Lorinz; *D:* Eric L. Schlagman. VHS $79.98 VID 𝕚𝕚

Punchline
An ostensible look into the life of stand-up comics, following the career ups-and-downs of an embittered professional funny-man and a frustrated housewife hitting the stage for the first time. Written by Seltzer. Some very funny and touching moments and some not-so-funny and touching as the movie descends into melodrama without a cause.
1988 (R) 100m/C Tom Hanks, Sally Field, John Goodman, Mark Rydell, Kim Greist, Barry Sobel, Paul Mazursky, Pam Matteson, George Michael McGrath, Taylor Negron, Damon Wayans; *D:* David Seltzer. VHS, Beta, LV $19.95 COL 𝕚𝕚

The Punisher
Lundgren portrays Frank Castle, the Marvel Comics anti-hero known as the Punisher. When his family is killed by the mob Castle set his eyes on revenge. Filmed in Australia.

1990 (R) 92m/C Dolph Lundgren, Louis Gossett Jr., Jeroen Krabbe, Kim Miyori; *D:* Mark Goldblatt. VHS, Beta, LV $92.95 LIV 𝕚

Punk Rock Movie
The musical explosion known as punk rock is documented here in its early days (circa 1977) at the Roxy in England. Includes a look at leading punk rock artists such as the Sex Pistols, the Clash, Slits, and others, and at the entire counter-culture that was punk.
1978 80m/C VHS, Beta $19.95 MVD, SUN 𝕚

Punk Vacation
A gang of motorcycle mamas terrorize a small town. The usual biker stuff.
1990 90m/C Stephen Falchi, Roxanne Rogers, Don Martin, Sandra Bogan; *D:* Stanley Lewis. VHS, Beta, LV NO 𝕚

Puppet Master
Four psychics are sent to investigate a puppet maker who they think may have discovered the secret of life. Before they know it, they are stalked by evil puppets. Great special effects, not-so-great script.
1989 (R) 90m/C Paul LeMat, Jimmie F. Skaggs, Irene Miracle, Robin Rates, Barbara Crampton, William Hickey; *D:* David Schmoeller. VHS, Beta, LV $14.95 PAR 𝕚𝕚½

Puppet Master 2
Puppets on a rampage turn hotel into den of special effects. Less effective string pulling than in original. Long live Pinocchio.
1991 (R) 90m/C Elizabeth MacLellan, Collin Bernsen, Greg Webb, Charlie Spradling, Nita Talbot, Steve Welles, Jeff Weston; *D:* David Allen; *W:* David Pabian. VHS, Beta, LV $14.95 PAR 𝕚𝕚

Puppet Master 3: Toulon's Revenge
Prequel about the origin of the whole gory Puppet Master shebang, set in Nazi Germany. The weapon-hungry Third Reich tries to wrest secrets of artificial life from sorceror Andre Toulon, who sics his deadly puppets on them. Toulon's a good guy here, one of many contradictions in the series. Fine cast, but strictly for the followers.
1991 (R) 86m/C Guy Rolfe, Ian Abercrombie, Sarah Douglas; *D:* David DeCoteau. VHS, LV $14.95 PAR 𝕚𝕚

Puppet on a Chain
American narcotics officer busts an Amsterdam drug ring and the leader's identity surprises him. Slow-moving thriller based on the Alistair MacLean novel.
1972 (PG) 97m/C GB Sven-Bertil Taube, Barbara Parkins, Alexander Knox, Patrick Allen, Geoffrey Reeve; *D:* Geoffrey Reeve. VHS, Beta $59.95 PSM 𝕚𝕚

The Puppetoon Movie
A compilation of George Pal's famous Puppetoon cartoons from the 1940s, marking his stature as an animation pioneer and innovator. Hosted by Gumby, Pokey, Speedy Alka Seltzer and Arnie the Dinosaur in newly directed scenes.
1987 (G) 80m/C *D:* Arnold Leibovit. VHS, Beta, LV $19.95 FHE, IVE, WTA 𝕚𝕚

Pure Country
An easygoing movie about a familiar subject is held together by the charm of Strait (in his movie debut) and the rest of the cast. Strait plays a country music superstar, tired of the career glitz, who decides to get out and go back to his home in Texas. He falls in love with the spunky Glasser and decides to run his career his own way. Warren is effective as his tough manager and old-time cowboy Calhoun is finely weathered as Glasser's gruff dad.

1992 (PG) 113m/C George Strait, Isabel Glasser, Lesley Ann Warren, Rory Calhoun, Kyle Chandler, Molly McClure, John Doe; **D:** Christopher Cain. VHS, Beta, LV $94.99 WAR ♫♫½

The Pure Hell of St. Trinian's In this sequel to ''Blue Murder at St. Trinian's,'' a sheik who desires to fill out his harem tries recruiting at a rowdy girls' school. Although it isn't as funny as the first, due to the lack of Alistair Sim, it is still humorous. Followed by ''The Great St. Trinian's Train Robbery.'' Based on the cartoon by Ronald Searle.
1961 94m/B **GB** Cecil Parker, Joyce Grenfell, George Cole, Thorley Walters; **D:** Frank Launder. VHS FCT ♫♫½

Pure Luck A who-asked-for-it remake of a 1981 Franco-Italian film called ''La Chevre.'' The premise is the same: an accident-prone heiress disappears in Mexico, and her father tries to locate her using an equally clumsy accountant. The nebbish and an attendant tough private eye stumble and bumble south of the border until the plot arbitrarily ends. Pure awful.
1991 (PG) 96m/C Martin Short, Danny Glover, Sheila Kelley, Scott Wilson, Sam Wanamaker, Harry Shearer; **D:** Nadia Tass. VHS, Beta, LV $19.98 MCA, PIA ♫½

Purgatory While travelling abroad, two innocent women find themselves unjustly jailed. During their confinement they are tortured and raped.
1989 90m/C Tanya Roberts, Julie Pop; **D:** Ami Artzi. VHS, Beta, LV NO ♫

Purlie Victorious Presentation of the award-winning Broadway hit, which takes a look at racial integration.
1963 93m/C Ossie Davis, Ruby Dee, Godfrey Cambridge, Alan Alda; **D:** Nicholas Webster. VHS, Beta NO ♫♫

The Purple Heart An American Air Force crew is shot down over Tokyo and taken into brutal POW camps. Intense wartime melodramatics.
1944 99m/B Dana Andrews, Richard Conte, Farley Granger, Donald (Don ''Red'') Barry, Sam Levene, Kevin O'Shea, Tala Birell, Nestor Paiva, Benson Fong, Marshall Thompson, Richard Loo; **D:** Lewis Milestone. VHS, Beta $19.98 FOX ♫♫½

Purple Hearts Wahl stars as a Navy doctor who falls in love with nurse Ladd against the backdrop of the Vietnam war. Overlong and redundant.
1984 (R) 115m/C Cheryl Ladd, Ken Wahl, Stephen Lee, Annie McEnroe, Paul McCrane, Cyril O'Reilly; **D:** Sidney J. Furie. VHS, Beta $19.98 WAR ♫½

The Purple Monster Strikes A martian plots to conquer Earth to save his dying planet. Serial in fifteen episodes.
1945 188m/B Dennis Moore, Linda Stirling, Roy Barcroft; **D:** Spencer Gordon Bennet. VHS $29.98 REP, VCN, MLB ♫

Purple People Eater The alien of the title descends to earth to mix with young girls and rock 'n roll. Based on the song of the same name whose performer, Sheb Wooley, appears in the film. Harmless, stupid fun for the whole family.
1988 (PG) 91m/C Ned Beatty, Shelley Winters, Neil Patrick Harris, Kareem Abdul-Jabbar, Little Richard, Chubby Checker, Peggy Lipton; **D:** Linda Shayne. VHS, Beta, LV $79.95 MED ♫

Purple Rain A quasi-autobiographical video showcase for the pop-star Prince. Film tells the tale of his struggle for love, attention, acceptance, and popular artistic recognition in Minneapolis. Not a bad film, for such a monumentally egotistical movie.
1984 (R) 113m/C Prince, Apollonia, Morris Day, Olga Karlatos, Clarence Williams III; **D:** Albert Magnoli. VHS, Beta, LV $19.98 MVD, WAR ♫♫½

The Purple Rose of Cairo A diner waitress, disillusioned by the Depression and a lackluster life, escapes into a film playing at the local movie house where a blond film hero, tiring of the monotony of his role, makes a break from the celluloid to join her in the real world. The ensuing love story allows director-writer Allen to show his knowledge of old movies and provide his fans with a change of pace. Farrow's film sister is also her real-life sister Stephanie, who went on to appear in Allen's ''Zelig.''
1985 (PG) 82m/C Mia Farrow, Jeff Daniels, Danny Aiello, Dianne Wiest, Van Johnson, Zoe Caldwell, John Wood, Michael Tucker, Edward Herrmann, Milo O'Shea, Glenne Headly; **D:** Woody Allen. Academy Awards '85 Nominations: Best Original Screenplay; British Academy Awards '85: Best Film; Cesar Awards '86: Best Foreign Film. VHS, Beta, LV $19.98 LIV, VES, HMV ♫♫♫

The Purple Taxi Romantic drama revolving around several wealthy foreigners who have taken refuge in beautiful southern Ireland. From Michel Deon's bestselling novel.
1977 (R) 93m/C **FR** Fred Astaire, Charlotte Rampling, Peter Ustinov, Philippe Noiret, Edward Albert; **D:** Yves Boisset. VHS, Beta $59.95 COL ♫♫½

Purple Vigilantes The Three Mesquiteers uncover a gang of vigilantes. Part of the series. **AKA:** The Purple Riders.
1938 54m/B Bob Livingston, Ray Corrigan, Max Terhune. VHS, Beta VCN, DVT ♫½

Pursued Excellent performances by Mitchum and Wright mark this suspenseful Western drama of a Spanish-American war veteran in search of his father's killer.
1947 101m/B Teresa Wright, Robert Mitchum, Judith Anderson, Dean Jagger, Alan Hale Jr., Harry Carey Jr., John Rodney; **D:** Raoul Walsh. VHS $14.95 REP, HEG ♫♫

Pursuit A terrorist threatens to release a toxic nerve gas throughout a city hosting a political convention. Tension mounts as federal agents must beat the extremists' countdown to zero. Based on the novel by Crichton.
1972 73m/C Ben Gazzara, E.G. Marshall, Martin Sheen, Joseph Wiseman, William Windom; **D:** Michael Crichton; **M:** Jerry Goldsmith. VHS, Beta $69.95 REP ♫♫♫

Pursuit A mercenary comes out of retirement to join a renegade team recovering stolen gold. But they turn on him, stealing the treasure and taking a hostage. Now he must track them down, or there's no movie.
1990 (R) 94m/C James Ryan, Andre Jacobs; **D:** John H. Parr. VHS $89.99 HBO ♫♫

The Pursuit of D.B. Cooper Based on an actual hijacking that occurred on Thanksgiving Eve in 1971 in which J.R. Meade (alias D.B. Cooper) parachuted out of an airliner with $200,000 of stolen money. Although his fate and whereabouts have remained a mystery, this story speculates about what may have happened.
1981 (PG) 100m/C Robert Duvall, Treat Williams, Kathryn Harrold, Ed Flanders; **D:** Roger Spottiswoode. VHS, Beta, LV $29.98 LIV, VES ♫♫

The Pursuit of Happiness An idealistic man is convicted of manslaughter after accidentally running down a woman. Once in prison, he's faced with the decision to try to escape.

1970 (PG) 85m/C Michael Sarrazin, Arthur Hill, E.G. Marshall, Barbara Hershey, Robert Klein; **D:** Robert Mulligan. VHS, Beta $69.95 RCA ♫♫½

Pursuit of the Graf Spee Three small British ships destroy the mighty Graf Spee, a World War II German battleship. **AKA:** The Battle of the River Plate.
1957 106m/C **GB** Anthony Quayle, Peter Finch, Ian Hunter; **D:** Michael Powell. VHS, Beta NO ♫♫½

Pursuit to Algiers The modernized Holmes and Watson guard over the King of fictional Rovenia during a sea voyage, during which assassins close in.
1945 65m/B Basil Rathbone, Nigel Bruce, Martin Kosleck, Marjorie Riordan, Rosalind Iven, John Abbott; **D:** Roy William Neill. VHS, Beta $14.98 FOX ♫♫½

Pushed to the Limit Harry Lee, the most feared gangster in Chinatown, is about to meet his match in martial-arts queen Lesseos. She's out for revenge when she learns that Lee is responsible for her brother's murder but first she must get by Lee's lethal bodyguard, the equally skilled Inga.
1992 (R) 88m/C Mimi Lesseos. VHS $89.95 IMP ♫½

Puss 'n Boots From ''Faerie Tale Theatre'' comes the story of a cat who makes his poor master a rich land-owning nobleman.
1984 60m/C Ben Vereen, Gregory Hines; **D:** Robert Iscove. VHS, Beta $14.98 KUI, FOX, FCT ♫½

Putney Swope Comedy about a token black ad man mistakenly elected Chairman of the board of a Madison Avenue ad agency who turns the company upside-down. A series of riotous spoofs on commercials is the highpoint in this funny, though somewhat dated look at big business.
1969 (R) 84m/B Arnold Johnson, Laura Greene, Stanley Gottlieb, Mel Brooks; **D:** Robert Downey. VHS, Beta $14.95 CUL, PTB ♫♫♫

Puzzle Franciscus searches for the urn that contains the remains of Buddha but instead finds danger and intrigue. Made for television.
1978 90m/C **AU** James Franciscus, Wendy Hughes, Robert Helpmann, Peter Gwynne, Gerald Kennedy, Kerry McGuire; **D:** Gordon Hessler. VHS $19.95 ACA ♫♫½

Pygmalion Oscar-winning film adaptation of Shaw's play about a cockney flower-girl who is transformed into a ''lady'' under the guidance of a stuffy phonetics professor. Shaw himself aided in writing the script in this superbly acted comedy that would be adapted into the musical, ''My Fair Lady,'' first on Broadway in 1956 and for the screen in 1964.
1938 96m/B **GB** Leslie Howard, Wendy Hiller, Wilfred Lawson, Marie Lohr; **D:** Leslie Howard, Anthony Asquith. Academy Awards '38: Best Adapted Screenplay; Nominations: Best Actor (Howard), Best Actress (Hiller), Best Picture; Venice Film Festival '38: Best Actor (Howard). VHS, Beta, LV $14.95 COL, NOS, SUE ♫♫♫½

Pyrates Real life husband-wife team of Bacon and Sedgwick try to provide fireworks as hot, hot lovers in the forgettable one. For the price of this one you can buy a newspaper and chewing gum instead. Use both at the same time and you'll be ahead of everyone involved in this senseless hoot.
1991 (R) 98m/C Kevin Bacon, Kyra Sedgwick, Bruce Martin Payne, Kristin Datillo; **D:** Noah Stern. VHS $89.98 VES, LIV ♫

Python Wolf It's non-stop action in South Africa as a counter-terrorist group sets out to thwart a drug smuggler's plans to export plutonium. As usual, intense pacing from director Friedkin. Made for television. Sequel to "C.A.T. Squad" (1986). *AKA:* C.A.T. Squad: Python Wolf.
1988 (R) 100m/C Joe Cortese, Jack Youngblood, Steve James, Deborah Van Valkenburgh, Miguel Ferrer, Alan Scarfe; *D:* William Friedkin; *M:* Ennio Morricone. **VHS, LV** $19.95 STE, VMK *ⁿⁿ*

The Pyx Canadian suspense thriller about the murder of a prostitute with satanic overtones. Poice sargeant investigates the crime and enters a world of devil worship and decadence. Based on the novel by John Buell. *AKA:* The Hooker Cult Murders.
1973 (R) 111m/C CA Karen Black, Christopher Plummer, Donald Pilon; *D:* Harvey Hart. **VHS** $39.95 PSM *ⁿⁿⁿ*

Q & A Semi-taut thriller with Nolte playing a totally corrupt, hair-trigger cop trying to make his murder of a drug dealer look like self-defense. Assigned to the case is an ex-cop turned assistant DA (Hutton) who's supposed to sweep the case under the rug. Then he finds out another dealer (Assante) is a witness and he happens to be romancing Hutton's former girlfriend (film debut of director Lumet's daughter). Lots of violence and raw language.
1990 (R) 132m/C Nick Nolte, Timothy Hutton, Armand Assante, Patrick O'Neal, Lee Richardson, Luis Guzman, Charles S. Dutton, Jenny Lumet, Paul Calderone, Fyvush Finkel; *W/ D:* Sidney Lumet. **VHS, Beta, LV** $19.98 HBO *ⁿⁿ*

Q Ships Silent German drama about a submarine commander who has inner conflicts with his country's war effort.
1928 78m/B GE J.P. Kennedy, Roy Travers, Johnny Butt, Philip Hewland; *D:* Geoffrey Barkas. **VHS, Beta** $19.95 NOS, DVT, GLV *ⁿⁿ½*

Q (The Winged Serpent) A cult of admirers surrounds this goony monster flick about dragonlike Aztec god Quetzlcoatl, summoned to modern Manhattan by gory human sacrifices, and hungry for rooftop sunbathers and construction teams. Direction and special effects are pretty ragged, but witty script helps the cast shine, especially Moriarty as a lowlife crook who's found the beast's hidden nest. Also called "Q: The Winged Serpent."
1982 (R) 92m/C Michael Moriarty, Candy Clark, David Carradine, Richard Roundtree; *D:* Larry Cohen. **VHS, Beta** $14.98 MCA *ⁿⁿⁿ*

QB VII A knighted physician brings a suit for libel against a novelist for implicating him in war crimes. Hopkins as the purportedly wronged doctor and Gazzara as the writer are both superb. Ending is stunning. Adapted from the novel by Leon Uris. Over five hours long; made for TV. Available only as a three-cassette set.
1974 313m/C Anthony Hopkins, Ben Gazzara, Lee Remick, Leslie Caron, Juliet Mills, John Gielgud, Anthony Quayle; *D:* Tom Gries; *M:* Jerry Goldsmith. **VHS, Beta, LV** $139.95 COL, SWC *ⁿⁿⁿ½*

Quackser Fortune Has a Cousin in the Bronx An Irish fertilizer salesman meets an exchange student from the U.S., who finds herself attracted to this unlearned, but not unknowing, man. An original love story with drama and appeal. *AKA:* Fun Loving.
1970 88m/C IR Gene Wilder, Margot Kidder; *D:* Waris Hussein. **VHS, Beta, LV** $19.95 UHV *ⁿⁿⁿ*

Quadrophenia Pete Townshend's excellent rock opera about an alienated youth looking for life's meaning in Britain's rock scene circa 1963. Music by The Who is powerful and apt. Fine performance by Sting in his acting debut.
1979 (R) 115m/C GB Phil Daniels, Mark Wingett, Philip Davis, Leslie Ash, Sting; *D:* Franc Roddam. **VHS, Beta, LV** $19.95 MVD, COL, RHI *ⁿⁿⁿ*

Quake Railsback stars as a stalker who takes advantage of the 1990 San Franscisco earthquake to finally obtain the woman of his dreams. A surveillance expert, he's after a beautiful lawyer (Anderson) and when the earthquake leaves her trapped he rushes to rescue her—only to hold her captive himself.
1992 (R) 83m/C Steve Railsback, Erika Anderson, Eb Lottimer, Dick Miller; *D:* Louis Morneau; *W:* Mark Evan Schwartz. **VHS** $89.95 COL *ⁿ½*

Quality Street English lovers Tone and Hepburn are separated when he leaves to fight in the Napoleonic Wars. When Tone returns years later, he's forgotten his erstwhile heartthrob. He also fails to recognize that the 16-year old coquette who's caught his eye is his old beloved in disguise. Cast works hard to overcome the absurd premise, based on the play by Sir James Barrie.
1937 84m/B Katharine Hepburn, Franchot Tone, Fay Bainter, Eric Blore, Cora Witherspoon, Estelle Winwood, Florence Lake, Bonita Granville; *D:* George Stevens; *W:* Sir James Barrie. **VHS, LV** $19.98 NOS, FCT, TTC *ⁿⁿ*

Quarantine Quarantine camps for carriers of a fatal virus are the serious measures taken by the nation. The solution is clear to a rebel and an inventor; all must be liberated or exterminated.
1989 (R) 92m/C Beatrice Boepple, Garwin Sanford, Jerry Wasserman, Charles Wilkinson. **VHS** $89.98 REP *ⁿⁿ½*

Quarterback Princess Workaday made-for-TV telling of the real-life girl who goes out for football and becomes homecoming queen. Heartwarming, if you like that kinda stuff, but not exciting.
1985 96m/C Helen Hunt, Don Murray, John Stockwell, Daphne Zuniga; *D:* Noel Black. **VHS, Beta** $59.98 FOX *ⁿⁿ*

Quartet A young French women is taken in by an English couple after her husband goes to prison. The husband seduces her, and she becomes trapped emotionally and socially. Superbly acted, claustrophobic drama based on a Jean Rhys novel.
1981 (R) 101m/C GB FR Isabelle Adjani, Alan Bates, Maggie Smith, Anthony Higgins; *D:* James Ivory. **VHS, Beta** $19.98 WAR *ⁿⁿⁿ*

Quatermass 2 In the well-made sequel to "Quatermass Experiment," (also known as "The Creeping Unknown") Professor Quatermass battles blobs and brainwashed zombies to rescue government officials whose bodies have been invaded by aliens. "Five Million Years to Earth" concluded the trilogy. *AKA:* Enemy from Space.
1957 84m/B GB Brian Donlevy, John Longden, Sidney James, Bryan Forbes, William Franklyn, Vera Day, John Van Eyssen, Michael Ripper, Michael Balfour; *D:* Val Guest. **VHS, Beta, LV** $54.95 FCT, CTH, SNC *ⁿⁿⁿ*

Quatermass Conclusion An elderly British scientist comes out of retirement to stop an immobilizing death ray from outer space from destroying Earth. Edited version of a television miniseries continues earlier adventures of Quatermass on film and television.

1979 105m/C GB John Mills, Simon MacCorkindale, Barbara Kellerman, Margaret Tyzack; *D:* Piers Haggard. **VHS, Beta** $59.99 HBO *ⁿⁿ*

The Quatermass Experiment Excellent British production about an astronaut who returns to Earth carrying an alien infestation that causes him to turn into a horrible monster. Competent acting and tense direction. Followed by "Enemy From Space." *AKA:* The Creeping Unknown.
1956 78m/B GB Brian Donlevy, Margia Dean, Jack Warner, Richard Wordsworth; *D:* Val Guest. **VHS** $19.95 NOS, SNC *ⁿⁿⁿ*

Quatorze Juliet A taxi driver and a flower girl meet on Bastille Day and fall in love. When he becomes involved with gangsters, she steers him back to virtue in this minor French relic from director Clair.
1932 85m/B FR Anabella Rigaud, Jorge Rigaud; *D:* Rene Clair. **VHS** $29.95 VDM, FCT *ⁿⁿ½*

Que Viva Mexico Eisenstein's grand unfinished folly on the history of Mexico, reconstructed and released in 1979 by his protege, Grigori Alexandrov. Divided into four sections: "Sandunga" covers the Tehuantepec jungles and its inhabitants; "Manguei" is about a peasant and his bride; "Fiesta" devotes itself to bullfighting and romance; and "Soldadera" depicts the 1910 Mexican revolution through frescoes. Along with "Greed" and "Napoleon," it remains as one of cinema's greatest irrecoverable casualties. Russian narration with English subtitles.
1932 85m/B RU *D:* Sergei Eisenstein, Grigori Alexandrov. **VHS, Beta** $59.95 KIV *ⁿⁿⁿ*

Queen Boxer A female kick-boxer beats up those who reprehensibly enslaved her family.
1973 (R) 92m/C Judy Lee, Peter Yang Kwan. **VHS, Beta** $12.95 LIV *ⁿ*

Queen Christina A stylish, resonant star vehicle for Garbo, portraying the 17th-century Swedish queen from ascension to the throne to her romance with a Spanish ambassador. Alternately hilarious and moving, it holds some of Garbo's greatest and most memorable moments. Gilbert's second to last film and his only successful outing after the coming of sound.
1933 101m/B Greta Garbo, John Gilbert, Lewis Stone, C. Aubrey Smith, Ian Keith, Reginald Owen, Elizabeth Young; *D:* Rouben Mamoulian. **VHS, Beta, LV** $19.98 MGM *ⁿⁿⁿ½*

Queen for a Day Three differing vignettes, based on a rather notorious radio/TV game show of the time, in which "deserving" (or sufficiently pathetic) working-class women were rewarded for their selflessness. Part one concerns a perfect suburban family whose son contracts polio. Part two has a teen spooking his immigrant parents by working as a carnival high diver to earn college cash. The finale is a Dorothy Parker farce about a homely but kindhearted nurse caring for the child of an unappreciative couple. So popular was this segment that the film was retitled after the main character. Overall, not bad considering the source. *AKA:* Horsie.
1951 107m/B Phyllis Avery, Darren McGavin, Tristram Coffin, Adam Williams, Tracey Roberts, Jack Bailey, Jim Morgan, Fort Pearson; *D:* Arthur Lubin. **VHS** $19.95 NOS *ⁿ½*

Queen Kelly The popularly known, slapdash version of von Stroheim's famous final film, in which an orphan goes from royal marriage to white slavery to astounding wealth. Never really finished, the film is the edited first half of the intended project,

prepared for European release after von Stroheim had been fired. Even so, a campy, extravagant and lusty melodrama. Silent.
1929 113m/B Gloria Swanson, Walter Byron, Seena Owen, Tully Marshall, Madame Sul Te Wan; *D:* Erich von Stroheim. **VHS, Beta, LV, 8mm $19.95** *NOS, KIV, VYY 444*

Queen of Diamonds A woman pulls off the biggest diamond heist of all time.
198? 90m/C Claudia Cardinale, Stanley Baker, Henri Charriere. **VHS, Beta** *NO 44*

Queen of Diamonds The "Queen of Diamonds" is an alienated blackjack dealer in Vegas who, in between dealing cards, casually searches for her missing husband and looks after an old man in a motel.
1991 77m/C Tinka Menkes; *W/D:* Nina Menkes. **VHS $59.95** *FCT 44*

Queen of Hearts Excellent, original romantic comedy is a directorial triumph for Amiel in his first feature. An Italian couple defy both their families and marry for love. Four children later, we find them running a diner in England. Humorous, dramatic, sad—everything a move can and should be. Fine performances.
1989 (PG) 112m/C *GB* Anita Zagaria, Joseph Long, Eileen Way, Vittorio Duse, Vittorio Amandola, Ian Hawkes; *D:* Jon Amiel. **VHS, Beta, LV** *NO 444½*

The Queen of Mean Tabloid TV-movie based on Ransdell Pierson's scandal-sheet bio of the hotel magnate and convicted tax cheat. See Leona connive. See Leona bitch. See Leona get hers. What's the point? If you ask that you're too bright to watch. *AKA:* Leona Helmsley: The Queen of Mean.
1990 94m/C Suzanne Pleshette, Lloyd Bridges, Bruce Weitz, Joe Regalbuto; *D:* Richard Michaels. **VHS $64.95** *FRH 4½*

Queen of Outer Space Notorious male-chauvinist sci-fi cheapie starts out slow, but then the laughs keep coming as the cast plays the hyperdumb material straight. Space cadets crash on Venus, and it ruled by women—and the dolls have wicked plans in store for mankind. Don't be surprised if you've seen the sets before since they were borrowed from "Forbidden Planet," "World Without End," and "Flight to Mars."
1958 80m/C Zsa Zsa Gabor, Eric Fleming, Laurie Mitchell, Paul Birch, Barbara Darrow, Dave Willcock, Lisa Davis, Patrick Waltz, Marilyn Buferd, Marjorie Durant, Lynn Cartwright, Gerry Gaylor; *D:* Edward L. Bernds. **VHS, Beta $14.98** *FXV Woof!*

The Queen of Spades Mystical drama about a Russian soldier who ruins his life searching for winning methods of card playing. Well-made version of the Pushkin story.
1949 95m/B *GB* Anton Walbrook, Edith Evans, Ronald Howard, Mary Jerrold, Yvonne Mitchell, Anthony Dawson; *D:* Thorold Dickinson. **VHS, LV $79.99** *HBO 444*

Queen of the Amazons A girl searches for her fiance and finds him reluctantly held captive by a tribe of women who rule the jungle.
1947 60m/B Robert Lowery, Patricia Morison, J. Edward Bromberg, John Miljan. **VHS, Beta, LV $16.95** *SNC, NOS, WGE 4½*

Queen of the Jungle Re-edited adventure serial featuring a white woman cast off in a hot-air balloon and landing in Africa, where she is hailed as a Queen. High camp, starring ex-Our Ganger Kornman.
1935 85m/B Mary Kornman, Reed Howes; *D:* Robert Hill. **VHS, Beta, 8mm $26.95** *SNC, NOS, MLB 4*

Queen of the Road A feisty Aussie schoolteacher starts a new life as a tractor-trailer driver.
1984 96m/C *AU* Joanne Samuel, Amanda Muggleton; *D:* Bruce Best. **VHS, Beta $69.98** *LIV, VES 44*

Queen of the Stardust Ballroom Well-made television drama about a lonely widow who goes to a local dance hall, where she meets a man and begins an unconventional late love.
1975 98m/C Maureen Stapleton, Charles Durning, Michael Strong, Charlotte Rae, Sam O'Steen; *D:* Michael Brandon. **Beta $11.95** *PSM 444*

Queenie Television miniseries Loosely based on the life of actress Merle Oberon, exploring her rise to stardom. Based on the best-selling novel by Michael Korda, Oberon's nephew by marriage. Many long, dry passages fit for leaving the room for snacks.
1987 233m/C Mia Sara, Kirk Douglas, Martin Balsam, Claire Bloom, Chaim Topol, Joel Grey, Sarah Miles, Joss Ackland; *D:* Larry Peerce. **VHS $29.95** *STE, NWV 44½*

Queens Logic Ensemble comedy in the tradition of "The Big Chill" featuring the trials and tribulations of the "old-neighborhood" gang, who gather again on hometurf and reminisce. Most of the film centers around Olin and girlfriend Webb and whether or not he will chicken out of their wedding. Not bad comedy, with Mantegna delivering most of the good lines.
1991 (R) 116m/C John Malkovich, Kevin Bacon, Jamie Lee Curtis, Linda Fiorentino, Joe Mantegna, Ken Olin, Tom Waits, Chloe Webb, Ed Marinaro, Kelly Bishop; *D:* Steve Rash. **VHS, LV $92.98** *LIV 44½*

Querelle Querelle, a handsome sailor, finds himself involved in a bewildering environment of murder, drug smuggling, and homosexuality in the port of Brest. Highly stylized and erotic sets, along with a dark look, give the film an interesting feel. Nice performances by Davis, Nero, and Moreau. Fassbinder's controversial last film, based on the story by Jean Genet. Strange, difficult narrative (such as it is), alternately boring and engrossing.
1983 (R) 106m/C *GE* Brad Davis, Jeanne Moreau, Franco Nero, Laurent Malet; *D:* Rainer Werner Fassbinder. **VHS, Beta $59.95** *COL, APD, GLV 44½*

The Quest Australian film never released theatrically in the United States. A young boy (Thomas, of "E.T." fame) raised in the outback investigates a local Aboriginal superstition about a monster living in an ancient cemetery. Not bad, just dull.
1986 (PG) 94m/C *AU* Henry Thomas, Tony Barry, John Ewart, Rachel Friend, Tamsin West, Dennis Miller, Katya Manning; *D:* Brian Trenchard-Smith. **VHS, Beta $9.98** *NLC 44*

Quest for Fire An interesting story sans the usual dialogue thing. A group of men during the Ice Age must wander the land searching for fire after they lose theirs fending off an attack. During their quest, they encounter and battle various animals and tribesmen in order to survive. The special language they speak was developed by Anthony Burgess, while the primitive movements were Desmond "The Naked Ape" Morris. Perlman went on to become the Beast in TV's "Beauty and the Beast"; Chong is the daughter of Tommy Chong of the comic duo Cheech and Chong.
1982 (R) 75m/C *FR* Everett McGill, Ron Perlman, Nameer El-Kadi, Rae Dawn Chong; *D:* Jean-Jacques Annaud. **VHS, Beta, LV $69.98** *FOX, TAM 444*

Quest for Love Quirky sci-fi story of a man who passes through a time warp and finds himself able to maintain two parallel lives. Based on John Wyndham's short story.
1971 90m/C *GB* Joan Collins, Tom Bell, Denholm Elliott, Laurence Naismith; *D:* Ralph Thomas. **VHS, Beta** *NO 44½*

Quest for the Mighty Sword A warrior battles dragons, demons and evil wizards.
1990 (PG-13) 94m/C Eric Allen Kramer, Margaret Lenzey, Donald O'Brien, Dina Marrone, Chris Murphy; *D:* David Hills. **VHS, Beta, LV $79.95** *COL 4*

Question of Faith A happily married woman is diagnosed with a rare form of cancer. Much to her family's dismay, she turns to some unconventional medical therapies in order to heal herself. Based on a true story. Basically noble, Archer and Neill lift this tearjerker out of most of its maudlin aspects.
1993 90m/C Anne Archer, Sam Neill, Frances Lee McCain, James Tolkan, James Hong, CCH Pounder, Louis Giambalvo, Norman Parker, Michael Constantine; *D:* Stephen Gyllenhaal; *W:* Bruce Hart. **VHS $89.95** *WOV 44½*

A Question of Guilt When her child turns up dead, a free-wheeling divorcee is the prime suspect. Made-for-television soaper.
1978 100m/C Tuesday Weld, Ron Leibman, Peter Masterson, Alex Rocco, Viveca Lindfors, Lana Wood; *D:* Robert Butler. **VHS $39.95** *LIV 44*

Question of Honor Under governmental pressures, an honest narcotics cop decides to inform on his department's corruption. Co-written and produced by ex-cop Sonny Grosso, on who "The French Connection" was based. Made for television and based on the book, "Point Blank," by Grosso and Philip Rosenberg, with script by Budd Schulberg.
1980 134m/C Ben Gazzara, Paul Sorvino, Robert Vaughn, Tony Roberts, Danny Aiello, Anthony Zerbe; *D:* Judd Taylor. **VHS, Beta** *NO 44½*

A Question of Love Fine performances in this well-done television movie about two lesbians—one of whom is fighting her ex-husband for custody of their child.
1978 100m/C Gena Rowlands, Jane Alexander, Ned Beatty, Clu Gulager, Bonnie Bedelia, James Sutorius, Jocelyn Brando; *D:* Jerry Thorpe. **VHS** *NO 444*

Question of Silence Three women, strangers to each other, stand trial for a murdering a man. Intricately analyzed courtroom drama with much to say about male domination. In Dutch with English subtitles or dubbed. *AKA:* De Stilte Rond Christine M.
1983 (R) 92m/C *NL* Cox Habrema, Nelly Frijda, Henriette Tol, Edda Barends; *D:* Morleen Gorris. **VHS, Beta $59.95** *SUE, TAM 444*

Question 7 The fifteen-year-old son of a pastor who lives behind the iron curtain faces a dilemma: should he answer a political question the way his teacher wants or the way he believes? *AKA:* Frage 7.
1963 107m/B **VHS, Beta** *VGD 444*

Qui Etes Vous, Mr. Sorge? The story of German journalist Richard Sorge, who was hanged by the Japanese in 1944 for being a Soviet spy. Uninteresting docudrama which focuses on the opinions of various witnesses as to the accuracy of the espionage charge. In French with English subtitles.
1961 130m/B *FR* Thomas Holtzman, Keiko Kishi; *D:* Andre Girard. **VHS, Beta $19.95** *KRT, TAM 44*

The Quick and the Dead Based on a Louis L'Amour story, this made-for-cable western features a lone gunslinger who protects a defenseless settler's family from the lawless West, only to become a source of sexual tension for the wife.
1987 91m/C Sam Elliott, Tom Conti, Kate Capshaw, Kenny Morrison, Matt Clark; *D:* Robert Day. VHS, Beta $79.95 *LHV, WAR* ✗

Quick Change Murray, Davis, and Quaid form bumbling trio of New York bank robbers who can't seem to exit the Big Apple with loot. Based on Jay Cronley's book, it's Murray's directing debut (with help from screenwriter Franklin). Engaging minor caper comedy displaying plenty of NYC dirty boulevards.
1990 (R) 89m/C Bill Murray, Geena Davis, Randy Quaid, Jason Robards Jr., Bob Elliott, Victor Argo, Kathryn Grody; *D:* Bill Murray. VHS, Beta, LV, 8mm $19.98 *WAR* ✗✗½

Quick, Let's Get Married Quick, let's not watch this movie. Even the people who made it must have hated it: they waited seven years to release it. Rogers runs a whorehouse; Eden is a gullible, pregnant prostitute; Gould in his big-screen debut(!) is a deaf-mute. A must-not see. *AKA:* Seven Different Ways; The Confession.
1971 96m/C Ginger Rogers, Ray Milland, Barbara Eden, Carl Schell, Michael Ansara, Walter Abel, Scott Meyer, Cecil Kellaway, Elliott Gould; *D:* William Dieterle. VHS, Beta, LV *NO Woof!*

Quicker Than the Eye When a magician gets mixed up in an assassination plot, he must use his wit, cunning, and magic to get out of it.
1988 94m/C Ben Gazzara, Mary Crosby, Catherine Jarrett, Ivan Desny, Eb Lottimer, Sophie Carle, Wolfram Berger, Dinah Hinz, Jean Yanne; *D:* Nicolas Gessner. VHS, Beta $79.95 *ACA* ✗✗

Quicksand Mechanic Rooney borrows $20 from his boss's cash register, intending to return it. One thing leads to another, the plot thickens, and it's downhill (for Rooney) from there. Good, tense suspense drama.
1950 79m/B Mickey Rooney, Peter Lorre, Jeanne Cagney; *D:* Irving Pichel. VHS, Beta $14.95 *NOS, QNE, MRV* ✗✗½

Quicksand: No Escape Scott Reinhardt (Matheson) is a successful architect whose partner decides to secure a building contract by bribing a city official. When his partner is murdered Reinhardt is approached by a former cop (Sutherland) asking a lot of money for some incriminating evidence. Reinhardt is then drawn ever deeper into the illicit dealings, endangering his life.
1991 (PG-13) 93m/C Tim Matheson, Donald Sutherland, Jay Acovone, Timothy Carhart, John Finn, Marc Alaimo, Felicity Huffman, Al Pugliese; *D:* Michael Pressman. VHS, Beta, LV $89.98 *MCA* ✗✗

Quicksilver A young stockbroker loses all, then quits his job to become a city bicycle messenger. Pointless, self-indulgent yuppie fantasy. Songs by Roger Daltrey and Ray Parker, Jr.
1986 (PG) 106m/C Kevin Bacon, Jami Gertz, Paul Rodriguez, Rudy Ramos, Andrew Smith, Gerald S. O'Loughlin, Larry Fishburne, Louie Anderson; *D:* Tom Donnelly. VHS, Beta, LV $79.95 *COL* ✗½

Quiet Cool When his former girlfriend's family is killed, a New York cop travels to a sleepy California town run by a pot-growing tycoon. He subsequently kills the bad guys in a Rambo-like fit of vengeance. Dopey exercise in sleepy-eyed bloodshed.

1986 (R) 80m/C James Remar, Daphne Ashbrook, Adam Coleman Howard, Jared Martin, Fran Ryan; *D:* Clay Borris. VHS, Beta, LV $79.95 *COL* ✗

Quiet Day In Belfast Tragedy occurs when northern Irish patriots and British soldiers clash in an Irish betting parlor. Kidder plays a duel role: an Irish woman in love with a British soldier and the woman's twin sister. Convincingly adapted from a Canadian stage play.
1974 92m/C *CA* Barry Foster, Margot Kidder; *D:* Milad Bessada. VHS, Beta $59.95 *MED* ✗✗✗

The Quiet Earth Serious science fiction film about a scientist who awakens to find himself seemingly the only human left on earth as the result of a misfired time/space government experiment. He later finds two other people, a girl and a Maori tribesman, and must try to repair the damage in order to save what's left of mankind.
1985 (R) 91m/C *NZ* Bruno Lawrence, Alison Routledge, Peter Smith; *D:* Geoff Murphy. VHS, Beta, LV $19.98 *FOX* ✗✗✗

Quiet Fire A health-club owner tries to get the goods on the arms-dealing congressman who killed his best friend. Hilton-Jacobs looks properly pumped up since his sweathog days on TV's "Welcome Back Kotter."
1991 (R) 100m/C Lawrence Hilton-Jacobs, Robert Z'Dar, Nadia Marie, Karen Black, Lance Lindsey; *D:* Lawrence Hilton-Jacobs. VHS $79.95 *PMH* ✗½

The Quiet Man The classic incarnation of Hollywood Irishness, and one of Ford's best, and funniest films. Wayne is Sean Thornton, a weary American ex-boxer who returns to the Irish hamlet of his childhood and tries to take a spirited lass as his wife, despite the strenuous objections of her brawling brother (McLaglen). Thornton's aided by the leprechaun-like Fitzgerald and the local parish priest, Bond. A high-spirited and memorable film filled with Irish stew, wonderful banter, and shots of the lush countryside. Listen for the Scottish bagpipes at the start of the horse race, a slight geographic inaccuracy.
1952 129m/C John Wayne, Maureen O'Hara, Barry Fitzgerald, Victor McLaglen, Arthur Shields, Jack MacGowran, Ward Bond, Mildred Natwick; *D:* John Ford. Academy Awards '52: Best Color Cinematography, Best Director (Ford); Nominations: Best Art Direction/Set Decoration (Color), Best Picture, Best Screenplay, Best Sound, Best Supporting Actor (McLaglen); National Board of Review Awards '52: 10 Best Films of the Year; Venice Film Festival '52: Best Director (Ford). VHS, LV $19.98 *REP, TLF, CCB* ✗✗✗✗

Quiet Thunder A hard-drinking bush pilot in Africa and a beautiful senator's wife are thrown together on the run after both witness an assassination. Mindless, thoroughly derivative "adventure."
1987 (PG-13) 94m/C Wayne Crawford, June Chadwick, Victor Steinbach; *D:* David Rice. VHS, Beta, LV $79.95 *LIV* ✗

Quigley Down Under A Western sharpshooter moves to Australia in search of employment. To his horror, he discovers that he has been hired to kill aborigines. Predictable action is somewhat redeemed by the terrific chemistry between Selleck and San Giacomo and the usual enjoyable theatrics from Rickman as the landowner heavy.
1990 (PG-13) 121m/C *AU* Tom Selleck, Laura San Giacomo, Alan Rickman, Chris Haywood, Ron Haddrick, Tony Bonner, Roger Ward, Ben Mendelsohn; *D:* Simon Wincer. VHS, Beta, LV, 8mm $19.98 *MGM* ✗✗½

The Quiller Memorandum An American secret agent travels to Berlin to uncover a deadly neo-Nazi gang. Refreshingly different from other spy tales of its era. Good screenplay by Harold Pinter taken from Adam Hall's novel, "The Berlin Memorandum."
1966 103m/C George Segal, Senta Berger, Alec Guinness, Max von Sydow, George Sanders; *D:* Michael Anderson Sr.; *M:* John Barry. VHS, Beta $59.98 *FOX* ✗✗✗

Quilombo The title refers to a legendary settlement of runaway slaves in 17th-century Brazil; an epic chronicles its fortunes as leadership passes from a wise ruler to a more militant one who goes to war against the government. Stunning scenery, tribal images, and folk songs, but the numerous characters seldom come to life as personalities. One of Brazil's most expensive films, in Portuguese with English subtitles.
1984 114m/C *BR* Vera Fischer, Antonio Pompeo, Zeze Motta, Toni Tornado; *W/D:* Carlos Diegues. VHS $79.95 *NYF, FCT, TAM* ✗✗½

Quintet Atypical Altman sci-fi effort. The stakes in "Quintet," a form of backgammon, are high—you bet your life. Set during the planet's final ice age. Newman and wife Fossey wander into a dying city and are invited to play the game, with Fossey losing quickly. Bizarre and pretentious, with heavy symbolic going.
1979 118m/C Paul Newman, Bibi Andersson, Fernando Rey, Vittorio Gassman, David Langton, Nina Van Pallandt, Brigitte Fossey; *D:* Robert Altman. VHS, Beta $19.98 *FOX* ✗✗

Quo Vadis One of the first truly huge Italian silent epics. The initial adaptation of the Henryk Sienkiewicz novel about Nero and ancient Rome. Probably the cinema's first great financial success.
1912 45m/B *D:* Enrico Guazzoni. VHS, Beta $89.95 *FCT* ✗✗½

Quo Vadis Larger-than-life production about Nero and the Christian persecution. Done on a giant scale: features exciting fighting scenes, romance, and fabulous costumes. Definitive version of the classic novel by Henryk Siekiewicz. Remade for Italian television in 1985.
1951 171m/C Robert Taylor, Deborah Kerr, Peter Ustinov, Patricia Laffan, Finlay Currie, Abraham Sofaer, Marina Berti, Buddy Baer, Felix Aylmer, Nora Swinburne; *Cameos:* Sophia Loren, Elizabeth Taylor; *D:* Mervyn LeRoy; *M:* Miklos Rozsa. Academy Awards '51 Nominations: Best Art Direction/Set Decoration (Color), Best Color Cinematography, Best Costume Design (Color), Best Film Editing, Best Picture, Best Supporting Actor (Genn, Ustinov), Best Original Score; Golden Globe Awards '52: Best Supporting Actor (Ustinov). VHS, Beta $29.98 *MGM, APD, IGP* ✗✗✗

Quo Vadis Third screen version of Henryk Sienkiewicz's book. See the other two first. This one is slow and perfunctory. Brandauer is memorable as Nero; Quinn (in the lead) is the son of Anthony.
1985 (R) 122m/C *IT* Klaus Maria Brandauer, Frederic Forrest, Christina Raines, Maria Therese Relin, Francesco Quinn, Barbara de Rossi, Phillipe LeRoy, Max von Sydow; *D:* Franco Rossi. VHS, Beta, LV $89.95 *PSM, APD* ✗✗½

Rabbit Test In Rivers' first directorial effort, a clumsy virginal guy becomes the world's first pregnant man. So irreverent it's almost never in good taste, and so poorly written it's almost never funny.
1978 (PG) 86m/C Billy Crystal, Roddy McDowall, Imogene Coca, Paul Lynde, Alex Rocco, George Gobel; *D:* Joan Rivers. VHS, Beta, LV $9.95 *COL, SUE* ✗½

Rabid A young girl undergoes a radical plastic surgery technique and develops a strange and unexplained lesion in her armpit. She also finds she has an unusual craving for human blood. *AKA:* Rage.
1977 (R) 90m/C *CA* Marilyn Chambers, Frank Moore, Joe Silver; *D:* David Cronenberg. **VHS, Beta** $29.98 *WAR* ♫♫½

Rabid Grannies Wicked satire about two aging sisters who receive a surprise birthday gift from their devilworshipping nephew. The gift turns their party into a gorefest as they rip into various family members—literally. Any humor will be lost on any but the most diehard Troma fans. Dubbed.
1989 (R) 89m/C *BE* Catherine Aymerie, Caroline Brackman, Danielle Daven, Raymond Lescot, Anne Marie Fox, Richard Cotica, Patricia Davie; *W/D:* Emmanuel Kervyn. **VHS, Beta, LV** $79.95 *MED* Woof!

Race for Glory A young motorcyclist builds a super-bike he hopes will help him win a world championship race. Will he win? Can you stand the suspense? Let's just say there's a happy ending.
1989 (R) 102m/C Alex McArthur, Peter Berg, Pamela Ludwig; *D:* Rocky Lang. **VHS, Beta** $89.99 *HBO* ♫½

Race for Life A race car driver attempts to make a comeback despite objections from his wife. He races around Europe (great scenery); she leaves him; he tries to win her back and salvage his career. Standard, ungripping story. Car scenes are great. *AKA:* Mask of Dust.
1955 69m/B *GB* Richard Conte, Mari Aldon, George Coulouris; *D:* Terence Fisher. **VHS, Beta, LV** *NO* ♫½

Race for Your Life, Charlie Brown Another in the popular series of "Peanuts" character films. This one features Charlie Brown, Snoopy, and all the gang spending an exciting summer in the American wilderness.
1977 (G) 76m/C **VHS, Beta, LV** $14.95 *PAR, WTA* ♫♫½

Race to the Yankee Zephyr Bad guy Peppard and good guys Pleasance and Wahl race to recover $50 million in gold from a downed World War II plane. Confused, ill plotted and predictable.
1981 108m/C *AU NZ* Ken Wahl, Lesley Ann Warren, Donald Pleasence, George Peppard, Bruno Lawrence, Grant Tilly; *D:* David Hemmings. **VHS** *VES* ♫♫

Race with the Devil Vacationers are terrorized by devil worshippers after they witness a sacrificial killing. Heavy on car chases; light on plot and redeeming qualities. Don't waste your time.
1975 (PG) 88m/C Peter Fonda, Warren Oates, Loretta Swit, Lara Parker; *D:* Jack Starrett. **VHS, Beta** $14.98 *FOX, FCT* ♫½

The Racers Douglas brings power to the role of a man determined to advance to the winners' circle. Exciting European location photography, but not much plot. *AKA:* Such Men are Dangerous.
1955 112m/C Gilbert Roland, Kirk Douglas, Lee J. Cobb, Cesar Romero, Bella Darvi; *D:* Henry Hathaway. **VHS** $39.98 *FOX, FCT* ♫♫½

Rachel and the Stranger A God-fearing farmer declares his love for his wife when a handsome stranger (Mitchum) nearly woos her away. Well-cast, well-paced, charming Western comedy-drama.
1948 93m/B Loretta Young, Robert Mitchum, William Holden, Gary Gray; *D:* Norman Foster. **VHS, Beta, LV** $19.95 *MED, TTC* ♫♫♫

The Rachel Papers Based on the Martin Amis novel, this is the funny/sad tale of an Oxford youth who plots via his computer the seduction of a beautiful American girl. For anyone who has ever loved someone just out of their reach.
1989 (R) 92m/C Dexter Fletcher, Ione Skye, James Spader, Jonathan Pryce, Bill Paterson, Michael Gambon; *D:* Damien Harris. **VHS, Beta** $79.98 *FOX* ♫♫♫

Rachel, Rachel Rachel teaches by day, wearing simple, practical dresses and her hair up. By night she caters to her domineering mother by preparing refreshments for her parties. This sexually repressed, spinster schoolteacher, however, gets one last chance at romance in her small Connecticut town. Woodward mixes just the right amounts of loneliness and sweetness in the leading role. A surprising award-winner that was an independent production of Newman. Based on Margaret Laurence's "A Jest of God."
1968 (R) 102m/C Joanne Woodward, James Olson, Estelle Parsons, Geraldine Fitzgerald, Donald Moffatt; *D:* Paul Newman. Academy Awards '68 Nominations: Best Actress (Woodward), Best Adapted Screenplay, Best Picture, Best Supporting Actress (Parsons); Golden Globe Awards '69: Best Actress—Drama (Woodward), Best Director (Newman); New York Film Critics Awards '68: Best Actress (Woodward), Best Director (Newman). **VHS, Beta** $19.98 *WAR* ♫♫♫½

Rachel River A divorced radio personality struggles to make something of her life in her small Minnesota town.
1989 (PG-13) 88m/C Pamela Reed, Craig T. Nelson, Viveca Lindfors, James Olson. **VHS, LV** $89.95 *ACA* ♫♫½

Rachel's Man A big-screen version of the Biblical love story of Jacob and Rachel.
1975 115m/C Mickey Rooney, Rita Tushingham, Leonard Whiting; *D:* Moshe Mizrahi. **VHS, Beta** $59.95 *LIV* ♫

Racing Luck While working at a race track, a man is framed and forced to work for another stable. *AKA:* Red Hot Tires.
1935 56m/B William Boyd, Barbara Worth, George Ernest, Esther Muir, Dick Curtis; *D:* Sam Newfield. **VHS, Beta** $9.95 *GPV* ♫♫

Racing with the Moon Sweet, nostalgic film about two buddies awaiting induction into the Marines in 1942. They have their last chance at summer romance. Benjamin makes the most of skillful young actors and conventional story. Great period detail. Keep your eyes peeled for glimpses of many rising young stars including Hannah and Carvey.
1984 (PG) 108m/C Sean Penn, Elizabeth McGovern, Nicolas Cage, John Karlen, Rutanya Alda, Max Showalter, Crispin Glover, Suzanne Adkinson, Page Hannah, Michael Madsen, Dana Carvey, Carol Kane, Michael Talbott; *D:* Richard Benjamin; *W:* Steven Kloves; *M:* Dave Grusin. **VHS, Beta, LV** $14.95 *PAR* ♫♫♫

The Racket Police captain Mitchum tries to break up mob racket of gangster Ryan. Internecine strife on both sides adds complexity. Mitchum and especially Ryan are super; fine, tense melodrama.
1951 88m/B Robert Ryan, Robert Mitchum, Lizabeth Scott, Ray Collins, William Conrad, Don Porter; *D:* John Cromwell. **VHS, Beta, LV** $19.98 *MED, TTC* ♫♫♫

Racket Squad, Vol. 12 Features two episodes of the popular crime-drama. Includes "Staff of Life" and "Perfect Match."
1951 ?m/C Reed Hadley. **VHS** $16.95 *SNC* ♫♫♫

The Racketeer A racketeer falls in love with a pretty girl and attempts to win her over. As part of his plan, the gangster arranges to help the girl's boyfriend begin his musical career in exchange for the girl's promise to marry him.
1929 68m/B Carole Lombard, Robert Armstrong, Hedda Hopper; *D:* Howard Higgin. **VHS, Beta, 3/4U, Special order formats** $16.95 *SNC, NOS, CAB* ♫♫½

Racketeers of the Range Cattleman fights a crooked attorney who wants to sell his client's stock to a large meat packing company.
1939 62m/B George O'Brien, Marjorie Reynolds, Chill Wills, Ray Whitley; *D:* Ross Lederman. **VHS, Beta** *MED* ♫½

Racquet Tennis pro Convy searches for true love and a tennis court of to call his own in Beverly Hills. Lame, sophomoric, and unfunny.
1979 87m/C Bert Convy, Edie Adams, Lynda Day George, Phil Silvers, Bobby Riggs, Bjorn Borg, Tanya Roberts; *D:* David Winters. **VHS, Beta** *NO* ♫

Rad Teenage drama revolving around BMX racing and such dilemmas as: can the good guys beat the bad guys, who's got the fastest bike, must you cheat to win, and should our hero miss his SAT tests to compete in "the big race.." Directed by stunt-expert Needham.
1986 (PG) 94m/C Bill Allen, Bart Conner, Talia Shire, Jack Weston, Lori Loughlin; *D:* Hal Needham. **VHS, Beta, LV** $9.98 *SUE, NLC* ♫½

Radar Men from the Moon Commando Cody, with his jet-pack, fights to defend the earth from invaders from the moon. Twelve-episode serial on two tapes. Silly sci-fi. *AKA:* Retik, the Moon Menace.
1952 152m/B George Wallace, Aline Towne, Roy Barcroft, William Bakewell, Clayton Moore; *D:* Fred Brannon. **VHS, LV** $49.95 *NOS, REP, SNC* ♫½

Radar Secret Service Two servicemen witness the hijacking of a truck loaded with nuclear material.
1950 59m/B John Howard, Adele Jergens, Tom Neal, Ralph Byrd. **VHS, Beta, LV** *NO* ♫½

The Radical Spacek is convincing as a middle class student who becomes involved with a radical political group, eventually becoming a terrorist. *AKA:* Katherine.
1975 100m/C Julie Kavner, Hector Elias, Jenny Sullivan, Sissy Spacek, Art Carney, Henry Winkler, Jane Wyatt; *W:* Jeremy Paul Kagan. **VHS** $9.95 *SIM* ♫½

Radio Days A lovely, unpretentious remembrance of the pre-television radio culture. Allen tells his story in a series of vignettes centering around his youth in Brooklyn, his eccentric extended family, and the legends of radio they all followed. The ubiquitous Farrow is a young singer hoping to make it big.
1987 (PG) 96m/C Mia Farrow, Dianne Wiest, Julie Kavner, Michael Tucker, Wallace Shawn, Josh Mostel, Tony Roberts, Jeff Daniels, Kenneth Mars, Seth Green, William Magerman, Diane Keaton, Renee Lippin, Danny Aiello, Gina DeAngelis, Kitty Carlisle, Mercedes Ruehl; *W/D:* Woody Allen. **VHS, Beta, LV** $19.95 *HBO* ♫♫♫

Radio Flyer It's 1969 and Mike and Bobby have just moved to northern California with their divorced mom. Everything would be idyllic if only their mother hadn't decided to marry a drunken child abuser who beats Bobby whenever the mood strikes him. Mike decides to help Bobby escape by turning their Radio Flyer wagon into a magic rocketship that will carry Bobby to safety, but

ultimately proves tragic. Appealing version of childhood dreams sans the child abuse angle (toned down though it was), which is abruptly and unsatisfactorily handled.
1992 (PG-13) 114m/C Elijah Wood, Joseph Mazzello, Lorraine Bracco, Adam Baldwin, John Heard, Ben Johnson; **D:** Richard Donner. **VHS, LV** COL ✰✰

Radio Patrol Plenty of action and thrills abound in this complete collection of all the chapters of this vintage serial. Pinky Adams, radio cop, is assisted by his trusty canine partner, Irish (Silverwolf). A cop's best friend is his dog.
1937 235m/B Mickey Rentschler, Adrian Morris, Monte Montague, Silver Wolf, Grant Withers, Catherine Hughes; **D:** Ford Beebe. **VHS, Beta $49.95** NOS, VDM, MLB ✰½

Radio Ranch Autry and friends are up against an underground world of robots and death rays. Movie version of the serial "Phantom Empire." **AKA:** The Phantom Empire.
1935 80m/B Gene Autry, Frankie Darro, Betsy King Ross, Smiley Burnette; **D:** Otto Brower; **W:** B. Reeves Eason. **VHS, Beta $19.95** NOS, VYY, DVT ✰½

Radioactive Dreams Surreal, practically senseless fantasy wherein two men, trapped in a bomb shelter for 15 years with nothing to read but mystery novels, emerge as detectives into a post-holocaust world looking for adventure.
1986 (R) 94m/C John Stockwell, Michael Dudikoff, Lisa Blount, George Kennedy, Don Murray, Michelle Little; **D:** Albert Pyun. **VHS, Beta, LV $79.98** LIV, VES ✰✰

Rafferty & the Gold Dust Twins Two women kidnap a motor vehicle inspector at gunpoint in Los Angeles and order him to drive to New Orleans. En route, they become pals. Wandering, pointless female buddy flick. **AKA:** Rafferty and the Highway Hustlers.
1975 (R) 91m/C Alan Arkin, Sally Kellerman, MacKenzie Phillips, Charles Martin Smith, Harry Dean Stanton; **D:** Dick Richards. **VHS, Beta $19.98** WAR ✰½

Rage Scott's directorial debut. A military helicopter sprays peace-loving rancher Scott and his son with nerve gas. The son's death is covered up; the rancher embarks on a vengeful rampage. Scott's sudden transformation to avenging killer is implausible and overwrought.
1972 (PG) 100m/C George C. Scott, Richard Basehart, Martin Sheen, Barnard Hughes, Kenneth Tobey, Ed Lauter, Nicholas Beauvy, Dabbs Greer; **D:** George C. Scott. **VHS, Beta $19.98** WAR ✰✰

Rage Well-acted, well-written, nerve-wracking drama about a convicted rapist who finds help through difficult therapy. Focuses on how the sex-offender discovers the "whys" behind his assaults. Made for television.
1980 100m/C David Soul, James Whitmore, Yaphet Kotto, Caroline McWilliams, Vic Tayback, Sharon Farrell, Craig T. Nelson, Garry Walberg; **D:** William A. Graham. **VHS, Beta $59.95** WAR ✰✰✰

Rage and Honor Rothrock stars as Kris Fairfield, a high-school teacher who spends her spare time tutoring students in the martial-arts. Her present students are a group of cops, including Aussie visitor Preston Michaels. When Michaels witnesses a drug deal, he gets set-up by the dealers for a murder he didn't commit and only Kris can help him prove his innocence.
1992 (R) 93m/C Cynthia Rothrock, Richard Norton, Brian Thompson, Terri Treas, Catherine Bach, Alex Datcher; **W/D:** Terence H. Winkless. **VHS, LV $89.95** COL, PMS ✰✰

Rage at Dawn An outlaw gang is tracked by a special agent who must "bend" the rules a little in order to get the bad guys. Not surprisingly, he gets his girl as well. A solid standard of the genre, with some clever plot twists. **AKA:** Seven Bad Men.
1955 87m/C Randolph Scott, Forrest Tucker, Mala Powers, J. Carroll Naish, Edgar Buchanan; **D:** Tim Whelan. **VHS $13.95** NOS, GHV, MRV ✰✰½

A Rage in Harlem The crime novels of Chester A. Himes were translated into the best movies of the early '70s blaxploitation era. Now, a Himes story gets the big budget Hollywood treatment with juice and aplomb. A voluptuous lady crook enters Harlem circa 1950 with a trunkful of stolen gold sought by competing crooks, and the chase is on, with one virtuous soul (Whitaker) who only wants the girl. Great cast and characters, much humor, but unsparing in its violence. heart out.
1991 (R) 108m/C Forest Whitaker, Gregory Hines, Robin Givens, Zakes Mokae, Danny Glover; **D:** Bill Duke. **VHS, LV $19.98** HBO, FCT ✰✰✰

Rage of Angels Lengthy television mini-iseries adaptation of the Sidney Sheldon novel about an ambitious female attorney, her furs, and her men. Followed by "Rage of Angels: The Story Continues" (1986).
1983 192m/C Jaclyn Smith, Ken Howard, Armand Assante, Ronald Hunter, Kevin Conway, George Coe, Deborah May; **D:** Buzz Kulik. **VHS, Beta $19.95** COL ✰✰

Rage of Angels: The Story Continues In this sequel to the Sidney Sheldon trash-with-flash television miniseries, Smith reprises her role as the beautiful lady lawyer who always gets involved with the wrong men. This time she tries to hide the fact of her illegitimate son from his father, who's about to become Vice President of the United States.
1986 200m/C Jaclyn Smith, Ken Howard, Michael Nouri, Susan Sullivan, Brad Dourif, Angela Lansbury, Mason Adams; **D:** Paul Wendkos. **VHS** STE ✰✰½

Rage of Honor A high-kicking undercover cop seeks vengeance on bad guys for his partner's murder. Standard of its type; why bother?
1987 (R) 92m/C Sho Kosugi, Lewis Van Bergen, Robin Evans, Gerry Gibson; **D:** Gordon Hessler. **VHS, Beta $19.95** MED ✰

The Rage of Paris Scheming ex-actress and head waiter hope to gain by helping a beautiful French girl (Darrieux) snag a rich hubby. She comes to her senses, realizing that love, true love, matters more than wealth. Well-acted, quaint comedy.
1938 78m/B Danielle Darrieux, Douglas Fairbanks Jr., Mischa Auer, Helen Broderick; **D:** Henry Koster. **VHS, Beta, 3/4U, Special order formats $19.95** NOS, DVT, CAB ✰✰✰

Rage of the Master During the Ching dynasty, good and bad guys bound about, kicking each other and themselves in the head and temples.
197? 100m/C Ng Ming Tsai, Tiger Yang. **VHS, Beta $19.95** UHV ✰

Rage of Wind Master boxer seeks revenge on a Japanese commandant who kidnaps his wife during WWII.
1982 97m/C Chen Hsing, Yasuka Kurata, Irene Ryder. **VHS, Beta** WVE ✰

Rage to Kill Jingoistic retelling of the 1982 Grenada invasion, complete with helpless American med students. Good-guy race car driver whips them into shape to fight the Soviet-supplied general (he's the bad guy). Guess who wins.
1988 (R) 94m/C Oliver Reed, James Ryan, Henry Cele, Cameron Mitchell; **D:** David Winters. **VHS, Beta $29.95** AIP ✰½

Raggedy Ann and Andy: A Musical Adventure Here are the fun-filled exploits of America's favorite fictional dolls, transformed into an enchanting animated musical. Includes 16 songs by Joe Raposo.
1977 (G) 87m/C D: Richard Williams; **V:** Didi Conn, Joe Silver. **VHS, Beta $14.98** FOX ✰½

Raggedy Man Spacek in her signature role as a lonely small-town woman. Here she's raising two sons alone in a small Texas town during World War II. Spacek's strong acting carries a well-scripted story, unfortunately marred by an overwrought ending.
1981 (PG) 94m/C Sissy Spacek, Eric Roberts, Sam Shepard, Tracy Walter, William Sanderson, Henry Thomas; **D:** Jack Fisk; **M:** Jerry Goldsmith. **VHS, Beta, LV $59.95** MCA ✰✰✰

The Raggedy Rawney A young Army deserter dresses in women's clothing and hides out as a mad woman with a band of gypsies. Good first directing effort by English actor Bob Hoskins. Unpretentious and engaging.
1990 (R) 102m/C Bob Hoskins, Dexter Fletcher, Zoe Nathenson, David Hill, Ian Dury, Zoe Wanamaker; **W/D:** Bob Hoskins. **VHS $19.98** CAN ✰✰½

Ragin' Cajun Retired kickboxer is forced into a death match to save his girlfriend.
1990 91m/C David Heavener, Charlene Tilton, Sam Bottoms, Samantha Eggar, Dr. Death; **D:** William B. Hillman. **VHS $79.95** AIP, HHE ✰

Raging Bull Scorsese's depressing but magnificent vision of the dying American Dream and suicidal macho codes in the form of the rise and fall of middleweight boxing champ Jake LaMotta, a brutish, dull-witted animal who can express himself only in the ring and through violence. A photographically expressive, brilliant drama, with easily the most intense and brutal boxing scenes ever filmed. De Niro provides a vintage performance, going from the young LaMotta to the aging has-been, and is ably accompanied by Moriarty as his girl and Pesci as his loyal, much beat-upon bro. Script by Paul Schrader and Mardik Martin.
1980 (R) 128m/B Robert De Niro, Cathy Moriarty, Joe Pesci, Frank Vincent, Nicholas Colasanto; **D:** Martin Scorsese; **W:** Paul Schrader, Mardik Martin. Academy Awards '80: Best Actor (De Niro), Best Film Editing; Nominations: Best Cinematography, Best Director (Scorsese), Best Picture, Best Sound, Best Supporting Actor (Pesci), Best Supporting Actress (Moriarty); Golden Globe Awards '81: Best Actor—Drama (De Niro); Los Angeles Film Critics Association Awards '80: Best Actor (De Niro), Best Film; National Board of Review Awards '80: Best Actor (De Niro), Best Supporting Actor (Pesci). **VHS, Beta, LV, 8mm $19.98** MGM, FOX, VYG ✰✰✰✰

Rags to Riches A wealthy Beverly Hills entrepreneur decides to improve his public image by adopting six orphan girls. TV pilot.
1987 96m/C Joseph Bologna, Tisha Campbell. **VHS, Beta $19.95** STE, NWV ✰

Ragtime The lives and passions of a middle class family weave into the scandals and events of 1906 America. A small, unthinking act represents all the racist attacks on one man, who refuses to back down this

time. Wonderful period detail. Music composed by Randy Newman. From the E.L. Doctorow novel, but not nearly as complex. Features Cagney's last film performance.
1981 (PG) 156m/C Howard E. Rollins Jr., Kenneth McMillan, Brad Dourif, Mary Steenburgen, James Olson, Elizabeth McGovern, Pat O'Brien, James Cagney, Debbie Allen, Jeff Daniels, Moses Gunn, Donald O'Connor, Mandy Patinkin, Norman Mailer; **D:** Milos Forman. **VHS, Beta, LV** $29.95 PAR, FCT ✐✐✐

Raid on Entebbe Dramatization of the Israeli rescue of passengers held hostage by terrorists at Uganda's Entebbe Airport in 1976. A gripping actioner all the more compelling because true. Finch received an Emmy nomination in this, his last film. Made for television.
1977 (R) 113m/C Charles Bronson, Peter Finch, Horst Buchholz, John Saxon, Martin Balsam, Jack Warden, Yaphet Kotto, Sylvia Sidney; **D:** Irvin Kershner. **VHS, Beta** $69.95 HBO ✐✐✐

Raid on Rommel A British soldier (Burton) poses as a Nazi and tries to infiltrate Rommel's team with his rag-tag brigade of misfits. Predictable drivel. Contains action footage from the 1967 film "Tobruk."
1971 (PG) 98m/C Richard Burton, John Colicos, Clinton Greyn, Wolfgang Preiss; **D:** Henry Hathaway. **VHS, Beta** $19.95 MCA ✐✐½

Raiders in Action Tale following the activities of a band of allied commandos in the closing days of the war.
1971 89m/C Paul Smith. **VHS, Beta** $59.95 TWE ✐

Raiders of Atlantis Battles break out when the lost continent surfaces in the Caribbean. The warriors in these apocalyptic frays deploy atomic arsenals.
1983 100m/C Christopher Connelly; **D:** Roger Franklin. **VHS, Beta** $69.95 PSM ✐

Raiders of Red Gap A cattle company tries running homesteaders off their land to get control of it. The Lone Rider saves the day.
1943 56m/B Al "Fuzzy" St. John, Bob Livingston. **VHS, Beta** $19.98 DVT, VYY, VCN ✐½

Raiders of Sunset Pass Wartime western quickie makes an interesting novelty today. With most cowboys off fighting the Axis, the ladies form the Women's Army of the Plains to watch out for 4-F rustlers.
1943 57m/B Eddie Dew, Smiley Burnette, Jennifer Holt, Roy Barcroft, Mozelle Cravens, Beverly Aadland, Nancy Worth, Kenne Duncan, Jack Rockwell, Budd Buster, Jack Ingram; **D:** John English. **VHS** $19.95 NOS, HEG ✐

Raiders of the Border A white-hatted cowboy must prevent the takeover of a trading post.
1944 55m/B Johnny Mack Brown, Raymond Hatton, Ellen Hall. **VHS, Beta** $19.95 VDM ✐

Raiders of the Buddhist Kung Fu Conspiracy to restore Manchu dynasty results in deadly duel between Nat Kit of the Manchu dynasty and Wong Lung of the new Buddhist government.
1984 40m/C VHS, Beta $14.95 NEG ✐✐

Raiders of the Lost Ark Breathless neo-classic '30s-style adventure made the now-ubiquitous Ford a household name. Intrepid archeologist Indiana Jones in his first and best adventure battles mean Nazis, decodes hieroglyphics and hates snakes in his search for the biblical Ark of the Covenant. He stops in Kathmandu en route to Egypt and teams up with old flame Allen who says, "Indiana Jones. I always knew some day you'd come walkin' back into my life." "I'm making it up as I go along," he admits to her once when they're in a bind; the whole

story is wonderfully, playfully picaresque. Every chase and stunt tops the last, though "Raiders" avoids the excess and gore of its sequel, "Indiana Jones and the Temple of Doom." Allen is fetching as the feisty gal. Of course there's romance, and of course the good guys win (sort of).
1981 (PG) 115m/C Harrison Ford, Karen Allen, Wolf Kahler, Paul Freeman, John Rhys-Davies, Denholm Elliott; **D:** Steven Spielberg; **M:** John Williams. Academy Awards '81: Best Art Direction/Set Decoration, Best Film Editing, Best Sound, Best Visual Effects; Nominations: Best Cinematography, Best Director (Spielberg), Best Picture, Best Original Score; People's Choice Awards '82: Best Film. **VHS, Beta, LV, 8mm** $19.95 PAR ✐✐✐✐

Raiders of the Sun After the Earth has been ruined in a biological disaster, a futuristic warrior arrives to help restore world peace and order. Cheap "Mad Max" ripoff.
1992 (R) 80m/C Richard Norton, Rick Dean, William Steis, Blake Boyd, Brigitta Stenberg; **D:** Cirio H. Santiago. **VHS** $89.98 NHO ✐

Railroaded The police seek a demented criminal who kills his victims with perfumed-soaked bullets. Tense, excellent noir Anothony Mann crime drama.
1947 72m/B John Ireland, Sheila Ryan, Hugh Beaumont, Ed Kelly; **D:** Anthony Mann. **VHS, Beta, LV** $19.95 STE, NOS, NWV ✐✐

Railroader Buster Keaton as the railroader in this slapstick short fumbles his way across Canada. As in the days of the silents, he speaks not a word.
1965 25m/C Buster Keaton. **VHS, Beta** NFC ✐✐✐

Railway Children At the turn of the century in England, the father of three children is framed and sent to prison during Christmas. The trio and their mother must survive on a poverty stricken farm near the railroad tracks. They eventually meet a new friend who helps them prove their father's innocence. Wonderfully directed by Jeffries. From the classic Edith Nesbitt children's novel.
1970 104m/C GB Jenny Agutter, William Mervyn, Bernard Cribbins, Dinah Sheridan, Iain Cuthbertson; **D:** Lionel Jeffries. **VHS, Beta** $79.99 HBO ✐✐✐½

The Railway Station Man Set in present-day Ireland. Christie plays a widowed artist struggling to put her life back together after her husband's death in a terrorist bombing. She meets a mysterious American (Sutherland) who's working on restoring the local railway station and finds herself falling in love. When she stumbles upon an IRA bombing plot she also finds out some unpleasant truths about her new lover. Wonderful performances, tragic story. Shot on location in County Donegal, Northern Ireland. Based on the novel by Jennifer Johnston. Made for cable television.
1992 93m/C Julie Christie, Donald Sutherland, John Lynch, Mark Tandy, Frank McCusker; **D:** Michael Whyte; **W:** Shelagh Delaney. **VHS, Beta, LV** $89.98 TTC ✐✐✐

Rain W. Somerset Maugham's tale of a puritanical minister's attempt to reclaim a "lost woman" on the island of Pago Pago. Crawford and Huston work up some static. Remake of the 1928 silent film "Sadie Thompson." Remade again in 1953 as "Miss Sadie Thompson."
1932 92m/B Joan Crawford, Walter Huston, William Gargan, Guy Kibbee, Beulah Bondi, Walter Catlett; **D:** Lewis Milestone. **VHS, Beta, 3/4U, Special order formats** $8.95 NEG, NOS, UHV ✐✐½

The Rain Killer Big city cop and fed don goloshes to track serial killer who slays rich ladies during heavy precipitation. Soggy story.
1990 (R) 94m/C Ray Sharkey, David Beecroft, Maria Ford, Woody Brown, Tania Coleridge; **D:** Ken Stein; **W:** Ray Cunneff. **VHS, LV** $89.95 COL ✐

Rain Man When his father dies, ambitious and self-centered Charlie Babbit finds he has an older autistic brother who's been institutionalized for years. Needing him to claim an inheritance, he liberates him from the institution and takes to the road, where both brothers undergo subtle changes. The Vegas montage is wonderful. Critically acclaimed drama and a labor of love for the entire cast. Cruise's best performance to date as he goes from cad to recognizing something wonderfully human in his brother and himself. Hoffman is exceptional.
1988 (R) 128m/C Dustin Hoffman, Tom Cruise, Valeria Golino, Jerry Molen, Jack Murdock, Michael D. Roberts, Ralph Seymour, Lucinda Jenney, Bonnie Hunt, Kim Robillard, Beth Grant; **D:** Barry Levinson. Academy Awards '88: Best Actor (Hoffman), Best Director (Levinson), Best Original Screenplay, Best Picture; Nominations: Best Art Direction/Set Decoration, Best Cinematography, Best Film Editing, Best Original Score; Berlin International Film Festival '88: Golden Berlin Bear; Directors Guild of America Awards '88: Best Director (Levinson); Golden Globe Awards '89: Best Actor—Drama (Hoffman), Best Film—Drama; People's Choice Awards '89: Best Film—Drama. **VHS, Beta, LV, 8mm** $19.98 MGM, BTV, JCF ✐✐✐½

The Rain People Pregnant housewife Knight takes to the road in desperation and boredom; along the way she meets retarded ex-football player Caan. Well directed by Coppola from his original script. Pensive drama.
1969 (R) 102m/C Shirley Knight, James Caan, Robert Duvall; **D:** Francis Ford Coppola. **VHS, Beta** $19.98 WAR ✐✐✐

Rainbow Broadway's "Annie" is badly miscast as Judy Garland from her early years in vaudeville to her starring years at M.G.M. Based on the book by Christopher Finch. Made for television; directed by sometime Garland flame Jackie Cooper.
1978 100m/C Andrea McArdle, Jack Carter, Don Murray; **D:** Jackie Cooper. **VHS, Beta, LV** NO ✐✐

The Rainbow Mature, literate rendering of the classic D.H. Lawrence novel about a young woman's sexual awakening. Beautiful cinematography. Companion/prequel to director Russell's earlier Lawrence adaptation, "Women in Love" (1969).
1989 (R) 104m/C GB Sammi Davis-Voss, Amanda Donohoe, Paul McGann, Christopher Gable, David Hemmings, Glenda Jackson, Kenneth Colley; **D:** Ken Russell. **VHS, LV** $49.95 VES, IME ✐✐✐

Rainbow Bridge The adventures of a group of hippies searching for their consciousness in Hawaii. Features concert footage from Jimi Hendrix's final performance.
1971 (R) 74m/C D: Chuck Wein. **VHS, Beta** $19.95 RHI, FCT ✐

Rainbow Drive Made for cable tv cop thriller promises great things but fails to deliver. Weller is a good cop trapped in the political intrigues of Hollywood. He discovers five dead bodies; when the official count is four, he detects funny business. Music by Tangerine Dream. From the novel by Roderick Thorp.

1990 (R) 93m/C Peter Weller, Sela Ward, Bruce Weitz; *D:* Bobby Roth; *W:* Roderick Thorp, Bill Phillips, Bennett Cohen; *M:* Tangerine Dream. VHS $89.95 BTV, VMK ♫♫½

The Rainbow Gang A trio of unlikely prospectors heads into a legendary mine in search of riches and fame.
1973 90m/C Donald Pleasence, Don Calfa, Kate Reid. VHS, Beta $19.95 STE, NWV ♫

Rainbow Parade 2 A collection of three animated classics from Burt Gillette including "Molly Moo Cow and Robinson Crusoe," "Trolley Ahoy," and "Waifs Welcome."
1936 21m/C VHS, Beta CCB ♫

Rainbow Ranch A Navy boxer returns home to his ranch to find murder and corruption. Needless to say, he rides off to seek revenge.
1933 54m/B Rex Bell, Cecilia Parker, Robert Kortman, Henry Hall, Gordon DeMain; *D:* Harry Fraser. VHS $19.95 NOS, DVT, HEG ♫½

Rainbow's End Gibson must defend Gale, the female rancher, from an evil adversary who is trying to run Gale and her invalid father off of their land. Things get complicated when Gibson discovers that Stark works for his father!
1935 54m/B Hoot Gibson, June Gale, Oscar Apfel, Ada Ince, Charles Hill, Warner Richmond; *D:* Norman Spencer. VHS $19.95 NOS, DVT ♫♫

The Rainmaker Reminiscent of "Elmer Gantry" in his masterful performance, Lancaster makes it all believable as a con man who comes to a small midwestern town and works miracles not only on the weather but on spinster Hepburn, although both were a little long in the tooth for their roles. Written by Nash from his own play.
1956 121m/C Burt Lancaster, Katharine Hepburn, Wendell Corey, Lloyd Bridges, Earl Holliman, Cameron Prudhomme, Wallace Ford; *D:* Joseph Anthony; *W:* N. Richard Nash. Academy Awards '56 Nominations: Best Actress (Hepburn), Best Original Score; Golden Globe Awards '57: Best Supporting Actor (Holliman). VHS, LV $14.95 PAR, CCB ♫♫♫

Raintree County A lavish, somewhat overdone epic about two lovers caught up in the national turmoil of the Civil War. An Indiana teacher marries a southern belle just after the outbreak of war. The new wife battles mental illness. Producers had hoped this would be another "Gone With the Wind." Adapted from the novel.
1957 175m/C Elizabeth Taylor, Montgomery Clift, Eva Marie Saint, Lee Marvin, Nigel Patrick, Rod Taylor, Agnes Moorehead, Walter Abel; *D:* Edward Dmytryk. VHS, Beta, LV $29.98 MGM, PIA ♫♫½

Rainy Day A successful actress' return home for her father's funeral brings back unpleasant childhood memories that force her to face the truth about herself.
1979 35m/C Mariette Hartley. VHS, Beta LCA ♫♫

Raise the Red Lantern Set in 1920s China, Zhang explores its claustrophobic world of privilege and humiliation. Songlian, an educated 19-year-old beauty, is forced into marriage as the fourth wife of a wealthy and powerful old man. She discovers that the wives have their own separate quarters and servants, and spend most of their time battling to attract their husband's attention. Over the course of a year, Songlian's fury and resentment grow until self-defeating rebellion is all she has. Gong Li is exquisite as the young woman struggling for dignity in a portrayal which is both haunting and tragic.
1991 (PG) 125m/C CH Gong Li, Ma Jingwu, He Caifei, Cao Cuifeng, Jin Shuyuan, Kong Lin, Ding Weimin; *D:* Zhang Yimou. Academy Awards '91 Nominations: Best Foreign Language Film; New York Film Critics Awards '92: Best Foreign Film. VHS, LV $79.98 ORI, TAM ♫♫♫½

Raise the Titanic A disaster about a disaster. Horrible script cannot be redeemed by purported thrill of the ship's emergence from the deep after 70 years. It's a shame, because the free world's security hangs in the balance. Based on Clive Cussler's best seller.
1980 (PG) 112m/C Jason Robards Jr., Richard Jordan, Anne Archer, Alec Guinness, J.D. Cannon; *D:* Jerry Jameson; *M:* John Barry. VHS, Beta, LV $29.98 FOX Woof!

A Raisin in the Sun Outstanding story of a black family trying to make a better life for themselves in an all-white neighborhood in Chicago. The characters are played realistically and make for a moving story. Each person struggles with doing what he must while still maintaining his dignity and sense of self. Based on the Broadway play by Lorraine Hansberry.
1961 128m/B Diana Sands, John Fiedler, Ivan Dixon, Louis Gossett Jr., Sidney Poitier, Claudia McNeil, Ruby Dee; *D:* Daniel Petrie. VHS, Beta, LV $14.95 COL, HMV ♫♫♫♫

A Raisin in the Sun An "American Playhouse," made for television presentation of the Lorraine Hansberry play about a black family threatened with dissolution by the outside forces of racism and greed when they move into an all-white neighborhood in the 1950s.
1989 171m/C Danny Glover, Esther Rolle, Starletta DuPois; *D:* Bill Duke. VHS, Beta $69.95 FRH ♫♫♫

Raising Arizona Hi's an ex-con and the world's worst hold-up man. Ed's a policewoman. They meet, fall in love, marry, and kidnap a baby (one of a family of quints). Why not? Ed's infertile and the family they took the baby from has "more than enough," so who will notice? But unfinished furniture tycoon Nathan Arizona wants his baby back, even if he has to hire an axe-murderer on a motorcycle to do it. A brilliant, original comedy written by Coen and brother Ethan. Narrated in notorious loopy deadpan style by Cage. Innovative camerawork by Barry Sonnenfeld. Wild, surreal and hilarious.
1987 (PG-13) 94m/C Nicolas Cage, Holly Hunter, John Goodman, William Forsythe, Randall "Tex" Cobb, Trey Wilson, M. Emmet Walsh, Frances McDormand; *W/D:* Joel Coen; *W:* Ethan Coen. VHS, Beta, LV $19.98 FOX ♫♫♫½

Raising Cain Thriller evoking poor man's Hitchcock about a child psychiatrist who just happens to be nuts features Lithgow in five roles. Seems his supposedly dead Norwegian father has come to the United States and needs his son's help to steal babies for a child development experiment, so the son's alter ego, Cain, shows up to commit the nasty deed. Unfortunately Lithgow also catches his wife with another man, and that's when the bodies start piling up.
1992 (R) 95m/C John Lithgow, Lolita Davidovich, Steven Bauer, Frances Sternhagen, Cindy Girard, Tom Bower, Mel Harris, Gabrielle Carteris, Barton Heyman; *W/D:* Brian DePalma. VHS, Beta, LV MCA ♫♫

Ramblin' Man Selleck and Reed are on their way from Montana to Nashville when they stumble across a missing persons case and a blackmailer's schemes. *AKA:* Concrete Cowboys.
1979 (R) 100m/C Tom Selleck, Jerry Reed, Morgan Fairchild, Barbara Mandrell, Claude Akins, Ray Stevens; *D:* Burt Kennedy; *W:* Jimmy Sangster. VHS EDV, HHE, MTX ♫♫

Rambling Rose Dern is Rose, a free-spirited, sexually liberated before her time young woman taken in by a Southern family in 1935. Rose immediately has an impact on the male members of the clan, father Duvall and son Haas, thanks to her insuppressible sexuality. This causes consternation with the strait-laced patriarch, who attempts to control his desire for the girl. Eventually Rose decides she must try to stick to one man, but this only causes further problems. Dern gives her best performance yet in this excellent period piece, and solid support is offered from the rest of the cast, in particular Duvall and Dern's real-life mother Ladd.
1991 (R) 115m/C Laura Dern, Diane Ladd, Robert Duvall, Lukas Haas, John Heard, Kevin Conway, Robert Burke, Lisa Jakub, Evan Lockwood; *D:* Martha Coolidge. Academy Awards '91 Nominations: Best Actress (Dern), Best Supporting Actress (Ladd); Independent Spirit Awards '92: Best Actress (Ladd), Best Director (Coolidge), Best Film; National Board of Review Awards '91: 10 Best Films of the Year. VHS, LV $19.98 LIV ♫♫♫

Rambo: First Blood, Part 2 If anyone can save Our Boys still held prisoner in Asia it's John Rambo. Along the way he's tortured, flexes biceps, grunts, and then disposes of the bad guys by the dozen in one of filmdom's bigger dead body parades. Mindless action best enjoyed by testosterone-driven fans of the genre. Sequel to "First Blood" (1982); followed by "Rambo 3" (1988).
1985 (R) 93m/C Sylvester Stallone, Richard Crenna, Charles Napier, Steven Berkoff, Julia Nickson-Soul, Martin Kove; *D:* George P. Cosmatos; *M:* Jerry Goldsmith. VHS, Beta, LV $14.95 HBO, LIV ♫♫

Rambo 3 John Rambo, the famous Vietnam vet turned Buddhist monk, this time invades Afghanistan to rescue his mentor. Meets up with orphan and fights his way around the country. Typically exploitative, kill now, ask questions later Rambo attack, lacking the sheer volume of no-brainer action of the first two Rambos. At the time, the most expensive film ever made, costing $58 million. Filmed in Israel. Co-scripted by Stallone.
1988 (R) 102m/C Sylvester Stallone, Richard Crenna, Marc De Jonge, Kurtwood Smith, Spiros Focas; *D:* Peter McDonald; *M:* Jerry Goldsmith. VHS, Beta, LV $14.95 LIV ♫½

Rampage Seemingly all-American guy Charles Reece (McArthur) goes on a murder spree, killing and then mutilating his victims. Fraser (Biehn) is a liberal district attorney who questions his own views as he argues during the trial that Reece was sane when he committed the murders and deserves the death penalty. Director Friedkin makes no bones about his concerns that the criminal insanity defense often spares the perpetrator while denying justice to the victims. Adapted from the book by William P. Wood and loosely based on killer Richard Chase. Filmed in 1987, the movie wasn't released until 1992 due to the production company's financial difficulties.
1987 (R) 92m/C Michael Biehn, Alex McArthur, Nicholas Campbell, Deborah Van Valkenburgh, John Harkins, Art LaFleur; *W/D:* William Friedkin; *M:* Ennio Morricone. VHS, Beta $92.95 PAR, BTV ♫♫

Ramparts of Clay A young woman in Tunisia walks the line between her village's traditional way of life and the modern world just after her country's independence from France. Brilliantly shot on location; exquisitely poignant. In Arabic with English subtitles.
1971 (PG) 87m/C *FR D:* Jean-Louis Bertucelli. **VHS, Beta $59.95** *COL, TAM* 🐾🐾🐾

Ramrod Lake is a tough ranch owner at odds with her father, who is being manipulated by a big-time cattleman into trying to put them out of business. She fights back, and McCrea is caught in the middle as the only good guy. Nothing special.
1947 94m/B Veronica Lake, Joel McCrea, Arleen Whelan, Don DeFore, Preston Foster, Charlie Ruggles, Donald Crisp, Lloyd Bridges; *D:* Andre de Toth. **VHS $14.95** *REP* 🐾🐾

The Ramrodder An adult western spoof. *AKA:* Ramrodders.
1969 92m/C **VHS, Beta $19.95** *VDM* 🐾

Ran The culmination of Kurosawa's life's work stands as his masterpiece. Loosely adapting Shakespeare's "King Lear," with plot elements from "Macbeth," he's fashioned an epic, heartbreaking statement about honor, ambition and the futility of war. Aging medieval warlord Hidetora gives control of his empire to his oldest son, creating conflict with the other two sons. Soon Hidetora is an outcast, as ambition and greed seize two of his sons. Stunning battle scenes illuminate the full-blown tragedy of Kurosawa's vision. The acting is superb, with Harada a scene-stealer as the revenge-minded Lady Kaede; award-winning period costumes took three years to create. Written by Kurosawa, Hideo Oguni, and Masato Ide. In Japanese with English subtitles.
1985 (R) 160m/C *JP FR* Tatsuya Nakadai, Akira Terao, Jinpachi Nesu, Daisuke Oka, Meiko Harada, Hisashi Igawa; *D:* Akira Kurosawa. Academy Awards '85: Best Costume Design; Nominations: Best Art Direction/Set Decoration, Best Cinematography, Best Director (Kurosawa); New York Film Critics Awards '85: Best Foreign Film; National Society of Film Critics Awards '85: Best Film. **VHS, Beta, LV $19.98** *FOX, APD, TAM* 🐾🐾🐾🐾

Rana: The Legend of Shadow Lake Gold at the bottom of a lake is guarded by a frog-monster, but treasure hunters try to retrieve it anyway.
1975 96m/C Alan Ross, Karen McDiarmid, Jerry Gregoris. **VHS, Beta $24.95** *AHV* 🐾

Ranch An executive who loses everything inherits a dilapidated ranch and renovates it into a health spa.
1988 (PG-13) 97m/C Andrew Stevens, Gary Fjellgaard, Lou Ann Schmidt, Elizabeth Keefe; *D:* Stella Stevens. **VHS, Beta $14.95** *HMD* 🐾🐾

Rancho Deluxe Off-beat western spoof starring Bridges and Waterston as two carefree cowpokes. Cult favorite written by talented McGuane and featuring music by Buffett, who also appears in the film.
1975 93m/C Jeff Bridges, Sam Waterston, Elizabeth Ashley, Charlene Dallas, Clifton James, Slim Pickens, Harry Dean Stanton, Richard Bright, Jimmy Buffett; *D:* Frank Perry; *W:* Thomas McGuane; *M:* Jimmy Buffett. **VHS $19.98** *MGM* 🐾🐾🐾

Rancho Notorious Kennedy, on the trail of his girlfriend's murderer, falls for dance hall girl Dietrich. Fine acting. A "period" sample of 50's westerns, but different. A must for Dietrich fans.
1952 89m/C Marlene Dietrich, Arthur Kennedy, Mel Ferrer, William Frawley, Jack Elam, George Reeves; *D:* Fritz Lang. **VHS, Beta, LV $15.95** *UHV* 🐾🐾🐾

Random Harvest A masterful, tearjerking film based on the James Hilton novel. A shell-shocked World War I amnesiac meets and is made happy by a beautiful music hall dancer. He regains his memory and forgets about the dancer and their child. This is Garson's finest hour, and a shamelessly potent sobfest.
1942 126m/B Greer Garson, Ronald Colman, Reginald Owen, Philip Dorn, Susan Peters, Henry Travers, Margaret Wycherly, Bramwell Fletcher; *D:* Mervyn LeRoy. **VHS, Beta $19.98** *MGM* 🐾🐾🐾

Randy Rides Alone Very young Wayne is good in this slappable but pleasant B effort. Wayne single-handedly cleans up the territory and rids the land of a passel o'bad guys.
1934 53m/B John Wayne, Alberta Vaughn, George "Gabby" Hayes; *D:* Harry Fraser. **VHS, Beta, 3/4U, Special order formats $9.98** *REP, NOS, VCN* 🐾

Range Busters 🐾🐾 Range Busters are called in to find the identity of the phantom killer.
1940 55m/B Ray Corrigan, Max Terhune. **VHS, Beta $19.95** *NOS, VCN, DVT* 🐾

Range Feud Wayne is a ranch owner's son falsely accused of murder. Just as he's about to hang, Jones, as the heroic sheriff, saves the day and reveals the real killer's identity.
1931 58m/B Buck Jones, John Wayne, Susan Fleming, William Walling, Wallace MacDonald, Harry Woods, Ed LeSaint; *D:* Ross Lederman. **VHS $14.95** *COL* 🐾½

The Range Feud/Two Fisted Law Two early, short Wayne oaters which reveal the Duke developing the drawl, gait and pleasingly profane style that would carry him to fame. In "Feud" he is a young rancher accused of murdering a cattle rustler. "Law" finds him playing a character named Duke who loses his land and girl to a neighboring land grabber.
1931 112m/B Buck Jones, Tim McCoy, John Wayne, Susan Fleming, Alice Faye, Walter Brennan; *D:* Ross Lederman. **VHS $19.95** *COL* 🐾🐾

Range Law Another entry in the infamous Maynard series of horseplay, cliche, and repetitive plot elements.
1931 60m/B Ken Maynard. **VHS, Beta $19.95** *NOS, UHV, DVT* 🐾

Range Rider Eight episodes of the series are on four tapes, including "Greed Rides the Range," "Silver Blade" and "Fatal Bullet."
1952 60m/B Jock Mahoney. **VHS, Beta** *DVT* 🐾

Range Riders A gunman poses as a wimp and cleans out an outlaw gang.
1935 46m/B Buddy Roosevelt. **VHS, Beta** *NO* 🐾

Rangeland Empire Shamrock and Lucky are at it again, implicated as being members of an outlaw gang until that gang attacks them.
1950 59m/B James Ellison, Russell Hayden, Stanley Price, John Cason. **VHS, Beta, LV** *NO* 🐾

Rangeland Racket The Lone Rider (Houston) has been wrongly accused of a crime.
1941 60m/B George Houston, Hillary Brooke, Al "Fuzzy" St. John. **VHS, Beta** *VYY* 🐾½

Ranger and the Lady Texas Ranger Rogers romances the woman who is the leader of a wagon train.
1940 54m/B Roy Rogers, George "Gabby" Hayes; *D:* Joseph Kane. **VHS, Beta $19.95** *NOS, DVT, KRT* 🐾½

Ranger's Roundup The Rangers prove their courage by rounding up an outlaw gang.

1938 57m/B Fred Scott, Al "Fuzzy" St. John. **VHS, Beta $19.95** *NOS, DVT* 🐾

Rangers Take Over Gunlords are driven out by the Texas Rangers.
1943 62m/B Dave O'Brien, James Newill. **VHS, Beta $19.95** *NOS, VYY, DVT* 🐾½

Ransom A group of wealthy citizens decides to take on an assassin who stalks a resort town. *AKA:* Maniac; Assault on Paradise.
1984 90m/C Oliver Reed, Deborah Raffin, Stuart Whitman, John Ireland; *D:* Richard Compton. **VHS, Beta $69.98** *LIV, VES* 🐾

Ransom Money A kidnapping scheme involving millions of dollars, in and around the Grand Canyon, backfires.
1988 87m/C Broderick Crawford, Rachel Romen, Gordon Jump, Randy Whipple; *D:* DeWitt Lee. **VHS, Beta $9.95** *SIM* 🐾½

Ranson's Folly Barthelmess makes a wager that he can impersonate a famous outlaw well enough to rob a stage with only a pair of scissors. When the army paymaster is killed, guess who gets caught with his swash unbuckled?
1926 80m/B Richard Barthelmess, Dorothy Mackaill, Anders Randolf, Pat Hartigan, Brooks Benedict; *D:* Sidney Olcott. **VHS, Beta** *NO* 🐾🐾½

Rap Master Ronnie Reagan-era social phenomena are targeted in a series of musical sketches/parodies. Based on an off-Broadway hit.
1988 60m/C Jim Morris, Carol Kane, Jon Cryer, Dick Smothers, Tom Smothers; *D:* Jay Dubin. **VHS, Beta $39.99** *HBO, TLF* 🐾🐾½

Rape Two guys investigate a third pal's mysterious death. They discover that his supernatural-power-imbued girlfriend is at the root of the matter.
1987 90m/C Rick Joss, Gil Vidal. **VHS, Beta** *NO* 🐾

Rape and Marriage: The Rideout Case The true story of an Oregon wife who accused her husband of rape. Thoughtfully explores the legal and moral questions raised by the case. Interpreted well enough, though not superbly, by a decent cast. although Rourke is a little too intense. Made for television.
1980 96m/C Mickey Rourke, Linda Hamilton, Rip Torn, Eugene Roche, Conchata Ferrell, Gail Strickland, Bonnie Bartlett, Alley Mills; *D:* Peter Levin. **VHS, Beta $49.95** *LIV* 🐾🐾½

Rape of Love The story begis with one of the most chilling rape scenes on film and then attempts to analyze the emotional impact of rape on its victim. Well-acted and directed. In French with English subtitles.
1979 117m/C *FR* Nathalie Nell, Alain Foures; *D:* Yannick Bellon. **VHS, Beta $59.95** *COL, TAM* 🐾🐾½

The Rape of the Sabines The story of Romulus, king of Rome, and how he led the Romans to capture the women of Sabina. The battles rage, the women plot, and Romulus fights and lusts. Dubbed in English. *AKA:* El Rapto de las Sabinas; The Mating of the Sabine Women; Shame of the Sabine Women.
1961 101m/C *IT FR* Roger Moore, Mylene Demongeot, Jean Marais; *D:* Richard Pottier. **VHS, Beta $29.95** *UNI* Woof!

Rapid Fire Cheap, made-for-video quickie about a good guy U.S. agent who battles terrorists. Easy to skip.
1989 90m/C Joe Spinell, Michael Wayne, Ron Waldron; *D:* David A. Prior. **VHS, Beta $79.95** *AIP* 🐾

Rapid Fire Lee (son of martial arts cult film star Bruce Lee) is a Chinese-American art student who also happens to be a martial arts expert. He's tapped by the police to help stem the violence between the Asian and Italian gangs fighting for control over Chicago's drug trade. Typical martial arts movie is made better by uniquely choreographed action sequences and Lee's attractive presence.
1992 (R) 96m/C Brandon Lee, Powers Boothe, Nick Mancuso, Raymond J. Barry, Kate Hodge, Tzi Ma; **D:** Dwight Little. **VHS, LV $94.98** FXV ⅊⅊½

Rappaccini's Daughter Adaptation of a Nathaniel Hawthorne short story about a doctor's daughter who is cursed with the ability to kill anything she touches. Made for television.
1980 59m/C Kathleen Beller, Kris Tabori, Michael Egan; **D:** Dezso Magyar. **VHS, Beta $24.95** MON, MTI, KAR ⅊½

Rappin' Ex-con Van Peebles gets into it with the landlord and a street gang leader. Forgettable action/music drivel. ♫Rappin'; Two of a Kind; Call Me; Born to Love; Killer; Itching for a Scratch; Snack Attack; Dodge; Golly Gee; Colors; Lady Alcohol; Flame in the Fire; First Love Never Dies; The Game; FU12; Courtroom; Finale.
1985 (PG) 92m/C Mario Van Peebles, Tasia Valenza, Harry Goz, Charles Flohe; **D:** Joel Silberg. **VHS, Beta $79.95** MGM ⅊

The Rapture A beautiful telephone operator engages in indiscrimate sexual adventures to relieve the boredom of her job and life. She becomes curious by, and eventually converted to, evangelical Christianity, which leads her to a contented marriage and the birth of a daughter. When her husband is tragically killed she becomes convinced that she and her child will be taken by God into heaven if she only waits for the proper sign.
1991 (R) 100m/C Mimi Rogers, David Duchovny, Patrick Bauchau, Will Patton; **W/D:** Michael Tolkin. **VHS, LV** NLC ⅊⅊

Rapunzel A beautiful young woman locked in a tall tower who is saved by the handsome prince who climbs her golden tresses. Part of Shelly Duvall's "Faerie Tale Theatre" series.
1982 60m/C Shelley Duvall, Gena Rowlands, Jeff Bridges. **VHS, Beta, LV $14.95** KUI, FOX, FCT ⅊⅊

The Rare Breed Plodding but pleasant Western. A no-strings ranch hand (Stewart) agrees to escort a Hereford Bull to Texas, where the widow of an English breeder plans to crossbreed the bull with longhorn cattle. The widow (O'Hara) insists that she and her daughter accompany Stewart on the trip, which features every kind of western calamity imaginable. When all others believe the attempt to crossbreed them has failed, Stewart sets out to prove them wrong.
1966 97m/C James Stewart, Maureen O'Hara, Brian Keith, Juliet Mills, Jack Elam, Ben Johnson; **D:** Andrew V. McLaglen; **M:** John Williams. **VHS, Beta $19.95** MCA ⅊⅊½

A Rare Breed Real-life story of a kidnapped horse in Italy and a young girl's quest to retrieve it. Directed by David Nelson of television's "Ozzie and Harriet" fame, this movie is cute and old-fashioned.
1981 (PG) 94m/C George Kennedy, Forrest Tucker, Tracy Vaccaro, Tom Hallick, Don DeFore; **D:** David Nelson. **VHS, Beta $19.95** STE, LIV ⅊½

Rascal Dazzle Montage-like tribute to that best-loved group of children, the Our Gang kids. Narrated by Jerry Lewis. Includes scenes with Spanky, Alfalfa, Darla and the rest of the gang.
1981 100m/B VHS, Beta, LV $39.98 SUE ⅊½

The Rascals An irrepressible youth at a rural Catholic boys' school comes of age.
1981 (R) 93m/C FR Thomas Chabrol; **D:** Bernard Revon. **VHS, Beta $29.98** SUE ⅊⅊½

Rashomon In 12th century Japan, two travelers attempt to discover the truth about an ambush/rape/murder. They get four completely different versions of the incident from the three people involved in the crime and the single witness. An insightful masterpiece that established Kurosawa and Japanese cinema as major artistic forces. Fine performances, particularly Mifune as the bandit. Visually beautiful and rhythmic. Remade as a western, "The Outrage," in 1964. In Japanese with English subtitles. **AKA:** In the Woods.
1951 83m/B JP Machiko Kyo, Toshiro Mifune, Masayuki Mori; **D:** Akira Kurosawa. Academy Awards '51: Best Foreign Language Film; Nominations: Best Art Direction/Set Decoration (B & W); National Board of Review Awards '51: 5 Best Foreign Films of the Year, Best Director (Kurosawa). **VHS, Beta, LV $29.98** SUE, CRC, VYG ⅊⅊⅊⅊

Rasputin The long-censored and banned film of the story of the mad monk and his domination of the royal family before the Russian Revolution. Petrenko is superb. First released in the United States in 1988. In Russian with English subtitles. **AKA:** Agoniya.
1985 104m/C RU Alexei Petrenko, Anatoly Romashin, Velta Linne, Alice Freindlikh; **D:** Elem Klimov. **VHS, Beta $79.95** WBF, TAM ⅊⅊⅊

Rasputin and the Empress Lavish historical epic which teamed the three Barrymore siblings for the first and only time, as they vied for scene-stealing honors. Ethel plays Empress Alexandra of Russia, tied to the weak-willed Nicholas II (Morgan) and under the spell of Rasputin, played by Lionel. John plays a nobleman who seeks to warn the Russian rulers of their perilous perch on the throne, made only worse by Rasputin's spreading power and corruption. John seeks to kill off Lionel, finally accomplishing the deed, and gets to ride off into the sunset with a beautiful lady-in-waiting (Wynyard), still leaving Nicholas and Alexandra in willful ignorance of their fate. Ethel's first talkie and the first film role for Wynyard. Uncredited director Charles Brabin was replaced by Boleslawski due to his incompatability with the imperious Ethel. **AKA:** Rasputin: The Mad Monk.
1932 123m/B Ethel Barrymore, John Barrymore, Lionel Barrymore, Ralph Morgan, Diana Wynyard, Tad Alexander, C. Henry Gordon, Edward Arnold, Gustav von Seyffertitz, Anne Shirley, Jean Parker, Henry Kolker; **D:** Richard Boleslawski; **W:** Charles MacArthur. **VHS $19.98** MGM, MOV ⅊⅊⅊

Rat Pfink a Boo-Boo Parody on "Batman" in which a bumbling superhero and his sidekick race around saving people. Notoriously inept. Title story is legendary—it was misspelled accidentally and Steckler didn't have the cash to fix it.
1966 72m/B Vin Saxon, Carolyn Brandt, Titus Moede, Mike Kannon; **D:** Ray Dennis Steckler. **VHS, Beta** NO Woof!

The Rat Race A dancer and a musician venture to Manhattan to make it big, and end up sharing an apartment. Their relationship starts pleasantly and becomes romantic. Enjoyable farce. Well photographed and scripted, with the supporting characters stealing the show.
1960 105m/C Tony Curtis, Debbie Reynolds, Jack Oakie, Kay Medford, Don Rickles, Joe Bushkin; **D:** Robert Mulligan. **VHS** PAR ⅊⅊⅊

Ratboy An unscrupulous woman attempts to transform a boy with a rat's face into a celebrity, with tragic results. First directorial effort by Locke that gradually loses steam.
1986 (PG-13) 105m/C Sondra Locke, Sharon Baird, Robert Townsend; **D:** Sondra Locke. **VHS, Beta $79.95** WAR ⅊⅊½

Rate It X Sexism in a variety of national institutions, from pornography to consumerism, is revealed through the average man on the street via microphone interviews.
1986 (R) 95m/C **D:** Lucy Winer, Paula de Koenigsberg. **VHS, Beta $59.95** LIV ⅊⅊½

Ratings Game A bitter, out-of-work actor and a woman who works at the ratings service manage to mess up the television industry. Early directorial effort by DeVito is uneven but funny. Made for cable television. **AKA:** The Mogul.
1984 102m/C Danny DeVito, Rhea Perlman, Gerrit Graham, Kevin McCarthy, Jayne Meadows, Steve Allen, Ronny Graham, George Wenolt; **D:** Danny DeVito. **VHS, Beta, LV $79.95** PAR ⅊⅊

Rats In 2225, the beleaguered survivors of a nuclear holocaust struggle with a mutant rodent problem.
1983 100m/C Richard Raymond, Richard Cross; **D:** Vincent Dawn. **VHS, Beta** NO ⅊⅊

The Rats are Coming! The Werewolves are Here! Low budget schlock revolves around a family of werewolves and the daughter who decides to put an end to the curse. Imaginative title promises much more than movie delivers. The killer rats were thrown in as an afterthought to increase the run time.
1972 (R) 92m/C Hope Stansbury, Jackie Skarvellis, Noel Collins, Joan Ogden, Douglas Phair, Bernard Kaler; **W/D:** Andy Milligan. **VHS, Beta** NO Woof!

Rattle of a Simple Man A naive, chaste, middle-aged bachelor (Corbett) who lives in London must spend the night with a waitress (Cilento) to win a bet. She knows of the bet and kindly obliges. Enjoyable sex comedy.
1964 91m/B GB Harry H. Corbett, Diane Cilento, Michael Medwin, Thora Hird; **D:** Muriel Box. **VHS, Beta $59.99** HBO ⅊⅊½

Rattler Kid Cavalry sergeant wrongly accused of murdering his commanding officer escapes from prison and finds the real killer.
197? 86m/C Richard Wyler, Brad Harris. **VHS, Beta $49.95** UNI ⅊

Rattlers Made for television movie featuring poisonous rattlesnakes who attack at random.
1976 (PG) 82m/C Sam Chew, Elizabeth Chauvet, Dan Priest; **D:** John McCauley. **VHS, Beta** NO ⅊

The Raven An early, eccentric pseudo-biography of author Edgar Allan Poe. The film opens with a look at Poe's ancestors and follows the author to maturity when he turns to alcohol for solace. His drunken stupor produces hallucinations that lead to his tale of "The Raven." Silent with added music track.
1915 80m/B Henry B. Walthall, Wanda Howard; **D:** Charles Brabin. **VHS $29.95** FCT, HEG ⅊⅊

The Raven A lunatic surgeon (Lugosi), who has a dungeon full of torture gadgets inspired by Edgar Allan Poe's stories, is begged by a man to save his daughter's life.

The surgeon does, and then falls in love with the girl. But when she rejects his love (she's already engaged), he plans revenge in his chamber of horrors. Karloff plays the criminal who winds up ruining the mad doctor's plans. Lugosi is at his prime in this role, and any inconsistencies in the somewhat shaky script can be overlooked because of his chilling performance.
1935 62m/B Boris Karloff, Bela Lugosi, Irene Ware, Lester Matthews, Samuel S. Hinds; **D:** Lew Landers. VHS, LV $14.98 MCA 🐾🐾🐾

The Raven This could-have-been monumental teaming of horror greats Karloff, Lorre and Price is more of a satire than a true horror film. One of the more enjoyable of the Corman/Poe adaptations, the movie takes only the title of the poem. As for the storyline: Price and Karloff play two rival sorcerers who battle for supremacy, with Lorre as the unfortunate associate turned into the bird of the title.
1963 86m/C Vincent Price, Boris Karloff, Peter Lorre, Jack Nicholson, Hazel Court; **D:** Roger Corman. VHS, Beta, LV MLB 🐾🐾🐾

Ravishing Idiot An unemployed bank clerk becomes mixed up with Soviet spies. **AKA:** Agent 38-24-36; Adorable Idiot; The Warm-Blooded Spy; Bewitching Scatterbrain.
1964 99m/B FR Brigitte Bardot, Anthony Perkins; **D:** Edouard Molinaro. VHS, Beta NO 🐾

Raw Courage Three long-distance runners relax in New Mexico, but are kidnapped by vigilantes. Loosely based on a James Dickey novel. **AKA:** Courage.
1984 90m/C Ronny Cox, Lois Chiles, Art Hindle, Tim Maier, M. Emmet Walsh; **D:** Robert L. Rosen. VHS, Beta, LV $9.95 NWV, STE 🐾

Raw Deal Don't ever give Schwarzenegger a raw deal! FBI agent Schwarzie infiltrates the mob and shoots lots of people.
1986 (R) 106m/C Arnold Schwarzenegger, Kathryn Harrold, Darren McGavin, Sam Wanamaker, Paul Shenar, Steven Hill; **D:** John Irvin. VHS, Beta, LV $14.95 HBO, TLF 🐾 1/2

Raw Force Three karate buffs visit an island inhabited by a sect of cannibalistic monks who have the power to raise the dead (it could happen). They fix the villains by kicking them all in the head. **AKA:** Shogun Island.
1981 (R) 90m/C PH Cameron Mitchell, Geoffrey Binney, John Dresden, John Locke, Ralph Lombardi; **D:** Edward Murphy. VHS, Beta $49.95 MED 🐾

Raw Nerve A cast with possibilities can't overcome this poorly reasoned suspenser. A young man has visions of the local serial killer, but when he reports them to police he becomes the suspect. There are a few twists beyond that, none too thrilling.
1991 (R) 91m/C Glenn Ford, Traci Lords, Sandahl Bergman, Randall "Tex" Cobb, Ted Prior, Jan-Michael Vincent. VHS, Beta, LV $89.98 AIP 🐾

Raw Power Two thrill-seeking rich kids get their greedy hands on a super-car that defies any known power and gets them in loads of trouble. Some kids never learn.
19?? (R) 90m/C VHS PMH 🐾

Rawhead Rex An ancient demon is released from his underground prison in Ireland by a plowing farmer, and begins to decapitate and maim at will. Adapted by Clive Barker from his own short story. But Barker later disowned the film, so make your own judgment.
1987 (R) 89m/C David Dukes, Kelly Piper; **D:** George Pavlou. VHS, Beta $19.98 LIV, VES 🐾 1/2

Rawhide Rancher's Protection Association forces landowners to knuckle under resulting in friction. Gehrig plays a rancher in a western released the year before he died. Bandleader Ballew could be more gripping in the lead.
1938 60m/B Lou Gehrig, Smith Ballew, Evelyn Knapp; **D:** Ray Taylor. VHS, Beta $19.98 NOS, CCB, DVT 🐾🐾

Rawhide Four escaped convicts hijack a stagecoach way station and hold hostages while waiting for a shipment of gold. A suspenseful B-grade western with a bang-up ending. Well paced and cast with an abundance of good talent. A remake of "Show Them No Mercy" (1938). **AKA:** Desperate Siege.
1950 86m/B Tyrone Power, Susan Hayward, Hugh Marlowe, Jack Elam, Dean Jagger, George Tobias, Edgar Buchanan, Jeff Corey; **D:** Henry Hathaway. VHS, Beta $19.98 FOX 🐾🐾🐾

Rawhide Mail Extremely rare "B" western.
193? ?m/C Jack Perrin. VHS $15.95 LOO 🐾🐾

Rawhide Romance Bill finds justice and love in this chap-slappin' opus, which finds him neglecting the thieves operating on the ranch as he romances his girl. Naturally he comes to his senses and goes after the crooks.
1934 47m/B Buffalo Bill Jr., Genee Boutell, Lafe McKee, Si Jenks; **D:** Victor Adamson. VHS, Beta, LV $24.95 VYY, WGE 🐾

Razorback Young American travels to the Australian outback in search of his missing journalist wife. During his quest, he encounters a giant killer pig that has been terrorizing the area. Firmly establishes that pigs, with little sense of natural timing, make lousy movie villains.
1984 (R) 95m/C AU Gregory Harrison, Bill Kerr, Arkie Whiteley, Judy Morris, Chris Haywood; **D:** Russell Mulcahy. VHS, Beta $19.98 WAR 🐾

The Razor's Edge Adaptation of the W. Somerset Maugham novel. A rich young man spends his time between WWI & WWII searching for essential truth, eventually landing in India. A satisfying cinematic version of a difficult novel, supported by an excellent cast. Remade in 1984 with Bill Murray in the lead role.
1946 146m/B Tyrone Power, Gene Tierney, Anne Baxter, Clifton Webb, Herbert Marshall, John Payne, Elsa Lanchester; **D:** Edmund Goulding. Academy Awards '46: Best Supporting Actress (Baxter); Nominations: Best Interior Decoration, Best Picture, Best Supporting Actor (Webb); Golden Globe Awards '47: Best Supporting Actor (Webb), Best Supporting Actress (Baxter). VHS, Beta, LV $59.98 FOX, BTV 🐾🐾🐾

The Razor's Edge A beautifully filmed but idiosyncratic version of the W. Somerset Maugham novel. WWI-ravaged Larry Darrell combs the world in search of the meaning of life. Murray is a little too old and sardonic to seem really tortured. Russell is great as the loser he rescues. Subtly unique, with real shortcomings.
1984 (PG-13) 129m/C Bill Murray, Catherine Hicks, Theresa Russell, Denholm Elliott, James Keach, Peter Vaughan, Saeed Jaffrey, Brian Doyle-Murray; **D:** John Byrum; **M:** Jack Nitzsche. VHS, Beta, LV $79.95 COL 🐾🐾 1/2

The Re-Animator Based on an H.P. Lovecraft story, this grisly film deals with a medical student who re-animates the dead. It has quickly turned into a black humor cult classic. Also available in an "R" rated version, and followed by "Bride of Re-animator."
1985 86m/C Jeffrey Combs, Bruce Abbott, Barbara Crampton, David Gale, Robert Sampson; **D:** Stuart Gordon. VHS, Beta, LV $19.98 LIV, VES 🐾🐾🐾

Reach for the Sky WW II flying ace loses both legs in an accident and learns to fly again. He becomes a hero during the Battle of Britain, then is shot down over France and held prisoner by the Germans. At war's end he returns to England to lead 3,000 planes over London in a victory flight. Inspirationaly told true story.
1956 136m/B GB Kenneth More, Alexander Knox, Nigel Green; **D:** Lewis Gilbert. VHS, Beta LCA 🐾🐾 1/2

Reaching for the Moon A daydreaming department store employee finds himself in the unlikely position of ruling a kingdom. Vintage Fairbanks fun, based on a story by Anita Loos. Silent.
1917 91m/B Douglas Fairbanks Sr., Eileen Percy, Millard Webb; **D:** John Emerson. VHS, Beta, 8mm $29.95 VYY 🐾🐾 1/2

Reaching for the Moon Fairbanks is a businessman who falls for liquor and Daniels on a transatlantic cruise. Dull and cruel; not as light-hearted as it intends. One Irving Berlin song sung by Crosby.
1931 62m/B Douglas Fairbanks Sr., Bebe Daniels, Bing Crosby, Edward Everett Horton; **D:** Edmund Goulding. VHS, Beta, 8mm, 3/4U, Special order formats $19.95 NOS, VYY, CAB 🐾🐾 1/2

Reactor A low-budget sci-fi film about kidnapped scientists, alien ships and an activated nuclear reactor.
1985 90m/C Yanti Somer, Melissa Long, James R. Stuart, Robert Barnes, Nick Jordan. VHS, Beta NO 🐾

A Real American Hero Made for television story of Tennessee sheriff Buford Pusser, the subject of three "Walking Tall" films. Here, he battles moonshiners, with the usual violence. **AKA:** Hard Stick.
1978 94m/C Brian Dennehy, Brian Kerwin, Forrest Tucker; **D:** Lou Antonio. VHS, Beta $9.99 STE, PSM 🐾 1/2

Real Bruce Lee Contains actual early films of Bruce Lee, once feared lost but recently discovered in the Chinese film archives, (the movies, not Bruce).
1979 (R) 108m/C Bruce Lee. VHS, Beta $24.95 GEM, SUN 🐾 1/2

The Real Buddy Holly Story Documentary serves as a tribute to the rock 'n' roll legend who met an untimely death in 1959.
1987 90m/C VHS, Beta, LV $19.95 SMV, IME, VTK 🐾 1/2

Real Bullets Stunt team performs the real thing when two members get imprisoned in a bad guy's desert castle.
1990 86m/C John Gazarian, Martin Landau; **D:** Lance Lindsay. VHS, Beta, LV $89.95 VMK 🐾

Real Genius Brainy kids in California work with lasers on a class project that is actually intended for use as an offensive military weapon. When they learn of the scheme, they use their brilliant minds to mount an amusingly elaborate strategic defense initiative of their own. Eccentric characters and an intelligent script provide a bevy of laughs for the family.
1985 (PG) 108m/C Val Kilmer, Gabe Jarret, Jonathan Gries, Michelle Meyrink, William Atherton, Patti D'Arbanville, Severn Darden; **D:** Martha Coolidge. VHS, Beta, LV $14.95 COL 🐾🐾🐾

The Real Glory After the U.S. capture of the Philippine islands during the Spanish-American war, an uprising of Moro tribesmen spreads terror. After most of the islands are evacuated only a small group of Army officers is left to lead the Filipino soldiers against the rebels. Cooper plays the heroic doctor, who is not afraid to fight, especially when he comes to the rescue of the beseiged Army fort. Great action sequences and paticularly good performances by Cooper and Niven. **1939 95m/B** Gary Cooper, Andrea Leeds, David Niven, Reginald Owen, Broderick Crawford; *D:* Henry Hathaway. VHS $19.98 *MGM* 𝄞𝄞𝄞

Real Life Writer/comedian Brooks's first feature sags in places, but holds its own as a vehicle for his peculiar talent. Brooks plays a pompous director whose ambition is to make a documentary of a "typical" American family. Good, intelligent comedy. **1979 (R) 99m/C** Charles Grodin, Frances Lee McCain, Albert Brooks; *D:* Albert Brooks. VHS, Beta $19.95 *PAR* 𝄞𝄞𝄞

The Real Malcolm X: An Intimate Portrait of the Man A look at the controversial and charismatic leader of the civil rights movement. Includes footage of Malcolm X, excerpts from his speeches, and interviews with his widow and contemporaries as well as younger artists who discuss his legacy. **1992 60m/C** VHS $19.98 *FXV, BTV, FCT* 𝄞𝄞𝄞

Real Men The junior Belushi brother is a spy forced to recruit ordinary guy Ritter to help him negotiate with aliens to save the world. Bizarre premise shows promise, but spy spoof doesn't fire on all comedic pistons. Nice try. **1987 (PG-13) 86m/C** James Belushi, John Ritter, Barbara Barrie; *D:* Dennis Feldman. VHS, Beta, LV $79.98 *FOX* 𝄞 ½

The Real Patsy Cline The story of Patsy Cline's brilliant rise to stardom and her tragic death at the pinnacle of her career. **1990 60m/C** Patsy Cline, Loretta Lynn, Carl Perkins, Dottie West. VHS $14.95 *MVD, CAF* 𝄞 ½

Really Weird Tales Several SCTV alumni highlight this three-story movie, which is science fiction with a satirical edge. **1986 85m/C** John Candy, Martin Short, Joe Flaherty, Catherine O'Hara. VHS, Beta $7.00 *VTR* 𝄞𝄞 ½

Reap the Wild Wind DeMille epic about salvagers off the Georgia coast in the 1840s featuring Wayne as the captain and Milland and a giant squid as the villains. Good cast, lesser story, fine underwater photography. **1942 123m/C** Ray Milland, John Wayne, Paulette Goddard, Raymond Massey, Robert Preston, Lynne Overman, Susan Hayward, Charles Bickford, Walter Hampden, Louise Beavers, Martha O'Driscoll, Elisabeth Risdon, Hedda Hopper, Raymond Hatton; *D:* Cecil B. DeMille. Academy Awards '42: Best Special Effects; Nominations: Best Color Cinematography, Best Interior Decoration. VHS, Beta $14.98 *MCA* 𝄞𝄞 ½

Rear Window A newspaper photographer with a broken leg (Stewart) passes the time recuperating by observing his neighbors through the window. When he sees what he believes to be a murder, he decides to solve the crime himself. With help from his beautiful girlfriend and his nurse, he tries to catch the murderer without getting killed himself. Top-drawer Hitchcock blends exquisite suspense with occasional on-target laughs. **1954 112m/C** James Stewart, Grace Kelly, Thelma Ritter, Wendell Corey, Raymond Burr; *D:* Alfred Hitchcock. Academy Awards '54 Nominations: Best Director (Hitchcock), Best Screenplay, Best Sound; Edgar Allan Poe Awards '54: Best Screenplay. VHS, Beta, LV $19.95 *MCA, TLF, HMV* 𝄞𝄞𝄞𝄞

Reason to Die Bounty hunter uses his own girlfriend as a decoy to trap a psychotic prostitute killer. **1990 (R) 86m/C** Liam Cundill, Wings Hauser, Anneline Kriel, Arnold Vosloo; *D:* Tim Spring. VHS, LV $89.95 *VMK* 𝄞

A Reason to Live, A Reason to Die A bland Italian-French-German-Spanish western in which a group of condemned men attempt to take a Confederate fort. *AKA:* Massacre at Fort Holman; Una Ragione Per Vivere e Una Per Morire. **1973 90m/C** James Coburn, Telly Savalas, Bud Spencer, Robert Burton; *D:* Tonino Valerii. VHS, Beta $9.95 *NO* 𝄞𝄞

Rebecca Based on Daphne Du Maurier's best-selling novel about a young unsophisticated girl who marries a moody and prominent country gentleman haunted by the memory of his first wife. Fontaine and Olivier turn in fine performances as the unlikely couple. Suspenseful and surprising. Hitchcock's first American film and only Best Picture Oscar. Laserdisc features: rare screen tests of Vivien Leigh, Anne Baxter, Loretta Young, and Joan Fontaine, footage from Rebecca's winning night at the Academy Awards, original radio broadcasts of film by Orson Welles and David O. Selznick, and commentary of film with interview excerpts with Hitchcock. **1940 130m/B** Joan Fontaine, Laurence Olivier, Judith Anderson, George Sanders, Nigel Bruce, Florence Bates, Gladys Cooper, Reginald Denny, Leo G. Carroll; *D:* Alfred Hitchcock. Academy Awards '40: Best Black and White Cinematography, Best Picture; Nominations: Best Actor (Olivier), Best Actress (Fontaine), Best Adapted Screenplay, Best Director (Hitchcock), Best Film Editing, Best Interior Decoration, Best Supporting Actress (Anderson), Best Original Score; National Board of Review Awards '40: 10 Best Films of the Year. VHS, Beta, LV $19.98 *FOX, VYG, HMV* 𝄞𝄞𝄞𝄞

Rebecca of Sunnybrook Farm The original film version of the tale about an orphan who spreads sunshine and good cheer to all those around her. Silent with organ score by Gaylord Carter. Based on the popular novel by Kate Douglas Wiggin; remade with Shirley Temple in 1938. **1917 77m/B** Mary Pickford, Eugene O'Brien, Marjorie Daw, Helen Jerome Eddy; *D:* Marshall Neilan. VHS, Beta, LV $19.98 *CCB* 𝄞𝄞

Rebecca of Sunnybrook Farm Temple becomes a radio star over her aunt's objections in this bouncy musical that has nothing to do with the famous Kate Douglas Wiggin novel. Temple sings a medley of her hits, and dances the finale with Bill "Bojangles" Robinson. ♫On the Good Ship Lollipop/When I'm With You/Animal Crackers medley; Crackly Corn Flakes; Alone With You; Happy Ending; Au Revoir; An Old Straw Hat; Come and Get Your Happiness; Parade of the Wooden Soldiers. **1938 80m/B** Shirley Temple, Randolph Scott, Jack Haley, Phyllis Brooks, Gloria Stuart, Slim Summerville, Bill Robinson, Helen Westley, William Demarest; *D:* Allan Dwan. VHS, Beta, LV $19.98 *FOX, MLB, MLT* 𝄞𝄞 ½

Rebel Mumbling student radical must decide between his love for a country girl and his loyalty to an underground terrorist organization. Notable (or not) for display of early Stallone. **1973 (PG) 80m/C** Sylvester Stallone, Anthony Page, Rebecca Grimes. VHS, Beta *PGN* 𝄞 ½

Rebel A U.S. Marine falls in love with a Sydney nightclub singer and goes AWOL during World War II. Stylish but empty and badly cast.

1985 (R) 93m/C *AU* Matt Dillon, Debbie Byrne, Bryan Brown, Bill Hunter, Ray Barrett; *D:* Michael Jenkins. VHS, Beta, LV $79.98 *LIV, VES* 𝄞 ½

Rebel High Hijinks occur at a high school where youngsters study guerilla warfare and teachers wear bullet-proof vests. **1988 (R) 92m/C** Harvey Berger, Stu Trivax, Larry Gimple, Shawn Goldwater; *D:* Harry Jacobs. VHS, Beta $29.95 *ACA* 𝄞 ½

Rebel Love Love grows between a northern widow and a Confederate spy. In better hands it might have been a good story. Here, it's overwrought and embarrassing historical melodrama. **1985 84m/C** Terence Knox, Jamie Rose, Fred Ryan; *D:* Milton Bagby Jr. VHS, Beta $79.98 *LIV, VES* 𝄞

Rebel Rousers A motorcycle gang wreaks havoc in a small town where a drag-race is being held to see who will get the pregnant girlfriend of Dern's high-school buddy as the prize. Young Nicholson in striped pants steals the show. **1969 81m/C** Jack Nicholson, Cameron Mitchell, Diane Ladd, Bruce Dern, Harry Dean Stanton; *D:* Martin B. Cohen. VHS, Beta $29.95 *MED* 𝄞𝄞

The Rebel Set The owner of a beat generation coffeehouse plans an armed robbery with the help of some buddies. Genuinely suspenseful, competently directed. *AKA:* Beatsville. **1959 72m/B** Gregg Palmer, Kathleen Crowley, Edward Platt, John Lupton, Ned Glass, Don Sullivan, Vicki Dougan, I. Stanford Jolley; *D:* Gene Fowler. VHS, Beta $16.95 *SNC* 𝄞𝄞 ½

Rebel Storm A group of freedom fighters team up to rescue America from the totalitarian rulers that are in charge in 2099 A.D. **1990 (R) 99m/C** Zach Galligan, Wayne Crawford, June Chadwick, Rod McCary, John Rhys-Davies, Elizabeth Kiefer; *D:* Francis Schaeffer. VHS, Beta, LV $29.95 *ACA* 𝄞

Rebel Vixens Even though the war is over, ex-confederate soldiers continue looting and raping, until a brothel-full of prostitutes concoct a plan that has a lot to do with softcore sex. **1985 94m/C** Maria Lease, Roda Spain. VHS, Beta $29.95 *MED* Woof!

Rebel Without a Cause James Dean's most memorable screen appearance. In the second of his three films, he plays a troubled teenager from the right side of the tracks. Dean's portrayal of Jim Stark, a teen alienated from both his parents and peers, is excellent. He befriends outcasts Wood and Mineo in a police station and together they find a common ground. Superb young stars carry this in-the-gut story of adolescence. All three leads met with real-life tragic ends. **1955 111m/C** James Dean, Natalie Wood, Sal Mineo, Jim Backus, Nick Adams, Dennis Hopper, Ann Doran; *D:* Nicholas Ray. VHS, Beta, LV $19.98 *WAR* 𝄞𝄞𝄞𝄞

The Rebellious Reign In an effort to resurrect the Ming Dynasty, a single soldier seeks to unseat the sovereign power, the Ching Dynasty. **19?? (R) 100m/C** Jimmy Lee, Tsui Siu Keung. VHS, Beta $49.95 *OCE* 𝄞

The Rebels In the sequel to the television mini series "The Bastard," Philip Kent (Stevens) continues his Revolutionary War battle on the side of American independence. He is assisted by Southerner Judson Fletcher (Johnson) in thwarting an assassination attempt on George Washington. In addition to Bosley's Ben Franklin, "The Rebels" offers Backus as John Hancock. Followed by "The

Seekers;'' based on the novel by John Jakes.
1979 190m/C Andrew Stevens, Don Johnson, Doug McClure, Jim Backus, Richard Basehart, Joan Blondell, Tom Bosley, Rory Calhoun, MacDonald Carey, Kim Cattrall, William Daniels, Anne Francis, Peter Graves, Pamela Hensley, Wilfrid Hyde-White, Nehemiah Persoff, William Smith, Forrest Tucker, Tanya Tucker, Robert Vaughn, Debi Richter; **D:** Russ Mayberry. **VHS** $29.98 *MCA ✶✶*

Reborn A faith healer and a talent scout hire actors to be cured of fake ailments.
1978 91m/C Dennis Hopper, Michael Moriarty, Francisco Rabal, Antonella Murgia. **VHS, Beta** $69.95 *VES ✶✶*

Reckless Harlow, in a role originally intended for Joan Crawford, plays a showgirl coveted by a millionaire and secretly loved by her manager. Unfortunately, Harlow couldn't pull off the acting (much less the singing and dancing), although the plot strangely paralleled her own life. Songs include ''Reckless,'' ''Ev'rything's Been Done Before,'' ''Trocadero,'' ''Hear What My Heart Is Saying'' and ''Cyclone.''
1935 96m/B Jean Harlow, William Powell, Franchot Tone, May Robson, Ted Healy, Nat Pendleton, Rosalind Russell; **D:** Victor Fleming. **VHS, LV** $19.98 *MGM ✶✶*

Reckless A sincere movie about a ''good'' girl who finds herself obsessed with a rebel from the wrong side of her small town. Differs from 1950s' wrong-side-of-the-track flicks only in updated sex and music.
1984 (R) 93m/C Aidan Quinn, Daryl Hannah, Kenneth McMillan, Cliff DeYoung, Lois Smith, Adam Baldwin, Dan Hedaya, Jennifer Grey, Pamela Springsteen; **D:** James Foley. **VHS, Beta, LV** $14.95 *MGM ✶✶½*

Reckless Disregard A doctor whose career is ruined by a news report accusing him of involvement in a drug scam sues the newscaster. Made for television saga based on Dan Rather's ''60 Minutes'' story and ensuing lawsuit.
1984 92m/C Leslie Nielsen, Tess Harper, Ronny Cox, Kate Lynch; **D:** Harvey Hart. **VHS, Beta** $69.98 *LIV, VES ✶½*

Reckless Moment A mother commits murder to save her daughter from an unsavory older man, and finds herself blackmailed. Gripping, intense thriller.
1949 82m/B James Mason, Joan Bennett, Geraldine Brooks; **D:** Max Ophuls. **VHS, Beta** *LCA ✶✶*

The Reckless Way A young woman struggles for her big break into the movies.
1936 72m/B Marion Nixon, Kane Richmond, Inez Courtney, Malcolm McGregor, Harry Harvey, Arthur Howard; **D:** Raymond K. Johnson. **VHS, Beta** *GPV ✶½*

Recruits Sophomoric gagfest about an inept Californian police force. Typical 80's-style mindless ''comedy;'' dumb gags ensue from perfunctory premise.
1986 (R) 81m/C Alan Deveau, Annie McAuley, Lolita David; **D:** Rafal Zeilinski. **VHS, Beta, LV** $79.98 *LIV, VES ✶*

Red Alert Good, suspenseful, topical made for television thriller about nuclear meltdown. Will Minneapolis be saved? Usually Barbeau's name in the credits is a red alert, but this one is better than most.
1977 95m/C William Devane, Ralph Waite, Michael Brandon, Adrienne Barbeau; **D:** Billy Hale. **VHS, Beta** $19.95 *PAR ✶✶½*

The Red and the Black A big budgeted French adaptation of the classic Stendhal novel. A young man from the country seeks success, first in the Church and later in the employment and seduction of the gentry.

In French with English subtitles. *AKA:* Le Rouge et le Noir.
1957 134m/B *FR* Danielle Darrieux, Gerard Philippe; **D:** Claude Autant-Lara. **VHS, Beta** $69.95 *TAM, IVY, MRV ✶✶✶*

The Red and the White Epic war drama about the civil war between the Red Army and the non-communist Whites in Russia in 1918. Told from the perspective of Hungarians who fought alongside the Reds. Little dialogue. In Hungarian with English subtitles. *AKA:* Csillagosok, Katonak.
1968 92m/B *HU* **D:** Miklos Jancso. **VHS, LV** $79.95 *KIV, TAM ✶✶✶*

The Red Badge of Courage John Huston's adaptation of the Stephen Crane Civil War novel is inspired, despite cutting room hatchet job by the studio. A classic study of courage and cowardice. Sweeping battle scenes and intense personal drama.
1951 69m/B Audie Murphy, Bill Mauldin, Douglas Dick, Royal Dano, Andy Devine; **D:** John Huston. **VHS, Beta** $24.95 *KUI, MGM, HMV ✶✶✶½*

The Red Balloon The story of Pascal, a lonely French boy who befriends a wondrous red balloon which follows him everywhere. Lovely, finely done parable of childhood, imagination and friendship.
1956 34m/C *FR* Pascal Lamorisse; **D:** Albert Lamorisse. **VHS, Beta, LV, 8mm** $14.95 *COL, HHT, DVT ✶✶✶½*

Red Balloon/Occurrence at Owl Creek Bridge Two classic award-winning shorts have been combined on one tape: ''The Red Balloon'' (color, 1956) and ''An Occurrence at Owl Creek Bridge.'' The former is a children's story about a balloon on the loose; the latter is a perfectly rendered adaptation of the Ambrose Bierce short story of the same title, a taut narration of a Civil War hanging.
1962 60m/C *FR* Pascal Lamorisse, Roger Jacquet; **D:** Robert Enrico, Albert Lamorisse. **VHS, Beta, 3/4U, Special order formats** *SUE, VYY, WFV ✶✶✶½*

Red Balloon/White Mane The two classic, award-winning children's films by the French master, released only on laserdisc in pristine transfers.
1956 72m/C **D:** Albert Lamorisse. **Beta, LV** *CRC ✶✶✶½*

Red Barry A comic strip detective tries to track down criminals who threaten the world. Thirteen episodes on one videotape.
1938 ?m/B Buster Crabbe, Frances Robinson, Edna Sedgwick, Cyril Delevanti, Frank Lackteen; **D:** Ford Beebe, Alan James. **VHS** $49.95 *NOS, MLB ✶✶✶*

Red Beard An uncharacteristic drama by Kurosawa, about a young doctor in feudal Japan awakening to life and love under the tutelage of a compassionate old physician. Highly acclaimed; in Japanese with English subtitles. *AKA:* Akahige.
1965 185m/B *JP* Toshiro Mifune, Yuzo Kayama, Yoshio Tsuchiya, Reiko Dan; **D:** Akira Kurosawa. **VHS, Beta, LV** $59.95 *TAM, VYG, CRC ✶✶✶*

Red Blooded American Girl A scientist develops a virus that turns people into vampires. Those infected hit the streets in search of blood.
1990 (R) 89m/C *CA* Christopher Plummer, Andrew Stevens, Heather Thomas, Kim Coates; **D:** David Blyth. **VHS, Beta, LV** $29.95 *PSM ✶*

Red Dawn During World War III, Russian invaders overrun America's heartland and take over the country. Eight small-town teenagers, calling themselves the Wolverines, hide out in the rugged countryside and fight the Russians. Swayze and Grey met again in ''Dirty Dancing.''

1984 (PG-13) 114m/C Patrick Swayze, C. Thomas Howell, Harry Dean Stanton, Powers Boothe, Lea Thompson, Charlie Sheen, Ben Johnson, Jennifer Grey, Ron O'Neal, William Smith; **D:** John Milius. **VHS, Beta, LV** $19.95 *MGM ✶✶*

Red Desert The Pecos Kid is sent to track down the theft of a shipment of gold.
1950 60m/B Jack Holt, Donald (Don ''Red'') Barry, Tom Neal, Joseph Crehan, Tom London; **D:** Charles Marquis Warren. **VHS, Beta, LV** *NO ✶*

The Red Desert Antonioni's first color film, depicting an alienated Italian wife who searches for meaning in the industrial lunar landscape of northern Italy, to no avail. Highly acclaimed, and a masterpiece of visual form. Cinematography by Carlo di Palma. In Italian with English subtitles.
1964 120m/C *IT* Monica Vitti, Richard Harris, Carlos Chionetti; **D:** Michelangelo Antonioni. **VHS, Beta** $79.95 *FCT, TAM ✶✶✶*

Red Desert Penitentiary A spoof of movie-making featuring caricatures of industry-types.
1983 104m/C James Michael Taylor, Cathryn Bissell, Will Rose; **D:** George Sluizer. **VHS, Beta** *NO ✶✶✶*

Red-Dragon Two FBI agents are in Hong Kong trying to find out who has been smuggling electrical supplies to the communists. Unimaginative, but the scenery in Hong Kong is great. Based on the story ''La Riviere des Trois Jonques'' by Georges Godefroy.
1967 89m/C *IT GE* Stewart Granger, Rosanna Schiaffino, Harald Juhnke, Paul Klinger; **D:** Ernest Hofbauer. **VHS** $16.95 *SNC ✶✶*

Red Dragons of Shaolin Acrobats/kung-fu performers are caught up in a bloodbath. Warriors teach them how to spill a little blood of their own.
19?? 90m/C **VHS** $49.95 *OCE ✶*

Red Dust The overseer of a rubber plantation in Indochina causes all kinds of trouble when he falls in love with a young engineer's wife. Filled with free-spirited humor and skillfully directed; remarkably original. Remade in 1940 as ''Congo Maisie'' and in 1954 as ''Mogambo.''
1932 83m/B Clark Gable, Jean Harlow, Mary Astor, Gene Raymond, Donald Crisp; **D:** Victor Fleming. **VHS, Beta** $19.98 *MGM ✶✶✶*

Red Flag: The Ultimate Game Pilots rival for success in battle simulation training with terrible consequences. Fine performances cover plot weaknesses. Well-written dialogue. Made for television.
1981 100m/C Barry Bostwick, William Devane, Joan VanArk, Fred McCarren, Debra Feuer, George Coe, Linden Chiles, Arlen Dean Snyder; **D:** Don Taylor. **VHS, Beta** $39.95 *LIV ✶✶½*

The Red Fury Young Indian boy struggles to overcome prejudice and caring for his horse shows him the way. Family stuff.
197? 105m/C William Jordan, Katherine Cannon. **VHS** $59.95 *TPV, HHE ✶✶*

Red Garters A musical parody of old-time westerns which doesn't quite come off. Mitchell plays the cowpoke who comes to town to avenge the death of his brother with Clooney as the saloon singer who uses him to make boyfriend Carson jealous. The adequate songs include ''Red Garters,'' ''Man and Woman,'' ''A Dime and a Dollar,'' and ''Vaquero.''
1954 91m/C Guy Mitchell, Rosemary Clooney, Jack Carson, Gene Barry, Pat Crowley, Joanne Gilbert, Frank Faylen, Reginald Owen, Buddy Ebsen; **D:** George Marshall; **W:** Michael Fessier; **M:** Jay Livingston, Ray Evans. **VHS** $14.95 *PAR ✶✶½*

R

The Red Half-Breed A lonely half-breed Indian, wrongly accused of murder, discovers the real killer while running from the law.
1970 103m/C Daniel Pilon, Genevieve Deloir; D: Gilles Carle. **VHS, Beta** $59.95 NWV ✠½

Red Headed Stranger Willie Nelson vehicle based on his 1975 album. Nelson is a gun-totin' preacher who kills his wife and is led to salvation by a good farm woman. But honestly: Morgan Fairchild as Willie Nelson's wife? Please.
1987 (R) 108m/C Willie Nelson, Katharine Ross, Morgan Fairchild; D: Bill Wittliff. **VHS, Beta, LV** $9.98 NLC ✠½

Red Headed Woman Harlow plays an unscrupulous woman who charms her way into the lives of influential men. She causes her boss to divorce his wife and marry her while she sleeps with the chauffeur (Boyer) and others. Audiences loved the scandalous material, but the Hays Office objected to the fact that the immoral woman goes unpunished. Boyer's small but important role salvaged his floundering American film career. Harlow is sultry and funny.
1932 79m/B Jean Harlow, Chester Morris, Lewis Stone, Leila Hyams, Una Merkel, Henry Stephenson, May Robson, Charles Boyer, Harvey Clark; D: Jack Conway. **VHS, Beta** $19.98 MGM, FCT ✠✠✠

Red Heat Blair is a tourist in East Germany mistakenly arrested and sent to a rough women's prison. Her fiance tries to free her. Meanwhile, she has to deal with tough-lady fellow jail bird Kristel. Familiar and marginal.
1985 104m/C Linda Blair, Sylvia Kristel, Sue Kiel, William Ostrander; D: Robert Collector. **VHS, Beta, LV** $19.98 LIV, VES ✠½

Red Heat Two cops—one from the Soviet Union, one from Chicago—team up to catch the Eastern Bloc's biggest drug czar. Lots of action, but at times it seems too similar to Hill's earlier hit "48 Hours." Film claims to be the first major U.S. production shot in Red Square, Moscow.
1988 (R) 106m/C Arnold Schwarzenegger, James Belushi, Peter Boyle, Ed O'Ross, Larry Fishburne, Gina Gershon, Richard Bright; D: Walter Hill. **VHS, Beta, LV** $14.95 LIV, TLF ✠✠

The Red House Robinson plays a crippled farmer who, after his daughter brings home a suitor, attempts to keep everyone from a mysterious red house located on his property. Madness and murder prevail. Strange film noir about tangled relationships and unsuccessful attempts to bury the horrid past. Based on the novel by George Agnew Chamberlain.
1947 100m/B Edward G. Robinson, Lon McCallister, Judith Anderson, Allene Roberts, Rory Calhoun, Ona Munson; D: Delmer Daves. **VHS, Beta, 3/4U, Special order formats** $9.95 NEG, NOS, SNC ✠✠✠

Red Kimono Exploitative silent melodrama about a young woman ditched by her husband. She becomes a prostitute, but is redeemed by true love. Interesting slice of its period.
1925 95m/B Tyrone Power Sr., Priscilla Boner, Nellie Bly Baker, Mary Carr; D: Walter Lang. **VHS, Beta** $19.95 NOS, VYY, DVT ✠✠

Red King, White Knight An assassin tries to kill Mikhail Gorbachev during superpower peace talks. Ex-spook Skerritt returns to duty to thwart him. Better than most "topical" thrillers. Made for cable television.
1989 (R) 106m/C Tom Skerritt, Max von Sydow, Helen Mirren; D: Geoff Murphy. **VHS, Beta** $89.99 HBO ✠✠½

Red Kiss In 1952 Paris, Nadia, a 15-year-old French-Jewish Stalinist of Polish descent falls in love with an older, apolitical photographer. She's torn between love and politics; he's worried (rightly) about her being underage; and to make matters more complicated, her Polish mother has been reunited with her first love and Nadia's family may be split apart. The sensual Valandrey is a real find in her difficult coming-of-age role. In French with English subtitles. *AKA:* Rouge Baiser.
1985 110m/C FR Charlotte Valandrey, Lambert Wilson, Marthe Keller, Gunter Lamprecht, Laurent Terzieff; D: Vera Belmont. **VHS, LV** $79.95 FXL, FCT, TAM ✠✠✠

The Red Light Sting A Justice Department rookie (Bridges) and a call girl (Fawcett) reluctantly team up to con the Mafia in order to convict a San Francisco rackets czar. Goes down easy, but also easily forgotten or skipped.
1984 96m/C Farrah Fawcett, Beau Bridges, Harold Gould, Paul Burke, Sunny Johnson; D: Rod Holcomb. **VHS, Beta** $39.95 MCA ✠

Red Line 7000 High stakes auto racers drive fast cars and date women. Excellent racing footage in otherwise routine four-wheel fest.
1965 110m/C James Caan, Laura Devon, Gail Hire, Charlene Holt, John Crawford, Marianna Hill, George Takei; D: Howard Hawks. **VHS** $39.95 PAR, FCT ✠✠

Red Lion A bumbling horse-tender in feudal Japan impersonates a military officer to impress his family, only to be swept into leading a liberating revolution. In Japanese with English subtitles. *AKA:* Akage.
1969 115m/C JP Toshiro Mifune, Shima Iwashita; D: Kihachi Okamoto. **VHS, Beta** $49.95 TAM, VDA ✠✠½

The Red Menace Anti-Communist propaganda, made with unknown actors in documentary style has little to offer today's viewers other than unintentional laughs. Picture the Commies offering naive Americans money and sex to join the party, and you'll have an idea of the intellectual talent that went into this one.
1949 87m/B Robert Rockwell, Hanne Axman, Shepard Menken, Betty Lou Gerson, Barbara Fuller; D: R.G. Springsteen. **VHS, LV** $19.98 REP, FCT Woof!

Red Nightmare Anti-communist propaganda produced for the Department of Defense by Warner Brothers features the cast of "Dragnet." The story dramatizes the Red Menace, with communists conspiring to take over America, and shows what would happen to life in a small American town if the Commies took over.
1962 30m/B Jack Webb, Jack Kelly, Jeanne Cooper, Peter Brown. **VHS, Beta, 3/4U** $19.95 VYY, IHF ✠½

Red Nights A country boy goes to Hollywood seeking success and finds instead corruption, decadence, and dishonesty. Excellent soundtrack by Tangerine Dream.
1987 90m/C Christopher Parker, Jack Carter, Brian Matthews; D: Izhak Hanooka. **VHS, Beta** $19.98 TWE ✠

The Red Pony A young boy escapes from his family's fighting through his love for a pet pony. Based on the novel by John Steinbeck, with musical score by Aaron Copeland. Remade for television in 1976. Timeless classic that the whole family can enjoy.
1949 89m/C Myrna Loy, Robert Mitchum, Peter Miles, Louis Calhern, Sheppard Strudwick, Margaret Hamilton, Beau Bridges; D: Lewis Milestone. **VHS, LV** $14.98 REP, KUI ✠✠✠

The Red Pony Excellent TV remake of a classic 1949 adaptation of John Steinbeck. Fonda is superb as a troubled young boy's difficult father.
1976 101m/C Henry Fonda, Maureen O'Hara; D: Robert Totten. **VHS, Beta, LV** $19.98 BFA ✠✠✠

The Red Raven Kiss-Off A seedy Hollywood detective becomes the key suspect in a movie-making murder. Based on the 1930s' Dan Turner mystery stories. Made for video.
1990 (R) 93m/C Marc Singer, Tracy Scoggins, Nicholas Worth, Arte Johnson; D: Christopher Lewis. **VHS, Beta** $19.95 FRH ✠

Red Riding Hood Musical version of story of wolf who has little girl fetish.
1988 81m/C Isabella Rossellini, Craig T. Nelson, Rocco Sisto. **VHS, Beta** $14.95 MGM, CAN ✠✠½

Red River The classic Hawks epic about a gruelling cattle drive and the battle of wills between father and son. Generally regarded as one of the best westerns ever made, and Wayne's shining moment as a reprehensible, obsessive man. Featuring Clift in his first film. Restored version has eight minutes of previously edited material. Remade for television in 1988 with James Arness and Bruce Boxleitner.
1948 133m/B John Wayne, Montgomery Clift, Walter Brennan, Joanne Dru; D: Howard Hawks. **VHS, Beta, LV** $19.98 MGM, TLF, RDG ✠✠✠✠

Red River Valley Autry and partner Burnette go undercover to find out who's plaguing a dam construction site with explosions. Not to be confused with a 1941 Roy Rogers pic bearing the same title.
1936 60m/B Gene Autry, Smiley Burnette, Frances Grant, Booth Howard, Sam Flint, George Cheseboro, Charles King, Eugene Jackson, Frank LaRue, Lloyd Ingraham, Champion; D: B. Reeves Eason. **VHS** $19.95 NOS ✠✠

Red Rock Outlaw A sleazy character tries to kill his twin brother and takes his place as an honest rancher.
1947 56m/B Lee White. **VHS, Beta, LV** NO ✠

The Red Rope A Western hero cuts his honeymoon short to track down some villains.
1937 56m/B Bob Steele, Lois January, Forrest Taylor, Charles King, Karl Hackett, Bobby Nelson; D: S. Roy Luby. **VHS** $19.95 NOS, DVT ✠½

Red Scorpion A Soviet soldier journeys to Africa where he is to assassinate the leader of a rebel group. Will he succeed or switch allegiances? Poor acting and directing abound.
1989 (R) 102m/C Dolph Lundgren, M. Emmet Walsh, Al White, T.P. McKenna, Carmen Argenziano, Brion James, Regopstann; D: Joseph Zito. **VHS, LV** $89.95 STE ✠

Red Shoe Diaries After a woman's suicide her grieving lover discovers her diaries and finds out she led a secret erotic life, revolving around her shoe-salesman lover and a pair of sexy red shoes. Made for cable television; also available in an unrated version.
1992 (R) 105m/C David Duchovny, Billy Wirth, Brigitte Bako; D: Zalman King. **VHS, LV** REP ✠✠

Red Shoe Diaries 2: Double Dare The erotic sequel to "Red Shoe Diaries" follows the libidinous fancies of three women. Severance begins a sexual affair with a stranger only to be torn between love and lust. Johnson gets naked to tease an office worker in the building next door. Crosby is a cop who is rejected by the man she desires—so she arrests and handcuffs

him in order to play some kinky games. Also available in an unrated version.
1992 (R) 92m/C Joan Severance, Laura Johnson, Denise Crosby, Steven Bauer, Arnold Vosloo, David Duchovny; **D:** Zalman King, Tibor Takacs. VHS, LV $89.98 *REP, PMS* 🐾🐾

The Red Shoes British classic about a young ballerina torn between love and success. Inspired by the Hans Christian Andersen fairy tale. Written by Powell and Pressburger. Noted for its lavish use of Technicolor.
1948 136m/C *GB* Anton Walbrook, Moira Shearer, Marius Goring, Leonide Massine, Robert Helpmann, Albert Basserman, Emeric Pressburger; **D:** Michael Powell. Academy Awards '48: Best Art Direction/Set Decoration (Color), Best Score; Nominations: Best Film Editing, Best Picture, Best Story; National Board of Review Awards '48: 10 Best Films of the Year. VHS, Beta, LV $19.95 *PAR, VTK, HMV* 🐾🐾🐾🐾

The Red Shoes The Children's Theatre Company and School of Minneapolis perform their own unique interpretation of the Hans Christian Andersen story.
1983 79m/C VHS, Beta $39.95 *MCA* 🐾🐾🐾🐾

Red Signals Mystery criminal makes trains collide.
1927 70m/B Wallace MacDonald, Earl Williams, Eva Novak, J.P. McGowan, Frank Rice; **D:** J.P. McGowan. VHS, Beta $24.95 *GPV, FCT* 🐾

Red Snow High in the Cascade Mountains, Kyle Lewis is the new snowboard instructor for the Hurricane Ridge Ski Resort. The job is fine in the beginning, until Kyle learns of the tragic fate of the last instructor. Before he knows it, Kyle is the next target and is framed for two murders. He secures the help of his fellow snowboard buddies in hopes of solving the mystery and getting the girl, too. High speed ski scenes and dangerous stunts are the film's only redeeming qualities.
1991 86m/C Carlo Scandiuzzi, Scott Galloway, Darla Slavens, Mitch Cox, Tamar Tibbs, Brian Mahoney; **D:** Phillip J. Roth. VHS $79.95 *VHE* 🐾

Red Sonja Two warriors join forces against an evil queen in this sword and sorcery saga. Big, beautiful bodies everywhere, with Bergman returning from her Conan adventures. Little humor, few special effects, and weak acting make this a poor outing.
1985 (PG-13) 89m/C Arnold Schwarzenegger, Brigitte Nielsen, Sandahl Bergman, Paul Smith; **D:** Richard Fleischer; **M:** Ennio Morricone. VHS, Beta, LV $19.98 *MGM, FOX* 🐾½

Red Sorghum A stunning visual achievement, this new wave Chinese film (and Yimou's directorial debut) succeeds on many levels—as an ode to the color red, as dark comedy, and as a sweeping epic with fairy tale overtones. A young woman traded for a donkey and betrothed to a leper in the rural China of the 1920s is reprieved when the leper is murdered, presumably by her lover. She marries her lover, and they take over the distillery owned by the leper. Further complications ensue when the Japanese invade. The sorghum plot nearby is a symbolic playing field in the movie's most stunning scenes. Here, people make love, murder, betray, and commit acts of bravery, all under the watchful eye of nature. In Mandarin with English subtitles.
1987 91m/C *CH* Gong Li, Jiang Wen, Ji Cun Hua; **D:** Zhang Yimou. VHS $79.95 *NYF, TAM* 🐾🐾🐾½

The Red Stallion Good film for animal lovers, but it loses something when it comes to human relationships. A young boy raises his pony into an award-winning racehorse that saves the farm when it wins the big race. Good outdoor photography.
1947 82m/B Robert Paige, Noreen Nash, Ted Donaldson, Jane Darwell; **D:** Lesley Selander. VHS $19.95 *NOS, MOV, HEG* 🐾½

Red Sun A gunfighter, a samurai, and a French bandit fight each other in various combinations in the 1860s. Ludicrous and boring.
1971 115m/C *FR IT SP* Charles Bronson, Toshiro Mifune, Alain Delon, Ursula Andress; **D:** Terence Young. VHS, Beta $24.95 *GEM* 🐾🐾

Red Surf Action abounds in this surfer film. A couple of hard-nosed wave-riders get involved with big money drug gangs and face danger far greater than the tide.
1990 (R) 104m/C George Clooney, Doug Savant, Dedee Pfeiffer, Gene Simmons, Rick Najera, Philip McKeon; **D:** H. Gordon Boos. VHS, Beta, LV $29.95 *ACA* 🐾

Red Tent A robust, sweeping man-versus-nature epic based on the true story of the Arctic stranding of Italian explorer Umberto Nobile's expedition in 1928. Music by Ennio Morricone. A Russian-Italian co-production. *AKA:* Krasnaya Palatka.
1969 (G) 121m/C Sean Connery, Claudia Cardinale, Peter Finch, Hardy Kruger, Massimo Girotti, Luigi Vannucchi; **D:** Mikhail Kalatozov; **M:** Ennio Morricone. Beta, LV, Q $19.95 *PAR* 🐾🐾🐾

Red, White & Busted Amnesty or prison? That is the scorching, virtually unanswerable question asked by indictment of America. We follow three friends during the Vietnam War and see how they were affected by the events, whether or not they went. *AKA:* Outside In.
1975 85m/C Darrell Larson, Heather Menzies, Dennis Oliveri, John Bill. VHS, Beta, LV *NO* 🐾

Red Wind Kris Morrow is a psychotherapist whose latest patient, Lila, has a number of disturbing sadomasochistic fantasies. When Kris feels she's getting too close to the situation, she refers Lila to another therapist. But Lila calls and tells Kris she's already acted out one of her fantasies by killing her husband. In order to stop Lila from killing again, Kris goes on a dangerous search for her deadly patient.
1991 (R) 93m/C Lisa Hartman, Deanna Lund, Philip Casnoff, Christopher McDonald; **D:** Alan Metzger. VHS *MCA* 🐾🐾

The Redeemer Group of adults at their high school reunion play the children's game of hide-and-seek, with deadly results.
1976 80m/C F.G. Finkbinder, Damien Knight, Jeanetta Arnetta; **D:** Constantine S. Gochis. VHS, Beta *GHV* 🐾

Redneck Implausible, distasteful purported "thriller" about criminals on the run.
1973 92m/C *IT GB* Telly Savalas, Franco Nero, Mark Lester, Ely Galleani, Dulio Del Prete, Maria Michi; **D:** Silvio Narizzano. VHS, Beta *NO* 🐾

Redneck Zombies A bunch of backwoods rednecks become zombies after chug-a-lugging some radioactive beer. Eating local tourists becomes a hard habit to break. Betcha can't have just one!
1988 (R) 83m/C Floyd Piranha, Lisa DeHaven, W.E. Benson, William W. Decker, James Housely, Zoofoot, Tyrone Taylor, Perieles Lewnes. VHS, Beta $79.95 *TWE* 🐾

Reds The recreation of the life of author John Reed ("Ten Days that Shook the World"), his romance with Louise Bryant, his efforts to start an American Communist party, and his reporting of the Russian Revolution. A sweeping, melancholy epic using dozens of "witnesses" who reminisce about what they saw. Won several Oscars, including Best Director for Beatty.
1981 (PG) 195m/C Warren Beatty, Diane Keaton, Jack Nicholson, Edward Herrmann, Maureen Stapleton, Gene Hackman, Jerzy Kosinski, George Plimpton, Paul Sorvino, William Daniels, M. Emmet Walsh, Dolph Sweet, Josef Sommer; **D:** Warren Beatty. Academy Awards '81: Best Cinematography, Best Director (Beatty), Best Supporting Actress (Stapleton); Nominations: Best Actor (Beatty), Best Actress (Keaton), Best Art Direction/Set Decoration, Best Costume Design, Best Film Editing, Best Original Screenplay, Best Picture, Best Sound, Best Supporting Actor (Nicholson); Directors Guild of America Awards '81: Best Director (Beatty); Golden Globe Awards '82: Best Director (Beatty); New York Film Critics Awards '81: Best Film. VHS, Beta, LV $29.95 *PAR, BTV* 🐾🐾🐾

Reefer Madness Considered serious at the time of its release (it was originally titled "Tell Your Children"), this low-budget depiction of the horrors of marijuana has become an underground comedy favorite. Overwrought acting and lurid script contribute to the fun. *AKA:* Tell Your Children.
1938 (PG) 67m/B Dave O'Brien, Dorothy Short, Warren McCollum, Lillian Miles, Thelma White, Carleton Young; **D:** Louis Gasnier. VHS, Beta $16.95 *SNC, NOS, HHT* 🐾🐾

Reet, Petite and Gone All-Black musical featuring the music of neglected jive singer Louis Jordan, and his band, The Tympany Five. A girl's mother dies; sneaky lawyer tries to cheat her. Slick and enjoyable.
1947 75m/B Louis Jordan, June Richmond; **D:** William Forest Crouch. VHS, Beta $19.95 *MVD, NOS, VYY* 🐾🐾

The Reflecting Skin In a 1950s prairie town a small boy sees insanity, child-murder, and radiation sickness, leading him to fantasize that the tormented young widow next door is a vampire. The pretentious drama/freak show rationalizes its ghastly events as symbolizing the hero's loss of youthful innocence. But the Hound knows the score; this is "Faces of Death" for the arts crowd, a grotesque menagerie that dares you to watch. The exploding-frog opener is already notorious. Beautiful photography, with vistas inspired by the painting of Andrew Wyeth.
1991 116m/C Viggo Mortensen, Lindsay Duncan, Jeremy Cooper; **W/D:** Philip Ridley. VHS, LV *NO* 🐾🐾

A Reflection of Fear Lame psychothriller about a young girl's jealously of her father's girlfriend, with family members dying of supernatural causes. *AKA:* Labyrinth.
1972 (PG) 90m/C Robert Shaw, Sally Kellerman, Sondra Locke, Mary Ure; **D:** William A. Fraker. VHS, Beta $69.95 *COL* 🐾🐾

Reflections in a Golden Eye Huston's film adaptation of Carson McCullers novel about repressed homosexuality, madness, and murder at a Southern Army base in 1948. Star-studded cast cannot consistently pull off convoluted lives of warped characters; not for everyone, though it holds some interest.
1967 109m/C Elizabeth Taylor, Marlon Brando, Brian Keith, Julie Harris; **D:** John Huston. VHS, Beta $19.98 *WAR* 🐾🐾½

Reflections of Murder Evil schoolteacher's wife and mistress decide to kill him off and then are plagued by his phantom. Well done made for television remake of the French film "Diabolique." Suspenseful, with a great ending.

1974 97m/C Tuesday Weld, Joan Hackett, Sam Waterston, Lucille Benson, R.G. Armstrong, Michael Lerner, Ed Bernard, Lance Kerwin; **D:** John Badham. VHS $14.98 REP 🐾🐾½

Reform School Girl A young girl ends up behind bars when her boyfriend steals a car to go joy-riding and is involved in a hit-and-run murder. Extremely cheap production and incredulous story. Look for Kellerman in a bit part in her first screen appearance. **1957** 71m/B Gloria Castillo, Ross Ford, Edward Byrnes, Ralph Reed, Jack Kruschen, Sally Kellerman; **W/D:** Edward L. Bernds. VHS $9.95 NLC 🐾

Reform School Girls Satiric raucous women's prison film, complete with tough lesbian wardens, brutal lesbian guards, sadistic lesbian inmates, and a single, newly convicted heterosexual heroine. Wendy O. Williams as a teenager? Come on. Overdone, over-campy, exploitative. **1986** (R) 94m/C Linda Carol, Wendy O. Williams, Pat Ast, Sybil Danning, Charlotte McGinnis, Sherri Stoner; **D:** Tom De Simone. VHS, Beta, LV $19.95 STE, NWV 🐾

Refuge of Fear Drama set in a post-nuclear-holocaust world. **198?** 90m/C VHS, Beta NO 🐾

Regarding Henry A cold-hearted lawyer gets shot in the head during a holdup and survives with memory and personality erased. During recovery the new Henry displays compassion and conscience the old one never had. Though too calculated in its yuppie-bashing ironies, the picture works thanks to splendid acting and low-key, on-target direction. **1991** (PG-13) 107m/C Harrison Ford, Annette Bening, Bill Nunn, Mikki Allen; **D:** Mike Nichols. VHS, Beta, LV $19.95 PAR 🐾🐾🐾

Reggie Mixes In Wealthy man brawls in bar room and falls for barmaid. Taking a job to be near his beloved, he wipes out local thugs while tending to her welfare. Exhilarating fight scenes in which Fairbanks fists it out with real life boxers. **1916** 58m/B Douglas Fairbanks Sr., Bessie Love, Joseph Singleton, William E. Lowery, Wilbur Higby, Frank Bennett; **D:** Christy Cabanne. VHS, Beta $24.95 GPV, FCT 🐾🐾🐾

Regina A woman controls all the activities of her husband and son. At age 36, her son is ready to leave home and she refuses to let him. Fine performances in this strange and disturbing film. **1983** 86m/C IT Anthony Quinn, Ava Gardner, Ray Sharkey, Anna Karina; **D:** Jean-Yves Prate. VHS, Beta $69.95 VMK 🐾🐾½

Reg'lar Fellers A gang of kids save the town and soften the heart of their grandmother. Production is sloppy. Based on a comic strip by Gene Byrnes. **1941** 66m/B Billy Lee, Carl "Alfalfa" Switzer, Buddy Boles, Janet Dempsey, Sarah Padden, Roscoe Ates; **D:** Arthur Dreifuss. VHS $19.95 NOS, FMT, VYY 🐾🐾

Rehearsal for Murder Movie star Redgrave is murdered on the night of her Broadway debut. Seems it might have been someone in the cast. Brought to you by the creative team behind "Columbo." Challenging made for television whodunit with a twist. Good cast. **1982** 96m/C Robert Preston, Lynn Redgrave, Patrick Macnee, Lawrence Pressman, Madolyn Smith, Jeff Goldblum, William Daniels; **D:** David Greene. VHS, Beta $59.95 REP 🐾🐾½

Reign of Terror British-made adventure set during the French Revolution, with everyone after the black book that holds the names of those arch-fiend Robespierre plans to guillotine in his ruthless bid for power. Well-mounted, but historical personages and events are reduced to cartoon form. **AKA:** The Black Book. **1949** 89m/B Robert Cummings, Arlene Dahl, Richard Hart, Arnold Moss, Richard Basehart; **D:** Anthony Mann. VHS $19.95 NOS, MRV, VEC 🐾🐾

Reilly: Ace of Spies Covers the exploits of the real-life superspy and womanizer Sydney Reilly who uncovers Russian secrets in 1901, allowing the Japanese to sink the Russian fleet and invade China. After a lively spying career for the British, Reilly eventually plots against the Bolsheviks and comes close to overthrowing Lenin and installing himself as the new leader of the Russian government. Eleven episodes on four cassettes. **1987** 572m/C GB Sam Neill, Sebastian Shaw, Jeananne Crowley; **D:** Jim Goddard. VHS, Beta, LV $179.00 SIG, HBO, FCT 🐾🐾🐾

The Reincarnate Cult guarantees lawyer will live forever if he can find a new body. Enter gullible sculptor; lawyer uses skill at persuasion. **1971** (PG) 89m/C CA Jack Creley, Jay Reynolds, Trudy Young, Terry Tweed; **D:** Don Haldane. VHS, Beta NO 🐾

The Reincarnation of Golden Lotus In this highly erotic story of love and revenge, Wong escapes China for decadent Hong Kong by marrying a wealthy but foolish man. She has numerous sadomasochistic affairs and begins having flashbacks, revealing her to be the reincarnation of Golden Lotus, a courtesan of ancient China. In Mandarin Chinese with English subtitles. **1989** 99m/C HK Joi Wong, Eric Tsang, Lam Chen Yen; **D:** Clara Law. VHS $79.95 CVC, TAM 🐾🐾🐾🐾

The Reincarnation of Peter Proud A college professor has nightmares which lead him to believe the spirit of a murdered man is now possessing him. Kinda scary, but predictable. Screenplay adapted by Max Ehrlich from his novel. **1975** (R) 105m/C Michael Sarrazin, Jennifer O'Neill, Margot Kidder, Cornelia Sharpe; **D:** J. Lee Thompson; **M:** Jerry Goldsmith. VHS, Beta, LV $29.98 LIV, VES 🐾🐾

The Reivers Young boy and two adult pals journey from small town Mississippi (circa 1905) to the big city of Memphis in a stolen car. Picaresque tale is delightful on-screen, as in William Faulkner's enjoyable last novel. **1969** (PG) 107m/C Steve McQueen, Sharon Farrell, Will Geer, Michael Constantine, Rupert Crosse; **D:** Mark Rydell; **M:** John Williams. VHS, Beta $14.98 FOX 🐾🐾🐾½

The Rejuvenator Also known as "Rejuvenatrix." An oft-told film story: an aging actress discovers a "youth" serum but finds out that the serum affects things other than her aging. Well-done. **AKA:** Rejuvenatrix. **1988** (R) 90m/C Marcus Powell, John MacKay, James Hogue, Vivian Lanko, Jessica Dublin; **D:** Brian Thomas Jones. VHS, LV $79.95 SVS 🐾🐾½

Relentless Twisted psycho Nelson, once rejected by the LAPD Academy on psychological grounds takes his revenge by murdering people and using his police training to cover his tracks. Good acting keeps sporadically powerful but cliched thriller afloat. **1989** (R) 92m/C Judd Nelson, Robert Loggia, Meg Foster, Leo Rossi, Pat O'Bryan, Mindy Seeger, Angel Tompkins, Ken Lerner, George Flower; **D:** William Lustig. VHS, Beta, LV $19.95 COL 🐾🐾

Relentless 2: Dead On Rossi, the detective from the first film, tracks yet another murderer whose occult-style mutilations mask an international political conspiracy. So-so slaughter with artsy camerawork. Honestly, how many "Relentless" fans can you name who've been waiting with anticipation? **1991** (R) 93m/C Leo Rossi, Ray Sharkey, Meg Foster, Miles O'Keeffe; **D:** Michael Schroeder. VHS, LV $89.95 SVS, PIA 🐾🐾

The Reluctant Debutante Harrison and Kendall are the urbane parents of Dee who are trying to find a suitable British husband for their girl. It seems their choices just won't do however, and Dee falls for American bad boy musician Saxon. A very lightweight yet extremely enjoyable romantic comedy thanks to Harrison and in particular his real-life wife Kendall, who unfortunately died the following year. **1958** 96m/C Rex Harrison, Kay Kendall, John Saxon, Sandra Dee, Angela Lansbury, Diane Clare; **D:** Vincente Minnelli. VHS, Beta, LV $19.98 MGM 🐾🐾🐾

The Reluctant Dragon This is the classic Disney short about a fun-loving dragon, based on the Kenneth Grahame story; accompanied also by the Disney short "Morris, the Midget Moose." Not to be confused with the full-length 1941 Disney feature film. **1941** 28m/C **D:** Alfred Werker. VHS, Beta $12.99 DIS, KUI, WTA 🐾🐾🐾

Rembrandt Necessarily very visual biography of the great Dutch painter, Rembrandt. Superb acting by Laughton. **1936** 86m/B GB Charles Laughton, Elsa Lanchester, Gertrude Lawrence, Walter Hudd; **D:** Alexander Korda. VHS, Beta, LV $14.98 SUE 🐾🐾🐾

Rembrandt—1669 A recreation of the controversial artist's last year, with his egotism clashing with his artistic impulses. In Dutch with English subtitles. **1977** 114m/C NL Frans Stelling, Tom de Koff, Aye Fil; **D:** Jos Stelling. VHS $79.95 CVC, TAM 🐾🐾

Remedy for Riches The fourth "Dr. Christian" comedy, has the small-town doctor trying to uncover a real estate fraud before it bankrupts his community. Mildly funny. **1940** 66m/B Jean Hersholt, Dorothy Lovett, Edgar Kennedy, Jed Prouty, Walter Catlett; **D:** Erle C. Kenton. VHS, Beta, 8mm $19.95 NOS, VYY 🐾🐾

Remember Me Just as a woman is starting to gain control of her life, her husband returns home from the mental hospital. **1985** 95m/C Robert Grubb, Wendy Hughes, Richard Moir; **D:** Lex Marinos. VHS, Beta $59.95 MNC 🐾

Remembrance of Love A widower and his daughter attend the Jerusalem Gathering of Holocaust Survivors and he is reunited with his forty-years lost love. Romantic tale suffers from cliches. Made for television. **1982** 100m/C Kirk Douglas, Pam Dawber, Chana Eden, Robert Clary, Yoram Gall, Michael Goodwin, Eric Douglas; **D:** Jack Smight. VHS SWC 🐾🐾½

Remo Williams: The Adventure Begins Adaptation of "The Destroyer" adventure novel series with a Bond-like hero who can walk on water and dodge bullets after being instructed by a Korean martial arts master. Funny and diverting, and Grey is excellent (if a bit over the top) as the wizened oriental. The title's assumption is that the adventure will continue.

1985 (PG-13) 121m/C Fred Ward, Joel Grey, Wilford Brimley, Kate Mulgrew; **D:** Guy Hamilton. **VHS, Beta, LV** $14.99 *HBO* ♫♫

Remote Thirteen-year-old Randy is a whiz designing high-tech remote-control gadgets. When one of his toys wipes out a friend's science project, Randy's parents try to put a halt to his tinkering but the kid has other plans. Innocuous rip-off of "Honey, I Shrunk the Kids" with some "Home Alone" thrown in as well.
1993 (PG) 80m/C Chris Carrara, Jessica Bowman, John Diehl, Derya Ruggles, Tony Longo, Stuart Fratkin; **D:** Ted Nicolaou; **W:** Mike Farrow; **M:** Richard Band. **VHS, Beta** *PAR* ♫♫½

Remote Control A circulating videotape of a 1950's sci-fi flick is turning people into murderous zombies, thanks to some entrepreneurial aliens. Silly, but performed by young actors with gusto.
1988 (R) 88m/C Kevin Dillon, Deborah Goodrich, Christopher Wynne, Jennifer Tilly; **D:** Jeff Lieberman. **VHS, Beta, LV** $79.95 *LIV, IME* ♫♫

Rendez-Moi Ma Peau A modern-day witch transposes two people's personalities with comic results. In French with subtitles.
1981 82m/C *FR* **D:** Patrick Schulmann. **VHS, Beta** *FCT* ♫♫½

Rendez-vous A racy, dark film about the sensitive balance between sex and exploitation, the real world and the stage world. Some may be disturbed by chillingly explicit scenes. Impressive tour de force of imagination, direction, and cinematography. In French with English subtitles.
1985 (R) 82m/C *FR* Juliette Binoche, Lambert Wilson, Wadeck Stanczak, Jean-Louis Trintignant; **D:** Andre Techine. **VHS, LV** $29.95 *CVC, TAM* ♫♫♫

Renegade Girl A special agent is sent west to capture the female head of a band of outlaws.
1946 65m/B Alan Curtis, Ann Savage, Edward Brophy, Ray Corrigan; **D:** William Berke. **VHS, Beta, LV** $19.95 *NOS, RXM, WGE* ♫♫

Renegade Monk Invincible warrior-monk dispenses his own brand of justice with his fists of aluminum foil.
1982 90m/C Liu Chang Liang, Huang Hsing Shaw, Ko Shou Liang, Lang Shih Chia, Hsu Chung Hsing. **VHS, Beta** $59.95 *GEM* ♫½

Renegade Ninja A man whose father was murdered kicks everyone within reach in his quest for revenge.
1983 109m/C Kensaku Marita; **D:** Sadao Nakajima. **VHS, Beta** $79.95 *PSM* ♫

Renegade Ranger/Scarlet River A western double feature: A Texas Ranger and his singing sidekick attempt to help out a woman accused of murder in the "The Renegade Ranger," and a cowboy tries to free his sweetheart from a band of cattle rustlers in "Scarlet River."
1938 113m/B Rita Hayworth, Tim Holt, George O'Brien, Ray Whitley, Tom Keene, Lon Chaney Jr., Myrna Loy, Bruce Cabot, Betty Furness; **D:** David Howard. **VHS, Beta** $34.95 *RKO, TTC* ♫½

Renegade Trail Hopalong Cassidy helps a marshall and a pretty widow round up ex-cons and rustlers. The King's Men, radio singers of the era, perform a fistful of songs.
1939 61m/B William Boyd, George "Gabby" Hayes, Russell Hayden, Charlotte Wynters, Russell Hopton, Sonny Bupp, Jack Rockwell, Roy Barcroft, Eddie Dean; **D:** Lesley Selander. **VHS** $19.95 *NOS* ♫♫

Renegades A young cop from Philadelphia and a Lakota Indian begrudgingly unite to track down a gang of ruthless crooks. Good action, and lots of it; not much story.

1989 (R) 105m/C Kiefer Sutherland, Lou Diamond Phillips, Rob Knepper, Jami Gertz, Bill Smitrovich; **D:** Jack Sholder. **VHS, Beta, LV** $19.95 *MCA* ♫♫

Renfrew of the Royal Mounted A Canadian Mountie goes after counterfeiters and sings a few songs in this mild adaptation of a popular kids' radio serial. Newill was a popular tenor of the day, but the Hound thinks Renfrew's dog 'Lightning' should have been the star.
1937 57m/B Carol Hughes, James Newill, Kenneth Harlan; **D:** Al Herman. **VHS, Beta** *DVT, GPV, HEG* ♫♫

Renfrew on the Great White Trail A frustrated fur trader takes off after a pack of thieves. **AKA:** On the Great White Trail; Renfrew of the Royal Mounted on the Great White Trail.
1938 58m/B James Newill, Terry Walker, Robert Frazer, Richard Alexander; **D:** Al Herman. **VHS** $19.95 *NOS, DVT* ♫½

Reno and the Doc Enjoyable comedy about two endearingly cranky middle-aged men battling mid-life crises join together and test their mettle in the world of professional skiing.
1984 88m/C *CA* Ken Walsh, Henry Ramer, Linda Griffiths; **D:** Charles Dennis. **VHS, Beta** $19.95 *STE, NWV* ♫♫½

Renoir Shorts Two early silent Renoir fantasies: "The Little Matchgirl," a lyrical adaptation of the Hans Christian Anderson fairy tale, and "Charleston," in which a space-traveling African and Parisian girl dance comically.
1927 50m/B Catherine Hessling; **D:** Jean Renoir. **VHS, Beta** $24.95 *NOS, FCT* ♫♫♫

Rent-A-Cop A cop (Reynolds) is bounced from the force after he survives a drug-bust massacre under suspicious circumstances. He becomes a security guard and continues to track down the still-at-large killer with help from call girl Minnelli.
1988 (R) 95m/C Burt Reynolds, Liza Minnelli, James Remar, Richard Masur, Bernie Casey, John Stanton, John P. Ryan, Dionne Warwick, Robby Benson; **D:** Jerry London; **M:** Jerry Goldsmith. **VHS, Beta, LV** $14.99 *HBO* ♫♫

Rentadick A precursor to the Monty Python masterpieces, written by Graham Chapman and John Cleese. Private eye spoof isn't as funny as later Python efforts; but it is an indication of what was yet to come and fans should enjoy it.
1972 94m/C *GB* James Booth, Julie Ege, Ronald Fraser, Donald Sinden, Michael Bentine, Richard Briers, Spike Milligan; **D:** Jim Clark. **VHS** *NO* ♫♫

Rented Lips Two documentary film makers sell out, taking over the production of a porno film at the request of a public television producer who promises to help their careers. Mull and Shawn are well supported by an impressive cast, but everyone's effort is wasted in unfunny attempt at comedy.
1988 (R) 82m/C Martin Mull, Dick Shawn, Jennifer Tilly, Kenneth Mars, Edy Williams, Robert Downey Jr., June Lockhart, Shelley Berman, Mel Welles, Pat McCormick, Eileen Brennan; **D:** Robert Downey. **VHS, Beta, LV** $9.99 *CCB, IVE* ♫

Repentance A popular, surreal satire of Soviet and Communist societies. A woman is arrested for repeatedly digging up a dead local despot, and put on trial. Wickedly funny and controversial; released under the auspices of glasnost. In Russian with English subtitles. **AKA:** Pokayaniye; Confession.

1987 (PG) 151m/C *RU* Avtandil Makharadze, Zeinab Botsvadze, Ia Ninidze, Edisher Giorgobiani; **D:** Tenghiz Abuladze. **VHS, Beta, LV** $79.95 *MED* ♫♫

Repo Jake Jake Baxter learns the myth of the carefree life of a repossession man in this action thriller. His illusion is destroyed by angry clients, pornography, a deadly underworld racetrack, and a sinister crime boss.
1990 90m/C Dan Haggerty, Robert Axelrod. **VHS** $19.95 *PMH* ♫

Repo Man An inventive, perversely witty portrait of sick modern urbanity, following the adventures of a punk rocker taking a job as a car repossessor in a barren city. The landscape is filled with pointless violence, no-frills packaging, media hypnosis and aliens. Executive producer: none other than ex-Monkee Michael Nesmith.
1983 (R) 93m/C Emilio Estevez, Harry Dean Stanton, Sy Richardson, Tracy Walter, Olivia Barash, Fox Harris, Jennifer Balgobin, Vonetta McGee, Angelique Pettyjohn; **D:** Alex Cox. **VHS, Beta, LV** $19.95 *MCA* ♫♫♫½

The Report on the Party and the Guests A controversial, widely banned political allegory, considered a masterpiece from the Czech new wave. A picnic/lawn party deteriorates into brutality, fascist intolerance and persecution. Many Czech film makers, some banned at the time, appear. In Czech with English subtitles.
1966 71m/B *CZ* Jiri Nemec, Evald Schorm, Ivan Vyskocil, Jan Klusak, Zdena Skvorecka, Pavel Bosek; **D:** Jan Nemec. **VHS, Beta** $59.95 *FCT* ♫♫♫♫

Report to the Commissioner A rough, energetic crime-in-the-streets cop thriller. A young detective accidentally kills an attractive woman who turns out to have been an undercover cop, then is dragged into the bureaucratic cover-up. **AKA:** Operation Undercover.
1974 (R) 112m/C Michael Moriarty, Yaphet Kotto, Susan Blakely, Hector Elizondo, Richard Gere, Tony King, Michael McGuire, Stephen Elliott; **D:** Milton Katselas. **VHS, Beta** $29.95 *MGM* ♫♫♫

Repossessed A corny, occasionally funny takeoff on the human-possessed-by-the-devil films with Blair, as usual, as the afflicted victim. Nielsen, in another typecast role, plays the goofy man of the cloth who must save the day. Numerous actors appear in brief comedy sequences which lampoon current celebrities and constitute the film's highlights. For fans of "Airplane" and "The Naked Gun"; not necessarily for others.
1990 (PG-13) 89m/C Linda Blair, Ned Beatty, Leslie Nielsen, Anthony Starke, Jesse Ventura; **W/D:** Bob Logan; **M:** Charles Fox. **VHS, LV** $89.95 *LIV* ♫♫

Repulsion Character study of a young French girl who is repulsed and attracted by sex. Left alone when her sister goes on vacation, her facade of stability begins to crack, with violent and bizarre results. Polanski's first film in English and his first publicly accepted full-length feature. Suspenseful, disturbing and potent.
1965 105m/B *GB* Catherine Deneuve, Yvonne Furneaux, Ian Hendry, John Fraser, Patrick Wymark, James Villers; **D:** Roman Polanski. **VHS, Beta** $29.95 *VDM, VCN, MRV* ♫♫♫½

Requiem for a Heavyweight The original television version of the story about an American Indian heavyweight boxer played by Palance who risks blindness in order to help his manager pay off bookies. Highly acclaimed teleplay written by Rod Sterling for "Playhouse 90."

1956 90m/B Jack Palance, Keenan Wynn, Ed Wynn, Kim Hunter, Ned Glass; **D:** Ralph Nelson. **VHS, Beta** $14.95 *WKV* 👁👁👁

Requiem for Dominic A Communist-bloc country in the midst of revolution accuses a man of terrorist activities. Can his friend, exiled for years, help him discover the truth? Interesting and timely premise matched with outstanding ensemble acting make for a superior thriller. Amnesty International receives partial proceeds from all sales of this video. In German with English subtitles. *AKA:* Requiem fur Dominic.
1991 (R) 88m/C *GE* Felix Mitterer, Viktoria Schubert, August Schmolzer, Angelica Schutz; **D:** Robert Dornhelm. **VHS, LV** $79.95 *HMD, TAM* 👁👁👁½

The Rescue An elite team of U.S. Navy Seals is captured after destroying a disabled submarine. When the U.S. government writes off the men, their children decide to mount a rescue. Puerile, empty-headed trash for teens.
1988 (PG) 97m/C Marc Price, Charles Haid, Kevin Dillon, Christina Harnos, Edward Albert; **D:** Ferdinand Fairfax. **VHS, Beta, LV** $89.95 *TOU, HHE* 👁½

Rescue Force A crack team of anti-terrorists, led by Lt. Col. Steel, takes on the kidnappers of an American ambassador. Action filled excitement.
1990 85m/C Richard Harrison. **VHS** *NO* 👁👁

The Rescuers Bernard and Miss Bianca, two mice who are members of the Rescue Aid Society, attempt to rescue an orphan named Penny from the evil Madame Medusa, who's after the world's biggest diamond. They are aided by comic sidekick, Orville the albatross, and a group of lovable swamp creatures. Very charming in the best Disney tradition. Based on the stories of Margery Sharp. Followed by "The Rescuers Down Under."
1977 (G) 76m/C D: Wolfgang Reitherman, John Lounsbery; **V:** Bob Newhart, Eva Gabor, Geraldine Page, Jim Jordan, Joe Flynn, Jeanette Nolan, Pat Buttram. **VHS, LV** $24.99 *DIS, OM* 👁👁👁

The Rescuers Down Under 'Crocodile' Dundee goes Disney; the followup to "The Rescuers" places its characters in Australia with only mild results for a Magic Kingdom product. Heroic mice Bernard and Bianca protect a young boy and a rare golden eagle from a poacher. The great bird closely resembles the logo of Republic Pictures.
1990 (G) 77m/C D: Hendel Butoy, Mike Gabriel; **V:** Bob Newhart, Eva Gabor, John Candy, Tristan Rogers, George C. Scott. **VHS, Beta, LV** $29.99 *DIS, OM* 👁👁½

Reservoir Dogs Writer/director/actor Tarantino comes up with an ultraviolent tale of honor among thieves. Six professional criminals known by code names to protect their identities (Misters Pink, White, Orange, Blonde, Blue, and Brown) are assembled by Tierney to pull off a diamond heist. But two of the gang are killed in a police ambush. The survivors regroup in an empty warehouse and try to discover the informer in their midst. Psychotic Mr. Pink (Madsen) has the foresight to take a cop hostage and, in probably the most stomach-churning scene (there is some competition here), tortures the officer just for the heck of it to the tune of the Stealers Wheel "Stuck in the Middle with You." Unrelenting; auspicious debut for Tarantino with strong ensemble cast anchored by Keitel as the very professional Mr. White.
1992 (R) 100m/C Harvey Keitel, Tim Roth, Michael Madsen, Steve Buscemi, Christopher Penn, Lawrence Tierney, Quentin Tarantino; **W/D:** Quentin Tarantino. **VHS, LV** $92.98 *LIV* 👁👁👁½

The Respectful Prostitute Sartre's tale of hooker who is cajoled into providing false testimony as a witness in the trial of a member of a prominent family. English language version of French drama.
1952 75m/B *FR* Ivan Desny, Barbara Laage, Walter Bryan; **D:** Marcel Pagliero, Charles Brabant; **W:** Jean-Paul Sartre. **VHS** $39.95 *FCT, TAM* 👁👁½

Rest In Pieces A young woman inherits a Spanish mansion, and weird things begin to happen. It seems a cult of Satan worshippers is already living on the estate. As one might infer from the title, quite a bit of hacking and slashing ensues.
1987 (R) 90m/C Scott Thompson Baker, Lorin Jean, Dorothy Malone; **D:** Joseph Braunstein. **VHS, Beta** $14.95 *LIV* 👁

Restless A restless homemaker begins an affair with a childhood friend. Director Cosmatos later oversaw "Rambo." *AKA:* The Beloved.
1972 75m/C *GR* Raquel Welch, Richard Johnson, Jack Hawkins, Flora Robson; **D:** George P. Cosmatos. **VHS, Beta** $79.95 *VMK* 👁

The Restless Breed Son is restless after dad, a secret service agent, is slain by gunrunners. Routine oater-revenge epic done in by listless script.
1958 81m/C Scott Brady, Anne Bancroft, Jay C. Flippen, Rhys Williams, Jim Davis; **D:** Allan Dwan. **VHS, LV** $19.95 *FRH, IME* 👁

The Resurrected One of the best recent H.P. Lovecraft horror adaptations, a fairly faithful try at "The Case of Charles Dexter Ward." Ward learns he has a satanic ancestor who possessed the secret of resurrection and eternal life—but, as the warlock says, it is very messy. Surprisingly tasteful even with occasional gore and truly ghastly monsters; in fact this pic could have used a bit more intensity.
1991 (R) 108m/C John Terry, Jane Sibbet, Chris Sarandon; **D:** Dan O'Bannon. **VHS** $89.98 *LIV* 👁👁½

Resurrection After a near-fatal car accident, a woman finds she has the power to heal others by touch. She denies that God is responsible, much to her Bible Belt community's dismay. Acclaimed and well-acted.
1980 (PG) 103m/C Ellen Burstyn, Sam Shepard, Roberts Blossom, Eva Le Gallienne, Clifford David, Richard Farnsworth, Pamela Payton-Wright; **D:** Daniel Petrie. Academy Awards '80 Nominations: Best Actress (Burstyn), Best Supporting Actress (Le Gallienne); National Board of Review Awards '80: 10 Best Films of the Year, Best Supporting Actress (Le Gallienne). **VHS, Beta** $59.95 *MCA* 👁👁👁½

Resurrection of Zachary Wheeler A presidential candidate, who narrowly escaped death in an auto crash, is brought to a mysterious clinic in New Mexico. A reporter sneaks into the clinic and discovers the horrors of cloning.
1971 (G) 100m/C Angie Dickinson, Bradford Dillman, Leslie Nielsen, Jack Carter, James Daly; **D:** Bob Wynn. **VHS, Beta** $29.95 *UHV* 👁👁½

Retreat, Hell! Korean War drama about the retreat from the Changjin Reservoir. Standard gun-ho military orientation with dismal results.
1952 95m/B Frank Lovejoy, Richard Carlson, Russ Tamblyn, Anita Louise; **D:** Joseph H. Lewis. **VHS** $19.98 *REP* 👁👁

Retribution Struggling artist survives suicide attempt only to find himself possessed by the spirit of a criminal who was tortured to death. Seeing the hood's gruesome demise in his dreams, the survivor sets out to bring his murderers face-to-face with their maker.
1988 (R) 106m/C Dennis Lipscomb, Hoyt Axton, Leslie Wing, Suzanne Snyder; **D:** Guy Magar. **VHS, Beta, LV** *NO* 👁½

Retrievers Young man and a former CIA agent team up to expose the unsavory practices of the organization.
1982 90m/C Max Thayer, Roselyn Royce. **VHS, Beta** $69.98 *VES* 👁

The Return Vincent and Shepherd meet as adults and discover that they had both, as children, been visited by aliens who had given technology to a cattle-mutilating prospector. A mess with no idea of what sort of film it wants to be. *AKA:* The Alien's Return.
1980 (PG) 91m/C Cybill Shepherd, Raymond Burr, Jan-Michael Vincent, Martin Landau, Vincent Schiavelli, Zachary Vincent, Farah Bunch, Neville Brand, Susan Kiger; **D:** Greydon Clark. **VHS, Beta** $19.99 *HBO Woof!*

Return A woman believes that the man she loves is the reincarnation of her dead grandfather. Interesting concept, but overall, a disappointing mystery.
1988 (R) 78m/C Frederic Forrest, Anne Francis, Karlene Crockett, John Walcutt, Lisa Richards; **D:** Andrew Silver. **VHS, Beta, LV** $79.95 *ACA* 👁

Return Engagement A lonely middle-aged ancient history professor falls in love with one of her students.
1978 76m/C Elizabeth Taylor, Joseph Bottoms, Peter Donat, James Ray; **D:** Joseph Hardy. **VHS, Beta** *NO* 👁½

Return Fire A former employee of the government finds that he must now fight the system if he wants to save his son. Trivial action fare.
1991 (R) 97m/C Adam West, Ron Marchini. **VHS** $79.95 *AIP* 👁½

Return from Witch Mountain A pair of evil masterminds use a boy's supernatural powers to place Los Angeles in nuclear jeopardy. Sequel to Disney's ever-popular "Escape to Witch Mountain."
1978 (G) 93m/C Christopher Lee, Bette Davis, Ike Eisenmann, Kim Richards, Jack Soo; **D:** John Hough. **VHS, Beta** *DIS* 👁½

The Return of a Man Called Horse Sequel to "A Man Called Horse" tells the story of an English aristocrat who was captured and raised by Sioux Indians, and then returned to his native homeland. Contains more of the torture scenes for which this series is famous, but not much of Harris.
1976 (PG) 125m/C Richard Harris, Gale Sondergaard, Geoffrey Lewis; **D:** Irvin Kershner. **VHS, Beta** $59.98 *FOX* 👁👁

The Return of Boston Blackie The oft-filmed crook/detective tries to retrieve an heiress's stolen jewels. Silent.
1927 77m/B Raymond Glenn, Corliss Palmer, Strongheart, Rosemary Cooper, Coit Albertson; **D:** Harry Hoyt. **VHS, Beta, 8mm** $29.95 *VYY* 👁½

Return of Bruce No one is quite sure if Bruce Le was ever here before, but he claims to be returning now. Slam-bang, chop-socky action.
1982 90m/C Bruce Le. **VHS, Beta** $29.99 *BFV* 👁½

Return of Captain Invincible Arkin is a derelict super-hero persuaded to fight crime again in this unique spoof. One liners fly faster than a speeding bullet. Lee gives one of his best performances as the mad scientist. Musical numbers by Rocky Horror's O'Brien and Hartley sporadically interrupt. Made on a shoe-string budget, offbeat film is entertaining but uneven. *AKA:* Legend in Leotards.
1983 (PG) 90m/C *AU* Alan Arkin, Christopher Lee, Kate Fitzpatrick, Bill Hunter, Graham Kennedy, Michael Pate, Hayes Gordon, Max Phipps, Noel Ferrier; *D:* Philippe Mora. **VHS, Beta, LV** NO 🎞🎞½

The Return of Casey Jones Early adventure film featuring lots of great railroad action. *AKA:* Train 2419.
1934 64m/B Charles Starrett, Ruth Hall, George "Gabby" Hayes, Robert Elliott, Margaret Seddon, Jackie Searl; *D:* John P. McCarthy. **VHS $12.95** GPV 🎞🎞

Return of Chandu This serial in 12 chapters features Bela Lugosi as Chandu, who exercises his magical powers to conquer a religious sect of cat worshippers inhabiting the island of Lemuria. In the process, he fights to save the Princess Nadji from being sacrificed by them.
1934 156m/B Bela Lugosi, Maria Alba, Clara Kimball Young; *D:* Ray Taylor. **VHS, Beta, 3/4U, Special order formats $24.95** DVT, NOS, SNC 🎞🎞

The Return of Count Yorga The vampire Count returns, taking up residence in a decrepit mansion nearby an orphanage. There he spies the toothsome Cynthia and Yorga decides to make her a vampiric bride. But the Count reckons without Cynthia's noble boyfriend who wants to keep his honey on this side of the grave. Preceded by "Count Yorga, Vampire."
1971 (R) 97m/C Robert Quarry, Mariette Hartley, Roger Perry, Yvonne Wilder, Rudy DeLuca, George Macready, Walter Brooke; *W/D:* Bob Kelljan; *W:* Yvonne Wilder. **VHS $9.98** ORI 🎞🎞

The Return of Dr. Mabuse The evil doctor is back, this time sending his entranced slaves to attack a nuclear power plant. Frobe, the inspector, and Barker, the FBI man, team up to thwart him. Fun for fans of serial detective stories. *AKA:* Im Stahlnetz Des Dr. Mabuse; Phantom Fiend.
1961 88m/B *GE FR IT* Gert Frobe, Lex Barker, Daliah Lavi, Wolfgang Preiss, Fausto Tozzi, Rudolph Forster; *D:* Harald Reinl. **VHS, Beta $16.95** SNC 🎞🎞½

Return of Draw Egan Vintage silent western wherein Hart is an outlaw-turned-greenhorn sheriff of a lawless town. Music score.
1916 64m/B William S. Hart, Louise Glaum; *D:* William S. Hart. **VHS, Beta, 8mm $29.95** GPV, VYY 🎞½

Return of Fist of Fury A kung-fu film featuring Bruce Le.
1977 88m/C Bruce Le. **VHS, Beta $29.99** BFV 🎞

Return of Frank Cannon Portly private eye Frank Cannon comes out of retirement to investigate the alleged suicide of an old friend. Made for television.
1980 96m/C William Conrad, Diana Muldaur, Joanna Pettet, Allison Argo, Arthur Hill, Ed Nelson; *D:* Corey Allen. **VHS, Beta $39.95** WOV 🎞🎞

Return of Frank James One of Lang's lesser Hollywood works, this is nonetheless an entertaining sequel to 1939's "Jesse James." Brother Frank tries to go straight, but eventually has to hunt down the culprits who murdered his infamous outlaw sibling. Tierney's first film.

1940 92m/C Henry Fonda, Gene Tierney, Jackie Cooper, Henry Hull, John Carradine, Donald Meek, J. Edward Bromberg; *D:* Fritz Lang. **VHS, Beta, LV $19.98** FOX 🎞🎞

The Return of Grey Wolf A wild dog must fight for survival in Northern Quebec and is befriended by a fur trapper. An intelligent hound, he repays the trapper's generosity by helping him put the moves on some fur thieves. Silent.
1922 62m/B Helen Lynch, Henry Pierce. **VHS, Beta, 8mm** VYY 🎞🎞

Return of Jesse James Look-alike of dead outlaw Jesse James joins in with some former members of the James Gang, leading townsfolk to believe the notorious bank robber never died. It's up to brother Frank James, now an upstanding citizen, to set the record straight. A little slow moving at times, but still worth viewing.
1950 77m/B John Ireland, Ann Dvorak, Reed Hadley, Henry Hull, Hugh O'Brian, Tommy Noonan, Peter Marshall; *D:* Arthur Hilton. **VHS, Beta** NO 🎞🎞

The Return of Josey Wales No match for the original featuring Clint Eastwood, the title character is played woodenly by Parks. This installment finds Wales pitted against a bumbling lawman. Sequel to 1976's "The Outlaw Josey Wales."
1986 (R) 90m/C Michael Parks, Rafael Campos, Bob Magruder, Paco Vela, Everett Sifuentes, Charlie McCoy; *D:* Michael Parks. **VHS** HHE 🎞

The Return of Martin Guerre In this medieval tale, a dissolute village husband disappears soon after his marriage. Years later, someone who appears to be Martin Guerre returns, allegedly from war, and appears much kinder and more educated. Starring in a love story of second chances, Depardieu does not disappoint, nor does the rest of the cast. In French with English subtitles. Based on an actual court case. Remade in 1993 as "Sommersby."
1983 111m/C *FR* Gerard Depardieu, Roger Planchon, Maurice Jacquemont, Barnard Pierre Donnadieu, Nathalie Baye; *D:* Daniel Vigne. **VHS, Beta, LV $29.98** SUE, APD, HMV 🎞🎞½

Return of Our Gang Contains three vintage silent Pathe "Our Gang" shorts: "The School Play (Stage Fright)," "Summer Daze (The Cobbler)," and "Dog Days."
1925 57m/B Joe Cobb, Ernie Morrison, Mickey Daniels, Farina Hoskins, Mary Kornman, Jackie Condon, Jack Davis, Jannie Hoskins, Andy Samuola, Eugene Jackson, Pete the Pup. **VHS, Beta, 8mm $24.95** VYY 🎞½

The Return of Peter Grimm Man returns from death to try to tidy up the mess he left behind. Enjoyable if trite fantasy based on a play by David Belasco.
1935 82m/B Lionel Barrymore, Helen Mack, Edward Ellis, Donald Meek, George Breakston, James Bush; *D:* George Nichols. **VHS $19.98** TTC, FCT 🎞🎞

The Return of Spinal Tap Cult-fave mock rock group Spinal Tap is back with a feature-length video of performance and backstage footage from its recent reunion concert tour promoting their album "Break Like the Wind." Sequel to "This is Spinal Tap" features lots of heavy metal songs including the title track, "Majesty of Rock," "Bitch School," "Diva Fever," "Clam Caravan," and "Stinkin' Up the Great Outdoors." Not as great as the original satire, but will appeal to Spinal Tap fans.
1992 110m/C Christopher Guest, Michael McKean, Harry Shearer, Rick Parnell, C.J. Vanston; *Cameos:* Paul Anka, Jeff Beck, Jamie Lee Curtis, Richard Lewis, Martha Quinn, Kenny Rogers, Martin Short, Mel Torme; *W:*

Christopher Guest, Michael McKean, Harry Shearer. **VHS, LV $89.98** MPI, MVD 🎞🎞½

Return of Superfly Man with insect moniker pesters drug dealers and cops in Harlem. Long-awaited sequel to urban epic "Superfly," with music again by Curtis Mayfield.
1990 (R) 94m/C Margaret Avery, Nathan Purdee, Sam Jackson; *M:* Ice-T, Curtis Mayfield. **VHS $92.95** VMK 🎞

The Return of Swamp Thing The DC Comics creature rises again out of the muck to fight mutants and evil scientists. Tongue-in-cheek, and nothing at all like the literate, ecologically-oriented comic from which it was derived.
1989 (PG-13) 95m/C Louis Jourdan, Heather Locklear, Sarah Douglas, Dick Durock; *D:* Jim Wynorski. **VHS, Beta, LV $14.95** COL 🎞½

Return of the Aliens: The Deadly Spawn Aliens infect the earth and violently destroy humans. Extremely violent and gory. Watch out for those officious offspring.
1983 (R) 90m/C Charles George Hildebrandt; *D:* Douglas McKeown. **VHS** NO 🎞

Return of the Ape Man Campy fun with Carradine and Lugosi. A mad scientist transplants Carradine's brain into the body of the "missing link." Hams galore.
1944 51m/B Bela Lugosi, John Carradine, George Zucco, Judith Gibson, Michael Ames, Frank Moran, Mary Currier; *D:* Phil Rosen. **VHS $59.95** MED 🎞🎞

Return of the Bad Men Scott is a retired marshall who must fight against a gang of outlaws lead by the Sundance Kid. Sequel to "Badman's Territory." *AKA:* Return of the Badmen.
1948 90m/C Randolph Scott, Robert Ryan, Anne Jeffreys, George "Gabby" Hayes, Jason Robards Jr., Jacqueline White; *D:* Ray Enright. **VHS, Beta $19.98** RKO, CCB, MED 🎞🎞

Return of the Chinese Boxer Samurai and ninja warriors fight, usually to the death.
1974 93m/C Jimmy Wang Yu, Lung Fei, Cheung Ying Chen, Chin Kang. **VHS, Beta $39.95** UNI 🎞

Return of the Dinosaurs A comet is about to collide with the Earth. Never fear! The dinosaur patrol will interfere (and ultimately save the planet).
1983 82m/C **VHS, Beta $39.95** TWE 🎞

Return of the Dragon In Lee's last picture, a Chinese restaurant in Rome is menaced by gangsters who want to buy the property. On behalf of the owners, Lee duels an American karate champ in the Roman forum. The battle scenes between Lee and Norris are great and make this a must-see for martial arts fans.
1973 (R) 91m/C *CH* Bruce Lee, Nora Miao, Chuck Norris; *D:* Bruce Lee. **VHS, Beta, LV $19.98** FOX, GEM 🎞🎞½

Return of the Dragon For vengeance's sake, a wronged karate master goes on a rampage of abundant whacking, slashing and head kicking. Not to be confused with the 1973 film of the same name that marked Bruce Lee's final appearance.
1984 110m/C Ramon Zanora, Lotis Key, Leila Hermosa; *D:* ? **VHS, Beta $49.98** WWV 🎞

Return of the Evil Dead The sightless dead priests return to attack still more 1970s' Europeans in this second installment of the "blind dead" trilogy. Preceded by "Tombs of the Blind Dead" and followed by "Horror of the Zombies." Not to be confused with Raimi's "Evil Dead" slasher flicks. *AKA:* Return of the Blind Dead.

1975 85m/C *SP PT* Tony Kendall, Esther Roy, Frank Blake; *D:* Armando de Ossorio. **VHS** $59.95 *JEF ✍*

Return of the Family Man A mass murderer seems unstoppable as he continues to slash whole families at a time...the family man is redefined in this bloody gorefest.
1989 90m/C Ron Smerczak, Liam Cundill, Terence Reis, Michelle Constant; *D:* John Murlowski. **VHS** *NO ✍*

Return of the Fly The son of the scientist who discovered how to move matter through space decides to continue his father's work, but does so against his uncle's wishes. He soon duplicates his dad's experiments with similar results. This sequel to "The Fly" doesn't buzz like the original. Followed by "Curse of the Fly."
1959 80m/B Vincent Price, Brett Halsey, John Sutton, Dan Seymour, David Frankham; *D:* Edward L. Bernds. **VHS, Beta, LV** $14.98 *FOX, FCT ✍✍*

Return of the Jedi Third film in George Lucas' popular space saga. Against seemingly fearsome odds, Luke Skywalker battles such worthies as Jabba the Hutt and heavy-breathing Darth Vader to save his comrades and triumph over the evil Galactic Empire. Han and Leia reaffirm their love and team with C3PO, R2-D2, Chewbacca, Calrissian, and a bunch of furry Ewoks to aid in the annihilation of the Dark Side. The special effects are still spectacular, even the third time around. Sequel to "Star Wars" (1977) and "The Empire Strikes Back" (1980).
1983 (PG) 132m/C Mark Hamill, Carrie Fisher, Harrison Ford, Billy Dee Williams, David Prowse, James Earl Jones, Kenny Baker, Denis Lawson, Anthony Daniels, Peter Mayhew; *D:* Richard Marquand; *M:* John Williams; *V:* Alec Guinness, Frank Oz. Academy Awards '83: Best Visual Effects; Nominations: Best Art Direction/Set Decoration, Best Sound, Best Original Score; People's Choice Awards '84: Best Film. **VHS, Beta, LV** $19.98 *FOX, RDG, HMV ✍✍✍½*

Return of the Killer Tomatoes The man-eating plant-life from 1980's "Attack of the Killer Tomatoes" is back, able to turn into people due to the slightly larger budget. Astin is mad as the scientist. Not as bad as "Attack," representing a small hurdle in the history of filmdom.
1988 (PG) 98m/C Anthony Starke, George Clooney, Karen Mistal, Steve Lundquist, John Astin, Charlie Jones, Rock Peace, Frank Davis, C.J. Dillon, Teri Weigel; *D:* John DeBello. **VHS, Beta, LV** $19.95 *STE, NWV ✍*

The Return of the King The third and final animated episode of J.R.R Tolkien's Middle Earth Trilogy. This saga features Frodo, relative to Hobbit Bilbo Baggins, and his faithful servant, making middle Earth safe from Orcs, Gollums and other ooky creatures.
1980 120m/C *D:* Arthur Rankin Jr., Jules Bass; *V:* Orson Bean, Roddy McDowall, John Huston, Theodore Bikel, William Conrad, Glen Yarborough, Paul Frees, Casey Kasem, Sonny Melendrez. **VHS** $9.99 *XVC, VTR, FFF ✍*

Return of the Lash Lash LaRue once again defends settlers' rights from ruthless outlaws.
1947 53m/B Lash LaRue, Al "Fuzzy" St. John, Mary Maynard, George Cheseboro; *D:* Ray Taylor. **VHS, Beta** $12.95 *COL, SVS ✍*

Return of the Living Dead Poisonous gas revives a cemetery and a morgue rendering an outrageous spoof on the living-dead sub-genre with fast-moving zombies, punk humor, and exaggerated gore. Its humor does not diminish the fear factor, how-

ever. Sequel follows. Directed by "Alien" writer O'Bannon.
1985 (R) 90m/C Clu Gulager, James Karen, Linnea Quigley, Don Calfa, Jewel Shepard; *D:* Dan O'Bannon. **VHS, Beta, LV** $14.95 *HBO, HMD ✍✍½*

Return of the Living Dead Part 2 An inevitable sequel to the original Dan O'Bannon satire about George Romero-esque brain-eating zombies attacking suburbia with zest and vigor.
1988 (R) 89m/C Dana Ashbrook, Marsha Dietlein, Philip Bruns, James Karen, Thom Mathews; *D:* Ken Weiderhorn. **VHS, Beta, LV** $14.95 *LHV, WAR ✍½*

Return of the Man from U.N.C.L.E. Those dashing super agents Napoleon Solo and Illya Kuryakin come out of retirement to settle an old score with their nemesis THRUSH. Made for television.
1983 96m/C Robert Vaughn, David McCallum, Patrick Macnee, Gayle Hunnicutt, Geoffrey Lewis; *D:* Ray Austin. **VHS, Beta** $69.95 *TWE ✍✍*

Return of the Pink Panther Bumbling Inspector Clouseau is called upon to rescue the Pink Panther diamond stolen from a museum. Sellers manages to produce mayhem with a vacuum cleaner and other devices that, in his hands, become instruments of terror. Clever opening credits. Fourth installment in the Pink Panther series but the first with Sellers since 1964's "A Shot In The Dark."
1974 (G) 113m/C Peter Sellers, Christopher Plummer, Catherine Schell, Herbert Lom, Victor Spinetti; *D:* Blake Edwards. **VHS, Beta, LV** $19.95 *FOX, FCT, TVC ✍✍½*

Return of the Rebels Made for television fluff with Eden as a motorcycle matron whose campground is rid of riff-raff by the crow-lined participants in a 25-year reunion of a biker gang.
1981 100m/C Barbara Eden, Robert Mandan, Jamie Farr, Patrick Swayze, Don Murray, Christopher Connelly; *D:* Noel Nosseck. **VHS** *NO ✍✍*

Return of the Red Tiger Kung-Fu master Bruce Lee displays one of the most exciting styles of kung-fu: The Tiger.
1981 82m/C Bruce Lee. **VHS, Beta** *NO ✍½*

Return of the Scorpion Big trouble abounds as that crazy kung fu guy, the "Scorpion," comes back to town.
1980 90m/C Yang Pan Pan, Lam Men Wei, Philip Ko. **VHS, Beta** *NO ✍*

Return of the Secaucus 7 Centers around a weekend reunion of seven friends who were activists during the Vietnam War in the turbulent '60s. Now turning 30, they evaluate their present lives and progress. Writer and director Sayles plays Howie in this excellent example of what a low-budget film can and should be. A less trendy predecessor of "The Big Chill" (1983) which, perhaps, was a few years ahead of its time.
1980 110m/C Mark Arnott, Gordon Clapp, Maggie Cousineau-Arndt, David Strathairn; *D:* John Sayles. **VHS, Beta** $59.95 *COL ✍✍✍½*

Return of the Seven The first sequel to "The Magnificent Seven" features the group liberating a compatriot who is held hostage. Yawn. *AKA:* Return of the Magnificent Seven.
1966 97m/C Yul Brynner, Warren Oates, Robert Fuller, Claude Akins; *D:* Burt Kennedy. **VHS, Beta** $19.98 *MGM ✍✍*

Return of the Soldier A shell-shocked World War I veteran has no memory of his marriage, leaving his wife, his childhood flame, and an unrequited love to vie for

his affections. Adapted from the novel by Rebecca West.
1984 101m/C *GB* Glenda Jackson, Julie Christie, Ann-Margret, Alan Bates, Ian Holm, Frank Finlay; *D:* Alan Bridges. **VHS, Beta** $79.99 *HBO ✍✍✍*

Return of the Tall Blond Man With One Black Shoe Sequel to 1972's "The Tall Blond Man With One Black Shoe." Again a "klutz" is mistaken for a master spy and becomes unknowingly involved in the world of international intrigue. In French with English subtitles. Not quite as good as the original.
1974 84m/C *FR* Pierre Richard, Mireille Darc, Michael Duchaussoy, Jean Rochefort, Jean Carmet; *D:* Yves Robert. **VHS, Beta** $49.95 *PSM, TAM ✍✍½*

Return of the Tiger The Hovver Night Club in Bangkok fronts the operations of an international narcotics group headed by an American. When a rival Chinese gang tries to dominate the drug market, conflict and lots of kicking ensue.
1978 95m/C Bruce Li, Paul Smith, Chaing I, Angela Mao; *D:* Jimmy Shaw. **VHS, Beta** $29.95 *MED ✍½*

Return of the Vampire A Hungarian vampire and his werewolf servant seek revenge on the family who drove a spike through his heart two decades earlier.
1943 69m/B Bela Lugosi, Nina Foch, Miles Mander, Matt Willis, Frieda Inescort, Roland Varno; *D:* Lew Landers, Kurt Neumann. **VHS, Beta, LV** $9.95 *GKK, MLB ✍✍*

Return of Wildfire Two sisters are left to run the family horse ranch when their brother is killed. A drifter aids the sisters in bringing the murderer to justice.
1948 83m/B Richard Arlen, Patricia Morison, Mary Beth Hughes. **VHS, Beta** *NO ✍½*

Return to Africa Rebels threaten the familial paradise of the tightknit Mallory clan.
1989 95m/C Stan Brock, Anne Collings, David Tors, Ivan Tors, Peter Tors, Steven Tors; *D:* Leslie Martinson. **VHS, Beta** $59.95 *PSM ✍✍*

Return to Boggy Creek Townspeople in a small fishing village learn from a photographer that a "killer" beast, whom they thought had disappeared, has returned and is living in Boggy Creek. Some curious children follow the shutterbug into the marsh, despite hurricane warnings, and the swamp monster reacts with unusual compassion. OK for the kiddies. Fictitious story unlike other "Boggy Creek" films, which are billed as semi-documentaries. Sequel to "Legend of Boggy Creek." Features Mary Ann from "Gilligan's Island" and written by Dave Woody.
1977 (PG) 87m/C Dawn Wells, Dana Plato, Louise Belaire, John Hofeus; *D:* Thomas Moore. **VHS, Beta** $19.98 *FOX ✍✍*

Return to Earth Made for television drama deals with the self-doubts faced by Apollo 11 astronaut Buzz Aldrin after his triumphant return to Earth. Based on Aldrin's own novel.
1976 74m/C Cliff Robertson, Shirley Knight, Ralph Bellamy, Stefanie Powers, Charles Cioffi; *D:* Judd Taylor. **VHS, Beta** $19.98 *TWE ✍✍*

Return to Eden A young woman falls in love with her philosophy tutor, but he can't return her affections. An interesting comparison between the passion of the primitive and the tangle of modern-day romance.
1989 90m/C Sam Bottoms, Edward Binns, Renee Coleman; *D:* William Olsen. **VHS** *NO ✍✍*

Return to Fantasy Island Boss, boss, it's da plane! The second full-length television treatment of the once popular series wherein three couples get their most cherished fantasy fulfilled by Mr. Roarke. and company.

1977 100m/C Ricardo Montalban, Herve Villechaize, Adrienne Barbeau, Pat Crowley, Joseph Campanella, Karen Valentine, Laraine Day, George Maharis, Horst Buchholz, France Nuyen, Joseph Cotten, Cameron Mitchell, George Chakiris; **D:** George McCowan. **VHS, Beta** $79.95 *PSM* ♫♫½

Return to Horror High A horror movie producer makes a film in an abandoned and haunted high school, where a series of murders occurred years earlier. As in most "return" flicks, history repeats itself.
1987 (R) 95m/C Alex Rocco, Vince Edwards, Philip McKeon, Brendan Hughes, Lori Lethin, Scott Jacoby; **D:** Bill Froehlich. **VHS, Beta** $19.95 *STE, NWV* ♫

Return to Macon County Tale of three young, reckless youths who become involved with drag racing and a sadistic law enforcement officer. Nolte turns in a good performance in his first film, as does Johnson, despite a mediocre script and dialogue. Sequel to 1974's "Macon County Line."
1975 90m/C Nick Nolte, Don Johnson, Robin Mattson; **D:** Richard Compton. **VHS, Beta** $69.98 *LIV, VES* ♫

Return to Mayberry Andy Taylor returns to Mayberry after 20 years to obtain his old job as sheriff. Sixteen of the original actors reappeared for this nostalgia-fest. Made for television.
1985 95m/C Andy Griffith, Ron Howard, Don Knotts; **D:** Bob Sweeney. **VHS, Beta** $29.98 *MCG* ♫♫

Return to Oz Picking up where "The Wizard of Oz" left off, Auntie Em and Uncle Ed place Dorothy in the care of a therapist to cure her "delusions" of Oz. A natural disaster again lands her in the land of the yellow brick road, where the evil Nome King and Princess Mombi are spreading terror and squalor. Based on a later L. Frank Baum book. Enjoyable for the whole family although some scenes may frighten very small children.
1985 (PG) 109m/C Fairuza Balk, Piper Laurie, Matt Clark, Nicol Williamson, Jean Marsh; **D:** Walter Murch. **VHS, Beta, LV** $29.95 *DIS* ♫♫½

Return to Peyton Place A young writer publishes novel exposing town as virtual Peyton Place, and the townsfolk turn against her and her family. Sequel to the scandalously popular '50s original and inspiration for the just-as-popular soap opera. Astor is excellent as the evil matriarch.
1961 122m/C Carol Lynley, Jeff Chandler, Eleanor Parker, Mary Astor, Robert Sterling, Lucianna Paluzzi, Tuesday Weld, Brett Halsey, Bob Crane; **D:** Jose Ferrer. **VHS** $39.98 *FOX, FCT* ♫♫½

Return to Salem's Lot Enjoyable camp sequel to the Stephen King tale, this time involving a cynical scientist and his son returning to the town only to find it completely run by vampires.
1987 (R) 101m/C Michael Moriarty, Ricky Addison Reed, Samuel Fuller, Andrew Duggan, Evelyn Keyes, Jill Gatsby, June Havoc, Ronee Blakley, James Dixon, David Holbrook; **D:** Larry Cohen. **VHS, Beta** $14.95 *WAR* ♫♫

Return to Snowy River Continues the love story of the former ranch hand and the rancher's daughter in Australia's Victoria Alps that began in "The Man From Snowy River." Dennehy takes over from Kirk Douglas as the father who aims to keep the lovers apart. The photography of horses and the scenery is spectacular, making the whole film worthwhile.

1988 (PG) 99m/C *AU* Tom Burlinson, Sigrid Thornton, Brian Dennehy, Nicholas Eadie, Mark Hembrow, Bryan Marshall; **D:** Geoff Burrowes. **VHS, Beta, LV** $19.99 *DIS, TVC* ♫♫♫

Return to the Blue Lagoon Neither the acting nor the premise has improved with age. Another photogenic adolescent couple experiences puberty on that island; for continuity, the young woman is the daughter of the lovers in the first "Blue Lagoon." Breathtaking scenery—just turn down the sound.
1991 (PG-13) 102m/C Milla Jovovich, Brian Krause, Lisa Pelikan; **D:** William A. Graham. **VHS, LV** $19.95 *COL, PIA* ♫

Return to Waterloo A psychological mystery concerning the fantasies and flashbacks of a businessman traveling by train to London. He may be cheating on his wife, he may be abusing his daughter, he may be a rapist wanted by the police. Surreal musical interludes highlight the ambiguity of the story. Written and directed by "Kinks" frontman, Davies.
1985 57m/C Kenneth Colley; **W/D:** Ray Davies. **VHS** $12.98 *LTY* ♫♫

Reuben, Reuben Brilliant, but drunken poet Conti turns himself around when he falls in love with earthy college girl McGillis in her film debut. The student's dog Reuben unwittingly alters Conti's progress, however, in the film's startling conclusion. Based on the writings of Peter DeVries.
1983 (R) 100m/C Tom Conti, Kelly McGillis, Roberts Blossom, E. Katherine Kerr, Cynthia Harris, Joel Fabiani, Kara Wilson, Lois Smith; **D:** Robert Ellis Miller. **VHS, Beta** $59.98 *FOX* ♫♫♫

Reunion Well-heeled young Jewish boy is sent to the U.S. for safety in the 1930s, while his friend, an ambassador's son, remains in Germany. Fifty years later, he returns to Stuttgart on business and encounters his old friend, a shock for both. Thoughtful and well-acted though occasionally plodding drama written by Harold Pinter and based on Fred Uhlman's novel.
1988 (PG-13) 120m/C Jason Robards Jr.; **D:** Jerry Schatzberg; **W:** Harold Pinter. **VHS, Beta, LV** $29.95 *FRH, IME, FCT* ♫♫♫

Reunion in France Parisian dress designer sacrifices her lifestyle to help an American flier flee France after the Nazis invade. Dated patriotic flag-waver. **AKA:** Mademoiselle France; Reunion.
1942 104m/B Joan Crawford, John Wayne, Philip Dorn, Reginald Owen, Albert Basserman, John Carradine, Henry Daniell, Moroni Olsen, Howard da Silva, Ava Gardner, John Considine; **D:** Jules Dassin. **VHS, Beta** $19.98 *MGM* ♫♫

Revealing of Elsie A young dancer goes from bed to bed in her rise to the top. Previously titled "Strip for Action."
1986 70m/C Christa Free, Marianne Dupont. **VHS, Beta** $29.95 *MED* ♫

Revenge The parents of a girl who was brutally killed take the law into their own hands in this bloody, vengeful thriller. **AKA:** Terror under the House; After Jenny Died; Inn of the Frightened People.
1971 89m/C *GB* Joan Collins, James Booth, Ray Barrett, Sinead Cusack, Kenneth Griffith; **D:** Sidney Hayers. **VHS, Beta** $29.95 *SUE, MRV* ♫½

Revenge Sequel to "Blood Cult" about a cult led by horror king Carradine. Seems these dog worshippers want McGowan's land and Senator Carradine will stop at nothing to get it. Woofer filled with gratuitous violence.

1986 (R) 104m/C Patrick Wayne, John Carradine, Bennie Lee McGowan, Josef Hanet, Stephanie Kropke; **D:** Christopher Lewis. **VHS, Beta** $19.95 *UHV* Woof!

Revenge Retired pilot Costner makes the mistake of falling in love with another man's wife. Quinn gives a first-rate performance as the Mexican crime lord who punishes his spouse and her lover, beginning a cycle of vengeance. Sometimes contrived, but artfully photographed with tantalizing love scenes. Based on the Jim Harrison novel.
1990 (R) 123m/C Kevin Costner, Anthony Quinn, Madeleine Stowe, Sally Kirkland, Joe Santos, Miguel Ferrer, James Gammon, Tomas Milian; **D:** Tony Scott; **M:** Jack Nitzsche. **VHS, Beta, LV, 8mm** $19.95 *COL* ♫♫

Revenge in the House of Usher House holds grudge.
1982 90m/C Howard Vernon, Dan Villers; **D:** Jess (Jesus) Franco. **VHS** $29.99 *MOV* ♫♫

Revenge of a Kabuki Actor When Kabuki actor Kazuo Hasegawa's parents are viciously murdered, he seeks their killer with a vengeance. In Japanese with English subtitles.
1963 114m/C *JP* **D:** Kon Ichikawa. **VHS** $59.95 *FST, FCT* ♫♫

Revenge of Doctor X A man/beast lies waiting for the pretty reporter who seeks her shipwrecked father in the jungles of an uncharted island.
198? 90m/C John Ashley, Ronald Remy, Angelique Pettyjohn. **VHS, Beta** NO Woof!

Revenge of Fist of Fury Kung fu masters beat one another to a pulp in tribute to Bruce Lee.
1977? 93m/C VHS, Beta $39.95 *UNI* ♫

Revenge of the Barbarians As the barbarians descend on Rome, Olympus must decide whether to save the empire or the beautiful Gallo, the woman he loves. Decisions, decisions.
1964 99m/C Robert Alda, Anthony Steele. **Beta** $39.95 *AIP* ♫

Revenge of the Barbarians A Scandinavian adventure about a young Celt seeking revenge against the Viking hordes that killed his family.
1985 95m/C D: Hrafn Gunnlaugsson. **Beta** NO ♫

Revenge of the Cheerleaders The cheerleaders pull out all the stops to save their school from a ruthless land developer. What spirit.
1976 (R) 86m/C Jerii Woods, Cheryl "Rainbeaux" Smith, Helen Lang, Patrice Rohmer, Susie Elene, Eddra Gale, William Bramley, Carl Ballantine, David Hasselhoff; **D:** Richard Lerner. **VHS, Beta** $69.98 *LIV* ♫

Revenge of the Dead European archeological team discovers the existence of a powerful force that allows the dead to return to life.
1984 (R) 100m/C *IT* Gabriele Lavia, Anne Canoras; **D:** Pupi Avati. **VHS, Beta** $69.98 *LIV* ♫

Revenge of the Living Zombies Teens on a Halloween hayride run headlong into flesh-craving zombies. Available in a slightly edited version.
1988 (R) 85m/C Bill Hinzman, John Mowod, Leslie Ann Wick, Kevin Kindlan; **D:** Bill Hinzman. **VHS, Beta** NO ♫

Revenge of the Nerds When nerdy college freshmen are victimized by jocks, frat boys and the school's beauties, they start their own fraternity and seek revenge. Carradine and Edwards team well as the geeks in this better than average teenage sex comedy. Guess who gets the girls? Sequel was much worse.

1984 (R) 89m/C Robert Carradine, Anthony Edwards, Timothy Busfield, Andrew Cassese, Curtis Armstrong, Larry B. Scott, Brian Tochi, Julia Montgomery, Michelle Meyrink, Ted McGinley, John Goodman, Bernie Casey; *D:* Jeff Kanew. **VHS, Beta, LV** $14.98 *FOX* 🐾🐾½

Revenge of the Nerds 2: Nerds in Paradise
The nerd clan from the first film (minus Edwards who only makes a brief appearance) travels to Fort Lauderdale for a fraternity conference. They fend off loads of bullies and jocks with raunchy humor. Boy can Booger belch. Not as good as the first Nerds movie; a few laughs nonetheless.
1987 (PG-13) 89m/C Robert Carradine, Curtis Armstrong, Timothy Busfield, Andrew Cassese, Ed Lauter, Larry B. Scott, Courtney Thorne-Smith, Anthony Edwards, James Hong; *D:* Joe Roth. **VHS, Beta, LV** $89.98 *FOX* 🐾🐾

Revenge of the Nerds 3: The Next Generation
Adams College has nerd-loathing trustee Downey, Jr. mobilizing those frat boys against the bespectacled geeks, who turn to founding nerd Carradine to save them. Cookie-cutter characters and the gags won't hold your attention. Let's hope this is the last in the series.
1992 ?m/C Robert Carradine, Curtis Armstrong, Ted McGinley, Morton Downey Jr., Julia Montgomery. **VHS** *FXV* 🐾½

Revenge of the Ninja
Ninja Kosugi hopes to escape his past in Los Angeles. A drug trafficker, also ninja-trained, prevents him. The two polish off a slew of mobsters before their own inevitable showdown. Better-than the standard chop-socky fest from Cannon with amusing surreal touches like a battling grandma ninja. Written by James R. Silke. Sequel to "Enter the Ninja," followed by "Ninja III."
1983 (R) 90m/C Sho Kosugi; *D:* Sam Firstenberg. **VHS, Beta** $14.95 *MGM* 🐾🐾½

Revenge of the Pink Panther
Inspector Clouseau survives his own assassination attempt, but allows the world to think he is dead in order to pursue an investigation of the culprits in his own unique, bumbling way. The last "Pink Panther" film before Sellers died, and perhaps the least funny.
1978 (PG) 99m/C Peter Sellers, Herbert Lom, Dyan Cannon, Robert Webber, Burt Kwouk, Robert Loggia; *D:* Blake Edwards. **VHS, Beta, LV** $19.98 *FOX, PIA, FCT* 🐾🐾½

Revenge of the Radioactive Reporter
Nuclear plant honchos don't like journalist who's about to hang their dirty laundry, so they toss him into vat of nuclear waste. He returns as a reporter with a cosmetic peel.
1991 90m/C David Scammell, Kathryn Boese, Randy Pearlstein, Derrick Strange; *D:* Craig Pryce. **VHS** *NO* 🐾🐾

Revenge of the Stepford Wives
Made for television sequel to the Ira Levin fantasy about suburban husbands who create obedient robot replicas of their wives. In this installment, the wives are not robots, but are simply made docile by drugs. Strange casting pairs Johnson and Kavner as husband and stepford wife. Begat "The Stepford Children."
1980 95m/C Sharon Gless, Julie Kavner, Don Johnson, Audra Lindley, Mason Adams, Arthur Hill; *D:* Robert Fuest. **VHS, Beta** $9.98 *SUE, NLC* 🐾½

Revenge of the Teenage Vixens from Outer Space
A low-budget film about three sex starved females from another planet who come to earth to find men. When the ones they meet do not live up to their expectations, the frustrated females

turn the disappointing dudes are turned into vegetables.
1986 84m/C Lisa Schwedop, Howard Scott; *D:* Jeff Ferrell. **VHS, Beta** *NO* 🐾🐾

Revenge of the Virgins
A tribe of topless 'Indian' women protect their sacred land from the white man. Exhumed exploitation for bad-film junkies, narrated by Kenne Duncan, an Ed Wood cohort.
1962 53m/B Jewell Morgan, Charles Veltman, Jodean Russo, Stanton Pritchard; *D:* Paul Perri. **VHS** $19.95 *NOS, SMW, VDM* 🐾

Revenge of the Zombies
In this sequel of sorts to "King of the Zombies," Carradine is creating an army of the undead for use by an evil foreign entity.
1943 61m/B John Carradine, Robert Lowery, Gale Storm, Veda Ann Borg, Mantan Moreland; *D:* Steve Sekely. **VHS** *MLB* 🐾½

Revenge of the Zombies
Kung-fu exploitation film featuring man-eating alligators, zombies, mad magicians, and more.
1981 (R) ?m/C Ti Lung, Lily Tu. **VHS** $15.95 *LOO* 🐾½

The Revenge Rider
Orphan McCoy goes after the villains who killed his parents. Good performance from McCoy in an otherwise average film.
1935 60m/B Tim McCoy, Robert Allen, Billie Seward, Edward Earle, Jack Clifford, Lafe McKee; *D:* David Selman. **VHS** $19.95 *DVT, HEG* 🐾🐾

The Revenger
A framed man returns from prison and finds that a mobster has kidnapped his wife and wants $50,000 to give her back.
1990 91m/C Oliver Reed, Frank Zagarino; *D:* Cedric Sundstrom. **VHS, Beta** $79.95 *AIP* 🐾

Reversal of Fortune
True tale of wealthy socialite Claus von Bulow (Irons) accused of deliberately giving his wife Sunny (Close) a near-lethal overdose of insulin. Comatose Close narrates history of the couple's courtship and married life, a saga of unhappiness and substance abuse, while Silver (as lawyer Dershowitz) et al prepare von Bulow's defense. An unflattering picture of the idle rich that never spells out what really happened. Irons is excellent as the eccentric and creepy defendant and richly deserved his Best Actor Oscar. From the novel by Dershowitz.
1990 (R) 112m/C Jeremy Irons, Glenn Close, Ron Silver, Annabella Sciorra, Uta Hagen, Fisher Stevens, Julie Hagerty, Jack Gilpin, Christine Baranski; *D:* Barbet Schroeder. Academy Awards '90: Best Actor (Irons); Nominations: Best Adapted Screenplay, Best Director (Schroeder); Golden Globe Awards '91: Best Actor—Drama (Irons). **VHS, Beta, LV, 8mm** $19.98 *WAR, PIA, FCT* 🐾🐾🐾½

The Revolt of Job
An elderly Jewish couple adopts an 8-year-old Gentile boy although it is illegal in World War II-torn Hungary and against the beliefs of the orthodox community. Moving story with fine performances. *AKA:* Job Lazadasa.
1984 98m/C *GE HU* Fereno Zenthe, Hedi Tenessy; *D:* Imre Gyongyossy, Barna Kabay. **VHS, Beta** $79.95 *MGM, SWC* 🐾🐾🐾

The Revolt of Mother
Mary E. Wilkins Freeman story of two hard-working farmers. Set in 1890 New England.
1988 60m/C Amy Madigan, Jay O'Saunders. **VHS** $24.95 *MON, KAR* 🐾🐾🐾½

Revolt of the Barbarians
Ancient Rome is plagued by barbarian invasion and piracy. A consul travels to Gaul to try to put an end to their misdeeds.
1964 ?m/C *IT* Roland Carey, Grazia Maria Spina, Mario Feliciani. **VHS, Beta** $16.95 *SNC* 🐾

Revolt of the Dragon
Martial arts expert visits friends in his hometown and finds himself battling a ruthless gang that terrorizes the people.
1975 (R) 90m/C **VHS, Beta** $54.95 *HHT* 🐾

Revolt of the Zombies
A mad scientist learns the secret of bringing the dead to life and musters the zombies into a unique, gruesome military unit during World War I. Strange early zombie flick looks silly by today's standards.
1936 65m/B Dorothy Stone, Dean Jagger, Roy D'Arcy, Robert Noland, George Cleveland; *D:* Victor Halperin; *W:* Howard Higgin. **VHS, Beta** $14.95 *SNC, QNE, MLB* 🐾

Revolution
Documentary of hippie life in San Francisco during the turbulent '60s.
1969 90m/C Today Malone; *D:* Jack O'Connell. **VHS** *WAR* 🐾

Revolution
The American Revolution is the setting for this failed epic centering on an illiterate trapper and his son who find themselves caught up in the fighting. Long and dull, which is unfortunate, because the story had some potential. The cast is barely believable in their individual roles. Where did you get that accent, Al?
1985 (R) 125m/C *GB* Al Pacino, Donald Sutherland, Nastassia Kinski, Annie Lennox, Joan Plowright, Steven Berkoff, Dave King; *D:* Hugh Hudson. **VHS, Beta, LV** $19.98 *WAR* 🐾

Revolution! A Red Comedy
A group of students are lured away from their revolutionary tendencies by materialistic indulgences. This satirical comedy is in color and black and white.
1991 84m/B Kimberly Flynn, Christopher Renstrom, Georg Osterman; *W/D:* Jeff Kahn. **VHS** $69.95 *TAM* 🐾🐾🐾

Revolver
FBI agent Nick Sastro is paralyzed by an assassin's bullet when he tries to stop Aldo Testi, an arms and drug smuggler. But Nick decides to come out of retirement when a chance to nail Testi comes his way.
1992 (R) 96m/C Robert Urich, Dakin Matthews, Steven Williams, Assumpta Serna; *D:* Gary Nelson. **VHS** $79.95 *COL* 🐾

Rhapsody
Taylor plays a wealthy woman torn between a famous young violinist and an equally talented pianist in this long and overdrawn soap opera. Although Taylor gives a superb performance, it's not enough to save this sugarcoated musical romance. Includes lush European scenery and sequences of classical music dubbed in by Claudio Arrau and Michael Rabin. Based on the adaptation of the Henry Handel Richardson novel "Maurice Guest."
1954 115m/C Elizabeth Taylor, Vittorio Gassman, John Ericson, Louis Calhern, Michael Chekhov, Barbara Bates, Celia Lovsky; *D:* Charles Vidor; *W:* Michael Kanin, Fay Kanin. **VHS** $19.98 *MGM* 🐾🐾½

Rhapsody in Blue
Standard Hollywood biography of the great composer features whitewashed and non-existent characters to deal with the spottier aspects of Gershwin's life. Still, the music is the main attraction and it doesn't disappoint. ♫Rhapsody in Blue; Concerto in F; The Cuban Overture; Fascinatin' Rhythm; The Man I Love; Yankee Doodle Blues; Somebody Loves Me; Swanee; Mine; Lady Be Good; Clap Yo' Hands; Bindin' My Time; Love Walked In; Someone To Watch Over Me; S'Wonderful; I Got Rhythm; My One and Only; Delicious; Embraceable You; Variations on "I Got Rhythm" (instrumental); An American in Paris (instrumental); Summertime; I Got Plenty O'Nuttin'; Liza; Blue Monday Blues; Oh Lady Be Good.

1945 139m/B Robert Alda, Joan Leslie, Alexis Smith, Charles Coburn, Julie Bishop, Albert Basserman, Morris Carnovsky, Rosemary DeCamp, Herbert Rudley, Charles Halton, Robert Shayne, Johnny Downs; **D:** Irving Rapper; **W:** Howard Koch; **M:** George Gershwin, Ira Gershwin. **VHS, LV $29.98** *FOX, PIA, FCT* ✍✍✍

Rhinestone A country singer claims she can turn anyone, even a cabbie, into a singing sensation. Stuck with Stallone, Parton prepares her protege to sing at New York City's roughest country-western club, The Rhinestone. Only die-hard Dolly and Rocky fans should bother with this bunk. Some may enjoy watching the thick, New York accented Stallone learn how to properly pronounce dog ("dawg") in country lingo. Yee-haw.
1984 (PG) 111m/C Sylvester Stallone, Dolly Parton, Ron Leibman, Richard Farnsworth, Tim Thomerson; **D:** Bob Clark. **VHS, Beta, LV $79.98** *FOX* ✍

Rhodes The story of Cecil Rhodes, a man who was instrumental in the Boer War in Africa and established the Rhodes Scholarships with $10 million, is told in this biography. Fine performance by Huston and Homolka. **AKA:** Rhodes of Africa.
1936 91m/B *GB* Walter Huston, Oscar Homolka, Basil Sydney, Frank Cellier, Peggy Ashcroft, Renne De Vaux, Percy Parsons, Bernard Lee, Ndanisa Kumalo; **D:** Berthold Viertel. **VHS, CV $19.95** *NOS, SNC* ✍✍½

Rhythm Parade A woman takes off for Hawaii, leaving her infant in the care of an L.A. nightclub singer. A jealous rival of the singer takes the opportunity to cause problems. The thin plot serves as a vehicle for lots of singing. ♫Tootin' My Own Horn; Petticoat Army; Mimi From Tahiti; You're Drafted; Wait Till the Sun Shines Nellie; Sweet Sue; 'Neath the Yellow Moon In Old Tahiti.
1943 68m/B Nils T. Granlund, Gale Storm, Robert Lowery, Margaret Dumont, Chick Chandler, Cliff Nazarro, Jane Wiley, Candy Candido, The Mills Brothers, Yvonne De Carlo; **D:** Howard Bretherton. **VHS $19.95** *NOS, MLB* ✍✍

The Ribald Tales of Robin Hood The Robin Hood legend is satirized in this comedy which concentrates on Prince John and his favorite pastimes: rape, pillage and plunder.
1980 (R) 83m/C **VHS, Beta $49.95** *MED* ✍✍

Ricco A young man swears vengeance against the mobsters who killed his father. He kidnaps the daughter of a mafia kingpin and the battle begins. **AKA:** Summertime Killer.
1974 (PG) 90m/C *FR IT SP* Chris Mitchum, Karl Malden, Olivia Hussey, Raf Vallone, Claudine Auger, Gerard Tichy; **D:** Antonio Isasi. **VHS, Beta** *NO* ✍✍

Rich and Famous The story of the 25-year friendship of two women, through college, marriage, and success. George Cukor's last film.
1981 (R) 117m/C Jacqueline Bisset, Candice Bergen, David Selby, Hart Bochner, Meg Ryan, Steven Hill, Michael Brandon, Matt Lattanzi; **D:** George Cukor. **VHS, Beta, LV $79.95** *MGM* ✍✍

Rich and Strange Early Hitchcock movie is not in the same class as his later thrillers. A couple inherits a fortune and journeys around the world. Eventually the pair gets shipwrecked. **AKA:** East of Shanghai.
1932 92m/B *GB* Henry Kendall, Joan Barry, Betty Amann, Percy Marmont, Elsie Randolph; **D:** Alfred Hitchcock. **VHS, LV $19.95** *NOS, SNC, MLB* ✍✍½

Rich Girl A winsome, wealthy wench hides her millions by going to work in a rock'n'roll bar and falls in love with the local Bruce Springsteen wannabee. Despite the thick coating of music, sex, drugs and profanity, this consists of cliches that were old before talkies. Too earnestly-acted to be campy fun. Poor movie.
1991 (R) 96m/C Jill Schoelen, Don Michael Paul, Ron Karabatsos, Sean Kanan, Willie Dixon, Paul Gleason; **D:** Joel Bender. **VHS, LV $89.95** *COL, PIA* ✍

Rich Hall's Vanishing America Funnyman Hall travels across the country looking for the mail-order company that promised to give him a genuine Wilt Chamberlain basketball hoop.
1986 50m/C Rich Hall, M. Emmet Walsh, Peter Isacksen, Harry Anderson, Wilt Chamberlain; **D:** Steve Rash. **VHS, Beta $29.95** *PAR* ✍

Rich in Love Light-hearted look at the changes a Southern family experiences following the voluntary departure of matriarch Helen Odom (Clayburgh). Warren "Rich" Odom (Finney), although shaken, adjusts quite well to the situation. He rekindles an affair with local hairdresser Laurie and perceives anew his 17-year-old daughter Lucille's (Erbe) coming of age, who helps him put the pieces of his life back together. Warren's elder daughter Amis, unexpectedly pregnant, decides to move back home forcing her fiance and her father to come to terms with each other. Finney's inspired performance overcomes a mediocre script. Based on the novel by Josephine Humphreys.
1993 (PG-13) 105m/C Albert Finney, Jill Clayburgh, Kathryn Erbe, Kyle MacLachlan, Piper Laurie, Ethan Hawke, Suzy Amis, Alfre Woodard; **D:** Bruce Beresford; **W:** Alfred Uhry; **M:** Georges Delerue. **VHS, LV $94.99** *MGM, RTV* ✍✍½

Rich Kids A young girl trying to cope with the divorce of her parents is aided by a boyfriend whose parents have already split.
1979 (PG) 97m/C John Lithgow, Kathryn Walker, Trini Alvarado, Paul Dooley, David Selby, Jill Eikenberry, Olympia Dukakis; **D:** Robert M. Young. **VHS, Beta $59.95** *MGM* ✍✍½

Rich, Young and Pretty Light-hearted, innocuous musical starring Powell as a Texas gal visiting Paris with her rancher father (Corey). Powell finds romance with Damone (in his screen debut) and a secret— the mother she has never known (Darrieux). Lamas (in his American screen debut) plays Darrieux's new heartthrob. ♫Dark is the Night; L'Amour Toujours, Tonight For Sure; Wonder Why; I Can See You; Paris; We Never Talk Much; How Do You Like Your Eggs in the Morning?; There's Danger in Your Eyes, Cherie; The Old Piano Roll Blues; Deep In the Heart of Texas; Wonder Why.
1951 95m/C Jane Powell, Danielle Darrieux, Wendell Corey, Vic Damone, Fernando Lamas, Marcel Dalio, Una Merkel, Richard Anderson, Jean Murat, Hans Conried; **D:** Norman Taurog; **W:** Sidney Sheldon, Dorothy Cooper; **M:** Sammy Cahn, Nicholas Brodszky. **VHS $19.98** *MGM* ✍✍

Richard II In the 14th century, a rebellion against even the most corrupt monarch was viewed as an uprising against heaven itself. Shakespeare's "Richard II" is the story of just such a momentous rebellion. Part of the BBC television series "The Shakespeare Plays."
1979 157m/C *GB* Derek Jacobi, Jon Finch, John Gielgud. **VHS, Beta** *TLF* ✍✍✍

Richard III This landmark film version of the Shakespearean play features an acclaimed performance by Laurence Olivier, who also directs. The plot follows the life of the mentally and physically twisted Richard of Gloucester and his schemes for the throne of England.
1955 138m/C *GB* Laurence Olivier, Cedric Hardwicke, Ralph Richardson, John Gielgud, Stanley Baker, Michael Gough, Claire Bloom; **D:** Laurence Olivier. Academy Awards '56 Nominations: Best Actor (Olivier); British Academy Awards '55: Best Actor (Olivier), Best Director (Olivier), Best Film; Golden Globe Awards '57: Best Foreign Film. **VHS, Beta $14.95** *COL, SUE, HMV* ✍✍½

Richard III Shakespeare's play about Richard's quest for the British throne is performed in this BBC television production.
1982 120m/C *GB* Martin Shaw, Brian Protheroe. **VHS, Beta $14.98** *TLF* ✍✍½

Richard Petty Story The biography of race car driver Petty, played by himself, and his various achievements on the track.
1972 (G) 83m/C Richard Petty, Darren McGavin, Kathi Browne, Lynn Marta, Noah Beery Jr., L.Q. Jones. **VHS, Beta $59.95** *GEM* ✍

Richard Pryor: Here and Now Filmed at the Saenger Theater in New Orleans, Pryor's sharp, witty commentaries are delivered with a unique piercing humor.
1983 (R) 83m/C Richard Pryor; **D:** Richard Pryor. **VHS, Beta, LV $14.95** *COL* ✍

Richard Pryor: Live and Smokin' Richard Pryor displays his comedic talents in this 1971 performance where he does his classic "The Wino and the Junkie" routine.
1971 47m/C Richard Pryor; **D:** Michael Blum. **VHS, Beta, LV $19.98** *LIV, VES* ✍

Richard Pryor: Live in Concert Richard Pryor demonstrates his unique brand of humor before an enthusiastic audience. Extremely vulgar.
1979 (R) 78m/C Richard Pryor; **D:** Jeff Margolis. **VHS, Beta $19.95** *VES, FCT* ✍

Richard Pryor: Live on the Sunset Strip Filmed live at the Hollywood Palladium, this program captures Richard Pryor at his funniest, including his segment about "Pryor on Fire."
1982 82m/C Richard Pryor; **D:** Joe Layton. **VHS, Beta, LV $14.95** *COL* ✍

Richard's Things A man's wife and his girlfriend find love and comfort in each other after his death. Screenplay by Frederic Raphael, from his novel. Very slow and dreary, with a weak performance from Ullman.
1980 (R) 104m/C *GB* Liv Ullmann, Amanda Redman; **D:** Anthony Harvey. **VHS, Beta $69.98** *SUE* ✍✍

Richie Experiments with drugs lead a young man's family life down a dead end. Performances are good, script gets sappy. Made for TV; based on a Thomas Thompson story. **AKA:** The Death of Richie.
1977 (R) 86m/C Ben Gazzara, Eileen Brennan, Robby Benson; **D:** Paul Wendkos. **VHS, Beta $59.95** *PSM, LCA* ✍✍

Rickisha Kuri A rickshaw boy gets mad and kicks everyone within reach.
197? 98m/C **VHS, Beta** *UNI* ✍

Ricky 1 Mumbling pugilist spoof. Da Mob wants to make Ricky da fall guy, but uh, he's not as dumb as he looks.
1988 90m/C Michael Michaud, Maggie Hughes, James Herbert, Lane Montano; **D:** Bill Naud. **VHS $69.99** *TPV, HHE* ✍½

Ricochet Rookie cop Washington causes a sensation when he singlehandedly captures notorious psychopath Lithgow. But this particular criminal is a twisted genius, and from his prison cell he comes up with a plan to destroy the young cop. Teaming up with old friend Ice-T, the rookie tries to outwit his evil arch-nemesis, but to do so may cost him his very life. A genuinely scary, tense and violent thriller.
1991 (R) 104m/C Denzel Washington, John Lithgow, Ice-T, Jesse Ventura, Kevin Pollak; *D:* Russell Mulcahy. **VHS, LV, 8mm $19.98** *HBO, CCB* 🐾🐾🐾

Riddance The second of Meszaros' trilogy, about a Hungarian couple, an upper-class male student, and a factory-working young woman, and their difficulties in meshing their lives together. In Hungarian with English subtitles.
1973 84m/B *HU D:* Marta Meszaros. **VHS, Beta $69.95** *KIV, TAM* 🐾🐾🐾

The Riddle of the Sands Two English yachtsmen in 1903 inadvertently stumble upon a German plot to invade England by sea. British film based on the Erskine Childers spy novel.
1984 99m/C *GB* Michael York, Jenny Agutter, Simon MacCorkindale, Michael York, Alan Badel; *D:* Tony Maylam. **VHS, Beta $39.95** *BVG, VID, BMV* 🐾🐾½

Ride a Wild Pony A poor Australian farmer's son is allowed to pick a horse of his own from a neighboring rancher's herd. After he trains and grows to love the pony, the rancher's daughter, a handicapped rich girl, decides to claim it for herself. Enjoyable Disney story is based on the tale "Sporting Proposition," by James Aldridge.
1975 (G) 86m/C *AU* John Meillon, Michael Craig, Robert Bettles, Eva Griffith, Graham Rouse; *D:* Don Chaffey. **VHS, Beta $69.95** *DIS* 🐾🐾🐾

Ride 'Em Cowboy Two peanut and hotdog vendors travel west to try their hand as cowpokes. Usual Abbott and Costello fare with a twist—there are lots of great musical numbers. 🎵A Tisket, A Tasket; I'll Remember April; Wake Up Jacob; Beside the Rio Tonto; Rock 'n' Reelin'; Give Me My Saddle; Cow Boogie.
1942 86m/B Bud Abbott, Lou Costello, Anne Gwynne, Samuel S. Hinds, Dick Foran, Richard Lane, Johnny Mack Brown, Ella Fitzgerald, Douglas Dumbrille; *D:* Arthur Lubin. **VHS $14.98** *MCA* 🐾🐾½

Ride 'Em Cowgirl Singing cowgirl, Page, enters a horse race to expose the crook who cheated her father.
1941 51m/B Dorothy Page, Vince Barnett, Milton Frome; *D:* Samuel Diege. **VHS, 3/4U** *VCN* 🐾🐾

Ride in a Pink Car When a Vietnam vet returns home, he discovers that his welcoming committee is really a lynch mob.
1974 (R) 83m/C Glenn Corbett, Morgan Woodward, Ivy Jones; *D:* Robert Emery. **VHS, Beta $19.95** *ACA* 🐾

Ride in the Whirlwind Three cowboys are mistaken for members of a gang by a posse. Screenplay for the offbeat western was by Nicholson.
1967 83m/C Jack Nicholson, Cameron Mitchell, Millie Perkins, Katherine Squire, Harry Dean Stanton; *D:* Monte Hellman. **Beta, LV, CDV $19.99** *MED, HHT, DVT* 🐾🐾

Ride, Ranger, Ride Texas Ranger Autry is out to stop a group of Comanches from raiding a wagon train.
1936 56m/B Gene Autry, Smiley Burnette, Kay Hughes, Max Terhune, Monte Blue, Chief Thundercloud; *D:* Joseph Kane. **VHS, Beta $19.95** *NOS, MED, VYY* 🐾½

Ride the High Country The cult classic western about two old friends who have had careers on both sides of the law. One, Joel McCrea, is entrusted with a shipment of gold, and the other, Randolph Scott, rides along with him to steal the precious cargo. Although barely promoted by MGM, became a critics' favorite. Grimacing and long in the tooth, McCrea and Scott enact a fitting tribute and farewell to the myth of the grand ol' West. Wonderfully photographed by Lucien Ballard. The laserdisc edition carries the film in widescreen format along with the original movie trailer. *AKA:* Guns in the Afternoon.
1962 93m/C Randolph Scott, Joel McCrea, Mariette Hartley, Edgar Buchanan, R.G. Armstrong, Ronald Starr, John Anderson, James Drury, L.Q. Jones, Warren Oates; *D:* Sam Peckinpah. **VHS, Beta, LV $19.98** *MGM, PIA* 🐾🐾🐾🐾

Ride the Man Down Story of a murderous land war between neighboring landowners tells the same old story: Greed knows no boundaries.
1953 90m/C Brian Donlevy, Chill Wills, Jack LaRue, Rod Cameron, Ella Raines; *D:* Joseph Kane. **VHS $19.98** *REP* 🐾½

Ride the Wild Surf It's fun in the sun when surfers Fabian, Hunter, and Brown head to Hawaii in search of the ultimate waves. Throw in a little romance and a cool title song by Jan and Dean and you've got your better than average beach movie. The surfing footage is excellent. Cowabunga!
1964 101m/C Fabian, Tab Hunter, Barbara Eden, Peter Brown, Susan Hart, Shelley Fabares, James Mitchum; *D:* Don Taylor. **VHS $19.95** *COL* 🐾🐾½

Ride the Wind "Bonanza" gang goes to the aid of the Pony Express.
1966 120m/C Michael Landon, Lorne Greene, Dan Blocker. **VHS, Beta $14.95** *REP* 🐾🐾

Ride to Glory In 1886, a cavalry officer deserts his troops to seek revenge on the Apaches that brutally killed his family. Hearing this, a general offers to pardon him if he will lead a dangerous group of men on a mission against the Apaches. Fast-paced and very bloody. *AKA:* The Deserter; La Spina Dorsale del Diavolo.
1971 90m/C Bekim Fehmiu, Richard Crenna, Chuck Connors, Ricardo Montalban, Ian Bannen, Slim Pickens, Woody Strode, Patrick Wayne, John Huston; *D:* Burt Kennedy. **VHS $19.95** *SIM, PAR, HHE* 🐾🐾

Rider from Tucson Two rodeo riders head out to Colorado for a friend's wedding. They find out the bride has been kidnapped by a bunch of claim jumpers after control of a gold mine.
1950 60m/B Tim Holt, Richard Martin, Elaine Riley, Douglas Fowley; *D:* Lesley Selander. **VHS, Beta** *RKO* 🐾🐾

Rider of the Law A government agent poses as a greenhorn easterner to nab a gang of outlaws.
1935 56m/B Bob Steele. **VHS, Beta** *NO* 🐾

Rider on the Rain A young housewife is viciously raped by an escaped sex maniac. She kills him and disposes of his body, not knowing that he is being relentlessly pursued by mysterious American Bronson. Suspenseful, French-made thriller featuring one of Bronson's best performances. *AKA:* Lepassager de la Pluie.
1970 115m/C *FR* Marlene Jobert, Charles Bronson, Jill Ireland; *D:* Rene Clement. **VHS, Beta $19.95** *MON* 🐾🐾🐾

Riders of Death Valley Splendid western action serial in 15 thirteen-minute episodes. Foran, Jones, and Carillo head a passel o'men watching for thieves and claim jumpers in a mining area.
1941 195m/B Dick Foran, Buck Jones, Leo Carrillo, Lon Chaney Jr.; *D:* Ford Beebe, Ray Taylor. **VHS, Beta $49.95** *NOS, VCN, DVT* 🐾🐾🐾

Riders of Destiny Wayne plays a government agent sent to find out who is stealing water from the local farmers. Very early Wayne has the Duke looking awfully young as an agent securing water rights for ranchers.
1933 59m/B John Wayne, George "Gabby" Hayes, Cecilia Parker, Forrest Taylor, Al "Fuzzy" St. John; *D:* Robert North Bradbury. **VHS $9.98** *REP, NOS, SVS* 🐾🐾½

Riders of the Desert Steele tracks down the loot from a stagecoach robbery.
1932 57m/B Bob Steele. **VHS, Beta $24.95** *VYY, VCN* 🐾½

Riders of the Range Sheep invade the cattle range and a range war flares up between those who would herd and the ranchers. Silent flick of interest because of the stars.
1924 62m/B Edmund Cobb, Helen Hayes, Dolly Dale; *D:* Otis Thayer. **VHS, Beta** *GPV* 🐾🐾

Riders of the Range Cowboy rides into town just in time to save a girl's brother from gamblers.
1949 60m/B Tim Holt, Richard Martin. **VHS, Beta** *RKO* 🐾

Riders of the Range/Storm Over Wyoming A double feature package of Tim Holt Westerns.
1950 120m/B Tim Holt, Richard Martin, Jacqueline Wells. **VHS, Beta $39.95** *RKO, TTC* 🐾½

Riders of the Rockies An honest cowboy turns rustler in order to trap a border gang. One of Ritter's very best cowboy outings; good fun, and a very long fistfight with King.
1937 60m/B Tex Ritter, Yakima Canutt, Louise Stanley, Charles King, Snub Pollard; *D:* Robert North Bradbury. **VHS, Beta $19.95** *NOS, UHV, VCN* 🐾🐾🐾

Riders of the Storm A motley crew of Vietnam vets runs a covert television broadcasting station from an in-flight B-29, jamming America's legitimate airwaves. Interesting premise with boring result. *AKA:* The American Way.
1988 (R) 92m/C Dennis Hopper, Michael J. Pollard, Eugene Lipinski, James Aubrey, Nigel Pegram; *D:* Maurice Phillips. **VHS, Beta, LV $19.98** *SUE, NLC* 🐾½

Riders of the Timberline Unusual for a Hopalong Cassidy programmer in that it puts him in timber country. Yes, he's a lumberjack and he's okay, as he fights against land-grabbing crooks all day.
1941 59m/B William Boyd, Brad King, Andy Clyde, J. Farrell MacDonald, Elaine Stewart, Anna Q. Nilsson, Hal Taliaferro, Tom Tyler, Victor Jory; *D:* Lesley Selander. **VHS $19.95** *NOS* 🐾🐾

Riders of the West An honest cowpoke fights off a band of rustlers.
1942 58m/B Buck Jones, Tim McCoy, Raymond Hatton, Sarah Padden, Harry Woods; *D:* Howard Bretherton. **VHS $19.95** *NOS, DVT* 🐾

Riders of the Whistling Pines Our ever-so-bland hero solves a murder perpetrated by a passel of lumber thieves and saves the day for yet another damsel in distress.

1949 70m/B Gene Autry, Patricia White, Jimmy Lloyd.; *D:* John English. **VHS, Beta** $19.95 *NOS, MED, DVT* ♂♂

Riders of the Whistling Skull
The Three Mesquiteers are guiding an expedition to an ancient Indian city. A gang of rustlers looting the city are holding an archeology professor hostage, and the Mesquiteers must rescue him. Swell cast; nifty, creepy plot; solid-as-usual leads. *AKA:* The Golden Trail.
1937 58m/B Bob Livingston, Ray Corrigan, Max Terhune, Yakima Canutt, Roland Winters; *D:* Mack V. Wright. **VHS, Beta** $12.95 *SNC, NOS, VCN* ♂♂½

Riders to the Seas
A mother envisions the death of her last son in the same manner her other sons died—by drowning.
1988 90m/C Geraldine Page, Amanda Plummer, Sachi Parker, Barry McGovern; *D:* Ronan O'Leary. **VHS, Beta** *NO* ♂½

Ridin' on a Rainbow
Has-been performer on a steamboat decides to rob a bank in the hopes of starting a new life for himself and his daughter. The money he robs had just been deposited by some cattlemen, one of whom joins the steamboat's crew, wins the daughter's heart, and gets to the father. Slow and dull, with too much singing, and too little plot and scenery.
1941 79m/B Gene Autry, Smiley Burnette, Mary Lee; *D:* Lew Landers. **VHS, Beta** $39.98 *REP, CCB, VCN* ♂½

Ridin' the California Trail
The Cisco Kid is wanted dead or alive in several states.
1947 40m/B Gilbert Roland. **VHS, Beta** $24.95 *DVT* ♂½

Ridin' the Lone Trail
Steele attempts to stop some criminals who've been harassing a stagecoach line. Republic was better than this weak western would lead us to believe. Steele, who went on to better things, is a bright spot in a film that sounds and looks bad. Keep your ears open for the sound of airplanes—apparently Newfield forgot they hadn't been invented in the time of the wild west. From a story by E.B. Mann.
1937 56m/B Bob Steele, Claire Rochelle, Charles King, Ernie Adams, Lew Meehan, Julian Rivero; *D:* Sam Newfield; *W:* Charles Francis Royal. **VHS** $19.95 *NOS, DVT* Woof!

Ridin' the Trail
Scott stars as a cowboy out to rid the countryside of bad guys in this western.
1940 60m/B Fred Scott, Iris Lancaster, Harry Harvey, Jack Ingram, John Ward; *D:* Raymond K. Johnson. **VHS, Beta** $19.95 *NOS, DVT* ♂

Ridin' Thru
Another Tom Tyler western, in which the hero does battle with unscrupulous villains.
1935 60m/B Tom Tyler, Ruth Hiatt, Lafe McKee, Philo McCullough, Lew Meehan, Bud Osborne; *D:* Harry S. Webb. **VHS, Beta** $16.95 *NOS, DVT, HEG* ♂♂

The Riding Avenger
To gain the love of a beautiful lady, a cowboy vows never to fight again, but is forced to break his promise when the town is terrorized. Aw, shucks.
1936 56m/B Hoot Gibson, Ruth Mix, Buzz Barton. **VHS, Beta** $19.95 *VCN* ♂½

Riding Bean
Animated Japanese feature aimed at a mature audience. An adventure about a kidnapping blamed on an innocent courier. In Japanese with English subtitles.
1991 46m/C *JP* **VHS, LV** $34.95 *CPM, TAM, WTA* ♂½

Riding High
It's a battle for supremacy between the kings of the motorcycle stunt world. Made for television movie's soundtrack includes songs from The Police, Dire Straits, Jerry Lee Lewis, and more.
1978 92m/C Murray Salem, Marella Oppenheim, Eddie Kidd, Irene Handl; *D:* Ross Cramer. **VHS, Beta** $39.95 *LIV* ♂

Riding On
Hayseed falls for the daughter of his father's arch rival. While his father battles it out over cattle, he pines for his enemy's daughter. Lots of action which is typical fare in mediocre western production.
1937 59m/B Tom Tyler, Germaine Greer, Rex Lease, John Elliott, Earl Dwire; *D:* Harry S. Webb. **VHS** $19.95 *NOS, DVT* ♂♂

Riding on Air
Small-town newspaper editor Brown discovers that his bumbling methods get him the right results. Smugglers and crazy inventions in a ho-hum Brown entry.
1937 58m/B Joe E. Brown; *D:* Edward Sedgwick. **VHS, Beta** $19.95 *NOS, KRT, FCT* ♂♂

Riding Speed
Our hero breaks up a gang of smugglers along the Mexican border.
1935 50m/B Buffalo Bill Jr. **VHS, Beta, LV** *NO* ♂

Riding the Edge
Teenage motocross rider rescues his scientist dad from Middle Eastern terrorists. Thoroughly unoriginal.
1990 (R) 100m/C **VHS, LV** $89.99 *HBO* ♂

Riding with Death
A man who can become invisible, thanks to a military experiment, uses his power to uncover a dastardly plot by a mad scientist. So-so TV pilot.
1976 97m/C Ben Murphy, Andrew Prine, Katherine Crawford, Richard Dysart; *D:* Alan J. Levi. **VHS, Beta** $39.95 *MCA* ♂

Riel
The story of Louis Riel, a half-French, half-Indian visionary who challenged the Canadian army in his fight for equality and self-rule.
1979 150m/C Raymond Cloutier, Arthur Hill, William Shatner, Christopher Plummer, Leslie Nielsen; *D:* George Bloomfield. **VHS, Beta** $49.95 *PSM* ♂♂

Riff Raff
Melodramatic story about the relationship of two waterfront workers in the tuna fishing business. Confusing script saddled with too many characters, but there is some good sharp dialogue between the leads. Also features the scenic California waterfront. *AKA:* Riffraff.
1935 80m/B Jean Harlow, Spencer Tracy, Joseph Calleia, Una Merkel, Mickey Rooney, Victor Kilian, J. Farrell MacDonald, Roger Imhof; *D:* J. Walter Ruben. **VHS** $19.98 *MGM* ♂♂

Riff-Raff
Various dramatic and comic complications arise when a dying man gives Panama City con man O'Brien a map to oil deposits. Interesting and quick-moving melodrama.
1947 80m/B Pat O'Brien, Walter Slezak, Anne Jeffreys, Jason Robards Sr., Percy Kilbride, Jerome Cowan; *D:* Ted Tetzlaff. **VHS, Beta** $19.98 *TTC* ♂♂½

Riff Raff
Unsparing black comedy about the British working-class by director Loach. Ex-con Stevie comes to London from Scotland to look for work and escape his thieving past. He finds a nonunion job on a construction site, takes up squatter's rights in an abandoned apartment, and finds a girlfriend in equally struggling singer Susie, who turns out to be a junkie. Loach's characters deal with their unenviable lot in life through rough humor and honest sentiment. Regional accents are so thick that the film is subtitled.

1992 96m/C *GB* Robert Carlyle, Emer McCourt, Jimmy Coleman, George Moss, Ricky Tomlinson, David Finch, Bill Jesse; *D:* Ken Loach; *W:* Bill Jesse; *M:* Stewart Copeland. **VHS, LV** *NLC, COL, IME* ♂♂♂

Rififi
Perhaps the greatest of all "heist" movies. Four jewel thieves pull off a daring caper, only to fall prey to mutual distrust. The long scene of the actual theft, completely in silence, will have your heart in your throat. In French with English subtitles. *AKA:* Du Rififi Chez les Hommes.
1954 115m/B *FR* Jean Servais, Carl Mohner, Robert Manuel, Jules Dassin; *D:* Jules Dassin. **VHS, Beta, 3/4U, Special order formats** $29.95 *NOS, VYY, HHT* ♂♂♂

The Right Hand Man
A brother and sister must deal with their crusty patriarch's demise in the Victorian-era Australian outback. Disappointing and overwrought.
1987 (R) 101m/C *AU* Rupert Everett, Hugo Weaving, Arthur Dignam; *D:* Di Drew. **VHS, Beta** $9.99 *STE, NWV* ♂½

Right of Way
Stewart plays an elderly man who makes a suicide pact with his wife (Davis) when he learns of her terminal illness. Davis and Stewart's first film together is disappointing and stodgy, with an abrupt ending that looks like bad editing by a frightened studio. Made for TV.
1984 102m/C James Stewart, Bette Davis, Priscilla Morrill, Melinda Dillon; *D:* George Schaefer. **VHS, Beta** *NO* ♂♂½

The Right Stuff
A rambunctious adaptation of Tom Wolfe's nonfiction book about the beginnings of the U.S. space program, from Chuck Yeager's breaking of the sound barrier to the last of the Mercury missions. Featuring an all-star cast and an ambitious script. Rowdy, imaginative, and thrilling, though broadly painted and oddly uninvolving. Former astronaut John Glenn was running for president when this was out.
1983 (PG) 193m/C Ed Harris, Dennis Quaid, Sam Shepard, Scott Glenn, Fred Ward, Charles Frank, William Russ, Kathy Baker, Barbara Hershey, Levon Helm, David Clennon, Kim Stanley, Mary Jo Deschanel, Veronica Cartwright, Pamela Reed, Jeff Goldblum, Harry Shearer, Donald Moffatt, Scott Paulin, Lance Henriksen, Scott Wilson, John P. Ryan, Royal Dano; *D:* Philip Kaufman; *M:* Bill Conti. Academy Awards '83: Best Film Editing, Best Sound, Best Original Score; Nominations: Best Art Direction/Set Decoration, Best Cinematography, Best Picture, Best Supporting Actress (Shepard). **VHS, Beta, LV** $29.98 *WAR* ♂♂♂

Rikisha-Man
A tragic melodrama about a rickshaw puller who helps raise a young boy after his father has died, and loves the boy's mother from afar. Also called "Rickshaw Man" and "Muhomatsu no Issho." Inagaki's remake of his original 1943 version. In Japanese with English subtitles.
1958 105m/B *JP* Toshiro Mifune; *D:* Hiroshi Inagaki. **VHS, Beta** $59.95 *FCT, AUD* ♂♂♂½

Rikky and Pete
An engaging Australian comedy about a bizarre, precociously eccentric brother and sister. He's a Rube Goldberg-style mentor; she's a scientist-cum-country singer. They move together to the outback and meet a score of weird characters. A worthy follow-up to director Tass's "Malcolm."
1988 (R) 103m/C *AU* Nina Landis, Stephen Kearney, Tetchie Agbayani, Bruce Spence, Bruno Lawrence, Bill Hunter, Dorothy Allison, Don Reid; *D:* Nadia Tass, David Parker. **VHS, Beta, LV** $79.98 *MGM, FOX* ♂♂½

Rikyu
Set in 16th century Japan, Rikyu is a Buddhist priest who elevated the tea ceremony to an art form. To him it is a spiritual experience, to his master, Lord Hideyoshi

Toiiyotomi, the ruler of Japan, mastery of the ceremony is a matter of prestige. Conflict arises between Rikyu's ideal of profound simplicity, symbolized by the ceremony, and Toiiyotomi's planned conquest of China, which Rikyu opposes. In Japanese with English subtitles.
1990 116m/C JP Rentaro Mikuni, Tsutomu Yamazaki; **D:** Hiroshi Teshigahara. **VHS, LV $79.95** CTL, TAM, LUM &&

Rim of the Canyon Autry has a dual role as a lawman tracking villains who were jailed by his father years before.
1949 70m/B Gene Autry, Nan Leslie, Thurston Hall, Clem Bevans, Walter Sande, Jock Mahoney, Alan Hale Jr., Denver Pyle; **D:** John English. **VHS, Beta $19.95** NOS, DVT &&1/2

Rimfire An undercover agent tracks down some stolen U.S. Army gold, aided by the ghost of a wrongly-hanged gambler. Fun B western.
1949 65m/B Mary Beth Hughes, Henry Hull, Fuzzy Knight, James Millican, Victor Kilian, Margia Dean, Jason Robards Sr., Reed Hadley; **D:** B. Reeves Eason. **VHS, Beta, LV** WGE &&1/2

Rin Tin Tin, Hero of the West In one of his last adventures, the famous German Shepherd proves his courage and hyper-canine intelligence. Colorized.
1955 75m/C James Brown, Lee Aaker, Rin Tin Tin. **VHS, Beta $24.95** MON &

The Ring Very early Hitchcock about boxer who marries carnival girl, loses carnival girl, and wins carnival girl back again. Standard romantic punch and roses yarn interesting as measure of young director's developing authority.
1927 82m/B GB Carl Brisson, Lillian Hall-Davies, Ian Hunter, Gordon Harker; **D:** Alfred Hitchcock. **VHS $19.98** VEC, MLB &&1/2

The Ring Poignant early fight movie that gives a lesson in prejudice against Chicanos. The main character feels that the only way to get respect from the world is to fight for it. Well-directed and perceptive.
1952 79m/B Gerald Mohr, Rita Moreno, Kiri Te Kanawa, Robert Arthur, Art Aragon, Jack Elam; **D:** Kurt Neumann. **VHS, CV** MOV, DVT, HEG &&1/2

Ring of Bright Water Well done story of a pet otter from Gavin Maxwell's autobiography. The film stars the couple that made the delightful "Born Free." Beautiful Scottish Highlands photography adds to this captivating and endearing tale of a civil servant who purchases an otter from a pet store and moves to the country.
1969 (G) 107m/C GB Bill Travers, Virginia McKenna, Peter Jeffrey, Archie Duncan; **D:** Charles Lamont. **VHS, Beta** FCT, SIG, TVC &&&

Ring of Death A tough cop investigating a routine case becomes a hunted man after someone kills the man he is following.
1972 93m/C Franco Nero, Florinda Bolkan, Adolfo Celi. **VHS, Beta $59.95** GEM, MRV &1/2

Ring of Fire Wilson is one of very few modern American kung-fu heroes of Asian descent, and he works messages against prejudice into this interracial Romeo-and-Juliet chopsocky tale. What foot through yonder window breaks?
1991 (R) 100m/C Don "The Dragon" Wilson, Maria Ford, Vince Murdocco, Dale Jacoby, Michael Delano, Eric Lee; **D:** Richard W. Munchkin. **VHS, LV $89.95** IMP, HMV &

Ring of Fire 2: Blood and Steel Wilson returns as Dr. Johnny Wu in this martial-arts actioner which finds the good doctor the witness to a robbery. When one of the robbers is killed, the gang's leader kidnaps Johnny's fiance and holds her for

ransom. He decides to bypass the police and use his own expertise to rescue her.
1992 (R) 94m/C Don "The Dragon" Wilson, Maria Ford, Sy Richardson, Michael Delano, Dale Jacoby, Vince Murdocco, Evan Lorie, Gary Robbins, Charlie Ganis, Ron Yuan; **D:** Richard W. Munchkin. **VHS $89.95** PMH &1/2

Ring of Terror College boy who wants to join a fraternity must survive the initiation rights, which include stealing a ring from a corpse. Unfortunately, this seemingly invincible guy has a deadly terror of the dead. Cheaply made flop alledgedly based on a composite of actual hazing incidents.
1962 72m/B George Mather, Esther Furst, Austin Green, Joseph Conway; **D:** Clark Paylow. **VHS $16.95** NOS, SNC &

Ringside A concert pianist turns boxer to avenge his brother who was blinded in a fight.
1949 64m/B Donald (Don "Red") Barry, Sheila Ryan, Tom Brown. **VHS, Beta, LV $16.95** SNC &1/2

The Rink Chaplin plays a waiter who spends his lunch hour on roller skates. Silent with musical soundtrack added.
1916 20m/B Charlie Chaplin; **D:** Charlie Chaplin. **VHS, Beta, 3/4U, Special order formats** CAB &&&

Rink/Immigrant Two Chaplin shorts: "The Rink" (1916), in which Charlie defends his girlfriend's honor at a local roller skating rink; "The Immigrant" (1917), features Charlie as a newcomer to America.
191? 56m/B Charlie Chaplin, Mack Swain, Edna Purviance. **VHS, Beta $29.95** VYY &&&

Rio Bravo The sheriff of a Texas border town (Wayne) takes a brutal murderer into custody and faces a blockade of hired gunmen determined to keep his prisoner from being brought to justice. Long, but continually entertaining. Generally regarded as an American film classic, with an all-star cast, didn't impress the critics at the time. Sequel: "El Dorado." Semi-remake was called "Assault on Precinct 13."
1959 140m/C John Wayne, Dean Martin, Angie Dickinson, Ricky Nelson, Walter Brennan, Ward Bond, Claude Akins, Bob Steele, John Russell; **D:** Howard Hawks. **VHS, Beta $19.98** WAR, TLF &&&1/2

Rio Conchos Nifty nonstop action in this western set in Texas after the Civil War. Three Army buddies search for 2,000 stolen rifles. Boone is understated, O'Brien is good, and Brown memorable in his debut.
1964 107m/C Richard Boone, Stuart Whitman, Edmond O'Brien, Anthony (Tony) Franciosa, Jim Brown; **D:** Gordon Douglas; **M:** Jerry Goldsmith. **VHS, Beta $19.98** FOX &&&

Rio Diablo Country Western singers abound in—what else—a made-for-TV Western movie. A bounty hunter (Rogers) and newlywed groom (Tritt) set off after a gang of thieving kidnappers who have snatched the young bride (Harring). Judd shows up as the owner of a desert hostelry, who happens to cross paths with the hunters. Watch out—this could be more fun than a Partridge Family reunion.
1993 120m/C Kenny Rogers, Travis Tritt, Naomi Judd, Stacy Keach, Brion James, Bruce Greenwood, Laura Harring. **VHS** CAF &&1/2

Rio Grande The last entry in Ford's cavalry trilogy following "Fort Apache" and "She Wore a Yellow Ribbon." A U.S. cavalry unit on the Mexican border conducts an unsuccessful campaign against marauding Indians. The commander (Wayne) has an unhappy wife and is estranged from his son, a new recruit. Featuring an excellent Victor

Young score and several songs by the Sons of the Pioneers.
1950 105m/B John Wayne, Maureen O'Hara, Ben Johnson, Claude Jarman Jr., Harry Carey Jr., Victor McLaglen, Chill Wills, J. Carroll Naish; **D:** John Ford. **VHS, LV $19.98** REP, TLF, RXM &&&

Rio Grande Raiders A Stagecoach driver discovers that his kid brother is working for a crooked rival stage company.
1946 54m/B Sunset Carson, Linda Stirling, Bob Steele. **VHS, Beta $29.95** DVT, RXM &

Rio Hondo An ex-gunfighter comes back to his home town only to find it filled with outlaws.
1947 90m/B Carlos Cortez, Elsa Cardenas, Alfonso Mejias, Alfredo Leal. **VHS, Beta $39.95** MAD &&

Rio Lobo Hawks's final film takes place after the Civil War, when Union Colonel Wayne goes to Rio Lobo to take revenge on two traitors. Disappointing. The Duke has to carry weak supporting performances on his brawny shoulders—and nearly does.
1970 (G) 114m/C John Wayne, Jorge Rivero, Jennifer O'Neill, Jack Elam, Chris Mitchum, David Huddleston, George Plimpton; **D:** Howard Hawks; **M:** Jerry Goldsmith. **VHS, Beta, LV $19.98** FOX &&1/2

Rio Rattler A vintage fast-shooting matinee western.
1935 60m/B Tom Tyler, Marion Shilling, Eddie Gribbon, William Gould, Tom London; **D:** Bernard B. Ray. **VHS, Beta $27.95** VCN &1/2

Rio Rita Abbott & Costello are working on a ranch and somehow become involved with Nazi spies. Provides a few original comic bits for the duo but is otherwise mediocre. An updated remake of the 1929 Wheeler & Woolsey comedy.
1942 91m/B Bud Abbott, Lou Costello, Kathryn Grayson, John Carroll, Patricia Dane, Tom Conway, Peter Whitney; **D:** Sylvan Simon. **VHS $19.98** MGM &&1/2

Riot Men in cages throw tantrums until warden returns from vacation. Filmed in Arizona State Prison with real convicts as extras. Strong performances by fullback Brown and durable Hackman. Screenplay by James Poe based on story by ex-con Frank Elli. Too oft played theme song sung by Bill Medley of the Righteous Brothers.
1969 (R) 97m/C Gene Hackman, Jim Brown, Mike Kellin, Ben Carruthers, Frank Eyman; **D:** Buzz Kulik. **VHS $14.95** PAR &&1/2

Riot in Cell Block 11 A convict leads four thousand prisoners in an uprising to improve prison conditions. Based on producer/ex-con Walter Wanger's own experience. Powerful and still timely. Filmed at Folsom Prison.
1954 80m/B Neville Brand, Leo Gordon, Emile Meyer, Frank Faylen; **D:** Don Siegel. **VHS, Beta $19.98** REP &&&

Riot Squad An intern poses as a doctor in order to find out who was responsible for putting a mob hit on a police captain.
1941 55m/B Richard Cromwell, Rita Quigley, John Miljan, Mary Ruth, Herbert Rawlinson, Mary Gordon, Arthur Space; **D:** Edward Finney. **VHS, Beta $16.95** SNC, RXM &&

Rip-Off Two Greek wanderers enter the American way of life via sex, drugs, syndicated crime, and terrorism.
1977 78m/C Michael Benet, Michelle Simone, James Masters, Johnny Dark; **D:** Manolis Tsafos. **VHS, Beta $49.95** UNI &

The Rip Off A colorful gang of hoodlums goes for the biggest heist of their lives—six million bucks in diamonds!

1978 (R) 99m/C Lee Van Cleef, Karen Black, Robert Alda, Edward Albert; *D:* Anthony M. Dawson. **VHS, Beta** $49.95 *WOV* 🎞️

Rip Roarin' Buckaroo A fighter sets out to avenge himself when he is framed in a dishonest fight.
1936 51m/B Tom Tyler, B.J. Quinn Jr., Beth Marion, Charles King; *D:* Robert Hill. **VHS, Beta** $19.95 *NOS, DVT, RXM* 🎞️

Rip van Winkle 🎞️ Sleepy Coppola adaptation of the Washington Irving story about a man who falls asleep for twenty years after a group of ghosts get him drunk. From the "Faerie Tale Theatre" series.
1985 60m/C Harry Dean Stanton, Talia Shire; *D:* Francis Ford Coppola. **VHS, Beta** $14.95 *KUI, FOX, FCT* 🎞️🎞️

Ripley's Believe It or Not! Each episode of this series outlines incredible facts based on the long-running newspaper feature. New volumes are being added to this on-going series on a regular basis. Volumes are available separately.
1985 80m/C **VHS, Beta, Special order formats** *NO* 🎞️

The Ripper The spirit of Jack-the-Ripper possesses a university professor's body. Ultra-violent. Shot on videotape for the video market.
1986 90m/C Wade Tower, Tom Schreir, Mona Van Pernis, Andrea Adams; *D:* Christopher Lewis. **VHS, Beta** $24.95 *NEG* Woof!

Ripping Yarns Three episodes of the popular British comedy series written by Monty Python's Terry Jones and Michael Palin: "Tomkinson's Schooldays," "Escape from Stalag Luft 112B," and "Golden Gordon." The subsequent episodes are released as "More Ripping Yarns" and "Even More Ripping Yarns."
1975 90m/C *GB* Michael Palin, Gwen Watford, Ian Ogilvy, Roy Kinnear, Bill Fraser; *D:* Terry Hughes, Jimmy Franklin, Alan Bell; *W:* Michael Palin, Terry Jones. **VHS, Beta** $14.98 *FOX* Woof!

The Rise and Fall of Legs Diamond Not quite historically accurate but fast-paced and entertaining gangster bio of legendary booze trafficker Legs Diamond. Danton's debut.
1960 101m/B Ray Danton, Karen Steele, Jesse White, Simon Oakland, Robert Lowery, Elaine Stewart; *D:* Budd Boetticher. **VHS, LV** $59.99 *WAR, PIA, FCT* 🎞️🎞️½

Rise and Fall of the Third Reich A pictorial record which tracks Adolf Hitler's path through the years between 1920 and 1945. Some segments are in black and white.
1968 120m/C **VHS, Beta** $59.95 *MGM* 🎞️🎞️½

The Rise & Rise of Daniel Rocket A exceptional young boy believes he can fly without the aid of a flying machine. From the "American Playhouse" series.
1986 90m/C Tom Hulce, Timothy Daly, Valerie Mahaffey; *D:* Emile Ardolino. **VHS, Beta** $59.95 *ACA, PBS* 🎞️🎞️

The Rise of Louis XIV A masterful docudrama detailing the life and court intrigues of Louis XIV of France. Successfully captures the attitudes and mores of the royalty at the time. One of a series of historical films directed by Rossellini. Made for French television. In French with English subtitles. *AKA:* La Prise de Pouvoir Par Louis XIV.
1966 100m/C *FR* Jean-Marie Patte, Raymond Jourdan, Dominique Vincent, Silvagni, Pierre Barrat; *D:* Roberto Rossellini. **VHS** $59.95 *HTV, TAM, FCT* 🎞️🎞️🎞️

Rising Son A family man who loves his job faces trauma when his factory closes at the same time his son informs him he's quitting medical school. Solid family drama and parable of economic hard times of the early '80s, sustained by top-drawer performances by Dennehy, Damon, and Laurie. Well directed by Coles. Made for cable.
1990 92m/C Brian Dennehy, Matt Damon, Piper Laurie, Graham Beckel, Ving Rhames, Jane Adams, Richard Jenkins, Emily Longstreth; *D:* John Coles. **VHS, Beta** $79.98 *TTC* 🎞️🎞️🎞️

Rising Sun When a prostitute is found murdered in the boardroom of a powerful Japanese-owned corporation, seasoned cop (and Japanese expert) Connery and partner Snipes are sent to investigate. Based on the book by Michael Crichton, which offered ominous theories about international politics and business. These aspects had the film labeled as Japan-bashing, one of the reasons the script was rewritten to focus more on the murder mystery.
1993 (R) 120m/C Sean Connery, Wesley Snipes, Tia Carrere, Harvey Keitel, Kevin Anderson, Stan Egi, Mako, Cary-Hiroyuki Tagawa, Ray Wise; *W/D:* Philip Kaufman; *W:* David Mamet, Michael Crichton; *M:* Toru Takemitsu. **VHS** 🎞️🎞️🎞️

Risky Business Fortune-seeking mother disapproves of daughter's doctor fiance, and educates girl in marital woes. Video includes early Pollard short "Sold at Auction."
1928 104m/B Vera Reynolds, ZaSu Pitts, Ethey Clayton; *D:* Alan Hale Jr. **VHS, Beta, LV** $18.95 *GPV, FCT, WAR* 🎞️🎞️

Risky Business With his parents out of town and awaiting word from the college boards, a teenager becomes involved in unexpected ways with a quick-thinking prostitute, her pimp, and assorted others. Cruise is likeable, especially when dancing in his underwear. Funny, well-paced, stylish prototypical '80s teen flick reintroduced Ray-Bans as the sunglasses for the wannabe hip. What a party!
1983 (R) 99m/C Tom Cruise, Rebecca DeMornay, Curtis Armstrong, Bronson Pinchot, Joe Pantoliano, Kevin Anderson, Richard Masur, Raphael Sbarge, Nicholas Pryor, Janet Carroll; *D:* Paul Brickman. **VHS, Beta, LV, 8mm** $19.98 *WAR* 🎞️🎞️🎞️

Rita Hayworth: The Love Goddess Made for television drama details the tragic life of the beautiful film star. Carter, lovely though she is, plays Rita weakly and without depth.
1983 100m/C Lynda Carter, Michael Lerner, Alejandro Rey, John Considine; *D:* James Goldstone. **VHS, Beta** $39.95 *LIV* 🎞️½

Rita, Sue & Bob Too A middle-aged Englishman gets involved in a menage a trois with two promiscuous teenagers, until the whole town gets wind of it. A raunchy, amoral British comedy. Written by Andrea Dunbar.
1987 (R) 94m/C *GB* Michelle Holmes, George Costigan, Siobhan Finneran; *D:* Alan Clarke. **VHS, Beta, LV** $79.95 *LHV, WAR* 🎞️🎞️🎞️

Rituals Group of five calm, rational men suddenly turn desperate after a chain of nightmarish events on a camping trip. Yet another low-budget "Deliverance" rip off. *AKA:* The Creeper.
1979 100m/C *CA* Hal Holbrook, Lawrence Dane; *D:* Peter Carter. **VHS, Beta** $24.98 *SUE* 🎞️½

The Ritz Weston tries to get away from his gangster brother-in-law by hiding out in a gay bathhouse in New York. Moreno plays a talentless singer Googie Gomez, who performs in the bathhouse while waiting for her big break. Moreno is great reprising her Tony-winning stage role, and Lester's direction is spiffy. Written by Terence McNally from his play.
1976 (R) 91m/C Rita Moreno, Jack Weston, Jerry Stiller, Kaye Ballard, Treat Williams, F. Murray Abraham; *D:* Richard Lester. **VHS, Beta, LV** $19.98 *WAR* 🎞️🎞️🎞️

Rivals Shallow, unconvincing drama about a stepfather challenged by his stepson, who wants to kill this new contender for his mother's love. Nice handling of cast credits, but other details—like acting, directing and photography—leave much to be desired.
1972 (R) 103m/C Robert Klein, Joan Hackett, Scott Jacoby; *D:* Krishna Shah. **VHS** $54.95 *TPI* 🎞️½

Rivals of the Dragon/ Magnificent Shaolin Fist Fighter Two action-packed oriental martial arts movies are crammed onto one tape, fairly bursting with head-kicking pleasure.
1979 176m/C **VHS, Beta** $7.00 *VTH* 🎞️½

Rivals of the Silver Fox Young kickers prove no match for their hoary, hard-chopping elder.
1980 90m/C Casanova Wong, Barry Lam, Chen Shao Ping, Lee Fat Yuen. **VHS, Beta** *NO* 🎞️½

The River A massively lauded late film by Renoir about three British girls growing up in Bengal, India, all developing crushes on a one-legged American vet. Lyrical and heartwarming, with hailed cinematography by Claude Renoir. Based on a novel by Rumer Godden; script by Godden and director Renoir. Satyajit Ray, who assisted Renoir, is one of India's greatest filmmakers.
1951 99m/C *FR* Patricia Walters, Adrienne Corri, Nora Swinburne, Radha, Arthur Shields, Thomas E. Breen; *D:* Jean Renoir. **VHS, Beta, LV** $79.95 *TAM, VYG, CRC* 🎞️🎞️🎞️

The River Farmers battle a river whose flood threatens their farm. Spacek, as always, is strong and believable as the wife and mother, but Gibson falters. Beautiful photography. The third in an onslaught of films in the early '80s that dramatized the plight of the small American farmer. "The River" isn't as strong as "Country" and "Places in the Heart" which managed to convey important messages less cloyingly.
1984 (PG) 124m/C Mel Gibson, Sissy Spacek, Scott Glenn, Billy Green Bush; *D:* Mark Rydell; *M:* John Williams. **VHS, Beta, LV** $19.95 *MCA* 🎞️🎞️

River Beat A woman aboard an American freighter is unwittingly used as diamond smuggler, and is arrested when the ship docks in London. An inspector does his best to clear the hapless woman.
1954 70m/B Phyllis Kirk, John Bentley, Robert Ayres, Lenny White, Glyn Houston, Charles Lloyd Pack; *D:* Guy Green. **VHS, Beta** $16.95 *SNC* 🎞️

The River Niger Jones is riveting, and Tyson is good in an otherwise muddling adaptation of the Tony-award winning play about black ghetto life. Realistic emotions and believable characters.
1976 (R) 105m/C James Earl Jones, Cicely Tyson, Glynn Turman, Louis Gossett Jr., Roger E. Mosley, Jonelle Allen; *D:* Krishna Shah. **VHS** *NO* 🎞️🎞️½

River of Death Absurd adventure, based on an Alistair McLean novel, about a white man entering the Amazon jungle world of a forgotten tribe in search of wealth, tripping over Neo-Nazi scientists and war criminals. Too complex to be harmlessly enjoyable; too mindless for the complexity to be worth unraveling.

1990 (R) 103m/C Michael Dudikoff, Robert Vaughn, Donald Pleasence, Herbert Lom, L.Q. Jones, Cynthia Erland, Sarah Maur-Thorp; *D:* Steve Carver. **VHS, Beta, LV** $14.95 *MGM, WAR* 🎬½

River of Diamonds A daring adventurer, with the standard beautiful woman at his side, battles evil curses and Nazis buried alive to find a fortune in diamonds. Yeah, sure. Another miserable "Indiana Jones" rip off.
1990 88m/C Dack Rambo, Angela O'Neill, Ferdinand "Ferdy" Mayne, Graham Clark, David Sherwood, Tony Caprari, Dominique Tyawa; *D:* Robert J. Smawley. **VHS, Beta** $79.98 *TTC* 🎬

River of Evil Action/adventure in which a young girl travels through the Amazon jungle searching for clues to her father's death.
1964 ?m/C Barbara Rutting, Harald Leipnitz. **VHS** $16.95 *SNC* 🎬½

River of No Return During the gold rush, an itinerant farmer and his young son help a heart-of-gold saloon singer search for her estranged husband. Rather crummy script is helped by the mere presence of Mitchum and Monroe. Marilyn sings the title song, "Down in the Meadow," and "I'm Going to File My Claim."
1954 91m/C Robert Mitchum, Marilyn Monroe, Tommy Rettig, Rory Calhoun, Murvyn Vye, Douglas Spencer; *D:* Otto Preminger. **VHS, Beta, LV** $14.98 *FOX* 🎬🎬½

River of Unrest Remarkable visual expressiveness and emotional power mark this depiction of terrorism and open warfare during the Irish Rebellion. Based on a play, hence slow; but good acting pulls it up half a bone. *AKA:* Ourselves Alone.
1937 69m/B John Lodge, John Loder, Antoinette Cellier. **VHS, Beta** $29.95 *VYY* 🎬🎬½

The River Rat Ex-con Jones is reunited with his daughter after spending thirteen years in prison. There's something in there about stashed loot that should have been jettisoned in favor of more getting-to-know-you father-daughter drama, which is good.
1984 (PG) 93m/C Tommy Lee Jones, Brian Dennehy, Martha Plimpton, Shawn Smith, Melissa Davis; *D:* Tom Rickman. **VHS, Beta, LV** $14.95 *PAR* 🎬🎬½

A River Runs Through It Contemplative exploration of family ties and coming of age with impact falling just short of the novel's is another well-crafted American tale directed by Redford. Set in Montana during the early part of the century, a Presbyterian minister teaches his two sons, one troubled and one on his way to success, about life and religion via fly-fishing. Based on the novel by Norman Maclean. The laser disc version includes commentary by Redford.
1992 (PG) 123m/C Craig Sheffer, Brad Pitt, Tom Skerritt, Brenda Blethyn, Emily Lloyd, Edie McClurg, Stephen Shellan; *D:* Robert Redford; *W:* Richard Friedenberg; *M:* Mark Isham. Academy Awards '92: Best Cinematography; Nominations: Best Adapted Screenplay, Best Original Score. **VHS, LV, 8mm** $94.95 *COL, CRC* 🎬🎬🎬½

Riverbend A renegade black Army major escapes a rigged court martial only to be persecuted by racist whites in a small Southern town. Made for television.
1989 (R) 106m/C Steve James, Tony Frank, Julius Tennon, Margaret Avery; *D:* Sam Firstenberg. **VHS, Beta** $89.95 *PAR* 🎬🎬

River's Edge A drug-addled high school student strangles his girlfriend and casually displays the corpse to his apathetic group of friends, who leave the murder unreported for days. Harrowing and gripping; based on a true story. Aging biker Hopper is splendid.

1987 (R) 99m/C Keanu Reeves, Crispin Glover, Daniel Roebuck, Joshua Miller, Dennis Hopper, Ione Skye, Roxana Zal; *D:* Tim Hunter. **VHS, Beta, LV, 8mm** $14.98 *SUE, NLC* 🎬🎬🎬

Road Agent Hoxie is the Kansas Kid, a fugitive hired by a crooked lawyer to pose as the long-lost heir to a ranching fortune. Only the Kid develops a soft spot for his "family" and may not be able to go through with the evil plot. *AKA:* Texas Road Agent.
1926 70m/B Al Hoxie; *D:* J.P. McGowan. **VHS, Beta** $19.95 *NOS, DVT, MLB* 🎬½

Road Games Trucker Keach is drawn into a web of intrigue surrounding a series of highway "Jack the Ripper"-style murders. Curtis is a hitchhiker. Nothing special. Director Franklin later helmed "Psycho II."
1981 (PG) 100m/C *AU* Stacy Keach, Jamie Lee Curtis; *D:* Richard Franklin. **VHS, Beta** $9.95 *COL, SUE, NLC* 🎬🎬

Road House Nightclub singer Lupino inspires noir feelings between jealous road house owner Widmark and his partner Wilde. Widmark sets up Wilde to take the fall for a faked robbery, convinces the law to release him into his custody, then dares him to escape.
1948 95m/B Richard Widmark, Ida Lupino, Cornel Wilde, Celeste Holm, O.Z. Whitehead; *D:* Jean Negulesco. **VHS, Beta** $19.98 *FOX, FCT* 🎬🎬½

Road House Bouncer Swayze is hired to do the impossible: clean up the toughest bar in Kansas City. When he lays down his rules he makes a lot of enemies, including ex-bar employees and local organized crime. Ample violence; an example of formula filmmaking at its most brain-numbing, with a rock soundtrack.
1989 (R) 115m/C Patrick Swayze, Sam Elliott, Kelly Lynch, Ben Gazzara, Kevin Tighe, Marshall Teague, Julie Michaels, Jeff Healey; *D:* Rowdy Herrington. **VHS, Beta, LV, 8mm** $19.98 *MGM* 🎬½

Road Lawyers and Other Briefs Several recent comedic shorts. "Road Lawyers," the title short, is a hilarious look at lawyers in a post-apocalyptic world that won major awards at film festivals in New York, Houston, Australia, and Chicago. Also included are: "Escape from Heaven," about a nun with an attitude problem; "Radar Men on the Moon," a comic reworking of an old "Commander Cody" serial; and "Hairline."
1989 79m/C **VHS** $79.95 *AIP* 🎬🎬½

Road Racers The roar of the engine, fast cars, and family ties combine in this movie about the thrill of speed.
1959 73m/B Joel Lawrence, Marian Collier, Skip Ward; *D:* Arthur Swerdloff; *W:* Stanley Kalis, Ed Lasko. **VHS** $9.95 *COL* 🎬🎬

The Road Runner vs. Wile E. Coyote: Classic Chase Wile E. Coyote engages in a battle of wits against the Road Runner in this collection of eight classic cartoons. Watching this entire tape straight through is almost a religious experience in the Zen of Futility.
1963 54m/C *D:* Chuck Jones. **VHS, Beta** $12.95 *WAR* 🎬🎬🎬

Road Show Menjou stars as a young man wrongfully committed to an insane asylum. He escapes and joins a bankrupt carnival owned by Landis. Some really zany stuff keeps this from being just standard fare. Co-written by silent film comic Harry Langdon.

1941 87m/B Adolphe Menjou, Carole Landis, John Hubbard, Charles Butterworth, Patsy Kelly, George E. Stone, Polly Ann Young, Edward Norris, Marjorie Woodworth, Florence Bates; *D:* Hal Roach. **VHS** $19.95 *NOS* 🎬🎬½

Road to Avonlea Based on Lucy Maud Montgomery's books, these endearing tales are set in Nova Scotia at the turn of the century, and focus on the heroine Sarah, who lives with her aunt, uncle, and cousins in a small country town. Beautiful cinematography and costuming enhance the stories which include characters from Montgomery's "Anne of Green Gables." Available on two tapes.
1990 120m/C *CA* **VHS** $150.00 *DCL* 🎬🎬🎬

The Road to Bali Sixth Bob-n-Bing road show, the only one in color, is a keeper. The boys are competing for the love of— that's right—Lamour. She must be some gal, cuz they chase her all the way to Bali, where they meet cannibals and other perils, including the actual Humphrey Bogart. Jones's debut, in a bit role. ♫Moonflowers; Chicago Style; Hoots Mon; To See You; The Merry-Go-Runaround; Chorale for Brass, Piano, and Bongo (instrumental).
1953 90m/C Bob Hope, Bing Crosby, Dorothy Lamour, Murvyn Vye, Ralph Moody, Jane Russell, Jerry Lewis, Dean Martin, Carolyn Jones; *D:* Hal Walker. **VHS, Beta** $29.95 *UNI, DVT, MLB* 🎬🎬🎬

The Road to Hong Kong Last of the Crosby/Hope team-ups shows some wear, but still manages charm and humor. Lamour appears only briefly in this twisted comedy of hustlers caught in international espionage and cosmic goings-on. ♫Teamwork; Let's Not Be Sensible; It's The Only Way to Travel; We're On the Road to Hong Kong; Warmer Than a Whisper.
1962 91m/B Bob Hope, Bing Crosby, Joan Collins, Dorothy Lamour, Peter Sellers; *D:* Norman Panama. **VHS** $19.98 *MGM, BTV, FCT* 🎬🎬½

The Road to Lebanon An original musical comedy featuring many stars, spoofing the famous Hope-Crosby "Road" films.
1960 50m/B Danny Thomas, Bing Crosby, Bob Hope, Hugh Downs, Claudine Auger, Sheldon Leonard. **VHS, Beta** $24.95 *NOS, VYY, DVT* 🎬🎬

The Road to Morocco The third in the road movie series finds Hope and Crosby in Morocco, stranded and broke. To get some money, Crosby sells Hope into slavery to be the princess's (Lamour) personal plaything. Feeling guilty, Crosby returns to the palace to rescue Hope, only to find that he and the princess are getting married because the royal astrologer said it was in the stars. Crosby then tries to woo Lamour and, when the astrologer discovers the stars were mistaken, those two decide to marry. Quinn, however, also wants her and hilarious scenes ensue when the boys rescue Lamour from him. One of the funniest in the series. Watch for the camel at the end. ♫Constantly; Moonlight Becomes You; Ain't Got a Dime to My Name; Road to Morocco.
1942 83m/C Bing Crosby, Bob Hope, Dorothy Lamour, Anthony Quinn, Dona Drake, Vladimir Sokoloff, Yvonne De Carlo; *D:* David Butler. **VHS, LV** $14.98 *MCA* 🎬🎬🎬½

Road to Nashville An agent travels to Nashville to enlist talent for a new musical. Why do so many of these semi-musicals insist on having a plot? Good music.
1967 (G) 110m/C Marty Robbins, Johnny Cash, Doodles Weaver, Connie Smith, Richard Arlen; *D:* Robert Patrick. **VHS, Beta** $29.95 *UHV* 🎬🎬

Road to 1984 Biodrama about futuristic author George Orwell centers on his classic "1984."
19?? 86m/C *GB* Edward Fox. **VHS $19.99** *PAR ♂♂½*

The Road to Rio The wisecracking duo travel to Rio De Janeiro to prevent Spanish beauty Lamour (there she is again) from going through with an arranged marriage. Top-notch entry; fifth in the "Road" series. ♫But Beautiful; You Don't Have To Know the Language; For What?; Experience; Apalachicola, Florida; Cavaquinho; Brazil.
1947 100m/B Bing Crosby, Bob Hope, Dorothy Lamour, Gale Sondergaard, Frank Faylen, The Andrews Sisters, The Wiere Brothers; *D:* Norman Z. MacLeod. **VHS, Beta $14.95** *COL ♂♂♂½*

The Road to Ruin The evils of smoking and drinking plummet a girl into a life of prostitution in this melodramatic, moralistic tale. An unintentional laugh-riot right up there with "Reefer Madness." Silent.
1928 45m/B Helen Foster, Grant Withers, Virginia Roye; *D:* Norton S. Parker. **VHS, Beta $16.95** *SNC, NOS, VYY ♂♂*

Road to Ruin A rich playboy pretends to lose all his money to see if his girlfriend loves him for himself or for his wealth. But when his business partner embezzles his fortune, he must regain both his money and his girlfriend's trust.
1991 (R) 94m/C Peter Weller, Carey Lowell, Michael Duchaussoy; *D:* Charlotte Brandstrom. **VHS $89.95** *LIV ♂♂*

Road to Salina A drifter is mistaken for (and might actually be) a desert-restaurant owner's long-lost son. He plays along, eventually seducing the family's daughter, who might be his sister.
1968 (R) 97m/C *FR* Robert Walker Jr., Rita Hayworth, Mimsy Farmer, Ed Begley Sr.; *D:* Georges Lautner. **VHS, Beta $59.95** *NLC ♂♂♂*

The Road to Singapore This is the movie that started it all. Crosby and Hope decide to swear off women and escape to Singapore to enjoy the free life. There they meet Lamour, a showgirl who is abused by Quinn. The boys rescue Lamour, but soon find they are both falling for her. She's in love with one of them, but won't reveal her feelings. Who will get the girl? Not as funny as some of the other road movies, but it's great for a first try. ♫Captain Custard; The Moon and the Willow Tree; Sweet Potato Piper; Too Romantic; Kaigoon.
1940 84m/C Bing Crosby, Bob Hope, Dorothy Lamour, Charles Coburn, Judith Barrett, Anthony Quinn, Jerry Colonna, Johnny Arthur, Pierre Watkin; *D:* Victor Schertzinger. **VHS, LV $14.98** *MCA ♂♂½*

The Road to Utopia Fourth of the "Road" films, wherein the boys wind up in Alaska posing as two famous escaped killers in order to locate a secret gold mine. One of the series' funniest and most spontaneous entries, abetted by Benchley's dry, uppercrust comments. ♫Put It There, Pal; Welcome to My Dreams; Would You?; Personality; Sunday, Monday, or Always?; Goodtime Charlie; It's Anybody's Spring.
1946 90m/B Bing Crosby, Bob Hope, Dorothy Lamour, Jack LaRue, Robert Benchley, Douglas Dumbrille, Hillary Brooke; *D:* Hal Walker. **VHS, Beta, LV $29.95** *MCA ♂♂♂*

The Road to Yesterday Two couples together on a crashing train are somehow thrown into the eighteenth century in roles parallel to their own lives. DeMille's first independent film; intriguing action/melodrama. Silent with musical soundtrack.

1925 136m/B Joseph Schildkraut, William Boyd, Jetta Goudal, Vera Reynolds, Iron Eyes Cody; *D:* Cecil B. DeMille. **VHS, Beta $49.95** *VYY, GPV ♂♂½*

Road to Yesterday/The Yankee Clipper Four train passengers are transported back to previous lives in "The Road to Yesterday." "The Yankee Clipper" races the British Lord of the Isles from China to New England to capture the tea trade. Both of these pictures are abridged versions. Silent.
1927 56m/B William Boyd, Elinor Fair, Joseph Schildkraut, Jetta Goudal, Vera Reynolds; *D:* Cecil B. DeMille. **VHS, Beta $29.95** *CCB ♂♂½*

The Road to Zanzibar After selling a fake diamond mine to a criminal, Crosby and Hope flee to Zanzibar, where they meet up with Lamour and Merkel. The guys put up the money for a safari, supposedly to look for Lamour's brother, but they soon discover that they too have been tricked. Deciding to head back to Zanzibar, Crosby and Hope find themselves surrounded by hungry cannibals. Will they survive, or will they be someone's dinner? Not as funny as the other road movies, but amusing nonetheless. ♫It's Always You; You're Dangerous; On the Road to Zanzibar; You Lucky People You; Birds of a Feather; African Etude.
1941 92m/C Bing Crosby, Bob Hope, Dorothy Lamour, Una Merkel, Eric Blore, Iris Adrian, Lionel Royce; *D:* Victor Schertzinger. **VHS, LV $14.98** *MCA ♂♂*

The Road Warrior The first sequel to "Mad Max" takes place after nuclear war has destroyed Australia. Max helps a colony of oil-drilling survivors defend themselves from the roving murderous outback gangs and escape to the coast. The climactic chase scene is among the most exciting ever filmed; this film virtually created the "action-adventure" picture of the 1980s.
1982 95m/C Mel Gibson, Bruce Spence, Emil Minty, Vernon Wells; *D:* George Miller. **VHS, Beta, LV $19.98** *WAR, PIA ♂♂♂½*

Roadhouse Girl A sexy woman kindles a romance with one of her husband's employees and the result is murder. Reminiscent of "The Postman Always Rings Twice," but with poor production values and performances. *AKA:* Marilyn.
1953 70m/B *GB* Maxwell Reed, Sandra Dorne, Leslie Dwyer, Hope, Ferdinand "Ferdy" Mayne; *W/D:* Wolf Rilla. **VHS, Beta $16.95** *SNC ♂*

Roadhouse 66 Utterly unoriginal brokedown-in-a-hick-town nonsense. Snooty Reinhold and scruffy Dafoe go through the motions, and of course find a pair of female companions. Soundtrack features Los Lobos, the Pretenders, and Dave Edmunds.
1984 (R) 90m/C Willem Dafoe, Judge Reinhold, Karen Lee, Kate Vernon, Stephen Elliott; *D:* John Mark Robinson. **VHS, Beta $79.98** *FOX ♂½*

Roadie Supposedly a look at the backstage world of rock n' roll, but the performances and direction leave a lot to be desired. Meatloaf is a roadie who desperately wants to meet Alice Cooper, and spends the movie trying to do so. Features Art Carney, and musical names like Blondie, Roy Orbison, Hank Williams, Jr. and Don Cornelius (of "Soul Train" fame).
1980 (PG) 105m/C Meatloaf, Kaki Hunter, Alan Carney, Art Carney, Gailard Sartain, Alice Cooper, Blondie, Roy Orbison, Hank Williams Jr., Ramblin' Jack Elliot; *D:* Alan Rudolph. **VHS $14.95** *MVD ♂½*

Roadkill Cheap thriller about Ramona (Buhagiar), a concert promoter who tries to find a lost band, "The Children of Paradise," in the Canadian north woods. Along the way,

she meets a would-be serial killer and other assorted weirdos.
1989 85m/B *CA* Valerie Buhagiar, Don McKellar, Bruce McDonald; *D:* Bruce McDonald; *W:* Don McKellar. **VHS $100.00** *CPL ♂*

Roads to the South One-time Spanish revolutionary turned screenwriter returns to his homeland to fight fascism, but finds himself attracted to his son's beautiful girlfriend. Much soul searching. In French with English subtitles.
1978 100m/C *FR* Yves Montand, Miou-Miou; *D:* Joseph Losey. **VHS, LV $59.95** *CVC, IME, FCT ♂♂½*

Roadside Prophets Counter-culture road trip, striving to be the '90s version of "Easy Rider," follows factory worker/biker Joe (Doe) on his mission to transport the ashes of a fellow biker to Nevada. He is accompanied by the pesky younger Sam (Horovitz), and together they meet up with lots of eccentrics and stay at lots of cheap motels. Interesting cast meanders through sentimental and slow-moving buddy flick from debut director Wool, who wrote "Sid and Nancy." Cusack completes the cameo hat trick, with appearances here and in 1992's "The Player" and "Shadows and Fog."
1992 (R) 96m/C John Doe, Adam Horovitz, David Carradine, Timothy Leary, Arlo Guthrie, Barton Heyman, Jennifer Balgobin; *Cameos:* John Cusack; *W/D:* Abbe Wool. **VHS, LV** *NLC ♂*

The Roamin' Cowboy In a town where the local ranchers are being threatened, a drifter comes to their rescue and wins both a girl and a job.
1937 56m/B Fred Scott, Al "Fuzzy" St. John, Lois January, Forrest Taylor, Roger Williams; *D:* Robert Hill. **VHS $19.95** *NOS, DVT ♂♂*

Roamin' Wild Exciting, action-packed early western with marshal Tyler saving a lady's stagecoach line from unsavory varmints.
1936 60m/B Tom Tyler, Carol Wyndham, Al Ferguson, George Chesebro, Max Davidson, Fred Parker; *D:* Bernard B. Ray. **VHS, Beta $19.95** *NOS, DVT ♂♂½*

Roanoak A dramatization in three parts of the mysterious fate of the early English settlement of Roanoak in North Carolina, which disappeared without a trace. Long, but intriguing. Made for PBS: "American Playhouse."
1986 180m/C Will Sampson, Victoria Racimo, Porky White, Adrian Sparks, Patrick Kilpatrick; *D:* Jan Egleson. **Beta $150.00** *PBS ♂♂½*

Roarin' Lead Three Mesquiteers fight with a gang of rustlers while helping the orphans' and cattlemen's associations.
1937 54m/B Bob Livingston, Ray Corrigan, Max Terhune. **VHS, Beta $19.95** *VCN ♂½*

Roaring City A hard-boiled detective searches for the person behind the murders of gangsters and prize fighters.
1951 58m/B Hugh Beaumont, Edward Brophy, Richard Travis; *D:* William Berke. **VHS, Beta, LV** *NO ♂½*

Roaring Fire Martial arts thriller set against the backdrop of exotic Japan.
1982 95m/C Sonny Chiba. **VHS, Beta $69.99** *HBO ♂½*

Roaring Guns An unflappable McCoy rides in to thwart a despicable landowner trying to drive all the small ranchers out of business. Low-budget fun.
1936 66m/B Tim McCoy, Rex Lease, Wheeler Oakman; *D:* Sam Newfield. **VHS, Beta $19.95** *NOS, VCN, DVT ♂♂½*

The Roaring Road Romantic comedy about a car salesman named Toodles, who drives for his company in a big race. Vintage racing footage; silent with original organ music.
1919 57m/B Wallace Reid, Ann Little, Theodore Roberts; *D:* James Cruze. **VHS, Beta, 8mm $24.99** *VYY, GPV ∦∦½*

Roaring Roads An heir to a fortune acquires a lust for race car driving, and his family thinks, a reckless death wish.
1935 60m/B Gertrude Messinger, David Sharpe. **VHS, Beta, LV** *NO ∦*

Roaring Six Guns Maynard protects his property against his crooked partner and his fiancee's father.
1937 60m/B Kermit Maynard, Mary Hayes, John Merton, Edward Cassidy. **VHS, Beta $19.95** *NOS, DVT, VCN ∦½*

Roaring Speedboats Bakewell is a speedboat racer up against crooks who want to con him out of his money by tinkering with his invention. *AKA:* Mile a Minute Love.
1937 62m/B William Bakewell, Arletta Duncan, Duncan Renaldo, Vivien Oakland, Wilfrid Lucas; *D:* Elmer Clifton. **VHS, Beta, 8mm $24.95** *VYY ∦*

The Roaring Twenties Three World War I buddies find their lives intersecting unexpectedly in Prohibition-era New York. Cagney becomes a bootlegger and vies with Bogart for status as crime boss. Lynn is the attorney working to prosecute them. Greatest of all gangster flicks established director Walsh's reputation. Cheesy script delivered with zest by top pros.
1939 106m/B James Cagney, Humphrey Bogart, Jeffrey Lynn, Priscilla Lane, Gladys George, Frank McHugh; *D:* Raoul Walsh. **VHS, Beta, LV $19.98** *MGM, FOX, PIA ∦∦∦½*

Rob Roy—The Highland Rogue In the early 18th century, Scottish Highlander Rob Roy must battle against the King of England's secretary, who would undermine the MacGregor clan to enact his evil deeds. Dull Disney drama. *AKA:* Rob Roy.
1953 84m/C Richard Todd, Glynis Johns, James Robertson Justice, Michael Gough; *D:* Harold French. **VHS, Beta $69.95** *DIS ∦½*

Robbers of the Sacred Mountain TV rip-off of "Raiders of the Lost Ark," loosely based on Arthur Conan Doyle's story "Challenger's Gold." Adventurers seek meteorites in the Mexican jungle. Billed as the first made for cable movie. *AKA:* Falcon's Gold.
1983 95m/C John Marley, Simon MacCorkindale, Louise Vallance, George Touliatos; *D:* Bob Schulz. **VHS, Beta $49.95** *PSM ∦∦*

Robbery Unoriginal but competent rendition of the hackneyed British Royal Mail robbery. Thieves plan and execute a heist of a late-night mail train carrying $10 million.
1967 113m/C *GB* Stanley Baker, James Booth, Joanna Pettet, Frank Finlay, Barry Foster; *D:* Peter Yates. **VHS, Beta $9.98** *NLC ∦∦½*

Robbery A six-man platoon of Vietnam war veterans endeavors to assault and rob a mob of shiftless bookies.
1985 91m/C John Sheerin, Tony Rickards, Tim Hughes; *D:* Michael Thornhill. **VHS, Beta $69.98** *LIV ∦*

Robbery Under Arms From Australia in the 1800s, similar to the American wild west, comes a tale of love and robbery. Finch is the leader of a band of outlaws. Rather dull story redeemed by excellent photography of beautiful landscape.
1957 83m/C *GB* Peter Finch, Ronald Lewis, Laurence Naismith, Maureen Swanson, David McCallum, Jill Ireland; *D:* Jack Lee. **VHS $79.95** *IMP ∦∦½*

Robby A young white boy and a young black boy shipwrecked on an island form a strong friendship that sees them through a series of adventures.
1968 60m/C Warren Raum, Ryp Siani, John Garces; *D:* Ralph Blumke. **VHS, Beta** *FCT ∦∦*

Robby the Rascal The evil Mr. Bullion devises a plan to steal a cybot, Robby the Rascal, from his inventor Dr. Rumplechips.
1985 90m/C VHS, Beta $24.95 *PAR, WTA ∦∦*

The Robe This moving, religious portrait follows the career and religious awakening of drunken and dissolute Roman tribune Marcellus (Burton), after he wins the robe of the just-crucified Christ in a dice game. Mature plays Burton's slave surprisingly well, and reprised the role in the sequel, "Demetrius and the Gladiators"; Burton is wooden. "The Robe" was the first movie to be filmed in CinemaScope. Based on the novel by Lloyd C. Douglas.
1953 133m/C Richard Burton, Jean Simmons, Victor Mature, Michael Rennie, Richard Boone, Dean Jagger, Jeff Morrow, Jay Robinson, Dawn Addams, Ernest Thesiger; *D:* Henry Koster. Academy Awards '53: Best Art Direction/Set Decoration (Color), Best Costume Design (Color); Nominations: Best Actor (Burton), Best Color Cinematography, Best Picture; Golden Globe Awards '54: Best Film—Drama; National Board of Review Awards '53: 10 Best Films of the Year, Best Actress (Simmons). **VHS, Beta, LV $19.98** *FOX, IGP ∦∦½*

Robert et Robert Two 'ineligible' bachelors resort to using a computerized matrimonial agency to find the girls of their dreams. They become friends while they wait for their dates. Sensitive tale of loneliness and friendship. Warm and witty with fine performances throughout. French with English subtitles.
1979 95m/C *FR* Charles Denner, Jacques Villeret, Jean-Claude Brialy; *D:* Claude Lelouch. **VHS, Beta $59.95** *COL ∦∦∦*

Robert Kennedy and His Times Another look at the Kennedy clan, this time from the Bobby angle. Good acting. Based on the book by Arthur Schlesinger.
1990 335m/C Brad Davis, Veronica Cartwright, Cliff DeYoung, Ned Beatty, Beatrice Straight, Jack Warden; *D:* Marvin J. Chomsky. **VHS $59.95** *COL ∦∦½*

Roberta A football player inherits his aunt's Parisian dress shop and finds himself at odds with an incognito Russian princess. Dumb plot aside, this is one of the best Astaire-Rogers efforts. A later remake was titled "Lovely to Look At." ♫Let's Begin; Yesterdays; Smoke Gets in Your Eyes; I'll Be Hard to Handle; I Won't Dance; Lovely To Look At; Back Home Again in Indiana; The Touch of Your Hand; You're Devasting; Don't Ask Me Not To Sing.
1935 85m/B Fred Astaire, Ginger Rogers, Irene Dunne, Lucille Ball, Randolph Scott; *D:* William A. Seiter. **VHS, Beta $19.98** *MGM ∦∦*

Robin and Marian After a separation of twenty years, Robin Hood is reunited with Maid Marian, who is now a nun. Their dormant feelings for each other are reawakened as Robin spirits her to Sherwood Forest. In case you wanted to see Robin Hood robbed of all magic, spontaneity, and fun. Connery is dull, dull, dull, working with an uninspired script.
1976 (PG) 106m/C *GB* Sean Connery, Audrey Hepburn, Robert Shaw, Richard Harris; *D:* Richard Lester; *M:* John Barry. **VHS, Beta, LV $19.95** *COL, FOX ∦∦*

Robin and the Seven Hoods Runyon-esque Rat Pack version of 1920s Chicago, with Frank and the boys as do-good gangsters in their last go-round. Fun if not unforgettable. ♫Bang! Bang!; Style; Mister Booze; Don't Be a Do-Badder; My Kind of Town.
1964 124m/C Frank Sinatra, Bing Crosby, Dean Martin, Sammy Davis Jr., Peter Falk, Barbara Rush, Allen Jenkins; *D:* Gordon Douglas. **VHS, Beta, LV $19.98** *WAR, PIA ∦∦½*

Robin Hood Extravagant production casts Fairbanks as eponymous gymnastic swashbuckler who departs for Crusades as Earl of Huntington and returns as the hooded one to save King Richard's throne from the sinister Sheriff of Nottingham. Best ever silent swashbuckling. *AKA:* Douglas Fairbanks in Robin Hood.
1922 110m/B Douglas Fairbanks Sr., Wallace Beery, Sam DeGrasse, Enid Bennett, Paul Dickey, William E. Lowery, Roy Coulson, Bill Bennett, Merrill McCormick, Wilson Benge, Willard Louis, Alan Hale Jr., Maine Geary, Lloyd Talman; *D:* Allan Dwan. **VHS, Beta $19.95** *NOS, GPV, FCT ∦∦∦½*

Robin Hood This time the Sherwood Forest crew are portrayed by appropiate cartoon animals, hence, Robin is a fox, Little John a bear, etc. Good family fare, but not as memorable as other Disney features.
1973 83m/C *D:* Wolfgang Reitherman; *V:* Roger Miller, Brian Bedford, Monica Evans, Phil Harris, Andy Devine, Carol Shelley, Peter Ustinov, Terry-Thomas, Pat Buttram, George Lindsey, Ken Curtis. **VHS, Beta, LV $24.99** *DIS, FCT, RDG ∦∦∦*

Robin Hood An animated version of the classic legend.
1985 60m/C VHS, Beta *NO ∦∦∦*

Robin Hood Dark version of the medieval tale. Bergin's Prince of Thieves is well developed and Thurman is a graceful Marion. Three studios announced plans to remake "Robin Hood" in 1990 and two were completed, including this one which was scaled down for cable television.
1991 116m/C Patrick Bergin, Uma Thurman, Juergen Prochnow, Edward Fox, Jeroen Krabbe; *D:* John Irvin. **VHS, Beta, LV $89.98** *FXV, FCT ∦∦∦*

Robin Hood: Men in Tights Brooksian rendition of the classic legend inspires guffaws, but doesn't hit the bullseye on all it promises. Hood afficiandos will appreciate the painstaking effort taken to spoof the 1938 Errol Flynn classic while leaving plenty of room to poke fun at the more recent Costner non-classic "Robin Hood: Prince of Thieves." Elwes, last seen swinging swords in "The Princess Bride," is well cast as the Flynn look-alike. Expect the usual off-color humor that's so prevalent in all Brooks outings. *AKA:* Men in Tights.
1993 (PG-13) ?m/C Cary Elwes, Richard Lewis, Roger Rees, Amy Yasbeck, Dave Chappelle, Isaac Hayes, Tracy Ullman, Mark Blankfield, Megan Cavanagh, Eric Allen Kramer, Tony Griffin, Dick Van Patten, Mel Brooks; *W/D:* Mel Brooks; *W:* J. David Shapiro; *M:* Hummie Mann. **VHS** *NYR ∦∦½*

Robin Hood of Texas Autry finds his calm life disturbed when he is falsely accused of robbing a bank. Pretty good plot for once, in Autry's last Republic western, and plenty of action.
1947 71m/B Gene Autry, The Cass County Boys, Lynn (Mary Hart) Roberts, Sterling Holloway, Adele Mara; *D:* Lesley Selander. **VHS, Beta $29.95** *CCB, VCN ∦½*

Robin Hood of the Pecos Ex-Confederate soldier takes on northern post-war politicians and carpetbaggers. Decent Rogers/Hayes outing.
1941 56m/B Roy Rogers, George "Gabby" Hayes, Marjorie Reynolds, Jay Novello, Roscoe Ates; *D:* Joseph Kane. **VHS, Beta $19.95** NOS, DVT, VYY ☾☾½

Robin Hood: Prince of Thieves Costner is the politically correct Rebel with a Cause, but a thinker, not a doer—and therein lies the problem. His quiet thoughtfulness doesn't add up to leadership. Rickman easily overpowers him as the wicked, crazed Sheriff of Nottingham. Freeman is excellent as a civilized Moor who finds England, and its people, inhospitable, dangerous, and not a little stupid. Mastrantonio, a last minute choice, excels as the lovely Lady Marian. Great action sequences, a gritty and morbid picture of the Middle Ages, and some fun scenes with the Merry Men. Revisionist in its ideas about the times and people, critics generally disapproved of the changes in the story and Costner's performance, though their comments about his lack of an English accent seem nitpicky in light of some basic plot problems. Still has lots of fun for lovers of action, romance and fairy tales.
1991 (PG-13) 144m/C Kevin Costner, Morgan Freeman, Mary Elizabeth Mastrantonio, Christian Slater, Alan Rickman, Geraldine McEwan, Micheal McShane, Brian Blessed, Michael Wincott, Nick Brimble, Harold Innocent, Jack Wild; *Cameos:* Sean Connery; *D:* Kevin Reynolds; *W:* Pen Densham, John Watson; *M:* Michael Kamen. Academy Awards '91 Nominations: Best Song ("(Everything I Do) I Do It for You"); British Academy Awards '92: Best Supporting Actor (Rickman); MTV Movie Awards '92: Best Song ("(Everything I Do) I Do for You"). **VHS, LV $19.98** WAR, PIA, RDG ☾☾½

Robin Hood: The Movie A colorized and re-mixed version of several episodes of the British television series adds up to a fine version of the classic tale. Excellent cast, clever editing and stunning colorization.
1955 90m/C *GB* Richard Greene, Bernadette O'Farrell, Alan Wheatley; *D:* Ralph Smart, Daniel Birt, Terence Fisher. **VHS $14.99** GKK ☾☾½

Robin Hood...The Legend: Herne's Son When Robin Hood is killed by the Sheriff of Nottingham, he begs Robert of Huntington (Connery) to continue his work. Connery refuses, the band dissolves, Maid Marion is kidnapped, and they reunite to save her. Good entry in the BBC series.
1985 101m/C *GB* Jason Connery, Oliver Cotton, Michael Craig, Nickolas Grace, George Baker; *D:* Robert M. Young. **VHS, Beta $14.98** FOX, FCT, TVC ☾☾½

Robin Hood...The Legend: Robin Hood and the Sorcerer Robin Hood is chosen by the mystical Herne the Hunter to thwart the evil Sheriff of Nottingham and protect the English peasantry. He must defeat the supernatural powers of a sorcerer and gather together his men in this introduction to the made for British television series.
1983 115m/C *GB* Michael Praed, Anthony Valentine, Nickolas Grace, Clive Mantle, Peter Williams; *D:* Ian Sharp. **VHS $14.98** FOX, FCT, TVC ☾☾½

Robin Hood...The Legend: The Swords of Wayland A wicked sorceress provides a supernatural threat to Robin and his merry men. Second entry in the BBC series. Convoluted, breathless plot makes for swashbuckling fun and much derring-do.
1983 115m/C *GB* Michael Praed, Rula Lenska, Nickolas Grace; *D:* Robert M. Young. **VHS, Beta $14.98** FOX, FCT ☾☾½

Robin Hood...The Legend: The Time of the Wolf Robin Hood finds out that an old enemy is about to release his evil doings on the world and only he can stop him, while Maid Marian comes to a momentous decision.
1985 105m/C *GB* Jason Connery, Nickolas Grace, Richard O'Brien; *D:* Syd Roberson. **VHS, Beta $14.98** FOX, FCT, TVC ☾☾½

Robinson Crusoe A real oddity: a British silent film originally made in 1927, re-edited ten years later. Music and sound effects were added, along with a narration by children's radio personality Carney. Follows the plot of the famous adventure story by Daniel Defoe.
1936 34m/B VHS, Beta $11.98 VYY ☾☾

Robinson Crusoe The classic survival story by Daniel Defoe is retold with animation.
1972 48m/C VHS, Beta $19.95 MGM, WTA ☾☾

Robinson Crusoe An animated adaptation of the classic Daniel Defoe story about a man marooned on a small island.
1978 86m/C VHS, Beta $11.95 FHE ☾☾

Robinson Crusoe & the Tiger A tiger tells the famous story of how Robinson Crusoe became stranded on a desert island.
1972 (G) 109m/C Hugo Stiglitz, Ahui; *D:* Rene Cardona Jr. **VHS, Beta $29.98** SUE ☾½

Robinson Crusoe of Clipper Island Fourteen-episodes serial featuring the investigative expertise of Mala, a Polynesian in the employ of the U.S. Intelligence Service. Each episode runs 16 minutes. Shortened version titled "Robinson Crusoe of Mystery Island."
1936 256m/B Ray Mala, Rex, Buck, Kate Greenfield, John Ward, Tracy Lane, Robert Kortman, Herbert Rawlinson; *D:* Mack V. Wright. **VHS, LV $26.95** SNC, NOS, REP ☾☾

Robinson Crusoe of Mystery Island A Polynesian employed by the U.S. Intelligence Service investigates saboteurs on a mysterious island. Would-be cliffhanger is a yawner; where are the chills and thrills? Edited from the serial "Robinson Crusoe of Clipper Island."
1936 100m/B Mala, Rex, Buck, Herbert Rawlinson, Ray Taylor; *D:* Mack V. Wright. **VHS, Beta $27.95** VCN ☾☾

Robo-Chic A woman who is part cop, part machine, becomes a defender of justice.
1989 90m/C Kathy Shower, Jack Carter, Julie Newmar, Burt Ward, Lyle Waggoner. **VHS, Beta** AIP ☾☾

RoboCop A nearly dead Detroit cop is used as the brain for a crime-fighting robot in this bleak vision of the future. Humor, satire, action, and violence keep this moving in spite of its underlying sadness. Slick animation techniques from Phil Tippet. Verhoeven's first American film.
1987 (R) 103m/C Peter Weller, Nancy Allen, Ronny Cox, Kurtwood Smith, Ray Wise, Miguel Ferrer; *D:* Paul Verhoeven. **VHS, Beta, LV, SVS $14.98** ORI, SUP ☾☾☾

RoboCop 2 Grimer, more violent sequel to the initial fascinating look at the future, where police departments are run by corporations hungry for profit at any cost. A new and highly addictive drug has made Detroit more dangerous than ever. Robocop is replaced by a stronger cyborg with the brain of a brutal criminal. When the cyborg goes berserk, Robocop battles it and the drug lords for control of the city. Dark humor and graphic savagery, with little of the tenderness and emotion of the original.

1990 (R) 117m/C Peter Weller, Nancy Allen, Belinda Bauer, Dan O'Herlihy, Tommy Noonan, Gabriel Damon, Galyn Gorg, Felton Perry, Patricia Charbonneau; *D:* Irvin Kershner. **VHS, Beta, LV $14.98** ORI ☾☾

Roboman American scientist gets in car crash in Soviet Union. When he returns to the States as a cyborg, his friends seem to notice a change. *AKA:* Who?.
1975 (PG) 91m/C *GB GE* Elliott Gould, Trevor Howard, Joe Bova, Ed Grover, James Noble, John Lehne; *D:* Jack Gold. **VHS** ACE, MTX ☾☾½

Robot Holocaust Somewhere in the doomed future, after the Earth is laid waste by robots with superior intelligence, a human survivor dares to challenge them. If you're doomed to watch this, you just might survive; it's so-so, unsurprisingly sci-fi.
1987 79m/C Norris Culf, Nadine Hart, Joel von Ornsteiner, Jennifer Delora, Andrew Howarth, Angelika Jager, Rick Gianasi; *W/D:* Tim Kincaid. **VHS, Beta $69.95** UHV ☾☾

Robot Jox Two futuristic warriors battle to the finish in giant mechanical robots. Preteen fare.
1989 (PG) 84m/C Gary Graham, Anne-Marie Johnson, Paul Koslo, Robert Sampson, Danny Kamekona, Hilary Mason, Michael Allredge; *D:* Stuart Gordon. **VHS, LV $14.95** COL, PIA ☾½

Robot Monster Ludicrous cheapie is widely considered one of the worst films of all time, as a single alien dressed in a moth-eaten gorilla suit and diving helmet conspires to take over the Earth from his station in a small, bubble-filled California cave. Available in original 3-D format. *AKA:* Monsters From the Moon.
1953 62m/B George Nader, Claudia Barrett, Gregory Moffett, Selena Royle; *D:* Phil Tucker. **VHS, Beta, LV $12.95** RHI, SVS, FCT ☾☾½

Robot Ninja A comic-book ninja comes to life to destroy criminals. Good genre cast.
1989 (R) 90m/C Michael Todd, Linnea Quigley, Burt Ward. **VHS** PHX ☾½

Robot Pilot Tucker stars as a WWII test pilot trying to promote a friend's invention. Along the way, he's involved in a subplot with enemy agents who steal a bomber. He also finds time to become romantically entangled with the boss' spoiled daughter. *AKA:* Emergency Landing.
1941 68m/B Forrest Tucker, Carol Hughes, Evelyn Brent, Emmett Vogan, William Halligan; *D:* William Beaudine. **VHS, Beta, 8mm $29.95** VYY, SNC ☾

The Robot vs. the Aztec Mummy Grade-Z Mexican horror film pits a jealous mummy who guards a tomb against tomb robbers and the robot they invent. Special effects are laughable today—the robot's ears are lightbulbs—but true mummy movie fans might want to watch this one. Everyone else will probably be better off skipping it. *AKA:* El Robot Humano; La Momia Azteca Contra el Robot Humano; The Aztec Mummy.
1959 65m/B *MX* Ramon Gay, Rosita Arenas, Crox Alvarado, Luis Aceves Cantaneda, Emma Rolden; *D:* Rafael Portillo; *W:* Alfredo Salazar. **VHS, Beta $19.98** SNC, AOV, MRV Woof!

Robot Wars When what seems to be the last mega-robot on earth falls into enemy hands, a renegade pilot unearths another with the help of an engineer and archeologist to fight for the future of mankind.
1993 (PG) 106m/C Don Michael Paul, Barbara Crampton, James Staley, Lisa Rinna, Danny Kamekona, Yuji Okumoto, J. Downing, Peter Haskell; *D:* Albert Band. **VHS, Beta, LV** PAR ☾☾

Robotix This is a feature-length animated film starring a bunch of robots who struggle to save the universe from evil forces.
1986 90m/C VHS, Beta $69.98 *LIV, VES, WTA* 🐾🐾

Robotman & Friends 2: I Want to be Your Robotman This is another entry in the children's animated series about robots who fight the denizens of evil.
1986 42m/C VHS, Beta $19.98 *LIV, WTA* 🐾🐾

Rocco and His Brothers A modern classic from top director Visconti, about four brothers who move with their mother from the Italian countryside to Milan. Very long, sometimes ponderous, but engrossing, complex drama. Available shortened to 90 minutes, but the unedited version is much more rewarding. In Italian with English subtitles.
AKA: Rocco et Ses Freres.
1960 175m/B *IT* Alain Delon, Renato Salvatori, Annie Girardot, Katina Paxinou, Claudia Cardinale, Roger Hanin; *D:* Luchino Visconti.
VHS, LV $29.95 *VDM, TAM* 🐾🐾🐾½

Rock-a-Doodle Little Edmond is knocked out during a storm and has Elvis-influenced vision. He sees Chanticleer, the sun-raising rooster, tricked into neglecting his duties by an evil barnyard owl. Humiliated and scorned, earnest young fowl leaves the farm and winds up in a Las Vegas-like city as an Elvis-impersonating singer (complete with pompadour) where he meets with success and all its trappings, including a hound-dog pal, an unscrupulous manager, and a cute little chick as a girlfriend. Meanwhile, back at the farm things aren't going so well, and Chanticleer's friends realize that he is the only one who can help. Mildly amusing, but bland by today's standards of animation, with music which is certainly nothing to crow about.
1992 (G) 77m/C *D:* Don Bluth; *W:* David A. Weiss; *V:* Glen Campbell, Christopher Plummer, Phil Harris, Sandy Duncan, Ellen Greene, Charles Nelson Reilly, Eddie Deezen, Sorrell Booke. VHS, LV $24.98 *HBO, WTA* 🐾🐾½

Rock All Night Typically trashy Corman quickie (filmed in five days on one set) about some wild fifties teens and, in this case, a couple of murderers. Seems Cloud Nine, the local teen hangout, is invaded by a couple of murderers who hold the kids hostage. It's up to the hipster bartender, known as Shorty because he's five-foot-one, to save the day. Unrelated concert footage of The Platters and The Blockbusters opens the film.
1957 62m/B Dick Miller, Abby Dalton, Russell Johnson, Jonathan Haze, Robin Morse; *D:* Roger Corman. VHS $9.95 *COL, MOV* 🐾🐾

Rock & Roll Cowboys Set in the near-future. Mickey LaGrange is a roadie who has dreams of playing his own songs and becoming a rock and roll star himself. When he meets the mysterious Damien Shard he just may get the opportunity and a lot more besides. Shard is the inventor of an instrument that taps directly into the brain to transform thought into music. When Mickey uses the instrument he becomes an instant success—until he notices some horrifying side effects.
1992 83m/C Peter Phelps, David Franklin, John Doyle; *D:* Robert Stewart. VHS $59.95 *HMD, MOV* 🐾

Rock & Rule Animated sword & sorcery epic with a rock soundtrack. Voices are provided by Deborah Harry, Cheap Trick, Lou Reed, and Iggy Pop.
1983 85m/C *D:* Clive A. Smith; *M:* Deborah Harry, Cheap Trick, Lou Reed, Iggy Pop; *V:* Paul LeMat, Catherine O'Hara. VHS, Beta, LV $79.95 *MGM* 🐾🐾

Rock & the Money-Hungry Party Girls A struggling musician battles against Gabor-sister-worshiping bimbos in an effort to find unpublished songs by a '50s music legend.
1989 90m/C Paul Sercu, Adam Small, Judi Durand, Mary Baldwin, Debra Lamb; *D:* Kurt MacCarley. VHS, Beta *NO* 🐾

Rock, Baby, Rock It Weak and silly rock-and-roll crime drama about teens trying to fight the Mafia in Dallas in 1957. Features performances by many regional bands including Kay Wheeler, the Cell Block Seven, Johnny Carroll, Preacher Smith and the Deacons, and the Five Stars. If you grew up in Dallas in the '50s, the musical groups may bring back some fond memories; otherwise, this obscure film probably isn't worth your time.
1957 84m/B Kay Wheeler, John Carroll; *D:* Murray Douglas Sporup. VHS, Beta $59.95 *RHI* 🐾

Rock House When an L.A. narcotics officer's wife is murdered by drug runners he goes on an obsessive revenge mission to destroy the city's cocaine operations.
1992 97m/C Joseph Jennings, Michael Robbin, Alan Shearer; *W/D:* Jack Vacek. VHS $89.95 *CHV, HMD* 🐾🐾

Rock 'n' Roll High School The music of the Ramones highlights this non-stop high-energy cult classic about a high school out to thwart the principal at every turn. If it had been made in 1957, it would have been the ultimate rock 'n' roll teen movie. As it is, its 1970s' milieu works against it, but the performances are perfect for the material and the Ramones are great. Songs include "Teenage Lobotomy," "Blitzkrieg Bop," "I Wanna Be Sedated" and the title track, among others. Followed less successfully by "Rock 'n' Roll High School Forever."
1979 (PG) 94m/C The Ramones, P.J. Soles, Vincent Van Patten, Clint Howard, Dey Young, Mary Woronov, Alix Elias, Dick Miller, Paul Bartel; *D:* Allan Arkush. VHS, Beta $64.95 *MVD* 🐾🐾🐾

Rock 'n' Roll High School Forever Jesse Davis and his band just want to rock 'n' roll, but the new principal doesn't share their enthusiasm. Way late, way lame sequel to "Rock 'n' Roll High School" doesn't even come close to the originality that made it a cult classic. Soundtrack includes music from The Divinyls, Dee Dee Ramone, Mojo Nixon, Will and the Bushmen, The Pursuit of Happiness, and more.
1991 (PG-13) 94m/C Corey Feldman, Mary Woronov, Mojo Nixon, Evan Richards, Michael Cerveris, Michael Ceveris, Mojo Nixon, Patrick Malone, Patrick Malone, Larry Linville, Sarah Buxton; *W/D:* Deborah Brock. VHS, Beta, LV $89.95 *LIV, IME* 🐾

Rock 'n' Roll Nightmare A rock band is pursued by demons from another dimension. The usual lame garbage. *AKA:* The Edge of Hell.
1985 (R) 89m/C *CA* Jon Mikl Thor, Paula Francescatto, Rusty Hamilton; *D:* John Fasano. VHS, Beta $29.95 *ACA* 🐾½

Rock, Pretty Baby Early rock-'n'-roll movie about a teenage band and high school riots.
1956 89m/B Sal Mineo, John Saxon, Rod McKuen, Luanna Patten, Fay Wray, Edward Platt; *D:* Richard Bartlett. VHS, Beta $14.95 *KRT* 🐾

Rock River Renegades The Range Busters capture a band of renegades and restore peace to the territory once more.
1942 59m/B Ray Corrigan, John "Dusty" King. VHS, Beta $19.95 *NOS, DVT* 🐾

Rock, Rock, Rock A young girl tries to earn enough money for a prom gown after her father closes her charge account. Screen debut of Tuesday Weld. Ultra-low-budget, but a classic after a fashion. Includes classic musical numbers performed by Chuck Berry and other rock'n'roll pioneers.
1956 78m/B Alan Freed, Chuck Berry, Fats Domino, Tuesday Weld, Frankie Lymon & the Teenagers; *D:* Will Price. VHS, Beta $12.95 *MVD, MED, MRV* 🐾🐾½

Rocket Attack U.S.A. Antiquated and ridiculous tale of nuclear warfare about the time of Sputnik, with Russia's first strike blowing up New York City and environs. Mercifully short, with time for a little romance. Everything about this movie is so bad it's good for a laugh.
1958 70m/B Monica Davis, John McKay, Dan Kern, Edward Czerniuk, Art Metrano; *D:* Barry Mahon. VHS, Beta $14.95 *SVS* Woof!

Rocket Gibraltar On the occasion of a crusty patriarch's birthday, a large family unites on his remote estate to carry out his special birthday wish. Fine performance by Lancaster. Supported by a solid cast, overcomes a slim story, Culkin, later of "Home Alone," is loveable as the precocious five-year-old. Picturesque Long Island scenery.
1988 (PG) 92m/C Burt Lancaster, Bill Pullman, John Glover, Suzy Amis, Macaulay Culkin; *D:* Daniel Petrie; *W:* Amos Poe. VHS, Beta $14.95 *COL* 🐾🐾🐾

Rocket to the Moon An adaptation of the Clifford Odets story about the mundane life of a 30-year-old Manhattan dentist and how he comes to terms with his life. From the PBS "American Playhouse" series.
1986 118m/C Judy Davis, John Malkovich, Eli Wallach; *D:* John Jacobs. VHS, Beta $59.95 *ACA, PBS* 🐾🐾

The Rocketeer Lightheaded fun. A stunt flyer in the 1930s finds a prototype jet backpack sought by Nazi spies. Donning a mask, he becomes a flying superhero. Breezy family entertainment with stupendous effects; even better if you know movie trivia, as it brims with Hollywood references, like a great villain (Dalton) clearly based on Errol Flynn.
1991 (PG) 109m/C Bill Campbell, Jennifer Connelly, Alan Arkin, Timothy Dalton, Paul Sorvino; *D:* Joe Johnston. VHS, Beta, LV $19.99 *DIS, CCB, IME* 🐾🐾🐾

Rocketship Flash Gordon battles sea monsters, ray guns, and robots in this sci-fi adventure.
1936 ?m/B Buster Crabbe, Jean Rogers, Charles Middleton. VHS $15.95 *LOO, HEG* 🐾🐾

Rocketship X-M A lunar mission goes awry and the crew lands on Mars, where they discover ancient ruins. Well acted and nicely photographed. Contains footage, a tinted sequence and previews of coming attractions from classis science fiction files. *AKA:* Expedition Moon.
1950 77m/B Lloyd Bridges, Osa Massen, John Emery, Hugh O'Brian, Noah Beery Jr.; *D:* Kurt Neumann. VHS, Beta, LV $19.95 *MED, RXM* 🐾🐾½

Rockin' Road Trip A guy meets a girl in a Boston bar, and finds himself on a drunken, slapstick road trip down the Eastern seaboard with a rock band.
1985 (PG-13) 101m/C Garth McLean, Katherine Harrison, Margeret Currie, Steve Boles. VHS, Beta $79.98 *FOX* 🐾

Rockin' Ronnie A rough, sophomoric, uproarious send-up of President Reagan, using news footage of him and of Queen Elizabeth, Ayatollah Khomeini, Jayne Mansfield, and other figures.
1987 45m/C VHS, Beta $19.98 *MPI* 🎬🎬½

The Rocking Horse Winner Poignant tale of a young boy who tries to keep his parents from splitting up by predicting horse race winners. His mother's greed spurs tragedy. Based on the short story by D.H. Lawrence.
1950 91m/B Kenneth More; *D:* Peter Meda. **VHS, Beta, 3/4U $59.95** *LCA, FLI* 🎬🎬½

Rocktober Blood A convicted and executed rock star comes back from the grave and starts killing people all over again. Yet another gorefest.
1985 (R) 88m/C Donna Scoggins, Tray Loren, Nigel Benjamin, Beverly Sebastian; *D:* Ferd Sebastian. **VHS, Beta $19.98** *LIV, VES* 🎬½

Rockula Teen rock comedy about a young-yet-300-year-old vampire looking to lose his virginity. Recommended only for hard-core Diddley fans.
1990 (PG-13) 90m/C Dean Cameron, Bo Diddley, Tawny Fere, Susan Tyrrell, Thomas Dolby, Toni Basil; *D:* Luca Bercovici. **VHS, Beta, LV $14.95** *MGM, WAR* 🎬½

Rocky Box office smash about a young man from the slums of Philadelphia who dreams of becoming a boxing champion. Stallone wrote the script and plays Rocky, the underdog hoping to win fame and self-respect. Rags-to-riches story seems to parallel Stallone's life; he had been previously virtually unknown before this movie. Intense portrayal of the American Dream; loses strength in the subsequent (and numerous) sequels. Powerful score by Bill Conti.
1976 (PG) 125m/C Sylvester Stallone, Talia Shire, Burgess Meredith, Burt Young, Carl Weathers; *D:* John G. Avildsen; *M:* Bill Conti. Academy Awards '76: Best Director (Avildsen), Best Film Editing, Best Picture; Nominations: Best Actor (Stallone), Best Actress (Shire), Best Original Screenplay, Best Song ("Gonna Fly Now"), Best Sound, Best Supporting Actor (Meredith, Young); Directors Guild of America Awards '76: Best Director (Avildsen); Golden Globe Awards '77: Best Film—Drama; Los Angeles Film Critics Association Awards '76: Best Film; National Board of Review Awards '76; 10 Best Films of the Year, Best Supporting Actress (Shire). **VHS, Beta, LV, 0mm $19.98** *MGM, FOX, BTV* 🎬🎬½

Rocky 2 Time-marking sequel to the box office smash finds Rocky frustrated by the commercialism which followed his match to Apollo, but considering a return bout. Meanwhile, his wife fights for her life. The overall effect is to prepare you for the next sequel.
1979 (PG) 119m/C Sylvester Stallone, Talia Shire, Burt Young, Burgess Meredith, Carl Weathers; *D:* Sylvester Stallone. **VHS, Beta, LV $19.98** *MGM, FOX* 🎬½

Rocky 3 Rocky is beaten by big, mean Clubber Lang (played to a tee by Mr. T). He realizes success has made him soft, and has to dig deep to find the motivation to stay on top. Amazingly, Stallone regains his underdog persona here, looking puny next to Mr. T, who is the best thing about the second-best "Rocky" flick.
1982 (PG) 103m/C Sylvester Stallone, Talia Shire, Burgess Meredith, Carl Weathers, Mr. T, Leif Erickson, Burt Young; *D:* Sylvester Stallone. **VHS, Beta, LV $19.98** *MGM, FOX* 🎬🎬½

Rocky 4 Rocky travels to Russia to fight the Soviet champ who killed his friend during a bout. Will Rocky knock the Russkie out? Will Rocky get hammered on the head a great many times and sag around the ring? Will Rocky ever learn? Lundgren isn't nearly as much fun as some of Rocky's former opponents and Stallone overdoes the hyper-patriotism and relies too heavily on uplifting footage from earlier "Rocky" movies.
1985 (PG) 91m/C Sylvester Stallone, Talia Shire, Dolph Lundgren, Brigitte Nielsen, Michael Pataki, Burt Young, Carl Weathers; *D:* Sylvester Stallone. **VHS, Beta, LV $19.98** *MGM, FOX* 🎬½

Rocky 5 Brain damaged and broke, Rocky finds himself back where he started on the streets of Philadelphia. Boxing still very much in his blood, Rocky takes in a protege, training him in the style that made him a champ (take a lickin' and keep on tickin'). However an unscrupulous promoter has designs on the young fighter and seeks to wrest the lad from under the former champ's wing. This eventually leads to a showdown between Rocky and the young boxer in a brutal streetfight. Supposedly the last "Rocky" film, it's clear the formula has run dry.
1990 (PG) 105m/C Sylvester Stallone, Talia Shire, Burt Young, Sage Stallone, Tom Morrison, Burgess Meredith; *D:* John G. Avildsen; *W:* Sylvester Stallone; *M:* Bill Conti. **VHS, Beta, LV, 8mm $19.98** *MGM* 🎬🎬

The Rocky Horror Picture Show When a young couple take refuge in a haunted castle, they find themselves the unwilling pawns in a warped scientist's experiment. Cult camp classic has been a midnight movie favorite for years and has developed an entire subculture built around audience participation. The tape includes a seven-minute short detailing the story behind the movie's popularity. May not be as much fun watching it on the little screen unless you bring the rice and squirt guns. 🎵The Time Warp; Science Fiction Double Feature; Wedding Song; Sweet Transvestite; The Sword of Damocles; Charles Atlas Song; Whatever Happened to Saturday Night; Touch-a Touch-a Touch Me; Eddie's Teddy; Planet Schmanet; Over at the Frankenstein Place; It Was Great When It All Began; I'm Going Home; Super-Heroes.
1975 (R) 105m/C Tim Curry, Susan Sarandon, Barry Bostwick, Meatloaf, Little Nell, Richard O'Brien; *D:* Jim Sharman; *M:* John Barry. **VHS, LV $19.98** *FOX, FCT, PMS* 🎬🎬🎬

Rocky Jones, Space Ranger This syndicated space series followed the adventures of Rocky Jones, commander of the spaceship Orbit Jet, who worked for the United Worlds. The first three half-hour television episodes chronicle the story of how Rocky met his beautiful assistant Vena. Entitled "Beyond the Curtain of Space." Additional episodes available.
1954 78m/B Richard Crane, Sally Mansfield, Scotty Beckett. **VHS, Beta $22.50** *MVC, MOV* 🎬🎬🎬

Rocky Jones, Space Ranger: Renegade Satellite Nostalgia freaks may embrace this revived edition of the infamous early live-TV space cadet show. Rocky squares off against enemies of the United Solar System like Dr. Reno and Rudy DeMarco. Really cheap.
1954 69m/B Richard Crane, Sally Mansfield, Maurice Cass. **VHS $19.95** *VDM* 🎬½

Rocky Mountain Rangers The Three Mesquiteers do what they do best: save a town from bad guys.
1940 58m/B Bob Livingston, Raymond Hatton, Duncan Renaldo, Leroy Mason, Dennis Moore, John St. Polis; *D:* George Sherman. **VHS $19.95** *NOS* 🎬🎬

Rodan A gigantic prehistoric bird is disturbed from his slumber by H-bomb tests. He awakens to wreak havoc on civilization. Big bugs also run amok. From the director of "Godzilla" and a host of other nuclear monster movies. *AKA:* Radon; Radon the Flying Monster.
1956 74m/C JP Kenji Sahara, Yumi Shirakawa; *D:* Inoshiro Honda. **VHS, Beta, LV** *PAR, MLB, VES* 🎬🎬

Rodeo Girl Ross is a restless housewife who joins the rodeo in this television drama based on the life of cowgirl Sue Pirtle. Particularly strong supporting cast of Hopkins, Clark, and Brimley.
1980 100m/C Katharine Ross, Bo Hopkins, Candy Clark, Jacqueline Brookes, Wilford Brimley, Parley Baer; *D:* Jackie Cooper. **VHS, Beta $39.95** *LIV* 🎬🎬½

Rodrigo D.: No Future Gritty, realistic portrayal of the youth-killing culture of Medellin, Columbia. Minimal plot involves a young drummer and his drug-running friends. The actors used are actual untrained street kids, several of whom died after the film's completion. In Spanish with English subtitles. *AKA:* Rodrigo D.: No Futuro.
1991 92m/C Ramiro Meneses, Carlos Mario Resrepo; *D:* Victor Gaviria. **VHS $79.95** *KIV, TAM* 🎬🎬

Roe vs. Wade Hunter is excellent as the single woman from Texas who successfully challenged the nation's prohibitive abortion laws in a landmark Supreme Court case. Television drama based on the actual 1973 case of Norma McCorvey.
1989 92m/C Holly Hunter, Amy Madigan, Terry O'Quinn, Stephen Tobolowsky, Dion Anderson, Kathy Bates, James Gammon, Chris Mulkey; *D:* Gregory Hoblit. **VHS, Beta, LV $14.95** *PAR* 🎬🎬🎬

Roger & Me The hilarious, controversial and lauded atypical semi-documentary. Details Moore's protracted efforts to meet General Motors president Roger Smith and confront him with the poverty and despair afflicting Flint, Michigan, after GM closed its plants there. Includes some emotionally grabbing scenes: a Flint family is evicted just before Christmas; a woman makes a living by selling rabbits for food or pets; and a then soon-to-be Miss America addresses the socioeconomic impact of GM's decision. One of the highest-grossing non-fiction films ever released, and Moore's first.
1989 (R) 91m/C Michael Moore, Bob Eubanks, Pat Boone, Anita Bryant; *D:* Michael Moore. **VHS, Beta, LV $19.95** *WAR* 🎬🎬🎬½

Rogue The Rogue is a ruthless man who can make beautiful women do anything that he desires; so, of course, he does.
1976 (R) 87m/C Milan Galvonic, Barbara Bouchet, Margaret Lee; *D:* Gregory Simpson. **VHS, Beta** *NO* 🎬

Rogue Lion A quasi-incompetent game warden more than meets his match when a voraciously carnivorous lion begins stalking an African community.
1975 89m/C VHS, Beta $59.95 *UHV* 🎬½

Rogue of the Range A lawman pretends that he is a bandit in order to track down an outlaw gang.
1936 60m/B Johnny Mack Brown. **VHS, Beta $19.95** *NOS, DVT, RXM* 🎬

Rogue of the Rio Grande Musical western in which the renowned bandit El Malo arrives in the peace-loving town of Sierra Blanca. One of Loy's earlier films. 🎵Argentine Moon; Carmita; Song of the Bandoleros.

1930 60m/B Myrna Loy, Jose Bohr, Raymond Hatton, Carmelita Geraghty. **VHS, Beta $27.95** VCN *Ⅱ*½

Rogue's Gallery A reporter and photographer covering the story of an inventor and his latest device are caught up in intrigue when he is found murdered.
1944 60m/B Frank Jenks, Robin Raymond, H.B. Warner, Ray Walker, Davison Clark, Robert E. Homans, Frank McGlynn, Pat Gleason, Edward Keane; *D:* Albert Herman. **VHS, Beta $16.95** SNC, RXM *ⅡⅡ*

Rogue's Tavern In this grade B curio, a blood-thirsty killer stalks the occupants of a country inn.
1936 70m/B Wallace Ford, Joan Woodbury; *D:* Bob Hill. **VHS, Beta $24.95** NOS, DVT, HEG *ⅡⅡ*

Rogue's Yarn An investigator probes the death of a woman, ostensibly the result of a boating accident. Gradually he uncovers a plot involving the woman's husband and his mistress in this semi-entertaining British mystery.
1956 80m/B GB Nicole Maurey, Derek Bond, Elwyn Brook-Jones, Hugh Latimer; *D:* Vernon Sewell. **VHS, Beta $16.95** SNC *ⅡⅡ*

Roland and Rattfink Five cartoons starring the good/evil cartoon characters, including "Hawks and Doves," "Sweet and Sourdough" and "Flying Feet." In HiFi.
1969 32m/C **VHS, Beta $14.95** MGM, WTA *ⅡⅡ*

Roland the Mighty Muscular, Herculeanesque hero takes on all comers in this sword and sandal epic set in the Asian steppes.
1958 ?m/C IT Rick Battaglia. **VHS, Beta $16.95** SNC *Ⅱ*½

Roll Along Cowboy A vintage sagebrush saga about a cowboy caught by love. Based on Zane Grey's "The Dude Ranger."
1937 55m/B Smith Ballew, Cecilia Parker, Buster Fite & his Saddle Tramps; *D:* Gus Meins. **VHS, Beta $19.95** NOS, CCB, VDM *Ⅱ*½

Roll of Thunder, Hear My Cry A black family struggles to survive in Depression-era Mississippi in this inspiring, if somewhat predictable, television production. Look for the always impressive Freeman in a supporting role. Set in the South of 1933 and based on the novels of Mildred Taylor.
1978 110m/C Claudia McNeil, Janet MacLachlan, Morgan Freeman; *D:* Jack Smight. **VHS, Beta $14.98** LIV, LCA *ⅡⅡ*½

Roll on Texas Moon A cowpoke is hired to prevent a feud between the sheep men and the cattle ranchers.
1946 68m/B Roy Rogers, George "Gabby" Hayes, Dale Evans, Dennis Hoey; *D:* William Witney. **VHS $19.95** NOS, DVT, MTX *Ⅱ*

Roll, Wagons, Roll Tex Ritter leads a wagon train to Oregon.
1939 52m/B Tex Ritter; *D:* Al Herman. **VHS, Beta $19.95** NOS, VCN *Ⅱ*½

Roller Blade In a post-holocaust world a gang of Amazon-style nuns, who worship a "have a nice day" happy face, battle the forces of evil with martial arts and mysticism. Has to be seen to be believed. Extremely low-budget outing.
1985 88m/C Suzanne Solari, Jeff Hutchinson, Shaun Mitchelle; *D:* Donald G. Jackson. **VHS, Beta $19.95** NWV *Ⅱ*

Roller Blade Warriors: Taken By Force Roller babes battle evil mutant while balancing on big boots with small wheels.
1990 90m/C Kathleen Kinmont, Rory Calhoun, Abby Dalton, Elizabeth Kaitan. **VHS** NO *ⅡⅡ*

Roller Boogie A truly awful film made at the time of the mercifully brief roller-disco craze. Blair runs away from home and winds up helping some friends thwart a businessman looking to close the local roller rink. Everything about this one reeks amateur.
1979 (PG) 103m/C Linda Blair, Jim Bray, Beverly Garland, Roger Perry, James Van Patten, Kimberly Beck, Mark Goddard, Stoney Jackson, Sean McClory; *D:* Mark L. Lester. **VHS $14.95** MGM *Woof!*

Rollerball Caan is utterly convincing in this futuristic tale in which a brutal sport assumes alarming importance to a sterile society. Flashy, violent, sometimes exhilirating.
1975 (R) 123m/C James Caan, John Houseman, Maud Adams, Moses Gunn; *D:* Norman Jewison. **VHS, Beta, LV $29.95** MGM *ⅡⅡ*½

Rollercoaster A deranged extortionist threatens to sabotage an amusement park ride. Plucky Segal must stop him. Video renters will be spared the nauseating effects of film's original "Sensurround."
1977 (PG) 119m/C George Segal, Richard Widmark, Timothy Bottoms, Henry Fonda, Susan Strasberg, Harry Guardino; *D:* James Goldstone. **VHS, Beta, LV $59.95** MCA *ⅡⅡ*

Rollin' Plains A Texas Ranger tries to settle a feud between cattlemen and sheepmen over water rights.
1938 60m/B Tex Ritter; *D:* Al Herman. **VHS, Beta $19.95** NOS, VCN, UHV *Ⅱ*

Rolling Home Tame tale about aging cowpoke, his grandson, and a really swell horse. Saddle up and snooze.
1948 71m/B Jean Parker, Russell Hayden, Pamela Blake, Buss Henry, Raymond Hatton. **VHS, Beta, LV** NO *ⅡⅡ*

Rolling Thunder Vietnam vet turns vigilante when he arrives home from POW camp and sees his family slaughtered. Graphically violent, potentially cathartic. Typical of screenwriter Paul Schrader.
1977 (R) 99m/C William Devane, Tommy Lee Jones, Linda Haynes; *D:* John Flynn. **VHS, Beta, LV $79.98** LIV, VES *ⅡⅡ*½

Rolling Vengeance Enterprising fellow constructs powerful truck to better facilitate the extermination of gang members who earlier slaughtered his family. Keep on truckin'.
1987 (R) 90m/C Don Michael Paul, Ned Beatty, Lawrence Dane, Lisa Howard; *D:* Steven Hilliard Stern. **VHS, Beta, LV $19.98** NLC *Ⅱ*

Rollover Turgid big-budget drama about Arab undermining of American economy. Kristofferson is lifeless, Fonda is humorless. Supporting players Sommer and Cronyn fare better.
1981 (R) 117m/C Jane Fonda, Kris Kristofferson, Hume Cronyn, Bob Gunton, Josef Sommer, Martha Plimpton; *D:* Alan J. Pakula. **VHS, Beta $39.98** WAR *Ⅱ*½

Roman Holiday Hepburn's first starring role is a charmer as a princess bored with her official visit to Rome who slips away and plays at being an "average Jane." A reporter discovers her little charade and decides to cash in with an exclusive story. Before they know it, love calls. Blacklisted screenwriter Trumbo was "fronted" by Ian McLellan Hunter, who accepted screen credit and the Best Story Oscar in Trumbo's stead. The Academy voted to posthumously award Trumbo his own Oscar in 1993.
1953 118m/B Audrey Hepburn, Gregory Peck, Eddie Albert, Tullio Carminati; *D:* William Wyler; *W:* Dalton Trumbo. Academy Awards '53: Best Actress (Hepburn), Best Costume Design (B & W), Best Story; Nominations: Best Art Direction/Set Decoration (B & W), Best Black and White Cinematography, Best Director (Wyler), Best Film

Editing, Best Picture, Best Screenplay, Best Supporting Actor (Albert); British Academy Awards '53: Best Actress (Hepburn); Golden Globe Awards '54: Best Actress—Drama (Hepburn); New York Film Critics Awards '53: Best Actress (Hepburn). **VHS, Beta, LV, 8mm $14.95** PAR, BTV, HMV *ⅡⅡ*½

Roman Scandals A penniless young man daydreams himself back to ancient Rome with uproarious results. Lucille Ball appears as one of the Goldwyn Girls. Dance sequences were choreographed by Busby Berkeley. ♫No More Love; Build A Little Home; Keep Young and Beautiful; Rome Wasn't Built in a Day; Put a Tax on Love.
1933 91m/B Eddie Cantor, Ruth Etting, Gloria Stuart, Edward Arnold, Lucille Ball, Busby Berkeley; *D:* Frank Tuttle. **VHS, Beta $19.98** SUE, HBO *ⅡⅡ*½

Roman Spring of Mrs. Stone An aging actress determines to revive her career in Rome but finds romance with a gigolo instead in this adaptation of Tennessee Williams's novella. Leigh and Beatty are compelling, but Lenya nearly steals the show as Leigh's distinctly unappealing confidant. *AKA:* The Widow and the Gigolo.
1961 104m/C Warren Beatty, Vivien Leigh, Lotte Lenya, Bessie Love, Jill St. John; *D:* Jose Quintero. **VHS, Beta $19.98** WAR, FHE *ⅡⅡⅡ*

Romance In only her second talkie, Garbo stars as an Italian opera star who seduces a young priest. Poor story and weak acting from everyone with the exception of Garbo. Even SHE can't save this one. Adapted from the play "Signora Cacllini."
1930 77m/B Greta Garbo, Lewis Stone, Gavin Gordon, Elliott Nugent, Florence Lake, Clara Blandick; *D:* Clarence Brown. **VHS $19.98** MGM *ⅡⅡ*

Romance in Manhattan Recent immigrant to New York struggles to build new life, in spite of unemployment, language barriers, and loneliness. He meets Broadway chorine Rogers and song and dance ensues. America, ain't it a great place?
1934 78m/B Ginger Rogers, Francis Lederer, J. Farrell MacDonald; *D:* Pandro S. Berman. **VHS $19.98** TTC, FCT *ⅡⅡ*

Romance of a Horsethief Brynner leads this entertaining but slow-paced "Fiddler on the Roof" comedic romp without the music. In 1904 Poland, a Cossack captain takes horses for the Russo-Japanese war. The residents of the town rise up, goaded on by Birkin.
1971 (PG) 100m/C YU Yul Brynner, Eli Wallach, Jane Birkin, Oliver Tobias, Lainie Kazan, David Opatoshu; *D:* Abraham Polonsky. **VHS** ACE, MOV *ⅡⅡ*½

Romance on the High Seas A woman is scheduled to take a cruise vacation but skips the boat when she believes her husband is cheating on her. Her husband believes she is taking the cruise to cheat on him and hires a private detective to follow her. Pleasant comedy features the film debut of Doris Day. ♫It's Magic; It's You or No One; The Tourist Trade; Put 'Em in a Box, Tie 'Em with a Ribbon, and Throw 'Em in the Deep Blue Sea; Two Lovers Met in the Night; Run, Run, Run; I'm in Love; Cuban Rhapsody.
1948 99m/C Jack Carson, Janice Paige, Don DeFore, Doris Day, Oscar Levant, S.Z. Sakall, Eric Blore, Franklin Pangborn, Leslie Brooks, William Bakewell; *W:* Julius J. Epstein. **VHS, LV $29.98** FOX, FCT *ⅡⅡ*

Romance on the Orient Express Sparks fly when former lovers meet again on the Orient Express. Don't expect any flesh, though, as film was made for television.

1989 96m/C Cheryl Ladd, Stuart Wilson, John Gielgud; **D:** Lawrence Gordon Clark. **VHS, Beta** $9.98 *TTC ♂♂½*

Romance on the Range
Rogers sets out to trap a gang of fur thieves and finds romance.
1942 60m/B Roy Rogers, George "Gabby" Hayes, Sally Payne. **VHS** $19.95 *NOS, VCN, REP ♂♂½*

Romance with a Double Bass
When a musician and a princess take a skinny dip in the royal lake and get their clothes stolen, comic complications arise. Reminiscent of Cleese's sojourn as a Monty Python member, with surreal, frequently raunchy humor.
1974 40m/C *GB* John Cleese, Connie Booth, Graham Crowden, Desmond Jones, Freddie Jones, Andrew Sachs; **D:** Robert Young. **VHS, Beta, LV** $19.95 *PAV ♂♂*

Romancing the Stone
Uptight romance novelist lives out her fantasies after she receives a mysterious map from her murdered brother-in-law and her sister is kidnapped in South America—the ransom being the map. Out to rescue her sister, she's helped and hindered by an American soldier of fortune (Douglas) whose main concern is himself and the hidden treasure described in the map. Great chemistry between the stars and loads of clever dialogue in this appealing adventure comedy. First outing with Turner, Douglas, and DeVito. Followed by "The Jewel of the Nile."
1984 (PG) 106m/C Michael Douglas, Kathleen Turner, Danny DeVito, Zack Norman, Alfonso Arau, Ron Silver; **D:** Robert Zemeckis. Academy Awards '84 Nominations: Best Film Editing; Golden Globe Awards '85: Best Actress—Musical/Comedy (Turner), Best Film—Musical/Comedy. **VHS, Beta, LV** $19.98 *FOX, HMV ♂♂♂*

Romantic Comedy
Writing duo doesn't seem to synchronize their desires for each other in this dull comedy. Engaging stars don't inspire each other much, and supporting cast can't make up the difference. Adapted from the Bernard Slade play.
1983 (PG) 102m/C Dudley Moore, Mary Steenburgen, Frances Sternhagen, Ron Leibman; **D:** Arthur Hiller. **VHS, Beta** $14.95 *MGM, FOX ♂♂*

Romantic Encounters
See what happens after people call a sexy singles hotline.
199? 90m/C Bonnie Torture, Guy Lane, Karen Grey, Don Larsen. **VHS** $49.99 *CEL ♂*

Romantic Englishwoman
Literate comedy-drama about the intertwined lives of several sophisticated and restrained Brits. Caine is a successful novelist with writer's block whose wife falls for another man while on a trip alone. He then invites his wife's lover to stay with them in order to generate his writing.
1975 (R) 117m/C *GB* Glenda Jackson, Michael Caine, Helmut Berger, Kate Nelligan; **D:** Joseph Losey; **W:** Tom Stoppard, Thomas Wiseman. **VHS, Beta** *WAR, OM ♂♂♂*

Rome Adventure
Spinster librarian Pleshette takes Roman vacation hoping to meet handsome prince. Donahue takes shine to her while girlfriend Dickinson is away, as does suave Roman Brazzi. Soapy, ill-paced romance. *AKA:* Lovers Must Learn.
1962 119m/C Troy Donahue, Angie Dickinson, Suzanne Pleshette, Rossano Brazzi, Constance Ford, Al Hirt, Chad Everett; **W/D:** Delmer Daves; **M:** Max Steiner. **VHS, LV** $59.99 *PAR, PIA, FCT ♂♂*

Rome '78
Acclaimed underground film centered around Caligula and the Queen of Sheba in ancient Rome.
1978 60m/C Eric Mitchell; **D:** James Nares. **VHS** $59.95 *MWF ♂♂½*

Romeo and Juliet
One of MGM producer Irving Thalberg's pet projects (and starring Thalberg's wife, Norma Shearer), this Shakespeare classic was given the spare-no-expense MGM treatment. Physically too old to portray teen-age lovers, both Howard and Shearer let their acting ability supply all necessary illusions. Also notable is Barrymore's over-the-top portrayal of Mercutio.
1936 126m/B Leslie Howard, Norma Shearer, John Barrymore, Basil Rathbone, Edna May Oliver; **D:** George Cukor. **VHS, LV** $19.98 *MGM, CCB ♂♂♂½*

Romeo and Juliet
Unfulfilling adaptation of Shakespeare's timeless drama of young love cast against family antagonism. Peculiar supporting cast features both Cabot and ubiquitous master Gielgud.
1954 138m/C *IT* Laurence Harvey, Susan Shantall, Aldo Zollo, Sebastian Cabot, Flora Robson, Mervyn Johns, Bill Travers, John Gielgud; **D:** Renato Castellani. **VHS, Beta** $29.95 *SUE, LCA ♂♂*

Romeo and Juliet
Young couple share love despite prohibitive conflict between their families in this adaptation of Shakespeare's classic play. Director Zeffirelli succeeds in casting relative novices Whiting and Hussey in the leads, but is somewhat less proficient in lending air of free-wheeling sixties appeal to entire enterprise. Kudos, however, to cinematographer Pasquale de Santis and composer Nina Rota. Also available in a 45-minute edited version.
1968 (PG) 138m/C *GB IT* Olivia Hussey, Leonard Whiting, Michael York, Milo O'Shea; **D:** Franco Zeffirelli. Academy Awards '68: Best Cinematography, Best Costume Design; Nominations: Best Director (Zeffirelli), Best Picture; Golden Globe Awards '69: Best Foreign Film; National Board of Review Awards '68: 10 Best Films of the Year, Best Director (Zeffirelli). **VHS, Beta, LV** $19.95 *PAR, HMV, PBC ♂♂♂½*

Romeo and Juliet
Entertaining enactment of 400-year-old Shakespearean classic about the passion and tragedy of a family feud and young star-crossed lovers. Part of the BBC television series "The Shakespeare Plays."
1979 167m/C *GB* John Gielgud, Rebecca Saire, Patrick Ryecart. **VHS, Beta** *TLF ♂♂♂*

Romero
Julia is riveting as the Salvadoran archbishop who championed his destitute congregation despite considerable political opposition. A stirring biography financed by the United States Roman Catholic Church, with a screenplay by John Sacret Young of television's "China Beach."
1989 102m/C Raul Julia, Richard Jordan, Ana Alicia, Eddie Velez, Alejandro Bracho, Tony Plana, Lucy Reina, Harold Gould, Al Ruscio, Robert Viharo; **D:** John Duigan. **VHS, Beta, LV** $29.95 *VMK ♂♂½*

Romola
Silent adventure. After Powell and his father are attacked by pirates, Powell escapes. But instead of rescuing his father, he opts for a life of corruption. Dad eventually escapes and returns to exact vengeance. A rather expensive film in its day, troubled by modern-day sights in what was supposed to be old Florence. Gish's drowning scene had to be re-shot because she wouldn't sink. Colman arranged for his then-wife Raye to have a bit part, but they were divorced soon after the film was finished.
1925 120m/B Lillian Gish, Dorothy Gish, William H. Powell, Ronald Colman, Charles Lane, Herbert Grimwood, Bonaventure Ibanez, Frank Puglia, Thelma Raye; **D:** Henry King. **VHS, Beta** *NO ♂♂½*

Rona Jaffe's Mazes & Monsters
Geeky collegians get more than they bargain for when they become preoccupied with a fantasy game. Early Hanks appearance is among this television film's few assets. *AKA:* Mazes and Monsters; Dungeons and Dragons.
1982 103m/C Tom Hanks, Chris Makepeace, Lloyd Bochner, Anne Francis, Susan Strasberg, Murray Hamilton, Vera Miles, Louise Sorel; **D:** Steven Hilliard Stern. **VHS, Beta** $19.98 *WAR, LHV ♂♂½*

The Roof
Uninteresting outing about a young couple who married against their families' wishes and find that setting up a home of their own is more difficult than they thought. In Italian with English subtitles.
1956 98m/B *IT* Gabriella Pallotti, Giorgio Listuzzi; **D:** Vittorio De Sica. **VHS, Beta** $24.95 *NOS, HHT, APD ♂♂*

Rooftops
Peculiar but predictable, centering on love between Hispanic girl and white youth who has mastered martial arts dancing. Director Wise is a long way from his earlier "West Side Story." See this one and be the only person you know who has.
1989 (R) 108m/C Jason Gedrick, Troy Beyer, Eddie Velez, Tisha Campbell; **D:** Robert Wise. **VHS, Beta, LV** $19.95 *LIV ♂♂½*

The Rookie
Routine cop drama has worldly veteran and wide-eyed newcomer team to crack stolen-car ring managed by Germans. Eastwood and Sheen are reliable, but Hispanics Julia and Braga, though miscast, nonetheless steal this one as the German villains.
1990 (R) 121m/C Clint Eastwood, Charlie Sheen, Raul Julia, Sonia Braga, Lara Flynn Boyle, Pepe Serna, Marco Rodriguez, Tom Skerritt, Roberta Vasquez; **D:** Clint Eastwood. **VHS, Beta, LV, 8mm** $19.90 *WAR, PIA ♂♂*

Rookie of the Year
Klutzy 12-year-old baseball fanatic Henry dreams of making the big leagues. Chasing a fly, he falls, breaks his arm, and his dreams dashed for the summer. But talk about your lucky breaks: the arm heals and Henry finds himself able to throw fastballs at more than 100 mph. So of course, the Cubs, supreme victims of baseball bad kharma, sign the lad. Busey is the over-the-hill vet who shows him the ropes and romances his single ma, Morton. Stern adds to the fun as a coach who's taken a few too many hardballs to the noggin. Unbilled Candy does play by play, while real-life baseball stars Bobby Bonds, Pedro Guerrero, and others step to the plate to face the rookie. Enjoyable family fare by rookie director Stern, who looks like he'll make the big show.
1993 (PG) ?m/C Thomas Ian Nicholas, Daniel Stern, Gary Busey, Dan Hedaya; **D:** Daniel Stern; **W:** Sam Harper; **M:** Bill Conti. **VHS** *NYR ♂♂♂*

The Room
Altman takes on Pinter in this brooding mini-play about two young strangers who try to rent the room already occupied by a disconnected woman and her semi-catatonic husband. Made for television.
1987 48m/C Julian Sands, Linda Hunt, Annie Lennox, David Hemblen, Donald Pleasence; **D:** Robert Altman; **W:** Harold Pinter. **VHS, Beta** $79.95 *PSM ♂♂½*

Room at the Top
Ambitious factory man forsakes true love and marries boss's daughter instead in this grim drama set in industrial northern England. Cast excels, with Harvey and Sears as the worker and his wife. Signoret is also quite compelling as the abandoned woman. Adapted from John Braine's novel and followed by "Life at the Top" and "Man at the Top."

1959 118m/B *GB* Laurence Harvey, Simone Signoret, Heather Sears, Hermione Baddeley, Anthony Elgar, Donald Wolfit; *D:* Jack Clayton. Academy Awards '59: Best Actress (Signoret), Best Adapted Screenplay; Nominations: Best Actor (Harvey), Best Director (Clayton), Best Picture, Best Supporting Actress (Baddeley); British Academy Awards '58: Best Actress (Signoret), Best Film; Cannes Film Festival '59: Best Actress (Signoret). **VHS** *AVT* ♫♫♫

Room 43 Campy fable about a British cab driver who falls in love with a French girl, and stumbles onto a white-slavery ring when she falls victim to it. Features a young Caine and future novelist Collins in bit parts. *AKA:* Passport to Shame.
1958 93m/B *B* Diana Dors, Herbert Lom, Eddie Constantine, Michael Caine, Jackie Collins; *D:* Alvin Rakoff. **VHS, Beta $19.95** *VDM* ♫ ½

Room Service The Marx Brothers provide less than the usual mayhem here with Groucho as penniless theatrical producer determined to remain in his hotel room until he can secure funds for his next play. Ball doesn't help matters much either. Not bad, but certainly not up to Marxian Standards.
1938 78m/B Groucho Marx, Harpo Marx, Chico Marx, Lucille Ball, Ann Miller, Frank Albertson, Donald MacBride; *D:* William A. Seiter. **VHS, Beta, LV $19.95** *RKO, VID, CCB* ♫♫ ½

Room to Let An elderly woman and her daughter take in boarders in Victorian England. They rent a room to a man who claims to be a doctor, but the two women eventually become prisoners of fear, believing the man is actually Jack the Ripper. Will there be a vacancy soon? Occasionally suspenseful.
1949 68m/B *GB* Jimmy Hanley, Valentine Dyall, Christine Silver, Merle Tottenham, Charles Hawtrey, Connie Smith, Laurence Naismith; *D:* Godfrey Grayson. **VHS, Beta $16.95** *NOS, SNC* ♫♫

A Room with a View Engaging adaptation of E.M. Forster's novel of requited love. Carter stars as the feisty British idealist who rejects dashing Sands for supercilious Day Lewis, then repents and finds (presumably) eternal passion. A multi-Oscar nominee, with great music (courtesy of Puccini), great scenery (courtesy of Florence), and great performances (courtesy of practically everybody, but supporters Smith, Dench, Callow, and Elliott must be particularly distinguished). Truly romantic, and there's much humor too.
1986 117m/C *GB* Helena Bonham Carter, Julian Sands, Denholm Elliott, Maggie Smith, Judi Dench, Simon Callow, Daniel Day-Lewis, Rupert Graves; *D:* James Ivory; *W:* Ruth Prawer Jhabvala. Academy Awards '86: Best Adapted Screenplay, Best Art Direction/Set Decoration, Best Costume Design; Nominations: Best Cinematography, Best Director (Ivory), Best Picture, Best Supporting Actor (Elliott), Best Supporting Actress (Smith); British Academy Awards '86: Best Actress (Smith), Best Film, Best Supporting Actress (Dench); Independent Spirit Awards '87: Best Foreign Film; National Board of Review Awards '86: 10 Best Films of the Year. **VHS, Beta, LV $19.98** *FOX, HMV* ♫♫♫♫

Roommate A valedictorian church-goer and a rebellious iconoclast room together at Northwestern University in 1952, with the expected humorous results. Public television presentation based on a John Updike story.
1984 96m/C Lance Guest, Barry Miller, Elaine Wilkes, Melissa Ford, David Bachman; *D:* Neil Cox. **VHS, Beta $69.98** *LIV, VES* ♫♫ ½

Rooster Cogburn Bible-thumping schoolmarm joins up with a hard-drinking, hard-fighting marshal in order to capture gang of outlaws who killed her father. Tired sequel to "True Grit" helped by chemistry between Wayne and Hepburn.
1975 (PG) 107m/C John Wayne, Katharine Hepburn, Richard Jordan, Anthony Zerbe, John McIntire, Strother Martin, Paul Koslo; *D:* Stuart Millar. **VHS, Beta, LV $19.95** *MCA, TLF* ♫♫ ½

Rooster: Spurs of Death! An expose on cock fighting, in which a young idealist tries to stop the thriving sport in a small southern town. Dog of a movie that (not surprisingly) went straight to video.
1983 (PG) 90m/C Vincent Van Patten, Ty Hardin, Kristine DeBell, Ruta Lee. **VHS, Beta $59.95** *WWV* Woof!

Rootin' Tootin' Rhythm All's not quiet on the range, but Autry comes along to sing things back to normal. Goofy, clumsy, ubiquitous sidekick Burnette is a symbol for this whole effort. *AKA:* Rhythm on the Ranch.
1938 55m/B Gene Autry, Smiley Burnette, Monte Blue; *D:* Mack V. Wright. **VHS, Beta $19.95** *NOS, VYY, DVT* ♫

Roots The complete version of Alex Haley's made for television saga following a black man's search for his heritage, revealing an epic panorama of America's past. Available on six tapes, complete at 570 minutes.
1977 90m/C Ed Asner, Lloyd Bridges, LeVar Burton, Chuck Connors, Lynda Day George, Lorne Greene, Burl Ives, O.J. Simpson, Cicely Tyson, Ben Vereen, Sandy Duncan; *D:* David Greene; *M:* Quincy Jones. **VHS, Beta $64.95** *WAR, KUI, MOV* ♫♫♫♫

Roots of Evil This erotic thriller follows a cop on the trail of a murderer who specializes in killing Hollywood's most beautiful prostitutes. Also available in unrated and Spanish-language versions.
1991 (R) ?m/C Alex Cord, Delia Sheppard, Charles Dierkop, Jillian Kesner; *D:* Gary Graver. **VHS $89.99** *CAN* ♫ ½

Roots: The Gift It's Christmas, 1770, and Kunte Kinte (Burton) and Fiddler (Gossett) try to escape slavery via the Underground Railroad. In their attempt, they wind up giving the gift of freedom to several of their fellow slaves. A made for television movie based on the Alex Haley characters.
1988 94m/C Louis Gossett Jr., LeVar Burton, Michael Learned, Avery Brooks, Kate Mulgrew, Shaun Cassidy, John McMartin; *D:* Kevin Hooks. **VHS $59.99** *WAR, FCT* ♫♫

Roots: The Next Generation Sequel to the landmark television miniseries continuing the story of author Alex Haley's ancestors from the Reconstruction era of the 1880s to 1967, culminating with Haley's visit to West Africa where he is told the story of Kunta Kinte. On seven tapes.
1979 685m/C Georg Stanford Brown, Lynne Moody, Henry Fonda, Richard Thomas, Marc Singer, Olivia de Havilland, Paul Koslo, Beah Richards, Stan Shaw, Harry Morgan, Irene Cara, Dorian Harewood, Ruby Dee, Paul Winfield, James Earl Jones, Debbie Allen; *Cameos:* Al Freeman Jr., Marlon Brando. **VHS $149.99** *MOV* ♫♫♫

Rope In New York City, two gay college students murder a friend for kicks and store the body in a living room trunk. They further insult the dead by using the trunk as the buffet table and inviting his parents to the dinner party in his honor. Very dark humor is the theme in Hitchcock's first color film, which he innovatively shot in uncut ten-minute takes, with the illusion of a continuous scene maintained with tricky camera work. Based on the Patrick Hamilton play and on the Leopold-Loeb murder case; script by Arthur Laurents.
1948 (PG) 81m/C James Stewart, John Dall, Farley Granger, Cedric Hardwicke, Constance Collier; *D:* Alfred Hitchcock. **VHS, Beta, LV $19.95** *MCA* ♫♫♫ ½

Rorret "Rorret" is "terror" spelled backwards—a good indication of the psychological and physical terror Mr. Rorret, the owner of the Peeping Tom Cinema, inflicts upon his female patrons. The Cinema is devoted to the horror film and Rorret himself dresses like Peter Lorre in "M;" lives behind the movie screen, watching the films in mirror image; and enjoys the frightened reactions of his female patrons. He enjoys their reactions so much that he later stalks the women for real. Highlighted by recreated sequences from such psycho-terror classics as "Psycho," "Dial M for Murder," "Strangers on a Train," and "Peeping Tom." In Italian with English subtitles.
1987 105m/C *IT* Lou Castel, Anna Galiena, Massimo Venturiello; *W/D:* Fulvio Wetzl. **VHS $79.95** *NYF, TAM* ♫♫♫

Rosalie A gridiron great from West Point falls for a mysterious beauty from Vassar. He soon learns that her father reigns over a tiny Balkan nation. Expensive, massive, imperfect musical; exotic romantic pairing fails to conceal plot's blah-ness. Oh well, the music's good. Score by Cole Porter. ♫I've a Strange New Rhythm in My Heart; Why Should I Care?; Spring Love Is in the Air; Rosalie; It's All Over But the Shouting; Who Knows?; In the Still of the Night; To Love or Not to Love; Close (instrumental); In the Still of the Night.
1938 118m/B Nelson Eddy, Eleanor Powell, Frank Morgan, Ray Bolger, Ilona Massey, Reginald Owen, Edna May Oliver, Jerry Colonna; *D:* Woodbridge S. Van Dyke. **VHS, Beta $19.98** *MGM* ♫♫ ½

Rosalie Goes Shopping Satire about American consumerism hiding behind slapstick comedy, and it works, most of the time. Misplaced Bavarian (Sagebrecht) moves to Arkansas and begins spending wildly and acquiring "things." Twisty plot carried confidently by confident wackiness from Sagebrecht and supporters.
1989 (PG-13) 94m/C *GE* Marianne Sagebrecht, Brad Davis, Judge Reinhold, Willie Harlander, Alex Winter; *D:* Percy Adlon. **VHS, LV $89.95** *VMK, TAM* ♫♫♫

The Rosary Murders Based on the William X. Kienzle mystery about a serial killer preying on nuns and priests. Father Koesler (Sutherland) must betray the confessional to stop him. Interesting, though sometimes muddled and too rarely tense. Screenplay co-written by Elmore Leonard and Fred Walton. Filmed on location in Detroit.
1987 (R) 105m/C Donald Sutherland, Charles Durning, Belinda Bauer, Josef Sommer; *D:* Fred Walton. **VHS, Beta, LV** *NO* ♫♫

The Rose Modeled after the life of Janis Joplin, Midler plays a young, talented and self-destructive blues/rock singer. Professional triumphs don't stop her lonely restlessness and confused love affairs. The best exhibition of the rock and roll world outside of documentaries. Electrifying film debut for Midler features an incredible collection of songs. ♫Fire Down Below; I've Written A Letter to Daddy; Let Me Call You Sweetheart; The Rose; Stay With Me; Camellia; Sold My Soul To Rock 'n' Roll; Keep On Rockin'; When A Man Loves a Woman; Whose Side Are You On?; Midnight in Memphis; The Night We Said Goodbye; Evil Lies; Love Me With a Feeling.

1979 (R) 134m/C Bette Midler, Alan Bates, Frederic Forrest, Harry Dean Stanton, David Keith; **D:** Mark Rydell. Academy Awards '79 Nominations: Best Actress (Midler), Best Film Editing, Best Sound, Best Supporting Actor (Forrest); Golden Globe Awards '80: Best Actress—Musical/Comedy (Midler). **VHS, Beta, LV $19.98** FOX 🐾🐾🐾

The Rose and the Jackal Fun, intriguing fictionalization about the founder of the Pinkerton detective agency. During the Civil War, bearded, Scottish Reeve tries to persuade a wealthy Southern lady to help save the Union. Made for cable television. **1990 94m/C** Christopher Reeve, Madolyn Smith, Granville Van Dusen, Carrie Snodgress, Kevin McCarthy; **D:** Jack Gold. **VHS, Beta $79.98** TTC 🐾🐾

The Rose Garden In modern Germany, a Holocaust survivor is put on trial for assaulting an elderly man. The victim, it turns out, was a Nazi guilty of heinous war crimes. Ullmann and Schell lend substance, though treatment of a powerful theme is inadequate. **1989 (PG-13) 112m/C** Liv Ullmann, Maximilian Schell, Peter Fonda; **D:** Fons Rademakers; **W:** Paul Hengge. **VHS, Beta, LV $89.95** CAN 🐾🐾 ½

Rose Marie An opera star falls in love with the mountie who captured her escaped convict brother. Hollywood legend has it that when a British singer was presented with the first line in "Indian Love Song," which is "When I'm calling you-oo-oo-oo-oo-oo-oo," the confused performer sang, "When I'm calling you, double oh, double oh, double oh..." Maybe true, maybe not, but funny anyway. Classic MacDonald-Eddy operetta; Rudolf Friml score. Remade in 1954. ♫Indian Love Call; Pardon Me, Madame; The Mounties; Rose Marie; Totem Tom Tom; Just For You; Tex Yeux; St. Louis Blues; Dinah; Three Blind Mice; Some of These Days. **AKA:** Indian Love Call. **1936 112m/B** Jeanette MacDonald, Nelson Eddy, James Stewart, Allan Jones, David Niven, Reginald Owen; **D:** Woodbridge S. Van Dyke. **VHS, Beta, LV $19.95** MGM, PIA 🐾🐾🐾

Rose Marie Blyth is a lonely Canadian woman wooed by a mean spirited fur trapper and a gallant mountie. Unremarkable remake of the Eddy/MacDonald musical is saved by specatular technicolor and CinemaScope photography. Choreography by Busby Berkeley. ♫Rose Marie; Indian Love Call; Totem Tom Tom; The Mounties; I Have the Love; The Right Place For A Girl; Free to be Free; The Mountie Who Never Got His Man. **1954 (G) 115m/C** Ann Blyth, Howard Keel, Fernando Lamas, Bert Lahr, Marjorie Main, Joan Taylor, Chief Yowlachie, Abel Fernandez, Al Ferguson, Dabbs Greer, Lumsden Hare; **D:** Mervyn LeRoy. **VHS, LV** MGM, MLB 🐾🐾

Rose of Rio Grande A western musical about a Mexican gang that avenges the deaths of members of the upper strata. **1938 60m/B** John Carroll, Movita, Antonio Moreno, Lena Basquette, Duncan Renaldo; **D:** William Nigh. **VHS, Beta** GPV 🐾

The Rose Tattoo Magnani, in her U.S. screen debut, is just right as a Southern widow who cherishes her husband's memory, but falls for virile trucker Lancaster. Williams wrote this play and screenplay specifically for Magnani, who was never as successful again. Interesting character studies, although Lancaster doesn't seem right as an Italian longshoreman. **1955 117m/B** Anna Magnani, Burt Lancaster, Marisa Pavan, Ben Cooper, Virginia Grey, Jo Van Fleet; **D:** Daniel Mann; **W:** Tennessee Williams, Hal Kanter. Academy Awards '55: Best Actress (Magnani), Best Art Direction/Set Decoration (B & W), Best Black and White

Cinematography; Nominations: Best Costume Design (B & W), Best Film Editing, Best Picture, Best Supporting Actress (Pavan); British Academy Awards '56: Best Actress (Magnani); Golden Globe Awards '56: Best Actress—Drama (Magnani), Best Supporting Actress (Pavan). **VHS, Beta, LV $19.95** PAR, PIA, FCT 🐾🐾🐾 ½

Rosebud Beach Hotel Wimpy loser tries his hand at managing a run-down hotel in order to please his demanding girlfriend. Camp is okay, but this soft-porn excuse is horrible in every other way. **AKA:** The Big Lobby. **1985 (R) 82m/C** Colleen Camp, Peter Scolari, Christopher Lee, Fran Drescher, Eddie Deezen, Chuck McCann, Hank Garrett, Hamilton Camp, Cherie Currie; **D:** Harry Hurwitz. **VHS, Beta, LV $79.98** LIV, VES 🐾

Roseland Three interlocking stories, set at New York's famous old Roseland Ballroom, about lonely people who live to dance. Not fully successful, but strong characters, especially in the second and third stories, make it worth watching, although it lacks energy. **1977 (PG) 103m/C** Christopher Walken, Geraldine Chaplin, Joan Copeland, Teresa Wright, Lou Jacobi; **D:** James Ivory; **W:** Ruth Prawer Jhabvala. **VHS, Beta $59.95** VES, CVC, TAM 🐾🐾🐾

Rosemary's Baby A young woman, innocent and religious, and her husband, ambitious and agnostic, move into a new apartment. Soon the woman is pregnant, but she begins to realize that she has fallen into a coven of witches and warlocks, and that they claim the child as the antichrist. Gripping and powerful, subtle yet utterly horrifying, with luminous performances by all. Polanski's first American film; from Levin's best-seller. **1968 (R) 134m/C** Mia Farrow, John Cassavetes, Ruth Gordon, Maurice Evans, Patsy Kelly, Elisha Cook Jr., Charles Grodin, Sidney Blackmer, William Castle, **D:** Roman Polanski. Academy Awards '68: Best Supporting Actress (Gordon); Nominations: Best Adapted Screenplay; Golden Globe Awards '69: Best Supporting Actress (Gordon). **VHS, Beta, LV $14.95** PAR, MLB, BTV 🐾🐾🐾🐾

Rosencrantz & Guildenstern Are Dead Playwright Stoppard adapted his own absurdist 1967 play to film—which makes as much sense as a "Swan Lake" ballet on radio. Two tragicomic minor characters in "Hamlet" squabble rhetorically and misperceive Shakespeare's plot tightening fatally around them. Uprooted from the stage environment, it's affected, arcane and pointless for all but fervent Stoppard fans and Bard completists. **1990 (PG) 118m/C** Gary Oldman, Tim Roth, Richard Dreyfuss, Iain Glen; **W/D:** Tom Stoppard. **VHS, Beta, LV $92.95** BVV, FCT 🐾🐾

Roses Bloom Twice When a middle-aged widow decides to make up for some of the wild living that she missed during her marriage, she shocks her children. **1977 87m/C** Glynis McNicoll, Michael Craig, Diane Craig, John Allen, Jennifer West; **D:** David Stevens. **VHS, Beta** PGN 🐾🐾

Rosie: The Rosemary Clooney Story Above average biography of Clooney's up-and-down career. Locke lip-synches Clooney's voice in songs. Orlando doesn't help matters portraying Jose Ferrer. Made for television. **1982 100m/C** Sondra Locke, Tony Orlando, Penelope Milford, Katherine Helmond, Kevin McCarthy, John Karlen, Cheryl Anderson, Robert Ridgely, Joey Travolta; **D:** Jackie Cooper; **Performed by:** Rosemary Clooney. **VHS, Beta $39.95** LIV 🐾🐾 ½

R.O.T.O.R. R.O.T.O.R. (Robotic Officer of Tactical Operations Research) is a law enforcement robot that is supposed to stop criminals. But watch out! It might go beserk and wreck your town. **1988 90m/C** Richard Gesswein, Margaret Trigg, Jayne Smith; **D:** Cullen Blaine. **VHS $79.95** IMP 🐾

Rouge A young prostitute enlists the aid of a journalist in helping her find her lover, who recovered from their attempted double suicide years before. Set in China of the 1930s. In Cantonese with English subtitles. **AKA:** Yanzhi Kou. **1987 99m/C** HK Anita Mui, Leslie Cheung; **D:** Stanley Kwan. **VHS $39.95** FCT 🐾

Rough Cut American diamond thief Reynolds lives in London, pursued by an aging Scotland Yard detective who wants to end his career in a blaze of glory. A beautiful lady is the decoy. Good chemistry; lousy script. **1980 (PG) 112m/C** Burt Reynolds, Lesley-Anne Down, David Niven, Timothy West, Joss Ackland, Patrick Magee; **D:** Don Siegel. **VHS, Beta, LV $14.95** PAR 🐾🐾

Rough Justice Spaghetti western about a lone gunfighter tracking down three killers. Kinski is a sexually aroused bad guy in this miserable excuse. What could he have been thinking? **1987 95m/C** IT Klaus Kinski, Steven Tedd; **D:** Mario Costa. **VHS, Beta $59.95** TWE 🐾 ½

Rough Riders of Cheyenne Sunset Carson ends the feud between the Carsons and the Sterlings. **1945 54m/B** Sunset Carson, Peggy Stewart. **VHS, Beta** MED 🐾 ½

Rough Riders' Roundup Roy and the boys rid a mining town of its crooked manager. Less yodeling than later Roger's outings; also better all around. **1934 54m/B** Roy Rogers, Raymond Hatton, Lynn (Mary Hart) Roberts, Dorothy Sebastian, Duncan Renaldo, George Montgomery; **D:** Joseph Kane. **VHS, Beta $9.95** NOS, VDM, DVT 🐾🐾

Rough Riding Rangers Threatening letters plague a western ranch family. **AKA:** The Secret Stranger. **1935 57m/B** Rex Lease, Janet Chandler. **VHS, Beta $27.95** VCN 🐾 ½

Roughnecks A team of Texas oil drillers attempt to dig the deepest oil well in history and chase women on the side. Too long, and not particularly action-packed or gripping. Made for television. **1980 240m/C** Sam Melville, Cathy Lee Crosby, Vera Miles, Harry Morgan, Steve Forrest, Stephen McHattie, Wilford Brimley; **D:** Bernard McEveety. **VHS, Beta $69.95** PSM 🐾 ½

Round Midnight An aging, alcoholic black American jazz saxophonist comes to Paris in the late 1950s seeking an escape from his self-destructive existence. A devoted young French fan spurs him to one last burst of creative brilliance. A moody, heartfelt homage to such expatriate bebop musicians as Bud Powell and Lester Young. In English and French with English subtitles. Available in a Spanish-subtitled version. **1986 (R) 132m/C** FR Dexter Gordon, Lonette McKee, Francois Cluzet, Martin Scorsese, Herbie Hancock, Sandra Reaves-Phillips; **D:** Bertrand Tavernier. Academy Awards '86: Best Original Score; Nominations: Best Actor (Gordon). **VHS, Beta, LV $19.98** MVD, WAR, TAM 🐾🐾🐾

Round Numbers Judith Schweitzer believes her husband "Big Al the Muffler King" is having an affair with the gorgeous Muffler Mate of the Month, Mitzi (Playboy Playmate Hope Marie Carlton). Determined to get

revenge, Judith books herself into the same health spa that Mitzi attends and the result is pure comedy.
1991 (R) 98m/C Kate Mulgrew, Samantha Eggar, Marty Ingels, Hope Marie Carlton, Shani Wallis, Natalie Barish, Debra Christofferson; *W/D:* Nancy Zala. **VHS $89.95** HMD ♫ ½

Round Trip to Heaven Party guy Larry (Feldman) and his innocent cousin (Galligan) take off in a borrowed Rolls Royce to go meet Larry's dream centerfold in a super model contest. Unfortunately, the Rolls' trunk is loaded with stolen money and Stoneface (Sharkey), the felon who stashed the cash, wants the money back. With Stoneface in pursuit these guys are in for the ride of their lives. For the teen set only. Also available with Spanish subtitles.
1992 (R) 97m/C Corey Feldman, Zach Galligan, Julie McCullough, Rowanne Brewer, Ray Sharkey; *D:* Alan Roberts. **VHS, LV $89.95** PSM ♫♫

The Round Up Brutal tale spins a realistic political web of fear. Set in 1868 in a prison camp, suspected Hungarian subversives, largely peasants and herdsmen, are thrown into jail and tortured. A direct and shocking exploration of life under dehumanizing, totalitarian rule. In Hungarian with English subtitles. *AKA:* Szegenylegenyek Nehezeletuck; The Hopeless Ones; The Poor Outlaws.
1966 90m/B *HU* Janos Gorbe, Tibor Molnar, Andras Kozak; *D:* Miklos Jancso; *W:* Gyula Hernadi. **VHS $59.95** FST, HTV ♫♫ ½

Round-Up Time in Texas Autry delivers a herd of horses to his diamond-prospector brother in South Africa and has to deal with bandits after the jewels. Typical early Autry entry, with singin' on the side.
1937 54m/B Gene Autry, Smiley Burnette; *D:* Joseph Kane. **VHS, Beta $19.95** NOS, VCN, VYY ♫♫

The Rounders Two aging, no-account cowboys (Ford and Fonda) dream of giving up their bronco-busting ways to open a bar in Tahiti where they can watch the world go by. But they have a habit of blowing all their money on women, whiskey, and bad bets. An ornery unbreakable horse may be the key to changing their luck. Mild-mannered comedy with beautiful Arizona scenery.
1965 85m/C Glenn Ford, Henry Fonda, Sue Ann Langdon, Hope Holiday, Chill Wills, Edgar Buchanan, Kathleen Freeman, Joan Freeman, Denver Pyle; *W/D:* Burt Kennedy. **VHS $19.98** MGM ♫♫ ½

Rounding Up the Law Good guy dupes bad guy while organ plays.
1922 62m/B Russell Gordon, Chet Ryan, Patricia Palmer, William McCall, Guinn Williams; *D:* Charles Seeling. **VHS, Beta, 8mm $24.95** VYY, GPV ♫♫ ½

Roustabout A roving, reckless drifter joins a carnival and romances the owner's daughter. Elvis rides on good support from Stanwyck et al. Welch has a bit part in her film debut; look for Terri Garr as a dancer. ♫Roustabout; Poison Ivy League; One Track Heart; Little Egypt; Wheels on My Heels; It's a Wonderful World; It's Carnival Time; Hard Knocks; There's a Brand New Day on the Horizon; Big Love, Big Heartache; Carny Town.
1964 101m/C Elvis Presley, Barbara Stanwyck, Joan Freeman, Leif Erickson, Sue Ann Langdon, Pat Buttram, Joan Staley, Dabbs Greer, Steve Brodie, Jack Albertson, Marianna Hill, Beverly Adams, Billy Barty, Raquel Welch; *D:* John Rich. **VHS, Beta $14.98** FOX, MVD ♫♫ ½

The Rousters Descendants of Wyatt Earp run a carnival in a small Western town. Comic misadventures arise when a modern varmint named Clayton comes looking for action. Stephen J.Cannell (of "The A-Team" and "Riptide" fame) wrote and produced—with his usual extraordinary mix of the absurd and the dangerous. Unusual vehicle for Rogers, but she keeps her style and humor. Made for TV.
1990 (PG) 72m/C Jim Varney, Mimi Rogers, Chad Everett, Maxine Stuart, Hoyt Axton; *W/D:* E.W. Swackhamer. **VHS, LV $79.95** VMK ♫♫ ½

Rover Dangerfield Lovable Las Vegas hound Rover Dangerfield searches for respect but finds none. The results are hilarious. Quality animation from a project developed by Rodney Dangerfield and Harold Ramis.
1991 (G) 78m/C *V:* Rodney Dangerfield. **VHS, LV, 8mm $19.98** WAR, PIA ♫♫

Roxanne A modern comic retelling of "Cyrano de Bergerac." The romantic triangle between a big nosed, small town fire chief, a shy fireman and the lovely astronomer they both love. Martin gives his most sensitive and believable performance. Don't miss the bar scene where he gets back at a heckler. A wonderful adaptation for the modern age, memorably written by Martin.
1987 (PG) 107m/C Steve Martin, Daryl Hannah, Rick Rossovich, Shelley Duvall, Michael J. Pollard, Fred Willard; *D:* Fred Schepisi. **VHS, Beta, LV, 8mm $14.95** COL ♫♫♫

The Royal Bed King Eric's queen really wears the pants in the family, and when she leaves on a trip, he's left helpless and hapless. A revolution erupts, and his daughter announces she plans to marry a commoner. What's a king to do? *AKA:* The Queen's Husband.
1931 74m/B Lowell Sherman, Nance O'Neill, Mary Astor, Anthony Bushell, Gilbert Emery, Robert Warwick, J. Carroll Naish; *D:* Lowell Sherman. **VHS, Beta $29.95** VYY ♫♫ ½

Royal Wedding Astaire and Powell play a brother-and-sister dance team who go to London during the royal wedding of Princess Elizabeth, and find their own romances. Remembered for the inspired songs and Astaire's incredible dancing on the ceiling and walls, this film was Alan Jay Lerner's first screenplay. The idea came from Adele Astaire's recent marriage to a British Lord. ♫Too Late Now; Sunday Jumps; How Can You Believe Me When I Said I Love You When You Know I've Been A Liar All My Life?; You're All the World to Me; The Happiest Day of My Life; Open Your Eyes; Ev'ry Night at Seven; I Left My Hat in Haiti; What A Lovely Day For A Wedding; How About You?; The Devonshire Regiment. *AKA:* Wedding Bells.
1951 93m/C Fred Astaire, Jane Powell, Peter Lawford, Keenan Wynn, Sarah Churchill; *D:* Stanley Donen. **VHS, Beta, LV, 3/4U, Special order formats $19.98** MGM, NOS, CAB ♫♫♫

R.P.M.* (*Revolutions Per Minute) Another chance to relive the sixties. Student activists force the university hierarchy to appoint their favorite radical professor president. Hip prof-turned-prez Quinn is between a rock and a hard place, and allows police to crack down. Could have been intriguing, but loses steam; in any case, the script and direction both stink.
1970 (R) 90m/C Anthony Quinn, Paul Winfield, Gary Lockwood, Ann-Margret; *D:* Stanley Kramer. **VHS, Beta $59.95** COL ♫ ½

R.S.V.P. Hollywood party honoring a writer turns tragic when a body is found in the guest of honor's pool. Most interesting part is watching the porn stars who make up most of the cast fail at acting while dressed.
1984 (R) 87m/C Harry Reems, Lynda Wiesmeier; *D:* Lem Amero. **VHS, Beta, LV $69.98** LIV, VES ♫♫ ½

Rub a Dub Dub A jazzy score backs this modernization of classic Mother Goose tales. Animated.
1983 60m/C VHS, Beta $29.95 MED ♫ ½

Rub a Dub Dub—There's a Zoo in This Tub!, Vol. 2 Another volume of songs & rhymes animated for children.
1987 60m/C VHS, Beta $29.95 MED ♫ ½

Rubin & Ed Ed is a real estate groupie who bribes the eccentric Rubin to attend a get-rich-quick seminar. Rubin decides to cash in on the favor by taking Ed on the road in search of the perfect gravesite for Rubin's long-dead feline. If that sounds wacky, just wait—the fun really begins when the duo is stranded in Death Valley and begins to suffer from sunstroke and hallucinations. Those who dream of weirdos bonding in the desert may be enthused but other viewers may thirst for something more.
1992 (PG-13) 82m/C Crispin Glover, Howard Hesseman, Karen Black, Michael Greene, Brittney Lewis; *D:* Trent Harris; *W:* Trent Harris. **VHS, LV $89.95** COL, FCT ♫♫

Ruby A young woman, christened in blood and raised in sin, has a love affair with the supernatural and murders up a storm at a drive-in. Confused, uneven horror a step up from most similar flicks.
1977 (R) 85m/C Roger Davis, Janet Baldwin, Piper Laurie, Stuart Whitman; *D:* Curtis Harrington. **VHS, Beta $14.95** NEG ♫♫

Ruby Another in the increasing number of Kennedy assassination and conspiracy dramas—this one told from the viewpoint of Jack Ruby, Lee Harvey Oswald's killer. Ruby (Aiello) is a Dallas strip club owner, a mob hanger-on, and also a minor informant to both the Dallas police and the FBI. The jist is that Ruby assassinated Oswald to expose a mob and CIA conspiracy to get Kennedy. Candy Cane (Fenn) is a Marilyn Monroe look-alike, working as a stripper in Ruby's club, who has a tryst with President Kennedy. Confusing plot, somewhat redeemed by the performances of Aiello and Fenn. Combines actual footage of Ruby shooting Oswald with black-and-white filmed scenes. Based on the play "Love Field" by Stephen Davis.
1992 (R) 100m/C Danny Aiello, Sherilyn Fenn, Arliss Howard, Tobin Bell, David Duchovny, Richard Sarafian, Joe Cortese, Marc Lawrence; *D:* John MacKenzie. **VHS, LV $19.95** COL ♫♫ ½

Ruby Cairo Talented cast is wasted in an old-fashioned mystery that lacks a coherent script. MacDowell is married to Mortensen, the owner of an aircraft salvage company. He's supposedly killed in a plane crash but she thinks he's just done a bunk and sets off to track him down. MacDowell discovers her hubby has lots of secret bank accounts and her travels take her to Panama, the Bahamas, Germany, Greece, and finally to Cairo, Egypt where she meets Neeson. Together they discover Mortensen's scam involves smuggling poison gas and the duo then try to outwit the hoods on their trail. The locations are pretty.
1992 (R) 110m/C Andie MacDowell, Liam Neeson, Viggo Mortensen, Jack Thompson, Jeff Corey, Miriam Reed, Luis Cortes, Paco Mauri; *D:* Graeme Clifford; *W:* Robert Dillon, Michael Thomas; *M:* John Barry. ♫ ½

Ruby Gentry White-trash girl Jones, cast aside by man-she-loves Heston, marries wealthy Malden to spite him, then seeks revenge. Classic Southern theme of comeuppance, good direction and acting lift it a notch.
1952 82m/B Charlton Heston, Jennifer Jones, Karl Malden; *D:* King Vidor. VHS, Beta $59.98 FOX ⅛⅛½

Ruby's Dream A bowling alley and nightclub owner dreams of making it big in Las Vegas. After his dreams crash to the ground, however, he realizes what is truly important in life.
19?? 100m/C Joe Pesci. VHS $9.99 QVD ⅛⅛

Ruckus A Vietnam vet uses his training to defend himself when he runs into trouble in a small Alabama town. Less obnoxious than "First Blood," (which came later), but basically the same movie. *AKA:* The Loner.
1981 (PG) 91m/C Dirk Benedict, Linda Blair, Ben Johnson, Richard Farnsworth, Matt Clark; *D:* Max Kleven. VHS, Beta PGN ⅛⅛

Ruddigore The Lords of Ruddigore have been bound for centuries by a terribly inconvenient curse; they must commit a crime every day or die a horribly painful death. When the Lord of Ruddigore passes his mantle on to the new heir, the young heir loses both his good reputation and his proper fiancee. A new version of Gilbert and Sullivan's opera.
197? 112m/C Vincent Price, Keith Michell, Sandra Dugdale. VHS, Beta $49.98 FOX ⅛⅛

Rude Awakening A real estate agent is tortured by bizarre nightmares which lead to an unusual series of events. Part of the "Thriller Video" series.
1981 60m/C Denholm Elliott, James Laurenson, Pat Heywood; *D:* Peter Sasdy. VHS, Beta $29.95 LIV ⅛⅛½

Rude Awakening Hippies Cheech and Roberts (where's Chong?) settled in a South American commune 20 years ago. Now they're back, and don't know what to make of old pals Carradine and Hagerty who have become - that's right - yuppies. Rip Van Winkle-ian farce draws a few yuks, but could have been much funnier. Points for trying.
1989 (R) 100m/C Eric Roberts, Cheech Marin, Julie Hagerty, Robert Carradine, Buck Henry, Louise Lasser, Cindy Williams, Andrea Martin, Cliff DeYoung; *D:* Aaron Russo, David Greenwalt. VHS, Beta, LV $89.99 HBO ⅛⅛

Rudolph & Frosty's Christmas in July More animated adventures of Rudolph and friends. This time they are transported to a glittering, sunny seashore for a magical summer weekend that almost turns into tragedy.
1982 97m/C *V:* Red Buttons, Ethel Merman, Mickey Rooney, Jackie Vernon, Shelley Winters. VHS, Beta $12.95 LIV, TLF, WTA ⅛⅛

Rudolph the Red-Nosed Reindeer The durable Christmas story of the nasally enhanced reindeer who saved the holiday; colorful stop-motion animation and character voices bring it to life, with a memorable guest visit from an abominable snowman. Made for television.
1964 53m/C *D:* Larry Roemer. VHS, Beta, LV, 8mm $14.95 FHE, WTA ⅛⅛

Rudolph's Shiny New Year A puppet-animated Christmas special, showing Rudolph rescuing the Baby New Year from certain peril. Made for television.
1979 50m/C *V:* Red Skelton, Frank Gorshin. VHS, Beta $12.95 LIV, WTA ⅛⅛

Rudyard Kipling's Classic Stories Three Kipling stories come to animated life: "How the Elephant Got His Trunk," "How the Whale Got His Throat" and "How the First Letter Was Written."
1970 25m/C VHS, Beta $14.95 NWV ⅛⅛

The Rue Morgue Massacres A modern reprise of the Poe story with touches of Frankensteinia thrown in; plenty of gore.
1973 (R) 90m/C SP Paul Naschy, Rossana Yanni, Maria Perschy, Vic Winner, Mary Ellen Arpon; *D:* Javier Aguirre. VHS, Beta NO ⅛½

The Ruggles of Red Gap Classic comedy about an uptight British butler who is "won" by a barbarous American rancher in a poker game. Laughton as the nonplussed manservant is hilarious; supporting cast excellent. Third and far superior filming of Harry Leon Wilson story. One of the all-time great comedies, the film was remade musically with Bob Hope and Lucille Ball as "Fancy Pants" (1950).
1935 90m/B Charles Laughton, Mary Boland, Charlie Ruggles, ZaSu Pitts, Roland Young, Leila Hyams, James Burke, Maude Eburne; *D:* Leo McCarey. Academy Awards '35 Nominations: Best Picture; National Board of Review Awards '35: 10 Best Films of the Year; New York Film Critics Awards '35: Best Actor (Laughton). VHS, Beta $14.98 MCA ⅛⅛⅛

Rulers of the City Young gangster avenges his father's death.
1971 91m/C Jack Palance, Edmund Purdom, Al Cliver, Harry Baer. VHS, Beta $19.98 VDC ⅛

The Rules of the Game Renoir's masterpiece, in which a group of French aristocrats, gathering for a weekend of decadence and self-indulgence just before World War II, becomes a metaphor for human folly under siege. The film was banned by the French government, pulled from distribution by the Nazis, and not restored to its original form until 1959, when it premiered at the Venice Film Festival. A great, subtle, ominous film landmark. In French with English subtitles. The laserdisc version includes a commentary by director Peter Bogdanovich. Heavily copied and poorly remade in 1989 as "Scenes from the Class Struggle in Beverly Hills." *AKA:* Le Regle du Jeu.
1939 110m/B FR Marcel Dalio, Nora Gregor, Jean Renoir, Mila Parely, Julien Carette, Gaston Modot, Roland Toutain; *D:* Jean Renoir. VHS, Beta, LV, 8mm $19.95 NOS, SUE, HHT ⅛⅛⅛

The Ruling Class The classic cult satire features O'Toole as the unbalanced 14th Earl of Gurney, who believes that he is either Jesus Christ or Jack the Ripper. Tongue-in-cheek look, complete with dance and music, at eccentric upper-class Brits and their institutions. Uneven, chaotic, surreal and noteworthy.
1972 (PG) 154m/C GB Peter O'Toole, Alastair Sim, Arthur Lowe, Harry Andrews, Coral Browne, Nigel Green; *D:* Peter Medak. Academy Awards '72 Nominations: Best Actor (O'Toole); National Board of Review Awards '72: 10 Best Films of the Year, Best Actor (O'Toole). VHS, Beta, LV $19.98 SUE, NLC ⅛⅛⅛½

Rumble Fish A young street punk worships his gang-leading older brother, the only role model he's known. Crafted by Coppola into an important story of growing up on the wrong side of town, from the novel by S.E. Hinton. Atmospheric musical score by Stewart Copeland. Ambitious and experimental; in black and white.
1983 (R) 94m/B Matt Dillon, Mickey Rourke, Dennis Hopper, Diane Lane, Vincent Spano, Nicolas Cage, Diana Scarwid, Christopher Penn, Tom Waits; *D:* Francis Ford Coppola. VHS, Beta, LV $59.95 MCA ⅛⅛⅛

The Rumor Mill The careers and titanic rivalry of influential Hollywood gossip writer Hedda Hopper and Louella Parsons, played with verve by Taylor and Alexander. Fictionalized script by Jacqueline Feather and David Seidler based on the book "Hedda and Louella" by George Eels. Made for TV. *AKA:* Malice in Wonderland.
1986 94m/C Elizabeth Taylor, Jane Alexander, Richard Dysart, Joyce Van Patten; *D:* Gus Trikonis. VHS, Beta, LV $79.95 VMK ⅛⅛½

A Rumor of War The first big Vietnam drama for TV is a triumph, portraying the real-life experience of author Philip Caputo (based on his bestseller), from naive youth to seasoned soldier to bitter murder suspect at court martial. Succeeds where Stone's later, much-ballyhooed "Born on the Fourth of July" fails. Adapted by John Sacret Young.
1980 195m/C Brad Davis, Keith Carradine, Michael O'Keefe, Stacy Keach, Steve Forrest, Richard Bradford, Brian Dennehy, John Friedrich, Perry Lang, Chris Mitchum, Dan Shor, Jeff Daniels; *D:* Richard T. Heffron. VHS, Beta $14.95 FRH ⅛⅛⅛½

Rumpelstiltskin From "Faerie Tale Theatre" comes the story of a woman who can spin straw into gold (Duvall) and the strange man who saves her life (Villechaize). Enjoyable for the whole family.
1982 60m/C Bud Cort, Ned Beatty, Shelley Duvall, Herve Villechaize, Paul Dooley; *D:* David Irving. VHS, Beta, LV $14.98 KUI, FOX, FCT ⅛⅛⅛½

Rumpelstiltskin Musical retelling of the classic Brother Grimm fairy tale. Irving plays a young girl who says she can spin straw into gold. Barty is a dwarf who helps her. The catch: she must give up her first born to pay him. Lackluster direction and uninspired acting make this version a yawner. Irving's real-life mother (Pointer) and brother have roles too.
1986 (G) 84m/C Amy Irving, Billy Barty, Robert Symonds, Priscilla Pointer, Clive Revill, John Moulder-Brown; *D:* David Irving. VHS, Beta, LV $19.98 MED ⅛⅛

Rumpole of the Bailey John Mortimer's famed British barrister comes to life in McKern's portrait In two episodes taken from the television series. In "Rumpole and the Genuine Article," Rumpole is called on to defend an embittered artist in a forgery case. "Rumpole and the Old Boy Network" has the barrister drawn into blackmail and deception when a brothel is discovered in a respectable London neighborhood. Additional episodes available.
198? 104m/C GB Leo McKern. VHS $49.95 MOV, SIG, TVC ⅛⅛

Rumpole of the Bailey: Rumpole's Return A feature-length film based on the popular British television series. A middle aged barrister refuses to settle for less than justice. Based on the character created by John Mortimer.
1990 106m/C GB Leo McKern. VHS $59.99 FCT, TAM ⅛⅛½

Run A high energy action cartoon, with little plot but lots of stunts. Dempsey is a super-smart law student hired to drive a car to Atlantic City. A stop on the way starts trouble. Instant romance with a local girl balances mayhem from crime boss. Expect no more than physical feats and you'll be happy with this lightweight fare.
1991 (R) 91m/C Patrick Dempsey, Kelly Preston, Ken Pogue, Alan C. Peterson, Sean McCann; *D:* Geoff Burrowes. VHS, Beta, LV $19.99 HPH ⅛½

Run, Angel, Run! Ex-biker Angel is on the run from his former gang after he helps expose them in a magazine article. He settles on a sheep ranch with his girl and then the gang shows up with revenge in mind. Prime drive-in fare with title song sung by none other than Ms. Tammy Wynette.
1969 (R) 90m/C William Smith, Margaret Markov, Valerie Starrett; *D:* Jack Starrett. **VHS, Beta $29.98** *VID* ⚖️½

Run for the Roses "National Velvet" clone about a young Puerto Rican boy and a champion race horse in Kentucky. Cheery family fare. *AKA:* Thoroughbred.
1978 (PG) 93m/C Lisa Eilbacher, Vera Miles, Stuart Whitman, Sam Groom; *D:* Henry Levin. **VHS, Beta $59.98** *LIV* ⚖️½

Run If You Can A woman sees a brutal murderer killing his victims on her television. Will she be next?
1987 (R) 92m/C Martin Landau, Yvette Nipar, Jerry Van Dyke; *D:* Virginia Lively Stone. **Beta $79.95** *ALL* ⚖️

Run of the Arrow Rather than surrender to the North at the end of the Civil War, an ex-Confederate soldier (Steiger) joins the Sioux nation, engaged in war against the white man. Steiger's Irish brogue is weird and distracting, and the intriguing premise fails to satisfy, but the cast is competent and interesting. *AKA:* Hot Lead.
1956 85m/C Rod Steiger, Brian Keith, Charles Bronson, Ralph Meeker, Tim McCoy; *D:* Samuel Fuller. **VHS, Beta, LV $54.95** *UHV* ⚖️⚖️⚖️

Run, Rebecca, Run Interesting family adventure yarn for the family about a South American refugee who tries to stop a young girl from leaving from an Australian island where they are both stranded. She eventually befriends him, and attempts to get permission for him to enter the country.
1981 90m/C *AU* Simone Buchanan, Henri Szeps; *D:* Peter Maxwell. **VHS, Beta $14.98** *VID* ⚖️⚖️½

Run Silent, Run Deep Submarine commander Gable battles his officers, especially the bitter Lancaster who vied for the same command, while stalking the Japanese destroyer that sunk his former command. Top-notch World War II sub action, scripted from Commander Edward L. Beach's novel.
1958 93m/B Burt Lancaster, Clark Gable, Jack Warden, Don Rickles, Brad Dexter; *D:* Robert Wise. **VHS, Beta $19.95** *FOX, FCT* ⚖️⚖️⚖️

Run, Stranger, Run The inhabitants of a seaside house in Nova Scotia are paralyzed with fear when a number of brutal murders occur. A couple of sicko slasher scenes, but hard to swallow. *AKA:* Happy Mother's Day, Love, George.
1973 (PG) 110m/C Ron Howard, Patricia Neal, Cloris Leachman, Bobby Darin; *D:* Darren McGavin. **VHS $59.95** *COL* ⚖️

Run Virgin Run The village women find a beautiful virgin to marry the blacksmith so he will stay in town and they will still be able to enjoy him.
1990 (R) 90m/C Cheryl Ross, Kyle Coleman, Suzanne Baron. **VHS, Beta $39.95** *MON* ⚖️

Runaway A cop and his sidekick track down a group of killer robots wreaking havoc. Self-serious, sorry sci-fi. Features Simmons of the rock group KISS.
1984 (PG-13) 100m/C Tom Selleck, Cynthia Rhodes, Gene Simmons, Stan Shaw, Kirstie Alley; *D:* Michael Crichton; *M:* Jerry Goldsmith. **VHS, Beta, LV $14.95** *COL* ⚖️½

Runaway A boy blames himself for his friend's accidental death and runs away to live in the subway tunnels of New York City. After four months of life underground, a

disabled veteran and a waitress lend the boy a hand. Adapted from the novel "Slake's Limbo" by Felice Holman. Made for PBS and aired as part of the "Wonderworks" series.
1989 58m/C Charles S. Dutton, Jasmine Guy, Gavin Allen; *D:* Gilbert Moses. **VHS $29.95** *PME, HMV, COL* ⚖️½

The Runaway Barge Tiresomely ordinary TV yarn about three adventurers earning their living on a riverboat. The usual cliches are present, including a gang of bad guys.
1975 78m/C Bo Hopkins, Tim Matheson, Jim Davis, Nick Nolte, Devon Ericson, Christina Hart, James Best; *D:* Boris Sagal. **VHS $29.95** *LIV* ⚖️⚖️

The Runaway Bus Filled with the requisite motley crew of passengers, including a gold-carrying thief and the ever-befuddled Margaret Rutherford, a bus gets lost between airports and ends up in a deserted village. Would-be wacky comedy.
1954 78m/B *GB* Frankie Howerd, Margaret Rutherford, Petula Clark, George Coulouris; *D:* Val Guest. **VHS, Beta $29.95** *VYY, FCT* ⚖️⚖️

Runaway Island, Part 1 Episode: "Quest for Jamie McLeod." In 1830's Australia, two youths battle corruption when their father leaves for England.
19?? 96m/C Miles Buchanan, Simone Buchanan. **VHS, Beta $59.95** *SVS* ⚖️⚖️

Runaway Island, Part 2 Episode: "The Exiles." When their father dies, the McLeod children realize their only hope of obtaining his property is to find his hidden will.
19?? 103m/C Miles Buchanan, Simone Buchanan. **VHS, Beta $59.95** *SVS* ⚖️⚖️

Runaway Island, Part 3 Episode: "The Bushranger." Jamie and Jemma McLeod continue the search for their father's will, but are captured by a gang of terrorists.
19?? 101m/C Miles Buchanan, Simone Buchanan. **VHS, Beta $59.95** *SVS* ⚖️⚖️

Runaway Island, Part 4 Episode: "Treasure of the Conquistadors." Having found the missing portion of the map that will lead them to their father's will, the McLeod children encounter a band of pirates, Aborigines and other dangers that might prevent them from staking their claim.
19?? 104m/C Miles Buchanan, Simone Buchanan. **VHS, Beta $59.95** *SVS* ⚖️⚖️

Runaway Nightmare Two western worm ranchers are kidnapped by a female gang whose members torture and initiate them, then talk about their plan to steal from organized criminals. Just another typical worm rancher flick.
1984 104m/C Michael Cartel, Al Valletta; *D:* Michael Cartel. **VHS** *NO* ⚖️

Runaway Train A tough jailbird and his sidekick break out of the hoosegow and find themselves trapped aboard a brakeless freight train heading for certain derailment in northwestern Canada. Harrowing existential action drama based on a screenplay by Akira Kurosawa. Voight is superb.
1985 (R) 112m/C Jon Voight, Eric Roberts, Rebecca DeMornay, John P. Ryan, T.K. Carter, Kenneth McMillan; *W/D:* Andrei Konchalovsky. Academy Awards '85 Nominations: Best Actor (Voight), Best Film Editing, Best Supporting Actor (Roberts); Golden Globe Awards '86: Best Actor—Drama (Voight). **VHS, Beta, LV $14.98** *MGM* ⚖️⚖️⚖️

The Runaways A boy runs away from an unhappy foster home situation and becomes friends with a leopard that has escaped from an animal park. Sentimental but well-done family fun.

1975 76m/C Dorothy McGuire, John Randolph, Neva Patterson, Josh Albee; *D:* Harry Harris. **VHS, Beta** *NO* ⚖️

Runaways A corrupt politician's wife falls in love with the man who saved her when she attempted suicide. The two try to escape her husband's wrathful vengeance.
1984 95m/C Steve Oliver, Sondra Currie, John Russell. **VHS, Beta** *NO* ⚖️

The Runestone After the eponymous viking relic is unearthed, an archaeologist's meddling frees a long-imprisoned wolf-beast that terrorizes New York. An adequate horror flick that taps the seldom-explored vein of Norse mythology. Based on a novel by Mark E. Rogers.
1991 (R) 105m/C Peter Riegert, Joan Severance, William Hickey, Tim Ryan, Chris Young, Alexander Godunov; *D:* Willard Carroll. **VHS, LV $89.98** *LIV* ⚖️⚖️

The Runner Stumbles Dated melodrama about a priest who goes on trial for murdering the nun with whom he fell in love in a mining town in the 1920s. Based on a true incident, from the play by Milan Stiff. Van Dyke in an unwanted serious role is miserably grim and wooden.
1979 (R) 109m/C Dick Van Dyke, Kathleen Quinlan, Maureen Stapleton, Ray Bolger, Beau Bridges, Tammy Grimes; *D:* Stanley Kramer. **VHS, Beta $59.98** *FOX* ⚖️½

The Runnin' Kind A yuppie expecting to inherit his father's Ohio law firm goes on a wild spree with an all-girl rock band. Sexy drummer Howard shows him the sights of certain parts of L.A. Original, fun comedy. Independent.
1989 (R) 89m/C David Packer, Pleasant Gehman, Brie Howard, Susan Strasberg; *D:* Max Tash. **VHS, Beta $79.98** *FOX* ⚖️⚖️½

Running Against Time A teacher tries to change history (and erase his brother's Vietnam War death) by time-warping back to 1963 and preventing JFK's murder. The made for cable TV movie takes an offhanded gee-whiz approach to a tantalizing premise, as temporal paradoxes multiply in "Back to the Future" style. No assassination-conspiracy theories, by the way, but Lyndon Johnson fans may not like his portrayal here. Based on the novel "A Time to Remember" by Stanley Shapiro.
1990 (PG) 93m/C Robert Hays, Catherine Hicks, Sam Wanamaker; *D:* Bruce Seth Green; *W:* Robert Glass. **VHS $79.95** *MCA* ⚖️⚖️½

Running Away Bittersweet story of WWII romance, with a twist of adventure. Strong cast creates good chemistry, but somehow the story is not engaging. Loren and Penny are mother and daughter, leaving Rome for the hills and encountering dangers.
1989 (PG-13) 101m/C Sophia Loren, Sydney Penny, Robert Loggia, Andrea Occhipinti; *D:* Dino Risi. **VHS, LV $89.95** *PSM, PAR, FCT* ⚖️⚖️

Running Blind Espionage/adventure thriller has a double agent and a beautiful woman on the run in Iceland.
197? 120m/C *GB* Stuart Wilson, Heidi Steindorsittir. **VHS $49.95** *FCT* ⚖️⚖️

Running Brave The true story of Billy Mills, a South Dakota Sioux Indian who won the Gold Medal in the 10,000 meter run at the 1964 Tokyo Olympics. Not bad, but hokey in the way of many of these plodding true-story flicks.
1983 (PG) 90m/C Robby Benson, Claudia Cron, Pat Hingle, Denis Lacroix; *D:* D.S. Everett. **VHS, Beta, LV** *DIS* ⚖️⚖️

Running Hot Seventeen-year-old convicted murderer Stoltz gets love letter in prison from older woman Carrico. When he escapes, they flee the law together. Quick-paced and entertaining. *AKA:* Highway to Hell; Lucky 13.
1983 (R) 88m/C Monica Carrico, Eric Stoltz, Stuart Margolin, Virgil Frye, Richard Bradford, Sorrels Pickard, Juliette Cummins; *W/D:* Mark Griffiths. VHS, Beta $69.98 LIV, VES ✶✶½

The Running Kind A young man set to inherit a law firm drops it all to manage an all-girl rock band. His new career takes him into the L.A. punk-scene in this clever comedy.
1989 (R) 100m/C David Packer, Pleasant Gehman, Brie Howard, Susan Strasberg; *D:* Max Tash. VHS, Beta $79.98 FOX ✶✶½

The Running Man Special-effects-laden adaptation of the Stephen King novel about a futuristic television game show. Convicts are given a chance for pardon—all they have to do is survive an on going battle with specially-trained assassins in the bombed-out sections of Los Angeles. Sci-fi with an attitude.
1987 (R) 101m/C Arnold Schwarzenegger, Richard Dawson, Maria Conchita Alonso, Yaphet Kotto, Mick Fleetwood, Dweezil Zappa, Jesse Ventura; *D:* Paul Michael Glaser. VHS, Beta, LV $14.98 LIV, VES ✶✶½

Running Mates Occasionally intriguing drama of two teens who fall in love, but are kept apart by their fathers' local political rivalry. Could have been better, but cardboard characters abound.
1986 (PG-13) 90m/C Greg Webb, Barbara Howard, J. Don Ferguson, Clara Dunn; *D:* Thomas L. Neff. VHS, Beta $19.95 STE, NWV ✶✶

Running Mates Cynically amusing political satire about a bachelor politician and his too intelligent lady love. Harris is Hugh, a U.S. senator looking forward to the presidential primaries when he meets widowed children's novelist Aggie (Keaton). She hates politics and he's Mr. Slick, although decent enough behind the political expediency. Aggie, however, has a potentially damaging secret in her past which causes the scandal-scenting pack of press hounds to bay in salivating anticipation. Will Hugh stick by Aggie and will Aggie overcome her natural political distaste for everything to end happily? A well-played romp. Made for cable television.
1992 (PG-13) 88m/C Ed Harris, Diane Keaton, Ed Begley Jr., Ben Masters, Russ Tamblyn; *D:* Michael Lindsay-Hogg; *W:* A.L. Appling. VHS, LV $89.99 HBO ✶✶✶

Running on Empty Two 1960s radicals are still on the run in 1988 for a politically motivated Vietnam War-era crime. Though they have managed to stay one step ahead of the law, their son wants a "normal" life, even if it means never seeing his family again. Well-performed, quiet, plausible drama.
1988 (PG-13) 116m/C Christine Lahti, River Phoenix, Judd Hirsch, Martha Plimpton, Jonas Arby, Ed Crowley, L.M. Kit Carson, Steven Hill, Augusta Dabney, David Margulies, Sidney Lumet; *D:* Sidney Lumet. Academy Awards '88 Nominations: Best Original Screenplay, Best Supporting Actor (Phoenix); National Board of Review Awards '88: Best Supporting Actor (Phoenix). VHS, Beta, LV, 8mm $19.95 WAR ✶✶✶

Running Out of Luck A light, song-packed story about a rock star very much like Jagger who is abandoned in South America and believed dead, until he returns to his world. Features songs from Jagger's solo album "She's the Boss".
1986 (R) 88m/C Mick Jagger, Dennis Hopper, Jerry Hall, Rae Dawn Chong; *D:* Julien Temple. VHS, Beta, LV $19.95 MVD, FOX ✶✶½

Running Scared Two young men, returning from military service as stowaways aboard an Army cargo plane, are caught by an intelligence agent and thought to be spies, because Reinhold has unknowingly photographed a secret US base wire his stolen Army-issue camera. Not-bad spy thriller with a twist - the "spies" are hapless nobodies, now on the lam.
1979 (PG) 92m/C Ken Wahl, Judge Reinhold, John Saxon, Annie McEnroe, Bradford Dillman, Pat Hingle; *D:* Paul Glickler. VHS, Beta, LV $59.99 HBO ✶✶

Running Scared Hip, unorthodox Chicago cops Hines and Crystal have to handle an important drug arrest before taking an extended vacation in Key West. Not as relentless as "48 Hrs.," but more enjoyable in some ways. Ever wonder what it's like to ride in a car at high speed on the tracks? Find out here.
1986 (R) 107m/C Gregory Hines, Billy Crystal, Dan Hedaya, Jimmy Smits, Darlanne Fluegel, Joe Pantoliano, Steven Bauer; *D:* Peter Hyams. VHS, Beta, LV $14.98 MGM ✶✶½

Running Wild Early silent comedy starring mustachioed Fields as an eternal coward who suddenly turns into a lion by hypnosis. Odd, often unfunny Fields entry sometimes hits the mark. He's awfully mean, though. Music score by Gaylord Carter.
1927 68m/B W.C. Fields, Mary Brian, Claud Buchanan; *D:* Gregory La Cava. VHS, Beta $29.95 PAR ✶✶

Running Wild A free-lance photographer becomes involved in a dispute to save a corral of wild mustang horses. The usual great Colorado scenery enhances a good, family-view story.
1973 (G) 102m/C Lloyd Bridges, Dina Merrill, Pat Hingle, Gilbert Roland, Morgan Woodward. VHS, Beta $19.95 MED ✶✶½

Rush A post-nuclear world war movie in which a rebel named Rush battles the rulers of a slave colony.
1984 83m/C IT Conrad Nichols, Gordon Mitchell, Laura Trotter, Rita Furlan; *D:* Tonino Ricci. VHS NO ✶

Rush Texas drug culture, circa 1975, is portrayed in this bleak cop drama. Rookie narcotics officer Kristen Cates (Leigh) goes undercover with the experienced Raynor (Patric) to catch a big-time dealer, menacingly played by Allman, and their bosses don't much care how they do it. Cates falls in love with Raynor and is drawn ever deeper into the drug-addicted world they are supposed to destroy. Fine performances and a great blues score by Eric Clapton. The directorial debut of Zanuck. Based on ex-narcotics cop Kim Wozencraft's autobiographical novel.
1991 (R) 120m/C Jason Patric, Jennifer Jason Leigh, Gregg Allman, Max Perlich; *D:* Lili Fini Zanuck; *W:* Pete Dexter; *M:* Eric Clapton. VHS $19.98 MGM ✶✶✶

Rush It Scriptwriters ponder possible plots over capucino: "I've got it! 'Bike Messengers in Love'!" "Nah. The title's too obvious. Why don't we call it 'Rush It'?" Much hard work and many months later, the result is forgettable.
1977 78m/C Tom Berenger, Jill Eikenberry. VHS, Beta $49.95 UNI ✶½

Rush Week Dead coeds populate campus during frat week. Greg Allman has bit part and the Dickies perform two songs.
1988 (R) 93m/C Dean Hamilton, Gregg Allman, Kathleen Kinmont, Roy Thinnes, Pamela Ludwig; *D:* Bob Bravler. VHS, LV $79.95 COL ✶

The Russia House Russian scientist Brandauer attempts to publish book debunking Soviet Union's claims of military superiority by passing it through ex-lover Pfeiffer to British editor Connery, apparently unaware of impending glasnost. Star-studded spy thriller directed by Aussie Schepisi aspires to heights it never quite reaches. Adapted by Tom Stoppard from John Le Carre's novel. Beautiful on-location photography. Stoppard's screenplay is very fine, actually making some aspects of the novel work better.
1990 (R) 122m/C Sean Connery, Michelle Pfeiffer, Roy Scheider, James Fox, John Mahoney, Klaus Maria Brandauer, Ken Russell, J.T. Walsh, Michael Kitchen; *D:* Fred Schepisi; *W:* Tom Stoppard; *M:* Jerry Goldsmith. VHS, LV, 8mm $94.99 MGM, PIA, FCT ✶✶½

Russian Roulette The Russian premier is visiting Vancouver in 1970, and the Mounties must prevent a dissident KGB terrorist from assassinating him. Un-thrilling spy yarn fails to deliver on intriguing premise.
1975 100m/C George Segal, Christina Raines, Bo Brundin, Denholm Elliott, Louise Fletcher; *D:* Lou Lombardo. VHS, Beta $59.98 FOX ✶✶

The Russian Terminator An FBI agent is up against a one-man "death squad."
1990 (R) 90m/C Helena Michaelson, Frederick Offrein, Harley Melin, Tina Tjung; *W/D:* Mats Helge. VHS $79.95 XVC, PHX ✶

The Russians are Coming, the Russians are Coming Based on the comic novel "The Off-Islanders" by Nathaniel Benchley, this is the story of a Russian sub which accidentally runs aground off the New England coast. The residents falsely believe that the nine-man crew is the beginning of a Soviet invasion, though the men are only looking for help. A memorable set of silly events follows the landing, engineered by a gung-ho police chief and a town filled with overactive imaginations.
1966 126m/C Alan Arkin, Carl Reiner, Theodore Bikel, Eva Marie Saint, Brian Keith, Paul Ford, Jonathan Winters, Ben Blue, Tessie O'Shea, Doro Merando, John Phillip Law; *D:* Norman Jewison. Academy Awards '66 Nominations: Best Actor (Arkin), Best Picture, Best Story & Screenplay; Golden Globe Awards '67: Best Actor—Musical/Comedy (Arkin), Best Film—Musical/Comedy; National Board of Review Awards '66: 10 Best Films of the Year. VHS, Beta $19.95 FOX, MLB ✶✶✶

Russkies A jolly comedy about three adorable American kids who capture, and eventually grow to like, a stranded Russian sailor. Friendly and peace-loving, but dull.
1987 (PG) 98m/C Leaf Phoenix, Whip Hubley, Peter Billingsley, Stefan DeSalle; *D:* Rick Rosenthal. VHS, Beta, LV $19.98 LHV, WAR ✶½

Rustler's Hideout One of numerous westerns starring Crabbe as cowboy do-gooder Billy Carson, here plodding through standard histrionics against rustlers, a card-sharp, and a business fraud. *AKA:* Rustler's Roundup.
1944 60m/C Buster Crabbe, Al "Fuzzy" St. John, Charles King, John Merton, Lane Chandler, Hal Price, Edward Cassidy, Bud Osborne; *D:* Sam Newfield. VHS, Beta GPV ✶

Rustler's Paradise Carey seeks revenge on the man who stole his wife and daughter.
1935 59m/B Harry Carey Sr., Gertrude Messinger, Edmund Cobb; *D:* Harry Fraser. VHS, Beta, LV $19.95 NOS ✶

Rustler's Rhapsody A singing cowboy rides into a small western town and encounters all kinds of desperados in this earnest would-be satire of '40s B-movie westerns.
1985 (PG) 89m/C Tom Berenger, Patrick Wayne, G.W. Bailey, Andy Griffith, Marilu Henner; **D:** Hugh Wilson. **VHS, Beta, LV** $14.95 PAR ♫♫

Rustler's Valley Hopalong Cassidy is a ranch foreman who tries to save his employer from the clutches of a crooked lawyer. Pretty fun ordinary range-ridin' saga.
1937 59m/B William Boyd, George "Gabby" Hayes, Lee J. Cobb; **D:** Nate Watt. **VHS, Beta** $24.95 VYY ♫♫

The Rutanga Tapes Soviet bloc country has representatives in Africa producing deadly chemicals used for war and a dissident has taped evidence of native deaths. Reporter babe Simpson wants an exclusive, Petersen wants the dissident, Libyan agents want the tapes, and you'll want to fast forward to the end.
1990 (R) 88m/C Henry Cele, Arnold Vosloo, Wilson Dunster, David Dukes, Susan Anspach; **D:** David Lister. **VHS** NO ♫ ½

The Rutherford County Line A tough small-town sheriff searches for the killer of his deputies.
1987 98m/C Earl Owensby; **D:** Thom McIntyre. **VHS, Beta** $59.95 MCA ♫

The Ruthless Four Quartet of unlikely mining partners match wills and wits and battle the elements. Not-so-hot spaghetti western, with good lead from Heflin. **AKA:** Every Man For Himself; Each One For Himself; Sam Cooper's Gold; Each Man For Himself.
1970 97m/C IT Van Heflin, Klaus Kinski, Gilbert Roland, George Hilton; **D:** Giorgio Capitani. **VHS, Beta** $24.95 MON ♫

Ruthless People DeVito and his mistress spend a romantic evening plotting his obnoxious wife's untimely demise. Before he can put his plan into action, he's delighted to discover she's been kidnapped by some very desperate people—who don't stand a chance with Bette. High farcical entertainment script by Dale Lanner; variation on the story "The Ransom of Red Chief," by O. Henry.
1986 (R) 93m/C Bette Midler, Danny DeVito, Judge Reinhold, Helen Slater, Anita Morris, Bill Pullman; **D:** Jim Abrahams, David Zucker. **VHS, Beta, LV** $19.95 TOU ♫♫♫

Ryan's Daughter Irish woman (Miles) marries a man she does not love and then falls for a shell-shocked British major who arrives during the 1916 Irish uprising to keep the peace. Not surprisingly, she is accused of betraying the local IRA gunrunners to her British lover. Tasteful melodrama with lots of pretty scenery that goes on a bit too long.
1970 (PG) 194m/C GB Sarah Miles, Robert Mitchum, John Mills, Trevor Howard, Christopher Jones, Leo McKern; **D:** David Lean; **W:** Robert Bolt. Academy Awards '70: Best Cinematography, Best Supporting Actor (Mills); Nominations: Best Actress (Miles), Best Sound; National Board of Review Awards '70: 10 Best Films of the Year. **VHS, Beta, LV** $29.98 MGM, PIA, BTV ♫♫ ½

Ryder P.I. P.I Ryder and his sidekick fight crime and solve weird cases in the big city.
1988

Sabaka Adventure set in India about a scary religious cult. Karloff and the cast of stalwart "B" movie performers have fun with this one, and you should, too. **AKA:** The Hindu.
1955 81m/C Boris Karloff, Reginald Denny, Victor Jory, Lisa Howard, Jeanne Bates, Jay Novello, June Foray; **D:** Frank Ferrin. **VHS** $16.95 SNC ♫♫

Sabotage Early Hitchcock thriller based on Conrad's "The Secret Agent". A woman who works at a movie theater (Sidney) suspects her quiet husband (Homolka) might be the terrorist planting bombs around London. Numerous sly touches of the Master's signature humor. **AKA:** A Woman Alone; The Woman Alone.
1936 81m/B Oscar Homolka, Sylvia Sidney, John Loder; **D:** Alfred Hitchcock. **VHS, Beta, LV, 8mm, 3/4U, Special order formats** $16.95 SNC, NOS, HHT ♫♫♫

Saboteur A man wrongly accused of sabotaging an American munitions plant during World War II sets out to find the traitor who framed him. Hitchcock uses his locations, including Boulder Dam, Radio City Music Hall, and the Statue of Liberty, to greatly intensify the action. Stunning resolution.
1942 108m/B Priscilla Lane, Robert Cummings, Otto Kruger, Alan Baxter, Norman Lloyd; **D:** Alfred Hitchcock. **VHS, Beta, LV** $19.95 MCA ♫♫♫

Sabre Jet Run-of-the-mill wartime drama of hubbies flying combat missions in Korea and long-suffering spouses on the home front.
1953 90m/C Robert Stack, Amanda Blake, Louis King; **D:** Louis King. **VHS, Beta** $39.95 VCD ♫♫

Sabrina Two wealthy brothers, one an aging businessman and the other a dissolute playboy, vie for the attention of their chauffeur's daughter, who has just returned from a French finishing school. Typically acerbic, in the Wilder manner, with Bogart and Holden cast interestingly against type. Written by Wilder from the play "Sabrina Fair" by Samuel Taylor. **AKA:** Sabrina Fair.
1954 113m/B Audrey Hepburn, Humphrey Bogart, William Holden, Walter Hampden, Francis X. Bushman, John Williams, Martha Hyer, Marcel Dalio; **D:** Billy Wilder. Academy Awards '54: Best Costume Design (B & W); Nominations: Best Actress (Hepburn), Best Art Direction/Set Decoration (B & W), Best Black and White Cinematography, Best Director (Wilder), Best Screenplay; Directors Guild of America Awards '54: Best Director (Wilder); National Board of Review Awards '54: 10 Best Films of the Year, Best Supporting Actor (Williams). **VHS, Beta, LV** $19.95 PAR ♫♫♫

Sabrina, the Teenage Witch What happens when a pretty teenage girl is also a witch? If it's Sabrina, you know you're in for plenty of amazing, amusing and action-packed adventures. Join her and her pals Archie, Betty, Veronica and Jughead for magical fun at Riverdale High. Nine volumes available.
1969 57m/C **V:** Jane Webb. **VHS, Beta** $39.98 SUE ♫♫♫

Sacco & Vanzetti Two Italian immigrants and acknowledged anarchists are caught amidst communist witch-hunts and judicial negligence when they are tried and executed for murder in 1920s America. Based on the true-life case, considered by some a flagrant miscarriage of justice and political martyrdom, by others, honest American judicial-system proceedings. Well-made and acted. Joan Baez sings the title song "The Ballad of Sacco and Vanzetti." **AKA:** Sacco e Vanzetti.
1971 (PG) 120m/C Gian Marie Volonte, Riccardo Cucciolla, Milo O'Shea, Cyril Cusack, Geoffrey Keen; **D:** Guiliano Montaldo; **M:** Ennio Morricone. **VHS, Beta** $59.95 UHV ♫♫

The Sacketts Follows the adventures of three Tennessee brothers who migrate to the West after the Civil War. Based on two Louis L'Amour novels. Made for television.
1979 198m/C Jeffery Osterhage, Tom Selleck, Sam Elliott, Glenn Ford, Ben Johnson, Mercedes McCambridge, Ruth Roman, Jack Elam, Gilbert Roland; **D:** Robert Totten. **VHS, Beta** $14.99 WAR, HHE ♫♫ ½

Sacred Ground A trapper and his pregnant Apache wife unknowingly build shelter on the Paiute Indians' sacred burial ground. When the wife dies in childbirth, the pioneer is forced to kidnap a Paiute woman who has just buried her own deceased infant. Average western drama.
1983 (PG) 100m/C Tim McIntire, Jack Elam, L.Q. Jones, Mindi Miller; **D:** Charles B. Pierce. **VHS, Beta** $59.98 FOX ♫♫

Sacred Mountain/White Flame Two short films starring Riefenstahl, featuring mostly fluid dance sequences and Teutonic mountain boy/girl plots. Silent.
1931 60m/B GE Leni Riefenstahl. **VHS, Beta** $34.95 FCT, GLV, MRV ♫♫♫

The Sacrifice Tarkovsky's enigmatic final film, released after his death. Deals with a retired intellectual's spiritually symbolic efforts at self-sacrifice in order to save his family on the eve of a nuclear holocaust. Stunning cinematography by Sven Nykvist. Acclaimed, but sometimes slow going; not everyone will appreciate Tarkovsky's visionary spiritualism. In Swedish with English subtitles.
1986 (PG) 145m/C FR SW Erland Josephson, Susan Fleetwood, Valerie Mairesse, Allan Edwall, Gudrun Gisladottir, Sven Wollter, Filippa Franzen; **D:** Andrei Tarkovsky. **VHS, Beta, LV** $29.95 PAV, TAM ♫♫♫

Sacrilege A nun and a nobleman engage in a hot love affair that fosters scandal, murder and, revenge. Cynical use of religious theme masks otherwise ordinary sex/romance flick. Controversial Italian-made erotic drama.
1986 104m/C IT Myriem Roussel, Alessandro Gassman; **D:** Luciano Odorisio. **VHS, Beta** $79.95 PSM ♫ ½

The Sad Sack A bumbling hero with a photographic memory winds up in Morocco as a member of the French Foreign Legion. Although a success at the box office, Lewis's second movie (without partner Dean Martin) seems jerky and out of sorts today. Based on the comic strip character by George Baker, but not effectively. Hal David and Burt Bacharach wrote the music.
1957 98m/B Jerry Lewis, Phyllis Kirk, David Wayne, Peter Lorre, Gene Evans, Mary Treen; **D:** George Marshall. **VHS** COL ♫♫

Sadat Gossett, Jr. well plays his title role of Egyptian leader and Nobel Peace Prize winner, Anwar el Sadat. But the controversial life and peace efforts of the president (assassinated in 1981) are given a quick overview in this average drama. Made for television.
1983 (PG) 191m/C Louis Gossett Jr., John Rhys-Davies, Jeremy Kemp, Nehemiah Persoff, Madolyn Smith, Anne Heywood, Jeffrey Tambor, Barry Morse; **D:** Richard Michaels. **VHS** $59.95 COL ♫♫ ½

Saddle Buster A rodeo cowboy loses his nerve after being thrown by a tough horse, but gets it back again by the end of the hour. Actual rodeo footage is incorporated into this low-budget bronco saga.
1932 59m/B Tom Keene, Helen Foster, Charles Quigley, Marie Quillen, Robert Frazer, Charles "Slim" Whitaker; **D:** Fred Allen. **VHS** $19.95 NOS, HEG ♫♫

Saddle Mountain Round-Up The Range Busters are on the trail again as they smoke out a murderer.
1941 61m/B Ray Corrigan, John "Dusty" King, Max Terhune. **VHS, Beta** $19.95 *NOS, DVT, RXM* ✰

Sadie McKee A melodrama with Crawford as a maid searching for love in the big city. She falls for a self-destructive ne'er-do-well, marries an alcoholic millionaire, and eventually finds true love with the wealthy Tone (who would become Crawford's third husband). Professional acting and directing elevate the story.
1934 90m/B Joan Crawford, Franchot Tone, Gene Raymond, Edward Arnold; *D:* Clarence Brown. **VHS** $19.98 *BTV* ✰✰✰

Sadie Thompson Swanson plays a harlot with a heart of gold, bawdy and good-natured, in the South Seas. A zealot missionary (Barrymore) arrives and falls in love with her. The last eight minutes of footage have been recreated by using stills and the original title cards, to replace the last reel which had decomposed. Remade as "Rain," "Dirty Gertie From Harlem," and "Miss Sadie Thompson." Based on W. Somerset Maugham's "Rain."
1928 97m/B Gloria Swanson, Lionel Barrymore, Raoul Walsh, Blanche Frederici, Charles Lane, James Marcus; *D:* Raoul Walsh. **VHS, LV** $29.95 *KIV, MOV* ✰✰✰

The Sadist Three teachers on their way to Dodger Stadium find themselves stranded at a roadside garage and terrorized by a snivelling lunatic. Tense and plausible. Cinematography by Vilmos Zsigmond. *AKA:* The Profile of Terror.
1963 95m/B Arch Hall Jr., Helen Hovey, Richard Alden, Marilyn Manning; *W/D:* James Landis. Beta $16.95 *SNC, RHI* ✰✰½

Safari 3000 "Playboy" writer is assigned to do a story on a three-day, 3,000 kilometer car race in Africa. Doesn't take itself too seriously, and neither should we. Dumb, dull, and disjointed.
1982 (PG) 91m/C Stockard Channing, David Carradine, Christopher Lee; *D:* Harry Hurwitz. **VHS, Beta** $59.95 *MGM* ✰½

Saga of Death Valley Rogers battles a band of outlaws and discovers that their leader is his own brother. Exciting and likeable early Rogers western.
1939 56m/B Roy Rogers, George "Gabby" Hayes, Donald (Don "Red") Barry, Doris Day; *D:* Joseph Kane. **VHS, Beta, 3/4U, Special order formats** $19.95 *NOS, VDM, VCN* ✰✰½

The Saga of the Draculas An aging vampire wishes to continue his bloodline and seeks to convert his niece's baby to his bloodsucking ways. *AKA:* Dracula Saga; Dracula: The Bloodline Continues...; The Saga of Dracula.
1972 (R) 90m/C SP Narciso Ibanez Menta, Tina Sainz, Tony Isbert, Maria Koski, Cristina Suriani, Helga Line; *D:* Leon Klimovsky. **VHS** $19.98 *SNC* ✰

Saga of the Vagabond Arranged by master director Akira Kurosawa. A band of ruthless outlaws careen across a civil war-torn countryside. With English subtitles. *AKA:* Sengoku Gunto-Den.
1959 115m/C JP Toshiro Mifune, Michiyo Aratama; *D:* Toshio Sugie. **VHS, Beta** $59.95 *VDA* ✰✰½

Sagebrush Trail Wayne's second-ever western, complete with all sorts of tumbleweed and white-hat cliches. Our hero is wrongly accused of killin' a man, and busts out of the hoosegow to clear his name. Interesting plot twists makes for fun, compelling viewing.
1933 53m/B John Wayne, Yakima Canutt, Wally Wales; *D:* Armand Schaefer. **VHS, LV, 3/4U, Special order formats** $8.95 *NEG, REP, NOS* ✰✰✰

Sahara A British-American unit must fight the Germans for their survival in the Libyan desert during World War II. Plenty of action and suspense combined with good performances makes this one a step above the usual war movie.
1943 97m/B Humphrey Bogart, Dan Duryea, Bruce Bennett, Lloyd Bridges, Rex Ingram, J. Carroll Naish, Richard Nugent; *D:* Zoltan Korda. **VHS, Beta** $9.95 *COL* ✰✰✰

Sahara Disappointing "Perils of Pauline" type adventure. Shields disguises herself as a man (sure) to complete a race across the desert in honor of her late father, and a sheik captures her.
1983 (PG) 111m/C Brooke Shields, Lambert Wilson, Horst Buchholz, John Rhys-Davies, Ronald Lacey, John Mills, Steve Forrest, Perry Lang, Cliff Potts; *D:* Andrew V. McLaglen; *W:* James R. Silke; *M:* Ennio Morricone. **VHS, Beta, LV** $14.95 *MGM* Woof!

Saigon Commandos Commandos, on the eve of the fall of Saigon in the 1970s, attempt to prevent heroin dealers from toppling the already-shaky government. So-so war/action flick.
1988 (R) 84m/C Richard Young, P.J. Soles, John Allen Nelson, Jimi B Jr.; *D:* Clark Henderson. **VHS, Beta, LV** $79.95 *MED* ✰

Saigon: Year of the Cat A made for British television drama about an American ambassador, a CIA operative, and a British bank clerk who try to leave Saigon in 1974 before the Vietcong enter the city.
1987 106m/C GB Frederic Forrest, E.G. Marshall, Judi Dench; *D:* Stephen Frears; *W:* David Hare. **VHS, Beta** $89.99 *HBO* ✰

Sailing Along British musical about a young starlet who sacrifices her career for true love.
1938 80m/B GB Jessie Matthews, Barry Mackay, Jack Whiting, Roland Young, Noel Madison, Athene Seyler, Patrick Barr; *D:* Sonnie Hale. **VHS** $29.95 *FCT* ✰✰

Sailor-Made Man/Grandma's Boy Silent comedy shorts. In "A Sailor-Made Man" (1921) Lloyd joins the Navy. As shy "Grandma's Boy" (1922), he is given courage and good advice to win the hand of a girl and defeat a bully.
192? 83m/B Harold Lloyd. **VHS, Beta** *TLF* ✰✰✰

The Sailor Who Fell from Grace with the Sea Perverse tale of a disillusioned sailor who rejects the sea for the love of a lonely young widow and her troubled son. Graphic sexual scenes. Based on the novel by Yukio Mishima, the film suffers from the transition of Japanese culture to an English setting.
1976 (R) 105m/C GB Sarah Miles, Kris Kristofferson, Jonathan Kahn, Margo Cunningham; *D:* Lewis John Carlino. **VHS, Beta, LV** *FOX, SUE* ✰✰

The Saint Moore is Simon Templar, Leslie Charteris' mysterious British detective/hero in this adventure tale that takes him to Naples. Revival of and improvement on earlier movie series, and based on the very popular British television show.
1968 98m/C GB Roger Moore, Ian Hendry. **VHS** $59.98 *FOX* ✰✰

St. Benny the Dip Three con-men evade police by posing as clergymen, and end up going straight after a series of adventures in a skid row mission. Funny in parts but extremely predictable. Still, good for a few laughs. *AKA:* Escape If You Can.
1951 80m/B Dick Haymes, Nina Foch, Roland Young, Lionel Stander, Freddie Bartholomew; *D:* Edgar G. Ulmer. **VHS** $19.95 *NOS, FCT, HEG* ✰✰½

St. Elmo's Fire Seven Georgetown graduates confront adult problems during their first post-graduate year. Reminiscent of "The Big Chill," but a weak story wastes lots of talent and time.
1985 (R) 110m/C Rob Lowe, Demi Moore, Andrew McCarthy, Judd Nelson, Ally Sheedy, Emilio Estevez, Mare Winningham, Martin Balsam, Joyce Van Patten, Andie MacDowell, Anna Maria Horsford, Jenny Wright; *D:* Joel Schumacher; *M:* David Foster. **VHS, Beta, LV** $12.95 *COL* ✰✰½

St. Helen's, Killer Volcano A young man and an old man develop a deep friendship amid the devastation, fear, greed, and panic surrounding the eruption of the Mt. St. Helen's volcano. Based on the true story of Harry Truman (!), who refused to leave his home. Pretty good.
1982 95m/C Art Carney, David Huffman, Cassie Yates, Bill McKinney, Ron O'Neal, Albert Salmi, Cesare Danova; *D:* Ernie Pintoff. **VHS, Beta** $69.95 *VES* ✰✰½

Saint in London The Saint investigates a gang trying to pass counterfeit banknotes. The third in "The Saint" series.
1939 72m/B George Sanders, Sally Gray; *D:* John Paddy Carstairs. **VHS, Beta** *MED* ✰✰

The Saint in New York The Saint, Simon Templar, turns Robin Hood to help the Civic Committee clean up a gang of desperados. First of "The Saint" series.
1938 71m/B Louis Hayward, Kay Sutton, Jack Carson; *D:* Ben Holmes. **VHS, Beta** *MED* ✰✰

St. Ives Former police reporter Bronson agrees to recover some stolen ledgers and finds himself dealing with betrayal and murder. Bisset is sultry and the tale is slickly told, but dumb. Co-stars Travanti, later of TV's "Hill Street Blues."
1976 (PG) 94m/C Charles Bronson, Jacqueline Bisset, John Houseman, Harry Guardino, Maximilian Schell, Harris Yulin, Elisha Cook Jr., Daniel J. Travanti; *D:* J. Lee Thompson. **VHS, Beta** $59.95 *WAR* ✰✰

Saint Jack The story of a small-time pimp with big dreams working the pleasure palaces of late-night Singapore. Engrossing and pleasant. Based on Paul Theroux's novel.
1979 (R) 112m/C Ben Gazzara, Denholm Elliott, Joss Ackland, George Lazenby; *D:* Peter Bogdanovich. **VHS, Beta** $69.98 *LIV, VES* ✰✰✰

Saint Joan Film of the George Bernard Shaw play, adapted by Graham Greene, about the French Maid of Orleans at her trial. Otto Preminger went on a nationwide talent hunt for his leading actress and chose the inexperienced Seberg (her screen debut). A good thing for her career, but not for this ill-begotten, overambitious opus. Seberg doesn't fit. Also available colorized.
1957 110m/B Jean Seberg, Anton Walbrook, Richard Widmark, John Gielgud, Harry Andrews, Felix Aylmer, Richard Todd; *D:* Otto Preminger. **VHS, Beta** $29.95 *HRS, QNE* ✰✰

The Saint Strikes Back Sanders debuts as the mysterious Simon Templar in this competent series. On a trip to San Francisco, the Saint aims to clear the name of a murdered man. The second in the series.
1939 67m/B George Sanders, Wendy Barrie, Jonathan Hale, Jerome Cowan, Neil Hamilton, Barry Fitzgerald, Edward Gargan, Robert Strange; *D:* John Farrow. **VHS** $19.95 *MOV* ✰✰

Saint Strikes Back: Criminal Court A suspense double feature: The Saint helps a daughter clear the name of her murdered father, a San Francisco police commissioner in "The Saint Strikes Back," and a young lawyer becomes involved in murder in "Criminal Court."
1946 127m/B George Sanders, Wendy Barrie, Barry Fitzgerald, Tom Conway, Steve Brodie; **D:** John Farrow. **VHS, Beta $34.95** *RKO, TTC* ♂♂

The Saint Takes Over More adventures with the British mystery man; this time involving racetrack gambling. An original story that wasn't based on a Leslie Charteris novel as were the others.
1940 69m/B George Sanders, Jonathan Hale, Wendy Barrie, Paul Guilfoyle, Morgan Conway, Cy Kendall; **D:** Jack Hively. **VHS** *MOV* ♂♂

The St. Valentine's Day Massacre Corman's big studio debut recreates the events leading to one of the most violent gangland shootouts in modern history: the bloodbath between Chicago's Capone and Moran gangs on February 14, 1929. Uninspired and unremittingly violent. Watch for Jack Nicholson's bit part.
1967 100m/C Jason Robards Jr., Ralph Meeker, Jean Hale, Joseph Campanella, Bruce Dern, Clint Ritchie, Richard Bakalayan, George Segal; **D:** Roger Corman. **VHS, Beta $14.98** *FOX, FCT* ♂♂♂

The Saint's Double Trouble Leslie Charteris' suave detective becomes embroiled in another mystery, this one involving jewel thieves. Sanders plays a dual role as the hero and the crook. The fourth in the series.
1940 68m/B George Sanders, Helene Whitney, Jonathan Hale, Bela Lugosi, Donald MacBride, John Hamilton; **D:** Jack Hively. **VHS** *MED* ♂♂

The Saint's Vacation/The Narrow Margin A mystery double feature. In "The Saint's Vacation," Simon Templar prevents a valuable secret from getting into the wrong hands, and in "The Narrow Margin," strange things happen to a detective when he takes a train ride with a witness to Chicago. Sinclair took over the sleuth's role from George Sanders in this series.
1952 148m/B Hugh Sinclair, Sally Gray, Charles McGraw, Marie Windsor, Jacqueline White. **VHS, Beta $34.95** *RKO, TTC* ♂♂

Sakharov The true story of the Russian physicist who designed the H-bomb and then rose to lead the Soviet dissident movement and win the Nobel Peace Prize. Robards is excellent. Made for cable; topical and powerful.
1984 120m/C Glenda Jackson, Jason Robards Jr., Michael Bryant; **D:** Jack Gold. **VHS, Beta $69.95** *PSM* ♂♂♂

Sakura Killers Killer Ninjas steal a valuable gene-splicing formula and are hunted down by an American colonel.
1986 87m/C Chuck Connors, Mike Kelly, Brian Wong, Thomas Lung; **D:** Richard Ward. **VHS, Beta $59.98** *FOX* ♂

Salaam Bombay! A gritty film about a child street beggar in the slums of Bombay trying to raise enough money to return to his mother's house in the country. The boy experiences every variety of gutter life imaginable, from humiliation to love. Moving and successful directional debut for Nair. Filmed on location, with actual homeless children; In Hindi with subtitles.
1988 114m/C *IN GB* Shafiq Syed, Hansa Vithal, Chanda Sharma, Nana Patekar, Aneeta Kanwar; **D:** Mira Nair. **VHS, Beta, LV** *NO* ♂♂♂

The Salamander A French detective tries to find the assassin of the leaders of a neo-fascist underground movement in Italy and follows clues that lead back to World War II. Disappointing, overwrought adaptation of a Morris West novel.
1982 (R) 101m/C *GB* Franco Nero, Anthony Quinn, Martin Balsam, Sybil Danning, Christopher Lee, Cleavon Little, Paul Smith, Claudia Cardinale, Eli Wallach; **D:** Peter Zinner; **M:** Jerry Goldsmith. **VHS, Beta $59.95** *NLC* ♂ ½

Salammbo An early silent epic in the grand Italian tradition. Loosely based on Flaubert's novel about ancient Carthage.
1914 49m/B *IT* Ernesto Pagani; **D:** Giovanni Pastrone. **VHS, Beta $49.95** *FCT* ♂♂ ½

Salem's Lot Based on Stephen King's novel about a sleepy New England village which is infiltrated by evil. A mysterious antiques dealer takes up residence in a forbidding hilltop house—and it becomes apparent that a vampire is on the loose. Generally creepy; Mason is good, but Soul only takes up space in the lead as a novelist returning home. Also available in the original television miniseries version at 190 minutes on two cassettes. **AKA:** Blood Thirst.
1979 (PG) 112m/C David Soul, James Mason, Lance Kerwin, Bonnie Bedelia, Lew Ayres, Bo Fanders, Elisha Cook Jr., Reggie Nalder, Fred Willard, Kenneth McMillan, Marie Windsor; **D:** Tobe Hooper. **VHS, Beta, LV $14.95** *WAR* ♂♂ ½

Sallah A North African Jew takes his family to Israel in 1949 in hopes of making his fortune. He finds himself in a transit camp and runs up against the local bureaucracy in a quest for permanent housing as well as the European work ethic. Amusing and enjoyable satire. In Hebrew with English subtitles.
1963 105m/B *IS* Chaim Topol, Geula Noni, Gila Almagor, Arik Einstein, Shraga Friedman, Esther Greenberg; **D:** Ephraim Kishon. Academy Awards '64 Nominations: Best Foreign Language Film; Golden Globe Awards '65: Best Foreign Film. **VHS, Beta $79.99** *MOV, ERG, NCJ* ♂♂♂

Sally of the Sawdust W. C. Fields' first silent feature; he is a carnival barker who adopts a young woman. Allows him to demonstrate his talent for juggling, conning customers, and car chasing. Musical score. Interesting movie caught director Griffith on the decline and Fields on the verge of stardom. Remade as a talkie in 1936 entitled "Poppy."
1925 124m/B W.C. Fields, Carol Dempster, Alfred Lunt; **D:** D.W. Griffith. **VHS, Beta $19.95** *NOS, VYY, CCB* ♂♂ ½

Salo, or the 120 Days of Sodom Extremely graphic film follows sixteen children (eight boys and eight girls) who are kidnapped by a group of men in Fascist Italy. On reaching a secluded villa in the woods, the children are told to follow strict rules and then subjected to incredible acts of sadomasochism, rape, violence, and mutilation. This last film of Pasolini's was taken from a novel by the Marquis de Sade. Viewers are strongly recommended to use their utmost discretion when watching this controversial film. In Italian with English subtitles.
1975 117m/C *IT* Giorgio Cataldi, Umberto P. Quinavalle, Paolo Bonacelli; **D:** Pier Paolo Pasolini; **M:** Ennio Morricone. **VHS $89.95** *TAM, FCT, HHE* ♂♂

Salome Garish silent rendition of Oscar Wilde's scandalous tale.
1922 54m/B Alla Nazimova, Rose Dione, Mitchell Lewis, Earl Schenck; **D:** Charles Bryant. **VHS, Beta $19.95** *GPV, FCT* ♂♂ ½

Salome An over-costumed version of Oscar Wilde's Biblical story about King Herod's lascivious stepdaughter who danced her way to stardom and tried to save the life of John the Baptist. Talented cast can't overcome hokey script.
1953 103m/C Rita Hayworth, Stewart Granger, Charles Laughton, Judith Anderson, Cedric Hardwicke, Basil Sydney, Maurice Schwartz; **D:** William Dieterle. **VHS, Beta $19.95** *COL, CCB* ♂♂

Salome An updated and graphic version of the Oscar Wilde historical fantasy about the temptress Salome who helped topple Herod's Biblical kingdom with her dance of the Seven Veils. Photographed by Pasqualino De Santis. Not really a remake of the 1953 film since this is set during the 1940s.
1985 (R) 100m/C Jo Ciampa, Tomas Milian, Pamela Salem; **D:** Claude D'Anna. **VHS, Beta $79.95** *MGM* ♂ ½

Salome/Queen Elizabeth Two famous silent shorts: "Salome," (1923), an atmospheric adaptation of Oscar Wilde's tale, with sets designed after Aubrey Beardsley; and "Queen Elizabeth," (1912), Bernhardt's famous, and famously stilted, singular film appearance.
1923 91m/B Alla Nazimova, Sarah Bernhardt, Lou Tellegen, Mitchell Lewis, Nigel de Brulier; **D:** Charles Bryant, Henri Desfontaines, Louis Mercanton. **VHS, Beta, 8mm $29.95** *VYY* ♂ ½

Salome, Where She Danced Set during the Franco-Prussian war. A European dancer helps an American reporter in a spy scheme. She eventually relocates to America and becomes the toast of San Francisco. Somehow De Carlo managed to spring from this ridiculous camp outing to stardom.
1945 90m/C Yvonne De Carlo, Rod Cameron, David Bruce, Walter Slezak; **D:** Charles Lamont. **VHS, Beta $19.95** *NOS, KRT, DVT* ♂

Salome's Last Dance A theatrical, set-surreal adaptation of the Wilde story. Typically flamboyant Russell.
1988 (R) 113m/C Glenda Jackson, Stratford Johns, Nickolas Grace, Douglas Hodge, Imogen Millais Scott; **D:** Ken Russell. **VHS, Beta, LV $89.98** *LIV, IME, VES* ♂♂

Salsa An auto repairman would rather dance in this "Dirty Dancing" clone. Rosa was formerly a member of the pop group Menudo.
1988 (PG) 97m/C Robby Rosa, Rodney Harvey, Magali Alvarado, Miranda Garrison, Moon Orona; **D:** Boaz Davidson. **VHS, Beta, LV $19.98** *CAN* ♂♂

Salt of the Earth Finally available in this country after being suppressed for thirty years, this controversial film was made by a group of blacklisted filmmakers during the McCarthy era. It was deemed anti-American, communist propaganda. The story deals with the anti-Hispanic racial strife that occurs in a New Mexico zinc mine when union workers organize a strike.
1954 94m/B Rosaura Revueltas, Will Geer, David Wolfe; **D:** Herbert Biberman. **VHS, Beta, LV, 3/4U $19.95** *IHF, NOS, VYG* ♂♂♂ ½

Salty A lovable but mischievous sea lion manages to complicate two brothers' lives when they volunteer to help a friend renovate a Florida marina, which is threatened by a mortgage foreclosure. Straightforward and inoffensive tale.
1973 93m/C Clint Howard, Mark Slade, Nina Foch; **D:** Ricou Browning. **VHS, Beta** *NO* ♂♂

Salut l'Artiste Two bad actors try to make it in the industry. Delightfully funny with an excellent cast, especially Mastroianni. Snide and irreverant, yet loving and comic

look at the world of acting. In French with English subtitles.
1974 96m/C *FR* Marcello Mastroianni, Jean Rochefort, Francoise Fabian, Carla Gravina; *D:* Yves Robert. VHS $79.95 FCT, TAM 🐾🐾🐾

Salute John Citizen The life of an average English family during the early days of World War II is depicted, focusing on the deprivation and horror of the Nazi blitzkrieg.
1942 74m/B Peggy Cummins, Stanley Holloway, Dinah Sheridan, Jimmy Hanley. VHS, Beta $19.98 VYY 🐾🐾🐾

Salute to Chuck Jones Collection of eight Chuck Jones favorites including "Duck Dodgers in the 24 1/2th Century," "One Froggy Evening," "Rabbit Seasoning," and "Feed the Kitty."
1960 56m/C *D:* Chuck Jones; *V:* Mel Blanc. VHS, Beta $12.95 WAR, WTA 🐾🐾🐾~

Salute to Friz Freleng Several classic Friz Freleng cartoons, including the Academy Award winners "Speedy Gonzales" (1955), "Birds Anonymous" (1957), and "Knighty Knight Bugs" (1958).
1958 57m/C *D:* Friz Freleng; *V:* Mel Blanc. VHS, Beta $12.95 WAR, WTA 🐾🐾🐾

Salute to Mel Blanc This compilation pays tribute to the multi-talented Mel Blanc and features such memorable cartoons including "The Rabbit of Seville," "Little Boy Boo," "Robin Hood Daffy," and "Past Performances."
1958 58m/C *D:* Chuck Jones, Friz Freleng, Bob Clampett; *V:* Mel Blanc. VHS, Beta $12.95 WAR, WTA 🐾🐾🐾

Salute to the "King of the Cowboys," Roy Rogers Glimpses of Roy from song clips, home movies, trailers, out-takes, and other sources.
197? 60m/B Roy Rogers. VHS, Beta $29.95 DVT 🐾½

Salvador Photo journalist Richard Boyle's unflinching and sordid adventures in war-torn El Salvador. Boyle (Woods) must face the realities of social injustice. Belushi and Woods are hard to like, but excellent. Early critical success for director Stone.
1986 (R) 123m/C James Woods, James Belushi, John Savage, Michael Murphy, Elpidia Carrillo, Cynthia Gibb; *D:* Oliver Stone. Academy Awards '86 Nominations: Best Actor (Woods), Best Original Screenplay; Independent Spirit Awards '87: Best Actor (Woods). VHS, Beta, LV $29.98 LIV, IME, VES 🐾🐾🐾½

Salvation! A mean-tempered, timely satire about a money-hungry television evangelist beset by a family of fervent, equally money-hungry followers, who proceed to cheat, seduce and blackmail him. Occasionally quite funny, but sloppy and predictable. Underground director Beth B's first above-ground film. *AKA:* Salvation! Have You Said Your Prayers Today?.
1987 (R) 80m/C Stephen McHattie, Exene Cervenka, Dominique Davalos, Viggo Mortensen, Rockets Redglare, Billy Bastiani; *D:* Beth B. Beta NO 🐾🐾½

The Salzburg Connection A list of Nazi collaborators is discovered in Austria. A vacationing American lawyer is caught up in the battle for its possession. Filmed on location, it's still a poor, cheesy adaptation of the Helen MacInnes novel.
1972 94m/C Barry Newman, Anna Karina, Klaus Maria Brandauer, Karen Jensen, Lee H. Katzin; *D:* Lee H. Katzin. VHS, Beta $59.98 FOX 🐾½

Samantha Twenty-one year-old Samantha discovers she was left on her parents' doorstep in a basket and decides to find out where she came from. Good cast and high charm quotient help this film along.
1992 (PG) 101m/C Martha Plimpton, Dermot Mulroney, Hector Elizondo, Mary Kay Place, Ione Skye; *W/D:* Steven La Rocque; *W:* John Golden. VHS, Beta $89.95 ACA 🐾🐾½

Samar A liberal penal colony commandant rebels against his superiors by leading his prisoners through the Philippine jungles to freedom. Original action drama with an interesting premise.
1962 (PG) 89m/C George Montgomery, Gilbert Roland, Joan O'Brien, Ziva Rodann; *D:* George Montgomery. VHS, Beta $19.95 NOS 🐾🐾½

Samaritan: The Mitch Snyder Story Effective television drama based upon the true story of Vietnam vet Mitch Snyder (Sheen) who battles various government agencies and ultimately fasts to call national attention to his crusade against homelessness. Tyson appears as bag lady; Snyder eventually committed suicide.
1986 90m/C Martin Sheen, Roxanne Hart, Joe Seneca, Stan Shaw, Cicely Tyson; *D:* Richard T. Heffron. VHS, Beta $14.95 FRH 🐾🐾🐾

Same Time, Next Year A chance meeting between an accountant and a housewife results in a sometimes tragic, always sentimental 25-year affair in which they meet only one weekend each year. Well-cast leads carry warm, touching story based on the Broadway play by Bernard Slade.
1978 119m/C Ellen Burstyn, Alan Alda; *D:* Robert Mulligan. Academy Awards '78 Nominations: Best Actress (Burstyn), Best Adapted Screenplay, Best Cinematography, Best Song ("The Last Time I Felt Like This"); Golden Globe Awards '79: Best Actress—Musical/Comedy (Burstyn). VHS, Beta, LV $14.98 MCA 🐾🐾🐾

Sammy & Rosie Get Laid An unusual social satire about a sexually liberated couple living in London whose lives are thrown into turmoil by the arrival of the man's father - a controversial politician in India. Provides a confusing look at sexual and class collisions. From the makers of "My Beautiful Launderette."
1987 97m/C *GB* Shashi Kapoor, Frances Barber, Claire Bloom, Ayub Khan Din, Roland Gift, Wendy Gazelle, Meera Syal; *D:* Stephen Frears; *W:* Hanif Kureishi. VHS, Beta, LV $79.95 LHV, WAR 🐾🐾🐾

Sammy Bluejay Features two escapades—"Brainy Bluejay" and "Sammy's Revenge," starring Sammy Bluejay, Peter Cottontail, and Reddy the Fox.
1983 60m/C VHS, Beta $29.95 FHE, WTA 🐾🐾🐾

Sammy, the Way-Out Seal Two young boys bring a mischievous seal to live in their beach house and try to keep it a secret from their parents. Disney in its early '60s phase.
1962 89m/C Michael McGreevey, Billy Mumy, Patricia Barry, Robert Culp; *D:* Norman Tokar. VHS, Beta $69.95 DIS 🐾🐾

Sam's Son Sentimental, autobiographical tale about how a young man's athletic prowess opens the door for an acting career in Hollywood. Good performance by Wallach as the boy's father. Self-indulgent, though entertaining. Written and directed by Landon, who also appears briefly.
1984 (PG) 107m/C Eli Wallach, Anne Jackson, Timothy Patrick Murphy, Hallie Todd, James Karen, Allan Hayes, Joanna Lee, Michael Landon; *D:* Michael Landon. VHS, Beta $59.95 WOV 🐾🐾

Samson Samson attempts to keep wits and hair about him.
1961 90m/C *IT* Brad Harris, Brigitte Corey, Alan Steel, Serge Gainsbourg, Mara Berni; *D:* Gianfranco Parolini. VHS $14.99 SNC, MRV 🐾

Samson Against the Sheik Samson survives long enough to battle a sheik in the Middle Ages.
1962 ?m/C *IT* Ed Fury. VHS, Beta $16.95 SNC 🐾

Samson and Delilah The biblical story of the vindictive Delilah, who after being rejected by the mighty Samson, robbed him of his strength by shearing his curls. Delivered in signature DeMille style. Wonderfully fun and engrossing. Mature is excellent.
1950 128m/C Victor Mature, Hedy Lamarr, Angela Lansbury, George Sanders, Henry Wilcoxon, Olive Deering, Fay Holden; *D:* Cecil B. DeMille. Academy Awards '50: Best Art Direction/Set Decoration (Color), Best Costume Design (Color); Nominations: Best Color Cinematography, Best Original Score. VHS, Beta, LV $29.95 PAR, PIA 🐾🐾🐾

Samson and Delilah A made for television version of the Biblical romance, semi-based on DeMille's 1949 version. Original Samson (Mature) plays Samson's father. Too long but inoffensive; see the DeMille version instead.
1984 95m/C Anthony Hamilton, Belinda Bauer, Max von Sydow, Jose Ferrer, Victor Mature, Maria Schell; *D:* Lee Philips. VHS, Beta $9.99 STE, PSM 🐾🐾

Samson and His Mighty Challenge In this rarely seen muscle epic, Hercules, Maciste, Samson and Ursus all take part in a battle royale.
1964 ?m/C *IT* Alan Steel. VHS, Beta $16.95 SNC 🐾

Samson and the 7 Miracles of the World This time the hero known as Maciste (renamed Samson for Americans) is in the 13th century battling brutal Tartar warlords. The very Earth itself shakes when our hero goes into battle! *AKA:* Maciste Alla Corte Del Gran Khan; Maciste at the Court of the Great Khan; Goliath and the Golden City.
1962 80m/C *FR IT* Gordon Scott, Yoko Tani, Gabriele Antonini, Leonardo Severini, Valeri Inkizhinov, Helene Chanel; *D:* Riccardo Freda. VHS, Beta $16.95 SNC 🐾🐾

Samson in the Wax Museum Masked Mexican wrestling hero Santo (here called Samson) does battle with a scientist who has discovered a way to make wax monsters come to life. *AKA:* Santo en el Museo de Cera; Santo in the Wax Museum.
1963 92m/B *MX* Santo, Claudio Brook, Rueben Rojo, Norma Mora, Roxana Bellini; *D:* Alfonso Corona Blake. VHS $19.98 SNC, HHT 🐾🐾

Samson vs. the Vampire Women Santo (here called Samson) the masked hero and athlete, battles the forces of darkness as a horde of female vampires attempt to make an unsuspecting girl their next queen.
1961 89m/B *MX* Santo, Lorena Velasquez, Jaime Fernandez, Maria Duval; *D:* Alfonso Corona Blake. VHS, Beta $19.98 SNC, HHT 🐾½

Samurai Truly bad spy-exploitation film about a Japanese orphan who was raised in America, turns traitor, and helps plot the invasion of California.
1945 ?m/C Paul Fung, Luke Chan, David Chow. VHS $16.95 SNC 🐾

The Samurai An unstoppable ninja warrior seeks revenge against a sadistic clan of martial arts experts for the murder of his fiance's father. He will settle for nothing less than the decapitation of those who have destroyed his life.

19?? 90m/C Chung Wong, Tien Pang. **VHS** $49.95 *OCE* ✂

Samurai 1: Musashi Miyamoto
The first installment in the film version of Musashi Miyamoto's life, as he leaves his 17th century village as a warrior in a local civil war only to return beaten and disillusioned. Justly award-winning. In Japanese with English subtitles.
1955 92m/C *JP* Toshiro Mifune; *D:* Hiroshi Inagaki. **VHS, Beta, LV** $19.95 *NLC, SUE, TAM* ✂✂✂½

Samurai 2: Duel at Ichijoji Temple Inagaki's second film depicting the life of Musashi Miyamoto, the 17th century warrior, who wandered the disheveled landscape of feudal Japan looking for glory and love. In Japanese with English subtitles.
1955 102m/C *JP* Toshiro Mifune; *D:* Hiroshi Inagaki. **VHS, Beta, LV** $19.95 *NLC, SUE, TAM* ✂✂✂½

Samurai 3: Duel at Ganryu Island The final film of Inagaki's trilogy, in which Musashi Miyamoto confronts his life-long enemy in a climactic battle. Depicts Miyamoto's spiritual awakening and realization that love and hatred exist in all of us. In Japanese with English subtitles.
1956 102m/C *JP* Toshiro Mifune, Koji Tsurata; *D:* Hiroshi Inagaki. **VHS, Beta, LV** $29.98 *SUE, TAM, NLC* ✂✂✂½

Samurai Blood, Samurai Guts The wooden hag offers The Book of 9 Yin to the man who will retrieve the Devil Knight's head. Yet the man who would do so will risk his very blood, guts, and brains.
19?? 90m/C Kong Pun, Ng Pun, Lee Shue. **VHS, Beta** $29.95 *OCE* ✂

Samurai Death Bells Gory samurai sword fighting flick full of conspiracy and deceit.
19?? 90m/C Chung Wong, Lee Le Le, Miao Ko Sou. **VHS, Beta** $49.95 *OCE* ✂

Samurai Reincarnation After the Shogunate government kills 18,000 Christian rioters in the revolt of 1638, and publicly beheads the leader Shiro Amakusa, Shiro reincarnates during a monstrous thunderstorm. Consumed with hatred, he discards the teachings of Jesus Christ and seeks revenge. In Japanese with English subtitles.
1981 122m/C *JP D:* Kinji Fukasaku. **VHS** $59.95 *FCT* ✂

Samurai Sword of Justice A pair of gruelling samurai warriors seek and destroy their evil nemesis Chi. When they finally meet up with him, you can bet some guts and brains will be splattered about.
19?? 90m/C Kam Hon, Wong Kuan Hung, Mo Si Shing, Lee Shue. **VHS, Beta** $49.95 *OCE* ✂

San Antonio A bad girl working in a dance hall turns over a new leaf on meeting the good guy. Trite plot, but good production.
1945 105m/C Errol Flynn, Alexis Smith, S.Z. Sakall, Victor Francen, Florence Bates, John Litel, Paul Kelly; *D:* David Butler. **VHS, Beta** $19.98 *MGM, FCT, MLB* ✂✂

San Demetrio, London Set in 1940, the crew of a crippled tanker endures harrowing situations to reach port. A decent anti-war movie in its time, it's now showing its age. Based on a true story, the plot sags with unbelievable scenes and holes on the plot side.
1947 76m/B Walter Fitzgerald, Mervyn Johns, Ralph Michael, Robert Beatty, Charles Victor, Frederick Piper; *D:* Charles Frend. **VHS** $19.95 *NOS* ✂✂½

San Fernando Valley Also called "San Fernando". Another lawman-in-evil-town epic. Rogers received his first on-screen kiss in 1944's biggest western. Fairly typical, pleasant cowboy tale.
1944 54m/B Roy Rogers, Dale Evans. **VHS, Beta** $19.95 *NOS, DVT* ✂✂

San Francisco The San Francisco Earthquake of 1906 serves as the background for a romance between an opera singer and a Barbary Coast saloon owner. Somewhat overdone but gripping tale of passion and adventure in the West. Wonderful special effects. Finale consists of historic earthquake footage. Script by Anita Loos. Also available colorized. ♫San Francisco; A Heart That's Free; Would You?; Air des Bijoux; Sempre Libera.
1936 116m/B Jeanette MacDonald, Clark Gable, Spencer Tracy, Jack Holt, Jessie Ralph, Al Shear; *D:* Woodbridge S. Van Dyke. Academy Awards '36: Best Sound; Nominations: Best Actor (Tracy), Best Director (Van Dyke), Best Picture, Best Story. **VHS, Beta, LV** $19.98 *MGM* ✂✂✂½

Sanctuary of Fear A priest in New York City helps an actress subjected to a series of terrorizing incidents. Uninspired would-be TV pilot based on Chesterton's "Father Brown" series. *AKA:* Girl in the Park.
1979 98m/C George Hearn, Barnard Hughes, Kay Lenz; *D:* John Llewellyn Moxey. **VHS, Beta** $29.98 *FOX* ✂½

Sand and Blood A young matador who wishes to escape poverty and a young, cultivated doctor, who despises bullfighting, meet and eventually become friends. A woman enters the picture and completes the love triangle. Widely praised by critics. Interesting and moving. In French with English subtitles. *AKA:* Blood and Sand; De Sable et de Sang.
1987 101m/C *FR* Sami Frey, Andre Dussollier, Clementine Celarie, Patrick Catalifo, Maria Casares, Catherine Rouvel; *W/D:* Jeanne Labrune. **VHS, Beta** $29.95 *NYF, FCT, TAM* ✂✂½

The Sand Pebbles An American expatriate engineer, transferred to a gunboat in 1926, falls in love with a missionary teacher. As he becomes aware of the political climate of American imperialism, he finds himself at odds with his command structure; the treatment of this issue can be seen as commentary on the situation in Vietnam at the time of the film's release. Considered one of McQueen's best performances, blending action and romance.
1966 193m/C Steve McQueen, Richard Crenna, Richard Attenborough, Candice Bergen, Marayat Andriane, Gavin MacLeod, Larry Gates, Mako, Simon Oakland; *D:* Robert Wise; *M:* Jerry Goldsmith. Academy Awards '66 Nominations: Best Actor (McQueen), Best Art Direction/Set Decoration (Color), Best Color Cinematography, Best Film Editing, Best Picture, Best Sound, Best Supporting Actor (Mako), Best Original Score; Golden Globe Awards '67: Best Supporting Actor (Attenborough). **VHS, Beta, LV** $29.98 *FOX, FCT* ✂✂✂½

Sandakan No. 8 A Japanese woman working as a journalist befriends an old woman who was sold into prostitution in Borneo in the early 1900s. Justly acclaimed feminist story dramatizes the role of women in Japanese society. Japanese with English subtitles. *AKA:* Brothel 8; Sandakan House 8.
1974 121m/C *JP* Kinuyo Tanaka, Yoko Takakashi, Komake Kurihara, Eitaro Ozawa; *D:* Kei Kumai. Academy Awards '75 Nominations: Best Foreign Language Film; Berlin International Film Festival '75: Best Actress. **VHS, Beta** $59.95 *FCT* ✂✂✂

Sanders of the River A British officer in colonial Africa must work with the local chief to quell a rebellion. Tale of imperialism. Dated but still interesting and of value. Robeson is very good; superb location cinematography. *AKA:* Bosambo.
1935 80m/B *GB* Paul Robeson, Leslie Banks, Robert Cochran; *D:* Zoltan Korda. **VHS, Beta, 3/4U, Special order formats** $19.95 *NOS, SUE, VYY* ✂✂✂

Sandflow Well-made Western with Jones playing a man whose father has cheated many ranchers. Jones is out to avenge all of his father's misdeeds and build a new life for himself in this above-average oater.
1937 58m/B Buck Jones, Lita Chevret, Bob Kortman, Arthur Aylsworth, Robert Terry, Enrique DeRosas; *D:* Lesley Selander. **VHS** $9.95 *GPV* ✂✂½

The Sandlot Young Scotty (Guiry) moves to a new neighborhood in California in 1962 and tries to make friends despite not knowing anything about playing baseball. He endures their taunts during the course of the summer and is also tested by other mysteries including an unknown "beast" who lurks just beyond the left-field fence and the local beautiful lifeguard. His other scrappy teammates include the friendly Benny (Vitar), a chubby loud-mouthed catcher named Ham (Renna), and Squints (Leopardi), a would-be Lothario before his time. Can be seen as either slow-moving coming-of-age or as a nostalgic look at youthful innocence.
1993 (PG) 101m/C Patrick Renna, Tom Guiry, Mike Vitar, Chauncey Leopardi, Marty York, Brandon Adams, Art La Fleur, Marlee Shelton, Karen Allen, James Earl Jones; *D:* David Mickey Evans; *W:* David Mickey Evans, Robert Gunter; *M:* David Newman; *V:* Arliss Howard. **VHS** *NYR* ✂✂½

The Sandpiper Free-spirited artist Taylor falls in love with Burton, the married headmaster of her son's boarding school. Muddled melodrama offers little besides starpower. Filmed at Big Sur, California.
1965 117m/C Elizabeth Taylor, Richard Burton, Charles Bronson, Eva Marie Saint, Robert Webber, Morgan Mason; *D:* Vincente Minnelli. **VHS, Beta** $19.98 *MGM* ✂✂

Sands of Iwo Jima Wayne earned his first Oscar nomination as a tough Marine sergeant, in one of his best roles. He trains a squad of rebellious recruits in New Zealand in 1943. Later they are responsible for the capture of Iwo Jima from the Japanese—one of the most difficult campaigns of the Pacific Theater. Includes striking real war footage.
1949 109m/B John Wayne, Forrest Tucker, John Agar, Richard Jaeckel; *D:* Allan Dwan. **VHS, LV** $19.98 *REP, TLF, RDG* ✂✂✂½

Sandstone A pair of film-makers visit a California hedonist retreat and study the effects of nudity and free sexual expression on the modern psyche. Pretty lame and prurient.
1974 (R) 76m/C *D:* Jonathan, Bonny Peters. **VHS, Beta** $69.98 *VES* ✂½

Sanjuro In this offbeat, satiric sequel to "Yojimbo," a talented but lazy samurai comes to the aid of a group of naive young warriors. The conventional ideas of good and evil are quickly tossed aside; much less earnest than other Kurosawa Samurai outings. In Japanese with English subtitles. *AKA:* Tsubaki Sanjuro.
1962 96m/B *JP* Toshiro Mifune, Tatsuya Nakadai; *D:* Akira Kurosawa. **VHS, Beta, LV** $29.95 *NOS, SUE, HHT* ✂✂✂

Sans Soleil A female narrator reads and comments on the letters she receives from a friend, a freelance cameraman traveling through Japan, West Africa, and Iceland. The cameraman meditates on the cultural dislocation he feels and the meaning of his work and of life itself. Both narrator and cameraman remain unseen with the visuals being the cameraman's work in progress. *AKA:* Sunless.
1982 100m/C *FR W/D:* Chris Marker. **VHS $69.95** *NYF, BTV* ♫♫♫

Sanshiro Sugata Kurosawa's first film. A young man learns discipline in martial arts from a patient master. Climactic fight scene is early signature Kurosawa. In Japanese with English subtitles.
1943 82m/B *JP* Susumo Fusuita, Takashi Shimura; *D:* Akira Kurosawa. **VHS $59.95** *SVS, FCT, TAM* ♫♫♫

Sansho the Bailiff A world masterpiece by Mizoguchi about feudal society in 11th century Japan. A woman and her children are sold into prostitution and slavery. As an adult, the son seeks to right the ills of his society. Powerful and tragic, and often more highly esteemed than "Ugetsu." In Japanese with English subtitles. *AKA:* The Bailiff; Sansho Dayu.
1954 132m/B *JP* Kinuyo Tanaka, Yoshiaki Hanayagi, Kyoko Kagawa, Eitaro Shindo, Ichiro Sugai; *D:* Kenji Mizoguchi. **VHS, Beta $39.95** *SVS, TAM* ♫♫♫♫

Santa Claus Santa Claus teams up with Merlin the Magician to fend off an evil spirit who would ruin everyone's Christmas. Mexican camp classic.
1959 94m/C *MX* Jose Elias Moreno, Cesareo Quezadas, Rene Cardona Sr. **VHS, Beta $16.95** *SNC, MLB* Woof!

Santa Claus A kiddie fantasy about Saint Nick and his Arctic Playworld.
1985 90m/C VHS, Beta, LV $49.95 *UHV* ♫♫

Santa Claus Conquers the Martians A Martian spaceship comes to Earth and kidnaps Santa Claus and two children. Martian kids, it seems, are jealous that Earth tykes have Christmas. Features then-child star Pia Zadora. *AKA:* Santa Claus Defeats the Aliens.
1964 80m/C John Call, Pia Zadora, Leonard Hicks, Vincent Beck, Victor Stiles, Donna Conforti; *D:* Nicholas Webster. **VHS, Beta $19.95** *COL, SNC, SUE* ♫

Santa Claus is Coming to Town Kris Kringle takes you along on his quest to give toys to the citizens of Sombertown. An animated classic.
1970 53m/C *D:* Arthur Rankin Jr., Jules Bass; *V:* Mickey Rooney, Keenan Wynn, Paul Frees. **VHS, Beta, LV $14.95** *FHE, WTA* ♫

Santa Claus: The Movie A big-budgeted spectacle about an elf who falls prey to an evil toy maker and almost ruins Christmas and Santa Claus. Boring, 'tis-the-season fantasy-drama meant to warm our cockles.
1985 (PG) 112m/C Dudley Moore, John Lithgow, David Huddleston, Judy Cornwell, Burgess Meredith; *D:* Jeannot Szwarc. **VHS, Beta, LV $9.98** *MED* ♫♫

Santa Fe Bound Tyler must work to clear his name when he is falsely accused of having murdered a man.
1937 58m/B Tom Tyler, Jeanne Martel, Richard Cramer, Charles "Slim" Whitaker, Edward Cassidy, Lafe McKee, Dorothy Woods, Charles King; *D:* Harry S. Webb. **VHS $19.95** *DVT, HEG* ♫♫

Santa Fe Marshal The 27th Hopalong Cassidy movie, if anyone's counting. In the title job the Hopster goes undercover with a medicine show to smash a criminal gang. A little different than usual, right up to the surprise identity of the crooked mastermind.
1940 66m/B William Boyd, Russell Hayden, Marjorie Rambeau, Bernadene Hayes, Earle Hodgins, Kenneth Harlan, Eddie Dean; *D:* Lesley Selander. **VHS $19.95** *NOS* ♫♫

Santa Fe Stampede The Three Mesquiteers join an old prospector in his claim but when he is killed, one of them (Wayne) is framed. The photography makes up for the weak story line and direction.
1938 58m/B John Wayne, Ray Corrigan, Max Terhune, William Farnum, June Martel, Leroy Mason, Yakima Canutt, Curly Dresden; *D:* George Sherman. **VHS $19.95** *NOS* ♫♫½

Santa Fe Trail Historically inaccurate but entertaining tale about the pre-Civil War fight for "bloody Kansas." The action-adventure depicts future Civil War Generals J.E.B. Stuart (Flynn) and George Armstrong Custer (Reagan!) as they begin their military career (although Custer was really just a youth at this time). Good action scenes. Also available colorized.
1940 110m/B Errol Flynn, Olivia de Havilland, Ronald Reagan, Van Heflin, Raymond Massey, Alan Hale Jr.; *D:* Michael Curtiz. **VHS, Beta** *MGM, NOS, PSM* ♫♫½

Santa Fe Uprising Red Ryder has to save Little Beaver from kidnappers. Good first entry for Lane in the "Red Ryder" series.
1946 54m/B Allan "Rocky" Lane, Robert (Bobby) Blake. **VHS, Beta** *MED* ♫♫½

Santa Sangre A circus in Mexico City, a temple devoted to a saint without arms, and a son who faithfully dotes upon his mother are just a few of the things in Jodorowsky's fantastic film. Young Fenix witnesses his father's cavorting and subsequent suicide following a spousal fight which leaves his mother armless. After years in an insane asylum, Fenix's mother calls on him to help her out in her nightclub act. Fenix acts as his mother's arms, plays the piano and carries out any wish she desires. Eventually Fenix is forced to kill off any woman who comes into his mother's sight. Visually intoxicating film that may prove too graphic for some viewers. Not as rigorous as other Jodorowsky outings. Also available in an NC-17 version.
1990 (R) 123m/C *IT MX* Axel Jodorowsky, Sabrina Dennison, Guy Stockwell, Blanca Guerra, Thelma Tixou, Adan Jodorowsky, Faviola Tapia, Jesus Juarez; *D:* Alejandro Jodorowsky. **VHS, LV $19.98** *REP, FCT, TAM* ♫♫♫

Santee A father-son relationship develops between a bounty hunter and the son of a man he killed. Good, but not great, Western.
1973 (PG) 93m/C Glenn Ford, Dana Wynter, Jay Silverheels, John Larch; *D:* Gary Nelson. **VHS, Beta $49.95** *PSM, HHE* ♫♫

The Saphead Keaton's first outing as the rich playboy has him playing the none-to-bright son of a Wall Street mogul. Some great moments provide a glimpse of cinematic greatness to come from the budding comedic genius. Based on the play "The New Henrietta" by Winchell Smith and Victor Mapes. Silent.
1921 70m/B William H. Crane, Buster Keaton, Carol Holloway, Edward Connelly, Irving Cummings; *D:* Herbert Blache. **VHS $59.95** ♫♫½

Sapphire Two Scotland Yard detectives seek the killer of a beautiful black woman who was passing for white. Good mystery and topical social comment; remains interesting and engrossing. Superbly acting all around.
1959 92m/C *GB* Nigel Patrick, Yvonne Mitchell, Michael Craig, Paul Massie, Bernard Miles; *D:* Basil Dearden. **VHS, Beta** *NO* ♫♫♫

Saps at Sea A doctor advises Ollie to take a rest away from his job at a horn factory. He and Stan rent a boat, which they plan to keep tied to the dock, until an escaped criminal happens by and uses the boys (and their boat) for his getaway. Cramer is a good bad guy; Stan and Ollie cause too much trouble, as always.
1940 57m/B Stan Laurel, Oliver Hardy, James Finlayson, Ben Turpin, Richard Cramer; *D:* Gordon Douglas. **VHS, Beta, LV $12.98** *CCB, MED, CCB* ♫♫½

Sara Dane A strong young woman in the 18th century rises in the world through marriage and business acumen. Interesting but imperfect and slow.
1981 150m/C *AU* Harold Hopkins, Brenton Whittle, Barry Quin, Sean Scully; *D:* Rod Hardy, Gary Conway. **VHS, Beta $79.95** *PSM* ♫♫

Sarafina! Part coming-of-age saga, part political drama, part musical, and all emotionally powerful. Sarafina is a young girl in a township school in Soweto, South Africa in the mid-'70s, gradually coming into a political awakening amid the Soweto riots. Khumalo recreates her stage role as the glowing and defiant Sarafina with both Goldberg and Makeba good in their roles as Sarafina's outspoken and inspirational teacher and her long-suffering mother, respectively. Adapted from Ngema's stage musical.
1992 (PG-13) 98m/C Leleti Khumalo, Whoopi Goldberg, Miriam Makeba, John Kani, Mbongeni Ngema; *D:* Darrell Roodt; *W:* Mbongeni Ngema, William Nicholson. **VHS, Beta, LV $94.95** *TOU* ♫♫♫

Sarah & the Squirrel A young girl learns to survive in a forest after she becomes separated from her family during a war.
1983 74m/C *V:* Mia Farrow. **VHS, Beta $29.98** *FOX, WTA* ♫♫

Sarah Bailey Portrait of the Harlan County folk artist who teaches residents of an Elderhostel to make corn-shuck flowers and dolls.
1984 28m/C VHS, Beta, 3/4U $150.00 *AAI, APL* ♫½

Sarah, Plain and Tall New England school teacher (Close) travels to Kansas circa 1910 to care for the family of a widowed farmer who has advertised for a wife. Superior entertainment for the whole family. Adapted for television from Patricia MacLachlan's novel of the same name by MacLachlan and Carol Sobieski. Nominated for nine Emmy Awards. A "Hallmark Hall of Fame" presentation.
1991 (G) 98m/C Glenn Close, Christopher Walken, Lexi Randall, Margaret Sophie Stein, Jon DeVries, Christopher Bell; *D:* Glenn Jordan. **VHS, LV $14.98** *REP, PIA* ♫♫♫

Saratoga Gable plays a bookie and Harlow the daughter of an impoverished horse breeder in this romantic comedy centered around the race tracks. This was the final film appearance for Harlow, who died before the film's completion. Mary Dees was chosen as her stand-in and had to finish many of the scenes. "Saratoga" was released just a month after Harlow's death and became one of the biggest moneymakers of the year.
1937 94m/B Jean Harlow, Clark Gable, Lionel Barrymore, Walter Pidgeon, Frank Morgan, Una Merkel, Cliff Edwards, George Zucco, Hattie McDaniel, Jonathan Hale; *D:* Jack Conway; *W:*

Anita Loos, Robert Hopkins. VHS $19.98
MGM ✰✰½

Sardinia Kidnapped A beautiful girl is trapped in a clash between two powerful families while on vacation in Sardinia, where the peasants' custom is to kidnap a member of a rival family and then exchange the victim for land. Former documentary maker Mingozzi creates a realistic and uncompromising look at culture and change. In Italian; dubbed.
1975 95m/C IT Charlotte Rampling, Franco Nero; D: Gianfranco Mingozzi. VHS, Beta $24.95 AHV ✰✰½

Sartana's Here...Trade Your Pistol for a Coffin A soldier of fortune searches for a missing shipment of gold in the Old West.
1970 92m/C George Hilton, Charles Southwood, Erika Blanc, Linda Sini. VHS, Beta $49.95 UNI ✰

S.A.S. San Salvador A CIA agent tries to prevent a psychotic from running amok in El Salvador.
1984 95m/C Miles O'Keeffe, Dagmar Lassander, Catherine Jarrett. VHS, Beta $69.98 LIV, VES ✰

Sasquatch Purported "documentary" about the mythical creature Bigfoot. Includes "real" pictures of the "actual" monster. For those real stupid moods.
1976 94m/C D: Ed Ragozzini. VHS, Beta $19.95 UHV Woof!

Satan Met a Lady A weak adaptation of Dashiell Hammett's "Maltese Falcon." This version has Davis employing a private detective to track down a mysterious woman. The hunted woman is herself searching for a valuable collectible.
1936 74m/B Bette Davis, Warren William, Alison Skipworth, Arthur Treacher, Marie Wilson, Porter Hall, Olin Howland; D: William Dieterle. VHS $19.98 MGM, FCT ✰✰½

The Satanic Rites of Dracula Count Dracula is the leader of a satanic cult of prominent scientists and politicians who develop a gruesome plague virus capable of destroying the human race. Preceded by "Dracula A.D. 1972" and followed by "The 7 Brothers Meet Dracula." AKA: Count Dracula and His Vampire Bride.
1973 88m/C GB Christopher Lee, Peter Cushing, Michael Coles, William Franklyn, Freddie Jones, Joanna Lumley, Richard Vernon, Patrick Barr, Barbara Yo Ling; D: Alan Gibson. VHS $14.95 MLB ✰✰

Satanik A hideous old hag is turned into a lovely young woman by a satanic love potion, but it doesn't last long and she becomes a monster.
1969 (R) 85m/C IT SP Magda Konopka, Julio Pena, Luigi Montini, Armando Calvo, Umberto Raho; D: Piero Vivarelli. VHS $16.95 SNC ✰

Satan's Black Wedding The ghouls arrive at a Monterey monastery in their Sunday best to celebrate devildom's most diabolical ritual, the "Black Wedding."
1975 (R) 61m/C Greg Braddock, Ray Miles, Lisa Milano. VHS, Beta $39.95 WWV ✰

Satan's Blade The owner of an ancient talisman goes on a killing rampage at a remote mountain lodge.
1984 87m/C VHS, Beta $9.99 STE, PSM Woof!

Satan's Cheerleaders A demonic high school janitor traps a bevy of buxom cheerleaders at his Satanic altar for sacrificial purposes. The gals use all of their endowments to escape the clutches of the evil sheriff and his fat wife. Is it ever campy!

1977 (R) 92m/C John Carradine, John Ireland, Yvonne De Carlo, Kerry Sherman, Jacqulin Cole, Hilary Horan, Alisa Powell, Sherry Marks, Jack Kruschen, Sydney Chaplin; D: Greydon Clark. VHS, Beta $24.95 UHV Woof!

Satan's Harvest American detective inherits estate in Johannesburg, only to find the place is being used by drug smugglers. Sidesteps the political climate and shows the beauty of the land. And a good thing: the story is virtually nonexistent.
1965 88m/C George Montgomery, Tippi Hedren; D: Ferde Grofe Jr. VHS, Beta NO ✰½

Satan's Princess Satanic cult with a female leader runs amuck. Sloppy and forgettable.
1990 90m/C Robert Forster, Caren Kaye, Lydie Denier; D: Bert I. Gordon. VHS, Beta $29.95 PAR ✰

Satan's Sadists Tamblyn and his biker gang terrorize folks in the Southern California desert, including a retired cop, a Vietnam vet and a trio of vacationing coeds. Violent film will probably be best appreciated by Adamson completists.
1969 (R) 88m/C Russ Tamblyn, Regina Carrol, Gary Kent, Jackie Taylor, John Cardos, Kent Taylor, Dix Scott Brady, Evelyn Frank, Greydon Clark, Bill Bonner, Bobby Clark, Yvonne Stewart, Cheryl Anne, Randee Lynn, Bambi Allen, Breck Warwick; D: Al Adamson. VHS NO ✰

Satan's Satellites Space zombies invade Earth. Ironically, one of the evil aliens is played by Mr. Spock himself. Originally released in serial form. AKA: Zombies of the Stratosphere.
1958 70m/B Judd Holdren, John Crawford, Leonard Nimoy, Ray Boyle; D: Fred Brannon. VHS, Beta AOV ✰½

Satan's School for Girls When a young woman investigates the circumstances that caused her sister's suicide, it leads her to a satanic girl's academy. Dumb and puerile made for TV "horror."
1973 74m/C Pamela Franklin, Roy Thinnes, Kate Jackson, Lloyd Bochner, Jamie Smith-Jackson, Jo Van Fleet, Cheryl Ladd; D: David Lowell Rich. VHS, Beta $19.99 PSM ✰½

Satan's Touch A simpleton worships the Devil and gets burned for his trouble.
1984 (R) 86m/C James Lawless, Shirley Venard. VHS, Beta NO Woof!

Satanwar A fictional look at various forms of Satan worship.
1979 95m/C Bart LaRue, Sally Schermerhorn, Jimmy Drankovitch. VHS, Beta $59.95 UHV Woof!

Satisfaction An all-girl, high school rock band play out the summer before college. The Keatons should have sent Bateman to her room for this stunt.
1988 (PG-13) 93m/C Justine Bateman, Trini Alvarado, Britta Phillips, Julia Roberts, Scott Coffey, Liam Neeson, Deborah Harry; D: Joan Freeman. VHS, Beta, LV $19.98 FOX ✰

Saturday Night Fever Brooklyn teenager (Travolta), bored with his daytime job, becomes the nighttime king of the local disco. Based on a story published in "New York Magazine" by Nik Cohn. Acclaimed for its disco dance sequences, memorable soundtrack by the Bee Gees, and carefree yet bleak script; extremely dated, although it made its mark on society in its time. Followed by the sequel "Staying Alive." Also available in a 112-minute "PG" rated version. ♫Staying Alive; Night Fever; More Than a Woman; How Deep Is Your Love?.

1977 (R) 118m/C John Travolta, Karen Gorney, Barry Miller, Donna Pescow; D: John Badham. Academy Awards '77 Nominations: Best Actor (Travolta); National Board of Review Awards '77: 10 Best Films of the Year, Best Actor (Travolta). VHS, Beta, LV $29.95 PAR ✰✰½

Saturday Night Live Premiere episode of the late night classic, SNL. Guests Steve Martin and Elliott Gould join in these "best of" skits which feature the Killer Bees, the Blues Brothers, and a parody of "Star Trek," among other bits. Additional episodes are available.
197? 90m/C Dan Aykroyd, John Belushi, Jane Curtin, Garrett Morris, Chevy Chase, Gilda Radner, Laraine Newman. VHS, Beta $14.99 COL, MOV ✰✰½

Saturday Night Live: Best of Robin Williams The unpredictable Williams featured in "Proud Dad," "I Wuv You," "Shakespeare," "The Sweeney Sisters," and more.
19?? 90m/C VHS $14.99 STE, MOV ✰✰½

Saturday Night Serials A compilation of excerpts from four serials: "The Phantom Creeps," "The Phantom Empire," "Undersea Kingdom," and "Junior G-Men."
1940 90m/B Bela Lugosi, Gene Autry, Ray Corrigan, Lon Chaney Jr. VHS, Beta $29.98 RHI ✰✰½

Saturday Night Shockers Each volume in this series is comprised of two full-length horror flicks, featuring twisted twins, barbarous butchers and sinister snow creatures. Terror abounds.
1950 150m/B Daisy Hilton. VHS, Beta $49.95 RHI ✰✰½

Saturday Night Shockers, Vol. 2 Two horror film compilations, each with copious cartoons, film clips and trailers added. Volume 2 has "Human Gorilla" and "Manbeast" and some added clips and attractions.
1958 150m/B Tod Slaughter, Eric Portman, Richard Carlson. VHS, Beta $49.95 RHI ✰✰½

Saturday Night Shockers, Vol. 3 A double feature with "Murders in the Red Barn," and "Face at the Window," plus some added classic previews and shocking shorts.
19?? 150m/B VHS $39.95 RHI ✰✰½

Saturday Night Shockers, Vol. 4 Features "The Monsters from Piedras Blancas" and "Mesa of Lost Women."
19?? 145m/B VHS $39.95 RHI ✰✰½

Saturday Night Sleazies, Vol. 1 Two sleazy films. "College Girl Confidential" (1968) and "Suburban Confidential" (1966) are each directed by the man who helmed "Orgy of the Dead." Also includes sleazy short subjects.
1966 150m/B Marsha Jordan, Harvey Shane; W/ D: A.C. Stephen. VHS, Beta $49.95 RHI ✰

Saturday the 14th A parody of the popular axe-wielding-maniac genre, about a family inheriting a haunted mansion. Poorly made; not funny or scary. Followed by even worse sequel: "Saturday the 14th Strikes Back".
1981 (PG) 91m/C Richard Benjamin, Paula Prentiss, Severn Darden; D: Howard R. Cohen. VHS, Beta $19.98 SUE ✰½

Saturday the 14th Strikes Back Pathetic sequel to the horror film spoof of the "Friday the 13th" series.
1988 91m/C Ray Walston, Avery Schreiber, Patty McCormack, Julianne McNamara, Jason Presson; D: Howard R. Cohen. VHS, Beta $79.95 MGM ✰

Saturn 3 Two research scientists create a futuristic Garden of Eden in an isolated sector of our solar system, but love story turns to horror story when a killer robot arrives. Sporadically promising, but ultimately lame; dumb ending. For Farrah fans only.
1980 (R) 88m/C *GB* Farrah Fawcett, Kirk Douglas, Harvey Keitel, Ed Bishop; *D:* Stanley Donen; *M:* John Barry. **VHS, Beta, LV $19.98** FOX *♫♫½*

Saul and David Beautifully filmed story of David's life with King Saul, the battle with Goliath, and the tragic end of Saul. From the "Bible" series. *AKA:* Saul e David.
1968 120m/C Norman Wooland, Gianno Garko. **VHS, Beta $19.95** UHV, MOV *♫½*

Savage! A savage foreign mess with ex-baseball star Iglehardt killing people with grenades and guns, abetted by an army full of murderous models. Also on video as "Black Valor."
1973 (R) 81m/C *MX* James Iglehardt, Lada Edmund, Carol Speed, Rossana Ortiz, Sally Jordan, Aura Aurea, Vic Diaz; *D:* Cirio H. Santiago. **VHS, Beta $59.98** NLC, SIM *Woof!*

Savage Abduction Two girls visiting Los Angeles are kidnapped by a bizarre man.
1973 (R) 84m/C Tom Drake, Stephen Oliver, Sean Kenney; *D:* John Lawrence. **VHS, Beta $24.95** GHV *♫*

Savage Attraction True story of a 16-year-old girl forced to marry an ex-Nazi, and her hellish life thereafter. Frustrating because it could have been much better. *AKA:* Hostage: The Christine Maresch Story; Hostage.
1983 (R) 93m/C *AU* GE Kerry Mack, Ralph Schicha; *D:* Frank Shields. **VHS, Beta $19.95** STE, SUE *♫½*

Savage Beach A pair of well-endowed female federal agents battle assorted buccaneers on a remote Pacific isle over a rediscovered cache of gold from WWII. Exploitative, pornographic, and degrading to watch. Sequel to "Picasso Trigger."
1989 (R) 90m/C Dona Speir, Hope Marie Carlton, Bruce Penhall, Rodrigo Obregon, John Aprea, Teri Weigel, Lisa London; *D:* Andy Sidaris. **VHS, Beta, LV $79.95** COL *♫*

The Savage Bees A South American ship harbored at New Orleans during Mardi Gras unleashes killer bees into the celebratory crowds. Not bad, relatively exciting, TV thriller.
1976 90m/C Ben Johnson, Michael Parks, Paul Hecht, Horst Buchholz, Gretchen Corbett; *D:* Bruce Geller. **VHS, Beta $49.95** LIV *♫♫*

Savage Dawn In yet another desert town, yet another pair of combat-hardened vets are confronted by yet another vicious motorcycle gang. Haven't we seen this one before?
1984 (R) 102m/C George Kennedy, Karen Black, Richard Lynch, Lance Henriksen, William Forsythe; *D:* Simon Nuchtern. **VHS, Beta $59.95** MED *♫½*

Savage Drums Sabu returns to his South Seas island to help end tribal warfare there. Dated and dumb, but fun-to-watch melodrama/action.
1951 70m/B Sabu, Lita Baron; *D:* William Berke. **VHS, Beta, LV** NO *♫½*

Savage Fury Feature-length version of the popular movie serial. *AKA:* Call of the Savage.
1933 80m/B Noah Beery Jr., Dorothy Short. **VHS, Beta $19.95** NOS, DVT, HEG *♫*

The Savage Girl A hunter journeys through the darkest jungle in search of prey. Instead, he stumbles across a beautiful white jungle girl, falls in love with her and attempts to take her back with him.
1932 64m/B Rochelle Hudson, Walter Byron, Harry Myers, Ted Adams, Adolph Milar, Floyd Schackleford; *D:* Harry Fraser. **VHS $16.95** SNC, NOS, DVT *♫*

Savage Guns A gunslinger goes after his brother's murderer. *AKA:* Tierra Bru Tal.
1968 85m/C **VHS, Beta $39.95** TWE *♫♫½*

Savage Hunger Ten plane crash survivors struggle to survive in the Baja desert.
1984 90m/C Chris Makepeace, Scott Hylands, Anne Lockhart; *D:* Sparky Green. **VHS, Beta $69.95** VES *♫*

Savage Instinct A woman stumbles across a drug ring and becomes a target when they fear she could expose them. Only Mongo and his crew are even more surprised when she decides to fight back.
1991 95m/C Debra Sweaney, Brian Oldfield. **VHS $89.95** AIP, MOV *♫♫*

Savage Intruder A wandering opportunist worms his way into the heart and home of a rich ex-movie star. She soon discovers that he's a sexual deviant who mutilates and murders for fun. Twisted doings with Hopkins in her final role.
1968 (R) 90m/C John Garfield, Miriam Hopkins, Gale Sondergaard, Florence Lake, Joe Besser, Minta Durfee; *D:* Donald Wolfe. **VHS $59.95** UNI *♫*

Savage is Loose Drivel about a scientist, his wife, and their son stranded on a deserted island for 20 years. Not surprisingly, as junior matures he realizes there isn't a woman for him—or is there? Completely lacking in redeeming qualities. Absurd pseudo-Freudian claptrap produced by Scott.
1974 114m/C George C. Scott, Trish Van Devere, John David Carson, Lee Montgomery; *D:* George C. Scott. **VHS, Beta $29.95** MLB *Woof!*

Savage Island Women's prison in the tropics sets the scene for the usual exploitative goings-on. Blair is actually in the film only for a few minutes. Chopped-up, even worse version of "Escape From Hell."
1985 (R) 74m/C *SP* IT Nicholas Beardsley, Linda Blair, Anthony Steffen, Ajita Wilson, Christina Lai, Leon Askin; *D:* Edward Muller. **VHS** NO *♫½*

Savage Journey A wagon train of pioneers has difficulty on its westward journey. Simple story with no real appeal.
1983 (PG) 99m/C Richard Moll, Maurice Grandmaison, Faith Clift; *D:* Tom McGowan. **VHS, Beta $79.95** PSM, SIM *♫½*

Savage Justice A young woman seeks revenge against leftist rebels (boo, hiss) in a Southeast Asian country who killed her parents and raped her. She hooks up with an ex-Green Beret, and they fight and love their way through the jungle. The usual nudity and violence; derivative and dumb.
1988 90m/C Julia Montgomery, Steven Memel. **Beta** NO *♫*

Savage Run Reynolds is Papago Indian framed and imprisoned for his brother's murder. Sprung from the pen, he heads back to the reservation to find the real killers and to avenge his brother's death. Convincing made for televisiondrama. Stevens' last role before her suicide. *AKA:* Run, Simon, Run.
1970 73m/C Burt Reynolds, Inger Stevens, James Best, Rodolfa Acosta, Don Dubbins, Joyce Jameson, Barney Phillips, Eddie Little Sky; *D:* George McCowan. **VHS $9.95** SIM *♫♫♫*

Savage Sam Intended as a sequel to "Old Yeller." Sam, the offspring of the heroic dog named Old Yeller, tracks down some children kidnapped by Indians. Fun, but not fully successful.
1963 103m/C Tommy Kirk, Kevin Corcoran, Brian Keith, Dewey Martin, Jeff York, Marta Kristen; *D:* Norman Tokar. **VHS, Beta $69.95** DIS *♫♫*

The Savage Seven An underground classic where everyone loses. A motorcycle gang rides into an Indian town which is at the mercy of corrupt businessmen. The gang's leader becomes involved in the Indians' problems but the businessmen and the cops cause trouble for all concerned. Less than memorable. Produced by Dick Clark.
1968 96m/C Larry Bishop, Joanna Frank, Adam Roarke, Robert Walker Jr.; *D:* Richard Rush. **VHS** NO *♫♫*

Savage Streets Blair seeks commando-style revenge on the street gang that raped her deaf sister. Extended rape scene betrays the exploitative intentions, though other bits are entertaining, in a trashy kind of way.
1983 (R) 93m/C Linda Blair, John Vernon, Sal Landi, Robert Dryer, Debra Blee, Linnea Quigley; *D:* Danny Steinmann. **VHS, Beta, LV $29.98** LIV, VES *♫½*

Savage Weekend A killer behind a ghoulish mask stalks human prey in the boonies, of couse. Astoundingly, there is one interesting role—William Sanderson's looney. Otherwise, throw this one no bones. *AKA:* The Killer Behind the Mask; The Upstate Murders.
1980 (R) 88m/C Christopher Allport. **VHS, Beta $42.95** PGN *Woof!*

The Savage Woman Marianna escapes from a desperate situation and is found unconscious in the woods by Elysee. He nurses her back to health, learns her terrible secret, and tries to help Marianna decides whether to turn herself into the police or keep running. In French with English subtitles.
1991 100m/C *CA* Patricia Tulasne, Matthias Habich; *D:* Lea Pool. **VHS $79.95** WBF *♫♫*

Savages A group of savages descend on a palatial mansion, and after living there for some time, become refined ladies and gentlemen. The moral savages and "civilized" men are really the same.
1972 106m/C Lewis J. Stadlen, Anne Francine, Thayer David, Salome Jens, Susan Blakely, Kathleen Widdoes, Sam Waterston; *D:* James Ivory. **VHS** NO *♫♫*

Savages Griffith as a demented nut-case stalking another man in the desert? That's right, Opie. "The Most Dangerous Game" remade-sort of-for TV.
1975 74m/C Andy Griffith, Sam Bottoms, Noah Beery Jr.; *D:* Lee H. Katzin. **VHS, Beta $49.95** PSM *♫♫½*

Savages from Hell Greasy biker dude beats up a young farm guy because he was flirting with the biker's woman. The biker also tries to rape a migrant farmworker's daughter because he lusts after her. Trashy exploitation film. *AKA:* Big Enough and Old Enough.
1968 (R) 79m/C Bobbie Byers, Cyril Poitier, Diwaldo Myers, Viola Lloyd, William P. Kelley; *W/ D:* Joseph Prieto. **VHS $16.95** SNC *♫*

Savannah Smiles Poor little rich girl Anderson runs away from home, into the clutches of two ham-handed crooks. She melts their hearts, and they change their ways. Decent, sentimental family drama.

1982 (PG) 104m/C Bridgette Anderson, Mark Miller, Donovan Scott, Peter Graves, Chris Robinson, Michael Parks; **D:** Pierre De Moro. **VHS, Beta, LV** $14.98 SUE, NLC ✍✍½

Save the Lady Plucky kids fight city hall to save an old ferry, the Lady Hope, from the scrap heap. Nothing offensive here—just a pleasant family flick.
1982 76m/C Matthew Excell, Robert Clarkson, Miranda Cartledge, Kim Clifford; **D:** Leon Thau. **VHS, Beta** $14.98 VID ✍✍

Save the Tiger A basically honest middle-aged man sees no way out of his failing business except arson. The insurance settlement will let him pay off his creditors, and save face. David, as the arsonist, and Gilford, as Lemmon's business partner, are superb. Lemmon is also excellent throughout his performance.
1973 (R) 100m/C Jack Lemmon, Jack Gilford, Laurie Heineman, Patricia Smith, Norman Burton, Thayer David; **D:** John G. Avildsen. Academy Awards '73: Best Actor (Lemmon); Nominations: Best Story & Screenplay, Best Supporting Actor (Gilford). **VHS, Beta, LV** $69.95 PAR, BTV ✍✍✍

Saving Grace A tale of the fictional youngest Pope of modern times, Pope Leo XIV (Conti). Beset by duty, he decides to shed his robes and get in touch with the world's peasantry. Improbable, but that's okay; the mortal sin is that it's improbable and slow and boring.
1986 (PG) 112m/C Tom Conti, Fernando Rey, Giancarlo Giannini, Erland Josephson, Donald Hewlett, Edward James Olmos; **D:** Robert M. Young. **VHS, Beta, LV, 8mm** $14.98 SUE, NLC ✍✍

Sawdust & Tinsel Early Bergman film detailing the grisly, humiliating experiences of a traveling circus rolling across the barren Swedish countryside. Lonely parable of human relationships. In Swedish with English subtitles. **AKA:** The Naked Night; Sunset of a Clown; Gycklarnas Afton.
1953 85m/B SW Harriet Andersson, Ake Gronberg; **D:** Ingmar Bergman. **VHS, Beta, LV** $29.98 SUE, TAM, NLC ✍✍✍

Sawmill/The Dome Doctor Two silent comedies starring the inimitable klutz of the golden era, Larry Semon, whose name has been nearly forgotten today.
1922 71m/B Larry Semon, Dorothy Dwan. **VHS, Beta** $29.95 VYY ✍✍½

Say Anything A semi-mature, successful teen romance about an offbeat loner interested in the martial arts (Cusack, in a winning performance) who goes after the beautiful class brain of his high school. Things are complicated when her father is suspected of embezzling by the IRS. Joan Cusack, John's real-life sister, also plays his sister in the film. Works well on the romantic level without getting too sticky.
1989 (PG-13) 100m/C John Cusack, Ione Skye, John Mahoney, Joan Cusack, Lili Taylor, Richard Portnow; **D:** Cameron Crowe. **VHS, Beta, LV** $19.98 FOX ✍✍✍

Say Goodbye, Maggie Cole A widow goes to work as a doctor in a Chicago street clinic and becomes emotionally involved with a dying child. Hayward's final role in moving made-for-TV drama.
1972 78m/C Susan Hayward, Darren McGavin, Michael Constantine, Nichelle Nichols, Dane Clark; **D:** Judd Taylor. **VHS, Beta** $69.95 VMK ✍✍½

Say Hello to Yesterday A May-December romance that takes place entirely in one day. An unhappy housewife meets an exciting young traveler while both are in London. Cast and director try hard but fail to get the point across to the audience.

1971 (PG) 91m/C GB Jean Simmons, Leonard Whiting, Evelyn Laye; **D:** Alvin Rakoff. **VHS, Beta** $59.95 PSM ✍✍½

Say Yes! A nutty millionaire (Winters) bets $250 million that his inept nephew cannot get married within 24 hours. Three times the length of usual wacky sitcom, alas.
1986 (PG-13) 87m/C Jonathan Winters, Art Hindle, Logan Ramsey, Lissa Layng; **D:** Larry Yust. **VHS, Beta, LV** $79.95 RCA ✍½

Sayonara An Army major is assigned to a Japanese airbase during the Korean conflict at the behest of his future father-in-law. Dissatisfied with his impending marriage, he finds himself drawn to a Japanese dancer and becomes involved in the affairs of his buddy who, against official policy, marries a Japanese woman. Tragedy surrounds the themes of bigotry and interracial marriage. Based on the novel by James Michener.
1957 147m/C Marlon Brando, James Garner, Ricardo Montalban, Patricia Owens, Red Buttons, Miyoshi Umeki, Martha Scott; **D:** Joshua Logan. Academy Awards '57: Best Art Direction/Set Decoration, Best Sound, Best Supporting Actor (Buttons), Best Supporting Actress (Umeki); Nominations: Best Actor (Brando), Best Adapted Screenplay, Best Cinematography, Best Director (Logan), Best Film Editing, Best Picture. **VHS, Beta** $19.98 FOX, BTV ✍✍✍

The Scalawag Bunch Yet another retelling of Robin Hood and his Merry Men and their adventures in Sherwood Forest.
1975 100m/C IT Mark Damon, Luis Davila, Silvia Dionisio; **D:** George Ferron. **VHS, Beta** HHE ✍

Scalp Merchant Private investigator Cliff Rowan hunts for a missing payroll. Someone would rather see him dead than successful.
1977 108m/C Cameron Mitchell, John Waters, Elizabeth Alexander, Margaret Nelson; **D:** Howard Rubie. **VHS, Beta** PGN ✍

Scalpel After his daughter's death, a plastic surgeon creates her image on another woman to get an inheritance. Violent and graphic, with a surprise ending. Not too bad; interesting premise. **AKA:** False Face.
1976 (R) 95m/C Robert Lansing, Judith Chapman, Arlen Dean Snyder; **D:** John Grissmer. **VHS, Beta** $9.95 NLC ✍✍

The Scalphunters Semi-successful, semi-funny western about an itinerant trapper (Lancaster) who is forced by Indians to trade his pelts for an educated black slave (Davis); many chases and brawls ensue. Good performances.
1968 102m/C Burt Lancaster, Ossie Davis, Telly Savalas, Shelley Winters, Nick Cravat, Dabney Coleman, Paul Picerni; **D:** Sydney Pollack. **VHS, Beta** $19.98 MGM ✍✍½

Scalps Hunted Indian princess and man whose family was killed by Indians form uneasy alliance in old West.
1983 (R) 90m/C Karen Wood, Albert Farley, Benny Cardosa, Charlie Bravo, Vassili Garis; **D:** Werner Knox. **VHS, Beta** $79.95 IMP, HHE ✍

Scandal A dramatization of Britain's Profumo government sex scandal of the 1960s. Hurt plays a society doctor who enjoys introducing pretty girls to his wealthy friends. One of the girls, Christine Keeler, takes as lovers both a Russian government official and a British Cabinet Minister. The resulting scandal eventually overturned an entire political party, and led to disgrace, prison, and death for some of those concerned. Also available in an unedited 115-minute version which contains more controversial language and nudity. Top-notch performances make either version well worth watching.

1989 (R) 105m/C GB John Hurt, Joanne Whalley-Kilmer, Ian McKellan, Bridget Fonda, Jeroen Krabbe, Britt Ekland, Roland Gift; **D:** Michael Caton-Jones. **VHS, Beta, LV** $19.95 HBO ✍✍✍

Scandal A college co-ed has an affair with her professor and eventually ends up ruining his life.
198? 95m/C Glen Saxson, Melissa Long, Patricia Reed. **VHS, Beta** NO ✍✍

Scandal in a Small Town A cocktail waitress in a small town has to defend herself and her daughter from the town's critical eye and hateful actions. Self-righteous made for TV drama rehashes several earlier plots.
1988 90m/C Raquel Welch, Christa Denton, Peter Van Norden, Ronny Cox; **D:** Anthony Page. **VHS, LV** $9.99 STE, VMK ✍✍

Scandal Man A French photographer gets in over his head when he snaps the daughter of an American KKK leader embracing a black man in a nightclub. In French with English subtitles.
1967 86m/C Maurice Ronet; **D:** Richard Balducci. **VHS, Beta** $19.95 FCT, TAM ✍✍½

Scandalous A bumbling American television reporter becomes involved with a gang of British con artists. Starts well but peters out. Look for the scene where Gielgud attends a Bow Wow Wow concert.
1984 (PG) 93m/C Robert Hays, Pamela Stephenson, John Gielgud, Jim Dale, M. Emmet Walsh; **D:** Rob Cohen. **VHS, Beta, LV** $29.98 LIV, VES ✍½

Scandalous A duke and his uncle work together to find a secretary who disappeared after witnessing a murder.
1988 90m/C Albert Fortell, Lauren Hutton, Ursula Carven, Capucine; **D:** Robert W. Young. **VHS, Beta** $9.99 STE, PSM ✍

Scandalous John Comedy western about a last cattle drive devised by an aging cowboy (Keith) in order to save his ranch. Keith's shrewd acting as the ornery cattle man who won't sell to developers carries this one.
1971 (G) 113m/C Brian Keith, Alfonso Arau, Michele Carey, Rick Lenz; **D:** Robert Butler. **VHS, Beta** $69.95 DIS ✍

Scanners "Scanners" are telepaths who can will people to explode. One scanner in particular harbors Hitlerian aspirations for his band of psychic gangsters. Gruesome but effective special effects.
1981 (R) 102m/C CA Stephen Lack, Jennifer O'Neill, Patrick McGoohan, Lawrence Dane; **D:** David Cronenberg. **VHS, Beta, LV, SVS** $14.95 COL, SUE, SUP ✍✍½

Scanners 2: The New Order This not-bad sequel to the 1981 cult classic finds a power-mad police official out to build a psychic militia of captured Scanners. More story than last time, plus more and better special effects.
1991 (R) 104m/C CA David Hewlett, Deborah Raffin, Yvan Ponton, Isabelle Mejias, Valentin Trujillo, Tom Butler, Vlasta Vrana, Dorothee Berryman; **D:** Christopher Duguay. **VHS, Beta, LV** $92.98 MED, IME ✍✍½

Scanners 3: The Takeover The third sequel in which Scanner siblings battle for control of the world. Lacks the creativity and storyline of the first two films.
1992 (R) 101m/C CA Steve Parrish, Liliana Komorowska, Valerie Valois; **D:** Christian Duguay. **VHS, LV** $14.98 REP ✍½

The Scar A cunning criminal robs the mob, then hides by "stealing" the identity of a lookalike psychologist. But he's overlooked one thing...or two. Farfetched film noir show-

cases a rare villainous role for Henreid (who also produced). Based on a novel by Murray Forbes. **AKA:** Hollow Triumph.
1948 83m/B Paul Henreid, Joan Bennett, Eduard Franz, Leslie Brooks, John Qualen, Mabel Paige, Herbert Rudley; **D:** Steve Sekely. **VHS $19.98** *REP, FCT* ♫♫½

Scar of Shame Explores the ill-fated romance between a successful black concert pianist and the lower-class woman he marries. Gives a look at the color caste system and divisions within the black community of the era.
1927 90m/B Harry Henderson, Lucia Lynn Moses, Ann Kennedy, Norman Johnstone; **D:** Frank Peregini. **VHS $39.95** *FCT* ♫♫

Scaramouche Thrilling swashbuckler about a nobleman (Granger, very well cast) searching for his family during the French Revolution. To avenge the death of a friend, he joins a theater troupe where he learns swordplay and becomes the character "Scaramouche." Features a rousing six-and-a-half-minute sword battle.
1952 111m/C Stewart Granger, Eleanor Parker, Janet Leigh, Mel Ferrer, Henry Wilcoxon, Nina Foch, Richard Anderson, Robert Coote, Lewis Stone, Elisabeth Risdon, Howard Freeman; **D:** George Sidney. **VHS, LV** *VYG, FCT* ♫♫♫½

Scarecrow Two homeless drifters (Hackman and Pacino) walk across America, heading toward a car wash business they never reach. An oft-neglected example of the early 70s extra-realistic subgenre initiated by "Midnight Cowboy." Engrossing until the end, when it falls flat. Filmed on location in Detroit.
1973 (R) 112m/C Gene Hackman, Al Pacino, Ann Wedgeworth, Eileen Brennan, Richard Lynch; **D:** Jerry Schatzberg. **VHS, Beta $19.98** *WAR* ♫♫½

Scared Stiff Fleeing a murder charge, Martin and Lewis find gangsters and ghosts on a Caribbean island. Funny and scary, a good remake of "The Ghost Breakers," with cameos by Hope and Crosby. ♫San Domingo; Song of the Enchilada Man; Mama Yo Quiero; You Hit the Spot; I Don't Care If the Sun Don't Shine; I'm Your Pal; When Somebody Thinks You're Wonderful.
1953 108m/B Dean Martin, Jerry Lewis, Lizabeth Scott, Carmen Miranda, Dorothy Malone; *Cameos:* Bob Hope, Bing Crosby; **D:** George Marshall. **VHS $14.98** *REP, MLB* ♫♫♫

Scared Stiff Three people move into a mansion once owned by a sadistic slave trader. Once there, they become unwilling victims of a voodoo curse. Bad special effects and script, not redeemed by decent but unoriginal story.
1987 (R) 85m/C Andrew Stevens, Mary Page Keller; **D:** Richard S. Friedman. **VHS, LV $14.95** *REP, PIA* ♫

Scared to Death Begins with a woman dying of fright when shown the death mask of the man she framed. Dead woman then proceeds to narrate remainder of the story, which focuses on events leading up to her unfortunate, untimely, and fairly uninteresting demise. Memorable as Lugosi's only color film.
1947 70m/C Bela Lugosi, George Zucco, Douglas Fowley, Nat Pendleton, Joyce Compton; **D:** Walt Mattox. **VHS, Beta $19.95** *NOS, SNC, MWP* ♫½

Scared to Death A scientific experiment goes awry as a mutation begins killing off the residents of Los Angeles.
1980 (R) 93m/C John Stinson, Diana Davidson, David Moses, Kermit Eller; **D:** William Malone. **VHS, Beta $49.95** *MED* ♫

Scared to Death/Dick Tracy's Dilemma On one tape, two 40's programmers-Lugosi's only color film, about a psychotic magician who tortures a young girl, and a standard black-and-white Tracy entry.
1947 125m/C Bela Lugosi, George Zucco, Ralph Byrd, Kay Christopher, Ian Keith. **VHS, Beta** *AOV* ♫♫

Scarface The violent rise and fall of a 1930s Chicago crime boss (based on the life of notorious gangster Al Capone). Release was held back by censors due to the amount of violence and its suggestion of incest between the title character and his sister. Producer Howard Hughes recut and filmed an alternate ending, without director Hawks' approval, to pacify the censors, and both versions of the film were released at the same time. Almost too violent and intense at the time. Remains brilliant and impressive. Remade in 1983. **AKA:** Scarface: The Shame of a Nation.
1931 93m/B Paul Muni, Ann Dvorak, Karen Morley, Osgood Perkins, George Raft, Boris Karloff; **D:** Howard Hawks. **VHS, Beta, LV $19.95** *MCA* ♫♫♫

Scarface Al Pacino is a Cuban refugee who becomes powerful in the drug trade until the life gets the better of him. A remake of the 1932 classic gangster film of the same name, although the first film has more plot. Extremely violent, often unpleasant, but not easily forgotten.
1983 (R) 170m/C Al Pacino, Steven Bauer, Michelle Pfeiffer, Robert Loggia, F. Murray Abraham, Mary Elizabeth Mastrantonio, Harris Yulin, Paul Shenar, Oliver Stone; **D:** Brian DePalma. **VHS, Beta, LV $29.95** *MCA* ♫♫♫

Scarface Mob This is the original television pilot film for the popular series "The Untouchables," about Eliot Ness's band of good guys battling Chicago's crime lord, Al Capone. Still strong stuff. Narrated by Walter Winchell. **AKA:** Tueur de Chicago.
1962 120m/B Robert Stack, Neville Brand, Barbara Nichols; **D:** Phil Karlson. **VHS, Beta** *PAR* ♫♫

The Scarlet & the Black A priest clandestinely works within the shield of the Vatican's diplomatic immunity to shelter allied soldiers from the Nazis in occupied Rome. His efforts put him at odds with the Pope and target him for Gestapo assassination. Swashbuckling adventure at its second-best. Made for television. Based on the nonfiction book "The Scarlet Pimpernel of the Vatican" by J.P. Gallagher.
1983 145m/C Gregory Peck, Christopher Plummer, John Gielgud, Raf Vallone; **D:** Jerry London; **M:** Ennio Morricone. **VHS, Beta $59.98** *FOX, FCT, IGP* ♫♫½

The Scarlet Car Chaney is a bank cashier who discover his boss has been embezzling funds. A fight causes Chaney to believe he has killed his employer and he hides out in a remote cabin where guilt preys on his mind.
1917 50m/B Lon Chaney Sr., Franklin Farnum, Edith Johnson, Sam DeGrasse; **D:** Joseph DeGrasse. **VHS, Beta $16.95** *SNC, GPV, FCT* ♫♫

Scarlet Claw Holmes and Watson solve the bloody murder of an old lady in the creepy Canadian village of Le Mort Rouge. The best and most authentic of the Sherlock Holmes series. **AKA:** Sherlock Holmes and the Scarlet Claw.
1944 74m/B Basil Rathbone, Nigel Bruce, Miles Mander, Gerald Hamer, Kay Harding; **D:** Roy William Neill. **VHS, Beta $14.98** *FOX* ♫♫♫

The Scarlet Clue A better script and faster pacing improved this Monogram entry in the Chan series. Charlie investigates a series of mysterious deaths which lead to a plot to steal secret government radar plans.
1945 65m/B Sidney Toler, Benson Fong, Mantan Moreland, Robert E. Homans, Helen Devereaux; **D:** Phil Rosen. **VHS $19.98** *MGM* ♫♫

The Scarlet Letter Unlikely comic relief provides only measure of redemption for this poorly rendered version of Hawthorne's classic novel about sin and Hester Prynne. Actor Hale is Skipper from "Gilligan's Island".
1934 69m/B Colleen Moore, Hardie Albright, Henry B. Walthall, Alan Hale Jr., Cora Sue Collins, Betty Blythe; **D:** Robert G. Vignola. **VHS, Beta $19.95** *NOS, KRT, VYY* ♫♫

The Scarlet Letter A studied, thoughtful, international production of the Nathaniel Hawthorne classic about a woman's adultery which incites puritanical violence and hysteria in colonial America. Fine modernization by Wenders. In German with English subtitles.
1973 90m/C *SP GE* Senta Berger, Lou Castel, Yella Rottlaender, William Layton, Yelena Samarina, Hans-Christian Blech; **D:** Wim Wenders. **VHS, Beta $59.95** *FCT, GLV, TAM* ♫♫♫

The Scarlet Pimpernel "The Scarlet Pimpernel," supposed dandy of the English court, assumes a dual identity to outwit the French Republicans and aid innocent aristocrats during the French Revolution. Classic rendering of Baroness Orczy's novel, full of exploits, 18th century costumes, intrigue, damsels, etc. Produced by Alexander Korda, who fired the initial director, Rowland Brown. Remade for television in 1982. Available in colorized version.
1934 95m/B *GB* Leslie Howard, Joan Gardner, Merle Oberon, Raymond Massey, Anthony Bushell; **D:** Harold Young. **VHS, Beta, 3/4U, Special order formats $9.95** *NFG, NOS, PSM* ♫♫♫½

The Scarlet Pimpernel A British television remake of the classic about a British dandy who saved French aristocrats from the Reign of Terror guillotines during the French Revolution. Made for television version is almost as good as the original 1935 film, with beautiful costumes and sets and good performances from Seymour and Andrews.
1982 142m/C *GB* Anthony Andrews, Jane Seymour, Ian McKellan, James Villers, Eleanor David; **D:** Clive Donner. **VHS, Beta, LV $19.98** *LIV, VEG* ♫♫♫

Scarlet Spear Filmed in Nairobi National Park in Kenya. A great white hunter convinces a young African chief that the ancient practices of his people are uncivilized. Pathetically stated and culturally offensive by today's standards.
1954 78m/C John Bentley, Martha Hyer, Morasi; **D:** George Breakston, Roy Stahl. **VHS, Beta $39.95** *MSP* Woof!

Scarlet Street A mild-mannered, middle-aged cashier becomes an embezzler when he gets involved with a predatory, manipulating woman. Lang remake of Jean Renoir's "La Chienne" (1931). Set apart from later attempts on the same theme by excellent direction by Lang and acting. Also available Colorized.
1945 95m/B Edward G. Robinson, Joan Bennett, Dan Duryea, Samuel S. Hinds; **D:** Fritz Lang. **VHS, Beta, 3/4U, Special order formats $9.95** *NEG, NOS, HHT* ♫♫♫

Scarred Unwed teenage mother becomes prostitute to support baby. Predictable plot and acting pull this one down. **AKA:** Street Love; Red on Red.

1984 (R) 85m/C Jennifer Mayo, Jackie Berryman, David Dean; **W/D:** Rosemarie Turko. VHS, Beta $69.98 LIV, VES ℐ ½

The Scars of Dracula A young couple tangles with Dracula in their search for the man's missing brother. Gory, creepy, violent, sexy tale from the dark side. Don't see it late at night. Preceded by "Taste the Blood of Dracula" and followed by "Dracula A.D. 1972." Available on Laserdisc with "The Horror of Frankenstein."
1970 (R) 96m/C GB Christopher Lee, Jenny Hanley, Dennis Waterman, Wendy Hamilton, Patrick Troughton, Michael Gwynn, Anouska Hempel, Michael Ripper; **D:** Roy Ward Baker. VHS, Beta, LV $59.99 HBO, MLB ℐℐ½

Scavenger Hunt Action begins when a deceased millionaire's will states that his 15 would-be heirs must compete in a scavenger hunt, and whoever collects all the items first wins the entire fortune. Big cast wanders about aimlessly.
1979 (PG) 117m/C Richard Benjamin, James Coco, Ruth Buzzi, Cloris Leachman, Cleavon Little, Roddy McDowall, Scatman Crothers, Tony Randall, Robert Morley, Richard Mulligan, Dirk Benedict, Willie Aames, Vincent Price; **D:** Michael Schultz. VHS, Beta $59.98 FOX ℐ

Scavengers A man and a woman become involved in a spy plot and wind up in all sorts of danger. Pathetic excuse for a "thriller."
1987 (PG-13) 94m/C Kenneth Gilman, Brenda Bakke, Ken Gampu, Norman Anstey, Crispin De Nys; **D:** Duncan Maclachlan. VHS, Beta, LV $29.95 ACA ℐ

Scenario du Film Passion A classically self-analyzing video piece by Godard, in which he recreates on tape the scenario for his film "Passion," resulting in a reflexive, experimental essay on the process of image-making and conceptualizing films, especially Godard's. In French with English subtitles.
1982 54m/C **D:** Jean-Luc Godard, Anne-Marie Mieville, Barnard Menoud. VHS, Beta EAI ℐℐℐ

Scene of the Crime Three short mysteries, which the audience is asked to solve: "The Newlywed Murder," "Medium Is the Murder" and "Vote for Murder." Made for television.
1985 74m/C Markie Post, Alan Thicke, Ben Piazza; **D:** Andre Techine, Walter Grauman. VHS, Beta $39.95 MCA ℐℐ½

Scene of the Crime Beautiful widow, trapped in small French town, is sexually awakened by escaped convict hiding out near her home. Acclaimed, but sometimes distracting camera technique and slow pace undermine the film. In French with English subtitles.
1987 90m/C FR Catherine Deneuve, Danielle Darrieux, Wadeck Stanczak, Victor Lanoux, Nicolas Giraudi; **D:** Andre Techine. Beta NO ℐℐℐ

Scenes from a Mall Conspicuous consumers spend sixteenth wedding anniversary waltzing in mall while marriage unravels with few laughs. Surprisingly superficial comedy given the depth of talent of Allen and Midler.
1991 (R) 87m/C Woody Allen, Bette Midler, Bill Irwin, Daren Firestone, Rebecca Nickels; **Cameos:** Fabio Lanzoni; **W/D:** Paul Mazursky. VHS, Beta, LV $19.99 TOU, IME ℐℐ

Scenes from a Marriage Originally produced in six one-hour episodes for Swedish television, this bold and sensitive film excruciatingly portrays the painful, unpleasant, disintegration of a marriage. Ullman is superb. Realistic and disturbing. Dubbed.
1973 (PG) 168m/C SW Liv Ullmann, Erland Josephson, Bibi Andersson; **D:** Ingmar Bergman. VHS, Beta $89.95 COL ℐℐℐℐ

Scenes from a Murder A killer (Savalas) stalks a beautiful actress (Heywood). Dull excuse for a suspense flick.
1972 91m/C IT Telly Savalas, Anne Heywood, Giorgio Piazza; **D:** Alberto De Martino. VHS, Beta NO ℐ½

Scenes from the Class Struggle in Beverly Hills Social satire about the wealthy, their servants, and their hangers-on in two Hollywood households. Two chauffeurs spend their spare time lusting after their lovely employers, and bet to see who can accomplish reality first. All kinds of erotic capers result. Usually funny and irreverent; occasionally misfires or takes itself too seriously. Reunites the trio from cult classic "Eating Raoul": Bartel, Woronov, and Beltran. Remake of Renoir's "The Rules of the Game."
1989 (R) 103m/C Jacqueline Bisset, Ray Sharkey, Mary Woronov, Robert Beltran, Ed Begley Jr., Wallace Shawn, Paul Bartel, Paul Mazursky, Arnetia Walker, Rebecca Schaeffer; **Cameos:** Little Richard; **D:** Paul Bartel. VHS, Beta, LV NO ℐℐ

Scenes from the Goldmine A young woman joins a rock band and falls in love with its lead singer. Realistic but bland; music not memorable (performed mostly by the actors themselves).
1987 (R) 99m/C Catherine Mary Stewart, Cameron Dye, Joe Pantoliano, John Ford Coley, Steve Railsback, Timothy B. Schmit, Jewel Shepard, Alex Rocco, Lee Ving, Lesley-Anne Down; **D:** Marc Rocco. VHS, Beta, LV $19.98 NLC ℐ½

Scent of a Woman Pacino is a powerhouse (verging on caricature) in a story that, with anyone else in the lead, would be your run-of-the-mill, overly sentimental coming of age/redemption flick running 30 minutes too long. Even with Pacino giving acting lessons, it's probably 30 minutes too long. Blind, bitter, and semi-alcoholic Pacino is a retired army colonel under the care of his married niece. The colonel is home alone during Thanksgiving weekend, under the watchful eye of local prep school student Charlie (O'Donnell). After admonishments from the departing family about no 900 numbers and a four-drink-per-day limit, the colonel lets Charlie in on his plan: to go to New York City and live it up. What he doesn't mention is that this is to be his last hurrah. Just so happens, the innocent youth has problems of his own, which leads the two men to a rather predictable bonding scene. What is not predictable, however, is how Pacino's abrasive (though wonderfully intuitive and romantic) colonel makes an impact on viewers that lingers like a woman's scent long after the last tango. O'Donnell is competently understated in key supporting role, while the tango lesson between Pacino and Anwar dances to the tune of "classic." Box-office winner is a remake of 1975 Italian film "Profumo di Donna." The laserdisc version is available in letterbox format.
1992 (R) 149m/C Al Pacino, Chris O'Donnell, James Rebhorn, Gabrielle Anwar, Philip S. Hoffman, Richard Venture, Bradley Whitford, Rochelle Oliver, Margaret Eginton, Tom Riis Farrell; **D:** Martin Brest; **W:** Bo Goldman; **M:** Thomas Newman. Academy Awards '92: Best Actor (Pacino); Nominations: Best Adapted Screenplay, Best Director (Brest), Best Picture; Golden Globe Awards '93: Best Actor—Drama (Pacino), Best Film—Drama. VHS, LV $89.99 MCA, MOV, BTV ℐℐℐ

Scherzo One of McLaren's earliest films, an abstract meditation lost in 1939 and subsequently found and reconstructed in 1984.

1939 2m/C **D:** Norman McLaren. VHS, Beta NFC ℐℐℐ

Schizo Devious intentions abound as a middle-aged man is overcome by weird scenes and revelations, caused by the impending wedding of the figure skater he adores. Confusing tale of insanity, obsession, and skating. **AKA:** Amok; Blood of the Undead.
1977 (R) 109m/C Lynne Frederick, John Layton; **D:** Pete Walker. VHS, Beta $24.95 UHV, MED ℐ

Schizoid Advice-to-the-lovelorn columnist Hill receives a series of threatening letters causing her to wonder whether psychiatrist Kinski is bumping off his own patients. Boring blood dripper that's difficult to follow. **AKA:** Murder by Mail.
1980 (R) 91m/C Klaus Kinski, Marianna Hill, Craig Wasson; **D:** David Paulsen. VHS, Beta $19.98 MCA ℐ

Schlock Accurately titled horror parody is first directorial effort for Landis, who does double duty as a missing link who kills people and falls in love with blind girl. Look for cameo appearance by Forrest J. Ackerman; ape-makeup by Rick Baker. **AKA:** The Banana Monster.
1973 (PG) 78m/C John Landis, Saul Kahan, Joseph Piantadosi, Eliza Garrett; **Cameos:** Forrest J. Ackerman; **W/D:** John Landis VHS NO ℐℐ

Schnelles Geld A mild-mannered guy gets involved with a prostitute, and is plunged into a world of crime and drugs. In German with English subtitles.
1984 90m/C GE VHS, Beta $39.95 VCD, GLV ℐ½

School Daze Director/writer/star Lee's second outing is a rambunctious comedy (with a message, of course) set at an African-American college in the South. Skimpy plot revolves around the college's homecoming weekend and conflict among frats and sororities and African-Americans who would lose their racial identity and others who assert it. Entertaining and thought provoking. A glimpse at Lee's "promise," fulfilled in "Do the Right Thing."
1988 (R) 114m/C Spike Lee, Larry Fishburne, Giancarlo Esposito, Tisha Campbell, Ossie Davis, Joe Seneca, Art Evans, Ellen Holly, Branford Marsalis; **D:** Spike Lee. VHS, Beta, LV $14.95 COL, FCT ℐℐℐ

School for Scandal British television adaptation of Richard Sheridan's comedic play of the morals and manners of 18th century England.
1965 100m/B GB Joan Plowright, Felix Aylmer. VHS, Beta $29.95 VYY ℐℐ

School for Sex A young man starts a school to teach young girls how to marry well and divest their husbands of their money. Not satirical, but funny in places, relies heavily on slapstick. **AKA:** Nikutai No Gakko; School of Love.
1969 81m/C Derek Aylward, Rose Alba, Hugh Latimer, Cathy Howard. VHS, Beta $59.95 MON ℐ½

School Spirit A hormonally motivated college student is killed during a date. He comes back as a ghost to haunt the campus, disrupt the stuffy president's affair, and fall in love. Forgettable, lame, low-grade teen sex flick.
1985 (R) 90m/C Tom Nolan, Elizabeth Foxx, Larry Linville; **D:** Allan Holleb. VHS, Beta $79.95 MED ℐ

School Ties Encino man Fraser does a dramatic turn as a talented 1950's quarterback who gets a scholarship to the elite St. Matthew prep school. To conform with the

S

closed-mindedness of the McCarthy era, both his father and coach suggest that he hide his Jewish religion. Fraser's compliance results in his big-man-on-campus status, until his rival in football and his love interest both find out that he is Jewish, creating an ugly rift in the school. What easily could have been just another teen hunk flick looks at much more than just Fraser's pretty face in successful, unflinching treatment of anti-Semitism.
1992 (PG-13) 110m/C Brendan Fraser, Matt Damon, Chris O'Donnell, Randall Batinkoff, Anthony Rapp, Amy Locane, Ben Affleck, Andrew Lowery, Cole Hauser, Peter Donat, Kevin Tighe; **D:** Robert Mandel; **W:** Darryl Ponicsan, Dick Wolf; **M:** Maurice Jarre. **VHS, Beta, LV** PAR *ΖΖΖ*

Science Crazed A scientist creates a monster who could conceivably destroy the world.
19?? 90m/C Cameron Klein; **D:** Ron Switzer. **VHS, Beta** NO *ΖΖ* 1/2

Scissors Yes, this Hitchcock imitation needs trimming. An unstable young woman contends with a rapist, devious lookalikes, birds, and a prison-like apartment, not all of which are relevant to the plot. An unsharp stab at suspense from novelist/filmmaker DeFelitta.
1991 (R) 105m/C Sharon Stone, Steve Railsback, Michelle Phillips, Ronny Cox; **W/D:** Frank de Felitta. **VHS, Beta $14.95** PAR *ΖΖ* 1/2

Scorchers Back in the bayou, Splendid (Lloyd), a newlywed who won't sleep with her husband, and her cousin Talbot (Tilly), a preacher's daughter whose husband prefers the town whore Thais (Dunaway), find their lives intertwined because of their marital and sexual problems. A real "scorcher."
1992 (R) 81m/C Faye Dunaway, Denholm Elliott, James Earl Jones, Emily Lloyd, Jennifer Tilly, Leland Crooke, James Wilder, Anthony Geary; **W/D:** David Beaird. **VHS, Beta, LV $89.98** FXV *ΖΖ*

Scorchy Low-budget female cop action flick about a narcotics agent (Stevens) on the trail of a drug kingpin. Blood and guts, guns, and violence. Poor casting.
1976 (R) 100m/C Connie Stevens, William Smith, Cesare Danova, Marlene Schmidt; **D:** Hikmet Avedis. **VHS, Beta $29.98** LIV *Ζ*

Score A married couple introduces newlywed neighbors to the world of kinky sexual experiments. The two couples try all combinations. Director Metzger was well known in the '60s for soft-core porn.
1973 (R) 89m/C Claire Wilbur, Calvin Culver, Lynn Lowry; **D:** Radley Metzger. **VHS, Beta** NO *Ζ* 1/2

Scoring Battle between an all-women's basketball team and a men's team combining fun, sex, and athletic prowess, but missing film expertise. Ever so zany.
1980 90m/C Myra Taylor, Greg Perrie, Freya Crane, Pete Maravich. **VHS, Beta $49.95** VHE Woof!

Scorpio Okay cat-and-mouse espionage tale about a wily, veteran CIA agent (Lancaster) who may have turned traitor. He's set-up to be killed by a CIA boss but the assassin, code-name Scorpio (Delon), has some trouble fulfilling his assignment. Cross- and double-cross abound.
1973 (PG) 114m/C Burt Lancaster, Alain Delon, Paul Scofield, John Colicos, Gayle Hunnicutt, J.D. Cannon, Joanne Linville, Melvin Stewart, James B. Sikking, Vladek Sheybal, William Smithers, Celeste Yarnall; **D:** Michael Winner. **VHS $14.95** MGM *ΖΖ* 1/2

The Scorpio Factor Murder and mayhem follow microchip heist.

1990 87m/C Attila Bertalan, David Nerman, Wendy Dawn Wilson. **VHS** NO *ΖΖ*

Scorpion A karate-master and anti-terrorist expert defuses a skyjacking and infiltrates international assassination conspiracies. Ex-real life karate champ Tulleners is a ho-hum hero, and the story is warmed over.
1986 (R) 98m/C Tonny Tulleners, Allen Williams, Don Murray; **D:** William Reed. **VHS, Beta, LV $79.95** COL, HHE *Ζ*

Scorpion with Two Tails In an underworld of terror, people die grotesque deaths that a woman dreams of.
1982 99m/C John Saxon, Van Johnson. **VHS $59.98** CGH *Ζ*

The Scorpion Woman A female Viennese judge becomes entwined in an unusual case which partially parallels her own life. Her new young lover turns out to be bisexual. Not gripping. In German with English subtitles.
1989 101m/C GE Angelica Domrose, Fritz Hammel; **D:** Susanne Zanke. **VHS, Beta** NO *ΖΖ*

The Scorpion's Tail Graphic murder scenes rev up this early thriller by Martino filmed with plot twists and visual games. Dubbed in English.
1971 90m/C IT SP Evelyn Stewart, Anita Strindberg, George Hilton, Luigi Pistilli, Janine Reynaud; **D:** Sergio Martino; **W:** Sauro Scavolini, Ernesto Gastaldi; **M:** Bruno Nicolai. **VHS** VSM *Ζ*

Scotland Yard Inspector An American newspaperman (Romero) in London looks for a killer. Nothing special. **AKA:** Lady in the Fog.
1952 73m/B GB Cesar Romero, Bernadette O'Farrell; **D:** Sam Newfield. **VHS, Beta, LV $24.95** MLB *ΖΖ*

Scott of the Antarctic Drama of doomed British expedition of 1911 struggling to be the first group to reach the South Pole. Much of the stunning location filming was shot in the Swiss Alps. Story is authentic, but oddly uninvolving, as though seen from afar.
1948 111m/C John Mills, Christopher Lee, Kenneth More, Derek Bond; **D:** Charles Frend. **VHS, Beta $24.95** NOS, DVT, WES *ΖΖ* 1/2

Scoumoune The local "fixer" and heavy gets into trouble and no one comes to help. A movie that searches for honesty. Dubbed in English.
1974 87m/C FR Jean-Paul Belmondo, Claudia Cardinale. **VHS, Beta** NO *ΖΖ* 1/2

Scout's Honor An orphan (Coleman) is determined to become the best Cub Scout ever when he joins a troop led by an executive who dislikes children. Harmless, enjoyable family tale includes several former child stars as Scout parents. Made for television.
1980 96m/C Gary Coleman, Katherine Helmond, Wilfrid Hyde-White, Pat O'Brien, Joanna Moore, Meeno Peluce, Jay North, Harry Morgan, Angela Cartwright; **D:** Henry Levin. **VHS, Beta** NO *ΖΖ*

Scrambled Feet An uninhibited satire of the world of show business.
1983 100m/C Madeline Kahn. **VHS, Beta $39.95** RKO, TTC *ΖΖ* 1/2

Scream Vacationers on a raft trip down the Rio Grande are terrorized by a mysterious murderer. Hopelessly dull.
1983 (R) 86m/C Pepper Martin, Hank Warden, Alvy Moore, Woody Strode, John Ethan Wayne; **D:** Byron Quisenberry. **VHS, Beta $69.98** LIV, VES *Ζ*

Scream and Die A model is harassed by a murderous thief and is forced to run for her life.

1974 (R) 98m/C Andrea Allan, Karl Lanchbury, Maggie Walker, Judy Matheson; **D:** Joseph Larraz. **VHS, Beta $69.98** LIV Woof!

Scream and Scream Again Price is a sinister doctor who tries to create a super race of people devoid of emotions. Cushing is the mastermind behind the plot. Lee is the agent investigating a series of murders. Three great horror stars, a psychedelic disco, great '60s fashions; it's all here.
1970 (PG) 95m/C GB Vincent Price, Christopher Lee, Peter Cushing, Judy Huxtable, Alfred Marks, Anthony Newlands, Uta Levka, Judi Bloom, Yutte Stensgaard; **D:** Gordon Hessler. **VHS, Beta $69.98** LIV, VES *ΖΖ* 1/2

Scream, Baby, Scream An unsuccessful artist switches from sculpting clay to carving young models' faces into hideous deformed creatures. **AKA:** Nightmare House.
1969 86m/C Ross Harris, Eugenie Wingate, Chris Martell, Suzanne Stuart, Larry Swanson, Brad Grinter; **D:** Joseph Adler. **VHS, Beta** NO *Ζ*

Scream Blacula Scream Blacula returns from his dusty undoing in the original movie to once again suck the blood out of greater Los Angeles. A voodoo priestess (Grier) is the only person with the power to stop him. A weak follow up to the great "Blacula," but worth a look for Marshall and Grier.
1973 (R) 96m/C William Marshall, Don Mitchell, Pam Grier, Michael Conrad, Richard Lawson, Lynne Moody, Janee Michelle, Barbara Rhoades, Bernie Hamilton; **D:** Bob Kelljan. **VHS $59.98** ORI, FCT *ΖΖ*

Scream Bloody Murder A young boy grinds his father to death with a tractor but mangles his own hand trying to jump off. After receiving a steel claw and being released from a mental institution he continues his murderous ways in and around his home town. Inspiring.
1972 (R) 90m/C Fred Holbert, Leigh Mitchell, Robert Knox, Suzette Hamilton; **D:** Robert Emery. **VHS, Beta $19.95** UHV Woof!

Scream Dream A beautiful rock star uses her supernatural powers to control her fans, turning them into revenge-seeking monsters when she wants to. Heavy on the blood and skin; heavily exploitative.
1989 80m/C Melissa Moore, Carole Carr, Nikki Riggins, Jesse Ray; **W/D:** Donald Farmer. **VHS** NO *Ζ*

Scream for Help A young girl discovers that her cheating stepfather is plotting to murder her mother, but no one will believe her. Is she paranoid? So bad it's funny; otherwise, it's just bad, and far from suspenseful.
1986 (R) 95m/C Rachael Kelly, David Brooks, Marie Masters; **D:** Michael Winner. **VHS, Beta, LV $19.95** LHV, WAR *Ζ*

Scream of Fear A wheelchair-bound young woman goes to visit her father and new stepmother only to find her father is away on business. But she believes she sees her father's corpse. Is someone trying to drive her mad? Abounds in plot twists and mistaken identities. A truly spooky film, suspenseful, and well-made. **AKA:** Taste of Fear.
1961 81m/B GB Susan Strasberg, Ronald Lewis, Ann Todd, Christopher Lee; **D:** Seth Holt; **W:** Jimmy Sangster. **VHS, Beta $69.95** COL, MLB *ΖΖΖ*

Scream of the Demon Lover A young biochemist has a busy day as she works for a reclusive Baron. She fantasizes about him, tries to track down a murderer, and eventually discovers a mutant in the cellar. About as bad as they come, but short!

▲ 725 VIDEOHOUND'S GOLDEN MOVIE RETRIEVER

1971 (R) 75m/C Jennifer Hartley, Jeffrey Chase; **D:** J.L. Merino. **VHS, Beta** $59.98 *NLC* Woof!

Screamer A woman wants revenge after she is viciously attacked and raped. Now every man she sees is her attacker as she becomes more and more unbalanced.
1974 71m/C Pamela Franklin, Donal McCann. **VHS, Beta** NO *♂*

Screamers A mad scientist on a desert island gleefully turns escaped convicts into grotesque monstrosities. Gory and gratuitous. *AKA:* L'Isola Degli Uomini Pesce; Island of the Fishmen; Something Waits in the Dark.
1980 (R) 83m/C Richard Johnson, Joseph Cotten, Barbara Bach; **D:** Dan T. Miller, Sergio Martino. **VHS, Beta** $19.98 *SUE ♂*

The Screaming Dead Monsters rise from the tomb to do battle with planet Earth and each other. Not to be confused with the Al Adamson epic "Dracula vs. Frankenstein." *AKA:* Dracula vs. Frankenstein.
1972 84m/C *SP* Dennis Price, Howard Vernon, Alberto Dalbes, Mary Francis, Genevieve Deloir, Josianne Gibert, Fernando Bilbao; **D:** Jess (Jesus) Franco. **VHS** $69.95 *UHV ♂*

The Screaming Skull Man redecorates house with skulls in attempt to drive already anxious wife insane.
1958 68m/B William Hudson, Peggy Webber, Toni Johnson, Russ Conway, Alex Nicol; **D:** Alex Nicol. **VHS** $19.98 *NOS, SNC ♂½*

Screams of a Winter Night Ghostly tale of an evil monster from the lake and the terror he causes.
1979 (PG) 92m/C Matt Borel, Gil Glasco. **VHS, Beta** $54.95 *UHV ♂*

Screamtime Two fiendish friends filch a trilogy of horror tapes for home viewing. After the show, real scary things happen.
1983 (R) 89m/C Jean Anderson, Robin Bailey, Dora Bryan, David Van Day; **D:** Al Beresford. **VHS, Beta** $69.98 *LIV ♂*

Screen Test Oversexed silly teenagers arrange fake screen tests in order to meet girls.
1985 (R) 84m/C Michael Allan Bloom, Robert Bundy, Paul Lueken, David Simpatico; **D:** Sam Auster. **VHS, Beta, LV** $79.95 *COL* Woof!

Screwball Academy A beautiful female director makes a soft-core film on a secluded island, and gets trouble from thugs, evangelists, horny crew members and others. Former "SCTV" director John Blanchard understandably used a pseudonym to direct this lame effort.
1986 (R) 90m/C Colleen Camp, Kenneth Welsh, Christine Cattell; **D:** Reuben Rose. **VHS, Beta** $69.95 *TWE ♂½*

Screwball Hotel A beauty pageant is organized to help fund a nearly bankrupt hotel. Three bell hops are the saviors of this madcap motor inn. Exploitative skin flick.
1988 (R) 101m/C Michael C. Bendetti, Andrew Zeller, Corinne Alphen, Kelly Monteith; **D:** Rafal Zeilinski. **VHS, Beta** $89.95 *MCA ♂½*

Screwballs Freewheeling group of high school boys stirs up trouble for their snooty and virginal homecoming queen. Another inept teen sex comedy with no subtlety whatsoever. Sequel: "Loose Screws."
1983 (R) 80m/C Peter Keleghan, Lynda Speciale; **D:** Rafal Zeilinski. **VHS, Beta** $19.98 *WAR ♂*

Scrooge On Christmas Eve a miser changes his ways after receiving visits from the ghosts of Christmas past, present, and future. Based on the classic novel "A Christmas Carol" by Charles Dickens. Screenplay co-written by Hicks, who gives an interesting performance as Ebeneezer Scrooge.
1935 61m/B *GB* Seymour Hicks, Maurice Evans, Robert Cochran, Donald Calthrop, Mary Glynne, Oscar Asche; **D:** Henry Edwards. **VHS, Beta** $24.95 *VYY, CCB, DVT ♂♂♂*

Scrooge Well-done musical version of Charles Dickens' classic "A Christmas Carol," about a miserly old man who is faced with ghosts on Christmas Eve. Finney is memorable in the title role. ♫The Beautiful Day; Happiness; Thank You Very Much; A Christmas Carol; Christmas Children; I Hate People; Farver Chris'mas; See the Phantoms; December the 25th; You...You...; I Like Life; I'll Begin Again.
1970 (G) 86m/C *GB* Albert Finney, Alec Guinness, Edith Evans, Kenneth More; **D:** Ronald Neame. Academy Awards '70 Nominations: Best Art Direction/Set Decoration, Best Costume Design, Best Song ("Thank You Very Much"), Best Original Score; Golden Globe Awards '71: Best Actor—Musical/Comedy (Finney). **VHS, Beta, LV** $19.98 *FOX ♂♂½*

Scrooged Somewhat disjointed big-budgeted version of the hallowed classic. A callous television executive staging "A Christmas Carol" is himself visited by the three ghosts and sees the light. Music by Danny Elfman. Kane is terrific as one of the ghosts. Film is heavy-handed, Murray too sardonic to be believable.
1988 (PG-13) 101m/C Bill Murray, Carol Kane, John Forsythe, David Johansen, Bob Goldthwait, Karen Allen, Michael J. Pollard, Brian Doyle-Murray, Alfre Woodard, John Glover, Robert Mitchum, Buddy Hackett, Robert Goulet, Jamie Farr, Mary Lou Retton, Lee Majors; **D:** Richard Donner; **W:** Mitch Glazer, Michael O'Donoghue. **VHS, Beta, LV, 8mm** $89.95 *PAR ♂♂*

Scrubbers Young girl is sent to reform school where she's forced to survive in a cruel and brutal environment. Low-budget "reform school" movie with no point, but lots of lesbianism.
1982 (R) 93m/C *GB* Amanda York, Chrissie Cotterill, Elizabeth Edmonds, Kate Ingram, Debbie Bishop, Dana Gillespie; **D:** Mai Zetterling. **VHS, Beta** $69.99 *HBO ♂*

Scruffy An orphan and his dog survive with the help of two crooks who are reformed through their love for the little boy. Animated.
1980 72m/C *V:* Alan Young, June Foray, Hans Conried, Nancy McKeon. **VHS, Beta** $19.95 *WOV, GKK, WTA ♂*

Scruples Set in the glamorous, jet-setting world of Beverly Hills, this top-rated miniseries follows the career of Billy Ikehorn (Wagner) as she weds a wealthy industrialist and opens a clothing boutique named "Scruples." She caters to high society's haute couture, and meets unscrupulous individuals who threaten to dethrone her from her position of power and privilege. Based on the best-selling novel by Judith Krantz.
1980 279m/C Lindsay Wagner, Barry Bostwick, Kim Cattrall, Gavin MacLeod, Connie Stevens, Efrem Zimbalist Jr., Gene Tierney. **VHS, Beta** $79.99 *WAR ♂*

Scum Adapted from Roy Minton's acclaimed play, this British production looks at the struggle among three young men in a British Borstal (a prison for young convicts.) Portrays the physical, sexual, and psychological violence committed. Horrifying and powerful.
1979 96m/C *GB* Phil Daniels, Mick Ford, Ray Winstone; **D:** Alan Clarke. **VHS, Beta** $59.95 *PSM ♂♂♂*

Sea Chase An odd post-war sea adventure, wherein a renegade German freighter captain is pursued by British and German navies as he leaves Australia at the outbreak of World War II. A Prussian Wayne rivaled only by his infamous Genghis Khan in "The Conqueror" for strange character selection. Turner is on board as Wayne's girlfriend.
1955 117m/C John Wayne, Lana Turner, Tab Hunter, James Arness, Lyle Bettger, David Farrar, Richard Davalos, Claude Akins, John Qualen; **D:** John Farrow. **VHS, Beta, LV** $19.98 *WAR ♂♂½*

Sea Devils Sentenced to prison for a crime he didn't commit, a man escapes and joins a boatload of treasure hunters, but mutiny is afoot. Don't get soaked by this cheapie.
1931 77m/B Walter Long, Edmund Burns, Henry Otto, James Donnelly; **D:** Joseph Levering. **VHS** $16.95 *SNC, NOS ♂*

Sea Devils The tale of a sea captain and his lovely daughter who have differing opinions on whom she should marry. While her father would like her to marry a tame gentlemen under his command, she has her heart set on another beau. Sound predictable? It is, but fun.
1937 88m/B Victor McLaglen, Preston Foster, Ida Lupino, Donald Woods, Gordon Jones; **D:** Ben Stoloff. **VHS** $9.95 *MED ♂*

Sea Devils A smuggler and a beautiful spy come together during the Napoleonic Wars in this sea romance filled with intrigue and adventure.
1953 86m/C *GB* Rock Hudson, Yvonne De Carlo, Maxwell Reed; **D:** Raoul Walsh. **VHS, Beta** $9.95 *MED ♂♂*

Sea Gypsies A sailing crew of five is shipwrecked off the Aleutian Islands. They must escape before winter or learn to survive. Passable family drama.
1978 (G) 101m/C Robert F. Logan, Mikki Jamison-Olsen, Heather Rattray, Cjon Damitri; **D:** Stewart Raffill. **VHS, Beta** $19.98 *WAR ♂♂*

The Sea Hawk An English privateer learns the Spanish are going to invade England with their Armada. After numerous adventures, he is able to aid his queen and help save his country, finding romance along the way. One of Flynn's swashbuckling best. Available colorized.
1940 128m/B Errol Flynn, Claude Rains, Donald Crisp, Alan Hale Jr., Flora Robson, Brenda Marshall, Henry Daniell, Gilbert Roland, James Stephenson, Una O'Connor; **D:** Michael Curtiz. **VHS, Beta, LV** $19.98 *MGM, TTC, FOX ♂♂♂½*

Sea Hound A 15-part series set in the late 1940s that charts the voyage of a group of pirates searching for buried treasure. Everything goes well until Buster Crabbe emerges to wreck their hopes.
1947 ?m/B Buster Crabbe, Jimmy Lloyd, Pamela Blake, Ralph Hodges, Robert Barron; **D:** Walter B. Eason, Mack V. Wright. **VHS** *MLB ♂*

Sea Lion A vicious sea captain, embittered by a past romance, becomes sadistic and intolerable, until the truth emerges. Lots of action, but plodding, rehashed plot. Silent.
1921 50m/B Hobart Bosworth. **VHS, Beta** $29.95 *VYY ♂♂*

Sea of Dreams Don't expect much in the way of a script from this soft-core production.
1990 80m/C Jon Rodgers, Chad Scott, Jacky Peel, Renee O'Neil. **VHS, Beta** $39.95 *AHV, HHE ♂*

Sea of Love A tough, tightly wound thriller about an alcoholic cop with a mid-life crisis. While following the track of a serial killer, he begins a torrid relationship with one of his suspects. Pacino doesn't stand a chance when Barkin heats up the screen. Music by Trevor Jones.

1989 (R) 113m/C Al Pacino, Ellen Barkin, John Goodman, Michael Rooker, William Hickey, Richard Jenkins; **D:** Harold Becker; **W:** Richard Price. VHS, Beta, LV $19.95 MCA ♂♂♂½

Sea Prince and the Fire Child
Japanese animated film follows two young lovers who set off on an adventure to escape the disapproval of their parents.
1982 70m/C JP VHS, Beta $19.95 COL ♂♂

Sea Racketeers
Soggy old tribute to the Coast Guard inadvertently makes them look like a bunch of bumblers, as they belatedly uncover a fur-smuggling racket working under their noses from a floating nightclub.
1937 64m/B Weldon Heyburn, Jeanne Madden, Warren Hymer, Dorothy McNulty, J. Carroll Naish, Joyce Compton, Charles Trowbridge, Syd Saylor, Lane Chandler, Benny Burt; **D:** Hamilton MacFadden. VHS, Beta $16.95 SNC ♂½

The Sea Serpent
A young sea captain and a crusty scientist unite to search out a giant sea monster awakened by atomic tests. Not one of Millan's better films.
1985 92m/C SP Timothy Bottoms, Ray Milland, Jared Martin; **D:** Gregory Greens. VHS, Beta $69.98 LIV ♂½

The Sea Shall Not Have Them
A British bomber crashes into the North Sea during World War II. Film tells of the survivors' rescue by the Air-Sea Rescue Unit. Decent drama/adventure.
1955 92m/B Michael Redgrave, Dirk Bogarde; **D:** Lewis Gilbert. VHS $39.98 REP ♂♂½

The Sea Wolf
Jack London's adventure novel about brutal, canny Captain Wolf Larsen (Robinson) his rebellious crew, and some unexpected passengers. Knox and Lupino are shipwreck survivors, picked up by Robinson and forced into working aboard his ship, the aptly named "Ghost." Crewman Garfield falls for Lupino and tries to rally his shipmates into resisting the meglomaniacal Robinson. Fine performances by all, especially Robinson as the personification of malevolent ego. Screen debut of Knox. Director Curtiz filmed entirely in studio tanks, sets, and pervasive fog machines. The story was previously filmed three times and later remade as "Barricade" and "Wolf Larsen."
1941 90m/C Edward G. Robinson, Alexander Knox, John Garfield, Ida Lupino, Gene Lockhart, Barry Fitzgerald, Stanley Ridges, Francis McDonald, David Bruce, Howard da Silva, Frank Lackteen, Ralf Harolde; **D:** Michael Curtiz; **W:** Robert Rossen. VHS $19.98 MGM, MOV ♂♂♂½

Sea Wolves
True World War II story about a commando-style operation undertaken by a group of middle-aged, retired British calvarymen in India in 1943. Decent acting, though Peck's British accent fades in and out, with Moore as Bond.
1981 (PG) 120m/C GB Gregory Peck, Roger Moore, David Niven, Trevor Howard, Patrick Macnee; **D:** Andrew V. McLaglen. VHS, Beta $59.98 FOX, WAR ♂♂½

The Seagull
A pensive, sensitive adaptation of the famed Chekhov play about the depressed denizens of an isolated country estate. In Russian with English subtitles.
1971 99m/B Alla Demidova, Lyudmila Savelyeva, Yuri Yakovlev; **D:** Yuri Karasik. VHS, Beta $29.95 FCT, MRV, AUD ♂♂♂

Sealab 2020
Two animated episodes chronicling the underwater adventures a scientific expedition encounters in the year 2020.
1972 50m/C **V:** Ross Martin, Ann Jillian, Pamelyn Ferdin. VHS, Beta $19.95 TTC, WTA ♂♂♂

Seance on a Wet Afternoon
Dark, thoughtful film about a crazed pseudo-psychic who coerces her husband into a kidnapping so she can gain recognition by divining the child's whereabouts. Directed splendidly by Forbes, and superb acting from Stanley and Attenborough, who co-produced with Forbes.
1964 111m/B GB Kim Stanley, Richard Attenborough, Margaret Lacey, Maria Kazan, Mark Eden, Patrick Magee; **D:** Bryan Forbes; **M:** John Barry. Academy Awards '64 Nominations: Best Actress (Stanley); British Academy Awards '64: Best Actor (Attenborough); National Board of Review Awards '64: 10 Best Films of the Year, Best Actress (Stanley). VHS, Beta $29.95 VID ♂♂♂½

The Search
Clift, an American solider stationed in post-World War II Berlin, befriends a homeless nine-year-old amnesiac boy (Jandl) and tries to find his family. Meanwhile, his mother has been searching the Displaced Persons camps for her son. Although Clift wants to adopt the boy, he steps aside, and mother and son are finally reunited. "The Search" was shot on location in the American Occupied Zone of Germany. Jandl won a special juvenile Oscar in his first (and only) film role. This was also Clift's first screen appearance, although this movie was actually filmed after his debut in "Red River," it was released first.
1948 105m/B Montgomery Clift, Aline MacMahon, Ivan Jandl, Jarmila Novotna, Wendell Corey; **D:** Fred Zinneman. Academy Awards '48: Best Original Screenplay; Nominations: Best Actor (Clift), Best Director (Zinneman), Best Screenplay. VHS $19.98 MGM ♂♂♂½

Search and Destroy
Deadly vendetta is begun by a Vietnamese official during the war. It is continued in the U.S. as he hunts down the American soldiers he feels betrayed him. Sub-par, forgettable war/action flick. **AKA:** Striking Back.
1981 (PG) 93m/C Perry King, Don Stroud, Park Jong Soo, George Kennedy, Tisa Farrow; **D:** William Fruet. VHS, Beta, LV $69.95 VES ♂

Search and Destroy
Sci-fi action flick about the capture of a secret biological warfare research station. Lotsa action, that's for sure - where's the plot?
1988 (R) 87m/C Stuart Garrison Day, Dan Kuchuck, Peggy Jacobsen; **D:** J. Christian Ingvordsen. VHS, Beta $19.95 MCG ♂

The Search for Bridey Murphy
Long before channelers, Ramtha and New-Age profiteers, there was a Colorado housewife who under hypnosis described a previous life as an Irish girl. Her famous claim was never proven—but that didn't stop this well-acted but dull dramatization. Neither sensationalist, nor likely to persuade skeptics. Based on the book by Morey Bernstein, hypnotist in the case.
1956 84m/B Teresa Wright, Louis Hayward, Nancy Gates, Kenneth Tobey, Richard Anderson; **W/D:** Noel Langley. VHS $14.95 PAR, FCT ♂♂

Search for the Gods
A dig in the Southwest turns interesting when one of the archeologists comes across an exquisite ancient medallion that could answer questions about alien visitors. Pilot for a television series that didn't make it.
1975 100m/C Kurt Russell, Stephen McHattie, Ralph Bellamy, Victoria Racimo, Raymond St. Jacques; **D:** Judd Taylor. VHS $59.95 UNI, HHE ♂½

The Searchers
The classic Ford western, starring John Wayne as a hard-hearted frontiersman who spends years doggedly pursuing his niece, who was kidnapped by Indians. A simple western structure supports Ford's most moving, mysterious, complex film. Many feel this is the best western of all time.
1956 119m/C John Wayne, Jeffrey Hunter, Vera Miles, Natalie Wood, Ward Bond, John Qualen, Harry Carey Jr.; **D:** John Ford. VHS, Beta, LV $19.98 WAR, PIA, TLF ♂♂♂♂

Seaside Swingers
A group of teenagers at a seaside resort work to win a talent competition on television. But where is the talent? Dumb teen romance comedy with accidental plot. ♫All I Want Is You; A Girls Needs a Boy; Second Time Around; Indubitably Me; Love Me, Please; Now, Ain't That Somethin'—Caw Blimey; Romeo Jones; What's Cookin. **AKA:** Every Day's a Holiday.
1965 94m/C GB Michael Sarne, Grazina Frame, John Leyton, Freddie & the Dreamers; **D:** James Hill. VHS, Beta $59.98 NLC ♂½

Season for Assassins
Police commissioner Castroni is the only man who can stop a wave of violence enveloping Rome.
1971 102m/C Joe Dallesandro, Martin Balsam. VHS, Beta $29.95 LIV ♂½

Season of Fear
A young man visits his estranged father's home. Abandoned as a child, he's embroiled in a murder scheme engineered by his father's beautiful young wife. Intriguing premise, forgettable execution.
1989 (R) 89m/C Michael Bowen, Clancy Brown, Clare Wren, Ray Wise, Michael J. Pollard; **D:** Douglas Campbell. VHS, Beta $79.98 FOX ♂½

Season of the Witch
A frustrated housewife becomes intrigued with a neighboring witch and begins to practice witchcraft herself, through murder and seduction. Meant to be suspenseful, thrilling, and topical, it is none of these. Poorly acted at best. Originally 130 minutes! **AKA:** Hungry Wives; Jack's Wife.
1973 (R) 89m/C Jan White, Ray Laine, Bill Thunhurst, Joedida McClain, Virginia Greenwald; **D:** George A. Romero. Beta NO ♂½

Sebastian
A mathematics whiz is employed by the British to decipher codes. He falls in love with York, another code breaker, and becomes involved in international intrigue. A bit too fast-paced and busy, but enjoyable spy drama. Donald Sutherland has a small role. **AKA:** Mr. Sebastian.
1968 100m/C GB Dirk Bogarde, Susannah York, Lilli Palmer, John Gielgud, Margaret Johnston, Nigel Davenport; **D:** David Greene. VHS MOV ♂♂½

Sebastiane
An audacious film version of the legend of St. Sebastian, packed with homoerotic imagery and ravishing visuals. Honest, faithful rendering of the Saint's life and refusal to obey Roman authorities. Jarman's first film, in Latin with English subtitles. Music by Brian Eno.
1979 90m/C Leonardo Treviglio, Barney James, Richard James, Neil Kennedy; **D:** Derek Jarman. VHS, Beta $29.95 FCT, TAM ♂♂♂

Second Best Secret Agent in the Whole Wide World
A klutzy agent attempts to prevent a Swedish anti-gravity formula from falling into Russian hands. Surprisingly good early spoof of the James Bond genre. **AKA:** Licensed to Kill.
1965 93m/C GB Tom Adams, Veronica Hurst, Peter Bull, Karel Stepanek, John Arnatt; **D:** Lindsay Shonteff. VHS, Beta $59.98 NLC ♂♂½

Second Chance
A former prizefighter (Mitchum) travels to Mexico where he protects a gangster's moll (Darnell) targeted for murder. But Palance is on their tail. Originally released theatrically on a wide screen in 3-D. Good melodrama.

1953 82m/C Robert Mitchum, Linda Darnell, Jack Palance, Reginald Sheffield, Roy Roberts; **D:** Rudolph Mate. **VHS, Beta, LV** $19.95 MED ♂♂1/2

Second Chance When a woman finds her husband is in love with another, her marital happiness is shattered. She leaves her betrayer and struggles to adapt to life as a single mother. Made for British television.
1980 270m/C *GB* Susannah York, Ralph Bates; **D:** Gerry Mill, Richard Handford. **VHS** $79.95 SVS ♂♂1/2

Second Chorus Rivalry of two trumpet players for a girl and a job with Artie Shaw Orchestra. Music, dance, and romance. Nothing great, but pleasant. ♫Would You Like to Be the Love of My Life?; Poor Mr. Chisholm; (I Ain't Help to That Step) But I'll Dig It; Swing Concerto; Sweet Sue; I'm Yours.
1940 83m/B Fred Astaire, Paulette Goddard, Burgess Meredith, Artie Shaw, Charles Butterworth; **D:** H.C. Potter. **VHS, Beta, LV, 3/ 4U, Special order formats** $19.95 NOS, HHT, CAB ♂♂1/2

Second City Insanity The famed Second City improvisational troupe performs their unique brand of humor.
1981 60m/C Fred Willard, John Candy. **VHS, Beta** LHV ♂♂

Second Coming of Suzanne Young actress encounters a hypnotic film director. Her role: to star in a crucifixion—which may be more real than she imagines. Winner of two international film festivals.
1980 90m/C Sondra Locke, Richard Dreyfuss, Gene Barry; **D:** Michael Barry. **VHS, Beta** $19.95 GEM ♂♂1/2

Second Sight A detective (Larroquette) and a goofy psychic (Pinchot) set out to find a kidnapped priest. Flick is sidetracked along the way by such peculiarities as a pixieish nun for romantic, not religious, intrigue. Remember this one? No? That's because you blinked when it was released to theaters. Eminently missable.
1989 (PG) 84m/C John Larroquette, Bronson Pinchot, Bess Armstrong, James Tolkan, Christine Estabrook, Cornelia Guest, Stuart Pankin, William Prince, John Schuck; **D:** Joel Zwick. **VHS, Beta, LV** $19.95 WAR ♂

Second Thoughts Frustrated woman attorney divorces her stuffy husband and takes up with an aging hippie. She comes to regret her decision when it becomes obvious that her new man has his head firmly stuck in the 60s. Comedy-drama lacking real laughs or drama.
1983 (PG) 109m/C Lucie Arnaz, Craig Wasson, Ken Howard, Joe Mantegna; **D:** Lawrence Turman. **VHS, Beta** $59.99 HBO ♂

Second Time Lucky The devil makes a bet with God that if the world began all over again Adam and Eve would repeat their mistake they made in the Garden of Eden. Bites a lot, but has no teeth nor laughs.
1984 98m/C *AU NZ* Diane Franklin, Roger Wilson, Robert Morley, Jon Gadsby, Bill Ewens; **D:** Michael Anderson Sr. **VHS, Beta** $14.95 HMD, LHV ♂

Second Victory Major Mark Hanlon has been appointed an Occupation Officer in the winter of 1945. He expects this will be his chance to work for peace but when a good friend is brutally murdered all his thoughts turn to revenge. Based on the novel by Morris West.
1987 (PG) 95m/C Anthony Andrews, Max von Sydow, Renee Soutendijk; **D:** Gerald Thomas. **VHS** $89.95 AIP ♂♂1/2

Second Wind Wagner and Naughton are trying to settle into their new life together, but find they must make a variety of difficult choices.
1990 (PG) 93m/C Lindsay Wagner, James Naughton. **VHS** $79.98 VID ♂

Second Woman An architect, suffering from blackouts and depression, believes himself responsible for the death of his fiancee. Well-done psycho-drama. **AKA:** Here Lies Love; Twelve Miles Out.
1951 91m/B Robert Young, Betsy Drake, John Sutton; **D:** James V. Kern. **VHS, Beta** $14.95 NOS, QNE, UHV ♂♂1/2

Secret Admirer A teenager's unsigned love letter keeps falling into the wrong hands. Intends to be funny, and sometimes is; too often, though, it surrenders to obviousness and predictability.
1985 (R) 98m/C C. Thomas Howell, Cliff DeYoung, Kelly Preston, Dee Wallace Stone, Lori Loughlin, Fred Ward, Casey Siemaszko, Corey Haim, Leigh Taylor-Young; **D:** David Greenwalt. **VHS, Beta, LV** $19.99 HBO ♂♂

The Secret Adversary Set in 1920s London. Ace detectives Tommy and Tuppence Beresford must find a secret treaty before it falls into the wrong hands. Pilot for the "Partners in Crime" series. Based on the characters created by Agatha Christie.
1983 120m/C *GB* Francesca Annis, James Warwick; **W:** Agatha Christie. **VHS, Beta** $19.95 PAV ♂♂

The Secret Agent Presumed dead, a British intelligence agent (Gielgud) reappears and receives a new assignment. Using his faked death to his advantage, he easily journeys to Switzerland where he is to eliminate an enemy agent. Strange Hitchcockian melange of comedy and intrigue; atypical, but worthy offering from the Master.
1936 83m/B *GB* Madeleine Carroll, Peter Lorre, Robert Young, John Gielgud, Lilli Palmer; **D:** Alfred Hitchcock. **VHS, Beta, LV, 3/4U, Special order formats** $16.95 SNC, NOS, HHT ♂♂

Secret Agent Secret agent John Drake embarks upon dangerous and exciting assignments around the world in this mystery-adventure series, which ran during 1965 and 1966. All but two episodes are in black and white.
1964 60m/B Patrick McGoohan, Niall MacGinnis, Dawn Addams, Lelia Goldoni; **D:** Don Chaffey. **VHS, Beta** $19.99 MPI, MOV ♂♂♂

Secret Agent 00 A master criminal plans to blackmail the western world and only special Secret Agent 00 can stop him. Bad spy genre ripoff, interesting only as the screen debut of Sean Connery's brother. **AKA:** Operation Kid Brother.
1967 (R) 97m/C *IT* Neil Connery, Daniela Bianchi, Adolfo Celi; **D:** Alberto De Martino; **M:** Ennio Morricone. **VHS** NO ♂

Secret Agent Super Dragon The CIA calls in the agent known as "Super Dragon" when it is discovered that a Venezuelan drug czar plans to spike U.S. gum and candy with an LSD-like drug. Less than competent production offers some unintended laughter. **AKA:** Super Dragon.
1966 95m/C *FR IT GE* Ray Danton, Marisa Mell, Margaret Lee, Jess Hahn, Carol D'Angelo, Andriana Ambesi; **D:** Calvin Jackson Padget. **VHS, Beta** $16.95 SNC ♂

Secret Beyond the Door A wealthy heiress marries a widower and soon discovers that he murdered his first wife. Understandably, she wonders what plans he might have for her. Capably done chiller, but the plot is hackneyed pseudo-Hitchcock.

1948 99m/B Joan Bennett, Michael Redgrave, Barbara O'Neil, Anne Revere; **D:** Fritz Lang. **VHS** $19.98 REP ♂

Secret Ceremony An aging prostitute and a young, aimless waif resemble each other's dead mother and dead daughter, respectively, and the relationship goes on, strangely, from there. This original big-screen version is very good Freudian psycho-drama; 101-minute TV version is unfortunately greatly diluted.
1969 109m/C Elizabeth Taylor, Robert Mitchum, Mia Farrow, Pamela Brown, Peggy Ashcroft; **D:** Joseph Losey. **VHS, Beta** $14.95 KRT ♂♂1/2

The Secret Cinema A woman is caught between reality and a cinematic nightmare in this bizarre first film by famed cult director Bartel.
19?? 37m/C **D:** Paul Bartel. **VHS** $19.95 RHI ♂

The Secret Diary of Sigmund Freud Spoofy look at the early years of Sigmund Freud, the father of modern psychoanalysis. Freud (Cort) has an affair with lisping nurse Kane while tending to patient Shawn and answering to mama Baker, who's carrying on with mad doctor Kinski. Talented cast falls asleep on couch.
1984 129m/C Bud Cort, Carol Kane, Carroll Baker, Klaus Kinski, Marisa Berenson, Dick Shawn, Ferdinand "Ferdy" Mayne; **D:** Danford B. Greene. **VHS, Beta** $79.98 FOX ♂

Secret Executioners A singular, lone, almost defenseless guy battles the mob's assassins with his feet.
197? 90m/C Wong Chen-Li, Jim Norris, Peggy Min. **VHS, Beta** NO ♂

Secret Fantasy Musician overcomes his fears of inferiority as he makes his fantasies a reality by having other men admire his wife's beautiful body. A lesson in self-esteem.
1981 (R) 88m/C Laura Antonelli. **VHS, Beta** $54.95 MED ♂

Secret File of Hollywood A down-and-out private eye gets a job taking photos for a sleazy Hollywood scandal sheet and finds himself in the midst of a blackmail plot masterminded by his editor. An often childish potboiler, perhaps inspired by the once-feared Confidential Magazine. **AKA:** Secret File: Hollywood.
1962 85m/B Robert Clarke, Francine York, Syd Mason, Maralou Gray, John Warburton; **D:** Ralph Cushman. **VHS** $15.95 NOS, LOO ♂1/2

The Secret Four Three young men seek to avenge the death of their friend at the hands of British traitors, and become involved in a plot to sabotage the Suez canal. Poorly adapted from the novel by Edgar Wallace. **AKA:** The Four Just Men.
1940 79m/B *GB* Hugh Sinclair, Griffith Jones, Francis L. Sullivan, Frank Lawton, Anna Lee, Alan Napier, Basil Sydney; **D:** Walter Forde. **VHS, Beta** $16.95 SNC ♂♂

Secret Games An unhappily married woman (Brin) is searching for relief from her restrictive marriage. At the "Afternoon Demitasse," an exclusive brothel where women are paid for fulfilling their ultimate fantasies, she meets a man (Hewitt) who pushes her beyond her sexual limits and threatens to totally possess her.
1992 (R) 90m/C Martin Hewitt, Michele Brin, Delia Sheppard, Billy Drago; **D:** Alexander Gregory Hippolyte. **VHS** $89.95 IMP ♂1/2

The Secret Garden The well-loved Frances Hodgson Burnett story has been remade and even revamped as a Broadway musical, but this is considered the definitive version. An orphan girl arrives at her uncle's

S

somber Victorian estate. She starts tending a long-forgotten garden, and with its resurrection joy returns to the household. O'Brien leads an outstanding cast in one of her final juvenile roles. In black and white, with Technicolor for later garden scenes.
1949 92m/B Margaret O'Brien, Herbert Marshall, Dean Stockwell, Gladys Cooper, Elsa Lanchester, Brian Roper; **D:** Fred M. Wilcox. **VHS $19.98** MGM ✂✂✂

The Secret Garden Orphaned Mary Lennox is sent to live with her mysterious uncle after her parents die. Mary is willful and spoiled and her uncle's house holds a number of secrets, including a crippled cousin. When Mary discovers a mysteriously abandoned locked garden she makes it her mission to restore the garden to life. Based on the children's classic by Frances Hodgson Burnett. Made for British television.
1984 107m/C GB Sarah Hollis Andrews, David Patterson; **D:** Katrina Murray. **VHS $19.95** MOV, 3IG, TVC ✂✂½

The Secret Garden Mary Lennox is a lonely orphan who is sent to live with her unknown uncle in England after her parent's deaths. Mary, who has grown up in India, is selfish and unhappy until she discovers two secrets on her uncle's estate. One is her crippled cousin, as demanding as Mary, and the other is a walled, neglected garden. With the aid of Dickon, the gardener's boy, Mary begins to transform the garden into a living area once again, and the garden works its wonders not only on Mary but on her family as well. A prologue and afterword to the story (showing Mary as an adult) are unnecessary additions but this is a class production with wonderful performances. Based on the children's classic by Frances Hodgson Burnett. Made for television as a "Hallmark Hall of Fame" special.
1987 (PG) 100m/C Gennie James, Barret Oliver, Jadrien Steele, Michael Hordern, Derek Jacobi, Billie Whitelaw, Lucy Gutteridge, Julian Glover, Colin Firth, Alan Grint. **VHS, LV $14.98** REP ✂✂✂

The Secret Garden Rekindled interest in Frances Hodgon Burnett's classic tale has prompted a Broadway musical, two TV movies, and now the big screen version. Mary Lennox is an orphan sent to live in her uncle's forbidding mansion filled with secrets, including a cousin she didn't know she had. She discovers a secret garden with her new friends and together they nurse it back to health.
1993 ?m/C Maggie Smith, Kate Maberly, Haydon Prowse, Andrew Knott; **D:** Agnieszka Holland; **W:** Caroline Thompson. **VHS** NYR ✂✂½

Secret Honor Idiosyncratic, single-set, one-man film version adapted by Donald Freed and Arnold Stone from their stage play about Richard Nixon coping with the death of his presidency on the night he's decided to blow his brains out. Made with students at the University of Michigan, and carried by the ranting and raving of Hall as a tragic Shakespearean Nixon with plenty of darkly humorous lines. **AKA:** Lords of Treason; Secret Honor: The Last Testament of Richard M. Nixon; Secret Honor: A Political Myth.
1985 90m/C Philip Baker Hall; **D:** Robert Altman. **VHS, Beta, LV $29.98** LIV, VES, CRC ✂✂✂

Secret Ingredient A legendary cognac recipe is the secret formula of the monks of St. Celare, whose monastery is located in the mountains of Yugoslavia. A wealthy American sends his flighty heiress daughter to pry the secret recipe from the monks but she runs into more than she bargains for when she falls for a handsome friar and gets

caught up with a band of bumbling gypsies and the inept state police.
1988 95m/C Rick Rossovich, Catherine Hicks, Gary Kroeger, Jeff Corey, Brad Dexter, Sam Wanamaker; **D:** Slobodan Shijan. **VHS $89.95** HMD ✂½

Secret Life of an American Wife A bored housewife (Jackson) tries to seduce a client of her husband's, with less than hilarious results. Too much dialogue, not enough genuine humor. Disappointing inversion of director Axelrod's "The Seven Year Itch."
1968 97m/C Walter Matthau, Anne Jackson, Patrick O'Neal, Edy Williams; **D:** George Axelrod. **VHS, Beta $59.98** FOX ✂✂

The Secret Life of Walter Mitty An entertaining adaptation of the James Thurber short story about a meek man (Kaye) who lives an unusual secret fantasy life. Henpecked by his fiancee and mother, oppressed at his job, he imagines himself in the midst of various heroic fantasies. While Thurber always professed to hate Kaye's characterization and the movie, it scored at the box office and today stands as a comedic romp for Kaye. Available with digitally remastered stereo and original movie trailer.
1947 110m/C Danny Kaye, Virginia Mayo, Boris Karloff, Ann Rutherford, Fay Bainter, Florence Bates; **D:** Norman Z. MacLeod. **VHS, Beta, LV $19.98** HBO, SUE ✂✂✂

Secret Obsession A love triangle among a father, his illegitimate son, and the woman they both love, set in North Africa in 1955. Sounds intriguing, but don't be fooled. Slow, dull, and poorly acted.
1988 (PG) 82m/C Julie Christie, Ben Gazzara, Patrick Bruel, Jean Carmet; **D:** Henri Vart. **VHS, Beta $79.95** VMK ✂

The Secret of El Zorro Don Diego's friend, Don Ricardo, threatens to unmask Zorro's secret identity when he challenges the legendary swordsman to a duel.
1957 75m/B Guy Williams. **VHS, Beta $39.95** DIS ✂½

The Secret of My Success Country bumpkin Fox goes to the Big Apple to make his mark. He becomes the corporate mailboy who rises meteorically to the top of his company (by impersonating an executive) in order to win the love of an icy woman executive. He spends his days running frantically between his real job in the mailroom and his fantasy position, with various sexual shenanigans with the boss's wife thrown in to keep the viewer alert. Fox is charismatic while working with a cliche-ridden script that ties up everything very neatly at the end. Written by top guns Jim Cash and Jack Epps, Jr., with an assist by Carothers.
1987 (PG-13) 110m/C Michael J. Fox, Helen Slater, Richard Jordan, Margaret Whitton; **D:** Herbert Ross; **M:** David Foster. **VHS, Beta, LV $19.95** MCA ✂✂

The Secret of Navajo Cave Fair family adventure. Two young friends explore the mysterious Navajo cave, where one can be assured that a secret awaits. **AKA:** Legend of Cougar Canyon.
1976 (G) 84m/C Holger Kasper, Steven Benally Jr., Johnny Guerro; **D:** James T. Flocker. **VHS $39.95** XVC, UHV ✂✂

Secret of NIMH Animated tale, produced by a staff of Disney-trained artists led by "American Tail's" Bluth; concerns a newly widowed mouse who discovers a secret agency of superintelligent rats (they've escaped from a science lab) who aid her in protecting her family. As is usually the case with Bluth films, the animation is superb

while the socially aware plot struggles to keep pace. That aside, it's still an interesting treat for the youngsters. Adapted from Robert C. O'Brien's "Mrs. Frisby and the Rats of N.I.M.H."
1982 (G) 84m/C D: Don Bluth; **M:** Jerry Goldsmith; **V:** John Carradine, Derek Jacobi, Dom DeLuise, Elizabeth Hartman, Peter Strauss, Aldo Ray, Edie McClurg, Wil Wheaton. **VHS, Beta, LV, 8mm $19.98** MGM, WTA ✂✂✂

Secret of Tai Chi A young man uses his wits and martial arts to battle an evil Chinese general.
19?? 90m/C VHS, Beta $49.95 OCE ✂

Secret of the Black Trunk Chilling Edgar Wallace story about a series of murders at a famed English hotel. Filmed in Great Britain.
1962 96m/C GE Joachim Hansen, Senta Berger, Hans Reiser, Leonard Steckel, Peter Carsten; **D:** Werner Klinger. **VHS $16.95** SNC ✂✂½

The Secret of the Golden Eagle A boy and his new adventurer friend are on a quest to find the strange "Golden Statue" that causes people to grow old before their time. They must take it from criminals who are using it for evil purposes. A good adventure/fantasy for the entire family.
1991 90m/C Michael Berryman, Brandon McKay; **D:** Cole McKay. **VHS $79.95** WLA ✂✂

Secret of the Ice Cave A motley band of explorers, hijackers and mercenaries go after a secret treasure in the remote mountains.
1989 (PG-13) 106m/C Michael Moriarty, Sally Kellerman, David Mendenhall, Virgil Frye, Gerald Anthony, Norbert Weisser; **D:** Radu Gabrea. **VHS, Beta $14.99** MOV ✂

The Secret of the Loch Scottish scientist claims to have seen Loch Ness Monster but everyone thinks his bagpipe's blown a reed.
1934 80m/B GB Seymour Hicks, Nancy O'Neil, Gibson Gowland, Frederick Peisley; **D:** Milton Rosmer. **VHS $19.98** NOS, SNC ✂½

The Secret of the Snake and Crane Resistance group relies on ancient fighting techniques to battle the rule of the Ching Dynasty in this kung fu adventure.
19?? 90m/C VHS, Beta NO ✂½

The Secret of the Telegian Rare Japanese sci-fi flick about a soldier who uses a teleportation device to kill fellow soldiers who tried to kill him. He could find his victims wherever they hid. Also known as "The Telegian."
1961 85m/C JP Koji Tsurata, Yumi Shirakawa, Akihiko Hirata, Tadao Nakamura; **D:** Jun Fukuda. **VHS $16.95** SNC ✂✂½

Secret of Yolanda Steamy romance about a young deaf-mute whose guardian and riding instructor both fall for her.
1982 (R) 90m/C Aviva Ger, Asher Zarfati, Shraga Harpaz. **VHS, Beta $59.95** MGM ✂

The Secret Passion of Robert Clayton When Robert Clayton Jr. (Valentine) returns to his home town to take the position of D.A., he is forced to go head to head in a lurid murder trial with the defense attorney (Mahoney), who also happens to be his own father.
1992 (R) 92m/C John Mahoney, Scott Valentine, Eve Gordon, Kevin Conroy; **D:** E.W. Swackhamer; **W:** Brian Ross. **VHS $58.03** PAR ✂✂

Secret Passions A young couple are haunted by a dark, romance-novel-type secret. Made for television.
1978 99m/C John James, Susan Lucci; **D:** Michael Pressman. **VHS, Beta** NO ✂½

Secret Places On the brink of World War II, a German girl in an English school finds friendship with a popular classmate. Touching and involving, but somehow unsatisfying.
1985 (PG) 98m/C *GB* Maria Therese Relin, Tara MacGowan, Claudine Auger, Jenny Agutter; *D:* Zelda Barron. **VHS, Beta** $79.98 *FOX* 𝘐𝘐½

The Secret Policeman's Other Ball Engaging live performance by most of the Monty Python troupe and guest rock artists, staged for Amnesty International. Follows 1979's "The Secret Policeman's Ball," and followed by 1987's "The Secret Policeman's Third Ball."
1982 (R) 101m/C *GB* John Cleese, Graham Chapman, Michael Palin, Terry Jones, Pete Townsend, Sting, Billy Connolly, Bob Geldof, Jeff Beck, Eric Clapton; *D:* Julien Temple. **VHS, Beta, LV** $14.95 *MGM* 𝘐𝘐½

Secret Policeman's Private Parts Various sketches and performances from the various Secret Policeman occasions, featuring classic Python sketches including "I'm a Lumberjack and I'm OK." Also featured are performances by Phil Collins, Pete Townshend, Donovan, and Bob Geldof. Thank you very much.
1981 77m/C *GB* John Cleese, Michael Palin, Terry Jones, Pete Townsend, Julien Temple; *D:* Roger Graef. **VHS, Beta, LV** $59.95 *MED* 𝘐𝘐½

A Secret Space Story of a young man, born of secular parents, searching for the meaning of his Jewish roots as he nears his Bar Mitzvah. He is helped along by a group of Jews who are also searching for this meaning.
1988 80m/C Robert Klein, Phyllis Newman, John Matthews, Sam Schacht, Virginia Graham; *D:* Roberta Hodes. **VHS, Beta** $79.95 *ERG* 𝘐½

Secret Squirrel Here are eight episodes of adventure with the clever secret agent.
1965 53m/C **VHS, Beta** $19.95 *TTC, WTA* 𝘐𝘐½

Secret Squirrel's Undercover Capers The world's only animated undercover rodent, Secret Squirrel battles a motley crew of zany villains with his cohorts Winsome Witch and Squiddley Diddley.
1966 52m/C **VHS, Beta** $19.95 *TTC, WTA* 𝘐𝘐½

The Secret War of Harry Frigg Non-conformist WWII Private Harry Frigg is promoted to general as part of a scheme to help five Allied generals escape from the custody of the Germans. Rare Newman bomb; dismal comedy.
1968 (R) 123m/C Paul Newman, Sylva Koscina, John Williams, Tom Bosley, Andrew Duggan; *D:* Jack Smight. **VHS, Beta** $49.95 *MCA* 𝘐½

Secret Weapon An Israeli technician flees his country with atomic secrets and a beautiful government agent is sent to induce him to return. Based on the true case of Mordecai Vanunu. Slow-paced and not very suspenseful. Made for cable.
1990 95m/C Griffin Dunne, Karen Allen, Stuart Wilson, Jeroen Krabbe, Brian Cox, John Rhys-Davies, Ian Mitchell; *D:* Ian Sharp. **VHS, Beta** $19.98 *TTC* 𝘐𝘐

Secret Weapons Sexy Russian babes are KGB-trained to get any secret from any man. Strains credibility as well as patience. Made for TV. *AKA:* Secrets of the Red Bedroom.
1985 100m/C Linda Hamilton, Sally Kellerman, Hunt Block, Viveca Lindfors, Christopher Atkins, Geena Davis, James Franciscus; *D:* Don Taylor. **VHS** $69.95 *SVS* 𝘐½

Secrets A wife, her husband, and her daughter each have a sexual experience which they must keep secret. Bisset's nude love scene is an eye-opener. Fast forward through the rest of this dull, overwrought drama.
1971 (R) 86m/C Jacqueline Bisset, Per Oscarsson, Shirley Knight Hopkins, Robert Powell, Tarka Kings, Martin C. Thurley; *D:* Philip Saville. **VHS, CV** $59.95 *PSM* 𝘐½

Secrets An unhappy young bride starts having numerous affairs when her mother dies. Made for television. Hardly worth the effort.
1977 100m/C Susan Blakely, Roy Thinnes, Joanne Linville, John Randolph, Anthony Eisley, Andrew Stevens; *D:* Paul Wendkos. **VHS** *MGM* 𝘐

Secrets British drama about the confused life of an innocent schoolgirl who's the victim of a mess of authoritative misunderstandings. Written by Noella Smith; one of David Puttnam's "First Love" series.
1982 79m/C *GB* Helen Lindsay, Anna Campbell-Jones, Daisy Cockburn; *D:* Gavin Millar. **VHS, Beta** $59.95 *MGM* 𝘐𝘐

Secrets in the Dark A small-town group of womanizers get together and engage in soft-core "fun."
1983 84m/C Viktor Lange, Ulrike Butz, Logena Marks, Martha Meding. **VHS, Beta** $29.95 *MED* 𝘐

Secrets of a Married Man A married man's philandering ways are his ruination when he falls hard for a beautiful prostitute. Shatner and Shepherd contain their laughter as they make their way through this hyper-earnest family drama.
1984 96m/C William Shatner, Cybill Shepherd, Michelle Phillips, Glynn Turman; *D:* William A. Graham. **VHS, Beta** $29.98 *LIV* 𝘐

Secrets of a Soul A visually impressive presentation of Freudian psychoanalytic theory, in which a professor, wanting a child and jealous of his wife's childhood sweetheart, moves toward madness (we did say Freudian) and is cured through dream interpretation. Great dream sequences bring out the arm-chair psychoanalyst. Silent.
1925 94m/B *GE* Werner Krauss, Ruth Weyher, Jack Trevor; *D:* G.W. Pabst. **VHS, Beta** $49.95 *FCT* 𝘐𝘐½

Secrets of Life Documentary captures the various ways that organisms on earth respond to the challenges of survival and reproduction. An installment of the Disney "True-Life Adventures" series.
1956 69m/C *D:* James Algar. **VHS, Beta** $69.95 *DIS* 𝘐𝘐½

Secrets of Sweet Sixteen Gag-fest about budding sexuality in high school.
1974 (R) 84m/C Suzie Atkins. **VHS, Beta** $59.95 *WWV* Woof!

Secrets of Three Hungry Wives When a multi-millionaire is killed, the women with whom he was having affairs are suspected. Tacky made for television flick.
1978 97m/C Jessica Walter, Gretchen Corbett, Eve Plumb, Heather MacRae, James Franciscus, Craig Stevens; *D:* Gordon Hessler. **VHS** *NO* 𝘐

Secrets of Women A rare Bergman comedy about three sisters-in-law who tell about their affairs and marriages as they await their husbands at a lakeside resort. His first commercial success, though it waited nine years for release (1961). In Swedish with English subtitles. *AKA:* Kvinnors Vantan; Waiting Women.
1952 108m/B *SW* Anita Bjork, Karl Arne Homsten, Eva Dahlbeck, Maj-Britt Nilsson, Jarl Kulle; *W/D:* Ingmar Bergman. **VHS, Beta** $29.98 *SUE, NLC* 𝘐𝘐𝘐

The Secrets of Wu Sin A suicidal news writer in Chinatown is given a reason to live by a news editor who gives her a job. She starts investigating a ring smuggling Chinese workers, with the trail leading to, of course, Chinatown. Low-budget crime thriller.
1932 65m/B Lois Wilson, Grant Withers, Dorothy Revier, Robert Warwick, Toshia Mori; *D:* Richard Thorpe. **VHS** $12.95 *SNC, NOS, DVT* 𝘐𝘐

Seduced When a rich businessman turns up dead, the ambitious politician who was involved with his wife must find the killer. Not memorable or exceptional, but not boring or offensive either. Made for television.
1985 100m/C Gregory Harrison, Cybill Shepherd, Jose Ferrer, Adrienne Barbeau, Michael C. Gwynne, Karmin Murcelo, Paul Stewart; *D:* Jerrold Freedman. **VHS** $9.99 *STE, PSM* 𝘐

Seduced and Abandoned A lothario seduces his fiancee's young sister. When the girl becomes pregnant, he refuses to marry her. Family complications abound. A comic look at the Italian code of honor. In Italian with English subtitles. *AKA:* Sedotta e Abbandonata.
1964 118m/B *IT* Saro Urzi, Stefania Sandrelli, Aldo Puglisi; *D:* Pietro Germi. **VHS, Beta** $24.95 *NOS, HHT, HEG* 𝘐𝘐𝘐

The Seducer Things get dangerous when a playboy's goals turn from love to death.
1982 (R) 72m/C Christopher Mathews; *D:* Donovan Winters. **VHS** *NO* 𝘐𝘐

The Seducers An acid-dropping mother takes her shy, withdrawn son on a Mediterranean cruise and asks along some of her girlfriends in the hopes of stoking his libido. However, she finds it difficult to control her own impulses. The boy gets a chance when the ship runs aground on a remote island and he meets an innocent native girl. His mother, though, has designs of her own. Dubbed from Italian.
1970 84m/C *GE* Rosalba (Sara Bay) Neri, Edwige Fenech, Maud de Belleroche, Maurizio Bonuglia, Ruggero Miti, Ewa Thulin; *D:* Ottavio Alessi. **VHS** $23.00 *SMW* 𝘐

Seducers Wealthy, middle-aged man unsuspectingly allows two young lesbians to use his telephone. A night of bizarre mayhem and brutal murder begins. They tease him, tear apart his house, and generally make him miserable. Why? Good question. *AKA:* Death Game.
1977 (R) 90m/C Sondra Locke, Colleen Camp, Seymour Cassel; *D:* Peter S. Traynor. **VHS, Beta** $59.95 *GEM* 𝘐

The Seduction Superstar television anchorwoman is harassed by a psychotic male admirer. Usual run of the mill exploitive "B" thriller with no brains behind the camera.
1982 (R) 104m/C Morgan Fairchild, Michael Sarrazin, Vince Edwards, Andrew Stevens, Colleen Camp, Kevin Brophy; *D:* David Schmoeller. **VHS, Beta** $9.98 *MED* 𝘐

The Seduction of Joe Tynan Political drama about a young senator (Alda) torn between his family, his political career, and his mistress (Streep). Alda also wrote the thin screenplay, which reportedly is loosely based on the remarkable life of Ted Kennedy. Relatively shallow treatment of the meaty themes of power, hypocrisy, sex, and corruption in our nation's capital.
1979 (R) 107m/C Alan Alda, Meryl Streep, Melvyn Douglas, Barbara Harris, Rip Torn; *D:* Jerry Schatzberg; *W:* Alan Alda. **VHS, Beta, LV** $69.95 *MCA* 𝘐𝘐½

Seduction of Mimi Comic farce of politics and seduction about a Sicilian laborer's escapades with the Communists and the local Mafia. Giannini is wonderful as the stubborn immigrant to the big city who finds himself in trouble. One of the funniest love scenes on film. Basis for the later movie ''Which Way is Up?''
1974 (R) 92m/C *IT* Giancarlo Giannini, Mariangela Melato; *D:* Lina Wertmuller. **VHS, Beta** *FOX, OM* 🌀🌀🌀

Seduction: The Cruel Woman A curiously uninvolving look at sexual games and fantasies. Wanda is a dominatrix, who also owns a sado-masochistic gallery where her various friends and current and formers lovers act out their basest desires. Stylized, with some graphic sex. Based on the novel ''Venus in Furs'' by Leopold Sacher-Masoch. In German with English subtitles.
1989 84m/C *GE* Mechthild Grossmann, Carola Regnier, Udo Kier, Shella McLaughlin; *W/D:* Elfi Mikesch, Monika Treut. **VHS** $59.95 *TAM* 🌀🌀

See How She Runs Running becomes a central and redefining experience for a 40-year-old divorced schoolteacher (Woodward). Her training culminates with a run in the Boston marathon. Her loved ones, though concerned for her health and sanity, cheer her on. Excellent made for TV drama. Screen daughter Newman is also Woodward's real-life daughter.
1978 92m/C Joanne Woodward, John Considine, Lissy Newman, Barbara Manning; *D:* Richard T. Heffron. **VHS, Beta** *NO* 🌀🌀🌀

See No Evil A blind girl gradually discovers the murdered bodies of her uncle's family. Trapped in the family mansion, she finds herself pursued by the killer. Chilling and well crafted. *AKA:* Blind Terror.
1971 (PG) 90m/C Mia Farrow, Dorothy Allison, Robin Bailey; *D:* Richard Fleischer. **VHS, Beta, LV** $39.95 *COL* 🌀🌀🌀

See No Evil, Hear No Evil Another teaming for Pryor and Wilder, in which they portray a blind man and a deaf man both sought as murder suspects. Pryor and Wilder deserve better. Music by Stewart Copeland.
1989 (R) 103m/C Gene Wilder, Richard Pryor, Joan Severance, Anthony Zerbe; *D:* Arthur Hiller. **VHS, Beta, LV, 8mm** $14.95 *COL* 🌀🌀

See You in the Morning Ill-conceived romantic comedy-drama about a divorced psychiatrist and a widow, both of whom had unhappy marriages, who meet and marry. They must cope with their respective children, family tragedies, and their own expectations, in order to make this second marriage work. Director Pakula also wrote the disappointing screenplay.
1989 (PG-13) 119m/C Jeff Bridges, Alice Krige, Farrah Fawcett, Drew Barrymore, Lukas Haas, Macaulay Culkin, David Dukes, Frances Sternhagen, Theodore Bikel, George Hearn, Linda Lavin; *D:* Alan J. Pakula. **VHS, Beta, LV** $19.98 *WAR* 🌀½

Seedpeople Mindless horror flick has bloodthirsty plants inhabiting peaceful Comet Valley after their seeds fall from outer space and germinate. These ''seedpeople'' possess tremendous powers and soon have the rural residents transformed into zombies. Bears an uncanny resemblance to ''Invasion of the Bodysnatchers,'' and is so bad it's almost good. Also available with Spanish subtitles.
1992 87m/C Sam Hennings, Andrea Roth, Dane Witherspoon, Sal Dunard, Holly Fields, Bernard Kates; *D:* Peter Manoogian; *W:* Jackson Barr. **VHS, Beta** $19.95 *PAR* 🌀🌀½

Seeds of Evil Warhol alumnus Dallesandro is a strange gardener who grows flowers that can kill. He can also turn himself into a tree and figures to seduce rich and bored housewife Houghton (niece of Katherine Hepburn) after he finishes tending her garden. Strange, quirky horror flick. *AKA:* The Gardener.
1976 (R) 97m/C Katherine Houghton, Joe Dallesandro, Rita Gam; *D:* James H. Kay. **VHS, Beta** $29.95 *UNI* 🌀

The Seekers The story of the Kent family continues, as Abraham Kent, his wife and young son are forced to leave the safety of Boston for the rugged, untamed Pacific Northwest. TV movie based on the novel by John Jakes; preceded by ''The Bastard'' and ''The Rebels.''
1979 200m/C Randolph Mantooth, Edie Adams, Neville Brand, Delta Burke, John Carradine, George DeLoy, Julie Gregg, Roosevelt Grier, George Hamilton, Alex Hyde-White, Brian Keith, Ross Martin, Gary Merrill, Martin Milner, Vic Morrow, Timothy Patrick Murphy, Hugh O'Brian, Robert Reed, Allen Rich, Barbara Rush, Sarah Rush, Stuart Whitman, Ed Harris, Jeremy Licht, Eric Stoltz; *D:* Sidney Hayers. **VHS** $29.98 *MCA* 🌀

Seems Like Old Times A sweet lawyer (Hawn) finds herself helping her ex-husband (Chase) when two robbers force him to hold up a bank. Grodin is the new spouse threatened by Chase's appearance and by the heavies he's trying to escape. Better-than-average Simon script. Funny, with appealing characters.
1980 (PG) 102m/C Goldie Hawn, Chevy Chase, Charles Grodin, Robert Guillaume, Harold Gould, George Grizzard, J.K. Carter; *D:* Jay Sandrich; *W:* Neil Simon. **VHS, Beta, LV** $19.95 *COL* 🌀🌀½

Seize the Day A man approaching middle age (Williams) feels that he is a failure. Brilliant performances by all, plus a number of equally fine actors in small roles. Based on the short novel by Saul Bellow.
1986 93m/C Robin Williams, Joseph Wiseman, Jerry Stiller, Glenne Headly, Tony Roberts; *D:* Fielder Cook. **VHS, Beta, LV** $19.99 *HBO* 🌀🌀🌀

Selzure Three demonic creatures from a writer's dreams come to life and terrorize him and his housequests at a weekend party. Slick but disjointed; Stone's directorial debut. Interesting cast includes Tattoo from ''Fantasy Island.''
1974 (PG) 93m/C *CA* Jonathan Frid, Herve Villechaize, Christina Pickles; *D:* Oliver Stone. **VHS, Beta** $9.99 *STE, PSM* 🌀½

Seizure: The Story of Kathy Morris The real-life anguish and struggle of a young music student who must have brain surgery and comes out of it unable to read or count. Workaday dramatization.
1982 104m/C Leonard Nimoy, Penelope Milford; *D:* Gerald I. Isenberg. **VHS, Beta** *TLF* 🌀

Self-Defense When a city's police force goes on strike, the citizens band together into vigilante troops.
1988 (R) 85m/C Tom Nardini, Brenda Bazinet. **VHS, Beta, LV** $79.95 *MED* 🌀½

Sell Out A former spy living in Jerusalem is called out of retirement; his protege, who defected to the Soviets, now wants out.
1976 (PG) 102m/C Richard Widmark, Oliver Reed, Gayle Hunnicutt, Sam Wanamaker; *D:* Peter Collinson. **VHS, Beta** $59.95 *MED* 🌀🌀½

Semaforo en Rojo Five men who are planning a robbery run into trouble from some ex-lovers.
1947 95m/B *MX* Jose Galvez, Enrique Ponton, Jaime Velasquez, German Robles. **VHS, Beta** $44.95 *MAD* 🌀🌀

Semi-Tough Likeable, still current social satire involving a couple of pro-football buddies and their mutual interest in their team owner's daughter. Romantic comedy, satire of the sports world, zany highjinks—it's all here, though not enough of any of these. Pleasant and enjoyable. Based on the novel by Dan Jenkins.
1977 (R) 107m/C Burt Reynolds, Kris Kristofferson, Jill Clayburgh, Lotte Lenya, Robert Preston, Bert Convy, Richard Masur, Carl Weathers, Brian Dennehy, John Matuszak, Ron Silver; *D:* Michael Ritchie. **VHS, Beta, LV** $19.95 *MGM, FOX* 🌀🌀½

The Senator was Indiscreet A farcical comedy concerning a slightly loony senator with presidential aspirations. He thinks he can win the nomination because he keeps a diary that would prove embarrassing to numerous colleagues. The diary then falls into the hands of a journalist. Powell is wonderful as the daffy politician. Playwright Kaufman's only directorial effort. *AKA:* Mr. Ashton was Indiscreet.
1947 75m/B William Powell, Ella Raines, Hans Conried; *D:* George S. Kaufman. **VHS** $19.98 *REP* 🌀🌀🌀

Send Me No Flowers Vintage Hudson-Day comedy. Hudson plays a hypochondriac who thinks his death is imminent. He decides to provide for his family's future by finding his wife a rich husband. She thinks he's feeling guilty for having an affair.
1964 100m/C Rock Hudson, Doris Day, Tony Randall, Paul Lynde; *D:* Norman Jewison. **VHS, Beta** $14.95 *MCA, CCB* 🌀🌀🌀

The Sender An amnesiac young man is studied by a psychiatrist. She discovers that her patient is a ''sender,'' who can transmit his nightmares to other patients at a hospital.
1982 (R) 92m/C *GB* Kathryn Harrold, Zeljko Ivanek, Shirley Knight, Paul Freeman, Sean Hewitt; *D:* Roger Christian. **VHS, Beta, LV** $19.95 *PAR* 🌀🌀

Senior Trip New York City will never be the same after a bunch of rowdy Midwestern high school seniors tear up the town on their graduation trip. Made for television.
1981 96m/C Scott Baio, Mickey Rooney, Faye Grant, Vincent Spano, Jane Hoffman; *D:* Kenneth Johnson. **VHS, Beta** $39.95 *WOV* 🌀

Senior Week A batch of girl-hungry teens have a wacky time on their Florida vacation just before graduation.
1988 97m/C Michael St. Gerard, Devon Skye, Leesa Bryte; *D:* Stuart Goldman. **VHS, Beta** $29.98 *LIV, VES* Woof!

The Seniors A group of college students decide to open a phony sex clinic, but the joke is on them when the clinic becomes a success. Better than it sounds. Pretty good acting and much harmless goofiness.
1978 (R) 87m/C Dennis Quaid, Priscilla Barnes, Jeffrey Byron, Gary Imhoff; *D:* Rod Amateau. **VHS, Beta** $29.98 *VES* 🌀🌀

Senora Tentacion Musical melodrama about a composer who fights to leave his mother, sister, and girlfriend in order to flee with Hortensia, a famous singer. In Spanish with English subtitles.
1949 82m/B David Silva, Susana Guizar, Ninon Sevilla. **VHS, Beta** $29.95 *VYY, APD, TAM* 🌀🌀

Sensations A woman and a man who aren't exceptionally fond of one another share a lottery ticket and win. Vincent is best known as a former director of porno flicks, and he manages to work in sexual overtones.

1987 (R) 91m/C Rebecca Lynn, Blake Bahner, Jennifer Delora, Rick Savage, Loretta Palma, Frank Stewart; **D:** Chuck Vincent. **VHS, Beta** $29.95 ACA *ℐℐ*

Sensations of 1945 A press agent turns his firm over to one of his clients, a dancer with some wild promotional ideas. Brings together numerous variety and musical acts. W. C. Fields has a cameo in his last film role. Mostly unremarkable, occasionally fun musical. *AKA:* Sensations.
1944 86m/B Eleanor Powell, Dennis O'Keefe, C. Aubrey Smith, Eugene Pallette, Cab Calloway, Sophie Tucker, Woody Herman, Lyle Talbot, Marie Blake; *Cameos:* W.C. Fields; **D:** Andrew L. Stone. **VHS, Beta** $19.95 VDM *ℐℐ½*

Sense & Sensibility BBC miniseries adaptation of Jane Austen's first novel concerning two sisters striving for happiness in their well-ordered lives.
1985 174m/C *GB* Irene Richard, Tracey Childs; **D:** Rodney Bennett. **VHS, Beta** $29.98 FOX, TVC, HMV *ℐℐ*

A Sense of Freedom A hopeless racketeering criminal is thrust from institution to institution until the Scottish authorities decide on an innovative style of reform. Based on Jimmy Boyle's autobiographical book. Excellent and disturbing.
1978 (R) 81m/C *GB* David Hayman, Alex Norton, Jake D'Arcy, Sean Scanlan, Fulton Mackay; **D:** John MacKenzie. **VHS, Beta** $79.99 HBO *ℐℐℐ*

Senso Tragic story of romance and rebellion as Italian patriots battle the Austro-Hungarian empire for independence in 1866. An Italian noblewoman betrays her marriage, and almost her country, to be with a cynical Austrian soldier in this visually stunning piece of cinematography. *AKA:* The Wanton Contessa.
1968 125m/C *IT* Alida Valli, Massimo Girotti, Heinz Moog, Farley Granger; **D:** Luchino Visconti. **VHS** $29.95 APD *ℐℐℐ*

The Sensual Man Hot-blooded Italian falls in love and gets married only to find out that his wife cannot consummate their marriage. Exploitative, misogynistic, and unfunny.
1974 (R) 90m/C Giancarlo Giannini, Rossana Podesta, Lionel Stander; **D:** Marco Vicario. **VHS, Beta** $59.95 COL *ℐ½*

Sensual Partners Young actresses are lured to Tangier by a fake movie producer and sold as sex slaves. Emphasis on soft-focus, soft-core flesh.
1987 87m/C Gina Jansen, Eric Falk. **VHS, Beta** $29.95 MED *Woof!*

Sensuous Caterer Marc Stevens hosts a video Valentine's Day orgy and invites an uninhibited crowd of erotic stars and starlets to come and show their stuff. Soft porn for the soft minded.
1982 60m/C Marc Stevens. **VHS, Beta** NO *ℐ*

The Sensuous Nurse Italian comedy about a beautiful nurse hired by the greedy, treacherous relatives of a weak-hearted count in hopes that her voluptuousness will give him a heart attack. It doesn't, and she falls in love. Mindless, but fun and sexy. Dubbed in English.
1976 (R) 79m/C *IT* Ursula Andress, Mario Pisu, Dulio Del Prete, Jack Palance; **D:** Nello Rosati. **VHS, Beta** $59.98 FOX *ℐℐ*

Sensuous Summer When Bobby returns home to the town of Elk Lake he finds the family business, run by his brother Nick, is in deep trouble. It seems Alex, an unscrupulous banker, wants to foreclose. But business comes second to pleasure when Bobby

is reunited with old flame Jill and Nick takes up again with ex-girlfriend Cindy.
1993 (R) 80m/C Tom Case, Christina Campbell, Brittany McGrea, Gina Jorand. **VHS** $79.95 CEL *ℐ½*

The Sensuous Teenager Overwhelmingly erotic and uncontrollably seductive, a teenage girl aims to please by releasing all the sensuality within her. *AKA:* Libido; Forbidden Passions.
1970 (R) 80m/C Sandra Jullien, Janine Reynaud, Michel Lemoine; **D:** Max Pecas. **VHS** SUN *Woof!*

The Sentinel A model, who has moved into a New York City brownstone, encounters an aging priest and some unusual neighbors. When she investigates strange noises she finds out that the apartment building houses the doorway to hell - and that she's intended to be the next doorkeeper. Modest suspense film with a good cast and enough shock and special effects to keep the viewer interested.
1976 (R) 92m/C Chris Sarandon, Christina Raines, Ava Gardner, Jose Ferrer, Sylvia Miles, John Carradine, Burgess Meredith, Tom Berenger, Beverly D'Angelo, Jeff Goldblum; **D:** Michael Winner. **VHS, Beta** $14.98 MCA *ℐℐ*

Separate But Equal One of TV's greatest history lessons, a powerful dramatization of the 1954 Brown vs. the Board of Education case that wrung a landmark civil rights decision from the Supreme Court. Great care is taken to humanize all the participants, from the humblest schoolchild to NAACP lawyer Thurgood Marshall (Poitier). On two cassettes.
1991 (PG) 194m/C Sidney Poitier, Burt Lancaster, Richard Kiley, Cleavon Little, John McMartin, Graham Beckel, Lynne Thigpen, Albert Hall; **W/D:** George Stevens. **VHS, LV** $19.98 REP, PIA, FCT *ℐℐℐ½*

A Separate Peace Two young men in a New England prep school during World War II come to grips with the war, coming of age, and a tragic accident. Cheap rendition of a not-so-great novel by John Knowles.
1973 (PG) 104m/C John Heyl, Parker Stevenson, William Roerick; **D:** Larry Peerce. **VHS, Beta** $45.95 PAR, HMV *ℐℐ*

Separate Tables Adaptation of the Terence Rattigan play about a varied cast of characters living out their personal dramas in a British seaside hotel. Guests include a matriarch and her shy daughter, a divorced couple, a spinster, and a presumed war hero. Their secrets and loves are examined in grand style. Fine acting all around.
1958 98m/B Burt Lancaster, David Niven, Rita Hayworth, Deborah Kerr, Wendy Hiller, Rod Taylor, Gladys Cooper, Felix Aylmer, Cathleen Nesbitt; **D:** Delbert Mann. Academy Awards '58: Best Actor (Niven), Best Supporting Actress (Hiller); Nominations: Best Actress (Kerr), Best Adapted Screenplay, Best Black and White Cinematography, Best Picture, Best Original Score; National Board of Review Awards '58: 10 Best Films of the Year; New York Film Critics Awards '58: Best Actor (Niven). **VHS, Beta** $19.98 MGM, FOX, FCT *ℐℐℐ½*

Separate Tables A remake of the 1958 film adapted from Terence Rattigan's play. Separated into two parts, "Table by the Window" and "Table Number Seven." The lives of the lonely inhabitants of a hotel are dramatized through wonderful acting by Christie and Bates. Made for cable television.
1983 (PG) 50m/C Julie Christie, Alan Bates, Claire Bloom, Irene Worth; **D:** John Schlesinger. **VHS, Beta** $59.95 MGM *ℐℐ½*

Separate Vacations A married man leaves his wife and kids to take a separate vacation, hoping he'll find exciting sex. Wife and kids end up at a ski resort, where romance comes her way. A lightweight, old story.
1986 (R) 91m/C David Naughton, Jennifer Dale, Mark Keyloun; **D:** Michael Anderson Sr. **VHS, Beta** $79.98 LIV *ℐℐ*

Separate Ways Unhappily married couple involved in various affairs split up in order to deal with themselves and their marriage. Good cast; bad script wandering down Maudlin Lane.
1982 92m/C Karen Black, Tony LoBianco, David Naughton, Sybil Danning; **D:** Howard Avedis. **VHS, Beta, LV** $79.95 VES *ℐ½*

Sepia Cinderella A songwriter, who finds himself with a hit, abandons his current life and love to try high society. He finds out it's not what he wants after all.
1947 67m/B Sheila Guyse, Rubel Blakely, Freddie Bartholomew, The John Kirby Sextet, Sid Catlett, Deke Wilson. **VHS, Beta** $29.95 NOS, DVT, FCT *ℐℐ*

September Woody does Bergman again with a shuttered, claustrophobic drama about six unhappy people trying to verbalize their feelings in a dark summer house in Vermont. Well-acted throughout and interesting at first, but the whining and angst attacks eventually give way to boredom. Of course, the Woodman went on to "Crimes and Misdemeanors," blending his dark and comedic sides masterfully, so the best way to look at this is as a training film. Nice music by Art Tatum.
1988 (PG-13) 82m/C Mia Farrow, Dianne Wiest, Denholm Elliott, Sam Waterston, Elaine Stritch, Jack Warden; **D:** Woody Allen. **VHS, Beta, LV** $89.98 ORI *ℐℐ½*

September Affair A married engineer and a classical pianist miss their plane from Naples. When the plane crashes, they're presumed dead, and they find themselves free to continue their illicit love affair. They find they cannot hide forever and must make peace with their pasts. Features the hit "September Song," recorded by Walter Huston.
1950 104m/B Joseph Cotten, Joan Fontaine, Francoise Rosay, Jessica Tandy, Robert Arthur; **D:** William Dieterle. **VHS, LV** $14.95 PAR *ℐℐℐ½*

September Gun A nun hires an aging gunfighter to escort her and a group of Apache children to a church school two hundred miles away. Preston is excellent as the ornery varmint in this enjoyable, pleasant western comedy. Made for television.
1983 94m/C Robert Preston, Patty Duke, Christopher Lloyd, Geoffrey Lewis, Sally Kellerman; **D:** Don Taylor. **VHS, Beta** $39.95 WOV *ℐℐ½*

September 30, 1955 A college undergrad (Thomas) in a small Arkansas town is devastated when he learns of the death of his idol, James Dean. (The title refers to the day Dean died.) Jimmy gathers a group of friends together for a vigil which turns into a drinking-binge, resulting in police chases and, finally, tragedy. Film debut of Quaid. Also known as "9/30/55."
1977 (PG) 107m/C Richard Thomas, Lisa Blount, Deborah Benson, Tom Hulce, Dennis Christopher, Dennis Quaid, Susan Tyrrell; **W/D:** James Bridges. **VHS** MCA *ℐℐℐ½*

Sergeant Matlovich vs. the U.S. Air Force A serviceman fights to remain in the Air Force after admitting his homosexuality. Compelling theme (from a true story) and good lead performance from Dourif are not enough to carry a rather flat made for TV script.

1978 100m/C Brad Dourif, Marc Singer, Frank Converse, William Daniels, Stephen Elliott, David Spielberg, Rue McClanahan, Mitchell Ryan, David Ogden Stiers; **D:** Paul Leaf. **VHS $59.95** LIV 🎬🎬½

Sgt. Pepper's Lonely Hearts Club Band "Rip-off" would be putting it kindly. A classic album by one of the greatest rock bands of all time deserves the respect of not having a star-studded extravaganza "filmization" made of it. Gratuitous, weird casting, bad acting give it a surreal feel. And the Bee Gees? Please. A nadir of seventies popular entertainment. 🎵Sgt. Pepper's Lonely Hearts Club Band; With a Little Help From My Friends; Fixing a Hole; Getting Better; Here Comes the Sun; I Want You (She's So Heavy); Good Morning, Good Morning; Nowhere Man; Polythene Pam; She Came Through the Bathroom Window; Mean Mister Mustard; She's Leaving Home; Lucy in the Sky With Diamonds; Oh Darling; Maxwell's Silver Hammer; Because; Strawberry Fields Forever; Being for the Benefit of Mr. Kite; You Never Give Me Your Money; Got to Get You Into My Life; When I'm 64; Come Together; Golden Slumbers; Carry That Weight; The Long and Winding Road; A Day in the Life; Get Back.

1978 (PG) 113m/C Peter Frampton, The Bee Gees, Steve Martin, Aerosmith, Earth Wind & Fire, George Burns, Donald Pleasence; **D:** Michael Schultz. **VHS, Beta, LV $29.95** MCA 🎬½

Sergeant Rutledge The story of a court-martial, told in flashback, about a black calvary officer on trial for rape and murder. A detailed look at overt and covert racism handled by master director Ford. It is always apparent Strode (as Rutledge) is a heroic, yet human, figure who refuses to be beaten down by circumstances. The courtroom setting is deliberately oppressive but does make the film somewhat static. Based on the novel "Captain Buffalo" by James Warner Bellah.

1960 112m/C Woody Strode, Jeffrey Hunter, Constance Towers, Billie Burke, Juano Hernandez, Carleton Young, Charles Seel, Jan Styne, Mae Marsh; **D:** John Ford; **W:** Willis Goldbeck, James Warner Bellah; **M:** Howard Jackson. **VHS $29.98** WAR 🎬🎬🎬

Sergeant Ryker Confident lead acting from Marvin as a U.S. serviceman accused of treason during the Korean War carries this otherwise blah army/courtroom drama. Remake of 1963 TV film "The Case Against Sergeant Ryker." Dillman is good as Marvin's energetic lawyer.

1968 85m/C Lee Marvin, Bradford Dillman, Vera Miles, Peter Graves, Lloyd Nolan, Murray Hamilton; **D:** Buzz Kulik; **M:** John Williams. **VHS $9.95** CAR 🎬🎬½

Sergeant York Timely and enduring war movie based on the true story of Alvin York, the country boy from Tennessee drafted during World War I. At first a pacifist, Sergeant York (Cooper, well cast in an Oscar-winning role) finds justification for fighting and becomes one of the war's greatest heros. Gentle scenes of rural life contrast with horrific battlegrounds. York served as a consultant.

1941 134m/B Gary Cooper, Joan Leslie, Walter Brennan, Dickie Moore, Ward Bond, George Tobias, Noah Beery Jr., June Lockhart, Abe Finkel; **D:** Howard Hawks; **W:** Harry Chandler. Academy Awards '41: Best Actor (Cooper), Best Film Editing; Nominations: Best Black and White Cinematography, Best Director (Hawks), Best Interior Decoration, Best Original Screenplay, Best Picture, Best Sound, Best Supporting Actor (Brennan), Best Supporting Actress (Wycherly),

Best Original Score. **VHS, Beta $19.98** MGM, FOX, BTV 🎬🎬🎬

Serial Fun spoof of hyper-trendiness—open marriage, health foods, fad religions, navel-gazing—in Marin County, the really cool place to live across the Golden Gate from San Francisco. Mull in his first lead is the oddly normal guy surrounded by fruits and nuts. Based on Cyra McFadden's novel.

1980 (R) 90m/C Martin Mull, Sally Kellerman, Tuesday Weld, Tom Smothers, Bill Macy, Peter Bonerz, Barbara Rhoades, Christopher Lee; **D:** Bill Persky. **VHS, Beta, LV $49.95** PAR 🎬🎬🎬

The Serpent and the Rainbow A good, interesting book (by Harvard ethnobotanist Wade Davis) offering serious speculation on the possible existence and origin of zombies in Haiti has been hacked and slashed into a cheap Wes Craven-ized screen semblance of itself. And a shame it is: the result is racist, disrespectful, exploitative, and superficial. From the director of "Nightmare on Elm Street."

1987 (R) 98m/C Bill Pullman, Cathy Tyson, Zakes Mokae, Paul Winfield, Conrad Roberts, Badja Djola, Theresa Merritt; **D:** Wes Craven. **VHS, Beta, LV $19.95** MCA Woof!

Serpent Island Two seamen fight over a Caribbean woman amid voodoo rituals, sea monsters and buried treasure.

1954 63m/C Sonny Tufts. **VHS, Beta $59.95** MED 🎬½

The Serpent of Death An archaeologist uncovers a statue and a curse which changes his life. Horror and adventure rolled into one.

1990 (R) 90m/C VHS, Beta, LV $79.95 PAR 🎬🎬

The Serpent's Egg Big disappointment from the great Bergman in his second film in English. Ullman is not sultry and Carradine is horrible. Big budget matched by big Bergman ego, making a big, bad parody of himself. The plot concerns a pair of Jewish trapeze artists surviving in Berlin during Hitler's rise to power by working in a grisly and mysterious medical clinic. **AKA:** Das Schlangenei.

1978 (R) 119m/C GE David Carradine, Liv Ullmann, Gert Frobe, James Whitmore; **D:** Ingmar Bergman. **VHS, Beta $79.98** LIV, TAM 🎬½

Serpico Based on Peter Maas's book about the true-life exploits of Frank Serpico, a New York undercover policeman who exposed corruption in the police department. Known as much for his nonconformism as for his honesty, the real Serpico eventually retired from the force and moved to Europe. South Bronx-raised Pacino gives the character reality and strength. Excellent New York location photography.

1973 (R) 130m/C Al Pacino, John Randolph, Jack Kehoe, Barbara Eda-Young, Cornelia Sharpe, F. Murray Abraham, Tony Roberts; **D:** Sidney Lumet. Academy Awards '73: Nominations: Best Actor (Pacino), Best Adapted Screenplay; Golden Globe Awards '74: Best Actor—Drama (Pacino). **VHS, Beta, LV $14.95** PAR 🎬🎬🎬

The Servant A dark, intriguing examination of British class hypocrisy and the master-servant relationship. A rich, bored playboy is ruined by his socially inferior but crafty and ambitious manservant. Playwright Harold Pinter wrote the adaptation of Robin Maugham's novel in his first collaboration with director Losey. The best kind of British societal navel-gazing.

1963 112m/B GB Dirk Bogarde, James Fox, Sarah Miles, Wendy Craig; **D:** Joseph Losey. **VHS, Beta $59.95** HBO 🎬🎬🎬½

Servants of Twilight Religious zealots target a small boy for assassination because their cult leader says he's the anti-Christ. Adaptation of the Dean R. Koontz novel. Packed with action, its spell on the viewer hinges on a cruel shock ending that undercuts what came before. Made for cable television.

1991 (R) 95m/C Bruce Greenwood, Belinda Bauer, Grace Zabriskie, Richard Bradford, Jarrett Lennon, Carel Struycken, Jack Kehoe, Kelli Maroney; **D:** Jeffrey Obrow. **VHS $89.98** VMK 🎬🎬

Sesame Street Presents: Follow That Bird Television's Big Bird suffers an identity crisis, and leaves Sesame Street to join a family of real birds. He soon misses his home, and returns, in a danger-filled journey. **AKA:** Follow That Bird.

1985 (G) 92m/C Sandra Bernhard, John Candy, Chevy Chase, Joe Flaherty, Dave Thomas, Waylon Jennings, Jim Henson's Muppets; **D:** Ken Kwapis. **VHS, Beta, LV $19.98** WAR 🎬🎬

A Session with the Committee Collection of skits performed by a Los Angeles comedy troupe.

1969 90m/C Peter Bonerz, Barbara Bosson, Garry Goodrow, Carl Gottlieb, Jessica Myerson, Christopher Ross, Melvin Stewart, Melvin Sturdy; **D:** Jack Del. **VHS $59.95** PAV 🎬🎬

Sessions Mentally exhausted by her roles as sister, single parent, lover, exercise enthusiast, and high-priced prostitute, Leigh Churchill (Hamel) seeks professional counselling. Hamel's first role after "Hill Street Blues" is only average in this made for TV drama.

1983 96m/C Veronica Hamel, Jeffrey DeMunn, Jill Eikenberry, David Marshall Grant, George Coe, Henderson Forsythe, Deborah Hedwall; **D:** Richard Pearce. **VHS, Beta** NO 🎬🎬

The Set-Up Excellent, original if somewhat overwrought morality tale about integrity set in the world of boxing. Filmed as a continuous narrative covering only 72 minutes in the life of an aging fighter (Ryan). Told to throw a fight, he must battle gangsters when he refuses. Powerful, with fine performances, especially from Ryan in the lead. Inspired by Joseph Moncure March's narrative poem.

1949 72m/B Robert Ryan, Audrey Totter, George Tobias, Alan Baxter, James Edwards, Wallace Ford; **D:** Robert Wise. **VHS, Beta, LV $19.95** CCB, MED 🎬🎬🎬½

Seven Freelance desperado Smith takes $7 million of your tax dollars at work from the feds to get rid of Hawaiian gangsters. Might be tongue in cheek, though sometimes it's hard to tell. Fun action pic unfortunately characterized by bad camera work and overearnest direction. Features the original of a gag made famous in "Raiders of the Lost Ark."

1979 (R) 100m/C William Smith, Barbara Leigh, Guich Koock, Art Metrano, Martin Kove, Richard Le Pore, Susan Kiger; **D:** Andy Sidaris. **VHS, Beta $59.95** LIV 🎬🎬½

Seven Alone Family adventure tale (based on Monroe Morrow's book "On to Oregon," based in turn on a true story) about seven siblings who undertake a treacherous 2000-mile journey from Missouri to Oregon, after their parents die along the way. Inspiring and all that; good family movie. **AKA:** House Without Windows.

1975 (G) 85m/C Dewey Martin, Aldo Ray, Anne Collins, Dean Smith, Stewart Peterson; **D:** Earl Bellamy. **VHS, Beta** NO 🎬🎬½

Seven Beauties Very dark war comedy about a small-time Italian crook in Naples with seven ugly sisters to support. He survives a German prison camp and much else;

unforgettably, he seduces the ugly commandant of his camp to save his own life. Good acting and tight direction. *AKA:* Pasqualino Settebellezze; Pasqualino: Seven Beauties.
1976 116m/C IT Giancarlo Giannini, Fernando Rey, Shirley Stoler; *D:* Lina Wertmuller. **VHS, Beta, LV $59.95** COL, APD 𝔛𝔛𝔛𝔛

Seven Blows of the Dragon The Chinese novel, "All Men Are Brothers," is the basis for this spectacular martial arts epic.
1973 (R) 81m/C David Chiang. **VHS, Beta** WAR 𝔛𝔛½

Seven Brides for Seven Brothers The eldest of seven fur-trapping brothers in the Oregon Territory brings home a wife. She begins to civilize the other six, who realize the merits of women and begin to look for romances of their own. Thrilling choreography by Michael Kidd - don't miss "The Barn Raising." Charming performances by Powell and Keel, both in lovely voice. Based on Stephen Vincent Benet's story. Thrills, chills, singin', dancin'—a classic Hollywood good time. ♫When You're In Love; Spring, Spring, Spring; Sobbin' Women; Bless Your Beautiful Hide; Goin' Co'tin; Wonderful, Wonderful Day; June Bride; Lonesome Polecat Lament.
1954 103m/C Howard Keel, Jane Powell, Russ Tamblyn, Julie Newmar, Jeff Richards, Tommy Rall, Virginia Gibson; *D:* Stanley Donen. Academy Awards '54: Best Score; Nominations: Best Color Cinematography, Best Film Editing, Best Picture, Best Screenplay; National Board of Review Awards '54: 10 Best Films of the Year. **VHS, Beta, LV, 8mm $19.98** MGM, HMV 𝔛𝔛𝔛½

The 7 Brothers Meet Dracula Seven siblings meet guy with dental anomaly. *AKA:* Legend of the Seven Golden Vampires.
1973 110m/C GB Peter Cushing, David Chang, Robin Stewart, Julie Ege; *D:* Roy Ward Baker. **VHS** NO 𝔛½

Seven Chances Silent classic that Keaton almost didn't make, believing instead that it should go to Harold Lloyd. Lawyer Keaton finds that he can inherit $7 million if he marries by 7:00 p.m. After his girlfriend turns down his botched proposal, chaos breaks loose when he advertises for someone—anyone—to marry him and make him rich. Suddenly he finds what seems to be hundreds of women willing to make the sacrifice, setting up one of the great film pursuits. Memorable boulder sequence was added after preview audience indicated climax was lacking that certain something.
1925 60m/B Buster Keaton, T. Roy Barnes, Snitz Edwards, Ruth Dwyer, Frankie Raymond; *D:* Buster Keaton. **VHS** NO 𝔛𝔛𝔛½

Seven Cities of Gold An expedition of Spanish conquistadors and missionaries descend on 18th-century California, looking for secret Indian caches of gold. Semi-lavish costume epic.
1955 103m/C Anthony Quinn, Michael Rennie, Richard Egan, Rita Moreno, Jeffrey Hunter, Eduardo Noriega, John Doucette; *D:* Robert D. Webb. **VHS, Beta $19.98** FOX 𝔛𝔛

Seven Days Ashore/Hurry, Charlie, Hurry A comedy double feature. In "Seven Days Ashore," three merchant marines on leave in San Francisco become romantically involved with three women. In "Hurry, Charlie, Hurry," a henpecked husband finds himself in a lot of trouble.
1944 141m/B Gordon Oliver, Virginia Mayo, Dooley Wilson, Margaret Dumont, Leon Errol, Mildred Coles. **VHS, Beta $34.95** RKO, TTC 𝔛𝔛

Seven Days in May Topical but still gripping Cold War nuclear-peril thriller. An American general plans a military takeover because he considers the president's paci-

fism traitorous. Screenplay by Rod Serling of "Twilight Zone" fame. Highly suspenseful, with a breathtaking climax. Houseman's film debut in a small role.
1964 117m/B Burt Lancaster, Kirk Douglas, Edmond O'Brien, Fredric March, Ava Gardner, John Houseman; *D:* John Frankenheimer; *M:* Jerry Goldsmith. Academy Awards '64 Nominations: Best Art Direction/Set Decoration (B & W), Best Supporting Actor (O'Brien); Golden Globe Awards '65: Best Supporting Actor (O'Brien). **VHS, Beta, LV $19.98** WAR 𝔛𝔛𝔛½

Seven Days' Leave Radio star-crammed musical comedy about a soldier who must marry a certain already betrothed gal (Ball) within a week so he can inherit a fortune. Songs include "Can't Get Out of this Mood," "A Touch of Texas," and "Baby, You Speak My Language." Following the completion of the film, Mature joined the Coast Guard. Lively but not memorable.
1942 87m/B Victor Mature, Lucille Ball, Harold Peary, Mary Cortes, Ginny Simms, Marcy McGuire, Peter Lind Hayes, Wallace Reed, Wallace Ford, Arnold Stang, Buddy Clark, Charles Victor; *D:* Tim Whelan. **VHS, Beta $19.98** TTC 𝔛𝔛

Seven Deadly Sins A collection of tales concerning destructive emotions and the downfalls they cause. Contains shorts from some of Europe's finest directors (five French and two Italian). Stories and their directors are "Avarice and Anger" (de Filippo), "Sloth" (Dreville), "Lust" (Allegret), "Envy" (Rossellini), "Gluttony" (Rim), "Pride" (Autant-Lara) and "The Eighth Sin" (Lacombe).
1953 127m/B FR IT Eduardo de Filippo, Isa Miranda, Jacqueline Plessis, Louis de Funes, Paolo Stoppa, Frank Villard, Jean Richard, Francoise Rosay, Jean Debucourt, Louis Seigner; *D:* Eduardo de Filippo, Jean Dreville, Yves Allegret, Roberto Rossellini, Carlo Rim, Claude Autant-Lara, Georges Lacombe. **VHS** IVY 𝔛𝔛𝔛

Seven Deaths in the Cat's Eye A ravenous beast slaughters people in a small Scottish village. This flick reveals a little-known fact about felines.
1972 90m/C IT Anton Diffring, Jane Birkin; *D:* Anthony M. Dawson. **VHS, Beta $79.95** PSM 𝔛𝔛

Seven Doors of Death A young woman inherits a possessed hotel. Meanwhile, hellish zombies try to check out. Chilling Italian horror flick. *AKA:* The Beyond.
1982 (R) 80m/C IT Katherine MacColl, David Warbeck, Farah Keller, Tony St. John; *D:* Louis Fulller. **VHS, Beta $39.95** LIV 𝔛𝔛

Seven Doors to Death Young architect tries to solve a crime to avoid being placed under suspicion. The suspects are six shop owners in this low-budget attempt at a murder mystery.
1944 70m/B Chick Chandler, June Clyde, George Meeker, Gregory Gay, Edgar Dearing; *D:* Elmer Clifton. **VHS, Beta $14.95** UHV, MRV, SNC 𝔛

Seven Faces of Dr. Lao Dr. Lao is the proprietor of a magical circus that changes the lives of the residents of a small western town. Marvelous special effects and makeup (Randall plays seven characters) highlight this charming family film in the Pal tradition. Charles Finney adapted from his novel.
1963 101m/C Tony Randall, Barbara Eden, Arthur O'Connell, Lee Patrick, Noah Beery Jr., John Qualen; *D:* George Pal. **VHS, Beta, LV $59.95** MGM 𝔛𝔛𝔛

Seven Hours to Judgment When the punks who murdered his wife go free, a psychotic man (Liebman) decides to take justice into his own hands. He kidnaps the

wife of the judge in charge (Bridges, who also directed) and leads him on a wild goose chase. Liebman steals the film as the psycho. Ex-Springsteen spouse Phillips plays the judge's wife. Ambitious but credulity-stretching revenge/crime drama.
1988 (R) 90m/C Beau Bridges, Ron Leibman, Julianne Phillips, Al Freeman Jr., Reggie Johnson; *D:* Beau Bridges. **VHS, Beta, LV $19.95** MED 𝔛𝔛

Seven Indignant A group of elite fighters is China's only hope against the invading Japanese.
19?? ?m/C Kong Hoi. **VHS, Beta** OCE 𝔛

The Seven Little Foys Enjoyable musical biography of Eddie Foy (played ebulliently by Hope) and his famed vaudevillian troupe. Cagney's appearance as George M. Cohan is brief, but long enough for a memorable dance duet with Hope. ♫Mary's a Grand Old Name; I'm a Yankee Doodle Dandy; I'm the Greatest Father of Them All; Nobody; Comedy Ballet; I'm Tired; Chinatown, My Chinatown.
1955 95m/C Bob Hope, Milly Vitale, George Tobias, Angela Clark, James Cagney; *D:* Melville Shavelson. **VHS, Beta $14.95** COL 𝔛𝔛𝔛

Seven Magnificent Gladiators Seven gladiators team up to save a peaceful Roman village from total annihilation. Dismal effort at a remake of "The Seven Samurai"—see the original instead, please. Ferrigno was "The Incredible Hulk" on TV.
1984 (PG) 86m/C Lou Ferrigno, Sybil Danning, Brad Harris, Dan Vadis, Carla Ferrigno; *D:* Bruno Mattei. **VHS, Beta $59.95** MGM 𝔛

Seven Miles from Alcatraz/Flight from Glory Dramatic double feature: Two escaped convicts discover a hideout for Nazi spies in "Seven Miles From Alcatraz," and an evil man tries to recruit pilots to fly planes over the Andes Mountains in "Flight From Glory."
1943 127m/B James Craig, Bonita Granville, Chester Morris, Van Heflin, Onslow Stevens; *D:* Edward Dmytryk. **VHS, Beta $34.95** RKO, TTC 𝔛𝔛

Seven Minutes in Heaven Sensitive love story about a 15-year-old girl who invites her platonic male friend to live in her house, and finds it disturbs her boyfriend, as these things will. Ever so tasteful (unlike most other teen comedies), with gentle comedy—but forgettable.
1986 (PG) 90m/C Jennifer Connelly, Byron Thames, Maddie Corman; *D:* Linda Feferman. **VHS, Beta $19.98** WAR 𝔛𝔛

The Seven Percent Solution Dr. Watson persuades Sherlock Holmes to meet with Sigmund Freud to cure his cocaine addiction. Holmes and Freud then find themselves teaming up to solve a supposed kidnapping. Adapted by Nicholas Meyer from his own novel. One of the most charming Holmes films; well-cast, intriguing blend of mystery, drama, and fun.
1976 (PG) 113m/C Alan Arkin, Nicol Williamson, Laurence Olivier, Robert Duvall, Vanessa Redgrave, Joel Grey, Samantha Eggar, Jeremy Kemp, Charles Gray, Regine; *D:* Herbert Ross. Academy Awards '76 Nominations: Best Adapted Screenplay, Best Costume Design; National Board of Review Awards '76: 10 Best Films of the Year. **VHS, Beta, LV $34.98** MCA 𝔛𝔛𝔛

Seven Samurai Kurosawa's masterpiece, set in 16th-century Japan. A small farming village, beset by marauding bandits, hires seven professional soldiers to rid itself of the scourge. Wanna watch a samurai movie? This is the one. Sweeping, complex human drama with all the ingredients: action, suspense, comedy. Available in several ver-

sions of varying length, all long—and all too short. Splendid acting. In Japanese with English subtitles. *AKA:* Shichinin No Samurai; The Magnificent Seven.
1954 204m/B JP Toshiro Mifune, Takashi Shimura, Yoshio Inaba, Kuninori Kodo; *D:* Akira Kurosawa. Academy Awards '56 Nominations: Best Art Direction/Set Decoration (B & W), Best Costume Design (B & W); Venice Film Festival '54: Silver Prize. **VHS, Beta, LV, 3/4U, Special order formats $24.95** NOS, SUE, HHT �►☄☄

Seven Sinners A South Seas cabaret singer (Dietrich) attracts sailors like flies, resulting in bar brawls, romance, and intrigue. Manly sailor Wayne falls for her. A good-natured, standard Hollywood adventure. Well cast; performed and directed with gusto. *AKA:* Cafe of the Seven Sinners.
1940 83m/B Marlene Dietrich, John Wayne, Albert Dekker, Broderick Crawford, Mischa Auer, Billy Gilbert, Oscar Homolka; *D:* Tay Garnett. **VHS, Beta $16.95** SNC, NOS, KRT ☄☄☄

Seven Sixgunners A western from the book by Nelson Nye.
1987 60m/C *D:* George Potter; *W:* Nelson Nye. **VHS** NO ☄☄

Seven Thieves Charming performances and nice direction make this tale of the perfect crime especially watchable. Robinson, getting on in years, wants one last big heist. With the help of Collins and Steiger, he gets his chance. From the Max Catto novel "Lions at the Kill." Surprisingly witty and light-hearted for this subject matter, and good still comes out ahead of evil.
1960 102m/C Joan Collins, Edward G. Robinson, Eli Wallach, Rod Steiger; *D:* Henry Hathaway. **VHS $39.98** FOX, FCT ☄☄☄

The Seven-Ups An elite group of New York City detectives seeks to avenge the killing of a colleague and to bust crooks whose felonies are punishable by jail terms of seven years or more. Unoriginal premise portends ill; plotless cop action flick full of car chases. Scheider tries hard. Directed by the producer of "The French Connection."
1973 (PG) 109m/C Roy Scheider, Tony LoBianco, Larry Haines, Jerry Leon; *D:* Phil D'Antoni. **VHS, Beta, LV $59.98** FOX ☄½

The Seven Year Itch Classic, sexy Monroe comedy. Stunning blonde model (who else?) moves upstairs just as happily married guy Ewell's wife leaves for a long vacation. Understandably, he gets itchy. Monroe's famous blown skirt scene is here, as well as funny situations and appealing performances.
1955 105m/C Marilyn Monroe, Tom Ewell, Evelyn Keyes, Sonny Tufts, Victor Moore, Doro Merande, Robert Strauss, Oscar Homolka, Carolyn Jones; *D:* Billy Wilder. **VHS, Beta, LV $14.98** FOX ☄☄☄

Seven Years Bad Luck French comic Linder has the proverbial seven years' bad luck all in one day (!) after he breaks a mirror. Original and quite funny; full of fetching sophisticated sight gags. Silent with music score.
1920 67m/B Max Linder. **VHS, Beta $16.95** GPV, VYY ☄☄☄

1776 A musical comedy about America's first Continental Congress. The delegates battle the English and each other trying to establish a set of laws and the Declaration of Independence. Adapted from the Broadway hit with many members of the original cast. Available in widescreen format on laserdisc. ♫The Lees of Old Virginia; He Plays the Violin; But, Mr. Adams; Sit Down John; Till Then; Piddle, Twiddle and Resolve; Yours, Yours, Yours; Mama, Look Sharp; The Egg; Is Anybody There?; Molasses to Rum.

1972 (G) 141m/C William Daniels, Howard da Silva, Ken Howard, Donald Madden, Blythe Danner, Ronald Holgate, Virginia Vestoff, Stephen Nathan, Ralston Hill; *D:* Peter Hunt. Academy Awards '72 Nominations: Best Cinematography; National Board of Review Awards '72: 10 Best Films of the Year. **VHS, Beta, LV $19.95** COL, PIA, FCT ☄☄☄

The Seventeenth Bride Set in a Czechoslovakian town; a strong-willed young woman is slowly destroyed by the insanity of war and racism.
1984 92m/C Lisa Hartman, Rosemary Leach; *D:* Israeli Nadav Levitan. **VHS $79.95** SVS ☄☄

Seventh Cavalry A somewhat different look at Custer's defeat at the Little Big Horn. A soldier who was branded a coward for not taking part in the festivities tries to assuage his guilt by heading up the burial detail. The muddled ending tries to tell us that the Indians were afraid of Custer's horse.
1956 75m/C Randolph Scott, Barbara Hale, Jay C. Flippen, Jeanette Nolan, Frank Faylen, Leo Gordon, Denver Pyle, Harry Carey Jr., Michael Pate, Donald Curtis, Frank Wilcox, Pat Hogan, Russell Hicks; *D:* Joseph H. Lewis. **VHS $19.95** NOS ☄☄½

The 7th Commandment Unlikely melodrama about a man afflicted with amnesia following an auto accident. He becomes a successful evangelist only to be blackmailed by an old girlfriend. Don't you just hate when that happens?
1961 82m/B Jonathan Kidd, Lynn Statten; *D:* Irvin Berwick. **VHS $15.95** NOS, LOO ☄½

The Seventh Cross Tracy stars as one of seven men who escape from a German concentration camp. When it is discovered they're gone, the commandant nails seven crosses to seven trees, intending them for the seven escapees. Watch for Tandy ("Driving Miss Daisy") in her first screen appearance. Effective war-time drama. From the novel by Anna Seghers.
1944 110m/B Spencer Tracy, Signe Hasso, Hume Cronyn, Jessica Tandy, Agnes Moorehead, Herbert Rudley, Felix Bressart, Ray Collins, Alexander Granach, George Macready, Steve Geray, Karen Verne, George Zucco; *D:* Fred Zinneman. **VHS $19.98** MGM ☄☄☄

The Seventh Seal As the plague sweeps through Europe a weary knight convinces "death" to play one game of chess with him. If the knight wins, he and his wife will be spared. The game leads to a discussion of religion and the existence of God. Considered by some Bergman's masterpiece. Von Sydow is stunning as the knight. In Swedish with English subtitles. Also available on laserdisc with a filmography of Bergman's work and commentary by film historian Peter Cowie. *AKA:* Det Sjunde Inseglet.
1956 96m/B SW Gunnar Bjornstrand, Max von Sydow, Bibi Andersson, Bengt Ekerot, Nils Poppe, Gunnel Lindblom; *D:* Ingmar Bergman. **VHS, Beta, LV, 8mm $19.95** VDM, SUE, VYG ☄☄☄☄

The Seventh Sign A pregnant woman realizes that the mysterious stranger boarding in her house and the bizarre events that accompany him are connected to Biblical prophesy and her unborn child. Tries hard, but it's difficult to get involved in the supernatural goings-on.
1988 (R) 105m/C Demi Moore, Juergen Prochnow, Michael Biehn, John Heard, Peter Friedman, Manny Jacobs, John Taylor, Lee Garlington, Akosua Busia; *D:* Carl Schultz; *M:* Jack Nitzsche. **VHS, Beta, LV $14.95** COL ☄☄

Seventh Veil A concert pianist loses the use of her hands in a fire, and with it her desire to live. Through the help of her friends and a hypnotizing doctor, she regains her love for life. Superb, dark psycho-drama. Todd as the pianist and Mason as her guardian are both unforgettable. Wonderful music and staging.
1946 91m/B GB James Mason, Ann Todd, Herbert Lom, Hugh McDermott, Albert Lieven; *D:* Compton Bennett. **VHS, Beta $29.95** VID ☄☄☄½

The Seventh Victim Another Val Lewton-produced low-budget exercise in shadowy suggestion, dealing with a woman searching for her lost sister, who'd gotten involved with Satanists. The Hays Office's squeamishness regarding subject matter makes the film's action a bit cloudy but it remains truly eerie.
1943 71m/B Kim Hunter, Tom Conway, Jean Brooks, Hugh Beaumont, Erford Gage, Isabel Jewell, Evelyn Brent; *D:* Mark Robson. **VHS, Beta, LV $14.95** RKO, TTC ☄☄☄

The Seventh Voyage of Sinbad Sinbad seeks to restore his fiancee from the midget size to which an evil magician (Thatcher) has reduced her. Ray Harryhausen works his animation magic around a well-developed plot and engaging performances by the real actors. Herrmann's score is great, as is fun, fast-moving plot.
1958 (G) 94m/C Kerwin Mathews, Kathryn Grant, Torin Thatcher, Richard Eyer; *D:* Nathan Juran; *W:* Kenneth Kolb; *M:* Bernard Herrmann. **VHS, Beta, LV $14.95** COL, MLB, CCB ☄☄☄

Severance An ex-pilot attempts to save his daughter from the world of drugs and violence.
1988 93m/C Lou Liotta, Lisa Nicole Wolpe, Linda Christian-Jones; *D:* David Max Steinberg. **VHS, Beta $79.95** MNG ☄

The Severed Arm Trapped in a cave, five men are compelled to cut off the arm of a companion in order to ward off starvation. Then as luck would have it, they're rescued. Years later, one-by-one they meet a bloody demise. Is it the one-armed man?
1973 (R) 89m/C Deborah Walley, Marvin Kaplan, Paul Carr, John Crawford, David Cannon; *D:* Thomas Alderman. **VHS, Beta $59.95** GEM, MRV Woof!

Severed Ties Brilliant genetic scientist experiments with human limb regeneration in order to re-grow his accidentally severed arm. His strange mixture of lizard and serial-killer genes results in a repulsive reptilian limb with a nasty habit of slithering out of his shoulder. His mother discovers his experiments and tries to sell his discovery to the Nazis but her son escapes into a bizarre subterranean society and vows revenge. So bad it's just bad.
1992 (R) 95m/C Billy Morrissette, Elke Sommer, Oliver Reed, Garrett Morris; *D:* Damon Santostefano. **VHS $89.95** COL ☄½

Sewing Woman The story of the life of a Chinese woman who uses her sewing machine to represent the passage of time.
1981 60m/C VHS, Beta NO ☄½

Sex Interesting dated relic. Morality play about a Broadway star who uses her charms to destroy a marriage only to dump her lover for richer prospects. The businessman she lands then shamelessly betrays her. What a title, especially for its time!
1920 87m/B Adrienne Renault, Louise Glaum, Irving Cummings, Peggy Pearce, Myrtle Stedman; *D:* Fred Niblo. **VHS, Beta $19.98** CCB, GPV ☄☄½

Sex Adventures of the Three Musketeers Soft-core spoof of the Dumas classic. Dubbed.

198? 79m/C Inga Steeger, Achim Hammer, Peter Graf, Jurg Coray. **VHS, Beta** $29.95 *MED Woof!*

Sex and Buttered Popcorn Stylish and entertaining documentary of the Hollywood sexploitation moguls, and their films, from the 1920s through the 1950s. These films shamelessly catered to audience's prurient interests, but typically delivered saccharin-coated morality messages and stock footage of routine baby births or the horrible effects of sexually transmitted diseases. Hosted by Ned Beatty, and featuring clips from the actual films, plus an interview with the widow of Kroger Babb, the most notorious of the exploiteers. A real hoot.
1991 (R) 70m/C David Friedman; *D:* Sam Harrison. **VHS** $29.95 *CPM, FCT Woof!*

Sex and the College Girl Folks talk about their relationship problems while vacationing in Puerto Rico. Tame talkfest providing Grodin with his first role. Included as part of Joe Bob Brigg's "Sleaziest Movies in the History of the World" series, probably just for the title.
1964 ?m/C Charles Grodin, Richard Arlen, Luana Anders; *D:* Joseph Adler. **VHS** *SVI √*

Sex and the Office Girl Advertising agency turns into an after-hours pleasure dome of erotic complications.
197? 76m/C **VHS, Beta** $19.95 *MED √*

Sex and the Other Woman A series of vignettes depicting how women manipulate men into sexual submission.
1979 (R) 80m/C Richard Wattis, Maggie Wright, Felicity Devonshire, Jane Carder. **VHS, Beta** $69.95 *VID √*

Sex and the Single Girl Curtis is a reporter for a trashy magazine who intends to write an expose on "The International Institute of Advanced Marital and Pre-Marital Studies," an organization run by Wood. Curtis poses as a man having marital trouble, using his neighbor's name and marital problems, in order to get close to Wood. Things get sticky when Wood wants to meet Curtis' wife and three women show up claiming to be her. This confusing but amusing tale twists and turns until it reaches a happy ending. Loosely based on the book by Helen Gurley Brown.
1964 114m/C Tony Curtis, Natalie Wood, Henry Fonda, Lauren Bacall, Mel Ferrer, Fran Jeffries, Leslie Parrish, Edward Everett Horton, Larry Storch; *D:* Richard Quine; *M:* Count Basie. **VHS, LV** $19.98 *WAR √√½*

Sex and the Single Parent St. James and Farrell, both divorced, both with kids, have a relationship. Complications set in—just how does one be a single parent and have a fulfilling sex life in this day and age? Some of these made for TV efforts are so formulaic!
1982 98m/C Susan St. James, Mike Farrell, Dori Brenner, Warren Berlinger, Julie Sommars, Barbara Rhoades; *D:* Jackie Cooper. **VHS, Beta** *TLF √√½*

Sex Appeal Another smut comedy depicting the sex-gathering adventures of a horny young man.
1986 (R) 84m/C Brian Bonanno, Tally Brittany, Marcia Karr, Jerome Brenner, Marie Sawyer, Philip Campanaro, Jeff Eagle, Gloria Leonard, Molly Morgan; *D:* Chuck Vincent. **VHS, Beta** $79.98 *LIV, VES √*

Sex Crimes A tough female judge is brutally raped and she keeps the attack a secret. However, she does ask a friendly police detective to teach her how to use a gun. He's suspicious of her reasons and decides to trail her as she sets out for revenge on her attacker. Predictable actioner.
1992 90m/C Jeffery Osterhage, Maria Richwine, Fernando Garzon, Craig Alan, Grace Morley; *D:* David Garcia. **VHS** $89.95 *ATV √√*

Sex, Drugs, and Rock-n-Roll Several girls frequent a rock club looking for all the action they can get their hands on.
1984 90m/C Jeanne Silver, Sharon Kane, Tish Ambrose, Josey Duval. **VHS, Beta** *NO Woof!*

sex, lies and videotape Acclaimed, popular independent film by first-timer Soderbergh, detailing the complex relations among a childless married couple, the wife's adulterous sister, and a mysterious college friend of the husband's obsessed with videotaping women as they talk about their sex lives. Heavily awarded, including first prize at Cannes. Confidently uses much (too much?) dialogue and slow (too slow?) pace. Available on laserdisc with a deleted scene and interviews with the director; also includes two theatrical trailers and a short film by Soderbergh.
1989 (R) 101m/C James Spader, Andie MacDowell, Peter Gallagher, Laura San Giacomo, Ron Vawter, Steven Brill; *D:* Steven Soderberg. Academy Awards '89 Nominations: Best Original Screenplay; Cannes Film Festival '89: Best Actor (Spader), Best Film; Independent Spirit Awards '90: Best Actress (MacDowell), Best Director (Soderberg), Best Film, Best Supporting Actress (San Giacomo). **VHS, Beta, LV, 8mm** $19.95 *COL, VYG √√√*

The Sex Machine In the year 2037, a scientist finds two of the world's greatest lovers and unites them so he can transform their reciprocating motion into electricity. It worked on paper.
1976 (R) 80m/C Agostina Belli. **VHS, Beta** $19.95 *MED Woof!*

Sex Madness Then—deadly serious, now—campy educational melodrama about the "madness" of sex and the peril of syphilis. Quaint, to say the least, in view of all that has intervened—and all the onscreen sex—since 1937.
1937 50m/B **VHS, Beta** $19.95 *NOS, HHT, MRV Woof!*

Sex O'Clock News Fervently paced series of comedy skits. Made for television. Meant to be zany and ireverent; succeeds only in being dull and dorky.
1985 (R) 80m/C Doug Ballard, Lydia Mahan, Wayne Knight, Don Pardo, Kate Weiman, Joy Bond; *D:* Roman Vanderbes. **VHS, Beta** $79.95 *PSM √*

Sex on the Brain A PhD student gets a little too involved with her research on prostitution.
197? 90m/C Pilar Velasquez. **VHS, Beta** $59.95 *MPI √√*

Sex on the Run Love-starved wife of an oil-rich sheik, stimulated by the idea of having Casanova for her lover, teases her master into delivering him, but Casanova finds peace in the arms of three convent lovelies. Disgusting, amateurish, and offensive. *AKA:* Cassanova and Co.; Some Like it Cool.
1978 (R) 88m/C Tony Curtis, Marisa Berenson, Britt Ekland; *D:* Francois Legrand. **VHS, Beta, LV** $69.95 *VES Woof!*

Sex Ray Inexplicable light ray zaps everyone's clothing and trepidations. A sex frolic ensues.
19?? 90m/C **VHS** *NO Woof!*

Sex Surrogate A psychologist/sex surrogate gets very involved in her work.
1988 81m/C Marilyn Chambers. **Beta** *NO Woof!*

Sex Through a Window TV reporter becomes an obsessive voyeur after filing a report on high tech surveillance equipment. Flimsy premise is a yucky, lame excuse to show skin. *AKA:* Extreme Close-Up.
1972 (R) 81m/C James McMullan, James A. Watson Jr., Kate Woodville, Bara Byrnes, Al Checco, Antony Carbone; *D:* Jeannot Szwarc. **VHS, Beta** $69.98 *LIV, VES √*

Sex with a Smile Five slapstick episodes by five different directors with lots of sexual satire pointed at religion and politics in Italy. Don't know much about Italy? Then you'll be left out of the joke here. And really, only one episode is funny anyway (the one with Feldman of "Young Frankenstein" fame).
1976 (R) 100m/C *IT* Marty Feldman, Edwige Fenech, Alex Marino, Enrico Monterrano, Giovanna Ralli; *D:* Sergio Martino. **VHS, Beta** $59.95 *GEM √*

Sex with the Stars In order to get a feel for his newspaper column, a horoscope writer conducts interviews with a beautiful woman born under each astrological sign.
1981 90m/C Martin Burrows, Faith Davkin, Suzannah Willis, Jada; *D:* Anwar Kawadri. **VHS, Beta** $19.98 *TWE √*

Sexcetera A Playboy Video program featuring sex-related news items.
1984 63m/C **VHS, Beta** $59.98 *FOX √*

Sexo Y Crimen Two lovers find themselves inextricably tangled in a violent situation.
1987 90m/C *MX* Enrique Lizalde, Emily Cranz, Enrique Rambal, Yoland Ciani. **VHS, Beta** $54.95 *MAD √√*

Sexpot A voluptuous woman's rich husbands mysteriously keep dying, but not before they leave their fortunes to her.
1988 (R) 95m/C Ruth Collins, Troy Donahue, Joyce Lyons, Gregory Patrick, Frank Stewart, Jack Carter; *D:* Chuck Vincent. **VHS, Beta** $29.95 *ACA √*

Sextette Lavish film about an elderly star who is constantly interrupted by former spouses and well-wishers while on a honeymoon with her sixth husband. West unwisely came out of retirement for this last film role, based on her own play. Exquisitely embarrassing to watch. Interesting cast.
1978 (PG) 91m/C Mae West, Timothy Dalton, Ringo Starr, George Hamilton, Dom DeLuise, Tony Curtis, Alice Cooper, Keith Moon, George Raft, Rona Barrett, Walter Pidgeon; *D:* Ken Hughes. **VHS, Beta** $9.95 *MED, MLB Woof!*

Sexton Blake and the Hooded Terror Sexton Blake a British private detective a la Holmes, is after "The Snake," a master criminal, and his gang The Hooded Terror. One of a series of melodramatic adventures interesting chiefly for Slaughter's performance as the gangleader.
1938 70m/B *GB* Tod Slaughter, Greta Gynt, George Culzon, George King. **VHS, Beta** $29.95 *SNC, VYY, MRV √√*

Sexual Response Eve, a radio talk show "sexologist," is ironically unhappy in her marriage but scoffs at her producer's suggestion of an affair. That is until she meets a brash sculptor and they begin a torrid, and increasingly obsessive, romance. Her lover suggests that her husband have an "accident" with his hunting rifle, but Eve refuses and throws him out. The sculptor, however, breaks into the husband's loft to steal the rifle and finds some news clippings about the man's past that could ruin the lives of many. Little more than an excuse for torrid love scenes. Also available in an unrated version.

1992 (R) 87m/C Shannon Tweed, Catherine Oxenberg, Vernon Wells, Emile Levisetti; **D:** Yaky Yosha. VHS, LV $19.95 COL *ℐℐ*

Shack Out on 101 A waitress (Moore) in an isolated cafe on a busy highway notices suspicious doings among her customers. What could they be up to? Communist subversion, of course. Of-its-era anti-pinko propoganda, but with a twist: Moore uncovers commie plots, pleases her customers, and fends off unwelcome lecherous advances all in 80 minutes, on a single set! 1955 80m/B Lee Marvin, Terry Moore, Keenan Wynn, Frank Lovejoy, Whit Bissell; **D:** Edward Dein. VHS $29.95 REP *ℐℐ*

Shades of Love: Champagne for Two I really love him—but I want a career too! What's a gal to do? Vintage eighties yuppie self-involvement brought to the big screen. 1987 80m/C Kirsten Bishop, Nicholas Campbell. VHS, Beta $9.98 LHV, WAR *ℐ½*

Shades of Love: Echoes in Crimson Woman must deal with new career at art gallery and former lover who wants her back. 1987 90m/C Greg Evigan, Patty Talbot. VHS $9.98 LHV, WAR *ℐℐ*

Shades of Love: The Ballerina & the Blues A ballerina attempts to start her own dance company but runs into trouble when she must choose between two loves. 1987 90m/C Rex Smith, Tamara Chaplin. VHS $9.98 LHV, WAR *ℐℐ*

Shadey The premise for this oddball comedy came to someone in the wee hours: I've got it! Mild-mannered mechanic can film people's thoughts; wants to use his gift only for good, but needs money for a sex-change operation. Assorted bad guys want to use him for evil purposes. Strange, but not bad; Helmond's character is memorable. 1987 (PG-13) 90m/C GB Anthony Sher, Billie Whitelaw, Patrick Macnee, Katherine Helmond; **D:** Philip Saville. VHS, Beta $79.98 FOX *ℐℐ½*

The Shadow Scotland Yard pulls out all the stops to track down a murderous extortionist, enlisting the aid of a novelist in their efforts. Long on talk and short on action. 1936 63m/B GB Henry Kendall, Elizabeth Allan, Jeanne Stuart, Felix Aylmer, Cyril Raymond; **D:** George Cooper. VHS, Beta $16.95 NOS, SNC *ℐ½*

The Shadow Box Three terminally ill people at a California hospice confront their destinies. Pulitzer Prize-winning play by Michael Cristofer is actually improved by director Newman and a superb, well-chosen cast. Powerful. 1980 96m/C Joanne Woodward, Christopher Plummer, Robert Urich, Valerie Harper, Sylvia Sidney, Melinda Dillon, Ben Masters, John Considine, James Broderick; **D:** Paul Newman. VHS, Beta KAR *ℐℐℐ*

Shadow Dancing The proprietor of the auspicious Beaumont Theater of Dance is haunted by one of his former dancers who died unexpectedly during a performance of "Medusa." Now, over fifty years later, Jessica, the pick for the lead in a new production, begins to take on her predecessor's mannerisms and spirit as she faces her impending doom. Surprisingly believable and suspenseful—and scary! 1988 (PG) 100m/C Nadine Van Der Velde, James Kee, John Colicos, Shirley Douglas, Christopher Plummer; **D:** John Furey. VHS, Beta $89.95 SGE *ℐℐℐ*

Shadow Force Homicide detective Rick Kelly is investigating the murders of a district attorney and a police sergeant. With the help of Mary, the usual beautiful female journalist, he uncovers a plot to assassinate key law enforcement officers. 1992 ?m/C Dirk Benedict, Lance LeGault, Lise Cutter, Jack Elam, Glenn Corbett, Bob Hastings; **D:** Darrell Davenport. VHS $89.95 IMP *ℐ½*

Shadow Killers There's no time to fear your own shadow, for there is a far more terrifying darkness stalking the city. 1980 90m/C Chen Ching, Chang Wu Lang, Chen Chiang. VHS, Beta NO *ℐ½*

The Shadow Man A casino operator in London (Romero) is accused of killing a former girlfriend and works to clear himself. Family conventional action mystery: nothing to write home about. **AKA:** Street of Shadows. 1953 76m/B GB Cesar Romero, Simone Silva, Kay Kendall, John Penrose, Edward Underdown; **D:** Richard Vernon. VHS, Beta, LV NO *ℐℐ*

Shadow Man A mysterious thief, a master of disguise, sets out to steal the Treasure of the Knights Templar and nothing will stand in his way. 1975 (PG) 89m/C Josephine Chaplin, Gert Frobe, Gayle Hunnicutt. VHS, Beta $59.95 MED *ℐℐ*

Shadow of a Doubt Uncle Charlie has come to visit his relatives in Santa Rosa. Although he is handsome and charming, his young niece slowly comes to realize he is a wanted mass murderer - and he comes to recognize her suspicions. Hitchcock's personal favorite movie; a quietly creepy venture into Middle American menace. Good performances, especially by Cronyn. Co-written by Thornton Wilder, and score by Dmitri Tiomkin. From the story by Gordon McConnell. 1943 108m/B Teresa Wright, Joseph Cotten, Hume Cronyn, MacDonald Carey, Henry Travers, Wallace Ford; **D:** Alfred Hitchcock. VHS, Beta, LV $19.95 MCA *ℐℐℐ½*

Shadow of Chikara A Confederate Army Captain and an orphan girl encounter unexpected adventures as they search for a fortune in diamonds hidden in a river in northern Arkansas. **AKA:** Thunder Mountain; The Curse of Demon Mountain. 1977 (PG) 96m/C Joe Don Baker, Sondra Locke, Ted Neely, Slim Pickens. VHS, Beta, LV $19.95 STE, NWV *ℐ*

Shadow of China A young man struggles for power and love in Hong Kong, while an English beauty and an Oriental activist hold the keys to his future and a past which could destroy him. Excellent acting, stunning location photography. Exotic and intense. Based on the Japanese best-seller "Snakehead." 1991 (PG-13) 100m/C John Lone, Sammi Davis-Voss, Vivian Wu; **D:** Mitsuo Yanagimachi. VHS, LV $89.99 COL, NLC *ℐℐℐ*

Shadow of Chinatown Mad scientist creates wave of murder and terror in Chinatown. 1936 70m/B Bela Lugosi, Herman Brix, Joan Barclay. VHS, Beta $27.95 NOS, SNC, VCN *ℐ½*

Shadow of the Eagle The intrigue and mystery of carnival life. Twelve chapters, 13 minutes each. 1932 226m/B John Wayne, Dorothy Gulliver; **D:** Ford Beebe. VHS, Beta $24.95 NOS, VYY, VCN *ℐ½*

Shadow of the Thin Man In the fourth "Thin Man" film, following "Another Thin Man," Nick and Nora stumble onto a murder at the racetrack. The rapport between Powell and Loy is still going strong, providing us with some wonderful entertainment. Followed by "The Thin Man Goes Home." 1941 97m/B William Powell, Myrna Loy, Barry Nelson, Donna Reed, Sam Levene, Alan Baxter, Dickie Hall, Loring Smith, Joseph Anthony, Henry O'Neill; **D:** Woodbridge S. Van Dyke. VHS, Beta $19.98 MGM *ℐℐℐ*

Shadow of the Wolf Phillips is as Agaguk, the son of the village leader, in this epic saga of survival set against the wilderness of the Arctic. Agaguk decides he cannot accept the white man's intrusion, so he sets out on his own. His father believes his departure to be the ultimate betrayal and casts upon him the "curse of the white wolf." Now Agaguk and his companion (Tilly) must face the harsh tundra alone and struggle to stay alive in the Great White North. Based on the novel "Agaguk" by Yves Theriault. 1992 (PG-13) 108m/C Lou Diamond Phillips, Donald Sutherland, Jennifer Tilly, Toshiro Mifune; **D:** Jacques Dorfman; **W:** Rudy Wurlitzer, Evan Jones. VHS, LV COL *ℐℐ*

Shadow on the Sun The life of Beryl Markham, pioneer female aviator and adventurer of the 1930s. Way too long and boring made for TV answer to "Out of Africa." On two cassettes. 1988 192m/C Stefanie Powers, Claire Bloom, Frederic Forrest, James Fox, John Rubinstein, Jack Thompson; **D:** Tony Richardson. VHS $29.95 STE, NWV *ℐ½*

Shadow Play A successful female playwright is haunted by visions of a past lover. Her life slowly falls apart, but not before this film does. 1986 (R) 98m/C Dee Wallace Stone, Cloris Leachman; **D:** Susan Shadburne. VHS, Beta $19.95 STE, NWV *ℐ½*

The Shadow Riders Two brothers who fought on opposite sides during the Civil War return home to find their brother's fiancee kidnapped by a renegade Confederate officer who plans to use her as ransom in a prisoner exchange, and they set out to rescue the woman. Preceded by "The Sacketts" and based on the works of Louis L'Amour. Made for television. **AKA:** Louis L'Amour's "The Shadow Riders". 1982 (PG) 96m/C Tom Selleck, Sam Elliott, Ben Johnson, Katharine Ross, Jeffery Osterhage, Gene Evans, R.G. Armstrong, Marshall Teague, Dominique Dunne, Joanetta Arnetta; **D:** Andrew V. McLaglen. VHS $79.98 VMK *ℐℐ*

The Shadow Strikes Adaptation of the radio serial. The sleuth pursues a killer and a gangster. Meanwhile, the police try to pin a robbery on the "Shadow." Who did it? The Shadow knows! 1937 61m/B Rod LaRocque, Lynn Anders. VHS, Beta, 3/4U, Special order formats $16.95 SNC, NOS, CAB *ℐ½*

Shadow World A small boy transforms himself into a superhero and battles alien evil. Animated. 1983 77m/C VHS, Beta $9.95 MED, WTA *ℐ*

Shadowhunter Glenn stars as a burned-out big city detective who is sent to a Navajo reservation in Arizona to bring a murder suspect back to Los Angeles. When the alleged killer escapes custody Glenn must track him across forbidding desert territory and face his suspect's unusual mystical powers. 1993 (R) 98m/C Scott Glenn. VHS, LV $89.98 REP *ℐℐ*

Shadowlands A look at the later life of bachelor-scholar C.S. Lewis. A devout proponent of Christianity, the middle-aged Lewis fell in love and married Joy Gresham, a divorced American poet with two young sons. Joy was diagnosed with cancer and her illness provided Lewis with the clearest test of his faith. Wonderful performances by both Ackland and Bloom. *AKA*: C.S. Lewis Through the Shadowlands.
1985 90m/C GB Joss Ackland, Claire Bloom, Rupert Baderman; *D:* Norman Stone. **VHS** **$29.95** *FRV, VGD, KAR ������*

Shadows A Chinese laundryman (Chaney) lives with a group of his countrymen in a New England seacoast village. All is peaceful until the local minister decides to convert the "heathen" Chinese. Ludicrous but worth seeing for Chaney's fun performance. Silent with music score.
1922 70m/B Lon Chaney Sr., Harrison Ford. **VHS, Beta, 8mm $16.95** *SNC, NOS, CCB ������*

Shadows and Fog Offbeat, unpredictable Allen film that is little more than an exercise in expressionistic visual stylings. The action centers around a haunted, alienated clerk (Allen) who is awakened in the middle of the night to join a vigilante group searching the streets for a killer. Although reminiscent of a silent film, Carlo Di Palma's black and white cinematography is stunning. Several stars appear briefly throughout this extremely unfocused comedy.
1992 (PG-13) 85m/C Woody Allen, Kathy Bates, John Cusack, Mia Farrow, Jodie Foster, Fred Gwynne, Julie Kavner, Madonna, John Malkovich, Kenneth Mars, Kate Nelligan, Donald Pleasence, Lily Tomlin, Philip Bosco, Robert Joy, Wallace Shawn, Kurtwood Smith, Josef Sommer, David Ogden, Michael Kirby, Anne Lange; *W/D:* Woody Allen. **VHS, LV $67.40** *ORI ������*

Shadows in the Storm A librarian/poet retreats to a secluded forest after losing his job. There he meets an exotically beautiful young woman who becomes his lover. With her love, she brings blackmail, murder, and mystery.
1988 (R) 90m/C Ned Beatty, Mia Sara, Michael Madsen; *D:* Terrell Tannen. **VHS, LV** *VMK ������*

Shadows of Death Crabbe is the hero who must track down a gang of outlaws who kill to grab the land along the path of a new railroad. One of the "Billy Carson" series.
1945 60m/B Buster Crabbe, Al "Fuzzy" St. John. **VHS, Beta $27.95** *VCN, UHV ������*

Shadows of Forgotten Ancestors Set in rural Russia in the early 20th century. Brings to expressive life the story of a man whose entire life has been overtaken by tragedy. Folk drama about a peasant who falls in with the daughter of his father's killer, then marries another woman. Strange, resonant and powerful with distinctive camera work. In Ukrainian with English subtitles. *AKA*: Tini Zabutykh Predkiv; Shadows of Our Ancestors; Shadows of Our Forgotten Ancestors.
1964 99m/C RU Ivan Micholaichuk, Larisa Kadochnikova; *D:* Sergei Paradjanov. **VHS, Beta $29.95** *CVC, TAM, AUD ������*

Shadows of the Orient Two detectives are out to smash a Chinese smuggling ring.
1937 70m/B Regis Toomey, Esther Ralston. **VHS $16.95** *SNC, NOS, DVT ������*

Shadows on the Stairs A creepy boarding house is the scene of a number of mystery-drenched murders. A bizarre assortment of suspects make things even crazier.

1941 63m/B Frieda Inescort, Paul Cavanagh, Heather Angel, Bruce Lester, Miles Mander, Lumsden Hare, Turhan Bey; *D:* Ross Lederman. **VHS, Beta $16.95** *SNC ������*

Shadows Over Shanghai This adventure relic was set during the Japanese invasion of China prior to WWII and uses much newsreel footage of that infamy. As for the plot, it's a groaner about good guys and bad skulking around the eponymous port in search of a treasure.
1938 66m/B James Dunn, Ralph Morgan, Linda Gray, Robert Barratt, Paul Sutton, Edward Woods; *D:* Charles Lamont. **VHS $19.95** *NOS, LOO ������*

Shadows Run Black A police detective must save a college coed from the clutches of a maniac wielding a meat cleaver. Ordinary slash-em-up. Bet Costner's embarrassed now about this early role - like Stallone's porno role in "The Italian Stallion."
1984 89m/C William J. Kulzer, Elizabeth Trosper, Kevin Costner; *D:* Howard Heard. **VHS, Beta** *NO ������*

Shadowzone As a result of NASA experiments in dream travel, an interdimensional monster invades our world in search of victims. Begins well, with slightly interesting premise, but degenerates into typical monster flick. Good special effects.
1990 88m/C Louise Fletcher, David Beecroft, James Hong, Shawn Weatherly, Lu Leonard; *D:* J.S. Cardone. **VHS, Beta, LV $19.95** *PAR ������*

Shaft A black private eye is hired to find a Harlem gangster's kidnapped daughter. Lotsa sex and violence; suspenseful and well directed. Great ending. Academy Award winning theme song by Isaac Hayes, the first music award from the Academy to an African American. Adapted from the novel by Ernest Tidyman. Followed by "Shaft's Big Score" and "Shaft in Africa."
1971 (R) 98m/C Richard Roundtree, Moses Gunn, Charles Cioffi; *D:* Gordon Parks. Academy Awards '71: Best Song ("Theme from Shaft"); Nominations: Best Original Score. **VHS, Beta $19.95** *MGM ������*

Shaft's Big Score This first sequel to the extremely successful "Shaft" has Roundtree's detective trying to mediate between several mobsters while investigating a friend's murder. Lots of action and an exciting Brooklyn chase scene involving cars, helicopters, and boats but still routine when compared to the original. Followed by "Shaft in Africa."
1972 (R) 105m/C Richard Roundtree, Moses Gunn, Joseph Macolo, Drew Bundi Brown, Wally Taylor, Kathy Imrie, Julius W. Harris, Rosalind Miles, Joe Santos; *D:* Gordon Parks; *W:* Ernest Tidyman; *M:* Gordon Parks. **VHS $19.98** *MGM ������*

Shag: The Movie The time is 1963, the setting Myrtle Beach, South Carolina, the latest craze shaggin' when four friends hit the beach for one last weekend together. Carson (Cates) is getting ready to marry staid Harley (Power); Melaina (Fonda) wants to be discovered in Hollywood; and Pudge (Gish) and Luanne (Hannah) are off to college. They encounter lots of music, boys, and dancing in this delightful film. Not to be confused with other "teen" movies, this one boasts a good script and an above average cast.
1989 (PG) 96m/C Phoebe Cates, Annabeth Gish, Bridget Fonda, Page Hannah, Scott Coffey, Robert Rusler, Tyrone Power Jr., Jeff Yagher, Carrie Hamilton; *D:* Zelda Barron; *W:* Robin Swicord, Lanier Laney, Terry Sweeney. **VHS, Beta, LV $89.99** *HBO ������*

The Shaggy D.A. Wilby Daniels is getting a little worried about his canine alter ego as he is about to run for District Attorney. Fun sequel to "The Shaggy Dog."
1976 (G) 90m/C Dean Jones, Tim Conway, Suzanne Pleshette, Keenan Wynn; *D:* Robert Stevenson. **VHS, Beta** *DIS, OM ������*

The Shaggy Dog When young Wilby Daniels utters some magical words from the inscription of an ancient ring he turns into a shaggy dog, causing havoc for family and neighbors. Disney slapstick is on target at times, though it drags in places. Followed by "The Shaggy D.A." and "Return of the Shaggy Dog."
1959 (G) 101m/B Fred MacMurray, Jean Hagen, Tommy Kirk, Annette Funicello, Tim Considine, Kevin Corcoran; *D:* Charles T. Barton. **VHS, Beta, LV $19.99** *DIS ������*

Shaka Zulu British miniseries depicting the career of Shaka, king of the Zulus (Cele). Set in the early 19th century during British ascendency in Africa. Good, absorbing cross-cultural action drama would have been better with more inspired directing by Faure.
1983 300m/C GB Edward Fox, Robert Powell, Trevor Howard, Christopher Lee, Fiona Fullerton, Henry Cele; *D:* William C. Faure. **VHS, Beta $14.99** *STE, PSM, FCT ������*

Shake Hands with Murder Three people spend their time bailing criminals out of jail for profit. One is murdered, and the other two become implicated in comedy.
1944 63m/B Iris Adrian, Frank Jenks, Douglas Fowley, Jack Raymond, Claire Rochelle, Herbert Rawlinson, Forrest Taylor; *D:* Albert Herman. **VHS, Beta $16.95** *SNC ������*

Shake Hands with the Devil It's the Irish Republican Army against the British Black and Tans as Ireland fights for independence in 1921. Cagney is a teaching surgeon who is secretly a militant, obsessed with the idea of gaining Irish freedom. He urges his students to join with him, which Irish-American Murray does. When Murray learns that Cagney is out to sabotage a peace treaty, he must decide whether to betray Cagney in order to stop further violence. Cagney is excellent as the hard-bitten revolutionary who can't see beyond his own ideals. Filmed on location in Dublin, which further heightens the film's tension.
1959 110m/B James Cagney, Don Murray, Dana Wynter, Glynis Johns, Michael Redgrave, Sybil Thorndike, Harry Brogan, Robert Brown; *D:* Michael Anderson Sr. **VHS $19.98** *MGM ������*

Shake, Rattle and Rock A deejay wants to open a teen music club playing rock 'n' roll, which has all the conservative parents up in arms. A court case follows (which the kids win). Incidental plot to the great music by Fats Domino, Joe Turner, Annita Ray, and Tommy Charles. Songs include "Ain't It a Shame," "Honey Chile," "I'm in Love Again," "Feelin' Happy," and "Sweet Love on My Mind."
1957 76m/C Mike Connors, Lisa Gaye, Sterling Holloway, Margaret Dumont, Raymond Hatton, Douglas Dumbrille; *D:* Edward L. Cahn; *W:* Lou Rusoff. **VHS $9.95** *COL, MOV ������*

Shakedown Power-packed action film. An overworked attorney and an undercover cop work together to stop corruption in the N.Y.P.D. Although lacking greatly in logic or plot, the sensational stunts make this an otherwise entertaining action flick.
1988 (R) 96m/C Sam Elliott, Peter Weller, Patricia Charbonneau, Antonio Fargas, Blanche Baker, Richard Brooks, Jude Ciccolella, George Loros, Tom Waits, Shirley Stoler, Rockets Redglare; *D:* James Glickenhaus. **VHS, Beta, LV $19.98** *MCA ������*

Shaker Run A stunt car driver and his mechanic transport a mysterious package. They don't know what to do—they're carrying a deadly virus that every terrorist wants! Car chases galore, and not much else. However, if you like chase scenes...
1985 91m/C *NZ* Leif Garrett, Cliff Robertson, Lisa Harrow; *D:* Bruce Morrison. VHS, Beta, LV $19.98 *SUE, NLC* 🎞🎞½

Shakes the Clown Chronicles the rise and fall of Shakes, an alcoholic clown wandering through the all-clown town of Palukaville. Framed for the murder of his boss by his archrival, Binky, Shakes takes it on the lam in order to prove his innocence, aided by his waitress girlfriend Judy, who dreams of becoming a professional bowler. Meant as a satire of substance-abuse recovery programs and the supposed tragedies of a performer's life, the film is sometimes zany, but more often merely unpleasant and unamusing. Williams has an uncredited role as a mime.
1992 (R) 83m/C Bob Goldthwait, Julie Brown, Blake Clark, Adam Sandler, Tom Kenny, Sydney Lassick, Paul Dooley, Tim Kazurinsky, Florence Henderson, LaWanda Page; *Cameos:* Robin Williams; *W/D:* Bob Goldthwait. VHS, LV *COL* 🎞

Shakespeare Wallah Tender, plausible drama of romance and postcolonial relations in India. A troupe of traveling Shakespeareans quixotically tours India trying to make enough money to return to England. Wonderfully acted and exquisitely and sensitively directed by Ivory.
1965 120m/B Laura Liddell, Geoffrey Kendal, Felicity Kendal, Shashi Kapoor, Madhur Jaffrey; *W/D:* James Ivory; *W:* Ruth Prawer Jhabvala. VHS, Beta $29.98 *SUE, TAM, NLC* 🎞🎞🎞½

The Shakiest Gun in the West Don Knotts isn't Bob Hope, but he's pretty funny in the same bumbling way. Remake of Hope's "Paleface" has Philadelphia dentist Knotts unwittingly taking on bad guys and sultry Rhoades.
1968 101m/C Don Knotts, Barbara Rhoades, Jackie Coogan, Donald (Don "Red") Barry, Ruth McDevitt; *D:* Alan Rafkin. VHS, LV *MCA* 🎞🎞½

Shaking the Tree Group of four high school buddies are still in quest of self-fulfillment ten years after high school as they grapple with problems in the real world of adulthood, seeking distraction in adventure, romance, friendship and sex.
1992 (PG-13) 97m/C Arye Gross, Gale Hansen, Doug Savant, Courteney Cox; *D:* Duane Clark; *W:* Duane Clark, Steven Wilde. VHS $89.95 *ACA* 🎞🎞½

Shakma A group of medical researchers involved with experiments on animal and human tendencies toward aggression take a night off to play a quiet game of "Dungeons and Dragons." The horror begins when their main experimental subject comes along and turns things nasty!
1989 101m/C Roddy McDowall, Christopher Atkins, Amanda Wyss, Ari Meyers; *D:* Hugh Parks. VHS $29.95 *HHE* 🎞½

Shalako Connery/Bardot pairing promises something special, but fails to deliver. European aristocrats on a hunting trip in New Mexico, circa 1880, are menaced by Apaches. U.S. Army scout tries to save captured countess Bardot. Strange British attempt at a Euro-western. Poorly directed and pointless. Based on a Louis L'Amour story.
1968 113m/C Brigitte Bardot, Sean Connery, Stephen Boyd, Jack Blackman, Woody Strode, Alexander Knox; *D:* Edward Dmytryk. VHS, Beta $19.98 *FOX* 🎞🎞

Shall We Dance And shall we ever! Seventh Astaire-Rogers pairing has a famous ballet dancer and a musical-comedy star embark on a promotional romance and marriage, to boost their careers, only to find themselves truly falling in love. Score by George and Ira Gershwin includes memorable songs. Thin, lame plot—but that's okay. For fans of good singing and dancing, and especially of this immortal pair. 🎵Slap That Bass; Beginner's Luck; Let's Call the Whole Thing Off; Walking the Dog; They All Laughed; They Can't Take That Away From Me; Shall We Dance.
1937 116m/B Fred Astaire, Ginger Rogers, Edward Everett Horton, Eric Blore; *D:* Mark Sandrich; *M:* George Gershwin, Ira Gershwin. VHS, Beta, LV $14.98 *TTC, RKO, CCB* 🎞🎞🎞

Shallow Grave Four coeds en route to Florida witness a murder in rural Georgia and then are pursued relentlessly by the killer, a local sheriff. Decent premise and talented cast could have offered something better, given a meatier script.
1987 (R) 90m/C Tony March, Lisa Stahl, Tom Law, Carol Cadby; *D:* Richard Styles. VHS, Beta $14.95 *PSM, PAR* 🎞½

The Shaman Members of a family succumb to the hypnotic spell of the Shaman as he searches for the perfect one to inherit his powers.
1987 (R) 88m/C Michael Conforti, Elvind Harum, James Farkas, Lynn Weaver; *D:* Michael Yakub. VHS, Beta $79.95 *IMP* 🎞½

Shame Strangely unsuccessful low-budget Corman effort, starring pre-"Star Trek" Shatner as a freelance bigot who travels around Missouri stirring up opposition to desegregation. Moralistic and topical but still powerful. Adapted from the equally excellent novel by Charles Beaumont. Uses location filming superbly to render a sense of everydayness and authenticity. *AKA:* The Intruder; I Hate Your Guts; The Stranger.
1961 84m/B William Shatner, Frank Maxwell, Jeanne Cooper, Robert Emhardt, Leo Gordon; *D:* Roger Corman. VHS, Beta, LV $19.95 *NOS, DVT, FCT* 🎞🎞🎞½

The Shame A Bergman masterpiece focusing on the struggle for dignity in the midst of war. Married concert musicians Ullmann and von Sydow flee a bloody civil war for a small island off their country's coast. Inevitably, the carnage reaches them and their lives become a struggle to endure and retain a small measure of civilized behavior as chaos overtakes them. Deeply despairing and brilliantly acted. In Swedish with English subtitles.
1968 (R) 103m/C *SW* Max von Sydow, Liv Ullmann, Gunnar Bjornstrand, Sigge Furst, Brigitta Valberg, Hans Alfredson, Ingvar Kjellson; *W/D:* Ingmar Bergman. VHS $19.98 *MGM* 🎞🎞🎞

Shame Strange Australian revenge drama about a female lawyer/biker who rides into a small town and finds herself avenging the rape of a 16-year-old girl. Is it a genuinely feminist movie about justice and a strong woman taking charge? Or is it exploitative trash using a politically correct theme and "message" as a peg for much - very much - gratuitous violence? Hard to tell. Cultish for sure; made on a B budget.
1987 95m/C *AU* Deborra-Lee Furness, Tony Barry, Simone Buchanan, Gillian Jones; *D:* Steve Jodrell. VHS, LV $89.99 *REP* 🎞🎞

Shame of the Jungle Animated spoof on Tarzan featuring the voices of John Belushi, Bill Murray, and Johnny Weissmuller, Jr.

1990 (R) 73m/C *D:* Boris Szulzinger, Picha; *V:* Johnny Weissmuller Jr., John Belushi, Bill Murray, Brian Doyle-Murray, Christopher Guest, Andrew Duncan. VHS $79.95 *JEF* 🎞🎞

Shame, Shame on the Bixby Boys Somewhere in the Old West, outside a small town, lives a band of misfits who persist in rustling cattle. The Bixby Boys and their Pa have made a bad habit into a family tradition.
1982 90m/C Monte Markham, Sammy Jackson; *D:* Anthony Bowers. VHS, Beta *TLF* 🎞½

The Shaming Puritanical schoolteacher is raped by a janitor, then develops a voracious sexual appetite. Horrible script, offensive premise can't be saved by good cast. Based on a novel by William Inge. *AKA:* The Sin; Good Luck, Miss Wyckoff.
1971 (R) 90m/C Anne Heywood, Donald Pleasence, Robert Vaughn, Carolyn Jones; *D:* Marvin J. Chomsky. VHS, Beta $14.95 *QNE* 🎞½

Shampoo A satire of morals (and lack thereof) set in Southern California, concerning a successful hairdresser (Beatty) and the many women in his life. A notable scene with Julie Christie is set at a 1968 presidential election-night gathering. Fisher's screen debut, only one year before "Star Wars" made her famous. Beatty and Robert Towne wrote the script. Has a healthy glow in places and a perky bounce, but too many split ends.
1975 (R) 112m/C Warren Beatty, Julie Christie, Goldie Hawn, Jack Warden, Lee Grant, Tony Bill, Carrie Fisher, William Castle, Howard Hesseman; *D:* Hal Ashby; *W:* Warren Beatty, Robert Towne; *M:* John Barry. Academy Awards '75: Best Supporting Actress (Grant); Nominations: Best Art Direction/Set Decoration, Best Original Screenplay, Best Supporting Actor (Warden). VHS, Beta, LV $14.95 *COL, VYG, CRC* 🎞🎞½

Shamus Private dick Reynolds investigates a smuggling ring, beds a sultry woman, gets in lotsa fights. Classic Burt vehicle meant as a send-up. Unoriginal but fun.
1973 (PG) 91m/C Burt Reynolds, Dyan Cannon, John P. Ryan; *D:* Buzz Kulik; *M:* Jerry Goldsmith. VHS, Beta $9.95 *GKK* 🎞🎞

Shane A retired gunfighter, now a drifter, comes to the aid of a homestead family threatened by a land baron and his hired gun. Ladd is the mystery man who becomes the idol of the family's young son. Classic, flawless western. Pulitzer prize-winning western novelist A.B. Guthrie, Jr. adapted from the novel by Jack Schaefer. Long and stately; worth savoring.
1953 117m/C Alan Ladd, Jean Arthur, Van Heflin, Brandon de Wilde, Jack Palance, Ben Johnson, Elisha Cook Jr., Edgar Buchanan; *D:* George Stevens. Academy Awards '53: Best Color Cinematography; Nominations: Best Director (Stevens), Best Picture, Best Screenplay, Best Supporting Actor (de Wilde, Palance); National Board of Review Awards '53: 10 Best Films of the Year, Best Director (Stevens). VHS, Beta, LV $14.95 *PAR, TLF* 🎞🎞🎞🎞

The Shanghai Cobra Below-average mystery has Chan hired by the government to investigate several supposed cobra bite murders. All motives lead to stealing a supply of radium.
1945 64m/B Sidney Toler, Benson Fong, Mantan Moreland, Walter Fenner, James B. Cardwell, Joan Barclay, James Flavin; *D:* Phil Karlson. VHS $19.98 *MGM* 🎞½

The Shanghai Gesture A wildly baroque, subversive melodrama. An English financier tries to close a gambling den, only to be blackmailed by the female proprietor—who tells him not only is he a man's daughter heavily indebted to her, but that she is the wife he abandoned long ago. Based on a

notorious Broadway play. Von Sternberg had to make numerous changes to the script in order to get it past the Hays censors; the director's final Hollywood work, and worthy of his oeuvre, but oddly unsatisfying.
1942 97m/B Walter Huston, Gene Tierney, Victor Mature, Ona Munson, Albert Basserman, Eric Blore, Maria Ouspenskaya, Phyllis Brooks, Mike Mazurki; **D:** Josef von Sternberg. **VHS, Beta, LV $29.95** *MFV* ⚔️⚔️½

Shanghai Massacre It's a violent battle when two Chinese gangs vie for control of the underworld.
19?? 83m/C D: Lee Tso Nan. **VHS, Beta $42.95** *PGN* ⚔️

Shanghai Surprise Tie salesman Penn and missionary Madonna (yeah, right) are better than you'd think, and the story (of opium smuggling in China in the '30s) is intrepid and wildly fun, but indifferently directed and unsure of itself. Executive producer George Harrison wrote the songs and has a cameo.
1986 (PG-13) 90m/C Sean Penn, Madonna, Paul Freeman, Richard Griffiths; **Cameos:** George Harrison; **D:** Jim Goddard. **VHS, Beta, LV $79.98** *LIV, VES* ⚔️½

Shanty Tramp Small-town tramp puts the moves on an evangelist, a motorcycle gang, and a young black man, who risks his life trying to save her from her loose morals. Another cheesy flick made for the drive-in crowd.
1967 72m/B Lee Holland, Bill Rogers, Lawrence Tobin; **D:** Joseph Prieto. **VHS $16.95** *SNC* ⚔️

The Shaolin: Blood Mission/ Deadly Shaolin Long Fist Two full-length kung fu spectaculars with double the head-kicking and rib-crunching fun.
1975 172m/C VHS, Beta $7.00 *VTR* ⚔️½

The Shaolin Brothers The brothers earn their living by putting on street gymnastics exhibitions. Foolishly, a Shaolin rebel attempts to disrupt one of their performances. Thus begins the battle between the rebels and the brothers.
198? ?m/C VHS $29.95 *OCE* ⚔️½

Shaolin Challenges Ninja Ninja and shaolin masters kick it out over honor and their respective orders.
198? 107m/C Liu Chia Hui. **Beta** *NO* ⚔️

Shaolin Death Squad Ruthless Japanese premier murders a statesman as the first step in his plan to become Emperor. The murdered man's daughter swears vengeance and enlists the Shaolin Death Squad to help.
1983 (R) 90m/C VHS, Beta $16.50 *OCE, FOX* ⚔️

Shaolin Devil/Shaolin Angel To prevent more needless kick murders, two warriors learn the dreaded Dammoth Kung Fu and kick everyone anyway.
197? 87m/C VHS, Beta $29.95 *UNI* ⚔️

Shaolin Disciple Kung Fu action-adventure featuring real monks.
19?? 90m/C Ku Feng. **VHS $49.95** *OCE* ⚔️

Shaolin Drunk Fighter When a nasty spate of intemperance plagues the Shaolin training grounds, the temple masters seek new cures to an old problem.
1969 95m/C VHS, Beta $29.95 *TWE* ⚔️

The Shaolin Drunk Monkey The dreaded Shaolin Drunk Monkey faces his enemies in a veritable array of fights and lethal kicks.
1985 85m/C VHS, Beta $14.95 *SVS* ⚔️

Shaolin Ex-Monk Renegade Shaolin Monk is pursued by a Kung Fu master and his disciple.
1982 94m/C John Liu, Ko Shou Liang, Huang Hsing Shaw. **VHS, Beta** *WVE* ⚔️

Shaolin Executioner Several generations of Shaolin defend the Shaolin Temple against all high-kicking odds.
198? 104m/C Chen Kuan-Tai, Lo Lieh; **D:** Lu Chia-Liang. **Beta** *NO* ⚔️

Shaolin Fox Conspiracy This kung-fu epic features unusual moves, including the Mantis Strike, the Dragon Claw and the Crescent Kick.
1985 75m/C VHS, Beta $14.95 *SVS* ⚔️

Shaolin Incredible Ten A Shaolin abbot and his daughters kick a great many Manchu warriors in their helmeted heads.
197? 87m/C Sue Lee, Elton Chong, Eagle Han. **VHS, Beta** *NO* ⚔️

The Shaolin Invincibles Shaolin buddies team up to fight the evil Emperor Yung Ching eventually coming to final blows with him in the Forbidden City Golden Palace.
198? ?m/C VHS *OCE* ⚔️½

Shaolin Kids Shaolin warriors discover a conspiracy and kick it to death.
1977 91m/C VHS, Beta $29.95 *UNI* ⚔️

Shaolin Kung Fu Mystagogue In this action-packed chop-fest, the mysterious "Floating in Blood" weapon enlivens the battle between the Ching Dynasty and Ming rebels.
1984 90m/C D: Chang Peng-I. **VHS, Beta $49.95** *WWV* ⚔️

The Shaolin Kung Fu Mystagogue/Iron Ox, the Tiger's Killer Double your pleasure, double your fun, with two martial arts flicks in one.
19?? 180m/C VHS $9.99 *VTR* ⚔️

Shaolin Red Master/Two Crippled Heroes Kung Fu is back, choppin' 'em down and spreadin' 'em around in this double feature, martial arts adventure.
19?? 180m/C VHS $9.99 *VTR* ⚔️

Shaolin Temple Strikes Back The protective inhabitants of the Shaolin temple defend themselves against invading Manchu Barbarians.
1972 90m/C Chen Chien Chang, Sho Kosugi, Chang Shan, Lung Fei; **D:** Joseph Kuo. **VHS, Beta $29.95** *TWE* ⚔️

Shaolin Thief A traitor gives the invading Japanese a priceless treasure and the loyal Chinese troops must fight to get it back.
19?? 90m/C VHS $29.95 *OCE* ⚔️

Shaolin Traitor Exotic weapons and dazzling martial-arts action are featured in this exciting tale of intrigue and mystery.
1982 (R) 99m/C Carter Wong, Shangkuan Ling-Feng, Lung Chun-Eng, Chang Yi, Lung Fei. **VHS, Beta $59.95** *GEM* ⚔️½

Shaolin Vengence Framed for murder and deceived into accepting guilt for the crime, a man does penance in a Shaolin temple. When he learns of the deception, he uses his newly learned Shaolin boxing skills to relentlessly pound the creeps who set him up.
1982 ?m/C Chen Sing. **VHS $24.50** *OCE* ⚔️½

Shaolin vs. Lama A group of Shaolin Kung Fu fighters participates in a series of battles against Tibetan Monks.
1984 90m/C VHS, Beta $39.95 *WWV* ⚔️

Shaolin vs. Manchu A Manchu spy infiltrates a Shaolin temple, and causes much head-splitting on both sides.
198? 91m/C Romy Tso. **VHS, Beta** *NO* ⚔️

Shaolin Warrior A young man must battle an evil Tartar warlord who massacred his family.
19?? 90m/C Kam Kong, Chan Wai, Chen Sing. **VHS, Beta $29.95** *OCE* ⚔️

Shaolin Wooden Men A young man vows revenge, and gets it, on the masked ninja who killed his father.
19?? 90m/C Jackie Chan; **D:** Lo Wei. **VHS, Beta** *NO* ⚔️

Shark! American gun smuggler Reynolds, stranded in a tiny seaport in Africa, joins the crew of a marine biologist's boat. He soon discovers the boat's owner and his wife are trying to retrieve gold bullion that lies deep in shark-infested waters. Typical Reynoldsian action-infested dumbness. Like "Twilight Zone: The Movie", earned notoriety because of on-location tragedy: a stunt diver really was killed by a shark. Edited without the consent of Fuller, who disowned it. **AKA:** Man-Eater; Un Arma de Dos Filos.
1968 (PG) 92m/C Burt Reynolds, Barry Sullivan, Arthur Kennedy; **D:** Samuel Fuller. **VHS, Beta $24.95** *REP, MRV* ⚔️½

Shark Attack Rodney Fox, a businessman left scarred and bitter from an attack by a great white shark, recuperates and kills the shark to satisfy his thirst for revenge. Later, having overcome his fear of the "White Death," he realizes that sharks are people too, so to speak.
197? 30m/C Jean-Michel Cousteau. **VHS, Beta $29.95** *VVI* ⚔️

Shark Hunter Shark hunter gets ensnared in the mob's net off the Mexican coast as they race for a cache of sunken millions. The usual garden-variety B-grade adventure.
1984 (PG) 95m/C Franco Nero, Jorge Luke, Mike Forrest. **VHS, Beta $49.95** *PSM, MRV* ⚔️

Shark River A man attempts to get his brother, a Civil War veteran accused of murder, through the Everglades and send him to safety in Cuba. Good photography of the great swamp; disappointing story.
1953 80m/C Steve Cochran, Carole Matthews, Warren Stevens; **D:** John Rawlins. **VHS, Beta** *NO* ⚔️½

Shark's Paradise A madman threatens to set sharks loose on a popular Australian surf coast if his demands are not met.
1986 93m/C VHS, Beta $59.95 *WOV* ⚔️

Sharks' Treasure A band of escaped convicts commandeer a boat filled with gold. Old fashioned sunken-treasure tale unexceptional except as a virtual one man show by writer/actor/director/producer/fitness nut Wilde.
1975 (PG) 96m/C Cornel Wilde, Yaphet Kotto, John Neilson, Cliff Osmond, David Canary, David Gilliam; **D:** Cornel Wilde. **VHS, Beta $59.95** *MGM* ⚔️½

Sharky's Machine A tough undercover cop (Reynolds) is hot on the trail of a crooked crime czar. Meanwhile he falls for a high-priced hooker. Well done but overdone action, with much violence. Based on the William Diehl novel.
1981 (R) 119m/C Burt Reynolds, Rachel Ward, Vittorio Gassman, Brian Keith, Charles Durning, Bernie Casey, Richard Libertini, Henry Silva, John Fiedler, Earl Holliman; **D:** Burt Reynolds. **VHS, Beta, LV $19.98** *WAR* ⚔️⚔️½

Sharma & Beyond A teenage would-be science fiction writer falls in love with the daughter of a famous sci-fi author.
1984 85m/C Suzanne Burden, Robert Urquhart, Michael Maloney; **D:** Brian Gilbert. **VHS, Beta $59.95** *MGM* ⚔️

Sharp Fists in Kung Fu The cruel son of a gentle man returns to terrorize his hometown. Strictly for fans of the genre.
19?? 90m/C VHS, Beta $49.95 *OCE Woof!*

Shattered Finch plays Harry, a man blamed for a failed marriage, held hostage in his home by his own paranoia, and driven to bouts of drinking. Slowly his tenuous grip on sanity slips and at any moment his fragile and crumbling life may be shattered. Tired, overwrought domestic drama. *AKA: Something to Hide.*
1972 (R) 100m/C *GB* Peter Finch, Shelley Winters, Colin Blakely; *D:* Alastair Reid. **VHS, Beta** $24.95 *MED �½*

Shattered An architect recovering from a serious automobile accident tries to regain the memory that he has lost. As he begins to put together the pieces of his life, some parts of the puzzle don't quite fit. For example, he recalls his now loving wife's affair as well as his own. He remembers that he hired a private detective to follow his wife and shockingly, he remembers that he once believed his wife had planned to kill him. Are these memories the real thing, or are they all part of some mad, recuperative nightmare? Who knows.
1991 (R) 98m/C Tom Berenger, Bob Hoskins, Greta Scacchi, Joanne Whalley-Kilmer, Corbin Bernsen, Theodore Bikel; *W/D:* Wolfgang Petersen. **VHS, Beta, LV, 8mm** $94.99 *MGM ☰☰*

Shattered Innocence Journey through beauty, sensuality, and innocence revolving around a 16-year-old ballet dancer's first stirrings of sexuality. Soft porn. *AKA: Laura.*
1979 (R) 95m/C Maud Adams, Dawn Dunlap. **VHS, Beta** $9.95 *SIM, SUE ☰*

Shattered Silence A woman is tormented by phone calls that seem to be coming from her dead son as her life is torn apart by divorce. Leaves unanswered the question: Will there be any suspense? Made for TV. Worthless and dumb. *AKA: When Michael Calls.*
1971 73m/C Elizabeth Ashley, Ben Gazzara, Michael Douglas, Karen Pearson; *D:* Philip Leacock. **VHS** $9.99 *CCB ☰½*

Shattered Spirits A quiet family man cracks and goes on a rampage through his normally peaceful suburban neighborhood.
1991 (PG-13) 93m/C Martin Sheen, Melinda Dillon, Matthew Laborteaux, Roxana Zal, Lukas Haas. **VHS** $89.98 *VMK ☰½*

Shattered Vows A young nun struggles with her love for a priest and her desire for a child. Bertinelli is convincing as the confused teen in otherwise ordinary TV drama. Adapted from the true story of Dr. Mary Gilligan Wong as told in her book, "Nun: A Memoir."
1984 95m/C Valerie Bertinelli, David Morse, Caroline McWilliams, Patricia Neal, Millie Perkins, Leslie Ackerman, Lisa Jane Persky; *D:* Jack Bender. **VHS, Beta** $14.95 *FRH ☰☰*

She H. Rider Haggard's famous story about the ageless Queen Ayesha, (Blythe), who renews her life force periodically by walking through a pillar of cold flame. Story and titles by Haggard. Blythe is a stirringly mean queen, and the story remains fresh and fun. Silent film with music score.
1921 69m/B Betty Blythe, Carlyle Blackwell, Mary Odette. **VHS, Beta** $19.95 *NOS, VYY, DVT ☰☰½*

S*H*E A flashy made for TV spy thriller. The female agent S*H*E (Securities Hazards Expert) must save the world's oil; good locations, nifty plot and looker Sharpe as the she-Bond add up to a reasonably fun time. Written by Richard Maibaum, late of several Bond scripts.
1979 100m/C Cornelia Sharpe, Robert Lansing, William Taylor, Isabella Rye, Anita Ekberg; *Cameos:* Omar Sharif; *D:* Robert Lewis. **VHS, Beta** $59.95 *PSM ☰☰*

She A beautiful female warrior rules over the men in a post-holocaust world. She is kidnapped by a wealthy merchant who uses her to fight evil mutants. Utter rubbish vaguely based on the Haggard novel.
1983 90m/C Sandahl Bergman, Harrison Muller, Quin Kessler, David Goss; *D:* Avi Nesher. **VHS, Beta** $29.98 *LIV ☰*

She and He Hani's look at the oppression of women, marital and spiritual discontent, and class divisions. Naoko is a bored housewife, living in a sterile high-rise apartment with her equally dissatisfied husband, and yearning for something to express her inner feelings. She accidentally meets an old classmate of her husband's who has become a poor ragpicker and tries to aid him. But all her efforts only lead to further tragedies. In Japanese with English subtitles.
1963 110m/C *JP* Sachiko Hidari, Eiji Okada, Kikuji Yamashita; *D:* Susumu Hani. **VHS** $39.95 *FCT ☰☰½*

The She-Beast Burned at the stake in 18th-century Transylvania, a witch returns in the body of a beautiful young English woman on her honeymoon (in Transylvania?!), and once again wreaks death and destruction. Caution, Barbara Steele fans: she appears for all of fifteen minutes. Sporadically funny. *AKA: Il Lago di Satana; The Revenge of the Blood Beast.*
1965 74m/C *IT YU* Barbara Steele, Ian Ogilvy, Mel Welles, Lucretia Love; *D:* Michael Reeves. **VHS, Beta** $59.95 *SNC, MPI ☰½*

She Came on the Bus Young thugs break into a well-kept suburban home and terrorize the housewife through rape and torture. Then they kidnap a bus and pose as the drivers until they can find more victims. Contains scenes of graphic violence which would be considered offensive even by today's standards.
1969 58m/C *D:* Harry Vincent. **VHS** $23.00 *SMW Woof!*

She Came to the Valley A tough pioneer woman becomes embroiled in political intrigue during the Spanish-American War. Based on Cleo Dawson's book. *AKA: Texas in Flames.*
1977 (PG) 90m/C Ronee Blakley, Dean Stockwell, Scott Glenn, Freddy Fender. **VHS, Beta** $69.95 *MED, QVD ☰*

She Couldn't Say No A wealthy oil heiress (Simmons) with good intentions plans to give her money away to those friends who had helped her when she was struggling. Things don't go quite as planned; her philanthropy leads to unexpected mayhem in her Arkansas hometown. Passable, but not memorable comedy. Mitchum as a small-town doctor? *AKA: Beautiful But Dangerous.*
1952 88m/B Robert Mitchum, Jean Simmons, Arthur Hunnicutt, Edgar Buchanan, Wallace Ford; *D:* Lloyd Bacon. **VHS, Beta** *CCB ☰☰*

She Demons Pleasure craft loaded with babes crashes into a remote island controlled by a mad ex-Nazi scientist who transforms pretty girls into rubber-faced Frankensteins. Incomprehensible, to say the least.
1958 68m/B Irish McCalla, Tod Griffin, Victor Sen Yung; *D:* Richard Cunha. **VHS, Beta** $9.95 *RHI, SNC, MWP Woof!*

She-Devil A comic book version of the acidic Fay Weldon novel "The Life and Loves of a She-Devil"; a fat, dowdy suburban wife (Arnold) becomes a vengeful beast when a smarmy romance novelist steals her hus-band. Uneven comedic reworking of a distinctly unforgiving feminist fiction. Arnold is given too much to handle (her role requires an actual range of emotions); Streep's role is too slight, though she does great things with it.
1989 (PG-13) 100m/C Meryl Streep, Roseanne (Barr) Arnold, Ed Begley Jr., Linda Hunt, Elizabeth Peters, Bryan Larkin, A. Martinez, Sylvia Miles; *D:* Susan Seidelman. **VHS, Beta, LV** $14.98 *ORI ☰☰½*

She Devils in Chains A group of traveling female athletes are kidnapped by a groups of sadists who torture and beat them. In the end, however, the girls get their revenge, and it's bloody.
19?? (R) 82m/C Colleen Camp, Rosanne Katon, Sylvia Anderson, Ken Washington, Leo Martinez; *D:* Cirio H. Santiago. **VHS** $9.95 *SIM ☰☰*

She-Devils on Wheels Havoc erupts as an outlaw female motorcycle gang, known as "Maneaters on Motorbikes," terrorizes a town—especially the men. Really, really bad biker flick finely honed by Lewis.
1968 83m/C Betty Connell, Christie Wagner, Pat Poston, Nancy Lee Noble, Ruby Tuesday; *D:* Herschell Gordon Lewis. **VHS, Beta** $19.95 *SVI, WWV Woof!*

She Done Him Wrong West stars as Lil, an 1890s saloon singer in the screen version of her Broadway hit "Diamond Lily," and imparts on the negligible plot her usual share of double entendres and racy comments. Grant is likeable as the hapless sap she beds. ♫Silver Threads Among the Gold; Masie, My Pretty Daisy; Easy Rider; I Like a Guy What Takes His Time; Frankie and Johnny.
1933 65m/B Mae West, Cary Grant, Owen Moore, Noah Beery Sr., Gilbert Roland, Louise Beavers; *D:* Lowell Sherman. Academy Awards '33 Nominations: Best Picture; National Board of Review Awards '33: 10 Best Films of the Year. **VHS, Beta, LV** $14.98 *MCA, MLB ☰☰☰*

She-Freak Remake of Tod Brownings' "Freaks." A cynical waitress burns everyone in a circus and gets mauled by the resident freaks. Pales beside its unacknowledged, classic original. *AKA: Alley of Nightmares.*
1967 87m/C Claire Brennan, Lynn Courtney, Bill McKinney, Lee Raymond, Madame Lee; *D:* Byron Mabe. **VHS, Beta** *NO ☰*

She Gods of Shark Reef Typical no-budget Corman exploitation tale of two brothers shipwrecked on an island inhabited by beautiful pearl-diving women. Filmed in Hawaii. *AKA: Shark Reef.*
1956 63m/C Bill Cord, Don Durant, Lisa Montell, Carol Lindsay, Jeanne Gerson; *D:* Roger Corman. **VHS** $16.95 *SNC, MRV, HEG ☰*

She Goes to War King's first part-sound effort that takes place in the milieu of World War I. Boardman plays a spoiled rich girl who grows up fast when confronted with the horrors of the frontline while working in a canteen.
1929 50m/B Eleanor Boardman, Alma Rubens, Al "Fuzzy" St. John; *D:* Henry King. **VHS, Beta, 8mm** $19.95 *NOS, GVV, DVT ☰☰*

She Likes You, Charlie Brown Romantic travails for Charlie Brown and the gang. Animated.
1986 41m/C VHS, Beta $14.95 *KRT, WTA ☰☰*

She Shall Have Music A magnate hires a dance band to broadcast from a cruise ship. Features music by Jack Hylton and his band, one of Britain's most popular orchestras of the 1930s.
1936 76m/B Jack Hylton, June Clyde, Claude Dampier, Bryan Lawrence, Gwen Farrar. **VHS, Beta** *MWP ☰½*

She Shoulda Said No Exploitation film focusing on the horrors of marijuanna.
1949 ?m/C Lila Leeds, Lyle Talbot, Alan Baxter, Jack Elam. **VHS $16.95** *SNC* ⅃⅃½

She Waits When a newlywed couple moves into an old house, the bride becomes possessed by the spirit of her husband's first wife. Unoriginal and mediocre horror. Made for television.
1971 74m/C Dorothy McGuire, Patty Duke, David McCallum; *D:* Delbert Mann. **VHS, Beta $59.95** *PSM* ⅃⅃

She Wore a Yellow Ribbon An undermanned cavalry outpost makes a desperate attempt to repel invading Indians. Wayne shines as an officer who shuns retirement in order to help his comrades. Excellent color photography by Winston C. Hoch. Still fun and compelling. The second chapter in director Ford's noted cavalry trilogy, preceded by "Fort Apache" and followed by "Rio Grande."
1949 93m/C John Wayne, Joanne Dru, John Agar, Ben Johnson, Harry Carey Jr., Victor McLaglen, Mildred Natwick, George O'Brien; *D:* John Ford. **VHS, Beta, LV $19.95** *TTC, RKO, VID* ⅃⅃⅃½

Sheba, Baby A female dick (Grier) heads to Louisville where someone is trying to threaten her rich father and his loan company. Oddly non-violent for action-flick vet Grier; poorly written and directed.
1975 (PG) 90m/C Pam Grier, Rudy Challenger, Austin Stoker, D'Urville Martin, Charles Kissinger; *D:* William Girdler. **VHS, Beta $59.98** *ORI, FCT* ⅃⅃

Sheena Television sportscaster aids a jungle queen in defending her kingdom from being overthrown by an evil prince. Horrid bubble-gum "action" fantasy.
1984 (PG) 117m/C Tanya Roberts, Ted Wass, Donovan Scott, Elizabeth Toro; *D:* John Guillermin. **VHS, Beta, LV $12.95** *GKK* Woof!

The Sheep Has Five Legs Quintuplet brothers return from around the world for a reunion in their small French village. Fernandel plays the father and all five sons; otherwise, comedy is only average-to-good. In French with English subtitles.
1954 96m/B *FR* Fernandel, Edouard Delmont, Louis de Funes, Paulette Dubost; *D:* Henri Verneuil. **VHS, Beta, 8mm $24.95** *NOS, DVT, VYY* ⅃⅃½

Sheer Madness Focuses on the intense friendship between a college professor and a troubled artist, both women. Engrossing and subtle exposition of a relationship. Ambiguous ending underscores film's general excellence. Subtitled.
1984 105m/C *GE FR* Hanna Schygulla, Angela Winkler; *D:* Margarethe von Trotta. **VHS, Beta** *MGM* ⅃⅃⅃

The Sheik High camp Valentino has English woman fall hopelessly under the romantic spell of Arab sheik who flares his nostrils. Followed by "Son of the Sheik."
1921 80m/B Agnes Ayres, Rudolph Valentino, Adolphe Menjou, Walter Long, Lucien Littlefield, George Waggner, Patsy Ruth Miller; *D:* George Melford. **VHS, Beta $19.95** *PAR, GPV* ⅃⅃

She'll Be Wearing Pink Pajamas Eight women volunteer for a rugged survival course to test their mettle. The intense shared experience gives them all food for thought. Well acted from a pretty thin story.
1984 90m/C Julie Walters, Anthony Higgins; *D:* John Goldschmidt. **VHS, Beta $59.95** *LHV* ⅃⅃

Shell Shock Four GIs fight off the Germans and the longings for home during World War II.
198? 90m/C *D:* John Hayes. **VHS, Beta** *NO* ⅃½

Shelley Duvall's Bedtime Stories A series of stories based on popular children's books, narrated by celebrities. Each tape is available individually and contains at least two stories. Nominated for cable's ACE award and an Emmy award. Originally produced for cable television.
1992 25m/C **VHS, LV $12.98** *MCA* ⅃½

The Sheltering Sky American couple Winger and Malkovich flee the plasticity of their native land for a trip to the Sahara desert where they hope to renew their spirits and rekindle love. Accompanied by socialite acquaintance Scott with whom Winger soon has an affair, their personalities and belief systems deteriorate as they move through the grave poverty of North Africa in breathtaking heat. Based on the existential novel by American expatriate Paul Bowles who narrates and appears briefly in a bar scene. Overlong but visually stunning, with cinematography by Vittorio Storaro.
1990 (R) 139m/C Debra Winger, John Malkovich, Campbell Scott, Jill Bennett, Timothy Spall, Eric Vu-An; *D:* Bernardo Bertolucci; *M:* Ryuichi Sakamoto, Richard Horowitz. **VHS, Beta, LV $19.98** *WAR, PIA, FCT* ⅃⅃⅃

Shenandoah A Virginia farmer (Stewart, in a top-notch performance) who has raised six sons and a daughter, tries to remain neutral during the Civil War. War takes its toll as the daughter marries a Confederate soldier and his sons become involved in the fighting. Screen debut for Ross.
1965 105m/C James Stewart, Doug McClure, Glenn Corbett, Patrick Wayne, Rosemary Forsyth, Katharine Ross, George Kennedy; *D:* Andrew V. McLaglen. **VHS, Beta, LV $19.95** *MCA* ⅃⅃⅃

Shep Comes Home Shep the wonder canine accompanies an orphan through the Midwest where he nabs a band of bankrobbers. Sequel to "My Dog Shep."
1949 62m/B Robert Lowery, Sheldon Leonard, Flame. **VHS, Beta, LV** *NO* ⅃

Sheriff of Tombstone Trouble begins when a "judge" takes a sharpshooter in a poker game.
1941 60m/B Roy Rogers. **VHS, Beta $19.95** *NOS, DVT, RXM* ⅃½

Sherlock Holmes: A Study in Scarlet Holmes and Watson have only one clue to go on when they investigate the murder of an American tourist in London.
1984 49m/C *V:* Peter O'Toole. **VHS, Beta, LV $14.95** *PAV, WTA* ⅃½

Sherlock Holmes and the Deadly Necklace Once again, Holmes and Watson are up against their old nemesis Moriarty. This time, Moriarty wants to get his hands on a necklace stolen from Cleopatra's tomb. Not only does Scotland Yard not consider him a suspect, they seek his advice. Enter Holmes and Watson, and the game's afoot. The offbeat casting and direction help make this one of the odder versions of Conan Doyle's work. *AKA:* Sherlock Holmes Und Das Halsband des Todes; Valley of Fear.
1962 84m/B *GE* Christopher Lee, Senta Berger, Hans Sohnker, Hans Nielsen, Ivan Desny, Leon Askin, Thorley Walters; *D:* Terence Fisher. **VHS $19.95** *NOS, SNC* ⅃⅃½

Sherlock Holmes and the Incident at Victoria Falls A substandard Holmes excursion brings the Baker Street sleuth out of retirement to transport the world's largest diamond from Africa to London. The resulting mystery involves Teddy Roosevelt, the inventor of radio, and poor plotting. *AKA:* Incident at Victoria Falls.
1991 120m/C *GB* Christopher Lee, Patrick Macnee, Jenny Seagrove; *D:* Bill Corcoran. **VHS $89.98** *VES* ⅃½

Sherlock Holmes and the Secret Weapon Based on "The Dancing Men" by Sir Arthur Conan Doyle. Holmes battles the evil Moriarty in an effort to save the British war effort. Good Holmes mystery with gripping wartime setting. Hoey is fun as bumbling Inspector Lestrade. Available colorized. *AKA:* Secret Weapon.
1942 68m/B Basil Rathbone, Nigel Bruce, Karen Verne, William Post Jr., Dennis Hoey, Holmes Herbert, Mary Gordon, Henry Victor, Philip Van Zandt, George Eldridge, Leslie Denison, James Craven, Paul Fix, Hugh Herbert, Lionel Atwill; *D:* Roy William Neill. **VHS, LV $14.98** *REP, MED, AOV* ⅃⅃

Sherlock Holmes Faces Death Dead bodies are accumulating in a mansion where the detecting duo are staying. Underground tunnels, life-size dress boards, and unanswered mysteries... Top-notch Holmes. Peter Lawford appears briefly as a sailor. Also available with "Hound of the Baskervilles" on Laser Disc.
1943 68m/B Basil Rathbone, Nigel Bruce, Hillary Brooke, Milburn Stone, Halliwell Hobbes, Arthur Margetson, Gavin Muir; *D:* Roy William Neill. **VHS, Beta, LV $14.98** *FOX* ⅃⅃⅃

Sherlock Holmes in Washington A top-secret agent is murdered; seems it's those blasted Nazis again! Holmes and Watson rush off to Washington, D.C. to solve the crime and to save some vitally important microfilm. Heavily flag-waving Rathbone-Bruce episode. Dr. Watson is dumbfounded by bubble gum.
1943 71m/B Basil Rathbone, Nigel Bruce, Henry Daniell, George Zucco, Marjorie Lord, John Archer; *D:* Roy William Neill. **VHS, Beta $14.98** *FOX* ⅃⅃½

Sherlock Holmes: The Baskerville Curse Animated feature film with Peter O'Toole as the voice of Sherlock Holmes.
1984 70m/C *V:* Peter O'Toole. **VHS, Beta, LV $14.95** *PAV, WTA* ⅃⅃

Sherlock Holmes: The Sign of Four Sherlock Holmes must find the man who murdered Bartholomew Sholto with a poison dart in the neck.
1984 48m/C *V:* Peter O'Toole. **VHS, Beta $14.95** *PAV, WTA, PMS* ⅃⅃

Sherlock Holmes: The Silver Blaze Sherlock Holmes mystery about the theft of a racehorse known as "The Silver Blaze." Remade in 1977.
1941 70m/B Arthur Wontner, Ian Fleming, Lyn Harding. **VHS, Beta $19.95** *NOS, KRT, MWP* ⅃½

Sherlock Holmes: The Silver Blaze Sherlock Holmes, with Dr. Watson, in one of the legendary detective's most famous adventures involving the theft of a racehorse and the mysterious murder of his trainer. Remake of a 1941 film.
1977 31m/C Christopher Plummer, Thorley Walters; *D:* John Davies. **VHS, Beta $24.98** *LCA* ⅃⅃

Sherlock Holmes: The Valley of Fear Sherlock Holmes and Dr. Watson investigate a man who faked his own death to escape retribution from an American secret society.
1984 49m/C *V:* Peter O'Toole. **VHS, Beta $14.95** *PAV, WTA* ⅃½

Sherlock Holmes: The Voice of Terror Holmes and Watson try to decode German radio messages during World War II. First Rathbone-as-Holmes effort for Univer-

sal, and first in which we are asked to believe the Victorian sleuth and his hairdo could have lived in this century. Patriotic and all that—and lots of fun.
1942 65m/B Basil Rathbone, Nigel Bruce, Hillary Brooke, Reginald Denny, Evelyn Ankers, Montagu Love; **D:** John Rawlins. **VHS, Beta, LV $14.98** FOX 🎬🎬½

Sherlock Hound: Tales of Mystery Sherlock, Watson and Moriarty are all dogs in this animated children's adaptation of the popular Arthur Conan Doyle stories. Well worth a howl.
1990 115m/C VHS, Beta JFK 🎬🎬½

Sherlock's Rivals & Where's My Wife Double feature includes a detective movie in which two used car dealers become amateur sleuths and a comedy in which a man has a hard time enjoying his weekend at a seashore resort.
1927 53m/B Milburn Morante, Monty Banks. **VHS, Beta $19.95** VYY 🎬🎬½

She's a Good Skate, Charlie Brown Snoopy becomes Peppermint Patty's ice-skating coach, and he helps her train for the local competition.
1980 30m/C D: Phil Roman. **VHS, Beta $14.95** VTR, HSE, WTA 🎬½

She's Back Murderee Fisher pesters hubby Joy from beyond the grave to avenge her death at the hands of a motorcycle gang. Uneven, but occasionally funny.
1988 (R) 89m/C Carrie Fisher, Robert Joy; **D:** Tim Kincaid. **VHS, Beta, LV $79.98** VES, LIV 🎬½

She's Dressed to Kill Beautiful models are turning up dead during a famous designer's comeback attempt at a mountain retreat. Who could be behind these grisly deeds? Suspenseful in a made for TV kind of way, but not memorable. **AKA:** Someone's Killing the World's Greatest Models.
1979 100m/C Eleanor Parker, Jessica Walter, John Rubinstein, Connie Sellecca; **D:** Gus Trikonis. **VHS $29.95** LIV 🎬🎬

She's Gotta Have It Lee wrote, directed, edited, produced and starred in this romantic comedy about an independent-minded black girl in Brooklyn and the three men and one woman who compete for her attention. Full of rough edges, but vigorous, confident, and hip. Filmed entirely in black and white except for one memorable scene. Put Lee on the film-making map.
1986 (R) 84m/B Spike Lee, Tommy Redmond Hicks, Raye Dowell; **D:** Spike Lee. **VHS, Beta $19.95** FOX, FCT 🎬🎬🎬

She's Having a Baby Newlyweds Bacon and McGovern tread the marital waters with some difficulty, when news of an impending baby further complicates their lives. Told from Bacon's viewpoint as the tortured young writer/husband, who wonders if the yuppie life they lead is trapping him. Hughes' first venture into the adult world isn't as satisfying as his teen angst flicks, although the charming leads help. Major drawbacks are the arguably sexist premise and dull resolution. Great soundtrack; observant viewers will notice the beemer's license plate is the title's acronym: "SHAB."
1988 (PG-13) 106m/C Kevin Bacon, Elizabeth McGovern, William Windom, Paul Gleason, Alec Baldwin, Cathryn Damon, Holland Taylor, James Ray, Isabel Lorca, Dennis Dugan, Edie McClurg; **D:** John Hughes; **W:** John Hughes. **VHS, Beta, LV, 8mm $19.95** PAR 🎬🎬½

She's in the Army Now Farce about military life. Two bubble-headed females undergo basic training. Made for TV "Private Benjamin" ripoff was meant as a series pilot.
1981 97m/C Jamie Lee Curtis, Kathleen Quinlan, Melanie Griffith, Susan Blanchard, Julie Carmen, Janet MacLachlan; **D:** Hy Averback. **VHS, Beta $9.98** SUE, NLC 🎬

She's Out of Control Dad Danza goes nuts when teen daughter Dolenz (real-life daughter of Monkee Mickey Dolenz) takes the advice of Dad's girlfriend on how to attract boys. Formulaic plot could almost be an episode of "Who's the Boss?" Danza is appealing, but not enough to keep this one afloat.
1989 95m/C Tony Danza, Catherine Hicks, Wallace Shawn, Dick O'Neill; **D:** Stan Dragoti. **VHS, Beta, LV, 8mm $19.95** COL 🎬½

Shifting Sands Compelling film tells the tale of a young girl looking to be a successful artist. Her landlord makes constant overtures towards her. She refuses, so he has her thrown in jail for prostitution as an act of revenge. She fears her past may prevent her from obtaining true love.
1918 52m/B Gloria Swanson, Joe King, Lillian Langdon. **VHS, Beta, 8mm $14.95** GPV, VYY 🎬½

Shin Heike Monogatari Mizoguchi's second to last film, in which a deposed Japanese emperor in 1137 endeavors to win back the throne from the current despot, who cannot handle the feudal lawlessness. Acclaimed; his second film in color. In Japanese with English subtitles. Also called "New Tales of the Taira Clan."
1955 106m/C JP Raizo Ichikawa, Ichijiro Oya, Michiyo Kogure, Eijiro Yanagi, Tatsuya Ishiguro, Yoshiko Kuga; **D:** Kenji Mizoguchi. **VHS, Beta $29.95** FCT 🎬🎬🎬

Shinbone Alley Animated musical about Archy, a free-verse poet reincarnated as a cockroach, and Mehitabel, the alley cat with a zest for life. Based on the short stories by Don Marquis.
1970 (G) 83m/C D: John D. Wilson; **V:** Carol Channing, Eddie Bracken, John Carradine, Alan Reed. **VHS, Beta $14.95** SIM, GEM, KAR 🎬🎬🎬🎬

Shine on, Harvest Moon Rogers brings a band of outlaws to justice and clears an old man suspected of being their accomplice. Title bears no relation to storyline.
1938 60m/B Roy Rogers, Lynn (Mary Hart) Roberts, Stanley Andrews; **D:** Joseph Kane. **VHS, Beta $19.95** NOS, VYY, VDM 🎬🎬

The Shining Very loose adaptation of the Stephen King horror novel about a writer and his family, snowbound in a huge hotel, who experience various hauntings caused by either the hotel itself or the writer's dementia. Technically stunning, and pretty dang scary, but too long, pretentious and implausible. Nicholson is excellent as the failed writer gone off the deep end.
1980 (R) 143m/C Jack Nicholson, Shelley Duvall, Scatman Crothers, Danny Lloyd, Joe Turkel, Barry Nelson; **D:** Stanley Kubrick. **VHS, Beta, LV $19.98** WAR, PIA 🎬🎬½

The Shining Hour A compelling melodrama in which Crawford portrays a New York night club dancer who is pursued by the rather conservative Douglas. His brother tries to persuade him from marrying Crawford, but then he soon finds himself attracted to her. A devastating fire wipes out all problems of family dissension in this intelligent soap opera.
1938 76m/B Joan Crawford, Margaret Sullavan, Melvyn Douglas, Robert Young, Fay Bainter, Allyn Joslyn; **D:** Frank Borzage; **W:** Ogden Nash, Jane Murfin. **VHS $19.98** MGM 🎬🎬

A Shining Season Tearjerker about a potential-packed long-distance runner, John Baker, stricken with cancer. He spends his last year training a girls' track team to a championship. Earnest, well-performed and involving. Based on a true story. Made for TV.
1979 100m/C Timothy Bottoms, Rip Torn, Allyn Ann McLerie, Ed Begley Jr., Benjamin Bottoms, Mason Adams, Constance Forslund, Ellen Geer; **D:** Stuart Margolin. **VHS, Beta $59.95** BTV 🎬🎬🎬

Shining Star A recording company is run by the mob. Potentially interesting film is hampered by quality of sound and photography and general lack of purpose or direction. Music by Earth, Wind and Fire. **AKA:** That's the Way of the World.
1975 (PG) 100m/C Harvey Keitel, Ed Nelson, Cynthia Bostick, Bert Parks; **D:** Sig Shore. **VHS $39.95** LIV 🎬½

Shining Through Baby-voiced Griffith as a spy sent behind enemy lines without training? Douglas as a spy sent behind enemy lines without speaking German? Old-fashioned blend of romance, espionage, and derring-do where noble hero saves spunky heroine from nasty Nazis in WWII Germany works despite thin plot. Series of flash-forwards to an aged Griffith is annoying and tends to stop action cold, but everyone tries hard and period flavor is authentic. Adapted from best-selling Susan Isaacs novel, but bears little resemblance to book.
1992 (R) 133m/C Michael Douglas, Melanie Griffith, Liam Neeson, Joely Richardson, John Gielgud, Francis Guinan, Patrick Winczewski, Sylvia Syms; **W/D:** David Seltzer. **VHS $19.98** FXV 🎬🎬½

Shinobi Ninja Last-surviving member of Koga ninja clan returns to Japan from U.S. to save his homeland from enemy ninja clan. Mediocre pseudo ninja antics. Badly dubbed.
1984 103m/C JP Tadashi Yamashita, Eric Lee, Karen Lee Sheperd. **VHS, Beta $24.95** AHV 🎬

Shiokari Pass A man has a divine revelation at the pass. In Japanese with English subtitles.
1977 60m/C JP **D:** Novuru Nakamuru. **VHS $29.95** REP, VBL 🎬½

Ship Ahoy Songs, comedy, a spy spoof, and some patriotism thrown in for good measure. Powell plays a dancer who works with Tommy Dorsey and his orchestra. They're on their way to Puerto Rico, via ocean liner, along with her pulp fiction writer boyfriend (Skelton). Emery, posing as an FBI man, convinces Powell to smuggle a package for him but he's really a spy and the whole thing's a con which turns out to be based on one of Skelton's potboiler plots. An uncredited Frank Sinatra is the singer with the Dorsey band, along with drummer Buddy Rich and trumpeter Ziggy Elman who provide some great musical solos. 🎵Last Call For Love; Poor You; On Moonlight Bay; Tampico; I'll Take Tallulah; Cape Dance; Ship Ahoy.
1942 95m/B Eleanor Powell, Red Skelton, Bert Lahr, Virginia O'Brien, John Emery, William Post Jr.; **D:** Edward Buzzell; **W:** Harry Kurnitz, Harry Clork, Irving Brecher. **VHS $19.98** MGM 🎬🎬½

Ship of Fools A group of passengers sailing to Germany in the '30s find mutual needs and concerns, struggle with early evidence of Nazi racism, and discover love on their voyage. Twisted story and fine acting maintain interest. Appropriate tunes written by Ernest Gold. Based on the Katherine Ann Porter novel. Leigh's last film role; she died two years later. Kramer grapples with civil rights issues in much of his work.

1965 149m/B Vivien Leigh, Simone Signoret, Jose Ferrer, Lee Marvin, Oskar Werner, Michael Dunn, Elizabeth Ashley, George Segal, Jose Greco, Charles Korvin, Heinz Ruehmann; *D:* Stanley Kramer. Academy Awards '65: Best Art Direction/Set Decoration (B & W), Best Black and White Cinematography; Nominations: Best Actor (Werner), Best Actress (Signoret), Best Adapted Screenplay, Best Costume Design (B & W), Best Picture, Best Supporting Actor (Dunn); National Board of Review Awards '65: 10 Best Films of the Year, Best Actor (Marvin). **VHS, Beta, LV** $19.95 *COL, SWC* 🎬🎬🎬

Ships in the Night Logan is the plucky heroine who is searching for her missing brother who has been captured by pirates. She is aided in her search by handsome hero Mower.
1928 86m/B Frank Moran, Jacqueline Logan, Jack Mower, Andy Clyde. **VHS, Beta** *FCT, GPV, SNC* 🎬🎬

Shipwreck Island Eight boys are shipwrecked on a deserted island, then make their way to another island where they must survive against wild animals and the elements for two years.
1961 93m/C **VHS** $19.95 *HTV, FCT* 🎬🎬

Shipwrecked Kiddie swashbuckler based on the 1873 popular novel "Haakon Haakonsen." *AKA:* Haakon Haakonsen.
1990 (PG) 93m/C *NO* Gabriel Byrne, Stian Smestad, Louisa Haigh; *D:* Nils Gaup. **VHS, LV** $19.99 *BVV* 🎬🎬½

Shirley Temple Festival A collection of four Shirley Temple short subjects from the 30s: "Dora's Dunkin Doughnuts," "Pardon My Pups," "War Babies" and "Kid N' Africa."
1933 55m/B Shirley Temple, Andy Clyde. **VHS, Beta** $19.95 *WWV, MRV* 🎬🎬½

Shirley Valentine A lively middle-aged English housewife gets a new lease on life when she travels to Greece without her husband. Collins reprises her London and Broadway stage triumph. The character frequently addresses the audience directly to explain her thoughts and feelings; her energy and spunk carry the day. Good script by Willy Russell from the people who brought us "Educating Rita."
1989 108m/C *GB* Pauline Collins, Tom Conti, Alison Steadman, Julia McKenzie; *D:* Lewis Gilbert. Academy Awards '89 Nominations: Best Actress (Collins), Best Song ("The Girl Who Used to Be Me"); British Academy Awards '89: Best Actress (Collins). **VHS, LV, 8mm** $14.95 *PAR, TVC, HMV* 🎬🎬🎬

Shirt Tales This is a series of cartoons featuring the animated crime-stoppers.
1985 45m/C **VHS, Beta** $19.95 *TTC, WTA* 🎬🎬🎬

Shiver, Gobble & Snore Series of animations based on stories by Mary Winn: "The Kings of Snark," "The Town That Had No Policemen," "The Fisherman Who Needed a Knife," and the title tale.
1970 45m/C **VHS, Beta** $19.95 *NWV* 🎬🎬🎬

The Shock Crippled low-life Chaney becomes restored spiritually by a small-town girl and rebels against his Chinese boss. This causes an unfortunate string of melodramatic tragedies, including the San Francisco earthquake of 1906. Silent. Odd, desultory tale with bad special effects is worth seeing for Chaney's good acting.
1923 96m/B Lon Chaney Sr., Virginia Valli; *D:* Lambert Hillyer. **VHS, Beta** $16.95 *SNC, NOS, HEG* 🎬🎬½

Shock! A psychiatrist is called on to treat a woman on the edge of a nervous breakdown. He then discovers she saw him murder his wife, and tries to keep her from

remembering it. Interesting premise handled in trite B style. Price's first starring role.
1946 70m/B Vincent Price, Lynn Bari, Frank Latimore, Anabel Shaw; *D:* Alfred Werker. **VHS, Beta, 3/4U, Special order formats** $16.95 *SNC, NOS, KRT* 🎬

Shock Corridor A reporter, dreaming of a Pulitzer Prize, fakes mental illness and gets admitted to an asylum, where he hopes to investigate a murder. He is subjected to disturbing experiences, including shock therapy, but does manage to solve the murder. However, he suffers a mental breakdown in the process and is admitted for real. Disturbing and lurid.
1963 101m/B Peter Breck, Constance Towers, Gene Evans, Hari Rhodes, James Best, Philip Ahn; *D:* Samuel Fuller. **VHS, LV** $79.95 *CRC, VYG* 🎬🎬🎬

Shock 'Em Dead A devil worshipper trades his life to Lucifer for a chance at rock and roll fame and beautiful Miss Lords. Sexy thriller, with a good share of violence and tension. Ironically, ex porn great Lords is one of the few starlets who doesn't disrobe in the film.
1990 (R) 94m/C Traci Lords, Aldo Ray, Troy Donahue, Stephen Quadros; *D:* Mark Freed. **VHS, LV** $19.95 *ACA* 🎬🎬

Shock! Shock! Shock! Another low-budget slasher flick, with a homicidal lunatic wielding a butcher knife. Space alien jewel thieves add an element, for what it's worth. Makes one ponder the cosmic question: What's the diff between a bad slasher flick and a spoof of a bad slasher flick? Whichever this one is, it's really bad!
1987 60m/B Brad Issac, Cyndy McCrossen, Allen Rickman, Brian Fuorry; *D:* Todd Rutt, Arn McConnell. **VHS, Beta** $29.95 *RHI, MWF* 🎬

A Shock to the System Business exec. Caine is passed over for a long-deserved promotion in favor of a younger man. When he accidentally pushes a panhandler in front of a subway in a fit of rage, he realizes how easy murder is and thinks it may be the answer to all his problems. Tries to be a satire take on corporate greed, etc., but somehow loses steam. Excellent cast makes the difference; Caine adds class.
1990 (R) 88m/C Michael Caine, Elizabeth McGovern, Peter Riegert, Swoosie Kurtz, Will Patton, Jenny Wright; *D:* Jan Egleson. **VHS, Beta, LV** $89.99 *HBO* 🎬🎬🎬

Shock Treatment Seldom-seen mediocre semi-sequel to the cult classic, "The Rocky Horror Picture Show" (1975). Brad and Janet, now married and portrayed by different leads, find themselves trapped on a TV gameshow full of weirdos. Same writers, same director, and several original cast members do make an appearance. *AKA:* Traitement de Choc.
1981 (PG) 94m/C Richard O'Brien, Jessica Harper, Cliff DeYoung, Patricia Quinn, Charles Gray, Ruby Wax; *D:* Jim Sharman. **VHS, Beta** $19.98 *FOX* 🎬½

Shock Waves A group of mutant-underwater-zombie-Nazi-soldiers terrorizes stranded tourists staying at a deserted motel on a small island. Cushing is the mad scientist intent on recreating the Nazi glory days with the seaweed-attired zombies. Odd B-grade, more or less standard horror flick somehow rises (slightly) above badness. *AKA:* Death Corps; Almost Human.
1977 (PG) 90m/C Peter Cushing, Brooke Adams, John Carradine, Luke Halprin; *D:* Ken Wiederhorn. **VHS, Beta** $9.99 *STE, PSM* 🎬🎬

Shocker Another Craven gore-fest. A condemned serial killer is transformed into a menacing electrical force after being fried in the chair. Practically a remake of Craven's original "Nightmare on Elm Street." Great special effects, a few enjoyable weird and sick moments. What's Dr. Timothy Leary doing here?
1989 (R) 111m/C Michael Murphy, Peter Berg, Cami Cooper, Mitch Pileggi, Richard Price; *D:* Wes Craven, Timothy Leary. **VHS, Beta, LV** $19.98 *MCA* 🎬🎬½

Shocking Asia For the eye-covering delight of Western audiences, Mr. Fox compiles gruesome Asian oddities.
1975 94m/C *GE D:* Emerson Fox. **VHS, Beta** *HHE* 🎬½

The Shoes of the Fisherman Morris West's interesting, speculative best seller about Russian Pope brought to the big screen at much expense, but with little care or thought. Siberian prison-camp vet Quinn, elected Pope, tries to arrest nuclear war. Director Anderson wasted the prodigious talents of Olivier, Gielgud, et al. Sloppy use of good cast and promising plot.
1968 (G) 160m/C Anthony Quinn, Leo McKern, Laurence Olivier, John Gielgud, Vittorio De Sica, Oskar Werner, David Janssen; *D:* Michael Anderson Sr. **VHS, Beta, LV** $29.99 *MGM, PIA, FCT* 🎬½

Shoeshine Two shoeshine boys struggling to survive in post-war Italy become involved in the black market are eventually caught and imprisoned. Prison scenes detail the sense of abandonment and tragedy that destroys their friendship. A rich, sad achievement in neo-realistic drama. In Italian with English subtitles.
1947 90m/B *IT* Franco Interlenghi, Rinaldo Smordoni, Anniello Mele, Bruno Ortensi, Pacifico Astrologo; *D:* Vittorio De Sica; *W:* Cesare Zavattini, Sergio Amidei, Adolfe Franci, C.G. Viola. Academy Awards '47 Nominations: Best Original Screenplay; National Board of Review Awards '47: 10 Best Films of the Year. **VHS, Beta** *FCT* 🎬🎬🎬🎬

Shogun Television miniseries chronicling the saga of a shipwrecked English navigator who becomes the first Shogun, or Samurai warrior chief, from the Western world. Colorfully adapted from the James Clavell bestseller. Also released in a two-hour version, but this full-length version is infinitely better.
1980 550m/C Richard Chamberlain, Toshiro Mifune, Yoko Shimada, John Rhys-Davies, Damien Thomas; *D:* Jerry London. **VHS, Beta, LV** $249.95 *TAM, PAR* 🎬🎬🎬½

Shogun Assassin Story of a proud samurai named Lone Wolf who served his Shogun master well as the Official Decapitator, until the fateful day when the aging Shogun turned against him. Extremely violent, with record-breaking body counts. Edited from two other movies in a Japanese series called "Sword of Vengeance"; a tour de force of the cutting room. The samurai pushes his son's stroller through much of the film-sets it aside to hack and slash.
1980 (R) 89m/C *JP* Tomisaburo Wakayama; *D:* Kenji Misumi, Robert Houston. **VHS, Beta, LV** *MCA, OM* 🎬🎬½

Shogun's Ninja In 16th-century Japan, an age-old rivalry between two ninja clans sparks a search for a dagger which will lead to one clan's hidden gold. Martial arts performed and directed by Sonny Chiba. In Japanese with usual poor English dubbing.
1983 115m/C Henry Sanada, Sue Shiomi, Sonny Chiba; *D:* Noribumi Suzuki. **VHS, Beta** $49.95 *MED* 🎬½

Shoot Five hunting buddies fall prey to a group of crazed killers after one man is shot by accident. What's the message: Anti-gun? Anti-hunting? Silly, unbelievable, irresponsibly moralistic, and gratuitously violent.
1985 (R) 98m/C Ernest Borgnine, Cliff Robertson, Henry Silva, Helen Shaver; **D:** Harvey Hart. **VHS, Beta $59.98** SUE *ℐ*

Shoot It Black, Shoot It Blue Rogue cop shoots a black purse snatcher and thinks he has gotten away with it. Unknown to him, a witness has filmed the incident and turns the evidence over to a lawyer.
1974 93m/C Michael Moriarty. **VHS, Beta $69.99** HBO *ℐ½*

Shoot Loud, Louder, I Don't Understand! A sculptor who has a hard time separating reality from dreams thinks he witnessed a murder. Shenanigans follow. Meant to be a black comedy, but when not dull, it is confusing. Welch looks good, as usual, but doesn't show acting talent here. In Italian with English subtitles. **AKA:** Spara Forte, Piu Forte...Non Capisco.
1966 101m/C *IT* Marcello Mastroianni, Raquel Welch; **D:** Eduardo de Filippo. **VHS, Beta $59.95** NLC *ℐ½*

Shoot the Living, Pray for the Dead While travelling through Mexico, the leader of a band of killers promises his guide half of a share in stolen gold if he can lead them to it.
1973 90m/C Klaus Kinski. **VHS, Beta $19.95** NEG *ℐℐ*

Shoot the Moon A successful writer, married and with four children, finds his life unrewarding and leaves his family to take up with a younger woman. The wife must learn to deal with her resentment, the fears of her children, and her own attempt at a new love. Fine acting but a worn-out story.
1982 (R) 124m/C Diane Keaton, Albert Finney, Karen Allen, Peter Weller, Dana Hill, Viveka Davis, Tracey Gold, Tina Yothers; **D:** Alan Parker. **VHS, Beta, LV $19.99** MGM *ℐℐ½*

Shoot the Piano Player Former concert pianist (Aznavour, spendidly cast) changes his name and plays piano at a low-class Paris cafe. A convoluted plot ensues; he becomes involved with gangsters, though his girlfriend wants him to try a comeback. Lots of atmosphere, character development, humor, and romance. A Truffaut masterpiece. In French with English subtitles. **AKA:** Tirez sur le Pianiste; Shoot the Pianist.
1962 92m/B *FR* Charles Aznavour, Marie DuBois, Nicole Berger; **D:** Francois Truffaut. **VHS, Beta, LV, 3/4U, Special order formats $39.95** HMV, HHT, WFV *ℐℐℐℐ*

Shoot the Sun Down Four offbeat characters united in a search for gold turn against each other. "Gilligan's Island"-style assortment of characters (Indian; gunfighter; girl; sea captain) are cast away in a pointless plot from which they never escape. Too bad: talented cast could have done better.
1981 (PG) 102m/C Christopher Walken, Margot Kidder, Geoffrey Lewis, Bo Brundin, Sacheen Little Feather; **D:** David Leeds. **VHS, Beta $19.95** VID *ℐ½*

Shoot to Kill B-grade noir-esque mystery about a crooked D.A. and a gangster who bite the dust. Suspenseful, dark, street-level crime drama uncovered by ambitious journalist Ward.
1947 64m/B Russell Wade, Susan Walters, Nestor Paiva, Edmund MacDonald, Vince Barnett; **D:** William Berke. **VHS, Beta, LV $19.99** SNC, WGE, VYY *ℐℐ½*

Shoot to Kill A city cop (Poitier, better than ever after 10 years off the screen) and a mountain guide (Berenger) reluctantly join forces to capture a killer who is part of a hunting party traversing the Pacific Northwest and which is being led by the guide's unsuspecting girlfriend (Alley). Poitier may be a bit old for the role, but he carries the implausible plot on the strength of his performance. Good action.
1988 (R) 110m/C Sidney Poitier, Tom Berenger, Kirstie Alley, Clancy Brown, Richard Masur, Andrew Robinson; **D:** Roger Spottiswoode. **VHS $19.99** TOU *ℐℐℐ*

Shooters A wacky platoon of misfits is paired off against a group of vicious killers in a "war game" training session. Not completely unfunny or worthless.
1989 84m/C Ben Schick, Robin Sims, Aldo Ray. **VHS, Beta $79.95** AIP *ℐℐ½*

Shootfighter: Fight to the Death Two boys become experts in the martial arts and constant rivals. Now grown-up they take their rivalry to a deadly level in a "shootfight," a game which has no rules and is so brutal it's banned as a sport. Not that this stops them. An unrated version is also available.
1993 (R) 94m/C Bolo Yeung, Martin Kove, William Zabka, Michael Bernardo, Maryam D'Abo, Edward Albert; **D:** Pat Alan; **W:** Judd B. Lynn, Larry Feliz Jr., Peter Shaner. **VHS, LV** COL, VIS *ℐℐ½*

The Shooting A mysterious woman, bent on revenge, persuades a former bounty hunter and his partner to escort her across the desert, with tragic results. Offbeat, small film filled strong by performances of Nicholson and Oates. Filmed concurrently with "Ride in the Whirlwind," with the same cast and director. Bang-up surprise ending.
1966 82m/C Warren Oates, Millie Perkins, Jack Nicholson, Will Hutchins; **D:** Monte Hellman. **VHS, Beta, LV** MED, DVT, HHT *ℐℐℐ*

Shooting Three boys run away when they think they have killed a man in a hunting accident.
1982 60m/C Lynn Redgrave, Lance Kerwin, Barry Primus. **VHS, Beta** NO *ℐ*

Shooting Elizabeth A fed-up husband decides to shut his loudmouthed wife up—permanently. Before he can kill her, she disappears. The police don't buy it and want to charge him with murder. Can he find his wife before things really get serious?
1992 (PG-13) 96m/C Jeff Goldblum, Mimi Rogers. **VHS, LV** LIV *ℐ½*

The Shooting Party A group of English aristocrats assemble at a nobleman's house for a bird shoot on the eve of World War I. Splendid cast crowned Mason in his last role. Fascinating crucible class anxieties, rich wit social scheming, personality conflicts, and things left unsaid. Julian Bond wrote the script from Isabel Colegate's novel.
1985 97m/C *GB* James Mason, Dorothy Tutin, Edward Fox, John Gielgud, Robert Hardy, Cheryl Campbell, Judi Bowker; **D:** Alan Bridges. **VHS, Beta $69.99** HBO *ℐℐℐ*

Shooting Stars Two actors who play private eyes on television are pushed out of their jobs by a jealous co-star. They take to the streets as "real" crime-fighting dicks. Interesting premise goes nowhere. Made for TV.
1985 96m/C Billy Dee Williams, Parker Stevenson, Efrem Zimbalist Jr., Edie Adams; **D:** Richard Lang. **VHS, Beta $24.95** AHV *ℐ*

The Shootist Wayne, in a support last role, plays a legendary gunslinger afflicted with cancer, who seeks peace and solace in his final days. Town bad guys Boone and O'Brian aren't about to let him rest and are determined to gun him down to avenge past deeds. One of Wayne's best and most dignified performances about living up to a personal code of honor. Stewart and Bacall head excellent supporting cast. Based on Glendon Swarthout's novel.
1976 (PG) 100m/C John Wayne, Lauren Bacall, Ron Howard, James Stewart, Richard Boone, Hugh O'Brian, Bill McKinney, Harry Morgan, John Carradine, Sheree North, Scatman Crothers; **D:** Don Siegel. Academy Awards '76 Nominations: Best Art Direction/Set Decoration; National Board of Review Awards '76: 10 Best Films of the Year. **VHS, Beta, LV $14.95** PAR, TLF *ℐℐℐ½*

Shop Angel A department store dress designer encounters romance and scandal in this low-budget drama of intrigue and romance. She falls in love with the fiance of her boss's daughter, and schemes to blackmail him (the boss). Competently rendered if unexceptional tale.
1932 66m/B Marion Shilling, Holmes Herbert, Creighton Hale; **D:** Mason Hopper. **VHS, Beta, 8mm** VYY *ℐℐ*

The Shop Around the Corner A low-key romantic classic in which Stewart and Sullavan are feuding clerks in a small Budapest shop, who unknowingly fall in love via a lonely hearts club. Charming portrayal of ordinary people in ordinary situations. Excellent script adapted by Simon Raphaelson, from the play "Parfumerie" by Nikolaus Laszlo. Later made into a musical called "In the Good Old Summertime" and, on Broadway, "She Loves Me."
1940 99m/B Margaret Sullavan, James Stewart, Frank Morgan, Joseph Schildkraut, Sara Haden, Felix Bressart; **D:** Ernst Lubitsch. **VHS, LV $19.98** MGM, PIA *ℐℐℐℐ½*

The Shop on Main Street During World War II, a Slovak takes a job as an "Aryan comptroller" for a Jewish-owned button shop. The owner is an old deaf woman; they slowly build a friendship. Tragedy ensues when all of the town's Jews are to be deported. Sensitive and subtle. Surely among the most gutwrenching portrayals of human tragedy ever on screen. Exquisite plotting and direction. In Czechoslovakian with English subtitles. **AKA:** The Shop on High Street; Obch Od Na Korze.
1965 111m/B *CZ* Ida Kaminska, Josef Kroner, Hana Slivkoua, Elmar Klos; **D:** Jan Kadar, Elmar Klos. Academy Awards '65: Best Foreign Language Film; Nominations: Best Actress (Kaminska); New York Film Critics Awards '66: Best Foreign Film. **VHS, Beta, LV $19.98** COL, TAM, SWC *ℐℐℐℐ*

Shore Leave Dressmaker Mackaill isn't getting any younger. Tough-guy sailor Bilge Smith (Barthelmess, in top form) meets her on shore leave; little does he realize her plans for him! She owns a dry-docked ship, you see, and it (and she) will be ready for him when he comes ashore next. Lovely, fun (if rather plodding) romantic comedy. Later made into musicals twice, as "Hit the Deck" and "Follow the Fleet."
1925 74m/B Richard Barthelmess, Dorothy Mackaill; **D:** John S. Robertson. **VHS $19.95** GPV, VYY *ℐℐ*

Short Circuit A newly-developed robot designed for the military is hit by lightning and begins to think it's alive. Sheedy and Guttenberg help it hide from the mean people at the weapons lab who want to take it home. Followed two years later, save

Sheedy and Guttenberg, by the lame "Short Circuit 2."
1986 (PG) 98m/C Steve Guttenberg, Ally Sheedy, Austin Pendleton, Fisher Stevens, Brian McNamara; *D:* John Badham. **VHS, Beta, LV** $19.98 FOX 🎬🎬

Short Circuit 2 A sequel to the first adorable-robot-outwits-bad-guys tale. The robot, Number Five, makes his way through numerous plot turns without much human assistance or much purpose. Harmless (unless you have to spend time watching it), but pointless and juvenile. Very occasional genuinely funny moments.
1988 (PG) 95m/C Fisher Stevens, Cynthia Gibb, Michael McKean, Jack Weston, David Hemblen; *D:* Kenneth Johnson. **VHS, Beta, LV** $19.95 COL 🎬 ½

Short Eyes When a child molester (Davison) enters prison, the inmates act out their own form of revenge against him. Filmed on location at New York City's Men's House of Detention, nicknamed "The Tombs." Script by Manuel Pinero from his excellent play; he also acts in the film. Top-notch performances and respectful direction from Young bring unsparingly realistic prison drama to the screen. Title is prison jargon for child molester. *AKA:* The Slammer.
1979 (R) 100m/C Bruce Davison, Miguel Pinero, Nathan George, Donald Blakely, Curtis Mayfield, Jose Perez, Shawn Elliott; *D:* Robert M. Young. **VHS, Beta** $69.98 LIV 🎬🎬🎬½

A Short Film Festival A festive collection of short animated films. Includes Oscar nominee "The Family That Lived Apart," and "Hot Stuff."
1990 57m/C VHS, Beta $29.95 WTA, FCT 🎬🎬½

Short Films of D.W. Griffith, Vol. 1 Three early shorts by the great silent-film director. "The Battle" is a lavish Civil War drama. "The Female of the Species" stars pickford McDowell and Bernard as pioneers struggling to survive hardship and each other's company in the desert. "The New York Hat" is a comedy (written by Anita Loos, aged 14!) starring Pickford as a girl who endures the malice of her peers when she is given a nice hat. Landmark early films from a master director.
1912 59m/B Mary Pickford, Charles West, Blanche Sweet, Claire McDowell; *D:* D.W. Griffith. **VHS, Beta** $24.95 VYY, DVT, HEG 🎬🎬🎬🎬

Short Films of D.W. Griffith, Vol. 2 Five early silent shorts by Griffith, with original organ music and some familiar faces in the casts: "A Corner in Wheat," "The Revenue Man and his Girl," "The Musketeers of Pig Alley," "A Girl and her Trust" and "The Battle of Elderbush Gulch."
1909 112m/B Lillian Gish, Bobby Harron, Mae Marsh, Lionel Barrymore, Dorothy Gish, Henry B. Walthall, Kate Bruce, James Kirkwood, Harry Carey Sr. **VHS, Beta, 8mm** $29.99 VYY, DVT, HEG 🎬🎬½

Short Fuse A Washington, D.C. reporter uncovers the truth behind the rape and murder of a nurse. Interesting "go-go" music from the Washington D.C. ghetto aids an otherwise uninteresting film. *AKA:* Good to Go.
1988 (R) 91m/C Art Garfunkel, Robert DoQui, Harris Yulin, Richard Brooks, Reginald Daughtry; *D:* Blaine Novak. **VHS, Beta** $79.95 VMK 🎬½

Short Time Somewhere between "Tango & Cash" and "Airplane" is where you'll find "Short Time." Non-stop action/comedy stars Dabney Coleman and Teri Garr as partners in crime and humor. Coleman is a cop days from retirement; wrongly told he is dying, he tries hard to get killed so his family will be provided for. Coleman is wonderful. Garr, no longer the long-suffering wife of "Oh, God" and "Close Encounters," is appealing here as the indulgent sidekick.
1990 (PG-13) 100m/C Dabney Coleman, Teri Garr, Matt Frewer, Barry Corbin, Joe Pantoliano, Xander Berkeley; *D:* Gregg Champion. **VHS, LV** $14.95 IME, LIV 🎬🎬🎬

A Shot in the Dark A minister suspects murder when a despised miser is thought to have committed suicide. He takes it on himself to investigate in this routine mystery.
1933 53m/B GB Dorothy Boyd, O.B. Clarence, Jack Hawkins, Russell Thorndike, Michael Shepley; *D:* George Pearson. **VHS, Beta** $16.95 SNC 🎬½

A Shot in the Dark When his son is murdered at a New England college, a distraught dad takes it on himself to investigate. Former movie cowboy Starrett plays the sleuthing pop in this undistinguished mystery.
1935 69m/B Charles Starrett, Robert Warwick, Edward Van Sloan, Marion Shilling, Doris Lloyd, Helen Jerome Eddy, James Bush; *D:* Charles Lamont. **VHS, Beta** $16.95 NOS, SNC 🎬🎬

A Shot in the Dark Second and possibly the best in the classic "Inspector Clouseau-Pink Panther" series of comedies. The bumbling Inspector Clouseau (Sellers, of course) investigates the case of a parlor maid (Sommer) accused of murdering her lover. Clouseau's libido convinces him she's innocent, even though all the clues point to her. Classic gags, wonderful Henry Maucini music. After this film, Sellers as Clouseau disappears until 1975's "Return of the Pink Panther" (Alan Arkin played him in "Inspector Clouseau," made in 1968 by different folks).
1964 101m/C Peter Sellers, Elke Sommer, Herbert Lom, George Sanders, Bryan Forbes; *D:* Blake Edwards. **VHS, Beta, LV** $19.98 FOX, FCT 🎬🎬🎬½

Shotgun A sheriff on the trail of a killer is accompanied by a girl he's saved from Indians. Average western cowritten by western actor Rory Calhoun, who had hoped to star in the film, but was turned down by the studio.
1955 81m/C Sterling Hayden, Zachary Scott, Yvonne De Carlo; *D:* Lesley Selander. **VHS** $29.95 PAR 🎬🎬½

Shotgun The main character, "Shotgun," is out to avenge a prostitute's murder. Along the way, he has to deal with sex, drugs, and violence.
1989 90m/C Stuart Chapin, Katie Caple. **VHS** $29.95 PMH 🎬

The Shout From a strange Robert Graves story, an even stranger film. A lunatic befriends a young couple, moves in with them, and gradually takes over their lives. The movie's title refers to the man's ability to kill by shouting, a power he learned from his Australian aboriginal past.
1978 (R) 88m/C GB Alan Bates, Susannah York, John Hurt, Tim Curry; *D:* Jerzy Skolimowski. **VHS, Beta** $39.98 COL, VID 🎬🎬🎬

Shout Romance and rebellion set in a sleepy Texas town during the 1950s. Jesse Tucker's (Walters) rebellious ways land him in the Benedict Home for Boys and he seems lost until Jack Cabe (Travolta) enters town. Jack introduces Jesse and the gang to the exciting new sounds of rock 'n' roll. Been done before and better.
1991 (PG-13) 93m/C John Travolta, James Walters, Heather Graham, Richard Jordan, Linda Fiorentino; *D:* Jeffrey Hornaday. **VHS, Beta, LV** $19.98 MCA 🎬🎬

Shout at the Devil English officer Moore and Irish-American adventurer Marvin seek to blow up a German battleship out for repairs in East Africa before the outbreak of WWI. There's also some intrigue about ivory smuggling. From the novel by Wilbur Smith and based on an actual incident, but that doesn't make the comedy adventure any more palatable. Marvin's hamming is ludicrous, Moore is unusually wooden, and the big budget permits any number of fairly pointless action-oriented excursions and explosions.
1976 (PG) 128m/C GB Lee Marvin, Roger Moore, Barbara Parkins, Ian Holm; *D:* Peter Hunt. **VHS, Beta, LV** $29.98 LIV, VES 🎬½

Show Boat The second of three film versions of the Jerome Kern/Oscar Hammerstein musical, filmed previously in 1929, about a Mississippi showboat and the life and loves of its denizens. Wonderful romance, unforgettable music. Director Whale also brought the world "Frankenstein." The laser edition includes a historical audio essay by Miles Kreuger, excerpts from the 1929 version, Ziegfeld's 1932 stage revival, "Life Aboard a Real Showboat" (a vintage short), radio broadcasts, and a 300-photo essay tracing the history of showboats. Screenplay by Hammerstein. As is this version was not the end-all, it was filmed yet again 15 years later. ♫Ol' Man River; Ah Still Suits Me; Bill; Can't Help Lovin' Dat Man; Only Make Believe; I Have the Room Above Her; You Are Love; Gallivantin' Around; Cotton Blossom; Cap'n Andy's Ballyhoo; Where's the Mate For Me?; Mis'ry's Comin' Around; Why Do I Love You; Goodbye, My Lady Love; At A Georgia Camp Meeting; Washington Post March; Make Believe; After the Ball.
1936 110m/B Irene Dunne, Allan Jones, Paul Robeson, Helen Morgan, Hattie McDaniel, Charles Winninger, Donald Cook; *D:* James Whale. **VHS, Beta, LV** $29.95 CRC, MLB 🎬🎬🎬🎬

Show Boat Third movie version of Jerome Kern and Oscar Hammerstein II's 1927 musical play about the life and loves of a Mississippi riverboat theater troupe. Young girl raised as a showboat entertainer falls in love with a gambler. Heartache follows. Terrific musical numbers, with fun dance from Champion who went on to great fame as a choreographer. Grayson is somewhat vapid, but lovely to look at and hear. Gardner didn't want to do the part of Julie, although she eventually received fabulous reviews. Her singing was dubbed by Annette Warren. The 171-foot "Cotton Blossom" boat was built on the Tarzan lake on the MGM back lot at a cost of $126,468.00—a lot of money in 1951. Warfield's film debut—his "Ole Man River"—was recorded in one take. Laserdisc version features the original motion picture trailer, excerpts from "Broadway," "Silent Film," and radio Version of "Show Boat," a documentary featuring life on a real show boat, and a commentary on the performers, the film, and the history of show boats. ♫Make Believe; Can't Help Lovin' Dat Man; I Might Fall Back On You; Ol' Man River; You Are Love; Why Do I Love You?; Bill; Life Upon the Wicked Stage; After the Ball.
1951 107m/C Kathryn Grayson, Howard Keel, Ava Gardner, William Warfield, Joe E. Brown, Agnes Moorehead; *D:* George Sidney. **VHS, Beta, LV** $19.98 MGM, VYG, TLF 🎬🎬🎬

Show Business Historically valuable film record of classic vaudeville acts, especially Cantor and Davis. A number of vaudevillians recreate their old acts for director Marin—unforgettable slapstick and songs. All this pegged on a plot that follows Cantor's rise to

fame with the Ziegfeld Follies. ♫Alabamy Bound; I Want a Girl (Just Like the Girl Who Married Dear Old Dad); It Had to Be You; Making Whoopee; Why Am I Blue; They're Wearing 'Em Higher in Hawaii; The Curse of an Aching Heart; While Strolling in the Park One Day; You May Not Remember; The Daughter of Rosie O'Grady.
1944 92m/B Eddie Cantor, Joan Davis, George Murphy; **D:** Edwin L. Marin. **VHS, Beta, LV** $19.98 *CCB, TTC* 🎞🎞🎞

A Show of Force Reporter Irving investigates the coverup of a murder with political ramifications. Brazilian director Barreto cast (surprise!) his girlfriend in the lead; she doesn't exactly carry the day. Phillips is good, but you'll end up feeling cheated if you expect to see much of highly-billed Duvall or Garcia. Based on a real incident of 1978, but hardly believable as political realism or even moralism.
1990 (R) 93m/C Erik Estrada, Amy Irving, Andy Garcia, Robert Duvall, Lou Diamond Phillips; **D:** Bruno Barreto. **VHS, Beta, LV** $19.95 *PAR* 🎞🎞

Show People A pretty girl from the boonies tries to make it big in Tinseltown. But as a slapstick star?! She wanted to be a leading lady! Enjoyable, fun silent comedy shows Davies's true talents. Interesting star cameos, including director Vidor at the end.
1928 82m/B Marion Davies, William Haines, Dell Henderson, Paul Ralli; **Cameos:** King Vidor; **D:** King Vidor. **VHS** $29.95 *MGM* 🎞🎞🎞

Show Them No Mercy A couple and their baby out for a drive unwittingly stumble into a kidnapping that doesn't go as planned. Tense gangster drama reincarnated as the Western "Rawhide." **AKA:** Tainted Money.
1935 76m/B Rochelle Hudson, Cesar Romero, Bruce Cabot, Edward Norris, Edward Brophy, Warren Hymer, Herbert Rawlinson; **D:** George Marshall. **VHS** $19.98 *FOX, FCT* 🎞🎞🎞

The Showdown The title actually refers to a tricky poker game, the highlight of yet another Hopalong Cassidy versus hoss thieves quickie epic. Kermit Maynard is the brother of cowboy hero Ken Maynard.
1940 65m/B William Boyd, Russell Hayden, Britt Wood, Morris Ankrum, Jan Clayton, Roy Barcroft, Kermit Maynard; **D:** Howard Bretherton. **VHS** $19.95 *NOS* 🎞🎞

The Showdown Elliott plays trail boss Shad Jones who knows one of his fellow cowhands has murdered his brother. Jones is determined to find out who it is and even the score. Brennan is cast against type as a greedy cattle baron. Elliott's last film for Republic.
1950 86m/B Wild Bill Elliott, Walter Brennan, Marie Windsor, Henry Morgan, Rhys Williams, Jim Davis, Leif Erickson, Yakima Canutt; **W/D:** Stuart E. McGowan, Dorrell McGowan. **VHS** $9.98 *REP* 🎞🎞½

Showdown A woman comes between two men and sends them their separate ways. One becomes a sheriff and must pursue the other, who is now a criminal. Seaton's final film is mediocre.
1973 (PG) 99m/C Rock Hudson, Dean Martin, Susan Clark, Donald Moffatt, John McLiam; **D:** George Seaton. **VHS** 🎞🎞

Showdown at Boot Hill A U.S. Marshal (Bronson) kills a wanted murderer but cannot collect the reward because the townspeople will not identify the victim.
1958 76m/B Charles Bronson, Robert Hutton, John Carradine; **D:** Gene Fowler. **VHS** $19.98 *REP* 🎞🎞

Showdown at the Equator Chinese cops are trained to kill criminals with their feet, and they do.

1983 (R) 95m/C Lo Lieh, Bruce Liang, Nora Miao, Lee Kan Kwun. **VHS, Beta** $24.95 *GEM* 🎞

Showdown at Williams Creek A graphic Canadian Western set in the old Montana territory, where an outcast settler goes on trial for killing an old man. Testimony recounts a shocking history of greed and betrayal. The dark side of the Gold Rush, generally well-acted. Inspired by an actual incident. **AKA:** Kootenai Brown.
1991 (R) 97m/C CA Tom Burlinson, Donnelly Rhodes, Raymond Burr; **D:** Allen Kroeker. **VHS** $89.98 *REP* 🎞🎞½

Showdown in Little Tokyo Lundgren stars as a martial arts master/L.A. cop who was raised in Japan, and has all the respect in the world for his "ancestors" and heritage. Brandon Lee (son of Bruce) is Lundgren's partner, and he's a bona fide American-made, pop-culture, mall junkie. Together, they go after a crack-smuggling gang of "yakuza" (Japanese thugs). Lots of high-kicking action and the unique angle on stereotypes make this a fun martial arts film.
1991 (R) 78m/C Dolph Lundgren, Brandon Lee, Tia Carrere, Cary-Hiroyuki Tagawa; **D:** Mark L. Lester. **VHS, Beta, LV, 8mm** $19.98 *WAR* 🎞🎞

Shredder Orpheus Rock star Orpheus skateboards through hell to stop deadly television transmissions and rescue his wife.
1989 93m/C Jesse Bernstein, Robert McGinley, Vera McCaughan, Megan Murphy, Carlo Scandiuzzi; **D:** Robert McGinley. **VHS, Beta** $79.95 *AIP* 🎞

Shriek in the Night Two rival reporters (Rogers and Talbot, previously paired in "The Thirteenth Guest") turn detective to solve a string of apartment murders. Made on a proverbial shoestring, but not bad.
1933 66m/B Ginger Rogers, Lyle Talbot, Harvey Clark; **D:** Albert Ray. **VHS, Beta** $12.95 *SNC, NOS, KRT* 🎞🎞½

Shriek of the Mutilated An anthropological expedition on a deserted island turns into a night of horror as a savage beast kills the members of the group one by one.
1974 (R) 85m/C Alan Brock, Jennifer Stock, Michael Harris; **D:** Michael Findlay. **VHS, Beta** $59.98 *LIV, SNC* Woof!

The Shrieking Black magic women hang out with biker types in Nebraska in 1919. **AKA:** Hex.
1973 (PG) 93m/C Keith Carradine, Christina Raines, Gary Busey, Robert Walker Jr., Dan Haggerty, John Carradine, Scott Glenn; **D:** Leo Garen. **VHS, Beta, LV** $29.95 *PSM, WAR* 🎞

The Shrimp on the Barbie When daddy refuses to bless her marriage to dim bulb boyfriend, Australian Samms hires L.A. low life Marin to pose as new beau. Another pseudonymous Smithee effort.
1990 (R) 86m/C Cheech Marin, Emma Samms, Vernon Wells, Bruce Spence, Carole Davis; **D:** Alan Smithee. **VHS, Beta, LV** $89.98 *MED* 🎞½

Shy People An urbanized New York journalist and her spoiled daughter journey to the Louisiana bayou to visit long-lost relatives in order to produce an article for "Cosmopolitan." They find ignorance, madness, and ancestral secrets and are forced to examine their motives, their relationships and issues brought to light in the watery, murky, fantastic land of the bayous. Well-acted melodrama with an outstanding performance by Hershey as the cajun matriarch. Music by Tangerine Dream; cinematography by Chris Menges.
1987 (R) 119m/C Jill Clayburgh, Barbara Hershey, Martha Plimpton, Mare Winningham, Merritt Butrick, John Philbin; **D:** Andrei Konchalovsky. **VHS, Beta, LV** $19.89 *WAR* 🎞🎞🎞

The Sibling Two sisters become involved in the accidental murder of a man who was a husband to one woman and lover to the other. Of course, one sister has just been released from the mental rehabilitation clinic. **AKA:** Psycho Sisters; So Evil, My Sister.
1972 (PG) 85m/C Susan Strasberg, Faith Domergue, Sydney Chaplin, Steve Mitchell; **D:** Reginald LeBorg. **VHS, Beta** $9.95 *SIM, PSM, HHE* 🎞🎞

Sibling Rivalry Repressed doctor's wife (redundant) Alley rolls in hay with soon to be stiff stranger upon advice of footloose sister. Stranger expires from heart attack in hay and Alley discovers that the corpse is her long-lost brother-in-law. Slapstick cover-up ensues.
1990 (PG-13) 88m/C Kirstie Alley, Bill Pullman, Carrie Fisher, Sam Elliott, Jami Gertz, Ed O'Neill, Scott Bakula, Frances Sternhagen, Bill Macy; **D:** Carl Reiner. **VHS, Beta, LV, 8mm** $19.95 *COL, SUE, NLC* 🎞🎞

The Sicilian Adapted from the Mario Puzo novel and based on the life of Salvatore Giuliano. Chronicles the exploits of the men who took on the government, the Catholic Church, and the Mafia in an effort to make Sicily secede from Italy and become its own nation in the 1940s. Pretentious, overdone, and confused. This long, uncut version was unseen in America, but hailed by European critics; the 115-minute, R-rated American release is also available, but isn't as good. See "Salvatore Giuliano" (Francesco Rosi, 1962) instead of either version.
1987 146m/C Christopher Lambert, John Turturro, Terence Stamp, Joss Ackland, Barbara Sukowa; **D:** Michael Cimino. **VHS, Beta, LV** $14.98 *LIV, VES* 🎞½

Sicilian Connection A narcotics agent poses as a nightclub manager to bust a drug-smuggling organization.
1974 100m/C IT Ben Gazzara, Silvia Monti, Fausto Tozzi. **VHS, Beta** $79.95 *VCD* 🎞½

The Sicilian Connection Two brothers in the mob serve out vendettas and generally create havoc wherever they go. **AKA:** The Pizza Connection.
1985 (R) 117m/C Michele Placido, Mark Switzer, Simona Cavallari. **VHS, Beta** $79.95 *MGM* 🎞

Sid & Nancy The tragic, brutal, true love story of The Sex Pistols' Sid Vicious and American groupie Nancy Spungen, from the director of "Repo Man." Remarkable lead performances in a very dark story that manages to be funny at times. Depressing but engrossing; no appreciation of punk music or sympathy for the self-destructive way of life is required. Oldman and Webb are superb. Music by Joe Strummer, the Pogues, and Pray for Rain.
1986 (R) 111m/C Gary Oldman, Chloe Webb, Debbie Bishop, David Hayman; **D:** Alex Cox. **VHS, Beta, LV** $14.95 *MVD, SUE, NLC* 🎞🎞🎞½

Side By Side In the same vein as "Cocoon," three senior citizens who aren't ready to retire decide to start their own business and launch a sportswear company designed for seniors. A witty portrayal of graceful aging that is uneven at times.
1988 100m/C Milton Berle, Sid Caesar, Danny Thomas; **D:** Jack Bender. **VHS, Beta** $79.95 *TRI* 🎞🎞

Side Out The first major film about volleyball!? What a claim! What a bore. Midwestern college guy spends summer in Southern Cal. working for slumlord uncle; instead enters "the ultimate" beach volleyball touring. Bogus. Don't see it, dude.

1990 (PG-13) 100m/C C. Thomas Howell, Peter Horton, Kathy Ireland, Sinjin Smith, Randy Stoklos, Courtney Thorne-Smith, Harley Jane Kozak, Christopher Rydell; **D:** Peter Israelson. **VHS, Beta, LV** $89.95 COL ♂♂½

Side Show A runaway teen joins the circus, witnesses a murder, and must use his wits to stay out of reach of the killer. Forced "suspense" and "drama" of the bad made for TV ilk.
1984 98m/C Lance Kerwin, Red Buttons, Anthony (Tony) Franciosa, Connie Stevens; **D:** William Conrad. **VHS, Beta** $19.98 TWE ♂

Sideburns The Pushkin Club, a group of reactionaries who try to remove the western influence from Russia, attack first a rock band, then innocent civilians as they act as a social cleaning service. Uses humor to try and warn people against the rising fascism in Russia because of the battle between conservative and reformist forces. In Russian with English subtitles.
1991 110m/C RU **D:** Yurii Mamin. **VHS** $59.95 FCT ♂♂

Sidekicks Cutesy ego vehicle for executive producer Norris. (Brandis) is bullied by the kids at school and doesn't find much support at home from his well-meaning but ineffectual dad. He has a severe case of hero-worship for Norris, who appears as himself in a series of daydream karate sequences, saving the good guy and maiming the bad. Brandis takes up karate himself and gains self-respect at the same time, which is when his high school dream girl suddenly becomes interested in him. Director Norris is actor Norris' brother. Predictable and sappy.
1993 (PG) 100m/C Chuck Norris, Jonathan Brandis, Beau Bridges, Mako, Julia Nickson-Soul, Danica McKellar, Richard Moll, Joe Piscopo; **D:** Aaron Norris; **W:** Donald W. Thompson, Lou Illar; **M:** Alan Silvestri. **VHS** NYR ♂♂

Sidewalks of London Laughton's a sidewalk entertainer who takes in homeless waif Leigh and puts her in his act and in his heart. Harrison steals her away and before long she's a star in the music halls. Meanwhile, Laughton has fallen on hard times. Memorable performances. **AKA:** St. Martin's Lane.
1940 86m/B GB Charles Laughton, Vivien Leigh, Rex Harrison; **D:** Tim Whelan. **VHS, Beta, 3/4U, Special order formats** $19.95 NOS, HHT, CAB ♂♂♂

Sidewinder One Motocross racing is the setting for a romance between a racer and an heiress. Good racing footage, but where's the plot? If you like cars a whole lot .
. .
1977 (PG) 97m/C Michael Parks, Marjoe Gortner, Susan Howard, Alex Cord, Charlotte Rae; **D:** Earl Bellamy. **VHS, Beta** $59.98 NLC ♂

Sidney Sheldon's Bloodline Wealthy businesswoman Hepburn finds she is marked for death by persons unknown. Exquisitely bad trash from another Sheldon bestseller. **AKA:** Bloodline.
1979 (R) 116m/C Audrey Hepburn, Ben Gazzara, James Mason, Michelle Phillips, Omar Sharif, Irene Papas, Romy Schneider, Gert Frobe, Maurice Ronet, Beatrice Straight; **D:** Terence Young; **M:** Ennio Morricone. **VHS, Beta** PAR Woof!

The Siege of Firebase Gloria Story of the Marines who risked their lives defending an outpost against overwhelming odds during the 1968 Tet offensive in Vietnam. Purportedly patriotic war drama made by an Australian director; lead Hauser is a disgusting sadist, and plot is hopelessly hackneyed.

1989 95m/C Wings Hauser, Lee Ermey; **D:** Brian Trenchard-Smith. **VHS, Beta, LV** $29.95 FRH ♂½

Siegfried Half of Lang's epic masterpiece "Der Niebelungen," based on German mythology. Title hero bathes in the blood of a dragon he has slain. He marries a princess, but wicked Queen Brumhilde has him killed. Part two, in which Siegfried's widow marries Attila the Hun, is titled "Kriemheld's Revenge." These dark, brooding, archetypal tours de force were patriotic tributes, and were loved by Hitler. Silent with music score. **AKA:** Siegfrieds Tod; Siegfried's Death.
1924 100m/B GE Paul Richter, Margareta Schoen; **D:** Fritz Lang. **VHS, LV** $16.95 SNC, NOS, GPV ♂♂♂♂

Siempre Hay una Primera Vez The different loves of two women are contrasted.
1987 94m/C MX Ana Martin, Ana Louisa Peluffo, Helena Rojo. **VHS, Beta** $47.95 MAD ♂♂

Siesta Barkin is a professional stunt woman who leaves her current lover/manager, played by Sheen, and returns to visit her former lover and trainer, Byrne, on the eve of his marriage to another woman. Her trip, marked by flashbacks and flights of seemingly paranoid fantasy, leads to the discovery of murder, but she cannot remember who, when, why, or where. The film distorts time, reality, and perception in a sometimes fascinating, sometimes frustrating psychological mystery. Attractively filmed by video director Lambert with music by Miles Davis. Barkin and Byrne were married in real life a year after the film's release.
1987 (R) 97m/C Ellen Barkin, Gabriel Byrne, Jodie Foster, Julian Sands, Isabella Rossellini, Martin Sheen, Grace Jones, Alexei Sayle; **D:** Mary Lambert. **VHS, Beta, LV** $89.95 LHV, WAR ♂♂½

Sifted Evidence Woman archeologist who becomes involved with a man promises to show him an obscure archeological site in Mexico.
1983 42m/C 3/4U, **Special order formats** NO ♂

The Sign of Four Sherlock Holmes and the ever-faithful Watson are hired by a young woman who has been anonymously sent an enormous diamond. An inept production which looks good but that's all.
1983 97m/C GB Ian Richardson, David Healy, Thorley Walters, Cherie Lunghi; **D:** Desmond Davis. **VHS, Beta** $59.95 PAR ♂½

Sign of the Wolf Features ten chapters of the rare, early talking serial.
1930 ?m/B Rex Lease, Virginia Brown Faire. **VHS** $16.95 SNC ♂½

The Sign of Zorro Adventures of the masked swordsman as he champions the cause of the oppressed in early California. Full-length version of the popular late-50s Disney television series.
1960 89m/C Guy Williams, Henry Calvin, Gene Sheldon, Romney Brent, Britt Lomond, George Lewis, Lisa Gaye; **D:** Norman Foster, Lewis R. Foster. **VHS, Beta** $69.95 DIS ♂♂

Signal 7 An improvised, neo-verite document of a night in the lives of two San Francisco taxi drivers. Nilsson's first major release and a notable example of his unique scriptless, tape-to-film narrative technique.
1983 89m/C Bill Ackridge, Dan Leegant; **D:** Rob Nilsson. **VHS, Beta** $39.98 WAR ♂♂

Signals Through the Flames A film by Sheldon Rochlin and Maxine Harris outlining the tumultuous history of the famous experimental group, The Living Theatre.

1983 97m/C Julian Beck, Judith Malina, Maxine Harris, Living Theatre Company; **D:** Sheldon Rochlin. **VHS, Beta** $29.95 MFV ♂♂♂

Signs of Life A boat-building company in Maine closes its doors after centuries in business; the employees and families whose lives have been defined by it for generations learn to cope. Wonderful performances compensate only partly for a week script. An episode on PBS's "American Playhouse." **AKA:** One for Sorrow, Two for Joy.
1989 (PG-13) 95m/C Beau Bridges, Arthur Kennedy, Vincent D'Onofrio, Kevin J. O'Connor, Will Patton, Kate Reid; **D:** John David Coles. **VHS, Beta, LV** $89.95 LIV ♂♂½

Silas Marner Superb made for British television adaptation of the 1861 George Eliot classic about an itinerant weaver subjected to criminal accusation, poverty, and exile. Wonderful detail and splendid acting. Shot on location in the Cotswold district of England.
1985 92m/C GB Ben Kingsley, Jenny Agutter, Patrick Ryecart, Patsy Kensit; **D:** Giles Foster. **VHS, Beta** $29.98 FOX, TVC, HMV ♂♂♂

The Silence A brutal, enigmatic allegory about two sisters, one a nymphomaniac, the other a violently frustrated lesbian, traveling with the former's young son to an unnamed country beset by war. Fascinating and memorable but frustrating and unsatisfying: What is it about? What is it an allegory of? Where is the narrative? The third in Bergman's crisis-of-faith trilogy following "Through a Glass Darkly" and "Winter Light." In Swedish with English subtitles or dubbed. **AKA:** Tystnaden.
1963 95m/B SW Ingrid Thulin, Gunnel Lindstrom, Birger Malmsten; **D:** Ingmar Bergman. **VHS, Beta, LV** $29.98 SUE, TAM, NLC ♂♂♂

Silence An autistic boy gets lost in the wilderness and faces an array of difficulties while his foster parents search for him. **AKA:** Crazy Jack and the Boy.
1973 (G) 82m/C Will Geer, Ellen Geer, Richard Kelton, Ian Geer Flanders, Craig Kelly; **D:** John Korty. **VHS, Beta** NO ♂♂

Silence Like Glass Diagnosed with life-threatening illness, two young women struggle to overcome their anger at their fate. They find friendship and together, search for reasons to live. Fine performances, with pacing that keeps the melodrama to a minimum.
1990 (R) 102m/C Jami Gertz, Martha Plimpton, George Peppard, Rip Torn, James Remar; **D:** Carl Schenkel. **VHS, Beta, LV** $89.98 MED ♂♂½

Silence of the Heart Mother copes with aftermath of suicide of teenage son following her recent divorce. Scripted by Phil Penningroth.
1984 100m/C Mariette Hartley, Dana Hill, Howard Hesseman, Chad Lowe, Charlie Sheen; **D:** Richard Michaels. **VHS** $29.95 PMH, HHE ♂♂♂

The Silence of the Lambs Foster is FBI cadet Clarice Starling, a woman with ambition, a cum laude degree in psychology, and a traumatic childhood. When a serial killer begins his ugly rounds, the FBI wants psychological profiles from other serial killers. Starling's sent to collect a profile from one who's exceptionally clever—psychiatrist Hannibal Lector, a vicious killer prone to dining on his victims. He trades clues for intimate details of Starling's life and those clues point her at a head-on collision with the mad man. Brilliant performances from Foster and Hopkins, finely detailed supporting characterizations, and elegant pacing from Demme. Some brutal visual effects. Excellent portrayals of women who refuse to be victims. Based on the Thomas Harris novel. **1991 (R) 118m/C** Jodie Foster, Anthony Hopkins, Scott Glenn, Ted Levine, Brooke Smith, Charles Napier, Roger Corman, Anthony Heald, Diane Baker, Chris Isaak; *D:* Jonathan Demme; *W:* Ted Tally. Academy Awards '91: Best Actor (Hopkins), Best Actress (Foster), Best Adapted Screenplay, Best Director (Demme), Best Picture; Nominations: Best Film Editing, Best Sound; British Academy Awards '91: Best Actor (Hopkins), Best Actress (Foster); Directors Guild of America Awards '91: Best Director (Demme); Golden Globe Awards '92: Best Actress—Drama (Foster); National Board of Review Awards '91: 10 Best Films of the Year, 10 Best Films of the Year, Best Director (Demme); People's Choice Awards '92: Best Film—Drama. **VHS, Beta, LV $19.98** *CCB, ORI, FCT* 🐾🐾🐾½

Silence of the North A widow (Burstyn) with three children struggles to survive under rugged pioneer conditions on the Canadian frontier. The scenery is, not surprisingly, stunning. Based on a true but generic story. **1981 (PG) 94m/C** *CA* Ellen Burstyn, Tom Skerritt; *D:* Allan Winton King. **VHS, Beta $59.95** *MCA* 🐾🐾½

The Silencer Walden stars as Harley-riding Angel who is out to stop a slavery and prostitution ring that abuses young runaways. Video-arcades hold the clues, and Angel must learn to kill without a conscience. Every time she kills, Angel seeks comfort in the arms of anonymous lovers. However, what she doesn't know is that her demented ex-boyfriend is watching. **1992 (R) 85m/C** Lynette Walden, Chris Mulkey, Paul Ganus, Morton Downey Jr.; *W/D:* Amy Goldstein; *W:* Scott Kraft. **VHS $89.95** *ACA* 🐾🐾

Silent Assassins Fists and bullets fly when a scientist is kidnapped in order to gain secrets to biological warfare. Chong and Rhee, real-life owners of a martial arts studio, produced and choreographed the film. Blair is here, but doesn't figure much. A notch up from most similar martial arts pics. **1988 92m/C** Sam Jones, Linda Blair, Jun Chong, Phillip Rhee; *D:* Scott Thomas, Lee Doo-yong. **VHS $79.98** *MCG* 🐾🐾

Silent Code A Mountie is framed for the murder of a young miner. **1935 55m/B** Tom Tyler. **VHS, Beta** *NO* 🐾

The Silent Enemy The true-life exploits of British frogmen battling Italian foes during World War II. Suspenseful and engrossing; good performances and good rendering of underwater action. Video release snips twenty minutes from the original and adds color. **1958 91m/C** *GB* Laurence Harvey, John Clements, Michael Craig, Dawn Addams, Sidney James, Alec McCowen, Nigel Stock; *D:* William Fairchild. **VHS, Beta $7.00** *VTR* 🐾🐾½

Silent Killers A scientist is responsible for the deaths of many people because of his research in germ warfare. He's haunted by the ghosts of his victims. Is he losing his mind or is it a sinister plot? **197? 90m/C** Stephen Soul, Daniel Garfield. **VHS** *MOV* 🐾½

Silent Laugh Makers, No. 1 Four hilarious short movies from the silent era: "Looking for Sally," about an immigrant in search of his best girlfriend; "Lucky Dog," with the young Laurel and Hardy; "His Night Out," about a wild evening with Charlie Chaplin and Ben Turpin; and "Hop-a-Long." Non-stop side-splitting fun. **1915 50m/B** Charley Chase, Stan Laurel, Oliver Hardy, Charlie Chaplin, Ben Turpin, Arthur Lake. **VHS, Beta $29.95** *VYY* 🐾🐾🐾

Silent Laugh Makers, No. 2 Several short funny films of the silent picture era: "Fluttering Hearts," "Long Live the King," about a king who just can't get along with his nobles, starring Chase and Hardy; and "A Sea Dog Tale." All are unremittingly hilarious. **1917 50m/B** Charley Chase, Oliver Hardy, Billy Bevan. **VHS, Beta $29.95** *VYY* 🐾🐾🐾

Silent Laugh Makers, No. 3 Four comedy shorts: "Picking Peaches" (1924), directed by Frank Capra, Langdon's first for Mack Sennett; "All Tied Up" (1925), featuring "A Ton of Fun"-four rotund comedians; "Don't Shove" (1919), featuring Harold Lloyd wooing Bebe Daniels; and "Some Baby" (1922), with Snub Pollard, written by Hal Roach. **1919 55m/B** Harry Langdon, Harold Lloyd, Bebe Daniels, Snub Pollard. **VHS, Beta $24.95** *VYY* 🐾🐾🐾

Silent Madness A psychiatrist must stop a deranged killer, escaped from an asylum, from slaughtering helpless college coeds in a sorority house. Meanwhile, hospital execs send orderlies to kill the patient, to conceal their mistake. Ludicrous. **1984 (R) 93m/C** Belinda J. Montgomery, Viveca Lindfors, Sydney Lassick; *D:* Simon Nuchtern. **VHS, Beta $59.95** *MED* 🐾

The Silent Mr. Sherlock Holmes These two silent shorts are a rare treat for Holmes fans. "The Copper Beeches" was produced with the "personal supervision of Arthur Conan Doyle." In "The Man with the Twisted Lip," Holmes is hired to find out whether a banker was murdered. **1912 68m/B** *GB* Ellie Norwood. **VHS** *VYY* 🐾🐾

Silent Motive Laura is a Hollywood screenwriter who's shocked to discover that a killer is using her recent script as an outline for a series of film-industry murders. She's even more unnerved when a detective makes Laura his number one suspect. **1991 90m/C** Patricia Wettig, Mike Farrell, Ed Asner, Rick Springfield, David Packer; *D:* Lee Philips. **VHS $89.95** *WOV* 🐾🐾½

Silent Movie A has-been movie director (Brooks) is determined to make a comeback and save his studio from being taken over by a conglomerate. Hilarious at times but uneven. An original idea; not as successful as it could have been. Has music and sound effects, but only one word of spoken dialogue by famous mime Marceau. **1976 (PG) 88m/C** Mel Brooks, Marty Feldman, Dom DeLuise, Burt Reynolds, Anne Bancroft, James Caan, Liza Minnelli, Paul Newman, Sid Caesar, Bernadette Peters, Harry Ritz, Marcel Marceau; *D:* Mel Brooks. **VHS, Beta, LV $19.98** *FOX* 🐾🐾½

Silent Movies...Just For the Fun of It! Three short silent films: "The Iron Mule" (1925), "For Sadie's Sake" (1926), and "Hazel from Hollywood" (1918). **1926 56m/B** Jimmie Adams, Dorothy Devore, Al "Fuzzy" St. John. **VHS, Beta, 8mm $24.95** *VYY* 🐾🐾½

Silent Night, Bloody Night An escaped lunatic terrorizes a small New England town, particularly a mansion that was once an insane asylum. Not great, but well done by director Gershuny, with some nail-biting suspense and slick scene changes. *AKA:* Night of the Dark Full Moon; Death House. **1973 (R) 83m/C** Patrick O'Neal, John Carradine, Walter Abel, Mary Woronov, Astrid Heeren, Candy Darling; *D:* Theodore Gershuny. **VHS $42.95** *PGN* 🐾🐾

Silent Night, Deadly Night A psycho ax-murders people while dressed as jolly old St. Nick. Violent and disturbing, to say the least. Caused quite a controversy when it was released to theaters. Santa gimmick sold some tickets at the time, but resist the urge to rent it: it's completely devoid of worth, whatever the killer's outfit. As if one were not enough, we've been blessed with four sequels. **1984 (R) 92m/C** Lilyan Chauvin, Gilmer McCormick, Toni Nero; *D:* Charles E. Sellier. **VHS, Beta, LV $14.95** *LIV, IME* 🐾

Silent Night, Deadly Night 2 The psychotic little brother of the psychotic, Santa Claus-dressed killer from the first film exacts revenge, covering the same bloody ground as before. Almost half this sequel consists of scenes lifted whole from the original. **1987 (R) 88m/C** Eric Freeman, James Newman, Elizabeth Cayton, Jean Miller; *D:* Lee Harry. **VHS, Beta, LV $14.95** *LIV* 🐾

Silent Night, Deadly Night 3: Better Watch Out! The now grown-up psycho goes up against a young blind woman. Santa is no longer the bad guy, thank goodness. The least bad of the lot, with black humor—though not enough to make it worth seeing. **1989 (R) 90m/C** Richard Beymer, Bill Moseley, Samantha Scully, Eric Dare, Laura Herring, Robert Culp; *D:* Monte Hellman. **VHS, Beta, LV $14.95** *LIV* 🐾½

Silent Night, Deadly Night 4: Initiation A secret L.A. cult of she-demons use the slasher Ricky for their own ends—making for more mayhem and horror. Has virtually nothing to do with its three "sequels"—which is not to say it's very good. **1990 (R) 90m/C** Maud Adams, Allyce Beasley, Clint Howard, Reggie Bannister; *D:* Brian Yuzna. **VHS, LV $14.95** *MOV* 🐾

Silent Night, Deadly Night 5: The Toymaker A young boy's Christmas is overrun by murderous Santas and vicious stuffed animals. Definitely for fans of the genre only. **1991 90m/C** Mickey Rooney, William Thorne, Jane Higginson. **VHS $89.95** *LIV* 🐾🐾

Silent Night, Lonely Night Two lonely middle-aged people (Bridges and Jones) begin an affair at Christmas to stem the pain of their separately disintegrating marriages. Poignant but not successfully credible. Based on the play by Robert Anderson. Made for television. **1969 98m/C** Lloyd Bridges, Shirley Jones, Jeff Bridges, Cloris Leachman, Carrie Snodgress, Lynn Carlin; *D:* Daniel Petrie. **VHS, Beta $39.95** *MCA* 🐾🐾

The Silent One Featuring underwater photography by Ron and Valerie Taylor, this is the odd story of a mysterious Polynesian boy who has a nautical relationship with a sea turtle. **1986 96m/C** *NZ* Telo Malese, George Henare; *D:* Yvonne Mackay. **VHS, Beta $69.95** *VID* 🐾½

The Silent Partner A bank teller (Gould) foils a robbery, but manages to take some money for himself. The unbalanced robber (Plummer) knows it and wants the money. Good script by Curtis Hansen and well directed by Duke, with emphasis on suspense and detail. Unexpectedly violent at times. Early, non-comedic role for big guy Candy. **1978 103m/C** *CA* Elliott Gould, Christopher Plummer, Susannah York, John Candy; *D:* Daryl Duke. **VHS, Beta, LV $29.98** *VES* 🐾🐾🐾

The Silent Passenger Amateur sleuth Lord Peter Wimsey makes cinematic debut investigating murder and blackmail on the British railway. Dorothy Sayer's character later inspired BBC mystery series.
1935 75m/B *GB* John Loder, Peter Haddon, Mary Newland, Austin Trevor, Donald Wolfit, Leslie Perrins, Aubrey Mather, Ralph Truman; **D:** Reginald Denham. **VHS, Beta $16.95** NOS, SNC 🎞🎞½

Silent Rage Sheriff Norris of a small Texas town must destroy killer Libby who has been made indestructible through genetic engineering. Chuck Norris meets Frankenstein, sort of. Nice try, but still thoroughly stupid and boring.
1982 (R) 100m/C Chuck Norris, Ron Silver, Steven Keats, Toni Kalem, Brian Libby; **D:** Michael Miller. **VHS, Beta, LV, 8mm $9.95** COL, PIA 🎞

Silent Raiders A commando unit is sent to France in 1943 to knock out a Nazi communications center.
1954 72m/B Richard Bartlett, Earle Lyon, Jeanette Bordeau. **VHS, Beta $39.95** SVS 🎞

Silent Rebellion A Greek immigrant (Savalas) and his son return to Greece, where they reunite with mother and brother and re-discover their heritage and each other. Cross-cultural misunderstandings abound; could have been interesting, but the story is just too generic and uninspired.
1982 90m/C Telly Savalas, Keith Gordon, Michael Constantine, Yula Gavala. **VHS, Beta** NO 🎞½

Silent Running Members of a space station orbiting Saturn care for the last vegetation of a nuclear-devastated earth. When orders come to destroy the vegetation, Dern takes matters into his own hands. Speculative sci-fi at its best. Trumbull's directorial debut; he created special effects for "2001" and "Close Encounters." Screenplay written by Michael Cimino ("The Deerhunter"), Steven Bochco ("Hill Street Blues") and Deric Washburn. Peter Schickele did the strange music.
1971 (G) 90m/C Bruce Dern, Cliff Potts, Ron Rifkin; **D:** Douglas Trumbull. **VHS, Beta, LV $19.95** MCA 🎞🎞🎞

Silent Scream College kids take up residence with the owners of an eerie mansion complete with obligatory murders. Obvious to the point of being gratuitous—and just plain uninteresting.
1980 (R) 87m/C Rebecca Balding, Cameron Mitchell, Avery Schreiber, Barbara Steele, Steve Doubet, Brad Reardon, Yvonne De Carlo; **D:** Denny Harris. **VHS, Beta $29.95** MED 🎞½

Silent Scream A former Nazi concentration camp commandant collects unusual animals and humans as a hobby.
1984 60m/C *GB* Peter Cushing, Brian Cox, Elaine Donnelly; **D:** Alan Gibson. **VHS, Beta $29.95** LIV 🎞

Silent Valley Adventure of the Old West with American cowboy star Tom Tyler.
1935 60m/B Tom Tyler. **VHS, Beta $19.95** NOS, VCN, DVT 🎞

Silent Victim Greene stars as Bonnie Jackson, a Georgia housewife whose marriage has not only gone wrong but turned violent. She takes a drug overdose in a suicide attempt but it results only in a miscarriage. Her furious husband sues her for the murder of their unborn child while an ambitious district attorney petitions the state to charge Bonnie with committing an illegal abortion. Bonnie's torment soon becomes a media circus as she goes on trial. Based on a true story.

1992 (R) 116m/C Michelle Greene, Kyle Secor, Ely Pouget, Alex Hyde-White, Dori Brenner, Leann Hunley; **D:** Menahem Golan; **W:** Nelly Adnil, Jonathan Platnick; **M:** William T. Stromberg. **VHS $89.95** COL 🎞🎞½

Silent Victory: The Kitty O'Neil Story Genuinely stirring real-life-overcoming-adversity story of the deaf woman who became a top stunt woman in Hollywood and holder of the land speed record for women. Channing is very good as O'Neil. Made for television.
1979 96m/C Stockard Channing, Brian Dennehy, Colleen Dewhurst, Edward Albert, James Farentino; **D:** Lou Antonio. **Beta $69.95** VID 🎞🎞🎞

Silent Witness A woman (Bertinelli) witnesses her brother-in-law and his friend rape a young woman. She must decide whether to testify against them or keep the family secret. Exploitative and weakly plotted. Rip-off of the much-discussed Massachusetts barroom rape case. Made for television.
1985 (R) 97m/C Valerie Bertinelli, John Savage, Chris Nash, Melissa Leo, Pat Corley, Steven Williams, Jacqueline Brookes, Alex McArthur, Katie McCombs; **D:** Michael Miller. **VHS, Beta $79.95** ACA 🎞

Silhouette Detained in a small Texas town, a woman witnesses the murder of a local girl—but in silhouette, so the killer's identity takes a feature-length running time to resolve. A fair but contrived made for cable TV thriller that the leading lady co-produced.
1991 (R) 89m/C Faye Dunaway, David Rasche, John Terry, Carlos Gomez, Ron Campbell, Margaret Blye, Talisa Soto, Ritch Brinkley; **D:** Carl Schenkel. **VHS $79.95** MCA 🎞

Silk A beautiful and bloodthirsty detective cuts a swath through local heroin rings.
1986 (R) 84m/C Cec Verrell, Bill McLaughlin, Fred Bailey; **D:** Cirio H. Santiago. **VHS, Beta $79.95** MGM 🎞

Silk 2 A foreign-made sequel, in which a beautiful cop stops crime in Honolulu. Ludicrous plot, bad acting, lots of skin and violence—what more could you want? Dreadful.
1989 85m/C Monique Gabrielle, Peter Nelson, Jan Merlin, Maria Clair; **D:** Cirio H. Santiago. **VHS, Beta $44.98** MGM 🎞

The Silk Road Set in the 11th-century, the ancient trading route leads to Dun Huang, a desert city that is the last Chinese outpost on the road. A young scholar, Zhao, travels in a caravan which is attacked by Chinese mercenaries. The leader of the group takes a liking to the young man and makes him his protege so that Zhao may witness history unfolding. When Zhao's new home of Dun Huang is attacked by a neighboring nation, Zhao is there to conveniently hide the city's treasures in some nearby caves. (This is based on the Thousand Buddha Caves, where a treasure of Buddhist icons and scrolls were discovered in 1900.) Billed as an epic, there's lots of pageantry and some impressive battle scenes but the film is too stately to be more than merely interesting. Adapted from a novel by Yashushi Inoue. In Japanese with English subtitles.
1992 (PG-13) 99m/C *CH JP* Koichi Sato, Toshiyuki Nishida, Anna Nakagawa, Tsunehiko Watase, Daijiro Harada; **D:** Junya Sato. **VHS, LV $89.95** VMK, TAM 🎞🎞½

Silk Stockings Splendid musical comedy adaptation of "Ninotchka," with Astaire as a charming American movie man, and Charisse as the cold Soviet official whose commie heart he melts. Music and lyrics by Cole Porter highlight this film adapted from George S. Kaufman's hit Broadway play.

Director Mamoulian's last film. 🎵Too Bad; Paris Loves Lovers; Fated to Be Mated; The Ritz Roll 'n Rock; Silk Stockings; Red Blues; All of You; Stereophonic Sound; Josephine; Satin and Silk; Without Love; Chemical Reaction; Siberia; Red Blues.
1957 117m/C Fred Astaire, Cyd Charisse, Janice Paige, Peter Lorre, George Tobias; **D:** Rouben Mamoulian. **VHS, Beta, LV $29.95** MGM, TTC 🎞🎞🎞

Silkwood The story of Karen Silkwood, who died in a 1974 car crash under suspicious circumstances. She was a nuclear plant worker and activist who was investigating shoddy practices at the plant. Streep acts up a storm, disappearing completely into her character. Cher surprises with her fine portrayal of a lesbian co-worker, and Russell is also good. Nichols has a tough time since we already know the ending, but he brings top-notch performances from his excellent cast.
1983 (R) 131m/C Meryl Streep, Kurt Russell, Cher, Diana Scarwid, Bruce McGill, Fred Ward, David Strathairn, Ron Silver, Josef Sommer, Craig T. Nelson; **D:** Mike Nichols. Academy Awards '83 Nominations: Best Actress (Streep), Best Director (Nichols), Best Film Editing, Best Original Screenplay, Best Supporting Actress (Cher); Golden Globe Awards '84: Best Supporting Actress (Cher). **VHS, Beta, LV $9.98** SUE 🎞🎞🎞

Silver Bandit A bookkeeper is sent to investigate a mine theft. Along the way he sings country and western songs.
1947 54m/B Spade Cooley. **VHS, Beta, LV $19.95** NOS 🎞

Silver Bears Caine is an unlikely mobster in this comedy. He's sent to Switzerland to buy a bank for laundering purposes and ends up being swindled himself. So-so entry adapted from the novel by Paul Erdman.
1978 (PG) 114m/C Michael Caine, Cybill Shepherd, Louis Jourdan, Stephane Audran, David Warner, Tom Smothers, Martin Balsam, Jay Leno, Charles Gray, Joss Ackland; **D:** Ivan Passer. **VHS, Beta** NO 🎞

Silver Bullet Adapted from Stephen King's "Cycle of the Werewolf," about a town whose inhabitants are being brutally murdered. It finally dawns on them the culprit is a werewolf. Action moves along at a good clip and the film has its share of suspense. **AKA:** Stephen King's Silver Bullet.
1985 (R) 95m/C Corey Haim, Gary Busey, Megan Follows, Everett McGill; **D:** Daniel Attias. **VHS, LV $14.95** PAR 🎞🎞

The Silver Chalice Newman's career somehow survived his movie debut in this bloated, turgid Biblical epic about the momentous events that befall a young Greek sculptor who fashions the cup that will be used at the Last Supper. Newman later took out an ad in Variety to apologize for the film, in which Greene also made his debut. Based on the novel by Thomas Costain with a music score by Franz Waxman.
1954 135m/C Paul Newman, Virginia Mayo, Pier Angeli, Jack Palance, Natalie Wood, Joseph Wiseman, Lorne Greene, E.G. Marshall; **D:** Victor Saville. **VHS, Beta $19.98** WAR 🎞

Silver City A saga depicting the plight of Polish refugees in Australia in 1949. A pair of lovers find each other in a crowded refugee camp. He's married to her friend. Too-complex, slow but earnest effort.
1984 (PG) 110m/C *AU* Gosia Dobrowolska, Ivar Kants; **D:** Sophia Turkiewicz. **VHS, Beta $59.95** LHV 🎞

Silver City Kid A foreman for a silver mine exposes a corrupt local banker as a thief.

1945 56m/B Allan "Rocky" Lane. **VHS, Beta** $24.95 *DVT* 🎬

Silver Dream Racer An English grease monkey wants to win the World Motorcycle Championship title away from an American biker. He's also after someone else's girlfriend. Boring, stilted, unoriginal "Big Race" flick. Essex also wrote and performed the music.
1983 (PG) 103m/C Beau Bridges, David Essex, Christina Raines, Diane Keen, Harry H. Corbett; *D:* David Wickes. **VHS, Beta** $69.98 *LIV, VES* 🎬½

Silver Hermit from Shaolin Temple/The Devil's Assignment Two kung fu thrillers on one action-filled tape.
1981 175m/C **VHS, Beta** $7.00 *VTR* 🎬½

Silver Lode A man accused of murder on his wedding day attempts to clear his name while the law launches an intensive manhunt for him. Ordinary story improved by good, energetic cast.
1954 92m/C John Payne, Dan Duryea, Lizabeth Scott, Stuart Whitman; *D:* Allan Dwan. **VHS, Beta** *NO* 🎬🎬

Silver Queen A woman finds out her father has gambled away a silver mine and left her with debts. She opens a saloon, only to have her fiance use the money to hunt for more silver.
1942 81m/B Priscilla Lane, George Brent, Bruce Cabot, Eugene Pallette; *D:* Lloyd Bacon. **VHS, Beta** *NO* 🎬🎬

Silver River Average western that marked the final collaboration between director Walsh and star Flynn. It never even comes close to their previous works. Flynn plays a no-good, power-hungry cad who will stop at nothing to get what he wants. He happens to want Sheridan, who is married to Bennett, so Flynn schemes to get rid of him. Overall, Flynn acts as though he really isn't interested in the material and had to make a pact with Walsh that he would stay sober until five in the afternoon while filming. Based on an unpublished novel by Stephen Longstreet.
1948 108m/B Errol Flynn, Ann Sheridan, Thomas Mitchell, Bruce Bennett, Tom D'Andrea, Barton MacLane, Monte Blue, Jonathan Hale; *D:* Raoul Walsh; *W:* Stephen Longstreet, Harriet Frank Jr. **VHS** $19.98 *MGM* 🎬½

Silver Spurs Villain tries to get some oil-rich property by murdering the ranch's owner. Ranch foreman Rogers saves the day.
1943 60m/B Roy Rogers, Jerome Cowan, John Carradine, Phyllis Brooks, Smiley Burnette, Joyce Compton; *D:* Joseph Kane. **VHS, Beta** $19.95 *NOS, VCN, DVT* 🎬½

Silver Stallion Thunder the Wonder Horse plays the title character, who fights rattlesnakes, wild dogs and hoss thieves. Too bad he doesn't give acting lessons to the humans in the this frail family western with nice scenery and action scenes.
1941 59m/C David Sharpe, Carol Hughes, Leroy Mason, Walter Long; *D:* Edward Finney. **VHS, Beta** $24.95 *VYY, GPV* 🎬½

Silver Star Man elected sheriff of a western town turns down the job because he is a pacifist. He changes his mind when his defeated opponent hires a trio of killers to come after him.
1955 73m/B Jimmy Wakely, Edgar Buchanan, Marie Windsor. **VHS, Beta** *NO* 🎬🎬

The Silver Streak The sickly son of a diesel train designer needs an iron lung—pronto. A rival's super-fast locomotive is the only hope for the boy. Murders, runaway

engines, and a crew that would rather walk enliven this race against time.
1934 72m/B Sally Blane, Charles Starrett, Arthur Lake, Edgar Kennedy, William Farnum; *D:* Thomas Atkins. **VHS, Beta** $17.95 *CCB* 🎬🎬

The Silver Streak Pooped exec Wilder rides a train from L.A. to Chicago, planning to enjoy a leisurely, relaxing trip. Instead he becomes involved with murder, intrigue, and a beautiful woman. Energetic Hitchcock parody action comedy written by Colin Higgins; successful first pairing of Wilder and Pryor.
1976 (PG) 113m/C Gene Wilder, Richard Pryor, Jill Clayburgh, Patrick McGoohan, Ned Beatty, Ray Walston, Richard Kiel, Scatman Crothers; *D:* Arthur Hiller. **VHS, Beta, LV** $14.98 *FOX* 🎬🎬🎬

Silverado Affectionate pastiche of western cliches has everything a viewer could ask for--except Indians. The straightforward plot finds four virtuous cowboys rising up against a crooked lawman in a blaze of six guns. No subtlety from the first big Western in quite a while, but plenty of fun and laughs. Special laser disc edition features a wide screen film-to-tape transfer monitored by the photography director. Also included are set photos, release trailers, and other publicity hoohah as well as a special time-lapse sequence of the set construction, and interviews with the stars and director Kasdan. Letterboxed laserdisc version is available with dolby surround sound.
1985 (PG-13) 132m/C Kevin Kline, Scott Glenn, Kevin Costner, Danny Glover, Brian Dennehy, Linda Hunt, John Cleese, Jeff Goldblum, Rosanna Arquette, Jeff Fahey; *D:* Lawrence Kasdan. **VHS, Beta, LV** $14.95 *COL, VYG, CRC* 🎬🎬🎬

Simba A young Englishman arrives at his brother's Kenyan farm to find him murdered in a local skirmish between the Mau Maus and white settlers. Well made, thoughtful look at colonialism, racial animosity, and violence.
1955 98m/C *GB* Dirk Bogarde, Donald Sinden, Virginia McKenna, Orlando Martins; *D:* Brian Desmond Hurst. **VHS, Beta, LV** *NO* 🎬🎬🎬

Simon A group of bored demented scientists brainwash a college professor into believing he is an alien from a distant galaxy, whereupon he begins trying to correct the evil in America. Screwball comedy, or semi-serious satire of some kind? Hard to tell. Some terrific set pieces but the movie as a whole doesn't quite hold together. Directorial debut of Marshall Brickman, who previously worked as a scriptwriter with Woody Allen ("Sleeper," etc.).
1980 (PG) 97m/C Alan Arkin, Madeline Kahn, Fred Gwynne, Adolph Green, Wallace Shawn, Austin Pendleton; *D:* Marshall Brickman. **VHS, Beta** $19.98 *WAR* 🎬🎬½

Simon Blanco A hero of the Mexican Revolution is tricked by men who want to kill him and steal his wife.
1987 145m/C *MX* Antonio Aguilar, Jacqueline Andere, Mario Almada, Valentin Trujillo. **VHS, Beta** $59.95 *MAD* 🎬🎬

Simon Bolivar The title character leads the Venezuelan revolution in 1817.
1969 110m/C Maximilian Schell, Rosanna Schiaffino. **VHS, Beta** $49.95 *UNI* 🎬🎬½

Simon, King of the Witches An L.A. warlock who lives in a sewer drain finds himself the center of attention when his spells actually work. This interesting hippie/witchcraft entry bogs down now and then but Prine's performance is droll and lively.
1971 (R) 90m/C Andrew Prine, Brenda Scott, George Paulsin, Norman Burton, Ultra Violet; *D:* Bruce Kessler. **VHS, Beta** $59.95 *UNI* 🎬🎬½

Simon of the Desert Not Bunuel's very best, but worthy of the master satirist. An ascetic stands on a pillar in the desert for several decades—closer to God, farther from temptation. Pinal is a gorgeous devil that tempts Simon. Hilarious, irreverent, sophisticated. What's with the weird ending, though? In Spanish with English subtitles.
1966 43m/B *D:* Luis Bunuel. **VHS, Beta, 3/4U, Special order formats** $68.00 *NOS, HHT, DVT* 🎬🎬🎬½

Simple Justice Mindless, justice-in-own-hands anti-liberal hogwash. Overwrought, smug, and violent story of a young couple beaten by robbers who remain at large.
1989 (R) 91m/C Cesar Romero, John Spencer, Doris Roberts, Candy McClain; *D:* Deborah Del Prete. **VHS** $59.95 *JTC* 🎬½

Simple Men Odd-ball brothers Bill (a petty criminal) and Dennis (a shy college student) decide to track down their missing father in this fractured comedy. Dad, a former big-league baseball player who bombed the Pentagon in the '60s, is a long-time fugitive hiding out somewhere in the wilds of Long Island. Their search leads them to two equally opposite women, the wary Kate, whom Bill immediately falls for, and the sexy Elina, who turns out to know dear old dad quite well. Deliberately deadpan and cliched, Hartley's quirky style can either irritate or illuminate via the weird turnings of his characters' lives.
1992 (R) 105m/C Robert Burke, William Sage, Karen Sillas, Elina Lowensohn, Martin Donovan, Mark Chandler Bailey, John Alexander MacKay; *W/D:* Hal Hartley. **VHS, LV** *COL, IME, NLC* 🎬🎬🎬

A Simple Story A woman faces her 40th birthday with increasing uneasiness, though her life seems perfect from the outside. She evaluates her chances at love, child-bearing, and friendship, after having an abortion and breaking up with her lover. Schneider's performance is brilliant in this gentle, quiet drama. In French with English subtitles. *AKA:* Une Histoire Simple.
1979 110m/C *FR* Romy Schneider, Bruno Cremer, Claude Brasseur; *D:* Claude Sautet. **VHS, Beta** $59.95 *COL, TAM* 🎬🎬🎬

The Simple Truth A woman's romance novel is dramatized, dealing with a receptionist who has a fling with the company president.
1985 90m/C **Beta** $14.95 *PSM* Woof!

The Simpsons Christmas Special America's favorite cartoon family celebrates Christmas as only they can; Bart gets a tattoo, Homer works as a mall Santa and the Christmas spirit arrives in the unlikely package of a greyhound named "Santa's Little Helper."
1989 30m/C *V:* Dan Castellaneta, Julie Kavner, Harry Shearer, Maggie Roswell, Nancy Cartwright, Yeardley Smith. **VHS** $9.98 *FXV, WTA* Woof!

Sin of Adam & Eve The story of Adam and Eve in the Garden of Eden and their fall from grace. Voice-over narrator is only sound in this strange dialogue-less story of the Adam and Eve, how they got kicked out of the Garden of Eden, and how they lose and then find each other outside. Ancient plot, to say the least.
1972 (R) 72m/C Candy Wilson, Jorge Rivero; *D:* Michael Zachary. **VHS, Beta** $19.95 *VDM, UHV* 🎬½

The Sin of Harold Diddlebock A man gets fired from his job, stumbles around drunk, and wins a fortune gambling. He then buys a circus and uses a lion to frighten

investors into backing him. Inventive comedy, but missing the spark and timing of "The Freshman" (1925), of which it is a sequel. The final feature film for Lloyd, made it at the urging of director Sturges, who did all his own stunts. **AKA:** Mad Wednesday.
1947 89m/B Harold Lloyd, Margaret Hamilton, Frances Ramsden, Edgar Kennedy, Lionel Stander, Rudy Vallee, Franklin Pangborn; **D:** Preston Sturges. **VHS, Beta $14.95** ONE, NOS, KRT ♫♫½

The Sin of Madelon Claudet Hayes plays common thief who works her way into upper crust of Parisian society only to tumble back into the street, all in the name of making a better life for her illegitimate son. Very sudsy stuff, with an outstanding performance by Hayes. **AKA:** The Lullaby.
1931 74m/B Helen Hayes, Lewis Stone, Neil Hamilton, Robert Young, Cliff Edwards, Jean Hersholt, Marie Prevost, Karen Morley, Charles Winninger, Alan Hale Jr.; **D:** Edgar Selwyn. **VHS $19.98** MGM, FCT ♫♫♫

Sin Salida A man is chased through Mexico City by the Mafia.
1987 97m/C *MX* Jorge Rivero, Nadia Milton, Mario Almada, Daniela Rosen. **VHS, Beta $58.95** MAD ♫

Sin Takes a Holiday A woman marries her boss to save him from his girl friend. On a trip to Paris, she is wooed by a refined European gentleman, but finds that she really does love her husband. By today's standards, it doesn't sound like much, but in the '30s, it was pretty sophisticated stuff.
1930 81m/B Constance Bennett, Kenneth MacKenna, Basil Rathbone, Rita La Roy, ZaSu Pitts, Fred Walton, Richard Carle, Helen Johnson; **D:** Paul Stein. **VHS $19.95** NOS, HEG ♫♫½

Sin You Sinners Aging stripper gets ahold of an amulet that allows her to look youthful and manipulate the lives of others. When she loses the amulet, however, bad things happen. Twisted ending.
1963 73m/B June Colbourne, Dian Lloyd, Derek Murcott, Beverly Nazarow, Charles Clements; **D:** Anthony Farrar. **VHS $16.95** SNC ♫

Sinai Commandos The story of a group of commandos in the Israeli Six-Day War in 1967 who are assigned to destroy important Arab radar installations. Includes actual combat footage. **AKA:** Sinai Commandos: The Story of the Six Day War; Ha'Matarah Tiran.
1968 99m/C Robert Fuller; **D:** Raphael Nussbaum. **VHS $29.95** ATL, FCT ♫♫½

Sinatra Made for television biopic chronicles the stormy life of crooner Frank Sinatra. Begins with his childhood in Hoboken, New Jersey and works its way through his big band tours, bobby soxer days, career skids, and triumphant comeback with his Oscar-winning performance in "From Here to Eternity," as well as his three marriages, "Rat Pack" friends, and mob connections. Executive Producer Tina Sinatra, Frank's daughter, doesn't gloss over her father's less savory character points and Casnoff does well with his leading role. Songs are lip-synched to classic Sinatra tunes with a few early, unavailable recordings redone by actor Tom Burlinson and Frank Sinatra, Jr.
1992 245m/C Philip Casnoff, Olympia Dukakis, Joe Santos, Gina Gershon, Nina Siemaszko, Marcia Gay Harden, Rod Steiger, Bob Gunton, David Raynr, James F. Kelly, Matthew Posey, Jay Robinson, Robin Gammell, Todd Waring, Joris Stuyck, Danny Gans; **D:** James Sadwith; **W:** William Mastrosimone. **VHS, Beta, LV $29.98** WAR ♫♫½

Sinbad A sardonic portrait of an aging hedonist as he tries to hold onto the pleasures of drink, sex and gluttony. In Magyar (Hungarian), with English subtitles.
1971 98m/C *HU* **D:** Zoltan Huszarik. **VHS, Beta $69.95** KIV, FCT ♫♫♫

Sinbad and the Eye of the Tiger The swashbuckling adventures of Sinbad the Sailor as he encounters the creations of Ray Harryhausen's special effects magic. Don't see this one for the plot, which almost doesn't exist. Otherwise, mildly fun.
1977 (G) 113m/C *GB* Patrick Wayne, Jane Seymour, Taryn Power, Margaret Whiting; **D:** Sam Wanamaker; **W:** Beverly Cross. **VHS, Beta, LV $14.95** COL, CCB ♫♫

Sinbad of the Seven Seas Italian muscle epic based on the ancient legends. Ferrigno isn't green, but he's still a hulk, and he still can't act. It's poorly dubbed, which makes little difference; it would be stupid regardless. Italian muscle epic based on the ancient legends.
1989 90m/C *IT* Lou Ferrigno, John Steiner, Leo Gullotta, Teagan Clive; **D:** Enzo G. Castellari. **VHS, Beta, LV $89.95** WAR, OM ♫½

Sinbad the Sailor Fairbanks fits well in his luminent father's swashbuckling shoes, as he searches for the treasure of Alexander the Great. Self-mocking but hamhanded, and confusing if you seek the hidden plot. Still, it's all in fun, and it is fun.
1947 117m/C Douglas Fairbanks Jr., Maureen O'Hara, Anthony Quinn, Walter Slezak, George Tobias, Jane Greer, Mike Mazurki, Sheldon Leonard; **D:** Richard Wallace. **VHS, Beta, LV $24.95** RKO, MED, VID ♫♫♫

Since You Went Away An American family copes with the tragedy, heartache and shortages of wartime in classic mega-tribute to the home front. Be warned: very long and bring your hankies. Colbert is superb, as is the photography. John Derek unobtrusively made his film debut, as an extra. Script by producer David O. Selznick.
1944 172m/B Claudette Colbert, Jennifer Jones, Shirley Temple, Joseph Cotten, Agnes Moorehead, Monty Woolley, Guy Madison, Lionel Barrymore, Robert Walker, Hattie McDaniel, Keenan Wynn, Craig Stevens, Albert Basserman, Alla Nazimova, Lloyd Corrigan, Terry Moore, Florence Bates, Ruth Roman, Andrew V. McLaglen, Dorothy Dandridge, Rhonda Fleming; **D:** John Cromwell; **M:** Max Steiner. Academy Awards '44: Best Score; Nominations: Best Supporting Actress (Jones); Academy Awards '44: Best Actress (Colbert), Best Black and White Cinematography, Best Film Editing, Best Interior Decoration, Best Picture, Best Supporting Actor (Woolley). **VHS, Beta, LV $39.98** FOX ♫♫♫½

Sincerely Charlotte Huppert directs her sister in this film about a beautiful singer framed for her boyfriend's murder. She enlists an old lover to help her flee across the countryside. Love story/thriller is pleasingly odd and absorbing. In French with English subtitles. **AKA:** Signe Charlotte.
1986 92m/C *FR* Isabelle Huppert, Niels Arestrup, Christine Pascal; **D:** Caroline Huppert. **VHS, Beta, LV $79.95** COL, TAM ♫♫♫

Sincerely Yours Liberace wisely stayed away from acting after inauspiciously debuting in this horrible, maudlin remake of "The Man Who Played God." He plays a pianist who loses his hearing and decides to become a philanthropist to help those less fortunate than himself. Laughably cheesy. Script by Irving Wallace. Thirty-one musical numbers, including Liberace's inimitable arrangement of "Chopsticks."
1956 116m/C Liberace, Joanne Dru, Dorothy Malone, William Demarest; **D:** Gordon Douglas. **VHS, Beta, LV $19.98** WAR Woof!

The Sinful Bed A bed tells of its witnessed liasons over the years.
1978 84m/C *GB* **VHS, Beta $19.95** ACA, HHE Woof!

Sinful Life A strained, offbeat, B-grade comedy about an odd, infantile mother fighting to keep her unusual child from being taken away. Definitely not a must-see; can be irritating and obnoxious, depending on viewer and mood. Morris is at her oddball comedic best as the mother and former show dancer. Adult Tefkin plays her little girl. Based on the play "Just Like the Pom Pom Girls."
1989 (R) 112m/C Anita Morris, Rick Overton, Dennis Christopher, Blair Tefkin, Mark Rolston, Cynthia Szigeti; **D:** William Schreiner. **VHS, Beta, LV $89.95** COL ♫♫

Sing The students in the real-life Brooklyn public school "Sing" program endure the trials of adolescence while putting together a musical revue. Hurtles over the edge into cheesiness from the start, with way too much (cheesy) music. From the creator of "Fame" and "Footloose."
1989 (PG-13) 111m/C Lorraine Bracco, Peter Dobson, Jessica Steen, Louise Lasser, George DiCenzo, Patti LaBelle; **D:** Richard Baskin. **VHS, Beta, LV $89.95** COL ♫½

Sing, Cowboy, Sing Decent adventure story about a wagon train heading west that runs into a band of outlaws doing outlaw stuff and must somehow get through.
1937 60m/B Tex Ritter. **VHS, Beta $19.95** NOS, DVT ♫♫

Sing Sing Nights A world-famous journalist is killed with three bullets. Three men have confessed, but only one could have actually done it. A professor sets out to solve the case. **AKA:** Reprieved.
1935 60m/B Conway Tearle, Mary Doran, Hardie Albright, Patricia "Boots" Mallory, Ferdinand Gottschalk, Berton Churchill, Jameson Thomas; **D:** Lewis Collins. **VHS $16.95** SNC ♫½

Sing Your Worries Away Songwriter Ebsen inherits 3 million dollars and finds the money causes him nothing but trouble. Band of crooks cause the requisite wacky complications. Fun, harmless musical comedy. ♫It Just Happened to Happen; Sally, My Dear Sally; Sing Your Worries Away; Cindy Lou McWilliams; How Do You Fall in Love.
1942 71m/B Buddy Ebsen, Bert Lahr, June Havoc, Patsy Kelly, Margaret Dumont; **D:** Edward Sutherland. **VHS, Beta** CCB ♫♫

Singin' in the Rain One of the all-time great movie musicals—an affectionate spoof of the turmoil that afflicted the motion picture industry in the late 1920s during the changeover from silent films to sound. Co-director Kelly and Hagen lead a glorious cast. Music and lyrics by Arthur Freed and Nacio Herb Brown. Served as basis of story by Betty Comden and Adolph Green. Also available on laserdisc with the original trailer, outtakes, behind the scenes footage, and commentary by film historian Ronald Haver. Later a Broadway musical. ♫All I Do is Dream of You; Should I?; Singin' in the Rain; Wedding of the Painted Doll; Broadway Melody; Would You; I've Got a Feelin' You're Foolin'; You Are My Lucky Star; Broadway Rhythm; Beautiful Girl; Fit as a Fiddle; Make 'Em Laugh; Good Morning; You Were Meant For Me.
1952 103m/C Gene Kelly, Donald O'Connor, Jean Hagen, Debbie Reynolds, Rita Moreno, King Donovan, Millard Mitchell, Cyd Charisse; **D:** Gene Kelly, Stanley Donen; **W:** Adolph Green,

Betty Comden. Academy Awards '52 Nominations: Best Supporting Actress (Hagen), Best Original Score; Golden Globe Awards '53: Best Actor—Musical/Comedy (O'Connor); National Board of Review Awards '52: 10 Best Films of the Year. **VHS, Beta, LV $19.98** *MGM, PIA, VYG* ✂✂✂✂

The Singing Blacksmith A relic of American Yiddish cinema, adapting popular 1909 play by David Pinski. A married blacksmith is wooed by another woman and falls victim to alcoholism. Overlong, but Oysher and his rich baritone voice still shine. In Yiddish with English subtitles.
1938 95m/B *PL* Miriam Riselle, Florence Weiss, Moishe Oysher; *D:* Edgar G. Ulmer. **VHS $79.95** *ERG, TAM* ✂✂½

Singing Buckaroo Dastardly bandits try to pilfer money from pretty blonde damsel and have to battle with yodelin' cowboy. B-level western good guy Scott belts out a few numbers and saves the day. Innocuously pleasant.
1937 58m/B Fred Scott, Victoria Vinton, Cliff Nazarro; *D:* Tom Gibson. **VHS, Beta $19.95** *NOS, VYY* ✂✂

The Singing Nun The true story of a Belgian nun who takes a liking to a motherless little boy. She writes a song for him, and a kind-hearted priest talks to a record producer to see about getting the song to go somewhere. The song soon becomes an international hit, and the nun ends up on the "Ed Sullivan Show." Sentimental and sugary sweet, but a big box-office hit.
1966 98m/C Debbie Reynolds, Ricardo Montalban, Greer Garson, Agnes Moorehead, Chad Everett, Katharine Ross, Juanita Moore, Ricky Cordell, Michael Pate, Tom Drake; *D:* Henry Koster. **VHS $19.98** *MGM* ✂✂

Singing the Blues in Red Dark, pessimistic character study of a protest singer/songwriter who leaves his native East Germany to escape repression and finds his loyalties divided. A moving personal story, as well as insightful, subtle social commentary. In English and German with subtitles. Cinematography by Chris Menges.
1987 110m/C *GE* Gerulf Pannach, Fabienne Babe, Cristine Rose, Trevor Griffiths; *D:* Ken Loach; *W:* Trevor Griffiths. **VHS, Beta** *NO* ✂✂✂

Single Bars, Single Women Utterly formulaic made for TV comedy-drama based on Dolly Parton's song is not entirely without merit. Lonely people gather in a local pickup joint and share their miseries and hopes.
1984 96m/C Shelley Hack, Christine Lahti, Tony Danza, Mare Winningham, Keith Gordon, Paul Michael Glaser; *D:* Harry Winer. **VHS, Beta $79.95** *PSM, PAR* ✂½

Single Fighter A martial arts expert in China seeks out traitors who collaborated with the Japanese during World War II.
1978 (R) 79m/C Tu Chiang; *D:* Lee Chin-Chuan. **VHS $49.95** *PGN* ✂

Single Room Furnished The fall of a buxom blonde from uncorrupted innocence through pregnancies to desperate prostitution. Fails to demonstrate any range of talent in Mansfield, who died before it was completed. Exploitative and pathetic.
1968 93m/C Jayne Mansfield, Dorothy Keller; *D:* Matt Cimber, Matteo Ottaviano. **VHS, Beta $29.95** *UHV, HEG* ✂½

The Single Standard San Francisco deb Garbo flings with artsy Asther and finds out the Hayes Code is just around the corner.
1929 93m/B Greta Garbo, Nils Asther, Johnny Mack Brown, Dorothy Sebastian, Lane Chandler, Zeffie Tilbury; *D:* John S. Robertson. **VHS $29.99** *MGM, FCT* ✂✂

Single White Female Psycho thriller casts Fonda as chic Manhattan computer consultant, Allison Jones, who advertises for a roommate after a falling out with her boyfriend. Leigh is the frumpy, shy, bookstore clerk Hedra who answers the ad and moves into Allie's great Upper West Side apartment. Their friendship grows steadily until Allie gradually notices Hedy beginning to emulate many of her characteristics. The last straw comes when Hedy gets her hair cut and dyed just like Allison's. Witnessing Hedy grow increasingly creepy, Allison tries to shake her, but Hedy's obsessive devotion is already out of hand. Derivative, though bonus points for creative murder implements and interesting performances throughout, including Friedman as Allie's gay upstairs neighbor. Based on the novel "SWF Seeks Same" by John Lutz.
1992 (R) 107m/C Bridget Fonda, Jennifer Jason Leigh, Steven Weber, Peter Friedman, Stephen Tobolowsky; *D:* Barbet Schroeder; *W:* Don Roos. **VHS, Beta, LV, 8mm $94.95** *COL* ✂✂½

Singles The Seattle music scene sets the background for this lighthearted film of twentysomethings meeting and mating. Dillon is the lead singer of an alternative band, Citizen Dick (played by real life band Pearl Jam), who lives in the same apartment building as an eclectic group of singles whose lives slowly become interwoven. Soundtrack features the hot Seattle sounds of Alice in Chains, Soundgarden, and Mudhoney. Thanks to Crowe's tight script and a talented cast, this charming comedy works; anyone who is twentysomething and single will smile knowingly at its portrayals. The video contains six extra minutes of footage after the movie's end credits which director Crowe edited out for the feature version. Scenes include a newsstand sequence and his "French Club" scene.
1992 (PG-13) 100m/C Matt Dillon, Bridget Fonda, Campbell Scott, Kyra Sedgwick, Sheila Kelley, Jim True; *W/D:* Cameron Crowe. **VHS, Beta, LV $94.99** *WAR, PMS* ✂✂✂

Singleton's Pluck Touching British comedy about a determined farmer who must walk his 500 geese 100 miles to market because of a strike. He becomes a celebrity when the TV stations start covering his odyssey. *AKA:* Laughterhouse.
1984 89m/C *GB* Ian Holm, Penelope Wilton, Bill Owen, Richard Hope; *D:* Richard Eyre. **VHS, Beta $19.95** *STE, NWV* ✂✂✂

The Sinister Invasion A turn-of-the-century scientist (Karloff) discovers a death ray. Aliens, who would like a closer peek at what makes it work, use a sex-fiend's body to do so. One of Karloff's last four films, made simultaneously in Mexico. The great horror master's final offering. Excruciating. *AKA:* Alien Terror; The Incredible Invasion.
1968 95m/C *MX* Boris Karloff, Enrique Guzman, Jack Hill; *D:* Juan Ibanez. **VHS, Beta $49.95** *SNC* ✂

The Sinister Urge Vice cops Duncan and Moore search for the murderer of three women. Seems the disturbed slayer is unbalanced because he's been looking at pictures of naked ladies. Was this meant to be taken seriously at the time? The last film by camp director Wood, maker of the infamous "Plan 9 From Outer Space." A must see for Wood fans. *AKA:* The Young and the Immortal; Hellborn.
1960 82m/B Kenne Duncan, Duke Moore, Jean Fontaine; *D:* Edward D. Wood Jr. **VHS, Beta $59.98** *AOV, SNC* Woof!

Sink the Bismarck British navy sets out to locate and sink infamous German battleship during WWII. Good special effects with battle sequences in this drama based on real incidents. One of the better of the plethora of WWII movies, with stirring naval battles and stylish documentary-style direction.
1960 97m/B Kenneth More, Dana Wynter, Karel Stepanek, Carl Mohner, Laurence Naismith, Geoffrey Keen, Michael Hordern, Maurice Denham, Esmond Knight; *D:* Lewis Gilbert. **VHS, Beta $19.98** *FOX, HMV* ✂✂✂

Sinners Outrageous portrait of an Italian family in the Big Apple trying to come to terms with the violence that surrounds their neighborhood.
1989 90m/C Joey Travolta, Robert Gallo, Joe Palese, Lou Calvelli, Angie Daglas, Sabrina Ferrand; *D:* Charles Kanganis. **VHS, Beta $29.95** *PMH* ✂

Sinner's Blood Bikers terrorize and torture a small town.
1970 (R) 81m/C Stephen Jacques, Crusty Beal, Nancy Sheldon, Parker Herriott, Julie Connors; *D:* Neil Douglas. **VHS, Beta $24.95** *GHV* Woof!

Sinners in Paradise An assortment of trouble-plagued characters alternately hide and face up to their mysterious pasts when their plane crashes on a deserted island. Interesting "crucible" premise runs out of steam, but plucky, resourceful cast and competent direction keep it going.
1938 64m/B Madge Evans, John Boles, Bruce Cabot, Marion Martin, Gene Lockhart, Dwight Frye, Charlotte Wynters, Nana Bryant, Milburn Stone, Donald (Don "Red") Barry, Morgan Conway; *D:* James Whale. **VHS, Beta $16.95** *SNG, MLB* ✂✂

Sins On her way up the ladder of success in the fashion industry, Helene has stepped on a few toes. Those rivals and her over-increasing acquisition of power and money make this film an exciting drama.
1985 336m/C Joan Collins, Timothy Dalton, Catherine Mary Stewart, Gene Kelly, James Farentino; *D:* Douglas Hickox. **VHS, Beta $29.95** *STE, NWV, HHE* ✂✂

Sins of Desire Highly erotic thriller with Roberts going undercover as a nurse in a sex therapy clinic. It seems her sister was a former patient at the clinic and has since died a mysterious death. Linking up with private eye Cassavetes, Roberts sets out to investigate the doctors who treated her sister, searching for clues to her untimely death.
1992 90m/C Tanya Roberts, Jay Richardson, Delia Sheppard, Nick Cassavetes, Jan-Michael Vincent; *D:* Jim Wynorski; *W:* Mark McGee, Peter Liapis. **VHS $89.95** *COL, VMK, PMS* ✂✂

The Sins of Dorian Gray A modernized adaptation of "The Portrait of Dorian Grey" by Oscar Wilde, with Dorian as a beautiful woman who remains young for 30 years, while a video screen test ages, like the original character's mirror image. Might have been intriguing and stylish; instead, only disappointing and incompetent. Made for television.
1982 (PG) 95m/C Belinda Bauer, Joseph Bottoms, Anthony Perkins; *D:* Tony Maylam. **VHS, Beta $59.98** *FOX* ✂

Sins of Jezebel Biblical epic about Jezebel, who worships an evil god. She marries the king of Israel and brings the kingdom nothing but trouble.
1954 74m/C Paulette Goddard, George Nader, John Hoyt, Eduard Franz; *D:* Reginald LeBorg. **VHS, Beta, LV** *NO* ✂

Sins of Rome Spartacus risks it all in a bold attempt to free his fellow slaves. Not nearly the equal of Kirk Douglas's "Spartacus," but much better than later Italian adventure epics.
1954 75m/B *IT* Ludmila Tcherina, Massimo Girotti, Giana Maria Canale, Yves Vincent; *D:* Riccardo Freda. VHS $16.95 SNC ✍✍

Sinthia: The Devil's Doll A little girl is thought to be possessed by a demon after she has horrible dreams about killing her father.
1970 ?m/C Shula Roan, Diane Webber; *D:* Ray Dennis Steckler. VHS $16.95 SNC ✍✍

Sioux City Sue Talent scouts looking to cast a western musical find Autry, then trick him into being the voice of a singing donkey in an animated production. But, the yodelin' cowboy belts out a number or two, and the poobahs give him the lead. Singin' and fancy ridin' abound in Autry's first post-WWII role.
1946 69m/B Gene Autry, Lynn (Mary Hart) Roberts, Sterling Holloway. VHS, Beta $29.98 CCB, VCN ✍✍

Sirocco An American gun-runner (Bogart) stuck in Syria in 1925 matches wits with a French intelligence officer amid civil war and intrigue. About the underbelly of human affair.
1951 111m/B Humphrey Bogart, Lee J. Cobb, Zero Mostel, Everett Sloane, Gerald Mohr; *D:* Curtis Bernhardt. VHS, Beta, LV $9.95 COL ✍✍ ½

Sister Act Surprising box office hit casts Goldberg as Deloris, a Reno lounge singer. She inadvertently witnesses a mob murder and is hidden by the police in a convent where she's as comfortable in a habit as a fish is out of water. Much to the dismay of poker-faced Mother Superior Smith, she promptly takes over the rag-tag choir and molds them into a swinging, religious version of a '60s girls group. The choir's overwhelming popularity blows her cover and she winds up back in Reno, accompanied by her nun pals, and with the mob hot on her trail. Stock characters and situations are deflected by some genuinely funny moments and good performances, especially by Najimy as the plump and jolly sister and Makkena as the shy novice. Coached by the very clever Shaiman, Whoopie handles her singing bits with gusto, highlight of which is "My God," sung to the tune of "My Guy."
1992 (PG) 100m/C Whoopi Goldberg, Maggie Smith, Harvey Keitel, Bill Nunn, Kathy Najimy, Wendy Makkena, Mary Wickes, Robert Miranda, Richard Portnow, Joseph Maher; *D:* Emile Ardolino; *W:* Joseph Howard; *M:* Marc Shaiman. VHS, Beta, LV $19.99 TOU, PMS ✍✍ ½

Sister Dora An idealistic young woman joins a nursing sisterhood in 19th century England but she questions her vocation when she falls in love. Adapted from a popular romance novel.
1977 147m/C *GB* Dorothy Tutin, James Grout, Peter Cellier; *D:* Mark Miller. VHS $59.95 SVS ✍✍ ½

The Sister-in-Law Shady dealings, seduction, and adultery run rampant. Savage (who also wrote and sings the folk score) reluctantly agrees to deliver a package across the Canadian border for his brother. Intriguing.
1974 (R) 80m/C John Savage, Anne Saxon, W.G. McMillan, Meredith Baer; *D:* Joseph Rubin. VHS, Beta $79.95 PSM ✍✍

Sister Kenny Follows the story of a legendary Australian nurse crusading for the treatment of infantile paralysis. Stirring, well-made screen biography. Co-scripted by Mary McCarthy. Based on Elizabeth Kenny's memoir, "And They Shall Walk."
1946 116m/B Rosalind Russell, Dean Jagger, Alexander Knox, Philip Merivale, Beulah Bondi; *D:* Dudley Nichols. Academy Awards '46 Nominations: Best Actress (Russell); Golden Globe Awards '47: Best Actress—Drama (Russell). VHS, Beta, LV $19.98 NOS, CCB, TTC ✍✍✍

Sister, Sister A Congressional aide on vacation in Louisiana takes a room in an old mansion. He gradually discovers the secret of the house and its resident sisters. Dark Southern gothicism, full of plot surprises, with a twisted ending.
1987 (R) 91m/C Eric Stoltz, Judith Ivey, Jennifer Jason Leigh, Dennis Lipscomb, Anne Pitoniak, Natalija Nogulich; *D:* Bill Condon. VHS, Beta, LV $19.95 STE, NWV ✍✍

Sister Street Fighters Boy meets girl, boy and girl terrorize the neighborhood. Typical martial arts fest.
1976 (R) 82m/C Sonny Chiba; *D:* Kazuhiko Yamaguchi. VHS UHV ✍

The Sisterhood A pair of amazons fight for women's rights in a post-nuclear future. Cheap feminist theme laid over warmed-over sci-fi plot.
1988 (R) 75m/C Rebecca Holden, Chuck Wagner, Lynn-Holly Johnson, Barbara Hooper; *D:* Cirio H. Santiago. VHS, Beta, LV $79.95 MED ✍

The Sisters Lavish film of three sisters and their marital problems in turn of the century San Francisco. Davis gives a great performance as the oldest sister with the most trouble—notably in the form of unreliable sports reporter Flynn. Look for Susan Hayward in a bit role, as well as Bogart's wife, Mayo Methot. Based on the bestselling novel by Myron Brinig.
1938 98m/B Bette Davis, Errol Flynn, Anita Louise, Jane Bryan, Ian Hunter, Henry Travers, Beulah Bondi, Donald Crisp, Dick Foran, Patric Knowles; *D:* Anatole Litvak. VHS $19.98 MGM ✍✍✍

Sisters Siamese twins are separated surgically, but one doesn't survive the operation. The remaining sister is scarred physically and mentally with her personality split into bad and good. The bad side commits a murder, witnessed (or was it?) by an investigative reporter. And then things really get crazy. DePalma's first ode to Hitchcock, with great music by Hitchcock's favorite composer, Bernard Herrmann. Scary and suspenseful.
1973 (R) 93m/C Margot Kidder, Charles Durning, Barnard Hughes; *D:* Brian DePalma. VHS, Beta $29.98 WAR, OM ✍✍✍

Sisters of Death Five members of a sorority gather together for a reunion in a remote California town. Little do they know, a psychopath is stalking them, one by one. Could it have something to do with the terrible secret they each keep? Good, cheap thrills and some Bicentennial fashions to boot.
1976 (PG) 87m/C Arthur Franz, Claudia Jennings, Cheri Howell, Sherry Boucher, Paul Carr; *D:* Joseph Mazzuca. VHS, Beta $29.95 UHV ✍✍

Sisters of Gion Mizoguchi's most famous and arguably best pre-war film. Two geisha sisters in Tokyo's red-light district reflect the tension in Japanese culture by waging a quiet battle of tradition vs. progressiveness. Highly acclaimed. In Japanese with English subtitles.
1936 69m/B *JP* Isuzu Yamada, Yoko Umemura; *D:* Kenji Mizoguchi. VHS, Beta FCT ✍✍✍ ½

Sisters of Satan The nuns of the infamous convent St. Archangelo choose to survive by trading God for the devil.
1975 91m/C *MX* Claudio Brook, David Silva, Tina Romero, Susana Kamini; *D:* Juan Montezuma. VHS, Beta $19.95 ACA, MPI ✍✍ ½

Sitting Ducks Mild-mannered accountant and lecherous pal rip off and then attempt to outrun the mob—all while swapping songs and confessions. Emil and Norman make it up as they go along; their hilarious repartee is largely improvised. They pick up a gorgeous lady (Townsend) and go about their way.
1980 (R) 88m/C Michael Emil, Zack Norman, Patrice Townsend, Richard Romanus, Irene Forrest, Henry Jaglom; *D:* Henry Jaglom. VHS, Beta $19.95 MED ✍✍✍

The Situation Two years of life and death in El Salvador's civil war. Also the tale of an American film crew who spent the time with a Salvadoran family covering the events. Many events in the movie "Salvador" were inspired by incidents portrayed here.
1987 91m/C Richard Boyle; *M:* Bob Dylan, Peter, Paul & Mary, Paul & Mary. Beta VDE ✍✍✍

Six Fois Deux/Sur et Sous la Communication A six-part experimental series made for French television, in which Godard and Mieville analyze modern culture and socioeconomics via a free-form essay format, combining interviews, screened text, self-referential devices and news footage. In French with English voice-over.
1976 100m/C *FR D:* Jean-Luc Godard, Anne-Marie Mieville. VHS, Beta EAI ✍✍✍

Six Gun Gospel Hatton masquerades as a preacher to investigate some shady dealings. Laughs come when the women of the congregation prevail upon him to sing, and he croons a ballad about Jesse James!
1943 59m/B Johnny Mack Brown, Raymond Hatton, Inna Gest, Eddie Dew, Roy Barcroft, Kenneth MacDonald, Bud Osborne; *D:* Lambert Hillyer. VHS $19.95 DVT, HEG ✍✍

Six Gun Rhythm Novelty western plot has football player traveling to Texas to avenge his father's murder.
1939 59m/B Tex Fletcher. VHS, Beta $19.95 NOS, VDM, HEG ✍ ½

633 Squadron A skilled R.A.F. pilot attempts to lead his squadron on a mission deep into the fjords of Norway in search of a Nazi fuel plant. Robertson tries hard, as always, but is really not British officer material. Well-made war flick, based on a true story. Script co-written by James Clavell.
1964 102m/C Cliff Robertson, George Chakiris, Maria Perschy, Harry Andrews; *D:* Walter Grauman. VHS, Beta $19.98 MGM ✍✍ ½

Six Pack The Gambler goes auto racing. Rogers, in his theatrical debut, stars as Brewster Baker, a former stock car driver. He returns to the racing circuit with the help of six larcenous orphans (the six-pack, get it?) adept at stripping cars. Kinda cute if you're in the mood for sugar-powered race car story.
1982 (PG) 108m/C Kenny Rogers, Diane Lane, Erin Gray, Barry Corbin, Anthony Michael Hall; *D:* Daniel Petrie. VHS, Beta $14.98 FOX ✍ ½

Six Shootin' Sheriff A cowboy framed for bank robbery is released and seeks to rid his town of all evil. And he gets the girl!
1938 59m/B Ken Maynard, Marjorie Reynolds, Walter Long; *D:* Harry Fraser. VHS, Beta $47.95 UHV, VYY, VCN ✍✍

Six Weeks A young girl dying of leukemia brings together her work-driven mother and an aspiring married politician. Manipulative hanky-wringer has good acting from both Moores but oddly little substance.
1982 (PG) 107m/C Dudley Moore, Mary Tyler Moore, Katherine Healy; **D:** Tony Bill. **VHS, Beta, LV $12.95** COL ✍✍

Six Wives of Henry VIII Michell has been called the definitive Henry VIII, and this BBC Classic Television Series (shown as part of ''Masterpiece Theatre'' on PBS) was perhaps the most praised series on British TV. Henry's wives were: Catherine of Aragon, Anne Boleyn, Jane Seymour, Anne of Cleves, Catherine Howard, and Catherine Parr. Each episode tells of their, sometimes tragic, fates as pawns in Henry's quest for an heir, and his changes from an eager young man to aged, bitter monarch. The 90-minute videos are available individually or as a boxed set.
197? 540m/C GB Keith Michell, Annette Crosble, Dorothy Tutin, Anne Stallybrass, Elvi Hale, Angela Pleasence, Rosalie Crutchley. **VHS $129.95** SIG, FCT, BFS ✍✍✍

Sixteen A naive country lass is attracted to the glitter and hum of the outside world. Her determination and optimism help her triumph. **AKA:** Like a Crow on a June Bug.
1972 (R) 84m/C Mercedes McCambridge, Parley Baer, Ford Rainey, Beverly Powers, John Lozier, Simone Griffeth, Maddie Norman; **D:** Lawrence Dobkin. **VHS, Beta $19.95** STE, NWV ✍

Sixteen Candles Hughes gathers his stable of young stars again for one of his best films. Every girl's sixteenth birthday is supposed to be special, but in the rush of her sister's wedding nobody remembers Ringwald's. After that, everything seems to go downhill in hilarious fashion. Ringwald and Hall are especially charming in this humorous look at teenage traumas. Title song performed by The Stray Cats.
1984 (PG) 93m/C Molly Ringwald, Justin Henry, Michael Schoeffling, Haviland Morris, Gedde Watanabe, Anthony Michael Hall, Paul Dooley, Carlin Glynn, Blanche Baker, Edward Andrews, Carole Cook, Max Showalter, Liane Curtis, John Cusack, Joan Cusack, Brian Doyle-Murray, Jami Gertz, Cinnamon Idles, Zelda Rubenstein; **W/D:** John Hughes. **VHS, Beta, LV $19.95** MCA ✍✍✍

Sixteen Fathoms Deep A sponge fisherman risks it all, including his love, when a mean businessman threatens his operation. Good underwater photography, but otherwise undistinguished.
1934 57m/B Lon Chaney Jr., Sally O'Neil, George Regas, Maurice Black, Russell Simpson; **D:** Armand Schaefer. **VHS $16.95** SNC, NOS, DVT ✍✍

'68 A Hungarian family struggles with the generation gap in 1968 America.
1987 (R) 99m/C Eric Larson, Terra Vandergaw, Neil Young; **D:** Steven Kovacks. **VHS, Beta, LV $19.95** STE, NWV ✍

Sizzle When her boyfriend is murdered by the mob, nightclub singer Anderson, newly arrived from Hicksville in Roaring '20s Chicago, stops at nothing to get revenge. Bad-guy gangster Forsythe falls for her charms. Fun but unsophisticated. Made for TV.
1981 100m/C Loni Anderson, John Forsythe, Leslie Uggams, Roy Thinnes, Richard Lynch, Michael Goodwin; **D:** Don Medford. **VHS, Beta $59.95** PSM ✍✍

Sizzle Beach U.S.A. Three young women who want a shot at becoming famous travel to Los Angeles and play on the beach with little budget and no particular purpose. Also available in an unrated version.

Although released in 1986, this was made in 1974. Kevin Costner's film debut.
1986 (R) 90m/C Terry Congie, Leslie Brander, Roselyn Royce, Kevin Costner; **D:** Richard Brander. **VHS, Beta, LV $19.95** STE, VMK ✍

Skag Disabled following a stroke, a Pittsburgh steel worker confronts a change in family roles and long-ignored family problems during his convalescence. Malden is exceptional and believable as a Joe Lunchbucket in this well-written, well-cast TV outing, pilot for the NBC series.
1979 145m/C Karl Malden, Piper Laurie, Craig Wasson, Leslie Ackerman, Peter Gallagher, Kathryn Holcomb, Powers Boothe; **D:** Frank Perry. **VHS, Beta $49.95** IVE ✍✍✍

Skateboard A down-and-out Hollywood agent creates a pro skateboarding team and enters them in a race worth $20,000. Quickie premise executed lamely.
1977 (PG) 97m/C Allen Garfield, Kathleen Lloyd, Chad McQueen, Leif Garrett, Richard Van Der Wyk, Tony Alva, Antony Carbone. **VHS, Beta** NO ✍

Skeezer A dog becomes a key factor in a sympathetic doctor's efforts to communicate with emotionally unstable children. Based on reality, and a good cast makes it believable and moving. Quality family fare.
1982 100m/C Karen Valentine, Dee Wallace Stone, Tom Atkins, Mariclare Costello, Leighton Greer, Justine Lord; **D:** Peter Hunt. **VHS $39.95** LIV ✍✍

Skeleton Coast Borgnine plays a retired U.S. Marine colonel who organizes a Magnificent Seven-like group of tough mercenaries to go into eastern Africa to save hostages held by Angolan terrorists. Cliches abound, including a token large-breasted woman, Mulford, getting her t-shirt ripped open. No plot and a bad script. Also called ''Fair Trade.''
1989 (R) 94m/C Ernest Borgnine, Robert Vaughn, Oliver Reed, Herbert Lom, Daniel Greene, Nancy Mulford, Leon Isaac Kennedy; **D:** John Cardos. **VHS, LV $19.98** SUE, NLC ✍

Sketch Artist Jack Whitfield is a police sketch artist whose latest rendering of a murder suspect looks suspiciously like his wife. Jack decides to keep this information to himself while he does some quiet investigating but he may not have any time. The police have a new murder suspect in mind—Jack! Made for cable television.
1992 (R) 89m/C Jeff Fahey, Sean Young, Drew Barrymore, Frank McRae, Tcheky Karyo, James Tolkan, Charlotte Lewis; **D:** Phedon Papamichael. **VHS, Beta, LV $89.98** FXV ✍✍

Sketches of a Strangler A psychotic art student sketches, then murders prostitutes. Interesting lead character but hardly chilling—just horrible to watch. Made for TV.
1978 91m/C Allen Garfield, Meredith MacRae; **D:** Paul Leder. **VHS, Beta $59.95** MED ✍½

Ski Bum A ski bum discovers corruption and violence at a Colorado Rockies resort. Eminently forgettable trash. Scantily based on a novel by Romain Gary.
1975 (R) 94m/C Charlotte Rampling, Zalman King, Dimitra Arliss, Anna Karina; **D:** Bruce Clark. **VHS, Beta $59.98** NLC ✍

Ski Patrol Wacky ski groupies try to stop an evil developer. Good ski action in a surprisingly plotful effort from the crazy crew that brought the world ''Police Academy.''
1989 (PG) 85m/C Roger Rose, Yvette Nipar, T.K. Carter, Leslie Jordan, Ray Walston, Martin Mull; **D:** Richard Correll. **VHS, Beta, LV $19.95** COL ✍✍

Ski School Rival ski instructors compete for jobs and babes. Brow lowering.

1991 (R) 89m/C Ava Fabian, Dean Cameron, Tom Breznahan, Stuart Fratkin; **D:** Damian Lee. **VHS, LV $19.98** HBO ✍

Ski Troop Attack During World War II, an American ski patrol is sent behind Nazi lines to blow up a German railway bridge. Unexceptional low-budget Corman outing; not among the greatest of war movies.
1960 61m/B Michael Forest, Frank Wolff, Sheila Carol. **VHS, Beta $16.95** SNC, NOS, DVT ✍✍

Skier's Dream This spectacular action-packed film focuses on a young executive in search of the ultimate run. Shot on the most exotic ski locations in the world; covers freestyle skiing, powder skiing, snowboarding, extreme skiing, cliff jumping, paragliding, and wave riding.
1988 75m/C John Eaves, Ian Boyd; **M:** Jimi Hendrix, Tom Cochrane. **VHS $14.95** COL, RAP ✍✍

Skin Deep A boyish Don Juan tries everything to win back his ex-wife. Ritter whines about his mid-life crisis and seduces women, this substitutes for plot. A few funny slapstick scenes still don't make this worth watching.
1989 (R) 102m/C John Ritter, Vincent Gardenia, Julianne Phillips, Alyson Reed, Nina Foch, Chelsea Field, Denise Crosby; **D:** Blake Edwards. **VHS, Beta, LV $9.99** CCB, MED ✍½

Skin Game Two British families feud over land rights. Not thrilling; not characteristic of working with Hitchcock. Way too much talking in excruciating, drawn-out scenes. Adapted from the play of the same name.
1931 87m/B GB Phyllis Konstam, Edmund Gwenn, Frank Lawton, C.V. France, Jill Esmond, Helen Hayes; **D:** Alfred Hitchcock. **VHS, Beta $16.95** SNC, NOS, MLB ✍½

Skin Game A fast talking con-artist (Garner) and his black partner (Gossett) travel throughout the antebellum South setting up scams—Gossett is sold to a new owner by Garner, who helps him escape. Garner and Gossett make a splendid comedy team in this different kind of buddy flick. All is well until Asner turns the tables on them. Finely acted comedy-drama.
1971 (PG) 102m/C James Garner, Louis Gossett Jr., Susan Clark, Ed Asner, Andrew Duggan; **D:** Paul Bogart. **VHS, Beta $19.98** WAR ✍✍✍

Skinheads: The Second Coming of Hate Neo-fascists run rampant. Exploitative effort from schlock-doyen Clark.
1988 (R) 93m/C Chuck Connors, Barbara Bain, Brian Brophy, Jason Culp, Elizabeth Sagal; **D:** Greydon Clark. **VHS** NO ✍

Skinned Alive A woman and her children travel cross-country to sell leather goods. When a detective discovers where the leather comes from he's hot on their trail.
1989 90m/C Mary Jackson, Scott Spiegel; **W/D:** Jon Killough. **VHS, Beta** NO Woof!

Skinner's Dress Suit Meek, hen-pecked office clerk tells domineering wife he got a raise so she'll get off his back. She quickly insinuates them into upper crusty social circle, until the fib pays off big. Remake of the 1917 version based on Henry Irving Dodge's novel.
1926 79m/C Reginald Denny, Laura LaPlante, Arthur Lake, Hedda Hopper; **D:** William A. Seiter. **VHS, Beta $19.95** GPV ✍✍½

Skirts Ahoy! Williams, Evans, and Blaine are three WAVES who have their eyes set on three handsome men. To get them, of course, they must sing and dance a lot, and Williams must perform one of her famous water ballets. ♫Oh By Jingo; Hold Me Close to You; What Makes a WAVE?; What Good is a Gal Without a Guy?; Skirts Ahoy!; Glad

to Have You Aboard; The Navy Waltz; I Get a Funny Feeling; We Will Fight; Hilda Matilda.
1952 109m/C Esther Williams, Joan Evans, Vivian Blaine, Barry Sullivan, Keefe Brasselle, Billy Eckstine, Debbie Reynolds; **D:** Sidney Lanfield. **VHS $19.98** *MGM* ♫♫

The Skull Horror abounds when Cushing gets his hands on the skull of the Marquis de Sade that has mysterious, murderous powers. Based on a story by Robert Bloch.
1965 83m/C Peter Cushing, Patrick Wymark, Christopher Lee, Nigel Green, Jill Bennett, Michael Gough, George Coulouris, Patrick Magee; **D:** Freddie Francis. **VHS** *PAR* ♫♫

Skull: A Night of Terror A cop vows not to use guns after a tragic accident, then single-handed and unarmed, takes on terrorists who kidnap his family.
1988 (R) 80m/C Nadia Capone, Robert Bideman, Robbie Fox, Paul Sanders; **D:** Robert Bergman. **VHS, Beta $79.95** *ACA* ♫♫

Skull & Crown Rin Tin Tin, Jr. helps the hero break up a group of smugglers. A favorite of Tin fans everywhere.
1938 58m/B Rin Tin Tin Jr, Regis Toomey, Jack Mulhall, James Murray. **VHS, Beta $24.95** *NOS, DVT, HEG* ♫♫

Skullduggery When a peaceful race of blond ape-people are discovered in New Guinea, a courtroom battle ensues to prevent their slaughter at the hands of developers. Interesting premise sadly flops.
1970 (PG) 105m/C Burt Reynolds, Susan Clark, Roger C. Carmel, Chips Rafferty, Edward Fox, Wilfrid Hyde-White, Rhys Williams; **D:** Gordon Douglas. **VHS, Beta** *MED* ♫ ½

Skullduggery Costume-store minion Haverstock carries a curse that makes him kill and mutilate. The usual unspeakable horror ensues for a group of medieval-game players. *AKA:* Warlock.
1979 (PG) 95m/C Thom Haverstock, Wendy Crewson, David Calderisi; **D:** Ota Richter. **VHS, Beta $59.95** *MED* Woof!

The Sky Above, the Mud Below An acclaimed documentary following a band of explorers transversing New Guinea in 1959, and their confrontations with native rituals, heretofore unknown cannibal tribes and physical calamities. French title: "Le Ciel et la Boue." In HiFi.
1961 90m/C D: Pierre-Dominique Gaisseau. **VHS, Beta** *LHV, WAR, FCT* Woof!

Sky Bandits Mounties uncover the mystery of a disappearing plane carrying gold from a Yukon mine. Last of the "Renfrew of the Mounties" pictures.
1940 56m/B James Newill, Dave O'Brien, Louise Stanley. **VHS, Beta, 8mm $14.95** *NOS, SNC, VCN* ♫ ½

Sky Hei$t Criminals plan robbery of police helicopter carrying fortune in gold bullion. Made for television.
1975 96m/C Stefanie Powers, Joseph Campanella, Don Meredith, Larry Wilcox, Frank Gorshin, Shelley Fabares, Ken Swofford, Ray Vitte, Nancy Belle Fuller, Suzanne Somers; **D:** Lee H. Katzin. **VHS $29.95** *UNI* ♫♫

Sky High A spy at an Air Force base is trying to get hold of the plans to a secret plane. A GI is recruited to catch him.
1951 60m/B Sid Melton, Mara Lynn, Douglas Evans. **VHS, Beta, LV** *NO* ♫

Sky High Three college students become immersed in international intrigue when the C.I.A. and the K.G.B. pursue them through Greece looking for a secret Soviet tape.
1984 103m/C Daniel Hirsch, Clayton Norcross, Frank Schultz, Lauren Taylor; **D:** Nico Mastorakis. **VHS, Beta $79.98** *LIV* ♫

The Sky is Gray A young black Louisiana boy journeys with his mother to the dentist, and on the way is confronted with prejudice and poverty. Set in the 1940s. Based on a story by Ernest Gaines. Made for television, with an introduction by Henry Fonda.
1980 46m/C Olivia Cole, James Bond III, Margaret Avery, Cleavon Little; **D:** Stan Lathan. **VHS, Beta $24.95** *MON, KAR, FCT* ♫♫♫

Sky Liner An FBI agent is trailing a spy who has taken secret documents aboard a west-bound flight.
1949 62m/B Richard Travis, Pamela Blake. **VHS, Beta, LV** *NO* ♫

The Sky Pilot Young clergyman sets up a parish on North Pacific coast and finds he must prove himself to the cowboys. He saves young woman from stampede, but her father blames him for her maimed legs and sets the preacher's church on fire, providing girl with excuse to overcome handicap.
1921 63m/B John Bowers, Colleen Moore, David Butler, Donald Ian Macdonald; **D:** King Vidor. **VHS, Beta $29.95** *GPV, FCT* ♫♫ ½

Sky Pirates Space epic deals about pieces of ancient stone left by prehistoric extraterrestrials, now lost in a time warp. Bad stunts, bad script and notably bad acting make it a woofer in any era.
1987 88m/C *AU* John Hargreaves, Max Phipps, Meredith Phillips; **D:** Colin Eggleston. **VHS, Beta $79.98** *FOX* Woof!

Sky Riders Hang-gliders risk it all to take on a group of political kidnappers. Fine hang-gliding footage and glorious Greek locations make up for garden-variety plot.
1976 (PG) 93m/C James Coburn, Susannah York, Robert Culp, Charles Aznavour, Harry Andrews, John Beck; **D:** Douglas Hickox. **VHS** *FOX* ♫♫ ½

Skylark In a sequel to Hallmark Hall of Fame's hugely successful "Sarah, Plain and Tall," the whole Kansas crew shows up for more of their little-farm-on-the-prairie life. After two years in America's squarest state, mail-order bride Sarah (Close) loves Jacob (Walken), but not the scenery and still yearns for the lush greenery of Maine. When drought and fire threaten the farm, Jacob fears for the family's health and safety, and sends them back East for a visit. Close's "tough Yankee" expression grows a bit tiresome in a plot that is a tad predictable, yet the simplistic charm and nostalgia are unresistable and work to propel this quality Hallmark production.
1993 (G) 98m/C Glenn Close, Christopher Walken, Lexi Randall, Christopher Bell, Tresa Hughes, Lois Smith, Lee Richardson, Elizabeth Wilson, Margaret Sophie Stein, James Rebhorn, Woody Watson; **D:** Joseph Sargent; **W:** Patricia MacLachlan. **VHS $89.98** *REP, BTV* ♫♫ ½

Skyline A Spanish photographer comes to New York City to work for a magazine. Quietly funny, with a startling ending. Partly in Spanish with English subtitles. *AKA:* La Linea Del Cielo.
1984 (R) 84m/C *SP* Antonio Resines, Beatriz Perez-Porro, Jaime Nos, Roy Hoffman; **D:** Fernando Colombo. **VHS, Beta, LV $29.95** *PAV, KIV* ♫♫♫

The Sky's the Limit Astaire spends his leave in Manhattan and falls in love with fetching journalist Leslie. He's in civvies, so little does she know he's a war hero. Nothing-special semi-musical, with Fred-Ginger spark missing. ♫One For My Baby; My Shining Hour; I've Got a Lot in Common With You.

1943 89m/B Fred Astaire, Joan Leslie, Robert Benchley, Robert Ryan, Elizabeth Patterson; **D:** Edward H. Griffith. **VHS, Beta $19.95** *RKO, VYY, MED* ♫♫ ½

Skyscraper Souls William stars as David Dwight, a ruthless businessman who manipulates stock prices and double-crosses lovers in order to have complete control of a 100-story office building. He sacrifices everything and everyone in this story of big business. Based on the novel "Skyscraper" by Faith Baldwin.
1932 98m/B Warren William, Maureen O'Sullivan, Gregory Ratoff, Anita Page, Verree Teasdale, Norman Foster, Jean Hersholt, Wallace Ford; **D:** Edgar Selwyn. **VHS $19.98** *MGM* ♫♫♫

Slacker Defines a new generation: Overwhelmed by the world and it's demands, "Slackers" react by retreating into lives of minimal expectations. Filmed as a series of improvisational stories about people living on the fringes of the working world and their reactions (or lack thereof) to the life swirling around them. First feature for writer/director Linklater on a budget of $23,000; filmed on location in Austin, Texas with a cast of primarily non-professional actors.
1991 (R) 97m/C Richard Linklater; **W/D:** Richard Linklater. **VHS $79.95** *TAM, ORI* ♫♫♫

Slamdance A struggling cartoonist is framed for the murder of a beautiful young woman while being victimized by the real killer. A complicated murder mystery with a punk beat and visual flash. But the tale is unoriginal - and where's the slamdancing?
1987 (R) 99m/C Tom Hulce, Virginia Madsen, Mary Elizabeth Mastrantonio, Harry Dean Stanton, Adam Ant, John Doe; **D:** Wayne Wang. **VHS, Beta, LV $19.95** *FOX* ♫ ½

Slammer Girls In this sex-drenched, unfunny spoof on women's prison films, the inmates of Loch Ness Penitentiary try to break out using their sexual wiles. The actresses are pseudonymous porn stars.
1987 (R) 82m/C Tally Brittany, Jane Hamilton, Jeff Eagle, Devon Jenkin; **D:** Chuck Vincent. **VHS, Beta, LV $19.95** *LIV* ♫

The Slap French teens learn about love the French way.
1976 (PG) 103m/C *FR* Isabelle Adjani, Lino Ventura; **D:** Claude Pinoteau. **VHS, CDV** *SUE* ♫

Slap Shot A profane satire of the world of professional hockey. Over-the-hill player-coach Newman gathers an odd-ball mixture of has-beens and young players and reluctantly initiates them, using violence on the ice to make his team win. The strip-tease on ice needs to be seen to be believed. Charming in its own bone-crunching way.
1977 (R) 123m/C Paul Newman, Michael Ontkean, Jennifer Warren, Lindsay Crouse, Jerry Houser, Melinda Dillon, Strother Martin; **D:** George Roy Hill. **VHS, Beta, LV $19.95** *MCA* ♫♫♫

Slapstick An anthology of great moments from Mack Sennett comedy shorts, featuring many great stars in some of their earliest film appearances.
193? 76m/B Charlie Chaplin, Harold Lloyd, Charley Chase, Buster Keaton, Ben Turpin, Stan Laurel. **VHS, Beta $39.95** *REP* ♫♫♫

Slapstick of Another Kind Lewis and Kahn play dual roles as an alien brother and sister and their adoptive Earth parents, who are being pursued by U.S. agents. Rather miserable rendition of a Kurt Vonnegut novel.
1984 (PG) 85m/C Jerry Lewis, Madeline Kahn, Marty Feldman, Jim Backus, Pat Morita, Samuel Fuller, Orson Welles; **D:** Steven Paul. **VHS, Beta, LV $79.98** *LIV, VES* ♫ ½

Slash Each of four people caught in a political takeover harbors a secret that could harm one of the others. Extremely violent.
1987 90m/C Romano Kristoff, Michael Monty, Gwen Hung; **D:** John Gale. **VHS, Beta** *NO* ✂️ ½

Slashdance A really pathetic thriller follows a lady cop undercover in a chorus line to find out who's been murdering the dancers. The acting is on the level of pro wrestling. Don't be fooled by the naked babes on the cassette box - there's no nudity.
1989 83m/C Cindy Maranne, James Carroll Jordan, Queen Kong, Joel von Ornsteiner, Jay Richardson; **W/D:** James Shyman. **VHS, Beta** $9.95 *SIM Woof!*

Slashed Dreams Hippie couple travels to California wilderness in search of friend. A pair of woodsmen assault them and rape the woman, which really messes with their heads. Retitled and packaged as slasher movie. Mountain men Keach and Pritchard wrote the screenplay. **AKA:** Sunburst.
1974 (R) 74m/C Peter Hooten, Katherine Baumann, Ric Carrott, Anne Lockhart, Robert Englund, Rudy Vallee, James Keach, David Pritchard, Peter Brown; **D:** James Polakof. **VHS** $19.95 *ACA* ✂️✂️

The Slasher A policeman must find the madman who has been killing off unfaithful married women. Miserably gory, pointless slasher (hence the title) interesting only as an early example of its kind.
1974 88m/C Farley Granger, Sylva Koscina, Susan Scott. **VHS, Beta** $59.95 *MON Woof!*

Slate, Wyn & Me Two bank-robbing, kidnapping brothers flee cross-country from the law, and fall in love with the girl they've snatched. Pointless, and pointlessly violent and vulgar.
1987 90m/C Sigrid Thornton, Simon Burke, Martin Sacks; **D:** Don McLennan. **VHS, Beta** $19.98 *SUE, NLC* ✂️

Slaughter After his parents are murdered, a former Green Beret goes after their killers. Plenty of brutality. Followed by "Slaughter's Big Ripoff."
1972 (R) 92m/C Jim Brown, Stella Stevens, Rip Torn, Cameron Mitchell, Don Gordon, Marlene Clark; **D:** Jack Starrett. **VHS, Beta, LV** $59.98 *FOX* ✂️

Slaughter High A high school nerd is accidentally disfigured by a back-firing prank. Five years later, he returns to exact bloody revenge. Available in an unrated version.
1986 (R) 90m/C Caroline Munro, Simon Scuddamore, Kelly Baker; **D:** George Dugdale. **VHS, Beta** $79.98 *LIV, VES* ✂️

Slaughter Hotel An asylum already inhabited by extremely bizarre characters is plagued by a series of gruesome murders. Lots of skin and lots of blood; Neri shines as a nymphomaniacal lesbian nurse. **AKA:** Asylum Erotica; La Bestia Uccide a Sangue Freddo.
1971 (R) 72m/C Klaus Kinski, Rosalba (Sara Bay) Neri, Margaret Lee, John Ely; **D:** Fernando Di Leo. **VHS, Beta** *MPI, GRG* ✂️

Slaughter in San Francisco A Chinese-American cop leads a one-man fight against corruption in the department in Daly City, near San Francisco. Norris is the bad guy; made in 1973 but not released until he had an established following. Plenty of kicking and karate chops. **AKA:** Chuck Norris vs. the Karate Cop.
1981 92m/C *CH* Chuck Norris, Don Wong; **D:** William Lowe. **VHS, Beta** $9.95 *SUE, RHI* ✂️

The Slaughter of the Vampires Newlyweds meet a bloodthirsty vampire in a Viennese chalet. Real, real bad horror flick, poorly dubbed. **AKA:** Curse of the Blood-Ghouls; Curses of the Ghouls.
1962 81m/C *IT* Walter Brandi, Dieter Eppler, Graziella Granta; **W/D:** Robert Mauri. **VHS, Beta** $39.95 *SNC Woof!*

Slaughter Trail Rancher-turned-stage robber Young shoots two Indians and cavalry colonel Donlevy has to deal with the fallout. Peace returns when Young dies. Ordinary western with balladeer device helping the plot along, or trying to.
1951 78m/C Brian Donlevy, Gig Young, Virginia Grey, Andy Devine, Robert Hutton; **D:** Irving Allen. **VHS, Beta** $19.98 *TTC* ✂️

Slaughterday An innocent woman is caught in the middle of an ex-con's elaborate scheme to commit the largest heist of his life.
1977 (R) 87m/C Rita Tushingham, William Berger, Frederick Jaeger, Michael Hauserman, Gordon Mitchell; **D:** Peter Patzak. **VHS, Beta** *GHV* ✂️ ½

Slaughterhouse A rotund, pig-loving country boy kills, maims, and eats numerous victims. Features the requisite dumb teens and plenty of blood.
1987 (R) 87m/C Joe Barton, Sherry Bendorf, Don Barrett; **D:** Rick Roessler. **VHS, Beta** $14.98 *NLC Woof!*

Slaughterhouse Five A suburban optometrist becomes "unstuck" in time and flits randomly through the experiences of his life, from the Dresden bombing to an extraterrestrial zoo. Noticed at Cannes but not in theatres; ambitious failure to adapt Kurt Vonnegut's odd novel.
1972 (R) 104m/C Michael Sacks, Valerie Perrine, Ron Leibman, Eugene Roche, Perry King; **D:** George Roy Hill. **VHS, Beta, LV** $19.95 *MCA* ✂️

Slaughterhouse Rock A rock star goes on a cannibalistic rampage after being possessed by an evil spirit. Music group Devo did the score for this flick.
1988 (R) 90m/C Nicholas Celozzi, Donna Denton, Toni Basil, Hope Marie Carlton; **D:** Dimitri Logothetis; **M:** Devo. **VHS, Beta** $14.95 *SVS Woof!*

Slaughter's Big Ripoff Slaughter is back battling the Mob with guns, planes and martial arts. This undistinguished sequel features McMahon as a mob boss.
1973 (R) 92m/C Jim Brown, Brock Peters, Don Stroud, Ed McMahon, Art Metrano, Gloria Hendry; **D:** Gordon Douglas. **VHS, Beta** $59.98 *FOX* ✂️ ½

Slave Girls from Beyond Infinity In this B-movie spoof, two beautiful intergalactic slave girls escape their penal colony, land on a mysterious planet, and meet a cannibalistic despot. Fun spoof of '50s "B" sci-fi movies.
1987 80m/C Elizabeth Cayton, Cindy Beal, Brinke Stevens; **D:** Ken Dixon. **VHS, Beta, LV** *NO* ✂️✂️

A Slave of Love Poignant love story set in the Crimea as the Bolshevik Revolution rages around a film crew attempting to complete a project. Interesting as ideological cinema but also enjoyable romantic drama. In Russian with English subtitles.
1978 94m/C *RU* Elena Solovei, Rodion Nakhapetov, Alexander Kalyagin; **D:** Nikita Mikhalkov. **VHS, Beta** $29.95 *COL, AUD, TAM* ✂️✂️✂️

Slave of the Cannibal God Beautiful Andress is captured by "native" cannibals; Keach must save her. **AKA:** Il Montagna di Dio Cannibale; Mountain of Cannibal Gods.
1979 (R) 86m/C *IT* Stacy Keach, Ursula Andress, Claudio Cassinelli; **D:** Sergio Martino. **VHS, Beta** $49.95 *VES Woof!*

Slave Trade in the World Today Slavery practices in the modern world are shown, including actual scenes of a sheik's harem, slave auctions, and the kidnapping and selling of young women.
1964 87m/C **D:** Roberto Malenotti. **VHS, Beta** $19.95 *VDC* ✂️

Slavers Detailed depiction of the 19th century African slave trade with a little romance thrown in.
1977 (R) 102m/C *GE* Trevor Howard, Britt Ekland, Ron Ely, Cameron Mitchell, Ray Milland; **D:** Jurgen Goslar. **VHS, Beta** $69.95 *VCD* ✂️✂️

Slaves in Bondage Young, country girls are lured into the big city and initiated into a life of ill repute in this exploitation classic. A must for camp fans of the 30's.
1937 ?m/C Lona Andre, Wheeler Oakman. **VHS** $16.95 *SNC* ✂️

Slaves of Love Two men, stranded on a desert island, discover it is inhabited by sex-starved females.
1969 86m/C Peter Owen, Tina Brown. **VHS, Beta** $59.95 *MED, MOV* ✂️

Slaves of New York Greenwich Village artists worry about life and love in the '80s and being artistic enough for New York. Adapted from the stories of Tama Janowitz, who also wrote the screenplay and appears as Abby. Disastrous adaptation of a popular novel.
1989 (R) 115m/C Bernadette Peters, Chris Sarandon, Mary Beth Hurt, Madeleine Potter, Adam Coleman Howard, Nick Corri, Mercedes Ruehl, Joe Leeway, Charles McCaughan, John Harkins, Anna Katarina, Tama Janowitz; **D:** James Ivory; **W:** Tama Janowitz. **VHS, Beta, LV** $89.95 *COL* ✂️ ½

The Slayer It's movies like this that give getting back to nature a bad name. That horrible monster is after those nice young people again! This time it's on an island off the coast of Georgia. **AKA:** Nightmare Island.
1982 (R) 95m/C **D:** J.S. Cardone. **VHS, Beta** *NO Woof!*

The Slayer/The Scalps Double feature. "Scalps" is a slasher set in a Native American burial ground. "The Slayer" is about vacationing couples who run into more than they bargained for on their island retreat.
1982 (R) 150m/C **D:** J.S. Cardone. **VHS, Beta** *NO* ✂️

Slayground Man, distraught at the accidental death of his daughter, hires a hitman to exact revenge. Excruciating adaptation of the novel by Richard Stark (Donald E. Westlake).
1984 (R) 85m/C *GB* Peter Coyote, Mel Smith, Billie Whitelaw, Philip Sayer, Kelli Maroney; **D:** Terry Bedford. **VHS, Beta** $69.95 *HBO* ✂️ ½

Sleazemania Compilation of trailers 'n bits reviews some of the sleazier, sicker, and sexier selections of celluloid from the past 50 years.
1985 60m/C **VHS, Beta** $19.95 *RHI* ✂️✂️

Sleazemania III: The Good, the Bad & the Sleazy Another compilation of the cheapest, funniest and scurviest moments, from grade-Z horror films, including "Mondo Psycho" and "Smut Peddler Meets Emmanuel."
1986 90m/B **VHS, Beta** $39.95 *RHI* ✂️✂️

The Sleazy Uncle A successful but bored businessman is energized by an encounter with his vice-ridden uncle, a mooching, womanizing beatnik poet who knows how to enjoy life. An energetic but rather formulaic comedy. In Italian with English subtitles. *AKA: Lo Zio Indegno.*
1989 104m/C *IT* Giancarlo Giannini, Vittorio Gassman, Andrea Ferreol, Stefania Sandrelli; *D:* Franco Brusati. VHS, Beta $89.95 *TAM, TRI* ✓✓

Sledgehammer A madman is wreaking havoc on a small town, annihilating young women with a sledgehammer.
1983 87m/C Ted Prior, Doug Matley, Steven Wright. VHS, Beta $9.95 *WVV* Woof!

Sleep of Death Young Englishman's pursuit of a blue-blooded woman seems to set off a series of bizarre and mysterious murders. A gothic thriller based on Sheridan Le Fanu's short story.
1979 90m/C Brendan Price, Marilu Tolo, Patrick Magee, Curt Jurgens, Per Oscarsson; *D:* Calvin Floyd. VHS, Beta $59.95 *PSM* ✓½

Sleepaway Camp Crazed killer hacks away at the inhabitants of a peaceful summer camp in this run-of-the-mill slasher.
1983 (R) 88m/C Mike Kellin, Jonathan Tiersten, Felissa Rose, Christopher Collet. VHS, Beta $9.95 *MED* ✓

Sleepaway Camp 2: Unhappy Campers A beautiful camp counselor is actually a blood-thirsty, murdering madwoman. Sequel to the 1983 slasher, "Sleepaway Camp."
1988 (R) 82m/C Pamela Springsteen, Renee Estevez, Walter Gotell, Brian Patrick Clarke; *D:* Michael A. Simpson. VHS, Beta $14.98 *SUE, NLC* ✓½

Sleepaway Camp 3: Teenage Wasteland This second sequel is as bad as the first two movies. Another disturbed camper hacks up another bevy of teenagers. Better luck at the Motel Six.
1989 (R) 80m/C Pamela Springsteen, Tracy Griffith, Michael J. Pollard; *D:* Michael A. Simpson. VHS, Beta, LV $19.98 *SUE, NLC* Woof!

Sleeper Hapless nerd Allen is revived two hundred years after an operation gone bad. Keaton portrays Allen's love interest in a futuristic land of robots and giant vegetables. He learns of the hitherto unknown health benefits of hot fudge sundaes; discovers the truth about the nation's dictator, known as The Leader; and gets involved with revolutionaries seeking to overthrow the government. Hilarious, fast-moving comedy, full of slapstick and satire. Don't miss the "orgasmatron."
1973 (PG) 88m/C Woody Allen, Diane Keaton, John Beck, Howard Cosell; *D:* Woody Allen. VHS, Beta, LV $19.98 *MGM, FOX* ✓✓✓½

Sleeping Beauty Classic Walt Disney version of the famous fairy tale is set to the music of Tchaikovsky's ballet. Lavishly produced. With the voices of Mary Copsta, Bill Shirley, and Vera Vague.
1959 (G) 75m/C *D:* Clyde Geronimi, Eric Larson, Wolfgang Reitherman, Les Clark. VHS, Beta, LV *DIS, OM* ✓✓✓

Sleeping Beauty Peters is the princess put to sleep by evil queen Kellerman. Handsome prince Reeve comes to the rescue in this classy retelling of the Sleeping Beauty legend. Combines live action and animation. From Shelley Duvall's "Faerie Tale Theatre."
1983 60m/C Christopher Reeve, Bernadette Peters, Beverly D'Angelo. VHS, Beta, LV $14.95 *FOX, FCT, WKV* ✓✓✓

Sleeping Beauty Live action version of the beloved fairy tale, with Welch in the title role.
1989 92m/C Tahnee Welch, Morgan Fairchild, Nicholas Clay, Sylvia Miles. VHS $14.95 *MGM, PSM* ✓✓½

The Sleeping Car A vindictive ghost haunts a group of people living in an old railway car. Fairly fun, fairly competent horror.
1990 87m/C David Naughton, Judie Aronson, Kevin McCarthy, Jeff Conaway, Dani Minnick, John Carl Buechler; *D:* Douglas Curtis. VHS, LV $89.95 *VMK* ✓✓

Sleeping Car to Trieste Conspirators in the theft of a diplomat's diary ride the Orient Express, as a wily detective on board tries to piece together murder clues. Based on the story "Rome Express" by Clifford Grey.
1945 95m/B Jean Kent, Albert Lieven, David Tomlinson, Finlay Currie; *D:* John Paddy Carstairs. VHS, Beta *LCA* ✓✓

Sleeping Dogs A man in near-future New Zealand finds it hard to remain neutral when he is caught between a repressive government and a violent resistance movement. The first New Zealand film ever to open in the U.S., and a fine debut for director Donaldson.
1982 107m/C *NZ* Sam Neill, Ian Mune, Nevan Rowe, Dona Akersten, Warren Oates; *D:* Roger Donaldson. VHS, Beta $69.95 *VID* ✓✓½

Sleeping Fist A young man learns the sleeping fist style of Kung fu in order to save the girl he loves from a ruthless gang of marauders.
198? 85m/C Yuan Hsiao-Tien, Liang Chia-Yen. VHS, Beta $39.95 *TWE* ✓

The Sleeping Tiger A thief breaks into the home of a psychiatrist, who captures him. In exchange for his freedom, the thief agrees to become a guinea pig for the doctor's rehabilitation theories with ultimately tragic results. Director Losey was originally compelled to release the film under a pseudonym, "Victor Hanbury," because he had been blacklisted by Hollywood during the 1950s red scare. First pairing of Losey and Bogarde, who collaborated on several later films, including "Modesty Blaise" (1966) and "Accident" (1967).
1954 89m/B Alexis Smith, Alexander Knox, Dirk Bogarde, Hugh Griffith; *D:* Joseph Losey. VHS $16.95 *NOS, SNC* ✓✓½

Sleeping with the Enemy Roberts escapes from abusive husband by faking death, flees to Iowa, falls for drama professor, and, gasp, is found by psycho husband. Occasionally chilling but oft predictable thriller based on novel by Nancy Price.
1991 (R) 99m/C Julia Roberts, Kevin Anderson, Patrick Bergin, Elizabeth Lawrence, Kyle Secor, Claudette Nevins; *D:* Joseph Ruben. VHS, Beta, LV $19.98 *FXV, IME, FCT* ✓✓½

Sleepless in Seattle Unhappy Seattle widower Hanks is convinced that a great love occurs but once in a lifetime. More pragmatic, his son believes otherwise, and calls a national talk radio show on Christmas Eve to voice his wish that his dad will find a new wife, and therefore be happy. Ryan, a newly engaged journalist in Baltimore, hears the show and begins to wonder if she's settling for the available when the best might still be unknown. Witty, sweet, and unashamedly about love and romance, add this one to the list of new Hollywood date movies. Ephron's screenplay is full of one-liners reminiscent of "When Harry Met Sally" and adds a twist: the couple doesn't meet until the end.

O'Donnell shines in her supporting role as Ryan's best friend and Malinger (in his debut) is appropriately real as Hanks' sometimes loving, sometimes frustrating 8-year-old. Watch for the wonderful "An Affair to Remember" vs. "The Dirty Dozen" scene that underscores the difference between the movies that women and men love. Watch too, for Hanks real-life wife Wilson in that scene. Sven Nykvist's camera work is always interesting, capturing the luminous beauty of Seattle, Chicago, and particularly, New York City. And this is a movie full of fine detail, from the graphic layout of the opening credits to the great score put together by Shaiman, a soundtrack destined to be loved by millions.
1993 (PG) 100m/C Tom Hanks, Meg Ryan, Bill Pullman, Ross Malinger, Rosie O'Donnell, Gaby Hoffman, Victor Garber, Rita Wilson, Barbara Garrick, Carey Lowell, Rob Reiner, Sarah Trigger; *D:* Nora Ephron; *W:* Jeffrey Arch, Larry Atlas, David S. Ward, Nora Ephron; *M:* Marc Shaiman. VHS *NYR* ✓✓✓½

Sleepwalk Odd independent effort about a bored New York desk worker who is given an ancient text of Chinese fairy tales to translate, and finds they're manifesting themselves in dangerous ways in real life. Cinematography by Jim Jarmusch and Franz Prinzi.
1988 (R) 78m/C Suzanne Fletcher, Ann Magnuson; *D:* Sara Driver. VHS, Beta, LV $19.98 *SUE, NLC* ✓

Sleepwalkers When Mary and her son Charles arrive in the small town of Travis, Indiana, ugly things begin to happen. And no wonder, it seems the deadly duo are sleepwalkers—fiendish, cat-like vampire creatures who can only survive by sucking the life force out of unsuspecting virgins. Gory but not without some humor, particularly in Krige's portrayal of the sexy and too-loving mother. Not nearly as good as some of King's other horror classics. Also known as "Stephen King's Sleepwalkers."
1992 (R) 91m/C Brian Krause, Madchen Amick, Alice Krige, Jim Haynie, Cindy Pickett, Lyman Ward, Ron Perlman; *Cameos:* Dan Martin, Glenn Shadix, Joe Dante, John Landis, Clive Barker, Tobe Hooper, Stephen King, Mark Hamill; *D:* Mick Garris; *W:* Stephen King. VHS, LV $19.85 *COL* ✓✓

The Slender Thread Based on a true story, Poitier plays a college student who volunteers at a crisis center and must keep would-be suicide Bancroft on the phone until the police can find her. Filmed on location in Seattle. First film for director Pollack.
1965 98m/C Sidney Poitier, Anne Bancroft, Telly Savalas, Steven Hill; *D:* Sydney Pollack; *W:* Sterling Silliphant. VHS $14.95 *PAR* ✓✓✓

Sleuth A mystery novelist and his wife's lover face off in ever shifting, elaborate, and diabolical plots against each other, complete with red herrings, traps, and tricks. Playful, cerebral mystery thriller from top director Mankiewicz. Script by Anthony Schaffer, who also scripted "Frenzy" for Hitchcock, from his play.
1972 (PG) 138m/C Laurence Olivier, Michael Caine; *D:* Joseph L. Mankiewicz. Academy Awards '72 Nominations: Best Actor (Caine), Best Actor (Olivier), Best Director (Mankiewicz), Best Original Score; Edgar Allan Poe Awards '72: Best Screenplay. VHS, Beta, LV $19.95 *MED, HMV* ✓✓✓½

Slightly Honorable A lawyer gets involved in political scandals and becomes a murder suspect. Snappy comedy-drama with good performances but too many subplots. Based on the novel "Send Another Coffin" by F. G. Presnell.

1940 75m/B Pat O'Brien, Broderick Crawford, Edward Arnold, Eve Arden, Evelyn Keyes, Phyllis Brooks; **D:** Tay Garnett. **VHS, Beta** $19.95 NOS, VYY, KRT �½

A Slightly Pregnant Man Comic complications abound as a construction worker becomes the world's first pregnant man. Surprise ending saves this simple and not very exciting film.
1979 (PG) 92m/C Catherine Deneuve, Marcello Mastroianni; **D:** Jacques Demy. **VHS, Beta** $19.98 VID ⅛

Slightly Scarlet Small-time hood Payne carries out an assignment from boss DeCorsia to smear a law-and-order politico running for mayor. He falls in love with the candidate's secretary, tries to go straight, and ends up running the mob when DeCorsia flees town. A spiffy, low-budget noir crime drama.
1956 99m/C Rhonda Fleming, Arlene Dahl, John Payne, Kent Taylor, Ted DeCorsia; **D:** Allan Dwan. **VHS, Beta** NO ⅛½

Slime City The widow of an alchemist poisons her tenants so they will join her husband in the hereafter. Very low-budget; occasionally funny.
1989 90m/C Robert C. Sabin, Mary Huner, T.J. Merrick, Dick Biel; **D:** Gregory Lamberson. **VHS, Beta** NO ⅛

The Slime People Huge prehistoric monsters are awakened from long hibernation by atomic testing in Los Angeles. They take over the city, creating the fog they need to live. Thank goodness for scientist Burton, who saves the day. Filmed in a butcher shop in Los Angeles.
1963 76m/B Robert Hutton, Robert Burton, Susan Hart, William Boyce, Les Tremayne; **D:** Robert Hutton. **VHS, Beta** $19.95 NOS, GEM, RIII Woof!

Slipping into Darkness Three spoiled, rich college girls are held responsible for a retarded local boy's death. Honest and overwrought.
1988 (R) 86m/C Belle Mitchell, Laslo Papas, Rigg Kennedy, Beverly Ross, T.J. McFadden, Michelle Johnson, John DiAquino; **D:** Eleanor Gaver. **VHS, Beta, LV** $24.95 GHV, HHE ⅛½

Slipstream "Turgid" and "gloomy" are the words for this romantic drama set in remote Alberta. The minor plot concerns a young woman who teaches a lonely disc jockey a lesson about life and love. This film feels like a long Canadian winter.
1972 93m/C CA Julie Askew, Patti Oatman, Eli Rill. **VHS, Beta** $19.95 TWE ⅛

Slipstream A sci-fi adventure set on a damaged Earthscape where people seek to escape a giant jetstream. While tracking down a bounty hunter gone bad, a futuristic cop follows his quarry into the dangerous river of wind. Ambitious "Blade Runner" clone with big names (Hamill is good) was never released theatrically in the US. Musical score by Elmer Bernstein.
1989 (PG-13) 92m/C GB Mark Hamill, Bill Paxton, Bob Peck, Eleanor David, Kitty Aldridge, Robbie Coltrane, Ben Kingsley, F. Murray Abraham; **D:** Steven Lisberger. **VHS, Beta, LV** NO ⅛

Slither Caan and Boyle become wrapped up in a scheme to recover $300,000 in cash, stolen seven years previously. Along the way they pick up speed freak Kellerman, who assists them in a variety of loony ways. Frantic chase scenes are the highlight.
1973 (PG) 97m/C James Caan, Peter Boyle, Sally Kellerman, Louise Lasser, Allen Garfield, Richard B. Shull, Alex Rocco; **D:** Howard Zieff. **VHS, Beta** $19.98 MGM ⅛⅛⅛

Slithis Slithis, the nuclear-waste creature, is the menace of Venice, California. Keep your pets (and yourself) indoors!
1978 (PG) 86m/C Alan Blanchard, Judy Motulsky; **W/D:** Stephen Traxler. **VHS, Beta** $19.95 MED Woof!

Sliver Another voyeuristic thriller starring Stone. She plays Carly Norris, a lonely book editor who moves into one of Manhatten's toothpick thin buildings (the "sliver" of the title). Carly meets pulp novelist Jack (Berenger), whose libido is as overheated as his prose, but she gets involved in a steamy affair with handsome, rich neighbor Zeke (Baldwin), a computer whiz who also owns the building. Carly soon discovers Zeke has installed video cameras in every unit (revealing lots of intimate secrets) and that a series of murders has recently plagued the building. Is Zeke responsible for them as well? Lots of sex but this time Baldwin gets to be the object of desire. Murky and underdeveloped and the ending, which was reshot, still leaves much to be desired. Lots of hype, little to recommend.
1993 (R) 106m/C Sharon Stone, William Baldwin, Tom Berenger, Martin Landau, Polly Walker, Colleen Camp, CCH Pounder, Nina Foch, Keene Curtis; **D:** Phillip Noyce; **W:** Joe Eszterhas; **M:** Howard Shore. **VHS** PAR ⅛½

Sloane Typical sleazy sex and violence flick. For the record: organized crime baddies kidnap good guy Resnick's girlfriend and he seeks revenge.
1984 95m/C Robert Resnick, Debra Blee, Paul Aragon; **D:** Dan Rosenthal. **VHS, Beta** $69.98 LIV, VES Woof!

Slow Burn An ex-reporter tries some detective work in the seamy side of Palm Springs, and becomes embroiled in the standard drug, kidnapping, murder routine. Based on the novel "Castles Burning" by Arthur Lyons. Made for cable television.
1986 92m/C Eric Roberts, Beverly D'Angelo, Dan Hedaya, Dennis Lipscomb; **D:** Matthew Chapman. **VHS, Beta** $59.95 MCA ⅛

Slow Burn The Mafia and Chinese Triads are having troubles and a tired cop attempts to reach a peaceful solution.
1990 (R) 90m/C William Smith, Anthony James, Ivan Rogers. **VHS** $79.95 XVC, PHX ⅛

Slow Moves Slow story of slow people who meet slowly, have sluggish affair, and find tragedy eventually.
1984 93m/C Roxanne Rogers; **D:** Jon Jost. **VHS, Beta** $69.95 FCT ⅛½

The Slugger's Wife The marriage between an Atlanta Braves outfielder and a rock singer suddenly turns sour when their individual careers force them to make some tough choices. **AKA:** Neil Simon's The Slugger's Wife.
1985 (PG-13) 105m/C Michael O'Keefe, Rebecca DeMornay, Martin Ritt, Randy Quaid, Loudon Wainwright III, Rene Lefevre; **D:** Hal Ashby; **W:** Neil Simon. **VHS, Beta, LV** $79.95 COL ⅛½

Slugs A health inspector discovers that spilled toxic waste is being helpfully cleaned up by the slug population, saving Uncle Sam countless dollars. But wait! The slugs are mutating into blood-thirsty man-eaters. Is this the answer to military cut-backs?
1987 (R) 90m/C Michael Garfield, Kim Terry, Philip Machale; **D:** J.P. Simon. **VHS, Beta, LV** $19.95 STE, NWV Woof!

Slumber Party '57 At a slumber party, six girls get together and exchange stories of how they lost their virginity. Lots of great music by the Platters, Big Bopper, Jerry Lee Lewis, the Crewcuts, and Paul and Paula but complete schlock otherwise.

1976 (R) 89m/C Noelle North, Bridget Hollman, Debra Winger, Mary Ann Appleseth, Cheryl "Rainbeaux" Smith, Janet Wood, R.L. Armstrong, Rafael Campos, Larry Gelman, Will Hutchins, Joyce Jillson, Victor Rogers, Joe E. Ross, Bill Thurman; **D:** William A. Levey. **VHS, Beta, LV** $14.95 MGM, VES ⅛½

The Slumber Party Massacre A psychotic killer with a power drill terrorizes a high school girls' slumber party. Contrived and forced, but not always unfunny.
1982 (R) 84m/C Michele Michaels, Robin Stille, Andre Honore, Michael Villela, Debra Deliso, Gina Mari, Brinke Stevens; **D:** Amy Jones, Aaron Lipstadt; **W:** Rita Mae Brown. **VHS, Beta** $14.98 SUE ⅛½

Slumber Party Massacre 2 Drowsy babes in lingerie are drilled to death by a perverse madman. Another disappointing sequel.
1987 75m/C Crystal Bernard, Kimberly McArthur, Juliette Cummins, Patrick Lowe; **D:** Deborah Brock. **VHS, Beta, LV** $14.98 SUE, NLC Woof!

Slumber Party Massacre 3 Parents: Don't let your daughters have any slumber parties! Yes, it's a drill—for the third time.
1990 (R) 76m/C Keely Christian, Brittain Frye, M.K. Harris, David Greenle, Hope Marie Carlton, Maria Ford; **D:** Sally Mattison. **VHS, Beta** $79.98 MGM Woof!

The Small Back Room A crippled World War II munitions expert leads a tormented existence and laments government bureaucracy. Powerfully presented adult storyline. **AKA:** Hour of Glory.
1949 106m/B Emeric Pressburger, David Farrar, Jack Hawkins, Cyril Cusack, Kathleen Byron, Anthony Bushell, Michael Gough, Robert Morley; **D:** Michael Powell. **VHS** $39.95 NOS, LOO, FCT ⅛⅛⅛

Small Change Pudgy, timid Desmouceaux and scruffy, neglected Goldman lead a whole pack of heartwarming tykes. A realistically and tenderly portrayed testament to the great director's belief in childhood as a "state of grace." Criticized for sentimentality, "Small Change" followed Truffaut's gloomy "The Story of Adele H." Steven Spielberg suggested the English translation of "L'Argent de Poche." In French with English subtitles.
1976 (PG) 104m/C FR Geory Desmouceaux, Philippe Goldman, Jean-Francois Stevenin, Chantal Mercier, Francis Devlaeminck; **D:** Francois Truffaut. **VHS, Beta, LV** $19.99 MGM, FCT, TAM ⅛⅛⅛⅛

A Small Circle of Friends Three Harvard students struggle through their shifting relationships during their college years in the 1960s.
1980 (R) 112m/C Brad Davis, Jameson Parker, Karen Allen, Shelley Long; **D:** Rob Cohen. **VHS, Beta** $59.98 FOX ⅛½

Small Hotel After discovering that he is to be replaced as headwaiter by a young woman, Harker plots to save his job through espionage, blackmail and cajolery. Average comedy, adapted from a popular British stage play as a star vehicle for Harker.
1957 59m/B Gordon Harker, Marie Lohr, John Loder, Irene Handl, Janet Munro, Billie Whitelaw, Francis Matthews, Dora Bryan; **D:** David MacDonald. **VHS** $19.95 NOS ⅛½

A Small Killing An undercover cop and a college professor pose as a wino and a bag lady, when trying to put the tabs on a druglord. Made for TV mystery/romance based on "The Rag Bag Clan" by Richard Barth.

1981 100m/C Ed Asner, Jean Simmons, Sylvia Sidney, Andrew Prine, Pat O'Malley, Anne Ramsey; *D:* Steven Hilliard Stern. **VHS, Beta** $59.95 *LIV* 🎞🎞

Small Sacrifices The true story of Diane Downs, an Oregon woman who may have murdered her own three children in 1983. Fine performance from Fawcett, who seems to like made for TV tales of true-life domestic violence as an antidote to her earlier ditzy persona as a Charlie's Angel. Gripping; superb script by Joyce Eliason. 1989 159m/C Farrah Fawcett, Ryan O'Neal, John Shea; *D:* David Greene. **VHS, Beta, LV** $19.95 *FRH* 🎞🎞½

Small Town Boy The cast does what they can with the brief, hackneyed story of a guy whose personality changes for the worse when he finds a "fortune" (one thousand pre-inflationary dollars). 1937 61m/B Stuart Erwin, Joyce Compton, Jed Prouty, Clara Blandick, James "Doc" Blakely; *W/D:* Glenn Tryon. **VHS** $19.95 *NOS, LOO* 🎞🎞

Small Town Girl Typical romantic musical of the era, as a city slicker picked up for speeding in a hick town is pursued by the sheriff's daughter. Several Busby Berkeley blockbuster musical numbers are shoehorned incongruously into the rural doings. ♫Take Me To Broadway; I've Got To Hear That Beat; My Flaming Heart; Fine, Fine, Fine; The Fellow I'd Follow; Lullaby of the Lord; Small Towns Are Smile Towns; My Gaucho. *AKA:* One Horse Town. 1953 93m/C Jane Powell, Farley Granger, Bobby Van, Ann Miller, Billie Burke, Robert Keith, S.Z. Sakall, Fay Wray, Nat King Cole, Chill Wills; *D:* Leslie Kardos. **VHS, Beta** $19.98 *MGM* 🎞🎞½

A Small Town in Texas An ex-con returns home looking for the sheriff who framed him on a drug charge, and who has stolen his woman. Not-too-violent, predictable revenge flick. 1976 (PG) 96m/C Timothy Bottoms, Susan George, Bo Hopkins; *D:* Jack Starrett. **VHS, Beta** $69.98 *VES, LIV* 🎞🎞

The Smallest Show on Earth A couple inherit not only an old movie house, but the three people who work there as well. Very funny and charming, with a wonderful cast. Sellers is delightful as the soused projectionist. *AKA:* Big Time Operators. 1957 80m/B *GB* Bill Travers, Virginia McKenna, Margaret Rutherford, Peter Sellers, Bernard Miles, Leslie Phillips; *D:* Basil Dearden. **VHS** $19.95 *NOS, FCT, VEC* 🎞🎞🎞

Smart-Aleck Kill An episode of the cable television-produced Phillip Marlowe series involving the drug-related murder of a Hollywood actor in the 20s. 1985 53m/C Powers Boothe, Michael J. Shannon, Liza Ross; *D:* Peter Hunt. **VHS, Beta** $39.98 *FOX* 🎞🎞🎞

Smart Alecks The Bowery Boys get involved with gangsters when Jordan helps capture a crook. The usual wise-cracking from Hall and Gorcey helps keep things moving. 1942 88m/B Leo Gorcey, Huntz Hall, Gabriel Dell, Gale Storm, Roger Pryor Jr., Walter Woolf King, Herbert Rawlinson, Joe Kirk, Marie Windsor; *D:* Wallace Fox. **VHS** $19.95 *NOS* 🎞½

Smart Money A wrongly-jailed man enlists the help of his oddball pals to get revenge on the real thief who committed the computer fraud that put him behind bars. They get even while padding their pockets. 1988 88m/C Spencer Leigh, Alexandra Pigg, Ken Campbell. **VHS** $79.95 *SVS* 🎞🎞½

Smash Palace A compelling drama of a marriage jeopardized by his obsession with building a race car and her need for love and affection. Melodramatic, but worth watching. Robson as their young daughter is wonderful. 1982 100m/C *NZ* Bruno Lawrence, Anna Jemison, Greer Robson, Keith Aberdein; *D:* Roger Donaldson. **VHS, Beta, LV** $69.98 *LIV, VES* 🎞🎞

Smash-Up: The Story of a Woman A famous nightclub singer gives up her career for marriage and a family, only to become depressed when her husband's career soars. She turns to alcohol and her life falls apart. When her husband sues for divorce and custody of their child, she fights to recover from alcoholism. Screenplay by John Howard Lawson; Hayward's first major role. *AKA:* A Woman Destroyed. 1947 103m/B Susan Hayward, Lee Bowman, Marsha Hunt, Eddie Albert; *D:* Stuart Heisler. **VHS, Beta** $19.95 *NOS, PSM, DVT* 🎞🎞🎞

Smile Barbed, merciless send-up of small-town America focusing on a group of naive California girls who compete for the "Young American Miss" crown amid rampant commercialism, exploitation and pure middle-class idiocy. Hilarious neglected '70s-style satire. Early role for Griffith. 1975 (PG) 113m/C Bruce Dern, Barbara Feldon, Michael Kidd, Nicholas Pryor, Geoffrey Lewis, Colleen Camp, Joan Prather, Annette O'Toole, Melanie Griffith, Denise Nickerson; *D:* Michael Ritchie; *W:* Jerry Belson. **VHS, Beta, LV** $19.95 *MGM* 🎞🎞🎞

Smile, Jenny, You're Dead Janssen discovers that close friend's son-in-law has been murdered, and falls in love with the daughter, the main suspect. Pilot for Janssen's "Harry-O" detective series. 1974 100m/C David Janssen, John Anderson, Howard da Silva, Martin Gabel, Clu Gulager, Zalman King, Jodie Foster, Barbara Leigh; *D:* Jerry Thorpe. **VHS** $59.95 *UNI* 🎞🎞

Smiles of a Summer Night The best known of Bergman's rare comedies; sharp satire about eight Swedish aristocrats who become romantically and comically intertwined over a single weekend. Inspired Sondheim's successful Broadway musical "A Little Night Music," and Woody Allen's "A Midsummer Night's Sex Comedy." In Swedish with English subtitles. *AKA:* Sommarnattens Leende. 1955 108m/B *SW* Gunnar Bjornstrand, Harriet Andersson, Ulla Jacobsson, Eva Dahlbeck, Jarl Kulle, Margit Carlquist; *D:* Ingmar Bergman. **VHS, Beta, LV** $29.95 *SUE, VYG, DVT* 🎞🎞🎞½

Smilin' Through Third filming, second with sound, first in color, of a popular melodrama. An embittered man whose wife was murdered on their wedding day raises an orphaned niece, only to have her fall in love with the son of her aunt's murderer. Made MacDonald into a singing star. Songs include title tune and "A Little Love, a Little Kiss." 1941 101m/C Jeanette MacDonald, Brian Aherne, Gene Raymond, Ian Hunter, Frances Robinson; *D:* Frank Borzage. **VHS, Beta** $19.98 *MGM* 🎞🎞½

Smiling Madame Beudet/The Seashell and the Clergyman Two famous shorts by Dulac; the second scripted by Antonin Artaud. Both are pioneering examples of surrealistic film. Silent. 1928 62m/B *FR* Alix Allin; *D:* Germaine Dulac. **VHS, Beta** $19.95 *FCT* 🎞🎞🎞½

Smith! Naive but well intentioned look at present-day treatment of Native Americans. Rancher Ford becomes embroiled in the trial of murder suspect Ramirez. Based on Paul St. Pierre's novel "Breaking Smith's Quarter Horse." 1969 (G) 101m/C Glenn Ford, Frank Ramirez, Keenan Wynn; *D:* Michael O'Herlihy. **VHS, Beta** $69.95 *DIS* 🎞🎞½

Smithereens Working-class girl leaves home for New York's music scene. Rugged, hip character study. Director Seidelman's first feature. 1984 90m/C Susan Berman, Brad Rinn, Richard Hell; *D:* Susan Seidelman. **VHS, Beta, LV** $59.95 *MED, FCT* 🎞🎞½

Smoke A young boy nurses a lost German shepherd back to health with the help of his new stepfather, whom he learns to trust. Then he runs away with the dog when the original owners show up. Made for television Disney fare starring Opie/Richie (and later successful director) Howard. 1970 89m/C Earl Holliman, Ron Howard, Andy Devine; *D:* Vincent McEveety. **VHS, Beta** $69.95 *DIS* 🎞🎞½

Smoke in the Wind Subpar western about men accused of complicity with the Union in postbellum Arkansas. Minor role for Brennan was his last; also director Kane's last film. 1975 (PG) 93m/C John Ashley, Walter Brennan, John Russell, Myron Healey; *D:* Joseph Kane. **VHS, Beta** $49.95 *PSM* 🎞½

Smokescreen A young ad exec meets the girl of his dreams, and finds himself working for her gangster boyfriend. Competently made and acted, but phoney ending wrecks it. 1990 (R) 91m/C Kim Cattrall, Dean Stockwell, Matt Craven, Kim Coates, Brian George, Michael Hogan; *D:* Martin Lavut. **VHS, LV** $89.95 *COL* 🎞🎞½

Smokey and the Bandit If you don't know how to end a movie, you call for a car chase. The first and best of the horrible series about bootlegger Reynolds is one long car chase. Reynolds makes a wager that he can have a truck load of Coors beer—once unavailable east of Texas—delivered to Atlanta from Texas in 28 hours. Gleason is the "smokey" who tries to stop him. Field is the hitchhiker Reynolds picks up along the way. Great stunts; director Needham was a top stunt man. 1977 (PG) 96m/C Burt Reynolds, Sally Field, Jackie Gleason, Jerry Reed, Mike Henry, Paul Williams, Pat McCormick; *D:* Hal Needham. **VHS, Beta, LV** $19.95 *MCA* 🎞🎞

Smokey and the Bandit, Part 2 Pathetic sequel to "Smokey and the Bandit" proved a box-office winner, grossing $40 million. The Bandit is hired to transport a pregnant elephant from Miami to the Republican convention in Dallas. Sheriff Buford T. Justice and family are in hot pursuit. *AKA:* Smokey and the Bandit Ride Again. 1980 (PG) 101m/C Burt Reynolds, Sally Field, Jackie Gleason, Jerry Reed, Mike Henry, Dom DeLuise, Pat McCormick, Paul Williams; *D:* Hal Needham. **VHS, Beta, LV** $19.95 *MCA* 🎞

Smokey and the Bandit, Part 3 You thought the second one was bad? Another mega car chase, this time sans Reynolds and director Needham. 1983 (PG) 88m/C Burt Reynolds, Jackie Gleason, Jerry Reed, Paul Williams, Pat McCormick, Mike Henry, Colleen Camp; *D:* Dick Lowry. **VHS, Beta, LV** $59.95 *MCA* 🎞

Smokey & the Hotwire Gang A convoy of truckers try to track down a beautiful woman driving a stolen car.
1979 85m/C James Keach, Stanley Livingston, Tony Lorea, Alvy Moore, George Barris. **VHS, Beta $49.95** WWV ⅂½

Smokey & the Judge Police officer has his hands full with a trio of lovely ladies.
1980 (PG) 90m/C Gene Price, Wayde Preston, Juanita Curiel. **VHS** SUN ⅂

Smokey Bites the Dust Car-smashing gag-fest about a sheriff's daughter kidnapped by her smitten beau. Near-plotless and literally unoriginal: lifted footage from several other Corman-produced flicks, a technique that can aptly be called garbage picking.
1981 (PG) 87m/C Janet Julian, Jimmy McNichol, Patrick Campbell, Kari Lizer, John Blythe Barrymore; **D:** Charles B. Griffith. **VHS, Beta $19.98** NLC ⅂

Smokey Smith Ubiquitous Hayes and steely Steele hunt down the slayers of an elderly couple. Ordinary oater directed by Steele's father, Bradbury.
1936 59m/B Bob Steele; **D:** Robert North Bradbury. **VHS, Beta $27.95** VCN ⅂½

A Smoky Mountain Christmas Dolly gets away from it all in a secluded cabin that has been appropriated by a gang of orphans. Innocuous seasonal country fun. Dolly sings a half dozen songs and co-wrote the script. Winkler's TV directing debut.
1986 94m/C Dolly Parton, Bo Hopkins, Dan Hedaya, Gennie James, David Ackroyd, Rene Auberjonois, John Ritter, Anita Morris, Lee Majors; **D:** Henry Winkler. **VHS, Beta $79.98** FOX ⅂⅂

Smooth Talk An innocent, flirtatious teenager catches the eye of a shady character, played by Williams. Disturbing and thought-provoking film that caused some controversy when it opened. Dern gives a brilliant performance as the shy, sheltered girl. Based on the Joyce Carol Oates story of the same name. Made for PBS' "American Playhouse" series.
1985 (PG-13) 92m/C Laura Dern, Treat Williams, Mary Kay Place, Levon Helm; **D:** Joyce Chopra. **VHS, Beta, LV $29.98** LIV, VES ⅂⅂⅂

Smooth Talker A serial killer stalks the women of a 976 party line. Bad acting, bad dialog, not a scare to be found.
1990 (R) 89m/C Joe Guzaldo, Peter Crombie, Stuart Whitman, Burt Ward, Sydney Lassick, Blair Weickgenant; **D:** Tom Milo. **VHS $89.95** ACA Woof!

Smouldering Fires A tough businesswoman falls in love with an ambitious young employee, who is fifteen years her junior. After they marry, problems arise in the form of the wife's attractive younger sister. Surprisingly subtle melodrama, if that's not an oxymoron.
1925 100m/B Pauline Frederick, Laura La Plante, Tully Marshall; **D:** Clarence Brown. **VHS, Beta $29.95** VYY ⅂⅂½

Smugglers Opportunistic smugglers take advantage of the Russian Revolution to sack the land and make a bundle. *AKA:* Lover of the Great Bear.
1975 110m/C IT Senta Berger, Giuliano Gemma; **D:** Valentino Orsini. **VHS, Beta $59.95** VCD ⅂

Smugglers' Cove Gorcey wrongly believes he has inherited a mansion. He and the Bowery Boys move in, only to stumble across a smuggling ring. Plenty of slapsticks; the boys at their best.
1948 66m/B Leo Gorcey, Huntz Hall, Gabriel Dell; **D:** William Beaudine. **VHS $14.95** VID ⅂⅂⅂

Smuggler's Cove A young boy doggedly pursues a mysterious trawler captain despite warnings from his parents.
1983 75m/C AU VHS, Beta $14.98 VID ⅂½

Snake and Crane Arts of Shaolin There's plenty of action and battles going on in this martial arts film.
1980 93m/C VHS, Beta NO ⅂

Snake Dancer Softcore epic concerning the gyrations of a particular dancer.
19?? 87m/C Glenda Kemp, Peter Elliott, Christine Basson; **D:** Dirk DeVilliers. **VHS $29.95** ACA ⅂

Snake Fist Dynamo A kick-throwin' fight takes place over some valuable jewels.
1984 86m/C Eric Yee, Nancy Leung, Dick Lee. **VHS, Beta** NO ⅂

Snake Fist Fighter In one of the highest grossing martial arts movies of all time, Jackie Chan uses the deadly "snake fist" technique against the bad guys.
1981 (R) 83m/C Jackie Chan. **VHS, Beta** NO ⅂½

Snake Fist of the Buddhist Dragon In medieval China, a peaceful Buddhist goes mad and hits everyone around him in the head.
197? 88m/C Martial Lee, Lee King, Debbie Lam. **VHS, Beta** NO ⅂

The Snake Hunter Strangler A young girl is rescued after fifteen years from an evil cult of snake people.
1966 65m/C Guy Madison, Ivan Desny; **D:** Luigi Capuano. **VHS, Beta** NO ⅂

Snake in the Eagle's Shadow 2 Three champions of self-defense mount a major offensive and win battle after battle.
1983 89m/C Wang Tao, Cheng Shing, Lung Fei; **D:** Chang Shinn I. **VHS, Beta $39.95** TWE ⅂

Snake in the Monkey's Shadow Martial arts expert demonstrates the deadliest fighting techniques.
1982 (R) 85m/C VHS, Beta $39.95 TWE ⅂

The Snake People A police captain investigates a small island littered with LSD-experimenting scientists, snake-worshippers, and voodoo. One of the infamous quartet of Karloff's final films, all made in Mexico. *AKA:* Isle of the Snake People; Cult of the Dead; La Muerte Viviente; Isle of the Living Dead.
1968 90m/C MX Boris Karloff, Julissa, Carlos East; **D:** Enrique Vergara. **VHS, Beta $49.95** SNC, MPI, HEG ⅂

The Snake Pit One of the first films to compassionately explore mental illness and its treatment. Following an emotional collapse de Havilland is placed in a mental institution by her husband. The severity of her depression causes her sympathetic doctor to try such treatments as electric shock, hydrotherapy, and drugs, along with the psychoanalysis which gradually allows her to accept her fears and make her recovery. Tour-de-force performance by de Havilland. Based on the novel by Mary Jane Ward.
1948 108m/B Olivia de Havilland, Mark Stevens, Leo Genn, Celeste Holm, Glenn Langan, Helen Craig, Leif Erickson, Beulah Bondi; **D:** Anatole Litvak; **W:** Frank Partos, Millen Brand; **M:** Alfred Newman. Academy Awards '48: Best Sound; Nominations: Best Actress (de Havilland), Best Picture; Academy Awards '48: Best Director (Litvak), Best Screenplay, Best Original Score. **VHS $19.99** FXV, MOV ⅂⅂⅂½

The Snake Woman A herpetologist working in a small English village during the 1890s is conducting strange experiments to try to cure his wife's madness. He tries injecting his pregnant wife with snake venom and she gives birth to a cold-blooded daughter, who, when she grows up, has the ability to change herself into a deadly snake. She promptly begins killing the local male populace until Scotland Yard is called in to investigate. The curvy Travers is appropriately snakey but this movie is dull.
1961 68m/C GB John P. McCarthy, Susan Travers, Arnold Marle; **D:** Sidney J. Furie. **VHS** CNM ⅂

SnakeEater Loner cop tracks down swine who killed his parents and kidnapped his sister. "Rambo" rip-off with little plot, but lots of action. Followed by two sequels.
1989 (R) 89m/C Lorenzo Lamas, Larry Csonka, Ron Palillo; **D:** George Erschbamer. **VHS, Beta $89.95** MED ⅂

SnakeEater 2: The Drug Buster A cop goes nuts and kills four drug dealers. As a result he is committed to an institution. Iron bars don't make a prison for this guy though, and he's soon back on the streets fighting crime with his pal "Speedboat." Silly sequel is quite bad; followed by yet another.
1989 (R) 93m/C Lorenzo Lamas, Larry B. Scott, Michelle Scarabelli, Harvey Atkin, Jack Blum, Kathleen Kinmont; **D:** George Erschbamer. **VHS, Beta $14.95** PAR ⅂

SnakeEater 3: His Law Tough cop Jack Kelly (Lamas), aka SnakeEater, is out to avenge a woman's beating by a gang of thug bikers. Lots of action and violence, not much plot; based on W. Glenn Duncan's novel "Rafferty's Rules."
1992 (R) 109m/C Lorenzo Lamas, Minor Mustain, Tracy Cook, Holly Chester, Scott "Bam Bam" Bigelow; **D:** George Erschbamer; **W:** John Dunning. **VHS, Beta $14.95** PAR ⅂

Snapshot Typical grade 2 sex comedy; a free-lance photographer ogles lots of variously dishabilled young women through his lens.
1977 (R) 84m/C Jim Henshaw, Susan Petrie. **VHS, Beta $19.95** UHV ⅂

Snatched The wives of three wealthy men are held for ransom, but one man doesn't want to pay, while one of the victims needs insulin. Standard made for television fare.
1972 73m/C Howard Duff, Leslie Nielsen, Sheree North, Barbara Parkins, Robert Reed, John Saxon, Tisha Sterling; **D:** Sutton Roley. **VHS $79.95** REP ⅂⅂

Sneakers Competent thriller about five computer hackers with questionable pasts and an equally questionable government job. Redford is the head of a group of security analysts who is also wanted for a youthful dalliance in computer fraud. The way the government sees it, this puts him in a position for a bargain: they will drop the warrant if Redford agrees to steal the ultimate code-breaking machine from the mathematician who designed it. Here is the twist: nothing is as it seems. The government agents may not be actually working for the government, Redford is framed for murder, and everyone is in way over their heads as they try to recover the code-breaker from a mystery man. Rather slow-going considering the talents and suspense involved but includes enough turns to keep a viewer's interest.
1992 (PG-13) 125m/C Robert Redford, Sidney Poitier, River Phoenix, Dan Aykroyd, Ben Kingsley, David Strathairn, Mary McDonnell, Timothy Busfield, George Hearn, Eddie Jones, James Earl Jones; **D:** Phil Alden Robinson. **VHS, Beta, LV** MCA, PMS ⅂⅂½

Sniper Suspenseful television drama based on true story of Charles Whitman, who shot at University of Texas students from Texas Tower on a summer day in 1966. Disney alumnus Russell breaks type as mass killer, with fine support by Yniguez as a police officer on the scene and Beatty as the passerby who lends a hand. Finely crafted recreation of disturbing, true event. *AKA*: The Deadly Tower.
1975 85m/C Kurt Russell, Richard Yniguez, John Forsythe, Ned Beatty, Pernell Roberts, Clifton James, Paul Carr, Alan Vint, Pepe Serna; *D*: Jerry Jameson. **VHS $39.95** *XVC* ♪♪♪

The Sniper A law-abiding citizen becomes a vigilante killer after witnessing a violent crime.
1987 90m/C Claudia Cardinale. **VHS, Beta** NO ♪ ½

Sniper Less than compelling shoot-'em-up set in Panama. Lead characters include Sgt. Beckett (Berenger), a seasoned assassin who gets a rush from killing. Also assigned to the case is Richard Miller (Zane), a newcomer who knows his guns but not his jungles. Together they go in search of their target, a politician planning a coup with the help of a druglord. Action is poorly choreographed and plot is cursory at best. The laserdisc version is available letterboxed.
1992 (R) 99m/C Tom Berenger, Billy Zane, J.T. Walsh, Aden Young, Ken Radley, Reinaldo Arenas, Carolos Alvarez, Roy Edmonds; *D*: Luis Llosa; *W*: Michael Frost Beckner, Crash Leyland; *M*: Gary Chang. **VHS, LV, 8mm** COL ♪ ½

Sno-Line A New York gangster moves to Texas and begins to wipe out the competition on his way to building his drug and gambling dynasty. Bo-ring excuse for entertainment. No hope, no redemption, no titillation: just ultra-"realistic" depiction of organized crime, poorly acted.
1985 (R) 89m/C Vince Edwards, Paul Smith, June Wilkinson; *D*: Douglas F. Oneans. **VHS, Beta $69.98** LIV ♪

Snoopy, Come Home Snoopy leaves Charlie Brown to visit his former owner Lila in the hospital and returns with her to his apartment house. From Charles Schultz's popular comic strip "Peanuts."
1972 (G) 80m/C *D*: Bill Melendez; *W*: Charles M. Schulz. **VHS, Beta, LV $14.98** FOX ♪♪♪

Snoopy's Getting Married, Charlie Brown An animated Peanuts adventure wherein Snoopy prepares to get married.
1985 30m/C **VHS, Beta $14.95** KRT ♪♪♪

Snoopy's Getting Married, Charlie Brown/You're In Love, Charlie Brown Two episodes of the famed Peanuts gang.
1985 55m/C **VHS $14.95** KRT, WTA ♪♪♪

Snow Country Romantic drama of an unsuccessful, married artist from Tokyo who travels to a mountain resort to find himself. He requests a Geisha for the evening and, when none are available, the beautiful adopted daughter of the local music teacher is sent to him instead. Based on the novel by Nobel Prize winner Yasunari Kawabata. In Japanese with English subtitles. Remade in 1965.
1957 104m/B *JP* Ryo Ikebe, Keiko Kishi, Akira Kubo; *D*: Shiro Toyoda. **VHS, Beta $29.95** CVC, TAM ♪♪ ½

The Snow Creature Stupid troop of explorers bring back a snow creature from the Himalayas. Critter escapes in L.A. and terrorizes all in its path before blending in with club crowd. Very bad monster epic (the first about a snow monster) that strains

credibility frame by frame. Occasionally, depending upon camera angle, light, and viewer mood, monster appears to be something other than guy in bad suit sweating. Directed by Billy Wilder's brother and another argument against genetic consistency.
1954 72m/B Paul Langton, Leslie Denison; *D*: W. Lee Wilder. **VHS, Beta $19.95** NOS, SNC, UHV Woof!

Snow Kill Five city-dwellers travel into the mountains for a fun survival training weekend, but the fun turns deadly when they accidentally come across a murderous drug gang. Pseudo - '30s suspense adventure fails to thrill or surprise. Made for cable.
1990 90m/C Terence Knox, Patti D'Arbanville, David Dukes; *D*: Thomas J. Wright. **VHS, Beta $29.95** PAR, TTC ♪ ½

Snow Queen Music by Glazunov, Mussorgsky and Rimsky-Korsakov combines with Jean Pierre Bonnefoux's ice choreography in this setting of the Hans Christian Andersen tale.
1982 85m/C Janet Lynn, John Curry, Sandra Bezic, Jo Jo Starbuck, Dorothy Hamill, Toller Cranston; *D*: John Thompson. **VHS, Beta** NO ♪♪

The Snow Queen From "Fairie Tale Theatre" comes this adaptation of the Hans Christian Andersen tale. A boy and girl who grow up together are separated by evil when the boy is held captive in the icy palace of the Snow Queen. The girl sets out to rescue him.
1983 60m/C Lauren Hutton, Linda Manz, David Hemmings, Melissa Gilbert, Lee Remick, Lance Kerwin; *D*: Peter Medak. **VHS, Beta $14.98** KUI, FOX, FCT ♪♪

Snow Queen An animated version of the Hans Christian Andersen story about a young girl who battles the evil Snow Queen for possession of her young boy friend.
1990 60m/C **VHS $9.95** AIP ♪♪

Snow: The Movie Rates creative zero for title, though there is snow, as well as skiing, growing up, romance, and good times among the young people involved. Filmed in Australia.
1983 83m/C David Argue, Lance Curtis; *D*: Robert Gibson. **VHS, Beta $59.95** VCD ♪

Snow Treasure With the help of an underground agent, Norwegian children smuggle gold out of the country right under the noses of the Nazis. Based on the novel by Marie McSwigan.
1967 (G) 96m/C James Franciscus, Paul Anstad; *D*: Irving Jacoby. **VHS, Beta $29.95** LIV ♪

Snow White and the Seven Dwarfs Definitive, classic adaptation of the Grimm Brothers fairy tale about an orphan servant named Snow White—the fairest of them all. The vain, evil Queen plots to destroy Snow White, is warned by her would be assassin and flees deep into the woods. Enter the dwarfs who befriend her: Doc, Happy, Sneezy, Sleepy, Bashful, Grumpy, and Dopey. The Queen, furious that Snow White still lives, decides to kill her Ms. White by giving her a poisoned apple. Falling into a deep sleep, Snow is mourned by her new friends. Seems that only the kiss of a certain Prince Charming can awaken the sleeping Snow. Walt Disney took an unprecedented gamble by releasing this, the first ever animated feature-length film, a project which took over two years to create and $1.5 million to make. Lifelike animation was based on real stars, Margery Belcher (later Champion) posed for Snow, Louis Higtower was the Prince and Lucille LaVerne gave the Queen her look. Along with their earlier animated cartoons, it established Disney studios as the premier animator, a title which they still hold

today. Rereleased to the theaters in July 1993 for the 8th time and never released on video—we've added it due to regular reader questions on the issue and with the high hopes that Disney relents. Heigh Ho, heigh ho, it's off to video we go. ♫Some Day My Prince Will Come; One Song; With a Smile and a Song; Whistle While You Work; Bluddle-Uddle-Um-Dum; The Dwarfs' Yodel Song; Heigh Ho; I'm Wishing; Isn't This a Silly Song?.
1937 (G) 83m/C *D*: David Hand; *W*: Ted Sears, Otto Englander, Earl Hurd, Dorothy Blank, Richard Creedon, Dick Richard, Merrill De Maris, Webb Smith; *M*: Frank Churchill, Paul Smith, Larry Morey, Leigh Harline; *V*: Adriana Caseloti, Harry Stockwell, Lucille LaVerne, Moroni Olsen, Billy Gilbert, Pinto Colvig, Otis Harlan, Scotty Matraw, Roy Atwell, Stuart Buchanan, Marion Darlington, Jim Macdonald. **VHS** NYR ♪♪♪♪

Snow White and the Seven Dwarfs From cable television's "Faerie Tale Theatre" comes the story of a princess who befriends seven little men to protect her from the jealous evil queen.
1983 60m/C Elizabeth McGovern, Rex Smith, Vincent Price, Vanessa Redgrave; *D*: Peter Medak. **VHS, Beta, LV $14.98** KUI, FOX, FCT ♪♪♪♪

Snow White and the Three Stooges The Stooges fill in for the Seven Dwarfs when they go off prospecting in King Solomon's mines. Alas, see any Stooge movie but this one. *AKA*: Snow White and the Three Clowns.
1961 107m/C Moe Howard, Curly Howard, Larry Fine, Carol Heiss, Patricia Medina; *D*: Walter Lang. **VHS, Beta $14.98** FOX, FCT ♪♪

Snowball Express When a New York City accountant inherits a hotel in the Rocky Mountains, he decides to move his family west to attempt to make a go of the defunct ski resort, only to find that the place is falling apart. Run-of-the-mill Disney comedy, based on the novel "Chateau Bon Vivant" by Frankie and John O'Rear.
1972 (G) 120m/C Dean Jones, Nancy Olson, Harry Morgan, Keenan Wynn; *D*: Norman Tokar. **VHS, Beta $69.95** DIS ♪♪

Snowballin' A ski instructor gives private lessons to a bunch of snow bunnies.
1985 90m/C Seline Lomez, Daniel Pilon. **VHS, Beta $59.95** JEF ♪

Snowballing Part of the polluted wave of teen-sex flicks of the 1980s, this is very mild for the genre but still no prize. Lusty high schoolers at a skiing competition look for action on and off the slopes, end up exposing a resort fraud.
1985 (PG) 96m/C Mary McDonough, Bob Hastings. **VHS, Beta $79.95** PSM ♪

Snowbeast The residents of a ski resort are being terrorized by a half-human, half-animal beast leaving a path of dead bodies in its wake. "Jaws" hits the slopes. Not scary or even funny. Made for TV.
1977 96m/C Bo Svenson, Yvette Mimieux, Sylvia Sidney, Clint Walker, Robert F. Logan; *D*: Herb Wallerstein. **VHS, Beta $9.95** WOV ♪ ½

Snowblind Two ski gondolas derail, placing the passengers in jeopardy. Among the passengers is a mobster being pursued by an assassin. *AKA*: Ski Lift to Death.
1978 98m/C Deborah Raffin, Charles Frank, Howard Duff, Don Galloway, Gail Strickland, Don Johnson, Veronica Hamel, Clu Gulager, Lisa Reeves, Suzy Chaffee; *D*: William Wiard. **VHS $9.95** SIM ♪♪

The Snows of Kilimanjaro Called by Hemingway "The Snows of Zanuck," in reference to the great producer, this film is actually an artful pastiche of several Hemingway short stories and novels. The main story, "The Snows of Kilimanjaro," acts as a framing device, in which the life of a successful writer is seen through his fevered flashbacks as he and his rich wife, while on safari, await a doctor to save his gangrenous leg. Superbly scripted by Casey Robinson. **1952 117m/C** Gregory Peck, Susan Hayward, Ava Gardner, Hildegarde Neff, Leo G. Carroll, Torin Thatcher, Ava Norring, Helene Stanley, Marcel Dalio, Vincente Gomez, Richard Allen, Leonard Carey; *D:* Henry King. **Beta $7.50** NOS, GKK, VEC ⅃⅃⅃

Snuff-Bottle Connection Russian envoy is spying for the government while delivering a gift to a Ching dynasty emperor. **1982 96m/C** Hwang Jang Lee, John Liu, Roy Horan. **VHS, Beta** WVE ⅃

Snuffy Smith, Yard Bird The pint-sized moonshiner finds himself in the Army, clashing with his sergeant. Followed by "Hillbilly Blitzkrieg" later the same year. Duncan is perfect for the part, and Kennedy is right on as his foil. *AKA:* Private Snuffy Smith; Snuffy Smith. **1942 67m/B** Bud Duncan, Edgar Kennedy, Sarah Padden, Doris Linden, J. Farrell MacDonald, Frank Austin, Jimmie Dodd; *D:* Eddie Cline. **VHS $19.95** NOS, VYY ⅃½

So Dear to My Heart A farm boy and his misfit black sheep wreak havoc at the county fair. Several sequences combine live action with animation. Heartwarming and charming; straightforward and likeable but never sentimental. Wonderful, vintage Disney. ♫Sourwood Mountain; Billy Boy; So Dear To My Heart; County Fair; Stick-To-It-Ivity; Ol' Dan Patch; It's Whatcha Do With Watcha Got; Lavender Blue (Dilly Dilly). **1949 82m/C** Bobby Driscoll, Burl Ives, Beulah Bondi, Harry Carey Sr., Luanna Patten; *D:* Harold Schuster. **VHS, Beta, LV $69.95** DIS, WTA ⅃⅃⅃½

So Ends Our Night German scorns Nazi ideology, flees Austria, and meets young Jewish couple seeking asylum. Fine adaptation of Erich Maria Remarque's novel "Flotsam," with splendid performances from Sullavan (on loan from Universal) and young Ford. **1941 117m/B** Fredric March, Margaret Sullavan, Frances Dee, Glenn Ford, Anna Sten, Erich von Stroheim; *D:* John Cromwell. **VHS** IVY ⅃⅃⅃

So Fine Absent-minded English professor O'Neal tries to rescue his father's clothing business from going bottom-up. He accidentally invents peek-a-boo bottomed jeans, which become an immediate hit and make him rich. Comedy smorgasbord, setting out ing from sometime novelist Bergman, hits and misses. O'Neal is memorable, as is the ubiquitous Warden and his sidekick. **1981 (R) 91m/C** Ryan O'Neal, Jack Warden, Mariangela Melato, Richard Kiel; *D:* Andrew Bergman; *M:* Ennio Morricone. **VHS, Beta $19.98** WAR ⅃⅃½

So I Married an Axe Murderer Combination comedy/romance/thriller. Charlie (Myers) is a hip bookstore owner with a commitment problem. Once he finally falls in love with a woman who's a butcher, he comes to suspect she's a serial killer and he's in line as her next victim. He brings her home to meet her parents Stuart and May (Myers again and Fricker), Scottish transplants who mortify Charlie as they regale Harriet with embarrassing stories of his childhood. Dual role for Myers allows him a chance to be fanatically Scottish as Stuart and somewhat more restrained as the angst-ridden Charlie. **1993 (PG-13) ?m/C** Mike Myers, Nancy Travis, Anthony LaPaglia, Amanda Plummer, Brenda Fricker, Alan Arkin, Michael Richards, Phil Hartman, Charles Grodin, Matt Doherty; *D:* Thomas Schlamme; *W:* Mike Myers, Robbie Fox, Neil Mullarkey. **VHS** NYR ⅃⅃½

So This is Paris Roguish pre-Hayes Code dancing duo seeks spice through alternative lovemates. Classic sophisticated Lubitsch, with outstanding camerawork and a bit of jazz. **1926 68m/B** Monte Blue, Patsy Ruth Miller, Lilyan Tashman, Andre de Beranger, Myrna Loy; *D:* Ernst Lubitsch. **VHS, Beta $29.95** GPV, FCT ⅃⅃⅃

So This is Washington The comedy team go to Washington with wacky inventions to help the war effort. Turns out there's too entirely too much nonsense going around, and the boys give 'em a piece of their mind. Fun, featherweight wartime comedy. **1943 70m/B** Lum & Abner, Alan Mowbray. **VHS, Beta $24.95** NOS, DVT, HEG ⅃⅃½

Soapdish The back stage lives of a daytime soap opera, "The Sun Also Sets," and its cast. When the soap's ratings fall, a character written out of series via decapitation is brought back to give things a lift. While the writer struggles to make the reincarnation believable, the cast juggles old and new romances, and professional jealousies abound. Some genuinely funny moments as film actors spoof the genre that gave many of them a start. **1991 (PG-13) 97m/C** Sally Field, Kevin Kline, Robert Downey Jr., Cathy Moriarty, Whoopi Goldberg, Elisabeth Shue, Carrie Fisher, Garry Marshall, Teri Hatcher, Paul Johansson, Costas Mandylor, Stephen Nichols, Kathy Najimy, Sheila Kelley; *Cameos:* Leeza Gibbons, John Tesh, Garry Marshall; *D:* Michael Hoffman; *W:* Andrew Bergman, Robert Harling; *M:* Alan Silvestri. **VHS, Beta, LV, 8mm $19.95** PAR, PIA ⅃⅃⅃

S.O.B. Blake Edwards' bitter farce about Hollywood and the film industry wheelers and dealers who inhabit it. When a multi-million dollar picture bombs at the box office, the director turns suicidal, until he envisions re-shooting it with a steamy, X-rated scene starring his wife, a star with a goody-two-shoes image. Edwards used his real-life wife, Julie ("Mary Poppins") Andrews, for the scene in which she bared her breasts. Oft-inspired, but oft-terrible. Zestfully vengeful. William Holden's last film. **1981 (R) 121m/C** William Holden, Robert Preston, Richard Mulligan, Julie Andrews, Robert Webber, Shelley Winters, Robert Vaughn, Larry Hagman, Stuart Margolin, Loretta Swit, Craig Stevens, Larry Storch, Jennifer Edwards, Robert Loggia, Rosanna Arquette, Marisa Berenson; *D:* Blake Edwards. **VHS, Beta, LV $19.98** FOX, WAR ⅃⅃½

Social Error An heiress mistakes her guards for a group of kidnappers. **1935 60m/B** Gertrude Messinger, David Sharpe. **VHS, Beta, LV $19.95** NOS ⅃⅃

The Social Secretary Driven from the rat race by lecherous men, Talmadge gets new job as rich woman's secretary, where she down-dresses to avoid further lewd encounters. She falls for her boss's son, but isn't considered marriage material until she proves herself. **1916 56m/B** Norma Talmadge, Kate Lester, Helen Weir, Gladden James, Herbert Frank; *D:* John Emerson. **VHS, Beta $19.95** GPV, FCT ⅃⅃½

Society A teenager wonders if his visions are real or hallucinations when he believes his family, and everyone else around him, are flesh-eating predators. The puzzle isn't much but wait for the special-effects ladened ending to get your fill of gore. **1992 (R) 99m/C** Billy Warlock, Devin Devasquez, Evan Richards; *D:* Brian Yuzna. **VHS $89.98** REP ⅃

Sodom and Gomorrah The Italian-made, internationally produced epic about Lot, the Hebrews and the destruction of the two sinful biblical cities. Moderately entertaining—but ponderous, to say the least, and very long. *AKA:* Sodome et Gomorrhe; The Last Days of Sodom and Gomorrah. **1962 154m/C** *IT* Stewart Granger, Stanley Baker, Pier Angeli, Anouk Aimee, Rossana Podesta; *D:* Robert Aldrich. **VHS, Beta, LV $19.98** FOX, IME ⅃⅃

Soft and Hard Made for English television, this video by Godard and Mieville intends to address the role of media and television in everyday life via a seemingly informal look at the couple's daily existence and the propensity for image production in it. In French with English subtitles. **1985 48m/C** *FR D:* Anne-Marie Mieville, Jean-Luc Godard. **VHS, Beta** EAI ⅃⅃½

The Soft Skin A classic portrayal of marital infidelity by the master director. A writer and lecturer has an affair with a stewardess. After the affair ends, his wife confronts him, with tragic results. Cliche plot is forgivable; acted and directed to perfection. Frequent Truffaut star Jean-Pierre Leaud served here as an apprentice director. In French with English subtitles. *AKA:* Le Peau Douce; Silken Skin. **1964 120m/B** *FR* Jean Desailly, Nelly Benedetti, Francoise Dorleac; *D:* Francois Truffaut. **VHS, Beta $39.95** HMV, FOX ⅃⅃⅃

Soggy Bottom U.S.A. A sheriff has his hands full trying to keep the law enforced in a small Southern town. Quite-good cast keeps the plot from disappearing altogether. **1984 (PG) 90m/C** Don Johnson, Ben Johnson, Dub Taylor, Ann Wedgeworth, Lois Nettleton, Anthony Zerbe; *D:* Theodore J. Flicker. **VHS, Beta $9.99** STE, PSM, HHE ⅃⅃

Sois Belle et Tais-Toi A police detective tracks jewel thieves and falls in love with a young waif. Several interesting and later famous actors have small parts. Light-hearted adventure. Subtitled in English. **1958 110m/B** *FR* Henri Vidal, Mylene Demongeot, Jean-Paul Belmondo, Alain Delon; *D:* Marc Allegret. **VHS, Beta $19.95** KRT ⅃⅃½

Solar Crisis Eye-popping special effects highlight this Earth-on-the-edge-of-destruction sci-fi. In 2050 the sun has gone on self-destruct and begins throwing off giant solar flares which turn the Earth extra-crispy. A space team is sent to divert the flares but the mission may become a victim of sabotage. **1992 (PG-13) 111m/C** Tim Matheson, Charlton Heston, Peter Boyle, Annabel Schofield, Jack Palance, Corin "Corky" Nemec; *M:* Maurice Jarre. **VHS, LV $92.95** VMK ⅃⅃½

Solarbabies Rollerskating youths in a drought-stricken future vie for a mysterious power that will replenish the Earth's water. Shades of every sci-fi movie you've ever seen, from "Mad Max" to "Ice Pirates." Pathetic. **1986 (PG-13) 95m/C** Richard Jordan, Sarah Douglas, Charles Durning, Lukas Haas, Jami Gertz, Jason Patric; *D:* Alan Johnson. **VHS, Beta, LV $14.95** MGM ⅃

Solaris With this the USSR tried to eclipse "2001: A Space Odyssey" in terms of cerebral science-fiction. Some critics thought they succeeded. You may disagree now that the lumbering effort is available on tape. Adapted from a Stanislaw Lem novel, it depicts a dilapidated space lab orbiting the planet Solaris, whose ocean, a vast fluid "brain," materializes the stir-crazy cosmonauts' obsessions—usually morose ex-girlfriends. Talk, talk, talk, minimal special effects. In Russian with English subtitles. In a two-cassette package, with a letterbox format preserving Tarkovsky's widescreen compositions.
1972 167m/C *RU* Donatas Banionis, Natalya Bondarchuk; *D:* Andrei Tarkovsky. **VHS, LV** $79.95 *FXL, FCT, TAM* ⚔️⚔️

Soldat Duroc...Ca Va Etre Ta Fete! Days after the 1944 liberation of Paris, a French soldier crosses back over the French lines to see his lover, and is caught as a German sympathizer by American troops. *AKA:* Soldier Duroc.
196? 105m/C *FR* Pierre Tornade, Robert Webber, Michel Galabru, Roger Carel. **VHS, Beta** *NO* ⚔️⚔️

The Soldier The Russians are holding the world at ransom with a pile of stolen plutonium, and a soldier finds himself in the position to carry out an unauthorized and dangerous plan to preserve the balance of world power. Wildly implausible, gratuitously violent spy trash. *AKA:* Codename: The Soldier.
1982 (R) 90m/C Ken Wahl, Klaus Kinski; *D:* James Glickenhaus. **VHS, Beta** $14.95 *COL, SUE* ⚔️

Soldier Blue Two survivors of an Indian attack make their way back to an army outpost. The cavalry then seeks revenge on the Cheyenne tribe accused of the attack. Gratuitously violent Vietnam-era western hits hard on racial themes. Based on the novel "Arrow in the Sun" by Theodore V. Olsen on the Sand Creek Indian massacre.
1970 (R) 109m/C Candice Bergen, Peter Strauss, Donald Pleasence, Dana Elcar, Jorge Rivero; *D:* Ralph Nelson. **VHS, Beta** $14.95 *COL, SUE* ⚔️⚔️

Soldier in Love Teleplay from "George Schaefer's Showcase Theatre" is based on the life of John Churchill, first Duke of Marlborough, and his wife Sarah. The ambitious young couple held the favor of Queen Anne for a time, until political intrigue brought about their downfall.
1967 76m/C Jean Simmons, Claire Bloom, Keith Michell; *D:* George Schaefer. **VHS, Beta** *FHS* ⚔️⚔️

Soldier in the Rain An unusual friendship develops between career sergeant Gleason and wheeler-dealer McQueen. Gleason is in good form, but McQueen is listless, and the story (set in a Southern army camp) is unsatisfying. Weld is the comely teen who makes for an intriguing love triangle. From the novel by William Goldman.
1963 88m/B Steve McQueen, Jackie Gleason, Tuesday Weld, Tony Bill, Tom Poston, Ed Nelson. **VHS, Beta** $59.98 *FOX* ⚔️⚔️½

Soldier of Fortune A woman (Hayward) enlists mercenaries to help find her lost husband in Red China. Late Gable vehicle with the formula beginning to feel the postwar strain and the star looking a trifle long in the tooth. Still, a fun adventure from a top star. Hayward had been among the myriad starlets vying for the Scarlett O'Hara roles nearly two decades earlier.

1955 96m/C Clark Gable, Susan Hayward, Gene Barry, Alexander D'Arcy, Michael Rennie, Tom Tully, Anna Sten, Russell Collins, Leo Gordon, Jack Kruschen, Robert Quarry; *D:* Edward Dmytryk. **VHS, Beta** $39.98 *FOX* ⚔️⚔️½

Soldier of Orange The lives of six Dutch students are forever changed by the World War II invasion of Holland by the Nazis. Based on the true-life exploits of Dutch resistance leader Erik Hazelhoff. Exciting and suspenseful; cerebral; carefully made and well acted. Made Rutger Hauer an international star.
1978 144m/C *NL* Rutger Hauer, Jeroen Krabbe, Edward Fox, Susan Penhaligon; *D:* Paul Verhoeven. **VHS, Beta, LV** $59.95 *MED* ⚔️⚔️⚔️

Soldier of the Night Toy-store worker by day, vigilante killer by night. Israeli thriller set in Tel Aviv lacks vim and is badly dubbed.
1984 89m/C *D:* Dan Wolman. **VHS, Beta** $59.95 *MGM* ⚔️½

Soldier's Fortune A traveling gun for hire leaves the combat of Central America for the jungles of Los Angeles, only to find out that his daughter had been taken hostage. That's the last thing these kidnappers will ever do when they are found by this tough guy looking for his child.
1991 (R) 96m/C Gil Gerard, Charles Napier, Dan Haggerty, P.J. Soles, Barbara Bingham, Janus Blythe; *D:* Arthur N. Mele. **VHS** $89.98 *REP* ⚔️½

Soldier's Revenge A Vietnam vet has a hard time adjusting to life at home.
197? 92m/C John Savage. **VHS, Beta** $19.98 *TWE* ⚔️⚔️

A Soldier's Story A black army attorney is sent to a Southern base to investigate the murder of an unpopular sergeant. Features World War II, Louisiana, jazz and blues, and racism in and outside the corps. From the Pulitzer-prize winning play by Charles Fuller, with most of the Broadway cast. Fine performances from Washington and Caesar.
1984 (PG) 101m/C Howard E. Rollins Jr., Adolph Caesar, Denzel Washington, Patti LaBelle, Robert Townsend, Scott Paulin, Wings Hauser, Art Evans, Larry Riley, David Alan Grier; *D:* Norman Jewison. Academy Awards '84 Nominations: Best Adapted Screenplay, Best Picture, Best Supporting Actor (Caesar); Edgar Allan Poe Awards '84: Best Screenplay. **VHS, Beta, LV** $14.95 *COL, FCT* ⚔️⚔️⚔️

Soldier's Tale Igor Stravinsky's "The Soldier's Tale" is animated by New Yorker cartoonist R.O. Bleechman with the voices provided by Max Von Sydow and Andre Gregory.
1984 60m/C *V:* Max von Sydow, Andre Gregory. **VHS, Beta, LV** $39.95 *MGM* ⚔️⚔️⚔️

A Soldier's Tale During WWII, a menage-a-trois develops that can only lead to tragedy, yet the participants find themselves unable to resist.
1991 (R) 96m/C Gabriel Byrne, Marianne Basler, Judge Reinhold, Paul Wyett; *D:* Larry Parr. **VHS** $89.94 *REP* ⚔️⚔️

Sole Survivor A group of zombies are searching for a beautiful advertising executive who was the sole survivor of a plane crash.
1984 (R) 85m/C Anita Skinner, Kurt Johnson, Caren Larkey; *D:* Thom Eberhardt. **VHS, Beta** $79.98 *LIV, VES* ⚔️½

The Solitary Man Glum look at a family breakup, from the husband's point of view. Holliman is good, but the exercise at large is regularly blues-inducing, and not especially inspiring or artful. Made for TV.

1982 96m/C Earl Holliman, Carrie Snodgress, Lara Parker, Lane Smith, Nicholas Coster, Michelle Pfeiffer; *D:* John Llewellyn Moxey. **VHS, Beta** *TLF* ⚔️⚔️

Solo Young hitchhiker Peers enters the lives of fire patrol pilot Gil and his teenage son. A plotless friendship develops, headed nowhere—like this movie. Great New Zealand scenery might be worth the price of rental.
1977 (PG) 90m/C Vincent Gil, Perry Armstrong, Martyn Sanderson, Lisa Peers; *D:* Tony Williams. **VHS, Beta** *VES, HHE* ⚔️⚔️

Solo Voyage: The Revenge A Russian "Rambo" goes on a murderous rampage, the likes of which humanity has not yet seen.
1990 91m/C *RU* Mikhail Nojkine, Alexandre Fatiouchine; *D:* Mikhail Toumanichulli. **VHS** *NO* ⚔️⚔️

Solomon and Sheba King Solomon's brother and the Egyptian Pharaoh send the Queen of Sheba to Israel to seduce King Solomon so they may gain his throne. Tyrone Power had filmed most of the lead role in this silly, overwrought epic when he died of a heart attack. The role was reshot, with Brynner (with a full head of hair) replacing him. Director Vidor's unfortunate last film. Shot on location in Spain.
1959 139m/C Yul Brynner, Gina Lollobrigida, Marisa Pavan, George Sanders, Alejandro Rey; *D:* King Vidor. **VHS, Beta, LV** $59.98 *FOX* ⚔️⚔️

The Sombrero Kid The Kid unwittingly gets involved in a murder and is nearly hanged before his friends help him discover the real culprits. Plenty of action in this straight forward, fun western.
1942 54m/B Donald (Don "Red") Barry, Lynn Merrick, Rand Brooks; *D:* George Sherman. **VHS, Beta** $19.95 *VDM* ⚔️⚔️

Some Call It Loving Bad, pretentious modern version of Sleeping Beauty, set in L.A. King buys the sleeping girl (Farrow) from a carnival show, but she doesn't live up to his ideal.
1973 (R) 103m/C Zalman King, Carol White, Tisa Farrow, Richard Pryor, Pat Priest; *D:* James B. Harris. **VHS** $39.95 *IVE* ⚔️

Some Came Running James Jones's follow-up novel to "From Here to Eternity" does not translate nearly as well to the screen. Overlong and with little plot, the action centers around a would-be writer, his floozy girl friend, and the holier-than-thou characters which populate the town in which he grew up and to which he has now returned. Strong performances by all.
1958 136m/C Frank Sinatra, Dean Martin, Shirley MacLaine, Martha Hyer, Arthur Kennedy, Nancy Gates; *D:* Vincente Minnelli. **VHS, Beta, LV** $19.98 *MGM* ⚔️⚔️⚔️

Some Girls A man goes to Quebec to see his college girlfriend who informs him that she is not in love with him anymore. But she has two sisters ready to comfort him! Strange black comedy; Gregory as the girl's father elevates so-so story. *AKA:* Sisters.
1988 (R) 104m/C Patrick Dempsey, Andre Gregory, Lila Kedrova, Florinda Bolkan, Jennifer Connelly; *D:* Michael Hoffman. **VHS, Beta** $89.95 *MGM* ⚔️⚔️½

Some Kind of Hero A Vietnam prisoner of war returns home to a changed world. Pryor tries hard, but can't get above this poorly written, unevenly directed film.
1982 97m/C Richard Pryor, Margot Kidder, Ray Sharkey, Ronny Cox, Lynne Moody, Olivia Cole; *D:* Michael Pressman. **VHS, Beta, LV** $14.95 *PAR* ⚔️⚔️

Some Kind of Wonderful A high-school tomboy has a crush on a guy who also happens to be her best friend. Her feelings go unrequited as he falls for a rich girl with snobbish friends. In the end, true love wins out. Deutch also directed (and John Hughes also produced) the teen flick "Pretty in Pink," which had much the same plot, with the rich/outcast characters reversed by gender. OK, but completely predictable.
1987 (PG-13) 93m/C Eric Stoltz, Lea Thompson, Mary Stuart Masterson, Craig Sheffer, John Ashton, Elias Koteas, Molly Hagan; **D:** Howard Deutch. **VHS, LV $19.95** PAR ✰✰

Some Like It Hot Two unemployed musicians witness the St. Valentine's Day massacre in Chicago. They disguise themselves as women and join an all-girl band headed for Miami to escape the gangsters' retaliation. Flawless cast includes a fetching Monroe at her best; hilarious script. Curtis does his Cary Grant impression. Classic scenes between Lemmon in drag and Joe E. Brown as a smitten suitor. Brown also has the film's famous closing punchline. Monroe sings "I Wanna Be Loved By You," "Running Wild," and "I'm Through With Love." One of the very funniest movies of all time.
1959 120m/B Marilyn Monroe, Tony Curtis, Jack Lemmon, George Raft, Pat O'Brien, Nehemiah Persoff, Edward G. Robinson; **D:** Billy Wilder. Academy Awards '59: Best Costume Design (B & W); Nominations: Best Actor (Lemmon), Best Adapted Screenplay, Best Art Direction/Set Decoration (B & W), Best Black and White Cinematography, Best Director (Wilder); British Academy Awards '59: Best Actor (Lemmon); Golden Globe Awards '60: Best Actor—Musical/Comedy (Lemmon), Best Actress—Musical/Comedy (Monroe), Best Film—Musical/Comedy; National Board of Review Awards '59: 10 Best Films of the Year. **VHS, Beta, LV $19.95** MGM, FOX, VYG ✰✰✰✰

Somebody Has to Shoot the Picture Photographer Scheider is hired by a convicted man to take a picture of his execution. Hours before the event, Scheider uncovers evidence that leads him to believe the man is innocent. He then embarks in a race against time to save him. Adapted by Doug Magee from his book "Slow Coming Dark." Unpretentious, tough drama. Made for cable.
1990 (R) 104m/C Roy Scheider, Bonnie Bedelia, Robert Carradine, Andre Braugher, Arliss Howard; **D:** Frank Pierson; **W:** Doug Magee. **VHS, Beta, LV $79.98** MCA ✰✰✰

Somebody Up There Likes Me Story of Rocky Graziano's gritty battle from his poor, street-wise childhood to his prison term and his eventual success as the middle-weight boxing champion of the world. Adapted from Graziano's autobiography. Superior performance by Newman (in his third screen role, after the miserable "The Silver Chalice" and forgettable "The Rack"); screen debuts for McQueen and Loggia.
1956 113m/B Paul Newman, Pier Angeli, Everett Sloane, Eileen Heckart, Sal Mineo, Robert Loggia, Steve McQueen; **D:** Robert Wise. Academy Awards '56: Best Art Direction/Set Decoration (B & W), Best Black and White Cinematography; Nominations: Best Film Editing. **VHS, Beta $19.98** MGM ✰✰✰

Someday You'll Find Her, Charlie Brown Charlie Brown tries to find a beautiful girl he saw on tv.
1981 24m/C VHS $14.95 WTA ✰✰✰

Someone at the Door Reporter Medwin arranges to be suspected of killing his sister, thus providing him with a good story and advancing his career. His plan almost backfires, when he is almost executed. Remake of a 1936 film of the same name.
1950 65m/B GB Michael Medwin, Garry Marsh, Yvonne Owen, Hugh Latimer; **D:** Francis Searle. **VHS, Beta $16.95** SNC ✰✰

Someone Behind the Door Evil brain surgeon Perkins implants murderous suggestions into psychopathic amnesia victim Bronson's mind, then instructs him to kill his (the surgeon's) wife and her lover. *AKA:* Two Minds for Murder; Quelqu' Un Derriere la Porte.
1971 (PG) 97m/C Charles Bronson, Anthony Perkins, Jill Ireland, Henri Garcin; **D:** Nicolas Gessner. **VHS, Beta, LV $39.95** UNI ✰1/2

Someone I Touched Way-overdone melodrama starring Leachman as a finally-pregnant woman who learns her husband and a teenager he slept with have venereal disease.
1975 74m/C Cloris Leachman, James Olson, Glynnis O'Connor, Andy Robinson, Allyn Ann McLerie; **D:** Lou Antonio. **VHS, Beta $34.95** WOV ✰1/2

Someone to Love Rootless filmmaker gathers all his single friends together and interviews them about their failed love lives. Welles's last film as an actor. Wildly uneven, interesting experiment.
1987 (R) 110m/C Henry Jaglom, Orson Welles, Sally Kellerman, Andrea Marcovicci, Michael Emil, Oja Kodar, Stephen Bishop, Ronee Blakley, Kathryn Harrold, Monte Hellman; **D:** Henry Jaglom. **VHS, Beta, LV $79.95** PAR ✰✰

Someone to Watch Over Me After witnessing the murder of a close friend, a beautiful and very wealthy woman must be protected from the killer. The working-class New York detective assigned the duty is more than taken with her, despite the fact that he has both a wife and son at home. A highly watchable, stylish romantic crime thriller. Music by Michael Kamen.
1987 (R) 106m/C Tom Berenger, Mimi Rogers, Lorraine Bracco, Jerry Orbach, Andreas Katsulas, Tony DiBenedetto, James Moriarty, John Rubinstein; **D:** Ridley Scott. **VHS, Beta, LV $19.95** COL ✰✰✰

Something for Everyone A corrupt footman uses sex and murder in an attempt to take over the estate of an aristocratic Bavarian family in post-World War II Germany. He nearly succeeds in marrying the countess (Lansbury), but someone has been keeping tabs on him. Funny, ambitious black comedy. From the novel "The Code" by Harry Kressing. *AKA:* The Rook; Black Flowers for the Bride.
1970 (R) 112m/C Angela Lansbury, Michael York, Anthony Corlan, Heidelinde Weis; **D:** Harold Prince. **VHS, Beta $59.98** FOX ✰✰1/2

Something in Common A woman discovers her 22-year-old son is having an affair with a woman her own age. Nicely done comedy; Burstyn and Weld both make good use of a solid script by Susan Rice. Made for TV.
1986 94m/C Ellen Burstyn, Tuesday Weld, Don Murray, Patrick Cassidy, Eli Wallach; **D:** Glenn Jordan. **VHS, Beta $19.95** STE, NWV ✰✰1/2

Something of Value Good ensemble performances in a serious colonial story about the Mau Mau rebellion in Kenya. Hudson and Poitier are torn between their friendship and their opposing loyalties. Drama solidly grounded in fact from the book by Robert Ruark.
1957 113m/B Rock Hudson, Sidney Poitier, Wendy Hiller, Dana Wynter, Juano Hernandez; **D:** Richard Brooks. **VHS, Beta $24.95** MGM ✰✰✰

Something Short of Paradise The owner of a Manhattan movie theater has an on again/off again romance with a magazine writer. Would-be Allenesque romantic comedy is too talky and pretentious.
1979 (PG) 87m/C David Steinberg, Susan Sarandon, Jean-Pierre Aumont, Marilyn Sokol; **D:** David Helpern. **VHS, Beta $29.98** LIV, VES ✰1/2

Something Special A fourteen-year-old girl has her wish come true when she is turned into a boy. Charming, original fantasy-comedy is fun for young and old. *AKA:* Willy Milly; I Was a Teenage Boy.
1986 (PG-13) 93m/C Pamela Segall, Patty Duke, Eric Gurry, John Glover, Seth Green; **D:** Paul Schneider. **VHS, LV** NO ✰✰1/2

Something to Sing About Musical melodrama about a New York bandleader's attempt to make it big in Hollywood. Allows Cagney the opportunity to demonstrate his dancing talents; he also sings. Rereleased in 1947. Also available colorized. Frawley was Fred on "I Love Lucy." ♫Any Old Love; Right or Wrong; Loving You; Out of the Blue; Something to Sing About. *AKA:* Battling Hoofer.
1936 84m/B James Cagney, William Frawley, Evelyn Daw, Gene Lockhart; **D:** Victor Schertzinger. **VHS, Beta, LV, 3/4U, Special order formats $19.95** NOS, VHE, CAB ✰✰

Something Weird McCabe is disfigured horribly in an electrical accident. A seemingly beautiful witch fixes his face, on condition that he be her lover. The accident also gave him ESP—and it gets cheesier from there.
1968 80m/C Tony McCabe, Elizabeth Lee; **D:** Herschell Gordon Lewis. **VHS, Beta $29.95** VMK, VDM, TWE Woof!

Something Wicked This Way Comes Two young boys discover the evil secret of a mysterious traveling carnival that visits their town. Ray Bradbury wrote the screenplay for this much-anticipated, expensive adaptation of his own novel. Good special effects, but disappointing. Clayton earlier directed "The Great Gatsby."
1983 (PG) 94m/C Jason Robards Jr., Jonathan Pryce, Diane Ladd, Pam Grier, Richard Davalos, James Stacy; **D:** Jack Clayton. **VHS, Beta, LV $14.99** DIS ✰✰

Something Wild Mild-mannered business exec Daniels is picked up by an impossibly free-living vamp with a Louise Brooks hairdo, and taken for the ride of his up-till-then staid life, eventually leading to explosive violence. A sharp-edged comedy with numerous changes of pace. Too-happy ending wrecks it, but it's great until then. Look for cameos from filmmakers John Waters and John Sayles.
1986 (R) 113m/C Jeff Daniels, Melanie Griffith, Ray Liotta, Margaret Colin, Tracy Walter, Dana Peru, Jack Gilpin, Su Tissue, Kenneth Utt, Sister Carol East; *Cameos:* John Sayles, John Waters; **D:** Jonathan Demme. **VHS, Beta, LV $19.99** HBO ✰✰1/2

Sometimes a Great Notion Trouble erupts in a small Oregon town when a family of loggers decide to honor a contract when the other loggers go on strike. Newman's second stint in the director's chair; Fonda's first role as an old man. Based on the novel by Ken Kesey. *AKA:* Never Give an Inch.
1971 (PG) 115m/C Paul Newman, Henry Fonda, Lee Remick, Richard Jaeckel, Michael Sarrazin; **D:** Paul Newman. **VHS, Beta $59.95** MCA ✰✰✰

Sometimes Aunt Martha Does Dreadful Things Another deranged-slasher movie, this one featuring a female psychopath.
1988 95m/C VHS, Beta NO ✰

Sometimes It Works, Sometimes It Doesn't A film in two parts, the first being interviews with Merce Cunningham and John Case about their work together, the second being the filmdance "Channels/Inserts," in its entirety.
1983 63m/C VHS, Beta NO ♂♂½

Sometimes They Come Back Another Stephen King tale of terror. Matheson plays a man haunted by the tragedy in his past. A witness to his brother's death, he also witnesses the fiery crash of his brother's killers. Only now the killers have returned from the dead, to take their revenge on him. Made for television.
1991 (R) 97m/C Tim Matheson, Brooke Adams, Robert Rusler. VHS, LV $89.95 VMK ♂♂

Somewhere I'll Find You Clark and Turner heat up the screen as correspondents running all over the war-torn world in their second film together. ("Honky Tonk" was their first.) Notable mainly because Gable's beloved wife, Carole Lombard, was killed in a plane crash only three days into production. Lombard was returning from a war bonds drive when the twin-engine plane she was flying in crashed into the side of a cliff shortly after takeoff. Gable forced himself to finish the film and it became one of the studios biggest hits. Although critics applauded his determination to complete the film, many felt his performance was subdued and strained. Film debut of Keenan Wynn. Based on a story by Charles Hoffman.
1942 108m/B Clark Gable, Lana Turner, Robert Sterling, Reginald Owen, Lee Patrick, Charles Dingle, Tamara Shayne, Leonid Kinskey, Diana Lewis, Molly Lamont, Patricia Dane, Sara Haden; D: Wesley Ruggles; W: Walter Reisch, Marguerite Roberts. VHS $19.98 MGM ♂♂♂

Somewhere in Time Playwright Reeve (in his first post-Clark Kent role) falls in love with a beautiful woman in an old portrait. Through self-hypnosis he goes back in time to 1912 to discover what their relationship might have been. The film made a star of the Grand Hotel, located on Mackinac Island in Michigan, where it was shot. Drippy rip-off of the brilliant novel "Time and Again" by Jack Finney. Reeve is horrible; Seymour is underused. All in all, rather wretched.
1980 (PG) 103m/C Christopher Reeve, Jane Seymour, Christopher Plummer, Teresa Wright; D: Jeannot Szwarc; M: John Barry. VHS, Beta, LV $19.95 MCA ♂♂½

Somewhere Tomorrow A lonely, fatherless teenage girl is befriended by the ghost of a young man killed in a plane crash. Charming and moving, if not perfect.
1985 (PG) 91m/C Sarah Jessica Parker, Nancy Addison, Tom Shea; D: Robert Wiemer. VHS, Beta $59.95 MED ♂♂½

Sommersby A too-good-to-be-true period romance based on the film "The Return of Martin Guerre." A Civil War veteran (Gere) returns to his wife's (Foster) less-than-open arms. However, she soon warms up to his kind, sensitive and caring manner. She can't quite believe the change that the war has brought in him. Neither can the neighbors, especially the one (Pullman) who had his own eye on Laurel Sommersby. So is he really Jack Sommersby or an all too clever imposter? When Sommersby goes on trial for murder the truth will have to come out (maybe). Lots of hankies needed for the tender-hearted. Strong performance by Foster. Filmed in Virginia (passing for the state of Tennessee.) The laserdisc version is available in letterbox format.
1993 (PG-13) 114m/C Richard Gere, Jodie Foster, Bill Pullman, James Earl Jones, William Windom; D: Jon Amiel; W: Nicholas Meyer, Sarah Kernochan; M: Danny Elfman. VHS, Beta, LV, 8mm $94.99 WAR ♂♂½

Somos Novios Publicity agent and his friend, along with a salesclerk in a record store, find themselves at the top of the music charts. In Spanish. AKA: In Love and Engaged.
1968 100m/C MX Angelica Maria, Armando Manzanero, Palito Ortega, Olga Zubarry, Raul Ross; D: Enrique Carreras. VHS, Beta $69.95 MAD ♂

Son-in-Law Surfer-dude comic Shore's a laconic fish out of water as a city-boy rock 'n' roller who falls in love with a country beauty, marries her, and visits the family farm to meet the new in-laws. Once there, he weirds out family and neighbors before showing everyone how to live, Pauly style. Silly entertainment best appreciated by Shore fans.
1993 (PG-13) 95m/C Pauly Shore, Carla Gugino, Lane Smith, Cindy Pickett, Mason Adams, Patrick Renna, Dennis Burkley, Dan Gauthier, Tiffani-Amber Thiessen; D: Steve Rash; W: Shawn Schepps, Fax Bahr, Adam Small; M: Richard Gibbs. VHS NYR ♂½

Son of a Gun A loveable but ornery cowboy gets banished from the county for disturbing the peace. However, he wins the favor of the townspeople when he stands up to a gang of gambling swindlers. Silent.
1919 68m/B Billy Anderson. VHS, Beta $19.95 NOS, DVT, RXM ♂½

Son of Blob A scientist brings home a piece of frozen blob from the North Pole; his wife accidentally revives the dormant gray mass. It begins a rampage of terror by digesting nearly everyone within its reach. A host of recognizable faces make for fun viewing. Post-Jeannie, pre-Dallas Hagman directed this exercise in zaniness. AKA: Beware! The Blob.
1972 (PG) 87m/C Robert Walker Jr., Godfrey Cambridge, Carol Lynley, Shelley Berman, Larry Hagman, Burgess Meredith, Gerrit Graham, Dick Van Patten; D: Larry Hagman. VHS, Beta $19.95 GEM ♂♂

Son of Captain Blood The son of the famous pirate meets up with his father's enemies on the high seas. The son of the famous actor Errol Flynn—Sean—plays the son of the character the elder Flynn played in "Captain Blood." Let's just say the gimmick didn't work. AKA: Il Figlio del Capitano Blood.
1962 (G) 90m/C IT SP Sean Flynn, Ann Todd; D: Tulio Demicheli. VHS, Beta $59.95 PSM, MLB ♂½

Son of Dracula In this late-coming sequel to the Universal classic, a stranger named Alucard is invited to America by a Southern belle obsessed with eternal life. It is actually Dracula himself, not his son, who wreaks havoc in this spine-tingling chiller. AKA: Young Dracula.
1943 80m/B Lon Chaney Jr., Evelyn Ankers, Frank Craven, Robert Paige, Louise Allbritton, J. Edward Bromberg, Samuel S. Hinds; D: Robert Siodmak. VHS, Beta, LV $14.95 MCA ♂♂♂

Son of Flubber Sequel to "The Absent Minded Professor" finds Fred MacMurray still toying with his prodigious invention, Flubber, now in the form of Flubbergas, which causes those who inhale it to float away. Disney's first-ever sequel is high family wackiness.
1963 96m/C Fred MacMurray, Nancy Olson, Tommy Kirk, Leon Ames, Joanna Moore, Keenan Wynn, Charlie Ruggles, Paul Lynde; D: Robert Stevenson. VHS, Beta DIS ♂♂½

Son of Frankenstein The second sequel (after "The Bride of Frankenstein") to the 1931 version of the horror classic. The good doctor's skeptical son returns to the family manse and becomes obsessed with his father's work and with reviving the creature. Full of memorable characters and brooding ambience. Karloff's last appearance as the monster.
1939 99m/C Basil Rathbone, Bela Lugosi, Boris Karloff, Lionel Atwill, Josephine Hutchinson, Donnie Dunagan, Emma Dunn, Edgar Norton, Lawrence Grant; D: Rowland V. Lee. VHS, Beta, LV $14.98 MCA ♂♂♂

Son of God's Country Utterly hackneyed, near-comic attempt at a western. Good-guy U.S. Marshall poses as a crook to get the lowdown on the varmints.
1948 60m/B Monte Hale, Pamela Blake, Adrian Booth. VHS, Beta $29.95 DVT ♂½

Son of Godzilla Dad and junior protect beauty Maeda from giant spiders on a remote island ruled by a mad scientist. Fun monster flick with decent special effects. AKA: Gojira no Musuko.
1966 86m/C JP Tadao Takashima, Akira Kubo; D: Jun Fukuda. VHS, Beta $19.95 PSM, HHT, DVT ♂♂

Son of Hercules vs. Venus Mortals battle the gods in this low budget action-adventure.
19?? 93m/C VHS, Beta $19.99 BFV ♂

Son of Ingagi Lonely ape-man kidnaps woman in search of romance. Early all-black horror film stars Williams of "Amos 'n' Andy."
1940 70m/B Zack Williams, Laura Bowman, Alfred Grant, Spencer Williams Jr.; D: Richard C. Kahn; W: Spencer Williams Jr. VHS $19.98 NOS, SNC, MLB ♂½

Son of Kong King Kong's descendant is discovered on an island amid prehistoric creatures in this often humorous sequel to RKO's immensely popular "King Kong." Hoping to capitalize on the enormous success of its predecessor, director Schoedsack quickly threw this together. As a result, its success at the box office did not match the original's, and didn't deserve to, but it's fun. Nifty special effects from Willie O'Brien, the man who brought them to us the first time!
1933 70m/B Robert Armstrong, Helen Mack; D: Ernest B. Schoedsack. VHS, Beta, LV $19.98 NOS, MED, FCT ♂♂½

Son of Lassie It seems that Lassie's son Laddie just isn't quite as smart as his mother. After the dog sneaks onto his master's plane during WWII, the plane gets shot down, and Lawford parachutes out with Laddie in his arms. The dog goes to get help because Lawford is hurt, but he brings back two Nazis! A sequel to "Lassie Come Home."
1945 102m/C Peter Lawford, Donald Crisp, June Lockhart, Nigel Bruce, William Severn, Leon Ames, Donald Curtis, Nils Asther, Robert Lewis; D: Sylvan Simon. VHS MGM ♂♂½

The Son of Monte Cristo Illegitimate offspring of the great swashbuckler with Robert Donat proves they made pathetic, pointless sequels even back then.
1941 102m/B Louis Hayward, Joan Bennett, George Sanders, Florence Bates, Montagu Love, Ralph Byrd, Clayton Moore; D: Rowland V. Lee. VHS, Beta, LV, 3/4U, Special order formats $19.95 DVT, KRT, CAB ♂♂½

Son of Paleface Hilarious sequel to the original Hope gag-fest, with the Harvard-educated son of the original character (again played by Hope) heading west to claim an inheritance. Hope runs away with every

cowboy cliche and even manages to wind up with the girl. Songs include "Buttons and Bows" (reprised from the original), "There's a Cloud in My Valley of Sunshine," and "Four-legged Friend."
1952 95m/C Bob Hope, Jane Russell, Roy Rogers, Douglass Dambrille, Iron Eyes Cody, Bill Williams, Harry von Zell, Trigger; *D:* Frank Tashlin. VHS, Beta, LV **$14.95** *COL* 🎬🎬🎬½

Son of Samson Man with large pectoral muscles puts an end to the evil Queen of Egypt's reign of terror *AKA:* Le Geant de la Vallee Das Rois.
1962 89m/C *FR IT YU* Mark Forest, Chelo Alonso, Angelo Zanolli, Vira Silenti, Frederica Ranchi; *D:* Carlo Campogalliani. VHS **$19.98** *SNC* 🎬½

Son of Sinbad Sinbad, captured by the Khalif of Baghdad, must bring him the secret of Greek fire to gain his freedom and free the city from the forces of mighty Tamerlane. About three dozen nubile young women wear very little and gambol with our hero herein; much-anticipated skinfest caused a scandal, nurtured by Howard Hughes for profit. *AKA:* Nights in a Harem.
1955 88m/C Dale Robertson, Sally Forrest, Vincent Price, Lili St. Cyr, Mari Blanchard; *D:* Ted Tetzlaff. VHS, Beta **$15.95** *UHV* 🎬🎬

Son of the Morning Star Lavish made for TV retelling of Custer's famed-butt kicking. Complex characterizations and unusual points of view, based on the book by Evan S. Connell.
1991 (PG-13) 186m/C Gary Cole, Rosanna Arquette, Dean Stockwell, Rodney Grant; *D:* Mike Robe. VHS, LV **$19.98** *REP, PIA, FCT* 🎬🎬🎬

Son of the Sheik A desert sheik abducts an unfaithful dancing girl. Valentino's well-done, slightly self-mocking last film. Silent. Sequel to "The Sheik" (1921).
1926 62m/B Rudolph Valentino, Vilma Banky, Agnes Ayres; *D:* George Fitzmaurice. VHS, Beta, LV, 3/4U, Special order formats **$19.95** *NOS, CCB, VCN* 🎬🎬🎬

Son of Zorro Zorro takes the law into his own hands to protect ranchers from bandits. A serial in thirteen chapters.
1947 164m/B George Turner, Peggy Stewart, Roy Barcroft, Edward Cassidy. VHS **$27.95** *REP, VCN, MLB* 🎬🎬🎬

A Song is Born A group of music professors try to trace the history of music. Kaye is in charge of a U.S. music foundation whose research has led him up to ragtime. He is soon, however, thrust into the sometimes seedy world of jazz joints and night spots, all in the name of research. Enter love interest Mayo, a woman on the run from her gangster boyfriend who hides out at the foundation. Not one of Kaye's funniest or best, but if you enjoy big band music, you'll love this. Includes music by Louis Armstrong and his orchestra, Tommy Dorsey and his orchestra, and Charlie Barnet and his orchestra. This was Kaye's last film for Goldwyn. 🎵A Song is Born; Bach Boogie; Anitra's Dance; I'm Getting Sentimental Over You; Blind Barnabas; Mockin' Bird; Redskin Rhumba; The Goldwyn Stomp; Daddy-O; Stealin' Apples; Longhair Jam Session; Oh, Genevieve; Guadeamas Igitur; Joshua Fit De Battle O' Jericho; Anvil Chorus; Flyin' Home; Muskrat Ramble.
1948 113m/B Danny Kaye, Virginia Mayo, Benny Goodman, Hugh Herbert, Steve Cochran, J. Edward Bromberg, Felix Bressart; *D:* Howard Hawks. VHS *HBO* 🎬🎬🎬

Song O' My Heart An early musical starring popular Irish tenor McCormack as a singer forced to abandon his career when he marries a woman he does not love. A tour de force for the lead in his movie debut. 🎵Little Boy Blue; Paddy Me Lad; I Hear You Calling Me; A Fair Story by the Fireside; Just For a Day; Kitty My Love; The Rose of Tralee; A Pair of Blue Eyes; I Feel You Near Me; Song O' My Heart; Then You'll Remember Me; Loughi Sereni E Cari; Ireland, Mother Ireland.
1929 91m/B John McCormack, Maureen O'Sullivan, John Garrick, J.M. Kerrigan, Tommy Clifford, Alice Joyce; *D:* Frank Borzage. VHS, Beta **$39.95** *VAI, FCT, TVC* 🎬🎬🎬

Song of Arizona Rogers and the Sons of the Pioneers arrive to aid their pal Hayes against a gang of bank robbers in this modern-day oater. Eight songs perpetually punctuate the perfunctory plot, particularly "Will Ya Be My Darling," "Half-a-Chance Ranch," and the title tune.
1946 54m/B Roy Rogers, Dale Evans, George "Gabby" Hayes, Lyle Talbot, Bob Nolan, The Pioneers; *D:* Frank McDonald. VHS, Beta **$19.95** *NOS, VCN, DVT* 🎬🎬

The Song of Bernadette Depicts the true story of a peasant girl who sees a vision of the Virgin Mary in a grotto at Lourdes in 1858. The girl is directed to dig at the grotto for water that will heal those who believe in its powers, much to the astonishment and concern of the townspeople. Based on Franz Werfel's novel. Directed with tenderness and carefully cast, and appealing to religious and sentimental susceptibilities, it was a box-office smash.
1943 156m/B Charles Bickford, Lee J. Cobb, Jennifer Jones, Vincent Price, Anne Revere, Gladys Cooper; *D:* Henry King; *M:* Alfred Newman. Academy Awards '43: Best Actress (Jones), Best Black and White Cinematography, Best Interior Decoration, Best Interior Decoration, Best Score; Nominations: Best Director (King), Best Film Editing, Best Picture, Best Screenplay, Best Sound, Best Supporting Actor (Bickford), Best Supporting Actress (Cooper); Golden Globe Awards '44: Best Actress—Drama (Jones), Best Director (King), Best Film—Drama. VHS, Beta, LV **$19.98** *FOX, IGP, BTV* 🎬🎬🎬

Song of Freedom The story of a black dockworker whose gift of voice is discovered by an opera impresario. After realizing a career as a concert performer, Robeson ventures to Africa to investigate his ancestry and finds he has royal roots. Robeson turns in a fine performance in what is otherwise an average film.
1938 70m/B *GB* Paul Robeson, Elizabeth Welch, George Mozart; *D:* J. Elder Wills. VHS, Beta, 3/4U, Special order formats **$29.95** *NOS, HHT, VYY* 🎬🎬½

Song of Nevada Rogers woos the high-society daughter (Evans, of course) of a rancher (Hall). Quintessential Roy-n-Dale. 🎵It's Love, Love, Love; New Moon Over Nevada; Hi Ho Little Dogies; The Harum Scarum Baron of the Harmonium; What Are We Going to Do?; A Cowboy Has to Yodel in the Morning.
1944 60m/B Roy Rogers, Dale Evans, Mary Lee; *D:* Joseph Kane. VHS, Beta **$9.95** *NOS, HHT, DVT* 🎬🎬½

Song of Norway A dramatization of the early life of the beloved Norwegian Romantic composer Edvard Grieg. Filmed against the beautiful mountains, waterfalls, and forests of Norway and based on the popular '40s stage production. The scenery is the best thing because Grieg's life was dull—even with cinematic liberties taken. 🎵Strange Music; The Song of Norway; The Little House; Be a Boy Again; Three There Were; A Rhyme and a Reason; Wrong to Dream; I Love You; The Solitary Wanderer; Hill of Dreams; Opening Concerto—The Life of the Wife of the Sailor; Solvejg's Song—Norwegian National

Anthem; Betrothal Hymn; Midsummer's Eve; A Welcome Toast; Freddie and His Fiddle; In the Hall of the Mountain King; At Christmas Time; Ribbons and Wrappings; When We Wed; John Heggerstrom.
1970 (G) 143m/C Toralv Maurstad, Florence Henderson, Edward G. Robinson, Christina Schollin, Frank Porretta, Oscar Homolka, Robert Morley, Harry Secombe; *D:* Andrew L. Stone. VHS, Beta **$59.98** *FOX* 🎬🎬

Song of Old Wyoming Three of those songs are presented in the course of an ordinary western about a spunky widow driving badmen out of Wyoming territory. La Rue plays the villainous Cheyenne Kid; this was before he got his own series as the heroic "Lash" La Rue.
1945 65m/C Eddie Dean, Sarah Padden, Lash LaRue, Jennifer Holt, Emmett Lynn, John Carpenter, Ian Keith, Bob Barron; *D:* Robert Tansey. VHS **$19.95** *NOS, HEG* 🎬½

Song of Texas When a young woman journeys west to visit her father at "his" ranch, Roy and his pals must keep the father's secret that he is just another hired hand. Whenever possible, everyone breaks into song.
1943 54m/B Roy Rogers, Harry Shannon, Pat Brady, Barton MacLane, Arline Judge; *D:* Joseph Kane. VHS, Beta **$19.95** *NOS, VYY, VCN* 🎬🎬

Song of the Exile A Chinese/Japanese student living in London in the early 1970's faces racial job discrimination and decides to return to her native Hong Kong. But on the home front, she and her family clash emotionally until daughter and mother come to a gradual understanding of how the past affects the present. In Cantonese and Japanese with with English subtitles.
1990 100m/C *CH* Maggie Cheung, Shwu-Fen Chang; *D:* Ann Hui. VHS **$79.95** *KIV, FCT, TAM* 🎬🎬½

Song of the Gringo Tex Ritter stars in his first singing western as a sheriff going after a gang of claim jumpers. *AKA:* The Old Corral.
1936 57m/B Tex Ritter, Monte Blue, Joan Woodbury, Fuzzy Knight, Richard Adams, Warner Richmond; *D:* John P. McCarthy. VHS, Beta **$19.95** *NOS, UHV, VCN* 🎬🎬

Song of the Islands Landing families in Hawaii feud over a beach, while the son of one (Mature) and the daughter of the other (Grable) fall in love. Plenty of songs, and dancing to display Grable's legs. Of course happiness and concord reign at the end. Songs include "O'Brien Has Gone Hawaiian," "Sing Me a Song of the Islands," and "What's Buzzin', Cousin?"
1942 75m/C Betty Grable, Victor Mature, Jack Oakie, Thomas Mitchell, Billy Gilbert; *D:* Walter Lang. VHS, Beta, LV **$19.98** *FOX, MLB* 🎬🎬½

Song of the Thin Man The sixth and final "Thin Man" mystery. This time Nick and Nora Charles (Powell and Loy) investigate the murder of a bandleader. Somewhat more sophisticated than its predecessor, due in part to its setting in the jazz music world. Sequel to "The Thin Man Goes Home."
1947 86m/B William Powell, Myrna Loy, Keenan Wynn, Dean Stockwell, Philip Reed, Patricia Morison, Gloria Grahame, Jayne Meadows, Don Taylor, Leon Ames, Ralph Morgan, Warner Anderson; *D:* Edward Buzzell. VHS, Beta **$19.98** *MGM* 🎬🎬

Song of the Trail Our hero saves an old man hornswoggled at cards.
1936 65m/B Kermit Maynard, George "Gabby" Hayes, Fuzzy Knight, Wheeler Oakman, Evelyn Brent, Andrea Leeds; *D:* Russell Hopton. VHS, Beta **$19.95** *NOS, VDM, VCN* 🎬½

A Song to Remember With music performed by Jose Iturbi, this film depicts the last years of the great pianist and composer Frederic Chopin, including his affair with famous author George Sand, the most renowned French woman of her day. Typically mangled film biography. ♫Valse in D Flat (Minute Waltz); Mazurka In B Flat, Opus 7, No. 1; Fantasie Impromptu, Opus 66; Etude In A Flat, Opus 25, No. 1 (partial); Polonaise In A Flat, Opus 53 (partial); Scherzo In B Flat Minor; Etude In C Minor, Opus 10, No. 12; Nocturne In C Minor, Opus 48, No. 1; Nocturn In E Flat, Opus 9, No. 2; Valse In A Flat, Opus 34, No. 1; Ballade In A Flat, Opus 47; Waltz In C Sharp Minor, Opus 64, No. 2; Berceuse In D Flat, Opus 57; Etude in E, Opus 10, No. 3.
1945 112m/C Cornel Wilde, Paul Muni, Merle Oberon, Nina Foch, George Coulouris; **D:** Charles Vidor. **VHS, Beta, LV** $19.95 COL, RDG, TVC *♪♪♪*

Song Without End This musical biography of 19th century Hungarian pianist/composer Franz Liszt is given the Hollywood treatment. The lavish production emphasizes Liszt's scandalous exploits with married women and his life among the royal courts of Europe rather than his musical talents. Features music from several composers including Handel, Beethoven, Bach and Schumann. This film marked the debut of Capucine. Director Vidor died during filming and Cukor stepped in, so there is a noticeable change in style. Although there is much to criticize in the story, the music is beautiful. ♫Mephisto Waltz; Spozalizio; Sonata In B Minor; Un Sospiro; Fantasy on Themes From "Rigoletto"; Consolation in D Flat; Liebestraum; Les Preludes; Piano Concerto No. 1; Hungarian Fantasy; Venezia e Napoli; Valse Oubliee; Pilgrim's Chorus; La Campanella; Rakoczy March; Pathetique Symphony; Rondo Capriccioso; Largo; Passacaglia In C Minor.
1960 130m/C Dirk Bogarde, Capucine, Genevieve Page, Patricia Morison, Ivan Desny, Martita Hunt, Lou Jacobi; **D:** Charles Vidor; **M:** Morris Stoloff, Harry Sukman. **VHS** $19.95 COL, TVC *♪♪½*

Songs and Bullets The Hound loves the zen-like simplicity of that title. The songs total five in number, the bullets somewhat more as hero cowboys battle rustlers in routine fashion. One of a handful of films (westerns and comedies) produced by funnyman Stan Laurel.
1938 57m/B Fred Scott, Al "Fuzzy" St. John, Alice Ardell, Charles King, Karl Hackett, Frank LaRue, Budd Buster; **D:** Sam Newfield. **VHS** $19.95 NOS, HEG *♪½*

Songwriter A high-falutin' look at the lives and music of two popular country singers with, aptly, plenty of country tunes written and performed by the stars. Singer-businessman Nelson needs Kristofferson's help keeping a greedy investor at bay. Never mind the plot; plenty of good music. ♫How Do You Feel About Foolin' Around?; Songwriter; Who'll Buy My Memories; Write Your Own Songs; Nobody Said It Was Going To Be Easy; Good Times; Eye of the Storm; Crossing the Border; Down to Her Socks; Under the Gun; Final Attraction.
1984 (R) 94m/C Willie Nelson, Kris Kristofferson, Rip Torn, Melinda Dillon, Lesley Ann Warren; **D:** Alan Rudolph. **VHS, Beta, LV** $12.95 COL *♪♪½*

Sonny and Jed An escaped convict and a free-spirited woman travel across Mexico pillaging freely, followed determinedly by shiny-headed lawman Savalas. Lame rip-off of the Bonnie and Clyde legend. **AKA:** La Banda J.&S. Cronaca Criminale del Far West.
1973 (R) 85m/C *IT* Tomas Milian, Telly Savalas, Susan George, Rosanna Janni, Laura Betti; **D:** Sergio Corbucci; **M:** Ennio Morricone. **VHS, Beta** $9.95 NO *♪*

Sonny Boy A transvestite and a psychopath adopt a young boy, training him to do their bidding, which includes murder.
1987 (R) 96m/C *IT* David Carradine, Paul Smith, Brad Dourif, Conrad Janis, Sydney Lassick, Savina Gersak, Alexandra Powers, Steve Carlisle, Michael Griffin; **D:** Robert Martin Carroll; **W:** Graeme Whifler. **VHS, Beta, LV** $89.98 TWE, MED Woof!

Sonora Stagecoach Okay sagebrush saga with an interesting lineup; two cowboys, a heroic Indian and a tough gal pilot escort a murder suspect in the title conveyance and manage to clear him when the real bad guys attack.
1944 61m/B Hoot Gibson, Bob Steele, Chief Thundercloud, Rocky Camron, Betty Miles, Glenn Strange, George Eldridge, Karl Hackett; **D:** Robert Tansey. **VHS** $19.95 NOS, HEG *♪♪*

Sons A Vietnam veteran's son joins the military, causing strains within the family.
1991 ?m/C VHS $79.95 LRP *♪♪*

Sons of Hercules in the Land of Darkness Hercules' sons kill dragons, fight titans, and generally flex up a storm.
1955 74m/B Dan Vadis. **VHS, Beta** $29.95 VYY *♪*

Sons of Katie Elder After their mother's death, four brothers are reunited. Wayne is a gunman; Anderson is a college graduate; silent Holliman is a killer; and Martin is a gambler. When they learn that her death might have been murder, they come together to devise a way to seek revenge on the killer. The town bullies complicate matters; the sheriff tells them to lay off. Especially strong screen presence by Wayne, in his first role following cancer surgery. One of the Duke's most popular movies of the '60s.
1965 122m/C John Wayne, Dean Martin, Earl Holliman, Michael Anderson Jr., Martha Hyer; **D:** Henry Hathaway. **VHS, Beta, LV** $14.95 PAR, TLF *♪♪♪*

Sons of Steel Two brothers, owners of a steel mill, lead vastly different lives. They raise their sons in their own images, causing problems.
1935 65m/B Charles Starrett, Polly Ann Young, William Bakewell, Walter Walker, Aileen Pringle, Holmes Herbert, Florence Roberts, Adolf Millar, Lloyd Ingraham; **D:** Charles Lamont. **VHS** $19.95 NOS *♪♪*

Sons of the Desert Laurel and Hardy in their best-written film. The boys try to fool their wives by pretending to go to Hawaii to cure Ollie of a bad cold when in fact, they are attending their lodge convention in Chicago. Also includes a 1935 Thelma Todd/Patsy Kelly short, "Top Flat." **AKA:** Sons of the Legion; Convention City; Fraternally Yours.
1933 73m/B Stan Laurel, Oliver Hardy, Mae Busch, Charley Chase, Dorothy Christy; **D:** William A. Seiter. **VHS, Beta** $19.95 MED, MLB, FFF *♪♪♪*

Sons of the Pioneers Small town sheriff Hayes hires cowboy Roy to rid town of outlaws.
1942 61m/B Roy Rogers, George "Gabby" Hayes, Maris Wrixon, Forrest Taylor; **D:** Joseph Kane. **VHS** $12.98 REP *♪♪*

Sooner or Later 13-year-old girl passes herself off as 16 with a local rock idol and must decide whether to go all the way.

1978 100m/C Rex Smith, Judd Hirsch, Denise Miller, Morey Amsterdam, Lynn Redgrave; **D:** Bruce Hart. **VHS, Beta** $19.95 STE, NWV *♪♪½*

Sophia Loren: Her Own Story Bio of Sophia Loren, watching her grow from a spindly child in working-class Naples to a world-renowned movie star, beauty queen, and mother. Loren plays herself and her mother in this tedious account. Scripted by Joanna Crawford from A.E. Hotchner's biography. Made for TV.
1980 150m/C Sophia Loren, Armand Assante, Ed Flanders, John Gavin; **D:** Mel Stuart. **VHS, Beta** $69.95 HBO *♪♪*

Sophie's Choice A haunting modern tragedy about Sophie Zawistowska, a beautiful Polish Auschwitz survivor settled in Brooklyn after World War II. She has intense relationships with a schizophrenic genius and an aspiring Southern writer. An artful, immaculately performed and resonant drama, with an astonishing, commanding performance by the versatile Streep; a chilling portrayal of the banality of evil. From the best-selling, autobiographical novel by William Styron.
1982 (R) 157m/C Meryl Streep, Kevin Kline, Peter MacNicol, Rita Karin, Stephen D. Newman, Josh Mostel; **D:** Alan J. Pakula. Academy Awards '82: Best Actress (Streep); Nominations: Best Adapted Screenplay, Best Cinematography, Best Costume Design, Best Original Score; Golden Globe Awards '83: Best Actress—Drama (Streep); Los Angeles Film Critics Association Awards '82: Best Actress (Streep); National Board of Review Awards '82: Best Actress (Streep); New York Film Critics Awards '82: Best Actress (Streep); National Society of Film Critics Awards '82: Best Actress (Streep). **VHS, Beta, LV** $19.98 FOX, SWC *♪♪♪½*

Sophisticated Gents Nine boyhood friends, members of a black athletic club, reunite after 25 years to honor their old coach and see how each of their lives has been affected by being black men in American society. Based on the novel "The Junior Bachelor Society" by John A. Williams. Originally made for television.
1981 200m/C Paul Winfield, Roosevelt Grier, Bernie Casey, Raymond St. Jacques, Thalmus Rasulala, Dick Anthony Williams, Ron O'Neal, Rosalind Cash, Denise Nicholas, Alfre Woodard, Melvin Van Peebles; **D:** Harry Falk; **W:** Melvin Van Peebles. **VHS** $89.95 XVC *♪♪♪*

Sorcerer To put out an oil fire, four men on the run in South America agree to try to buy their freedom by driving trucks loaded with nitroglycerin over dangerous terrain—with many natural and man-made obstacles to get in their way. Remake of "The Wages of Fear" is nowhere as good as the classic original, but has exciting moments. Puzzlingly retitled, which may have contributed to the box-office failure, and the near demise of Friedlein's directing career. **AKA:** Wages of Fear.
1977 (PG) 121m/C Roy Scheider, Bruno Cremer, Francisco Rabal, Souad Amidou, Ramon Bieri; **D:** William Friedkin. **VHS, LV** $79.95 MCA *♪♪½*

Sorcerer's Apprentice The classic fairy tale of a young boy who is hired by an evil sorcerer and eventually challenges him to a duel of magic.
1980 27m/C VHS, Beta $95.00 PYR *♪♪½*

Sorceress The Harris girls are sisters who use their powers of sorcery and fighting skills to battle demons, dragons, and evil. Yeah, sure. Really, they're just a pair of babes parading for the camera.
1982 (R) 83m/C Leigh Anne Harris, Lynette Harris, Bob Nelson, David Milbern, Bruno Rey, Anna De Sade; **D:** Brian Stuart. **VHS, Beta** $19.99 HBO Woof!

Sorceress A friar in medieval Europe feels insecure in his religious beliefs after encountering a woman who heals through ancient practices. Historically authentic and interestingly moody. Written, produced, and directed by two women: an art history professor and a collaborator of Francois Truffaut's. In French with English subtitles or dubbed.
1988 98m/C Tcheky Karyo, Christine Boisson, Jean Carmet; *D:* Suzanne Schiffman; *W:* Pamela Berger, Pamela Berger, Suzanne Schiffman. VHS $29.95 *MFV, TAM* 🎞🎞🎞

Sorority Babes in the Slimeball Bowl-A-Rama An ancient gremlin-type creature is released from a bowling alley, and the great-looking sorority babes have to battle it at the mall, with the help of a wacky crew of nerds. Horrible horror spoof shows plenty of skin.
1987 (R) 80m/C Linnea Quigley, Brinke Stevens, Andras Jones, John Wildman; *D:* David DeCoteau. Beta, LV *NO* 🎞🎞

Sorority Girl Camp classic in which beautiful co-ed Cabot is presented as a malicious rich kid involved in everything from petty fights to blackmail. Cheap production from the Corman factory.
1957 60m/B Susan Cabot, Dick Miller, Barbara Crane, June Kenney, Fay Baker, Jeane Wood; *D:* Roger Corman. VHS $9.95 *NLC* 🎞½

Sorority House Massacre A knife-wielding maniac stalks a sorority girl while her more elite sisters are away for the weekend. Yawn—haven't we seen this one before? Unfortunately for us we'll see it again because this one's followed by a sequel.
1986 (R) 74m/C Angela O'Neill, Wendy Martel, Pamela Ross, Nicole Rio; *D:* Carol Frank. VHS, Beta $79.95 *WAR* Woof!

Sorority House Massacre 2: Nighty Nightmare Another no-brainer with a different cast and director. This time around three lingerie-clad lovelies are subjected to the terrors of a killer their first night in their new sorority house. College just keeps getting tougher all the time.
1992 80m/C Melissa Moore, Robyn Harris, Stacia Zhivago, Dana Bentley; *D:* Jim Wynorski. VHS $89.98 *NHO* Woof!

Sorority House Scandals These strippers have nothing whatsoever to do with a sorority, unless you believe the on-stage announcer, who claims they're pledges. The only pledge these girls have taken is to wear as little as possible as often as possible.
1986 60m/C *D:* Tony Christopher. VHS, Beta $19.95 *AHV* Woof!

The Sorrow and the Pity A classic documentary depicting the life of a small French town and its resistance during the Nazi occupation. Lengthy, but totally compelling. A great documentary that brings home the atrocities of war. In French with English narration.
1971 265m/B *FR D:* Marcel Ophuls. VHS, Beta *COL, OM* 🎞🎞🎞½

Sorrowful Jones A ''Little Miss Marker'' remake, in which bookie Hope inherits a little girl as collateral for an unpaid bet. Good for a few yuks, but the original is much better.
1949 88m/B Bob Hope, Lucille Ball, William Demarest, Bruce Cabot, Thomas Gomez, Mary Jane Saunders; *D:* Sidney Lanfield. VHS, Beta $14.98 *MCA* 🎞🎞

Sorrows of Gin Eight-year-old girl searches for a sense of family amid her parents' lives. Her efforts to deal with alienation and emotional isolation lead her to run away from home. From a short story by John Cheever.

1979 60m/C Edward Herrmann, Sigourney Weaver, Mara Hobel, Eileen Heckart, Rachel Roberts. VHS, Beta *FLI* 🎞🎞½

The Sorrows of Satan Dempster and Cortez star as writers in love with each other, but Cortez can't take his poverty and the rejection of publishers. As he is about to end it all, the devil appears to him in disguise and makes an offer he can hardly refuse. He is introduced to London society and winds up marrying a fortune hunter. When he discovers this he goes back to Dempster, who still loves him, and vows to give up everything for her. Menjou then reveals himself to be the devil but Dempster's faith is so strong that the evil is vanquished.
1926 111m/B Adolphe Menjou, Carol Dempster, Ricardo Cortez, Lya de Putti; *D:* D.W. Griffith. VHS, Beta $32.95 *GPV* 🎞🎞🎞

Sorry, Wrong Number A wealthy, bedridden wife overhears two men plotting a murder on a crossed telephone line, and begins to suspect that one of the voices is her husband's. A classic tale of paranoia and suspense. Based on a radio drama by Louise Fletcher, who also wrote the screenplay. Remade for television in 1989.
1948 89m/B Barbara Stanwyck, Burt Lancaster, Ann Richards, Wendell Corey, Harold Vermilyea, Ed Begley Sr.; *D:* Anatole Litvak. VHS, Beta, LV $19.95 *PAR* 🎞🎞🎞½

Sorry, Wrong Number Cable remake of the 1948 Barbara Stanwyck thriller about a bed-ridden woman trying to get help after she realizes she's being stalked by a killer. Offers a new twist (drug dealing), but doesn't even approach the Stanwyck original. From the story by Lucille Fletcher.
1989 90m/C Loni Anderson, Hal Holbrook, Patrick Macnee, Miguel Fernandez, Carl Weintraub; *D:* Tony Wharmby; *W:* Ann Louise Bardach. VHS, Beta, LV $79.95 *PAR* 🎞½

S.O.S. Coast Guard A fiendish scientist creates a disintegrating gas and the U.S. Coast Guard must stop him from turning it over to unfriendly foreigners. Loads of action in this 12-part serial.
1937 224m/B Ralph Byrd, Bela Lugosi, Maxine Doyle. VHS, LV $29.98 *NOS, SNC, REP* 🎞🎞½

S.O.S. Pacific A seaplane crashes on a nuclear-test island and the survivors find that they have only five hours before they get nuked. Even though there is plenty of the usual action one would expect from such a film, the story really revolves around the characters. The British and U.S. versions have different endings.
1960 91m/B *GB* Eddie Constantine, Pier Angeli, Richard Attenborough, John Gregson, Eva Bartok; *D:* Guy Green. VHS $19.95 *NOS* 🎞🎞

S.O.S. Titanic The story of the Titanic disaster, recounted in flashback, in docudrama style. James Costigan's teleplay of the familiar story focuses on the courage that accompanied the horror and tragedy. Thoroughly professional, absorbing made-for-TV drama.
1979 98m/C David Janssen, Cloris Leachman, Susan St. James, David Warner, Ian Holm, Helen Mirren, Harry Andrews; *D:* Billy Hale. VHS, Beta $59.99 *HBO* 🎞🎞½

Sotto, Sotto A minor Wertmuller comedy about an Italian businessman who is constantly suspicious of his wife's fidelity. As it happens, she's attracted to another woman (de Santis). Massimo Wertmuller is Lina's nephew. Entertaining. In Italian with English subtitles.
1985 (R) 104m/C *IT* Enrico Montesano, Veronica Lario, Massimo Wertmuller, Luisa de Santis; *D:* Lina Wertmuller. VHS, Beta $69.95 *COL, APD, TAM* 🎞🎞½

Soul-Fire South Pacific high seas induce Cupid's arrow. Silent.
1925 100m/B Richard Barthelmess, Bessie Love, Walter Long, Arthur Metcalfe; *D:* John S. Robertson. VHS, Beta $24.95 *GPV, FCT* 🎞🎞

Soul Hustler A con man becomes rich and famous as a tent-show evangelist. Pathetic drivel.
1976 (PG) 81m/C Fabian, Casey Kasem, Larry Bishop, Nai Bonet; *D:* Burt Topper. VHS, Beta $39.95 *LIV, MON* Woof!

Soul Man Denied the funds he expected for his Harvard tuition, a young white student (Howell) masquerades as a black in order to get a minority scholarship. As a black student at Harvard, Howell learns about racism and bigotry. Pleasant lightweight comedy with romance thrown in (Chong is the black girl he falls for), and with pretensions to social satire that it never achieves.
1986 (PG-13) 101m/C C. Thomas Howell, Rae Dawn Chong, James Earl Jones, Leslie Nielsen, Arye Gross; *D:* Steve Miner. VHS, Beta, LV $9.95 *NWV, STE* 🎞🎞

Soul of Samurai Duo searches for the essence of kung fu but finds terror instead.
19?? 90m/C Kong Pun. VHS, Beta $29.95 *OCE* 🎞

Soul of the Beast An elephant repeatedly saves Bellamy from the villainous Beery. Silent with original organ score.
1923 77m/B Madge Bellamy, Cullen Landis, Noah Beery Sr. VHS, Beta, 8mm $29.99 *VYY, GPV* 🎞½

Soul Patrol Black newspaper reporter clashes with the all-white police department in a racist city.
1980 (R) 90m/C Nigel Davenport, Ken Gampu, Peter Dyneley; *D:* Christopher Rowley. VHS, Beta *SUN* 🎞

Soul Vengeance Black man is jailed and brutalized for crime he didn't commit and wants revenge when he's released. Many afros and platform shoes. Vintage blaxploitation. *AKA:* Welcome Home Brother Charles.
1975 91m/C Marlo Monte, Reatha Grey, Stan Kamber, Tiffany Peters, Ven Bigelow, Jake Carter; *W/D:* Jamaa Fanaka. VHS $39.95 *XVC* 🎞

Soultaker The title spirit is after a young couple's souls, and they have just an hour to reunite with their bodies after a car crash. Meanwhile, they're in limbo (literally) between heaven and earth. The ending's OK, if you can make it that far.
1990 (R) 94m/C Joe Estevez, Vivian Schilling, Gregg Thomsen, David Shark, Jean Reiner, Chuck Williams, Robert Z'Dar; *D:* Michael Rissi; *W:* Vivian Schilling. VHS, LV $89.95 *AIP* 🎞½

Sound of Horror The Hound usually admires creative efforts to keep budgets down, but this is too much (or too little). A dinosaur egg hatches, and out lashes an invisible predator. Yes, you'll have to use your imagination as archaeologists are slashed to bits by the no-show terror. *AKA:* El Sonido de la Muerte; Sound From a Million Years Ago; The Prehistoric Sound.
1964 85m/B *SP* James Philbrook, Arturo Fernandez, Soledad Miranda, Ingrid Pitt; *D:* Jose Antonio Nieves-Conde. VHS $15.95 *NOS, LOO* 🎞½

Sound of Love The mutual attraction between a deaf female hustler and a deaf race car driver leads to a deep relationship where they both learn about their own fears and desires.
1977 74m/C Celia de Burgh, John Jarratt. VHS, Beta $49.98 *SUE* 🎞

Sound of Murder A successful children's book writer wants to exact revenge on his adulterous wife, but is himself murdered before he can "execute" his plan.
1982 114m/C Michael Moriarty, Joanna Miles. **VHS, Beta $59.95** LIV ✍

The Sound of Music The classic film version of the Rodgers and Hammerstein musical based on the true story of the singing von Trapp family of Austria and their escape from the Nazis just before World War II. Beautiful Salzburg, Austria location photography and an excellent cast. Andrews, fresh from her Oscar for "Mary Poppins," is effervescent, in beautiful voice, but occasionally too good to be true. Not Rodgers & Hammerstein's most innovative or lyrical score, but lovely to hear and see. Plummer's singing was dubbed by Bill Lee. Marni Nixon, behind-the-scenes songstress for "West Side Story" and "My Fair Lady," makes her on-screen debut as one of the nuns. ♫I Have Confidence In Me; Something Good; The Sound of Music; Preludium; Morning Hymn; Alleluia; How Do You Solve A Problem Like Maria?; Sixteen, Going on Seventeen; My Favorite Things; Climb Every Mountain; The Lonely Goatherd; Do Re Mi; Edelweiss; So Long, Farewell; How Can Love Survive?.
1965 174m/C Julie Andrews, Christopher Plummer, Eleanor Parker, Peggy Wood, Charmian Carr, Heather Menzies, Marni Nixon; **D:** Robert Wise; **W:** Ernest Lehman; **M:** Richard Rodgers, Oscar Hammerstein. Academy Awards '65: Best Adapted Score, Best Director (Wise), Best Film Editing, Best Picture, Best Sound; Nominations: Best Actress (Andrews), Best Art Direction/Set Decoration (Color), Best Color Cinematography, Best Costume Design (Color), Best Supporting Actress (Wood); Directors Guild of America Awards '65: Best Director (Wise); Golden Globe Awards '66: Best Actress—Musical/Comedy (Andrews), Best Film—Musical/Comedy; National Board of Review Awards '65: 10 Best Films of the Year. **VHS, Beta, LV $24.98** FOX, BTV, RDG ✍✍✍✍

Sounder The struggles of a family of black sharecroppers in rural Louisiana during the Depression. When the father is sentenced to jail for stealing in order to feed his family, they must pull together even more, and one son finds education to be his way out of poverty. Tyson brings strength and style to her role, with fine help from Winfield. Moving and well made, with little sentimentality and superb acting from a great cast. Adapted from the novel by William Armstrong. Score was written by Taj Mahal. Director Ritt works well in this Southern-struggles genre; he went on to direct "Norma Rae" in 1979.
1972 (G) 105m/C Paul Winfield, Cicely Tyson, Kevin Hooks, Taj Mahal, Carmin Mathews, Carmen Best, Janet MacLachlan; **D:** Martin Ritt. Academy Awards '72 Nominations: Best Actor (Winfield), Best Actress (Tyson), Best Adapted Screenplay, Best Picture; National Board of Review Awards '72: 10 Best Films of the Year; National Society of Film Critics Awards '72: Best Actress (Tyson). **VHS, Beta, LV $14.95** KUI, PAR, PTB ✍✍✍✍

Sounds of Silence A young deaf boy fears that a killer arsonist may be at large—but can he prove it? One of a number of obscure oddities featuring former youth idol Donahue.
1991 108m/C Troy Donahue, Peter Nelson. **VHS, Beta** NO ✍✍

Soup for One Writer-director Kaufer's first film is a solid entry in the Woody Allenesque Manhattanite's angst genre. Young Jewish guy Rubinek pines for the woman of his dreams, finds her, is rejected, persists, gets her, wonders if she's what he wants

after all. If you like Woody Allen, this is worth seeing.
1982 (R) 84m/C Saul Rubinek, Marcia Strassman, Gerrit Graham, Richard Libertini, Andrea Martin; **D:** Jonathan Kaufer. **VHS, Beta $19.98** WAR ✍✍½

Sourdough Fur trapper Perry escapes the hustle and bustle of modern life by fleeing to the Alaskan wilderness. Near-plotless travelog depends heavily on scenery—and there's plenty of that, for sure.
1977 94m/C Gil Perry. **VHS, Beta** NO ✍✍

South Beach Two ex-football players turned private eyes are living the good life and partying it up in Miami Beach. However, their leisurely lifestyles are soon disrupted when they accept a mysterious challenge from the beautiful Vanity.
1992 93m/C Fred Williamson, Gary Busey, Vanity, Peter Fonda; **D:** Fred Williamson; **W:** Mark Montgomery; **M:** Joe Renzetti. **VHS $89.95** PSM ✍✍

South Bronx Heroes A police officer helps two children when they discover their foster home is the headquarters for a pornography ring. **AKA:** The Runaways; Revenge of the Innocents.
1985 (R) 105m/C Brendan Ward, Mario Van Peebles, Megan Van Peebles, Melissa Esposito, Martin Zurla, Jordan Abeles; **D:** William Szarka. **VHS, Beta** NO ✍½

South Central A low-budget urban drama set in a gang-infested L.A. neighborhood. Bobby is a young black man, and former gang leader, who has spent ten years in prison for murder. His wife has become a drug addict and his young son Jimmie has begun running with his dad's old gang. Now paroled, Bobby hopes to re-establish the bond with his son—enough to protect him from following in his nowhere-to-go-but-down footsteps. Worthy effort with an emotional ending. Feature debut of director Anderson. Based on the novel "Crips" by Donald Bakeer.
1992 (R) 99m/C Glenn Plummer, Carl Lumbly, Christian Coleman, LaRita Shelby, Byron Keith Minns; **W/D:** Steve Anderson. **VHS, Beta, LV $92.99** WAR, PMS ✍✍

South of Hell Mountain On the run from a gold mine robbery where they left 20 dead, the McHenry brothers meet a mother-daughter team that slows them down.
1970 (R) 87m/C Ann Stewart, Sam Hall, Nicol Britton; **D:** William Sachs, Louis Leahman. **VHS, Beta $59.95** MGM ✍½

South of Monterey Western adventure with the Cisco kid.
1947 63m/B Gilbert Roland, Martin Garralaga, Frank Yaconelli, Marjorie Riordan; **D:** William Nigh. **VHS, Beta $29.95** VCN ✍½

South of Pago Pago The unsuspecting natives of a tropical isle are exploited by a gang of pirates searching for a seabed of rare pearls. A notch up from most similar adventure outings, with great violent action and excellent cinematography. Leading lady Farmer was thought to be a rising star, but retired at 29 in 1942 because of alcoholism and spent some time in mental institutions. "Frances" (1982), with Jessica Lange, is based on her life.
1940 98m/B Victor McLaglen, Jon Hall, Frances Farmer, Gene Lockhart; **D:** Alfred E. Green. **VHS, Beta $12.95** LIV, MED ✍✍½

South of Reno A man living a secluded life in the desert dreams of moving to Reno and learns his wife is cheating on him. Odd, minimal plot. Impressive first feature for Polish director Rezyka, who cut his teeth on music videos.

1987 (R) 98m/C Jeffery Osterhage, Lisa Blount, Joe Phelan, Lewis Van Bergen, Julia Montgomery, Brandis Kemp, Danitza Kingsley, Mary Grace Canfield, Bert Remsen; **D:** Mark Rezyka. **VHS, LV $79.98** REP ✍✍½

South of St. Louis A peaceful cattle rancher turns renegade gunrunner during the Civil War when his stock is destroyed by Union guerrillas. Overplotted but exciting and action-packed western, with Smith dazzling in a plethora of costumes.
1948 88m/C Joel McCrea, Zachary Scott, Victor Jory, Douglas Kennedy, Alexis Smith, Alan Hale Jr., Dorothy Malone; **D:** Ray Enright. **VHS $14.95** REP ✍✍½

South of Santa Fe Mexican rebels give the hero a hard time in this standard Western.
1932 60m/B Bob Steele, Janis Elliott, Chris-Pin Martin, Jack Clifford, Eddie Dunn, Robert Burns, Hank Bell, Allan Garcia; **D:** Bert Glennon. **VHS $19.95** NOS ✍

South of Santa Fe Rogers and friends take on the mob—yes, the mob, armed with machine guns and airplanes—after they are falsely implicated in a crime. In lulls between the rootin' tootin' gunfights, Rogers belts out "We're Headin' for the Home Corral," "Down the Trail," and "Open Range Ahead."
1942 60m/B Roy Rogers, George "Gabby" Hayes, Linda Hayes, Paul Fix, Judy Clark; **D:** Joseph Kane. **VHS, Beta, 3/4U, Special order formats $19.95** NOS, DVT, CAB ✍✍

South of the Border Autry and Burnette are government agents sent to Mexico to investigate a possible revolution instigated by foreign agents. Propaganda-heavy singing western appeared just before the U.S. entered World War II; did well at the box office and boosted Autry's career.
1939 70m/B Gene Autry, Smiley Burnette. **VHS, Beta $19.88** CCB, VCN ✍½

South of the Rio Grande The Cisco Kid rides again as he comes to the aid of a rancher whose horses were stolen. Garden-variety law-and-order western.
1945 60m/B Duncan Renaldo; **D:** Lambert Hillyer. **VHS, Beta $12.95** UHV ✍½

South Pacific A young American Navy nurse and a Frenchman fall in love during World War II. Expensive production included much location shooting in Hawaii. Based on Rodgers and Hammerstein's musical; not as good as the play, but pretty darn good still. The play in turn was based on James Michener's novel "Tales of the South Pacific." ♫My Girl Back Home; Dites-Moi; Bali Ha'i; Happy Talk; A Cockeyed Optimist; Soliloquies; Some Enchanted Evening; Bloody Mary; I'm Gonna Wash That Man Right Out of My Hair; There Is Nothing Like a Dame; Younger Than Springtime; Honey Bun; You've Got To Be Carefully Taught; I'm In Love With a Wonderful Guy; This Nearly Was Mine; Two Soliloquies; Wonderful Guy.
1958 167m/C Mitzi Gaynor, Rossano Brazzi, Ray Walston, France Nuyen, John Kerr, Juanita Hall, Tom Laughlin; **D:** Joshua Logan; **M:** Richard Rodgers, Oscar Hammerstein; **V:** Giorgio Tozzi. Academy Awards '58: Best Sound; Nominations: Best Color Cinematography; Academy Awards '58: Best Original Score. **VHS, Beta, LV $19.98** FOX, RDG, HMV ✍½

South Seas Massacre A cop and a prisoner, shackled together, try to survive modern-day pirates, natives, and each other. They may make it through, but viewers may wish they didn't.
19?? 60m/C Troy Donahue; **D:** Pablo Santiago. **VHS, Beta $59.95** PSM Woof!

Southern Comfort A group of National Guardsmen are on weekend maneuvers in the swamps of Louisiana. They run afoul of some of the local Cajuns, and are marked for death in this exciting and disturbing thriller. Booth is excellent in a rare exploration of a little-understood way of life. Lots of blood. If you belong to the National Guard, this could make you queasy.
1981 (R) 106m/C Powers Boothe, Keith Carradine, Fred Ward, Franklyn Seales, Brion James, T.K. Carter, Peter Coyote; *D:* Walter Hill. **VHS, Beta, LV** $29.95 SUE, HHE 🎞🎞🎞

A Southern Yankee Skelton plays a bumbling bellboy who ends up as a Union spy during the Civil War. Enjoyable comedy, thanks largely to the off-screen input of Buster Keaton. *AKA:* My Hero.
1948 90m/B Red Skelton, Brian Donlevy, Arlene Dahl, George Coulouris, Lloyd Gough, John Ireland, Minor Watson, Charles Dingle, Art Baker, Reed Hadley, Arthur Space, Addison Richards, Joyce Compton, Paul Harvey, Jeff Corey; *D:* Edward Sedgwick. **VHS, Beta** $19.98 MGM 🎞🎞½

The Southerner A man used to working for others is given some land by an uncle and decides to pack up his family and try farming for himself. They find hardships as they struggle to support themselves. A superb, naturalistic celebration of a family's fight to survive amid all the elements. From the story "Hold Autumn in Your Hand," by George Sessions Perry. The great novelist William Faulkner had an uncredited hand in the script. He thought Renoir the best contemporary director, and later said "The Southerner" gave him more pleasure than any of his other Hollywood work (though this is faint praise; Faulkner is said to have hated Hollywood).
1945 91m/B Zachary Scott, Betty Field, Beulah Bondi, Norman Lloyd, Bunny Sunshine, Jay Gilpin, Estelle Taylor, Blanche Yurka, Percy Kilbride, J. Carroll Naish; *D:* Jean Renoir. Academy Awards '45 Nominations: Best Director (Renoir), Best Sound, Best Original Score; National Board of Review Awards '45: Best Director (Renoir); Venice Film Festival '46: Best Film. **VHS, Beta, 8mm, 3/4U, Special order formats** $19.95 NOS, PSM, VYY 🎞🎞🎞🎞

Southward Ho! In the first western to team Rogers with sidekick Gabby Hayes, they portray ranchers investigating bloodshed in their valley. Roy meanwhile yodelin' four tunes. Fun outing.
1939 56m/B Roy Rogers, George "Gabby" Hayes. **VHS, Beta, 3/4U, Special order formats** $19.95 NOS, VCN, CAB 🎞🎞

Souvenir A German soldier returns to France after World War II to find the woman he left behind and the daughter he never saw. Might have been good, but too melodramatic and overwrought, with lukewarm acting.
1988 (R) 93m/C Christopher Plummer, Catherine Hicks, Christopher Cazenove, Michael Lonsdale; *D:* Geoffrey Reeve. **VHS, Beta, LV** PAR 🎞🎞

Soviet Spy A French docu-drama written by Hans Otto Meissner, Chief of Protocol at the German Embassy in Tokyo during WWII, about the journalist Richard Sorge, a German hanged in 1944 for supplying information to the Soviets. In French with subtitles.
1961 130m/B FR **VHS, Beta** $19.95 FCT 🎞🎞

Soy un Golfo A lazy bum is inspired to do something with his life by a pretty girl who he later finds out is his brother's fiancee.
1965 90m/B MX Adalberto "Resortes" Martinez, Luz Maria Aguilar, Che Reyes. **VHS, Beta** $39.95 MAD 🎞🎞

Soylent Green In the 21st Century, hard-boiled police detective Heston investigates a murder and discovers what soylent green—the people's principal food—is made of. Robinson's final film is a disappointing end to a great career. Its view of the future and of human nature is relentlessly dark. Don't watch it with kids.
1973 (PG) 95m/C Charlton Heston, Leigh Taylor-Young, Chuck Connors, Joseph Cotten, Edward G. Robinson, Brock Peters; *D:* Richard Fleischer. **VHS, Beta, LV** $59.95 MGM 🎞🎞½

Space Monster Really bad, low-budget flick with a rubber monster and a climactic crash into a "sea of monsters" which is really a fish tank full of crabs. Ultra cheap production with handed down cast and props. *AKA:* First Woman Into Space; Voyage Beyond the Sun.
1964 ?m/B **VHS** $20 SMW Woof!

Space Mutiny Spaceship falls under the attack of the mutinous Kalgan. To keep everyone from being sold into slavery, a small band of loyal passengers strike back. Will they be successful in thwarting the attack? Who cares?
1988 (PG) 93m/C Reb Brown, James Ryan, John Phillip Law, Cameron Mitchell; *D:* David Winters. **VHS, Beta** $79.95 AIP 🎞

Space: 1999 Landau and Bain star as the leaders of Moonbase Alpha, a scientific outpost which is hurled out of orbit by a nuclear explosion. In "Voyager's Return" the crew of Moonbase Alpha discover the original Voyager probe and excitedly prepare to extract its vast knowledge of the universe. To their horror, they discover that it has somehow been transformed into a planet-destroying monster. Bitter aliens are coming to exact their revenge on the machine and the crew is caught in the middle! Additional episodes available.
1975 52m/C GB Martin Landau, Barbara Bain, Barry Morse, Nick Tate, Jeremy Kemp, Barry Stokes, Alex Scott, Lawrence Trimble; *D:* Bob Kellett. **VHS, LV** $14.99 MOV 🎞

Space: 1999—Alien Attack After an explosion on the moon, Moonbase Alpha loses contact with Earth forever. Pilot episode of the popular British sci-fi series.
1979 109m/C GB Martin Landau, Barbara Bain, Barry Morse, Nick Tate, Roy Dotrice, Philip Madoc, Lou Satton, Eric Carte; *D:* Lee H. Katzin. **VHS, Beta** $39.95 LIV 🎞🎞🎞

Space Ninja: Sword of the Space Ark A young fighter pilot returns home to find his planet under siege and his family dead. He vows to seek revenge and sets out to destroy the evil emperor who is wreaking such havoc.
1981 75m/C *D:* Bunker Jenkins. **VHS, Beta** $39.95 LIV 🎞½

Space Patrol Buzz Corey, Commander-in-Chief of the Space Patrol, tries to maintain interplanetary peace and protect the people of Earth's neighboring planets. These episodes television series include previews of coming attractions from classic science fiction films. Additional episodes are available.
1950 120m/B Edward Kemmer, Lyn Osborn. **VHS, Beta** $19.95 RHI, MED, MOV 🎞½

Space Rage A criminal sentenced to life on a prison planet leads a revolt of the inmates. Lame, formula western set in outer space.
1986 (R) 78m/C Michael Pare, Richard Farnsworth, John Laughlin, Lee Purcell; *D:* Conrad Palmisano. **VHS, Beta** $19.98 LIV 🎞

Space Raiders A plucky 10-year-old blasts off into a futuristic world of intergalactic desperados, crafty alien mercenaries, starship battles and cliff-hanging dangers. Recycled special effects (from producer Corman's movie factory) and plot (lifted near-whole from "Star Wars"). *AKA:* Star Child.
1983 (PG) 84m/C Vince Edwards, David Mendenhall; *D:* Howard R. Cohen. **VHS, Beta** $19.98 WAR 🎞🎞

Space Riders Action-adventure about the world's championship motorcycle race, with a rock soundtrack featuring Duran Duran, Simple Minds and Melba Moore.
1983 (PG) 93m/C Barry Sheene, Gavan O'Herlihy, Toshiya Ito, Stephanie McLean, Sayo Inaba; *D:* Joe Massot. **VHS, Beta** $79.99 HBO Woof!

Space Soldiers Conquer the Universe From the "Flash Gordon" serial. The evil Emperor Ming introduces a horrible plague from outer space called "The Purple Death." Dr. Zarkov, Dale, and Flash Gordon travel from the frozen wastes of Frigia to the palaces of Mongo and must take risk after risk. Twelve chapters at 20 minutes each.
1940 240m/B Buster Crabbe, Charles Middleton, Carol Hughes. **VHS, Beta, 3/4U, Special order formats** $49.95 NOS, CAB 🎞🎞

Spaceballs A humorous Brooks parody of recent science fiction pictures, mostly notably "Star Wars," with references to "Alien," the "Star Trek series," and "The Planet of the Apes." Disappointingly tame and tentative, but chuckle-laden enough for Brooks fans. The great man himself appears in two roles, including puny wise man/wise guy Yogurt.
1987 (PG) 96m/C Mel Brooks, Rick Moranis, John Candy, Bill Pullman, Daphne Zuniga, Dick Van Patten, John Hurt, George Wyner, Joan Rivers, Lorene Yarnell, Sal Viscuso, Stephen Tobolowsky, Dom DeLuise; *D:* Mel Brooks. **VHS, Beta, LV** $19.95 MGM 🎞🎞½

SpaceCamp Gang o'teens and their instructor at the US Space Camp are accidentally launched on a space shuttle, and then must find a way to return to Earth. Hokey plot, subpar special effects; why bother? Well, it is "inspirational".
1986 (PG) 115m/C Kate Capshaw, Tate Donovan, Leaf Phoenix, Kelly Preston, Larry B. Scott, Tom Skerritt, Lea Thompson, Terry O'Quinn; *D:* Harry Winer; *M:* John Williams. **VHS, Beta, LV** $29.98 LIV, VES, IME 🎞🎞

Spaced Invaders Five ultra-cool aliens crash-land in a small midwestern town at Halloween. Local denizens mistake them for trick-or-treaters. Poorly made and a waste of time.
1990 (PG) 102m/C Douglas Barr, Royal Dano, Ariana Richards, Kevin Thompson, Jimmy Briscoe, Tony Cox, Debbie Lee Carrington, Tommy Madden; *D:* Patrick Read Johnson. **VHS, Beta, LV** $19.99 TOU 🎞½

Spaced Out Naughty sci-fi sex comedy that parodies everything from "Star Wars" to "2001," though not very well. The sultry female aliens are visually pleasing, though. Watch this one with the sound turned off. *AKA:* Outer Reach.
1980 (R) 85m/C Barry Stokes, Glory Annen; *D:* Norman J. Warren. **VHS, Beta** $19.99 HBO Woof!

Spacehunter: Adventures in the Forbidden Zone Galactic bounty hunter agrees to rescue three damsels held captive by a cyborg. Strauss ain't no Harrison Ford. Filmed in 3-D, but who cares?

1983 (PG) 90m/C *CA* Peter Strauss, Molly Ringwald, Michael Ironside, Ernie Hudson, Andrea Marcovicci; *D:* Lamont Johnson. **VHS, Beta, LV** $12.95 *COL* ✰✰½

Spaceship Misguided attempt to spoof creature-features. Mad scientist tries to protect kindly monster from crazed crew. Not very funny, with the exception of the song-and-dance routine by the monster. *AKA:* The Creature Wasn't Nice.
1981 (PG) 88m/C Cindy Williams, Bruce Kimmel, Leslie Nielsen, Gerrit Graham, Patrick Macnee, Ron Kurowski; *D:* Bruce Kimmel. **VHS** $69.98 *LIV* ✰✰½

Spaceways Scientist Duff is beset by all sorts of troubles: his experimental rockets explode, his wife has an affair with an ambitious scientist, and when they disappear together, he's accused of killing them and placing their bodies in the exploded rocket. All in all, a pretty bad (and long) day for our hero. Why should we suffer through it with him?
1953 76m/B Howard Duff, Eva Bartok, Cecile Cheyreau, Andrew Osborn; *D:* Terence Fisher. **VHS, Beta, LV** *MLB* ✰✰½

Spaghetti House A handful of waiters are held hostage by ruthless killers in this innocuous but worthless Italian comedy. Dubbed.
1982 103m/C *IT* Nino Manfredi, Rita Tushingham; *D:* Giullo Paradisi. **VHS, Beta** $29.95 *TAM* ✰½

Spaghetti Western A farmer and a publisher take on the vile oil baron who is taking over the town. A parody-or is it?—of Eastwoodian B-grade spaghetti westerns. No director credited.
1969 90m/C Franco Nero, Martin Balsam, Sterling Hayden. **VHS, Beta** $19.98 *VDC* ✰½

Spalding Gray: Terrors of Pleasure The ultra-cool Gray tells the story of one man's dream to own land in his own inimitable way. HBO comedy special.
1988 60m/C Spalding Gray; *D:* Thomas Schlamme. **VHS, Beta** $39.99 *HBO* ✰✰✰

Spangles Silent circus drama.
1926 58m/B Marion Nixon, Hobart Bosworth, Pat O'Malley, Gladys Brockwell; *D:* Frank O'Connor. **VHS, Beta** $14.95 *GPV* ✰

The Spaniard's Curse When a man is convicted for a murder he did not commit, he puts a curse on the judge and jury responsible. Mysteriously, the marked people begin dying. Is he responsible? Then he dies and the mystery thickens. Intriguing but sloppy murder mystery.
1958 80m/B *GB* Tony Wright, Lee Patterson, Michael Hordern, Ralph Truman, Henry Oscar; *D:* Ralph Kemplen. **VHS, Beta** $16.95 *SNC* ✰✰½

The Spanish Gardener A boy in a prominent family spends more time with the gentle gardner than with the domineering father, so dad arranges for his rival to be framed and sent to prison. An affecting British adaptation of the A.J. Cronin novel, turned into a showcase for Bogarde in the title role.
1957 95m/C Dirk Bogarde, Jon Whiteley, Michael Hordern, Cyril Cusack, Maureen Swanson, Lyndon Brook, Josephine Griffin, Bernard Lee; *D:* Philip Leacock. **VHS** $19.95 *NOS, VEC* ✰✰✰

The Spanish Main Typical, gusto-laden swashbuckler, RKO's first in Technicolor. Evil Spanish governor Slezak captures Dutch crew led by Henreid. They escape and kidnap his fiancee (O'Hara) off a ship coming from Mexico. Henreid forces her to marry him, but his crew uses the might of the

armada and returns O'Hara to Slezak behind Henreid's back. Wow!
1945 100m/C Paul Henreid, Maureen O'Hara, Walter Slezak, Binnie Barnes, John Emery, Barton MacLane; *D:* Frank Borzage. **LV** $39.95 *IME* ✰✰½

Spare Parts Guests at a remote hotel discover that it is run by black marketeers who kill guests and sell the body parts. Of course, they don't bother signing out.
1985 108m/C Judith Speidel, Wolf Roth. **VHS, Beta** $69.95 *VMK* Woof!

Sparkle The saga of three singing sisters struggling to rise to the top of the charts in the 1950s. Sound familiar? Well done but cliched fictional version of the Supremes' career. McKee shines. Alcohol, drugs, and mobsters get in the way. Curtis Mayfield wrote the excellent musical score.
1976 (PG) 98m/C Irene Cara, Lonette McKee, Dwan Smith, Philip Michael Thomas, Mary Alice, Dorian Harewood, Tony King; *D:* Sam O'Steen. **VHS, Beta** $39.98 *WAR* ✰✰½

Sparrows Set to William Perry's score, a woman cares for nine orphan children on an impoverished farm, warding off starvation and kidnappers. Silent melodrama features notable performance by Pickford.
1926 81m/B Mary Pickford, Roy Stewart, Gustav von Seyffertitz; *D:* William Beaudine. **VHS, Beta, LV** $19.95 *NOS, CCB, DVT* ✰✰✰

Spartacus The true story of a gladiator who leads other slaves in a rebellion against the power of Rome in 73 B.C. The rebellion is put down and the rebels are crucified. Douglas, whose political leanings are amply on display herein, also served as executive producer, surrounding himself with the best talent available. Magnificent climactic battle scene features 8,000 real, live Spanish soldiers to stunning effect. A version featuring Kubrick's "director's cut" is also available, featuring a restored, controversial homoerotic bath scene with Olivier and Curtis. A box-office triumph that gave Kubrick much-desired financial independence.
1960 (PG-13) 196m/C Kirk Douglas, Laurence Olivier, Jean Simmons, Tony Curtis, Charles Laughton, Herbert Lom, Nina Foch, Woody Strode, Peter Ustinov, John Gavin, John Ireland; *D:* Stanley Kubrick. Academy Awards '60: Best Art Direction/Set Decoration (Color), Best Color Cinematography, Best Costume Design (Color), Best Supporting Actor (Ustinov); Nominations: Best Film Editing. **VHS, Beta, LV** $14.95 *MCA, APD, BTV* ✰✰✰

Spasms Reed is the unfortunate big game hunter who encounters The Demon Serpent, known as N'Gana Simbu, the deadliest snake in the world. Lame-brained horror fantasy; the producers should have released the nifty Tangerine Dream soundtrack and chucked the movie. *AKA:* Death Bite.
1982 (R) 92m/C *CA* Peter Fonda, Oliver Reed; *D:* William Fruet. **VHS, Beta** $19.99 *HBO* Woof!

The Spawning The sequel to "Piranha." At Club Elysium the main course is the vacationers themselves.
1982 (R) 88m/C Steve Marachuk; *D:* James Cameron. **VHS, Beta, LV** *NO* ✰

Speak Easily Keaton is bored with his dull life as a college professor. Durante tries to spice things up with a phony inheritance letter, and Keaton decides to spend his supposed money backing a stage show. Keaton is the star, but Durante steals the show. Great supporting cast.
1932 82m/B Buster Keaton, Jimmy Durante, Ruth Selwyn, Thelma Todd, Hedda Hopper, Sidney Toler, Lawrence Grant, Henry Armetta, Edward Brophy; *D:* Edward Sedgwick. **VHS** $19.95 *MGM, GPV, NOS* ✰✰½

Speak of the Devil A New Orleans evangelist who seduces his followers moves to Los Angeles and strikes a bargain with Satan. Exploitative, unthinking spoof of Swaggart/Bakker scandals of recent years.
1990 99m/C Robert Elarton, Jean Miller, Bernice Tamara Gor, Louise Sherill, Walter Kay, Shawn Patrick Greenfield. **VHS** $79.95 *AIP* ✰

Speaking Parts VCR-obsessed laundry worker and another woman battle for the attention of bit-part actor McManus who works in ritzy hotel. Scripted by Canadian director Egoyan, it's a telling picture of the inextricable nature of modern technology.
1989 92m/C *CA* Michael McManus, Arsinee Khanjian, David Hemblen; *D:* Atom Egoyan. **VHS, LV** $79.95 *FXL, FCT, TAM* ✰✰✰

Special Bulletin A pacifistic terrorist threatens to blow up Charleston, South Carolina with a nuclear warhead. Done quite well in docu-drama style as a TV news bulletin. Interesting examination of the media's treatment of dramatic events written by director Zwick (of "thirtysomething")and Marshall Herskovitz. Top-notch made-for-TV fare.
1983 105m/C Ed Flanders, Christopher Allport, Kathryn Walker, Roxanne Hart; *D:* Edward Zwick. **VHS, Beta** $59.95 *KRT, LHV, WAR* ✰✰✰

A Special Day The day of a huge rally celebrating Hitler's visit to Rome in 1939 serves as the backdrop for an affair between weary housewife Loren and lonely, unhappy homosexual radio announcer Mastroianni. Good performances from two thorough pros make a depressing film well worth watching. In Italian with English subtitles or dubbed. *AKA:* Una Giornata Speciale; The Great Day.
1977 105m/C *IT* Sophia Loren, Marcello Mastroianni; *D:* Ettore Scola. Academy Awards '77 Nominations: Best Actor (Mastroianni), Best Foreign Language Film; Golden Globe Awards '78: Best Foreign Film; National Board of Review Awards '77: 5 Best Foreign Films of the Year. **VHS, Beta, LV** $59.95 *COL, APD, TAM* ✰✰✰

Special Delivery Three unemployed Vietnam veterans decide to rob a bank but their getaway plans go awry. Svenson, the only robber who escapes, stashes the cash in a mailbox only to have it discovered by nutty artist, Shepherd, and crooked barkeep Gwynne.
1976 (PG) 99m/C Bo Svenson, Cybill Shepherd, Vic Tayback, Michael C. Gwynne, Tom Atkins, Sorrell Booke, Deidre Hall, Gerrit Graham, Jeff Goldblum; *D:* Paul Wendkos. **VHS, Beta** $69.98 *LIV, VES* ✰✰½

Special Effects A desperate movie director murders a young actress, then makes a movie about her death. Solid, creepy premise sinks in the mire of flawed execution; a good film about Hollywood ego trips and obsession is lurking inside overdone script.
1985 (R) 103m/C Zoe Tamerlis, Eric Bogosian, Brad Rijn, Bill Oland, Richard Greene; *W/D:* Larry Cohen. **VHS, Beta** $24.98 *SUE, NLC* ✰✰

Special Forces Eight specially trained soldiers drop behind enemy lines to rescue prisoners of war in World War II. *AKA:* Hell in Normandy.
1968 90m/C Peter Lee Lawrence, Guy Madison, Erika Blanc, Tony Norton. **VHS, Beta** *NO* ✰

Special Olympics A father attempts to care for his three sons, one of whom is mentally retarded, following the death of his wife. Made for television.
1978 104m/C Charles Durning, Philip Brown, George Parry, Irene Tedrow, Mare Winningham, Herb Edelman, Debra Winger, Constance McCashin; *D:* Lee Philips. **VHS, Beta** $59.95 *GEM* ✰

The Specialist Lawyer West thinks he has seduced stunning Capri, but she has lured him into her clutches—she's been hired to kill him. Campy crud. It's old home week for '60s TV alums: West was Batman; bailiff Moore was Mr. Kimbell on Green Acres.
1975 (R) 93m/C Adam West, John Anderson, Anna Capri, Alvy Moore; *D:* Hikmet Avedis. **VHS, Beta $19.95** *VID* ✍½

The Speckled Band Set in 1930, this early talkie is a Sherlock Holmes adventure wherein the great detective must solve the mysterious death of a young woman. Massey makes his screen debut as Holmes, making the sleuth cynical, unhappy and pessimistic. Interesting prototypical Holmes case, faithful to the like-titled Conan Doyle story.
1931 84m/B Raymond Massey, Lyn Harding, Athole Stewart, Angela Baddeley, Nancy Price; *D:* Jack Raymond. **VHS, Beta, 8mm $16.95** *SNC, NOS, VYY* ✍✍✍

Specters Archaeologists excavating the Roman catacombs break open the gates of hell. Hellishly confused plot is unoriginal, to boot; decent production values hardly compensate. *AKA:* Spettri.
1987 95m/C Donald Pleasence, John Pepper, Erna Schurer; *D:* Marcello Avallone. **VHS, Beta $79.95** *IMP* ✍

The Spectre of Edgar Allen Poe The horridly fictionalized writer of horror fiction visits the asylum where his love Lenore is being held, and discovers murder and torture. Based very loosely on Poe's own torments. Dorky, rip-off horror.
1973 87m/C Cesar Romero, Robert Walker Jr., Tom Drake; *D:* Mohy Quandour. **VHS, Beta $49.95** *UNI* ✍½

Spectre of the Rose Strange film set in the world of ballet. An impressario contends with an over-the-hill ballerina and a young male dancer with a deadly affinity for knives. Written, directed, and produced by Hecht.
1946 90m/B Judith Anderson, Michael Chekhov, Ivan Kirov, Viola Essen, Lionel Stander; *W/D:* Ben Hecht. **VHS, LV $19.98** *REP* ✍✍½

The Speed Spook Silent ghost races car and steals documents.
1924 85m/B Johnny Hines, Warner Richmond; *D:* Charles Hines. **VHS, Beta $19.95** *GPV* ✍

Speed Zone Comic celebrities take over a high speed auto race when a redneck cop locks up the real drivers. Unfunny sequel to "Cannonball Run."
1988 (PG) 96m/C Melody Anderson, Peter Boyle, Tim Matheson, Donna Dixon, John Candy, Eugene Levy, Joe Flaherty, Matt Frewer, Shari Belafonte-Harper, Tom Smothers, Dick Smothers, Brooke Shields, Lee Van Cleef, Jamie Farr, John Schneider, Michael Spinks; *D:* Jim Drake. **VHS, Beta, LV $89.95** *MED* ✍

Speeding Up Time An angry man wants to ice the dudes who torched his mother's tenement.
1971 (R) 90m/C Winston Thrash, Pamela Donegan. **VHS, Beta** *NO* ✍

Speedtrap Typical chase scenes and cross-gender sparring characterize this tale of a private detective and a police officer pursuing car thieves. Good cast and fun chemistry between the leads; weak, typical script.
1978 (PG) 101m/C Joe Don Baker, Tyne Daly, Richard Jaeckel, Robert Loggia, Morgan Woodward, Timothy Carey; *D:* Earl Bellamy. **VHS, Beta $69.95** *MED* ✍✍

Speedway Elvis the stock car driver finds himself being chased by Nancy the IRS agent during an important race. Will Sinatra keep to the business at hand? Or will the King melt her heart? Some cameos by real-life auto racers. Songs include "Speedway," "He's Your Uncle, Not Your Dad," and "There Ain't Nothing Like a Song." Watch for a young Teri Garr. Movie number 27 for Elvis.
1968 90m/C Elvis Presley, Nancy Sinatra, Bill Bixby, Gale Gordon, William Schallert, Carl Ballantine, Ross Hagen; *Cameos:* Richard Petty, Cale Yarborough, Teri Garr; *D:* Norman Taurog. **VHS, Beta $19.95** *MGM* ✍✍

Speedy Lloyd comes to the rescue when the last horse car in New York City, operated by his fiance's grandfather, is stolen by a gang. Thoroughly phoney, fun pursuit/action comedy shot on location. Look for a brief appearance by Babe Ruth.
1928 72m/B Harold Lloyd, Bert Woodruff, Ann Christy; *D:* Ted Wilde. **VHS, Beta** *TLF* ✍✍✍

The Spell An obese fifteen-year-old girl has the power to inflict illness and death on the people she hates. Necessarily mean-spirited, if we're being asked to sympathize with the main character. Therein lies the rub. Made for TV.
1977 86m/C Lee Grant, James Olson, Susan Myers, Barbara Bostock, Lelia Goldoni, Helen Hunt; *D:* Lee Philips. **VHS, Beta $14.99** *GKK, WOV* ✍

The Spellbinder L.A. lawyer Daly falls in love with a woman he saves from an attacker, then discovers she's a fugitive from a satanic cult that wants her back. Unoriginal, but slickly made.
1988 (R) 96m/C Timothy Daly, Kelly Preston, Rick Rossovich, Audra Lindley; *D:* Janet Greek. **VHS, Beta $19.98** *FOX* ✍½

Spellbound Broken-hearted over dead girlfriend, young college student attempts to contact her through spiritualism, succeeds, and suffers nervous breakdown. *AKA:* The Spell of Amy Nugent.
1941 75m/B *GB* Derek Farr, Vera Lindsay, Frederick Leister, Hay Petrie, Felix Aylmer; *D:* John Harlow. **VHS $19.98** *SNC* ✍✍

Spellbound Peck plays an amnesia victim accused of murder. Bergman plays the psychiatrist who uncovers his past through Freudian analysis and ends up falling in love with him. One of Hitchcock's finest films of the 1940s, with a riveting dream sequence designed by Salvador Dali. Full of classic Hitchcock plot twists and Freudian imagery. Based on Francis Bleeding's novel "The House of Dr. Edwardes."
1945 111m/B Ingrid Bergman, Gregory Peck, Leo G. Carroll, Michael Chekhov, Wallace Ford, Rhonda Fleming, Regis Toomey; *D:* Alfred Hitchcock; *M:* Miklos Rozsa. Academy Awards '45: Best Score; Nominations: Best Actor (Chekhov), Best Black and White Cinematography, Best Director (Hitchcock), Best Picture. **VHS, Beta, LV $19.98** *FOX, IME, TLF* ✍✍✍½

Spellcaster An evil wizard invites a DJ and a band of rock 'n roll fanatics to his thousand-year-old Italian castle for an evil and bloodcurdling treasure hunt.
1991 (R) 83m/C Richard Blade, Gail O'Grady, Harold Pruett, Bunty Bailey, Rafal Zeilinski, Adam Ant; *D:* Rafal Zeilinski. **VHS, LV $79.95** *COL* ✍

Spetters Four Dutch teenagers follow the motorcycle racing circuit and motocross champ Hauer. Misdirected youth film with a spicy performance from Soutendijk. Plenty of violence, sex, and gripping photography. Verhoeven went on to direct "Robocop" and "Total Recall."

1980 (R) 108m/C *NL* Rutger Hauer, Renee Soutendijk; *D:* Paul Verhoeven. **VHS, Beta, LV $29.98** *SUE* ✍✍½

The Sphinx A murderer causes havoc for his deaf-mute twin (Atwill, good in a dual role) when he frames him for his own crimes. Remade as "The Phantom Killer."
1933 63m/B Lionel Atwill, Theodore Newton, Sheila Terry, Paul Hurst, Luis Alberni, George "Gabby" Hayes; *D:* Phil Rosen. **VHS $16.95** *SNC* ✍✍½

Sphinx Woman archaeologist searches for hidden riches in the tomb of an Egyptian king. The scenery is impressive, but otherwise, don't bother. Based on the novel by Robin Cook.
1981 (PG) 117m/C Lesley-Anne Down, Frank Langella, John Gielgud, Maurice Ronet, John Rhys-Davies; *D:* Franklin J. Schaffner; *W:* John Byrum. **VHS, Beta $19.98** *WAR* Woof!

Spices Poor woman Sonbai revolts against the sexist mores of rural colonial India in the 1940s. Features actress Patil in her final role. In Hindi with English subtitles.
1986 98m/C *IN* Smita Patil; *D:* Ketan Mehta. **VHS $29.95** *MFV, FCT, TAM* ✍✍✍

Spider Baby A tasteless horror-comedy about a chauffeur who takes care of a psychotic family. Theme song sung by Lon Chaney. *AKA:* The Liver Eaters; Spider Baby, or the Maddest Story Ever Told; Cannibal Orgy, or the Maddest Story Ever Told.
1964 86m/B Lon Chaney Jr., Mantan Moreland, Carol Ohmart, Sid Haig; *D:* Jack Hill. **VHS, Beta $19.98** *VEC, SNC, AOV* ✍

Spider Woman A modernized Holmes and Watson adventure as the duo track down a woman responsible for a series of murders. His adversary uses poisonous spiders to do her work. Zestful, superior Holmes. *AKA:* Sherlock Holmes and the Spider Woman.
1944 62m/B Basil Rathbone, Nigel Bruce, Gale Sondergaard, Dennis Hoey; *D:* Roy William Neill. **VHS, Beta $14.98** *FOX* ✍✍✍

Spider-Woman A collection of Spider-Woman's most daring escapades.
1982 100m/C VHS, Beta *MCA* ✍✍✍

Spiderman: The Deadly Dust A live-action episode of Spider-Man, as he attempts to prevent a city-destroying plutonium accident.
1978 93m/C Nicholas Hammond, Robert F. Simon, Chip Fields; *D:* Ron Satlof. **VHS, Beta** *FOX* ✍✍✍

Spiders Directed by Fritz Lang, this is one of his earliest surviving films, and predates Indiana Jones by almost 60 years. In these first two chapters ("The Golden Lake" and "The Diamond Ship") of an unfinished 4-part thriller, Carl deVogt battles with the evil Spider cult for a mystically powerful Incan diamond. Restored version has original color-tinted scenes. Silent with organ score by Gaylord Carter.
1918 137m/B *GE* Lil Dagover; *D:* Fritz Lang. **VHS, Beta, LV $29.95** *KIV, IME, GLV* ✍✍✍

The Spider's Stratagem Thirty years after his father's murder by the facists, a young man returns to a small Italian town to learn why his father was killed. The locals resist his efforts, and he is trapped in a mysterious web where history and lies exert a stranglehold on the truth. Intriguing, high literate thriller; outrageously lovely color photography. Based on a short story by Jorge Luis Borges. In Italian with English subtitles.
1970 97m/C *IT* Giulio Brogi, Alida Valli; *D:* Bernardo Bertolucci. **VHS $59.95** *NYF, FCT, APD* ✍✍✍

Spies A sly criminal poses as a famous banker to steal government information and create chaos in the world in this silent Lang masterpiece. Excellent entertainment, tight plotting and pacing, fine performances. Absolutely relentless intrigue and tension. *AKA:* Spione.
1928 88m/B *GE* Rudolf Klein-Rogge, Lupo Pick, Fritz Rasp, Gerda Maurus, Willy Fritsch; *D:* Fritz Lang. **VHS, Beta, LV** $29.95 *KIV, NOS, VYY* ⅃⅃⅃½

Spies, Lies and Naked Thighs A pair of crackpot CIA agents find themselves in a whirlpool of comedic madness when they are assigned to track down a deadly assassin. The problem? The assassin happens to be the ex-wife of one of the guys. Can he go another round with her and this time come out on top? Who cares?
1991 90m/C Harry Anderson, Ed Begley Jr., Rachel Ticotin, Linda Purl, Wendy Crewson; *D:* James Frawley. **VHS, LV** $19.95 *COL, NLC* ⅃½

Spies Like Us Chase and Aykroyd meet while taking the CIA entry exam. Caught cheating on the test, they seem the perfect pair for a special mission. Pursued by the Soviet government, they nearly start World War III. Silly, fun homage to the Bing Crosby-Bob Hope "Road" movies that doesn't capture those classics' quota of guffaws, but comes moderately close. Look for several cameos by film directors.
1985 (PG) 103m/C Chevy Chase, Dan Aykroyd, Steve Forrest, Bruce Davison, William Prince, Bernie Casey, Tom Hatton, Donna Dixon, Frank Oz; *Cameos:* Michael Apted, Constantin Costa-Gavras, Terry Gilliam, Ray Harryhausen, Joel Coen, Martin Brest, Bob Swaim; *D:* John Landis. **VHS, Beta, LV** $19.98 *WAR* ⅃⅃½

Spike of Bensonhurst A Brooklyn street kid dreams of becoming a championship boxer. He tries to gain the mob's help by courting the local Don's daughter. Hip-but-stereotyped Morrissey effort is helped by great cast.
1988 (R) 101m/C Sasha Mitchell, Ernest Borgnine, Maria Pitillo, Talisa Soto, Sylvia Miles; *D:* Paul Morrissey. **VHS, Beta, LV** *NO* ⅃⅃½

Spinout A pouty traveling singer decides to drive an experimental race car in a rally. Usual Elvis fare with the King being pursued by an assortment of beauties. ♫Adam and Eve; Stop, Look, Listen; All That I Am; Am I Ready; Smorgasbord; Never Say Yes; Beach Shack; I'll Be Back; Spinout. *AKA:* California Holiday.
1966 93m/C Elvis Presley, Shelley Fabares, Carl Betz, Diane McBain, Cecil Kellaway, Jack Mullaney, Deborah Walley, Una Merkel, Warren Berlinger, Will Hutchins, Dodie Marshall; *D:* Norman Taurog. **VHS, Beta** $19.95 *MGM* ⅃⅃

The Spiral Staircase A mute servant, working in a creepy Gothic mansion, may be the next victim of a murderer preying on women afflicted with deformities, especially when the next murder occurs in the mansion itself. Great performance by McGuire as the terrified victim. Remade for television in 1975.
1946 83m/B Dorothy McGuire, George Brent, Ethel Barrymore, Kent Smith, Rhonda Fleming, Gordon Oliver, Elsa Lanchester, Sara Allgood; *D:* Robert Siodmak. **VHS, LV** $39.95 *FOX* ⅃⅃⅃

Spiral Staircase Mild TV remake of the 1946 classic about a mute servant who is menaced by a psychopathic killer. Why didn't they just show the original?
1975 99m/C *GB* Jacqueline Bisset, Christopher Plummer, John Phillip Law, Mildred Dunnock, Sam Wanamaker, Gayle Hunnicutt; *D:* Peter Collinson. **VHS, Beta** $59.95 *WAR* ⅃½

Spirit of St. Louis A lavish Hollywood biography of famous aviator Charles Lindbergh and his historic transatlantic flight from New York to Paris in 1927, based on his autobiography. Intelligent; Stewart shines as the intrepid airman. Inexplicably, it flopped at the box office. Musical score by Franz Waxman.
1957 137m/C James Stewart, Patricia Smith, Murray Hamilton, Marc Connelly; *D:* Billy Wilder. **VHS, Beta** $19.98 *WAR, HMV* ⅃⅃⅃

Spirit of '76 In the 22nd century, the Earth faces certain disaster as a magnetic storm wipes out all of American culture. Now time travellers must return to 1776 to reacquire the Constitution to fix things up. But when their computer goes on the blink, the do-gooders land, not in 1776, but in 1976 at the beginning of disco fever!
1991 (PG-13) 82m/C David Cassidy, Olivia D'Abo, Leif Garrett, Geoff Hoyle, Jeff McDonald, Steve McDonald, Liam O'Brien, Barbara Bain, Julie Brown, Thomas Chong, Devo, Iron Eyes Cody, Kipper Kids, Don Novello, Carl Reiner, Rob Reiner, Moon Zappa; *W/D:* Lucas Reiner. **VHS, LV** $89.95 *SVS* ⅃½

Spirit of the Beehive An acclaimed and haunting film about a young Spanish girl enthralled by the 1931 "Frankenstein," embarking on a journey to find the creature in the Spanish countryside. One of the best films about children's inner life; in Spanish with subtitles. *AKA:* El Espiritu de la Colmena.
1973 95m/C *SP* Fernando Gomez, Teresa Gimpera, Ana Torrent; *D:* Victor Erice. **VHS, Beta, LV** $29.95 *CVC, TAM* ⅃⅃⅃

Spirit of the Eagle Man and young son wander in mountains and make friends with feathered creature. Then boy is kidnapped, creating problems for dad. Somnolent family fare.
1990 (PG) 93m/C Dan Haggerty, Bill Smith, Don Shanks, Jeri Arrendondo, Trever Yarrish; *W/D:* Boon Collins. **VHS, LV** *IME* ⅃⅃

Spirit of the West Rodeo star Gibson and his ranch foreman brother work together to save a fair damsel's land from a gang of rustlers. Routine western of its era.
1932 61m/B Hoot Gibson, Hooper Atchley; *D:* Otto Brower. **VHS, Beta** $19.95 *NOS, DVT, UHV* ⅃½

The Spirit of West Point The true story of West Point's two All-American football greats, Doc Blanchard and Glenn Davis (who play themselves), while on leave after graduation from the title school.
1947 77m/B Felix "Doc" Blanchard, Glenn Davis, Tom Harmon, Alan Hale Jr., Anne Nagel, Robert Shayne; *D:* Ralph Murphy. **VHS, Beta, LV** $19.95 *STE, NWV* ⅃½

The Spirit of Youth Joe Louis supports his family with menial jobs until he shows his knack as a fighter. When he's knocked down, his gal appears at ringside to inspire him, and does.
1937 70m/B Joe Louis, Mantan Moreland. **VHS, Beta** $29.95 *NOS, VYY, VCN* ⅃⅃

Spiritism Mother uses one of her three wishes to bring back her dead son. Adapted from the "Monkey's Paw." *AKA:* Espiritismo.
1961 85m/B *MX* Nora Veyran, Jose Luis Jimenez, Jorge Mondragon, Rene Cardona Jr.; *D:* Benito Alazraki. **VHS** $19.98 *SNC* ⅃⅃

Spirits A priest tormented by his lust-filled dreams breaks his vows of chastity with a woman who turns out to be a murderer. Bad luck.

1990 (R) 88m/C Erik Estrada, Carol Lynley, Robert Quarry, Brinke Stevens, Oliver Darrow, Kathrin Lautner; *D:* Fred Olen Ray. **VHS** $89.98 *VMK* ⅃½

Spirits of the Dead Three Edgar Allan Poe stories adapted for the screen and directed by three of Europe's finest. "Metzengerstein," directed by Roger Vadim stars the Fonda siblings in a tale of incestuous lust. "William Wilson" finds Louis Malle directing Delon and Bardot in the story of a vicious Austrian army officer haunted by a murder victim. Finally, Fellini directs "Never Bet the Devil Your Head" or "Toby Dammit" in which Stamp plays a drunken British film star who has a gruesome date with destiny. Although Fellini's segment is generally considered the best (and was released on its own) all three provide an interesting, atmospheric vision of Poe. *AKA:* Histoires Extraordinaires.
1968 (R) 117m/C *IT FR* Jane Fonda, Peter Fonda, Carla Marlier, Francoise Prevost, James Robertson Justice, Brigitte Bardot, Alain Delon, Katia Christine, Terence Stamp, Salvo Randone; *D:* Roger Vadim, Louis Malle, Federico Fellini. **VHS** $18.00 *FRG, MLB* ⅃⅃⅃

Spiritual Kung Fu A young man masters the art of spiritual kung fu and uses it to take on a roving band of warriors.
1978 97m/C Jackie Chan. **VHS, Beta** *NO* ⅃

Spite Marriage When Sebastian's lover dumps her like yesterday's garbage, she marries Keaton out of spite. Much postnuptual levity follows. Keaton's final silent.
1929 82m/B Buster Keaton, Dorothy Sebastian, Edward Earle, Leila Hyams, William Bechtel, Hank Mann; *D:* Edward Sedgwick. **VHS, Beta, LV** $29.99 *MGM, FCT* ⅃⅃⅃

Spitfire Sentimental comedy drama starring Hepburn as a hillbilly faith healer from the Ozarks who falls into a love triangle. One in a string of early box-office flops for Hepburn. She wanted to play a role other than patrician Eastern Seaboard, and did, but audiences didn't buy it.
1934 90m/B Katharine Hepburn, Robert Young, Ralph Bellamy, Sidney Toler; *D:* John Cromwell. **VHS, Beta, 8mm** $44.95 *NO* ⅃⅃⅃

Spitfire True story of Reginald J. Mitchell, who designed "The Spitfire" fighter plane, which greatly assisted the Allies during World War II. Howard's last film. Heavily propagandist but enjoyable and uncomplicated biography. Splendid score by composer William Walton. *AKA:* The First of the Few.
1942 88m/B *GB* Leslie Howard, David Niven, Rosamund John, George King, Jon Stafford, Adrian Brunel; *D:* Leslie Howard. **VHS, Beta, 3/4U, Special order formats** $9.95 *NEG, NOS, HHT* ⅃⅃⅃

Spittin' Image After falling from her mean-spirited father's wagon, a young girl befriends a kind mountain man. She learns the ways of the wilderness and tobacco spitting.
1983 92m/C Sunshine Parker, Trudi Cooper, Sharon Barr, Karen Barr; *D:* Russell Kern. **VHS, Beta** $59.95 *PSM* ⅃

Splash A beautiful mermaid ventures into New York City in search of a man she's rescued twice when he's fallen overboard. Now it's her turn to fall—in love. Charming performances by Hanks and Hannah. Well-paced direction from Howard, with just enough slapstick. Don't miss the lobster scene.
1984 109m/C Tom Hanks, Daryl Hannah, Eugene Levy, John Candy, Dody Goodman, Shecky Greene, Richard B. Shull, Bobby DiCicco, Howard Morris; *D:* Ron Howard. **VHS, Beta, LV, 8mm** $79.95 *TOU, BVV* ⅃⅃½

S

Splatter University A deranged killer escapes from an asylum and begins to slaughter and mutilate comely coeds at a local college. Abysmally motiveless killing and gratuitous sex. Also available in a 78-minute ''R'' rated version.

1984 79m/C Francine Forbes, Dick Biel, Cathy Lacommaro, Ric Randing, Dan Eaton; **D:** Richard W. Haines. **VHS, Beta $69.98** *LIV, VES Woof!*

Splendor in the Grass A drama set in rural Kansas in 1925, concerning a teenage couple who try to keep their love on a strictly intellectual plane and the sexual and family pressures that tear them apart. After suffering a mental breakdown and being institutionalized, the girl returns years later in order to settle her life. Film debuts of Beatty, Dennis, and Diller. William Inge wrote the screenplay specifically with Beatty in mind, after the actor appeared in one of Inge's stage plays. Filmed not in Kansas, but on Staten Island and in upstate New York.

1961 124m/C Natalie Wood, Warren Beatty, Audrey Christie, Barbara Loden, Zohra Lampert, Phyllis Diller, Sandy Dennis; **D:** Elia Kazan; **W:** William Inge. Academy Awards '61: Best Story & Screenplay; Nominations: Best Actress (Wood). **VHS, Beta, LV $19.98** *WAR, PIA ♪♪♪*

Split Humanoids from another dimension manipulate earth activity.

1990 85m/C John Flynn, Timothy Dwight, Chris Shaw, Joan Bechtel; **D:** Chris Shaw. **VHS $79.95** *AIP ♪*

Split Decisions An Irish family of boxers, dad and his two sons, slug it out emotionally and physically, as they come to terms with career choices and each other. Good scenes in the ring but the drama leans toward melodrama. Decent family drama, but somewhat of a ''Rocky'' rip-off.

1988 (R) 95m/C Gene Hackman, Craig Sheffer, Jeff Fahey, Jennifer Beals, John McLiam, Eddie Velez, Carmine Caridi, James Tolkan; **D:** David Drury. **VHS, LV, 8mm $19.95** *WAR ♪♪*

Split Image An all-American boy comes under the spell of a cult. His parents then hire a deprogrammer to bring the boy back to reality. Exceptional performances by Dennehy and Woods. This is a worthwhile film that spent far too little time in theatres.

1982 (R) 113m/C Michael O'Keefe, Karen Allen, Peter Fonda, Brian Dennehy, James Woods; **D:** Ted Kotcheff. **VHS, Beta $24.98** *SUE ♪♪♪*

Split Second An escaped prisoner holds hostages in a Nevada atomic bomb testing area. Powell's directorial debut, and a script by William Bowers and Irving Wallace. McNally's excellent performance as the kidnapper, in addition to strong supporting performances, enhance a solid plot.

1953 85m/B Paul Kelly, Richard Egan, Jan Sterling, Alexis Smith, Stephen McNally; **D:** Dick Powell. **VHS, Beta $39.95** *RKO, TTC ♪♪½*

Split Second Hauer is a futuristic cop tracking down a vicious alien serial killer in London in the year 2008. The monster rips out the hearts of his victims and then eats them in what appears to be a satanic ritual in this blood-soaked thriller wanna-be. Hauer gives a listless performance and overall, the action is quite dull. The music soundtrack also manages to annoy with the Moody Blues song ''Nights in White Satin'' playing at the most inappropriate times. A British/American co-production.

1992 (R) 91m/C *GB* Rutger Hauer, Kim Cattrall, Neil Duncan, Michael J. Pollard, Alun Armstrong, Peter Postlethwaite, Ian Dury, Roberta Eaton; **D:** Tony Maylam. **VHS $92.99** *HBO ♪½*

Splitting Heirs Idle stars as the offspring of titled parents who is accidentally abandoned in a restaurant as an infant and raised by poor Pakistanis. (His mother winds up claiming the wrong abandoned baby.) When he discovers he's actually the 15th Duke of Bournemouth he plots, ineffectually, to kill off the present unknowing imposter, a nitwit American (Moranis). Cleese pops in as a shabby lawyer hired by Idle to help him claim the title with Hershey as Idle's real mother, the addle-brained and sex-starved Duchess. Convoluted plot, bland comedy.

1993 (PG-13) 87m/C Eric Idle, Rick Moranis, Barbara Hershey, John Cleese, Catherine Zeta Jones, Sadie Frost, Stratford Johns, Brenda Bruce, William Franklyn, Jeremy Clyde; **D:** Robert M. Young; **W:** Eric Idle; **M:** Michael Kamen. *♪♪½*

Splitz An all-girl rock band agrees to help out a sorority house by participating in a series of sporting events.

1984 (PG-13) 89m/C Robin Johnson, Patti Lee, Shirley Stoler, Raymond Serra; **D:** Domonic Paris. **VHS, Beta $79.98** *LIV, VES Woof!*

The Spoilers Virtually unstaged account of gold hunting in the Alaskan wilderness enhanced by gritty film quality. Was a gold mine when released.

1914 110m/B William Farnum, Thomas Santschi, Kathlyn Williams, Bessie Eyton, Frank Clark, Wheeler Oakman; **D:** Colin Campbell. **VHS, Beta $19.95** *GPV ♪♪½*

The Spoilers Two adventurers in the Yukon are swindled out of their gold mine and set out to even the score. A trademark scene of all versions of the movie (and there are many) is the climactic fistfight, in this case between hero Wayne and bad-guy Scott. One of the better films adapted from the novel by Rex Beach. William Farnum, who starred in both the 1914 and the 1930 versions, has a small part.

1942 84m/B John Wayne, Randolph Scott, Marlene Dietrich, Margaret Lindsay, Harry Carey Sr., Richard Barthelmess; **D:** Ray Enright. **VHS, Beta, LV $19.95** *MCA, MLB ♪♪♪*

Spontaneous Combustion A grisly horror film detailing the travails of a hapless guy who has the power to inflict the title phenomenon on other people.

1989 (R) 97m/C Brad Dourif, Jon Cypher, Melinda Dillon, Cynthia Bain, William Prince; **D:** Tobe Hooper. **VHS, Beta, LV $89.98** *LIV ♪♪*

Spook Busters The Bowery Boys take jobs as exterminators, only to find themselves assigned the unenviable task of ridding a haunted house of ghosts. To make matters worse, the resident mad scientist wants to transplant Sach's brain into a gorilla. Essential viewing for anyone who thought ''Ghostbusters'' was an original story.

1946 68m/B Leo Gorcey, Huntz Hall, Douglas Dumbrille, Bobby Jordan, Gabriel Dell, Billy Benedict, David Gorcey, Bernard Gorcey, Tanis Chandler, Maurice Cass, Charles Middleton; **D:** William Beaudine. **VHS $14.98** *WAR ♪♪½*

The Spook Who Sat By the Door A black CIA agent organizes an army of inner-city youths and launches a revolution. Based on the novel by Sam Greenlee.

1973 (PG) 95m/C Lawrence Cook, Paula Kelly, J.A. Preston; **D:** Ivan Dixon. **VHS, Beta $69.95** *VCD ♪½*

Spookies An old master sorcerer who lives in a run-down haunted house sacrifices humans to give eternal life to his unconscious bride. He needs only a few more vitims when a group of teenagers come along to explore the house.

1985 (R) 85m/C Felix Ward, Dan Scott, Maria Pechukas, Brendan Faulkner, Eugine Joseph; **D:** Thomas Doran. **VHS, Beta, LV $14.95** *SVS Woof!*

Spooks Run Wild The East Side Kids seek refuge in a spooky mansion owned by the eerie Lugosi. A fun horror-comedy with the Kids' antics playing off Lugosi's scariness quite well. Co-scripter Carl Foreman later co-wrote ''High-Noon,'' ''The Bridge on the River Kwai,'' and ''The Guns of Navarone.'' *AKA:* Ghosts on the Loose.

1941 64m/B Huntz Hall, Leo Gorcey, Bobby Jordan, Sammy Morrison, Dave O'Brien, Dennis Moore, Bela Lugosi; **D:** Phil Rosen. **VHS, Beta $19.95** *NOS, SNC, VYY ♪♪½*

Spoon River Anthology This film is based on Edgar Lee Master's poetry in which we can sense the complexity of American life as it entered the twentieth century. Masters probes human strengths and weaknesses.

1976 21m/C VHS, Beta *BFA ♪♪½*

The Sporting Club A semi-gothic melodrama about a strict all men's club which, during a 100th anniversary party, reverts to savagery and primitive rites.

1972 (R) 104m/C Robert Fields, Margaret Blye, Nicholas Coster, Ralph Waite, Jack Warden, Linda Blair; **D:** Larry Peerce. **VHS, Beta $24.98** *NLC Woof!*

Spotlight Scandals A barber and a vaudevillian team up and endure the ups and downs of showbiz life in this low-budget musical from prolific B-movie director Beaudine. ♫The Restless Age; Goodnight Now; The Lilac Tree; Tempo of the Trail; Oh Johnny.

1943 79m/B Billy Gilbert, Frank Fay, Bonnie Baker; **D:** William Beaudine. **VHS $19.95** *NOS, LOO ♪♪*

Spraggue A Boston professor and his eccentric aunt put the moves on a doctor who may have committed murder. Served as a TV pilot for a series that never materialized.

1984 78m/C Michael Nouri, Glynis Johns, James Cromwell, Mark Herrier, Patrick O'Neal, Andrea Marcovicci; **D:** Larry Elikann. **VHS $59.95** *LIV ♪♪*

The Spring Two archaeologists search Florida for the fountain of youth after they find new clues to its whereabouts. However, a greedy industrialist and an evil priest are both on their trail, fighting to keep the secret for themselves at any cost.

1989 110m/C Dack Rambo, Gedde Watanabe, Shari Shattuck, Steven Keats; **D:** John D. Patterson. **VHS** *NO ♪½*

Spring Break Four college students go to Fort Lauderdale on their spring vacation and have a wilder time that they bargained for, though viewer is deprived of excitement.

1983 (R) 101m/C Perry Lang, David Knell, Steve Bassett, Paul Land, Jayne Modean, Corinne Alphen; **D:** Sean S. Cunningham. **VHS, Beta, LV $14.95** *COL ♪*

Spring Fever Heartaches of the junior tennis circuit are brought to the screen in this sports comedy. Previews promised a lot more than this film could ever hope to deliver. Even tennis fans will be disappointed.

1981 93m/C *CA* Susan Anton; **D:** Joseph L. Scanlan. **VHS, Beta $69.98** *LIV, VES ♪½*

Spring Symphony A moody, fairy-tale biography of composer Robert Schumann, concentrating on his rhapsodic love affair with pianist Claire Weick. Kinski is very good as the rebellious daughter, while the music is even better. Reasonably accurate in terms of history; dubbed. *AKA:* Fruhlingssinfonie.

1986 (PG-13) 102m/C *GE* Nastassia Kinski, Rolf Hoppe, Herbert Gronemeyer; **D:** Peter Schamoni. **VHS, Beta $79.98** *LIV ♪♪½*

Springhill The true story of a mining disaster in which seven miners fought to survive the elements while buried 13,000 feet underground.
197? 90m/C VHS, Beta $49.95 TWE *½*

Springtime in the Rockies Autry is a cattle-ranch foreman whose employer decides to try raising sheep. This doesn't set well with the other ranchers, but Autry manages to save the day and sing a little too.
1937 60m/B Gene Autry, Polly Rowles, Smiley Burnette; *D:* Joseph Kane. VHS, Beta $19.98 NOS, VCN, DVT *½½*

Springtime in the Rockies A Broadway duo just can't get along despite being in love with each other. Top-notch musical, with a touch of romantic tension and comedy. Beautifully filmed in the Canadian Rockies. ♫I Had the Craziest Dream; Run Little Rainrop Run; A Poem Set to Music; Pan American Jubilee; I Like to Be Love by You; Chattanooga Choo Choo; Tic Tac Do Meu Coracao.
1942 91m/C Betty Grable, John Payne, Carmen Miranda, Cesar Romero, Charlotte Greenwood, Edward Everett Horton, Jackie Gleason; *D:* Irving Cummings. VHS, LV $19.95 FOX, MLB *½½½*

Springtime in the Sierras Rogers and Devine band together to fight a gang of poachers who prey on the wildlife of a game preserve. Features a number of songs by Rogers and The Sons of the Pioneers. *AKA:* Song of the Sierra.
1947 54m/B Roy Rogers, Andy Devine, Jane Frazee, Stephanie Bachelor; *D:* William Whitney. VHS, Beta, 3/4U, Special order formats $19.95 NOS, CAB, DVT *½½½*

The Sprinter (Der Sprinter) A young homosexual, while trying to submerge his confusion in professional track and field, gets to know a homely shot-putter and is seduced by her. In German with English subtitles.
1984 90m/C VHS, Beta $39.95 VCD, GLV *½½½*

Spurs A rodeo star takes on a whole gang of rustlers and their imposing machine gun. This transitional western was made both with and without sound.
1930 60m/B Hoot Gibson, Robert E. Homans; *D:* Hoot Gibson. VHS $19.95 NOS, DVT, HEG *½½*

Sputnik A Frenchman, amnesiac after a car crash, comes up against Russian scientists, space-bound dogs, and weightlessness. Pleasant and charming family fun though clearly dated. Another fine performance from Auer. Dubbed. *AKA:* A Dog, a Mouse, and a Sputnik.
1961 80m/B FR Noelia Noel, Mischa Auer, Denise Gray; *D:* Jean Dreville. VHS, Beta $39.95 SVS, TAM *½½*

Spy A former spy who knows too much becomes the target of a renegade agency. Made for television.
1989 88m/C Ned Beatty, Tim Choate, Bruce Greenwood, Catherine Hicks, Jameson Parker, Michael Tucker; *D:* Philip Frank Messina. VHS, Beta, LV $79.95 PAR *½½*

Spy in Black A German submarine captain returns from duty at sea during World War I and is assigned to infiltrate one of the Orkney Islands and obtain confidential British information. Known in the U.S. as "U-Boat 29," this film is based on a J. Storer Clouston novel. This was the first teaming of director Powell and writer Pressburger, who followed with "Contraband" in 1940 .
1939 82m/B GB Conrad Veidt, Valerie Hobson, Sebastian Shaw, Marius Goring, June Duprez, Helen Hayes, Cyril Raymond, Hay Petrie; *D:* Michael Powell. VHS, Beta, LV $19.95 NOS, VYY, DVT *½½½*

Spy of Napoleon A French aristocrat agrees to marry the illegitimate daughter of Emperor Napoleon III and finds himself working to uncover traitors to the throne. Based on Baroness Orczy's novel.
1936 77m/B GB Richard Barthelmess, Dolly Hass, Francis L. Sullivan. VHS, Beta $29.95 VYY *½½*

Spy Smasher Returns The exciting 12-part serial "Spy Smasher" was cut and edited into feature length and released under this title. The masked marvel and his twin brother battle enemy agents during World War II. This new version is just as exciting as the original cliffhanger.
1942 185m/B Kane Richmond, Marguerite Chapman, Sam Flint, Hans Schumm, Tristram Coffin; *D:* William Witney. VHS $29.98 REP, MLB *½½*

Spy Story A Cold War conflict, counter-intelligence, conspiracy, and a nuclear sub chase highlight this tale by Len Deighton.
1986 105m/C VHS, Beta $69.95 VCD, MOV *½½*

Spy Trap Four junior-high school friends concoct bogus military plans using futuristic toys for blueprints. The "secret" plans get sold to the Russians and the kids find themselves chased by the unhappy KGB and the CIA. Family adventure.
1992 96m/C Elya Baskin, Danielle Du Clos, Jason Kristofer, Cameron Johann, Devin Ratray, Kimble Joyner; *D:* Arthur Sherman. VHS $89.95 HMD *½½*

The Spy Who Came in from the Cold The acclaimed adaptation of the John Le Carre novel about an aging British spy who attempts to infiltrate the East German agency. Prototypical Cold War thriller, with emphasis on de-glamorizing espionage. Gritty and superbly realistic with a documentary style which hampered it at the box office.
1965 110m/B Richard Burton, Oskar Werner, Claire Bloom, Sam Wanamaker, Peter Van Eyck, Cyril Cusack, Rupert Davies, Michael Hordern; *D:* Martin Ritt. Academy Awards '65 Nominations: Best Actor (Burton); British Academy Awards '66: Best Film; Edgar Allan Poe Awards '65: Best Screenplay; Golden Globe Awards '66: Best Supporting Actor (Werner). VHS, Beta, LV $19.95 PAR *½½½½*

The Spy Who Loved Me James Bond teams up with female Russian Agent XXX to squash a villain's plan to use captured American and Russian atomic submarines in a plot to destroy the world. The villain's henchman, 7'2" Kiel, is the steel-toothed Jaws. Carly Simon sings the memorable, Marvin Hamlisch theme song, "Nobody Does It Better."
1977 (PG) 136m/C GB Roger Moore, Barbara Bach, Curt Jurgens, Richard Kiel, Caroline Munro, Walter Gotell, Geoffrey Keen, Valerie Leon, Bernard Lee, Lois Maxwell, Desmond Llewelyn; *D:* Lewis Gilbert; *M:* Marvin Hamlisch. VHS, Beta, LV $19.98 MGM, FOX, TLF *½½½*

Spy with a Cold Nose A sporadically funny spy spoof about a bugged dog passed between British and Soviet intelligence. Hard-working cast keeps it from collapsing.
1966 93m/C GB Laurence Harvey, Daliah Lavi, Lionel Jeffries; *D:* Daniel Petrie. VHS, Beta $59.95 NLC *½½*

Spymaker: The Secret Life of Ian Fleming Fictionalized account of the creator of the ultimate spy James Bond and his early days in the British Secret Service. Fans of the Bond movies will appreciate the numerous inside jokes. Connery is the son of Sean. Made for British television. *AKA:* Spymaker.

1990 100m/C GB Jason Connery, Kristin Scott Thomas, Joss Ackland, Patricia Hodge, David Warner, Fiona Fullerton, Richard Johnson; *D:* Ferdinand Fairfax. VHS TTC *½½*

S*P*Y*S An attempt to cash in on the success of "M*A*S*H," this unfunny spy spoof details the adventures of two bumbling CIA men who botch a Russian defection, and get both sides after them. Usually competent director Kershner had a bad day.
1974 (PG) 87m/C Donald Sutherland, Elliott Gould, Joss Ackland, Zouzou, Shane Rimmer, Vladek Sheybal, Nigel Hawthorne; *D:* Irvin Kershner; *M:* Jerry Goldsmith. VHS, Beta $59.98 FOX *½*

Squadron of Doom Government troubleshooter Ace Drummond battles enemy agents out to steal a mountain of jade. *AKA:* Ace Drummond.
1936 70m/B John "Dusty" King, Jean Rogers, Noah Beery Jr. VHS, Beta $19.95 NOS, VCN, DVT *½½*

Square Dance A Texas teenager leaves the farm where she's been raised by her grandfather to live in the city with her promiscuous mother (Alexander, cast against type) where she befriends a retarded young man (yes, it's Lowe, also cast against type). Too slow, but helped by good acting. *AKA:* Home is Where the Heart Is.
1987 (PG-13) 118m/C Jane Alexander, Jason Robards Jr., Rob Lowe, Winona Ryder; *D:* Daniel Petrie. VHS, Beta, LV $19.95 PAV *½½½*

Square Dance Jubilee Television scouts hit Prairie City in search of cowboy stars, and stumble onto cattle rustlers. Twenty-one C & W tunes support a near-invisible plot, suitable for fridge runs.
1951 78m/B Mary Beth Hughes, Donald (Don "Red") Barry, Wally Vernon, John Eldridge; *D:* Paul Landres. VHS, Beta, LV NO *½½*

Square Shoulders Adventures of young military school student with geometric anatomy (Coghlan).
1929 58m/B Frank "Junior" Coghlan, Louis Wolheim, Anita Louise, Montague Shaw; *D:* E. Mason Hopper. VHS, Beta $19.95 GPV, FCT *½*

The Squeaker Good Edgar Wallace mystery about a disgraced inspector trying to clear his name. *AKA:* Murder on Diamond Row.
1937 ?m/C Edmund Lowe, Sebastian Shaw. VHS $16.95 SNC *½½*

The Squeaker Complicated but interesting thriller about the underworld goings-on after a big-time diamond heist. German remake of an early (1930) British talkie, also done in 1937, based on the Edgar Wallace novel.
1965 95m/B GE Heinz Drache, Eddi Arent, Klaus Kinski, Barbara Rutting; *D:* Alfred Vohrer. VHS SNC *½½*

The Squeeze Scotland Yard detective Keach, fired for drunkenness, gets a chance to reinstate himself when his ex-wife is caught up in a brutal kidnapping scheme. Slim script gives good cast uphill work. Ordinary thriller. Available with Spanish subtitles.
1977 (R) 106m/C Stacy Keach, Carol White, David Hemmings, Edward Fox, Stephen Boyd; *D:* Michael Apted. VHS, Beta, LV $19.98 WAR *½½*

The Squeeze An aging safecracker is hired for a final job, but learns that his cohorts plan to kill him when the heist is finished. Blah revenge thriller. Dawson is a pseudonym for Antonio Margheriti.
1980 93m/C IT Lee Van Cleef, Karen Black, Edward Albert, Lionel Stander, Robert Alda; *D:* Anthony M. Dawson. Beta NO *½*

The Squeeze Keaton is wasted in this attempt at a comedy about a small-time con artist who discovers a Mafia plan to fix a lottery electromagnetically.
1987 (PG-13) 101m/C Michael Keaton, Rae Dawn Chong, John Davidson, Ric Abernathy, Bobby Bass, Joe Pantoliano, Meatloaf, Paul Herman; *D:* Roger Young. VHS, Beta, LV $14.99 HBO Woof!

Squeeze Play Group of young women start a softball team and challenge the boy-friends to a game. Standard battle of the sexes takes place, with a wet T-shirt con-test thrown in for good measure. Cheap, plotless, offensive trash from Troma.
1979 92m/C Al Corley, Jenni Hetrick, Jim Metzler; *D:* Samuel Weil. VHS, Beta, LV $19.99 HBO, PIA Woof!

Squiddly Diddly Compilation of "Squiddly Diddly" cartoons, about a star-struck squid hoping to break into show business.
196? 55m/C VHS, Beta $19.95 TTC, WTA Woof!

Squirm Storm disrupts a highly charged power cable, electrifying a host of garden-variety worms. The worms then turn them into giant monsters that terrorize a small town in Georgia. The opening credits claim it's based on an actual 1975 incident. Okay entry in giant worm genre written by Lieber-man.
1976 (R) 92m/C Don Scardino, Patricia Pearcy, Jean Sullivan; *D:* Jeff Lieberman. VHS, Beta, LV $59.98 LIV, VES 🐾🐾

Squizzy Taylor The rise and fall of real-life Australian mob boss Squizzy Taylor in the 1920s. Colorful period gangster drama loses steam about halfway through.
1984 82m/C AU Jacki Weaver, Alan Cassell, David Atkins; *D:* Kevin Dobson. VHS, Beta $69.95 VID 🐾🐾

S.S. Experiment Camp 2 Hitler's elite corps of sadists get their kicks torturing and maiming prisoners during the dark days of World War II.
1986 90m/C John Braun, Macha Magal. VHS, Beta NO 🐾

SS Girls After the assassination attempt of July 1944, Hitler does not trust the Wermacht and extends the power of the SS over Germany. General Berger entrusts Hans Schillemberg to recruit a specially chosen group of prostitutes who must test the fighting spirit and loyalty of the generals. Seedy exploitation.
1978 82m/C Gabriele Carrara, Marina Daunia, Vassilli Karis, Macha Magal, Thomas Rudy, Lucic Bogoljub Benny, Ivano Staccioli. VHS, Beta MED 🐾

S.S. Love Camp No. 27 A beautiful young girl's life is torn to shreds when she is imprisoned in a Nazi brothel.
197? 90m/C VHS, Beta VCD 🐾

Stacey Ex-Playmate Randall stars as Sta-cey Hansen, a beautiful, implausibly talented private detective. Hyper-convoluted plot, too much sex and violence detract from a poten-tially not-wretched whodunit. *AKA:* Stacey and Her Gangbusters.
1973 (R) 87m/C Anne Randall, Marjorie Bennett, Anitra Ford, Alan Landers, James Westmoreland, Christina Raines; *D:* Andy Sidaris. VHS, Beta $59.95 GEM 🐾1/2

Stacking In the 1950s, a Montana family is threatened with losing their farm. Typical, boring '80s farmland tragedy with coming of age tale. *AKA:* Season of Dreams.
1987 (PG) 111m/C Christine Lahti, Megan Follows, Frederic Forrest, Peter Coyote, Jason Gedrick; *D:* Martin Rosen. VHS, Beta, LV $14.95 NLC 🐾🐾

Stacy's Knights A seemingly shy girl happens to have an uncanny knack for blackjack. With the odds against her and an unlikely group of "knights" to aid her, she sets up an implausible "sting" operation. Blah TV fodder for the big screen. *AKA:* Double Down.
1983 (PG) 95m/C Kevin Costner, Andra Millian; *D:* Jim Wilson. VHS, Beta $29.98 LIV, VES 🐾🐾

Stage Door An energetic ensemble peek at the women of the theater. A boarding house for potential actresses houses a wide variety of talents and dreams. Patrician Hep-burn and wisecracking Rogers make a good team in a talent-packed ensemble. Realistic look at the sub-world of Broadway aspira-tions includes dialogue taken from idle chat among the actresses between takes. Based on the play by Edna Ferber and George S. Kaufman, who suggested in jest a title change to "Screen Door," since so much had been changed. Watch for young stars-to-be like Ball, Arden and Miller.
1937 92m/B Katharine Hepburn, Ginger Rogers, Lucille Ball, Eve Arden, Andrea Leeds, Jack Carson, Adolphe Menjou, Gail Patrick; *D:* Gregory La Cava. Academy Awards '37 Nominations: Best Director (La Cava), Best Picture, Best Screenplay, Best Supporting Actress (Leeds); National Board of Review Awards '37: 10 Best Films of the Year. VHS, Beta $19.98 TTC, CCB, MED 🐾🐾🐾1/2

Stage Door Canteen The Stage Door Canteens were operated by the American Theatre Wing during World War II for service-men on leave. They were staffed by some of the biggest stars of the day, 65 of whom are featured here. The slight, hokey plot con-cerns three soldiers who fall for canteen workers while on furlough in New York City. Many musical numbers, cameos, and walk-ons by a plethora of stars. ♫We Mustn't Say Goodbye; Bombshell From Brooklyn; The Machine Gun Song; Sleep, Baby, Sleep in Your Jeep; Quick Sands; You're Pretty Ter-rific Yourself; Don't Worry Island; We Meet in the Funniest Places; A Rookie and His Rhythm; American Boy; The Girl I Love to Leave Behind; Marching Through Berlin; Deutschland Uber Alles; Why Don't You Do Right?; The Lord's Prayer; Bugle Call Rag; Ave Maria; Flight of the Bumble Bee.
1943 135m/B Cheryl Walker, William Terry, Marjorie Riordan, Lon McCallister, Sunset Carson, Tallulah Bankhead, Merle Oberon, Katharine Hepburn, Paul Muni, Ethel Waters, Judith Anderson, Ray Bolger; *Cameos:* Helen Hayes, Harpo Marx, Gertrude Lawrence, Ethel Merman, Edgar Bergen, George Raft, Benny Goodman, Peggy Lee, Count Basie, Kay Kyser, Guy Lombardo, Xavier Cugat, Johnny Weissmuller; *D:* Frank Borzage. VHS, Beta, LV, 3/4U, Special order formats $9.95 NEG, NOS, PSM 🐾🐾1/2

Stage Fright Wyman will stop at nothing to clear her old boyfriend, who has been accused of murdering the husband of his mistress, an actress (Dietrich). Disguised as a maid, she falls in love with the investigating detective, and discovers her friend's guilt. Dietrich sings "The Laziest Gal in Town." The Master's last film made in England until "Frenzy" (1971).
1950 110m/B GB Jane Wyman, Marlene Dietrich, Alastair Sim, Sybil Thorndike, Michael Wilding, Kay Walsh; *D:* Alfred Hitchcock. VHS, Beta, LV $19.98 WAR, MLB 🐾🐾🐾

Stage Fright Bashful actress is trans-formed into a homicidal killer after a latent psychosis in her becomes active.
1983 82m/C Jenny Neumann, Gary Sweet. VHS, Beta $19.98 VID 🐾

Stage Struck Strasberg reprises the role made famous by Katharine Hepburn as a determined, would-be actress in this medio-cre remake of "Morning Glory" (1933). Chris-topher Plummer's screen debut shows little of his later talent.
1957 95m/B Henry Fonda, Susan Strasberg, Christopher Plummer, Herbert Marshall, Joan Greenwood; *D:* Sidney Lumet. VHS, Beta, LV $29.95 UHV, IME 🐾🐾

Stage to Mesa City Marshall LaRue must find out who is behind the pesky attacks on the stage line to Mesa City. Cheseboro, as usual, is a good bad guy. A few chuckles between fist fights and shoot-em-ups.
1948 52m/B Lash LaRue, Al "Fuzzy" St. John, George Cheseboro, Jennifer Holt, Russell Arms; *D:* Ray Taylor. VHS, Beta $12.95 COL, SVS 🐾🐾

Stagecoach A varied group of characters with nothing in common are stuck together inside a coach besieged by bandits and Indians. Considered structurally perfect, with excellent direction by Ford, it's the film that made Wayne a star as the Ringo Kid, an outlaw looking to avenge the murder of his brother and father. The first pairing of Ford and Wayne changed the course of the mo-dern western. Stunning photography by Bert Glennon and Ray Binger captured the mythi-cal air of Monument Valley, a site that Ford was often to revisit. Based on the story "Stage to Lordsburg" by Ernest Haycox. Remade miserably with Ann-Margaret, Red Buttons, and Bing Crosby as the drunken doctor, in 1966 and again—why?—as a TV movie in 1986.
1939 100m/B John Wayne, Claire Trevor, Thomas Mitchell, George Bancroft, John Carradine, Andy Devine, Donald Meek; *D:* John Ford. Academy Awards '39: Best Supporting Actor (Mitchell), Best Score; Nominations: Best Black and White Cinematography, Best Director (Ford), Best Film Editing, Best Interior Decoration, Best Picture; National Board of Review Awards '39: 10 Best Films of the Year; New York Film Critics Awards '39: Best Director (Ford). VHS, Beta, LV $19.98 WAR, VES, PIA 🐾🐾🐾🐾

Stagecoach A forgettable made-for-tele-vision remake of the classic 1939 western about a motley crew of characters in a cross-country coach beset by thieves and Indians.
1986 95m/C Willie Nelson, Waylon Jennings, Johnny Cash, Kris Kristofferson, John Schneider, Elizabeth Ashley, Mary Crosby, Anthony Newley, Anthony (Tony) Franciosa; *D:* Ted Post. VHS, Beta $19.95 STE, VMK 🐾

Stagecoach to Denver Lane as Red Ryder investigates a stagecoach wreck and uncovers a land-grabbing plot led by-who else?—the pillar of the community (Barcroft). Well-directed "Red Ryder" episode.
1946 53m/B Allan "Rocky" Lane, Roy Barcroft, Robert (Bobby) Blake, Peggy Stewart, Martha Wentworth; *D:* R.G. Springsteen. VHS, Beta, 3/4U, Special order formats $19.95 NOS, CAB, VCN 🐾🐾

Stagefright A maniacal serial killer tries to cover his trail by joining the cast of a play about mass murder. The other actors soon have more to worry about than remembering their lines. Typical low-grade horror.
1987 95m/C David Brandon, Barbara Cupisti, Robert Gligorov; *D:* Michele (Michael) Soavi. VHS, Beta $79.95 IMP 🐾

Stakeout An ex-con tries to start life anew, but every time he finds a good job, his past catches up with him. A return to the life of crime looks tempting. Predictable and familiar plot, but performances are sincere.

1962 81m/B Bing Russell, Billy Hughes, Bill Hale, Jack Harris; **W/D:** James Landis. **VHS** $16.95 *SNC* ✍✍

Stakeout A sometimes violent comedy-thriller about a pair of detectives who stake out a beautiful woman's apartment, hoping for a clue to the whereabouts of her psycho boyfriend who has broken out of prison. One of them (Dreyfuss) then begins to fall in love with her. Natural charm among Estevez, Dreyfuss, and Stowe that adds to the proceedings, which are palpably implausible and silly.
1987 (R) 117m/C Richard Dreyfuss, Emilio Estevez, Madeleine Stowe, Aidan Quinn, Forest Whitaker; **D:** John Badham. **VHS, Beta, LV, 8mm** $89.95 *TOU* ✍✍½

Stakeout 2 Sequel six years after the original finds Dreyfuss and Estevez partnered again for another stakeout, this time to keep an eye on Moriarty, a reluctant witness against the Mob. The two spying detectives find themselves in an upscale neighborhood where blending in is a hard thing to do. O'Donnell is a breath of fresh air as a wisecracking assistant district attorney assigned to play Dreyfuss's wife. Writer Kouf reportedly had difficulty penning the script. *AKA:* Another Stakeout.
1993 ?m/C Richard Dreyfuss, Emilio Estevez, Rosie O'Donnell, Cathy Moriarty, Madeleine Stowe, John Rubinstein, Marcia Strassman, Dennis Farina, Miguel Ferrer; **D:** John Badham; **W:** Jim Kouf. **VHS** *NYR* ✍✍½

Stalag 17 A group of American G.I.s in a German POW camp during World War II suspects the opportunistic Holden of being the spy in their midst. One of the very best American movies of the 1950's, adapted from the play by Donald Bevan and Edmund Trzcinski. Wilder, so good at comedy, proved himself equally adept at drama, and brought a top-drawer performance out of Holden. Superb photography from Ernest Laszlo and a wonderful score from Franz Waxman.
1953 120m/B William Holden, Don Taylor, Peter Graves, Otto Preminger, Harvey Lembeck, Robert Strauss, Sig Rumann; **D:** Billy Wilder. Academy Awards '53: Best Actor (Holden); Nominations: Best Director (Wilder), Best Supporting Actor (Strauss); National Board of Review Awards '53: 10 Best Films of the Year. **VHS, Beta, LV** $14.95 *PAR, TLF, BTV* ✍✍✍✍

Stalin The story of the leader of the Soviet Union who ruled with an iron fist from 1924-1953. One of the most feared men of the 20th century, he wrenched the largest country in the world singlehandedly from a backward, pastoral farmland to an industrial landscape. He was also responsible for the feared purges of the late 1930s where more than a million people were executed. Also explored is the dictator's relationships with his family, including how marriage to a cunning, sadistic, paranoid tyrant affected his wife. Filmed at actual historical locations in Russia. Made for cable television.
1992 173m/C Robert Duvall, Julia Ormond, Jeroen Krabbe, Joan Plowright, Maximilian Schell, Frank Finlay, Roshan Seth, Daniel Massey, Miriam Margolyes, Jim Carter, Joanna Roth, Andras Balint; **D:** Ivan Passer; **W:** Paul Monash. **VHS, LV** $92.99 *MGM* ✍✍½

Stalk the Wild Child Well-intentioned but unconvincing American remake of Truffaut's "The Wild Child," about a child psychologist's efforts to rehabilitate a boy raised by wolves. TV pilot inspired "Lucan," a short-lived series.
1976 78m/C David Janssen, Trish Van Devere, Benjamin Bottoms, Joseph Bottoms; **D:** William Hale. **VHS** *WOV* ✍✍½

Stalker A meteorite, crashing to Earth, has caused a wasteland area known as the Zone. The Zone is forbidden to anyone except special guides called Stalkers. Three Stalkers enter the region searching for its center, which contains a room that supposedly reveals fantasies. From the Soviet team that made "Solaris." Filmed with both color and black-and-white sequences. Suspenseful atmosphere due to the director's use of long takes, movement, and color. In Russian with English subtitles.
1979 160m/C *RU* Alexander Kaidanovsky, Nikolai Grinko, Anatoli Solonitzin, Alice Freindlikh; **D:** Andrei Tarkovsky. **VHS** $89.95 *FXL, FCT* ✍✍✍

Stalking Danger A secret government group must terminate an assassination plot by a terrorist organization. *AKA:* C.A.T. Squad.
1988 (PG) 97m/C Joe Cortese, Steve James, Patricia Charbonneau, Jack Youngblood; **D:** William Friedkin; **M:** Ennio Morricone. **VHS, Beta, LV** $19.95 *STE, VMK* ✍✍

The Stalking Moon Indian scout Peck, ready to retire, meets a woman and her half-breed son who have been captives of the Apaches for 10 years. He agrees to help them escape but learns that the woman's Indian husband is hunting them down. Skeletal plot with little meat on it; great scenery but you wouldn't know it.
1969 (G) 109m/C Gregory Peck, Eva Marie Saint, Robert Forster, Noland Clay; **D:** Robert Mulligan. **VHS** *ACE, WAR* ✍✍½

Stallion A city slicker brings his reputation as a womanizer to a small town.
1988 90m/C Alberto Rojas, Fernando Lujan, Leticia Perdigon, Charly Valentino, Luis Aguilar, Hilda Aguirre. **VHS, Beta** $79.95 *MED* ✍

Stamp Day for Superman Based on the "Superman" television series, this program was made to promote defense savings stamps for kids. A "Superman" cartoon is also included.
1953 25m/B George Reeves, Jack Larson, Robert Shayne. **VHS, Beta** $19.95 *VDM* ✍✍

Stamp of a Killer A tough cop tries to decipher the pattern of a rampaging serial killer. Made for television.
1987 (PG) 95m/C Jimmy Smits, Judith Light, Audra Lindley, Michael Parks, Billy Sullivan, Rhea Perlman; **D:** Larry Elikann. **VHS** $19.95 *STE, NWV* ✍

Stan Without Ollie, Vol. 1 Three silent comedy shorts featuring Laurel on his own, years before teaming with Ollie: "Kill or Cure," "Oranges & Lemons," and "The Noon Whistle."
1923 53m/B Stan Laurel. **VHS, Beta** $24.95 *VYY* ✍

Stan Without Ollie, Vol. 2 Three silent shorts from Laurel before he met the big guy.
1923 55m/B Stan Laurel. **VHS, Beta** $24.95 *VYY* ✍

Stan Without Ollie, Vol. 3 Three early Laurel shorts: "White Wings," "Man About Town," and "Smithy."
1923 51m/B Stan Laurel, James Finlayson. **VHS, Beta** $24.95 *VYY* ✍

Stan Without Ollie, Vol. 4 Three classic pre-Hardy shorts featuring Laurel: "Half a Man," "Yes, Yes, Nanette," and "Save the Ship."
1925 64m/B Stan Laurel, Blanche Payson, James Finlayson. **VHS, Beta, 8mm** $29.95 *VYY* ✍

Stand Alone World War II vet Durning battles local dope dealers in his New York neighborhood. Self-serious anti-drug flick miscasts Durning (overweight and looking silly in fight scenes) and Grier.
1985 (R) 94m/C Charles Durning, Pam Grier, James Keach; **D:** Alan Beattie. **VHS, Beta** $19.95 *NWV, STE* ✍✍

Stand and Deliver War vet joins Greek ranks for the smell of gunpowder in the morning and meets woman of his dreams. Kidnapped by infamous outlaws, he pledges allegiance to them before turning them over to the authorities, and he's free to live happily ever after with heartthrob.
1928 57m/B Rod La Rocque, Lupe Velez, Warner Oland, James Dime, Frank Lanning, Donald Crisp; **D:** Donald Crisp. **VHS, Beta** $14.95 *GPV* ✍✍

Stand and Deliver A tough teacher inspires students in an East L.A. barrio to take the Advanced Placement Test in calculus. A superb, inspirational true story, with a wonderful performance from Olmos.
1988 (PG) 105m/C Edward James Olmos, Lou Diamond Phillips, Rosana De Soto, Andy Garcia; **D:** Ramon Menendez. Academy Awards '88 Nominations: Best Actor (Olmos); Independent Spirit Awards '89: Best Actor (Olmos), Best Director (Menendez), Best Film, Best Screenplay, Best Supporting Actor (Phillips), Best Supporting Actress (De Soto). **VHS, LV, 8mm** $19.98 *WAR, HMV* ✍✍✍

Stand By Me A sentimental, observant adaptation of the Stephen King novella "The Body." Four 12-year-olds trek into the Oregon wilderness to find the body of a missing boy, learning about death and personal courage. Told as a reminiscence by narrator "author" Dreyfuss with solid performances from all four child actors. Too much gratuitous obscenity, but a very good, gratifying film from can't-miss director Reiner.
1986 (R) 87m/C River Phoenix, Wil Wheaton, Jerry O'Connell, Corey Feldman, Kiefer Sutherland, Richard Dreyfuss, Casey Siemaszko, John Cusack; **D:** Rob Reiner; **M:** Jack Nitzsche. **VHS, Beta, LV, 8mm** $14.95 *COL* ✍✍✍

Stand-In When a Hollywood studio is threatened with bankruptcy, the bank sends in timid efficiency expert Howard to save it. Satire of studio executives and big-budget movie making. Bogart is interestingly cast and effective in his first comedy role, playing a drunken producer in love with star Shelton.
1937 91m/B Humphrey Bogart, Joan Blondell, Leslie Howard, Marla Shelton, Alan Mowbray, Jack Carson; **D:** Tay Garnett. **VHS, Beta** *NO* ✍✍✍

Stand-In A strange comedy-action film that takes a behind-the-scenes look at sleaze films and organized crime.
1985 87m/C Danny Glover; **D:** Robert Zagone. **VHS, Beta** *NO* ✍

Stand Off Two young hoodlums with guns take eighteen girls hostage in a dormitory. In Hungarian with English subtitles.
1989 97m/C *HU* Ary Beri, Gabor Svidrony, Zbigniew Zapassiewicz, Istvan Szabo; **D:** Gyula Gazdag. **VHS** $79.95 *EVD, FCT, TAM* ✍½

Stand Up and Cheer The new federal Secretary of Entertainment organizes a huge show to raise the country's depressed spirits. Near-invisible plot, fantastic premise are an excuse for lots of imagery, dancing, and comedy, including four-year-old Temple singing "Baby Take a Bow." Also available colorized. ♫I'm Laughing; We're Out of the Red; Broadway's Gone Hillbilly; Baby Take a Bow; This Is Our Last Night Together; She's Way Up Thar; Stand Up and Cheer.

1934 80m/B Shirley Temple, Warner Baxter, Madge Evans, Nigel Bruce, Stepin Fetchit, Frank Melton, Lila Lee, James Dunn, John Boles; **D:** Hamilton MacFadden; **W:** Will Rogers, Ralph Spence. VHS, Beta $19.98 FOX ♫♫½

Standing Tall A small-time cattle rancher takes on a high-class land baron in this average, made-for-TV western set during the Depression. Playing a "half-breed," Forster carries an otherwise mediocre effort.
1978 100m/C Robert Forster, Linda Evans, Will Sampson, L.Q. Jones; **D:** Harvey Hart. VHS $14.98 WOV ♫♫

Stanley Seminole Vietnam veteran Robinson uses rattlesnakes as his personal weapon of revenge against most of mankind. Thoroughly wretched effort in the gross-pets vein of "Willard" and "Ben."
1972 108m/C Chris Robinson, Alex Rocco, Susan Carroll; **D:** William Grefe. VHS, Beta $14.98 VID ♫½

Stanley An animated featurette about a duckling named Stanley who's searching for his identity.
1983 30m/C VHS, Beta $19.95 ISS ♫½

Stanley and Iris Blue collar recent widow Fonda meets co-worker De Niro, whose illiteracy she helps remedy. Romance follows, inevitably but excruciatingly. Leads' strong presence helps along a very slow, underdeveloped plot.
1990 (PG-13) 107m/C Jane Fonda, Robert De Niro, Swoosie Kurtz, Martha Plimpton, Harley Cross, Jamey Sheridan, Feodor Chaliapin, Zohra Lampert; **D:** Martin Ritt; **M:** John Williams. VHS, Beta, LV $14.95 MGM, FCT ♫♫½

Stanley and Livingstone The classic Hollywood kitsch version of the Victorian legend-based-on-fact. American journalist Tracy sets out into darkest Africa to locate a long lost Brisith explorer. Lavish, dramatically solid fictionalized history. (The real Stanley did not become a missionary—but hey, this is the movies). Tracy is excellent, as usual, and low-key.
1939 101m/B Spencer Tracy, Cedric Hardwicke, Nancy Kelly, Walter Brennan, Richard Greene, Charles Coburn, Henry Hull, Henry Travers, Miles Mander, Holmes Herbert, Paul Stanton, Brandon Hurst, Joseph Crehan, Russell Hicks; **D:** Henry King; **M:** Alfred Newman. VHS, Beta $39.98 FOX ♫♫♫

The Star Chamber A conscientious judge (Douglas) sees criminals freed on legal technicalities and wonders if he should take justice into his own hands. He finds a secret society that administers justice extra-legally. Implausible yet predictable.
1983 (R) 109m/C Michael Douglas, Hal Holbrook, Yaphet Kotto, Sharon Gless; **D:** Peter Hyams. VHS, Beta, LV $19.98 FOX ♫♫

Star Crash Trio of adventurers (woman, man, and robot) sent by emperor Plummer square off against interstellar evil (Spinnell) by using their wits and technological wizardry. Semi-funny and cheesy sci-fi, done with style beyond its limited budget. Soundtrack by John Barry. **AKA:** Stella Star.
1978 (PG) 92m/C IT Caroline Munro, Marjoe Gortner, Christopher Plummer, David Hasselhoff, Robert Tessier, Joe Spinell, Nadia Cassini, Judd Hamilton; **D:** Lewis (Luigi Cozzi) Coates; **M:** John Barry. VHS, Beta, LV $19.98 NLC ♫♫½

Star Crystal Aboard a spaceship, an indestructible alien hunts down the human crew. Cheap imitation of "Alien."
1985 (R) 93m/C C. Jutson Campbell, Faye Bolt, John W. Smith; **D:** Lance Lindsay. VHS, Beta $14.95 NWV, STE, HHE ♫

Star 80 Based on the true-life tragedy of Playmate of the Year Dorothy Stratten and her manager-husband Paul Snider as they battle for control of her body, her mind, and her money, with gruesome results. Roberts is overpowering as the vile Snider, but the movie is generally unpleasant. Fosse's last film.
1983 (R) 104m/C Mariel Hemingway, Eric Roberts, Cliff Robertson, David Clennon, Josh Mostel, Roger Rees, Carroll Baker; **D:** Bob Fosse. VHS, Beta, LV $79.95 WAR ♫♫½

A Star is Born A movie star declining in popularity marries a shy girl and helps her become a star. Her fame eclipses his and tragic consequences follow. Shows Hollywood-behind-the-scenes machinations. Stunning ending is based on the real-life tragedy of silent film star Wallace Reid, who died of a morphine overdose in 1923 at age 31. Remade twice, in 1954 and 1976.
1937 111m/C Janet Gaynor, Fredric March, Adolphe Menjou, May Robson, Andy Devine, Lionel Stander, Franklin Pangborn; **W/D:** William A. Wellman; **D:** David O. Selznick, Dorothy Parker. Academy Awards '37: Best Story; Nominations: Best Actor (March), Best Actress (Gaynor), Best Director (Wellman), Best Picture, Best Screenplay; National Board of Review Awards '37: 10 Best Films of the Year. VHS, Beta, LV, 3/4U, Special order formats $9.95 NEG, NOS, VYY ♫♫♫½

A Star is Born Aging actor helps a young actress to fame. She becomes his wife, but alcoholism and failure are too much for him. She honors his memory. Remake of the 1937 classic was Garland's triumph, a superb and varied performance. Newly restored version reinstates over 20 minutes of long-missing footage, including three Garland musical numbers. ♫I'll Get By; You Took Advantage of me; Black Bottom; Peanut Vendor; My Melancholy Baby; Swanee; It's A New World; Gotta Have Me Go With You; Somewhere There's Someone; Here's What I'm Here For; Shampoo Commercial; Lose That Long Face.
1954 (PG) 175m/C Judy Garland, James Mason, Jack Carson, Tommy Noonan, Charles Bickford, Emerson Treacy; **D:** George Cukor. Academy Awards '54 Nominations: Best Actor (Mason), Best Actress (Garland), Best Art Direction/Set Decoration (Color), Best Costume Design (Color), Best Song ("The Man That Got Away"), Best Original Score; Golden Globe Awards '55: Best Actor—Musical/Comedy (Mason), Best Actress—Musical/Comedy (Garland). VHS, Beta, LV $19.95 WAR ♫♫♫½

A Star is Born Miserable update of the 1937 and 1954 classics permitting Ms. Streisand to showcase her hit song "Evergreen." The tragic story of one rock star (the relentlessly un-hip Streisand) on her way to the top and another (good old boy Kristofferson) whose career is in decline. Kristofferson is miscast, Streisand eventually numbing, but film may interest those looking into big-budget, big-star misfires. ♫Watch Closely Now; Spanish Lies; Hellacious Acres; With One More Look At You; Woman in the Moon; Queen Bee; Everything; Crippled Cow; I Believe in Love; Lost Inside of You; Evergreen.
1976 (R) 140m/C Barbra Streisand, Kris Kristofferson, Paul Mazursky, Gary Busey, Sally Kirkland, Oliver Clark; **D:** Frank Pierson. Academy Awards '76: Best Song ("Evergreen"); Nominations: Best Cinematography, Best Sound, Best Original Score; Golden Globe Awards '77: Best Actor—Musical/Comedy (Kristofferson), Best Actress—Musical/Comedy (Streisand), Best Film—Musical/Comedy (Streisand). VHS, Beta $19.98 WAR ♫♫

Star of Midnight A lawyer/detective becomes involved in the disappearance of the leading lady in a Broadway show and the murder of a columnist. Powell and Rogers take on characters similar to Nick and Nora Charles, but the pizazz of the "Thin Man" series is missing.
1935 90m/B Ginger Rogers, William Powell, Paul Kelly; **D:** Stephen Roberts. VHS, Beta, LV $39.95 RKO, TTC ♫♫

The Star Packer Wayne puts on a marshal's badge, straightens out a gang of crooks, and still finds time for romance. Implausible and kind of dull early Wayne vehicle.
1934 53m/B John Wayne, George "Gabby" Hayes, Earl Dwire, Yakima Canutt; **D:** Robert North Bradbury. VHS, Beta, 3/4U, Special order formats $9.98 REP, COL, NOS ♫♫

Star Quest A genetically engineered woman fights for freedom from her corporate creators. Mediocre effects and some pointless action; done much better by Ridley Scott in "Blade Runner." **AKA:** Beyond the Rising Moon; Space 2074.
1989 90m/C Tracy Davis, Hans Bachman, Michael Mack; **D:** Phillip Cook. VHS, Beta, LV $79.98 VID ♫

Star Reporter A son takes over his father's newspaper when dad is killed by gangsters. The son uses the paper in an attempt to destroy the underworld, but stumbles on some startling personal information that could drastically backfire on him. Generally interesting plot, but has some implausibility and too-broad characterization.
1939 62m/B Warren Hull, Marsha Hunt, Morgan Wallace, Clay Clement, Wallis Clark, Virginia Howell, Paul Fix, Joseph Crehan; **D:** Howard Bretherton. VHS, Beta $16.95 SNC ♫½

Star Slammer A beautiful woman is unjustly sentenced to a brutal intergalactic prison ship. She leads the convicts to escape amid zany situations. Unevenly funny sci-fi comedy.
1987 (R) 85m/C Ross Hagen, John Carradine, Sandy Brooke, Aldo Ray; **D:** Fred Olen Ray. VHS, Beta, LV $79.95 VMK ♫½

Star Spangled Girl One of Neil Simon's lesser plays, one of his least movies. A pert, patriotic young lady captures the hearts of two left-wing alternative-newspaperguys next door; their political conflicts never rise above bland sitcom level.
1971 (G) 94m/C Sandy Duncan, Tony Roberts, Todd Susman, Elizabeth Allan; **D:** Jerry Paris; **W:** Neil Simon. VHS $14.95 PAR ♫½

Star Time Henry is a mentally ill loser who wants to be as happy and famous as his favorite TV stars. Deciding to kill himself, Henry is stopped by the mysterious Sam Bones, who offers him TV stardom—at a steep price. Henry achieves his 15 minutes of fame as a serial killer and his only link to reality is a female social worker.
1992 85m/C Michael St. Gerard, John P. Ryan, Maureen Teefy; **W/D:** Alexander Cassini. VHS $89.95 MNC ♫

Star Trek: The Motion Picture The Enterprise fights a strange alien force that threatens Earth in this first film adaptation of the famous television series. Very slow moving; followed by numerous sequels. Twelve additional minutes of previously unseen footage have been added to this home video version of the theatrical feature. The laserdisc edition offers the film in widescreen format.
1980 (G) 143m/C William Shatner, Leonard Nimoy, DeForest Kelley, James Doohan, Stephen Collins, Persis Khambatta, Nichelle Nichols, Walter Koenig, George Takei; **D:** Robert Wise;

M: Jerry Goldsmith. **VHS, Beta, LV** $14.95 PAR, PIA ☾☾ ½

Star Trek 2: The Wrath of Khan
Picking up from the 1967 Star Trek episode "Space Seed," Admiral James T. Kirk and the crew of the Enterprise must battle Khan, an old foe out for revenge. Warm and comradly in the nostalgic mode of its successors. Introduced Kirk's former lover and unknown son to the series plot, as well as Mr. Spock's "death," which led to the next sequel (1984's "The Search for Spock"). Can be seen in widescreen format on laserdisc.
1982 (PG) 113m/C William Shatner, Leonard Nimoy, Ricardo Montalban, DeForest Kelley, Nichelle Nichols, James Doohan, George Takei, Walter Koenig, Kirstie Alley, Merritt Butrick, Paul Winfield; D: Nicholas Meyer. **VHS, Beta, LV, SVS, 8mm** $14.95 PAR, PIA ☾☾☾

Star Trek 3: The Search for Spock
Captain Kirk hijacks the USS Enterprise and commands the aging crew to go on a mission to the Genesis Planet to discover whether Mr. Spock still lives (supposedly he died in the last movie). Klingons threaten, as usual. Somewhat slow and humorless, but intriguing. Third in the series of six (so far) Star Trek movies. The laserdisc edition carries the film in widescreen format.
1984 (PG) 105m/C William Shatner, Leonard Nimoy, DeForest Kelley, James Doohan, George Takei, Walter Koenig, Mark Lenard, Robin Curtis, Merritt Butrick, Christopher Lloyd, Judith Anderson, John Larroquette, James B. Sikking, Nichelle Nichols, Cathie Shirriff, Miguel Ferrer, Grace Lee Whitney; D: Leonard Nimoy. **VHS, Beta, LV, 8mm** $14.95 PAR, PIA ☾☾ ½

Star Trek 4: The Voyage Home
Kirk and the gang go back in time (to the 1980s, conveniently) to save the Earth of the future from destruction. Filled with hilarious moments and exhilarating action; great special effects enhance the timely conservation theme. Watch for the stunning going-back-in-time sequence. Spock is particularly funny as he tries to fit in and learn the 80s lingo! Can be seen in widescreen format on laserdisc. Also available as part of Paramount's "director's series," in which Nimoy discusses various special effects aspects in the making of the film. The best in the six-part (so far) series.
1986 (PG) 119m/C William Shatner, DeForest Kelley, Catherine Hicks, James Doohan, Nichelle Nichols, George Takei, Walter Koenig, Mark Lenard; D: Leonard Nimoy. **VHS, Beta, LV, 8mm** $14.95 PAR, PIA ☾☾☾

Star Trek 5: The Final Frontier
A renegade Vulcan kidnaps the Enterprise and takes it on a journey to the mythic center of the universe. Shatner's big-action directorial debut (he also co-wrote the script) is a poor follow-up to the Nimoy-directed fourth entry in the series. Heavy-handed and pretentiously pseudo-theological. Available in widescreen format on laserdisc.
1989 (PG) 107m/C William Shatner, Leonard Nimoy, DeForest Kelley, James Doohan, Laurence Luckinbill, Walter Koenig, George Takei, Nichelle Nichols, David Warner; D: William Shatner; M: Jerry Goldsmith. **VHS, Beta, LV, 8mm** $14.95 PAR, PIA ☾ ½

Star Trek 6: The Undiscovered Country
The final chapter in the long running Star Trek series is finally here. The Federation and the Klingon Empire are preparing a much-needed peace summit but Captain Kirk has his doubts about the true intentions of the Federation's longtime enemies. When a Klingon ship is attacked, Kirk and the crew of the Enterprise, who are accused of the misdeed, must try to find the real perpetrator. Has an exciting, climactic ending. As is typical of the series, the film highlights current events—glasnost—in its plotlines. Meyer also directed Star Trek movies 2 ("The Wrath of Khan") and 4 ("The Voyage Home").
1991 (PG) 110m/C William Shatner, Leonard Nimoy, DeForest Kelley, James Doohan, George Takei, Walter Koenig, Nichelle Nichols, Christopher Plummer, Kim Cattrall, Iman, David Warner; D: Nicholas Meyer. **VHS, Beta** $14.95 PAR ☾☾ ½

Star Trek Bloopers
The television cast of "Star Trek" appears in these flubs and goofs that were edited out of the actual episodes. The blooper reels from all three seasons are included on this tape.
1969 25m/C William Shatner, Leonard Nimoy, DeForest Kelley, Nichelle Nichols, James Doohan, George Takei, Walter Koenig, Frank Gorshin. **VHS, Beta** $24.95 MOV

Star Trek: The Cage
This cult series only ran from 1966-1969 but it's impact has been lasting. Join Captain Kirk and the crew of the starship Enterprise on its voyages of discovery. Additional episodes available. In this original pilot episode for the series Captain Chris Pike of the Enterprise faces the challenge of his life when he is captured by the telepathic aliens of Talos IV. Never telecast in its original form and later edited to form the flashback sequences of the two-part episode "Menagerie." Some portions are in black and white. Version was long believed to be lost, but was reconstituted from original color footage.
1965 73m/C Jeffrey Hunter, Leonard Nimoy, Susan Oliver, Majel Barrett, Meg Wyllie, John Hoyt, Gene Roddenberry; D: Robert Butler. **VHS, Beta, LV** $12.95 PAR, PIA, MOV ☾☾

Star Trek the Next Generation: Encounter at Farpoint
Gene Roddenberry, the creator of the original "Star Trek" television series, spearheaded this episodic reincarnation for network syndication. This series, set 80 or so years beyond the original, enjoys an entirely new crew and a modernized vessel. Also, the new series places less emphasis on violent solutions to conflicts than the original TV series. In this first installment, entitled "Encounter at Farpoint, Parts 1 and 2," a powerful life force named "Q" threatens the lives of Captain Jean-Luc Picard and his crew as they attempt to figure out what's going on at Farpoint Station. Look for a cameo appearance by DeForest Kelly, "Bones" from the original series, as a very old man waxing nostalgic about the old U.S.S. Enterprise. Excellent production values, including fine special effects. Additional episodes available.
1987 96m/C Patrick Stewart, Michael Dorn, Jonathon Frakes, Gates McFadden, Marina Sirtis, Denise Crosby, Brent Spiner, Wil Wheaton, LeVar Burton; Cameos: DeForest Kelley; W: Gene Roddenberry. **VHS, LV** $19.95 PAR, PIA, MOV ☾☾

Star Trek 25th Anniversary Special
Shatner and Nimoy are joined by other members of the original series as well as cast from "Star Trek: The Next Generation" in this tribute to the enduring popularity of the television/film series. Includes commentary by "Star Trek" creator Gene Roddenberry, highlights from the films and television series, bloopers, and a behind-the-scenes look at "Star Trek VI: The Undiscovered Country."
1991 100m/C Gene Roddenberry. **VHS, Beta** $14.95 PAR

Star Wars
The first of Lucas's "Star Wars" trilogy and one of the biggest box-office hits of all time. A young hero, a captured princess, a hot-shot pilot, cute robots, a vile villain, and a heroic and mysterious Jedi knight blend together with marvelous special effects to make you care about the rebel forces engaged in a life-or-death struggle with the tyrant leaders of the Galactic Empire. Musical score composed by John Williams. Followed by "The Empire Strikes Back" (1980) and "Return of the Jedi" (1983).
1977 (PG) 121m/C Mark Hamill, Carrie Fisher, Harrison Ford, Alec Guinness, Peter Cushing, Kenny Baker, James Earl Jones, David Prowse; D: George Lucas; M: John Williams. Academy Awards '77: Best Art Direction/Set Decoration, Best Costume Design, Best Film Editing, Best Sound, Best Visual Effects, Best Original Score; Nominations: Best Director (Lucas), Best Original Screenplay, Best Picture, Best Supporting Actor (Guinness); Los Angeles Film Critics Association Awards '77: Best Film; National Board of Review Awards '77: 10 Best Films of the Year; People's Choice Awards '78: Best Film. **VHS, Beta, LV** $19.98 FOX, RDG, HMV ☾☾☾☾

Starbird and Sweet William
On a solo plane flight, a young Native American crashes in the wilderness. He must fight for survival in the harsh woods with his only friend, a bear cub. Good family fare.
1973 (G) 95m/C A. Martinez, Louise Fitch, Dan Haggerty, Skip Homeier; D: Jack B. Hively. **VHS** $79.95 UHV ☾☾

Starbirds
Animated sci-fi epic featuring warriors, robots and battles for the supremacy of Earth and the universe.
1982 75m/C **VHS, Beta** $9.95 MED, WTA ☾ ½

Starchaser: The Legend of Orin
Animated fantasy about a boy who must save the world of the future from malevolent hordes.
1985 (PG) 107m/C D: Steven Hahn. **VHS, Beta, LV** $14.95 PAR ☾☾ ½

Stardust Memories
Allen's "8 1/2." A comic filmmaker is plagued with creative blocks, relationships, modern fears and fanatical fans. The last film in Allen's varying self-analysis, with explicit references to Fellini and Antonioni.
1980 (PG) 88m/B Woody Allen, Charlotte Rampling, Jessica Harper, Marie-Christine Barrault, Tony Roberts, Helen Hanft, Cynthia Gibb, Amy Wright, Daniel Stern; D: Woody Allen. **VHS, Beta, LV** $14.95 MGM, FOX ☾☾ ½

The Starfighters
Air Force Lieutenant Dornan must prove his courage to his disapproving war hero Congressman father. Dornan flies his F-104 through a dangerous storm, thereby earning his father's respect, which leads them to form a bond.
1963 84m/C Robert Dornan, Richard Jordahl, Shirley Olmstead. **VHS, Beta** $59.95 WWV ☾ ½

Starflight One
A space shuttle is called on to save the world's first hypersonic airliner trapped in an orbit above earth. Also called "Starflight: The Plane That Couldn't Land." The film features good special effects, but also a predictable "rescue-mission" plot.
1983 155m/C Ray Milland, Lee Majors, Hal Linden, Lauren Hutton, Robert Webber, Terry Kiser; D: Jerry Jameson. **VHS, Beta** $69.98 LIV, VES ☾ ½

Starhops
A trio of buxom young women attract business to their drive-in restaurant by wearing skimpy outfits. Surprisingly inoffensive for an "R" rating.
1978 (R) 92m/C Dorothy Buhrman, Sterling Frazier, Jillian Kesner, Peter Paul Liapis, Paul Ryan, Anthony Mannino, Dick Miller; D: Barbara Peeters; W: Stephanie Rothman. **VHS** NO ☾ ½

Stark Wichita detective journeys to Las Vegas in an effort to locate his missing sister. During his search, he finds himself taking on the mob. A television pilot for a series that never happened, and Ernest Tidyman's last screenplay. A sequel "Stark: Mirror Image," was made in 1986.
1985 94m/C Nicolas Surovy, Dennis Hopper, Marilu Henner, Seth Jaffe; D: Rod Holcomb. VHS, Beta $59.98 FOX ℤ½

Starlet Soft-core romp wherein a young actress sleeps her way to the top of the Hollywood ladder.
1987 80m/C Shari Mann, Stuart Lancaster, John Alderman. VHS, Beta $29.95 MED Woof!

Starlight Hotel An unhappy teenage girl sets off to find her father, with the help of a shellshocked veteran wrongly accused of a crime. Set in New Zealand during the Depression. Lovely scenery and good acting highlight nice story of odd friendship.
1990 (PG) 90m/C NZ Greer Robson, Peter Phelps, Marshall Napier, Mr. Wizard; D: Sam Pillsbury. VHS, LV $79.95 REP, VTK, PIA ℤℤ½

Starman An alien from an advanced civilization lands in Wisconsin. He hides beneath the guise of a grieving young widow's recently deceased husband. He then makes her drive him across country to rendezvous with his spacecraft so he can return home. Well-acted, interesting twist on the "Stranger in a Strange Land" theme. Bridges is fun as the likeable starman; Allen is lovely and earthy in her worthy follow-up to "Raiders of the Lost Ark." Available in widescreen format on laserdisc.
1984 (PG) 115m/C Jeff Bridges, Karen Allen, Charles Martin Smith, Richard Jaeckel; D: John Carpenter; M: Jack Nitzsche. VHS, Beta, LV $12.95 COL, PIA ℤℤℤ

Starring Bugs Bunny! Bug Bunny teams up with Yosemite Sam and others in some of these great hits. Friz Freleng's "Buccaneer Bunny" and "Hare Force," as well as Chuck Jones' "Hare Tonic."
1948 54m/C D: Friz Freleng, Chuck Jones, Robert McKimson. VHS $14.95 MGM, WTA ℤℤℤ½

Starring the Barkleys Two more episodes from the cartoon series where Arnie Barkley puts his paw in his mouth once again.
1973 44m/C VHS, Beta $39.95 TWE ℤℤℤ½

Stars and Bars O'Connor misfire strands Day-Lewis in the midst of hillbillies. A stuffy English art expert travels from New York to Georgia to price a Renoir, and happens on a bizarre backwoods family marginally run by Stanton. Stereotypical pursuit of humor teeters precariously on the edge of black comedy without actually being funny. Stinky script dooms fine cast to just act weird in a "Deliverance" sort of way. Based on the novel by William Boyd.
1988 (R) 95m/C Daniel Day-Lewis, Harry Dean Stanton, John Cusack, Joan Cusack, Spalding Gray, Will Patton, Martha Plimpton, Glenne Headly, Laurie Metcalf, Maury Chaykin; D: Pat O'Connor. VHS, Beta, LV $79.95 COL ℤℤ

Stars and Stripes Forever Sumptious, Hollywoodized bio of composer John Phillip Sousa, based on his memoir "Marching Along," but more concerned with the romantic endeavors of young protege Wagner. Accuracy aside, it's solid entertainment even if you're not mad about march music. ♫Stars and Stripes Forever; El Capitan; Washington Post; King Cotton; The Battle Hymn of the Republic; Dixie; Light Cavalry; Turkey in the Straw; Hail to the Chief; The Bowery. AKA: Marching Along.

The Stars Look Down A mine owner forces miners to work in unsafe conditions in a Welsh town and disaster strikes. Redgrave is a miner's son running for office, hoping to improve conditions, and to escape the hard life. Forceful, well-directed effort suffered at the box office, in competition with John Ford's similar classic "How Green Was My Valley." From the novel by A.J. Cronin.
1939 96m/B GB Michael Redgrave, Margaret Lockwood, Emlyn Williams, Cecil Parker; D: Carol Reed. VHS, Beta, 3/4U, Special order formats $19.95 NOS, HHT, CAB ℤℤℤ

Starship British sci-fi seems to be an oxymoron. To wit, this lame "Star Wars" ripoff is about human slaves on a planet run by evil robots.
1987 (PG) 91m/C GB John Tarrant, Cassandra Webb, Donough Rees, Deep Roy, Ralph Cotterill; D: Roger Christian. VHS, Beta HHE ℤ

Starship Invasions Lee leads a group of bad aliens seeking to take over the Earth. He's thwarted by UFO expert Vaughn, who is aided by a group of good aliens. Cheesy special effects have this one looking like a bad sci-fi serial from the '40s.
1977 (PG) 89m/C CA Christopher Lee, Robert Vaughn, Daniel Pilon, Helen Shaver, Henry Ramer, Victoria (Vicki) Johnson; W/D: Edward Hunt. VHS $19.98 WAR ℤ

Starstruck Fun-loving folly about a teen who tries to help his talented cousin make it as a singer. Playfully tweeks Hollywood musicals. Enjoyable and fun.
1982 95m/C AU Jo Kennedy, Ross O'Donovan, Pat Evison; D: Gillian Armstrong. VHS $69.98 SUE ℤℤ½

Start the Revolution Without Me Hilarious, Moliere-esque farce about two sets of identical twins (Wilder and Sutherland) separated at birth, who meet 30 years later, just before the French Revolution. About as hammy as they come; Wilder is unforgettable. Neglected when released, but now deservedly a cult favorite.
1970 (PG) 91m/C Gene Wilder, Donald Sutherland, Orson Welles, Hugh Griffith, Jack MacGowran, Billie Whitelaw, Victor Spinetti, Ewa Aulin; D: Bud Yorkin. VHS, Beta $19.98 WAR ℤℤℤ

Starting Over His life racked by divorce, Phil Potter learns what it's like to be single, self-sufficient, and lonely once again. When a blind date grows into a serious affair, the romance is temporarily halted by his hang-up for his ex-wife. Enjoyable love-triangle comedy loses direction after a while, but Reynolds is subtle and charming, and Bergen good as his ex, a very bad songwriter. Based on a novel by Dan Wakefield.
1979 (R) 106m/C Burt Reynolds, Jill Clayburgh, Candice Bergen, Frances Sternhagen, Austin Pendleton, Mary Kay Place, Kevin Bacon, Daniel Stern; D: Alan J. Pakula; W: James L. Brooks. VHS, Beta, LV $14.95 PAR ℤℤℤ

State Department File 649 Insipid spy drama set in northern China. Mongolian rebels hold U.S. agent Lundigan captive; he hopes to capture a Chinese warlord.
1949 87m/C Virginia Bruce, William Lundigan; D: Peter Stewart. VHS, Beta $16.95 SNC, NOS, DVT ℤ½

State Fair The second version of the glossy slice of Americana about a family at the Iowa State Fair, featuring plenty of great songs by Rodgers and Hammerstein. Screenplay by Hammerstein from the 1933 screen version of Phil Strong's novel. Re-

made again in 1962. ♫It Might as Well Be Spring; It's a Grand Night for Singing; That's For Me; Isn't It Kinda Fun?; All I Owe Iowa; Our State Fair. AKA: It Happened One Summer.
1945 100m/C Charles Winninger, Jeanne Crain, Dana Andrews, Vivian Blaine, Dick Haymes, Fay Bainter, Frank McHugh, Percy Kilbride, Donald Meek; William Marshall, Harry Morgan; D: Walter Lang; M: Richard Rodgers, Oscar Hammerstein. Academy Awards '45: Best Song ("It Might as Well Be Spring"); Nominations: Best Original Score. VHS, Beta $19.98 FOX ℤℤℤ

State Fair The third film version of the story of a farm family who travel to their yearly state fair and experience life. The original songs are still there, but otherwise this is a letdown. Texas setting required dropping the song "All I Owe Iowa." ♫Our State Fair; It's a Grand Night For Singing; That's For me; It Might as Well Be Spring; Isn't It Kinda Fun?; More Than Just a Friend; It's the Little Things in Texas; Willing and Eager; This Isn't Heaven.
1962 118m/C Pat Boone, Ann-Margret, Bobby Darin, Tom Ewell, Alice Faye, Pamela Tiffin, Wally Cox; D: Jose Ferrer. VHS, Beta $19.98 FOX ℤℤ

State of Grace Irish hood Penn returns to old NYC neighborhood as undercover cop and becomes involved with an Irish Westies mob in a fight for survival as urban renewal encroaches on their Hell's Kitchen turf. Shrinking client base for shakedown schemes and protection rackets forces them to become contract killers for the Italian mafia, which mixes as well as Bushmills and chianti. Fine performances, with Penn tense but restrained, gang honcho Harris intense, and Oldham chewing up gritty urban scenery as psycho brother of Harris, but the story is long and meandering. Well-choreographed violence.
1990 (R) 134m/C Sean Penn, Ed Harris, Gary Oldman, Robin Wright, John Turturro, Burgess Meredith; D: Phil Joanou; W: Dennis McIntyre; M: Ennio Morricone. VHS, LV $14.98 ORI ℤℤℤ

State of Siege Third pairing of Montand and Costa-Gavras, about the real-life death of USAID employee Daniel Mitrione, suspected to be involved in torture and murder in Uruguay in the '60s. Quietly suspenseful, with snazzy editing; conspiracy-theory premise is similar to Stone's "JFK," and similarly disturbing, whether you believe it or not. Dubbed. AKA: Etat de Siege.
1973 119m/C FR Yves Montand, Renato Salvatori, O.E. Hasse, Jacques Perrin; D: Constantin Costa-Gavras. VHS, Beta, LV $59.95 COL, TAM ℤℤℤ

State of the Union Tracy is a liberal multimillionaire seeking the Republican presidential nomination. His estranged wife (Hepburn) is asked to return so they can masquerade as a loving couple for the sake of his political career. Hepburn tries to help Tracy, as the backstage political machinations erode his personal convictions. From a highly successful, topical Broadway play whose writers changed dialogue constantly to reflect the news. Capra and his partners at Liberty Pictures originally hoped to cast Gary Cooper and Claudette Colbert. Hepburn and Menjou were at odds politically (over communist witch hunts in Hollywood at the time) and on the set, but are fine together onscreen. AKA: The World and His Wife.
1948 124m/B Spencer Tracy, Katharine Hepburn, Angela Lansbury, Van Johnson, Adolphe Menjou, Lewis Stone, Howard Smith; D: Frank Capra. VHS, Beta, LV $39.95 MCA ℤℤℤ½

State of Things Ostensibly a mystery involving a film crew trying to remake a B-movie, "The Most Dangerous Man On Earth," but also an in-depth look at the process of filmmaking, a scathing look at nuclear warfare and an homage to Roger Corman and Hollywood at large. An enigmatic, complex film from Wenders prior to his American years. In German with English subtitles; some dialogue in English.
1982 120m/B *GE* Patrick Bauchau, Allen Garfield, Isabelle Weingarten, Viva, Samuel Fuller, Paul Getty III, Roger Corman; **D:** Wim Wenders. **VHS, Beta, LV $59.95** *PAV, GLV, TAM* 🎞🎞🎞

Stateline Motel Cheap Italian ripoff of "The Postman Always Rings Twice," with a surprise ending but little of great interest. **AKA:** Last Chance For a Born Loser.
1975 (R) 86m/C *IT* Eli Wallach, Ursula Andress, Fabio Testi, Barbara Bach; **D:** Maurizio Lucidi. **VHS, Beta $24.95** *NO* 🎞½

State's Attorney A burned-out attorney finds himself falling in love with the least likely person, a prostitute he is defending. Contrived, improbable story succumbs to star-quality lead acting from Barrymore. Remade in 1937 with Lee Tracy as "Criminal Lawyer." **AKA:** Cardigan's Last Case.
1931 79m/B John Barrymore, Jill Esmond, William Boyd, Helen Twelvetrees; **D:** George Archainbaud. **VHS, Beta $19.98** *TTC* 🎞🎞½

Static A strange, disquieting independent film about an eccentric youth who claims to have built a machine through which one can see heaven. Uneven, with some dull stretches. Co-written by Romanek and Gordon.
1987 (PG-13) 89m/C Keith Gordon, Amanda Plummer, Bob Gunton; **D:** Mark Romanek. **VHS, Beta, LV $19.98** *MCG* 🎞🎞½

Station A Japanese detective's love affair is corrupted by his ruthless search for a bloodthirsty cop killer. With English subtitles.
1981 130m/C *JP* Ken Takakura, Chieko Baisho; **D:** Yasuo Furuhata. **VHS, Beta** *NO* 🎞🎞½

The Station A sophisticated woman, who has just abandoned her fiancee, waits in a tiny station for an early train. The only person around is the young and ordinary stationmaster. Gradually the two are drawn together in a number of charming and comic romantic fantasies. In Italian with English subtitles.
1992 92m/C *IT* Margherita Buy, Ennio Fantastichini; **W/D:** Sergio Rubini. **VHS $89.95** *FXL* 🎞🎞

Station West A disguised Army officer is sent to uncover a mystery of hijackers and murderers. Along the way, he meets up with and falls for a beautiful woman who may be involved in the treachery. Good, solid western with a fine cast and plenty of fun action shot against the requisite beautiful western landscapes. Based on the Luke Short story. Also available colorized.
1948 92m/B Dick Powell, Jane Greer, Agnes Moorehead, Burl Ives, Tom Powers, Raymond Burr; **D:** Sidney Lanfield. **VHS, Beta $19.95** *RKO, CCB, TTC* 🎞🎞🎞

The Statue Famed sculptress unveils a nude rendering of her Nobel Prize-winning husband. Much hilarity in the British vein is meant to ensue, but doesn't. Niven is OK, but this empty, plotless farce should have been much shorter.
1971 (R) 84m/C *GB* David Niven, Virna Lisi, Robert Vaughn, Ann Bell, John Cleese; **D:** Rod Amateau. **VHS, Beta $59.95** *PSM* 🎞

Stavisky Sumptuously lensed story of Serge Stavisky, a con-artist and bon-vivant whose machinations almost brought down the French government when his corruption

was exposed in 1934. Belmondo makes as charismatic an antihero as you could find, and Stephen Sondheim's musical score complements the visuals. In French with English subtitles.
1974 117m/C Jean-Paul Belmondo, Anny Duperey, Charles Boyer, Francois Perier, Gerard Depardieu; **D:** Alain Resnais. **VHS $59.95** *TAM, INT* 🎞🎞

Stay As You Are Aging French architect Mastroianni has designs on a teenager who may be his illegitimate daughter from an earlier affair.
1978 95m/C *FR* Marcello Mastroianni, Nastassia Kinski, Francisco Rabal; **D:** Alberto Lattuada. **VHS, Beta $19.98** *WAR, OM* 🎞½

Stay Awake A demon stalks, haunts and tortures eight young girls sleeping together at a secluded Catholic school. Title might be addressed to the viewer, who will be tempted to snooze.
1987 (R) 90m/C *SA* Shirley Jane Harris, Tanya Gordon, Jayne Hutton, Heath Porter; **D:** John Bernard. **VHS, Beta, LV $19.98** *SUE, NLC* 🎞

Stay Away, Joe The King is a singing half-breed rodeo star who returns to his reservation where he finds love and trouble. Utterly cliche, embarrassing, and stupid even by Elvis-movie standards.
1968 98m/C Elvis Presley, Burgess Meredith, Joan Blondell, Thomas Gomez, L.Q. Jones, Katy Jurado, Henry Jones; **D:** Peter Tewkesbury. **VHS, Beta $19.95** *MGM* 🎞

Stay Hungry A wealthy southerner (Bridges) is involved in a real estate deal which depends on the sale of a gym where a number of body builders hang out. He becomes immersed in their world and finds himself in love with the working-class Field. Big Arnold's first acting role. Offbeat and occasionally uneven comedy-drama based on a novel by Charles Gaines is a sleeper.
1976 (R) 102m/C Jeff Bridges, Sally Field, Arnold Schwarzenegger, Robert Englund, Scatman Crothers; **D:** Bob Rafelson. **VHS, Beta, LV $14.95** *MGM, FOX* 🎞🎞🎞

Stay Tuned Suburban yuppie couple buys a large-screen TV and satellite dish from Hellvision salesman, are sucked into their dish, and wind up starring in hellish TV shows such as "Wayne's Underworld," "Northern Overexposure," "Sadistic Home Videos," and "My Three Sons of Bitches." If they can survive for 24 hours, they'll be able to return to their normal lives. Clever idea for a film is wasted as this one never really gets off the ground; viewers may not want to stay tuned to the low comedy and frantic yucks.
1992 (PG-13) 90m/C John Ritter, Pam Dawber, Jeffrey Jones, Eugene Levy, David Tom, Heather McComb; **D:** Peter Hyams. **VHS, LV $19.98** *WAR* 🎞

Stay Tuned for Murder A sexy news reporter gets caught in a web of financial wrongdoings and corruption. The financiers, lawyers, and other sinister types she's investigating decide to give her a story she will never forget—if she ever gets the chance to tell it!
1988 92m/C Terry Reeves Wolf, Christopher Ginnaven; **D:** Gary Jones. **VHS, Beta $79.95** *IME* 🎞½

Staying Alive "Saturday Night Fever" was the ultimate cheesy 70's musical, hence likeable in a dorky way. This pathetic sequel (directed by Stallone from a Rocky-esque script about beating the odds, etc.) is utterly predictable and forgettable. Music mostly by Frank Stallone, the great heir to Rogers and Hammerstein. 🎵The Woman In You; I Love You Too Much; Breakout; Someone Belonging to Someone; Life Goes On; Far From

Over; Devils and Seducers; (We Dance) So Close to the Fire; Hope We Never Change; Moody Girl; I'm Never Gonna Give You Up; The Winning End; Waking Up.
1983 (PG) 96m/C John Travolta, Cynthia Rhodes, Finola Hughes; **D:** Sylvester Stallone. **VHS, Beta, LV $19.95** *PAR* 🎞½

Staying On Based on the Paul Scott novel, this English drama follows the life of a post-colonial British colonel and his wife who chose to remain in India.
1980 87m/C *GB* Trevor Howard, Celia Johnson; **D:** Irene Shubik. **VHS, Beta $19.95** *MTI* 🎞🎞½

Staying Together Three midwestern brothers go into a panic when their father decides to sell the restaurant they've worked at all their adult lives. Somehow they manage the transition and learn about life. Sloppy comedy-drama with way too many unresolved subplots.
1989 (R) 91m/C Dermot Mulroney, Tim Quill, Sean Astin, Stockard Channing, Melinda Dillon, Daphne Zuniga; **D:** Lee Grant. **VHS, Beta, LV $89.99** *HBO* 🎞½

Steagle The threat of the Cuban missile crisis lets a fantasizing professor loose to enact his wildest dreams. Odd Mitty-esque fantasy comedy might have worked, but ends up confusing and frustrating.
1971 (R) 101m/C Richard Benjamin, Cloris Leachman; **D:** Paul Sylbert. **VHS, Beta $9.98** *NLC* 🎞

Steal the Sky Israeli agent Hemingway seduces Iraqi pilot Cross and persuades him to steal a Soviet MIG jet and defect to Israel. Unlikely plot but swell flying scenes. Hemingway is poorly cast, as she often is. Made for cable television.
1988 110m/C Mariel Hemingway, Ben Cross, Etta Ankri; **D:** John Hancock. **VHS, Beta, LV $89.99** *HBO* 🎞🎞

Stealing Heaven Based on the lives of Abelard and Heloise. In 12th-century Paris, a theologian and teacher falls in love with a beautiful young woman, and the two must defend their bond from all comers, including her righteous uncle. Steamy; trimmed to 108 minutes after threatened X rating. Attractive and cerebral. Available in a 115 minute-uncut, unrated version.
1988 (R) 108m/C *GB YU* Derek De Lint, Kim Thomson, Denholm Elliott; **D:** Clive Donner. **VHS, Beta, LV** *NO* 🎞🎞

Stealing Home A washed-up baseball player learns his former babysitter (who was also his first love and inspiration), has committed suicide. Their bittersweet relationship is told through flashbacks. Foster's superb performance steals the show in this quiet sleeper.
1988 (PG-13) 98m/C Mark Harmon, Jodie Foster, William McNamara, Blair Brown, Harold Ramis, Jonathan Silverman, John Shea, Helen Hunt; **D:** Steven Kampmann, Will Aldis; **M:** David Foster. **VHS, LV $19.98** *WAR* 🎞🎞½

Steamboat Bill, Jr. City-educated student returns to his small home-town and his father's Mississippi river boat, where he's an embarrassment to dad. But bond they do, to ward off the owner of a rival riverboat, whose daughter Keaton falls for. Engaging look at small-town life and the usual wonderful Keaton antics, including braving the big tornado.
1928 75m/B Buster Keaton, Ernest Torrence, Marion Byron, Tom Lewis; **D:** Charles Riesner. **VHS, Beta, LV $19.95** *NOS, CCB, DVT* 🎞🎞🎞½

Steaming Six women get together in a London bathhouse and review their various troubles with men. Unfortunate adaptation of the good play by Nell Dunn. Where are the laughs—and what happened to the dramatic tension? The last film of Dors and director Losey.

1986 (R) 102m/C *GB* Vanessa Redgrave, Sarah Miles, Diana Dors; *D:* Joseph Losey. VHS, Beta $19.95 STE, NWV *⊿⊿*

Steel Construction workers on a mammoth skyscraper face insurmountable odds and strong opposition. Will they finish their building? Worth watching, if you don't have anything else to do. *AKA:* Look Down and Die; Men of Steel.

1980 (R) 100m/C Lee Majors, Jennifer O'Neill, Art Carney, George Kennedy, Harris Yulin, Terry Kiser, Richard Lynch, Roger E. Mosley, Albert Salmi, R.G. Armstrong; *D:* Steve Carver. VHS, Beta, LV $69.95 VES *⊿⊿*

Steel and Lace Davison is the scientist brother of a classical pianist who commits suicide after being raped. He revives her as a cyborg, which promptly sets out to enact its revenge. Depressing, morbid sci-fi.

1990 (R) 92m/C Bruce Davison, Clare Wren, Stacy Haiduk, David Naughton, David Lander; *D:* Ernest Farino; *W:* Joseph Dougherty, Dave Edison. VHS, Beta, LV $89.95 FRH *⊿ ½*

Steel Arena Several real life stunt-car drivers appear in this action-packed film, crammed with spins, jumps, explosions and world-record-breaking, life risking stunts.

1972 (PG) 99m/C Dusty Russell, Gene Drew, Buddy Love; *D:* Mark L. Lester. VHS, Beta $69.98 LIV, VES *⊿*

The Steel Claw One-handed ex-Marine Montgomery organizes guerilla forces against the Japanese in the Philippines in World War II. Good location shooting and plenty of action.

1961 95m/C George Montgomery, Charito Luna, Mario Barri; *D:* George Montgomery. VHS, Beta NO *⊿⊿*

Steel Cowboy With his marriage, sanity, and livelihood on the line, an independent trucker agrees to haul a hot herd of stolen steers. Passable made-for-TV macho adventure.

1978 100m/C James Brolin, Rip Torn, Jennifer Warren, Strother Martin, Melanie Griffith, Lou Frizzell; *D:* Harvey Laidman. VHS, Beta NO *⊿⊿*

Steel Dawn Another "Mad Max" clone: A leather-clad warrior wields his sword over lots of presumably post-apocalyptic desert terrain. Swayze stars with his real-life wife Niemi in unfortunate follow-up to "Dirty Dancing."

1987 (R) 90m/C Patrick Swayze, Lisa Niemi, Christopher Neame, Brett Hool, Brion James, Anthony Zerbe; *D:* Lance Hool. VHS, Beta, LV $14.98 LIV, VES *⊿ ½*

Steel Fisted Dragon Son seeks revenge on the gang who murdered his mother and burned her house to the ground.

1982 (R) 85m/C Stephen Lee, Johnny Kong Kong, Peter Chan. VHS, Beta $69.99 HBO *⊿*

The Steel Helmet Hurriedly made Korean War drama stands as a top-notch war film. Brooding and dark, GIs don't save the world for democracy or rescue POWs; they simply do their best to survive a horrifying situation. Pointless death, confused loyalties and cynicism abound in writer-director Fuller's scathing comment on the madness of war.

1951 84m/B Gene Evans, Robert Hutton, Steve Brodie, William Chun, James Edwards, Richard Loo, Sid Melton; *W/D:* Samuel Fuller. VHS, Beta, LV $14.95 RXM *⊿⊿⊿ ½*

Steel Magnolias Julia Roberts plays a young woman stricken with severe diabetes who chooses to live her life to the fullest despite her bad health. Much of the action centers around a Louisiana beauty shop

where the women get together to discuss the goings-on of their lives. Screenplay by R. Harling, based on his partially autobiographical play. Sweet, poignant, and often hilarious, yet just as often overwrought. MacLaine is funny as a bitter divorcee; Parton is sexy and fun as the hairdresser. But Field and Roberts go off the deep end and make it all entirely too weepy.

1989 (PG) 118m/C Sally Field, Dolly Parton, Shirley MacLaine, Daryl Hannah, Olympia Dukakis, Julia Roberts, Tom Skerritt, Sam Shepard, Dylan McDermott, Kevin J. O'Connor, Bil McCurcheon, Ann Wedgeworth; *D:* Herbert Ross. Academy Awards '89 Nominations: Best Supporting Actress (Wiest); Golden Globe Awards '90: Best Supporting Actress (Roberts); People's Choice Awards '90: Best Film—Drama. VHS, Beta, LV, 8mm $19.95 COL *⊿⊿⊿*

Steele Justice A tough 'Nam vet takes on the whole Vietnamese Mafia in Southern California after his friend is murdered. One of those head-scratchers: Should I laugh, or be offended?

1987 96m/C Martin Kove, Sela Ward, Ronny Cox, Bernie Casey, Joseph Campanella, Sarah Douglas; *D:* Robert Boris. VHS, Beta, LV $19.95 PAR *⊿*

Steele's Law A loner cop is forced to take the law into his own hands in order to track down an insane international assassin.

1991 (R) 90m/C Fred Williamson, Bo Svenson, Doran Inghram, Phyllis Cicero; *D:* Fred Williamson, Fred Williamson. VHS, LV $89.95 ACA *⊿⊿*

Steelyard Blues A motley-crew comedy about a wacky gang that tries to steal an abandoned WW II airplane. Zany pranks abound. Technically flawed direction from Myerson mars a potentially hilarious story. *AKA:* The Final Crash.

1973 (PG) 93m/C Jane Fonda, Donald Sutherland, Peter Boyle, Howard Hesseman, John Savage; *D:* Alan Myerson. VHS, Beta $19.98 WAR *⊿⊿ ½*

Stella Mercouri's film debut has her as a free-spirited bar singer who gets involved in a tragic romantic triangle with a middle-class writer and a local football hero. Melodramatic but Mercouri's earthy joie de vivre is already apparent. In Greek with English subtitles.

1955 94m/B *GR* Melina Mercouri, Yiorgo Fountas, Aiekos Alexandrikis, Sophia Vembo; *D:* Michael Cacoyannis; *M:* Manos Hadjidakis. VHS $59.95 FCT *⊿⊿ ½*

Stella Anachronistic remake update of "Stella Dallas" casts Midler as a single mother who sacrifices everything to give her daughter a better life. Barbara Stanwyck did it much better in 1937. Based on Olive Higgins Prouty's novel.

1989 (PG-13) 109m/C Bette Midler, John Goodman, Stephen Collins, Eileen Brennan, Ben Stiller, Trini Alvarado, Marsha Mason; *D:* John Erman. VHS, Beta, LV $12.95 TOU *⊿ ½*

Stella Dallas An uneducated woman lets go of the daughter she loves when she realizes her ex-husband can give the girl more advantages. What could be sentimental turns out believable and worthwhile under Vidor's steady hand. Stanwyck never makes a wrong step. From a novel by Olive Higgins Prouty. Remade in 1989 as "Stella," starring Bette Midler.

1937 106m/B Barbara Stanwyck, Anne Shirley, John Boles, Alan Hale Jr., Marjorie Main; *D:* King Vidor. VHS, Beta, LV $14.98 SUE *⊿⊿⊿*

Stella Maris Pickford plays tattered waif who's a slave to an alcoholic who's married to the man she loves. But he's in love with Pickford playing a sheltered rich invalid.

Brimming with the tragic consequences of love.

1918 70m/B Mary Pickford, Conway Tearle, Camille Ankewich, Ida Waterman; *D:* Marshall Neilan. VHS, Beta $24.95 GPV, FCT *⊿⊿⊿*

Step Lively A young playwright tries to recover the money he lent to a fast-talking Broadway producer and is forced to take the leading role in his play. Lively musical remake of "Room Service" (1938) was Sinatra's first starring role. Look for Dorothy Malone as a brunette switchboard operator. ♫Some Other Time; As Long As There's Music; Where Does Love Begin?; Come Out, Come Out, Wherever You Are; Why Must There Be an Opening Song?; And Then You Kissed Me; Ask the Madame.

1944 88m/B Frank Sinatra, Gloria de Haven, George Murphy, Walter Slezak, Adolphe Menjou, Anne Jeffreys; *D:* Tim Whelan. VHS, Beta, LV $19.98 RKO, CCB *⊿⊿ ½*

The Stepfather Creepy thriller about a seemingly ordinary stepfather who is actually a homicidal maniac searching for the "perfect family." An independently produced sleeper tightly directed by Ruben and well written by Donald E. Westlake. Followed by two inferior sequels.

1987 (R) 89m/C Terry O'Quinn, Shelley Hack, Jill Schoelen; *D:* Joseph Ruben. VHS, Beta, LV $14.95 COL, SUE *⊿⊿⊿*

Stepfather 2: Make Room for Daddy A poor sequel to the suspenseful sleeper, wherein the psychotic family man escapes from an asylum and woos another suburban family, murdering anyone who may suspect his true identity. Followed by yet another sequel.

1989 (R) 93m/C Terry O'Quinn, Meg Foster, Caroline Williams, Jonathan Brandis; *D:* Jeff Burr. VHS, Beta, LV $89.99 HBO *⊿ ½*

Stepfather 3: Father's Day The father from Hell is back! Escaping from the loony bin with a surgically altered face, the stepfather settles in a small town and gets a job at a nursery (the plant kind, not the children kind). His favorite gardening tool fast becomes the mulch machine, and soon locals are fertilizing the garden. Well below the original, but it may please fans of this genre.

1992 (R) 110m/C Robert Wightman, Priscilla Barnes, Season Hubley; *D:* Guy Magar. VHS, LV $92.95 VMK *⊿*

Stephen King's Golden Years Stephen King creates a semi-chilling vision of scientific progress gone awry in this techno thriller. After being accidentally exposed to exotic chemicals in a lab explosion, an aging janitor undergoes an extraordinary transformation and the government will sacrifice anything to learn more about it. Originally a made-for-television miniseries.

1991 232m/C Keith Szarabajka, Frances Sternhagen, Ed Lauter, R.D. Call. VHS, LV $89.95 WOV *⊿⊿*

Stephen King's It A group of small town children, who were terrorized by an evil force in their youth, are traumatized again some thirty years later, when they learn a new series of child murders occurred in their Eastern home town. The adults, who now all have successful and diverse careers, must come to terms with the terrible secret they share, as "IT" has returned to wreak havoc in their New England home town. Based on horror master King's bestselling novel of the same name.

1990 193m/C Tim Reid, Richard Thomas, John Ritter, Annette O'Toole, Richard Masur, Dennis Christopher, Harry Anderson, Olivia Hussey, Tim Curry; *D:* Tommy Lee Wallace; *W:* Stephen King. VHS, Beta, LV $79.99 WAR *⊿⊿ ½*

Stepmonster A boy tries to convince his father that his new stepmother is a monster—literally. Doesn't work any better that "My Stepmother Is an Alien."
1992 (PG-13) ?m/C Alan Thicke, Robin Riker, Corey Feldman, John Astin, Ami Dolenz, George Gaynes. VHS $89.98 NHO ♪1/2

The Stepmother Yet another Hitchcock ripoff story involving an evil stepmother. Rey is passable, but there's not much else to recommend this dredge.
1971 100m/C Alejandro Rey, John Anderson, Katherine Justice, John Garfield, Marlene Schmidt, Claudia Jennings, Larry Linville; D: Hikmet Avedis. VHS $19.95 ACA ♪1/2

Steppenwolf Static, enigmatic film version of the famous Herman Hesse novel about a brooding writer searching for meaning and self-worth. Interesting to watch, but the offbeat novel doesn't translate to the screen; leaves you flat.
1974 (PG) 105m/C Max von Sydow, Dominique Sanda; D: Fred Haines. VHS, Beta, LV $59.95 VMK, GLV ♪♪1/2

Stepping Out Minnelli stars as a would-be Broadway dancer who gives tap dancing lessons in an old church to an assortment of offbeat and interesting characters. When the troupe is asked to perform for a local charity, they make the most of their opportunity. A warm and touching ensemble piece that avoids over-sentimentalizing and utilizes its cast to best advantage.
1991 (PG) 113m/C Liza Minnelli, Shelley Winters, Bill Irwin, Ellen Greene, Julie Walters, Robyn Stevan, Jane Krakowski, Sheila McCarthy, Andrea Martin, Carol Woods, Nora Dunn; D: Lewis Gilbert. VHS, Beta, LV $14.95 PAR ♪♪♪

Stepsisters Murderous double-crosses occur among a pilot, his wife, and her sister.
1985 75m/C Hal Fletcher, Sharyn Talbert, Bond Gideon. VHS, Beta NO Woof!

The Sterile Cuckoo An aggressive co-ed pursues a shy freshman who seems to embody her romantic ideal. Minnelli's performance is outstanding; Burton as the naive young man is also fine. Pakula's splendid first directing job. AKA: Pookie.
1969 (PG) 108m/C Liza Minnelli, Wendell Burton, Tim McIntire; D: Alan J. Pakula. VHS, Beta, LV $49.95 PAR ♪♪♪

Steve Martin Live Martin shows veteran comedians his famous Universal Amphitheatre performance and his short "The Absent-Minded Waiter."
1985 58m/C Steve Martin, Teri Garr, Buck Henry, David Letterman, Paul Simon. VHS, Beta, LV $14.98 LIV, VES ♪♪1/2

Stevie Jackson brings her flawless skill to the role of British poet Stevie Smith. Excellent performance from Washbourne as Stevie's spinster aunt. Wooden, lifeless screen rendition for the Hugh Whitemore stage play is helped greatly by good performances, but is too talky and, frankly, rather dull and self-absorbed.
1978 102m/C GB Glenda Jackson, Mona Washbourne, Alec McCowen, Trevor Howard; D: Robert Enders. VHS $29.95 UAV, SUE ♪♪

Stewardess School Airline spoof aims at wackiness, but misses the runway. Generic title betrays probable badness which turns out to be all too real. An utter woofer.
1986 (R) 84m/C Sandahl Bergman, Wendie Jo Sperber, Judy Landers, Julia Montgomery, Corinne Bohrer; D: Ken Blancato. VHS, Beta, LV $9.95 RCA Woof!

The Stewardesses The notorious 3-D spectacle of 56 stewardi and their lusty, druggy, rude activities during an 18-hour layover. Legendary sexploitation pasted together from peep-show loops by a San Francisco porn entrepeneur.
1969 90m/C VHS $19.95 VDM ♪

Stick Ex-con Stick (Reynolds, directing himself) wants to start a new life for himself in Miami. Lots of drug dealers and guns don't help the interest level in this dull underworld tale. Based upon the Elmore Leonard novel.
1985 (R) 109m/C Burt Reynolds, Candice Bergen, George Segal, Charles Durning, Dar Robinson; D: Burt Reynolds. VHS, Beta, LV $19.95 MCA ♪1/2

The Stick-Up In 1935, a young American traveling in Great Britain is introduced to some rather illegal fun. Rather sorry attempt at romance/comedy/adventure. AKA: Mud.
1977 101m/C David Soul, Pamela McMyler; D: Jeffrey Bloom. VHS, Beta $79.98 CGH, HHE ♪

Stickfighter The oppressive reign of an evil Spanish ruler of the Philippines is challenged by the world's best stickfighter.
1989 (PG) 102m/C PH Dean Stockwell, Nancy Kwan, Alejandro Rey, Roland Dantes; D: Luis Nepomuceno. VHS $59.95 PSM ♪

Sticks of Death When a man is left near death by gangsters, his grandfather teaches him the ancient martial art of the sticks of death.
1984 90m/C VHS, Beta NO ♪

Sticky Fingers Two female musicians, asked to watch nearly a million bucks in drug money, go on a mega shopping spree. Completely incredible, unlikeable and mean-spirited attempt at zany comedy. Co-written by Mayron and Adams.
1988 (PG-13) 89m/C Melanie Mayron, Helen Slater, Eileen Brennan, Carol Kane, Christopher Guest, Danitra Vance, Gwen Welles, Stephen McHattie; D: Catlin Adams. VHS, Beta, LV $19.95 MED ♪

Stigma "Miami Vice" star Thomas (then 23; later to restore his middle name, Michael) is a young doctor who treats a syphilis epidemic in a small town. He's indistinguishable, but better than anything else here. Ever seen close-ups of advanced syphilis? Here's your chance—but it's not pretty.
1973 93m/C Philip Michael Thomas, Harlan Cary Poe; D: David E. Durston. Beta NO ♪1/2

Stiletto Good cast is wasted in this mediocre depiction of the trouble encountered by a contract Mafia assassin when he decides to change careers. Based on the usual pulp cheese by Harold Robbins.
1969 (R) 101m/C Alex Cord, Britt Ekland, Patrick O'Neal, Joseph Wiseman, Barbara McNair, Roy Scheider, M. Emmet Walsh; Cameos: Raul Julia; D: Bernard L. Kowalski. VHS, Beta $59.98 SUE ♪1/2

Still Life The press has dubbed him "the Art Killer," a serial murderer who makes sculptures out of his victims. He's a sensation—and not ready to stop. This sicko's next "Still Life" may just be a struggling young musician.
1992 (PG-13) 83m/C Jason Gedrick, Jessica Steen, Stephen Shellan; D: Graeme Campbell; M: Michael Danna. VHS $79.95 PSM ♪♪

Still of the Night A Hitchcock-style thriller about a psychiatrist infatuated with a mysterious woman who may or may not be a killer.
1982 (PG) 91m/C Meryl Streep, Roy Scheider, Jessica Tandy, Joe Grifasi, Sara Botsford, Josef Sommer; D: Robert Benton. VHS, Beta, LV $14.95 MGM ♪♪

The Stilts From modern Spanish cinema's preeminent director, this is a study of sexual dynamics revolving around a doomed love triangle. Aging professor Gomez wants young Del Sol to commit to him, but she won't; she has another, younger lover. Overwrought at times, but well acted. In Spanish with English subtitles.
1984 95m/C SP Laura Del Sol, Francisco Rabal, Fernando Gomez; D: Carlos Savrat. VHS, Beta $24.95 XVC, MED, TAM ♪♪♪

The Sting Newman and Redford together again in this sparkling story of a pair of con artists in 1930s Chicago. They set out to fleece a big-time racketeer, pitting brain against brawn and pistol. Very inventive, excellent acting, Scott Joplin's wonderful ragtime music adapted by Marvin Hamlisch. The same directorial and acting team from "Butch Cassidy and the Sundance Kid" triumphs again.
1973 (PG) 129m/C Paul Newman, Robert Redford, Robert Shaw, Charles Durning, Eileen Brennan, Harold Gould, Ray Walston; D: George Roy Hill. Academy Awards '73: Best Adapted Score, Best Art Direction/Set Decoration, Best Costume Design, Best Director (Hill), Best Film Editing, Best Picture, Best Story & Screenplay; Nominations: Best Actor (Redford), Best Cinematography, Best Sound; Directors Guild of America Awards '73: Best Director (Hill); People's Choice Awards '75: Best Film. VHS, Beta, LV $14.95 MCA, BTV ♪♪♪1/2

The Sting 2 Complicated comic plot concludes with the final con game, involving a fixed boxing match where the stakes top a million dollars and the payoff could be murder. Lame sequel to "The Sting" (1973).
1983 (PG) 102m/C Jackie Gleason, Mac Davis, Teri Garr, Karl Malden, Oliver Reed; D: Jeremy Paul Kagan. VHS, Beta, LV $69.95 MCA ♪1/2

Sting of the Dragon Masters Martial arts adventure featuring Bruce Lee's female Kung-Fu counterpart, Angela Mao.
1974 (R) 96m/C Angela Mao, Thoon Rhee, Carter Huang; D: Huang Feng. VHS, Beta $19.95 UHV ♪

Sting of the West Journeyman con artist swindles his way across the Wild West.
1976 (PG) 90m/C Jack Palance, Timothy Brent, Lionel Stander. VHS, Beta $59.95 MPI ♪

Stingiest Man in Town Dickens' tale inspires celebrity voices to break into frequent musical numbers.
1978 50m/C V: Tom Bosley, Walter Matthau, Paul Frees, Theodore Bikel, Robert Morse, Dennis Day. VHS $12.95 WAR ♪

Stingray Two guys buy a Corvette, not knowing it's loaded with stolen heroin. Gangsters with an interest in the dope come after them, and the chase is on. Very violent and not all that funny.
1978 (PG) 105m/C Chris Mitchum, Sherry Jackson, Les Lannom; D: Richard Taylor. VHS, Beta $14.95 COL, SUE ♪1/2

Stir Crazy Two down-on-their luck losers find themselves convicted of a robbery they didn't commit and sentenced to 120 years behind bars with a mean assortment of inmates.
1980 (R) 111m/C Richard Pryor, Gene Wilder, Nicholas Coster, Lee Purcell, Craig T. Nelson, JoBeth Williams; D: Sidney Poitier. VHS, Beta, LV $14.95 COL ♪♪1/2

Stitches Adolescent comedy about med students playing practical jokes on the dean using laboratory specimens. So bad the director (actually Rod Holcomb) allegedly did not want his name associated with it.
1985 (R) 92m/C Eddie Albert, Parker Stevenson, Geoffrey Lewis, Brian Tochi; D: Alan Smithee. VHS, Beta $19.95 MED ♪

Stocks and Blondes The world of industrial finance is used as a background for some raunchy sex humor.

1985 (R) 79m/C VHS, Beta $69.98 *LIV, VES Woof!*

The Stolen Children Highly acclaimed Italian neo-realist film that tells the story of a shy carabiniere and two children who have been placed in his care. They are an emotionally battered 11-year-old girl who was forced into prostitution by her mother and her sullen 9-year-old brother. As they journey from Milan to Sicily and gradually get to know each other, all three of the characters undergo a slight transformation. Gracefully executed, this haunting masterpiece explores the overriding themes of guilt and innocence and keeps you thinking about them long after the movie's over. *AKA:* Il Ladro di Bambini.
1993 108m/C *IT* Enrico Lo Verso, Valentina Scalici, Giuseppe Ieracitano, Florence Darel, Marina Golovine, Fabio Alessandrini; *W/D:* Gianni Amelio; *W:* Sandro Petraglia, Stefano Rulli; *M:* Franco Piersanti. **VHS** 🎬🎬🎬½

A Stolen Face Creepy, implausible drama of a plastic surgeon, spurned by a beautiful concert pianist, who transforms a female convict to look just like her. The convict runs away, but perhaps there's hope in the future with the pianist.
1952 71m/B *GB* Paul Henreid, Lizabeth Scott, Andre Morell, Susan Stephen, John Wood; *D:* Terence Fisher. **VHS, Beta, LV** *WGE, MLB* 🎬🎬

Stolen Identity A Viennese cabbie sees his American dream dashed for lack of the proper papers. When an American businessman is murdered in his cab he is quick to seize the moment...and the dead man's identity. In no time at all he finds himself involved with the widow, entangled with the murderer and under suspicion for the killing. Predictable and sluggish, the story inches its way to the foregone conclusion.
1953 81m/B Francis Lederer, Donald Buka, Joan Camden, Adrienne Gessner; *D:* Gunther Fritsch. **VHS, Beta $16.95** *SNC* 🎬½

Stolen Kisses Sequel to "The 400 Blows," the story of Antoine Doinel: his unsuccessful career prospects as a detective in Paris, and his initially awkward but finally successful adventures with women. Made during Truffaut's involvement in a political crisis involving the sack of Cinematique Francais director Henri Lauglois. Truffaut dedicated the film to Lauglois and the Cinematique, but it is a thoroughly apolitical, small-scale, charming (some say too charming) romantic comedy, Truffaut-style. Followed by "Bed and Board." *AKA:* Baisers Voles.
1968 90m/C *FR* Jean-Pierre Leaud, Delphine Seyrig; *D:* Francois Truffaut. Academy Awards '68 Nominations: Best Foreign Language Film; National Board of Review Awards '69: 5 Best Foreign Films of the Year; National Society of Film Critics Awards '69: Best Director (Truffaut). **VHS, Beta $59.95** *COL* 🎬🎬🎬

A Stolen Life Remake of 1939 film of the same title starring Elizabeth Berguer. Oddly, Davis chose this as her first and last producing effort. Implausible tale of an evil twin (Davis) who takes her sister's (Davis) place so she can have the man they both love. Davis pulls it off as both twins; Ford is good as the hapless hubby.
1946 107m/B Bette Davis, Glenn Ford, Dane Clark, Walter Brennan, Charlie Ruggles, Bruce Bennett, Esther Dale, Peggy Knudsen; *D:* Curtis Bernhardt. **VHS, Beta $19.95** *MGM* 🎬🎬

Stolen Painting A man's wife is kidnapped by an evil gang while having her portrait painted. Her husband rescues her, and they, in turn, are chased by the kidnappers.
1979 11m/C VHS, Beta *BFA* 🎬½

The Stone Boy A boy accidentally kills his older brother on their family's Montana farm. The family is torn apart by sadness and guilt. Sensitive look at variety of reactions during a crisis, with an excellent cast led by Duvall's crystal-clear performance.
1984 (PG) 93m/C Glenn Close, Robert Duvall, Jason Presson, Frederic Forrest, Wilford Brimley, Linda Hamilton; *D:* Christopher Cain. **VHS, Beta $59.98** *FOX* 🎬🎬🎬½

Stone Cold Flamboyant footballer Bosworth made his acting debut in this sensitive human document, playing the usual musclebound, one-punk-army terminator cop, out to infiltrate a sadistic band of fascist biker barbarians engaged in drug running and priest shooting. Profane, lewd, gory, self-deifying; a crash course (accent on crashes) in everything despicable about modern action pics.
1991 (R) 91m/C Brian Bosworth, Lance Henriksen, William Forsythe, Arabella Holzbog, Sam McMurray; *D:* Craig R. Baxley. **VHS, Beta, LV, 8mm $64.99** *COL, PIA Woof!*

Stone Cold Dead Rugged cop Crenna battles crime lord Williams (Paul Williams? Yeah, sure) over a prostitution ring. Meanwhile, a sniper starts killing hookers. Unoriginal and thoroughly dull would-be thriller.
1980 (R) 100m/C Richard Crenna, Paul Williams, Linda Sorensen, Belinda J. Montgomery; *D:* George Mendeluk. **VHS, Beta $59.95** *MED* 🎬½

Stone Fox Heartwarming family drama in which a young man must win a dogsled race to save the family farm. Based on John Reynolds Gardiner's popular children's book.
1987 96m/C Buddy Ebsen, Joey Cramer, Belinda J. Montgomery, Gordon Tootoosis; *D:* Harvey Hart. **VHS $14.98** *WOV* 🎬🎬

The Stone Killer Bronson stars as a tough plainclothes cop in this action-packed drama about a Mafia plot to use Vietnam vets in a mass killing. Violent but tense and action-packed revenge adventure set in the underworlds of New York and Los Angeles.
1973 (R) 95m/C Charles Bronson, Martin Balsam, Norman Fell, Ralph Waite, John Ritter; *D:* Michael Winner. **VHS, Beta, LV $59.95** *COL* 🎬🎬½

Stoner Martial arts adventure featuring a showdown between special agents and a depraved crime lord.
1980 88m/C VHS, Beta *NO* 🎬

Stones of Death An aboriginal curse is invoked when a subdivision is built too close to an ancient burial site. Teenagers begin having all-too-real nightmares about death.
1988 (R) 90m/C Tom Jennings, Natalie McCurray, Zoe Carides, Eric Oldfield; *D:* James Bagle. **VHS, Beta $79.95** *SVS* 🎬

Stoogemania A nerd becomes so obsessed with the Three Stooges that they begin to take over his life and ruin it. Harmless except as a waste of time. Includes actual Stooge footage including some colorized—but see an old Stooges movie instead.
1985 95m/C Josh Mostel, Melanie Chartoff, Sid Caesar; *D:* Chuck Workman. **VHS, Beta $19.95** *PAR* 🎬

The Stoogephile Trivia Movie A program of trivia points, quizzes and clips about Larry, Moe, Curly and Shemp for Stooges fanatics.
1986 55m/C VHS, Beta $19.95 *MPI* 🎬

Stooges Shorts Festival This collection of shorts includes "Disorder in the Court" (1936), "Sing a Song of Six Pants" (1947), and "Malice in the Palace" (1949).
194? 55m/B VHS, Beta $34.95 *HHT* 🎬

The Stooges Story "The Stooges Anthology" presents a history of the comedy team, from their vaudevillian beginnings to their television resurgence in the 60s. "Disorder in the Court" finds the trio making a mockery of the United States justice system, and in "Brideless Groom," Shemp must find a bride within forty-eight hours in order to collect an inheritance.
1990 90m/B Moe Howard, Larry Fine, Curly Howard, Shemp Howard. **VHS $9.95** *SIM* 🎬🎬🎬

Stop Making Sense The Talking Heads perform eighteen of their best songs in this concert filmed in Los Angeles. Considered by many to be the best concert movie ever made. The band plays with incredible energy and imagination, and Demme's direction and camera work is appropriately frenzied and original. Features such Talking Heads songs as "Burning Down the House," "Psycho Killer," and "Once in a Lifetime." Band member Tina Weymouth's Tom Tom Club also performs for the audience.
1984 99m/C David Byrne, Tina Weymouth, Chris Franz, Jerry Harrison; *D:* Jonathan Demme. **VHS, Beta, LV $19.95** *MVD, COL* 🎬🎬½

Stop! or My Mom Will Shoot Getty is an overbearing mother paying a visit to her cop son (Stallone) in Los Angeles. When mom witnesses a crime she has to stay in town longer than intended, which gives her time to meddle in her son's work and romantic lives. If Stallone wants to change his image this so-called comedy isn't the way to do it—because the joke is only on him. Viewers who rent this may find the joke is on them.
1992 (PG-13) 87m/C Sylvester Stallone, Estelle Getty, JoBeth Williams, Roger Rees, Martin Ferrero, Gailard Sartain, Dennis Burkley; *D:* Roger Spottiswoode. **VHS, Beta, LV $19.98** *MCA* 🎬

Stop That Cab Sloppy crooks accidentally leave precious jewels in the back seat of a taxi, and pursue and torture the cabby who found and hid them. Rather mean-spirited, uninteresting comedy.
1951 56m/B Sid Melton, Iris Adrian, Tom Neal. **VHS, Beta** *NO* 🎬½

Stopover Tokyo An American intelligence agent uncovers a plot to assassinate the American ambassador while on leave in Japan. Nice location shooting and scenery; limp story and characters. Based on a novel by John P. Marquand.
1957 100m/C Robert Wagner, Joan Collins, Edmond O'Brien, Ken Scott; *D:* Richard L. Breen. **VHS, Beta $59.98** *FOX* 🎬🎬

The Stork Club A little song, a little dance, will Betty Hutton find romance? The actors manage to rise above the script in this silly, overdone fable. Hutton stars as the poor but spunky hatcheck girl who unwittingly saves the life of a cynical billionaire. His expressions of gratitude are less than appreciated by her G.I. beau. Done mainly as a vehicle for Hutton's promotion, so Betty's die-hard fans may find it to their liking. 🎵Doctor, Lawyer, Indian Chief; Baltimore Oriole; I'm a Square in the Social Circle; If I Had a Dozen Hearts; Love Me; China Boy; In the Shade of the Old Apple Tree.
1945 98m/B Betty Hutton, Barry Fitzgerald, Don DeFore, Robert Benchley, Bill Goodwin, Iris Adrian, Noel Neill, Andy Russell; *D:* Hal Walker. **VHS $19.95** *NOS* 🎬

Storm Uneven thriller finds college students on a camping trip who must fight for their lives when they are confronted by killer thieves. Somewhat contrived, but interesting ending to this low-budget outing.

1987 (PG-13) 99m/C *CA* David Palfy, Stan Kane, Harry Freedman, Lawrence Elion, Tom Schioler; *D:* David Winning. **VHS** $17.95 *WAR* ⅃⅃½

Storm and Sorrow Molly Higgins is known as the "Spiderwoman of the Rockies" for her legendary mountain climbing abilities. Then she joins a team looking to scale the 24,000-foot peaks of Russia's Pamir Mountains. The group meets deadly hazards—both natural and those caused by the ego-driven rivalries of the group's members. A fact-based drama based on the novel by Richard Craig.
1990 96m/C Lori Singer, Todd Allen, Steve Anderson, Jay Baker. **VHS** $89.98 *WOV* ⅃⅃

Storm in a Teacup A reporter starts a campaign to save a sheepdog that the town magistrate has ordered killed because the owner, an old woman, is unable to pay the license tax. As the dog's fate hangs in the balance, this often humorous film provides an interesting look at British society of the 1930s.
1937 80m/B *GB* Vivien Leigh, Rex Harrison, Cecil Parker, Sara Allgood; *D:* Victor Saville. **VHS, Beta** $19.95 *NOS, KRT, DVT* ⅃⅃½

Storm Over Asia A Mongolian trapper is discovered to be descended from Genghis Khan and is made puppet emperor of a Soviet province. Beautiful and evocative. Silent masterpiece. *AKA:* The Heir to Genghis Khan.
1928 70m/B *RU* I. Inkizhinov, Valeri Inkizhinov, A. Christiakov; *D:* Vsevolod Pudovkin. **VHS, Beta, 3/4U** $35.95 *IHF, FST, TAM* ⅃⅃⅃⅃

Storm Over Wyoming The old sheep-and-cattle battle again; Holt and Martin find themselves haplessly embroiled in a Wyoming range war. Action-packed but thin, ordinary western.
1950 60m/B Tim Holt, Richard Martin. **VHS, Beta** $39.95 *RKO* ⅃⅃

Storm Rider A gunman hired to protect a group of ranchers from a powerful rancher falls in love with a local widow. After his job is done, however, he leaves her behind. Typical western fare.
1957 70m/B Scott Brady, Mala Powers, Bill Williams, Olin Howland, William Fawcett, John Goddard; *W/D:* Edward L. Bernds. **VHS** *NO* ⅃⅃

Stormquest Deep in the jungle, a band of women warriors live without men. When it is discovered that one of the group has a male lover, she is sentenced to death. Her man tries to rescue her, and it turns into a war of the sexes—literally. In Spanish with subtitles.
1987 90m/C *SP* Kai Baker, Brent Huff; *D:* Alex Sessa. **VHS** $79.95 *MED* Woof!

Stormy Monday An American developer conspires to strike it rich in Newcastle, England real estate by resorting to violence and political manipulations. Sting plays the jazz club owner who opposes him. Slow plot, but acted and directed well; interesting photography.
1988 (R) 108m/C Melanie Griffith, Tommy Lee Jones, Sting, Sean Bean; *D:* Mike Figgis. **VHS, Beta, LV, 8mm** *PAR, OM* ⅃⅃½

Stormy Trails Bell battles bellicose bad guys who are after his property. At least all the gunfights should keep a viewer awake!
1936 59m/B Rex Bell. **VHS, Beta** $27.95 *VCN* ⅃⅃

Stormy Waters A romantic French drama about a sea captain falling in love with a woman he rescues from a storm. He goes back to his wife, however, when she becomes critically ill. Director Gremillon insisted

on realistic footage of storms at sea; production was delayed because of the difficulties of the German occupation. Dubbed. *AKA:* Remorques.
1941 75m/B *FR* Jean Gabin, Michele Morgan, Madeleine Renaud; *D:* Jean Gremillon. **VHS, Beta** $29.95 *VYY, TAM* ⅃⅃½

Stormy Weather In this cavalcade of black entertainment the plot takes a back seat to the nearly non-stop array of musical numbers, showcasing this stellar cast at their performing peak. ♫There's No Two Ways About Love; Stormy Weather; Ain't Misbehavin'; Rhythm Cocktail; Rang Tang Tang; Dat, Dot, Dah; That Ain't Right; I Can't Give You Anything But Love, Baby; Digga Digga Doo; I Lost My Sugar in Salt Lake City; Geechy Joe; Jumpin' Jive; My, My, Ain't That Somethin'?; De Camptown Races; At A Georgia Camp Meeting; Linda Brown; Nobody's Sweetheart; Beale Street Blues; Basin Street Blues.
1943 77m/B Lena Horne, Bill Robinson, Fats Waller, Dooley Wilson, Cab Calloway, Nicholas Brothers, Katherine Dunham & Her Dance Troupe; *D:* Andrew L. Stone. **VHS, Beta, LV** $19.98 *FOX, PTB, FCT* ⅃⅃½

Story in the Temple Red Lily Insurrectionists capture the Prince and Princess of the Sung Dynasty and only one man can save them in this Kung Fu bonanza.
197? 88m/C **VHS, Beta** $24.50 *OCE* ⅃

Story of a Cowboy Angel On the Christmas Mountain Ranch, a cowboy angel descends to Earth to bestow various beneficences.
1981 90m/C Slim Pickens. **VHS, Beta** $69.98 *LIV, VES* ⅃

The Story of a Love Story Bates plays a writer whose imagination gets the better of him when he attempts an extra-marital affair. Was he with her or not? Unusual concept doesn't stand up in the long run. Fine cast is under-utilized. *AKA:* Impossible Object.
1973 110m/C *FR* Alan Bates, Dominique Sanda, Evans Evans, Lea Massari, Michel Auclair, Laurence De Monaghan; *D:* John Frankenheimer; *W:* Alan Bates. **VHS** *NO* ⅃⅃½

The Story of a Three Day Pass A black American GI falls in love with a French girl he meets in peacetime Paris. With English subtitles. Made on a low budget and flawed, but poignant and impressive. *AKA:* La Permission.
1968 87m/B Harry Baird, Nicole Berger, Pierre Doris; *D:* Melvin Van Peebles. **VHS, Beta** $24.95 *DVT, FCT, HEG* ⅃⅃½

Story of Adele H. The story of Adele Hugo, daughter of Victor Hugo, whose love for an English soldier leads to obsession and finally to madness after he rejects her. Sensitive and gentle unfolding of characters and story. Beautiful photography. In French with English subtitles. *AKA:* L'Histoire d'Adele H.
1975 (PG) 97m/C *FR* Isabelle Adjani, Bruce Robinson; *D:* Francois Truffaut. Academy Awards '75 Nominations: Best Actress (Adjani); National Board of Review Awards '75: 5 Best Foreign Films of the Year, Best Actress (Adjani); National Society of Film Critics Awards '75: Best Actress (Adjani). **VHS, Beta, LV** $19.98 *MGM, FCT, TAM* ⅃⅃⅃

The Story of Boys & Girls Two very different families come together for the wedding feast of their children, during which family secrets are revealed and we come to know and care for everyone present. A twenty-course meal rivals the food scenes in "Babette's Feast" and is guaranteed to make your mouth water. Fine ensemble of actors, well directed, with a vivid evocation of

1930s Italy. In Italian with English subtitles. *AKA:* Storia de Ragazzi e di Ragazze.
1991 92m/C *IT* Lucrezia Lante della Rovere, Massimo Bonetti, Davide Bechini; *W/D:* Pupi Avati. **VHS, LV** $89.95 *FXL, TAM* ⅃⅃⅃

The Story of David Well-done Old Testament Bible drama about the shepherd boy who slew Goliath, overcame the Philistines, and united Israel. Then, as King David, he winds up involved in an illicit love affair with Bathsheba that threatens to destroy his kingdom. Fine acting and a literate script highlight this made for television production. On two cassettes.
1976 (PG) 192m/C Timothy Bottoms, Anthony Quayle, Jane Seymour, Keith Michell, Susan Hampshire; *D:* Alex Segal; *W:* Ernest Kinoy. **VHS** $59.95 *COL* ⅃⅃⅃

The Story of Drunken Master A drunken kung fu master? That's the premise for this film.
19?? 90m/C Yang Pan Pan, Chi Hsiao Fu. **VHS** $49.95 *OCE* ⅃

The Story of Fausta An unhappily married cleaning woman in the slums of Rio entices all the money and gifts she can out of an elderly widower. Decidely grim comedy-drama, well-done but unsparing in its depiction of overwhelming greed. In Portuguese with English subtitles. *AKA:* Romance da Empregada.
1988 (R) 90m/C *BR* Betty Faria, Daniel Filho, Brandao Filho; *D:* Bruno Barreto; *M:* Ruben Blades. **VHS** $79.95 *FXL, TAM* ⅃⅃½

The Story of Jacob & Joseph Fine Biblical drama finds brothers Jacob and Esau fighting over their birthright, tearing apart their family for twenty years. When the brothers finally reconcile it's only to cast an envious eye on youngest brother Joseph, whom they sell into slavery. Taken to Egypt Joseph uses his talents to become the Pharoah's chief advisor but he can never forget his family or what was done to him. All-around good acting, directing and writing. Made for television.
1974 (R) 96m/C Keith Michell, Tony LoBianco, Julian Glover, Colleen Dewhurst, Herschel Bernardi, Harry Andrews; *D:* Michael Cacoyannis; *W:* Ernest Kinoy. **VHS** $59.95 *COL* ⅃⅃⅃

The Story of Louis Pasteur Formulaic Hollywood biopic raised a notch or two by Muni's superb portrayal of the famous scientist and his career leading up to his most famous discoveries. Acclaimed in its time; excellent despite low budget.
1936 85m/B Paul Muni, Josephine Hutchinson, Anita Louise, Fritz Leiber, Donald Woods, Porter Hall, Akim Tamiroff, Walter Kingsford; *D:* William Dieterle. Academy Awards '36: Best Actor (Muni), Best Story & Screenplay; Nominations: Best Picture; National Board of Review Awards '36: 10 Best Films of the Year. **VHS, Beta** $19.98 *MGM, BTV* ⅃⅃⅃

The Story of O A young woman's love for one man moves her to surrender herself to many men, in order to please him. Softcore porn with bondage and S&M beautified by camera work. Based on the classic Freudian-erotic novel by Pauline Reage.
1975 97m/C Corinne Clery, Anthony Steel; *D:* Just Jaeckin. **VHS, Beta, LV** $39.95 *HHE* ⅃⅃

The Story of O, Part 2 A sort-of sequel to the erotic classic, in which the somewhat soiled vixen takes over an American conglomerate by seducing everyone in it.
1987 107m/C Sandra Wey, Carole James. **Beta, LV** $69.98 *LIV, VES, HHE* ⅃

The Story of Robin Hood & His Merrie Men Well-made swashbuckler based on the English legend was Disney's second live action feature. Almost, but not quite, as memorable as the 1938 Micheal Curtiz "Adventures of Robin Hood." Curtiz's version had Errol Flynn, after all. *AKA:* The Story of Robin Hood.
1952 83m/C Richard Todd, Joan Rice, Peter Finch, Martita Hunt; *D:* Ken Annakin. **VHS, Beta** **$19.99** *DIS ♫♫♫*

The Story of Ruth Biblical saga of adventures of Ruth as she denounces her pagan gods and flees to Israel. Typically "epic" with overwrought performances. Alternately not too bad to downright boring.
1960 132m/C Elana Eden, Viveca Lindfors, Peggy Wood, Tom Tryon, Stuart Whitman, Jeff Morrow, Thayer David, Eduard Franz; *D:* Henry Koster. **VHS, Beta** **$19.98** *FOX, IGP ♫♫*

The Story of Seabiscuit The famous racing winner Seabiscuit is featured in a fluffy story of a racetrack romance. Temple is in love with a jockey (McCallister) but wants him to give up racing. Her uncle (Fitzgerald), who is Seabiscuit's trainer, has other other things in mind. *AKA:* Pride of Kentucky.
1949 93m/C Shirley Temple, Barry Fitzgerald, Lon McCallister, Rosemary DeCamp; *D:* David Butler. **VHS** **$19.98** *MGM, BTV ♫♫½*

Story of the Dragon How Bruce Lee developed the martial arts technique of Jeet Kune Do.
1982 93m/C Bruce Li, Hwang Jang Lee, Carter Wong, Roy Horan. **VHS, Beta** *WVE ♫♫*

The Story of the Late Chrysanthemum Classic drama about the son of a Kabuki actor who falls in love with a servant girl against his father's wishes. Their doomed affair is the center of the plot. Acclaimed and sensitive drama, in Japanese with English subtitles.
1939 115m/B *JP* Shotaro Hanayagi, Kakuo Mori, Kokichi Takada, Gonjuro Kawarazaki, Yoko Umemura; *D:* Kenji Mizoguchi. **VHS, Beta** **$79.95** *FCT ♫♫♫½*

Story of the Silent Serials Girls in Danger These two selections capture the best of more than fourteen silent serials. Featured are Swanson tied to the railroad tracks by Beery, Marsh threatened with death (or worse) in caveman times, and other classic cliffhanger situations. Narration and musical score.
19?? 54m/B Gloria Swanson, Mae Marsh, Wallace Beery. **VHS, Beta** **$29.98** *CCB ♫♫½*

The Story of Vernon and Irene Castle In this, their last film together for RKO, Astaire and Rogers portray the internationally successful ballroom dancers who achieved popularity in the early 1900s. Irene Castle served as technical advisor for the film and exasperated everyone on the set by insisting that Rogers be a brunette. Still fun, vintage Fred and Ginger. ♫Only When You're In My Arms; Missouri Waltz; Oh, You Beautiful Doll; Nights of Gladness; By the Beautiful Sea; Glow, Little Glow Worm; Destiny Waltz; Row, Row, Row; The Yama Yama Man; Hello, Hello, Who's Your Lady Friend?; Take Me Back to New York Town; It's A Long Way to Tipperary; Come, Josephine in My Flying Machine; By the Light of the Silvery Moon; Cuddle Up a Little Closer; Way Down Yonder in New Orleans; Texas Tommy; The Darktown Strutters' Ball; While They Were Dancing Around; Rose Room; Hello, Frisco, Hello; Tres Jolie Waltz; You're Here and I'm Here; Syncopated Walk; Maxixe Dengozo; Little Brown Jug; Too Much Mustard; Waitin' for the Robert E. Lee.

1939 93m/B Fred Astaire, Ginger Rogers, Edna May Oliver, Lew Fields, Jack Perrin, Walter Brennan; *D:* H.C. Potter. **VHS, Beta, LV** **$14.98** *TTC, MED ♫♫♫*

Story of William S. Hart/Sad Clowns Features William S. Hart as a cowboy in "Hell's Hinges," and Chaplin in "Tumbleweeds" (1925). From "The History of the Motion Picture" series.
192? 50m/B William S. Hart, Charlie Chaplin, Buster Keaton, Harry Langdon. **VHS, Beta** **$29.98** *CCB ♫♫♫*

Story of Women Riveting factual account of a woman (Huppert) who was guillotined for performing abortions in Nazi-occupied France. In French with English subtitles.
1988 110m/C *FR* Isabelle Huppert, Francois Cluzet, Marie Trintignant; *D:* Claude Chabrol. **VHS** **$79.95** *NYF, TAM ♫♫♫*

Storytime Classics A collection of popular fairy tales narrated by Katharine Hepburn.
1983 78m/C VHS, Beta *VES ♫♫♫*

Storyville Love and music overcome prostitution and poverty in this turn-of-the-century New Orleans jazz drama, but tragedy prevails.
1974 (PG) 96m/C Tim Rooney, Jeannie Wilson, Butch Benit, Wayne Mack, Bond Gideon, Oley Sassone; *D:* Jack Weis. **VHS, Beta** *NO ♫½*

Storyville Southern Gothic tale set in New Orleans about a feckless young lawyer running for a local congressional seat. Neither Cray nor his family are strong candidates for the family values vote. Cray is separated from his wife and willingly indulges in an affair with a beautiful and mysterious young woman. This leads to a blackmail plot when he finds out his lover has been videotaping their antics. There's also a murder investigation and a host of family skeletons rattling around. Robards is fine as the crafty uncle but Spader's low-key attitude works against the story. Directorial debut of Frost.
1992 (R) 112m/C James Spader, Joanne Whalley-Kilmer, Jason Robards Jr., Charlotte Lewis, Michael Warren, Piper Laurie, Michael Parks, Chuck McCann, Woody Strode, Charles Haid; *W/D:* Mark Frost; *W:* Lee Reynolds. **VHS, LV** *COL ♫♫*

Stowaway After her missionary parents are killed in a Chinese revolution, Shirley stows away on a San Francisco-bound liner and plays cupid to a bickering couple who adopt her. ♫Good Night, My Love; One Never Knows, Does One; You Gotta S-M-I-L-E to Be H-A-P-P-Y; I Wanna Go To the Zoo; That's What I Want For Christmas.
1936 86m/B Shirley Temple, Robert Young, Alice Faye, Eugene Pallette, Helen Westley, Arthur Treacher, Astrid Allwyn; *D:* William A. Seiter. **VHS, Beta** **$19.98** *FOX ♫♫*

Straight for the Heart Photojournalist Pierre returns to Montreal after a harrowing assignment in Nicaragua. His homecoming is less than happy when he discovers both his lovers, David and Sarah, have deserted him. Pierre takes to wandering the Montreal streets, taking pictures, hoping they will help him make some sense of his life and help him re-establish a connection with beauty and humanity. In French with English subtitles.
1988 92m/C *CA* Matthias Habich; *D:* Lea Pool. **VHS** **$79.95** *WBF ♫♫*

Straight Line T.S. Turner is a private investigator who goes after street gangs in order to prevent further violence in this action-packed story.
1988 95m/C Mr. T, Sean Roberge, Ron Ryan. **VHS** **$49.95** *CAF, MOV ♫♫*

Straight Out of Brooklyn A bleak, nearly hopeless look at a struggling black family in a Brooklyn housing project. The son seeks escape through crime, his father in booze. An up-close and raw look at part of society seldom shown in mainstream film, its undeniable power is sapped by ragged production values and a loose narrative prone to melodrama. Rich (seen in a supporting role) was only 19 years old when he completed this, funded partly by PBS-TV's "American Playhouse."
1991 (R) 91m/C George T. Odis, Ann D. Sanders, Lawrence Gilliard, Mark Malone Jr., Reana E. Drummond, Barbara Sanon; *W/D:* Matty Rich. **VHS** **$19.98** *HBO, FCT ♫♫*

Straight Shooter An early sagebrush programmer.
1940 60m/B Tim McCoy. **VHS, Beta** **$19.95** *NOS, DVT ♫*

Straight Shootin' Ford's first major effort launched both Carey and Gibson to national fame. Prototypical western; great action, great scenery. Silent.
1917 53m/B Harry Carey Sr., Hoot Gibson, Mollie Malone; *D:* John Ford. **VHS, Beta** **$27.95** *GPV, VCN, DVT ♫♫½*

Straight Talk Shirlee (Parton) is a down-home girl and former dance teacher from Arkansas who heads for Chicago to start life anew. She finds a job as a receptionist at WNDY radio, but she is mistaken for the new radio psychologist. Her homespun advice ("Get off the cross. Somebody needs the wood") becomes hugely popular and soon "Dr." Shirlee is the toast of the town. An investigative reporter (Woods), however, is looking for a scandal by trying to prove that she holds no degrees, but he soon falls in love with her. Parton's advice is the funniest part of this flimsy movie, but she is helped immensely by Dunne and Orbach. Woods, however, is not in his element in a romantic comedy, and holds the movie down.
1992 (PG) 88m/C Dolly Parton, James Woods, Griffin Dunne, Michael Madsen, Deidre O'Connell, John Sayles, Teri Hatcher, Spalding Gray, Jerry Orbach, Philip Bosco, Charles Fleischer, Jay Thomas; *D:* Barnet Kellman. **VHS, Beta** **$19.99** *HPH ♫♫½*

Straight Time Ex-con Hoffman hits the streets for the first time in six years and finds himself again falling into a life of crime. Well-told, sobering story flopped at the box office and has never received the recognition it deserved. Convincing, realistic portrayal of a criminal. Hoffman was the original director, but gave the reins to Grosbard. Based on the novel "No Beast So Fierce" by Edward Bunker.
1978 (R) 114m/C Dustin Hoffman, Harry Dean Stanton, Gary Busey, Theresa Russell, M. Emmet Walsh; *D:* Ulu Grosbard. **VHS, Beta** **$19.98** *WAR ♫♫♫*

Straight to Hell A wildly senseless, anachronistic western spoof about a motley, inept gang of frontier thieves. An overplayed, indiscriminating punk spaghetti oat-opera.
1987 (R) 86m/C Dennis Hopper, Joe Strummer, Elvis Costello, Grace Jones, Jim Jarmusch, Dick Rude, Courtney Love, Sy Richardson; *D:* Alex Cox. **VHS, Beta** *OM ♫½*

Straight Up A musical f/x-ridden attempts to warn MTV-era children about drugs, but visual gimmicks often overwhelm the message. Gossett sings nicely as a cosmic sage of abstinence, who cautions a boy against substance abuse. The smartest segment lambasts cigarette and alcohol ads.
1990 75m/C Chad Allen, Louis Gossett Jr. **VHS, Beta** *RHI ♫½*

Strait-Jacket After Crawford is released from an insane asylum where she was sent 20 years for axing her husband and his mistress, mysterious axe murders begin to occur in the neighborhood. Coincidence? Aging axist Crawford is the prime suspect, and even she cannot say for sure who's doing it. Daughter Baker is there to help her adjust. Moderately creepy grade B+ slasher is lifted somewhat by Crawford. Written by Robert Bloch ("Psycho"). Never one to miss a gimmick, director Castle arranged for the distribution of cardboard "bloody axes" to all theater patrons attending the movie.
1964 89m/B Joan Crawford, Leif Erickson, Diane Baker, George Kennedy; *D:* William Castle. VHS, Beta $59.95 COL *ℐℐ*½

Stranded A group of aliens escaping interplanetary persecution land on Earth and enlist the aid of an Earth family. Solid characters make it more than sci-fi; sort of a parable of intolerance, human (and alien) goodness, etc.
1987 (PG-13) 80m/C Maureen O'Sullivan, Ione Skye, Cameron Dye; *D:* Tex Fuller. VHS, Beta, LV $79.95 COL *ℐℐ*

The Strange Affair of Uncle Harry Small-town gothic with fine acting by Sanders, an aging bachelor who plots murder when his romance is threatened by a jealous sister. A title card asks you not to reveal the 'surprise' ending—a hackneyed twist that appeased the censors but made producer Joan Harris resign in protest. Based on a play by Robert Job. Tape suffers from poor film-video transfer. *AKA:* Uncle Harry.
1945 80m/B George Sanders, Geraldine Fitzgerald, Ella Raines, Sara Allgood, Moyna MacGill, Samuel S. Hinds, Harry von Zell; *D:* Robert Siodmak. VHS, LV $19.98 REP, PIA, FCT *ℐℐ*½

A Strange and Deadly Occurence Strange things start to happen to a family when they move to a house in a remote area. Made-for-television.
1974 74m/C Robert Stack, Vera Miles, L.Q. Jones, Herb Edelman; *D:* John Llewellyn Moxey. VHS, Beta $34.95 WOV *ℐ*½

Strange Awakening Traveling in France while recuperating from amnesia, Barker is trapped in a plot of fraud and theft. Confused and contrived.
1958 75m/B GB Lex Barker, Carole Mathews, Nora Swinburne, Richard Molinos, Peter Dyneley; *D:* Montgomery Tully. VHS $16.95 SNC *ℐ*

Strange Behavior In a small Midwestern town, the police chief follows the clues from a series of murders to the experimental lab of the local college. Seems there's a mad scientist involved... Grisly and creepy, but unduly ballyhooed when it appeared. Shot on location in New Zealand. *AKA:* Dead Kids; Small Town Massacre.
1981 (R) 105m/C Michael Murphy, Louise Fletcher, Dan Shor, Fiona Lewis, Arthur Dignam, Marc McClure, Scott Brady; *D:* Michael Laughlin. Beta $59.95 COL, RHI *ℐℐ*

Strange Brew The screen debut of the SCTV alumni's characters Doug & Bob MacKenzie, the Great White North duo. They do battle with a powerful, megalomaniacal brew master over - what else? - a case of beer. Dumb, but what did you expect? Watch it, or be a hoser.
1983 (PG) 91m/C Rick Moranis, Dave Thomas, Max von Sydow, Paul Dooley; *D:* Rick Moranis, Dave Thomas. VHS, Beta, LV $19.98 MGM *ℐℐ*½

Strange Cargo Convicts escaping from Devil's Island are mystically entranced by a Christ-like fugitive en route to freedom. An odd, pretentious Hollywood fable waiting for a cult following. Gable and Crawford's eighth and final pairing. Adapted by Anita Loos from the book "Not Too Narrow...Not Too Deep" by Richard Sale.
1940 105m/B Clark Gable, Joan Crawford, Ian Hunter, Peter Lorre, Paul Lukas, Albert Dekker, J. Edward Bromberg, Eduardo Ciannelli, Frederick Worlock; *D:* Frank Borzage. VHS, Beta $19.98 MGM *ℐℐ*½

Strange Case of Dr. Jekyll & Mr. Hyde An adaptation of the classic Robert Louis Stevenson book about a scientist who conducts experiments on himself to separate good from evil. Palance is oddly but appealingly cast; Jarrott's bad direction wrecks it. Made for TV.
1968 128m/C Jack Palance, Leo Genn, Oscar Homolka, Billie Whitelaw, Denholm Elliott; *D:* Charles Jarrott. VHS, Beta $49.95 LIV *ℐℐ*

Strange Case of Dr. Jekyll & Mr. Hyde The Robert Louis Stevenson classic, with Hyde portrayed as an icy, well-dressed sociopath. In Shelley Duvall's "Nightmare Classics" series. More psychological than special effect-y. Made for cable.
1989 60m/C Anthony Andrews, Laura Dern, George Murdock, Nicholas Guest; *D:* Michael Lindsay-Hogg. VHS, Beta $59.95 WAR, OM *ℐℐ*½

The Strange Countess A girl is almost murdered and no apparent motive can be found until a 20-year old murder is uncovered in this Edgar Wallace story.
1961 96m/C GE Joachim Fuchsberger, Lil Dagover, Marianne Hoppe, Brigitte Grothum; *D:* Josef von Baky. VHS $16.95 SNC *ℐℐ*

Strange Fruit Based on Lillian Smith's novel, this program tells the story of a black painter in Georgia, 1948, who faces racism. At first avoiding voter registration, he becomes involved and is killed. His death serves as an inspiration to his community.
1979 33m/C VHS, Beta LCA *ℐℐ*

Strange Illusion Unbalanced teen Lydon believes his mother, about to remarry, was responsible for his father's death. He feigns insanity in a plan to catch her, but is sent to an asylum, where he nearly goes insane for real. Slow and implausible, but creepy enough to hold your interest. *AKA:* Out of the Night.
1945 87m/B Jimmy Lydon, Warren William, Sally Eilers, Regis Toomey, Charles Arnt, George Reed; *D:* Edgar G. Ulmer. VHS, Beta $16.95 SNC *ℐℐ*½

Strange Interlude Shearer is at her best in screen adaptation of talky Eugene O'Neill play in which she portrays a young wife who wants a child, but discovers that insanity runs in her husband's family. Doing the only sensible thing, she decides to have a child by another man (Gable). Interesting because the characters' thoughts are revealed to the audience through voice-overs. *AKA:* Strange Interval.
1932 110m/B Norma Shearer, Clark Gable, May Robson, Ralph Morgan, Robert Young, Mary Alden, Maureen O'Sullivan, Henry B. Walthall; *D:* Robert Z. Leonard. VHS $19.98 MGM *ℐℐ*

Strange Interlude Slow PBS production of Eugene O'Neill's famous drama covering two decades of the lives and loves of an upper-class family. Excellent performances help to make up for talkiness. On two cassettes.
1990 190m/C Glenda Jackson, Jose Ferrer, David Dukes, Ken Howard, Edward Petherbridge; *D:* Herbert Wise. VHS $29.95 FRH, TVC *ℐℐ*½

Strange Invaders Body-snatchers-from-space sci-fi with an attitude—fun spoof of '50s alien flicks. Space folks had taken over a midwestern town in the '50s, assuming the locals' appearance and attire before returning to their ship. Seems one of them married an earthling—but divorced and moved with her half-breed daughter to New York City. So the hicksters from space arrive in Gotham wearing overalls...
1983 (PG) 94m/C Paul LeMat, Nancy Allen, Diana Scarwid, Michael Lerner, Louise Fletcher, Wallace Shawn, Fiona Lewis, Kenneth Tobey, June Lockhart, Charles Lane, Dey Young, Mark Goddard; *D:* Michael Laughlin. VHS, Beta, LV $79.95 VES *ℐℐℐ*

The Strange Love of Martha Ivers Douglas is good in his screen debut as the wimpy spouse of unscrupulous Stanwyck. Stanwyck shines as the woman who must stay with Douglas because of a crime she committed long ago... Tough, dark melodrama; classic film noir.
1946 117m/B Barbara Stanwyck, Van Heflin, Kirk Douglas, Lizabeth Scott, Judith Anderson; *D:* Lewis Milestone. VHS, Beta, LV $19.95 NOS, KRT, DVT *ℐℐℐ*

Strange New World Three astronauts awake from 188 years in the fridge to find cloning has arrived. Made for TV as a pilot for a hoped-for series that might have been even worse.
1975 100m/C John Saxon, Kathleen Miller, Keene Curtis, Martine Beswick, James Olson, Catherine Bach, Richard Farnsworth, Ford Rainey; *D:* Robert Butler. VHS $59.95 UNI *ℐ*½

Strange Shadows in an Empty Room Sleuth Whitman wants answers about the murder of his kid sis. He beats lots of people up, and the viewer leaves the empty living room to look at the inside of the fridge, which is more interesting. *AKA:* Blazing Magnums; Shadows in an Empty Room.
1976 (R) 97m/C Stuart Whitman, John Saxon, Martin Landau, Tisa Farrow, Carole Laure, Gayle Hunnicutt; *D:* Martin Herbert. VHS, Beta $69.95 VES *ℐ*

Strange Tales A collection of fantasy shorts, including "Twilight Journey," "The Crystal Quest" and "The Visitant."
198? 60m/C VHS, Beta VDC *ℐ*

Strange Tales/Ray Bradbury Theatre An anthology of thrillers based on Bradbury stories: "Banshee," "The Screaming Woman," and "The Town Where No One Got Off."
1986 (R) 86m/C Jeff Goldblum, Peter O'Toole, Drew Barrymore, Charles Martin Smith. VHS, Beta $19.99 HBO *ℐℐ*½

The Strange Woman Uneventful Hollywood costume drama. Lamarr stalks man after man, but never creates much excitement in spite of Ulmer's fancy camera work and intense pace.
1946 100m/B Hedy Lamarr, George Sanders, Louis Hayward, Gene Lockhart, Hillary Brooke, June Storey; *D:* Edgar G. Ulmer. VHS $29.95 NOS, FCT *ℐℐ*

The Strangeness Miners in search of gold release a "strange" creature from far beneath the earth—eek! Made on a negative budget.
1985 90m/C Dan Lunham, Terri Berland; *D:* David Michael Hillman. VHS, Beta $49.95 TWE Woof!

The Stranger Notably conventional for Welles, but swell entertainment nonetheless. War crimes tribunal sets Nazi thug Shayne free hoping he'll lead them to his superior, Welles. Robinson trails Shayne through Europe and South America to a small town in

Connecticut. Tight suspense made on a tight budget saved Welles's directorial career.
1946 95m/B Edward G. Robinson, Loretta Young, Martha Wentworth, Konstantin Shayne, Richard Long, Orson Welles; **D:** Orson Welles. **VHS, Beta $9.95** *NEG, NOS, PSM* 𝄞𝄞𝄞½

The Stranger Corbett crash-lands on a planet an awful lot like Earth - and must stay on the run. Uneven fugitive thriller in sci-fi drag. Made for TV.
1973 100m/C Cameron Mitchell, Glenn Corbett, Sharon Acker, Lew Ayres, George Coulouris, Dean Jagger; **D:** Lee H. Katzin. **VHS** *NO* 𝄞½

The Stranger Amnesiac car-wreck victim Bedelia begins regaining her memory, and realizes she witnessed several grisly murders. Is her shrink (Riegert) helping her remember, or keeping something from her? Good, neglected thriller.
1987 (R) 93m/C *AR* Bonnie Bedelia, Peter Riegert, Barry Primus, David Spielberg, Julio de Grazia, Celia Roth; **D:** Adolfo Aristarain. **VHS, Beta, 8mm $79.95** *COL* 𝄞𝄞𝄞

A Stranger Among Us A missing jeweler turns up dead and more than $1 million in diamonds has disappeared. NYPD Detective Emily Eden (Griffith) is called in to solve the case, and she decides she must go undercover in a community of Hasidic Jews to find the perpetrator. She not only finds the criminal, but she also falls in love with one of the group's most devout residents. Griffith is out of her element as a tough cop with her baby voice and cutesy style, but other actors, including Thal (in his movie debut) and Sara, perform splendidly, even though they are held back by a cumbersome script that is similar in many respects to "Witness."
1992 (PG-13) 109m/C Melanie Griffith, Eric Thal, John Pankow, Tracy Pollan, Lee Richardson, Mia Sara, Jamey Sheridan; **D:** Sidney Lumet; **W:** Robert J. Avereen. **VHS, Beta, LV $94.95** *HPH* 𝄞𝄞

The Stranger and the Gunfighter The baddest spaghetti western of all time - or is it a kung fu movie? Alcoholic cowpoke Van Cleef and kung fu master Lieh pair up to find hidden treasure. There is a map, but parts are printed on the assorted fannies of various women.
1976 106m/C Patty Shepard, Lee Van Cleef, Lo Lieh; **D:** Anthony M. Dawson **VHS, Beta, LV $59.95** *COL* 𝄞𝄞

The Stranger from Pecos Brown fights a cheater who swindles people at poker and then uses the money to buy their mortgages. Meanwhile, his pal Hatton finds a novel way to help a robbery victim buy back his property.
1945 55m/B Johnny Mack Brown, Raymond Hatton, Kirby Grant, Christine McIntyre, Steve Clark, Kermit Maynard; **D:** Lambert Hillyer. **VHS $19.95** *DVT, HEG* 𝄞𝄞

The Stranger from Venus "The Day the Earth Stood Still" warmed over. Venusian Dantine tells earth lady Neal he's worried about the future of her planet. Real low budget. Includes previews of coming attractions from classic sci-fi. **AKA:** Immediate Disaster; The Venusian.
1954 78m/C Patricia Neal, Helmut Dantine, Derek Bond. **VHS, Beta $19.95** *MED, MLB* Woof!

Stranger in Paso Bravo A distraught drifter returns to a strange Italian town to avenge the murders of his wife and daughter years before. Dubbed.
1973 92m/C *IT* Anthony Steffen, Giulia Rubini, Eduardo Fajardo, Adriana Ambesi. **VHS, Beta $57.95** *UNI* 𝄞

Stranger in Town A young journalist looks into the murder of an American composer in a sleepy English village. He discovers blackmail and intrigue. So-so thriller. Based on the novel "The Uninvited" by Frank Chittenden.
1957 73m/B *GB* Alex Nicol, Ann Page, Mary Laura Wood, Mona Washbourne, Charles Lloyd Pack; **D:** George Pollock. **VHS, Beta $16.95** *SNC* 𝄞𝄞

A Stranger is Watching Rapist-murderer Torn holds his victim's 10-year-old daughter hostage, along with a New York television anchorwoman. Complicated and distasteful. Made for TV.
1982 (R) 92m/C Rip Torn, Kate Mulgrew, James Naughton; **D:** Sean S. Cunningham. **VHS, Beta $79.95** *MGM* 𝄞½

Stranger on the Third Floor Reporter McGuire's testimony helped convict cabbie Cook of murder, but he begins to have doubts. Odd, shadowy psycho-thriller considered by some the first film noir. The reporter comes to be suspected of the crime...and his fiancee pounds the pavement to prove him innocent. Average acting, but great camera work gives the whole a deliciously menacing feel.
1940 64m/B Peter Lorre, John McGuire, Elisha Cook Jr., Margaret Tallichet; **D:** Boris Ingster. **VHS, Beta, LV $19.95** *CCB, MED* 𝄞𝄞𝄞

Stranger than Paradise Regular guy, nerdy sidekick and Hungarian girl cousin traipse around America being bored and having fun and adventure. New York, then - on to Cleveland! The thinking person's mindless flick. Inventive, independent comedy made on quite a low budget was acclaimed at Cannes.
1984 (R) 90m/B *GE* Richard Edson, Eszter Balint, John Lurie; **D:** Jim Jarmusch. **VHS, Beta, LV $79.98** *FOX* 𝄞𝄞𝄞

The Stranger Who Looks Like Me Adoptees Baxter and Bridges set out to find their real parents. Not-bad TV fare. Blake is Baxter's real-life mom. Look for a young Patrick Duffy.
1974 74m/C Meredith Baxter Birney, Beau Bridges, Whitney Blake; **D:** Larry Peerce. **VHS, Beta $29.95** *WOV* 𝄞𝄞

The Stranger Within Made-for-TV "Rosemary's Baby" rip-off. Eden is in a family way, though hubby Grizzard is impotent. The stranger within begins commanding her to do its bidding, just as if she were a genie.
1974 74m/C Barbara Eden, George Grizzard, Joyce Van Patten, Nehemiah Persoff; **D:** Lee Philips. **VHS, Beta $49.95** *LIV* 𝄞½

The Stranger Wore a Gun Hoping to remove a black mark against his name, Jeff Travis (Scott) goes to Arizona and ends up foiling a stagecoach robbery. Features a great action sequence in a burning saloon. Originally shot in 3-D, this is based on the novel "Yankee Gold" by John M. Cunningham.
1953 83m/C Randolph Scott, Claire Trevor, Joan Weldon, George Macready, Alfonso Bedoya, Lee Marvin, Ernest Borgnine, Pierre Watkin, Joseph Vitale; **D:** Andre de Toth. **VHS $19.95** *COL* 𝄞𝄞

Strangers Australian horror film revolves around a man in a troubled marriage who fools around with another woman, only to realize she is dead set on mating for life. When he hesitates, she vows to murder his wife. Very similar to the smash hit "Fatal Attraction."
1990 83m/C *AU* James Healey, Anne Looby; **D:** Craig Lahiff. **VHS $29.95** 𝄞𝄞

Strangers Features three provocative vignettes that take place far from home. Fiorentino, Chen, and Hutton each star in an erotic story played out in a foreign land.
1991 (R) 85m/C Linda Fiorentino, Joan Chen, Timothy Hutton; **D:** Joan Tewkesbury. **VHS, LV $89.98** *PSM* 𝄞𝄞

Stranger's Gold A mysterious gunslinger eliminates corruption in a western mining town.
1971 90m/C John Garko, Antonio Vilar, Daniela Giordano. **VHS, Beta $19.95** *GEM* 𝄞

Strangers in Good Company A loving metaphor to growing older. Director Scott uses non-actors for every role in this quiet little film about a bus-load of elderly women lost in the Canadian wilderness. They wait for rescue without hystrionics, using the opportunity instead to get to know each other and nature. Beautifully made, intelligent, uncommon and worthwhile. **AKA:** The Company of Strangers.
1991 (PG) 101m/C *CA* Alice Diabo, Mary Meigs, Cissy Meddings, Beth Webber, Winifred Holden, Constance Garneau, Catherine Roche, Michelle Sweeney; **D:** Cynthia Scott. **VHS, Beta $94.95** *TOU* 𝄞𝄞𝄞

Strangers in Paradise A scientist who had cryogenically frozen himself to escape the Nazis is thawed out in the present, and his powers are used by a delinquent-obsessed sociopath.
1986 81m/C **W/D:** Ulli Lommel. **VHS, Beta $69.98** *LIV, VES* 𝄞½

Strangers in the City Puerto Ricans newly arrived in New York try to make their way. Serious but slightly overwrought immigrant-family melodrama.
1962 80m/B Robert Gentile, Camilo Delgado, Rosita De Triana; **D:** Rick Carrier. **VHS, Beta $59.98** *NLC* 𝄞𝄞

Strangers Kiss Circa 1955· Hollywood director encourages his two leads to have an off-screen romance to bring reality to his film. Conflict arises when the leading lady's boyfriend, the film's financier, gets wind of the scheme. Intriguing, fun, slightly off-center. Based on Stanley Kubrick's film "Killer Kiss."
1983 (R) 93m/C Peter Coyote, Victoria Tennant, Blaine Novak, Dan Shor, Richard Romanus, Linda Kerridge, Carlos Palomino; **D:** Matthew Chapman. **VHS, Beta $69.99** *HBO* 𝄞𝄞½

Strangers of the Evening In its day this dark comedy/mystery caught flak for its gruesomeness. There's been a mixup at the undertaker's, and the wrong body was buried— possibly alive. Good photography and acting make the humor work, intentionally or not. Based on the novel "The Illustrious Corpse," by Tiffany Thayer.
1932 70m/B ZaSu Pitts, Eugene Pallette, Lucien Littlefield, Tully Marshall, Miriam Seegar, Theodore von Eltz; **D:** H. Bruce Humberstone. **VHS $12.95** *SNC, NOS* 𝄞𝄞

Strangers on a Train Long before there was "Throw Momma from the Train," there was this Hitchcock super-thriller about two passengers who accidentally meet and plan to "trade" murders. Amoral Walker wants the exchange and the money he'll inherit by his father's death; Granger would love to end his stifling marriage and wed Roman, a senator's daughter, but finds the idea ultimately sickening. What happens is pure Hitchcock. Screenplay co-written by murder-mystery great Raymond Chandler. Patricia Hitchcock, the director's only child, plays Roman's sister. The concluding "carousel" scene is a masterpiece. From the novel by Patricia Highsmith.

1951 101m/B Farley Granger, Robert Walker, Ruth Roman, Leo G. Carroll, Patricia Hitchcock; *D:* Alfred Hitchcock. Academy Awards '51 Nominations: Best Black and White Cinematography; National Board of Review Awards '51: 10 Best Films of the Year. **VHS, Beta, LV** $19.98 *WAR, MLB* 🐾🐾🐾🐾

Strangers: The Story of a Mother and Daughter Rowlands is the long-estranged daughter of Davis, who won an Emmy for her portrayal of the embittered widow. The great actress truly is at her recent best in this made-for-TV tearjerker, and Rowlands keeps pace.
1979 88m/C Bette Davis, Gena Rowlands, Ford Rainey, Donald Moffatt; *D:* Milton Katselas. **VHS, Beta** $69.95 *TLF* 🐾🐾🐾

Strangers When We Meet A married architect and his equally married neighbor begin an affair. Their lives become a series of deceptions. Lavish but uninvolving soaper. Written by Evan Hunter and based on his novel.
1960 117m/B Kirk Douglas, Kim Novak, Ernie Kovacs, Walter Matthau, Barbara Rush, Virginia Bruce, Kent Smith; *D:* Richard Quine. **VHS, Beta** $19.95 *COL* 🐾🐾½

The Strangler A confused, mother-fixated psychopath strangles young women. Made at the time the Boston Strangler was terrorizing Beantown. The film slayer strangles ten lasses before his love of dolls gives him away.
1964 89m/B Victor Buono, David McLean, Diane Sayer, Ellen Corby, Jeanne Bates; *D:* Burt Topper. **VHS, Beta** $14.98 *FXV, FOX, FCT* 🐾🐾½

Strangler of Blackmoor Castle Someone is murdering people at an old English castle and Scotland Yard sends an investigator to track down the killer.
1963 ?m/C *GE* Karin Dor, Ingmar Zeisberg. **VHS** $16.95 *SNC* 🐾🐾

Strangler of the Swamp The ghost of an innocent man wrongly hanged for murder returns to terrorize the village where he was lynched. Decidedly B-grade horror features an out-of-focus ghost and Edwards—on the other side of the camera—as one of his would-be victims.
1946 60m/B Rosemary La Planche, Blake Edwards, Charles Middleton, Robert Barratt; *D:* Frank Wisbar. **VHS, Beta** $14.95 *COL, SVS* 🐾½

Strangler of the Tower Edgar Wallace thriller made in Germany.
1964 ?m/C *GE* **VHS** $20 *SMW* 🐾½

Strapless Just-turned-40 American doctor Brown lives and works in London. She has just ended a long-term romance, and takes up with suave foreigner Ganz. Her young sister Fonda, arrives for a visit. Good, interesting if sometimes plodding story of adult relationships.
1990 (R) 99m/C Blair Brown, Bridget Fonda, Bruno Ganz, Alan Howard, Michael Gough, Hugh Laurie, Suzanne Burden, Camille Coduri; *D:* David Hare. **VHS, Beta, LV** $79.95 *COL* 🐾🐾½

Strategic Air Command A classic post-World War II chunk of Air Force patriotism. Veteran third baseman Stewart is recalled to flight duty at the hint of a nuclear war. He's already put in his time in the Big One and thinks he's being singled out now, but he answers his Uncle Sam's call. Allyson plays Stewart's wife for the third time.
1955 114m/C James Stewart, June Allyson, Frank Lovejoy, Barry Sullivan; *D:* Anthony Mann. **VHS, Beta, LV** $14.95 *PAR* 🐾🐾½

Straw Dogs An American mathematician, disturbed by the predominance of violence in American society, moves with his wife to an isolated Cornish village. He finds that primi-

tive savagery exists beneath the most peaceful surface. After his wife is raped, Hoffman's character seeks revenge. Hoffman is good, a little too wimpy at times. A violent, frightening film reaction to the violence of the 1960s.
1972 (R) 118m/C *GB* Dustin Hoffman, Susan George, Peter Vaughan, T.P. McKenna, David Warner; *D:* Sam Peckinpah. **VHS, Beta, LV, CDV** $59.98 *FOX* 🐾🐾🐾

Strawberry Blonde A romantic comedy set in the 1890s, with Cagney as a would-be dentist infatuated with money-grubbing Hayworth (the strawberry blonde of the title), who wonders years later whether he married the right woman (chestnut brunette de Havilland). Attractive period piece remade from 1933's "One Sunday Afternoon," and revived yet again in 1948 by Raoul Walsh.
1941 100m/B James Cagney, Olivia de Havilland, Rita Hayworth, Alan Hale Jr., George Tobias, Jack Carson, Una O'Connor, George Reeves; *D:* Raoul Walsh. **VHS, Beta** $19.98 *MGM* 🐾🐾🐾

Strawberry Roan Maynard plays a stubborn rodeo cowboy, out to prove he ain't whipped yet. One of Maynard's most popular films. Gene Autry bought the story to help him out in later years; the 1948 Autry "remake" uses only the title.
1933 59m/B Ken Maynard, Ruth Hall; *D:* Ken Maynard. **VHS** $19.95 *NOS, DVT, HEG* 🐾🐾

The Strawberry Statement Dated message film about a campus radical who persuades a college student to take part in the student strikes on campus during the '60s. Ambitious anti-violence message is lost in too many subplots. Soundtrack features songs by Crosby, Stills, Nash and Young and John Lennon.
1970 (R) 109m/C Kim Darby, Bruce Davison, Bud Cort, James Coco, Kristina Holland, Bob Balaban, James Dukes, Jeannie Berlin; *D:* Stuart Hagmann. **VHS, Beta** $69.95 *MGM* 🐾🐾

Stray Dog A tense, early genre piece by Kurosawa, about a police detective who has his revolver picked from his pocket on a bus, and realizes soon after it's being used in a series of murders. Technically somewhat flawed, but tense and intense. Mifune's pursuit of the criminal with his gun becomes metaphorically compelling. In Japanese with English subtitles.
1949 122m/B *JP* Toshiro Mifune, Takashi Shimura; *D:* Akira Kurosawa. **VHS, Beta** $24.95 *SVS, TAM, COL* 🐾🐾🐾

Strays Here kitty kitty! A young couple move into their dream home, convinced it is the perfect place to raise their daughter. What they don't know is that the area is populated by a pack of wild cats. Before they can get rid of the kitties, one has marked their bedroom as his territory and they find themselves battling a swarm of mean kitties during a bad storm.
1991 (R) 83m/C Kathleen Quinlan, Timothy Busfield, Claudia Christian; *D:* John McPherson; *W:* Shaun Cassidy. **VHS, LV** $79.98 *MCA* 🐾🐾

Streamers Six young soldiers in a claustrophobic army barracks tensely await the orders that will send them to Vietnam. Written by David Rabe from his play. Well acted but downbeat and drawn out.
1983 (R) 118m/C Matthew Modine, Michael Wright, Mitchell Lichenstein, George Dzundza; *D:* Robert Altman. **VHS, Beta, LV** $69.95 *MED, IME, FCT* 🐾🐾

The Street A dark classic of German Kammerspiel film, notable for its expressionist treatment of Paris street life. A middle-aged man decides to abandon his wife and job to see what excitement he can find. He is duped by a prostitute, accused of murder,

imprisoned, and nearly commits suicide before being rescued. Silent.
1923 87m/B *GE W/D:* Karl Grune. **VHS, Beta** $29.95 *VYY, TAM* 🐾🐾½

Street Asylum Real-life Watergate spook Liddy is pathetically bad as an evil genius who cooks up a scheme to rid the streets of deadbeats and scumbags by implanting cops with a gizmo that makes them kill. Also available in a 94-minute unrated version.
1990 (R) 94m/C Wings Hauser, Alex Cord, Roberta Vasquez, G. Gordon Liddy, Marie Chambers, Sy Richardson, Jesse Doran, Jesse Aragon, Brion James; *D:* Gregory Brown. **VHS, Beta, LV** *NO* 🐾

Street Crimes A street-wise cop convinces gang members to put down their weapons and settle their grudges in the boxing ring. But when a gang leader starts shooting down the police and civilians, the cop and his young partner must work together to keep the neighborhood safe.
1992 (R) ?m/C Dennis Farina, Max Gail, Mike Worth; *W/D:* Stephen Smoke. **VHS, LV** $89.95 *PMH* 🐾🐾

Street Fighter Local hoodlum engages in fast-paced marital arts action.
1975 (R) 77m/C Sonny Chiba. **VHS, Beta** *FOX* 🐾

The Street Fighter's Last Revenge The theft of a formula for synthetic heroin brings martial artist Sonny Chiba to the rescue. Lots of action, not much acting.
1979 (R) 80m/C Sonny Chiba, Sue Shiomi; *D:* Sakae Ozawa. **VHS** $49.98 *UHV* 🐾

Street Fighters, Part 2/Masters of Tiger Crane Martial arts action abounds in these two movies on one tape.
1985 176m/C **VHS, Beta** $7.00 *VTR* 🐾½

Street Girls A father enters the world of urban drugs and prostitution to find his runaway daughter.
1975 77m/C Carol Case, Christine Souder, Paul Pompian; *D:* Michael Miller. **VHS, Beta** $59.98 *NLC* 🐾

Street Hawk A government agent operates an experimental, crime-fighting motorcycle in battling against a high-powered drug smuggling ring.
1984 60m/C Rex Smith, Jayne Modean, Richard Venture, Christopher Lloyd. **VHS, Beta** $39.95 *MCA* 🐾

Street Hero A young thug is torn between familial common sense and Mafia connections.
1984 102m/C Vince Colosimo, Sigrid Thornton, Sandy Gore. **VHS, Beta** $69.98 *LIV, VES* Woof!

Street Hitz Two brothers in the South Bronx find their family loyalties tested. Joey wants to finish college and get away from the violence in the streets while his brother Junior turns to the gangs to survive.
1992 92m/C Angelo Lopez, Melvin Muza, Lyota Ramirez; *D:* Joseph P. Vasquez. **VHS** $89.95 *AIP* 🐾½

Street Hunter Former cop turned freelance fighter quit the force when his integrity was questioned, but he still helps out now and then. Scumbag drug dealers line up a thug to waste him; epic kung fu battle ensues.
1990 (R) 120m/C Steve James, Reb Brown, John Leguizamo, Valarie Pettiford, Frank Vincent, Richie Havens; *D:* John A. Gallagher. **VHS, LV** $79.95 *COL* Woof!

Street Justice Over-complex tale of a CIA agent on the lam. Returning from years of Russian imprisonment, Ontkean finds his wife remarried, his daughter grown and both battling the corrupt town government. Good performances can't help the confusion of too many characters too flatly developed.
1989 (R) 94m/C Michael Ontkean, Joanna Kerns, Catherine Bach, J.D. Cannon, Jeanette Nolan, Richard Cox, William Windom; *D:* Richard Sarafian. **VHS, Beta $19.98** *WAR* ⅆ½

Street Knight Gang warfare in L.A. in a routine actioner. Jake is an ex-cop who gets drawn into a battle between two rival gangs when their truce is broken by mysterious murders on both sides. Seems there's an unsuspected third party involved—a paramilitary band of professional killers that want the gang violence to divert police interest from their own nefarious operations.
1993 (R) 88m/C Jeff Speakman, Christopher Neame, Lewis Van Bergen, Bernie Casey, Jennifer Gatti, Richard Coca; *D:* Albert Magnoli. **VHS, LV $92.99** *WAR* ⅆⅆ

Street Law Vivid and violent study of one man's frustrated war on crime.
1979 (R) 77m/C Franco Nero, Barbara Bach, Reno Palmer. **VHS, Beta $14.98** *VID* ⅆ

Street Music The elderly people living in an old hotel join forces with a young couple to organize a protest that may save their building. Well-directed urban comedy-drama; good location shooting in San Francisco's Tenderloin.
1981 88m/C Larry Breeding, Elizabeth Daily, Ned Glass; *D:* Jenny Bowen. **VHS, Beta $69.98** *LIV, VE3* ⅆⅆ½ ⅛

Street of Crocodiles The decrepit caretaker of an equally decrepit museum is transformed into another being by a Kinetoscope machine. An avant-garde animated classic by the Quay Brothers.
1986 21m/C VHS, 3/4U *ICA* ⅆ½

Street of Forgotten Women Hollywood, in one of its periodic morality binges, came up with this purported expose on prostitution. An innocent girl is seduced and brutalized by a theatrical agent and eventually finds herself walking the pavement for less than moral purposes. Lots of shots of scantily clad showgirls and our heroine in her undies.
1925 55m/B VHS $16.95 *SNC, VYY* ⅆ

Street of Shame A portrayal of the abused lives of six Tokyo prostitutes. Typically sensitive to the roles and needs of women and critical of the society that exploits them, Mizoguchi creates a quiet, inclusive coda to his life's work in world cinema. Kyo is splendid as a hardened hooker and has a memorable scene with her father. Kogure is also good. The great director's last finished work was instrumental in the outlawing of prostitution in Japan. Written by Masaichi Narusawa. In Japanese with English subtitles.
1956 88m/B *JP* Machiko Kyo, Aiko Mimasu; *D:* Kenji Mizoguchi. **VHS, Beta $29.98** *SUE, TAM, NLC* ⅆⅆⅆ½

Street People Gratuitous car chases and violence do not a movie make, as in this case in point. Utter woofer has Brit Moore cast as a mafiosa. Yeah, right.
1976 (R) 92m/C Roger Moore, Stacy Keach, Ivo Garrani, Ettore Manni; *D:* Maurizio Lucidi. **VHS, Beta $29.98** *LIV, VES Woof!*

Street Scene Life in a grimy New York tenement district, circa 1930. Audiences nationwide ate it up when Elmer Rice adapted his own Pulitzer Prize-winning play and top

helmsman Vidor gave it direction. Fine score by Alfred Newman.
1931 80m/B Sylvia Sidney, William Collier Jr., Estelle Taylor, Beulah Bondi, David Landau; *D:* King Vidor. **VHS, Beta, 8mm, 3/4U, Special order formats $19.95** *NOS, HHT, CAB* ⅆⅆⅆ

Street Smart Reeve was blah as Superman (let's be frank), and he's blah here as a desperate New York freelance writer who fakes a dramatic story about prostitution. When his deception returns to haunt him, he's in trouble with pimps and murderers, as well as the D.A. Freeman and Baker are both superb. Based on screenwriter David Freeman's own experience with "New York" magazine.
1987 (R) 97m/C Christopher Reeve, Morgan Freeman, Kathy Baker, Mimi Rogers, Andre Gregory, Jay Patterson, Anna Maria Horsford; *D:* Jerry Schatzberg. Academy Awards '87 Nominations: Best Supporting Actor (Freeman); Independent Spirit Awards '88: Best Supporting Actor (Freeman). **VHS, Beta, LV $19.95** *MED, IME* ⅆⅆ½

Street Soldiers Martial artists are out to take back the streets from the punks and scum who now rule them.
1991 (R) 98m/C Jun Chong, Jeff Rector, David Homb, Jonathan Gorman, Joon Kim, Katherine Armstrong, Joel Weiss; *D:* Lee Harry. **VHS, Beta, LV $19.95** *ACA* ⅆ½

Street Trash In Brooklyn, a strange poisonous liquor is being sold cheap to bums, making them melt and explode. A gross, cheap, tongue-in-cheek shocker from the makers of "The Toxic Avenger."
1987 91m/C R.L. Ryan, Vic Noto, Miriam Zucker, Bill Chepil, Mike Lackey; *D:* Jim Muro. **VHS, Beta $79.98** *LIV Woof!*

Street War A cop pursues the Mob in the name of revenge as well as duty.
197? 90m/C James Mason, Cyril Cusack, Raymond Pellegrin. **VHS, Beta** *NO* ⅆ

Street Warriors Ostensibly "serious" look at juvenile crime. Actually miserable, exploitative, offensive junk.
1987 105m/C Christa Leem, Nadia Windell, Victor Petit, Francisco (Frank) Brana; *D:* Jose Antonio De La Loma. **VHS, Beta** *NO Woof!*

Street Warriors, Part 2 Even worse than its predecessor, and that's saying something. Horrible dubbing from Spanish would be laughable, if the rapes weren't so graphic.
1987 105m/C Angel Fernandez, Paul Ramirez, Teresa Giminez, Veronica Miriel, Conrad Tortosa; *D:* Jose Antonio De La Loma. **VHS, Beta** *NO Woof!*

The Street with No Name In followup to "Kiss of Death," Widmark confirms rep as one disturbed guy playing psychotic career criminal whose life is grisly trail of murder and brutality.
1948 93m/B Mark Stevens, Richard Widmark, Lloyd Nolan, Barbara Lawrence, Ed Begley Sr., Donald Buka, Joseph Pevney; *D:* William Keighley. **VHS $19.98** *FOX, FCT* ⅆⅆⅆ

A Streetcar Named Desire Powerful film version of Tennessee Williams' play about a neurotic southern belle with a hidden past who comes to visit her sister and is abused and driven mad by her brutal brother-in-law. Grim New Orleans setting for terrific performances by all, with Malden, Leigh, and Hunter winning Oscars, and Brando making highest impact on audiences. Brando disliked the role, despite the great impact it had on his career. Great jazz score by Alex North. Remade for television in 1984.

1951 122m/B Vivien Leigh, Marlon Brando, Kim Hunter, Karl Malden; *D:* Elia Kazan. Academy Awards '51: Best Actress (Leigh), Best Art Direction/Set Decoration (B & W), Best Supporting Actor (Malden), Best Supporting Actress (Hunter); Nominations: Best Actor (Brando), Best Director (Kazan), Best Picture; Academy Awards '51: Best Black and White Cinematography, Best Costume Design (B & W), Best Screenplay, Best Sound, Best Original Score; Golden Globe Awards '52: Best Supporting Actress (Hunter); National Board of Review Awards '51: 10 Best Films of the Year; New York Film Critics Awards '51: Best Actress (Leigh), Best Director (Kazan), Best Film. **VHS, Beta, LV, CDV $19.98** *RCA, FOX, WAR* ⅆⅆⅆⅆ

Streetfight Semi-animated racist exploitation from the creator of "Fritz the Cat." Features some superb animation. *AKA:* Coonskin.
1975 (R) 89m/C Philip Michael Thomas, Scatman Crothers; *D:* Ralph Bakshi. **VHS, Beta $29.95** *ACA, WTA* ⅆ½

Streets Applegate (of Fox TV's "Married...With Children") is believable as an illiterate runaway teen. Good drama set in Venice, California about life on the streets is flawed by near-gratuitous pairing with story of a crazy prostitute-killing cop.
1990 (R) 90m/C Christina Applegate, David Mendenhall, Eb Lottimer; *D:* Katt Shea Ruben. **VHS, Beta $89.99** *MGM* ⅆⅆ

Streets of Fire A soldier of fortune rescues his ex-girlfriend, now a famous rock singer, after she's been kidnapped by a malicious motorcycle gang. Violently energetic in its insistent barrage of imagery. Director Hill's never-never land establishes a retro-futuristic feel, set to the music of Ry Cooder and beautifully photographed, however vacuous the ending may be.
1984 93m/C Michael Pare, Diane Lane, Rick Moranis, Amy Madigan, Willem Dafoe, Deborah Van Valkenburgh, Richard Lawson, Rick Rossovich, Bill Paxton, Lee Ving, Stoney Jackson, Robert Townsend, Grand Bush, Mykel T. Williamson, Elizabeth Daily, Lynne Thigpen, Marine Jahan, Ed Begley Jr., John Dennis Johnston, Olivia Brown; *D:* Walter Hill. **VHS, Beta, LV $19.95** *MCA* ⅆⅆ½

Streets of Gold Brandauer is good as a Soviet boxer who defected and now washes dishes in Brooklyn. He trains a pair of street youngsters in the hope of beating his old coach in the Olympics. "Rocky"-like in the boxing, and in the rags-to-riches optimism.
1986 (R) 94m/C Klaus Maria Brandauer, Adrian Pasdar, Wesley Snipes; *D:* Joe Roth; *M:* Jack Nitzsche. **VHS, Beta, LV $79.98** *LIV, VES* ⅆⅆ½

The Streets of L.A. A frustrated middle-aged woman teaches some punks from an L.A. barrio a thing or two about pride and motivation when she demands reimbursement for the tires they slashed. Without thoroughly professional Woodward to carry it, there would not be much of a movie. Woodward's character is resourceful, and so is the actress. Made for TV.
1979 94m/C Joanne Woodward, Robert Webber, Michael C. Gwynne; *D:* Jerrold Freedman. **VHS, Beta** *NO* ⅆⅆ½

The Streets of San Francisco The pilot that spawned the popular TV series. A streetwise old cop and his young college-boy partner (who else but Malden and Douglas as Stone and Keller) investigate the murder of a young woman. Adapted from "Poor, Poor Ophelia" by Carolyn Weston.
1972 120m/C Karl Malden, Robert Wagner, Michael Douglas, Andrew Duggan, Tom Bosley, Kim Darby, Mako; *D:* Walter Grauman. **VHS, Beta $14.99** *GKK* ⅆⅆⅆ

Streets of Sin Written and produced by Ida Lupino, this film tells the story of a naive girl's tribulations when she becomes infatuated with a musician and allows herself to become pregnant by him. *AKA:* Not Wanted.
1949 91m/B Sally Forrest, Keefe Brasselle, Leo Penn, Dorothy Adams, Rita Lupino; *D:* Elmer Clifton; *W:* Ida Lupino. VHS $19.95 NOS 𝒁𝒁½

Streetwalkin' Life in the Big Apple isn't always rosy for a brother and sister who must contend with prostitutes, drug dealers, and tough cops. She turns to prostitution to get by. Miserable, exploitative trash.
1985 (R) 86m/C Melissa Leo, Dale Midkiff, Leon Robinson, Julie Newmar, Randall Batinkoff, Annie Golden, Antonio Fargas; *D:* Joan Freeman. VHS, Beta, LV $79.98 LIV, VES 𝒁

Streetwise Eye-opening and candid documentary inspired by a "Life" magazine article. Frank and honest look at homeless children making a living on the streets. Seattle provides the backdrop to the story as the filmmakers hang around with the kids, earning their trust, and receive the truth from them. Cruel, funny, enraging, but always sobering look into a population of homeless in America. A deservedly acclaimed, terrifying vision of urban America.
1985 92m/C *D:* Martin Bell; *M:* Tom Waits. VHS, Beta, LV $19.95 STE, NWV 𝒁𝒁𝒁½

Strictly Ballroom Offbeat, cheerfully tacky dance/romance amusingly turns every movie cliche slightly askew. Scott (Mercurio) has been in training for the Pan-Pacific ballroom championships since the age of six. While talented, he also refuses to follow convention and scandalizes the stuffy dance establishment with his new steps. When his longtime partner leaves him, Scott takes up with a love-struck beginner (Morice), with some surprises of her own. Ballet dancer Mercurio (in his film debut) is appropriately arrogant yet vulnerable, with Morice as the plain Jane turned steel butterfly. Wonderful supporting cast; great debut for director Luhrmann.
1992 (PG) 94m/C *AU* Paul Mercurio, Tara Morice, Bill Hunter, Pat Thomsen, Barry Otto, Gia Carides, Peter Whitford, John Hannan, Sonia Kruger-Tayler, Kris McQuade, Pip Mushin, Leonie Page, Antonio Vargas, Armonia Benedito; *D:* Baz Luhrmann; *W:* Craig Pearce, Baz Luhrmann; *M:* David Hershfelder. VHS NYR 𝒁𝒁½

Strictly Business An upwardly mobile black broker has his career aspirations in order until he meets a beautiful club promoter who finds him square and boring. Wanting to impress her he asks the advice of a young man who works in the mail room for the proper way to dress and talk. A low-rent Pygmalion story.
1991 (PG-13) 83m/C Halle Berry, Tommy Davidson, Joseph C. Phillips; *D:* Kevin Hooks. VHS $94.99 WAR, FCT 𝒁½

Strictly G.I. A collection of war-time patriotic shorts, including "All Star Bond Rally." The support and perception of World War II is historically intriguing.
1944 45m/B Bing Crosby, Frank Sinatra, Betty Grable, Judy Garland, Harpo Marx, Harry James, Bob Hope, Jerry Colonna. VHS, Beta $19.95 NOS, DVT, HEG 𝒁½

Strike Eisenstein's debut, and a silent classic. Stirring look at a 1912 clash between striking factory workers and Czarist troops.
1924 78m/B *RU D:* Sergei Eisenstein. VHS, Beta, 3/4U $24.95 NOS, KIV, IHF 𝒁𝒁𝒁½

Strike Back A convict escapes from prison to find the girl he loves, and is hounded by the police and the mob.
1980 89m/C Dave Balko, Brigette Wollner; *D:* Carl Schenkel. VHS, Beta $69.98 LIV, VES 𝒁𝒁

Strike Commando Cheap, exploitative ripoff of the expensive, exploitative mega-action thriller "Rambo." Sleepwalking actors; horrible, overwrought script.
1987 (R) 92m/C Reb Brown, Christopher Connelly, Locs Kamme; *D:* Vincent Dawn. VHS, Beta $9.99 CCB, IVE Woof!

Strike Force A New York City cop, a Federal agent and a state trooper work together to battle a large drug ring. Failed made-for-TV pilot. Early Gere appearance; not related to later Robert Stack film with the same title. *AKA:* Crack.
1975 74m/C Cliff Gorman, Richard Gere, Donald Blakely; *D:* Barry Shear. VHS, Beta $24.95 VMK 𝒁

Strike Force The jurors on an embezzlement case turn up bloody and headless around town, so a special criminal strike force is brought in to solve the murders. Why do the murders happen only on Tuesdays? Made for TV.
1981 90m/C Robert Stack, Dorian Harewood, Herb Edelman; *D:* Richard Lang. VHS, Beta $24.95 AHV 𝒁𝒁

Strike It Rich A honeymooning couple find themselves resorting to the Monte Carlo gambling tables in order to raise money for the ride home. Lightweight fluff unfortunately adapted from Graham Greene's short novel "Loser Takes All." Only for hard-core Gielgudites. *AKA:* Loser Take All.
1990 (PG) 86m/C Molly Ringwald, Robert Lindsay, John Gielgud, Max Wall, Simon de la Brosse; *D:* James Scott. VHS, Beta, LV $89.99 HBO 𝒁½

Strike of Thunderkick Tiger Two gang members kill their leader, and then have a go at each other.
198? 84m/C Casanova Wong, Charles Han, Lisa Lee. VHS, Beta NO 𝒁

Strike Up the Band A high school band turns to hot swing music and enters a national radio contest. Rooney and Garland display their usual charm in this high-energy stroll down memory lane. ♫Over the Waves; The Light Cavalry Overture; Walkin Down Broadway; Five Foot Two, Eyes of Blue; After the Ball; Nobody; Strike Up the Band.
1940 120m/B Judy Garland, Mickey Rooney, Paul Whiteman, William Tracy, June Preisser; *D:* Busby Berkeley. Academy Awards '40: Best Sound; Nominations: Best Song ("Our Love Affair"), Best Score. VHS, Beta, LV $19.98 MGM 𝒁𝒁½

Strikeback A young boy comes painfully of age in West Berlin.
1984 88m/C VHS, Beta $69.98 VES 𝒁𝒁

Striker Mercenary John "Striker" Slade is sent to Nicaragua to free a captured American journalist, not knowing his superiors have betrayed him to the Contras and the Sandinistas. He battles it out with both groups while seeking revenge on the businessmen who set him up.
1988 (R) 90m/C Frank Zagarino, Melanie Rogers, Paul Werner; *D:* Stephen M. Andrews. VHS, Beta $39.95 AIP 𝒁𝒁

Striker's Mountain Story of a sports enthusiast who creates heliskiing and builds it into a business. Great ski scenes, but skip the rest.
1987 99m/C Bruce Greenwood, Mimi Kuzyk, Leslie Nielsen, August Schellenberg; *D:* Allen Simmonds. VHS $9.95 SIM, CGH 𝒁½

Striking Back Fed up citizens decline to turn other cheek.
1981 91m/C Perry King, Tisa Farrow, Don Stroud, George Kennedy, Park Jong Soo; *D:* William Fruet. VHS NO 𝒁½

Stripes Feeling like losers and looking to straighten out their lives, two friends enlist in the Army under the mistaken impression that military life is something like a summer camp for grownups. A box-office success (despite a poorly written and directed script) due in large part to Murray's charm and his verbal and sometimes physical sparring with Oates, who is good as the gruff-tempered platoon sergeant. Often humorous, it includes performances by various "Second City" players, including fat slob Candy, whom Murray turns into a "lean, mean fighting machine."
1981 (R) 105m/C Bill Murray, Harold Ramis, P.J. Soles, Warren Oates, John Candy, John Larroquette, Judge Reinhold, Sean Young, Dave Thomas, Joe Flaherty; *D:* Ivan Reitman. VHS, Beta, LV $29.95 COL 𝒁𝒁½

Stripped to Kill A female cop goes undercover to lure a psycho killing strippers. Not-bad entry from Corman and cohorts. Followed by—you guessed it—"Stripped to Kill II."
1987 (R) 88m/C Kay Lenz, Greg Evigan, Norman Fell; *D:* Katt Shea Ruben. VHS, Beta $79.95 MGM 𝒁

Stripped to Kill II: Live Girls A young woman with extra-sensory powers dreams of murders which she discovers are all too real. A weak sequel, despite the interesting premise.
1989 83m/C Maria Ford, Eb Lottimer, Karen Mayo Chandler, Marjean Holden, Birke Tan, Debra Lamb; *D:* Katt Shea Ruben. VHS, Beta $79.95 MGM 𝒁

The Stripper A middle-aged stripper in a traveling show returns to the small Kansas town of her youth. Left stranded, she moves in with an old friend whose teenage son promptly falls in love with her. Based on the play "A Loss of Roses" by William Inge. *AKA:* Woman of Summer.
1963 95m/B Joanne Woodward, Richard Beymer, Claire Trevor, Carol Lynley, Robert Webber, Gypsy Rose Lee; *D:* Franklin J. Schaffner; *M:* Jerry Goldsmith. VHS, Beta $39.95 FOX 𝒁𝒁½

Stripper A good under-the-covers glimpse of the life and work of several real-life strippers, culminating in the First Annual Stripper's Convention in 1984.
1986 (R) 90m/C Janette Boyd, Sara Costa, Kimberly Holcomb; *D:* Jerome Gary; *M:* Jack Nitzsche. VHS, Beta $79.98 FOX 𝒁𝒁½

Striptease A slew of slowly-declothing women do their thing.
198? 60m/C VHS, Beta $59.95 JEF 𝒁

Stroke of Midnight Souped-up Cinderella with Lowe as egotistic high fashion designer, Grey as struggling shoe designer and a pumpkin-colored VW Bug.
1990 (PG) 102m/C Rob Lowe, Jennifer Grey, Andrea Ferreol; *D:* Tom Clegg. VHS, Beta, LV $89.98 MED 𝒁𝒁

Stroker Ace Flamboyant stock car driver tries to break an iron-clad promotional contract signed with a greedy fried-chicken magnate. Off duty, he ogles blondes as dopey as he is. One of the worst from Reynolds—and that's saying something.
1983 (PG) 96m/C Burt Reynolds, Ned Beatty, Jim Nabors, Parker Stevenson, Loni Anderson, Bubba Smith; *D:* Hal Needham. VHS, Beta $19.98 WAR Woof!

Stromboli Bergman is a Czech refugee who marries an Italian fisherman in order to escape from her displaced persons camp. He brings her to his home island of Stromboli where she finds the life bleak and isolated and her marriage a trial. In Italian with English subtitles. The melodrama was even greater

off-screen than on; this is the movie which introduced Bergman and Rossellini and began their (then) scandalous affair.
1950 81m/B *IT* Ingrid Bergman, Mario Vitale, Renzo Cesana; **D:** Roberto Rossellini. **VHS, Beta $19.95** *UHV, TAM* ✗✗½

Strong Man A World War I veteran, passing himself off as an unlikely circus strongman, searches an American city for the girl whose letters gave him hope during the war. Perhaps Langdon's best full-length film. With a new score by Carl Davis.
1926 78m/B Harry Langdon, Gertrude Astor, Tay Garnett; **D:** Frank Capra. **VHS, Beta, LV $39.99** *HBO, IME* ✗✗✗

Strong Medicine Strange, avant-garde film about a strange, off-written young woman. Cleverly directed experiment that's not for everyone.
1984 84m/C Carol Kane, Raul Julia, Wallace Shawn, Kate Manheim, David Warrilow; **D:** Guy Green. **VHS, Beta** *NO* ✗✗½

Stroszek Three German misfits—a singer, a prostitute and an old man—tour the U.S. in search of their dreams. Touching, hilarious comedy-drama with a difference and an attitude. One of Herzog's easiest and also best films. In English and German with English subtitles.
1977 108m/C *GE* Eva Mattes, Bruno S, Clemens Scheitz; **D:** Werner Herzog. **VHS $79.95** *NYF, FCT, TAM* ✗✗✗

Struggle Through Death Two young men escape the clutches of evil Ching Kue and attempt to free their fellow prisoners so they can overthrow the despot.
197? 93m/C **VHS, Beta** *NO* ✗

Stryker The ever-lovin' nuclear holocaust has occurred, and good guys and bad guys battle it out for scarce water. If you liked "Mad Max," go see it again; don't watch this miserable effort.
1983 (R) 86m/C *PH* Steve Sandor, Andria Fabio; **D:** Cirio H. Santiago. **VHS, Beta $19.98** *SUE, STE* *Woof!*

Stuck on You Couple engaged in a palimony suit takes their case to a judge to work out their differences. Wing-clipped angel Gabriel (Corey) comes to earth to help them patch it up. Never mind.
1984 (R) 90m/C Prof. Irwin Corey, Virginia Penta, Mark Mikulski; **D:** Samuel Weil, Michael Herz. **VHS, Beta $9.98** *SUF* ✗

Stuckey's Last Stand A group of camp counselors prepare to take 22 children on a nature hike they will never forget. Mindless teen fodder.
1978 95m/C Whit Reichert, Tom Murray, Rich Casentino. **VHS, Beta** *NO* ✗

The Stud Owner of a fashionable "after hours" dance spot hires a young, handsome stud to manage the club and attend to her personal needs. Low-budget look and seemingly scriptless. Faithfully adapted by sister Jackie Collins from her novel.
1978 90m/C *GB* Joan Collins, Oliver Tobias; **D:** Quentin Masters. **VHS, Beta $19.99** *HBO Woof!*

Student Affairs A bunch of highschool misfits vie for roles in a movie about a bunch of high school misfits.
1988 (R) 92m/C Louie Bonanno, Jim Abele, Alan Fisler, Deborah Blaisdell; **D:** Chuck Vincent. **VHS, Beta $79.98** *LIV, VES Woof!*

Student Bodies A "Halloween"-style spoof of high-school horror films, except it's not funny. And what's so funny about bloody murder anyway? When the on-the-set problems and strife arose (which they did), why didn't everyone just cut their losses and go home?
1981 (R) 86m/C Kristen Riter, Matthew Goldsby, Richard Brando, Joe Flood; **D:** Mickey Rose. **VHS, Beta, LV $72.95** *PAR Woof!*

The Student Body Every boy on campus hopes to win the heart (and everything that goes with it) of the lustiest girl on campus.
1976 (R) 85m/C Jillian Kesner, Janice Heiden. **VHS, Beta** *NO Woof!*

The Student Body/Jailbait Babysitter Double cassette containing "The Student Body" and "Jailbait Babysitter." In our first feature, three girls recently released from the local reform school, participate in a psychological experiment. In the second feature, a 17-year-old discovers her sexual awakening can be fun.
197? (R) 150m/C **VHS, Beta** *NO Woof!*

Student Confidential A Troma-produced spoof of seedy high school youth movies, new and old, involving four students who are led into the world of adult vices by a mysterious millionaire. Badly made and dull. Douglas and Jackson both have brothers named Michael.
1987 (R) 99m/C Eric Douglas, Marlon Jackson, Susan Scott, Ronee Blakley, Elizabeth Singer; **D:** Richard Horian. **VHS, Beta $79.95** *MED* ✗

The Student Nurses The adventures, amorous and otherwise, of four last-year nursing students. Followed by four sequels: "Private Duty Nurses," "Night Call Nurses," "The Young Nurses," and "Candy Stripe Nurses." Better than average exploitation fare. First release from Roger Corman's New World studios; it goes down hill from there.
1970 (R) 89m/C Elaine Giftos, Karen Carlson, Brioni Farrell, Barbara Leigh, Reni Santoni, Richard Rust, Lawrence Casey, Darrell Larson, Paul Camen, Richard Stahl, Scottie MacGregor, Pepe Serna; **D:** Stephanie Rothman. **VHS, Beta $59.98** *NLC* ✗✗

Student of Prague Early silent classic based on the German Faust legend: a student makes a pact with the devil to win a beautiful woman. Poor fellow. With either German or English title cards. Music track.
1913 60m/B *GE* Lothar Koemer, Grete Berger, Paul Wegener; **D:** Paul Wegener, Stellan Rye. **VHS, Beta $39.95** *FST, DVT, GLV* ✗✗✗

The Student Prince Delightful rendition of Sigmund Romberg's famous operetta in which Purdom stars as the Prince of Heidelberg who falls for barmaid Blyth. Lanza recorded the soundtrack, but could not star in this film because of his weight problem. Previously filmed in 1919 and 1927 without music. ♪♪ Golden Days; Serenade; Deep in My Heart; To the Inn We're Marching; Drink, Drink, Drink; Come Boys, Let's All Be Gay, Boys; Summertime in Heidelberg; Beloved; I Walk With God.
1954 107m/C Ann Blyth, Edmund Purdom, John Ericson, Louis Calhern, Edmund Gwenn, S.Z. Sakall, Betta St. John; **D:** Richard Thorpe. **VHS $19.98** *MGM* ✗✗

The Student Prince in Old Heidelberg Prince Karl Heinrich silently falls in love with lowly barmaid. **AKA:** Old Heidelberg.
1927 102m/B Ramon Novarro, Norma Shearer; **D:** Ernst Lubitsch. **VHS $29.98** *MGM, FCT* ✗✗½

The Student Teachers Yet another soft-core Corman product. Three student teachers sleep around, on screen.
1973 79m/C Susan Damante Shaw, Brooke Mills, Bob Harris, John Cramer, Chuck Norris; **D:** Jonathan Kaplan. **VHS, Beta $59.98** *SUE* ✗½

Studs Lonigan Drifting, too artsy rendering a James T. Farrell's trilogy about an Irish drifter growing up in Chicago in the twenties. Good period detail, but oddly off-kilter and implausible as history.
1960 96m/B Christopher Knight, Frank Gorshin, Jack Nicholson; **D:** Irving Lerner; **M:** Jerry Goldsmith. **VHS, Beta $24.95** *MGM* ✗✗

A Study in Scarlet Owen played Watson the previous year in "Sherlock Holmes;" here he's not perfect as Holmes. The plot is not the same as in the Conan Doyle story of the same title. Owen wrote much of the script for this one.
1933 77m/B Reginald Owen, Alan Mowbray, Anna May Wong, June Clyde, Alan Dinehart; **D:** Edwin L. Marin. **VHS, Beta, 3/4U, Special order formats $16.95** *SNC, NOS, CAB* ✗✗

A Study in Terror A well-appointed Sherlock Holmes thriller. The second Holmes film in color. Premise has a young, athletic Holmes in pursuit of a well-educated Jack the Ripper in the atmosphere of London in the 1880s. **AKA:** Sherlock Holmes Grosster Fall; Fog.
1966 94m/C *GE GB* John Neville, Donald Houston, Judi Dench, Anthony Quayle, Robert Morley, Frank Finlay, Cecil Parker; **D:** James Hill. **VHS, Beta, LV $69.95** *COL* ✗✗✗

The Stuff Surreal horror semi-spoof about an ice cream mogul and a hamburger king who discover that the new, fast-selling confection in town zombifies its partakers. Forced, lame satire from producer/director/ writer Cohen.
1985 (R) 93m/C Michael Moriarty, Andrea Marcovicci, Garrett Morris, Paul Sorvino, Danny Aiello, Brooke Adams; **D:** Larry Cohen. **VHS, Beta $9.95** *NWV, STE* ✗½

Stuff Stephanie in the Incinerator A Troma gagfest about wealthy cretins who torture and kill young women. "Funny" title betrays utter, exploitive mindlessness.
1989 (PG-13) 97m/C Catherine Dee, William Dame, M.R. Murphy, Dennis Cunningham; **D:** Don Nardo. **VHS, Beta, LV $79.95** *LIV* ✗

The Stunt Man A marvelous and unique exercise in meta-cinematic manipulation. O'Toole, in one of his very best roles, is a power-crazed movie director; Railsback is a fugitive sheltered by him from sherrif Rocco. When a stunt man is killed in an accident, O'Toole prevails on Railsback to replace him. Railsback wonders if O'Toole wants him to die . . . a labor of love for director-producer Rush, who spent nine years working on it, and waited two years to see it released, by Fox.
1980 (R) 129m/C Peter O'Toole, Steve Railsback, Barbara Hershey, Allen Garfield, Alex Rocco; **D:** Richard Rush. Academy Awards '80 Nominations: Best Actor (O'Toole), Best Adapted Screenplay, Best Director (Rush); Montreal World Film Festival '80: Best Film; National Board of Review Awards '80: 10 Best Films of the Year; National Society of Film Critics Awards '80: Best Actor (O'Toole). **VHS, Beta, LV $19.98** *FOX* ✗✗✗

Stunt Pilot A young man takes a job at a film studio as a stunt pilot and finds mayhem and romance on and off the ground. One in the "Tailspin Tommy" series. Well-paced and fun to watch.
1939 61m/C John Trent, Marjorie Reynolds, Milburn Stone, Jason Robards Sr., Pat O'Malley; **D:** George Waggner. **VHS $19.95** *NOS, MOV* ✗✗

Stunt Rock A feature film combining rock music, magic, and some of the most incredible stunts ever attempted.
1980 (PG) 90m/C **VHS, Beta** *NO* ✗✗

Stunts See "The Stunt Man" instead. OK script hides near-invisible plot; stunt man engage in derring-doo. *AKA:* Who is Killing the Stuntman.
1977 (PG) 90m/C Robert Forster, Fiona Lewis, Joanna Cassidy, Darrell Fetty, Bruce Glover, James Luisi; *D:* Mark L. Lester. **VHS, Beta** $69.99 *HBO ⅛⅛*

Stuntwoman Welch plays a stuntwoman whose death-defying job interferes with her love life. What ever shall she do?
1981 95m/C Raquel Welch, Jean-Paul Belmondo; *D:* Claude Zidi. **VHS** $14.95 *LPC ⅛½*

Submarine Seahawk When a group of Japanese warships mysteriously disappear, allied intelligence suspect a big battle is brewing. An inexperienced commander who has been tracking the movement of the Japanese ships is put in charge of the submarine Seahawk, even though the crew lacks faith in his command abilities. His own men may prove a bigger obstacle than any of the Japanese. Lots of action and stock World War II footage.
1959 83m/B John Bentley, Brett Halsey, Wayne Heffley, Steve Mitchell, Henry McCann, Frank Gerstle; *D:* Spencer Gordon Bennet. **VHS** $9.95 *COL ⅛⅛*

Submission A pharmacist's sensuality is reawakened when she has a provocative affair with a clerk in her shop.
1977 (R) 107m/C *IT* Franco Nero, Lisa Gastoni; *D:* Salvatore Samperi. **VHS, Beta** $59.95 *PSM ⅛½*

Subspecies New improved vampire demons descend on earth. The first full-length feature film shot on location in Transylvania. For horror buffs only.
1991 (R) 90m/C Laura Tate, Michael Watson, Anders Hove, Michelle McBride, Irina Movila, Angus Scrimm; *D:* Ted Nicolaou. **VHS, LV, 8mm** $19.95 *PAR, PIA, BTV ⅛½*

Substitute Teacher Every guy on campus is falling for the science department's latest experiment—the most beautiful teacher on campus.
19?? 90m/C Dayle Haddon. **VHS, Beta** *NO ⅛½*

Subterfuge When a special American security agent goes to England for a "vacation," his presence causes speculation and poses several serious questions for both British Intelligence and the underworld. Nothing special, with the occasional suspenseful moment.
1968 89m/C *GB* Joan Collins, Gene Barry, Richard Todd; *D:* Peter Graham Scott. **VHS, Beta** *REP ⅛⅛*

Suburban Commando A goofy, muscular alien mistakenly lands on Earth while on vacation. He does his best to remain inconspicuous, resulting in numerous hilarious situations. Eventually he is forced to confront his arch, interstellar nemesis in order to defend the family who befriended him. A harmless, sometimes cute vehicle for wrestler Hogan, which will certainly entertain his younger fans.
1991 (PG) 88m/C Hulk Hogan, Christopher Lloyd, Shelley Duvall, Larry Miller, William Ball, JoAnn Dearing, Jack Elam, Roy Dotrice, Christopher Neame, Tony Longo; *D:* Burt Kennedy. **VHS, LV** $14.95 *COL, NLC, SVS ⅛⅛*

Suburban Roulette "Adults only" feature from splattermaster Lewis caters to the prurient. Groovy themes like wife swapping and other very daring subjects. Totally sixties. Presented as part of Joe Bob Brigg's "Sleaziest Movies in the History of the World" series.
1967 91m/C *D:* Herschell Gordon Lewis. **VHS** $19.98 *SVI ⅛*

Suburbia When a group of punk rockers move into a condemned suburban development, they become the targets of a vigilante group. Low budget, needless violent remake of anyone of many '50s rebellion flicks that tries to have a "message." *AKA:* The Wild Side.
1983 (R) 99m/C Chris Pederson, Bill Coyne, Jennifer Clay, Timothy Eric O'Brien, Andrew Pece, Don Allen; *D:* Penelope Spheeris. **VHS, Beta, LV** $29.98 *LIV, VES ⅛*

Subway Surreal, MTV-esque vision of French fringe life from the director of "Le Dernier Combat." A spike-haired renegade escapes the law by plunging into the Parisian subway system. Once there, he encounters a bizarre subculture living under the city. Plenty of angry-youth attitude, but where's the point? And frankly, too much bad New Wave music.
1985 (R) 103m/C *FR* Christopher Lambert, Isabelle Adjani; *D:* Luc Besson. **VHS, Beta, LV** $79.98 *FOX ⅛*

Subway to the Stars Young saxophonist Fontes searches the back streets of Rio for his missing girlfriend. Realistic and sometimes depressing, if aimless at times. Overall, an intriguing "underworld" flick from Brazil. *AKA:* Un Trem Para as Estrelas.
1987 103m/C *BR* Guilherme Fontes, Milton Goncalves, Taumaturgo Ferreira, Ze Trindade, Ana Beatriz Wiltgen; *D:* Carlos Diegues. **VHS** $19.95 *STE, NWV ⅛⅛*

Success is the Best Revenge A Polish film director living in London struggles with his rebellious teenage son. Both struggle with questions of exile and identity. Uneven but worthwhile and based on Skolimowski's own experiences. His better earlier film is "Moonlighting."
1985 95m/C *GB* Michael York, Michel Piccoli, Anouk Aimee, John Hurt, Jane Asher, Joanna Szerbic, Michael Lyndon, George Skolimowski; *D:* Jerzy Skolimowski. **VHS, LV** *IME ⅛⅛*

Sucker Money Newspaper reporter works to expose phony spiritualist. Good title; little else. Boring. *AKA:* Victims of the Beyond.
1934 59m/B Mischa Auer, Phyliss Barrington, Earl McCarthy, Ralph Lewis, Mae Busch; *D:* Dorothy Reid. **VHS, Beta, LV** $16.95 *NOS, SNC, WGE ⅛½*

Sudden Death Shamrock and Lucky are back as cowboys posing as hired gunmen in order to foil a wealthy, homesteader-hating land baron.
1950 55m/B James Ellison, Russell Hayden, Stanley Price, Raymond Hatton, Betty Adams. **VHS, Beta, LV** *NO ⅛*

Sudden Death Two professional violence merchants put themselves up for hire.
1977 (R) 84m/C Robert Conrad, Felton Perry, Don Stroud, Bill Raymond, Ron Vawter, Harry Roskolenko; *D:* Richard Foreman. **VHS, Beta** $49.95 *MED ⅛*

Sudden Death A beautiful businesswoman decides to kill every rapist she can find after she herself has been attacked. Exploitative in its own fashion; fueled and felled by rage.
1985 (R) 95m/C Denise Coward, Frank Runyeon, Jamie Tirelli; *D:* Sig Shore. **VHS, Beta** $29.98 *LIV, VES ⅛*

Sudden Impact Eastwood directs himself in this formula thriller, the fourth "Dirty Harry" entry. This time "Dirty Harry" Callahan tracks down a revenge-obsessed murderess and finds he has more in common with her than he expected. Meanwhile, local mobsters come gunning for him. This is the one where he says, "Go ahead. Make my day." Followed by "The Dead Pool."
1983 (R) 117m/C Clint Eastwood, Sondra Locke, Pat Hingle, Bradford Dillman; *D:* Clint Eastwood. **VHS, Beta, LV, 8mm** $19.98 *WAR, PIA, TLF ⅛⅛½*

Sudden Terror The murder of an African dignitary is witnessed by a young boy who has trouble convincing his parents and the police about the incident. Suspenseful but less than original. Shot on location in Malta. *AKA:* Eyewitness.
1970 (PG) 95m/C *GB* Mark Lester, Lionel Jeffries, Susan George, Tony Bonner; *D:* John Hough. **VHS, Beta** *FOX ⅛⅛*

Suddenly Crazed gunman Sinatra (following his Oscar role in "From Here to Eternity") holds a family hostage in the hick town of Suddenly, California, as part of a plot to kill the president, who is passing through town. Tense thriller well displays Sinatra's acting talent, as does "The Manchurian Candidate." Unfortunately hard to find (as was "The Manchurian Candidate," which was re-released in 1987), because Sinatra forced United Artists to take them out of distribution after hearing that Kennedy assassin Lee Harvey Oswald had watched "Suddenly" only days before November 22, 1963. Really, Ol' Blue Eyes should have stuck with making top-notch thrillers like this one, instead of degenerating into the world's greatest lounge singer.
1954 75m/B Frank Sinatra, Sterling Hayden, James Gleason, Nancy Gates, Paul Frees; *D:* Lewis Allen. **VHS, Beta** $16.95 *SNC, NOS, VEC ⅛⅛⅛½*

Suddenly, Last Summer A brain surgeon is summoned to the mansion of a rich New Orleans matron who wishes him to perform a lobotomy on her niece, who has supposedly suffered a mental breakdown. The doctor seeks to learn the truth about the young woman and her family. Based on the play by Tennessee Williams. Although soft-pedaled for the censors, this movie's themes of homosexuality, insanity and murder, its characterizations of evil and its unusual settings, presage many movies of the next two decades. Extremely fine performances from Hepburn and Taylor. Clift, having never completely recovered from his automobile accident two years before, and struggling with his own mental health, does not come across with the strength of purpose really necessary in his character. Still, fine viewing.
1959 114m/B Elizabeth Taylor, Katharine Hepburn, Montgomery Clift, Mercedes McCambridge, Albert Dekker; *D:* Joseph L. Mankiewicz. Academy Awards '59 Nominations: Best Actress (Hepburn), Best Actress (Taylor), Best Art Direction/Set Decoration (B & W); Golden Globe Awards '60: Best Actress—Drama (Taylor); National Board of Review Awards '59: 10 Best Films of the Year. **VHS, Beta, LV** $19.95 *COL ⅛⅛⅛½*

Sudie & Simpson Heart-tugging tale of friendship set in rural 1940s Georgia. Twelve-year-old white Sudie's forbidden friendship with the adult black Simpson provides a lot of talk in their small town. Racial barriers finally cause Simpson to be accused of child molestation and the odds of his survival, despite his innocence, don't seem great. Based on Sara Flanigan Carter's autobiographical novel. Made for cable television.
1990 95m/C Sara Gilbert, Louis Gossett Jr., Frances Fisher, John Jackson, Paige1 Danahy, Ken Strong; *D:* Joan Tewkesbury; *W:* Sara Flanigan Carter, Ken Koser. **VHS** $89.95 *WOV ⅛⅛⅛*

S

Suds Pickford is tragic laundress with major crush on a guy who left his shirt at the laundry.
1920 75m/B Mary Pickford, William Austin, Harold Goodwin, Rose Dione, Theodore Roberts; *D:* Jack Dillon. **VHS, Beta, LV** $19.95 *GPV ✂✂½*

Suffering Bastards Buddy and Al have never worked a day in their lives—Mom's nightclub always gave them something to do and a regular paycheck. But when Mom's swindled out of the family business, they decide it's time to take charge. Soon they're caught between bullets, babes, and belly laughs in this action-filled comedy.
1990 95m/C Eric Bogosian, John C. McGinley, David Warshofsky. **VHS** $89.95 *AIP ✂✂½*

Sugar Cane Alley After the loss of his parents, an 11-year-old orphan boy goes to work with his grandmother on a sugar plantation. She realizes that her young ward's only hope is an education. Set in Martinique in the 1930s among black workers. Poignant and memorable. *AKA:* Rue Cases Negres.
1983 (PG) 106m/C *FR* Garry Cadenat, Darling Legitimus, Douta Seck; *D:* Euzhan Palcy. **VHS, Beta, LV** $29.95 *MED ✂✂✂*

Sugar Cookies Erotic horror story in which young women are the pawns as a satanic satyr and an impassioned lesbian play out a bizarre game of vengeance, love, and death.
1977 (R) 89m/C Mary Woronov, Lynn Lowry, Monique Van Vooren; *D:* Michael Herz. **VHS, Beta** $29.98 *VID Woof!*

Sugarbaby An acclaimed German film about a fat mortuary attendant living in Munich who transforms herself (but doesn't lose weight) in order to seduce a young, handsome subway conductor. Touching and warm film that introduced Sagebrecht to American audiences. A bit too cutting-edge cinematographically. In German with English subtitles. Remade as "Babycakes." Sagebrecht and director Adlon team up again for "Bagdad Cafe" and "Rosalie Goes Shopping." *AKA:* Zuckerbaby.
1985 (R) 103m/C *GE* Marianne Sagebrecht, Eisi Gulp, Toni Berger, Will Spendler, Manuela Denz; *D:* Percy Adlon. **VHS, Beta** $29.95 *LHV, GLV, APD ✂✂✂*

The Sugarland Express To save her son from adoption, a young woman helps her husband break out of prison. In their flight to freedom, they hijack a police car, holding the policeman hostage. Speilberg's first feature film is a moving portrait of a couple's desperation. Based on a true story, adapted by Hal Barwood and Matthew Robbins.
1974 (PG) 109m/C Goldie Hawn, Ben Johnson, Michael Sacks, William Atherton; *D:* Steven Spielberg; *M:* John Williams. **VHS, Beta, LV** $59.95 *MCA ✂✂✂*

Suicide Battalion/Hell Squad A war movie double feature. In "Suicide Battalion," American troops must sneak through enemy territory to destroy a captured American command outpost in the Philippines during World War II. Five American soldiers are lost in the North African desert in "Hell Squad." After a series of fights with various enemies, one soldier survives, only to nearly be doublecrossed by a Nazi he meets in the desert.
1958 150m/B Mike Connors, John Ashley, Russ Bender, Jewell Lain, Bing Russell, Wally Campo, Brandon Carroll, Frederic Galvin; *D:* Edward L. Cahn; *W/D:* Burt Topper. **VHS** $14.95 *COL ✂✂*

The Suicide Club A wealthy, depressed young woman joins a club filled with affluent people who play mysterious games. She finds that winning their games means more than she bargained for. Hemingway looks great in her off-kilter way, but really, there's no point, and the on-screen decadence gets tiresome.
1988 (R) 92m/C Mariel Hemingway, Robert Joy, Lenny Henry, Madeleine Potter, Michael O'Donoghue, Anne Carlisle; *D:* James Bruce. **VHS, Beta, LV** $29.95 *ACA ✂½*

Suicide Cult A CIA employee predicts the second coming of Christ, and a battle ensues between the forces of good and evil for possession of the child.
1977 82m/C **VHS, Beta** *NO Woof!*

Suicide Patrol A small band of saboteurs patrols a German-controlled Mediterranean island during World War II.
197? 90m/C Gordon Mitchell, Pierre Richard, Max Dean. **VHS, Beta** $57.95 *UNI, MOV ✂*

The Suitors When a group of Iranians decide to sacrifice a lamb in their apartment, the New York police send in SWAT team assuming they're terrorists. First time effort by Ebrahimian, in Farsi with English subtitles.
1988 106m/C *D:* Ghasem Ebrahimian. **VHS** $59.95 *FCT, TAM ✂*

Sullivan's Travels Sturges' masterpiece is a sardonic, whip-quick romp about a Hollywood director tired of making comedies who decides to make a serious, socially responsible film and hits the road masquerading as a hobo in order to know hardship and poverty. Beautifully sustained, inspired satire that mercilessly mocked the ambitions of Depression-era social cinema. Gets a little over-dark near the end before the happy ending; Sturges insisted on 20-year-old Lake as The Girl; her pregnancy forced him to rewrite scenes and design new costumes for her. As ever, she is stunning.
1941 90m/B Joel McCrea, Veronica Lake, William Demarest, Robert Warwick, Franklin Pangborn, Porter Hall, Eric Blore, Byron Foulger, Robert Greig, Torben Meyer, Jimmy Conlin, Margaret Hayes, Chester Conklin; *D:* Preston Sturges. **VHS, Beta, LV** $14.98 *MCA ✂✂✂✂*

Summer The fifth and among the best of Rhomer's "Comedies and Proverbs" series. A romantic but glum young French girl finds herself stuck in Paris during the tourist season searching for true romantic love. Takes time and patience to seize the viewer; moving ending makes it all worthwhile. In French with English subtitles. *AKA:* Le Rayon Vert; The Green Ray.
1986 (R) 90m/C *FR* Marie Riviere, Lisa Heredia, Beatrice Romand, Eric Hamm, Rosette, Isabelle Riviere; *D:* Eric Rohmer. **VHS, Beta, LV** $29.95 *PAV, FCT, TAM ✂✂✂½*

Summer Affair Two young lovers run away from their bickering parents and get shipwrecked on a desert island.
1979 90m/C *IT* Ornella Muti, Les Rannow; *D:* George S. Casorati. **VHS, Beta** *NO ✂½*

Summer and Smoke Repressed, unhappy Page falls for handsome doctor Harvey. A tour de force for Page, but that's all; adapted clumsily from the overwrought Tennessee Williams play.
1961 118m/C Laurence Harvey, Geraldine Page, Rita Moreno, Una Merkel, John McIntire, Thomas Gomez, Pamela Tiffin, Lee Patrick, Casey Adams, Earl Holliman, Harry Shannon, Pattee Chapman; *D:* Peter Glenville. Academy Awards '61 Nominations: Best Actress (Page), Best Art Direction/Set Decoration (Color), Best Supporting Actress (Merkel), Best Original Score; Golden Globe Awards '62: Best Actress—Drama (Page). **VHS, Beta, LV** $19.95 *PAR, PIA, FCT ✂✂½*

Summer Camp Ten-year reunion at a summer camp is the inane excuse for a bizarre weekend of co-ed football, midnight panty-raids, coupling couples and a wild disco party.
1978 (R) 85m/C John McLaughlin, Matt Michaels, Colleen O'Neil. **VHS, Beta** $54.95 *MED Woof!*

Summer Camp Nightmare See "Lord of the Flies" instead. A young fascist incites children at two summer camps to overthrow and imprison the adults. Barbarism rears its ugly head. Self-serious and anticlimatic. Based on the novel "The Butterfly Revolution" by William Butler. *AKA:* The Butterfly Revolution.
1986 (PG-13) 89m/C Chuck Connors, Charles Stratton, Harold Pruett, Tom Fridley, Adam Carl; *D:* Bert L. Dragin. **VHS, Beta, LV** $19.95 *SUE, NLC ✂✂*

Summer City Fun-and-sun surfing movie complete with romance, hot rods, murder and great shots of the sea features Gibson in his debut. Ever wonder what Australian surf bums do on weekends? The same as their California counterparts—except they talk funny. *AKA:* Coast of Terror.
1977 83m/C *AU* Mel Gibson, Phillip Avalon, John Jarratt, Christopher Fraser. **VHS, Beta** $59.95 *VCD ✂½*

Summer Dog A family falls in love with an abandoned dog they adopt and their landlord tries to evict them.
1978 (G) 88m/C James Congdon, Elizabeth Eisenman; *D:* John Clayton. **VHS, Beta** $19.95 *STE, VES ✂½*

Summer Fantasy Mindless TV surf saga about a curvy teen who would rather watch the beach hunks then go to medical school.
1984 96m/C Julianne Phillips, Ted Shackleford, Michael Gross, Dorothy Lyman; *D:* Noel Nosseck. **VHS, Beta** $79.95 *SVS ✂*

Summer Heat When a young man spends his summer with his hypnotic aunt, we are taken on a no-holds-barred tour through the steamy world of the rich and the restless.
1973 71m/C Bob Garry, Nicole Avril, Pat Pascal. **VHS, Beta** $19.95 *VID ✂*

Summer Heat In rural, mid-Depression North Carolina, a young, lonely wife and mother is seduced by a drifter and together they plot murder. Her husband neglects her, and you should neglect to see this utter yawner. Based on a Louise Shivers novel.
1987 (R) 80m/C Lori Singer, Anthony Edwards, Bruce Abbott, Kathy Bates; *D:* Michie Gleason. **VHS, Beta, LV** $19.95 *PAR ✂✂*

Summer Holiday Rooney comes of age with a vengeance during summer vacation in musical rendition of "Ah, Wilderness." Undistinguished musical numbers, inferior to the original, but jazzy Technicolor cinematography. Ended up in the red by over $1.5 million, lotsa money back then. ♫It's Our Home Town; Afraid to Fall in Love; All Hail, Danville High; The Stanley Steamer; It's Independence Day; I Think You're the Sweetest Kid I've Ever Known; Weary Blues.
1948 92m/C Mickey Rooney, Gloria DeHaven, Walter Huston, Frank Morgan, Jackie "Butch" Jenkins, Marilyn Maxwell, Agnes Moorehead, Selena Royle, Anne Francis; *D:* Rouben Mamoulian. **VHS** $19.98 *MGM, TTC, FCT ✂✂½*

A Summer in St. Tropez Photographer David Hamilton's erotic and lyrical study of a household of girls in their first stages of womanhood living outside of society in the south of France.
1981 60m/C **VHS, Beta** $19.99 *HBO ✂✂*

Summer Interlude A ballerina recalls a romantic summer spent with an innocent boy, who was later tragically killed. Contains many earmarks and visual ideas of later Bergman masterpieces. In Swedish with English subtitles. *AKA:* Illicit Interlude; Summerplay.
1950 95m/B *SW* Maj-Britt Nilsson, Birger Malmsten, Alf Kjellin; *D:* Ingmar Bergman. **VHS, Beta $19.98** *SUE, TAM, NLC* 🎬🎬🎬½

Summer Job A group of college kids work and play at a decadent resort. In the "alleged comedy" genre, and among the very worst.
1988 (R) 92m/C Sherrie Rose, Fred Boudin, Dave Clouse, Kirk Earhardt; *D:* Paul Madden. **VHS, Beta, LV $14.95** *SVS, COL* Woof!

Summer Lovers Summer vacation finds young couple traveling to the exotic Greek island of Santorini. They meet up with a fun-loving woman and discover three-way sexual tension, but little in the way of plot, dialogue, or acting. From the director of "Grease" and "Blue Lagoon" and best watched late at night while half conscious.
1982 (R) 98m/C Peter Gallagher, Daryl Hannah, Valerie Quennessen; *D:* Randal Kleiser. **VHS, Beta, LV $9.95** *COL, SUE* 🎬

Summer Magic An impecunious recent widow is forced to leave Boston and settle her family in a small town in Maine. Typical, forgettable Disney drama; early Mills vehicle. A remake of "Mother Carey's Chickens."
1963 116m/C Hayley Mills, Burl Ives, Dorothy McGuire, Deborah Walley, Una Merkel, Eddie Hodges; *D:* James Neilson. **VHS, Beta $69.95** *DIS* 🎬🎬

Summer Night A female tycoon who is concerned for the environment decides to strike out at the terrorists who are destroying it. This caper turns into one big comedy. In Italian with English subtitles.
1987 (R) 94m/C *IT* Mariangela Melato, Michele Placido, Roberto Herlitzka, Massimo Wertmuller; *D:* Lina Wertmuller. **VHS, Beta $79.95** *LIV* 🎬🎬

Summer Night Fever A pair of young males go girl crazy near the end of their summer vacation.
1979 101m/C Stephanie Hillel, Olivia Pascal, Betty Verges; *D:* Siggi Gotz. **VHS, Beta $19.98** *TWE* 🎬

Summer Night with Greek Profile, Almond Eyes & Scent of Basil A wealthy woman tycoon hires an ex-CIA man to kidnap a wealthy, professional terrorist and hold him for ransom. An ironic battle of the sexes follows. In Italian with English subtitles.
1987 (R) 94m/C *IT* Mariangela Melato, Michele Placido, Roberto Herlitzka; *D:* Lina Wertmuller. **VHS, Beta $19.95** *IVE, TAM* 🎬

Summer of Fear A happy young woman must overcome evil forces when her cousin comes to live with her family. Based on a novel by Lois Duncan. Pretty scary if ordinary, dumb made-for-TV horror from later-famous Craven. *AKA:* Stranger in Our House.
1978 94m/C Linda Blair; *D:* Wes Craven. **VHS, Beta $59.99** *HBO* 🎬🎬

Summer of '42 Touching if sentimental story about a 15-year-old boy's sexual coming of age during his summer vacation on an island off New England. While his friends are fumbling with girls their own age, he falls in love with a beautiful 22-year-old woman whose husband is off fighting in the war.
1971 (R) 102m/C Jennifer O'Neill, Gary Grimes, Jerry Houser, Oliver Conant; *D:* Robert Mulligan. Academy Awards '71: Best Original Score; Nominations: Best Cinematography, Best Film

Editing, Best Story & Screenplay. **VHS, Beta, LV $19.98** *WAR* 🎬🎬🎬

The Summer of Miss Forbes A governess rules over two young boys with an iron hand by day and cavorts nude and drunk by night. The boys fantasize about her murder, but fate has different plans. In Spanish with English subtitles. *AKA:* El Verano de la Senora Forbes.
1988 85m/C *SP* Hanna Schygulla, Alexis Castaneras, Victor Cesar Villalobos, Guadalupe Sandoval, Fernando Balzaretti, Yuriria Munguia; *D:* Jaime Humberto Hermosillo. **VHS, LV $79.95** *FXL, FCT, TAM* 🎬🎬

The Summer of My German Soldier A young Jewish girl befriends an escaped German prisoner of war in a small town in Georgia during World War II. Occasionally sentimental but more often genuinely moving made for TV drama. Rolle won a deserved Emmy as the housekeeper. Adapted from Bette Green's novel.
1978 98m/C Kristy McNichol, Esther Rolle, Bruce Davison; *D:* Michael Tuchner. **VHS, Beta $14.95** *MTI* 🎬🎬🎬

Summer of Secrets Young couple get more than they bargained for when they make love in a demented doctor's beach house.
1976 (PG) 100m/C **VHS, Beta $14.98** *VID* 🎬

A Summer Place Melodrama about summer liaisons amid the young and middle-aged rich on an island off the coast of Maine. Too slick; romantic drama is little more than skin-deep, and dialogue is excruciating. Donahue's first starring role. Based on the novel by Sloan Wilson. Featuring "Theme from a Summer Place," which was a number-one hit in 1959.
1959 130m/C Troy Donahue, Richard Egan, Sandra Dee, Dorothy McGuire, Arthur Kennedy, Constance Ford, Beulah Bondi; *D:* Delmer Daves; *M:* Max Steiner. **VHS, Beta, LV $19.98** *WAR* 🎬🎬

Summer Rental That John Candy just can't win, can he? Here, as a hopeless, harried air traffic controller, he tries to have a few days to relax in sunny Florida. Enter mean rich guy Crenna. Candy can add something hefty to the limpest of plots, and does so here. Watch the first hour for yuks, then rewind.
1985 (PG) 87m/C John Candy, Rip Torn, Richard Crenna, Karen Austin, Kerri Green, John Larroquette, Pierrino Mascarino; *D:* Carl Reiner. **VHS, Beta, LV, 8mm $19.95** *PAR* 🎬🎬

Summer School A teenaged boy's girlfriend will stop at nothing to prevent him from going out with the pretty new girl in town.
1977 (R) 80m/C John McLaughlin, Steve Rose, Phoebe Schmidt. **VHS, Beta $19.95** *AHV* 🎬

Summer School A high-school teacher's vacation plans are ruined when he gets stuck teaching remedial English in summer school. It seems all these students are interested in is re-enacting scenes from "The Texas Chainsaw Massacre." Actually, one of the better films of this genre.
1987 (PG-13) 98m/C Mark Harmon, Kirstie Alley, Nels Van Patten, Courtney Thorne-Smith, Lucy Lee Flippin, Shawnee Smith; *D:* Carl Reiner. **VHS, Beta, LV $14.95** *PAR* 🎬🎬½

Summer School Teachers Three sultry femmes bounce about Los Angeles high school and make the collective student body happy. Typical Corman doings; sequel to "The Students Teachers."
1975 (R) 87m/C Candice Rialson, Pat Anderson, Rhonda Leigh Hopkins, Christopher Wales; *D:* Barbara Peeters. **VHS, Beta $59.98** *NLC* Woof!

Summer Solstice Fonda and Loy are splendid as a couple married half a century who revisit the beach where they first met. Fonda especially shines, as a crusty old artist. Yes, it is an awful lot like "On Golden Pond." Made for TV.
1981 75m/C Henry Fonda, Myrna Loy, Lindsay Crouse, Stephen Collins; *D:* Ralph Rosenblum. **VHS, Beta $59.99** *HBO, MTT* 🎬🎬½

Summer Stock Garland plays a farm owner whose sister arrives with a summer stock troupe, led by Kelly, to rehearse a show in the family barn. Garland agrees, if the troupe will help her with the farm's harvest. When her sister decamps for New York, leaving the leading lady role open, guess who steps into the breach. Slim plot papered over with many fun song-and-dance numbers. Also features Garland's first MGM short, "Every Sunday," made in 1936 with Deanna Durbin. 🎵Friendly Star; Mem'ry Island; Dig-Dig-Dig For Your Dinner; If You Feel Like Singing, Sing; Howdy Neighbor; Blue Jean Polka; Portland Fancy; You, Wonderful You; Get Happy; If You Feel Like Singing, Sing; Happy Harvest; Heavenly Happy. *AKA:* If You Feel Like Singing.
1950 109m/C Judy Garland, Gene Kelly, Gloria de Haven, Carleton Carpenter, Eddie Bracken, Phil Silvers, Hans Conried, Marjorie Main, Ray Collins, Deanna Durbin; *D:* Charles Walters. **VHS, Beta, LV $19.98** *MGM, TTC* 🎬🎬🎬

A Summer Story Superbly acted, typically British period drama about beautiful farm girl Stubbs and city lawyer Wilby, who fall in love. But can they overcome difference of social class? From the story "The Apple Tree" by John Gaslworthy.
1988 (PG-13) 97m/C *GB* James Wilby, Imogen Stubbs, Susannah York, Sophie Ward; *D:* Piers Haggard. **VHS, Beta $79.98** *MED* 🎬🎬🎬

Summer Switch A boy and his father magically switch bodies and learn about each other. Originally made for television.
1983 46m/C Robert Klein. **VHS, Beta $19.95** *NWV* 🎬

A Summer to Remember A five-year-old boy spends a summer with his stepfather on a Soviet collective farm. The two become deeply attached. Scenes of collective life will be of more interest to Westerners than the near-sentimental story. Star Bondarchuk later directed the epic, award-winning "War and Peace." *AKA:* Seryozha.
1961 80m/B *RU* Borya Barkhazov, Sergei Bondarchuk, Irana Skobtseva. **VHS, Beta** *NO* 🎬🎬🎬

A Summer to Remember A deaf boy (played by Gerlis, himself deaf since birth) develops a friendship with an orangutan through sign language. Bad guys abduct the friendly ape - but all is right in the end. Nice, innocuous family viewing. Made for TV.
1984 (PG) 93m/C Tess Harper, James Farentino, Burt Young, Louise Fletcher, Sean Gerlis, Bridgette Anderson; *D:* Robert Lewis. **VHS, Beta $39.95** *MCA* 🎬🎬½

Summer Vacation: 1999 Four boys are left behind at boarding school during their summer vacation. They experience all the early pangs of adolescence from love to jealousy. Their summer is then disturbed by the arrival of another boy who appears to be the reincarnation of a dead friend. Romantic look at youth caught between innocence and awareness. In Japanese with English subtitles. *AKA:* 1999—Nen No Natsu Yasumi.
1988 90m/C *JP* Eri Miyagima, Miyuki Nakano, Tomoko Otakra, Rie Mizuhara; *D:* Shusuke Kaneko. **VHS, Beta $69.95** *NYF, FCT, TAM* 🎬🎬

Summer Wishes, Winter Dreams
Woodward and Balsam are a materially prosperous middle-aged couple with little but tedium in their lives—a tedium accurately replicated, in what feels like real life, in this slow, dull film. The two leads and Sidney—in her first screen role in 17 years—are all excellent, but the story of regret and present unhappiness wears the viewer down.
1973 (PG) 95m/C Joanne Woodward, Martin Balsam, Sylvia Sidney, Dori Brenner, Ron Richards; D: Gilbert Cates; W: Stewart Stern. Academy Awards '73 Nominations: Best Actress (Woodward), Best Supporting Actress (Sidney); British Academy Awards '74: Best Actress (Woodward); National Board of Review Awards '73: Best Supporting Actress (Sidney); New York Film Critics Awards '73: Best Actress (Woodward). VHS, Beta $59.95 COL ♫♫

Summerdog
Harmless family tale about vacationers who rescue a cheerful, lovable mutt named Hobo. And a good thing they found him: He saves them from many perils. Thanks, Hobo!
1978 (G) 90m/C James Congdon, Elizabeth Eisenman, Oliver Zabriskie, Tavia Zabriskie; D: John Clayton. VHS, Beta $29.95 GEM ♫♫

Summer's Children
Man who suffers from amnesia as a result of a car crash becomes the target of a mysterious killer. Forget about it.
1984 90m/C Tom Haoff, Pauly Jardine, Kate Lynch. VHS, Beta $49.95 TWE ♫

Summer's Games
Buxom girls cavort on the beach, competing in various games designed specifically to expose as much flesh as possible—mud wrestling, bikini boxing, wet T-shirting and more.
1987 60m/C VHS, Beta, LV NO ♫♫

Summertime
Spinster Hepburn vacations in Venice and falls in love with Brazzi. She is hurt when inadvertently she learns he is married, but her life has been so bleak she is not about to end her one great romance. Moving, funny, richly photographed in a beautiful Old World city. From Arthur Laurents' play "The Time of the Cuckoo." AKA: Summer Madness.
1955 98m/C Katharine Hepburn, Rossano Brazzi; D: David Lean. Academy Awards '55 Nominations: Best Actress (Hepburn), Best Director (Lean); National Board of Review Awards '55: 10 Best Films of the Year; New York Film Critics Awards '55: Best Director (Lean). VHS, Beta, LV $14.98 SUE, VYG, CRC ♫♫♫½

Summertree
Douglas stars as a young musician in the 1960s trying to avoid the draft and the wrath of his parents. Contrived and heavy-handed. Produced by Douglas pere, Kirk. Adapted from the play by Ron Cower.
1971 (PG) 88m/C Michael Douglas, Jack Warden, Brenda Vaccaro, Barbara Bel Geddes, Kirk Calloway, Bill Vint; D: Anthony Newley. VHS, Beta WAR, OM ♫♫

The Sun Shines Bright
Heavily stereotyped, contrived tale of a Southern judge with a heart of gold who does so many good deeds (defending a black man accused of rape; helping a desperate prostitute) that he jeopardizes his re-election. Set during Reconstruction. An unfortunate remake of Ford's own 1934 "Judge Priest," starring Will Rogers.
1953 92m/B Charles Winninger, Arleen Whelan, John Russell, Stepin Fetchit, Milburn Stone, Russell Simpson; D: John Ford. VHS $19.98 REP ♫♫

Sun Valley Serenade
Wartime musical fluff about a band that adopts a Norwegian refugee waif as a publicity stunt. She turns out to be a full-grown man-chaser who stirs up things at a ski resort. Fun, but it ends abruptly—because, they say, Henie fell during the huge skating finale, and Darryl Zanuck wouldn't greenlight a reshoot. One of only two feature appearances by Glenn Miller and his Orchestra (the other was "Orchestra Wives"), on video with a soundtrack restored from original dual-track recordings. ♫Chattanooga Choo Choo; I Know Why And So Do You; It Happened In Sun Valley; The Kiss Polka; In The Mood.
1941 86m/C Sonja Henie, John Payne, Glenn Miller, Milton Berle, Lynn Bari, Joan Davis, Dorothy Dandridge; D: H. Bruce Humberstone. VHS $19.98 FXV, FCT, MLB ♫♫½

Sunburn
Insurance investigator Grodin hires model Fawcett to pretend to be his wife to get the scoop on a suicide/murder case of a rich guy in Acapulco. Made-for-TV drivel.
1979 (PG) 110m/C Farrah Fawcett, Charles Grodin, Joan Collins, Art Carney, William Daniels; D: Richard Sarafian. VHS, Beta $49.95 PAR ♫½

Sundance
Surf dudes get together on the beaches of Hawaii and California for some romance and, of course, plenty of wave riding.
1972 87m/C VHS, Beta NO ♫

Sundance and the Kid
Two brothers try to collect an inheritance against all odds. Originally known as "Sundance Cassidy and Butch the Kid."
1976 (PG) 84m/C John Wade, Karen Blake; D: Arthur Pitt. VHS, Beta NO ♫♫

Sunday, Bloody Sunday
Adult drama centers around the intertwined love affairs of the homosexual Finch, the heterosexual Jackson, and self-centered bisexual artist Head, desired by both. Fully-drawn characters brought to life by excellent acting make this difficult story well worth watching—though Head's central character is sadly rather dull. Day-Lewis makes his first (brief) screen appearance as a car vandalizing teenager. Powerful, sincere and sensitive.
1971 (R) 110m/C GB Glenda Jackson, Peter Finch, Murray Head, Daniel Day-Lewis; D: John Schlesinger. Academy Awards '71 Nominations: Best Actor (Finch), Best Actress (Jackson), Best Director (Schlesinger), Best Story & Screenplay; British Academy Awards '71: Best Actor (Finch), Best Actress (Jackson), Best Director (Schlesinger), Best Film; Golden Globe Awards '72: Best Foreign Film; National Society of Film Critics Awards '71: Best Actor (Finch). VHS, LV $59.98 FOX ♫♫♫

Sunday Daughters
A teenage girl kept in a detention home constantly tries to escape and find some kind of familial love. Stronge performances mix with keen direction. In Hungarian with English subtitles.
1980 100m/C HU Julianna Nyako; D: Janosz Rozsa. VHS, Beta $59.95 FCT ♫♫♫

A Sunday in the Country
A lush, distinctively French affirmation of nature and family life. This character study with a minimal plot takes place during a single summer day in 1910 France. An elderly impressionist painter-patriarch is visited at his country home by his family. Highly acclaimed, though the pace may be too slow for some. Beautiful location photography. In French with English subtitles. AKA: Un Dimanche a la Campagne.
1984 (G) 94m/C FR Louis Ducreux, Sabine Azema, Michel Aumont; D: Bertrand Tavernier. VHS, Beta $19.98 MGM ♫♫♫½

Sunday in the Park with George
Taped theatrical performance of the Tony, Grammy, and Pulitzer Prize-winning musical play, which is based upon impressionist Georges Seurat's painting "A Sunday Afternoon on the Island of Grande Jatte." The celebrated music score was composed by Stephen Sondheim.
1986 120m/C Mandy Patinkin, Bernadette Peters, Barbara Byrne, Charles Kimbrough; D: James Lapine. VHS, Beta, LV $19.98 LHV, WAR, STS ♫♫♫

Sunday Too Far Away
The rivalries between Australian sheep shearers and graziers leads to an ugly strike at a remote outback area in 1955. An uncomplicated story and a joy to watch.
1974 100m/C AU Jack Thompson; D: Ken Hannam. VHS, Beta $59.98 SUE ♫♫♫

Sundays & Cybele
A ragged war veteran and an orphaned girl develop a strong emotional relationship, which is frowned upon by the townspeople. Warm and touching. In French with English subtitles. AKA: Les Dimanches de Ville d'Avray; Cybele.
1962 110m/B FR Hardy Kruger, Nicole Courcel; D: Serge Bourguignon. VHS, Beta $24.95 NOS, HHT, DVT ♫♫♫½

Sundown
In Africa at the beginning of World War II, a local girl aids the British against a German plot to run guns to the natives and start a rebellion. Engaging performances and efficient direction keep it above the usual cliches. Also available in a colorized version.
1941 91m/B Gene Tierney, Bruce Cabot, George Sanders, Harry Carey Sr., Cedric Hardwicke, Joseph Calleia, Dorothy Dandridge, Reginald Gardiner; D: Henry Hathaway. VHS, Beta $19.95 NOS, VYY, DVT ♫♫½

Sundown
An ambitious shot at a vampire western fails because it drains almost all vampire lore and winds up resembling a standard oater. Carradine plays a reformed vampire king (guess who) running a desert clinic that weans bloodsuckers away from preying on humans. But undead renegades attack using sixguns and wooden bullets. The climax may outrage horror purists.
1991 (R) 104m/C David Carradine, Bruce Campbell, Deborah Foreman, Maxwell Caulfield, Morgan Brittany; D: Anthony Hickox. VHS $89.98 VES ♫½

Sundown Fury
Young cowboy fights against a group of bandits to hold a telegraph office.
1942 56m/B Donald (Don "Red") Barry. VHS, Beta $27.95 VCN ♫

Sundown Kid
A Pinkerton agent goes undercover to break up a counterfeiting operation. Routine western.
1943 55m/B Donald (Don "Red") Barry. VHS, Beta DVT ♫½

Sundown Riders
Cowhands are victimized by noose-happy outlaws. Filmed in just over a week on a $30,000 budget and originally shot on 16mm to make it accessible to hospitals and schools with basic viewing equipment. The lesson here: it takes time and money to make a good western.
1948 56m/B Russell Wade, Andy Clyde, Jay Kirby; D: Lambert Hillyer. VHS, Beta, LV NO ♫

Sundown Saunders
A standard oater about a cowboy whose prize for winning a horse race is a ranch. Trouble is, an outlaw wants the homestead as well.
1936 64m/B Bob Steele; D: Robert North Bradbury. VHS, Beta $19.95 NOS, WGE, VYY ♫

The Sundowners Slow, beautiful, and often moving epic drama about a family of Irish sheepherders in Australia during the 1920s who must continually uproot themselves and migrate. They struggle to save enough money to buy their own farm and wind up training a horse they hope will be a money-winner in racing. Well-acted by all, with Johns and Ustinov providing some humorous moments. Adapted from the novel by Jon Cleary, with music by Dimitri Tiomkin. Filmed in Australia and London studios. **1960** 133m/C Deborah Kerr, Robert Mitchum, Peter Ustinov, Glynis Johns, Dina Merrill, Chips Rafferty, Michael Anderson Jr., Lola Brooks, Wylie Watson; **D:** Fred Zinneman. Academy Awards '60 Nominations: Best Actress (Kerr), Best Adapted Screenplay, Best Director (Zinneman), Best Picture, Best Supporting Actress (Johns); National Board of Review Awards '60: 10 Best Films of the Year, Best Actor (Mitchum). **VHS, Beta, LV $19.98** *WAR, PIA, CCB ♂♂♂1/2*

Sunny Another glossed-over, love-conquers-all musical with Neagle as a circus star who falls for a wealthy car maker's son. Dad and crew disapprove, putting a damper on the romance. In spite of the weak storyline and flat direction, Kerns' music and Bolger's dancing make it enjoyable. ♫Who?; D'ya Love Me?; Sunny; Two Little Bluebirds. **1941** 98m/B Anna Neagle, Ray Bolger, John Carroll, Edward Everett Horton, Frieda Inescort, Helen Westley, Benny Rubin, Richard Lane, Martha Tilton; **D:** Herbert Wilcox. **VHS $19.95** *NOS ♂♂*

Sunny Side Up As stress of pickle factory work takes toll on woman's friend, she makes heroic effort to help her to the country to recover. **1928** 66m/B Vera Reynolds, ZaSu Pitts. **VHS, Beta $16.95** *GPV ♂♂1/2*

Sunny Skies Bargain-basement retread has Lease donating a pint of blood. ♫Sunny Days; I Must Have You; Wanna Find a Boy; Must Be Love. **1930** 75m/B Benny Rubin, Marceline Day, Rex Lease, Marjorie Kane, Wesley Barry; **D:** Norman Taurog. **VHS $19.95** *NOS ♂*

Sunnyside Travolta plays a street kid trying to bring an end to the local gang warfare so he can move to Manhattan. Features a host of pop tunes in an attempt to ride the coattails of brother John's successful "Saturday Night Fever." Laughably bad. **1979 (R)** 100m/C Joey Travolta, John Lansing, Stacey Pickren, Andrew Rubin, Michael Tucci, Talia Balsam, Joan Darling; **D:** Timothy Galfas. **VHS $19.98** *AIP, FOX Woof!*

Sunrise Magnificent silent story of a simple country boy who, prodded by an alluring city woman, tries to murder his wife. Production values wear their age well. Gaynor won an Oscar for her stunning performance. Remade as "The Journey to Tilsit." **AKA:** Sunrise—A Song of Two Humans. **1927** 110m/B George O'Brien, Janet Gaynor, Bodil Rosing, Margaret Livingston, J. Farrell MacDonald; **D:** F. W. Murnau. Academy Awards '28: Best Actress (Gaynor), Best Cinematography; Nominations: Best Interior Decoration. **VHS** *VTR, GPV ♂♂♂♂*

Sunrise at Campobello A successful adaptation (with Bellamy and Donehue repeating their roles) of the Tony award-winning play that chronicles Franklin D. Roosevelt's battle to conquer polio and ultimately receive the Democratic presidential nomination in 1924. Garson gives an excellent performance as Eleanor Roosevelt. Screenplay by Dore Schary, who adapted from his own play (and also produced). **1960** 143m/C Ralph Bellamy, Greer Garson, Hume Cronyn, Jean Hagen, Jack Perrin, Lyle Talbot; **D:** Vincent J. Donehue. Academy Awards '60 Nominations: Best Actress (Garson), Best Art Direction/Set Decoration (Color), Best Costume Design (Color), Best Sound; Golden Globe Awards '61: Best Actress—Drama (Garson); National Board of Review Awards '60: 10 Best Films of the Year, Best Actress (Garson). **VHS, Beta $59.95** *WAR ♂♂♂*

Sunset Edwards wanders the range in this soft-centered farce about a couple of Western legends out to solve a mystery. On the backlots of Hollywood, silent screen star Tom Mix (Willis) meets aging marshall Wyatt Earp (Garner) and participates in a time-warp western circa 1927. They encounter a series of misadventures while trying to finger a murderer. Garner ambles enjoyably, lifting him a level above the rest of the cast. **1988 (R)** 101m/C Bruce Willis, James Garner, Mariel Hemingway, Darren McGavin, Jennifer Edwards, Malcolm McDowell, Kathleen Quinlan, M. Emmet Walsh, Patricia Hodge, Richard Bradford, Joe Dallesandro, Dermot Mulroney; **D:** Blake Edwards. **VHS, Beta, LV $14.95** *COL ♂♂*

Sunset Boulevard Famed tale of Norma Desmond (Swanson), aging silent film queen, who refuses to accept that stardom has ended for her and hires a young down-on-his-luck screenwriter (Holden) to help engineer her movie comeback. The screenwriter, who becomes the actress' kept man, assumes he can manipulate her, but finds out otherwise. Reality was almost too close for comfort, as Swanson, von Stroheim (as her major domo), and others very nearly play themselves. A darkly humorous look at the legacy and loss of fame with witty dialog, stellar performances, and some now-classic scenes. **1950** 100m/B Gloria Swanson, William Holden, Erich von Stroheim, Nancy Olson, Buster Keaton, Jack Webb, Cecil B. DeMille, Fred Clark; **D:** Billy Wilder. Academy Awards '50: Best Art Direction/Set Decoration (B & W), Best Story & Screenplay, Best Score; Nominations: Best Actor (Holden), Best Actress (Swanson), Best Black and White Cinematography, Best Director (Wilder), Best Film Editing, Best Picture, Best Supporting Actor (von Stroheim), Best Supporting Actress (Olson); Golden Globe Awards '51: Best Actress—Drama (Swanson), Best Director (Wilder), Best Film—Drama. **VHS, Beta, LV $14.95** *PAR, HMV ♂♂♂1/2*

Sunset Grill While investigating his wife's murder, detective Ryder Hart (Weller) discovers a pattern of grisly killings. Sexy singer Loren Duquesne (Singer) leads him south of the border to her boss and his bloody money-making scheme. Unrated version also available. **1992 (R)** 103m/C Peter Weller, Lori Singer, Alexandra Paul, John Rhys-Davies, Michael Anderson Jr., Stacy Keach; **D:** Kevin Connor. **VHS $89.95** *NLC, PMS ♂♂*

Sunset Heat Former drug dealer (Pare) returns to his home in Los Angeles with a legit job as a photojournalist. He stays with an old friend who turns out to be involved with the obsessed drug czar that Pare used to work for. Trouble comes along when the drug lord is robbed and blames Pare for the crime. Action-packed, with some good plot twists. An unrated version contains two additional minutes of footage. **AKA:** Midnight Heat. **1992 (R)** 94m/C Michael Pare, Dennis Hopper, Adam Ant, Daphne Ashbrook, Charlie Schlatter; **D:** John Nicolella. **VHS $89.95** *NLC ♂♂*

Sunset in El Dorado Roy and Dale thwart a villainous scheme to defraud farmers of their land. **1945** 56m/B Roy Rogers, Dale Evans. **VHS, Beta $27.95** *VCN ♂♂1/2*

Sunset Limousine An out-of-work stand-up comic gets thrown out by his girlfriend, then takes a job as a chauffeur. Standard vehicle with occasional bursts of speed. **1983** 92m/C John Ritter, Martin Short, Susan Dey, Paul Reiser, Audrie Neehan, Lainie Kazan; **D:** Terry Hughes. **VHS, Beta $59.95** *LIV ♂♂1/2*

Sunset on the Desert Rogers gets to wear a white hat and a black hat as both the leader of a gang of outlaws and the hero who brings them to justice. A poor man's Western omelette. **1942** 53m/B Roy Rogers, George "Gabby" Hayes, Trigger, Lynne Carver, Frank M. Thomas, Bob Nolan, Beryl Wallace, Glenn Strange, Douglas Fowley, Roy Bancroft, Pat Brady; **D:** Joseph Kane. **VHS, Beta $24.95** *VYY ♂1/2*

Sunset Range The "World's All-Around Champion Cowboy" of 1912 stars in this chaps-slappin', bit-chompin', dust-raisin' saga of the plains. **1935** 59m/B Hoot Gibson. **VHS, Beta $19.95** *NOS, VCN, UHV ♂1/2*

Sunset Serenade Roy and Gabby outwit murderous duo who plan to eliminate the new heir to a ranch. **1942** 60m/B Roy Rogers, Trigger, George "Gabby" Hayes, Helen Parrish; **D:** Joseph Kane. **VHS, Beta $19.95** *NOS, MED, HEG ♂♂*

Sunset Strip A photographer investigates a friend's murder, and enters the seamy world of drugs and rock and roll in L.A. **1985** 83m/C Tom Elpin, Cheri Cameron Newell, John Mayall. **VHS, Beta $69.98** *LIV, VES ♂*

Sunset Strip A young dancer finds a job in a strip club and competes against the other women there to find the man of her dreams. The women take their jobs very seriously—even attending ballet classes to improve their performances. However, the viewer probably won't take this movie very seriously since it is just another excuse to show women in as little clothing as possible. **1991 (R)** 95m/C Jeff Conaway, Michelle Foreman, Shelley Michelle; **D:** Paul G. Volk. **VHS, LV $29.95** *PMH Woof!*

Sunset Trail Routine Maynard sagebrush saga with the hero protecting a woman rancher from outlaws. **1932** 60m/B Ken Maynard. **VHS, Beta $19.95** *NOS, UHV, DVT ♂*

The Sunshine Boys Two veteran vaudeville partners, who have shared a love-hate relationship for decades, reunite for a television special. Adapted by Neil Simon from his play. Matthau was a replacement for Jack Benny, who died before the start of filming. Burns, for his first starring role since "Honolulu" in 1939, won an Oscar. **1975 (PG)** 111m/C George Burns, Walter Matthau, Richard Benjamin, Lee Meredith, F. Murray Abraham, Carol Arthur, Howard Hesseman; **D:** Herbert Ross; **W:** Neil Simon. Academy Awards '75: Best Supporting Actor (Burns); Nominations: Best Actor (Matthau), Best Adapted Screenplay, Best Art Direction/Set Decoration; Golden Globe Awards '76: Best Actor—Musical/Comedy (Matthau), Best Film—Musical/Comedy, Best Supporting Actor (Benjamin). **VHS, Beta, LV $14.95** *MGM, BTV ♂♂♂*

Sunshine Run Two escaped slaves and a young widow search for Spanish treasure in the Everglades. Also on video as "Black Rage."

1979 (PG) 102m/C Chris Robinson, Ted Cassidy, David Legge, Phyllis Robinson; *D:* Chris Robinson. **VHS, Beta** *NO* 🎬½

Sunstroke Seymour plays a desperate mother searching for her kidnapped child through the Arizona desert. Framed for murder, she cannot contact the police but must track the kidnappers herself, until she meets a drifter with secrets of his own.
1992 (R) 91m/C Jane Seymour, Stephen Meadows, Steve Railsback, Ray Wise, Don Ameche; *D:* James Keach; *W:* Duane Poole. **VHS, Beta** *PAR* 🎬🎬

The Super Pesci stars as a slumlord who faces a prison sentence thanks to his terminal neglect. The option given to him is to live in his own rat hole until he provides reasonable living conditions. This he does, and predictably learns a thing or two about his own greed and the people who suffer as a result of it. Pesci as always gives an animated performance but poor scripting laden with stereotypes and cliches successfully restricts effort.
1991 (R) 86m/C Joe Pesci, Vincent Gardenia, Madolyn Smith, Ruben Blades; *D:* Rod Daniel. **VHS** $19.98 *FXV, CCB* 🎬½

Super Bitch Nasty, cold, and uncaring woman uses men to keep up her expensive habits, then ruthlessly tosses them aside when she is done. She purposely entangles them in her drug trade and thinks nothing of their deaths. Proving once again that you get what you pay for. *AKA:* Mafia Junction.
1989 90m/C Stephanie Beacham, Patricia Hayes, Gareth Thomas; *D:* Massimo Dallamano. **VHS** $79.95 *ATL* 🎬½

Super Brother The feared and respected leader of an oppressed people is imprisoned, much to everyone's regret.
1990 (R) 90m/C Woody Strode. **VHS, Beta** *ELE* 🎬

Super Dragons/Mafia vs. Ninja The baddest of the bad and the best of the good battle for ultimate control in two, full-length martial arts films.
19?? 180m/C Alexander Lou, Pad Yku La, Wang Hsia. **VHS** $9.99 *VTR* 🎬

Super Dynamo An orphaned child is raised by monks, who teach him kung fu as part of his spiritual training and discipline. Once grown, the young man fights to stem the tide of smuggling rings and crime societies in Asia.
19?? 90m/C **VHS** $19.95 *OCE* 🎬

Super Fuzz Rookie policeman develops super powers after being accidentally exposed to radiation. Somewhat ineptly, he uses his abilities to combat crime. Somewhat ineptly acted, written, and directed as well. *AKA:* Supersnooper.
1981 (PG) 97m/C Terence Hill, Joanne Dru, Ernest Borgnine; *D:* Sergio Corbucci. **VHS, Beta** $69.98 *SUE* 🎬½

Super Gang Abounding fists and feet punctuate this tale of colliding gangs.
1985 75m/C Bruce Lee. **VHS, Beta** $59.95 *SVS* 🎬

Super Kung Fu Kid A kung fu hero is pursued by countless villains out to murder him but no one knows why.
19?? 90m/C Nan Kung Fan, Chung Lick, Yeung Si, Kong Yeh. **VHS** $29.95 *OCE* 🎬

Super Mario Bros. Big-budget ($42 million) adventure fantasy produced by Roland Joffe and based on the Nintendo video game featuring the two Italian plumber brothers from Brooklyn, Mario and Luigi Mario. Apprentice Luigi falls for student paleontologist Daisy who's digging in New York for bones but she's really a princess from a parallel world of lizard people who evolved from dinosaurs after a big meteorite crashed into Earth and created a separate dino world and somehow or another her mom the queen passed into our world and dropped the egg that would be Daisy off with nuns who watch it hatch with subtle interest. Holding the key (actually, a chunk of the meteorite) to uniting the two worlds, she's kidnapped and taken back to Dinohattan, a fungi-infested, garbage-strewn, rat-hole version of Manhattan (how is that different from real life?). The Mario Brothers are in hot pursuit, finding much surreal adventure as they try to rescue Princess Daisy from the clutches of chief slimebucket Hopper (and when we say slimebucket, we mean literally). As King Koopa, Hopper is the chief adult delight, doing a gleeful reptilian version of Frank Booth from "Blue Velvet." Mario bros Hoskins and Leguizamo act gamely in broad Nintendo style while enthusiastically partaking in high-tech wizardry and the many gags. Hits bullseye of target audience—elementary and junior high kids—with frenetic pace, gaudy special effects, oversized sets, and animatronic monsters. Vital dialogue to live by: "Trust the fungus."
1993 (PG) 104m/C Bob Hoskins, John Leguizamo, Samantha Mathis, Fisher Stevens, Richard Edson, Dana Kaminsky, Dennis Hopper, Fiona Shaw; *D:* Rocky Morton, Annabel Jankel; *W:* Edward Solomon, Parker Bennett, Terry Runte; *M:* Alan Silvestri. **VHS** *NYR* 🎬🎬½

Super Ninja A modern day ninja must battle modern-day bad guys.
19?? 90m/C Yu Jin Boa, Yi Dao Dao, Alexander Lou, Lou Mei, Wang Qiang, Yang Song, Yau Jin Tomas. **VHS** $59.95 *OCE* 🎬

Super Ninjas A ninja battles evil hordes of like-trained ninja warriors, and wins over and over again.
198? 104m/C Cheng Tien Chi, Lung Tien Hsiang, Chen Pei Hsi. **VHS, Beta** *NO* 🎬

Super Seal An injured seal pup disrupts a family's normal existence after the young daughter adopts him.
1977 (G) 95m/C Foster Brooks, Sterling Holloway, Sarah Brown; *D:* Michael Dugan. **VHS, Beta** $39.95 *UHV* 🎬

Super Soul Brother A lazy no-goodnik accidentally ingests a strange potion which turns him into a master thief.
198? 80m/C Wildman Steve. **VHS** $39.95 *XVC* 🎬

Superargo A wrestler becomes a superhero with psychic powers and a bulletproof leotard. He fights against a madman who is turning athletes into robots. Successful Italian hero who wouldn't last two minutes in the ring with Batman. *AKA:* Il Re Dei Criminali; Superargo the Giant; The King of Criminals.
1967 95m/C *IT SP* Guy Madison, Ken Wood, Liz Barrett, Diana Loris; *D:* Paul Maxwell. **VHS, Beta** $19.98 *SNC, MAD* 🎬

Superboy Join Superboy and his dog Krypto as they fight crime in this collection of eight animated adventures.
1966 60m/C **VHS, Beta** $12.95 *WAR, WTA* 🎬🎬

Superbug Super Agent Dodo, the wonder car puts the brakes on crime in this silly action-adventure tale. A lemon in a lot full of Herbies.
1976 90m/C Robert Mark, Heidi Hansen, George Goodman. **VHS, Beta** $59.95 *JEF* 🎬½

Superchick Mild-mannered stewardess by day, sexy blonde with karate blackbelt by night. In addition to stopping a skyjacking she regularly makes love to men around the world. A superbomb that never gets off the ground.

1971 (R) 94m/C Joyce Jillson, Louis Quinn, Thomas Reardon; *D:* Ed Forsyth. **VHS, Beta** $19.95 *PSM* *Woof!*

Superdad A middle-aged parent is determined to bridge the generation gap by trying his hand at various teenage activities. Disney family fare that's about as complicated as a television commercial. The adolescents are two-dimensional throwbacks to the fun-loving fifties.
1973 (G) 94m/C Bob Crane, Kurt Russell, Joe Flynn, Barbara Rush, Kathleen Cody, Dick Van Patten; *D:* Vincent McEveety. **VHS, Beta** *DIS* 🎬

Superfly Controversial upon release, pioneering blaxploitation has Harlem dope dealer finding trouble with gangs and police as he attempts to establish retirement fund from one last deal. Excellent period tunes by Curtis Mayfield. Two lesser sequels.
1972 (R) 98m/C Ron O'Neal, Carl Lee, Sheila Frazier, Julius W. Harris; *D:* Gordon Parks Jr.; *M:* Curtis Mayfield. **VHS, Beta** $19.98 *WAR* 🎬🎬½

Superfly T.N.T. This confusing sequel to "Superfly" finds O'Neal returning as Youngblood Priest. The now ex-drug dealer has retired with his girlfriend to Rome where he is approached by an African gun-runner (Browne) for help in a revolution against an oppressive government. Cheap exploitation. *AKA:* Super Fly T.N.T.
1973 (R) 87m/C Ron O'Neal, Roscoe Lee Browne, Sheila Frazier, Robert Guillaume, Jacques Sernas, William Berger; *D:* Ron O'Neal; *W:* Alex Haley. **VHS** $14.95 *PAR* *Woof!*

Supergirl Big-budget bomb in which Slater made her debut and nearly killed her career, with the help of Kryptonite. Unexciting and unsophisticated story of a young woman, cousin to Superman, with super powers, based on the comic book series. She's in pursuit of a magic paperweight, but an evil sorceress wants it too. Dunaway is a terrifically vile villainess with awesome black magic powers. Slater is great to look at, but is much better in almost any other film.
1984 (PG) 114m/C *GB* Faye Dunaway, Helen Slater, Peter O'Toole, Mia Farrow, Brenda Vaccaro, Marc McClure, Simon Ward, Hart Bochner, Maureen Teefy, David Healy, Matt Frewer; *D:* Jeannot Szwarc; *M:* Jerry Goldsmith. **VHS, Beta, LV** $19.95 *LIV* 🎬½

Supergrass A low-brow British farce about a nebbish who poses as a drug smuggler to impress his girlfriend, and is then mistaken for a real one by the authorities.
1987 (R) 105m/C Adrian Edmondson, Peter Richardson, Nigel Planer, Jennifer Saunders, Ronald Allen, Dawn French; *D:* Peter Richardson. **VHS, Beta** $19.98 *NLC* 🎬🎬

Superman: The Movie The DC Comics legend comes alive in this wonderfully entertaining saga of Superman's life from a baby on the doomed planet Krypton to Earth's own Man of Steel. Hackman and Beatty pair marvelously as super criminal Lex Luthor and his bumbling sidekick. Award winning special effects and a script (written by Mario Puzo, Robert Benton, and David Newman) that doesn't take itself too seriously make this great fun. Followed by three sequels.
1978 (PG) 144m/C Christopher Reeve, Margot Kidder, Marlon Brando, Gene Hackman, Glenn Ford, Susannah York, Ned Beatty, Valerie Perrine, Jackie Cooper, Marc McClure, Trevor Howard, Sarah Douglas, Terence Stamp, Jack O'Halloran, Phyllis Thaxter; *D:* Richard Donner; *M:* John Williams. Academy Awards '78: Best Visual Effects; Nominations: Best Film Editing, Best Sound, Best Original Score; National Board of Review Awards '78: 10 Best Films of the Year. **VHS, Beta, LV** $19.95 *WAR* 🎬🎬🎬½

Superman 2 The sequel to "the movie" about the Man of Steel. This time, he has his hands full with three super-powered villains from his home planet of Krypton. The romance between reporter Lois Lane and our superhero is made believable and the storyline has more pace to it than the original. A sequel that often equals the first film—leave it to Superman to pull off the impossible. **1980 (PG) 127m/C** Christopher Reeve, Margot Kidder, Gene Hackman, Ned Beatty, Jackie Cooper, Sarah Douglas, Jack O'Halloran, Susannah York, Marc McClure, Terence Stamp, Valerie Perrine, E.G. Marshall; **D:** Richard Lester; **M:** John Williams. **VHS, Beta, LV** $19.98 *WAR, PIA* 𝄫𝄫𝄫

Superman 3 Villainous businessman Vaughn tries to conquer Superman via the expertise of bumbling computer expert Pryor and the judicious use of Red Kryptonite. Superman explores his darker side after undergoing transformation into sleaze ball. Promising satiric start ultimately defeated by uneven story and direction and boring physical comedy. Notable is the absence of Lois Lane as a main character. Followed by "Superman 4." **1983 (PG) 123m/C** Christopher Reeve, Richard Pryor, Annette O'Toole, Jackie Cooper, Margot Kidder, Marc McClure, Annie Ross, Robert Vaughn; **D:** Richard Lester; **M:** John Williams. **VHS, Beta, LV** $19.98 *WAR* 𝄫𝄫

Superman 4: The Quest for Peace The third sequel, in which the Man of Steel endeavors to rid the world of nuclear weapons, thereby pitting himself against nuclear-entrepreneur Lex Luthor and his superpowered creation, Nuclear Man. Special effects are dime-store quality and it appears that someone may have walked off with parts of the plot. Reeve deserves credit for remaining true to character through four films. **1987 (PG) 90m/C** Christopher Reeve, Gene Hackman, Jon Cryer, Marc McClure, Margot Kidder, Mariel Hemingway, Sam Wanamaker; **D:** Sidney J. Furie; **M:** John Williams; **V:** Susannah York. **VHS, Beta, LV** $19.98 *WAR, APD* 𝄫

Superman & the Mole Men The cast of the popular 1950s' television show made this rarely seen feature as a "pilot" for the series. Superman faces the danger threatened by the invasion of radioactive mole-men who make their way to the surface world from the bowels of the earth through an oil-well shaft. Simple fun. **AKA:** Superman and the Strange People. **1951 58m/C** George Reeves, Phyllis Coates, Phyllis Coates, Jeff Corey; **D:** Lee Sholem. **VHS, Beta** $19.98 *WAR* 𝄫𝄫½

Superman: The Cartoons Eight of the comic book hero's adventures from 1942 are featured along with a 1953 black and white short called "Stamp Day for Superman," starring the cast of the television show. **1942 89m/C V:** Bud Collyer, Joan Alexander. **VHS, Beta** $14.98 *AOV* 𝄫𝄫½

Superman: The Complete Cartoon Collection This tape features all 17 Superman cartoons made by the Max Fleischer Studios from 1941 to 1943. Several are in black & white. **1943 141m/C VHS, Beta** $19.95 *VDM, WTA* 𝄫𝄫½

Superman: The Serial, Vol. 1 Superman was first seen in live action in this 15-part theatrical serial that has been rarely shown since its original release. **1948 248m/B** Kirk Alyn, Noel Neill, Pierre Watkin, Tommy "Butch" Bond, Thomas Carr; **D:** Spencer Gordon Bennet. **VHS, Beta** $29.95 *WAR* 𝄫𝄫½

The Supernaturals Confederate Civil War-era ghosts, bent on avenging their deaths, haunt a wooded area in which modern Yankee army maneuvers are practiced. Antebellum boredom. **1986 (R) 85m/C** Maxwell Caulfield, LeVar Burton, Nichelle Nichols; **D:** Armand Mastroianni. **VHS, Beta** $19.98 *SUE, NLC* 𝄫½

Supersonic Man Incoherent shoestring-budget Superman spoof with a masked hero fighting to save the world from the evil intentions of a mad scientist. **1978 (PG) 85m/C SP** Michael Coby, Cameron Mitchell, Diana Polakov; **D:** Piquer Simon. **VHS, Beta** $59.95 *UHV Woof!*

Superstar: The Life and Times of Andy Warhol Even if you didn't grok Andy's 'pop' artwork and self-created celebrity persona, this ironic, kinetic, oft-rollicking documentary paints a vivid picture of the wild era he inspired and exploited. Interviewees range from Warhol cohorts like Dennis Hopper to proud executives at the Campbell Soup plant. One highlight: a Warhol guest shot on "The Love Boat." **1990 87m/C VHS** $89.98 *VES* 𝄫𝄫𝄫

Superstition A reverend and his family move into a vacant house despite warnings about a curse from the townsfolk. Some people never learn. **AKA:** The Witch. **1982 85m/C** James Houghton, Albert Salmi, Lynn Carlin; **D:** James Robertson Justice. **VHS, Beta** $79.98 *LIV* 𝄫½

Supervixens True to Meyer's low-rent exploitation film canon, this wild tale is filled with characteristic Amazons, sex and violence. A gas station attendant is framed for the grisly murder of his girlfriend and hustles out of town, meeting a succession of well-endowed women during his travels. As if it needed further problems, it's hampered by a tasteless storyline and incoherent writing. **1975 105m/C** Shari Eubank, Charles Napier; **D:** Russ Meyer. **VHS** $59.99 *RMF* 𝄫𝄫

Support Your Local Gunfighter Garner plays a western con man with his tongue firmly in his cheek. He comes to the small town of Purgatory and is thought to be a notorious gunfighter. He decides to go with the mistaken identity and use it to his profitable advantage. Elam is his bumbling sidekick and Pleshette the love interest. A delightful, deliberately cliche-filled western. A follow-up, not a sequel, to "Support Your Local Sheriff" (1969). **1971 (G) 92m/C** James Garner, Jack Elam, Suzanne Pleshette, Harry Morgan, Dub Taylor, John Dehner, Joan Blondell, Ellen Corby, Henry Jones; **D:** Burt Kennedy. **VHS** $19.98 *MGM* 𝄫𝄫𝄫

Support Your Local Sheriff Amiable, irreverent western spoof with more than its fair share of laughs. When a stranger stumbles into a gold rush town, he winds up becoming sheriff. Garner is perfect as the deadpan sheriff, particularly in the scene where he convinces Dern to remain in jail, in spite of the lack of bars. Neatly subverts every western cliche it encounters, yet keeps respect for formula western. Written and produced by William Bowers. Followed by "Support Your Local Gunfighter." **1969 (G) 92m/C** James Garner, Joan Hackett, Walter Brennan, Bruce Dern, Jack Elam, Harry Morgan; **D:** Burt Kennedy. **VHS, Beta** $19.98 *FOX, MGM* 𝄫𝄫½

Suppose They Gave a War and Nobody Came? A small Southern town battles with a local army base in this entertaining but wandering satire. The different acting styles used as the producers wavered on making this a comedy or drama were more at war with one another than the characters involved. **AKA:** War Games. **1970 (G) 113m/C** Tony Curtis, Brian Keith, Ernest Borgnine, Suzanne Pleshette, Ivan Dixon, Bradford Dillman, Don Ameche; **D:** Hy Averback. **VHS** $59.98 *FOX* 𝄫𝄫½

Surabaya Conspiracy Mystery and intrigue surround a quest for gold in Africa. **1975 90m/C** Michael Rennie, Richard Jaeckel, Barbara Bouchet, Mike Preston; **D:** Roy Davis. **VHS, Beta** *NO* 𝄫½

The Sure Thing College students who don't like each other end up travelling to California together, and of course, falling in love. Charming performances make up for predictability. Can't-miss director (and ex-Meathead) Reiner's second direct hit at the box office. **1985 (PG-13) 94m/C** John Cusack, Daphne Zuniga, Anthony Edwards, Boyd Gaines, Lisa Jane Persky, Viveca Lindfors, Nicollette Sheridan, Tim Robbins; **D:** Rob Reiner. **VHS, Beta, LV, 8mm** $14.95 *COL, SUE* 𝄫𝄫𝄫

Surf Nazis Must Die A piece of deliberate camp in the Troma mold, about a group of psychotic neo-Nazi surfers taking over the beaches of California in the wake of a devastating earthquake. Tongue-in-cheek, tasteless and cheap, but intentionally so. **1987 83m/C** Barry Brenner, Gail Neely, Michael Sonye, Dawn Wildsmith, Tom Shell, Bobbie Bresee; **D:** Peter George. **VHS, Beta** $19.98 *MED* 𝄫

Surf Party Romance among the sands of Malibu with Vinton as the owner of a surf shop. Risque in 1964; utterly campy today. Songs include, "If I Were an Artist," "That's What Love Is," and "Pearly Shells." **1964 68m/C** Bobby Vinton, Jackie De Shannon, Patricia Morrow, Kenny Miller; **D:** Maury Dexter. **VHS** $39.95 *MOV* 𝄫

Surf 2 A most excellent group of surfers get sick from drinking tainted Buzz Cola concocted by demented chemist Deezen in most heinous effort to obliterate surfer population from Southern California. Bogus, dude. No, you didn't miss "Surf 1" (there's not one), the title is the sort of in-joke this exercise in mental meltdown perpetuates as comedy. Ha. **AKA:** Surf 2: The End of the Trilogy. **1984 (R) 91m/C** Morgan Paull, Cleavon Little, Lyle Waggoner, Ruth Buzzi, Linda Kerridge, Carol Wayne, Eddie Deezen, Eric Stoltz, Lucinda Dooling, Brandis Kemp, Terry Kiser; **D:** Randall Badat. **VHS, Beta** $59.95 *MVD, MED Woof!*

Surfacing A girl braves the hostile northern wilderness to search for her missing father. This pseudo-psychological, sex-driven suspense flick makes little sense. **1984 90m/C** Joseph Bottoms, Kathleen Beller, R.H. Thompson, Margaret Dragu; **D:** Claude Jutra. **VHS, Beta** *NO Woof!*

Surprise Attack The Spanish Civil War forms the backdrop for this action opus. **197? 124m/C** Simon Andrew, Danny Martin, Patty Shepard; **D:** Joseph Loman. **VHS, Beta** $19.95 *NEG* 𝄫

Surrender A struggling woman artist and a divorced author fall in love but won't admit it for fear of being hurt again. Jumbled plot, unfortunate casting. Available in a Spanish-subtitled version.

1987 (PG) 95m/C Michael Caine, Sally Field, Steve Guttenberg, Peter Boyle, Jackie Cooper, Julie Kavner, Louise Lasser, Iman; *D:* Jerry Belson. VHS, Beta, LV $19.98 WAR ♂♂½

Surrogate A young couple fights to keep their marriage afloat by turning to a sex surrogate. Strong cast helps carry odd, confusing script, with plenty of (you guessed it) sex, and a mystery to solve.
1988 100m/C *CA* Art Hindle, Shannon Tweed, Carole Laure, Michael Ironside, Marilyn Lightstone; *D:* Don Carmody. VHS, Beta MED ♂♂

Survival Earth After civilization collapses, humans begin reverting back to a primitive way of life. A young couple and a soldier of fortune fight against it, hoping for a better existence.
19?? 90m/C VHS NO ♂

Survival Game A young combat expert (Chuck Norris's son) gets involved with some ex-hippies in search of a $2 million cache. High-kickin' action.
1987 91m/C Mike Norris, Deborah Goodrich, Seymour Cassel; *D:* Herb Freed. VHS, Beta $79.95 MED ♂

Survival of a Dragon A medieval Chinese warrior is transported into the future, where he goes on a kicking rampage.
19? 88m/C Squall Hung, Jaguar Lee. VHS, Beta NO ♂

Survival of Spaceship Earth Man, his world and the protection of its ecology are discussed in this beautiful and fascinating film. Winner of numerous international awards due to the strength of its production values and writing. Nominated for 10 Emmy awards, winner of 2 Emmys.
1990 63m/C Rue McClanahan; *W/D:* Dirk Summers. VHS, Special order formats $24.95 CPM, FCT, CRY ♂

Survival Quest Students in a Rocky Mountain survival course cross paths with a band of bloodthirsty mercenaries-in-training. A battle to the death ensues; you'll wish they'd all put each other out of their misery a lot sooner.
1989 (R) 90m/C Lance Henriksen, Dermot Mulroney, Mark Rolston, Steve Antin, Paul Provenza, Ben Hammer, Traci Lin, Catherine Keener, Reggie Bannister; *D:* Don A. Coscarelli. VHS, Beta $89.98 FOX ♂♂½

Survival Run Six California teenagers become stranded in the Mexican desert, where they witness Graves and Millard making a shady deal. The chase is on, the story is lame, the gory parts aren't gory—so why bother?
1980 (R) 90m/C Peter Graves, Ray Milland, Vincent Van Patten; *D:* Larry Spiegel. VHS, Beta $54.95 MED ♂

Survival Zone Nuclear holocaust survivors battle a violent band of marauding motorcyclists on the barren ranches of the 21st century. Advice to director Rubens and cohorts: Next time, find a plot that's not growing mold.
1984 (R) 90m/C Gary Lockwood, Morgan Stevens, Camilla Sparv; *D:* Percival Rubens. VHS, Beta $9.99 PSM, STE Woof!

The Survivalist An arms-ready survivalist nut defends his family and supplies against a panicked society awaiting nuclear war. Poorly acted, little tension, and ineffective plotting make boredom seem a more critical issue than survival.
1987 (R) 96m/C Steve Railsback, Susan Blakely, Marjoe Gortner, David Wayne, Cliff DeYoung; *D:* Sig Shore. VHS, Beta, LV $79.98 VES ♂

Surviving Desire Donovan plays Jude, a neurotic, romantic English professor who falls madly in love with an independently-minded student, Sophie. Unfortunately, Sophie is more interested in how the seduction will advance her writing than how it will affect her life. The lovers explore their brief affair by analyzing every emotion and motive in a series of quirky conversations. Intelligent, amusing, and stylized film from director Hartley. The tape also includes two Hartley shorts: "Theory of Achievement" and "Ambition."
1991 86m/C Martin Donovan, Mary Ward, Matt Malloy, Rebecca Nelson; *D:* Hal Hartley. VHS $89.95 FXL, TAM ♂♂♂

Survivor A jetliner crashes, leaving but one survivor, the pilot, who is then plagued by visions, tragedies, and ghosts of dead passengers. Viewers also suffer.
1980 91m/C *AU* Robert Powell, Jenny Agutter, Joseph Cotten, Angela Punch McGregor; *D:* David Hemmings. VHS, Beta $19.95 LHV, WAR ♂

Survivor A lone warrior on a post-nuclear holocaust wasteland battles a megalomaniac ruler. Moll as the evil villian is watchable, but overall the film is a wasteland, too.
1987 92m/C Chip Mayer, Richard Moll, Sue Kiel; *D:* Michael Shackleton. VHS, Beta, LV $19.98 LIV, VES ♂♂

Survivors Two unemployed men find themselves the target of a hit man, whom they have identified in a robbery attempt. One of the men goes gun-crazy protecting himself. Uneven comedy with wild Williams and laid-back Matthau.
1983 (R) 102m/C Robin Williams, Walter Matthau, Jerry Reed, John Goodman; *D:* Michael Ritchie. VHS, Beta, LV $12.95 COL ♂♂

Susan and God A selfish socialite returns from Europe and starts practicing a new religion, much to the dismay of her friends and family. Despite her preaching, her own domestic life is falling apart and she realizes that her preoccupation and selfish ways have caused a strain on her marriage and her relationship with her daughter. An excellent script and a fine performance from Crawford make this a highly satisfying film. *AKA:* The Gay Mrs. Trexel.
1940 115m/B Joan Crawford, Fredric March, Ruth Hussey, John Carroll, Rita Hayworth, Nigel Bruce, Bruce Cabot, Rose Hobart, Rita Quigley, Marjorie Main, Gloria de Haven; *D:* George Cukor; *W:* Anita Loos. VHS $19.98 MGM ♂♂♂

Susan Lenox: Her Fall and Rise Garbo, the daughter of an abusive farmer, falls into the arms of the handsome Gable to escape an arranged marriage. Both stars are miscast, but the well-paced direction keeps the melodrama moving. *AKA:* The Rise of Helga; Rising to Fame.
1931 84m/B Greta Garbo, Clark Gable, Jean Hersholt, John Miljan, Alan Hale Jr., Hale Hamilton; *D:* Robert Z. Leonard. VHS, Beta $19.98 MGM, FCT ♂♂½

Susan Slept Here While researching a movie on juvenile delinquents, a Hollywood script writer (Powell) is given custody of a spunky 18-year-old delinquent girl (Reynolds) during the Christmas holidays. Cute sex comedy. Based on the play "Susan," by Alex Gottlieb and Steve Fisher.
1954 98m/C Dick Powell, Debbie Reynolds, Anne Francis; *D:* Frank Tashlin. VHS, Beta, LV $15.95 UHV ♂♂½

Susana Minor though still interesting Bunuel, in which a sexy delinquent young girl is rescued from vagrancy by a Spanish family, and how she subsequently undermines the family's structure through sexual allurement and intimidation. In Spanish with English subtitles.
1951 87m/B *MX* Rosita Quintana, Fernando Soler, Victor Manuel Mendoza, Matilde Palou; *D:* Luis Bunuel. VHS, Beta $24.95 XVC, TAM, APD ♂♂♂

Susanna Pass Oil deposits underneath a fish hatchery lake attract bad guys. They set off explosions to destroy the fishery, but game warden Rogers investigates. Minor outing for Roy.
1949 67m/C Roy Rogers, Dale Evans, Estelita Rodriguez, Martin Garralaga, Robert Emmett Keane, Lucien Littlefield, Douglas Fowley; *D:* William Witney. VHS $12.98 REP ♂

Susannah of the Mounties An adorable young girl is left orphaned after a wagon train massacre and is adopted by a Mountie. An Indian squabble gives Shirley a chance to play little peacemaker and teach Scott how to tap dance, too. Could she be any cuter? Available colorized.
1939 78m/B Shirley Temple, Randolph Scott, Margaret Lockwood, J. Farrell MacDonald, Moroni Olsen, Victor Jory; *D:* William A. Seiter. VHS, Beta $19.98 FOX ♂♂½

Suspect An overworked Washington, DC, public defender (Cher) is assigned to a controversial murder case in which her client is a deaf-mute, skid-row bum. A cynical lobbyist on the jury illegally researches the case himself. They work together to uncover a far-reaching conspiracy. Unrealistic plot, helped along by good performances and tight direction.
1987 (R) 101m/C Dennis Quaid, Cher, Liam Neeson, E. Katherine Kerr, Joe Mantegna; *D:* Peter Yates. VHS, Beta, LV, 8mm $14.95 COL ♂♂½

Suspended Alibi British crime-drama about an adulterous man unjustly accused when his alibi is murdered. Overlook the convenient coincidence. *AKA:* Suspected Alibi.
1956 64m/B *GB* Patrick Holt, Honor Blackman, Andrew Keir, Valentine Dyall; *D:* Alfred Shaughnessy. VHS $16.95 NOS, SNC ♂½

Suspicion Alfred Hitchcock's suspense thriller about a woman who gradually realizes she is married to a killer and may be next on his list. An excellent production unravels at the end due to RKO's insistence that Grant retain his "attractive" image. This forced the writers to leave his guilt or innocence undetermined. Available colorized.
1941 99m/B Cary Grant, Joan Fontaine, Cedric Hardwicke, Nigel Bruce, May Whitty, Leo G. Carroll, Heather Angel; *D:* Alfred Hitchcock. Academy Awards '41: Best Actress (Fontaine); Nominations: Best Picture. VHS, Beta, LV $19.98 RKO, VID, MED ♂♂♂½

Suspicion Remake of the chilling Hitchcock tale. Newlywed bride is consumed with fears about her wealthy new husband. The suspense builds as she comes to suspect that she is married to a cold-blooded killer. Curtin in way over her head.
1987 97m/C Jane Curtin, Anthony Andrews; *D:* Andrew Grieve. VHS, Beta $79.95 MED ♂♂

Suspiria An American dancer enters a weird European ballet academy and finds they teach more than movement as bodies begin piling up. Sometimes weak plot is aided by great-but-gory special effects, fine photography, good music, and a chilling opening sequence. Also available in unrated version.
1977 (R) 92m/C *IT* Jessica Harper, Joan Bennett, Alida Valli, Udo Kier; *D:* Dario Argento. VHS, Beta, LV HHE, QVD ♂♂♂

Suzanne Set in 1950s Quebec, the story of a good woman whose criminal boyfriend leaves her pregnant when he is sent to prison. Ten years later, he returns, threatening her happy marriage. Confused script can't be saved by valiant cast.
1980 (R) 90m/C Sondra Locke, Richard Dreyfuss, Gene Barry. **VHS, Beta $69.98** VES *♫* ½

Suzy Harlow's fourth film and her only one with Grant is a mixture of romance, action, and comedy set during World War I. Grant plays a French flier who falls in love with Harlow, although she is married to Tone. Excellent air footage and some good funny scenes keep this film moving right along. Even has Grant singing hit song, "Did I Remember?"
1926 99m/B Jean Harlow, Franchot Tone, Cary Grant, Benita Hume, Lewis Stone, Inez Courtney; **D:** George Fitzmaurice. **VHS $19.98** MGM *♫♫* ½

Svengali A music teacher uses his hypnotic abilities to manipulate one of his singing students and make her a star. Soon the young woman is singing for sell-out crowds, but only if her teacher is present. Barrymore in a hypnotic performance. Adapted from "Trilby" by George Du Maurier. Remade in 1955 and 1983.
1931 76m/B John Barrymore, Marian Marsh, Donald Crisp; **D:** Archie Mayo. **VHS, Beta, 3/4U, Special order formats $19.95** NOS, GPV, SNC *♫♫♫*

Svengali Limp remake of the 1931 film about Trilby, an artist's model, falling under the mesmerizing spell of the title character, who is determined to make her into a famous singer. Chiefly notable for its visuals which were based on the illustrations from the original novel "Trilby" by George du Maurier.
1955 82m/C *GB* Hildegarde Neff, Donald Wolfit, Terence Morgan, Derek Bond, Paul Rogers, David Kossoff; **W/D:** Noel Langley. **VHS** NO *♫♫* ½

Svengali Flamboyant but faded music star O'Toole mentors Foster, a young pop singer looking for stardom. Boring, made for television remake of the Barrymore classic.
1983 96m/C Peter O'Toole, Jodie Foster, Elizabeth Ashley, Larry Joshua, Pamela Blair, Barbara Byrne, Holly Hunter; **D:** Anthony Harvey; **M:** John Barry. **VHS** NO *♫♫* ½

Swamp Fire Mississippi river-boat captain Weismuller, wrestles aligators and battles with Crabbe for the woman he loves in this turgid drama. Look for Janssen in an early screen performance.
1946 69m/B Johnny Weissmuller, Virginia Grey, Buster Crabbe, Carol Thurston, Edwin Maxwell, Pedro de Cordoba, Pierre Watkin, David Janssen; **D:** William H. Pine. **VHS, Beta $19.95** NOS, SNC *♫* ½

Swamp of the Lost Monster An incredible Mexican horror/western/musical that features a mouse-like monster that'll scare the cheese out of you.
1965 88m/B *MX* Gaston Santos, Sarah Cabrera, Manuel Donde; **D:** Rafael Baledon. **VHS, Beta $24.95** NOS, SNC, GHV *♫*

Swamp Thing Overlooked camp drama about scientist accidentally turned into tragic half-vegetable, half-man swamp creature, with government agent Barbeau caught in the middle, occasionally while topless. A vegetarian nightmare or ecology propaganda? You be the judge. Adapted from the comic book by Craven.
1982 (PG) 91m/C Adrienne Barbeau, Louis Jourdan, Ray Wise, Adam West; **D:** Wes Craven. **VHS, Beta, LV $14.95** COL, SUE *♫♫* ½

Swamp Women Four escaped women convicts, known as the "Nardo Gang," chase after a stash of diamonds in this super cheap, super bad action adventure from cult director Corman. **AKA:** Swamp Diamonds; Cruel Swamp.
1955 73m/C Mike Connors, Marie Windsor, Beverly Garland, Carole Matthews, Susan Cummings; **D:** Roger Corman. **VHS $16.95** SNC *♫*

The Swan Princess' arranged marriage with a prince is complicated by a poor man also in love with her. Classic romantic comedy of the silent era. Remade in 1956. Based on a play by Ferenc Molnar.
1925 50m/B Adolphe Menjou, Ricardo Cortez, Frances Howard; **D:** Dimitri Buchowetzki. **VHS, Beta $19.95** NOS, DVT *♫♫* ½

The Swan A twist on the Cinderella story with Kelly (in her last film before her marriage) as the charming beauty waiting for her prince. Both Guinness, as the crown prince, and Jourdan, as her poor tutor, want her hand (and the rest of her). Attractive cast, but story gets slow from time to time. Remake of a 1925 silent film. The laser disc version also includes "Wedding in Monaco," the news short showing Kelly's wedding to Prince Rainier.
1956 112m/C Grace Kelly, Louis Jourdan, Alec Guinness, Jessie Royce Landis, Brian Aherne, Estelle Winwood; **D:** Charles Vidor. **VHS, LV $19.98** MGM *♫♫♫*

Swan Lake Prince searches for a bride. The swan that bears the golden crown possesses magical powers that hold the key.
1982 75m/C **VHS, Beta $9.95** MED, WTA *♫♫*

Swann in Love A handsome, wealthy French aristocrat makes a fool of himself over a beautiful courtesan who cares nothing for him. Elegant production lacks spark. Based upon a section of Marcel Proust's "Remembrance of Things Past." In French with English subtitles or an English language version. **AKA:** Un Amour De Swann.
1984 (R) 110m/C *FR GE* Jeremy Irons, Ornella Muti, Alain Delon, Fanny Ardant, Marie-Christine Barrault; **D:** Volker Schlondorff. **VHS, Beta $24.95** XVC, MED, TAM *♫♫*

Swans A brother and sister battle an evil spell that keeps them apart and controls their little village. From the Hans Christian Andersen story.
1990 60m/C **VHS $9.95** AIP *♫♫* ½

The Swap Ex-con searches for his brother's killer. Muddled story uses clips from early De Niro film "Sam's Song."
1971 (R) 120m/C Robert De Niro, Jered Mickey, Jennifer Warren, Terrayne Crawford, Martin Kelley; **D:** Jordan Leondopoulos. **VHS $14.95** MGM, CAN *♫*

Swap Meet Wacky teen sex comedy about shenanigans at a small town swap meet. Strictly bargain basement.
1979 (R) 86m/C Ruth Cox, Debi Richter, Danny Goldman, Cheryl Rixon, Jonathan Gries; **D:** Brice Mack. **VHS** UHV *♫*

The Swarm Low-brow insect contest as scientist Caine fends off a swarm of killer bees when they attack metro Houston. The bees are really just black spots painted on the film. And the acting is terrible. "B" movie on bees, but it's still better than "The Bees."
1978 (PG) 116m/C Michael Caine, Katharine Ross, Richard Widmark, Lee Grant, Richard Chamberlain, Olivia de Havilland, Henry Fonda, Fred MacMurray, Patty Duke, Ben Johnson, Jose Ferrer, Slim Pickens, Bradford Dillman, Cameron Mitchell; **D:** Irwin Allen; **M:** Jerry Goldsmith. **VHS, Beta $59.95** WAR *♫*

Swashbuckler Jaunty pirate returns from sea to find his friends held captive by dastardly dictator for their political views. He rescues them, and helps them overthrow the erstwhile despot. **AKA:** Scarlet Buccaneer.
1976 (PG) 101m/C Robert Shaw, James Earl Jones, Peter Boyle, Genevieve Bujold, Beau Bridges, Geoffrey Holder; **D:** James Goldstone. **VHS, LV $79.95** MCA, PIA *♫*

Swashbuckler Eighteenth-century pirate fracas that can't compete with Errol Flynn. **AKA:** The Scarlet Buccaneer.
1984 100m/C *FR* Jean-Paul Belmondo, Marlene Jobert, Laura Antonelli, Michel Auclair, Julien Guiomar; **D:** Jean-Paul Rappeneau. **VHS** MCA *♫* ½

Sweater Girls Sex comedy about two girls starting their own club called the "Sweater Girls." Terrible teen exploitaiton film.
1978 (R) 90m/C Charlene Tilton, Harry Moses, Meegan King, Noelle North, Kate Sarchet, Carol Seflinger, Tamara Barkley, Julie Parsons; **D:** Don Jones. **VHS, Beta** NO Woof!

Swedenhielms A poor Swedish scientist struggles to support his family while hoping to win a Nobel prize. Fine performances by Ekman and the 20-year-old Bergman (in her third film). In Swedish with English subtitles.
1935 92m/B *SW* Gosta Ekman, Karin Swanstrom, Bjorn Berglund, Hakan Westergren, Tutta Rolf, Ingrid Bergman, Sigurd Wallen; **D:** Gustaf Molander. **VHS, Beta, LV $29.95** WAC, LUM, TAM *♫♫* ½

Swedish Wildcats Three eccentric ladies run a brothel specializing in live theatrical productions.
19?? 90m/C Diana Dors. **VHS, Beta $59.95** JEF *♫♫* ½

Sweeney Todd: The Demon Barber of Fleet Street A filmed performance of the Tony-winning Broadway musical by Stephen Sondheim, directed by Harold Prince. Creepy thriller about a demon barber, his razor, and his wife's meatpies.
1984 139m/C *GB* Angela Lansbury, George Hearn; **D:** Harold Prince. **VHS, Beta, LV $39.95** MVD, RKO, VTK *♫♫* ½

Sweet Adeline Smalltime hayseed makes it big in the music business while brother steals his girl back home. Not easily put off, young songster perseveres.
1926 60m/B Charles Ray, Gertrude Olmsted, Jack Clifford, Ida Lewis; **D:** Jerome Storm. **VHS, Beta $19.95** GPV, FCT *♫*

Sweet Adeline Dunne attracts all the men in her father's Hoboken beer garden but Woods plays the songwriter with whom she finds real love. Wonderful score by Kern and Hammerstein. *♫*Play Us a Polka, Dot; Here Am I; We Were So Young; Why Was I Born?; Mollie O'Donahue; Lonely Feet; 'Twas Not So Long Ago; Don't Ever Leave Me.
1935 87m/B Irene Dunne, Donald Woods, Hugh Herbert, Ned Sparks, Joseph Cawthorn, Louis Calhern; **D:** Mervyn LeRoy. **VHS $19.98** MGM *♫♫* ½

Sweet Beat A young woman gets a chance to become a singer when she reaches the finals of a British beauty contest. Pedestrian story enlivened by music from popular British bands of the time. **AKA:** The Amorous Sex.
1962 66m/B Julie Amber, Sheldon Lawrence, Irv Bauer, Billy Myles. **VHS, Beta $19.95** NOS, INC *♫*

Sweet Bird of Youth An acclaimed adaptation of the Tennessee Williams play about Chance Wayne, a handsome drifter who travels with an aging movie queen to his small Florida hometown, hoping she'll get him started in a movie career. However, coming home turns into a big mistake, as the town boss wants revenge on Chance for seducing his daughter, Heavenly. Williams' original stage ending was cleaned up, providing a conventional "happy" movie ending for the censors. Remade for television in 1989 with Elizabeth Taylor and Mark Harmon in the lead roles.

1962 120m/C Paul Newman, Geraldine Page, Ed Begley Sr., Mildred Dunnock, Rip Torn, Shirley Knight, Madeline Sherwood; **D:** Richard Brooks. Academy Awards '62: Best Supporting Actor (Begley); Nominations: Best Actress (Page), Best Supporting Actress (Knight); Golden Globe Awards '63: Best Actress—Drama (Page). **VHS, Beta, LV $19.95** *MGM, BTV* 🎬🎬🎬

Sweet Charity An ever-optimistic dime-a-dance girl has a hard time finding a classy guy to marry. MacLaine is appealing in this big-budget version of the popular Broadway musical by Neil Simon (derived from Fellini's "Notti di Cabiria"). Bob Fosse's debut as film director. Bud Cort plays a flower child. ♫My Personal Property; It's a Nice Face; Hey, Big Spender; Rich Man's Frug; If My Friends Could See Me Now; There's Gotta Be Something Better Than This; Rhythm of Life; Sweet Charity; I'm a Brass Band; I Love To Cry at Weddings; Where Am I Going?.

1969 148m/C Shirley MacLaine, Chita Rivera, John McMartin, Paula Kelly, Sammy Davis Jr., Ricardo Montalban; **D:** Bob Fosse. **VHS, Beta, LV $19.95** *MCA* 🎬🎬½

Sweet Country During the overthrow of the Allende government in Chile, the lives of a Chilean family and an American couple intertwine. Heavy-going propaganda is a cross between tragedy and unintentional comedy. Made by the director of "Zorba the Greek."

1987 (R) 147m/C Jane Alexander, John Cullum, Carole Laure, Franco Nero, Joanna Pettet, Randy Quaid, Irene Papas, Jean-Pierre Aumont, Pierre Vaneck, Katia Dandoulaki; **D:** Michael Cacoyannis. **VHS, Beta, LV** *NO* 🎬½

Sweet Country Road A rock singer journeys to Nashville to try to cross over into country music.

1981 95m/C Buddy Knox, Kary Lynn, Gordy Trapp, Johnny Paycheck, Jeanne Pruett. **VHS, Beta $19.95** *STE, NWV* 🎬½

Sweet Creek County War Retired sheriff must leave his quiet ranch to battle a greedy businessman.

1982 90m/C Richard Egan, Albert Salmi, Nita Talbot, Slim Pickens. **VHS, Beta** *PGN* 🎬

Sweet Dirty Tony Tale about renegade CIA agent plotting to assassinate Fidel Castro. Key West scenery is pretty. **AKA:** Assignment Kill Castro; Cuba Crossing; The Mercenaries.

1981 90m/C Sybil Danning, Michael Gazzo, Caren Kaye, Raymond St. Jacques, Woody Strode, Robert Vaughn, Stuart Whitman; **D:** Chuck Workman. **VHS, Beta $79.95** *JEF* 🎬

Sweet Dreams Biography of country singer Patsy Cline, focusing mostly on her turbulent marriage. Her quick rise to stardom ended in an early death. Fine performances throughout. Cline's original recordings are used. ♫Walking After Midnight; Crazy; Sweet Dreams; San Antonio Rose; Blue Moon of Kentucky; Lovesick Blues; Seven Lonely Days; Foolin' Around; Your Cheatin' Heart; Walking After Midnight; I Fall to Pieces; She's Got You.

1985 (PG-13) 115m/C Jessica Lange, Ed Harris, Ann Wedgeworth, David Clennon; **D:** Karel Reisz. **VHS, Beta, LV $19.99** *HBO* 🎬🎬½

Sweet Ecstasy Wealthy shenanigans on the French Riviera. Pezy is the upright young man who can't sleep with anyone unless he's in love, much to Sommer's dismay. **AKA:** Douce Violence; Sweet Violence.

1962 75m/B *FR* Elke Sommer, Pierre Brice, Christian Pezy, Claire Maurier; **D:** Max Pecas. **VHS $29.95** *NO* 🎬½

Sweet 15 A young Hispanic girl learns that there is more to growing up than parties when she learns her father is an illegal alien. Originally aired on PBS as part of the "Wonderworks" family movie series.

1990 120m/C Karla Montana, Panchito Gomez, Tony Plana, Jenny Gago, Susan Ruttan; **D:** Victoria Hochberg. **VHS $29.95** *PME, HMV* 🎬½

Sweet Georgia Soft-core star Jordan is a lusty wife whose husband is an alcoholic, so she has a roll in the hay with almost every other cast member. Lots of action, too, including a pitchfork fight. Ride 'em cowboy.

1972 80m/C Marsha Jordan. **VHS $19.95** *VDM* 🎬

Sweet Hearts Dance Parallel love stories follow two long-time friends, one just falling in love, the other struggling to keep his marriage together. Charming performances from all, but a slow pace undermines the film. Written by Ernest Thompson.

1988 (R) 95m/C Don Johnson, Jeff Daniels, Susan Sarandon, Elizabeth Perkins, Justin Henry; **D:** Robert Greenwald; **W:** Ernest Thompson. **VHS, Beta, LV $89.95** *COL* 🎬🎬

Sweet Hostage Escaped mental patient kidnaps uneducated farm girl and holds her captive in a remote cabin. Blair and Sheen turn in good performances. Adaptation of Nathaniel Benchley's "Welcome to Xanadu." Made-for-television.

1975 93m/C Linda Blair, Martin Sheen, Jeanne Cooper, Lee DeBroux, Dehl Berti, Bert Remsen; **D:** Lee Philips. **VHS** *IMP* 🎬🎬½

Sweet Justice This time its the women who get to be commandos, have all the adventures, and get revenge on various scum. The nominal plotline has Sunny Justice (Carter) and her group of gal-warriors avenging the sadistic murder of a friend. Martial arts, weapons, and action galore.

1992 (R) 92m/C Finn Carter, Kathleen Kinmont, Marc Singer, Frank Gorshin; **Cameos:** Mickey Rooney; **W/D:** Allen Plone; **W:** Jim Tabilio. **VHS $89.95** *TRI* 🎬½

Sweet Liberty Alda's hometown is overwhelmed by Hollywood chaos during the filming of a movie version of his novel about the American Revolution. Pleasant but predictable.

1986 (PG) 107m/C Alan Alda, Michael Caine, Michelle Pfeiffer, Bob Hoskins, Lillian Gish; **D:** Alan Alda. **VHS, Beta, LV $19.95** *MCA* 🎬🎬

Sweet Lies An insurance investigator tracking a scam artist in Paris is preyed upon by a group of single women betting one another that any man can be seduced. Slow comedy.

1988 (R) 86m/C Treat Williams, Joanna Pacula, Julianne Phillips, Laura Manszky, Norbert Weisser, Marilyn Dodd-Frank; **D:** Nathalie Delon. **VHS, Beta $79.98** *FOX* 🎬½

Sweet Light in a Dark Room A student in Prague during the Nazi Occupation hides a Jewish girl. He falls in love with her but becomes the suspect in the murder of a Nazi officer. Directed by the great Czech filmmaker Weiss who was himself forced to leave his country during Nazi occupation. In Czech with English subtitles. **AKA:** Romeo, Julia a Tma; Romeo, Juliet and Darkness.

1960 93m/B *CZ* Ivan Mistrik, Dana Smutna; **D:** Jiri Weiss. **VHS $29.95** *FCT, DVT, HEG* 🎬🎬🎬

Sweet Lorraine A bittersweet, nostalgic comedy about the staff and clientele of a deteriorating Catskills hotel on the eve of its closing.

1987 (PG-13) 91m/C Maureen Stapleton, Lee Richardson, Trini Alvarado, Freddie Roman, John Bedford Lloyd, Giancarlo Esposito; **D:** Steve Gomer. **VHS, Beta $79.98** *PAR* 🎬🎬🎬

Sweet Love, Bitter The downfall of a black jazz saxophonist in the 1950's. The character is loosely based on the life of legendary musician Charlie "Bird" Parker. Alto sax man Charles McPherson dubs Gregory's solos. Adapted from the novel "Night Song" by John A. Williams. **AKA:** It Won't Rub Off, Baby; Black Love, White Love.

1967 92m/C Dick Gregory, Don Murray, Diane Varsi, Robert Hooks; **W/D:** Herbert Danska; **W:** Lewis Jacobs; **M:** Mal Waldron. **VHS $59.95** *RHP, MVD, FCT* 🎬🎬½

Sweet Movie A provocative cult classic concerning a South African tycoon who purchases a virgin bride and then exploits her sexually. In English and French with subtitles.

1975 120m/C *YU* Carole Laure, Pierre Clementi, Sami Frey; **D:** Dusan Makavejev. **VHS, Beta $79.95** *FCT, MOV* 🎬🎬

Sweet Perfection Jackson plans a big promotion for her beauty contest. Who will be voted the "Perfect Woman?" Tired premise, but it has its moments.

1990 (R) 90m/C Stoney Jackson, Anthony Norman McKay, Catero Colbert, Liza Crusat, Reggie Theus, Tatiana Tumbtzen. **VHS $59.95** *XVC, HHE* 🎬🎬

Sweet Poison Bobby Stiles is a ruthless criminal who has just broken out of prison. He wants to get home and settle the score with his brother, who actually committed the crime Bobby was imprisoned for. Henry and Charlene Odell are traveling cross-country when Bobby crosses their path and forces them to drive him home. Bobby's not too busy eluding the police to notice that his captives marriage is a little shaky—and that Charlene is attractive and sexy. As Bobby and Charlene get closer husband Henry just becomes another problem.

1991 (R) 101m/C Steven Bauer, Patricia Healy, Edward Herrmann; **D:** Brian Grant. **VHS $79.98** *MCA* 🎬🎬

Sweet Revenge TV journalist kidnapped by a white slavery ring in the Asian jungles. After escaping, she returns for vegeance. Meok drama.

1987 (R) 79m/C Ted Shackleford, Nancy Allen, Martin Landau; **D:** Mark Sobel. **VHS, Beta $79.95** *MED* 🎬🎬

Sweet Revenge When a judge tells a divorced couple that the woman must pay the man alimony, she hires an actress to marry her ex. The tables are turned in this way-out marriage flick, reminiscent of the screwball comedies of the 1940s.

1990 89m/C Rosanna Arquette, Carrie Fisher, John Sessions; **D:** Charlotte Brandstrom. **VHS, Beta $79.98** *TTC* 🎬½

Sweet Sea A fantastical children's animated adventure about good and evil battling it out under the sea.

1986 30m/C **VHS, Beta $19.98** *LIV, WTA* 🎬🎬

Sweet 16 Serial killings in Texas town begin to set off muffled alarms in big head of sheriff Hopkins. Sixteen-year-old Melissa has recently moved into town. She's beautiful, mysterious, and promiscuous, and she has a big problem—all her boyfriends end up dead. No real puzzle.

1981 (R) 90m/C Susan Strasberg, Bo Hopkins, Don Stroud, Dana Kimmell, Patrick Macnee, Larry Storch; *D:* Jim Sotos. **VHS, Beta $69.95** VES 🐾🐾

Sweet Smell of Success Evil New York City gossip columnist J.J. Hunsecker (Lancaster) and sleazy press agent (Curtis) cook up smear campaign to ruin career of jazz musician in love with J.J.'s sister. Engrossing performances, great dialogue. Music by Oscar winner Elmer Bernstein.
1957 96m/C Burt Lancaster, Tony Curtis, Martin Milner, Barbara Nichols, Sam Levene; *D:* Alexander MacKendrick; *W:* Ernest Lehman, Clifford Odets. **VHS, LV $19.98** MGM 🐾🐾🐾½

Sweet Smell of Woman An acclaimed dark comedy that may be an acquired taste for some. A blinded military officer and his valet take a sensual tour of Italy, the sightless man seducing beautiful women on the way. But at the end of the journey awaits a shock, and the real point of the tale, based on a novel by Giovanni Arpino. In Italian with English subtitles. Remade in 1992 as "Scent of a Woman." *AKA:* Scent of a Woman; Profumo di Donna.
1975 103m/C *IT* Vittorio Gassman; *D:* Dino Risi. **VHS $59.95** FST 🐾🐾½

Sweet Spirits Soft-sell European fluff about a modern mannequin having a raucous affair with an artist.
198? 87m/C Erika Blanc, Farley Granger. **VHS, Beta $29.95** MED Woof!

Sweet Sugar Slave girls try to escape from a Costa Rican sugar cane plantation and its cruel owner. Needless to say, vulgar exploitation runs hither and yon in this film. *AKA:* Chaingang Girls; Captive Women 3: Sweet Sugar.
1972 (R) 90m/C Phyllis E. Davis, Ella Edwards, Pamela Collins, Cliff Osmond, Timothy Brown; *D:* Michel Levesque. **VHS** NO 🐾½

Sweet Sweetback's Baadasssss Song A black pimp kills two policemen who beat up a black militant. He uses his streetwise survival skills to elude his pursuers and escape to Mexico. A thriller, but racist, sexist, and violent.
1971 97m/C Melvin Van Peebles, Simon Chuckster, John Amos; *D:* Melvin Van Peebles. **VHS, Beta $59.98** SUN 🐾

Sweet Talker Following his release from prison, a charming con man shows up in a small coastal village, thinking the townsfolk will be ripe for the picking. What he doesn't know is they can do some sweet talking of their own, and he soon finds himself caring for a pretty widow and her son. Enjoyable light comedy works thanks to likable leads.
1991 (PG) 91m/C *AU* Bryan Brown, Karen Allen, Chris Haywood, Bill Kerr, Bruce Spence, Bruce Myles, Paul Chubb, Peter Hehir, Justin Rosniak; *D:* Michael Jenkins. **VHS, LV $89.98** LIV 🐾🐾½

Sweet Trash A vice cop, having an affair with a 17-year-old prostitute, is blackmailed by an underworld figure. Lives up to its name.
1989 (R) 80m/C Sebastian Gregory, Sharon Matt, Luke Perry, Bonnie Clark, Gene Blackey; *D:* John Hayes. **VHS** NO Woof!

Sweet William A philandering and seemingly irresistible young man finds that one sensitive woman hasn't the patience or time for his escapades. Adult comedy concerned with sex without displaying any on the screen.
1979 (R) 88m/C *GB* Sam Waterston, Jenny Agutter, Anna Massey, Arthur Lowe; *D:* Claude Whatham. **VHS, Beta $59.95** PSM 🐾🐾🐾

Sweet Young Thing Young students at a French girls' school receive all sorts of attention from the male staff.
19?? 83m/C Jean Tolzac, Bernard Musson. **VHS, Beta** MED 🐾🐾🐾

Sweetheart! Biography of Hal Banks, convicted for strong-arming shipping unions in an effort to destroy them.
19?? 115m/C Maury Chaykin. **VHS** NO 🐾½

Sweetheart of the Navy Sailors help a cafe singer out of a jam, with one of them almost giving up his career for her. Standard fare, but Parker is well worth listening to.
1937 63m/B Eric Linden, Cecilia Parker, Roger Imhof, Bernadene Hayes, Jason Robards Sr., Don Barclay; *D:* Duncan Mansfield. **VHS $19.95** NOS 🐾½

Sweethearts MacDonald and Eddy star as married stage actors trying to get some time off from their hectic schedule in this show-within-a-show. Trouble ensues when their conniving producer begs, pleads and tricks them into staying. Lots of well-staged musical numbers. 🎵Wooden Shoes; Every Lover Must Meet His Fate; Sweethearts; Pretty as a Picture; Summer Serenade; On Parade.
1938 114m/C Jeanette MacDonald, Nelson Eddy, Frank Morgan, Florence Rice, Ray Bolger, Mischa Auer; *D:* Woodbridge S. Van Dyke. **VHS, LV $19.98** MGM 🐾🐾🐾

Sweetie Bizarre, expressive Australian tragicomedy about a pair of sisters—one a withdrawn, paranoid Plain Jane, the other a dangerously extroverted, overweight sociopath who re-enters her family's life and turns it upside down. Campion's first feature.
1989 (R) 97m/C *AU* Genevieve Lemon, Karen Colston, Tom Lycos, Jon Darling, Dorothy Barry, Michael Lake, Andre Pataczek; *D:* Jane Campion. **VHS, Beta, LV $89.95** LIV 🐾🐾🐾

Sweetwater An independent woman and a feisty young orphan find each other amid society's rejections.
1984 30m/C VHS, Beta LCA 🐾🐾

Swept Away... A rich and beautiful Milanese woman is shipwrecked on a desolate island with a swarthy Sicilian deck hand, who also happens to be a dedicated communist. Isolated, the two switch roles, with the wealthy woman dominated by the crude proletarian. Sexy and provocative. Scripted by Wertmuller. *AKA:* Swept Away...By an Unusual Destiny in the Blue Sea of August.
1975 (R) 116m/C *IT* Giancarlo Giannini, Mariangela Melato; *D:* Lina Wertmuller. **VHS, Beta, LV $59.95** COL, APD 🐾🐾🐾

Swift Justice Mayor of a small town thinks he's gotten away with murder after leaving a young girl for dead in a junk yard. However, the mayor and his violent pals are soon hunted by an ex-Green Beret with a penchant for justice.
1988 90m/C Jon Greene, Sindi Rome, Cameron Mitchell, Aldo Ray, Chuck "Porky" Mitchell, Wilson Dunster, Ted Leplat; *D:* Harry Hope. **VHS, Beta $79.95** TWE 🐾🐾

Swifty A cowpoke is accused of murder but escapes to track down the real culprit and win the hand of the girl he loves.
1936 60m/B Hoot Gibson. **VHS, Beta $27.95** VCN 🐾½

Swim Team New coach for a terminally inept school swimming team whips them into shape. Doesn't hold much water.
1979 81m/C Stephen Furst, James Daughton, Jenny Neumann, Kim Day, Buster Crabbe; *D:* James Polakof. **VHS, Beta $9.99** STE, PSM 🐾

Swimmer A lonely suburbanite swims an existential swath through the pools of his neighborhood landscape in an effort at self-discovery. A surreal, strangely compelling work based on a story by John Cheever.
1968 (PG) 94m/C Burt Lancaster, Janice Rule, Janet Landgard; *D:* Frank Perry. **VHS, Beta, LV $9.95** GKK 🐾🐾🐾½

Swimming Pool Two men and two women spend a weekend in a villa on the French Riviera, manipulating each other, playing sexual games, and changing partners. Their escapades end in murder. Romantic melodrama is sensuous if slow-moving. French film dubbed in English.
1970 (PG) 85m/C *FR* Romy Schneider, Alain Delon, Maurice Ronet, Jane Birkin; *D:* Jacques Deray. **VHS, Beta $59.95** NLC 🐾🐾½

Swimming to Cambodia Gray tells the story of his bit part in "The Killing Fields," filmed in Cambodia, and makes ironic observations about modern life. It works. Music by Laurie Anderson.
1987 87m/C Spalding Gray; *D:* Jonathan Demme. **VHS, Beta, LV $19.98** LHV, WAR 🐾🐾🐾

Swimsuit: The Movie A young ad executive decides to revitalize a swimsuit company's failing business by sponsoring a contest for the perfect swimsuit model. Made-for-television fluff.
1989 100m/C William Katt, Catherine Oxenberg, Cyd Charisse, Nia Peeples, Tom Villard, Cheryl Pollak, Billy Warlock, Jack Wagner; *D:* Chris Thomson; *W:* Robert Schiff. **VHS $79.95** AIP 🐾½

The Swindle Three Italian conmen pull capers in Rome trying to make a better life for themselves. Dark overtones permeate one of Fellini's lesser efforts. Good cast can't bring up the level of this film. In Italian with English subtitles. *AKA:* Il Bidone.
1955 92m/C *IT* Broderick Crawford, Giulietta Masina, Richard Basehart, Franco Fabrizi; *D:* Federico Fellini. **VHS, LV $69.95** TAM, IME 🐾🐾

Swindle Two life-long friends set up scam after scam in their quest for sex and money. Their latest con involves a phony marriage broker business, which provides the opportunity to meet a lot of lovely ladies. Only it turns out the hustlers may be the ones getting hustled.
1992 85m/C Robby West, Britt Houston, Elaina Dunn, Samantha Fong, Bobby Tess, Donna Thomas; *D:* J. Holt. **VHS $79.95** CEL 🐾

Swing An all-black musical revue.
1947 80m/B VHS, Beta $29.95 NOS, DVT 🐾

Swing High, Swing Low A trumpet player fights the bottle and the dice to become a hit in the jazz world and marry the woman he loves. Solid drama. From the stage play "Burlesque." Made first as "The Dance of Life," then as "When My Baby Smiles At Me."
1937 95m/B Carole Lombard, Fred MacMurray, Charles Butterworth, Dorothy Lamour; *D:* Mitchell Leisen. **VHS, Beta, 3/4U, Special order formats $19.95** NOS, HHT, DVT 🐾🐾½

Swing It, Professor A stodgy music professor refuses to recognize jazz as a valid musical form and subsequently loses his job. During his unemployment, he wanders into a nightclub and discovers jazz isn't so bad after all. Nice camera work. 🎵I'm Sorta Kinda Glad I Met You; An Old-Fashioned Melody; Richer Than A Millionaire. *AKA:* Swing It Buddy.
1937 62m/B Pinky Tomlin, Paula Stone, Mary Kornman, Milburn Stone, Pat Gleason; *D:* Maurice Conn. **VHS $24.95** NOS, DVT, HEG 🐾🐾½

Swing It, Sailor! Two footloose sailors go after the same woman while on shore leave. Decent screwball comedy.
1937 61m/B Wallace Ford, Ray Mayer, Isabel Jewell, Mary Treen; **D:** Raymond Connon. **VHS, Beta** $24.95 NOS, VYY *½*

Swing Kids Drama with lots of music set in 1939 Germany about a group of American-big-band-loving teens who persist in dancing to these forbidden sounds. The trio of young rebels include the sensitive Leonard, whose father has disappeared at the hands of the Nazis; Whaley, the most musically knowledgeable and defiant; and Bale, seduced by Nazi power. Although the premise is based in historic fact, there is still something disturbingly silly about the entire production. Dance sequences are lively and well-choreographed. Branagh (in an uncredited role) plays a smooth-talking Gestapo chief who admires Leonard's mother (Hershey) and takes a fatherly interest in the son. Filmed on location in Prague, Poland (as a substitute for Hamburg, Germany).
1993 (PG-13) 114m/C Robert Sean Leonard, Christian Bale, Frank Whaley, Barbara Hershey, Tushka Bergen, David Tom, Kenneth Branagh; **D:** Thomas Carter; **W:** Jonathan Marc Feldman. **VHS, Beta, LV** $94.95 HPH *½*

Swing Parade of 1946 One of the multitude of 1940s musicals. Young songwriter falls in love with club owner. Highlights include an appearance by the Three Stooges. ♫Stormy Weather; Just a Little Fond Affection; Don't Worry About the Mule; A Tender Word Will Mend It All; On the Sunny Side of the Street; Oh, Brother; After All This Time; Caledonia.
1946 74m/B Gale Storm, Phil Regan, Moe Howard, Edward Brophy, Connee Boswell; **D:** Phil Karlson. **VHS** NO *½*

Swing Shift When Hawn takes a job at an aircraft plant after her husband goes off to war, she learns more than riveting. Lahti steals the film as her friend and co-worker. A detailed reminiscence of the American home front during World War II that never seems to gel. Produced by Hawn.
1984 (PG) 100m/C Goldie Hawn, Kurt Russell, Ed Harris, Christine Lahti, Holly Hunter, Chris Lemmon, Belinda Carlisle, Fred Ward, Roger Corman, Lisa Pelikan; **D:** Jonathan Demme. **VHS, Beta, LV** $19.98 WAR *½*

Swing Time Astaire, a dancer who can't resist gambling, is engaged to marry another woman, until he meets Ginger. One of the team's best efforts. The score is by Jerome Kern and Dorothy Fields. Laserdisc version includes: production photos and stills, commentary on Fred Astaire and musical films, and excerpts from "Hooray for Love" featuring Bill "Bojangles" Robinson and Fats Waller. ♫The Way You Look Tonight; Waltz in Swing Time; Never Gonna Dance; Pick Yourself Up; A Fine Romance; Bojangles of Harlem.
1936 103m/B Fred Astaire, Ginger Rogers, Helen Broderick, Betty Furness, Eric Blore, Victor Moore; **D:** George Stevens. **VHS, Beta, LV** $14.98 TTC, RKO, MED *½*

A Swingin' Summer A bunch of groovy guys and gals go-go to the beach for a vacation of fun and sun and end up starting a rock 'n' roll concert series. Everybody gets part of the action...even the bespectacled Welch, who gets a chance to sing. Performances from the Righteous Brothers and rock semi-legends Donnie Brooks, Gary Lewis and the Playboys, and the Rip Chords. ♫Red Hot Roadster; Justine; Penny the Poo; Out to Lunch; Nitro; Ready to Groove.

1965 81m/C James Stacy, William Wellman Jr., Quinn O'Hara, Martin West, Mary Mitchell, Allan Jones, Raquel Welch; **D:** Robert Sparr. **VHS** NO *½*

The Swinging Cheerleaders A group of amorous cheerleaders turn on the entire campus in this typical sexploiter.
1974 (PG) 90m/C Cheryl "Rainbeaux" Smith, Colleen Camp, Jo Johnston; **D:** Jack Hill. **VHS, Beta** $29.95 MON *½*

Swinging Ski Girls Group of free-loving university co-eds spend a wild weekend at a ski lodge.
197? 85m/C Cindy Wilton, Dick Cassidy. **VHS, Beta** $44.95 MED *½*

Swinging Sorority Girls Intimate glimpse behind the closed doors of a sorority house during a wild homecoming weekend.
197? 73m/C Susie Carlson, Anne Marlie. **VHS, Beta** MED *½*

Swinging Wives Ribald humor for the discriminating viewer.
1979 (R) 84m/C Gale Mayberrie, Ron James. **VHS, Beta** $39.95 WWV *½*

Swiss Conspiracy Against the opulent background of the world's richest financial capital and playground of the wealthy, one man battles to stop a daring and sophisticated blackmailer preying on the secret bank account set. Fast-paced, if sometimes confusing.
1977 (PG) 92m/C GE David Janssen, Senta Berger; **D:** Jack Arnold. **VHS, Beta** $49.95 UHV *½*

The Swiss Family Robinson A family, seeking to escape Napoleon's war in Europe, sets sail for New Guinea, but shipwrecks on a deserted tropical island. There they build an idyllic life, only to be confronted by a band of pirates. Lots of adventure for family viewing. Filmed on location on the island of Tobago. Based on the novel by Johann Wyss.
1960 126m/C John Mills, Dorothy McGuire, James MacArthur, Tommy Kirk, Janet Munro, Sessue Hayakawa; **D:** Ken Annakin. **VHS, Beta, LV** $19.99 DIS, IGP *½½½*

The Swiss Family Robinson An animated version of the classic adventure epic.
1972 49m/C **VHS, Beta** $19.95 MGM *½½½*

Swiss Miss Stan and Ollie are mousetrap salesmen on the job in Switzerland. Highlights include Stan's tuba serenade and the gorilla-on-the-bridge episode. Also included on this tape is a 1935 Thelma Todd/Patsy Kelly short, "Hot Money."
1938 97m/B Stan Laurel, Oliver Hardy, Della Lind, Walter Woolf King, Eric Blore, Thelma Todd, Patsy Kelly; **D:** John Blystone. **VHS, Beta** $14.98 CCB, MED, FCT *½½*

The Switch An escaped convict takes the place of a talented conman and chaos ensues.
1989 (R) ?m/C Anthony Quinn, Adriano Celentano, Capucine, Corinne Clery. **VHS** NO *½½*

Switch A chauvinist louse, slain by the girlfriends he misused, is sent back to Earth as an alluring female to learn the other side's point of view. The plot may lack urgency, but this is a sparkling adult comedy that scores as it pursues the gimmicky concept to a logical, outrageous and touching conclusion. Barkin's act as swaggering male stuck in a woman's body is a masterwork of physical humor.
1991 (R) 104m/C Ellen Barkin, Jimmy Smits, JoBeth Williams, Lorraine Bracco, Perry King; **W/D:** Blake Edwards; **M:** Henry Mancini. **VHS, LV** $92.99 HBO, PIA, WAR *½½½*

Switchblade Sisters Crime gang of female ex-cons wreaks pseudo-feminist havoc. Bruce is Lenny Bruce's daughter. **AKA:** The Jezebels; Playgirl Gang.
1975 90m/C Robbie Lee, Joanne Nail, Monica Gayle, Kitty Bruce; **D:** Jack Hill. **VHS, Beta** $59.95 MON, HHE Woof!

Switched at Birth A fact-based made for television drama about two girls, switched in a hospital nursery at birth. Only when one girl dies, a decade later, do her parents discover that she could not have been their biological child. Their search for their daughter leads to an emotional conflict between the girl, the family that raised her, and the biological parents who seek to claim her.
1991 (PG) 200m/C Bonnie Bedelia, Brian Kerwin, Ed Asner, Caroline McWilliams, John M. Jackson, Lois Smith, Eve Gordon, Judith Hoag, Ariana Richards; **D:** Waris Hussein. **VHS** COL, PMS *½½*

Switching Channels A modernized remake of "His Girl Friday," and therefore the fourth version of "The Front Page." Beautiful television anchorwoman (Turner) wants to marry handsome tycoon (Reeve), but her scheming ex-husband (Reynolds) gets in the way. Weak performances from everyone but Beatty and lackluster direction render this off-told story less funny than usual.
1988 (PG) 108m/C Burt Reynolds, Kathleen Turner, Christopher Reeve, Ned Beatty, Henry Gibson; **D:** Ted Kotcheff. **VHS, Beta, LV** $14.95 COL *½½½½*

Swoon Kalin's directorial debut is a stylish rendering of the sensational 1924 kidnapping and murder of Bobby Franks by Richard Loeb and Nathan Leopold Jr. and their subsequent trial and imprisonment. Core elements of the case remain but Kalin imposes contemporary styles and morals on the past, particularly his protest against the homophobic attitudes influencing the trial while acknowledging the jaded and dispassionate behavior of the two young men. Previous cinematic versions of the murder case include "Rope" and "Compulsion" but Kalin graphically portrays the characters homosexuality, which was only hinted at in the earlier films.
1991 95m/B Daniel Schlachet, Craig Chester, Ron Vawter, Michael Kirby; **W/D:** Tom Kalin. **VHS, LV** NLC, IME *½½½*

The Sword and the Cross A grade-B adventure about the life of Mary Magdelene.
1958 93m/B Yvonne De Carlo, George Mistral; **D:** Carlo L. Bragaglia. **VHS, Beta** NO *½½*

Sword & the Dragon A young warrior must battle any number of giant mythical creatures. **AKA:** Ilya Mourometz.
1956 81m/C RU Boris Andreyer, Andrei Abrikosov; **D:** Alexander Ptushko. **VHS, Beta** $59.95 UHV, SNC *½½*

The Sword & the Rose Mary Tudor, sister of King Henry VIII, shuns the advances of a nobleman for the love of a commoner. Johns is an obstinate princess; Justice, a fine king. Based on the book "When Knighthood Was in Flower." **AKA:** When Knighthood Was in Flower.
1953 91m/C Richard Todd, Glynis Johns, Michael Gough, Jane Barrett, James Robertson Justice; **D:** Ken Annakin. **VHS, Beta, LV** $19.99 DIS, HHE *½½½*

Sword & the Sorcerer Young prince strives to regain control of his kingdom, now ruled by an evil knight and a powerful magician. Mediocre script and acting is enhanced by decent special effects.

1982 (R) 100m/C Lee Horsely, Kathleen Beller, George Maharis, Simon MacCorkindale, Richard Lynch, Richard Moll, Robert Tessier, Nina Van Pallandt, Anna Bjorn, Jeff Corey; **D:** Albert Pyun. **VHS, Beta, LV** $24.95 *MCA* 🎞️½

The Sword in the Stone The Disney version of the first volume of T.H. White's "The Once and Future King" wherein King Arthur, as a boy, is instructed in the ways of the world by Merlin and Archimedes the owl. Although not in the Disney masterpiece fold, boasts the usual superior animation and a gripping mythological tale.
1963 (G) 79m/C **D:** Wolfgang Reitherman, Wolfgang Reitherman; **V:** Ricky Sorenson, Sebastian Cabot, Karl Swenson, Junius Matthews, Alan Napier, Norman Alden, Martha Wentworth, Barbara Jo Allen. **VHS, Beta, LV** $24.99 *DIS, KUI, HMV* 🎞️🎞️🎞️

Sword of Doom A rousing samurai epic detailing the training of an impulsive, blood-lusting warrior by an elder expert. In Japanese with English subtitles. *AKA:* Daibosatsu Toge.
1967 120m/B *JP* Tatsuya Nakadai, Toshiro Mifune; **D:** Kihachi Okamoto. **VHS, Beta** $29.98 *SUE, TAM, NLC* 🎞️🎞️🎞️

The Sword of El Cid Not much dash and very little daring-do in this poorly plotted, overly dramatic saga of good vs. evil, Spanish style. Rightful heir to the crown threatens, challenges and enevitably crosses swords with the pretender to his throne. Costume mavens may find something to hold their interest. *AKA:* La Spada del Cid.
1962 86m/C *SP IT* Roland Carey, Sandro Moretti, Chantal Deberg, Iliana Grimaldi, Jose Luis Pellicena, Daniela Bianchi; **D:** Miguel Iglesias. **VHS, Beta** $16.95 *SNC* 🎞️½

Sword of Fury I How Musashi Miyamoto became Japan's greatest samurai. With English subtitles. Followed by a sequel.
1973 90m/C *JP* Hideki Takahashi, Jiro Tamiya. **VHS, Beta** *NO* 🎞️½

Sword of Fury II The sequel. Two samurai fight to the death to determine who will become the premier swordsman of all Japan. With English subtitles.
1973 77m/C *JP* Hideki Takahashi, Jiro Tamiya. **VHS, Beta** *NO* 🎞️½

Sword of Gideon An action packed and suspenseful made for television film about an elite commando group who set out to avenge the Munich Olympic killings of 1972. Adapted from "Vengeance" by George Jonas.
1986 148m/C Steven Bauer, Michael York, Rod Steiger, Colleen Dewhurst, Robert Joy, Laurent Malet, Lino Ventura, Leslie Hope; **D:** Michael Anderson Sr. **VHS** $79.99 *HBO* 🎞️🎞️½

Sword of Heaven Forged from a meteorite in the 15th century, a sword holds magical powers. When it is stolen, a young warrior pursues the villains.
1981 87m/C *JP* Tadashi Yamashita. **VHS, Beta** $69.95 *TWE* 🎞️

Sword of Lancelot A costume version of the Arthur-Lancelot-Guinevere triangle, with plenty of swordplay and a sincere respect for the old legend. *AKA:* Lancelot and Guinevere.
1963 115m/C *GB* Cornel Wilde, Jean Wallace, Brian Aherne, George Baker; **D:** Cornel Wilde. **VHS, Beta** $59.95 *MCA* 🎞️½

Sword of Monte Cristo Masked female avenger, seeking the liberty of the French people, discovers a valuable sword that holds the key to a vast fortune. But the sword is also desired by an evil government minister.
1951 80m/C George Montgomery, Paula Corday; **D:** Maurice Geraghty. **VHS, Beta** $29.95 *VHE* 🎞️½

Sword of Sherwood Forest The Earl of Newark plots the murder of the Archbishop of Canterbury in yet another rendition of the Robin Hood legend. Peter Cushing is truly evil as the villain.
1960 80m/C *GB* Richard Greene, Peter Cushing, Niall MacGinnis, Richard Pasco, Jack Gwillim, Sarah Branch, Nigel Green, Oliver Reed; **D:** Terence Fisher. **VHS** *COL, MLB* 🎞️🎞️½

Sword of the Valiant The Green Knight arrives in Camelot to challenge Gawain. Remake of "Gawain And The Green Knight." Connery adds zest to a minor epic.
1983 (PG) 102m/C *GB* Sean Connery, Miles O'Keeffe, Cyrielle Claire, Leigh Lawson, Trevor Howard, Peter Cushing, Wilfrid Brambell, Lila Kedrova, John Rhys-Davies; **D:** Stephen Weeks. **VHS, Beta** $69.95 *MGM* 🎞️🎞️

Sword of Venus Uninspired production finds the son of the Count of Monte Cristo the victim in a scheme to deprive him of his wealth. *AKA:* Island of Monte Cristo.
1953 73m/B Robert Clarke, Catherine McLeod, Dan O'Herlihy, William Schallert; **D:** Harold Daniels. **VHS** $29.95 *FCT* 🎞️

Swords of Death Final film by Uchida, released posthumously, deals with the adventurous period exploits of the irrepressible Miyamoto Musashi. With English subtitles.
1971 76m/C *JP* Kinnosuke Nakamura, Rentaro Mikuni; **D:** Tomu Uchida. **VHS, Beta** *VDA* 🎞️🎞️

The Swordsman The quest to return the stolen sword of the legendary Alexander the Great to a museum is muscular detective Lamas' assignment. Turns out the detective and his evil millionaire antagonist have been chasing each other through time in their endless quest for revenge and power.
1992 (R) 98m/C Lorenzo Lamas, Claire Stansfield, Michael Champion; **W/D:** Michael Kennedy. **VHS, LV** $89.98 *REP* 🎞️🎞️½

Sybil Fact-based story of a woman who developed 16 distinct personalities, and the supportive psychiatrist who helped her put the pieces of her ego together. Excellent made-for-television production with Field's Emmy-winning performance.
1976 122m/C Sally Field, Joanne Woodward, Brad Davis, Martine Bartlett, Jane Hoffman; **D:** Daniel Petrie. **VHS, Beta** $19.98 *FOX* 🎞️🎞️🎞️

Sylvester A 16-year-old girl and a cranky stockyard boss team up to train a battered horse named Sylvester for the National Equestrian trials. Nice riding sequences and good performances can't overcome familiar plot, but the kids will enjoy this one.
1985 (PG) 104m/C Melissa Gilbert, Richard Farnsworth, Michael Schoeffling, Constance Towers; **D:** Tim Hunter. **VHS, Beta, LV** $79.95 *COL* 🎞️🎞️

Sylvester & Tweety's Crazy Capers Sylvester keeps on the tail of Tweety Pie in this collection of eight classic cartoons that include "Tweet and Lovely," "Tree for Two," and "Hyde and Go Tweet."
1961 54m/C **D:** Friz Freleng, Chuck Jones; **V:** Mel Blanc. **VHS, Beta** $12.95 *WAR, WTA* 🎞️🎞️

Sylvia Biography of author/educator Sylvia Ashton-Warner, and her efforts to teach Maori children in New Zealand to read via unorthodox methods. David is a marvel. Based on Ashton-Warner's books "Teacher" and "I Passed This Way."
1986 (PG) 99m/C *NZ* Eleanor David, Tom Wilkinson, Nigel Terry, Mary Regan; **D:** Michael Firth. **VHS, Beta** $79.98 *FOX* 🎞️🎞️½

Sylvia and the Phantom A charming French comedy about a lonely young girl who is befriended by the ghost of a man killed decades earlier in a duel over the girl's grandmother. Based on the play by Alfred Adam. In French with English subtitles. *AKA:* Sylvia and the Ghost.
1945 97m/B *FR* Odette Joyeux, Jacques Tati, Francois Perier; **D:** Claude Autant-Lara. **VHS, Beta** $29.98 *SUE, TAM, NLC* 🎞️🎞️

Sylvia Scarlett An odd British comedy about a woman who masquerades as a boy while on the run with her father, who causes all kinds of instinctive confusion in the men she meets.
1935 94m/B Katharine Hepburn, Cary Grant, Brian Aherne, Edmund Gwenn, Natalie Paley, Dennis Moore, Lennox Pawle, Daisy Belmore, Nola Luxford; **D:** George Cukor. **VHS, Beta, LV** $19.95 *RKO, FCT, TTC* 🎞️🎞️½

Sympathy for the Devil Rolling Stones provide music for confused, revolutionary documentary. Episodic jumble is odd, sometimes fascinating. *AKA:* One Plus One.
1970 110m/C *FR* Mick Jagger, Rolling Stones; **D:** Jean-Luc Godard. **VHS, Beta** *FOX, OM* 🎞️🎞️

Symphony in the Mountains An early German sound romance, where an Austrian singing teacher falls in love with the sister of one of his student's. Featuring choral work by the Vienna Boys' Choir. In German with English subtitles.
1935 75m/B *GE V:* The Vienna Boys Choir. **VHS, Beta, 3/4U** $35.95 *FCT, IHF, GLV* 🎞️🎞️½

Symphony of Living Intended heartwarmer about a man's bitter betrayal by his family and the hardship and tragedy he experiences.
1935 73m/B **VHS, Beta** $29.95 *VYY* 🎞️½

Syngenor Syngenor stands for Synthesized Genetic Organism, to differentiate it from all other organisms. Created by science, it escapes, and a crack team of scientists and gung-ho military types are mobilized to track it down.
1990 (R) 98m/C Starr Andreeff, Michael Laurence, David Gale, Charles Lucia, Riva Spier, Jeff Doucette, Bill Gratton, Lewis Arquette, Jon Korkes, Melanie Shatner; **D:** George Elanjian Jr. **VHS** $14.95 *HMD* 🎞️½

T-Bird Gang A high school student goes undercover to infiltrate a teen gang. When his cover is blown, things get hairy. Laughable sleazebag production.
1959 75m/B Ed Nelson, John Brinkley, Pat George, Beach Dickerson, Tony Miller; **D:** Richard Harbinger; **M:** Shelley Manne. **VHS** $19.98 *SNC* 🎞️½

T Bone N Weasel Hines and Lloyd play not-so-ex-cons who steal a car and try to lead a life of ease. Crime doesn't pay. Made for cable television.
199? (PG-13) 94m/C Gregory Hines, Christopher Lloyd. **VHS, LV** $89.98 *TTC* 🎞️🎞️

T-Men Two agents of the Treasury Department infiltrate a counterfeiting gang. Filmed in semi-documentary style, exciting tale serves also as an effective commentary on the similarities between the agents and those they pursue. Mann and cinematographer John Alton do especially fine work here.
1947 96m/B Alfred Ryder, Dennis O'Keefe, June Lockhart, Mary Meade, Wallace Ford, Charles McGraw; **D:** Anthony Mann. **VHS, Beta, LV** $29.95 *MED* 🎞️🎞️

Table for Five A divorced father takes his children on a Mediterranean cruise and while sailing, he learns that his ex-wife has died. The father and his ex-wife's husband struggle over who should raise the children. Sentimental and well-acted.

1983 (PG) 120m/C Jon Voight, Millie Perkins, Richard Crenna, Robbie Kiger, Roxana Zal, Son Hoang Bui, Marie-Christine Barrault, Kevin Costner; **D:** Robert Lieberman. **VHS, Beta, LV** $14.98 *FOX* 🞰🞰½

Table Settings A taped performance of James Lapines' comedy about the lives of three generations of a Jewish family.
1984 90m/C Robert Klein, Stockard Channing, Dinah Manoff, Eileen Heckart. **VHS, Beta** $39.95 *RKO* 🞰

Tabloid! Unorthodox woman prints and sells racy trash for enquiring minds.
1988 99m/C Scott Davis, Glen Cobum; **D:** Bret McCormick, Matt Shaffen. **VHS** *TPV, HHE* 🞰½

Tabu: A Story of the South Seas Fascinating docudrama about a young pearl diver's ill-fated romance. The gods have declared the young woman he desires ''taboo'' to all men. Filmed on location in Tahiti. Authored and produced by Murnau and Flaherty. Flaherty left in mid-production due to artistic differences with Murnau, who was later killed in an auto accident one week before the premiere of film. Oscar-winning cinematography by Floyd Crosby.
1931 81m/B **D:** Robert Flaherty, F. W. Murnau. **VHS, Beta** $39.95 *MIL, GVV, LUM* 🞰🞰🞰½

Tacos al Carbon A singer falls in love with a beautiful woman.
1987 103m/C *MX* Vicente Fernandez, Nadia Milton, Sonia Amelio, Ana Martin, Sergio Ramos. **VHS, Beta** $59.95 *MAD* 🞰🞰

Taffin An Irish bill collector battles a group of corrupt businessmen who want to replace the local soccer field with a hazardous chemical plant. Pretty dull fare, overall, with Brosnan much less charismatic than usual.
1988 (R) 96m/C *GB* Pierce Brosnan, Ray McAnally, Alison Doody, Patrick Bergin, Patrick Bergin; **D:** Francis Megahy. **VHS, Beta, LV** $79.95 *MGM* 🞰½

Tag: The Assassination Game An exciting new game has been discovered by a group of university students. Players act as spies and assassins, ''killing'' each other to make points. But a school newspaper sportswriter finds the game has become more real than make-believe. Timely topic in the early '80s when Dungeons and Dragons and other ''war'' games were popular on college campuses across the nation.
1982 (PG) 92m/C Robert Carradine, Linda Hamilton, Michael Winslow, Kristine DeBell, Perry Lang; **D:** Nick Castle. **VHS, Beta** $59.98 *SUE* 🞰½

Tagget A former CIA operative who has erased his nightmarish stint in Vietnam gradually begins to recall his past. When pieces of the puzzle begin to come together, he remembers a few things that the government would prefer he forget. Soon, CIA men are on his trail and their mission is to see that he forgets his past—permanently. Made for cable television.
1990 (PG-13) 89m/C Daniel J. Travanti, William Sadler, Roxanne Hart, Stephen Tobolowsky, Peter Michael Goetz, Sarah Douglas, Noel Harrison; **D:** Richard T. Heffron. **VHS** $79.95 *MCA* 🞰

Tai-Pan A 19th century Scottish trader and his beautiful Chinese mistress are the main characters in this confusing attempt to dramatize the story of Hong Kong's development into a thriving trading port. Too many subplots and characters are introduced in a short time to do justice to James Clavell's novel of the same name, the basis for the movie. The first American production completely filmed in China.

1986 (R) 130m/C Joan Chen, John Stanton, Kyra Sedgwick, Tim Guinee, Bryan Brown; **D:** Daryl Duke. **VHS, Beta, LV** $79.98 *VES* 🞰½

Tailspin: Behind the Korean Airline Tragedy Made-for-TV docudrama on the 1983 downing of Korean Aire flight 007 in Soviet airspace. Purports to show the U.S. government's reaction to what became a major international incident.
1989 82m/C Michael Moriarty, Michael Murphy, Chris Sarandon, Harris Yulin, Gavan O'Herlihy, Ed O'Ross; **D:** David Darlow. **VHS, Beta, LV** *PSM, PAR* 🞰🞰

Tailspin Tommy Features twelve chapters of the great action serial.
1934 ?m/B Maurice Murphy, Noah Beery Jr., Walter Miller, Patricia Farr, Grant Withers, John Davidson, William Desmond, Charles A. Browne. **VHS** $24.95 *GPV* 🞰🞰

Tainted Small-town woman tries to endure after being raped. Both her husband and the attacker are killed, and she is forced to conceal their deaths. Poorly scripted.
1988 90m/C Shari Shattuck, Park Overall, Gene Tootle, Magilla Schaus, Blaque Fowler; **D:** Orestes Matacena. **VHS, Beta** *NO* 🞰½

Tainted Image Artist woman starts to lose sanity with help of boyfriend, psycho neighbor and rash of bizarre deaths. She turns to canvas for solace and decides she needs secret ingredient that can't be found in art supply store to complete masterpiece.
1991 95m/C Tom Saunders, Sandra Frances, Annetta Arpin, Ken La Mothe, Heidi Emerich, Steve Kornacki. **VHS** $79.95 *HHT, PHX* 🞰

The Take Recovering alcoholic cop faces wrath of drug lord and marriage on the rocks.
1990 (R) 91m/C Ray Sharkey, Lee Ermey, Lisa Hartman, Larry Manetti, Joe Lala; **D:** Leon Ichaso; **W:** Edward Anhalt, Handel Glassberg. **VHS** $79.95 *MCA* 🞰🞰

Take a Hard Ride Dull spaghetti western about a cowboy transporting money to Mexico, evading bandits and bounty hunters.
1975 (R) 103m/C Jim Brown, Lee Van Cleef, Fred Williamson, Jim Kelly, Barry Sullivan; **D:** Anthony M. Dawson; **M:** Jerry Goldsmith. **VHS, Beta** $19.98 *FOX* 🞰½

Take Down Hermann is charming as a high school English teacher turned reluctant wrestling coach.
1979 96m/C Lorenzo Lamas, Kathleen Lloyd, Maureen McCormick, Edward Herrmann; **D:** Keith Merrill. **VHS, Beta** $29.95 *UNI* 🞰🞰

Take It Big Uninspired B-musical starring the Tin Man from the ''Wizard of Oz.'' Haley is an impoverished actor who inherits a ranch and saves it by—surprise—putting on a show. 🎵Sunday, Monday, and Always; Love and Learn; Life Can Be Beautiful; Take It Big; I'm a Big Success with You.
1944 75m/B Jack Haley, Harriet Hilliard Nelson, Mary Beth Hughes, Arline Judge, Nils T. Granlund, Fuzzy Knight, Ozzie Nelson; **D:** Frank McDonald. **VHS, Beta** $19.95 *NOS, VYY, DVT* 🞰½

Take Me Back to Oklahoma Musical western with comedy.
1940 64m/B Tex Ritter, Terry Walker, Karl Hackett, George Eldridge; **D:** Al Herman. **VHS, Beta** $19.95 *NOS, VCN, VYY* 🞰

Take Me Out to the Ball Game Williams manages a baseball team, locks horns with players Sinatra and Kelly, and wins them over with song. Naturally, there's a water ballet scene. Contrived and forced, but enjoyable. 🎵Take Me Out to the Ball Game; The Hat My Father Wore on St. Patrick's Day; O'Brien to Ryan to Goldberg; The Right Girl for Me; It's Fate, Baby, It's Fate; Yes, Indeedy; Strictly U.S.A. *AKA:* Everybody's Cheering.

1949 93m/C Frank Sinatra, Gene Kelly, Esther Williams, Jules Munshin, Betty Garrett, Edward Arnold, Tom Dugan, Richard Lane; **D:** Busby Berkeley. **VHS, Beta, LV** $19.98 *MGM* 🞰🞰½

Take the Money and Run Allen's directing debut; he also co-wrote and starred. ''Documentary'' follows a timid, would-be bank robber who can't get his career off the ground and keeps landing in jail. Little plot, but who cares? Nonstop one-liners and slapstick.
1969 (PG) 85m/C Woody Allen, Janet Margolin, Marcel Hillaire, Louise Lasser; **D:** Woody Allen. **VHS, Beta, LV** $19.98 *FOX* 🞰🞰🞰

Take This Job & Shove It The Johnny Paycheck song inspired this story of a hot-shot efficiency expert who returns to his hometown to streamline the local brewery. Encounters with old pals inspire self-questioning. Alternately inspired and hackneyed. Cameos by Paycheck and other country stars.
1981 (PG) 100m/C Robert Hays, Art Carney, Barbara Hershey, David Keith, Martin Mull, Eddie Albert, Penelope Milford; *Cameos:* Johnny Paycheck, David Allen Coe, Charlie Rich, Lacy J. Dalton; **D:** Gus Trikonis. **VHS, Beta** $14.95 *COL, SUE* 🞰🞰

Take Two A woman has an affair with her husband's twin brother. Interesting metaphysically: Are you my husband or my lover? But is an adultery/murder drama with Frank Stallone worth 101 minutes of your time?
1987 (R) 101m/C Grant Goodeve, Robin Mattson, Frank Stallone, Warren Berlinger, Darwyn Swalve, Nita Talbot; **D:** Peter Rowe. **VHS, Beta, LV** $29.95 *ACA* 🞰

Take Your Best Shot Standard TV fare about an out-of-work actor struggling with his low self-esteem and his failing marriage. Made-for-television comedy.
1982 96m/C Robert Urich, Meredith Baxter Birney, Jeffrey Tambor, Jack Bannon, Claudette Nevins; **D:** David Greene. **VHS, Beta** $39.95 *LIV* 🞰

Takin' It All Off In this sequel to ''Takin' It Off,'' Kitten does it again with unbelievable bumps and grinds.
1987 90m/C Francesca ''Kitten'' Natavidad; **D:** Ed Hansen. **VHS** $69.98 *LIV, VES* 🞰½

Takin' It Off Exotic dancer's agent advises her to trim down her well-endowed figure in order to become a serious actress.
1984 90m/C Francesca ''Kitten'' Natavidad, Adam Hadum, Ashley St. John, Angelique Pettyjohn. **VHS, Beta, LV** $69.98 *LIV, VES* Woof!

Taking Care of Business Too familiar tale of switched identity has crazed Cubs fan Belushi find Grodin's Filofax, allowing him to pose as businessman. Old jokes and a story full of holes. *AKA:* Filofax.
1990 (R) 108m/C James Belushi, Charles Grodin, Anne De Salvo, Loryn Locklin, Veronica Hamel, Hector Elizondo, Mako, Gates McFadden, Stephen Elliott; **D:** Arthur Hiller. **VHS, Beta, LV** $19.99 *HPH* 🞰½

Taking Care of Terrific A young babysitter takes the naive boy she is caring for out into the streets to visit with a street musician. The trio plan an evening to help the homeless in this entry in the ''Wonderworks'' series.
1988 55m/C Melvin Van Peebles, Joanne Vannicola, Jackie Burroughs. **VHS** $29.95 *PME, HMV, BTV* 🞰½

Taking it to the Street It's an all-out high-stakes battle between good and evil.
19?? 90m/C **VHS** *NO* 🞰½

Taking My Turn A taped performance of the off Broadway musical revue about growing old gracefully.

The Taking of Beverly Hills Deranged billionaire Bat Masterson designs a bogus toxic spill that leaves the wealth of Beverly Hills his for the taking. Football hero Boomer Hayes teams up with renegade cop Ed Kelvin to try and stop Masterson and save the city of Beverly Hills.
1991 (R) 96m/C Ken Wahl, Matt Frewer, Robert Davi, Harley Jane Kozak, Lee James, Branscombe Richmond, Lyman Ward, Michael Bowen, William Prince, Ken Swofford, George Wyner; *D:* Sidney J. Furie. **VHS, LV** $19.95 *COL, NLC* 🎞️½

The Taking of Flight 847: The Uli Derickson Story Wagner plays the stewardess who acted as a go-between for the passengers during a 1985 terrorist hijacking, saving all but one life. True-story drama is suspenseful and entertaining, nominated for several Emmys. Made-for-television drama. *AKA:* The Flight.
1988 100m/C Laurie Walters, Sandy McPeak, Ray Wise, Leslie Easterbrook, Lindsay Wagner, Eli Danker; *D:* Paul Wendkos. **VHS, LV** *IME* 🎞️🎞️🎞️

The Taking of Pelham One Two Three A hijack team, lead by the ruthless Shaw, seizes a New York City subway car and holds the 17 passengers for one million dollars ransom. Fine pacing keeps things on the edge. New cinematic techniques used by cameraman Owen Roizman defines shadowy areas like never before.
1974 (R) 105m/C Robert Shaw, Walter Matthau, Martin Balsam, Hector Elizondo, James Broderick; *D:* Joseph Sargent. **VHS, Beta** $14.95 *MGM, FOX* 🎞️🎞️🎞️

The Tale of Ruby Rose Living in the mountains of Tasmania, Ruby Rose, her husband Henry, and their adopted son Gem, struggle to survive the '30s depression by hunting and trapping. Having spent all her life in the mountains, Ruby Rose has a very superstitious view of life and a terror of nightfall. But after an argument with her husband, Ruby Rose sets out on a cross-country journey to find her grandmother and discover the secrets of her past.
1987 (PG) 101m/C *AU* Melita Jurisic, Chris Haywood; *W/D:* Roger Sholes. **VHS** $89.95 *HMD* 🎞️🎞️🎞️

A Tale of Springtime This comedy-romance is the first film in Rohmer's planned new series, the "Tales of the Four Seasons," not to be confused with his "Six Moral Tales" or his "Comedies and Proverbs." The story centers around Jeanne, a high school philosophy teacher; Natacha, a young student; and Igor, Natacha's father. Igor has been living with a young woman named Eve, and Natacha has been seeing William, who is nearly as old as Igor. To further complicate matters, Natacha views Eve as a rival, and thus, tries to set Jeanne up with her father. As characteristic of Rohmer films, texture and character largely overshadow linear plots and social messages. However, the efficiency and directness of his camerawork make it a pleasure to watch.
1992 (PG) 107m/C *FR* Anne Teyssedre, Hugues Quester, Florence Darel, Eloise Bennett; *W/D:* Eric Rohmer. **VHS** $19.98 *ORI* 🎞️🎞️½

The Tale of the Frog Prince Superb edition of Shelley Duvall's "Faerie Tale Theatre" finds Williams the victim of an angry fairy godmother's spell. Garr to the rescue as the self-centered princess who saves him with a kiss. Directed and written by Idle of Monty Python fame.
1983 60m/C Robin Williams, Teri Garr; *W/D:* Eric Idle. **VHS, Beta, LV** $14.98 *FOX* 🎞️🎞️🎞️½

A Tale of Two Chipmunks Three Chip 'n' Dale Disney cartoons: "Chicken in the Rough," "The Lone Chipmunks" and "Chips Ahoy."
1953 (G) 24m/C **VHS, Beta, LV** $14.95 *DIS* 🎞️🎞️🎞️½

A Tale of Two Cities Lavish production of the Dickens' classic set during the French Revolution, about two men who bear a remarkable resemblance to each other, both in love with the same girl. Carefree lawyer Sydney Carton (Colman) roused to responsibility, makes the ultimate sacrifice. A memorable Madame DeFarge from stage star Yurka in her film debut, with assistance from other Dickens' film stars Rathbone, Oliver and Walthall.
1935 128m/B Ronald Colman, Elizabeth Allan, Edna May Oliver, Reginald Owen, Isabel Jewell, Walter Catlett, H.B. Warner, Donald Woods, Basil Rathbone, Blanche Yurka; *D:* Jack Conway. **VHS, Beta** $24.95 *MGM, KUI, IGP* 🎞️🎞️🎞️🎞️

A Tale of Two Cities A well-done British version of the Dickens' classic about a lawyer who sacrifices himself to save another man from the guillotine during the French Reign of Terror. The sixth remake of the tale.
1958 117m/B *GB* Dirk Bogarde, Dorothy Tutin, Christopher Lee, Donald Pleasence, Ian Bannen, Cecil Parker; *D:* Ralph Thomas. **VHS, Beta** $19.98 *SUE, LCA, FHS* 🎞️🎞️🎞️🎞️

A Tale of Two Cities Impressive looking but bloodless adaptation of the Dickens novel set in the French Revolution. Sarandon takes on the dual role of sacrificing English lawyer Carton and French nobleman Darnay, with Krige as the lovely woman caught between the two. Made for television.
1980 156m/C Chris Sarandon, Alice Krige, Peter Cushing, Kenneth More, Barry Morse, Flora Robson, Billie Whitelaw; *D:* Jim Goddard; *W:* John Gay. **VHS** $19.98 *LIV* 🎞️🎞️½

A Tale of Two Cities A cartoon adaptation of the Dickens classic. A man sacrifices his own life for his friend's to ensure the happiness of the woman they both love.
1984 72m/C **VHS, Beta** *NO* 🎞️🎞️½

A Tale of Two Cities Masterpiece Theatre production of the classic Dickens tale. The French revolution was a time of revenge and brutality, but also provided the proving ground for a love greater than life. Terrific cast and perfectly detailed production. On two cassettes.
1991 240m/C John Mills. **VHS** $39.95 *PBS, PAV, TVC* 🎞️🎞️🎞️

Tale of Two Cities/In the Switch Tower A package of two medium-length silent films, the latter featuring a rare acting appearance by director Borzage.
1915 70m/B Walter Edwards, Maurice Costello, Florence Turner, Frank Borzage, Norma Talmadge, Leo Delaney. **VHS, Beta, 8mm** $29.95 *VYY* 🎞️½

Tale of Two Sisters Sheen narrates sensual drama about two beautiful, ambitious sisters.
1989 90m/C Valerie Breiman, Claudia Christian, Sydney Lassick, Jeff Conaway. **VHS** *NO* 🎞️🎞️½

Talent for the Game A slight but handsomely produced baseball pleasantry about a talent scout who recruits a phenomenonal young pitcher, then sees the kid exploited by the team owner. More like an anecdote than a story, with an ending that aims a little too hard to please. Good for sports fans and family audiences.
1991 (PG) 91m/C Edward James Olmos, Lorraine Bracco, Jeff Corbett; *D:* Robert M. Young. **VHS, Beta, LV** $19.95 *PAR* 🎞️🎞️½

Tales from the Crypt A collection of five scary stories from the classic EC comics that bear the movie's title. Richardson tells the future to each of five people gathered in a cave, each tale involving misfortune and, of course, gore.
1972 (PG) 92m/C *GB* Ralph Richardson, Joan Collins, Peter Cushing, Richard Greene, Ian Hendry; *D:* Freddie Francis. **VHS, Beta** $59.95 *PSM* 🎞️🎞️🎞️

Tales from the Crypt Three contemporary tales of the macabre, "The Man Who Was Death," "'Twas the Night Before," and "Dig That Cat...He's Real Gone," linked together by a special-effects host. Ry Cooder provides the musical score for the second episode. Based on stories published by William M. Gaines in EC Comics; made-for-cable-television.
1989 81m/C Bill Sadler, Mary Ellen Trainor, Larry Drake, Joe Pantoliano, Robert Wuhl, Gustav Vintas; *D:* Walter Hill, Robert Zemeckis, Richard Donner. **VHS, Beta, LV** $89.99 *HBO* 🎞️🎞️🎞️

Tales from the Crypt, Vol. 3 Three more tales of terror from the made-for-cable-television series. "Dead Right" has Moore as a golddigger who takes a fortuneteller's advice and marries a penniless slob. "Cutting Cards" has Tighe and Hendricksen involved in a very high stakes game. "The Switch" features Hickey as a wealthy old man bartering for a new body to woo the beautiful Preston.
1990 80m/C Demi Moore, William Hickey, Kelly Preston, Jeffrey Tambor, Rick Rossovich, Lance Henriksen, Kevin Tighe; *D:* Arnold Schwarzenegger, Walter Hill, Howard Deutch. **VHS, Beta** $19.98 *WAR, MOV* 🎞️🎞️🎞️

Tales from the Darkside Each episode of this series features several short Twilight Zone-esque stories of fantasy and suspense. Additional tapes available.
1985 70m/C **VHS, Beta, LV** $29.95 *LIV, MOV* 🎞️🎞️½

Tales from the Darkside: The Movie Three short stories in the tradition of the ghoulish TV show are brought to the big screen, with mixed results. The plot centers around a boy who is being held captive by a cannibal. In order to prolong his life, he tells her horror stories. The tales were written by Sir Arthur Conan Doyle, Stephen King, and Michael McDowell.
1990 (R) 93m/C Deborah Harry, Christian Slater, David Johansen, William Hickey, James Remar, Rae Dawn Chong, Julianne Moore, Robert Klein; *D:* John Harrison. **VHS, Beta, LV** $14.95 *PAR* 🎞️🎞️🎞️

Tales from the Snow Zone "Tales from the Snow Zone" is the latest feature length ski film from RAP producers Jon Long and James Angrove. Filmed entirely in the 1991 ski season, this film captures the essence of the sport and lifestyle. "Tales" covers true extreme skiing, radical free skiing, moguls, downhill ski racing, telemarking, snowboarding, and monoskiing. Filmed in Europe and North America, "Tales" features skiers from the United States, Canada, France, Sweden, and Australia.
1991 70m/C **VHS** *RAP* 🎞️🎞️🎞️

Tales of Beatrix Potter The Royal Ballet Company of England performs in this adaptation of the adventures of Beatrix Potter's colorful and memorable creatures. Beautifully done. *AKA:* Peter Rabbit and Tales of Beatrix Potter.
1971 (G) 90m/C *GB D:* Reginald Mills. **VHS** $29.95 *HMV* 🎞️🎞️🎞️½

The Tales of Hoffman A ballet-opera consisting of three stories by Jacques Offenbach covering romance, magic and mystery arising out of a poet's misadventures in love. Lavishly designed and highly stylized.
1951 138m/C Robert Rounseville, Robert Helpmann, Moira Shearer; **D:** Michael Powell, Emeric Pressburger; **M:** Royal Philharmonic Orchestra. VHS $39.95 *HMV, PME ♫♫½*

Tales of Ordinary Madness Gazzara as a poet who drinks and sleeps with assorted women. Based on the stories of Charles Bukowski. Pretentious and dull.
1983 107m/C Ben Gazzara, Ornella Muti, Susan Tyrrell, Tanya Lopert, Roy Brocksmith, Katya Berger; **D:** Marco Ferreri. VHS, Beta $69.98 *LIV, VES ♫*

Tales of Robin Hood A low-budget depiction of the Robin Hood legend.
1952 59m/B Robert Clarke, Mary Hatcher; **D:** James Tinling. VHS, Beta, LV *NO ♫½*

Tales of Terror Three tales of terror based on stories by Edgar Allan Poe: "Morella," "The Black Cat," and the "The Case of M. Valdemar." Price stars in all three segments and is excellent as the bitter and resentful husband in "Morella." **AKA:** Poe's Tales of Terror.
1962 90m/C Vincent Price, Peter Lorre, Basil Rathbone, Debra Paget, Joyce Jameson; **D:** Roger Corman. VHS, Beta *MLB ♫♫*

Tales of the Klondike: In a Far Country An adaptation of Jack London's story exploring the fears, dangers, and joys experienced by prospectors in the harsh wilderness of northwest Canadian gold country.
1987 60m/C Robert Carradine, Scott Hylands; **D:** Janine Manatis. VHS, Beta $19.95 *AHV ♫♫*

Tales of the Klondike: Race for Number One Two men compete in a highly contested dog-sled race—the goal of which is to be the first to reach a tract of gold-laden land. Adapted from a story by Jack London.
1987 60m/C David Ferry, John Ireland; **D:** David Cobham. VHS, Beta $19.95 *AHV ♫♫*

Tales of the Klondike: The Scorn of Women An available man is enthusiastically courted by every single woman in Dawson City, Alaska. From a story by Jack London.
1987 60m/C Tom Butler, Eva Gabor; **D:** Claude Fournier. VHS, Beta $19.95 *AHV ♫♫*

Tales of the Klondike: The Unexpected Five gold prospectors grow rich, but lose all that is most valuable through overwhelming greed. Adapted from a story by Jack London.
1987 60m/C John Candy, Cherie Lunghi; **D:** Peter Pearson. VHS, Beta $19.95 *AHV ♫♫*

Tales of the Unexpected Four tales designed to startle the senses and provoke the imagination. Episodes include "People Don't Do Such Things," about a marriage gone awry, "Youth from Vienna," about a weird fountain of youth, "Skeleton in the Cupboard," which tells of a man desperately trying to hide some strange secret and finally, "Bird of Prey," in which a pet parrot leaves its owners an enormous egg before dying.
1991 101m/C Arthur Hill, Samantha Eggar, Don Johnson, Dick Smothers, Sharon Gless, James Carroll Jordan, Charles Dance, Zoe Wanamaker, Sondra Locke, Frank Converse; **D:** Gordon Hessler, Norman Lloyd, Paul Annett, Ray Danton. VHS, Beta, LV $69.95 *PSM, IME ♫♫½*

Tales of Washington Irving Animated adaptations of Irving's famous tales including "Legend of Sleepy Hollow" and "Rip Van Winkle."
1970 48m/C VHS, Beta $19.95 *MGM ♫♫½*

Tales That Witness Madness An asylum is the setting for four tales of horror, as a doctor tells a visitor how four patients ended up in his clinic. Stories are "Mr. Tiger," "Penny Farthing," "Mel" and "Luau." At the time this was Novak's first film appearance in four years.
1973 (R) 90m/C *GB* Jack Hawkins, Donald Pleasence, Suzy Kendall, Joan Collins, Kim Novak, Mary Tamm, Georgia Brown, Donald Houston, David Wood, Peter McEnery; **D:** Freddie Francis. VHS $14.95 *PAR ♫♫½*

Talion A western revenge movie that features two disabled men, a rancher and a bounty hunter, who team up to find the gang that slaughtered the rancher's family. **AKA:** An Eye for an Eye.
1966 (PG) 92m/C Robert Lansing, Slim Pickens, Patrick Wayne; **D:** Michael Moore. VHS, Beta $9.95 *COL, NLC, QVD ♫♫*

Talk of the Town A brilliantly cast, strange mixture of screwball comedy and lynch-mob melodramatics co-written by Irwin Shaw. An accused arsonist, a Supreme Court judge and the girl they both love try to clear the former's name and evade the cops.
1942 118m/B Ronald Colman, Cary Grant, Jean Arthur, Edgar Buchanan, Glenda Farrell, Rex Ingram, Emma Dunn; **D:** George Stevens. VHS, Beta, LV $69.95 *COL ♫♫♫*

Talk Radio Riveting Stone adaptation of Bogosian's one-man play. An acidic talk radio host confronts America's evil side and his own past over the airwaves. The main character is loosely based on the life of Alan Berg, a Denver talk show host who was murdered by white supremacists.
1988 (R) 110m/C Eric Bogosian, Alec Baldwin, Ellen Greene, John Pankow, John C. McGinley, Michael Wincott, Leslie Hope; **D:** Oliver Stone; **W:** Eric Bogosian, Oliver Stone. VHS, Beta, LV $19.95 *MCA ♫♫♫*

Talk to Me A successful New York accountant checks into the Hollins Communication Institute to cure his stuttering. While there, he meets and falls in love with a squirrel-hunting stuttering woman from Arkansas.
1982 90m/C Austin Pendleton, Michael Murphy, Louise Fletcher, Brian Backer, Clifton James. VHS, Beta $59.98 *FOX ♫♫½*

Talkin' Dirty After Dark Sexy comedy starring Lawrence as a suave comedian who will do anything to get a late-night spot at Dukie's comedy club.
1991 (R) 89m/C Martin Lawrence, Jedda Jones, Phyllis Stickney, Darryl Sivad; **W/D:** Topper Carew. VHS $14.95 *NLC, FCT ♫♫*

The Talking Parcel An animated film about a parrot sweeping a young girl off to a fantasy world. Based on the book by Gerald Durrell.
1984 40m/C VHS, Beta $12.99 *HBO ♫♫*

Talking Walls A college sociology student uses high-tech surveillance equipment to spy on the clients of a seedy motel, in order to complete his thesis on human sexuality. **AKA:** Motel Vacancy.
1985 85m/C Stephen Shellan, Marie Laurin, Barry Primus, Sally Kirkland; **D:** Stephen Verona. VHS, Beta $19.95 *STE, NWV ♫½*

The Tall Blond Man with One Black Shoe A violinist is completely unaware that rival spies mistakenly think he is also a spy, and that he is the center of a plot to booby-trap an overly ambitious agent at the French Secret Service. A sequel followed called "Return of the Tall Blond Man with One Black Shoe" which was followed by a disappointing American remake, "The Man with One Red Shoe." In French with English subtitles or dubbed. **AKA:** Le Grand Blond Avec Une Chaussure Noire.
1972 (PG) 90m/C *FR* Pierre Richard, Bernard Blier, Jean Rochefort, Mireille Darc, Jean Carmet; **D:** Yves Robert. VHS, Beta, 8mm $59.95 *CVC, COL, VYY ♫♫♫*

The Tall Guy Goldblum is a too-tall actor who tries the scene in London and lands the lead in a musical version of 'The Elephant Man,' becoming an overnight success. Not consistently funny, but good British comedy, including an interesting sex scene.
1989 (R) 92m/C Jeff Goldblum, Emma Thompson, Rowan Atkinson, Geraldine James; **D:** Mel Smith; **W:** Richard Curtis. VHS, LV $89.95 *COL, FCT ♫♫♫*

Tall in the Saddle A misogynist foreman (Wayne) finds himself accused of murder. Meanwhile, he falls in love with his female boss's niece. An inoffensive and memorable western.
1944 79m/B John Wayne, Ella Raines, George "Gabby" Hayes, Ward Bond; **D:** Edwin L. Marin. VHS, Beta, LV $19.95 *MED, TTC ♫♫½*

Tall Lie A student quits a fraternity hazing exercise. He's pursued by a psychotic bunch of his fraternity brothers and is killed in a smash-up. A local doctor goes onto an anti-hazing campaign in the aftermath. **AKA:** For Men Only.
1953 93m/B Paul Henreid, Robert Sherman; **D:** Paul Henreid. VHS, Beta, LV *NO ♫♫*

The Tall Men Standard western features frontier hands on a rough cattle drive confronting Indians, outlaws, and the wilderness while vying with each other for the love of Russell.
1955 122m/C Clark Gable, Jane Russell, Robert Ryan, Cameron Mitchell, Mae Marsh; **D:** Raoul Walsh. VHS, Beta $19.98 *FOX ♫♫*

Tall Story Perkins is a star basketball player who must pass a crucial test in order to continue to play the game. In addition to the pressure of the exam, he is being pressured by gamblers to throw a game against the Russians. Fonda makes her screen debut as a cheerleader who is so awe-struck by Perkins that she takes the same classes just to be close to him. Based on the play by Howard Lindsay and Russel Crouse, and the novel "The Homecoming Game" by Howard Nemerov.
1960 91m/C Anthony Perkins, Jane Fonda, Ray Walston, Marc Connelly, Anne Jackson, Tom Laughlin; **D:** Joshua Logan. VHS, LV $19.98 *WEA ♫♫*

The Tall T A veteran rancher (Pat) stumbles onto big trouble when by chance he catches a stage coach that is eventually overrun by an evil band of cut-throats. After killing everyone on the coach except Pat and the daughter of a wealthy copper mine owner (Doretta), the renegades decide to leave the seen with the unfortunate two as hostages. Pat and Doretta, although in dire straights, find time to fall in love and devise an intricate plan for their escape. Regarded in certain western-lover circles as a cult classic.
1957 77m/B Randolph Scott, Richard Boone, Maureen O'Sullivan, Arthur Hunnicutt, Skip Homeier, Henry Silva, Robert Burton, Robert Anderson; **D:** Budd Boetticher; **W:** Burt Kennedy. VHS *GKK ♫♫*

Tall, Tan and Terrific Things really go crazy when the owner of a nightclub in Harlem is accused of murder.
1946 40m/C Mantan Moreland, Monte Hawley, Francine Everett, Dots Johnson; **D:** Bud Pollard. **VHS, Beta** $24.95 NOS *½*

Tall Texan A motley crew seeks gold in an Indian burial ground in the desert. Flawed but interesting and suspenseful. Greed, lust, Indians and desert heat.
1953 82m/B Lloyd Bridges, Lee J. Cobb, Marie Windsor, George Steele; **D:** Elmo Williams. **VHS, Beta, LV** RXM *½½*

Talons of the Eagle Martial arts adventure centers around three undercover agents who go up against crimelord Mr. Li (Hong). To impress Li, martial arts champion Tyler Wilson (Blanks) and vice detective Michael Reeds (Merhi) enter a deadly martial arts tournament. They later hook up with beautiful agent Cassandra Hubbard (Barnes), who has already investigated Li's drug, gambling, and prostitution rings. Features the most advanced fighting techniques ever filmed.
1992 (R) 96m/C Billy Blanks, Jalal Merhi, James Hong, Priscilla Barnes, Matthias Hues; **D:** Michael Kennedy; **W:** J. Stephen Maunder. **VHS, LV** MCA *½½*

Tamango A confusing drama set on a slave ship travelling from Africa to Cuba in 1830. Jurgens is the ship's captain who takes the black Dandridge as his mistress. Meanwhile, the slaves are plotting a revolt, with Dandridge as a conspirator. Will Jurgens quell the rebellion and still keep his mistress? The interracial romance does takes a secondary role to the racial conflicts. The title refers to the leader of the slave revolt, played by Cressan. Filmed in both English- and French-language versions.
1959 98m/C FR Curt Jurgens, Dorothy Dandridge, Jean Servais, Alex Cressan; **D:** John Berry. **VHS** $29.95 IVY *½½*

The Tamarind Seed Andrews and Sharif are star-crossed lovers kept apart by Cold War espionage. Dated, dull and desultory.
1974 123m/C Julie Andrews, Omar Sharif, Anthony Quayle, Dan O'Herlihy, Sylvia Syms; **D:** Blake Edwards; **M:** John Barry. **VHS, Beta** $24.98 SUE *½½*

The Tamer of Wild Horses A parody of the mechanized world.
1967 8m/C **VHS, Beta** NO *½½*

The Taming of the Shrew Historically interesting early talkie featuring sole (if perhaps unfortunate) pairing of Pickford and Fairbanks. Features the legendary credit line "By William Shakespeare, with additional dialogue by Sam Taylor." Re-edited in 1966; 1967 Zeffirelli remake featured Taylor and Burton.
1929 66m/B Mary Pickford, Douglas Fairbanks Sr., Edwin Maxwell, Joseph Cawthorn; **D:** Sam Taylor. **VHS, Beta, LV** $19.95 NOS, CCB *½½½*

The Taming of the Shrew A lavish screen version of the classic Shakespearean comedy. Burton and Taylor are violently physical and perfectly cast as the battling Katherine and Petruchio. At the time the film was made, Burton and Taylor were having their own marital problems, which not only added an inner fire to their performances, but sent the interested moviegoers to the theatres in droves.
1967 122m/C IT Elizabeth Taylor, Richard Burton, Michael York, Michael Hordern, Cyril Cusack; **D:** Franco Zeffirelli. Academy Awards '67 Nominations: Best Art Direction/Set Decoration, Best Costume Design; National Board of Review Awards '67: 10 Best Films of

the Year. **VHS, Beta, LV** $19.95 COL, TVC *½½½*

The Taming of the Shrew The classic Shakespearean comedy about the battle of the sexes where Petruchio attempts to tame his fiery, free-spirited wife, Kate.
1981 152m/C **D:** Peter Dews. **VHS, Beta** $59.95 SUE *½½*

Tammy and the Bachelor A backwoods Southern girl becomes involved with a romantic pilot and his snobbish family. They don't quite know what to make of her but she wins them over with her down-home philosophy. Features the hit tune, "Tammy." Charming performance by Reynolds.
1957 89m/C Debbie Reynolds, Leslie Nielsen, Walter Brennan, Fay Wray, Sidney Blackmer, Mildred Natwick, Louise Beavers; **D:** Joseph Pevney. **VHS, Beta** $14.98 MCA *½½*

Tammy and the Doctor Sandra Dee reprises Debbie Reynolds's backwoods gal ("Tammy and the Bachelor"). Dee becomes a nurse's aide and is wooed by doctor Fonda, in his film debut.
1963 88m/C Sandra Dee, Peter Fonda, MacDonald Carey; **D:** Harry Keller. **VHS, Beta** $14.98 MCA *½½*

Tampopo A hilarious, episodic Japanese comedy. A widowed noodle shop owner is coached by a ten-gallon-hatted stranger in how to make the perfect noodle. Popular, free-form hit that established Itami in the West. In Japanese with English subtitles.
1986 114m/C JP Ken Watanabe, Tsutomu Yamazaki, Nobuko Miyamoto, Koji Yakusho, Rikiya Yasuoka, Kinzo Sakura, Shoji Otake; **D:** Juzo Itami. **VHS, LV** $79.95 REP, TAM *½½½*

Tangiers The disappearance of a British intelligence agent in Gibraltar sets off a chain-reaction of violent incidents.
1983 82m/C Ronny Cox. **VHS** WAR *½*

Tango An early melodrama follows the ups and down of a chorus girl and the guy who sticks with her through thick and thin and poorly-filmed dance routines. Based on a novel by Vida Hurst.
1936 66m/B Marion Nixon, Chick Chandler, Matty Kemp, Marie Prevost, Warren Hymer, Herman Bing, Franklin Pangborn, George Meeker; **D:** Phil Rosen. **VHS** $15.95 NOS, LOO *½½*

Tango and Cash Stallone and Russell are L.A. cops with something in common: they both think they are the best in the city. Forced to work together to beat drug lord Palance, they flex their muscles a lot. Directing completed by Albert Magnoli, after Andrei Konchalovsky left in a huff.
1989 (R) 104m/C Sylvester Stallone, Kurt Russell, Jack Palance, Brion James, Teri Hatcher, Michael J. Pollard, James Hong, Marc Alaimo, Robert Z'Dar; **D:** Andrei Konchalovsky. **VHS, Beta, LV, 8mm** $19.98 WAR *½½*

Tango Bar A romantic triangle between a tango dancer who leaves Argentina during a time of political unrest, his former partner, and his wife, who both stay behind. They are reunited after years of separation. Gives the viewer a detailed vision of the historical and cultural significance of the tango. Charming, interesting and very watchable. In Spanish with English subtitles.
1988 90m/C AR Raul Julia, Valeria Lynch, Ruben Juarez; **D:** Marcos Zurinaga. **VHS, Beta** $79.95 WAR, TAM *½½½*

Tank Retired Army officer Garner's son is thrown into jail on a trumped-up charge by a small town sheriff. Dad comes to the rescue with his restored Sherman tank. Trite and unrealistic portrayal of good versus bad made palatable by Garner's performance.

1983 (PG) 113m/C James Garner, Shirley Jones, C. Thomas Howell, Mark Herrier, Sandy Ward, Jenilee Harrison, Dorian Harewood, G.D. Spradlin; **D:** Marvin J. Chomsky. **VHS, Beta, LV** $19.95 MCA *½½*

Tank Commando Mediocre World War II actioner, set in Italy, about a demolition squad of battle-hardened Americans trying to locate a secret German crossing point. It turns out to be an underwater bridge and an Italian orphan is the only one, besides the Germans, to know its location. Can the Americans persuade the kid to talk?
1959 79m/B Robert Barron, Wally Campo, Maggie Lawrence, Donato Farretta, Leo V. Metranga, Jack Sowards, Anthony Rich, Larry Hudson; **W/D:** Burt Topper. **VHS** $9.95 COL *½*

Tanks a Million Despite the title, tanks aren't even mentioned in this. Tracy stars as a wacky genius who gets drafted. His excellent memory keeps getting him into one predicament after another. Though he gets promoted quickly, he shows himself no leader. Lots of time-worn gags, but they still work.
1941 50m/B William Tracy, James Gleason, Noah Beery Jr., Joe Sawyer, Elyse Knox, Douglas Fowley, Frank Faylen, Dick Wessel, Frank Melton, Harold Goodwin, William Gould, Norman Kerry; **D:** Fred Guiol. **VHS** $19.95 NOS *½½*

Tanner '88 Murphy is excellent as a longshot politician on the trail of the Democratic presidential nomination. Story by Gary Trudeau of Doonesbury fame. A precise political satire made for cable. **AKA:** Tanner: A Political Fable.
1988 120m/C Michael Murphy, Pamela Reed, Cynthia Nixon; **D:** Robert Altman. **VHS, LV** $79.99 PAV, HBO, TAM *½½½*

Tanya's Island Abused girlfriend fantasizes about life on deserted island and romance with an ape. Vanity billed as D.D. Winters.
1981 (R) 100m/C Vanity, Richard Sargent, Mariette Levesque, Don McCleod; **D:** Alfred Sole. **VHS, Beta** NO *½½½*

Taoism Drunkard It's alcoholism at its funniest as a juice-guzzling martial artist goes nuts.
19?? 100m/C Yuen Tat Chor, Yuen Cheung Yan, Chu Hai Ling. **VHS, Beta** $49.95 OCE *½½*

Tap The son of a famous tap dancer, a dancer himself, decides to try to get away from his former life of crime by helping an aging hoofer revitalize the art of tap dancing. Fun to watch for the wonderful dancing scenes. Davis' last big screen appearance. Hines is sincere in this old-fashioned story, and dances up a storm. Captures some never-before filmed old hoofers.
1989 (PG-13) 106m/C Gregory Hines, Sammy Davis Jr., Suzanne Douglas, Joe Morton; **D:** Nick Castle. **VHS, Beta, LV** $14.95 COL *½½½*

Tapeheads Silly, sophomonic, sexy comedy starring Cusack and Robbins as young wannabe rock-video producers who strike it big. Many big-name cameos; good soundtrack; laughs.
1989 (R) 93m/C John Cusack, Tim Robbins, Mary Crosby, Connie Stevens, Susan Tyrrell, Lyle Alzado, Don Cornelius, Katy Boyer, Doug McClure, Clu Gulager, Jessica Walter; **Cameos:** Stiv Bators, Sam Moore, Junior Walker, Martha Quinn, Ted Nugent, Don Cornelius, Weird Al Yankovic; **D:** Bill Fishman. **VHS, Beta, LV** $19.95 PAV *½½*

T

Taps Military academy students led by Hutton are so true to their school they lay siege to it to keep it from being closed. An antiwar morality play about excesses of zeal and patriotism. Predictable but impressive.
1981 (PG) 126m/C Timothy Hutton, George C. Scott, Ronny Cox, Sean Penn, Tom Cruise; D: Harold Becker. VHS, Beta $19.98 FOX ⅃⅃½

Tarantula If you're into gigantic killer insect movies this is one of the best with nifty special effects and some good action. Carroll plays a scientist working on a growth formula which he's testing on a spider when it accidentally gets loose. This eight-legged horror grows to 100 feet high and causes havoc in the Arizona desert until the Air Force napalms the sucker. Look for Eastwood in the final sequence as an Air Force pilot.
1955 81m/B Leo G. Carroll, John Agar, Mara Corday, Nestor Paiva, Ross Elliott, Clint Eastwood; D: Jack Arnold; W: Robert M. Fresco, Martin Berkeley. VHS $14.98 MCA ⅃⅃⅃

Tarantulas: The Deadly Cargo Eek! Hairy spiders terrizing our sleepy town and destroying our orange crop! Made-for-TV cheapie not creepy; will make you sleepy.
1977 100m/C Claude Akins, Charles Frank, Deborah Winters, Pat Hingle, Sandy McPeak, Bert Remsen, Howard Hesseman, Tom Atkins, Charles Siebert; D: Stuart Hagmann. VHS $49.95 LIV ⅃

Taras Bulba Well-photographed costume epic on the 16th century Polish revolution. Brynner as the fabled Cossack; Curtis plays his vengeful son. Good score. Shot on location in Argentina. Based on the novel by Nikolai Gogol.
1962 122m/C Tony Curtis, Yul Brynner, Christine Kaufmann, Sam Wanamaker, George Macready, Vladimir Sokoloff, Perry Lopez; D: J. Lee Thompson. VHS, LV $24.95 MGM ⅃⅃½

Target Normal dad/hubby Hackman slips into a figurative phone booth and emerges as former CIA when his better half is kidnapped in Paris. Good action scenes, but poorly scripted and too long. Matt Dillon is the teenaged son.
1985 117m/C Gene Hackman, Matt Dillon, Gayle Hunnicutt, Josef Sommer; D: Arthur Penn. VHS, Beta, LV $19.98 FOX ⅃⅃

Target Eagle Spanish police chief von Sydow hires mercenary Rivero to infiltrate drug ring. Good performances; ho-hum story.
1984 99m/C SP MX Max von Sydow, George Peppard, Maud Adams, Chuck Connors, George Rivero, Susana Dosamantes; D: J. Anthony Loma. VHS, Beta NO ⅃⅃

Target: Favorite Son An attractive, ammunition-laden woman sharp-shoots her way to power in this made-for-TV movie.
1987 (R) 115m/C Linda Kozlowski, Harry Hamlin, Robert Loggia, Ronny Cox, James Whitmore. VHS $89.95 VMK ⅃⅃

Targets Bogdanovich's suspenseful directorial debut. An aging horror film star plans his retirement, convinced that real life is too scary for his films to have an audience. A mad sniper at a drive-in movie seems to prove he's right. Some prints still have anti-gun prologue, which was added after Robert Kennedy's assassination.
1969 (PG) 90m/C Boris Karloff, James Brown, Tim O'Kelly; D: Peter Bogdanovich. VHS, Beta $44.95 PAR ⅃⅃⅃

Tarka the Otter The story of Tarka the Otter who encounters many dangers as he pursues his favorite eel meals.
198? 91m/C VHS, Beta $39.95 TWE ⅃⅃⅃

Taro, the Dragon Boy A young boy searches for his mother who has been turned into a dragon.
1985 75m/C VHS, Beta $19.95 COL, WTA ⅃⅃⅃

Tartuffe Popular French leading man Depardieu makes directorial debut with Moliere classic about religious hypocrisy and an imposter taking advantage of a wealthy merchant and his family. In French with English subtitles.
1984 140m/C FR Gerard Depardieu, Francois Perier, Elisabeth Depardieu; D: Gerard Depardieu. VHS, LV $79.95 CVC, FCT, APD ⅃⅃½

Tartuffe Moliere's famous comedy has Tartuffe posing as a holy man who has attracted the incredulous merchant Orgon. Orgon is willing to give Tartuffe anything—money, social position, even his daughter—and Tartuffe is more than happy to accept.
1990 110m/C Anthony Sher, Nigel Hawthorne, Alison Steadman; D: Bill Alexander. VHS, Beta $39.95 TTC, TAM ⅃⅃½

Tarzan and His Mate Second entry in the lavishly produced MGM Tarzan series. Weissmuller and O'Sullivan cohabit in unmarried bliss before the Hays Code moved them to a tree house with twin beds. Many angry elephants, nasty white hunters, and hungry lions. Laserdisc includes the original trailer.
1934 93m/B Johnny Weissmuller, Maureen O'Sullivan, Neil Hamilton, Paul Cavanagh; D: Jack Conway. VHS, LV $19.98 MGM, FCT ⅃⅃⅃

Tarzan and the Green Goddess Tarzan searches for a statue that could prove dangerous if in the wrong hands. AKA: New Adventures of Tarzan.
1938 72m/B Herman Brix, Ula Holt, Frank Baker; D: Edward Kull. VHS, Beta $19.95 HHT, SNC ⅃⅃

Tarzan and the Trappers Bad-guy trappers and would-be treasure-seekers wish they hadn't messed with the ape man.
1958 74m/B Gordon Scott, Eve Brent, Ricky Sorenson, Maurice Marsac, Cheetah; D: H. Bruce Humberstone. VHS, Beta $16.95 SNC, NOS, VYY ⅃½

Tarzan Escapes Jane is tricked by evil hunters into abandoning her fairy tale life with Tarzan, so the Ape Man sets out to reunite with his one true love. The third entry in MGM's Weissmuller/O'Sullivan series is still among the better Tarzan movies thanks to the leads, but the Hays Office made sure Jane was wearing a lot more clothes this time around.
1936 95m/B Johnny Weissmuller, Maureen O'Sullivan, John Buckler, Benita Hume, William Henry; D: Richard Thorpe. VHS $19.98 FOX, FCT ⅃⅃⅃

Tarzan Finds a Son Weissmuller and O'Sullivan returned to their roles after three years with the addition of the five-year-old Sheffield as Boy. He's an orphan whose awful relatives hope he stays lost so they can collect an inheritance. Jane and Tarzan fight to adopt the tyke and when the new family are captured by a wicked tribe only an elephant stampede can save them!
1939 90m/B Johnny Weissmuller, Maureen O'Sullivan, Johnny Sheffield, Ian Hunter, Henry Stephenson, Frieda Inescort, Henry Wilcoxon; D: Richard Thorpe. VHS $19.98 MGM ⅃⅃⅃

Tarzan of the Apes Brawny Lincoln is the original screen Tarzan. Silent film well done and more faithful to the book than later versions.
1917 63m/B Elmo Lincoln, Enid Markey; D: Scott Sidney. VHS, Beta, 3/4U, Special order formats $19.95 NOS, VYY, WFV ⅃⅃

Tarzan, the Ape Man The definitive Tarzan movie; the first Tarzan talkie; the original of the long series starring Weissmuller. Dubiously faithful to the Edgar Rice Burroughs story, but recent attempts to remake, update or improve it (notably the pretentious 1984 Greystoke) have failed to near the original's entertainment value or even its technical quality. O'Sullivan as Jane and Weissmuller bring style and wit to their classic roles.
1932 99m/B Johnny Weissmuller, Maureen O'Sullivan, Neil Hamilton; D: Woodbridge S. Van Dyke. VHS, Beta, LV $19.98 MGM, FCT ⅃⅃⅃

Tarzan, the Ape Man Plodding, perverted excuse to see Derek cavort nude in jungle. So bad not even hard-core Tarzan fans should bother.
1981 (R) 112m/C Bo Derek, Richard Harris, John Phillip Law, Miles O'Keeffe; D: John Derek. VHS, Beta, LV $79.95 MGM Woof!

Tarzan the Fearless Tarzan (Crabbe) helps a young girl find her missing father.
1933 84m/B Buster Crabbe, Jacqueline Wells, F Allen Warren, Eddie Woods, Philo McCullough, Matthew Betz; D: Robert Hill. VHS, Beta, 3/4U, Special order formats $16.95 SNC, NOS, CAB ⅃½

Tarzan the Tiger Series of 15 chapters is loosely based on the Edgar Rice Burroughs novel entitled "Tarzan and the Jewels of Opar." These chapters were filmed as silent pieces, and were later released with a musical score and synchronized sound effects. Here Merrill is the first to sound the cry of the bull ape, Tarzan's trademark.
1929 ?m/B Frank Merrill, Natalie Kingston, Lilian Worth, Al Ferguson; D: Henry MacRae. VHS $49.95 NOS, FCT, MOV ⅃½

Tarzan's New York Adventure O'Sullivan's final appearance as Jane is a so-so adventure with some humorous moments when Tarzan meets the big city. When Boy is kidnapped by an evil circus owner, Tarzan, Jane, and Cheta head out to rescue him. Tarzan shows off his jungle prowess by climbing skyscrapers and diving off the Brooklyn Bridge into the Hudson River. Lincoln, the screen's first Tarzan, has a cameo.
1942 70m/B Johnny Weissmuller, Maureen O'Sullivan, Johnny Sheffield, Virginia Grey, Charles Bickford, Paul Kelly, Chill Wills, Russell Hicks, Cy Kendall; Cameos: Elmo Lincoln; D: Richard Thorpe. VHS $19.98 MGM ⅃⅃½

Tarzan's Revenge Morris is a better Olympic runner than actor; Holm is horrible. Only for serious Tarzan fans.
1938 70m/B Glenn Morris, Eleanor Holm, Hedda Hopper; D: Ross Lederman. VHS, Beta $16.95 SNC, NOS, VYY ⅃

Tarzan's Secret Treasure Tarzan saves an expedition from a savage tribe only to be repaid by having the greedy hunters hold Jane and Boy hostage. They want Tarzan's help in finding a secret cache of gold. But Tarzan doesn't take kindly to threats to his family and teaches those evildoers a lesson!
1941 81m/B Johnny Weissmuller, Maureen O'Sullivan, Johnny Sheffield, Reginald Owen, Barry Fitzgerald, Tom Conway, Philip Dorn; D: Richard Thorpe. VHS $19.98 MGM ⅃⅃½

A Taste for Flesh and Blood A monster from outer space comes to earth and is delighted with the easy pickings for his insatiable appetite. A brave boy and girl, and a NASA commander must join forces to take the alien out. This one is billed as a campy salute to '50s B movies.
1990 (R) 84m/C Rubin Santiago, Lori Karz, Tim Ferrante. VHS NO ⅃⅃½

A Taste for Killing Two boys, both from well-to-do families, decide to take summer jobs on an offshore Texas oil rig. The best friends think a summer of adventure awaits them; however, their lives are made miserable by their blue-collar boss, who is resentful of their high society background. Then they meet Bo Landry, who befriends them and helps them survive. Unfortunately, Bo turns out to be anything but a friend as he reveals himself as a deadly con-artist in this intense psychological thriller.
1992 (R) 87m/C Jason Bateman, Henry Thomas, Michael Biehn, Blue Deckert, Helen Cates; **D:** Lou Antonio; **W:** Dan Bronson. **VHS, LV $89.98** *MCA* �ⅈ

Taste of Death A youth discovers his courage within when he stands up to the bandits invading his village.
1977 90m/C John Ireland. **VHS, Beta** *WWV* ⅈ

A Taste of Hell Two American soldiers fight a guerilla outfit in the Pacific during World War II. A low-budget film with few redeeming characteristics.
1973 (PG) 90m/C William Smith, John Garwood. **VHS, Beta $19.95** *NWV, STE* ⅈ

A Taste of Honey A plain working-class girl falls in love with a black sailor. When she becomes pregnant, a homosexual friend helps her out. A moving film with strong, powerful performances. Based on the London and Broadway hit play by She-lagh Delaney.
1961 100m/B *GB* Rita Tushingham, Robert Stephens, Dora Bryan, Murray Melvin, Paul Danquah; **D:** Tony Richardson. **VHS** *NO* ⅈⅈⅈ

Taste the Blood of Dracula Lee's Dracula only makes a brief appearance in this Hammer horror film which has three children taking over from the bloodsucker. Three Victorian dandies have killed the wizard who revived Dracula and he seeks their deaths by using their own children as the means of his revenge. Not enough Lee but still creepy. Preceded by "Dracula Has Risen from the Grave" and followed by "Scars of Dracula."
1970 (PG) 91m/C *GB* Christopher Lee, Ralph Bates, Geoffrey Keen, Gwen Watford, Linda Hayden, John Carson, Peter Sallis, Isla Blair, Martin Jarvis, Roy Kinnear; **D:** Peter Sasdy. **VHS $19.98** *WAR* ⅈⅈ½

Tatie Danielle Pitch-black comedy from the director of "Life Is a Long Quiet River" sees a bitter, elderly widow moving in with her young nephew and making his life a hell. In French with yellow English subtitles.
1991 114m/C *FR* Tsilla Chelton, Catherine Jacob, Isabelle Nanty, Neige Dolsky, Eric Prat, Laurence Fevrier; **D:** Etienne Chatiliez. **VHS, LV $19.98** *LIV, TAM* ⅈⅈⅈ

The Tattered Web A police sergeant confronts and accidently kills the woman with whom his son-in-law has been cheating. He's then assigned the case. When he tries to frame a wino for the murder, things get more and more messy. Fine performances aid this made-for-television story.
1971 74m/C Lloyd Bridges, Frank Converse, Broderick Crawford, Murray Hamilton, Sallie Shockley; **D:** Paul Wendkos. **VHS, Beta $59.95** *LHV* ⅈⅈ

Tattoo A model becomes the object of obsession for a crazy tattoo artist. He relentlessly pursues her, leaving behind all his other more illustrated clients. Starts out fine, but deteriorates rapidly. Controversial love scene between Dern and Adams.
1981 (R) 103m/C Bruce Dern, Maud Adams, Leonard Frey, Rikke Borge, John Getz; **D:** Bob Brooks. **VHS, Beta $19.98** *FOX* ⅈⅈ

Tattoo Connection A gang of lethal Oriental diamond thieves is pursued with whip-snapping flamboyance by a taciturn kung-fu investigator.
1978 (R) 95m/C Jim Kelly; **D:** Luk Pak Sang. **VHS, Beta $9.98** *SUE* ⅈ

Tattooed Dragon Even the dumbest of grisly gangs should know better than to toy with the Tattooed Dragon, but they don't.
1982 (R) 91m/C Jimmy Wang Yu; **D:** Lo Wei. **VHS, Beta $9.98** *SUE* ⅈ

Tattooed Hit Man Japanese gangster violence in a revenge-doesn't-pay action story.
1976 81m/C *JP* Mayumi Nagisa, Bunta Sugawara, Tsunehiko Watase. **VHS, Beta $59.95** *MED* ⅈ

Tax Season A small-time businessman buys a Hollywood tax service sight-unseen, and finds it employing a hooker, a bookie and a variety of other unconventional types.
1990 (PG-13) 93m/C Fritz Bronner, James Hong, Jana Grant, Toru Tanaka, Dorie Krum, Kathryn Knotts, Arte Johnson, Rob Slyker; **D:** Tom Law. **VHS, Beta $29.95** *PAR* ⅈⅈ

Taxi Blues A political allegory with the two protagonists representing the new and old Soviet Union. A hard-working, narrow-minded cabdriver keeps the saxophone of a westernized, Jewish, jazz-loving musician who doesn't have his fare. The two strike up a wary friendship as each tries to explain his view of life to the other. Good look at the street life of Moscow populated by drunks, punks, and black marketeers. Directorial debut of Lounguine. In Russian with English subtitles.
1990 110m/C *RU* Piotr Mamonov, Piotr Zaitchenko, Natalia Koliakanova, Vladimir Kachpour; **W/D:** Pavel Lounguine. **VHS $89.95** *NYF, TAM* ⅈⅈⅈ½

Taxi Driver A psychotic New York City taxi driver tries to save a child prostitute and becomes infatuated with an educated political campaigner. He goes on a violent rampage when his dreams don't work out. Repellant, frightening vision of alienation and urban catharsis. On-target performances from Foster and De Niro. The laserdisc version is slightly longer, with commentary by Scorsese and screenwriter Paul Schrader, storyboards, complete screenplay, and Scorsese's production photos.
1976 (R) 112m/C Robert De Niro, Jodie Foster, Harvey Keitel, Cybill Shepherd, Peter Boyle, Albert Brooks; **D:** Martin Scorsese; **W:** Paul Schrader. Academy Awards '76 Nominations: Best Actor (De Niro), Best Picture, Best Supporting Actress (Foster), Best Original Score; British Academy Awards '76: Best Supporting Actress (Foster); Cannes Film Festival '76: Best Film; Los Angeles Film Critics Association Awards '76: Best Actor (De Niro); New York Film Critics Awards '76: Best Actor (De Niro); National Society of Film Critics Awards '76: Best Actor (De Niro), Best Director (Scorsese), Best Supporting Actress (Foster). **VHS, Beta, LV, 8mm $14.95** *COL, VYG* ⅈⅈⅈ

The Taxi Mystery Guy saves Broadway starlet from band of ne'er-do-wells thanks to deserted taxi, then tries to figure out who she is, unaware that her sinister understudy plans to do her in.
1926 50m/B Edith Roberts, Robert Agnew, Virginia Pearson, Phillips Smalley; **D:** Fred Windermere. **VHS, Beta $16.95** *GPV* ⅈ

Taxi zum Klo An autobiographical semi-documentary about the filmmaker's aimless existence and attempts at homosexual affairs after being fired from his job as a teacher. Explicit. In German with English subtitles. Sordid sexual situations.

1981 98m/C *GE* Bernd Broaderup, Frank Ripploh; **D:** Frank Ripploh. **VHS, Beta $79.95** *FCT, GLV, CCN* ⅈⅈⅈ

A Taxing Woman Satiric Japanese comedy about a woman tax collector in pursuit of a crafty millionaire tax cheater. Followed by the equally hilarious "A Taxing Woman's Return." In Japanese with English subtitles. **AKA:** Marusa No Onna.
1987 127m/C *JP* Nobuko Miyamoto, Tsutomu Yamazaki; **D:** Juzo Itami. **VHS, Beta, LV $39.95** *LUM, TAM, FXL* ⅈⅈⅈ½

A Taxing Woman Returns Funny, sophisticated, action-packed. Miyamoto returns as the dedicated tax investigator to fight industrialists, politicians, and other big swindlers, who have contrived to inflate Tokyo's real estate values. Sequel to "A Taxing Woman." In Japanese with English subtitles. **AKA:** Marusa No Onna II.
1988 127m/C *JP* Nobuko Miyamoto, Rentaro Mikuni, Masahiko Tsugawa, Tetsuro Tamba, Toru Masuoka, Takeya Nakamura, Hosei Komatsu, Mihoko Shibata; **W/D:** Juzo Itami. **VHS, LV $79.95** *NYF, TAM* ⅈⅈⅈ

Tchao Pantin An acclaimed French film noir about an ex-cop being drawn into drug smuggling underground via a young Arab. English subtitles. Finely drawn characters skillfully portrayed make this a winner.
1984 100m/C *FR* Coluche, Richard Anconina, Agnes Soral; **D:** Claude Berri. **VHS, Beta $29.98** *SUE* ⅈⅈⅈ

Tea and Sympathy A young prep school student, confused about his sexuality, has an affair with an older woman, his teacher's wife. The three leads recreate their Broadway roles in this tame adaption of the Robert Anderson play which dealt more openly with the story's homosexual elements.
1956 122m/C Deborah Kerr, John Kerr, Leif Erickson, Edward Andrews, Darryl Hickman, Norma Crane, Dean Jones; **D:** Vincente Minnelli. **VHS, LV $19.98** *MGM, FCT* ⅈⅈⅈ

Tea For Three Sexual trio develops and seeks therapy after a fledgling doctor has been having sexual relationships with two women, and the females finally meet.
1984 (R) 89m/C Iris Berben, Mascha Gonska, Heinz Marecek; **D:** Gerhard Janda. **VHS, Beta** *MED* ⅈ

Tea for Two This take-off on the Broadway play "No, No, Nanette" features Day as an actress who takes a bet that she can answer "no" to every question for twenty-four hours (life was less complex back then). If she can, she gets to finance and star in her own Broadway musical. ♫I Know That You Know; Crazy Rhythm; Charleston; I Only Have Eyes For You; Tea For Two; I Want to be Happy; Oh Me, Oh My; The Call of the Sea; Do Do Do; No, No, Nanette.
1950 98m/C Doris Day, Gordon MacRae, Gene Nelson, Patrice Wymore, Eve Arden, Billy DeWolfe, S.Z. Sakall, Bill Goodwin, Bill Gibson, Virginia Gibson, Crauford Kent, Harry Harvey; **D:** David Butler. **VHS $19.98** *WAR, CCB* ⅈⅈ

The Teacher TV's "Dennis the Menace" (North) has an affair with his high school teacher; the pair is menaced by a deranged killer. Cheap but enjoyable. **AKA:** The Seductress.
1974 (R) 97m/C Angel Tompkins, Jay North, Anthony James; **D:** Hikmet Avedis. **VHS, Beta, LV $29.98** *VID* ⅈⅈ

Teachers A lawsuit is brought against a high school for awarding a diploma to an illiterate student. Comedy-drama starts slowly and seems to condemn the school system, never picking up strength or resolving any

T

issues, though Nolte is fairly intense. Shot in Columbus, Ohio.
1984 (R) 106m/C Nick Nolte, JoBeth Williams, Lee Grant, Judd Hirsch, Ralph Macchio, Richard Mulligan, Royal Dano, Morgan Freeman, Laura Dern, Crispin Glover, Madeline Sherwood, Zohra Lampert; **D:** Arthur Hiller. VHS, Beta, LV $14.95 MGM, FOX 🎬🎬

Teacher's Pet This charming comedy features a cynical newspaper editor who enrolls in a night college journalism course, believing that it won't teach anything of substance. He later becomes enamored of his instructor. Well written script and superb performance by Young as Gable's rival for Day.
1958 120m/B Clark Gable, Doris Day, Mamie Van Doren, Gig Young, Nick Adams; **D:** George Seaton; **W:** Fay Kanin, Michael Kanin. VHS, Beta $14.95 PAR, KRT 🎬🎬🎬

The Teahouse of the August Moon An adaptation of the John Patrick play. Post-war American troops are assigned to bring civilization to a small village in Okinawa and instead fall for Okinawan culture and romance. Lively cast keeps it generally working, but assessments of Brando's comedic performance vary widely.
1956 123m/C Glenn Ford, Marlon Brando, Eddie Albert, Paul Ford, Machiko Kyo, Henry Morgan; **D:** Daniel Mann. VHS, Beta, LV $19.98 MGM 🎬🎬½

Teamster Boss: The Jackie Presser Story A well-done made-for-cable-television movie powered by a riveting performance by Dennehy. Presser followed Jimmy Hoffa as president of the Teamsters and was equally caught between the mob and the government as he tried to do what he considered best for the union.
1992 (R) 111m/C Brian Dennehy, Jeff Daniels, Maria Conchita Alonso, Eli Wallach; **D:** Alastair Reid. VHS, LV $89.99 HBO, PMS 🎬🎬

Tearaway Australian story of a street punk with an alcoholic father. Story has potential, but ends up going nowhere.
1987 (R) 100m/C NZ AU Matthew Hunter, Mark Pilisi, Peter Bland, Kim Willoughby, Rebecca Saunders; **D:** Bruce Morrison. VHS, Beta $79.95 LHV, WAR 🎬½

Ted & Venus Cort plays Ted, an oddball cult poet in love with Linda, a beach beauty who finds him repulsive. The more she rejects him, the more obsessed about her Ted gets, especially when his equally oddball friends offer him romantic advice.
1993 (R) 100m/C Bud Cort, Kim Adams, Rhea Perlman, James Brolin, Carol Kane; **Cameos:** Gena Rowlands, Martin Mull, Woody Harrelson, Andrea Martin; **W/D:** Bud Cort; **W:** Paul Ciotti. VHS $89.95 COL 🎬🎬

Teddy at the Throttle Teddy, the Great Dane, must rescue Gloria Swanson from a villain who has tied up her boyfriend. Silent.
1916 20m/B Bobby Vernon, Gloria Swanson, Wallace Beery; **D:** Clarence Badger. VHS, Beta CCB 🎬🎬

Teddy at the Throttle/Speeding Along A silent comedy about stealing fortunes from innocent heroines and another about racing cars in a farm area.
1917 54m/B Gloria Swanson, Wallace Beery, Bobby Vernon. VHS, Beta $29.95 VYY 🎬🎬

Teen Alien On Halloween, a young boy and his friends run into a hostile alien. It could happen.
1988 (PG) 88m/C Vern Adix, Michael Dunn. VHS, Beta $79.95 PSM 🎬

Teen Lust Two girls look for an exciting summer job. They get all the action they can handle when they work as undercover prostitutes for the local police department.
1978 (R) 90m/C Kirsten Baker, Perry Lang, Richard Singer. VHS, Beta $69.98 LIV 🎬

Teen Mothers Bittersweet story of two unwed teenagers forced to take their child and leave home for the tenements of New York. **AKA:** Seed of Innocence.
1980 (R) 91m/C VHS, Beta PGN 🎬🎬

Teen Vamp Dorky high schooler is bitten by a prostitute; becomes a cool vampire. Mindless "comedy."
1988 87m/C Clu Gulager, Karen Carlson, Angela Brown; **D:** Samuel Bradford. VHS, Beta $19.95 STE, NWV 🎬

Teen Witch A demure high schooler uses black magic to woo the most popular guy in school.
1989 (PG-13) 94m/C Robin Lively, Zelda Rubinstein, Dan Gauthier, Joshua Miller, Dick Sargent; **D:** Dorian Walker. VHS, Beta $89.95 MED 🎬🎬

Teen Wolf A nice, average teenage basketball player begins to show werewolf tendencies which suddenly make him popular at school when he leads the team to victory. The underlying message is to be yourself, regardless of how much hair you have on your body. Lighthearted comedy carried by the Fox charm; followed by subpar "Teen Wolf Too."
1985 (PG) 92m/C Michael J. Fox, James Hampton, Scott Paulin, Susan Ursitti; **D:** Rod Daniel. VHS, Beta, LV, 8mm $14.95 PAR 🎬🎬½

Teen Wolf Too The sequel to "Teen Wolf" in which the Teen Wolf's cousin goes to college on a boxing scholarship. More evidence that the sequel is rarely as good as the original.
1987 (PG) 95m/C Jason Bateman, Kim Darby, John Astin, Paul Sand; **D:** Christopher Leitch. VHS, Beta $14.95 PAR 🎬🎬

Teenage Low budget juvenile schlock film that tries to figure out what's wrong with modern youth. Pure camp.
1944 ?m/C Herbert Heyes, Wheeler Oakman. VHS $16.95 SNC 🎬

Teenage Bad Girl A woman who edits a magazine for teenagers can't control her own daughter. The kid does time in the pen after staying out all night and generally running around with the wrong crowd. Syms first lead performance is memorable in an otherwise routine teensploitation flick. **AKA:** Bad Girl; My Teenage Daughter.
1959 100m/B Anna Neagle, Sylvia Syms, Norman Wooland, Wilfrid Hyde-White, Kenneth Haigh, Julia Lockwood; **D:** Herbert Wilcox. VHS, Beta $16.95 SNC 🎬🎬½

Teenage Caveman A teenage boy living in a post-apocalypse yet prehistoric world journeys across the river, even though he was warned against it, and finds an old man who owns a book about past civilizations in the 20th Century. Schlocky, and one of the better bad films around. The dinosaur shots were picked up from the film "One Million B.C." **AKA:** Out of the Darkness; Prehistoric World.
1958 66m/B Robert Vaughn, Darrah Marshall, Leslie Bradley, Frank DeKova; **D:** Roger Corman. VHS $9.95 COL 🎬🎬

Teenage Crime Wave Route 66 provides thrills for a couple of teen punks, but things get out of hand when they blow a sheriff's head off. They scoop up a couple of babes and hightail it with the police close

behind, ultimately confronting their destiny at a mountain top observatory.
1955 77m/B Tommy Cook, Mollie McCart, Sue England, Frank Griffin, James Bell, Kay Riehl; **D:** Fred F. Sears. VHS, Beta $16.95 SNC, AOV 🎬

Teenage Devil Dolls A cheap exploitation teenage flick wherein an innocent girl is turned on to reefer and goofballs, and eventually ends up on the street.
1953 70m/C Barbara Marks, Bramlef L. Price Jr.; **D:** B. Lawrence Price. VHS, Beta $9.95 RHI 🎬

Teenage Frankenstein A descendent of Dr. Frankenstein makes his own scramble-faced monster out of a teenage boy. Lurid '50s drive-in fare (companion to "I Was a Teenage Werewolf") is campy fun in small doses only.
1958 72m/B Whit Bissell, Phyllis Coates, Robert Burton, Gary Conway, George Lynn, John Cliff; **D:** Herbert L. Strock. VHS $29.95 COL 🎬½

Teenage Mother A Swedish sex education teacher comes to town and poisons the minds of the local high school kids. Naturally one becomes pregnant and has to try to trick the father into marrying her. More awful stuff from the director of "Girl On a Chain Gang."
1967 78m/C Arlene Sue Farber, Frederick Riccio, Julie Ange, Howard Le May, George Peters; **D:** Jerry Gross. VHS, Beta $16.95 SNC Woof!

Teenage Mutant Ninja Turtles: The Movie Four sewer-dwelling turtles that have turned into warrior ninja mutants due to radiation exposure take it upon themselves to rid the city of crime and pizza. Aided by a television reporter and their ninja master, Splinter the Rat, the turtles encounter several obstacles, including the evil warlord Shredder. A most excellent live-action version of the popular comic book characters which will hold the kids' interest. Much headkicking and rib-crunching action as Leonardo, Donatello, Raphael, and Michelangelo fight for the rights of pre-adolescents everywhere. Combines real actors with Jim Henson creatures.
1990 (PG) 95m/C Judith Hoag, Elias Koteas; **D:** Steven Barron; **V:** Robbie Rist, Corey Feldman. VHS, Beta, LV, 8mm $24.99 FHE, LIV, WTA 🎬🎬½

Teenage Mutant Ninja Turtles 2: The Secret of the Ooze Amphibious pizza-devouring mutants search for the toxic waste that turned them into marketable martial artist ecologically correct kid idols. Same formula as the first go-round with some new characters tossed in. Animatronic characters from the laboratory of Jim Henson, first screen appearance by rapper Vanilla Ice. Marked end of pre-teen turtle craze.
1991 (PG) 88m/C Francois Chau, David Warner, Paige Turco, Ernie Reyes Jr., Vanilla Ice; **D:** Michael Pressman. VHS, Beta $22.98 COL, NLC 🎬🎬

Teenage Mutant Ninja Turtles 3 Check it out dudes; the Teenage Mutant Ninja Turtles hit 17th century Japan to rescue loyal friend, reporter April O'Neil. Plenty of smoothly executed, blood-free martial arts moves keep the pace rolling, while the turtles battle an evil lord and English pirates. Seeing the TMNT's use a little more of their reptilian grey matter, and snarf a little less pizza should contribute to a relatively high adult tolerance level (considering the genre), and loads of good clean fun for the kiddies.
1993 (PG) 95m/C Elias Koteas, Paige Turco, Stuart Wilson, Sab Shimono, Vivian Wu; **W/D:** Stuart Gillard; **M:** John Du Prez; **V:** Randi Mayem Singer, Matt Hill, Jim Raposa, David Fraser. VHS, LV NLC, COL, IME 🎬🎬

Teenage Seductress A young girl connives her way into the life of a writer and finds ways to distract him from his work.
19?? 84m/C Sondra Currie, Chris Warfield. **VHS, Beta** *NO* Woof!

Teenage Strangler A homicidal teen terrorizes his school. Cheap film features drag races, rumbles, dances, babes, rock 'n' roll and more. One for the "bad enough to be fun" category.
1964 61m/C Bill A. Bloom, Jo Canterbury, John Ensign; *D:* Bill Posner. **VHS, Beta** $16.95 *SNC, SMW* Woof!

Teenage Wolfpack Boring film about German juvenile delinquents, robbery, violence, and murder.
1957 90m/C *GE* Horst Buchholz, Karin Baal, Christian Doermer; *D:* Georg Tressier. **VHS** $16.95 *SNC* ♂♂½

Teenage Zombies Mad scientist on remote island kidnaps teenagers and uses her secret chemical formula to turn them into zombies as part of her plan to enslave the world. Not as good as it sounds. Written by Jacques Le Cotier.
1958 71m/B Don Sullivan, Katherine Victor, Chuck Niles; *D:* Jerry Warren. **VHS, Beta** $19.95 *NOS, SNC, VYY* Woof!

Teenager Three desperate, reckless individuals, all caught up in making a low budget movie, interact and eventually self-destruct.
1974 (R) 91m/C Andrea Cagan, Reid Smith, Susan Bernard; *D:* Gerald Seth Sindell. **VHS, Beta** $19.95 *STE, NWV* ♂

Teenagers from Outer Space A low-budget sci-fi film in which extraterrestrial youngsters come to conquer the earth and find food for their "monstrous pets" (they're really lobster shadows.) So cheaply made and melodramatic that it just may be good for a laugh. *AKA:* The Gargon Terror.
1959 86m/B Tom Graeff, Dawn Anderson, Harvey B. Dunn, Bryant Grant, Tom Lockyear; *D:* Tom Graeff. **VHS** $16.95 *SNC* Woof!

Tekkaman, the Space Knight A Japanese-produced giant-robot-saves-the-universe cartoon series.
1986 30m/C **VHS, Beta** $19.95 *WVV* Woof!

Tekkaman, the Space Knight: Vol. 2 Human space pilot Barry Gallagher dons a suit of space armor made from "tekka," an indestructible alloy, and fights the evil robots that have invaded the world of 2037. Although this film was produced in the United States, it employs Japanese animation techniques.
199? 86m/C **VHS** $19.95 *LDV* Woof!

Telefon Suspenseful, slick spy tale. Soviet agents battle a lunatic comrade who tries to use hypnotized Americans to commit sabotage. Daly, later of TV's "Cagney and Lacey," is memorable.
1977 (PG) 102m/C Charles Bronson, Lee Remick, Donald Pleasence, Tyne Daly, Patrick Magee, Sheree North; *D:* Don Siegel; *W:* Sterling Silliphant, Peter Hyams. **VHS, Beta** $19.95 *MGM* ♂♂

The Telephone A neurotic out-of-work actress begins a comedic chain of events via a few prank phone calls. Goldberg has managed to salvage some bad material with the strength of her comedic performances, but not so here. In fact, she sued to prevent this version from ever seeing the light of day. Too bad she didn't have a better lawyer. Torn's directorial debut.
1987 (R) 96m/C Whoopi Goldberg, Elliott Gould, John Heard, Amy Wright; *D:* Rip Torn. **VHS, Beta, LV** $19.95 *STE, NWV* Woof!

Tell It to the Judge Russell plays the exuberant ex-wife of lawyer Cummings. They repeatedly try reconciling but ditzy blonde McDonald always manages to catch Cummings eye. Fed up Russell takes off for a holiday in the mountains where she meets Young. When her ex-hubby follows her, she decides to try and make him jealous using Young as the bait.
1949 87m/B Rosalind Russell, Robert Cummings, Gig Young, Marie McDonald, Harry Davenport, Louise Beavers; *D:* Norman Foster. **VHS** $19.95 *FCT* ♂♂½

Tell Me a Riddle A dying woman attempts to reconcile with her family in this poignant drama about an elderly couple rediscovering their mutual love after 47 years of marriage. Fine acting; Grant's directorial debut.
1980 (PG) 94m/C Melvyn Douglas, Lila Kedrova, Brooke Adams, Peter Coyote; *D:* Lee Grant. **VHS, Beta** $19.95 *MED* ♂♂½

Tell Me That You Love Me A tear-jerking portrait of a disintegrating modern marriage.
1984 (R) 88m/C Nick Mancuso, Barbara Williams, Belinda J. Montgomery; *D:* Tzipi Trope. **VHS, Beta** $59.98 *LIV, VES* ♂½

Tell Me Where It Hurts A middle-aged housewife changes her life when she forms a women's consciousness-raising group with her friends. The script won an Emmy. Stapleton's performance is redeeming in this otherwise slow movie.
1974 78m/C Maureen Stapleton, Paul Sorvino; *D:* Paul Bogart. **VHS, Beta** *LCA* ♂♂

The Tell-Tale Heart Daydreaming author fantasizes about falling for major babe and killing his best friend for her. Adapted Poe tale. *AKA:* The Hidden Room of 1,000 Horrors.
1962 78m/B *GB* Laurence Payne, Adrienne Corri, Dermot Walsh, Selma Vaz Dias, John Scott, John Martin, Annette Carell, David Lander; *D:* Ernest Morris. **VHS** $19.98 *NOS, SNC, LOO* ♂♂½

Tell Them Willie Boy Is Here Western drama set in 1909 California about a Paiute Indian named Willie Boy and his white bride. They become the objects of a manhunt (led by the reluctant local sheriff, Redford) after Willie kills his wife's father in self-defense. This was once-blacklisted Polonsky's first film in 21 years.
1969 (PG) 98m/C Robert Redford, Katharine Ross, Robert (Bobby) Blake, Susan Clark, Barry Sullivan, John Vernon, Charles McGraw; *D:* Abraham Polonsky. **VHS, Beta, LV** $39.95 *MCA* ♂♂♂

The Temp Unbelievably bad attempt at horror in the corporate workplace. Beautiful, mysterious Kris takes a job as a temporary assistant to Hutton, a junior executive at the Mrs. Appleby baked goods company. Almost too good to be true, she soon has everything organized and running smoothly. Once she's hired permanently, Kris begins her rapid ascension through the ranks. Meanwhile, strange accidents continue to eliminate her coworkers. Pyscho-drama has pyscho, lacks drama, and suffers from a lack of direction, lack of plot development, lack of intelligent dialogue, and lack of anything resembling motive, never establishing how evil or powerful Kris should be. While Hutton is tolerable, ex-Twin Peaker Boyle enters bad acting hall of shame as the conniving psycho with deadly career ambition.
1993 (R) 99m/C Timothy Hutton, Lara Flynn Boyle, Faye Dunaway, Dwight Schultz, Oliver Platt, Steven Weber, Scott Coffey, Colleen Flynn, Dakin Matthews, Maura Tierney; *D:* Tom Holland; *W:* Kevin Falls. **VHS, Beta** *PAR* Woof!

The Tempest A Russian peasant soldier rises through the ranks to become an officer, only to be undone by his love for the daughter of his commanding officer. Silent with musical score.
1928 105m/B John Barrymore, Louis Wolheim; *D:* Sam Taylor. Academy Awards '28: Best Interior Decoration; Nominations: Best Cinematography. **VHS, Beta** $9.95 *NOS, CCB, VYY* ♂♂♂

The Tempest Shakespeare's classic tale of the fantasy world of spirits, sorcerers, maidens, monsters, and scheming noblemen is brought to life in George Schaefer's ethereal production.
1963 76m/C Maurice Evans, Richard Burton, Roddy McDowall, Lee Remick, Tom Poston; *D:* George Schaefer. **VHS, Beta** $34.95 *TVC, FHS* ♂♂½

The Tempest The lust for power is ultimately overcome by the need for love in this play, one of Shakespeare's most dramatic and emotional romances. Part of the "Shakespeare Plays" series.
1980 150m/C *GB* **VHS, Beta** *TLF* ♂♂♂

The Tempest A New York architect, fed up with city living, chucks it all and brings his daughter to live with him on a barren Greek island. Based on Shakespeare's play of the same name. Well-written, thoughtfully acted, and beautifully filmed.
1982 (PG) 140m/C John Cassavetes, Gena Rowlands, Susan Sarandon, Vittorio Gassman, Molly Ringwald, Paul Stewart, Sam Robards, Raul Julia; *D:* Paul Mazursky. **VHS, Beta, LV** *COL* ♂♂♂

The Tempest/The Eagle A Russian soldier during the Revolution is betrayed and humiliated by the woman he loves in "The Tempest." In "The Eagle," an outcast guardsman becomes the Russian version of Robin Hood.
1927 56m/B John Barrymore, Camilla Horn, Rudolph Valentino, Louise Dressler; *D:* Sam Taylor, Clarence Brown. **VHS, Beta** $29.98 *CCB* ♂♂♂

Temporada Salvaje Three criminals try to steal a fortune in platinum. Also known as Savage Season. *AKA:* Savage Season.
1987 90m/C *MX* Armando Silvestre, Isela Vega, Ron Harper, Diane McBain. **VHS, Beta** $77.95 *MAD* ♂♂½

The Tempter Mirrors the gruesomeness of "The Exorcist," with story following an invalid's adventures with witchcraft, bestiality, and Satanism.
1974 (R) 96m/C *IT* Mel Ferrer, Carla Gravina, Arthur Kennedy, Alida Valli, Anita Strindberg, George Coulouris; *D:* Alberto De Martino; *M:* Ennio Morricone. **VHS, Beta** $24.98 *SUE* ♂

The Temptress A doctor attempting to find a cure for polio is coerced by an irresistible woman into murder and blackmail. Well-told story, if somewhat grim.
1949 85m/B *GB* Joan Maude, Arnold Bell, Don Stannard, Shirley Quentin, John Stuart, Ferdinand "Ferdy" Mayne; *D:* Oswald Mitchell. **VHS, Beta** $16.95 *SNC* ♂♂½

10 A successful songwriter who has everything finds his life is incomplete without the woman of his dreams, the 10 on his girl-watching scale. His pursuit brings surprising results. Music by Henry Mancini; also popularizes Ravel's "Bolero."

1979 (R) 121m/C Dudley Moore, Julie Andrews, Bo Derek, Dee Wallace Stone, Brian Dennehy, Robert Webber; **D:** Blake Edwards. **VHS, Beta, LV** $19.98 *WAR, FCT 𝄞𝄞½*

Ten Brothers of Shao-lin Martial arts adventure from the days of warlords and warriors, when men were fierce and strong and struggles to the death occurred several times a day.
1987 90m/C Chia Ling, Wang Tao, Chang Yi. **VHS, Beta** *NO 𝄞*

Ten Commandments The silent epic that established DeMille as a popular directorial force and which he remade 35 years later as an even bigger epic with sound. Follows Moses' adventures in Egypt, plus a modern story of brotherly love and corruption. Features a new musical score by Gaylord Carter. Remade in 1956.
1923 146m/B Theodore Roberts, Richard Dix, Rod La Rocque, Edythe Chapman; **D:** Cecil B. DeMille. **VHS, Beta** $19.95 *PAR 𝄞𝄞½*

The Ten Commandments DeMille's remake of his 1923 silent classic is a lavish Biblical epic that tells the life story of Moses, who turned his back on a privileged life to lead his people to freedom outside of Egypt. Exceptional cast. Parting of Red Sea rivals any modern special effects. Available in widescreen on laserdisc. A 35th Anniversary Collector's Edition is available in widescreen format in Dolby Surround stereo, and 1,000 copies of an Autographed Limited Edition that includes an engraved bronze plaque and an imprinted card written and personally signed by Charlton Heston are also available.
1956 (G) 219m/C Charlton Heston, Yul Brynner, Anne Baxter, Yvonne De Carlo, Nina Foch, John Derek, H.B. Warner, Henry Wilcoxon, Judith Anderson, John Carradine, Douglas Dumbrille, Cedric Hardwicke, Martha Scott, Vincent Price, Debra Paget; **D:** Cecil B. DeMille. Academy Awards '56: Best Special Effects; Nominations: Best Art Direction/Set Decoration (Color), Best Color Cinematography, Best Costume Design (Color), Best Film Editing, Best Picture, Best Sound. **VHS, Beta, LV** $35.00 *PAR, IGP, RDG 𝄞𝄞𝄞*

Ten Days That Shook the World Silent Russian epic details the events that culminated in the Russian Revolution of October 1917, using actual locations and many actual participants. Based on the book by American author John Reed by the same name. Some of Eisenstein's most striking work. **AKA:** October.
1927 104m/B Nikandrov, N. Popov, Boris Livanov; **D:** Sergei Eisenstein, Grigori Alexandrov. **VHS, Beta** $29.95 *VYY, IHF, WFV 𝄞𝄞½*

Ten Days Wonder Mystery/drama focuses on the patriarch of a wealthy family (Welles), his young wife, and his adopted son (Perkins), who is having an affair with his stepmother. It also turns out that Perkins is certifiable and is trying to break all of the Ten Commandments, which he succeeds in doing before killing himself (gruesomely). Based on the mystery novel by Ellery Queen.
1972 (PG) 101m/C *FR* Orson Welles, Anthony Perkins, Marlene Jobert, Michel Piccoli, Guido Alberti; **D:** Claude Chabrol. **VHS** $39.95 *TAM, MOV 𝄞𝄞½*

Ten Little Indians Ten people are gathered in an isolated inn under mysterious circumstances. One by one they are murdered, each according to a verse from a children's nursery rhyme. British adaptation of the novel and stage play by Agatha Christie. **AKA:** And Then There Were None.
1975 (PG) 98m/C *GB* Herbert Lom, Richard Attenborough, Oliver Reed, Elke Sommer, Charles Aznavour, Stephane Audran, Gert Frobe, Adolfo Celi, Orson Welles; **D:** Peter Collinson; **W:**

Agatha Christie. **VHS, Beta, LV** $59.98 *NLC 𝄞𝄞½*

Ten Little Indians A group of prize-winning vacationers find themselves embarking on an African adventure. They all wind up at the same camp, and realize that they are being murdered one by one. Based on the work of Agatha Christie. **AKA:** Agatha Christie's Ten Little Indians.
1989 (PG) 100m/C Donald Pleasence, Brenda Vaccaro, Frank Stallone, Herbert Lom, Sarah Maur-Thorp; **D:** Alan Birkinshaw; **W:** Agatha Christie. **VHS, Beta, LV** $89.95 *CAN 𝄞𝄞*

The Ten Million Dollar Getaway True story of the 1978 Lufthansa robbery at Kennedy Airport in which the criminals were forced to leave ten of their twenty-million-dollar heist behind when a pick-up van didn't show. Standard made-for-cable fare produced to cash in on the same scenario played out in "Goodfellas."
1991 (PG-13) 93m/C John Mahoney, Karen Young, Tony LoBianco, Gerry Bamman, Joseph Carberry, Terrence Mann, Kenneth John McGregor, Christopher Murney; **D:** James A. Contner. **VHS, Beta** *PAR 𝄞𝄞*

Ten Nights in a Bar Room The evils of alcohol are dramatized when they ruin a man's life. One of many propaganda films about alcohol and the problems that it caused that were made during the prohibition era. Silent, with a musical score. Remade in 1931.
1913 68m/B Robert Lawrence, Marie Trado. **VHS, Beta** $29.95 *VCN 𝄞𝄞*

Ten Nights in a Bar-Room A turn-of-the-century mill owner succumbs to alcoholism and ruins his life and family. Later, he sees the error of his ways and gives up drinking. This was one of many films made during this era that chronicled the evils of alcohol and fanned the flames of the prohibition debate. Remake of the 1913 silent film.
1931 60m/B William Farnum, Thomas Santschi, John Darrow, Robert Frazer. **VHS, Beta** $24.95 *VYY 𝄞*

Ten North Frederick A shrewish wife (Fitzgerald) forces her gentle lawyer husband (Cooper) into cut-throat politics. He consoles himself in the arms of a much younger woman. Good performances, hokey script, based on the John O'Hara novel.
1958 102m/B Gary Cooper, Diane Varsi, Suzy Parker, Geraldine Fitzgerald, Tom Tully, Stuart Whitman; **D:** Philip Dunne. **VHS** *TCF 𝄞𝄞½*

10 Rillington Place A grimy, upsetting British film about the famed serial killer John Christie and the man wrongly hanged for his crimes, the incident that led to the end of capital punishment in England. Impeccably acted. One of Hurt's earliest films.
1971 (PG) 111m/C *GB* Richard Attenborough, John Hurt, Judy Geeson, Gabrielle Daye, Andre Morell; **D:** Richard Fleischer. **VHS, Beta, LV** $59.95 *COL 𝄞𝄞𝄞*

Ten Speed Two advertising executives compete in a 400-mile bicycle race from San Francisco to Malibu.
1976 89m/C William Woodbridge, Patricia Hume, David Clover. **VHS, Beta** $69.98 *LIV 𝄞𝄞*

Ten Tigers of Shaolin Kicks and chops are dished out freely in this martial arts epic.
1977 90m/C **VHS, Beta** $29.95 *UNI 𝄞*

Ten to Midnight Vigilante Bronson is on the prowl again, this time as a police officer after a kinky serial murderer. The psychotic killer stalks his daughter and Dad's gonna stop him at any cost.

1983 (R) 101m/C Charles Bronson, Wilford Brimley, Lisa Eilbacher, Andrew Stevens; **D:** J. Lee Thompson. **VHS, Beta, LV** $14.95 *MGM 𝄞𝄞*

10 Violent Women Ten women who take part in a million dollar jewelry heist are tossed into a women's prison where brutal lesbian guards subject them to degradation and brutality.
1979 (R) 97m/C Sherri Vernon, Dixie Lauren, Sally Gamble; **D:** Ted V. Mikels. **VHS, Beta** $49.95 *WWV Woof!*

Ten Wanted Men A successful cattle baron is confronted by a pistol-wielding landowner determined to ruin him. Standard fare, with better than average performances from Scott and Boone.
1954 80m/C Randolph Scott, Jocelyn Brando, Richard Boone, Skip Homeier, Leo Gordon, Jack Perrin, Donna Martell; **D:** H. Bruce Humberstone. **VHS, Beta, LV** $69.95 *COL 𝄞*

Ten Who Dared Ten Civil War heroes brave the Colorado River in an effort to chart its course. Although it's based on an actual historic event, the film is poorly paced and lacks suspense.
1960 92m/C Brian Keith, John Beal, James Drury; **D:** William Beaudine. **VHS, Beta** $69.95 *DIS 𝄞𝄞*

The Tenant Polanski co-wrote the screenplay, directed, and starred in this disturbing film about a hapless office worker who moves into a spooky Paris apartment house. Once lodged inside its walls, he becomes obsessed with the previous occupant—a suicide—and the belief that his neighbors are trying to kill him. Based on a novel by Roland Topor. **AKA:** Le Locataire.
1976 (R) 126m/C *FR* Roman Polanski, Isabelle Adjani, Melvyn Douglas, Jo Van Fleet, Bernard Fresson, Shelley Winters; **D:** Roman Polanski. **VHS, Beta** $49.95 *PAR 𝄞𝄞𝄞½*

The Tender Age Troubled 18-year-old girl gets out of a detention home and is put on probation. She captivates her idealistic probation officer, whose interest may extend beyond professional concern. Fine idea, but under-played. **AKA:** The Little Sister.
1984 103m/C John Savage, Tracy Pollan, Roxanne Hart, Richard Jenkins; **W/D:** Jan Egleson. **VHS, Beta** $79.98 *LIV 𝄞𝄞*

Tender Comrade Flag-waving violin-accompanied tearjerker about five women who live together to make ends meet while their men do manly things during WWII. Intended to puff your heart up with patriotic gusto. Ironically, thanks to the girls' communal living arrangement, director Dmytryk was later accused of un-American activities.
1943 101m/B Ginger Rogers, Robert Ryan, Ruth Hussey, Patricia Collinge, Mady Christians, Kim Hunter, Jane Darwell, Mary Forbes, Richard Martin; **D:** Edward Dmytryk. **VHS** $19.98 *TTC, FCT 𝄞𝄞*

Tender Is the Night A television-special adaptation of the F. Scott Fitzgerald classic, set in the roaring '20s, in which a psychiatrist marries one of his patients and then heads down the road to ruin, driven by his marriage and the times in which he lives. An entry from the "Front Row Center" series.
1955 60m/B Mercedes McCambridge, James Daly. **VHS, Beta** $24.95 *NOS, DVT 𝄞𝄞½*

Tender Loving Care Three nurses dispense hefty doses of T.L.C. in their hospital, and the patients aren't the only ones on the receiving end.
1973 72m/C Donna Desmond, Leah Simon, Anita King; **D:** Don Edmonds. **VHS, Beta** $39.98 *SUE 𝄞*

Tender Mercies A down-and-out country western singer finds his life redeemed by the love of a good woman. Aided by Horton Foote's script, Duvall, Harper and Barkin keep this from being simplistic and sentimental. Duvall wrote as well as performed the songs in his Oscar-winning performance. Wonderful, life-affirming flick.
1983 (PG) 93m/C Robert Duvall, Tess Harper, Betty Buckley, Ellen Barkin, Wilford Brimley; *D:* Bruce Beresford; *W:* Horton Foote Jr. Academy Awards '83: Best Actor (Duvall), Best Original Screenplay; Nominations: Best Director (Beresford), Best Picture, Best Song ("Over You"); Golden Globe Awards '83: Best Actor—Drama (Duvall). VHS, Beta, LV $19.99 HBO, BTV, HMV ✻✻✻

The Tender Trap Charlie Reader (Sinatra) is a bachelor not content with the many women in his life. He meets the innocent Julie Gillis (Reynolds) and falls head over heels for her. He then torments himself over a marriage proposal, unwilling to let go of his freedom.
1955 111m/C Frank Sinatra, Debbie Reynolds, Celeste Holm, David Wayne, Carolyn Jones, Lola Albright, Tom Helmore, Howard St. John, Willard Sage, James Drury, Benny Rubin, Frank Sully, David White; *D:* Charles Walters. VHS, LV $19.98 MGM, MOV ✻✻½

The Tender Warrior A beautifully photographed animal adventure with Haggerty as the woodsman.
1971 (G) 85m/C Dan Haggerty, Charles Lee, Liston Elkins; *D:* Stewart Raffill. VHS, Beta $59.95 VCD ✻

The Tender Years Sentimental drama of a minister trying to outlaw dog fighting, spurred on by his son's fondness for a particular dog.
1947 81m/B Reb Brown, Richard Lyon, Noreen Nash, Charles Drake, Josephine Hutchinson; *D:* Harold Schuster. VHS, Beta $12.95 TCF ✻✻

Tendres Cousines Comedy follows the exploits of two cousins coming of age in the French countryside. Along with the rest of their relatives and friends, they become entwined in a web of unrequited love and intricate relationships.
1983 (R) 90m/C FR VHS, Beta $59.98 VES ✻✻

Tenement Unspeakably violent story of urban low-lifes, frightened slum-dwellers, and revenge. *AKA:* Game of Survival.
1985 94m/C VHS, Beta NO ✻

Tennessee Stallion A low-class horse-trainer breaks into the world of aristocratic thoroughbred racing.
1978 87m/C Audrey Landers, Judy Landers, James Van Patten. VHS, Beta $69.98 LIV, VES ✻

Tennessee's Partner Enjoyable, unexceptional buddy Western. Reagan intervenes in an argument and becomes Payne's pal. Adapted from a story by Bret Harte.
1955 87m/C Ronald Reagan, Rhonda Fleming, John Payne; *D:* Allan Dwan. VHS, Beta NO ✻✻

Tension at Table Rock Accused of cowardice, a lone gunman must prove he killed in self-defense. Well-cast serious Western.
1956 93m/C Richard Egan, Dorothy Malone, Cameron Mitchell; *D:* Charles Marquis. VHS, Beta UHV ✻✻

Tentacles Cheesy Italian version of "Jaws" lacking only the suspense and cogent storytelling. Huston slums as the investigator charged with finding the octopus gone mad, while Fonda collects check and makes a quick exit. Hopkins is in charge of the killer whales that save the day. You'll cheer when Winters is devoured by sea pest. From the director of an "Exorcist" rip-off,

"Beyond the Door" (that's not a recommendation).
1977 (PG) 90m/C IT John Huston, Shelley Winters, Bo Hopkins, Henry Fonda, Cesare Danova; *D:* Oliver Hellman. VHS, Beta $59.98 LIV, VES Woof!

The Tenth Man Hopkins stars as a wealthy French lawyer, captured by the Nazis and sentenced to death. He discovers a fellow prisoner who is willing to take his place in exchange for Hopkins' wealth going to support the man's family. After his release, Hopkins returns to his old home, now occupied by the dead man's family, but doesn't reveal his true identity. When an imposter appears, claiming to be Hopkins, another twist is added. Slow-going but the usual excellent performances by Hopkins and Jacobi. Based on a novella by Graham Greene. Made for television.
1988 99m/C Anthony Hopkins, Kristin Scott Thomas, Derek Jacobi, Cyril Cusack, Brenda Bruce, Paul Rogers; *D:* Jack Gold. VHS, LV $79.99 MGM ✻✻½

Tenth Month Carol Burnett plays a divorced, middle-aged woman who becomes pregnant by a married man. She refuses help, choosing instead to live alone and keep an ever hopeful vigil for the birth of her child. Sappy but touching made-for-TV drama.
1979 123m/C Carol Burnett, Keith Mitchell, Dina Merrill; *D:* Joan Tewkesbury. VHS, Beta $59.95 TLF ✻✻

10th Victim Sci-fi cult film set in the 21st century has Mastroianni and Andress pursuing one another in a futuristic society where legalized murder is used as the means of population control. Intriguing movie where Andress kills with a double-barreled bra, the characters hang out at the Club Masoch, and comic books are considered literature. Based on "The Seventh Victim" by Robert Sheckley. *AKA:* La Decima Vittima; La Dixieme Victime.
1965 92m/C IT Ursula Andress, Marcello Mastroianni, Elsa Martinelli, Salvo Randone, Massimo Serato; *D:* Elio Petri. VHS, Beta $14.95 SUE, NLC ✻✻✻

Teorema A scathing condemnation of bourgeois complacency. Stamp, either a devil or a god, mysteriously appears and enters into the life of a well-to-do Milanese family and raises each member's spirituality by sleeping with them. Ultimately, the experience leads to tragedy. In Italian with English subtitles.
1968 98m/C IT Terence Stamp, Silvana Mangano, Massimo Girotti, Anna Wiazemsky, Laura Betti, Andres Jose Cruz; *D:* Pier Paolo Pasolini; *M:* Ennio Morricone. VHS $39.95 TAM ✻✻✻

Tequila Sunrise Writer-director Robert Towne's twisting film about two lifelong friends and a beautiful woman. Gibson is a (supposedly) retired drug dealer afraid of losing custody of his son to his nagging ex-wife. Russell is the cop and old friend who's trying to get the lowdown on a drug shipment coming in from Mexico. Pfeiffer runs the poshest restaurant on the coast and is actively pursued by both men. Questions cloud the plot: Is Gibson involved in the upcoming drug deal? Will Russell catch the notorious Mexican drug kingpin? Will beautiful Pfeiffer ever make up her mind about which man she loves? Loaded with double-crosses, intrigue and surprises around every corner. Steamy love scene between Pfeiffer and Gibson.
1988 (R) 116m/C Mel Gibson, Kurt Russell, Michelle Pfeiffer, Raul Julia, Arliss Howard, Arye Gross, J.T. Walsh, Ann Magnuson; *D:* Robert Towne. VHS, Beta, LV, 8mm $19.95 WAR ✻✻½

Teresa Venerdi An unusual Italian comedy about a man and his financial difficulties. His mistress, his fiance and a young girl make his troubles more confusing. Unusually sweet and humorous DeSica.
1941 90m/B IT D: Vittorio De Sica. VHS, Beta, 3/4U, Special order formats $49.95 CIG ✻✻✻

Tereza In politically chaotic Czechoslovakia, a female police detective tries to solve an intricate murder mystery. In Czech with English subtitles.
1961 91m/B CZ Jirina Svorcova; *D:* Pavel Blumenfeld. VHS, Beta, 3/4U $39.95 FCT, IHF ✻✻✻

Terminal Bliss Teen heartthrob Perry stars as a spoiled rich druggie in this "Less Than Zero" knock-off. Perry and childhood pal Owen grow up sharing everything—lacrosse, girlfriends, and drugs. However, their friendship is really put to the test when a beautiful new girl (Chandler) moves to town just before graduation. Release was delayed, but obviously wants to capitalize on Perry's popularity.
1991 (R) 94m/C Luke Perry, Timothy Owen, Estee Chandler; *D:* Jordan Allen. VHS, LV $19.98 WAR ✻½

Terminal Choice Staff at a hospital conduct a betting pool on patients' life expectancies. Someone decides he should win more often and uses a computer to help hedge his bets. Wasted cast on this unsuspenseful and bloody film.
1985 (R) 98m/C Joe Spano, Diane Venora, David McCallum, Ellen Barkin; *D:* Sheldon Larry. VHS, Beta $79.95 VES ✻½

Terminal Entry Teen computer geeks accidentally find a terrorist online network, and inadvertently begin transmitting instructions to destroy U.S. targets. The premise is intriguing but poorly done.
1987 (R) 95m/C Edward Albert, Yaphet Kotto, Kabir Bedi; *D:* John Kincade. VHS, Beta $79.95 CEL ✻½

Terminal Exposure Predictable but likeable comedy-mystery. A pair of Venice, CA, beach denizens capture a murder on film and try to solve it.
1989 (R) 105m/C Steve Donmyer, John Vernon, Ted Lange, Joe Phelan, Hope Marie Carlton, Mark Hennessy, Scott King; *D:* Nico Mastorakis. VHS, Beta, LV $79.98 LIV, VES ✻✻

Terminal Force Stupid, poorly executed story of kidnapping and the mob. So bad it never saw the inside of a theater; went straight to video.
1988 (R) 83m/C Troy Donahue, Richard Harrison, Dawn Wildsmith; *D:* Fred Olen Ray. VHS, LV $19.95 STE, NWV ✻

Terminal Island Tough southern California penal colony is crowded with inmates from death row. When prison becomes coed, violence breaks out. Exploitative and unappealing.
1973 (R) 88m/C Phyllis E. Davis, Tom Selleck, Don Marshall, Ena Hartman, Marta Kristen; *D:* Stephanie Rothman. VHS, Beta $29.95 UHV ✻½

The Terminal Man A slick, visually compelling adaptation of the Michael Crichton novel. A scientist plagued by violent mental disorders has a computer-controlled regulator implanted in his brain. The computer malfunctions and he starts a murdering spree. Futuristic vision of man-machine symbiosis gone awry. Well acted, but still falls short of the novel.
1974 (R) 107m/C George Segal, Joan Hackett, Jill Clayburgh, Richard Dysart, James B. Sikking, Norman Burton; *D:* Mike Hodges. VHS, Beta $19.98 WAR ✻✻½

T

The Terminator A futuristic cyborg is sent to present-day Earth. His job: kill the woman who will conceive the child destined to become the great liberator and arch-enemy of the Earth's future rulers. The cyborg is also pursued by another futuristic visitor, who falls in love with the intended victim. Cameron's pacing is just right in this exhilarating, explosive thriller which displays Arnie as one cold-blooded villain. Followed by "Terminator 2: Judgment Day."
1984 (R) 108m/C Arnold Schwarzenegger, Michael Biehn, Linda Hamilton, Paul Winfield, Lance Henriksen, Bill Paxton, Rick Rossovich, Dick Miller; *D:* James Cameron. VHS, Beta, LV, SVS $19.95 HBO, HMD ⅛⅛⅛

Terminator 2: Judgment Day Arnold returns as the lethal android from the future, now programmed not to destroy but protect a boy who will be mankind's postnuke resistance leader. But the T-1000, a shape-changing, ultimate killing machine, is also on the boy's trail, bent on terminating him. Twice the mayhem, five times the special effects, ten times the budget of the first "Terminator," but without Arnold it'd be half the movie. The word hasn't been invented to describe the special effects, particularly THE scariest nuclear holocaust scene yet. While it was a worldwide megahit, a hundred-million dollar budget nearly ruined the studio; Arnold accepted his $12 million in the form of a jet. Laserdisc features include Pan and Scan, Widescreen and a "Making of T-2" short.
1991 (R) 139m/C Arnold Schwarzenegger, Linda Hamilton, Edward Furlong, Robert Patrick, Earl Boen, Joe Morton; *D:* James Cameron. Academy Awards '91: Best Makeup, Best Sound, Best Sound Effects Editing, Best Visual Effects; Nominations: Best Cinematography, Best Sound; MTV Movie Awards '92: Best Actor (Schwarzenegger), Best Actress (Hamilton), Best Film, Breakthrough Performance (Furlong), Most Desirable Female (Hamilton), Best Action Sequence; People's Choice Awards '92: Best Film. VHS, LV, 8mm LIV, PIA ⅛⅛⅛½

Termini Station Dewhurst gives an excellent performance as the alcoholic matriarch of a small-town Canadian family. She drinks all day and dreams of traveling to Italy, while her children work and believe there is something more to life than their mundane existence. When they finally do leave, they discover an intriguing new world. Dewhurst and Follows also appear together in "Anne of Green Gables" and "Anne of Avonlea."
1991 105m/C Colleen Dewhurst, Megan Follows, Gordon Clapp, Hannah Lee; *D:* Allen King. VHS $79.95 MNC ⅛⅛½

Terms of Endearment A weeper following the changing relationship between a young woman and her mother, over a thirty-year period. Beginning as a comedy, turning serious as the years go by, this was Brooks' debut as screenwriter and director. Superb supporting cast headed by Nicholson's slyly charming neighbor/astronaut, with stunning performances by Winger and MacLaine as the two women who often know and love each other too well. Adapted from Larry McMurtry's novel.
1983 (PG) 132m/C Shirley MacLaine, Jack Nicholson, Debra Winger, John Lithgow, Jeff Daniels, Danny DeVito; *D:* James L. Brooks. Academy Awards '83: Best Actress (MacLaine), Best Adapted Screenplay, Best Director (Brooks), Best Picture, Best Supporting Actor (Nicholson); Nominations: Best Actress (Winger), Best Art Direction/Set Decoration, Best Film Editing, Best Sound, Best Supporting Actor (Lithgow), Best Original Score; Golden Globe Awards '84: Best Actress—Drama (MacLaine), Best Film—Drama,

Best Supporting Actor (Nicholson). VHS, Beta, LV $19.95 PAR, BTV, HMV ⅛⅛⅛

Terraces TV series pilot about high-rise tenants whose balconies are their only common ground. Good performances.
1977 90m/C Lloyd Bochner, Eliza Garrett, Julie Newmar, Tim Thomerson; *D:* Lila Garrett. VHS, Beta WOV ⅛⅛

Terronauts When man begins space exploration, Earth is attacked by aliens. The defenders are taken to an out-dated fortress where they learn that their forebears were similarly attacked. Juvenile, lackluster, contrived, and really dumb.
1967 77m/C *GB* Simon Oates, Zena Marshall, Charles Hawtrey, Stanley Meadows; *D:* Montgomery Tully. VHS, Beta $59.98 NLC Woof!

The Terror A hostelry is the scene of a number of brutal murders. Remake of a 1928 film and based on a play by Edgar Wallace. Good story, but weak version of it.
1938 63m/B *GB* Wilfred Lawson, Bernard Lee, Arthur Wontner, Linden Travers, Henry Oscar, Alastair Sim; *D:* Richard Bird. VHS, Beta $16.95 SNC ⅛⅛

The Terror A lieutenant in Napoleon's army chases a lovely maiden and finds himself trapped in a creepy castle by a mad baron. Movie legend has it Corman directed the movie in 3 days as the sets (from his previous movie "The Raven") were being torn down around them. *AKA:* Lady of the Shadows.
1963 81m/C Boris Karloff, Jack Nicholson, Sandra Knight; *D:* Roger Corman. VHS, Beta $19.95 NOS, SNC, PSM ⅛⅛

The Terror After 100 years, a man reveals in a film that his family killed a witch. Friends who see the film are attacked by supernatural forces. Originally double-billed with "Dracula's Dog."
1979 (R) 86m/C John Nolan, Carolyn Courage, James Aubrey; *D:* Norman J. Warren. VHS, Beta $19.95 UHV, VCD, HHE Woof!

Terror at London Bridge London Bridge is transported brick by brick to Arizona. It carries its history with it, including the havoc-wreaking spirit of Jack the Ripper. Campy made-for-TV effort. *AKA:* Bridge Across Time; Arizona Ripper.
1985 96m/C David Hasselhoff, Stephanie Kramer, Adrienne Barbeau, Randolph Mantooth; *D:* E.W. Swackhamer. VHS, Beta $29.95 FRH ⅛⅛

Terror at Red Wolf Inn Young woman wins a vacation; finds she's been invited for dinner, so to speak. Not campy enough to overcome stupidity. *AKA:* Club Dead; Terror House; The Folks at Red Wolf Inn.
1972 (R) 90m/C Linda Gillin, Arthur Space, John Neilson, Mary Jackson, Janet Wood, Margaret Avery; *D:* Bud Townsend. VHS, Beta $29.95 ACA ⅛⅛

Terror at Tenkiller Two girls vacationing in the mountains are seemingly surrounded by a rash of mysterious murders. Made for video.
1986 87m/C Mike Wiles, Stacey Logan. VHS, Beta $19.95 UHV ⅛

Terror at the Opera A bizarre staging of Verdi's "Macbeth" is plagued by depraved gore murders. But the show must go on, as one character chirps in badly-dubbed English. Italian horrormeister Argento's everfluid camera achieves spectacular shots, but the lurid, ludicrous script make this one for connoisseurs only. The operatic scenes employ the voice of Maria Callas. Available in an edited "R" rated version.

1988 (R) 107m/C Christina Marsillach, Ian Charleson, Urbano Barberini, William McNamara, Antonella Vitale, Barbara Cupisti, Coralina Cataldi Tassoni, Daria Nicolodi; *W/D:* Dario Argento. VHS $89.98 FCT ⅛½

Terror Beach A doctor and his bride move to a coastal village, only to find it enmeshed in witchcraft and devil worship.
198? 90m/C Victor Petit, Julie James, Mary Costi, Sandra Mozar. VHS, Beta NO ⅛

Terror Beneath the Sea A mad scientist wants to rule the world with his cyborgs. American and Japanese scientists unite to fight him. Fine special effects, especially the transformation from human to monster. *AKA:* Kaitei Daisenso; Water Cyborgs.
1966 85m/C *JP* Sonny Chiba, Peggy Neal, Franz Gruber, Gunther Braun, Andrew Hughes, Mike Daneen; *D:* Hajime Sato. VHS, Beta $39.95 DVT ⅛⅛½

Terror by Night Holmes and Watson attempt to solve the murder of the owner of a gigantic, beautiful jewel. Their investigation must be completed before their train arrives at its destination, where the murderer can escape.
1946 60m/B Basil Rathbone, Nigel Bruce; *D:* Roy William Neill. VHS, LV, 3/4U, Special order formats $14.95 NEG, REP, FOX ⅛⅛½

Terror by Night/Meeting at Midnight In "Terror by Night" (1946), Sherlock Holmes and Dr. Watson board a train to protect a fabulous diamond. In "Meeting at Midnight" (1944), Charlie Chan becomes involved in magic and murder.
1946 122m/B Basil Rathbone, Nigel Bruce, Sidney Toler; *D:* Roy William Neill. VHS, Beta MED ⅛⅛

Terror Creatures from the Grave Husband summons medieval plague victims to rise from the grave to drop in on his unfaithful wife. Should've been better.
1966 85m/C *IT* Barbara Steele, Riccardo Garrone, Walter Brandi; *D:* Ralph Zucker. VHS $19.98 SNC ⅛

Terror Eyes Spoof-thriller revolves around an "agent from Hell," sent to Earth to recruit writers for a horror film.
1987 (PG-13) 90m/C Daniel Roebuck, Vivian Schilling, Dan Bell, Lance August. VHS, Beta $39.95 AIP ⅛½

Terror in Beverly Hills When the President's daughter is kidnapped, it's up to an ex-marine to save her. The trouble is, the head terrorist hates the marine's guts as he blames him for the deaths of his wife and children. So incredibly bad it's campy and fun.
1990 88m/C Frank Stallone, Cameron Mitchell, William Smith; *W/D:* John Myhers. VHS, Beta, LV $79.95 AIP Woof!

Terror in Paradise Jason and Vickie think they're going to have a romantic holiday on a beautiful island paradise. But they've picked the wrong spot to vacation. It seems the island harbors a terrorist group and when they see more than they should the lovers become the next targets.
19?? (R) ?m/C Joanna Pettet, Gary Lockwood, David Anthony Smith, Leslie Ryan; *D:* Peer J. Oppenheimer. VHS $89.98 NHO ⅛½

Terror in the Haunted House Newlyweds move into an old house. The bride remembers it from her nightmares. First release featured the first use of Psychorama, a technique in which scary words or advertising messages were flashed on the screen for a fraction of a second—just long enough to cause subliminal response. The technique was banned later in the year.

1958 90m/C Gerald Mohr, Cathy O'Donnell, William Ching; *D:* Harold Daniels. **VHS, Beta** $9.95 *RHI, MLB, CCB* ⓛⓛ½

Terror in the Jungle Plane crashes in Peruvian wilds and young boy survivor meets Jivaro Indians who think he's a god. Much struggling to survive and battling with horrible script.
1968 (PG) 95m/C Jimmy Angle, Robert Burns, Fawn Silver; *D:* Tom De Simone. **VHS** $19.95 *ACA* ⓛ

Terror in the Swamp When not hanging out in the local murky waters, a swamp creature terrorizes the residents of a small town.
1985 (PG) 89m/C Billy Holliday; *D:* Joe Catalanotto. **VHS, Beta, LV** $9.95 *NWV, STE* ⓛ

Terror in the Wax Museum The owner of a wax museum is killed while mulling over the sale of the museum. The new owner has little better luck as the bodies continue to pile up. Production uses every out-of-work horror film actor of the time. The most suspenseful part of this low-budget flick is waiting to see how long the "wax dummies" can hold their breath.
1973 (PG) 94m/C Ray Milland, Broderick Crawford, Elsa Lanchester, Louis Hayward, Maurice Evans, John Carradine; *D:* Georg Fenady. **VHS, Beta** $69.98 *LIV Woof!*

Terror in Toyland Once again a knife-wielding lunatic dresses as Santa Claus to strike terror and death into the hearts of children. *AKA:* Christmas Evil; You Better Watch Out.
1985 90m/C Brandon Maggart, Jeffrey DeMunn; *D:* Lewis Jackson. **VHS, Beta** $19.95 *ACA* ⓛ½

Terror is a Man A mad scientist attempts to turn a panther into a man on a secluded island. Early Filipino horror attempt inspired by H.G. Wells' "The Island of Doctor Moreau." *AKA:* Blood Creature.
1959 89m/B *PH* Francis Lederer, Greta Thyssen, Richard Derr, Oscar Keesee; *D:* Gerardo (Gerry) De Leon. **VHS** $16.95 *SNC* ⓛⓛ

Terror of Mechagodzilla It's monster vs. machine in the heavyweight battle of the universe as a huge mechanical Godzilla built by aliens is pitted against the real thing. The last Godzilla movie made until "Godzilla 1985." *AKA:* Monsters from the Unknown Planet; The Escape of Megagodzilla; Mekagojira No Gyakushu.
1978 (G) 79m/C *JP* Katsuhiko Sasakai, Tomoko Ai. **VHS, Beta** $19.95 *PAR* ⓛ½

Terror of Rome Against the Son of Hercules Muscle-bound gladiators battle it out in this low-budget Italian action flick. Dubbed.
1964 100m/C *FR IT* Mark Forest, Marilu Tolo; *D:* Mario Ciano. **VHS, Beta** $16.95 *SNC, NLC* ⓛ

Terror of the Bloodhunters A French author is sentenced to Devil's Island for a crime he didn't commit. The warden's daughter takes a liking to him and arranges for him and a friend to escape, but numerous perils await them in the jungle.
1962 60m/B Robert Clarke, Steve Conte, Dorothy Haney; *W/D:* Jerry Warren. **VHS, Beta** $16.95 *SNC* ⓛ

Terror of the Steppes Yet another sword and sandal extravaganza in which a musclebound hero conquers all.
1964 ?m/C *IT* Kirk Morris. **VHS, Beta** $16.95 *SNC* ⓛ

Terror of Tiny Town Main characteristic of this musical/western is its entire midget cast, all members of Jed Buell's Midgets. Otherwise the plot is fairly average and features a bad guy and the good guy

who finally teaches him a lesson. Newfield plays up the cast's short stature—they walk under saloon doors and ride Shetland ponies.
1938 65m/B Bill Curtis, Yvonne Moray; *D:* Sam Newfield. **VHS, Beta** $16.95 *SNC, NOS, DVT* ⓛⓛ

Terror on Alcatraz The only prisoner to successfully escape from Alcatraz returns to retrieve the safety deposit box key he needs to get his stolen loot. And anyone who gets in his way is in for trouble.
1986 96m/C Veronica Porsche Ali, Sandy Brooke, Aldo Ray, Scott Ryder; *D:* Philip Marcus. **VHS** $79.95 *TWE, HHE* ⓛ

Terror on the 40th Floor Seven people make an attempt to escape from the 40th floor of an inflamed skyscraper. Poorly done re-hash of "Towering Inferno." Uninspired.
1974 98m/C John Forsythe, Anjanette Comer, Don Meredith, Joseph Campanella; *D:* Jerry Jameson. **VHS, Beta** $49.95 *PSM* ⓛ

Terror on Tour The Clowns, a rock group on their way up, center their stage performance around sadistic, mutilating theatrics. When real murders begin, they become prime suspects. Exploitive, bloody, disgusting.
1983 90m/C Dave Galluzzo, Richard Styles, Rick Pemberton; *D:* Don Edmonds. **VHS, Beta** $54.95 *MED Woof!*

Terror Out of the Sky A scientist must disguise himself as one of the insects to divert the attention of a horde of killing bees from a busload of elementary children. Sub-par sequel to "The Savage Bees."
1978 95m/C Efrem Zimbalist Jr., Dan Haggerty; *D:* Lee H. Katzin. **VHS, Beta** $49.95 *LIV* ⓛ½

Terror Ship Three people find an abandoned yacht which they believe was used for smuggling. While searching it, they find that it was used to transport stolen uranium. Before the police can arrive, the thieves show up. Not a very good handling of what was actually an interesting idea. Released as "Dangerous Voyage" in Great Britain.
1954 72m/B *GB* William Lundigan, Naomi Chance, Vincent Ball, Jean Lodge, Richard Stewart; *D:* Vernon Sewell. **VHS** $19.95 *NOS* ⓛⓛ

Terror Squad An unsuspecting high school population is put under siege by Libyan terrorists. The students get a hands-on lesson in revolution and guerrilla war tactics.
1987 95m/C Kerry Brennan, Bill Calvert, Chuck Connors, Greer Brodie; *D:* Peter Maris. **VHS** $79.98 *MCG* ⓛ

Terror Stalks the Class Reunion Kay (Nelligan) is a teacher who disappears at a class reunion. Police dismiss the case as a runaway wife, except for Virginia, a young detective (Beals) who doesn't accept that theory. And she's right—Kay is held hostage in a remote cabin by an obsessed former student (Davies). Kay needs all her wits to fend off her deranged and possibly deadly suitor while Virginia races to find her. Based on the novel by Mary Higgins Clark.
1993 (PG-13) 95m/C Kate Nelligan, Jennifer Beals, Geraint Wyn Davies. **VHS** $89.98 *REP* ⓛⓛ½

Terror Street An Air Force pilot's wife is murdered. He has 36 hours to clear his name and find the killer.
1954 84m/B Dan Duryea, Elsy Albiin, Ann Gudrun, Eric Pohlmann. **VHS, Beta, LV** *NO* ⓛ

Terror Trail As usual, Mix uses guns and fists to bring bad guys to justice, and gets the girl in the bargain.

1933 62m/B Tom Mix, Naomi Judge, Arthur Rankin, Raymond Hatton, Francis McDonald, Robert Kortman, John St. Polis, Lafe McKee, Buffalo Bill Jr.; *D:* Armand Schaefer. **VHS** $19.98 *DVT, HEG* ⓛ½

Terror Train A masquerade party is held on a chartered train. But someone has more than mask-wearing in mind as a series of dead bodies begin to appear. Copperfield provides magic, Curtis provides screams in this semi-scary slasher movie. *AKA:* Train of Terror.
1980 (R) 97m/C Jamie Lee Curtis, Ben Johnson, Hart Bochner, David Copperfield, Vanity; *D:* Roger Spottiswoode. **VHS, Beta, LV** $79.98 *FOX* ⓛ

The Terror Within Reptilian mutants hit the streets searching for human women to breed with. Have the Teenage Mutant Ninja Turtles grown up?
1988 (R) 90m/C George Kennedy, Andrew Stevens, Starr Andreeff, Terri Treas; *D:* Thierry Notz. **VHS, Beta** $79.95 *MGM* ⓛ

The Terror Within 2 In a world destroyed by biological warfare, a warrior and the woman he rescued traverse the badlands occupied by hideous mutants. What they don't know is that the real terror comes from within. How can they possibly survive? Not without decent dialogue, that's for sure.
1991 (R) 90m/C Andrew Stevens, Stella Stevens, Chick Vennera, Lee Ermey; *D:* Andrew Stevens. **VHS** $89.98 *VES* ⓛ½

Terrorgram Not a very special delivery. An offscreen James Earl Jones introduces three lesser tales of terror. Best seg: a sleazy filmmaker gets trapped in the world of his own exploitation scripts. The other two are bloody but negligible revenge-from-the-grave yarns. All start off with the receipt of a sinister package, hence a postal motif.
1990 (R) 88m/C Michael Hartson, J.T. Wallace. **VHS** $29.95 *MNC* ⓛ

The Terrorists Just as later he was a Scottish Lithuanian sub-commander in "The Hunt for Red October" (1990), here Connery is a Scottish Norwegian security chief. Good cinematography and premise are wasted; generic title betrays sloppy execution.
1974 (PG) 89m/C Sean Connery, Ian McShane, John Quentin; *D:* Caspar Wrede; *M:* Jerry Goldsmith. **VHS, Beta** $59.98 *FOX* ⓛ½

Terrorists An Army investigator discovers a plot to assassinate the President. It's up to him to move quickly enough to stop it. Brutal action.
1983 61m/C Marland Proctor, Irmgard Millard. **VHS, Beta** $59.95 *WWV* ⓛ

The Terrornauts Astronomer inadvertently contacts alien race and his entire building is transported across the galaxy. Supposed nuclear precautionary.
1967 75m/C *GB* Simon Oates, Zena Marshall, Charles Hawtrey, Patricia Hayes; *D:* Montgomery Tully. **VHS** *NLC* ⓛ½

Terrorvision OUR TV GAVE BIRTH TO SPACE ALIENS! It's amazing what modern technology can do: Suburban family buys a fancy satellite dish; bad black comedy and gory special effects result.
1986 (R) 84m/C Gerrit Graham, Mary Woronov, Diane Franklin, Bert Remsen, Alejandro Rey; *D:* Ted Nicolaou. **VHS, Beta** $79.98 *LIV Woof!*

The Terry Fox Story In the spring of 1980, a young man who had lost his right leg to cancer dipped his artificial limb into the Atlantic Ocean and set off on a fund-raising "Marathon of Hope" across Canada, drawing national attention. Inspiring made-for-TV true story is well-scripted and avoids cor-

niness. Good acting from real-life amputee Fryer and, as usual, from Duvall.
1983 96m/C Eric Fryer, Robert Duvall, Chris Makepeace, Michael Zelniker, Rosalind Chao; **D:** Ralph L. Thomas. **VHS, Beta** $69.95 VES 🎬🎬🎬

Tess Sumptuous adaptation of a Thomas Hardy novel. Kinski is wonderful as an innocent poor girl who marries into the aristocracy, where she is sexually and socially out of her depth. Polanski's direction is faithful and artful. Nearly three hours long, but worth every minute. Multiple Oscar winner.
1980 (PG) 170m/C GB FR Nastassia Kinski, Peter Firth, Leigh Lawson, John Collin; **D:** Roman Polanski. Academy Awards '80: Best Art Direction/Set Decoration, Best Cinematography, Best Costume Design; Nominations: Best Director (Polanski), Best Picture, Best Original Score; Cesar Awards '80: Best Director (Polanski), Best Film; Golden Globe Awards '81: Best Foreign Film; Los Angeles Film Critics Association Awards '80: Best Director (Polanski); National Board of Review Awards '80: 10 Best Films of the Year. **VHS, Beta, LV** $14.95 COL 🎬🎬🎬

Test of Donald Norton Good early Western. A young man raised by Indians finds work with the Hudson's Bay Company and does well, but is haunted by suspicions that he is a half-breed.
1926 68m/B George Walsh, Tyrone Power Sr., Eugenia Gilbert, Robert Graves, Virginia True Boardman; **D:** B. Reeves Eason. **VHS, Beta, 8mm** $16.95 GPV, VYY 🎬🎬½

A Test of Love Incorrectly diagnosed as retarded, a young woman with cerebral palsy struggles to adjust to life outside an institution. Predictable but touching and well-acted. **AKA:** Annie's Coming Out.
1984 (PG) 93m/C AU Angela Punch McGregor, Drew Forsythe, Tina Arhondis; **D:** Gil Brealey. **VHS, Beta** $69.95 MCA 🎬🎬

Test Pilot Gable and Spencer star as daring test pilot and devoted mechanic respectively. When Gable has to land his experimental craft in a Kansas cornfield, he meets and falls in love with farm girl Loy. The two marry and raise a family, all the while she worries over his dangerous profession. When the Air Force asks him to test their new B-17 bomber, she refuses to watch, thinking the test will end in tragedy. Superb aviation drama featuring excellent cast.
1938 118m/B Clark Gable, Myrna Loy, Spencer Tracy, Lionel Barrymore, Samuel S. Hinds; **D:** Victor Fleming. **VHS, Beta** $19.98 MGM, TLF, CCB 🎬🎬🎬½

Test Tube Babies A married couple's morals begin to deteriorate as they mourn the fact they can't have a child. The day is saved, however, when they learn about the new artificial insemination process. Amusing, campy propaganda in the vein of "Reefer Madness."
1948 83m/B Dorothy Duke, Timothy Farrell, William Thompson; **D:** W. Merle Connell. **VHS, Beta** $19.95 GVV Woof!

Test Tube Babies Exploitative and campy account of a childless couple who sink into despair until they learn about artificial insemination. Rereleased in 1967 as "The Pill" with extra scenes featuring Monica Davis and John Maitland.
1953 ?m/C Dorothy Duke, William Thomason, Timothy Farrell; **D:** W. Merle Connell. **VHS** $16.95 SNC 🎬

Testament Well-made and thought-provoking story of the residents of a small California town struggling to survive after a nuclear bombing. Focuses on one family who tries to accept the reality of post-holocaust life. We see the devastation but it never sinks

into sensationalism. An exceptional performance from Alexander.
1983 (PG) 90m/C Jane Alexander, William Devane, Ross Harris, Roxana Zal, Kevin Costner, Rebecca DeMornay; **D:** Lynne Littman. **VHS, Beta, LV** $14.95 PAR 🎬🎬🎬

The Testament of Dr. Cordelier A strange, experimental fantasy about a Jekyll and Hyde-type lunatic stalking the streets and alleys of Paris. Originally conceived as a television play, Renoir attempted to create a new mise-en-scene, using multiple cameras covering the sequences as they were performed whole. In French with English subtitles.
1959 95m/C FR Jean-Louis Barrault; **D:** Jean Renoir. **VHS, Beta** $29.95 FCT 🎬🎬🎬

Testament of Dr. Mabuse The director of an asylum is controlled by the evil genius, Dr. Mabuse, who hypnotizes him in this well-done remake of Lang's 1933 classic. **AKA:** The Crimes of Dr. Mabuse; The Last Will of Dr. Mabuse.
1962 ?m/C Gert Frobe, Wolfgang Preiss, Senta Berger. **VHS** $16.95 SNC, LSV 🎬🎬½

The Testament of Orpheus Superb, personal surrealism; writer-director Cocteau's last film. Hallucinogenic, autobiographical dream-journey through time. Difficult to follow, but rewarding final installment in a trilogy including "The Blood of the Poet" and "Orpheus." In French with English subtitles.
1959 80m/B FR Jean Cocteau, Edouard Dermithe, Maria Casares, Francois Perier, Yul Brynner, Jean-Pierre Leaud, Daniel Gelin, Jean Marais, Pablo Picasso, Charles Aznavour; **D:** Jean Cocteau. **VHS, Beta** $29.95 NOS, FCT, TAM 🎬🎬🎬½

Tetsuo: The Iron Man A weird live-action science-fiction cartoon about a white-collar Japanese worker who finds himself being gradually transformed into a walking metal collection of cables, drills, wires, and gears. The newly-formed metal creature then faces off with an equally bizarre metals fetishist (played by the director). In Japanese with English subtitles.
1992 67m/B JP Tomoroh Taguchi, Kei Fujiwara, Shinya Tsukamoto; **W/D:** Shinya Tsukamoto. **VHS** $79.95 FXL 🎬🎬

Tevye Sholom Aleichem's story of Jewish family life, intermarriage, and turmoil in Poland. When Khave, the daughter of Tevye the dairyman, seeks to marry a Ukrainian peasant, Tevye must come to terms with his love for his daughter and his faith and loyalty to tradition. Also the basis for the musical "Fiddler on the Roof." In Yiddish with English subtitles. **AKA:** Tevye der Milkhiker.
1939 96m/B Maurice Schwartz, Miriam Riselle; **D:** Maurice Schwartz. **VHS, Beta** $89.95 ERG, NCJ, TAM 🎬🎬½

Tex Fatherless brothers in Oklahoma come of age. Dillon is excellent. Based on the novel by S.E. Hinton.
1982 (PG) 103m/C Matt Dillon, Jim Metzler, Meg Tilly, Bill McKinney, Frances Lee McCain, Ben Johnson, Emilio Estevez; **D:** Tim Hunter. **VHS, Beta, LV** DIS, OM 🎬🎬½

Tex Avery's Screwball Classics, Vol. 1 Collection of eight classic cartoons compiled by renowned MGM director Avery.
194? 60m/C **D:** Tex Avery. **VHS, Beta, LV** $14.95 MGM, WTA 🎬🎬🎬

Tex Avery's Screwball Classics, Vol. 2 More Averian cartoon classics, bearing the master's unmistakable stamp: "One Ham's Family," "Happy Go Nutty," "Slap Happy Lion," "Wild and Wolfy," "Ventriloquist Cat," "Big Heel Watha," "North-

west Hounded Police" and the semi-rare, long-banned "Red Hot Riding Hood."
194? 60m/C **D:** Tex Avery. **VHS, Beta** $14.95 MGM, WTA 🎬🎬½

Tex Avery's Screwball Classics, Vol. 3 Hilarious cartoons from the man responsible for Bugs Bunny and other animated nuts.
194? 60m/C **VHS, Beta** $12.98 MGM, FCT, WTA 🎬🎬½

Tex Rides with the Boy Scouts Scouts aid Ritter in capturing gold bandits with a little bit of singing thrown in for good measure.
1937 60m/B Tex Ritter. **VHS, Beta** $19.95 NOS, DVT 🎬½

Texas Two friends wander through the West after the Civil War getting into scrapes with the law and eventually drifting apart. Ford takes a job on a cattle ranch run by Trevor and discovers Holden has joined a gang of rustlers aiming to steal her herd. The two men vie for Trevor's affections. Although friends, a professional rivalry also existed between the two leading actors and they competed against each other, doing their own stunts during filming. Well-acted, funny, and enthusiastic Western.
1941 94m/B William Holden, Glenn Ford, Claire Trevor, Edgar Buchanan, George Bancroft; **D:** George Marshall. **VHS, Beta** $9.95 COL 🎬🎬🎬

Texas Carnival Williams and Skelton star as carnival performers who operate the dunk tank. When Skelton is mistaken for an oil tycoon, he lives high on the hog until the mistake is discovered. Believe it or not, this musical has only one water ballet sequence. Songs include "It's Dynamite," "Whoa! Emma," and "Young Folks Should Get Married."
1951 77m/C Esther Williams, Red Skelton, Howard Keel, Ann Miller, Paula Raymond, Keenan Wynn, Tom Tully; **D:** Charles Walters. **VHS** $19.98 MGM 🎬🎬

The Texas Chainsaw Massacre The movie that put the "power" in power tools. An idyllic summer afternoon drive becomes a nightmare for a group of young people pursued by a chainsaw-wielding maniac. Made with tongue firmly in cheek, this is nevertheless a mesmerizing saga of gore, flesh, mayhem, and violence.
1974 (R) 86m/C Marilyn Burns, Allen Danzinger, Paul A. Partain, William Vail, Teri McMinn, Edwin Neal, Jim Siedow, Gunnar Hansen, John Dugan, Jerry Lorenz; **W/D:** Tobe Hooper; **W:** Kim Henkel. **VHS, Beta, LV** $39.95 MED 🎬🎬½

Texas Chainsaw Massacre, Part 2 A tasteless, magnified sequel to the notorious blood-bucket extravaganza, about a certain family in southern Texas who kill and eat passing travelers. Followed by "Leatherface: Texas Chainsaw Massacre III."
1986 (R) 90m/C Dennis Hopper, Caroline Williams, Bill Johnson, Jim Siedow; **D:** Tobe Hooper. **VHS, Beta, LV** $19.95 MED Woof!

Texas Cyclone A stranger rides into a town that turns out to be incredibly friendly. Later he realizes the entire town thinks he is a prominent citizen who disappeared years ago.
1932 58m/B Tim McCoy, Wheeler Oakman, Shirley Grey, Walter Brennan, John Wayne, Wallace MacDonald, Vernon Dent, Mary Gordon; **D:** Irving Briskin. **VHS** $14.95 COL, DVT, NOS 🎬🎬

Texas Detour On a trip across country, a trio of young Californians have their van stolen. They decide to take the law into their own hands when the redneck sheriff gives them no help. Dull, undistinguished "action" flick.

1977 90m/C Cameron Mitchell, Priscilla Barnes, Patrick Wayne, Mitch Vogel, Lindsay Bloom, R.G. Armstrong; *D:* Hikmet Avedis. VHS, Beta $59.95 *PSM* ⅋

Texas Gunfighter Your basic western from the Maynard series, with everything a western could have.
1932 60m/B Ken Maynard. VHS, Beta $19.95 *NOS, UHV, DVT* ⅋⅋

Texas Guns A gritty western about an old-time gunman (Nelson) and his quest for one last robbery, killing those who stand in his way and some just for fun. Also watch for Cassidy's comeback. *AKA:* Once Upon a Texas Train.
1990 (PG) 96m/C Willie Nelson, Richard Widmark, Shaun Cassidy, Angie Dickinson, Kevin McCarthy, Royal Dano, Chuck Connors, Ken Curtis, Dub Taylor. VHS, LV $89.95 *VMK* ⅋⅋

Texas John Slaughter: Geronimo's Revenge An Indian-loving rancher frets and fights when Geronimo attacks innocent settlers. Compiled fom Walt Disney television episodes.
1960 77m/C Tom Tryon, Darryl Hickman, Betty Lynn; *D:* Harry Keller. VHS, Beta $69.95 *DIS* ⅋⅋

Texas John Slaughter: Stampede at Bitter Creek Good guy Texas John Slaughter meets a variety of threatening obstacles when he tries to move his cattle herd into New Mexico. Originally from the "Walt Disney Presents" television series.
1962 90m/C Tom Tryon; *D:* Harry Keller. VHS, Beta $69.95 *DIS* ⅋⅋

Texas Justice The "Lone Rider" cavorts around in the desert, dispensing justice in the guise of a monk.
1942 60m/B George Huston, Al "Fuzzy" St. John, Dennis Moore, Wanda McKay, Claire Rochelle; *D:* Sam Newfield. VHS, Beta $19.95 *NOS, DVT* ⅋ ½

Texas Kid A typical western. Hero helps a vengeance-minded kid catch the robbergang who robbed and killed his father. Yee-Haw.
1943 53m/B Johnny Mack Brown, Kermit Maynard. VHS, Beta $19.95 *VDM* ⅋ ½

Texas Lady When a woman wins $50,000 gambling, she buys a Texas newspaper on the stipulation that she can edit it in this standard fare western. Good vehicle for Colbert to look beautiful, but the plot and script are average and uninspired.
1956 86m/C Claudette Colbert, Barry Sullivan, Gregory Walcott; *D:* Tim Whelan. VHS $19.98 *REP* ⅋⅋

Texas Layover Impossible-to-describe western/exploitation entry from trashmeister Adamson involving multiple stewardesses and the remnants of the Ritz Brothers.
1975 88m/C Yvonne De Carlo, Bob Livingston, Donald (Don "Red") Barry, Connie Hoffman, Regina Carrol, Jimmy Ritz, Harry Ritz; *D:* Al Adamson. VHS *NO Woof!*

Texas Legionnaires Roy comes back to his home town and gets caught between feuding cattle and sheep herders. *AKA:* Man from Music Mountain.
1943 71m/B Roy Rogers, Ruth Terry, Paul Kelly, Anne Gillis, George Cleveland, Pat Brady; *D:* Joseph Kane. VHS $19.95 *NOS, DVT* ⅋⅋

Texas Lightning Innocuous B-grade touching movie about a father and son and their family woes.
1981 (R) 93m/C Cameron Mitchell, Channing Mitchell, Maureen McCormick, Peter Jason. VHS, Beta $49.95 *MED* ⅋ ½

Texas Masquerade Standard good cowboys versus land-grabbers action filler. William Boyd plays Hopalong Cassidy. Andy Clyde plays California Carson. Jimmy Rogers plays...Jimmy Rogers.
1944 59m/B William Boyd, Andy Clyde, Jimmy Rogers, Mady Correll, Don Costello, Russell Simpson, Nelson Leigh, Francis McDonald, J. Farrell MacDonald; *D:* George Archainbaud. VHS $19.95 *NOS* ⅋⅋

Texas Pioneers A frontier scout is sent to an outpost town besieged by crooks. *AKA:* The Blood Brother.
1932 54m/B Bill Cody. VHS, Beta $19.95 *VDM* ⅋ ½

The Texas Rangers A prisoner is given the opportunity to capture the notorious Sam Bass gang in exchange for freedom. Good B Western; lotsa shootin'.
1951 68m/C George Montgomery, Gale Storm, Jerome Courtland, Noah Beery Jr.; *D:* Phil Karlson. VHS, Beta *GKK* ⅋⅋

Texas Terror Young Wayne resigns his badge when he mistakenly believes he has shot and killed his friend. He later rescues his friend's sister, learns the truth, and (naturally) finds true love.
1935 50m/B John Wayne, George "Gabby" Hayes, Lucille Browne. VHS $9.98 *REP, NEG, NOS* ⅋⅋

Texas to Bataan The Range Busters ship horses to the Philippines and encounter enemy spies. Part of the "Range Busters" series.
1942 56m/B Range Busters, John "Dusty" King, David Sharpe, Max Terhune; *D:* Robert Tansey. VHS, Beta $24.95 *VYY* ⅋ ½

Texas Trouble Standard matinee fare with cowboy Bob Steele.
193? 0m/B Bob Steele. VHS, Beta $27.95 *VCN* ⅋ ½

Texas Wildcats A cowboy helps make sure that sinister adversaries are brought to justice on the American Frontier.
1939 60m/B Tim McCoy. VHS, Beta $19.95 *NOS, DVT, MOV* ⅋ ½

Texasville Sequel to "The Last Picture Show" finds the characters still struggling after 30 years, with financial woes from the energy crisis, mental illness inspired by the Korean War, and various personal tragedies. Lacks the melancholy sensitivity of its predecessor, but has some of the wit and wisdom that comes with age. Based again on a Larry McMurtry novel. Not well received during its theatrical release.
1990 (R) 120m/C Timothy Bottoms, Jeff Bridges, Annie Potts, Cloris Leachman, Eileen Brennan, Randy Quaid, Cybill Shepherd, William McNamara; *D:* Peter Bogdanovich. VHS, LV $19.95 *COL, VMK* ⅋⅋ ½

Thank God It's Friday Episodic and desultory disco-dancing vehicle which won the Best Song Oscar for Donna Summer's rendition. Life is irony. Co-produced by Motown. ♫Last Dance; After Dark; Find My Way; It's Serious; Let's Make A Deal; Romeo and Juliet; You're the Reason I Feel Like Dancing; From Here to Eternity; Dance All Night; Love Masterpiece; I'm Here Again; Disco Queen; Trapped in a Stairway; Thank God It's Friday; You are the Most Precious Thing in My Life; I Wanna Dance; Meco's Theme; Floyd's Theme; Down to Lovetown; Lovin', Livin', and Givin'; Do You Want the Real Thing?; You Can Always Tell a Lady by the Company She Keeps.
1978 (PG) 100m/C Valerie Landsburg, Teri Nunn, Chick Vennera, Jeff Goldblum, Debra Winger; *D:* Robert Klane. VHS, Beta $12.95 *COL* ⅋ ½

Thank You & Good Night Director Oxenberg gathers members of her own family around a purple armchair of grandma's to talk about life, love, and family memories, including grandma's illness and recent death.
1991 81m/C *W/D:* Jan Oxenberg. VHS $79.95 *FXL* ⅋ ½

Thank Your Lucky Stars A lavish, slap-dash wartime musical that emptied out the Warner's lot for an array of uncharacteristic celebrity turns. Features Shore in her movie debut. ♫They're Either Too Young or Too Old; Blues in the Night; Hotcha Cornia; Ridin' For A Fall; We're Staying Home Tonight; Goin' North; Love Isn't Born, It's Made; No You, No Me; Ice Cold Katie; The Dreamer; How Sweet You Are; Good Night, Good Neighbor; Finale; Thank Your Lucky Stars; That's What You Jolly Well Get.
1943 127m/B Eddie Cantor, Dinah Shore, Joan Leslie, Errol Flynn, Bette Davis, Edward Everett Horton, Humphrey Bogart, John Garfield, Alan Hale Jr., Ann Sheridan, Ida Lupino, Jack Carson, Dennis Morgan, Olivia de Havilland; *D:* David Butler. VHS, Beta, LV $29.95 *MGM* ⅋⅋

Thanksgiving Story When John-Boy's college career is jeopardized by a freak accident, the Walton family gathers together for comfort. Very sentimental family-fare, originally shown as a holiday special from the popular television series "The Waltons."
1973 95m/C Richard Thomas, Ralph Waite, Michael Learned, Ellen Corby, Will Geer; *D:* Philip Leacock. VHS, Beta $59.95 *LHV, WAR, TVC* ⅋⅋ ½

Tharus Son of Attila A couple of sword-wielding barbarians battle each other and an evil emperor.
1987 89m/C Jerome Courtland, Rik von Nutter, Lisa Gastoni; *D:* Robert Montero. VHS, Beta $59.95 *TWE* ⅋

That Brennan Girl A maudlin soap opera about how a girl's upbringing by an inconsiderate mother makes her a devious little wench. Fortunately her second husband had a better mom, and redemption is at hand.
1946 95m/B James Dunn, Mona Freeman, William Marshall, June Duprez, Frank Jenks, Charles Arnt; *D:* Alfred Santell. VHS $19.95 *NOS* ⅋ ½

That Certain Thing Very early silent Capra comedy about a bachelor with a silver spoon in his mouth who loses his inheritance when he marries for love. It's got that certain Capra screwball feeling.
1928 65m/B Viola Dana, Ralph Graves, Burr McIntosh, Aggie Herring, Syd Crossley; *D:* Frank Capra. VHS, Beta $19.95 *GPV* ⅋⅋ ½

That Certain Woman Sentimental drama with Davis portraying a gangster's widow who wants to make a new life for herself. Fonda plays the rich playboy with whom she falls in love. Because of Davis' star power, she demanded that Fonda play opposite her. It seems Davis had a real life crush on him when they were both players in a stock company several years earlier. Remake of Goulding's "The Trespasser" which starred Gloria Swanson.
1937 91m/B Bette Davis, Henry Fonda, Ian Hunter, Anita Louise, Donald Crisp, Katherine Alexander, Minor Watson; *W/D:* Edmund Goulding. VHS $19.98 *MGM* ⅋⅋ ½

That Championship Season Long-dormant animosities surface at the reunion of a championship basketball team. Unfortunate remake of Miller's Pulitzer-prize winning play, with none of the fire which made it a Broadway hit.

1982 (R) 110m/C Martin Sheen, Bruce Dern, Stacy Keach, Robert Mitchum, Paul Sorvino, Jason Miller; D: Jason Miller. VHS, Beta $24.95 MGM ⅞⅞

That Cold Day in the Park Early Altman. An unhappy woman takes in a homeless young man from the park near her home. The woman (Dennis) is obsessive and odd; so is the film. Dennis is excellent. Reminiscent of ''The Collector.''
1969 (R) 91m/C Sandy Dennis, Michael Burns, Suzanne Benton, Michael Murphy; D: Robert Altman. VHS, Beta $14.98 REP, FCT ⅞⅞ ½

That Darn Cat Vintage Disney comedy about a Siamese cat that helps FBI Agent Jones thwart kidnappers. Could be shorter, but suspenseful and funny with characteristic Disney slapstick. Based on the book ''Undercover Cat'' by The Gordons.
1965 (G) 115m/C Hayley Mills, Dean Jones, Dorothy Provine, Neville Brand, Elsa Lanchester, Frank Gorshin; D: Robert Stevenson. VHS, Beta $19.99 DIS ⅞⅞ ½

That Darn Sorceress A child witch has grown up, and so has her power. To keep her disciples, she must perform increasingly horrible feats.
1988 89m/C Pauline Adams, Betty Page; D: Whitney Bain. VHS, Beta NO ⅞

That Forsyte Woman Based on the novel ''A Man of Property'' by John Galsworthy, a married Victorian woman falls for an architect engaged to be wed. Remade later, and better for BBC-television as ''The Forsythe Saga.'' AKA: The Forsyte Saga.
1950 112m/C Errol Flynn, Greer Garson, Walter Pidgeon, Robert Young, Janet Leigh, Harry Davenport, Stanley Logan, Lumsden Hare, Aubrey Mather, Matt Moore; D: Compton Bennett. VHS $19.98 MGM, CCB ⅞⅞

That Gang of Mine ''East Side Kids'' episode about gang member Mugg's ambition to be a jockey. Good racing scenes.
1940 62m/B Bobby Jordan, Leo Gorcey, Clarence Muse, Dave O'Brien; D: Joseph H. Lewis. VHS, Beta $24.95 NOS, DVT, HEG ⅞

That Girl from Paris An opera singer from Paris stows away on an ocean liner to be near the swing bandleader she has fallen in love with. An entertaining film with many songs; remade as ''Four Jacks and a Jill.'' ♫Una Voce Poco Fa; The Blue Danube; Love and Learn; The Call to Arms; Seal It With A Kiss; My Nephew From Nice; Moon Face; Tarantella.
1936 105m/B Lily Pons, Gene Raymond, Jack Oakie, Herman Bing, Lucille Ball, Mischa Auer, Frank Jenks; D: Leigh Jason. VHS, Beta $19.98 TTC ⅞⅞ ½

That Hamilton Woman Screen biography of the tragic 18th-century love affair between British naval hero Lord Nelson and Lady Hamilton. Korda exaggerated the film's historical distortions in order to pass the censor's production code about adultery. Winston Churchill's favorite film which paralleled Britain's heroic struggles in World War II. AKA: Lady Hamilton.
1941 125m/B Laurence Olivier, Vivien Leigh, Gladys Cooper, Alan Mowbray, Sara Allgood, Henry Wilcoxon; D: Alexander Korda. Academy Awards '41: Best Sound; Nominations: Best Black and White Cinematography, Best Interior Decoration. VHS, Beta, LV $19.98 HBO, SUE ⅞⅞⅞

That Long Night in '43 A gripping story of fascist terror during World War II.
1960 110m/B D: Florestano Vancini. VHS, Beta, 3/4U, Special order formats CIG ⅞⅞ ½

That Lucky Touch York is a reporter covering NATO games; Moore is Bond warmed over as an arms dealer. Sexual and professional tension becomes unlikely romance. Slight and dull. Cobb's last film.
1975 92m/C Roger Moore, Susannah York, Shelley Winters, Lee J. Cobb, Jean-Pierre Cassel, Raf Vallone, Sydne Rome; D: Christopher Miles. VHS, Beta $69.95 TWE ⅞⅞

That Man Is Pregnant NYPD detective gets the incredible news that he is pregnant. Viewers can't believe it, either.
1980 (PG) 80m/C VHS, Beta NO ⅞

That Midnight Kiss Glossy production of a musical romance featuring Lanza in his film debut. Thin plot has Lanza starring as a singing truck driver who is discovered by opera diva Grayson. ♫They Didn't Believe Me; I Know, I Know, I Know; Three O'Clock in the Morning; Santa Lucia; Down Among the Sheltering Palms; Revolutionary Etude; Cara Nome; Celeste Aida; Una Furtiva Lacrima; Mama Mia Che Vo Sape.
1949 96m/C Kathryn Grayson, Jose Iturbi, Ethel Barrymore, Mario Lanza, Keenan Wynn, J. Carroll Naish, Jules Munshin; D: Norman Taurog. VHS $19.98 MGM ⅞⅞ ½

That Naughty Girl The bored daughter of a nightclub owner decides to experience all life has to offer.
1958 77m/C FR Brigitte Bardot, Jean Bretonniere, Francoise Fabian; D: Michel Boisrond. VHS, Beta $69.95 JEF ⅞⅞

That Obscure Object of Desire Bunuel's last film, a comic nightmare of sexual frustration. A rich Spaniard obtains a beautiful girlfriend who, while changing physical identities, refuses to sleep with him. Based on a novel by Pierre Louys, which has been used as the premise for several other films, including ''The Devil is a Woman,'' ''La Femme et le Pantin,'' and ''The Female.'' Available with subtitles or dubbed. AKA: Cet Obscur Objet Du Desir.
1977 (R) 100m/C SP Fernando Rey, Carol Bouquet, Angela Molina; D: Luis Bunuel. Academy Awards '77 Nominations: Best Adapted Screenplay, Best Foreign Language Film; Los Angeles Film Critics Association Awards '77: Best Foreign Film; National Board of Review Awards '77: 5 Best Foreign Films of the Year, Best Director (Bunuel). VHS, Beta, LV $19.95 COL, VYG, APD ⅞⅞ ½

That Sinking Feeling A group of bored Scot teenagers decide to steal 90 sinks from a plumber's warehouse. One of Forsythe's early films, it was well received and is genuinely funny as the boys try to get rid of the sinks and turn a profit.
1979 (PG) 82m/C GB Robert Buchanan, John Hughes, Billy Greenlees, Alan Love; D: Bill Forsyth. VHS, Beta, LV $59.98 SUE ⅞⅞⅞

That Summer of White Roses Compelling action drama about a lifeguard working at a resort in Nazi-occupied Yugoslavia and his love for a woman resistance fighter and her child.
1990 (R) 98m/C Tom Conti, Susan George, Rod Steiger; D: Rajko Grlic. VHS, Beta, LV $89.98 MED, IME ⅞⅞

That Touch of Mink In New York City, an unemployed secretary finds herself involved with a business tycoon. On a trip to Bermuda, both parties get an education as they play their game of ''cat and mouse.'' Enjoyable romantic comedy.
1962 99m/C Cary Grant, Doris Day, Gig Young, Audrey Meadows, John Astin, Dick Sargent; D: Delbert Mann. Academy Awards '62 Nominations: Best Art Direction/Set Decoration (Color), Best Sound, Best Story & Screenplay;

Golden Globe Awards '63: Best Film—Musical/Comedy. VHS, LV $19.98 REP, MLB ⅞⅞ ½

That Uncertain Feeling Light comedy about a couple's marital problems increasing when she develops the hiccups and a friendship with a flaky piano player. A remake of the earlier Lubitsch silent film, ''Kiss Me Again.'' Available colorized.
1941 86m/B Merle Oberon, Melvyn Douglas, Burgess Meredith, Alan Mowbray, Eve Arden, Sig Rumann, Harry Davenport; D: Ernst Lubitsch. VHS, Beta $14.95 NOS, VYY, DVT ⅞⅞ ½

That Was Then...This Is Now Lame adaptation of S.E. Hinton teen novel (script by Estevez) about a surly kid who is attached to his adoptive brother and becomes jealous when the brother gets a girlfriend.
1985 (R) 102m/C Emilio Estevez, Craig Sheffer, Kim Delaney, Jill Schoelen, Barbara Babcock, Frank Howard, Larry B. Scott, Morgan Freeman; D: Christopher Cain; W: Emilio Estevez. VHS, Beta, LV $79.95 PAR ⅞⅞

That'll Be the Day The early rock 'n' roll of the 1950s is the only outlet for a frustrated young working-class Brit. Prequel to ''Stardust.'' Good, meticulous realism; engrossing story.
1973 86m/C Ringo Starr, Keith Moon, David Essex, Rosemary Leach; D: Claude Whatham. VHS, Beta, LV $14.95 HBO ⅞⅞ ½

That's Adequate Mock documentary about a fictional film studio. Lampoons just about every movie made in the last 60 years. Premise might have been adequate for a sketch, but hardly for a feature-length film. Zaniness gets old quickly.
1990 (R) 82m/C Tony Randall, Robert Downey, Rocky Aoki, Bruce Willis, Robert Townsend, James Coco, Jerry Stiller, Peter Riegert, Susan Dey, Richard Lewis, Robert Vaughn, Renee Taylor, Stuart Pankin, Brother Theodore, Anne Bloom, Chuck McCann, Anne Meara; D: Harry Hurwitz. VHS $14.95 HMD ⅞⅞

That's Dancing! This anthology features some of film's finest moments in dance from classical ballet to break-dancing.
1985 (G) 104m/C Fred Astaire, Ginger Rogers, Ruby Keeler, Cyd Charisse, Gene Kelly, Shirley MacLaine, Liza Minnelli, Sammy Davis Jr., Mikhail Baryshnikov, Ray Bolger, Jennifer Beals, Dean Martin; D: Jack Haley Jr. VHS, Beta, LV $19.98 MGM ⅞⅞

That's Entertainment A compilation of scenes from the classic MGM musicals beginning with ''The Broadway Melody'' (1929) and ending with ''Gigi'' (1958). Great fun, especially for movie buffs.
1974 (G) 132m/C Judy Garland, Fred Astaire, Frank Sinatra, Gene Kelly, Esther Williams, Bing Crosby; D: Jack Haley Jr. VHS, Beta, LV $19.98 MGM, PIA ⅞⅞

That's Entertainment, Part 2 A cavalcade of great musical and comedy sequences from MGM movies of the past. Also stars Jeanette MacDonald, Nelson Eddy, the Marx Brothers, Laurel and Hardy, Jack Buchanan, Ann Miller, Mickey Rooney, Louis Armstrong, Oscar Levant, Cyd Charisse, Elizabeth Taylor, Maurice Chavalier, Bing Crosby, Jimmy Durante, Clark Gable, and the Barrymores. Not as unified as its predecessor, but priceless nonetheless.
1976 (G) 133m/C Fred Astaire, Gene Kelly. VHS, Beta, LV $19.98 MGM ⅞⅞

That's Life! A lackluster semi-home movie starring Edwards' family and friends. A single weekend in the lives of a writer who's turning sixty, his singer wife who has been diagnosed with cancer, and their family.

1986 (PG-13) 102m/C Jack Lemmon, Julie Andrews, Sally Kellerman, Chris Lemmon, Emma Walton, Rob Knepper, Robert Loggia, Jennifer Edwards; **D:** Blake Edwards. **VHS, Beta, LV $14.98** CCB, LIV, VES 🎬🎬

That's My Baby! A man wants his girlfriend to have their baby, but the only thing she wants is a career. War between the sexes poorly done.
1988 (PG-13) 97m/C Sonja Smits, Timothy Webber; **D:** Edie Yolles, John Bradshaw. **VHS, Beta $79.98** TWE 🎬

That's My Hero! An animated film about Waldo Kitty, a cartoon cat who fantasizes about heroic adventures much like Thurber's Mitty.
1975 72m/C VHS, Beta SUE, OM 🎬

That's Singing: The Best of Broadway A tribute to the American musical theatre featuring performances of memorable songs from twenty Broadway shows.
1984 111m/C VHS, Beta, LV $19.98 LHV, VTK, WAR 🎬

Theatre of Blood Critics are unkind to Shakespearian ham Price, and he eliminates them by various Bard-inspired methods with the assistance of his lovely daughter. Top drawer comedy noir.
1973 (R) 104m/C GB Vincent Price, Diana Rigg, Ian Hendry, Robert Morley, Dennis Price, Diana Dors, Milo O'Shea; **D:** Douglas Hickox. **VHS, LV $59.95** MGM 🎬🎬

Theatre of Death Horror master Lee is back, this time as a theatre director in Paris. Meanwhile, police are baffled by a series of mysterious murders, each bearing a trace of vampirism. Well-plotted suspense. A racy voodoo dance sequence, often cut, is available on some video versions. **AKA:** Blood Fiend.
1967 90m/C Christopher Lee, Lelia Goldoni, Julian Glover, Evelyn Laye, Jenny Till, Ivor Dean; **D:** Samuel Gallu. **VHS, Beta $54.95** UHV, SNC 🎬🎬½

Thelma & Louise Hailed as the first "feminist-buddy" movie, Sarandon and Davis bust out as best friends hittin' the open road and heading directly into one of the better movies of the year. Davis plays the ditzy Thelma, a housewife rebelling against her dominating, unfaithful, abusive husband (who, rather than being disturbing, provides some of the best comic relief in the film). Sarandon is Louise, a hardened and world-weary waitress in the midst of an unsatisfactory relationship. These two hit the road for a respite from their mundane lives, only to find violence and a part of themselves they never knew existed. Outstanding performances from Davis and especially Sarandon. Laserdisc version features a letterboxed screen and Dolby surround sound. Director Scott has a fine eye for set details, although at times the film appears to be a travelogue made for MTV.
1991 (R) 130m/C Susan Sarandon, Geena Davis, Harvey Keitel, Christopher McDonald, Michael Madsen, Brad Pitt, Timothy Carhart; **D:** Ridley Scott; **W:** Callie Khouri. Academy Awards '91: Best Original Screenplay; Nominations: Best Actress (Davis), Best Actress (Sarandon), Best Cinematography, Best Director (Scott), Best Film Editing; National Board of Review Awards '91: 10 Best Films of the Year, Best Actress (Sarandon, Davis). **VHS, Beta, LV, 8mm $94.99** MGM, PIA 🎬🎬🎬

Them! A group of mutated giant ants wreak havoc on a southwestern town. The first of the big-bug movies, and far surpassing the rest, this is a classic fun flick. See how many names you can spot among the supporting cast.

1954 93m/B James Whitmore, Edmund Gwenn, Fess Parker, James Arness, Onslow Stevens, Jack Perrin; **D:** Gordon Douglas. **VHS, Beta, LV $19.98** WAR 🎬🎬🎬

There Goes Barder Constantine plays a con-man who's hired by a crooked ship owner to become a security agent.
1964 ?m/C FR Eddie Constantine, May Britt. **VHS $16.95** SNC 🎬🎬

There Goes the Neighborhood A dying convict tells prison psychiatrist Daniels where he has buried 8.5 million dollars—under the home of neighbor O'Hara. Daniels and O'Hara try to discreetly dig up the fortune but when the neighborhood finds out everyone wants a chance at the cash.
1992 (PG-13) 88m/C Jeff Daniels, Catherine O'Hara, Dabney Coleman, Hector Elizondo, Judith Ivey, Rhea Perlman; **W/D:** Bill Phillips. **VHS, Beta** PAR 🎬🎬½

There was a Crooked Man An Arizona town gets some new ideas about law and order when an incorruptible and innovative warden takes over the town's prison. The warden finds he's got his hands full with one inmate determined to escape. Offbeat western black comedy supported by an excellent and entertaining production, with fine acting all around.
1970 (R) 123m/C Kirk Douglas, Henry Fonda, Warren Oates, Hume Cronyn, Burgess Meredith, John Randolph, Arthur O'Connell, Alan Hale Jr., Lee Grant; **D:** Joseph L. Mankiewicz; **W:** Robert Benton. **VHS, Beta $19.98** WAR 🎬🎬🎬½

There's a Girl in My Soup Sellers is a gourmet who moonlights as a self-styled Casanova. Early post "Laugh-In" Hawn is the young girl who takes refuge at his London love nest when her boyfriend dumps her. Lust ensues. Has its funny parts, but not a highlight of anyone's career. Based on the hit play.
1970 (R) 95m/C GB Peter Sellers, Goldie Hawn, Diana Dors; **D:** Roy Boulting. **VHS, Beta $9.95** GKK 🎬🎬

There's No Business Like Show Business A top husband and wife vaudevillian act make it a family affair. Filmed in CinemaScope, allowing for full and lavish musical numbers. Good performances and Berlin's music make this an enjoyable film. 🎵When the Midnight Choo-Choo Leaves for Alabam; Let's Have Another Cup of Coffee; Play a Simple Melody; After You Get What You Want You Don't Want It; You'd Be Surprised; A Sailor's Not a Sailor; A Pretty Girl is Like a Melody; If You Believe Me; A Man Chases a Girl Until She Catches Him; Alexander's Ragtime Band.
1954 117m/C Ethel Merman, Donald O'Connor, Marilyn Monroe, Dan Dailey, Mitzi Gaynor, Frank McHugh, Hugh O'Brian; **D:** Walter Lang. **VHS, Beta, LV $19.98** FOX, FCT 🎬🎬🎬

There's No Time for Love, Charlie Brown An animated adventure with the Peanuts gang as they travel to a museum on a class trip.
1987 30m/C VHS, Beta $14.95 KRT 🎬🎬🎬

There's Nothing Out There A group of seven teenagers spends Spring Break at a secluded mountain cabin. It sounds wonderful, but one of the boys (who claims to have seen every horror movie on video) knows the signs of a horror movie just waiting to happen.
1990 91m/C Craig Peck, Wendy Bednarz, Mark Collver, Bonnie Bowers, John Carhart III, Claudia Flores, Jeff Dachis; **W/D:** Rolfe Kanefsky. **VHS, Beta, LV $49.95** PSM 🎬🎬

Therese Stylish biography of a young French nun and her devotion to Christ bordering on romantic love. Explores convent life. Real-life Therese died of TB and was made a saint. A directorial tour de force for Cavalier. In French with English subtitles.
1986 90m/C FR Catherine Mouchet, Aurore Prieto, Sylvie Habault, Ghislaine Mona; **D:** Alain Cavalier. **VHS, Beta $39.95** TAM, APD, MED 🎬🎬🎬

Therese & Isabelle Story of growing love and physical attraction between two French schoolgirls. On holiday together, they confront their mutual desires. Richly photographed soft porn. It's not vulgar, but certainly for adults. **AKA:** Therese Und Isabell.
1968 102m/C Essy Persson, Anna Gael, Barbara Laage, Anne Vernon; **D:** Radley Metzger. **VHS, Beta** NO 🎬½

These Girls Won't Talk Three female stars of early silent pictures are featured separately in: "Her Bridal Nightmare," "Campus Carmen," and "As Luck Would Have It."
192? 50m/B Colleen Moore, Carole Lombard, Betty Compson. **VHS, Beta $29.95** VYY 🎬🎬½

These Three A teenaged girl ruins the lives of two teachers by telling a malicious lie. Excellent cast. Script by Lillian Hellman, based on her play "The Children's Hour." Remade by the same director as "The Children's Hour" in 1961.
1936 92m/B Miriam Hopkins, Merle Oberon, Joel McCrea, Bonita Granville, Marcia Mae Jones, Walter Brennan, Margaret Hamilton; **D:** William Wyler. **VHS, Beta, LV $19.98** SUE 🎬🎬🎬½

They Beings from beneath the earth's crust take their first trip to the surface.
198? 88m/C Paul Dentzer, Debbie Pick, Nick Holt. **VHS, Beta** NO 🎬

They All Laughed Three detectives become romantically involved with the women they were hired to investigate. Essentially light-hearted fluff with little or no script. Further undermined by the real-life murder of Stratten before the film's release.
1981 (PG) 115m/C Ben Gazzara, John Ritter, Audrey Hepburn, Colleen Camp, Patti Hansen, Dorothy Stratten, Elizabeth Pena; **D:** Peter Bogdanovich. **VHS, Beta, LV $19.98** VES 🎬🎬

They Call Me Bruce? A bumbling Bruce Lee look-alike meets a karate-chopping Mafia moll in this farce. Silly premise creates lots of laughs. Followed by a sequel, "They Still Call Me Bruce." **AKA:** A Fist Full of Chopsticks.
1982 (PG) 88m/C Johnny Yune, Margaux Hemingway; **D:** Elliot Hong. **VHS, Beta $29.98** VES 🎬🎬

They Call Me Mr. Tibbs! Lieutenant Virgil Tibbs (Poitier) investigates the murder of a prostitute. The prime suspect is his friend, the Reverend Logan Sharpe (Landau). He is torn between his duty as a policeman, his concern for the reverend, and the turmoil of his domestic life. Less tense, less compelling sequel to "In the Heat of the Night."
1970 (R) 108m/C Sidney Poitier, Barbara McNair, Martin Landau, Juano Hernandez, Anthony Zerbe, Ed Asner, Norma Crane, Jeff Corey; **D:** Gordon Douglas. **VHS, Beta $14.95** MGM, FOX 🎬🎬

They Call Me Trinity Lazy drifter-gunslinger and his outlaw brother join forces with Mormon farmers to rout bullying outlaws. Spoofs every western cliche with relentless comedy, parodying "The Magnificent Seven" and gibing the spaghetti western. Followed by "Trinity is Still My Name." Dubbed. **AKA:** Lo Chiamavano Trinita.

1972 (G) 110m/C IT Terence Hill, Bud Spencer, Farley Granger, Steffen Zacharias; D: E.B. Clucher. VHS, Beta $14.95 CCB, SUE, HHE 𝐼𝐼½

They Came from Beyond Space Aliens invade the earth and possess the brains of humans. They only want a few slaves to help them repair their ship which crashed on the moon. The only person able to stop them is a scientist with a steel plate in his head. Silly and forgettable.
1967 86m/C Robert Hutton, Michael Gough; D: Freddie Francis. VHS, Beta $59.98 SUE 𝐼

They Came from Within The occupants of a high-rise building go on a sex and violence spree when stricken by an aphrodisiac parasite. Queasy, sleazy and weird. First major film by Cronenberg. AKA: Shivers; The Parasite Murders.
1975 (R) 87m/C CA Paul Hampton, Joe Silver, Lynn Lowry, Barbara Steele; D: David Cronenberg. VHS, Beta $69.98 LIV, VES 𝐼𝐼½

They Came to Cordura Mexico, 1916: a woman and six American soldiers—five heroes and one who has been branded a coward—begin a journey to the military headquarters in Cordura. Slow journey brings out personalities. Look for "Bewitched" hubby Dick York. Based on Glendon Swarthout's best-seller.
1959 123m/C Gary Cooper, Rita Hayworth, Van Heflin, Tab Hunter, Dick York, Richard Conte; D: Robert Rossen. VHS, Beta, LV $14.95 COL 𝐼𝐼½

They Died with Their Boots On The Battle of Little Big Horn is recreated Hollywood style. Takes liberties with historical fact, but still an exciting portrayal of General Custer's last stand. The movie also marks the last time de Havilland worked with Flynn. Also available colorized.
1941 141m/B Errol Flynn, Sydney Greenstreet, Anthony Quinn, Hattie McDaniel, Arthur Kennedy, Gene Lockhart, Regis Toomey, Olivia de Havilland, Charley Grapewin; D: Raoul Walsh. VHS, Beta $19.98 MGM, MLB, FOX 𝐼𝐼𝐼

They Drive by Night Two truck-driving brothers break away from a large company and begin independent operations. After an accident to Bogart, Raft is forced to go back to the company where Lupino, the boss's wife, becomes obsessed with him and kills her husband to gain the company and win Raft. When he rejects her, she accuses him of the murder. Well-plotted film with great dialogue. Excellent cast gives it their all. AKA: Road to Frisco.
1940 97m/B Humphrey Bogart, Ann Sheridan, George Raft, Ida Lupino, Alan Hale Jr., Gale Page, Roscoe Karns; D: Raoul Walsh. VHS, Beta $19.98 FOX, FCT 𝐼𝐼𝐼½

They Got Me Covered Two World War II-era journalists get involved in a comic web of murder, kidnapping and romance. Hope is very funny and carries the rest of the cast. Look for Doris Day in a bit part and listen for Bing Crosby singing whenever Hope opens his cigarette case.
1943 95m/B Bob Hope, Dorothy Lamour, Otto Preminger, Eduardo Ciannelli, Donald Meek, Walter Catleh; D: David Butler. VHS, Beta, LV $19.98 SUE 𝐼𝐼

They Knew What They Wanted A lonely San Francisco waitress begins a correspondence romance with a grape grower and agrees to marry him after he sends her a photo which shows him as being young and handsome. She arrives to discover Laughton had sent her a picture of another man. An accident, an affair, and a pregnancy provide further complications before a satisfactory ending is suggested. Flawed adaptation of

Sidney Howard's play still has strong performances from Lombard and Laughton.
1940 96m/B Charles Laughton, Carole Lombard, Harry Carey Sr., Karl Malden, William Gargan; D: Garson Kanin. VHS, Beta $34.95 RKO 𝐼𝐼𝐼

They Live A semi-serious science-fiction spoof about a drifter who discovers an alien conspiracy. They're taking over the country under the guise of Reaganism, capitalism and yuppiedom. Screenplay written by Carpenter under a pseudonym. Starts out fun, deteriorates into cliches and bad special effects makeup.
1988 (R) 88m/C Roddy Piper, Keith David, Meg Foster, George Flower, Peter Jason, Raymond St. Jacques, John Lawrence, Sy Richardson; D: John Carpenter. VHS, Beta, LV $19.95 MCA 𝐼𝐼½

They Live by Night A young fugitive sinks deeper into a life of crime thanks to his association with two hardened criminals. Classic film noir was Ray's first attempt at directing. Based on Edward Anderson's novel "Thieves Like Us," under which title it was remade in 1974. Compelling and suspenseful. AKA: The Twisted Road; Your Red Wagon.
1949 95m/B Cathy O'Donnell, Farley Granger, Howard da Silva, Jay C. Flippen, Helen Craig; D: Nicholas Ray. VHS, Beta, LV $59.95 HHT 𝐼𝐼𝐼½

They Made Me a Criminal A champion prizefighter, believing he murdered a man in a drunken brawl, runs away. He finds refuge in the West with the Dead End Kids. Remake of "The Life of Jimmy Dolan." Berkeley was best-known for directing and choreographing musicals and surprisingly did very well with this movie. AKA: I Became a Criminal; They Made Me a Fugitive.
1939 92m/B John Garfield, Ann Sheridan, Claude Rains, Leo Gorcey; D: Busby Berkeley. VHS, Beta, LV, 3/4U, Special order formats $9.95 NEG, NOS, PSM 𝐼𝐼½

They Meet Again The final segment of the Dr. Christian series. The country doctor sets out to prove the innocence of a man who has been wrongly accused of stealing money. Slow moving and not particularly exciting.
1941 68m/B Jean Hersholt, Dorothy Lovett; D: Erle C. Kenton. VHS, Beta, 8mm $19.95 NOS, VYY, KRT 𝐼𝐼

They Might Be Giants Woodward is a woman shrink named Watson who treats retired judge Scott for delusions that he is Sherlock Holmes. Scott's brother wants him committed so the family loot will come to him. Very funny in places; Woodward and Scott highlight a solid cast.
1971 (G) 98m/C George C. Scott, Joanne Woodward, Jack Gilford, Eugene Roche, Kitty Winn, F. Murray Abraham, M. Emmet Walsh; D: Anthony Harvey; M: John Barry. VHS, Beta $12.95 MCA 𝐼𝐼𝐼

They Never Come Back A boxer is thrown in jail and then stages a comeback.
1932 62m/B Regis Toomey, Dorothy Sebastian. VHS, Beta, LV $16.95 SNC, WGE 𝐼½

They Only Kill Their Masters Garner plays a California police chief investigating the death of a wild beach town resident, supposedly killed by her doberman pinscher. He discovers the woman was actually drowned and there are any number of secrets to uncover. Mild whodunit.
1972 (PG) 98m/C James Garner, Katharine Ross, June Allyson, Hal Holbrook, Harry Guardino, Christopher Connelly, Tom Ewell, Peter Lawford, Edmond O'Brien, Arthur O'Connell, Ann Rutherford, Art Metrano; D: James Goldstone. VHS $19.98 MGM 𝐼𝐼½

They Paid with Bullets: Chicago 1929 The story of one man's rise to power, and eventual downfall as a Mafia consigliatore.
197? 88m/C Peter Lee Lawrence, Ingrid Schoeller. VHS, Beta $19.95 NEG 𝐼½

They Saved Hitler's Brain Fanatical survivors of the Nazi holocaust gave eternal life to the brain of their leader in the last hours of the war. Now it's on a Caribbean island giving orders again. One of the truly great "bad" movies. Shot in pieces in the U.S., the Philippines, and elsewhere, with chunks of other films stuck in to hold the "story" together. AKA: Madmen of Mandoras; The Return of Mr. H.
1964 91m/B Walter Stocker, Audrey Caire; D: David Bradley. VHS, Beta, 8mm $29.95 VYY, UHV Woof!

They Shall Have Music A poverty-stricken child hears a concert by violinist Heifetz and decides to become a musician. He joins Brennan's nearly bankrupt music school and persuades Heifetz to play at a benefit concert. Hokey but enjoyable Goldwyn effort to bring classical music to the big screen. ♫ Rondo Capriccioso; Hora Staccato; Estrellita; Melody; Concerto in E Minor for Violin and Orchestra; Waltz in D Flat, Opus 64, No. 1; Cara Nome; Casta Diva. AKA: Melody of Youth; Ragged Angels.
1939 101m/B Walter Brennan, Joel McCrea, Gene Reynolds, Jascha Heifetz, Marjorie Main, Porter Hall, Andrea Leeds, Terence Kilburn; D: Archie Mayo. VHS, Beta $19.98 SUE, HBO 𝐼𝐼

They Shoot Horses, Don't They? Powerful period piece depicting the desperation of the Depression Era. Contestants enter a dance marathon in the hopes of winning a cash prize, not realizing that they will be driven to exhaustion. Fascinating and tragic.
1969 (R) 121m/C Jane Fonda, Michael Sarrazin, Susannah York, Gig Young, Red Buttons, Bonnie Bedelia, Bruce Dern, Allyn Ann McLerie, Chaing I; D: Sydney Pollack. Academy Awards '69: Best Supporting Actor (Young); Nominations: Best Actress (Fonda), Best Adapted Screenplay, Best Art Direction/Set Decoration, Best Costume Design, Best Director (Pollack), Best Film Editing, Best Supporting Actress (York), Best Original Score; British Academy Awards '70: Best Supporting Actress (York); Golden Globe Awards '70: Best Supporting Actor (Young). VHS, LV ABC, OM 𝐼𝐼𝐼½

They Still Call Me Bruce A Korean searches for the American who saved his life when he was young and instead becomes big brother to an orphan. Supposedly a sequel to "They Call Me Bruce," but has little in common with it. Poorly done and not particularly entertaining.
1986 (PG) 91m/C Johnny Yune, Robert Guillaume, Pat Paulsen; D: Johnny Yune. VHS, Beta $14.95 NWV, STE 𝐼

They Went That-a-Way & That-a-Way Two bumbling deputies pose as convicts in this madcap prison caper. Script by Conway. Terrible re-hash of Laurel-and-Hardy has nothing going for it. Lackluster.
1978 (PG) 96m/C Tim Conway, Richard Kiel; D: Edward Montagne. VHS, Beta $69.98 SUE Woof!

They Were Expendable Two American captains pit their PT boats against the Japanese fleet. Based on the true story of a PT boat squadron based in the Philippines during the early days of World War II. One of the best (and most underrated) World War II films. Also available in a colorized version.

1945 135m/B Robert Montgomery, John Wayne, Donna Reed, Jack Holt, Ward Bond, Cameron Mitchell, Leon Ames, Marshall Thompson; *D:* John Ford. **VHS, Beta $19.95** *MGM* ♨♨½

They Were So Young European models become the pawns of wealthy Brazilian magnates when they are sent to South America. They are threatened with death if they do not cooperate. The scenes were shot in Italy and Berlin. Well acted and believable, although rather grim story.
1955 78m/B *GE* Scott Brady, Johanna Matz, Raymond Burr; *D:* Kurt Neumann. **VHS, Beta, LV** *NO* ♨♨½

They Were Ten Ten Soviet Jews make Palestine their home in the 1800s despite Arab and Turkish persecution and pressures among themselves. In Hebrew with English subtitles.
1961 105m/B *IS* Ninette, Oded Teomi, Leo Filer, Yosef Safra; *D:* Baruch Dienar. **VHS, Beta** $79.95 *ERG, FCT, TAM* ♨♨½

They Won't Believe Me A man plots to kill his wife, but before he does, she commits suicide. He ends up on trial for her "murder." Interesting acting by Young and Hayward against type. Surprising, ironic ending.
1947 95m/B Robert Young, Susan Hayward, Rita Johnson, Jane Greer; *D:* Irving Pichel. **VHS, Beta, LV** $19.98 *MED, TTC* ♨♨♨

They Won't Forget When a young girl is murdered in a southern town, personal interests take precedence over justice. Turner is excellent in her first billed role, as are the other actors. Superbly scripted by Robert Rossen and Aben Kandel. Expert direction by LeRoy pulls it all together. Based on Ward Greene's "Death in the Deep South."
1937 95m/B Claude Rains, Otto Kruger, Lana Turner, Allyn Joslyn, Elisha Cook Jr., Edward Norris; *D:* Mervyn LeRoy. **VHS** *WAR, OM* ♨♨♨½

They're Playing with Fire An English teacher seduces a student and gets him involved in a murder plot to gain an inheritance. Turns out someone else is beating them to the punch. Sleazy semi-pornographic slasher.
1984 (R) 96m/C Sybil Danning, Eric Brown, Andrew Prine, Paul Clemens, K.T. Stevens, Alvy Moore; *D:* Howard Avedis. **VHS, Beta $19.95** *STE, HBO* Woof!

The Thief An American commits treason and is overcome by guilt. Novel because there is not one word of dialogue, though the gimmick can't sustain the ordinary story. A product of the Communist scare of the 1950s, it tends to be pretentious and melodramatic.
1952 84m/C Ray Milland, Rita Gam, Martin Gabel, Harry Bronson, John McKutcheon; *D:* Russel Rouse. **VHS, Beta $19.95** *UHV* ♨♨

Thief A successful businessman (Crenna) attempts to put his criminal past behind him. He's trapped when looking for a quick way to get some money to pay off a gambling debt. Made for television drama that's well-written and directed with tepid acting.
1971 74m/C Richard Crenna, Angie Dickinson, Cameron Mitchell, Hurd Hatfield, Robert Webber; *D:* William A. Graham. **VHS, Beta $59.95** *LHV* ♨♨

Thief A big-time professional thief likes working solo, but decides to sign up with the mob in order to make one more big score and retire. He finds out it's not that easy. Taut and atmospheric thriller with score by Tangerine Dream. Director Mann's feature film debut. *AKA:* Violent Streets.

1981 (R) 126m/C James Caan, Tuesday Weld, Willie Nelson, James Belushi, Elizabeth Pena, Robert Prosky; *D:* Michael Mann. **VHS, Beta, LV** $19.95 *MGM, FOX* ♨♨♨

The Thief of Baghdad The classic silent crowd-pleaser, about a roguish thief who uses a genie's magic to outwit Baghdad's evil Caliph. With famous special effects in a newly struck print, and a new score by Carl Davis based on Rimsky-Korsakov's "Scheherezade." Remade many times.
1924 153m/B Douglas Fairbanks Sr., Snitz Edwards, Charles Belcher, Anna May Wong, Etta Lee, Brandon Hurst, Sojin, Julanne Johnston; *D:* Raoul Walsh. **VHS, Beta, LV, 3/4U, Special order formats** $19.98 *HBO, SNC, NOS* ♨♨♨

Thief of Baghdad A wily young thief enlists the aid of a powerful genie to outwit the Grand Vizier of Baghdad. An Arabian Nights spectacular with lush photography, fine special effects, and striking score by Miklos Rozsa. Outstanding performance by Ingram as the genie.
1940 106m/C Sabu, Conrad Veidt, June Duprez, Rex Ingram, Tim Whelan, Michael Powell; *D:* Ludwig Berger. **VHS, Beta, LV** $14.98 *SUE, MLB* ♨♨♨½

Thief of Baghdad An Arabian Nights fantasy about a thief in love with a Sultan's daughter who has been poisoned. He seeks out the magical blue rose which is the antidote. Not as lavish as the previous two productions by this title, nor as much fun. *AKA:* Il Ladro Di Bagdad; Le Voleur De Bagdad.
1961 89m/C *IT* Georgia Moll, Steve Reeves; *D:* Arthur Lubin. **VHS, Beta $59.98** *SUE* ♨♨

The Thief of Baghdad A fantasy-adventure about a genie, a prince, beautiful maidens, a happy-go-lucky thief, and magic. Easy to take, but not an extraordinary version of this oft-told tale. Ustinov is fun as he tries to marry off his daughter. Made for television.
1978 (G) 101m/C Peter Ustinov, Roddy McDowall, Terence Stamp, Frank Finlay, Ian Holm; *D:* Clive Donner. **VHS, Beta $29.95** *GEM* ♨♨½

Thief of Hearts A thief steals a woman's diary when he's ransacking her house. He then pursues the woman, using his secret knowledge. Slick, but too creepy. Re-edited with soft porn scenes in some video versions. Stewart's first film.
1984 (R) 101m/C Steven Bauer, Barbara Williams, John Getz, Christine Ebersole, George Wendt; *D:* Douglas Day Stewart. **VHS, Beta, LV** $14.95 *PAR* ♨♨

The Thief Who Came to Dinner A computer analyst and a wealthy socialite team up to become jewel thieves and turn the tables on Houston's high society set. Comedy plot gets complex, though O'Neal and Bisset are likeable. Early Clayburgh role as O'Neal's ex. Based on a novel by Terence Lore Smith, music by Henry Mancini.
1973 (PG) 103m/C Ryan O'Neal, Jacqueline Bisset, Warren Oates, Jill Clayburgh, Ned Beatty, Gregory Sierra, Michael Murphy, Austin Pendleton, John Hillerman, Charles Cioffi; *D:* Bud Yorkin; *W:* Walter Hill. **VHS, Beta $19.98** *WAR* ▲

Thieves of Fortune Former Miss Universe stars as a contestant in a high stakes fortune hunt that spans half the globe. She meets with more than her share of action-packed encounters among the ruffians who compete for the $28 million purse. Implausible; horrible script; cliched.
1989 (R) 100m/C Michael Nouri, Lee Van Cleef, Shawn Weatherly. **VHS, Beta, LV** $29.95 *ACA* Woof!

The Thin Blue Line The acclaimed docudrama about the 1977 shooting of a cop in Dallas County, and the incorrect conviction of Randall Adams for the crime. A riveting, spellbinding experience. Due to the film's impact and continued lobbying by Morris, Adams is now free. Music by Philip Glass.
1988 101m/C *D:* Errol Morris. **VHS, Beta, LV** $19.98 *HBO, CCB* ♨♨♨½

The Thin Man Married sleuths Nick and Nora Charles investigate the mysterious disappearance of a wealthy inventor. Charming and sophisticated, this was the model for all husband-and-wife detective teams that followed. Don't miss Asta, their wire-hair terrier. Based on the novel by Dashiell Hammett. Its enormous popularity triggered five sequels, starting with "After the Thin Man."
1934 90m/B William Powell, Myrna Loy, Maureen O'Sullivan, Cesar Romero, Porter Hall, Nat Pendleton, Minna Gombell, Natalie Moorhead, Edward Ellis; *D:* Woodbridge S. Van Dyke. **VHS, Beta, LV** $19.95 *MGM, HMV* ♨♨♨½

The Thin Man Goes Home Married sleuths Nick and Nora Charles solve a mystery with Nick's disapproving parents looking on in the fifth film from the "Thin Man" series. Despite a three-year gap and slightly less chemistry between Powell and Loy, audiences welcomed the skinny guy. Sequel to "Shadow of the Thin Man;" followed by "Song of the Thin Man."
1944 100m/B William Powell, Myrna Loy, Lucile Watson, Gloria DeHaven, Anne Revere, Harry Davenport, Helen Vinson, Lloyd Corrigan, Donald Meek, Edward Brophy; *D:* Richard Thorpe. **VHS, Beta $19.98** *MGM* ♨♨½

The Thing One of the best of the Cold War allegories and a potent lesson to those who won't eat their vegetables. In the original version of this science fiction classic, an alien craft and creature (Arness in monster drag) are discovered by an Arctic research team. They take it back to the base where the creature is accidentally thawed. The creature then wreaks havoc, sucking the blood from sled dog and scientist alike. The scientists soon discover they have a giant seed-dispersing vegetable running amuck, little affected by missing body parts, bullets, or cold. In other words, Big Trouble. Excellent direction, assisted substantially by producer Hawks, and supported by strong performances. Available colorized; remade in 1982. Loosely based on "Who Goes There?" by John Campbell; adapted by Charles Lederer; score by Dimith Tiomkin. *AKA:* The Thing From Another World.
1951 87m/B James Arness, Kenneth Tobey, Margaret Sheridan, Dewey Martin; *D:* Christian Nyby; *W:* Howard Hawks. **VHS, Beta, LV** $14.98 *MED, TTC, MLB* ♨♨♨½

The Thing A team of scientists at a remote Antarctic outpost discover a buried spaceship with an unwelcome alien survivor still alive. Bombastic special effects overwhelm the suspense and the solid cast. Less a remake of the 1951 science fiction classic than a more faithful version of the original novel, since the seeds/spores take on human shapes.
1982 (R) 127m/C Kurt Russell, Wilford Brimley, T.K. Carter, Richard Masur, Keith David, Richard Dysart, David Clennon, Donald Moffatt, Thomas G. Waites, Charles Hallahan; *D:* John Carpenter; *M:* Ennio Morricone. **VHS, Beta, LV** $19.95 *MCA* ♨♨½

The Thing Called Love Take last year's surprise hit "Singles" and replace grunge rock and Seattle with Country/Western and Nashville for this heartwarming tale of four twentysomething singles trying to

make their mark in the world of country music. The idea for the plot comes from the real-life Bluebird Cafe—the place where all aspiring singers and songwriters want to perform. Phoenix, Mathis, Mulroney, and Bullock did their own singing; look for Oslin as the Cafe owner.
1993 (PG-13) ?m/C River Phoenix, Samantha Mathis, Sandra Bullock, Dermot Mulroney, Trisha Yearwood; **Cameos:** K.T. Oslin; **D:** Peter Bogdanovich; **W:** Allan Moyle, Carol Heikkinen. **VHS** *NYR* 🐾🐾½

Things A man creates a monster during his freakish experiments with artificial insemination. The monster returns to his house seeking revenge, and the man's visiting brother and a friend disappear, probably a clever move given their lackluster circumstances.
198? 90m/C Barry Gillis, Amber Lynn, Doug Bunston, Bruce Roach; **D:** Andrew Jordan. **VHS, Beta** *NO* 🐾

Things Change An old Italian shoeshine agrees, for a fee, to be a fall guy for the Mafia. A lower-echelon mob hood, assigned to watch over him, decides to give the old guy a weekend of fun in Vegas before going to jail. Mamet's second film as director; he co-wrote the screenplay with Silverstein, best-known for his children's books ("Where the Sidewalk Ends," "The Giving Tree"). Combines charm and menace with terrific performances, especially from Ameche and Mantegna.
1988 (PG) 114m/C Joe Mantegna, Don Ameche, Robert Prosky, J.J. Johnston, Ricky Jay; **D:** David Mamet; **W:** David Mamet, Shel Silverstein. **VHS, Beta, LV** $14.95 *COL* 🐾🐾🐾

Things Happen at Night Scientist and insurance investigator determine that friendly ghost has possessed a family's youngest daughter. Not much happens.
1948 79m/B **GB** Gordon Harker, Alfred Drayton, Robertson Hare, Olga Lindo, Wylie Watson; **D:** Francis Searle. **VHS, Beta** $16.95 *NOS, SNC* 🐾

Things in Their Season Made for TV melodrama about the imminent death of the mother of a Wisconsin farm family who makes those around her realize the value of happiness. Neal is excellent, rest of cast better than average in a well-told and sincere film.
1974 79m/C Patricia Neal, Ed Flanders, Marc Singer, Meg Foster; **D:** James Goldstone. **VHS, Beta** *LCA* 🐾🐾½

The Things of Life A car crash makes a man re-evaluate his life, goals, and loves. In the end he must choose the course of his future and decide between his wife and mistress. In French with English subtitles. **AKA:** Les Choses De La Vie.
1970 90m/C **FR** Romy Schneider, Michel Piccoli, Lea Massari; **D:** Claude Sautet. **VHS, Beta, LV** $79.95 *CVC, TAM* 🐾🐾🐾

Things to Come Using technology, scientists aim to rebuild the world after a lengthy war, followed by a plague and other unfortunate events. Massey and Scott each play two roles, in different generations. Startling picture of the world to come, with fine sets and good acting. Based on an H.G. Wells story, "The Shape of Things to Come."
1936 92m/B **GB** Raymond Massey, Ralph Richardson, Cedric Hardwicke, Derrick DeMarney; **D:** William Cameron Menzies. **VHS, Beta, 3/4U, Special order formats** $19.95 *NOS, PSM, SNC* 🐾🐾🐾½

Think Big Former professional wrestlers, the Pauls are truck drivers in this silly, enjoyable comedy. They pick up a brilliant teenager running from bad guys. Mayhem ensues.
1990 (PG-13) 86m/C Peter Paul, David Paul, Martin Mull, Ari Meyers, Richard Kiel, David Carradine, Richard Moll, Peter Lupus. **VHS, Beta, LV** $89.98 *LIV* 🐾🐾½

Think Dirty Lascivious comedy about advertising executive Feldman's attempt to develop a series of sexy commercials to sell cereal. At the same time his wife forms a "clean up television" group. Not very interesting or funny. **AKA:** Every Home Should Have One.
1970 (R) 93m/C **GB** Marty Feldman, Judy Cornwell, Shelley Berman; **D:** Jim Clark. **VHS, Beta** $59.95 *COL* 🐾🐾

Thinkin' Big Guys and gals cavort on the Texas coast, except for one lonely fat guy who tries to increase his sexual prowess. The usual teen sex frenzy.
1987 (R) 96m/C Bruce Anderson, Kenny Sargent, Randy Jandt, Nancy Buechler, Darla Ralston; **D:** S.F. Brownrigg. **VHS, Beta** $9.99 *STE, PSM* 🐾

Third Degree Burn A made-for-cable-television mystery about a small-time detective hired by a businessman to follow a woman, only to become a suspect when the woman's real husband is killed.
1989 97m/C Treat Williams, Virginia Madsen, Richard Masur; **D:** Roger Spottiswoode. **VHS, Beta, LV** $14.95 *PAR* 🐾🐾

The Third Key A solid British crime drama follows a dogged detective as he probes serial safe-crackings, with a climax set at London's Festival Hall. Based on the book by Robert Barr, who co-scripted. **AKA:** The Long Arm.
1957 96m/B Jack Hawkins, Dorothy Allison, Geoffrey Keen, Richard Leech, Ian Bannen; **D:** Charles Frend. **VHS** $19.95 *NOS* 🐾🐾½

The Third Man An American writer of pulp westerns (Cotten) arrives in post-war Vienna to take a job with an old friend, but discovers he has been murdered. Or has he? Based on Graham Greene's mystery, this classic film noir thriller plays on national loyalties during the Cold War. Welles is top-notch as the manipulative Harry Lime, black-market drugdealer extraordinare. The underground sewer sequence is not to be missed. With a haunting (sometimes irritating) theme by Anton Karas on unaccompanied zither. Special edition features trailer.
1949 104m/B Joseph Cotten, Orson Welles, Alida Valli, Trevor Howard, Bernard Lee, Wilfrid Hyde-White; **D:** Carol Reed. Academy Awards '50: Best Black and White Cinematography; Nominations: Best Director (Reed), Best Film Editing; British Academy Awards '49: Best Film; Cannes Film Festival '49: Best Film; Directors Guild of America Awards '49: Best Director (Reed); National Board of Review Awards '50: 5 Best Foreign Films of the Year. **VHS, Beta, LV, 8mm, 3/4U, Special order formats** $16.95 *SNC, REP, MED* 🐾🐾🐾🐾

Third Man on the Mountain A family epic about mountain climbing, shot in Switzerland and based on James Ramsey Ullman's "Banner in the Sky." A young man is determined to climb the "Citadel" as his ancestors have. He finds there's more to climbing than he imagined. Look for Helen Hayes (MacArthur's mother) in a cameo. Standard Disney adventure drama. **AKA:** Banner in the Sky.
1959 (G) 106m/C James MacArthur, Michael Rennie, Janet Munro, James Donald, Herbert Lom, Laurence Naismith; **Cameos:** Helen Hayes; **D:** Ken Annakin. **VHS, Beta** $69.95 *DIS* 🐾🐾½

The Third Sex One of the first films to deal with homosexuality in which parents try to "straighten out" their gay son.
1959 ?m/C Paul Dahlke, Paula Wesley. **VHS** $16.95 *SNC* 🐾

Third Solution An Italian-made film about the discovery of a secret pact made between the Kremlin and the Vatican that may start World War III. Well-cast, but poorly conceived spook drama, with music by Vangelis. **AKA:** Russicum.
1989 (R) 93m/C **IT** Treat Williams, F. Murray Abraham, Danny Aiello, Nigel Court, Rita Rusic, Rossano Brazzi; **D:** Pasquale Squitieri. **VHS, Beta, LV** $79.95 *COL* 🐾🐾

Third Walker A desperate woman sacrifices her marriage to immerse herself in efforts to reunite her twin sons, who were inadvertently separated at birth. An original and intriguing directorial debut by McLuhan.
1979 85m/C William Shatner, Colleen Dewhurst; **D:** Marshall McLuhan. **VHS, Beta** *NO* 🐾

Thirst A girl is abducted by a secret society that wants her to become their new leader. There is just one catch: she has to learn to like the taste of human blood. Chilling but weakly plotted.
1987 (R) 96m/C David Hemmings, Henry Silva, Chantal Contouri; **D:** Rod Hardy. **VHS, Beta** $79.95 *MED* 🐾🐾

The Thirsty Dead Maybe they could learn to like Gatorade. An eternally young jungle king is looking for a wife. She can be young forever too, if she's not above vampirism and sacrificing virgins. In spite of the jungle vampire slant, this Filipino-made movie is a woofer. Also released on video, as "Blood Hunt." **AKA:** The Blood Cult of Shangri-La.
1974 (PG) 90m/C **PH** John Considine, Jennifer Billingsley, Judith McConnell, Fredricka Meyers, Tani Phelps Guthrie; **D:** Terry Becker. **VHS, Beta** $59.95 *WWV, SIM* Woof!

13 Ghosts A dozen ghosts need another member to round out their ranks. They have four likely candidates to choose from when a family moves into the house inhabited by the ghoulish group. Originally viewed with "Illusion-O," a technology much like 3-D, which allowed the viewing of the ghosts only through a special pair of glasses.
1960 88m/C Charles Herbert, Jo Morrow, Martin Milner, Rosemary DeCamp, Donald Woods, Margaret Hamilton; **D:** William Castle. **VHS, Beta** $9.95 *GKK* 🐾🐾½

13 Rue Madeleine Cagney plays a World War II spy who infiltrates Gestapo headquarters in Paris in order to find the location of a German missile site. Actual OSS footage is used in this fast-paced early postwar espionage propaganda piece. Rex Harrison rejected the part taken by Cagney.
1946 95m/B James Cagney, Annabella, Richard Conte, Frank Latimore, Walter Abel, Sam Jaffe, Melville Cooper, E.G. Marshall, Karl Malden, Red Buttons; **D:** Henry Hathaway. **VHS, Beta** $19.98 *FOX, FCT* 🐾🐾

Thirteenth Day of Christmas A made-for-British-television yarn about a psychotic boy left alone by his parents on Christmas night.
1985 60m/C **GB** Patrick Allen, Elizabeth Spiggs. **VHS, Beta** $59.95 *PSM* 🐾🐾🐾

The 13th Floor A young girl fuses with the spirit of a young boy her father ruthlessly killed years before, and together they wreak havoc.
1988 (R) 86m/C Lisa Hensley, Tim McKenzie, Miranda Otto; **D:** Chris Roach. **VHS, Beta** $89.99 *PAR* 🐾

13th Guest Two people try to solve a murder that occurred at a dinner party. An incredibly creaky early talkie melodrama that created some of the cliches of the genre. *AKA:* Lady Beware.
1932 70m/B Ginger Rogers, Lyle Talbot, J. Farrell MacDonald, Paul Hurst; *D:* Albert Ray. **VHS, Beta $12.95** *SNC, NOS, VYY ⅛⅛*

The Thirteenth Man When a journalist investigating the murder of a district attorney is also killed, the paper's gossip columnist takes the case. Entertaining, fast-paced mystery.
1937 70m/B Weldon Heyburn, Inez Courtney, Selmer Jackson, Milburn Stone, Matty Fain; *D:* William Nigh. **VHS, Beta $16.95** *NOS, SNC, MLB ⅛⅛½*

The 13th Mission A low-budget overseas combat adventure, no better than the first twelve.
1991 95m/C Robert Marius, Jeff Griffith, Michael Monty, David Morisson, Paul Home, John Falch, Albert Bronski, Chantal Manz; *D:* Antonio Perez. **VHS** *KBE ⅛½*

Thirteenth Reunion A newspaperwoman uncovers a bizarre secret society when she does a routine story on a health spa.
1981 60m/C Julia Foster, Dinah Sheridan, Richard Pearson; *D:* Peter Sasdy. **VHS, Beta $29.95** *LIV ⅛*

30-Foot Bride of Candy Rock A junk dealer invents a robot, catapults into space and causes his girlfriend to grow to 30 feet in height. Lightweight, whimsical fantasy was Costello's only solo starring film, and his last before his untimely death.
1959 73m/B Lou Costello, Dorothy Provine, Gale Gordon; *D:* Sidney Miller. **VHS, Beta $9.95** *GKK ⅛*

30 Is a Dangerous Age, Cynthia Dudley Moore stars as a nightclub pianist who spends a lot of his time daydreaming about being rich, famous and married to a beautiful woman. Moore determines to attain all these dreams before his thirtieth birthday, which is only six weeks away. Light-hearted fun. Moore wrote the score and co-wrote the screenplay.
1968 85m/C *GB* Dudley Moore, Suzy Kendall, Eddie Foy Jr.; *D:* Joseph McGrath. **VHS, Beta $59.95** *RCA ⅛⅛½*

The 39 Steps The classic Hitchcock mistaken-man-caught-in-intrigue thriller, featuring some of his most often copied setpieces and the surest visual flair of his prewar British period. The laserdisc version includes a twenty-minute documentary tracing the director's British period. Remade twice, in 1959 and 1979.
1935 81m/B *GB* Robert Donat, Madeleine Carroll, Godfrey Tearle, Lucie Mannheim, Peggy Ashcroft; *D:* Alfred Hitchcock. **VHS, Beta, LV, 8mm, 3/4U, Special order formats $8.95** *NEG, NOS, SUE ⅛⅛⅛⅛*

The Thirty-Nine Steps Hitchcock remake is a visually interesting, but mostly uninvolving, mystery. Powell is the man suspected of stealing plans to begin World War I. Above average, but not by much.
1979 98m/C *GB* Robert Powell, David Warner, Eric Porter, Karen Dotrice, John Mills, Andrew Keir; *D:* Don Sharp. **VHS, Beta $14.95** *MED ⅛⅛½*

Thirty Seconds Over Tokyo Written by Dalton Trumbo and based on a true story. Dated but still interesting classic wartime flagwaver details the conception and execution of the first bombing raids on Tokyo by Lt. Col. James Doolittle and his men. Look for Blake Edwards, as well as Steve Brodie in

his first screen appearance. Received an Oscar for Best Special Effects.
1944 138m/B Spencer Tracy, Van Johnson, Robert Walker, Robert Mitchum, Phyllis Thaxter, Scott McKay, Stephen McNally, Louis Jean Heydt, Leon Ames, Paul Langton; *D:* Mervyn LeRoy. Academy Awards '44: Best Special Effects; Nominations: Best Black and White Cinematography. **VHS, Beta $19.98** *MGM, FCT, TLF ⅛⅛⅛*

Thirty-Six Hours of Hell A troop of Marines battle Japanese forces in the South Pacific during World War II. Dubbed.
1977 95m/C Richard Harrison, Pamela Tudor; *D:* Roberto Marrtero. **VHS, Beta $59.95** *UNI ⅛½*

36 Fillete Intellectually precocious 14-year old French girl (dress size 36 fillete) discovers her sexuality. Critically acclaimed.
1988 88m/C *FR* Delphine Zentout, Etienne Chicot, Oliver Parniere, Jean-Pierre Leaud; *D:* Catherine Breillat. **VHS $79.95** *FXL, TAM ⅛⅛⅛*

'38: Vienna Before the Fall Wartime Vienna explodes with love and politics. Academy Award Nominee for best foreign language film. In German with English subtitles.
1988 97m/C *GE* Tobias Engel, Sunnyi Melles; *D:* Wolfgang Gluck. **VHS, LV $34.95** *LUM ⅛⅛½*

This Boy's Life Carolyn (Barkin) and her son Toby (DiCaprio) flee Florida in search of a new life, far from Carolyn's abusive exboyfriend. They end up in Seattle, where Carolyn meets Dwight (DeNiro), a suave mechanic and ex-military man who may be able to tame her rebellious son. Successfully wooing her, Dwight marries Carolyn. After their first night together, Carolyn knows that she has made a tragic error when Dwight reveals his true colors. Tyranical, mean-spirited, and demented, he is a man who relishes mentally tormenting his new family, especially Toby, a confused teenager who is divided between his dream of prep school and attraction to the going-nowhere crowd. All performances are finely crafted, especially newcomer DiCaprio's. Based on the memoirs of Tobias Wolff; director Caton-Jones masterfully depicts the skewed understanding of masculinity in the 1950s.
1993 (R) 115m/C Robert De Niro, Ellen Barkin, Leonardo DiCaprio, Jonah Blechman, Eliza Dushku, Chris Cooper; *D:* Michael Caton-Jones; *W:* Robert Getchell; *M:* Carter Burwell. **VHS** *NYR ⅛⅛⅛*

This Could Be the Night Rocco and Tony are two small-fry gangsters who run a nightclub. Anne is a prim schoolteacher who takes a part-time job as their secretary. She falls for the handsome Tony much to the dismay of Rocco who knows his partner's less-than-sterling character. Sweet but minor comedy. Franciosa's first film. ♫This Could Be The Night; Hustlin' News Gal; I Got It Bad; I'm Gonna Live Till I Die; Taking a Chance on Love; Trumpet Boogie; Mamba Combo; Blue Moon; Dream Dancing; The Tender Trap.
1957 105m/B Jean Simmons, Paul Douglas, Anthony (Tony) Franciosa, Joan Blondell, Julie Wilson, Neile Adams, J. Carroll Naish, Rafael Campos, ZaSu Pitts, Tom Helmore; *D:* Robert Wise. **VHS, LV $19.98** *MGM, MOV ⅛⅛½*

This Gun for Hire In his first major film role, Ladd plays a hired gun seeking retribution from a client who betrays him. Preston is the cop pursuing him and hostage Lake. Ladd's performance as the cold-blooded killer with a soft spot for cats is stunning; his train-yard scene is an emotional powerhouse. Based on Graham Greene's novel "A Gun for Sale." Remade as "Short Cut to Hell." The first of several films using the

Ladd-Lake team, but the only one in which Ladd played a villain.
1942 81m/B Alan Ladd, Veronica Lake, Robert Preston, Laird Cregar; *D:* Frank Tuttle. **VHS, Beta, LV $39.95** *MCA ⅛⅛⅛*

This Gun for Hire A professional assassin finds that he has been duped into killing a powerful political figure, whom he was told was a New Orleans mobster. Now on the run, he takes a nightclub performer hostage, unaware that she is the fiance of the FBI agent who is after him. All odds are against him, but the special relationship he forms with the woman may just be his ticket out. Adapted from novel by Graham Greene.
1990 (R) 89m/C Robert Wagner, Nancy Everhard, Frederic Lehne, John Harkins; *D:* Lou Antonio. **VHS $79.95** *MCA ⅛⅛*

This Happy Breed A celebrated film version of Noel Coward's classic play depicts the changing fortunes of a large family in England between the world wars. Happiness, hardships, triumph and tragedy mix a series of memorable episodes, including some of the most cherished moments in popular British cinema, though its appeal is universal. Narrated by Laurence Olivier.
1947 114m/C *GB* Robert Newton, Celia Johnson, John Mills, Kay Walsh, Stanley Holloway; *W/D:* David Lean. **VHS $39.95** *HMV, FCT ⅛⅛⅛½*

This Happy Feeling Reynolds is a young woman who is romantically attracted to both Jurgens, a sophisticated retired actor, and Saxon, a younger suitor who is Jurgens' neighbor. Good acting all around. Charming telling of old tale.
1958 83m/C Curt Jurgens, Debbie Reynolds, John Saxon, Alexis Smith, Mary Astor, Estelle Winwood; *D:* Blake Edwards. **VHS, Beta $14.95** *KRT, FCT ⅛⅛½*

This is a Hijack Gambler hijacks the plane carrying his wealthy boss to help pay his debts. What it lacks in suspense, it lacks in performance and direction as well.
1975 (PG) 90m/C Adam Roarke, Neville Brand, Jay Robinson, Lynn Borden, Dub Taylor. **VHS, Beta** *NO ⅛*

This is Elvis The life of Elvis, combining documentary footage with dramatizations of events in his life. Includes more than three dozen songs. Generally seen as an attempt to cash in on the myth, but was well-received by his fans.
1981 (PG) 144m/C Elvis Presley; *D:* Malcolm Leo. **VHS, Beta $19.95** *MVD, WAR ⅛⅛*

This is My Life The story of a working mother torn between her skyrocketing career as a stand-up comic and her two daughters. Kavner plays the divorced mom who is determined to chuck her cosmetic sales job for comic success. Her career starts to really take off; she hires an agent and makes appearances on talk shows. As offers pour in, she eventually realizes that her girls are suffering as a result of her success. Good performances highlight an otherwise average drama.
1992 (PG-13) 105m/C Julie Kavner, Samantha Mathis, Carrie Fisher, Dan Aykroyd, Gaby Hoffman; *D:* Nora Ephron; *W:* Nora Ephron, Delia Ephron. **VHS $19.98** *FXV ⅛⅛*

This is Not a Test When news comes of an impending nuclear attack, a state trooper at a roadblock offers sanctuary to passing travellers. The effectiveness of the film's social commentary is hindered by its small budget.
1962 72m/B Seamon Glass, Mary Morlass, Thayer Roberts, Aubrey Martin; *D:* Frederic Gadette. **VHS, Beta $16.95** *SNC ⅛⅛*

This is Spinal Tap Pseudo-rockumentary about heavy-metal band Spinal Tap, profiling their career from "England's loudest band" to an entry in the "where are they now file." Hilarious satire, featuring music performed by Guest, McKean, Shearer, and others. Included are Spinal Tap's music video "Hell Hole," and an ad for their greatest hits album, "Heavy Metal Memories." Features great cameos, particularly David Letterman's Paul Schaefer as a record promoter and Billy Crystal as a surly mime. First feature for Reiner (Meathead on "All in the Family"). Followed by "The Return of Spinal Tap." *AKA:* Spinal Tap.
1984 (R) 82m/C Michael McKean, Christopher Guest, Harry Shearer, Tony Hendra, Bruno Kirby, Rob Reiner, June Chadwick, Howard Hesseman, Dana Carvey, Ed Begley Jr., Patrick Macnee, Anjelica Huston; *Cameos:* Billy Crystal, Paul Schaffer; *D:* Rob Reiner. VHS, Beta, LV, 8mm $14.95 MVD, SUE, NLC ♪♪♪½

This is the Army A robust tribute to the American soldier of World War II based on the hit play by Irving Berlin. Murphy, who later was a senator from California, played Reagan's father. ♪Your Country and My Country; My Sweetie; Poor Little Me, I'm on K.P.; We're On Our Way to France; What Does He Look Like?; This is the Army, Mr. Jones; I'm Gettin' Tired So I Can Sleep; Mandy; Ladies of the Chorus; That What the Well-Dressed Man in Harlem Will Wear; How About a Cheer for the Navy; I Left My Heart at the Stage Door Canteen; With My Head in the Clouds; American Eagles; Oh, How I Hate to Get Up in the Morning; This Time is the Last Time; The Army's Made a Man Out of Me; God Bless America.
1943 105m/C George Murphy, Joan Leslie, Ronald Reagan, Alan Hale Jr., Kate Smith, George Tobias, Irving Berlin, Joe Louis; *D:* Michael Curtiz. Academy Awards '43: Best Score; Nominations: Best Interior Decoration, Best Sound, 3/4U, Special order formats $19.95 NOS, DVT, CAB ♪♪♪½

This Island Earth The planet Metaluna is in desperate need of uranium to power its defense against enemy invaders. A nuclear scientist and a nuclear fission expert from Earth are kidnapped to help out. The first serious movie about interplanetary escapades. Bud Westmore created pulsating cranium special effects make-up.
1955 86m/C Jeff Morrow, Faith Domergue, Rex Reason, Russell Johnson; *D:* Joseph M. Newman. VHS, Beta, LV $19.95 MCA, MLB ♪♪½

This Land is Mine A timid French schoolteacher gathers enough courage to defy the Nazis when they attempt to occupy his town. Laughton's characterization is effective as the meek fellow who discovers the hero within himself in this patriotic wartime flick.
1943 103m/B Charles Laughton, Maureen O'Hara, George Sanders, Walter Slezak, George Coulouris, Una O'Connor; *D:* Jean Renoir. VHS, Beta, LV $19.98 RKO, TTC ♪♪♪

This Lightning Always Strikes Twice An elegant murder mystery made for British television.
1985 60m/C GB Claire Bloom, Trevor Howard, Charles Dance. VHS, Beta $59.95 PSM ♪♪♪

This Man Must Die A man searches relentlessly for the driver who killed his young son in a hit-and-run. When found, the driver engages in a complex cat-and-mouse chase. Another stunning crime and punishment tale from Chabrol. *AKA:* Que La Bete Meure; Uccidero Un Uomo.
1970 (PG) 112m/C FR Michael Duchaussoy, Caroline Cellier, Jean Yanne; *D:* Claude Chabrol. VHS, Beta $59.95 FOX ♪♪♪½

This Nude World A campy "expose" of the secret world of nudist colonies, including a look at volleyball players in Camp Olympia, New York.
1932 55m/B VHS, Beta $24.95 NOS, VDM, MLB ♪♪

This Property is Condemned The lure of steamy sex fills a southern boardinghouse when a mother offers her daughter (Wood) to a wealthy tenant (Harding). But the daughter loves another man (Redford). Based on the Tennessee Williams play; the author was reportedly unhappy with the script and wanted his name removed from the film.
1966 109m/C Robert Redford, Natalie Wood, Charles Bronson, Kate Reid, Mary Badham, Jon Provost, Robert (Bobby) Blake, John Harding; *D:* Sydney Pollack; *W:* Francis Ford Coppola, Edith Sommer, Fred Coe. VHS, Beta, LV $19.95 PAR, PIA ♪♪

This Special Friendship Powerful, if overdone French drama about an emotionally sensitive young man at a Catholic boarding school. His sexual relationship with another boy leads to tragedy. Based on the novel by Roger Peyrefitte. *AKA:* Les Amities Particulieres.
1967 99m/B FR Francis Lacombrade, Didier Haudepin, Lucien Nat, Louis Seigner, Michel Bouquet, Francois Leccia; *D:* Jean Delannoy. VHS, Beta FCT ♪♪½

This Sporting Life A gritty, depressing portrait of a former coal miner who breaks into the violent world of professional rugby, and whose inability to handle social differences causes problems. He begins an affair with the widow from whom he rents a room but finds they are capable of only a physical attachment. One of the best of the British early 60s working-class angry young man melodramas. Written by David Storey.
1963 134m/B GB Richard Harris, Rachel Roberts, Alan Badel, William Hartnell, Colin Blakely, Vanda Godsell, Arthur Lowe; *D:* Lindsay Anderson. Academy Awards '63 Nominations: Best Actor (Harris), Best Actress (Roberts); British Academy Awards '63: Best Actress (Roberts); Cannes Film Festival '63: Best Actor (Harris); National Board of Review Awards '63: 10 Best Films of the Year. VHS, Beta $19.95 PAR ♪♪♪

This Stuff'll Kill Ya! A backwoods preacher who believes in free love and moonshining runs into trouble with the locals when a series of gruesome religious murders are committed. Southern drive-in material from one of the genre's masters. Holt's last film.
1971 (PG) 100m/C Jeffrey Allen, Tim Holt, Gloria King, Ray Sager, Eric Bradly, Terence McCarthy; *W/D:* Herschell Gordon Lewis. VHS $29.95 TWE, FRG Woof!

This Time I'll Make You Rich Two American hoodlums work out a drug-ring heist in the Far East.
1975 (PG) 97m/C Tony Sabato, Robin McDavid; *D:* Frank Kramer. VHS, Beta $59.98 NLC ♪

Thomas Crown Affair A multi-millionaire (McQueen) decides to plot and execute the perfect theft, a daring daylight robbery of a bank. Dunaway is the gorgeous and efficient insurance investigator determined to nab him. One of the best visual scenes is the chess match between the two as they begin to fall in love. Strong production with Oscar-winning theme "Windmills of Your Mind." *AKA:* Thomas Crown and Company; The Crown Caper.
1968 (R) 102m/C Steve McQueen, Faye Dunaway, Jack Weston, Yaphet Kotto; *D:* Norman Jewison. VHS, Beta $19.98 MGM, FCT, FOX ♪♪♪

Thomas Graal's Best Film The famous comical adventures of a film scriptwriter wooing his secretary, followed by "Thomas Graal's First Child." Silent.
1917 70m/B SW Victor Sjostrom, Karin Molander; *D:* Mauritz Stiller. VHS, Beta $49.95 FCT ♪♪♪

Thomas Graal's First Child The sequel to "Thomas Graal's Best Film." The comical screenwriter and actress couple attempt to raise a baby. Silent.
1918 70m/B Victor Sjostrom, Karin Molander; *D:* Mauritz Stiller. VHS, Beta $49.95 FCT ♪♪♪

Thompson's Last Run Boyhood friends grow up on either side of the law. They come face-to-face, though, when one is assigned to transport the other to prison. Made for television.
1990 95m/C Robert Mitchum, Wilford Brimley, Kathleen York, Susan Tyrrell; *D:* Jerrold Freedman. VHS, Beta, LV NO ♪½

Thor and the Amazon Women The mighty Thor leads his enslaved men on an attack against the evil Queen Nera and her female-dominated Amazon society.
1960 85m/C Joe Robinson, Susy Anderson. VHS $39.95 AIP ♪

Thor el Conquistador The mighty Thor risks it all in a savage prehistoric land to avenge the slaying of his parents.
1986 90m/C MX Maria Romano, Malisa Lang, Ralf Falcone, Christopher Holm. VHS, Beta $59.95 MED ♪

Thorn The Virgin Mary and Joseph try to raise Jesus Christ in the modern world.
1973 (R) 90m/C Bette Midler, John Bassberger. VHS, Beta NO ♪½

The Thorn Birds Pioneers find danger and romance in the Australian outback as they struggle to begin a dynasty. Charismatic priest sometimes hurts, sometimes helps them. One of Stanwyck's last performances; Ward's American television debut. Originally a ten-hour television epic based on Colleen McCullough novel. Emmy nominations for Actor Chamberlain, Supporting Actor(s) Brown and Plummer, Supporting Actress Laurie, direction, photography, music, costume design, and editing. On four cassettes.
1983 486m/C Rachel Ward, Richard Chamberlain, Jean Simmons, Ken Howard, Mare Winningham, Richard Kiley, Piper Laurie, Bryan Brown, Christopher Plummer, Barbara Stanwyck; *D:* Daryl Duke. VHS, Beta $199.92 WAR, MOV, TVC ♪♪♪

Thoroughbreds Don't Cry Rooney plays a jockey who throws a race so his no-good father can win enough money to pay for his supposed medical problems. The owner of the horse then drops dead from a heart attack. Rooney feels guilty, so he asks his father to loan the owner's grandson $1,000 to run in another race. His father says no, so Rooney steals the money from him, and when the father finds out he tells the track officials that Rooney threw the race. Garland is Rooney's best friend and moral support, and she sings a few songs too! A fairly good horse racing story.
1937 80m/B Judy Garland, Mickey Rooney, Sophie Tucker, C. Aubrey Smith, Ronald Sinclair, Forrester Harvey; *D:* Alfred E. Green. VHS $19.98 MGM, MVD ♪♪½

Thoroughly Modern Millie Andrews is a young woman who comes to New York in the early 1920s where she meets another newcomer, the innocent Moore. Andrews

decides to upgrade her image to that of a "modern" woman, a flapper, and sets out to realize her ambition, to become a stenographer and marry the boss. Meanwhile, Moore has become an object of interest to Lillie, who just happens to run a white-slavery ring. Lots of frantic moments and big production numbers in this campy film. Channing and Lillie are exceptional in it. ♫Thoroughly Modern Millie; The Tapioca; Jimmy; The Jewish Wedding Song; Baby Face; Do It Again; Poor Butterfly; Rose of Washington Square; I Can't Believe That You're In Love With Me; I'm Sitting on Top of the World; Stumbling; Japanese Sandman; Charmaine; Jazz Baby.
1967 (G) 138m/C Julie Andrews, Carol Channing, Mary Tyler Moore, John Gavin, Beatrice Lillie, James Fox, Pat Morita; *D:* George Roy Hill. Academy Awards '67: Best Original Score; Nominations: Best Art Direction/Set Decoration, Best Costume Design, Best Song ("Thoroughly Modern Millie"), Best Supporting Actress (Channing), Best Original Score; Golden Globe Awards '68: Best Supporting Actress (Channing). **VHS, Beta, LV $19.95** *MCA ♪♪½*

Those Calloways A small town family attempts to establish a sanctuary for the flocks of wild geese who fly over the woods of Swiftwater, Maine. Fine Disney family fare, with good cast. Based on Paul Annixter's novel "Swiftwater."
1965 (PG) 131m/C Brian Keith, Vera Miles, Brandon de Wilde, Walter Brennan, Ed Wynn, John Qualen, Linda Evans; *D:* Norman Tokar. **VHS, Beta $69.95** *DIS ♪♪½*

Those Daring Young Men in Their Jaunty Jalopies Daring young men in noisy slow cars trek 1500 miles across country in the 1920s and call it a race. *AKA:* Monte Carlo or Bust; Quei Temerari Sulle Loro Pazze, Scatenate, Scalcinate Carriole.
1969 (G) 125m/C *GB* Tony Curtis, Susan Hampshire, Terry-Thomas, Eric Sykes, Gert Frobe, Peter Cook, Dudley Moore, Jack Hawkins; *D:* Ken Annakin. **VHS $39.95** *PAR, FCT ♪♪*

Those Endearing Young Charms Romance develops between a young Air Corps mechanic and a salesgirl. Complications arise when another man enters the scene. Light romantic comedy. Based on the play by Edward Chodorov.
1945 82m/B Robert Young, Laraine Day, Anne Jeffreys, Lawrence Tierney; *D:* Lewis Allen. **VHS, Beta** *CCB ♪♪*

Those Fantastic Flying Fools A mad race to be the first on the moon brings hilarious results. Loosely based on a Jules Verne story. *AKA:* Blast-Off; Jules Verne's Rocket to the Moon.
1967 95m/C *GB* Burl Ives, Troy Donahue, Gert Frobe, Terry-Thomas, Hermione Gingold, Daliah Lavi, Lionel Jeffries; *D:* Don Sharp. **VHS $79.95** *HBO ♪♪½*

Those Glory, Glory Days An English woman, secure in her position as an outstanding sports journalist, reminisces about the days when she and her friends idolized the boys on the soccer team. Nothing extraordinary, but nicely made.
1983 92m/C *GB* Zoe Nathenson, Liz Campion, Cathy Murphy; *D:* Philip Saville. **VHS, Beta $59.95** *MGM ♪½*

Those Krazy Klassic Kolor Kartoons: Vol. 1 A compilation of classic cartoons such as "Felix the Cat" and "Old Mother Hubbard" that the whole family can enjoy.
1985 58m/C VHS, Beta $29.95 *MPI ♪½*

Those Lips, Those Eyes A pre-med student takes a job as a prop boy in a summer stock company and winds up falling in love with the company's lead dancer. Subplot about aging actor is more interesting, better played by Langella. O'Conner is appropriately lovely. Nicely made, charming sleeper of a film.
1980 106m/C Frank Langella, Tom Hulce, Glynnis O'Connor, Jerry Stiller, Kevin McCarthy; *D:* Michael Pressman. **VHS, Beta $59.95** *MGM ♪♪½*

Those Magnificent Men in Their Flying Machines In 1910, a wealthy British newspaper publisher is persuaded to sponsor an air race from London to Paris. Contestants come from all over the world and shenanigans, hijinks, double-crosses, and romance are found along the route. Skelton has fun in prologue, while Terry-Thomas is great as the villain. Fun from start to finish.
1965 138m/C *GB* Stuart Whitman, Sarah Miles, Robert Morley, Alberto Sordi, James Fox, Gert Frobe, Jean-Pierre Cassel, Flora Robson, Sam Wanamaker, Terry-Thomas, Irina Demick, Benny Hill, Gordon Jackson, Millicent Martin, Red Skelton; *D:* Ken Annakin. **VHS, Beta, LV $79.98** *FOX ♪♪♪*

Thou Shalt Not Kill...Except A Vietnam vet seeks revenge on the violent cult who kidnapped his girlfriend.
1987 84m/C Brian Schulz, Robert Rickman, John Manfredi, Tim Quill, Cheryl Hansen, Sam Raimi. **VHS, Beta $9.99** *STE, PSM ♪*

Thoughts are Free A young soldier, wounded in World War II, escapes from the train that is transporting him and his comrades to a Soviet labor camp and rejoins his family. Under the repressive communist regime, he plots his family's escape to the West but his plans are thwarted when the Berlin Wall is erected, leaving him in the West and his wife and daughter in the East. As the years go by, they can get together only by outwitting the bureaucrats. The film's title is taken from an old German folk song "Die Gedanken sind frei," sung here by Heino.
1984 (PG) 93m/C Herbert Ludwig, Kathrin Kratzer; *D:* Josef Sommer. **VHS, Beta $29.95** *ZBI ♪♪♪½*

A Thousand Clowns A nonconformist has resigned from his job as chief writer for an obnoxious kiddie show in order to enjoy life. But his independence comes under fire when he becomes guardian for his young nephew and social workers have a dim view of his lifestyle. Balsam won an Oscar for his role as Robard's agent brother. Adapted from Herb Gardner's Broadway comedy.
1965 118m/B Jason Robards Jr., Barry Gordon, William Daniels, Barbara Harris, Gene Saks, Martin Balsam; *D:* Fred Coe. Academy Awards '65: Best Supporting Actor (Balsam); Nominations: Best Adapted Screenplay, Best Picture, Best Original Score; National Board of Review Awards '65: 10 Best Films of the Year. **VHS, Beta $19.98** *MGM, FOX, BTV ♪♪♪*

The Thousand Eyes of Dr. Mabuse Lang's last film is a return to his pre-war German character, the evil Dr. Mabuse. A series of strange murders occur in a Berlin hotel and police believe the killer thinks he's a reincarnation of the doctor. Disorienting chiller. *AKA:* The Secret of Dr. Mabuse; The Diabolical Dr. Mabuse; The Shadow Versus the Thousand Eyes of Dr. Mabuse.
1960 103m/B *GE* Dawn Addams, Peter Van Eyck, Gert Frobe, Wolfgang Preiss; *D:* Fritz Lang. **VHS $39.95** *FCT ♪♪½*

Thousand Mile Escort Chinese peasants struggle to survive amid poverty and power-mad warlords. Dubbed.
19?? 86m/C *CH* Pak Ying. **VHS, Beta** *NO ♪*

Thousand Pieces of Gold A young Chinese woman is sold by her father to a marriage broker, but instead of a respectable marriage she is shipped to America and expected to work as a prostitute in an Idaho mining town. Instead she works taking in laundry as she tries to make her way in a man's world, finding a sweet romance of opposites along the way. Based on a true story. Excellent performances by Chao and Cooper.
1991 (PG-13) 105m/C Rosalind Chao, Dennis Dun, Michael Paul Chan, Chris Cooper, Jimmie F. Skaggs, William Oldham, David Hayward, Beth Broderick; *D:* Nancy Kelly. **VHS, LV $89.95** *HMD, TAM ♪♪♪*

Thousands Cheer A flag-waving wartime musical about a tap-dancing Army private who falls in love with the colonel's daughter, culminating with an all-star (MGM) USO show. Songs include "Honeysuckle Rose," sung by Horne, and "The Joint Is Really Jumping Down at Carnegie Hall," sung by Garland.
1943 126m/C Gene Kelly, Kathryn Grayson, Judy Garland, Mickey Rooney, Mary Astor, John Boles, Lucille Ball, Eleanor Powell, Virginia O'Brien, Margaret O'Brien, Red Skelton, Lionel Barrymore, June Allyson, Frank Morgan, Kay Kyser, Bob Crosby, Lena Horne, Donna Reed; *D:* George Sidney. **VHS, Beta, LV $19.98** *MGM ♪♪½*

Thrashin' A new-to-L.A. teen must prove himself to a tough gang on skateboards by skateboarding a certain treacherous race. For skateboarding fans only.
1986 (PG-13) 93m/C Josh Brolin, Pamela Gidley, Robert Rusler, Chuck McCann; *D:* David Winters. **VHS, Beta** *NO ♪*

Threads The famed dramatic recreation of the effects of nuclear war on a British city and two of its families. A disturbing, uncompromising, and somewhat plausible drama. Made for British television.
1985 110m/C *GB* Karen Meagher, Rita May, David Brierly, Reece Dinsdale, Harry Beety; *D:* Mick Jackson. **VHS, Beta $59.95** *WWV ♪♪♪*

Threat A killer escapes from jail and returns to settle the score with those who convicted him. Tense, fast-moving thriller.
1949 66m/B Michael O'Shea, Virginia Grey, Charles McGraw; *D:* Felix Feist. **VHS, Beta $34.95** *RKO ♪♪½*

Three Ages A parody of D.W. Griffith's 1916 film "Intolerance." Keaton's first feature film casts him in prehistoric days, ancient Rome, and in modern times. Silent with musical score.
1923 59m/B Wallace Beery, Oliver Hardy, Buster Keaton; *D:* Buster Keaton, Eddie Cline. **VHS, Beta $19.95** *NOS, VDM, DVT ♪♪♪*

Three Amigos Three out-of-work silent screen stars are asked to defend a Mexican town from bandits; they think it's a public appearance stint. Spoof of Three Stooges and Mexican bandito movies that at times falls short, given the enormous amount of comedic talent involved. Generally enjoyable with some very funny scenes. Co-written by Martin, songwriter Randy Newman (who also appears in the film), and former "Saturday Night Live" producer Lorne Michaels. Short's first major film appearance.
1986 (PG) 105m/C Chevy Chase, Steve Martin, Martin Short, Joe Mantegna, Patrice Martinez, Jon Lovitz, Alfonso Arau, Randy Newman; *D:* John Landis. **VHS, Beta, LV $14.99** *HBO ♪♪*

Three Avengers Trouble abounds when two kung fu masters and an American Chinese boy open a martial arts school. **1980 (R) 93m/C VHS, Beta $9.98** *SUE* 🎬

Three Broadway Girls Three gold-diggers go husband-hunting. Well-paced, very funny telling of this old story. Remade many times, including "How to Marry a Millionaire," "Three Blind Mice," "Moon Over Miami," and "Three Little Girls in Blue." **AKA:** The Greeks Had a Word for Them. **1932 78m/B** Joan Blondell, Ina Claire, Madge Evans, David Manners, Lowell Sherman; **D:** Lowell Sherman. **VHS, Beta, 3/4U, Special order formats $19.95** *NOS, CAB, KRT* 🎬🎬🎬

Three Brothers An acclaimed Italian film by veteran Rosi about three brothers summoned to their small Italian village by a telegram saying their mother is dead. Sensitive and compassionate. In Italian with English subtitles. Adapted from Platonov's story "The Third Son." **1980 (PG) 113m/C** *IT* Philippe Noiret, Charles Vanel, Michele Placido, Vittorio Mezzogiorno, Andrea Ferreol; **D:** Francesco Rosi. **VHS, Beta $29.98** *SUE, APD* 🎬🎬🎬

Three Bullets for a Long Gun Two prairie renegades battle bandits as they search for an inherited gold mine. Written by Van Der Wat. **1973 (PG) 89m/C** Keith Van Der Wat, Beau Brummel, Patrick Munhardt; **D:** Peter Henkel. **VHS, Beta $14.95** *COL, NLC, SIM* 🎬½

Three by Hitchcock Condensed versions of three of Hitchcock's early films (1927-28). Consists of "The Ring," "Champagne," and "The Manxman," his last silent film. **1928 90m/B D:** Alfred Hitchcock. **VHS, Beta $60.50** *GVV* 🎬🎬

The Three Caballeros Donald Duck stars in this journey through Latin America. Full of music, variety, and live-action/animation segments. Songs include "The Three Caballeros" and "Baia." Stories include "Pablo the Penguin," "Little Gauchito," and adventures with Joe Carioca, who was first introduced in Disney's "Saludos Amigos." Today this film stands as one of the very best pieces of animation ever created. Great familyfare. **1945 71m/C V:** Sterling Holloway, Aurora Miranda. **VHS, Beta, LV $24.99** *DIS, APD, WTA* 🎬🎬½

Three Came Home Colbert is an American married to a British administrator in the Far East during WWII. Conquering Japanese throw the whole family into a brutal POW concentration camp, and their confinement is recounted in harrowing and unsparing detail. Superior drama, also laudable for a fairly even-handed portrayal of the enemy captors. Based on an autobiographical book by Agnes Newton-Keith. **1950 106m/B** Claudette Colbert, Patric Knowles, Sessue Hayakawa; **D:** Jean Negulesco. **VHS $19.95** *NOS, HEG* 🎬🎬🎬

Three Charlies and One Phoney! Three of Charlie Chaplin's best comedy shorts, plus one featuring his best-known imitator — Billy West. Included are "Recreation" ("Fun is Fun") ("Spring Fever"), "His Musical Career" ("The Piano Movers") ("Musical Sracps"), "The Bond" (featuring Charlie in a Liberty Bond appeal) and "His Day Out" with Billy West imitating Chaplin. All but "His Day Out" were written and directed by Chaplin.

1918 69m/B Charlie Chaplin, Mack Swain, Charley Chase, Edna Purviance, Sydney Chaplin, Albert Austin; **W/D:** Charlie Chaplin. **VHS, Beta, 8mm $29.95** *VYY* 🎬🎬🎬

Three Coins in the Fountain Three women throw money into fountain and get romantically involved with Italian men. Outstanding CinemaScope photography captures beauty of Italian setting. Sammy Cahn theme song sung by Frank Sinatra. **1954 102m/C** Clifton Webb, Dorothy McGuire, Jean Peters, Louis Jourdan, Maggie McNamara, Rossano Brazzi; **D:** Jean Negulesco. **VHS, Beta $59.98** *FOX* 🎬🎬½

Three Comrades Taylor, Tone, and Young play three friends, reunited in bleak, post-WWI Germany. They soon meet and befriend Sullavan, a tubercular beauty who's looked after by the wealthy Atwill. Reluctant to marry because of her health, she's finally persuaded to wed Taylor, amidst the country's increasing unrest. Tragedy soon strikes both Sullavan and the politicized Young, with the two remaining comrades facing an uncertain future. Bleak but forceful and passionate drama with a superb performance by Sullavan. Based on the novel by Erich Maria Remarque. Fitzgerald's script was heavily rewritten because both Sullavan and producer Mankiewicz found much of his dialog unspeakable and his approach too literary for such a visual medium. **1938 99m/B** Robert Taylor, Margaret Sullavan, Robert Young, Franchot Tone, Lionel Atwill, Guy Kibbee, Henry Hull, George Zucco, Monty Woolley, Charley Grapewin, Spencer Charters, Sarah Padden; **D:** Frank Borzage; **W:** F. Scott Fitzgerald, Edward Paramore; **M:** Franz Waxman. **VHS $19.98** *MGM, MOV* 🎬🎬🎬

Three Days in Beirut A soldier of fortune and a beautiful interpreter join forces against a backdrop of Middle Eastern politics, espionage, and violence. **1983 (PG) 94m/C** Diana Sands, Calvin Lockhart; **D:** Michael Schultz. **VHS, Beta $59.95** *PSM* 🎬

Three Days of the Condor CIA researcher Redford finds himself on the run from unknown killers when he is left the only survivor of the mass murder of his office staff. Good performance by Dunaway as the photographer who shelters him. Excellent suspense tale. Based on "Six Days of the Condor" by James Grady. **1975 (R) 118m/C** Robert Redford, Faye Dunaway, Cliff Robertson, Max von Sydow, John Houseman; **D:** Sydney Pollack. Academy Awards '75 Nominations: Best Film Editing; Edgar Allan Poe Awards '75: Best Screenplay. **VHS, Beta, LV $24.95** *PAR, PIA* 🎬🎬🎬

Three Days to a Kill Calvin Sims is a mercenary hired to rescue a kidnapped ambassador—by any means necessary. **1991 (R) 90m/C** Fred Williamson, Bo Svenson, Henry Silva, Chuck Connors, Van Johnson, Sonny Landham; **D:** Fred Williamson. **VHS, LV $89.99** *HBO* 🎬🎬

Three Desperate Men Three brothers accused of murder become outlaws. Not innovative, but satisfactory tale of the Old West. **1950 71m/B** Preston Foster, Virginia Grey, Jim Davis; **D:** Sam Newfield. **VHS, Beta** *NO* 🎬🎬

The Three Faces of Eve An emotionally disturbed woman seeks the help of a psychiatrist, who discovers she has three distinct personalities. Powerful performances highlight this fascinating study based on a true story. **1957 91m/B** Joanne Woodward, David Wayne, Lee J. Cobb, Nancy Kulp, Vince Edwards; **D:** Nunnally Johnson. **VHS, LV $19.98** *FXV* 🎬🎬🎬½

Three Faces West A dust bowl community is helped by a Viennese doctor who left Europe to avoid Nazi capture. He's aided by the Duke in this odd combination of Western frontier saga and anti-Nazi propaganda. Works only part of the time. **AKA:** The Refugee. **1940 79m/B** John Wayne, Charles Coburn, Sigrid Gurie, Sonny Bupp, Russell Simpson; **D:** Bernard Vorhaus. **VHS $14.98** *REP* 🎬🎬

3:15—The Moment of Truth A vicious high school gang is confronted by an angry ex-member in this so-so teen delinquent film. **1986 (R) 86m/C** Adam Baldwin, Deborah Foreman, Rene Auberjonois, Danny De La Paz; **D:** Larry Gross. **VHS, Beta $19.95** *MED* 🎬🎬

Three for Bedroom C A movie star and a scientist make romance on a train bound for Los Angeles. Swanson's follow-up to "Sunset Boulevard." **1952 74m/C** Gloria Swanson, Fred Clark, Steve Brodie, Hans Conried, Margaret Dumont; **D:** Milton Bren. **VHS, Beta $12.95** *LIV* 🎬🎬

Three for the Road A young aspiring political aide and his roommate must escort a Senator's ill-mannered and spoiled daughter to a reform institution. On the road, they run into more than a few surprises. Good performances elevate a bland script. Sheen made this movie before his riveting performance as a young GI in "Platoon." **1987 (PG) 98m/C** Charlie Sheen, Kerri Green, Alan Ruck, Sally Kellerman; **D:** B.W.L. Norton. **Beta, LV** *NO* 🎬🎬

Three Fugitives An ex-con holdup man determined to go straight is taken hostage by a bungling first-time bank robber, who is only attempting the holdup in order to support his withdrawn young daughter. Ex-con Nolte winds up on the lam with the would-be robber and his daughter. The comedy is fun, the sentimental moments too sweet and slow. Remake of French "Les Fugitifs." **1989 (PG-13) 96m/C** Nick Nolte, Martin Short, James Earl Jones, Kenneth MacMillan, Sarah Rowland Doroff, Alan Ruck; **D:** Francis Veber. **VHS, Beta, LV $19.99** *TOU* 🎬🎬

Three Godfathers A sweet and sentimental western has three half-hearted outlaws on the run, taking with them an infant they find in the desert. Dedicated to western star and Ford alumni Harry Carey, Sr. (whose son is one of the outlaws in the film), who died of cancer the year before. Ford had first filmed the tale with Carey Sr. as "Marked Men" in 1919. **1948 82m/C** John Wayne, Pedro Armendariz Sr., Harry Carey Jr., Ward Bond, Mae Marsh, Jane Darwell, Ben Johnson, Mildred Natwick, Guy Kibbee; **D:** John Ford. **VHS, Beta $19.98** *MGM* 🎬🎬🎬

Three Guys Named Mike Wyman plays an overly enthusiastic airline stewardess who finds herself the object of affection from three guys named Mike, including an airline pilot, an advertising man, and a scientist. A cute comedy. **1951 89m/B** Jane Wyman, Van Johnson, Barry Sullivan, Howard Keel, Phyllis Kirk, Jeff Donnell; **D:** Charles Walters. **VHS $19.95** *VDM* 🎬🎬

The 317th Platoon An emotionally gripping war drama of the French-Vietnemese War in which the 317th Platoon of the French Army, consisting of 4 French commanders and 41 Laotians, is ordered to retreat to camp Dien Bien Phu. The men begin their march and slowly succomb to the elements and ambushes. Days later, when what is left of the platoon finally reaches Dien Bien Phu, the camp is in enemy hands and

the remnants of the 317th Platoon are killed in cold blood. Director Shoendoerffer portrays this struggle, conflict, and the quiet haunting tension of war with great skill. In French with English subtitles.
1965 100m/B FR Jacques Perrin, Bruno Cremer, Pierre Fabre, Manuel Zarzo; W/D: Pierre Shoendoerffer. VHS, LV $49.95 INT, IME, FCT ⅔⅔⅔

357 Magnum Jonathan Hightower, the CIA's special investigator in the Far East, speaks softly and carries a very big gun.
1977 71m/C Marland T. Stewart, James Whitworth, Kathryn Hayes. VHS, Beta $59.95 WWV ⅔

Three Husbands A deceased playboy leaves letters for the title characters incriminating their wives in extramarital affairs. The men's reactions are pure farce—even though this same concept was played straight with a sex change in the earlier "A Letter to Three Wives."
1950 79m/B Eve Arden, Ruth Warrick, Vanessa Brown, Howard da Silva, Sheppard Strudwick, Jane Darwell; D: Irving Reis. VHS $19.95 NOS, VDM ⅔⅔½

Three in the Attic A college student juggles three girlfriends at the same time. When the girls find out they are being two-timed, they lock their boyfriend in an attic and exhaust him with forced sexual escapades. Then they talk. Limited trashy and foolish appeal.
1968 (R) 92m/C Christopher Jones, Yvette Mimieux, John Beck; D: Richard Wilson. VHS, Beta $9.98 SUE, MLB ⅔½

Three in the Cellar A disgruntled college student seeks revenge on the school president by seducing his wife, daughter and mistress. Good screenplay helps carry it off. AKA: Up in the Cellar.
1970 (R) 92m/C Wes Stern, Joan Collins, Larry Hagman, Judy Pace; D: Theodore J. Flicker. VHS $79.95 HBO ⅔⅔

Three in the Saddle Ritter and the Texas Rangers fight for law and order.
1945 61m/B Tex Ritter, Dave O'Brien, Charles King; D: Harry Fraser. VHS, Beta $19.95 NOS, VCN ⅔½

Three Kinds of Heat Three Interpol agents track down a warring Oriental crime lord. Alternately tongue-in-cheek and silly. Never released in theaters, it found a home on video. Stevens created "The Outer Limits" for television.
1987 (R) 88m/C Robert Ginty, Victoria Barrett, Shakti; D: Leslie Stevens. VHS, Beta $19.98 WAR ⅔

Three Legionnaires Three soldiers cavort in a post-World War I Siberian tank town. AKA: Three Crazy Legionnaires.
1937 67m/B Robert Armstrong, Lyle Talbot, Fifi d'Orsay, Anne Nagel, Donald Meek. VHS, Beta, LV NO ⅔⅔½

The Three Little Pigs From "Faerie Tale Theatre" comes the story of three little pigs, the houses they lived in and the wolf that tried to do them in.
1984 60m/C Billy Crystal, Jeff Goldblum, Valerie Perrine; D: Howard Storm. VHS, Beta $14.98 KUI, FOX, FCT ⅔⅔½

Three Little Words A musical biography of songwriting team Harry Ruby and Bert Kalmar, filled with Kalmar-Ruby numbers. June Haver (famous for her boop-boop-de-boops) dubbed "I Wanna Be Loved By You" for Reynolds. A musical in the best MGM tradition. ♪I Wanna Be Loved By You; Who's Sorry Now?; Three Little Words; I Love You So Much; She's Mine, All Mine; So-Long, Oo-Long; Hooray for Captain Spauld-

ing; Up In the Clouds; All Alone Monday; Where Did You Get That Girl?; My Sunny Tennessee; Come On Papa; You Are My Lucky Star; Thinking of You; Mr. and Mrs. Hoofer at Home; Nevertheless; All Alone Monday.
1950 102m/C Fred Astaire, Red Skelton, Vera-Ellen, Arlene Dahl, Keenan Wynn, Gloria de Haven, Debbie Reynolds, Gale Robbins; D: Richard Thorpe. Academy Awards '50 Nominations: Best Original Score; Golden Globe Awards '51: Best Actor—Musical/Comedy (Astaire). VHS, Beta $19.98 MGM ⅔⅔½

The Three Lives of Thomasina In turn-of-the-century Scotland, a veterinarian orders his daughter's beloved cat destroyed when the pet is diagnosed with tetanus. After the cat's death (with scenes of kitty heaven), a beautiful and mysterious healer from the woods is able to bring the animal back to life and restore the animal to the little girl. Lovely Disney fairy tale with good performances by all.
1963 (PG) 95m/C Patrick McGoohan, Susan Hampshire, Karen Dotrice, Matthew Garber; D: Don Chaffey. VHS, Beta $19.99 DIS, TVC ⅔⅔⅔

Three Men and a Baby The arrival of a young baby forever changes the lives of three sworn bachelors living in New York. Well-paced, charming and fun, with good acting from all. A remake of the French movie "Three Men and a Cradle."
1987 (PG) 102m/C Tom Selleck, Steve Guttenberg, Ted Danson, Margaret Colin, Nancy Travis, Philip Bosco, Celeste Holm; D: Leonard Nimoy. VHS, Beta, LV, 8mm $19.99 TOU, BVV ⅔⅔⅔

Three Men and a Cradle Remade in the U.S. in 1987 as "Three Men and a Baby," this French film is about three bachelors living together who suddenly find themselves the guardians of a baby girl. After the initial shock of learning how to take care of a child, they fall in love with her and won't let her go. Fans of the American version may find themselves liking the original even more. In French with English subtitles. AKA: Trois Hommes et un Couffin.
1985 (PG-13) 100m/C FR Roland Giraud, Michel Boujenah, Andre Dussollier; D: Coline Serreau. Academy Awards '85 Nominations: Best Foreign Language Film; Cesar Awards '86: Best Film, Best Supporting Actor (Boujenah). VHS, LV $19.98 LIV, MGM, TAM ⅔⅔⅔½

Three Men and a Little Lady In this sequel to "Three Men and a Baby," the mother of the once abandonded infant decides that her child needs a father. Although she wants Selleck, he doesn't get the message and so she chooses a snooty British director. The rest of the movie features various semi-comic attempts to rectify the situation.
1990 (PG) 100m/C Tom Selleck, Steve Guttenberg, Ted Danson, Nancy Travis, Robin Weisman, Christopher Cazenove, Leona Shaw; D: Emile Ardolino. VHS, Beta, LV $19.99 TOU ⅔⅔½

Three Men on a Horse Comedy classic about mild-mannered McHugh's ability to predict horse races and the bettors that try to take advantage of him. Blondell is great as the Brooklynese girlfriend of one of the bettors. Lots of laughs, but don't watch for the horse-racing scenes, because there aren't many.
1936 88m/B Frank McHugh, Joan Blondell, Carol Hughes, Allen Jenkins, Guy Kibbee, Sam Levene; D: Mervyn LeRoy. VHS $19.98 MGM ⅔⅔⅔

The Three Musketeers One of the many movie adaptation of Alexandre Dumas' adventure, but this one comes from the hand of famed movie pioneer Ince. D'Artagnan joins the title characters in saving France's Queen Anne from a nefarious plot. Silent with the original organ score. AKA: D'Artagnan.
1916 74m/B Orin Johnson, Dorothy Dalton, Louise Glaum, Walt Whitman; D: Thomas Ince. VHS, Beta, 8mm $29.95 VYY, GPV, DVT ⅔⅔

The Three Musketeers D'Artagnan swashbuckles silently amid stylish sets, scores of extras and exquisite costumes. Relatively faithful adaptation of Alexandre Dumas novel, slightly altered in favor of D'Artagnan's lover. Classic Fairbanks, who also produced.
1921 120m/B Douglas Fairbanks Sr., Leon Barry, George Siegmann, Eugene Pallette, Boyd Irwin, Thomas Holding, Sidney Franklin, Charles Stevens, Nigel de Brulier, Willis Robards; D: Fred Niblo. VHS, Beta, LV $29.95 GPV, FCT ⅔⅔⅔½

Three Musketeers Modern adaptation of the classic tale by Alexander Dumas depicts the three friends as members of the Foreign Legion. Weakest of Wayne serials, in 12 parts.
1933 215m/B John Wayne, Raymond Hatton, Lon Chaney Jr. VHS, Beta $24.95 NOS, VCN, VDM ⅔⅔

Three Musketeers Three swordsmen, loyal to each other, must battle the corrupt Cardinal Richelieu. Generally regarded as the least exciting adaptation of Alexander Dumas' classic tale. The first talking version.
1935 95m/B Walter Abel, Paul Lukas, Moroni Olsen, Ian Keith, Margot Grahame, Heather Angel, Onslow Stevens, Miles Mander; D: Rowland V. Lee. VHS, Beta, LV $29.95 RKO, IME, TTC ⅔⅔

Three Musketeers The three musketeers who are "all for one and one for all" join forces with D'Artagnan to battle the evil Cardinal Richelieu in this rambunctious adaptation of the classic tale by Alexander Dumas. Good performances by the cast, who combined drama and comedy well. Turner's first color film.
1948 126m/C Lana Turner, Gene Kelly, June Allyson, Gig Young, Angela Lansbury, Van Heflin, Keenan Wynn, Robert Coote, Reginald Owen, Frank Morgan, Vincent Price; D: George Sidney. VHS, Beta, LV $19.98 MGM, CCB ⅔⅔½

Three Musketeers Extravagant and funny version of the Dumas classic. Three swashbucklers and their country cohort, who wishes to join the Musketeers, set out to save the honor of the French Queen. To do so they must oppose the evil cardinal who has his eyes on the power behind the throne. A strong cast leads this winning combination of slapstick and high adventure.
1974 (PG) 105m/C Richard Chamberlain, Oliver Reed, Michael York, Raquel Welch, Frank Finlay, Christopher Lee, Faye Dunaway, Charlton Heston, Geraldine Chaplin, Simon Ward, Jean-Pierre Cassel; D: Richard Lester. VHS, Beta COL ⅔⅔⅔½

3 Ninjas Lively kid's actioner about three brothers who are trained as ninjas by their grandpa. When a group of bad guys tries to kidnap the boys, they're in for trouble. Sort of a cross between "The Karate Kid" and "Home Alone" that is suitable for family viewing.
1992 (PG) 84m/C Victor Wong, Michael Treanor, Max Elliott Slade, Chad Power, Rand Kingsley, Alan McRae, Margarita Franco, Toru Tanaka; D: Jon Turteltaub. VHS, Beta, LV $19.99 TOU, PMS ⅔⅔½

T

Three Nuts in Search of a Bolt Three neurotics send a surrogate to a comely psychiatrist for help, but the shrink thinks the surrogate's a three-way multiple personality. Raunchy monkey-shines ensue. Includes Van Doren's infamous beer bath scene.
1964 (R) 78m/C Mamie Van Doren, Tommy Noonan, Paul Gilbert, Alvy Moore; D: Tommy Noonan. VHS, Beta $9.95 WGE ♂♂½

Three O'Clock High A nerdy high school journalist is assigned a profile of the new kid in school, who turns out to be the biggest bully, too. He approaches his task with great unease. Silly teen-age farce is given souped-up direction by Spielberg protege Joanou. Features decent work by the young cast.
1987 (PG) 97m/C Casey Siemaszko, Anne Ryan, Stacey Glick, Jonathan Wise, Richard Tyson; D: Phil Joanou. VHS, Beta, LV $79.95 MCA ♂♂½

Three of a Kind A compilation of the best skits and satires from the British comedy series.
198? 84m/C GB Tracy Ullman, David Copperfield, Lenny Henry. VHS, Beta $14.98 FOX ♂♂½

Three of Hearts Slick look at love in contemporary downtown New York. Connie's bisexual girlfriend Ellen (Fenn) has just dumped her. She hires male escort Joe (Baldwin) to seduce Ellen and then break her heart, causing her to fall back on Connie's sympathetic shoulder. Guess what happens. Hiply superficial plot is transparent although the three leads are likeable, especially Lynch as the lanky lovelorn Connie.
1993 (R) 102m/C Kelly Lynch, William Baldwin, Sherilyn Fenn, Joe Pantoliano, Gail Strickland, Cec Verrell, Claire Callaway, Tony Amendola; D: Yurek Bogayevicz; W: Philip C. Epstein, Adam Greenman; M: Richard Gibbs. VHS NYR ♂½

Three on a Match An actress, a stenographer and a society woman get together for a tenth year reunion. They become embroiled in a world of crime when Blondell's gangster boyfriend takes a liking to Dvorak. She leaves her husband and takes up with the crook. The results are tragic. Bogart's first gangster role.
1932 64m/B Joan Blondell, Warren William, Ann Dvorak, Bette Davis, Lyle Talbot, Humphrey Bogart, Patricia Ellis, Grant Mitchell; D: Mervyn LeRoy. VHS, Beta $19.98 MGM, FCT ♂♂♂

Three on a Meathook When a young man and his father living on an isolated farm receive female visitors, bloodshed is quick to follow. Essentially a remake of "Psycho," and very loosely based on the crimes of Ed Gein. Filmed in Louisville, Kentucky.
1972 85m/C Charles Kissinger, James Pickett, Sherry Steiner, Carolyn Thompson; W/D: William Girdler. VHS, Beta NO Woof!

The Three Penny Opera Mack the Knife presides over an exciting world of thieves, murderers, beggars, prostitutes and corrupt officials in a seedy section of London. Based on the opera by Kurt Weill and Bertold Brecht, which was based on "The Beggar's Opera" by John Gay. Remake of "The Threepenny Opera" (1931). AKA: Die Dreigroschenoper.
1962 124m/C GE Curt Jurgens, Hildegarde Neff, Gert Frobe, June Ritchie, Lino Ventura, Sammy Davis Jr. VHS, Beta, LV $29.98 MVD, VYG, FCT ♂♂♂

Three Secrets A plane crashes and the only survivor is a five-year-old boy. Three women, each with a secret, seek to claim him as the child each gave up for adoption five years before. Tearjerker with good cast.
1950 98m/B Eleanor Parker, Patricia Neal, Ruth Roman, Frank Lovejoy, Leif Erickson; D: Robert Wise. VHS $19.98 REP ♂♂½

Three Sovereigns for Sarah Witchhunters tortured and toasted Sarah's two sisters for practicing witchcraft in the past. Now, accused of witchery herself, she struggles to prove the family's innocence. Excellent, made-for-PBS. Fine performances from all, especially Redgrave.
1985 152m/C Vanessa Redgrave, Phyllis Thaxter, Patrick McGoohan; D: Philip Leacock. VHS, Beta $79.95 PSM, PBS ♂♂½

Three Stooges Comedy Capers: Vol. 1 Compilation includes: "Disorder in the Court" (1936), "Malice in the Palace" (1949), "Sing a Song of Six Pants" (1947), and "The Brideless Groom" (1947).
194? 80m/B Moe Howard, Larry Fine, Curly Howard, Shemp Howard. VHS, Beta $9.95 NOS, MED ♂♂½

Three Stooges Comedy Classics The antics of the Stooges are featured in this collection of five original shorts, along with an early Ted Healy comedy that features all four Stooges: "Hollywood on Parade," "Disorder in the Court," "Malice in the Palace," "Brideless Groom," and "Sing a Song of Six Pants."
1949 79m/B Moe Howard, Larry Fine, Curly Howard, Shemp Howard, Ted Healy. VHS $19.95 REP ♂♂½

Three Stooges: Cookoo Cavaliers and Other Nyuks The boys star in "Cookoo Cavaliers," "Busy Buddies," and "Booby Dupes."
1940 55m/B Moe Howard, Curly Howard, Larry Fine. VHS $14.95 COL ♂♂½

Three Stooges Festival Three original shorts by the comedy trio, including: "Disorder in the Court" (1936-Curly), "Sing a Song of Six Pants" (1949-Shemp) and "Malice in the Palace" (1949-Shemp).
1949 60m/B Moe Howard, Larry Fine, Shemp Howard, Curly Howard. VHS, Beta $29.95 AOV, VYY ♂♂½

Three Stooges: From Nurse to Worse and Other Nyuks The irrepressible Stooges star in "From Nurse to Worse," "Crash Goes the Hash," and "G.I. Wanna Go Home."
1945 55m/B Moe Howard, Larry Fine, Curly Howard. VHS $14.95 COL ♂♂½

Three Stooges: Half-Wit's Holiday and Other Nyuks Includes, "Half-Wit's Holiday," "Horse Collars," and "How High Is Up?"
1935 55m/B Moe Howard, Curly Howard, Larry Fine. VHS $14.95 COL ♂♂½

Three Stooges: Idiots Deluxe and Other Nyuks Curly, Larry and Moe star in, "Idiots Deluxe," "I Can Hardly Wait," and "Idle Roomers."
1940 55m/B Moe Howard, Curly Howard, Larry Fine. VHS $14.95 COL ♂♂½

Three Stooges Meet Hercules The Three Stooges are transported back to ancient Ithaca by a time machine when a young scientist and his girlfriend. When the girl is captured, they enlist the help of Hercules to rescue her.
1961 80m/B Moe Howard, Larry Fine, Joe DeRita, Vicki Trickett, Quinn Redeker; D: Edward L. Bernds. VHS, Beta $9.95 GKK ♂♂½

Three Stooges: Nutty but Nice and Other Nyuks The boys star in "Nutty but Nice," "The Sitter-Downers," and "Slippery Silks."

1936 55m/B Moe Howard, Curly Howard, Larry Fine. VHS $14.95 COL ♂♂½

Three Stooges: They Stooge to Conga and Other Nyuks World War II madness from the Stooges in "They Stooge to Conga," "You Natzy Spy!" and "I'll Never Heil Again."
1940 55m/B Moe Howard, Curly Howard, Larry Fine. VHS $14.95 COL ♂♂½

Three Stops to Murder An FBI agent investigates the murder of a beautiful model in this early, unspectacular Hammer production.
1953 76m/B GB Tom Conway, Mila Parely, Naomi Chance, Eric Pohlmann, Andrew Osborn, Richard Wattis, Eileen Way, Delphi Lawrence; D: Terence Fisher. VHS, Beta $16.95 SNC, MLB ♂

Three Strange Loves Men and women struggle with loneliness, old age, and sterility. Sometimes disjointed, but for the most part, well-made. Finely acted. In Swedish with English subtitles. AKA: Thirst.
1949 88m/B SW Eva Henning, Brigit Tengroth, Birger Malmsten; D: Ingmar Bergman. VHS, Beta $29.98 NOS, HHT, SUE ♂♂♂

3:10 to Yuma In order to collect $200 he desperately needs, a poor farmer has to hold a dangerous killer at bay while waiting to turn the outlaw over to the authorities arriving on the 3:10 train to Yuma. Stuck in a hotel room with the outlaw's gang gathering outside, the question arises as to who is the prisoner. Farmer Heflin is continually worked on by the outlaw Ford, in a movie with more than its share of great dialogue. Suspenseful, well-made action western adapted from an Elmore Leonard story.
1957 92m/B Glenn Ford, Van Heflin, Felicia Farr, Richard Jaeckel; D: Delmer Daves; M: Frankie Laine. VHS, Beta, LV $9.95 GKK ♂♂♂½

Three Texas Steers A circus owner inherits some land that the government wants for a water project and her manager tries to get it for himself. Enter the terrific trio to set things right. Last of the series for Terhune. The scenes of the circus fire were taken from "Circus Girl" (1937). AKA: Danger Rides the Range.
1939 59m/B John Wayne, Ray Corrigan, Max Terhune, Carole Landis, Ralph Graves, Roscoe Ates; D: George Sherman. VHS $19.95 NOS ♂½

Three the Hard Way An insane white supremacist has a plan to eliminate blacks by contaminating water supplies. A big blaxploitation money maker and the first to team Brown, Williamson, and Kelly, who would go on to make several more pictures together.
1974 (R) 93m/C Jim Brown, Fred Williamson, Jim Kelly, Sheila Frazier, Jay Robinson, Alex Rocco; D: Gordon Parks. VHS $39.95 XVC ♂♂½

Three Violent People Family feud set in post-Civil War Old West features Heston and Baxter impulsively marrying and returning to run the family ranch. Heston's brother (Tryon) wants to sell the ranch in order to get his share of the inheritance and then Heston finds out Baxter was once a prostitute. In this case family squabbles don't make for an exciting film.
1957 100m/C Charlton Heston, Anne Baxter, Gilbert Roland, Tom Tryon, Forrest Tucker, Elaine Stritch, Bruce Bennett, Barton MacLane; D: Rudolph Mate; W: James Edward Grant; M: Walter Scharf. VHS $14.95 PAR ♂♂

Three Warriors Young Native American boy is forced to leave the city and return to the reservation, where his contempt for the traditions of his ancestors slowly turns to appreciation and love.

1977 100m/C Charles White Eagle, Lois Red Elk, McKee "Kiko" Red Wing, Christopher Lloyd, Randy Quaid. **VHS, Beta** $59.99 *HBO* 🎬🎬½

Three Way Weekend Two young girls set off on a back-packing trip through the mountains of Southern California to enjoy camping and romance.
1981 (R) 78m/C Dan Diego, Jody Lee Olhava, Richard Blye, Blake Parrish; *D:* Emmett Alston. **VHS, Beta** $19.95 *ACA* 🎬

The Three Weird Sisters Title characters maintain life of luxury through murder and inheritance. Dylan Thomas co-wrote script.
1948 82m/B *GB* Nancy Price, Mary Clare; *D:* Daniel Birt; *W:* Dylan Thomas. **VHS** $19.95 *VDM, SNC, VMK* 🎬🎬

Three Word Brand Hart plays three roles in this film, a homesteader who is killed by Indians and his twin sons, who are separated after their father's death and reunited many years later. Silent with musical score.
1921 75m/B William S. Hart, Jayne Navak, S.J. Bingham; *D:* Lambert Hillyer. **VHS, Beta** $29.95 *GPV, VYY* 🎬🎬

The Three Worlds of Gulliver A colorful family version of the Jonathan Swift classic about an Englishman who discovers a fantasy land of small and giant people. Visual effects by Ray Harryhausen. *AKA:* The Worlds of Gulliver.
1959 100m/C Kerwin Mathews, Jo Morrow, Basil Sydney, Mary Ellis; *W/D:* Jack Sher; *W:* Arthur Ross; *M:* Bernard Herrmann. **VHS, Beta, LV** $14.95 *COL, MLB, CCB* 🎬🎬½

The Threepenny Opera A musical about the exploits of gangster Mack the Knife. Adapted from Bertolt Brecht's play and John Gay's "The Beggar's Opera." In German with English subtitles. *AKA:* Die Dreigroschenoper; L'Opera De Quat'Sous; Beggars' Opera.
1931 107m/B Rudolph Forster, Lotte Lenya, Carola Neher, Reinhold Schunzel, Fritz Rasp, Valeska Gert; *D:* G.W. Pabst. **VHS** $14.95 *VDM, AUD, TAM* 🎬🎬🎬

Three's Trouble A middle-class family erupts when a young male babysitter enters to care for its three mischievous sons.
1985 93m/C *AU* John Waters, Jacki Weaver, Steven Vidler; *D:* Chris Thomson. **VHS, Beta** $19.95 *STE, NWV* 🎬🎬

Threshold An internationally-acclaimed research biologist is frustrated by his inability to save a dying 20-year-old woman born with a defective heart. She becomes the recipient of the first artificial heart. Solid performances.
1983 (PG) 97m/C *CA* Donald Sutherland, Jeff Goldblum, John Marley, Mare Winningham; *D:* Richard Pearce. **VHS, Beta** $59.98 *FOX* 🎬🎬½

The Thrill Killers Young murderous thugs rampage through Los Angeles suburbs, killing indiscriminately. Pretentious and exploitative. Sometimes shown with Hallucinogenic Hypo-Vision—a prologue announcing the special effect would be shown before the film, and on cue, hooded ushers would run through the theatre with cardboard axes. Weird. *AKA:* The Monsters Are Loose; The Maniacs Are Loose.
1965 82m/C Cash Flagg, Liz Renay, Brick Bardo, Carolyn Brandt, Atlas King; *D:* Ray Dennis Steckler. **VHS, Beta** *NO* Woof!

Thrill of a Romance Johnson, an Army hero, meets Williams, a swimming instructor of all things, at a resort in the Sierra Nevadas. The only problem is that she's married. Typical swim-romance vehicle. 🎵Please Don't Say No, Say Maybe; I

Should Care; Lonely Night; Vive L'Amour; Schubert's Serenade; The Thrill of a Romance.
1945 105m/C Esther Williams, Van Johnson, Frances Gifford, Henry Travers, Spring Byington, Lauritz Melchior; *D:* Richard Thorpe. **VHS** $19.98 *MGM* 🎬🎬

The Thrill of It All! An average housewife becomes a star of television commercials, to the dismay of her chauvinist husband, a gynecologist. Fast and funny, with numerous acidic jokes about television sponsors and programs. Written by Carl Reiner.
1963 108m/C James Garner, Doris Day, Arlene Francis, Edward Andrews, Carl Reiner, Elliott Reid, Reginald Owen, ZaSu Pitts; *D:* Norman Jewison. **VHS, Beta** $14.98 *MCA* 🎬🎬½

Thrilled to Death An utterly naive husband and wife get caught in the middle of a lethal game when they befriend a scheming couple.
1988 (R) 90m/C Blake Bahner, Rebecca Lynn, Richard Maris, Christine Moore; *D:* Chuck Vincent. **VHS** $79.98 *REP* 🎬½

Thrillkill A young girl is enmeshed in a multi-million-dollar burglary scheme after her computer-whiz/embezzler sister disappears.
1984 88m/C Robin Ward, Gina Massey, Anthony Kramroither; *D:* Anthony D'Andrea. **VHS, Beta** $9.95 *MED* 🎬

Throne of Blood Kurosawa's masterful adaptation of "Macbeth," transports the story to medieval Japan and the world of the samurai. Mifune and Chiaki are warriors who have put down a rebellion and are to be rewarded by their overlord. On their way to his castle they meet a mysterious old woman who prophesizes that Mifune will soon rule but his reign will be short. She is dismissed as crazy but her prophesies come to pass. Mifune's ambitions soon overwhelm him and his paranoia causes him to have his old friend Chiaki killed. Chiaki's son then seeks revenge against the tyrant. So steeped in Japanese style that it bears little resemblance to the Shakespearean original, this film is an incredibly detailed vision in its own right. In Japanese with English subtitles. *AKA:* Kumonosujo, Kumonosu-djo; Cobweb Castle; The Castle of the Spider's Web.
1957 105m/B *JP* Toshiro Mifune, Isuzu Yamada, Takashi Shimura, Minoru Chiaki, Akira Kubo; *D:* Akira Kurosawa. **VHS, Beta, LV, 3/4U** $35.95 *IHF, TAM, VYG* 🎬🎬🎬🎬

Throne of Fire A mighty hero battles the forces of evil to gain control of the powerful Throne of Fire. Dubbed.
1982 91m/C *IT* Peter McCoy, Sabrina Siami; *D:* Franco Prosperi. **VHS, Beta** $59.95 *MGM* Woof!

Throne of Vengeance Prince Sandokan's bride, his kingdom, and even his life are in danger when the nefarious "Leopard" plans to take over.
19?? 86m/C **VHS** *NO* 🎬

Through a Glass Darkly Oppressive interactions within a family sharing a holiday on a secluded island: a woman recovering from schizophrenia, her husband, younger brother, and her psychologist father. One of Bergman's most mysterious, upsetting and powerful films. In Swedish with English subtitles. Part of Bergman's Silence-of-God trilogy followed by "Winter Light" and "The Silence."
1961 91m/B *SW* Harriet Andersson, Max von Sydow, Gunnar Bjornstrand, Lars Passgard; *D:* Ingmar Bergman. Academy Awards '61: Best Foreign Language Film; Nominations: Best Story & Screenplay; National Board of Review Awards '62: 5 Best Foreign Films of the Year. **VHS, Beta** $24.95 *NOS, SUE, TAM* 🎬🎬🎬

Through Naked Eyes Made-for-television thriller about two people who spy on each other. They witness a murder and realize that someone else is watching them. What a coincidence.
1987 91m/C David Soul, Pam Dawber; *D:* John Llewellyn Moxey. **VHS, Beta** $79.95 *MED* 🎬🎬½

Through the Breakers Heartbroken woman suffers silently on South Pacific isle.
1928 55m/B Margaret Livingston, Holmes Herbert, Clyde Cook, Natalie Joyce. **VHS, Beta** $19.95 *GPV, FCT* 🎬½

Throw Momma from the Train DeVito plays a man, henpecked by his horrific mother, who tries to persuade his writing professor (Crystal) to exchange murders. DeVito will kill Crystal's ex-wife and Crystal will kill DeVito's mother. Only mama isn't going to be that easy to get rid of. Fast-paced and entertaining black comedy. Ramsey steals the film. Inspired by Hitchcock's "Strangers on a Train."
1987 (PG-13) 88m/C Danny DeVito, Billy Crystal, Anne Ramsey, Kate Mulgrew; *D:* Danny DeVito. **VHS, Beta, LV** $19.98 *ORI* 🎬🎬🎬

Thumb Tripping A dated sixties/hippie film. Two flower children hitchhike and encounter all kinds of other strange people in their travels on the far-out roads.
1972 (R) 94m/C Meg Foster, Michael Burns, Bruce Dern, Marianna Hill, Michael Conrad, Joyce Van Patten; *D:* Quentin Masters. **VHS, Beta** $59.98 *NLC* 🎬🎬

Thumbelina From "Faerie Tale Theatre" comes the story of a tiny girl who gets kidnapped by a toad and a mole, but meets the man of her dreams in the nick of time. Adapted from the classic tale by Hans Christian Andersen. Made for television.
1982 60m/C Carrie Fisher, William Katt, Burgess Meredith; *D:* Michael Lindsay-Hogg. **VHS, Beta, LV** $14.98 *KUI, FOX, FCT* 🎬🎬🎬

Thumbelina An animated version of the Hans Christian Andersen fairy tale about a little girl who's only as tall as a thumb.
1984 (G) 45m/C **VHS, Beta** $19.95 *COL, WTA* 🎬🎬🎬

Thunder Alley In middle America, two friends and their rock group struggle for success. One of the friends dies after an accidental overdose and the other's grief propels him to stardom. 🎵Can't Look Back; Just Another Pretty Boy; Sometimes in the Night; Heart to Heart; Can You Feel My Heart Beat; Do You Feel Alright?; Danger, Danger; Surrender; Gimme Back My Heart; Country Waltz; Thunder Alley; Dogs and Cats; K.T. Country; Drivin' Blues; Nowhere to Run.
1985 102m/C Roger Wilson, Leif Garrett, Jill Schoelen; *D:* J.S. Cardone. **VHS, Beta** $79.95 *MGM* 🎬½

Thunder and Lightning A mismatched young couple chase a truckload of poisoned moonshine. Action-packed chases ensue. Nice chemistry between Carradine and Jackson.
1977 (PG) 94m/C David Carradine, Kate Jackson, Roger C. Carmel, Sterling Holloway; *D:* Corey Allen. **VHS, Beta** $59.98 *FOX* 🎬🎬

Thunder & Mud Female mud wrestlers battle over their favorite rock band. Hahn's attempt to cash in on her notoriety after the Bakker scandal.
1989 90m/C Jessica Hahn; *D:* Penelope Spheeris. **VHS, Beta, LV** $59.95 *COL* 🎬🎬

Thunder Bay Stewart and Duryea are a pair of Louisiana wildcat oil drillers who believe there is oil at the bottom of the Gulf of Mexico off the coast of the town of Port Felicity. They decide to construct an oil

platform which the shrimp fisherman of the town believe will interfere with their livelihoods. Tensions rise between the two groups and violence seems likely. Action packed, with timely storyline as modern oil drillers fight to drill in waters that have historically been off-limits.
1953 82m/C James Stewart, Joanne Dru, Dan Duryea, Gilbert Roland, Marcia Henderson; **D:** Anthony Mann. **VHS, Beta $19.95** MCA ℐℐℐ

Thunder County Federal agents and drug runners are after a group of four convicts who have just escaped from prison.
1974 78m/C Mickey Rooney, Ted Cassidy, Chris Robinson. **VHS, Beta $49.95** PSM ℐ ½

Thunder in God's Country A dishonest gambler eyes a peaceful western town as the next Vegas-like gambling capital. Before this occurs he is exposed as a cheat.
1951 67m/B Rex Allen, Mary Ellen Kay. **VHS, Beta $24.95** DVT ℐ

Thunder in the City Robinson is an intense American promoter in the sales game who is sent to London by his employers to learn a more subdued way of doing business. Instead, he meets a pair of down-on-their-luck artistocrats whose only asset is an apparently worthless Rhodesian mine. Robinson, however, comes up with a way to promote the mine and get enough capital together to make it profitable. Good satire with Robinson well cast. Robinson wasn't taken with the script in its original form and persuaded his friend, playwright Robert Sherwood, to re-write it.
1937 85m/B GB Edward G. Robinson, Nigel Bruce, Ralph Richardson, Constance Collier; **D:** Marion Gering. **VHS, Beta $19.95** NOS, DVT, KRT ℐℐℐ

Thunder in the Desert A cowhand joins an outlaw gang in order to catch his uncle's killer.
1938 56m/C Bob Steele, Louise Stanley, Don Barclay, Charles King, Lew Meehan, Budd Buster; **D:** Sam Newfield. **VHS, Beta $19.95** NOS, DVT ℐ

Thunder in the Pines Two lumberjack buddies send for the same French girl to marry, unbeknownst to each other. When she arrives, the dismayed men agree to a contest to see who will marry her. Meanwhile the French girl falls for the local saloon owner and his jilted girlfriend vows to get even. She does, with the help of the lumberjacks.
1949 61m/B Denise Darcel, George Reeves, Ralph Byrd, Lyle Talbot, Michael Whalen, Roscoe Ates, Vince Barnett; **D:** Robert Edwards. **VHS, Beta, LV** NO ℐ

Thunder Mountain Zane Grey's novel about two prospectors who are bushwhacked on their way to file a claim comes to life on the screen.
1935 56m/B George O'Brien. **VHS, Beta $24.95** DVT, HHE, MLB ℐ ½

Thunder Over Texas The cowboy hero gets embroiled in a railroad scandal that involves a kidnapping. Directed by Edgar G. Ulmer, who used the alias John Warner because he was moonlighting. His first western; previously he was best known for "The Black Cat."
1934 52m/B Marion Shilling, Helen Westcott, Victor Potel, Tiny Skelton; **D:** Edgar G. Ulmer. **VHS, Beta $19.95** VDM ℐ

Thunder Pass Gold and greed are the motives for murder as two young brothers become separated when their wagon train is attacked and their family is slaughtered. One brother searches for the other and finds him several years later. Based on the novel

"Arizona Ames" by Zane Grey. Also released as "Thunder Trail."
1937 58m/B Charles Bickford, Marsha Hunt, Gilbert Roland, Monte Blue; **D:** Charles T. Barton. **VHS $14.95** NOS, VDM, DVT ℐℐ

Thunder River Feud The Rangebusters help two ranchers avoid a range war. Part of "The Rangebusters" series.
1942 58m/B Ray Corrigan, John "Dusty" King, Max Terhune. **VHS, Beta $19.95** NOS, VCN, DVT ℐℐ

Thunder Road Mitchum comes home to Tennessee from Korea and takes over the family moonshine business, fighting both mobsters and federal agents. An exciting chase between Mitchum and the feds ends the movie with the appropriate bang. Robert Mitchum not only produced, wrote and starred in this best of the moonshine-running films, but also wrote the theme song "Whippoorwill" (which later became a radio hit). Mitchum's son, James, made his film debut, and later starred in a similar movie "Moonrunners." A cult favorite, still shown in many drive-ins around the country.
1958 (PG) 92m/B Robert Mitchum, Jacques Aubuchon, Gene Barry, Keely Smith, Trevor Bardette, Sandra Knight, Jim Mitchum, Betsy Holt, Frances Koon; **D:** Arthur Ripley; **W:** Robert Mitchum. **VHS, Beta $19.98** MGM ℐℐℐ

Thunder Run When a load of uranium needs to be transferred across Nevada, a retired trucker takes on the job. The trip is made more difficult since terrorists are trying to hijack the shipment to use for a bomb.
1986 (PG-13) 84m/C Forrest Tucker, John Ireland, John Shepherd, Jill Whitlow, Wally Ward, Cheryl Lynn; **D:** Gary Hudson. **VHS, Beta $79.95** MED ℐ

Thunder Score Evil crime boss and his ruthless ninja hitmen are out to steal a fortune in gold.
19?? 92m/C Jack Fox, Stuart Lyne. **VHS $39.95** TWE ℐℐ½

Thunder Warrior A young Indian turns into a one-man army determined to punish the local authorities who are abusing his fellow tribe members. **AKA:** Thunder.
1985 (R) 84m/C Raymond Harmstorf, Bo Svenson, Mark Gregory; **D:** Larry Ludman. **VHS, Beta $79.95** TWE ℐ

Thunder Warrior 2 A tough Native American is provoked to violence by small-town prejudice.
1985 (PG-13) 114m/C IT Mark Gregory, Karen Reel, Bo Svenson; **D:** Larry Ludman. **VHS, Beta $79.95** TWE ℐ

Thunder Warrior 3 The Indian Thunder has vowed to live in peace, but forswears the oath when his wife is kidnapped and family is terrorized. Revenge is the top priority as he torments the bad guys.
1988 90m/C Mark Gregory, John Phillip Law, Ingrid Lawrence, Werner Pochat, Horts Schon; **D:** Larry Ludman. **VHS $79.95** IMP ℐ

Thunderball The fourth installment in Ian Fleming's James Bond series finds 007 on a mission to thwart SPECTRE, which has threatened to blow up Miami by atomic bomb if 100 million pounds in ransom is not paid. One of the more tedious Bond entries but a big box-office success. Tom Jones sang the title song. Remade as "Never Say Never Again" in 1983 with Connery reprising his role as Bond after a 12-year absence.
1965 (PG) 125m/C GB Sean Connery, Claudine Auger, Adolfo Celi, Lucianna Paluzzi, Rik von Nutter, Martine Beswick, Molly Peters, Guy Doleman, Bernard Lee, Lois Maxwell, Desmond Llewelyn; **D:** Terence Young; **M:** John Barry. **VHS, Beta, LV $19.98** MGM, TLF ℐℐ½

Thunderbolt & Lightfoot Eastwood is an ex-thief on the run from his former partners (Kennedy and Lewis) who believe he's made off with the loot from their last job, the robbery of a government vault. He joins up with drifter Bridges, who helps him to escape. Later, Eastwood manages to convince Kennedy he doesn't know where the money is. Bridges then persuades the men that they should plan the same heist and rob the same government vault all over again, which they do. But their getaway doesn't go exactly as planned. All-around fine acting; notable is Bridges' scene dressed in drag. First film for director Cimino.
1974 (R) 115m/C Clint Eastwood, Jeff Bridges, George Kennedy, Geoffrey Lewis, Gary Busey; **D:** Michael Cimino. **VHS, Beta, LV $19.98** MGM ℐℐℐ

Thunderfist A police detective, who is also a Kung Fu expert, goes after thieves who have stolen a precious jade pagoda.
1973 (PG) 82m/C Alex Lung, Steve Yu. **VHS $59.95** ACA ℐ

Thunderground A beautiful con artist teams with a fighter and together they travel to New Orleans to arrange a bout with the king of bare-knuckled fighting.
1989 (R) 92m/C Paul Coufos, Margaret Langrick, Jesse Ventura, M. Emmet Walsh; **D:** David Mitchell. **VHS, LV** IME ℐ

Thunderheart A young FBI agent (Kilmer) is sent to an Oglala Sioux reservation to investigate a murder. He is himself part Sioux, but is so assimilated that he resents being chosen for the assignment because of his forgotten heritage. Aided by a veteran partner (Shepard), Ray learns, professionally and personally, from a shrewd tribal police officer (well played by Greene). Set in the late 70's the film is loosely based on actual events plaguing the violence-torn Native American community at that time. Great cinematography by Roger Deakins. Filmed on the Pine Ridge Reservation in South Dakota. Director Apted deals with the actual incidents this film is based on in his documentary about Leonard Peltier, "Incident at Oglala."
1992 (R) 118m/C Val Kilmer, Sam Shepard, Graham Greene, Fred Ward, Fred Dalton Thompson, Sheila Tousey, Chief Ted Thin Elk, John Trudell, Dennis Banks, David Crosby; **D:** Michael Apted. **VHS, LV $19.95** COL, FCT, BTV ℐℐℐ

Thundering Forest Australian actioneer pitting loggers against saboteurs.
1941 ?m/C AU Frank Leighton. **VHS $15.95** LOO ℐ

Thundering Gunslingers A group of gunmen terrorizing townspeople finally meet their match in this Western.
1940 61m/B Buster Crabbe. **VHS, Beta $19.95** NOS, DVT ℐ

Thundering Mantis Rousing martial arts film with a shattering climax that features the thundering mantis style of Kung-fu. Okay, try martial arts effort that ends eventually featuring thundering mantis chop-socky.
1976 85m/C VHS, Beta $39.95 TWE ℐ

Thundering Ninja Three secret agents fight off an army of ninjas. Plenty of heel-to-head antics.
198? 89m/C Bernard Geurts, Joe Redner, Klaus Mutter, Ken Kerr, Jimmy Wang Yu; **D:** Joseph Kong. **VHS, Beta $59.95** TWE ℐ ½

Thundering Trail Two cowboys encounter plenty of trouble before they take the President's newly appointed territorial governor to his office. **AKA:** Thunder on the Trail.

1951 55m/B Lash LaRue, Al "Fuzzy" St. John, Sally Anglim, Archie Twitchell, Ray Bennett. **VHS, Beta $19.95** NOS, DVT ☾

Thundersquad Mercenaries help a South American rebel leader rescue his kidnapped son.
1985 90m/C Sal Borgese, Julia Fursich, Anthony Sabato. **VHS, Beta** NO ☾

Thursday's Child A child's success in films causes trouble for her family. Melodramatic and sappy, but Howes, as the kid, is excellent. One of Granger's early supporting roles.
1943 95m/B Stewart Granger, Sally Ann Howes; D: Rodney Ackland. **VHS, Beta $24.95** NOS, DVT, HEG ☾☾

Thursday's Game Two crisis-besieged businessmen meet every Thursday, using poker as a ruse to work on their business and marital problems. Wonderful cast; intelligently written and directed by James L. Brooks. Made for television.
1974 (PG) 99m/C Gene Wilder, Ellen Burstyn, Bob Newhart, John Mills, Cloris Leachman, Nancy Walker, Valerie Harper, Rob Reiner; W/D: James L. Brooks. **VHS, Beta, LV $69.95** VMK ☾☾☾

THX 1138 In the dehumanized world of the future, people live in underground cities run by computer, are force-fed drugs to keep them passive, and no longer have names— just letter/number combinations (Duvall is THX 1138). Emotion is also outlawed and when the computer-matched couple THX 1138 and LUH 3417 discover love, they must battle the computer system to escape. George Lucas' first film, which was inspired by a student film he did at USC. The laserdisc format carries the film in widescreen.
1971 (PG) 88m/C Robert Duvall, Donald Pleasence, Maggie McOmie; D: George Lucas. **VHS, Beta, LV $19.98** WAR ☾☾☾

Tiara Tahiti Intrigue, double-cross, romance, and violence ensue when two old army acquaintances clash in Tahiti. Very fine performances from the two leading men.
1962 100m/C James Mason, John Mills, Claude Dauphin, Rosenda Monteros, Herbert Lom; D: Ted Kotcheff. **VHS, Beta $59.98** SUE ☾☾

Ticket of Leave Man London's most dangerous killer fronts a charitable organization designed to help reform criminals. It actually steers them into a crime syndicate that cheats philanthropists out of their fortunes.
1937 71m/B Tod Slaughter, John Warwick, Marjorie Taylor. **VHS, Beta $29.95** SNC, VYY ☾☾

Ticket to Heaven A young man, trying to deal with the painful breakup of a love affair, falls under the spell of a quasi-religious order. His friends and family, worried about the cult's influence, have him kidnapped in order for him to be de-programmed. Mancuso is excellent, as are his supporting players Rubinek and Thomson.
1981 (PG) 109m/C Nick Mancuso, Meg Foster, Kim Cattrall, Saul Rubinek, R.H. Thomson; D: Ralph L. Thomas. **VHS, Beta $79.95** MGM ☾☾

Ticket to Tomahawk A gunslinger is hired by a stagecoach company to sabotage a railroad. Look for Marilyn Monroe as a chorus girl in a musical number.
1950 90m/C Anne Baxter, Rory Calhoun, Walter Brennan, Charles Kemper, Connie Gilchrist, Arthur Hunnicutt, Victor Sen Yung; D: Richard Sale. **VHS** TCF ☾☾½

Tickle Me An unemployed rodeo star finds work at an all-girl health spa and dude ranch. He falls in love with a young lady who has a treasure map and keeps her safe from the evil men who want her fortune. For die-

hard Elvis fans only. ♫(It's a) Long, Lonely Highway; Night Rider; It Feels So Right; Dirty, Dirty Feeling; (Such an) Easy Question; Put the Blame on Me; I'm Yours; I Feel That I'v Known You Forever; Slowly but Surely.
1965 90m/C Elvis Presley, Julie Adams, Jack Mullaney; D: Norman Taurog. **VHS, Beta $14.98** FOX, MVD ☾½

Tidal Wave Scientists discover that Japan is slowly sinking and order the island to be evacuated. Originally a popular Japanese production, the American version is a poorly dubbed, re-edited mess. AKA: Nippon Chiubotsu; The Submersion of Japan; Japan Sinks.
1975 (PG) 82m/C JP Lorne Greene, Keiju Kobayashi, Rhonda Leigh Hopkins, Hiroshi Fujioka, Shiro Moriana; D: Andrew Meyer. **VHS** NWV ☾½

Tides of War In the twilight of the second world war, a German officer begins to question his role in a proposed missile attack on Washington in light of the S.S. brutality he witnesses.
1990 90m/C Yvette Heyden, Rodrigo Obregon, David Soul, Bo Svenson; D: Neil Rossati. **VHS** NO ☾½

Tidy Endings A man who died from AIDS leaves behind his male lover and his ex-wife. The two form a friendship as they both try to cope with the man's death. Based on the play by Fierstein.
1988 54m/C Harvey Fierstein, Stockard Channing; D: Gavin Millar. **VHS, Beta $79.95** PSM ☾½

Tie Me Up! Tie Me Down! A young psychiatric patient kidnaps a former porno actress he has always had a crush on, and holds her captive, certain that he can convince her to love him. Black comedy features a fine cast and is well directed. At least one fairly explicit sex scene and the bondage theme caused the film to be X-rated, although it was released unrated by the distributor. In Spanish with English subtitles.
1990 105m/C SP Victoria Abril, Antonio Banderas, Loles Leon, Francisco Rabal, Julieta Serrano, Maria Barranco, Rossy di Palma; D: Pedro Almodovar; M: Ennio Morricone. **VHS, LV $14.95** COL, TAM ☾☾½

Tiefland Melodrama based on the libretto for D'Abert's opera about a gypsy dancer and her loves. Unreleased until 1954, this film is the last of Riefenstahl's career; she subsequently turned to still photography. In German with English subtitles.
1944 98m/B GE Leni Riefenstahl, Franz Eichberger, Bernard Minetti, Maria Koppenhofer, Luise Rainer; D: Leni Riefenstahl. **VHS, Beta $24.95** NOS, FCT, GLV ☾☾½

Tiffany Jones Tiffany Jones is a secret agent who has information that presidents and revolutionaries are willing to kill for.
1975 (R) 90m/C Anouska Hempel, Ray Brooks, Eric Pohlmann, Martin Benson, Susan Sneers; D: Pete Walker. **VHS, Beta $39.95** MON ☾

Tiger and the Pussycat A successful Italian businessman's infatuation with an attractive American art student leads to marital and financial woes. AKA: Il Tigre.
1967 (R) 110m/C Ann-Margret, Vittorio Gassman, Eleanor Parker; D: Dino Risi. **VHS, Beta $59.98** SUE, HHE ☾☾½

Tiger Bay A young Polish sailor, on leave in Cardiff, murders his unfaithful girlfriend. Lonely ten-year-old Gillie sees the crime and takes the murder weapon, thinking it will make her more popular with her peers. Confronted by a police detective, she convincingly lies but eventually the sailor finds Gillie and kidnaps her, hoping to keep her

quiet until he can get aboard his ship. A delicate relationship evolves between the child and the killer as she tries to help him escape and the police close in. Marks Hayley Mills' first major role and one of her finest performances.
1959 107m/B GB John Mills, Horst Buchholz, Hayley Mills, Yvonne Mitchell; D: J. Lee Thompson. **VHS, Beta $19.95** PAR ☾☾☾

Tiger Claws The pretty, petite Rothrock has been called the female Bruce Lee. Perhaps, but at least he got a good script every once in a while. This time Rothrock's a kung-fu cop investigating the strange ritual-murders of martial-arts champions.
1991 (R) 93m/C Cynthia Rothrock, Bolo Yeung, Jalal Merhi; D: Kelly Markin. **VHS, Beta, LV $19.98** MCA ☾½

Tiger Fangs When Nazis threaten the Far East rubber production with man-eating tigers, real-life big game hunter Frank Buck comes to the rescue.
1943 57m/B Frank Buck, June Duprez, Duncan Renaldo; D: Jack Schwartz. **VHS $16.95** SNC, NOS, DVT ☾½

Tiger Joe There's trouble in Southeast Asia, and the U.S. military confuses things even more.
1985 96m/C Alan Collins, David Warbeck; D: Anthony M. Dawson. **VHS $69.98** LIV ☾

Tiger of the Seven Seas A female pirate takes over her father's command and embarks on adventures on the high seas. Generous portions of action, intrigue, and romance. Sequel to "Queen of the Pirates."
1962 90m/C IT FR Giana Maria Canale, Anthony Steel, Grazia Maria Spina, Ernesto Calindri; D: Luigi Capuano. **VHS, EJ** ☾

Tiger Town A baseball player, ending an illustrious career with the Detroit Tigers, sees his chance of winning a pennant slipping away. A young fan, however, proves helpful in chasing that elusive championship. Made for the Disney cable station.
1983 (G) 76m/C Roy Scheider, Justin Henry, Ron McLarty, Bethany Carpenter, Noah Moazezi; D: Alan Shapiro. **VHS, Beta $69.95** DIS ☾☾½

Tiger vs. Dragon The Hungry Tiger, undercover agent, takes on Chinese boxing expert The Crazy Dragon.
198? 88m/C **VHS, Beta $59.95** SVS ☾

A Tiger Walks A savage tiger escapes from a circus and local children start a nationwide campaign to save its life. Notable for its unflattering portrayal of America's heartland and small town dynamics. Radical departure from most Disney films of the period.
1964 88m/C Sabu, Pamela Franklin, Brian Keith, Vera Miles, Kevin Corcoran, Peter Brown, Una Merkel, Frank McHugh, Edward Andrews; D: Norman Tokar. **VHS, Beta $69.95** DIS ☾☾½

Tiger Warsaw A young man returns to the town where he once lived, before he shot his father. He hopes to sort out his life and repair family problems. Muddled and sappy. AKA: The Tiger.
1987 (R) 92m/C Patrick Swayze, Barbara Williams, Piper Laurie, Bobby DiCicco, Kaye Ballard, Lee Richardson, Mary McDonnell; D: Amin Q. Chaudhri. **VHS, Beta, LV $14.95** SVS, COL ☾½

Tigers at the Top More Kung-Fu brutality and hi jinks.
1985 75m/C **VHS, Beta $59.95** SVS ☾

Tiger's Claw Shen roves the country honing his Kung Fu technique, obsessed by his fanatical desire to challenge Kuo, the finest warrior in China.
197? 90m/C Chin Long. **VHS, Beta** NO ☾½

Tigers Don't Cry An unusual friendship develops between a male nurse and the African dignitary he kidnaps.
1981 105m/C Anthony Quinn. **VHS, Beta $59.95** MPI �›½

Tigers in Lipstick Seven short vignettes featuring the beautiful actresses as aggressive women and the men that they influence. *AKA:* Wild Beds.
1980 (R) 88m/C *IT* Laura Antonelli, Monica Vitti, Ursula Andress, Sylvia Kristel; *D:* Luigi Zampa. **VHS, Beta $39.95** MON �›½

A Tiger's Tale A middle-aged divorced nurse begins an affair with her daughters's ex-boyfriend.
1987 (R) 97m/C Ann-Margret, C. Thomas Howell, Charles Durning, Kelly Preston, Ann Wedgeworth, Tim Thomerson, Steven Kampmann, Traci Lin, Angel Tompkins; *D:* Peter Douglas. **VHS, Beta, LV** KRT, OM �›½

Tigershark A martial arts expert goes to Southeast Asia to rescue his girlfriend, who has been kidnapped by communist forces and held captive for arms and ammunition. Strictly for fans of the martial arts.
1987 (R) 97m/C Mike Stone, John Quade, Pamela Bryant; *D:* Emmett Alston; *W:* Ivan Rogers. **VHS, Beta** NO ⅐

Tightrope Police inspector Wes Block pursues a killer of prostitutes in New Orleans' French Quarter. The film is notable both as a thriller and as a fascinating vehicle for Eastwood, who experiments with a disturbing portrait of a cop with some peculiarities of his own.
1984 (R) 115m/C Clint Eastwood, Genevieve Bujold, Dan Hedaya, Jennifer Beck, Alison Eastwood, Randi Brooks, Regina Richardson, Jamie Rose; *D:* Richard Tuggle. **VHS, Beta, LV $19.98** WAR, TLF ⅔⅔⅔

The Tigress In 1920s Berlin two con artists set out to scam a rich American using sex as a lure. Things don't go as planned. Also available in an unrated version.
1993 (R) 89m/C Valentina Vargas, James Remar, George Peppard. **VHS, LV $92.95** VMK ⅳ½

Till Death Do Us Part Three married couples spend a weekend at a counseling retreat, unaware that the proprietor is a murderous maniac.
1972 (PG) 77m/C James Keach, Claude Jutra, Matt Craven; *D:* Timothy Brand. **VHS, Beta $69.95** VES ⅳ½

Till Death Do Us Part An ex-cop turns into an evil killer who seduces unsuspecting women and murders them for their insurance money. Contains footage not seen in the TV movie. Based on a true story and the book by Vincent Bugliosi.
1992 (R) 93m/C Treat Williams, Arliss Howard, Rebecca Jenkins; *D:* Yves Simoneau. **VHS, Beta $89.95** TRI ⅳ½

Till Marriage Do Us Part An innocent couple discover on their wedding night that they are really brother and sister. Since they can't in good conscience get a divorce or consummate their marriage, they must seek sexual gratification elsewhere. Antonelli is deliciously tantalizing in this silly satire. *AKA:* Dio Mio, Come Sono Caduta in Basso; How Long Can You Fall?.
1974 (R) 97m/C *IT* Laura Antonelli, Alberto Lionello, Jean Rochefort, Michele Placido, Karin Schubert; *D:* Luigi Comencini. **VHS, Beta, LV $59.95** VES, TAM ⅳ½

Till the Clouds Roll By An all-star, high-gloss musical biography of songwriter Jerome Kern, that, in typical Hollywood fashion, bears little resemblance to the compos-

er's life. Filled with wonderful songs from his Broadway hit. ♫Showboat Medley; Till the Clouds Roll By; Howja Like to Spoon with Me?; The Last Time I Saw Paris; They Didn't Believe Me; I Won't Dance; Why Was I Born?; Who?; Sunny; One More Dance; Smoke Gets in Your Eyes; Yesterdays; She Didn't Say Yes; Look for the Silver Lining; Leave It to Jane; Cleopatterer; Long Ago and Far Away; A Fine Romance; The Land Where the Good Songs Go; Kalua; Polka; Ol' Man River; Make Believe; Can't Help Lovin' dat Man; All The Things You Are.
1946 137m/C Robert Walker, Van Heflin, Judy Garland, Frank Sinatra, Lucille Bremer, Kathryn Grayson, June Allyson, Dinah Shore, Lena Horne, Virginia O'Brien, Tony Martin; *D:* Richard Whorf. **VHS, Beta, LV, 3/4U, Special order formats $19.98** NEG, NOS, MGM ⅔⅔½

Till the Clouds Roll By/A Star Is Born Ostensibly concerns the life and career of songwriter Jerome Kern. Highlighted by stellar performances from a number of musical stars of the day. Maudlin and unconcerned with factual accuracy, the film nonetheless is an exuberant celebration of Kern's talent.
1946 249m/C Judy Garland, Frank Sinatra, Robert Walker, Fredric March, Janet Gaynor, Andy Devine, Lionel Stander, Franklin Pangborn, Van Heflin, Lucille Bremer, Kathryn Grayson, Lena Horne, Tony Martin, Angela Lansbury, Dinah Shore, Virginia O'Brien, Cyd Charisse, Adolphe Menjou; *D:* William A. Wellman, Richard Whorf. **VHS, Beta $29.95** DVT ⅔⅔⅔

Till the End of Time Three GIs have trouble adjusting to civilian life in their home town after World War II. Fine performances and excellent pacing. Popular title song. Adapted from "They Dream of Home" by Niven Busch.
1946 105m/C Robert Mitchum, Guy Madison, Bill Williams, Dorothy McGuire, William Gargan, Tom Tully; *D:* Edward Dmytryk. **VHS, Beta, LV $19.98** RKO, TTC ⅔⅔½

Till There was You A struggling musician travels to a faraway tropical isle to solve the mystery of his brother's death.
1991 (PG-13) 94m/C Mark Harmon, Deborah Unger, Jeroen Krabbe, Shane Briant; *D:* John Seale. **VHS $19.98** MCA ⅐

Tillie's Punctured Romance The silent comedy which established Chaplin and Dressler as comedians. Chaplin, out of his Tramp character, is the city slicker trying to put one over on farm girl Dressler, who pursues revenge. First feature length comedy film. Followed by "Tillie's Tomato Surprise" and "Tillie Wakes Up," which starred Dressler but not Chaplin.
1914 73m/B Charlie Chaplin, Marie Dressler, Mabel Normand, Mack Swain, Chester Conklin; *D:* Mack Sennett. **VHS, Beta, LV $12.95** NOS, CCB, HHT ⅔⅔

Tilt Flimsy storyline concerns a young runaway's adventures with an aspiring rock star. Shields' pinball expertise eventually leads her to a match against pinball champ Durning.
1978 (PG) 111m/C Charles Durning, Ken Marshall, Brooke Shields, Geoffrey Lewis; *D:* Rudy Durand. **VHS** NO ⅐

Tim Follows the relationship between a handsome, mentally retarded young man and an attractive older businesswoman. Sappy storyline is redeemed by Gibson's fine debut performance. Based on Colleen McCullough's first novel.
1979 94m/C *AU* Mel Gibson, Piper Laurie, Peter Gwynne, Alwyn Kurts, Pat Evison; *D:* Michael Pate. **VHS, Beta** MED, OM ⅔⅔½

Tim Tyler's Luck Lost but not forgotten serial in its twelve-chapter entirety. The fearless Tim Tyler uses whatever he can to do battle with the sinister Spider Web gang.
1937 235m/B Frankie Thomas, Frances Robinson, Al Shear, Norman Willis, Earl Douglas; *D:* Ford Beebe. **VHS, Beta $29.95** NOS, GPV, FCT ⅔⅔½

Timber Queen A WWII flier comes home and aids his best friend's widow, who must make a quota of timber or lose her sawmill to gangsters. Old-fashioned.
1944 66m/B Richard Arlen, Mary Beth Hughes, June Havoc, Sheldon Leonard, George E. Stone, Dick Purcell; *D:* Frank McDonald. **VHS $19.95** NOS, LOO ⅔⅔

Timber Terrors A Mountie investigates his partner's murder. *AKA:* Morton of the Mounted.
1935 50m/B VHS, Beta NO ⅐

Time After Time In Victorian London, circa 1893, H.G. Wells is experimenting with his time machine. He discovers the machine has been used by an associate, who turns out to be Jack the Ripper, to travel to San Francisco in 1979. Wells follows to stop any further murders and the ensuing battle of wits is both entertaining and imaginative. McDowell is charming as Wells and Steenburgen is equally fine as Well's modern American love interest. Notable score by Miklos Rozsa.
1979 (PG) 112m/C Malcolm McDowell, David Warner, Mary Steenburgen, Patti D'Arbanville, Charles Cioffi; *D:* Nicholas Meyer. **VHS, Beta, LV $19.98** WAR ⅔⅔⅔

Time Bandits A group of dwarves help a young boy to travel through time and space with the likes of Robin Hood, Napoleon, Agamemnon, and other time-warp playmates. Epic fantasy from Monty Python alumni.
1981 (PG) 110m/C *GB* John Cleese, Sean Connery, Shelley Duvall, Katherine Helmond, Ian Holm, Michael Palin, Ralph Richardson, Kenny Baker, Peter Vaughan, David Warner; *D:* Terry Gilliam. **VHS, Beta, LV $19.95** PAR ⅔⅔½

Time Burst—The Final Alliance A man fights for his soul to protect the secret of immortality at any cost.
1989 93m/C VHS, Beta AIP ⅔⅔½

Time Fighters A time machine has the ability to travel at the speed of light from prehistoric times to the distant future. This is a great help to the Time fighters.
1985 60m/C VHS, Beta SUE ⅐½

Time Flies When You're Alive A made-for-cable-television presentation of actor Linke's performance monologue detailing the traumas and experiences he and his family underwent as his wife Francesca slowly died of cancer.
1989 79m/C Paul Linke; *D:* Roger Spottiswoode. **VHS, Beta $79.99** HBO ⅔½

A Time for Miracles Dramatic biography of the first native-born American saint, Elizabeth Bayley Seton, who was canonized in 1975. Made for television.
1980 97m/C Kate Mulgrew, Lorne Greene, Rossano Brazzi, John Forsythe, Jean-Pierre Aumont, Milo O'Shea; *D:* Michael O'Herlihy. **VHS, Beta $9.98** NLC ⅐½

Time for Murder A series of British dramatizations of famous murder mystery stories. Made for television.
198? 60m/C *GB* Beta PSM ⅐½

Time for Revenge A demolitions worker attempts to blackmail his corrupt employer by claiming a workplace explosion made him speechless. He finds himself in a contest of

silence and wits. In Spanish with English subtitles.
1982 112m/C *AR* Federico Luppi, Haydee Padilla, Julio de Grazia, Ulises Dumont; **D:** Adolfo Aristarain. **VHS, Beta $24.95** *XVC, MED, AUD* 🎞🎞½

The Time Guardian Time-travelers of the future arrive in the Australian desert in 1988, intent on warning the local populace of the impending arrival of killer cyborgs from the 40th century. Muddled and confusing.
1987 (PG) 89m/C Tom Burlinson, Carrie Fisher, Dean Stockwell, Nikki Coghill; **D:** Brian Hannant; **W:** Brian Hannant, John Baxter. **VHS, Beta, LV, 8mm $14.95** *COL, SUE, NLC* 🎞½

Time is Running Out A man races against the clock in this taut thriller.
1952 ?m/C Dave Clark, Mike Smith, Lenny Davidson. **VHS $16.95** *SNC* 🎞🎞

Time Lock An expert safecracker races against time to save a child who is trapped inside a bank's pre-set time-locked vault. Canada is the setting, although the film was actually made in England. Based on a play by Arthur Hailey.
1957 73m/B *GB* Sean Connery, Robert Beatty, Lee Patterson, Betty McDowall, Vincent Winter; **D:** Gerald Thomas. **VHS, Beta $39.95** *MON* 🎞🎞

The Time Machine English scientist living near the end of the 19th century invents time travel machine and uses it to travel into various periods of the future. Rollicking version of H.G. Wells' classic cautionary tale boasts Oscar-winning special effects. Remade in 1978.
1960 103m/C Rod Taylor, Yvette Mimieux, Whit Bissell, Sebastian Cabot, Alan Young; **D:** George Pal. **VHS, Beta, LV $19.95** *MGM, MLB* 🎞🎞🎞

Time Machine Yet another adaptation of H.G. Wells' classic novel about a scientist who invents a machine that enables him to travel through time. Inferior remake of the 1960 version.
1978 (G) 99m/C John Beck, Priscilla Barnes, Andrew Duggan; **D:** Henning Schellerup. **VHS, Beta $19.95** *UHV, LME* 🎞½

A Time of Destiny During World War II, an American soldier vows to kill his brother-in-law, who he believes caused his father's death. Meanwhile, the two men have become good friends in the army, never realizing their connection. A strange, overblown family saga from the director of "El Norte." Music by Ennio Morricone. Beautiful photography, terrific editing.
1988 (PG-13) 118m/C William Hurt, Timothy Hutton, Melissa Leo, Stockard Channing, Megan Follows, Francisco Rabal; **D:** Gregory Nava; **W:** Anna Thomas; **M:** Ennio Morricone. **VHS, Beta, LV, 8mm $14.95** *COL, SUE* 🎞🎞

Time of Indifference Based on the novel by Alberto Moravia. Tale of the disintegration of values in 1920s Italy is unable to take full advantage of its fine cast or potentially thought-provoking themes. **AKA:** Gli Indifferenti; Les Deux Rivales.
1964 84m/B *IT* Rod Steiger, Shelley Winters, Claudia Cardinale, Paulette Goddard, Tomas Milian; **D:** Francesco Maselli. **VHS** *GKK* 🎞🎞

Time of Tears A young boy, grieving after his grandfather's death, meets a lonely old man and they fill each other's emotional needs.
1987 (PG) 95m/C, Beta $19.95 *STE, NWV* 🎞½

Time of the Apes A Japanese-made horror film about a woman and two kids thrust into an underground world ruled by intelligent gorillas.
1987 98m/C *JP* **VHS, Beta $39.95** *CEL* 🎞

Time of the Gypsies Acclaimed Yugoslavian saga about a homely, unlucky Gypsy boy who sets out to steal his way to a dowry large enough to marry the girl of his dreams. Beautifully filmed, magical, and very long. In the Gypsy language, Romany, it's the first feature film made in the Gypsy tongue. **AKA:** Dom Za Vesanje.
1990 (R) 136m/C *YU* Davor Dujmovic, Sinolicka Trpkova, Ljubica Adzovic, Hunsija Hasimovic, Bora Todorovic; **D:** Emir Kusturica. **VHS, Beta, LV $79.95** *COL, TAM* 🎞🎞🎞

The Time of Their Lives A pair of Revolutionary War-era ghosts haunt a modern country estate. One of the best A & C comedies. **AKA:** The Ghost Steps Out.
1946 82m/B Bud Abbott, Lou Costello, Marjorie Reynolds, Binnie Barnes, Gale Sondergaard, John Shelton; **D:** Charles T. Barton. **VHS, Beta $14.95** *MCA* 🎞🎞½

The Time of Your Life The only Cagney film that ever lost money. A simple but engaging story of people trying to live their dreams. Cagney is delightful as a barroom philosopher who controls the world around him from his seat in the tavern. Although it was not very popular with audiences at the time, the critics hailed it as an artistic achievement. Based on William Saroyan's play.
1948 109m/B James Cagney, William Bendix, Jeanne Cagney, Broderick Crawford, Ward Bond, James Barton, Paul Draper, Natalie Schafer; **D:** H.C. Potter. **VHS $19.95** *NOS, VEC, HEG* 🎞🎞🎞½

Time Out for Love An American girl travels to Paris in search of romance, but discovers more than she bargained for. In French with English subtitles. **AKA:** Les Grandes Personnes; Five Day Lover.
1961 91m/B *IT FR* Jean Seberg, Micheline Presle, Maurice Ronet, Francoise Prevost, Annabelle Ninchi, Fernando Bruno; **D:** Jean Valere. **VHS $29.95** *DVT, HEG* 🎞🎞½

Time Runner It's 2022 and the Earth is being used as target practice by alien invaders. Space captain Hamill manages to find a hole in time and slip back to 1992 where he can battle the first of the alien infiltrators and maybe change Earth's destiny. The time-travel theme (including Hamill watching his own birth) is fun and the special effects are well done.
1992 (R) 90m/C Mark Hamill, Brion James, Rae Dawn Chong; **D:** Michael Mazo. **VHS, LV $89.95** *NLC, COL* 🎞🎞

Time Stands Still Two brothers experience troubled youth in Budapest. Artful, somberly executed, with American pop soundtrack. Subtitled in English.
1982 99m/C *HU* Istvan Znamenak, Henrik Pauer, Aniko Ivan, Sander Soth, Peter Galfy; **D:** Peter Gothar. **VHS, Beta $59.95** *COL* 🎞🎞🎞

Time to Die WWII victim of heinous war crimes, obsessed with revenge, stalks his prey for a final confrontation, while eluding U.S. intelligence. Disappointing despite good cast working with Mario Puzo story. **AKA:** Seven Graves for Rogan.
1983 (R) 89m/C Edward Albert, Rex Harrison, Rod Taylor, Raf Vallone; **D:** Matt Cimber. **VHS, Beta $59.95** *MED* 🎞½

A Time to Die Lords plays a police photographer who, well, photographs the police. But her camera catches one in the act of murder. Routine crime thriller. **AKA:** Seven Graves for Rogan.
1991 (R) 93m/C Traci Lords, Jeff Conaway, Richard Roundtree, Bradford Bancroft, Nitchie Barrett; **W/D:** Charles Kanganis; **M:** Ennio Morricone. **VHS, LV $89.95** *PMH* 🎞½

Time to Kill A young soldier in Africa wanders away from his camp and meets a woman whom he rapes and kills. But when he returns to his outfit he finds he can't escape his tormenting conscience. **AKA:** Tempo di Uccidere.
1989 (R) 110m/C Nicolas Cage, Giancarlo Giannini, Robert Liensol; **D:** Guiliano Montaldo; **M:** Ennio Morricone. **VHS, LV $19.98** *REP* 🎞½

Time to Live Made-for-television adaptation of Mary Lou Weisman's "Intensive Care" about a family's adjustment to a young boy's fight with Muscular Dystrophy. Minnelli's first appearance in a television movie.
1985 97m/C Liza Minnelli, Jeffrey DeMunn, Swoosie Kurtz, Corey Haim, Scott Schwartz; **D:** Rick Wallace. **Beta** *NO* 🎞½

A Time to Love & a Time to Die Lush adaptation of Erich Maria Remarque novel about WWII German soldier who falls in love with a young girl during furlough. The two are married, only to be separated when he is forced to return to the Russian front. Sympathetic treatment of Germans opposed to Hitler's policies.
1958 133m/C John Gavin, Lilo (Liselotte) Pulver, Jock Mahoney, Keenan Wynn, Klaus Kinski, Jim Hutton, Dana J. Hutton; **D:** Douglas Sirk. **VHS, Beta $14.95** *KRT* 🎞🎞½

A Time to Remember Sticky with sentiment, this family film tells of a boy with a gift for singing, encouraged by a priest, discouraged by his father. At one point the kid loses his voice—he probably choked on the pathos.
1990 90m/C Donald O'Connor, Morgana King. **VHS $29.95** *IGP* 🎞½

Time Trackers A Roger Corman cheapie about a race through time, from present-day New York to medieval England, to recover a time machine before it alters the course of history.
1988 (PG) 87m/C Kathleen Beller, Ned Beatty, Will Shriner; **D:** Howard R. Cohen. **VHS, Beta $79.95** *MGM* 🎞

The Time Travelers Scientists discover and pass through a porthole leading to earth's post-armageddon future where they encounter unfriendly mutants. Frightened, they make a serious effort to return to the past. Remade as "Journey to the Center of Time." **AKA:** Time Trap.
1964 82m/C Preston Foster, Phil Carey, Merry Anders, John Hoyt, Joan Woodbury, Dolores Wells, Dennis Patrick; **D:** Ib Melchior. **VHS, Beta $69.95** *HBO* 🎞🎞

Time Troopers In another post-nuke society, special police must execute anyone who has misused their allotted "energy clips" for illicit behavior. Dime-store budget sci-fi. **AKA:** Morgen Grauen; Morning Terror.
1989 (R) 90m/C *AT* Albert Fortell, Hannelore Elsner; **D:** L.E. Neiman. **VHS, Beta $59.95** *PSM* 🎞

Time Walker An archaeologist unearths King Tut's coffin in California. An alien living inside is unleashed and terrorizes the public.
1982 (PG) 86m/C Ben Murphy; **D:** Tom Kennedy. **VHS, Beta $19.98** *NLC* 🎞

Timebomb When someone attempts to kill Biehn, he turns to a beautiful psychiatrist for help. She triggers flashbacks that send her hunted patient on a dangerous, perhaps deadly, journey into his past.
1991 (R) 96m/C Michael Biehn, Patsy Kensit, Tracy Scoggins, Robert Culp, Richard Jordan, Raymond St. Jacques; **W/D:** Avi Nesher. **VHS, Beta, LV $19.98** *MGM* 🎞🎞½

Timepiece This tape features one of Jim Henson's earlier films about an overworked, young executive.
1965 10m/C Jim Henson. **VHS, Beta** FLL ⅔⅔

Timerider Motorcyclist riding through the California desert is accidentally thrown back in time to 1877, the result of a scientific experiment that went awry. There he finds no gas stations and lots of cowboys. Co-written and co-produced by Michael Nesmith, best known for his days with the rock group "The Monkees." **AKA:** The Adventure of Lyle Swan.
1983 (PG) 93m/C Fred Ward, Belinda Bauer, Peter Coyote, Richard Masur, Ed Lauter, L.Q. Jones, Tracy Walter; **D:** William Dear. **VHS, Beta, LV** $19.95 PAV ⅔½

Times of Harvey Milk A powerful and moving documentary about the life and career of San Francisco supervisor and gay activist Harvey Milk. The film documents the assassination of Milk and Mayor George Moscone by Milk's fellow supervisor, Dan White. Highly acclaimed by both critics and audiences, the film gives an honest and direct look at the murder and people's reactions. News footage of the murders and White's trial is included.
1983 90m/C D: Robert Epstein. **VHS, Beta, LV** $59.95 PAV ⅔½

Times Square A 13-year-old girl learns about life on her own when she teams up with a defiant, anti-social child of the streets. Unappealing and unrealistic, the film features a New Wave music score. Film critic Jacob Brackman wrote the script.
1980 (R) 111m/C Tim Curry, Trini Alvarado, Robin Johnson, Peter Coffield, Elizabeth Pena, Anna Maria Horsford; **D:** Allan Moyle. **VHS, Beta** $59.99 HBO ⅔½

Times to Come Taut thriller reminiscent of bleak futuristic movies like "Clockwork Orange." Three people try to survive in a desolate, aggressive, and unstable future. In Spanish with English subtitles. **AKA:** Lo Que Vendra.
1981 98m/C AR Hugo Soto, Juan Leyrado, Charly Garcia; **D:** Gustavo Mosquera. **VHS** $79.95 CCN, FCT, TAM ⅔⅔⅔

Timestalkers A college professor's infatuation with a young woman is complicated by their pursuit of a criminal from the 26th century into the past. Mildly entertaining adventure. Tucker's last film. Made for television.
1987 100m/C William Devane, Lauren Hutton, Klaus Kinski, John Ratzenberger, Forrest Tucker, Gail Youngs; **D:** Michael Schultz. **VHS** $29.95 FRH ⅔⅔½

Timothy and the Angel A young man with a deep desire to be a ranger must pass up the rival temptations of a baseball scholarship and a life of speed and drugs offered by a motorcyclist.
1979 29m/C VHS, Beta LCA ⅔½

The Tin Drum German child in the 1920s wills himself to stop growing in response to the increasing Nazi presence in Germany. He communicates his anger and fear by pounding on a tin drum. Memorable scenes, excellent cast. In German with English subtitles. Adapted from the novel by Gunter Grass. From the novel by Gunter Grass. **AKA:** Die Blechtrommel.
1979 (R) 141m/C GE David Bennent, Mario Adorf, Angela Winkler, Daniel Olbrychski; **D:** Rainer Werner Fassbinder, Volker Schlondorff. **VHS, Beta** $59.95 WAR, APD, GLV ⅔⅔⅔

Tin Man Garage mechanic born totally deaf designs and builds a computer that can both hear and speak for him. His world is complicated, however, when a young speech therapist introduces him to new and wonderful sounds and unscrupulous and exploitative computer salesmen. Interesting premise and nice performances.
1983 95m/C Timothy Bottoms, Deana Jurgens, Troy Donahue; **D:** John G. Thomas. **VHS, Beta** $59.95 MED ⅔⅔½

Tin Men Set in Baltimore in the 1960s, this bitter comedy begins with two aluminum-siding salesmen colliding in a minor car accident. They play increasingly savage pranks on each other until one seduces the wife of the other, ruining his marriage. Like "Diner," the movie is full of Levinson's idiosyncratic local Baltimore color.
1987 (R) 112m/C Richard Dreyfuss, Danny DeVito, Barbara Hershey, John Mahoney, Jackie Gayle; **D:** Barry Levinson. **VHS, Beta, LV** $19.95 TOU ⅔⅔½

Tin Star Perkins is the young sheriff who persuaded veteran bounty hunter Fonda to help him rid the town of outlaws. Excellent Mann western balances humor and suspense.
1957 93m/B Henry Fonda, Anthony Perkins, Betsy Palmer, Neville Brand, Lee Van Cleef, John McIntire, Michel Ray; **D:** Anthony Mann. **VHS, Beta** $14.95 PAR, KRT ⅔⅔⅔

Tintorera...Tiger Shark Three shark hunters attempt to discover why buxom swimmers are disappearing. Phony takeoff of "Jaws." **AKA:** Tintorera; Tintorera...Bloody Waters.
1978 (R) 91m/C GB MX Susan George, Fiona Lewis, Jennifer Ashley, D. Dene Cardona, Jr. **VHS, Beta** $54.95 MED Woof!

Tiny Toon Adventures: How I Spent My Vacation How the tiny toons of Acme Acres spend their summer vacation in this animated adventure that spoofs several popular films and amusements. Plucky Duck and Hampton Pig journey to "Happy World Land" (a takeoff on Walt Disney World), Babs and Buster Bunny's water adventure parodies "Deliverance," there's a spoof of "The Little Mermaid," and the Road Runner even makes a cameo appearance. Parents will be equally entertained by the level of humor and the fast-paced action. Based on the Steven Spielberg TV cartoon series, this is the first made-for-home-video animated feature ever released in the United States.
1991 80m/C VHS, Beta, LV, 8mm $19.95 WAR ⅔⅔⅔

The Tip-Off Lovable boxer (Armstrong) and vivacious girlfriend (Rogers) save less-than-bright friend from getting involved with mean mobster's girlfriend. Major chemistry between Rogers and Armstrong.
1931 75m/B Eddie Quillan, Robert Armstrong, Ginger Rogers, Joan Peers, Ernie Adams; **D:** Albert Rogell. **VHS** $19.98 TTC, FCT ⅔⅔½

'Tis a Pity She's a Whore A brother and sister engage in an incestuous affair. She becomes pregnant and is married off. Her husband, however, becomes infuriated when he learns of his wife's pregnancy. Photography is by Vittorio Storaro in this highly stylized drama set in Renaissance Italy. **AKA:** Addio, Fratello, Crudele.
1973 (R) 102m/C IT Charlotte Rampling, Oliver Tobias, Fabio Testi, Antonio Falsi, Rick Battaglia, Angela Luce, Rino Imperio; **D:** Giuseppe Patroni Griffi; **M:** Ennio Morricone. **VHS, Beta** $19.95 ACA ⅔⅔½

Title Shot A crafty manager convinces a millionaire to bet heavily on the guaranteed loss of his heavyweight contender in an upcoming fight. He doesn't realize the boxer is too stupid to throw the fight.
1981 (R) 88m/C Tony Curtis, Richard Gabourie, Susan Hogan, Robert Delbert; **D:** Les Rose. **VHS, Beta** $69.98 LIV ⅔

TNT Jackson A kung fu mama searches for her brother while everyone in Hong Kong tries to kick her out of town.
1975 (R) 73m/C Jeanne Bell; **D:** Cirio H. Santiago. **VHS, Beta** $19.95 NLC Woof!

To All a Goodnight Five young girls and their boyfriends are planning an exciting Christmas holiday until a mad Santa Claus puts a damper on things. Total gorefest, with few, if any, redeeming virtues.
1980 (R) 90m/C Jennifer Runyon, Forrest Swanson, Linda Gentile, William Lover; **D:** David Hess. **VHS, Beta** MED Woof!

To All My Friends on Shore A made-for-television story about a father dealing with his young son's sickle cell anemia. Fine performances, realistic script make this an excellent outing.
1971 74m/C Bill Cosby, Gloria Foster, Dennis Hines; **D:** Gilbert Cates. **VHS, Beta** NO ⅔⅔⅔

To Be a Rose Poignant rendering of the person behind the prostitute. In-depth story following one woman's evening at work, from her point of view. Wonderful sense of her defenses and her feelings.
1974 (R) 92m/C Rose Kilpatrick; **D:** William A. Levey. **VHS, Beta** $69.95 TWE ⅔⅔

To Be or Not to Be Sophisticated black comedy set in wartime Poland. Lombard and Benny are Maria and Josef Tura, the Barrymores of the Polish stage, who use the talents of their acting troupe against the invading Nazis. The opening sequence is regarded as a cinema classic. One of Benny's finest film performances, the movie marks Lombard's final screen appearance. Classic Lubitsch. Remade in 1983.
1942 102m/B Carole Lombard, Jack Benny, Robert Stack, Sig Rumann, Lionel Atwill, Felix Bressart, Helmut Dantine, Tom Dugan; **D:** Ernst Lubitsch. **VHS, Beta** $59.95 VES, WAR ⅔⅔⅔½

To Be or Not to Be In this remake of the 1942 film, Bancroft and Brooks are actors in Poland during World War II. They accidentally become involved with the Polish Resistance and work to thwart the Nazis. Lots of laughs, although at times there's a little too much slapstick.
1983 (PG) 108m/C Mel Brooks, Anne Bancroft, Charles Durning, Jose Ferrer, Tim Matheson, Christopher Lloyd; **D:** Alan Johnson. **VHS, Beta, LV** $19.98 FOX ⅔⅔½

To Be the Best Eric, a member of the U.S. Kickboxing Team, lets his love for the beautiful Cheryl and his hot temper get the best of him. When a ruthless gambler threatens to kill Cheryl if Eric doesn't throw his big match, he joins with his family, fellow teammates, and most feared opponent, to set things right.
1993 (R) 99m/C Michael Worth, Martin Kove, Phillip Troy, Brittney Powell, Alex Cord, Steven Leigh; **D:** Joseph Merhi; **W:** Michael January. **VHS** $89.95 PMH ⅔½

To Catch a Killer A chilling performance by Dennehy highlights this true-crime tale of a detective's relentless pursuit of serial killer John Wayne Gacy, who preyed on young men and hid the bodies in his home. Made for television.
1992 95m/C Brian Dennehy, Michael Riley, Margot Kidder, Meg Foster; **D:** Eric Till. **VHS, LV** $89.95 WOV ⅔⅔⅔

To Catch a King Garr is a singer working in Wagner's nightclub in 1940s' Lisbon. The pair becomes involved in trying to foil the Nazi plot to kidnap the vacationing Duke and Duchess of Windsor. Average made-for-cable fare.
1984 120m/C Robert Wagner, Teri Garr, Horst Janson, Barbara Parkins, John Standing; *D:* Clive Donner. **VHS, Beta** $49.95 *PSM* ⅓

To Catch a Thief On the French Riviera, a reformed jewel thief falls for a wealthy American woman, who suspects he's up to his old tricks when a rash of jewel thefts occur. Oscar-winning photography by Robert Burks, a notable fireworks scene, and snappy dialogue. A change of pace for Hitchcock, this charming comedy-thriller proved to be as popular as his other efforts. Kelly met future husband Prince Ranier during shooting in Monaco.
1955 103m/C Cary Grant, Grace Kelly, Jessie Royce Landis, John Williams; *D:* Alfred Hitchcock. Academy Awards '55: Best Color Cinematography; Nominations: Best Art Direction/Set Decoration (Color), Best Costume Design (Color). **VHS, Beta, LV** $19.95 *PAR, MLB, HMV* ⅓⅓⅓

To Die for A vampire stalks, woos, and snacks on a young real estate woman.
1989 (R) 99m/C Brendan Hughes, Scott Jacoby, Duane Jones, Steve Bond, Sydney Walsh, Amanda Wyss, Ava Fabian; *D:* Deran Sarafian. **VHS, Beta, LV** $29.95 *ACA* ⅓½

To Die for 2 This far outclasses part one in terms of acting and production values, but the plot still isn't back from the grave. Strange, because all the vampires are; despite their fiery deaths last time they flock around the adoptive mother of a baby secretly sired by a bloodsucker.
1991 (R) 95m/C Rosalind Allen, Steve Bond, Scott Jacoby, Michael Praed, Jay Underwood, Amanda Wyss, Remy O'Neill; *D:* David F. Price. **VHS** $89.95 *VMK* ⅓½

To Die Standing Two mavericks team up to do what the D.E.A. and cops simply cannot... capture a dangerous international drug lord. High action.
1991 (R) 87m/C Cliff DeYoung, Robert Beltran, Jamie Rose, Gerald Anthony, Orlando Sacha, Michael Ford; *D:* Louis Morneau; *W:* Ross Bell, Daryl Haney. **VHS, LV** $89.95 *COL, PIA* ⅓½

To Forget Venice Portrays the sensitive relationships among four homosexuals, and their shared fears of growing older. Dubbed in English.
1979 90m/C *IT* Erland Josephson, Mariangela Melato, David Pontremoli, Elenora Giorgi; *D:* Franco Brusati. **VHS, Beta** $59.95 *COL* ⅓⅓½

To Have & Have Not Martinique charter boat operator gets mixed up with beautiful woman and French resistance fighters during World War II. Top-notch production in every respect. Classic dialogue and fiery romantic bouts between Bogart and Bacall. Bacall's first film. Based on a story by Ernest Hemingway. Remade in 1950 as "The Breaking Point" and in 1958 as "The Gun Runners."
1944 100m/B Humphrey Bogart, Lauren Bacall, Walter Brennan, Hoagy Carmichael, Marcel Dalio, Dolores Moran, Sheldon Leonard, Dan Seymour; *D:* Howard Hawks. **VHS, Beta, LV** $19.95 *MGM* ⅓⅓⅓

To Heal a Nation The story of veteran Jan Scruggs, who spearheaded the movement to build the Vietnam Veterans memorial. The then little-known Ross Perot provided major financial support for Scruggs' dream. Made for television.
1988 ?m/C Eric Roberts, Conrad Bachmann. **VHS** $89.98 *TTC* ⅓⅓½

To Hell and Back Adaptation of Audie Murphy's autobiography. Murphy plays himself, from his upbringing to World War II, where he was the most-decorated American soldier. Features realistic battle sequences punctuated with grand heroics.
1955 106m/C Audie Murphy, Marshall Thompson, Jack Kelly; *D:* Jesse Hibbs. **VHS, Beta** $19.95 *MCA, TLF* ⅓⅓½

To Joy The rocky marriage of a violinist and his wife illuminate the problems of the young in Swedish society. Early Bergman. In Swedish with English subtitles or dubbed.
1950 90m/B *SW D:* Ingmar Bergman. **VHS, Beta, LV** $29.98 *SUE, TAM* ⅓⅓⅓

To Kill a Clown Painter and his wife working to save their marriage are trapped on an isolated island and terrorized by a crazed Vietnam veteran. This helps pull them together. Some holes in the plot, but generally effective.
1972 (R) 82m/C Alan Alda, Blythe Danner, Heath Lamberts; *D:* George Bloomfield. **VHS, Beta** $9.95 *MED* ⅓⅓

To Kill a Mockingbird Faithful adaptation of powerful Harper Lee novel, both an evocative portrayal of childhood innocence and a denunciation of bigotry. Peck's performance as southern lawyer defending a black man accused of raping a white woman is flawless. Duvall debuted as the dim-witted Boo Radley. Lee based her characterization of "Dill" on Truman Capote, a childhood friend. Script by Horton Foote and a score by Elmer Bernstein.
1962 129m/B Gregory Peck, Brock Peters, Phillip Alford, Mary Badham, Robert Duvall, Rosemary Murphy, William Windom, Alice Ghostley; *D:* Robert Mulligan; *W:* Horton Foote. Academy Awards '62: Best Actor (Peck), Best Adapted Screenplay, Best Art Direction/Set Decoration (B & W); Nominations: Best Black and White Cinematography, Best Director (Mulligan), Best Picture, Best Supporting Actress (Badham), Best Original Score; Golden Globe Awards '63: Best Actor—Drama (Peck). **VHS, Beta, LV** $14.95 *KUI, MCA, BTV* ⅓⅓⅓⅓

To Kill a Priest Based on the true story of Father Jerzy Popieluszko, a young priest in 1984 Poland who defies his church and speaks out publicly on Solidarity. He is killed by the government as a result. Harris is good as the menacing police official.
1989 (R) 110m/C Christopher Lambert, Ed Harris, David Suchet, Tim Roth, Joanne Whalley-Kilmer, Peter Postlethwaite, Cherie Lunghi, Joss Ackland; *D:* Agnieszka Holland. **VHS, Beta, LV** $89.95 *COL* ⅓⅓

To Kill a Stranger A beautiful pop singer is stranded in a storm, and then victimized by a mad rapist/murderer.
197? 100m/C Donald Pleasence, Dean Stockwell, Angelica Maria, Aldo Ray, Sergio Aragones. **VHS, Beta** *NO* ⅓

To Kill with Intrigue After his entire family is brutally slaughtered, a young lord learns new fighting techniques and embarks on a mission of vengeance.
1985 107m/C Jackie Chan. **VHS, Beta** *NO* ⅓

To Live and Die in Hong Kong Two sailors arrive in Hong Kong for a little R & R, until they are mistaken for spies by both the Hong Kong police and the Chinese mob. Action-packed tale.
1989 98m/C Rowena Cortes, Lawrence Jan, Mike Kelly, Laurens C. Postma; *D:* Lau Shing Hon. **VHS** *ELV* ⅓½

To Live & Die in L.A. Fast-paced, morally ambivalent tale of cops and counterfeiters in L.A. After his partner is killed shortly before his retirement, a secret service agent sets out to track down his ruthless killer. Lots of violence; some nudity. Notable both for a riveting car chase and its dearth of sympathetic characters.
1985 (R) 114m/C William L. Petersen, Willem Dafoe, John Pankow, Dean Stockwell, Debra Feuer, John Turturro, Darlanne Fluegel, Robert Downey Jr.; *D:* William Friedkin. **VHS, Beta, LV** $9.99 *LIV, VES* ⅓⅓

To Love Again A middle-aged love story about a reclusive college professor and the campus handyman.
1980 96m/C Lynn Redgrave, Brian Dennehy, Conchata Ferrell; *D:* Joseph Hardy. **VHS, Beta** $9.98 *NLC* ⅓½

To Paris with Love A British man and his son fall in love with a shop girl and her boss while on vacation in Paris. Charming and humorous, with a witty performance from Guinness.
1955 75m/C Alec Guinness, Odile Versuis, Vernon Gray; *D:* Robert Hamer. **VHS, Beta** $19.98 *VID* ⅓⅓½

To Play or To Die The introverted Kees attends an all-boy school where powerful bullies and sadomasochistic games are the rule. Kees is fascinated by the handsome Charel, the bullies leader. He invites Charel to his home, intending to turn the tables on his tormentor, but nothing goes as planned. Intense and controversial look at gay teens. Directorial debut of Krom. In Dutch with English subtitles.
1991 50m/C *NL* Geert Hunaerts, Tjebbo Gerritsma; *W/D:* Frank Krom; *W:* Anne Van De Putte. **VHS** $39.95 *WBF* ⅓⅓

To Protect and Serve When crooked cops start getting killed, two young cops are assigned to investigate. Suspicion points to a rookie (Howell), who just may have decided to clean things up his own way.
1992 (R) 93m/C C. Thomas Howell, Leslie Deane, Richard Romanus, Joe Cortese; *D:* Eric Weston. **VHS** $49.98 *LIV* ⅓⅓

To Race the Wind Blind man wants to be treated like a normal person as he struggles through Harvard Law School. Based upon Harold Krents' autobiography "Butterflies Are Free." Made for television.
1980 97m/C Steve Guttenberg, Lisa Eilbacher, Randy Quaid, Barbara Barrie; *D:* Walter Grauman. **VHS, Beta** $39.95 *UNI* ⅓⅓

To See Such Fun Hilarious excerpts from 80 years of the greatest British movie comedies.
1981 90m/C *GB* Peter Sellers, Marty Feldman, Benny Hill, Eric Idle, Alec Guinness, Margaret Rutherford, Dirk Bogarde, Spike Milligan. **VHS, Beta** $59.95 *PAV* ⅓

To Sir, with Love Teacher in London's tough East End tosses books in the wastebasket and proceeds to teach his class about life. Skillful and warm performance by Poitier as idealistic teacher; supporting cast also performs nicely. Based on the novel by E.R. Braithwaite. LuLu's title song was a big hit in 1967-68.
1967 105m/C *GB* Sidney Poitier, Lulu, Judy Geeson, Christian Roberts, Suzy Kendall, Faith Brook; *D:* James Clavell. **VHS, Beta** $14.95 *COL* ⅓⅓½

To Sleep with a Vampire A Los Angeles bloodsucker is tired of his violent existence and craves the one thing he can't have—daylight. As he stalks his latest victim, a stripper, he decides to take her home and have her tell him about living in daytime. When she realizes what's going on, the intended victim decides to fight for her life. Action and eroticism raises this one above the norm. Remake of "Dance of the Damned."

1992 (R) 90m/C Scott Valentine, Charlie Spradling, Richard Zobel, Ingrid Vold, Stephanie Hardy; *D:* Adam Friedman. **VHS $89.98** NHO ♫♫

To Sleep with Anger At first a comic, introspective look at a black middle-class family going about their business in the heart of Los Angeles. Sly charmer Glover shows up and enthralls the entire family with his slightly sinister storytelling and a gnawing doom gradually permeates the household. Insightful look into the conflicting values of Black America. Glover's best performance.
1990 (PG) 105m/C Danny Glover, Mary Alice, Paul Butler, Richard Brooks, Carl Lumbly, Vonetta McGee, Sheryl Lee Ralph; *W/D:* Charles Burnett. **VHS, Beta $19.95** COL, FCT, IME ♫♫♫½

To Subdue the Evil In a tale of brutality and betrayal, twin brothers oppose each other after being separated at birth.
19?? 90m/C Lung Chunem, Chen Hung Lieh, Tien Pang. **VHS $49.95** OCE ♫

To the Camp & Back A romantic novel transposed to tape, with equal amounts of unfettered sentiment, fantasy, and style.
1985 60m/C Jan Niklas. **Beta $11.95** PSM ♫½

To the Devil, A Daughter A nun is put under a spell by a priest who has been possessed by Satan. She is to bear his child. A writer on the occult intervenes. Based on the novel by Dennis Wheatley. One of Kinski's early films. *AKA:* Child of Satan.
1976 (R) 93m/C Richard Widmark, Christopher Lee, Nastassia Kinski, Honor Blackman, Denholm Elliott, Michael Goodliffe; *D:* Peter Sykes. **VHS, Beta $19.95** MLB ♫

To the Last Man An early Scott sagebrush epic, about two feuding families. Temple is seen in a small role. Based on Zane Grey's novel of the same name.
1933 70m/B Randolph Scott, Esther Ralston, Jack LaRue, Noah Beery Sr., Buster Crabbe, Gail Patrick, Barton MacLane, Fuzzy Knight, John Carradine, Jay Ward, Shirley Temple; *D:* Henry Hathaway. **VHS, Beta $9.95** NOS, DVT, MLB ♫

To the Lighthouse A proper British holiday turns into a summer of disillusionment in this adaptation of the Virginia Woolf novel.
1983 115m/C Rosemary Harris, Michael Clough, Suzanne Bertish, Lynsey Baxter. **VHS, Beta** NO ♫♫

To the Shores of Hell Leaving his sweetheart behind, Major Greg Donahue attacks Da Nang and plots to rescue his brother from the Viet Cong.
1965 82m/C Marshall Thompson, Kiva Lawrence, Richard Jordahl. **VHS, Beta $42.95** PGN ♫♫

To the Shores of Tripoli Wartime propaganda in the guise of drama, in which a smarmy playboy is transformed into a Marine in boot camp.
1942 82m/C John Payne, Maureen O'Hara, Randolph Scott, Nancy Kelly, Henry Morgan, Maxie Rosenbloom, William Tracy, Minor Watson, Alan Hale Jr., Hugh Beaumont, Hillary Brooke; *D:* H. Bruce Humberstone. **VHS, Beta $14.98** FOX, MLB ♫♫

The Toast of New Orleans A poor fisherman rises to stardom as an opera singer. Likable, though fluffy production features a plethora of musical numbers. ♫Be My Love; Tina Lina; I'll Never Love You; The Toast of New Orleans; Song of the Bayou; Boom Biddy Boom Boom.
1950 97m/C Kathryn Grayson, Mario Lanza, David Niven, Rita Moreno, J. Carroll Naish; *D:* Norman Taurog. **VHS, Beta $19.98** MGM ♫♫½

Toast of New York Arnold plays Jim Fisk, a New England peddler who rises to become one of the first Wall Street giants of industry. Atypical Grant performance.
1937 109m/B Edward Arnold, Cary Grant, Frances Farmer, Jack Oakie, Donald Meek, Billy Gilbert; *D:* Rowland V. Lee. **VHS, Beta, LV $19.98** RKO, TTC ♫♫♫

Tobor the Great Sentimental and poorly executed, this film tells the tale of a boy, his grandfather, and Tobor the robot. Villainous communists attempt to make evil use of Tobor, only to be thwarted in the end.
1954 77m/B Charles Drake, Billy Chapin, Karin Booth, Taylor Holmes, Joan Gerber, Steve Geray; *D:* Lee Sholem. **VHS, LV $19.98** REP ♫½

Tobruk American GI's endeavor to knock out the guns of Tobruk, to clear the way for a bombing attack on German fuel supply depots of North Africa in this World War II actioner.
1966 110m/C Rock Hudson, George Peppard, Guy Stockwell, Nigel Green; *D:* Arthur Hiller. **VHS, Beta $19.95** MCA ♫♫

Toby & the Koala Bear A little boy and his pet koala bear leave a convict colony in Australia. They befriend an Aborigine boy who teaches them to survive in the woods.
1983 77m/C VHS, Beta $29.98 FOX, WTA ♫♫

Toby McTeague A story about an Alaskan family that breeds Siberian Huskies. When his father is injured, the youngest son tries to replace him in the regional dog-sled race.
1987 (PG) 94m/C Winston Rekert, Wannick Bisson, Timothy Webber; *D:* Jean-Claude Lord. **VHS, Beta, LV $14.95** COL, NLC ♫♫

Toby Tyler A boy runs off to join the circus, and teams up with a chimpanzee. A timeless and enjoyable Disney film that still appeals to youngsters. Good family-fare.
1959 (G) 93m/C Kevin Corcoran, Henry Calvin, Gene Sheldon, Bob Sweeney, Mr. Stubbs; *D:* Charles T. Barton. **VHS, Beta $69.95** DIS ♫♫♫

Today I Hang A man is framed for murder and sentenced to hang. His buddies on the outside do their best to prove his innocence. Meanwhile, in prison, the accused encounters any number of interesting characters.
1942 67m/B Walter Woolf King, Mona Barrie, William Farnum, Harry Woods, James Craven; *D:* Oliver Drake. **VHS, Beta $16.95** SNC ♫♫

Today We Kill, Tomorrow We Die A rancher is unjustly sent to prison; when his sentence is over he hires a gang to relentlessly track down the culprit who framed him.
1971 (PG) 95m/C Montgomery Ford, Bud Spencer, William Berger, Tatsuya Nakadai, Wayde Preston; *D:* Tonino Cervi. **VHS, Beta $59.95** PSM ♫

The Todd Killings A psychotic young man commits a series of murders involving young women. Sleazy, forgettable picture wastes a talented cast. *AKA:* A Dangerous Friend; Skipper.
1971 (R) 93m/C Robert F. Lyons, Richard Thomas, Barbara Bel Geddes, Ed Asner, Sherry Miles, Gloria Grahame, Belinda J. Montgomery; *D:* Barry Shear. **VHS $59.95** WAR ♫½

Toga Party Fraternity house throws a wild toga party in this raunchy low-rent depiction of college life.
1979 (R) 82m/C Bobby H. Charles, Mary Mitchell. **VHS, Beta $59.95** MON ♫

Together Divorced woman and a male chauvinist test the limits of their sexual liberation as well as viewer patience.

1979 (R) 91m/C *IT* Maximilian Schell, Jacqueline Bisset, Terence Stamp, Monica Guerritore; *D:* Armena Balducci. **VHS, Beta $24.98** SUE ♫½

Togetherness Two wealthy, good-for-nothing playboys chase after the same blonde, a Communist, in Greece.
1970 101m/C George Hamilton, Peter Lawford, Olinka Berova, John Banner, Jesse White; *D:* Arthur Marks. **VHS, Beta, LV** NO ♫½

Tokyo-Ga Impelled by his love for the films of Yasujiro Ozu, Wenders traveled to Tokyo and fashioned a caring document of both the city and of Ozu's career, using images that recall and comment on Ozu's visual motifs.
1985 92m/C *D:* Wim Wenders. **VHS, Beta $59.95** PAV, TAM ♫♫½

Tokyo Joe A war hero/nightclub owner returns to Tokyo and becomes ensnared in blackmail and smuggling while searching for his missing wife and child. Slow-moving tale has never been considered one of Bogart's better movies.
1949 88m/B Humphrey Bogart, Florence Marly, Alexander Knox, Sessue Hayakawa, Jerome Courtland, Lora Lee Michel; *D:* Stuart Heisler. **VHS, Beta, LV $69.95** COL ♫½

Tokyo Olympiad A monumental sports documentary about the 1964 Olympic Games in its entirety. Never before available for home viewing. Letterboxed with digital sound. In Japanese with English subtitles.
1966 170m/C *JP D:* Kon Ichikawa. **VHS, Beta, LV, 3/4U $99.95** TPV, WFV, CRC ♫½

Tokyo Pop A punk rocker travels to Japan to find stardom and experiences a series of misadventures. Enjoyable in its own lightweight way.
1988 (R) 99m/C Carrie Hamilton, Yutaka Tadokoro, Tetsuro Tamba, Taiji Tonoyama, Masumi Harukawa; *D:* Fran Rubel Kazui. **VHS, LV $19.95** WAR ♫♫½

Tokyo Story Poignant story of elderly couple's journey to Tokyo where they receive little time and less respect from their grown children. Masterful cinematography, and sensitive treatment of universally appealing story. In Japanese with English subtitles.
1953 134m/B *JP* Chishu Ryu, Chieko Higashiyama, So Yamamura, Haruko Sugimura, Sotsuko Hara; *D:* Yasujiro Ozu. **VHS $69.95** NYF, FCT, TAM ♫♫♫♫

Tol'able David A simple tale of mountain folk, done in the tradition of Mark Twain stories. A family of hillbillies is embroiled in a feud with a clan of outlaws. When the community's mail is stolen by the troublesome ruffians, the family's youngest member, who harbors dreams of becoming a mail driver, comes to the rescue. Silent film.
1921 79m/B Richard Barthelmess, Gladys Hulette, Ernest Torrence; *D:* Henry King. **VHS, Beta $19.95** NOS, VYY, CCB ♫♫

Toll Gate Quick on the draw outlaw Hart risks capture to rescue drowning child, and consequently gets involved with the boy's mother. Silent classic.
1920 55m/B William S. Hart, Anna Q. Nilsson, Jack Richardson, Joseph Singleton; *D:* Lambert Hillyer. **VHS, Beta $27.95** GPV, VCN ♫♫½

Toll of the Desert A lawman learns that his father is a ruthless, back-stabbing renegade. Now he must try and catch him.
1935 58m/B Roger Williams, Ted Adams, Edward Cassidy, Tom London, John Elliott, Earl Dwire, Betty Mack, Fred Kohler Jr.; *D:* William Berke. **VHS, Beta, LV $19.95** NOS, DVT ♫

Tom & Jerry: Starring Maniacal entertainment from the legendary cat and mouse team.
1988 60m/C Tom & Jerry. **VHS, Beta $14.95** MGM, WTA ♫♫♫

Tom and Jerry: The Movie Everybody's favorite animated cat/mouse duo hit the big screen. For "Tom and Jerry" lovers of all ages. Based on the popular TV cartoon.
1993 (G) ?m/C VHS NYR ✗✗

Tom Brown's School Days Depicts life among the boys in an English school during the Victorian era. Based on the classic novel by Thomas Hughes. Remade in 1951. *AKA:* Adventures at Rugby.
1940 86m/B *GB* Cedric Hardwicke, Jimmy Lydon, Freddie Bartholomew; *D:* Robert Stevenson. VHS, Beta, 3/4U, Special order formats $19.95 NOS, HHT, PSM ✗✗½

Tom Brown's School Days Tom enrolls at Rugby and is beset by bullies in classic tale of English school life. British remake of the 1940 version. Based on the novel by Thomas Hughes.
1951 93m/B *GB* Robert Newton, John Howard Davies, James Hayter; *D:* Gordon Parry. VHS, Beta $19.95 UHV ✗✗✗

Tom, Dick, and Harry Dreamy girl is engaged to three men and unable to decide which to marry. It all depends on a kiss. Remade as "The Girl Most Likely."
1941 86m/B Ginger Rogers, George Murphy, Burgess Meredith, Alan Marshal, Phil Silvers; *D:* Garson Kanin. Academy Awards '41 Nominations: Best Story; National Board of Review Awards '41: 10 Best Films of the Year. VHS, Beta, LV $19.98 CCB, TTC, FCT ✗✗½

Tom Edison: The Boy Who Lit Up the World This is the story of Tom Edison's life and how he changed the world.
1978 49m/C David Huffman, Adam Arkin, Michael Callan; *D:* Henning Schellerup. VHS, Beta $9.98 VID ✗

Tom Horn The final days of one of the Old West's legends. Gunman Tom Horn, hired by Wyoming ranchers to stop cattle rustlers, goes about his job with a zeal that soon proves embarrassing to his employers. Beautifully photographed and authentic in its attention to details of the period, the film nonetheless takes liberties with the facts of Horn's life and is lacking in other aspects of production.
1980 (R) 98m/C Steve McQueen, Linda Evans, Richard Farnsworth, Billy Green Bush, Slim Pickens; *D:* William Wiard. VHS, Beta $19.98 WAR ✗✗

Tom Jones Bawdy comedy based on Henry Fielding's novel about a rustic playboy's wild life in 18th century England. Hilarious and clever with a grand performance by Finney. One of the sexiest eating scenes ever. Redgrave's debut. Theatrically released at 129 minutes, the film was recut by the director, who decided it needed tightening before its 1992 re-release on video.
1963 121m/C *GB* Albert Finney, Susannah York, Hugh Griffith, Edith Evans, Joan Greenwood, Diane Cilento, George Devine, David Tomlinson, Joyce Redman, Lynn Redgrave, Julian Glover; *D:* Tony Richardson; *W:* John Osborne. Academy Awards '63: Best Adapted Screenplay, Best Director (Richardson), Best Picture, Best Original Score; Nominations: Best Actor (Finney), Best Art Direction/Set Decoration (Color), Best Supporting Actor (Griffith), Best Supporting Actress (Cilento, Evans, Redman); British Academy Awards '63: Best Film; Directors Guild of America Awards '63: Best Director (Richardson); Golden Globe Awards '64: Best Film—Musical/Comedy, Best Foreign Film. VHS, Beta, LV $19.98 HBO, FOX, PIA ✗✗✗

Tom Mix Compilation 1 This compilation of six "Great American Cowboy" films from Tom Mix's early period includes: "Jimmy Hayes and Muriel," "The Stagecoach Driver and the Girl," "Sagebrush Tom," "An Arizona Wooing," "Roping a Bride" and "Local Color."
1916 60m/B Tom Mix. VHS, Beta GVV ✗✗✗✗

Tom Mix Compilation 2 Five films from Tom Mix's early period include "Never Again," "An Angelic Attitude," "A Western Masquerade," "A $5,000 Elopement," and "Local Color."
1916 60m/B Tom Mix. VHS, Beta GVV ✗✗✗✗

Tom Sawyer Winning adaptation of Mark Twain's oft told tale of boyhood in Hannibal, Missouri. Cast reprised their roles the following year in "Huckleberry Finn."
1930 86m/B Jackie Coogan, Mitzie Green, Lucien Littlefield, Tully Marshall; *D:* John Cromwell. VHS, Beta $19.98 MGM ✗✗✗

Tom Sawyer Musical version of the Mark Twain tale of the boisterous Tom, his friend Becky Thatcher, and various adventures, including the fence whitewashing. Amusing kid fare shot on location in Missouri. ♫River Song; Gratification; Tom Sawyer; Freebootin'; Aunt Polly's Soliloquy; If'n I Was God; A Man's Gotta Be What He's Born To Be; How Come?; Hannibal, Mo.
1973 (G) 104m/C Johnny Whitaker, Jodie Foster, Celeste Holm, Warren Oates, Jeff East; *D:* Don Taylor; *M:* John Williams. VHS $19.98 MGM ✗✗½

tom thumb Diminutive boy saves village treasury from bad guys. Adapted from classic Grimm fairy tale. Special effects combine live actors, animation, and puppets.
1958 92m/C *GB* Russ Tamblyn, Peter Sellers, Terry-Thomas; *D:* George Pal. VHS, Beta, LV $39.95 MGM ✗✗✗

Tomb Fortune seekers disturb the slumber of a magical, sadistic princess much to their everlasting regret. Adapted from a Bram Stoker novel.
1986 106m/C Cameron Mitchell, John Carradine, Sybil Danning; *D:* Fred Olen Ray. VHS, Beta $19.98 TWE ✗

Tomb of Ligeia The ghost of a man's first wife expresses her displeasure when groom and new little missus return to manor. One of the better Corman adaptations of Poe. Written by Robert Towne. Also available with "The Conqueror Worm" on Laser Disc. *AKA:* Tomb of the Cat.
1964 82m/C *GB* Vincent Price, Elizabeth Shepherd, John Westbrook, Oliver Johnston, Richard Johnson; *D:* Roger Corman. VHS, Beta, LV $59.99 HBO, MLB ✗✗✗

Tomb of the Undead The sadistic guards of a prison camp are rudely awakened by the prisoners they tortured to death when they return as flesh-eating zombies looking to settle the score.
1972 60m/C *GB* Duncan McLeod, Lee Frost, John Dennis; *D:* John Hayes. VHS, Beta $19.95 NOS, INC ✗½

Tomb of Torture Murdered countess is reincarnated in the body of a newspaperman's mistress. Together they investigate monster reports in a murder-ridden castle. The butler may have something to do with it. Filmed in Sepiatone and dubbed. *AKA:* Metempsycose.
1965 88m/B Annie Albert, Thony Maky, Mark Marian, Queen Elizabeth; *D:* William Grace. VHS, Beta $39.99 MSP Woof!

The Tomboy A young woman behaves boyishly in Colonial America.
1924 64m/B Dorothy Devore, Lotta Williams, Herbert Rawlinson, Harry Gibbon, Lee Moran; *D:* David Kirkland. VHS, Beta $19.95 GPV, FCT ✗½

Tomboy Shy country boy and a not-so-shy city girl meet, fall in love, and overcome obstacles that stand in their path.
1940 70m/B Jackie Moran, Marcia Mae Jones. VHS, Beta $29.95 VYY ✗

Tomboy A pretty auto mechanic is determined to win not only the race but the love and respect of a superstar auto racer.
1985 (R) 91m/C Betsy Russell, Eric Douglas, Jerry Dinome, Kristi Somers, Richard Erdman, Toby Iland; *D:* Herb Freed. VHS, Beta $79.98 LIV, VES Woof!

Tomboy & the Champ Despite many obstacles, a music-loving calf becomes a prize winner with the help of its loving owner. Kids will love it, but adults will find this one a little sugary.
1958 82m/C Candy Moore, Ben Johnson, Jesse White; *D:* Francis D. Lyon. VHS, Beta $29.95 UHV ✗✗

Tombs of the Blind Dead Blinded by crows for using human sacrifice in the thirteenth century, zombies rise from the grave to wreak havoc upon 20th-century Spaniards. Atmospheric chiller was extremely popular in Europe and spawned three sequels. Originally titled "The Blind Dead." The sequels, also on video, are "Return of the Evil Dead" and "Horror of the Zombies." *AKA:* The Blind Dead; La Noche dell Terror Ciego.
1972 (PG) 86m/C *SP PT* Caesar Burner, Lone Fleming, Helen Harp; *D:* Armando de Ossorio. VHS, Beta $42.95 PGN ✗✗½

Tombstone Canyon Death rides the range until Maynard and his horse Tarzan put a halt to it.
1935 60m/B Ken Maynard, Sheldon Lewis, Cecilia Parker. VHS, Beta $12.95 SNC, NOS, RXM ✗½

Tombstone Terror A cowboy is beleaguered by a case of mistaken identity.
1934 55m/B Bob Steele. VHS, Beta NO ✗

Tomcat: Dangerous Desires Tom (Grieco) suffers from a rare degenerative condition and agrees to become a guinea pig in a secret, genetic imprinting experiment that has him injected with feline RNA. Tom's health is restored but the side effects give him the predatory instincts of a cat and the need to kill to stay alive.
1993 (R) 96m/C Richard Grieco, Maryam D'Abo, Natalie Radford. VHS, LV $89.98 REP ✗✗

Tommy Peter Townshend's rock opera as visualized in the usual hyper-Russell style about the deaf, dumb, and blind boy who becomes a celebrity due to his amazing skill at the pinball machines. A parade of rock musicians perform throughout the affair, with varying degrees of success. Despite some good moments, the film ultimately falls prey to ill-conceived production concepts and miscasting. ♫Underture; Captain Walker Didn't Come Home; It's A Boy; '51 is Going to Be A Good Year; What About the Boy?; The Amazing Journey; Christmas; See Me, Feel Me; Eyesight to the Blind; The Acid Queen; Do You Think It's All Right; Cousin Kevin; Fiddle About; Sparks; Pinball Wizard; Today It Rained Champagne; There's A Doctor; Go to the Mirror; Tommy Can You Hear Me?; Smash the Mirror; I'm Free; Miracle Cure; Sensation; Sally Simpson; Welcome; Deceived; Tommy's Holiday Camp; We're Not Gonna Take It; Listening To You.
1975 (PG) 108m/C Ann-Margret, Elton John, Oliver Reed, Tina Turner, Roger Daltrey, Eric Clapton, Keith Moon, Pete Townsend, Jack Nicholson, Robert Powell; *W/D:* Ken Russell. Academy Awards '75 Nominations: Best Actress (Ann-Margret), Best Original Score; Golden Globe Awards '76: Best Actress—Musical/Comedy (Ann-Margret). VHS, Beta, LV $14.95 COL, MVD, WME ✗✗

Tomorrow Powerful tale of the love of two lonely people. Outstanding performance by Duvall as lumber mill worker who falls for a pregnant woman. Based on neglected Faulkner story with screenplay by Horton Foote.
1983 (PG) 102m/B Robert Duvall, Olga Bellin, Sudie Bond; *D:* Joseph Anthony; *W:* Horton Foote Jr. VHS, Beta $24.95 *MON* ⊿⊿⊿

Tomorrow at Seven A mystery writer is determined to discover the identity of the Ace of Spades, a killer who always warns his intended victim, then leaves an ace of spades on the corpse as his calling card.
1933 62m/B Chester Morris, Vivienne Osborne, Frank McHugh, Allen Jenkins, Henry Stephenson; *D:* Ray Enright. VHS, Beta $12.95 *SNC, NOS, VYY* ⊿⊿½

Tomorrow is Forever Welles and Colbert marry shortly before he goes off to fight in World War I. Badly wounded and disfigured, he decides to stay in Europe while Colbert, believing Welles dead, eventually marries Brent. Fast forward to World War II when Brent, a chemical manufacturer, hires a new scientist to work for him in the war effort (guess who). This slow-moving melodrama wastes a good cast. Six-year-old Wood debuts as Colbert's daughter.
1946 105m/B Claudette Colbert, Orson Welles, George Brent, Lucile Watson, Richard Long, Natalie Wood; *D:* Irving Pichel. VHS $19.98 *MGM* ⊿⊿½

Tomorrow Never Comes When he discovers his girlfriend has been unfaithful, a guy goes berserk and eventually finds himself in a stand-off with the police. Violent.
1977 109m/C Oliver Reed, Susan George, Raymond Burr, John Ireland, Stephen McHattie, Donald Pleasence; *D:* Peter Collinson. VHS, Beta $79.95 *UNI, HHE* ⊿½

Tomorrow's Child Made-for-television drama about in vitro fertilization (test-tube babies) and surrogate motherhood.
1982 100m/C Stephanie Zimbalist, William Atherton, Bruce Davison, Ed Flanders, Salome Jens, James Shigeta, Susan Oliver, Arthur Hill; *D:* Joseph Sargent. VHS, Beta $59.98 *FOX* ⊿⊿

Tomorrow's Children An alarmist melodrama warning against the threat of government-induced female sterilization asks the question: if a woman's family is weird, should her tubes be tied?
1934 55m/B Sterling Holloway, Diana Sinclair, Sarah Padden, Don Douglas; *D:* Crane Wilbur. VHS, Beta $16.95 *SNC, NOS, VYY* ⊿

The Tongfather The Tongfather is a ruthless crime boss who leads a Chinese opium ring. An undercover agent sets out to bring him down.
1978 (R) 92m/C VHS *NO* ⊿

Tongs: An American Nightmare Chinese-American street gangs in Chinatown battle over turf and drug shipments.
1988 (R) 80m/C Ian Anthony Leung, Christopher O'Conner, Simon Yam; *D:* Philip Chan. VHS, Beta $29.95 *ACA* ⊿

Toni An Italian worker falls for his landlady and they make plans to marry. A grim turn of events, however, brings tragic consequences. Based on the lives of several townsfolk in the village of Les Martiques, the film was shot in the town and members of the local populace were used as characters. In French with English subtitles.
1934 90m/B *FR* Charles Blavette, Jenny Helia, Edouard Delmont, Celia Montalvan; *D:* Jean Renoir. VHS, Beta $24.95 *DVT* ⊿⊿½

Tonight and Every Night Cabaret singer and RAF pilot fall in love during World War II. Her music hall post puts her in the midst of Nazi bombing, and her dedication to

her song and dance career puts a strain on the romance. Imaginative production numbers outweigh pedestrian storyline. ♫Cry and You Cry Alone; What Does an English Girl Think of a Yank; Anywhere; The Boy I Left Behind; You Excite Me; Tonight and Every Night.
1945 92m/C Rita Hayworth, Lee Bowman, Janet Blair, Marc Platt, Leslie Brooks; *D:* Victor Saville. VHS, Beta $19.95 *COL* ⊿⊿½

Tonight for Sure Coppola made this nudie, his first film, as a student at UCLA. Two men, one who spies on women and the other who imagines nude women everywhere, plan an escapade. Music by Carmine Coppola.
1961 66m/B *D:* Francis Ford Coppola. VHS, Beta $29.95 *VYY* ⊿½

Tonio Kroger A young writer travels through Europe in search of intellectual and sensual relationships and a home that will suit him. He must balance freedom and responsibility. Works best if one is familiar with the Thomas Mann novel on which film is based. In German with English subtitles.
1965 92m/B *GE* Jean-Claude Brialy, Nadja Tiller, Gert Frobe; *D:* Rolf Thiele. VHS, Beta $29.95 *VYY, APD, GLV* ⊿⊿

Tonka A children's story about a wild horse tamed by a young Indian, only to have it recruited for the Battle of Little Bighorn. Mineo is fine as the Indian brave determined to be reunited with his steed. The film also makes a laudable effort to portray the Indians as a dignified race. The movie, however, stumbles at its conclusion and is contrived throughout. *AKA:* A Horse Named Comanche.
1958 97m/C Sal Mineo, Phil Carey, Jerome Courtland; *D:* Lewis R. Foster. VHS, Beta $69.95 *DIS* ⊿⊿½

The Tonto Kid Action-packed western featuring Rex Bell.
1935 56m/B Rex Bell, Ruth Mix, Buzz Barton, Joseph Girard, Jack Rockwell, Murdock McQuarrie; *D:* Harry Fraser. VHS, Beta $19.95 *NOS, DVT, VDM* ⊿

Tony Draws a Horse An eight-year old draws an anatomically correct horse on the door of his father's office, leading to a rift between the parents as they argue how to handle the heartbreak of precociousness. Somewhat uneven but engaging comedy, based on a play by Lesley Storm.
1951 90m/B Cecil Parker, Anne Crawford, Derek Bond, Barbara Murray, Mervyn Johns, Barbara Everest, David Hurst; *D:* John Paddy Carstairs. VHS $19.95 *NOS* ⊿⊿

Tony Rome The Marvin H. Albert private eye agency investigates a millionaire's daughter's disappearance and her involvement in organized crime. Entertaining and complex plot, although the cast is a numbingly large one.
1967 110m/C Frank Sinatra, Jill St. John, Simon Oakland, Gena Rowlands, Richard Conte, Lloyd Bochner, Jeffrey Lynn, Sue Lyon; *D:* Gordon Douglas. VHS, Beta $59.98 *FOX* ⊿⊿½

Too Beautiful for You A successful car salesman, married for years to an extraordinarily beautiful woman, finds himself head over heels for his frumpy secretary. Depardieu plays the regular guy who finds he's never believed in the love and fidelity of a woman he thinks is too beautiful for him. In French with English subtitles. *AKA:* Trop Belle Pour Toi.
1988 (R) 91m/C *FR* Gerard Depardieu, Josiane Balasko, Carol Bouquet, Roland Blanche; *W/D:* Bertrand Blier. VHS $79.95 *ORI, FXL, FCT* ⊿⊿

Too Hot to Handle Two rival photographers searching for a beautiful lady-pilot's missing brother wind up in Brazil, where they encounter a dangerous tribe of voodoo types. Amusing, if exaggerated, picture of the lengths to which reporters will go for a story. Classic Gable.
1938 105m/B Clark Gable, Myrna Loy, Walter Pidgeon, Walter Connolly, Leo Carrillo, Virginia Weidler; *D:* Jack Conway. VHS $19.98 *MGM, FCT* ⊿⊿⊿

Too Hot to Handle Voluptuous lady contract killer fights against the mob with all the weapons at her disposal. Filmed on location in Manila.
1976 88m/C Cheri Caffaro, Aharon Ipale, Vic Diaz, Corinne Calvet; *D:* Don Schain. VHS, Beta $39.98 *WAR* ⊿

Too Late for Tears An honest husband and his not so honest wife stumble on a load of mob-stolen cash and become entangled in a web of deceit and murder as the wife resorts to increasingly desperate measures to keep her newfound fortune. Atmospheric and entertaining film noir albeit sometimes confusing. *AKA:* Killer Bait.
1949 99m/B Lizabeth Scott, Don DeFore, Dan Duryea, Arthur Kennedy, Kristine Miller, Barry Kelley, Denver Pyle; *D:* Byron Haskin. VHS, Beta $16.95 *SNC, VDM, NOS* ⊿⊿⊿

Too Late the Hero Unlikely band of allied soldiers battle Japanese force entrenched in the Pacific during WWII. Rousing adventure, fine cast. *AKA:* Suicide Run.
1970 (PG) 133m/C Michael Caine, Cliff Robertson, Henry Fonda, Ian Bannen, Harry Andrews, Denholm Elliott; *D:* Robert Aldrich. VHS, Beta $14.98 *FOX* ⊿⊿⊿

Too Many Crooks A British spoof of crime syndicate films. Crooks try to extort, but bungle the job. Terry-Thomas is fun, as always.
1959 85m/B *GB* Terry-Thomas, Brenda de Banzie, George Cole; *D:* Mario Zampi. VHS, Beta *NO* ⊿⊿

Too Many Girls Beautiful heiress goes to a small New Mexico college to escape from a cadre of gold-digging suitors. Passable adaptation of the successful Rodgers and Hart Broadway show, with many original cast members and the original stage director. Lucy and Desi met while making this film, and married shortly after. ♫Spic and Spanish; Heroes in the Fall; Pottawatomie; 'Cause We All Got Cake; Love Never Went to College; Look Out; I Didn't Know What Time It Was; The Conga; You're Nearer.
1940 85m/B Lucille Ball, Richard Carlson, Eddie Bracken, Ann Miller, Desi Arnaz Sr., Hal LeRoy, Libby Bennett, Frances Langford, Van Johnson; *D:* George Abbott; *M:* Richard Rodgers, Lorenz Hart. VHS, Beta, LV $14.98 *RKO, TTC* ⊿⊿½

Too Much Sun A dying man can prevent his fortune from falling into the hands of a corrupt priest simply by having one of his two children produce an heir. The problem is, they're both gay!
1990 (R) 97m/C Robert Downey Jr., Ralph Macchio, Eric Idle, Andrea Martin, Laura Ernst, Jim Haynie; *D:* Robert Downey. VHS, LV $89.95 *COL* ⊿½

Too Pretty to Be Honest Four French girls witness a robbery. When they discover the thief's identity they decide to rip him off. In French with subtitles.
1972 95m/C *FR* Jane Birkin, Bernadette LaFont; *D:* Richard Balducci. VHS, Beta $39.95 *FCT* ⊿⊿

Too Scared to Scream Policeman and an undercover agent team up to solve a bizarre series of murders at a Manhattan apartment house.

1985 (R) 104m/C Mike Connors, Anne Archer, Leon Isaac Kennedy, John Heard, Ian McShane, Maureen O'Sullivan, Murray Hamilton; **D:** Tony LoBianco. **VHS, Beta** $79.98 *LIV, VES* ℤ½

Too Shy to Try A incredibly shy man meets his dream girl, and enrolls in a psychology course to overcome his ineptitude. A ribald, slapstick French comedy.
1982 (PG) 89m/C *FR* Pierre Richard, Aldo Maccione; **D:** Pierre Richard. **VHS, Beta** $29.98 *SUE* ℤℤ

Too Wise Wives A story of would-be marital infidelity and misunderstandings. Silent.
1921 90m/C Louis Calhern, Claire Windsor; **D:** Lois Weber. **VHS, Beta** $57.95 *GVV* ℤℤ

The Toolbox Murders Unknown psychotic murderer brutally claims victims one at a time, leaving police mystified and townsfolk terrified. Sick and exploitative, with predictably poor production values.
1978 (R) 93m/C Cameron Mitchell, Pamelyn Ferdin, Wesley Eure, Nicholas Beauvy, Aneta Corseaut, Tim Donnelly, Evelyn Guerrero; **D:** Dennis Donnelly. **VHS, Beta** $19.95 *UHV, VTR* ℤ

Tootsie A stubborn, unemployed actor disguises himself as a woman to secure a part on a soap opera. As his popularity on television mounts, his love life becomes increasingly soap operatic. Hoffman is delightful, as is the rest of the stellar cast. Laserdisc version features audio commentary by director Sidney Pollack, behind the scenes footage and photographs, and complete coverage of Tootsie's production.
1982 (PG) 110m/C Dustin Hoffman, Jessica Lange, Teri Garr, Dabney Coleman, Bill Murray, Charles Durning, Geena Davis; **D:** Sydney Pollack. Academy Awards '82: Best Supporting Actress (Lange); Nominations: Best Actor (Hoffman), Best Cinematography, Best Director (Pollack), Best Film Editing, Best Original Screenplay, Best Picture, Best Song ("It Might Be You"), Best Sound, Best Supporting Actress (Garr); British Academy Awards '83: Best Actor (Hoffman); Golden Globe Awards '83: Best Actor—Musical/Comedy (Hoffman), Best Film—Musical/Comedy, Best Supporting Actress (Lange). **VHS, Beta, LV** $29.95 *COL, VYG, CRC* ℤℤℤℤ

Top Gun Young Navy pilots compete against one another on the ground and in the air at the elite Fighter Weapons School. Cruise isn't bad as a maverick who comes of age in Ray Bans, but Edwards shines as his buddy. Awesome aerial photography and high-cal beefcake divert from the contrived plot and stock characters. The Navy subsequently noticed an increased interest in fighter pilots. Features Berlin's Oscar-winning song "Take My Breath Away."
1986 (PG) 109m/C Tom Cruise, Kelly McGillis, Val Kilmer, Tom Skerritt, Anthony Edwards, Meg Ryan, Rick Rossovich, Michael Ironside, Barry Tubb, Whip Hubley, John Stockwell, Tim Robbins; **D:** Tony Scott. Academy Awards '86: Best Song ("Take My Breath Away"); Nominations: Best Film Editing, Best Sound; People's Choice Awards '87: Best Film. **VHS, Beta, LV, SVS, 8mm** $14.95 *PAR* ℤℤ½

Top Hat Ginger isn't impressed by Fred's amorous attentions since she's mistaken him for a friend's other half. Many believe it to be the duo's best film together. Score by Irving Berlin makes this one a classic Hollywood musical. Look for a young Lucille Ball as a clerk in a flower shop. ♫Cheek to Cheek; Top Hat, White Tie and Tails; Isn't This A Lovely Day; The Piccolino; No Strings.
1935 97m/B Fred Astaire, Ginger Rogers, Erik Rhodes, Helen Broderick, Edward Everett Horton, Eric Blore, Lucille Ball; **D:** Mark Sandrich. **VHS, Beta, LV, 8mm** $14.98 *TTC, RKO, VID* ℤℤℤℤ

Top of the Heap A cop is denied a promotion and gets angry. Deciding to chuck the laws of due process, he goes on a criminal-killing rampage.
1972 (R) 91m/C Christopher St. John, Paula Kelly, Patrick MacVey; **D:** Christopher St. John. **VHS, Beta** *NO* ℤ

Top Secret! Unlikely musical farce parodies spy movies and Elvis Presley films. Young American rock Nick Rivers star goes to Europe on goodwill tour and becomes involved with Nazis, the French Resistance, an American refugee, and more. Sophisticated it isn't. From the creators of "Airplane!"
1984 (PG) 90m/C Val Kilmer, Lucy Gutteridge, Christopher Villiers, Omar Sharif, Peter Cushing, Jeremy Kemp, Michael Gough; **D:** Jim Abrahams, Jerry Zucker, David Zucker. **VHS, Beta, LV** $14.95 *PAR* ℤℤℤ

Topaz American CIA agent and French intelligence agent combine forces to find information about Russian espionage in Cuba. Cerebral and intriguing, but not classic Hitchcock. Based on the novel by Leon Uris. Laser disc video release includes two alternate endings.
1969 (PG) 126m/C John Forsythe, Frederick Stafford, Philippe Noiret, Karin Dor, Michel Piccoli; **D:** Alfred Hitchcock. **VHS, Beta, LV** $19.95 *MCA* ℤℤℤ

Topaze A shy, depressed teacher is fired from his job at a private school and takes a new job, unaware that his boss is being him in a business scam. From the French play by Marcel Pagnol. An American version was also filmed in 1933; Pagnol produced his own version in '51. In French with English subtitles.
1933 92m/B *FR* Louis Jouvet, Edwige Feuillere, Marcel Vallee; **D:** Louis Gasnier; **W:** Marcel Pagnol. **VHS, Beta** $59.95 *INT, FOX, TAM* ℤℤℤ

Topaze American adaptation of the Marcel Pagnol play, about an innocent, doltish schoolmaster who becomes the unknowing front for a baron's illegal business scam. Remade in two French versions, in 1933, and in 1951 by Pagnol.
1933 127m/B John Barrymore, Myrna Loy, Jobyna Howland, Jackie Searl; **D:** Harry D'Abbadie D'Arrast. **VHS, Beta, LV** $39.98 *FOX* ℤℤℤ

Topaze After losing his job, a pathetic school teacher gets involved with the mob and winds up a powerful businessman. Remake of two earlier versions, one French and one American. Based on the play by director Pagnol. In French with English subtitles.
1951 95m/B *FR* Fernandel, Helen Perdriere, Pierre Larquey; **D:** Marcel Pagnol. **VHS, Beta** $29.95 *DVT, APD, TAM* ℤℤℤ½

Topkapi An international bevy of thieves can't resist the treasures of the famed Topkapi Palace Museum, an impregnable fortress filled with wealth and splendor. Comic thriller based on Erie Ambler's "The Light of Day."
1964 122m/C Melina Mercouri, Maximilian Schell, Peter Ustinov, Robert Morley, Akim Tamiroff; **D:** Jules Dassin. **VHS, Beta** $59.98 *FOX* ℤℤℤ

Topper George and Marion Kerby return as ghosts after a fatal car accident, determined to assist their pal Cosmo Topper. Immensely popular at the box office, followed by "Topper Takes a Trip" and "Topper Returns." The series uses trick photography and special effects to complement the comedic scripts. Inspired a television series and remade in 1979 as television movie. Also available colorized.

1937 97m/B Cary Grant, Roland Young, Constance Bennett, Billie Burke, Eugene Pallette; **D:** Norman Z. MacLeod. **VHS, Beta** $9.95 *MED, CCB* ℤℤℤ½

Topper Returns Cosmo Topper helps ghost find the man who mistakenly murdered her and warns her friend, the intended victim. Humorous conclusion to the trilogy preceded by "Topper" and "Topper Takes a Trip." Followed by a television series. Also available colorized.
1941 87m/B Roland Young, Joan Blondell, Dennis O'Keefe, Carole Landis, Eddie Anderson, H.B. Warner, Billie Burke; **D:** Roy Del Ruth. **VHS, Beta, LV, 3/4U, Special order formats** $16.95 *SNC, NOS, CAB* ℤℤℤ

Topper Takes a Trip Cosmo Topper and his wife have falling out and ghosts Kerby help them get back together. The special effects sequences are especially funny. Followed by "Topper Returns." Also available colorized.
1939 85m/B Constance Bennett, Roland Young, Billie Burke, Franklin Pangborn, Alan Mowbray; **D:** Norman Z. MacLeod. **VHS, Beta** $14.95 *MED* ℤℤℤ

Topsy Turvy A comedy about reckless romance and not much else.
1984 (R) 90m/C Lisbet Dahl, Ebbe Rode; **D:** Edward Fleming. **VHS, Beta** $69.98 *LIV, VES* ℤℤ½

Tor Medieval barbarian endeavors to free an enslaved village from a band of murderous hoodlums.
1964 94m/C Joe Robinson, Bella Cortez, Harry Baird; **D:** Antonio Leonuiola. **VHS, Beta** $59.95 *TWE* ℤ½

Tora! Tora! Tora! The story of events leading up to December 7, 1941, is retold by three directors from both Japanese and American viewpoints in this tense, large-scale production. Well-documented and realistic treatment of the Japanese attack on Pearl Harbor that brought the US into WWII; notable for its good photography but lacks a storyline equal to its epic intentions.
1970 (G) 144m/C Martin Balsam, Soh Yomamura, Joseph Cotten, E.G. Marshall, Tatsuya Mihashi, Wesley Addy, Jason Robards Jr., James Whitmore, Leon Ames, George Macready; **D:** Richard Fleischer, Toshio Masuda, Kinji Fukasaku; **M:** Jerry Goldsmith. Academy Awards '70: Best Visual Effects; Nominations: Best Art Direction/Set Decoration, Best Cinematography, Best Film Editing; National Board of Review Awards '70: 10 Best Films of the Year. **VHS, Beta, LV** $14.98 *FOX, TLF, HMV* ℤℤ

Torch Song In this muddled melodrama, a tough, demanding Broadway actress meets her match when she is offered true love by a blind pianist. Contains a couple of notoriously inept musical numbers. Made to show off Crawford's figure at age 50. Crawford's singing in the movie is dubbed.
1953 90m/C Joan Crawford, Michael Wilding, Marjorie Rambeau, Gig Young, Harry Morgan, Dorothy Patrick, Benny Rubin, Nancy Gates; **D:** Charles Walters. **VHS, LV** $19.98 *MGM* ℤℤ

Torch Song Trilogy Adapted from Fierstein's hit Broadway play about a gay man who "just wants to be loved." Still effective, but the rewritten material loses something in the translation to the screen. Bancroft heads a strong cast with a finely shaded performance as Fierstein's mother.
1988 (R) 126m/C Anne Bancroft, Matthew Broderick, Harvey Fierstein, Brian Kerwin, Karen Young, Charles Pierce; **D:** Paul Bogart. **VHS, Beta, LV** *COL* ℤℤ½

Torchlight A young couple's life begins to crumble when a wealthy art dealer teaches them how to free base cocaine. Heavy-handed treatment of a subject that's been tackled with more skill elsewhere.
1985 (R) 90m/C Pamela Sue Martin, Steve Railsback, Ian McShane, Al Corley, Rita Taggart; *D:* Thomas J. Wright. **VHS, Beta, LV $19.98** *SUE* ✂️

Torero A young man becomes a bullfighter to overcome his fear of bulls. *AKA:* Bullfighter.
1956 89m/B *MX* Luis Procuna, Manolete, Dolores Del Rio, Carlos Arruza; *D:* Carlos Velo. **VHS, Beta $44.95** *MAD* ✂️

Torment Tragic triangle has young woman in love with fellow student and murdered by sadistic teacher. Atmospheric tale hailed by many as Sjoberg's finest film. Ingmar Bergman's first filmed script. In Swedish with English subtitles. *AKA:* Hets; Frenzy.
1944 90m/B *SW D:* Alf Sjoberg; *W:* Ingmar Bergman. **VHS, Beta $69.95** *SUE, TAM, NLC* ✂️✂️✂️

Torment A mild-mannered fellow is secretly a mass murderer specializing in young lovers. He struggles to hide his secret as his daughter approaches dating age and a relentless detective gets closer to the truth. A low-budget slasher.
1985 (R) 85m/C Taylor Gilbert, William Witt, Eve Brenner; *D:* Samson & Hopkins, John Aslanian. **VHS, Beta $19.95** *STE, NWV* ✂️

Tormented Man pushes his mistress out of a lighthouse, killing her. Her ethereal body parts return to haunt him.
1960 75m/B Richard Carlson, Susan Gordon, Juli Reding; *D:* Bert I. Gordon. **VHS $16.95** *SNC* ✂️½

The Tormentors Vaguely neo-Nazi gangs rape and murder a man's family, and he kills them all in revenge.
198? (R) 78m/C James Craig, Anthony Eisley, Chris Nole; *D:* Boris Eagle. **VHS, Beta** NO Woof!

Torn Allegiance An Australian anti-war epic set in the Boer War about the effects of war on one family and their fight for survival on the veldt.
1984 102m/C *AU* **VHS, Beta $79.95** *PSM, FCT* ✂️

Torn Apart Traditional Middle East hatreds undermine the love affair between two young people. Excellent performances from the principals highlight this drama. Adapted from the Chayin Zeldis novel "A Forbidden Love."
1989 (R) 95m/C Adrian Pasdar, Cecilia Peck, Machram Huri, Arnon Zadok, Barry Primus; *D:* Jack Fisher. **VHS, Beta $89.95** *WAR, BTV* ✂️✂️

Torn Between Two Lovers A beautiful married woman has an affair with an architect while on a trip. Remick is enjoyable to watch, but it's a fairly predictable yarn. Made for television.
1979 100m/C Lee Remick, Joseph Bologna, George Peppard, Giorgio Tozzi; *D:* Delbert Mann. **VHS $59.95** *LIV* ✂️

Torn Curtain American scientist poses as a defector to East Germany in order to uncover details of the Soviet missile program. He and his fiancee, who follows him behind the Iron Curtain, attempt to escape to freedom. Derivative and uninvolving.
1966 125m/C Paul Newman, Julie Andrews, Lila Kedrova, David Opatoshu; *D:* Alfred Hitchcock. **VHS, Beta, LV $19.95** *MCA* ✂️✂️

Tornado An army sergeant revolts against his superiors and the enemy when his captain leaves him stranded in Vietnam.
1983 90m/C Timothy Brent, Tony Marsina, Alan Collins. **VHS, Beta $69.98** *LIV* ✂️

Torpedo Alley A guilt-ridden WWII Navy pilot feels responsible for the deaths of his crew. After the war, he joins a submarine crew and gradually learns to deal with his guilt. Average drama with plenty of submarine footage.
1953 84m/B Dorothy Malone, Mark Stevens, Charles Winninger, Bill Williams; *D:* Lew Landers. **VHS $19.98** *REP* ✂️✂️

Torpedo Attack Greek sailors, in an outdated submarine, bravely but hopelessly attack Mussolini's Italy during World War II.
1972 88m/C *GR* John Ferris, Sidney Kazan; *D:* George Law. **VHS, Beta $39.95** *LIV* ✂️

Torpedo Run Standard submarine melodramatics, about a U.S. sub that must torpedo a Japanese aircraft carrier which holds some of the crew's family members. Sometimes slow, generally worthwhile.
1958 98m/C Glenn Ford, Ernest Borgnine, Dean Jones, Diane Brewster, L.Q. Jones; *D:* Joseph Pevney. **VHS, Beta $19.98** *MGM* ✂️✂️

Torrents of Spring Based on an Ivan Turgenev story, this lavishly filmed and costumed drama concerns a young Russian aristocrat circa 1840 who is torn between two women. Predictably, one is a good-hearted innocent, the other a scheming seductress.
1990 (PG-13) 102m/C Timothy Hutton, Nastassia Kinski, Valeria Golino, William Forsythe, Urbano Barberini, Francesca De Sapio, Jacques Herlin; *D:* Jerzy Skolimowski. **VHS, Beta, LV $89.99** *HBO* ✂️✂️

Torso Crazed psychosexual killer stalks beautiful women and dismembers them. Fairly bloodless and uninteresting, in spite of lovely Kendall. Italian title translates: The Bodies Showed Signs of Carnal Violence— quite an understatement for people missing arms and legs. Screenplay by Ernesto Gastaldi and Sergio Martino. *AKA:* I Corpi Presentano Tracce Di Violenza Carnale.
1973 (R) 91m/C *IT* Suzy Kendall, Tina Aumont, John Richardson; *D:* Sergio Martino. **VHS, Beta $79.95** *MPI, PSM* Woof!

Tortilla Flat Based on the John Steinbeck novel of the same name, two buddies, Tracy and Garfield, struggle to make their way on the wrong side of the tracks in California. Garfield gets a break by inheriting a couple of houses, Tracy schemes to rip-off a rich, but eccentric, dog owner. In the meantime, both fall for the same girl, Lamarr, in perhaps the finest role of her career. Great performances from all, especially Morgan.
1942 105m/B Spencer Tracy, Hedy Lamarr, John Garfield, Frank Morgan, Akim Tamiroff, Sheldon Leonard, John Qualen, Donald Meek, Connie Gilchrist; *D:* Victor Fleming. **VHS $19.98** *MGM, CCB* ✂️✂️✂️

Torture Chamber of Baron Blood Baron with gorgeous thirst for the red stuff is reanimated and lots of innocent bystanders meet a grisly fate in this spaghetti gorefest. Familiar story has that certain Bava feel. *AKA:* Baron Blood.
1972 (PG) 90m/C *IT* Joseph Cotten, Elke Sommer, Massimo Girotti, Rada Rassimov; *D:* Mario Bava. **VHS, Beta $19.99** *HBO* ✂️✂️½

The Torture Chamber of Dr. Sadism Decapitated and drawn and quartered for sacrificing twelve virgins, the evil Count Regula is pieced together forty years later to continue his wicked ways. Great fun, terrific art direction. Very loosely based on Poe's "The Pit and the Pendulum." Beware of the heavily edited video version. *AKA:* Blood Demon; Castle of the Walking Dead; Die Schlangengrube und das Pendel.

1969 120m/C *GE* Christopher Lee, Karin Dor, Lex Barker, Carl Lange, Vladimir Medar, Christiane Rucker, Dieter Eppler; *D:* Harald Reinl. **VHS, Beta** NO ✂️✂️½

Torture Dungeon Director Milligan tortures audience with more mindless medieval pain infliction from Staten Island.
1970 (R) 80m/C Jeremy Brooks, Susan Cassidy; *D:* Andy Milligan. **VHS** NO ✂️

Torture Garden A sinister man presides over an unusual sideshow where people can see what is in store if they allow the evil side of their personalities to take over. Written by Robert Bloch ("Psycho") and based on four of his short stories.
1967 93m/C *GB* Jack Palance, Burgess Meredith, Peter Cushing, Beverly Adams; *D:* Freddie Francis. **VHS, Beta, LV $59.95** *COL* ✂️✂️

The Torture of Silence A simple little drama about a doctor's neglected wife seeking out the doctor's best friend for love, remade by Gance again in 1932; both originally titled "Mater Dolorosa." Silent. *AKA:* Master Dolorosa.
1917 55m/B *D:* Abel Gance. **VHS, Beta $44.95** *FCT* ✂️✂️½

Torture Ship Director Halperin, who earlier made the minor horror classic "White Zombie," was all at sea in this becalmed thriller about a mad doctor who uses convicts for glandular experiment in his shipboard laboratory. Based on the short story "A Thousand Deaths" by Jack London.
1939 57m/B Lyle Talbot, Irving Pichel, Jacqueline Wells, Sheila Bromley; *D:* Victor Halperin. **VHS $15.95** *NOS, LOO* ✂️½

Torture Train Mayhem, murder and knife-wielding psychosis occurs on board a train.
1983 (R) 78m/C Patty Edwards, Kay Beal. **VHS, Beta $59.95** *JEF* ✂️½

Total Exposure Total idiocy involving unclad babes and hormonally imbalanced men in blackmail and murder. 1990 Playboy Playmate Deborah Driggs proves there is life of sorts after playmatedom.
1991 (R) 96m/C Michael Nouri, Season Hubley, Christian Bocher, Robert Prentiss, Deborah Driggs, Jeff Conaway; *D:* John Quinn. **VHS, LV $89.95** *NCP, PIA* ✂️

Total Recall Mind-bending sci-fi movie set in the 21st century. Construction worker Schwarzenegger travels to Mars to discover his true identity after learning that his memories have been artificially altered. Intriguing plot and spectacular special effects. Laced with graphic violence. Based on Phillip K. Dick's "We Can Remember It For You Wholesale."
1990 (R) 113m/C Arnold Schwarzenegger, Rachel Ticotin, Sharon Stone, Michael Ironside, Ronny Cox, Roy Brocksmith, Marshall Bell, Mel Johnson Jr.; *D:* Paul Verhoeven; *W:* Gary Goldman; *M:* Jerry Goldsmith. Academy Awards '90: Best Visual Effects; Nominations: Best Sound. **VHS, Beta, LV, 8mm $19.95** *IME, LIV, TLF* ✂️✂️✂️

Toto le Heros A bitter old man, who as a child fantasized that he was a secret agent named Toto, harbors deep resentment over not living the life he is convinced he should have had. He still maintains his childhood fantasy that he and his rich neighbor, who was born on the same day in the same hospital, were switched at birth in the confusion of a fire in the maternity ward. He was so convinced of this as a child that he even barged into his neighbors birthday party demanding that he be recognized as an heir and given the boy's birthday presents. A series of flashbacks and fast forwards show

glimpses of his life, not necessarily as it was, but how he perceived it. He also pines over his long-dead sister and her look-alike, a love whom he lost to the rich neighbor. Although this film sounds complex, it is actually very clear and fluid. A mix of comedy and tragedy, lots of ironic twists, and precise visuals. In French with English subtitles. *AKA:* Toto the Hero.
1991 (PG-13) 90m/C *FR* Michel Bouquet, Jo De Backer, Thomas Godet, Mireille Perrier, Sandrine Blancke, Didier Ferney, Hugo Harold Harrisson; *W/D:* Jaco Van Dormael. **VHS, Beta $89.95** *PAR, BTV 𝔍𝔍𝔍*

The Touch Straightforward story of a woman who is satisfied with her husband until the arrival of a stranger. The stranger soon has her yearning for a life she has never known. Bergman's first English film lacks the sophistication of his earlier work. *AKA:* Be Roringen.
1971 (R) 112m/C *SW* Bibi Andersson, Elliott Gould, Max von Sydow; *D:* Ingmar Bergman. **VHS, Beta** *FOX 𝔍 ½*

Touch & Go Three beautiful women commit grand larceny in order to raise funds for underprivileged children.
1980 (PG) 92m/C *AU* Wendy Hughes; *D:* Peter Maxwell. **VHS, Beta $29.95** *VID 𝔍*

Touch and Go Sentimental drama about a self-interested hockey pro who learns about love and giving through a young delinquent and his attractive mother.
1986 (R) 101m/C Michael Keaton, Maria Conchita Alonso, Ajay Naidu, Maria Tucci, Max Wright; *D:* Robert Mandel. **VHS, Beta, LV $14.99** *HBO 𝔍 ½*

Touch Me Not A neurotic secretary is used by an industrial spy to gain information on her boss. Weak thriller. *AKA:* The Hunted.
1974 (PG) 84m/C *GB* Lee Remick, Michael Hinz, Ivan Desny, Ingrid Garbo; *D:* Douglas Fifthian. **VHS** *NO 𝔍𝔍*

A Touch of Class Married American insurance adjustor working in London plans quick and uncommitted affair but finds his heart doesn't obey the rules. Jackson and Segal create sparkling record of a growing relationship.
1973 (PG) 105m/C George Segal, Glenda Jackson, Paul Sorvino, Hildegarde Neil, K. Callan, Mary Barclay, Cec Linder; *D:* Melvin Frank. Academy Awards '73: Best Actress (Jackson); Nominations: Best Picture, Best Song ("All That Love Went to Waste"), Best Story & Screenplay, Best Original Score; Golden Globe Awards '74: Best Actor—Musical/Comedy (Segal), Best Actress—Musical/Comedy (Jackson). **VHS, Beta $9.99** *MED 𝔍𝔍𝔍*

Touch of Evil Stark, perverse story of murder, kidnapping and police corruption in Mexican border town. Welles portrays a police chief who invents evidence to convict the guilty. Filled with innovative photography reminiscent of "Citizen Kane." (Filmed by Russell Metty). Score by Henry Mancini.
1958 108m/B Charlton Heston, Orson Welles, Janet Leigh, Joseph Calleia, Akim Tamiroff, Marlene Dietrich, Ray Collins, Dennis Weaver, Zsa Zsa Gabor, Joseph Cotten, Mercedes McCambridge; *D:* Orson Welles. **VHS, Beta, LV $29.95** *MCA 𝔍𝔍𝔍𝔍*

The Touch of Satan Lost on the road, a young man meets a lovely young woman and is persuaded to stay at her nearby farmhouse. Things there are not as they seem, including the young woman—who turns out to be a very old witch. *AKA:* The Touch of Melissa; Night of the Demon; Curse of Melissa.
1970 (PG) 90m/C Michael Berry, Emby Mallay, Lee Amber, Yvonne Wilson, Jeanne Gerson; *D:* Don Henderson. **VHS, Beta** *NO 𝔍*

Touched Two young people struggle with the outside world after their escape from a mental institution. Although melodramatic and poorly scripted, the film is saved by fine performances by Hays and Beller.
1982 (R) 89m/C Robert Hays, Kathleen Beller, Ned Beatty, Gilbert Lewis; *D:* John Flynn. **VHS, Beta $59.95** *MED 𝔍𝔍*

Touched by Love The true story of a handicapped child who begins to communicate when her teacher suggests she write to Elvis Presley. Sincere and well performed. *AKA:* To Elvis, With Love.
1980 (PG) 95m/C Deborah Raffin, Diane Lane, Christina Raines, Clu Gulager, John Amos; *D:* Gus Trikonis; *M:* John Barry. **VHS, Beta $59.95** *COL 𝔍𝔍 ½*

Tough Assignment A reporter in the West discovers and infiltrates a gang of organized rustlers who are forcing butchers to buy inferior meat.
1949 64m/B Donald (Don "Red") Barry, Marjorie Steele, Steve Brodie. **VHS, Beta, LV** *𝔍*

Tough Enough A country-western singer and songwriter decides to finance his fledgling singing career by entering amateur boxing matches. Insipid and predictable, with fine cast wasted.
1987 (PG) 107m/C Dennis Quaid, Charlene Watkins, Warren Oates, Pam Grier, Stan Shaw, Bruce McGill, Wilford Brimley; *D:* Richard Fleischer. **VHS, Beta $59.98** *FOX 𝔍𝔍*

Tough Guy Based on the play by Bruce Walker, a London hood carouses, mugs, breaks hearts and personifies his generation's anxiety.
1953 73m/B *GB* James Kenney, Hermione Gingold, Joan Collins; *D:* Lewis Gilbert. **VHS, Beta $19.95** *UNI 𝔍*

Tough Guy Two undercover policemen battle local gangsters in a bid to smash their crime ring.
197? 90m/C Chen Ying, Charlie Chiang; *D:* Chieng Hung. **VHS, Beta** *NO 𝔍*

Tough Guys Two aging ex-cons, who staged America's last train robbery in 1961, try to come to terms with modern life after many years in prison. Amazed and hurt by the treatment of the elderly in the 1980s, frustrated with their inability to find something worthwhile to do, they begin to plan one last heist. Tailor-made for Lancaster and Douglas, who are wonderful. Script becomes cliched at end.
1986 (PG) 103m/C Burt Lancaster, Kirk Douglas, Charles Durning, Eli Wallach, Lyle Alzado, Dana Carvey; *D:* Jeff Kanew. **VHS, Beta, LV $19.95** *TOU 𝔍𝔍 ½*

Tough Guys Don't Dance Mailer directed this self-satiric mystery thriller from his own novel. A writer may have committed murder—but he can't remember. So he searches for the truth among various friends, enemies, lovers, and cohorts.
1987 (R) 110m/C Ryan O'Neal, Isabella Rossellini, Wings Hauser, Debra Sandlund, John Bedford Lloyd, Lawrence Tierney, Clarence Williams III; *D:* Norman Mailer; *M:* Angelo Badalamenti. **VHS, Beta, LV $19.95** *MED, CVS 𝔍𝔍 ½*

Tough Kid A bad kid with gang connections attempts to shield his boxer brother from corruption at the hands of the same gang. Poor production all around.
1939 61m/B Frankie Darro, Dick Purcell, Judith Allen, Lillian Elliot; *D:* Howard Bretherton. **VHS, Beta $16.95** *SNC 𝔍*

Tough to Handle ...And no picnic to watch, either. A reporter cracks a criminal racket that rips off lottery sweepstakes winners. A laughably inept production.

1937 58m/B Frankie Darro, Kane Richmond, Phyllis Fraser, Harry Worth; *D:* S. Roy Luby. **VHS $15.95** *NOS, LOO 𝔍 ½*

Tougher than Leather The rap triumvirate battles criminals, vigilante-style, in their home neighborhood. Poorly executed and exploitative fare.
1988 (R) 92m/C Run DMC, The Beastie Boys, Slick Rick, Richard Edson, Jenny Lumet; *D:* Rick Rubin. **VHS, Beta $89.95** *COL 𝔍*

Toughlove The parents of a juvenile delinquent organize a tough parental philosophy and a support group for other parents having a difficult time with their teens. Made for television.
1985 100m/C Lee Remick, Bruce Dern, Piper Laurie, Louise Latham, Dana Elcar, Jason Patric, Eric Schiff, Dedee Pfeiffer; *D:* Glenn Jordan. **VHS, Beta $39.95** *FRH 𝔍*

Tour of Duty Follows the trials that the members of an American platoon face daily during the Vietnam war. The pilot movie for a television series.
1987 93m/C Terence Knox, Stephen Caffrey, Joshua Maurer, Ramon Franco; *D:* Bill L. Norton. **VHS, Beta, LV $59.95** *NWV, HHE 𝔍𝔍 ½*

Tourist Trap While traveling through the desert, a couple's car has a flat. A woman's voice lures the man into an abandoned gas station, where he discovers that the voice belongs to a mannequin. Or is it? Not very interesting or suspenseful.
1979 (PG) 90m/C Tanya Roberts, Chuck Connors, Robin Sherwood; *D:* David Schmoeller. **VHS, Beta, LV $79.95** *PAR 𝔍*

Tournament Renoir's second-to-last silent film, in which Protestants and Catholics joust out their differences in era of Catherine de Medici. French title: "Le Tournoi dans la Cite."
1929 90m/B *FR* Aldo Nadi; *D:* Jean Renoir. **VHS, Beta $29.95** *FCT 𝔍𝔍 ½*

Toute Une Nuit Assorted people stumble melodramatically in and out of one another's lives on steamy summer night in Brussels. Fine combination of avant-garde technique and narrative. In French with English subtitles. *AKA:* All Night Long.
1982 90m/C *BE FR* Aurore Clement, Tcheky Karyo, Veronique Silver, Angelo Abazoglou, Natalia Akerman; *D:* Chantal Akerman; *W:* Andra Akers. **VHS $29.95** *WAC, FCT, TAM 𝔍𝔍𝔍*

Tower of Evil Anthropologists and treasure hunters unite in search of Phoenician hoard on Snape Island. Suddenly, inanimate bodies materialize. Seems the island's single inhabitant liked it quiet. Cult favorite despite uneven performances. So bad it's not bad. *AKA:* Horror on Snape Island; Beyond the Fog.
1972 (R) 86m/C *GB* Bryant Halliday, Jill Haworth, Jack Watson, Mark Edwards, George Coulouris; *D:* James O'Connolly. **VHS, Beta $59.95** *MPI Woof!*

The Tower of London Tells the story of Richard III (Rathbone), the English monarch who brutally executed the people who tried to get in his way of the throne. This melodrama was considered extremely graphic for its time, and some of the torture scenes had to be cut before it was released.
1939 93m/B Basil Rathbone, Boris Karloff, Barbara O'Neil, Ian Hunter, Vincent Price, Nan Grey, John Sutton, Leo G. Carroll, Miles Mander; *D:* Rowland V. Lee. **VHS $14.98** *MCA 𝔍𝔍 ½*

Tower of London A deranged lord (Price) murdering his way to the throne of England is eventually crowned Richard III. Sophisticated and well-made Poe-like thriller. More interesting as historic melodrama than as horror film. A remake of the 1939 version

T

starring Basil Rathbone, in which Price played a supporting role.
1962 79m/B Vincent Price, Michael Pate, Joan Freeman, Robert Brown; **D:** Roger Corman. **VHS, Beta** NO *J*

Tower of Screaming Virgins The Queen of France maintains a tower in which she has her lovers killed—after she makes love to them. An extremely loose adaptation of a Dumas novel; with English subtitles.
1968 89m/C GE Terry Torday, Jean Piat. **VHS, Beta, 8mm** $14.95 *VYY, VDM, SNC J*

Tower of Terror Woman escapes from a German concentration camp and takes refuge in a lighthouse. The proprietor sees in her an uncanny resemblance to his late wife, whom he killed, and soon plots to do away with her. Story hampered by poor acting.
1942 (NC-17) 62m/B GB Wilfred Lawson, Movita, Michael Rennie, Morland Graham, John Longden, George Woodbridge; **D:** Lawrence Huntington. **VHS, Beta** $16.95 *NOS, SNC J½*

The Towering Inferno Raging blaze engulfs the world's tallest skyscraper on the night of its glamorous dedication ceremonies. Allen had invented the disaster du jour genre two years earlier with "The Poseidon Adventure." Features a new but equally noteworthy cast.
1974 (PG) 165m/C Steve McQueen, Paul Newman, William Holden, Faye Dunaway, Fred Astaire, Jennifer Jones, Richard Chamberlain, Susan Blakely, O.J. Simpson, Robert Vaughn, Robert Wagner; **D:** John Guillermin, Irwin Allen; **M:** John Williams. Academy Awards '74: Best Cinematography, Best Film Editing, Best Song ("We May Never Love Like This Again"); Nominations: Best Art Direction/Set Decoration, Best Picture, Best Sound, Best Supporting Actor (Astaire), Best Original Score; Golden Globe Awards '75: Best Supporting Actor (Astaire). **VHS, Beta, LV** $19.98 *FOX JJ*

A Town Called Hell Two men hold an entire town hostage while looking for "Aguila," the Mexican revolutionary. Greed, evil, and violence take over. Shot in Spain. Whatever you call it, just stay out of it. **AKA:** A Town Called Bastard.
1972 (R) 95m/C GB SP Robert Shaw, Stella Stevens, Martin Landau, Telly Savalas, Fernando Rey; **D:** Robert Parrish. **VHS, Beta** $24.95 *WWV, GEM J*

A Town Like Alice An Australian miniseries based on a novel by Nevil Shute. The story follows women prisoners of war during World War II. Jean Paget is a British prisoner in the camps of Malaya when she meets and falls in love with a fellow prisoner, the rugged Australian, Joe. Separated by their captors, they reunite years later and try to see if their love has survived. Remake of a 1951 film of the same name that is also known as "Rape of Malaya."
1985 301m/C AU Bryan Brown, Helen Morse, Gordon Jackson; **D:** David Stevens. **VHS, Beta** $29.95 *SIG, NWV, IME JJ½*

Town that Dreaded Sundown A mad killer is on the loose in a small Arkansas town. Based on a true story, this famous 1946 murder spree remains an unsolved mystery.
1976 (R) 90m/C Ben Johnson, Andrew Prine, Dawn Wells; **D:** Charles B. Pierce. **VHS, Beta** $19.98 *WAR, OM JJ½*

Toxic Avenger Tongue-in-cheek, cult fave has 98-pound weakling fall into barrel of toxic waste to emerge as a lumbering, bloodthirsty hulk of sludge and mire. Two sequels followed: "Toxic Avenger Part II" and "Toxic Avenger Part III: The Last Temptation of Toxie."
1986 (R) 90m/C Mitchell Cohen, Andree Maranda, Jennifer Baptist; **D:** Michael Herz. **VHS, Beta, LV** $29.98 *VES, LIV JJ*

Toxic Avenger, Part 2 Sequel to "Toxic Avenger." Hulky slimer targets Japanese corporations that built toxic chemical dump in Tromaville. Followed by "Toxic Avenger Part III: The Last Temptation of Toxie."
1989 (R) 90m/C Ron Fazio, Phoebe Legere, Rick Collins; **D:** Michael Herz, Lloyd Kaufman. **VHS, Beta, LV** $14.95 *WAR J½*

Toxic Avenger, Part 3: The Last Temptation of Toxie Unemployed superhero is tempted by Devil to become greedy capitalist. Also available in an unrated version.
1989 (R) 102m/C Ron Fazio, Phoebe Legere, Rick Collins, Lisa Gaye, Jessica Dublin, John Altamura; **D:** Michael Herz, Lloyd Kaufman. **VHS** $89.98 *VES, LIV J½*

Toxic Zombies Pot farmers become crazy cannibals when the marijuana is sprayed with an untested chemical.
1989 90m/C **VHS, Beta** $99.97 *MON J*

The Toy Penniless reporter finds himself the new "toy" of the spoiled son of a multimillionaire oil man. Unfortunate casting of Pryor as the toy owned by Gleason, with heavy-handed lecturing about earning friends. Slow and terrible remake of the Pierre Richard comedy "Le Jouet."
1982 (PG) 99m/C Richard Pryor, Jackie Gleason, Ned Beatty, Wilfrid Hyde-White; **D:** Richard Donner. **VHS, Beta, LV, 8mm** $9.95 *COL J½*

Toy Soldiers A group of college students are held for ransom in a war-torn Central American country. When they escape, they join forces with a seasoned mercenary who leads them as a vigilante force.
1984 (R) 85m/C Cleavon Little, Jason Miller, Tim Robbins, Tracy Scoggins; **D:** David Fisher. **VHS, Beta, LV** $9.95 *NWV, STE J½*

Toy Soldiers This unlikely action tale stops short of being laughable but still has a fair share of silliness. South American narco-terrorists seize an exclusive boys' school. The mischievous students turn their talent for practical jokes to resistance fighting. Orbach has an uncredited cameo. Based on a novel by William P. Kennedy.
1991 (R) 104m/C Sean Astin, Wil Wheaton, Keith Coogan, Andrew Divoff, Denholm Elliott, Louis Gossett Jr.; **Cameos:** Jerry Orbach; **W/D:** Daniel Petrie. **VHS, Beta, LV, 8mm** $92.95 *COL, PIA JJ*

Toys Disappointingly earnest comedy about Leslie (Williams), the whimsical son of a toy manufacturer who must fight to keep the playful spirit of the factory alive after it passes into the hands of his deranged uncle (Gambon). This uncle is a general who attempts to transform the factory into an armaments plant. Leslie receives assistance in this battle from his sister Alsatia (Cusack) and his cousin Patrick (L.L. Cool J). Flat characters; generally falls short by trying too hard to send a message to viewers about the folly of war. Does have extremely vivid and intriguing visuals and special effects.
1992 (PG-13) 121m/C Robin Williams, Joan Cusack, Michael Gambon, L.L. Cool J., Robin Wright; **Cameos:** Donald O'Connor; **W/D:** Barry Levinson; **W:** Valerie Curtin. **VHS** $94.98 *FXV J½*

Toys in the Attic A man returns to his home in New Orleans with his child bride, where they will live with his two impoverished, spinster sisters. Toned-down version of the Lillian Hellman play.
1963 88m/B Dean Martin, Geraldine Page, Yvette Mimieux, Wendy Hiller, Gene Tierney, Nan Martin, Larry Gates, Frank Silvera; **D:** George Roy Hill; **W:** James Poe. **VHS** $19.98 *MGM JJ½*

Traces of Red Set in affluent Palm Beach, and filled with dead bodies, colorful suspects, and red herrings. The complex plot, often so serious it's funny, leads viewers through a convoluted series of events. Cop Jack Dobson (Belushi) is found dead in the opening scene; in homage to "Sunset Boulevard," his corpse acts as the narrator, a vehicle which unfortunately doesn't work as well here. He promises to recount the events leading up to his death which circle around a series of murders, and the people in his life who are possible suspects. Although Belushi's performance is average, Goldwyn, as Dobson's partner, shows off the talent he displayed in "Ghost."
1992 (R) 105m/C James Belushi, Lorraine Bracco, Tony Goldwyn, William Russ, Michelle Joyner, Joe Lisi, Jim Piddock; **D:** Andy Wolk. **VHS, LV** $92.99 *HBO JJ*

Track of the Moonbeast An American Indian uses mythology to capture the Moonbeast, a lizard-like creature that is roaming the deserts of New Mexico.
1976 90m/C Chase Cordell, Donna Leigh Drake; **D:** Richard Ashe. **VHS, Beta** $49.95 *PSM JJ*

Track of the Vampire Half an hour of leftover footage from a Yugoslavian vampire movie stuck into the story of a California painter who kills his models. Gripping and atmospheric, but disjointed. **AKA:** Blood Bath.
1966 80m/B YU William Campbell, Jonathan Haze, Sid Haig, Marissa Mathes, Lori Saunders, Sandra Knight; **D:** Stephanie Rothman, Jack Hill. **VHS** *SNC, GNS J½*

Track 29 A confusing black comedy about a lonely woman, her husband who has a model train fetish, and a stranger who claims to be her son. Filmed in North Carolina.
1988 (R) 90m/C Theresa Russell, Gary Oldman, Christopher Lloyd, Colleen Camp, Sandra Bernhard, Seymour Cassel, Leon Rippy, Vance Colvig; **D:** Nicolas Roeg. **VHS** $14.95 *MGM, CAN J½*

The Tracker HBO western about a retired gunman/tracker who must again take up arms. His college-educated son joins him as he searches for a murdering religious fanatic. Fairly decent for the genre. Made for cable television. **AKA:** Dead or Alive.
1988 102m/C Kris Kristofferson, Scott Wilson, Mark Moses, David Huddleston; **D:** John Guillermin. **VHS, Beta** $89.99 *HBO JJ½*

The Trackers A frontier man searches for the people who kidnapped his daughter and killed his son. He is joined by a cocky black tracker. Borgnine brings strength to his character as the rancher seeking revenge. Made for television.
1971 73m/C Sammy Davis Jr., Ernest Borgnine, Julie Adams, Connie Kreski, Jim Davis; **D:** Earl Bellamy. **VHS, Beta** $19.98 *FOX J½*

Tracks Vietnam veteran accompanies the body of a buddy on a long train ride home. He starts suffering flashbacks from the war and begins to think some of the passengers are out to get him.
1976 (R) 90m/C Dennis Hopper, Dean Stockwell, Taryn Power; **D:** Henry Jaglom. **VHS, Beta** $39.95 *PAR J½*

Trade Secrets Special investigator Jerry Morrison is assigned to probe the mysterious death of an heiress to a wine fortune. His investigation leads to the secrets and private fantasies of the woman's family and friends.

199? 91m/C Sam Waterston, Marisa Berenson, Lauren Hutton, Arielle Dombasle; *W/D:* Claude Feraldo. **VHS $89.95** *TRI &Z*

Trader Tom of the China Seas A young island trader and a shipwrecked beauty get involved in espionage while helping the UN to safeguard the Asian corridor. Double cassette.
19?? 167m/B VHS **$29.98** *REP &Z*

Trading Hearts Over-the-hill baseball player falls for an unsuccessful singer and single mom at a Florida training camp set in the 1950s. Written by Frank Deford.
1987 (PG) 88m/C Beverly D'Angelo, Raul Julia, Jerry Lewis, Parris Buckner, Robert Gwaltney; *D:* Neil Leifer. **VHS, Beta, LV $14.95** *LIV &Z*

Trading Places Two elderly businessmen wager that environment is more important than heredity in creating a successful life, using a rich nephew and an unemployed street hustler as guinea pigs. Curtis is winning as a hooker-with-a-heart-of-gold who helps the hapless Aykroyd. Oft-told tale succeeds thanks to strong cast. Murphy's second screen appearance.
1983 (R) 118m/C Eddie Murphy, Dan Aykroyd, Jamie Lee Curtis, Ralph Bellamy, Don Ameche, Denholm Elliott, Paul Gleason, James Belushi; *D:* John Landis. Academy Awards '83 Nominations: Best Original Score; British Academy Awards '83: Best Supporting Actor (Elliott), Best Supporting Actress (Curtis). **VHS, Beta, LV, 8mm $14.95** *PAR &Z 1/2*

Traenen in Florenz A woman involved in a car accident winds up falling in love with the man who injured her, only to discover later that they are actually brother and sister, long separated. In German with English subtitles. *AKA:* Tears in Florence.
1984 90m/C GE *D:* Marianne Schafer. **VHS, Beta $39.95** *VCD, APD, GLV &*

Traffic in Souls A silent melodrama dealing with white slavery. Immigrants and gullible country girls are lured into brothels where they are trapped with no hope of escape until, in a hail of bullets, the police raid the dens of vice and rescue them.
1913 74m/B Matt Moore, Jane Gail, William Welsh; *D:* George Tucker. **VHS, Beta $24.95** *GPV &ZZ*

Traffik A tense, unnerving look at the international world of heroin smuggling. The British drama follows the lives of three men involved in the drug trade: a farmer in the poppy fields of Pakistan, a drug smuggler in Hamburg, and a Tory cabinet minister who heads his government's anti-drug cabinet and then comes to realize his own daughter is an addict. On three cassettes. Made for British television.
199? 360m/C GB Lindsay Duncan, Bill Paterson. **VHS $99.95** *SIG, TVC &*

The Tragedy of a Ridiculous Man The missing son of an Italian cheese manufacturer may or may not have been kidnapped by terrorists. Lesser Bertolucci effort may or may not have a point. In Italian with English subtitles. *AKA:* La Tragedia di un Uomo Ridicolo.
1981 (PG) 116m/C IT Ugo Tognazzi, Anouk Aimee, Victor Cavallo, Ricardo Tognazzi, Laura Morante; *D:* Bernardo Bertolucci; *M:* Ennio Morricone. **VHS $59.99** *WAR, FCT, TAM &Z*

Tragedy of Flight 103: The Inside Story Dramatization of the events surrounding the destruction of Pan Am flight 103 over Lockerbie, Scotland, due to a terrorist-planted bomb.
1991 (PG) 89m/C Ned Beatty, Peter Boyle, Vincent Gardenia, Timothy West, Michael Wincott; *D:* Leslie Woodhead. **VHS $89.95** *MGM &ZZ*

The Tragedy of King Richard II Shakespeare's tale of the fight for the English crown between the current king, Richard II, and the usurper, Henry Bolingbroke, who seizes the throne. Made for television.
1982 180m/C David Birney, Paul Shenar. **VHS, Beta** *NO &Z*

Trail Beyond A cowboy and his sidekick go on the trek to the northwest to find a girl and a gold mine.
1934 57m/B John Wayne, Noah Beery Sr., Verna Hillie; *D:* Robert North Bradbury. **VHS $19.95** *COL, REP, NOS &Z 1/2*

Trail Drive Adventures of a cowboy during a big cattle drive.
1935 63m/B Ken Maynard. **VHS, Beta, 3/4U, Special order formats $19.95** *NOS, VCN, CAB &*

Trail of Robin Hood Rogers sees to it that poor families get Christmas trees, in spite of the fact that a big business wants to raise the prices. Features a number of western stars, including Holt playing himself.
1950 67m/C Roy Rogers, Penny Edwards, Gordon Jones, Jack Holt, Emory Parnell, Rex Allen, Allan "Rocky" Lane, Clifton Young, Monte Hale, Kermit Maynard, Tom Keene, Ray Corrigan, William Farnum; *D:* William Witney. **VHS $12.98** *REP &Z 1/2*

Trail of Terror G-Man poses as an escaped convict to get the goods on a gang.
1935 60m/B Bob Steele. **VHS, Beta, LV** *NO &*

Trail of the Hawk Saga of frontier justice and love on the plains.
1937 50m/B Yancey Lane, Betty Jordan, Dick Jones; *D:* Edward Dmytryk. **VHS, Beta $19.95** *NOS, DVT, RXM &*

Trail of the Mounties A Mountie gallops smack into a murdering slew of fur thieves.
1947 41m/B Donald (Don "Red") Barry, Robert Lowery, Tom Neal, Russell Hayden. **VHS, Beta, LV** *WGE &*

Trail of the Pink Panther The sixth in Sellers' "Pink Panther" series. Inspector Clouseau disappears while he is searching for the diamond known as the Pink Panther. Notable because it was released after Sellers' death, using clips from previous movies to fill in gaps. Followed by "Curse of the Pink Panther."
1982 (PG) 97m/C Peter Sellers, David Niven, Herbert Lom, Capucine, Burt Kwouk, Robert Wagner, Robert Loggia; *D:* Blake Edwards. **VHS, Beta, LV** *FOX &Z*

Trail of the Royal Mounted Western adventure serial made up of ten 15-minute episodes.
1934 150m/B Robert Frazer. **VHS, Beta, 3/4U, Special order formats $27.95** *VCN, CAB &Z 1/2*

Trail of the Silver Spurs A lone man remaining in a ghost town discovers gold and becomes rich. Part of the "Range Busters" series.
1941 57m/B Ray Corrigan, John "Dusty" King, Max Terhune, I. Stanford Jolley, Dorothy Short; *D:* S. Roy Luby. **VHS $19.95** *NOS, DVT &Z 1/2*

Trail Riders The Range Busters set a trap to capture a gang of outlaws who killed the son of the town marshal during a bank robbery. Part of the "Range Busters" series.
1942 55m/B John "Dusty" King, David Sharpe, Max Terhune, Evelyn Finley, Forrest Taylor, Charles King. **VHS, Beta $19.95** *NOS, VYY, DVT &Z 1/2*

Trail Street Scott is Bat Masterson, the western hero. He aids the struggle of Kansans as they conquer the land and local ranchers.
1947 84m/B Randolph Scott, Robert Ryan, Anne Jeffreys, George "Gabby" Hayes, Madge Meredith, Jason Robards Jr.; *D:* Ray Enright. **VHS, Beta $34.95** *CCB, MED &Z 1/2*

Trailing Double Trouble A corrupt attorney murders a rancher to pursue a business scheme. Three ranch hands kidnap the rancher's orphaned baby to keep her safe from the attorney. The second entry in the "Range Busters" series.
1940 56m/B Ray Corrigan, John "Dusty" King, Max Terhune. **VHS, Beta $19.95** *NOS, VDM, VYY &Z 1/2*

Trailing Trouble Cattle driver is robbed of his money while selling cattle. He also finds time to vie for a young woman's heart. Basic low-budget oater.
1937 60m/B Ken Maynard. **VHS, Beta $19.95** *NOS, VYY, VCN &Z 1/2*

Trails West Western adventure starring Steele.
194? ?m/B Bob Steele. **VHS, Beta $27.95** *VCN &*

The Train During the German occupation of Paris in 1944, a German general (Scofield) is ordered to ransack the city of its art treasures and put them on a train bound for Germany. Word gets to the French Resistance who then persuade the train inspector (Lancaster) to sabotage the train. An elaborate ruse is planned, which works but ultimately causes the Nazi general to take hostages and demand the art shipment reach its destination. A battle of wills ensues between Scofield and Lancaster as each becomes increasingly obsessed with outwitting the other—though the cost to all turns out to be as irreplaceable as the art itself. Filmed on location in France. Frankenheimer used real locomotives, rather than models, throughout the film, even in the spectacular crash sequences. *AKA:* Le Train; Il Treno.
1965 133m/C Burt Lancaster, Paul Scofield, Jeanne Moreau, Michel Simon, Suzanne Flon, Wolfgang Preiss, Albert Remy; *D:* John Frankenheimer. **VHS $19.98** *MGM &ZZZ*

The Train Killer A mad Hungarian is bent on destroying the Orient Express.
1983 90m/C Michael Sarrazin; *D:* Sandor Simo. **VHS, Beta $69.98** *VES &*

Train of Events An interesting look at lives affected by a train wreck just outside London, taking the form of four short episodes. Three are frankly somber, depressing tales of the ill-fated train driver, a murderer and an escaped prisoner-of-war. The fourth segment is a refreshingly lighthearted piece about romantic jealousies in a traveling orchestra. A precursor to the later swarm of crass disaster movies, except here emphasis is on character over special effects.
1949 89m/C Jack Warner, Gladys Henson, Susan Shaw, Patric Doonan, Miles Malleson, Leslie Phillips, Joan Dowling, Laurence Payne, Valerie Hobson, John Clements, Peter Finch, Mary Morris, Laurence Naismith, Michael Hordern; *D:* Sidney Cole, Basil Dearden, Charles Crichton. **VHS $29.95** *NOS, FCT &ZZ*

Train Robbers A widow employs the services of three cowboys to help her recover some stolen gold in order to clear her late husband's name. At least that's what she says.
1973 (PG) 92m/C John Wayne, Ann-Margret, Rod Taylor, Ben Johnson, Christopher George, Ricardo Montalban, Bobby Vinton, Jerry Gatlin; *D:* Burt Kennedy. **VHS, Beta, LV $19.98** *WAR &Z*

Train Station Pickups Trashy film about young girls who hook at a local train depot, until something goes wrong.
197? 96m/C Marco Knoger, Katja Carrol, Ingeborg Steinbach, Benjamin Carwath; **D:** Walter Boos. **VHS $29.95** ACN ♂

Train to Hollywood Marilyn Monroe-obsessed young Polish girl daydreams incessantly as she works on dining car. Funny and surreal. Polish dialogue with English subtitles.
1986 96m/C PL D: Radoslaw Piwowarski. **VHS $49.98** FCT ♂♂♂

Train to Tombstone A train running from Albuquerque to Tombstone carries a motley mob of the usual characters.
1950 60m/B Donald (Don "Red") Barry, Judith Allen, Robert Lowery, Tom Neal; **D:** Charles F. Reisner. **VHS, Beta, LV** NO ♂

Trained to Kill, U.S.A. Vietnam veteran relives his war experiences when a gang of terrorists threaten his hometown.
1983 (R) 88m/C Stephen Sander, Heidi Vaughn, Rockne Tarkington. **VHS, Beta** PGN ♂ 1/2

The Traitor Undercover man joins a gang of bandits.
1936 57m/B Tim McCoy; **D:** Sam Newfield. **VHS, Beta $19.95** NOS, UHV, VCN ♂ 1/2

Traitors of the Blue Castle Two samurai must preserve the honor of the emperor in 19th-century Japan.
1958 100m/C JP Kanjuro Aroshi, Ryuzaburo Nakamura. **VHS, Beta $54.00** VDA ♂

Tramp & a Woman Two shorts made for the Essanay Company in 1915 which offer the Little Tramp wooing Purviance in typical Chaplin fashion. Silent with musical score.
1915 45m/B Charlie Chaplin, Edna Purviance. **VHS, Beta $24.95** VYY ♂♂

Tramp at the Door Delightful drama about a wandering, magical man who enters the lives of an embittered family. He helps them sort the skeletons in their closets, and works wonders on their relationships.
1987 81m/C Ed McNamara, August Schellenberg, Monique Mercure, Eric Peterson; **D:** Allen Kroeker. **VHS, Beta $79.98** CGH ♂♂ 1/2

Tramplers A rebel father and son split over the hanging of a Yankee during the Civil War. Italian made spaghetti western without much plot and lots of gratuitous gunplay.
1966 103m/C IT Joseph Cotten, Gordon Scott; **D:** Albert Band, Mario Sequi. **VHS, Beta $9.95** COL, SUE, HHE ♂

Trancers A time-traveling cult from the future goes back in time to 1985 to meddle with fate. Only Jack Deth, defender of justice, can save mankind. Low-budget "Blade Runner." Followed by two sequels. **AKA:** Future Cop.
1985 (PG-13) 76m/C Tim Thomerson, Michael Stefoni, Helen Hunt, Art LaFleur, Telma Hopkins; **D:** Charles Band. **VHS, Beta, LV $19.98** LIV, VES ♂♂

Trancers 2: The Return of Jack Deth Retro cop is back from the future again, but seems to have lost his wit and nerve in between sequels. Ward is miscast and the pacing undermines whatever suspense that might have been.
1991 (R) 85m/C Tim Thomerson, Helen Hunt, Megan Ward, Biff Manard, Martine Beswick, Jeffrey Combs, Barbara Crampton, Richard Lynch; **D:** Charles Band. **VHS, Beta, LV $19.95** PAR, PIA ♂

Trancers 3: Deth Lives In the third film of the "Trancers" series, time-traveling cop Jack Deth fights the deadliest form of government-sponsored Trancer yet—it has a brain.
1992 (R) 83m/C Tim Thomerson, Melanie Smith, Andrew Robinson, Tony Pierce, Dawn Ann Billings, Helen Hunt, Megan Ward, Stephen Macht, Telma Hopkins; **W/D:** C. Courtney Joyner. **VHS, Beta, LV** PAR ♂ 1/2

Transatlantic Merry-Go-Round An early semi-musical mystery about an eclectic assortment of passengers aboard a luxury liner. ♫It Was Sweet of You; Rock and Roll; Moon Over Monte Carlo; Oh Leo, It's Love; If I Had a Million Dollars.
1934 90m/B Jack Benny, Gene Raymond, Nancy Carroll, Boswell Sisters, Ralph Morgan, Sidney Blackmer; **D:** Ben Stoloff. **VHS, Beta $12.95** IVE ♂♂

Transatlantic Tunnel An undersea tunnel from England to America is attempted, despite financial trickery and undersea disasters. Made with futuristic sets which were advanced for their time. **AKA:** The Tunnel.
1935 94m/B GB Richard Dix, Leslie Banks, Madge Evans, Helen Vinson, C. Aubrey Smith, George Arliss, Walter Huston; **D:** Maurice Elvey. **VHS, Beta, 3/4U, Special order formats $44.95** GPV, SNC, HHT ♂♂

Transformations An interplanetary pilot battles a deadly virus that threatens life throughout the universe. Obscure space jetsam.
1988 (R) 84m/C Rex Smith, Patrick Macnee. **VHS, LV $19.95** STE ♂ 1/2

Transformers: The Movie A full-length animated film featuring the universe-defending robots fighting the powers of evil. These robots began life as real toys, so there's some marketing going on.
1986 (G) 85m/C **D:** Nelson Shin; **V:** Orson Welles, Eric Idle, Judd Nelson, Leonard Nimoy, Robert Stack. **VHS, Beta $19.95** FHE ♂

Transmutations A mad scientist harbors a bevy of mind-expanding, drug-addicted, disfigured victims in his underground lab, who eventually rebel. **AKA:** Underworld.
1986 (R) 103m/C GB Denholm Elliott, Steven Berkoff, Miranda Richardson, Nicola Cowper; **D:** George Pavlou; **W:** Clive Barker. **VHS, Beta, LV $79.98** LIV, VES ♂ 1/2

Transport from Paradise Follows the story of Jewish life in the Terezin ghetto before the inhabitants are imprisoned and shipped off to Auschwitz as part of Hitler's final solution. Based on a novel by Arnold Lustig. In Czech with English subtitles. **AKA:** Transport Z Raje.
1965 93m/B CZ D: Zbynek Brynych. **VHS, Beta $59.95** FCT ♂♂ 1/2

Transylvania 6-5000 Agreeably stupid horror spoof about two klutzy reporters who stumble into modern-day Transylvania and encounter an array of comedic creatures. Shot in Yugoslavia.
1985 (PG) 93m/C Jeff Goldblum, Joseph Bologna, Ed Begley Jr., Carol Kane, John Byner, Geena Davis, Jeffrey Jones, Norman Fell; **D:** Rudy DeLuca. **VHS, Beta, LV $19.95** STE, NWV ♂

Transylvania Twist Moronic comedy about vampires, teenage vampire hunters and half-naked babes.
1989 (PG-13) 90m/C Robert Vaughn, Teri Copley, Steve Altman, Ace Mask, Angus Scrimm, Jay Robinson, Brinke Stevens; **D:** Jim Wynorski. **VHS, Beta $79.95** MGM ♂ 1/2

The Trap Chaney kidnaps the son of a man he's sent to prison on false charges. Rather than give up the kid when the man is released, he plans a trap.
1922 ?m/C Lon Chaney Sr., Alan Hale Sr., Irene Rich. **VHS $16.95** SNC ♂♂

The Trap In trying to escape justice, a ruthless crime syndicate boss holds a small desert town in a grip of fear. **AKA:** The Baited Trap.
1959 84m/C Richard Widmark, Tina Louise, Lee J. Cobb, Earl Holliman, Lorne Greene, Carl Benton Reid; **D:** Norman Panama. **VHS, Beta $19.95** KRT ♂♂ 1/2

Trap A trapper buys a mute girl as his wife. Together they try to make a life for themselves in the Canadian wilderness. Fine telling of interesting western tale. Unusual and realistic. **AKA:** L'Aventure Sauvage.
1966 106m/C GB CA Rita Tushingham, Oliver Reed, Rex Sevenoaks; **D:** Sidney Hayers. **VHS, Beta** NO ♂

Trap on Cougar Mountain A young boy begins a crusade to save his animal friends from the traps and bullets of hunters.
1972 (G) 97m/C Erik Larsen, Keith Larsen, Karen Steele; **D:** Keith Larsen. **VHS, Beta, LV $9.95** NWV, STE ♂

Trap Them & Kill Them American group traveling through the Amazon jungle encounter a terrifying aborigine tribe. Point of trip undergoes considerable reexamination.
1984 90m/C Gabriele Tinti, Susan Scott, Donald O'Brien. **VHS, Beta $59.95** TWE ♂

Trapeze Lancaster is a former trapeze artist, now lame from a triple somersault accident. Curtis, the son of an old friend, wants Lancaster to teach him the routine. Lollobrigida, an aerial acrobat, is interested in both men. Exquisite European locations, fine camera work. The actors perform their own stunts.
1956 105m/C Burt Lancaster, Tony Curtis, Gina Lollobrigida, Katy Jurado; **D:** Carol Reed. **VHS, Beta $19.98** MGM, FOX ♂♂♂

Trapped Semi-documentary crime drama shows in semi-documentary style how the feds hunt down a gang of counterfeiters by springing one of their comrades from prison. Well-paced, suspenseful and believable.
1949 78m/B Lloyd Bridges, Barbara Payton, John Hoyt, James Todd; **D:** Richard Fleischer. **VHS $19.95** NOS, DVT, HEG ♂♂ 1/2

Trapped A woman working late in her high-rise office is stalked by a killer and must rely on her ingenuity to outwit him. Made-for-cable-television thriller.
1989 (R) 93m/C Kathleen Quinlan, Bruce Abbott, Katy Boyer, Ben Loggins; **D:** Fred Walton. **VHS, Beta $79.95** MCA ♂

Trapped by the Mormons Mormons seduce innocent young girls to add to their harems. An interesting piece of paranoid propaganda. Silent with original organ music. **AKA:** The Mormon Peril.
1922 97m/B Evelyn Brent, Lewis Willoughby. **VHS, Beta, 8mm $19.95** NOS, VYY, GPV ♂♂

Trapped in Silence Young Sutherland, abused since childhood, stops speaking to protect himself mentally and physically. Psychologist Mason is determined to break down the walls to help him confront his pain. Interesting cameo by Silver as a gay counselor forced out of his job when his sexual preference is discovered. Mildly melodramatic made-for-TV message drama.
1986 94m/C Marsha Mason, Kiefer Sutherland, John Mahoney, Amy Wright; **Cameos:** Ron Silver; **D:** Michael Tuchner. **VHS $59.98** TTC ♂♂

Trapper County War A city boy and a Vietnam vet band together to rescue a young woman held captive by a backwoods clan.
1989 (R) 98m/C Robert Estes, Bo Hopkins, Ernie Hudson, Betsy Russell, Don Swayze; **D:** Worth Keeter. **VHS, LV $9.98** REP 🎞

Trash Andy Warhol's profile of a depraved couple (Warhol-veteran Dallesandro and female impersonater Woodlawn) living in a lower east side basement and scouting the streets for food and drugs. Not for those easily offended by nymphomaniacs, junkies, lice, and the like; a must for fans of underground film and the cinema verite style.
1970 110m/C Joe Dallesandro, Holly Woodlawn, Jane Forth, Micael Sklar, Geri Miller, Bruce Pecheur; **D:** Paul Morrissey. **VHS, Beta** PAR 🎞🎞

Trauma A girl suffers amnesia after the trauma of witnessing her aunt's murder. She returns to the mansion years later to piece together what happened. A sometimes tedious psychological thriller.
1962 93m/C John Conte, Lynn Bari, Lorrie Richards, David Garner, Warren Kemmerling, William Bissell, Bond Blackman, William Justine; **D:** Robert M. Young. **VHS, Beta** VES 🎞½

Traveling Companions The beautiful, young owner of a truck stop has all the local truckers vying for her via macho contests.
1986 80m/C Elizabeth Turner, Nikki Gentile. **VHS, Beta $29.95** MED Woof!

Traveling Man A made-for-cable-television drama about a veteran traveling salesman who's assigned an eager young apprentice when his sales go down. Lithgow gives a great performance as the burnt-out traveling salesman.
1989 105m/C John Lithgow, Jonathan Silverman, Margaret Colin, John Glover; **D:** Irvin Kershner. **VHS, Beta $89.99** HBO 🎞🎞

Travelling North A belligerent retiree falls in love with a divorcee and they move together to a rustic retreat. They have an idyllic existence until the man discovers he has a serious heart condition. Adaptation of David Williamson's play has fine performances.
1987 (PG-13) 97m/C AU Leo McKern, Julia Blake; **D:** Carl Schultz; **W:** David Williamson. **VHS, Beta** NO 🎞🎞

Travels with My Aunt A banker leading a mundane life is taken on a wild, whirlwind tour of Europe by an eccentric woman claiming to be his aunt. Based on Graham Greene's best-selling novel.
1972 (PG) 109m/C Maggie Smith, Alec McCowen, Louis Gossett Jr., Robert Stephens, Cindy Williams; **D:** George Cukor; **W:** Jay Presson Allen. Academy Awards '72: Best Costume Design; Nominations: Best Actress (Smith), Best Art Direction/Set Decoration, Best Cinematography. **VHS, LV** MGM 🎞🎞½

Traxx Satire about an ex-cop soldier of fortune. Not surprisingly, Stevens doesn't do much with this lame script.
1987 (R) 84m/C Shadoe Stevens, Priscilla Barnes, William E. Pugh, John Hancock, Robert Davi, Rick Overton; **D:** Jerome Gary. **VHS, Beta $79.99** HBO 🎞

Treacherous Crossing When her husband disappears on their honeymoon cruise heiress Wagner tries to get the ship's crew to help her. They think she's crazy, but aided by new friend Dickinson, Wagner intends to find out just what's going on. Based on the radio play "Cabin B-13" by John Dickson Carr.
1992 (PG) 88m/C Lindsay Wagner, Angie Dickinson, Grant Show, Joseph Bottoms, Karen Medak, Charles Napier, Jeffrey DeMunn; **D:** Tony Wharmby. **VHS, Beta** PAR, PMS 🎞🎞

Treasure Island Fleming's adaptation of Robert Louis Stevenson's eighteenth century English pirate tale of Long John Silver is a classic. Beery is great as the pirate; Cooper has trouble playing the boy. Also available colorized. Multitudinous remakes.
1934 102m/B Wallace Beery, Jackie Cooper, Lionel Barrymore, Lewis Stone, Otto Kruger, Douglas Dumbrille, Chic Sale, Nigel Bruce; **D:** Victor Fleming. **VHS, Beta, LV $19.98** MGM, TLF, HMV 🎞🎞🎞½

Treasure Island Spine-tingling Robert Louis Stevenson tale of pirates and buried treasure, in which young cabin boy Jim Hawkins matches wits with Long John Silver. Some editions excise extra violence. Stevenson's ending is revised. Full Disney treatment, excellent casting.
1950 (PG) 96m/C Bobby Driscoll, Robert Newton, Basil Sydney, Walter Fitzgerald, Denis O'Dea, Ralph Truman, Finlay Currie; **D:** Byron Haskin. **VHS, Beta, LV $19.99** DIS, IGP 🎞🎞🎞½

Treasure Island Unexceptional British reheat of familiar pirate tale. Welles' interpretation of Long John Silver may be truer to Stevenson, but it's one heckuva blustering binge. **AKA:** La Isla Del Tersoro.
1972 (G) 94m/C GB Orson Welles, Kim Burfield, Walter Slezak, Lionel Stander; **D:** John Hough; **W:** Orson Welles. **VHS $79.95** BTV 🎞🎞

Treasure Island Excellent made for cable version of the classic Robert Louis Stevenson pirate tale with Heston as Long John Silver. Written, produced and directed by Fraser Heston, son of Charlton.
1989 131m/C Charlton Heston, Christian Bale, Julian Glover, Richard Johnson, Oliver Reed, Christopher Lee, Clive Wood, Nicholas Amer, Michael Halsey; **W/D:** Fraser Heston. **VHS $79.98** TTC 🎞🎞½

Treasure of Arne A 16th century Scottish mercenary kills and loots the estate of rich, well-to-do property owner Sir Arne. Famous early Swedish silent that established Stiller as a director.
1919 78m/B SW **D:** Mauritz Stiller. **VHS, Beta $49.95** FCT 🎞½

The Treasure of Bengal Sabu attempts to stop his chief from trading the village's precious gem (the largest ruby in the world) for firearms.
1953 72m/C Sabu. **VHS** NO 🎞½

Treasure of Bruce Le Bruce Le beats up on Samurai to avenge a friend's death.
1976 80m/C Bruce Le. **VHS, Beta $19.99** BFV 🎞🎞

Treasure of Fear A bungling newspaper reporter gets involved with four jade chessmen once owned by Kubla Khan. A few laughs in this contrived haunted house story. **AKA:** Scared Stiff.
1945 66m/B Jack Haley, Barton MacLane, Ann Savage; **D:** Frank McDonald. **VHS, Beta $16.95** SNC, NOS, FCT 🎞½

The Treasure of Jamaica Reef Adventurers battle sharks and other nasty fish as they seek a sunken Spanish galleon and its cache of golden treasure.
1974 (PG) 96m/C Cheryl Ladd, Stephen Boyd, Roosevelt Grier, David Ladd, Darby Hinton; **D:** Virginia Lively Stone. **VHS, Beta $39.95** WWV 🎞½

The Treasure of Matecumbe A motley crew of adventurers led by a young boy search for buried treasure as they are pursued by Indians and other foes. Filmed in the Florida Key Islands.
1976 (G) 107m/C Billy Attmore, Robert Foxworth, Joan Hackett, Peter Ustinov, Vic Morrow; **D:** Vincent McEveety. **VHS, Beta $69.95** DIS 🎞🎞

Treasure of Monte Cristo A woman marries a seaman said to be an ancestor of the Count for his inheritance. Instead, she finds love and mystery.
1950 78m/B GB Adele Jergens, Steve Brodie, Glenn Langan; **D:** William Berke. **VHS, Beta, LV** NO 🎞

Treasure of Pancho Villa An American adventurer plots a gold heist to help Villa's revolution. He encounters every obstacle in the West while on his way to help the Mexican rebel.
1955 96m/C Rory Calhoun, Shelley Winters, Gilbert Roland; **D:** George Sherman. **VHS, Beta $15.95** UHV 🎞½

The Treasure of the Amazon Three fortune hunters embark on a perilous search for wealth in the South American jungles. Silly and unnecessarily violent. **AKA:** El Tesoro del Amazones.
1984 105m/C MX Stuart Whitman, Donald Pleasence, Ann Sydney, Bradford Dillman, John Ireland; **D:** Rene Cardona Jr. **VHS, Beta $69.98** LIV, VES 🎞½

Treasure of the Four Crowns Aging history professor hires a team of tough commandos to recover four legendary crowns containing the source of mystical powers. The crowns are being held under heavy guard by a crazed cult leader.
1982 (PG) 97m/C SP Tony Anthony, Anna Obregon, Gene Quintano; **D:** Ferdinando Baldi; **M:** Ennio Morricone. **VHS, Beta $59.95** MGM 🎞

Treasure of the Golden Condor A swashbuckler heads to the jungles of 18th-century Guatemala in search of ancient treasure. Contains interesting footage of Mayan ruins, but otherwise ordinary. A remake of "Son of Fury."
1953 93m/C Cornel Wilde, Connie Smith, Fay Wray, Anne Bancroft, Leo G. Carroll, Robert (Bobby) Blake; **D:** Delmer Daves. **VHS** TCF 🎞🎞½

Treasure of the Lost Desert A Green Beret crushes a terrorist operation in the Middle East.
1983 93m/C Bruce Miller, Susan West, Larry Finch; **D:** Tony Zarindast. **VHS, Beta $69.98** LIV 🎞½

Treasure of the Moon Goddess A dizzy nightclub singer is mistaken by Central American pirates and natives for the earthly manifestation of their Moon Goddess.
1988 (R) 90m/C Don Calfa, Joann Ayres, Asher Brauner; **D:** Joseph Louis Agraz. **VHS, Beta $79.95** VMK Woof!

Treasure of the Sierra Madre Three prospectors in search of gold in Mexico find suspicion, treachery and greed. Bogart is superbly believable as the paranoid, and ultimately homicidal, Fred C. Dobbs. Huston directed his father and wrote the screenplay, based on a B. Traven story.
1948 126m/B Humphrey Bogart, Walter Huston, Tim Holt, Bruce Bennett, Barton MacLane, Robert (Bobby) Blake; **W/D:** John Huston. Academy Awards '48: Best Director (Huston), Best Screenplay, Best Supporting Actor (Huston); Nominations: Best Picture; National Board of Review Awards '48: 10 Best Films of the Year, Best Actor (Huston). **VHS, Beta, LV $19.98** MGM, FOX, TLF 🎞🎞🎞

Treasure of the Yankee Zephyr Trio join in the quest for a plane that has been missing for 40 years... with a cargo of $50 million. They have competition in the form of Peppard and cronies. Decent cast muddles through. **AKA:** Race For the Yankee Zephyr.
1983 (PG) 97m/C Ken Wahl, George Peppard, Donald Pleasence, Lesley Ann Warren; **D:** David Hemmings. **VHS, Beta $69.98** LIV, VES, SIM 🎞🎞

The Treasure Seekers Four rival divers set off on a perilous Caribbean expedition in search of the legendary treasure of Morgan the Pirate.
1979 88m/C Rod Taylor, Stuart Whitman, Elke Sommer, Keenan Wynn, Jeremy Kemp. **VHS, Beta $59.95** MGM ⅛

A Tree Grows in Brooklyn Sensitive young Irish lass growing up in turn-of-the-century Brooklyn tries to rise above her tenement existence. Based on the novel by Betty Smith. Kazan's directorial debut.
1945 128m/B Peggy Ann Garner, James Dunn, Dorothy McGuire, Joan Blondell, Lloyd Nolan, Ted Donaldson, James Gleason, John Alexander; **D:** Elia Kazan; **M:** Jerry Goldsmith. Academy Awards '45: Best Supporting Actor (Dunn), Special Achievement Award (Garner); Nominations: Best Screenplay. **VHS, Beta, LV $19.98** KUI, FOX, BTV ⅛⅛⅛½

The Tree of Wooden Clogs Epic view of the lives of four peasant families working on an estate in turn of the century Northern Italy. Slow moving and beautiful, from former industrial filmmaker Olmi. In Italian with English subtitles. **AKA:** L'Albero Degli Zoccoli.
1978 185m/C IT Luigi Ornaghi, Francesca Moriggi, Omar Brignoll, Antonio Ferrari; **W/D:** Ermanno Olmi. **VHS, Beta, LV $79.95** FXL, APD, TAM ⅛⅛⅛½

Tremors A tiny desert town is attacked by giant man-eating worm-creatures. Bacon and Ward are the handymen trying to save the town. Amusing, with good special effects.
1989 (PG-13) 96m/C Kevin Bacon, Fred Ward, Finn Carter, Michael Gross, Reba McEntire, Bibi Besch; **D:** Ron Underwood. **VHS, Beta, LV $19.95** MCA ⅛⅛½

Trenchcoat Aspiring mystery writer travels to Malta to research her new novel and is drawn into a real-life conspiracy. Silly and contrived spoof of the detective genre.
1983 95m/C Margot Kidder, Robert Hays; **D:** Michael Tuchner. **VHS, Beta** DIS, OM ⅛½

Trespass Violent crime tale set in East St. Louis, Illinois. Two redneck firemen learn about stolen gold artifacts supposedly hidden in an abandoned building and go on a treasure hunt. When they witness a murder they also get involved in a battle between two crime lords—who want these interlopers dead. What follows is a deadly game of cat-and-mouse. Lots of action but it's all fairly routine. Original release date of summer 1992 was delayed until the winter because of unfortunate similarities to the L.A. riots. **AKA:** Looters.
1992 (R) 104m/C Ice Cube, Ice-T, William Sadler, Bill Paxton, Art Evans; **D:** Walter Hill; **W:** Robert Zemeckis, Bob Gale; **M:** Ry Cooder. **VHS, Beta, LV** MCA ⅛⅛

Trespasser A painter has an affair with a young woman. He comes to regret destroying his family and their life together. Based on a D.H. Lawrence novel.
1985 90m/C Alan Bates, Dinah Stabb, Pauline Morgan, Margaret Whiting. **VHS, Beta** NO ⅛⅛

Trespasses A rape victim and a cattleman get involved and become the target of her husband's revenge. Murder and lust in a small Texas town in this tedious film.
1986 90m/C Lou Diamond Phillips, Robert Kuhn, Ben Johnson, Adam Roarke, Mary Pillot, Van Brooks; **D:** Lauren Bivens. **VHS, Beta $29.95** ACA, MTX ⅛

Triad Savages Triad war with the Mafia.
19?? 90m/C Chow Yung Fat, Ko Chun Hsiung, Lam Wai. **VHS $49.95** OCE ⅛

The Trial Expressionistic Welles adaptation of classic Kafka novella about an innocent man accused, tried, and convicted of an unknown crime in an unnnamed exaggeratedly bureaucratic country. Another Welles project that met with constant disaster in production, with many lapses in continuity. **AKA:** Le Proces; Der Prozess; Il Processo.
1963 118m/B FR Anthony Perkins, Jeanne Moreau, Orson Welles, Romy Schneider, Akim Tamiroff, Elsa Martinelli; **D:** Orson Welles. **VHS, Beta, 3/4U, Special order formats $39.95** CVC, NOS, HHT ⅛⅛⅛

Trial of Bernhard Goetz A re-enactment of the celebrated vigilante's trial, taken from the actual court transcripts.
1988 135m/C **VHS, Beta $59.95** ALL ⅛⅛

The Trial of Billy Jack Billy Jack takes on the feds and beats the hell out of a lot of people to prove that the world can live in peace. Awful, pretentious film.
1974 (PG) 175m/C Tom Laughlin, Delores Taylor, Victor Izay, Terasa Laughlin, William Wellman Jr.; **D:** Frank Laughlin. **VHS** NO Woof!

The Trial of Lee Harvey Oswald What would've happened if Jack Ruby had not shot Oswald. Oswald's trial and its likely results are painstakingly created. In 2 volumes. Made for television.
1977 192m/C Ben Gazzara, Lorne Greene, John Pleshette, Lawrence Pressman; **D:** Gordon Davidson. **VHS, Beta $69.95** WOV ⅛⅛

Trial of the Catonsville Nine Riveting political drama that focuses on the trial of nine anti-war activists, including Father Daniel Berrigan, during the Vietnam War days of the late 1960s. Imperfect, but involving.
1972 (PG) 85m/C Ed Flanders, Douglas Watson, William Schallert, Peter Strauss; **D:** Gordon Davidson. **VHS, Beta $59.95** COL ⅛⅛½

The Trial of the Incredible Hulk The Hulk returns to battle organized crime and is aided by his blind superhero/lawyer friend Daredevil. Followed by "The Death of the Incredible Hulk." Made for television.
1989 96m/C Bill Bixby, Lou Ferrigno, Rex Smith, John Rhys-Davies, Marta DuBois, Nancy Everhard, Nicholas Hormann; **D:** Bill Bixby. **VHS $19.95** STE ⅛⅛

The Triangle Factory Fire Scandal Based on the true-life Triangle factory fire at the turn of the century. The fire killed 145 garment workers and drastically changed industrial fire and safety codes. Made for television.
1979 100m/C Tom Bosley, David Dukes, Tovah Feldshuh, Janet Margolin, Stephanie Zimbalist, Lauren Frost, Stacey Nelkin, Ted Wass, Charlotte Rae, Milton Selzer, Valerie Landsburg; **D:** Mel Stuart. **VHS $59.95** LIV ⅛⅛

Tribes A made-for-television movie about a hippie drafted into the Marines. Despite the furious efforts of his drill sergeant, he refuses to conform to military life. Soon his bootcamp mates are trying his methods of defiance and survival. Well-made mix of comedy and social commentary. **AKA:** The Soldier Who Declared Peace.
1970 90m/C Jan-Michael Vincent, Darren McGavin, Earl Holliman; **D:** Joseph Sargent. **VHS, Beta $59.98** MGM, FOX ⅛⅛½

Tribute A dying man is determined to achieve a reconciliation with his estranged son. Adapted by Bernard Slade from his play.
1980 (PG) 125m/C CA Jack Lemmon, Robby Benson, Lee Remick, Kim Cattrall; **D:** Bob Clark. **VHS, Beta, LV $19.98** VES, FCT ⅛⅛

A Tribute to the Boys An all-star salute to the comedy of Laurel & Hardy featuring clips from more than 30 of their comedies, including scenes from their silent film days. Guests include Johnny Carson, Steve Allen, Walter Mathau, Rich Little, Henny Youngman, Robert Klein, Bronson Pinchot, and The Smothers Brothers.
1992 85m/C **VHS $59.95** CAF ⅛⅛

Tricheurs Scam artists hit largest casino in the world and look forward to golden years of retirement. From the director of "Reversal of Fortune." In French with English subtitles. **AKA:** Cheaters.
1984 95m/C FR Jacques Dutronc, Bulle Ogier, Kurt Raab, Virgilio Teixeira, Steve Baes; **D:** Barbet Schroeder. **VHS, Beta $59.99** WAR, BTV, FCT ⅛⅛

Trick or Treat A high school student is helped to exact violent revenge against his bullying contemporaries. His helper is the spirit of a violent heavy metal rock star who he raises from the dead. Sometimes clever, not terribly scary.
1986 (R) 97m/C Tony Fields, Marc Price, Ozzy Osbourne, Gene Simmons; **D:** Charles Martin Smith. **VHS, Beta $19.98** LHV, WAR ⅛½

Trick or Treats Young boy's pranks on his terrified babysitter backfire on Halloween night. His deranged father, escaped from an asylum, shows up to help him "scare" her. Giroux doesn't look very frightened in this extremely tedious film from Welles' best camera man.
1982 (R) 90m/C Carrie Snodgress, David Carradine, Jackie Giroux, Steve Railsback; **D:** Gary Graver. **VHS, Beta $69.98** LIV, VES Woof!

Tricks of the Trade Goody-two-shoe housewife and hooker accomplice search for husband's murderer. Racy made-for-television fodder.
1988 (R) 100m/C Cindy Williams, Markie Post, Chris Mulkey, James Whitmore Jr., Scott Paulin, John Ritter, Apollonia; **D:** Jack Bender. **VHS, LV $19.95** ACA, SFR ⅛⅛

Trident Force International counter-terrorism team is ordered to destroy the Palestinian Revolutionary Legion by any means possible.
1988 90m/C Anthony Alonzo, Mark Gil, Nanna Anderson, Steve Rogers, Eddie M. Gaerlan; **D:** Richard Smith. **VHS, Beta** NO ⅛

Trifles Five people enter a farmhouse kitchen in the bleak Midwest plains where a man was murdered upstairs. Whodunit? The solution lies in piecing together certain "trifles" that seem even more trivial later.
1979 21m/C **VHS, Beta** BFA ⅛½

Trigger, Jr. Rogers and Evans team up to battle an extortion ring and a murderous stallion.
1950 68m/C Roy Rogers, Dale Evans, Pat Brady, Gordon Jones, Grant Withers; **D:** William Witney. **VHS $12.98** REP ⅛⅛

Trigger Pals Jarrett stars in this basic oater about bringing a gang of rustlers to justice. Besides the usual gunplay, he also attempts to sing a few songs.
1939 58m/B Art Jarrett, Lee Powell, Al "Fuzzy" St. John, Ted Adams; **D:** Philip Krasne. **VHS, Beta $27.95** VCN ⅛½

Trigger Trio Rancher with diseased cattle kills a ranch inspector. The Three Mesquiteers are called in to crack the case.
1937 54m/B Ray Corrigan, Max Terhune, Ralph Byrd, Robert Warwick, Cornelius Keefe; **D:** William Witney. **VHS, Beta $19.95** VCN, DVT ⅛½

Trilby Original screen production of Du Maurier's classic tale of Svengali.

1917 59m/B Clara Kimball Young, Wilton Lackaye, Chester Barnett; *D:* Maurice Tourneur. **VHS, Beta** $19.95 *GPV, FCT ♂♂♂*

Trilogy of Terror Black shows her versatility as she plays a tempting seductress, a mousy schoolteacher and the terrified victim of an African Zuni fetish doll in three horror shorts penned by Richard Mathes. Made for television.
1975 78m/C Karen Black, Robert Burton, John Karlen, Gregory Harrison; *D:* Dan Curtis. **VHS, Beta** $59.95 *MPI ♂♂½*

Trinity is Still My Name Sequel to "They Call Me Trinity." Insouciant bumbling brothers Trinity and Bambino, oblivious to danger and hopeless odds, endure mishaps and adventures as they try to right wrongs. A funny parody of Western cliches that never becomes stale. *AKA:* Continuavamo A Chiamarlo Trinita.
1975 (G) 117m/C *IT* Bud Spencer, Terence Hill, Harry Carey Jr.; *D:* E.B. Clucher. **VHS, Beta, LV** $9.99 *CCB, SUE, HHE ♂♂½*

Trio Sequel to "Quartet," featuring the W. Somerset Maugham stories "The Verger," "Mr. Knowall" and "Sanatorium Acclaimed." Cinematography by Geoffrey Unsworth and Reg Wyer.
1950 88m/B Jean Simmons, Michael Rennie, Bill Travers, James Hayter, Kathleen Harrison, Felix Aylmer, Nigel Patrick, Finlay Currie, John Laurie; *D:* Ken Annakin, Harold French. **VHS, Beta** *NO ♂♂♂*

The Trip A psychedelic journey to the world of inner consciousness, via drugs. A television director, unsure where his life is going, decides to try a "trip" to expand his understanding. Hopper is the drug salesman, Dern, the tour guide for Fonda's trip through sex, witches, torture chambers and more. Great period music. Screenplay by Jack Nicholson.
1967 85m/C Peter Fonda, Dennis Hopper, Susan Strasberg, Dick Miller, Peter Bogdanovich, Bruce Dern; *D:* Roger Corman; *W:* Jack Nicholson. **VHS, Beta** $29.98 *LIV, VES ♂♂*

The Trip to Bountiful An elderly widow, unhappy living in her son's fancy modern home, makes a pilgrimage back to her childhood home in Bountiful, Texas. Based on the Horton Foote play. Fine acting with Oscar-winning performance from Page.
1985 (PG) 102m/C Geraldine Page, Rebecca DeMornay, John Heard, Carlin Glynn, Richard Bradford; *D:* Peter Masterson. Academy Awards '85: Best Actress (Page); Nominations: Best Adapted Screenplay; Independent Spirit Awards '86: Best Actress (Page), Best Screenplay; National Media Owl Awards '87: First Prize. **VHS, Beta, LV, 8mm** $14.95 *COL, BTV, SUE ♂♂♂*

Triple Cross Plummer is a British safecracker imprisoned on the channel islands at the outbreak of World War II. When the Germans move in, he offers to work for them if they set him free. The Germans buy his story and send him to England, but once there he offers his services to the British as a double agent. Based on the exploits of Eddie Chapman, adapted from his book, "The Eddie Chapman Story."
1967 91m/C *FR GB* Christopher Plummer, Romy Schneider, Trevor Howard, Gert Frobe, Yul Brynner, Claudine Auger, Georges Lycan, Jess Hahn, Howard Vernon; *D:* Terence Young. **VHS, Beta** $39.99 *ACE, MOV, HHE ♂♂♂*

Triple Echo A young woman falls for an army deserter who is hiding from the military police by dressing as a woman. Mistrust and deception get the best of some of the involved parties. *AKA:* Soldier in Skirts.

1977 (R) 90m/C *GB* Glenda Jackson, Oliver Reed, Brian Deacon; *D:* Michael Apted. **VHS, Beta** $42.95 *PGN ♂♂*

Triple Impact Hall, Cook, and Riley are three martial-arts experts who join forces against illegal gambling syndicates who are staging full-contact bloodmatches. Their alliance leads them to Asia where the prize is death—or a fortune in gold.
1992 97m/C Dale "Apollo" Cook, Ron Hall, Bridgett "Baby Doll" Riley, Robert Marius, Steve Rogers, Nick Nicholson, Ned Hourani, Mike "Cobra" Cole; *D:* David Hunt; *W:* Steve Rogers. **VHS** $89.95 *AIP ♂*

Triple Trouble/Easy Street Two of Chaplin's classic two-reel silent comedy shorts are shown on video.
1918 60m/B Charlie Chaplin, Edna Purviance, Eric Campbell. **VHS, Beta, 8mm** $24.95 *VYY ♂*

TripleCross Three former cops strike it rich and although they love the money, they miss the game, so they get involved in a murder case. These wealthy detectives encounter high-level gangsters, a baseball scandal, and a hit man in their race to solve the perfect crime.
1985 97m/C Ted Wass, Markie Post, Gary Swanson; *D:* David Greene. **VHS, Beta** $79.95 *PSM ♂♂½*

Tripods: The White Mountains Sci-fi thriller about the takeover of earth by alien tripods. The conquerors start controlling human minds, but not until after they are sixteen years old. Two boys seek to end the terror.
1984 150m/C John Shackley, Jim Baker, Cari Seel; *D:* Graham Theakston. **VHS, Beta, LV** $79.95 *SVS, IME ♂♂½*

Tripwire A vengeance-crazed government agent tracks down the terrorist who murdered his wife.
1989 (R) 120m/C Terence Knox, David Warner, Charlotte Lewis, Isabella Hoffman, Yaphet Kotto, Thomas Chong, Meg Foster; *D:* James Lemmo. **VHS, Beta, LV** $89.95 *COL ♂½*

Tristana The allegorical tale of a beautiful girl (Deneuve) who moves in with a hypocritical benefactor following the death of her mother. She is quickly exploited and seduced by the one who would protect her, but runs away with an artist in pursuit of love. The affair fails and Deneuve, after developing a tumor and losing a leg, returns and marries the benefactor, who despite her lack of feeling for him, can support and care for her. Searing in its commentary on Catholicism, death, lust, and the woebegone place of humanity in the world, the movie is also widely seen as a depiction of fascist Spain's attempt to find its place in the twentieth century. Based on the novel by Benito Perez Galdos. In Spanish with English subtitles.
1970 (PG) 98m/C *SP IT FR* Catherine Deneuve, Fernando Rey, Franco Nero, Lola Gaos, Antonio Casas; *D:* Luis Bunuel. **VHS** $59.95 *HTV, TAM ♂♂♂♂*

The Triumph of Sherlock Holmes Wontner and Fleming teamed for an early series of Holmesian romps. In one of their best outings, Sherlock Holmes comes out of retirement as a series of bizarre murders of Pennsylvania coal miners lure him back into action. From "The Valley of Fear" by Sir Arthur Conan Doyle.
1935 84m/B *GB* Arthur Wontner, Ian Fleming; *D:* Leslie Hiscott. **VHS, Beta, 3/4U, Special order formats** $16.95 *SNC, NOS, CAB ♂♂½*

Triumph of the Son of Hercules All other victories pale when compared to this, the Son of Hercules' greatest!

1963 ?m/C *IT* Kirk Morris, Cathia Caro. **VHS, Beta** $16.95 *SNC ♂♂½*

Triumph of the Spirit Gritty account of boxer Salamo Arouch's experiences in Auschwitz. The boxer became champion in matches between prisoners conducted for the amusement of Nazi officers. Filmed on location in Auschwitz.
1989 (R) 115m/C Willem Dafoe, Robert Loggia, Edward James Olmos, Wendy Gazelle; *D:* Robert M. Young. **VHS, Beta, LV** $89.95 *COL ♂♂♂*

Triumph of the Will Director Riefenstahl's formidable, stunning film, documenting Hitler and the Sixth Nazi Party Congress in 1934 in Nuernberg, Germany. The greatest and most artful propaganda piece ever produced. German dialogue. Includes English translation of the speeches.
1934 115m/B *GE D:* Leni Riefenstahl. **VHS, Beta, 3/4U** $24.95 *NOS, SUE, VYY ♂♂♂*

Triumphs of a Man Called Horse An Indian must save his people from prospectors in order to keep his title as Peace, Chief of the Yellow Hand Sioux. Inadequate sequel to two previous films: "A Man Called Horse" and "The Return of a Man Called Horse."
1983 (R) 91m/C *MX* Richard Harris; *D:* John Hough. **VHS, Beta** $69.99 *HBO ♂♂*

Troilus & Cressida Here love is mocked and heroism made absurd in a powerful play revealing the darker side of Shakespeare.
1982 190m/C Anton Lesser, Suzanne Burden. **VHS, Beta** *TLF ♂♂½*

Trojan Women Euripides' tragedy on the fate of the women of Troy after the Greeks storm the famous city. The play does not translate well to the screen, in spite of tour-de-force acting.
1971 (G) 105m/C Katharine Hepburn, Vanessa Redgrave, Irene Papas, Genevieve Bujold, Brian Blessed, Patrick Magee; *D:* Michael Cacoyannis. **VHS, Beta** $39.95 *FHS ♂♂*

Troll A malevolent troll haunts an apartment building and possesses a young girl in hopes of turning all humans into trolls. Sometimes imaginative, sometimes embarrassing. Followed by a sequel.
1985 (PG-13) 86m/C Noah Hathaway, Gary Sandy, Anne Lockhart, Sonny Bono, Shelley Hack, June Lockhart, Michael Moriarty; *D:* John Carl Buechler. **VHS, Beta, LV** $79.98 *LIV, VES ♂½*

Troll 2 A young boy can only rely on his faith in himself when no one believes his warnings about an evil coming to destroy his family. Entering into a nightmare world, Joshua must battle witches' spells and the evil trolls who carry out their bidding.
1992 (PG-13) 95m/C Michael Stephenson, Connie McFarland; *D:* Drago Floyd. **VHS** $79.95 *COL ♂½*

Troma's War The survivors of an air crash find themselves amid a tropical terrorist-run civil war. Also available in a 105-minute, unrated version. Devotees of trash films shouldn't miss this one; Weil is an alias used by Michael Herz and Lloyd Kaufman.
1988 (R) 90m/C Ara Romanoff, Michael Ryder, Carolyn Beauchamp, Sean Bowen; *D:* Michael Herz, Samuel Weil. **VHS, Beta** $19.98 *MED Woof!*

Tromba, the Tiger Man A circus tiger tamer uses a special drug that hypnotizes the critters into obeying his every whim. When he tries the same drug on women, things get out of hand. *AKA:* Tromba.

1952 62m/B **GE** Rene Deltgen, Angelika Hauff, Gustav Knuth, Hilde Weissner, Grethe Weiser, Gardy Granass, Adrian Hoven; **D:** Helmut Weiss. **VHS, Beta** $16.95 *SNC* ⅛½

Tron A video game designer enters into his computer, where he battles the computer games he created and seeks revenge on other designers who have stolen his creations. Sounds better than it plays. Terrific special effects, with lots of computer-created graphics.
1982 (PG) 96m/C Jeff Bridges, Bruce Boxleitner, David Warner, Cindy Morgan, Barnard Hughes, Dan Shor; **D:** Steven Lisberger. **VHS, Beta, LV** $19.99 *DIS* ⅛⅛

Troop Beverly Hills When spoiled housewife Long is chosen to lead her daughter's Girl Scout troop from posh Beverly Hills, everyone gets lessons deviating from the standard fare. From "camp-outs" at exclusive hotels to minks in the rain, the troop of unwilling, uncooperative little brats must eventually learn to work together to survive the wilderness and come out on top. Silly, light fun.
1989 (PG) 105m/C Shelley Long, Craig T. Nelson, Betty Thomas, Mary Gross, Stephanie Beacham; **D:** Jeff Kanew. **VHS, Beta, LV, 8mm** $14.95 *COL* ⅛⅛½

Trop Jolie pour Etre Honette Four women sharing an apartment witness a robbery and begin to suspect their neighbor is the culprit. So they decide to steal the money from him. In French with English subtitles. *AKA:* Too Pretty to Be Honest.
1967 95m/C **FR** Jane Birkin, Serge Gainsbourg, Bernadette LaFont. **VHS, Beta** *NO* ⅛⅛

Tropic Heat An exploitative voodoo/ancient taboo adventure with plenty to avoid.
1984 90m/C Tudi Wiggins, Christopher St. John, Greer St. John, Sabra Welles. **VHS, Beta** $19.98 *VDC, MOV* Woof!

Tropic of Desire A gigolo is swept up into a number of meaningless affairs in Key West, Florida. Based on Darwin Porter's novel "Butterflies in Heat."
1987 87m/C Matt Collins, Eartha Kitt, Pat Carroll, Tom Ewell, Barbara Baxley. **VHS** $69.95 *SVS* ⅛

Tropical Heat When the Maharajah is killed on safari, his grieving widow (D'Abo) files a five-million-dollar insurance claim before returning to India. She's followed by an investigator (Rossovich) who becomes infatuated with the lovely D'Abo. Through palaces, primitive villages, and ancient jungle temples, they are drawn into a mystery involving blackmail and murder. Based on a story by Jag Mundhra, Michael W. Potts, and Simon Levy.
1993 (R) 86m/C Rick Rossovich, Maryam D'Abo, Lee Ann Beaman, Asha Siewkumar; **D:** Jag Mundhra; **W:** Michael W. Potts; **M:** Del Casher. **VHS** $89.95 *PSM* ⅛

Tropical Snow A pair of lovers living poorly in Colombia decide to enter the drug trade in exchange for passage to the U.S. offered to them by drug kingpin Carradine. Unfortunately, they get more than they bargained for. Shot on location.
1988 (R) 87m/C David Carradine, Madeleine Stowe, Nick Corri, Argemiro Catiblanco; **D:** Ciro Duran. **VHS, Beta, LV** $34.95 *PAR* ⅛

Trouble Along the Way Wayne, in an uncharacteristically sentimental role, stars as a once big-time college football coach who takes a coaching job at a small, financially strapped Catholic college in an effort to retain custody of his young daughter. He uses some underhanded methods to recruit good players (with poor scholastic records),

promising them they will get a share of parking fees and concessions. Once the rector of the school finds out, he fires Wayne, even though the team won its first game. Reed, the probation officer, thus won't file a favorable report for Wayne. At the custody trial, however, the rector shows up, says the whole fiasco was his fault, and offers Wayne his job back. Good family fare proves that Wayne can handle comedy as well as action.
1953 110m/B John Wayne, Donna Reed, Charles Coburn, Tom Tully, Sherry Jackson, Marie Windsor, Tom Helmore, Dabbs Greer, Leif Erickson, Douglas Spencer; **D:** Michael Curtiz. **VHS** $19.98 *WAR* ⅛⅛½

Trouble Bound Madsen is Harry, a guy just out of prison, on his way to Nevada with trouble dogging him every step. He's got a dead body in the car trunk, drug dealers after him, and when he offers a lift to a pretty cocktail waitress (Arquette) his luck only gets worse. She plans to kill a Mob boss and it's no secret. Chases and violence.
1992 (R) 90m/C Michael Madsen, Patricia Arquette, Florence Stanley, Seymour Cassel, Sal Jenco; **D:** Jeff Reiner; **W:** Darrell Fetty, Francis Delia; **M:** Vinnie Golia. **VHS, LV** $89.98 *FXV* ⅛⅛

Trouble Busters Troubled locals worry about who to call when oil is discovered in their town, bringing evil profiteers with it. The Trouble Busters come into town to set things straight.
1933 51m/B Jack Hoxie, Lane Chandler; **D:** Lewis Collins. **VHS, Beta** $19.95 *NOS, DVT* ⅛

Trouble in Mind Stylized romance is set in the near future in a rundown diner. Kristofferson is an ex-cop who gets involved in the lives of a young couple looking for a better life. Look for Divine in one of her/his rare appearances outside of John Waters' works.
1986 (R) 111m/C Kris Kristofferson, Keith Carradine, Genevieve Bujold, Lori Singer, Divine, Joe Morton; **D:** Alan Rudolph. **VHS, Beta, LV, 8mm** $14.95 *COL, NLC* ⅛⅛⅛

Trouble in Paradise Welch stars as a widow stranded in a tropical island paradise with an Australian sailor. The two must struggle as they are stalked by a gang of drug smugglers, hence the title. Made for television.
1988 92m/C Raquel Welch, Jack Thompson, Nicholas Hammond, John Gregg; **D:** Di Drew. **VHS** *CAF* ⅛⅛

Trouble in Paris Softcore trash about two wives going to Paris without their husbands and having sex all over the place.
1987 83m/C **VHS, Beta** $29.95 *MED* ⅛⅛

Trouble in Store A bumbling department store employee stumbles on a gangster's plot. Fun gags and a good cast.
1953 85m/B Margaret Rutherford, Norman Wisdom, Moira Lister, Megs Jenkins; **D:** John Paddy Carstairs. **VHS** *REP* ⅛⅛½

Trouble in Texas Outlaws go to a rodeo and try to steal the prize money. Tex wants to find out who killed his brother and in his spare time, sings and tries to stop the crooks. Notable because it is the last film Hayworth made under her original stage name (Rita Cansino).
1937 65m/B Tex Ritter, Rita Hayworth, Earl Dwire, Yakima Canutt; **D:** Robert North Bradbury. **VHS, Beta** $19.95 *NOS, DVT, UHV* ⅛⅛

Trouble in the Glen A Scottish-American soldier returns to his ancestral home and becomes involved in a dispute between the town residents and a lord over a closed road. Uneven script undermines comic idea.

1954 91m/C Orson Welles, Victor McLaglen, Forrest Tucker, Margaret Lockwood; **D:** Herbert Wilcox. **VHS** $19.98 *REP* ⅛⅛½

The Trouble with Angels Two young girls turn a convent upside down with their endless practical jokes. Russell is everything a Mother Superior should be: understanding, wise, and beautiful.
1966 112m/C Hayley Mills, June Harding, Rosalind Russell, Gypsy Rose Lee, Binnie Barnes; **D:** Ida Lupino; **M:** Jerry Goldsmith. **VHS, Beta, LV** $59.95 *COL* ⅛⅛½

The Trouble with Dick An ambitious young science fiction writer's personal troubles begin to appear in his writing. Although the box cover displays a "Festival Winner" announcement, don't be fooled! Story becomes tedious after first five minutes.
1988 (R) 86m/C Tom Villard, Susan Dey; **D:** Gary Walkow. **VHS, Beta** $29.95 *ACA* ⅛

The Trouble with Father Erwin starred in the classic comedy series about a bumbling father which aired from 1950-1955. Two episodes per tape. On this tape: "Yvette," a 1954 episode in which Stu tries to surprise June with a lifelike female mannequin as an anniversary gift and the 1952 episode "What Paper Do you Read" when June enrolls in Stu's evening government classes. *AKA:* The Stu Erwin Show.
1950 50m/B Stuart Erwin, June Collyer Erwin, Sheila James, Ann Todd, Martin Milner, Willie Best. **VHS, Beta** $19.95 *NOS, MOV, DVT* ⅛

The Trouble with Girls (and How To Get Into It) A 1920s traveling show manager tries to solve a local murder. Not as much singing as his earlier films, but good attention is paid to details. This is definitely one of the better Elvis vehicles. ♫Almost; Clean Up Your Own Back Yard. *AKA:* The Chautauqua.
1969 (G) 99m/C Elvis Presley, Marlyn Mason, Nicole Jaffe, Sheree North, Edward Andrews, John Carradine, Vincent Price, Joyce Van Patten, Dabney Coleman, John Rubinstein, Anthony Teague; **D:** Peter Tewkesbury. **VHS, Beta** $19.95 *MGM* ⅛⅛

The Trouble with Harry When a little boy finds a dead body in a Vermont town, it causes all kinds of problems for the community. No one is sure who killed Harry and what to do with the body. MacLaine's film debut and Bernard Hermann's first musical score for Hitchcock.
1955 (PG) 90m/C John Forsythe, Shirley MacLaine, Edmund Gwenn, Jerry Mathers, Mildred Dunnock, Mildred Natwick, Royal Dano; **D:** Alfred Hitchcock. **VHS, Beta, LV** $19.95 *MCA, HMV* ⅛⅛⅛

The Trouble with Spies A bumbling British spy goes to locate a Russian agent, makes a million mistakes and wins anyway. A loser of a film, wasted a fine cast. Made in 1984; no one bothered to release it for 3 years.
1987 (PG-13) 91m/C Donald Sutherland, Malcolm Morley, Lucy Gutteridge, Ruth Gordon, Ned Beatty, Michael Hordern, Robert Morley; **D:** Burt Kennedy. **VHS, Beta** $79.99 *HBO* ⅛

Truck Stop This truck stop has all a trucker needs—including the owner, voluptuous Pamela.
197? 80m/C Nikki Gentile, Elizabeth Turner; **D:** Jean Marie Pallardy. **VHS** *MED* ⅛

Truck Stop Women Female truckers become involved in smuggling and prostitution at a truck stop. The mob wants a cut of the business and will do anything to get their way. Better than it sounds.

1974 (R) 88m/C Claudia Jennings, Lieux Dressler, John Martino, Dennis Fimple, Dolores Dorn, Gene Drew, Paul Carr, Jennifer Burton; **D:** Mark L. Lester. **VHS, Beta** $59.95 *VES* 🐾🐾

Truck Turner He's a bounty hunter, he's black and he's up against a threadbare plot. Hayes methodically eliminates everyone involved with his partner's murder while providing groovy soundtrack. Quintessential blaxploitation.
1974 (R) 91m/C Isaac Hayes, Yaphet Kotto, Annazette Chase, Nichelle Nichols, Scatman Crothers, Dick Miller; **D:** Jonathan Kaplan; **M:** Isaac Hayes. **VHS** $59.95 *ORI, FCT* 🐾½

Trucker's Woman Man takes a job driving an 18-wheel truck in order to find the murderers of his father.
1983 (R) 90m/C Michael Hawkins, Mary Cannon; **D:** Will Zens. **VHS, Beta** $42.95 *PGN* 🐾

True Believer Cynical lawyer, once a '60s radical, now defends rich drug dealers. Spurred on by a young protege, he takes on the hopeless case of imprisoned Asian-American accused of gang-slaying. Tense thriller with good cast.
1989 (R) 103m/C James Woods, Robert Downey Jr., Yuji Okumoto, Margaret Colin, Kurtwood Smith, Tom Bower, Miguel Fernandez, Charles Hallahan; **D:** Joseph Ruben. **VHS, Beta, LV** $14.95 *COL* 🐾🐾½

True Blood A man returns to his home turf to save his brother from the same ruthless gang who set him up for a cop's murder.
1989 (R) 100m/C Chad Lowe, Jeff Fahey, Sherilyn Fenn; **D:** Peter Maris. **VHS, Beta, LV** $29.95 *FRH, IME* 🐾🐾

True Colors A woman fights for her homeland of France in order to save the country from being taken over by Hitler.
1987 (PG-13) 160m/C Noni Hazlehurst, John Waters, Patrick Ryecart, Shane Briant, Alan Andrews; **D:** Pina Amenta. **VHS, Beta** $29.95 *ACA* 🐾🐾½

True Colors Law school buddies take divergent paths in post grad real world. Straight and narrow Spader works for Justice Department while dropout Cusack manipulates friends and acquaintances to further his position as Senator's aid. Typecast, predictable and moralizing.
1991 (R) 111m/C John Cusack, James Spader, Imogen Stubbs, Mandy Patinkin, Richard Widmark; **D:** Herbert Ross. **VHS, LV** $19.95 *PAR* 🐾🐾

True Confessions Tale of corruption pits two brothers, one a priest and the other a detective, against each other. Nice 1940s period look, with excellent performances from De Niro and Duvall. Based on a true case from the Gregory Dunne novel, with screenplay by the author and Joan Didion.
1981 (R) 110m/C Robert De Niro, Robert Duvall, Kenneth McMillan, Charles Durning, Cyril Cusack, Ed Flanders, Burgess Meredith, Louisa Moritz; **D:** Ulu Grosbard. **VHS, Beta, LV** $19.98 *MGM* 🐾🐾🐾

The True Game of Death A story of the circumstances behind the death of superstar Bruce Lee.
197? 90m/C Bruce Lee, Shou Lung. **VHS, Beta** *NO* 🐾🐾🐾

True Grit Hard-drinking U.S. Marshal Rooster Cogburn (Wayne) is hired by a young girl (Darby) to find her father's killer. Won Wayne his only Oscar. Based on the Charles Portis novel. Prompted sequel, "Rooster Cogburn."
1969 (G) 128m/C John Wayne, Glen Campbell, Kim Darby, Robert Duvall; **D:** Henry Hathaway. Academy Awards '69: Best Actor (Wayne); Nominations: Best Song ("True Grit"); Golden

Globe Awards '70: Best Actor—Drama (Wayne); National Board of Review Awards '69: 10 Best Films of the Year. **VHS, Beta, LV** $14.95 *PAR, HHE, TLF* 🐾🐾🐾

True Heart Susie A simple, moving story about a girl who is in love with a man who marries another girl from the city. Silent.
1919 87m/B Lillian Gish, Robert Harring; **D:** D.W. Griffith. **VHS, Beta** $19.95 *NOS, VYY, DVT* 🐾🐾½

True Identity Henry, a comic superstar in England, stars as an innocent black man marked for death by the Mafia. He hides by disguising himself as white and gets a taste of life on the other side of the color line. The interesting premise was based on a classic Eddie Murphy sketch on "Saturday Night Live," but isn't treated with sufficient imagination or humor here.
1991 (R) 94m/C Lenny Henry, Frank Langella, Anne-Marie Johnson; **D:** Charles Lane. **VHS, Beta** $94.95 *TOU, FCT* 🐾🐾

True Love Low-budget, savagely observed comedy follows the family and community events leading up to a Bronx Italian wedding. Authentic slice-of-life about two young people with very different ideas about what marriage and commitment mean. Acclaimed script and performances.
1989 (R) 104m/C Annabella Sciorra, Ron Eldard, Aida Turturro, Roger Rignack, Michael J. Wolfe, Star Jasper, Kelly Cinnante, Rick Shapiro, Suzanne Costallos, Vinny Pastore; **D:** Nancy Savoca. **VHS, Beta, LV** $89.95 *MGM* 🐾🐾

True Romance Misfits Slater and Arquette meet at a John Woo film in Detroit, accidentally lift a suitcase full of drugs, and hit the road to L.A. with the Mob and the cops in pursuit. Bad guys Hopper and Oldman are Slater's character likes to talk to Elvis (Kilmer) in times of stress. Horrific violence mixed with very black humor (courtesy of a script by pre "Reservoir Dogs" Tarantino and "Last Boy Scout" director Scott).
1993 (R) ?m/C Christian Slater, Patricia Arquette, Gary Oldman, Brad Pitt, Val Kilmer, Dennis Hopper, Christopher Walken, Samuel L. Jackson, Christopher Penn, Bronson Pinchot, Michael Rappaport, Saul Rubinek, Conchata Ferrell, James Gandolfini; **D:** Tony Scott; **W:** Quentin Tarantino; **M:** Hans Zimmer. **VHS** 🐾🐾🐾

True Stories Quirky, amusing look at the eccentric denizens of a fictional, off-center Texas town celebrating its 150th anniversary. Notable are Kurtz as the Laziest Woman in America and Goodman as a blushing suitor. Directorial debut of Byrne. Co-written with playwright Beth Henley. Music by Byrne and the Talking Heads. Worth a look.
1986 (PG) 89m/C David Byrne, John Goodman, Swoosie Kurtz, Spalding Gray, Annie McEnroe, Pops Staples, Tito Larriva; **D:** David Byrne. **VHS, Beta, LV** $19.98 *MVD, WAR* 🐾🐾🐾½

True West Filmed performance of the acclaimed Sam Shepard play about two mismatched brothers. Made for Television.
1986 110m/C John Malkovich, Gary Sinise; **D:** Allan Goldstein. **VHS, Beta** $59.95 *ACA, VTK* 🐾🐾🐾

Truly, Madly, Deeply The recent death of her lover drives a young woman into despair and anger, until he turns up at her apartment one day. Tender and well written tale of love and the supernatural, with believable characters and plot-line. Playwright Minghella's directorial debut.
1991 (PG) 107m/C Juliet Stevenson, Alan Rickman, Bill Paterson, Michael Maloney; **W/D:** Anthony Minghella. **VHS** *TOU* 🐾🐾🐾

The Trumpet and I An eight-year-old boy inherits magical powers when he plays a "silver sounding" trumpet.
1985 53m/C VHS, Beta $29.95 *GEM* 🐾🐾½

Trumps Startling relationship between man and woman has dire consequences. **AKA:** Enormous Changes at the Last Minute.
1988 (R) 90m/C Ellen Barkin, Kevin Bacon, Maria Tucci, Ron McLarty, Zvee Scooler. **VHS** $29.95 *HHE* 🐾🐾

Trust An obnoxious girl, tossed out by her family after becoming pregnant, forms a loving bond with a strange, possibly deranged guy from an abusive household. Similar in style and theme to Hartley's "The Unbelievable Truth" - a peculiar sardonic comedy/drama not for every taste.
1991 (R) 107m/C Adrienne Shelly, Martin Donovan, Merritt Nelson, Edie Falco, John McKay; **W/D:** Hal Hartley. **VHS, LV** $19.98 *REP* 🐾🐾

Trust Me A cynical L.A. art dealer decides to promote a young artist's work and then kill him off to increase the value of his paintings. Satirical view of the Los Angeles art crowd.
1989 (R) 94m/C Adam Ant, Talia Balsam, David Packer, Barbara Bain, Joyce Van Patten, William DeAcutis; **D:** Bobby Houston. **VHS, Beta, LV** *NO* 🐾🐾

Truth About Women An old aristocrat recounts his youthful adventures to his son-in-law. A pale British comedy of manners.
1958 107m/C GB Laurence Harvey, Julie Harris, Mai Zetterling, Eva Gabor, Wilfrid Hyde-White, Derek Farr; **D:** Muriel Box. **VHS, Beta** $19.95 *NOS, DWE* 🐾🐾

Truth or Dare? The childhood game of truth or dare turns deadly in this violent thriller.
1986 87m/C John Brace, Mary Fanaro, Geoffrey Lewis Miller; **D:** Yale Wilson. **VHS, Beta** $49.95 *PII, HHE* 🐾

Truth or Dare A quasi-concert-documentary—here is music superstar Madonna tarted up in fact, fiction, and fantasy—exhibitionism to the nth power. Tacky, self-conscious and ultimately, if you are a Madonna fan, moving. On camera Madonna stings ex-boyfriend Warren Beatty, disses admirer Kevin Costner, quarrels with her father, reminisces, and does sexy things with a bottle. Oh yes, she occasionally sings and dances. Both those who worship and dislike the Material Girl will find much to pick apart here. Available in Widescreen format on laserdisc. **AKA:** In Bed with Madonna; Madonna Truth or Dare.
1991 (R) 118m/C Madonna; **D:** Alek Keshishian. **VHS, LV** $92.95 *LIV, FCT, PIA* 🐾🐾½

Truth or Die This trite, cliched TV movie chronicles the life of convict Jerry Rosenberg, the first prisoner to earn a law degree from his cell. Still, an uncharacteristic role for sitcom guy Danza. Based on Rosenberg's book "Doing Life." **AKA:** Doing Life.
1986 (PG-13) 96m/C Tony Danza, Jon DeVries, Lisa Langlois, Rocco Sisto; **D:** Gene Reynolds. **VHS, LV** *VMK* 🐾🐾

Try and Get Me A small town is incited into a manhunt for kidnappers who murdered their victim. Suspenseful melodrama analyzes mob rule and the criminal mind. **AKA:** Sound of Fury.
1950 91m/B Lloyd Bridges, Kathleen Ryan, Richard Carlson, Frank Lovejoy, Katherine Locke; **D:** Cy Endfield. **VHS** $19.95 *REP* 🐾🐾

The Tsar's Bride A lovely young woman is chosen to be the bride of the horrible Tsar Glebov but when the Tsar's bodyguard falls for her, romantic difficulties ensue. A

hybrid of the 1899 Rimsky-Korsakov opera and an 1849 play. **AKA:** Tsarskaya Nevesta.
1966 95m/B *RU* Raisa Nedashkovskaya, Natalya Rudnaya, Otar Koberidze; *D:* Vladimir Gorikker. **VHS** $49.95 *KUL, MVD, PME* ♫♫½

Tucker and the Horse Thief A girl dresses and lives like a boy for safety's sake during the California Gold Rush.
1985 45m/C VHS, Beta *NO* ♫♫

Tucker: The Man and His Dream Portrait of Preston Tucker, entrepreneur and industrial idealist, who in 1946 tried to build the car of the future and was effectively run out of business by the powers-that-were. Ravishing, ultra-nostalgic lullaby to the American Dream. Watch for Jeff's dad, Lloyd, in a bit role. Musical score by Joe Jackson.
1988 (PG) 111m/C Jeff Bridges, Martin Landau, Dean Stockwell, Frederic Forrest, Mako, Joan Allen, Christian Slater, Lloyd Bridges; *D:* Francis Ford Coppola. Academy Awards '88 Nominations: Best Art Direction/Set Decoration, Best Costume Design, Best Supporting Actor (Landau); Golden Globe Awards '89: Best Supporting Actor (Landau). **VHS, Beta, LV, 8mm** $14.95 *PAR* ♫♫♫

Tuff Turf The new kid in town must adjust to a different social lifestyle and a new set of rules when his family is forced to move to a low-class section of Los Angeles. He makes enemies immediately when he courts the girlfriend of one of the local toughs. Fast-paced with a bright young cast. Music by Jim Carroll, Lene Lovich, and Southside Johnny.
1985 (R) 113m/C James Spader, Kim Richards, Paul Mones, Matt Clark, Olivia Barash, Robert Downey Jr., Catya Sassoon; *D:* Fritz Kiersch. **VHS, Beta, LV** $9.95 *NWV, STE* ♫♫

Tulips Would-be suicide takes a contract out on himself, and then meets a woman who makes life worth living again. Together they attempt to evade the gangland hit man. Limp comedy.
1981 (PG) 91m/C *CA* Gabe Kaplan, Bernadette Peters, Henry Gibson; *D:* Stan Ferris. **VHS, Beta** $19.95 *SUE* ♫½

Tulsa High-spirited rancher's daughter begins crusade to save her father's oil empire when he's killed. Having become ruthless and determined to succeed at any cost, she eventually sees the error of her ways. Classic Hayward.
1949 96m/C Susan Hayward, Robert Preston, Chill Wills, Ed Begley Sr.; *D:* Stuart Heisler. **VHS, Beta, 3/4U, Special order formats** $19.95 *NOS, QNE, MED* ♫♫♫

Tumbledown Ranch in Arizona After a rodeo accident, an unconscious college student dreams of adventure out west. Part of the "Range Busters" series.
1941 60m/B Ray Corrigan, John "Dusty" King, Max Terhune, Sheila Darcy, Marian Kerby; *D:* S. Roy Luby. **VHS** $19.95 *NOS, DVT* ♫

Tumbleweed Trail Action-packed thundering western.
1942 57m/B William Boyd, Art Davis, Lee Powell, Jack Rockwell; *D:* Sam Newfield. **VHS, Beta** $27.95 *VCN* ♫½

Tumbleweeds William S. Hart's last western. Portrays the last great land rush in America, the opening of the Cherokee Strip in the Oklahoma Territory to homesteaders. Preceded by a sound prologue, made in 1939, in which Hart speaks for the only time on screen, to introduce the story. Silent, with musical score.
1925 114m/B William S. Hart, Lucien Littlefield, Barbara Bedford; *D:* King Baggott. **VHS, Beta, LV** $44.95 *VYY, CCB* ♫♫♫

Tundra Quasi adventure-drama/documentary set in the Alaskan tundra. A young man, known only as the "Flying Doctor," tends to the sick in small villages throughout the wilderness. But his own survival is at stake when his small plane crashes. Filmed on location. **AKA:** The Mighty Thunder.
1936 72m/B Del Cambre; *D:* Norman Dawn. **VHS** $29.95 *VYY* ♫♫½

Tune in Tomorrow Lovesick young Keanu wants to woo divorced babe aunt Hershey and is counseled by wacky soap opera writer Falk. Seems even soap operas draw on real life, and his story's immortalized on the silver screen. Sometimes funny, sometimes not. Adapted from the novel "Aunt Julia and the Scriptwriter."
1990 (PG-13) 90m/C Barbara Hershey, Keanu Reeves, Peter Falk, Bill McCutcheon, Patricia Clarkson, Peter Gallagher, Dan Hedaya, Buck Henry, Hope Lange, John Larroquette, Elizabeth McGovern, Robert Sedgwick, Henry Gibson; *D:* Jon Amiel; *M:* Wynton Marsalis. **VHS, LV** $92.98 *HBO* ♫♫♫

Tunes of Glory Guinness and Mills are wonderful in this well made film about a brutal, sometimes lazy colonel and a disciplined and educated man moving up through the ranks of the British military. York's film debut. From the novel by James Kennaway, who adapted it for the screen. Laserdisc version contains interview with director Neame.
1960 107m/C *GB* Alec Guinness, John Mills, Dennis Price, Kay Walsh, Susannah York; *D:* Ronald Neame. **VHS, Beta, LV** $19.98 *SUE, VYG, NLC* ♫♫♫½

Tunes of Glory/Horse's Mouth Guinness double feature. First, "Tunes of Glory" looks at the relationship between good and bad soldiers vying for the same rank. "Horse's Mouth" takes a much lighter tone. Guinness plays a truly obsessed painter who creates his work on public property. Wildly humorous.
1960 305m/C Alec Guinness, Kay Walsh, Renco Houston, John Mills, Robert Coote; *D:* James Kennaway, Ronald Neame. **VHS, Beta** $69.95 *CHC* ♫♫♫½

The Tunnel Obsessive romance film with a trace of suspense. Artist sees the woman of his dreams at a showing of his work. Her marriage, and her trepidation, don't keep his obsession from consuming him.
1989 (R) 99m/C Jane Seymour, Peter Weller, Fernando Rey; *D:* Antonio Drove. **VHS, Beta, LV** $79.98 *VES, IME* ♫♫½

The Tunnel of Love Day and Widmark are a married couple who find themselves over their heads in red tape when they try to adopt a baby. A beautiful, disapproving adoption investigator also causes more problems for the couple when she believes Widmark is less than ideal father material. Widmark is not in his element at comedy but Day and Young (as their next-door neighbor) are fine in this lightweight adaptation of the Joseph Fields-Peter DeVries play.
1958 98m/B Doris Day, Richard Widmark, Gig Young, Gia Scala, Elisabeth Fraser, Elizabeth Wilson; *D:* Gene Kelly. **VHS, LV** $19.98 *MGM, MOV* ♫♫½

Tunnelvision A spoof of television comprised of irreverent sketches. Fun to watch because of the appearances of several now-popular stars.
1976 (R) 70m/C Chevy Chase, John Candy, Laraine Newman, Joe Flaherty, Howard Hesseman, Gerrit Graham, Al Franken, Tom Davis, Ron Silver; *D:* Neal Israel. **VHS, Beta** *NO* ♫♫½

Turf Boy Desperate for cash, a boy and his uncle try to get an old horse into prime condition for racing. A minor equine melodrama, just the right length for an old-time matinee double-feature. **AKA:** Mr. Celebrity.
1942 68m/B Robert "Buzzy" Henry, James Seay, Doris Day, William Halligan, Gavin Gordon; *D:* William Beaudine. **VHS** $15.95 *NOS, LOO* ♫♫

Turk 182! The angry brother of a disabled fireman takes on City Hall in order to win back the pension that he deserves. He attacks through his graffiti art. Hutton is too heavy for the over-all comic feel of this mostly silly film.
1985 (PG-13) 96m/C Timothy Hutton, Robert Culp, Robert Urich, Kim Cattrall, Peter Boyle, Darren McGavin, Paul Sorvino; *D:* Bob Clark. **VHS, Beta** $79.98 *FOX* ♫½

Turkish Delights Free spirit sculptor falls in love with free spirit gal from bourgeois family and artsy soft porn ensues. That is until a brain tumor brings an end to their fun, and he's left to wallow in flashbacks and more artsy soft porn. Dubbed. Verhoeven later became big box office in the U.S. with "Total Recall."
1973 100m/C *NL* Monique Van De Ven, Rutger Hauer, Tonny Huurdeman, Wim Van Den Brink; *D:* Paul Verhoeven. **VHS** *NO* ♫♫½

The Turn of the Screw Supernatural powers vie with a young governess for control of the souls of the two children in her charge. Redgrave does well in this chilling film adapted from the Henry James story. Remade in 1989.
1974 120m/C Lynn Redgrave, Jasper Jacobs, Eva Griffith; *D:* Dan Curtis. **VHS, Beta, LV** $29.95 *LIV* ♫♫

The Turn of the Screw The young charges of an English nanny are sought for their souls by a dark, unimaginable evil in the mansion. Another version of the Henry James classic.
1989 (R) 60m/C Amy Irving, David Hemmings; *D:* Graeme Clifford. **VHS, Beta, LV** $59.95 *CAN* ♫♫

The Turn of the Screw Yet another version of the Henry James classic as a young governess struggles with sexual obsession and the two children in her care who are possessed by evil.
1992 (R) 95m/C Julian Sands, Patsy Kensit. **VHS, LV** $89.98 *LIV* ♫♫

Turnaround Unusual action/suspense film set in a small town. Relentless gang rampages the citizens. Finally, a man decides he's had enough, and turns on the heathens with his knowledge of magic.
1987 (R) 97m/C Doug McKeon, Tim Maier, Eddie Albert, Gayle Hunnicutt; *D:* Ola Solum. **VHS, Beta** $79.98 *CGH* ♫♫

Turner and Hooch A dog witnesses a murder, and a fussy cop is partnered with the drooling mutt and a weak script in his search for the culprit. Drool as a joke will only go so far, but Hanks is his usual entertaining self.
1989 (PG) 99m/C Tom Hanks, Mare Winningham, Craig T. Nelson, Scott Paulin, J.C. Quinn; *D:* Roger Spottiswoode. **VHS, Beta, LV** $19.99 *TOU* ♫♫

The Turning Point A woman who gave up ballet for motherhood must come to terms as her daughter launches a ballet career and falls for the lead male dancer. The mother finds herself threatened by her daughter's affection toward an old friend who sacrificed a family life for the life of a ballerina. Baryshnikov's film debut. Melodramatic ending and problems due to ballet sequences.

1977 (PG) 119m/C Shirley MacLaine, Anne Bancroft, Tom Skerritt, Leslie Browne, Martha Scott, Marshall Thompson, Mikhail Baryshnikov; *D:* Herbert Ross. Academy Awards '77 Nominations: Best Actress (Bancroft), Best Actress (MacLaine), Best Art Direction/Set Decoration, Best Cinematography, Best Director (Ross), Best Film Editing, Best Original Screenplay, Best Picture, Best Sound, Best Supporting Actor (Baryshnikov), Best Supporting Actress (Browne); Golden Globe Awards '78: Best Director (Ross), Best Film—Drama; Los Angeles Film Critics Association Awards '77: Best Director (Ross); National Board of Review Awards '77: 10 Best Films of the Year, Best Actress (Bancroft), Best Supporting Actor (Skerritt). **VHS, Beta $19.98** *FOX* ⅅⅅ½

Turtle Diary Two lonely Londoners collaborate to free giant turtles from the city aquarium with the aid of a zoo-keeper, and the turtles' freedom somehow frees them as well. Jackson and Kingsley are stunning. Adapted by Harold Pinter from the Russell Hoban book.
1986 (PG) 90m/C *GB* Ben Kingsley, Glenda Jackson, Richard Johnson, Michael Gambon, Rosemary Leach, Jeroen Krabbe, Eleanor Bron; *D:* John Irvin. **VHS, Beta, LV $79.98** *LIV, VES* ⅅⅅⅅ

Turumba A quiet satire about a family of papier-mache animal makers in a Philippine village who get a gargantuan order in time for the Turumba holiday, and desperately try to fill it. In Tagalog with English subtitles.
1984 94m/C *PH* *D:* Kidlat Tahimik. **VHS, Beta $59.95** *FFM, FCT* ⅅⅅⅅ

Tusks A ruthless hunter tries to kill elephants. *AKA:* Fire in Eden.
1989 (R) 99m/C Andrew Stevens, John Rhys-Davies, Lucy Gutteridge, Julian Glover; *D:* Tara Hawkins Moore. **VHS, Beta, LV** *NO* ⅅ½

Tut & Tuttle Young dabbler in magic is transported to ancient Egypt where he is able to demonstrate courage and wits against the evil Horemheb, who has kidnapped Prince Tut.
1982 97m/C Christopher Barnes, Eric Greene, Hans Conried, Vic Tayback. **VHS, Beta** *TLF* ⅅ½

The Tuttles of Tahiti The Tuttles lead a life of leisure in the South Seas. Laughton's child becomes enamoured of his rival's offspring, causing problems between the two families. More interesting than it sounds.
1942 91m/C Charles Laughton, Jon Hall, Peggy Drake, Victor Francen, Gene Reynolds, Florence Bates, Mala, Alma Ross, Curt Bois; *D:* Charles Vidor. **VHS, Beta, LV $19.95** *HHT* ⅅⅅⅅ

Tuxedo Warrior Set in South Africa, this film involves the adventures of a well-dressed mercenary who is caught between the police, diamond thieves, and an old girlfriend's bank robbing.
1982 93m/C John Wyman, Carol Royle, Holly Palance; *D:* Andrew Sinclair. **VHS, Beta $19.95** *STE, NWV* ⅅ½

TV's Best Adventures of Superman This first package of episodes from the original television series, which ran from 1951-1957, contains "Superman on Earth," the black & white series pilot about the Man of Steel's childhood on Krypton and Earth, and "All That Glitters," the series' final episode, wherein Lois Lane and Jimmy Olsen acquire super powers. Also includes the 1941 animated cartoon "Superman," the first-ever screen appearance of the superhero. Additional episodes available.
1951 62m/C George Reeves, Phyllis Coates, Noel Neill, Jack Larson, John Hamilton, Robert Shayne. **VHS, Beta $19.98** *WAR, MOV* ⅅ½

Tweety & Sylvester A compilation of pre-1948 Tweety and Sylvester cartoons.

1948 60m/C *D:* Robert McKimson, Friz Freleng, Chuck Jones. **VHS, Beta $14.95** *MGM, WTA* ⅅ½

Twelfth Night With its practical jokes, lyrics, poetry, and haunting songs, "Twelfth Night" is the most subtle of Shakespeare's comedies. An aristocratic country house and its inhabitants set the stage for a portrayal of the varieties of love. Part of the television series "The Shakespeare Plays."
1980 124m/C *GB* Alec McCowen, Trevor Peacock, Felicity Kendal. **VHS, Beta, LV** *TLF* ⅅⅅⅅ

Twelve Angry Men Fonda sounds the voice of reason as a jury inclines toward a quick-and-dirty verdict against a boy on trial. Excellent ensemble work. Lumet's feature film debut, based on a television play by Reginald Rose.
1957 95m/B Henry Fonda, Martin Balsam, Lee J. Cobb, E.G. Marshall, Jack Klugman, Robert Webber, Ed Begley Sr., John Fiedler, Jack Warden, George Voskovec, Edward Binns, Joseph Sweeney; *D:* Sidney Lumet. Academy Awards '57 Nominations: Best Adapted Screenplay, Best Director (Lumet), Best Picture; Berlin International Film Festival '57: Golden Berlin Bear; British Academy Awards '57: Best Actor (Fonda); Edgar Allan Poe Awards '57: Best Screenplay; National Board of Review Awards '57: 10 Best Films of the Year. **VHS, Beta, LV $19.98** *MGM, FOX, VYG* ⅅⅅⅅ

Twelve Chairs Take-off on Russian folk-tale first filmed in Yugoslavia in 1927. A rich matron admits on her deathbed that she has hidden her jewels in the upholstery of one of twelve chairs that are no longer in her home. A Brooksian treasure hunt ensues.
1970 (PG) 94m/C Mel Brooks, Dom DeLuise, Frank Langella, Ron Moody, Bridget Brice; *D:* Mel Brooks. **VHS, Beta, LV $59.95** *MED* ⅅⅅⅅ

Twelve Months An animated tale of a young girl who learns by trial and error that kindness is always rewarded.
1985 90m/C **VHS, Beta $19.95** *COL, WTA* ⅅⅅⅅ

Twelve O'Clock High Epic drama about the heroic 8th Air Force, with Peck as bomber-group commander sent to shape up a hard-luck group, forced to drive himself and his men to the breaking point. Compelling dramatization of the strain of military command. Includes impressive footage of actual WWII battles. Best-ever flying fortress movie.
1949 132m/B Gregory Peck, Hugh Marlowe, Gary Merrill, Millard Mitchell, Dean Jagger, Paul Stewart; *D:* Henry King. Academy Awards '49: Best Sound, Best Supporting Actor (Jagger); Nominations: Best Actor (Peck), Best Picture. **VHS, Beta, LV $19.98** *FOX, FCT, BTV* ⅅⅅⅅ½

12 Plus 1 A man sells 13 chairs left to him by his aunt, only to find that one of them contained a hidden fortune. He chases across Europe in search of each of them. Some good cameos help move this re-make of a Russian folk-tale along, but it remains lightweight. Tate's last movie, before her death at the hands of Manson and his "family." *AKA:* The Thirteen Chairs.
1970 (R) 94m/C *FR IT* Sharon Tate, Orson Welles, Vittorio Gassman, Mylene Demongeot, Terry-Thomas, Tim Brooke; *Cameos:* Vittorio De Sica; *D:* Nicolas Gessner. **VHS, Beta** *NO* ⅅⅅ½

Twentieth Century Maniacal Broadway director Barrymore transforms shop girl Lombard into a smashing success adored by public and press. Tired of Barrymore's manic-excessive ways, she heads for the Hollywood hills, pursued by the Profile in fine form. Scripted by Hecht and MacArthur.
1934 91m/B Carole Lombard, John Barrymore, Walter Connolly, Roscoe Karns, Edgar Kennedy, Ralph Forbes, Charles Lane, Etienne Girardot, Snow Flake; *D:* Howard Hawks; *W:* Charles MacArthur, Ben Hecht. **Beta $19.95** *COL* ⅅⅅⅅⅅ

Twenty-One Modern morality tale of a young English woman who moves to the U.S. to make a new start, but falls into the same old habits. Kensit is frank and charming, in spite of difficulties with her drug addict boyfriend and the illegal alien she marries. Director Boyd leaves it to the viewer to decide between right and wrong and where Kensit fits.
1991 (R) 92m/C Patsy Kensit, Jack Shepherd, Patrick Ryecart, Maynard Eziashi, Rufus Sewell, Sophie Thompson, Susan Wooldridge; *D:* Don Boyd. **VHS, LV $89.95** *SVS* ⅅⅅ½

21 Hours at Munich Made-for-TV treatment of the massacre of Israeli athletes by Arab terrorists at the 1972 Olympics. Well-done. The film was produced using the actual Munich locations.
1976 100m/C William Holden, Shirley Knight, William Knight, Franco Nero, Anthony Quayle, Noel Willman; *D:* William A. Graham. **VHS** *MOV* ⅅⅅⅅ

23 1/2 Hours Leave Amusing WWI service comedy as a barracks wiseacre bets that by the following morning he'll be breakfasting with a general. It's a song-filled remake of a 1919 film, whose star Douglas MacClean later produced this.
1937 73m/B James Ellison, Terry Walker, Morgan Hill, Arthur Lake, Paul Harvey; *D:* John Blystone. **VHS $15.95** *NOS, LOO* ⅅ½

Twenty-Four Eyes Free-thinking teacher takes on a school of traditionally-taught students on the eve of Japan's invasion of Manchuria in the late 1920s. Much lauded in its native country; in Japanese with English subtitles.
1954 158m/B *JP* Hideko Takamine, Chishu Ryu, Toshiko Kobayashi; *D:* Keisuke Kinoshita. **VHS, Beta $29.95** *SVS, TAM* ⅅⅅⅅ

24 Hours in a Woman's Life A girl in love with an irresponsible guy hears a cautionary tale from grandma Bergman, who once had a whirlwind romance with a young gambler and naively thought she could reform him. A static TV adaptation of an oft-filmed Stefan Zweig novel, unusually lavish for its time but on the dull side. Script by John Mortimer.
1961 90m/C Ingrid Bergman, Rip Torn, John Williams, Lili Darvas, Jerry Orbach; *D:* Silvio Narizzano. **VHS $29.95** *FCT* ⅅⅅ

24 Hours to Midnight A widow uses her ninja skills to wipe out the crime bosses and henchmen who killed her husband.
1992 91m/C Cynthia Rothrock, Stack Pierce; *D:* Leo Fong. **VHS $89.95** *AIP* ⅅ½

25 Fireman's Street An evocative drama about the residents of an old house in Hungary which is about to be torn down, and their evening of remembrances of life before, during and after World War II. In Hungarian with English subtitles.
1973 97m/C Rita Bekes, Peter Muller, Lucyna Winnicka; *D:* Istvan Szabo. **VHS, Beta $69.95** *KIV, TAM* ⅅⅅⅅ

The 27 Day Temperate cold war allegory has aliens deliver five mysterious capsules to five Earthlings from different countries. Each capsule, if opened, is capable of decimating the population of the entire planet, but is rendered ineffective after 27 days or upon the death of the holder. Wild ending. Based on John Mantley novel.
1957 75m/B Gene Barry, Valerie French, George Voskovec, Arnold Moss, Stefan Schnabel, Ralph Clanton, Friedrich Ledebur, Mari Tsien. **VHS $14.98** *MOV, MLB* ⅅⅅ½

29th Street Compelling comedy-drama based on the true story of Frank Pesce, a New York actor who won six million dollars in that state's first lottery. Great performance from Aiello, as usual, but the direction falters in the dramatic sequences. Based on the book by Frank Pesce and James Franciscus.
1991 (R) 101m/C Danny Aiello, Anthony LaPaglia, Lainie Kazan, Frank Pesce, Donna Magnani, Rick Aiello; **W/D:** George Gallo. VHS $19.98 FXV, CCB ✞✞½

Twenty Dollar Star Steamy thriller about an prominent actress who leads a double life as a cheap hooker, and consequent occupational hazards. The title may as well refer to the budget.
1991 (R) 92m/C Rebecca Holden, Bernie White, Eddie Barth, Marilyn Hassett, Dick Sargent; **D:** Paul Leder. VHS PAR ✞½

20 Million Miles to Earth A spaceship returning from an expedition to Venus crashes on Earth, releasing a fast-growing reptilian beast that rampages throughout Athens. Another entertaining work of stop-motion animation master Ray Harryhausen's work, offering a classic battle between the monster and an elephant.
1957 82m/B William Hopper, Joan Taylor, Frank Puglia, Joan Zaremba; **D:** Nathan Juran. LV $49.98 PIA ✞✞½

20,000 Leagues Under the Sea Outstanding silent adaptation of Jules Verne's "20,000 Leagues Under the Sea" and "The Mysterious Island" filmed with a then revolutionary underwater camera. Much octopus fighting. Look for newly mastered edition.
1916 105m/B Matt Moore, Allen Holubar, June Gail, William Welsh, Chris Benton, Dan Hamlon; **W/D:** Stuart Paton. VHS, Beta $19.98 KIV, GPV, DVT ✞✞✞

20,000 Leagues Under the Sea From a futuristic submarine, Captain Nemo wages war on the surface world. A shipwrecked scientist and sailor do their best to thwart Nemo's dastardly schemes. Buoyant Disney version of the Jules Verne fantasy.
1954 127m/C Kirk Douglas, James Mason, Peter Lorre, Paul Lukas, Robert J. Wilke, Carleton Young; **D:** Richard Fleischer. Academy Awards '54: Best Art Direction/Set Decoration (Color), Best Special Effects; Nominations: Best Film Editing; National Board of Review Awards '54: 10 Best Films of the Year. VHS, Beta, LV $19.99 DIS ✞✞✞½

Twice a Judas An amnesiac is swindled and has his family killed by a ruthless renegade. He wants to get even, even though he can't remember who anyone is.
196? 90m/C Klaus Kinski. VHS, Beta $49.95 UNI, MOV ✞

Twice a Woman Man and woman divorce, and then both fall in love with the same provocative young woman. It's complicated.
1979 90m/C Bibi Andersson, Anthony Perkins, Sandra Dumas. VHS, Beta $59.95 PSM ✞

Twice Dead A family moves into a ramshackle mansion haunted by a stage actor's angry ghost. The ghost helps them battle some attacking delinquent boys. Uninteresting story, poorly done. Never released in theaters.
1988 94m/C Tom Breznahan, Jill Whitlow, Sam Melville, Brooke Bundy, Todd Bridges, Jonathan Chapin, Christopher Burgard; **D:** Bert L. Dragin. VHS, Beta, LV $19.98 SUE, NLC Woof!

Twice in a Lifetime Middle-aged man takes stock of his life when he's attracted to Ann-Margret. Realizing he's married in name only, he moves in with his new love while his

former wife and children struggle with shock, disbelief, and anger. Well-acted, realistic, and unsentimental.
1985 (R) 117m/C Gene Hackman, Ellen Burstyn, Amy Madigan, Ann-Margret, Brian Dennehy, Ally Sheedy; **D:** Bud Yorkin. VHS, Beta, LV $79.98 LIV, VES ✞✞✞

Twice-Told Tales Horror trilogy based loosely on three Nathaniel Hawthorne tales, "Dr. Heidegger's Experiment," "Rappaccini's Daughter," and "The House of Seven Gables." Price is great in all three of these well-told tales. **AKA:** Nathaniel Hawthorne's "Twice Told Tales".
1963 120m/C Vincent Price, Sebastian Cabot, Brett Halsey; **D:** Sidney Salkow. VHS, Beta $19.95 MGM, MLB ✞✞✞

Twigs Taped performance of George Furthis' Tony Award-winning drama about a mother and her three daughters who meet the day before Thanksgiving.
1984 138m/C Cloris Leachman. VHS, Beta $39.95 RKO ✞½

Twilight in the Sierras Lots of heroics and music in this action-packed western. An ex-outlaw gone straight is kidnapped for his notorious criminal finesse. Rogers must come to rescue.
1950 67m/C Roy Rogers, Dale Evans, Estelita Rodriguez, Pat Brady, Russ Vincent, George Meeker; **D:** William Witney. VHS $12.98 REP ✞✞½

Twilight of the Cockroaches Mr. Saito is a slovenly bachelor who winds up leaving the remains of his meals for the anthropomorphic cockroaches that infest his apartment. The cockroaches have had it so good for so long that they don't know about insecticides and fearing humans. That is, until Mr. Saito's fastidious new girlfriend makes her appearance and declares war on the vermin. A lifelessly animated tale too dumb for both children and adults and with decidedly unpleasant subject matter, despite the singing, dancing insects. In Japanese with English subtitles. **AKA:** Gokiburi.
1990 105m/C JP **D:** Hiroaki Yoshida; **V:** Kaoru Kobayashi, Setsuko Karamsumarau. VHS, LV $34.95 FCT, STP, LUM ✞½

Twilight on the Rio Grande Autry runs into a female knife thrower and some jewel smugglers in this far-fetched western.
1941 54m/B Gene Autry, Sterling Holloway, Adele Mara, Bob Steele; **D:** Frank McDonald. VHS, Beta $27.95 VCN ✞

Twilight on the Trail Cattle rustlers disappear and Hopalong Cassidy and his sidekicks become "dude" detectives to solve the crime.
1941 54m/B William Boyd, Brad King, Andy Clyde, Jack Rockwell, Wanda McKay, Howard Bretherton. VHS, Beta GVV ✞✞

Twilight People When a mad scientist's creations turn on him for revenge, he runs for his life. Boring, gory, with bad make-up and even poorer acting. This one should fade away into the night. **AKA:** Beasts.
1972 (PG) 84m/C PH John Ashley, Pat Woodell, Jan Merlin, Pam Grier; **D:** Eddie Romero. VHS, Beta $29.95 UHV Woof!

The Twilight Zone Travel through another dimension in Rod Serling's classic science fiction series. Two episodes per tape. On this tape: "The Invaders," written by Richard Matheson, sees a farm house inhabited by a mute woman become the destination of strange, miniature space travelers. In "Nothing in the Dark," written by George Clayton Johnson, an elderly woman is given an interesting lesson regarding her fear of death.

1961 50m/B Agnes Moorehead, Douglas Heyes, Gladys Cooper, Robert Redford, R.G. Armstrong; **D:** Lamont Johnson. VHS, Beta, LV $14.98 FXV, FOX, MOV Woof!

Twilight Zone: The Movie Four short horrific tales are anthologized in this film as a tribute to Rod Sterling and his popular television series. Three of the episodes, "Kick the Can," "It's a Good Life" and "Nightmare at 20,000 Feet," are based on original "Twilight Zone" scripts. Morrow was killed in a helicopter crash during filming.
1983 (PG) 101m/C Dan Aykroyd, Albert Brooks, Vic Morrow, Kathleen Quinlan, John Lithgow, Billy Mumy, Scatman Crothers, Kevin McCarthy, Bill Quinn, Selma Diamond, Abbe Lane, John Larroquette, Jeremy Licht, Patricia Barry, William Shallert, Burgess Meredith, Cherie Currie; **D:** John Landis, Steven Spielberg, George Miller, Joe Dante; **M:** Jerry Goldsmith. VHS, Beta, LV $19.98 WAR ✞✞½

Twilight's Last Gleaming A maverick general takes a SAC missile base hostage, threatening to start World War III if the U.S. government doesn't confess to its Vietnam policies and crimes. Gripping film, with good performances. Based on a novel by Walter Wager, "Viper Three."
1977 (R) 144m/C Burt Lancaster, Charles Durning, Richard Widmark, Melvyn Douglas, Joseph Cotten, Paul Winfield, Burt Young; **D:** Robert Aldrich. VHS, Beta, LV $59.98 FOX ✞✞½

Twin Dragon Encounter Two kickboxing twins go on vacation with their girlfriends. When terrorized by slavering criminals, they place many an instep to many a temple.
198? (PG) 79m/C Michael McNamara; **D:** Paul Dunlop. VHS, Beta $79.95 VMK ✞

Twin Peaks Sketchy home video distillation of the eccentric TV series. It preserves much of the setup episode (the murder of teen-queen Laura Palmer and nest of small-town weirdness it reveals), then rushes piecemeal through the rest of the season. There's an altered quasi-solution to the enigma and a bizarre backward sequence not broadcast in the US. In this compressed form it's best for initiates of the TP cult; others won't be converted.
1990 113m/C Kyle MacLachlan, Michael Ontkean, Sherilyn Fenn, Lara Flynn Boyle, Joan Chen, Peggy Lipton, Piper Laurie, Michael Horse, Russ Tamblyn, Richard Beymer, Madchen Amick, Catherine Coulson, Warren Frost, Everett McGill, Jack Nance, Ray Wise, Eric Da Re, Harry Goaz, Sheryl Lee; **D:** David Lynch; **M:** Angelo Badalamenti. VHS, LV $79.99 WAR, FCT ✞✞

Twin Peaks Premiere episode of David Lynch's bizarre TV drama. In this episode, Agent Cooper and Sheriff Truman begin the investigation into the death of prom queen, Laura Palmer. All seven episodes are available in a boxed set.
1990 50m/C Michael Ontkean, Kyle MacLachlan, Joan Chen, Piper Laurie, Sherilyn Fenn, Peggy Lipton, Madchen Amick, Lara Flynn Boyle, Michael Horse, Russ Tamblyn, Richard Beymer, Dana Ashbrook, Warren Frost, Everett McGill, Jack Nance, Ray Wise, Eric Da Re, Catherine Coulson, Harry Goaz, Sheryl Lee; **D:** David Lynch; **M:** Angelo Badalamenti. VHS $14.99 WOV, MOV ✞✞

Twin Peaks: Fire Walk with Me Lynch's prequel to the cult TV series is a weird and frustrating account chronicling the week before Laura Palmer's death. Suspense is definitely lacking in a story with a preordained outcome, but Lynch manages to intrigue the audience with his dream-like sequences and interestingly offbeat characters. On the other hand, it's exploitative and violent enough to alienate fans of the series.

Includes extremely brief and baffling cameos by Bowie as an FBI agent and Stanton as the manager of a trailer park. Several of the show's regular players are missing here, and others (MacLachlan, Amick, and Lipton) appear and disappear so quickly that it's pointless. On the plus side, the sounds of Badalamenti's famous theme music diffuses throughout and Isaak appears as an FBI agent with amazingly acute powers of observation.
1992 (R) 135m/C Kyle MacLachlan, Sheryl Lee, Moira Kelly, Chris Isaak, Ray Wise, Kiefer Sutherland, Peggy Lipton, Dana Ashbrook, James Marshall, David Lynch; *Cameos:* David Bowie, Harry Dean Stanton; *W/D:* David Lynch; *M:* Angelo Badalamenti. **VHS, LV $19.95** *NLC* ✗✗

Twins A genetics experiment gone awry produces twins rather than a single child. One is a genetically-engineered superman, the other a short, lecherous petty criminal. Schwarzenegger learns he has a brother, and becomes determined to find him, despite their having been raised separately. The two meet and are immediately involved in a contraband scandal. Amusing pairing of Schwarzenegger and DeVito.
1988 (PG) 107m/C Arnold Schwarzenegger, Danny DeVito, Kelly Preston, Hugh O'Brian, Chloe Webb, Bonnie Bartlett; *D:* Ivan Reitman. **VHS, Beta, LV $19.95** *MCA* ✗✗½

Twins of Evil Beautiful female twins fall victim to the local vampire, and their God-fearing uncle is out to save/destroy them. Hammer sex and blood-sucking epic starring the Collinsons, who were featured in the October 1970 issue of Playboy as that magazine's first twin Playmates. Written by Tudor Gates.
1971 86m/C *GB* Madeleine Collinson, Mary Collinson, Peter Cushing, Kathleen Bryon, Dennis Price, Damien Thomas, David Warbeck, Katya Wyeth, Maggie Wright, Luan Peters, Kristen Lindholm, Judy Matheson; *D:* John Hough. **VHS, Beta $14.98** *VID, MLB* ✗✗½

Twinsanity Evil twins are charged with the murder of a man who attempted to blackmail them. *AKA:* Goodbye Gemini.
1970 (R) 91m/C *GB* Judy Geeson, Martin Potter, Alexis Kanner, Michael Redgrave, Freddie Jones, Peter Jeffrey; *D:* Alan Gibson. **VHS, Beta $59.95** *PSM* ✗

Twirl Satirical look at the cutthroat world of baton twirling. Parents apply relentless pressure on their daughters to win a contest. Decent made-for-TV movie.
1981 100m/C Stella Stevens, Charles Haid, Lisa Whelchel, Erin Moran, Edd Byrnes, Sharon Spelman, Matthew Tobin, Donna McKechnie, Rosalind Chao, Heather Locklear, Debi Richter, Jamie Rose, Tracy Scoggins; *D:* Gus Trikonis. **VHS, Beta $39.95** *LIV* ✗

Twist A tepid French drama chronicling the infidelities of various wealthy aristocrats; dubbed. The aristocrats are boring, as is the film. In French and English versions. *AKA:* Folies Bourgeoises.
1976 105m/C *FR* Bruce Dern, Stephane Audran, Ann-Margret, Sydne Rome, Jean-Pierre Cassel, Curt Jurgens, Maria Schell, Charles Aznavour; *D:* Claude Chabrol. **VHS, Beta $49.95** *LIV* ✗½

Twist & Shout Sequel to the popular Danish import "Zappa," in which two teenage lovers discover sex and rock and roll. Transcends the teens discovering sex genre. Danish with English subtitles. Profanity, nudity, and sex. *AKA:* Hab Og Karlighed.
1984 (R) 107m/C *DK* Lars Simonsen, Adam Tonsberg, Ulrikke Juul Bondo, Camilla Soeberg; *D:* Bille August. **VHS, Beta $79.99** *HBO* ✗✗✗

Twisted This curio from Slater's early career came out on tape to take advantage of his rising stardom. He's properly creepy as a brilliant but evil teen using electronics, psychology, and swordplay to terrorize victims. The suspense isn't too bad when direction doesn't go overboard, which unfortunately is half the time. Based on the play "Children! Children!" by Jack Horrigan.
1986 (R) 87m/C Lois Smith, Christian Slater, Tandy Cronyn, Brooke Tracy, Dina Merrill, Dan Ziskie, Karl Taylor, Noelle Parker, John Cunningham, J.C. Quinn; *D:* Adam Holender. **VHS $79.95** *HMD* ✗✗

Twisted Brain An honor student develops a serum that makes him half man and half beast. Now he can exact revenge on all the jocks and cheerleaders who have humiliated him in the past. Cardi is okay, the rest of the cast is awful. Silly, horrific teen monster epic. *AKA:* Horror High.
1974 (R) 89m/C Pat Cardi, Austin Stoker, Rosie Holotik, John Niland, Joyce Hash, Jeff Alexander, Joe "Mean Joe" Greene; *D:* Larry N. Stouffer. **VHS, Beta $29.95** *UHV* ✗

Twisted Justice Set in 2020, Heavener is a cop determined to stop a ruthless killer. Matters become complicated, however, when his gun is taken away. Now he's forced to rely on his cunning to outwit his sadistic opponent.
1989 90m/C David Heavener, Erik Estrada, Jim Brown, Shannon Tweed, James Van Patten, Don Stroud, Karen Black, Lori Warren; *W/D:* David Heavener. **VHS $79.95** *KBE* ✗½

Twisted Nightmare The people responsible for a young retarded boy's death are hunted by a strange figure lurking in the shadows.
1987 (R) 95m/C Rhonda Gray, Cleve Hall, Brad Bartrum, Robert Padilla; *D:* Paul Hunt. **Beta** *TWE* ✗

Twisted Obsession A man becomes passionately obsessed with a woman, and it leads to murder.
1990 (R) 109m/C *IT* Jeff Goldblum, Miranda Richardson, Anemone, Dexter Fletcher, Daniel Ceccaldi, Liza Walker, Jerome Natali, Arielle Dombasle; *D:* Fernando Trueba. **VHS, Beta, LV $89.95** *LIV* ✗✗

Twister An intriguing independent feature about a bizarre midwestern family, its feverish eccentricities and eventual collapse. Awaiting a cult following.
1989 (PG-13) 93m/C Dylan McDermott, Crispin Glover, Harry Dean Stanton, Suzy Amis, Jenny Wright, Lindsay Christman, Lois Chiles; *D:* Michael Almereyda. **VHS, Beta, LV $89.98** *LIV, VES* ✗✗

Twister Kicker When the woman he loves is in jeopardy, an invincible man battles the best of fighters from three continents. Despite all this action, it's pretty ho-hum.
1985 93m/C Wang Hoi, Yeung Oi Wa, Po Pei. **VHS $39.95** *WWV* ✗

Twitch of the Death Nerve A bevy of vacationers are hacked up by a crazy with a sickle. A superior inspiration to the "Friday the 13th" series. *AKA:* Bay of Blood; Last House on the Left, Part 2.
1972 (R) 87m/C *IT* Claudine Auger, Chris Avran; *D:* Mario Bava. **VHS, Beta $79.95** *MPI* ✗✗

Two Assassins in the Dark Martial arts adventure about a pair of kung-fu killers who fight in the dark.
198? 90m/C Wang Tao, Chang Yi, Lung Chun-Eng. **VHS, Beta** *NO* ✗

Two by Forsyth Two short films based on stories by Frederick Forsyth, one dealing with a dying millionaire's clever efforts to prevent his fortune from being inherited by

greedy relatives, the other about a mild-mannered stamp dealer who avenges himself on a nasty gossip columnist.
1986 60m/C Dan O'Herlihy, Cyril Cusack, Milo O'Shea, Shirley Anne Field. **VHS, Beta $59.95** *PSM* ✗✗

Two Can Play This is a taped production of Trevor Rhone's play about political upheaval in Jamaica in the 1970's.
1983 105m/C **VHS, Beta** *KET* ✗✗

Two Champions of Shaolin Sure, there are two champions now, but after the battle royale, only one will be left standing!
19?? ?m/C **VHS $59.98** *NO* ✗✗

Two Daughters Director Ray wrote the scripts for two stories based on the writings of Nobel Prize winner Rabindranath Tagore, one about the relationship between an orphan and a postman, the other about a young man who declines to marry the girl arranged to be his intended. In Hindi with English subtitles. *AKA:* Teen Kanya.
1961 114m/B *IN D:* Satyajit Ray. **VHS, Beta $29.98** *SUE, TAM, NLC* ✗✗✗

Two Dragons Fight Against the Tiger Kung fu equals survival in this martial arts adventure. Several men strike a gold vein in a Chinese mine. They wind up fighting against corruption and greed.
19?? 90m/C Kao Tien Chu, Wang Luan Hsiung, Tse Lan, Huang I Lung. **VHS $49.95** *OCE* ✗

Two English Girls A pre-World War I French lad, with a possessive mother, loves two English sisters, one an impassioned, reckless artist, the other a repressed spinster. Tenderly delineates the triangle's interrelating love and friendship over seven years. Based on the novel "Les Deux Anglaises et le Continent" by Henri-Pierre Roche. In French with English subtitles. *AKA:* Les Deux Anglaises et le Continent.
1972 (R) 108m/C *FR* Jean-Pierre Leaud, Kika Markham, Stacey Tendeter, Sylvia Marriott, Marie Mansert, Philippe Leotard; *D:* Francois Truffaut. **VHS, Beta $39.95** *HMV, FOX, APD* ✗✗✗½

Two Evil Eyes Horror kings Romero and Argento each direct an Edgar Allan Poe tale in this release, hence the title. Barbeau, the scheming younger wife of a millionaire, hypnotizes her husband with the help of a her lover in "The Facts in the Case of M. Valdemar." When hubby dies too soon to validate changes made in his will, the lovers decide to freeze him for two weeks in order that death can be recorded at the correct time. In "Black Cat" a crime photographer used to photographing gore adopts a feline friend and starts getting sick on the job. *AKA:* Due Occhi Diabolici.
1990 (R) 121m/C *IT* Adrienne Barbeau, Ramy Zada, Harvey Keitel, Madeleine Potter; *D:* George A. Romero, Dario Argento. **VHS, Beta, LV $92.98** *FXV* ✗✗

Two-Faced Woman Garbo, in her last film, attempts a ruse when she finds her husband may be interested in an old flame. Pretending to be her twin sister in an attempt to lure Douglas away from the other woman, she's fooled a little herself. Romantic comedy unfortunately miscasts Garbo as an Americanized ski bunny.
1941 90m/B Greta Garbo, Melvyn Douglas, Constance Bennett, Roland Young, Ruth Gordon, Robert Sterling, George Cleveland, Frances Carson; *D:* George Cukor. **VHS, Beta $19.98** *MGM* ✗✗✗

The Two Faces of Evil A family's vacation turns into a night of unbearable terror when they pick up a sinister hitchhiker.

1982 60m/C Anna Calder-Marshall, Gary Raynmond, Denholm Elliott, Pauline Delany, Philip Latham; *D:* Peter Sasdy, Alan Gibson. VHS, Beta $29.95 *LIV ₤*

Two Fathers' Justice Two dads, one tough and one a wimp, seek revenge on the men who killed their kids. Made for television.
1985 100m/C Robert Conrad, George Hamilton, Brooke Bundy, Catherine Corkill, Whitney Kershaw, Greg Terrell; *D:* Rod Holcomb. VHS $19.98 *MCG ₤*

Two Fisted Justice A cowboy protects a town against a daring and deadly Indian attack. From the "Range Busters" series.
1931 45m/B Tom Tyler. VHS, Beta $19.95 *VDM ₤*

Two-Fisted Justice The Range Busters do their part to maintain law and order in the old West.
1943 55m/B John "Dusty" King, David Sharpe, Max Terhune. VHS, Beta $19.95 *NOS, DVT ₤*

Two-Fisted Law McCoy plays a rancher who borrows big bucks from the corrupt Oakman, who's actually a land grabber. McCoy then teams up with a posse to bring the evildoer to justice. Early (and small) screen roles for Wayne and Brennan.
1932 58m/B Tim McCoy, Tully Marshall, Wheeler Oakman, Alice Day, Wallace MacDonald, John Wayne, Walter Brennan; *D:* Ross Lederman. VHS $14.95 *COL ₤½*

Two for the Road After over a decade of marriage, Finney and Hepburn look back and find only fragments of their relationship. Mancini score adds poignancy to the couple's reflections on their stormy life. Touching and well-acted. Scipted by Frederic Raphael.
1967 112m/C Audrey Hepburn, Albert Finney, Eleanor Bron, William Daniels, Claude Dauphin, Nadia Gray, Jacqueline Bisset; *D:* Stanley Donen. VHS, LV $19.98 *FXV ₤₤₤½*

Two for the Seesaw Mitchum stars as a Nebraska attorney who comes to New York and gets involved with MacLaine. Humorous and touching comedy-drama worked better on stage, because the large screen magnified the talkiness of Gibson's play. Unusual casting of Mitchum as a Midwest lawyer and MacLaine as a New York Jewish bohemian.
1962 119m/B Robert Mitchum, Shirley MacLaine, Edmond Ryan, Elisabeth Fraser, Eddie Firestone, Billy Gray, Vic Lundin; *D:* Robert Wise; *W:* Isobel Lennart. VHS, LV $19.98 *MGM ₤₤₤*

Two Girls and a Sailor Wartime musical revue loosely structured around a love triangle involving a sailor on leave. Vintage hokum with lots of songs. ♫Paper Doll; The Young Man with a Horn; Concerto for Index Finger; Take it Easy; Ritual Fire Dance; Inka Dinka Doo; My Mother Told Me; A Love Like Ours; In A Moment of Madness; Sweet and Lovely; Granada; Estrellita; A-Tisket-A-Tasket; Did You Ever Have the Feeling?; Castles in the Air; Who Will Be With You When I'm Far Away?; Flash; Charmaine; Babalu; The Thrill of a New Romance; You Dear; Dardanella; My Wonderful One Let's Dance.
1944 124m/B June Allyson, Gloria de Haven, Van Johnson, Xavier Cugat, Jimmy Durante, Tom Drake, Lena Horne, Harry James, Gracie Allen, Virginia O'Brien, Jose Iturbi, Carlos Ramirez, Donald Meek, Ava Gardner, Buster Keaton; *D:* Richard Thorpe. VHS, Beta, LV $19.98 *MGM ₤₤₤*

Two Graves to Kung-Fu Young kung-fu student is framed for murder. When the real murderers kill his teacher, he escapes from prison to seek revenge.
1982 (R) 95m/C Liu Chia-Yung, Shek Kin, Chen Hung-Lieh. VHS, Beta $59.95 *GEM ₤*

The Two Great Cavaliers A Ming warrior has a hard time with the Manchurian army, fending it off as he must with only his bare instep, heel, and wrist.
1973 95m/C Chen Shing, Mao Ying; *D:* Yeung Ching Chen. VHS, Beta $39.95 *UNI ₤*

Two Gun Man America's first singing cowboy, Ken Maynard, performs hair-raising stunts in this old oater. One of the first "talkies!"
1931 60m/B Ken Maynard, Lafe McKee, Charles King, Tom London, Lucille Powers; *D:* Phil Rosen. VHS, Beta $19.95 *NOS, VCN, DVT ₤½*

Two-Gun Man from Harlem Big city guy travels to the wild West in search of a little truth.
1938 60m/B Herbert Jeffries, Marguerite Whitten, Mantan Moreland, Matthew "Stymie" Beard; *D:* Richard C. Kahn. VHS $24.95 *NOS, TPV ₤½*

Two-Gun Troubador A masked singing cowboy struggles to uncovers his father's murderer. *AKA:* The Lone Troubador.
1937 59m/B Fred Scott, Claire Rochelle, John Merton. VHS, Beta $19.95 *NOS, KRT, HEG ₤*

200 Motels Rambling, non-narrative self-indulgent video album by and about Frank Zappa and the Mothers of Invention, as they document a long and especially grueling road tour. For fans only.
1971 (R) 99m/C Frank Zappa, Ringo Starr, The Mothers of Invention; *D:* Frank Zappa. VHS, Beta $19.95 *MVD, MGM ₤½*

2 Idiots in Hollywood Two unapologetically moronic dimwits make their mark on Tinseltown amid underwear jokes, exaggerated leering and contrived subplots.
1988 (R) 87m/C Jeff Doucette. VHS, Beta, LV $19.95 *STE, NWV ₤*

The Two Jakes Ten years have passed and Jake Gittes is still a private investigator in this sequel to 1974's "Chinatown." When a murder occurs while he's digging up dirt on an affair between the wife of a real estate executive and the executive's partner, Jake must return to Chinatown to uncover the killer and face the painful memories buried there. Despite solid dialogue and effective performances, it's unreasonably difficult to follow if you haven't seen "Chinatown." Outstanding photography by Vilmos Zsigmond.
1990 (R) 137m/C Jack Nicholson, Harvey Keitel, Meg Tilly, Madeleine Stowe, Eli Wallach, Ruben Blades, Frederic Forrest, David Keith, Richard Farnsworth, Tracy Walter; *D:* Jack Nicholson, Vilmos Zsigmond; *W:* Robert Towne; *M:* Van Dyke Parks. VHS, Beta, LV $19.95 *PAR, FCT ₤₤*

Two Kinds of Love Adapted from Peggy Mann's novel "There Are Two Kinds of Terrible" this is the story of a young boy who learns to love his distant, workaholic father after his protective mother suddenly dies. Made for television.
1985 94m/C Rick Schroder, Lindsay Wagner, Peter Weller; *D:* Jack Bender. VHS, Beta $59.98 *FOX ₤₤*

Two Lost Worlds A young hero battles monstrous dinosaurs, pirates, and more in this cheapy when he and his shipmates are shipwrecked on an uncharted island. Don't miss the footage from "Captain Fury," "One Billion B.C.," and "Captain Caution" and Arness long before his Sheriff Dillon fame, and his "big" role in "The Thing."

1950 63m/B James Arness, Laura Elliott, Bill Kennedy; *D:* Norman Dawn. VHS, Beta $39.95 *SVS Woof!*

Two Men & a Wardrobe Polanski's project while a student at the Polish Film Institute. Consideration of modern man's lack of privacy and made without dialogue. Two men emerge from the sea carrying nothing but a large piece of furniture. Absurd and funny.
1958 19m/B *D:* Roman Polanski. VHS, Beta *IHF Woof!*

Two Minute Warning A sniper plans to take out the president of the United States at an NFL playoff game in this boring, pointless, disaster film that goes on forever. Features all the ready-made characters inherent in the genre, but, until its too late, precious little of the mayhem. To get caught watching the TV version, which features more characters and an additional subplot, would be truly disastrous.
1976 (R) 116m/C Charlton Heston, John Cassavetes, Martin Balsam, Beau Bridges, Marilyn Hassett, David Janssen, Jack Klugman, Walter Pidgeon, Gena Rowlands; *D:* Larry Peerce. VHS, LV $89.95 *MCA ₤*

The Two Mrs. Carrolls Bogart is a psycho-killer/artist who paints portraits of his wives as the Angel of Death—and then kills them. The married Bogart falls for Stanwyck, poisons his current wife, and the two marry. After a few years, Bogart falls for Smith and decides to rid himself of Stanwyck in the same manner as his first killing. Stanwyck, however, becomes increasingly suspicious and calls on an old beau for help. Melodrama cast Bogart against type (not always successfully). Filmed in 1945, but was unreleased until 1947.
1947 99m/B Humphrey Bogart, Barbara Stanwyck, Alexis Smith, Nigel Bruce, Pat O'Moore, Ann Carter; *D:* Peter Godfrey. VHS $19.98 *MGM ₤₤½*

Two Moon Junction A soon-to-be-wed Southern debutante enters into a wild love affair with a rough-edged carnival worker. Poorly acted, wildly directed, with many unintentional laughs.
1988 (R) 104m/C Sherilyn Fenn, Richard Tyson, Louise Fletcher, Burl Ives, Kristy McNichol, Millie Perkins, Don Galloway, Herve Villechaize, Dabbs Greer, Jay Hawkins; *D:* Zalman King. VHS, Beta, LV $14.95 *COL ₤½*

Two Mules for Sister Sara American mercenary in 19th century Mexico gets mixed up with a cigar-smoking nun and the two make plans to capture a French garrison. MacLaine and Eastwood are great together. Based on a Boetticher story, scripted by Maltz. Filmed by Gabriel Figueroa.
1970 (PG) 105m/C Clint Eastwood, Shirley MacLaine; *D:* Don Siegel; *W:* Budd Boetticher, Albert Maltz; *M:* Ennio Morricone. VHS, Beta $19.95 *MCA ₤₤₤*

Two Nights with Cleopatra A piece of Italian pizza involving Cleopatra's double (also played by Loren) falling in love with one of the guards. Notable only for the 19-year-old Sophia's brief nudity. *AKA:* Due Notti Con Cleopatra.
1954 77m/C *IT* Sophia Loren, Ettore Manni, Alberto Sordi, Paul Muller, Alberto Talegalli, Rolf Tasna, Gianni Cavalieri, Fernando Bruno, Riccardo Garrone, Carlo Dale; *D:* Mario Mattoli; *W:* Nino Maccari, Ettore Scola. VHS, Beta $29.95 *VDM ₤½*

Two of a Kind In his television movie debut, Burns plays an elderly man whose mentally handicapped grandson helps him put the starch back in his shirt. Sensitively produced and performed.

1982 102m/C George Burns, Robby Benson, Cliff Robertson, Barbara Barrie, Frances Lee McCain, Geri Jewell, Ronny Cox; **D:** Roger Young. **VHS, Beta** $49.95 *FOX, IVE* 🎬🎬½

Two of a Kind Angels make a bet with God—two selfish people will redeem themselves or God can blow up the Earth. Bad acting, awful direction, and the script needs divine intervention.
1983 (PG) 88m/C John Travolta, Olivia Newton-John, Charles Durning, Beatrice Straight, Scatman Crothers, Oliver Reed; **D:** John Herzfeld. **VHS, Beta, LV** $19.98 *FOX* 🎬

Two of Us Young Jewish boy flees Nazi-occupied Paris to live in the country with an irritable, bigoted guardian. Sensitive, eloquent movie about racial prejudice and anti-Semitism. In French with English subtitles. *AKA:* Le Vieil Homme Et L'Enfant; Claude; The Old Man and the Boy.
1968 86m/B *FR* Michel Simon, Alain Cohen, Luce Fabiole, Roger Carel, Paul Preboist, Charles Denner; **D:** Claude Berri. **VHS** $59.95 *NO* 🎬🎬🎬½

Two Reelers: Comedy Classics
1 Includes a 1944 Edgar Kennedy short, "Feather Your Nest" (RKO), and two 1933 films, "How Comedies Are Born" and "Dog Blight."
1933 54m/B Edgar Kennedy, Harry Gribbon, Harry Sweet, Jack Norton, Maxine Jennings, Willie Best. **VHS, Beta** $24.95 *VYY* 🎬🎬🎬½

Two Reelers: Comedy Classics
2 Three vintage shorts: "Chicken Feed" (1939) with Billy Gilbert, "Twin Husbands" (1946) with Leon Errol, and Edgar Kennedy in "False Roomers" (1938).
1946 53m/B Leon Errol, Dorothy Granger, Billy Gilbert, Edgar Kennedy. **VHS, Beta** $24.95 *VYY* 🎬🎬🎬½

Two Reelers: Comedy Classics
3 More laughs, with two Edgar Kennedy shorts, "A Merchant of Menace" (1933), and "Social Terrors" (1946). Also, Jed Prouty is featured in "Coat Tales" (193).
1933 52m/B Edgar Kennedy, Jed Prouty. **VHS, Beta** $24.95 *VYY* 🎬🎬🎬½

Two Reelers: Comedy Classics
4 "Bridal Bail" (1934), "No More West" (Educational-1934) with Bert Lahr singing and clowning, and "Bad Medicine" (1936) with crooner Gene Austin comprise this comedy package.
1936 56m/B Bert Lahr, Gene Austin, June Brewster, Carol Tevis, Grady Sutton. **VHS, Beta** $24.95 *VYY* 🎬🎬🎬½

Two Reelers: Comedy Classics
5 A compilation of three vintage comedy shorts by popular stars of the 1930's: "Dear Deer" (1942) with Leon Errol, "Hotel Anchovy" (1934) with the Ritz Brothers and "Love Your Neighbor" (1930) with Charlotte Greenwood.
1938 55m/B Leon Errol, The Ritz Brothers, Charlotte Greenwood. **VHS, Beta** $24.95 *VYY* 🎬🎬🎬½

Two Reelers: Comedy Classics
6 Three vintage comedy shorts: "LePutt, The Specialist," "Dumb Luck," and "Our Gang Follies of 1938."
1935 59m/B Charles Sale, Goodman Ace. **VHS, Beta** $24.95 *VYY* 🎬🎬🎬½

Two Reelers: Comedy Classics
7 Three more comedy shorts from the '30s: "Dumb Dicks," "Love and Onions," and "Julius Sizzler."
1938 56m/B Benny Rubin, Harry Gribbon, Johnny Johnson, Pat Rooney Jr. **VHS, Beta** $24.95 *VYY* 🎬🎬🎬½

Two Reelers: Comedy Classics
8 Three comedy shorts from the zany 30's.
1933 57m/B Billy Bevan, Tom Patricola, Charles Judels, Dorothy Sebastian, William Farnum, Mack Swain. **VHS, Beta** $24.95 *VYY* 🎬🎬🎬½

Two Reelers: Comedy Classics
9 Three early comedy shorts featuring several stars-to-be. Includes "A Slip at the Switch" (directed by Mark Sandrich), "No Sleep on the Deep," and "Going Spanish."
1934 57m/B Bob Hope, Leah Ray, Betty Compson, Robert Warwick, Chic Sale, George Hay. **VHS, Beta, 8mm** $24.95 *VYY* 🎬🎬🎬½

Two Reelers: Comedy Classics
10 Three shorts: "The Stolen Jools" stars more than 40 name performers and was produced by the Masquers Club of Hollywood. The plot has Shearer's jewels being stolen after a party and each of her illustrious guests is a suspect. "Easy on the Eyes" features Pangborn as a millionaire who has a romantic rival for his pretty fiance. "Knight Duty" portrays Langdon as a simpleton vagrant in constant trouble with a brawny cop.
1931 59m/B Norma Shearer, Franklin Pangborn, Harry Langdon, Vernon Dent. **VHS** $24.95 *VYY* 🎬🎬🎬½

Two Rode Together A Texas marshal and an army lieutenant negotiate with the Comanches for the return of captives, but complications ensue.
1961 109m/C James Stewart, Richard Widmark, Shirley Jones, Linda Cristal, Andy Devine, John McIntire; **D:** John Ford. **VHS, Beta, LV** $14.95 *RCA, COL* 🎬🎬½

The Two Sisters Goldstein, in her only film role, plays an older sister who sacrifices everything for the younger. The younger thanks her by stealing her fiance. In Yiddish with English subtitles.
1937 70m/B Jenney Goldstein, Michael Rosenberg. **VHS** $89.95 *ALD* 🎬🎬½

2000 Maniacs One of cult director Lewis' most enjoyably watchable films. A literal Civil War "ghost town" takes its revenge 100 years after being slaughtered by renegade Union soldiers by luring unwitting "yankee" tourists to their centennial festival. The hapless Notherners are then chopped, crushed, ripped apart etc. while the ghostly rebels party. Quite fun in a cartoonishly gruesome sort of way. Filmed in St. Cloud, FL.
1964 75m/C Thomas Wood, Connie Mason, Jeffrey Allen, Ben Moore, Gary Bakeman, Jerome Eden, Shelby Livingston, Michael Korb, Yvonne Gilbert, Mark Douglas, Linda Cochran, Vincent Santo, Andy Wilson; **W/D:** Herschell Gordon Lewis. **VHS, Beta** $29.95 *RHI* 🎬🎬

2000 Year Old Man An animated version of the Brooks-Reiner classic comedy routine, featuring the reminiscences of the bemused patriarch of the past, the 2000 Year Old Man.
1982 (G) 25m/C **V:** Carl Reiner, Mel Brooks. **VHS, Beta** $19.95 *MED* 🎬🎬

2001: A Space Odyssey A space voyage to Jupiter turns into chaos when a computer, HAL 9000, takes over. Seen by some as a mirror of man's historical use of machinery and by others as a grim vision of the future, the special effects and music are still stunning. Critically acclaimed and well accepted by the public. Written by Kubrick and Clarke from Clarke's novel "The Sentinel." Followed by a sequel "2010: The Year We Make Contact." The laser disc edition is presented in letterbox format and features a special supplementary section on the making of "2001," a montage of images from the film, production documents, memos and photos. Also included on the disc is a NASA film entitled "Art and Reality," which offers footage from the Voyager I and II flybys of Jupiter.
1968 139m/C *GB* Keir Dullea, Gary Lockwood, William Sylvester, Dan Richter; **W/D:** Stanley Kubrick; **W:** Arthur C. Clarke; **V:** Douglas Raines. Academy Awards '68: Best Visual Effects; Nominations: Best Art Direction/Set Decoration, Best Director (Kubrick), Best Story & Screenplay; National Board of Review Awards '68: 10 Best Films of the Year. **VHS, Beta, LV** $19.98 *MGM, VYG, CRC* 🎬🎬🎬🎬

2010: The Year We Make Contact The film version of Arthur C. Clarke's novel "The Sentinel" continues in this sequel to "2001: A Space Odyssey." Americans and Russians unite to investigate the abandoned starship Discovery's decaying orbit around Jupiter and try to determine why the HAL 9000 computer sabotaged its mission years before, while signs of cosmic change are detected on and around the giant planet.
1984 (PG) 116m/C Roy Scheider, John Lithgow, Helen Mirren, Bob Balaban, Keir Dullea, Madolyn Smith, Mary Jo Deschanel; **D:** Peter Hyams; **V:** Douglas Raines. **VHS, Beta, LV** $19.95 *MGM* 🎬🎬🎬

2020 Texas Gladiators In the post-nuclear holocaust world, two groups, one good, one evil, battle for supremacy.
1985 (R) 91m/C *IT* Harrison Muller, Al Cliver, Daniel Stephen, Peter Hooten, Al Yamanouchi, Sabrina Santi; **D:** Kevin Mancuso. **VHS, Beta** $59.95 *MED* Woof!

2069: A Sex Odyssey Team of beautiful, sensuous astronauts are sent to Earth to obtain male sperm which they must bring back to Venus. Tongue-in-cheek soft core sci-fi spoof.
1978 (R) 73m/C Alena Penz, Nina Fredric, Gerti Sneider, Raul Retzer, Catherine Conti, Heidi Hammer, Michael Mein, Herb Heesel; **D:** George Keil. **VHS, Beta** $19.95 *ACA, HHE* 🎬½

Two Tickets to Broadway A small-town singer and a crooner arrange a hoax to get themselves on Bob Crosby's television show. Appealing but lightweight. Full of songs by Jule Stein and Leo Robin. 🎵Let the Worry Bird Worry For You; Pagliacci; There's No Tomorrow; Manhattan; Big Chief Hole in the Ground; The Closer You Are; Baby, You'll Never Be Sorry; Pelican Falls High; It Began In Yucatan; Are You a Beautiful Dream?; Let's Make Comparisons.
1951 106m/C Tony Martin, Janet Leigh, Gloria de Haven; **D:** James V. Kern; **Performed by:** Smith & Dale. **VHS, Beta** *TTC* 🎬🎬½

Two to Tango A hired assassin goes to Buenos Aires to kill a crime boss, and falls in love with his tango-dancing mistress. Based on the novel by J.P. Feinman.
1988 (R) 87m/C *AR* Don Stroud, Adrienne Sachs; **D:** Hector Olivera. **VHS, Beta** *NO* 🎬½

Two Top Bananas A Las Vegas-style burlesque show, featuring song, dance, sketch comedy, and impersonations.
1987 45m/C Don Rickles, Don Adams, Carol Wayne, Sandy O'Hara, Murray Langston, Dorit Stevens. **VHS, Beta** $11.95 *PSM* 🎬🎬

Two-Way Stretch Three prison inmates in a progressive jail plan to break out, pull a diamond heist, and break back in, all in the same night. Fast-paced slapstick farce.
1960 84m/B *GB* Peter Sellers, Wilfrid Hyde-White, Liz Fraser, David Lodge; **D:** Robert Day. **VHS, Beta** $19.98 *HBO* 🎬🎬½

Two Weeks in Another Town
Douglas and Robinson are a couple of Hollywood has-beens who set out to make a comeback picture but meet with adversity at every turn. Extremely sappy melodrama is based on Irwin Shaw's trashy novel and represents one of director Minelli's poorer efforts. Laserdisc features a letterboxed screen and the original movie trailer.
1962 107m/C Kirk Douglas, Edward G. Robinson, Cyd Charisse, George Hamilton, Daliah Lavi, Claire Trevor, James Gregory, Rosanna Schiaffino, George Macready, Stefan Schnabel, Vito Scotti, Leslie Uggams; **D:** Vincente Minnelli. **VHS, LV** MGM, PIA 🐾🐾

Two Weeks to Live The comedy team inherits a railroad line, only to find it's a pile of junk.
1943 60m/B Lum & Abner, Franklin Pangborn. **VHS, Beta** $24.95 NOS, DVT, HEG 🐾½

Two Weeks with Love Reynolds and family wear funny bathing suits in the Catskills in the early 1900s while the Debster sings songs and blushes into young adulthood. ♫ Aba Daba Honeymoon; The Oceana Roll; A Heart That's Free; By the Light of the Silvery Moon; My Hero; Row, Row, Row; That's How I Need You; Beautiful Lady.
1950 92m/C Debbie Reynolds, Jane Powell, Ricardo Montalban, Louis Calhern, Ann Harding, Phyllis Kirk, Carleton Carpenter, Clinton Sundberg, Gary Gray; **D:** Roy Rowland. **VHS** $19.98 MGM, FCT 🐾🐾

Two Women A mother and her 13-year-old daughter travel war-torn Italy during World War II and must survive lack of food, crazed monks and brutal soldiers. Tragic, moving, well-directed. Loren received well-deserved Oscar. In Italian with English subtitles or dubbed. **AKA:** La Ciociara.
1961 99m/B IT Sophia Loren, Raf Vallone, Eleonora Brown, Jean-Paul Belmondo; **D:** Vittorio De Sica. **VHS, Beta** $19.95 COL, APD, BTV 🐾🐾🐾🐾

Two Women in Gold Two sexy housewives seduce everyone around, until a bird salesman has a coronary in their living room. A laugh riot.
1970 (R) 90m/C Louise Turcot, Monique Mercure, Donald Pilon, Marcel Sabourin. **VHS, Beta** $59.95 NWV Woof!

Two Wondrous Tigers Awesome Kung-fu gang terrorizes a small town until a local dares to out-chop the bullies.
1979 74m/C John Chang; **D:** Wilson Tong. **VHS, Beta** $39.95 TWE 🐾

The Two Worlds of Jenny Logan A woman travels back and forth in time whenever she dons a 19th century dress she finds in her old house. She is also able to fall in love twice, in different centuries. Made for television and adapted from "Second Sight," a novel by David Williams. Stylish and well made.
1979 97m/C Lindsay Wagner, Marc Singer, Alan Feinstein, Linda Gray, Constance McCashin, Henry Wilcoxon, Irene Tedrow, Joan Darling, Allen Williams, Pat Corley, Gloria Stuart; **D:** Frank de Felitta. **VHS, Beta** $14.95 FRH, LIV 🐾🐾½

Two Wrongs Make a Right A quiet nightclub owner beats and clubs his way through his tough neighborhood to protect himself and his woman.
1989 85m/C Ivan Rogers, Ron Blackstone, Rich Komenich; **D:** Robert Brown. **VHS, Beta** $79.95 UNI 🐾

Tycoon Wayne goes to Latin America to build a road for an American industrialist. When the industrialist insists on a shorter but more dangerous route, Wayne must satisfy his own sense of honor. Meanwhile, he's

found romance with the industrialist's half-Spanish daughter. Long, but well-acted.
1947 129m/C John Wayne, Laraine Day, Cedric Hardwicke, Judith Anderson, James Gleason, Anthony Quinn; **D:** Richard Wallace. **VHS, Beta, LV** $19.95 CCB, RKO, TTC 🐾🐾½

Typhoon Treasure Whilst recovering his sunken treasure, the hero battles bad guys, savage natives and a crocodile, all of whom could probably have made a more sophisticated film.
1939 68m/B AU Campbell Copelin, Gwen Munro, Joe Valli, Douglas Herald; **D:** Noel Monkman. **VHS** $15.95 NOS, LOO 🐾

Tyrant of Lydia Against the Son of Hercules Hercules' son takes on a wicked king in this startling adventure.
1963 ?m/C IT Gordon Scott, Massimo Serato. **VHS, Beta** $16.95 SNC 🐾

Ub Iwerks Cartoonfest There are seven delightful cartoons by one of the pioneering geniuses of animation. Includes: "The Brave Tin Soldier," "Happy Days," "Fiddlesticks," "Jack and the Beanstalk," "The Headless Horseman," and "The Little Red Hen."
193? 57m/C **VHS, Beta** $19.98 CCB, WTA 🐾

Ub Iwerks Cartoonfest 2 Here are more cartoons from the pen of the immortal Iwerks. Six color masterpieces of such great tales as "Tom Thumb," "Jack Frost," "Aladdin and the Wonderful Lamp," "Ali Baba," "Sinbad," and "Spooks."
193? 46m/C **VHS, Beta** $19.98 CCB 🐾

Ub Iwerks Cartoonfest 3 A compilation of Iwerks classics: "Simple Simon" (1935), "Puss in Boots" (1934), "Dick Whittington's Cat" (1936), and "Don Quixote" (1934).
193? 30m/C **VHS, Beta** $19.98 CCB 🐾

Ub Iwerks Cartoonfest 4 Another collection of enjoyable cartoons from the pen of Ub Iwerks. Included are "The Valiant Tailor," "Mary's Little Lamb," "The Bremen-town Musicians," and "Balloonland," all from 1934-35.
1935 30m/C **VHS, Beta** $19.98 CCB 🐾🐾½

Ub Iwerks Cartoonfest 5 Three more fabulous Cinecolor cartoons from the Ub Iwerks studio are combined on this tape: "Queen of Hearts" (1934), "Old Mother Hubbard" (1935), and "Humpty Dumpty" (1935), all from the Comicolor Cartoons series.
193? 23m/C **VHS, Beta** $19.98 CCB 🐾🐾½

Ubu and the Great Gidouille Animation from one of the world's most exciting animators, based on the play by Alfred Jarry. Ubu captures the Polish throne and spreads chaos across the land. When the people revolt, he flees to Paris and successfully spreads his message around the world. Strong black humor. In French with English subtitles.
1979 80m/C FR **D:** Jan Lenica. **VHS** $49.95 FCT, WTA 🐾🐾½

L'Udienza A bizarre black comedy about a guy who does anything he can, at any criminal cost, to obtain an audience with the Pope. In Italian with subtitles.
1971 111m/C IT Claudia Cardinale, Ugo Tognazzi; **D:** Marco Ferreri. **VHS, Beta** $49.95 FCT 🐾🐾

UFO: Target Earth Scientist attempts to fish flying saucer out of lake and costs studio $70,000.
1974 (G) 80m/C Nick Plakias, Cynthia Cline, Phil Erickson; **D:** Michael de Gaetano. **VHS** $14.98 MOV 🐾

Uforia Two rival evangelists meet up with a UFO-infatuated girl. Under her guidance, they wait for UFO encounters they intend to use to milk their revivalist audiences. Sometimes clumsy, but more often fun.
1981 92m/C Cindy Williams, Harry Dean Stanton, Fred Ward; **D:** John Binder. **VHS, Beta** $59.95 MCA 🐾🐾

Ugetsu The classic film that established Mizoguchi's reputation outside of Japan. Two 16th century Japanese peasants venture from their homes in pursuit of dreams, and encounter little more than their own hapless folly and a bit of the supernatural. A wonderful mix of comedy and action with nifty camera movement. Based on the stories of Akinara Ueda. In Japanese with English subtitles. **AKA:** Ugetsu Monogatari.
1953 96m/B JP Machiko Kyo, Masayuki Mori, Kinuyo Tanaka, Sakae Ozawa; **D:** Kenji Mizoguchi. Academy Awards '55 Nominations: Best Costume Design (B & W); Venice Film Festival '53: Silver Prize. **VHS, Beta, LV, 8mm** $29.98 NOS, SUE, WFV 🐾🐾🐾½

The Ugly American A naive American ambassador to a small, civil-war-torn Asian country fights a miniature Cold War against northern communist influence. Too preachy, and the "Red Menace" aspects are now very dated, but Brando's performance is worth watching. Based on the William J. Lederer novel.
1963 120m/C Marlon Brando, Sandra Church, Eiji Okada, Pat Hingle, Arthur Hill; **D:** George Englund. **VHS, Beta** $19.95 MCA 🐾🐾½

The Ugly Dachshund Jones and Pleshette are married dog lovers who raise Dachshunds. When Ruggles convinces them to take a Great Dane puppy, the fun begins! The Great Dane thinks he is a Dachshund because he has been raised with them—just imagine what happens when such a large dog acts as if he is small! Kids will love this wacky Disney film.
1965 93m/C Dean Jones, Suzanne Pleshette, Charlie Ruggles, Kelly Thordsen, Parley Baer; **D:** Norman Tokar. **VHS, Beta** DIS, OM 🐾🐾½

Ugly Little Boy Nurse is placed in charge of a child brought back through time from the Neanderthal age. Problems occur when the scientists involved ignore the fact that he is human.
1977 26m/C Kate Reid; **D:** Barry Morse, Don Thompson. **VHS, Beta** LCA 🐾½

UHF A loser is appointed manager of a bargain-basement UHF television station. He turns it around via bizarre programming ideas. Some fun parodies of TV enhance this minimal story. Developed solely as a vehicle for Yankovic.
1989 (PG-13) 97m/C Weird Al Yankovic, Kevin McCarthy, Victoria Jackson, Michael Richards, David Bowie, Anthony Geary; **D:** Jay Levey. **VHS, Beta, LV** $19.98 ORI 🐾🐾

Ulterior Motives P.I. Jack Blaylock agrees to protect a pretty reporter from Japanese gangsters. He finds himself caught up in deception and betrayal and uses all his considerable, and violent, skills to make certain he does his job.
1992 (R) ?m/C Thomas Ian Griffith, Mary Page Keller, Joe Yamanaka, Ellen Crawford, Ken Howard, Tyra Ferrell; **D:** James Becket. **VHS** $89.95 IMP 🐾½

Ultimate Desires When a high class hooker is brutally killed, beautiful Scoggins puts on what there is of the victim's clothes in order to solve the mystery. But trouble lies in wait as she actually begins to enjoy her funky new double life. Can she solve the

crime before becoming lost in her own hot fantasy world?
1991 (R) 93m/C Tracy Scoggins, Brion James, Marc Singer, Marc Baur, Marc Bennett, Suzy Joachim, Jason Scott, Frank Wilson; **D:** Lloyd A. Simandl. **VHS, Beta $89.95** *PSM* ✂✂

The Ultimate Imposter A secret agent acquires voluminous knowledge through a computer brain linkup, but can only retain the knowledge for 72 hours. In that timespan he has to rescue a defecting Russian from hordes of assassins. Made for television.
1979 97m/C Keith Andes, Erin Gray, Joseph Hacker, Macon McCalman; **D:** Paul Stanley. **VHS, Beta $39.95** *MCA* ✂

The Ultimate Ninja Two pseudo ninjas wearing official ninja headbands get together and batter the evil enemy with foot and sword. Poorly dubbed and incomprehensible.
1985 92m/C *HK* Stuart Smith, Bruce Baron, Sorapong Chatri; **W/D:** Godfrey Ho. **VHS, Beta $59.95** *TWE* Woof!

The Ultimate Ninja Challenge A police officer, disheartened by the corruption of his fellow officers, is alone in his integrity, refusing to accept the "fringe benefits" of drug-busting. To combat the evil, he forms a sort of vigilante group of wrongly accused illegal aliens.
1989 90m/C VHS, Beta *NO* ✂

The Ultimate Teacher Japanese animated adventure in which a new teacher is assigned to the most violent school in the world. This dude will do anything, including insulting the underwear of the students, to keep law and order.
1992 60m/C *JP* **VHS** *CPM* ✂

The Ultimate Thrill Businessman's paranoia about his wife's affairs leads him to follow her to Colorado on a ski holiday and stalk her lovers. Well-filmed skiing scenes and not much else. Also known as "The Ultimate Chase."
1974 (PG) 84m/C Britt Ekland, Barry Brown, Michael Blodgett, John Davis Chandler, Eric Braeden; **D:** Robert Butler. **VHS, Beta $19.95** *GEM, WWV* ✂ ½

The Ultimate Warrior Yul Brynner must defend the plants and seeds of a pioneer scientist to help replenish the world's food supply in this thriller set in 2012.
1975 (R) 92m/C Yul Brynner, Max von Sydow, Joanna Miles, Richard Kelton, Lane Bradbury, William Smith; **D:** Robert Clouse. **VHS, Beta $59.95** *WAR* ✂✂ ½

Ultra Flash A fantasy that is performed to some of today's hottest dance music. In stereo
1983 60m/C VHS, Beta $39.98 *LIV, VES* ✂✂ ½

Ultra Warrior A basic post-apocalyptic adventure tale of a radioactive earth, mutants, and various battles by the good guys to save the planet.
199? (R) 80m/C Dack Rambo, Meshach Taylor, Clare Beresford. **VHS $89.98** *NHO* ✂ ½

Ulysses An Italian made version of the epic poem by Homer, as the warrior returns to his homeland and the ever-faithful Penelope after the Trojan war. Ambitious effort provides for the ultimate mixed review. Douglas is good in the role and his stops along the ten-year way are well visualized. Sometimes sluggish with poor dubbing. Seven writers helped bring Homer to the big screen. *AKA:* Ulisse.
1955 104m/C *IT* Kirk Douglas, Silvana Mangano, Anthony Quinn, Rossana Podesta; **D:** Mario Camerini. **VHS, Beta $39.98** *WAR, OM* ✂✂ ½

Ulysses James Joyce's probably unfilmable novel was given a noble effort in this flawed film covering a day in the life of Leopold Bloom as he wanders through Dublin. Shot in Ireland with a primarily Irish cast.
1967 140m/B Milo O'Shea, Maurice Roeves, T.P. McKenna, Martin Dempsey, Sheila O'Sullivan, Barbara Jefford; **D:** Joseph Strick. **VHS, LV $29.95** *MFV* ✂✂ ½

Ulzana's Raid An aging scout and an idealistic Cavalry lieutenant lock horns on their way to battling a vicious Apache chieftain. A violent, gritty western that enjoyed critical re-evaluation years after its first release.
1972 (R) 103m/C Burt Lancaster, Bruce Davison, Richard Jaeckel, Lloyd Bochner, Jorge Luke; **D:** Robert Aldrich. **VHS, Beta, LV $19.95** *MCA* ✂✂✂

Umberto D A government pensioner, living alone with his beloved dog, struggles to keep up a semblance of dignity on his inadequate pension. De Sica considered this his masterpiece. A sincere, tender treatment of the struggles involved with the inevitability of aging. In Italian with English subtitles. Laser edition features letterboxed print.
1955 89m/B *IT* Carlo Battista, Maria Pia Casilio, Lina Gennari; **D:** Vittorio De Sica. Academy Awards '56 Nominations: Best Story; New York Film Critics Awards '55: Best Foreign Film. **VHS, Beta, LV, 8mm $29.98** *NOS, SUE, HHT* ✂✂✂✂

Umbrellas of Cherbourg A bittersweet film operetta with no spoken dialog. Deneuve is the teenaged daughter of a widow who owns an umbrella shop. She and her equally young boyfriend are separated by his military duty in Algeria. Finding she is pregnant, the girl marries a wealthy man, and when her former lover returns, he too marries someone else. But when they meet once again will their love be rekindled? Lovely photography and an evocative score enhance the story. In French with subtitles; also available dubbed in English (not with the same effectiveness). Oscar nominee for cinematography and story. *AKA:* Les Parapluies De Cherbourg; Die Regenschirme Von Cherbourg.
1964 90m/C *FR* Catherine Deneuve, Nino Castelnuovo, Anne Vernon, Ellen Farner, Marc Michel, Mireille Perrey, Jean Champion, Alfred Wolff, Dorothee Blanck; **W/D:** Jacques Demy; **M:** Michel Legrand. Academy Awards '65 Nominations: Best Foreign Language Film, Best Song ("I Will Wait for You"), Best Story & Screenplay, Best Original Score; Cannes Film Festival '64: Best Film. **VHS, Beta $39.95** *LIV, APD* ✂✂✂ ½

Un Chien Andalou Masterful surrealist short features a host of classic sequences, including a razor across an eye, a severed hand lying in the street, ants crawling from a hole in a man's hand, priests, dead horses, and a piano dragged across a room. A classic. Score features both Wagner and tango.
1928 20m/B *FR* Pierre Batcheff, Simone Marevil, Jaime Miravilles; **D:** Luis Bunuel, Salvador Dali. **VHS, Beta $34.95** *HHT, GVV, APD* ✂✂✂✂

Un Singe en Hiver A young wanderer (Belmondo) befriends a crusty old alcoholic (Gabin) who has kept his vow to abstain since his village survived the German bombing of World War II. Moving tale of regret and the passage of time. In French with English subtitles. *AKA:* A Monkey in Winter; It's Hot in Hell.
1962 105m/B *FR* Jean-Paul Belmondo, Jean Gabin, Suzanne Flon, Paul Frankeur; **D:** Henri Verneuil. **VHS, Beta $19.95** *KRT, TAM* ✂✂ ½

Una Vez en la Vida A young farm girl travels to the big city, where she becomes a nightclub dancer and gets involved with a shady character. In Spanish.
1949 75m/B *SP* Libertad Lamarque, Luis Aldas, Raimundo Pastore. **VHS, Beta $29.95** *VYY, APD* ✂

The Unapproachable A rendition of the Polish director's two one-act plays concerning a reclusive aging stage star being manipulated by her hangers-on.
1982 92m/C *PL* Leslie Caron, Daniel Webb, Leslie Malton; **D:** Krzysztof Zanussi. **VHS, Beta $59.95** *MGM* ✂✂ ½

The Unbearable Lightness of Being Tomas (Day Lewis), a young Czech doctor in the late 1960s, leads a sexually and emotionally carefree existence with a number of women, including a provocative artist, played by Olin. When he meets the fragile Binoche, he may be falling in love for the first time. On the eve of the 1968 Russian invasion of Czechoslovakia the two flee to Switzerland, but Binoche can't reconcile herself to exile and returns, followed by the reluctant doctor who has lost his position because of his new-found political idealism. The two find themselves leading an increasingly simple life, drawn ever closer together. The haunting ending caps off superb performances. Based on the novel by Milan Kundra.
1988 (R) 172m/C Daniel Day-Lewis, Juliette Binoche, Lena Olin, Derek De Lint, Erland Josephson, Pavel Landovsky, Daniel Olbrychski, Stellan Skarsgard; **W/D:** Philip Kaufman; **W:** Jean-Claude Carriere. Academy Awards '88 Nominations: Best Adapted Screenplay, Best Cinematography; Independent Spirit Awards '89: Best Cinematography; National Society of Film Critics Awards '88: Best Director (Kaufman), Best Film. **VHS, Beta, LV $89.98** *ORI, TAM* ✂✂✂ ½

The Unbeaten 28 A group of kung fu masters is forced to fight for their lives against evil criminals.
1987 90m/C Lisa Chang, Meng Fei, Lung Sikar; **D:** Joseph Kuo. **VHS, Beta $39.95** *MPI* ✂

The Unbelievable Truth Ex-con Robocop-to-be Burke meets armageddon-obsessed model and sparks fly until bizarre murder occurs. Quirky black comedy shot in less than two weeks.
1990 (R) 100m/C Adrienne Shelly, Robert Burke, Christopher Cooke, Julia Mueller; **D:** Hal Hartley. **VHS, LV $89.95** *VMK* ✂✂ ½

The Unborn An infertile wife gets inseminated at unorthodox clinic. But once pregnant she suspects that her unborn baby is a monstrous being. Tasteless B-movie with an A-performance from Adams; if the rest had been up to her standard this could have been another "Stepford Wives." Instead it cops out with cheap gore.
1991 (R) 85m/C Brooke Adams, Jeff Hayenga, James Karen, K. Callan, Jane Cameron; **D:** Rodman Flender. **VHS, LV $89.95** *COL* ✂ ½

The Unbreakable Alibi A wealthy young man asks Tommy and Tuppence Beresford to help him prove that one of two alibis an Australian journalist created is false. Based on the mysteries by Agatha Christie. Made for television.
1983 51m/C *GB* Francesca Annis, James Warwick; **W:** Agatha Christie. **VHS, Beta $14.95** *PAV* ✂✂

Uncaged Five beautiful young prostitutes hit Sunset Strip, each of them dreaming of a better life. When a crazy pimp brutally murders one of their friends, they set out to avenge that girl, and her broken dreams. *AKA:* Angel in Red.

U

1991 (R) 78m/C Leslie Bega, Jeffrey Dean Morgan, Pamella O'Pella, Gregory Millar, Henry Brown, Jason Oliver, Elena Sahagun; *D:* William Duprey. VHS, LV *$79.95 COL, CCV, PIA* �18

The Uncanny Horror anthology of three tales concerned with feline attempts to control the world. Waste of good cast and cats on silly stories. Not released in the U.S.
1978 85m/C *GB* Peter Cushing, Ray Milland, Samantha Eggar, Donald Pleasence; *D:* Denis Heroux. VHS, Beta *$49.95 MED Woof!*

Uncensored This fast-paced comedy special features dozens of hilarious skits and sketches.
1985 60m/C Murray Langston, Cassandra Peterson, John Paragon, Ben Powers. VHS, Beta *$29.95 WWV* �18

The Unchastened Woman A married couple is torn apart by infidelity despite their impending parenthood, and wife Bara heads overseas to run wild and have the baby. She returns with a foreign flame, whom she dumps when erstwhile husband finds fatherly feelings in his heart. One of Bara's last films.
1925 52m/B Theda Bara, Wyndham Standing, Dale Fuller, John Miljan; *D:* James Young. VHS, Beta *$19.95 GPV, FCT* �18

Uncle Buck When Mom and Dad have to go away suddenly, the only babysitter they can find is good ol' Uncle Buck, a lovable lout who spends much of his time smoking cigars, trying to make up with his girlfriend, and enforcing the teenage daughter's chastity. More intelligent than the average slob/teen comedy with a heart, due in large part to Candy's dandy performance. Memorable pancake scene.
1989 (PG) 100m/C John Candy, Amy Madigan, Jean Kelly, Macaulay Culkin, Jay Underwood; *D:* John Hughes. VHS, Beta, LV *$19.95 MCA* �18�18�18

Uncle Moses The clash of old-world values and new-world culture in a story of East European Jewish immigrants transplanted to turn of the century New York's Lower East Side. Patriarch Uncle Moses struggles to keep traditional family values as romantic difficulties and labor union struggles intrude. Based on the novel by Sholem Asch. In Yiddish with English subtitles.
1932 87m/B Maurice Schwartz, Rubin Goldberg; *D:* Sidney Goldin, Aubrey Scotto. VHS *$72.00 NCJ* �18�18½

Uncle Sam Magoo Mr. Magoo provides a history lesson in his own unmatchable style.
1970 53m/C *V:* Jim Backus. VHS, Beta *$12.95 PAR, FCT, WTA* �18�18½

Uncle Tom's Cabin Satisfying version of Harriet Beecher Stowe's tale from the view of a founder of the underground railroad. Lucas was the first black actor to garner a lead role.
1914 54m/C Mary Eline, Irving Cummings, Sam Lucas; *D:* William Robert Daly. VHS, Beta *$19.95 GPV, FCT, DVT* �18�18

Uncle Tom's Cabin Ambitious adaptation of Harriet Beecher Stowe's stirring book about the Southern slavery and the famous underground railroad devised to aid those most determined to reach freedom. The film has the habit of drifting away from the facts. Though set in Kentucky, the picture was filmed in Yugoslavia with an international cast. *AKA:* Onkel Toms Hutte; La Case de L'Oncle Tom; Cento Dollari D'Odio; Cica Tomina Koliba.

1969 (G) 120m/C *FR IT YU GE* Herbert Lom, John Kitzmiller, O.W. Fischer, Eleanora Rossi-Drago, Mylene Demongeot, Juliette Greco; *D:* Geza von Radvanyi; *V:* Ella Fitzgerald. VHS, Beta *$39.95 XVC, AFR* �18½

Uncle Tom's Cabin The first American sound version of this film. Excellent cast and interestingly adapted script are perfect for a message that is still socially relevant today. Based on the novel by Harriet Beecher Stowe. Made for television.
1987 110m/C Avery Brooks, Kate Burton, Bruce Dern, Paula Kelly, Phylicia Rashad, Kathryn Walker, Edward Woodward, Frank Converse, George Coe, Albert Hall; *D:* Stan Lathan. VHS, WOV �18�18½

Uncle Was a Vampire Lee stars as Count Dracula in this vampire story.
1959 ?m/C Christopher Lee, Kay Fisher. VHS *$16.95 SNC* �18�18

Uncommon Valor After useless appeals to the government for information on his son listed as "missing in action" in Vietnam, Colonel Rhodes takes matters into his own hands. Hackman is solid and believable as always, surrounded with good cast in generally well-paced film.
1983 (R) 105m/C Gene Hackman, Fred Ward, Reb Brown, Randall "Tex" Cobb, Robert Stack, Patrick Swayze, Harold Sylvester, Tim Thomerson; *D:* Ted Kotcheff. VHS, Beta, LV, 8mm *$14.95 PAR* �18�18½

The Undaunted Wu Dang Set in 19th-century China, this film follows the adventures of the beautiful young daughter of a Chinese martial arts master seeking to avenge the murders of her father and brother.
1989 95m/C VHS, Beta *NO* �18

The Undead A prostitute is accidentally sent back to the Middle Ages as the result of a scientific experiment and finds herself condemned to die for witchcraft. Early Corman script filled with violence and heaving bosoms.
1957 75m/B Pamela Duncan, Richard Garland, Allison Hayes, Mel Welles; *D:* Roger Corman. VHS *$19.95 NOS, AIP, MLB* �18�18�18

Undeclared War Suspenseful espionage thriller that takes you behind the scenes of an international terrorist plot, which has been cleverly disguised as a bloody global revolution. Intense action heightened by conflicts between worldwide intelligence networks, the news media and terrorist organizations.
1991 (R) 103m/C Vernon Wells, David Hedison, Olivia Hussey, Peter Lapis; *D:* Ringo Lam. VHS *$89.95 IMP* �18

The Undefeated A Confederate and Yankee find they must team up on the Rio Grande. They attempt to build new lives in the Spanish held Mexico territory, but are caught in the battle for Mexican independence. Standard fare made palatable only by Wayne and Hudson.
1969 (G) 119m/C John Wayne, Rock Hudson, Lee Meriwether, Merlin Olsen, Bruce Cabot, Ben Johnson, Jan-Michael Vincent, Harry Carey Jr., Antonio Aguilar, Roman Gabriel; *D:* Andrew V. McLaglen. VHS, Beta, LV *$19.98 FOX* �18

Under California Stars Shady gang making a living rounding up wild horses decides they can make more money by capturing Rogers' horse, Trigger. *AKA:* Under California Skies.
1948 71m/C Roy Rogers, Andy Devine, Jane Frazee, The Pioneers; *D:* William Witney. VHS, Beta *$19.95 NOS, VYY, DVT* �18�18

Under Capricorn Bergman is an Irish lass who follows her convict husband Cotten out to 1830s Australia where he makes a fortune. She turns to drink, perhaps because of his neglect, and has her position usurped by a housekeeper with designs on her husband. When Bergman's cousin (Wilding) arrives, Cotten may have cause for his violent jealousy. There's a plot twist involving old family skeletons, but this is definitely lesser Hitchcock. Adapted from the Helen Simpson novel. Remade in 1982.
1949 117m/C *GB* Ingrid Bergman, Joseph Cotten, Michael Wilding, Margaret Leighton, Jack Watling, Cecil Parker, Denis O'Dea; *D:* Alfred Hitchcock. VHS, Beta, LV *$14.98 VES, VID* �18�18½

Under Capricorn An Australian remake of the 1949 Hitchcock film about family secrets, an unhappy marriage, and violence set in 1830's Australia.
1982 120m/C *AU* Lisa Harrow, John Hallam, Peter Cousens, Julia Blake, Catherine Lynch; *D:* Rod Hardy. VHS, Beta *$59.95 PSM* �18�18

Under Fire Three foreign correspondents, old friends from the past working together, find themselves in Managua, witnessing the 1979 Nicaraguan revolution. In a job requiring objectivity, but a situation requiring taking sides, they battle with their ethics to do the job right. Fine performances, including Camp as a mercenary. Interesting view of American media and its political necessities.
1983 (R) 128m/C Gene Hackman, Nick Nolte, Joanna Cassidy, Ed Harris, Richard Masur, Hamilton Camp, Jean-Louis Trintignant; *D:* Roger Spottiswoode; *W:* Ron Shelton, Clayton Frohman; *M:* Jerry Goldsmith. VHS, Beta, LV *$19.98 VES* �18�18�18½

Under Milk Wood An adaptation of the Dylan Thomas play about the lives of the residents of a village in Wales. Burton and O'Toole are wonderful in this uneven, but sometimes engrossing film.
1973 (PG) 90m/C *GB* Richard Burton, Elizabeth Taylor, Peter O'Toole, Glynis Johns, Vivien Merchant; *D:* Andrew Sinclair. VHS, Beta *$59.98 FOX* �18�18½

Under Montana Skies An early talkie western features music and comedy in abundance, relegating the action to second place. A singing cowboy protects a travelling burlesque show from evildoers.
1930 55m/B Kenneth Harlan, Dorothy Gulliver, Lafe McKee, Ethel Wales, Slim Summerville; *D:* Dave Thorpe. VHS, Beta *GPV* �18½

Under Nevada Skies Fairly good matinee-era western centers on a missing map to a uranium deposit, climaxing with Rogers heading a posse of Indian allies to the rescue. The Sons of the Pioneers contribute songs.
1946 69m/B Roy Rogers, George "Gabby" Hayes, Dale Evans, Douglas Dumbrille, Tristram Coffin, Rudolph Anders, Iron Eyes Cody; *D:* Frank McDonald. VHS *$19.95 NOS, HEG* �18�18½

Under Satan's Sun A rural priest is tortured by what he sees as his sins and failings to his parishioners. He is further tempted from the straight path by a beautiful murderess, a worldly priest, and, perhaps by Satan in disguise. Stylized film is not easily accessible, but Depardieu's performance is worth the effort. Based on the Georges Bernanos book "Diary of a Country Priest." In French with English subtitles. *AKA:* Under the Sun of Satan; Sous le Soleil de Satan.
1987 97m/C *FR* Gerard Depardieu, Sandrine Bonnaire, Yann Dedet, Alain Artur, Maurice Pialat; *D:* Maurice Pialat. VHS *$79.95 TAM, FCT* �18�18�18

Under Siege The USS Missouri becomes the battleground for good-guy-with-a-secret-past Seagal. He's up against the deranged Jones, as an ex-Special Forces leader, and Busey, a corrupt naval officer looking to steal the battleship's nuclear arsenal. May be predictable (especially the graphic violence) but the action is fast, the villains swaggering, and Seagal efficient at dispatching the enemy. Work for "Die Hard 3" was reportedly scrapped after Warner announced this film because DH's John McClane was supposed to save the passengers of a boat from terrorists. Sound familiar?
1992 (R) 100m/C Steven Seagal, Tommy Lee Jones, Gary Busey, Patrick O'Neal, Erika Eleniak; **D:** William Webb; **W:** J.F. Lawton. **VHS, Beta, LV, 8mm $94.99** WAR ✍✍

Under Suspicion Christmas 1959 in Brighton, England finds seedy private eye Tony Aaron doing his usual divorce work. He and wife/partner Hazel stage phony adultery cases for those desperate to get around England's strict divorce laws. Hazel checks into a hotel with the male client and after a suitable time, Tony bursts in to snap incriminating photos. Only this time, Tony finds both his wife and their client, a famous artist, murdered. Suspects include Angeline, the artist's mistress and his jealous wife, Selina. Even Tony is a suspect and as he works to clear his name, he also falls into a heated, if mistrustful, affair with the sultry Angeline. Conventional melodrama well-acted by Neeson as the charmingly sleazy Tony; San Giacomo is, however, miscast as the femme fatale. Theatrical feature debut for director Moore.
1992 (R) 99m/C GB Liam Neeson, Laura San Giacomo, Alphonsia Emmanuel, Kenneth Cranham, Maggie O'Neill; **W/D:** Simon Moore. **VHS, LV** COL ✍✍½

Under the Biltmore Clock F. Scott Fitzgerald's story, "Myra Meets His Family," is the basis for this American Playhouse installment for PBS television. It is outwit or be outwitted in this tale of a fortune-hunting '20s flapper who is outsmarted by the man she has set her sights on when he hires actors to play his eccentric "family."
1985 70m/C Sean Young, Lenny Von Dohlen, Barnard Hughes; **D:** Neal Miller. **VHS, Beta, LV, 8mm $19.98** SUE, NLC ✍✍

Under the Boardwalk A pair of star-crossed teenage lovers struggle through familial and societal differences in 1980s California. This is, like, bogus, ya know.
1989 (R) 102m/C Keith Coogan, Danielle von Zernaeck, Richard Joseph Paul, Hunter von Leer, Tracy Walter, Roxana Zal, Dick Miller, Sonny Bono, Corky Carroll; **D:** Fritz Kiersch. **VHS, Beta, LV $19.95** STE, NWV ✍½

Under the Cherry Moon Prince portrays a fictional musician of the 1940s who travels to the French Riviera, seeking love and money. Songs include "Under the Cherry Moon," "Kiss," "Anotherloverholeinyouhead," "Sometimes It Snows in April," and "Mountains." A vanity flick down to its being filmed in black and white.
1986 (PG-13) 100m/B Prince, Jerome Benton, Francesca Annis, Kristin Scott Thomas; **D:** Prince. **VHS, Beta, LV $19.98** MVD, WAR, FCT ✍½

Under the Doctor A silly British comedy about a psychiatrist who fantasizes about his gorgeous female patients who only want to talk about their sexual problems.
1976 (R) 84m/C GB **D:** Gerry Poulson. **VHS, Beta $29.95** ACA Woof!

Under the Earth An Argentine-Czech co-production, depicting the plight of a family of Polish Jews forced to live underground for two years to avoid the Nazis. Harrowing and critically well-received. In Spanish with subtitles. **AKA:** Debajo del Mundo.
1986 (R) 100m/C SP Victor Laplace; **D:** Beda Ocampo Feijoo, Juan Bautista Stagnaro. **VHS, Beta, LV $19.95** STE, NWV, SWC ✍✍

Under the Gun A cop recruits a lawyer to help him find the man who murdered his brother. Action drives this formulaic plot along.
1988 (R) 89m/C Sam Jones, Vanessa Williams, John Russell, Michael Halsey; **D:** James Sbardellati. **VHS, LV $79.89** IME ✍✍

Under the Rainbow Comic situations encountered by a talent scout and a secret service agent in a hotel filled with Munchkins during filming of "The Wizard of Oz." Features midgets, spies, and a prevailing lack of taste. International intrigue adds to the strange attempt at humor.
1981 (PG) 97m/C Chevy Chase, Carrie Fisher, Eve Arden, Joseph Maher, Robert Donner, Mako, Pat McCormick, Billy Barty, Zelda Rubinstein; **D:** Steve Rash. **VHS, Beta $19.98** WAR Woof!

Under the Red Robe A French soldier of fortune is trapped into aiding Cardinal Richelieu in his persecution of the Huguenots and winds up falling in love with the sister of his intended victim. Good costume adventure-drama. Sjostrom's last film as a director.
1936 82m/B GB Raymond Massey, Conrad Veidt, Annabella, Romney Brent; **D:** Victor Sjostrom. **VHS, Beta $19.95** NOS, HHT, WFV ✍✍½

Under the Roofs of Paris An early French sound film about the lives of young Parisian lovers. A gentle, highly acclaimed melodrama. In French with English subtitles. **AKA:** Sous les Toits de Paris.
1929 95m/B FR Albert Prejean, Pola Illery, Gaston Modot; **D:** Rene Clair. **VHS, Beta, 3/4U, Special order formats $29.95** NOS, VYY, CAB ✍✍✍½

Under the Sheets Four zany medical students would rather undress the nurses than hit the books.
1986 87m/C SP Karin Schubert. **VHS** NO ✍✍✍½

Under the Volcano An alcoholic British ex-consul finds his life further deteriorating during the Mexican Day of the Dead in 1939. His half-brother and ex-wife try to save him from himself, but their affair sends him ever-deeper into his personal hell. Finney's performance is pathetic and haunting. Adapted from the novel by Malcolm Lowry.
1984 112m/C Albert Finney, Jacqueline Bisset, Anthony Andrews, Katy Jurado; **D:** John Huston. **VHS, Beta, LV $79.95** MCA ✍✍✍

Under Western Stars Roy's first starring vehicle. A newly elected congressman goes to Washington and fights battles for his constituents, caught in the middle of the Dust Bowl and drought.
1945 83m/B Roy Rogers, Trigger, Smiley Burnette; **D:** Jean Yarborough. **VHS, Beta, 3/4U, Special order formats $19.95** NOS, DVT, VCN ✍

The Underachievers A night school is the scene for typical libido-oriented gags, but this time instead of teenagers it's adult education providing the plot. Only a few real laughs in this one.
1988 (R) 90m/C Barbara Carrera, Edward Albert, Michael Pataki, Vic Tayback, Garrett Morris, Susan Tyrrell; **D:** Jackie Kong. **VHS, Beta $79.98** LIV, VES ✍

Undercover Routine cop action film in which an eastern detective finds himself undercover in a southern high school in search of a cop-murdering drug ring. Plagued with cliches. Director Stockwell is appropriately better known for his role as "Cougar" in "Top Gun."
1987 (R) 92m/C David Neidorf, Jennifer Jason Leigh, Barry Corbin, David Harris, Kathleen Wilhoite; **D:** John Stockwell. **VHS $79.98** WAR ✍1½

Undercover Blues Comedy-thriller starring Turner and Quaid as married spies Jane and Jeff Blue, retired from the espionage biz, only to return to it because of the financial demands new parenthood has placed on them (and it's all they know how to do). Their assignment is to stop an international terrorist group dealing in stolen weapons. Sound familiar? Basically an updated version of Nick and Nora Charles from the "Thin Man."
1993 (PG-13) ?m/C Kathleen Turner, Dennis Quaid; **D:** Herbert Ross. **VHS** NYR ✍✍½

Undercover Man A Wells Fargo agent goes undercover to expose a crooked sheriff.
1936 57m/B Johnny Mack Brown, Suzanne Karen, Ted Adams, Lloyd Ingraham, Horace Murphy; **D:** Albert Ray. **VHS $19.95** NOS, DVT, RXM ✍1½

Undercover Vixens Undercover Israeli beauties battle and seduce enemy agents.
1987 78m/C Monica Gayle, Sherrie Land. **VHS, Beta $29.95** MED Woof!

The Underdog After the bank forecloses, a farm family must move to the city. The family's young son has only his loyal dog to turn to for friendship, but the gallant animal proves his mettle by rounding up a gang of spies plotting some WWII sabotage. Believe it if you dare.
1943 65m/B Barton MacLane, Bobby Larson, Jane Wiley; **D:** William Nigh. **VHS, Beta, 8mm** VYY ✍1½

Undergrads A bright generational Disney comedy with Carney, estranged from his stick-in-the-mud son, deciding to attend college with his free-thinking grandson. Made for television.
1985 102m/C Art Carney, Chris Makepeace, Jackie Burroughs, Len Birman; **D:** Steven Hilliard Stern. **VHS, Beta $59.95** DIS ✍✍

Underground Aces A group of parking lot attendants transforms a sheik into an attendant in order to help him meet the girl of his dreams. A bad "Car Wash" spinoff.
1980 (PG) 93m/C Dirk Benedict, Melanie Griffith, Frank Gorshin, Jerry Orbach, Robert Hegyes, Audrey Landers; **D:** Robert Butler. **VHS, Beta $69.98** LIV, VES Woof!

Underground Rustlers The Range Busters are commissioned by the government to stop unscrupulous gold-marketeers.
1941 58m/B Ray Corrigan, Max Terhune, John "Dusty" King; **D:** S. Roy Luby. **VHS, Beta $19.95** VDM ✍

Underground Terror A gang of murderers, organized by a psychopath, rampages through the New York City subway system. One cop enthusiastically tries to snuff out each one.
1988 91m/C Doc Dougherty, Lenny Y. Loftin; **D:** James McCalmont. **VHS $79.95** SVS ✍

Underground U.S.A. Street hustler picks up a has-been underground movie star at the chic New York new wave disco, The Mudd Club.
1984 85m/C Patti Astor, Eric Mitchell; **D:** Eric Mitchell. **VHS, Beta** NO ✍

Undersea Kingdom Adventure beneath the ocean floor. In twelve chapters of thirteen minutes each; the first chapter runs twenty minutes. Later re-edited into one film, "Sharad of Atlantis."
1936 226m/B Ray Corrigan, Lon Chaney Jr.; *D:* B. Reeves Eason. **VHS, LV $29.98** *NOS, SNC, VCN* ⅛

Understudy: The Graveyard Shift 2 Vampire survives poorly directed cliche-riddled original to be cast as a vampire cast as a vampire in a horror movie within a horrible sequel.
1988 (R) 88m/C Wendy Gazelle, Mark Soper, Silvio Oliviero; *D:* Gerard Ciccoritti. **VHS, Beta, LV** *NO* ⅛½

The Undertaker and His Pals Undertaker teams up with diner owners in murder scheme to improve mortician's business and expand restaurateurs' menu. Pretty violent stuff, with some good laughs and a campy flare, but not for every one's palate.
1967 70m/C Ray Dannis, Brad Fulton, Larrene Ott, Robert Lowery, Sally Frei; *D:* David C. Graham. **VHS** *MTH* ⅛

Underwater A team of skin divers faces danger when they try to retrieve treasure from a Spanish galleon. The second film after "The Outlaw" masterminded by Howard Hughes, primarily to show off Russell's figure.
1955 99m/C Jane Russell, Richard Egan, Gilbert Roland, Jayne Mansfield; *D:* John Sturges. **VHS, Beta, LV $19.98** *MED, TTC* ⅛

Underworld Underground mutants kidnap a prostitute in order to get a life-sustaining drug. A gangland boss hires a gunman to save her. Based on a Clive Barker novel.
1985 100m/C Denholm Elliott, Steven Berkoff, Larry Lamb, Nicola Cowper; *D:* George Pavlou. **VHS** *VES, LIV* ⅛½

Underworld Scandal An editor attempts to break up a ring of basketball game fixers.
1947 ?m/C Philip Reed, Hillary Brooke. **VHS $16.95** *SNC* ⅛⅛

The Underworld Story Big city journalist at large moves to smalltown New England after losing job for unethical reporting and uncovers scheme to frame innocent man for murder. Solid performances.
1950 90m/B Dan Duryea, Herbert Marshall, Gale Storm, Howard da Silva, Michael O'Shea, Mary Anderson, Gar Moore, Melville Cooper, Frieda Inescort, Art Baker, Harry Shannon, Alan Hale Jr., Steve Dunne, Roland Winters; *D:* Cy Endfield. **VHS $19.98** *FOX, FCT* ⅛⅛½

Underworld, U.S.A. A man infiltrates a tough crime syndicate to avenge his father's murder, which winds up with him caught between the mob and the feds. A well-acted and directed look at the criminal underworld.
1960 99m/B Cliff Robertson, Dolores Dorn, Beatrice Kay, Robert Emhardt, Larry Gates, Paul Dubov; *W/D:* Samuel Fuller. **VHS, Beta $69.95** *COL* ⅛⅛⅛

The Undying Monster Upper crusty Brit is werewolf with insatiable appetite. Familiar story with lots of atmosphere and style. Photography by Lucien Ballard. *AKA:* The Hammond Mystery.
1942 63m/B James Ellison, Heather Angel, John Howard, Bramwell Fletcher, Heather Thatcher, Aubrey Mather, Halliwell Hobbes, Heather Wilde; *D:* John Brahm. **VHS $19.98** *MOV* ⅛⅛

Une Jeunesse A middle-aged French couple reminisce about their meeting and courtship. In French with English subtitles.
1983 100m/C *FR* **VHS, Beta $29.95** *FCT* ⅛⅛⅛

The Unearthly A mad scientist is trying to achieve immortality through his strange experiments, but all he winds up with is a basement full of mutants. When his two latest about-to-be victims fall in love, the doctor's mutant assistant decides enough is enough and things come to an unpleasant end. Carradine is typecast. Absurd, but fun.
1957 76m/B John Carradine, Tor Johnson, Allison Hayes, Myron Healey; *D:* Brooke L. Peters. **VHS, Beta $9.95** *RHI, SNC, DVT* ⅛½

The Unearthly Stranger Earth scientist marries woman and decides she's from another planet. Not a nineties style gender drama; seems she's part of an invading alien force, but really does love her earth man. Surprisingly good low-budget sci-fi. *AKA:* The Unearthly Stranger.
1964 75m/B *GB* John Neville, Gabriella Licudi, Philip Stone, Patrick Newell, Jean Marsh, Warren Mitchell; *D:* John Krish. **VHS $19.98** *MOV* ⅛⅛½

Uneasy Terms Rennie is a detective investigating the murder of one of his own clients. Evidence points to stepchildren and inheritance money but things may not be as they seem. Written for the screen by Peter Cheyney, adapted from his own novel.
1948 91m/B *GB* Michael Rennie, Moira Lister, Faith Brook, Joy Shelton, Patricia Goddard, Barry Jones; *D:* Vernon Sewell. **VHS, Beta $16.95** *SNC* ⅛

Unexplained Laughter A cynical journalist vacations in Wales with her timid vegetarian friend and stumbles across a mystery in this darkly comic British TV-movie.
1989 85m/C *GB* Diana Rigg, Elaine Page, Jon Finch. **VHS $49.95** *FCT* ⅛⅛

Unfaithfully Yours A conductor suspects his wife is cheating on him and considers his course of action. He imagines punishment scenarios while directing three classical works. Well-acted by all, but particularly by Harrison as the egotistical and jealous husband. Another of Sturges' comedic gems. Remade in 1984.
1948 105m/B Rex Harrison, Linda Darnell, Kurt Kreuger, Rudy Vallee, Lionel Stander, Edgar Kennedy; *D:* Preston Sturges. **VHS, Beta, LV $59.98** *FOX* ⅛⅛⅛½

Unfaithfully Yours A symphony conductor suspects his wife of fooling around with a musician; in retaliation, he plots an elaborate scheme to murder her with comic results. No match for the 1948 Preston Sturges film it's based on.
1984 (PG) 96m/C Dudley Moore, Nastassia Kinski, Armand Assante, Albert Brooks, Cassie Yates, Richard Libertini, Richard B. Shull; *D:* Howard Zieff. **VHS, Beta, LV $79.98** *FOX* ⅛⅛

Unfinished Business A 17 year-old girl leads a troubled adolescent life with her divorced parents. She decides running away will ease her problems—not a smart move. Sequel to "Nobody Waved Goodbye."
1989 88m/C *CA* Isabelle Mejias, Peter Kastner, Leslie Toth, Peter Spence; *D:* Don Owen. **VHS, Beta $79.95** *JEF* ⅛⅛½

An Unfinished Piece for a Player Piano A general's widow invites family and friends to a weekend house party in 1910 Russia. Romantic and familial entanglements begin to intrude in a lyrical adaptation of Chekov's play "Platonov." In Russian with English subtitles.
1977 100m/C *RU* Alexander Kalyagin, Elena Solovei, Antonina Shuranova, Oleg Tabakov, Yuri Bogatyrev, Nikita Mikhalkov; *D:* Nikita Mikhalkov. **VHS, Beta $69.95** *FCT, TAM, CVC* ⅛⅛⅛½

The Unforgiven A western family is torn asunder when it is suspected that the eldest daughter is of Indian birth. Film takes place in 1850s' Texas. One of Huston's weakest ventures, but viewed in terms of 1950s' prejudices it has more resonance. Fine acting from all the cast, especially Gish. Watch for the stunning Indian attack scene.
1960 123m/C Burt Lancaster, Audrey Hepburn, Lillian Gish, Audie Murphy, John Saxon, Charles Bickford, Doug McClure, Joseph Wiseman, Albert Salmi; *D:* John Huston. **VHS, Beta, LV $19.98** *MGM* ⅛⅛⅛

Unforgiven Will Munny (Eastwood) lives a quiet life with his stepchildren on his failing pig farm. His desperado past catches up with him with the arrival of the Schofield Kid, who wants Munny to join him in bounty hunting two cowhands. Munny needs the money and reluctantly agrees, mistakenly believing that once the killing is through he can take up his peaceful ways again. Their destination is Big Whiskey, run by sadistic sheriff Little Bill Daggett (Hackman), who doesn't want any gunmen messing up his town. Eastwood uses his own status as a screen legend to full advantage as the aging gunman who realizes too late that his past can never be forgotten. Director Eastwood is also in top form with his well-seasoned cast and myth-defying Old West realism. A surprising critical and box office hit. The laserdisc version is available in letterbox format.
1992 (R) 131m/C Clint Eastwood, Gene Hackman, Morgan Freeman, Richard Harris, Jaimz Woolvett, Saul Rubinek, Frances Fisher, Anna Thomson, David Mucci, Rob Campbell, Anthony James; *D:* Clint Eastwood; *W:* David Peoples. Academy Awards '92: Best Director (Eastwood), Best Film Editing, Best Picture, Best Supporting Actor (Hackman); Nominations: Best Actor (Eastwood), Best Art Direction/Set Decoration, Best Cinematography, Best Original Screenplay, Best Sound; Directors Guild of America Awards '92: Best Director (Eastwood); Golden Globe Awards '93: Best Director (Eastwood), Best Supporting Actor (Hackman); New York Film Critics Awards '92: Best Supporting Actor (Hackman); National Society of Film Critics Awards '92: Best Director (Eastwood), Best Film, Best Supporting Actor (Hackman). **VHS, Beta, LV, 8mm $99.99** *WAR, MOV, BTV* ⅛⅛⅛½

Unforgotten Crime A small town murder mystery.
1941 ?m/C George E. Stone, Dennis O'Keefe. **VHS $16.95** *SNC* ⅛⅛

The Unholy A New Orleans priest battles a demon that's killing innocent parishioners. Confusing and heavy-handed.
1988 (R) 100m/C Ben Cross, Hal Holbrook, Trevor Howard, Ned Beatty, William Russ, Jim Carroll; *D:* Camilo Vila. **VHS, Beta, LV $19.98** *LIV, VES, HHE* ⅛½

Unholy Four An amnesiac returns home after three years to attempt to find out which of his three fishing buddies left him for dead. Confusing at times, but has some suspenseful moments. British title was "A Stranger Came Home."
1954 80m/B *GB* Paulette Goddard, Paul Carpenter, William Sylvester, Patrick Holt, Russell Napier; *D:* Terence Fisher. **VHS, Beta, LV** *WGE* ⅛½

Unholy Rollers Jennings stars as a factory worker who makes it big as a tough, violent roller derby star. Typical "Babes-on-Wheels" film that promises nothing and delivers even less. *AKA:* Leader of the Pack.
1972 (R) 88m/C Claudia Jennings, Louis Quinn, Betty A. Rees, Roberta Collins, Alan Vint, Candice Roman; *D:* Vernon Zimmerman. **VHS $79.95** *HBO* ⅛

The Unholy Three Ventriloquist Chaney, working with other carnival cohorts, uses his talent to gain entrance to homes which he later robs. Things go awry when two of the gang strike out on their own and the victim is killed. When the wrong man is accused, his girl, one of Chaney's gang, begs Chaney to get him free, which he does by using his vocal talents. Chaney decides being a criminal is just too hard and goes back to his ventriloquism.
1925 70m/B Lon Chaney Sr., Harry Earles, Victor McLaglen, Mae Busch, Matt Moore, Matthew Betz, William Humphreys; **D:** Tod Browning. **VHS** *NO* ♂♂♂½

The Unholy Three Chaney remade his silent hit of 1925 for his first and only talking picture (he died before the film was released). The story is essentially the same. Chaney is a ventriloquist who, with his circus friends, work as scam artists and thieves. When an innocent man is accused of their crimes Chaney tries his ventriloquist tricks to come to his aid, only in this version Chaney is exposed as a fraud and is sent to prison. Rumors that Chaney was a mute had him agreeing to appear in a "talkie" and he actually used five different voices for his various roles.
1930 75m/B Lon Chaney Sr., Lila Lee, Elliott Nugent, Harry Earles, John Miljan; **D:** Jack Conway. **VHS $29.95** *FCT* ♂♂♂

Unholy Wife A young woman plans to murder her wealthy husband, but her plan goes awry when she accidentally kills someone else. Muddled and heavy-handed, with Steiger chewing scenery.
1957 94m/C Rod Steiger, Diana Dors, Tom Tryon, Marie Windsor, Beulah Bondi; **D:** John Farrow. **VHS, Beta $15.95** *UHV, HHE* ♂♂½

Unicorn A small boy hears the legend that if one rubs the horn of a Unicorn his wishes will come true. Mistakenly he buys a one-horned goat and sets out to fulfill his dreams.
1983 29m/C *GB* Diana Dors, David Kossoff, Celia Johnson; **D:** Carol Reed. **VHS, Beta $24.95** *SUE, NLC* ♂♂

Unidentified Flying Oddball An astronaut and his robotic buddy find their spaceship turning into a time machine that throws them back into Arthurian times and at the mercy of Merlin the magician. Futuristic version of Twain's "A Connecticut Yankee at King Arthur's Court."
1979 (G) 92m/C Dennis Dugan, Jim Dale, Ron Moody, Kenneth More, Rodney Bewes; **D:** Russ Mayberry. **VHS, Beta $69.95** *DIS* ♂♂½

The Uninvited A brother and sister buy a house in England, only to find it is haunted. Doors open and close by themselves, strange scents fill the air, and they hear sobbing during the night. Soon they are visited by a woman with an odd link to the house—her mother is the spirit who haunts the house. Chilling and unforgettable, this is one of the first films to deal seriously with ghosts.
1944 99m/B Ray Milland, Ruth Hussey, Donald Crisp, Cornelia Otis Skinner, Gail Russell; **D:** Lewis Allen. **VHS, LV $14.98** *MCA* ♂♂♂

The Uninvited A mutant cat goes berserk onboard a luxury yacht, killing the passengers one by one with big, nasty, pointy teeth.
1988 89m/C George Kennedy, Alex Cord, Clu Gulager, Toni Hudson, Eric Larson, Shari Shattuck, Austin Stoker; **D:** Greydon Clark. **VHS, Beta, LV** *NO* Woof!

Union City Deborah "Blondie" Harry's husband gets a little edgy when someone steals the milk. Murder ensues, and they're on the run from the law. Intended as a film noir spoof, and not without some good moments.
1981 (R) 82m/C Deborah Harry, Everett McGill, Dennis Lipscomb, Pat Benatar; **D:** Mark Reichart. **VHS, Beta, LV $59.95** *COL* ♂♂

Union Station Holden plays the chief of the railway police for Chicago's Union Station. He learns the station is to be used as a ransom drop in a kidnapping; but for all his security, the main thug gets away with the money, and the hunt is on. Good acting raises this film above the ordinary.
1950 80m/B William Holden, Barry Fitzgerald, Nancy Olson, Jan Sterling, Lee Marvin, Allene Roberts, Lyle Bettger; **D:** Rudolph Mate. **VHS, Beta $19.95** *KRT* ♂♂

Universal Soldier A reporter discovers a secret government project to design perfect robo-soldiers by using the bodies of dead GIs, including tough guys Lundgren and Van Damme who were killed in Vietnam. But the knowledge is going to get her killed until Van Damme has flashbacks of his past (the soldier's memories have supposedly been erased) and agrees to help her. Lundgren doesn't have the same compassion and goes after them both. Big-budget thriller with some good action sequences and a lot of violence.
1992 (R) 98m/C Jean-Claude Van Damme, Dolph Lundgren, Ally Walker, Ed O'Ross, Jerry Orbach; **D:** Roland Emmerich. **VHS, LV $94.98** *LIV, PMS* ♂♂

The Unkissed Bride A young newlywed couple are driven to distraction by the husband's inexplicable fainting spells and his strange obsession with Mother Goose. **AKA:** Mother Goose A Go-Go.
1966 (PG) 82m/C Tommy Kirk, Anne Helm, Danica D'Hondt, Henny Youngman; **D:** Jack H. Harris. **VHS, Beta $19.95** *STE, NWV* ♂

The Unknown Typically morbid Chaney fare has him working as a circus freak while trying to win the heart of his assistant. After drastic romancing he's still rejected by her, so he plots to kill the object of her intentions. Ghoulish as it is, the picture is really top-notch.
1927 60m/B Lon Chaney Sr., Norman Kerry, Joan Crawford, Nick De Ruiz, Frank Lanning, John St. Polis; **D:** Tod Browning. **VHS $24.95** *FCT* ♂♂♂½

Unknown Island Scientists travel to a legendary island where dinosaurs supposedly still exist. Bogus dinosaurs and cliche script.
1948 76m/C Virginia Grey, Philip Reed, Richard Denning, Barton MacLane; **D:** Jack Bernhard. **VHS $19.95** *NOS, MOV, HEG* Woof!

Unknown Powers Science and drama are combined to examine ESP and magic. Are they gifts or curses, and how are peoples' lives affected by them? Members of the cast introduce various sections of this totally inept film.
1980 (PG) 97m/C Samantha Eggar, Jack Palance, Will Geer, Roscoe Lee Browne; **D:** Don Como. **VHS, Beta $39.95** *GEM* Woof!

Unknown World A group of scientists tunnel to the center of the Earth to find a refuge from the dangers of the atomic world. Big sharp winds down fast.
1951 73m/B Bruce Kellogg, Marilyn Nash, Victor Kilian, Jim Bannon; **D:** Terrell O. Morse. **VHS, Beta $19.95** *NOS, PSM, SNC* ♂

Unlawful Entry When the home of Karen and Michael Carr is broken into, they naturally call the cops. Handsome, polite policeman Pete Davis responds to the call and agrees to help burglar-proof their home. But Pete has some definite quirks—he falls for the beauteous Karen and begins stalking the couple, deciding to get rid of Michael in order to have his wife. A lurid combination of the worst moments of "Internal Affairs" and "Fatal Attraction" undermines this usually-talented cast.
1992 (R) 110m/C Kurt Russell, Ray Liotta, Madeleine Stowe, Roger E. Mosley, Ken Lerner, Deborah Offner, Carmen Argenziano, Andy Romano, Barry W. Blaustein, Dick Miller; **D:** Jonathan Kaplan. **VHS, LV $94.98** *FXV* ♂♂

Unmarried Mothers A number of young ladies engage in sex before marriage and must suffer the consequences.
1955 ?m/C *SW* **VHS $16.95** *SNC* ♂

An Unmarried Woman Suddenly divorced by her husband of 17 years, a woman deals with change. She enters the singles scene, copes with her daughter's growing sexuality, and encounters a new self-awareness. Mazursky puts real people on screen from start to finish.
1978 124m/C Jill Clayburgh, Alan Bates, Cliff Gorman, Michael Murphy; **D:** Paul Mazursky. Academy Awards '78 Nominations: Best Actress (Clayburgh), Best Original Screenplay, Best Picture; Cannes Film Festival '78: Best Actress (Clayburgh); National Board of Review Awards '78: 10 Best Films of the Year. **VHS, Beta $69.98** *FOX* ♂♂♂

Unmasked Part 25 A second-generation serial killer takes up where dad left off. This one is intended to be a parody of slasher films, but it's still very bloody.
1988 85m/C *GB* Gregory Cox, Fiona Evans, Edward Brayshaw, Debbie Lee London; **D:** Anders Palm. **VHS, Beta $79.95** *ACA* ♂½

Unmasking the Idol A suave hero with tongue firmly in check battles Ninja warlords. Sequel to "Order of the Black Eagle."
1986 90m/C *GB* Ian Hunter, William T. Hicks, Charles K. Bibby; **D:** Worth Keeter. **VHS, Beta $19.95** *CEL* ♂

The Unnamable The adaptation of the H.P. Lovecraft story about a particular New England ancestral home haunted by a typically Lovecraftian bloodthirsty demon borne of a woman hundreds of years before. College students, between trysts, investigate the myths about it. Uncut version, unseen in theaters, available only on video good for a few giggles and thrills.
1988 87m/C Charles King, Mark Kinsey Stephenson, Alexandra Durrell; **D:** Jean-Paul Ouellette. **VHS, Beta, LV $19.95** *STE, VMK* ♂

The Unnamable 2: The Statement of Randolph Carter Randolph Carter is investigating a series of murders at Miskatonic University. Evidence leads Carter back to a 17th-century warlock who had the misfortune to summon an evil creature known as Alyda. The half-demon, half-woman now wants to permanently return to the mortal plane and every new victim just helps her evil purpose along. Based on a story by H.P. Lovecraft.
1992 (R) 104m/C Mark Kinsey Stephenson, John Rhys-Davies, David Warner, Julie Strain, Maria Ford; **D:** Jean-Paul Ouellette. **VHS, LV $89.95** *PSM* ♂½

Unnatural A mad scientist creates a souless child from the genes of a murderer and a prostitute. The child grows up to be the beautiful Neff, who makes a habit of seduc-

ing and destroying men. Dark, arresting film from a very popular German story.
1952 90m/B Hildegarde Neff, Erich von Stroheim, Karl-Heinz Boehm, Harry Meyen, Harry Helm, Denise Vernanc, Julia Koschka; *D:* Arthur Maria Rabenalt. **VHS $19.98** *SNC* 🎦🎦½

Unnatural Causes A dying Vietnam vet believes that his illness is the result of exposure to Agent Orange. With the help a VA counselor, they lobby for national programs to assist other veterans who have been exposed to the chemical and together bring publicity to the issue. A made-for-television drama that is exceptionally well-acted.
1986 96m/C John Ritter, Patti LaBelle, Alfre Woodard, Lamont Johnson; *W/D:* John Sayles. **VHS, Beta, LV** *NO* 🎦🎦🎦

An Unremarkable Life Two aging sisters live symbiotically together, until one views the other's romantic attachment to a charming widower as destructive to her own life.
1989 (PG) 97m/C Shelley Winters, Patricia Neal, Mako, Rochelle Oliver, Charles S. Dutton, Lily Knight; *D:* Amin Q. Chaudhri. **VHS, Beta $14.95** *SVS, IME, COL* 🎦🎦

Unsane A mystery novelist realizes that a series of bizarre murders strangely resembles the plot of his latest book. Bloody fun from Argento. *AKA:* Tenebrae.
1982 91m/C *IT* Anthony (Tony) Franciosa, John Saxon, Daria Nicolodi, Giuliano Gemma, Christian Borromeo, Mirella D'Angelo, Veronica Lario; *D:* Dario Argento. **VHS $9.95** *MED* 🎦🎦½

The Unseen Three young women from a television station are covering a story in a remote area of California. Before nightfall, two are horribly killed, leaving the third to come face to face with the terror.
1980 91m/C Barbara Bach, Sydney Lassick, Stephen Furst; *D:* Peter Foleg. **VHS, Beta $19.98** *VID* 🎦½

Unsettled Land Young Israeli settlers try to survive the elements and Bedouin attackers in Palestine during the 1920s.
1988 (PG) 109m/C *IS* Kelly McGillis, John Shea, Arnon Zadok, Christine Boisson; *D:* Uri Barbash. **VHS, Beta, LV, 8mm $19.98** *SUE, NLC* 🎦🎦

The Unsinkable Molly Brown A spunky backwoods girl is determined to break into the upper crust of Denver's high society and along the way survives the sinking of the Titanic. This energetic version of the Broadway musical contains many Meredith Wilson (Music Man) songs and lots of hokey, good-natured fun. 🎵Colorado Is My Home; Leadville Johnny Brown (Soliloquy); I Ain't Down Yet; Belly Up to the Bar, Boys; He's My Friend; I've Already Started; The Beautiful People of Denver; I May Never Fall in Love with You; Up Where the People Are; Dolce Far Niente; I'll Never Say No to You.
1964 128m/C Debbie Reynolds, Harve Presnell, Ed Begley Sr., Martita Hunt, Hermione Baddeley; *D:* Charles Walters. **VHS, Beta, LV $19.98** *MGM* 🎦🎦🎦

The Unstoppable Man The son of an American businessman is kidnapped while they are in London. No pushover he, dad develops his own plan to destroy the criminals, eventually pursuing them with a flame thrower.
1959 68m/B *GB* Cameron Mitchell, Marius Goring, Harry H. Corbett, Lois Maxwell, Denis Gilmore; *D:* Terry Bishop. **VHS, Beta $16.95** *NOS, SNC* 🎦½

Unsuitable Job for a Woman Independent Cordelia Gray, following the death of her boss, takes over his detective agency and gets involved with murder. Based on the novel by P.D. James.
1982 94m/C *GB* Pippa Guard, Paul Freeman, Billie Whitelaw; *D:* Christopher Petit. **VHS, Beta** *NO* 🎦🎦½

The Untamable Unusual silent about volatile woman suffering from schizophrenia.
1923 65m/B Gladys Walton, Malcolm McGregor, John Seinpolis, Etta Lee; *D:* Herbert Blache. **VHS, Beta $19.95** *GPV, FCT* 🎦🎦

Untamed Heart Adam (Slater) the painfully shy busboy with a heart condition loves Caroline (Tomei) the bubbly waitress from afar. She doesn't notice him until he saves her from some would-be rapists and their love blooms in the coffee shop where they both work. Tomei and Slater are both strong in the leads and Perez, as Caroline's best buddy Cindy, hurls comic barbs with ease. Charmingly familiar surroundings help set this formulaic romance apart. Filmed on location in Minneapolis. Laserdisc version is in letterbox format.
1993 (PG-13) 102m/C Christian Slater, Marisa Tomei, Rosie Perez, Kyle Secor, Willie Garson; *D:* Harold Ramis; *W:* Tom Sierchio; *M:* Cliff Eidelman. **VHS, LV $94.99** *MGM* 🎦🎦½

Until September An American tourist becomes stranded in Paris. She meets and falls in love with a married banker while she is stuck in her hotel. Routine romance.
1984 (R) 96m/C Karen Allen, Thierry Lhermitte, Christopher Cazenove, Johanna Pavlis; *D:* Richard Marquand; *M:* John Barry. **VHS, Beta $14.95** *MGM* 🎦🎦

Until The End of The World Convoluted road movie set in 1999 follows the travails of Sam Farber (Hurt) through 15 cities in 8 countries on 4 continents. Mystery woman Claire (Dommartin) winds up with the loot from a bank robbery as she drives to Paris. She picks up Sam, who promptly steals half the money and disappears. Claire tells her novelist/lover Gene (Neill) that she's going after Sam. Sam is chased by Claire, who is followed by a bounty hunter, a private detective, the bank robbers, and Gene, until all wind up in the Australian outback where Sam goes to see his parents (von Sydow and Moreau). And this is only the first half of the movie. For true cinematic satisfaction, don't expect logic and just go with the flow of the movie. Visually stunning, unexpectedly humorous, with excellent performances from an international cast. Footage created with high definition (HDTV) video technology is also a technological first. The soundtrack, which is successfully integrated into the film, features Lou Reed, David Byrne, U2, and others.
1991 (R) 158m/C William Hurt, Solveig Dommartin, Sam Neill, Max von Sydow, Ruediger Vogler, Ernie Dingo, Jeanne Moreau; *D:* Wim Wenders; *W:* Wim Wenders, Peter Carey. **VHS, Beta, LV $92.99** *WAR* 🎦🎦🎦½

Until They Get Me Northern Mountie rides horse in silence as he tracks criminal to the edge of the earth.
1918 58m/B Pauline Starke, Joe King. **VHS, Beta $24.95** *GPV, FCT* 🎦½

Until They Sail Soap opera set in New Zealand during World War II. Plot centers around the lives of four sisters involved in love and murder. Dee's film debut. Based on a story by James Michener.
1957 95m/B Jean Simmons, Joan Fontaine, Paul Newman, Piper Laurie, Charles Drake, Sandra Dee, Wally Cassell, Alan Napier; *D:* Robert Wise; *W:* Robert Anderson. **VHS $19.98** *MGM* 🎦🎦

The Untouchables Big-budget, fast-paced and exciting re-evaluation of the famous television series about the real-life battle between Treasury officer Eliot Ness and crime boss Al Capone in 1920s' Chicago. Costner shows us the change in Ness from naive idealism to steely conviction. Splendid performances by De Niro as Capone and Connery as the cop playing mentor to Ness. Imaginative and beautifully filmed with excellent special effects. Music by Ennio Morricone and script by David Mamet.
1987 (R) 119m/C Kevin Costner, Sean Connery, Robert De Niro, Andy Garcia, Charles Martin Smith, Billy Drago, Richard Bradford, Jack Kehoe; *D:* Brian DePalma; *M:* Ennio Morricone. Academy Awards '87: Best Supporting Actor (Connery); Nominations: Best Art Direction/Set Decoration, Best Costume Design, Best Original Score; Golden Globe Awards '88: Best Supporting Actor (Connery); National Board of Review Awards '87: 10 Best Films of the Year, Best Supporting Actor (Connery). **VHS, Beta, LV, 8mm $14.95** *PAR, PIA, BTV* 🎦🎦🎦½

Up Against the Wall A black kid from the Chicago projects attends school in the affluent suburbs, but there too he must resist temptation, crime and violence. A well-intentioned but didactic cautionary drama, adapted from the book by African-American author/commentator Dr. Jawanza Kunjufu.
1991 (PG-13) 103m/C Marla Gibbs, Stoney Jackson, Catero Colbert, Ron O'Neal, Salli Richardson; *D:* Ron O'Neal. **VHS $79.99** *BMG* 🎦🎦

Up from the Depths Something from beneath the ocean is turning the paradise of Hawaii into a nightmare. Prehistoric fish are returning to the surface with one thing on their minds—lunch. "Jaws" rip-off played for humor.
1979 (R) 85m/C Sam Bottoms, Suzanne Reed, Virgil Frye; *D:* Charles B. Griffith; *W:* Alfred Sweeny. **VHS, Beta $59.98** *LIV, VES* 🎦½

Up in Arms Danny Kaye's first film presents a typical Kaye scenario: he plays a twitching hypochondriac who is drafted into the Army and sneaks his girlfriend aboard the troopship bound for the Pacific. Features an appearance by the Goldwyn Girls. Remake of the film "The Nervous Wreck." 🎵Theatre Lobby Number; Now I Know; All Out for Freedom; Tess's Torch Song; Melody in 4-F.
1944 105m/C Danny Kaye, Dinah Shore, Constance Dowling, Dana Andrews, Margaret Dumont, Goldwyn Girls, Lyle Talbot, Louis Calhern; *D:* Elliott Nugent. **VHS, Beta $19.98** *SUE* 🎦🎦

Up in the Air Darro and Moreland have ambitions as radio comedians, and their friend Reynolds wants to be a singer. Their break comes when other performers are murdered on the air. First, though, they must solve the killings.
1940 62m/B Frankie Darro, Marjorie Reynolds, Mantan Moreland, Gordon Jones, Tristram Coffin, John Holland, Carleton Young; *D:* Howard Bretherton. **VHS $19.95** *NOS* 🎦🎦

Up Periscope Garner is a demolitions expert unwillingly assigned to a submarine commanded by O'Brien. His mission: to sneak onto a Japanese-held island and steal a top-secret code book. Trouble is, O'Brien may not wait for Garner to complete his mission before taking the sub back underwater. A routine submarine film.
1959 111m/C James Garner, Edmond O'Brien, Andra Martin, Alan Hale Jr., Carleton Carpenter, Frank Gifford, Richard Bakalayan; *D:* Gordon Douglas. **VHS, LV** *WAR* 🎦🎦½

Up River Wealthy land baron rapes and murders the wife of a simple pioneer, who is beaten and whose homestead is burned by the baron as well. The pioneer lives to seek terrible vengeance.
1979 90m/C Jeff Corey, Morgan Stevens, Debbie AuLuce; *D:* Carl Kitt. VHS *NO ✂*

Up the Academy Four teenaged delinquents are sent to an academy for wayward boys where they encounter a sadistic headmaster and a gay dance instructor. Sometimes inventive, often tasteless fare from "Mad" magazine. *AKA:* Mad Magazine's Up the Academy; The Brave Young Men of Weinberg.
1980 (R) 88m/C Ron Leibman, Ralph Macchio, Barbara Bach, Tom Poston, Stacey Nelkin, Wendell Brown, Tom Citera; *D:* Robert Downey. VHS, Beta $19.98 *WAR ✂*

Up the Creek Crazy antics abound in this tale of an old British destroyer, a black-market scheme run by the crew, and the new skipper whose hobby is rocket building. Followed by "Further Up the River."
1958 83m/B *GB* David Tomlinson, Wilfrid Hyde-White, Peter Sellers, Vera Day, Michael Goodliffe, Lionel Jeffries; *D:* Val Guest. VHS, Beta $39.95 *MON ✂✂*

Up the Creek Four college losers enter a whitewater raft race to gain some respect for their school. The soundtrack features songs by Heart, Cheap Trick and The Beach Boys. Routine.
1984 (R) 95m/C Tim Matheson, Jennifer Runyon, Stephen Furst, John Hillerman, James B. Sikking, Julia Montgomery, Jeana Tomasina; *D:* Robert Butler. VHS, Beta, LV $29.98 *LIV, VES ✂✂*

Up the Down Staircase A naive, newly trained New York public school teacher is determined to teach the finer points of English literature to a group of poor students. She almost gives up until one student actually begins to learn. Good production and acting. Based on Bel Kaufman's novel.
1967 124m/C Sandy Dennis, Patrick Bedford, Eileen Heckart, Ruth White, Jean Stapleton, Sorrell Booke; *D:* Robert Mulligan. VHS *WAR, OM ✂✂✂*

Up the Sandbox A bored housewife fantasizes about her life in order to avoid facing her mundane existence. Fine acting from Streisand, with real problems of young mothers accurately shown.
1972 (R) 98m/C Barbra Streisand, David Selby, Jane Hoffman, Barbara Rhoades; *D:* Irvin Kershner. VHS, Beta $19.98 *WAR ✂✂*

Up Your Alley A female reporter, pursuing a story on homelessness, and a skidrow bum find romance. Langston, who produced and co-wrote the film, is better known as "The Unknown Comic."
1989 (R) 90m/C Linda Blair, Murray Langston, Ruth Buzzi, Johnny Dark, Bob Zany, Yakov Smirnoff; *D:* Bob Logan. VHS, Beta, LV $89.95 *LIV ✂✂*

Up Your Anchor Two hyperactive nerds enlist in the Navy, and pursue every sexual fantasy within their reach.
1985 89m/C *IS* Yftach Katzur, Zachi Nay; *D:* Dan Wolman. VHS, Beta $79.95 *MGM* Woof!

Uphill All the Way A couple of card-cheatin' good old boys are pursued by posses and cavalry alike, and end up killing real outlaws. Made for television.
1985 91m/C Roy Clark, Mel Tillis, Glen Campbell, Trish Van Devere, Burl Ives, Burt Reynolds; *D:* Frank Q. Dobbs. VHS, Beta $19.95 *NWV, STE ✂✂*

Upper Crust Boring tale of corruption and greed that takes place at the highest levels of American business and government.
1988 95m/C Frank Gorshin, Broderick Crawford, Nigel Davenport. VHS, Beta *NO ✂½*

The Uprising A Nicaraguan drama filmed just months after the 1979 Sandinista revolution, wherein a young guard of Somoza retains his job for the money, while his father is active in the revolutionary forces. In Spanish with English subtitles.
1981 96m/C *SP D:* Peter Lilienthal. VHS, Beta $69.95 *KIV, TAM ✂✂✂*

Uptown Angel A young woman is determined to work her way out of her home on the wrong side of town. Black cast brings new life to old premise.
1990 (R) 90m/C Caron Tate, Cliff McMullen, Gloria Davis Hill, Tracy Hill; *W/D:* Joy Shannon. VHS $59.95 *XVC ✂✂*

Uptown New York A young man pressured by his family marries a rich girl instead of the woman he loves, who in turn marries a man she does not love. Routine melodrama.
1932 81m/B Jack Oakie, Shirley Green, Leon Waycoff, Shirley Grey, George Cooper, Raymond Hatton; *D:* Victor Schertzinger. VHS, Beta $19.95 *NOS, FCT, DVT ✂✂*

Uptown Saturday Night Two working men attempt to recover a stolen lottery ticket from the black underworld after being ripped off at an illegal gambling place. Good fun, with nice performances from both leads and from Belafonte doing a black "Godfather" parody of Brando. Followed by "Let's Do It Again."
1974 (PG) 104m/C Sidney Poitier, Bill Cosby, Harry Belafonte, Flip Wilson, Richard Pryor, Calvin Lockhart; *D:* Sidney Poitier. VHS, Beta $19.98 *WAR ✂✂½*

The Uranium Conspiracy A secret agent and a mercenary soldier try to stop a shipment of uranium out of Zaire from falling into enemy hands. It won't be easy.
1978 (PG) 100m/C Fabio Testi, Janet Agren, Assaf Dayan. VHS, Beta $42.95 *PGN ✂½*

Uranus After WWII a French provincial town has been liberated from Nazi invaders—but not its own suspicions, as citizens try to rebuild knowing some of them collaborated with the enemy. An important subject is heavily talked over in static fashion, with a robust Depardieu either a standout or a ham as the earthy saloon-keeper. Based on a novel by Marcel Ayme, himself accused of pro-Vichy leanings during the era. In French with English subtitles.
1991 (R) 100m/C *FR* Gerard Depardieu, Michel Blanc, Jean-Pierre Marielle, Philippe Noiret, Gerard Desarthe, Michel Galabru, Fabrice Luchini; *D:* Claude Berri. VHS, LV $89.99 *HBO, TAM ✂✂✂*

Urban Cowboy A young Texas farmer comes to Houston to work in a refinery. After work he hangs out at Gilley's, a roadhouse bar. Here he and his friends, dressed in their cowboy gear, drink, fight, and prove their manhood by riding a mechanical bull. Film made Winger a star, was an up in Travolta's roller coaster career, and began the craze for country western apparel and dance and then there mechanical bulls. Ride 'em, cowboy!
1980 (PG) 135m/C John Travolta, Debra Winger, Scott Glenn, Madolyn Smith, Barry Corbin; *D:* James Bridges. VHS, Beta, LV *PAR ✂✂½*

Urban Warriors Savage barbarians roam and pillage a post-nuclear war Earth, but one invincible warrior ushers them out.
1975 90m/C Karl Landgren, Alex Vitale, Deborah Keith; *D:* Joseph Warren. VHS, Beta $59.95 *CAN ✂*

Urge to Kill A man returning from a mental hospital after pleading temporary insanity to the murder of his girlfriend returns to her town and tries to uncover the truth, with the help of her younger sister. Made for television.
1984 (PG) 96m/C Karl Malden, Holly Hunter, William Devane, Alex McArthur; *D:* Mike Robe. VHS, Beta $59.98 *FOX, VTR ✂*

Urotsukidoji: Legend of the Overfiend Legend has it that the world is made up of Humans, Man-Beasts, and Monster-Demons. Every 3000 years superfiend Chojin is supposed to unite the three into a single Land of Eternity. However, the heroic Amano discovers this land will be a nightmare world and unless he can successfully battle Chojin humanity may not survive. Ultra-violent and sexually explicit. Animated; dubbed into English.
19?? (NC-17) 108m/C *JP* VHS $39.95 *CPM ✂✂*

Ursus in the Valley of the Lions Ursus attempts to rescue love from druids but is dismayed to find that she has taken up homicide in her free time. *AKA:* The Mighty Ursus; Ursus.
1962 92m/C *IT SP* Ed Fury, Luis Prendes, Moira Orfei, Cristina Gajoni, Maria Luisa Merlo; *D:* Carlo Campogalliani. VHS $19.98 *SNC ✂½*

Urusei Yatsura 1: Only You The animated adventures of Ataru Moroboshi, one of the most unlucky teenagers in the world. In Japanese with English subtitles.
1992 100m/C *JP* VHS $39.95 *CPM ✂½*

Urusei Yatsura 2: Beautiful Dreamer Unlucky teenager Ataru Moroboshi and his classmates at Tomobiki High School find themselves reliving the day before the School Festival over and over again. Funny and dreamlike. In Japanese with English subtitles.
1992 90m/C *JP D:* Oshii Mamoru. VHS, LV $39.95 *CPM, TAM ✂½*

Urusei Yatsura 3: Remember My Love More animated fun with unlucky teen Ataru Moroboshi and his high school friends. In Japanese with English subtitles.
1992 100m/C *JP* VHS $39.95 *CPM ✂½*

Used Cars A car dealer is desperate to put his jalopy shop competitors out of business. The owners go to great lengths to stay afloat. Sometimes too obnoxious, but often funny.
1980 (R) 113m/C Kurt Russell, Jack Warden, Deborah Harmon, Gerrit Graham, Joe Flaherty, Michael McKean; *D:* Robert Zemeckis. VHS, Beta, LV, 8mm $12.95 *COL ✂✂*

Used People A study in ethnicity and characterization, three Oscar-winning actresses lead a talented cast playing a Jewish family living in Queens in 1969. When the father dies, Joe (Mastroianni), an old friend with an old torch the widow, Pearl (MacLaine), shows up at the funeral and manages to charm her into a date for coffee. Pearl's new relationship with her Italian suitor affects each of the somewhat off-balance family members and washes the whole clan with a sense of hope and renewal. Adapted from screenwriter Graff's play "The Grandma Plays" that was based on memories of his grandmother. Director Kidron's American debut.
1992 (PG-13) 116m/C Shirley MacLaine, Marcello Mastroianni, Bob Dishy, Kathy Bates, Jessica Tandy, Marcia Gay Harden, Sylvia Sidney, Joe Pantoliano, Doris Roberts, Helen Hanft; *D:* Beeban Kidron; *W:* Todd Graff. VHS, LV $94.98 *FXV ✂✂½*

Users Small-town girl who worked as a prostitute meets a faded film star and becomes involved in the movie business. Ode to decadent Hollywood. Based on the Joyce Haber novel. Made for television.
1978 125m/C Jaclyn Smith, Tony Curtis, John Forsythe, Red Buttons, George Hamilton; **D:** Joseph Hardy. **VHS, Beta** $49.95 PSM *ℐℐ*

Utah A musical comedy star who inherits a ranch wishes to sell it to finance one of her shows. She is persuaded not to by Rogers, the ranch foreman.
1945 54m/B Roy Rogers, Dale Evans, George "Gabby" Hayes; **D:** John English. **VHS, Beta** $19.95 NOS, VDM, VCN *ℐℐ*

Utah Trail Lawman Ritter is hired to stop a gang of cattle rustlers. Cheapie oater made for Grand National, which went bankrupt soon after.
1938 57m/B Tex Ritter; **D:** Al Herman. **VHS, Beta** $19.95 NOS, VCN, DVT *ℐ*

Utilities A frustrated social worker enlists the help of his friends in his efforts to impress an attractive policewoman by taking on a large corporate utility. **AKA:** Getting Even.
1983 (PG) 94m/C CA Robert Hays, Brooke Adams, John Marley, Ben Gordon, Helen Burns; **D:** Harvey Hart. **VHS, Beta, LV** $79.98 LIV, VES *ℐ½*

Utopia Laurel and Hardy inherit an paradisiacal island, but their peace is disturbed when uranium is discovered. Final screen appearance of the team is diminished by poor direction and script. **AKA:** Atoll K; Robinson Crusoeland; Escapade.
1951 82m/B FR Stan Laurel, Oliver Hardy, Suzy Delair, Max Elloy; **D:** Leo Joannon. **VHS, Beta** QNE, MRV, VYY *ℐℐ*

Utu A Maori tribesman serving with the colonizing British army in 1870 explodes into ritual revenge when his home village is slaughtered. Filmed in New Zealand.
1983 (R) 104m/C NZ Anzac Wallace, Kelly Johnson, Tim Elliot, Bruno Lawrence; **D:** Geoff Murphy. **VHS, Beta** $79.98 FOX *ℐℐℐ*

The Vagabond The Little Tramp is a pathetic fiddler making a scanty living who rescues a damsel in distress. Silent with musical soundtrack added.
1916 20m/B Charlie Chaplin, Edna Purviance, Eric Campbell, Albert Austin; **D:** Charlie Chaplin. **VHS, Beta, 3/4U, Special order formats** CAB *ℐℐℐ*

Vagabond Bleak, emotionally shattering, powerful and compelling, this film traces the peripatetic life of an amoral and selfish young French woman who has no regard for social rules and tremendous fear of responsibility in her drifting yet inexorable journey into death. Told via flashbacks from the moment when she is found dead, alone, and unaccounted for by the roadside, this film will not leave you unscathed. Written by New Wave director Varda. In French with English subtitles. **AKA:** Sans Toit Ni Loi.
1985 105m/C FR Sandrine Bonnaire, Macha Meril, Stephane Freiss, Elaine Cortadellas, Marthe Jarnias, Yolanda Moreau; **D:** Agnes Varda. **VHS, Beta, LV** $29.95 PAV, TAM *ℐℐℐ½*

Vagabond Lover The amusing tale of the loves, hopes, and dreams of an aspiring saxophone player. Rudy croons through his megaphone in his movie debut. Appealing, with Dressler sparkling in the role of the wealthy aunt. ♫If You Were the Only Girl in the World; A Little Kiss Each Morning; Heigh Ho Everybody; I Love You; I'll Be Reminded of Vienna; I'm Just a Vagabond Lover.

1929 66m/B Rudy Vallee, Sally Blane, Marie Dressler; **D:** Marshall Neilan. **VHS, Beta** $29.95 VYY, RXM *ℐℐ½*

The Vagrant Run-of-the-mill creeper with a mind-game playing derelict inhabiting the home of a young exec. A series of murders has this wimp yuppie wondering how to get rid of his unwelcome intruder.
1992 (R) 91m/C Bill Paxton, Michael Ironside, Marshall Bell, Stuart Pankin; **D:** Chris Walas. **VHS** $89.99 MGM *ℐ*

Valdez is Coming Though not a world-class western, this filmed-in-Spain saga does feature a probing script (based on an Elmore Leonard novel) on the nature of race relations. Fine performance by Lancaster as a Mexican-American who ignites the passions of a town, and ultimately confronts the local land baron.
1971 (PG) 90m/C Burt Lancaster, Susan Clark, Jon Cypher, Barton Heyman, Richard Jordan, Frank Silvera, Hector Elizondo; **D:** Edwin Sherin. **VHS** $19.98 MGM *ℐℐ½*

Valentino Returns A kid in 1955 California buys a pink Cadillac he nicknames "Valentino Returns," thinking it will help him meet girls, as his parents undergo a stormy divorce. Weak script fades fast from fine premise, good start. Nice period feel.
1988 (R) 97m/C Frederic Forrest, Veronica Cartwright, Jenny Wright, Barry Tubb; **D:** Peter Hoffman. **VHS, Beta, LV** $29.95 VMK *ℐℐ*

Valet Girls Two Hollywood parking services engage in comedic competitive warfare by offering "special service" to their customers.
1986 89m/C Meri D. Marshall, April Stewart, Mary Kohnert, Christopher Weeks. **VHS, Beta, LV** $79.98 LIV, VES *ℐ*

The Valley Hipsters search for Utopia in New Guinea and find sex, spirits, and Pink Floyd. Dated groovy road tripper with beautiful photography. In French with English subtitles.
1972 106m/C **D:** Barbet Schroeder. **VHS, Beta** $59.99 WAR, BTV, TAM *ℐℐ*

Valley Girl Slight but surprisingly likeable teen romantic-comedy inspired by Frank Zappa novelty tune. Title stereotype falls for a leather-jacketed rebel. Really. It may look like a music video, but the story is straight from "Romeo and Juliet" via Southern California. Helped launch Cage's career. Music by Men at Work, Culture Club, and others.
1983 (R) 95m/C Nicolas Cage, Deborah Foreman, Colleen Camp, Frederic Forrest; **D:** Martha Coolidge. **VHS, Beta, LV** $29.98 VES *ℐℐ½*

Valley of Fire Autry is the mayor of a boom town that suffers from a lack of women. He decides to import a caravan of brides for the men in town but villains attempt to kidnap the women.
1951 63m/B Gene Autry, Gail Davis, Pat Buttram; **D:** John English. **VHS, Beta** $29.98 CCB *ℐℐ*

The Valley of Gwangi One of the best prehistoric-monster-westerns out there. Cowboys discover a lost valley of dinosaurs and try to capture a vicious, carnivorous allosaurus. Bad move, kemosabe! The creatures move via the stop-motion model animation by f/x maestro Ray Harryhausen, here at his finest.
1969 (G) 95m/C James Franciscus, Gila Golan, Richard Carlson, Laurence Naismith, Freda Jackson; **D:** James O'Connolly. **VHS, Beta, LV** $19.98 WAR, PIA *ℐℐℐ*

Valley of Terror Maynard is framed for cattle rustling. Can he prove his innocence?

1938 59m/B Kermit Maynard, Rocky the Horse, Harley Wood, John Merton, Jack Ingram, Dick Curtis, Roger Williams; **D:** Al Herman. **VHS, Beta** $19.98 NOS, CCB, DVT *ℐ½*

Valley of the Dolls A camp/trash classic that's rated as a bomb by many critics but it's really of the so-bad-it's-good variety. Tate, Duke, and Perkins are three beauties who dream of Hollywood stardom but fall victim to Hollywood excess, including drug dependency (the "dolls" of the title). There's unhappy love affairs, porno parts, health risks, and hysterics of various kinds—all designed to have you dropping your jaw in disbelief. The bathroom scene between Duke and Hayward involving a wig is not to be missed. Based on the novel by Jacqueline Susann who has a bit part as a reporter. Remade for television as "Jacqueline Susann's Valley of the Dolls" in 1981.
1967 (PG) 123m/C Barbara Parkins, Patty Duke, Sharon Tate, Paul Burke, Tony Scotti, Martin Milner, Susan Hayward, Charles Drake, Lee Grant, Alex Davion, Robert Harris, Robert Viharo, Joey Bishop, George Jessel; *Cameos:* Jacqueline Susann; **D:** Mark Robson; **W:** Dorothy Kingsley, Helen Deutch; **M:** John Williams. **VHS** $19.98 FXV, BTV *ℐℐ*

Valley of the Eagles When his wife and partner take off into the Lapland wilderness with his new invention, a scientist leads the police across the tundra in pursuit. Setting is at least a plus.
1951 83m/B GB Jack Warner, Nadia Gray, John McCallum, Martin Boddeg, Christopher Lee; **D:** Terence Young. **VHS, Beta** $39.95 MSP *ℐ½*

Valley of the Lawless A cowboy rides into trouble aplenty while out searching for treasure. A routine western for Brown fans only.
1936 59m/B Johnny Mack Brown; **W/D:** Robert North Bradbury. **VHS, Beta, LV** NO *ℐ*

Valley of the Sun A government agent tracks a crooked Indian liaison to prevent an Indian uprising in Arizona. Ball, well before her "Lucy" days, plays the restaurant owner both men romance. Better than average, with good cast, some laughs, and lots of excitement.
1942 84m/B Lucille Ball, James Craig, Cedric Hardwicke, Dean Jagger, Peter Whitney, Billy Gilbert, Tom Tyler, Antonio Moreno, George Cleveland, Hank Bell; **D:** George Marshall. **VHS, Beta** RKO, TTC *ℐℐ*

Valley of Wanted Men Three cons escape during a jailbreak and one uses his wits and nerve to prove another was framed.
1935 56m/B Frankie Darro. **VHS, Beta, 8mm** $24.95 VYY *ℐ½*

Valmont Another adaptation of the Choderlos de Laclos novel "Les Liaisons Dangereuses." Various members of the French aristocracy in 1782 mercilessly play each other for fools in a complex game of lust and deception. Firth and Bening are at first playfully sensual, then the stakes get too high. They share an interesting bathtub scene. Well-acted, the 1988 Frears version, "Dangerous Liaisons," is edgier. Seeing the two films together makes for interesting comparisons of characters and styles.
1989 (R) 137m/C Colin Firth, Meg Tilly, Annette Bening, Fairuza Balk, Sian Phillips, Jeffrey Jones, Fabia Drake, Henry Thomas, Vincent Schiavelli, T.P. McKenna, Ian McNeice; **D:** Milos Forman. **VHS, Beta, LV** $89.98 ORI, TAM *ℐℐℐ*

The Vals The glibly hip lethargy which is characteristic of four southern California teenaged girls turns to socially conscious resolve when a local orphanage is threatened. Like, for sure.

1985 (R) 100m/C Jill Carroll, Elana Stratheros, Gina Calabrese, Michelle Laurita, Chuck Connors, Sonny Bono, John Carradine, Michael Leon; *D:* James Polakof. VHS, Beta $69.98 *LIV, VES* ✗✗½

Vamp Two college freshmen encounter a slew of weird, semi-vampiric people in a seamy red-light district nightclub. Starts cute but goes kinky. Jones is great as the stripping vampire.
1986 (R) 93m/C Grace Jones, Chris Makepeace, Robert Rusler, Gedde Watanabe; *D:* Richard Wenk. VHS, Beta, LV $19.95 *NWV, STE* ✗✗½

Vamping Struggling musician plans to burglarize a wealthy widow's home. Once inside, he finds himself attracted to his proposed victim. Tedious going.
1984 (PG) 110m/C Patrick Duffy, Catherine Hyland, Rod Arrants, Fred A. Keller; *D:* Frederick King Keller. VHS, Beta $59.98 *FOX* ✗✗½

The Vampire Pale man with big teeth attempts to swindle a beautiful babe out of fortune. Followed by "The Vampire's Coffin." *AKA:* Mark of the Vampire.
1957 95m/B Abel Salazar, Ariadne Welter, German Robles, Carmen Montejo, Jose Luis Jimenez; *D:* Fernando Mendez. VHS $19.98 *SNC* ✗

Vampire at Midnight Fairly stupid homicide detective stalks a rampaging vampire in Los Angeles. Occasional moments of gratitious sex thrown in for good measure.
1988 93m/C Jason Williams, Gustav Vintas, Jeanie Moore, Christina Whitaker, Leslie Milne; *D:* Gregory McClatchy. VHS, Beta $79.98 *FOX* ✗½

The Vampire Bat A mad scientist and a vampire bat and its supernatural demands set the stage for murders in a small town. Sets and actors borrowed from Universal Studios in this low-budget flick that looks and plays better than it should. Weird and very exploitative for 1932, now seems dated.
1932 69m/B Lionel Atwill, Fay Wray, Melvyn Douglas, Dwight Frye, Maude Eburne, George E. Stone; *D:* Frank Strayer. VHS, Beta, 3/4U, Special order formats $16.95 *NOS, SNC, WFV* ✗✗½

Vampire Circus A circus appears in an isolated Serbian village in the 19th century but instead of bringing joy and happiness, this circus brings only death, mutilation and misery. It seems all the members are vampires who have the unique ability to transform themselves into animals. They intend to take revenge on the small town, whose inhabitants killed their evil ancestor 100 years previously. Excellent Hammer production.
1971 (R) 84m/C *GB* Adrienne Corri, Laurence Payne, Thorley Walters, John Moulder-Brown, Lynne Frederick, Elizabeth Seal, Anthony Corlan, Richard Owens, Domini Blythe, David Prowse; *D:* Robert Young. VHS $18.00 *FRG, MLB* ✗✗½

Vampire Cop A vampire cop (not to be confused with zombie, maniac, midnight, psycho, future or Robo) teams up with a beautiful reporter to 'collar' a drug kingpin.
1990 (R) 89m/C Melissa Moore, Ed Cannon, Terence Jenkins. VHS $79.95 *ATL* ✗½

The Vampire Happening An actress discovers to her chagrin that her ancestors were vampires and so is she.
1971 (R) 90m/C *GE* Ferdinand "Ferdy" Mayne; *D:* Freddie Francis. VHS, Beta $24.95 *NEG* ✗½

The Vampire Hookers Man in makeup recruits bevy of beautiful bloodsuckers to lure warm blooded victims to his castle. High ham performance by Carradine. *AKA:* Cemetary Girls; Sensuous Vampires; Night of the

Bloodsuckers; Twice Bitten.
1978 (R) 82m/C *PH* John Carradine, Bruce Fairbairn, Trey Wilson, Karen Stride, Lenka Novak, Katie Dolan, Lex Winter; *D:* Cirio H. Santiago. VHS, Beta *NO* ✗

The Vampire Lovers An angry father goes after a lesbian vampire who has ravished his daughter and other young girls in a peaceful European village. Innovative story was soon used in countless other vampire vehicles. Hammer Studio's first horror film with nudity, another addition to the genre which spread rapidly. Based on the story "Carmilla" by Sheridan Le Fanu. Followed by, "Lust for a Vampire."
1970 (R) 91m/C *GB* Ingrid Pitt, Pippa Steele, Madeleine Smith, Peter Cushing, George Cole, Dawn Addams, Kate O'Mara, Ferdinand "Ferdy" Mayne; *D:* Roy Ward Baker. VHS, Beta $9.98 *ORI, MLB, SUE* ✗✗✗½

Vampire Over London Lugosi gives an outstanding performance as a maniac who thinks he's a vampire in this British horror-comedy. Watch it for him only. *AKA:* "Old Mother Riley Meets the Vampire." Released in the United States as "My Son, the Vampire."
1951 74m/B *GB* Bela Lugosi, Arthur Lucan; *D:* John Gilling. VHS $16.95 *SNC* ✗

The Vampire People A dwarf-assisted vampire attempts to save the life of his true love by transplanting his sister's heart. Typical Filipino vampire movie. In color and sepia-tone. *AKA:* The Blood Drinkers.
1966 (PG) 79m/C *PH* Ronald Remy, Amalia Fuentes, Eddie Fernandez, Eva Montez; *D:* Gerardo (Gerry) De Leon. VHS, Beta $16.95 *SNC* ✗½

Vampire Princess Miyu A medium investigates vampire murders in a Japanese city and discovers the Vampire Princess and her demon slave. In Japanese with English subtitles.
1990 60m/C VHS, LV $39.95 *CPM, TAM, FCT* ✗½

Vampire Raiders—Ninja Queen The white ninjas versus the black ninjas. The evil black ninjas are plotting to infiltrate the hotel industry. The white ninjas come to the rescue.
1989 90m/C Agnes Chan, Chris Peterson; *D:* Bruce Lambert. VHS $59.95 *TWE* Woof!

The Vampire's Coffin Count Lavud is relieved when faithful servant removes stake implanted in his heart. *AKA:* El Ataud Del Vampiro; El Ataud Del Coffin.
1958 86m/B *MX* Abel Salazar, Ariadne Welter, German Robles; *D:* Fernando Mendez. VHS $19.98 *SNC* ✗✗½

The Vampire's Ghost A 400-hundred-year-old vampire/zombie, doomed to walk the earth forever, heads the African underworld. He can't be killed and can even go out during the day if he wears sunglasses. His future's so bright he's just gotta wear shades.
1945 59m/B John Abbott, Peggy Stewart; *D:* Lesley Selander. VHS $24.95 *NOS, DVT, HEG* ✗

Vampire's Kiss Cage makes this one worthwhile; his twisted transformation from pretentious post-val dude to psychotic yuppie from hell is inspired. If his demented torment of his secretary (Alonso) doesn't give you the creeps, his scene with the cockroach will. Cage fans will enjoy his facial aerobics; Beals fans will appreciate her extensive sucking scenes (she's the vamp of his dreams). More for psych majors than horror buffs.

1988 (R) 103m/C Nicolas Cage, Elizabeth Ashley, Jennifer Beals, Maria Conchita Alonso, Kasi Lemmons, Bob Lujan; *D:* Robert Bierman. VHS, Beta, LV $89.99 *HBO* ✗✗✗

Vampyr Dreyer's classic portrays a hazy, dreamlike world full of chilling visions from the point of view of a young man who believes himself surrounded by vampires and who dreams of his own burial in a most disturbing way. Evil lurks around every corner as camera angles, light and shadow sometimes overwhelm plot. A high point in horror films based on a collection of horror stories by Sheridan le Fanu. Music by Wolfgang Zeller. In German with English subtitles. *AKA:* Vampyr, Ou L'Etrang e Aventure De David Gray; Vampyr, Der Traum Des David Gray; Not Against the Flesh; Castle of Doom; The Strange Adventure of David Gray; The Vampire.
1931 75m/B *GE* Julien West, Sybille Schmitz, Harriet Gerard; *D:* Carl Theodor Dreyer. VHS, Beta, 3/4U, Special order formats $29.95 *KIV, NOS, SNC* ✗✗✗✗

Vampyres Alluring female vampires coerce unsuspecting motorists to their castle for a good time, which ends in death. Anulka was the centerfold girl in Playboy's May 1973 issue. *AKA:* Vampyres, Daughters of Dracula; Blood Hunger; Satan's Daughters.
1974 (R) 90m/C *GB* Marianne Morris, Anulka, Murray Brown, Brian Deacon, Sally Faulkner; *D:* Joseph Larraz. VHS, Beta *NO* ✗✗½

The Van A recent high school graduate passes on the college scene so he can spend more time picking up girls in his van. A lame sex (and sexist) comedy. *AKA:* Chevy Van.
1977 92m/C Stuart Getz, Deborah White, Danny DeVito, Harry Moses, Maurice Barkin; *D:* Sam Grossman. VHS, Beta $9.95 *NO* ✗

Van Nuys Blvd. The popular boulevard is the scene where the cool southern California guys converge for cruising and girl watching, so naturally it's where a country hick comes to test his drag racing skills and check out the action.
1979 (R) 93m/C Bill Adler, Cynthia Wood, Dennis Bowen, Melissa Prophet; *D:* William Sachs. VHS, Beta $9.99 *STE, UHV* ✗

Vanessa Story of an innocent young girl's introduction to the erotic pleasures of the Orient.
1977 (X) 90m/C VHS, Beta $34.95 *VID* ✗

Vanina Vanini An acclaimed Rossellini historical drama about the daughter of an Italian aristocrat in 1824 who nurses and falls in love with a wounded patriot hiding in her house. Based on a Stendhal short story. In Italian with English subtitles.
1961 113m/B *IT* Sandra Milo, Laurent Terzieff; *D:* Roberto Rossellini. VHS, Beta $59.95 *FCT, TAM* ✗✗✗½

The Vanishing When his wife suddenly disappears, a young husband finds himself becoming increasingly obsessed with finding her. Three years down the road, his world has become one big, mad nightmare. Then, just as suddenly, the answer confronts him, but the reality of it may be too horrible to face. Well-made dark thriller based on "The Golden Egg" by Time Krabbe. In French and Dutch with English subtitles. Remade by Sluizer in 1992. *AKA:* Spoorloos.
1988 107m/C *NL FR* Barnard Pierre Donnadieu, Johanna Ter Steege, Gene Bervoets; *D:* George Sluizer. VHS $89.95 *FXL, TAM* ✗✗✗

The Vanishing Director Sluizer remakes his own 1988 Dutch film "Spoorloos" to lesser effect. Tense thriller is about the disappearance of a woman (Bullock) at a

highway rest stop. The abductor is a disarmingly rumpled scientist (Bridges) with a psychotic streak. The woman's boyfriend (Sutherland) becomes obsessed with locating her, searching for some three years. He continues to be haunted by her memory, despite a new partner (Travis). As he is about to let go of her memory, the scientist baits him with clues to her whereabouts. Unlike the Dutch original, the remake resorts to a clumsy ending designed for feel-good appeal. Based on the novel "The Golden Egg" by Tim Krabbe.
1993 (R) 110m/C Jeff Bridges, Kiefer Sutherland, Nancy Travis, Sandra Bullock, Park Overall, Lisa Eichhorn, George Hearn; *D:* George Sluizer; *W:* Todd Graff; *M:* Jerry Goldsmith. VHS $94.98 *FXV* 🐾🐾½

Vanishing Act While on his honeymoon, Harry Kenyon reports his wife missing to the local police. Within a short period of time his wife is found, but Harry says the women is an impostor. This thriller follows Harry's desperate attempt to get to the truth. Made for television.
1988 (PG) 94m/C Mike Farrell, Margot Kidder, Elliott Gould, Fred Gwynne, Graham Jarvis; *D:* David Greene. VHS, Beta $89.95 *VMK* 🐾🐾½

Vanishing American The mistreatment of the American Indian is depicted in this sweeping Western epic. Musical score.
1926 114m/B Richard Dix, Noah Beery Sr.; *D:* George B. Seitz. VHS, Beta $49.95 *GPV, VYY* 🐾🐾

Vanishing Legion Western serial with outdoor action and gunplay. Twelve chapters, 13 minutes each.
1931 156m/B Frankie Darro, Rin Tin Tin Jr, Harry Carey Sr.; *D:* B. Reeves Eason. VHS, Beta $24.95 *GPV, NOS, VCN* 🐾🐾

Vanishing Point An ex-racer makes a bet to deliver a souped-up car from Denver to San Francisco in 15 hours. Taking pep pills along the way, he eludes police, meets up with a number of characters, and finally crashes into a roadblock. Rock score helps attract this film's cult following.
1971 (PG) 98m/C Barry Newman, Cleavon Little, Gilda Texler, Dean Jagger, Paul Koslo, Robert Donner, Severn Darden, Victoria Medlin; *D:* Richard Sarafian. VHS, Beta, LV $59.98 *FOX* 🐾🐾

Vanishing Prairie This documentary examines the wonders of nature that abound in the American prairie. From the "True-Life Adventures" series.
1954 60m/C *D:* James Algar. VHS, Beta $69.95 *DIS* 🐾🐾🐾

The Vanishing Westerner A cowboy, falsely accused of murder, works to vindicate himself and uncovers a series of robberies. This one has enough plot twists to take it out of the routine.
1950 60m/B Monte Hale, Arthur Space, Aline Towne, Paul Hurst, Roy Barcroft, Richard Anderson, William Phipps, Rand Brooks; *D:* Philip Ford. VHS, Beta $24.95 *DVT* 🐾🐾

Vanishing Wilderness This documentary looks at the wild animals roaming across North America.
1973 (G) 90m/C *D:* Arthur Dubs. VHS, Beta $9.98 *MED, VTK* 🐾🐾

Vanity Fair Loy stars in this tale of a wily and manipulative woman looking for the perfect marriage. This was the 58th film for the 27-year-old Loy, but even she couldn't save it. Of course, none of the three films based on the story by Thackery have done it justice.

1932 67m/B Myrna Loy, Conway Tearle, Barbara Kent, Walter Byron, Anthony Bushell, Billy Bevan, Montagu Love, Mary Forbes; *D:* Chester M. Franklin. VHS $19.95 *NOS, HEG* 🐾🐾

Varan the Unbelievable A chemical experiment near a small island in the Japanese archipelago disturbs a prehistoric monster beneath the water. The awakened monster spreads terror on the island. Most difficult part of this movie is deciding what the rubber monster model is supposed to represent. *AKA:* Daikaiju Baran; The Monster Baran.
1961 70m/B *JP* Myron Healey, Tsuruko Kobayashi; *D:* Inoshiro Honda. VHS, Beta $19.95 *NOS, UHV* 🐾

Varieties on Parade A vaudeville show on film, featuring an array of second-rate comics and musical personalities. Sad to watch its demise.
1952 55m/B Jackie Coogan, Eddie Garr, Tom Neal, Iris Adrian. VHS, Beta, LV *NO* 🐾

Variety Simple and tragic tale of a scheming young girl and the two men of whom she takes advantage. The European circus in all its beautiful sadness is the setting. Extraordinary cast and superb cinematography. Silent.
1925 104m/B *GE* Emil Jannings, Lya de Putti, Warwick Ward, Werner Krauss; *D:* E.A. Dupont. VHS, Beta $29.95 *NOS, VYY, DVT* 🐾🐾🐾🐾

Variety A girl takes a job selling tickets in a Times Square porn theater. Her initial loathing for the genre gives way to a fascination with its clients, one of whom is a gangster, and she becomes drawn to the seamy world inside. An independently made feature.
1983 101m/C Sandy McLeod, Will Patton, Richard Davidson; *D:* Delta Gordon. VHS, Beta $69.95 *MED* 🐾🐾½

Variety Lights Fellini's first (albeit joint) directorial effort, wherein a young girl runs away with a travelling vaudeville troupe and soon becomes its main attraction as a dancer. Filled with Fellini's now-familiar delight in the bizarre and sawdust/tinsel entertainment. In Italian with English subtitles. *AKA:* Luci Del Varieta; Lights of Variety.
1951 93m/B *IT* Giulietta Masina, Peppino de Filippo, Carla Del Poggio, Folco Lulli; *D:* Federico Fellini, Alberto Lattuada. VHS, Beta $29.95 *CVC, TAM, APD* 🐾🐾🐾½

Vasectomy: A Delicate Matter A mother of eight issues a final decree to her husband about their sex life. He must get a vasectomy or there won't be any. As good as it sounds. *AKA:* Vasectomy.
1986 (PG-13) 92m/C Paul Sorvino, Abe Vigoda, Cassandra Edwards, Lorne Greene, Ina Balin, June Wilkinson, William Marshall; *D:* Robert Burge. VHS, Beta *WOV* Woof!

Vatican Conspiracy The members of the Vatican's College of Cardinals do everything in their power to discredit a newly-appointed radical pontiff.
1981 90m/C Terence Stamp; *D:* Marcello Aliprandi. VHS, Beta *NO* 🐾½

Vault of Horror A collection of five terrifying tales based on original stories from the E.C. comic books of the 1950s. Stories include, "Midnight Mess," "Bargain in Death," "This Trick'll Kill You," "The Neat Job" and "Drawn and Quartered." *AKA:* Tales from the Crypt II.
1973 (R) 86m/C *GB* Terry-Thomas, Curt Jurgens, Glynis Johns, Dawn Addams, Daniel Massey, Tom Baker, Michael Craig, Anna Massey, Denholm Elliott; *D:* Roy Ward Baker; *W:* Milton Subotsky. VHS, Beta *MED* 🐾🐾½

Vegas A private detective, with Las Vegas beauties as assistants and pursuers, solves the murder of a teenage runaway girl. Pilot for television series. Script by Michael Mann who went on to do "Miami Vice."
1978 74m/C Robert Urich, June Allyson, Tony Curtis, Will Sampson, Greg Morris; *D:* Richard Lang. VHS, Beta $49.95 *PSM* 🐾

The Vegas Strip Wars Rival casino owners battle it out in the land of lady luck. Unmemorable except for Jones's Don King impersonation and the fact that it was Hudson's last TV movie.
1984 100m/C Rock Hudson, James Earl Jones, Pat Morita, Sharon Stone, Robert Costanzo; *D:* George Englund. VHS *NO* 🐾🐾

Velnio Nuotaka (The Devil's Bride) A popular Lithuanian musical based on the play "Baltargio Malunas" by K. Boruta. English subtitles.
1975 78m/C *LI* VHS, Beta *IHF* 🐾🐾½

Velvet Smooth A protection agency's sultry boss, Velvet Smooth, gets involved solving the problems of a numbers racket.
1976 (R) 89m/C Johnnie Hill; *D:* Janace Fink. VHS $42.95 *PGN* 🐾

Velvet Touch Well-engineered thriller about an actress who craftily murders her producer. A theater-loving police detective winds up accusing the wrong woman—sending the overwrought murderess into a moral tailspin. Things don't work out as you may expect. Fine acting.
1948 97m/B Rosalind Russell, Leo Genn, Claire Trevor, Sydney Greenstreet, Leon Ames, Frank McHugh, Walter Kingsford, Dan Tobin, Lex Barker, Nydia Westman; *D:* John Gage; *W:* Leo Rosten. VHS, Beta *RKO, TTC* 🐾🐾🐾

The Velvet Vampire Yarnall is a sexy, sun-loving, dune buggy-riding vampiress who seduces a young, sexy, swinging, Southern California couple in her desert home. Lots of atmosphere to go along with the blood and nudity. *AKA:* Cemetary Girls; Through the Looking Glass.
1971 (R) 82m/C Michael Blodgett, Sherry Miles, Celeste Yarnall, Gene Shane, Jerry Daniels, Sandy Ward, Paul Prokop, Chris Woodley, Robert Tessier; *D:* Stephanie Rothman. VHS, Beta, LV $9.95 *SIM, SUE* 🐾🐾

Vendetta A woman gets herself arrested and sent to the penitentiary in order to exact revenge there for her sister's death. Better than average sexploitation film works because of acting and pacing.
1985 89m/C Karen Chase, Sandy Martin, Durga McBroom, Kin Shriner; *D:* Bruce Logan. VHS, Beta $79.98 *LIV, VES* 🐾½

Vendetta for the Saint A feature-length episode of the television series "The Saint," in which Simon Templar pursues a Sicilian mobster on a personal vendetta.
1968 98m/C *GB* Roger Moore; *D:* James O'Connolly. VHS, Beta $59.98 *FOX* 🐾

Vengeance A police officer resigns in shame after failing to thwart a holdup. He attempts to redeem himself by working on his own to infiltrate the same gang.
1937 61m/B Lyle Talbot, Wendy Barrie, Wally Albright, Marc Lawrence; *D:* Del Lord. VHS $24.95 *VYY, MOV* 🐾

Vengeance Four burglars take hostages after their robbery is bungled, but they won't get away—especially after the hostages die.
1980 92m/C Sally Lockett, Nicholas Jacquez, Bob Elliott; *D:* Bob Blizz. VHS, Beta *NO* 🐾

Vengeance A low-budget film about rebels fighting off an authoritarian government.
1986 114m/C Jason Miller, Lea Massari; *D:* Antonio Isasi. VHS, Beta $69.95 *TWE* 🐾

Vengeance A bereaved young man strikes out against the injustice of his parents' murder. His revenge against the killers takes him several steps beyond the law, and he's not so sure it was the right idea. Made for television. *AKA:* Vengeance: The Story of Tony Cimo.
1989 (R) 90m/C Brad Davis, Roxanne Hart, Brad Dourif, William Conrad; *D:* Marc Daniels. **VHS, LV $39.95** *IME ♪♪*

Vengeance Is Mine Told in flashbacks, the film focuses on the life of a habitual criminal whose life of deprivation leads to murder. Contains violence and nudity. Based on a true story. In Japanese with English subtitles.
1979 129m/C *JP* Ken Ogata; *D:* Shohei Imamura. **VHS, LV $59.95** *SVS, FCT, TAM ♪♪♪*

Vengeance Is Mine A demented farmer captures three criminals and tortures them in horrifyingly sadistic ways. Gratuitously grisly.
1984 (R) 90m/C Ernest Borgnine, Michael J. Pollard, Hollis McLaren; *D:* John Trent. **VHS, Beta, LV $9.99** *VTR, GEM, VYG Woof!*

Vengeance of the Snowmaid Some Kung Fu creepies raped her mom. Now nobody can get a sword in edgewise on the Snow Maid as she seeks revenge.
197? 82m/C Mo Ka Kei, Chen Chen. **VHS, Beta** *NO ♪ ½*

Vengeance of the Zombies A madman seeks revenge by setting an army of walking corpses to stalk the streets of London.
1972 90m/C *SP* Paul Naschy; *D:* Leon Klimovsky. **VHS, Beta $19.95** *SNC ♪ ½*

Vengeance Valley Lancaster and Walker are foster brothers with Walker being an envious weasel who always expects Lancaster to get him out of scrapes. Lancaster is even accused of a crime committed by Walker and must work to clear himself. Good cast is let down by uneven direction.
1951 83m/C Burt Lancaster, Joanne Dru, Robert Walker, Sally Forrest, John Ireland, Hugh O'Brian; *D:* Richard Thorpe. **VHS, Beta, 3/4U, Special order formats $14.95** *NOS, QNE, DVT ♪♪*

Venom Deadly black mamba is loose in an elegant townhouse, terrorizing big-name cast. The snake continually terrorizes an evil kidnapper, his accomplices and his kidnapped victim. Participants walk through tired cliches with that far-away look in their eyes—like they wish they were anywhere else. Original director Tobe Hooper was replaced.
1982 (R) 92m/C *GB* Sterling Hayden, Klaus Kinski, Sarah Miles, Nicol Williamson, Cornelia Sharpe, Susan George, Michael Gough, Oliver Reed; *D:* Piers Haggard. **VHS, Beta $59.95** *VES Woof!*

Venus Against the Son of Hercules Our hero must use all his genetically procured musculature in his battle against the lovely but deadly Venus.
1962 ?m/C *IT* Roger Brown, Jackie Lane. **VHS, Beta $16.95** *SNC Woof!*

Venus in Furs Jazz musician working in Rio de Janeiro becomes obsessed with a mysterious woman; she resembles a murder victim whose body he discovered months earlier. Weird mix of horror, sadism, black magic, and soft porn. *AKA:* Paroxismus; Puo Una Morta Rivivere Per Amore?; Venus in Peltz.
1970 (R) 90m/C *GB* James Darren, Klaus Kinski, Barbara McNair, Dennis Price, Maria Rohm; *D:* Jess (Jesus) Franco. **VHS, Beta $39.98** *NO ♪ ½*

Venus on Fire A photography crew searches for the perfect woman for their suntan oil ads on a tropical island, and one magically appears. French softcore, dubbed in English.
1984 91m/C *FR* Odile Michel, Nadege Clair, Francois Blanchard. **VHS, Beta $29.95** *MED ♪*

Venus the Ninja A comely female Ninja battles an evil warlord.
198? 90m/C Pearl Cheung, Meng Fei; *D:* Sze Ma Peng. **VHS, Beta $39.95** *TWE ♪*

Vera Cruz Two soldiers of fortune become involved in the Mexican Revolution of 1866, a stolen shipment of gold, divided loyalties, and gun battles. Less than innovative plot is made into an exciting action flick.
1953 94m/C Gary Cooper, Burt Lancaster, Denise Darcel, Cesar Romero, George Macready, Ernest Borgnine, Charles Bronson; *D:* Robert Aldrich. **VHS, Beta, LV $19.98** *MGM, FOX, FCT ♪♪ ½*

Verboten! In post-war occupied Berlin, an American G.I. falls in love with a German girl. Good direction maintains a steady pace.
1959 93m/B James Best, Susan Cummings, Tom Pittman, Paul Dubov; *D:* Samuel Fuller. **VHS** *IME ♪♪ ½*

Verdi The story of the Italian operatic composer and the loves of his life. Dubbed in English.
1953 80m/C *IT* Pierre Cressoy. **VHS $29.95** *FCT ♪♪*

The Verdict Newman plays an alcoholic failed attorney reduced to ambulance chasing. A friend gives him a supposedly easy malpractice case which turns out to be a last chance at redeeming himself and his career. Screenplay by David Mamet, from the novel by Barry Reed. One of Newman's finest performances.
1982 (R) 122m/C Paul Newman, James Mason, Charlotte Rampling, Jack Warden, Milo O'Shea, Lindsay Crouse; *D:* Sidney Lumet; *W:* David Mamet. **VHS, Beta, LV $19.98** *FOX ♪♪♪*

Verne Miller A film of the true story of Verne Miller, Al Capone's hit man. After rescuing a friend from the Feds, Miller is hunted down by both the cops and the mob.
1988 (R) 95m/C Scott Glenn, Barbara Stock, Thomas G. Waites, Lucinda Jenney, Sonny Carl Davis; *D:* Rob Hewitt. **VHS, Beta, LV $19.98** *SUE, NLC ♪♪*

Vernon, Florida A quixotic, eccentric documentary by Morris dealing simply with the backwater inhabitants of the small Florida town of the title, each speaking openly about his or her slightly strange lifestyle, dreams and life experiences.
1982 72m/C Beta $79.95 *COL ♪♪♪*

The Vernonia Incident Urban guerillas invade a small town, killing the police chief. The townspeople gather up their shotguns and fight back. That's entertainment.
1989 95m/C David Jackson, Shawn Stevens, Floyd Ragner, Ed Justice, Robert Louis Jakson; *W/D:* Ray Etheridge. **VHS, Beta $9.95** *SIM ♪ ½*

Veronico Cruz Despite its sincerity, Pereira's feature debut offers muddled response to the human waste incurred by the Falklands War. Set in a tiny remote village in the Argentinean mountains, the film's narrative is derived from the growing friendship between a shepherd boy and a teacher from the city. Well-meaning anti-war movie. In Spanish with English subtitles. *AKA:* La Dueda Interna; The Debt.
1987 96m/C *AR GB* Juan Jose Camero, Gonzalo Morales, Rene Olaguivel, Guillermo Delgado; *D:* Miguel Pereira. **VHS $79.95** *CCN ♪♪ ½*

Veronika Voss Highlights the real life of fallen film star Sybille Schmitz who finally took her own life out of despair. Played by Zech, Voss is exploited by her physician to turn over all of her personal belongings for morphine. A lover discovers the corruption and reveals it to the authorities. This causes great upheaval resulting in Voss' suicide. Highly metaphoric and experimental in its treatment of its subject. In German with English subtitles. *AKA:* Die Sehns Ucht Der Veronika Voss.
1982 (R) 105m/C *GE* Conny Froboess, Anna Marie Duringer, Volker Spengler; *D:* Rainer Werner Fassbinder. **VHS $48.00** *APD, FCT, TAM ♪♪♪*

Vertigo Hitchcock's romantic story of obsession, manipulation and fear. Stewart plays a detective forced to retire after his fear of heights causes the death of a fellow policeman and, perhaps, the death of a woman he'd been hired to follow. The appearance of her double (Novak), whom he compulsively transforms into the dead girl's image, leads to a mesmerizing cycle of madness and lies. Haunting music by Bernard Herrmann.
1958 (PG) 126m/C James Stewart, Kim Novak, Barbara Bel Geddes, Tom Helmore, Ellen Corby; *D:* Alfred Hitchcock. **VHS, Beta, LV $19.95** *MCA, TLF ♪♪♪*

A Very Brady Christmas Many of the original Bradys returned for this yuletide special. After Mike and Carol's vacation plans go awry, they decide to invite the whole bunch home for a family reunion. This was the highest rated television movie in 1989. Spawned yet another unsuccessful "Brady" series sequel.
1988 94m/C Florence Henderson, Robert Reed, Ann B. Davis, Maureen McCormick, Eve Plumb, Jennifer Runyon, Barry Williams, Christopher Knight, Michael Lookinland, Jerry Houser, Caryn Richman; *D:* Peter Baldwin. **VHS** *PAR ♪♪*

A Very British Coup McAnally plays Harry Perkins, a former steelworker who gets involved in British politics. Although a left-wing radical, the charismatic Perkins is actually elected Prime Minister. However, his radical policies cause the entrenched government officials to conspire to bring him down. And you thought American politics were dirty! Made for British television.
199? 180m/C *GB* Ray McAnally. **VHS $59.95** *SIG, TVC ♪♪♪*

Very Close Quarters Thirty people face many trials and tribulations as they share an apartment in Moscow. Interesting cast is wasted in this mostly un-funny flick.
1984 97m/C Shelley Winters, Paul Sorvino, Theodore Bikel, Farley Granger; *D:* Vladmir Rif. **VHS, Beta $69.98** *LIV, VES ♪*

A Very Curious Girl A peasant girl realizes she is being used by the male population of her village, and decides to charge them for sex, creating havoc. In French with English subtitles. *AKA:* La Fiancee du Pirate; Dirty Mary; Pirate's Fiancee.
1969 (R) 105m/C *FR* Bernadette LaFont; *D:* Nelly Kaplan. **VHS, Beta** *SUE, OM ♪♪ ½*

The Very Edge A pregnant woman suffers a miscarriage after being brutally attacked. The repercussions nearly destroy her marriage until her attacker is caught. A disturbing psycho-drama.
1963 90m/C *GB* Anne Heywood, Richard Todd, Jeremy Brett; *D:* Cyril Frankel. **VHS, Beta $59.95** *VID ♪♪ ½*

V

A Very Merry Cricket An adventurous cricket learns about the spirit of Christmas. Sequel to "The Cricket in Times Square."
1973 30m/C **D:** Chuck Jones; **V:** Mel Blanc. VHS, Beta $14.95 *FHE, WTA* ♪♪½

A Very Old Man with Enormous Wings An angel, battered during a hurricane, seeks refuge on a tiny Caribbean island. There, two men keep him and charge an increasingly curious world admission to view the creature. A colorful, musical expose of human failings based on a story by Gabriel Garcia Marquez. In Spanish with English subtitles. *AKA:* Un Senor Muy Viejo Con Unas Alas Enormes.
1988 90m/C *SP IT* Daisy Granados, Asdrubal Melendez, Luis Alberto Ramirez, Fernando Birri; **D:** Fernando Birri. VHS, LV $79.95 *FXL, FCT, TAM* ♪♪

A Very Private Affair A movie star finds that she has no privacy from the hordes of fans and paparazzi who flock to her side. The glare of publicity helps to destroy her relationship with a married director, and to fuel her desire for privacy, a desire that ends tragically. An appealing, better-than-average Bardot vehicle, it is nonetheless below-average (early) Malle. In French with English subtitles. *AKA:* La Vie Privee; Vita Privata.
1962 95m/C *FR* Marcello Mastroianni, Brigitte Bardot; **D:** Louis Malle. VHS, Beta $19.98 *MGM* ♪♪½

V.I. Warshawski The filmmakers seem to think they can slum with the oldest cliches in detective shows just as long as the tough gumshoe is a woman. They're wrong. Turner is terrific as the leggy shamus of the title (from a popular series of books by Sara Paretsky), but the plot is nothing special, featuring stock characters in the killing of a pro athlete and a real-estate deal.
1991 (R) 89m/C Kathleen Turner, Jay O. Sanders, Angela Goethals, Charles Durning; **D:** Jeff Kanew. VHS, Beta, LV $19.99 *HPH* ♪♪

Vibes Two screwball psychics are sent on a wild goose chase through the Ecuadorean Andes in search of cosmic power and, of course, fall in love. Flat offering from the usually successful team of writers, Lowell Ganz and Babaloo Mandel ("Splash" and "Night Shift"). Lauper's first starring role (and so far, her last).
1988 (PG) 99m/C Jeff Goldblum, Cyndi Lauper, Julian Sands, Googy Gress, Peter Falk, Elizabeth Pena; **D:** Ken Kwapis. VHS, Beta $89.95 *COL* ♪

Vice Academy Two females join the Hollywood vice squad. Allen was a former porn queen.
1988 (R) 90m/C Linnea Quigley, Ginger Lynn Allen, Karen Russell, Jayne Hamil, Ken Abraham, Stephen Steward, Jeannie Carol; **D:** Rick Sloane. VHS, Beta, LV $79.95 *PSM* ♪♪

Vice Academy 2 Two vice cop babes try to stop a female crime boss from dumping aphrodesiacs in the city's water supply.
1990 (R) 90m/C Linnea Quigley, Ginger Lynn Allen, Jayne Hamil, Scott Layne, Jay Richardson, Joe Brewer, Marina Benvenga, Teagan Clive; **D:** Rick Sloane. VHS, Beta $29.95 *PSM* ♪

Vice Academy 3 The worst of the series, and not just because cult actress Linnea Quigley is absent. Wit, pacing and even sets are nonexistent as the girls battle a toxic villainess called Malathion.
1991 (R) 88m/C Ginger Lynn Allen, Elizabeth Kaitan, Julia Parton, Jay Richardson, Johanna Grika, Steve Mateo; **W/D:** Rick Sloane. VHS, Beta $79.95 *PSM Woof!*

Vice Squad Lukas is forced to turn police informer to save his own neck, which almost ruins him. Just when he thinks he's free of the cops they come back threatening the woman he loves unless he plays stoolie again. Rather flat, but the different cop/criminal angle makes for some unusual twists.
1931 80m/B Paul Lukas, Kay Francis, Helen Johnson, William B. Davidson, Esther Howard; **D:** John Cromwell. VHS, Beta, LV $19.98 *SUE* ♪♪

Vice Squad Violent and twisted killer-pimp goes on a murderous rampage, and a hooker helps a vice squad plainclothesman trap him. Sleazy and disturbing, with little to recommend it.
1982 (R) 97m/C Wings Hauser, Season Hubley, Gary Swanson, Cheryl "Rainbeaux" Smith; **D:** Gary Sherman. VHS, Beta, LV $19.98 *SUE, NLC Woof!*

Vice Versa Another 80s comedy about a workaholic father and his 11-year-old son who switch bodies, with predictable slapstick results. Reinhold and Savage carry this, appearing to have a great time in spite of over-done story.
1988 (PG) 97m/C Judge Reinhold, Fred Savage, Swoosie Kurtz, David Proval, Corinne Bohrer, Jane Kaczmarek, William Prince, Gloria Gifford; **D:** Brian Gilbert. VHS, Beta, LV $14.95 *COL* ♪♪♪

Vicious A bored young woman falls in with people your mother warned you about and soon their high school hi-jinks turn into murder. Graphic violence.
1988 88m/C Tamblyn Lord, Craig Pearce, Tiffany Dowe; **D:** Karl Zwicky. VHS $79.95 *SVS* ♪

The Vicious Circle A prominent London physician becomes involved in murder and an international crime ring when he agrees to perform an errand for a friend. Good performances and tight pacing. *AKA:* The Circle.
1957 84m/B *GB* John Mills, Wilfrid Hyde-White, Rene Ray, Lionel Jeffries, Noelle Middleton; **D:** Gerald Thomas. VHS, Beta *NO* ♪♪

Victim A successful married English barrister (Bogarde) with a hidden history of homosexuality is threatened by blackmail after the death of his ex-lover. When the blackmailers, who are responsible for his lover's suicide, are caught, Bogarde decides to prosecute them himself, even though it means revealing his hidden past. One of the first films to deal straightforwardly with homosexuality. Fine performances.
1962 100m/C *GB* Dirk Bogarde, Sylvia Syms, Dennis Price, Peter McEnery; **D:** Basil Dearden. VHS, Beta $19.98 *SUE* ♪♪♪½

The Victim Chan Wing meets up with Master Leung and decides to become his follower. Intent on impressing the master, Chan proves an inept chopsocker.
19?? 90m/C Samo Hung. VHS, Beta $24.50 *OCE* ♪♪

Victim of Beauty A small-town girl comes to the big city and becomes a successful model. However, she then becomes the victim of a fatal attraction killer as all her would-be suitors get killed off one by one. Made for cable television.
1991 90m/C Jennifer Rubin, Sally Kellerman, Stephen Shellan, Peter Outerbridge; **Cameos:** Michael Ironside; **D:** Paul Lynch. VHS $89.95 *WOV, PMS* ♪♪

Victim of Love A therapist doesn't know whom to believe when she finds out she and one of her more neurotic patients are sharing the same boyfriend. Only the patient claims the man murdered his wife to be with his lover. Who will be the next victim? Made for television.

1991 (PG-13) 92m/C Pierce Brosnan, JoBeth Williams, Virginia Madsen, Georgia Brown; **D:** Jerry London. VHS, Beta, LV $19.95 *ACA* ♪♪

Victimless Crimes The seemingly victimless crime of robbing art galleries turns deadly when betrayal and murder enter the picture.
1990 (R) 85m/C Debra Sandlund, Craig Bierko, Larry Brandenburg, Peggy Dunne, Richard Redlin, Cheryl Lynn Bruce; **D:** Peter Hawley. VHS $89.95 *SVS* ♪

Victims Four young women head out for a weekend in the country not realizing that a host of freaks await them.
19?? (R) 85m/C VHS $59.95 *NO* ♪½

Victims of the Assassin Two lovers are sentenced to decapitation but they use their martial arts skills to escape and wreak vengeance on those who would destroy them.
1988 ?m/C VHS $19.95 *OCE* ♪½

Victor/Victoria An unsuccessful actress in Depression-era Paris impersonates a man impersonating a woman and becomes a star. Luscious music and sets. Warren as femme fatale and Preston as Andrews' gay mentor are right on target; Garner is charming as the gangster who falls for the woman he thinks she is. ♫You and Me; The Shady Dame from Seville; Le Jazz Hot; Crazy World; Chicago Illinois; Gay Peree.
1982 (PG) 133m/C Julie Andrews, James Garner, Robert Preston, Lesley Ann Warren, Alex Karras, John Rhys-Davies; **D:** Blake Edwards; **M:** Henry Mancini. Academy Awards '82: Best Score; Nominations: Best Actress (Andrews), Best Adapted Screenplay, Best Art Direction/Set Decoration, Best Costume Design, Best Supporting Actor (Preston), Best Supporting Actress (Warren); Cesar Awards '83: Best Foreign Film; Golden Globe Awards '83: Best Actress—Musical/Comedy (Andrews). VHS, Beta, LV $19.95 *MGM* ♪♪♪

Victoria Regina In a succession of vignettes, the life of Queen Victoria is viewed, from her ascension to the throne of England in 1837 through the celebration of her Diamond Jubilee. A presentation from "George Schaefer's Showcase Theatre." Made for television.
1961 76m/C Julie Harris, James Donald, Felix Aylmer, Pamela Brown, Basil Rathbone; **D:** George Schaefer. VHS, Beta *FHS* ♪♪

Victorian Fantasies A softcore comedy about Victorian adults unleashing wild sexual fantasies.
1986 90m/C Ollie Soltoft, Sue Longhurst, Diana Dors. VHS, Beta $29.95 *MED* ♪½

Victory Soccer match between WWII American prisoners of war and a German team is set up so that the players can escape through the sewer tunnels of Paris. Of course they want to finish the game first. Not particularly believable as either a soccer flick (even with Pele and other soccer stars) or a great escape, but watchable.
1981 (PG) 116m/C Sylvester Stallone, Michael Caine, Max von Sydow, Pele, Carole Laure, Bobby Moore, Daniel Massey; **D:** John Huston. VHS, Beta $19.98 *FOX, WAR* ♪♪½

The Victory In 1967 Montreal, an American college exchange student falls in love with a French-Canadian co-ed. Can love survive their different cultures?
1988 (PG) 95m/C Vincent Van Patten, Cloris Leachman, Eddie Albert, Claire Pimpare, Nicholas Campbell, Jack Wetherall, Jacques Godin, Marthe Mercure; **D:** Larry Kent. VHS, Beta $9.99 *STE, PSM* ♪♪

Video Americana A collection of seven video shorts by various avant-garde artists depicting the absurdities of modern life.
1985 60m/C VHS, Beta *NO* 🎬🎬

Video Baby The joys and frustrations of parenting a video child can be yours without the mess, expense or longterm responsibility. Watch baby laugh, cry and sleep on command.
1989 13m/C VHS, Beta $9.98 *LIV, VTK* 🎬

The Video Dead Gore-farce in which murderous zombies emerge from a possessed television and wreak havoc.
1987 (R) 90m/C Roxanna Augesen, Rocky Duvall, Michael St. Michaels; *D:* Robert Scott. VHS, Beta $19.98 *SUE, NLC Woof!*

Video Murders A police detective tracks down a rapist/murderer who tapes all his own crimes.
1987 90m/C Eric Brown, Virginia Loridans, John Ferita. VHS, Beta $19.98 *TWE* 🎬

Video Violence A gory spoof about a video store owner who discovers that his customers have grown bored with the usual Hollywood horror movies and decide to shoot some flicks of their own. Followed by a sequel.
1987 90m/C Art Neill, Jackie Neill, William Toddie, Bart Sumner; *D:* Gary P. Cohen. VHS, Beta *NO* 🎬

Video Violence Part 2...The Exploitation! Two sickos named Howard and Eli run a cable television network where talk show guests are spindled and mutilated.
1987 90m/C Uke, Bart Sumner, Lee Miller; *D:* Gary P. Cohen. VHS, Beta *NO* 🎬

Video Vixens A television executive shakes up a restrained society by producing the most erotic awards show ever seen on television. Basic soft-core nudie.
1984 85m/C Robyn Hilton, Sandy Dempsey. VHS, Beta $69.98 *LIV, VES Woof!*

Video Wars Video games explode randomly. A wicked computer whiz is behind it all in a blackmail scheme.
1984 90m/C George Diamond. VHS $19.99 *BFV Woof!*

Videodrome Woods is a cable TV programmer with a secret yen for sex and violence, which he satisfies by watching a pirated TV show. "Videodrome" appears to show actual torture and murder, and also seems to control the thoughts of its viewers—turning them into human VCRs. Cronenberg's usual sick fantasies are definitely love 'em or leave 'em. Special effects by Rick Baker.
1983 87m/C CA James Woods, Deborah Harry, Sonja Smits, Peter Dvorsky; *D:* David Cronenberg. VHS, Beta, LV $19.95 *MCA* 🎬🎬

Vietnam: Chronicle of a War Drawing upon the resources of the CBS News archives, this CBS News Collectors Series program presents a retrospective portrait of American military involvement as witnessed by on-the-scene correspondents and camera crews. Some portions are in black-and-white.
1981 88m/C VHS, Beta $49.98 *FOX, KUI* 🎬🎬

Vietnam, Texas Vietnam vet leaves his past to become a priest. But he returns to violence when he discovers his Vietnamese daughter is in the hands of Houston's most relentless gangster.
1990 (R) 101m/C Robert Ginty, Haing S. Ngor, Tamlyn Tomita, Tim Thomerson; *D:* Robert Ginty. VHS, Beta, LV $89.95 *COL* 🎬

Vietnam War Story 1 Three hard-hitting Vietnam War stories on tape. "The Mine," "Home," and "The Pass." Each is an intimate account straight from the men who lived them. Poignant and action-packed. Made for television.
1988 87m/C Eriq La Salle, Nicholas Cascone, David Harris, Tom Fridley. VHS $79.99 *HBO* 🎬

Vietnam War Story 2 Three short, made-for-television war stories set in Vietnam: "An Old Ghost Walks the Earth," "R & R," and "The Fragging."
1988 90m/C Tim Guinee, Tate Donovan, Cynthia Bain, Wesley Snipes, David Niedorf. VHS, Beta $79.99 *HBO* 🎬

Vietnam War Story 3 Three episodes of the television series: "Separated," "Dusk to Dawn" and "The Promise."
1989 90m/C Tom Hodges, Todd Graff, Gregory Cooke, Francois Chau, Stacy Edwards, Laura Harrington, Raymond Cruz. VHS, Beta $79.99 *HBO* 🎬

A View to a Kill This James Bond mission takes him to the United States, where he must stop the evil Max Zorin from destroying California's Silicon Valley. Feeble and unexciting plot with unscary villain. Duran Duran performs the catchy title tune. Moore's last appearance as 007.
1985 (PG) 131m/C GB Roger Moore, Christopher Walken, Tanya Roberts, Grace Jones, Patrick Macnee, Lois Maxwell, Dolph Lundgren, Desmond Llewelyn; *D:* John Glen; *M:* John Barry. VHS, Beta, LV $19.98 *FOX, TLF* 🎬🎬

Vigil A stark, dreamy parable about a young girl, living on a primitive farm in a remote New Zealand valley, who watches her family collapse after a stranger enters their territory. Visually ravishing and grim; Ward's first American import. Predecessor to "The Navigator."
1984 90m/C NZ Penelope Stewart, Bill Kerr, Fiona Kay, Gordon Shields, Frank Whitten; *D:* Vincent Ward. VHS, Beta $79.95 *PSM* 🎬🎬🎬

Vigilante Frustrated ex-cop, tired of seeing criminals returned to the street, joins a vigilante squad dedicated to law and order. Often ridiculous and heavy handed. *AKA:* Street Gang.
1983 (R) 91m/C Carol Lynley, Robert Forster, Rutanya Alda; *D:* William Lustig. VHS, Beta $79.98 *LIV, VES Woof!*

The Vigilantes are Coming "The Eagle" sets out to avenge his family and upsets a would-be dictator's plot to establish an empire in California. In twelve chapters; the first is 32 minutes, and additional chapters are 18 minutes each.
1936 230m/B Bob Livingston, Kay Hughes, Guinn Williams; *D:* Mack V. Wright, Ray Taylor. VHS, Beta $49.95 *NOS, VCN, MED* 🎬🎬

Vigilantes of Boom Town A championship prize fight is the cover for a bank robbery which must be foiled by Red Ryder.
1946 54m/B Allan "Rocky" Lane, Robert (Bobby) Blake, Peggy Stewart, Martha Wentworth, Roscoe Karns, Roy Barcroft, George Turner, John Dehner; *D:* R.G. Springsteen. VHS, Beta $9.99 *NOS, VCN, MED* 🎬½

Viking Massacre Brutal ax-bearing Vikings ruin the days of hundreds in this primitive story of courage and desperation. John Hold is the pseudonym for director Mario Bava. *AKA:* Knives of the Avenger; I Coltelli Del Vendicatore.
197? 90m/C IT Cameron Mitchell; *D:* John Hold. VHS, Beta *WWV* 🎬½

The Vikings A Viking king and his son kidnap a Welsh princess and hold her for ransom. Depicts the Vikings' invasion of England. Great location footage of both Norway and Brittany. Basic costume epic with good action scenes. Narrated by Welles.
1958 116m/C Kirk Douglas, Ernest Borgnine, Janet Leigh, Tony Curtis, James Donald, Alexander Knox; *D:* Richard Fleischer. VHS, Beta $19.98 *MGM* 🎬🎬½

Villa Rides A flying gun-runner aids Francisco "Pancho" Villa's revolutionary Mexican campaign. Considering the talent involved, this one is a disappointment. Co-written by Sam Peckinpah. Check out Brynner's hair.
1968 125m/C Yul Brynner, Robert Mitchum, Charles Bronson, Herbert Lom, Jill Ireland, Robert Towne; *D:* Buzz Kulik; *W:* Robert Towne, Sam Peckinpah. VHS, Beta $19.95 *KRT* 🎬🎬

Village of the Damned A group of unusual children are born in a small English village. They avoid their fathers and other men, except for the one who is their teacher. He discovers they are the vanguard of an alien invasion and leads the counter-attack. Exciting and bone-chilling low-budget thriller. From the novel, "The Midwich Cuckoos," by John Wyndham. The sequel, "The Children of the Damned" (1964) is even better.
1960 78m/B GB George Sanders, Barbara Shelley, Martin Stephens, Laurence Naismith, Michael C. Goetz; *D:* Wolf Rilla. VHS, Beta, LV $14.95 *MGM, MLB* 🎬🎬🎬

Village of the Giants A group of beer-guzzling teenagers become giants after eating a mysterious substance invented by a twelve-year-old genius. Fun to pick out all the soon-to-be stars. Totally silly premise with bad special effects and minimal plot follow-through. Based on an H.G. Wells story.
1965 82m/C Ron Howard, Johnny Crawford, Tommy Kirk, Beau Bridges, Freddy Cannon, Beau Brummel; *D:* Bert I. Gordon; *M:* Jack Nitzsche. VHS, Beta $59.98 *SUE, MLB* 🎬🎬

Village on Fire A young guy whose family was slaughtered inexplicably wants retribution, and is willing to kick anything to get it.
1987? 86m/C VHS, Beta $59.95 *SVS* 🎬

The Villain An unfunny spoof of "B" westerns that is almost like a live-action "Roadrunner" cartoon. Douglas plays Cactus Jack, a highwayman who keeps trying to kidnap fair damsel Ann-Margaret. Hero Schwarzenegger keeps rescuing her. Lynde is amusing as the uptight Indian chief Nervous Elk. *AKA:* Cactus Jack.
1979 (PG) 93m/C Kirk Douglas, Ann-Margret, Arnold Schwarzenegger, Paul Lynde, Foster Brooks, Ruth Buzzi, Jack Elam, Strother Martin, Robert Tessier, Mel Tillis; *D:* Hal Needham. VHS $14.95 *COL* 🎬½

The Villain Still Pursued Her A poor hero and rich villain vie for the sweet heroine in this satire of old-fashioned temperance melodrama. Keaton manages to shine as the hero's sidekick.
1941 67m/B Anita Louise, Alan Mowbray, Buster Keaton, Hugh Herbert; *D:* Eddie Cline. VHS, Beta $19.95 *NOS, VYY, DVT* 🎬🎬

Vincent & Theo The story of Impressionist painter Vincent van Gogh, and his brother Theo, a gallery owner who loved his brother's work, yet could not get the public to buy it. Increasing despair and mental illness traps both men, as each struggles to create beauty in a world where it has no value. Altman has created a stunning portrait of "the artist" and his needs. The exquisite cinematography will make you feel as if you stepped into van Gogh's work.
1990 (PG-13) 138m/C Tim Roth, Paul Rhys, Johanna Ter Steege, Wladimir Yordanoff; *D:* Robert Altman. VHS, Beta, LV $19.95 *HMD, TAM, TVC* 🎬🎬🎬½

Vincent, Francois, Paul and the Others Three middle-aged Frenchmen rely on their friendships to endure a host of mid-life crises. In French with English subtitles.
1976 113m/C FR Yves Montand, Gerard Depardieu, Michel Piccoli, Stephane Audran; D: Claude Sautet. VHS, Beta, LV $79.95 FCT, TAM ⫬⫬⫬

Vincent: The Life and Death of Vincent van Gogh Van Gogh's work and creativity is examined in a documentary manner through his life and his letters. Thoughtful and intriguing production. Narrated by John Hurt as van Gogh.
1987 99m/C AU D: Paul Cox; V: John Hurt. VHS, LV $89.95 FCT, PIA, SIG ⫬⫬⫬

The Vindicator A scientist killed in a lab accident is transformed into a cyborg who runs amok and murders indiscriminately. A modernized Frankenstein, with interesting special effects and well drawn characters. AKA: Frankenstein '88.
1985 (R) 92m/C CA Terri Austin, Richard Cox, David McIlwraith, Pam Grier; D: Jean-Claude Lord. VHS, Beta $79.98 FOX ⫬⫬

The Vineyard Hapless victims are lured to a Japanese madman's island, where he drinks their blood and maintains a questionable immortality.
1989 (R) 95m/C James Hong, Karen Witter, Michael Wong; D: James Hong, Bill Rice. VHS, Beta, LV $19.95 STE, NWV ⫬

Vintage Cartoon Holiday A tape of eight cartoons from the major animation studios of the 1930s and 40s that cannot be shown on TV because of extreme violence, racial slurs or ethnic stereotypes; from the Fleischer Brothers, Warners and Ub Iwerks.
1935 60m/B VHS, Beta, 3/4U $19.00 MVC, IHF ⫬

Violated A detective endeavors to implicate a local businessman in the rapes of two beautiful women. Exploitative and dreary.
1984 88m/C John Heard, J.C. Quinn, April Daisy White, Samantha Fox; D: Richard Cannistraro. VHS, Beta $69.98 LIV, VES Woof!

The Violation of Laura Love triangle pits mother against daughter as they vie for the affections of Fernando. By the way, there is no reference to a "Laura" in this film. Provocative fare for the mature. Spanish with subtitles.
1972 93m/C SP IT Lucia Bose, Ornella Muti, Glen Lee; W/D: Claudio Guerin Hill; W: Leonardo Martin, Miguel Rubio, Giovanni Simonelli; M: Francesco DeMasi. VHS $27.90 VSM ⫬

Violence at Noon Highly disturbing film in which two women protect a brutal sex murderer from the law. Living among a quiet community of intellectuals, this conspiracy ends in a shocking finale in Oshima's stylized masterpiece. In Japanese with English subtitles.
1966 99m/B JP Saeda Kawaguchi, Akiko Koyama; D: Nagisa Oshima. VHS $79.95 KIV, TAM ⫬⫬⫬

Violent Blood Bath Justice takes on a terrifying new meaning. A grisly death romp occurs after one judge becomes a bit too interested by his own most despicable cases. He sheds his robe to try a life of crime on for size.
19?? 91m/C Fernando Rey. VHS $14.98 VID ⫬⫬⫬

Violent Breed A CIA operative is sent on a mission to put a black marketeer out of business.
1983 91m/C IT Henry Silva, Harrison Muller, Woody Strode; D: Fernando Di Leo. VHS, Beta $59.95 MGM ⫬

The Violent Men Big-time land baron Robinson is trying to push out all other landowners in the valley, including Ford. At first Ford refuses to fight back, but after one of Robinson's henchmen kills one of his hired hands, he starts an all-out war against Robinson to save his land. Stanwyck as Robinson's wife and Keith as his brother are wicked as the two urging him on and having an affair behind his back. Based on the novel "Rough Company" by Donald Hamilton. AKA: Rough Company.
1955 95m/C Glenn Ford, Barbara Stanwyck, Edward G. Robinson, Dianne Foster, Brian Keith, May Wynn; D: Rudolph Mate. VHS, LV $19.95 COL ⫬⫬½

Violent Ones Three men who are suspected of raping a young girl are threatened with lynching by an angry mob of townspeople. Badly acted, poorly directed, uneven and feeble.
1968 96m/C Fernando Lamas, David Carradine; D: Fernando Lamas. VHS, Beta REP Woof!

Violent Professionals Suspended cop runs into resistance inside and outside the force when he infiltrates the mob to get the goods on a crime boss.
1982 100m/C IT Richard Conte, Luc Merenda; D: Sergio Martino. VHS, Beta $42.95 PGN ⫬½

Violent Women Five female convicts escape and embark on a bloody journey through the countryside, pursued by the authorities. Shows women can be just as brutal as any man.
1959 61m/C Jennifer Slater, Jo Ann Kelly, Sandy Lyn, Eleanor Blair, Pati Magee; D: Barry Mahon. VHS, Beta $29.95 VMK ⫬

The Violent Years Spoiled high-school debutantes form a vicious all-girl gang and embark on a spree that includes murder, robbery, and male rape. Justice wins out in the end. Exploitive trash written by Wood, who directed the infamous "Plan 9 from Outer Space." AKA: Female.
1956 60m/B Jean Moorehead, Barbara Weeks, Glenn Corbett; D: Franz Fichorn; W/D: Edward D. Wood Jr. VHS, Beta $16.95 SNC, RHI, AOV Woof!

Violent Zone Mercenaries go on a supposed rescue mission in the wilderness.
1989 92m/C John Douglas, Chad Hayward, Christopher Weeks; D: John Garwood. VHS $69.95 SGE ⫬

Violets Are Blue Two high-school sweethearts are reunited in their hometown years later and try to rekindle their romance—even though the man is married.
1986 (PG-13) 86m/C Kevin Kline, Sissy Spacek, Bonnie Bedelia; D: Jack Fisk. VHS, Beta, LV $79.95 COL ⫬⫬½

Violette Fascinating true-life account of a nineteen-year-old French girl in the 1930s who, bored with her life and wanting to be with her lover, decides to poison her parents so she can receive her inheritance. Her mother survives but her father dies, and the girl is sent to prison for murder. Extraordinary performance by Huppert and the film is visually stunning. AKA: Violette Noziere.
1978 (R) 122m/C FR Isabelle Huppert, Stephane Audran, Jean Carmet, Jean Francoise, Bernadette LaFont; D: Claude Chabrol. VHS NYF ⫬⫬⫬

Vip, My Brother Superman The Vips are modern-day descendants of superbeings about to become legends in their own times. SuperVip is broad of chest and pure in spirit while his brother MiniVip possesses only limited powers. From the creator of "Allegro Non Troppo" comes this enticing, amusing piece of animation.

1990 90m/C D: Bruno Bozzetto. VHS $59.95 EXP ⫬⫬⫬

Viper A woman battles a cryptic anti-terrorist band to avenge the murder of her husband.
1988 96m/C Linda Purl, Chris Robinson, James Tolkan; D: Peter Maris. VHS $29.95 FRH ⫬

The V.I.P.'s Slick, sophisticated drama set in the V.I.P. lounge of a British airport. Trapped by fog, several of the passengers get acquainted and are forced to face their problems as they spend the night in the airport lounge. Taylor stars as Frances Andros, a wealthy young woman leaving her husband (Burton) for life in the U.S. with her lover, Jourdan. A movie tycoon, an Australian entrepreneur, his secretary, and a duchess are among the other passengers grounded by the fog. Both Rutherford and Smith give excellent performances and it was a tossup as to which actress would be nominated for the Oscar.
1963 119m/C GB Elizabeth Taylor, Richard Burton, Louis Jourdan, Elsa Martinelli, Margaret Rutherford, Maggie Smith, Rod Taylor, Orson Welles, Linda Christian, Dennis Price; D: Anthony Asquith; W: Terence Rattigan. VHS $19.98 MGM ⫬⫬⫬

Virgin Among the Living Dead Young woman travels to remote castle when she hears of relative's death. Once there, she finds the residents a tad weird and has bad dreams in which zombies chase her. Bizarre even for Franco, who seems to have been going through a "Pasolini" phase while making this one.
1971 (R) 90m/C SP Christina von Blanc, Britt Nichols, Howard Vernon, Anne Libert, Rose Kiekens, Paul Muller; D: Jess (Jesus) Franco. VHS, Beta NO ⫬

The Virgin and the Gypsy An English girl brought up in a repressive household in 1920s England falls in love with a gypsy. Based on the novel by D.H. Lawrence. Directorial debut of Miles.
1970 (R) 92m/C GB Joanna Shimkus, Franco Nero, Honor Blackman, Mark Burns; D: Christopher Miles. VHS NO ⫬⫬½

Virgin High Three young men sneak into an all-girls Catholic boarding school with hilarious consequences. Ward (TV's Robin, from "Batman") makes a special appearance in bondage in this sex farce.
1990 (R) 90m/C Burt Ward, Linnea Quigley, Tracy Dali, Richard Gabai, Catherine McGuiness, Chris Dempsey; W/D: Richard Gabai; W: Jeff Neal. VHS, LV $79.95 COL ⫬

The Virgin of Nuremberg A young woman enters her new husband's ancestral castle and is stalked by the specter of a legendary sadist. AKA: Horror Castle; Terror Castle; Castle of Terror; Castle of the Living Dead; La Vergine de Norimberga.
1965 82m/C IT Rossana Podesta, George Riviere, Christopher Lee, Jim Dolen; D: Anthony Dawson. VHS, Beta NO ⫬½

The Virgin Queen Davis stars in this historical drama, which focuses on the stormy relationship between the aging Queen and Sir Walter Raleigh. Collins is the lady-in-waiting who is the secret object of Raleigh's true affections. Previously, Davis played Queen Elizabeth I in "Elizabeth and Essex." Davis holds things together.
1955 92m/C Bette Davis, Richard Todd, Joan Collins, Herbert Marshall, Dan O'Herlihy, Jay Robinson, Romney Brent; D: Henry Koster. VHS, Beta $19.98 FOX ⫬⫬⫬

Virgin Queen of St. Francis High Two high school foes make a bet that one of them can take the "virgin" title away from gorgeous Christensen by summer's end. She has to fight off their advances, but grows to like Straface.
1988 (PG) 89m/C CA Joseph R. Straface, Stacy Christensen, J.T. Wotton; **D:** Francesco Lucente. VHS, Beta, LV $79.95 MED ℐ

Virgin Sacrifice A great white hunter looking for zoo-bound jaguars confronts the virgin-sacrificing, Tiger God-revering natives of Guatemala.
1959 67m/C David Dalie, Antonio Gutierrez, Angelica Morales, Fernando Wagner; **D:** Fernando Wagner. VHS, Beta, LV NO ℐ

The Virgin Soldiers A British comedy about greenhorn military recruits stationed in Singapore, innocent of women as well as battle, and their struggles to overcome both situations. A good cast raises this above the usual low-brow sex farce. Based on the novel by Leslie Thomas. Followed by "Stand Up Virgin Soldiers."
1969 (R) 96m/C GB Hywel Bennett, Nigel Davenport, Lynn Redgrave, Nigel Patrick, Rachel Kempson, Jack Shepherd, Tsai Chin; **D:** John Dexter. VHS, Beta $69.95 COL ℐℐ½

The Virgin Spring Based on a medieval ballad and set in 14th-century Sweden. The rape and murder of a young innocent spurs her father to vengeance and he kills her attackers. Over the girl's dead body, the father questions how God could have let any of it happen, but he comes to find solace and forgiveness. Stunning Bergman compositions. In Swedish with English subtitles; also available in dubbed version. **AKA:** Jungfrukallan.
1959 88m/B SW Max von Sydow, Brigitta Valberg, Gunnel Lindblom, Brigitta Pattersson, Axel Duborg; **D:** Ingmar Bergman. Academy Awards '60: Best Foreign Language Film; Nominations: Best Costume Design (B & W); Golden Globe Awards '61: Best Foreign Film. VHS, Beta $29.98 SUE, TAM ℐℐℐ½

The Virgin Witch Two beautiful sisters are sent to the British countryside, ostensibly for a modeling job. They soon find themselves in the midst of a witches' coven however, and discover one of them is to be sacrificed. The Michelles were "Playboy" magazine's first sister centerfolds. **AKA:** Lesbian Twins.
1970 (R) 89m/C GB Anne Michelle, Vicki Michelle, Patricia Haines, Keith Buckley, James Chase, Neil Hallett; **D:** Ray Austin. VHS, Beta $59.95 PSM ℐ½

Virginia City Action-packed western drama set during the Civil War. Flynn is a Union soldier who escapes from a Confederate prison run by Scott, after learning of a gold shipment being sent by Southern sympathizers to aid the Confederacy. He ends up in Virginia City (where the gold-laden wagon train is to leave from) and falls for a dance-hall girl (Hopkins) who turns out to be a Southern spy working for Scott but who falls for Flynn anyway. Bogart is miscast as a half-breed outlaw who aids Scott but wants the gold for himself. Considered a follow-up to "Dodge City."
1940 121m/C Errol Flynn, Miriam Hopkins, Randolph Scott, Humphrey Bogart, Frank McHugh, Alan Hale Sr., Guinn Williams, Douglas Dumbrille; **D:** Michael Curtiz. VHS $19.98 MGM ℐℐℐ

The Virginia Hill Story Fictionalized biography of mobster Bugsy Siegel's girl-friend who, in the mid-fifties, was subpoenaed to appear before the Kefauver investigation on crime in the U.S. As the examining

lawyer presents questions regarding her background and connections with the under-world, we see the story of her life. Made for television.
1976 90m/C Dyan Cannon, Harvey Keitel, Robby Benson, Allen Garfield, John Vernon; **D:** Joel Schumacher. VHS, Beta LME ℐℐ

The Virginian The second silent version of Owen Wister's classic western novel, inferior to both the 1914 Cecil B. DeMille silent and the 1929 Victor Fleming talkie. Harlan plays the title role as the cowpoke who leads a posse against cattle rustlers and falls in love with a schoolteacher.
1923 79m/B Kenneth Harlan, Florence Vidor, Russell Simpson, Pat O'Malley, Raymond Hatton; **D:** Tom Forman. VHS GPV ℐℐ½

The Virginian A classic early-talkie western about a ranch-hand defeating the local bad guys. One line of dialogue has become, with modification, a standard western cliche: "If you want to call me that, smile." Based on the novel by Owen Wister. With this starring role, Cooper broke away from the juvenile lovers he had been playing to the laconic, rugged male leads he would be known for. Huston is perfectly cast as the outlaw leader.
1929 95m/B Gary Cooper, Walter Huston, Richard Arlen, Chester Conklin, Eugene Pallette; **D:** Victor Fleming. VHS, Beta $14.95 KRT ℐℐℐ

Virgins of Purity House A group of chaste maidens decide to go all out to change their lifestyles.
1979 90m/C Juan Carlos Dual, Jorge Martinez, Elena Sedova, Patricia Dal. VHS, Beta $39.95 MED Woof!

Viridiana An innocent girl, with strong ideas about goodness, visits her worldly uncle before she takes her vows as a nun. Her uncle has developed a sick obsession for her, but after drugging the girl he finds he cannot violate her purity. He tells her, however, she is no longer chaste so she will not join the church. After her uncle's suicide, Viridiana learns she and his illegitimate son Jorge have inherited her uncle's rundown estate. Viridiana opens the house to all sorts of beggars, who take shameless advantage, while Jorge works slowly to restore the estate and improve the lives of those around him. Considered to be one of Bunuel's masterpieces and a bitter allegory of Spanish idealism versus pragmatism and the state of the world. In Spanish with English subtitles.
1961 90m/B SP MX Silvia Pinal, Francisco Rabal, Fernando Rey, Margarita Lozano, Victoria Zinny; **D:** Luis Bunuel. VHS, Beta $68.00 NOS, HHT, DVT ℐℐℐℐ

Virtue's Revolt A small-town girl is corrupted by the sleazy world of showbiz. Silent.
1924 51m/B Edith Thornton, Crauford Kent. VHS, Beta $19.95 NO ℐ½

Virus After nuclear war and plague destroy civilization, a small group of people gather in Antarctica and struggle with determination to carry on life. A look at man's genius for self-destruction and his endless hope. **AKA:** Fukkatsu no Hi.
1982 (PG) 102m/C JP George Kennedy, Sonny Chiba, Glenn Ford, Robert Vaughn, Stuart Gillard, Stephanie Faulkner, Ken Ogata, Bo Svenson, Olivia Hussey, Chuck Connors, Edward James Olmos; **D:** Kinji Fukasaku. VHS, Beta $19.95 STE, MED ℐℐ

The Vision Suspenseful British production about televangelists who attempt to control their viewers' minds through world-wide satellite broadcasting.

1987 103m/C GB Lee Remick, Dirk Bogarde, Helena Bonham Carter, Eileen Atkins; **D:** Norman Stone. VHS, Beta $79.95 SVS ℐℐ

Vision Quest A high school student wants to win the Washington State wrestling championship and the affections of a beautiful older artist. He gives it his all as he trains for the meet and goes after his "vision-quest." A winning performance by Modine raises this above the usual teen coming-of-age movie. Madonna sings "Crazy for You" in a nightclub. Based on novel by Terry Davis. **AKA:** Crazy for You.
1985 (R) 107m/C Matthew Modine, Linda Fiorentino, Ronny Cox, Roberts Blossom, Daphne Zuniga, Charles Hallahan, Michael Schoeffling; **D:** Harold Becker; **Performed by:** Madonna. VHS, Beta, LV $19.98 WAR ℐℐ½

Visions A man's ability to "see" murders before they happen leads police to suspect him of committing them, and he must clear himself.
1990 90m/C Joe Balogh, Alice Villarreal, Tom Taylor, A.R. Newman, J.R. Pella; **D:** Stephen E. Miller. VHS $79.95 MNC ℐ½

Visions of Evil A young woman, recently released from a mental institution, is plagued by a series of terrifying visions when she moves into a house where a brutal axe murder took place.
1973 85m/C Lori Sanders, Dean Jagger. VHS, Beta $49.95 PSM ℐ

Visitants Aliens descend irreverently on a small town in the 1950s, with unexpected comedic results.
1987 93m/C Marcus Vaughter, Johanna Grika, Joel Hile, Nicole Rio; **D:** Rick Sloane. VHS, Beta $69.95 TWE ℐ

Visiting Hours Psycho-killer slashes his female victims and photographs his handi-work. Grant is one of his victims who doesn't die, so the killer decides to visit the hospital and finish the job. Fairly graphic and generally unpleasant. **AKA:** The Fright; Get Well Soon.
1982 (R) 101m/C CA Lee Grant, William Shatner, Linda Purl, Michael Ironside; **D:** Jean-Claude Lord. VHS, Beta $59.98 FOX ℐ

The Visitor Affluent handsome doctor and mate conspire with grisly devil worshippers to conceive devil child.
1980 (R) 90m/C Mel Ferrer, Glenn Ford, Lance Henriksen, John Huston, Shelley Winters, Joanne Nail, Sam Peckinpah; **D:** Giullo Paradisi. VHS $29.95 UAV, HHE ℐ½

Visitor from the Grave When an American heiress and her boyfriend dispose of a dead man's body, his spirit comes back to haunt them. This annoys them.
1981 60m/C Simon MacCorkindale, Kathryn Leigh Scott, Gareth Thomas, Mia Nadasi. VHS, Beta $29.95 LIV ℐ

The Visitors Ghosts come to stay at a young family's dream house in Sweden. Not exactly a novel treatment or a novel premise.
1989 (R) 102m/C SW Keith Berkeley, Lena Endre, John Force, John Olsen, Joanna Berg, Brent Landiss, Patrick Ersgard; **D:** Joakim Ersgard. VHS, Beta, LV $79.95 VMK ℐ½

Vital Signs Hackneyed drama about six medical students enduring the tribulations of their profession.
1990 (R) 102m/C Adrian Pasdar, Diane Lane, Jack Gwaltney, Laura San Giacomo, Jane Adams, Tim Ransom, Bradley Whitford, Lisa Jane Persky, William Devane, Norma Aleandro, Jimmy Smits, James Karen, Telma Hopkins; **D:** Marisa Silver. VHS, Beta, LV $19.98 FOX ℐ

Viva Chihuahua (Long Live Chihuahua) Supposed to be one of the greatest achievements of Tin Tan.

1947 95m/B MX German Valdes, Miguel Aceves Mejia, Norma Mora, Marcelo Chavez. **VHS, Beta** $44.95 MAD ♫♫½

Viva Knievel Crooks plan to sabotage Knievel's daredevil jump in Mexico and then smuggle cocaine back into the States in his coffin. Unintentionally campy. *AKA:* Seconds to Live.
1977 (PG) 106m/C Evel Knievel, Gene Kelly, Lauren Hutton, Red Buttons, Leslie Nielsen, Cameron Mitchell, Marjoe Gortner, Albert Salmi, Dabney Coleman; *D:* Gordon Douglas. **VHS, Beta** $59.95 WAR Woof!

Viva Las Vegas Race care driver Elvis needs money to compete against rival Danova in the upcoming Las Vegas Grand Prix. He takes a job in a casino and romances fellow employee Ann-Margaret, who turns out to be his rival for the grand prize in the local talent competition. Good pairing between the two leads, and the King does particularly well with the title song. ♫The Lady Loves Me; Viva Las Vegas; What'd I Say; I Need Somebody to Lean On; Come On, Everybody; Today, Tomorrow and Forever; If You Think I Don't Need You; Appreciation; My Rival; The Climb; The Yellow Rose of Texas; The Eyes of Texas Are Upon You. *AKA:* Love in Las Vegas.
1963 85m/C Elvis Presley, Ann-Margaret, William Demarest, Jack Carter, Cesare Danova, Nicky Blair, Larry Kent; *D:* George Sidney. **VHS, Beta, LV** $19.95 MGM ♫♫½

Viva Max A blundering modern-day Mexican general and his men recapture the Alamo, and an equally inept American force, headed by Winters, is sent to rout them out. Mostly works, with some very funny scenes. Ustinov is great.
1969 93m/C Peter Ustinov, Jonathan Winters, John Astin, Pamela Tiffin, Keenan Wynn; *D:* Jerry Paris. **VHS** $14.98 REP ♫♫½

Viva Villa! Exciting action biography of Mexican revolutionary Pancho Villa, well-portrayed by the exuberant Beery. The film follows the early Robin Hood-like exploits of Villa and his men who soon join Walthall and his peasant army in overthrowing the government. But Villa's bandito instincts and ego cause problems and a power struggle ensues. Director Howard Hawks went uncredited for his work on the film, being fired by the studio after an incident while on location in Mexico.
1934 115m/B Wallace Beery, Fay Wray, Stuart Erwin, Leo Carrillo, Donald Cook, George E. Stone, Joseph Schildkraut, Henry B. Walthall, Katherine DeMille, David Durand, Frank Puglia; *D:* Jack Conway; *W:* Ben Hecht. **VHS, LV** $19.98 MGM, MOV ♫♫♫

Viva Zapata! John Steinbeck's screenplay of the life of Mexican revolutionary Emiliano Zapata. Brando is powerful as he leads the peasant revolt in the early 1900s, only to be corrupted by power and greed. Quinn well deserved his Best Supporting Actor Oscar for his performance as Zapata's brother. Based on the novel "Zapata the Unconquered" by Edgcumb Pinchon.
1952 112m/B Marlon Brando, Anthony Quinn, Jean Peters, Margo, Arnold Moss, Joseph Wiseman, Mildred Dunnock; *D:* Elia Kazan. Academy Awards '52: Best Supporting Actor (Quinn); Nominations: Best Actor (Brando), Best Art Direction/Set Decoration (B & W), Best Story & Screenplay, Best Original Score; British Academy Awards '52: Best Actor (Brando); Cannes Film Festival '52: Best Actor (Brando). **VHS, Beta, LV** $19.98 FOX, BTV ♫♫♫♫

Vivacious Lady Romantic comedy about a mild-mannered college professor who marries a chorus girl. Problems arise when he must let his conservative family and

his former fiancee in on the marriage news. Good performances. Appealing.
1938 90m/B Ginger Rogers, James Stewart, James Ellison, Beulah Bondi, Charles Coburn, Jack Carson, Franklin Pangborn; *D:* George Stevens. **VHS, Beta** $39.95 CCB, MED ♫♫♫

Vivo o Muerto Action and adventure abound in this shoot 'em up Spanish-language film.
1987 100m/B MX Manuel Capetillo, Flor Silvestre, Aldo Monti, Wolf Rubinskis. **VHS, Beta** $44.95 MAD ♫

Vogues of 1938 As a lark, a rich girl takes a job as a fashion model and incurs the displeasure of Baxter, the owner of the chic fashion house where she works. An early Technicolor fashion extravaganza. ♫That Old Feeling; Lovely One; Turn On the Red Hot Heat (Burn the Blues Away); King of Jam. *AKA:* All This and Glamour Too; Vogues.
1937 110m/C Joan Bennett, Warner Baxter, Helen Vinson, Mischa Auer, Hedda Hopper, Penny Singleton, Alan Mowbray; *D:* Irving Cummings. **VHS, Beta** NO ♫

Voice of Hollywood Some of Hollywood's great stars are caught off guard in this collection of short subjects.
1929 60m/B Buster Keaton, Ken Maynard, Johnny Mack Brown. **VHS, Beta** $19.95 VDM, DVT ♫½

Volere Volare Shy sound engineer Nichetti shares a studio with his brother. The brother employs a bevy of beauties to dub sound effects onto soft-core porn films while Nichetti works on dubbing classic cartoons. He becomes so involved in his work he actually turns into a cartoon figure, which does nothing for his love life. Then he meets Martina, who's strangely attracted to this cartoon figure. Quirky comedy mixes animation and live action with too many gimmicks and not enough heart.
1992 (R) 92m/C IT Maurizio Nichetti, Angela Finocchiaro, Mariella Valentini, Patrizio Roversi; *D:* Maurizio Nichetti, Guido Manuli; *W:* Maurizio Nichetti, Guido Manuli. **VHS, LV** COL ♫♫½

Volpone A classic adaptation of Ben Jonson's famous tale. A greedy merchant pretends he is dying, leaving a fortune behind, in order see what his family will do to become his heir. In French with English subtitles.
1939 95m/B FR Harry Baur, Louis Jouvet, Fernand Ledoux; *D:* Maurice Tourneur. **VHS, Beta** $24.95 NOS, HHT, APD ♫♫♫

Voltus 5 Five children stand against an alien race invading earth. Animated.
1983 75m/C **VHS, Beta** $14.95 MED, WTA ♫½

Volunteers Ivy League playboy joins the newly formed Peace Corps to escape gambling debts and finds himself on a bridge-building mission in Thailand. Has its comedic moments, especially with Candy.
1985 (R) 107m/C Tom Hanks, John Candy, Rita Wilson, Tim Thomerson, Gedde Watanabe, George Plimpton, Ernest Harada; *D:* Nicholas Meyer. **VHS, Beta, LV** $19.99 HBO ♫♫

Volver, Volver, Volver! A beautiful woman is abused by the brother of her dead husband.
1987 90m/C Antonio Aguilar, Jorge Rivero, Claudia Islas, Consuelo Frank, Bruno Rey. **VHS, Beta** $59.95 MAD ♫

Von Ryan's Express An American Air Force colonel leads a group of prisoners-of-war in taking control of a freight train in order to make their exciting escape from a World War II P.O.W. camp in Italy. Strong cast.

1965 117m/C Frank Sinatra, Trevor Howard, Brad Dexter, Raffaella Carra, Sergio Fantoni, John Leyton, Vito Scotti, Edward Mulhare, Adolfo Celi, James Brolin; *D:* Mark Robson; *M:* Jerry Goldsmith. **VHS, Beta, LV** $19.98 FOX, FCT ♫♫♫

Voodoo Black Exorcist Some 3000 years ago, a black prince was buried alive for messin' with another man's woman. Now he's back...and he's mad—real mad. He's prepared to kill just about everyone. Can he be stopped before all in the modern world are dead??
1989 ?m/C Aldo Sambrel, Tenyeka Stadle, Fernando Sancho. **VHS** $19.95 HHE ♫

Voodoo Dawn Two New Yorkers travel to the Deep South to visit a friend who, it turns out, is the latest victim in a series of really gross voodoo murders. A beautiful girl is written into the plot, and the New York guys have an excuse to stay in voodooville, even though bimbolina's southern accent comes and goes for no discernable reason. Filmed near Charleston, South Carolina. Co-written by John Russo of "Night of the Living Dead" fame.
1989 (R) 83m/C Raymond St. Jacques, Theresa Merritt, Gina Gershon, Kirk Baily, Billy "Sly" Williams, J. Grant Albrecht, Tony Todd; *D:* Steven Fierberg. **VHS** $19.95 ACA ♫♫

Voodoo Woman An innocent girl is lured into the jungle by an evil scientist who is trying to create the perfect woman to commit murders. He turns the girl into an ugly monster in an attempt to get her to obey his telepathic commands. A campy classic that's as bad as it sounds.
1957 77m/B Marla English, Tom Conway, Mike Connors, Lance Fuller; *D:* Edward L. Cahn. **VHS** $9.95 COL, HAR ♫

Vortex Punk/film noir style in which a female private eye becomes immersed in corporate paranoia and political corruption.
1981 87m/C Lydia Lunch, James Russo, Bill Rice; *D:* Scott B, Beth B. **VHS, 3/4U** ICA ♫½

Voulez-Vous Danser Avec Moi? A young bride endeavors to clear her husband of murder charges and find the real killer. In French with English subtitles. *AKA:* Come Dance with Me; Do You Want to Dance with Me?.
1959 90m/C FR Brigitte Bardot, Henri Vidal; *D:* Michel Boisrond. **VHS, Beta** $19.95 KRT, TAM ♫♫

Voyage en Balloon This is the delightful story of a young boy (played by the star of "The Red Balloon") who stows away on his grandfather's hot air balloon for an adventurous trip across France.
1959 82m/C FR Pascal Lamorisse, Andre Gille, Maurice Baquet; *W/D:* Albert Lamorisse. **VHS, Beta** $14.95 COL, TAM, SUE ♫♫½

The Voyage of Tanai A young Polynesian battles nature's snarls on his quest to save his village.
1975 (G) 90m/C *D:* John Latos. **VHS, Beta** NO ♫

Voyage of Terror: The Achille Lauro Affair Recounting of the 1985 Italian cruise-ship hijacking by four Palestinians. Lancaster is the wheelchair-bound Leon Klinghoffer and Saint is wife Marilyn. Shot on the actual ship and route where the tragedy occurred. Originally a made-for-television miniseries.
1990 120m/C Burt Lancaster, Eva Marie Saint, Robert Culp, Brian Bloom, Dominique Sanda, Rebecca Schaeffer, Joseph Nasser; *D:* Alberto Negrin. **VHS** $79.95 PSM ♫♫½

Voyage of the Damned The story of one of the most tragic incidents of World War II. In 1939, 1,937 German-Jewish refugees fleeing Nazi Germany are bound for Cuba aboard the Hamburg-America liner S.S. St. Louis. They are refused permission to land in Cuba (and everywhere else) and must sail back to Germany and certain death. Based on the novel by Gordon Thomas and Max Morgan-Witts.
1976 (G) 134m/C Faye Dunaway, Max von Sydow, Oskar Werner, Malcolm McDowell, Orson Welles, James Mason, Lee Grant, Katharine Ross, Ben Gazzara, Lynne Frederick, Wendy Hiller, Jose Ferrer, Luther Adler, Sam Wanamaker, Denholm Elliott, Nehemiah Persoff, Julie Harris, Maria Schell, Janet Suzman; **D:** Stuart Rosenberg. Academy Awards '76 Nominations: Best Adapted Screenplay, Best Supporting Actress (Grant), Best Original Score; Golden Globe Awards '77: Best Supporting Actress (Ross). **VHS, Beta $79.98** FOX *Ⅲ*

Voyage of the Heart An aging fisherman meets up with a sexy college girl and the passion begins.
1990 88m/C Bill Aldrij, Dunja Djordjenic. **VHS $79.95** AIP *Ⅱ*

Voyage of the Rock Aliens A quasi-satiric space farce about competing alien rock stars.
1987 97m/C Pia Zadora, Tom Nolan, Craig Sheffer, Rhema, Ruth Gordon, Michael Berryman, Jermaine Jackson; **D:** James Fargo. **VHS, Beta $79.95** PSM *Ⅱ*

The Voyage of the Yes Two teenagers, one white and one black, in a small sailboat hit rough weather and battle the elements while learning about themselves. Average made-for-television movie.
1972 (PG) 100m/C Desi Arnaz Jr., Mike Evans, Beverly Garland, Skip Homeier, Della Reese, Scoey Mitchell; **D:** Lee H. Katzin. **VHS** NO *Ⅱ*

A Voyage' Round My Father John Mortimer's adaptation of his semi-autobiographical stage play. Olivier is the eccentric, opinionated blind barrister-father and Bates the exasperated son as both try to come to terms with their stormy family relationship. Well-acted and directed. Made for television.
1989 85m/C GB Laurence Olivier, Alan Bates, Jane Asher, Elizabeth Sellars; **D:** Alvin Rakoff. **VHS, Beta $89.99** HBO *Ⅲ*

Voyage-Suprise A slapstick comedy about a crazy old man who runs a mystery tour from a dilapidated bus as he takes an unknowing mob of tourists on a cross-country escapade through a brothel, a wedding, criminals, police, terrorists and the Haute-Provence. In French with English subtitles.
1946 108m/B FR Martine Carol, Sioel; **D:** Pierre Prevert. **VHS, Beta $59.95** FCT, FST *Ⅲ*

Voyage to Italy An unhappy couple, on the verge of divorce, inherit a house in Italy and make a trip to see it. In Italy, they dally with other people but realize their attachment to each other demands they attempt to salvage their marriage. Not the best of the Rossellini-Bergman collaborations. Poor editing and directing undermine weak script. Sanders and Bergman do their best.
1953 87m/B Ingrid Bergman, George Sanders; **D:** Roberto Rossellini. **VHS, Beta $29.95** NOS, FCT *Ⅱ½*

Voyage to the Bottom of the Sea The crew of an atomic submarine must destroy a deadly radiation belt which has set the polar ice cap ablaze. Fun stuff, with good special effects and photography. Later became a television show.

1961 106m/C Walter Pidgeon, Joan Fontaine, Barbara Eden, Peter Lorre, Robert Sterling, Michael Ansara, Frankie Avalon; **D:** Irwin Allen. **VHS, Beta, LV $14.98** FOX, FCT *Ⅲ*

Voyage to the Planet of Prehistoric Women Astronauts journey to Venus, where they discover a race of gorgeous, sea-shell clad women led by Van Doren, as well as a few monsters. Incomprehensible but fun. The third film incorporating the Russian "Planeta Burg" footage. Directed (and narrated) by Bogdanovich under the pseudonym Derek Thomas. **AKA:** Gill Woman; Gill Women of Venus.
1968 78m/C Mamie Van Doren, Mary Mark, Paige Lee; **D:** Peter Bogdanovich. **VHS $16.95** SNC **Woof!**

Voyage to the Prehistoric Planet In the year 2020, an expedition to Venus is forced to deal with dinosaurs and other perils. In the making of this movie, Roger Corman edited in special effects and additional footage from a recently acquired Russian film, "Planeta Burg," and his own "Queen of Blood." **AKA:** Voyage to a Prehistoric Planet.
1965 80m/C Basil Rathbone, Faith Domergue, Marc Shannon, Christopher Brand; **D:** John Sebastian. **VHS $16.95** NOS, SNC *Ⅱ½*

Voyager Restless, middle-aged engineer Walter Faber (Shepherd) tells his life story in a series of flashbacks. Twenty years before (the film starts in 1957) he abandons his pregnant girlfriend who promises to get an abortion. He laters hears she married, had a child, and divorced. While sailing to New York from France Walter falls in love with a young student, Sabeth (Delpy), and after an idyllic interlude Walter agrees to accompany her to Greece to visit her mother. Shepherd's is a glum, repressed performance (in keeping with the character) while Delpy personifies youthful sweetness. Based on the novel "Homo Faber" by Max Frisch.
1991 (PG-13) 110m/C FR GE Sam Shepard, Julie Delpy, Barbara Sukowa, Dieter Kirchlechner, Traci Lin, Deborra-Lee Furness, August Zirner, Thomas Heinze; **D:** Volker Schlondorff. **VHS, LV $89.95** ACA, TAM *Ⅲ*

Vulcan God of Fire A foreign film featuring various Steve Reeves style musclemen portraying the gods of Olympus.
19?? 76m/C Rob Flash, Gordon Mitchell, Bella Cortez. **VHS, Beta $59.95** TWE **Woof!**

Vulture In an attempt to carry out a curse on the descendants of the man who killed his forefather, a scientist tries an atomic transmutation experiment and winds up combining himself with a bird.
1967 91m/C Robert Hutton, Akim Tamiroff, Broderick Crawford, Diane Clare, Philip Friend, Patrick Holt, Annette Carell; **D:** Lawrence Huntington. **VHS, Beta $14.95** NEG *Ⅱ*

Vultures A dying patriarch summons his predatory family to his home in order to straighten out the distribution of inheritance. One by one, they fall victim to a mysterious murderer.
1984 101m/C Yvonne De Carlo, Stuart Whitman, Jim Bailey, Meredith MacRae, Aldo Ray; **D:** Paul Leder. **VHS, Beta $79.95** PSM *Ⅰ*

W A woman and her husband are terrorized and must find out why. A single letter "W" is found at the scene of the crimes. Notable only as model Twiggy's first film. **AKA:** I Want Her Dead.
1974 (PG) 95m/C Twiggy, Dirk Benedict, John Vernon, Eugene Roche; **D:** Richard Quine. **VHS, Beta $69.98** LIV, VES *Ⅰ½*

W Hour A tragic story of young Polish soldiers participating in the Warsaw uprisings of 1944.
19?? 85m/C PL **VHS $39.99** FCT *Ⅱ½*

Wackiest Ship in the Army A completely undisciplined warship crew must smuggle an Australian spy through Japanese waters during World War II. Odd, enjoyable mixture of action and laughs. Became a TV series. In the middle of the war effort, Nelson straps on a guitar and sings "Do You Know What It Means to Miss New Orleans."
1961 99m/C Jack Lemmon, Ricky Nelson, Chips Rafferty, John Lund, Mike Kellin, Patricia Driscoll; **D:** Richard Murphy. **VHS, Beta, LV $14.95** COL *Ⅱ½*

Wackiest Wagon Train in the West Hapless wagon master is saddled with a dummy assistant as they guide a party of five characters across the West. Based on the minor TV sitcom "Dusty's Trail." Produced by the same folks who delivered the similarly premised TV series "Gilligan's Island" and "The Brady Bunch."
1977 (G) 86m/C Bob Denver, Forrest Tucker, Jeannine Riley. **VHS, Beta $19.95** MED *Ⅰ*

Wacko Group of nymphettes and tough guys get caught up in a wild Halloween-pumpkin-lawnmower murder. This spoof of the "Halloween" series works too hard for as few laughs as it gets.
1983 (PG) 84m/C Stella Stevens, George Kennedy, Joe Don Baker, Andrew Dice Clay; **D:** Greydon Clark. **VHS, Beta, LV** VES **Woof!**

The Wacky World of Mother Goose All the familiar Mother Goose characters are brought together in a delightful animated tale of secret agents and sinister surprises.
1967 81m/C V: Margaret Rutherford. **VHS, Beta $14.95** COL, SUE **Woof!**

The Wacky World of Wills & Burke Comedy based on the adventures of Wills and Burke, the two 19th-century explorers who led the first unsuccessful expedition across the outback—the Lewis and Clark of Australia, if you will. In real life they died during the adventure, a less than wacky finale. "Burke and Wills," out the same year, was a serious treatment of the same story.
1985 102m/C AU Garry McDonald, Kim Gyngell, Peter Collingwood, Jonathon Hardy, Mark Little; **D:** Bob Weis. **VHS, Beta $79.95** MNC *Ⅱ*

Wager of Love While vacationing on their annual pleasure cruise, four women bet on their individual power of seduction. They find themselves competing for passion as each woman's erotic adventure unravels in this exciting and sensual tale.
1990 75m/C Steve Landers, Shelly Johnson, Elliot Silverman, Lisa Cook; **D:** Jason Holt. **VHS $49.95** CEL *Ⅱ*

Wages of Fear An American oil company controls a desolate Central American town. Its denizens desperately want out—so desperately that four are willing to try a suicide mission to deliver tow truckfuls of nitroglycerin to put out a well-fire raging 300 miles away. The company's cynical head has offered $2,000 to each man—enough to finance escape from the hell-hole they live in. Complex, multi-dimensional drama. Second half focuses on the truck rides, but the first half, concentrating on character development, is crucial to the film's greatness. This is the restored version. Remade by William Friedkin as "Sorcerer" in 1977. Based on a novel by Georges Arnaud. In French with English subtitles. **AKA:** Le Salaire De La Peur.

1955 138m/B *FR* Yves Montand, Charles Vanel, Peter Van Eyck; **W/D:** Henri-Georges Clouzot. **VHS, Beta, LV** $24.95 *HHT, SNC, VYY* &&&&

Wagner: The Complete Epic The unedited version of the epic made-for-television miniseries dramatizing the life of German composer Richard Wagner. The excellent photography does justice to the elaborate production, shot on some 200 different locations. The actors cringe in the presence of the subject's grandeur; Burton, a shell of his former cinematic self, is painful to watch in his last released film. Frankly, this is way too long. Music conducted by Sir Georg Solti. 1985 540m/C *GB HU* Richard Burton, Vanessa Redgrave, Ralph Richardson, John Gielgud, Laurence Olivier; **D:** Tony Palmer; **M:** George Solti. **VHS, Beta** $124.95 *MVD, KUL* &&

Wagner: The Movie Slightly half it's original length, the world's biggest biopic is still huge, sweeping, and long. Incoherent and over-acted. Wagner's music is conducted by Sir Georg Soltl. Made for television. 1985 300m/C *GB HU* Richard Burton, Vanessa Redgrave, John Gielgud, Franco Nero, Laurence Olivier; **D:** Tony Palmer. **VHS, Beta** $29.95 *MVD, SUE, GLV* &½

Wagon Master Two cowboys are persuaded to guide a group of Mormons, led by Bond, in their trek across the western frontier. They run into a variety of troubles, including a band of killers who joins the wagon train to escape a posse. Sensitively directed, realistic and worthwhile. Inspired the TV series "Wagon Train." Also available colorized. 1950 85m/B Ben Johnson, Joanne Dru, Harry Carey Jr., Ward Bond, Jane Darwell, James Arness; **D:** John Ford. **VHS, Beta, LV** $19.95 *MED, TTC* &&&

Wagon Trail The sheriff's son is blackmailed into helping a gang of robbers, with terrible consequences for himself and his father (Carey), who is fired from his job after the son breaks jail. The new sheriff is secretly chief of the outlaw band. Carey rides back into town and eventually virtue triumphs. Good, tense—but not too tense—western. 1935 59m/B Harry Carey Sr.; **D:** Harry Fraser. **VHS, Beta** $27.95 *VCN* &&½

Wagon Wheels Recycling was in vogue in '34, when unused footage from "Fighting Caravans" (1931) with Gary Cooper was used to remake the very same plot. The result is biodegradable. Settlers heading to Oregon are ambushed by bad guy Blue, employed by fur traders. Blue sics Injuns on them too, but don't worry, they make it. Adapted from Zane Grey's novel "Fighting Caravans." **AKA:** Caravans West. 1934 54m/B Randolph Scott, Gail Patrick, Billy Lee; **D:** Charles T. Barton. **VHS, Beta** $9.95 *NOS, DVT* &&

Waikiki Two private eyes set out to prove that their friend is not the "cane field murderer" who is terrorizing the Hawaiian island of Oahu. Harmless but pointless TV pilot. 1980 96m/C Dack Rambo, Steve Marachuk, Donna Mills, Cal Bellini, Darren McGavin; **D:** Ron Satlof. **VHS, Beta** $59.95 *LHV* &½

Wait Till Your Mother Gets Home "Mr. Mom"-like zaniness abounds as a football coach care for the kids and does chores while his wife takes her first job in 15 years. Almost too darn cute, but well written. Made for television. 1983 97m/C Paul Michael Glaser, Dee Wallace Stone, Peggy McKay, David Doyle, Raymond Buktencia, James Gregory, Joey Lawrence, Lynne Moody; **D:** Bill Persky. **VHS, Beta** $9.99 *STE, PSM* &&

Wait Until Dark A photographer unwittingly smuggles a drug-filled doll into New York, and his blind wife, alone in their apartment, is terrorized by murderous crooks in search of it. A compelling thriller based on the Broadway hit by Frederick Knott, who also wrote "Dial M for Murder." The individual actors' performances were universally acclaimed in this spinetingler. Music by Henry Mancini. 1967 105m/C Audrey Hepburn, Alan Arkin, Richard Crenna, Efrem Zimbalist Jr., Jack Weston; **D:** Terence Young. **VHS, Beta** $59.95 *WAR* &&&

Wait Until Spring, Bandini A flavorful immigrant tale about a transplanted Italian family weathering the winter in 1925 Colorado, as seen through the eyes of a young son. Alternately funny and moving, with one of Dunaway's scenery-chewing performances as a local temptation for the father. Based on the autobiographical novel by John Fante, co-produced by Francis Ford Coppola. 1990 (PG-13) 104m/C Joe Mantegna, Faye Dunaway, Burt Young; **D:** Dominique Deruddere. **VHS** $19.98 *WAR* &&½

Waiting for the Light When a woman takes over a small-town diner, she gets the surprise of her life. Seems an angel has made his home there and now the townsfolk are flocking to see him. MacLaine is wonderful and Garr is fetching and likeable. Set during the Cuban missile crisis. Enjoyable, tame comedy. 1990 (PG) 94m/C Shirley MacLaine, Teri Garr, Vincent Schiavelli, John Bedford Lloyd; **W/D:** Christopher Monger. **VHS, LV, 8mm** $19.95 *COL, PIA* &&½

Waiting for the Moon Hunt as Alice B. Toklas is a relative treat in this ponderous, frustrating biopic about Toklas and Gertrude Stein, her lover. Made for "American Playhouse" on PBS. 1987 (PG) 88m/C Linda Hunt, Linda Bassett, Andrew McCarthy; **D:** Jill Godmilow. **VHS, Beta** $79.98 *FOX* &½

Waitress Three beautiful girls are waitresses in a crazy restaurant where the chef gets drunk, the kitchen explodes, and the customers riot. Awful premise, worse production. **AKA:** Soup to Nuts. 1981 (R) 85m/C Jim Harris, Carol Drake, Carol Bever; **D:** Samuel Weil. **VHS, Beta** $19.99 *HBO* Woof!

Wake Island After Pearl Harbor, a small group of Marines face the onslaught of the Japanese fleet on a small Pacific Island. Although doomed, they hold their ground for 16 days. Exciting, realistic, and moving. The first film to capitalize on early "last stands" of WWII; also among the most popular war movies. Shown to soldiers in training camps with great morale-raising success. 1942 88m/B Robert Preston, Brian Donlevy, William Bendix, William Bendix, MacDonald Carey, Albert Dekker, Walter Abel, Rod Cameron; **D:** John Farrow. Academy Awards '42 Nominations: Best Director (Farrow), Best Original Screenplay, Best Picture, Best Supporting Actor (Bendix); New York Film Critics Awards '42: Best Director (Farrow). **VHS, Beta** $19.95 *MCA, TLF* &&&

Wake of the Red Witch Wayne captains the ship of the title and battles shipping tycoon Adler for a fortune in pearls and the love of a beautiful woman (Russell). Wayne shows impressive range in a non-gun-totin' role. 1949 106m/B John Wayne, Gail Russell, Gig Young, Luther Adler, Henry Daniell; **D:** Edward Ludwig. **VHS, Beta** $14.98 *REP* &&½

Walk, Don't Run Romantic comedy involving a British businessman (Grant) unable to find a hotel room in Tokyo due to the crowds staying for the 1964 summer Olympic Games. He winds up renting a room from an Embassy secretary (Eggar) and then meets and invites Hutton, a member of the U.S. Olympic walking team, also without a place to stay, to share it with him. Grant then proceeds to play matchmaker, despite the fact that Eggar has a fiance. Grant's last film. Innocuous, unnecessary remake of "The More the Merrier." 1966 114m/C Cary Grant, Samantha Eggar, Jim Hutton, John Standing, Miiko Taka; **D:** Charles Walters. **VHS, Beta** $69.95 *COL* &&½

Walk in the Spring Rain The bored wife of a college professor follows him to rural Tennessee when he goes on sabbatical, where she meets the married Quinn and the two begin an affair. When Quinn's disturbed son learns of the affair, he attacks the woman, with tragic results. Fine cast should have had better effect on low-key script by Stirling Silliphant. 1970 (PG) 98m/C Ingrid Bergman, Anthony Quinn, Fritz Weaver, Katherine Crawford, Tom Fielding, Virginia Gregg; **D:** Guy Green. **VHS, Beta** $59.95 *HCA* &&½

A Walk in the Sun The trials of a group of infantrymen in World War II from the time they land in Italy to the time they capture their objective, a farmhouse occupied by the Germans. Excellent ensemble acting shows well the variety of civilians who make up any fighting force and explores their fears, motivations, and weaknesses. Producer and director Milestone also made "All Quiet on the Western Front" and the Korean War masterpiece "Pork Chop Hill." Released in the final days of the war, almost concurrently with two other WWII films of the first echelon, "The Story of G.I. Joe" and "They Were Expendable." **AKA:** Salerno Beachhead. 1946 117m/B Dana Andrews, Richard Conte, John Ireland, Lloyd Bridges, Sterling Holloway; **D:** Lewis Milestone; **W:** Robert Rossen. **VHS, Beta, LV, 8mm** $19.95 *LUM, NOS, DVT* &&&½

Walk into Hell A mining engineer and his assistant searching for oil meet the primitive natives of New Guinea. Tedious at times and dated, but pleasant enough. 1957 91m/C *AU* Chips Rafferty, Francoise Christophe, Reg Lye; **D:** Lee Robinson. **VHS, Beta** $59.95 *NLC, VYY* &&

Walk Like a Man In a take-off of Tarzan movies, Mandel plays a man raised by wolves. Comic problems arise when he is found by his mother and the family attempts to civilize him. Juvenile script wastes fine cast. 1987 (PG) 86m/C Howie Mandel, Christopher Lloyd, Cloris Leachman, Colleen Camp, Amy Steel; **D:** Melvin Frank. **VHS, Beta** $79.95 *MGM* &½

Walk on the Wild Side In 1930s New Orleans, a man searches for his long-lost love, finds her working in a whorehouse and fights to save her from the lesbian madame Stanwyck. Melodrama, based only loosely on the Nelson Algren novel and adapted by cult novelist John Fante, with Edmund Morris. Much-troubled on the set, and it shows. 1962 114m/B Jane Fonda, Laurence Harvey, Barbara Stanwyck, Capucine, Anne Baxter; **D:** Edward Dmytryk. **VHS, Beta** $69.95 *COL* &&

Walk Softly, Stranger Two-bit crook is reformed by the love of an innocent peasant girl. If you can stand the cliche masquerading as a plot, the performances are good.

1950 81m/B Alida Valli, Joseph Cotten, Spring Byington, Paul Stewart, Jack Paar, Jeff Donnell, John McIntire; *D:* Robert Stevenson. **VHS, Beta** $19.98 *TTC* 𝟚𝟚

Walker Slapdash, tongue-in-cheek historical pastiche about the real-life American William Walker (played previously in "Burn!" by Marlon Brando), and how he led a revolution in Nicaragua in 1855 and became its self-declared president. A bitter, revisionist farce never for a moment attempting to be accurate. Matlin's unfortunate, though fortunately brief, follow-up to her Oscar-winning performance. Music by Joe Strummer. 1987 (R) 95m/C Ed Harris, Richard Masur, Peter Boyle, Rene Auberjonois, Marlee Matlin, Miguel Sandoval; *D:* Alex Cox; *W:* Rudy Wurlitzer. **VHS, Beta** $79.95 *MCA* 𝟚𝟚

Walking Back Troubled teens go for joyride and bash mirthmobile to smithereens. The body shop agrees to give them a different car, but they find themselves in the middle of a heist at a plant belonging to the father of one of the boys. 1926 53m/B Sue Carol, Richard Walling, Ivan Lebedeff, Robert Edeson, Florence Turner, Arthur Rankin; *D:* Rupert Julian. **VHS, Beta** $19.95 *GPV, FCT* 𝟚𝟚½

Walking on Air Ray Bradbury's story comes to life as a handicapped boy dreams of completing a real space walk. Originally aired on PBS as part of the "Wonderworks" series. 1987 60m/C Lynn Redgrave, Jordan Marder, James Treuer, Katheryn Trainor; *D:* Ed Kaplan. **VHS** $29.95 *PME, HMV* 𝟚𝟚

Walking Tall A Tennessee sheriff takes a stand against syndicate-run gambling and his wife is murdered in response. Ultra-violent crime saga wowed the movie going public and spawned several sequels and a TV series. Based on the true story of folk-hero Buford Pusser, admirably rendered by Baker. 1973 (R) 126m/C Joe Don Baker, Elizabeth Hartman, Noah Beery Jr., Gene Evans, Rosemary Murphy, Felton Perry; *D:* Phil Karlson. **VHS, Beta, LV** $29.98 *LIV* 𝟚𝟚½

Walking Tall: Part 2 Club-wielding Tennessee sheriff Buford Pusser, this time played less memorably by Svenson, attempts to find the man who killed his wife. Even more violent than the original. 1975 (PG) 109m/C Bo Svenson, Noah Beery Jr., Angel Tompkins, Richard Jaeckel; *D:* Earl Bellamy. **VHS, Beta, LV** $29.98 *LIV, VES* 𝟚𝟚

Walking Tall: The Final Chapter The final months in the life of Tennessee sheriff Buford Pusser and the mystery surrounding his death. It wasn't the final chapter. Still to come: a TV flick and series. 1977 (PG) 112m/C Bo Svenson, Forrest Tucker, Leif Garrett, Morgan Woodward; *D:* Jack Starrett. **VHS, Beta, LV** $29.98 *LIV* 𝟚½

Walking the Edge A widow hires a taxi driver to help her seek vengeance against the men who killed her husband and her son. Forster does what he can with the lousy story and script. 1983 (R) 94m/C Robert Forster, Nancy Kwan, Joe Spinell, Aarika Wells; *D:* Norbert Meisel. **VHS, Beta** $79.98 *LIV* 𝟚½

Walking Through the Fire A young woman's real-life struggle with Hodgkin's disease. Her fight for her own and her unborn baby's survival is a stirring testament to the power of faith. Absorbing made-for-television drama. 1980 143m/C Bess Armstrong, Tom Mason, Bonnie Bedelia, Richard Masur, Swoosie Kurtz, J.D. Cannon, June Lockhart; *D:* Robert Day. **VHS, Beta** *TLF* 𝟚𝟚½

The Wall The last film by Guney, author of "Yol," about orphaned boys in prison in the Turkish capitol of Ankara trying to escape and/or rebel after ceaseless rapings, beatings and injustice. An acclaimed, disturbing film made from Guney's own experience. He died in 1984, three years after escaping from prison. Brutal and horrifying. In Turkish with English subtitles. *AKA:* Guney's The Wall; Le Mur; Duvar. 1983 117m/C *TU* Ayse Emel Mesci, Saban, Sisko; *W/D:* Yilmaz Guney. **VHS, Beta** $69.95 *KIV, TAM* 𝟚𝟚𝟚½

Wall Street Stone's energetic, high-minded big business treatise in which naive, neophyte stockbroker Sheen is seduced into insider trading by sleek entrepreneur Douglas, much to his blue-collar father's chagrin. A fast-moving drama of 80's-style materialism with a mesmerizing, award-winning performance by Douglas as greed personified. Expert direction by Stone, who co-wrote the not-very-subtle script. His father, to whom this film is dedicated, was a broker. Look for Stone in a cameo. 1987 (R) 126m/C Michael Douglas, Charlie Sheen, Martin Sheen, Daryl Hannah, Sean Young, James Spader, Hal Holbrook, Terence Stamp, Richard Dysart, John C. McGinley; *Cameos:* Oliver Stone; *D:* Oliver Stone. **VHS, Beta, LV** $19.98 *FOX, BTV* 𝟚𝟚𝟚

Wall Street Cowboy When his land is threatened, a cowboy fights big business in the big city. 1939 54m/B Roy Rogers. **VHS, Beta** $9.99 *NOS, DVT* 𝟚

Wallaby Jim of the Islands The singing captain of a pearl fishing boat must protect his treasure from marauding pirates. Pleasant enough musical adventure. 1937 61m/B George Houston, Douglas Walton; *D:* Bud Barsky. **VHS** $24.95 *NOS, DVT, HEG* 𝟚𝟚

The Walloping Kid A B-western with photography done in Monument Valley. Silent with original organ music. 1926 67m/B Kit Carson; *D:* Pauline Curley. **VHS, Beta, 8mm** $29.95 *VYY* 𝟚½

Walls of Glass An aging New York cabby tries to make it as an actor. Effective performances by all override the thin plot. Slow and uneven, but involving. Also called "Flanagan." 1985 (R) 85m/C Geraldine Page, Philip Bosco, William Hickey, Olympia Dukakis, Brian Bloom, Linda Thorson; *D:* Scott Goldstein. **VHS, Beta** $79.95 *MED* 𝟚𝟚

Walpurgis Night Soapy Swedish drama about abortion was racy for its time. Office gal Bergman secretly loves her boss (Hanson). His wife refuses to have children and goes through an abortion. An unscrupulous fellow blackmails her with this knowledge. Bergman bides her time. Stay tuned... Interesting document on the mores of another time. In Swedish with English subtitles. *AKA:* Valborgmassoafton. 1941 82m/B *SW* Lars Hanson, Karin Carlsson, Victor Sjostrom, Ingrid Bergman, Erik Berglund, Sture Lagerwall, Georg Rydeberg, Georg Blickingberg; *D:* Gustaf Edgren. **VHS, Beta** $29.95 *WAC, TAM* 𝟚𝟚

The Waltons: The Children's Carol Heart-warming made-for-TV holiday special involving the Appalachian family on the farm for a yuletide celebration. 1978 94m/C Will Geer, Michael Learned, Richard Thomas, Judy Norton-Taylor, Ralph Waite. **VHS** $14.95 *VTK, WAR, TVC* 𝟚𝟚𝟚

Waltz Across Texas Young oil man Farnsworth and good-lookin' rock scientist Place at first don't take to each other, but there's something in the air, and romance blossoms. Not great, but enjoyable. Farnsworth and Place cowrote and coproduced, and cohabitate as real-life spouses offscreen. 1983 100m/C Mary Kay Place, Richard Farnsworth, Terry Jastrow, Anne Archer; *D:* Ernest Day. **VHS, Beta** $69.95 *VES* 𝟚𝟚½

Waltz King Typically hokey Disney biography of the young composer Johann Strauss during his Old Viennese heyday. Fine music, pretty German locations. Well-made family fare. 1963 94m/C Kerwin Mathews, Senta Berger, Brian Aherne; *D:* Steve Previn. **VHS, Beta** $69.95 *DIS* 𝟚𝟚½

Waltz of the Toreadors Retired general Sellers doesn't care for his wealthy, shrewish wife and tries to re-kindle a 17-year-old romance with a French woman. It doesn't work out (seems his illegitimate son also has a soft spot for the lady), but the general decides to keep his eyes open for other possibilities. Interestingly cast adaptation of Jean Anouilh's play. Sellers is hilarious, as usual. *AKA:* The Amorous General. 1962 105m/C *GB* Peter Sellers, Dany Robin, Margaret Leighton, Cyril Cusack; *D:* John Guillermin. **VHS, Beta** $19.98 *VID* 𝟚𝟚𝟚

A Waltz Through the Hills Two orphans head into the Australian outback and experience many adventures en route to the coast where they can set sail for England and their grandparents. Aired on PBS as part of the "Wonderworks" series. 1988 116m/C Tina Kemp, Andre Jansen, Ernie Dingo, Dan O'Herlihy; *D:* Frank Arnold. **VHS** $29.95 *PME, HMV* 𝟚𝟚

Wanda Nevada Gambler Fonda wins nubile young Shields in a poker game, so her drags her with him to the Grand Canyon to look for gold. Director/star Fonda sure picked a lemon for his only screen appearance with dad Henry (a grizzled old varmint appearing briefly). Shields is in her usual form—stellar for a shampoo commercial. 1979 (PG) 105m/C Peter Fonda, Brooke Shields, Henry Fonda, Fiona Lewis, Luke Askew, Ted Markland, Severn Darden, Paul Fix; *D:* Peter Fonda. **VHS, Beta** *NO* 𝟚½

Wanda, The Sadistic Hypnotist A comely vixen hypnotizes an innocent pedestrian, ties him up and whips him to indulge her whims. Despite the "victim's" protests, she unleashes a gang of sexually playful women on him, and he is subjected to a multitude of "tortures." 1967 70m/C Katharine Shubeck, Janice Sweet, Dick Dangerfield, Daryl Cobinot; *D:* Gregory Corarito. **VHS** $23.00 *SMW* 𝟚

The Wanderer Two friends fall in love—Frantz with Valentine and his friend Augustin with Frantz's sister, Yvonne. When the two women disappear on Frantz's wedding day, the two men begin a search to find both the women and the reasons for their disappearance. In French with English subtitles. *AKA:* Le Grand Meaulnes. 1967 108m/C *FR* Brigitte Fossey, Jean Blaise, Alain Noury, Juliette Villard; *D:* Jean-Gabriel Albicocco. **VHS** $79.95 *TAM* 𝟚

Wanderers Richard Price's acclaimed novel about youth gangs coming of age in the Bronx in 1963. The "Wanderers," named after the Dion song, are a gang of Italian-American teenagers about to graduate high school, who prowl the Bronx with the feeling that something is slipping away from them.

Fascinating, funny and touching. Manz is unforgettable as a scrappy gal. A wonderful 60s soundtrack (Dion, the Four Seasons) colors this "coming of age the hard way" film.
1979 (R) 113m/C Ken Wahl, John Friedrich, Karen Allen, Linda Manz; *Cameos:* Richard Price; *D:* Philip Kaufman. **VHS, Beta** $19.98 *WAR* ♫♫♫½

Wandering Jew An excellent print of the rare Austrian film version of the classic legend, one of at least three silent versions. A Jew is condemned to wander the earth for eternity.
1920 65m/B Rudolf Schildkraut, Joseph Schildkraut. **VHS, Beta** *GVV* ♫♫½

The Wannsee Conference A startling, important film depicting, in real time, the conference held at the Wannsee on January 20, 1942, during which 14 members of the Nazi hierarchy decided in 85 minutes the means and logistics of effecting the Final Solution. Recreated from the original secretary's notes. Horrifying and chilling. Along with "Shoah," a must-see for understanding the Holocaust and the psychology of genocide. In German with English subtitles. *AKA:* Wannseekonferenz.
1984 87m/C *GE* Dietrich Mattausch, Gerd Brockmann, Friedrich Beckhaus; *D:* Heinz Schirk. **VHS, Beta, LV** $79.95 *PSM, APD, GLV* ♫♫♫½

Wanted: Babysitter A young student accidentally becomes involved by her roommate in a plot to kidnap the child she is babysitting. Schneider is truly awful; Italian comic Pazzetto is at sea in a bad role as her boyfriend. Also released as "The Babysitter."
1975 90m/C Robert Vaughn, Vic Morrow, Maria Schneider, Renato Pozzetto, Nadja Tiller, Carl Mohner, Sydne Rome; *D:* Rene Clement. **VHS, Beta** $24.95 *AHV* Woof!

Wanted: Dead or Alive This western series, which ran from 1958-1961, launched the career of McQueen who starred as bounty hunter Josh Randall. In this episode, "Reunion for Revenge," Randall must protect the man in his custody from escaped criminals with vengeance on their mind. Also available colorized. Additional episodes available.
1959 22m/B Steve McQueen, Wright King, Jane Burns, James Coburn, Cloris Leachman, John Baer, Ralph Meeker; *D:* Thomas Carr, Richard Donner. **VHS, Beta** $9.98 *VID, MOV* Woof!

Wanted Dead or Alive Ex-CIA agent Hauer is now a high-tech bounty hunter assigned to bring in an international terrorist. When the terrorist kills Hauer's friend and girlfriend, he forgets the $50,000 bonus for bringing him in alive. Official "sequel" to the Steve McQueen television series with Hauer as the McQueen character's great-grandson. The link is meaningless, and the plot is a thin excuse for much violence and anti-terrorist flag-waving.
1986 (R) 104m/C Rutger Hauer, Gene Simmons, Robert Guillaume, William Russ, Jerry Hardin, Mel Harris; *D:* Gary Sherman. **VHS, Beta, LV** $14.95 *NWV, STE* ♫½

Wanted: The Perfect Guy Danny and Melanie try to find Mister Right for their divorced Mom (Kahn). An Emmy Award winner about single parents and their children.
1990 45m/C Madeline Kahn, Melanie Mayron. **VHS** $99.95 *AIM* ♫♫½

The Wanton Contessa In 1866, as the Austrians prepare for war with Italy, a love affair arises between an Italian countess and an Austrian lieutenant. This deeply romantic saga dwells on the complexities in an affair that cross lines of war, nation, and social class. Lush photography. Dubbed. *AKA:* Senso.
1955 125m/C *IT* Alida Valli, Farley Granger, Massimo Girotti, Heinz Moog; *D:* Luchino Visconti. **VHS, Beta** $59.95 *VCD* ♫♫♫

War & Love Two Jewish teenagers in Warsaw are torn apart by WWII and Nazi persecution. After the war they search for each other. Sincere, but not adequately developed, drama based on the book "The Survivors" by film's producer Jack Eisner.
1984 (PG-13) 112m/C Sebastian Keneas, Kyra Sedgwick; *D:* Moshe Mizrahi. **VHS, Beta** $79.95 *MGM, SWC* ♫♫

War and Peace Lengthy adaptation of Tolstoy's great (and likewise lengthy) novel about three families caught up in Russia's Napoleonic Wars from 1805 to 1812; filmed in Rome. Bad casting and confused script (by six writers) are somewhat overcome by awesome battle scenes and Hepburn. Score by Nino Rota. Remade in 1968.
1956 208m/C Audrey Hepburn, Mel Ferrer, Henry Fonda, Anita Ekberg, Vittorio Gassman, John Mills, Oscar Homolka, Herbert Lom, Helmut Dantine; *D:* King Vidor. Academy Awards '56 Nominations: Best Color Cinematography, Best Costume Design (Color), Best Director (Vidor); Golden Globe Awards '57: Best Foreign Film; National Board of Review Awards '56: 5 Best Foreign Films of the Year. **VHS, Beta, LV** $14.95 *PAR* ♫♫½

War and Peace The massive Russian production of Leo Tolstoy's masterpiece, adapting the classic tome practically scene by scene. All of the production took place in the Soviet Union. So painstaking that it took more than five years to finish, no other adaptation can touch it. Hugely expensive ($100 million, claimed the Russians), wildly uneven production. Great scenes of battle and aristocratic life. Though this version is far from perfect, one asks: is it humanly possible to do screen justice to such a novel? In Russian with English subtitles. On four tapes. (Beware the two-part, poorly dubbed version that was also released.)
1968 373m/C *RU* Lyudmila Savelyeva, Sergei Bondarchuk, Vyacheslav Tihonor, Hira Ivanov-Golarko, Irina Gubanova, Antonina Shuranova; *D:* Sergei Bondarchuk. Academy Awards '68: Best Foreign Language Film; Nominations: Best Art Direction/Set Decoration; Golden Globe Awards '69: Best Foreign Film; National Board of Review Awards '68: 5 Best Foreign Films of the Year; New York Film Critics Awards '68: Best Foreign Film. **VHS, Beta, LV** $99.95 *VTK, KUL, TAM* ♫♫♫

War & Remembrance, Part 1 Tedious sequel to the epic television mini-series "The Winds of War," based on the novel by Herman Wouk. Historical fiction is created around the events of World War II, including Nazi persecution and naval battles in the Pacific. Seven cassette series. Followed by "War and Remembrance: The Final Chapter."
1988 120m/C Robert Mitchum, Jane Seymour, Hart Bochner, Victoria Tennant, Barry Bostwick, Polly Bergen, David Dukes, Michael Woods, Sharon Stone, Robert Morley, Sami Frey, Chaim Topol, John Rhys-Davies, Ian McShane, William Schallert, Jeremy Kemp, Steven Berkoff, Robert Hardy, Ralph Bellamy, John Gielgud; *D:* Dan Curtis. **VHS, Beta** $139.98 *MPI, MOV* ♫½

War & Remembrance, Part 2 The final installments of the excruciatingly boring and long mini-series. Herman Wouk's historical fiction concerning the last years of World War II. Six cassettes, in Hi-Fi stereo.
1989 120m/C Robert Mitchum, Jane Seymour, Hart Bochner, Ralph Bellamy, Victoria Tennant, Barry Bostwick, John Gielgud, Polly Bergen, David Dukes, Michael Woods; *D:* Dan Curtis. **VHS, Beta** *MPI* ♫½

War & Remembrance, Part 3 A brief glimmer of hope appears in this volume involving the lovers' reunion in Hawaii and the military power's changing of hands due to command of the Americans following the infamous Midway battle.
1988 120m/C Robert Mitchum, Jane Seymour, Hart Bochner, Victoria Tennant, Polly Bergen, David Dukes, Michael Woods; *D:* Dan Curtis. **VHS, Beta** *MPI* ♫½

War & Remembrance, Part 4 The middle part of 1942 sees its way through the American infiltration of Guadacanal, the treacherous stranglehold of Nazi Germany on Europe and other parts of the world, and the defiance toward defeat of the Russian Army.
1988 120m/C Robert Mitchum, Jane Seymour, Hart Bochner, Victoria Tennant, Polly Bergen, David Dukes, Michael Woods; *D:* Dan Curtis. **VHS, Beta** *MPI* ♫½

War & Remembrance, Part 5 As 1942 draws to a close, Wouk's well-known character, Pug, finds himself heading for a new assignment. North Africa welcomes the Allies in lieu of the Nazis. Stalingrad is mortified by an ever-strong Nazi invasion.
1988 120m/C Robert Mitchum, Jane Seymour, Hart Bochner, Victoria Tennant, Polly Bergen, David Dukes, Michael Woods; *D:* Dan Curtis. **VHS, Beta** *MPI* ♫½

War & Remembrance, Part 6 After leaving his dear cruiser behind, Pug says hello to Russia. The Ally leaders meet with much to discuss. Hitler is getting stronger and shrewder.
1988 120m/C Robert Mitchum, Jane Seymour, Hart Bochner, Victoria Tennant, Polly Bergen, David Dukes, Michael Woods; *D:* Dan Curtis. **VHS, Beta** *MPI* ♫½

War & Remembrance, Part 7 The Sicilian win by Patton brings about the devastation of Mussolini. Hitler's henchman are getting nervous and tired of battle. Germany succumbs to Allied troops in North Africa.
1988 120m/C Robert Mitchum, Jane Seymour, Hart Bochner, Victoria Tennant, Polly Bergen, David Dukes, Michael Woods; *D:* Dan Curtis. **VHS, Beta** *MPI* ♫½

War & Remembrance: The Final Chapter, Part 8 The final episodes of Herman Wouk's sweeping saga, following "The Winds of War" and "War and Remembrance," deal with the struggle of a Jewish family in war-torn Europe. Natalie and her son, Louis, are trapped in a ghetto under the reign of a vicious Nazi, who considers a bribe for the sake of the mother and son. On 5 cassettes.
1989 120m/C Robert Mitchum, Jane Seymour, Hart Bochner, Victoria Tennant, Polly Bergen, David Dukes, Michael Woods, Sharon Stone, Robert Morley, Sami Frey, Chaim Topol, John Rhys-Davies, Ian McShane, William Schallert, Jeremy Kemp, Steven Berkoff, Robert Hardy, Ralph Bellamy, John Gielgud; *D:* Dan Curtis. **VHS, Beta** $99.98 *MPI, MOV* ♫½

War & Remembrance: The Final Chapter, Part 9 Both D-Day and an assasination of Hitler are in the works. Natalie and Louis are still in a desperate situation with the tyrannical Nazi endangering them constantly.

1989 120m/C Robert Mitchum, Jane Seymour, Hart Bochner, Victoria Tennant, Polly Bergen, David Dukes, Michael Woods; **D:** Dan Curtis. **VHS, Beta** MPI 𝄞½

War & Remembrance: The Final Chapter, Part 10 Though Louis becomes gravely ill, Natalie and Aaron are shipped to Auschwitz. Hitler lives in spite of the botched assasination threat, but the allies are closing in rapidly.
1989 120m/C Robert Mitchum, Jane Seymour, Hart Bochner, Victoria Tennant, Polly Bergen, David Dukes, Michael Woods; **D:** Dan Curtis. **VHS, Beta** MPI 𝄞½

War & Remembrance: The Final Chapter, Part 11 The infamous Battle of the Bulge takes place. Louis is taken away in the Nazi retreat. Natalie and Aaron continue to defy death in Auschwitz.
1989 120m/C Robert Mitchum, Jane Seymour, Hart Bochner, Victoria Tennant, Polly Bergen, David Dukes, Michael Woods; **D:** Dan Curtis. **VHS, Beta** MPI 𝄞½

War & Remembrance: The Final Chapter, Part 12 The climax culminates into the death of both FDR and Hitler, whose suicide shocked and relieved an entire world. The Nazi reign of terror crumbles, and the allies are victorious. But this series ends on the note of displacement and the effort of rebuilding what has so quickly and deftly been destroyed.
1989 120m/C Robert Mitchum, Jane Seymour, Hart Bochner, Victoria Tennant, Polly Bergen, David Dukes, Michael Woods; **D:** Dan Curtis. **VHS, Beta** MPI 𝄞½

War Between the Tates A college professor's affair with a female student is the basis for a tension filled stand-off with his wife. Mediocre made for television adaptation of the Allison Lurie novel, somewhat redeemed by Ashley's performance.
1976 90m/C Richard Crenna, Elizabeth Ashley, Granville Van Dusen; **D:** Lee Philips; **M:** John Barry. **VHS, Beta** TLF 𝄞𝄞

The War Boy Difficulties encountered by a young Canadian boy as he grows up in Central Europe during WWII. Not to be compared with ''Empire of the Sun'' or ''Hope and Glory,'' both of which were released later; successful in its modest ambitions. Beautiful performance from 12-year-old star Hopely.
1985 (R) 86m/C CA Helen Shaver, Kenneth Welsh, Jason Hopely; **D:** Allan Eastman. **VHS** $79.98 HHE 𝄞𝄞½

War Brides Civil War brides confront life after the war. Low-budget drama.
198? 100m/C Elizabeth Richardson, Sharry Fleet, Sonja Smits. **VHS, Beta** $49.95 TWE 𝄞

War Bus Commando A fully loaded bus is the only way out when soldiers are caught behind enemy lines in Afghanistan. A case of the spoof coming first: The plot is almost exactly the same as ''Stripes''—only this one isn't funny. In Hi-Fi.
1989 90m/C IT Savina Gersak, Mark Gregory, John Vernon; **D:** Frank Valenti. **VHS** NO 𝄞

War Games A young computer whiz, thinking that he's sneaking an advance look at a new line of video games, breaks into the country's NORAD missile-defense system and challenges it to a game of Global Thermonuclear Warfare. The game might just turn out to be the real thing. Slick look at the possibilities of an accidental start to World War III. Entertaining and engrossing, but with a B-grade ending.
1983 (PG) 110m/C Matthew Broderick, Dabney Coleman, John Wood, Ally Sheedy; **D:** John Badham. **VHS, Beta, LV** $19.98 FOX 𝄞𝄞½

War in Space Powerful U.N. Space Bureau Starships and UFOs band together to battle alien invaders among the volcanoes and deserts of Venus.
1977 91m/C JP Kensaku Marita, Yuko Asano, Ryo Ikebe. **VHS, Beta** VDA 𝄞

War in the Sky Director William Wyler's documentary account of the Army Air Corps in action. Extraordinary footage of the Thunderbolt, the P47 Fighter, and the B17 Bomber.
1982 90m/C **D:** William Wyler. **VHS, Beta** $59.95 GEM 𝄞𝄞𝄞

War Kill A man fights for his country in this violent war saga.
1968 99m/C Tom Drake, George Montgomery; **D:** Ferde Grofe Jr. **VHS, Beta** NO 𝄞

The War Lord Set in the 11th century, Heston stars as Chrysagon, a Norman knight and war lord who commands a peasant village. While battling his enemies, he becomes enamored of a peasant girl named Bronwyn (Forsyth), who is unfortunately engaged to someone else. Pulling rank, Chrysagon uses an ancient law that allows noblemen the first night with a bride and the two fall in love. The two vow to never part, but that sets the stage for even more bloody battles. Fine acting and great production values make this a well-adapted version of the play ''The Lovers'' by Leslie Stevens.
1965 121m/C Charlton Heston, Richard Boone, Rosemary Forsyth, Guy Stockwell, Niall MacGinnis, Henry Wilcoxon, James Farentino, Maurice Evans, Michael Conrad; **D:** Franklin J. Schaffner; **W:** John Collier, Millard Kaufman. **VHS, Beta** $19.98 MCA 𝄞𝄞𝄞

War Lover An American daredevil flying captain and his co-pilot find themselves vying for the affections of a woman during WWII in England. Seeks human frailty beneath surface heroism. McQueen is impressive, no thanks to mediocre script, and featuring one of only a very few serviceable WWII B-17s then remaining. Based on John Hersey's novel.
1962 105m/B GB Steve McQueen, Robert Wagner, Shirley Anne Field, Bill Edwards, Gary Cockrell; **D:** Philip Leacock. **VHS, Beta, LV** $9.95 GKK 𝄞𝄞½

The War of the Colossal Beast This sequel to ''The Amazing Colossal Man'' finds the seventy-foot Colonel Manning even angrier at the attempts to kill him than he was in the first film. So he wreaks more havoc until scolded by his sister into committing suicide for being such a troublemaker. Cheesy special effects but good for a laugh. **AKA:** The Terror Strikes.
1958 68m/B Dean Parkin, Sally Fraser, Russ Bender, Roger Pace, Charles Stewart; **D:** Bert I. Gordon. **VHS** $9.95 COL 𝄞½

War of the Gargantuas Tokyo is once again the boxing ring for giant monsters. This time it's a good gargantua (half human, half monster) against a bad gargantua. This is a strange one. **AKA:** Furankenshutain No Kaijusanda Tai Gailah; Sanda Tai Gailah; Duel of the Gargantuas.
1970 (G) 92m/C JP Russ Tamblyn, Kimi Mizuno, Kipp Hamilton, Yu Fujiki. **VHS** PAR 𝄞

War of the Robots A dying alien civilization kidnaps two brilliant Earth scientists in the hope that they'll help it survive.
1978 99m/C Antonio Sabato, Melissa Long, James R. Stuart. **VHS, Beta, LV** $59.95 UHV 𝄞

The War of the Roses Acidic black comedy about a well-to-do suburban couple who can't agree on a property settlement in their divorce so they wage unreserved and ever-escalating combat on each other, using

their palatial home as a battleground. Expertly and lovingly (if that's the word) directed by DeVito, who plays the lawyer. Turner and Douglas are splendid. Laserdisc version includes previously deleted scenes and commentary from DeVito.
1989 (R) 116m/C Michael Douglas, Kathleen Turner, Danny DeVito, Marianne Sagebrecht, Sean Astin, G.D. Spradlin, Peter Donat; **D:** Danny DeVito. **VHS, Beta, LV** $12.00 FOX, IME 𝄞𝄞𝄞

War of the Shaolin Temple In 14th century China, a young boy is the only hope against a band of raiding Manchu warriors. Jammed with action.
19?? 90m/C Chan Kin Cheong. **VHS, Beta** OCE 𝄞½

War of the Wildcats Fast-moving western with Wayne as a tough cowboy battling a powerful land baron. They fight over land, oil and a woman. Unusual because Wayne's character acts on behalf of the Indians to drill and transport oil. **AKA:** In Old Oklahoma.
1943 102m/B John Wayne, Martha Scott, Albert Dekker, George ''Gabby'' Hayes, Sidney Blackmer; **D:** Albert Rogell. **VHS** $14.98 REP 𝄞𝄞½

War of the Wizards Low-budget sci-fi thriller about an alien woman with supernatural powers who comes to take over the Earth. But, lucky for all earthlings, she's challenged by a hero-type just in the nick of time. **AKA:** The Phoenix.
1981 (PG) 90m/C Richard Kiel; **D:** Richard Caan. **VHS, Beta** NO 𝄞½

The War of the Worlds H.G. Wells's classic novel of the invasion of Earth by Martians, updated to 1950s California, with spectacular special effects of destruction caused by the Martian war machines. Pretty scary and tense; based more on Orson Welles's radio broadcast than on the book. Still very popular; hit the top 20 in sales when released on video. Classic thriller later made into a TV series. Produced by George Pal, who brought the world much sci-fi, including ''The Time Machine,'' ''Destination Moon,'' and ''When Worlds Collide,'' and who appears here as a street person.
1953 85m/C Gene Barry, Ann Robinson, Les Tremayne, Lewis Martin, Robert Cornthwaite, Sandro Giglio; **D:** Byron Haskin. Academy Awards '53: Best Special Effects; Nominations: Best Film Editing, Best Sound. **VHS, Beta, LV** $14.95 PAR 𝄞𝄞𝄞½

War Party During a 100-year commemoration of an Indian massacre in the Midwest, a murder occurs and a lynch mob chases a pack of young Blackfeet into the mountains before the inevitable showdown. A feeble attempt at portraying the unfair treatment of Native Americans. Un-subtle, Hollywood style, this time in favor of the Indians, and therefore un-serious. Too bad; the premise had potential.
1989 (R) 99m/C Kevin Dillon, Billy Wirth, Tim Sampson, M. Emmet Walsh; **D:** Franc Roddam. **VHS, Beta, LV** $89.99 HBO 𝄞

War Victims Drama about Japanese POW prisons in World War II.
1985 90m/C IT **VHS, Beta** $59.95 VCD 𝄞½

The War Wagon The Duke plans revenge on Cabot, the greedy mine owner who stole his gold claim and framed him for murder for which he spent years in prison. He assembles a gang to aid him, including a wise-cracking Indian (Keel) and the man sent by Cabot to kill him (Douglas). Wayne's plan is to steal the gold being shipped in Cabot's armor-plated stagecoach, the ''war wagon.''

Well-written, good performances, lots of action. Based on the book ''Badman'' by Clair Huffaker. The laserdisc version is available in letterbox format.
1967 101m/C John Wayne, Kirk Douglas, Howard Keel, Robert Walker Jr., Keenan Wynn, Bruce Dern, Bruce Cabot, Joanna Barnes; **D:** Burt Kennedy. **VHS, Beta, LV** $19.98 *MCA* 🎭🎭🎭

Warbirds American pilots are off to quell a revolution in a Middle East country. Too little action fails to support mediocre plot and characters.
1988 (R) 88m/C Jim Eldert, Cully Holland, Bill Brinsfield; **D:** Ulli Lommel. **VHS, Beta** $19.95 *STE, VMK* 🎭🎭

Warbus Marines lead a school bus load of Americans through war-torn Vietnam to safety. Decent action and surprisingly enjoyable characters. Otherwise mediocre.
1985 (R) 90m/C Daniel Stephen, Romano Kristoff, Urs Althaus; **D:** Ted Kaplan. **VHS, Beta** $19.98 *SUE, NLC* 🎭🎭

WarCat The daughter of a green beret fights for her life against a blood-thirsty gang. Also known as ''Angel of Vengeance.''
1988 78m/C Macka Foley, Jannina Poynter, David O'Hara, Carl Erwin; **D:** Ted V. Mikels. **VHS** $79.95 *TWE* 🎭

Ward Six An insane asylum is the setting for various analogies regarding the perception of reality as defined by societal values. When it is felt that the residing physician is no more sane than his patients, he is placed among them, in Ward Six. Adapted from a story by Anton Chekhov. In Serbian with English subtitles.
1977 93m/C *YU* **D:** Lucian Pintilie, **VHS, Beta** $59.95 *FCT* 🎭

Wardogs A man tries to rescue his brother from becoming one of an elite, brainwashed group of ex-Vietnam vets trained by the government as professional assassins. Might not have been quite so bad; promising inversion of many 'Nam cliches wrecked by unnecessary violence and bad acting. *AKA:* The Assassination Team.
1987 95m/C *SW* Tim Earle, Bill Redvers, Daniel Hubenbecker; **D:** Daniel Hubenbecker. **Beta** *NO* 🎭½

Warkill WWII action set in the jungles of the Philippines. Journalist who idolizes violent, hard-edged colonel, loses his illusions, but gains a more genuine respect for his men. Not-bad war flick.
1965 99m/C George Montgomery, Tom Drake, Eddie Infante; **W/D:** Ferde Grofe Jr. **VHS, Beta** $19.95 *AHV* 🎭🎭½

Warlock Claustrophic, resonant town-bound tale of a marshal (Fonda) and his adoring sidekick (Quinn) who clean up a town which then turns against him. Unusual story, fine performances carry this well beyond the run-of-the-mill cow flick. Fonda re-established himself at the box office as a western star, after ''Stage Struck'' and ''Twelve Angry Men.'' Script by Robert Alan Arthur from the novel by Oakley Hall. ''Bones'' McCoy from ''Star Trek'' has a small part.
1959 122m/C Henry Fonda, Anthony Quinn, Richard Widmark, Dorothy Malone, Wallace Ford, Richard Astin, Regis Toomey, DeForest Kelley; **D:** Edward Dmytryk; **M:** Jerry Goldsmith. **VHS, Beta** $19.98 *FOX* 🎭🎭🎭

Warlock It's 1691 and the most powerful warlock (Sands) in the New World is only hours away from execution. Luckily, his pal, Satan, whisks him (and witchhunter Grant, by mistake) three hundred years in the future to present-day Los Angeles, where he crash-lands in Singer's house. Surprisingly witty dialogue and neat plot twists outshine occasionally cheesy special effects.
1991 (R) 103m/C Richard E. Grant, Julian Sands, Lori Singer, Mary Woronov; **D:** Steve Miner. **VHS** $92.95 *VMK* 🎭🎭½

Warlock Moon Young woman is lured to a secluded spa and falls prey to a coven of witches.
1973 75m/C *MX* Laurie Walters, Joe Spano; **D:** Bill Herbert. **VHS, Beta** $49.95 *UNI* 🎭½

Warlords Lone soldier Carradine battles mutant hordes in a post-apocalyptic desert. Amateurish futuristic drivel.
1988 (R) 87m/C David Carradine, Sid Haig, Ross Hagen, Fox Harris, Robert Quarry, Victoria Sellers, Brinke Stevens, Dawn Wildsmith; **D:** Fred Olen Ray. **VHS, Beta, LV** $79.95 *VMK* 🎭½

Warlords from Hell Two young men motorcycling through Mexico are captured by a bloodthirsty gang and forced to do hard labor in the marijuana fields. We can only hope that they just learn to say no.
1987 (R) 76m/C Brad Henson, Jeffrey Rice; **D:** Clark Henderson. **VHS, Beta** *WAR* Woof!

Warlords of the 21st Century Bandit gang speed around the galaxy in an indestructible battle cruiser. Then the boys are challenged by a space lawman. Gratuitously violent action pic lacking real action. Filmed on planet New Zealand. *AKA:* Battletruck.
1982 91m/C Michael Beck, Annie McEnroe, James Wainwright; **D:** Harley Cokliss. **VHS, Beta** $19.98 *SUE* 🎭½

Warm Nights on a Slow-Moving Train A hot-blooded schoolteacher turns tricks for cash to support her brother on the Sunday-night train to Melbourne, until she meets a stranger who has a deadly masquerade of his own. Interestingly different; much sex, as you can imagine. Australian-made.
1987 (R) 90m/C *AU* Wendy Hughes, Colin Friels, Norman Kaye, John Clayton, Peter Whitford; **D:** Bob Ellis. **VHS, Beta, LV** $79.95 *PSM, PAR* 🎭🎭

Warm Summer Rain A young couple meet under unusual circumstances and develop a relationship in a desert cabin as they reflect on their unfulfilled pasts. Lust, self-doubt and longing for something to hold onto draw them together as the days pass. Thoroughly self-indulgent romantic comedy tht's oddly self-pitying and poorly directed.
1989 (R) 85m/C Kelly Lynch, Barry Tubb; **D:** Joe Gayton. **VHS, Beta, LV** $19.95 *COL* 🎭½

Warner Brothers Cartoon Festival 1 Includes ''Corny Concerto,'' ''Dover Boys,'' ''Hamateur Night,'' ''Wackiki Wabbit,'' ''Tale of Two Kitties,'' ''Daffy and the Dinosaur,'' and ''Falling Hare.''
194? 55m/C **D:** Chuck Jones, Bob Clampett, Friz Freleng. **VHS, Beta** $34.95 *HHT, DVT* 🎭½

Warner Brothers Cartoon Festival 2 Includes ''Wacky Wabbit,'' ''Daffy the Commando,'' ''Case of the Missing Hare,'' ''Jungle Jitters,'' ''All This and Rabbit Stew,'' ''Have You Got Any Castiles,'' ''Fresh Hare,'' and ''Inki and the Mina Bird.''
194? 55m/C **D:** Friz Freleng, Bob Clampett, Chuck Jones, Robert McKimson. **VHS, Beta** $34.95 *HHT, DVT* 🎭½

Warner Brothers Cartoon Festival 3 Includes ''Robin Hood Makes Good,'' ''Flop Goes the Weasel,'' ''Fony Fables,'' ''Pigs in a Polka,'' ''Fox Pop,'' ''Fifth Column Mouse,'' and ''Wabbit Who Came to Supper.''
194? 55m/C **D:** Chuck Jones, Friz Freleng, Robert McKimson, Bob Clampett. **VHS, Beta** $34.95 *HHT, DVT* 🎭½

Warner Brothers Cartoon Festival 4 Eight cartoons are included in this package, including ''Presto Change-O,'' ''Porky's Bare Facts,'' ''Get Rich Quick, Porky,'' ''Finn 'N Catty,'' ''Sheepish Wolf,'' ''Yankee Doodle Daffy,'' ''Porky's Railroad,'' and ''Bugs Bunny Bond Rally.''
194? 55m/C **D:** Chuck Jones, Bob Clampett, Friz Freleng. **VHS, Beta** $34.95 *HHT, DVT* 🎭½

The Warning A pair of proverbial honest cops investigate ties between the mob and the police department. Hard to follow.
1980 101m/C *IT* Martin Balsam, Giuliano Gemma, Giancarlo Zanetti; **D:** Damiano Damiani. **VHS, Beta** $49.95 *MED* 🎭

Warning from Space Aliens visit Earth to warn of impending cosmic doom. When it becomes apparent that the one-eyed starfish look is off-putting, they assume human form. Japanese sci fi. *AKA:* The Mysterious Satellite; The Cosmic Man Appears in Tokyo; Space Men Appear in Tokyo; Unknown Satellite Over Tokyo; Uchujin Tokyo Ni Arawaru.
1956 87m/B *JP* Toyomi Karita, Keizo Kawasaki, Isao Yamagata, Shozo Nanbu, Buntaro Miake, Mieko Nagai, Kiyoko Hirai; **D:** Koji Shima. **VHS** $19.98 *NOS, SMW, SNC* 🎭½

Warning Shadows Classic example of interior German Expressionism. Brilliantly portrays a jealous husband's emotions and obsessions through shadows. Innocent events seem to reek of sin. A seldom-seen study of the oft-precarious distinction between love and obsession; directly influenced by the classic ''The Cabinet of Dr. Caligari.'' Silent with German and English titles.
1923 93m/B *GE* Fritz Kortner; **D:** Arthur Robinson. **VHS, Beta, 8mm** $19.95 *GPV, FCT, VPR* 🎭🎭🎭

Warning Sign A high-tech thriller in which a small town is terrorized by the accidental release of an experimental virus at a research facility. Shades of ''The Andromeda Strain'' and ''The China Syndrome,'' though less originality and quality.
1985 (R) 99m/C Sam Waterston, Kathleen Quinlan, Yaphet Kotto, Richard Dysart, Rick Rossovich; **D:** Hal Barwood. **VHS, Beta** $79.98 *FOX* 🎭½

The Warrior A young warrior is trapped in a corrupt ring of competitive boxing and karate.
197? 50m/C Dennis Brown, Cheng Tien Chi. **VHS, Beta** $49.95 *OCE* 🎭

The Warrior & the Sorceress Mercenary Carradine offers his services to rival factions fighting for control of a water well in an impoverished desert village located on a planet with two suns. He attempts to aggravate the conflicts between the factions, playing the shifty go-between. The sorceress is topless throughout. ''A Fistful of Dollars'' goes to outer space. Inoffensive, except that better judgment is expected of Carradine.
1984 (R) 81m/C David Carradine, Luke Askew, Maria Socas, Harry Townes; **D:** John Broderick. **VHS, Beta, LV** $29.98 *LIV, VES* 🎭½

Warrior of the Lost World A warrior must destroy the evil Omega Force who tyrannically rules the world in the distant future, etcetera, etcetera. One-size-fits-all premise; horrible special effects; miserably directed. Only for really hard-core Pleasance fans.
1984 90m/C Robert Ginty, Persis Khambatta, Donald Pleasence; **D:** David Worth. **VHS, Beta** $69.99 *HBO* Woof!

Warrior Queen Long ago in ancient Rome, overly histrionic mayor Pleasance married porn queen with a wandering eye Fox, and much gratuitous sex and erupting volcanoes resulted. Even the score blows. Also available in an "Unrated" version. Brit pop star Fox is billed as Stasia Micula.
1987 (R) 69m/C Sybil Danning, Donald Pleasence, Richard Hill, Josephine Jacqueline Jones, Tally Chanel, Samantha Fox. **VHS, LV** $79.98 LIV, VES ♂

Warrior Within Eight Kung Fu greats pay tribute to the memory of Bruce Lee by kicking and jumping about.
1980 85m/C Chuck Norris, Dan Inosanto, Mike Stone, Fumio Demura, Ron Taganashi. **VHS, Beta** NO ♂

The Warriors Swashbuckling adventure about Prince Edward's valiant rescue of Lady Joan and her children from the clutches of the evil Count De Ville. Flynn looks old and pudgy, but buckles his way gallantly through intrepid adventure. Also the last Flynn to see: fun, but more or less completely derivative and familiar. Filmed in England. **AKA:** The Dark Avenger.
1955 85m/C GB Errol Flynn, Peter Finch, Joanne Dru, Yvonne Furneaux, Noel Willman, Michael Hordern; **D:** Henry Levin. **VHS, Beta** $59.98 FOX, MLB ♂♂½

The Warriors An action story about a turf battle between New York City street gangs that rages from Coney Island to the Bronx. Silly plot works because of fine performances and direction, excellent use of action and color, and nonstop pace. Fight scenes are very carefully, even obviously, choreographed.
1979 (R) 94m/C Michael Beck, James Remar, Deborah Van Valkenburgh, Thomas G. Waites, David Patrick Kelly; **D:** Walter Hill. **VHS, Beta, LV** $14.95 PAR ♂♂½

Warriors from Hell Western forces in a small African country battle rebel fighters who threaten the hapless native villagers.
1990 (R) 90m/C Deon Stewardson, Shayne Leith, Adrienne Pierce, Glen Gabela, Hector Manthanda, Ivan Dean, Connie Chume; **W/D:** Ronnie Isaacs. **VHS** $89.95 COL ♂½

Warriors of Fire A crime lord has a young girl killed, and her sister becomes a bloodthirsty ninja in order to wreak revenge.
198? 91m/C Glen Carson, Peter Davis, Joff Houston; **D:** Bruce Lambert. **VHS, Beta** $59.95 TWE ♂

Warriors of the Apocalypse After a nuclear holocaust, heavily sworded and loin-clothed men search for the secret of eternal life and instead find an Amazon realm in the jungle. A terrible waste of post-apocalyptic scenery. **AKA:** Searchers of the Voodoo Mountain; Time Raiders.
1985 (R) 96m/C Michael James, Debrah Moore, Ken Metcalfe, Franco Guerrero; **D:** Bobby Suarez. **VHS, Beta** $19.98 LIV Woof!

Warriors of the Sung Dynasty Warriors given amnesty by the Emperor are tricked into a bloody confrontation. Adaption of a classic Chinese tale.
19?? 90m/C Mu Huan Hu. **VHS** $34.95 OCE ♂

Warriors of the Wasteland It's the year 2019, and the world has been devastated by a nuclear war. The few survivors try to reach a distant land which emits radio signals indicating the presence of human life. They are hindered by attacks from the fierce homosexual Templars, led by a self-proclaimed priest called One. Mindless rip-off of "Road Warrior" and obviously made on the proverbial shoestring budget. Dubbed. **AKA:** The New Barbarians; I Nuovi Barbari.
1983 (R) 92m/C IT Fred Williamson, Timothy Brent, Anna Kanakis; **D:** Enzo G. Castellari. **VHS, Beta** $69.99 HBO, SIM Woof!

Warriors of the Wind An animated sword-and-sorcery tale about a magical land being fought over by the forces of good and evil.
1985 (PG) 85m/C JP **D:** Kazuo Komatsubara. **VHS, Beta** $9.95 NWV, STE, WTA ♂♂♂

The Wash Quiet domestic drama about a couple who drift apart after 40 years of marriage. Set interestingly among Japanese-Americans in California; treats social and cultural factors with intelligence. Superb cast takes it a notch higher.
1988 94m/C Mako, Nobu McCarthy, Sab Shimono; **D:** Michael Toshiyuki Uno. **VHS, Beta, LV** $79.95 ACA ♂♂♂

Washington Affair A tale of intrigue in the nation's capital. Sullivan is a businessman who uses women and blackmail to capture government contracts. Selleck is the hapless bureaucrat he preys on. Remake of Soloff's own "Intimacy" was not released until "Magnum P.I." became a hit.
1977 (PG) 90m/C Tom Selleck, Carol Lynley, Barry Sullivan; **D:** Victor Stoloff. **VHS, Beta** $69.98 SUE ♂♂

Washington Mistress Eminently ordinary made-for-TV grist about Capitol Hill aide Arnaz, politician Jordan, and their affair. Listless performances.
1981 96m/C Lucie Arnaz, Richard Jordan, Tony Bill; **D:** Peter Levin. **VHS** NO ♂½

The Wasp Woman In her quest for eternal beauty, a woman uses a potion made from wasp enzymes. Naturally, she turns into a wasp monster at night. Good fun, courtesy of Corman.
1949 84m/B Susan Cabot, Anthony Eisley, Barboura Morris, Michael Marks, William Roerick, Frank Gerstle, Bruno Ve Sota, Frank Wolff; **D:** Roger Corman. **VHS** $9.95 NOS, RHI, SNC ♂½

Watch It Four self-absorbed twenty-something guys share a house in Chicago for the summer. They pursue a post-adolescent game, consisting of increasingly complicated practical jokes, where the unsuspecting victim is set up for a "watch it" gag. The rivalry escalates, and turns increasingly unpleasant, when cousins John and Michael vie for the affections of Anne, who's wary of involvement because of male selfishness. A first-rate cast with recognizable situations and emotions.
1993 (R) 102m/C Jon Tenney, Peter Gallagher, Suzy Amis, John C. McGinley, Tom Sizemore, Lili Taylor, Cynthia Stevenson; **W/D:** Tom Flynn; **M:** Stanley Clarke. **VHS** PAR ♂♂½

Watch Me When I Kill We'd rather not. A young nightclub dancer stops by a drugstore seconds after the owner was killed. She doesn't see the killer's face, but his rasping voice remains to torment her and the viewer. Dubbed.
1981 (R) 95m/C IT Richard Stewart, Sylvia Kramer, Anthony Bido. **VHS, Beta** $19.99 HBO ♂

Watch on the Rhine A couple involved with the anti-Nazi underground has escaped the country, but is pursued and harassed by Nazi agents. Adapted by Lillian Hellman and Dashiell Hammett from Hellman's play. Performed on stage before the U.S. entered the war, it was the first American play and movie to portray the ugliness of fascism as an ideology, as opposed to the more devious evil of its practical side. The Production Code at the time required that a killer always be punished; the murderer (whose screen motives had been noble) refused to film the offending scene, which explains the tacked-on ending. Superb drama from a pair of highly gifted writers and a great cast. Shumlin also directed the play.
1943 114m/B Bette Davis, Paul Lukas, Donald Woods, Beulah Bondi, Geraldine Fitzgerald, George Coulouris, Henry Daniell; **D:** Herman Shumlin. Academy Awards '43: Best Actor (Lukas); Nominations: Best Picture, Best Screenplay, Best Supporting Actress (Watson); Golden Globe Awards '44: Best Actor—Drama (Lukas); National Board of Review Awards '43: 10 Best Films of the Year; New York Film Critics Awards '43: Best Actor (Lukas), Best Film. **VHS, Beta** $19.98 FOX, MGM, FCT ♂♂♂½

Watch Out, Crimson Bat! Blind swords-woman must deliver a sack containing a valuable secret which can win a war.
1969 87m/C Yoko Matsuyama, Goro Ibuki. **VHS, Beta** VDA ♂

Watch the Birdie It's Skelton three times over as cameraman, father, and grandfather! First, he accidentally films a scam that would send the lovely Miss Dahl filing for bankruptcy. Later a crazy chase scene unfolds, that will have viewers rolling, as Skelton the cameraman nabs the bad guys and turns them over to the cops. Light fun that will charm Skelton fans.
1950 70m/B Red Skelton, Arlene Dahl, Ann Miller, Leon Ames; **D:** Jack Donohue. **VHS, Beta** $19.98 MGM ♂♂½

Watched A former U.S. attorney, gone underground, has a nervous breakdown and kills the narcotics agent who has him under surveillance. Self-important, too serious social/political conspiracy drama of the Watergate era. Keach and Yulin are good, but not good enough to save it. Music score written and performed by the jazz/fusion band Weather Report.
1973 95m/C Stacy Keach, Harris Yulin, Bridgit Polk; **D:** John Parsons. **VHS, Beta** $69.98 LIV, VES, SIM ♂♂

Watcher in the Woods When an American family rents an English country house, the children are haunted by the spirit of a long-missing young girl. A very bland attempt at a ghost story.
1981 (PG) 83m/C Bette Davis, Carroll Baker, David McCallum, Ian Bannen, Lynn-Holly Johnson; **D:** John Hough. **VHS, Beta** $14.99 DIS ♂♂

Watchers From the suspense novel by Dean R. Koontz, a secret experiment goes wrong, creating half-human monsters. A boy and his extremely intelligent dog are soon pursued. Low-budget, Corman-influenced production is tacky but effective.
1988 (R) 99m/C Barbara Williams, Michael Ironside, Corey Haim; **D:** Jon Hess. **VHS, Beta, LV** $14.95 LIV ♂♂

Watchers 2 Sequel to "Watchers" follows the further adventures of a super-intelligent golden retriever who leads a Marine to an animal psychologist and then attempts to warn them both of a mutant killer. The dog says woof, but this movie doesn't quite. Fun for lovers of hounds or horror flicks.
1990 (R) 101m/C Marc Singer, Tracy Scoggins; **D:** Thierry Notz. **VHS, Beta, LV** $14.95 LIV ♂♂

Water The resident governor of a Caribbean British colony juggles various predatory interests when a valuable mineral water resource is found. The good cast is wasted in this all-too-silly effort.
1985 (PG-13) 89m/C GB Michael Caine, Brenda Vaccaro, Leonard Rossiter, Valerie Perrine, Jimmie Walker; **Cameos:** Eric Clapton, George Harrison, Fred Gwynne, Ringo Starr; **D:** Dick Clement. **VHS, Beta** $29.95 PAR ♂

Water Babies When a chimney sweep's 12-year-old apprentice is wrongly accused of stealing silver, the boy and his dog fall into a pond and eventually rescue some of the characters they find there. Combination of live-action and animated fairy-tale story set in nineteenth-century London. Boring, unless you're a young child with equivalent standards. Based on the book by Charles Kingsley. *AKA:* Slip Slide Adventures.
1979 93m/C *GB* James Mason, Billie Whitelaw, David Tomlinson, Paul Luty, Sammantha Coates; *D:* Lionel Jeffries. **VHS, Beta** $29.98 *SUE* 🎬🎬

Water Rustlers Unscrupulous land baron builds a dam on his side of the creek with the intention of drying out the cattle pastures. Heroine Page, whose pop has been rubbed out by varmints, and good guy/lover O'Brien save her property and avenge her father. Second of three Page westerns.
1939 55m/B Dorothy Page, Dave O'Brien; *D:* Samuel Diege. **VHS, Beta** $27.95 *VCN, VDM* 🎬½

The Waterdance Autobiographical film based on the experiences of screenwriter and co-director Jimenez. When writer Joel Garcia (Stolz) is paralyzed in a hiking accident he finds himself dealing with not only the rehab process itself but his feelings, the feelings of his married lover, and those of his fellow patients. These include Bloss, a white racist with a doting mother, and Hill, a womanizing black man with a fed-up wife. The film deals unsentimentally with all the physical adjustments, including the sexual ones. Resolutions may be predictable but the performances rise above any script weaknesses. The title refers to Hill's dream of dancing on water—and the fear of drowning if he stops.
1991 (R) 106m/C Eric Stoltz, Wesley Snipes, William Forsythe, Helen Hunt, Elizabeth Pena, Grace Zabriskie; *D:* Michael Steinberg; *W/D:* Neal Jimenez. **VHS, LV** *COL, PMS* 🎬🎬🎬

Waterfront Nazis coerce German-Americans into helping them in World War II-era San Francisco. Credulity defying spy doings, but that's okay. Fairly entertaining wartime drama about paranoia on the home front.
1944 68m/B John Carradine, J. Carroll Naish, Terry Frost, Maris Wrixon, Edwin Maxwell; *D:* Steve Sekely. **VHS, Beta** $16.95 *SNC, UHV* 🎬🎬

Waterfront Effective romantic drama set in Melbourne, Australia. Australian workers strike after taking forced pay cuts. As a result, Italian immigrants are hired as scabs to keep the docks going. Despite the tension, an Italian woman and an Australian man fall deeply in love, only to find that they must struggle to keep that love alive.
1983 294m/C *AU* Jack Thompson, Greta Scacchi, Frank Gallacher, Tony Rickards, Mark Little, Jay Mannering, Ray Barrett, Chris Haywood, Warren Mitchell, Noni Hazlehurst, John Karlsen, Elin Jenkins; *D:* Chris Thomson. **VHS, Beta** $79.95 *PSM, PAR* 🎬🎬½

Waterhole #3 Three Confederate army buddies steal a fortune in gold bullion from the Union Army and hide it in a waterhole in the desert. One of the funnier entries in the Western comedy genre.
1967 (PG) 95m/C James Coburn, Carroll O'Connor, Margaret Blye, Claude Akins, Bruce Dern, Joan Blondell, James Whitmore; *D:* William A. Graham. **VHS** $14.95 *PAR* 🎬🎬½

Waterland Meandering drama about a history teacher who tries to solve a personal crisis by using his class as a sounding board to describe his troubled past in England. Dark secrets abound, including incest, madness, murder, and the terrifying love between the teacher and his childhood bride. Melancholy, overwrought but partially re-deemed by the lead performances of Irons and his (real-life and cinematic) wife, Cusack. The film's setting has been unfortunately moved from London to Pittsburgh, destroying story links. Based on the novel by Graham Swift.
1992 (R) 95m/C Jeremy Irons, Ethan Hawke, Sinead Cusack, John Heard, Grant Warnock, Lena Headey, Peter Postlethwaite, Cara Buono; *D:* Stephen Gyllenhaal; *W:* Peter Prince; *M:* Carter Burwell. **VHS, LV** *NLC, COL* 🎬🎬

Waterloo Massive chronicle of Napoleon's European conquests and eventual defeat at the hands of Wellington. Filmed on location in Italy and the Ukraine, it bombed due largely to Steiger's bizarre rendition of Napoleon.
1971 (G) 122m/C *IT RU* Rod Steiger, Orson Welles, Virginia McKenna, Michael Wilding, Donal Donnelly, Christopher Plummer, Jack Hawkins, Dan O'Herlihy, Terence Alexander, Rupert Davies, Ivo Garrani, Gianno Garko; *D:* Sergei Bondarchuk. **VHS** $14.95 *PAR, FCT* 🎬🎬

Waterloo Bridge In London during World War I, a soldier from an aristocratic family and a ballet dancer begin a tragic romance when they meet by chance on the foggy Waterloo Bridge. When he's listed as dead, her despair turns her to prostitution. But then he returns from POW camp, they once again meet by accident on Waterloo Bridge, and their romance resumes. Four-hanky drama with fine performances by Leigh (her first after "Gone with the Wind") and Taylor.
1940 109m/B Vivien Leigh, Robert Taylor, Lucile Watson, C. Aubrey Smith, Maria Ouspenskaya, Virginia Field; *D:* Mervyn LeRoy. **VHS, Beta, LV** $19.98 *MGM* 🎬🎬

Watermelon Man The tables are turned for a bigoted white guy when he wakes up one morning to discover he has become a black man. Broad comedy with not much place to go is still engaging. Cambridge takes on both roles, appearing in unconvincing white makeup.
1970 (R) 97m/C Godfrey Cambridge, Erin Moran, Estelle Parsons, Howard Caine; *D:* Melvin Van Peebles. **VHS, Beta, LV** $59.95 *COL, FCT* 🎬🎬

Watership Down Wonderfully animated story based on Richard Adams's allegorical novel about how a group of rabbits escape fear and overcome oppression while searching for a new and better home. It's really an adult theme with sufficient violence to the poor wittle wabbits to scare the kiddies.
1978 (PG) 92m/C *GB D:* Martin Rosen; *V:* Ralph Richardson, Zero Mostel, John Hurt, Denholm Elliott, Harry Andrews, Michael Hordern, Joss Ackland. **VHS, Beta, 8mm** $14.95 *WAR, VTK, TVC* 🎬🎬½

Wavelength A rock star living in the Hollywood Hills with his girlfriend stumbles on an ultra-secret government project involving friendly aliens from outer space recovered from a recent UFO crash site. Fun, enthusiastically unoriginal cheap sci-fi. Soundtrack by Tangerine Dream.
1983 (PG) 87m/C Robert Carradine, Cherie Currie, Keenan Wynn; *W/D:* Mike Gray. **VHS, Beta, LV** $9.98 *SUE, STE* 🎬🎬½

Waxwork A wax museum opens up, and it is soon evident that the dummies are not what they seem. Garbled nonthriller. Available in a 100-minute unrated version.
1988 (R) 97m/C Zach Galligan, Deborah Foreman, Michelle Johnson, Dana Ashbrook, Miles O'Keeffe, Patrick Macnee, David Warner; *D:* Anthony Hickox. **VHS, Beta, LV** $14.98 *LIV, VES* 🎬½

Waxwork 2: Lost in Time A young couple (Galligan and Schnarre) barely escape with their lives when the infamous waxworks museum burns down. A severed hand also gets loose and follows Schnarre home and murders her stepfather, leaving her to take the blame. In order to prove her innocence, the couple must travel through a bizarre time machine. Extraordinary special effects, strange plot twists, and recreations of scenes from past horror movies make this a highly entertaining sequel.
1991 (R) 104m/C Zach Galligan, Alexander Godunov, Bruce Campbell, Michael Des Barres, Monika Schnarre; *D:* Anthony Hickox. **VHS** $49.98 *LIV* 🎬🎬½

Waxworks A major achievement in German Expressionism, in which a poet imagines scenarios in a wax museum fairground that involve Jack the Ripper, Ivan the Terrible and Haroun al-Rashid. Influential and considered ahead of its time. Silent.
1924 63m/B *GE* William Dieterle, Emil Jannings, Conrad Veidt, Werner Krauss, John Gottowt, Olga Belajeff; *D:* Paul Leni; *W:* Henrik Galeen. **VHS, Beta** $16.95 *SNC, NOS, LIV* 🎬🎬🎬

Way Back Home Man wants to adopt a boy to release him from the clutches of his cruel guardian. Minor role for the then-unknown Davis. *AKA:* Old Greatheart; Other People's Business.
1932 81m/B Phillips Lord, Frank Albertson, Bette Davis; *D:* William A. Seiter. **VHS, Beta** $19.98 *TTC, FCT* 🎬🎬

Way Down East Melodramatic silent drama of a country girl who is tricked into a fake marriage by a scheming playboy. The famous final scene of Gish adrift on the ice floes is in color. One of Griffith's last critical and popular successes. This tape includes the original Griffith-approved musical score. Remade in 1935 with Henry Fonda.
1920 107m/B Lillian Gish, Richard Barthelmess, Lowell Sherman, Creighton Hale; *D:* D.W. Griffith. **VHS, Beta** $19.95 *NOS, KRT, VYY* 🎬🎬🎬

Way Down South The orphan son of a plantation owner tries to take over his father's estate, only to find out that the place has been run into the ground by a corrupt lawyer and a cruel slave driver. Langston Hughes and Clarence Muse—both black—collaborated on the screenplay, but the film was released by a then-major distributor. German-born director Vorhaus was in his second year in Hollywood, after making his mark in Britain directing talkies. 🎵Good Ground; Louisiana; Nobody Know De Trouble I See; Sometimes I Feel Like a Motherless Child; Lord I You Can't Even Send One Angel Down.
1939 62m/B Bobby Breen, Alan Mowbray, Ralph Morgan, Clarence Muse, Steffi Duna, Sally Blane, Edwin Maxwell, Hall Johnson Choir; *D:* Bernard Vorhaus. **VHS** $24.95 *NOS* 🎬½

Way He Was A satirical re-enactment of the events that led up to the Watergate burglary and the coverup that followed.
1976 (R) 87m/C Steve Friedman, Al Lewis, Merrie Lynn Ross, Doodles Weaver. **VHS, Beta** $54.95 *UHV* 🎬🎬

Way of the Black Dragon When slave-trading drug traffickers threaten the moral fiber of our nation, two commandoes join forces to halt their operation.
1981 88m/C Ron Van Cliff, Carter Wang, Charles Bonet; *D:* Chan Wui Ngai. **VHS, Beta** $39.95 *TWE* 🎬

Way of the West Them durn pesky sheepherders are up to it again! Okay, so the cow/sheep thing is a classic western plot, but here it's offered perfunctorily.

1935 52m/B Wally Wales, William Desmond, Art Mix, Jim Sheridan, Bobby Nelson; **D:** Robert Emmett. **VHS, Beta $19.95** *NOS, DVT, RXM* ✍✍½

The Way Out Average crime drama starring Nelson as a fugitive accused of killing a bookie. **AKA:** Dial 999.
1956 90m/C *GB* Gene Nelson, Mona Freeman, John Bentley, Michael Goodliffe, Sydney Tafler; **D:** Montgomery Tully. **VHS $16.95** *SNC* ✍✍

Way Out West The classic twosome journey way out west to deliver the deed to a gold mine to the daughter of their late prospector pal. The obligatory romance is missing, but you'll be laughing so hard you won't notice. One of Stan and Ollie's best. Score includes the song "Trail of the Lonesome Pine." Also included on this tape is a 1932 Todd and Pitts short, "Red Noses." Available colorized.
1937 86m/B Stan Laurel, Oliver Hardy, Rosina Lawrence, James Finlayson, Sharon Lynne, ZaSu Pitts, Thelma Todd; **D:** James W. Horne. **VHS, Beta $19.95** *CCB, MED, MLB* ✍✍✍

The Way We Were Big box-office hit follows a love story between opposites from the 1930s to the 1950s. Streisand is a Jewish political radical who meets the handsome WASP Redford at college. They're immediately attracted to one another, but it takes years before they act on it and eventually marry. They move to Hollywood where Redford is a screenwriter and left-wing Streisand becomes involved in the Red scare and the blacklist, much to Redford's dismay. Though always in love, their differences are too great to keep them together. An old-fashioned and sweet romance, with much gloss. Hit title song sung by Streisand. Adapted by Arthur Laurents from his novel.
1973 (PG) 118m/C Barbra Streisand, Robert Redford, Bradford Dillman, Viveca Lindfors, Herb Edelman, Murray Hamilton, Patrick O'Neal, James Woods, Sally Kirkland; **D:** Sydney Pollack; **M:** Marvin Hamlisch. Academy Awards '73: Best Song ("The Way We Were"), Best Original Score; Nominations: Best Actress (Streisand), Best Art Direction/Set Decoration, Best Cinematography; Academy Awards '76: Best Costume Design; National Board of Review Awards '73: 10 Best Films of the Year. **VHS, Beta, LV, 8mm $19.95** *COL, PIA* ✍✍

The Way West A wagon train heads to Oregon. A poor and muddled attempt at recreating the style of a John Ford western. What really galls is that it's based on the Pulitzer-winning novel by A.B. Guthrie, Jr. Boy, is the book better than the movie. Field's first film.
1967 122m/C Kirk Douglas, Robert Mitchum, Richard Widmark, Lola Albright, Michael Witney, Stubby Kaye, Sally Field, Jack Elam; **D:** Andrew V. McLaglen. **VHS $14.95** *MGM* ✍½

Wayne Murder Case A fast-moving, cleverly constructed murder mystery. A rich old man dies just as he is about to sign a new will. Though no one was standing near him, a knife is found stuck in his back. **AKA:** Strange Adventure.
1938 61m/B June Clyde, Regis Toomey, Jason Robards Sr. **VHS, Beta $12.95** *SNC, VYY, WGE* ✍✍✍

Wayne's World Destined to become one of the top movies of all time—Not! This "Saturday Night Live" skit proved to be so popular that it got its own movie, not unlike the plot, which has slimy producer Lowe take the public access "Wayne's World" into the world of commercial television. The zany duo of Wayne and Garth are as much fun on the big screen as they are on SNL and there are many funny moments, several of which are destined to become comedy classics. The

movie was a box office hit and there's talk in Hollywood of a sequel.
1992 (PG-13) 93m/C Mike Myers, Dana Carvey, Rob Lowe, Tia Carrere, Brian Doyle Murray, Lara Flynn Boyle, Kurt Fuller, Colleen Camp, Donna Dixon, Ed O'Neill; **Cameos:** Alice Cooper, Meatloaf; **D:** Penelope Spheeris; **W:** Mike Myers. **VHS, LV $24.95** *PAR, FCT* ✍✍✍

Ways of Kung Fu Reincarnation and multi-generation vendettas spice up this martial arts festival.
197? 95m/C **VHS, Beta $29.95** *UNI* ✍

W.C. Fields Comedy Bag Compilation of three classic Fields shorts: "The Golf Specialist" (1930), "The Dentist" (1932) and "The Fatal Glass of Beer" (1933).
1933 56m/B W.C. Fields, Babe Kane, Dorothy Granger, George Chandler. **VHS, Beta $19.95** *KRT* ✍

W.C. Fields: Flask of Fields Three classic Fields shorts: "The Golf Specialist" (1930), in which J. Effington Bellweather finds himself teaching a lovely young lady how to play the game; "The Fatal Glass of Beer" (1933); and "The Dentist" (1932), in which Fields tackles a room filled with patients.
1930 61m/B W.C. Fields, Babe Kane, Elise Cavanna, Bud Jamison, Rosemary Theby. **VHS, Beta, 8mm $24.95** *VYY* ✍

We All Loved Each Other So Much Sensitive comedy follows three friends over 30 years, beginning at the end of World War II. All three have loved the same woman, an actress. Homage to friendship and to postwar Italian cinema. Includes a full-scale recreation of the fountain scene in "La Dolce Vita." In Italian with English subtitles.
1977 124m/C *IT* Vittorio Gassman, Nino Manfredi, Stefano Satta Flores, Stefania Sandrelli, Marcello Mastroianni, Federico Fellini; **D:** Ettore Scola. **VHS, Beta, LV $59.95** *COL, APD, TAM* ✍✍✍

We are the Children Cynical reporter covering the famine in Ethiopia meets an idealistic nurse who's been living there for years. Romance blossoms among the starving in made-for-TV drama co-produced by Danson.
1987 92m/C Ally Sheedy, Ted Danson, Judith Ivey, Zia Mohyeddi; **D:** Robert M. Young. **VHS, Beta $79.95** *PSM* ✍✍

We Dive at Dawn Interesting, tense British submarine drama. The "Sea Tiger" attempts to sink the German battleship "Brandenburg" off Denmark. Good cast. Mills prepared for the role by riding an actual submarine, turning "a pale shade of peagreen" when it crash-dived.
1943 98m/B *GB* Eric Portman, John Mills; **D:** Anthony Asquith. **VHS, Beta $19.95** *NOS, WWV, DVT* ✍✍✍

We of the Never Never In turn-of-the-century Australia a city-bred woman marries a cattle rancher and moves from civilized Melbourne to the barren outback of the Northern Territory. Based on the autobiographical story written by Jeannie Gunn, the first white woman to travel in the aboriginal wilderness. She finds herself fighting for her own rights as well as for those of the aborigines in this sincere, well-done film.
1982 (G) 136m/C Angela Punch McGregor, Arthur Dignam, Tony Barry; **D:** Igor Auzins. **VHS, Beta $59.95** *COL* ✍✍✍

We the Living The torpid long-lost and restored Italian version of Ayn Rand's unique political tome. Deals with a young Soviet woman in revolutionary Petrograd who is slowly ruined by the system and her affair with a romantic counter-revolutionary. Made

under the Fascists' nose during World War II. A fascinating dialectic between utopian melodrama and Rand dogma. In Italian with subtitles.
1942 174m/B *IT* Alida Valli, Rossano Brazzi, Fosco Giachetti; **D:** Goffredo Alessandrini. **VHS, Beta, LV $49.95** *LUM* ✍✍½

We Think the World of You When bisexual Oldman goes to prison, his lover Bates, whose feelings are unresolved and complex, finds friendship with Oldman's dog. Odd, oft-bitter comedy-drama of love and loyalty characterized by excellent acting and respectful, gentle direction. From the novel by Joseph R. Ackerly.
1988 (PG) 94m/C *GB* Alan Bates, Gary Oldman, Frances Barber, Liz Smith, Max Wall, Kerry Wise; **D:** Colin Gregg. **VHS, Beta, LV $19.98** *SUE, NLC* ✍✍½

We Will Not Enter the Forest Moral dilemmas afflict a group of French Resistance fighters during WWII when they must decide what to do with four German deserters they've captured. In French with subtitles.
1979 88m/C *FR* Marie-France Pisier; **D:** Georges Dumoulin. **VHS, Beta $39.95** *FCT* ✍✍✍

Weapons of Death Kung Fu expert Lee splatters his enemies all over San Francisco's Chinatown.
1983 90m/C Eric Lee, Bob Ramos, Ralph Catellanos. **VHS, Beta** *PGN* ✍

Weather in the Streets A young woman enters into an ill-fated love affair after spending a few moments with an aristocratic married man. Cliched drama set in England between the two world wars.
1984 (PG) 108m/C Michael York, Joanna Lumley, Lisa Eichhorn, Isabel Dean, Norman Pitt. **VHS, Beta** *NO* ✍½

Web of Deceit Defense lawyer Purl returns to her Southern hometown to defend an unjustly accused teenager. She falls in love with the prosecutor, but could he be the killer? Shades of "Jagged Edge." Good, suspenseful made-for-TV movie.
1990 (PG-13) 93m/C Linda Purl, James Read, Paul DeSouza, Larry Black, Len Birman, Barbara Rush; **W/D:** Sandor Stern. **VHS, Beta** *PAR* ✍✍½

Web of Deception A jewel thief disappears with five million dollars worth of jewels. When the case turns to murder, a private detective becomes the prime suspect.
19?? (R) 90m/C Thomas Hunter, Aelina Nathaniel, Gabriele Tinti. **VHS, Beta** *NO* ✍✍

Web of the Spider Kinski as Poe is really the only good thing about this run-of-the-mill horror outing. A man stays the night in a spooky house to prove it's not haunted. Remake of "Castle of Blood." **AKA:** Nella Stretta M Orsa Del Ragno; In the Grip of the Spider; Dracula in the Castle of Blood; And Comes the Dawn...But Colored Red.
1970 94m/C *GE FR IT* Anthony (Tony) Franciosa, Klaus Kinski, Michele Mercier, Peter Carsten, Karen Field; **D:** Anthony Dawson. **VHS $16.95** *SNC* ✍✍

A Wedding The occasion of a wedding leads to complications galore for the relatives and guests on the happy day. Silent film legend Gish's 100th screen role. Miserable, self-indulgent outing for Altman, who went through quite a dry spell after "Nashville."
1978 (PG) 125m/C Mia Farrow, Carol Burnett, Lillian Gish, Lauren Hutton, Viveca Lindfors, Geraldine Chaplin, Paul Dooley, Howard Duff, Dennis Christopher, Peggy Ann Garner, John Considine, Nina Van Pallandt, Dina Merrill, Pat McCormick, Vittorio Gassman, Desi Arnaz Jr.; **D:** Robert Altman. **VHS, Beta $59.98** *FOX* ✍½

Wedding Band Episodic comedy about a rock 'n roll band that plays all sorts of weddings. Thin and lame but inoffensive.
1989 95m/C William Katt, Joyce Hyser, Tino Insana, Fran Drescher, David Rasche, Joe Flaherty, Tim Kazurinsky, James Belushi; **D:** Daniel Raskov. **VHS, Beta, LV** $89.95 *COL ♂♂*

Wedding in Blood Two French lovers plot to kill their respective spouses, and proceed to do so amid calamity and much table-turning. Sharp social satire and suspenseful mystery. Based on a true story. In French with English subtitles.
1974 (PG) 98m/C *FR IT* Claude Pieplu, Stephane Audran, Michel Piccoli; **D:** Claude Chabrol. **VHS, Beta** $69.95 *COL ♂♂♂*

A Wedding in Galilee The elder of a Palestinian village is given permission to have a traditional wedding ceremony for his son if Israeli military officers can attend as the guests of honor. As the event approaches, conflicts arise among the villagers, the family, and the Israelis. Long but fascinating treatment of traditional culture in the modern world amidst political tension. In Arabic and Hebrew, with English subtitles. *AKA:* Noce In Galilee.
1987 113m/C *BE FR* Ali M. El Aleili, Nazih Akleh, Anna Achdian; **D:** Michel Khleifi. **VHS, LV** $79.95 *KIV, TAM ♂♂♂*

Wedding in White A rape and out-of-wedlock pregnancy trouble a poor British clan living in Canada during World War II. Sad, glum way to spend an evening. Kane is good in a non-comic role. Her screen father cares more for her honor than he does for her.
1972 (R) 103m/C *CA* Donald Pleasence, Carol Kane, Leo Phillips; **D:** William Fruet. **VHS, Beta** $39.95 *SUE ♂♂*

Wedding March Von Stroheim's famous silent film about romantic couplings in pre-World War I Vienna. The director also stars as a prince preparing to marry for money, who falls in love with a beautiful, but poor woman. Romance and irony, with a memorable finale. Like many of his other great films, it was taken from him and re-edited. Initially the first of two halves; the second, "The Honeymoon," has been lost. Next to "Greed," his most successful film. Score by Gaylord Carter.
1928 113m/B Erich von Stroheim, Fay Wray, ZaSu Pitts, George Fawcett, Maude George, Matthew Betz; **D:** Erich von Stroheim. **VHS, Beta** $29.95 *PAR ♂♂♂♂*

The Wedding Party Apprehensive groom is overwhelmed by his too-eager bride and her inquisitive relatives at a prenuptial celebration. Hokey, dull, would-be comedy. First screen appearances of both Clayburgh and De Niro (spelled DeNero in the credits).
1969 90m/C Jill Clayburgh, Robert De Niro, William Finley; **D:** Brian DePalma, Cynthia Munroe, Wilford Leach. **VHS, Beta** $14.98 *VID ♂♂½*

Wedding Rehearsal A young nobleman thwarts his grandmother's plans to marry him off by finding suitors for all the young ladies offered to him until he finally succumbs to the charms of his mother's secretary. Enjoyable, fun comedy. First featured roles for actresses Oberon, Barrie, and Gardner.
1932 84m/B Merle Oberon, Roland Young, John Loder, Wendy Barrie, Maurice Evans, Joan Gardner; **D:** Alexander Korda. **VHS, Beta, LV** $SUE ♂♂½*

Wee Wendy Wee Wendy and her people are aliens who land on earth and set up a village on an island in a lake, in this children's animated movie.
1989 100m/C **VHS, Beta** $14.95 *CEL, WTA ♂♂½*

Wee Willie Winkie A precocious little girl is taken in by a British regiment in India. Sugar-coated. If you're a cinematic diabetic, be warned. If you're a Temple fan, you've probably already seen it. If not, you're in for a treat. Inspired by the Rudyard Kipling story.
1937 99m/B Shirley Temple, Victor McLaglen, C. Aubrey Smith, June Lang, Michael Whalen, Cesar Romero, Constance Collier; **D:** John Ford. **VHS, Beta** $19.98 *FOX ♂♂♂*

Weeds A highly fictionalized account of the career of Rick Cluchey, who, as a lifer in San Quentin federal prison, wrote a play. He was eventually paroled and went on to form a theater group made up of ex-cons. Original and often enjoyable with a tight ensemble performance. Filmed on location at Stateville Correctional Center in Illinois, with inmates serving as extras.
1987 (R) 115m/C Nick Nolte, Rita Taggart, William Forsythe, Lane Smith, Joe Mantegna, Ernie Hudson, John Toles-Bey, Mark Rolston, Anne Ramsey; **D:** John Hancock; **M:** Angelo Badalamenti. **VHS, Beta, LV** $19.99 *HBO ♂♂♂*

Weekend A Parisian couple embark on a drive to the country. On the way they witness and are involved in horrifying highway wrecks. Leaving the road they find a different, equally grotesque kind of carnage. Godard's brilliant, surreal, hyper-paranoiac view of modern life was greatly influenced by the fact that his mother was killed in an auto accident in 1954 (he himself suffered a serious motorcycle mishap in 1971) In French with English subtitles.
1967 105m/C *FR IT* Mireille Darc, Jean Yanne, Jean-Pierre Kalfon, Valerie Lagrange, Jean-Pierre Leaud, Yves Beneyton; **W/D:** Jean-Luc Godard. **VHS** $79.95 *NYF, FCT, TAM ♂♂♂*

Weekend at Bernie's Two computer nerds discover embezzlement at their workplace after being invited to their boss's beach house for a weekend party. They find their host murdered. They endeavor to keep up appearances by (you guessed it) dressing and strategically posing the corpse during the party. Kiser as the dead man is memorable, and the two losers gamely keep the silliness flowing. Lots of fun. *AKA:* Hot and Cold.
1989 (PG-13) 101m/C Andrew McCarthy, Jonathan Silverman, Catherine Mary Stewart, Terry Kiser; **D:** Ted Kotcheff. **VHS, VHS, Beta** $14.95 *LIV ♂♂½*

Weekend at Bernie's 2 Unlikely but routine sequel to the original's cavorting cadaver slapstick, except now McCarthy and Silverman are frantically hunting for Bernie's (Kiser) cash stash, a quest that takes them and poor dead Bernie to the Caribbean. Also after the missing loot are company snoop Bostwick and Kiser's mob cohorts, who have employed the help of a Virgin Islands voodoo queen. See Bernie get stuffed in a suitcase, see Bernie hang glide, see Bernie tango, see Bernie attract the opposite sex. Thin script with one-joke premise done to death but fun for those in that certain mood for the post-mortem antics of a comedic stiff. Plenty of well-executed gags involving the well-preserved corpse (particularly one that's been dead for two films now) should lure back fans of the 1989 predecessor. Nice footage of St. Thomas and the U.S. Virgin Islands complements cadaver caprice.

1993 (PG) 90m/C Andrew McCarthy, Jonathan Silverman, Terry Kiser, Tom Wright, Steve James, Troy Beyer, Barry Bostwick; **D:** Robert Klane; **W:** Robert Klane; **M:** Peter Wolf. **VHS** *NYR ♂♂*

Weekend at the Waldorf Glossy, americanized remake of "Grand Hotel" set at the famous Park Avenue hotel, the Waldorf-Astoria, in New York City. Turner and Rogers star in the roles originated by Joan Crawford and Greta Garbo. Johnson and Pidgeon play their love interests. Combining drawing room comedy with slapstick and a touch of romance proved to be a hit, as this film was one of the top grossers of 1945 and was just what war-weary moviegoers wanted to see. Based on the play "Grand Hotel" by Vicki Baum.
1945 130m/B Ginger Rogers, Walter Pidgeon, Van Johnson, Lana Turner, Robert Benchley, Edward Arnold, Leon Ames, Warner Anderson, Phyllis Thaxter, Keenan Wynn, Porter Hall, Samuel S. Hinds; **D:** Robert Z. Leonard; **W:** Samuel Spewack, Bella Spewack, Guy Bolton. **VHS** $19.98 *MGM ♂♂♂*

Weekend of Shadows Confident, moralistic murder drama about a posse after an innocent immigrant they believe has killed a woman. Police sergeant Roberts is interested only in his reputation, not in justice. Posse member Waters begins to sympathize with the hunted man and defends his innocence. Intelligent, well-conceived, and professionally directed.
1977 94m/C John Waters, Melissa Jaffer, Graeme Blundell, Wyn Roberts, Barbara West, Graham Rouse; **D:** Tom Jeffry. **VHS, Beta** $49.98 *SUE ♂♂♂*

Weekend Pass Moronic rookie sailors who have just completed basic training are out on a weekend pass, determined to forget everything they have learned. They find this surprisingly easy to do.
1984 (R) 92m/C D.W. Brown, Peter Ellenstein, Phil Hartman, Patrick Hauser, Chip McAllister; **D:** Lawrence Bassoff. **VHS, Beta, LV** $79.98 *LIV, VES ♂*

Weekend War A group of National Guardsmen are sent to the Honduras for their annual tour of duty. But when a guerilla war between Honduras and Nicaragua breaks out, the Guardsmen are forced to fight for their lives. The "Bridge on the River Kwai" finale features the dilemma over a bridge linking the two countries. Made for television.
1988 (PG-13) 96m/C Daniel Stern, Stephen Collins, Charles Haid, Evan Mirand, Michael Beach, Scott Paulin; **D:** Steven Hilliard Stern. **VHS** $59.95 *COL ♂♂½*

Weekend Warriors Young film-studio employees evade the draft in 1961 by enlisting for National Guard weekend duty. Grade "C" dumb comedy from professional celebrity and first-time director Convy.
1986 (R) 88m/C Chris Lemmon, Lloyd Bridges, Daniel Greene, Tom Villard, Vic Tayback; **D:** Bert Convy. **VHS, Beta** $79.98 *LIV ♂½*

Weekend with the Babysitter Sordid teen drama about a weekend babysitter who goes to a film director's house and babysits everyone but the kids, running into a heroin-smuggling ring along the way. Casting-couch story with a twist. *AKA:* Weekend Babysitter.
1970 (R) 93m/C Susan Roman, George E. Carey, James Almanzar, Luanne Roberts; **D:** Don Henderson. **VHS, Beta** $59.95 *PSM Woof!*

Weird Science Hall is appealing, and Hughes can write dialogue for teens with the best of them. However, many of the jokes are in poor taste, and the movie seems to go

on forever. Hall and his nerdy cohort Mitchell-Smith use a very special kind of software to create the ideal woman who wreaks zany havoc in their lives from the outset.
1985 (PG-13) 94m/C Kelly Le Brock, Anthony Michael Hall, Ilan Mitchell-Smith, Robert Downey Jr., Bill Paxton; *W/D:* John Hughes. **VHS, Beta, LV** $19.95 *MCA* 🎬🎬

Weird World of LSD Cheap exploitation film featuring the evil effects of LSD.
1967 ?m/C Terry Tessem, Ann Lindsay, Yolanda Morino. **VHS** $16.95 *SNC* 🎬½

The Weirdo "The Jerk" meets Freddie Krueger. This film is absolutely wretched, even by horror movie standards.
1989 91m/C Steve Burlington, Jessica Straus; *D:* Andy Milligan. **VHS, Beta** *NO* 🎬

Welcome Back Mr. Fox An award-winning science fiction short wherein an obnoxious movie producer cheats death by being cryogenically frozen, and then wakes up years later no wiser for the experience. Suitably, he receives his comeuppance.
1983 21m/C E.D. Phillips, Gustav Vintas; *D:* Walter W. Pitt III. **VHS, Beta** *NO* 🎬

Welcome Home A missing-in-action Vietnam vet (Kristofferson) leaves his wife and children in Cambodia to return to America more than 15 years after he was reported dead. He finds his first wife remarried and discovers a teen-aged son he unknowingly fathered. This plotless, sporadically-moving film was Schaffner's last. Made for cable television.
1989 (R) 92m/C Kris Kristofferson, JoBeth Williams, Sam Waterston, Brian Keith, Trey Wilson, Thomas Wilson Brown; *D:* Franklin J. Schaffner. **VHS, Beta, LV** $89.98 *VES, LIV* 🎬🎬

Welcome Home, Roxy Carmichael Ryder, as a young misfit, is the bright spot in this deadpan, would-be satire. Hollywood star Roxy Charmichael returns to her small Ohio hometown and begins fantasizing that she is really her mother. It is obvious why this deadpan, hard-to-follow movie was a box-office flop.
1990 (PG-13) 98m/C Winona Ryder, Jeff Daniels, Laila Robins, Dinah Manoff, Ava Fabian, Robbie Kiger, Sachi Parker; *D:* Jim Abrahams. **VHS, Beta, LV, 8mm** $14.95 *PAR* 🎬🎬

Welcome to Blood City An anonymous totalitarian organization kidnaps a man and transports him electronically to a fantasy western town where the person who murders the most people becomes the town's "kill master." Amateurish and low-budget.
1977 96m/C Jack Palance, Keir Dullea, Samantha Eggar, Barry Morse. **VHS, Beta** $69.98 *LIV* 🎬½

Welcome to 18 Three girls, just out of high school, take summer jobs at a dude ranch, work a local casino, flirt, tease and get in trouble. The movie isn't funny in the least, and is filled with utter nonsense. Hargitay is the daughter of actress Jayne Mansfield.
1987 (PG-13) 91m/C Courtney Thorne-Smith, Mariska Hargitay, Jo Ann Willette, Christine Kaufmann; *D:* Terry Carr. **VHS, Beta** $19.95 *LIV* 🎬

Welcome to L.A. Rudolph's ambitious directorial debut focuses on the sexual escapades of a group of Southern Californians. Based on the music suite "City of the One Night Stands" by Richard Baskin, which also (unfortunately) serves as the soundtrack. Rudolph improved greatly after this initial effort.

1977 (R) 106m/C Sissy Spacek, Sally Kellerman, Keith Carradine, Geraldine Chaplin, Lauren Hutton, Viveca Lindfors, Harvey Keitel, John Considine; *D:* Alan Rudolph. **VHS, Beta** *FOX* 🎬🎬🎬

Welcome to Spring Break College co-eds are stalked by a killer on the beaches of Florida.
1988 (R) 92m/C John Saxon, Michael Parks. **VHS, Beta, LV** $9.99 *CCB, IVE* 🎬½

The Well A young black girl disappears and a white man (Morgan) is accused of kidnapping her. When it is discovered that the girl is trapped in a deep well, Morgan's expertise is needed to help free her.
1951 85m/B Richard Rober, Harry Morgan, Barry Kelley, Christine Larson; *D:* Leo Popkin, Russel Rouse. **VHS, Beta** *UHV* 🎬🎬🎬

Well-Digger's Daughter As her lover goes off to war, a well-digger's daughter discovers that she is pregnant causing both sets of parents to feud over who's to blame. This is the first film made in France after the end of World War II and marks the return of the French film industry. In French with English subtitles. *AKA:* La Fille Du Puisatier.
1946 142m/B *FR* Raimu, Josette Day, Fernandel, Charpin; *D:* Marcel Pagnol. **VHS, Beta** $29.95 *NOS, DVT, APD* 🎬🎬🎬

Wellington: The Duel Scandal A look at how the man who was Britain's greatest hero managed to garner the hatred of his countrymen in eighteen months.
19?? 60m/C *GB* **VHS** *QNE* 🎬🎬🎬

We're in the Legion Now Denny and Barnett star as a couple of American gangsters who join the French Foreign Legion to escape rival hoods from back home.
1937 56m/B Reginald Denny, Vince Barnett, Esther Ralston. **VHS, Beta, 8mm** $24.95 *VYY* 🎬½

We're No Angels Three escapees from Devil's Island hide out with the family of a kindly French storekeeper. One of Bogart's few comedies. From the French stage play of the same name. Claustrophobic and talky. Later remade with De Niro and Penn.
1955 103m/C Humphrey Bogart, Aldo Ray, Joan Bennett, Peter Ustinov, Basil Rathbone, Leo G. Carroll; *D:* Michael Curtiz. **VHS, Beta** $14.95 *PAR* 🎬🎬½

We're No Angels Two escaped cons disguise themselves as priests and get in the appropriate series of jams. De Niro and Penn play off each other well, turning in fine comic performances. Distantly related to the 1955 film of the same name and the David Mamet play.
1989 (R) 110m/C Robert De Niro, Sean Penn, Demi Moore, Hoyt Axton, Bruno Kirby, James Russo; *D:* Neil Jordan; *W:* David Mamet. **VHS, Beta, LV** $19.95 *PAR* 🎬🎬½

We're Not Married Five couples learn that they are not legally married when a judge realizes his license expired before he performed the ceremonies. The story revolves around this quintet of couples who now must cope with whether or not they really do want to be married. Although the episodes vary in quality, the Allen-Rogers sequence is excellent. Overall, the cast performs well in this lightweight comedy.
1952 85m/B Ginger Rogers, Fred Allen, Victor Moore, Marilyn Monroe, Paul Douglas, David Wayne, Eve Arden, Louis Calhern, Zsa Zsa Gabor, James Gleason, Jane Darwell, Eddie Bracken, Mitzi Gaynor; *D:* Edmund Goulding; *W:* Nunnally Johnson, Dwight Taylor. **VHS** $14.98 *FXV* 🎬🎬🎬

We're Talkin' Serious Money Sal and Charlie are a couple of loser scam-artists always after the elusive big score. They borrow $10,000 from the mob for another get-rich-quick scheme and wind up over their heads with both the mob and the FBI out to get them.
1992 (PG-13) 92m/C Dennis Farina, Leo Rossi, Fran Drescher, John Lamotta; *D:* James Lemmo. **VHS, LV** $89.95 *COL* 🎬🎬½

Werewolf in a Girl's Dormitory Girls' school headmaster undergoes dental transformation at night. Atrocious dubbing, with equally atrocious theme song "The Ghoul in School." *AKA:* Lycanthropus; The Ghoul in School.
1961 82m/B *IT* Barbara Lass, Carl Schell, Curt Lowens, Maurice Marsac; *D:* Richard Benson. **VHS** $19.95 *SMW, SNC* 🎬

Werewolf of London A scientist searching for a rare Tibetan flower is attacked by a werewolf. He scoffs at the legend, but once he's back in London, he goes on a murderous rampage every time the moon is full. Dated but worth watching as the first werewolf movie made.
1935 75m/B Henry Hull, Warner Oland, Valerie Hobson, Lester Matthews, Spring Byington; *D:* Stuart Walker. **VHS** $14.98 *MCA* 🎬🎬½

Werewolf of Washington Stockwell is a White House press secretary with a problem—he turns into a werewolf. And bites the President, among others. Sub-plot involves a short mad scientist who operates a secret monster-making lab in a White House bathroom. Occasionally engaging horror spoof and political satire made during Watergate era.
1973 (PG) 90m/C Dean Stockwell, Biff Maguire, Clifton James; *D:* Milton Moses Ginseberg. **VHS, Beta** *NO* 🎬🎬

The Werewolf vs. the Vampire Woman Hirsute Spanish wolfman teams with two female students in search of witch's tomb. One is possessed by the witch, and eponymous title results. *AKA:* The Werewolf vs. the Vampire Woman; Blood Moon.
1970 (R) 82m/C *SP GE* Paul Naschy, Gaby Fuchs, Barbara Capell, Patty Shepard, Valerie Samarine, Julio Pena, Andres Resino; *D:* Leon Klimovsky. **VHS** $19.98 *SNC, HEG* 🎬½

Werewolves on Wheels A group of bikers are turned into werewolves due to a Satanic spell. A serious attempt at a biker/werewolf movie, however, too violent and grim, not at all funny, and painful to sit through. McGuire had a hit with "Eve of Destruction."
1971 (R) 85m/C Stephen Oliver, Severn Darden, Donna Anderson, Duece Barry, Billy Gray, Barry McGuire; *D:* Michel Levesque. **VHS, Beta** $59.95 *UNI* Woof!

West and Soda Bozzetto, renowned artist and creator of "Allegro Non Troppo," presents animated tale about pincushion named Johnny who is the fastest gun in the West.
1990 ?m/C *D:* Bruno Bozzetto. **VHS** $59.95 *EXP* Woof!

West-Bound Limited A Romantic adventurer rescues a girl from certain death as a train is about to hit her, and the two fall in love. Lucky for him, she happens to be the boss' daughter. This film is a good example of classic silent melodrama with music score.
1923 70m/B John Harron, Ella Hall, Claire McDowell; *D:* Beta $29.95 *VYY* 🎬🎬½

West of Nevada A rare film, featuring the former Lieutenant Governor of Nevada (and Clara Bow's husband) in a fast-moving adventure about a band of Indians who must

protect their gold from thieves. Bell is the good guy who aids the Indians.
1936 59m/B Rex Bell, Joan Barclay, Al "Fuzzy" St. John, Steve Clark. **VHS, Beta, Special order formats $52.95** GVV 🐾🐾

West of Pinto Basin The Range Busters are riding around checking the territory for badmen in this tale of the old west. The music score includes "That Little Prairie Gal of Mine," "Rhythm of the Saddle," and "Ridin' the Trail Tonight."
1940 60m/B Ray Corrigan, Max Terhune, John "Dusty" King, Jack Perrin. **VHS, Beta $19.95** NOS, DVT 🐾🐾

West of the Divide A young cowboy (Wayne) impersonates an outlaw in order to hunt down his father's killer and find his missing younger brother. He saves a proud rancher and his feisty daughter along the way. A remake of "Partners of the Trail," and a solid early Wayne oater.
1934 53m/B John Wayne, George "Gabby" Hayes, Lloyd Whitlock, Yakima Canutt; **D:** Robert North Bradbury. **VHS, Beta, 3/4U, Special order formats $19.95** COL, REP, NOS 🐾🐾½

West of the Law A group of ranchers turn to lawmen for protection from a band of outlaws. Part of the Rough Riders series.
1942 60m/B Buck Jones, Tim McCoy, Raymond Hatton; **D:** Howard Bretherton. **VHS, Beta $19.95** NOS, VCN, DVT 🐾🐾

West of Zanzibar Chaney plays an ivory trader, ruling a jungle kingdom, who lives for revenge on the man who left him a cripple. He decides to ruin the man's daughter and turn her into a prostitute but his plan backfires. Chaney and director Browning offer a steamy atmosphere amidst a number of script flaws.
1928 63m/B Lon Chaney Sr., Lionel Barrymore, Warner Baxter, Mary Nolan; **D:** Tod Browning. **VHS $29.95** FCT 🐾🐾½

The West Point Story Cagney stars as an on-the-skids Broadway director offered a job staging a show at West Point. Seems cadet MacRae has written a musical and his uncle happens to be a producer. Cagney, with girlfriend Mayo, finds all the rules and regulations getting the better of his temper, so much so that he's told unless he can conform to academy standards the show won't go on! Day is the showgirl MacRae falls for. Cagney's energy and charm carry the too-long film but it's not one of his better musical efforts. ♫Ten Thousand Sheep; You Love Me; By the Kissing Rock; Long Before I Knew You; Brooklyn; It Could Only Happen in Brooklyn; Military Polka. **AKA:** Fine and Dandy.
1950 107m/B James Cagney, Virginia Mayo, Gordon MacRae, Doris Day, Roland Winters, Gene Nelson, Alan Hale Jr., Wilton Graff, Jerome Cowan; **D:** Roy Del Ruth; **W:** John Monks Jr., Charles Hoffman, Irving Wallace; **M:** Sammy Cahn, Jules Styne. **VHS $59.95** WAR 🐾🐾½

West Side Story Gang rivalry and ethnic tension on New York's West Side erupts in a ground-breaking musical that won ten Academy Awards. Loosely based on Shakespeare's "Romeo and Juliet," the story follows the Jets and the Sharks as they fight for their own turf while Tony and Maria fight for love. Frenetic and brilliant choreography by co-director Robbins, who also directed the original Broadway show, and a high-caliber score by Leonard Bernstein and Stephen Sondheim. Wood's voice was dubbed by Marni Nixon (she is also heard in "The King and I" and "My Fair Lady") and Jimmy Bryant dubbed Beymer's. The laserdisc version includes the complete story-

boards, production sketches, re-issue trailer, and an interview with Wise. It also utilizes letterboxing and digital stereo surround sound. ♫Prologue; Jet Song; Something's Coming; Dance at the Gym; Maria; America; Tonight; One Hand, One Heart; Gee, Officer Krupke; Quintet; Rumble; Cool; I Feel Pretty; Somewhere; A Boy Like That; I Have a Heart.
1961 151m/C Natalie Wood, Richard Beymer, Russ Tamblyn, Rita Moreno, George Chakiris, Simon Oakland, Ned Glass; **D:** Robert Wise, Jerome Robbins. Academy Awards '61: Best Art Direction/Set Decoration (Color), Best Color Cinematography, Best Costume Design (Color), Best Director (Wise), Best Film Editing, Best Picture, Best Sound, Best Supporting Actor (Chakiris), Best Supporting Actress (Moreno), Best Score; Nominations: Best Adapted Screenplay; Directors Guild of America Awards '61: Best Director (Wise), Best Director (Robbins). **VHS, Beta, LV $19.98** MGM, KUI, FOX 🐾🐾🐾½

West to Glory Glory isn't necessarily exciting, as the hero helps a Mexican rancher save his gold and jewels from evildoers in this slow-paced oater.
1947 61m/B Eddie Dean, Roscoe Ates, Dolores Castle, Gregg Barton, Alex Montoya, Harry Vejar; **D:** Ray Taylor. **VHS $19.95** NOS 🐾½

Western Double Feature 1 In "Utah" (1945, 55 minutes), Rogers foils a land swindle and helps a lady ranch owner; in "Man from Music Mountain" (1938, 60 minutes), Autry foils a worthless gold mining stock swindle. **AKA:** Utah; Man from Music Mountain.
1938 115m/B Roy Rogers, Dale Evans, George "Gabby" Hayes, Gene Autry, Smiley Burnette; **D:** Joseph Kane. **VHS, Beta $59.95** HHT 🐾🐾½

Western Double Feature 1: Wild Bill & Sunset Carson Double feature: in "Calling Wild Bill Elliot" (1943), Wild Bill comes to the aid of homesteaders; in "Santa Fe Saddlemates" (1945), Carson breaks up a diamond smuggling ring. **AKA:** Calling Wild Bill Elliot; Santa Fe Saddlemates.
194? 120m/B Wild Bill Elliott, Sunset Carson; **D:** Spencer Gordon Bennet. **VHS, Beta** MED 🐾½

Western Double Feature 2 Wayne and Hayes are teamed together in two hour-long B-westerns: "Star Packer" (1934) and "West of the Divide" (1933). **AKA:** Star Packer; West of the Divide.
1933 120m/B John Wayne, George "Gabby" Hayes; **D:** Robert North Bradbury. **VHS, Beta $59.95** HHT 🐾½

Western Double Feature 2: Wayne & Hale Double feature; in "Night Riders" (1939), Wayne battles injustice; in "Home on the Range" (1946, color), Hale protects a wild animal refuge. **AKA:** Nightriders; Home on the Range.
198? 120m/B John Wayne, Monte Hale; **D:** George Sherman. **VHS, Beta** MED 🐾½

Western Double Feature 3 Two Wayne westerns are on this tape: "Helltown" (1938, 59 minutes), in which Wayne catches a cattle rustler; and "Winds of the Wasteland" (1936, 54 minutes), where he plays an out-of-work Pony Express rider. **AKA:** Helltown; Winds of the Wasteland.
1936 113m/B John Wayne, Johnny Mack Brown, Marsha Hunt, Phyllis Fraser; **D:** Charles T. Barton, Mack V. Wright. **VHS, Beta $59.95** HHT 🐾½

Western Double Feature 3: Rogers & Allen Double feature. In "Twilight in the Sierras" (1950), Rogers catches a gang of crooks; in "Under Mexicali Stars" (1950), Allen is a cowboy who uncov-

ers a counterfeiting ring. **AKA:** Twilight in the Sierras; Under Mexicali Stars.
1950 134m/C Roy Rogers, Dale Evans, Rex Allen; **D:** William Witney. **VHS, Beta** MED 🐾½

Western Double Feature 4 Rogers plays a dual role in a case of mistaken identity in "Billy the Kid Returns" (1938, 56 minutes); in "Round Up Time in Texas" (1937, 56 minutes), Autry is framed on a charge of diamond smuggling. **AKA:** Billy the Kid Returns; Round Up Time in Texas.
1937 112m/B Roy Rogers, Gene Autry, Smiley Burnette; **D:** Joseph Kane. **VHS, Beta $59.95** HHT 🐾🐾½

Western Double Feature 4: Rogers & Evans In "Don't Fence Me In" (1945), Rogers helps out a woman reporter; in "Sheriff of Wichita" (1948), a frontier investigator solves a crime. **AKA:** Don't Fence Me In; Sheriff of Wichita.
194? 120m/B Roy Rogers, Dale Evans, Trigger, George "Gabby" Hayes, Allan "Rocky" Lane. **VHS, Beta** MED 🐾½

Western Double Feature 5 Wayne stars in both halves of this double feature: in "Desert Trail" (1935, 54 minutes), he plays a rodeo star; in "Man from Utah" (1934, 55 minutes), he brings a gang of murderers to justice. **AKA:** Desert Trail; Man from Utah.
1935 109m/B John Wayne, Polly Ann Young; **D:** Robert North Bradbury. **VHS, Beta $59.95** HHT 🐾½

Western Double Feature 5: Rogers & Autry "The Big Show" (1937) features songs, action, and horses; in "Home in Oklahoma" (1946), Roger tracks down a murderer. **AKA:** The Big Show; Home in Oklahoma.
1937 108m/B Gene Autry, Roy Rogers, Smiley Burnette, The Pioneers; **D:** Max Wright. **VHS, Beta** MED 🐾½

Western Double Feature 6: Rogers & Trigger "Trigger Jr." (1950) is the story of Trigger's colt; "Gangs of Sonora" (1941, black and white) deals with a fight to save a small frontier newspaper. **AKA:** Trigger, Jr.; Gangs of Sonora.
1950 120m/C Roy Rogers, Dale Evans, Trigger, Bob Livingston, Bob Steele; **D:** William Witney. **VHS, Beta** MED 🐾½

Western Double Feature 7: Wild Bill & Crabbe "Phantom of the Plains" deals with a plan to save a woman from a gigolo; "Prairie Rustlers" tells of the problems of a man who is the identical double of Billy the Kid. **AKA:** Phantom of the Plains; Prairie Rustlers.
1945 120m/B Wild Bill Elliott, Buster Crabbe. **VHS, Beta** MED 🐾½

Western Double Feature 8: Hale & Carradine In "Silver Spurs" (1943), ranchers wanting to get the right-of-way through oil land run into an ambitious resort owner; in "Out California Way" (1946), Hale is a young cowboy looking for work in Hollywood. **AKA:** Silver Spurs; Out California Way.
194? 121m/B Roy Rogers, Monte Hale, John Carradine. **VHS, Beta** MED 🐾½

Western Double Feature 9: LaRue & Beery In "Cheyenne Takes Over" (1947), LaRue battles outlaws; in "Tulsa Kid" (1940), a young man must face a gunfighter. **AKA:** Cheyenne Takes Over; Tulsa Kid.
194? 120m/B Lash LaRue, Donald (Don "Red") Barry, Noah Beery Sr. **VHS, Beta** MED 🐾½

Western Double Feature 10: Roy, Dale, & Trigger In "Bells of Coronado" (1950), Rogers must solve a murder and uranium ore theft; in "King of the Cowboys" (1943, black and white), Roy investigates a band of saboteurs.
198? 120m/C Roy Rogers, Dale Evans, Trigger; **D:** William Witney. **VHS, Beta** MED ♫½

Western Double Feature 11 Roy and Trigger act as modern day Robin Hoods to end crooked dealing in the West; Roy hides behind a smile and a song to capture murderers of a deputy and a ranch owner.
1950 121m/B Roy Rogers, Penny Edwards, Gordon Jones, Purple Sage, George "Gabby" Hayes. **VHS, Beta** MED ♫½

Western Double Feature 12 Red Ryder learns of a plot to scare ranchers into selling out before an oil strike is discovered; the Three Musketeers are sent to the Caribbean as U.S. envoys to sell Army horses.
1944 108m/B Bob Livingston, Wild Bill Elliott, Duncan Renaldo, Robert (Bobby) Blake. **VHS, Beta** MED ♫½

Western Double Feature 13 Red Ryder foils outlaws trying to swindle the Duchess' stage line in a small isolated town in "Wagon Wheels Westward" (1945). "Rocky Mountain Rangers" (1940), features the Three Mesquiteers pursuing the deadly Barton Gang.
194? 108m/B Red Ryder, Bob Livingston, Robert (Bobby) Blake. **VHS, Beta** MED ♫½

Western Double Feature 14 Outlaws, good guys, and romance on the old frontier. Amateur Robin Hoods steal back money wrongfully taken.
1952 123m/B Tim Holt, Jack Holt, Nan Leslie, Noreen Nash. **VHS, Beta** MED ♫½

Western Double Feature 15 Rogers breaks up a cattle rustling ring; the good guys try to bring law and order to a vast Wyoming territory plagued by a crooked political boss.
1950 122m/B Roy Rogers, Trigger, Penny Edwards, Donald (Don "Red") Barry, Lynn Merrick. **VHS, Beta** MED ♫½

Western Double Feature 16 Autry is sent to quell a revolution in Mexico; Rogers's horse Lady and Hayes's horse Golden Sovereign are the focal points of the second part of this double feature.
1946 108m/B Gene Autry, Smiley Burnette, Roy Rogers, George "Gabby" Hayes. **VHS, Beta** MED ♫½

Western Double Feature 17 Rogers stars in "The Golden Stallion" (1949). Roy battles diamond smugglers who use wild horses to transport the goods. "The Cherokee Flash" (1945), starring Carson, deals with a respectable citizen's outlaw past catching up to him.
194? 121m/C Roy Rogers, Sunset Carson; **D:** William Witney. **VHS, Beta** MED ♫½

Western Double Feature 18 A Rogers double feature: in "Eyes of Texas" (1948), a westerner turns his ranch into a camp for war-orphaned boys; in "Helldorado" (1946), Roy travels to Las Vegas.
194? 108m/B Roy Rogers, Andy Devine, Dale Evans; **D:** William Witney. **VHS, Beta** MED ♫½

Western Double Feature 19 Rogers helps a young woman foil a plot by crooks to swindle her inheritance. Roy appears in his first starring role (1938) and fights an outlaw gang.
1945 108m/B Roy Rogers, Dale Evans, Pat Brady, Trigger. **VHS, Beta** MED ♫½

Western Double Feature 20 "Night Time in Nevada" (1948), has Roy bringing a ruthless murderer to justice. "The Old Corral" (1937) features a clash between gangsters in limousines and deputies on horseback.
19?? 108m/B Roy Rogers, Gene Autry; **D:** Joseph Kane. **VHS, Beta** MED ♫½

Western Double Feature 21 Roy battles crooks in "Susanna Pass" (1949). In "Sheriff of Las Vegas" (1944), Red must find the murderer of Judge Blackwell.
194? 121m/C Roy Rogers, Red Ryder, Dale Evans, Robert (Bobby) Blake; **D:** William Witney. **VHS, Beta** MED ♫½

Western Double Feature 22 A Rogers double feature: "Under California Stars" (1948), Roy rounds up a gang of wild horse rustlers; "San Fernando Valley" (1944), Roy brings law and order to the valley.
194? 108m/B Roy Rogers; **D:** William Witney. **VHS, Beta** MED ♫½

Western Double Feature 23 In "Spoilers of the Plains" (1951), Roy finds cattle rustlers and sets out to capture the spoilers. "Lights of Old Santa Fe" (1947) features Roy as a cowboy who rescues a beautiful rodeo owner from bankruptcy.
19?? 122m/B Roy Rogers, Dale Evans. **VHS, Beta** MED ♫½

Western Double Feature 24 In "Cowboy and the Senorita" (1944), Roy solves the mystery of a missing girl. "Colorado Serenade" (1946) is a musical western in Cinecolor starring Dean.
194? 122m/C Roy Rogers, Dale Evans, Eddie Dean. **VHS, Beta** MED ♫½

Western Double Feature 25 In "Pals of the Golden West" (1951), Roy discovers how valuable Trigger is. "Springtime in the Sierras" (1947) features Roy raising and selling thoroughbreds.
19?? 122m/B Roy Rogers, Dale Evans, Andy Devine, The Pioneers; **D:** William Witney. **VHS, Beta** MED ♫½

Western Frontier Ordinary cowpoke Maynard is called on to lead the fight against a band of outlaws led by the Indian-raised sister he never knew he had. Action-packed, fast, and fun. Maynard's first outing for Columbia.
1935 56m/B Ken Maynard, Lucille Browne, Nora Lane, Robert "Buzzy" Henry, Frank Yaconelli; **D:** Al Herman. **VHS, Beta** $19.95 NOS, DVT ♫

Western Justice Good Guy Steele brings western-style justice to a lawless town. Ordinary oater with horses, etc., and a few chuckles on the side.
1935 56m/B Bob Steele; **D:** Robert North Bradbury. **VHS, Beta** $6.99 VTR, WGE, NOS ♫♫

Western Mail Yet another western in which the hero goes undercover so he can bring the bad guys to justice. Yaconelli plays a guitar tune, accompanied by his monkey.
1942 54m/B Tom Keene, Frank Yaconelli, Leroy Mason, Jean Trent, Fred Kohler Jr.; **D:** Robert Tansey. **VHS** $19.95 NOS, DVT ♫♫

Western Pacific Agent A Western Pacific agent chases an outlaw who has committed robbery and murder. The agent falls in love with the victim's sister and, of course, prevails. Rather violent.
1951 62m/B Kent Taylor, Sheila Ryan, Mickey Knox, Robert Lowery; **D:** Sam Newfield. **VHS, Beta, LV** NO ♫

Western Trails Forgettable western about the clean-up of a Wild West town terrorized by outlaws. Thin script, bad acting, and a little singin' and funnin' around.

1938 59m/B Bob Baker, Marjorie Reynolds, Robert Burns; **D:** George Waggner. **VHS, Beta** $19.95 NOS, DVT ♫

Western Union A lavish, vintage epic romantically detailing the political machinations, Indian warfare and frontier adventure that accompanied the construction of the Western Union telegraph line from Omaha, Nebraska, to Salt Lake City, Utah, during the Civil War. A thoroughly entertaining film in rich Technicolor. This was Lang's second western, following his personal favorite, "The Return of Frank James." Writer Carson utilized the title, but not the storyline, of a Zane Grey book. The German Lang showed himself a master of the most American of genres, yet made only one more western, "Rancho Notorious" (1952), another masterpiece.
1941 94m/C Randolph Scott, Robert Young, Dean Jagger, Slim Summerville, Virginia Gilmore, John Carradine, Chill Wills, Barton MacLane, Minor Watson, Charles Middleton, Irving Bacon; **D:** Fritz Lang. **VHS, Beta** $39.98 FOX, MLB ♫♫♫½

The Westerner A sly, soft-spoken drifter champions Texas border homesteaders in a land war with the legendary Judge Roy Bean. "The Law West of the Pecos" sentences drifter Cooper to hang, but Cooper breaks out of jail. He falls for damsel Davenport and stays in the area, advocating the rights of homesteaders to Brennan. Brennan's Bean is unforgettable and steals the show from Cooper. Film debuts of actors Tucker and Andrews. Amazing cinematography; Brennan's Oscar was his third, making him the first performer to pull a hat trick.
1940 100m/B Gary Cooper, Walter Brennan, Doris Davenport, Dana Andrews, Forrest Tucker; **D:** William Wyler. **Academy Awards '40:** Best Supporting Actor (Brennan); Nominations: Best Interior Decoration, Best Story. **VHS, Beta, LV** $19.98 HBO, SUE, BTV ♫♫♫½

Westfront 1918 A dogmatic anti-war film by the German master (his first talkie), about German and French soldiers on the fields of World War I, dying together without victory. Stunning in its portrayal of war's futility, with excellent photography that achieves a palpable realism. In German with English subtitles.
1930 90m/B GE Gustav Diesl, Fritz Kampers, Claus Clausen, Hans Joachim Moebis; **D:** G.W. Pabst. **VHS, Beta** $29.98 SUE, GLV, TAM ♫♫♫

Westward Ho Wayne is determined to bring to justice his parents' slayer. Haven't we seen this one before? Seems the bad guys have corrupted his brother. Wayne's group of vigilantes is called "The Singing Riders," so naturally he sings—or is made to appear to. He looks and sounds ridiculous.
1935 55m/B John Wayne, Sheila Manners; **D:** Robert North Bradbury. **VHS** $9.98 REP, VCN, NOS ♫½

Westward Ho, the Wagons! The promised land lies in the west, but to get there these pioneers must pass unfriendly savages, thieves, villains, and scoundrels galore. Suitable for family viewing, but why bother? Well, the cast does include four Mouseketeers.
1956 94m/B Fess Parker, Kathleen Crowley, Jeff York, Sebastian Cabot, George Reeves; **D:** William Beaudine. **VHS, Beta** $69.95 DIS ♫½

Westworld Crichton wrote and directed this story of an adult vacation resort of the future which offers the opportunity to live in various fantasy worlds serviced by lifelike robots. Brolin and Benjamin are businessmen who choose a western fantasy world. When an electrical malfunction occurs, the robots

begin to go berserk. Brynner is perfect as a western gunslinging robot whose skills are all too real.
1973 (PG) 90m/C Yul Brynner, Richard Benjamin, James Brolin, Dick Van Patten, Majel Barrett; **W/D:** Michael Crichton. **VHS, Beta, LV** $19.95 *MGM* 🎬🎬🎬

Wet Gold A beautiful young woman and three men journey to retrieve a sunken treasure. Nice scenery. Proves that it is possible to make "The Treasure of the Sierra Madre" without making a classic. John Huston, where are you? Made for television.
1984 90m/C Brooke Shields, Brian Kerwin, Burgess Meredith, Tom Byrd; **D:** Dick Lowry. **VHS, Beta** $9.99 *CCB, IVE* 🎬

Wetherby Playwright David Hare's first directorial effort, which he also wrote, about a Yorkshire schoolteacher whose life is shattered when a young, brooding stranger comes uninvited to a dinner party, and then shoots himself in her living room. Compelling but oh, so dark. Richardson, who plays a young Redgrave, is actually Redgrave's daughter.
1985 97m/C *GB* Vanessa Redgrave, Ian Holm, Judi Dench, Joely Richardson, Tim McInnery, Suzanna Hamilton; **D:** David Hare. **VHS, Beta** $19.98 *MGM* 🎬🎬🎬

Whale for the Killing An ecologist stranded in a remote Alaskan fishing village battles to save a beached humpbacked whale from a malicious Russian fisherman. Platitudinous and self-congratulatory, if well-meaning. Made for television from a book by Farley Mowat.
1981 145m/C Richard Widmark, Peter Strauss, Dee Wallace Stone, Bruce McGill, Kathryn Walker; **N:** Richard T. Heffron. **VHS, Beta** $59.98 *FOX* 🎬🎬½

Whale of a Tale A young boy trains a killer whale to appear in the big show in the main tank at "Marineland."
1976 (G) 90m/C William Shatner, Marty Allen, Abby Dalton, Andy Devine, Nancy O'Conner. **VHS, Beta** $39.95 *UHV, WTA* 🎬

Whales of August Based on the David Berry play, the story of two elderly sisters—one caring, the other cantankerous, blind, and possibly senile—who decide during a summer in Maine whether or not they should give up their ancestral house and enter a nursing home. Gish and Davis are exquisite to watch, and the all-star supporting cast is superb—especially Price as a suave Russian. Lovingly directed by Anderson in his first US outing.
1987 91m/C Lillian Gish, Bette Davis, Vincent Price, Ann Sothern, Mary Steenburgen, Harry Carey Jr.; **D:** Lindsay Anderson. Academy Awards '87 Nominations: Best Supporting Actress (Sothern); National Board of Review Awards '87: Best Actress (Gish); National Media Owl Awards '88: First Prize. **VHS, Beta, LV, 8mm** $14.98 *SUE, NLC* 🎬🎬½

What a Carve-Up! A group of relatives gather in an old, spooky mansion to hear the reading of a will. Tries too hard. Remake of "The Ghoul." **AKA:** No Place Like Homicide.
1962 87m/B *GB* Kenneth Connor, Sidney James, Shirley Eaton, Donald Pleasence, Dennis Price, Michael Gough; **D:** Pat Jackson. **VHS** $16.95 *SNC* 🎬🎬

What a Way to Die An evil assassin plots dispatching with a difference.
1970 (R) 87m/C William Berger, Anthony Baker, Helga Anders, Georgia Moll; **D:** Helmut Foernbacher. **VHS, Beta** *NO* 🎬½

What About Bob? Bob, a ridiculously neurotic patient, follows his psychiatrist on vacation, turning his life upside down. The psychiatrist's family find Bob entertaining and endearing. Murray is at his comedic best; Dreyfuss's overly excitable characterization occasionally wears thin.
1991 (PG) 99m/C Richard Dreyfuss, Bill Murray, Julie Hagerty, Charlie Korsmo, Tom Aldredge, Roger Bowen, Fran Brill; **D:** Frank Oz. **VHS, Beta, LV** $19.99 *BVV* 🎬🎬🎬

What Comes Around A good-ole-boy drama about a doped-up country singer who is kidnapped by his brother for his own good. The singer's evil manager sends his stooges out to find him. Might have been funny, but isn't. But is it meant to be? Good Reed songs; mildly interesting plot.
1985 (PG) 92m/C Jerry Reed, Bo Hopkins, Arte Johnson, Barry Corbin; **D:** Jerry Reed. **VHS, Beta, LV** $19.98 *NLC* 🎬🎬🎬

What Did You Do in the War, Daddy? Unfunny comedy set in World War II about a group of weary American soldiers trying to get a small town in Sicily to surrender. Things don't go smoothly thanks to a combination soccer game/wine festival, not to mention the Germans deciding to attack. Director Edwards comedic verve deserted him.
1966 119m/C Dick Shawn, James Coburn, Sergio Fantoni, Giovanna Ralli, Aldo Ray, Harry Morgan, Carroll O'Connor, Jay Novello, Vito Scotti; **D:** Blake Edwards; **W:** William Peter Blatty. **VHS** $14.95 *MGM* 🎬½

What Do You Say to a Naked Lady? Funt takes his Candid Camera to the streets to find out how people react when confronted by nude members of the opposite sex. Sporadically hilarious.
1970 92m/C **D:** Allen Funt. **VHS, Beta** *FOX* 🎬🎬½

What Ever Happened to Baby Jane? Davis and Crawford portray aging sisters and former child stars living together in a decaying mansion. When the demented Jane (Davis) learns of her now-crippled sister's (Crawford) plan to institutionalize her, she tortures the wheelchair-bound sis. Davis plays her part to the hilt, unafraid of Aldrich's unsympathetic camera, and the viciousness of her character. She received her tenth Oscar nomination for the role.
1962 132m/B Bette Davis, Joan Crawford, Victor Buono, Anna Lee, B.D. Merrill; **D:** Robert Aldrich. **VHS, Beta, LV** $19.98 *WAR* 🎬🎬🎬½

What Have I Done to Deserve This? A savage parody on Spanish mores, about a speed-addicted housewife who ends up selling her son and killing her husband with a ham bone. Black, black comedy, perverse and funny as only Almodovar can be. In Spanish with subtitles. Nudity and profanity. **AKA:** Que He Hecho Yo Para Merecer Esto?.
1985 100m/C Carmen Maura, Chus Lampreave; **D:** Pedro Almodovar. **VHS, Beta, LV** $79.95 *TAM, CCN* 🎬🎬🎬

What! No Beer? Two dim-bulb friends decide to put their money into a defunct brewery hoping for the end of Prohibition. They start up operations too soon and wind up attracting the unwelcome attentions of gangster bootleggers and the cops. Mediocre comedy and Keaton's last starring role as his own problems with alcohol affected his work.
1933 66m/B Buster Keaton, Jimmy Durante, Phyllis Barry, Roscoe Ates, John Miljan, Henry Armetta, Edward Brophy; **D:** Edward Sedgwick. **VHS** $19.98 *MGM* 🎬🎬

What Price Glory? Remake of the 1926 silent classic about a pair of comradely rivals for the affections of women in World War I France. Strange to have Ford directing an offbeat comedy, but it works: masterful direction, good acting. Demarest broke both legs in a motorcycle accident during shooting.
1952 111m/C James Cagney, Dan Dailey, Corinne Calvet, William Demarest, James Gleason, Robert Wagner, Casey Adams, Craig Hill, Marisa Pavan; **D:** John Ford. **VHS, Beta** $19.98 *FOX, FCT* 🎬🎬🎬

What Price Hollywood? Aspiring young starlet decides to crash film world by using an alcoholic director as her stepping stone. Bennett is lovely; Sherman is superb as an aging, dissolute man who watches his potential slip away. From a story by Adela Rogers St. John. Remade three times as "A Star is Born."
1932 88m/B Constance Bennett, Lowell Sherman, Neil Hamilton; **D:** George Cukor. **VHS, Beta, LV** $19.98 *CCB, TTC, FCT* 🎬🎬🎬

What the Peeper Saw The wife of a wealthy author finds her comfortable life turning into a terrifying nightmare when her young stepson starts acting funny. Juicy and terrifying. **AKA:** Night Hair Child; Child of the Night.
1972 97m/C Britt Ekland, Mark Lester, Hardy Kruger, Lilli Palmer. **VHS, Beta** $29.95 *UHV* 🎬🎬

What Waits Below A scientific expedition encounters a lost race living in caves in South America. Good cast, bad acting, and lousy script. Might have been much better.
1983 (PG) 88m/C Timothy Bottoms, Robert Powell, Lisa Blount; **D:** Don Sharp. **VHS, Beta** $69.98 *LIV* 🎬½

Whatever Happened to Aunt Alice? After murdering her husband to inherit his estate, a poor, eccentric widow develops an awful habit: she hires maids, only to murder them and steal their savings. The only evidence is the growing number of trees by the drive. Sleuth Ruth Gordon (of "Harold and Maude" fame, acting here just as odd) takes the job in hopes of solving the mystery. Thoroughly amusing.
1969 (PG) 101m/C Geraldine Page, Ruth Gordon, Rosemary Forsyth, Robert Fuller, Mildred Dunnock; **D:** Lee H. Katzin. **VHS, Beta** $59.98 *FOX, MLB* 🎬🎬🎬

Whatever Happened to Susan Jane? A bored housewife searches for an off-beat college friend, and enters into the seamy, strange world of San Francisco's lunatic fringe. Music by Tuxedo Moon, Indoor Life and other punk groups.
1984 90m/C **VHS, Beta** $39.95 *MPI* 🎬½

What's Love Got to Do With It? Energetic biopic of powerhouse songstress Tina Turner. Short sequences cover her early life before moving into her abusive relationship with Ike and solo comeback success. Bassett may not look like Tina, but her exceptionally strong performance leaves no question as to who she's supposed to be. And she's a professional lip syncher, giving depth and texture to the on-stage Tina. Some credibility is lost when the real Turner is shown in the final concert sequence—Gibson would have been wise to let Bassett finish what she started. Fishburne does a sympathetic but still chilling Ike, rising to the challenge of showing both Ike's initial charm and longtime cruelty. Based on "I, Tina" by Turner and Kurt Loder.
1993 (R) 118m/C Angela Bassett, Larry Fishburne, Vanessa Bell Calloway, Jenifer Lewis, Phyllis Stickney, Khandi Alexander, Pamela Tyson, Penny Johnson, Rae'ven Kelly; **D:** Brian Gibson; **W:** Kate Lanier; **M:** Stanley Clarke. **VHS** *NYR* 🎬🎬½

What's New Pussycat? A young engaged man, reluctant to give up the girls who love him, seeks the aid of a married psychiatrist who turns out to have problems of his own. Allen's first feature as both actor and screenwriter. Burt Bacharach and Hal David wrote the music which included the Oscar-nominated title song sung by Tom Jones. *AKA:* Quoi De Neuf, Pussycat?.
1965 108m/C Peter Sellers, Peter O'Toole, Romy Schneider, Paula Prentiss, Woody Allen, Ursula Andress, Capucine; *D:* Clive Donner. **VHS, Beta, LV** $19.98 FOX, FCT *♂♂♂*

What's the Matter with Helen? Two women, the mothers of murderous sons, move to Hollywood to escape their past and start a new life. They open a school for talented children, and seem to be adjusting to their new lives until strange things start happening. It is soon revealed that one of the mothers is a psychotic killer, and the other mother becomes part of an eerie finale. A fine starring vehicle for two aging actresses. Great score.
1971 (PG) 101m/C Debbie Reynolds, Shelley Winters, Dennis Weaver, Agnes Moorehead, Michael MacLiammoir; *D:* Curtis Harrington. **VHS** $19.98 MGM *♂♂½*

What's Up, Doc? A shy musicologist from Iowa (Ryan) travels to San Francisco with his fiance (Kahn) for a convention. He meets the eccentric Streisand at his hotel and becomes involved in a chase to recover four identical flight bags containing top secret documents, a wealthy woman's jewels, the professor's musical rocks, and Streisand's clothing. Bogdanovich's homage to the screwball comedies of the '30s. Kahn's feature film debut.
1972 (G) 94m/C Barbra Streisand, Ryan O'Neal, Kenneth Mars, Austin Pendleton, Randy Quaid; *D:* Peter Bogdanovich. **VHS, Beta** $19.98 WAR *♂♂♂*

What's Up Front Occasionally funny '60s gag-fest about an ogle-eyed bra salesman who decides to sell door-to-door in order to save a failing brassiere company. Filmed in "Girl-O-Rama" by the young Vilmos Zsigmond. Dated and weird, with camp value. No nudity. Costumes were done by Frederick's of Hollywood. *AKA:* The Fall Guy; A Fourth for Marriage.
1963 90m/C Tommy Holden, Marilyn Manning, Carolyn Walker, William Watters; *D:* Bob Whealing. **VHS, Beta** $59.95 RHI *♂½*

What's Up, Tiger Lily? This legitimate Japanese spy movie—"Kagi No Kag" (Key of Keys), a 1964 Bond imitation—was re-edited by Woody Allen, who added a new dialogue track, with hysterical results. Characters Terri and Suki Yaki are involved in an international plot to secure egg salad recipe; Allen's brand of Hollywood parody and clever wit sustain the joke. Music by the Lovin' Spoonful, who make a brief appearance.
1966 90m/C JP Woody Allen, Tatsuya Mihashi, Mie Hama, Akiko Wakabayashi; *D:* Woody Allen, Senkichi Taniguhi. **VHS, Beta, LV, 3/4U, Special order formats** $29.98 VES, CAB *♂♂♂*

Wheel of Fortune A shrewd small-town lawyer, working on a case in the big city, is forced to expose his girlfriend's father as a crooked politician. Strange to see the Duke here in the lead, but what the hey. Not great, but interesting. *AKA:* A Man Betrayed; Citadel of Crime.
1941 83m/B John Wayne, Frances Dee, Edward Ellis; *D:* John H. Auer. **VHS** $14.98 REP *♂♂*

The Wheeler Dealers Garner plays a supposedly penniless investor (actually a Texas millionaire) who comes to New York stock analyst Remick for investment advice.

Her shyster boss (Backus) tells her to sell the aw-shucks cowboy worthless stock which turns out to be worth a fortune. Zany spoof of Wall Street ethics. *AKA:* Separate Beds.
1963 100m/C James Garner, Lee Remick, Jim Backus, Phil Harris, Shelley Berman, Chill Wills, John Astin, Louis Nye; *D:* Arthur Hiller. **VHS** $19.98 MGM *♂♂♂*

Wheels of Fire The earth is a wasteland controlled by sadistic highway hoodlums. When they kidnap the hero's sister, he fights back in a flame-throwing car. Horrible "Road Warrior" rip-off. *AKA:* Vindicator; Wheels of Fire.
1984 (R) 81m/C Gary Watkins, Lynda Wiesmeier; *D:* Cirio H. Santiago. **VHS, Beta, LV** $79.98 LIV, VES *♂*

Wheels of Terror Possessed black car stalks children in isolated village. Bus driver Cassidy gets behind the wheel of V-8 super-charged school bus to initiate most interminable chase scene in screen history.
1990 (R) 86m/C Joanna Cassidy, Marcie Leeds, Carlos Cervantes, Arlen Dean Snyder; *D:* Christopher Cain. **VHS, Beta** $79.95 PAR *♂*

When a Man Rides Alone Tyler relieves trains of their gold shipments in order to reimburse swindled investors. Lovely Lacey frowns on his initiative, so he kidnaps her to keep her quiet. The two fall in love, and the man who rides alone works beside his beloved.
1933 60m/B Tom Tyler, Adele Lacey, Alan Bridge, Bob Burns, Frank Ball, Alma Chester, Bud Osborne; *D:* J.P. McGowan. **VHS** $19.99 NOS *♂♂*

When a Stranger Calls Babysitter is terrorized by threatening phone calls and soon realizes that the calls are coming from within the house. Story was expanded from director Walton's short film "The Sitter." Distasteful and unlikely, though the first half or so is tight and terrifying.
1979 (R) 97m/C Carol Kane, Charles Durning, Colleen Dewhurst, Rachel Roberts; *D:* Fred Walton. **VHS, Beta, LV** $64.95 COL *♂½*

When a Woman Ascends the Stairs Portrait of the troubled life of a Ginza bar hostess approaching the perilous professional age of 30. In Japanese with English subtitles. *AKA:* Onna Ga Kaidan O Agaru Toki.
1960 110m/B JP Hideko Takamine, Tatsuya Nakadai, Masayuki Mori; *D:* Mikio Naruse. **VHS** $79.95 WAC, TAM *♂♂*

When Angels Fly In this emotional tale of love and murder, a young woman sets out to find the exact circumstances surrounding the mysterious death of her sister.
1982 96m/C Jennifer Dale, Robin Ward. **VHS, Beta** $49.95 UNI, MOV *♂*

When Comedy was King A compilation of the greatest silent screen comedians, including Keaton, Chaplin, Langdon, and Turpin.
1959 81m/C Buster Keaton, Charlie Chaplin, Harry Langdon, Ben Turpin; *D:* Robert Youngson. **VHS, Beta, LV** VID *♂*

When Dinosaurs Ruled the Earth When "One Million Years B.C." ruled the box office the Brits cranked out a few more lively prehistoric fantasies. A sexy cavegirl, exiled because of her blond hair, acquires a cave-beau and a dinosaur guardian. Stop-motion animation from Jim Danforth, story by J.G. Ballard. Under the name Angela Dorian, Vetri was Playmate of the Year in 1968 (A.D.).

1970 (G) 96m/C GB Victoria Vetri, Robin Hawdon, Patrick Allen, Drewe Henley, Sean Caffrey, Magda Konopka, Imogen Hassall, Patrick Holt, Jan Rossini; *W/D:* Val Guest. **VHS, Beta, LV** $19.95 WAR, PIA, FCT *♂♂*

When Every Day was the Fourth of July A nine-year-old girl asks her father, a lawyer, to defend a mute handyman accused of murder, knowing this will bring on him the contempt of the community. Well handled, but see "To Kill a Mockingbird" first. Based on producer/director Curtis's childhood. Sequel: "The Long Days of Summer." Made for television.
1978 100m/C Katy Kurtzman, Dean Jones, Louise Sorel, Harris Yulin, Chris Peterson, Geoffrey Lewis, Scott Brady, Henry Wilcoxon, Michael Pataki; *D:* Dan Curtis. **VHS, Beta** $49.95 LIV *♂♂½*

When Father was Away on Business Set in 1950s Yugoslavia. A family must take care of itself when the father is sent to jail for philandering with a woman desired by a Communist Party official. The moving story of the family's day-to-day survival is seen largely through the eyes of the father's six-year-old son, who believes dad is "away on business." In Slavic with English subtitles.
1985 (R) 144m/C YU Moreno D'E Bartolli, Miki Manojlovic, Mirjana Karanovic; *D:* Emir Kusturica. **VHS** $89.95 FXL, TAM *♂♂♂½*

When Gangland Strikes A country lawyer, blackmailed by the mob, tries to protect his family without caving in. Unexceptional remake of "Main Street Lawyer."
1956 70m/B Raymond Greenleaf, Marjie Millar, Anthony Caruso, Jack Perrin, John Hudson; *D:* R.G. Springsteen. **VHS** $14.98 REP *♂♂*

When Harry Met Sally Romantic comedy follows the long relationship between two adults who try throughout the changes in their lives (and their mates) to remain platonic friends—and what happens when they don't. Wry and enjoyable script is enhanced by wonderful performances. Another directional direct hit for "Meathead" Reiner, and a tour de force of comic screenwriting for Ephron, with improvisational help from Crystal. Great songs by Sinatra soundalike Connick.
1989 (R) 96m/C Billy Crystal, Meg Ryan, Carrie Fisher, Bruno Kirby, Steven Ford, Lisa Jane Persky, Michelle Nicastro, Harley Jane Kozak; *D:* Rob Reiner; *W:* Nora Ephron; *M:* Harry Connick Jr., Marc Shaiman. **VHS, Beta, LV, SVS, 8mm** $19.95 COL, SUE, SUP *♂♂♂*

When Hell Broke Loose Routine World War II actioner about a small-time crook (Bronson) who joins the Army, changes his ways because of the love of a good woman, and gets a chance to be a hero when he stumbles upon a Nazi assassination plot against General Eisenhower.
1958 78m/B Charles Bronson, Violet Rensing, Richard Jaeckel, Arvid Nelson, Robert Easton; *D:* Kenneth Crane; *W:* Oscar Brodney. **VHS** $14.95 PAR *♂½*

When Hell Was in Session In more than seven years as a prisoner of the Viet Cong, Holbrook is subjected to torture, starvation, and psychological warfare to break his will. Based on the true story of Navy Commander Jeremiah Denton. Painful and violent. Made for TV.
1982 98m/C Hal Holbrook, Eva Marie Saint, Ronny Cox; *D:* Paul Krasny. **VHS, Beta** TLF *♂♂♂*

When He's Not a Stranger Date rape is the subject of this made-for-television drama. Lyn is a college freshman who goes to a campus party hosted by the football

team. When Ron, the star quarterback, invites Lyn to his dorm room, the situation gets out of hand. Only Lyn calls it rape and Ron calls her a liar. Intense performances are a highlight of this well-done story.
1989 100m/C Annabeth Gish, John Terlesky, Kevin Dillon, Paul Dooley; **D:** John Gray. **VHS** $89.95 TRI 🎞🎞🎞

When Knights were Bold An English nobleman living in India inherits a castle in his native land. Returning home, he is knocked unconscious by a falling suit of armor while trying to impress a young lady and dreams himself back to medieval days. Enjoyable comedy about that ubiquitous British class hierarchy.
1936 55m/B Fay Wray, Jack Buchanan, Martita Hunt. **VHS, Beta $24.95** VYY 🎞🎞½

When Ladies Meet Entertaining story of a love quadrangle that features several of MGM's top stars of the '40s. In this remake of the 1933 film, Crawford plays a novelist and an early proponent of the women's liberation movement. She falls in love with her publisher (Marshall), who just happens to be married to Garson. Meanwhile, Taylor, who is in love with Crawford, attempts to show her that he is a more suitable match for her than Marshall, but Crawford has yet to catch on. The lengthy dialogue on women's rights is badly dated, but the real-life rivalry between Crawford and Garson adds a certain bite to their witty exchanges. Also known as "Strange Skirts."
1941 105m/B Joan Crawford, Robert Taylor, Greer Garson, Herbert Marshall, Spring Byington; **D:** Robert Z. Leonard; **W/D:** Anita Loos, S.K. Lauren. **VHS $19.98** MGM 🎞🎞½

When Lightning Strikes Lightning the Wonder Dog prevents the owner of a rival lumber company from stealing his master's land. He gets to use his talents of running, swimming, barking, and smoking cigars. Proves that real woofers were made way back when, even though in 1934 they didn't feature scantily clad babes. Part of Video Yesteryear's Golden Turkey series.
1934 51m/B Francis X. Bushman, Lightning the Wonder Dog. **VHS, Beta $24.95** VYY Woof!

When Nature Calls A city family "gets back to nature" in this collection of mostly ineffective gags and poor satirical ideas. Probably your first and last chance to see Liddy and Mays on screen together.
1985 (R) 76m/C Davie Orange, Barbara Marineau, Nicky Beim, Tina Marie Stalano, Willie Mays, G. Gordon Liddy; **D:** Charles Kaufman. **VHS, Beta, LV $59.95** MED Woof!

When Taekwondo Strikes One brave Taekwondo master leads the Korean freedom fighters against the occupying army of WWII Japan.
1983 (R) 95m/C Jhoon Rhee, Ann Winton, Angela Mao, Huang Ing Sik; **D:** Raymond Chow. **VHS, Beta $9.98** SUE 🎞

When the Bough Breaks A psychologist helps the police with the case of a murder-suicide witnessed by a child. He finds one sick secret society at work in this unkinder, ungentler TV thriller, based on the novel by Jonathan Kellerman. Danson co-produced.
1986 100m/C Ted Danson, Richard Masur, Rachel Ticotin, David Huddleston, James Noble, Kim Miyori, Merritt Butrick; **D:** Waris Hussein. **VHS** WOV 🎞🎞

When the Clouds Roll By Psychosatire pits demented doctor against Fairbanks in experiment to make him suicidal basket case. Fairbanks seems to contract ferocious nightmares, passionate supersti-

tions, a spurning lover, and a warrant for his arrest, none of which suppresses his penchant for acrobatics.
1919 77m/B Douglas Fairbanks Sr., Herbert Grimwood, Kathleen Clifford, Frank Campeau, Ralph Lewis, Daisy Robinson, Albert MacQuarrie; **D:** Victor Fleming. **VHS, Beta $24.95** GPV, FCT 🎞🎞🎞½

When the Legends Die A Ute Indian strives to preserve his heritage in an often harsh modern world. Recorded in hi-fi.
1972 (PG) 105m/C Richard Widmark, Frederic Forrest; **D:** Stuart Millar. **VHS, Beta $19.98** FOX 🎞🎞🎞

When the Line Goes Through A drifter arrives in a small West Virginia town and changes the lives of two pretty sisters.
1971 90m/C Martin Sheen, Davey Davidson, Beverly Washburn. **VHS, Beta $39.95** NEG 🎞

When the North Wind Blows An old, lone trapper hunts for and later befriends the majestic snow tiger of Siberia in the Alaskan wilderness. A good family film.
1974 (G) 113m/C Henry Brandon, Herbert Nelson, Dan Haggerty; **D:** Stewart Raffill. **VHS, Beta $54.95** UHV, LME 🎞🎞

When the Screaming Stops A hunter is hired to find out who has been cutting the hearts out of young women who reside in a small village near the Rhine River. Turns out it's a she-monster who rules a kingdom beneath the river. Bad effects; gory gore; outlandish plot. All the ingredients, in other words, of a classic dog.
1973 (R) 86m/C SP Tony Kendall, Helga Line, Sylvia Tortosa; **D:** Armando de Ossorio. **VHS, Beta $59.98** LIV 🎞

When the Time Comes A woman dying of cancer wants to take her own life, but when her husband refuses, she seeks the help of a male friend. Excellent acting doesn't provide the needed depth. Less a disease-of-the-week TV movie, more of an ethical-dilemma-of-the-week, and just as trivial.
1991 (PG-13) 94m/C Bonnie Bedelia, Brad Davis, Terry O'Quinn, Karen Austin, Donald Moffatt, Wendy Schaal; **D:** John Erman; **M:** Marvin Hamlisch. **VHS $79.98** REP 🎞🎞

When the West Was Young An outdoor adventure about rounding up horses in the Old West. Based on a novel by Zane Grey; also titled "Wild Horse Mesa."
1932 58m/B Randolph Scott, Sally Blane, Guinn Williams; **D:** Henry Hathaway. **VHS, Beta $19.95** NOS, DVT, VYY 🎞½

When the Whales Came A conservationist fable about two children and a grizzled old codger living on a remote British isle during World War I. They try to avert disaster as mysterious narwhal whales descend on the island. Moralistic and uninvolving; poorly acted; slumber-inducing.
1989 (PG) 100m/C GB Paul Scofield, Helen Mirren, David Threlfall, David Suchet, Jeremy Kemp, Max Rennie; **D:** Clive Rees. **VHS, Beta, LV $14.98** FOX 🎞🎞½

When the Wind Blows An animated feature about a retired British couple when their peaceful—and naive—life in the country is destroyed by nuclear war. Poignant, sad, and thought-provoking, and just a little scary. Features the voices of Ashcroft and Mills; Roger Waters, David Bowie, Squeeze, Genesis, Hugh Cornell, and Paul Hardcastle all contribute to the soundtrack. Based on the novel by Raymond Briggs.
1986 80m/C GB D: Jimmy T. Murakami; **V:** Peggy Ashcroft, John Mills. **VHS, Beta, LV $79.95** LIV 🎞🎞🎞

When Thief Meets Thief A cat burglar finds his world turned upside down when he begins to fall in love with one of his victims. Not much happening except a few nice stunts by Fairbanks.
1937 85m/B GB Douglas Fairbanks Jr., Valerie Hobson, Alan Hale Jr., Jack Melford, Leo Genn, Ian Fleming; **D:** Raoul Walsh. **VHS, Beta $16.95** NOS, SNC 🎞½

When Time Ran Out A volcano erupts on a remote Polynesian island covered with expensive hotels and tourists with no way to escape. Contains scenes not seen in the theatrically released print of the film. A very good cast is wasted in this compilation of disaster film cliches.
1980 (PG) 144m/C Paul Newman, Jacqueline Bisset, William Holden, Ernest Borgnine, Edward Albert, Barbara Carrera, Valentina Cortese, Burgess Meredith, Pat Morita, Red Buttons; **D:** James Goldstone. **VHS, Beta $19.98** WAR 🎞

When Wolves Cry Tearjerker about an estranged father and young son reunited on a Corsican vacation. Their newfound joy sours when the lad is diagnosed with a fatal illness. **AKA:** The Christmas Tree.
1969 108m/C William Holden, Virna Lisi, Brook Fuller, Bourvil; **D:** Terence Young. **VHS, Beta $24.95** GEM 🎞½

When Women Had Tails A primitive comedy about prehistoric man's discovery of sex. And boy, did they ever discover it. Harmless (more or less), though not exactly cerebral. Followed by "When Women Lost Their Tails." **AKA:** Quando De Donne Avevando La Coda.
1970 (R) 99m/C IT Senta Berger, Frank Wolff; **D:** Pasquale Festa Campanile; **M:** Ennio Morricone. **VHS, Beta $16.95** SNC 🎞½

When Women Lost Their Tails Ostensible sequel to "When Women Had Tails" about prehistoric cavemen and their sexual habits.
1975 (R) 94m/C IT Senta Berger; **D:** Pasquale Festa Campanile; **M:** Ennio Morricone. **VHS, Beta $59.95** WWV 🎞

When Worlds Collide Another planet is found to be rushing inevitably towards earth, but a select group of people attempt to escape in a spaceship; others try to maneuver their way on board. Oscar-quality special effects and plot make up for cheesy acting and bad writing.
1951 (G) 81m/C Richard Derr, Barbara Rush, Larry Keating, Peter Hanson; **D:** Rudolph Mate. Academy Awards '51: Best Special Effects; Nominations: Best Color Cinematography. **VHS, Beta, LV $49.95** PAR 🎞🎞½

When Your Lover Leaves Alleged comedy about a woman, dumped by her married boyfriend, who gets involved in a short-lived relationship with a neighbor. When that also doesn't work out, she decides she must first do something to please herself. Here endeth the lesson. Produced by Fonzie and Richie of "Happy Days." Made for television.
1983 100m/C Valerie Perrine, Betty Thomas, David Ackroyd, Ed O'Neill, Dwight Schultz, Shannon Wilcox; **D:** Jeff Bleckner. **VHS $9.99** NWV, STE 🎞

When's Your Birthday? Brown stars in this comedy about a prize-fighter who is working his way through astrology school with his fighting skills. The stars, in turn, tell him when to fight. Lame zaniness (what other kind is there?) meant as a vehicle for Brown, though Kennedy is funnier. The opening sequence, an animated cartoon showing the influence of the moon over the planets, was filmed in Technicolor.

1937 77m/B Joe E. Brown, Marian Marsh, Edgar Kennedy; *D:* Harry Beaumont. **VHS, Beta $19.95** *NOS, VYY, JEF* ♪♪½

Where Angels Fear to Tread Another turn-of-the-century tale of the English in Italy from the pen of E.M. Forster. Widowed, fortyish Lilia (Mirren) is urged by her stuffy in-laws to spend some time in Italy chaperoned by the young Miss Abbott (Bonham Carter). Much to everyone's dismay Lilia impulsively marries a 21-year-old Italian and soon dies in childbirth. Her English relatives are loathe to leave the "beastly baby" with his father and Philip, the Italy-loving son (Graves) and his repressive sister Harriet (Davis) go to the child's rescue—with disasterous consequences. Based on Forster's first novel, published when he was 26, the characters are more stereotypical and the story less defined than his later works and the movies made from them. However, the impressive performances and beautiful settings make up for a somewhat lackluster direction.
1991 (PG) 112m/C *GB* Rupert Graves, Helena Bonham Carter, Judy Davis, Helen Mirren, Giovanni Guidelli, Barbara Jefford; *D:* Charles Sturridge. **VHS, LV $94.95** *NLC, TAM* ♪♪♪

Where Are the Children? Based on Mary Higgins Clark's bestseller. A woman who was cleared of murdering the children from her first marriage remarries. Then the children from her second marriage are kidnapped. Sustains suspense completely, until it falls apart.
1985 (R) 92m/C Jill Clayburgh, Max Gail, Barnard Hughes, Clifton James, Harley Cross, Elisabeth Harnois, Elizabeth Wilson, Frederic Forrest; *D:* Bruce Malmuth. **VHS, Beta $79.95** *COL* ♪½

Where Eagles Dare During World War II, a small group of Allied commandos must rescue an American general held by the Nazis in a castle in the Bavarian Alps. Relentless plot twists and action keep you breathless. Well-made suspense/adventure. Alistair MacLean adapted his original screenplay into a successful novel.
1968 (PG) 158m/C Clint Eastwood, Richard Burton, Mary Ure, Michael Hordern, Anton Diffring, Ingrid Pitt, Patrick Wymark, Robert Beatty; *D:* Brian G. Hutton. **VHS, Beta, LV $19.98** *MGM, TLF* ♪♪♪

Where East is East In Indochina a badly scarred trapper (Chaney) lives with his daughter (Velez) and sells wild animals to circuses. Velez falls in love with a circus owner's son but finds out her own mother, seeking revenge on her ex-husband, trying to seduce the young man. A gorilla figures in the plot as well. Chaney's makeup, which contributed to his "Man of a Thousand Faces" nickname, highlights a contrived movie.
1929 140m/B Lon Chaney Sr., Lupe Velez, Estelle Taylor, Lloyd Hughes. **VHS $29.95** *FCT* ♪♪½

Where Have All the People Gone? Solar explosion turns most of Earth's inhabitants to dust while the Anders family vacations in a cave. The family tries to return home amid the devastation. Bad timing, bad acting, bad script. Made for television.
1974 74m/C Peter Graves, Kathleen Quinlan, Michael-James Wixted, George O'Hanlon Jr., Verna Bloom; *D:* John Llewellyn Moxey. **VHS, Beta $59.95** *LHV* ♪

Where is My Child? Immigration to the New World brings only misfortune and betrayal in this tale of Jews in Eastern Europe between 1911 and 1937, as many

experience the loss of family ties and religion. In Yiddish with English subtitles.
1937 92m/B Celia Adler, Anna Lillian, Morris Strassberg; *D:* Abraham Leff, Harry Lynn. **VHS $54.00** *NCJ* ♪♪½

Where Sleeping Dogs Lie A struggling writer moves into an abandoned California home five years after a wealthy family was murdered there. While doing research for his novel on their brutal killings, he revives their ghosts as well as the very real presence of their killer.
1991 (R) 92m/C Dylan McDermott, Tom Sizemore, Sharon Stone; *D:* Charles Finch. **VHS $89.95** *COL, PMS* ♪♪

Where the Boys Are Four college girls go to Fort Lauderdale to have fun and meet boys during their Easter vacation. Features the film debuts of Francis, who had a hit single with the film's title song, and Prentiss. Head and shoulders above the ludicrous '84 remake.
1960 99m/C George Hamilton, Jim Hutton, Yvette Mimieux, Connie Francis, Paula Prentiss, Dolores Hart; *D:* Henry Levin. **VHS, Beta, LV $19.98** *MGM* ♪♪½

Where the Boys Are '84 Horrible remake of the 1960 comedy still features girls searching for boys during spring break in Fort Lauderdale. Telling about its era: charm gives way to prurience.
1984 (R) 95m/C Lisa Hartman, Wendy Schaal, Lorna Luft, Lynn-Holly Johnson; *D:* Hy Averback. **VHS, Beta $79.98** *FOX* Woof!

Where the Buffalo Roam Early starring role for Murray as the legendary "gonzo" journalist Hunter S. Thompson. Meandering satire based on Thompson's books "Fear and Loathing in Las Vegas" and "Fear and Loathing on the Campaign Trail '72." Either confusing or offensively sloppy, depending on whether you've read Thompson. Music by Neil Young, thank goodness, or this might be a woof.
1980 (R) 98m/C Bill Murray, Peter Boyle; *D:* Art Linson. **VHS, Beta $19.95** *MCA* ♪½

Where the Bullets Fly Fast-paced Bond spoof. A British spy takes on the intelligence forces of several governments in his search for a new fuel elixir. Fun, if not scintillating.
1966 88m/C *GB* Tom Adams, Dawn Addams, Michael Ripper, Tim Barrett; *D:* John Gilling. **VHS** *FOX* ♪♪

Where the Day Takes You Runaways on Hollywood Boulevard are depicted in an unfortunately heavy-handed drama. King (Mulroney) is the slightly older leader of a group of street kids who tries to discourage his friends from getting involved in the violence and drugs they see all around them. He falls in love with new runaway Heather (Boyle) but their love is blighted by the relentless bleakness of their lives. Among the other members of King's "family" are Astin, as a young druggie in thrall to his older dealer (MacLachlan) and Getty, as a young hustler drawn to violence. The story's predictability undercuts some convincing acting.
1992 (R) 105m/C Dermot Mulroney, Lara Flynn Boyle, Balthazar Getty, Sean Astin, Adam Baldwin, Kyle MacLachlan, Peter Dobson, Ricki Lake, James LeGros, Will Smith, Christian Slater, Laura San Giacomo, Leo Rossi; *W/D:* Marc Rocco; *W:* Kurt Voss. **VHS, LV** *COL* ♪♪½

Where the Eagle Flies Ersatz sixties rock'n'roll road movie shuffles together free spirited college coed, hobo with heart of gold, and rock and roller who's making a lane change out of the fast track. **AKA:** Pickup on 101.

1972 (PG) 93m/C Jack Albertson, Lesley Ann Warren, Martin Sheen, Michael Ontkean; *D:* John Florea. **VHS $39.99** *TPV* ♪♪

Where the Green Ants Dream A mining excavation in the Outback is halted by Aborigines who declare ownership of the sacred place where the mythical green ants are buried. A minor entry in the Herzog vision of modern-versus-primal civilization. Too obvious and somehow unsure of itself artistically. **AKA:** Wo Die Grunen Ameisen Traumen.
1984 99m/C *GE* Bruce Spence, Wandjuk Marika, Roy Marika, Ray Barrett, Norman Kaye, Colleen Clifford; *D:* Werner Herzog. **VHS, Beta $24.95** *XVC, MED, TAM* ♪♪½

Where the Heart Is Wealthy dad Coleman kicks his spoiled kids out on the streets to teach them the value of money. Meant as farce with a message. Flops in a big way; one senses it should have been much better.
1990 (R) 111m/C Dabney Coleman, Uma Thurman, Joanna Cassidy, Suzy Amis, Crispin Glover, Christopher Plummer; *D:* John Boorman. **VHS, LV $89.95** *TOU* ♪♪

Where the Hot Wind Blows The sexual scene in Sicily is sadly not succinctly summarized in this so-so cinematic soap. Cross-generational and cross-class couplings are constant. Think of it as "The Last Picture Show" in a similarly sorry setting, except boring. **AKA:** La Legge; La Loi; The Law.
1959 120m/C *FR IT* Gina Lollobrigida, Marcello Mastroianni, Yves Montand, Melina Mercouri, Paolo Stoppa; *D:* Jules Dassin. **VHS, Beta $39.95** *NOS, FCT* ♪♪

Where the Lilies Bloom The touching story of four backwoods children who are left orphans when their father dies. They don't report his death to authorities, because they are afraid the family will be separated and sent to an orphanage. Stanton is great as the crusty landlord the children gradually accept as a friend. Based on the book by Vera and Bill Cleaver.
1974 (G) 96m/C Julie Gholson, Jan Smithers, Matthew Burrill, Helen Harmon, Harry Dean Stanton, Rance Howard, Sudie Bond, Tom Spratley, Helen Bragdon, Alice Beardsley; *D:* William A. Graham. **VHS $14.95** *MGM* ♪♪♪

Where the North Begins A Mountie ransacks the Canadian countryside in search of crime.
1947 41m/B Russell Hayden, Jennifer Holt. **VHS, Beta, LV** *NO* ♪

Where the Red Fern Grows A young boy in Dust Bowl-era Oklahoma learns maturity from his love and responsibility for two Redbone hounds. Well produced, but tends to be hokey; good family fare. Followed by a sequel nearly twenty years later.
1974 (G) 97m/C James Whitmore, Beverly Garland, Jack Ging, Loni Chapman, Stewart Peterson; *D:* Norman Tokar. **VHS, Beta $14.98** *FHE, VES, HHE* ♪♪½

Where the Red Fern Grows: Part 2 Sequel to one of the most popular family movies of all time starring Brimley as Grandpa Coleman. Set deep in the Louisiana woods, this magical coming of age tale will touch the hearts of young and old viewers alike.
1992 (G) 105m/C Wilford Brimley, Doug McKeon, Lisa Whelchel, Chad McQueen. **VHS** *NO* ♪♪½

Where the River Runs Black An orphaned Indian child is raised in the Brazilian jungles by river dolphins. He is eventually befriended by a kindly priest who brings him into the modern world of violence and corruption. Slow pace is okay until the boy arrives at the orphanage, at which point the dolphin premise sadly falls by the wayside. **1986 (PG) 96m/C** Charles Durning, Peter Horton, Ajay Naidu, Conchata Ferrell, Alessandro Rabelo, Castulo Guerra; **D:** Christopher Cain. **VHS, Beta** $79.98 *FOX* ♫♫

Where the Sky Begins From the director of "Black Orpheus," this is a seven-part recreated history of turn-of-the-century aviation. **1984 420m/C** *FR* **D:** Marcel Camus. **VHS, Beta** $19.00 *VCD* ♫

Where the Spirit Lives Native children kidnapped by Canadian government agents are forced to live in dreadful boarding schools where they are abused emotionally and physically. St. John is a new arrival who refuses to put up with it and tries to escape. Engrossing and moving. **1989 (PG) 97m/C** *CA* Michelle St. John; **D:** Bruce Pittman. **VHS** $79.95 *BTV, HHE, UWA* ♫♫½

Where Time Began The discovery of a strange manuscript of a scientist's journey to the center of the earth leads to the decision to recreate the dangerous mission. Based on Jules Verne's classic novel "Journey to the Center of the Earth," but not anywhere near as fun or stirring. **1977 (PG) 87m/C** Kenneth More, Pep Munne, Jack Taylor; **D:** J.P. Simon. **VHS, Beta** $69.98 *SUE* ♫♫

Where Trails End Novel sci-fi western set during WWII with just about everything, including phosphorescent-clothed good guys, Nazis, scoundrels, literate horses, and Gallic sidekicks. Interestingly different. **1942 54m/B** Tom Keene, Joan Curtis, Charles King; **D:** Robert Tansey. **VHS, Beta** $12.95 *VDM, VYY* ♫♫

Where Were You When the Lights Went Out? A complicated, unsuccessful farce about a retiring Broadway actress, her jealous, possibly philandering husband, her greedy agent, an embezzler, and a citywide blackout. Film was actually not based on the 1965 New York City blackout but on a French play, "Monsieur Masure" by Claude Magnier, which was written nine years before. **1968 (PG) 94m/C** Doris Day, Patrick O'Neal, Robert Morse, Terry-Thomas, Lola Albright, Steve Allen, Jim Backus, Ben Blue, Pat Paulsen; **D:** Hy Averback. **VHS** $19.98 *MGM, MOV* ♫½

Where's Piccone A woman attempts, with the assistance of a two-bit hustler, to locate her missing husband, only to discover that he has led a double life in the Neapolitan underworld. Giannini as the sleazy hubby is perfectly cast. On-target social and political satire. In Italian with English subtitles. **1984 110m/C** *IT* Giancarlo Giannini, Lina Sastri, Aldo Guiffre, Clelia Rondinelli; **D:** Nanni Loy. **VHS, Beta** $59.95 *TAM, FCT, WBF* ♫♫♫

Where's Poppa? A Jewish lawyer's senile mother constantly ruins his love life, and he considers various means of getting rid of her, including dressing up as an ape to scare her to death. Filled with outlandish and often tasteless humor, befitting its reign as a black comedy cult classic. Adapted by Robert Klane from his novel. *AKA:* Going Ape. **1970 84m/C** George Segal, Ruth Gordon, Ron Leibman, Vincent Gardenia, Rob Reiner, Trish Van Devere; **D:** Carl Reiner. **VHS, Beta, LV** $19.95 *FOX* ♫♫♫

Where's Willie? Willie is a very bright boy; perhaps a little too bright. When he reveals his latest invention to the folks in his small town, everyone is out to get him. Find out why in this hilarious comedy.

1977 (G) 91m/C Guy Madison, Henry Darrow, Kate Woodville, Marc Gilpin; **D:** John Florea. **VHS, Beta** *NO* ♫♫♫

Which Way Home A Red Cross nurse attempts to flee Cambodia with four young orphans. An Australian smuggler befriends and helps her. Way too long and wandering, though like many a TV movie, it means well. **1990 141m/C** Cybill Shepherd, John Waters, Peta Toppano, John Ewart, Ruben Santiago-Hudson, Marc Gray; **D:** Carl Schultz; **W:** Michael Laurence. **VHS, Beta** $79.98 *TTC* ♫♫

Which Way Is Up? Pryor plays three roles in this story of an orange picker who accidentally becomes a union hero. He leaves his wife and family at home while he seeks work in Los Angeles. There he finds himself a new woman, starts a new family, and sells out to the capitalists. American version of the Italian comedy "The Seduction of Mimi" tries with mixed success for laughs. Pryor as a dirty old man is the high point. **1977 (R) 94m/C** Richard Pryor, Lonette McKee, Margaret Avery, Morgan Woodward, Marilyn Coleman; **D:** Michael Schultz. **VHS, Beta** $79.95 *MCA* ♫♫½

Which Way to the Front? Assorted Army rejects form a guerilla band and wage their own small-scale war during World War II. **1970 (G) 96m/C** Jerry Lewis, Jan Murray, John Wood, Steve Franken; **D:** Jerry Lewis. **VHS, Beta** $19.98 *WAR* ♫½

Whiffs A gullible man plays guinea pig in an Army experiment on germ warfare which leaves him with the intellect of a chimpanzee. Naturally, he then devises a plan to use the volatile gas in a chain of bank robberies. The title is appropriate—this movie is a stinker. **1975 (PG) 91m/C** Elliott Gould, Eddie Albert, Harry Guardino, Godfrey Cambridge, Jennifer O'Neill, Alan Manson; **D:** Ted Post. **VHS** $79.95 *MED* ♫

While I Live Woman meets female pianist with uncanny resemblance to sister who's been dead 25 years and rethinks her position on reincarnation. **1947 85m/B** *GB* Tom Walls, Clifford Evans, Carole Raye, Patricia Burke, Sonia Dresdel, John Warwick; **D:** John Harlow. **VHS, Beta** $16.95 *SNC* ♫½

While the City Sleeps Three newspaper reporters vie to crack the case of a sex murderer known as "The Lipstick Killer" with the editorship of their paper the prize. Good thriller-plus with the emphasis on the reporters' ruthless methods of gaining information rather than on the killer's motivations. Lang's last big success. Based on "The Bloody Spur" by Charles Einstein. **1956 100m/B** Dana Andrews, Rhonda Fleming, George Sanders, Howard Duff, Thomas Mitchell, Ida Lupino, Vincent Price, Mae Marsh; **D:** Fritz Lang. **VHS, Beta, LV** $15.95 *UHV* ♫♫

Whirlwind Horseman Substandard horse opera. Maynard's search for a gold prospector friend leads to a rancher and his pretty daughter. He beats up some bad guys, etcetera. **1938 60m/B** Ken Maynard, Joan Barclay, Bill Griffith; **D:** Bob Hill. **VHS, Beta** $19.95 *NOS, DVT, VCN* ♫

Whiskey Galore During World War II, a whiskey-less Scottish island gets a lift when a ship, carrying 50,000 cases of spirits, wrecks off the coast. A full-scale rescue operation and the evasion of both local and British government authorities ensue. The classic Ealing studio comedy is based on the actual wreck of a cargo ship off the Isle of Eriskay in 1941. *AKA:* Tight Little Island.

1948 81m/B *GB* Basil Radford, Joan Greenwood, Gordon Jackson, James Robertson Justice; **D:** Alexander MacKendrick. **VHS, Beta** $59.99 *HBO, HMV* ♫♫♫½

Whiskey Mountain Two couples go on a treasure hunt to Whiskey Mountain but instead find terror. **1977 (PG) 95m/C** Christopher George, Preston Pierce, Linda Borgeson, Roberta Collins, Robert Leslie; **D:** William Grefe. **VHS, Beta** $19.99 *BFV* ♫

A Whisper to a Scream An actress, in researching a film part, takes a job at a telephone sex service, creating different personas as she talks to keep herself interested. Soon, women resembling the personas are being murdered. Great premise fails to deliver fully, though there is some suspense. **1988 (R) 96m/C** *CA* Nadia Capone, Yaphet Kotto, Lawrence Bayne, Silvio Oliviero; **D:** Robert Bergman. **VHS, Beta, LV** *NO* ♫♫

Whispering City A female reporter receives an inside tip incriminating a prominent attorney in a murder committed several years earlier. She tries to get the evidence she needs before she becomes his latest victim. Highly suspenseful, thanks to competent scripting and directing. **1947 89m/B** *CA* Helmut Dantine, Mary Anderson, Paul Lukas; **D:** Fedor Ozep. **VHS, Beta** $16.95 *NOS, SNC* ♫♫

Whispering Shadow Serial starring the master criminal known as the "faceless whisperer." Twelve chapters, 13 minutes each. **1933 156m/B** Bela Lugosi, Robert Warwick; **D:** Al Herman, Colbert Clark. **VHS, Beta** $49.95 *NOS, SNC, VCN* ♫♫♫

Whispers Psycho Le Clerc repeatedly bothers writer Tennant even though she seems to have killed him. This dismays police guy Sarandon. Based on the novel by Dean R. Koontz. **1989 (R) 96m/C** Victoria Tennant, Chris Sarandon, Jean LeClerc; **D:** Douglas Jackson; **W:** Anita Doohan. **VHS, LV** $89.95 *LIV* ♫♫

Whispers in the Dark A psychiatrist counsels two odd patients—one is an ex-con turned painter with a violent streak, the other is a woman who reveals her kinky sexual experiences with a mystery man. Things get interesting when the doctor finds out her new lover is her patient's mystery man, and the patient turns up murdered. Confusing thriller seems forced but the experienced cast is worth watching. **1992 (R) 103m/C** Annabella Sciorra, Jamey Sheridan, Anthony LaPaglia, Jill Clayburgh, John Leguizamo, Deborah Unger, Alan Alda, Anthony Heald; **W/D:** Christopher Crowe. **VHS, Beta, LV** *PAR, PMS* ♫♫

The Whistle Blower A young government worker in England with a high-security position mysteriously dies. His father, a former intelligence agent, begins investigating his son's death and discovers sinister Soviet-related conspiracies. A lucid, complex British espionage thriller. Adapted from the John Hale novel by Julian Bond. **1987 98m/C** *GB* Michael Caine, Nigel Havers, John Gielgud, James Fox, Felicity Dean; **D:** Simon Langton. **VHS, Beta, LV** $19.98 *SUE, NLC* ♫♫♫

Whistle Down the Wind Three children of strict religious upbringing find a murderer hiding in their family's barn and believe him to be Jesus Christ. A well done and hardly grim or dull allegory of childhood innocence based on a novel by Mills's mother, Mary Hayley Bell. For a film relying heavily on child characters, it's important to portray

childhood well and realistically. That is done here, as in "To Kill a Mockingbird." Mills is perfect. The film is Forbes's directorial debut and Richard Attenborough's second production.
1962 98m/B *GB* Hayley Mills, Bernard Lee, Alan Bates; *D:* Bryan Forbes. **VHS, Beta** $19.98 SUE, NLC *♂♂♂½*

Whistle Stop A small-town girl divides her attentions between low-life gambler Raft, and villainous nightclub owner McLaglen, who plans a robbery-murder to get rid of any rivals. A forgettable gangster drama.
1946 85m/B George Raft, Ava Gardner, Victor McLaglen; *D:* Leonide Moguy. **VHS, Beta** $19.95 NOS, DVT, FCT *♂♂*

Whistlin' Dan Yet another lead cowpoke sets out to avenge the murder of a close relative. Maynard whistles while he walks (and rides) woodenly through this one.
1932 60m/B Ken Maynard, Joyzelle Joyner; *D:* Phil Rosen. **VHS, Beta** $19.95 NOS, UHV *♂♂*

Whistling Bullets Action galore in the story of an undercover Texas Ranger infiltrating a gang of thieves. The low budget doesn't detract from an exciting script and tight direction.
1936 58m/B Kermit Maynard, Jack Ingram; *D:* John English. **VHS, Beta** $19.95 NOS, DVT, RXM *♂♂½*

Whistling in Brooklyn Skelton again plays radio crime-solver Wally Benton in this third and last entry following "Whistling in the Dark" and "Whistling in Dixie." A cop-killer and the Brooklyn Dodgers baseball team figure in the mystery, which finds Skelton a suspect in the crimes.
1943 87m/B Red Skelton, Ann Rutherford, Jean Rogers, Rags Ragland, Ray Collins, Henry O'Neill, William Frawley, Sam Levene; *D:* Sylvan Simon. **VHS** $19.98 MGM *♂♂½*

Whistling in the Dark Skelton plays Wally Benton, a radio sleuth nicknamed "The Fox," in the first of a three-film series. Veidt (an always excellent villain) is the leader of a phony religious cult, after the money of one of his followers. He decides to kidnap Skelton and have him come up with a plan for the perfect murder but of course there are all sorts of comic complications. Skelton's first starring role is a clever comic mystery and a remake of the 1933 film. Followed by "Whistling in Dixie" and "Whistling in Brooklyn."
1941 78m/B Red Skelton, Ann Rutherford, Conrad Veidt, Virginia Grey, Rags Ragland, Eve Arden, Don Douglas, Don Costello, Paul Stanton, William Tannen, Reed Hadley; *D:* Sylvan Simon. **VHS** $19.98 MGM *♂♂♂*

Whitcomb's War Small town becomes a battleground among a host of comic characters who are unaware who really is in charge.
1988 67m/C Patrick Pankhurst, Leon Charles, Bill Morey, Robert Denison, Garnett Smith; *D:* Russell S. Doughten Jr. **VHS** MIV *♂½*

White Apache Emotionally charged saga of a man barred from both Indian and white societies, focusing on the impact of prejudice toward a white man raised by Apaches.
1988 90m/C **VHS, Beta** $79.95 IMP *♂♂*

The White Buffalo A strange, semi-surreal western parable about the last days of Wild Bill Hickok (Bronson) and his obsession with a mythical white buffalo that represents his fear of mortality. Something of a "Moby Dick" theme set in the Wild West. Clumsy but intriguing. *AKA:* Hunt to Kill.
1977 (PG) 97m/C Charles Bronson, Jack Warden, Will Sampson, Kim Novak, Clint Walker, Stuart Whitman, John Carradine, Slim Pickens, Cara Williams, Douglas Fowley; *D:* J. Lee

Thompson; *M:* John Barry. **VHS, Beta** $14.95 MGM *♂♂*

The White Butterfly Killer A young girl who witnesses her grandfather's murder by a group of ruthless opium dealers gets revenge by using her deadly kung fu.
19?? 90m/C Au Fong, Chee Fong, Wah Hon, Kwok H. Ting. **VHS, Beta** $49.95 OCE *♂*

White Cannibal Queen A young girl is captured by cannibals in the Amazon jungle, and her father spends years tracking her down.
1974 90m/C **VHS, Beta** $39.95 VCD Woof!

White Christmas Two ex-army buddies become a popular comedy team and play at a financially unstable Vermont inn at Christmas for charity's sake. Many swell Irving Berlin songs rendered with zest. Paramount's first Vista Vision film. Presented in widescreen on laserdisc. ♫The Best Things Happen While You're Dancing; Love, You Didn't Do Right By Me; Choreography; Count Your Blessings Instead of Sheep; What Can You Do With a General; Mandy; The Minstrel Show; Sisters; Heat Wave; Blue Skies; Let Me Sing; Abraham; Snow; The Old Man; Gee, I Wish I Was Back in the Army; White Christmas.
1954 120m/C Bing Crosby, Danny Kaye, Rosemary Clooney, Vera-Ellen, Dean Jagger; *D:* Michael Curtiz. **VHS, Beta, LV, 8mm** $14.95 PAR *♂♂♂*

The White Cliffs of Dover A prime example of a successful forties "women's weepie." Dunne is an American who comes to England in 1914 and promptly falls in love with the British Marshal. They marry but soon Marshal is off to war, where he is killed, never knowing about the son Dunne has given birth to. Dunne stays in England and as the boy grows a new threat looms with the rise of Hitler. Soon her now-grown son (Lawford) is off to do his duty and Dunne joins the Red Cross. She is later shocked to discover Lawford among the wounded, another victim of the ravages of war. Dunne is fine as the noble, sacrificing woman. McDowall plays the son's role as a boy with Taylor (with whom he'd already worked in "Lassie Come Home") as a childhood friend. Based on the poem by Alice Duer Miller. Bring the hankies.
1944 126m/B Irene Dunne, Alan Marshal, Frank Morgan, Peter Lawford, Gladys Cooper, May Whitty, C. Aubrey Smith, Roddy McDowall, Van Johnson, Elizabeth Taylor, June Lockhart, John Warburton, Jill Esmond, Norma Varden, Tom Drake, Arthur Shields; *D:* Clarence Brown. **VHS** $19.98 MGM, MOV *♂♂♂*

White Comanche Half-breed twins battle themselves and each other to a rugged climax.
1967 90m/C William Shatner, Joseph Cotten, Perla Cristal, Rossana Yanni; *D:* Gilbert Kay. **VHS, Beta** $19.95 NOS, UHV *♂½*

The White Dawn Three whalers are stranded in the Arctic in the 1890s and are taken in by an Eskimo vilage. They teach the villagers about booze, gambling, and other modern amenities. Resentment grows until a clash ensues. All three leads are excellent, especially Oates. Much of the dialogue is in an Eskimo language, subtitled in English, as in "Dances with Wolves."
1975 (PG) 110m/C Warren Oates, Timothy Bottoms, Louis Gossett Jr., Simonie Kopapik, Joanasie Salomonie; *D:* Philip Kaufman. **VHS, Beta, LV** $19.95 PAR *♂♂½*

White Eagle A white man who believes himself to be an Indian gets a job as a Pony Express rider and gets mixed up with horse rustlers. When he finds out who he really is, he is free to marry the white woman he's had his eye on. Interesting plot twist caused by the narrow-mindedness of the Hays Office.
1932 64m/B Buck Jones, Barbara Weeks, Robert Ellis, Jason Robards Sr., Robert Elliott, Jim Thorpe, Ward Bond; *D:* Lambert Hillyer. **VHS** $19.95 DVT, HEG *♂♂*

White Fang Boy befriends canine with big teeth and both struggle to survive in third celluloid rendition of Alaska during the Gold Rush. Beautiful cinematography. Based on Jack London book.
1991 (PG) 109m/C Klaus Maria Brandauer, Ethan Hawke, Seymour Cassel, James Remar, Susan Hogan; *D:* Randal Kleiser. **VHS, LV** $19.99 BVV, DIS, TVC *♂♂♂*

White Fang and the Hunter The adventures of a boy and his dog who survive an attack from wild wolves and then help to solve a murder mystery. Loosely based on the novel by Jack London.
1985 (G) 87m/C Pedro Sanchez, Robert Wood; *D:* Alfonso Brescia. **VHS, Beta** $19.95 STE, HHE *♂♂*

White Fire Brady, in search of his lost brother, gets involved in a smuggling ring. Seems the brother is falsely accused of murder and about to hang. Brady and bar singer Castle solve the case. Good photography; bad script. *AKA:* Three Steps to the Gallows.
1953 82m/C *GB* Scott Brady, Mary Castle, Ferdinand "Ferdy" Mayne; *D:* John Gilling. **VHS, Beta** $16.95 NOS, SNC *♂♂*

White Fire Two jewel thieves will stop at nothing to own White Fire, a two hundred-carat diamond.
1983 90m/C Robert Ginty, Fred Williamson. **VHS, Beta** $19.98 TWE *♂*

White Fury Couples on a campout are victimized by sleazy hoodlums during a snowstorm.
1990 89m/C Deke Anderson, Sean Holton, Douglas Hartier, Christine Shinn, Chastity Hammons; *D:* David A. Prior. **VHS** $79.95 AIP *♂*

White Ghost An Intelligence Officer who disappeared in the jungles of Asia 18 years ago is ready to come back to the United States, but not everyone wants to see him again.
1988 (R) 90m/C William Katt, Rosalind Chao, Martin Hewitt, Wayne Crawford, Reb Brown; *D:* B.J. Davis. **VHS, Beta** $19.98 TWE *♂*

White Gold Shepherd's son weds Mexican woman and his disgruntled father contrives apparent rendezvous between the wife and a ranch-hand, who's found dead in her bedroom. Seems no one believes the wife's story. Unprecedented, dark, silent drama.
1928 73m/B Jetta Goudal, Kenneth Thomson, George Bancroft, George Nichols, Clyde Cook; *D:* William K. Howard. **VHS, Beta** $19.95 GPV *♂♂♂*

White Gorilla A great white hunter sets out to kill a gigantic white gorilla that is terrorizing the black natives. Imperialist trash. On any informed person's list of all-time worst movies.
1947 62m/B Ray Corrigan, Lorraine Miller. **VHS, Beta, LV** NO Woof!

White Heat A classic gangster film with one of Cagney's best roles as a psychopathic robber/killer with a mother complex. The famous finale—perhaps Cagney's best-known scene—has Cagney trapped on top of a burning oil tank shouting "Made it, Ma! Top of the world!" before the tank explodes.

Cagney's character is allegedly based on Arthur "Doc" Barker and his "Ma," and his portrayal is breathtaking. Also available colorized.
1949 114m/B James Cagney, Virginia Mayo, Edmond O'Brien, Margaret Wycherly, Steve Cochran; *D:* Raoul Walsh. **VHS, Beta, LV $19.95** *MGM, FOX, PIA* 𝄞𝄞𝄞½

White Hot A young businessman loses his prestigious Wall Street job, and in order to live the good life, he resorts to selling drugs. Benson stars and directs.
1988 (R) 95m/C Robby Benson, Tawny Kitaen, Danny Aiello, Sally Kirkland, Judy Tenuta; *D:* Robby Benson. **VHS, Beta, LV $89.95** *ACA* 𝄞½

White Hot: The Mysterious Murder of Thelma Todd Thelma Todd was a Hollywood starlet found dead under strange circumstances in 1935. Buffs have sought a solution to the maybe-murder ever since; this treatment (based on the book "Hot Toddy" by Andy Edmunds) leaves too many loose ends for purists and isn't sufficiently gripping for the uninitiated.
1991 95m/C Loni Anderson, Robert Davi, Paul Dooley, Lawrence Pressman; *D:* Paul Wendkos. **VHS** *NO* 𝄞𝄞

White Hunter, Black Heart Eastwood casts himself against type as Huston-esque director who is more interested in hunting large tusked creatures than shooting the film he came to Africa to produce. Based on Peter Viertel's 1953 account of his experiences working on James Agee's script for Huston's "African Queen." Viertel scripted together with James Bridges and Burt Kennedy. Eastwood's Huston impression is a highlight, though the story occasionally wanders off with the elephants.
1990 (PG) 112m/C Clint Eastwood, Marisa Berenson, George Dzundza, Jeff Fahey, Timothy Spall, Charlotte Cornwell, Mel Martin, Alun Armstrong; *D:* Clint Eastwood. **VHS, Beta, LV, 8mm $19.98** *MGM, FCT, WAR* 𝄞𝄞𝄞

White Huntress Two brothers venturing into the jungle encounter a beautiful young woman, the daughter of a settlement leader. Meanwhile, a killer is on the loose. *AKA:* Golden Ivory.
1957 86m/C Robert Urquhart, John Bentley, Susan Stephen; *D:* George Breakston. **VHS, Beta $16.95** *SNC* 𝄞½

The White Legion Workers and engineers push their way through steaming jungles and reeking swamps while building the Panama Canal. Many fall victim to yellow fever. Physician Keith does some medical sleuthing and saves the day. Plodding, predictable drama.
1936 81m/B Ian Keith, Tala Birell, Snub Pollard; *D:* Karl Brown. **VHS, Beta $29.95** *VYY* 𝄞½

White Lie Len Madison, Jr. (Hines), a press secretary for the mayor of New York, receives an old photo of a lynched black man who he learns is his father, hung for raping a white woman. Madison returns to his Southern hometown to find out the truth behind his father's death, assisted by a white doctor (O'Toole) whose mother was a rape victim. They fall in love, adding to an already complicated situation, and incur the wrath of locals who are trying to keep the truth hidden. Based on the novel "Louisiana Black" by Samuel Charters.
1991 (PG-13) 93m/C Gregory Hines, Annette O'Toole, Bill Nunn; *D:* Bill Condon. **VHS $89.98** *MCA* 𝄞𝄞½

White Light "Flatliners" with a flatfoot; after a near-death experience a cop returns with memories of a beautiful woman. He tries to find out who she is/was in plodding

fashion. The voyage to the afterlife is represented by a jog through a storm sewer.
1990 (R) 96m/C Martin Kove, Allison Hossack, Martha Henry, Heidi von Palleske, James Purcell, Bruce Boa; *D:* Al Waxman. **VHS, LV $19.95** *ACA* 𝄞𝄞

White Lightning Good ol' boy Reynolds plays a moonshiner going after the crooked sheriff who murdered his brother. Good stunt-driving chases enliven the formula. The inferior sequel is "Gator." *AKA:* McKlusky.
1973 (PG) 101m/C Burt Reynolds, Ned Beatty, Bo Hopkins, Jennifer Billingsley, Louise Latham; *D:* Joseph Sargent. **VHS, Beta $29.95** *MGM* 𝄞𝄞½

White Line Fever A young trucker's search for a happy life with his childhood sweetheart is complicated by a corrupt group in control of the long-haul trucking business. Well-done action film of good triumphing over evil.
1975 (PG) 89m/C Jan-Michael Vincent, Kay Lenz, Slim Pickens, L.Q. Jones, John Garfield; *D:* Jonathan Kaplan. **VHS, Beta, LV $59.95** *COL* 𝄞𝄞½

White Mama A poor widow (Davis, in a splendid role) takes in a street-wise black kid (Harden) in return for protection from the neighborhood's dangers, and they discover friendship. Poignant drama, capably directed by Cooper, featuring sterling performances all around Made-for-TV drama at its best.
1980 96m/C Bette Davis, Ernest Harden, Eileen Heckart, Virginia Capers, Lurene Tuttle, Anne Ramsey; *D:* Jackie Cooper. **VHS, Beta $59.95** *LIV* 𝄞𝄞𝄞

White Mane The poignant, poetic story of a proud and fierce white stallion that continually eludes attempts by ranchers to capture it. In French with English subtitles.
1952 38m/B Alain Emery, Frank Silvera; *D:* Albert Lamorisse. **VHS, Beta, LV $14.95** *NLC, SUE, VYG* 𝄞𝄞𝄞

White Men Can't Jump Sometimes they can't act either. Small-time con man Harrelson stands around looking like a big nerd until someone dares him to play basketball and he proves to be more adept than he looks. After he beats Snipes, they become friends and start hustling together. Harrelson lays to rest the rumor that he can't act; here, he proves it. Fast-paced, obscenity-laced dialogue does not cover up for the fact that the story line hovers between dull and dismal, redeemed only by the surreal "Jeopardy" game show sequence and the convincing b-ball action. Snipes manages to rise above the material as well as the rim, while Perez, as wooden Woody's spitfire Hispanic girlfriend, is appropriately energetic.
1992 (R) 115m/C Wesley Snipes, Woody Harrelson, Rosie Perez, Tyra Ferrell, Cylk Cozart, Kadeem Hardison, Ernest Harden Jr., John Jones; *W/D:* Ron Shelton. **VHS $19.98** *FXV* 𝄞𝄞

White Mischief An alternately ghastly and hilarious indictment of the English upper class between the World Wars, and the decadence the English colonists perpetrated in Kenya, which came to world attention with the murder of the philandering Earl of Errol in 1941. Exquisitely directed and photographed. Acclaimed and grandly acted, especially by Scacchi; Howard's last appearance.
1988 (R) 108m/C Greta Scacchi, Charles Dance, Joss Ackland, Sarah Miles, John Hurt, Hugh Grant, Geraldine Chaplin, Trevor Howard, Murray Head, Susan Fleetwood, Alan Dobie; *D:* Michael Radford. **VHS, Beta, LV, SVS, 8mm $14.98** *SUE, SUP, NLC* 𝄞𝄞𝄞

White Nights Based on a love story by Dostoyevski. A young woman pines for the return of her sailor while a mild-mannered clerk is smitten by her. Both of their romantic fantasies are explored the dance-hall cadence is mixed with dreamy, fantastic flashbacks. In Italian with English subtitles. Equally good Soviet version made in 1959.
1957 107m/C *IT* Maria Schell, Jean Marais, Marcello Mastroianni; *D:* Luchino Visconti. **VHS $59.95** *FCT, TAM* 𝄞𝄞𝄞

White Nights A Russian ballet dancer who defected to the U.S. (Baryshnikov) is a passenger on a jet that crashes in the Soviet Union. With the aid of a disillusioned expatriate tap dancer (Hines), he plots to escape again. The excellent dance sequences elevate the rather lame story.
1985 (PG-13) 135m/C Mikhail Baryshnikov, Gregory Hines, Isabella Rossellini, Helen Mirren, Jerzy Skolimowski, Geraldine Page; *D:* Taylor Hackford. Academy Awards '85: Best Song ("Say You, Say Me"); Nominations: Best Song ("Separate Lives (Love Theme from White Nights)"). **VHS, Beta, LV $19.95** *COL* 𝄞𝄞

White of the Eye A murdering lunatic is on the loose in Arizona, and an innocent man must find him to acquit himself of the murders. A tense, effective thriller; dazzling technique recalls the experimental films of the 1960s.
1988 (R) 111m/C David Keith, Cathy Moriarty, Art Evans, Alan Rosenberg, Michael Greene, Alberta Watson; *D:* Donald Campbell. **VHS, Beta $14.95** *PAR* 𝄞𝄞𝄞

The White Orchid Romantic triangle ventures into the wilds of Mexico in search of Toltec ruins. Exceptional sets.
1954 81m/C William Lundigan, Peggy Castle, Armando Silvestre, Rosenda Monteros; *D:* Reginald LeBorg. **VHS, Beta $16.95** *SNC, DVT, HEG* 𝄞𝄞

White Palace Successful widowed Jewish lawyer Spader is attracted to older, less educated hamburger waitress Sarandon, and ethnic/cultural strife ensues, as does hot sex. Adapted from the Glenn Savan novel, it starts out with promise but fizzles toward the end.
1990 (R) 103m/C Susan Sarandon, James Spader, Jason Alexander, Eileen Brennan, Griffin Dunne, Kathy Bates, Steven Hill, Rachel Levin; *D:* Luis Mandoki. **VHS, LV $19.95** *MCA, FCT, CCB* 𝄞𝄞½

White Phantom: Enemy of Darkness Ninja warriors in modern day society battling against other evil ninjas.
1987 89m/C Page Leong, Jay Roberts Jr., Bo Svenson; *D:* Dusty Nelson; *W:* David Hamilton, Chris Gallagher. **VHS, Beta $79.95** *VMK* 𝄞

White Pongo A policeman goes undercover with a group of British biologists to capture a mythic white gorilla believed to be the missing link. A camp jungle classic with silly, cheap special effects.
1945 73m/B Richard Fraser, Maris Wrixon, Lionel Royce; *D:* Sam Newfield. **VHS, Beta $16.95** *SNC, NOS, HHT* Woof!

The White Rose An aspiring minister travels to see the world he intends to save, and winds up falling from grace. Complicated menage a trois is finally sorted out at the end. Silent.
1923 120m/B Mae Marsh, Carol Dempster, Ivor Novello, Neil Hamilton, Lucille LaVerne; *D:* D.W. Griffith. **VHS, Beta $27.95** *GPV* 𝄞𝄞𝄞

The White Rose The true story of a group of dissident students in Munich in 1942, who put their lives in danger by distributing leaflets telling the truth of what was going on in the concentration camps.

Hans Scholl was an Army officer who discovered the truth and told the others. In the end, most of the students were captured by the Gestapo and executed. "The White Rose" was the name of the group, but none survived to tell where the name came from. Verhoeven's film telling is engrossing and compelling, with excellent acting from the young cast. In German with English subtitles. 1983 108m/C GE Lena Stolze, Wulf Kessler, Oliver Siebert, Ulrich Tucker; D: Michael Verhoeven. VHS, Beta $79.00 MGM, GLV, SWC ���

White Sands When a dead man's body is found at a remote Indian reservation clutching a gun and a briefcase filled with $500,000, the local sheriff (Dafoe) takes his identity to see where the money leads. Using a phone number found on a piece of paper in the dead man's stomach, the sheriff follows clues until he finds himself mixed up with a rich woman (Mastrantonio) who sells black market weapons and uses the money to support "worthy" causes, and an FBI man (Jackson) who uses him as bait to lure a CIA turncoat/arms dealer (Rourke). Sound confusing? It is, and despite the strong cast and vivid scenery of the southwest United States, this film just doesn't cut it. 1992 (R) 101m/C Willem Dafoe, Mary Elizabeth Mastrantonio, Mickey Rourke, Mimi Rogers, Sam Jackson, M. Emmet Walsh, James Rebhorn, Maura Tierney, Beth Grant, Miguel Sandoval, John Lafayette; Cameos: Fred Dalton Thompson, John C. Ryan; D: Roger Donaldson. VHS, Beta, LV $94.99 WAR, FCT ��1/2

White Shadows in the South Seas Alcohol, drugs, and prostitution take their toll on the native population of Tahiti in this early talkie. Blue plays a western doctor who marries the daughter of a native chief. However, he finds greed for the island's pearl treasures drawing other unscrupulous westerners to destroy the unspoiled paradise. 1928 88m/B Monte Blue, Robert Anderson, Raquel Torres; D: Woodbridge S. Van Dyke. VHS $29.95 FCT ��1/2

The White Sheik Fellini's first solo effort. A newly wed bride meets her idol from the comic pages (made with photos, not cartoons; called fumetti) and runs off with him. She soon finds he's as ordinary as her husband. Brilliant satire in charming garb. Remade as "The World's Greatest Lover." Woody Allen's "The Purple Rose of Cairo" is in a similar spirt. In Italian with subtitles. AKA: Lo Sceicco Bianco. 1952 86m/B JP Alberto Sordi, Giulietta Masina, Brunella Bova, Leopoldo Trieste; D: Federico Fellini. VHS, Beta $29.95 NOS, CVC, TAM ��

The White Sin An innocent country girl hires on as maid of a rich woman and is seduced and abandoned by the woman's profligate son, but everything turns out all right by the end of the third handkerchief. Silent with original organ music. 1924 93m/B Madge Bellamy, John Bowers, Billy Bevan; D: William A. Seiter. VHS, Beta, 8mm $29.99 VYY ��

The White Sister Gish is an Italian aristocrat driven from her home by a conniving sister. When her true love (Colman) is reported killed she decides to become a nun and enters a convent. When her lover does return he tricks her into leaving the convent but before he can persuade her to renounce her vows Vesuvius erupts and he goes off to warn the villagers, dying for his efforts. Gish then re-dedicates herself to her faith. Colman's first leading role, which made him a romantic star. Filmed on location in Italy.

1923 108m/B Lillian Gish, Ronald Colman, Gail Kane, J. Barney Sherry, Charles Lane; D: Henry King. VHS, Beta $19.98 DVT, HEG ���1/2

White Slave An Englishwoman is captured by bloodthirsty cannibals and, rather than being eaten, is tormented and made a slave. AKA: Amazonia: The Catherine Miles Story. 1986 (R) 90m/C Elvire Avoray, Will Gonzales, Andrew Louis Coppola; D: Roy Garrett. VHS, Beta NO �

The White Tower Five men and a woman set out to scale the infamous White Tower in the Alps. Each person's true nature is revealed as he or she scales the peak, which has defied all previous attempts. Slightly overwrought, but exciting. Filmed in Technicolor on location in the Swiss Alps. 1950 98m/C Glenn Ford, Claude Rains, Cedric Hardwicke, Oscar Homolka, Lloyd Bridges; D: Ted Tetzlaff. VHS, Beta $19.98 HHT, TTC ���

White Water Summer A group of young adventurers trek into the Sierras, and find themselves struggling against nature and each other to survive. Bacon is the rugged outdoorsman (yeah, sure) who shows them what's what. Chances are it was never at a theater near you, and with good reason. AKA: Rites of Summer. 1987 (PG) 90m/C Kevin Bacon, Sean Astin, Jonathan Ward, Matt Adler; D: Jeff Bleckner. VHS, Beta, LV $29.95 COL �1/2

The White Zombie Lugosi followed his success in "Dracula" with the title role in this low-budget horror classic about the leader of a band of zombies who wants to steal a beautiful young woman from her new husband. Set in Haiti; the first zombie movie. Rich and dark, though ludicrous. Based on the novel "The Magic Island" by William Seabrook. 1932 73m/B Bela Lugosi, Madge Bellamy, John Harron; D: Victor Halperin. VHS, Beta, 3/4U, Special order formats $19.95 NOS, PSM, QNE ���

WhiteForce A secret agent tracks an enemy. His government tracks him. He runs around with a big machine gun and a couple of hand grenades. He fires the gun and throws the grenades. 1988 (R) 90m/C Sam Jones, Kimberly Pistone; D: Eddie Romero. Beta NO �

Whitewater Sam Whitewater Sam and his Siberian Husky, Sybar, embark on an exciting trip through the uncharted wilds of the Great Northwest. The likeable, intelligent hound steals the show. Good family adventure. Written, directed and coproduced by star Larsen. 1978 (G) 87m/C Keith Larsen. VHS, Beta MON ��1/2

Who Am I This Time? Two shy people can express their love for each other only through their roles in a local theater production of "A Streetcar Named Desire." Good cast responds well to competent direction from Demme; poignant, touching and memorable. Based on a story by Kurt Vonnegut, Jr. Made for television. 1982 60m/C Susan Sarandon, Christopher Walken, Robert Ridgely; D: Jonathan Demme. VHS, Beta, LV $24.95 MON ���

Who Done It? Average Abbott and Costello comedy about two would-be radio mystery writers, working as soda-jerks, who play detective after the radio station's president is murdered.

1942 77m/B Bud Abbott, Lou Costello, William Gargan, Patric Knowles, Louise Allbritton, Don Porter, Jerome Cowan, William Bendix, Mary Wickes; D: Erle C. Kenton. VHS, Beta $14.95 MCA ��

Who Framed Roger Rabbit? Technically marvelous, cinematically hilarious, eye-popping combination of cartoon and live action create a Hollywood of the 1940s where cartoon characters are real and a repressed minority working in films. A 'toon-hating detective is hired to uncover the unfaithful wife of 2-D star Roger, and instead uncovers a conspiracy to wipe out all 'toons. Special appearances by many cartoon characters from the past. Coproduced by Touchstone (Disney) and Amblin (Spielberg). Adapted from "Who Censored Roger Rabbit?" by Gary K. Wold. 1988 (PG) 104m/C Bob Hoskins, Christopher Lloyd, Joanna Cassidy, Alan Tilvern, Stubby Kaye; D: Robert Zemeckis; V: Charles Fleischer, Mae Questel, Kathleen Turner, Amy Irving, Mel Blanc, June Foray, Frank Sinatra. Academy Awards '88: Best Film Editing, Best Visual Effects; Nominations: Best Art Direction/Set Decoration, Best Cinematography, Best Sound; National Board of Review Awards '88: 10 Best Films of the Year. VHS, Beta, LV $19.99 TOU, WTA ���1/2

Who Has Seen the Wind? Two boys grow up in Saskatchewan during the Depression. So-so family viewing drama. Ferrer as a bootlegger steals the otherwise small-paced show. 1977 102m/C Jose Ferrer, Brian Painchaud, Charmion King, Helen Shaver. VHS, Beta SUE ��

Who is Killing the Great Chefs of Europe? A fast-paced, lightly handled black comedy. When a gourmand, well-played by Morley, learns he must lose weight to live, a number of Europe's best chefs are murdered according to their cooking specialty. A witty, crisp, international mystery based on Ivan and Nan Lyon's novel. AKA: Too Many Chefs; Someone is Killing the Great Chefs of Europe. 1978 (PG) 112m/C George Segal, Jacqueline Bisset, Robert Morley, Jean-Pierre Cassel, Philippe Noiret, Jean Rochefort, Joss Ackland, Nigel Havers; D: Ted Kotcheff. VHS $19.98 HBO, WAR ���

Who Is the Black Dahlia? In L.A. in 1947, a detective tries to find out who murdered a star-struck 22-year-old woman (Arnaz) nicknamed "The Black Dahlia." Well scripted by Robert W. Lenski and superb cast. Based on a famous unsolved murder case, the case was later the base for "True Confessions." Made for TV. 1975 96m/C Efrem Zimbalist Jr., Lucie Arnaz, Ronny Cox, MacDonald Carey, Linden Chiles; D: Joseph Pevney. VHS, Beta $29.95 WOV ���

Who Killed Baby Azaria? Parents are arrested for infanticide after they claim their baby was stolen by a wild dog while vacationing on a supposedly haunted Australian mountain, or was it an aboriginal spirit that absconded with the tyke? Less compelling than the American remake, "A Cry in the Dark." Made for Australian TV. 1983 96m/C AU Elaine Hudson, John Hamblin, Peter Carroll; D: Judy Rymer. VHS, Beta $59.95 PSM ��

Who Killed Doc Robbin? A group of youngsters try to clear their friend, Dan, the town handyman, when the sinister Dr. Robbin is murdered. The follow-up to "The Adventures of Curly and His Gang;" intended as part of a Roach kid-comedy series in the manner of "Our Gang." Fast pace and lots of slapstick give a first impression of spirited

juvenile hijinks, but not much is genuinely funny. And the names of the two black kids—"Dis" and "Dat"—aren't funny either. *AKA:* Sinister House; Curley and His Gang in the Haunted Mansion.
1948 50m/C Larry Olsen, Don Castle, Bernard Carr, Virginia Grey. **VHS, Beta** $16.95 *SNC, NOS, HHT ♂♂*

Who Killed Mary What's 'Er Name? A diabetic ex-fighter tracks a prostitute's killer through Greenwich Village. Illogical, incredible and disjointed attempt at comedy/mystery. Odd, unsatisfying ending, with the boxer going into a coma. Good supporting cast. *AKA:* Death of a Hooker.
1971 (PG) 90m/C Red Buttons, Sylvia Miles, Conrad Bain, Ron Carey, David Doyle, Sam Waterston; *D:* Ernie Pintoff. **VHS, Beta** $59.95 *GEM, PSM ♂♂*

Who Shot Pat? Funny, nostalgic, coming of age story set in fifties Brooklyn. Knight stars as Bic Bickham, the leader of a clean living "gang" of seniors at a Brooklyn vocational school. Memorable vintage soundtrack features hits by legendary artists Chuck Berry and Bo Diddly. *AKA:* Who Shot Patakango?.
1992 (R) 102m/C David Knight, Sandra Bullock, Kevin Otto, Aaron Ingram; *W/D:* Robert Brooks; *W:* Halle Brooks. **VHS** $89.99 *WAR ♂♂½*

Who Slew Auntie Roo? An updated twist on the Hansel and Gretel fairy tale. Features Winters as an odd, reclusive widow mistaken for the fairy tale's children-eating witch by one of the orphans at her annual Christmas party—with dire consequences. *AKA:* Whoever Slew Auntie Roo?; Gingerbread House.
1971 (PG) 90m/C Shelley Winters, Ralph Richardson, Mark Lester, Lionel Jeffries, Hugh Griffith; *D:* Curtis Harrington. **VHS, Beta** $69.95 *VES ♂♂½*

Whodunit The bad horror flicks always seem to have (usually young) characters murdered one at a time, often on a remote island. This loser is no exception.
1982 (R) 82m/C Rick Bean, Gary Phillips; *D:* Bill Naud. **VHS, Beta** $69.98 *LIV, VES ♂*

Whoever Says the Truth Shall Die A film portrait of the great Italian filmmaker Pier Paolo Pasolini, his work in film and letters, his life as a homosexual, anti-Fascist and Communist, until his murder in 1975. A highly acclaimed, searingly controversial documentary featuring interviews and copious clips from Pasolini's films. In English, Italian and French with English subtitles.
1981 60m/C Bernardo Bertolucci, Laura Betti, Pier Paolo Pasolini; *D:* Philo Bregstein. **VHS, Beta** $59.95 *FCT ♂*

The Whole Shootin' Match Two thirty something Texas nobodies chase the American Dream via a sure-fire invention called the Kitchen Wizard, after failing in the small-animal biz and polyurethane. Offbeat, very low-budget independent feature shot interestingly in sepia tones. Sympathetic and human.
1979 108m/C Matthew L. Perry, Sonny Davis, Doris Hargrave; *D:* Eagle Pennell. **VHS, 3/4U** *NO ♂♂♂*

Who'll Save Our Children? Two children are abandoned and left on the doorstep of a middle-aged, childless couple. Years later the natural parents, now reformed, attempt to reclaim their children. Well cast and topical. Made for TV.
1982 96m/C Shirley Jones, Len Cariou; *D:* George Schaefer. **VHS, Beta** *TLF ♂♂♂*

Who'll Stop the Rain? A temperamental Vietnam vet (Nolte) is enlisted in a smuggling scheme to transport a large amount of heroin into California. An excellent blend of drama, comedy, action, suspense, and tragedy. Based on Robert Stone's novel "Dog Soldiers" (also its alternate title). Outstanding period soundtrack by Creedence Clearwater Revival, including title song. Violent and compelling tale of late-'60s disillusionment. *AKA:* Dog Soldiers.
1978 (R) 126m/C Nick Nolte, Tuesday Weld, Michael Moriarty, Anthony Zerbe, Richard Masur, Ray Sharkey, David Opatoshu, Charles Haid, Gail Strickland; *D:* Karel Reisz. **VHS, Beta, LV** $14.95 *MGM ♂♂♂½*

Wholly Moses! Set in biblical times, this alleged comedy concerns a phony religious prophet who begins to believe that his mission is to lead the chosen. Horrible ripoff of "Life of Brian," released the previous year. What a cast—what a waste!
1980 (PG) 125m/C Dudley Moore, Laraine Newman, James Coco, Paul Sand, Dom DeLuise, Jack Gilford, John Houseman, Madeline Kahn, Richard Pryor, John Ritter; *D:* Gary Weiss. **VHS, Beta, LV** $9.95 *COL Woof!*

Whoopee! Cantor stars in his first sound picture as a rich hypochondriac sent out west for his health, where he encounters rugged cowboys and Indians. Filmed in two-color Technicolor and based on Ziegfeld's 1928 Broadway production with the same cast. Dances supervised by Busby Berkeley. ♫The Song of the Setting Sun; Mission Number; Makin' Whoopee; A Girlfriend of a Boyfriend of Mine; My Baby Just Cares for Me; I'll Still Belong to You; Stetson; Song of the Setting Sun.
1930 93m/C Eddie Cantor, Ethel Shutta, Paul Gregory, Eleanor Hunt, Betty Grable, George Olsen & His Orchestra; *D:* Thornton Freeland. **VHS, Beta** $19.98 *SUE, HBO ♂♂*

The Whoopee Boys A New York lowlife in Palm Beach tries to reform himself by saving a school for needy children so his rich girlfriend will marry him. Full of unfunny jokes and very bad taste, with no redeeming qualities whatever.
1986 (R) 89m/C Michael O'Keefe, Paul Rodriguez; *D:* John Byrum; *M:* Jack Nitzsche. **VHS, Beta, LV** $79.95 *PAR ♂*

Whoops Apocalypse Satiric account of events leading up to World War III. Invasion in South America leads British prime minister to suggest nuclear retaliation. Uneven but funny, though lacks Strangelovian bite. Based on the British hit television series and scripted by series writers Andrew Marshall and David Renwick.
1983 137m/C GB John Cleese, John Barron, Richard Griffiths, Peter Jones, Bruce Montague, Barry Morse, Rik Mayall, Ian Richardson, Alexei Sayle, Herbert Lom, Joanne Pearce; *D:* Tom Bussmann. **VHS, Beta** $59.95 *PAV ♂♂½*

Whoops Apocalypse America's first female president Swit, recently ensconced after the untimely death of the ex-circus clown previous president, is forced to contend with hotheaded superpowers who want to kick off WWIII with a bang. Uneven black comedic satire of holocaust genre. Based on the BBC TV series.
1988 (R) 93m/C Loretta Swit, Peter Cook, Michael Richards. **VHS, Beta** $14.95 *MGM ♂♂*

Whore Ken Russell's gritty night in the life of cynical prostitute Theresa Russell is strong medicine, a powerful antidote to sappy Hollywood films that glorify streetwalking. Also available in the 92-minute original uncut version, an 85-minute NC-17 version, and an

alternate R-Rated version titled "If You Can't Say It, Just See It."
1991 (R) 80m/C Theresa Russell, Antonio Vargas; *D:* Ken Russell. **VHS** $92.95 *VMK ♂♂*

Who's Afraid of Virginia Woolf? Nichols debuts as a director in this biting Edward Albee play. A teacher and his wife (Segal and Dennis) are invited to the home of a burned-out professor and his foul-mouthed, bitter, yet seductive wife (Burton and Taylor). The guests get more than dinner, as the evening deteriorates into brutal verbal battles between the hosts. Taylor and Dennis won Oscars; Burton's Oscar-nominated portrait of the tortured husband is magnificent. Richard and Liz's best film together.
1966 127m/B Richard Burton, Elizabeth Taylor, George Segal, Sandy Dennis; *D:* Mike Nichols. Academy Awards '66: Best Actress (Taylor), Best Art Direction/Set Decoration (B & W), Best Black and White Cinematography, Best Costume Design (B & W), Best Supporting Actress (Dennis); Nominations: Best Actor (Burton), Best Adapted Screenplay, Best Director (Nichols), Best Film Editing, Best Picture, Best Sound, Best Supporting Actor (Segal), Best Original Score; National Board of Review Awards '66: 10 Best Films of the Year, Best Actress (Taylor). **VHS, Beta, LV** $19.98 *WAR, PIA, BTV ♂♂♂♂*

Who's Got the Action? Martin and Turner are a husband and wife divided by his love of playing the ponies. In order to keep his gambling under control Turner schemes to become his new bookie. But when Martin suddenly goes on a winning streak, the new bookie is in trouble with her former competition, who just happen to be the Mob. Strained, flat comedy with Turner especially miscast.
1962 93m/C Lana Turner, Dean Martin, Walter Matthau, Eddie Albert, Nita Talbot, Margo, Paul Ford, John McGiver, Jack Albertson; *D:* Daniel Mann; *W:* Jack Rose. **VHS** $14.95 *PAR ♂♂½*

Who's Harry Crumb? Bumbling detective Candy can't even investigate a routine kidnapping! His incompetence is catching: the viewer can't detect a single genuinely funny moment. Candy is the only likeable thing in this all-around bad, mindless force.
1989 (PG-13) 95m/C John Candy, Jeffrey Jones, Annie Potts, Tim Thomerson, Barry Corbin, Shawnee Smith, Valri Bromfield, Renee Coleman, Joe Flaherty, Lyle Alzado, James Belushi, Stephen Young; *D:* Paul Flaherty. **VHS, Beta, LV** $14.95 *COL ♂½*

Who's Minding the Mint? A money checker at the U.S. Mint must replace $50,000 he accidentally destroyed. He enlists a retired money printer and an inept gang to infiltrate the mint and replace the lost cash, with predictable chaos resulting. Nonstop zaniness in this wonderful comedy that never got its due when released. Thieves who befriend Hutton include Denver of "Gilligan's Island" and Farr, later of "M*A*S*H."
1967 97m/C Jim Hutton, Dorothy Provine, Milton Berle, Joey Bishop, Bob Denver, Walter Brennan, Jamie Farr; *D:* Howard Morris. **VHS, Beta** $9.95 *GKK ♂♂♂*

Who's That Girl? A flighty, wrongly-convicted parolee kidnaps her uptight lawyer and they have wacky adventures as she goes in search of the crumb that landed her in the pokey. Plenty of Madonna tunes, if that's what you like; they briefly keep you from wondering why you're not laughing. Kind of a remake (a bad one) of "Bringing Up Baby" (1938).
1987 (PG) 94m/C Madonna, Griffin Dunne, John Mills, Haviland Morris; *D:* James Foley. **VHS, Beta, LV, 8mm** $19.98 *WAR ♂*

Who's That Knocking at My Door? Interesting debut for Scorsese, in which he exercises many of the themes and techniques that he polished for later films. An autobiographical drama about an Italian-American youth growing up in New York City, focusing on street life, Catholicism and adolescent bonding. Begun as a student film called "I Call First," later developed into a feature. Keitel's film debut. *AKA: J.R.; I Call First.*
1968 90m/B Harvey Keitel, Zena Bethune; *D:* Martin Scorsese. VHS, Beta $59.99 *DCL, FCT, WAR* ♫♫♫

Who's the Man? Two clowning companions who work in a barbershop in Harlem get recruited onto the police force to investigate a murder. Doctor Dre and Ed Lover (themselves) make use of their hip-hop music connections and full-throttle slapstick humor to enliven the search. The stars are the hosts of the hit MTV series "Yo! MTV Raps." Salt of "Salt 'n' Pepa," is the female lead and Ice-T plays a gangster. First-time director Demme works his star duo for both foolish and vulgar humor. Filming done mostly on location in Harlem. Includes a lengthy list of cameo appearances by several hip-hop performers. For fans; based on a story by Dre, Lover, and Seth Greenland.
1993 (R) 124m/C Dr. Dre, Ed Lover, Cheryl "Salt" James, Ice-T, Jim Moody, Colin Quinn, Kim Chan, Rozwill Young, Badja Djola, Richard Bright, Dennis Leary, Andre B. Blake, Bill Bellamy; *D:* Ted Demme; *W:* Seth Greenland; *M:* Andre Harrell. VHS *NYR* ♫♫

Whose Child Am I? A woman so desperately wants a child of her own that she doesn't mind who the father is. Ludicrous and vulgar.
1975 (R) 90m/C Kate O'Mara, Paul Freeman, Edward Judd, Felicity Devonshire; *D:* Lawrence Britten. VHS $59.95 *ATL* ♫

Whose Life Is It Anyway? Black humor abounds. Sculptor Dreyfuss is paralyzed from the neck down in an auto accident. What follows is his struggle to persuade the hospital authorities to let him die. Excellent cast headed impressively by Dreyfuss; Lahti as his doctor and hospital head Cassavetes also are superb. From Brian Clark's successful Broadway play, scripted by Clark and Reginald Rose.
1981 (R) 118m/C Richard Dreyfuss, John Cassavetes, Christine Lahti, Bob Balaban, Kenneth McMillan, Kaki Hunter, Thomas Carter; *D:* John Badham. VHS, Beta $79.95 *MGM* ♫♫♫½

Why Me? Two jewel thieves unknowingly steal an enormously valuable ruby ring and are in over their heads trying to evade the cops and everyone else. In the same vein as the much-funnier "Nuns on the Run," this caper is done in by bad acting and too much ill-conceived slapstick. Adapted by Donald E. Westlake from his own novel.
1990 (R) 96m/C Christopher Lambert, Christopher Lloyd, Kim Greist, J.T. Walsh, Michael J. Pollard, Tony Plana, John Hancock, Lawrence Tierney; *D:* Gene Quintano. VHS, LV $89.95 *COL* ♫♫

Why Shoot the Teacher A young teacher sent to a one-room schoolhouse in a small prairie town in Saskatchewan during the Depression gets a cold reception on the cold prairie. One of the more popular films at the Canadian box office. Cort was Harold in "Harold and Maude." Based on the novel by Max Braithwaite.
1979 101m/C *CA* Bud Cort, Samantha Eggar, Chris Wiggins; *D:* Silvio Narizzano. VHS, Beta $69.98 *SUE* ♫♫♫

The Wicked Though packaged as serious horror, this is a cheap, tacky spoof with folks stranded at the country residence of a vampire family. Sole point of interest: these Transylvanian cliches take place in the Australian outback. Kids might actually like this (gore isn't severe), if they can surmount the thick Down Under accents.
1989 87m/C Brett Cumo, Richard Morgan, Angela Kennedy, Maggie Blinco, John Doyle; *D:* Colin Eggleston. VHS $79.95 *HMD* ♫

The Wicked Lady Posh but lame costume drama about a bored 17th century noblewoman who takes to highway robbery to spice up her life. Credulity-stretcher extraordinaire. Based on "The Life and Death of Wicked Lady Skelton" by Magdalen King-Hall. Mason is cheeky as a fellow highwayman. Remade in 1983 with Faye Dunaway.
1945 103m/B *GB* James Mason, Margaret Lockwood, Patricia Roc, Michael Rennie, Felix Aylmer, Enid Stamp-Taylor, Griffith Jones; *D:* Louis Levy. VHS, Beta *NO* ♫♫

The Wicked Lady Remake of the 1945 costumer about a 17th-century noblewoman trying her hand at highway robbery. More noted for its low-cut costumes and racy humor than any talent involved.
1983 (R) 99m/C *GB* Faye Dunaway, John Gielgud, Denholm Elliott, Alan Bates, Glynis Barber, Oliver Tobias, Prunella Scales; *D:* Michael Winner. VHS, Beta $79.95 *MGM* ♫½

Wicked Stepmother A family discovers that an aged stepmother is actually a witch. Davis walked off the film shortly before she died, and was replaced by Carrera. Davis's move was wise; the result is dismal, and would have been had she stayed. As it is the newer wonders: How come the stepmother isn't Davis anymore? Davis's unfortunate last role.
1989 (PG-13) 90m/C Bette Davis, Barbara Carrera, Colleen Camp, Lionel Stander, David Rasche, Tom Bosley, Seymour Cassel, Evelyn Keyes, Richard Moll, Laurene Landon; *D:* Larry Cohen. VHS, Beta $79.95 *MGM* ♫

The Wicker Man The disappearance of a young girl leads a devoutly religious Scottish policeman to an island whose denizens practice bizarre pagan sexual rituals. An example of occult horror that achieves its mounting terror without gratuitous gore. The first original screenplay by playwright Anthony Shaffer. Beware shortened versions that may still lurk out there; the 103-minute restored director's cut is definitive.
1975 103m/C Edward Woodward, Britt Ekland, Diane Cilento, Ingrid Pitt, Christopher Lee; *D:* Robin Hardy. VHS, Beta $19.95 *MED* ♫♫♫½

Wide Open Faces Every crook in town is looking for some missing stolen loot. Soda jerk Brown outwits them all in his own inimitable way. The story may be predictable, but Brown's physical humor keeps things interesting.
1938 67m/B Joe E. Brown, Jane Wyman, Alison Skipworth, Alan Baxter, Lucien Littlefield, Sidney Toler, Berton Churchill, Barbara Pepper, Stanley Fields, Horace Murphy; *D:* Kurt Neumann. VHS $19.95 *NOS* ♫♫

The Widow A story about a woman slowly learning to deal with her own grief, her children's traumas and monetary worries after the death of her husband. Straightforward, passable made for TV domestic drama based on Lynn Caine's best-selling novel.
1976 99m/C Michael Learned, Farley Granger, Bradford Dillman, Robert Lansing; *D:* J. Lee Thompson. VHS, Beta *TLF, LME* ♫♫

Widow Couderc A provincial widow unknowingly includes an escaped murderer among her liaisons. Based on a novel by Georges Simenon. In French with English subtitles.
1974 92m/C *FR* Simone Signoret, Alain Delon; *D:* Pierre Granier-Deferre. VHS, Beta $59.00 *FCT* ♫♫♫

Widow's Nest Three widowed sisters live in a bizarre fantasy world when they lock themselves in a dingy mansion in Cuba of the 1930s. Filmed in Spain.
1977 90m/C Patricia Neal, Susan Oliver, Lila Kedrova, Valentina Cortese; *D:* Tony Navarro. VHS, Beta *NO* ♫♫

Wife Versus Secretary Excellent acting against type creates a near-perfect picture of romantic relationships. Harlow and Gable play a secretary and her boss who have a wonderful professional relationship, but Loy worries something else is afoot. Could have been a heavy-handed soap opera, but the witty dialogue and Brown's fine pacing make it much more. Stewart later claimed that he purposely messed up his romantic scenes with Harlow in order to spend more time in her arms.
1936 89m/B Clark Gable, Jean Harlow, Myrna Loy, May Robson, Hobart Cavanaugh, James Stewart, George Barbier, Gilbert Emery; *D:* Clarence Brown. VHS $19.98 *MGM* ♫♫♫½

Wifemistress In the early 1900s, an invalid wife resents her neglectful husband. When he goes into hiding because of a murder he didn't commit, she begins to drift into a world of sexual fantasies. Fine performances. Italian dialogue with English subtitles. *AKA: Mogliamante; Lover, Wife.*
1979 (R) 101m/C *IT* Marcello Mastroianni, Laura Antonelli; *D:* Marco Vicario. VHS, Beta $59.95 *COL* ♫♫½

The Wilby Conspiracy A political activist and an Englishman on the wrong side of the law team up to escape the clutches of a prejudiced cop in apartheid Africa. The focus of the film is on the chase, not the political uprising taking place around it. Well-done chase film with fine performances throughout.
1975 (PG) 101m/C Sidney Poitier, Michael Caine, Nicol Williamson, Prunella Gee, Persis Khambatta, Saeed Jaffrey, Rutger Hauer; *D:* Ralph Nelson. VHS $49.95 *MGM, FCT* ♫♫♫

The Wild Aces A relentless action flick with real documentary footage of the aerial war above Vietnam.
1985 58m/C VHS, Beta $24.95 *BVG, FGF, AVL* ♫½

The Wild and the Free Light-hearted comedy about research chimps. The lab-raised bunch become the instruments for radioactive experimenting. Scheming scientists return the chimps to their home to save them from their demise. Made for TV.
1980 100m/C Granville Van Dusen, Linda Gray, Bill Gribble; *D:* James Hill. VHS, Beta $39.95 *LIV* ♫♫

Wild & Wooly In 1903, a tough cowgirl and her friends must prevent the assassination of the President. Made for television.
1978 120m/C Chris DeLisle, Susan Bigelow, Elyssa Davalos, Jessica Walter, Doug McClure, David Doyle, Ross Martin, Vic Morrow, Charles Seibert, Sherry Bain, Paul Burke; *D:* Philip Leacock. VHS, Beta $59.95 *PSM* ♫½

The Wild Angels Excessively violent film but B-movie classic about an outlaw biker gang and the local townspeople. Typical Corman fodder was one of AIP's most successful productions.

1966 (PG) 124m/C Peter Fonda, Nancy Sinatra, Bruce Dern, Diane Ladd, Michael J. Pollard, Gayle Hunnicutt; **D:** Roger Corman; **W:** Charles B. Griffith. **VHS, Beta $9.98** SUE ✂✂½

Wild at Heart Dern and Cage are on the lam, going across country to escape her mother, his parole officer, and life. Humorous and frightening, sensual and evocative as only Lynch can be. Sweet love story of Sailor and Lula juxtaposed with the violent and bizarre, obsessive brand of love of the people they encounter. Unmistakable Wizard of Oz imagery sprinkled throughout, as are some scenes of graphic violence. Ladd is unnerving as Dern's on-screen mother (she also has the role off-screen).
1990 (R) 125m/C Nicolas Cage, Laura Dern, Diane Ladd, Willem Dafoe, Isabella Rossellini, Harry Dean Stanton, Crispin Glover, Grace Zabriskie, J.E. Freeman, Freddie Jones, Sherilyn Fenn, Sheryl Lee; **W/D:** David Lynch; **M:** Jerry Goldsmith. Academy Awards '90 Nominations: Best Supporting Actress (Ladd); Cannes Film Festival '90: Best Film; Independent Spirit Awards '91: Best Cinematography. **VHS, Beta, LV $19.98** CCB, MED, IME ✂✂✂½

The Wild Beasts Children and animals clash violently after drinking water tainted with PCP. Disgusting premise; unredeemably violent. **AKA:** Savage Beasts.
1985 92m/C John Aldrich, Lorraine De Selle; **D:** Franco Prosperi. **VHS, Beta $59.98** LIV Woof!

The Wild Bunch Acclaimed western about a group of aging outlaws on their final rampage, realizing time is passing them by. Highly influential in dialogue, editing style, and lyrical slow-motion photography of violence; Peckinpah's main claim to posterity. Holden and Ryan create especially memorable characters. Arguably the greatest western and one of the greatest American films of all times. Beware of shortened versions; after a pre-release showing to the East Coast critics, producer Feldman cut key scenes without Peckinpah's knowledge or consent.
1969 (R) 145m/C William Holden, Ernest Borgnine, Robert Ryan, Warren Oates, Strother Martin, L.Q. Jones, Albert Dekker, Bo Hopkins, Edmond O'Brien; **D:** Sam Peckinpah. **VHS, Beta, LV $19.98** WAR ✂✂✂✂

Wild Cactus Philip and Alexandria Marcus decide to take a romantic vacation at a desert resort where they meet up with a homicidal ex-con and his seductive girlfriend. The two couples find themselves entangled in some violent and kinky games. An unrated version is also available.
1992 (R) 92m/C David Naughton, India Allen, Gary Hudson, Michelle Moffett, Kathy Shower, Robert Z'Dar, Paul Gleason, Anna Karin, David Wells; **D:** Jag Mundhra; **W:** Carl Austin. **VHS $89.95** IMP ✂✂

The Wild Child The brilliant film based on the journal of a 19th century physician who attempts to educate and civilize a young boy who has been found living in the wilderness, without any comprehension of human life. Tenderly told coming of age tale, with surprising sensitivity for its subject. In French with English subtitles. **AKA:** L'Enfant Sauvage.
1970 (G) 85m/B FR **D:** Francois Truffaut. **VHS $19.99** MGM, TAM, FCT ✂✂✂½

Wild Country Tame western. A U.S. Marshall races to stop the bad guy from killing the late sheriff's daughter and snatching her ranch.
1947 57m/B Eddie Dean, Roscoe Ates, Peggy Wynn, Douglas Fowley, I. Stanford Jolley, Bill Fawcett; **D:** Ray Taylor. **VHS $19.95** NOS, HEG ✂½

The Wild Country Children's fare detailing the trials and tribulations of a Pittsburgh family moving into an inhospitable Wyoming ranch in the 1880s. Based on the novel "Little Britches" by Ralph Moody. **AKA:** The Newcomers.
1971 (G) 92m/C Steve Forrest, Ron Howard, Clint Howard; **D:** Robert Totten. **VHS, Beta $69.96** DIS ✂✂½

The Wild Duck A father discovers that his beloved daughter is illegitimate and turns against her. To regain her love, she plans to sacrifice her most prized possession. Irons overacts; Ullman almost disappears into the woodwork. Child star Jones is insufferable, and the whole family squeaks with "literary" pomposity. A horrid adaptation of the classic Ibsen play.
1984 (PG) 96m/C AU Jeremy Irons, Liv Ullmann, Lucinda Jones, Arthur Dignam; **D:** Henri Safran. **VHS, Beta $79.98** LIV, VES ✂

Wild Engine/Mistaken Orders The early screen daredevil Holmes stars in two railroad-and-betrayal epics
1923 48m/B Helen Holmes, Jack Hoxie, Hoot Gibson. **VHS, Beta $19.98** CCB ✂✂

Wild Frontier A rugged old lawman and his sons team up to rid a town of outlaws. Lane, playing a character with his own name for first time, takes over from his murdered father and roots out the evildoer (Holt, a pillar, as a bad guy for once). Decent, enjoyable, good-guys-win western.
1948 59m/B Allan "Rocky" Lane, Tim Holt. **VHS, Beta $29.95** DVT ✂✂½

Wild Geese The adventure begins when a veteran band of mercenaries land deep inside Africa to rescue the imprisoned leader of an emerging African nation, in the interest of protecting British commercial interest. Their mission meets an unexpected turn when they are betrayed by their financial backers. Too much training in the early part; too long; too much dialogue. Where's the action?
1978 (R) 132m/C GB Richard Burton, Roger Moore, Richard Harris, Hardy Kruger, Stewart Granger, Frank Finlay, Jeff Corey; **D:** Andrew V. McLaglen. **VHS, Beta, LV $59.98** FOX ✂✂

Wild Geese 2 Lame sequel to the flamed and overlong "Wild Geese," which depended on its name stars. More of the same, this time Sams Burton, Harris and Moore. Sure, it's got Olivier, but it still stinks.
1985 (R) 124m/C GB Laurence Olivier, Edward Fox, Scott Glenn, Barbara Carrera, Robert Webber; **D:** Peter Hunt. **VHS, Beta $14.95** MGM, HBO ✂½

Wild Guitar A swinging youth cycles into Hollywood and, improbably, becomes an instant teen idol. Considered a top contender for "Worst Picture of All Time" honors.
1962 92m/B Arch Hall Jr.; **D:** Ray Dennis Steckler. **VHS, Beta $24.95** RHI Woof!

Wild Gypsies A band of gypsies seek revenge against a renegade member who returned to rape and pillage. Without merit except for the good photography of Steven Burum, who has become respected doing cinematographically intriguing films like "Rumblefish."
1969 85m/C Todd Grange, Gayle Clark, Laurel Welcome. **VHS, Beta, LV $19.95** STE, NWV ✂

Wild Hearts Can't Be Broken Depicts the true-life story of Sonora Webster, a small town Georgia girl who runs away from a foster home to join a carnival in the early 1930s, hoping to become a stunt rider. She becomes a horse-diver (a Depression-era sideshow phenomena) and is blinded in a diving accident, but returns to find romance

and ride again. Storyline has little screen tension, but it doesn't detract from this fresh family film with a feisty heroine, a sweet romance, and horses. Nice U.S. screen debut for British actress Anwar.
1991 (G) 89m/C Gabrielle Anwar, Cliff Robertson, Dylan Kussman, Michael Schoeffling, Kathleen York, Frank Renzulli; **D:** Steve Miner; **W:** Oley Sassone; **M:** Mason Daring. **VHS, Beta $19.99** DIS ✂✂✂

Wild Horse Gibson is the lead (in his favorite talking role), but his magnificent mount Mut commands most of the attention. Interesting historically as an example of stars' (Gibson's in this case) difficulty adjusting to talking pictures. **AKA:** Silver Devil.
1931 68m/B Hoot Gibson, Stepin Fetchit, Edmund Cobb, Alberta Vaughn; **D:** Richard Thorpe, Sidney Algier. **VHS, Beta $19.95** NOS, GPV, VYY ✂½

Wild Horse Canyon Yakima Canutt, the man credited with creating the profession of stunt man, stars in this tale about a lady rancher who requires saving from her evil foreman. The climactic stampede scene gives Yakima a chance to demonstrate a high dive off a cliff and a somersault onto his horse. Silent, with musical score.
1925 68m/B Yakima Canutt, Edward Cecil, Helene Rosson, Jay Talbet. **VHS, Beta $19.95** NOS, GPV, VYY ✂½

Wild Horse Canyon One of those westerns designed to run as half of a double-feature, this one's shorter than most, but hardly notable. The hero goes after a rustler who shot his brother.
1939 57m/B Jack Randall, Dorothy Short, Frank Yaconelli, Dennis Moore, Warner Richmond, Charles King, Sherry Tansey; **D:** Robert Hill. **VHS $19.95** NOS ✂½

Wild Horse Hank A young woman risks everything to save a herd of wild mustangs from being slaughtered for use as dog food. Creena is good; otherwise, it's sentimental family fare. Based on the novel "The Wild Horse Killers" by Mel Ellis.
1979 94m/C CA Linda Blair, Richard Crenna, Michael Wincott, Al Waxman; **D:** Eric Till. **VHS, Beta $69.98** LIV, VES ✂✂

Wild Horse Phantom A Wild West banker plans to fake a robbery in a diabolical deception to part honest ranchers from their lands. Surely this man's not a member of the F.D.I.C. Okay sagebrush saga.
1944 56m/B Buster Crabbe, Al "Fuzzy" St. John, Charles King, John Merton, Lane Chandler, Edward Cassidy, Bud Osborne; **D:** Sam Newfield. **VHS, Beta** GPV ✂✂

Wild Horse Rodeo When a gunman appears at a rodeo, trouble starts. Part of "The Three Mesquiteers" series. Ordinary action-packed western, the good guys win. Actor Dick Weston, who sings, later gained fame as singing cowboy Roy Rogers.
1937 53m/B Ray Corrigan. **VHS, Beta $9.95** NOS, DVT ✂½

Wild Horses A man attempts to make a living by capturing and selling wild horses. Adventure fans will love this film which deals with the common theme of man against nature.
1982 88m/C NZ Keith Aberdein, John Bach, Robyn Gibbs; **D:** Derek Morton. **VHS, Beta $29.98** VES ✂✂

Wild Horses Ex-rodeo champ Rogers is hankering to escape his dull life. He joins a roundup of wild horses and with Dawber's help exposes a bureaucrat's scheme for them. Rogers is likable and sings, but the supporting cast carries this one. Made for TV.

1984 90m/C Kenny Rogers, Pam Dawber, Ben Johnson, Richard Masur, David Andrews, Karen Carlson; *D:* Dick Lowry. **VHS, Beta** $29.95 VID ♂♂

Wild in the Country Backwoods delinquent Presley is aided in his literary aspirations by woman psychiatrist Lange. Okay, so that's fairly novel. See, he's living with a crooked uncle whose daughter is sexy Weld which makes him fairly unique to begin with and Elvis he's had some problems with the law and he may have killed Ireland's son Lockwood but it was probably for good reason but Ireland happens to be the ex-lover of Lange who of course is the psychiatrist and she doesn't take this news too well but Elvis he's going to college and reading and writing and singing and playing his guitar though meanwhile Weld keeps wandering around seductively to provide that hint of Tennessee Williams ambience as interpreted by Clifford Odet but hey, who cares? Interesting if convoluted Elvis dramatic turn. ♫Wild in the Country; In My Way; I Slipped, I Stumbled, I Fell; Lonely Man.
1961 114m/C Elvis Presley, Hope Lange, Tuesday Weld, Millie Perkins, John Ireland, Gary Lockwood, Alan Napier; *D:* Philip Dunne. **VHS, Beta** $14.98 FOX, MVD ♂♂½

Wild in the Streets Satire set in the future, where a malcontent rock star becomes president after the voting age is lowered to 14. Adults over 30 are imprisoned and fed a daily dose of LSD. The president gets his comeuppance when challenged by even younger youths. Very groovy, very political in its own way, very funny.
1968 97m/C Shelley Winters, Christopher Jones, Hal Holbrook, Richard Pryor, Diane Varsi, Millie Perkins, Ed Begley Sr.; *D:* Barry Shear. **VHS, Beta, LV** $19.99 HBO ♂♂½

The Wild Life A recent high school graduate takes on a wild and crazy wrestler as his roommate in a swinging singles apartment complex. The same writer and producer as "Fast Times at Ridgemont High" but that film's commercial success. Just as adolescent, though.
1984 (R) 96m/C Christopher Penn, Randy Quaid, Rick Moranis, Hart Bochner, Eric Stoltz, Jenny Wright, Lea Thompson, Sherilyn Fenn, Lee Ving, Ashley St. John, Francesca "Kitten" Natavidad; *D:* Art Linson. **VHS, Beta, LV** $79.98 MCA ♂

Wild Man A Las Vegas gambling magnate with supernatural powers decides to avenge the murder of his friend and sets out on an adventure to find the killer. Crummy acting in yet another "ex-agent called back for one more mission" yarn.
1989 106m/C Ginger Lynn Allen, Michelle Bauer, Don Scribner, Kathleen Middleton; *D:* Fred J. Lincoln. **VHS, Beta** CEL ♂

Wild Mustang Sheriff's son (Gordon) joins some outlaws to help father (Carey) spring a trap. The plan is sidetracked, and Gordon is captured and nearly branded by the baddies. Don't worry, though; everything turns out all right. Good western.
1935 62m/B Harry Carey Sr.; *D:* Harry Fraser. **VHS, Beta** $19.95 NOS, VCN, DVT ♂♂½

The Wild One The original biker flick: two motorcycle gangs descend upon a quiet midwestern town and each other. Brando is the leader of one, struggling against social prejudices and his own gang's lawlessness to find love and a normal life. The classic tribute to 1950s rebelliousness. Based vaguely on a real incident in California. Quaint after nearly 40 years, but still the touchstone for much that has come since, and still a central role in Brando's now-long career. Brando himself believes it failed to explore

Motivations for youth gangs and violence, only depicting them. Banked in Britain until 1967.
1954 79m/B Marlon Brando, Lee Marvin, Mary Murphy, Robert Keith, Jerry Paris, Alvy Moore, Jay C. Flippen; *D:* Laslo Benedek. **VHS, Beta, LV** $19.95 COL ♂♂♂½

Wild Ones on Wheels A gang of teenage hot-rod punks meet an ex-con in the Mojave desert who is searching for the half-a-million bucks he buried there years earlier. Before they find out where the money is, they kill him. In an attempt to find the stash, they kidnap the dead con's wife, hoping she'll sing like a bird. Plenty of unintended laughter. *AKA:* Drivers to Hell.
1962 92m/B Francine York, Edmund Tontini, Robert Blair; *D:* Rudolph Cusumano. **VHS, Beta** $16.95 SNC Woof!

Wild Orchid One of the most controversial theatrical releases of 1990. Rourke is a mystery millionaire involved with two beautiful women in lovely Rio de Janeiro. Bisset is strange as an international real estate developer with unusual sexual mores. Very explicit sex scenes, but mostly boring and unbelievable. Rourke allegedly took his method-acting technique to the limit in the last love scene with Otis. Available in an unrated version as well. From the producers of "9 1/2 Weeks." Followed by a sequel.
1990 (R) 117m/C Mickey Rourke, Jacqueline Bisset, Carre Otis, Assumpta Serna, Bruce Greenwood; *D:* Zalman King. **VHS, Beta, LV** $19.95 COL, FCT ♂

Wild Orchid 2: Two Shades of Blue When Blue's jazz-musician, heroin-addicted father is violently killed, she is thrust into the world of prostitution. Taken into Elle's brothel, Blue fantasizes about Josh, a boy she met before her father's death, while she is working. Josh's father brings him to the brothel to lose his virginity and he chooses Blue, not realizing who she is because a geisha wig hides her blonde curls. Blue runs away from the brothel and tries to lead a normal teenage life. Another soft-core effort from the director of "9 1/2 Weeks" and "Two Moon Junction." This unrealistic film is available in rated and unrated versions and bears little resemblance to the original.
1992 (R) 107m/C Nina Siemaszko, Wendy Hughes, Brent Fraser, Robert Davi, Tom Skerritt, Joe Dallesandro, Christopher McDonald, Liane Curtis; *W/D:* Zalman King. **VHS** COL ♂

Wild Orchids A husband suspects his wife of infidelity when they take a business cruise to Java. One of Garbo's earliest silent films. Garbo is lushly surrounded with great scenery, costumes and sets, making the best of her as she makes the best of a cheery tale.
1928 119m/B Greta Garbo, Lewis Stone, Nils Asther; *D:* Sidney Franklin. **VHS, Beta** $29.99 MGM, FCT ♂♂½

The Wild Pair Two cops track down a cocaine smuggling ring and uncover a private army planning to conquer the United States. Lloyd Bridges is memorable as a rabid right-winger, and the wild pairing of Bubba and Beau inspires head-scatching. Otherwise, what we have here is a typical action epic, complete with car chases. Beau Bridges' inauspicious feature directing debut. *AKA:* Hollow Point; Devil's Odds.
1987 (R) 89m/C Beau Bridges, Bubba Smith, Lloyd Bridges, Gary Lockwood, Raymond St. Jacques; *D:* Beau Bridges. **VHS, Beta, LV** $19.95 MED, SIM ♂½

Wild Palms Lesson in weird style over substance. In 2007 Los Angeles, Harry (Belushi) accepts a television job at a station dealing in a revolutionary technology. Virtual reality provides at-home viewers with 3-D holographic programs, only this isn't benign technology. A group known as the Fathers, headed by sinister Senator Kreutzer (Loggia), plans to use it for mind-control. Delany is stuck in the thankless role of Harry's wife, Cattrall is his former lover and the Senator's new playmate, but Dickinson has the most fun as Harry's power-mad mother-in-law who's also a sadistic co-conspirator of the Senator's. Watching it doesn't make much more sense but, unlike "Twin Peaks" (to which the miniseries has been heavily compared) it at least has an ending. Executive producer Stone has a talk show cameo which concerns the JFK conspiracy. Based on the comic strip by Wagner. Available in two parts.
1993 ?m/C James Belushi, Robert Loggia, Dana Delany, Kim Cattrall, Angie Dickinson, Ernie Hudson, Bebe Neuwirth, Nick Mancuso, Charles Hallahan, Robert Morse, David Warner, Ben Savage, Bob Gunton, Brad Dourif, Charles Rocket; *Cameos:* Oliver Stone; *D:* Phil Joanou, Kathryn Bigelow; *W:* Bruce Wagner; *M:* Ryuichi Sakamoto. **VHS** $99.98 ABC ♂♂

The Wild Panther Kung Fu combat abounds in this story of spies, guerrillas and stolen military secrets.
1984 90m/C **VHS, Beta** $39.95 WWV ♂½

Wild Party It's 1929, a year of much frivolity in Hollywood. Drinking, dancing, maneuvering and almost every sort of romance are the rule of the night at silent film comic Jolly Grimm's sumptuous, star-studded party that climaxes with, among other things, a murder. Well performed but somehow hollow; ambitious Ivory effort unfortunately falls short. Based on Joseph Moncure March's poem, and loosely on the Fatty Arbuckle scandal.
1974 (R) 90m/C Raquel Welch, James Coco, Perry King, David Dukes, Royal Dano, Tiffany Bolling; *D:* James Ivory. **VHS, Beta** $9.98 SUE ♂♂½

Wild Pony A young boy spurns his new stepfather, preferring to live with his pony instead. Reversal of the evil-stepmother-and-girl-loves-horse theme.
1983 87m/C Marilyn Lightstone, Art Hindle, Josh Byrne; *D:* Kevin Sullivan. **VHS, Beta** $14.98 FHE, VES, LIV ♂

Wild Rapture The hunting and dissecting of an elephant and gorilla, a look at a tribe that practices lip-splitting, and other gruesome events abound in this shock-fest. Banned for 18 years.
1950 68m/B **VHS, Beta** $24.95 NOS, HEG ♂

Wild Rebels A two-faced member of a ruthless motorcycle gang informs the police of the gang's plans to rob a bank. Lots of bullet-flying action. Dumb, ordinary biker flick; star Pastrano was a former boxing champ in real life.
1971 90m/C Steve Alaimo, Willie Pastrano, John Vella, Bobbie Byers; *D:* William Grefe. **VHS, Beta** $59.95 ACA ♂

The Wild Ride Nicholson, in an early starring role, portrays a rebellious punk of the Beat generation who hotrods his way into trouble and tragedy. He kidnaps now-straight ex-buddy Bean's squeeze (Carter); kills a few cops; then is killed. Interesting only if you're interested in Nicholson.
1960 59m/B Jack Nicholson, Georgianna Carter, Robert Bean; *D:* Harvey Berman. **VHS, Beta** $16.95 SNC, NOS, VYY ♂♂

Wild Ride Ruthless bandits on horseback rape and pillage their way through a series of pioneer towns.
19?? 86m/C VHS NO *ℐℐ*

Wild Riders Two ruthless, amoral bikers molest, kidnap, rape, and beat two beautiful, naive young society ladies. Despicable story, with deplorable acting, but the ending, in which a husband slays a biker with a cello, surely is unique. *AKA:* Angels for Kicks.
1971 (R) 91m/C Alex Rocco, Elizabeth Knowles, Sherry Bain, Arell Blanton; *D:* Richard Kanter. VHS, Beta $19.95 *ACA* Woof!

Wild Rovers An aging cowboy and his younger colleague turn to bank robbing and are pursued by a posse in a wacky comedy-adventure from director Edwards. Uneven script and too much referential baggage (faint shades of "Butch Cassidy") doom this valiant effort, with the two stars hanging right in there all the way.
1971 (PG) 138m/C William Holden, Ryan O'Neal, Karl Malden, Lynn Carlin, Tom Skerritt, Joe Don Baker, Rachel Roberts, Moses Gunn; *D:* Blake Edwards; *M:* Jerry Goldsmith. VHS, Beta, LV $19.98 *MGM ℐℐ*

Wild Strawberries Bergman's landmark film of fantasy, dreams and nightmares. An aging professor, on the road to accept an award, must come to terms with his anxieties and guilt. Brilliant performance by Sjostrom, Sweden's first film director and star. Excellent use of flashbacks and film editing. An intellectual and emotional masterpiece. In Swedish with English subtitles. *AKA:* Smultron-Stallet.
1957 90m/B *SW* Victor Sjostrom, Bibi Andersson, Max von Sydow; *D:* Ingmar Bergman. Academy Awards '59 Nominations: Best Story & Screenplay; Golden Globe Awards '60: Best Foreign Film; National Board of Review Awards '59: 5 Best Foreign Films of the Year. VHS, Beta, LV, 8mm, 3/4U, Special order formats $29.95 *CVC, VYY, FOX ℐℐℐℐ*

Wild Style Zoro, a mild-mannered Bronx teenager, spends his evenings spray-painting subway cars. Intended as a depiction of urban street life, including graffiti, breakdancing and rap music. Mildly interesting social comment, but unconvincing as cinema. Too "realistic," with too little vision.
1983 82m/C Lee George Quinones, Fredrick Braithwaite, Dondi White; *D:* Charlie Ahearn. VHS, Beta $49.95 *WWV ℐℐ*

Wild Thing A modern variation on the Wild Child/Tarzan myth, as a feral kid stalks a crime-ridden ghetto. Is this the best scripter John Sayles, a usually imaginative writer and director, can do? of course, the Troggs' overplayed title hit is abused as the theme.
1987 (PG-13) 92m/C Kathleen Quinlan, Rob Knepper, Robert Davi, Betty Buckley, Maury Chaykin; *D:* Max Reid, Ken Cameron; *W:* John Sayles. VHS, Beta, LV *KRT, OM ℐℐ½*

Wild Times Too long but pleasant rendition of the life of High Candill, early Wild West showman. Based on the novel by Brian Garfield. Made for TV, originally in two parts.
1979 200m/C Sam Elliott, Trish Stewart, Ben Johnson, Dennis Hopper, Pat Hingle; *D:* Richard Compton. VHS, Beta $69.95 *PSM ℐℐ*

Wild Weed Funny smelling cigarettes ruin the lives of all who inhale. Viewers' advice: just say no. Leed's actual drug bust with Robert Mitchum got her the lead. *AKA:* The Devil's Weed; She Shoulda Said No; Marijuana the Devil's Weed.
1949 70m/B Lila Leeds, Alan Baxter, Lyle Talbot, Jack Elam, David Gorcey; *D:* Sam Newfield. VHS *SNC, AOV ℐ*

Wild West The hero and loyal companions (with names like Skinny, Stormy and Soapy) tackle desperadoes trying to stop telegraph line construction. More mild than wild, it was later trimmed and released under its alternate title, but here you're getting the original. *AKA:* Prairie Outlaws.
1946 73m/C Eddie Dean, Roscoe Ates, Lash LaRue, Robert "Buzzy" Henry, Sarah Padden, Louise Currie, Warner Richmond, Chief Yowlachie, Bud Osborne; *D:* Robert Tansey. VHS $19.95 *NOS, HEG ℐℐ*

Wild West A compilation of scenes from dozens of western films.
1987 90m/C John Wayne, Clint Eastwood, Steve McQueen, Charles Bronson. VHS, Beta *NO ℐℐ*

Wild Wheels A group of dune-buggy enthusiasts seek revenge against a gang of motorcyclists who have ravaged a small California beach town.
1975 (PG) 81m/C Casey Kasem, Dovie Beams, Terry Stafford, Robert Dix. VHS, Beta $59.95 *GEM* Woof!

Wild, Wild Planet Alien beings from a distant planet are miniaturizing Earth's leaders in a bid to destroy our planet, and a dubbed, wooden hero comes to the rescue. A rarely seen Italian SF entry, great fun for genre fans. A must for "robot girls in skin tight leather outfits" completists.
1965 93m/C *IT* Tony Russell, Lisa Gastoni, Massimo Serato, Franco Nero; *D:* Antonio Margheriti. VHS $20.00 *SMW ℐℐ½*

Wild, Wild West Revisited A feature-length reprise of the tongue-in-cheek western series. Irreverent and fun, in the spirit of its admirable predecessor-though it's probably just as well the proposed new series didn't see fruition. Made for television.
1979 95m/C Robert Conrad, Russ Martin, Harry Morgan, Rene Auberjonois; *D:* Burt Kennedy. VHS, Beta $59.98 *FOX ℐℐ½*

Wild, Wild World of Jayne Mansfield The life and times of Mansfield are explored in this unique documentary, which was unfinished at the time of her death. Jayne takes the viewer on a worldwide examination of sexual mores, from prostitution, nudist colonies, and the racy strip clubs of Europe, to the transvestite and topless bars of America. Perversely (but did you expect otherwise?), footage of her fatal car crash was included.
1968 89m/C Jayne Mansfield. VHS, Beta $19.99 *VDM, DVT ℐℐ*

Wild Women Extremely hilarious schlocker about a safari of white men captured by a savage tribe of jungle women. Total camp.
1953 ?m/C Lewis Wilson, Frances Dubay, Dana Wilson. VHS $16.95 *SNC, HEG ℐ*

Wild Women Five female convicts are released during the Texas/Mexico dispute to help smuggle arms to American forces. Innocuous western, original in a made-for-TV kind of way.
1970 90m/C Hugh O'Brian, Anne Francis, Marilyn Maxwell, Marie Windsor; *D:* Don Taylor. VHS, Beta $19.98 *FOX ℐ½*

Wild Women of Wongo The denizens of a primitive isle, essentially beautiful women and ugly men, meet the natives of a neighboring island, handsome men and ugly women. Not quite bad enough to be true camp fun, but stupidly silly in a low-budget way.
1959 73m/C Pat Crowley, Ed Fury, Adrienne Bourbeau, Jean Hawkshaw, Johnny Walsh; *D:* James L. Wolcott. VHS, Beta $19.98 *DVT, MED, HEG ℐ½*

The Wild World of Batwoman A campy cult film in which Batwoman and a bevy of Bat Girls are pitted against an evil doctor in order to find the prototype of an atomic hearing aid/nuclear bomb. Also released theatrically as "She Was a Hippy Vampire."
1966 70m/C Katherine Victor, George Andre, Steve Brodie, Lloyd Nelson; *D:* Jerry Warren. VHS, Beta $9.95 *RHI, SNC, DVT ℐℐ*

Wild Youth Juvenile delinquent trash about a wild gang of kids who fight over a doll filled with heroin.
1961 ?m/C Robert Arthur, Robert Hutton, Carol Ohmart. VHS $16.95 *SNC ℐℐ½*

Wild Zone An American ex-soldier combats mercenaries in Africa in order to rescue his kidnapped father.
1989 (R) 100m/C Edward Albert, Philip Brown, Carla Herd; *D:* Percival Rubens. VHS, Beta, LV $79.95 *COL ℐ*

Wildcard When a veteran pilot is killed in a helicopter crash, a friend suspects foul play. He calls in Preacher, a special forces veteran, to investigate and what he discovers is murder, greed, and corruption.
1992 (PG-13) 86m/C Powers Boothe, Cindy Pickett, Rene Auberjonois, Terry O'Quinn, M. Emmet Walsh, John Lacy; *D:* Mel Damski; *W:* Scobie Richardson. VHS, LV *MCA ℐℐ½*

Wildcat Crabbe, famous as the serials' Flash Gordon, is a villain in this petrochemical adventure. The hero overextends his credit when he buys an oil well and must produce a gusher or else.
1942 73m/B Richard Arlen, Arline Judge, Buster Crabbe, William Frawley, Arthur Hunnicutt, Elisha Cook Jr., Billy Benedict; *D:* Frank McDonald. VHS $19.95 *NOS ℐℐ*

Wildcats A naive female phys-ed teacher (Hawn) is saddled with the job of coach for a completely undisciplined, inner city, high school football team. Formulaic, connect-the-dots comedy; moderately funny, and of course Hawn triumphs in adversity, but at nearly two hours a very long sitcom episode.
1986 (R) 106m/C Goldie Hawn, James Keach, Swoosie Kurtz, Bruce McGill, M. Emmet Walsh, Woody Harrelson, Wesley Snipes; *D:* Michael Ritchie. VHS, Beta, LV $19.98 *WAR ℐℐ*

Wildest Dreams Released from its bottle by a lovely nebbish, a genie puts a love spell on one beautiful girl after another in order to find him the right one, resulting in a bevy of women clamoring for our hero's attention. *AKA:* Bikini Genie.
1990 (R) 84m/C James Davies, Heidi Paine, Deborah Blaisdell, Ruth Collins, Jane Hamilton, Jill Johnson; *D:* Chuck Vincent. VHS, Beta, LV $79.98 *LIV, VES ℐℐ*

The Wildest Office Party A sex-filled tape for and about wild, rowdy office parties.
1987 60m/C VHS, Beta $59.98 *LIV, VES* Woof!

Wildfire Two horse traders come to the aid of ranchers beset by horse thieves. Early color outing for Steele. Harmless, ordinary oater.
1945 60m/C Bob Steele, Sterling Holloway; *D:* Robert Tansey. VHS, Beta, LV $19.95 *NOS, VDM, DVT ℐℐ*

Wildfire As teenagers, Frank and Kay run away to get married but Frank is sent to prison for robbing a bank and Kay winds up making a new life for herself. Released from prison after eight years, Frank discovers Kay is married with two children and doesn't want anything further to do with him. But when Frank violates his parole, Kay discovers she can't leave him again and the two go on the run together.

1988 (PG) 98m/C Steven Bauer, Linda Fiorentino, Will Patton, Marshall Bell; *D:* Zalman King. VHS, LV *MCA* ⊿⊿

Wildflower Set in the Depression-era South, Alice is a 17 year-old partially deaf girl who also suffers from epilepsy. Her stepfather believes she's possessed and confines her to a shed. Growing up ignorant and abused Alice is befriended by a neighboring brother and sister who decide to rescue her. A three-hankie family picture with moving performances and inspirational themes. Based on the novel "Alice" by Sara Flanigan. Made for cable television.
1991 94m/C Patricia Arquette, Beau Bridges, Susan Blakely, William McNamara, Reese Witherspoon; *D:* Diane Keaton. VHS $89.98 *WOV* ⊿⊿⊿

Wilding A pair of cops are on the trail of a gang of kids who go "wilding," which involves sprees of killing, raping and looting. Exploitive fare based on horrible, recent events in New York. The filmmakers skirt controversy by making the criminals rich suburban kids.
1990 92m/C Wings Hauser, Joey Travolta, Karen Russell, Steven Cooke; *D:* Eric Louzil. VHS, Beta $79.95 *AIP* ⊿½

Wildrose Eichhorn is memorable as a recent divorcee who must assert herself among her otherwise all-male co-workers at a Minnesota strip mine. She finds a new love, and tries to put her life back together. Filmed on location.
1985 96m/C Lisa Eichhorn, Tom Bower, James Cada; *D:* John Hanson. VHS, Beta $69.98 *LIV* ⊿⊿⊿

Will: G. Gordon Liddy The life of the Watergate conspirator, based on his autobiography. Made for TV. Producer/star Conrad reportedly objected strongly to cuts from the original three-hour length, apparently with cause: the first half is superficial pap. The portrayal of Liddy's time in prison, though, is fascinating, and Conrad is excellent.
1982 100m/C Robert Conrad, Katherine Cannon, Gary Bayer, Peter Ratray, James Rebhorn, Red West, Maurice Woods, Danny Lloyd; *D:* Robert Lieberman. VHS $39.95 *LIV* ⊿⊿½

Will Penny Just back from a cattle drive, a range-wandering loner looks for work in the wrong place and offends a family of outlaws who come after him. His escape from them leads to another kind of trap—one set by a love-hungry woman (Hackett, in a strong performance). Heston considers this film his personal best, and he's probably right. Superbly directed western, with excellent cinematography and professional, realistic portrayals, flopped in theaters, moviegoers preferring simultaneous Heston outing "Planet of the Apes." Photography by Lucien Ballard. Music by Elmer Bernstein.
1967 109m/C Charlton Heston, Joan Hackett, Donald Pleasence, Lee Majors, Bruce Dern, Anthony Zerbe, Ben Johnson, Clifton James; *D:* Tom Gries. VHS, Beta, LV $14.95 *PAR* ⊿⊿⊿½

Willa Raffin, a hash-joint waitress with two kids and one in the pipeline, is deserted by her husband and determines to get ahead by becoming a trucker. Okay made-for-TV drama.
1979 95m/C Cloris Leachman, Deborah Raffin, Clu Gulager, John Amos, Diane Ladd; *D:* Claudio Guzman, Joan Darling; *M:* John Barry. VHS, Beta $39.95 *PSM* ⊿⊿

Willard Willard is a lonely, psychotic youngster who trains a group of rats, his only friends, to attack his enemies. Not as disgusting as it might have been (rated PG), but pretty weird and not redeemed by any sense of style or humor. Popular at the box office;

followed by inferior "Ben." Based on by Stephen Gilbert's novel "Ratman's Notebooks."
1971 (PG) 95m/C Bruce Davison, Ernest Borgnine, Elsa Lanchester, Sondra Locke; *D:* Daniel Mann. VHS, Beta, LV $59.95 *PSM, PAR* ⊿⊿

Willie & Phil At the start of the '70s, two buddies (Ontkean and Sharkey) fall for the same girl (Kidder). They become a threesome and are entangled in each other's lives for the rest of the decade. Insightful comedy-drama written and directed by Mazursky.
1980 (R) 111m/C Michael Ontkean, Margot Kidder, Ray Sharkey, Jan Miner, Julie Bovasso, Natalie Wood, Larry Fishburne, Louis Guss, Kaki Hunter, Kristine DeBell; *W/D:* Paul Mazursky. VHS, LV $59.98 *FXV* ⊿⊿½

The Willies Three youngsters gross each other out with juvenile tales of horror and scariness while camping out in the backyard. Pointless but not without a few yuks (in both senses of the term).
1990 (PG-13) 120m/C James Karen, Sean Astin, Kathleen Freeman, Jeremy Miller; *D:* Brian Peck. VHS, LV $29.95 *PSM* ⊿⊿

Willow Blockbuster fantasy epic combines the story of Moses with "Snow White," dwarves and all. Willow is the little Nelwyn who finds the lost baby Daikini and is assigned the task of returning her safely to her people. Willow discovers that the girl is actually a sacred infant who is destined to overthrow the evil queen Bavmorda and rule the land. As you might expect from executive producer George Lucas, there is much action and plenty of clever, high-quality special effects. But the "Star Wars"-esque story (by Lucas) is strangely predictable, and a bit too action-packed. Not really for children.
1988 (PG) 118m/C Warwick Davis, Val Kilmer, Jean Marsh, Joanne Whalley-Kilmer, Billy Barty, Pat Roach, Ruth Greenfield; *D:* Ron Howard. VHS, Beta, LV, 8mm $14.95 *COL* ⊿⊿½

Willy Wonka & the Chocolate Factory When the last of five coveted "golden tickets" falls into the hands of sweet but very poor Charlie, he and his Grandpa Joe get a tour of the most wonderfully strange chocolate factory in the world. The owner is the most curious hermit ever to hit the big screen. He leads the five young "winners" on a thrilling and often dangerous tour of his fabulous factory. Adapted from Roald Dahl's "Charlie and the Chocolate Factory," with a score by Anthony Newley-Leslie Brieusse. Without a doubt one of the best "kid's" movies ever made; a family classic worth watching again and again and... ♫Willy Wonka, the Candy Man; Cheer Up, Charlie; I've Got a Golden Ticket; Oompa-Loompa-Doompa-Dee-Doo; Pure Imagination.
1971 (G) 100m/C Gene Wilder, Jack Albertson, Denise Nickerson, Peter Ostrum, Roy Kinnear, Aubrey Woods, Michael Bollner, Ursula Reit, Leonard Stone, Dodo Denney; *D:* Mel Stuart. VHS, Beta, LV $19.98 *WAR, VTK, APD* ⊿⊿⊿½

Wilma Based on the true story of Wilma Rudolph, a young black woman who overcame childhood illness to win three gold medals at the 1960 Olympics. Plodding made-for-TV biography suffers from sub-par script and acting.
1977 100m/C Joe Seneca, Cicely Tyson, Shirley Jo Finney; *D:* Bud Greenspan. VHS, Beta $14.95 *COL, FCT* ⊿⊿

Wilson Biography of Woodrow Wilson from his days as the head of Princeton University, to the governorship of New York, and as U.S. President during World War I. After the war, Wilson conceives of the League of

Nations but is unable to sell it to a U.S. still bent on isolationism. This lavish film won critical plaudits but was a major money-loser.
1944 154m/C Alexander Knox, Charles Coburn, Geraldine Fitzgerald, Thomas Mitchell, Ruth Nelson, Cedric Hardwicke, Vincent Price, William Eythe, Mary Anderson, Sidney Blackmer, Stanley Ridges, Eddie Foy Jr.; *D:* Henry King; *W:* Lamar Trotti; *M:* Alfred Newman. Academy Awards '44: Best Color Cinematography, Best Film Editing, Best Interior Decoration, Best Original Screenplay, Best Sound; Nominations: Best Actor (Knox), Best Director (King), Best Picture, Best Original Score; Golden Globe Awards '45: Best Actor—Drama (Knox). VHS $19.99 *FXV, MOV* ⊿⊿⊿

Wimps A collegiate wimp is subjected to a brutal fraternity initiation, but eventually gets the girl. Cheap ripoff of Cyrano de Bergerac, turned into a teen sex flick.
1987 (R) 94m/C Louie Bonanno, Jim Abele, Deborah Blaisdell; *D:* Chuck Vincent. VHS, Beta $79.98 *LIV* ⊿

Win, Place, or Steal Lame comedy set at the racetrack about three grown men and their adolescent schemes to win big. Better you should scratch. *AKA:* The Big Payoff; Three For the Money; Just Another Day at the Races.
1972 (PG) 88m/C McLean Stevenson, Alex Karras, Dean Stockwell; *D:* Richard Bailey. VHS, Beta $69.98 *LIV, VES* ⊿½

Winchester '73 Superb acting and photography characterize this classic, landmark western. Simple plot—cowboy Stewart pursues his stolen state-of-the-art rifle as it changes hands—speeds along and carries the viewer with it, ending with an engrossing and unforgettable shoot-out. Almost single-handedly breathed new life into the whole genre. Laser videodisc version contains a special narration track provided by Stewart. Mann's and Stewart's first teaming.
1950 82m/C James Stewart, Shelley Winters, Stephen McNally, Dan Duryea, Millard Mitchell, John McIntire, Will Geer, Jay C. Flippen, Rock Hudson, Tony Curtis, Charles Drake; *D:* Anthony Mann. VHS, Beta, LV $19.95 *MCA* ⊿⊿⊿½

The Wind One of the last great silents still stands as a magnificent entertainment. Gish, in possibly her best role, is an innocent Easterner who finds herself married to a rough cowpoke and raped by a married man in a bleak frontier town. Director Sjostrom has a splendid feel for landscape, and the drama—climaxing with a tumultuous desert storm—is intense yet fully believable.
1928 74m/B Lillian Gish, Lars Hanson, Montagu Love, Dorothy Cumming, Edward Earle, William Orlamond; *D:* Victor Sjostrom. VHS, Beta $29.95 *MGM* ⊿⊿⊿⊿

The Wind Foster is terrorized by Hauser while attempting to write her next thriller in Greece. Let's hope her book is more exciting than this movie. Shot on location in Greece.
1987 92m/C Meg Foster, Wings Hauser, Steve Railsback, David McCallum, Robert Morley; *D:* Nico Mastorakis. VHS, Beta $79.98 *LIV* ⊿

Wind Will Parker (Modine) is a sailor who chooses the opportunity to be on the America's Cup sailing team over girlfriend Grey and then has the dubious honor of making a technical error that causes their loss. Undaunted, he locates Grey and her new engineer boyfriend (Skarsgard), convinces them to design the ultimate boat for the next set of races, and romances his former skipper's daughter (Miller) for financing. ESPN carried extensive coverage of the America's Cup races for the first time in the summer of '92 and viewers discovered that a little goes a long way. The same holds true for "Wind" which has stunning race footage, but little

else. The script lacks substance and was written as filming progressed, and it shows.
1992 (PG-13) 123m/C Matthew Modine, Jennifer Grey, Cliff Robertson, Jack Thompson, Stellan Skarsgard, Rebecca Miller, Ned Vaughn; **D:** Carroll Ballard; **W:** Rudy Wurlitzer, Mac Gudgeon; **M:** Basil Poledouris. **VHS, LV, 8mm** COL 𝄞𝄞½

The Wind and the Lion In turn-of-the-century Morocco, a sheik (Connery) kidnaps a feisty American woman (Bergen) and her children and holds her as a political hostage. President Teddy Roosevelt (Keith) sends in the Marines to free the captives, who are eventually released by their captor. Directed with venue and style by Milius. Highly entertaining, if heavily fictionalized. Based very loosely on a historical incident.
1975 (PG) 120m/C Sean Connery, Candice Bergen, Brian Keith, John Huston; **D:** John Milius; **M:** Jerry Goldsmith. **VHS, Beta, LV** **$59.95** MGM, PIA 𝄞𝄞𝄞

The Wind in the Willows "The Wind in the Willows," originally a part of the 1950 Disney feature "Ichabod and Mr. Toad," is the tale of J. Thaddeus Toad, who has a strange mania for fast cars. Based on a story by Kenneth Grahame. Also on this tape are two Disney cartoons with similar automotive themes, "Motor Mania" with Goofy and "Trailer Horn" with Donald Duck and Chip 'n' Dale.
1949 34m/C Eric Blore; **D:** Wolfgang Reitherman. **VHS, Beta $12.99** DIS, WTA, HMV 𝄞𝄞𝄞

The Wind That Walks Two girls trek into the New Jersey wilds after an unknown animal called by the Indians "the wind that walks."
1985 30m/C Beta NJN 𝄞𝄞𝄞

Windjammer Western star O'Brien took a break from the lone prairie to make this seafaring rescue drama. He is a deputy state's attorney who signs up for a yacht race in order to serve a subpoena. Bad guys arrive on the scene, and the initially moody yacht denizens rely on our trusty hero to save them. Decent adventure.
1931 75m/B George O'Brien, Constance Worth; **D:** Ewing Scott. **VHS $24.95** NOS, DVT, HEG 𝄞𝄞

Windmills of the Gods Glamor, romance, intrigue, and politics all mixed together in eastern Europe. Smith is named ambassador to Romania, finds the suave Wagner in residence, and becomes the target of assassins. Based on the novel by Sidney Sheldon. Made for television. **AKA:** Sidney Sheldon's Windmills of the Gods.
1988 95m/C Jaclyn Smith, Robert Wagner, Franco Nero, Christopher Cazenove, David Ackroyd, Jean-Pierre Aumont, Ruby Dee, Jeffrey DeMunn, Michael Moriarty, Ian McKellan, Susan Tyrrell; **D:** Lee Philips; **W:** John Gay. **VHS $79.98** LIV 𝄞𝄞½

Windom's Way Finch, in a strong role in this intriguing political drama, is an idealistic doctor in a remote village in Malaysia. He juggles a failing marriage and a budding romance, then finds himself caught in a local labor dispute. He works for a peaceful solution, but is captured by an insurgent army. Disillusioned, he plans to leave the country, but his wife persuades him to stay and tend the wounded. Based on a novel by James Ramsey Ullman.
1957 90m/B GB Peter Finch, Mary Ure; **D:** Ronald Neame. **VHS, Beta $19.98** VID 𝄞𝄞𝄞

The Window A little boy (Disney star Driscoll, intriguingly cast by director, Tetzlaff) has a reputation for telling lies, so no one believes him when he says he witnessed a murder...except the killers. Almost unbearably tense, claustrophobic thriller about the helplessness of childhood. Tetzlaff clearly learned more than a thing or two from the master, Hitchcock, for whom he photographed "Notorious." Based on "The Boy Who Cried Murder" by Cornell Woolrich, on whose writing "Rear Window" was also based. Driscoll was awarded a special miniature Oscar as Outstanding Juvenile for his performance.
1949 73m/B Bobby Driscoll, Barbara Hale, Arthur Kennedy, Ruth Roman; **D:** Ted Tetzlaff. Academy Awards '49 Nominations: Best Film Editing; Edgar Allan Poe Awards '49: Best Screenplay. **VHS, Beta, LV $19.95** MED 𝄞𝄞𝄞½

Window Shopping Multiple, confusing romances occur at the "Toison d' Or" shopping mall in Paris. A modern, French homage to the classic Hollywood musical. In French with English subtitles.
1986 96m/C FR Delphine Seyrig, Charles Denner, Fanny Cottencon, Miriam Boyer, Lio, Pascale Salkin, Jean-Francois Balmer; **W/D:** Chantal Akerman. **VHS $29.95** WAC, FCT, TAM 𝄞𝄞½

Windows A lonely lesbian (Ashley) becomes obsessed with her quiet neighbor (Shire) and concocts a plot to get close to her. Director Willis is known for his unbeatable cinematography, most notably for Woody Allen in "Manhattan." His debut in the chair is a miserable, offensive flop.
1980 (R) 93m/C Talia Shire, Joe Cortese, Elizabeth Ashley, Kay Medford, Linda Gillin; **D:** Gordon Willis; **M:** Ennio Morricone. **VHS** VID 𝄞

Windrider Simple love story made in Australia. A wind surfer and a rock star become lovers. Self-indulgent overwrought garbage with rare moments of promise.
1986 83m/C AU Tom Burlinson, Nicole Kidman, Charles Tingwell, Jill Perryman, Simon Chilvers; **D:** Vincent Monton. **VHS $79.95** MGM 𝄞½

Winds of Change A retelling of five ancient Greek myths, which features a disco-rock musical score. Written by Norman Corwin.
1979 90m/C **V:** Peter Ustinov. **VHS, Beta $19.95** COL, WTA 𝄞½

The Winds of Jarrah English woman runs from broken heart to Australia to become nanny for misogynist, and Harlequin code prevails. Based on a Harlequin romance novel.
1983 78m/C Terence Donovan, Susan Lyons; **D:** Mark Egerton. **VHS, Beta** NO 𝄞½

Winds of Kitty Hawk Visually interesting but talky account of the Wright brothers attempt to beat their rival Glenn Curtiss and his backer, phone man Alexander Graham Bell. Rule of thumb: Fast-forward through the parts when they are on the ground, or see Stacy Keach's public-TV version instead.
1978 96m/C Michael Moriarty, David Huffman, Kathryn Walker, Eugene Roche, John Randolph, Scott Hylands; **D:** E.W. Swackhamer. **VHS, Beta $14.95** FRH 𝄞𝄞

Winds of the Wasteland Would-be Pony Express contractors, Wayne and Chandler, race rivals to land government work. Competent western that put Wayne on the Hollywood map.
1936 54m/B John Wayne, Phyllis Fraser, Lane Chandler, Yakima Canutt; **D:** Mack V. Wright. **VHS $19.95** REP, NOS, VCN 𝄞𝄞½

The Winds of War On seven tapes, the excruciatingly long and dull television mini-series based on Herman Wouk's bestseller about World War II. The book was much better; Mitchum appears to be fighting sleep unsuccessfully for much of the show. Two follow-ups were produced: "War and Remembrance" and "War and Remembrance: The Final Chapter."
1983 900m/C Robert Mitchum, Ali MacGraw, Ralph Bellamy, Polly Bergen, Jan-Michael Vincent, David Dukes, John Houseman, Victoria Tennant, Peter Graves, Chaim Topol, Ben Murphy, Jeremy Kemp, Anton Diffring, Lawrence Pressman, Andrew Duggan, Barbara Steele; **D:** Dan Curtis. **VHS, Beta $139.95** PAR, MOV 𝄞𝄞

Windwalker Howard, the only cast member who is not a Native American, is an aged chief who shares the memories of his life with his grandchildren. Filmed in the Crow and Cheyenne Indian languages and subtitled in English throughout. A beautifully photographed, intelligent independent project.
1981 108m/C Trevor Howard, James Remar, Dusty Iron Wing McCrea; **D:** Keith Merrill. **VHS, Beta $59.98** FOX 𝄞𝄞𝄞

Windy City A group of seven childhood friends must come to terms with the harsh realities of their failed ambitions when they meet for a weekend in Chicago. Told from the point of view of one of the group, recounting the sorts of memories we all prefer to forget. Typical and overwrought '80s yuppie reunion/regret drama. Aren't these people too young to be unhappy?
1984 (R) 103m/C John Shea, Kate Capshaw, Josh Mostel, Jeffrey DeMunn, Lewis J. Stadlen, James Sutorius; **D:** Armyan Bernstein; **M:** Jack Nitzsche. **VHS, Beta, LV $79.98** FOX 𝄞𝄞

A Wing and a Prayer Better-than-average WWII Air Force action flick. Battles rage throughout the Pacific theater and the men aboard the aircraft carrier struggle to do their part to save the world for freedom. Fine cast receives Hathaway's excellent unsentimental direction.
1944 97m/B Don Ameche, Dana Andrews, William Eythe, Charles Bickford, Cedric Hardwicke, Kevin O'Shea, Richard Jaeckel, Harry Morgan; **D:** Henry Hathaway. **VHS $14.98** FXV 𝄞𝄞𝄞

Wings The silent classic about friends, Rogers and Arlen, their adventures in the Air Corps during WWI, and their rivalry for the hand of a woman. Contains actual footage of combat flying from the Great War. Won the very first Best Picture Oscar. Too-thin plot hangs on (barely) to the stirring, intrepid dogfight scenes.
1927 139m/B Clara Bow, Charles "Buddy" Rogers, Richard Arlen, Gary Cooper; **D:** William A. Wellman. **VHS, Beta, LV $14.95** BTV, PAR 𝄞𝄞½

Wings of Danger A pilot tries to save his friend from blackmailing gold smugglers. **AKA:** Dead on Course.
1952 72m/B Zachary Scott, Kay Kendall, Robert Beatty, Naomi Chance. **VHS, Beta, LV** MLB, RXM 𝄞

Wings of Desire An ethereal, haunting modern fable about one of many angels observing human life in and above the broken existence of Berlin, and how he begins to long to experience life as humans do. A moving, unequivocable masterpiece, with as many beautiful things to say about spiritual need as about the schizophrenic emptiness of contemporary Germany; Wenders' magnum opus. In German with English subtitles, and with black-and-white sequences. Magnificent cinematography by Henri Alekan. **AKA:** Der Himmel Uber Berlin.
1988 (PG-13) 130m/C GE Bruno Ganz, Peter Falk, Solveig Dommartin, Otto Sander, Curt Bois; **W/D:** Wim Wenders; **W:** Peter Handke. **VHS, Beta, LV $19.98** ORI, GLV, TAM 𝄞𝄞𝄞½

Wings of Eagles Hollywood biography of Frank 'Spig' Wead, a famous WWI aviation pioneer turned screenwriter. Veers wildly from comedy to stolid drama, though Bond's lampoon of Ford as ''John Dodge'' is justly famous.
1957 110m/C John Wayne, Ward Bond, Maureen O'Hara, Dan Dailey, Edmund Lowe, Ken Curtis, Kenneth Tobey, Sig Rumann; *D:* John Ford. VHS, Beta $19.98 MGM *ℐℐ*½

Winner Takes All A young college student during the Vietnam War comes to grips with maturity and growing pains.
1986 (R) 94m/C GB Jason Connery, Diane Cilento. VHS, Beta $59.95 NA *ℐℐ*

Winners of the West A landowner schemes to prevent a railroad from running through his property. The railroad's chief engineer leads the good guys in an attempt to prevent sabotage. A fun serial in thirteen chapters, full of shooting, blown-up bridges, locomotives afire, etc.; and of course, the requisite damsel in distress.
1940 169m/B Anne Nagel, Dick Foran, James Craig; *D:* Ford Beebe, Ray Taylor. VHS, Beta $49.95 NOS, VCN, VYY *ℐℐ*

Winners Take All A handful of friends compete in Supercross races. Spirited but thoroughly cliche sports flick.
1987 (PG-13) 103m/C Don Michael Paul, Kathleen York, Robert Krantz; *D:* Fritz Kiersch. VHS, Beta, LV $19.98 SUE, NLC *ℐ*

Winning A race car driver (Newman) will let nothing, including his new wife (Woodward), keep him from winning the Indianapolis 500. Newman does his own driving. Thomas' film debut.
1969 (PG) 123m/C Paul Newman, Joanne Woodward, Robert Wagner, Richard Thomas, Clu Gulager; *D:* James Goldstone. VHS, Beta, LV $49.95 MCA *ℐℐℐ*

Winning of the West Yodelin' ranger Autry vows to protect a crusading publisher from unscrupulous crooks, including his own dog-gone brothers. The brothers see the lights, and the two corral the varmints. Autry tunes include ''Cowboy Blues,'' ''Cowpoke Poking Along,'' and ''Find Me My 45.''
1953 57m/B Gene Autry, Smiley Burnette, Gail Davis, Richard Crane; *D:* George Archainbaud. VHS, Beta $24.95 CCB *ℐℐ*

The Winning Team Reagan stars in this biography of baseball legend Grover Cleveland Alexander and Day plays his dedicated wife. Some controversial issues were glossed over in the film, such as Alexander's real-life drinking problem and the fact that he had epilepsy. Although this was one of Reagan's favorite roles, he was upset by the studio's avoidance of all-too-human problems. Nonetheless, it's an entertaining enough movie about a very talented ballplayer.
1952 98m/B Doris Day, Ronald Reagan, Frank Lovejoy, Eve Miller, James Millican, Russ Tamblyn; *D:* Lewis Seiler. VHS, LV $19.98 WAR *ℐℐ*½

The Winslow Boy A cadet at the Royal Naval College is wrongly accused of theft and expelled. Donat as the boy's lawyer leads a splendid cast. Despite consequences for his family, the boy's father (Hardwicke) sues the government and fights his son's battle, as the case makes the papers and he approaches bankruptcy. Plot would seem far-fetched if it weren't based on fact. Absorbing. Based on a play by Terrence Rattigan, who co-wrote the script.
1948 112m/B GB Robert Donat, Cedric Hardwicke, Margaret Leighton, Frank Lawton, Basil Radford, Kathleen Harrison; *D:* Anthony Asquith. VHS, Beta $59.95 HBO, HEG *ℐℐℐ*½

Winter Flight A small, gentle British drama about an RAF recruit and a barmaid who quickly become lovers, and then are confronted with her pregnancy.
1984 105m/C GB Reece Dinsdale, Nicola Cowper, Gary Olsen; *D:* Roy Battersby. VHS, Beta $59.95 MGM *ℐℐ*

Winter Kills Distinctive political black comedy suffers a hilariously paranoid version of American public life. Bridges, the younger brother of a U.S. president assassinated 15 years earlier, uncovers the plot. Huston is delightful as Bridges' horny old father. Uneven, but well worth seeing; flopped at the box office, but was re-released in 1983. Taylor was not billed.
1979 (R) 97m/C Jeff Bridges, John Huston, Anthony Perkins, Richard Boone, Sterling Hayden, Eli Wallach, Ralph Meeker, Belinda Bauer, Dorothy Malone, Toshiro Mifune, Elizabeth Taylor, Donald Moffatt, Tisa Farrow, Brad Dexter, Joe Spinell; *D:* William Richert. VHS, Beta, LV $14.95 COL, SUE *ℐℐℐ*

The Winter Light The second film in Bergman's famous trilogy on the silence of God, preceded by ''Through a Glass Darkly'' and followed by ''The Silence.'' Bleak and disturbing view of a tortured priest who searches for the faith and guidance he is unable to give his congregation. Hard to swallow for neophyte Bergmanites, but challenging, deeply serious and rewarding for those accustomed to the Swede's angst. Polished and personal. In Swedish with English subtitles. *AKA:* Nattvardsgaesterna.
1962 80m/B SW Gunnar Bjornstrand, Ingrid Thulin, Max von Sydow; *D:* Ingmar Bergman. VHS, Beta $29.98 SUE, TAM, NLC *ℐℐℐ*½

Winter Meeting Overwrought drama with Bette Davis starring as a spinster poetess who falls in love with a war hero who wants to be a priest. Very talky script, of interest only as the sole romantic lead for James Davis, whose claim to fame was westerns and the TV series ''Dallas.''
1948 104m/B Bette Davis, Janice Paige, James Davis, John Hoyt, Florence Bates, Walter Baldwin, Ransom Sherman; *D:* Bretaigne Windust. VHS $19.98 MGM *ℐℐ*

The Winter of Our Dreams Down Under slice of seamy life as a heroin-addicted prostitute becomes involved with an unhappy bookshop owner. Davis shines in otherwise slow and confusing drama.
1982 89m/C AU Judy Davis, Bryan Brown, Cathy Downes, Baz Luhrmann, Peter Mochrie, Mervyn Drak, Margie McCrae, Marcie Deane-Johns; *D:* John Duigan. VHS, Beta $59.95 LIV *ℐℐ*½

Winter People A clock-making widower and a woman living alone with her illegitimate son experience tough times together with feuding families in a Depression-era Appalachian community. Silly, rehashed premise doesn't deter McGillis, who gamely gives a fine performance. Based on the novel by John Ehle.
1989 (PG-13) 109m/C Kurt Russell, Kelly McGillis, Lloyd Bridges, Mitchell Ryan, Jeffrey Meek; *D:* Ted Kotcheff. VHS, Beta, LV, 8mm $19.98 SUE, NLC *ℐℐ*½

Winterset A son seeks to clear his father's name of a falsely accused crime 15 years after his electrocution. Powerful at the time, though time has lessened its impact. Loosely based on the trial of Sacco and Vanzetti and adapted from Maxwell Anderson's Broadway play, with stars in the same roles. Meredith's film debut.

1936 85m/B Burgess Meredith, Margo, John Carradine; *D:* Alfred Santell. VHS, Beta, 3/4U, **Special order formats** $19.95 NOS, HHT, CAB *ℐℐ*½

Wired A justly lambasted, unintentionally hilarious biography of comic genius and overdose victim John Belushi, very loosely based on Bob Woodward's bestselling muckraking book. The chronicle of addiction and tragedy is tried here as a weird sort of comedy; was it meant as a tribute to its off-kilter subject? If so, it misses by a mile. And, we're sorry, but Chiklis doesn't cut is as Belushi—who would?!
1989 (R) 112m/C Michael Chiklis, Ray Sharkey, Patti D'Arbanville, J.T. Walsh, Gary Groomes, Lucinda Jenney, Alex Rocco, Jere Burns, Billy Preston; *D:* Larry Peerce. VHS, Beta, LV $89.95 LIV *ℐ*

Wired to Kill In a futuristic world, two teenagers seek justice for their parents' murder by building a remote-controlled erector set programmed for revenge. Laughably porous plot drops any pretence of credibility. Dizzyingly bad.
1986 (R) 96m/C Merritt Butrick, Emily Longstreth, Devin Hoelscher, Frank Collison; *D:* Franky Schaeffer. VHS, Beta $79.98 LIV Woof!

Wisdom Unemployed young guy (Estevez) becomes a bank robber with Robin Hood aspirations, coming to the aid of American farmers by destroying mortgage records. Estevez became the youngest person to star in, write, and direct a major motion picture. And, my goodness, it shows.
1987 (R) 109m/C Emilio Estevez, Demi Moore, Tom Skerritt, Veronica Cartwright; *D:* Emilio Estevez. VHS, Beta, LV $19.98 WAR *ℐ*½

Wise Blood Gothic drama about a drifter who searches for sin and becomes a preacher for a new religion, The Church Without Christ. Excellent cast in achingly realistic portrayal of ersatz religion, southern style. Many laughs are more painful than funny. Superb, very dark comedy from Huston. Adapted from the Flannery O'Connor novel.
1979 (PG) 106m/C Brad Dourif, John Huston, Ned Beatty, Amy Wright, Harry Dean Stanton; *D:* John Huston. VHS, Beta $59.95 MCA *ℐℐℐ*½

Wise Guys Two small-time hoods decide to rip off the mob. When their boss figures out their plan he decides to set them up instead. Lame black comedy that has too few moments.
1986 (R) 100m/C Joe Piscopo, Danny DeVito, Ray Sharkey, Captain Lou Albano, Dan Hedaya, Julie Bovasso, Patti LuPone; *D:* Brian DePalma. VHS, Beta $19.99 FOX, FCT *ℐ*½

Wish You Were Here Poignant yet funny slice of British postwar life roughly based on the childhood memoirs of famous madame, Cynthia Payne. A troubled and freedom-loving teenager expresses her rebellion in sexual experimentation. Mum is dead and Dad just doesn't understand, so what's a girl to do, but get the boys excited? Lloyd, in her first film, plays the main character with exceptional strength and feistiness. Payne's later life was dramatized in the Leland-scripted ''Personal Services.''
1987 92m/C GB Emily Lloyd, Tom Bell, Clare Clifford, Barbara Durkin, Geoffrey Hutchings, Charlotte Barker, Chloe Leland, Trudy Cavanagh, Jesse Birdsall, Geoffrey Durham, Pat Heywood; *D:* David Leland. VHS, Beta, LV $19.95 FRH, TVC *ℐℐℐ*

Wishful Thinking A lovelorn screenwriter rescues a peculiar man from mysterious assassins and receives a magical writing pad for his efforts. It seems that whatever Michael writes on the paper will come true, so

he decides to write himself into the life of the luscious Diane.
1992 94m/C Murray Langston, Michelle Johnson, Ruth Buzzi, Billy Barty, Johnny Dark, Ray ''Boom Boom'' Mancini, Vic Dunlop, Kip Addotta; **D:** Murray Langston. **VHS $89.95** HMD *ℐℐ*

The Wishing Ring Light and charming romance, beautifully filmed by Tourneur, based on Owen Davis' play. The son of an earl in Old England is expelled from college and told by his father he must earn half a crown on his own before the family will take him back. With the help of a minister's daughter, he sets things right.
1914 50m/B Vivian Martin, Alec B. Francis, Chester Barnett, Simeon Wiltsie, Walter Morton; **W/D:** Maurice Tourneur. **VHS, Beta** NO *ℐℐℐ*

The Wishmaker A young man squanders the three wishes granted to him for helping a strange old woman and her timid daughter.
1985 54m/C VHS, Beta $29.95 GEM *ℐℐℐ*

The Wistful Widow of Wagon Gap Lou, a traveling salesman, accidentally kills a man, and according to the law of the west he has to take care of the dead man's widow and children—all seven of them. Because the family is so unsavory, Lou knows that no other man will kill him, so he allows himself to be appointed sheriff and clears the town of lowlifes. Usual Abbott & Costello fare is highlighted with their zany antics. **AKA:** The Wistful Widow.
1947 78m/B Bud Abbott, Lou Costello, Marjorie Main, George Cleveland, Gordon Jones, William Ching, Peter Thompson, Glenn Strange, Olin Howland; **D:** Charles T. Barton. **VHS $14.98** MCA *ℐℐ*

The Witch Historian hired by family to assemble the late father's works falls in love with beautiful daughter. Seems she's no angel. **AKA:** La Strega in Amore; Aura.
1966 103m/B IT Rosanna Schiaffino, Richard Johnson, Sarah Ferrati, Gian Marie Volonte, Margherita Guzzinati; **D:** Damiano Damiani. **VHS $19.98** SNC *ℐℐ 1/2*

Witch Who Came from the Sea Witch terrorizes all the ships at sea, but doesn't exactly haunt the viewer.
1976 (R) 98m/C Millie Perkins, Loni Chapman, Vanessa Brown, Peggy Feury, Rick Jason; **D:** Matt Cimber. **VHS, Beta $49.95** UNI *ℐ 1/2*

A Witch Without a Broom Shoestring time travel fantasy. When an American professor catches the eye of a 15th century apprentice witch, the trip begins. Since the witch is only learning the ropes, they end up visiting a number of periods other than their own before the professor gets home. **AKA:** Una Bruja Sin Escoba.
1968 78m/C SP Jeffrey Hunter, Maria Perschy, Perla Cristal, Gustavo Rojo; **D:** Joe Lacy. **VHS** NO *ℐ 1/2*

Witchboard During a college party, a group of friends bring out the Ouija board and play with it for laughs. One of the girls discovers she can use the board to communicate with a small boy who died years before. In her effort to talk with him she unwittingly releases the evil spirit of an ax murderer who haunts and murders members of the group. An entertaining, relatively inoffensive member of its genre that displays some attention to characterization and plot.
1987 (R) 98m/C Todd Allen, Tawny Kitaen, Steven Nichols, Kathleen Wilhoite, Burke Byrnes, Rose Marie, James W. Quinn, Judy Tatum, Gloria Hayes, J.P. Luebsen, Susan Nickerson; **D:** Kevin S. Tenney. **VHS, Beta, LV** NO *ℐℐ 1/2*

Witchcraft A young mother meets a couple killed three centuries ago for performing witchcraft. They want her baby, of course, to be the son of the devil. ''Rosemary's Baby'' rip-off, that is thoroughly predictable.
1988 (R) 90m/C Anat ''Topol'' Barzilai, Gary Sloan, Lee Kisman, Deborah Scott; **D:** Robert Spera. **VHS, Beta, LV $29.95** ACA Woof!

Witchcraft 2: The Temptress A sensuous woman seduces an innocent young man into the rituals of witchcraft and the occult. Sequel to ''Witchcraft'' does not succeed where original failed, but does have a fair share of sex and violence.
1990 (R) 88m/C Charles Solomon, Mia Ruiz, Delia Sheppard; **D:** Mark Woods. **VHS, Beta, LV $29.95** ACA *ℐ*

Witchcraft 3: The Kiss of Death Once a master of the occult, William Spanner now seeks only to live a normal life. His plans are changed, however, when a sensual creature from Hell is sent to seduce him. More sex and violence, with an emphasis on sex. The best of the ''Witchcraft'' series, for those trying to plan a festive evening.
1990 (R) 85m/C Charles Solomon, Lisa Toothman, William L. Baker, Lena Hall; **D:** R.L. Tillmanns. **VHS $19.95** ACA *ℐℐ*

Witchcraft 4: Virgin Heart Supernatural horror continues as attorney Will Spanner sinks even deeper into his enemy's satanic trap in this shocking sequel to the popular series. His only hope is to use his own black magic powers and to enlist the help of a seductive stripper (Penthouse Pet Strain).
1992 (R) 92m/C Charles Solomon, Julie Strain, Clive Pearson, Jason O'Gulihar, Lisa Jay Harrington, Barbara Dow; **D:** James Merendino. VHS, LV $89.95 ACA *ℐ*

Witchcraft 5: Dance with the Devil This undistinguished horror series continues with several successful people finding the unpleasant loopholes in their satanic contracts. A demon named Cain is behind all the trouble. The horror special effects are cheap but there are several softcore sex scenes (pointless to the plot) which provide a minimal interest. An unrated version is also available.
1992 (R) 94m/C Marklen Kennedy, Carolyn Taye-Loren, Nicole Sassaman, Aysha Hauer; **D:** Talun Hsu. **VHS $89.95** ACA *ℐ*

Witchcraft Through the Ages The demonic Swedish masterpiece in which witches and victims suffer against various historical backgrounds. Nightmarish and profane, especially the appearance of the Devil as played under much make-up by Christiansen himself. Silent. **AKA:** Haxan.
1922 74m/B SW Maren Pedersen, Clara Pontoppidan; **D:** Benjamin Christiansen. **VHS, Beta $29.98** GPV, MPI, WFV *ℐℐℐ*

Witchery A photographer and his girlfriend vacation at a New England hotel where they discover a horrifying, satanic secret. One by one (as always, in this kind of bad flick, in the interest of ''suspense''), people are killed off. Seems it's a witch, bent on revenge. Forget room service and bar the door.
1988 96m/C David Hasselhoff, Linda Blair, Catherine Hickland, Hildegarde Knef, Leslie Cumming, Bob Champagne, Richard Farnsworth, Michael Manches; **D:** Fabrizio Laurenti. **VHS, Beta $79.95** VMK *ℐ*

The Witches Nine-year-old boy on vacation finds himself in the midst of a witch convention, and grand high witch Huston plans to turn all children into furry little creatures. The boy, with the help of his good witch grandmother, attempts to prevent the mass transmutation of children into mice. Top-notch fantasy probably too spooky for the training wheel set. Wonderful special effects; the final project of executive producer Jim Henson. Based on Roald Dahl's story.
1990 (PG) 92m/C Anjelica Huston, Mai Zetterling, Jasen Fisher, Rowan Atkinson, Charlie Potter, Bill Paterson, Brenda Blethyn, Jane Horrocks; **D:** Nicolas Roeg; **W:** Allan Scott. VHS, Beta, LV, 8mm $92.95 WAR, FCT *ℐℐℐ 1/2*

Witches' Brew Three young women try to use their undeveloped skills in witchcraft and black magic to help Garr's husband get a prestigious position at a university, with calamitous results. Oft-funny spoof is silly and oft-predictable. Turner's role is small as an older, experienced witch.
1979 (PG) 98m/C Teri Garr, Richard Benjamin, Lana Turner, Kathryn Leigh Scott; **D:** Richard Shorr, Herbert L. Strock. **VHS, Beta $59.98** SUE *ℐℐ*

Witches' Mountain A troubled couple is captured by a coven of witches in the Pyrenees. Dull and pointless.
1971 98m/C MX Patty Shepard, John Caffari, Monica Randall; **D:** Raul Artigot. **VHS, Beta $49.95** UNI, HEG *ℐ*

The Witches of Eastwick ''Mad Max'' director Miller meets Hollywood in this unrestrained, vomit-filled treatment of John Updike's novel about three lonely small-town New England women and their sexual liberation. A strange, rich, overweight and balding, but nonetheless charming man knows their deepest desires and makes them come true with decadent excess. Raunchy fun, with Nicholson over-acting wildly as the Mephisto. Miller lends a bombastic violent edge to the effort, sometimes at the expense of the story. Filmed on location in Cohasset, Massachusetts.
1987 (R) 118m/C Jack Nicholson, Cher, Susan Sarandon, Michelle Pfeiffer, Veronica Cartwright, Richard Jenkins, Keith Joakum, Carel Struycken; **D:** George Miller; **M:** John Williams. Academy Awards '87 Nominations: Best Sound, Best Original Score; Los Angeles Film Critics Association Awards '87: Best Actor (Nicholson); New York Film Critics Awards '87: Best Actor (Nicholson). **VHS, Beta, LV, 8mm $14.95** WAR *ℐℐ 1/2*

Witchfire After their pyschiatrist dies in an automobile accident, three maniacal women escape from an asylum and hide out in the woods. Winters then holds seances to contact the dead doctor, but instead captures a young, very much alive hunter. For dedicated fans of Winters.
1986 (R) 92m/C Shelley Winters, Gary Swanson, David Mendenhall, Corinne Chateau; **W/D:** Vincent J. Privitera. **VHS, Beta $79.98** LIV *ℐ*

The Witching Poorly made story of man's continuing quest for supernatural power. Welles slums as the high priest out to get victim Franklin. **AKA:** Necromancy.
1972 90m/C Orson Welles, Pamela Franklin, Michael Ontkean, Lee Purcell; **D:** Bert I. Gordon. **VHS, Beta $42.95** PGN Woof!

Witching Time Elvira presents this film, in which a young composer is visited by a horny 17th-century witch while his wife is away from home. When the wife returns, both women fight to possess him.
1984 60m/C Jon Finch, Prunella Gee, Patricia Quinn, Ian McCulloch; **D:** Don Leaver. **VHS, Beta $29.95** LIV *ℐ 1/2*

The Witchmaker Remote, crocodile-infested bayou in Louisiana is the scene of witchcraft and the occult as young girls are murdered in order for a group of witches to become youthful again. **AKA:** Legend of Witch Hollow; Witchkill.

1969 101m/C John Lodge, Alvy Moore, Thordis Brandt, Anthony Eisley, Shelby Grant, Robyn Millan; **W/D:** William O. Brown. **VHS, Beta** *NO* ⚜

The Witch's Curse Excellent fantasy in which an ancient witch places a curse on the surface world and Maciste travels into hell to find her.
1962 ?m/C Kirk Morris, Helene Chanel; **D:** Riccardo Freda. **VHS** $16.95 *SNC* ⚜⚜½

The Witch's Mirror A sorceress plots to destroy the murderer of her god- daughter. The murderer, a surgeon, begins a project to restore the disfigured face and hands of his burned second wife, and he doesn't care how he gets the materials. For true fans of good bad horror flicks. Badly dubbed (which adds to the charm); dark (of course); and offbeat (naturally).
1960 75m/B *MX* Rosita Arenas, Armando Calvo, Isabela Corona, Dina De Marco; **D:** Chano Urueto. **VHS, Beta** $59.95 *SNC, HHT* ⚜⚜

WitchTrap Lame sequel to "Witchboard." A mansion's new owner hires psychics to exorcise the disturbed ghost of his predecessor.
1989 (R) 87m/C James W. Quinn, Kathleen Bailey, Linnea Quigley; **D:** Kevin S. Tenney. **VHS, Beta, LV** *IME* ⚜

With Kit Carson Over the Great Divide A large-scale silent western about a doctor's family gone asunder and then reunited during the Fremont expeditions out of St. Louis in the 1840s. Snow's final screen appearance. Recently refound. Fun cinematic history (in two senses of the phrase). Beautiful landscape.
1925 72m/B Roy Stewart, Henry B. Walthall, Marguerite Snow, Sheldon Lewis, Earl Metcalfe; **D:** Frank S. Mattison. **VHS, Beta, 8mm** $29.95 *VYY* ⚜⚜½

With Six You Get Eggroll A widow with three sons and a widower with a daughter elope and then must deal with the antagonism of their children and even their dogs. Brady Bunch-esque family comedy means well, but doesn't cut it. Jamie Farr, William Christopher, and Vic Tayback have small parts. To date, Day's last big-screen appearance. *AKA:* A Man in Mommy's Bed.
1968 (G) 95m/C Doris Day, Brian Keith, Pat Carroll, Alice Ghostley; **D:** Howard Morris. **VHS, Beta** $59.98 *FOX* ⚜⚜

Withnail and I A biting and original black comedy about a pair of unemployed, nearly starving English actors during the late 1960s. They decide to retreat to a country house owned by Withnail's uncle, for a vacation and are beset by comic misadventures, particularly when the uncle, who is gay, starts to hit on his nephew's friend. Robinson, who scripted "The Killing Fields," makes his successful directorial debut, in addition to drafting the screenplay from his own novel. Co-produced by George Harrison and Richard Starkey (Ringo Starr).
1987 (R) 108m/C *GB* Richard E. Grant, Paul McGann, Richard Griffiths; **D:** Bruce Robinson. **VHS, Beta, LV** $79.95 *MED* ⚜⚜⚜½

Without a Clue Spoof of the Sherlock Holmes legend, in which Holmes is actually portrayed by a bumbling, skirt-chasing actor, and Watson is the sole crime-solving mastermind, hiring the actor to impersonate the character made famous by the doctor's published exploits. The leads have some fun and so do we; but laughs are widely spaced.
1988 (PG) 107m/C *GB* Michael Caine, Ben Kingsley, Jeffrey Jones, Lysette Anthony, Paul Freeman, Nigel Davenport, Peter Cook; **D:** Thom Eberhardt. **VHS, Beta, LV** $19.98 *ORI* ⚜⚜½

Without a Trace One morning, a six-year-old boy is sent off to school by his loving mother, never to return. The story of the mother's relentless search for her son. Cardboard characters, wildly unrealistic ending that is different from the real-life incident on which it's based. Scripted by Beth Gutcheon from her book "Still Missing." Jaffe's directorial debut.
1983 (PG) 119m/C Kate Nelligan, Judd Hirsch, Stockard Channing, David Dukes; **D:** Stanley R. Jaffe; **M:** Jack Nitzsche. **VHS, Beta** $59.98 *FOX* ⚜⚜

Without Honors A man seeks to restore the reputation of his dead brother, accused of murder and theft. He joins the Texas Rangers and brings the real criminals to justice. Excellent location shooting lifts ordinary early western.
1932 62m/B Harry Carey Sr., Mae Busch, Gibson Gowland, George "Gabby" Hayes; **D:** William Nigh. **VHS, Beta, LV** *NO* ⚜⚜

Without Love Tracy is a scientist, Hepburn, a woman with an empty basement for his laboratory. Since the neighbors would be scandalized by the idea of unmarried people living together, however platonically, they decide to get married, although each has sworn off romance. Snappy dialogue, expertly rendered by the Tracy/Hepburn team. Terrific supporting cast keeps this minimally plotted outing afloat. Adapted from the play of the same name by Philip Barry.
1945 113m/B Spencer Tracy, Katharine Hepburn, Lucille Ball, Keenan Wynn, Carl Esmond, Patricia Morison, Felix Bressart; **D:** Harold Bucquet; **W:** Donald Ogden Stewart. **VHS, Beta** $19.98 *MGM* ⚜⚜½

Without Love Ambitious young journalist experiences resentment from her peers because of her aggressive methods, and they decide to teach her a lesson by drawing her into a situation destined for disaster. In Polish with English subtitles.
1980 104m/C *PL* **D:** Barbara Sass. **VHS** $49.95 *FCT* ⚜⚜

Without Reservations Hollywood-bound novelist Colbert encounters Marine flyer Wayne and his pal (DeFore) aboard a train. She decides he would be perfect for her newest movie. They both dislike her famous book and don't realize they're traveling with the renowned author. Misadventures and misunderstandings abound as this trio make their way to Tinseltown. Of course, Colbert and Wayne fall in love. Box-office success with a tired script and too few real laughs. The Duke is interesting but miscast. Based on the novel "Thanks, God, I'll Take It From Here" by Jane Allen.
1946 101m/B Claudette Colbert, John Wayne, Don DeFore, Phil Brown, Frank Puglia; *Cameos:* Louella Parsons, Cary Grant, Jack Benny; **D:** Mervyn LeRoy. **VHS, Beta, LV** $19.98 *UHV, VCN, TTC* ⚜⚜½

Without Warning Inexperienced director and actors pull out a minor success in this fairly ordinary murder mystery, about a serial killer of beautiful blondes. *AKA:* The Story Without A Name.
1952 75m/C *FR* Maurice Ronet, Adam Williams, Gloria Franklin, Edward Binns; **D:** Arnold Laven. **VHS** *NO* ⚜⚜½

Without Warning: The James Brady Story White House Press Secretary Brady took a bullet in the brain during the 1981 shooting of President Reagan, and made a slow, grueling recovery. This fine made for cable TV film spares none of it, concentrating on the stricken man and his family, and opting out of disease-of-the-week cliches (though the pic's politics won't please

the gun-adorers). Based on Mollie Dickinson's biography "Thumbs Up."
1991 (R) 120m/C Beau Bridges, Joan Allen, David Strathairn; **D:** Michael Toshiyuki Uno; **W:** Robert Bolt. **VHS** $89.98 *HBO* ⚜⚜⚜

Without You I'm Nothing Comedienne Bernhard's stunning, intelligent, and hilarious one-person show explores three decades of American pop culture. Bernhard challenges audience expectations of societal norms by assuming sterotypical ideals from the 60's, 70's and 80's.
1990 (R) 90m/C Sandra Bernhard, John Doe, Lu Leonard, Cynthia Bailey; **D:** John Boskovich. **VHS** $89.98 *HBO* ⚜⚜⚜

Witness A young Amish boy traveling from his father's funeral witnesses a murder in a Philadelphia bus station. The investigating detective (Ford, in one of his best roles) soon discovers the killing is part of a conspiracy involving corruption in his department. He follows the child and his young widowed mother to their home in the country. A thriller with a difference, about the encounter of alien worlds, with a poignant love story. McGillis, in her first major role, is luminous as the Amish mother, while Ford is believable as both a cop and a sensitive man. An artfully crafted drama, richly focusing on the often misunderstood Amish lifestyle.
1985 (R) 112m/C Harrison Ford, Kelly McGillis, Alexander Godunov, Lukas Haas, Josef Sommer, Danny Glover, Patti LuPone; **D:** Peter Weir. Academy Awards '85: Best Film Editing, Best Original Screenplay; Nominations: Best Actor (Ford), Best Art Direction/Set Decoration, Best Cinematography, Best Director (Weir), Best Picture, Best Original Score; Edgar Allan Poe Awards '85: Best Screenplay. **VHS, Beta, LV, 8mm** $14.95 *PAR, HMV* ⚜⚜⚜½

Witness for the Prosecution An unemployed man is accused of murdering a wealthy widow whom he befriended. A straightforward court case becomes increasingly complicated in this energetic adaptation of an Agatha Christie story and stage play. Ailing defense attorney Laughton can't resist taking an intriguing murder case. Outstanding performances by Laughton, with excellent support by real life wife, Lanchester, as his patient nurse. Power, as the alleged killer, and Dietrich as a tragic woman are top-notch (see if you can detect Dietrich in an unbilled second role). Scripted by Wilder and Harry Kurnitz from Agatha Christie's novel.
1957 116m/B Charles Laughton, Tyrone Power, Marlene Dietrich, Elsa Lanchester, John Williams, Henry Daniell, Una O'Connor; **D:** Billy Wilder; Academy Awards '57 Nominations: Best Actor (Laughton), Best Director (Wilder), Best Film Editing, Best Picture, Best Sound, Best Supporting Actress (Lanchester); Golden Globe Awards '58: Best Supporting Actress (Lanchester). **VHS, Beta, LV** $19.98 *MGM, FOX, MLB* ⚜⚜⚜½

Wives Under Suspicion While prosecuting a man who murdered his wife out of jealousy, a district attorney finds his own home life filled with similar tension. Director Whale's unnecessary remake of his own earlier film, "The Kiss Before the Mirror." He is best known for "Frankenstein."
1938 75m/B Warren William, Gail Patrick, Constance Moore, William Lundigan; **D:** James Whale. **VHS, Beta** $24.95 *NOS, DVT, HEG* ⚜⚜½

The Wiz Black version of the long-time favorite "The Wizard of Oz," based on the Broadway musical. Ross plays a Harlem schoolteacher who is whisked away to a fantasy version of New York City in a search for her identity. Some good character performances and musical numbers, but generally an overblown and garish effort with Ross too

old for her role. Pryor is poorly cast, but Jackson is memorable as the Scarecrow. High-budget ($24 million) production with a ton of name stars, lost $11 million, and cooled studios on black films. Horne's number as the good witch is the best reason to sit through this one. ♫The Feeling That We HAve; Can I Go On Not Knowing; Glinda's Theme; He's the Wizard; Soon as I Get Home; You Can't Win; Ease on Down the Road; What Would I Do If I Could Feel?; Slide Some Oil to Me; I'm a Mean Old Lion; Poppy Girls; Be a Lion; Emerald City Ballet; Is This What Feeling Gets?; Don't Nobody Bring Me Bad News; Everybody Rejoice; Believe in Yourself; Brand New Day; So You Wanted to See the Wizard; He's the Wizard; Liberation Agitato; The Wiz; March of the Munchkins; Now Watch Me Dance; End of the Yellow Brick Road; A Sorry Phoney.
1978 (G) 133m/C Diana Ross, Michael Jackson, Nipsey Russell, Ted Ross, Mabel King, Thelma Carpenter, Richard Pryor, Lena Horne; *D:* Sidney Lumet. **VHS, Beta, LV $29.95** *MCA, FCT* 𝄞𝄞

The Wizard Facing the dissolution of his dysfunctional family, a youngster decides to take his autistic, video game-playing little brother across the country to a national video competition. Way too much plot in pretentious, blatantly commercial feature-length Nintendo ad, featuring the kid from "The Wonder Years." For teen video addicts only.
1989 (PG) 99m/C Fred Savage, Beau Bridges, Christian Slater, Luke Edwards, Jenny Lewis; *D:* Todd Holland. **VHS, Beta, LV $19.95** *MCA* 𝄞½

The Wizard of Gore The prototypical Lewis splatter party, about a magician whose on-stage mutilations turn out to be messily real. High camp and barrels of bright movie blood.
1970 (R) 96m/C Ray Sager, Judy Cler, Wayne Ratay, Phil Lauenson, Jim Rau, John Elliott, Don Alexander, Monika Blackwell, Corinne Kirkin; *D:* Herschell Gordon Lewis. **VHS, Beta** *RHI* 𝄞

The Wizard of Loneliness A disturbed young boy goes to live with his grandparents during WWII, and slowly discovers family secrets centering on his aunt. Excellent performances barely save an aimless plot with an overdone denouement. Based on the novel by John Nichols.
1988 (PG-13) 110m/C Lukas Haas, Lea Thompson, John Randolph, Lance Guest, Anne Pitoniak, Jeremiah Warner, Dylan Baker; *D:* Jenny Bowen. **VHS, Beta, LV** *NO* 𝄞½

The Wizard of Oz An early silent version of the L. Frank Baum fantasy, with notable plot departures from the book and later 1939 adaptation, starring long-forgotten comedian Semon as the Scarecrow, supported by a pre-Laurel Hardy as the Tin Woodman. With music score.
1925 93m/B Larry Semon, Dorothy Dwan, Bryant Washburn, Charles Murray, Oliver Hardy, Josef Swickard, Virginia Pearson; *D:* Larry Semon. **VHS, Beta, 8mm $19.95** *NOS, VYY, MLB* 𝄞𝄞½

The Wizard of Oz From the book by L. Frank Baum, a fantasy about a Kansas farm girl (Garland, in her immortal role) who rides a tornado to a brightly colored world over the rainbow, full of talking scarecrows, munchkins and a wizard who bears a strange resemblance to a Kansas fortune-teller. She must outwit the Wicked Witch if she is ever to go home. Delightful performances from Lahr, Bolger and Hamilton. Director Fleming originally wanted Deanna Durbin or Shirley Temple for the role of Dorothy, but settled for Garland who made the song "Somewhere Over the Rainbow" her own. She received a special Academy Award for her

performance. For the 50th anniversary of its release, "The Wizard of Oz" was restored and includes rare film clips of Bolger's "Scarecrow Dance" and the cut "Jitterbug" number, and shots by Buddy Ebsen as the Tin Man before he became ill and left the production. The laserdisc edition includes digital sound, commentary by film historian Ronald Haver, and test footage, trailers and stills, as well as Jerry Maren talking about his experiences as a Munchkin. ♫Munchkinland; Ding Dong the Witch is Dead; Follow the Yellow Brick Road; If I Only Had a Brain/a Heart/the Nerve; If I Were the King of the Forest; The Merry Old Land of Oz; Threatening Witch; Into the Forest of the Wild Beast; The City Gates are Open; At the Gates of the Emerald City; Magic Smoke Chords; Toto's Chase; On the Castle Wall; Delirious Escape; The Cornfields; Poppies; Optimistic Voices; The Witch's Castle; March of the Winkies; Dorothy's Rescue; Night on Bald Mountain; In the Shade of the Old Apple Tree; Come Out, Come Out Wherever you Are; It Really Was No Miracle; Lions and Tigers and Bears; You're Out of the Woods; Somewhere Over the Rainbow; We're Off to See the Wizard; Follow the Yellow Brick Road.
1939 101m/C Judy Garland, Margaret Hamilton, Ray Bolger, Jack Haley, Bert Lahr, Frank Morgan, Charley Grapewin, Clara Blandick, Mitchell Lewis, Billie Burke; *D:* Victor Fleming. Academy Awards '39: Best Song ("Over the Rainbow"), Best Original Score; Nominations: Best Color Cinematography, Best Interior Decoration, Best Picture, Best Special Effects. **VHS, Beta, LV $19.98** *MGM, VYG, APD* 𝄞𝄞𝄞𝄞

The Wizard of Speed and Time A special-effects wizard gets the break of his life when he's hired by a movie studio, but there's more to this particular studio than he realizes. Jittlov, a real special-effects expert, plays himself in this personally financed production. Although brimming with inside jokes and references, this self-indulgence succeeds with its enthusiasm and ambition, despite being rather obviously self-produced. Unique special effects make it memorable.
1988 95m/C Mike Jittlov, Richard Kaye, Page Moore, David Conrad, Steve Brodie, John Massari, Frank Laloggia, Philip Michael Thomas, Angelique Pettyjohn, Arnetia Walker, Paulette Breen; *D:* Mike Jittlov. **VHS, LV** *WTA* 𝄞𝄞½

Wizards A good, bumbling sorcerer battles for the sake of a magic kingdom and its princess against his evil brother who uses Nazi propaganda films to inspire his army of mutants. Profane, crude, & typically Bakshian fantasy with great graphics. Animated.
1977 (PG) 81m/C *D:* Ralph Bakshi. **VHS, Beta, LV $19.98** *FOX, WTA* 𝄞𝄞½

Wizards of the Lost Kingdom A boy magician, aided by various ogres and swordster Svenson battles an all-powerful wizard for control of his kingdom. Family fare a bit too clean and harmless.
1985 (PG) 76m/C Bo Svenson, Vidal Peterson, Thom Christopher; *D:* Hector Olivera. **VHS, Beta $19.95** *MED* 𝄞½

Wizards of the Lost Kingdom 2 A boy wizard is charged with vanquishing the evil tyrants from three kingdoms. Barely a sequel; no plot continuation or cast from earlier kiddie sword epic.
1989 (PG) 80m/C David Carradine, Bobby Jacoby, Lana Clarkson, Mel Welles, Susan Lee Hoffman, Sid Haig; *D:* Charles B. Griffith. **VHS, Beta $79.95** *MED* 𝄞

Wolf To everyone's lasting regret, an ex-Vietnam POW strives to rescue an American ambassador kidnapped by Central American rebels.

1986 95m/C J. Antonio Carreon, Ron Marchini; *D:* Charlie Ordonez. **VHS, Beta $79.95** *TWE* 𝄞

The Wolf at the Door A well-appointed, sincere biography of impressionist Paul Gauguin in the middle period of life, during his transition from the petty demands of his Parisian life to the freedom of Tahiti. Not definitive or compelling, but serves the purpose of a biography—arousing interest in the subject's life and art. Screenplay by Christopher Hampton.
1987 (R) 90m/C *DK FR* Donald Sutherland, Jean Yanne, Sofie Graboel, Ghita Norby, Max von Sydow, Merete Voldstedlund, Fanny Bastien; *D:* Henning Carlsen. **VHS, Beta $79.98** *FOX, TAM* 𝄞𝄞½

Wolf Call Carroll plays the son of a miner who travels with his devoted hound to see his father's old mine and start it working again. Gangsters and a beautiful Indian maiden get in his way. Master and pooch both find romance, and both sing. From the Jack London novel.
1939 62m/B John Carroll, Movita, Wheeler Oakman, Peter George Lynn; *D:* George Waggner. **VHS, Beta, 8mm $24.95** *VYY, FCT* 𝄞½

Wolf Dog A boy and his dog. Outdoor action and adventure. Twelve chapters, 13 minutes each.
1933 156m/B Rin Tin Tin Jr., Frankie Darro, Patricia "Boots" Mallory; *D:* Harry Fraser, Colbert Clark. **VHS, Beta $26.95** *SNC, VCN, MLB* 𝄞

Wolf Lake WWII veteran, whose son was killed in Vietnam, and a Vietnam army deserter clash with tragic consequences during their stay at a Canadian hunting lodge. Steiger gives it a go, but overwrought revenge pic resists quality upgrade.
1979 90m/C Rod Steiger, David Hoffman, Robin Mattson, Jerry Hardin, Richard Herd, Paul Mantu; *D:* Burt Kennedy. **VHS, Beta $9.99** *STE, PSM* 𝄞½

The Wolf Man Fun, absorbing classic horror with Chaney as a man bitten by werewolf Lugosi. His dad thinks he's gone nuts, his screaming gal pal just doesn't understand, and plants on the Universal lot have no roots. Ouspenskaya's finest hour as the prophetic gypsy woman. Ow-ooo! Chilling and thrilling.
1941 70m/B Lon Chaney Jr., Claude Rains, Maria Ouspenskaya, Ralph Bellamy, Bela Lugosi, Warren William, Patric Knowles, Evelyn Ankers; *D:* George Waggner. **VHS, Beta, LV $14.95** *MCA* 𝄞𝄞𝄞½

Wolfen Surrealistic menace darkens this original and underrated tale of super-intelligent wolf creatures terrorizing New York City. Police detective Finney tries to track down the beasts before they kill again. Notable special effects in this thriller, which covers environmental and Native American concerns while maintaining the tension. Feature film debuts of Hines and Venora. Based on the novel by Whitley Strieber. Available in widescreen on laserdisc.
1981 (R) 115m/C Albert Finney, Gregory Hines, Tommy Noonan, Diane Venora, Edward James Olmos; *D:* Michael Wadleigh. **VHS, Beta, LV $14.95** *WAR* 𝄞𝄞𝄞

Wolfen Ninja A girl is raised by wolves and is taught by them the secrets of Ninja fighting.
198? 92m/C **VHS, Beta $59.95** *TWE* 𝄞

Wolfheart's Revenge An honest cowboy, helped by Wolfheart the Wonder Dog, steps in when a sheep rancher is murdered. Silent film with original organ score.
1925 64m/B Guinn Williams. **VHS, Beta, 8mm $29.95** *VYY, GPV* 𝄞

The Wolfman In 1910, a young man learns that his family is heir to the curse of the Werewolf. Same old stuff.
1982 91m/C Earl Owensby, Kristina Reynolds; *D:* Worth Keeter. **VHS, Beta** $19.99 *HBO* 🐾

The Wolves Gosha shows the world of the yakuza (gangster) during the 1920s. Reminiscent of the samurai, the movie combines ancient Japanese culture with the rapidly changing world of 20th Century Japan. In Japanese with English subtitles.
1982 131m/C *JP* Tatsuya Nakadai; *D:* Hideo Gosha. **VHS, LV** $79.95 *TAM* 🐾🐾🐾

A Woman and a Woman Covers a ten-year period in the friendship of Barbara and Irena and how it survives their professional and personal conflicts. In Polish with English subtitles.
1980 99m/C *PL* Halina Labonarska, Anna Romantowska; *D:* Richard Bugajski. **VHS** $49.95 *FCT* 🐾🐾

A Woman Called Golda Political drama following the life and career of Golda Meir, the Israeli Prime Minister and one of the most powerful political figures of the 20th century. Davis portrays the young Golda, Bergman taking over as she ages. Superior made-for-television bio epic, scripted by Harold Gast and Steven Gethers.
1982 192m/C Ingrid Bergman, Leonard Nimoy, Anne Jackson, Ned Beatty, Robert Loggia, Judy Davis; *D:* Alan Gibson. **VHS, Beta** $69.95 *PAR* 🐾🐾🐾

A Woman Called Moses The story of Harriet Ross Tubman, who bought her freedom from slavery, founded the underground railroad, and helped lead hundreds of slaves to freedom before the Civil War. Wonderful performance by Tyson but the made-for-television film is bogged down by a so-so script. Based on the novel by Marcy Heidish.
1978 200m/C Cicely Tyson, Dick Anthony Williams, Will Geer, Robert Hooks, Hari Rhodes, James Wainwright; *D:* Paul Wendkos. **VHS** $89.95 *XVC, FCT* 🐾🐾½

Woman Condemned A reporter tries to clear a woman's name of murder.
1933 58m/B Mischa Auer, Lola Lane, Claudia Dell, Richard Hemingway. **VHS, Beta, LV** *NO* 🐾½

The Woman He Loved The infamous romance of Edward VIII, who gave up the throne of England for American divorcee, Wallis Warfield Simpson. Seymour and Andrews are fine in their roles but the made-for-television drama is slow-going.
1988 100m/C Anthony Andrews, Jane Seymour, Olivia de Havilland, Lucy Gutteridge, Julie Harris, Robert Hardy, Phyllis Calvert; *D:* Charles Jarrott. **VHS** *STE* 🐾🐾½

A Woman, Her Men and Her Futon A beautiful woman tries to find her identity by having a number of lovers but none can satisfy her every need.
1992 (R) 90m/C Jennifer Rubin, Lance Edwards, Grant Show, Michael Ceveris, Delaune Michel, Robert Lipton; *W/D:* Mussef Sibay. **VHS** $89.98 *REP* 🐾🐾

Woman Hunt Men kidnap women, then hunt them in the jungle for fun. So deeply offensive, we would give it negative bones if we could. "Hee Haw" bimbo Todd plays a sadistic lesbian. *AKA:* The Highest Bidder.
1972 (R) 81m/C John Ashley, Lisa Todd, Eddie Garcia, Laurie Rose; *D:* Eddie Romero. **VHS, Beta** $59.98 *NLC* Woof!

The Woman Hunter A wealthy woman recovering from a traffic accident in Mexico believes someone is after her for her jewels and possibly her life. Eden dressed well, if nothing else; suspense builds ploddingly to a "Yeah, sure" climax. Made for television.
1972 73m/C Barbara Eden, Robert Vaughn, Stuart Whitman, Sydney Chaplin, Larry Storch, Enrique Lucero; *D:* Bernard L. Kowalski. **VHS, Beta** $59.95 *QHV* 🐾½

Woman in Brown It's Hungary, 1882, and five Jewish men are on trial for the murder of a man who actually committed suicide. Despite the prejudice and hatred from the locals, their lawyer believes in and fights for their innocence. *AKA:* The Vicious Circle; The Circle.
1948 77m/B Conrad Nagel, Fritz Kortner, Reinhold Schunzel, Philip Van Zandt, Eddie LeRoy, Edwin Maxwell; *D:* W. Lee Wilder. **VHS, Beta** $16.95 *SNC* 🐾🐾½

A Woman in Flames A bored middle-class housewife leaves her overbearing husband and becomes a high-priced prostitute. She has a passionless affair with an aging bisexual gigolo. Dark and dreary tale of human relationships and the role of sex in people's lives. Interesting but depressing. *AKA:* Die Flambierte Frau.
1984 (R) 106m/C *GE* Gudrun Landgrebe, Robert Van Ackeren, Matthieu Carriere, Gabriele Lafari, Hanns Zischler; *D:* Robert Van Ackeren. **VHS, Beta** $39.98 *GLV* 🐾🐾

The Woman in Green Murder victims are found with missing index fingers, and it's up to Holmes and Watson to try to solve this apparently motiveless murder. Available colorized. *AKA:* Sherlock Holmes and the Woman in Green.
1945 68m/B Basil Rathbone, Nigel Bruce, Hillary Brooke, Henry Daniell, Paul Cavanagh, Frederick Worlock, Mary Gordon, Billy Bevan; *D:* Roy William Neill. **VHS, LV** $14.98 *SNC, REP, VYY* 🐾🐾

Woman in Grey A man and a woman battle wits when they attempt to locate and unravel the Army Code while staying one step ahead of J. Haviland Hunter, a suave villain after the same fortune. Silent.
1919 205m/B Arline Pretty, Henry Sell. **VHS, Beta** $49.98 *NOS, CCB, MLB* 🐾🐾

The Woman in Red Executive Wilder's life unravels when he falls hard for stunning Le Brock. Inferior Hollywood-ized remake of the ebulliant "Pardon Mon Affaire." Somehow the French seem to do the sexual force thing with more verve, but this one has its moments, and Wilder is likeable. Music by Stevie Wonder.
1984 (PG-13) 87m/C Gene Wilder, Charles Grodin, Kelly Le Brock, Gilda Radner, Judith Ivey, Joseph Bologna; *D:* Gene Wilder. **VHS, Beta, LV** $79.98 *LIV, VES* 🐾🐾

Woman in the Dunes Splendid, resonant allegorical drama. A scientist studying insects in the Japanese sand dunes finds himself trapped with a woman in a hut at the bottom of a pit. Superbly directed and photographed (by Hiroshi Segawa). Scripted by Kobo Abe from his acclaimed novel. In Japanese with English subtitles. *AKA:* Suna No Onna; Woman of the Dunes.
1964 123m/B *JP* Eiji Okada, Kyoko Kishida; *D:* Hiroshi Teshigahara. **VHS, Beta** $29.95 *CVC, NOS, VDM* 🐾🐾🐾🐾

Woman in the Moon Assorted people embark on a trip to the moon and discover water, and an atmosphere, as well as gold. Lang's last silent outing is nothing next to "Metropolis," with a rather lame plot (greedy trip bashers seek gold), but interesting as a vision of the future. Lang's predictions about space travel often hit the mark. Silent with music. *AKA:* By Rocket to the Moon; Girl in the Moon.
1929 115m/B *GE* Klaus Pohl, Willy Fritsch, Gustav von Wagenheim, Gerda Maurus; *D:* Fritz Lang. **VHS, Beta** $49.95 *IHF, VYY, LSV* 🐾🐾½

Woman in the Shadows A ex-con retreats to the woods for serenity and peace, but is assaulted by mysterious women, jealous lovers, and gun-slinging drunks, until he explodes. A man can only take so much. From a Dashiell Hammett story.
1934 70m/B Fay Wray, Ralph Bellamy, Melvyn Douglas, Roscoe Ates, Joe King. **VHS, Beta** $29.95 *VYY* 🐾🐾

The Woman Inside Low-budget gender-bender depicts the troubled life of a Vietnam veteran who decides on a sex-change operation to satisfy his inner yearnings. Blondell's unfortunate last role as his/her aunt. Cheesy like Limburger; almost too weird and boring even for camp buffs.
1983 (R) 94m/C *CA* Gloria Manon, Dave Clark, Joan Blondell; *D:* Joseph Van Winkle. **VHS, Beta** $24.95 *NO* 🐾½

A Woman is a Woman Godard's affectionate sendup of Hollywood musicals is a hilarious comedy about a nightclub dancer (Karina) who desperately wants a baby. When boyfriend Belmondo balks, she asks his best friend Brialy. Much ado is had, with the three leads all splendid. Great music by Legrand. Godard's first film shot in color and cinemascope. In French with English subtitles. *AKA:* Une Femme Est Une Femme; La Donna E Donna.
1960 88m/C *FR* Jean-Claude Brialy, Jean-Paul Belmondo, Anna Karina, Marie DuBois; *D:* Jean-Luc Godard. **VHS** $59.95 *INT, TAM* 🐾🐾🐾

The Woman Next Door One of Truffaut's last films before his sudden death in 1984. The domestic drama involves a suburban husband who resumes an affair with a tempestuous now-married woman after she moves next door, with domestic complications all around. An insightful, humanistic paean to passion and fidelity by the great artist, though one of his lesser works. Supported by strong outings from the two leads. In French with English subtitles. *AKA:* La Femme d'a Cote.
1981 (R) 106m/C *FR* Gerard Depardieu, Fanny Ardant, Michele Baumgartner, Veronique Silver, Roger Van Hool; *D:* Francois Truffaut. **VHS, Beta** $39.95 *HMV, FOX* 🐾🐾🐾

A Woman Obsessed Pathetic, overcooked drama about a woman obsessed with her long-lost son. "Ruth Raymond" is really porn-flick vet Georgina Spelvin. Soon-to-be camp classic takes itself with utter seriousness.
1988 (R) 105m/C Ruth Raymond, Gregory Patrick, Troy Donahue, Linda Blair; *D:* Chuck Vincent. **VHS, VHS, Beta** $29.95 *ACA* 🐾

A Woman of Affairs Garbo, who can't have the guy she really loves (Gilbert), marries scoundrel. When she finds out husband's true profession, he kills himself and Gilbert comes back. In order to preclude happy ending, she decides the affair wasn't meant to be and expires. Tragically. Silent.
1928 90m/B Greta Garbo, John Gilbert, Lewis Stone, Johnny Mack Brown, Douglas Fairbanks Jr., Hobart Bosworth, Dorothy Sebastian; *D:* Clarence Brown. **VHS** $29.98 *MGM, FCT* 🐾🐾

A Woman of Distinction Slapstick comedy with potential to be ordinary is taken over the top by a great, vivacious cast. Russell, the stuffy Dean of a women's college, is driven to distraction by a reporter linking her romantically to Milland, a visiting professor.

1950 85m/C Ray Milland, Rosalind Russell, Edmund Gwenn, Francis Lederer; *Cameos:* Lucille Ball; *D:* Edward Buzzell. VHS, Beta, LV $69.95 COL ♦♦♦

Woman of Paris/Sunnyside This double feature highlights the talents of Charlie Chaplin. "A Woman of Paris" is the tragic story of a French country girl who winds up a kept woman. Chaplin's only dramatic directional outing; he makes only a cameo appearance. Straightforward but hip story of sex and society. In "Sunnyside," an example of high Chaplin highjinks, the comic plays a hotel handyman who can't win.
1923 111m/B Adolphe Menjou, Edna Purviance, Carl Miller, Lydia Knott; *Cameos:* Charlie Chaplin; *D:* Charlie Chaplin. VHS, Beta $19.98 FOX ♦♦♦½

A Woman of Rome Standard Italian star vehicle, with Lollobrigida portraying a successful prostitute in Rome who decides to change her life. Dubbed. *AKA:* La Romana.
1956 93m/B *IT* Gina Lollobrigida, Daniel Gelin, Franco Fabrizi, Raymond Pellegrin; *D:* Luigi Zampa. VHS, Beta $24.95 NOS, FCT ♦♦

A Woman of Substance, Episode 1: Nest of Vipers The woman of the title, Emma Harte, rises from poverty to wealth and power through self-discipline. First episode in five three-cassette made for TV saga has our heroine working as a servant for the snooty Fairley family.
1984 100m/C Jenny Seagrove, Barry Bostwick, Deborah Kerr; *D:* Don Sharp. VHS, Beta $69.98 LIV ♦♦½

A Woman of Substance, Episode 2: The Secret is Revealed Emma Harte struggles to rise from a life of poverty to wealth and social acceptance. Second miniseries episode has Emma fighting to get by in the big city. Fun TV drama.
1984 100m/C Jenny Seagrove, Barry Bostwick, Deborah Kerr; *D:* Don Sharp. VHS, Beta $69.98 LIV ♦♦½

A Woman of Substance, Episode 3: Fighting for the Dream Third installment is pretty good romantic TV saga. Rags-to-riches Emma finds love and happiness—at last!
1984 100m/C Jenny Seagrove, Barry Bostwick, Deborah Kerr; *D:* Don Sharp. VHS, Beta $69.98 LIV ♦♦½

The Woman of the Town Frontier marshall and newspaperman Bat Masterson is portrayed convincingly by Dekker as a very human hero who seeks justice when the woman he loves, a dance hall girl who works in the town for social causes, is killed by an unscrupulous rancher. Fictionalized but realistic western shows "heroes" as good, ordinary people.
1944 90m/B Claire Trevor, Albert Dekker, Barry Sullivan, Henry Hull, Porter Hall, Percy Kilbride; *D:* George Archainbaud. VHS, Beta $19.95 NOS, HEG, FCT ♦♦½

Woman of the Year First classic Tracy/Hepburn pairing concerns the rocky marriage of a renowned political columnist and a lowly sportswriter. Baseball scene with Hepburn at her first game is delightful. Hilarious, rich entertainment that tries to answer the question "What really matters in life?" Tracy and Hepburn began a close friendship that paralleled their quarter-century celluloid partnership. Hepburn shepherded Kamin and Lardner's Oscar-winning script past studio chief Louis B. Mayer, wearing four-inch heels to press her demands. Mayer caved in; Tracy was freed from making "The Yearling;" and the rest is history.

1942 114m/B Spencer Tracy, Katharine Hepburn, Fay Bainter, Dan Tobin, Reginald Owen, Roscoe Karns, William Bendix, Minor Watson; *D:* George Stevens; *W:* Ring Lardner Jr. Academy Awards '42: Best Original Screenplay; Nominations: Best Actress (Hepburn). VHS, Beta, LV $19.95 MGM ♦♦♦♦

A Woman Rebels A young Victorian woman challenges Victorian society by fighting for women's rights. Excellent performance from Hepburn lifts what might have been a forgettable drama. Screen debut of Van Heflin. Based on Netta Syrett's "Portrait of a Rebel."
1936 88m/B Katharine Hepburn, Herbert Marshall, Elizabeth Allan, Donald Crisp, Van Heflin; *D:* Mark Sandrich. VHS, Beta $34.98 CCB ♦♦½

Woman Times Seven Italian sexual comedy: seven sketches, each starring MacLaine with a different leading man. Stellar cast and good director should have delivered more, but what they have provided has its comedic moments. *AKA:* Sept Fois Femme, Sette Volte Donna.
1967 (PG) 99m/C *IT FR* Shirley MacLaine, Peter Sellers, Rossano Brazzi, Vittorio Gassman, Lex Barker, Elsa Martinelli, Robert Morley, Alan Arkin, Michael Caine, Patrick Wymark, Anita Ekberg, Philippe Noiret; *D:* Vittorio De Sica. VHS, Beta $14.95 COL, SUE, NLC ♦♦½

A Woman Under the Influence Strong performances highlight this overlong drama about a family's disintegration. Rowlands is the lonely, middle-aged housewife who's having a breakdown and Falk is her blue-collar husband who can't handle what's going on.
1974 (R) 147m/C Gena Rowlands, Peter Falk, Matthew Cassel, Matthew Laborteaux, Christina Grisanti; *W/D:* John Cassavetes. Academy Awards '74 Nominations: Best Actress (Rowlands), Best Director (Cassavetes); Golden Globe Awards '75: Best Actress—Drama (Rowlands). VHS, Beta $94.95 TOU, FCT ♦♦♦

The Woman Who Came Back A young woman who believes she suffers from a witch's curse returns to her small hometown with unhappy results. Good cast; bad script. Indifference inducing.
1945 69m/B Nancy Kelly, Otto Kruger, John Loder, Ruth Ford, Jeanne Gail; *D:* Walter Colmes. VHS, Beta $14.95 COL, SVS ♦♦

The Woman Who Willed a Miracle Made-for-television drama has a devoted mother encouraging her mentally retarded son to pursue his interest in the piano.
1983 72m/C Cloris Leachman, James Noble; *D:* Sharron Miller. VHS, Beta NO ♦♦

A Woman Without Love A rarely seen film from Bunuel's Mexican period based on a classic Guy de Maupassant tale about a forbidden romance. Family tragedy results later when the husband "misbequeaths" his fortune. Minor but fascinating bug-the-bourgeoisie Bunuel. In Spanish with English subtitles.
1951 91m/C *MX* Rosario Granados, Julio Villareal, Tito Junco; *D:* Luis Bunuel. VHS, Beta $24.95 XVC, MED, TAM ♦♦♦

A Woman's Face An unpleasant, bitter woman with a hideous scar on her face contemplates murder. After plastic surgery, she becomes a nicer person and doubts her plan. Lean, tight suspense with a bang-up finale. In Swedish with English subtitles. Remade in Hollywood in 1941. *AKA:* En Kvinnas Ansikte.

1938 100m/B *SW* Ingrid Bergman, Anders Henrikson, Karin Carlsson, Georg Rydeberg, Goran Bernhard, Tore Svennberg; *D:* Gustaf Molander. VHS, Beta $29.95 WAC, TAM ♦♦♦

A Woman's Face A physically and emotionally scarred woman becomes part of a blackmail ring. Plastic surgery restores her looks and her attitude. Begins with a murder trial and told in flashbacks; tight, suspenseful remake of the 1938 Swedish Ingrid Bergman vehicle. Climax will knock you out of your chair.
1941 107m/B Joan Crawford, Conrad Veidt, Melvyn Douglas, Osa Massen, Reginald Owen, Albert Basserman, Marjorie Main, Donald Meek, Charles Quigley, Henry Daniell, George Zucco, Robert Warwick; *D:* George Cukor. VHS, Beta $19.98 MGM ♦♦♦

A Woman's Secret O'Hara admits to murder she didn't commit. Why? It's as indiscernible as why the plot should be muddled by flashbacks. RKO lost big bucks on this one.
1949 85m/C Maureen O'Hara, Melvyn Douglas, Gloria Grahame, Bill Williams, Victor Jory, Jay C. Flippen; *D:* Nicholas Ray; *W:* Herman J. Mankiewicz. VHS, Beta $19.98 TTC, FCT ♦♦

A Woman's Tale The superlative performance of Florance highlights this look at aging and death. Martha, 78, has been diagnosed with terminal lung cancer. She is looked after by a much-younger nurse and in turn looks after the older friends who share her apartment house. This gentle story quietly depicts the feisty, joyous Martha's last days and the simple pleasures she derives from her remaining time. Florance herself died from cancer not long after completing the film.
1992 (PG-13) 94m/C *AU* Sheila Florance, Gosia Dobrowolska, Norman Kaye, Chris Haywood, Myrtle Woods, Ernest Gray, Monica Maughan; *W/D:* Paul Cox. VHS, LV ORI ♦♦♦

Wombling Free An English girl makes friends with a race of tiny, litter-hating furry creatures called Wombles. The creatures are visible only to the little girl because she is the only one who believes. Together they try to clean up a dirty world. British society is less cutting-edge about social roles, etc. than our enlightened one; be prepared for retrograde characterizations. Fun scene with Kelly/Astaire-style dance number.
1977 86m/C *GB* Bonnie Langford, David Tomlinson; *D:* Lionel Jeffries. VHS, Beta $39.95 COL ♦♦

The Women A brilliant adaptation of the Clare Boothe Luce stage comedy about a group of women who destroy their best friends' reputations at various social gatherings. Crawford's portrayal of the nasty husband-stealer is classic, and the fashion-show scene in Technicolor is one not to miss. Hilarious bitchiness all around. Script co-written by Anita Loos. Remade semi-musically as "The Opposite Sex." Another in that long list of stellar 1939 pics.
1939 133m/B Norma Shearer, Joan Crawford, Rosalind Russell, Joan Fontaine, Mary Boland, Lucile Watson, Margaret Dumont, Paulette Goddard, Ruth Hussey, Marjorie Main; *D:* George Cukor. VHS, Beta, LV $19.98 MGM ♦♦♦½

The Women Sexy secretary seduces a world-weary writer. *AKA:* Les Femmes; The Vixen.
1969 86m/C *FR* Brigitte Bardot, Maurice Ronet. VHS, Beta, LV $59.95 UNI ♦♦½

Women & Men: Stories of Seduction Three famous short stories are brought to the screen in this made for TV collection. Mary McCarthy's "The Man in the Brooks Brothers Shirt," Dorothy Parker's

"Dusk Before Fireworks," and Hemingway's "Hills Like White Elephants" between them cover every aspect of male-female relationships. Since there are three casts and three directors, there is little to join the stories in style, calling attention to some flaws in pacing and acting ability; still, worth watching.
1990 90m/C James Woods, Melanie Griffith, Peter Weller, Elizabeth McGovern, Beau Bridges, Molly Ringwald; **D:** Ken Russell, Tony Richardson, Frederic Raphael. **VHS, LV $89.99** HBO, FCT ♫♫½

Women & Men: Stories of Seduction, Part 2 Made for cable extravaganza chronicling the relationships of three couples, each adapted from the short story of a renowned author. Irwin Shaw's "Return to Kansas City" tells of a young boxer who is prematurely pushed into a match by his ambitious wife. In Carson McCullers' "A Domestic Dilemma," a marriage begins to crumble thanks to an alcoholic wife. Finally, Henry Miller's "Mara" has an aging man and a young Parisian prostitute spending a revealing evening together.
1991 (R) 90m/C Matt Dillon, Kyra Sedgwick, Ray Liotta, Andie MacDowell, Scott Glenn, Juliette Binoche; **D:** Walter Bernstein, Kristi Zea, Mike Figgis. **VHS, LV $89.99** HBO ♫♫½

Women in Cell Block 7 Exploitative skinfest about women in prison suffering abuse from their jailers and each other. Seems that one of the prisoners knows the location of massive heroin stash. Badly dubbed. **AKA:** Diario Segreto Di Un Carcere Femminele.
1977 (R) 100m/C IT Anita Strindberg, Eve Czemeys, Olga Bisera, Jane Avril, Valeria Fabrizi, Jenny Tamburi; **D:** Rino Di Silvestro. **VHS, Beta $29.95** PGN Woof!

Women in Fury A woman is sentenced to imprisonment in a mostly lesbian Brazilian jail, and subsequently leads a breakout.
1984 94m/C BR Suzanne Carvalno, Gloria Cristal, Zeni Pereira, Leonardo Jose. **VHS, Beta $19.98** LIV Woof!

Women in Love Drama of two steamy affairs, based on D.H. Lawrence's classic novel. Deservedly Oscar-winning performance by Jackson; controversial nude wrestling scene with Bates and Reed is hard to forget. Plot is dumped on in favor of atmosphere. Followed nearly two decades later (1989) by a "prequel": "The Rainbow," also from Lawrence, also directed by Russell and starring Jackson.
1970 (R) 129m/C GB Glenda Jackson, Jennie Linden, Alan Bates, Oliver Reed, Michael Gough, Eleanor Bron; **D:** Ken Russell. Academy Awards '70: Best Actress (Jackson); Nominations: Best Adapted Screenplay, Best Cinematography, Best Director (Russell); Golden Globe Awards '71: Best Foreign Film; National Board of Review Awards '70: 10 Best Films of the Year, Best Actress (Jackson); National Society of Film Critics Awards '70: Best Actress (Jackson). **VHS, Beta, LV $19.98** MGM, FOX, BTV ♫♫♫

The Women of Brewster Place Seven black women living in a tenement fight to gain control of their lives. (Men in general don't come out too well.) Excellent, complex script by Karen Hall gives each actress in a fine ensemble headed by Winfrey (in her TV dramatic debut) time in the limelight. Pilot for the series "Brewster Place." Based on the novel by Gloria Naylor. Winfrey was executive producer.
1989 180m/C Oprah Winfrey, Mary Alice, Olivia Cole, Robin Givens, Moses Gunn, Jackee, Paula Kelly, Lonette McKee, Paul Winfield, Cicely Tyson; **D:** Donna Deitch. **VHS, Beta $79.95** JTC, FCT ♫♫♫

Women of the Prehistoric Planet On a strange planet, the members of a space rescue mission face deadly perils. Typical bad sci-fi of its era, with horrid special effects, including "giant" lizards. Get this: there's one woman, and she's not of the planet in question. See if you can last long enough to catch the amazing plot twist at the end.
1966 87m/C Wendell Corey, Irene Tsu, Robert Ito, Stuart Margolin, Lyle Waggoner, Adam Roarke, Merry Anders; **D:** Arthur C. Pierce. **VHS, Beta** PGN Woof!

Women of Valor During WWII, a band of American nurses stationed in the Philippines are captured by the Japanese and struggle to survive in a brutal POW camp. TV feature was made 40 years too late, adding up to a surreal experience.
1986 95m/C Susan Sarandon, Kristy McNichol, Alberta Watson, Valerie Mahaffey, Suzanne Lederer, Patrick Bishop, Terry O'Quinn, Neva Patterson; **D:** Buzz Kulik. **VHS, Beta $9.99** STE, PSM ♫½

Women on the Verge of a Nervous Breakdown Surreal and hilarious romp through the lives of film dubber Maura, her ex-lover, his crazed ex-mistress, his new lover, his son, and his son's girlfriend. There's also Maura's friend Barranco, who inadvertantly lent her apartment to Shiite terrorists and now believes the police are after her as an accomplice in an airline hijacking. They meet in a comedy of errors, missed phone calls, and rental notices, while discovering the truth and necessity of love. Fast-paced and full of black humor, with loaded gazpacho serving as a key element. Introduced Almodovar to American audiences. In Spanish with English subtitles. **AKA:** Mujeres al Borde de un Ataque de Nervios.
1988 (R) 88m/C SP Carmen Maura, Fernando Guillen, Julieta Serrano, Maria Barranco, Rossy de Palma, Antonio Banderas; **W/D:** Pedro Almodovar. Academy Awards '88 Nominations: Best Foreign Language Film; National Board of Review Awards '88: 5 Best Foreign Films of the Year; New York Film Critics Awards '88: Best Foreign Film. **VHS, Beta, LV $79.98** ORI, TAM ♫♫♫½

Women Unchained Five women escape from a maximum security prison and make a run for the Mexican border. Along the way, they shun civilized behavior. Much less-than-honorable entry in desperate women genre. Co-written by Clancy B. Grass III.
197? (R) 82m/C Carolyn Judd, Teri Guzman, Darlene Mattingly, Angel Colbert, Bonita Kalem; **W/D:** Kent Osborne. **VHS, Beta $59.95** GEM Woof!

Women's Club Table-turning sex comedy about a wealthy matron who patronizes a talented (?) young movie writer, but really wants—you know what. She begins lending his services to friends—and does he ever get worn out! This excuse may be intended to be uproarious, but it's hard to tell. And all that sex gets very perfunctory after awhile.
1987 (R) 89m/C Michael Pare, Maud Adams, Eddie Velez; **D:** Sandra Weintraub. **VHS, Beta $79.98** LIV, VES ♫½

Women's Prison Escape Four tough broads blow the pen and are forced to hightail it through the Everglades. They can't decide which is worse, the snakes and 'gators, or the corrupt and sleazy life they left behind. Only cinematic pairing of Rooney and Lurch. **AKA:** Cell Block Girls.
19?? 90m/C Ted Cassidy, Chris Robinson, Mickey Rooney; **D:** Chris Robinson. **VHS $9.99** QVD ♫½

Women's Prison Massacre Four male convicts temporarily detained at a woman's prison (why?) violently take hostages and generally make trouble for the authorities and the women. Horribly dubbed.
1985 89m/C IT Laura Gemser, Lorraine De Selle, Francoise Perrot, Ursula Flores, Gabriele Truti; **D:** Gilbert Roussel. **VHS, Beta $19.98** LIV, VES Woof!

Wonder Man When a brash nightclub entertainer (Kaye) is killed by gangsters, his mild-mannered twin brother (Kaye) takes his place to smoke out the killers. One of Kaye's better early films. The film debuts of Vera-Ellen and Cochran. Look for Mrs. Howell of "Gilligan's Island." ♫So In Love; Bali Boogie; Ortchi Chornya; Opera Number.
1945 98m/C Danny Kaye, Virginia Mayo, Vera-Ellen, Steve Cochran, S.Z. Sakall, Otto Kruger; **D:** H. Bruce Humberstone. Academy Awards '45: Best Special Effects; Nominations: Best Song ("So in Love"), Best Sound, Best Original Score. **VHS, Beta $19.98** HBO, SUE ♫♫½

The Wonderful World of the Brothers Grimm Big-budget fantasy based very loosely on the Grimm Brothers' lives and three of their stories: "The Dancing Princesses," "The Cobbler and the Elves," and "The Singing Bone." Good, fun Puppetoon scenes, but leaves much else to be desired. A megawatt cast and the ubiquitous hand of producer-director Pal are not enough to cover the flaws. The biographical parts are hokey, and the tales used are the wrong ones. Disappointing but historically interesting. The second-ever story film done in Cinerama. ♫The Theme From the Wonderful World of the Brothers Grimm; Gypsy Rhapsody; Christmas Land; Ah-Oom; Above the Stars; Dee-Are-A-Gee-O-En (Dragon).
1962 134m/C Laurence Harvey, Karl-Heinz Boehm, Claire Bloom, Buddy Hackett, Terry-Thomas, Russ Tamblyn, Yvette Mimieux, Oscar Homolka, Walter Slezak, Beulah Bondi, Martita Hunt, Otto Kruger, Barbara Eden, Jim Backus, Arnold Stang; **D:** Henry Levin, George Pal. Academy Awards '62: Best Costume Design (Color); Nominations: Best Art Direction/Set Decoration (Color), Best Color Cinematography, Best Original Score. **VHS, Beta, LV $19.98** MGM ♫♫½

Wonderland Campy thriller that follows two young gay boys in England. Charles recites lines in old movies while watching them and sidesteps his father's homophobic insults. His best friend, Michael, is restless and always looking for adventure. The two show up at a gay nightclub known as the "Fruit Machine" and are the only witnesses to the brutal murder of the club's transvestite-owner. The pair are soon taken in by a male opera singer they both find attractive and taken to a south seaside town. The murderer catches up with the boys and seeks to dispose of them before they can report him to the authorities. Fast paced, dreamy atmosphere makes up for the sometimes confusing plot. Often overlooked British import. **AKA:** The Fruit Machine.
1988 103m/C GB Emile Charles, Tony Forsyth, Robert Stephens, Clare Higgins, Bruce Payne, Robbie Coltrane; **D:** Philip Saville. **VHS, LV $79.98** LIV, VES ♫♫♫

Wonderland Cove Seafaring adventurer adopts five orphan children and embarks on journeys to exotic locales.
1975 78m/C Clu Gulager; **D:** Jerry Thorpe. **Beta $59.95** PSM ♫

The Wonders of Aladdin Slapstick comedy based on the ancient rubbed-lamp-and-genie chestnut. Kids'll love it; adults will yawn. **AKA:** Les Mille Et Une Nuits; Le Meraviglie Di Aladino.

W

1961 93m/C *IT FR* Donald O'Connor, Vittorio De Sica; *D:* Henry Levin, Mario Bava. **VHS, Beta** $59.95 *NLC* 🐾½

Wonderwall: The Movie Bizarre characters trip over themselves in love while groovy music plays in background.
1969 82m/C *GB* Jack MacGowran, Jane Birkin, Irene Handl; *D:* Joe Massot; *M:* George Harrison, Eric Clapton, Ravi Shankar. **VHS, Beta** $79.95 *FCT, MVD* 🐾½

Wonsan Operation U.N. soldiers plunge into the muddy depths of enemy territory in search of secret information that would end the Korean War. Dubbed.
1978 100m/C Lew Montania, Frederick Hill; *D:* Terrence Sul. **VHS, Beta** *VDA* 🐾

Woodchipper Massacre Aunt Tess is frozen in the freezer, waiting to be turned into whatever the fleshy equivalent of woodchips is by her three unloving relations, and her totally evil son has just broken out of prison looking to retrieve his inheritance. You think you have problems? You'll have one less if you leave this one on the shelf.
1989 90m/C Jon McBride, Patricia McBride; *D:* Jon McBride. **VHS, Beta** *DMP* Woof!

The Wooden Gun Conflicts arise between two teenage factions in 1950's Tel Aviv: native Israelis, and the children of Jews arrived from Europe since World War II. In Hebrew with English subtitles.
1979 91m/C *IS D:* Han Moshenson. **VHS, Beta** $79.95 *ERG, FCT, TAM* 🐾🐾½

Wooden Horse Lean thriller of British POWs escaping a Nazi camp through a tunnel beneath their exercise horse. Based on a true incident in 1943 and on "The Tunnel Escape" by Eric Williams; set the tone for all British prison-camp movies to follow: stiff upper lip and all that, and adolescent-style trickery reminiscent of English boarding schools.
1950 98m/C Anthony Steel, Leo Genn, David Tomlinson, Bryan Forbes, Peter Finch; *D:* Jack Lee. **VHS, Beta** $59.99 *HBO* 🐾🐾🐾

Woodstock Step into the way-back machine and return to the times of luv, peace and understanding. A powerful chronicle of the great 1969 Woodstock rock concert, celebrating the music and lifestyle of the late sixties. More than 400,000 spectators withstood lack of privacy, bathrooms, parking, and food while wallowing in the mud for four days to catch classic performances by a great number of popular rock performers and groups, including Joan Baez, Country Joe and the Fish, Joe Cocker, Crosby, Stills and Nash, Arlo Guthrie, Richie Havens, Jimi Hendrix, Jefferson Airplane, Santana, John Sebastian, Sly and the Family Stone, Ten Years After, and The Who. Martin Scorcese helped edit the documentary, which was trail-blazing in its use of split-screen montage.
1970 (R) 180m/C Canned Heat, Richie Havens, Roger Daltrey, Pete Townsend, Keith Moon, Joan Baez, Country Joe & the Fish, Jimi Hendrix, Carlos Santana, David Crosby, Stephen Stills; *D:* Michael Wadleigh. Academy Awards '70: Best Feature Documentary; Nominations: Best Film Editing, Best Sound. **VHS, Beta, LV** $29.95 *MVD, WAR, VTK* 🐾🐾🐾

The Word Intriguing premise has an archeologist finding a perviously unknown text purporting to be written by the younger brother of Jesus. If authentic and publicized, it would wreak theological havoc. Janssen is off to Italy to check up; he finds murder and skullduggery. Well-acted, interesting story.

1978 300m/C David Janssen, James Whitmore, Florinda Bolkan, Eddie Albert, Geraldine Chaplin, Hurd Hatfield, John Huston, Kate Mulgrew, Janice Rule, Nicol Williamson; *D:* Richard Long. **VHS, Beta, LV** $24.95 *FRH* 🐾🐾½

Words and Music Plot based on the careers of Rodgers and Hart is little more than a peg on which to hang lots of classic songs, sung by a parade of MGM stars: "Johnny One Note," "The Lady Is a Tramp," "Blue Moon," etc. Also includes Kelly's dance recreation of "Slaughter on Tenth Avenue." Good advice: if no one's singing or dancing, fast forward.
1948 122m/C Mickey Rooney, Tom Drake, Judy Garland, Gene Kelly, Lena Horne, Mel Torme, Cyd Charisse, Marshall Thompson, Janet Leigh, Betty Garrett, June Allyson, Perry Como, Vera-Ellen, Ann Sothern; *D:* Norman Taurog; *M:* Richard Rodgers, Lorenz Hart. **VHS, Beta** $29.95 *MGM* 🐾🐾½

Words by Heart An African American family in turn of the century Missouri faces issues of discrimination and prejudice. Twelve-year-old Lena wins a speech contest and begins to question their place in the community and their aspirations for a better life. Based on a book by Ouida Sebestyen. Aired by PBS as part of the "Wonderworks" family movie series.
1984 116m/C Charlotte Rae, Robert Hooks, Alfre Woodard; *D:* Robert Thompson. **VHS** $29.95 *PME, FCT, HMV* 🐾🐾½

Work/Police Two Chaplin two-reelers. In "Work (The Paper Hanger)" (1915), a family hires Charlie and cohorts Armstrong and Purviance to re-paper a house. Little did they know! In "Police" (1916), Charlie plays an ex-con released into the cruel world. Unremittingly hilarious. Silent with music score.
1916 54m/B Charlie Chaplin, Billy Armstrong, Charles Insley, Marta Golden, Edna Purviance; *D:* Charlie Chaplin. **VHS, Beta** $39.95 *VYY* 🐾🐾🐾½

Workin' for Peanuts A young man who sells beer at a baseball stadium falls in love with the stadium owner's daughter.
1985 52m/C Carl Marotte, Jessica Steer. **VHS, Beta** *NO* 🐾🐾🐾½

Working Girl Romantic comedy set in the Big Apple has secretary Griffith working her way to the top in spite of her manipulative boss (Weaver in a powerful parody). Griffith gets her chance to shine when Weaver breaks a leg. She meets Ford for business that turns to romance. A 1980s Cinderella story that's sexy, funny, and sharply written and directed. Nice work by Ford, but this is definitely Griffith's movie. And keep an eye on gal pal Cusack.
1988 (R) 115m/C Melanie Griffith, Harrison Ford, Sigourney Weaver, Joan Cusack, Alec Baldwin, Philip Bosco, Ricki Lake, Nora Dunn, Olympia Dukakis, Oliver Platt; *D:* Mike Nichols; *W:* Kevin Wade. Academy Awards '88: Best Song ("Let the River Run"); Nominations: Best Actress (Griffith), Best Director (Nichols), Best Picture, Best Supporting Actress (Cusack, Weaver); Golden Globe Awards '89: Best Actress—Musical/Comedy (Griffith), Best Film—Musical/Comedy, Best Supporting Actress (Weaver). **VHS, Beta, LV** $19.98 *FOX* 🐾🐾🐾

Working Girls Three girls who share an apartment in Los Angeles are willing to do anything for money. And they do. For lack of anything else to recommend, watch for the striptease by Peterson, better known as Elvira on TV.
1975 (R) 80m/C Sarah Kennedy, Laurie Rose, Mark Thomas, Cassandra Peterson; *D:* Stephanie Rothman. **VHS, Beta** $19.98 *UHV* 🐾

Working Girls An acclaimed, controversial look by independent filmmaker Borden into lives of modern brothel prostitutes over the period of one day. The sex is realistically candid and perfunctory; the docudrama centers on a prostitute who is a Yale graduate and aspiring photographer living with a female lover. Compelling, touching, and lasting, with sexually candid language and scenery.
1987 93m/C Amanda Goodwin, Louise Smith, Ellen McElduff; *D:* Lizzie Borden. **VHS, Beta** $14.95 *COL, NLC, HHE* 🐾🐾🐾

Working Winnie/Oh So Simple Two rare, second-echelon short silent comedies.
1922 61m/B Ethlyn Gibson, Bobby Ray. **VHS, Beta, 8mm** $24.95 *VYY* 🐾🐾🐾

The World According to Garp Comedy turns to tragedy in this relatively faithful version of John Irving's popular (and highly symbolic) novel, adapted by Steve Tesich. Chronicles the life of T.S. Garp, a struggling everyman beset by the destructive forces of modern society. Nevertheless, Garp maintains his optimism even as his life unravels around him. At the core of the film is a subplot involving a group of extreme feminists inspired in part by Garp's mother, the author of "A Sexual Suspect." Close and Lithgow (as a giant transsexual) are spectacular, while Williams is low-key and tender as the beleagured Garp. Ultimately pointless, perhaps, but effectively and intelligently so.
1982 (R) 136m/C Robin Williams, Mary Beth Hurt, John Lithgow, Glenn Close, Hume Cronyn, Jessica Tandy, Swoosie Kurtz, Amanda Plummer; *D:* George Roy Hill. **VHS, Beta, LV** $19.98 *WAR, PIA* 🐾🐾🐾

The World Accuses A woman takes a job in a nursery, unaware that one child is her own, put up for adoption after her wealthy husband died. Then, her ex-lover shows up in her attic after escaping from prison and takes her hostage. Whew! Everything works out, except that the viewer is left confused and incredulous.
1935 62m/B Vivian Tobin, Dickie Moore, Russell Hopton, Cora Sue Collins, Mary Carr; *D:* Charles Lamont. **VHS** $24.95 *NOS, DVT* 🐾½

A World Apart Cinematographer Menges' first directoral effort is a blistering, insightful drama told from the point of view of a 13-year-old white girl living in South Africa, oblivious to apartheid until her crusading journalist mother is arrested under the 90-Day Detention Act, under which she might remain in prison permanently. Political morality tale is also a look at the family-vs-cause choices activists must make. Heavily lauded, with good reason; the autobiographical script is based on Slovo's parents, persecuted South African journalists Joe Slovo and Ruth First.
1988 (PG) 114m/C *GB* Barbara Hershey, Jodhi May, Linda Mvusi, David Suchet, Jeroen Krabbe, Paul Freeman, Tim Roth; *D:* Chris Menges; *W:* Shawn Slovo. **VHS, Beta, LV** $9.98 *MED* 🐾🐾🐾½

The World Gone Mad During Prohibition, a tough reporter discovers the district attorney is the intended victim of a murder plot involving crooked Wall Street types. Full circle: this interesting drama of white-collar crime is again topical, though dialogue heavy and desultory. *AKA:* The Public Be Hanged; Public Be Damned.
1933 70m/B Pat O'Brien, Louis Calhern, J. Carroll Naish; *D:* Christy Cabanne. **VHS, Beta, 3/4U, Special order formats** $19.95 *NOS, CAB, DVT* 🐾🐾½

World Gone Wild Action yarn about a post-apocalyptic world of the future where an evil cult leader brainwashes his disciples. Together they battle a small band of eccentrics for the world's last water source. Stale rehash (with ineffective satiric elements) of the Mad Max genre, served with Ant for campy appeal.
1988 (R) 95m/C Bruce Dern, Michael Pare, Adam Ant, Catherine Mary Stewart, Rick Podell; D: Lee H. Katzin. **VHS, Beta, LV $89.95** MED ♪½

The World is Full of Married Men A philandering ad exec gets involved with a reckless model, inspiring his fed-up wife also to look for extramarital sex. Promiscuously raunchy melodrama was written by the queen of sleaze, Jackie Collins, based on her novel.
1980 (R) 106m/C GB Anthony (Tony) Franciosa, Carroll Baker, Sherrie Croon, Gareth Hunt, Paul Nicholas; D: Robert Young. **VHS, Beta $59.98** FOX Woof!

The World of Apu Finale of director Ray's acclaimed Apu trilogy (following "Pather Panchali" and "Aparajito"). Aspiring writer Apu drops out of the university for want of money and takes up with an old chum. An odd circumstance leads him to marry his friend's cousin, whom he comes to love. She dies in childbirth (though her baby boy lives); Apu is deeply distraught, destroys the novel he was working on, and becomes a wanderer. His friend finds him five years later and helps him begin again with his young son. Wonderfully human, hopeful story told by a world-class director. From the novel "Aparajito" by B. Bandopadhaya. In Bengali with English subtitles. AKA: Apu Sansat; Apur Sansar.
1959 103m/B IN Soumitra Chatterjee, Sharmila Tagore, Alok Charkravarty, Swapan Makerji; D: Satyajit Ray. **VHS, Beta $29.95** HHT, VVY, DVT ♪♪♪♪

World of Henry Orient Charming, eccentric comedy about two 15-year-old girls who, madly in love with an egotistical concert pianist, pursue him all around New York City. Sellers is hilarious, Walker and Spaeth are adorable as his teen groupies; Bosley and Lansbury are great as Walker's indulgent parents. For anyone who has ever been uncontrollably infatuated. Screenplay by the father/daughter team, Nora and Nunnally Johnson, based on Nora Johnson's novel. Music by Elmer Bernstein.
1964 106m/C Peter Sellers, Tippy Walker, Merrie Spaeth, Tom Bosley, Angela Lansbury, Paula Prentiss; D: George Roy Hill. **VHS, Beta, LV $59.98** FOX ♪♪♪½

A World of Strangers A harsh look at apartheid through the eyes of an Englishman who has traveled to South Africa to manage a publishing house. Filmed in strict secrecy in Johannesburg due to the film's aggressive condemnation of the practice. Based on a novel by Nadine Gordimer.
1962 89m/B DK Ivan Jackson, Zakes Mokae; D: Henning Carlsen. **VHS $59.95** CVC, TAM ♪♪♪

The World of Suzie Wong Asian prostitute Kwan plays cat-and-mouse with American painter Holden. She lies to him about her profession, her family, and herself. His association with her ruins relationships in his life. Why, then, does he not get a clue? Good question, not answered by this soap opera that would be a serious drama. Offensively sanitized picture of the world of prostitution in an Asian metropolis. On the other hand, it's all nicely shot, much of it on location in Hong Kong. Based on Paul Os-

born's play which was taken from Richard Mason's novel.
1960 129m/C GB William Holden, Nancy Kwan, Sylvia Syms, Michael Wilding, Laurence Naismith, Jackie Chan; D: Richard Quine. **VHS, Beta, LV $19.95** PAR ♪♪

World of the Vampires Evil count commands his vampire legions to wreak vengeance upon the family whose ancestors condemned him. Fairly miserable Mexican horror entry. Spanish title: "El Mundo de los Vampiros."
1960 75m/B MX Mauricio Garces, Erna Martha Bauman, Silvia Fournier, Guillermo Murray; D: Alfonso Corona Blake. **VHS, Beta $54.95** SNC, HHT, MAD Woof!

The World Owes Me a Living Melodrama about pilot Farrar losing his memory in a plane crash and Campbell trying to spark his recollection of the past.
1947 91m/B GB David Farrar, Judy Campbell, Jack Livesey, John Laurie; W/D: Vernon Sewell. **VHS $15.95** LOO ♪♪

World War III How's that for a title? A Russian plot is afoot to seize and destroy the Alaskan pipeline. When the plot is discovered, negotiation is needed to prevent world war. Executive branch showdown ensues between U.S. prez Hudson and Soviet chief Keith. Director Boris Sagal was killed on location, whereupon Greene took over, and shooting was moved indoors with dramatic tension lost in the transition. Made for TV.
1986 186m/C Brian Keith, David Soul, Rock Hudson, Cathy Lee Crosby, Katherine Helmond; D: David Greene. **VHS, Beta $79.98** FOX ♪♪½

The World's Greatest Athlete Lame Disney comedy about a Tarzan-like jungle-man (Vincent) recruited by an unsuccessful American college coach (Amos) and his bumbling assistant (Conway). Fun special effects, weak script add up to mediocre family fare. Cameo by Howard Cosell as—who else?—himself.
1973 (G) 89m/C Jan-Michael Vincent, Tim Conway, John Amos, Roscoe Lee Browne, Dayle Haddon; Cameos: Howard Cosell; D: Robert Scheerer. **VHS, Beta** DIS, OM ♪♪

World's Greatest Lover Milwaukee baker Rudi Valentine, played oft-hilariously by Wilder, tries to make it big in 1920s Hollywood. He has a screen test as a Hollywood movie sheik, but his wife (Kane) leaves him for the real McCoy. Episodic and uneven, it's alternately uproarious, touching and downright raunchy.
1977 (PG) 89m/C Gene Wilder, Carol Kane, Dom DeLuise, Fritz Feld, Carl Ballantine, Michael Huddleston, Matt Collins, Ronny Graham; W/D: Gene Wilder. **VHS, LV $59.98** FOX ♪♪½

The World's Oldest Living Bridesmaid Hokey romantic comedy about a successful woman attorney who just can't find Mr. Right. Brenda feels even worse when she attends yet another friend's wedding. However, when she hires a younger, male secretary (former model Wimmer) the romantic sparks fly. An appealing and attractive cast helps this made-for-television fare.
1992 100m/C Donna Mills, Brian Wimmer, Beverly Garland, Winston Reckert, Art Hindle, Laura Press; D: Joseph L. Scanlan. **VHS $89.95** AIP ♪♪½

The Worm Eaters Mean developers want to take over a reclusive worm farmer's land. He unleashes his livestock on them. The bad guys turn into—eeck!—"worm people." A truck runs over our hero nearly 75 minutes too late to save the viewer.
1977 (PG) 75m/C Herb Robins, Barry Hostetler, Lindsay Armstrong Black; W/D: Herb Robins. **VHS, Beta $19.95** WWV Woof!

The Worst of Hollywood: Vol. 1 Two really bad movies for your viewing displeasure. "Maniac" is a mad-scientist fest and "Protect Your Daughter" warns of the perils of the Flapper era.
1990 115m/B Bill Woods, Horace Carpenter, Phyllis Diller; D: Dwain Esper. **VHS, Beta $29.95** INC Woof!

The Worst of Hollywood: Vol. 2 A von Stroheim-fest of mediocrity. In "Fugitive Road" Erich plays an Austrian officer of the First World War. "The Crime of Dr. Crespi" has him portray a mad scientist.
1990 131m/B Erich von Stroheim, Dwight Frye; D: Erich von Stroheim. **VHS, Beta $29.95** INC Woof!

The Worst of Hollywood: Vol. 3 Two more awful, exploitive docudramas. "Nation Aflame" features many silent screen stars who teach the virtues of living in racial harmony. "Probation" boasts the first screen appearance of Grable, as a promiscuous woman who ends up in prison.
1990 140m/B Betty Grable. **VHS, Beta $29.95** INC Woof!

Worth Winning A notoriously eligible Philadelphia bachelor takes a bet to become engaged to three women within three months, and finds himself in hot water. A critically dead-in-the-water chucklefest.
1989 (PG-13) 103m/C Mark Harmon, Lesley Ann Warren, Madeleine Stowe, Maria Holvoe, Mark Blum, Andrea Martin, Alan Blumenfeld, Brad Hall, Tony Longo; D: Will MacKenzie. **VHS, Beta, LV $89.98** FOX ♪½

The Would-Be Gentleman The Comedie Francaise troupe performs Moliere's famous farce-comedy. Valuable as a record of the famous troupe on stage. When they're long gone, our grandkids can enjoy this. We can too (if we can't afford the trip to France), though it's less a film than a filming of a play. In French with English subtitles.
1958 93m/C FR Louis Seigner, Jean Meyer, Jean Piat. **VHS, Beta $24.95** DVT, TAM ♪♪½

Woyzeck Chilling portrayal of a man plunging into insanity. Mired in the ranks of the German Army, Woyzeck is harassed by his superiors and tortured in scientific experiments, gradually devolving into homicidal maniac. Based on Georg Buchner play. In German with English subtitles.
1978 82m/C GE Klaus Kinski, Eva Mattes, Wolfgang Reichmann, Josef Bierbichler; W/D: Werner Herzog. **VHS $59.95** NYF, TAM ♪♪♪

Woza Albert! An international hit play makes tries to transfer its appeal to film, not an easy feat. Set in South Africa and performed by black South Africans, (using their townships as a backdrop) it explores in stylized fashion events resulting from the second coming of Christ to a hypocritical nation.
1982 55m/C VHS, Special order formats $195.00 CAL, FLI ♪♪½

WR: Mysteries of the Organism Makavejev's breakthrough film, a surreal, essayist exploration of the conflict/union between sexuality and politics—namely, Wilheim Reich and Stalin. A raunchy, bitterly satiric non-narrative that established the rule-breaking Yugoslav internationally. In Serbian with English subtitles.
1971 84m/C Milena Dravic, Jagoda Kaloper, Tuli Kupferberg, Jackie Curtis; D: Dusan Makavejev. **VHS, Beta $79.95** FCT ♪♪♪

The Wraith Drag-racing Arizona teens find themselves challenged by a mysterious, otherworldly stranger. Hot cars; cool music; little else to recommend it. Lousy script; ludicrous excuse for a premise. Most of the

stars herein are related to somebody famous.
1987 (PG-13) 92m/C Charlie Sheen, Nick Cassavetes, Sherilyn Fenn, Randy Quaid, Matthew Barry, Clint Howard, Griffin O'Neal; **D:** Mike Marvin. **VHS, Beta, LV $14.98** *LIV* ✗✗½

Wrangler When an Australian rancher dies his daughter tries to hang on to the family ranch from a ruthless creditor. She also has to deal with the attentions of two men—one a businessman and the other a cattleman, both equally dashing and handsome. Beautiful scenery of the Australian Outback as well as romance and adventure.
1988 93m/C Jeff Fahey, Tushka Bergen, Steven Vidler, Richard Moir, Shane Briant, Drew Forsythe, Cornelia Frances, Sandy Gore, Frederick Parslow; **D:** Ian Barry; **W:** John Sexton; **M:** Mario Millo. **VHS, LV $89.95** *HMD* ✗✗½

The Wreck of the Mary Deare Slow-moving adventure drama focusing on the wreck of the freighter called the Mary Deare. Heston plays a ship salvager who comes upon a seemingly empty ship one night and Cooper is the only crew member on board. Special effects are the main attraction in this interesting sea drama. Film originally was to be directed by Hitchcock, but he turned down the offer to do "North by Northwest."
1959 105m/C *GB* Gary Cooper, Charlton Heston, Michael Redgrave, Emlyn Williams, Cecil Parker, Alexander Knox, Virginia McKenna, Richard Harris; **D:** Michael Anderson Sr. **VHS, LV $19.98** *MGM* ✗✗½

The Wrestler All-star wresting, which is fictional anyway, gets said treatment in the appropriate way. Honest promoter (yeah, sure) bumps heads with bad-guy crooks who want in on the action. Made-for-TV opportunity for Asner to slum.
1973 103m/C Ed Asner, Elaine Giftos, Verne Gagne, Harold Sakata. **VHS, Beta $19.95** *NWV, GTE* ✗

Wrestling Racket Girls An alleged white slavery expose, replete with seamy material that is only slightly laughable by modern terms, reducing overall camp appeal and increasing rating on boredom meter.
1939 72m/B VHS, Beta NO Woof!

Wrestling Women vs. the Aztec Ape An unclassifiable epic wherein female wrestlers battle a mad doctor and his Aztec robot gorilla. Dubbed badly, of course. Much anticipated follow-up to "Wrestling Women vs. the Aztec Mummy." **AKA:** Doctor of Doom.
1962 75m/C *MX* Elizabeth Campbell, Lorena Velasquez, Armando Silvestre, Roberto Canedo; **D:** Rene Cardona Sr. **VHS, Beta $19.95** *RHI, HHT, SNC Woof!*

Wrestling Women vs. the Aztec Mummy Women, broad of shoulder, wrestle an ancient Aztec wrestler who comes to life. Furnished with a new rock soundtrack.
1959 88m/C *MX* Lorena Velasquez, Armando Silvestre; **D:** Rene Cardona Sr. **VHS, Beta $54.95** *SNC, RHI, HHT Woof!*

Write to Kill A young mystery writer seeks revenge when his brother is murdered by a ring of counterfeiters.
1991 (R) 120m/C Scott Valentine, Chris Mulkey, Joan Severance, G.W. Bailey, Ray Wise; **D:** Ruben Preuss. **VHS, LV COL, PIA** ✗✗½

Writer's Block Fairchild is a successful thriller writer whose latest books feature a serial killer. She decides to kill the character off and is soon stalked by a psycho who is using her plots for some copy-cat killings.

Tepid made for cable television movie with San Diego locations the only highlight.
1991 (R) 90m/C Morgan Fairchild, Joe Regalbuto, Michael Praed, Cheryl Anderson, Mary Ann Pascal, Douglas Rowe, Ned Bellamy; **D:** Charles Correll; **W:** Elisa Bell. **VHS, Beta** *PAR* ✗✗

Written on the Wind Sirk's frenzied, melodrama-as-high-art dissection of both the American Dream and American movies follows a Texas oil family's self-destruction through wealth, greed and unbridled lust. Exaggerated depiction of and comment on American ambition and pretension, scripted by George Zuckerman from Robert Wilder's novel.
1956 99m/C Lauren Bacall, Rock Hudson, Dorothy Malone, Robert Stack, Robert Keith, Grant Williams, Edward Platt, Harry Shannon; **D:** Douglas Sirk. Academy Awards '56: Best Supporting Actress (Malone); Nominations: Best Song ("Written on the Wind"), Best Supporting Actor (Stack). **VHS, Beta $14.95** *MCA, BTV* ✗✗

The Wrong Arm of the Law Loopy gangster yarn about a trio of Aussie gangsters who arrive in London and upset the local crime balance when they dress up as cops and confiscate loot from apprehended robbers. General confusion erupts among the police, the local crooks, and the imposters. Riotous and hilarious, with Sellers leading a host of familiar faces.
1963 94m/B *GB* Peter Sellers, Lionel Jeffries, Nanette Newman, Bernard Cribbins, Dennis Price; **D:** Cliff Owen. **VHS, Beta $39.95** *MON* ✗✗✗

The Wrong Box Two elderly Victorian brothers try to kill each other so that one of them may collect the large inheritance left to them. Based on a Robert Louis Stevenson novel. Well-cast black comedy replete with sight gags, many of which flop.
1966 105m/C *GB* Peter Sellers, Dudley Moore, Peter Cook, Michael Caine, Ralph Richardson, John Mills; **D:** Bryan Forbes; **M:** John Barry. **VHS, Beta $59.95** *COL* ✗✗✗

The Wrong Guys Five giants of stand-up comedy star as a group of men who reunite their old boy scout pack and go camping. A crazed convict mistakes them for FBI agents. It's supposed to get zany after that, but succeeds only in being clumsy and embarrassing.
1988 (PG) 86m/C Richard Lewis, Richard Belzer, Louie Anderson, Tim Thomerson, Franklin Ajaye, John Goodman, Ernie Hudson, Timothy Van Patten; **D:** Danny Bilson. **VHS, Beta, LV $19.95** *STE, NWV* ✗

Wrong is Right A black action comedy about international terrorism, news reporting and the CIA. Connery is terrific, as usual, as a TV reporter in a head-scratching attempt at satire of our TV-influenced society. **AKA:** The Man With The Deadly Lens.
1982 (R) 117m/C Sean Connery, Katharine Ross, Robert Conrad, George Grizzard, Henry Silva, G.D. Spradlin, John Saxon, Leslie Nielsen, Robert Webber, Rosalind Cash, Hardy Kruger, Dean Stockwell, Ron Moody, Jennifer Jason Leigh; **D:** Richard Brooks. **VHS, Beta, LV $79.95** *COL* ✗✗

The Wrong Man Nightclub musician Fonda is falsely accused of a robbery and his life is destroyed. Taken almost entirely from the real-life case of mild-mannered bass player "Manny" Balestrero; probes his anguish at being wrongly accused; and showcases Miles (later to appear in "Psycho") and her character's agony. Harrowing, especially following more lighthearted Hitchcock fare such as "The Trouble with Harry." Part of the "A Night at the Movies" series, this tape

simulates a 1956 movie evening with a color Bugs Bunny cartoon, "A Star Is Bored," a newsreel and coming attractions for "Toward the Unknown."
1956 126m/B Henry Fonda, Vera Miles, Anthony Quayle, Nehemiah Persoff; **D:** Alfred Hitchcock. **VHS, Beta, LV $19.98** *WAR, MLB* ✗✗✗½

The Wrong Move A loose adaptation of Goethe's "Sorrows of Young Werther" by screenwriter Peter Handke. Justly acclaimed and engrossing, though slow. Kinski's first film. A young poet, searching for life's meaning, wanders aimlessly through Germany. In German with English subtitles.
1978 103m/C *GE* Nastassia Kinski, Hanna Schygulla, Ruediger Vogler, Hans-Christian Blech; **D:** Wim Wenders. **VHS, Beta $59.95** *FCT, GLV, TAM* ✗✗½

The Wrong Road A young couple embark on a robbery spree, and subsequently end up in prison. On their release, they search for the loot they had previously hidden, but find the man who was holding it for them has died. Will they ever recover their ill-gotten stash?
1937 62m/B Richard Cromwell, Helen Mack, Lionel Atwill, Horace McMahon, Russ Powell, Billy Bevan, Marjorie Main, Rex Evans; **D:** James Cruze. **VHS, Beta $16.95** *SNC* ✗½

Wuthering Heights The first screen adaptation of Emily Bronte's romantic novel about the doomed love between Heathcliff and Cathy on the Yorkshire moors. This film dynamically captures the madness and ferocity of the classic novel, remaining possibly the greatest romance ever filmed. Excellent performances from Wyler's sure direction, particularly Olivier's, which made him a star, and Oberon in her finest hour as the exquisite but selfish Cathy. Remade twice, in 1953 (by Luis Bunuel) and in 1970.
1939 104m/B Laurence Olivier, Merle Oberon, David Niven, Geraldine Fitzgerald, Flora Robson, Donald Crisp, Cecil Kellaway, Leo G Carroll, Miles Mander, Hugh Williams; **D:** William Wyler. Academy Awards '39: Best Black and White Cinematography; Nominations: Best Actor (Olivier), Best Director (Wyler), Best Interior Decoration, Best Picture, Best Screenplay, Best Supporting Actress (Fitzgerald), Best Original Score; National Board of Review Awards '39: 10 Best Films of the Year; New York Film Critics Awards '39: Best Film. **VHS, Beta, LV $19.98** *HBO, SUE, HMV* ✗✗✗✗

Wuthering Heights Bunuel tackles the Bronte classic during his Mexican period, and comes up with a film containing little passion, but much of the customary Bunuel manic cynicism. The 1939 version is far superior, but fans of Bunuel will probably enjoy this one. Loosely adapted; in Spanish with English subtitles. Remade in another English-language version in 1970. **AKA:** Abismos de Pasion.
1953 90m/B *MX* Irasema Dilian, Jorge Mistral, Lilia Prado, Ernesto Alonso; **D:** Luis Bunuel. **VHS, Beta $24.95** *XVC, MED, APD* ✗✗½

Wuthering Heights The third screening of the classic Emily Bronte romance about two doomed lovers. Fuest's version features excellent photography, and Calder-Marshall's and Dalton's performances are effective, but fail even to approach the intensity and pathos of the 1939 film original (or of the book). Filmed on location in Yorkshire, England.
1970 (G) 105m/C *GB* Anna Calder-Marshall, Timothy Dalton, Harry Andrews, Pamela Brown, Judy Cornwell, James Cossins, Rosalie Crutchley, Hilary Dwyer, Hugh Griffith, Ian Ogilvy; **D:** Robert Fuest. **VHS, Beta $9.95** *NEG, KAR, TVC* ✗✗½

Wyoming Outlaw Based on an actual incident, the story revolves around a small-town man who kills an outlaw. Barry, in the role that made him a western star, is forced into crime after a corrupt politician extorts money from him in exchange for a job. Lincoln, the screen's first Tarzan, appears in a supporting role.
1939 62m/B John Wayne, Ray Corrigan, Raymond Hatton, Donald (Don "Red") Barry, Adele Pearce, Leroy Mason, Charles Middleton, Elmo Lincoln, Jack Ingram, Yakima Canutt, Curly Dresden; **D:** George Sherman. **VHS $19.95** NOS, MLB ✻✻

X from Outer Space A space voyage to Mars brings back a giant rampaging creature. Badly dubbed.
1967 (PG) 85m/C JP Eiji Okada, Peggy Neal, Toshiya Wazaki, Itoko Harada, Shinichi Yanagisawa, Franz Gruber, Keisuke Sonoi, Mike Daning, Torahiko Hamada; **D:** Nazui Nihonmatsu. **VHS, Beta $19.98** ORI ✻

X Marks the Spot When a police sergeant is killed, his detective son investigates his murder. He's drawn into a crime ring which smuggles rubber (a scarce commodity during World War II). Quick pacing enlivens standard cliches.
1942 55m/B Damian O'Flynn, Helen Parrish, Dick Purcell, Jack LaRue, Neil Hamilton, Robert E. Homans, Anne Jeffreys, Dick Wessel, Vince Barnett; **D:** George Sherman. **VHS, Beta $16.95** SNC ✻✻

X: The Man with X-Ray Eyes First-rate Corman has Milland gain power to see through solid materials. Predates Little Caesars campaign. **AKA:** The Man With the X-Ray Eyes; X.
1963 79m/C Ray Milland, Diana Van Der Vlis, Harold J. Stone, John Hoyt, Don Rickles, Dick Miller, Jonathan Haze; **D:** Roger Corman. **VHS, Beta, LV $59.95** WAR ✻✻✻

X, Y & Zee A brassy, harsh version of the menage a trois theme, wherein the vicious wife (Taylor) of a philanderer (Caine) decides to avenge herself by seducing his mistress. An embarrassment for everyone involved. **AKA:** Zee & Co.
1972 (R) 110m/C Michael Caine, Elizabeth Taylor, Susannah York, Margaret Leighton; **D:** Brian G. Hutton; **W:** Edna O'Brien. **VHS, Beta $69.95** COL ✻✻ 1/2

Xanadu Dorky star-vehicle remake (of 1947's "Down to Earth") eminently of its era, which is now better forgotten. Newton-John is a muse who descends to Earth to help two friends open a roller disco. In the process she proves that as an actor, she's a singer. Kelly attempts to soft shoe some grace into the proceedings, though he seems mystified as anyone as to why he's in the movie. Don Bluth adds an animated sequence. ♫I'm Alive; The Fall; Don't Walk Away; All Over the World; Xanadu; Magic; Suddenly; Dancing; Suspended in Time; Whenever You're Away From Me.
1980 (PG) 96m/C Olivia Newton-John, Michael Beck, Gene Kelly, Sandahl Bergman; **D:** Robert Greenwald. **VHS, Beta, LV $79.95** MCA, MLB Woof!

Xtro An Englishman, abducted by aliens three years before, returns to his family with a deadly, transforming disease. Slime-bucket splatter flick notable for the scene where a woman gives birth to a full-grown man, and various sex slashings.
1983 (R) 80m/C GB Philip Sayer, Bernice Stegers, Danny Brainin, Simon Nash, Maryam D'Abo, David Cardy, Anna Wing, Peter Mandell, Robert Fyfe; **D:** Harry Bromley Davenport. **VHS, Beta, LV $19.95** NLC, HBO Woof!

Xtro 2: The Second Encounter A research facility conducts an experiment to transfer people to a parallel dimension. Out of the three researchers sent to the other side, only one returns, unconscious. Turns out that he is playing host to a biohazardous creature brought over from the other dimension who escapes into the air shafts and threatens to kill everyone in the research facility. Another problem arises. If the creature isn't killed, the computer system running the facility will fill the building with radiation. Sound familiar? It should, because this is a low-budget remake of "Alien." Good photography, adequate acting, but Vincent just isn't credible as a brillian scientist. A sequel to "Xtro" in name only.
1991 (R) 92m/C CA Jan-Michael Vincent, Paul Koslo, Tara Buckman, Jano Frandsen, Nicholas Lea, W.F. Wadden, Rolf Reynolds, Nic Amoroso, Tracy Westerholm; **D:** Harry Bromley Davenport. **VHS, LV $19.95** NLC ✻✻

Y Donde Esta el Muerto? (And... Where Is the Dead) This mystery/comedy centers around a weird gathering of people who are trying to find out if a man is really dead.
1987 34m/C MX Yvonne Fraissinet, Ricardo Fernandez, Nilda Munoz. **VHS, Beta $69.95** MAD ✻✻ 1/2

The Yakuza An ex G.I. (Mitchum) returns to Japan to help an old army buddy find his kidnapped daughter. He learns the daughter has been kidnapped by the Japanese version of the Mafia (the Yakuza) and he must call on old acquaintances to help free her. A westernized oriental gangster drama with a nice blend of buddy moments, action, ancient ritual, and modern Japanese locations. **AKA:** Brotherhood of the Yakuza.
1975 (R) 112m/C Robert Mitchum, Richard Jordan, Ken Takakura, Brian Keith, Herb Edelman; **D:** Sydney Pollack; **W:** Paul Schrader, Robert Towne. **VHS, Beta, LV $24.98** WAR, PIA ✻✻ 1/2

Yanco A young Mexican boy makes visits to an island where he plays his homemade violin. Unfortunately, no one can understand or tolerate his love for music, save for an elderly violinist, who gives him lessons on an instrument known as "Yanco." No dialogue. Not exactly riveting, but sensitively played.
1964 95m/B MX Ricardo Ancona, Jesus Medina, Maria Bustamante. **VHS, Beta $19.95** WFV, DVT, TAM ✻✻

A Yank in Australia Australian farce/war mystery/romance/documentary tells the story of two World War II newspaper reporters whose ship gets torpedoed, stranding them in the Australian outback, where they manage to foil a Japanese invasion.
1943 56m/B AU **VHS, Beta, 8mm $24.95** VYY ✻✻

Yank in Libya No, not the American bombing raid of Khadafy, rather a low-budget WWII adventure pitting an American man and an English girl against Libyan Arabs and Nazis.
1942 65m/B Walter Woolf King, John Woodbury, H.B. Warner, Parkyakarkus. **VHS, Beta** UHV ✻ 1/2

A Yank in the R.A.F. Power's enthusiastic performance as a brash American pilot boosts this dated WWII adventure. He and his British allies seem more concerned over who gets showgirl Betty Grable than in the Nazis, but climactic air attacks retain excitement. Produced by Darryl F. Zanuck to drum up American support for embattled Britain and France.
1941 98m/B Tyrone Power, Betty Grable, John Sutton, Reginald Gardiner; **D:** Henry King. **VHS, Beta $19.98** FOX, FCT ✻✻ 1/2

Yankee Clipper Deceit, treachery, and romance are combined in this depiction of a fierce race from China to New England between the American ship Yankee Clipper and the English ship Lord of the Isles. Silent.
1927 68m/B William Boyd, Elinor Fair, Frank "Junior" Coghlan, John Miljan, Walter Long; **D:** Rupert Julian. **VHS, Beta $29.95** CCB, GPV, VYY ✻✻ 1/2

Yankee Doodle A blacksmith and two Militiamen help Paul Revere complete his midnight ride.
1987? 30m/C VHS, Beta $6.95 STE, PSM ✻✻ 1/2

Yankee Doodle Dandy Nostalgic view of the Golden Era of show business and the man who made it glitter—George M. Cohan. His early days, triumphs, songs, musicals and romances are brought to life by the inexhaustible Cagney in a rare and wonderful song-and-dance performance. Told in flashback, covering the Irishman's struggling days as a young song writer and performer to his salad days as the toast of Broadway. Cagney, never more charismatic, dances up a storm, reportedly inventing most of the steps on ths spot. ♫Give My Regards to Broadway; Yankee Doodle Dandy; You're a Grand Old Flag; Over There; I Was Born in Virginia; Off the Record; You're a Wonderful Girl; Blue Skies, Grey Skies; Oh You Wonderful Girl; The Barber's Ball; The Warmest Baby in the Bunch; Little Nellie Kelly; In a Kingdom of Our Own; The Man Who Owns Broadway; Molly Malone; Billie; So Long Mary; The Love Nest; Harrigan; The Yankee Doodle Boy; I'll Be True to You; Mary's a Grand Old Name; Forty-five Minutes to Broadway.
1942 126m/B James Cagney, Joan Leslie, Walter Huston, Richard Whorf, Irene Manning, Rosemary DeCamp, Jeanne Cagney, S.Z. Sakall, Walter Catlett, Frances Langford, Eddie Foy Jr., Michael Curtiz; **D:** Michael Curtiz. Academy Awards '42: Best Actor (Cagney), Best Sound, Best Score; Nominations: Best Director (Curtiz), Best Picture, Best Story, Best Supporting Actor (Huston). **VHS, Beta, LV $29.98** MGM, FOX, FCT ✻✻✻✻

Yankee Doodle in Berlin A spoof of World War I dramas, with the hero dressing up as a woman and seducing the Kaiser into giving up his war plans. Typical Sennett slapstick with a music and effects score added to the silent film.
1919 60m/B Ford Sterling, Ben Turpin, Marie Prevost, Bothwell Browne. **VHS, Beta $14.95** GPV, CCB ✻✻ 1/2

Yanks An epic-scale but uneventful drama depicts the legions of American soldiers billeted in England during WWII, and their impact—mostly sexual—on the staid Britons. No big story, no big deal, despite a meticulous recreation of the era.
1979 139m/C Richard Gere, Vanessa Redgrave, William Devane, Lisa Eichhorn, Rachel Roberts, Chick Vennera, Arlen Dean Snyder, Annie Ross; **D:** John Schlesinger. **VHS, LV $79.95** MCA, PIA ✻✻✻

A Year in Provence Retired London executive Peter Mayle and his wife Annie decide to leave England to live in the south of France. They buy a 200-year-old farmhouse and experience all the trials and amusements of forging a new life in a different country, complete with different language and customs. They hoped for tranquility and what they got were eccentric neighbors, endless renovations, lots of company, and a taste for good food and drink. Based on Mayle's autobiographical novel and filmed on location. Made for British television. On four

cassettes, each depicting one season of the year.
1992 360m/C *GB* John Thaw, Lindsay Duncan, Bernard Spiegel, Jean-Pierre Delage, Maryse Kuster, Louis Lyonnet; **D:** David Tucker; **W:** Michael Sadler. **VHS, Beta $79.95** *AAE, SIG* ♫♫♫

The Year My Voice Broke Above average adolescent drama: a girl breaks a boy's heart by getting pregnant by a tougher, older boy; then leaves town. Blues-inducing, explicit, and not pleasant; but good acting from newcomers carries the day. Followed by ''Flirting.''
1987 (PG-13) 103m/C *AU* Noah Taylor, Loene Carmen, Ben Mendelsohn; **D:** John Duigan. **VHS, Beta, LV $89.95** *LIV* ♫♫♫

The Year of Living Dangerously Political thriller with a love interest features Gibson as an Australian journalist covering a political story in Indonesia, circa 1965. During the coup against President Sukarno, he becomes involved with a British attache (Weaver) at the height of the bloody fighting and rioting in Jakarta. Oscar-winning Hunt is excellent as male photographer Billy Swan, central to the action as the moral center. Rumored to be based on the activities of CNN's Peter Arnett, although the original source is a novel by C.J. Koch, who reportedly collaborated/battled with Weir on the screenplay. A fascinating, suspenseful film, set up brilliantly by Weir and shot on location in the Philippines (then moved to Sydney after cast and crew were threatened). The first Australian movie financed by a U.S. studio.
1982 (PG) 114m/C *AU* Mel Gibson, Sigourney Weaver, Linda Hunt, Michael Murphy; **D:** Peter Weir. **VHS, Beta, LV $19.98** *MGM, BTV* ♫♫♫½

Year of the Comet Amusing adventure/romantic comedy throws straightlaced Maggie (Miller) together with carefree Oliver (Daly) in a quest for a rare bottle of wine. Fine wine is Maggie's passion, and snagging this particular bottle will boost her status in the family business. Oliver is a pretzels and beer kind of guy, but his boss wants this bottle and will pay a lot to get it. Wants to be another ''Romancing the Stone,'' but plot and characters are too thin. Nice chemistry between Miller and Daly sort of saves this one despite a disappointing script from Goldman. Beautiful location shots of Scotland.
1992 (PG-13) 135m/C Penelope Ann Miller, Timothy Daly, Louis Jourdan, Art Malik, Ian Richardson, Ian McNeice, Timothy Bentinck, Julia McCarthy, Jacques Mathou; **D:** Peter Yates; **W:** William Goldman; **M:** Hummie Mann. **VHS, LV** *NLC* ♫♫

Year of the Dragon Polish police Captain Stanley White of the NYPD vows to neutralize the crime lords running New York's Chinatown. Brilliant cinematography, well-done action scenes with maximum violence, a racist hero you don't want to root for, murky script, and semi-effective direction are the highlights of this tour through the black market's underbelly and hierarchy. Based on Robert Daley's novel and adapted by Oliver Stone and Cimino.
1985 (R) 136m/C Mickey Rourke, John Lone, Ariane, Leonard Termo, Raymond J. Barry; **D:** Michael Cimino. **VHS, Beta, LV $14.95** *MGM* ♫♫½

Year of the Gun McCarthy is an American journalist in Rome who begins a novel based on the political instability around him, using the names of real people in his first draft. Soon, ambitious photojournalist Stone wants to collaborate with him, and the Red Brigade terrorist group wants to ''remove'' anyone associated with the book. Although

failing on occassion to balance the thin line it establishes between reality and perception, ''Gun'' aspires to powerful drama, offering a realistic look at the lives and priorities of political terrorists. Love scenes between Stone and McCarthy are torrid.
1991 (R) 111m/C Andrew McCarthy, Sharon Stone, Valeria Golino, John Pankow; **D:** John Frankenheimer. **VHS, LV, 8mm** *COL* ♫♫½

The Year of the Jellyfish An eighteen-year-old girl tries to seduce the local Monsieur Beefcake she meets on her vacation. When he doesn't return her interest, she decides to teach him a lesson. In French with English subtitles.
1984 (R) 110m/C *FR* Valerie Kaprisky, Bernard Giraudeau; **D:** Christopher Frank. **VHS $69.95** *TAM* ♫½

Year of the Quiet Sun A poignant, acclaimed love story about a Polish widow and an American soldier who find each other in the war-torn landscape of 1946 Europe. Beautifully rendered, with a confident sense of time and place, making this much more than a simple love story. In Polish with English subtitles.
1984 106m/C *PL GE* Scott Wilson, Maja Komorowska; **D:** Krzysztof Zanussi. **VHS, Beta, LV $29.98** *KRT, WAR, TAM* ♫♫♫½

The Yearling This family classic is a tearjerking adaptation of the Marjorie Kinnan Rawlings novel about a young boy's love for a yearling fawn during the post civil-war era. His father's encouragement and his mother's bitterness play against the story of unqualified love amid poverty and the boy's coming of age. Wonderful footage of Florida. Jarman was awarded a special Oscar as outstanding child actor.
1946 128m/C Gregory Peck, Jane Wyman, Claude Jarman Jr., Chill Wills, Henry Travers, Jeff York, Forrest Tucker, June Lockhart, Margaret Wycherly; **D:** Clarence Brown. Academy Awards '46: Best Color Cinematography, Best Interior Decoration; Nominations: Best Actor (Peck), Best Actress (Wyman), Best Director (Brown), Best Film Editing, Best Picture; Golden Globe Awards '47: Best Actor—Drama (Peck). **VHS, Beta, LV $19.98** *KUI, MGM, TLF* ♫♫♫½

The Yellow Cab Man Skelton plays a cab driver who is also an inventor of safety gadgets. When he invents unbreakable elastic glass he finds various crooks after him for the formula. Skelton's wacky inventions are amusing and the movie culminates in a breakneck chase through a home show exposition.
1950 85m/B Red Skelton, Gloria DeHaven, Walter Slezak, Edward Arnold, James Gleason, Jay C. Flippen, Paul Harvey; **D:** Jack Donohue. **VHS $19.98** *MGM* ♫♫½

Yellow Cargo Ingenious ''B'' movie about a pair of undercover agents who blow the lid off a smuggling scam. It seems that the smugglers have been masquerading as a movie crew, and use disguised Chinese ''extras'' to transport their goods. The agents pose as actors to infiltrate the gang.
1936 70m/B Conrad Nagel, Eleanor Hunt, Vince Barnett, Jack LaRue, Claudia Dell; **W/D:** Crane Wilbur. **VHS, Beta $16.95** *SNC* ♫♫

Yellow Emanuelle Exploitation film about a woman bound to an arranged marriage who falls in love with someone else.
197? 105m/C Chai Lee, Giuseppe Pambiere, Ilona Staller. **VHS, Beta $29.95** *UNI* ♫

Yellow Hair & the Fortress of Gold Princess who's part Indian and her sidekick fight bad guys and seek gold. Well-meaning, self-conscious parody. *AKA:* Yellow Hair and the Pecos Kid.

1984 (R) 102m/C *SP* Laurene Landon, Ken Robertson; **D:** Matt Cimber. **VHS, Beta $79.98** *LIV* ♫½

The Yellow Rose of Texas Rogers works as an undercover insurance agent (he's singing on a river boat) to clear the name of an old man falsely accused of a stagecoach robbery. The usual melodious Rogers lead.
1944 55m/B Roy Rogers, Dale Evans, Grant Withers, Harry Shannon; **D:** Joseph Kane. **VHS, Beta, 3/4U, Special order formats $19.95** *NOS, VCN, CAB* ♫♫

Yellow Submarine The acclaimed animated fantasy based on a plethora of mid-career Beatles songs, sees the Fab Four battle the Blue Meanies for the sake of Sgt. Pepper, the Nowhere Man, Strawberry Fields, and Pepperland. The first full-length British animated feature in 14 years features a host of talented cartoonists. Fascinating LSD-esque animation and imagery. Incidental music by George Martin, with a script assist by Love Story's Erich Segal. ♫Yellow Submarine; All You Need is Love; Hey, Bulldog; When I'm Sixty Four; Nowhere Man; Lucy in the Sky With Diamonds; Sgt. Pepper's Lonely Hearts Club Band; A Day in the Life; All Together Now; Eleanor Rigby; Only a Northern Song; It's All Too Much; March of the Meanies; Pepperland; Pepperland Laid Waste; Sea of Holes; Sea of Monsters; Sea of Time.
1968 (G) 87m/C *GB* **D:** Dick Emery, George Dunning; **V:** Paul McCartney, John Lennon, George Harrison, Ringo Starr. **VHS, Beta, LV $19.95** *MVD, MGM, WTA* ♫♫♫½

Yellowbeard An alleged comedy with a great cast who wander about with little direction. Follows the efforts of an infamous pirate (Chapman) to locate a buried treasure using the map tattooed on the back of his son's head. The final role for Feldman who died during production. Written by Chapman, Cook, and Bernard McKenna.
1983 (PG) 97m/C Graham Chapman, Peter Boyle, Cheech Marin, Thomas Chong, Peter Cook, Marty Feldman, Martin Hewitt, Michael Hordern, Eric Idle, Madeline Kahn, James Mason, John Cleese, Susannah York, David Bowie; **D:** Mel Damski. **VHS, Beta, LV $14.95** *VES* ♫½

Yellowneck A handful of Confederate Army soldiers desert, hoping to cross the Florida Everglades and eventually reach Cuba. The swamp takes its toll, however, and one by one the men fall by the wayside. A sole survivor reaches the coast. Will the escape boat be waiting for him?
1955 83m/C Lin McCarthy, Stephen Courtleigh, Berry Kroeger, Harold Gordon, Bill Mason; **D:** R. John Hugh. **VHS $29.95** *FCT* ♫♫

Yellowstone An ex-con is murdered at Yellowstone National Park, at the site of a hidden cache of money, of which assorted folks are in search. Uncomplicated, well-meaning mystery.
1936 65m/B Andy Devine, Ralph Morgan, Judith Barrett; **D:** Arthur Lubin. **VHS, Beta, 8mm $14.95** *NOS, DVT, HEG* ♫½

Yentl The famous Barbra adaptation of Isaac Bashevis Singer's story set in 1900s Eastern Europe about a Jewish girl who masquerades as a boy in order to study the Talmud, and who becomes enmeshed in romantic miscues. Lushly photographed, with a repetitive score by Alan and Marilyn Bergman and Michel Legrand that nevertheless won an Oscar. Singer was reportedly appalled by the results of Streisand's hyper-controlled project. ♫A Piece of Sky; No Matter What Happens; This Is One of Those Moments; Tomorrow Night; Where Is It Writ-

ten; No Wonder; The Way He Makes Me Feel; Papa, Can You Hear Me; Will Someone Ever Look at Me That Way?.
1983 (PG) 134m/C Barbra Streisand, Mandy Patinkin, Amy Irving, Nehemiah Persoff, Steven Hill, Allan Cordunner, Ruth Goring, David DeKeyser, Bernard Spear; **D:** Barbra Streisand. Academy Awards '83: Best Original Score; Nominations: Best Art Direction/Set Decoration, Best Song ("Papa, Can You Hear Me?", "The Way He Makes Me Feel"), Best Supporting Actress (Irving); Golden Globe Awards '84: Best Director (Streisand), Best Film—Musical/Comedy. **VHS, Beta, LV** $39.98 *MGM, IME* ♪♪½

Yes, Giorgio Opera singer Pavarotti in his big-screen debut. He has an advantage over other non-actors in trapped in similar situations (e.g., Hulk Hogan): He can sing (but of course, not wrestle). Lame plot (famous opera star falls for lady doctor) is the merest excuse to let the maestro belt out "If We Were in Love," "I Left My Heart in San Francisco," and arias by Verdi, Donizetti, and Puccini.
1982 (PG) 111m/C Luciano Pavarotti, Kathryn Harrold, Eddie Albert, James Hong; **D:** Franklin J. Schaffner; **M:** John Williams. **VHS, Beta, LV** $19.98 *MGM* ♪♪

Yes, Sir, Mr. Bones Entertaining but dated musical about a boy who wanders into a rest home and inspires the old folks there to reminisce about their days as riverboat minstrels. Written by Ormond. ♪I Want to Be a Minstrel Man; Stay Out of the Kitchen; Is Your Rent Paid Up in Heaven?; Flying Saucers; Memphis Bill; Southland.
1951 60m/B Pete Daily, Jimmy O'Brien, Sally Anglim, Cotton Watts, Chick Watts, Chet Davis, F.E. Miller, Scatman Crothers; **D:** Ron Ormond. **VHS, Beta** *NO* ♪♪½

The Yesterday Machine Camp sci-fi: A mad doctor tries to bring back Hitler. Don't worry, though: the good guys win. Predictable, dumb drivel.
1963 85m/B Tim Holt, James Britton, Jack Herman; **D:** Russ Marker. **VHS, Beta** $19.95 *SNC, VCD* Woof!

Yesterday, Today and Tomorrow Trilogy of comic sexual vignettes featuring Loren and her many charms. She plays a black marketeer, a wealthy matron, and a prostitute. Funny, and still rather racy. Loren at her best, in all senses; includes her famous striptease for Mastroianni. **AKA:** Ieri, Oggi E Domani; She Got What She Asked For.
1964 119m/C IT FR Sophia Loren, Marcello Mastroianni, Tony Pica, Giovanni Ridolfi; **D:** Vittorio De Sica. **VHS** $29.95 *JEF, HHE, TAM* ♪♪♪½

Yesterday's Hero A fading soccer star finds his career and love-life on the upswing. Poor production with equally lame pop music score. Written by Jackie Collins.
1979 95m/C GB Ian McShane, Suzanne Somers, Adam Faith, Paul Nicholas, Glynis Barber, Sandy Ratcliff; **D:** Neil Leifer. **VHS, Beta** $79.98 *CGH, HHE* ♪½

Yidl Mitn Fidl Disguised as a man, a young woman travels about the countryside with a group of musicians, revealing her female identity only after falling for a man. One of Picon's finest roles and Green's biggest successes. Vaudevillian fare in Yiddish with English subtitles. ♪Yiddle With His Fiddle; Arye With His Bass. **AKA:** Yiddle with a Fiddle; Castle in the Sky.
1936 92m/B PL Molly Picon, Simche Fostel, Max Bozyk, Leon Liebgold; **D:** Joseph Green. **VHS, Beta** $89.95 *ERG, DVT, TAM* ♪♪

Yin & Yang of Mr. Go A CIA operative must retrieve the stolen plans of an awesome weapons system. Set in Hong Kong, features a strong cast in a tangled tale of no particular merit. In addition to starring and directing, Meredith scripted this unworthy spoof of Oriental intrigue flicks.
1971 (R) 89m/C Jeff Bridges, James Mason, Broderick Crawford, Burgess Meredith; **D:** Burgess Meredith. **VHS, Beta** $9.95 *NO* ♪

Yodelin' Kid From Pine Ridge Autry tries to stop a war between cattlemen and woodsmen in Georgia. Standard horse opera notable for its location. **AKA:** The Hero of Pine Ridge.
1937 59m/B Gene Autry, Smiley Burnette, Betty Bronson, Tennessee Ramblers, Charles Middleton, Art Mix; **D:** Joseph Kane. **VHS, Beta** $19.95 *NOS, VCN, DVT* ♪♪

Yog, Monster from Space When a spaceship crashes somewhere near Japan, the aliens in it create monsters out of ordinary critters in order to destroy all the cities. A promoter gets a gleam in his eye and sees the potential for a vacation spot featuring the viscious creatures. Standard Japanese monster flick utilizing the usual out-of-synch dub machine. Dubbed. **AKA:** The Space Amoeba.
1971 (G) 105m/C JP Akira Kubo, Yoshio Tsuchiya; **D:** Inoshiro Honda. **VHS, Beta** $49.95 *SNC* ♪

Yogi's First Christmas Yogi Bear joins his friend, Huckleberry Hound, and others for a musical celebration of Christmas at the Jellystone Lodge.
1980 100m/C **D:** Ray Patterson; **V:** Daws Butler, Don Messick, John Stephenson, Janet Waldo, Hal Smith. **VHS, Beta, LV** $19.95 *TTC, IME, WTA* ♪

Yojimbo Two clans vying for political power bid on the services of a samurai (Mifune) who comes to town. The samurai sells his services to both parties, with devastating results for all. In Japanese with English subtitles or dubbed. Re-made by Sergio Leone as the western "A Fist Full of Dollars."
1961 110m/B JP Toshiro Mifune, Eijiro Tono, Suuzu Yamda; **D:** Akira Kurosawa. **VHS, Beta, LV, 8mm, 3/4U, Special order formats** $29.98 *NOS, SUE, HHT* ♪♪♪♪

Yol Five Turkish prisoners are granted temporary leave to visit their families. An acclaimed, heartfelt film, written by Yilmaz Guney while he himself was in prison. A potent protest against totalitarianism. In Turkish with English subtitles.
1982 (PG) 126m/C TU Tarik Akan, Serif Sezer; **D:** Serif Goren. **VHS, Beta** $19.98 *COL, AUD, TAM* ♪♪♪½

Yolanda and the Thief A charming, forgotten effort from the Arthur Freed unit about a con man who convinces a virginal South American heiress that he is her guardian angel. Songs by Freed and Harry Warren include a lengthy Dali-esque ballet built around "Will You Marry Me?". ♪This is the Day for Love; Angel; Yolanda; Coffee Time; Will You Marry Me.
1945 109m/C Fred Astaire, Lucille Bremer, Leon Ames, Mildred Natwick; **D:** Vincente Minnelli. **VHS, Beta** $19.98 *MGM* ♪♪½

Yongkari Monster of the Deep A giant burrowing creature is causing earthquakes and generally ruining scores of Japanese models. Dubbed. **AKA:** Dai Koesu Yongkari; Monster Yongkari; Great Monster Yongkari.
1967 (PG) 79m/C Oh Young Il, Nam Chung-Im; **D:** Kim Ki-dak. **VHS, Beta** $19.98 *ORI* ♪

Yor, the Hunter from the Future Lost in a time warp where the past and the future mysteriously collide, Yor sets out on a search for his real identity, with his only clue a golden medallion around his neck. **AKA:** Il Mondo Di Yor; The World of Yor.
1983 (PG) 88m/C IT Reb Brown, Corinne Clery, John Steiner; **D:** Anthony M. Dawson. **VHS, Beta, LV** $79.95 *COL* ♪

You Are Not Alone Boys in a small parochial school grow up and try to draw a defining line between friendship and love. In Danish with English subtitles.
1982 90m/C DK **VHS, Beta** *FCT* ♪♪

You are Not I After a multi-car accident a young woman escapes from psychiatric confinement and goes to her sister's house.
1984 50m/B **VHS, Beta** *NO* ♪♪

You Can't Cheat an Honest Man The owner of a misfit circus suffers a variety of headaches including the wisecracks of Charlie McCarthy. Contains Field's classic ping-pong battle and some of his other best work.
1939 79m/B W.C. Fields, Edgar Bergen, Constance Moore, Eddie Anderson, Mary Forbes, Thurston Hall; **D:** George Marshall. **VHS, Beta** $14.95 *KRT* ♪♪♪

You Can't Fool Your Wife Ball in two roles gives zip to this otherwise ordinary marital comedy. Previously blah hubby has a fling; previously blah better half wins him back with glamour.
1940 69m/C Lucille Ball, James Ellison, Robert Coote, Emma Dunn; **D:** Ray McCarey. **VHS, Beta** $19.98 *RKO, TTC* ♪♪

You Can't Hurry Love A jilted-at-the-altar Ohio bachelor moves to Los Angeles and flounders in the city's fast-moving fast lane. A dull film with Fonda, daughter of "Easy Rider" Peter, playing a minor role.
1988 (R) 92m/C David Leisure, Scott McGinnis, Sally Kellerman, Kristy McNichol, Charles Grodin, Anthony Geary, Bridget Fonda, David Packer, Frank Bonner; **D:** Richard Martini. **VHS, Beta, LV** $79.98 *LIV, VES* ♪

You Can't Take It with You The Capra version of the Kaufman-Hart play about an eccentric New York family and their non-conformist houseguests. Alice Sycamore (Arthur), the stable family member of an offbeat clan of free spirits, falls for Tony Kirby (Stewart), the down-to-earth son of a snooty, wealthy and not always quite honest family. Amidst the confusion over this love affair, the two families rediscover the simple joys of life.
1938 127m/B James Stewart, Jean Arthur, Lionel Barrymore, Spring Byington, Edward Arnold, Mischa Auer, Donald Meek, Samuel S. Hinds, Ann Miller, H.B. Warner, Halliwell Hobbes, Dub Taylor, Mary Forbes, Eddie Anderson, Harry Davenport, Lillian Yarbo; **D:** Frank Capra; **W:** Robert Riskin. Academy Awards '38: Best Director (Capra), Best Picture; Nominations: Best Cinematography, Best Film Editing, Best Screenplay, Best Sound, Best Supporting Actress (Byington). **VHS, Beta, LV** $19.95 *COL, PIA, BTV* ♪♪♪½

You Can't Take It with You Taped performance of the Kaufman and Hart comedy about the strange pastimes of the Sycamore family who must behave themselves to impress their daughter's boyfriend's stuffy family.
1984 116m/C Colleen Dewhurst, James Coco, Jason Robards Jr., Elizabeth Wilson, George Rose; **D:** Ellis Raab. **VHS, Beta, LV** $19.95 *COL, VES, LIV* ♪♪♪

You Light Up My Life Sappy sentimental story brought to you by Joseph Brooks, who wrote, directed, and produced. Young woman who sings tries to break into the music business. Premise of the movie was loosely taken from Debbie Boone's title song (also written by Brooks), which was a radio smash that drove many people over the edge.
1977 (PG) 91m/C Didi Conn, Michael Zaslow, Melanie Mayron; *D:* Joseph Brooks. VHS, Beta $14.95 COL Woof!

You Must Remember This When Uncle Buddy (Guillaume) receives a mysterious trunk, Ella's curiosity gets the best of her. She opens the trunk to discover a number of old movies made by W.B. Jackson—Uncle Buddy. Ella takes the films to a movie archive to find out about her uncle's past as an independent black filmmaker. After researching the history of black cinema, Ella convinces her uncle to be proud of his contribution to the film world. Includes a viewers' guide. Part of the "Wonderworks" series.
199? 110m/C Robert Guillaume, Tim Reid, Daphne Maxwell Reid, Vonetta McGee. VHS $29.95 PME, HMV, BTV Woof!

You Only Live Once Ex-con Fonda wants to mend his ways and tries to cross into Canada with his girlfriend in tow. Impressively scripted, but a glum and dated Depression-era tale.
1937 86m/B Henry Fonda, Sylvia Sidney, Ward Bond, William Gargan, Barton MacLane, Margaret Hamilton; *D:* Fritz Lang. VHS, Beta NO ✰✰1/2

You Only Live Twice 007 travels to Japan to take on arch-nemesis Blofeld, who has been capturing Russian and American spacecraft in an attempt to start World War III. Great location photography; theme sung by Nancy Sinatra. Implausible plot, however, is a handicap, even though this is Bond.
1967 (PG) 125m/C *GB* Sean Connery, Mie Hama, Akiko Wakabayashi, Tetsuro Tamba, Karin Dor, Charles Gray, Donald Pleasence, Tsai Chin, Bernard Lee, Lois Maxwell, Desmond Llewelyn; *D:* Lewis Gilbert; *M:* John Barry. VHS, Beta, LV, CDV $19.98 MGM, TLF ✰✰1/2

You Talkin' to Me? Fledgling actor who idolizes De Niro moves to the West Coast for his big break. He fails, so he dyes his hair blond and digs the California lifestyle. Embarrassingly bad.
1987 (R) 97m/C Chris Winkler, Jim Youngs, Faith Ford; *D:* Charles Winkler. VHS, Beta $79.95 MGM ✰

You Were Never Lovelier Charming tale of a father who creates a phony Romeo to try to interest his daughter in marriage. Astaire appears and woos Hayworth in the flesh. Splendid score by Jerome Kern and Johnny Mercer. The dancing, of course, is superb, and Hayworth is stunning. ♫Dearly Beloved; I'm Old Fashioned; Shorty George; Wedding in the Spring; You Were Never Lovelier.
1942 98m/B Fred Astaire, Rita Hayworth, Leslie Brooks, Xavier Cugat, Adolphe Menjou, Larry Parks; *D:* William A. Seiter. VHS, Beta, LV $19.95 COL ✰✰✰1/2

You'll Find Out A comic mix of music and mystery as Kay Kyser and his Band, along with a debutante in distress, are terrorized by Lugosi, Karloff, and Lorre. ♫The Bad Humor; Id' Know You Anywhere; You've Got Me This Way; Like the Fella Once Said; I've Got a One-Track Mind; Don't Think it Ain't Been Charming.
1940 97m/B Peter Lorre, Kay Kyser, Boris Karloff, Bela Lugosi, Dennis O'Keefe, Helen Parrish; *D:* David Butler. VHS, Beta $59.95 HHT, MLB ✰✰

You'll Never Get Rich A Broadway dance director is drafted into the Army, where his romantic troubles cause him to wind up in the guardhouse more than once. He of course gets the girl. Exquisitely funny. ♫Since I Kissed My Baby Goodbye; The A-stairable Rag; Shootin' the Works for Uncle Sam; Wedding Cake Walk; Dream Dancing; Boogie Barcarolle; So Near and Yet So Far.
1941 88m/B Fred Astaire, Rita Hayworth, Robert Benchley; *D:* Sidney Lanfield. VHS, Beta, LV $19.95 COL ✰✰✰

Young & Free Following the death of his parents, a young man must learn to face the perils of an unchartered wilderness alone. Ultimately he must choose between returning to civilization, or remain with his beloved wife and life in the wild.
1978 87m/C Erik Larson; *D:* Keith Larsen. VHS, Beta $59.95 MON ✰1/2

Young and Innocent Somewhat uneven thriller about a police constable's daughter who helps a fugitive prove he didn't strangle a film star. *AKA:* The Girl Was Young.
1937 80m/B *GB* Derrick DeMarney, Nova Pilbeam, Percy Marmont; *D:* Alfred Hitchcock. VHS, Beta, LV, 3/4U, Special order formats $16.95 SNC, NOS, VDM ✰✰✰

The Young and the Guilty Two star-crossed teenagers are frustrated in their romance when their parents find one of their love letters and hit the ceiling. Told not to see each other again, the two take to sneaking around, which adds an edge to their relationship. Moving performances by the two young leads.
1958 65m/B Phyllis Calvert, Andrew Ray, Edward Chapman, Janet Munro, Campbell Singer; *D:* Peter Cotes. VHS $19.95 NOS ✰✰

Young & Willing A group of struggling actors gets hold of a terrific play and tries various schemes to get it produced. Based on the Broadway Play "Out of the Frying Pan" by Francis Swann. Unexceptional but enjoyable comedy.
1942 83m/B William Holden, Susan Hayward, Eddie Bracken, Robert Benchley, Martha O'Driscoll; *D:* Edward H. Griffith. VHS, Beta NO ✰✰1/2

Young Aphrodites Two young teenagers of a primitive Greek tribe discover sexuality. An acclaimed film retelling the myth of Daphnis and Chloe. Narrated in English. *AKA:* Mikres Aphrodites.
1963 87m/B *GR* *D:* Nikos Koundouros. VHS, Beta $29.98 SUE, NLC ✰✰1/2

Young at Heart Fanny Hurst's lighthearted tale of a cynical hard-luck musician who finds happiness when he falls for a small town girl. A remake of the 1938 "Four Daughters." ♫Young at Heart; Someone to Watch Over Me; One for My Baby; Hold Me in Your Arms; Ready, Willing and Able; Till My Love Comes Back to Me; There's a Rising Moon For Every Falling Star; You, My Love.
1954 117m/C Frank Sinatra, Doris Day, Gig Young, Ethel Barrymore, Dorothy Malone, Robert Keith, Elisabeth Fraser, Alan Hale Jr.; *D:* Gordon Douglas. VHS $19.98 REP ✰✰1/2

Young Avengers/18 Jade Pearls Two full-length Kung Fu films packed with action, and an emphasis on self-defense.
19?? 180m/C VHS $9.99 VTR ✰✰1/2

Young Bill Hickok A Rogers vehicle in the form of a very fictionalized biography of the famous gunfighter.
1940 54m/B Roy Rogers, George "Gabby" Hayes. VHS, Beta $9.99 NOS, DVT ✰✰

Young Blood A cowboy robs from the rich to help the poor. He's also interested in a foreign actress having trouble bonding with the townfolk. Lots of old fashioned western violence.
1933 61m/B Bob Steele, Charles King, Helen Foster; *D:* Phil Rosen. VHS, Beta $19.95 NOS, DVT ✰✰

The Young Bruce Lee Bruce learns and uses the deadly skills that made him famous while only knee-high to a grasshopper.
19?? 90m/C Han Kwok Choi, Bruce Lee. VHS, Beta $19.95 OCE ✰✰

Young Buffalo Bill Buffalo Bill battles the Spanish land-grant patrons.
1940 54m/B Roy Rogers, George "Gabby" Hayes, Pauline Moore; *D:* Joseph Kane. VHS, Beta $19.95 NOS, DVT ✰✰

Young Caruso Dramatic biography of legendary tenor Enrico Caruso, following his life from childhood poverty in Naples to the beginning of his rise to fame. Dubbed in English.
1951 78m/B Gina Lollobrigida, Ermanno Randi, Mario del Monaco. VHS, Beta $29.95 MVD, NOS, VYY ✰✰

Young Catherine Made-for-TV account of Russia's strongest female ruler, the girl who would be Catherine the Great. Star-studded cast and excellent production values. Script and strong cast make Ormond look like a lightweight. Filmed in Leningrad. Also available in 186-minute version.
1991 150m/C Vanessa Redgrave, Christopher Plummer, Marthe Keller, Franco Nero, Julia Ormond, Maximilian Schell, Reece Dinsdale, Mark Frankel; *D:* Michael Anderson Sr. VHS, Beta $89.98 TTC ✰✰✰

Young Charlie Chaplin A British-made TV biography of the legendary silent screen comic.
1988 160m/C Ian McShane, Twiggy. VHS, Beta $39.99 HBO ✰✰

Young Doctors in Love Spoof of medical soap operas features a chaotic scenario at City Hospital, where the young men and women on the staff have better things to do than attend to their patients. Good cast keeps this one alive, though many laughs are forced. Includes cameos by real soap star, including then General Hospital star Moore. Director Marshall is from "Laverne and Shirley" fame.
1982 (R) 95m/C Dabney Coleman, Sean Young, Michael McKean, Harry Dean Stanton, Hector Elizondo, Patrick Macnee, Pamela Reed, Saul Rubinek; *Cameos:* Demi Moore, Janine Turner; *D:* Garry Marshall. VHS, Beta, LV $29.98 VES ✰✰

Young Dragon The Young Dragon's girlfriend is kidnapped by the underworld society, and he sets out to rescue her single-handedly.
1977 (R) 90m/C Yang Sze, Lo Lai, Yung Man Chi, Wong Ching, Nora Miao. VHS $54.95 SUN ✰1/2

Young Dragons: The Kung Fu Kids A kung fu master teaches his three grandsons the secrets of martial arts, which comes in handy on a trip to the big city. Followed by a sequel.
1987 95m/C *D:* Chang Mei Jun. VHS, Beta $59.95 CAN ✰

Young Dragons: The Kung Fu Kids 2 The Kung Fu Kids must choose between their beloved grandfather and their long-missing kung fu grandmother.
1989 100m/C D: Chen Che Hwa. **VHS, Beta** CAN *♂♂*

Young Eagles Serial with 12 chapters, 13 minutes each.
1934 156m/B Bobby Cox, Jim Vance, Carter Dixon. **VHS, Beta $49.95** NOS, VCN, MLB *♂♂*

Young Einstein A goofy, irreverent Australian farce starring, directed, co-scripted and co-produced by Serious, depicting Einstein as a young Outback clod who splits beer atoms and invents rock and roll. Winner of several Aussie awards. Fun for the kids.
1989 (PG) 91m/C AU Yahoo Serious, Odile Le Clezio, John Howard, Pee Wee Wilson, Su Cruickshank; **D:** Yahoo Serious. **VHS, Beta, LV $19.95** WAR *♂♂*

Young Frankenstein Young Dr. Frankenstein (Wilder), a brain surgeon, inherits the family castle back in Transylvania. He's skittish about the family business, but when he learns his grandfather's secrets, he becomes obsessed with making his own monster. Wilder and monster Boyle make a memorable song-and-dance team to Irving Berlin's "Puttin' on the Ritz," and Hackman's cameo as a blind man is inspired. Garr ("What knockers!" "Oh, sank you!") is adorable as a fraulein, and Leachman ("He's vass my—boyfriend!") is wonderfully scary. Wilder saves the creature with a switcheroo, in which the doctor ends up with a certain monster-sized body part. Hilarious parody.
1974 (PG) 108m/B Peter Boyle, Gene Wilder, Marty Feldman, Madeline Kahn, Cloris Leachman, Teri Garr, Kenneth Mars; *Cameos:* Gene Hackman; **D:** Mel Brooks. **VHS, Beta, LV $19.98** FOX, HMV *♂♂♂♂*

The Young Graduates Hormonally imbalanced teens come of age in spite of meandering plot. Features "Breaking Away" star Christopher in big screen debut.
1971 (PG) 99m/C Patricia Wymer, Steven Stewart, Gary Rist, Bruce Kirby, Jennifer Ritt, Dennis Christopher; **D:** Robert Anderson. **VHS $19.95** ACA *♂*

Young Guns A sophomoric Wild Bunch look-alike that ends up resembling a western version of the Bowery Boys. Provides a portrait of Billy the Kid and his gang as they move from prairie trash to demi-legends. Features several fine performances by a popular group of today's young stars.
1988 (R) 107m/C Emilio Estevez, Kiefer Sutherland, Lou Diamond Phillips, Charlie Sheen, Casey Siemaszko, Dermot Mulroney, Terence Stamp, Terry O'Quinn, Jack Palance; **D:** Christopher Cain. **VHS, Beta, LV $14.98** LIV, VES *♂♂ 1/2*

Young Guns 2 Brat Pack vehicle neo-Western sequel about Billy the Kid (Estevez) and his gang. This time they're making a run for the border with the law on their trail.
1990 (PG-13) 105m/C Emilio Estevez, Kiefer Sutherland, Lou Diamond Phillips, Christian Slater, William L. Petersen, Alan Ruck, R.D. Call, James Coburn, Balthazar Getty, Jack Kehoe, Rob Knepper, Jenny Wright, Tracy Walter, Ginger Lynn Allen, Jon Bon Jovi; **D:** Geoff Murphy. **VHS, LV $14.98** FXV, BTV, CCB *♂♂*

Young Hero The "Godfather of Chaos" has a town squashed under his thumb in this martial arts thriller. Enter Chang Ching, the new sheriff, and goodbye corruption. **AKA:** Deadly Strike.
1969 87m/C Huand Lund. **VHS, Beta $19.99** TWE *♂*

Young Hero of Shaolin When facing the fury of a thousand violent monks, one is forced to use the infamous "swastika" formation if one is to achieve "victory".
19?? 90m/C Guo Liang, Shih Bao Hwa. **VHS $49.95** OCE *♂*

Young Hero of the Shaolin Part 2 A mercenary and his gang commandeer a private yacht, kill the crew, and kidnap the owner's children.
19?? 90m/C Guo Liang. **VHS, Beta $49.95** OCE *♂*

The Young in Heart A lonely, old woman allows a family of con-artists into her life for companionship. Impressed by her sweet nature, the parasitic brood reforms. The cute comedy was a real crowd-pleaser in its day, especially after the bittersweet ending was replaced with a happier variety. Based on the novel "The Gay Banditti" by I.A.R. Wylie.
1938 90m/C Janet Gaynor, Douglas Fairbanks Jr., Paulette Goddard, Roland Young, Billie Burke, Minnie Dupree, Richard Carlson; **D:** Richard Wallace. **VHS $9.99** VTR *♂♂♂*

Young Lady Chatterly D.H. Lawrence meets "Debbie Does Houston." Cynthia Chatterly turns 20 and inherits Chatterly Estate, where servants are at her beck and call. Includes fifteen minutes of uncensored footage not found in the "Restricted" version.
1985 100m/C Harlee MacBride. **VHS $39.99** LIV *♂*

Young Lady Chatterly 2 A poor sequel to the popular MacBride film, with only the name of the Lawrence classic. Chatterly inherits the family mansion and fools around with the servants and any one else who comes along. Unrated version with 13 minutes of deleted footage is also available.
1985 87m/C Sybil Danning, Adam West, Harlee MacBride; **D:** Alan Roberts. **VHS, Beta, LV $79.98** LIV *♂ 1/2*

The Young Lions A cynical World War II epic following the experiences of a young American officer and a disillusioned Nazi in the war's last days. Martin does fine in his first dramatic role. As the Nazi, Brando sensitively considers the belief that the Hitler would save Germany. A realistic anti-war film.
1958 167m/B Marlon Brando, Montgomery Clift, Dean Martin, Hope Lange, Barbara Rush, Lee Van Cleef, Maximilian Schell; **D:** Edward Dmytryk. **VHS, Beta, LV $19.98** FOX *♂♂♂*

Young Love, First Love A made-for-television movie about a young woman who must decide whether to have sex with her boyfriend. Sound familiar? Pretty blah, earnest story, though well cast.
1979 100m/C Valerie Bertinelli, Leslie Ackerman, Timothy Hutton, Arlen Dean Snyder, Fionnula Flanagan; **D:** Steven Hilliard Stern. **VHS, Beta $59.95** LIV *♂ 1/2*

Young Love—Lemon Popsicle 7 Three hunks stalk the beaches in search of babes.
1987 (R) 91m/C Yftach Katzur, Zachi Noy, Jonathan Segall, Sonja Martin; **D:** Walter Bennett. **VHS, Beta $79.95** WAR *♂*

Young Man with a Horn Dorothy Baker's novel, which was loosely based on the life of jazz immortal Bix Beiderbecke, was even more loosely adapted for this film, featuring Kirk as an angst-ridden trumpeter who can't seem to hit that mystical "high note." ♫The Very Thought of You; I May be Wrong; The Man I Love; Too Marvelous for Words; With a Song in My Heart; Pretty Baby; I Only Have Eyes for You; Limehouse Blues; Melancholy Rhapsody; Lullaby of Broadway; Get Happy; Can't We Be Friends?.
1950 112m/B Kirk Douglas, Doris Day, Lauren Bacall, Hoagy Carmichael; **D:** Michael Curtiz. **VHS, Beta, LV $19.98** WAR *♂♂♂*

Young Mr. Lincoln A classy Hollywood biography of Lincoln in his younger years from log-cabin country boy to idealistic Springfield lawyer. Written by Lamar Trotti. A splendid drama, and one endlessly explicated as an American masterpiece by the French auteur critics in "Cahiers du Cinema."
1939 100m/B Henry Fonda, Alice Brady, Marjorie Weaver, Arleen Whelan, Eddie Collins, Ward Bond, Donald Meek, Richard Cromwell, Eddie Quillan; **D:** John Ford. Academy Awards '39 Nominations: Best Story; National Board of Review Awards '39: 10 Best Films of the Year. **VHS, Beta, LV $19.98** FOX *♂♂♂ 1/2*

The Young Nurses The fourth entry in the Roger Corman produced "nurses" series. Three sexy nurses uncover a drug ring run from their hospital, headed by none other than director Fuller. Also present is Moreland, in his last role. Preceded by "The Student Nurses," "Private Duty Nurses," "Night Call Nurses," followed by "Candy Stripe Nurses." Also on video as "Young L.A. Nurses 3." **AKA:** Nightingale.
1973 (R) 77m/C Jean Manson, Ashley Porter, Angela Gibbs, Zack Taylor, Dick Miller, Jack LaRue, William Joyce, Sally Kirkland, Allan Arbus, Mary Doyle, Don Keefer, Nan Martin, Mantan Moreland, Samuel Fuller; **D:** Clinton Kimbrough. **VHS, Beta $59.98** NLC *♂♂*

Young Nurses in Love Low-budget sex farce in which a foreign spy poses as a nurse to steal sperm from a sperm bank donated by world leaders, celebrities and geniuses.
1989 (R) 82m/C Jeanne Marie, Alan Fisher, Barbra Robb, James Davies; **D:** Chuck Vincent. **VHS, Beta $79.98** LIV, VES *♂*

The Young Ones Three episodes from the hilarious, offbeat British television sitcom about four violently eccentric college roommates. Episodes included are "Oil," "Boring," and "Flood."
1988 96m/C GB Rik Mayall, Ade Edmondson, Nigel Planer, Christopher Ryan, Alexei Sayle; **D:** Geoffrey Posner. **VHS, Beta $14.98** FOX *♂*

The Young Philadelphians Ambitious young lawyer Newman works hard at making an impression on the snobbish Philadelphia upper crust. As he schemes and scrambles, he woos debutante Rush and defends buddy Vaughn on a murder charge. Long, but worth it. Part of the "A Night at the Movies" series, this package simulates a 1959 movie evening with a Bugs Bunny cartoon, "People Are Bunny," a newsreel and coming attractions for "The Nun's Story" and "The Hanging Tree." **AKA:** The City Jungle.
1959 136m/B Paul Newman, Barbara Rush, Alexis Smith, Billie Burke, Brian Keith, John Williams, Otto Kruger, Robert Vaughn; **D:** Vincent Sherman. **VHS, Beta $69.95** WAR *♂♂♂*

Young Sherlock Holmes Holmes and Watson meet as schoolboys. They work together on their first case, solving a series of bizarre murders gripping London. Watch through the credits for an interesting plot twist. Promising "what if" sleuth tale crashes and burns, becoming a typical high-tech Spielberg film. Second half bears too strong a resemblance to "Indiana Jones and the Temple of Doom."

1985 (PG-13) 109m/C Nicholas Rowe, Alan Cox, Sophie Ward, Freddie Jones, Michael Hordern; *D:* Barry Levinson. VHS, Beta, LV, 8mm $14.95 PAR 🎬🎬

The Young Taoism Fighter The kung-fu film that tells it like it is—or was. Wacky shenanigans and zany pranks are the order of the day in a Taoist temple. Confucianism was never like this.
19?? 90m/C Yuen Tat Chor, Kwan Chung, Liu Hao Yi. VHS, Beta $49.95 OCE 🎬🎬

The Young Teacher A novice teacher finds out that trying to apply her college education to a real life elementary school environment isn't as easy as it sounds.
1985 90m/C VHS, Beta $29.95 GEM 🎬½

Young Tiger First a ninety-minute movie never before seen in the U.S. featuring an expert in martial arts who is accused of murder. Next is a twelve-minute documentary featuring Jackie Chan, kung-fu sensation, demonstrating his skills. What an evening.
1980 (R) 102m/C Jackie Chan. VHS, Beta $24.95 GEM 🎬🎬

Young Warlord Arthur roams western England in 500 AD, leading a band of guerrilla cavalrymen. When the Saxons invade, Arthur unites the tribe, holds off the attack and becomes king.
1975 97m/C Oliver Tobias, Michael Gothard, Jack Watson, Brian Blessed; *D:* Peter Sasdy. VHS, Beta $24.95 WWV 🎬🎬

Young Warriors Frat boys turn vigilante to avenge a street gang murder. Weird mix of teen sex comedy, insufferable self-righteous preachiness, and violence.
1983 (R) 104m/C Ernest Borgnine, James Van Patten, Richard Roundtree, Lynda Day George, Dick Shawn; *D:* Lawrence Foldes. VHS, Beta $59.95 MGM 🎬½

Young Winston Based on Sir Winston Churchill's autobiography "My Early Life: A Roving Commission." Follows him through his school days, journalistic career in Africa, early military career, and his election to Parliament at the age of 26. Ward is tremendous as the prime minister-to-be.
1972 (PG) 145m/C *GB* Simon Ward, Robert Shaw, Anne Bancroft, John Mills, Jack Hawkins, Ian Holm, Anthony Hopkins, Patrick Magee, Edward Woodward, Jane Seymour; *D:* Richard Attenborough. Academy Awards '72 Nominations: Best Art Direction/Set Decoration, Best Costume Design, Best Story & Screenplay; Golden Globe Awards '73: Best Foreign Film; VHS, Beta $19.95 COL, TVC 🎬🎬🎬

Youngblood An underdog beats the seemingly insurmountable odds and becomes a hockey champion. Some enjoyable hockey scenes although the success storyline is predictable.
1986 (R) 111m/C Rob Lowe, Patrick Swayze, Cynthia Gibb, Ed Lauter, George Finn, Fionnula Flanagan, Keanu Reeves; *D:* Peter Markle. VHS, Beta, LV $14.98 MGM 🎬🎬

Your Place or Mine Self-indulgent made-for-television yuppie pap about middle-aged singles trying to find the right mate.
1983 100m/C Bonnie Franklin, Robert Klein, Peter Bonerz, Tyne Daly, Penny Fuller; *D:* Robert Day. VHS, Beta $39.95 LIV 🎬½

Your Show of Shows The legendary variety program was a Saturday night fixture from 1950-1954 and featured the comedic talents of Sid Caesar, Imogene Coca, Carl Reiner, Howard Morris, and a bevy of guest stars. Additional episodes available.
1950 30m/B VHS, Beta $19.99 MOV, RDG, VYY 🎬½

Your Ticket Is No Longer Valid Prurient excuse for a serious drama. Impotent failed businessman has disturbing erotic dreams about his girlfriend. Adapted from a novel by Romain Gary.
1984 (R) 96m/C *CA* Richard Harris, George Peppard, Jeanne Moreau; *D:* George Kaczender. VHS, Beta $69.95 VES 🎬

Your Turn Darling French espionage thriller with Constantine once again playing Lemmy Caution, a U.S. secret agent involved with a gang of spies. *AKA:* A Toi De Faire; Mignonne.
1963 93m/C *FR* Eddie Constantine, Gaia Germani, Elga Andersen; *D:* Bernard Borderie. VHS $16.95 SNC 🎬🎬

You're a Big Boy Now Kastner, a virginal young man working in the New York Public Library, is told by his father to move out of his house and grow up. On his own, he soon becomes involved with man-hating actress Hartman and a discotheque dancer. A wild and weird comedy. Coppola's commercial directorial debut.
1966 96m/C Elizabeth Hartman, Geraldine Page, Peter Kastner, Julie Harris, Rip Torn, Michael Dunn, Tony Bill, Karen Black; *W/D:* Francis Ford Coppola. VHS, Beta $19.98 WAR 🎬🎬

You're a Good Man, Charlie Brown A filmed version of Charles Schulz's Broadway musical, based on his famous characters.
1987 60m/C VHS, Beta $14.95 KRT, KAR, WTA 🎬🎬🎬

You're Jinxed, Friend, You've Met Sacramento The tongue-in-cheek adventures of a cool-headed cowboy as he passes from town to colorful town. Great title, too.
1970 99m/C Ty Hardin, Christian Hay, Jenny Atkins; *D:* George Cristallini. VHS, Beta $57.95 UNI 🎬🎬

Yours, Mine & Ours Bigger, better, big screen version of "The Brady Bunch." It's the story of a lovely lady (Ball) with eight kids who marries a a widower (Fonda) who has ten. Imagine the zany shenanigans! Family comedy manages to be both wholesome and funny. Based on a true story.
1968 114m/C Lucille Ball, Henry Fonda, Van Johnson, Tim Matheson, Tom Bosley, Tracy Nelson; *D:* Melville Shavelson. VHS, Beta, LV $14.95 MGM 🎬🎬½

Youth on Parole Same old story: Boy gets paroled. Girl gets paroled. Parolee meets parolette and romance blossoms as they beat a further rap.
1937 60m/B Marian Marsh, Gordon Oliver. VHS LOO 🎬½

You've Got to Have Heart A young bridegroom's life gets complicated after he does not sexually satisfy his bride on their wedding night.
1977 (R) 98m/C Carroll Baker, Edwige French. VHS, Beta $49.95 PSM 🎬

Yukon Flight A Renfrew of the Mounties adventure. The hero finds illegal gold mining operations and murder in the Yukon.
1940 57m/B James Newill, Dave O'Brien. VHS, Beta $19.95 NOS, VCN 🎬🎬

The Yum-Yum Girls Pair of innocent girls arrive in New York City to pursue their dreams. Gives an inside looks at the fashion industry. Not as funny or as cute as it wants to be.
1978 (R) 89m/C Judy Landers, Tanya Roberts, Barbara Tully, Michelle Daw; *D:* Barry Rosen. VHS, Beta MCA 🎬½

Yuma An old-style made-for-television Western about a sheriff (Walker) who rides into town, cleans it up, and saves his own reputation from a plot to discredit him. Dull in places, but action-packed ending saves the day.
1970 73m/C Clint Walker, Barry Sullivan, Edgar Buchanan; *D:* Ted Post. VHS, Beta $19.98 FOX 🎬🎬

Yuri Nosenko, KGB Fact-based account of a KGB defector and the CIA agent who must determine if he's on the up-and-up. Made for British television.
1986 85m/C *GB* Tommy Lee Jones, Oleg Rudnik, Josef Sommer, Ed Lauter, George Morfogen, Stephen D. Newman; *D:* Mick Jackson. VHS $19.99 HBO 🎬🎬½

Z The assassination of a Greek nationalist in the 1960s and its aftermath are portrayed by the notorious political director as a gripping detective thriller. Excellent performances, adequate cinematic techniques, and important politics in this highly acclaimed film.
1969 128m/C *FR* Yves Montand, Jean-Louis Trintignant, Irene Papas, Charles Denner, Georges Geret; *D:* Constantin Costa-Gavras. Academy Awards '69: Best Film Editing, Best Foreign Language Film; Nominations: Best Adapted Screenplay, Best Director (Costa-Gavras), Best Picture; Cannes Film Festival '69: Best Actor (Trintignant); Edgar Allan Poe Awards '69: Best Screenplay; Golden Globe Awards '70: Best Foreign Film; New York Film Critics Awards '69: Best Director (Costa-Gavras), Best Film; National Society of Film Critics Awards '69: Best Film. VHS, Beta, LV $64.95 COL 🎬🎬🎬🎬

Zabriskie Point Antonioni's first U.S. feature. A desultory, surreal examination of the American way of life. Worthy but difficult. Climaxes with a stylized orgy in Death Valley.
1970 (R) 112m/C Mark Frechette, Daria Halprin, Paul Fix, Rod Taylor, Harrison Ford, G.D. Spradlin; *W/D:* Michelangelo Antonioni; *W:* Sam Shepard, Fred Gardner, Tonino Guerra, Clare Peploe. VHS, Beta, LV $59.95 MGM, MLB 🎬🎬🎬

Zachariah A semi-spoof 60s rock western, wherein two gunfighters given to pursuing wealth-laden bands of outlaws separate and experience quixotic journeys through the cliched landscape. Scripted by members of The Firesign Theater and featuring appearances by Country Joe and The Fish, The New York Rock Ensemble and The James Gang.
1970 (PG) 93m/C Don Johnson, John Rubinstein, Pat Quinn, Dick Van Patten, Country Joe & the Fish; *D:* George Englund. VHS, Beta $19.98 FOX 🎬🎬½

Zalmen or the Madness of God Elie Wiesel's mystical story about a rabbi's struggle against religious persecution in post-Stalin Russia.
1975 120m/C Joseph Wiseman, The Arena Stage Company. VHS, Beta WNE 🎬🎬½

Zandalee The sexual adventures of a bored sexy young woman who has a fling with her husband's friend. Bad script, graphic sex. Also available in an unedited NC-17 version.
1991 (R) 100m/C Nicolas Cage, Judge Reinhold, Erika Anderson, Viveca Lindfors, Aaron Neville, Joe Pantoliano; *D:* Sam Pillsbury; *W:* Mari Kornhauser. VHS, LV $89.95 LIV Woof!

Zandy's Bride Basic story about a rancher who sents for a mail-order bride. She's shocked by his ill-treatment of her and stands up to his bullying, thus winning his respect and love. Beautiful scenery, courtesy of Big Sur, California, but predictable all-around and essentially a waste of an experienced cast. Based on the novel "The Stranger" by Lillian Bos Ross.

1974 (PG) 97m/C Gene Hackman, Liv Ullmann, Eileen Heckart, Harry Dean Stanton, Joe Santos, Sam Bottoms, Susan Tyrrell, Frank Cady; **D:** Jan Troell; **W:** Marc Norman; **M:** Michael Franks. VHS $29.98 WAR ♫♫ ½

The Zany Adventures of Robin Hood Hackneyed spoof of the Robin Hood legend. Medieval man robs from the rich to help the poor. Not nearly as funny as Mel Brooks' TV series that spoofed "Robin Hood."
1984 95m/C George Segal, Morgan Fairchild, Roddy McDowall, Roy Kinnear, Janet Suzman, Tom Baker; **D:** Ray Austin. VHS, Beta $79.95 MED ♫

Zapped! Teen genius discovers he possesses telekinetic powers. He does the natural thing, using his talent to remove clothing from nearby females. A teen boy's dream come true.
1982 (R) 98m/C Scott Baio, Willie Aames, Robert Mandan, Felice Schachter, Scatman Crothers, Roger Bowen, Marya Small, Greg Bradford, Hilary Beane, Sue Ann Langdon, Heather Thomas, Merritt Butrick, LaWanda Page, Rosanne Katon; **D:** Robert J. Rosenthal. VHS, Beta, LV $14.98 SUE, NLC ♫

Zapped Again The lame-brained sequel to 1982's "Zapped" about a high schooler who has telekinetic powers and lust on his mind.
1989 (R) 93m/C Todd Eric Andrews, Kelli Williams, Reed Rudy, Linda Blair, Karen Black, Lyle Alzado; **D:** Douglas Campbell. VHS, Beta, LV, 8mm $14.95 COL, SUE ♫

Zardoz A surreal parable of the far future, when Earth society is broken into strict classes: a society of intellectuals, a society of savages, and an elite unit of killers who keep the order. Connery is the man who destroys the old order of things. Visually interesting but pretentious.
1973 105m/C Sean Connery, Charlotte Rampling, John Alderton, Sara Kestelman; **D:** John Boorman. VHS, Beta, LV $19.98 FOX ♫♫

Zatoichi: Master Ichi and a Chest of Gold A violent thriller about a blind gambler and former samurai who tries to clear his name after being framed for a gold robbery. Adapted from a novel by Kazuo Miyagawa. In Japanese with English subtitles.
1964 83m/C JP Shintaro Katsu; **D:** Kazuo Ikehiro. VHS $59.95 FCT ♫♫

Zatoichi: The Blind Swordsman and the Chess Expert Zatoichi, the blind gambler and former samurai, befriends a master chess player and gets involved with Japanese gangsters. In Japanese with English subtitles.
1965 87m/C JP Shintaro Katsu; **D:** Kenji Misumi. VHS $59.95 FCT ♫♫

Zatoichi: The Blind Swordsman's Vengeance Zatoichi defends a dying man against a group of gangsters who have taken over an isolated village. In Japanese with English subtitles.
1966 83m/C JP Shintaro Katsu, Shigeru Amachi, Kei Sato, Mayumi Ogawa; **D:** Tokuzo Tanaka. VHS $59.95 FCT ♫♫

Zatoichi vs. Yojimbo The legendary blind warrior-samurai, Zatoichi, wants to retire, but his village is being held captive by outlaws. He is forced to fight Yojimbo, the crude wandering samurai without a master, and the sparks really fly! This was a comic send-up of Akiro Kurosawa's "Yojimbo" with Mifune recreating his role here and playing it for laughs. Subtitled. **AKA:** Zatoichi Meets Yojimbo; Zato Ichi To Yojimbo.

1970 90m/C JP Toshiro Mifune, Shintaro Katsu, Osamu Takizawa; **D:** Kihachi Okamoto. VHS VDA ♫♫♫ ½

Zazie dans le Metro One of Malle's early movies, this is one of the best of the French New Wave comedies. A young girl, wise beyond her years, visits her drag queen uncle in Paris. She wants to ride the subway, but the ensuing hilarious adventures keep her from her goal. In French with English subtitles. **AKA:** Zazie in the Underground; Zazie in the Subway.
1961 92m/C FR Catherine Demonget, Philippe Noiret, Carla Marlier; **D:** Louis Malle. VHS $69.95 NYF, TAM ♫♫♫ ½

Zebra Force Group of army veterans embark on a personal battle against organized crime, using their military training with deadly precision. Non-distinguished substandard action-adventure.
1976 (R) 81m/C Mike Lane, Richard X. Slattery, Rockne Tarkington, Glenn Wilder, Anthony Caruso; **D:** Joe Tornatore. VHS, Beta $69.95 MED ♫

Zebra in the Kitchen A 12-year-old boy living in a small town is upset when he sees the run-down condition of the local zoo. So he decides to set all the animals free, which causes pandemonium in the town. Pleasant family fare.
1965 92m/C Jay North, Martin Milner, Andy Devine, Joyce Meadows, Jim Davis; **D:** Ivan Tors. VHS $19.98 MGM, BTV ♫♫ ½

Zebrahead Zack and Nikki are two high schoolers in love—which would be okay if Zack weren't white and Nikki weren't black. Their ill-fated interracial romance succumbs to the pressures of society in writer/director Drazan's expressive debut film. Outstanding performances by the young and largely unknown cast and a great musical score enrich the action. Filmed on location in Detroit.
1992 (R) 102m/C Michael Rappaport, N'Bushe Wright, Ray Sharkey, DeShonn Castle, Ron Johnson, Marsha Florence, Paul Butler, Abdul Hassan Sharif, Dan Ziskie; **W/D:** Tony Drazan; **M:** Taj Mahal. VHS, LV COL ♫♫♫

A Zed & Two Noughts A serio-comic essay by the acclaimed British filmmaker. Twin zoologists, after their wives are killed in an accident, explore their notions of death by, among other things, filming the decay of animal bodies absconded from the zoo. Heavily textured and experimental; Greenaway's second feature film.
1988 115m/C GB Eric Deacon, Brian Deacon, Joss Ackland, Andrea Ferreol; **D:** Peter Greenaway. VHS, Beta $29.95 PAV ♫♫♫

Zelig Documentary spoof stars Allen as Leonard Zelig, the famous "Chameleon Man" of the 1920s, whose personality was so vague he would assume the characteristics of those with whom he came into contact, and who had a habit of showing up among celebrities and at historic events. Filmed in black-and-white; intersperses bits of newsreel and photographs with live action. Allen-style clever filmmaking at its best.
1983 (PG) 79m/C Woody Allen, Mia Farrow, Susan Sontag, Saul Bellow, Irving Howe; **D:** Woody Allen. VHS, Beta, LV, 8mm $19.98 WAR ♫♫♫ ½

Zelly & Me A strange little drama about a young orphan living with her maniacally possessive grandmother, who forces the child into her own interior life through humiliation and isolation from anyone she cares for. Written by Rathborne, this is a well acted and interesting film that suffers from an overly introspective plot and confusing gaps in the narrative. Look for director Lynch on the other side of the camera. **AKA:** Phoebe.

1988 (PG) 87m/C Isabella Rossellini, Alexandra Johnes, David Lynch, Glynis Johns, Kaiulani Lee; **D:** Tina Rathborne; **W:** Tina Rathborne. VHS, Beta, LV $79.95 COL ♫♫♫

Zentropa Clever cinematic allusions and visuals mask what is essentially the plot of a conventional thriller. Leopold is a German-American pacifist who has traveled to Germany in 1945 to help in the postwar rebuilding. Through his uncle, Leopold finds work as a sleeping-car conductor for a giant railway system called Zentropa. When a beautiful woman summons him to her cabin, Leopold finds himself romancing the owner's daughter, the mysterious Katharina, who draws the hapless Leopold into an intrigue involving Nazi sympathizers. Director von Trier also uses the voice of Von Sydow as an omniscient narrator to address the audience and move the story along. Filmed primarily in black-and-white with bursts of color denoting dramatic moments. In English and German with English subtitles.
1992 (R) 112m/C GE Jean-Marc Barr, Barbara Sukowa, Udo Kier, Eddie Constantine; **W/D:** Lars von Trier; **W:** Niels Vorsel. VHS, Beta, LV $94.95 TOU ♫♫

Zeppelin During World War I, the British enlist the aid of York as a double agent. His mission is to steal Germany's plans for a super-dirigible. Accompanying the Germans on the craft's maiden voyage, York discovers they are actually on a mission to steal British treasures. Although the script is poor, the battle scenes and the blimp itself are very impressive.
1971 (G) 102m/C GB Michael York, Elke Sommer, Peter Carsten, Marius Goring, Anton Diffring, Andrew Keir, Rupert Davies, Alexandra Stewart; **D:** Etienne Perier. VHS, Beta, LV $19.98 WAR, FCT ♫♫ ½

Zero WWII story about the building of the zero fighter that was used to devastating effect in the invasion of Pearl Harbor.
1984 128m/C Yuzo Kayama, Tetsuro Tamba; **D:** Toshio Masuda. VHS, Beta $39.95 SVS ♫♫ ½

Zero Boys Teenage survivalists in the Californian wilderness are stalked by a murderous lunatic. Exploitative and mean-spirited.
1986 (R) 89m/C Daniel Hirsch, Kelli Maroney, Nicole Rio, Joe Phelan; **D:** Nico Mastorakis. VHS, Beta $19.98 LIV Woof!

Zero for Conduct Vigo's classic French fantasy about an outrageous rebellion of schoolboys against bureaucratic adults. More of a visual poem than a drama, it inspired Lindsay Anderson's "If...." One of only four films created by Vigo before his early death. Banned across Europe at release. In French with English subtitles. **AKA:** Zero de Conduite.
1933 49m/B FR Jean Daste; **D:** Jean Vigo. VHS, Beta $24.95 NOS, VYY, HHT ♫♫♫♫

Zero for Conduct/Taris/A Propos de Nice Three short films by the famed Jean Vigo. "Zero for Conduct" is a fascinating and fluid surrealist film about rebellion in a boy's prep school. "Taris" consists of underwater footage of the swimmer Jean Taris, and "A Propos de Nice" is a documentary that focuses on the great economic schism of the rich and the poor in the popular French vacation spot, Nice.
1991 75m/B FR **D:** Jean Renoir. VHS $39.95 FST ♫♫♫♫

Zero Pilot A Japanese film about the heroic fighter pilots of World War II.
1984 90m/C JP VHS, Beta VCD Woof!

Zero Population Growth In the 21st century the government has decreed that no babies may be born for a 30-year span in order to control the population. But Chaplin and Reed secretly have a child and when they are discovered are sent to be executed. Can they escape? Maudlin and simplistic. *AKA:* Z.P.G.
1972 95m/C Oliver Reed, Geraldine Chaplin, Diane Cilento, Don Gordon; *D:* Michael Campus; *W:* Frank de Felitta, Max Ehrlich. **VHS** $14.95 PAR *Ⅱ* ½

Zero to Sixty Newly divorced man finds his car has been repossessed for nonpayment. Seeking out the manager of the finance company, he gets a job as a repo man with a sassy 16-year-old girl as his assistant. Repartee develops, stuff happens, and the movie ends.
1978 (PG) 96m/C Darren McGavin, Sylvia Miles, Denise Nickerson, Joan Collins; *D:* Don Weis. **VHS, Beta** $69.98 SUF *Ⅱ*

Zertigo Diamond Caper Utilizing his heightened senses, a blind boy solves a diamond caper and proves his mother's innocence.
1982 50m/C Adam Rich, David Groh, Jane Elliot. **VHS, Beta** $29.95 GEM *Ⅱ*

Ziegfeld Follies A lavish revue of musical numbers and comedy sketches featuring many MGM stars of the World War II era. Highlights include Astaire and Kelly's only duet and a Astaire-Bremer ballet number. ♫Bring on Those Wonderful Men; Bring on Those Beautiful Girls; The Drinking Song; La Traviata; This Heart is Mine; Love; When Television Comes; There's Beauty Everywhere; The Babbitt and the Bromide; Here's to the Girls; Limehouse Blues; Libiamo Ne' Lieti Calici; Madame Crematon.
1946 109m/C Fred Astaire, Judy Garland, Gene Kelly, Red Skelton, Fanny Brice, William Powell, Jimmy Durante, Edward Arnold, Lucille Bremer, Hume Cronyn, Victor Moore, Lena Horne, Lucille Ball, Esther Williams; *D:* Vincente Minnelli. **VHS, Beta, LV** $19.98 MGM, MLB *Ⅱ* ½

Ziegfeld Girl Three star-struck girls are chosen for the Ziegfeld follies and move on to success and heartbreak. Lavish costumes and production numbers in the MGM style. ♫You Stepped Out of a Dream; I'm Always Chasing Rainbows; Minnie from Trinidad; Mr. Gallagher & Mr. Shean; You Never Looked So Beautiful.
1941 131m/B James Stewart, Judy Garland, Hedy Lamarr, Lana Turner, Tony Martin, Jackie Cooper, Ian Hunter, Charles Winninger, Al Shear, Edward Everett Horton, Philip Dorn, Paul Kelly, Eve Arden, Dan Dailey, Fay Holden, Felix Bressart, Mae Busch, Reed Hadley; *D:* Robert Z. Leonard. **VHS, Beta, LV** $19.98 MGM *ⅢⅢⅢ*

Zipperface A Palm Beach serial killer is making mincemeat of the local prostitutes. In order to capture the scum, the prerequisite beautiful police detective goes undercover only to find herself the killer's biggest thrill.
1992 90m/C Dona Adams, David Clover, John Dagnen; *D:* Mansour Pourmand. **VHS, LV** $89.95 AIP *Ⅱ*

Zis Boom Bah Musical-comedy star buys a cafe for her college son. He and his friends transform the place into a restaurant-theater with predictable results. ♫Annabella; It Makes No Difference When You're In the Army; Put Your Trust in the Moon; Zis Boom Bah; Good News Tomorrow; I've Learned to Smile Again.
1942 61m/B Peter Lind Hayes, Mary Healy, Grace Hayes, Huntz Hall, Benny Rubin. **VHS, Beta** $19.95 NOS, HEG, DVT *Ⅱ* ½

The Zodiac Killer Based on a true story, this tells the violent tale of the San Francisco murders that occurred in the late 1960s. Doesn't have the suspense it should.
1971 (R) 87m/C Tom Pittman, Hal Reed, Bob Jones, Ray Lynch; *D:* Tom Hanson. **VHS, Beta** $59.95 ACA *Ⅱ* ½

Zoltan...Hound of Dracula The vampire and his bloodthirsty dog go to Los Angeles to find the last of Count Dracula's living descendants. Campy and just original enough to make it almost worth watching. Written by co-producer Frank Ray Perilli. *AKA:* Dracula's Dog.
1977 85m/C Michael Pataki, Reggie Nalder, Jose Ferrer; *D:* Albert Band. **VHS, Beta** $69.99 HBO, UHV *Ⅱ* ½

Zombie Italian-made white-men-in-the-Caribbean-with-flesh-eating-zombies cheapie. *AKA:* Zombie Flesh Eaters.
1980 91m/C *IT* Tisa Farrow, Ian McCulloch, Richard Johnson, Al Cliver, Arnette Gay, Olga Karlatos, Stefania D'Amario; *D:* Lucio Fulci. **VHS, Beta, LV** VES *Ⅱ*

Zombie High Students at a secluded academy are being lobotomized by the school president. Mindless, In two senses of the word. *AKA:* The School That Ate My Brain.
1987 (R) 91m/C Virginia Madsen, Richard Cox, Kay E. Kuter, James Wilder, Sherilyn Fenn, Paul Williams; *D:* Ron Link. **VHS, Beta** $9.95 SIM *Ⅱ*

Zombie Island Massacre In this trying film, tourists travel to see a voodoo ritual, and then are systematically butchered by the rite-inspired zombies. Featuring former congressional wife and Playboy Magazine model Jenrette.
1984 (R) 89m/C Rita Jenrette, David Broadnax; *D:* John N. Carter. **VHS, Beta** $79.95 MED *Ⅱ*

Zombie Lake Killed in an ambush by villagers during WWII, a group of Nazi soldiers turned zombies reside in the town's lake, preying on unsuspecting swimmers, especially dog paddling nude young women. Laughable FX, almost bad enough to be good. From the team that produced "Oasis of the Zombies."
1984 90m/C *FR SP* Howard Vernon, Pierre Escourrou, Anouchka, Anthony Mayans, Nadine Pascale, Jean Rollin; *D:* J.A. Laser. **VHS** $59.95 UHV *Ⅱ*

Zombie Nightmare A murdered teenager is revived by a voodoo queen and slaughters his punk-teen assailants. Cheap and stupid just about sums this one up. Music by Motorhead, Death Mask, Girlschool and Thor.
1986 (R) 89m/C Adam West, Jon Mikl Thor, Tia Carrere, Frank Dietz, Linda Singer, Mandn E. Turbride, Hamibh McEwen; *D:* John Bravman. **VHS, Beta** $19.95 NWV, STE Woof!

Zombie vs. Ninja Guy who kicks and screams meets guy with bad complexion.
19?? ?m/C Wang Li, Keth Uh Land. **VHS** $59.95 LIV Woof!

Zombies of Moratau A diver and his girlfriend seek to retrieve an undersea treasure of diamonds protected by zombies. So boring you'll want to die.
1957 70m/B Gregg Palmer, Allison Hayes, Jeff Clark, Autumn Russel, Joel Ashley; *D:* Edward L. Cahn. **VHS, Beta** $59.95 COL, MLB Woof!

Zombies of the Stratosphere A serial in twelve chapters in which a cosmic policeman fights Zombies attempting to blow the Earth out of orbit. Also available in a 93 minute, colorized version. *AKA:* Satan's Satellites.
1952 152m/B Judd Holdren, Aline Towne, Leonard Nimoy; *D:* Fred Brannon. **VHS, LV** $14.98 REP, VCN, PIA Woof!

Zombies on Broadway Two press agents travel to the Caribbean in search of new talent, but find Lugosi performing experiments on people and turning them into sequel material. RKO hoped this would be equally successful follow-up to "I Walked with a Zombie." *AKA:* Loonies On Broadway.
1944 68m/B Wally Brown, Alan Carney, Bela Lugosi, Anne Jeffreys, Sheldon Leonard, Frank Jenks, Russell Hopton, Joseph Vitale, Ian Wolfe, Louis Jean Heydt, Darby Jones, Sir Lancelot; *D:* Gordon Douglas. **VHS, LV** $29.95 TTC, FCT, IME *Ⅱ* ½

Zombiethon A campy compilation of clips from cheapo zombie films, such as "Space Zombies," "Zombie Lake," and "The Invisible Dead."
1986 90m/C Dominique Singleton, Janelle Lewis, Tracy Burton. **VHS, Beta** NO *Ⅱ* ½

Zone of the Dead A mortician is using his morgue for other than embalming—and it isn't pretty!
1978 81m/C John Ericson, Ivor Francis, Charles Aidman, Bernard Fox. **VHS, Beta** $79.95 MNC *Ⅱ*

Zone Troopers Five American G.I.'s in World War II-ravaged Europe stumble upon a wrecked alien spacecraft and enlist the extraterrestrial's help in fending off the Nazis.
1985 (PG) 86m/C Timothy Van Patten, Tim Thomerson, Art LaFleur, Biff Manard; *D:* Danny Bilson. **VHS, Beta** $19.98 LIV *Ⅱ* ½

Zontar, the Thing from Venus Scientist is taken over by alien batlike thing from Venus, and attempts to take over the Earth. A parody of itself.
1966 68m/C John Agar, Anthony Huston; *D:* Larry Buchanan. **VHS** $19.98 SNC, VDM *Ⅱ*

The Zoo Gang A group of teens want to open a nightclub. Will they bring their dream to fruition, or will the mean rival gang foil their plans?
1985 (PG-13) 96m/C Jackie Earle Haley, Tiffany Helm, Ben Vereen, Jason Gedrick, Eric Gurry; *D:* John Watson, Pen Densham. **VHS, Beta** $9.99 NWV, STE *Ⅱ* ½

Zoo Radio Run by a wacky assortment of characters, a zany underground radio station embarks on a battle against bureaucracy.
1990 (R) 90m/C **VHS** $89.95 WAX *Ⅱ* ½

Zoot Suit Based on Luis Valdez' play, this murder mystery/musical is rooted in the historical Sleepy Lagoon murder in the 1940s. Valdez plays a Mexican-American accused of the crime. His friends (and defense lawyers) rally around him to fight this travesty of justice. Lots o'music and dancing.
1981 (R) 104m/C Edward James Olmos, Daniel Valdez, Tyne Daly, Charles Aidman, John Anderson; *W/D:* Luis Valdez. **VHS, LV** $14.98 MCA, FCT *ⅢⅢⅢ*

Zora Is My Name! The funny, moving story of Zora Neal Hurston, a Black writer known for her stories and folklore of the rural South of the '30s and '40s. From PBS's American Playhouse.
1990 90m/C Ruby Dee, Louis Gossett Jr. **VHS, LV** $19.95 PBS, PAV, KAR *Ⅱ* ½

Zorba the Greek A young British writer (Bates) comes to Crete to find himself by working his father's mine. He meets Zorba, an itinerant Greek laborer (Quinn), and they take lodgings together with an aging courtesan, who Zorba soon romances. The writer, on the other hand, is attracted to a lovely young widow. When she responds to him, the townsmen jealously attack her. Zorba

teaches the young man the necessary response to life and its tragedies. Based on a novel by Nicolai Kazantzakis. Masterpiece performance from Quinn. Beautifully photographed, somewhat overlong. Film later written for stage production. *AKA: Zormba.*
1964 142m/B Anthony Quinn, Alan Bates, Irene Papas, Lila Kedrova; *D:* Michael Cacoyannis. Academy Awards '64: Best Art Direction/Set Decoration (B & W), Best Black and White Cinematography, Best Supporting Actress (Kedrova); Nominations: Best Actor (Quinn), Best Adapted Screenplay, Best Director (Cacoyannis), Best Picture. **VHS, Beta, LV $19.98** *FXV, BTV* ♫♫♫½

Zorro Rides Again Zorro risks his life to outwit enemy agents endeavoring to secure ancestor's property. In twelve chapters, the first runs 30 minutes, the rest 17.
1937 217m/B John Carroll, Helen Christian, Noah Beery Sr., Duncan Renaldo; *D:* William Witney, John English. **VHS, Beta $27.95** *NOS, VCN, MED* ♫♫♫½

Zorro, the Gay Blade Tongue-in-cheek sword play with Hamilton portraying the swashbuckling crusader and his long-lost brother, Bunny Wigglesworth, in this spoof of the Zorro legend. The fashion-conscious hero looks his best in plum. Leibman is fun to watch.
1981 (PG) 96m/C George Hamilton, Lauren Hutton, Brenda Vaccaro, Ron Leibman; *D:* Peter Medak. **VHS, Beta $59.98** *FOX* ♫♫½

Zorro's Black Whip A young girl dons the mask of her murdered brother (Zorro) to fight outlaws in the old West. Serial in twelve episodes.
1944 182m/B George Lewis, Linda Stirling, Lucien Littlefield, Francis McDonald, Tom London; *D:* Spencer Gordon Bennet; *W:* Wallace Grissell. **VHS, LV $29.98** *NOS, GPV, MED* ♫♫½

Zorro's Fighting Legion Zorro forms a legion to help the president of Mexico fight a band of outlaws endeavoring to steal gold shipments. A serial in 12 chapters.
1939 215m/B Reed Hadley, Sheila Darcy; *D:* William Witney, John English. **VHS, LV, 3/4U, Special order formats $29.98** *NOS, VCN, VDM* ♫♫½

Zotz! The holder of a magic coin can will people dead by uttering "zotz"; spies pursue the mild-mannered professor who possesses the talisman. Russell wrote the screenplay from a Walter Karig novel. Typical William Castle fare; his gimic in the theatrical release of the movie was to distribute plastic "zotz" coins to the theatre patrons.
1962 87m/B Tom Poston, Julia Meade, Jim Backus, Fred Clark, Cecil Kellaway; *W/D:* Ray Russell. **VHS, Beta $59.95** *COL* ♫♫

Zou Zou Lavish backstage musical/drama of a laundress who fills in for the leading lady on opening night and becomes a hit. Baker's talking picture debut. In French with English subtitles.
1934 92m/B *FR* Josephine Baker, Jean Gabin; *D:* Marc Allegret. **VHS, LV $29.95** *MVD, KIV, APD* ♫♫½

Zulu In 1879, a small group of British soldiers try to defend their African outpost from attack by thousands of Zulu warriors. Amazingly, the British win. Dated colonial epic based on an actual incident; battle scenes are magnificent. Prequel "Zulu Dawn" (1979) depicts British mishandling of the situation that led to the battle.
1964 139m/C Michael Caine, Jack Hawkins, Stanley Baker, Nigel Green; *D:* Cy Endfield; *M:* John Barry. **VHS, Beta, LV $19.98** *NLC, VYG* ♫♫½

Zulu Dawn An historical epic about British troops fighting the Zulus at Ulandi in 1878. Shows the increasing tensions between the British colonial government and the Zulus. Stunning landscapes unfortunately don't translate to the small screen. Good but unoriginal colonial-style battle drama.
1979 (PG) 117m/C Burt Lancaster, Peter O'Toole, Denholm Elliott, Nigel Davenport, John Mills, Simon Ward, Bob Hoskins, Freddie Jones; *D:* Douglas Hickox. **VHS, Beta, LV $19.98** *TWE* ♫♫♫

Zvenigora Dovzhenko's first major film, and a lyrical revelation in the face of Soviet formality: a passionate, funny fantasy tableaux of 1,000 years of Ukrainian history, encompassing wild folk myths, poetic drama, propaganda and social satire. Silent.
1928 73m/B *RU* Mikola Nademsy, Alexander Podorozhny, Semyon Svashenko; *D:* Alexander Dovzhenko. **VHS, Beta $39.95** *FCT, TAM* ♫♫♫♫

The **CATEGORY INDEX** contains nearly 400 genre, sub-genre, thematic, or significant scene classifications, ranging from the very general (such as drama) to the fairly particular (such as phone terror). The terms are defined (more or less) below. While we've done our best to provide serious subject references, we've also had a bit of fun in the making of the various lists. No one list is inclusive; we're continually reclassifying, adding, and subtracting movies. Some 45 or so of the categories are new to this edition, and in some cases represent only a beginning. We're also trying to pare down some of the larger lists, like **Crime and Criminals**, by creating more targeted categories (such as **Crime Sprees, Crimes of Passion**). *VideoHound* invites readers to join in this sometimes fascinating pastime by sending in new titles for existing categories, as well as suggestions on new categories. With your suggestion, please list at least five movies that could be classified under the new category.

Action-Adventure: Adrenaline testers for those weary of the conventions of plot

Adoption & Orphans: Cute kids lacking permanent authority figures, ranging from *Annie* to *Wild Hearts Can't Be Broken*

Adventure Drama: Action with more attention to dramatic content—*Apocalypse Now* to *Robin Hood, Prince of Thieves*

Advertising: Corporate shenanigans at the agency—*How to Get Ahead in Advertising* to *The Horse in the Gray Flannel Suit*

Africa: Banana Republic franchise; *Out of Africa* to *Zulu Dawn*

AIDS: Someone usually dies; *An Early Frost* to *Longtime Companion*

Airborne: Contraptions up in the sky (see also Birds)

Alien Beings—Benign: Friendly space visitors, including *Howard the Duck* and little buddy E.T.

Alien Beings—Vicious: Not-so-friendly space visitors, notably the multi-jawed Alien continually harassing Sigourney Weaver

American South: Theatrics amid much brow mopping and drawling; *A Streetcar Named Desire* rattling down *Flamingo Road*

Amnesia: Phone call for Anastasia

Angels: Benevolent winged visitors from above: *Wings of Desire*

Animated Musicals: Boys, girls, dogs, ducks, birds, mice, and monkeys croon; many of Disney vintage, including *Aladdin* and *Sleeping Beauty*

Animation & Cartoons: Antics of Daffy, Donald, Bugs, Mickey, Chip, Dale, Tom, Jerry, Fred, Wilma, Charlie, and the rest of the gang

Anthology: More than one story to a cassette

Anti-War War Movies: *All Quiet on the Western Front* to *Glory* to **M*A*S*H* to *Full Metal Jacket*

Apartheid: Afrikaans term for racial segregation in South Africa

Art & Artists: They paint, pause, propagate with equal passion

Asia: *China White, Red Dust, Sand Pebbles*

Assassins & Assassination: Lincoln, JFK, *La Femme Nikita*, *Times of Harvey Milk*, and more

At the Movies: The movie within the movie or movies about watching the movies, from *Purple Rose of Cairo* to *Last Action Hero* to *Matinee*

Avant-garde: Ahead of its time or completely bewildering to most in the audience

Babysitting: Supervision of small-fry pranksters not your own; *Uncle Buck* to *Hand that Rocks the Cradle*

Ballet: On your toes—*The Turning Point*

Ballooning: Up, up and away, or *Around the World in 80 Days*

Baseball: Action on the diamond, ranging from *Bull Durham* to *A League of Their Own* to *Rookie of the Year*

Basketball: Roundball thrillers, including the memorable *The Fish that Saved Pittsburgh* and *White Men Can't Jump*

Beach Blanket Bingo: Annette, Frankie, sand, surf, bikinis

Behind the Scenes: Peek behind show business curtain, from *A Chorus Line* to *Truth or Dare*

Bicycling: Two wheels, no motor, much leg action and sweating

Big Battles: Big-budget (or at least illusion of such) clash of large, opposing military forces, from *Cromwell* to *Ran*

Big Budget Stinkers: Millions spent for no apparent reason

Big Daddies: Usually troublesome, with Freudian overtones

Big Digs: Anthropology and archaeology, from Indiana Jones to various mummy on-the-loose stories

Big Ideas: Philosophy, ideology and other semi-mental pursuits somehow translated to film

Bikers: Usually with a mean streak and traveling in leather-bound packs

Birds: Beaks, feathers, talons, bird #%!*; *The Birds, Beaks: The Movie, Howard the Duck*

Bisexuality: Going both ways—*Basic Instinct, Three of Hearts*

Black Comedy: Funny in a biting or despairing sort of way, from *The Addams Family* to *The Hospital*

Black Culture: Dominant African American themes, including blaxploitation: *House Party, Bingo Long, Superfly*

Black Gold: That's oil; aka *Oklahoma Crude*

Blindness: Can't see or sight impaired; *Afraid of the Dark*

Bloody Mayhem: Expanded scenes of arterial explosions, including *Blood Bride, Blood Cult, Blood Diner, Blood Feast, Blood Lake, Blood Legacy, Blood Mania,* and *Bloodbath in Psycho Town*

Body Guards: Costner looks after Whitney's personal business

Boxing: Yo, Adrian!

Bringing Up Baby: *Look Who's Talking* to *Raising Arizona,* plus infants with that little something different—*Alien 3, Enemy Mine, Basket Case 3: The Progeny*

Buddies: Butch and Sundance, Bill and Ted, Rubin and Ed, Thelma and Louise

Buddy Cops: Couple of police hanging together, usually practicing limited repartee at donut shop; *Lethal Weapon, Tango and Cash*

Camelot: *JFK Remembered*

Campus Capers: What really goes on at college—*Assault of the Party Nerds*

Canada: Renfrew the Mountie plus lots of wilderness and the occasional stray hockey puck

Cannibalism: People who eat people are the luckiest people; *Alive, Rabid Grannies, Cannibal Women in the Avocado Jungle of Death, The Cook, the Thief, His Wife & Her Lover*

Carnivals & Circuses: *Shakes the Clown* to *Rollercoaster,* plus *Big Top Pee Wee, State Fair,* and metaphoric circuses: *Brewster McCloud, La Strada*

Cats: Lesser vertebrate nonetheless much beloved by Hollywood

Central America: Mostly Latin warfare, with at least three sides to every conflict

Chases: Who are those guys? Someone's after someone else, usually at high-speed with transportation ranging from horses to autos to bikes to trains to trucks

Child Abuse: Not very funny at all—*Mommie Dearest, Fallen Angel*

Childhood Visions: Stories dominated by the kid point of view, or by an adult flashbacking to childhood; *Au Revoir Les Enfants, Home Alone*

China: *Last Emperor* to *Red Sorghum* to *The World of Suzie Wong*

Christmas: Reindeer, Santa, children make appearance amid much sentimentality

City Lights: Various urban sprawls used to good advantage; *L.A. Story; Last Tango in Paris; The Blues Brothers* (Chicago)

Civil Rights: Fighting for equality—*Autobiography of Miss Jane Pittman, Mississippi Burning*

Civil War: The Blue and the Gray

Classic Horror: Boris Karloff, Vincent Price, piercing screams

Cold Spots: Set in a frostbitten locale with lots of shivering; *Ice Station Zebra, Never Cry Wolf, Quest for Fire*

Comedy: *Yuck Yuck* fests not listed in other comedy categories—*Fletch, I Wanna Hold Your Hand, Tampopo*

Comedy Drama: Drama with a comedic touch or comedy underwired with drama—*Avalon, The Big Chill, Fried Green Tomatoes, One Flew Over the Cuckoo's Nest, Tootsie*

Comedy Performance: Stand-Ups; *Eddie Murphy: Raw, An Evening with Robin Williams, Without You I'm Nothing, Punchline*

Comic Adventure: *Romancing the Stone* to *Bird on a Wire* to *Crocodile Dundee*

Coming of Age: Hard-fought adolescent battle for adulthood, led by *American Graffiti, The Apprenticeship of Duddy Kravitz, Karate Kid*

Computers: Bits and bytes play major role

Contemporary Musicals: Thematically modern and made during last 20 years; *All That Jazz*

Cops: Police and pseudo-police work, including *Action Jackson, Blue Steel, The Choirboys, RoboCop, Lethal Weapon, National Lampoon's Loaded Weapon 1*

Corporate Shenanigans: Big Business runs amuck—*Barbarians at the Gate, Wall Street*

Crime & Criminals: Bad guys and gals, including the *Avenging Disco Godfather, The Grifters, In Cold Blood*

Crime Sprees: Boy meets girl and together begin life of crime and other tales of obsessional criminal activity, including *Bonnie & Clyde, The Boys Next Door*

Crimes of Passion: Love, sex, and death

Crop Dusters: Down on the farm: *Bitter Harvest, Pelle the Conqueror, Jean de Florette, The River*

Cult Items: Recognized for that something different by a relatively small group of people (at least initially); *Basket Case, Blood Simple, Harold and Maude, Mad Max,* and the greatest cult of them all—*The Rocky Horror Picture Show*

Cults: Something like a gang but more intense and usually governed by a state of mind similar to irrationality—*Helter Skelter*

Dance Fever: Whole lotta foot-tapping going on, including *An American in Paris, Daddy Long Legs,* and *Dirty Dancing*

Deafness: Can't hear or hearing impaired; *Bridge to Silence, The Miracle Worker*

Death & The Afterlife: Could be ghosts, could be voices from the beyond, could be any number of post-dead things—*Beetlejuice, Carnival of Souls, Flatliners, Poltergeist, Weekend at Bernie's*

Deep Blue: The sea around us, including *ffolkes* and *Splash*

Demons & Wizards: Swords, sorcery and wrinkled old men with wands—*The Alchemist*, *The Hobbit*, *Sword & the Sorcerer*

Dental Mayhem: Tooth-pickin' uproars; *Marathon Man*, *The Dentist*

Detective Spoofs: Putting together clues in humorous fashion—*Adventures of Sherlock Holmes Smarter Brother*, *Naked Gun*

Detectives: Clue happy but often grizzled and cynical—*The Drowning Pool*, *V.I. Warshawski*

Dinosaurs: *Jurassic Park* and other less life-like thundering lizards

Disaster Flicks: Natural and man-made, including 47 "Airport" sequels

Disease of the Week: Bulimia, anorexia, polio, cancer, and so on

Disorganized Crime: Stupid crime, including *Amos and Andrew*, *Dog Day Afternoon*, *Home Alone*, *Quick Change*

Divorce: Breaking up is hard to do; *Accidental Tourist*, *Heartburn*, *Kramer vs. Kramer*

Doctors & Nurses: Men and women in white concerned about health of complete strangers for profit, often to the dismay of the patient—*Autopsy*, *Candy Stripe Nurses*, *Dead Ringers*

Docudrama: *Thin Blue Line* between documentaries and drama

Documentary: Real life manipulated on film—*A Brief History of Time*, *The Last Waltz*, *Paris is Burning*, *Roger and Me*

Down Under: Australian, New Zealand settings—*Rescuers Down Under*, *Gallipoli*, *Man from Snowy River*, *The Thorn Birds*

Drama: Conflict, tension, climax, resolution

Dream Girls: Product of mid-life male crisis; *Battling Amazons*, *Cycle Vixens*, *The Doll Squad*, *The Woman in Red*

Edibles: Something's cooking—*Babette's Feast*, *Like Water for Chocolate*

Erotic Thrillers: Hot sex and murder, including *Basic Instinct*, *Body of Evidence*

Ethics & Morals: Examination of values (or lack of)—*Crimes & Misdemeanors*, *Judgment at Nuremberg*

Etiquette: Usually comedy of manners: *Educating Rita*, *My Fair Lady*

Exploitation: Rigged to take advantage of viewer, including historic treats like *Reefer Madness* and more recent ventures such as *Sleazemania*

Family Ties: Blood runs deep—*Back to the Future*, *Five Easy Pieces*, *The Godfather*, *Homeward Bound*, *Lorenzo's Oil*, *The Mosquito Coast*, *Rocket Gibraltar*

Family Viewing: Probably will not embarrass parents if viewing with children: *Bambi*, *Beethoven*, *Benji*, *Bingo*

Fantasy: Tales of the imagination, including Alice and her looking glass, E.T., *Ladyhawke*, *My Stepmother is an Alien*

Fast Cars: *Eat My Dust*; racing in the street or on the track; *The Last American Hero*

FBI Stories: Men and women of the Bureau, the Agency, or any national police organization with a dress code

Femme Fatale: She done him and him and him wrong

Film & Film History: *America at the Movies*; includes films about the making of films and movies important to film history

Film Noir: Dark and moody or tributes to dark and moody—*Farewell, My Lovely*, *The Postman Always Ring Twice*, *The Third Man*, *Who Framed Roger Rabbit?*

Film Stars: Movies or bios about cinema celebs, real or make-believe—*Bogie*, *Chaplin*, *Sinatra*

Firemen: *Backdraft*, *Fahrenheit 451*, and other tales of brave people with hoses

Fires: *Frankenstein*, *Quest for Fire*

Flower Children: The sixties are still alive at *Alice's Restaurant*—reflect on the *The Big Chill*, *The Doors*, and *Woodstock*; we all live on a *Yellow Submarine*

Folklore & Mythology: Age-old adult tales covering Atlantis, little people, Hercules, Ulysses

Football: Everything from terrorist attacks on the Superbowl (*Black Sunday*) to prison competition (*The Longest Yard*) plus *Diner*

Foreign Intrigue: Overseas mystery, with emphasis on accent and location

Frame-ups: *My Cousin Vinny*

France: *Dirty Rotten Scoundrels* to *The Moderns* to *Gigi* to *The Last Metro* to *Killer Tomatoes Eat France*

Front Page: *Citizen Kane*, *All the President's Men*, *The Philadelphia Story*, and other journalistic tales

Fugitives: On the lam: *Breathless*, *Nowhere to Hide*, *Posse*

Gambling: *Aces and Eights*, *The Color of Money*, *Eight Men Out*, *Honeymoon in Vegas*

Game Shows: *The Running Man* and *Queen for a Day*

Gangs: Criminally enterprising teens and adults running in packs: *State of Grace*, *Miller's Crossing*, *Public Enemy*, *Wanderers*

Gender Bending: *Crying Game*, *La Cage aux Folles*, *Her Life as a Man* and other instances of boys becoming girls and vice versa

Genetics: Fooling with the double helix—see *The Fly*

Genies: Aladdin finds magic lamp filled with compressed Robin Williams

Germany: *The Blue Angel*, *The Sound of Music*, *Wings of Desire*

Ghosts, Ghouls, & Goblins: *Ghostbusters*, *Topper*, *Poltergeist*

Giants: *The Amazing Colossal Man* visits *Village of the Giants*

Go Fish: Casting a line in the river that runs through it; *Man of Aran*, *A Fish Called Wanda*, *Captains Courageous*

Golf: Slow boring game best experienced on screen ("Be the ball, Danny")

Good Earth: Ecology, environment, nature, sod

Grand Hotel: Checkout time is noon; *Blame it on the Bellboy*

Great Britain: Thwarted royals (*Charles & Diana: A Palace Divided, Edward and Mrs. Simpson*), kings (*King Ralph*), queens (*The Naked Civil Servant*), class distinctions (*The Ruling Class*), vanished empires (*Cromwell, A Man for All Seasons*), criminals (*The Krays, The Long Good Friday*) plus multiple stiff upper lips, the Brontes, and Dickens

Great Death Scenes: Signing off with style: *Buffy the Vampire Killer, Bonnie and Clyde, Breaker Morant*

Great Depression: The era, not the state of mind—*Bound for Glory, Of Mice and Men, The Grapes of Wrath, Rambling Rose*

Great Escapes: Seizing the day for freedom—*The Big Doll House, Escape from Alcatraz, Papillon*

Growing Older: *On Golden Pond, *batteries not included, Cocoon, Driving Miss Daisy, The Shootist, The Wild Bunch*

Hard Knock Life: Poverty and bad luck: *City of Joy, The Match Factory Girl*

Heaven Sent: Visits or returns from the place where good souls and all dogs go—*Field of Dreams* to *Made in Heaven* to *Oh God!*

Heists: The big lift

Hell High School: Place where adolescents gather against their will; also known as *Rock 'n' Roll High School*

Historical Drama: Usually at least loosely based on an historic incident or personality

Hit Men: Armed with silencers; *Prizzi's Honor*

Hockey: *Slap Shot* and other icy tales of passing the puck

Holidays: Easter, Thanksgiving, New Year's, Halloween, but generally not Christmas

Holocaust: *Playing for Time*

Homeless: Street people with no homes

Homosexuality: Gay and lesbian themes—*Kiss of the Spider Woman, The Hunger, Cruising, Lianna, My Own Private Idaho*

Horror: Modern cut 'em up scare theater

Horror Comedy: Tongue-in-bloody cheek—*The Fearless Vampire Killers, Piranha, Sorority Babes in the Slimeball Bowl-A-Rama*

Horses: Whoa boy

Hospitals & Medicine: Dysfunctional institutional health care—*Article 99, The Hospital, One Flew Over the Cuckoo's Nest, Young Doctors in Love*

Hostage!: People held against their will for bargaining purposes

Hunting: Where's dat wascally wabbit? *Caddyshack, The Bear, White Hunter, Black Heart*

Identity: Who am I?

Immigration: Melting pot stories—*Avalon, Far and Away, Living on Tokyo Time*

India: On the road to Bombay

Insects: Bugs we have known; *The Applegates, Hellstrom Chronicle*

Interviews: When asked questions, people talk

Inventors & Inventions: Those wacky folks and their newfangled machines; *Chitty Chitty Bang Bang*

Ireland: Aye, make that a pint for take away: *The Field, Cal, The Playboys*

Islam: Religious themes

Island Fare: Thin, isolated stretch of land surrounded by water notorious for bringing out natural thing in men and women

Israel: *Cast a Giant Shadow, Exodus*

Italy: Passion, vino, lust, vino, Sophia Loren

Japan: Land of the Rising Sun, Godzilla, *Hiroshima, Mon Amour*

Judaism: *Fiddler on the Roof* meets *Funny Girl*

Jungle Stories: Tarzan, tribes, trees, treasure, temperature, temptresses, tigers

Kidnapped!: Held for ransom or just for the heck of it

Killer Appliances: Defrosted refrigerator goes on killing binge

Killer Beasts: Cloned dinosaurs run amuck in backyard, destroying patio

Killer Bugs: Giant and/or miserably mean spiders, ants, bees, worms, flies, slugs, and wasps

Killer Plants: Too much fertilizer produces killer tomatoes (stewed)

Killer Toys: Demented play things develop homicidal urges

Kindness of Strangers: Baffling altruistic behavior

King of Beasts (Dogs): Need we say more?

Korean War: *M*A*S*H* and friends

Labor & Unions: *Hoffa* and other working stiffs

Late Bloomin' Love: Better late than not bloomin' at all

Law & Lawyers: Tom Cruise joins *The Firm* and other realistic legal adventures

Loner Cops: *Dirty Harry* Syndrome

Macho, Macho Men: Ah-nold, The Duke, Van Damme, Stallone, Burt, Clint, Norris, Seagal, and many more cases of excessive testosterone

Mad Scientists: *The Brain That Wouldn't Die* spends an evening with *Frankenhooker*

Magic: Hocus pocus, often with evil intent

Marriage: Wedding bells, honeymoons, affairs, divorce, and growing old together, as well as the occasional unfortunate marital union with a blood-sucking vampire or knife-wielding satanist

Martial Arts: *Fists of Aluminum Foil*; much head-kicking, rib-crunching, chop-socky action

Martyred Pop Icons: For us, they gave their all: Buddy Holly, Elvis, Marilyn, James Dean, *Stardust Memories*

Mass Media: From *Network* to *Broadcast News* to *My Favorite Year*

Medieval Romps: Dirty peasants, deodorized and glorified kings and queens, splendid knights in shining armor, and one for all and all for one

Meltdown: Or how I learned to stop worrying and love the bomb; also bad wiring at local nuclear plants

Men: What is man? Is he neither fish nor fowl? Or perhaps not linoleum?

Men in Prison: Working on a chain gang; what we have here is a failure to communicate

Mental Retardation: Bill, Charly, Dominick, Lenny, Raymond (definitely)

Mexico: *South of Sante Fe* and *Against All Odds*

Middle East: Desert fare and camel close-ups ranging from *Ishtar* to *Lawrence of Arabia* to *The Jewel of the Nile*

Military Comedy: Marching to a different drummer, including *Stripes*, *M*A*S*H*, and *No Time for Sergeants*

Miners & Mining: Helmets with the little flashlights are nifty; *Matewan* and *McCabe & Mrs. Miller*

Missing Persons: People who disappear for a variety of reasons, sometimes because other people have taken them away

Missionaries: On a mission from God to save native populations

Misspelled Titles: Not proper Anglish

Mistaken Identity: You mean to say you're not the King of France?

Monsters, General: Not killer beasts, bugs, plants, appliances, aliens, toys, giants, vampires, werewolves, or politicians

Motor Vehicle Dept.: *Chitty Chitty Bang Bang* at the *Car Wash*, plus *Tucker*, *Herbie*, and the *Repo Man*

Mountaineering: Cliffhangers

Movie & TV Trailers: Snippets of stuff

Music: *Amadeus* meets the *Fabulous Baker Boys* and *The Commitments* after listening to *Mo' Better Blues* at *The Cotton Club*

Musical: High-energy singing and dancing, often for no particular reason

Musical Comedy: Laughter, singing, and dancing

Musical Drama: Singing and dancing, less laughter, more tension

Musical Fantasy: *Chitty Chitty Bang Bang*; *The Wizard of Oz*

Mystery & Suspense: Edge-of-the-couch thrillers and whodunits

Nashville Narratives: *Honkytonk Man* elopes with the *Coal Miner's Daughter*

Native Americans: Dancing with the wolves on *Pow Wow Highway*

Nazis & Other Paramilitary Slugs: *Boys from Brazil* and *The Dirty Dozen* plus SS she-wolf Ilsa and modern David Duke adaptations

Negative Utopia: Things seemed so perfect until...

New Age: New word for day dream

New Black Cinema: Spike is Godfather

Nifty '50s: *Grease*, *La Bamba*, *The Man in the Moon*, *Peggy Sue Got Married*, *School Ties* and 60 more from the Eisenhower era

Nightclubs: *Casablanca*, of course

Nuns & Priests: Collars and habits: *Agnes of God*, *The Cardinal*, *Going My Way*, *Nuns on the Run*, *Sister Act*

Occult: Witches, warlocks, devil worshippers, spell makers, spell breakers, haunted houses, and so on

Oldest Profession: It's not accounting

On the Rocks: Alcoholism, alcohol, barflies, moonshining, Prohibition—*Arthur*, *Days of Wine and Roses*, *Papa's Delicate Condition*, *My Favorite Year*

Only the Lonely: 50 ways to play solitaire—*The Cemetery Club*, *The Heart is a Lonely Hunter*, *Sleepless in Seattle*

Opera: Shouting in a melodic way while in costume

Order in the Court: Courtroom tales, including *The Accused*, *And Justice for All*, *A Few Good Men*, *Witness for the Prosecution*

Organized Crime: Gangsters with Franklin Planners

Outtakes & Bloopers: Inadvertent laugh riots

Pacific Islands: Hawaii, Tahiti, Philippines, etc.

Parades & Festivals: *Animal House* and *Ferris Bueller's Day Off*

Parenthood: Moms, dads, substitutes—*Dutch*, *Ma Barker's Killer Brood*, *Father of the Bride*, *Three Men and a Baby*, *Yours, Mine, and Ours*, *Raising Arizona*

Patriotism & Paranoia: Run the flag up the pole and salute it—*Rambo*, *Patton*, etc.

Peace: *Friendly Persuasion*, *Gandhi*

Performing Arts: *Fame*, *Swimming to Cambodia*

Period Piece: Costume epics or evocative of a certain time and place—*Bugsy*, *Cleopatra*, *Doctor Zhivago*, *The French Lieutenant's Woman*, *Swing Kids*

Persian Gulf War: Smart bombs away

Phone Terror: *Don't Answer the Phone*

Physical Problems: *My Left Foot*, *Coming Home*, *The Elephant Man*, *The Other Side of the Mountain*, *Untamed Heart*, *The Waterdance*

Pill Poppin': Life with a drugstore cowboy; consumption of drugs, mostly illegal or in extra-large dosages

Poetry: Not exactly a booming category, but think of *Poetic Justice*

Poisons: *Arsenic and Old Lace* and *D.O.A.*

Politics: *Bob Roberts*, *Mandela*, *Whoops Apocalypse*

Pool: *The Hustler*

Pornography: *Hardcore*, *Body Double*

Post Apocalypse: No more convenience stores

Postwar: After effects of war, generally WWI or WWII but sometimes the Civil War, the War of 1812, the Revolutionary War, and the Ohio Automobile Dealers War

POW/MIA: Captured by the enemy

Presidency: Mr. Lincoln, JFK, LBJ, FDR, and, of course, *Dave*

Price of Fame: What goes up...

Propaganda: Deliberately stretching the truth in order to persuade

Psycho-Thriller: It's all in your mind—*Bad Influence*, *House of Games*, *The Silence of the Lambs*

Psychotics/Sociopaths: *Killer Inside Me*, *Reservoir Dogs*, *The Stepfather*

Puppets: Usually with strings, but also muppets

Pure Ego Vehicles: Big stars doing their big star thing

Race Against Time: *China Syndrome*, *Lorenzo's Oil*

Race Relations: Black and white in color and other ethnic tales

Radio: *Choose Me*, *The Fisher King*, *Radio Days*, *Sleepless in Seattle*

Rags to Riches: Grit, determination, and hustling (or just pure dumb luck) lead to fortune—*Trading Places, Working Girls*

Rape: Victims and often their revenge

Rebel With a Cause: Bucking the establishment for a reason

Rebel Without a Cause: Bucking the establishment just because it's the establishment

Red Scare: Cold War and Communism—*The Commies are Coming, The Commies are Coming, Reds*

Religion: Charlton Heston parting the sea; *Witness, The Last Temptation of Christ*

Renegade Body Parts: Hands, fingers, eyes, brains with a life of their own

Restored Footage: Usually found in a vault or attic

Revenge: A key motivating factor—*Cape Fear, Death Wish, Hamlet*

Revolutionary War: Fought over tea

Road Trip: Escapism courtesy of two- and four-wheel vehicles—*Easy Rider, Coupe de Ville, Pee Wee's Big Adventure, Wild at Heart*

Robots/Androids: Mechanical but fascinating; *Blade Runner* and *The Terminator*

Rock Stars on Film: But can they act? Prince (Symbol), Sting, Elvis, Lennon, The Monkees, Whitney, and so on

Rodeos: Rope tricks with steers

Role Reversal: Vice versa; empathy test—*Freaky Friday, My Fair Lady, Switch, Soul Man*

Romantic Adventures: *The African Queen, Romancing the Stone*

Romantic Comedy: Falling in love has its hilarious moments—*Benny and Joon, Crossing Delancey, Modern Romance, Much Ado About Nothing*

Romantic Drama: Love thing leads to tension and anxiety—*Cyrano de Bergerac, Far and Away, Sommersby, Tender Mercies*

Roommates from Hell: *Single White Female*

Royalty: Emperors, kings, queens, princes, princesses, crowns, scepters

Running: Jogging, panting, collapsing

Russia: Back in what used to be the U.S.S.R.

Sail Away: Vessels on the water—*Mutiny on the Bounty, Erik the Viking, Mister Roberts*

Sanity Check: Inmates running the asylum; also deviant mental states

Satanism: *Speak of the Devil*

Satire & Parody: Biting social comment or genre spoofs, including *Being There, Airplane, Down and Out in Beverly Hills, I'm Gonna Git You Sucka, Monty Python's The Meaning of Life, The Player*

Savants: Half-minded geniuses: *Rain Man*

Scams, Stings & Cons: The hustle—*Billionaire Boys Club, The Color of Money, A Fish Called Wanda, The Grifters, The Sting*

Schmaltz: Extra cloying with sugar on top

School Daze: Education, school, and teachers—*Lean on Me, Dead Poet's Society, To Sir, with Love, Teachers*

Sci Fi: Imagination fueled by science and a vision of the future

Science & Scientists: *Altered States, Darkman, Them, They, Son of Flubber, The Story of Louis Pasteur*

Scotland: *Brigadoon, Local Hero, Whiskey Galore*

Screwball Comedy: Snappy repartee between sexes dueling in impossible situation

Scuba: Wet suits, including *The Abyss, Navy Seals*

Sea Critter Attack: Monsters from the deep (and not so deep) surface and surprise: *Jaws, Orca, Moby Dick*

Serial Killers: *Henry: Portrait of a Serial Killer, The Rosary Murders*

Serials: Heyday was in the 1930s; includes *Adventures of Red Ryder, Little Rascals, Flash Gordon*

Sex & Sexuality: Focus is on lust, for better or worse—*Alfie, Barbarella, Emmanuelle, Looking for Mr. Goodbar, Rambling Rose, She's Gotta Have It*

Sexploitation: Softcore epics usually lacking in plot but not skin—*The Erotic Adventures of Pinocchio*

Sexual Abuse: Victims and their stories—*Twin Peaks, Fire Walk with Me*

Shower & Bath Scenes: Encompassing bathtubs, hottubs, showers, sinks and toilets, including *Psycho, Fatal Attraction* and that poor fellow in *Jurassic Park*

Shrinks: Psychiatry or equivalent, with *The Prince of Tides, One Flew Over the Cuckoo's Nest*

Shutter Bugs: Photographers and their pictures—*Public Eye, Eyes of Laura Mars, Peeping Tom*

Silent Films: No small talk/no big talk/ no talk talk

Skateboarding: Teens on wheels—*Gleaming the Cube*

Skating: Roller and ice, including *The Cutting Edge, Xanadu*

Skiing: *Downhill Racer, Swinging Ski Girls*

Slapstick Comedy: Humor of the physical sort, including Abbott and Costello, Marx Brothers, sports comedies, Ernest, Pink Panther, *Home Alone*, Three Stooges

Slavery: *Roots, Spartacus*

Slice of Life: Charming small stories of life the way it might be—*The Bicycle Thief, Fried Green Tomatoes, Marty*

Soccer: *Victory, Ladybugs*

South America: *Aguirre, the Wrath of God, The Mission*

Southern Belles: *Blaze, Driving Miss Daisy, Steel Magnolias*

Space Exploration: Going where no spam has gone before—*Alien, Star Trek, 2001: A Space Odyssey*

Spaghetti Western: Clint with a squint, *A Fistful of Dollars, My Name is Nobody, Once Upon a Time in the West*

Spain: *Siesta*

Speculation: In search of…

Spies & Espionage: Trench coats, dark glasses, Bond, *North by Northwest*

Spousal Abuse: *Burning Bed, What's Love Got to Do With It?*

Stepparents: New spouse hiding either alien origins or sociopathic tendencies greets existing clan

Storytelling: *Amazing Stories, Grim Prairie Tales*

Strained Suburbia: Neighborhood is not what it seems—*Dennis the Menace, Neighbors, Edward Scissorhands*

Submarines: Deep sea diving; *Das Boot, Up Periscope, Run Silent, Run Deep, Hunt for Red October*

Suicide: Premature ends—*The Big Chill, Scent of a Woman, Romeo and Juliet*

Summer Camp: Where children go to misbehave, including *Meatballs* and *Sleepaway Camp*

Supernatural Horror: Forces from beyond terrorize people who are here

Surfing: Awesome wave, dude! *Mad Wax, The Surf Movie, Surf Nazis Must Die*

Survival: *Alive, The Bridge of the River Kwai, Testament*

Swashbucklers: Crossed swords, rope swinging including *Robin Hood,* Zorro, various Musketeers, *Captain Blood, Three Amigos*

Swimming: Ranging from *Gremlins* to *Jaws* to *The Swimmer* to *Cocoon*

Swingin' Singles: Not always swinging but still solidly single— *About Last Night, Singles, When Harry Met Sally*

Tearjerkers: Crying fests—*Love Story, Steel Magnolias, Old Yeller*

Technology—Rampant: Machines that wreak havoc—*Metropolis, Death Ray 2000, Blade Runner*

Teenage Angst: Adolescent anxieties, including *Baby It's You* and almost everything produced or directed by John Hughes

Tennis: Anyone?

Terror in Tall Buildings: *Die Hard*

Terrorism: Love affairs with hidden bombs

This Is Your Life: Biography and autobiography, including *The Babe Ruth Story, Amazing Howard Hughes, Amadeus, Catherine the Great, Great Balls of Fire, Raging Bull, What's Love Got to Do With It?*

3-D Flicks: Bring your special glasses

Time Travel: Fast forward or reverse with Bill and Ted, Dr. Who, *Back to the Future,* and *Peggy Sue Got Married*

Torrid Love Scenes: Steamy and/or sticky—*Angel Heart, Bull Durham, From Here to Eternity, Risky Business, The Unbearable Lightness of Being*

Toys: *Babes in Toyland, The Toy, Toys*

Track & Field: Running in circles

Tragedy: The fate of humankind, magnified—*King Lear, Madame Bovary, Tess, The World According to Garp*

Trains: Rhythm of the clackity clack—*Romance on the Orient Express, Throw Momma from the Train, Running Scared, The Silver Streak*

Treasure Hunt: Looking for hidden riches—*Klondike Fever, Treasure of Sierra Madre, Romancing the Stone*

Trees & Forests: Can't see one for the other, that wilderness paradox—includes *Mr. Sycamore* and *The Wizard of Oz*

True Crime: Based on fact, including *The Boston Strangler, The Executioner's Song, Helter Skelter*

True Stories: Approximations of real-life events often significantly fictionalized for the screen, including *All The President's Men, Chariot's of Fire, Cry Freedom, Heart Like a Wheel, The Killing Fields, Silkwood*

TV Movies: First shown on broadcast, cable, or foreign television (BBC, etc.)—*Adam, Autobiography of Miss Jane Pittman, Barbarians at the Gate, I, Claudius, Longtime Companion, The Day After*

TV Pilot Movies: Some became series; some did not

TV Series: Collections, anthologies, and individual episodes of memorable shows—*I Love Lucy, Star Trek, The Fugitive*

Urban Drama: *American Me* to *Boyz N the Hood* to *Grand Canyon* to *Zebrahead*

Vampire Spoof: Comedic blood suckers, including Buffy, *Andy Warhol's Dracula, Dracula Sucks*

Vampires: More serious vein of blood sucking varmint, including Dracula in his many manifestations

Variety: Little bit of everything

Veterans: *Alamo Bay* to *Who'll Stop the Rain*

Vietnam War: *Platoon, Hamburger Hill, Apocalypse Now, Good Morning, Vietnam*

Vigilantes: Individuals taking the law into their own hands—*Death Wish, The Outlaw Josie Wales*

Viva Las Vegas!: *Honeymoon in Vegas, Sister Act*

Volcanoes: Mountain blowing off steam, including *Joe Versus the Volcano*

War Between the Sexes: Men and women battle for supremacy—*It Happened One Night, The King and I, He Said, She Said, Romancing the Stone, When Harry Met Sally, The War of the Roses, Thelma & Louise*

War, General: Generally any conflict that defies other classification—*The Alamo, Gunga Din, The Last of the Mohicans*

Werewolves: Full moon wonders

Western Comedy: Gags and horses—*Ballad of Cable Hogue, Blazing Saddles, Rancho Deluxe, Support Your Local Sheriff*

Westerns: Cowboys, cowgirls, horses and jingle jangling spurs on the frontier

Wild Kingdom: Animals on their own and interacting with confused humans, including *The Bear, Dumbo, Born Free, Free Willy, Never Cry Wolf*

Wilderness: More trees than a forest, plus wild critters—*Life and Times of Grizzly Adams*

Women: Impressive women, less than impressive women, and issues concerning women—*Crimes of the Heart, My Brilliant Career, Passion Fish, Working Girls*

Women Cops: Female officers of the law

Women in Prison: The things that go on in the big doll house

Wonder Women: *Attack of the 50-Foot Woman,* Ripley, *La Femme Nikita, Supergirl*

World War I: *African Queen, Gallipoli, Grand Illusion*

World War II: The Last Big One, including *A Bridge Too Far, Guadalcanal Diary, The Guns of Navarone, Hope and Glory, Memphis Belle, Tora! Tora! Tora!*

Wrestling: Choreographed sports involving men and women—*No Holds Barred, All the Marbles, Wrestling Women vs. the Aztec Ape*

Wrong Side of the Tracks: Often involves relationship with someone on the right side—*Cannery Row, The Flamingo Kid, Pretty in Pink, White Palace*

Yuppie Nightmares: Young adults find best-laid plans for attaining wealth and privilege going astray—*Baby Boom, Desperately Seeking Susan, The Mighty Ducks, Pacific Heights, Something Wild, Wall Street*

Zombies: *I Walked with a Zombie, Night of the Living Dead*

CATEGORY INDEX

This list of cross-references for the categories is designed to provide alternatives for your search. For definitions and a full list of the categories, please refer to the preceding list for the category definitions.

Action Adventure (*see also* Adventure Drama, Comic Adventure, Disaster Films, Macho, Macho Men, Martial Arts, Romantic Adventures, Swashbucklers)

Adolescence **see** Coming of Age, Hell High School, Summer Camp, Teenage Angst

Adoption & Orphans (*see also* Hard Knock Life, Only the Lonely)

Advertising (*see also* Mass Media, Front Page)

Africa (*see also* Apartheid)

African Americans **see** Black Culture, Civil Rights, New Black Cinema, Race Relations

AIDS (*see also* Disease of the Week, Homosexuality)

Airplanes **see** Airborne

Alcoholism **see** On the Rocks

American Indians **see** Native Americans

American South (*see also* Nashville Narratives, Southern Belles)

Amnesia (*see also* Identity)

Angels (*see also* Heaven Sent)

Animals **see** Birds, Cats, Horses, King of Beasts (Dogs), Wild Kingdom

Animated Musicals (*see also* Animation & Cartoons)

Animation & Cartoons (*see also* Animated Musicals)

Anthology (*see also* Serials)

Anti-War War Movies (*see also* Satire & Parody)

Apartheid (*see also* Africa, Civil Rights, Race Relations)

Archaeology **see** Big Digs

Asia (*see also* China)

Assassinations (*see also* Camelot, Foreign Intrigue, Hit Men, Spies & Espionage)

Astronomy & Astrology **see** Star Gazing

At the Movies (*see also* Behind the Scenes)

Australia **see** Down Under

Automobiles **see** Fast Cars, Motor Vehicle Dept.

Babysitting (*see also* Bringing up Baby, Parenthood)

Ballet (*see also* Dance Fever)

Beach Blanket Bingo (*see also* Surfing, Swimming)

Behind Bars **see** Great Escapes, Men in Prison, Women in Prison

Behind the Scenes (*see also* At the Movies, Film & Film History)

Big Battles (*see also* War, General, specific war categories)

Big Budget Stinkers (*see also* Pure Ego Vehicles)

Big Ideas (*see also* Ethics & Morals)

Biography **see** This is Your Life

Bisexuality (*see also* Homosexuality)

Black Comedy (*see also* Comedy, Comedy Drama, Satire & Parody)

Black Culture (*see also* New Black Cinema)

Blindness (*see also* Physical Problems)

Bloody Mayhem (*see also* Horror)

Boating **see** Sail Away

Bringing Up Baby (*see also* Parenthood)

Buddy Cops (*see also* Cops, Crime & Criminals, Detectives)

Camelot (*see also* Assassinations, Presidency)

Campus Capers (*see also* Hell High School, School Daze)

Canada (*see also* Cold Spots, Hockey)

Cannibalism (*see also* Edibles, Horror)

Central America (*see also* Mexico, South America)

Chases (*see also* Road Trips)

Children **see** Animation & Cartoons, Animated Musicals, Childhood Visions, Family Viewing, Storytelling

China (*see also* Asia)

Christmas (*see also* Holidays)

CIA **see** FBI Stories, Spies & Espionage

Circuses **see** Carnivals & Circuses

Cities **see** City Lights, Urban Drama

Civil Rights (*see also* Race Relations, Slavery)

Civil War (*see also* American South)

Classic Horror (*see also* Horror)

Cold War **see** Red Scare

Comedy (*see also* Black Comedy, Comedy Drama, Comedy Performance, Comic Adventure, Horror Comedy, Military Comedy, Musical Comedy, Romantic Comedy, Satire & Parody, Slapstick Comedy, Screwball Comedy, Western Comedy)

Comedy Drama (*see also* Black Comedy)

Comic Adventure (*see also* Action Adventure, Comedy)

Coming of Age (*see also* Teenage Angst)

Communism **see** Red Scare

Computers (*see also* Robots/Androids, Technology Rampant)

Cooking **see** Edibles

Cops (*see also* Buddy Cops, Detectives, Killer Cops, Loner Cops, Women Cops)

Corporate Shenanigans (*see also* Advertising)

Courtroom Drama **see** Order in the Court

Crime & Criminals (*see also* Crime Sprees, Crimes of Passion, Disorganized Crime, Organized Crime, Serial Killers)

Cults (*see also* Occult, Satanism)

Dance Fever (*see also* Ballet)

Deafness (*see also* Physical Problems)

Death & the Afterlife (*see also* Angels, Great Death Scenes, Ghosts, Ghouls, & Goblins, Heaven Sent, Occult, Suicide)

Deep Blue (*see also* Go Fish, Sail Away, Submarines)

Demons & Wizards (*see also* Occult)

Detective Spoofs (*see also* Detectives)

Detectives (*see also* Cops)

Dinosaurs (*see also* Killer Beasts)

Disaster Flicks (*see also* Meltdown)

Disease of the Week (*see also* AIDS)

Disorganized Crime (*see also* Men in Prison)

Divorce (*see also* Marriage, Swingin' Singles)

Doctors & Nurses (*see also* AIDS, Disease of the Week, Hospitals & Medicine, Sanity Check, Shrinks)

Docudrama (*see also* Documentary)

Dogs **see** King of Beasts

Dolls That Kill **see** Killer Toys

Drama (*see also* Adventure Drama, Comedy Drama, Historical Drama, Musical Drama, Romantic Drama, Schmaltz, Tearjerkers, Tragedy)

Drugs **see** Pill Poppin'

Eating **see** Edibles, Cannibalism

Erotic Thrillers (*see also* Sex & Sexuality)

Ethics & Morals (*see also* Big Ideas)

Experimental **see** Avant-Garde

Exploitation (*see also* Sexploitation)

Family Ties (*see also* Parenthood)

Family Viewing (*see also* Animation & Cartoons, Fantasy, Musical Fantasy, Storytelling)

Fantasy (*see also* Animation & Cartoons, Musical Fantasy)

Fast Cars (*see also* Motor Vehicle Dept.)

FBI Stories (*see also* Detectives, Spies & Espionage)

Femme Fatale (*see also* Wonder Women)

Feminism **see** Women, Wonder Women

Firemen (*see also* Fires)

Flight **see** Airborne

Flying Saucers **see** Alien Beings, Space Exploration

Food **see** Edibles

Foreign Intrigue (*see also* Spies & Espionage)

Front Page (*see also* Mass Media, Shutterbugs)

Gambling (*see also* Viva Las Vegas!)

Gangs (*see also* Crime & Criminals, Organized Crime)

Gender Bending (*see also* Homosexuality, Role Reversal)

Genetics (*see also* Mad Scientists)

Genre Spoofs **see** Satire & Parody

Ghosts, Ghouls, & Goblins (*see also* Death & the Afterlife, Demons & Wizards, Occult)

Giants (*see also* Monsters, General)

Go Fish (*see also* Deep Blue, Sea Critter Attack)

Good Earth (*see also* Trees & Forests, Wilderness)

Great Britain (*see also* Ireland, Scotland)

Great Depression (*see also* Hard Knock Life, Homeless)

Great Escapes (*see also* Men in Prison, POW/MIA, Women in Prison, war categories)

Growing Older (*see also* Death & the Afterlife, Late Bloomin' Love)

Hard Knock Life (*see also* Great Depression, Homeless)

Hard Knuckle Sandwich **see** Boxing

Heaven Sent (*see also* Angels)

Heists (*see also* Scams, Stings, & Cons)

Hell High School (*see also* Campus Capers, School Daze, Teenage Angst)

Historical Drama (*see also* Medieval Romps, Period Piece)

Hit Men (*see also* Assassinations)

Hockey (*see also* Skating)

Holidays (*see also* Christmas)

Holocaust (*see also* Germany, Judaism, Nazis & Other Paramilitary Slugs, World War II)

Homeless (*see also* Great Depression, Hard Knock Life, Yuppie Nightmares)

Homosexuality (*see also* AIDS, Bisexuality, Gender Bending)

Horror (*see also* Bloody Mayhem, Cannibalism, Classic Horror, Horror Comedy, Killer Appliances, Killer Beasts, Killer Bugs, Killer Plants, Killer Toys, Mad

CATEGORY INDEX

The **CATEGORY INDEX** includes nearly 400 terms ranging from the orthodox to the slightly eccentric, allowing you to search for genres (Comedy), themes (Baseball), places (Great Britain), events (World War II), things (Killer Appliances), people (Doctors & Nurses), and more. Category definitions and cross-references precede the index; category terms are listed alphabetically.

Action Adventure

The Abductors
Above the Law
The Abyss
Aces: Iron Eagle 3
Across the Great Divide
Act of Vengeance
Action in Arabia
Action Jackson
Action U.S.A.
Adventure of the Action
    Hunters
The Adventurers
Adventures of Captain Fabian
Adventures of Captain Marvel
Adventures of Don Juan
The Adventures of Ford
    Fairlane
The Adventures of Frank and
    Jesse James
The Adventures of
    Huckleberry Finn
Adventures of Red Ryder
The Adventures of Rex &
    Rinty
The Adventures of Rin Tin Tin
The Adventures of Sinbad
Adventures of Smilin' Jack
The Adventures of Tartu
The Adventures of Tarzan
The Adventures of the
    Masked Phantom
The Adventures of Tom
    Sawyer
The Adventures of Ultraman
After the Fall of Saigon
Against All Flags
Ain't No Way Back
Alamut Ambush
Alice to Nowhere
Alien Private Eye
The Amateur
The Amazing Spider-Man
The Amazing Transparent
    Man
Amazon Jail
Amazons
American Autobahn
American Born
American Commandos
American Eagle
American Justice
American Ninja 3: Blood Hunt
Americano

The Amsterdam Kill
And Then You Die
Android
Angel 3: The Final Chapter
Angel of Death
Angel's Brigade
Angels Die Hard
Angels from Hell
Angels One Five
Angels' Wild Women
The Annihilators
Antarctica
Appointment in Honduras
Archer: The Fugitive from the
    Empire
Ark of the Sun God
Armed for Action
Armed Response
Around the World Under the
    Sea
Arrest Bulldog Drummond
Ashanti, Land of No Mercy
Assassin
Assault on a Queen
Assault on Agathon
Assault with a Deadly Weapon
Assignment Skybolt
At Gunpoint
At Sword's Point
Atlantis, the Lost Continent
Ator the Fighting Eagle
Attack Force Z
Avenged
The Avenger
Avenging Force
Baby Cart 4: Heart of a
    Parent...Heart of a Child
Back to Back
Back to Bataan
Background to Danger
Bad Guys
Badge 373
Bail Out
Balkan Express
Ballbuster
Band of the Hand
The Banker
Banzai Runner
Barbarian Queen
Barbarian Queen 2: The
    Empress Strikes Back
The Barbarians
The Barbary Coast
Bare Knuckles
Bat 21

Batman
Batman Returns
Battle of Neretva
Battle of the Commandos
Battle of Valiant
The Beast
Beasts
Bedford Incident
Bells of Coronado
The Belstone Fox
Berlin Tunnel 21
Best Revenge
Beyond Justice
Beyond the Call of Duty
Beyond the Carribean
Big Bad John
The Big Bust Out
Big Chase
The Big Doll House
Big Jim McLain
Big Steal
The Big Sweat
The Big Wheel
Billy the Kid in Texas
Bimini Code
Birds of Prey
Black Brigade
Black Caesar
The Black Cobra
Black Cobra 2
Black Cobra 3: The Manila
    Connection
The Black Coin
The Black Devils of Kali
Black Eliminator
Black Force
Black Force 2
Black Gestapo
Black Magic
Black Market Rustlers
Black Oak Conspiracy
The Black Pirate
The Black Raven
Black Shampoo
The Black Six
The Black Stallion
The Black Stallion Returns
Black Sunday
Black Terrorist
Black Water Gold
The Black Widow
Blackbeard the Pirate
Blackjack
Blade
Blade in Hong Kong

Blade Master
Blink of an Eye
Blonde in Black Leather
Blonde Savage
Blood Alley
Blood & Concrete: A Love
    Story
Blood and Guns
Blood Brothers
Blood Money
Blood Money: The Story of
    Clinton and Nadine
Blood on the Badge
Blood Ties
Bloodfist
Bloodfist 2
The Bloody Tattoo
Blue Jeans and Dynamite
The Blue Lightning
Blue Tornado
BMX Bandits
Bobbie Jo and the Outlaw
The Bold Caballero
Boomerang
Border Radio
Borderline
Born American
Born Killer
Born to Be Wild
Born to Race
Born to Ride
Bounty Hunters
Boxcar Blues
Boy of Two Worlds
Braddock: Missing in Action 3
Brady's Escape
Brannigan
The Brave Bunch
Breaking Loose
Breakout
Breathing Fire
A Breed Apart
The Bridge at Remagen
Bridge to Hell
The Bridge to Nowhere
The Bridges at Toko-Ri
Bring Me the Head of Alfredo
    Garcia
The Brotherhood of the Rose
Brothers Lionheart
The Buccaneer
Buffalo Stampede
Bulldog Drummond
Bulldog Drummond Escapes
Bulldog Drummond's Peril

Bulldog Drummond's Secret
    Police
Bulletproof
Bummer
Bunco
Burn 'Em Up Barnes
The Bushbaby
The Bushwackers
The C-Man
The Cage
Caged Fear
Caged Fury
Caged Heat
Caged Terror
Call Him Mr. Shatter
Camorra: The Naples
    Connection
Candleshoe
Cannonball
The Canon Operation
Canvas: The Fine Art of Crime
Captain America
Captain America 2: Death Too
    Soon
Captain Blood
Captain Kidd
Captain Scarlett
Captain Sinbad
Captive Rage
The Capture of Bigfoot
Captured in Chinatown
Car Crash
Carolina Skeletons
The Cary Grant Collection
Casey Jones and Fury (Brave
    Stallion)
Catch Me...If You Can
Ceiling Zero
Chain Gang Killings
Chained Heat
Chains
The Challenge
Challenge To Be Free
Challenge to White Fang
Chance
Chandu on the Magic Island
Chandu the Magician
Charlie and the Great Balloon
    Chase
Charlie Bravo
Charlie Grant's War
Charlie, the Lonesome Cougar
The Chase
The Cheaters

CATEGORY INDEX

Action

The Savage Girl
Savage Instinct
Savage Island
Scarface
The Scarlet & the Black
Sea Devils
Sea Hound
Sea Prince and the Fire Child
The Sea Wolf
Search and Destroy
Second Chance
Secret Agent Super Dragon
The Secret of El Zorro
Secret of the Ice Cave
Serpent Island
Sesame Street Presents:
    Follow That Bird
Seven Blows of the Dragon
Seven Magnificent Gladiators
Seven Sinners
The Seven-Ups
The Seventh Voyage of
    Sinbad
Shadow Man
Shadow of Chikara
Shadow of the Wolf
Shadow World
Shadowhunter
Shaft's Big Score
Shakedown
Shaker Run
Shamus
Shaolin Ex-Monk
Shaolin Vengence
Shark Attack
Shark Hunter
Shark River
Sharks' Treasure
Sharky's Machine
S*H*E
She Devils in Chains
Sheba, Baby
Sheena
The Sheik
Shep Comes Home
Ships in the Night
Shipwrecked
Shogun's Ninja
Shoot
Shoot the Sun Down
Shotgun
Showdown at the Equator
Sidekicks
Sidewinder One
Sign of the Wolf
The Sign of Zorro
Silk 2
Sinbad and the Eye of the
    Tiger
Sinbad of the Seven Seas
Sinbad the Sailor
633 Squadron
Sixteen Fathoms Deep
Skeleton Coast
Ski Bum
Ski Troop Attack
Skull: A Night of Terror
Skull & Crown
Sky Hei$t
Sky High
Sky Pirates
Slate, Wyn & Me
Slaughter
Slaughter's Big Ripoff
Slave of the Cannibal God
Sloane
Slow Burn
Smokey & the Hotwire Gang
Smuggler's Cove
SnakeEater
SnakeEater 2: The Drug
    Buster
SnakeEater 3: His Law
Soldier's Fortune
Solo Voyage: The Revenge
Son of Captain Blood

Son of Hercules vs. Venus
Son of Kong
The Son of Monte Cristo
Son of Samson
Son of Sinbad
Son of Zorro
S.O.S. Coast Guard
Sourdough
South Beach
South of Pago Pago
South Seas Massacre
Southern Comfort
Space Mutiny
Space Raiders
Space Riders
SpaceCamp
Spacehunter: Adventures in
    the Forbidden Zone
The Spanish Main
Spartacus
Speeding Up Time
Speedtrap
Spider-Woman
Spiderman: The Deadly Dust
Spiders
The Spirit of Youth
The Spoilers
Spy
Spy in Black
Spy Smasher Returns
The Spy Who Loved Me
Squadron of Doom
Stalking Danger
Stamp Day for Superman
Stand and Deliver
Star Quest
Starbird and Sweet William
Starchaser: The Legend of
    Orin
Starflight One
Steel Arena
Steel Dawn
Stone Cold
Storm and Sorrow
Stormquest
The Story of Robin Hood &
    His Merrie Men
Straight Line
Street Asylum
Street Hawk
Street Knight
Street Soldiers
Strike Back
Strike Commando
Striking Back
Stunt Pilot
Stunt Rock
Stunts
Subway
Sudden Death
Sudden Impact
Suicide Battalion/Hell Squad
Suicide Patrol
Summerdog
Sunshine Run
Super Dynamo
Super Mario Bros.
Superargo
Superbug Super Agent
Superchick
Superfly T.N.T.
Supergirl
Superman: The Movie
Superman 2
Superman 3
Superman 4: The Quest for
    Peace
Superman & the Mole Men
Supersonic Man
Supervixens
Surprise Attack
Survival Quest
Swamp Fire
Swamp Thing
Swamp Women
Swashbuckler

Sweet Dirty Tony
Sweet Justice
Sweet Revenge
Sweet Sugar
Sweet Trash
Swift Justice
The Switch
Switchblade Sisters
The Sword & the Rose
The Sword of El Cid
Sword of Fury I
Sword of Gideon
Sword of Lancelot
Sword of Monte Cristo
Sword of Sherwood Forest
Sword of Venus
The Swordsman
Taffin
Tailspin Tommy
The Take
Taking it to the Street
The Taking of Beverly Hills
Tales of Robin Hood
Tales of the Klondike: In a Far
    Country
Tales of the Klondike: Race
    for Number One
Tales of the Klondike: The
    Unexpected
Tangiers
Tango and Cash
Tank Commando
Target Eagle
Target: Favorite Son
Tarka the Otter
Tarzan and His Mate
Tarzan and the Green
    Goddess
Tarzan and the Trappers
Tarzan Finds a Son
Tarzan of the Apes
Tarzan, the Ape Man
Tarzan the Fearless
Tarzan the Tiger
Tarzan's New York Adventure
Tarzan's Revenge
Tarzan's Secret Treasure
A Taste of Hell
Tattooed Hit Man
Temporada Salvaje
Ten to Midnight
10 Violent Women
Ten Who Dared
The Tender Warrior
Terminal Island
The Terminator
Terminator 2: Judgment Day
Terror in Beverly Hills
Terror in Paradise
Terror in the Jungle
Terror of Rome Against the
    Son of Hercules
Terror of the Bloodhunters
Terror on Alcatraz
Terror on the 40th Floor
Terror Ship
Terror Squad
The Terrorists
Texas Detour
Tharus Son of Attila
Thieves of Fortune
Third Man on the Mountain
13 Rue Madeleine
The 13th Mission
This Gun for Hire
This is a Hijack
Thoughts are Free
Thrashin'
Three Days in Beirut
Three Days to a Kill
357 Magnum
Three Legionnaires
Three Musketeers
Throne of Fire
Thumb Tripping
Thunder Bay

Thunder County
Thunder Road
Thunder Run
Thunder Score
Thunder Warrior
Thunder Warrior 2
Thunderball
Thunderbolt & Lightfoot
Thundering Forest
Thundersquad
Tiara Tahiti
Tiffany Jones
Tiger Joe
Tiger of the Seven Seas
Tilt
Time Machine
Time to Die
The Time Travelers
Time Walker
Timebomb
Tintorera...Tiger Shark
To Die Standing
To Live and Die in Hong Kong
To Live & Die in L.A.
To Protect and Serve
To the Shores of Hell
Tobruk
Toby McTeague
Tokyo Joe
Tomorrow Never Comes
Tongs: An American
    Nightmare
Tonka
Top of the Heap
Tor
Tora! Tora! Tora!
Torero
The Tormentors
Total Exposure
Touch & Go
Tough Guy
Tougher than Leather
A Town Called Hell
Toy Soldiers
Trader Tom of the China Seas
Trap
Trap on Cougar Mountain
Trapper County War
Treasure Island
The Treasure of Bengal
The Treasure of Jamaica Reef
The Treasure of Matecumbe
Treasure of Monte Cristo
The Treasure of the Amazon
Treasure of the Four Crowns
Treasure of the Golden
    Condor
Treasure of the Sierra Madre
Treasure of the Yankee
    Zephyr
The Treasure Seekers
Trespass
The Trial of the Incredible Hulk
Trident Force
Triple Impact
Tripwire
Troma's War
Tropic Heat
Tropical Snow
Trouble Bound
Truck Stop Women
Truck Turner
Try and Get Me
Tucker and the Horse Thief
Tundra
Tusks
Tut & Tuttle
20,000 Leagues Under the
    Sea
Twilight's Last Gleaming
2020 Texas Gladiators
Two to Tango
Two Wrongs Make a Right
Typhoon Treasure
Ulterior Motives
Ultra Warrior

Ulysses
Undeclared War
Under Siege
Under the Gun
Under the Red Robe
Undercover
Undercover Vixens
Underground Terror
Underwater
Unholy Rollers
Universal Soldier
Unknown Island
Unmasking the Idol
Until They Get Me
The Uranium Conspiracy
Urban Warriors
Utu
Valley of the Eagles
Vengeance
Vera Cruz
The Vernonia Incident
V.I. Warshawski
Vice Squad
Vietnam, Texas
A View to a Kill
The Vigilantes are Coming
The Vikings
Violent Professionals
Violent Zone
Viper
Virgin Sacrifice
Viva Knievel
Viva Villa!
Vivo o Muerto
Voyage en Balloon
The Voyage of Tanai
The Voyage of the Yes
Wake of the Red Witch
Walk into Hell
Wanted Dead or Alive
War Bus Commando
War Party
Warbirds
Warbus
WarCat
Wardogs
Warlords from Hell
The Warriors
Warriors from Hell
Warriors of the Apocalypse
Warriors of the Wasteland
Web of Deception
Wet Gold
Wheels of Fire
When Hell Broke Loose
When Lightning Strikes
When the North Wind Blows
When Time Ran Out
Where Eagles Dare
Where the River Runs Black
White Cannibal Queen
The White Dawn
White Fang
White Fang and the Hunter
White Ghost
White Gorilla
White Huntress
White Lightning
White Line Fever
The White Orchid
White Pongo
White Slave
White Water Summer
WhiteForce
Whitewater Sam
Who Killed Mary What's 'Er
    Name?
The Wild Angels
Wild Geese
Wild Gypsies
Wild Horses
Wild Man
Wild Rebels
Wild Ride
Wild Women
The Wild World of Batwoman

Action

Wild Zone
Wilding
Willow
The Wind That Walks
Windjammer
Wings of Danger
Winners Take All
Wisdom
Wolf
Wolf Dog
Woman in Grey
Women in Fury
Women's Prison Escape
Women's Prison Massacre
Wonderland Cove
The Wreck of the Mary Deare
Write to Kill
The Yakuza
Yank in Libya
Yankee Clipper
Yellowstone
Yojimbo
Yor, the Hunter from the
  Future
You Only Live Twice
Young Eagles
Zatoichi: Master Ichi and a
  Chest of Gold
Zatoichi: The Blind
  Swordsman and the Chess
  Expert
Zatoichi: The Blind
  Swordsman's Vengeance
Zebra Force
Zero
Zipperface

Adoption &
Orphans

Across the Great Divide
Adoption
Aladdin
All Mine to Give
Angel in a Taxi
Anne of Green Gables
Annie
Babes on Broadway
Bachelor Mother
The Beniker Gang
Big Red
Blossoms in the Dust
Born Free
Born in America
The Boy with the Green Hair
The Children of An Lac
Christmas Lilies of the Field
A Cry from the Streets
Crystalstone
Daddy Long Legs
Dangerous Orphans
D.A.R.Y.L.
David Copperfield
Deadly Sanctuary
Defiant
Dick Tracy
Don't Cry, It's Only Thunder
Duelo en el Dorado
Eagle's Shadow
Earthling
Escape to Witch Mountain
A Far Off Place
The Father Clements Story
Fighting Father Dunne
Free Willy
Goldy: The Last of the Golden
  Bears
Goldy 2: The Saga of the
  Golden Bear
Great Expectations
Great Expectations: The
  Untold Story
Heaven on Earth
Hector's Bunyip
Home at Last
A Home of Our Own

Hoodoo Ann
Immediate Family
The Jack Knife Man
Jane Eyre
The Kid
The Kid/Idle Class
The Kid Who Loved Christmas
King, Queen, Knave
La Passante
Lady from Yesterday
The Land Before Time
Little Orphan Annie
A Little Princess
A Long Way Home
Love Without Fear
The Loves of Edgar Allen Poe
Mad Max Beyond
  Thunderdome
The Magic Christian
Man, Woman & Child
Manny's Orphans
Mighty Joe Young
Min & Bill
My Dog Shep
Mystery of the Million Dollar
  Hockey Puck
Napoleon and Samantha
Nice Girl Like Me
Nothing But the Night
The Odyssey of the Pacific
The Official Story
Oliver!
Oliver Twist
On the Right Track
One Good Cop
The Orphan
Orphan Train
Orphans
Orphans of the Storm
Paper Moon
Peck's Bad Boy
Penny Serenade
Pixote
Pollyanna
The Poor Little Rich Girl
The Prince of Central Park
Problem Child
Queen Kelly
Rags to Riches
Rebecca of Sunnybrook Farm
The Revolt of Job
Rikisha-Man
Sally of the Sawdust
Samantha
Scout's Honor
The Sea Serpent
Shep Comes Home
Sidewalks of London
Snow White and the Seven
  Dwarfs
Sois Belle et Tais-Toi
Sparrows
The Stranger Who Looks Like
  Me
Streetwise
Sugar Cane Alley
The Sugarland Express
Sundays & Cybele
Superman: The Movie
Susannah of the Mounties
Sweetwater
Tarzan Finds a Son
They Still Call Me Bruce
Three Secrets
The Tunnel of Love
Way Back Home
Where the River Runs Black
Which Way Home
Who'll Save Our Children?
Wild Hearts Can't Be Broken
The World Accuses
Young & Free

Adventure Drama

Ace of Aces

Act of Piracy
Action in the North Atlantic
The Adventures of Frontier
  Fremont
The Adventures of Huck Finn
The Adventures of
  Huckleberry Finn
The Adventures of Milo & Otis
The Adventures of Robin
  Hood
The Adventures of the
  Wilderness Family
The Adventures of Tom
  Sawyer
Air Force
Al Capone
The Alaska Wilderness
  Adventure
Alexander Nevsky
All the Rivers Run
Allan Quartermain and the
  Lost City of Gold
Alligator Alley
Aloha, Bobby and Rose
Amazon
The Amazons
American Empire
American Roulette
The American Scream
American Tiger
And I Alone Survived
Angels of the City
Anzacs: The War Down Under
Apocalypse Now
Appointment with Crime
The Arab Conspiracy
Archer's Adventure
Arizona Heat
Around the World in 80 Days
Assassination
Assault on Precinct 13
The Association
The Aviator
Back in the USSR
Backdraft
Backlash
Barbary Coast
The Baron
Bataan
Battle Hell
The Battle of El Alamein
Battle of the Eagles
The Battle of the Japan Sea
Battleforce
Bear Island
Beau Geste
The Beloved Rogue
Beneath the 12-Mile Reef
Benji the Hunted
The Berlin Conspiracy
Between Heaven and Hell
Beyond the Poseidon
  Adventure
Big Bad Mama
The Big Push
The Big Scam
Billy Budd
Black Arrow
The Black Arrow
Black Bikers from Hell
Black Moon Rising
Black Rain
Blackout
Blood and Sand
Blood Debts
Blood Money
Bloody Che Contra
Blowing Wild
The Blue and the Grey
Blue Fin
The Blue Lamp
Blue Thunder
Boiling Point
Bomb at 10:10
Bombardier
Border Heat

Botany Bay
The Bounty
Brighty of the Grand Canyon
Brotherhood of Death
A Bullet Is Waiting
Burke & Wills
Cadence
California Gold Rush
Call of the Wild
Camel Boy
Casablanca Express
Casualties of War
The Cat
Chain Reaction
Chains of Gold
The Challenge
Challenge of a Lifetime
The Charge of the Light
  Brigade
Children of the Wild
Children's Island
China Gate
Chrome Soldiers
Clarence, the Cross-eyed Lion
Claws
The Climb
The Coast Patrol
Code Name: Emerald
Cold Heat
Cold Justice
Command Decision
Commando Attack
Con Man
Coogan's Bluff
The Cop & the Girl
Cop-Out
Corsair
The Count of Monte Cristo
Courage Mountain
Courage of Black Beauty
Courage of Rin Tin Tin
Crime Story
Crimebusters
Crimson Romance
Dam Busters
Dangerous Moonlight
Dangerous Passage
Daring Game
Dark Before Dawn
Dark Mountain
The Darkside
The Dawson Patrol
The Day Will Dawn
Days of Thunder
Deadlock
Deadly Sanctuary
The Death Merchant
Death Stalk
The Deceivers
Deliverance
Desert Warrior
Destination Tokyo
Dick Tracy
Dick Turpin
Die Hard
Dillinger
Diplomatic Immunity
Dive Bomber
Down to the Sea in Ships
Dragonfly Squadron
Dust
Each Dawn I Die
The Eagle Has Landed
East of Borneo
Edge of Honor
84 Charlie Mopic
The Elusive Pimpernel
The Emerald Forest
Enchanted Island
Enemy Below
The Enforcer
Escape to Witch Mountain
Evel Knievel
The Expendables
Eye of the Octopus
Fangs of the Wild

Fantastic Balloon Voyage
Fantastic Seven
A Far Off Place
Farewell to the King
Ferry to Hong Kong
55 Days at Peking
The Fighting Prince of
  Donegal
Fire Alarm
Fire in the Night
Firepower
Flame Over India
The Flash
Flight of the Grey Wolf
Flipper
Flying Leathernecks
Flying Tigers
Follow Me
Forty Thousand Horsemen
The Four Feathers
F.P. 1
F.P. 1 Doesn't Answer
Free Grass
The Fugitive
Fury to Freedom: The Life
  Story of Raul Ries
Future Zone
Game for Vultures
Gente Violenta
God's Country
Goliath Awaits
Great Adventure
The Great Escape
The Great Escape 2: The
  Untold Story
The Great Locomotive Chase
The Great Train Robbery
The Green Glove
Greystoke: The Legend of
  Tarzan, Lord of the Apes
Grizzly Mountain
Guadalcanal Diary
Gun Cargo
Gunblast
Gunga Din
The Gunrunner
The Halls of Montezuma
Hamlet
Hangfire
Hard Knocks
Hard Rain-The Tet 1968
Harley
Hawk and Castile
Hell Commandos
Hell in the Pacific
Hell River
Hell Squad
Hell to Eternity
Hellcats of the Navy
Hellfighters
Hell's Angels
Hell's Brigade: The Final
  Assault
Here Come the Littles: The
  Movie
The Heroes of Desert Storm
Heroes Three
High Country Calling
Himatsuri
Hired to Kill
Hiroshima: Out of the Ashes
Hit!
Homeward Bound: The
  Incredible Journey
Hurricane Smith
Hustler Squad
Immortal Sergeant
Imperial Navy
In Harm's Way
In Love and War
In Search of a Golden Sky
In Which We Serve
Inferno in Paradise
The Iron Mask
Island of Adventure
Island of the Blue Dolphins

Animated

Behind

Sweet Liberty
Sweet Perfection
Teenager
Tootsie
Truth or Dare
Under the Rainbow
Users
Valley of the Dolls
Velvet Touch
A Very Private Affair
The West Point Story
What Price Hollywood?
Whodunit
Zou Zou

Bicycling

American Flyers
BMX Bandits
Breaking Away
Off the Mark
Pee-Wee's Big Adventure
Quicksilver
Rad
Rush It
Ten Speed

Big Battles

The Alamo
Alexander Nevsky
Alexander the Great
Aliens
Anzio
Apocalypse Now
Arena
Back to Bataan
Barry Lyndon
Battle Beyond the Sun
Battle of Britain
The Battle of El Alamein
Battle of the Bulge
The Battle of the Japan Sea
Battle of the Worlds
Battleground
The Battleship Potemkin
Ben-Hur
The Big Parade
The Big Red One
The Birth of a Nation
A Bridge Too Far
Captain Caution
Cromwell
Cross of Iron
Das Boot
Diamonds are Forever
Dragonslayer
El Cid
The Empire Strikes Back
Enemy Below
Excalibur
The Fall of the Roman Empire
The Fighting Sullivans
Gallipoli
The Giant of Marathon
Giants of Rome
Gladiators 7
Glory
Godzilla vs. the Smog
  Monster
Goldfinger
The Guns of Navarone
Heaven & Earth
Henry V
Highlander
The King of the Kickboxers
The Last Command
The Lighthorseman
The Long Riders
The Longest Day
The Man Who Would Be King
Midway
The Mongols
Monty Python and the Holy
  Grail
Moonraker
Motel Hell

Naked Warriors
A Nightmare on Elm Street
Patton
Raiders of the Lost Ark
Ran
Rawhide
Red Dawn
Return of the Jedi
Revolution
Ring of Fire
Robot Jox
Samson and His Mighty
  Challenge
The Sand Pebbles
Sands of Iwo Jima
The Siege of Firebase Gloria
The Silk Road
Son of the Morning Star
Star Crash
Star Wars
Street Hunter
Ten Days That Shook the
  World
They Died with Their Boots
  On
Thunderball
To Hell and Back
Tora! Tora! Tora!
Twelve O'Clock High
War and Peace
The War Lord
The Wild Bunch
Zulu
Zulu Dawn

Big Budget Stinkers

The Adventurers
Alexander the Great
American Anthem
Annie
Christopher Columbus: The
  Discovery
Cleopatra
The Conqueror
The Cotton Club
Dune
Harlem Nights
Heaven's Gate
Howard the Duck
Hudson Hawk
Ishtar
Last Action Hero
Midway
Moon in the Gutter
1941
One from the Heart
Pirates
Rambo 3
Santa Claus: The Movie
The Shoes of the Fisherman
The Silver Chalice
Summer Holiday
Supergirl
Tora! Tora! Tora!
Two Minute Warning
Two of a Kind
Waterloo

Big Daddies

All the King's Men
Big Country
Cat on a Hot Tin Roof
Fire in the Night
The Great Santini
The Learning Tree
The Long, Hot Summer
Man of Evil
Other People's Money
Papa's Delicate Condition
The Paper Chase
A Piece of Pleasure
Running Mates
Shaolin Incredible Ten
Smokey Bites the Dust

Sons of Hercules in the Land
  of Darkness
Stay As You Are
Sweet Bird of Youth
This Property is Condemned
Touch of Evil
Vultures
Where the Heart Is

Big Digs

The Curse of King Tut's Tomb
Deadly Intent
The Golden Salamander
Indiana Jones and the Last
  Crusade
Indiana Jones and the Temple
  of Doom
King of the Forest Rangers
March or Die
The Mask
The Mole People
The Mummy
The Mummy's Hand
Pimpernel Smith
Search for the Gods
The Serpent of Death
Sound of Horror
Specters
Tomb
The Word

Big Ideas

Barefoot in Athens
Blaise Pascal
The Incredible Shrinking Man
Jonathan Livingston Seagull
Judgment at Nuremberg
Meetings with Remarkable
  Men
The Messiah
Metropolitan
Mr. North
My Dinner with Andre
1900
The Occult Experience
The Razor's Edge
Return to Eden
Samurai 3: Duel at Ganryu
  Island
Sans Soleil
The Seventh Seal
Sorceress
Woman in the Dunes
The Wrong Move
Zabriskie Point

Bikers

The Acid Eaters
Adventures Beyond Belief
Angels Die Hard
Angels from Hell
Angels Hard as They Come
Angels' Wild Women
Black Bikers from Hell
Born Losers
Born to Ride
Breaking Loose
Bury Me an Angel
Chopper Chicks in
  Zombietown
Chrome and Hot Leather
Chrome Hearts
Chrome Soldiers
City Limits
Club Life
Crossing the Line
Cycle Psycho
Cycle Vixens
Cyclone
Danger Zone
Danger Zone 2
Danger Zone 3: Steel Horse
  War
Dark Rider

Darktown Strutters
Deadly Reactor
Devil's Angels
Dirt Bike Kid
Dirt Gang
Easy Rider
Easy Wheels
Easyriders Video Magazine
Eat the Peach
Electra Glide in Blue
Evel Knievel
Every Which Way But Loose
Eye of the Tiger
The Final Alliance
The Glory Stompers
Go for Broke
The Great Escape
Great Ride
The Great Skycopter Rescue
Greedy Terror
Harley
Harley Davidson and the
  Marlboro Man
Hellcats
Hellriders
Hell's Angels '69
Hell's Angels Forever
Hell's Angels on Wheels
Hog Wild
Hollywood Chaos
In Your Face
The Jesus Trip
Knightriders
The Losers
Loveless
Mad Max
The Masters of Menace
Master's Revenge
Motor Psycho
Motorcycle Gang
The Naked Angels
Nam Angels
Nomad Riders
Northville Cemetery Massacre
The Only Way Home
The Outlaw Bikers - Gang
  Wars
Outlaw Riders
Peacekillers
The Pink Angels
Pray for the Wildcats
Psychomania
Punk Vacation
Race for Glory
Raising Arizona
Raw Courage
Rebel Rousers
Return of the Rebels
Riding High
Riding the Edge
Roadside Prophets
Run, Angel, Run!
Satan's Sadists
Savage Dawn
The Savage Seven
Savages from Hell
Shame
She-Devils on Wheels
The Shrieking
Sidewinder One
Silver Dream Racer
Sinner's Blood
Space Riders
Spetters
Stone Cold
Street Hawk
Streets of Fire
Survival Zone
Timerider
Timothy and the Angel
Viva Knievel
Warlords from Hell
Werewolves on Wheels
The Wild Angels
Wild Guitar
The Wild One

Wild Rebels
Wild Riders
Wild Wheels
Winners Take All

Birds

Beaks: The Movie
Bill and Coo
Birdman of Alcatraz
The Birds
Blade Master
A Breed Apart
Brewster McCloud
Cockfighter
Continental Divide
El Gallo de Oro
Foghorn Leghorn's Fractured
  Funnies
The Giant Claw
High Anxiety
Howard the Duck
Mating Season
Million Dollar Duck
Rooster: Spurs of Death!
Sesame Street Presents:
  Follow That Bird
Spirit of the Eagle
The Talking Parcel
Vulture

Bisexuality

Basic Instinct
California Suite
Dog Day Afternoon
Dona Herlinda & Her Son
Happily Ever After
Les Biches
Liquid Sky
Mary, Mary, Bloody Mary
Pleasure Unlimited
Three of Hearts
A Woman in Flames

Black Comedy

Abigail's Party
The Addams Family
The Adjuster
After Hours
Age Isn't Everything
Alice
Alice Goodbody
All Over Town
Alone in the T-Shirt Zone
The Americanization of Emily
Angels Over Broadway
The Applegates
Ariel
Army Brats
Arnold
Arrivederci, Baby!
Arsenic and Old Lace
The Assassination Bureau
Assault of the Killer Bimbos
The Atomic Kid
Baby Face Morgan
Baby Love
Bad Charleston Charlie
Bambi Meets Godzilla and
  Other Weird Cartoons
Bare Hunt
Baring It All
Barton Fink
Battle of the Bullies
Beachballs
Beat the Devil
Beauties and the Beast
Bizarre Bizarre
Bliss
Brazil
Brewster McCloud
Buddy Buddy
Buffet Froid
The Cars That Ate Paris
Catch-22

Checking Out
Choice of Weapons
The Choirboys
The Comic
Consuming Passions
The Cook, the Thief, His Wife & Her Lover
Coup de Torchon
Crimes of the Heart
The Criminal Life of Archibaldo de la Cruz
The Dark Backward
A Day in the Death of Joe Egg
Death Becomes Her
Delicatessen
Divine
Don's Party
Eat the Rich
Eating Raoul
El: This Strange Passion
Ellie
The End
Enid is Sleeping
Entertaining Mr. Sloane
Exquisite Corpses
The Exterminating Angel
Female Trouble
A Fine Madness
The Firemen's Ball
A Fish Called Wanda
Four Bags Full
The 4th Man
The Funeral
Funny, Dirty Little War
The Garden of Delights
Gas-s-s-s!
Ghost Chase
Goodbye Cruel World
Grace Quigley
The Great Madcap
Greetings
Guilty as Charged
Harold and Maude
Hawks
Heart Condition
Heathers
Hexed
Hi, Mom!
High Heels
Highway 61
Homebodies
The Honey Pot
The Hospital
The Hot Rock
How to Get Ahead in Advertising
Husbands, Wives, Money, and Murder
I Love You to Death
I Ought to Be in Pictures
Infernal Trio
Into the Night
The Killing of Sister George
Kind Hearts and Coronets
King of Comedy
King, Queen, Knave
Ladykillers
The Laserman
Life is Sweet
Little Murders
Loot...Give Me Money, Honey!
The Loved One
Lucky Stiff
Mad Dog and Glory
Man Bites Dog
Marquis
Matador
A Matter of WHO
Miracle Mile
Mixed Blood
Monsieur Verdoux
Montenegro
Mortuary Academy
Mother, Jugs and Speed
Murphy's Fault
No Problem

No Surrender
Nuts in May
O Lucky Man
The Odd Job
Oh Dad, Poor Dad (Momma's Hung You in the Closet & I'm Feeling So Sad)
Out Cold
Over Her Dead Body
Pain in the A—
Parents
Passed Away
Paul Bartel's The Secret Cinema
Penn and Teller Get Killed
The Pornographers
Private Parts
Raising Arizona
Reuben, Reuben
Riff Raff
Rubin & Ed
Salvation!
Seven Beauties
3hadey
Shakes the Clown
She-Devil
Shoot Loud, Louder, I Don't Understand!
Sinful Life
So I Married an Axe Murderer
Some Girls
Something for Everyone
Something Wild
Stars and Bars
Steagle
Sticky Fingers
The Story of Fausta
Sweet Movie
Sweet Smell of Woman
Tatie Danielle
That Obscure Object of Desire
There was a Crooked Man
Throw Momma from the Train
Tie Me Up! Tie Me Down!
To Be or Not to Be
Toto le Heros
Transylvania Twist
L'Udienza
The Unbelievable Truth
Unexplained Laughter
Vampire's Kiss
The War of the Roses
What Have I Done to Deserve This?
Where's Piccone
Where's Poppa?
Who is Killing the Great Chefs of Europe?
Wise Guys
The Witches of Eastwick
Withnail and I
Women on the Verge of a Nervous Breakdown
The Wrong Box

Black Culture

Across 110th Street
Almos' a Man
Ashes and Embers
The Autobiography of Miss Jane Pittman
Avenging Disco Godfather
Beat Street
Bebe's Kids
Beware
Bingo Long Traveling All-Stars & Motor Kings
Black Brigade
Black King
Black Like Me
Black Vampire
Blaxploitation Cartoons
Blood of Jesus
Boardinghouse Blues
Body and Soul

Bronze Buckaroo
Bush Mama
Charlotte Forten's Mission: Experiment in Freedom
Christmas Lilies of the Field
Chuck Berry: Hail! Hail! Rock 'n' Roll
Come Back, Africa
Do the Right Thing
Double Deal
A Dream for Christmas
Drums O'Voodoo
The Five Heartbeats
For Us, the Living
Gang War
The George McKenna Story
Girl from Chicago
Glory
Go Down Death
The Great White Hope
Green Pastures
Guess Who's Coming to Dinner
Half Slave, Half Free
Hallelujah!
Harlem on the Prairie
A Hero Ain't Nothin' But a Sandwich
Hollywood Shuffle
Home Feeling
House Party
House Party 2: The Pajama Jam
How U Like Me Now?
I Know Why the Caged Bird Sings
Identity Crisis
I'm Gonna Git You Sucka
Imitation of Life
In the Heat of the Night
The Jackie Robinson Story
J.D.'s Revenge
Jericho
The Jesse Owens Story
Joe Louis Story
Joe's Bed-Stuy Barbershop: We Cut Heads
Juice
Just Another Girl on the I.R.T.
Keep Punching
Killing Floor
Livin' Large
Look Out Sister
Love Your Mama
Lying Lips
Malcolm X
Mandela
Miracle in Harlem
Monkey Hustle
Moon Over Harlem
New Faces of 1952
New Jack City
Paris is Burning
Perfume
Piece of the Action
Poetic Justice
Putney Swope
The Real Malcolm X: An Intimate Portrait of the Man
The Respectful Prostitute
Return of Superfly
The River Niger
Roots
Roots: The Gift
Roots: The Next Generation
Sarafina!
Scar of Shame
Sergeant Rutledge
Shaft
Shaft's Big Score
Shanty Tramp
Sophisticated Gents
South Central
Superfly
Superfly T.N.T.
Sweet Love, Bitter

Sweet Sweetback's Baadasssss Song
Truck Turner
Uncle Tom's Cabin
Way Down South
Words by Heart
A World of Strangers
You Must Remember This
Zebrahead

Black Gold

The Abyss
Black Gold
Blowing Wild
Boom Town
Comes a Horseman
Country Gentlemen
Dead Ahead: The Exxon Valdez Disaster
Devil's Crude
The Dive
Double Deal
Fighting Texans
Five Easy Pieces
The Formula
Gas Pump Girls
Giant
The Guns and the Fury
Hellfighters
Intruder Within
Legend of Frenchie King
Local Hero
Louisiana Story
The Madwoman of Chaillot
Mission in Morocco
Naked Gun 2 1/2: The Smell of Fear
'Neath the Arizona Skies
Oceans of Fire
Oklahoma Crude
Roughnecks
Thunder Bay
Tulsa
Waltz Across Texas
War of the Wildcats
Wildcat
Written on the Wind

Blindness

Afraid of the Dark
Against the Drunken Cat Paws
Alligator Eyes
Amy
Ballad in Blue
Blackout
Blind Fear
Blind Man's Bluff
Butterflies Are Free
Cactus
Can You Feel Me Dancing?
City for Conquest
City Lights
Don't Look Now
Eight Witnesses
Eighteen Jade Arhats
Elmer
Eye on the Sparrow
The Human Monster
Ice Castles
If You Could See What I Hear
Jennifer 8
The Killer
La Symphonie Pastorale
Last Game
Life on a String
Love at First Sight
Love Leads the Way
Marianela
Minnesota Clay
The Miracle Worker
Night Gallery
Night Is My Future
Octavia
On Dangerous Ground

Ordinary Heroes
A Patch of Blue
People Who Own the Dark
Places in the Heart
Proof
Return of the Evil Dead
Scent of a Woman
See No Evil
See No Evil, Hear No Evil
Sweet Smell of Woman
To Race the Wind
Until The End of The World
Wait Until Dark
Whales of August
Zertigo Diamond Caper

Bloody Mayhem

Alien
Anguish
Army of Darkness
The Art of Dying
The Avenger
Baby Cart 4: Heart of a Parent...Heart of a Child
Bad Blood
Bad Dreams
Ballbuster
The Banker
Barn of the Naked Dead
Basket Case
Basket Case 2
Basket Case 3: The Progeny
Bay of Blood
Beast of the Yellow Night
Between God, the Devil & a Winchester
Big Meat Eater
Bits and Pieces
Black Christmas
Black Shampoo
Blade of the Ripper
Blood and Black Lace
Blood Bride
Blood Cult
Blood Diner
Blood Feast
Blood Lake
Blood Legacy
Blood Mania
Blood of Ghastly Horror
Blood Orgy of the She-Devils
Blood Screams
Blood Sisters
Blood Tide
Blood Tracks
Bloodbath in Psycho Town
Bloodshed
Bloodstalkers
Bloody Birthday
Bloody Mama
The Bloody Tattoo
Body Count
Body Parts
The Body Shop
The Borrower
The Boys Next Door
The Brainiac
The Brides of Dracula
Bring Me the Head of Alfredo Garcia
Brothers in Arms
Brujo Luna
Burial Ground
Buried Alive
Cannibal Campout
Cardiac Arrest
Carnage
Carnival of Blood
The Carpathian Eagle
Carrie
Castle of the Creeping Flesh
Cataclysm
Challenge
The Channeler
Cheerleader Camp

Bloody

Bodyguards

Boxing

Buddies

Mean Frank and Crazy Tony
The Men's Club
Midnight Cowboy
Midnight Run
The Mighty Quinn
Mikey & Nicky
The Mission
Misunderstood
Moon Over Miami
Mortal Thoughts
My Beautiful Laundrette
My Best Friend's Girl
My Dinner with Andre
My Girl
Mystic Pizza
Naked Youth
The Naughty Nineties
Night Beat
Nightforce
The Nightingale
The Odd Couple
Old Explorers
Once Upon a Time in America
One Crazy Summer
One Sings, the Other Doesn't
The Opposite Sex and How to
    Live With Them
Pals
Papillon
Peck's Bad Boy with the
    Circus
The Penitent
Perfectly Normal
The Phantom of 42nd Street
P.K. and the Kid
Platoon
Playmates
A Pleasure Doing Business
Plunder Road
Portrait of a Showgirl
Racing with the Moon
Rafferty & the Gold Dust
    Twins
Ramblin' Man
Rape
The Red Balloon
The Reivers
Reno and the Doc
Requiem for Dominic
The Return of Grey Wolf
Return of the Secaucus 7
Revenge of the Nerds
Revenge of the Nerds 2:
    Nerds in Paradise
Rich and Famous
Ride the High Country
Rio Conchos
The Road to Hong Kong
The Road to Morocco
Roadside Prophets
Robby
Robert et Robert
Rubin & Ed
Running Scared
Russkies
St. Elmo's Fire
Salut l'Artiste
Seventh Veil
Shag: The Movie
Shaking the Tree
She Gods of Shark Reef
Showdown in Little Tokyo
Silence Like Glass
Snoopy's Getting Married,
    Charlie Brown
Snow White and the Seven
    Dwarfs
So This is Washington
Something of Value
Songwriter
Sophisticated Gents
Spies Like Us
Spittin' Image
Spotlight Scandals
Stand By Me

Star Trek 4: The Voyage
    Home
Starbird and Sweet William
Stealing Home
Steaming
The Steel Helmet
Stuckey's Last Stand
Sudden Death
Summer City
Sunny Skies
The Sunshine Boys
Ten Who Dared
Tendres Cousines
Tequila Sunrise
Terminal Bliss
That Sinking Feeling
Thelma & Louise
There's No Time for Love,
    Charlie Brown
Three Amigos
Three Legionnaires
Three Men and a Baby
Three Men and a Cradle
Three Musketeers
Thunder in the Pines
Thursday's Game
To Forget Venice
Top Gun
Tough Guys
Tour of Duty
True Colors
The Turning Point
Two Weeks to Live
Ugetsu
Unholy Four
Veronico Cruz
Vincent, Francois, Paul and
    the Others
Wayne's World
We're in the Legion Now
What Price Glory?
Whatever Happened to Susan
    Jane?
Where the River Runs Black
White Christmas
White Mama
White Men Can't Jump
White Nights
Who's the Man?
Why Me?
The Wild Life
Wild Rovers
Windy City
Winners Take All
Withnail and I
The Wrong Guys
The Wrong Road
The Yakuza
You Are Not Alone
Young Guns 2

Buddy Cops

Another 48 Hrs.
Arizona Heat
City Heat
Collision Course
48 Hrs.
The Hard Way
La Chevre
Lethal Weapon
Lethal Weapon 2
Lethal Weapon 3
Liberty & Bash
National Lampoon's Loaded
    Weapon 1
Night Children
Nighthawks
The Presidio
Red Heat
Renegades
The Rookie
Shakedown
Shoot to Kill
Stakeout
Stakeout 2

Tango and Cash

Camelot

Jacqueline Bouvier Kennedy
JFK
The JFK Conspiracy
JFK Remembered
Kennedy
The Kennedys Don't Cry
Prince Jack
PT 109
Robert Kennedy and His
    Times
Ruby

Campus Capers

Accident
All-American Murder
American Tiger
Animal Behavior
Assault of the Party Nerds
Attack of the Killer
    Refrigerator
Baby Love
Bachelor of Hearts
Back to School
Beware
Beyond Dream's Door
Black Christmas
Black Tower
Blood Cult
Blood Sisters
The Campus Corpse
Campus Knights
Campus Man
Carnal Knowledge
Catch Me...If You Can
The Cheerleaders
A Chump at Oxford
Class
Class of '44
College
College Swing
Computer Beach Party
The Computer Wore Tennis
    Shoes
The Cousins
Curse of the Alpha Stone
Deadly Obsession
Deadly Possession
Death Screams
Didn't You Hear?
Doctor in the House
Dorm That Dripped Blood
Escapade in Florence
Final Exam
First Affair
First Love
First Time
Fraternity Vacation
The Freshman
Fright Night 2
Ghoulies 3: Ghoulies Go to
    College
Girl Crazy
Girls Night Out
The Gladiator
Good News
Gotcha!
Gross Anatomy
Hamburger... The Motion
    Picture
Harrad Experiment
Harrad Summer
HauntedWeen
The Heart of Dixie
Hell Night
Higher Education
Horse Feathers
H.O.T.S.
The House on Sorority Row
House Party 2: The Pajama
    Jam
How I Got into College
I Don't Buy Kisses Anymore

Incoming Freshmen
The Initiation
Initiation of Sarah
Intimate Games
Jock Petersen
The Kid with the 200 I.Q.
A Killer in Every Corner
Killer Party
Knock Outs
Let's Go Collegiate
Little Sister
Lucky Jim
Making the Grade
A Matter of Degrees
Mazes and Monsters
Midnight Madness
The Misadventures of Merlin
    Jones
Monkey's Uncle
Mortuary Academy
Mugsy's Girls
Murder on the Campus
The Naked Witch
National Lampoon's Animal
    House
Naughty Co-Eds
A Night in the Life of Jimmy
    Reardon
Night of the Creeps
Nightwish
Odd Jobs
The Paper Chase
Party Animal
Pieces
Pledge Night
Preppies
Return Engagement
Revenge of the Nerds
Revenge of the Nerds 2:
    Nerds in Paradise
Revenge of the Nerds 3: The
    Next Generation
Ring of Terror
Rona Jaffe's Mazes &
    Monsters
Roommate
Rosalie
R.P.M.* (*Revolutions Per
    Minute)
Rush Week
Scandal
Scent of a Woman
School Daze
School Spirit
Scoring
The Seniors
Shallow Grave
Silent Madness
Silent Scream
Sky High
Slipping into Darkness
A Small Circle of Friends
Sniper
Sorority Babes in the Slimeball
    Bowl-A-Rama
Sorority Girl
Sorority House Massacre
Sorority House Massacre 2:
    Nighty Nightmare
Soul Man
Spellbound
The Spirit of West Point
Splatter University
Splitz
Spring Break
Star Spangled Girl
Stitches
The Student Body
The Sure Thing
Surviving Desire
Sweet Young Thing
Swinging Sorority Girls
Tag: The Assassination Game
Talking Walls
Tall Lie
Tall Story

Teen Wolf Too
Three in the Cellar
Toga Party
Undergrads
The Unnamable
Up the Creek
The Victory
War Between the Tates
When He's Not a Stranger
The Wild Life
Witchboard
Witches' Brew
Zero for Conduct
Zis Boom Bah

Canada

Anne of Avonlea
Anne of Green Gables
The Bay Boy
Big Red
Black Robe
Blood Clan
Canadian Capers...Cartoons:
    Vol. II
The Cariboo Trail
Clearcut
Cordelia
A Cry in the Wild
Danger Ahead
The Dawson Patrol
The Deserters
Explosion
Fighting Mad
Going Home
Heaven on Earth
House of the Living Dead
The Incredible Journey
Jaws of Justice
Ladies of the Lotus
Lassie's Great Adventure
Maria Chapdelaine
Men of Steel
Murder on the Yukon
Mystery Trooper
A Name for Evil
'Neath Canadian Skies
Nomads of the North
Obsessed
Phantom Patrol
Renfrew of the Royal
    Mounted
Renfrew on the Great White
    Trail
The Return of Grey Wolf
Riel
Road to Avonlea
Rose Marie
Silent Code
Slipstream
Some Girls
Strangers in Good Company
Tales of the Klondike: In a Far
    Country
Tales of the Klondike: Race
    for Number One
Tales of the Klondike: The
    Unexpected
Termini Station
Timber Terrors
Time Lock
Trail of the Mounties
Wedding in White
Where the North Begins
Who Has Seen the Wind?
Yukon Flight

Cannibalism

Adventures of Eliza Fraser
Alien Prey
Alive
Auntie Lee's Meat Pies
Back from Eternity
Beast of the Yellow Night
Black Werewolf
Blood Clan

Chases

Star Wars
Stephen King's Golden Years
The Sting
Stray Dog
The Sugarland Express
Sweet Sweetback's
  Baadasssss Song
Tagget
Teenage Crime Wave
Tell Them Willie Boy Is Here
The Terminator
Terror of the Bloodhunters
Thelma & Louise
The Third Man
This Man Must Die
Thunder and Lightning
Thunder Road
Thunderball
Thunderbolt & Lightfoot
Time After Time
To Live and Die in Hong Kong
To Live & Die in L.A.
Tom and Jerry: The Movie
Top Gun
Trouble Bound
12 Plus 1
Until The End of The World
Valley of the Eagles
Vanishing Point
Watch the Birdie
What's Up, Doc?
White Lightning
Who Framed Roger Rabbit?
Who Killed Mary What's 'Er
  Name?
The Wilby Conspiracy
Wolfen
Year of the Comet
You Only Live Twice

Child Abuse

Blind Fools
Close to Home
Fallen Angel
Fatal Confinement
Father Hood
Hush Little Baby, Don't You
  Cry
Impulse
Johnny Belinda
Judgment
Mommie Dearest
The Offence
Psychopath
A Question of Guilt
Radio Flyer
Raising Cain
Short Eyes
South Bronx Heroes
The Stolen Children
This Boy's Life
Where the Spirit Lives
Who Killed Baby Azaria?
Wildflower

Childhood Visions

Afraid of the Dark
All I Want for Christmas
Alsino and the Condor
And Now Miguel
Army Brats
Au Revoir Les Enfants
Beethoven Lives Upstairs
The Beniker Gang
Big
The Black Stallion
Born to Run
But Where Is Daniel Wax?
Cameron's Closet
Captain January
Careful, He Might Hear You
Casey's Shadow
The Cat
The Cellar
Chapter in Her Life

Child in the Night
The Children Are Watching Us
Children of Divorce
Child's Play
Chocolat
A Christmas Story
Cinema Paradiso
Cria
David Copperfield
Days of Heaven
Demons in the Garden
Desert Bloom
Deutschland im Jahre Null
Diva
Emma's Shadow
Empire of the Sun
Escapade
E.T.: The Extra-Terrestrial
The Fallen Idol
Fanny and Alexander
Far Away and Long Ago
Father
The Flame Trees of Thika
Flight of the Grey Wolf
Forbidden Games
Girl from Hunan
A Girl of the Limberlost
The Golden Seal
Grazuole
Home Alone
Home for Christmas
Hook
Hope and Glory
Hue and Cry
Invaders from Mars
Josh and S.A.M.
Journey for Margaret
The Kid from Left Field
The Kid with the Broken Halo
King of the Hill
The Kitchen Toto
The Lady in White
Lassie's Great Adventure
Last Action Hero
Le Grand Chemin
Les Violons du Bal
Lies My Father Told Me
Little Man Tate
Little Monsters
The Little Princess
The Littlest Horse Thieves
The Long Days of Summer
Lord of the Flies
Lost in Yonkers
Louisiana Story
Love Film
Magic of Lassie
The Mirror
Misty
Mosby's Marauders
My Childhood
My Friend Flicka
My Life as a Dog
My Mother's Castle
My Name is Ivan
National Velvet
New York Stories
Night of the Shooting Stars
Old Swimmin' Hole
An Orphan Boy of Vienna
Orphans
Our Gang
Parents
Peck's Bad Boy
Pelle the Conqueror
Pixote
Poltergeist
Poltergeist 2: The Other Side
A Poor Little Rich Girl
The Poor Little Rich Girl
Psycho 4: The Beginning
Radio Flyer
Railway Children
Real Genius
The Red Balloon
The Reflecting Skin

Return from Witch Mountain
Rock-a-Doodle
Roll of Thunder, Hear My Cry
Salaam Bombay!
Savage Sam
The Secret Garden
Shadow World
Sidekicks
The Silence of the Lambs
Small Change
Sounds of Silence
Spirit of the Beehive
Square Shoulders
Stealing Home
Sudden Terror
Sudie & Simpson
A Summer to Remember
Sunday Daughters
Taking Care of Terrific
Taps
The Tin Drum
To Kill a Mockingbird
Toto le Heros
Train to Hollywood
Treasure Island
Turf Boy
Unicorn
Voltus 5
Wait Until Spring, Bandini
The War Boy
When Father was Away on
  Business
Whistle Down the Wind
White Fang
The Wild Country
The Wizard of Loneliness
Wombling Free
A World Apart
The Yearling
Yes, Sir, Mr. Bones
Zazie dans le Metro
Zero for Conduct

China

Adventures of Smilin' Jack
Battle of China
Bethune
Beyond the Next Mountain
Bloody Fist
Bolo
China Cry
Chinese Gods
Dragon Seed
Eat a Bowl of Tea
Empire of the Sun
Fight to the Death
A Fist Full of Talons
The General Died at Dawn
Girl from Hunan
The Good Earth
A Great Wall
The Horse Thief
The Inn of the Sixth
  Happiness
Iron & Silk
Ju Dou
Kashmiri Run
The Keys of the Kingdom
The Killer
Lai Shi: China's Last Eunuch
The Last Emperor
The Leatherneck
The Mountain Road
Princess Yang Kwei Fei
Raiders of the Buddhist Kung
  Fu
Raise the Red Lantern
The Rebellious Reign
Red-Dragon
Red Sorghum
The Reincarnation of Golden
  Lotus
The Sand Pebbles
Seven Indignant
Sewing Woman

Shadows of the Orient
Shadows Over Shanghai
The Shaolin Invincibles
The Silk Road
Single Fighter
Soldier of Fortune
Tai-Pan
The Tongfather
The World of Suzie Wong

Christmas

ABC Stage 67: Truman
  Capote's A Christmas
  Memory
All I Want for Christmas
An American Christmas Carol
Babes in Toyland
Benji's Very Own Christmas
  Story
Bernard and the Genie
The Best Christmas Pageant
  Ever
The Bishop's Wife
Black Christmas
Bloodbeat
Bugs Bunny's Looney
  Christmas Tales
A Charlie Brown Christmas
Children's Carol
Child's Christmas in Wales
A Christmas Carol
The Christmas Coal Mine
  Miracle
Christmas Comes to Willow
  Creek
A Christmas Gift
Christmas in Connecticut
Christmas Lilies of the Field
The Christmas Messenger
Christmas Raccoons
A Christmas Story
The Christmas That Almost
  Wasn't
A Christmas to Remember
The Christmas Wife
A Christmas Without Snow
A Disney Christmas Gift
Don't Open Till Christmas
Dorm That Dripped Blood
Elves
Ernest Saves Christmas
A Family Circus Christmas
The Fat Albert Christmas
  Special
The First Christmas
Frosty the Snowman
The Gathering
The Gathering: Part 2
George and the Christmas
  Star
The Gift of Love
Gremlins
Here Comes Santa Claus
Hobo's Christmas
Holiday Affair
Holiday Inn
Home Alone
Home Alone 2: Lost in New
  York
Home for Christmas
Homecoming: A Christmas
  Story
A House without a Christmas
  Tree
How the Grinch Stole
  Christmas
It Came Upon a Midnight
  Clear
It's a Bundyful Life
It's a Wonderful Life
A Jetson Christmas Carol
The Kid Who Loved Christmas
La Pastorela
The Life and Adventures of
  Santa Claus

The Lion in Winter
The Little Drummer Boy
The Little Match Girl
Little Rascals Christmas
  Special
The Man in the Santa Claus
  Suit
March of the Wooden Soldiers
A Matter of Principle
Merry Christmas to You
Mickey's Christmas Carol
Miracle Down Under
Miracle in the Wilderness
Miracle on 34th Street
Mr. Corbett's Ghost
Mr. Magoo's Christmas Carol
The Muppet Christmas Carol
National Lampoon's
  Christmas Vacation
Nativity
The Night They Saved
  Christmas
Nutcracker, A Fantasy on Ice
The Nutcracker Prince
Nutcracker: The Motion
  Picture
One Magic Christmas
Pee-Wee's Playhouse
  Christmas Special
Prancer
Railway Children
Roots: The Gift
Rudolph & Frosty's Christmas
  in July
Rudolph the Red-Nosed
  Reindeer
Rudolph's Shiny New Year
Santa Claus
Santa Claus Conquers the
  Martians
Santa Claus is Coming to
  Town
Santa Claus: The Movie
Scrooge
Scrooged
Silent Night, Deadly Night
Silent Night, Deadly Night 2
Silent Night, Deadly Night 3:
  Better Watch Out!
Silent Night, Deadly Night 5:
  The Toymaker
Silent Night, Lonely Night
The Simpsons Christmas
  Special
A Smoky Mountain Christmas
Stingiest Man in Town
Susan Slept Here
Terror in Toyland
Thirteenth Day of Christmas
Three Godfathers
A Time to Remember
To All a Goodnight
Trail of Robin Hood
A Very Brady Christmas
A Very Merry Cricket
The Waltons: The Children's
  Carol
White Christmas
Who Slew Auntie Roo?
Yogi's First Christmas

City Lights

Abbott and Costello in
  Hollywood
Across 110th Street
Adventures in Babysitting
The Adversary
After Hours
Against All Odds
All the Lovin' Kinfolk
All the Vermeers in New York
Alone in the Neon Jungle
Assault on Precinct 13
Berlin Alexanderplatz
Beverly Hills Cop

Classic

Cold Spots

Comedy

Comedy

1941
Ninja Academy
Nobody's Perfect
Nobody's Perfekt
The Norman Conquests, Part 3: Round and Round the Garden
Norman Loves Rose
Norman's Awesome Experience
Now You See Him, Now You Don't
Nudity Required
Nudo di Donna
Nutcase
O.C. and Stiggs
Ocean Drive Weekend
Ocean's 11
The Odd Couple
The Odd Squad
Oddballs
Off the Mark
Oh, God!
Oh, God! Book 2
Oh, God! You Devil
Oh, Heavenly Dog!
Oh, Mr. Porter
Oklahoma Bound
Old Enough
Old Spanish Custom
Oldest Profession
On the Air Live with Captain Midnight
On the Right Track
On Top of the Whale
Once Upon a Crime
Once Upon a Honeymoon
Once Upon a Scoundrel
The One and Only
One Body Too Many
One Cooks, the Other Doesn't
One Crazy Summer
One More Saturday Night
One of Our Dinosaurs Is Missing
One-Punch O'Day
One Wish Too Many
Only Two Can Play
Open All Hours
Operation Dames
Operation Petticoat
Opportunity Knocks
Options
Our Gang
Our Gang Comedies
Our Gang Comedy Festival
Our Gang Comedy Festival 2
Our Hospitality
The Out-of-Towners
Out on a Limb
Outtakes
Packin' It In
Pals
Panic Button
Papa's Delicate Condition
Paper Lion
Paper Moon
Para Servir a Usted
Parade
Paradise Motel
Paradisio
Pardon Mon Affaire, Too!
The Parent Trap
Parlor, Bedroom and Bath
Party Animal
Party Camp
Party Favors
Party Incorporated
Party! Party!
Party Plane
Passionate Thief
Passport to Pimlico
Paternity
Paths to Paradise
Pauline at the Beach
Peck's Bad Boy

Peck's Bad Boy with the Circus
The Pee-Wee Herman Show
Pee-Wee's Big Adventure
Pee-Wee's Playhouse Christmas Special
Pee-Wee's Playhouse Festival of Fun
People Are Funny
People's Choice
Pepper and His Wacky Taxi
Personal Exemptions
Petit Con
Phantom Empire
Pick-Up Summer
The Pickwick Papers
Piece of the Action
The Pinchcliffe Grand Prix
The Pink Angels
Pink Motel
Plain Clothes
Planes, Trains & Automobiles
Playing Away
Playing for Keeps
Playing the Field
Playmates
Plaza Suite
Please Don't Eat My Mother
Please Don't Eat the Daisies
A Pleasure Doing Business
Pleasure Resort
The Plot Against Harry
Poison Ivy
Poker Alice
A Polish Vampire in Burbank
Pom Pom Girls
Pop Goes the Cork
The Pope Must Diet
Popeye Assorted Cartoons
Porky's
Porky's 2: The Next Day
Porky's Revenge
Porridge
Portrait of a White Marriage
Pot O' Gold
Pouvoir Intime
Prep School
Preppies
Pretty Smart
The Primitive Lover
Prince of Pennsylvania
Princess Academy
Private Affairs
The Private Eyes
Private Lessons
Private Popsicle
Private School
The Private Secretary
Prize Fighter
The Projectionist
The Promoter
Property
Prurient Interest
The Pure Hell of St. Trinian's
Pure Luck
Purlie Victorious
Pyrates
Queen for a Day
Rabbit Test
Race for Your Life, Charlie Brown
Radio Days
Rascal Dazzle
Ratings Game
Ravishing Idiot
Real Genius
Real Life
Really Weird Tales
Rebel High
Reg'lar Fellers
Remote
Rendez-Moi Ma Peau
Rented Lips
Repo Man
Return of Our Gang

Return of the Tall Blond Man With One Black Shoe
Return to Mayberry
Revenge of the Cheerleaders
Revenge of the Nerds
Revenge of the Nerds 2: Nerds in Paradise
Revenge of the Nerds 3: The Next Generation
Revenge of the Teenage Vixens from Outer Space
Rhinestone
Rich Hall's Vanishing America
Riders of the Storm
Riding on Air
Rikky and Pete
Rink/Immigrant
Ripping Yarns
Risky Business
Rita, Sue & Bob Too
Road Lawyers and Other Briefs
Road Show
Rock & the Money-Hungry Party Girls
Rockula
Roller Boogie
Rookie of the Year
Rosebud Beach Hotel
Rosencrantz & Guildenstern Are Dead
Ruddigore
The Ruggles of Red Gap
Run Virgin Run
The Runaway Bus
The Running Kind
The Russians are Coming, the Russians are Coming
Ryder P.I.
Sailor-Made Man/Grandma's Boy
St. Benny the Dip
Sally of the Sawdust
Salut l'Artiste
Samantha
Sammy, the Way-Out Seal
The Sandlot
Santa Claus Conquers the Martians
The Saphead
Sawmill/The Dome Doctor
Say Yes!
Scandalous
Scared Stiff
Scavenger Hunt
School Daze
School for Sex
Screwball Academy
Screwball Hotel
Second Sight
The Secret Life of Walter Mitty
The Secret War of Harry Frigg
Senior Trip
The Seniors
Sensations
Sensuous Caterer
Seven Chances
Sex and Buttered Popcorn
Sex and the Other Woman
Sex Appeal
Sex on the Brain
Sex on the Run
Sex Ray
Sexpot
Shadow of the Thin Man
The Shaggy D.A.
The Shaggy Dog
Shake Hands with Murder
She Couldn't Say No
The Sheep Has Five Legs
She's Out of Control
Shooting Elizabeth
Short Circuit 2
Side By Side
Silver Bears

Simple Men
The Sin of Harold Diddlebock
Singleton's Pluck
Sinners
Sister Act
Sitting Ducks
Skinner's Dress Suit
Skyline
The Slap
The Sleazy Uncle
Sleepaway Camp 2: Unhappy Campers
A Slightly Pregnant Man
Slumber Party '57
Small Change
Small Hotel
Smart Money
Snapshot
Snowball Express
Snowballing
Snuffy Smith, Yard Bird
So Fine
So This is Washington
Social Error
Soggy Bottom U.S.A.
Son-in-Law
Sorority House Scandals
Sorrowful Jones
Sotto, Sotto
Speak Easily
Splitting Heirs
Splitz
Squeeze Play
Story of William S. Hart/Sad Clowns
Strike It Rich
Summer Rental
Summer School
Summer Switch
The Super
Super Seal
The Sure Thing
Surf 2
Susan Slept Here
Swedish Wildcats
Sweet Liberty
Swimming to Cambodia
Swimsuit: The Movie
Swindle
A Swingin' Summer
Switch
Sylvia and the Phantom
Tabloid!
Takin' It Off
Taking Care of Business
Talkin' Dirty After Dark
Tall Story
Tampopo
Tax Season
Teen Wolf
Teen Wolf Too
The Telephone
That Gang of Mine
That Man Is Pregnant
That's Entertainment, Part 2
There Goes the Neighborhood
These Girls Won't Talk
Things Happen at Night
Think Dirty
Three Men on a Horse
Three Nuts in Search of a Bolt
Three O'Clock High
Three's Trouble
The Thrill of It All!
Tonight for Sure
Too Much Sun
Topper
Topper Returns
Topper Takes a Trip
The Toy
Trading Places
Troop Beverly Hills
The Trouble with Angels
True Identity
The Tunnel of Love
The Tuttles of Tahiti

Twelve Chairs
Twentieth Century
200 Motels
2000 Year Old Man
Two Top Bananas
The Ugly Dachshund
Uncle Buck
Under the Doctor
Undercover Blues
Undergrads
Unfaithfully Yours
Unidentified Flying Oddball
Used Cars
Varieties on Parade
Vasectomy: A Delicate Matter
A Very Brady Christmas
Victorian Fantasies
Video Vixens
Virgin High
Virgins of Purity House
Visitants
Viva Chihuahua (Long Live Chihuahua)
Voice of Hollywood
Volere Volare
Volunteers
The Wacky World of Wills & Burke
Water
A Wedding
Wedding Band
Wedding Rehearsal
Weekend Warriors
Weekend with the Babysitter
Weird Science
Welcome to 18
We're in the Legion Now
We're Talkin' Serious Money
What About Bob?
What Did You Do in the War, Daddy?
What Do You Say to a Naked Lady?
What's Up Front
The Wheeler Dealers
When Knights were Bold
When's Your Birthday?
Where's Willie?
Whiffs
Whiskey Galore
Whistling in Brooklyn
Whistling in the Dark
Who Framed Roger Rabbit?
Wholly Moses!
Who's Got the Action?
Who's Harry Crumb?
Who's Minding the Mint?
Who's the Man?
The Wild Life
Win, Place, or Steal
Women's Club
Working Winnie/Oh So Simple
The Wrong Guys
Y Donde Esta el Muerto? (And... Where Is the Dead)
You Can't Hurry Love
You Talkin' to Me?
Young Einstein
Young Love—Lemon Popsicle 7
Zazie dans le Metro
Zebra in the Kitchen
Zero to Sixty

Comedy Drama

Alice Doesn't Live Here Anymore
Alice's Restaurant
All I Want for Christmas
All My Good Countrymen
All Screwed Up
An Almost Perfect Affair
Aloha Summer
Always
Amarcord

Comedy

Only One Night
Only When I Laugh
Orphans
Other People's Money
Our Little Girl
Out
Outrageous!
Outside Chance of Maximillian Glick
Over the Brooklyn Bridge
Paddy
Palm Springs Weekend
Palooka
The Paper Chase
Parenthood
Patti Rocks
Perfect Timing
Perfumed Nightmare
Period of Adjustment
Pete 'n' Tillie
Peter's Friends
The Philadelphia Story
Ping Pong
Pink Cadillac
Pink Nights
P.K. and the Kid
Playboy of the Western World
Pocketful of Miracles
The Pointsman
Pollyanna
Popi
Portnoy's Complaint
Postcards from the Edge
Power
Powwow Highway
Preacherman
Pretty in Pink
Pride of the Bowery
The Prime of Miss Jean Brodie
Primrose Path
The Princess & the Call Girl
Prisoner of Second Avenue
Prisoners of Inertia
The Private History of a Campaign That Failed
Prizzi's Honor
Problem Child
Promised Land
Psychedelic Fever
Punchline
Purple People Eater
Quarterback Princess
Queen of Hearts
The Rachel Papers
Racquet
Rafferty & the Gold Dust Twins
Rags to Riches
The Rascals
Ratboy
The Red Light Sting
Remedy for Riches
Reno and the Doc
Return of the Secaucus 7
Rich and Famous
Ride the Wild Surf
Robert et Robert
Rocket Gibraltar
The Rocking Horse Winner
Romance of a Horsethief
Roommate
The Rules of the Game
The Runnin' Kind
Sadie McKee
Saving Grace
Say Anything
Scenes from a Mall
Scoumoune
Second Thoughts
Secrets of Women
Seduced and Abandoned
The Seducer
The Seven Percent Solution
Seven Thieves
Shadows and Fog

Shag: The Movie
Shirley Valentine
A Shock to the System
Shooters
Side Out
Signs of Life
Simon, King of the Witches
Single Bars, Single Women
Six Weeks
Sizzle Beach U.S.A.
Skin Game
Slap Shot
Slaves of New York
Slightly Honorable
The Slugger's Wife
Smart Alecks
Smugglers' Cove
Snoopy, Come Home
Soldier in the Rain
Some Kind of Hero
Some Kind of Wonderful
Something in Common
Something Special
Song of the Thin Man
Soul Man
Spike of Bensonhurst
Spitfire
Splash
Spook Busters
The Sprinter (Der Sprinter)
Stage Door
Star of Midnight
Star Spangled Girl
Stardust Memories
Starlight Hotel
Starting Over
Staying Together
Steamboat Bill, Jr.
Stoogemania
Storm in a Teacup
The Story of Seabiscuit
Stranger than Paradise
Strawberry Blonde
Street Music
Strong Man
Stroszek
Stuck on You
Student Confidential
Sugarbaby
The Sugarland Express
Summer Dog
Summer Fantasy
The Sunshine Boys
Suppose They Gave a War and Nobody Came?
Swedenhielms
Sweet Adeline
Sweet Hearts Dance
Sweet Lorraine
Sweet William
Sweetie
Swept Away...
Swing Shift
Sylvia Scarlett
T Bone N Weasel
Table Settings
Take Down
Take This Job & Shove It
Take Your Best Shot
A Tale of Springtime
Talking Walls
Taxi Blues
A Taxing Woman
Teachers
Teacher's Pet
Teddy at the Throttle
Teddy at the Throttle/ Speeding Along
10
Teresa Venerdi
Texasville
That's Life!
That's My Baby!
They Might Be Giants
The Thin Man Goes Home
Things Change

This is My Life
Those Lips, Those Eyes
A Thousand Clowns
Three for the Road
Three in the Attic
Three Men and a Baby
Three Men and a Cradle
Three Men and a Little Lady
Thunder in the City
Thursday's Child
Thursday's Game
A Tiger's Tale
The Time of Your Life
Timepiece
Tin Men
The Tip-Off
To Sleep with Anger
Toby Tyler
Tom Brown's School Days
Tom Sawyer
Tony Draws a Horse
Too Pretty to Be Honest
Tootsie
Topaze
Torch Song Trilogy
Toys
Trading Hearts
The Tragedy of a Ridiculous Man
Train to Hollywood
Travels with My Aunt
Trouble Along the Way
Trouble in the Glen
True Love
Truly, Madly, Deeply
Trust
Truth About Women
Tunes of Glory/Horse's Mouth
Turk 182!
Turkish Delights
Twelfth Night
Twenty-One
29th Street
Twister
Two for the Road
Two for the Seesaw
Ugetsu
Under the Biltmore Clock
Under the Boardwalk
An Unfinished Piece for a Player Piano
Up the Down Staircase
Up the Sandbox
Used People
The Vals
Very Close Quarters
The Virgin Soldiers
Volpone
Wait Until Spring, Bandini
Walls of Glass
We Think the World of You
Weekend at the Waldorf
Welcome Home, Roxy Carmichael
We're No Angels
Whatever Happened to Susan Jane?
When Your Lover Leaves
Where the Heart Is
Whitcomb's War
The Whole Shootin' Match
Whose Life Is It Anyway?
Wild in the Streets
Willie & Phil
Wings of Eagles
Winter Kills
Wired
Wise Blood
Wish You Were Here
The Wizard
The Women
The World According to Garp
World of Henry Orient
Woza Albert!
WR: Mysteries of the Organism

The Wrong Arm of the Law
A Yank in Australia
A Year in Provence
The Year My Voice Broke
Yesterday, Today and Tomorrow
You Are Not Alone
The Young in Heart
You're a Big Boy Now
A Zed & Two Noughts

Comedy Performance

American Fabulous
Benny Hill's Crazy World
The Best of Abbott & Costello Live
Best of Comic Relief
Best of Comic Relief '90
The Best of the Kids in the Hall
Bill Cosby, Himself
Bill Murray Live from the Second City
Billy Crystal: A Comic's Line
Billy Crystal: Midnight Train to Moscow
Bloodhounds of Broadway
Clark & McCullough
Eddie Murphy "Delirious"
Eddie Murphy: Raw
An Evening with Robin Williams
Gross Jokes
Hollywood Goes to War
Jo Jo Dancer, Your Life is Calling
Joe Piscopo: New Jersey Special
John Cleese on How to Irritate People
Lenny
Lenny Bruce Performance Film
Mr. Mike's Mondo Video
Monster in a Box
Monty Python Live at the Hollywood Bowl
Monty Python Meets Beyond the Fringe
National Lampoon's Class of '86
Punchline
Rap Master Ronnie
Richard Pryor: Here and Now
Richard Pryor: Live and Smokin'
Richard Pryor: Live in Concert
Richard Pryor: Live on the Sunset Strip
Scrambled Feet
Second City Insanity
The Secret Policeman's Other Ball
Secret Policeman's Private Parts
A Session with the Committee
Spalding Gray: Terrors of Pleasure
Steve Martin Live
Without You I'm Nothing
You Can't Take It with You

Comic Adventure

The Absent-Minded Professor
Adventures Beyond Belief
Adventures in Babysitting
Adventures in Spying
Adventures of a Private Eye
Adventures of a Taxi Driver
The Adventures of Bullwhip Griffin
Air America
Alien from L.A.

All the Lovin' Kinfolk
All the Way, Boys
The Amazing Dobermans
The Ambushers
Amenaza Nuclear
The Americano
Andy and the Airwave Rangers
Angel of H.E.A.T.
Angels Hard as They Come
Another 48 Hrs.
Avenging Disco Godfather
Baby on Board
Back Roads
Back to the Future
Back to the Future, Part 2
Back to the Future, Part 3
Bad Guys
Bagdad Cafe
The Balloonatic/One Week
The Baltimore Bullet
Bananas Boat
Behind the Front
Beverly Hills Cop
Beverly Hills Cop 2
The Big Slice
Big Zapper
Bingo
Bird on a Wire
Bloodstone
Blue Iguana
Body Trouble
Boris and Natasha: The Movie
Brink's Job
Bronx Cheers
Brothers O'Toole
Burglar
Bus Station
Butler's Dilemma
California Straight Ahead
Campus Knights
Cannibal Women in the Avocado Jungle of Death
Cannonball Run
Cannonball Run II
The Captain from Koepenick
Captain Swagger
Cartoon Collection, No. 3: Coal Black & de Sebben Dwarfs
Cartouche
Chan is Missing
Chu Chu & the Philly Flash
City Heat
Club Med
Collision Course
Crocodile Dundee
Crocodile Dundee 2
Dirt Bike Kid
Doctor Detroit
Dog Pound Shuffle
Dolemite 2: Human Tornado
The Double O Kid
Down to Earth
El Profesor Hippie
Every Girl Should Have One
Explosion
Fast Getaway
Feds
The Fifth Musketeer
Fifty Fifty
The Fighting American
Filthy Harry
Flatfoot
Flirting with Fate
Flush It
Forever Young
48 Hrs.
Foul Play
Free Ride
The Further Adventures of Tennessee Buck
Ghostbusters
Ghostbusters 2
Go for It
The Golden Child

The Gumshoe Kid
Hambone & Hillie
Having Wonderful Time/
    Carnival Boat
Hawthorne of the USA
Here We Go Again!
High Road to China
High Voltage
Highpoint
Hudson Hawk
Ice Pirates
In Like Flint
In 'n Out
It's in the Bag
Jake Speed
Jane & the Lost City
The Jewel of the Nile
Just Tell Me You Love Me
Kindergarten Cop
King Kung Fu
Kiss My Grits
Kuffs
La Petite Bande
Landlord Blues
Last Action Hero
Leonard Part 6
Lucky Devil
Lunch Wagon
Lust in the Dust
Mad About Money
Mademoiselle Striptease
Madigan's Millions
A Man Called Sarge
The Man in the Raincoat
The Man Who Wasn't There
The Man with One Red Shoe
Master Mind
The Masters of Menace
Memoirs of an Invisible Man
Massalina, Empress of Rome
Miami Supercops
Midnight Madness
Midnight Run
Miracles
Mr. Billion
Mr. Nanny
Mr. Robinson Crusoe
Mr. Superinvisible
Mitchell
Mo' Money
Mob Story
Mom and Dad Save the World
The Money
Monkey Hustle
Monkey's Uncle
Mutants In Paradise
My African Adventure
My Breakfast with Blassie
My Dog, the Thief
My Science Project
The Naked Sword of Zorro
Ninja Dragons
No Deposit, No Return
Oddball Hall
Odds and Evens
Our Man Flint
Over the Hill
Pippi Goes on Board
Pippi in the South Seas
Pippi Longstocking
Pippi on the Run
Pirates
Prehysteria
The Prince of Thieves
Ramblin' Man
Red Lion
Reggie Mixes In
The Reivers
Return of the Rebels
Riff-Raff
Romancing the Stone
Round Trip to Heaven
Running Scared
Russkies
Seven

Sherlock's Rivals & Where's
    My Wife
She's Back
Short Time
Shredder Orpheus
The Silver Streak
Ski Patrol
Sky High
Slither
Smokey and the Bandit
Smokey and the Bandit, Part
    2
Smokey and the Bandit, Part
    3
Smokey & the Judge
Smokey Bites the Dust
Spaghetti House
Special Delivery
Speed Zone
Speedy
Spies, Lies and Naked Thighs
Spy Trap
Spy with a Cold Nose
S*P*Y*S
The Squeeze
Stakeout
Stakeout 2
Stand-In
Star Trek 4: The Voyage
    Home
Steelyard Blues
Stepmonster
The Stick-Up
The Sting 2
Stingray
Stop! or My Mom Will Shoot
Stop That Cab
Stuntwoman
Suburban Commando
Suffering Bastards
The Suitors
Summer Night
Summer Night with Greek
    Profile, Almond Eyes &
    Scent of Basil
Sunburn
Super Fuzz
Super Kung Fu Kid
Super Soul Brother
Surf Nazis Must Die
Survivors
Swashbuckler
The Tall Blond Man with One
    Black Shoe
Tall, Tan and Terrific
A Taxing Woman Returns
Teenage Mutant Ninja Turtles:
    The Movie
Teenage Mutant Ninja Turtles
    2: The Secret of the Ooze
Teenage Mutant Ninja Turtles
    3
Terminal Exposure
That Sinking Feeling
That's My Hero!
The Thief Who Came to
    Dinner
Think Big
This Time I'll Make You Rich
Those Daring Young Men in
    Their Jaunty Jalopies
Those Fantastic Flying Fools
Those Magnificent Men in
    Their Flying Machines
Three Amigos
Three Fugitives
Three Kinds of Heat
Three Musketeers
3 Ninjas
Thunder and Lightning
Thunder in the Pines
Title Shot
Toga Party
Too Hot to Handle
Topkapi
Tough Guys

Treasure of the Moon
    Goddess
Trenchcoat
TripleCross
Trouble in Store
The Trouble with Spies
12 Plus 1
Twins
Under the Rainbow
Up the Creek
Uphill All the Way
Uptown Saturday Night
Van Nuys Blvd.
Vice Academy.
Vice Academy 2
Vice Academy 3
The Victim
Wackiest Ship in the Army
We're No Angels
When the Clouds Roll By
Who Killed Mary What's 'Er
    Name?
The Wild and the Free
World Gone Wild
Wrong is Right
Year of the Comet
The Yum-Yum Girls

Coming of Age

The Abe Lincoln of Ninth
    Avenue
Across the Great Divide
The Affairs of Annabel
Ah, Wilderness!
Alan & Naomi
All Fall Down
All the Right Moves
Aloha Summer
Alpine Fire
Amarcord
American Boyfriends
American Graffiti
An American Summer
Among the Cinders
Angele
Angelo My Love
Anne of Green Gables
Anthony Adverse
Aparajito
The Apprenticeship of Duddy
    Kravitz
Au Revoir Les Enfants
Baby It's You
Back Door to Heaven
Battling Bunyon
Big
The Big Bet
The Big Red One
Billy Bathgate
Billyboy
The Birch Interval
Blue Fin
Blue Jeans
The Blue Lagoon
Blue Velvet
Boss' Son
The Boys in Company C
Breaking Away
Breaking Home Ties
Brighton Beach Memoirs
Buddy's Song
Calendar Girl
Can You Feel Me Dancing?
Can't Buy Me Love
Carnal Knowledge
The Chicken Chronicles
Civil War Diary
Class
Class of '44
Closely Watched Trains
Cocktail
Cold Sassy Tree
The Color of Money
Come and See
Courage Mountain

Courtship
Crazy Moon
Cria
The Crossing
Crossing the Bridge
A Cry in the Wild
Cry of Battle
Culpepper Cattle Co.
Dakota
Dead Poets Society
December
The Deer Hunter
Desert Bloom
The Devil's Playground
Diner
Dirty Dancing
Dogfight
Dragstrip Girl
Dutch Girls
Edward Scissorhands
Emanon
Ernesto
Experience Preferred... But
    Not Essential
The Eyes of Youth
Eyes Right!
Family Prayers
Fandango
Fast Times at Ridgemont High
Father
Feelin' Screwy
Felicity
Fellini Satyricon
The Fire in the Stone
First Affair
First Love
The First Time
The Flamingo Kid
For Love Alone
Forever
Forever Young
The 400 Blows
Foxes
Freedom is Paradise
Friends Forever
Frogs!
Gas Food Lodging
A Generation
The Getting of Wisdom
Gidget
A Girl of the Limberlost
Goin' All the Way
The Gold & Glory
Goodbye Columbus
Goodbye, My Lady
The Graduate
The Great Santini
Gregory's Girl
Hairspray
Hangin' with the Homeboys
Happy Birthday, Gemini
Hard Choices
Heathers
Heaven Help Us
A Hero Ain't Nothin' But a
    Sandwich
Higher Education
Homeboy
Homework
The Horse
Horsemen
Hot Moves
Hour of the Star
How I Learned to Love
    Women
The Human Comedy
I Know Why the Caged Bird
    Sings
I Vitelloni
If Looks Could Kill
Il Sorpasso
In Praise of Older Women
In the Custody of Strangers
Indian Paint
Inga
The Inheritors

The Islander
Jacob Have I Loved
Joey
Johnny Be Good
Jory
The Journey of Natty Gann
Junior High School
The Karate Kid
The Karate Kid: Part 2
The Karate Kid: Part 3
King of the Gypsies
Kings Row
Kipperbang
The Kitchen Toto
La Boum
La Symphonie Pastorale
Labyrinth
The Last Prostitute
Late Summer Blues
The Lawrenceville Stories
Le Grand Chemin
The Learning Tree
Les Mistons
L'Homme Blesse
Little Ballerina
Little Lips
A Little Romance
Little Women
The Lords of Flatbush
Lost Legacy: A Girl Called
    Hatter Fox
Love Film
Lucas
Maid to Order
The Man from Snowy River
The Man in the Moon
A Man of Passion
The Mango Tree
Matinee
Mean Streets
The Member of the Wedding
Men of Ireland
Mickey
A Midnight Clear
Mirrors
Mischief
Monika
More American Graffiti
Mosby's Marauders
Murmur of the Heart
My American Cousin
My Apprenticeship
My Bodyguard
My Brilliant Career
My Girl
My Life as a Dog
My Tutor
My Universities
Mystic Pizza
Next Stop, Greenwich Village
Nicholas Nickleby
A Night in the Life of Jimmy
    Reardon
1969
No Regrets for Our Youth
No Secrets
No Time for Sergeants
Norman Loves Rose
A Nos Amours
Oddballs
Ode to Billy Joe
Oh, What a Night
Old Enough
One on One
Out of the Blue
The Outsiders
Over the Edge
Over the Summer
Palm Beach
The Paper Chase
Paradise
The Passing of Evil
Pather Panchali
Pauline at the Beach
Peck's Bad Boy

Coming

Crime

Cults

Dance Fever

Deafness

Death & the Afterlife

Detectives

Doctors

Men of Ireland
Mr. North
Monty Python's The Meaning of Life
Murder in Texas
Murder Once Removed
Murder or Mercy
My Father's Nurse
Night Call Nurses
Night Nurse
Nightbreaker
Nomads
Not as a Stranger
Nurse
Nurse Edith Cavell
Nurse on Call
Old Swimmin' Hole
One Flew Over the Cuckoo's Nest
The Ordeal of Dr. Mudd
Panic in Echo Park
Panic in the Streets
Paper Mask
Persona
Petulia
Praying Mantis
Private Duty Nurses
Promises in the Dark
Purple Hearts
The Raven
Reckless Disregard
Red Beard
Riot Squad
Say Goodbye, Maggie Cole
Scalpel
Sister Dora
Sister Kenny
Skeezer
Slaughter Hotel
Stigma
Stitches
The Student Nurses
Teenage Frankenstein
Tender Loving Care
Torture Ship
Tundra
The Unbearable Lightness of Being
Under the Sheets
The Vicious Circle
Vital Signs
We are the Children
Women of Valor
Young Doctors in Love
The Young Nurses

Docudrama

Above Us the Waves
Adam
After the Shock
Al Capone
The Amy Fisher Story
The Battle of Algiers
Beat Street
Blind Ambition
Bob Roberts
The Boston Strangler
Bound for Glory
Casimir the Great
Casualities of Love: The "Long Island Lolita" Story
Christian the Lion
Close to Home
Cocaine: One Man's Seduction
Conspiracy: The Trial of the Chicago Eight
The Courtesans of Bombay
Cruel Sea
A Cry in the Dark
Edge of the World
The General Line
Glen or Glenda
Henry: Portrait of a Serial Killer

Hostages
Immortal Battalion
In Cold Blood
In Search of Historic Jesus
Inside the Third Reich
Iron & Silk
James Dean
The Jayne Mansfield Story
Journey Through Rosebud
Kerouac
King
Lethal Lolita—Amy Fisher: My Story
The Lion Has Wings
Murder in Texas
The Naked City
Pickpocket
The Poppy is also a Flower
Prince of the City
Qui Etes Vous, Mr. Sorge?
The Red Menace
The Rise of Louis XIV
Shaka Zulu
S.O.S. Titanic
Soviet Spy
Special Bulletin
Tailspin: Behind the Korean Airline Tragedy
Teenage Devil Dolls
Ten Days That Shook the World
The Thin Blue Line
Times of Harvey Milk
Wellington: The Duel Scandal
The Wild Aces
Working Girls

Documentary

The American Gangster
Assassination of Trotsky
The Atomic Cafe
Battle of China
The Battle of Russia
The Battle of San Pietro
Beach Boys: An American Band
Born to Boogie
The Boys from Termite Terrace
A Brief History of Time
Bruce Lee: Curse of the Dragon
Burden of Dreams
Campaign in Poland
Caravaggio
The Carnivores
The Children of Theatre Street
Chuck Amuck: The Movie
Chuck Berry: Hail! Hail! Rock 'n' Roll
Ciao Federico! Fellini Directs Satyricon
The Civil War, Episode 1: The Cause—1861
The Civil War, Episode 2: A Very Bloody Affair—1862
The Civil War, Episode 3: Forever Free—1862
The Civil War, Episode 4: Simply Murder—1863
The Civil War, Episode 5: The Universe of Battle—1863
The Civil War, Episode 6: Valley of the Shadow of Death—1864
The Civil War, Episode 7: Most Hallowed Ground—1864
The Civil War, Episode 8: War is All Hell—1865
The Civil War, Episode 9: The Better Angels of Our Nature—1865
The Clowns
Come Back, Africa

Common Threads: Stories from the Quilt
Cyberpunk
Dance Hall Racket
Dear America: Letters Home from Vietnam
December 7th: The Movie
Decline of Western Civilization 1
Decline of Western Civilization 2: The Metal Years
Derby
D.O.A.: A Right of Passage
Don't Look Back
The Doors: Soft Parade, a Retrospective
Dracula: A Cinematic Scrapbook
Ebony Dreams
The Elvis Files
Elvis in the Movies
Elvis Memories
Elvis Presley's Graceland
Elvis: Rare Moments with the King
Elvis: The Echo Will Never Die
Emperor Jones/Paul Robeson: Tribute to an Artist
Empire of the Air: The Men Who Made Radio
Encounter with the Unknown
The Endless Summer
Epic That Never Was
Faces of Death, Part 2
Fallen Champ: The Untold Story of Mike Tyson
Fangoria's Weekend of Horrors
Flying Saucers Over Hollywood: The Plan 9 Companion
France/Tour/Detour/Deux/Enfants
Frankenstein: A Cinematic Scrapbook
Gimme Shelter
Gizmo!
Going Hollywood
Gotta Dance, Gotta Sing
Great American Cowboy
Grey Gardens
Guilty of Treason
Harlan County, U.S.A.
Hearts of Darkness: A Filmmaker's Apocalypse
Hell's Angels Forever
Hellstrom Chronicle
Here's Looking at You, Warner Bros.
Hide and Seek
Hollywood Clowns
Hollywood Home Movies
Hollywood Scandals and Tragedies
Hollywood Uncensored
The Horror of It All
Hugh Hefner: Once Upon a Time
Incident at Oglala: The Leonard Peltier Story
Indomitable Teddy Roosevelt
Irving Berlin's America
It Happened in the Park
James Dean
James Dean Story
The JFK Conspiracy
JFK Remembered
John F. Kennedy
The Kennedys Don't Cry
Kidco
Kino Pravda/Enthusiasm
The Lash of the Penitents
The Last Waltz
LBJ: A Biography
Le Joli Mai

The Legend of Valentino
Let It Be
Let's Get Lost
Lightning Over Water
Long Shadows
Louisiana Story
The Love Goddesses
Love Meetings
Love Without Fear
The Making of "A Brief History of Time"
The Making of a Legend: "Gone With the Wind"
Man in the Silk Hat
Man of Aran
The Man Who Skied Down Everest
The Man with a Movie Camera
Many Faces of Sherlock Holmes
Marilyn
Marjoe
Marlon Brando
Mein Kampf
Memphis Belle: A Story of a Flying Fortress
MGM: When the Lion Roars
Moana, a Romance of the Golden Age
Mondo Cane
Mondo Cane 2
Mondo Magic
Mysteries From Beyond Earth
October
Oscar's Greatest Moments: 1971-1991
Paris is Burning
Prelude to War
Pumping Iron
Pumping Iron 2: The Women
Punk Rock Movie
Rascal Dazzle
Rate It X
The Real Buddy Holly Story
The Real Malcolm X: An Intimate Portrait of the Man
Revolution
Rise and Fall of the Third Reich
Roger & Me
Sarah Bailey
Secrets of Life
Sex and Buttered Popcorn
Shocking Asia
Signals Through the Flames
The Situation
Slave Trade in the World Today
Soft and Hard
The Sorrow and the Pity
Streetwise
Stripper
Superstar: The Life and Times of Andy Warhol
Taxi zum Klo
Thank You & Good Night
The Thin Blue Line
Tokyo-Ga
Tokyo Olympiad
Triumph of the Will
Truth or Dare
Vanishing Prairie
Vanishing Wilderness
Vernon, Florida
Vietnam: Chronicle of a War
War in the Sky
Whoever Says the Truth Shall Die
Wild, Wild World of Jayne Mansfield
Woodstock

Down Under

Alvin Purple
Anzacs: The War Down Under

Around the World in 80 Ways
Between Wars
The Blue Lightning
Born to Run
Botany Bay
Burke & Wills
Caddie
The Cars That Ate Paris
Cass
Dark Age
Dead Easy
Death of a Soldier
The Desert Rats
Down Under
The Dunera Boys
Dusty
Eureka Stockade
Fast Talking
Forty Thousand Horsemen
Freedom
The Fringe Dwellers
Gallagher's Travels
Gallipoli
The Getting of Wisdom
The Good Wife
Great Gold Swindle
Ground Zero
Hurricane Smith
The Irishman
Kitty and the Bagman
The Lighthorseman
Little Boy Lost
The Long Weekend
Mad Dog Morgan
The Man from Snowy River
Miracle Down Under
Money Movers
Monkey Grip
Moving Out
My Brilliant Career
Ned Kelly
On the Beach
Over the Hill
Overlanders
Palm Beach
Phar Lap
Prince and the Great Race
Prisoners of the Sun
The Quest
Quigley Down Under
Rebel
The Rescuers Down Under
Return to Snowy River
Ride a Wild Pony
The Right Hand Man
Robbery Under Arms
Run, Rebecca, Run
Runaway Island, Part 1
Runaway Island, Part 2
Runaway Island, Part 3
Runaway Island, Part 4
Sara Dane
Savage Attraction
The Shrimp on the Barbie
Silver City
Sister Kenny
Squizzy Taylor
Stones of Death
Strictly Ballroom
The Sundowners
The Thorn Birds
Under Capricorn
The Wacky World of Wills & Burke
A Waltz Through the Hills
Waterfront
We of the Never Never
Where the Green Ants Dream
The Winds of Jarrah
The Winter of Our Dreams

Dream Girls

Alien Women
The Barbarians
Battling Amazons

Exploitation

Samurai
Satan's Cheerleaders
Saturday Night Sleazies, Vol. 1
Savages from Hell
Secrets of Sweet Sixteen
Sensual Partners
Sex Adventures of the Three Musketeers
Sexcetera
She Shoulda Said No
Sin You Sinners
Single Room Furnished
Slaughter
Slaughter's Big Ripoff
Slaves in Bondage
Sleazemania
Sleazemania III: The Good, the Bad & the Sleazy
Smile
S.O.B.
Something Weird
SS Girls
Star 80
Starlet
Street of Forgotten Women
Striptease
The Student Body/Jailbait Babysitter
Student Confidential
Summer Heat
Summer School Teachers
Sunset Strip
Swamp Women
Sweet Spirits
Takin' It Off
The Teacher
Teen Lust
Teenage Seductress
Test Tube Babies
Therese & Isabelle
They're Playing with Fire
The Third Sex
This Nude World
Three in the Attic
Thunder & Mud
Tomorrow's Children
Unmarried Mothers
Up Your Anchor
Vanessa
Venus on Fire
Victims
Warrior Queen
Weekend with the Babysitter
Weird World of LSD
Wild Rapture
Wild, Wild World of Jayne Mansfield
Woman Hunt
Women's Club
Wrestling Racket Girls
Yellow Emanuelle
Yesterday's Hero
Young Lady Chatterly
Young Lady Chatterly 2

Family Ties

ABC Stage 67: Truman Capote's A Christmas Memory
The Accidental Tourist
Adam Had Four Sons
The Addams Family
The Adventures of the Wilderness Family
An Affair in Mind
Affair in Trinidad
Afraid of the Dark
After Julius
Alberto Express
Alice
Alice Doesn't Live Here Anymore
All Fall Down
All I Want for Christmas

All Mine to Give
All My Sons
All the Kind Strangers
Alpha Beta
Alpine Fire
An American Christmas Carol
American Dream
American Flyers
American Gothic
American Samurai
And Baby Makes Six
And You Thought Your Parents Were Weird!
Andy Hardy Gets Spring Fever
Andy Hardy Meets Debutante
Andy Hardy's Double Life
Andy Hardy's Private Secretary
Angela
Anne of Green Gables
Applause
The Apprenticeship of Duddy Kravitz
Army Brats
The Arrangement
Arsenic and Old Lace
Ashanti, Land of No Mercy
Ask Any Girl
At Close Range
Atomic Attack
The Attic
Auntie Mame
Author! Author!
Autumn Marathon
Autumn Sonata
Avalon
Baba
The Baby
Baby Love
Baby of the Bride
Baby, the Rain Must Fall
Back to the Beach
Back to the Future
Backdraft
Bad Boy
The Bad Seed
The Badge
Bare Knees
The Baron and the Kid
Basket Case
Basket Case 2
Basket Case 3: The Progeny
Beast in the Cellar
The Beast Within
Beat Girl
Beau Geste
Beau Pere
Bed & Breakfast
Beethoven
Behind Prison Walls
Bellissima
Benny & Joon
The Best Christmas Pageant Ever
Best Enemies
The Betsy
Betsy's Wedding
Between Men
Between Two Women
Beulah Land
Beverly Hills Brats
Beyond Darkness
Beyond Obsession
Beyond the Door 2
Big Business
Big Country
Big Girls Don't Cry...They Get Even
The Big Rascal
The Big Showdown
A Bill of Divorcement
Billy Galvin
Billy Liar
The Birch Interval
Bittersweet Love
Black Eyes

Black Orchid
The Black Room
The Black Windmill
Blinded by the Light
Blood Mania
Blood Money: The Story of Clinton and Nadine
Blood Rage
Blood Red
Blood Relations
Blood Relatives
Blood Ties
Bloodbrothers
Bloodlink
Bloody Mama
The Blot
Blue City
Blue Fin
The Blue Yonder
Body Count
The Bodyguard
Bolero
Bon Voyage!
Bonjour Tristesse
Bonnie's Kids
Boomerang
Boss' Son
Bound by Honor
Bouquet of Barbed Wire
Branded a Coward
Breaking Home Ties
Breathing Fire
Bridge to Silence
Bright Angel
A Brivele der Mamen
Broadway Bound
Broadway Melody
Broken Angel
The Brothers Karamazov
Brussels Transit
The Buddy System
Buddy's Song
Butterfly
By the Light of the Silvery Moon
Cahill: United States Marshal
Call of the Forest
Call to Glory
Candles at Nine
Candleshoe
The Cantor's Son
Captain Ron
The Captive: The Longest Drive 2
The Capture of Grizzly Adams
Carbon Copy
Careful, He Might Hear You
Carolina Skeletons
Caroline?
Carousel
Carry Me Back
The Case of the Frightened Lady
Casey's Shadow
Cat Girl
Cat on a Hot Tin Roof
Cat People
Cathy's Curse
Cavalcade
Cavalcade of the West
Cavalry
The Champ
Chances Are
Charley and the Angel
Cheetah
The Children Are Watching Us
Children of Sanchez
The Chisholms
The Christmas Coal Mine Miracle
Christmas Comes to Willow Creek
A Christmas Story
A Christmas to Remember
The Christmas Tree
Cimarron

Cinderella Liberty
Circus World
Class Action
Clifford
Close to Home
The Closer
Clown
Cody
Cold Comfort
Cold Heat
Come and Get It
Coming Out Alive
Communion
Como Dos Gotas de Agua
Complex World
Consenting Adults
A Conspiracy of Love
Cookie
Coquette
The Corsican Brothers
Countdown
Country
Country Girl
Coupe de Ville
The Courtship of Eddie's Father
Cousin, Cousine
Cousins
Crazy in Love
Cries and Whispers
Crimes of the Heart
Crooked Hearts
Crossing Delancey
Cry from the Mountain
Cry, the Beloved Country
Curly Top
Da
Dad
Daddy's Boys
Daddy's Dyin'...Who's Got the Will?
Damage
The Dance Goes On
Daniel
The Dark Angel
Dark Horse
Dark Mirror
The Dark Room
D.A.R.Y.L.
Daughters of the Dust
A Day for Thanks on Walton's Mountain
Dead Men Walk
Dead Ringers
Deadly Blessing
Deadly Rivals
Deadly Sunday
Dear Dead Delilah
Dear Wife
Death Be Not Proud
Death Dreams
Death in the Shadows
Death of a Salesman
December Flower
Delightfully Dangerous
Demons in the Garden
Demons of the Mind
Demonstone
Demonstrator
Demonwarp
Desert Bloom
Desire Under the Elms
Desperados
Desperate Living
Desperate Motives
Detective Sadie & Son
Devi
Devil Dog: The Hound of Hell
Devil Woman
The Devil's Daughter
The Devil's Sleep
The Devil's Web
Diamond Head
Diamonds
Diary of a Mad Old Man
Diary of the Dead

Dias de Ilusion
Dick Tracy
Die! Die! My Darling!
Die Screaming, Marianne
Die Sister, Die!
Dim Sum: A Little Bit of Heart
Dimples
Dirty Hands
Disappearance
Disciple
Discontent
Distant Thunder
Distant Voices, Still Lives
Distortions
Divine Nymph
Dixie Dynamite
Dixie Lanes
Doctor Gore
Dr. Hackenstein
Doctor Phibes Rises Again
Dr. Seuss' Halloween Is Grinch Night
Doctor Who and the Daleks
Doin' Time on Planet Earth
The Dollmaker
Dominick & Eugene
Dona Herlinda & Her Son
Donde Duermen Dos...Duermen Tres
Donkey Skin
Donovan's Reef
Don't Drink the Water
Don't Go in the House
Don't Go to Sleep
Don't Mess with My Sister!
Don't Tell Daddy
Down & Dirty
A Dream of Kings
Dream Street
Drifting Weeds
Duel in the Sun
Duel of Champions
Dumbo
Duplicates
An Early Frost
Early Summer
East and West
East of Eden
East Side Kids
Eat a Bowl of Tea
Echoes
18 Again!
El Monte de las Brujas
El Norte
El Penon de las Animas
El Sabor de la Venganza
Eleni
Eli Eli
Elizabeth of Ladymead
Ellie
Embassy
The Emerald Forest
Emerald Jungle
Emissary
The Empire Strikes Back
Empty Canvas
Encore
The End of Innocence
Endless Love
Endplay
Enid is Sleeping
Enter the Panther
The Entertainer
Entertaining Mr. Sloane
Epitaph
The Equalizer: Memories of Manon
Equinox Flower
Erendira
Ernie Kovacs: Between the Laughter
Erotic Illusion
Escape
Escape Artist
Escape from Safehaven
Eternal Return

The Europeans
The Everlasting Secret Family
Everybody's Fine
The Executioner
Experiment in Terror
Eye of the Storm
Eyes of a Stranger
The Eyes of the Amaryllis
The Eyes, the Mouth
The Fabulous Baker Boys
Face to Face
The Fall of the House of Usher
Falling from Grace
The Family
Family Business
Family Prayers
Family Reunion
Family Secrets
Family Sins
Family Viewing
Fangs of the Living Dead
Fanny and Alexander
Far Away and Long Ago
Far North
Fast Talking
Fatal Justice
Father
Father Figure
Father Hood
Father of the Bride
Fathers and Sons
Father's Little Dividend
A Father's Revenge
Fear Strikes Out
Fearmaker
Feast for the Devil
The Feud
Field of Dreams
Fight for Your Life
Fighting Life
The Fighting Sullivans
Final Analysis
Final Embrace
Final Mission
Final Verdict
Fingers
Finish Line
Finishing School
The Fire Next Time
Firesign Theatre Presents
  Nick Danger in the Case of
  the Missing Yolks
First Born
Five Days One Summer
Five Easy Pieces
The Flame Trees of Thika
Flower Angel
Flowers in the Attic
The Flying Fool
Follow That Dream
Follow That Rainbow
Fool for Love
For Love or Money
For Richer, For Poorer
Force of Evil
Force on Thunder Mountain
Forever and a Day
Found Alive
Four Daughters
The Four Horsemen of the
  Apocalypse
Fourth Wish
Foxfire Light
Freedom is Paradise
Friendly Fire
Friendly Persuasion
Frightmare
The Fringe Dwellers
From the Terrace
Fulfillment
The Funeral
Funny About Love
Further Adventures of the
  Wilderness Family, Part 2
The Fury
Fuzz

The Game is Over
Garbo Talks
The Garden of Delights
Garden of the Finzi-Continis
Gas Food Lodging
The Gathering
The Gathering: Part 2
Generation
Gervaise
Ghosts Can't Do It
The Girl
A Girl on Her Own
Girly
The Go-Masters
The Godfather
The Godfather 1902-1959:
  The Complete Epic
The Godfather, Part 2
Goldengirl
The Good Earth
Good Morning, Babylon
Goodnight, Michelangelo
Grand Larceny
The Grapes of Wrath
The Grass is Always Greener
  Over the Septic Tank
Grave of the Fireflies
Grave of the Vampire
The Graveyard
Great Day
The Great Madcap
The Great Man Votes
The Great Outdoors
The Great Santini
A Great Wall
The Great Wallendas
Green Dolphin Street
Green Eyes
Green Horizon
The Green Promise
The Green Wall
Greenstone
Grown Ups
Guess Who's Coming to
  Dinner
Gun Play
Gypsy
Gypsy Colt
Halloween with the Addams
  Family
Hamlet
The Hand that Rocks the
  Cradle
Hannah and Her Sisters
Hard Frame
Hard Promises
Harry & Son
Harry and the Hendersons
The Hatfields & the McCoys
The Haunting of Barney
  Palmer
Head of the Family
Heart of a Nation
Heart of the Stag
Heidi
The Heiress
Held for Murder
Hell on Wheels
Hero
Hi Diddle Diddle
Hidden Guns
Hide in Plain Sight
The Hiding Place
High & Low
High Command
High Heels
High Tide
Hijazo de Mi Vidaza (Son of
  My Life)
His Private Secretary
The Hit List
Hobo's Christmas
Hobson's Choice
A Hole in the Head
Holiday in Mexico
The Holy Innocents

Home at Last
Home Feeling
Home for the Holidays
Home from the Hill
Home is Where the Hart is
Home to Stay
Homecoming: A Christmas
  Story
Homeward Bound
Homeward Bound: The
  Incredible Journey
Honey, I Blew Up the Kid
Honey, I Shrunk the Kids
Honor Thy Father
The Hoodlum
Hope and Glory
Horizons West
Horror Chamber of Dr.
  Faustus
The Horse
The Horse in the Gray Flannel
  Suit
Horsemen
Hot Lead & Cold Feet
Hot Spell
Hotel Colonial
House of Strangers
The House on Chelouche
  Street
The House that Bled to Death
A House without a Christmas
  Tree
Housekeeping
How Green was My Valley
How the West was Won
How to Commit Marriage
The Howards of Virginia
Hud
The Human Shield
I Accuse My Parents
I Could Go on Singing
I Live in Fear
I Live with Me Dad
I Met a Murderer
I Never Sang For My Father
I Ought to Be in Pictures
I Sent a Letter to My Love
The Ice Flood
I'd Give My Life
If Things Were Different
Immediate Family
The Imported Bridegroom
In Celebration
In Country
In Search of a Golden Sky
In Search of the Castaways
In the Custody of Strangers
In This Our Life
The Indian Runner
Indiana Jones and the Last
  Crusade
The Inheritance
Innocence Unprotected
Interiors
Intermezzo
Into Thin Air
Iphigenia
The Irishman
Iron Eagle
Ironweed
The Island
Islands in the Stream
It Could Happen to You
It's a Date
It's a Wonderful Life
It's in the Bag
Jack the Bear
The Jacksons: An American
  Dream
Jacob Have I Loved
Jazz Singer
Jenny's War
Joey
John and the Missus
Johnny Angel
Jory

Josh and S.A.M.
Journey of Hope
Jumpin' at the Boneyard
Juno and the Paycock
Keep the Change
Kid Vengeance
The Kid Who Loved Christmas
Kidnap Syndicate
Kidnapping of Baby John Doe
Killer with Two Faces
Killing of Randy Webster
Kind Hearts and Coronets
The King and Four Queens
King Lear
The King of Marvin Gardens
King of the Gypsies
King of the Hill
Kingfisher Caper
The Kiss
The Kissing Place
Kotch
Kramer vs. Kramer
The Krays
Kuffs
La Bamba
La Boum
La Cicada
La Symphonie Pastorale
La Terra Trema
Labyrinth
Ladies of the Chorus
Lady by Choice
Lady Mobster
The Lady Refuses
Lai Shi: China's Last Eunuch
Lantern Hill
The Last Days of Chez Nous
The Last Five Days
Last Resort
The Last Unicorn
Late Spring
Laughing at Life
Law of Desire
Legacy of Lies
The Legend of Black Thunder
  Mountain
The Legend of Hillbilly John
Les Bons Debarras
Les Comperes
Les Enfants Terrible
Les Violons du Bal
Lethal Weapon
Let's Dance
The Letter
Letter of Introduction
Letting the Birds Go Free
Liar's Edge
Liar's Moon
License to Kill
Lies My Father Told Me
Life is Sweet
Life with Father
Light of Day
Like Water for Chocolate
The Lion in Winter
The List of Adrian Messenger
Listen, Darling
Little Dorrit, Film 1: Nobody's
  Fault
Little Dorrit, Film 2: Little
  Dorrit's Story
Little House on the Prairie,
  Vol. 1
Little Nellie Kelly
Little Women
Long Day's Journey into Night
The Long, Hot Summer
The Long Riders
A Long Way Home
Looking for Miracles
Lorenzo's Oil
Los Dos Hermanos
The Lost Boys
The Lost Capone
Lost Honeymoon
Lost in Yonkers

The Lost Language of Cranes
Lots of Luck
Love
Love Crazy
Love Finds Andy Hardy
Love Laughs at Andy Hardy
Love Me Tender
Love on the Dole
Love Strange Love
Love Under Pressure
Love Without Fear
Love Your Mama
Lovers and Other Strangers
Lucky Stiff
Ma Barker's Killer Brood
Mac
Mad at the Moon
Mad Max
Madame X
M.A.D.D.: Mothers Against
  Drunk Driving
Made in America
Madhouse
Mafia Princess
Magic Adventure
The Magnificent Ambersons
The Maid
Make Room for Tomorrow
The Makioka Sisters
Mama Turns a Hundred
Mame
A Man About the House
Man & Boy
Man from Laramie
The Man in the Gray Flannel
  Suit
The Man in the Iron Mask
The Man in the Moon
The Man in the Santa Claus
  Suit
A Man of Passion
Man, Woman & Child
Mandy
Maniac
Mansfield Park
Maria Candelaria
Maria's Day
The Marshal's Daughter
Mask
The Mating Game
A Matter of Principle
May Fools
Maya
Maybe I'll Be Home in the
  Spring
Meet Me in St. Louis
Meet the Hollowheads
Meet the Parents
The Member of the Wedding
Memories of Me
Memory of Us
Menace on the Mountain
Midnight
Midnight Warning
Mildred Pierce
Miles from Home
Min & Bill
Mind Games
The Miniver Story
Miracle Down Under
Miracle on 34th Street
Mirele Efros
Miss Rose White
Mississippi Masala
Missouri Traveler
Mrs. Miniver
Mrs. Parkington
Mrs. Wiggs of the Cabbage
  Patch
Mr. & Mrs. Bridge
Mr. Hobbs Takes a Vacation
Mr. Saturday Night
Mr. Skitch
Misunderstood
Mob Boss
Mom & Dad

Family

Mon Oncle
Mon Oncle Antoine
Monsieur Verdoux
Moonstruck
The Mosquito Coast
Mother
Mother & Daughter: A Loving War
Mother Doesn't Always Know Best
Mother Lode
Mouchette
Moving
Murder-in-Law
Murder in the Doll House
Murder One
Murmur of the Heart
Mussolini & I
Mutual Respect
My Father is Coming
My Father's Glory
My Father's Nurse
My Grandpa is a Vampire
My Heroes Have Always Been Cowboys
My Mother's Castle
My Mother's Secret Life
My Old Man
My Old Man's Place
My Other Husband
My Outlaw Brother
My Sister Eileen
My Sister, My Love
My Twentieth Century
Naked Hills
Naked Paradise
Nancy Goes to Rio
National Lampoon's Christmas Vacation
National Lampoon's European Vacation
Natural Enemies
Never Too Young to Die
New York Stories
Next of Kin
Next Stop, Greenwich Village
Next Summer
Nicholas Nickleby
Night Crossing
'night, Mother
Night Moves
Night of Terror
The Night of the Hunter
Night Zoo
Nights and Days
Nightstalker
1900
Ninja Dragons
No Place to Hide
No Place to Run
Noon Wine
The Norman Conquests, Part 1: Table Manners
The Norman Conquests, Part 2: Living Together
The Norman Conquests, Part 3: Round and Round the Garden
Norman Loves Rose
Not My Kid
Nothing in Common
Nowhere to Hide
Nowhere to Run
Oh Dad, Poor Dad (Momma's Hung You in the Closet & I'm Feeling So Sad)
O'Hara's Wife
The Old Dark House
The Old Maid
Old Yeller
Oldest Living Graduate
Olivier, Olivier
Olly Olly Oxen Free
Omega Syndrome
On Golden Pond
On Moonlight Bay

On the Edge
On the Third Day
On the Waterfront
On Valentine's Day
Once Around
The One and Only, Genuine, Original Family Band
One Cooks, the Other Doesn't
One Good Cop
One More Chance
One Trick Pony
Onibaba
Only the Lonely
Only When I Laugh
Ordet
Ordinary People
Orphans
Orphans of the Storm
The Other
Our Little Girl
Our Town
Our Vines Have Tender Grapes
Out of Sight, Out of Her Mind
Out of the Blue
Out on a Limb
Outside Chance of Maximillian Glick
Over the Hill
Over the Top
Overboard
Overture to Glory
The Ox
Ozzie & Harriet
Paco
Padre Padrone
Panic in the Year Zero!
Paradise
Paradise Alley
The Parent Trap
Parenthood
Parents
Paris, Texas
Passed Away
Pathfinder
The Peasants
Peeping Tom
Peg O' My Heart
Peggy Sue Got Married
Penny Serenade
Perfect Family
The Perils of Gwendoline
Personal Exemptions
Pet Sematary
Pete Townsend: White City
Phantom Brother
Phar Lap
Phedre
Picture Mommy Dead
Pilgrim, Farewell
Ping Pong
The Pit and the Pendulum
The Pit & the Pendulum
Pitfall
Places in the Heart
Platinum High School
Please Don't Eat the Daisies
Poil de Carotte
Poison Ivy
Pollyanna
Pop Always Pays
The Pope of Greenwich Village
Popi
The Portrait
Portrait of a Stripper
Postcards from the Edge
Prehysteria
Pride and Prejudice
Prince of Pennsylvania
The Prince of Tides
Prizzi's Honor
The Prodigal
Promised a Miracle
Psycho Girls
Queen of Hearts

A Question of Love
The Quiet Man
Rachel, Rachel
Radio Flyer
Rage of Angels: The Story Continues
Raging Bull
Railway Children
Rain Man
Rainbow's End
A Raisin in the Sun
Raising Arizona
Ran
A Rare Breed
Rebecca of Sunnybrook Farm
Reckless Moment
The Red Pony
Red River
Regarding Henry
Regina
Remember Me
Return
Return of Jesse James
Return of the Family Man
Return of Wildfire
Return to Africa
Revenge
Revenge of Doctor X
Revenge of the Barbarians
The Revenger
The Revolt of Job
The Revolt of Mother
Revolution
Ricco
Rich in Love
Rich, Young and Pretty
Richie
Riding the Edge
The Right Hand Man
Rikky and Pete
Rivals
The River Niger
The River Rat
A River Runs Through It
Road Racers
Road to Salina
Robert Kennedy and His Times
Rocco and His Brothers
Rocket Gibraltar
Roll of Thunder, Hear My Cry
Rolling Home
Romeo and Juliet
Romola
Roses Bloom Twice
The Royal Bed
Rulers of the City
Rumble Fish
Running Mates
Running on Empty
The Sacketts
Sacred Ground
Sallah
Samantha
Sam's Son
Santa Sangre
The Saphead
Sardinia Kidnapped
Savage is Loose
Scandal in a Small Town
Scent of a Woman
Scream for Help
Sea Devils
The Search
Season of Fear
Secret Ceremony
The Secret Garden
The Secret Passion of Robert Clayton
Secrets of Women
Seduced and Abandoned
The Seducers
See How She Runs
See You in the Morning
The Seekers
Sense & Sensibility

Sensuous Summer
Separate Vacations
Separate Ways
Seven Alone
Seven Beauties
Seven Faces of Dr. Lao
Severance
Sex and the Single Parent
Shadow of a Doubt
The Shadow Riders
The Shanghai Gesture
Shaolin Death Squad
Shark River
The Sheep Has Five Legs
Shenandoah
The Shining Hour
Shoot the Moon
Shy People
The Sibling
Sibling Rivalry
The Sicilian Connection
The Silence
Silence
Silent Rebellion
Silent Witness
Simple Justice
Simple Men
The Sin of Madelon Claudet
Since You Went Away
Sinful Life
Sinners
The Sisters
Sisters
Sixteen Candles
'68
Skag
Skin Game
Skylark
The Sleazy Uncle
Slightly Scarlet
Small Sacrifices
Smoke
The Solitary Man
Sometimes a Great Notion
Son-in-Law
Son of Flubber
Son of Frankenstein
Song of the Exile
Song of the Islands
Sons
Sons of Katie Elder
Sons of Steel
Sorrows of Gin
The Sound of Music
South Central
South of Hell Mountain
The Southerner
Souvenir
The Spanish Gardener
Special Olympics
Spider Baby
Split Decisions
Split Image
State Fair
Stella
Stella Dallas
The Stepfather
Stepfather 2: Make Room for Daddy
Stepfather 3: Father's Day
Stepmonster
Stepsisters
The Stolen Children
The Stone Boy
Stop! or My Mom Will Shoot
The Story of Boys & Girls
The Story of Jacob & Joseph
Storyville
Strange Interlude
Strange Shadows in an Empty Room
Strangers in the City
Strangers: The Story of a Mother and Daughter
Strapless
Street Girls

Street Hero
Street Hitz
Street Justice
A Streetcar Named Desire
Stuck on You
Suddenly, Last Summer
Suffering Bastards
Sugar Cane Alley
Summer Holiday
Summer Magic
Summer of Fear
Summer Switch
Summer Wishes, Winter Dreams
A Sunday in the Country
The Sundowners
Susan and God
Susana
Suzanne
Swedenhielms
Sweet Smell of Success
Sweetie
The Swiss Family Robinson
Switched at Birth
Sylvester
Table Settings
The Tale of Ruby Rose
Tank
Tatie Danielle
The Tempest
Teorema
Termini Station
Terms of Endearment
Testament
Tevye
Tex
Texas Lightning
Thank You & Good Night
Thanksgiving Story
That Man Is Pregnant
That Was Then...This Is Now
There's No Business Like Show Business
Things in Their Season
Third Walker
This Boy's Life
This Happy Breed
This is My Life
This Property is Condemned
A Thousand Clowns
Threads
Three Brothers
The Three Lives of Thomasina
Three Men and a Cradle
3 Ninjas
Three Violent People
The Three Weird Sisters
Three's Trouble
Thrillkill
Through a Glass Darkly
Thursday's Child
Ticket to Heaven
Tiger Warsaw
Till Marriage Do Us Part
Till There was You
Time Flies When You're Alive
A Time of Destiny
Time Stands Still
Time to Live
'Tis a Pity She's a Whore
To All My Friends on Shore
To Die for 2
To Paris with Love
To Sleep with Anger
To Subdue the Evil
Toby McTeague
Tokyo Story
Toll of the Desert
Toughlove
Toys
Toys in the Attic
Track 29
Trade Secrets
Traenen in Florenz
Tramp at the Door
Travels with My Aunt

Treacherous Crossing
Treasure of the Sierra Madre
The Tree of Wooden Clogs
The Trip to Bountiful
True Blood
True Confessions
True Love
True West
Tucker and the Horse Thief
The Tuttles of Tahiti
29th Street
Twice in a Lifetime
Twister
Two Kinds of Love
The Two Sisters
The Ugly Dachshund
Uncle Buck
Uncle Moses
Uncommon Valor
Under the Boardwalk
Under the Volcano
Undergrads
Uneasy Terms
The Unforgiven
An Unremarkable Life
Until They Sail
Up the Sandbox
The Uprising
Used People
Vengeance
Vengeance Valley
A Very Brady Christmas
Vigil
Vincent & Theo
The Violation of Laura
Violette
Viridiana
Volver, Volver, Volver!
Voyage en Balloon
A Voyage' Round My Father
Voyage to Italy
Voyager
Vultures
Wait Till Your Mother Gets
   Home
Walk in the Spring Rain
War & Remembrance, Part 1
War & Remembrance, Part 2
War & Remembrance: The
   Final Chapter, Part 8
War & Remembrance: The
   Final Chapter, Part 9
Ways of Kung Fu
Wedding in White
Welcome Home
Whales of August
What About Bob?
What Ever Happened to Baby
   Jane?
What the Peeper Saw
When Nature Calls
When Wolves Cry
Where East is East
Where Have All the People
   Gone?
Where the Heart Is
Where the Lilies Bloom
Where's Poppa?
The White Cliffs of Dover
White Mane
Wicked Stepmother
Wild at Heart
The Wild Country
The Wild Duck
Wild Pony
Wild Zone
Wildflower
The Winds of War
Winter People
Winterset
The Wistful Widow of Wagon
   Gap
With Six You Get Eggroll
The Wizard
The Wizard of Loneliness
A Woman Under the Influence

Women on the Verge of a
   Nervous Breakdown
Woodchipper Massacre
The World Accuses
A World Apart
The World of Apu
You Can't Take It with You
Young Dragons: The Kung Fu
   Kids
Young Dragons: The Kung Fu
   Kids 2
Your Ticket Is No Longer Valid
Yours, Mine & Ours
Zertigo Diamond Caper

Family Viewing

The Absent-Minded Professor
Adventures in Spying
The Adventures of Bullwhip
   Griffin
The Adventures of
   Huckleberry Finn
The Adventures of Mark
   Twain
African Journey
Aladdin
Aladdin and His Wonderful
   Lamp
Almos' a Man
Almost Partners
The Amazing Dobermans
An American Tail
An American Tail: Fievel Goes
   West
Amy
And You Thought Your
   Parents Were Weird!
Animation Wonderland
Anne of Avonlea
Anne of Green Gables
Annie Oakley
The Apple Dumpling Gang
The Apple Dumpling Gang
   Rides Again
Babes in Toyland
Back to Hannibal: The Return
   of Tom Sawyer and
   Huckleberry Finn
The Ballad of Paul Bunyan
Bambi
The Barefoot Executive
Batman
Be My Valentine, Charlie
   Brown
Beauty and the Beast
Beethoven
Behave Yourself!
Bell, Book and Candle
Benji
Benji the Hunted
Benji's Very Own Christmas
   Story
Bernard and the Genie
The Best Christmas Pageant
   Ever
Best of Terrytoons
Big Red
The Billion Dollar Hobo
Bingo
The Black Arrow
Black Beauty
Black Beauty/Courage of
   Black Beauty
The Black Hole
Blackbeard's Ghost
The Blue Yonder
Bon Voyage!
Bongo
Born Free
Born to Run
A Boy Named Charlie Brown
The Boy Who Loved Trolls
The Brain
Breakin' Through
Brewster's Millions

Bridge to Terabithia
Brother Future
Bugs Bunny: Hollywood
   Legend
Bugs Bunny's Comedy
   Classics
Bugs Bunny's Looney
   Christmas Tales
Calacan
Candleshoe
The Canterville Ghost
The Capture of Grizzly Adams
The Care Bears Movie
The Care Bears Movie 2: A
   New Generation
Cartoon All-Stars to the
   Rescue
Casey at the Bat
The Castaway Cowboy
The Cat from Outer Space
Challenge to Lassie
Charley and the Angel
A Charlie Brown Christmas
Charlie Brown's All-Stars
Charlie, the Lonesome Cougar
Cheetah
Child of Glass
The Chronicles of Narnia
Cinderella
Clarence
Clarence, the Cross-eyed Lion
Clowning Around
The Computer Wore Tennis
   Shoes
Condorman
Courage Mountain
Courage of Lassie
Cross Creek
Cry from the Mountain
Daniel and the Towers
Darby O'Gill & the Little
   People
The Dark Crystal
Davy Crockett and the River
   Pirates
Davy Crockett, King of the
   Wild Frontier
A Day for Thanks on Walton's
   Mountain
The Devil & Max Devlin
Diamond's Edge
Diamonds on Wheels
Disney Beginnings
A Disney Christmas Gift
Disney's American Heroes
Disney's Halloween Treat
Disney's Storybook Classics
Dr. Seuss' Grinch Grinches
   the Cat in the Hat/Pontoffel
   Pock
Dr. Seuss' Halloween Is
   Grinch Night
Dr. Syn, Alias the Scarecrow
A Dog of Flanders
The Dogs Who Stopped the
   War
Donner Pass: The Road to
   Survival
DuckTales the Movie:
   Treasure of the Lost Lamp
Dumbo
Dusty
Emil and the Detective
The Enchanted Forest
The Enchanted Journey
Escapade in Florence
Escape to Witch Mountain
A Family Circus Christmas
Father of the Bride
Felix the Cat: The Movie
Ferngully: The Last Rain
   Forest
50 of the Greatest Cartoons
The Fig Tree
The Fighting Prince of
   Donegal

Flight of the Grey Wolf
Flight of the Navigator
The Flintstones: Dino & Juliet
The Flintstones Meet Rockula
   & Frankenstone
Flipper
Flipper's New Adventure
Flipper's Odyssey
Follow Me, Boys!
For the Love of Benji
Freaky Friday
Free Willy
Freeze Frame
Frog
Frogs!
Frosty the Snowman
Gay Purr-ee
George's Island
The Gift of Love
A Girl of the Limberlost
The Girl Who Spelled
   Freedom
Gnome-Mobile
Goin' Coconuts
Gone are the Days
The Good, the Bad, and
   Huckleberry Hound
The Great Land of Small
The Great Locomotive Chase
Greyfriars Bobby
Gryphon
Gus
Happily Ever After
The Haunting of Barney
   Palmer
Hector's Bunyip
Heidi
Herbie Goes Bananas
Herbie Goes to Monte Carlo
Herbie Rides Again
Here Comes Santa Claus
He's Your Dog, Charlie
   Brown!
The Hideaways
Hiroshima Maiden
The Hoboken Chicken
   Emergency
Hockey Night
Home at Last
Home for Christmas
Homeward Bound
Honey, I Blew Up the Kid
Honey, I Shrunk the Kids
The Horse in the Gray Flannel
   Suit
The Horse Without a Head
Horsemasters
Hot Lead & Cold Feet
The House of Dies Drear
How to Be a Perfect Person in
   Just Three Days
Huckleberry Finn
I Love Lucy
The Incredible Journey
Is This Goodbye, Charlie
   Brown?
The Island at the Top of the
   World
It Was a Short Summer,
   Charlie Brown
It's an Adventure, Charlie
   Brown!
It's the Great Pumpkin,
   Charlie Brown
Jack & the Beanstalk
Jacob Have I Loved
A Jetson Christmas Carol
The Jetsons Meet the
   Flintstones
Joe Panther
Johnny Appleseed
Johnny Shiloh
Johnny Tremain & the Sons of
   Liberty
Journey Back to Oz
The Journey of Natty Gann

Journey to Spirit Island
Jungle Book
The Jungle Book
Justin Morgan Had a Horse
Kid Colter
A Kid for Two Farthings
The Kid Who Loved Christmas
King of the Grizzlies
Konrad
The Land of Faraway
Lantern Hill
Lassie: Adventures of Neeka
Lassie: Well of Love
The Last Flight of Noah's Ark
The Lawrenceville Stories
Legend of Lobo
The Legend of Sleepy Hollow
Lt. Robin Crusoe, U.S.N.
The Light in the Forest
The Little Drummer Boy
Little Heroes
Little Miss Marker
Little Nemo: Adventures in
   Slumberland
The Little Princess
A Little Princess
Little Rascals Collector's
   Edition, Vol. 1-6
Little Rascals Comedy
   Classics, Vol. 1
Little Rascals Comedy
   Classics, Vol. 2
Little Rascals: Fish Hooky/
   Spooky Hooky
Little Rascals: Honkey
   Donkey/Sprucin' Up
Little Rascals: Little Sinner/
   Two Too Young
Little Rascals: Mush and Milk/
   Three Men in a Tub
Little Rascals on Parade
Little Rascals: Pups is Pups/
   Three Smart Boys
Little Rascals: Readin' and
   Writin'/Mail and Female
Little Rascals: Reunion in
   Rhythm/Mike Fright
Little Rascals: Spanky/Feed
   'Em and Weep
Little Rascals: The Pinch
   Singer/Framing Youth
Little Rascals Two Reelers,
   Vol. 1
Little Rascals Two Reelers,
   Vol. 2
Little Rascals Two Reelers,
   Vol. 3
Little Rascals Two Reelers,
   Vol. 4
Little Rascals Two Reelers,
   Vol. 5
Little Rascals Two Reelers,
   Vol. 6
Little Rascals, Vol. 1
Little Rascals, Vol. 2
The Littlest Horse Thieves
The Littlest Outlaw
Looking for Miracles
Lots of Luck
The Love Bug
Love Leads the Way
Magic of Lassie
The Magic Sword
Magical Wonderland
Maricela
Mark Twain and Me
Mary Poppins
Max Maven's Mindgames
Men of Boys Town
Menace on the Mountain
Mickey's Christmas Carol
The Mighty Ducks
The Mighty Pawns
Million Dollar Duck
Miracle at Moreaux
Miracle Down Under

Family

The Miracle of the White Stallions
The Misadventures of Merlin Jones
Mr. Superinvisible
Misty
Moby Dick & the Mighty Mightor
Monkeys, Go Home!
Monkey's Uncle
Moon Pilot
Moon-Spinners
Mooncussers
Mosby's Marauders
Mother Goose Rock 'n' Rhyme
Munchie
The Muppet Movie
Muppets Take Manhattan
My Darlin' Clementine
My Dog, the Thief
My Friend Flicka
The Mysterious Stranger
Napoleon and Samantha
Necessary Parties
Never a Dull Moment
The NeverEnding Story
The NeverEnding Story 2: Next Chapter
Newsies
Night Crossing
The Nightingale
Nikki, the Wild Dog of the North
The Nine Lives of Elfego Baca
No Deposit, No Return
No Grumps Allowed!
The North Avenue Irregulars
Now You See Him, Now You Don't
The Nutcracker Prince
Old Yeller
Once Upon a Forest
The One and Only, Genuine, Original Family Band
101 Dalmations
One Little Indian
One Magic Christmas
One of Our Dinosaurs Is Missing
The Out-of-Towners
Pecos Bill
Pete's Dragon
Pinocchio
Pippi Goes on Board
Pippi in the South Seas
Pippi Longstocking
Pippi on the Run
Pistol: The Birth of a Legend
Poco
Pollyanna
Prancer
Primo Baby
Prince and the Great Race
A Rare Breed
The Red Pony
The Reluctant Dragon
The Rescuers
The Rescuers Down Under
Return from Witch Mountain
The Return of the King
Return to Oz
Ride a Wild Pony
Ring of Bright Water
Road to Avonlea
Rob Roy—The Highland Rogue
Rock-a-Doodle
The Rocketeer
Rookie of the Year
Rover Dangerfield
Rudolph the Red-Nosed Reindeer
Rumpelstiltskin
Run for the Roses
Runaway

Runaway Island, Part 1
Runaway Island, Part 2
Runaway Island, Part 3
Runaway Island, Part 4
The Runaways
Sammy, the Way-Out Seal
Santa Claus
Santa Claus is Coming to Town
Santa Claus: The Movie
Sarah, Plain and Tall
Savage Sam
Savannah Smiles
Save the Lady
Scandalous John
The Secret Garden
The Secret of El Zorro
The Secret of Navajo Cave
The Secret of the Golden Eagle
Seven Alone
The Shaggy D.A.
The Shaggy Dog
She's a Good Skate, Charlie Brown
The Sign of Zorro
Skeezer
Sleeping Beauty
Smith!
Smoke
A Smoky Mountain Christmas
Snoopy, Come Home
Snow White and the Seven Dwarfs
Snowball Express
Son of Flubber
Spirit of the Eagle
Spy Trap
Starbird and Sweet William
Starring Bugs Bunny!
Stone Fox
The Story of Robin Hood & His Merrie Men
Summer Dog
Summer Magic
Superdad
Sweet 15
The Swiss Family Robinson
The Sword & the Rose
The Sword in the Stone
Taking Care of Terrific
Ten Who Dared
Tex Avery's Screwball Classics, Vol. 3
That Darn Cat
Thief of Baghdad
Third Man on the Mountain
Those Calloways
The Three Little Pigs
The Three Lives of Thomasina
Tiger Town
A Tiger Walks
Toby Tyler
Tom Sawyer
Tonka
Treasure Island
The Treasure of Matecumbe
The Ugly Dachshund
Unidentified Flying Oddball
Up Against the Wall
A Very Brady Christmas
A Very Merry Cricket
Walking on Air
Waltz King
A Waltz Through the Hills
Warner Brothers Cartoon Festival 3
Watcher in the Woods
Westward Ho, the Wagons!
Where the Lilies Bloom
Where the Red Fern Grows
Where the Red Fern Grows: Part 2
White Fang
Who Has Seen the Wind?
The Wild Country

Wild Hearts Can't Be Broken
Wild Horse Hank
The Wind in the Willows
The Witches
Words by Heart
The World's Greatest Athlete
Yankee Doodle
The Yearling
Yogi's First Christmas
You Must Remember This

Fantasy

The Acid Eaters
Adventures in Dinosaur City
The Adventures of Baron Munchausen
The Adventures of Mark Twain
The Adventures of Sinbad
The Adventures of Sinbad the Sailor
Afrita Hanen
Aladdin
Alice
Alice Through the Looking Glass
Alice's Adventures in Wonderland
Alien from L.A.
...Almost
Alone Against Rome
Amazing Mr. Blunden
The Amazing Spider-Man
Amazing Stories
Amazing Stories, Book 2
Amazing Stories, Book 4
Amazing Stories, Book 5
Amazons
America 3000
Angel on My Shoulder
Animation Wonderland
Atlantis, the Lost Continent
Atlas
Atlas in the Land of the Cyclops
Ator the Fighting Eagle
Baby...Secret of the Lost Legend
Barbarella
Barbarian Queen
Baron Munchausen
Batman
Batman Returns
*batteries not included
B.C. Rock
Beastmaster
Beastmaster 2: Through the Portal of Time
Beauty and the Beast
Beauty and the Beast: Once Upon a Time in New York
Beauty and the Beast: Though Lovers Be Lost
Benji's Very Own Christmas Story
Bernard and the Genie
Best of George Pal
Beyond Atlantis
Beyond Tomorrow
Big
Big Top Pee Wee
Big Trouble in Little China
Biggles
Bill and Coo
Bill & Ted's Excellent Adventure
The Bishop's Wife
Bladestorm
Blithe Spirit
The Blood of a Poet
The Blue Bird
The Blue Light
Blue Monkey
Blue Paradise
Boccaccio '70

The Boy God
The Boy Who Could Fly
The Boy Who Loved Trolls
Bridge to Terabithia
Brothers Lionheart
The Canterville Ghost
The Cat from Outer Space
Cave Girls
The Challenge
The Chambermaid's Dream
Charleston
Charley and the Angel
Child's Christmas in Wales
The Christmas That Almost Wasn't
The Chronicles of Narnia
Cinderella 2000
Circus Angel
The Clan of the Cave Bear
Clarence
Clash of the Titans
Cocoon
Cocoon: The Return
The Company of Wolves
Conan the Barbarian
Conan the Destroyer
A Connecticut Yankee
Conqueror of the World
Conquest
Conquest of Mycene
Coriolanus, Man without a Country
The Crazy Ray
Crystal Triangle
Curse of the Cat People
Darby O'Gill & the Little People
The Dark Crystal
The Day the Earth Froze
Daydreamer
Deathstalker
Deathstalker 2: Duel of the Titans
Deathstalker 3
Deathstalker 4: Clash of the Titans
Desperate Living
The Devil & Max Devlin
Devil of the Desert Against the Son of Hercules
Diary of Forbidden Dreams
Dias de Ilusion
Digby, the Biggest Dog in the World
Disney Beginnings
A Disney Christmas Gift
Disney's American Heroes
Disney's Halloween Treat
Dr. Seuss' Grinch Grinches the Cat in the Hat/Pontoffel Pock
Dr. Seuss' Halloween Is Grinch Night
Donkey Skin
Dos Cruces en Danger Pass
Dragonslayer
Dream a Little Dream
Dreamchild
Dreamscape
Dreamwood
Dungeonmaster
Early Russian Cinema, Vol. 3: Starewicz's Fantasies
Edward Scissorhands
El Cristo de los Milagros
Elle Voit des Nains Partout
Emmanuelle 4
The Enchanted Cottage
The Enchanted Journey
The Enchantress
Endgame
EPIC: Days of the Dinosaurs
Eraserhead
Ernest Saves Christmas
Erotic Escape
Erotic Illusion

Erotic Touch of Hot Skin
Escapes
E.T.: The Extra-Terrestrial
Eternal Return
The Ewok Adventure
The Ewoks: Battle for Endor
Excalibur
Explorers
Falcon
Fantasy Island
Field of Dreams
The Final Programme
Fire and Ice
Firesign Theatre Presents Nick Danger in the Case of the Missing Yolks
Flight of Dragons
Flight of the Navigator
Flights of Fancy
Flower Angel
Forbidden Impulse
Frank and I
French Quarter
Frogs!
From the Earth to the Moon
George's Island
The Ghost and Mrs. Muir
Ghost Chase
Ghost Writer
Ghosts Can't Do It
Ghostwarrior
The Giants of Thessaly
Gladiators 7
The Glass Slipper
Gnome-Mobile
Gnomes
Golden Voyage of Sinbad
The Golem
Goliath Against the Giants
Goliath and the Barbarians
Goliath and the Dragon
Goliath and the Sins of Babylon
Good Time with a Bad Girl
Gor
The Great Land of Small
Greenstone
Grendel, Grendel, Grendel
Gryphon
Gulliver's Travels
A Guy Named Joe
The Hanged Man
Harvey
Hawk the Slayer
Heartbreak Hotel
Hearts & Armour
Heaven Can Wait
Hector's Bunyip
Herbie Rides Again
Hercules
Hercules and the Captive Women
Hercules and the Princess of Troy
Hercules in the Haunted World
Hercules, Prisoner of Evil
Here Come the Littles: The Movie
Here Comes Mr. Jordan
Hey There, It's Yogi Bear
Highlander 2: The Quickening
His Majesty, the Scarecrow of Oz/The Magic Cloak of Oz
The Hobbit
Hobgoblins
The Holes
Hollywood Erotic Film Festival
Hook
Hoppity Goes to Town
Horrors of the Red Planet
A Hungarian Fairy Tale
Hyper-Sapien: People from Another Star
I Married a Witch
The Incredible Mr. Limpet

Fast Cars

The Naked City
Naked Kiss
Night and the City
Nightfall
Nocturne
On Dangerous Ground
Out of the Past
Pitfall
Plunder Road
The Postman Always Rings
  Twice
Postmark for Danger/
  Quicksand
The Public Eye
The Red House
Rendez-vous
The Scar
Shoot to Kill
Signal 7
Slow Moves
Station
Stormy Monday
Strange Illusion
The Strange Love of Martha
  Ivers
Sweet Smell of Success
Tchao Pantin
They Live by Night
The Third Man
Too Late for Tears
Touch of Evil
Vortex
Who Framed Roger Rabbit?
A Woman's Secret

Film Stars

Actor: The Paul Muni Story
Bela Lugosi Scrapbook
The Best of Bogart
Blonde Cobra/The Doctor's
  Dream
Bogie
Dombshell
Bruce Lee: Curse of the
  Dragon
Bud and Lou
Buster Keaton: The Great
  Stone Face
Calendar Girl
Chaplin
Committed
Count/Adventurer
Cult People
Dear Brigitte
Death at Love House
Death Becomes Her
Deep in My Heart
Duke: The Films of John
  Wayne
Emperor Jones/Paul
  Robeson: Tribute to an
  Artist
Frances
Hedda Hopper's Hollywood
Hepburn & Tracy
Hollywood Clowns
Hollywood Goes to War
Hollywood Home Movies
The Horror of It All
Hurricane Express
In Person
James Dean
The James Dean 35th
  Anniversary Collection
The Jayne Mansfield Story
The Josephine Baker Story
The King of Kings
Kisses
L.A. Goddess
Legend of Valentino
The Legend of Valentino
The Love Goddesses
Man of a Thousand Faces
Marlon Brando
The Meateater

My Favorite Year
My Wicked, Wicked Ways
The Oscar
Oscar's Greatest Moments:
  1971-1991
Overexposed
The Perils of Pauline
Play It Again, Sam
The Player
Power, Passion & Murder
The Purple Rose of Cairo
Queenie
Rainbow
Rascal Dazzle
Rita Hayworth: The Love
  Goddess
Sinatra
SnakeEater
Sophia Loren: Her Own Story
Superstar: The Life and Times
  of Andy Warhol
Targets
That's Entertainment
That's Entertainment, Part 2
Users
Veronika Voss
W.C. Fields: Flask of Fields
What Ever Happened to Baby
  Jane?
White Hot: The Mysterious
  Murder of Thelma Todd
Wild, Wild World of Jayne
  Mansfield
Work/Police

Firemen

Always
Backdraft
Club Paradise
Fahrenheit 451
Fire Alarm
Fireballs
Firehouse
The Fireman
The Firemen's Ball
Hellfighters
Inferno in Paradise
Roxanne
Trespass
Turk 182!

Fires

Always
Backdraft
Burning Rage
City on Fire
The Cremators
Dinosaurus!
Don't Go in the House
Endless Love
Erendira
Fire
Fire Alarm
Firehead
The Fireman
Firestarter
The Flaming Urge
Frankenstein
Island of the Burning Doomed
The Michigan Kid
Mighty Joe Young
Nice Girls Don't Explode
Oil
Pretty Poison
Pyrates
Quest for Fire
Save the Tiger
Sounds of Silence
Speeding Up Time
Spontaneous Combustion
Terror on the 40th Floor
The Towering Inferno
The Triangle Factory Fire
  Scandal

Flower Children

Adam at 6 A.M.
Alice's Restaurant
American Blue Note
Angels Hard as They Come
Best Enemies
Best Revenge
The Big Chill
The Big Fix
Bob & Carol & Ted & Alice
Born on the Fourth of July
Children Shouldn't Play with
  Dead Things
The Compleat Beatles
Conspiracy: The Trial of the
  Chicago Eight
The Crimson Cult
Dogfight
The Doors
Dreamwood
Dynamite Chicken
Easy Rider
Flashback
Four Friends
Free Grass
Fritz the Cat
Gimme Shelter
The Glory Stompers
Greetings
Hair
Head
High Hopes
I Drink Your Blood
I Love You, Alice B. Toklas
Mantis in Lace
Married to It
The Mod Squad
More
More American Graffiti
Off Limits
Out
Petit Con
Property
Psych-Out
Psychedelic Fever
Rainbow Bridge
The Rebel Set
Revolution
R.P.M.* (*Revolutions Per
  Minute)
Rude Awakening
The Sandpiper
Satan's Sadists
Sea Devils
Second Thoughts
Slashed Dreams
A Small Circle of Friends
The Snake People
The Strawberry Statement
There's a Girl in My Soup
Thumb Tripping
The Trip
Where the Eagle Flies
Who'll Stop the Rain?
Wild in the Streets
Woodstock
Yellow Submarine

Folklore & Mythology

Antonio Das Mortes
Atlantis, the Lost Continent
Atlas in the Land of the
  Cyclops
The Ballad of Paul Bunyan
Black Orpheus
Candyman
Chinese Gods
Clash of the Titans
Colossus and the Amazon
  Queen
Crossroads
Darby O'Gill & the Little
  People

Disney's American Heroes
Disney's Storybook Classics
Donkey Skin
Down to Earth
Dreamwood
Early Russian Cinema, Vol. 2:
  Folklore & Legend
Erik the Viking
Faust
Field of Dreams
The Fool Killer
Force on Thunder Mountain
The Fury of Hercules
The Giant of Marathon
The Giant of Metropolis
The Giants of Thessaly
Golden Voyage of Sinbad
Goliath Against the Giants
Goliath and the Barbarians
Goliath and the Dragon
Goliath and the Sins of
  Babylon
The Gorgon
Grendel, Grendel, Grendel
Hercules
Hercules 2
Hercules Against the Moon
  Men
Hercules and the Captive
  Women
Hercules in the Haunted World
Hercules Unchained
Invincible Gladiators
Invitation to the Dance
Iphigenia
Jason and the Argonauts
Johnny Appleseed
Kismet
Kriemhilde's Revenge
The Legend of Sleepy Hollow
The Legend of Suram
  Fortress
Life on a String
The Loves of Hercules
Maciste in Hell
Medea
Merlin and the Sword
Messalina vs. the Son of
  Hercules
A Midsummer Night's Dream
Monty Python and the Holy
  Grail
My Darlin' Clementine
Pancho Villa Returns
Pathfinder
Pecos Bill
Phedre
Phoenix
Rudyard Kipling's Classic
  Stories
The Secret of Navajo Cave
The Secret of the Loch
Siegfried
Son of Samson
Sons of Hercules in the Land
  of Darkness
Terror of Rome Against the
  Son of Hercules
Thor and the Amazon Women
Ulysses
Ursus in the Valley of the
  Lions
Winds of Change
Wonderful World of the
  Brothers Grimm
Young Aphrodites
Zvenigora

Football

All the Right Moves
Backfield in Motion
The Best of Times
Black Sunday
Brian's Song
Cheering Section

Cheerleaders' Beach Party
Cheerleaders' Wild Weekend
Diner
The Dropkick
Easy Living
Everybody's All American
First & Ten
First & Ten: The Team Scores
  Again
The Freshman
The Galloping Ghost
Good News
Grambling's White Tiger
Gus
Heaven Can Wait
Hold 'Em Jail
Horse Feathers
Jim Thorpe: All American
Johnny Be Good
Knute Rockne: All American
The Last Boy Scout
Last Game
The Longest Yard
Necessary Roughness
North Dallas Forty
One Night Only
Paper Lion
Quarterback Princess
Roberta
School Ties
Semi-Tough
The Spirit of West Point
Trouble Along the Way
Two Minute Warning
Wildcats

Foreign Intrigue

Above Suspicion
Ambassador Bill
American Roulette
Battle Beneath the Earth
Bulldog Drummond at Bay
Call Him Mr. Shatter
Catch Me a Spy
Chinese Boxes
Chinese Web
Cover-Up
Deadly Alliance
The Destructors
Devil Wears White
An Englishman Abroad
The Executioner
Federal Agent
The Fourth Protocol
Gunpowder
Jaguar Lives
Jumpin' Jack Flash
Overthrow
Postmark for Danger
Puzzle
Reilly: Ace of Spies
Saigon: Year of the Cat
Sebastian
Strangers
Sweet Country
The Third Man
Torn Curtain
Windmills of the Gods

Frame-Ups

Abbott & Costello Meet the
  Invisible Man
Another Pair of Aces: Three of
  a Kind
Backfire
Bedroom Eyes
Below the Deadline
Best Revenge
Big Score
The Big Sweat
The Big Switch
Blind Man's Bluff
The Blum Affair
Breakdown
Buried Alive

Hit Men

Hockey

Holidays

Holocaust

Homeless

Run, Stranger, Run
The Runestone
Rush Week
Sabaka
The Sadist
The Saga of the Draculas
Salem's Lot
Samson in the Wax Museum
Samson vs. the Vampire
  Women
The Satanic Rites of Dracula
Satanik
Satan's Black Wedding
Satan's Blade
Satan's Cheerleaders
Satan's Princess
Satan's School for Girls
Satan's Touch
Satanwar
Saturday Night Shockers
Saturday Night Shockers, Vol.
  2
Saturday Night Shockers, Vol.
  3
Saturday Night Shockers, Vol.
  4
The Savage Bees
Savage Intruder
Savage Weekend
Savages
Scalpel
Scanners
Scanners 2: The New Order
Scanners 3: The Takeover
Scared Stiff
Scared to Death
The Scars of Dracula
Schizo
Schizoid
Science Crazed
Scorpion with Two Tails
The Scorpion's Tail
Scream, Baby, Scream
Scream Blacula Scream
Scream Dream
Scream of Fear
Scream of the Demon Lover
Screamers
The Screaming Dead
The Screaming Skull
Screams of a Winter Night
Screamtime
Season of the Witch
The Secret Cinema
See No Evil
Seedpeople
Seeds of Evil
Seizure
The Sender
The Sentinel
The Serpent and the Rainbow
The Serpent of Death
Servants of Twilight
Seven Deaths in the Cat's Eye
Seven Doors of Death
The Seventh Victim
The Severed Arm
Severed Ties
Shadow of Chinatown
Shadows Run Black
Shakma
The Shaman
Shark's Paradise
The She-Beast
She Came on the Bus
She Demons
She-Freak
The Shining
Shock 'Em Dead
Shock! Shock! Shock!
Shock Waves
Shocker
Shriek of the Mutilated
The Sibling
Silent Madness
Silent Night, Bloody Night

Silent Night, Deadly Night
Silent Night, Deadly Night 2
Silent Night, Deadly Night 3:
  Better Watch Out!
Silent Night, Deadly Night 4:
  Initiation
Silent Night, Deadly Night 5:
  The Toymaker
Silent Scream
Silver Bullet
The Sinister Invasion
Sinner's Blood
The Sins of Dorian Gray
Sinthia: The Devil's Doll
Sisters
Sisters of Satan
Skinned Alive
The Skull
Skullduggery
Slashdance
Slaughter High
Slaughter Hotel
The Slaughter of the Vampires
Slaughterhouse
Slaughterhouse Rock
The Slayer
The Slayer/The Scalps
Sleazemania III: The Good,
  the Bad & the Sleazy
Sledgehammer
Sleep of Death
Sleepaway Camp
Sleepaway Camp 2: Unhappy
  Campers
Sleepaway Camp 3: Teenage
  Wasteland
Sleepwalkers
Slime City
The Slime People
Slithis
Slugs
The Slumber Party Massacre
Slumber Party Massacre 2
Slumber Party Massacre 3
The Snake Hunter Strangler
The Snake People
The Snake Woman
Snowbeast
Society
Sole Survivor
Something Weird
Sometimes Aunt Martha Does
  Dreadful Things
Sometimes They Come Back
Son of Blob
Sorority House Massacre
Sorority House Massacre 2:
  Nighty Nightmare
Sound of Horror
Sounds of Silence
Spasms
The Spawning
The Spectre of Edgar Allen
  Poe
The Spell
The Spellbinder
Spellcaster
Spiritism
Spirits
Spirits of the Dead
Splatter University
Spontaneous Combustion
Spookies
Squirm
Stage Fright
Stagefright
Stanley
Stay Awake
Stephen King's Golden Years
Stephen King's It
Stepsisters
Stones of Death
Strait-Jacket
Strange Behavior
Strange Case of Dr. Jekyll &
  Mr. Hyde

The Strangeness
Strangers
Strays
Stuff Stephanie in the
  Incinerator
Subspecies
Sugar Cookies
Suicide Cult
Summer of Fear
Summer of Secrets
Sundown
Superstition
Survivor
Suspiria
Swamp of the Lost Monster
The Swarm
Sweet 16
Tainted Image
Tales from the Crypt
Tales of Terror
Tales That Witness Madness
Tarantulas: The Deadly Cargo
Taste the Blood of Dracula
Teenage Strangler
Teenage Zombies
The Tell-Tale Heart
The Tempter
Tentacles
The Terror
Terror at Red Wolf Inn
Terror at Tenkiller
Terror at the Opera
Terror Beach
Terror Eyes
Terror in the Haunted House
Terror in the Swamp
Terror in the Wax Museum
Terror in Toyland
Terror on Tour
Terror Out of the Sky
Terror Train
The Terror Within
Terrorgram
Testament of Dr. Mabuse
The Texas Chainsaw
  Massacre
Texas Chainsaw Massacre,
  Part 2
That Darn Sorceress
Theatre of Death
They Came from Within
They Saved Hitler's Brain
Things
Thirst
The Thirsty Dead
The 13th Floor
Thirteenth Reunion
The Thousand Eyes of Dr.
  Mabuse
Three on a Meathook
Time of the Apes
To All a Goodnight
To Die for
To Die for 2
To Sleep with a Vampire
To the Devil, A Daughter
Tomb
Tomb of Ligeia
Tomb of the Undead
Tomb of Torture
Tombs of the Blind Dead
Tomcat: Dangerous Desires
The Toolbox Murders
Tormented
Torso
Torture Chamber of Baron
  Blood
The Torture Chamber of Dr.
  Sadism
Torture Dungeon
Torture Garden
Torture Train
The Touch of Satan
Tower of Evil
Tower of Screaming Virgins
Toxic Zombies

Track of the Moonbeast
Track of the Vampire
Transmutations
Trap Them & Kill Them
Trick or Treat
Trick or Treats
Trilogy of Terror
Troll
Troll 2
Truth or Dare?
Twice Dead
Twice-Told Tales
Twilight People
Twilight Zone: The Movie
Twins of Evil
Twinsanity
Twisted
Twisted Brain
Twisted Nightmare
Twitch of the Death Nerve
Two Evil Eyes
The Two Faces of Evil
2000 Maniacs
The Unborn
The Uncanny
Uncle Was a Vampire
The Undead
Understudy: The Graveyard
  Shift 2
Underworld
The Unearthly
The Unholy
The Uninvited
Unmasked Part 25
The Unnamable
The Unnamable 2: The
  Statement of Randolph
  Carter
The Unseen
Vampire at Midnight
Vampire Circus
Vampire Cop
The Vampire Hookers
The Vampire Lovers
Vampyres
Varan the Unbelievable
Vault of Horror
The Velvet Vampire
Vengeance Is Mine
Vengeance of the Zombies
Venom
Venus in Furs
Victims
The Video Dead
Video Violence
Video Violence Part 2...The
  Exploitation!
Videodrome
The Vindicator
The Vineyard
Violent Blood Bath
Virgin Among the Living Dead
The Virgin of Nuremberg
The Virgin Witch
Visions of Evil
The Visitor
Visitor from the Grave
Voodoo Black Exorcist
Voodoo Dawn
Voodoo Woman
Vulture
Wacko
Warlock
Warlock Moon
The Wasp Woman
Watch Me When I Kill
Watcher in the Woods
Watchers
Watchers 2
Waxwork
Web of the Spider
The Weirdo
Welcome to Spring Break
Werewolf in a Girl's Dormitory
Werewolf of Washington
Werewolves on Wheels

What a Carve-Up!
What Ever Happened to Baby
  Jane?
What the Peeper Saw
What's the Matter with Helen?
Wheels of Terror
When the Screaming Stops
Whiskey Mountain
Whispers
Who Slew Auntie Roo?
The Wicked
The Wicker Man
The Wild Beasts
Willard
The Willies
The Witch
Witch Who Came from the
  Sea
Witchboard
Witchcraft
Witchcraft 2: The Temptress
Witchcraft 3: The Kiss of
  Death
Witchcraft 5: Dance with the
  Devil
Witchery
Witches' Mountain
The Witching
Witching Time
The Witchmaker
The Witch's Mirror
WitchTrap
The Wizard of Gore
Wolfen
The Wolfman
Woodchipper Massacre
World of the Vampires
The Worm Eaters
Wrestling Women vs. the
  Aztec Ape
Wrestling Women vs. the
  Aztec Mummy
You are Not I
Zoltan...Hound of Dracula
Zombie
Zombie High
Zombie Island Massacre
Zombie Lake
Zombie Nightmare
Zombies of Moratau
Zombiethon
Zone of the Dead

Horror Comedy

Adventures of Eliza Fraser
Andy Warhol's Dracula
Andy Warhol's Frankenstein
Arachnophobia
Army of Darkness
Attack of the Killer
  Refrigerator
Attack of the Killer Tomatoes
Attack of the Robots
Auntie Lee's Meat Pies
Autopsy of a Ghost
Bad Channels
Bad Taste
Beauty on the Beach
Beetlejuice
Bela Lugosi Meets a Brooklyn
  Gorilla
Beverly Hills Bodysnatchers
Big Meat Eater
Billy the Kid Versus Dracula
Black Magic
Blood Beach
Blood Hook
Bloodbath at the House of
  Death
The Bone Yard
Brain Damage
Bride of Re-Animator
A Bucket of Blood
Carry On Screaming
C.H.U.D.

Killer

Creepers
Creepshow
Curse of the Black Widow
The Deadly Mantis
Doctor Who: The Ark in Space
Earth vs. the Spider
Empire of the Ants
Evil Spawn
Food of the Gods
The Giant Spider Invasion
Kingdom of the Spiders
Kiss of the Tarantula
The Lair of the White Worm
Monster from Green Hell
The Monster that Challenged
  the World
Mothra
Naked Jungle
The Nest
Parasite
Phase 4
Return of the Fly
The Savage Bees
The Scorpion's Tail
Slugs
Son of Godzilla
Spider Woman
Squirm
The Swarm
Tarantula
Tarantulas: The Deadly Cargo
Terror Out of the Sky
Them!
They Came from Within
The Wasp Woman
The Worm Eaters

Killer Plants

Attack of the Killer Tomatoes
Attack of the Mushroom
  People
Day of the Triffids
Dr. Terror's House of Horrors
The Freakmaker
Invasion of the Body
  Snatchers
Killer Tomatoes Eat France
Killer Tomatoes Strike Back
Little Shop of Horrors
Navy vs. the Night Monsters
Please Don't Eat My Mother
Return of the Killer Tomatoes
Seedpeople
Seeds of Evil

Killer Toys

Black Devil Doll from Hell
Child's Play
Child's Play 2
Child's Play 3
Dance of Death
Demonic Toys
Devil Doll
Devil's Gift
Dolls
Dolly Dearest
Halloween 3: Season of the
  Witch
House of Evil
Magic
Poltergeist
Puppet Master
Puppet Master 2
Puppet Master 3: Toulon's
  Revenge
Silent Night, Deadly Night 5:
  The Toymaker
Trilogy of Terror
Wired to Kill

Kindness of Strangers

Angels Over Broadway
The Big Push

Good Sam
Great Expectations
Lilies of the Field
Major Barbara
Mr. Deeds Goes to Town
Mr. Lucky
Mr. North
She Couldn't Say No
Sincerely Yours
Toll Gate
Touch & Go
The Vals

King of Beasts (Dogs)

The Accidental Tourist
Across the Bridge
The Adventures of Milo & Otis
The Adventures of Rex &
  Rinty
The Adventures of Rin Tin Tin
After the Thin Man
All Dogs Go to Heaven
The Amazing Dobermans
Antarctica
The Awful Truth
Baxter
Beethoven
Behave Yourself!
Benji
Benji the Hunted
Benji's Very Own Christmas
  Story
Big Red
Bingo
Bunnicula: Vampire Rabbit
Call of the Wild
Captured in Chinatown
Challenge To Be Free
Challenge to Lassie
Challenge to White Fang
A Charlie Brown Celebration
Children of the Wild
C.H.O.M.P.S.
Come Back Little Reba
Complex
Courage of Lassie
Courage of Rin Tin Tin
Courage of the North
A Cry in the Dark
Cujo
Danny Boy
Daring Dobermans
The Dawson Patrol
Devil Dog: The Hound of Hell
Digby, the Biggest Dog in the
  World
Dirkham Detective Agency
The Doberman Gang
A Dog of Flanders
Dog Pound Shuffle
Dogs of Hell
The Dogs Who Stopped the
  War
Down and Out in Beverly Hills
Dusty
Elmer
Eyes of Texas
Fabulous Joe
Famous Five Get Into Trouble
Fangs of the Wild
Flaming Signal
For the Love of Benji
Frankenweenie
George!
Git!
God's Country
The Good, the Bad, and
  Huckleberry Hound
Goodbye, My Lady
Great Adventure
Greyfriars Bobby
Hambone & Hillie
Heart of the Rockies
Here Comes Droopy

He's Your Dog, Charlie
  Brown!
Hollow Gate
Homeward Bound: The
  Incredible Journey
The Hound of the Baskervilles
Incredible Detectives
The Incredible Journey
Inside Information
It's a Dog's Life
It's a Mystery, Charlie Brown
K-9
K-9000
Kavik the Wolf Dog
Lady and the Tramp
Lassie: Adventures of Neeka
Lassie, Come Home
Lassie: The Miracle
Lassie: Well of Love
Lassie's Great Adventure
Laurel & Hardy: Laughing
  Gravy
Legend of the Northwest
Life is a Circus, Charlie
  Brown/You're the Greatest,
  Charlie Brown
Lightning Warrior
Little Heroes
The Lone Defender
Love Leads the Way
Magic of Lassie
Man Trouble
The Man Who Wagged His
  Tail
Man's Best Friend
The Meeting: Eddie Finds a
  Home
Million Dollar Haul
Milo & Otis
Mrs. Brown, You've Got a
  Lovely Daughter
Mr. Superinvisible
Mom, the Wolfman and Me
Mongrel
Monster Dog
My Dog Shep
My Dog, the Thief
The Night Cry
Nikki, the Wild Dog of the
  North
Oh, Heavenly Dog!
Old Yeller
101 Dalmations
The Pack
The Painted Hills
The Plague Dogs
Play Dead
Poco
Pound Puppies and the
  Legend of Big Paw
The Return of Grey Wolf
Return of Our Gang
Reuben, Reuben
Rin Tin Tin, Hero of the West
Rover Dangerfield
Savage Sam
Scruffy
Shadow of the Thin Man
The Shaggy D.A.
The Shaggy Dog
Shep Comes Home
Sherlock Hound: Tales of
  Mystery
Silver Stallion
Skeezer
Skull & Crown
Smoke
Son of Lassie
Song of the Thin Man
Sputnik
Spy with a Cold Nose
Storm in a Teacup
Summerdog
Teddy at the Throttle
The Tender Years
They Only Kill Their Masters

The Thin Man
The Thin Man Goes Home
Toby McTeague
Tom and Jerry: The Movie
Turner and Hooch
The Ugly Dachshund
Umberto D
The Underdog
Watchers
Watchers 2
We Think the World of You
When Lightning Strikes
Where the Red Fern Grows
Where the Red Fern Grows:
  Part 2
White Fang and the Hunter
Whitewater Sam
The Wizard of Oz
Wolf Dog
Wolfheart's Revenge
Zoltan...Hound of Dracula

Korean War

All the Young Men
Battle Circus
The Bridges at Toko-Ri
The Canon Operation
Dragonfly Squadron
Field of Honor
For the Boys
The Hunters
Iron Angel
Jet Attack/Paratroop
  Command
The Last Picture Show
MacArthur
The Manchurian Candidate
M*A*S*H
M*A*S*H: Goodbye, Farewell
  & Amen
Men in War
Men of the Fighting Lady
Mission Inferno
Mr. Walkie Talkie
One Minute to Zero
Operation Dames
Operation Inchon
Pork Chop Hill
Pueblo Affair
Retreat, Hell!
Sabre Jet
Sayonara
Sergeant Ryker
The Steel Helmet
Torpedo Alley
Wonsan Operation

Labor & Unions

Act of Vengeance
Black Fury
Blue Collar
Border Heat
Boxcar Bertha
Brother John
The Devil & Miss Jones
The Displaced Person
The End of St. Petersburg
Fame is the Spur
F.I.S.T.
The $5.20 an Hour Dream
Gung Ho
Hoffa
I'm All Right Jack
Joyride
Keeping On
Killing Floor
Last Exit to Brooklyn
Mac
Man of Marble
Matewan
Molly Maguires
Moonlighting
Never Steal Anything Small
Newsies
Norma Rae

North Dallas Forty
On the Waterfront
Pajama Game
Riff Raff
Salt of the Earth
Singleton's Pluck
Sons of Steel
Strike
Sweetheart!
Take This Job & Shove It
Teamster Boss: The Jackie
  Presser Story
The Triangle Factory Fire
  Scandal
Waterfront

Late Bloomin' Love

Adorable Julia
The African Queen
Ali: Fear Eats the Soul
Atlantic City
Bed & Breakfast
Breakfast in Paris
Brief Encounter
Cass Timberlane
Charly
The Christmas Wife
Circle of Two
Cold Sassy Tree
Crazy from the Heart
Devil in the Flesh
Doctor in Distress
End of August
A Fine Romance
Finnegan Begin Again
Forbidden Love
Foreign Affairs
Forty Carats
Gal Young 'Un
Gin Game
Harold and Maude
If Ever I See You Again
La Symphonie Pastorale
The Last Winters
Lonely Hearts
The Lonely Passion of Judith
  Hearne
Love Among the Ruins
Macaroni
A Man and a Woman
The Night of the Iguana
Other People's Money
The Pamela Principle
Players
Queen of the Stardust
  Ballroom
The Rainmaker
Roman Spring of Mrs. Stone
San Antonio
Shirley Valentine
The Shock
The Shop Around the Corner
Shore Leave
A Small Killing
Something in Common
Stay As You Are
Stormy Waters
Stroszek
To Love Again
Travelling North
24 Hours in a Woman's Life
Twice in a Lifetime
Used People
With Six You Get Eggroll

Law & Lawyers

Adam's Rib
Afterburn
Anatomy of a Murder
And Justice for All
Angel on My Shoulder
Beyond a Reasonable Doubt
Beyond the Silhouette
Bleak House
Blood Brothers

Martial

Chinese Connection 2
Chinese Stuntman
Circle of Iron
Clash of the Ninja
Cleopatra Jones
Cleopatra Jones & the Casino of Gold
Clones of Bruce Lee
The Cobra
Cobra
Cobra Against Ninja
Cold Blooded Murder
Counter Attack
Counter Destroyer
Crack Shadow Boxers
Crazy Kung Fu Master
Daggers 8
Dance of Death
Day of the Panther
The Deadliest Art: The Best of the Martial Arts Films
Deadly Bet
Deadly Kick
Deadly Strike
Death Beach
Death Challenge
Death Code Ninja
Death Duel of Mantis
Death Machines
Death Mask of the Ninja
Death Raiders
Death Ring
Death Warrant
The Demon Fighter
Desert Kickboxer
Diamond Ninja Force
Dirty Partners
The Divine Enforcer
Dolemite
Double Impact
The Dragon Fist
Dragon Force
Dragon from Shaolin
Dragon Lady Ninja/Devil Killer
Dragon Lee vs. the Five Brothers
The Dragon Lives Again
Dragon Lord
Dragon Princess
The Dragon Returns
Dragon Rider
The Dragon Strikes Back
Dragon: The Bruce Lee Story
Dragon the Odds
Dragon vs. Needles of Death
Dragon's Claw
The Dragon's Showdown
Dreadnaught
Dreadnaught Rivals
Dual Flying Kicks
Duel of Fists
Duel of the Brave Ones
Duel of the Iron Fist
Duel of the Masters
Duel of the Seven Tigers
Dynamo
Dynasty
Eagle Claws Champion
Eagle's Shadow
Edge of Fury
18 Bronzemen
Eighteen Jade Arhats
The Eliminators
Empire of Spiritual Ninja
Empire of the Dragon
Enter the Dragon
Enter the Game of Death
Enter the Ninja
Enter the Panther
Enter Three Dragons
Exit the Dragon, Enter the Tiger
An Eye for an Eye
Fantasy Mission Force
Fast Fists
The Fate of Lee Khan

Fearless Fighters
Fearless Hyena
Fearless Hyena: Part 2
The Fearless Young Boxer
Ferocious Female Freedom Fighters
Fight for Survival
Fight to the Death
Fighting Ace
Fighting Black Kings
Fighting Duel of Death
Fighting Life
Final Impact
Firecracker
A Fist Full of Talons
Fist of Death
Fist of Fear, Touch of Death
Fist of Vengeance
The Fist, the Kicks, and the Evils
Fists of Blood
Fists of Bruce Lee
Fists of Dragons
Fists of Fury
Fists of Fury 2
Fists of the White Lotus
Five Fighters from Shaolin
Flash Challenger
Force of One
Forced Vengeance
Forest Duel
Forgotten Warrior
The Four Hands of Death: Wily Match
Four Infernos to Cross
Four Robbers
From China with Death
Fugitive Samurai
Full Metal Ninja
The Furious
Furious
The Furious Avenger
Furious Slaughter
Fury in the Shaolin Temple
Fury of King Boxer
Futurekick
The Gambling Samurai
Game of Death
Gang Wars
Ghost of the Ninja
Ghostwarrior
Golden Destroyers
Golden Exterminators
Golden Ninja Invasion
Golden Ninja Warrior
Golden Sun
Goldfinger
Good Guys Wear Black
Grand Master of Shaolin Kung Fu
The Great Hunter
Great Massacre
The Greatest Fights of Martial Arts
Green Dragon Inn
Gymkata
Half a Loaf of Kung Fu
Hands of Death
Hard to Kill
Hell's Wind Staff
Hero and the Terror
Heroes in the Ming Dynasty
Hero's Blood
Hot Potato
The Hot, the Cool, and the Vicious
Hurricane Sword
Image of Bruce Lee
In Eagle Shadow Fist
In Your Face
Incredible Master Beggars
Instant Kung-Fu Man
The Instructor
Invasion U.S.A.
Invincible
Invincible Obsessed Fighter

Invincible Sword
Iron Dragon Strikes Back
Iron Thunder
Ironheart
Island Warriors
Jackie Chan's Police Force
Jaguar Lives
Japanese Connection
Jaws of the Dragon
The Karate Kid
The Karate Kid: Part 2
The Karate Kid: Part 3
Karate Killer
Karate Warrior
Karate Warriors
The Kick Fighter
Kick of Death: The Prodigal Boxer
Kickboxer
Kickboxer 2: The Road Back
Kickboxer 3: The Art of War
Kickboxer the Champion
Kill and Kill Again
Kill Factor
Kill Line
Kill or Be Killed
Kill Squad
Kill the Golden Goose
Killer Elephants
The Killing Machine
King Boxer
King Boxers
King of Kung-Fu
The King of the Kickboxers
Kingfisher the Killer
Kung Fu
Kung Fu Avengers
Kung Fu Commandos
Kung Fu for Sale
Kung Fu from Beyond the Grave
Kung Fu Genius
Kung Fu Hero
Kung Fu Hero 2
The Kung Fu Kid
The Kung Fu Kid from Peking
Kung Fu Kids
Kung Fu Massacre
Kung Fu of Eight Drunkards
Kung Fu Powerhouse
Kung Fu Rebels
Kung Fu Shadow
Kung Fu Strongman
Kung Fu Terminator
Kung Fu: The Movie
The Kung Fu Warrior
Kung Fu Zombie
Kung Fu's Hero
La Venganza del Kung Fu
Lady Dragon
Las Doce Patadas Mortales del Kung Fu
Last Challenge of the Dragon
The Last Dragon
Legend of Eight Samurai
Leopard Fist Ninja
Lightning Kung Fu
Lionheart
Little Big Master
Little Dragons
Little Heroes of Shaolin Temple
The Lost Samurai Sword
Low Blow
Machoman
Mafia vs. Ninja
The Magnificent
Magnificent Duo
The Magnificent Kick
Magnum Killers
Man Called Tiger
Manchurian Avenger
Mark of the Scorpion
Marked for Death
Martial Law
Martial Law 2: Undercover

Martial Monks of Shaolin Temple/Dragon Against Vampire
Marvelous Stunts of Kung Fu
Master Killer (The Thirty-Sixth Chamber)
The Master Killers
Master Ninja
Master Ninja 2
Master Ninja 3
Master Ninja 4
Master Ninja 5
Master of Death
Master of Kung Fu
Master's Revenge
Mean Streets of Kung Fu
Militant Eagle
Mission Kiss and Kill
Mission of Justice
Monkey in the Master's Eye
Monkey Kung Fu
Moonlight Sword & Jade Lion
Murder Masters of Kung Fu
My Lucky Stars
My Name Called Bruce
My Samurai
New Fist of Fury
Night Master
Night of the Kickfighters
Night of the Ninja
Night of the Warrior
9 1/2 Ninjas
Nine Deaths of the Ninja
Ninja 3: The Domination
Ninja Academy
Ninja: American Warrior
Ninja Avengers
Ninja Blacklist
Ninja Brothers of Blood
Ninja Champion
Ninja Checkmate
Ninja Commandments
Ninja Condors
Ninja Connection
Ninja Death Squad
Ninja Demon's Massacre
Ninja Destroyer
Ninja Dragon
The Ninja Empire
Ninja Enforcer
Ninja Exterminators
Ninja Fantasy
Ninja Force of Assassins
Ninja Holocaust
Ninja Hunt
The Ninja Hunter
Ninja in Action
Ninja in the Claws of the C.I.A.
Ninja in the Deadly Trap
Ninja in the U.S.A.
Ninja Kill
Ninja Knight Heaven's Hell
Ninja Massacre
Ninja Masters of Death
Ninja Mission
Ninja Nightmare
Ninja of the Magnificence
Ninja Operation: Licensed to Terminate
Ninja Phantom Heroes
The Ninja Pirates
Ninja Powerforce
Ninja Showdown
Ninja: Silent Assassin
Ninja Squad
Ninja Strike Force
Ninja Supremo
Ninja Swords of Death
Ninja Terminator
Ninja the Battalion
Ninja the Protector
Ninja, the Violent Sorcerer
Ninja Thunderbolt
Ninja Turf
Ninja USA
Ninja Vengeance

Ninja vs. Bruce Lee
Ninja vs. Ninja
Ninja vs. the Shaolin
Ninja Warriors
Ninja Wars
The Ninja Wolves
Ninja's Extreme Weapons
No Retreat, No Surrender
No Retreat, No Surrender 2
No Retreat, No Surrender 3: Blood Brothers
The Noble Ninja
Octagon
Of Cooks and Kung-Fu
Omega Cop
The One Arm Swordsmen
One Down, Two to Go!
One-Eyed Swordsman
Operation Orient
Out for Justice
Overkill
Passage of the Dragon
The Perfect Weapon
Phoenix the Ninja
The Power of the Ninjitsu
Powerforce
Pray for Death
Prodigal Boxer: The Kick of Death
Professional Killers 1
Protector
Pursuit
Pushed to the Limit
Queen Boxer
Rage and Honor
Rage of Honor
Rage of the Master
Rage of Wind
Ragin' Cajun
Raiders of the Buddhist Kung Fu
Rapid Fire
Raw Force
Real Bruce Lee
The Rebellious Reign
Red Dragons of Shaolin
Remo Williams: The Adventure Begins
Renegade Monk
Renegade Ninja
Retrievers
Return of Bruce
Return of Fist of Fury
Return of the Chinese Boxer
Return of the Dragon
Return of the Red Tiger
Return of the Scorpion
Return of the Tiger
Revenge of Fist of Fury
Revenge of the Ninja
Revolt of the Dragon
Rickisha Kuri
Ring of Fire
Ring of Fire 2: Blood and Steel
Rivals of the Dragon/ Magnificent Shaolin Fist Fighter
Rivals of the Silver Fox
Roaring Fire
Robot Ninja
Roller Blade
Sakura Killers
The Samurai
Samurai Blood, Samurai Guts
Samurai Death Bells
Samurai Sword of Justice
Sanshiro Sugata
Scorpion
Secret Executioners
Secret of Tai Chi
The Secret of the Snake and Crane
Seven Blows of the Dragon
The 7 Brothers Meet Dracula
Shadow Killers
Shanghai Massacre

Martyred Pop Icons

Mass Media

Medieval Romps

Meltdown

Mistaken

Support Your Local
    Gunfighter
Switched at Birth
10 Rillington Place
The Tenth Man
Texas Carnival
Texas Cyclone
They Knew What They
    Wanted
The Thin Blue Line
Things Change
The 39 Steps
Tombstone Terror
Top Hat
Toto le Heros
True Identity
The Unholy Three
The Well
We're No Angels
White Eagle
White of the Eye
Who's Harry Crumb?
Withnail and I
The Wrong Guys
Zertigo Diamond Caper

Monsters, General

The Astounding She-Monster
Atlas in the Land of the
    Cyclops
Barn of the Naked Dead
The Beast from Haunted Cave
Beast in the Cellar
Beast of the Yellow Night
The Beast of Yucca Flats
The Beast Within
The Being
The Best of the Monsters
Bio Hazard
Black Roses
Blackenstein
The Blob
Blood Tide
Boggy Creek II
The Boy Who Loved Trolls
Brain of Blood
The Brainiac
The Bride
Bride of the Gorilla
Bride of the Monster
Brides of the Beast
Cameron's Closet
Captain Sinbad
The Capture of Bigfoot
Carry On Screaming
Cast a Deadly Spell
Castle of Evil
The Cellar
The Channeler
C.H.U.D.
C.H.U.D. 2: Bud the Chud
The Crater Lake Monster
Creature of Destruction
Creeping Terror
Creepozoids
Creepshow
The Curse
Curse 2: The Bite
Curse 3: Blood Sacrifice
Curse of the Swamp Creature
Dagora, the Space Monster
The Daughter of Dr. Jekyll
Deepstar Six
The Demon
Demon of Paradise
Demons
Demons of Ludlow
Demonstone
Demonwarp
Destroy All Monsters
Devil Kiss
Devil Monster
Devil Rider
Dr. Orloff's Invisible Horror
Dr. Orloff's Monster

Doctor Who: Terror of the
    Zygons
Don't Be Afraid of the Dark
Emergency
Equinox
Evil Dead
Evil Dead 2: Dead by Dawn
The Evil of Frankenstein
Evil Town
Fiend Without a Face
Fire Maidens from Outer
    Space
Fire Monsters Against the Son
    of Hercules
Forbidden Planet
Frankenstein
Frankenstein: A Cinematic
    Scrapbook
Frankenstein '80
Frankenstein General Hospital
Frankenstein Island
Frankenstein Meets the
    Wolfman
Frankenstein Unbound
Frankenstein's Daughter
Gamera, the Invincible
Gamera vs. Barugon
Gamera vs. Gaos
Gamera vs. Guiron
Gamera vs. Zigra
Gammera the Invincible
Gappa the Trifibian Monster
Gate 2
Geek Maggot Bingo
Ghidrah the Three Headed
    Monster
The Giant Claw
Godzilla, King of the Monsters
Godzilla 1985
Godzilla on Monster Island
Godzilla Raids Again
Godzilla vs. Biollante
Godzilla vs. Gigan
Godzilla vs. Megalon
Godzilla vs. Monster Zero
Godzilla vs. Mothra
Godzilla vs. the Cosmic
    Monster
Godzilla vs. the Smog
    Monster
Godzilla's Revenge
Goliath and the Dragon
Gorgo
Half Human
Halloween Monster Madness
Harry and the Hendersons
Hideous Sun Demon
Horror Express
Horror of Party Beach
Howling 6: The Freaks
I Was a Teenage Zombie
The Incredible Two-Headed
    Transplant
Infra-Man
Intruder Within
Invasion of the Animal People
The Invisible Monster
Island of Dr. Moreau
It's Alive!
Jack the Giant Killer
Jason and the Argonauts
Jungle Heat
The Killer Shrews
The Kindred
King of Kong Island
Labyrinth
Lady Frankenstein
Legend of Boggy Creek
Little Monsters
Mad Doctor of Blood Island
The Mad Monster
Mad Monster Party
Man Beast
The Manster
Maxim Xul
Meteor Monster

The Milpitas Monster
Mirror, Mirror
The Monolith Monsters
The Monster and the Stripper
The Monster of Piedras
    Blancas
The Monster Squad
The Monster that Challenged
    the World
Monsters Crash the Pajama
    Party
Mutant
Mutants In Paradise
My Demon Lover
The People Under the Stairs
The Phantom Creeps
The Phantom from 10,000
    Leagues
The Prey
The Quatermass Experiment
The Quest
Rana: The Legend of Shadow
    Lake
Rawhead Rex
The Return of Swamp Thing
Return to Boggy Creek
Revenge of Doctor X
Revolt of the Zombies
Samson in the Wax Museum
Saturday the 14th Strikes
    Back
Science Crazed
Scream Dream
The Screaming Dead
The Secret of the Loch
Seven Doors of Death
Shadowzone
Silent Night, Deadly Night 5:
    The Toymaker
The Slayer
The Slime People
The Snake Hunter Strangler
The Snow Creature
Sons of Hercules in the Land
    of Darkness
Space Monster
Squirm
Stay Awake
Stepmonster
The Strangeness
Subspecies
Swamp of the Lost Monster
Tales from the Darkside: The
    Movie
Terror Beneath the Sea
Terror in the Swamp
Terror of Mechagodzilla
Terror of Rome Against the
    Son of Hercules
The Terror Within
The Terror Within 2
The Terrornauts
Things
Tomb of Torture
Track of the Moonbeast
Transmutations
20 Million Miles to Earth
Varan the Unbelievable
The Video Dead
Voodoo Woman
Voyage to the Planet of
    Prehistoric Women
War of the Gargantuas
Watchers
Watchers 2
Yog, Monster from Space
Yongkari Monster of the Deep

Motor Vehicle Dept.

Action Jackson
American Graffiti
Back to the Future
Bail Out
The Betsy
Black Moon Rising

The Blues Brothers
Cadillac Man
Car Trouble
Car Wash
Chitty Chitty Bang Bang
Comic Cabby
Corvette Summer
Coupe de Ville
Cry Panic
Dangerous Curves
Dark of the Night
D.C. Cab
Deadline Auto Theft
Dream Machine
Drive-In
Drive-In Massacre
The Driver
Driving Me Crazy
Duel
Ferris Bueller's Day Off
Firebird 2015 A.D.
Follow That Car
Ford: The Man & the Machine
Free Ride
Freedom
Freeway
Great American Traffic Jam
Gung Ho
The Hearse
Herbie Rides Again
High Rolling in a Hot Corvette
Hometown U.S.A.
Hot Wire
How I Learned to Love
    Women
Killing Cars
License to Drive
The Love Bug
Maximum Overdrive
Motorama
Motown's Mustang
Moving Violations
My Chauffeur
National Lampoon's Vacation
Night on Earth
One Deadly Owner
Pepper and His Wacky Taxi
Raw Power
Repo Jake
Repo Man
Roger & Me
Silkwood
Smokey & the Hotwire Gang
Steel Arena
Stingray
Sunset Limousine
Superbug Super Agent
This Man Must Die
Tomboy
Tucker: The Man and His
    Dream
Used Cars
Valet Girls
The Van
Vanishing Point
Wheels of Terror
Zero to Sixty

Mountaineering

Alpine Fire
The Challenge
Cliffhanger
The Climb
The Eiger Sanction
Five Days One Summer
God's Bloody Acre
Heidi
K2: The Ultimate High
The Mountain
My Side of the Mountain
Storm and Sorrow
Third Man on the Mountain
The White Tower

Movie & TV Trailers

Cinema Shrapnel
Cowboys of the Saturday
    Matinee
Dracula: A Cinematic
    Scrapbook
Frankenstein: A Cinematic
    Scrapbook
Hitchcock Classics Collection:
    Trailers on Tape
Hollywood Uncensored
It Came from Hollywood
La Jetee/An Occurrence at
    Owl Creek Bridge
Loose Shoes
1939, The Movies' Vintage
    Year: Trailers on Tape
The Professor
To See Such Fun

Music

All You Need Is Cash
Allegro Non Troppo
Amadeus
American Blue Note
Americathon
The Apple
Ballad in Blue
Basileus Quartet
Beach Boys: An American
    Band
Beat Street
The Beatniks
Beethoven
Beethoven Lives Upstairs
Beethoven's Nephew
The Benny Goodman Story
The Best of Kenny Everett
    Video Show
Beyond the Doors
Bird
Blame It on the Night
Bloodhounds of Broadway
Blueberry Hill
The Bodyguard
Born to Boogie
Bound for Glory
Broken Strings
Buddy's Song
Bummer
Burglar
Captain January
Carmen
Cartoon Classics, No. 1:
    Looney Tunes & Merrie
    Melodies
CB4: The Movie
Coal Miner's Daughter
Comeback
The Commitments
The Competition
The Compleat Beatles
Concrete Angels
Cool As Ice
Cool Mikado
The Cotton Club
The Courier
Crossroads
Dead Girls
Death Drug
Death Games
Deception
Decline of Western Civilization
    1
Decline of Western Civilization
    2: The Metal Years
Diner
Disorderlies
Diva
Divine Madness
Doctor Duck's Super Secret
    All-Purpose Sauce
Don't Look Back
The Doors

The Doors: Soft Parade, a
  Retrospective
Double Trouble
Dreaming Lips
Dubeat-E-O
Duet for One
The Duke is the Tops
Dutch Treat
Easyriders Video Magazine
Eddie and the Cruisers
Eddie and the Cruisers 2:
  Eddie Lives!
The Eddy Duchin Story
Edie in Ciao! Manhattan
Elvis and Me
Elvis Memories
Elvis on Tour
Elvis: One Night with You
Elvis: Rare Moments with the
  King
Elvis Stories
Elvis: The Lost Performances
Elvis: The Movie
Encounter at Raven's Gate
Escape Me Never
The Eternal Waltz
Eubie!
The Fabulous Baker Boys
The Fabulous Dorseys
Face the Music
Fantasia
Fastest Guitar Alive
The Fighting Legion
Fighting Mad
Fingers
Five Easy Pieces
The Five Heartbeats
The Five Pennies
FM
Follow Me, Boys!
Follow That Dream
For Those About to Rock:
  Monsters in Moscow
Forget Mozart
Frankie and Johnny
Fugitive Valley
The Gay Ranchero
The Gene Krupa Story
George and the Christmas
  Star
Get Crazy
Getting Over
Giant Steps
The Gig
Gimme Shelter
Give My Regards to Broad
  Street
The Glenn Miller Story
Good Morning, Vietnam
Gotta Dance, Gotta Sing
Great Balls of Fire
The Great Waltz
Green Card
Hard Day's Night
Hear My Song
Heartbreak Hotel
Hearts of Fire
Hi-De-Ho
Home Sweet Home
House Party
House Party 2: The Pajama
  Jam
Humoresque
I Wanna Hold Your Hand
Identity Crisis
Incident at Channel Q
Irving Berlin's America
It Couldn't Happen Here
I've Always Loved You
The Jacksons: An American
  Dream
Jazz Singer
Jazzman
Joey
Johnny Guitar
Johnny Suede

Kid from Gower Gulch
King of Jazz
Knights & Emeralds
Krush Groove
Lady Be Good
Lady Sings the Blues
Las Vegas Hillbillys
The Las Vegas Story
The Last Waltz
Le Cavaleur
Leningrad Cowboys Go
  America
Let It Be
Let It Rock
Let's Get Lost
Lisztomania
Los Apuros de Dos Gallos
Louis Armstrong: Chicago
  Style
Mahler
The Man and the Monster
A Matter of Degrees
Matters of the Heart
The Medium
Melody for Three
Mo' Better Blues
Monkey Grip
Monterey Pop
Moonlight Sonata
Moscow on the Hudson
Mozart: A Childhood
  Chronicle
The Mozart Brothers
The Mozart Story
The Music Lovers
The Music Teacher
My Pal Trigger
Mystery in Swing
Netherworld
New York, New York
Not Quite Love
Oklahoma Kid
On the Air Live with Captain
  Midnight
Otello
Outlaw Blues
Paris Blues
Party! Party!
Pete Kelly's Blues
Peter Pan
Phantom of the Paradise
The Pied Piper of Hamelin
Play Misty for Me
Play Murder for Me
Playing for Time
Point of Terror
Portfolio
Privates on Parade
Quadrophenia
The Real Buddy Holly Story
The Real Patsy Cline
Rhapsody
Rich Girl
River of No Return
Roadkill
Rock & Roll Cowboys
Rock & Rule
Rock & the Money-Hungry
  Party Girls
Rock, Baby, Rock It
Rock 'n' Roll High School
Rock 'n' Roll High School
  Forever
Rock, Pretty Baby
Rocktober Blood
Round Midnight
The Running Kind
Running Out of Luck
Satisfaction
Scenes from the Goldmine
Scream Dream
Sepia Cinderella
Seventh Veil
Shock 'Em Dead
Shoot the Piano Player
Shout

Sid & Nancy
Sinatra
Singles
Snow Queen
Soldier's Tale
Some Like It Hot
Sometimes It Works,
  Sometimes It Doesn't
Somos Novios
Son of Paleface
A Song is Born
Song of Arizona
A Song to Remember
Spellcaster
Splitz
Spring Symphony
A Star is Born
Sticky Fingers
Stunt Rock
Sundance
Sunset Strip
Sweet Country Road
Sweet Love, Bitter
Swing High, Swing Low
Swing It, Professor
Tapeheads
Terror on Tour
They Shall Have Music
This is Elvis
This is Spinal Tap
The Three Caballeros
Thunder Alley
Thunder & Mud
Tougher than Leather
Trick or Treat
The Trumpet and I
Twilight in the Sierras
Two-Gun Troubador
Underground U.S.A.
Unfaithfully Yours
Vagabond Lover
Verdi
Voyage of the Rock Aliens
Wagner: The Complete Epic
Wagner: The Movie
Waltz King
Who's the Man?
Wild Guitar
Wild Orchid 2: Two Shades of
  Blue
Woodstock
World of Henry Orient
Yanco
Young Man with a Horn
Zachariah

Musical

An American in Paris
Anchors Aweigh
Annie
Babes in Toyland
Bitter Sweet
Black Tights
Born to Dance
Breaking the Ice
Broadway Melody
Broadway Melody of 1938
Broadway Melody of 1940
By the Light of the Silvery
  Moon
Calamity Jane
Can't Stop the Music
Charm of La Boheme
Deep in My Heart
Dogs in Space
Dos Postolas Gemelas
Easter Parade
Easy to Love
Flying Down to Rio
Follies Girl
Follies in Concert
Follow the Fleet
Footlight Parade
Footlight Serenade
For Me and My Gal

Gaiety
Hair
Half a Sixpence
Hands Across the Border
Hans Brinker
Hans Christian Andersen
Harlem on the Prairie
Harvest Melody
Hats Off
Hawaii Calls
Hi-De-Ho
Higher and Higher
Hillbillies in a Haunted House
Incident at Channel Q
Invitation to the Dance
Junction 88
Killer Diller
Krush Groove
The Last Radio Station
Let's Sing Again
Little Johnny Jones
A Little Night Music
London Melody
Madam Satan
Manhattan Merry-Go-Round
Maytime
Meet Me in St. Louis
Meet the Navy
Mrs. Brown, You've Got a
  Lovely Daughter
Moon Over Harlem
Moon Over Miami
Music in My Heart
Music Shoppe
Oh! Calcutta!
On Moonlight Bay
Pagan Love Song
Pinocchio
Pippin
Private Buckaroo
Red Garters
Reet, Petite and Gone
Rhapsody
Rhythm Parade
Rich, Young and Pretty
Rosalie
Second Chorus
Sepia Cinderella
The Seven Little Foys
She Shall Have Music
Singin' in the Rain
South Pacific
Stage Door Canteen
Stormy Weather
The Story of Vernon and Irene
  Castle
The Student Prince
Sweeney Todd: The Demon
  Barber of Fleet Street
Sweet Adeline
Swing
Swing Parade of 1946
Take It Big
Taking My Turn
Terror of Tiny Town
Thank Your Lucky Stars
That Midnight Kiss
That's Dancing!
That's Entertainment
That's Entertainment, Part 2
That's Singing: The Best of
  Broadway
Thousands Cheer
Three Little Words
The Threepenny Opera
Thrill of a Romance
Till the Clouds Roll By
The Toast of New Orleans
Tonight and Every Night
The Trouble with Girls (and
  How To Get Into It)
Under the Cherry Moon
Vagabond Lover
Velnio Nuotaka (The Devil's
  Bride)
Viva Las Vegas

Window Shopping
Words and Music
Yes, Sir, Mr. Bones

Musical Comedy

Almost Angels
Amateur Night
Andy Hardy Meets Debutante
April In Paris
Around the World
Artists and Models
Athena
Babes in Arms
Babes on Broadway
Bathing Beauty
Beach Blanket Bingo
Beach Party
Because You're Mine
Bert Rigby, You're a Fool
Best Foot Forward
The Best Little Whorehouse in
  Texas
Bikini Beach
Billy Rose's Jumbo
The Blues Brothers
Boardinghouse Blues
The Boy Friend
Boy! What a Girl
Broadway Melody of 1936
Broadway Rhythm
Bundle of Joy
Bye, Bye, Birdie
Call Out the Marines
Captain January
Carefree
The Cocoanuts
College Swing
Como Dos Gotas de Agua
Copacabana
Court Jester
Cover Girl
Cry-Baby
Damee
Dance, Girl, Dance
Dangerous When Wet
Delightfully Dangerous
The Devil's Brother
Diplomaniacs
Disorderlies
Dixiana
Dixie Jamboree
Doll Face
DuBarry Was a Lady
Duchess of Idaho
Earth Girls are Easy
Easy Come, Easy Go
The Eighties
Escape to Paradise
Evergreen
Everybody Sing
Fashions of 1934
Feel the Motion
Femmes de Paris
Fiesta
Finian's Rainbow
The First Nudie Musical
Flirtation Walk
Flower Drum Song
Follow That Dream
Follow That Rainbow
Four Jacks and a Jill
Frankie and Johnny
The French Line
The French Way
Frolics on Ice
Fun in Acapulco
Funny Face
A Funny Thing Happened on
  the Way to the Forum
The Gay Divorcee
Gentlemen Prefer Blondes
George White's Scandals
G.I. Blues
Gigi
The Girl Can't Help It

Musical

Girl Crazy
Girl Happy
The Girl Most Likely
Girl of the Golden West
Girl Rush
Girls! Girls! Girls!
Give a Girl a Break
Glorifying the American Girl
Going Hollywood
Going My Way
Gold Diggers of 1933
Gold Diggers of 1935
The Goldwyn Follies
Good News
Grease
Grease 2
The Great American
    Broadcast
Guys and Dolls
Gypsy
Hairspray
Hallelujah, I'm a Bum
The Happiest Millionaire
Happy Go Lovely
The Harvey Girls
Head
Hello, Dolly!
Help!
Here Come the Girls
Here Comes the Groom
High Society
Hips, Hips, Hooray
Hit the Deck
Holiday in Havana
Holiday in Mexico
Holiday Inn
Hollywood Canteen
Honolulu
How to Succeed in Business
    without Really Trying
Huckleberry Finn
I Do! I Do!
I Dood It
I Dream of Jeannie
I Dream Too Much
I Love Melvin
I Married an Angel
In the Good Old Summertime
In the Navy
International House
It Happened in Brooklyn
It's a Date
It's a Great Feeling
It's Love Again
Jive Junction
Juke Joint
Jupiter's Darling
Keep 'Em Flying
Kid Galahad
Kid Millions
King Kelly of the U.S.A.
King of Jazz
Kiss Me Kate
Kissin' Cousins
La Marchanta
Lady Be Good
Latin Lovers
Le Million
Les Girls
Let's Dance
Let's Go Collegiate
Life Begins for Andy Hardy
Li'l Abner
Lili
Lily of Killarney
Little Nellie Kelly
Little Shop of Horrors
Live a Little, Love a Little
Look Out Sister
Louisiana Purchase
Lovely to Look At
Loving You
Lucky Me
Lullaby of Broadway
Make a Wish
Mame

Mamele
A Matter of Degrees
Maytime in Mayfair
Meet Me in Las Vegas
Melody Cruise
The Merry Widow
Mr. Music
The Muppet Christmas Carol
The Muppet Movie
Muppets Take Manhattan
Muscle Beach Party
My Dream is Yours
My Sister Eileen
My Song Goes Round the
    World
Nancy Goes to Rio
Naughty Marietta
Neptune's Daughter
Never a Dull Moment
New Faces of 1952
Newsies
No Time for Romance
Oklahoma!
On a Clear Day You Can See
    Forever
One from the Heart
One Touch of Venus
The Opposite Sex
Paint Your Wagon
Pajama Game
Pajama Party
Pal Joey
Panama Hattie
The Perils of Pauline
Phantom of the Paradise
Pin-Up Girl
The Pirate
The Pirates of Penzance
Popeye
Presenting Lily Mars
Rebecca of Sunnybrook Farm
The Road to Bali
The Road to Lebanon
The Road to Morocco
Road to Nashville
The Road to Rio
The Road to Singapore
The Road to Utopia
The Road to Zanzibar
Roadie
Roberta
Robin and the Seven Hoods
Rock 'n' Roll High School
Rock 'n' Roll High School
    Forever
Roman Scandals
Romance on the High Seas
Royal Wedding
Running Out of Luck
Sensations of 1945
Sgt. Pepper's Lonely Hearts
    Club Band
Seven Brides for Seven
    Brothers
Seven Days' Leave
The Seven Little Foys
1776
Sextette
Shake, Rattle and Rock
Shall We Dance
Ship Ahoy
Shock Treatment
Show Business
Silk Stockings
Sing Your Worries Away
Sioux City Sue
The Sky's the Limit
A Song is Born
Song of the Islands
Speedway
Spinout
Spotlight Scandals
Springtime in the Rockies
Starstruck
State Fair
Step Lively

The Stork Club
Strike Up the Band
Summer Holiday
Summer Stock
Sun Valley Serenade
Sunny
Sunny Skies
Sweethearts
Swing It, Professor
Swing Time
Take Me Out to the Ball Game
Tea for Two
Texas Carnival
Thank God It's Friday
That Girl from Paris
There's No Business Like
    Show Business
Thoroughly Modern Millie
Tickle Me
Tokyo Pop
Too Many Girls
Top Hat
23 1/2 Hours Leave
Two Girls and a Sailor
Two Tickets to Broadway
Two Weeks with Love
The Unsinkable Molly Brown
Up in Arms
Vogues of 1938
Wallaby Jim of the Islands
The West Point Story
White Christmas
Whoopee!
A Woman is a Woman
Wonder Man
Yes, Giorgio
Yidl Mitn Fidl
Yolanda and the Thief
You Were Never Lovelier
You'll Find Out
You'll Never Get Rich
Ziegfeld Follies
Zis Boom Bah

Musical Drama

Actor: The Paul Muni Story
The Band Wagon
The Barkleys of Broadway
Beatlemania! The Movie
The Belle of New York
Bells are Ringing
Beware
Blonde Venus
Blue Hawaii
Body Moves
Body Rock
Broadway Serenade
The Buddy Holly Story
Cabaret
Camelot
Can-Can
The Cantor's Son
Carmen Jones
Carnival Rock
The Cat and the Fiddle
The Chocolate Soldier
A Christmas Carol
Clambake
Club Havana
Coal Miner's Daughter
Concrete Angels
Congress Dances
Cool Mikado
The Cotton Club
Crossover Dreams
Curly Top
Daddy Long Legs
A Damsel in Distress
Dance Hall
Dance of Life
Dancing Lady
Dancing Pirate
A Date with Judy
Deadman's Curve
The Deputy Drummer

Dimples
Dogs in Space
Don Quixote
Double Trouble
Down Argentine Way
The Duke is the Tops
The Farmer Takes a Wife
Fast Forward
Fiddler on the Roof
The Firefly
Fisherman's Wharf
The Five Pennies
Flashdance
Footloose
The Forbidden Dance
42nd Street
Frankie and Johnny
Funny Girl
Funny Lady
Gangway
The Glenn Miller Story
Go, Johnny Go!
Goodbye, Mr. Chips
Graffiti Bridge
Great Balls of Fire
The Great Caruso
The Great Waltz
The Great Ziegfeld
Greek Street
Hard to Hold
The Harder They Come
Harmony Lane
Harum Scarum
Heart's Desire
Honeysuckle Rose
Honkytonk Nights
I Could Go on Singing
Idolmaker
If You Knew Susie
I'll Cry Tomorrow
I'll See You in My Dreams
The In Crowd
It Happened at the World's
    Fair
It's Always Fair Weather
Jailbird Rock
Jailhouse Rock
Jazz Singer
Jesus Christ, Superstar
Jolson Sings Again
The Jolson Story
Jubilee
Jungle Patrol
Just Around the Corner
The King and I
King Creole
Knights of the City
La Bamba
La Cucaracha
Ladies of the Chorus
Lady Sings the Blues
Lambada
Life of Verdi
Light of Day
The Little Colonel
Little Miss Broadway
The Littlest Angel
The Littlest Rebel
Los Tres Calaveras
Lottery Bride
Love Me or Leave Me
Love Me Tender
Mack the Knife
The Mambo Kings
Man of La Mancha
Marco
A Matter of Time
Melody Master
Miss Sadie Thompson
Motown's Mustang
Murder at the Vanities
Murder with Music
The Music Lovers
The Music Man
Musica Proibita
My Fair Lady

Never Steal Anything Small
New Moon
New York, New York
Night and Day
No, No Nanette
Northwest Outpost
The Old Curiosity Shop
Oliver!
The One and Only, Genuine,
    Original Family Band
One Night of Love
One Trick Pony
Opera do Malandro
Orchestra Wives
An Orphan Boy of Vienna
Paradise, Hawaiian Style
Paradise in Harlem
Paradise Island
Paris Blues
Pennies From Heaven
Pete Kelly's Blues
Pete Townsend: White City
Piaf
The Poor Little Rich Girl
Princess Tam Tam
Purple Rain
Quadrophenia
Rainbow
Rappin'
Reckless
The Red Shoes
Rhapsody in Blue
Rock, Baby, Rock It
Rock, Rock, Rock
Rooftops
The Rose
Rose Marie
Roustabout
Sailing Along
Salsa
Sarafina!
Satisfaction
Scrooge
Senora Tentacion
Shining Star
Shout
Show Boat
Sincerely Yours
Sing
Smilin' Through
Something to Sing About
Song O' My Heart
Song of Freedom
Song of Norway
Song Without End
Songwriter
The Sound of Music
Sparkle
Stars and Stripes Forever
Stay Away, Joe
Stepping Out
Stowaway
Sunday in the Park with
    George
Sweet Charity
Sweet Dreams
Sweetheart of the Navy
Tap
They Shall Have Music
This is the Army
The Three Penny Opera
Thunder Alley
Till the Clouds Roll By/A Star
    Is Born
Tommy
Transatlantic Merry-Go-Round
Umbrellas of Cherbourg
Una Vez en la Vida
Waltz King
Way Down South
West Side Story
What's Love Got to Do With
    It?
Yankee Doodle Dandy
Yentl
Young at Heart

Mystery

Death on the Nile
Death Rage
Death Sentence
Death Train
Death Valley
Death Warrant
Death Weekend
Deathmask
Deathtrap
Deceived
December Flower
Deceptions
The Deep
Deep Cover
Defense of the Realm
Defenseless
Delusion
Deranged
Descending Angel
Desire and Hell at Sunset
    Motel
Desperate
Desperate Hours
Desperate Motives
Desperately Seeking Susan
The Detective
Devil Diamond
The Devil Thumbs a Ride
The Devil Thumbs a Ride/
    Having Wonderful Crime
The Devil's Cargo
Devil's Party
The Devil's Undead
Devlin
Diabolically Yours
Dial Help
Dial ''M'' for Murder
Diamond Run
The Diamond Trap
Diamonds
Diamond's Edge
Diamonds on Wheels
Dias de Ilusion
Dick Tracy
Dick Tracy and the Oyster
    Caper
Dick Tracy, Detective
Dick Tracy, Detective/The
    Corpse Vanishes
Dick Tracy Double Feature #1
Dick Tracy Double Feature #2
Dick Tracy Meets Gruesome
Dick Tracy Returns
Dick Tracy: The Original
    Serial, Vol. 1
Dick Tracy: The Original
    Serial, Vol. 2
Dick Tracy: The Spider Strikes
Dick Tracy vs. Crime Inc.
Dick Tracy vs. Cueball
Dick Tracy's Dilemma
Die! Die! My Darling!
Die Screaming, Marianne
Die Sister, Die!
Dinner at the Ritz
Diplomatic Courier
Dirkham Detective Agency
Dirty Hands
Dirty Harry
Disappearance
Disconnected
Dishonored Lady
Distortions
Disturbance
Diva
The Dive
D.O.A.
Dr. Mabuse vs. Scotland Yard
Dr. Tarr's Torture Dungeon
Dog Day
Dog Day Afternoon
Dominique is Dead
The Domino Principle
Don't Bother to Knock
Don't Go in the House
Don't Look in the Attic

Don't Look Now
Don't Open the Door!
Doomed to Die
The Doomsday Flight
Door with the Seven Locks
Double Agents
Double Cross
Double Exposure
Double Face
Double Identity
Double Indemnity
Double Jeopardy
The Double McGuffin
The Double Negative
Double Threat
Double Vision
The Draughtsman's Contract
Dream Lover
Dream No Evil
Dress Gray
Dressed for Death
Dressed to Kill
The Drifter
Driven to Kill
Driver's Seat
The Dropkick
The Drowning Pool
Drums of Jeopardy
Duel
The Dummy Talks
Dust to Dust
Dying Room Only
The Dying Truth
Dynasty of Fear
Early Frost
Echo Murders
Echoes
Edge of Darkness
The Eiger Sanction
Eight Witnesses
El Libro de Piedra
El Tesoro de Chucho el Roto
Embassy
Emergency
Emil and the Detective
Emissary
The Empty Beach
Endangered Species
Endless Night
Enigma
Enrapture
The Equalizer: Memories of
    Manon
Equus
Escapade in Florence
Escape
Escapist
Estate of Insanity
Even Angels Fall
Everybody Wins
Everybody's Dancin'
Evil Under the Sun
Ex-Mrs. Bradford
The Executioner
Experiment in Terror
Experiment Perilous
Exposed
Exposure
Express to Terror
Exterminator
Extreme Close-Up
Eye of the Needle
Eyes of Laura Mars
Eyewitness
F/X
The Face at the Window
A Face in the Fog
Fail-Safe
Fake Out
The Falcon and the Snowman
The Falcon in Hollywood
The Falcon in Mexico
Falcon Takes Over/Strange
    Bargain
Falcon's Adventure/Armored
    Car Robbery

The Falcon's Brother
False Identity
Family Plot
The Fan
The Fantasist
Far from Home
Farewell, My Lovely
Fatal Attraction
Fatal Bond
Fatal Charm
Fatal Exposure
Fatal Games
The Fatal Hour
The Fatal Image
Fatal Instinct
FBI Girl
Fear
Fear City
Fear in the Night
Fearless
Fearmaker
The Female Jungle
Femme Fatale
Fer-De-Lance
Fever
Fiction Makers
The Fifth Floor
52 Pick-Up
The Fighting Westerner
Fin de Fiesta
Final Analysis
Final Assignment
Final Cut
Final Embrace
Final Notice
The Final Option
Finessing the King
Fingerprints Don't Lie
The Finishing Touch
The Firm
Flashpoint
Flatliners
Flowers in the Attic
Flying from the Hawk
Fog Island
Follow Me Quietly
The Fool Killer
Forbidden Sun
Foreign Correspondent
Forger of London
Forget Mozart
The Forgotten One
The Formula
Formula for a Murder
Fortress
Fourth Story
The Franchise Affair
Frantic
The French Detective
French Intrigue
Frenzy
Fresh Kill
Fright
From Hollywood to Deadwood
From the Dead of Night
Frozen Alive
Fu Manchu
Fugitive Lovers
Full Circle
Full Exposure: The Sex Tape
    Scandals
Full Fathom Five
Funeral in Berlin
The Game
A Game of Crime
Game of Seduction
Gangbusters
Gaslight
Gemidos de Placer
Get That Man
Getting Even
Ghost
The Ghost Camera
Ghost Ship
The Ghost Walks

Girl Hunters
The Girl in a Swing
The Girl in Lover's Lane
A Girl to Kill for
Girls Night Out
Glass
The Glass Key
Glass Tomb
Golden Lady
Golden Rendezvous
Gone to Ground
Goodnight God Bless
Gorky Park
Gotham
The Great Riviera Bank
    Robbery
Green Archer
Green for Danger
Green Ice
The Green Man
Grievous Bodily Harm
Ground Zero
Guest in the House
Guilty as Sin
Gunpowder
Half a Soldier
Hammett
Hands of a Stranger
Hanky Panky
Happily Ever After
Hard-Boiled Mahoney
Harper
The Harvest
Hat Box Mystery
The Haunted Castle
Haunted: The Ferryman
The Haunting of Barney
    Palmer
Haunting of Harrington House
The Haunting Passion
He Lives: The Search for the
    Evil One
Hear No Evil
Heartaches
The Heat of the Day
Heat Wave
Heatwave
The Heist
Hell Harbor
Hell's Harbor
Hell's Headquarters
Help!
Hi-Jacked
Hidden Agenda
Hidden City
Hidden Obsession
The Hidden Room
Hide in Plain Sight
High & Low
High Frequency
High Stakes
Highway 13
The Hillside Strangler
The Hit List
Hitchcock Classics Collection:
    Trailers on Tape
Hitchcock Collection
The Hitman
The Holcroft Covenant
Hollywood Stadium Mystery
Holocaust 2000
Home for the Holidays
Homicide
The Hooded Terror
The Horse Without a Head
Horseplayer
Hostage
Hostages
Hot Child in the City
Hotel Colonial
Hotel Reserve
Hotline
The Hound of the Baskervilles
Hour of Decision
House of Fear
The House of Lurking Death

House of Mystery
The House of Secrets
House of Shadows
The House of the Arrow
House of the Damned
House of the Rising Sun
The House on Carroll Street
House on Marsh Road
The Housekeeper
Human Gorilla
The Human Monster
Hunt the Man Down
Hunt the Man Down/
    Smashing the Rackets
Hunter
The Hunting
Hustle
Hysteria
I Am the Cheese
I Bury the Living
I Confess
I Killed That Man
I, Madman
I See a Dark Stranger
I Stand Condemned
I, the Jury
I Wake Up Screaming
I'd Give My Life
If It's a Man, Hang Up
If Looks Could Kill
I'll Get You
I'll Name the Murderer
Illegal
Illicit Behavior
Illusions
I'm the Girl He Wants to Kill
I'm the One You're Looking
    For
Image of Death
Impact
Impulse
In a Lonely Place
In a Stranger's Hand
In an Old Manor House
In the Cold of the Night
In the Heat of the Night
In the Line of Fire
In the Secret State
In the Spirit
Indecency
The Indian Scarf
Infamous Crimes
Inheritance
The Inheritor
The Inner Circle
Inner Sanctum
Innocent Victim
The Inquiry
Insanity
The Inside Man
Inspector Morse
Inspiration of Mr. Budd
The Instructor
Interface
Internal Affairs
International Crime
Internecine Project
Interrupted Journey
Intimate Obsession
Intimate Stranger
Into the Fire
Intrigue
Intruder
Invasion of Privacy
Investigation
Invincible Armor
The Invisible Avenger
The Invisible Killer
Invitation to Hell
The Ipcress File
Irish Luck
Island
Island Monster
Island of Adventure
Istanbul
It Could Happen to You

Mystery

Prey of the Chameleon
Prime Suspect
The Private Life of Sherlock Holmes
The Prize
Probe
Project: Eliminator
Project X
Promise to Murder
Prowler
Psychic
Psycho
Psycho 2
Psycho 3
Psycho Cop
Psychomania
Pulp
Pursuit
Pursuit to Algiers
Puzzle
Quake
Quicker Than the Eye
Quicksand: No Escape
The Quiller Memorandum
Rage
Railroaded
The Rain Killer
Raw Nerve
Rear Window
Rebecca
Reckless Moment
Red Alert
Red-Dragon
The Red House
Red King, White Knight
The Red Raven Kiss-Off
Red Wind
Redneck
Reflections of Murder
Regina
Rehearsal for Murder
Reilly: Ace of Spies
The Reincarnation of Peter Proud
Remember Me
Repulsion
Return
The Return of Boston Blackie
Return of Chandu
The Return of Dr. Mabuse
Return of Frank Cannon
Return to Waterloo
Revenge
Revenge of the Stepford Wives
Rich and Strange
Rider on the Rain
Riders to the Seas
Rififi
Ring of Death
Rising Sun
Road Games
Road to Salina
Roaring City
Roaring Fire
Rogue's Gallery
Rogue's Tavern
Rogue's Yarn
Room 43
Roots of Evil
Rope
The Rosary Murders
R.S.V.P.
Ruby Cairo
Rude Awakening
Run If You Can
Runaways
Russian Roulette
Sabotage
Saboteur
The Saint
Saint in London
The Saint in New York
The Saint Strikes Back
Saint Strikes Back: Criminal Court

The Saint Takes Over
The Saint's Double Trouble
The Saint's Vacation/The Narrow Margin
The Salamander
The Salzburg Connection
Sanctuary of Fear
Sanders of the River
Sapphire
Savages
Scalp Merchant
Scandal Man
Scandalous
Scared to Death/Dick Tracy's Dilemma
Scarlet Claw
The Scarlet Clue
Scarlet Street
Scavengers
Scene of the Crime
Scenes from a Murder
Schnelles Geld
Scissors
Scorpio
The Scorpio Factor
Scotland Yard Inspector
Scream
Scream and Die
Scream Bloody Murder
Scream for Help
Screamer
Sea of Love
Seance on a Wet Afternoon
Season of Fear
Second Woman
The Secret Adversary
Secret Agent 00
Secret of the Black Trunk
The Secret Passion of Robert Clayton
Seven Doors to Death
Seven Hours to Judgment
The Seven Percent Solution
The Seventh Sign
Sexo Y Crimen
Sexpot
Sexton Blake and the Hooded Terror
Sexual Response
The Shadow
Shadow Dancing
The Shadow Man
Shadow of a Doubt
Shadow of the Eagle
Shadow of the Thin Man
Shadow Play
The Shadow Strikes
Shadows on the Stairs
Shaft
Shallow Grave
The Shanghai Cobra
Shattered
Shattered Silence
She Waits
Sherlock Holmes: A Study in Scarlet
Sherlock Holmes and the Deadly Necklace
Sherlock Holmes and the Incident at Victoria Falls
Sherlock Holmes and the Secret Weapon
Sherlock Holmes Faces Death
Sherlock Holmes in Washington
Sherlock Holmes: The Baskerville Curse
Sherlock Holmes: The Sign of Four
Sherlock Holmes: The Silver Blaze
Sherlock Holmes: The Valley of Fear
Sherlock Holmes: The Voice of Terror
She's Dressed to Kill

Shock!
Shoot to Kill
A Shot in the Dark
The Shout
A Show of Force
Show Them No Mercy
Shriek in the Night
Side Show
Sidney Sheldon's Bloodline
The Sign of Four
The Silencer
Silent Assassins
Silent Killers
The Silent Mr. Sherlock Holmes
Silent Motive
The Silent Partner
The Silent Passenger
Silhouette
Sins of Desire
The Sister-in-Law
Sister, Sister
Sisters of Death
Sketch Artist
Sketches of a Strangler
Sky Liner
Slamdance
The Slasher
Slayground
Sleeping Car to Trieste
Sleepwalk
Sleuth
Slightly Honorable
Slightly Scarlet
Slipping into Darkness
Sliver
Slow Burn
Smart-Aleck Kill
Smile, Jenny, You're Dead
Smooth Talker
Snatched
Sneakers
Snow Kill
Snowblind
Sois Belle et Tais-Toi
Soldier of the Night
Somebody Has to Shoot the Picture
Someone Behind the Door
Someone to Watch Over Me
Song of the Thin Man
Sound of Murder
Spaceways
The Spaniard's Curse
Spare Parts
The Specialist
The Speckled Band
Spectre of the Rose
Spellbound
The Sphinx
Sphinx
Spider Woman
Spiders
The Spider's Stratagem
Sprague
Sputnik
Spy Story
The Spy Who Came in from the Cold
S*P*Y*S
The Squeaker
The Squeeze
Stacey
Stage Fright
Stamp of a Killer
Star of Midnight
Star Time
State Department File 649
State of Things
Station
Stay Tuned for Murder
The Stepmother
Stick
Still Life
Still of the Night
A Stolen Face

Stolen Painting
Stone Cold Dead
Stormy Monday
The Strange Affair of Uncle Harry
The Strange Countess
Strange Shadows in an Empty Room
Strange Tales/Ray Bradbury Theatre
The Stranger
A Stranger Among Us
Stranger in Town
A Stranger is Watching
Stranger on the Third Floor
The Stranger Within
Strangers
Strangers on a Train
The Strangler
Strangler of Blackmoor Castle
Strangler of the Swamp
Strangler of the Tower
Stray Dog
Strike Force
Stripped to Kill
Stripped to Kill II: Live Girls
A Study in Scarlet
A Study in Terror
Subterfuge
Sucker Money
Sudden Terror
Suddenly
Summer Heat
Summer's Children
Sunstroke
Surrogate
Suspect
Suspicion
Svengali
Swamp Thing
Swiss Conspiracy
Tag: The Assassination Game
Tagget
Take Two
Tales from the Darkside
Tales of the Unexpected
The Tall Blond Man with One Black Shoe
Tangiers
Target
The Tattered Web
The Taxi Mystery
The Teacher
Telefon
Ten Days Wonder
Ten Little Indians
10 Rillington Place
Tequila Sunrise
Tereza
Terminal Choice
Terminal Entry
The Terror
Terror at London Bridge
Terror by Night
Terror by Night/Meeting at Midnight
Terror Stalks the Class Reunion
Terror Street
Terrorists
They Call Me Mr. Tibbs!
They Meet Again
They Only Kill Their Masters
They Won't Believe Me
They're Playing with Fire
Thief
Thief of Hearts
The Thin Man
The Thin Man Goes Home
Third Degree Burn
The Third Key
The Third Man
Third Solution
13th Guest
The Thirteenth Man
The 39 Steps

The Thirty-Nine Steps
This is a Hijack
This Lightning Always Strikes Twice
This Man Must Die
Threat
Three by Hitchcock
Three Days of the Condor
Thrilled to Death
Thrillkill
Through Naked Eyes
Thundersquad
Tiara Tahiti
Ticket of Leave Man
Tiger Bay
Tightrope
Till Death Do Us Part
Till There was You
Time for Murder
Time for Revenge
Time is Running Out
A Time to Die
Times to Come
To Catch a King
To Catch a Thief
To Kill a Clown
To Kill a Stranger
The Todd Killings
Tomorrow at Seven
Tony Rome
Too Scared to Scream
Topaz
Torment
Torn Curtain
Total Exposure
Touch Me Not
Touch of Evil
Tough Assignment
Tough Guys Don't Dance
Tourist Trap
Town that Dreaded Sundown
Traces of Red
Track 29
Trade Secrets
The Train Killer
The Trap
Trapped
Trauma
Treacherous Crossing
Trespasses
Trifles
The Triumph of Sherlock Holmes
Tropical Heat
The Trouble with Harry
True Believer
Twenty Dollar Star
Twisted Obsession
Two by Forsyth
Two Fathers' Justice
The Two Jakes
Two Minute Warning
Ultimate Desires
The Ultimate Imposter
The Ultimate Thrill
The Unbreakable Alibi
Under Capricorn
Under Suspicion
Uneasy Terms
Unforgotten Crime
Unholy Four
Unholy Wife
Union City
Union Station
Unsane
Unsuitable Job for a Woman
Up in the Air
Urge to Kill
The Vagrant
Vamping
The Vanishing
Vanishing Act
Vatican Conspiracy
Vegas
Velvet Touch
Vertigo

Devil's Son-in-Law
Diary of a Madman
Dick Tracy, Detective
Doctor Faustus
Dr. Strange
Dominique is Dead
Dona Flor and Her Two
  Husbands
Donovan's Brain
Don't Be Afraid of the Dark
The Dreaming
Dreamscape
The Dunwich Horror
The Dybbuk
The Dying Truth
El Monte de las Brujas
Encounter with the Unknown
The Entity
Equinox
Erotic Dreams
Eternal Evil
The Evictors
The Evil
Evil Altar
Evil Dead
Evil Dead 2: Dead by Dawn
The Evil Mind
Evilspeak
Excalibur
Exorcism
The Exorcist
Exorcist 2: The Heretic
Eye of the Demon
Eyes of Fire
Feast for the Devil
Final Conflict
The First Power
The Fish that Saved
  Pittsburgh
Fright House
Full Circle
Genie of Darkness
Ghosts That Still Walk
The Girl in a Swing
God Told Me To
Grave Secrets
The Guardian
Half of Heaven
Hanussen
The Hearse
Horror Hotel
House of the Yellow Carpet
The House on Skull Mountain
The House that Bled to Death
I Don't Want to Be Born
I'm Dangerous Tonight
Inferno
Inner Sanctum
Into the Badlands
The Invasion of Carol Enders
Invasion of the Blood Farmers
Journey into the Beyond
Kill, Baby, Kill
Killing Hour
The Kiss
KISS Meets the Phantom of
  the Park
La Hora 24
Lady Terminator
The Lady's Maid's Bell
Land of the Minotaur
The Legacy
The Legend of Hell House
Leonor
The Living Head
Low Blow
The Magician
Making Contact
Manos, the Hands of Fate
Mardi Gras for the Devil
Mardi Gras Massacre
Maxim Xul
Medea
Men of Two Worlds
Midnight
Midnight Cabaret

Mirror, Mirror
Mirror of Death
Mirrors
Mrs. Amworth
The Monster Demolisher
Mystic Circle Murder
Natas...The Reflection
Necromancer: Satan's
  Servant
Necropolis
The Night Stalker: Two Tales
  of Terror
Ninja, the Violent Sorcerer
The Occult Experience
The Occultist
Omoo Omoo, the Shark God
One Step Beyond
The Oracle
Orgy of the Dead
Out on a Limb
Phantasm
Phantasm II
Poltergeist
Poltergeist 2: The Other Side
Poltergeist 3
Possession: Until Death Do
  You Part
The Power
The Psychic
Psychic
Psychic Killer
Psychomania
Puppet Master
Race with the Devil
The Raven
A Reflection of Fear
The Reincarnate
Rendez-Moi Ma Peau
Repossessed
Rest In Pieces
Retribution
Return
Return from Witch Mountain
Return of Chandu
Rosemary's Baby
Ruby
Run If You Can
The Runestone
Sabaka
Satan's Princess
Satan's Touch
Scared Stiff
Season of the Witch
Second Sight
Seizure
The Sentinel
The Seventh Sign
The Seventh Victim
The Shaman
Shock 'Em Dead
Silent Night, Deadly Night 3:
  Better Watch Out!
Sorceress
The Spaniard's Curse
Speak of the Devil
The Spellbinder
Spellbound
Spiritism
Student of Prague
Summer of Fear
Supergirl
Teen Witch
The Tempter
Terror Beach
Terror Creatures from the
  Grave
That Darn Sorceress
Three Sovereigns for Sarah
To the Devil, A Daughter
The Torture Chamber of Dr.
  Sadism
The Touch of Satan
Treasure of the Four Crowns
Tropic Heat
The Undead
Unknown Powers

Venus in Furs
Vibes
The Visitor
Warlock Moon
White Gorilla
The Wicker Man
Wild Man
Witch Who Came from the
  Sea
Witchboard
Witchcraft 2: The Temptress
Witchcraft 4: Virgin Heart
Witchcraft 5: Dance with the
  Devil
Witchcraft Through the Ages
The Witches of Eastwick
The Witching
Witching Time
The Witchmaker
The Witch's Mirror
The Wizard of Oz
Wizards
The Woman Who Came Back
Zapped Again
The Zodiac Killer

Oldest Profession

Accatone!
Alexa: A Prostitute's Own
  Story
Alexander: The Other Side of
  Dawn
Alien Warrior
The Allnighter
American Justice
American Nightmare
Amor Bandido
The Amsterdam Connection
Angel
Anna Christie
Auntie
Avenging Angel
Back Roads
The Balcony
Bellas de Noche
The Best Little Whorehouse in
  Texas
Beverly Hills Call Girls
Beverly Hills Madam
Beverly Hills Vamp
Blood Money: The Story of
  Clinton and Nadine
Bordello
Broken Mirrors
Butterfield 8
Candy Tangerine Man
Caravaggio
Catherine & Co.
The Cheyenne Social Club
Christiane F.
Cinderella Liberty
Class of 1984
Club Life
Coffy
Confessions of a Vice Baron
Cool it Carol
The Courtesans of Bombay
Crimes of Passion
Cross Country
Cry of a Prostitute: Love Kills
Dead End Street
Deadly Sanctuary
Death Shot
Death Target
Dedee d'Anvers
Diary of a Lost Girl
Diva
Dixie: Changing Habits
Doctor Detroit
Dr. Jekyll and Sister Hyde
Drying Up the Streets
The Duchess and the
  Dirtwater Fox
East End Hustle
8 Million Ways to Die

El Preprimido
Elmer Gantry
Emily
Emmanuelle & Joanna
Erendira
Escort Girls
Everybody Wins
Fall from Innocence
Flesh
For Pete's Sake
Foxy Brown
Frankenhooker
Frankie and Johnny
French Quarter
Full Exposure: The Sex Tape
  Scandals
Fyre
Get Rita
The Gift
Gigi
Girls of the White Orchid
Half Moon Street
The Happy Hooker
The Happy Hooker Goes
  Hollywood
The Happy Hooker Goes to
  Washington
High Stakes
Hollywood Chainsaw Hookers
Hollywood Vice Sqaud
Honky Tonk Girl
Hustle
Hustler Squad
Hustling
I Want to Live!
Impulse
Intimate Moments
Irma La Douce
Jack's Back
Just a Gigolo
Justine
Keetje Tippei
Kinjite: Forbidden Subjects
Kiss the Night
Kitty and the Bagman
Klute
La Chienne
L.A. Crackdown
L.A. Crackdown 2
Ladies of the Lotus
Lady of the Evening
Lady of the House
Lady of the Rising Sun
The Last Prostitute
Life of Oharu
A Life of Sin
Little Ladies of the Night
Lola Montes
Love Angels
Love by Appointment
Love Strange Love
Mack
Madame Rosa
Magdalene
Malibu High
Man of Flowers
Marriage Italian Style
Mayflower Madam
McCabe & Mrs. Miller
Miami Blues
Mid Knight Rider
Midnight Auto Supply
Midnight Cop
Midnight Cowboy
Miss Sadie Thompson
The Missionary
Mona Lisa
Mona's Place
Murderlust
Murphy's Law
My Life to Live
My Mother's Secret Life
My Own Private Idaho
My Pleasure Is My Business
Naked Kiss
Nana

Nanami, First Love
Never on Sunday
New York's Finest
Night Friend
Night of the Generals
Night Shift
Night Slasher
The Night They Robbed Big
  Bertha's
Nightmare in Badham County
Nights of Cabiria
The Ninja Empire
No One Cries Forever
No Prince for My Cinderella
The Nun
Nuts
Off Limits
Oldest Profession
Olivia
On the Block
One Night Only
Out of the Dark
The Owl and the Pussycat
Pandora's Box
Panic in Needle Park
Party Girls
The Passing of Evil
Pennies From Heaven
Personal Services
Poker Alice
Pretty Baby
Pretty Woman
Prettykill
Prime Cut
The Pyx
Queen Kelly
Quick, Let's Get Married
Rain
Reason to Die
Red Kimono
Risky Business
Room 43
Roots of Evil
Saint Jack
Sandakan No. 8
Sansho the Bailiff
Scarred
Schnelles Geld
Scorchers
Secret Games
Secrets of a Married Man
Sessions
Sex on the Brain
The Silencer
Single Room Furnished
Sisters of Gion
Sketches of a Stranger
SS Girls
S.S. Love Camp No. 27
Stone Cold Dead
Storyville
Street Girls
Street of Forgotten Women
Street of Shame
Street Smart
Streetwalkin'
Sweet Charity
Sweet Revenge
Sweet Sweetback's
  Baadasssss Song
Sweet Trash
The Sword and the Cross
Talons of the Eagle
Taxi Driver
Teen Lust
They Were So Young
Thousand Pieces of Gold
Tightrope
To Be a Rose
Trading Places
Traffic in Souls
Train Station Pickups
Tricks of the Trade
Truck Stop Women
Twenty Dollar Star

Oldest

Twin Peaks: Fire Walk with
  Me
Ultimate Desires
Uncaged
The Vampire Hookers
Vice Squad
Walk on the Wild Side
Warm Nights on a Slow-
  Moving Train
Warrior Queen
Waterloo Bridge
Whore
Wild Orchid 2: Two Shades of
  Blue
The Winter of Our Dreams
A Woman in Flames
A Woman of Rome
Working Girls
The World of Suzie Wong
Wrestling Racket Girls

On the Rocks

Arthur 2: On the Rocks
Barfly
The Big Hangover
Blue Heaven
Break of Hearts
Clean and Sober
Cocktail
Come Back, Little Sheba
Country Girl
A Cry for Love
Dance of Life
Danger in the Skies
Dangerous
Days of Wine and Roses
Desde el Abismo
Desert Bloom
The Devil at 4 O'Clock
The Devil Thumbs a Ride
The Devil Thumbs a Ride/
  Having Wonderful Crime
Dona Flor and Her Two
  Husbands
Drunken Angel
Educating Rita
El Dorado
The Electric Horseman
The Entertainer
Fat City
The Fire Within
Fish Hawk
The Flaming Teen-Age
Frances
A Free Soul
Gervaise
The Great Man Votes
The Green Man
Honkytonk Man
Hot Summer in Barefoot
  County
I Live with Me Dad
I'll Cry Tomorrow
The Informer
Ironweed
Izzy & Moe
Jack the Bear
Kill Cruise
The Last American Hero
Le Beau Serge
License to Kill
Long Day's Journey into Night
The Lost Weekend
M.A.D.D.: Mothers Against
  Drunk Driving
Marvin & Tige
Mean Dog Blues
Morning After
My Favorite Year
One Too Many
Only When I Laugh
Papa's Delicate Condition
The Pilot
Police Court
Reuben, Reuben

The Robe
Scent of a Woman
Shakes the Clown
The Sin of Harold Diddlebock
The Singing Blacksmith
Skin Deep
Smash-Up: The Story of a
  Woman
A Star is Born
Straight Up
Stranded
Strange Brew
Tales of Ordinary Madness
Ten Nights in a Bar Room
Ten Nights in a Bar-Room
Termini Station
Under Capricorn
Under the Volcano
What Price Hollywood?
Whiskey Galore
White Lightning
Willa
The Winning Team

Only the Lonely

Abducted
The Abduction of Kari
  Swenson
An Autumn Afternoon
Betrayal
Birdman of Alcatraz
The Body Shop
Breakfast in Paris
The Browning Version
The Cemetery Club
Choose Me
A Chorus of Disapproval
A Christmas Without Snow
Citizen Kane
Cotter
Cowboys Don't Cry
Cyrano de Bergerac
A Day in the Country
Desperately Seeking Susan
Didn't You Hear?
Dirty Dishes
Distant Thunder
Docks of New York
Doin' Time on Planet Earth
The Doll
A Doll's House
The Eclipse
El Super
An Empty Bed
Empty Suitcases
The Enchanted Cottage
Escapade in Japan
E.T.: The Extra-Terrestrial
Every Man for Himself & God
  Against All
Eye of the Needle
The Final Alliance
Full Moon in Blue Water
Full Moon in Paris
The Game of Love
The Gun in Betty Lou's
  Handbag
Harold and Maude
The Heart is a Lonely Hunter
Hell Hounds of Alaska
High Country
Hiroshima, Mon Amour
The Hunchback of Notre
  Dame
Husband Hunting
Husbands and Wives
I Don't Give a Damn
I Sent a Letter to My Love
In the White City
Inside Out
La Petite Sirene
La Vie Continue
Lana in Love
The Last Horror Film
Les Bons Debarras

Lonely Hearts
The Lonely Passion of Judith
  Hearne
Lonelyhearts
Looking for Mr. Goodbar
Lunatics: A Love Story
Luther the Geek
Man of Flowers
Marianela
Marty
The Match Factory Girl
Men Don't Leave
Miles to Go Before I Sleep
Mr. Kingstreet's War
Mouchette
976-EVIL
Ninotchka
None But the Lonely Heart
Once Around
Only the Lonely
Only You
Our Miss Brooks
Panic Station
The Passion of Anna
Persona
Priest of Love
The Prime of Miss Jean
  Brodie
The Prince of Central Park
The Pursuit of Happiness
Queen of the Stardust
  Ballroom
The Rachel Papers
Rachel, Rachel
The Red Desert
Red Kimono
Restless
Return Engagement
Robert et Robert
Roseland
Samurai 2: Duel at Ichijoji
  Temple
Scene of the Crime
Scream and Die
The Seagull
Secret Executioners
Secret Life of an American
  Wife
Seize the Day
Separate Tables
September
Shadows in the Storm
Single Bars, Single Women
Sleepless In Seattle
Slipstream
The Solitary Man
Someone to Love
South of Reno
Summer
Sweetwater
Tales of the Klondike: The
  Scorn of Women
Tenth Month
Terror at the Opera
That Cold Day in the Park
Tomorrow
Too Shy to Try
Turtle Diary
The Ultimate Ninja Challenge
Vagabond
When Your Lover Leaves
Wildest Dreams
Woman in the Shadows
The Young in Heart
Zelly & Me

Opera

Aria
Baritone
Broken Melody
Burlesque of Carmen
Carmen
Carmen Jones
The Chocolate Soldier
Elmer Fudd's Comedy Capers

Faust
Fitzcarraldo
Gentlemen of Titipu
The Great Caruso
The Great Waltz
I Dream Too Much
Jesus Christ, Superstar
Life of Verdi
The Magic Flute
The Medium
Meeting Venus
Midnight Girl
The Mozart Brothers
Musica Proibita
Naughty Marietta
A Night at the Opera
Otello
The Panther's Claw
Phantom of the Opera
Rose Marie
The Tales of Hoffman
Terror at the Opera
The Toast of New Orleans
The Tsar's Bride
Verdi
Wagner: The Complete Epic
Wagner: The Movie

Order in the Court

Absence of Malice
The Accused
Action for Slander
Adam's Rib
All God's Children
The Ambush Murders
Anatomy of a Murder
And Justice for All
The Andersonville Trial
As Summers Die
Beyond a Reasonable Doubt
Body of Evidence
Breaker Morant
The Caine Mutiny Court
  Martial
Carrington, V.C.
A Case of Libel
Clarence Darrow
Class Action
Clearcut
Cold Days
Conduct Unbecoming
Conspiracy: The Trial of the
  Chicago Eight
Convicted
Cordelia
The Court Martial of Billy
  Mitchell
Criminal Court
Cross Examination
A Cry in the Dark
Death of a Soldier
Death Sentence
The Defender
The Defense Never Rests
Defenseless
Delinquent Parents
The Devil & Daniel Webster
Dishonored Lady
The Drake Case
A Dry White Season
Ernest Goes to Jail
Eureka!
A Few Good Men
Final Verdict
A Free Soul
From the Hip
Gideon's Trumpet
The Good Father
The Good Fight
The Good Mother
Guilty as Sin
Guilty of Innocence
Hard Traveling
Hitz
How Many Miles to Babylon?

I Want to Live!
Illegally Yours
Inherit the Wind
It Could Happen to You
The Jagged Edge
Jailbait: Betrayed By
  Innocence
The Judge
The Judge and the Assassin
Judge Horton and the
  Scottsboro Boys
Judgment at Nuremberg
Judgment in Berlin
Justice
Killing in a Small Town
King of the Pecos
Knock on Any Door
L.A. Law
Last Innocent Man
The Last Wave
Les Assassins de L'Ordre
Little Gloria...Happy at Last
The Long Dark Hall
Madame X
Madeleine
Midnight
Mrs. R's Daughter
Monsieur Beaucaire
Murder
Murder or Mercy
Music Box
Naked Lie
Never Forget
Nuts
Outrage!
The Paradine Case
Penalty Phase
Perry Mason Returns
Perry Mason: The Case of the
  Lost Love
Presumed Innocent
Prisoners of the Sun
Question of Silence
Rampage
Red Kimono
The Respectful Prostitute
Reversal of Fortune
Riverbend
Roe vs. Wade
The Rose Garden
Rumpole of the Bailey
Rumpole of the Bailey:
  Rumpole's Return
The Runner Stumbles
Sacco & Vanzetti
The Scorpion Woman
The Secret Passion of Robert
  Clayton
Separate But Equal
Sergeant Rutledge
Sergeant Ryker
Silent Victim
Skullduggery
The Star Chamber
State's Attorney
Stuck on You
Suspect
Swoon
They Won't Believe Me
To Kill a Mockingbird
The Trial
Trial of Bernhard Goetz
The Trial of Lee Harvey
  Oswald
Trial of the Catonsville Nine
Twelve Angry Men
The Verdict
When Every Day was the
  Fourth of July
When Thief Meets Thief
The Winslow Boy
Witness for the Prosecution
Wives Under Suspicion
Woman in Brown
A Woman's Face
The Young Philadelphians

Organized Crime

Absence of Malice
Across 110th Street
Action U.S.A.
Agent on Ice
Almost Human
Alphabet City
American Born
The American Gangster
American Justice
The American Soldier
Angels with Dirty Faces
Armed for Action
Armed Response
Atlantic City
Baby on Board
Babyface Morgan
Backtrack
Bad Charleston Charlie
Bad Georgia Road
Ball of Fire
The Barber Shop
The Barcelona Kill
Bellas de Noche
Beverly Hills Bodysnatchers
Big Bad Mama 2
Big Boss
Big Combo
Big News
The Big Slice
The Big Sweat
The Big Switch
Big Town After Dark
Billy Bathgate
Black Belt Jones
Black Caesar
Black Godfather
Black Lemons
Black Lizard
Black Rain
Black Shampoo
Blackjack
Blind Fury
Blood Brothers
Blood Ties
Blood Vows: The Story of a
    Mafia Wife
Blown Away
Blue Money
Body Trouble
Boss Foreman
Brighton Rock
The Brotherhood
Bugsy
Bugsy Malone
California Casanova
Camorra: The Naples
    Connection
Capone
Car Crash
The Chinatown Murders: Man
    Against the Mob
Chu Chu & the Philly Flash
Cobra
Cohen and Tate
Cold Heat
Comfort and Joy
Cookie
Cop in Blue Jeans
Corleone
Corruption
The Cotton Club
Courier of Death
Crazy Streets
Crime Killer
Crime Story
Crime Story: The Complete
    Saga
Dagger Eyes
Dangerous Charter
Darker than Amber
Daughter of the Tong
Deadly Matrimony
Deadly Rivals
Deadly Vengeance

Deadly Weapons
Death Force
Delta Fox
Desperate
Dick Tracy
Dirty Work
Doctor Detroit
The Don is Dead
Double Deal
Drunken Angel
The Enforcer
Ernest Goes to Jail
Eureka!
Excessive Force
The Executioner
The Executioner, Part 2:
    Frozen Scream
An Eye for an Eye
Faith
Fake Out
The Family
A Family Matter
Fass Black
Fatal Chase
Fear in the City
The Fighting Rookie
Final Justice
Fingers
Fireback
The Firm
Fist of Honor
Five Miles to Midnight
The Freshman
Fugitive Lovers
Gang War
Gangster Wars
Gangsters
Gangster's Law
Get Rita
The Girl Who Had Everything
Gloria
The Godfather
The Godfather 1902-1959:
    The Complete Epic
The Godfather, Part 2
The Godfather, Part 3
Goodfellas
Gunblast
The Harder They Fall
Harlem Nights
Heat
Hell on Frisco Bay
Hell Up in Harlem
Heroes in Blue
Hiding Out
High Stakes
Hired to Kill
Hit Lady
The Hit List
Hit the Dutchman
Hollywood Cop
Hollywood Crime Wave
Hollywood Man
Hong Kong Nights
Honor Thy Father
Hooch
The Hunted Lady
Hurricane Smith
I Died a Thousand Times
I, Mobster
Innocent Blood
The Italian Connection
Jornada de Muerte
Kansas City Massacre
Keaton's Cop
Keeper of the City
The Key Man
Kill Me Again
The Kill Reflex
The Killer
Killer Bait
Killing in the Sun
The Killing of a Chinese
    Bookie

The King of the Roaring '20s:
    The Story of Arnold
    Rothstein
Kiss Tomorrow Goodbye
The Krays
Ladies of the Lotus
Lady Mobster
Lady of the Evening
Lady Scarface
The Last Contract
Last Exit to Brooklyn
Last Rites
Legacy of Lies
Lepke
Lethal Games
Little Caesar
Little Vegas
Loan Shark
The Long Good Friday
Lucky Luciano
Madigan's Millions
Mafia Princess
Mafia vs. Ninja
Making the Grade
Man on a String
The Manhandlers
Manhunt
Manhunter
Married to the Mob
Mean Machine
Mean Streets
Men of Respect
The Messenger
Mikey & Nicky
Mr. Majestyk
Mister Mean
Mob Boss
Mobsters
Moon Over Harlem
Movie...In Your Face
Moving Target
My Blue Heaven
The Narrow Margin
Never Steal Anything Small
New Mafia Boss
1931: Once Upon a Time in
    New York
Ninja Dragons
Nitti: The Enforcer
Odd Jobs
Once Upon a Time in America
Our Family Business
Out for Justice
The Outside Man
Overkill
Palais Royale
The Palermo Connection
Panic Button
Passion for Power
Payoff
Penthouse
Perfect Killer
Perfect Witness
The Plot Against Harry
Point Blank
The Pope Must Diet
Port of New York
Pray for Death
Prime Target
Prizzi's Honor
The Public Eye
Rapid Fire
Raw Deal
Red Heat
The Red Light Sting
The Revenger
Ricco
The Rise and Fall of Legs
    Diamond
Rock, Baby, Rock It
Ruby
Rulers of the City
Run
Scarface
Scarface Mob
Shaft's Big Score

Shoot to Kill
Sicilian Connection
The Sicilian Connection
Sitting Ducks
Sizzle
Slaughter
Slaughter's Big Ripoff
Sloane
Slow Burn
Smokescreen
Sno-Line
Squizzy Taylor
Stakeout 2
Stand-In
Stark
State of Grace
Stiletto
The Stone Killer
Street Hero
Street People
Street War
Sweet Dirty Tony
Terminal Force
They Call Me Bruce?
They Paid with Bullets:
    Chicago 1929
Thief
Things Change
This Could Be the Night
The Three Penny Opera
The Threepenny Opera
Ticket of Leave Man
The Tongfather
Tony Rome
The Trap
Triad Savages
TripleCross
True Identity
True Romance
Ulterior Motives
Underworld, U.S.A.
The Untouchables
Velvet Smooth
Vendetta for the Saint
Verne Miller
We're Talkin' Serious Money
What! No Beer?
White Heat
White Hot: The Mysterious
    Murder of Thelma Todd
White Sands
Who's Got the Action?
Wise Guys
The Wrestler
Zebra Force

Outtakes & Bloopers

Abbott and Costello
    Scrapbook
Bela Lugosi Scrapbook
Cinema Shrapnel
Hollywood Bloopers
Hollywood Outtakes & Rare
    Footage
Hollywood Uncensored
Salute to the "King of the
    Cowboys," Roy Rogers
Star Trek Bloopers
Voice of Hollywood
What Do You Say to a Naked
    Lady?
Zombiethon

Pacific Islands

Aloha Summer
Balboa
Blue Hawaii
Carlton Browne of the F.O.
Castaway
Cry of Battle
Dangerous Life
Enchanted Island
Ethan

Eye of the Octopus
Fighting Marines
Flaming Signal
Fog Island
Food of the Gods
From Hell to Borneo
From Here to Eternity
Hell in the Pacific
Hell Raiders
His Majesty O'Keefe
Hula
The Island
Island of Dr. Moreau
The Last Flight of Noah's Ark
The Last Warrior
Lt. Robin Crusoe, U.S.N.
Mad Doctor of Blood Island
The Mermaids of Tiburon
Midway
Miss Sadie Thompson
Mission Manila
Mr. Robinson Crusoe
Moana, a Romance of the
    Golden Age
Mysterious Island
Noon Sunday
Paradise, Hawaiian Style
Pardon My Sarong
Rain
Robinson Crusoe
South Pacific
Tabu: A Story of the South
    Seas
Till There was You
Tora! Tora! Tora!
Wackiest Ship in the Army
White Shadows in the South
    Seas
Windom's Way
The Year of Living
    Dangerously

Parades & Festivals

Easter Parade
Ferris Bueller's Day Off
Miracle on 34th Street
National Lampoon's Animal
    House
Sweet Beat

Parenthood

Adam
Alice in the Cities
Aliens
All the Kind Strangers
Amazing Grace
An Autumn Afternoon
Baby Boom
Baby Girl Scott
Bachelor Mother
Backfield in Motion
The Ballad of Narayama
Between Two Women
Big Girls Don't Cry...They Get
    Even
The Big Wheel
Blind Fools
Blue City
Boys Town
Bush Mama
Cahill: United States Marshal
Careful, He Might Hear You
Chapter in Her Life
The Children of Times Square
Cody
Cold River
Commissar
Cowboys Don't Cry
Crisscross
A Cry in the Dark
Da
Desde el Abismo
Distant Voices, Still Lives
Dona Herlinda & Her Son

Parenthood

Radio

Look Who's Laughing
The Man Who Came to Dinner
My Dream is Yours
The Next Voice You Hear
Night Rhythms
No Trace
Old Barn Dance
On the Air Live with Captain Midnight
Once Upon a Honeymoon
Open House
People Are Funny
People's Choice
The Phantom Broadcast
Pot O' Gold
Psycho 4: The Beginning
Pump Up the Volume
Rachel River
Radio Days
Rebecca of Sunnybrook Farm
Sexual Response
Sleepless In Seattle
Straight Talk
Strike Up the Band
Talk Radio
Up in the Air
Whistling in Brooklyn
Who Done It?
Zoo Radio

Rags to Riches

The Abe Lincoln of Ninth Avenue
Aladdin
All the King's Men
The Amorous Adventures of Moll Flanders
Better Late Than Never
Body Slam
Breaking Glass
Brewster's Millions
The Buddy Holly Story
Callie and Son
Can You Hear the Laughter? The Story of Freddie Prinze
Christmas in July
Citizen Kane
Coal Miner's Daughter
Covergirl
Craig's Wife
Daddy Long Legs
Dangerous When Wet
Darling
Dodsworth
Dreamer
Drifting Souls
Emperor Jones
Fifth Avenue Girl
Footlight Parade
For Richer, For Poorer
Give a Girl a Break
The Great Rupert
Hero
Honeyboy
I Love Melvin
Jailhouse Rock
The Jerk
Joseph Andrews
Kept Husbands
A Kid for Two Farthings
Kipps
La Violetera
Lady for a Day
Lady Grey
The Last American Hero
The Last Laugh
Laurel & Hardy: Below Zero
Lenny
Little Lord Fauntleroy
Livin' Large
Lots of Luck
Love Nest
Lucky Partners
Macario
The Mambo Kings

The Manions of America
Mannequin
Miss Melody Jones
Mrs. Parkington
Mr. Billion
My Fair Lady
New York's Finest
The Object of Beauty
One in a Million: The Ron LaFlore Story
Only One Night
The Patsy
The Pearl
Peddlin' in Society
Possessed
Power
Pride of the Clan
Princess Tam Tam
Rebecca of Sunnybrook Farm
Rocky
The Secret of My Success
Sepia Cinderella
The Sin of Harold Diddlebock
The Sin of Madelon Claudet
Sing Your Worries Away
Speak Easily
The Stork Club
Straight Talk
Striker's Mountain
Sweet Adeline
Sweet Hearts Dance
The Tall Guy
Tennessee Stallion
The Toast of New Orleans
Toast of New York
Trading Places
The Unsinkable Molly Brown
What Price Hollywood?
Working Girl
Ziegfeld Girl

Rape

The Accused
Act of Vengeance
The Adventurers
American Commandos
And Justice for All
The Awaken Punch
Awakening of Candra
Backlash
Bad Lieutenant
The Beast Within
Blind Justice
Blue Desert
Born Innocent
Broken Badge
Bullies
Caged Terror
Cast the First Stone
Casualties of War
Certain Sacrifice
Chain Gang Women
Class of 1984
Code of Honor
Convicted
Coward of the County
Deadline Assault
Deadly Darling
Deadly Twins
Death Blow
Death Wish
Deep in the Heart
Demented
The Desperados
Diary of a Lost Girl
Diary of a Teenage Hitchhiker
Emmanuelle's Daughter
The Entity
Extremities
Flesh and Blood
Forbidden Sun
Forced Entry
Free, White, and 21
From the Life of the Marionettes

The Furious Avenger
Gentle Savage
Guncrazy
Hands of a Stranger
Hannie Caulder
Heat of the Flame
His Name was King
Home Before Midnight
The Hooked Generation
The Hotel New Hampshire
I Spit on Your Grave
I'm the One You're Looking For
In Trouble
It's Alive
Jackson County Jail
Jailbait: Betrayed By Innocence
Judge Horton and the Scottsboro Boys
Ladies Club
Lethal Woman
Lipstick
Liquid Sky
Mrs. R's Daughter
Most Wanted
Motor Psycho
Ms. 45
Multiple Maniacs
Naked Vengeance
Necromancer: Satan's Servant
Night of the Demon
Northville Cemetery Massacre
Olivier, Olivier
Open Doors
A Passage to India
The Phantom of Soho
Positive I.D.
Purgatory
Rage
The Ramrodder
Rape and Marriage: The Rideout Case
Rape of Love
Rashomon
Rider on the Rain
Screamer
Sex Crimes
Shame
The Shaming
She Came on the Bus
Short Fuse
Silent Witness
Slashed Dreams
A Stranger is Watching
Straw Dogs
Streets
Sudden Death
Sudden Impact
Tainted
Time to Kill
To Kill a Mockingbird
To Kill a Stranger
The Tormentors
Trespasses
Vengeance of the Snowmaid
Violated
Violent Ones
The Violent Years
When He's Not a Stranger
Wild Riders

Rebel With a Cause

Acceptable Risks
The Accused
Ace High
The Adventures of Robin Hood
Afterburn
American Tiger
Ann Vickers
The Applegates
As Young As You Feel
Billy Jack

The Blob
Bloody Che Contra
Blue Collar
Born Losers
Boyz N the Hood
Brubaker
Burglar
The Burmese Harp
Courage
Courageous Dr. Christian
Crime of Honor
Dark Rider
Dead Poets Society
Deadly Business
Deadly Stranger
Die Hard
Die Hard 2: Die Harder
A Dream for Christmas
Dust
East of Eden
Easy Wheels
The Electric Horseman
Exiled in America
The Fighter
The Final Alliance
The Firing Line
The $5.20 an Hour Dream
Flesh and the Spur
Flight of the Intruder
The Fugitive
The Gambling Samurai
Game of Survival
Gandhi
Gorillas in the Mist
Hair
Hardcore
Hidden City
Iron Horsemen
Iron Thunder
James Dean Story
Jesse
Joe Kidd
Johnny Firecloud
Katherine
Killing of Randy Webster
Knights of the City
Kung Fu
La Marseillaise
The Last American Hero
Lawrence of Arabia
Legend of Billie Jean
Legend of Earl Durand
Legend of the Lone Ranger
Little Tough Guys
Lois Gibbs and the Love Canal
The Loneliness of the Long Distance Runner
Luther
Man of Marble
The Manhattan Project
Marie
Memories of Underdevelopment
Mr. Smith Goes to Washington
Mountain Man
Network
Night of Evil
Norma Rae
Northern Lights
Odd Man Out
One-Eyed Jacks
One Man Jury
One Man's War
Original Intent
Overdrawn at the Memory Bank
Paths of Glory
Patty Hearst
Plutonium Baby
The Principal
Punk Rock Movie
Quarantine
The Radical
Robin Hood: Prince of Thieves
Roe vs. Wade

Rooster: Spurs of Death!
Sakharov
Samaritan: The Mitch Snyder Story
The Sand Pebbles
Sansho the Bailiff
Save the Lady
The Scarlet Pimpernel
Serpico
The Shock
Silkwood
Sins of Rome
Somebody Has to Shoot the Picture
Stay Away, Joe
The Stranger Wore a Gun
Sympathy for the Devil
Taffin
This Land is Mine
Tin Star
To Kill a Priest
Trial of the Catonsville Nine
True Believer
The Ultimate Ninja Challenge
Under Western Stars
Vengeance
The Westerner
When a Man Rides Alone
Wisdom
Without You I'm Nothing

Rebel Without a Cause

Across the Tracks
All Night Long
Badlands
The Boys Next Door
Breathless
Cheech and Chong's Up in Smoke
A Clockwork Orange
Cool As Ice
The Cruel Story of Youth
Dino
Easy Rider
The Fugitive Kind
Fury to Freedom: The Life Story of Raul Ries
Girls' Town
Going Places
Gore Vidal's Billy the Kid
Great Missouri Raid
Guncrazy
Heart Beat
Hud
I Was a Teenage Werewolf
If...
James Dean
Just for the Hell of It
Leather Jackets
The Little Valentino
Lost Angels
On the Edge: The Survival of Dana
Over the Edge
Petit Con
Presumed Guilty
Pump Up the Volume
Rambo: First Blood, Part 2
Rambo 3
Rebel High
Rebel Rousers
Rebel Without a Cause
Road House
Rocky 4
September 30, 1955
sex, lies and videotape
Snow Kill
Suburbia
Summer Camp Nightmare
That Was Then...This Is Now
3:15—The Moment of Truth
Thunder Road
Top Gun
The Violent Years

The Wild Angels
The Wild One
The Wild Ride

Red Scare

Arsenal
Baltic Deputy
The Bamboo Saucer
Battle Beneath the Earth
Chapayev
China Cry
Coming Out of the Ice
The Commies are Coming, the
  Commies are Coming
Commissar
Conspirator
Death of a Bureaucrat
Earth
Eminent Domain
Fellow Traveler
The Great Armored Car
  Swindle
Guilty by Suspicion
Guilty of Treason
Hands Up
Hawthorne of the USA
The Inner Circle
The Interrogation
Invasion U.S.A.
Jet Pilot
Little World of Don Camillo
Man of Marble
Mandela
Mother Kusters Goes to
  Heaven
Mother of Kings
Nicholas and Alexandra
Night Crossing
Night Flight from Moscow
Oh, Bloody Life!
Open Doors
The Red Menace
Red Nightmare
Reds
Requiem for Dominic
Revolution! A Red Comedy
The She-Beast
Strike
Thoughts are Free
Tobor the Great
The Ugly American
Uranus
When Father was Away on
  Business

Religion

Abduction of St. Anne
Absolution
Androcles and the Lion
Angel Baby
Augustine of Hippo
Bernadette
The Birch Interval
The Blasphemer
Blood of Jesus
Body and Soul
Brother Sun, Sister Moon
Brothers in Arms
Caligari's Cure
Camila
Catholics
Chariots of Fire
The Church
Conquest of Space
The Courageous Mr. Penn
Crimes of Passion
Cry from the Mountain
Day of Judgment
Day of Triumph
Def by Temptation
Devi
The Devil at 4 O'Clock
The Disappearance of Aimee
Dr. Syn
Dr. Syn, Alias the Scarecrow

A Dream for Christmas
El Cid
El Cristo de los Milagros
El: This Strange Passion
Emanon
The Favor, the Watch, & the
  Very Big Fish
The Fiend
The First Christmas
The Flowers of St. Francis
Friendly Persuasion
The Ghoul
Glory! Glory!
Go Down Death
The Godfather, Part 3
God's Gun
Greaser's Palace
The Greatest Story Ever Told
Green Pastures
The Guyana Tragedy: The
  Story of Jim Jones
Hail Mary
Hallelujah!
Hazel's People
Heavens Above
Hellfire
In Search of Historic Jesus
Inherit the Wind
The Inquiry
Invasion of the Space
  Preachers
Iron Horsemen
Jesus
Jesus Christ, Superstar
Jesus of Nazareth
The Jesus Trip
Joan of Arc
Joni
The Last Temptation of Christ
Laughing Sinners
Leap of Faith
Leaves from Satan's Book
The Light of Faith
Little Church Around the
  Corner
The Littlest Angel
Love and Faith
Luther
Major Barbara
A Man Called Peter
Marjoe
Martin Luther
The Meeting: Eddie Finds a
  Home
The Milky Way
The Miracle
Miracle in Rome
Miracle of Our Lady of Fatima
Mohammed: Messenger of
  God
Monsieur Vincent
Monsignor Quixote
Monty Python's Life of Brian
A Mormon Maid
Moses
The Next Voice You Hear
The Night of the Iguana
Ordet
Pass the Ammo
The Passion of Joan of Arc
The Passover Plot
The Penitent
Pray TV
Prisoner of Rio
The Private Secretary
The Prodigal Planet
Promised a Miracle
Quo Vadis
Rain
The Rapture
Resurrection
The Robe
Romero
Sacrilege
St. Benny the Dip
Saint Joan

Salome
Salvation!
Sanctuary of Fear
Sebastiane
Shiokari Pass
The Sky Pilot
The Song of Bernadette
Susan and God
This Stuff'll Kill Ya!
Through a Glass Darkly
Tournament
Trapped by the Mormons
The Vision
Whistle Down the Wind
Whistling in the Dark
Whitcomb's War
The White Rose
Wholly Moses!
The Winter Light
Wise Blood
Witness
The Word

Religious Epics

The Agony and the Ecstasy
The Babylon Story from
  "Intolerance"
Barabbas
Ben-Hur
The Bible...In the Beginning
Cleopatra
David and Bathsheba
Day of Triumph
Demetrius and the Gladiators
The Egyptian
El Cid
Exodus
Fourth Wise Man
Gospel According to St.
  Matthew
Great Leaders of the Bibles
Herod the Great
In the Name of the Pope-King
The Inquiry
Jesus Christ, Superstar
Jesus of Nazareth
Joseph & His Brethren
King David
King of Kings
The King of Kings
The Last Supper
Legal Tender
Mary and Joseph: A Story of
  Faith
The Messiah
Moses
Nativity
Nefertiti, Queen of the Nile
Rachel's Man
The Robe
Salome
Samson and Delilah
Saul and David
The Silver Chalice
Sin of Adam & Eve
Sins of Jezebel
Sodom and Gomorrah
Solomon and Sheba
The Song of Bernadette
The Story of Ruth
Ten Commandments
The Ten Commandments

Renegade Body
Parts

The Beast with Five Fingers
Blood of Ghastly Horror
Body Parts
The Brain That Wouldn't Die
The Crawling Eye
The Crawling Hand
Demonoid, Messenger of
  Death
Doctor Butcher M.D.

The Hand
The Hands of Orlac
Mindkiller
Severed Ties
Waxwork 2: Lost in Time

Restored Footage

Beau Revel
Crimes of Passion
Dr. Jekyll and Mr. Hyde
Foolish Wives
Frankenstein
Isadora
Lawrence of Arabia
Lost Horizon
New York, New York
Que Viva Mexico
Red River
The Rules of the Game
Sadie Thompson
Spartacus
Spiders
A Star is Born
Star Trek: The Motion Picture
Star Trek: The Cage
Sunny Side Up
Tarzan and His Mate
Twelve O'Clock High
Two English Girls
Wages of Fear
When Time Ran Out

Revenge

Act of Aggression
Act of Passion: The Lost
  Honor of Kathryn Beck
Act of Vengeance
Adios, Hombre
The Adventurers
Against the Drunken Cat
  Paws
The Alchemist
Alien Seed
All Dogs Go to Heaven
American Commandos
American Eagle
American Samurai
Anatomy of a Psycho
Angel and the Badman
Angel Square
Angels from Hell
The Angry Dragon
Appointment with Crime
Archer: The Fugitive from the
  Empire
Arizona Terror
Asylum
Avenged
Avenging Angel
Avenging Force
Back to Back
Ballad of Cable Hogue
The Ballad of the Sad Cafe
Banzai Runner
The Baron
Basket Case
The Beast with Five Fingers
The Beguiled
Bell from Hell
Best of the Best 2
Betrayal and Revenge
Big Jake
The Big Showdown
Black Arrow
The Black Arrow
Black Cobra
Black Dragon's Revenge
The Black Hand
The Black Klansman
The Black Pirate
The Black Raven
The Black Six
Black Sunday
A Black Veil for Lisa
Blackbelt 2: Fatal Force

Blind Vengeance
Blood and Guns
Blood Avenger
Blood for a Silver Dollar
Blood on the Mountain
Blood Red
Blood Ring
Bloodfist
Bloodmatch
Bloody Birthday
The Bloody Fight
The Blue Knight
The Blue Lamp
Boiling Point
Bolo
Border Rangers
Born Invincible
Bounty Hunters
Branded a Coward
Bronze Buckaroo
Brotherhood of Justice
Bruce Li the Invincible
The Brute Man
Bulldance
Bulldog Courage
Bullet for Sandoval
Bullies
The Burning
Bury Me an Angel
Cadillac Man
Caged Terror
Cape Fear
The Caravan Trail
Carolina Skeletons
Carson City Kid
Cartouche
Certain Sacrifice
Chain Gang Women
The Chair
Challenge
Chan is Missing
The Chase
Chisum
Chrome and Hot Leather
Class of 1984
Clayton County Line
Cobra
Cobra Against Ninja
Code Name: Zebra
Code of Honor
Coffy
Cold Eyes of Fear
Cold Justice
Cold Steel
Cold Sweat
Cole Justice
Commando Invasion
Conqueror & the Empress
Cornered
The Count of Monte Cristo
The Count of the Old Town
The Courier
The Cowboys
Crack House
Crazed Cop
Creepers
Crimebusters
Cry Danger
Cry of the Innocent
Cry Vengeance
Curse of the Devil
Daddy-O
Daddy's Gone A-Hunting
Danger Zone 2
Dangerous Obsession
Dangerous Orphans
Dark August
Dark River: A Father's
  Revenge
Darkman
Daughter of the Dragon
DaVinci's War
Dawn Rider
The Day the Women Got Even
Dead on the Money
Deadly Darling

Revenge

Robots

Doctor Who: The Three Doctors
Doctor Who: The Troughton Years
Doctor Who: The War Games
Doctor Who: Tomb of the Cyberman
The Eliminators
The Empire Strikes Back
Eve of Destruction
Forbidden Planet
Future Cop
The Hitchhiker's Guide to the Galaxy
The Human Duplicators
Kronos
Mandroid
Megaville
Nemesis
Planets Against Us
Project: Shadowchaser
Prototype
Prototype X29A
Return of the Jedi
RoboCop
RoboCop 2
Roboman
Robot Holocaust
Robot Jox
Robot Monster
The Robot vs. the Aztec Mummy
Robot Wars
R.O.T.O.R.
Runaway
Short Circuit
Star Crash
Star Wars
Steel and Lace
Tekkaman, the Space Knight: Vol. 2
The Terminator
Terminator 2: Judgment Day
Terror of Mechagodzilla
Tobor the Great
War of the Robots
Westworld

Rock Stars on Film

All You Need Is Cash
Blow-Up
Blue Hawaii
The Bodyguard
Breaking Glass
The Bride
Carny
Caveman
Charro!
Chuck Berry: Hail! Hail! Rock 'n' Roll
Clambake
Double Trouble
Dune
Easy Come, Easy Go
Flaming Star
Follow That Dream
Frankie and Johnny
Freddy's Dead: The Final Nightmare
Fun in Acapulco
G.I. Blues
The Girl Can't Help It
Girl Happy
Girls! Girls! Girls!
Give My Regards to Broad Street
Go, Johnny Go!
Hard Day's Night
The Harder They Come
Harum Scarum
Head
Help!
How I Won the War
The Hunger

It Happened at the World's Fair
Jailhouse Rock
Jubilee
Kid Galahad
King Creole
KISS Meets the Phantom of the Park
Kissin' Cousins
La Bamba
The Last Temptation of Christ
The Legacy
Let It Be
Lisztomania
Live a Little, Love a Little
Love Me Tender
Loving You
The Magic Christian
Magical Mystery Tour
The Man Who Fell to Earth
Merry Christmas, Mr. Lawrence
Mrs. Brown, You've Got a Lovely Daughter
Monster Dog
Nomads
One Trick Pony
Paradise, Hawaiian Style
Pat Garrett & Billy the Kid
Performance
Pink Floyd: The Wall
Poetic Justice
Quadrophenia
Rock 'n' Roll High School
Roustabout
Speedway
Spinout
Stay Away, Joe
That'll Be the Day
This is Elvis
Tickle Me
Tommy
The Trouble with Girls (and How To Get Into It)
Viva Las Vegas
Wild in the Country
Woodstock
Yellow Submarine

Rodeos

The Adventures of Gallant Bess
Arizona Cowboy
Desert Trail
Feud of the West
Girl from Calgary
Goldenrod
Great American Cowboy
Junior Bonner
Kid from Gower Gulch
Lady Takes a Chance
Lights of Old Santa Fe
The Lusty Men
Luzia
Man from Utah
The Misfits
My Heroes Have Always Been Cowboys
Never a Dull Moment
Oklahoma Cyclone
Rider from Tucson
Rodeo Girl
Rolling Home
Saddle Buster
Trouble in Texas
Western Double Feature 5
Wild Horse
Wild Horse Rodeo

Role Reversal

Age Isn't Everything
All of Me
Anastasia
Anastasia: The Mystery of Anna

Angel
Angel on My Shoulder
Bad Manners
The Bank Dick
Before Morning
Belfast Assassin
Big
Biggles
Blood of Dracula
Bloodlink
The Captain from Koepenick
Captive Heart
Cheech and Chong's, The Corsican Brothers
Christmas in Connecticut
Cinderfella
Clambake
Class Act
Cleo/Leo
Coming to America
Como Dos Gotas de Agua
Condorman
The Couch Trip
Courage
Dave
The Deputy Drummer
Desperately Seeking Susan
Devil's Canyon
Dr. Black, Mr. Hyde
Doctor Detroit
Doctor Doolittle
Dr. Heckyl and Mr. Hype
Dr. Jekyll and Mr. Hyde
Doctors and Nurses
Donde Duermen Dos...Duermen Tres
Down and Out in Beverly Hills
Dream a Little Dream
A Dream of Passion
18 Again!
Extremities
The $5.20 an Hour Dream
For Ladies Only
48 Hrs.
Frank and I
Freaky Friday
Gentleman's Agreement
The Gladiator
The Grand Duchess and the Waiter
The Great Gabbo
Greystoke: The Legend of Tarzan, Lord of the Apes
Guest Wife
Gunfire
Heart Like a Wheel
Her Life as a Man
Hiding Out
Identity Crisis
The Incredible Mr. Limpet
Iron Maze
Johnny Guitar
Just One of the Guys
Kagemusha
Kim
Kings and Desperate Men
La Femme Nikita
La Ronde
The Lady Vanishes
Lady Vanishes
Ladybugs
Law and Order
Liana, Jungle Goddess
Like Father, Like Son
Liquid Sky
Lonely Wives
Maid to Order
Male and Female
The Man Who Haunted Himself
The Man Who Wagged His Tail
Man with Two Heads
Monkey Business
My Blue Heaven
My Fair Lady

My Neighborhood
Now, Voyager
Overboard
Panamint's Bad Man
Paris When It Sizzles
People's Choice
Performance
Persona
Pocketful of Miracles
Point of No Return
Posse
The Prince and the Pauper
Prisoner of Zenda
Psycho
Quicksilver
Rabbit Test
The Raggedy Rawney
Raid on Rommel
Red Lion
Red Rock Outlaw
Rendez-Moi Ma Peau
Rider of the Law
The Road to Yesterday
Roman Holiday
Satanik
Savages
Scalpel
The Scarlet Pimpernel
September Affair
The Shaggy Dog
The Shakiest Gun in the West
Showdown in Little Tokyo
Silent Night, Deadly Night
Slapstick of Another Kind
A Slightly Pregnant Man
Small Town Boy
Something Special
Sometimes Aunt Martha Does Dreadful Things
Song of Texas
Soul Man
A Stolen Face
Stoogemania
Summer Night with Greek Profile, Almond Eyes & Scent of Basil
Summer Switch
Super Soul Brother
Sweet Revenge
Switch
Sylvia Scarlett
Taking Care of Business
A Tale of Two Cities
That Man Is Pregnant
That's My Baby!
Tomboy
Trading Places
Triple Echo
True Identity
Ultimate Desires
Vice Versa
Victor/Victoria
Wait Till Your Mother Gets Home
Watermelon Man
White Sands
Wonder Man
Yentl
Yidl Mitn Fidl

Romantic Adventures

The African Queen
Baby...Secret of the Lost Legend
The Jewel of the Nile
Joe Versus the Volcano
Mogambo
Red Dust
Romancing the Stone

Romantic Comedy

Abdulla the Great
About Last Night...

Acqua e Sapone
Adam's Rib
The Admiral Was a Lady
Adorable Julia
The Adventures of Sadie
Aggie Appleby, Maker of Men
Alfredo, Alfredo
All Night Long
All the Way Down
The Allnighter
All's Fair
...Almost
Almost an Angel
Almost Pregnant
Almost You
The Ambassador's Daughter
American Dreamer
American Friends
The Amorous Adventures of Moll Flanders
And You Thought Your Parents Were Weird!
Animal Behavior
Anna Christie
Anna Karenina
Annabel Takes a Tour/Maid's Night Out
Annie Hall
Another Chance
Another Thin Man
The Apartment
April Fools
Are Parents People?
Arthur
Arthur 2: On the Rocks
Ask Any Girl
Baby Boom
Babycakes
Bachelor Apartment
Bachelor Bait
Bachelor Party
Back to the Beach
Bahama Passage
Baja Oklahoma
Ball of Fire
The Balloonatic/One Week
Bare Essentials
Barefoot in the Park
Barnaby and Me
The Bashful Bachelor
Battling Butler
Beachcomber
Bed & Breakfast
Bells are Ringing
Benny & Joon
Best Legs in the 8th Grade
Betsy's Wedding
Beyond Tomorrow
Birds & the Bees
Blame It on Rio
Blind Date
Blonde Crazy
Blue Country
Bobo
Bombshell
Boom Town
Boomerang
Born Yesterday
Boyfriends & Girlfriends
Breakfast at Tiffany's
Breath of Scandal
The Bride Came C.O.D.
Bull Durham
But Not for Me
The Butcher's Wife
Butterflies
Bye Bye Baby
Cactus Flower
Cafe Romeo
California Casanova
California Suite
Came a Hot Friday
The Cameraman
Can She Bake a Cherry Pie?
Can't Buy Me Love
Captain's Paradise

Romantic

Spite Marriage
Stand-In
State of the Union
The Station
The Sterile Cuckoo
Stolen Kisses
The Story of Boys & Girls
Straight Talk
Strictly Ballroom
Strictly Business
Stroke of Midnight
Summer School
Sunset Limousine
Surf Party
Surrender
Surviving Desire
Suzy
The Swan
Sweet Lies
Sweet Talker
The Tall Guy
The Taming of the Shrew
Tammy and the Bachelor
Tammy and the Doctor
The Teahouse of the August
  Moon
Ted & Venus
The Tender Trap
Tendres Cousines
That Certain Thing
That Lucky Touch
That Touch of Mink
That Uncertain Feeling
There's a Girl in My Soup
They All Laughed
They Got Me Covered
The Thing Called Love
The Things of Life
30 Is a Dangerous Age,
  Cynthia
This Could Be the Night
This Happy Feeling
Thomas Graal's Best Film
Thomas Graal's First Child
Those Endearing Young
  Charms
Three Broadway Girls
Three for Bedroom C
Three Guys Named Mike
Three Husbands
Three of Hearts
Three Way Weekend
Tiger and the Pussycat
Till Marriage Do Us Part
Tillie's Punctured Romance
Time of the Gypsies
To Paris with Love
Togetherness
Tom, Dick, and Harry
Tom Jones
Tomboy
Too Beautiful for You
Topsy Turvy
A Touch of Class
Tulips
Tune in Tomorrow
Two-Faced Woman
Two Nights with Cleopatra
Two of a Kind
Underground Aces
The Unkissed Bride
Up Your Alley
Utilities
Valley Girl
Victor/Victoria
Vivacious Lady
Waiting for the Light
Walk, Don't Run
Warm Summer Rain
Watch It
We All Loved Each Other So
  Much
The Wedding Party
We're Not Married
What's New Pussycat?
When Harry Met Sally

When Ladies Meet
Where the Boys Are
Who Am I This Time?
The Whoopee Boys
Wildest Dreams
Wimps
Wishful Thinking
With Six You Get Eggroll
Without Love
Without Reservations
The Woman in Red
Woman of the Year
The Women
Working Girl
The World's Oldest Living
  Bridesmaid
Worth Winning
The Year of the Jellyfish
You Can't Fool Your Wife
You Can't Take It with You
Your Place or Mine
You've Got to Have Heart

Romantic Drama

Aaron Loves Angela
The Accidental Tourist
The Adorable Cheat
The Affair
An Affair to Remember
The African Queen
After Julius
After Midnight
Algiers
Ali: Fear Eats the Soul
Alice
Alice Adams
All the Vermeers in New York
All This and Heaven Too
Always
Anatomy of a Seduction
And a Nightingale Sang
And Now My Love
Angel Square
The Animal Kingdom
Ann Vickers
Anna Karenina
Annapolis
The Annapolis Story
Anne of Avonlea
Another Time, Another Place
Anthony Adverse
Arch of Triumph
As Is
Aspen Extreme
Atalia
The Atonement of Gosta
  Berling
The Average Woman
Back Street
Backstreet Dreams
The Ballad of the Sad Cafe
Barbarian and the Geisha
The Barretts of Wimpole
  Street
Bayou Romance
Beau Revel
Beauty and the Beast
Beloved Enemy
Berlin Blues
Betty Blue
Beware of Pity
The Big Parade
Big Street
The Bigamist
Bird of Paradise
Birds of Paradise
Bitter Sweet
The Bitter Tears of Petra von
  Kant
The Black Marble
Black Orchid
Blind Husbands
Blood and Sand
Blood and Sand/Son of the
  Sheik

Blood Feud
The Blood of Others
The Bodyguard
Bolero
Bombay Talkie
Born to Be Bad
The Boss Is Served
Boy Takes Girl
Breakfast in Paris
Breathless
The Bride Wore Red
Brief Encounter
Buffalo Jump
Bullfighter & the Lady
Burning Secret
Buster and Billie
By Love Possessed
Bye Bye Blues
Cabiria
Cabo Blanco
Cactus in the Snow
Caddie
Camelia
Camila
Camille
Camille Claudel
Captive Hearts
Carmen
Carnival Story
The Carpetbaggers
Casablanca
Casino
Cass Timberlane
Castaway
The Castaway Cowboy
Caught
Chain Lightning
Chained
Chanel Solitaire
Chapter Two
Charles & Diana: A Palace
  Divided
The Children
Children of a Lesser God
Christopher Strong
Cinderella Liberty
Circle of Love
Circle of Two
Circus World
City for Conquest
City Girl
Clash by Night
Close My Eyes
Cobra
Cocktail
A Coeur Joie
Cold Sassy Tree
Collector's Item
Come See the Paradise
The Coming of Amos
The Competition
Conquest
Consolation Marriage
Corregidor
The Cousins
Cowboy & the Ballerina
The Cranes are Flying
The Crossing
Crystal Heart
The Cutting Edge
Cyrano de Bergerac
Damage
Dance
Dancers
Dangerous Liaisons
Dark Eyes
Dark Journey
Days and Nights in the Forest
Deception
A Dedicated Man
Deja Vu
Desert Hearts
Devil in the Flesh
Devil's Wanton
Devotion
Die Grosse Freiheit Nr. 7

A Different Kind of Love
The Divorcee
Doctor Zhivago
Dogfight
The Dolls
The Dolphin
Dos Chicas de Revista
A Dream of Kings
Dreams Lost, Dreams Found
Dressmaker
Dubarry
Duel of Hearts
Dying Young
Dynasty
East Side, West Side
Ecstasy
Edward and Mrs. Simpson
Effi Briest
84 Charing Cross Road
El
El Diputado
El Penon de las Animas
Elena and Her Men
Elephant Walk
Eliza's Horoscope
Empty Canvas
Enchanted April
End of August
Endless Love
Escape to Love
Ethan
Ethan Frome
Every Time We Say Goodbye
Everybody's All American
Ex-Lady
The Eyes, the Mouth
Falling in Love
The Family Man
Fanny
Far and Away
Far from the Madding Crowd
A Farewell to Arms
The Farmer Takes a Wife
Fatal Attraction
Fergie & Andrew: Behind
  Palace Doors
Fire and Ice
Fire and Sword
Fire with Fire
Fires Within
First Affair
First Love
Five Days One Summer
The Flame is Love
Flor Silvestre
The Flying Fool
Fool for Love
Fools
For Love Alone
For Love or Money
For the Love of Angela
Forbidden
Foreign Affairs
Forever
Forever Emmanuelle
Foxfire Light
Franz
The French Lieutenant's
  Woman
French Postcards
Fresh Horses
The Fugitive Kind
Fulfillment
Full Moon in Paris
Furia Pasional
Gal Young 'Un
Gamble on Love
The Game of Love
Georgia, Georgia
The Gift of Love
Girl in Black
The Girl in Blue
The Go-Between
Golden Demon
Gone with the Wind

Goodbye Again
The Gorgeous Hussy
Grand Isle
The Great Lie
Green Dolphin Street
Green Fields
Griffin and Phoenix: A Love
  Story
Guitarras Lloren Guitarras
The Hairdresser's Husband
Hanover Street
Harem
Havana
Head Over Heels
The Hearst and Davies Affair
Heart of Humanity
Heartbreakers
Heat and Dust
The Heiress
Heroes
Hide-Out
His Private Secretary
History is Made at Night
Hold the Dream
Holiday Affair
Holocaust
  Survivors...Remembrance
    of Love
The Home and the World
Home Before Midnight
Home Sweet Home
Homecoming
Honky
Humoresque
Husbands and Wives
I Can't Escape
I Conquer the Sea
I Live in Grosvenor Square
I Love All of You
I Love N.Y.
I Love You
I Never Sang For My Father
Ice Castles
Iguana
I'm a Fool
Image of Passion
In a Shallow Grave
In Dangerous Company
In Search of Anna
In Too Deep
An Indecent Obsession
Indecent Proposal
Independence Day
Indiscretion of an American
  Wife
Interval
Iron Cowboy
Island of Desire
Isle of Secret Passion
I've Always Loved You
Jacko & Lise
Jane Eyre
Jenny
Johnny Frenchman
Josepha
Jules and Jim
Jungle Fever
Just Between Friends
Katie's Passion
Kept Husbands
The Key
Killing Heat
The King's Rhapsody
The King's Whore
Kipperbang
Kitty Foyle
Knight Without Armour
Knights of the Round Table
La Bella Lola
La Carcel de Laredo
La Fuerza Inutil
La Grande Bourgeoise
La Mentira
La Petite Sirene
La Strada
Lady Chatterley's Lover

Roommates from Hell

Royalty

Royalty

Crow Hollow
Cutting Class
Dark Obsession
Dark Places
Dark Sanity
Dark Waters
Darkroom
A Day at the Races
Dead Man Out
Dead of Night
Dead Pit
Deadly Innocence
Deadly Intruder
Deadly Strangers
The Deadly Trap
Death Kiss
Death Nurse
Dementia 13
A Demon in My View
Demons of the Mind
Deranged
Despair
Desperate Living
Deutschland im Jahre Null
Devi
The Devil Bat
The Devil Bat's Daughter
Devil Doll
The Devil in Silk
Devil in the Flesh
Devil Times Five
Devil Wears White
Diary of a Mad Housewife
Diary of a Madman
Diary of a Young Comic
Diary of Forbidden Dreams
Dick Barton, Special Agent
Die! Die! My Darling!
Die Screaming, Marianne
Disturbance
Disturbed
The Doctor and the Devils
Doctor Blood's Coffin
Doctor Butcher M.D.
Dr. Caligari
Dr. Frankenstein's Castle of
    Freaks
Doctor Gore
Dr. Hackenstein
Dr. Jekyll and Mr. Hyde
Dr. Jekyll and the Wolfman
Dr. Mabuse the Gambler
Dr. Mabuse vs. Scotland Yard
Dr. Strangelove, or: How I
    Learned to Stop Worrying
    and Love the Bomb
Dr. Tarr's Torture Dungeon
Doctor X
Dog Day Afternoon
The Doll
Dominique is Dead
Don't Go in the Woods
Don't Look in the Basement
Don't Look Now
Don't Mess with My Sister!
Don't Open Till Christmas
Doom Asylum
A Double Life
Dream Lover
Dream No Evil
The Dream Team
Easy Rider
Eaten Alive
Echoes
Edge of Sanity
El: This Strange Passion
The End of Innocence
End of the Road
Endless Love
Endless Night
Entr'acte
Equus
Escape from Safehaven
Estate of Insanity
Europa '51
Exorcism's Daughter

Eyeball
The Eyes of the Amaryllis
The Fall of the House of Usher
False Identity
Fat Guy Goes Nutzoid
Fear Strikes Out
The Fifth Floor
The Fisher King
The Five of Me
Follow Me Quietly
Forced March
The 4th Man
Frances
Fright
From the Life of the
    Marionettes
Frozen Terror
The Girl in Room 2A
The Goalie's Anxiety at the
    Penalty Kick
The Hairdresser's Husband
Hamlet
Hammersmith is Out
Harvey
The Haunting
Haunting of Sarah Hardy
Haunts
Heart of Midnight
Heat and Sunlight
Henry IV
Heroes
Hider in the House
The Horrible Dr. Hichcock
Horror Chamber of Dr.
    Faustus
Horror Hospital
Horror House on Highway 5
Hotline
The Housekeeper
How to Get Ahead in
    Advertising
How to Make a Monster
Hysteria
I Am the Cheese
I Dismember Mama
I Never Promised You a Rose
    Garden
Icy Breasts
If Things Were Different
Illusions
Impulse
The Incredible Two-Headed
    Transplant
Innocent Victim
Insanity
Interiors
The Invisible Ghost
It Happened at Nightmare Inn
It's Alive!
Juggernaut
Keeper
Killer's Moon
The King of Hearts
Lassie from Lancashire
The Last of Philip Banter
The Last Ride
Lethal Weapon
Lethal Weapon 2
Let's Scare Jessica to Death
Lilith
The Lonely Sex
Lost Angels
Lower Level
Lunatics: A Love Story
Luther the Geek
Mad Love
Man Facing Southeast
Marat/Sade
Midnight Warning
Mind Games
Mine Own Executioner
Morgan!
Mother Kusters Goes to
    Heaven
My First Wife
Night of Bloody Horror

Night of Terror
The Night Visitor
Night Wars
Night Watch
The Ninth Configuration
Nobody's Perfekt
Nuts
October Man
Offerings
One Flew Over the Cuckoo's
    Nest
125 Rooms of Comfort
One Summer Love
The Onion Field
Out of Sight, Out of Her Mind
Overexposed
Pale Blood
Paperback Hero
Pay Off
Peeping Tom
Performance
A Piano for Mrs. Cimino
Picture Mommy Dead
Pigs
The Pink Panther Strikes
    Again
The Pit and the Pendulum
The Pit & the Pendulum
Poison
The Possessed
The President's Analyst
Prettykill
Prime Suspect
Private Parts
Psychic Killer
Psycho
Psycho 2
Psycho Cop
Psychos in Love
Question of Silence
Raising Cain
Rasputin
The Rejuvenator
Remember Me
Return of the Ape Man
Revolt of the Zombies
Richard III
Room to Let
The Ruling Class
Scissors
Scream Bloody Murder
Scream for Help
Screamer
Seance on a Wet Afternoon
Secret Beyond the Door
The Sender
Sessions
Seven Days in May
Shadow Play
Shattered
Shattered Silence
Shattered Spirits
The Shining
Shock Corridor
The Silence of the Lambs
Silent Night, Bloody Night
Sisters
Sketches of a Strangler
Slaughter Hotel
Sledgehammer
Sniper
Solaris
Sophie's Choice
South of Reno
Spectre of the Rose
Spellbound
Story of Adele H.
Strait-Jacket
Strange Illusion
Street Asylum
A Streetcar Named Desire
Strong Medicine
Summer of Secrets
The Survivalist
Svengali
Sybil

Tainted Image
Teenage Frankenstein
The Tenant
The Testament of Dr.
    Cordelier
They Might Be Giants
Three Nuts in Search of a Bolt
Torture Train
Touched
Tracks
Trapped in Silence
Twin Peaks: Fire Walk with
    Me
Twinsanity
Twister
Urge to Kill
Vampire's Kiss
Vengeance Is Mine
Ward Six
Watched
What About Bob?
What Ever Happened to Baby
    Jane?
Whatever Happened to Susan
    Jane?
What's the Matter with Helen?
While I Live
White Heat
The Wind
Witchfire
A Woman Under the Influence
You are Not I
Young Hero of the Shaolin
    Part 2
The Young Ones

Satanism

Alison's Birthday
Amazon Jail
Angel on My Shoulder
Asylum of Satan
Bad Dreams
Beast of the Yellow Night
Beyond the Door 3
The Black Cat
Black Roses
Black Sunday
The Blood on Satan's Claw
Blood Orgy of the She-Devils
The Bloodsuckers
The Brotherhood of Satan
Child of Darkness, Child of
    Light
The Chosen
The Crimson Cult
Damien: Omen 2
The Demon Lover
Demonoid, Messenger of
    Death
The Devil & Daniel Webster
Devil Rider
The Devils
The Devil's Daughter
The Devil's Eye
The Devil's Mistress
The Devil's Nightmare
The Devil's Partner
The Devil's Possessed
Devil's Rain
Devil's Son-in-Law
The Devil's Web
Disciple of Death
Doctor Faustus
El Monte de las Brujas
Equinox
Erotic Dreams
Eternal Evil
Evil Altar
Evilspeak
Exorcism
The Exorcist
Exorcist 2: The Heretic
Eye of the Demon
Fear No Evil
Final Conflict

Guardian of the Abyss
Hack O'Lantern
Halloween Night
Highway to Hell
House of the Black Death
I Don't Want to Be Born
I Drink Your Blood
Inferno
Invitation to Hell
Jaws of Satan
Land of the Minotaur
Leaves from Satan's Book
The Legend of Hillbilly John
Leonor
The Man and the Monster
Masque of the Red Death/
    Premature Burial
Maxim Xul
The Mephisto Waltz
Midnight
Midnight Cabaret
Mind, Body & Soul
Mysterious Doctor Satan
Necromancer: Satan's
    Servant
Night Visitor
976-EVIL
976-EVIL 2: The Astral Factor
The Occultist
Oh, God! You Devil
The Omen
Other Hell
Prime Evil
Prince of Darkness
The Pyx
Race with the Devil
Rest In Pieces
Revenge
Rosemary's Baby
The Satanic Rites of Dracula
Satan's Black Wedding
Satan's Blade
Satan's Cheerleaders
Satan's Princess
Satan's School for Girls
Satan's Touch
Satanwar
The Sentinel
Servants of Twilight
The Seventh Victim
Shock 'Em Dead
Sisters of Satan
Speak of the Devil
Specters
The Spellbinder
Sugar Cookies
Suicide Cult
The Tempter
Terror Beach
To the Devil, A Daughter
Tombs of the Blind Dead
The Visitor
Warlock
Witchcraft
Witchcraft 3: The Kiss of
    Death
Witchcraft 5: Dance with the
    Devil
WitchTrap

Satire & Parody

ABC's of Love & Sex,
    Australia Style
Abduction
The Act
The Adventures of
    Hairbreadth Harry
The Adventures of Picasso
The Adventures of Sherlock
    Holmes' Smarter Brother
The Affairs of Annabel
Airplane!
Airplane 2: The Sequel
Alex in Wonderland
Alien Women

Satire

All Through the Night
All You Need Is Cash
The Alphabet Murders
Amazon Women on the Moon
America 3000
American Drive-In
American Tickler
Americathon
And When She Was Bad...
Andy Warhol's Dracula
Angel City
Animal Farm
Animators from Allegro Non
   Troppo
Any Wednesday
The Apartment
As Young As You Feel
Auntie Mame
Bad Manners
Bad Medicine
Bambi Meets Godzilla
Bananas
Barry McKenzie Holds His
   Own
Basic Training
The Bawdy Adventures of
   Tom Jones
Beau Pere
Bebe's Kids
Being There
The Best Man
Beyond the Valley of the Dolls
Beyond Therapy
Big Bus
Big Deal on Madonna Street
The Big Picture
Big Trouble in Little China
Bill & Ted's Bogus Journey
Bill & Ted's Excellent
   Adventure
Bingo Inferno
Black and White in Color
Black Bird
Bob & Carol & Ted & Alice
Bob Roberts
The Bonfire of the Vanities
Boob Tube
Born in East L.A.
Boss
Boy Meets Girl
Britannia Hospital
Bullshot
Bullshot Crummond
The 'Burbs
The Candidate
Candide
Carry On Cleo
Carry On Dick
Casino Royale
Caveman
CB4: The Movie
Champagne for Caesar
The Cheap Detective
Clifford
The Clinic
Clockwise
A Clockwork Orange
Closet Cases of the Nerd Kind
The Coca-Cola Kid
Code Name: Chaos
Cold Turkey
The Committee
Coup de Grace
Crainquebille
Creature from the Haunted
   Sea
Crimewave
Cry Uncle
Curtain Up
Dark Habits
Dark Star
Darktown Strutters
Dead Men Don't Die
Dead Men Don't Wear Plaid
Deal of the Century
Death of a Bureaucrat

Deathrow Gameshow
Diary of a Chambermaid
Dirty Dishes
The Discreet Charm of the
   Bourgeoisie
Dr. Heckyl and Mr. Hype
Dr. Strangelove, or: How I
   Learned to Stop Worrying
   and Love the Bomb
Doctors and Nurses
Dope Mania
The Dove
Down & Dirty
Down and Out in Beverly Hills
Down to Earth
Down Under
Dracula Sucks
Dragnet
E. Nick: A Legend in His Own
   Mind
Easy Wheels
11 Harrowhouse
Ella Cinders
Erik the Viking
The Erotic Adventures of
   Pinocchio
The Extraordinary Adventures
   of Mr. West in the Land of
   the Bolsheviks
The Family Game
Fat and the Lean
Fatal Instinct
Ferocious Female Freedom
   Fighters
First Family
The Flaming Teen-Age
Flesh Gordon
Flicks
Footlight Frenzy
The Fortune Cookie
Frankenstein General Hospital
Frankenweenie
The French Touch
The Freshman
From Here to Maternity
The Front
Funny Money
Gabriel Over the White House
Galactic Gigolo
Galaxina
Ganjasaurus Rex
Gas
Geek Maggot Bingo
Genevieve
Gentlemen Prefer Blondes
Glory! Glory!
Going Berserk
Going Places
Greaser's Palace
Great American Traffic Jam
The Great Dictator
The Great Madcap
Great McGonagall
The Groove Tube
Grunt! The Wrestling Movie
Gulliver
Gumshoe
Gypsy
Hail
Hail the Conquering Hero
Hairspray
Half a Sixpence
Happiness
Hardware Wars & Other Film
   Farces
Heaven Can Wait
Heavens Above
Hell Comes to Frogtown
Hexed
High Anxiety
High Hopes
High Season
History of the World: Part 1
The History of White People in
   America

The History of White People in
   America: Vol. 2
Hollywood Harry
Home Movies
The Horror of Frankenstein
Hot Shots!
Hot Shots! Part Deux
The Hound of the Baskervilles
How I Got into College
I Love You, Alice B. Toklas
I Married a Vampire
I Was a Zombie for the FBI
The Icicle Thief
I'm All Right Jack
I'm Gonna Git You Sucka
The Incredible Shrinking
   Woman
Incredibly Strange Creatures
   Who Stopped Living and
   Became Mixed-Up Zombies
The Inspector General
Invasion Earth: The Aliens Are
   Here!
Is There Sex After Death?
It Couldn't Happen Here
It's a Bundyful Life
J-Men Forever!
Jabberwocky
Jekyll & Hyde...Together
   Again
Jet Benny Show
Johnny Dangerously
A Joke of Destiny, Lying in
   Wait Around the Corner
   Like a Bandit
Kentucky Fried Movie
The King of Hearts
La Casa de Madame Lulu
La Nueva Cigarra
The Ladies' Man
L'Age D'Or
The Last Polka
Let's Kill All the Lawyers
Lincoln County Incident
Lip Service
Look Out Sister
Loose Shoes
Love and Death
Love at Stake
Mad Mission 3
Mad Monster Party
Man Bites Dog
Man in the White Suit
Man Who Came to Dinner
Man Who Had Power Over
   Women
The Man with Bogart's Face
The Man with Two Brains
Marihuana
Men...
The Meteor Man
Mickey
The Milky Way
The Missionary
Mob Boss
Modern Times
Monster in a Box
Monty Python and the Holy
   Grail
Monty Python's Flying Circus
Monty Python's Life of Brian
Monty Python's Parrot Sketch
   Not Included
Monty Python's The Meaning
   of Life
More! Police Squad
The Mouse That Roared
Movers and Shakers
Movie, Movie
Murder by Death
Mutant on the Bounty
My Best Friend Is a Vampire
My Best Girl
Myra Breckinridge
The Naked Gun: From the
   Files of Police Squad

Naked Gun 2 1/2: The Smell
   of Fear
Nasty Habits
National Lampoon Goes to the
   Movies
National Lampoon's Animal
   House
National Lampoon's Loaded
   Weapon 1
Night Patrol
99 & 44/100 Dead
Nocturna
Northanger Abbey
The Nutty Professor
Oscar
Overdrawn at the Memory
   Bank
Pajama Tops
Pandemonium
Paramedics
Partners
Pass the Ammo
Personal Services
Phantom of Liberty
The Pink Chiquitas
The Player
Police Squad! Help Wanted!
The Positively True
   Adventures of the Alleged
   Texas Cheerleader-
   Murdering Mom
Pray TV
The President's Analyst
Prime Time
The Princess Bride
Prisoner of Rio
A Private Function
Prize of Peril
The Producers
A Propos de Nice
Putney Swope
The Ramrodder
Rat Pfink a Boo-Boo
Real Men
Really Weird Tales
Red Desert Penitentiary
Red Garters
Rentadick
Repentance
The Report on the Party and
   the Guests
Repossessed
Return of Captain Invincible
The Return of Spinal Tap
Revolution! A Red Comedy
The Ribald Tales of Robin
   Hood
Ricky 1
The Road to Lebanon
Robin Hood: Men in Tights
Rockin' Ronnie
The Rocky Horror Picture
   Show
Rosalie Goes Shopping
The Royal Bed
Rude Awakening
The Ruling Class
Running Mates
Sallah
Salvation!
Sammy & Rosie Get Laid
Saturday Night Live
Scenes from the Class
   Struggle in Beverly Hills
School for Scandal
Scrambled Feet
Scrooged
Second Time Lucky
The Secret Diary of Sigmund
   Freud
Seduction of Mimi
Serial
Sex Adventures of the Three
   Musketeers
Sex with a Smile

Shame of the Jungle
Shampoo
A Shock to the System
Sideburns
Silent Movie
Simon of the Desert
Slammer Girls
Sleeper
Smile
S.O.B.
Spaceballs
Spaced Out
Spaceship
Spirit of '76
State of Things
Stay Tuned
Straight to Hell
Strange Invaders
Streetfight
Sullivan's Travels
Sunset
Suppose They Gave a War
   and Nobody Came?
Surf Nazis Must Die
Sympathy for the Devil
The Tamer of Wild Horses
Tanner '88
Tapeheads
Tartuffe
A Taste for Flesh and Blood
That's Adequate
That's My Hero!
They Call Me Bruce?
They Live
They Still Call Me Bruce
This is Spinal Tap
Thorn
Three Ages
Three of a Kind
The Thrill of It All!
To Be or Not to Be
Too Many Crooks
Top Secret!
Transylvania 6-5000
Trash
Traxx
True Stories
Trust Me
Tunnelvision
Turumba
Uforia
UHF
Unmasking the Idol
Up from the Depths
Up the Academy
A Very Curious Girl
Victor/Victoria
The Villain Still Pursued Her
Virgin Hood
Voyage of the Rock Aliens
Walker
Watermelon Man
Way He Was
What's Up, Tiger Lily?
The Wheeler Dealers
When Nature Calls
Where the Buffalo Roam
Where the Bullets Fly
White Mischief
The White Sheik
Whoops Apocalypse
Wild, Wild West Revisited
Without a Clue
World Gone Wild
The Worm Eaters
The Worst of Hollywood: Vol.
   1
The Worst of Hollywood: Vol.
   2
The Worst of Hollywood: Vol.
   3
The Would-Be Gentleman
Yin & Yang of Mr. Go
You'll Find Out
Young Doctors in Love
Young Frankenstein

Science

Dam Busters
Dark Star
Darkman
The Day of the Dolphin
Dead Men Don't Wear Plaid
Deadly Friend
Demon Seed
Dick Barton, Special Agent
Dick Tracy, Detective/The
    Corpse Vanishes
Die Laughing
Die, Monster, Die!
Dr. Alien
Doctor Doolittle
The Eliminators
Fantastic Voyage
Fat Man and Little Boy
Feast for the Devil
The Fly
The Fly 2
Forbidden World
Four Sided Triangle
The 4D Man
From the Earth to the Moon
Geheimakte WB1
The Henderson Monster
Human Gorilla
Humanoid Defender
Illegal Entry: Formula for Fear
The Incredible Hulk Returns
International House
The Invisible Man Returns
Jupiter Menace
Jurassic Park
Last Day of the War
Link
Love Potion #9
The Man with Two Brains
Max Fleischer's Documentary
    Features
Medicine Man
Miracle Mile
Mr. Superinvisible
Monkey Boy
Monkey Business
Monkey's Uncle
My Science Project
My Stepmother Is an Alien
Neptune Factor
Phantom Empire
Project X
Prototype X29A
The Quiet Earth
Real Genius
Return of Captain Invincible
Return of the Ape Man
Return of the Fly
The Rocky Horror Picture
    Show
The Secret of the Telegian
The Sex Machine
Shaker Run
Shakma
Simon
Son of Flubber
Spaceways
Stephen King's Golden Years
The Story of Louis Pasteur
Substitute Teacher
Surf 2
Swamp Thing
The Thing
Things to Come
This Island Earth
Threshold
Tidal Wave
Time Trackers
The Time Travelers
Tomcat: Dangerous Desires
Underworld
Unknown Island
Unknown World
Where Time Began
The Wild and the Free
Woman in the Dunes
The Yesterday Machine

Scotland

Another Time, Another Place
The Big Man: Crossing the
    Line
Blood Clan
Bonnie Prince Charlie
Bonnie Scotland
Brigadoon
Challenge to Lassie
Comfort and Joy
Devil Girl from Mars
The Devil's Undead
Dreams Lost, Dreams Found
Escape
The Gospel According to Vic
Gregory's Girl
Greystoke: The Legend of
    Tarzan, Lord of the Apes
I Know Where I'm Going
Lady of the Lake
Little Minister
Local Hero
Madeleine
Mary of Scotland
The Master of Ballantrae
The Pointsman
Pride of the Clan
The Prime of Miss Jean
    Brodie
Ring of Bright Water
Rob Roy—The Highland
    Rogue
The Secret of the Loch
The Three Lives of Thomasina
Tragedy of Flight 103: The
    Inside Story
Trouble in the Glen
Whiskey Galore
Year of the Comet

Screwball Comedy

All in a Night's Work
Amazing Adventure
Ambassador Bill
America
And Baby Makes Six
Angel on My Shoulder
Antonio
As You Like It
As You Were
Assault of the Party Nerds
The Associate
Auntie
The Awful Truth
The Baby and the Battleship
The Bachelor and the Bobby-
    Soxer
Bachelor Mother
Bachelor of Hearts
Back to School
Bank Shot
Bedazzled
Bedtime Story
Beer
Best of W.C. Fields
Big Business
Blame It on the Bellboy
The Bliss of Mrs. Blossom
Blue Murder at St. Trinian's
Boeing Boeing
Boss Foreman
Bringing Up Baby
Bugs Bunny: Hollywood
    Legend
Bugs Bunny's Comedy
    Classics
Bullseye!
Buona Sera, Mrs. Campbell
Camp Cucamonga: How I
    Spent My Summer
    Vacation
Carry On Admiral
Chaplin: A Character Is Born

Chaplin: A Character Is Born/
    Keaton: The Great Stone
    Face
Chaplin Essanay Book 1
The Chaplin Revue
Charlie Chaplin Carnival, Four
    Early Shorts
Charlie Chaplin Cavalcade,
    Mutual Studios Shorts
Charlie Chaplin Centennial
    Collection
Charlie Chaplin Festival
Charlie Chaplin: Night at the
    Show
Charlie Chaplin: Rare Chaplin
Charlie Chaplin...Our Hero!
Charlie Chaplin's Keystone
    Comedies #1
Charlie Chaplin's Keystone
    Comedies #2
Charlie Chaplin's Keystone
    Comedies #3
Charlie Chaplin's Keystone
    Comedies #4
Charlie Chaplin's Keystone
    Comedies #5
The Circus
Combat Academy
The Couch Trip
The Count
Crackers
Days of Thrills and Laughter
Doctor in the House
Dr. Otto & the Riddle of the
    Gloom Beam
Doctor Takes a Wife
Don Juan, My Love
Donde Duermen
    Dos...Duermen Tres
Double Wedding
Doubting Thomas
Down Among the Z Men
Down the Drain
Easy Money
Easy Street
Egg and I
El Gendarme Desconocido
Ernest Saves Christmas
Ernest Scared Stupid
Everything You Always
    Wanted to Know About
    Sex (But Were Afraid to
    Ask)
The Favor, the Watch, & the
    Very Big Fish
Fireballs
The Fireman
Fit for a King
The Floorwalker
The Floorwalker/By the Sea
Forever Darling
Forsaking All Others
Fotografo de Senoras
The Geisha Boy
Get Crazy
Gold Rush/Payday
Halloween with the Addams
    Family
Hard Day's Night
Harvey
Her Husband's Affairs
He's My Girl
Holiday
Honey, I Blew Up the Kid
Honey, I Shrunk the Kids
Hot to Trot!
How I Learned to Love
    Women
How Sweet It Is!
I Love My...Wife
I Love You Again
I Wanna Be a Beauty Queen
Inspector Hornleigh
Italian Straw Hat
It's the Old Army Game
Joy of Living

La Chevre
Labyrinth of Passion
The Lady Eve
Libeled Lady
Life Stinks
Little Rascals Christmas
    Special
Lobster Man from Mars
The Long, Long Trailer
Lots of Luck
The Love Bug
Love Crazy
Lucky Partners
Lunatics & Lovers
Madhouse
Make Mine Mink
Makin' It
Malibu Beach
Malibu Bikini Shop
The Marriage Circle
The Marx Brothers in a
    Nutshell
The Mating Game
Mazurka
Me and Him
Meatballs
Meatballs 2
A Midsummer Night's Sex
    Comedy
Minsky's Follies
Miracle of Morgan's Creek
Mr. & Mrs. Smith
Modern Girls
The Money Pit
Monkey Business
Monkeys, Go Home!
Moon's Our Home
Morons from Outer Space
Mugsy's Girls
Munster's Revenge
My American Cousin
My Chauffeur
My Favorite Brunette
My Man Godfrey
Naked Is Better
National Lampoon's
    Christmas Vacation
National Lampoon's European
    Vacation
National Lampoon's Vacation
Noises Off
Not for Publication
Nothing Sacred
The Nude Bomb
One Woman or Two
The Palm Beach Story
Pick a Star
Pink Flamingos
Platinum Blonde
Police Academy
Police Academy 2: Their First
    Assignment
Police Academy 3: Back in
    Training
Police Academy 4: Citizens on
    Patrol
Police Academy 5:
    Assignment Miami Beach
Police Academy 6: City Under
    Siege
Polyester
Reaching for the Moon
Recruits
The Rink
Romance with a Double Bass
Running Wild
See No Evil, Hear No Evil
Simon
The Smallest Show on Earth
Some Like It Hot
Son of Flubber
A Southern Yankee
Spaceballs
Spaced Invaders
Spring Break
Stallion

Stan Without Ollie, Vol. 2
Stan Without Ollie, Vol. 3
Starhops
Starring Bugs Bunny!
Start the Revolution Without
    Me
The Statue
Stewardess School
Stir Crazy
Stitches
Stocks and Blondes
The Stoogephile Trivia Movie
Strange Brew
Stripes
Stroker Ace
Stuckey's Last Stand
Student Affairs
The Student Body
The Student Body/Jailbait
    Babysitter
The Student Teachers
Substitute Teacher
Summer Camp
Summer Job
Summer Night Fever
Summer School Teachers
Sundance
Superdad
Supergrass
Swap Meet
Sweet Revenge
Sweet Young Thing
Swing It, Sailor!
The Swinging Cheerleaders
Swinging Wives
Switching Channels
Takin' It All Off
Talk of the Town
Teen Lust
Teen Vamp
Teen Witch
Tell It to the Judge
Tex Avery's Screwball
    Classics, Vol. 3
That Darn Cat
That Naughty Girl
They Went That-a-Way &
    That-a-Way
Three in the Cellar
Three Stooges Meet Hercules
Thunder & Mud
Tigers in Lipstick
Tramp & a Woman
Traveling Companions
Tricks of the Trade
Triple Trouble/Easy Street
Trouble in Paris
Truck Stop
Turner and Hooch
Twist
2 Idiots in Hollywood
Two Reelers: Comedy
    Classics 10
Two Weeks to Live
Two Women in Gold
Under the Sheets
The Underachievers
Up Your Anchor
The Vagabond
Valet Girls
Vibes
Vice Versa
Waitress
Waltz of the Toreadors
Watch the Birdie
Wayne's World
W.C. Fields Comedy Bag
W.C. Fields: Flask of Fields
What's Up, Doc?
When Women Had Tails
When Women Lost Their Tails
Where Were You When the
    Lights Went Out?
Which Way Is Up?
Whoops Apocalypse
Who's That Girl?

Wild Women of Wongo
Witches' Brew
Woman of Paris/Sunnyside
Work/Police
World's Greatest Lover
You Can't Cheat an Honest
  Man
Zotz!

Scuba

The Abyss
Beneath the 12-Mile Reef
The Big Blue
Daring Game
The Deep
Easy Come, Easy Go
The Evil Below
ffolkes
Flipper
Flipper's New Adventure
Full Fathom Five
Isle of Forgotten Sins
Leviathan
The Man from Atlantis
Navy SEALS
Neptune Factor
Never Say Never Again
Night of the Sharks
Oceans of Fire
The Sea Serpent
Thunderball
The Treasure Seekers
Underwater

Sea Critter Attack

Alligator
Around the World Under the
  Sea
Attack of the Giant Leeches
Attack of the Swamp Creature
Barracuda
The Beach Girls and the
  Monster
The Beast from 20,000
  Fathoms
Beyond Atlantis
Blood Beach
Bloodstalkers
Creature from Black Lake
Creature from the Black
  Lagoon
Creature from the Haunted
  Sea
Creature of Destruction
Curse of the Swamp Creature
Deepstar Six
Demon of Paradise
Devil Monster
Devilfish
The Flesh Eaters
Godzilla vs. the Sea Monster
Gorgo
The Great Alligator
Horror of Party Beach
Island Claw
Jason and the Argonauts
Jaws
Jaws 2
Jaws 3
Jaws of Death
Jaws: The Revenge
Killer Fish
The Loch Ness Horror
The Man from Atlantis
The McConnell Story
Mean Streets
Memphis Belle
Moby Dick
Monster from the Ocean Floor
The Monster of Piedras
  Blancas
The Monster that Challenged
  the World
New York, New York
None But the Brave

Obsession
Octaman
Orca
The Phantom from 10,000
  Leagues
Piranha
Piranha 2: The Spawning
Reap the Wild Wind
Scorpion with Two Tails
Screams of a Winter Night
The Sea Serpent
Serpent Island
Shark!
Shark's Paradise
The Spawning
Tentacles
Terror in the Swamp
Tintorera...Tiger Shark
20,000 Leagues Under the
  Sea
Up from the Depths
What Waits Below

Serial Killers

Ambition
Amsterdamned
The Baby Doll Murders
The Banker
Bluebeard
Body Parts
The Boston Strangler
Broken Mirrors
The China Lake Murders
Cold Front
Cop
Cosh Boy
Dangerous Love
The Dark Ride
Dead Certain
Dead Girls
Deadly Force
Deadly Games
Deadly Neighbor
The Deliberate Stranger
A Demon in My View
Destroyer
The Element of Crime
Evil Laugh
Eyes of a Stranger
Eyes of Laura Mars
Eyes of the Beholder
Fatal Charm
Fathers and Sons
Fear
Final Notice
The First Power
The Freeway Maniac
Henry: Portrait of a Serial
  Killer
Hidden Obsession
The Hillside Strangler
Honeymoon Killers
The Horror Show
The Hunt for the Night Stalker
Impulse
Inn on the River
The Invisible Strangler
Jack the Ripper
The January Man
Jennifer 8
Kalifornia
L.A. Crackdown 2
Laser Moon
Laughing Policeman
M
The Mad Executioners
Man Bites Dog
Maniac Cop
Mr. Frost
Mortal Sins
Night Shadow
Night Stalker
Pale Blood
Prey of the Chameleon
Psychic

The Rosary Murders
The Silence of the Lambs
So I Married an Axe Murderer
Split Second
Stamp of a Killer
Star Time
Still Life
Strangler of Blackmoor Castle
10 Rillington Place
Ten to Midnight
Terror at London Bridge
To Catch a Killer
The Todd Killings
While the City Sleeps
Without Warning
Writer's Block
Zipperface

Serials

Ace Drummond
Adventures of Captain Marvel
The Adventures of Frank and
  Jesse James
Adventures of Red Ryder
The Adventures of Rex &
  Rinty
The Adventures of Tarzan
The Adventures of the Flying
  Cadets
The Adventures of the
  Masked Phantom
Amazing Stories
Amazing Stories, Book 2
Amazing Stories, Book 3
Amazing Stories, Book 4
Amazing Stories, Book 5
Battling with Buffalo Bill
The Black Coin
The Black Widow
Blake of Scotland Yard
Bugs Bunny Superstar
Burn 'Em Up Barnes
Captain America
Carmilla
Casey Jones and Fury (Brave
  Stallion)
Cheyenne Rides Again
The Clutching Hand
The Crimson Ghost
Custer's Last Stand
Cyclotrode "X"
D-Day on Mars
Daredevils of the Red Circle
Darkest Africa
Devil Horse
Dick Tracy
Dick Tracy Returns
Dick Tracy: The Original
  Serial, Vol. 1
Dick Tracy: The Original
  Serial, Vol. 2
Dick Tracy vs. Crime Inc.
Doctor Satan's Robot
Don Daredevil Rides Again
Don Winslow of the Coast
  Guard
Don Winslow of the Navy
Drums of Fu Manchu
East Side Kids/The Lost City
Federal Agents vs.
  Underworld, Inc.
Fighting Devil Dogs
Fighting Marines
Fighting with Kit Carson
Flaming Frontiers
Flash Gordon Conquers the
  Universe
Flash Gordon: Mars Attacks
  the World
Flash Gordon: Vol. 1
Flash Gordon: Vol. 2
Flash Gordon: Vol. 3
Flying Discman from Mars
G-Men Never Forget
G-Men vs. the Black Dragon

Genie of Darkness
Government Agents vs.
  Phantom Legion
Green Archer
The Green Hornet
Hawk of the Wilderness
Heroes of the West
Holt of the Secret Service
Hurricane Express
In Old New Mexico
The Invisible Monster
Jesse James Rides Again
Jungle Drums of Africa
Junior G-Men
Junior G-Men of the Air
King of the Congo
King of the Forest Rangers
King of the Kongo
King of the Rocketmen
King of the Texas Rangers
Last Frontier
The Last of the Mohicans
Law of the Wild
A Lawman is Born
Lightning Warrior
Little Rascals, Book 4
The Lone Defender
The Lone Ranger
Lone Ranger
The Lost City
Lost City of the Jungle
The Lost Jungle
Lost Planet Airmen
Manhunt in the African Jungle
Manhunt of Mystery Island
Mansfield Park
The Masked Marvel
Master Key
Masters of Venus
Miracle Rider: Vol. 1
Miracle Rider: Vol. 2
Mission: Monte Carlo
The Monster Demolisher
Mysterious Doctor Satan
Mystery Mountain
Mystery Squadron
Mystery Trooper
The New Adventures of
  Tarzan: Vol. 1
The New Adventures of
  Tarzan: Vol. 2
The New Adventures of
  Tarzan: Vol. 3
The New Adventures of
  Tarzan: Vol. 4
Nyoka and the Tigermen
Oregon Trail
The Original Flash Gordon
  Collection
Overland Mail
The Painted Stallion
The Perils of Pauline
Perils of the Darkest Jungle
The Phantom Creeps
The Phantom Empire
Phantom of the Air
Phantom of the West
The Phantom Rider
Pirates of the High Seas
The Purple Monster Strikes
Queen of the Jungle
Radar Men from the Moon
Radio Patrol
Radio Ranch
Red Barry
Return of Chandu
Riders of Death Valley
Robinson Crusoe of Clipper
  Island
Robinson Crusoe of Mystery
  Island
Saturday Night Serials
Savage Fury
Sea Hound
Shadow of the Eagle
Sign of the Wolf

Son of Zorro
S.O.S. Coast Guard
Space Soldiers Conquer the
  Universe
Spy Smasher Returns
Stone Cold Dead
Sunset on the Desert
Superman: The Serial, Vol. 1
Tailspin Tommy
Texas to Bataan
Three Musketeers
Tim Tyler's Luck
Tom Mix Compilation 1
Tom Mix Compilation 2
Trader Tom of the China Seas
Trail of the Royal Mounted
Trail of the Silver Spurs
Trail Riders
Tumbledown Ranch in
  Arizona
Undersea Kingdom
Vanishing Legion
The Vigilantes are Coming
Whispering Shadow
Winners of the West
Wolf Dog
Young Eagles
Zombies of the Stratosphere
Zorro Rides Again
Zorro's Black Whip
Zorro's Fighting Legion

Sex & Sexuality

ABC's of Love & Sex,
  Australia Style
Accident
The Adultress
Adventures of a Plumber's
  Helper
Adventures of a Private Eye
Adventures of a Taxi Driver
The Adventures of Sadie
After School
Alexa: A Prostitute's Own
  Story
Alfie
Alice Goodbody
All the Way Down
The Allnighter
Almost Pregnant
Alpine Fire
Alvin Purple
Alvin Rides Again
The Amazing Transplant
American Drive-In
American Gigolo
The Amorous Adventures of
  Moll Flanders
The Amy Fisher Story
And God Created Woman
And When She Was Bad...
Andy Warhol's Dracula
Andy Warhol's Frankenstein
Angel Heart
Angel of H.E.A.T.
Animal Instincts
Any Wednesday
The Apartment
Aphrodite
Appassionata
The Arousers
Arrivederci, Baby!
Assault
Baby Doll
The Baby Doll Murders
Baby Face
Baby Love
The Baby Maker
The Bachelor
Bachelor Party
Bad Girls from Mars
Bad Lieutenant
Ballyhoo Baby
Barbarella
Baring It All

Sexploitation

Cool It, Baby
Copenhagen Nights
Corruption
Dandelions
Deadly Embrace
Delinquent School Girls
Desert Passion
Devil's Wedding Night
Dirty Mind of Young Sally
Dr. Minx
Domino
Dracula Sucks
Ecstasy
Ecstasy Inc.
Emily
Emmanuelle
Emmanuelle 4
Emmanuelle 5
Emmanuelle 6
Emmanuelle & Joanna
Emmanuelle in Bangkok
Emmanuelle in Soho
Emmanuelle in the Country
Emmanuelle on Taboo Island
Emmanuelle, the Joys of a
  Woman
The Erotic Adventures of
  Pinocchio
Erotic Dreams
Erotic Escape
Erotic Illusion
Erotic Touch of Hot Skin
Erotica: Fabulous Female
  Fantasies
Escort Girls
Fanny Hill: Memoirs of a
  Woman of Pleasure
Fantasies
Feelin' Up
Firehouse
The First Nudie Musical
Flesh Gordon
Forbidden Impulse
Forever Emmanuelle
Frank and I
The French Woman
Ghosts Can't Do It
Gimme an F
Ginger
Good Time with a Bad Girl
Goodbye Emmanuelle
The Happy Gigolo
The Happy Hooker
The Happy Hooker Goes to
  Washington
Hardbodies
Hollywood Boulevard 2
Hollywood Erotic Film Festival
Hollywood High
Hollywood High, Part 2
Hollywood Hot Tubs
Hollywood Hot Tubs 2:
  Educating Crystal
Homework
Honkytonk Nights
Hot Moves
Hot T-Shirts
H.O.T.S.
Ilsa, She-Wolf of the SS
Ilsa, the Tigress of Siberia
Ilsa, the Wicked Warden
Infamous Daughter of Fanny
  Hill
Inferno in Paradise
Inhibition
Inn of Temptation
Intimate Games
Invasion of the Girl Snatchers
The Invisible Maniac
Joy of Sex
Kandyland
Kipling's Women
Knock Outs
Lady Godiva Rides
Lady of the Rising Sun
Last Dance

Let's Do It!
Liana, Jungle Goddess
The Lickerish Quartet
Liquid Dreams
Little Miss Innocence
Love Angels
Love Circles
Love Desperados
The Love Factor
Love Lessons
Love Notes
Lust for Freedom
Mistress Pamela
Modern Girls
Mona's Place
My Father's Wife
My Pleasure Is My Business
My Therapist
Mysterious Jane
The Naked Sword of Zorro
Naked Venus
Nature's Playmates
Naughty Knights
Night Call Nurses
The Night Evelyn Came Out of
  the Grave
The Night Porter
Nine Ages of Nakedness
Nude on the Moon
Nurse on Call
Orgy of the Dead
Paranoia
Party Favors
Party Plane
The Passion of Evelyn
Perfect Timing
The Perils of Gwendoline
Please Don't Eat My Mother
Pleasure Resort
Pleasure Unlimited
Preppies
The Prime Time
Private Duty Nurses
Private Passions
Rebel Vixens
Red Shoe Diaries 2: Double
  Dare
Return to the Blue Lagoon
Revealing of Elsie
Revenge of the Cheerleaders
Revenge of the Virgins
Romantic Encounters
Sacrilege
Saturday Night Sleazies, Vol.
  1
Screen Test
Sea of Dreams
Secrets in the Dark
The Seducers
Sensual Partners
Sensuous Caterer
The Sensuous Teenager
Sex Adventures of the Three
  Musketeers
Sex and Buttered Popcorn
Sex on the Brain
Sex Surrogate
Sex Through a Window
Shanty Tramp
She Came on the Bus
She Devils in Chains
Slammer Girls
Slumber Party Massacre 3
Snake Dancer
Snapshot
Snowballing
Sorority Babes in the Slimeball
  Bowl-A-Rama
Spaced Out
S.S. Love Camp No. 27
The Stewardesses
Stocks and Blondes
The Story of O, Part 2
Striptease
The Student Nurses
The Student Teachers

Submission
Suburban Roulette
Sugar Cookies
Superchick
Supervixens
Sweater Girls
Sweet Georgia
Sweet Young Thing
The Swinging Cheerleaders
Swinging Ski Girls
Swinging Sorority Girls
Swinging Wives
Takin' It All Off
Tender Loving Care
Texas Layover
Thinkin' Big
Train Station Pickups
Trouble in Paris
Truck Stop
Truck Stop Women
2069: A Sex Odyssey
Ultimate Desires
The Vampire Hookers
Vanessa
Venus in Furs
Venus on Fire
Vice Academy
Vice Academy 2
Vice Academy 3
Victorian Fantasies
Video Vixens
Wanda, The Sadistic
  Hypnotist
Wild Orchid 2: Two Shades of
  Blue
The Wildest Office Party
Witchcraft 2: The Temptress
Witchcraft 3: The Kiss of
  Death
Witchcraft 5: Dance with the
  Devil
The Young Nurses

Sexual Abuse

The Devils
Fall from Innocence
Fortune and Men's Eyes
Heart of the Stag
Ilsa, Harem Keeper of the Oil
  Sheiks
Mesmerized
The Night Porter
Twin Peaks: Fire Walk with
  Me

Shower & Bath
Scenes

About Last Night...
American Gigolo
Body Double
Breathless
Bull Durham
Club Paradise
Diabolique
Dressed to Kill
Fatal Attraction
Ghostbusters 2
High Anxiety
Hollywood Hot Tubs
Hollywood Hot Tubs 2:
  Educating Crystal
Jurassic Park
Jinxed
The Legacy
Married to the Mob
Mister Roberts
National Lampoon's Vacation
Porky's
The Postman Always Rings
  Twice
Psycho
Psycho 2
St. Elmo's Fire
Schizo

Silkwood
Snow White and the Seven
  Dwarfs
Stripes
Tequila Sunrise
Tie Me Up! Tie Me Down!
Valley Girl
Valmont

Shrinks

Agnes of God
Beauty on the Beach
Betrayal
Beyond Reason
Beyond Therapy
Blood Frenzy
Body Chemistry 2: Voice of a
  Stranger
Body of Influence
The Brain
Captain Newman, M.D.
The Cobweb
The Couch Trip
Dark Mirror
Dead Man Out
The Dream Team
Face to Face
Fear
Final Analysis
Final Approach
A Fine Madness
High Anxiety
Hollow Triumph
Home Movies
House of Games
Human Experiments
I Don't Buy Kisses Anymore
I Never Promised You a Rose
  Garden
Lies of the Twins
Lovesick
Lovey: A Circle of Children 2
The Man Who Loved Women
Mine Own Executioner
Mr. Frost
Norma
On a Clear Day You Can See
  Forever
One Flew Over the Cuckoo's
  Nest
Pressure Point
The Prince of Tides
Red Wind
Schizoid
Shock!
The Sleeping Tiger
Spellbound
Still of the Night
The Stranger
Sybil
They Might Be Giants
The Three Faces of Eve
Under the Doctor
Victim of Love
What's New Pussycat?
Whispers in the Dark
Wild in the Country

Shutterbugs

Adventures in Spying
Bikini Island
Blow-Up
The Corrupt Ones
Dagger Eyes
Darkroom
Dr. Mabuse vs. Scotland Yard
The Dolls
Don't Answer the Phone
Don't Change My World
Double Exposure
Double Exposure: The Story
  of Margaret Bourke-White
The Double Negative
Eyes Behind the Stars
Eyes of Laura Mars

Fatal Exposure
Fatal Images
The Favor, the Watch, & the
  Very Big Fish
Funny Face
Heat and Sunlight
High Season
I Love Melvin
Killer Image
Love & Murder
Love Crimes
Model Behavior
Not for Publication
The Outcasts
Peeping Tom
Perfect Timing
Photographer
Proof
The Public Eye
Return to Boggy Creek
Secret File of Hollywood
Shoot It Black, Shoot It Blue
Snapshot
Somebody Has to Shoot the
  Picture
Straight for the Heart
Sunset Heat
Sunset Strip
A Time to Die
The Unbearable Lightness of
  Being
Until The End of The World
Watch the Birdie

Silent Films

The Adorable Cheat
The Adventurer
The Adventures of
  Hairbreadth Harry
The Adventures of Tarzan
The Adventures of Walt
  Disney's Alice
Aelita: Queen of Mars
All Night Long/Smile Please
America/The Fall of Babylon
American Aristocracy
American Pluck
The Americano
The Americano/Variety
Annapolis
Are Parents People?
Arsenal
Assunta Spina
The Atonement of Gosta
  Berling
Avenging Conscience
The Average Woman
Baby Face Harry Langdon
The Babylon Story from
  "Intolerance"
Backfire
Backstairs
Bakery/Grocery Clerk
The Balloonatic/One Week
Bare Knees
The Bargain
Battle of Elderbush Gulch
The Battleship Potemkin
Battling Bunyon
Battling Butler
Beau Brummel
Beau Revel
Bed and Sofa
Behind the Front
Bellhop/The Noon Whistle
The Beloved Rogue
Below the Deadline
Ben-Hur
Ben Turpin: An Eye for an Eye
The Best of Chaplin
The Big Parade
Big Stakes
The Birth of a Nation
The Black Pirate

Silent

Skateboarding

Skating

Skiing

Slapstick Comedy

Spousal Abuse

Star Gazing

Stepparents

Storytelling

Strained Suburbia

Submarines

Suicide

And I Alone Survived
Antarctica
Attack of the Beast Creatures
The Aviator
Back from Eternity
Bat 21
Benjamin Argumedo
Black Rain
Born Killer
The Bridge on the River Kwai
Buffalo Rider
A Bullet Is Waiting
Caged in Paradiso
Captain January
Challenge To Be Free
Clearcut
Cliffhanger
Clown
Cold River
Cool Hand Luke
Damned River
Das Boot
The Dawson Patrol
The Day After
Dead Calm
Deadly Harvest
Deadly Prey
Death Hunt
Def-Con 4
Deliverance
Delos Adventure
Delusion
The Desert Tigers
Desperate Target
The Devil
The Devil at 4 O'Clock
Diamonds of the Night
The Dive
Earthling
Edge of Honor
Empire of the Sun
Endgame
Enemy Mine
Enemy Territory
Erendira
Eric
Escape from Hell
Escapist
Fight for Your Life
Firehawk
Five Came Back
Flight from Glory
Flight from Singapore
Flight of the Eagle
The Flight of the Phoenix
Fortress
Found Alive
Four Infernos to Cross
Gas-s-s-s!
The Ghost of Fletcher Ridge
Grave of the Fireflies
He is My Brother
Heroes for Sale
High Ice
High Noon
Hunter's Blood
The Incredible Journey
The Interrogation
The Island
The Island at the Top of the
    World
Island of the Blue Dolphins
Island of the Lost
Jeremiah Johnson
Jungle Inferno
Just Before Dawn
Kameradschaft
Killing at Hell's Gate
The Killing Fields
King Rat
Land That Time Forgot
The Last Chance
Last Exit to Brooklyn
The Last Flight of Noah's Ark
Le Dernier Combat
Legend of Alfred Packer

The Legend of Wolf Mountain
The Life and Death of Colonel
    Blimp
Lifeboat
Lily was Here
Little Dorrit, Film 1: Nobody's
    Fault
Little Dorrit, Film 2: Little
    Dorrit's Story
Lord of the Flies
Lost
Love on the Dole
Male and Female
Man in the Wilderness
Manon
Melody
Merry Christmas, Mr.
    Lawrence
Mr. Robinson Crusoe
The Mosquito Coast
The Most Dangerous Game
My Side of the Mountain
Mysterious Island
The Naked Prey
Nightmare at Bittercreek
Nightmare at Noon
Objective, Burma!
On the Beach
Once Before I Die
Osa
Out of Control
The Overlanders
Packin' It In
Panic in the Year Zero!
Paradise
Perfect Witness
Phone Call from a Stranger
Pioneer Woman
The Poseidon Adventure
Quest for Fire
The Return of Grey Wolf
Return of the Jedi
The Revolt of Job
Robby
Robinson Crusoe
Sahara
Savage Hunger
Savage Is Loose
Sea Gypsies
The Sea Shall Not Have Them
Seven Days in May
Shadow of the Wolf
She'll Be Wearing Pink
    Pajamas
Silence
Silence of the North
Skyline
Sniper
S.O.S. Pacific
Sourdough
SpaceCamp
Springhill
Stagecoach
Starbird and Sweet William
Storm and Sorrow
Survival of Spaceship Earth
Survival Quest
Survival Run
The Survivalist
Sweet Sweetback's
    Baadasssss Song
The Swiss Family Robinson
The Terror
Testament
Thief
Three Came Home
Trouble in Paradise
Tundra
Two Dragons Fight Against
    the Tiger
Unsettled Land
The Voyage of the Yes
Wagon Master
Warriors of the Apocalypse
The White Dawn
White Fang and the Hunter

White Water Summer

Swashbucklers

Abbott and Costello Meet
    Captain Kidd
Adventures of Captain Fabian
Adventures of Don Juan
The Adventures of Robin
    Hood
Against All Flags
Anthony Adverse
At Sword's Point
The Black Pirate
Blackbeard the Pirate
Blackbeard's Ghost
Bluebeard
The Bold Caballero
The Buccaneer
Captain Blood
Captain Horatio Hornblower
Captain Kidd
Captain Kronos: Vampire
    Hunter
Captain Ron
Cartouche
The Challenge
Cheech and Chong's, The
    Corsican Brothers
China Seas
Conqueror & the Empress
Corsair
The Corsican Brothers
The Count of Monte Cristo
Court Jester
Crimson Pirate
Dancing Pirate
Dr. Syn
Dr. Syn, Alias the Scarecrow
Don Q., Son of Zorro
The Elusive Pimpernel
Executioner of Venice
The Fifth Musketeer
Fighting Marines
The Fighting Prince of
    Donegal
A Fist Full of Talons
The Flame & the Arrow
The Four Musketeers
Ghost in the Noonday Sun
Gun Cargo
Gypsy
Hawk of the Caribbean
Hawk of the Wilderness
Hell Ship Mutiny
His Majesty O'Keefe
Hook
The Iron Mask
The Island
Island Trader
Ivanhoe
Kojiro
The Lamb
The Lives of a Bengal Lancer
Long John Silver
The Man in the Iron Mask
Marauder
Mark of Zorro
The Mark of Zorro
The Master of Ballantrae
Master of Dragonard Hill
Monty Python's The Meaning
    of Life
Mooncussers
Moonfleet
Moran of the Lady Letty
Morgan the Pirate
My Favorite Year
My Wicked, Wicked Ways
The Naked Sword of Zorro
Nate and Hayes
Naughty Marietta
New Moon
The Ninja Pirates
Old Ironsides
The Pirate

Pirate Movie
Pirate Warrior
Pirates
The Pirates of Penzance
Pirates of the Coast
Pirates of the Seven Seas
The Princess and the Pirate
The Princess Bride
Prisoner of Zenda
The Ribald Tales of Robin
    Hood
Robin Hood
Romola
Scaramouche
The Scarlet Pimpernel
The Sea Hawk
Sea Hound
The Secret of El Zorro
Shipwrecked
The Sign of Zorro
Sinbad and the Eye of the
    Tiger
Sinbad the Sailor
Smuggler's Cove
Son of Captain Blood
The Son of Monte Cristo
Son of Zorro
South of Pago Pago
South Seas Massacre
The Spanish Main
The Story of Robin Hood &
    His Merrie Men
Swashbuckler
The Swiss Family Robinson
Sword & the Sorcerer
Sword of Sherwood Forest
The Swordsman
Tharus Son of Attila
Three Amigos
The Three Musketeers
Three Musketeers
Tiger of the Seven Seas
Treasure Island
Treasure of the Golden
    Condor
Treasure of the Moon
    Goddess
Two Lost Worlds
Under the Red Robe
Wallaby Jim of the Islands
The Warriors
The Wicked Lady
Yellowbeard
Zorro, the Gay Blade

Swimming

Barracuda
Bathing Beauty
Cocoon
Dangerous When Wet
Dawn!
Easy to Love
Gremlins
Jaws
Lifeguard
The Man from Atlantis
Million Dollar Mermaid
Neptune's Daughter
Off the Mark
Swim Team
Swimmer
Thrill of a Romance

Swingin' Singles

About Last Night...
Breakfast at Tiffany's
He Said, She Said
Metropolitan
The Opposite Sex and How to
    Live With Them
Pillow Talk
St. Elmo's Fire
Shag: The Movie
Singles
Sleepless In Seattle

That Touch of Mink
The Thing Called Love
When Harry Met Sally
The Wild Life

Tearjerkers

Acorn People
After the Promise
All Fall Down
All Mine to Give
Another Time, Another Place
Baby Face
Balboa
Ballad in Blue
Bang the Drum Slowly
Beaches
Beyond Obsession
Big Bluff
Bittersweet Love
Black Eyes
Blood of Jesus
Bonjour Tristesse
Bouquet of Barbed Wire
Brian's Song
The Cabin in the Cotton
Carrie
Cast the First Stone
The Champ
The Cheat
Chinatown After Dark
The Christmas Tree
City That Never Sleeps
Claudia
Coquette
The Country Kid
The Courtney Affair
Craig's Wife
Dance Fools Dance
Dedee d'Anvers
Delinquent Parents
Easy Virtue
The Eddy Duchin Story
Escape Me Never
Fire Down Below
Flamingo Road
The Forbidden City
Fortune's Fool
Found Alive
Fourth Wish
Free Willy
Gangs, Inc.
The Garden of Allah
The Gathering
The Gathering: Part 2
Girl from Chicago
The Girl Who Had Everything
Goodbye, Mr. Chips
Goodbye, My Lady
Great Day
Harlow
Hearts of Humanity
Her Silent Sacrifice
High Gear
Honky Tonk
Hot Spell
Human Desire
Human Hearts
I Sent a Letter to My Love
If Ever I See You Again
In This Our Life
Inside Daisy Clover
Intermezzo
Jack the Bear
Johnny Belinda
Johnny Eager
Journey for Margaret
Keep Punching
The Kid with the Broken Halo
La Bete Humaine
La Chienne
Lady Caroline Lamb
The Lady Without Camelias
Le Jour Se Leve
Leper

Tearjerkers

Letter from an Unknown
 Woman
The Little Princess
The Love Flower
Love has Many Faces
Love in the Present Tense
Love Songs
Love Story
Loving
Lure of the Sila
Magnificent Obsession
Man of Evil
The Manxman
Matters of the Heart
Mildred Pierce
Miles to Go
Millie
Mimi
Miss Julie
Mr. Skeffington
Mistress
Moon Over Harlem
A Mormon Maid
The Night Cry
Night Life in Reno
Nomads of the North
Now, Voyager
Old Yeller
Only Angels Have Wings
The Other Side of the
 Mountain
The Other Side of the
 Mountain, Part 2
The Passing of the Third Floor
 Back
Pattes Blanches
Peg O' My Heart
Penny Serenade
A Place in the Sun
A Question of Guilt
Quicksand
The Racket
Random Harvest
Rebecca of Sunnybrook Farm
Red Kimono
Rikisha-Man
The Road to Ruin
Romola
Scar of Shame
Secrets of a Married Man
Seizure: The Story of Kathy
 Morris
Sex
She Goes to War
A Shining Season
The Shock
Silent Night, Lonely Night
The Sin of Madelon Claudet
Since You Went Away
Sparrows
Steel Magnolias
Stella
Stella Dallas
Stella Maris
Strangers: The Story of a
 Mother and Daughter
Stromboli
Suds
Summer and Smoke
A Summer Place
Susan Lenox: Her Fall and
 Rise
Tango
Tell Me That You Love Me
Tender Comrade
Terms of Endearment
Test Tube Babies
They Drive by Night
Things in Their Season
This Boy's Life
Three Secrets
Tiefland
Time to Live
Tomorrow's Children
Torch Song
Toute Une Nuit

Traffic in Souls
Trapped by the Mormons
Under the Roofs of Paris
The Underdog
The Unholy Three
Uptown New York
Walk on the Wild Side
Walpurgis Night
Waterloo Bridge
Way Down East
Welcome Home
West-Bound Limited
West of Zanzibar
Where East is East
Where the Red Fern Grows
The White Cliffs of Dover
The White Rose
Winter Meeting
Without a Trace
A Woman of Affairs
The World Accuses
The World is Full of Married
 Men
The World Owes Me a Living
Written on the Wind
X, Y & Zee
The Yearling

Technology-
Rampant

Assassin
Attack of the Killer
 Refrigerator
Attack of the Robots
Baby Girl Scott
Back to the Future
Best Defense
The Bionic Woman
Black Cobra 3: The Manila
 Connection
The Black Hole
Blade Runner
Blades
Bloodlust
Chandu the Magician
Charly
Chopping Mall
Circuitry Man
Colossus: The Forbin Project
Computer Beach Party
Computer Dreams
Computer Wizard
Crash and Burn
The Creation of the
 Humanoids
Cyberpunk
Death of the Rat
Death Ray 2000
Defense Play
Demon Seed
Diamonds are Forever
Dr. Goldfoot and the Bikini
 Machine
Dungeonmaster
Duplicates
Electric Dreams
The Eliminators
Eve of Destruction
Fail-Safe
Family Viewing
The Final Programme
The Fly
The Fly 2
Future Cop
Futureworld
Geheimakte WB1
Hide and Seek
Improper Channels
Interface
A Joke of Destiny, Lying in
 Wait Around the Corner
 Like a Bandit
A King in New York
The Lift

Lost Legacy: A Girl Called
 Hatter Fox
Maximum Overdrive
Metropolis
Microwave Massacre
Modern Times
Mon Oncle
Moonraker
Munster's Revenge
Murder by Phone
Murder by Television
Mutant Hunt
Night of the Kickfighters
A Nous la Liberte
One Deadly Owner
Out of Order
Panique
The Philadelphia Experiment
The Power Within
Project: Eliminator
Project: Shadowchaser
The Quiet Earth
Remote
RoboCop 2
Robot Holocaust
Robot Jox
Robot Ninja
Rock & Roll Cowboys
R.O.T.O.R.
Runaway
Search and Destroy
Shadowzone
Shaker Run
Shocker
Short Circuit
Short Circuit 2
Sneakers
Space: 1999
Speaking Parts
The Spy Who Loved Me
Stay Tuned
Steel and Lace
Strange New World
Street of Crocodiles
Tekkaman, the Space Knight
Terminal Choice
Terminal Entry
The Terminal Man
The Terminator
Terrorvision
Things to Come
Thrillkill
Tron
Twisted
2001: A Space Odyssey
The Ultimate Imposter
The Unborn
The Vindicator
War Games
Warning Sign
Weird Science
Westworld
Wild Palms
Wired to Kill
Wrestling Women vs. the
 Aztec Ape
Zardoz

Teen Angst

Across the Tracks
Adventures in Dinosaur City
Age Isn't Everything
Ah, Wilderness!
Almos' a Man
American Drive-In
American Graffiti
An American Summer
Amor Bandido
Andy Hardy Gets Spring Fever
Andy Hardy Meets Debutante
Andy Hardy's Double Life
Andy Hardy's Private
 Secretary
Angel
Angels with Dirty Faces

Baby It's You
The Bachelor and the Bobby-
 Soxer
Backstreet Dreams
Bad Boys
Bad Ronald
Battle of the Bullies
The Bay Boy
Beach House
The Beat
The Beniker Gang
Berserker
The Best Little Girl in the
 World
Better Off Dead
Beverly Hills 90210
Beverly Hills 90210: The
 Graduation
Beyond Innocence
The Big Bet
Big Girls Don't Cry...They Get
 Even
Big Town
Bikini Beach
Bill & Ted's Excellent
 Adventure
Blackboard Jungle
BMX Bandits
Book of Love
Born Innocent
Boy's Reformatory
Boyz N the Hood
The Breakfast Club
Breaking All the Rules
Breaking Away
Brotherhood of Justice
Buffy the Vampire Slayer
Burglar
Buster and Billie
Buying Time
Bye, Bye, Birdie
Can You Feel Me Dancing?
Can't Buy Me Love
Career Opportunities
Carrie
Cave Girl
The Chalk Garden
The Chicken Chronicles
Children of the Corn 2: The
 Final Sacrifice
Choices
The Choppers
Christine
Class
The Class of Miss MacMichael
Clayton County Line
Condemned to Hell
Coneheads
Corvette Summer
Cotton Candy
The Cruel Story of Youth
The Crush
Cry-Baby
A Cry in the Wild
A Dangerous Age
Dangerous Curves
Dangerously Close
Dark Horse
Date Bait
A Date with Judy
Daughter of Death
Dead End
Dead Poets Society
Deadly Weapon
Death Wish Club
Defense Play
The Defilers
Delinquent Daughters
Delivery Boys
Desert Bloom
Desperate Lives
The Devil on Wheels
The Devil's Sleep
The Diary of Anne Frank
Diner
Dino

Diving In
Dogs in Space
Doin' Time on Planet Earth
Don't Tell Mom the
 Babysitter's Dead
Dream Date
Dream Machine
Dream to Believe
Drive-In
Dudes
Dutch
Dutch Girls
East of Eden
East Side Kids
The Effect of Gamma Rays on
 Man-in-the-Moon Marigolds
Encino Man
Endless Love
Escape Artist
Escape from El Diablo
E.T.: The Extra-Terrestrial
Evils of the Night
Eyes of the Panther
Eyes Right!
Fame
Fast Talking
Fast Times at Ridgemont High
Fear No Evil
Fellini's Roma
Ferris Bueller's Day Off
Fire with Fire
The First Time
First Turn On
The Flamingo Kid
Flirting
Fly with the Hawk
Footloose
For Keeps
Force of Impulse
Forever
Foxes
The Franchise Affair
Freeze Frame
Friends
Friends Forever
Gas Food Lodging
Gate 2
Getting Lucky
Girl from Hunan
A Girl of the Limberlost
Girlfriend from Hell
Girls Just Want to Have Fun
Gleaming the Cube
Grease
Grease 2
Hadley's Rebellion
Hairspray
Halloween
Hang Tough
Hard Knocks
Hardcore
Harley
Heathers
The Heavenly Kid
Her Summer Vacation
Hide and Go Shriek
High School Caesar
High School Confidential
High School USA
Hollywood High
Hollywood High, Part 2
Hometown U.S.A.
Homework
Hoosiers
Hot Bubblegum
Hot Times
How I Got into College
I Accuse My Parents
I Am the Cheese
I Never Promised You a Rose
 Garden
I Wanna Hold Your Hand
I Was a Teenage Werewolf
If...
If Looks Could Kill
The In Crowd

Terrorism

Project: Alien
Pursuit
Python Wolf
The Radical
Raid on Entebbe
The Railway Station Man
Rebel
Rescue Force
Rollercoaster
The Rutanga Tapes
Secret Agent 00
Secret Agent Super Dragon
Skeleton Coast
Skull: A Night of Terror
Special Bulletin
Stalking Danger
Summer Night
The Taking of Flight 847: The Uli Derickson Story
The Taking of Pelham One Two Three
Terminal Entry
Terror in Beverly Hills
Terror in Paradise
Terror Squad
The Terrorists
Terrorists
Thunder Run
Thunderball
A Town Called Hell
Toy Soldiers
The Tragedy of a Ridiculous Man
Tragedy of Flight 103: The Inside Story
Trained to Kill, U.S.A.
Treasure of the Lost Desert
Trident Force
Troma's War
Turk 182!
21 Hours at Munich
Undeclared War
The Vernonia Incident
Viper
Voyage of Terror: The Achille Lauro Affair
Wanted Dead or Alive
Women on the Verge of a Nervous Breakdown
Wrong is Right
Year of the Gun
You Only Live Twice

This is Your Life

Abe Lincoln in Illinois
Abraham Lincoln
Actor: The Paul Muni Story
Agatha
Al Capone
Alex in Wonderland
Alexander the Great
All That Jazz
Amadeus
Amarcord
Amazing Howard Hughes
American Graffiti
Amin: The Rise and Fall
An Angel at My Table
Anita, Dances of Vice
The Ann Jillian Story
Annie Oakley
Antony and Cleopatra
Au Revoir Les Enfants
The Autobiography of Miss Jane Pittman
Babe!
The Babe
Babe Ruth Story
Bacall on Bogart
Barefoot in Athens
Barnum
The Barretts of Wimpole Street
Becoming Colette
Beethoven

Beethoven Lives Upstairs
The Benny Goodman Story
Bethune
Big Mo
The Big Red One
Bird
Blades of Courage
Blaze
Blind Ambition
Blossoms in the Dust
Bluebeard
Bogie
Bonnie & Clyde
Bonnie Prince Charlie
Born Again
Born on the Fourth of July
Bound for Glory
Boy in Blue
Bruce Lee: Curse of the Dragon
Bruce Lee: The Legend
Bruce Lee: The Man/The Myth
The Buccaneer
Bud and Lou
The Buddy Holly Story
Bugsy
Buster Keaton Rides Again/ The Railroader
Caddie
Calamity Jane
Camille Claudel
Can You Hear the Laughter? The Story of Freddie Prinze
Caravaggio
Casanova
Casimir the Great
Cast a Giant Shadow
Catherine the Great
Catholic Hour
Celeste
Chain Lightning
Champions
Chanel Solitaire
Chapayev
Chaplin
Chariots of Fire
Christopher Columbus
Christopher Columbus: The Discovery
Churchill and the Generals
Citizen Cohn
Coal Miner's Daughter
Committed
Conrack
The Courageous Mr. Penn
The Court Martial of Jackie Robinson
Crime Lords
Cromwell
Cross Creek
Damien: The Leper Priest
Dance with a Stranger
A Dangerous Man: Lawrence after Arabia
Daniel Boone
Dante's Inferno: Life of Dante Gabriel Rossetti
Dawn!
The Death of Adolf Hitler
Deep in My Heart
Dempsey
The Desert Fox
The Diary of Anne Frank
Dick Turpin
Dillinger
The Disappearance of Aimee
Disraeli
The Doctor
Don't Look Back: The Story of Leroy "Satchel" Paige
The Doors
Double Exposure: The Story of Margaret Bourke-White
Dragon: The Bruce Lee Story
Dreamchild
The Eddy Duchin Story

Edie in Ciao! Manhattan
Edison the Man
Edith & Marcel
The Education of Sonny Carson
Edward and Mrs. Simpson
Eleanor & Franklin
Eleanor: First Lady of the World
The Elegant Criminal
The Elephant Man
Elizabeth, the Queen
Elvis and Me
Elvis in the Movies
Elvis Memories
Elvis Presley's Graceland
Elvis: Rare Moments with the King
Elvis Stories
Elvis: The Echo Will Never Die
Elvis: The Movie
Enemy of Women
Enter Laughing
Ernie Kovacs: Between the Laughter
The Eternal Waltz
Eubie!
Europa, Europa
Evel Knievel
Exit the Dragon, Enter the Tiger
F. Scott Fitzgerald in Hollywood
The Fabulous Dorseys
Fallen Champ: The Untold Story of Mike Tyson
Fanny and Alexander
Fast Company
Final Shot: The Hank Gathers Story
The Five of Me
The Five Pennies
For Us, the Living
Forbidden Passion: The Oscar Wilde Movie
Ford: The Man & the Machine
Forever James Dean
The Fountainhead
1492: Conquest of Paradise
Frida
Funny Girl
Funny Lady
The Gallant Hours
Gandhi
The Gathering Storm
The Gene Krupa Story
Gentleman Jim
Give 'Em Hell, Harry!
The Glenn Miller Story
The Goddess
Going for the Gold: The Bill Johnson Story
Goodbye, Norma Jean
Goodnight, Sweet Marilyn
The Gorgeous Hussy
Gorillas in the Mist
Grambling's White Tiger
Greased Lightning
Great Balls of Fire
The Great Caruso
The Great Impostor
Great Missouri Raid
The Great Moment
The Great Wallendas
The Great Waltz
The Great White Hope
The Great Ziegfeld
The Greatest
The Greatest Story Ever Told
The Greek Tycoon
Grey Gardens
Gypsy
Hammett
The Happy Hooker Goes Hollywood
Harlow

Harmony Lane
Haunted Summer
Heart Beat
Heart Like a Wheel
Heart of a Champion: The Ray Mancini Story
Hedda Hopper's Hollywood
Henry & June
Hitler
Hitler: The Last Ten Days
Hoffa
Holy Terror
Home Sweet Home
Hoodoo Ann
Houdini
Hugh Hefner: Once Upon a Time
Hughes & Harlow: Angels in Hell
The Hunter
I Am a Fugitive from a Chain Gang
I Dream of Jeannie
I Shot Billy the Kid
Ike
I'll Cry Tomorrow
I'll See You in My Dreams
Imperial Venus
In Love and War
In Search of Historic Jesus
The Incredible Sarah
The Inn of the Sixth Happiness
Inside the Third Reich
Invincible Mr. Disraeli
Iris
The Iron Duke
Isadora
It's Good to Be Alive
J. Edgar Hoover
Jack Frost
Jack London
The Jackie Robinson Story
The Jacksons: An American Dream
Jacqueline Bouvier Kennedy
James Dean
James Dean Story
James Dean: The First American Teenager
James Joyce: A Portrait of the Artist as a Young Man
James Joyce's Women
Janis: A Film
The Jayne Mansfield Story
Jesse James Under the Black Flag
The Jesse Owens Story
Jesus
Jesus Christ, Superstar
Jim Thorpe: All American
Joan of Arc
Joe Louis Story
John & Yoko: A Love Story
John F. Kennedy
Johnny We Hardly Knew Ye
Jolson Sings Again
The Jolson Story
Joni
The Josephine Baker Story
Juarez
Judith of Bethulia
Kennedy
King
The King of Kings
The King of the Roaring '20s: The Story of Arnold Rothstein
Knute Rockne: All American
La Bamba
La Signora di Tutti
Lady Jane
Lady Sings the Blues
Lamp at Midnight
Last Days of Frank & Jesse James

The Last Days of Patton
The Last Emperor
Last Four Days
The Last of Mrs. Lincoln
Lawrence of Arabia
LBJ: The Early Years
The Learning Tree
The Left-Handed Gun
Legend of Valentino
The Legend of Valentino
Lenny
Lepke
Let's Get Lost
The Life and Assassination of the Kingfish
The Life and Loves of Mozart
Life & Times of Captain Lou Albano
The Life of Emile Zola
Life of Verdi
The Light in the Jungle
Lightning Over Water
Lillie
Lisztomania
The Loneliest Runner
The Long Gray Line
Long Journey Back
Louis Armstrong: Chicago Style
Love Affair: The Eleanor & Lou Gehrig Story
Love Me or Leave Me
The Loves of Edgar Allen Poe
Loyola, the Soldier Saint
Lucky Luciano
Lucy and Desi: Before the Laughter
Lust for Life
MacArthur
Madame Curie
Madman
Mae West
Mafia Princess
Magnificent Adventurer
Mahler
Malcolm X
A Man Called Peter
Man of a Thousand Faces
Mandela
Marciano
Marco
Marie Antoinette
Marilyn
Marilyn: The Untold Story
Marjoe
Marlon Brando
Martin Luther
Mary of Scotland
Mary White
A Matter of Life and Death
McVicar
Melody Master
The Miracle Worker
Mishima: A Life in Four Chapters
Mo' Better Blues
Moliere
Mommie Dearest
Monsieur Vincent
Moulin Rouge
Mozart: A Childhood Chronicle
The Mozart Story
Murderers Among Us: The Simon Wiesenthal Story
Murrow
The Music Lovers
Mussolini & I
My Apprenticeship
My Childhood
My Father's Glory
My Left Foot
My Universities
My Wicked, Wicked Ways
Nadia
The Naked Civil Servant

Volcanoes

The Last Days of Pompeii
Nutcase
St. Helen's, Killer Volcano

War Between the Sexes

Adam's Rib
The Adventures of Robin Hood
The African Queen
All of Me
All's Fair
Alternative
Always
America 3000
Anita de Montemar
Annie Hall
Around the World Under the Sea
Autumn Marathon
The Awful Truth
The Ballad of the Sad Cafe
Ballyhoo Baby
Bare Essentials
Basic Training
Behind Office Doors
Beware of Pity
The Bigamist
Blood and Sand
Blue Paradise
The Bodyguard
Boomerang
Bride Walks Out
Bringing Up Baby
Buffalo Jump
Bull Durham
Cannibal Women in the Avocado Jungle of Death
Carmen
Carmen Jones
Carrington, V.C.
Carry On Nurse
Casablanca
Casanova's Big Night
Castaway
Casual Sex?
Chained
Cold Heat
Con Mi Mujer No Puedo
Concrete Beat
The Cutting Edge
Dangerous Liaisons
Dear Murderer
Dear Wife
Designing Woman
Divorce His, Divorce Hers
Divorce—Italian Style
Dogfight
Don Juan, My Love
Easy Wheels
El Forastero Vengador
El: This Strange Passion
Far and Away
The Female Bunch
Fever
First Monday in October
Forever Darling
Frankie and Johnny
Fury is a Woman
A Girl in a Million
Gone with the Wind
The Good Father
Goodbye Love
The Happy Ending
Hardhat & Legs
Having It All
He Said, She Said
Heartburn
His Girl Friday
Housesitter
I, Claudius, Vol. 1: A Touch of Murder/Family Affairs
I Live My Life
I Love All of You
I Love My...Wife

I Love You
In the Good Old Summertime
In the Line of Fire
Intimate Story
Irreconcilable Differences
It Happened One Night
The Jewel of the Nile
Juliet of the Spirits
June Bride
Just Tell Me What You Want
Key Exchange
Kill My Wife...Please!
The King and I
Kiss Me Kate
La Diosa Arrodillada
L.A. Story
The Lady Says No
The Last Woman on Earth
Le Chat
Legion of Iron
Letters to an Unknown Lover
Lily in Love
The Lion in Winter
Love Crazy
Love in the Afternoon
Lover Come Back
Loyalties
Lucky Partners
Man of Destiny
The Man Who Guards the Greenhouse
Manhattan
Many Wonder
Maria's Lovers
The Marriage of Maria Braun
The Marrying Man
A Matter of Love
McLintock!
Men...
Menschenfrauen
A Midsummer Night's Dream
Moonlighting
Moonstruck
Mortal Thoughts
Much Ado About Nothing
Murphy's Law
My Brilliant Career
Near Misses
A New Leaf
9 to 5
Nothing in Common
One Woman or Two
The Opposite Sex and How to Live With Them
Pajama Tops
Pat and Mike
Patti Rocks
Pauline at the Beach
A Piece of Pleasure
Pillow Talk
Places in the Heart
Portrait of Teresa
The Practice of Love
Private Lives
Public Enemy
Queen of Outer Space
Question of Silence
The Quiet Man
Ramrod
Romancing the Stone
Rooster Cogburn
Running Mates
Sabrina
Scenes from a Mall
Seance on a Wet Afternoon
The Sensual Man
Sex and the College Girl
Shades of Love: Champagne for Two
She-Devil
Shore Leave
The Single Standard
The Social Secretary
Sotto, Sotto
Speedtrap
Spies, Lies and Naked Thighs

Star 80
The Story of Fausta
Summer Night with Greek Profile, Almond Eyes & Scent of Basil
Switch
Switching Channels
The Taming of the Shrew
A Taxing Woman
Teacher's Pet
Ted & Venus
That's My Baby!
Thelma & Louise
The Thing
Thor and the Amazon Women
Three of Hearts
Thunder in the Pines
Tiger and the Pussycat
To Have & Have Not
Tony Draws a Horse
True Love
Two-Faced Woman
Vasectomy: A Delicate Matter
War Between the Tates
The War of the Roses
When Harry Met Sally
When Ladies Meet
When Women Lost Their Tails
Who's Afraid of Virginia Woolf?
Wife Versus Secretary
The Witches of Eastwick
Without Love
A Woman of Distinction
Woman of the Year
Women & Men: Stories of Seduction
Women & Men: Stories of Seduction, Part 2
Women on the Verge of a Nervous Breakdown
The World According to Garp
Year of the Comet
Yesterday, Today and Tomorrow
You're a Big Boy Now

War, General

The Adventures of the Flying Cadets
The Alamo
The Alamo: Thirteen Days to Glory
Alexander Nevsky
Alexander the Great
Alone Against Rome
Alsino and the Condor
Anna Karenina
Atlas
The Avenger
Ay, Carmela!
Ballad of a Soldier
Battle Hell
The Battle of Algiers
The Battle of Austerlitz
The Beast
Beau Geste
Behind the Front
Behold a Pale Horse
Benjamin Argumedo
The Buccaneer
Bugles in the Afternoon
A Bullet for the General
By Dawn's Early Light
Captain Caution
Captain Horatio Hornblower
Carthage in Flames
Cast a Giant Shadow
Cavalry Command
Chapayev
The Charge of the Light Brigade
Civilization
Codename: Terminate
The Conqueror

Conquest of the Normans
Coup de Grace
The Court Martial of Billy Mitchell
Cromwell
Cup Final
Danton
Days of Hell
Deadline
The Desert of the Tartars
Devil Wears White
Distant Drums
Doctor Zhivago
Dragon Seed
Eagles Attack at Dawn
1860
El Cid
El Paso Stampede
El Rey
Elizabeth of Ladymead
Emissary
The Enchanted Cottage
The End of St. Petersburg
The Expendables
The Fall of the Roman Empire
Field of Honor
The Fighter
Fighting Marines
Fighting Pilot
The Fighting Prince of Donegal
The Finest Hour
Fire Over England
The Firing Line
Flor Silvestre
Forever and a Day
Fort Apache
Forty Days of Musa Dagh
The Four Feathers
F.P. 1
Funny, Dirty Little War
Guerilla Brigade
Gunga Din
Guns at Batasi
Hail the Conquering Hero
Harry's War
Heart of a Nation
Heartbreak Ridge
Hearts & Armour
Heaven & Earth
Hell in the Pacific
Hell on the Battleground
Hell Raiders
Henry V
The Hidden Fortress
Hill 24 Doesn't Answer
Holy Terror
Homecoming
How I Won the War
In the Name of the Pope-King
The Informer
The Invincible Gladiator
Johnny Got His Gun
Judith of Bethulia
Khartoum
Killers
Kolberg
La Chamuscada
La Marseillaise
La Nuit de Varennes
La Venganza del Rojo
The Last Command
The Last of the Mohicans
The Last Valley
Late Summer Blues
Latino
Laughing at Life
Legion of Missing Men
The Life and Death of Colonel Blimp
Lion of the Desert
The Lost Command
The Lost Idol/Shock Troop
Mademoiselle Fifi
Man from the Alamo
Massive Retaliation

Megaforce
Mercenary Fighters
Mission to Glory
Mission to Kill
The Mongols
The Moonraker
Mother
Mountain Fury
The Mouse That Roared
Napoleon
An Occurrence at Owl Creek Bridge/Coup de Grace
Old Gringo
One Night Stand
Orphans of the Storm
The Phantom Planet
Port Arthur
The Pride and the Passion
Project: Alien
Rage to Kill
The Rape of the Sabines
The Real Glory
A Reason to Live, A Reason to Die
The Rebellious Reign
The Red and the Black
The Red and the White
Red Dawn
Reds
Reign of Terror
Revenge of the Barbarians
Rhodes
Richard II
Ride to Glory
River of Unrest
Ryan's Daughter
Saga of the Vagabond
Salome, Where She Danced
Sanders of the River
Seven Indignant
The Seventeenth Bride
Shake Hands with the Devil
The Shame
She Wore a Yellow Ribbon
Simon Bolivar
Sinai Commandos
Smugglers
Something of Value
Striker
Surprise Attack
The Tempest/The Eagle
This Island Earth
The 317th Platoon
Tiger Joe
Time to Kill
Torn Allegiance
Treasure of the Lost Desert
Troilus & Cressida
The Ugly American
Under Fire
The Uprising
Vera Cruz
Villa Rides
Walker
The Wanton Contessa
War and Peace
War Bus Commando
Warbirds
Waterloo
Weekend War
Wild Geese 2
The World Owes Me a Living
World War III
Yank in Libya
Young Winston
Zulu Dawn

Werewolves

An American Werewolf in London
Black Werewolf
Blood of Dracula's Castle
Bride of the Gorilla
Children of the Full Moon
The Company of Wolves

The Craving
Cry of the Werewolf
Curse of the Devil
Curse of the Queerwolf
The Curse of the Werewolf
Deathmoon
Dr. Jekyll and the Wolfman
Dr. Jekyll vs. the Werewolf
Dr. Terror's House of Horrors
Dracula vs. Frankenstein
Face of the Screaming
    Werewolf
Frankenstein Meets the
    Wolfman
The Fury of the Wolfman
Hercules, Prisoner of Evil
House of Frankenstein
The Howling
Howling 2: Your Sister is a
    Werewolf
Howling 3: The Marsupials
Howling 4: The Original
    Nightmare
Howling 6: The Freaks
I Was a Teenage Werewolf
Legend of the Werewolf
The Legend of the Wolf
    Woman
Lone Wolf
The Mad Monster
Meridian: Kiss of the Beast
Monster Dog
The Monster Squad
Moon of the Wolf
My Mom's a Werewolf
Night of the Howling Beast
Orgy of the Dead
The Rats are Coming! The
    Werewolves are Here!
Return of the Vampire
Silver Bullet
Teen Wolf
Teen Wolf Too
The Undying Monster
Werewolf in a Girl's Dormitory
Werewolf of London
Werewolf of Washington
The Werewolf vs. the Vampire
    Woman
Werewolves on Wheels
The Wolf Man
Wolfen
The Wolfman

Western Comedy

Adios Amigo
Along Came Jones
The Apple Dumpling Gang
The Apple Dumpling Gang
    Rides Again
Bad Man's River
Ballad of Cable Hogue
Bang Bang Kid
The Beautiful Blonde from
    Bashful Bend
Blazing Saddles
Bordello
Border Phantom
Boss
Bowery Buckaroos
Branded Men
Bronco Billy
Bus Stop
Carry On Cowboy
Cat Ballou
Catlow
Check & Double Check
The Cheyenne Social Club
Cold Feet
Desperate Women
Destry Rides Again
The Duchess and the
    Dirtwater Fox
El Diablo Rides
Four Eyes and Six Guns

Four for Texas
The Frisco Kid
From Noon Till Three
Go West
Goin' South
Gold Raiders
Greaser's Palace
Great Scout & Cathouse
    Thursday
Gun Crazy
The Hallelujah Trail
Hangman's Knot
Hearts of the West
I'm from Arkansas
The Incredible Rocky
    Mountain Race
The Kid Brother
Life & Times of Judge Roy
    Bean
Lincoln County Incident
Local Badman
McLintock!
More Wild, Wild West
The Nervous Wreck
Oklahoma Kid
The Paleface
Pocket Money
Rancho Deluxe
Ride 'Em Cowboy
The Rounders
Rustler's Rhapsody
Scalphunters, The
Scandalous John
September Gun
The Shakiest Gun in the West
Shame, Shame on the Bixby
    Boys
Son of Paleface
Sting of the West
Support Your Local
    Gunfighter
Support Your Local Sheriff
Take Me Back to Oklahoma
Texas
Texas Layover
There was a Crooked Man
They Call Me Trinity
Three Godfathers
Ticket to Tomahawk
Trinity is Still My Name
Under Montana Skies
The Villain
Wackiest Wagon Train in the
    West
Waterhole #3
Way Out West
Wild & Wooly
Wild Horse Phantom
Wild Rovers
The Wistful Widow of Wagon
    Gap
Yellow Hair & the Fortress of
    Gold

Westerns

Abilene Town
Aces and Eights
Aces Wild
Across the Plains
Adios Gringo
Adios, Hombre
The Adventures of Gallant
    Bess
Adventures of Kit Carson
Adventures of Red Ryder
Against A Crooked Sky
The Alamo
Alias Billy the Kid
Alias John Law
Allegheny Uprising
Along the Great Divide
Along the Sundown Trail
Alvarez Kelly
Ambush at Tomahawk Gap
Ambush Trail

American Empire
Americano
And God Said to Cain
Angel and the Badman
Animal Called Man
Annie Oakley
Another Man, Another Chance
Another Pair of Aces: Three of
    a Kind
Any Gun Can Play
Apache
Apache Blood
Apache Chief
Apache Kid's Escape
Apache Rose
Apache Uprising
Apache Woman
Apaches Last Battle
Apocalipsis Joe
The Appaloosa
Arizona Badman
Arizona Bound
Arizona Bushwackers
Arizona Cowboy
Arizona Days
Arizona Gangbusters
Arizona Gunfighter
Arizona Kid
Arizona Raiders
Arizona Roundup
Arizona Stagecoach
Arizona Terror
Arizona Whirlwind
Arrowhead
At Gunpoint
Backfire
Bad Company
Bad Day at Black Rock
Bad Guys
Bad Jim
Bad Lands
Bad Man of Deadwood
The Badlanders
Badman's Territory
Badmen of Nevada
Ballad of a Gunfighter
Ballad of Gregorio Cortez
Bandera Bandits
Bandit Queen
Bandits
Bandolero!
Bar-20
Barbarosa
The Bargain
Baron of Arizona
Battle of Elderbush Gulch
Battling Marshal
Battling Outlaws
Battling with Buffalo Bill
Belle of San Fernando
Belle Starr Story
Bells of Coronado
Bells of Rosarita
Bells of San Angelo
Bells of San Fernando
Below the Border
Bend of the River
Beneath Arizona Skies/
    Paradise Canyon
Best of the Badmen
Between Fighting Men
Between God, the Devil & a
    Winchester
Between Men
Beyond the Law
Big Calibre
The Big Cat
Big Country
A Big Hand for the Little Lady
Big Jake
Big Show
The Big Sky
The Big Sombrero
Big Stakes
Big Trail
Big Valley

Billy the Kid in Texas
Billy the Kid Returns
Billy the Kid Trapped
Bite the Bullet
The Black Lash
Black Market Rustlers
Blazing Guns
Blood at Sundown
Blood for a Silver Dollar
Blood on the Moon
Bloody Trail
Blue
Blue Canadian Rockies
Blue Steel
Boiling Point
The Boldest Job in the West
Bonanza
Boot Hill Bandits
Boothill Brigade
Boots & Saddles
Border Badmen
Border Bandits
Border Devils
Border Feud
Border Patrol
Border Rangers
Border Romance
Border Roundup
Border Saddlemates
Border Shootout
Border Vigilantes
Bordertown Gunfighters
Born in America
Boss Cowboy
Boss of Rawhide
The Bounty Man
Brand of Hate
Brand of the Outlaws
Branded
Branded a Coward
Brandy Sheriff
The Bravados
Breakheart Pass
Breed of the Border
Broadway to Cheyenne
Broken Arrow
Broken Lance
Bronson's Revenge
Bronze Buckaroo
Brothers of the West
Brothers O'Toole
Buck and the Preacher
Buckeye and Blue
Buckskin
Buckskin Frontier
Buffalo Bill
Buffalo Bill & the Indians
Buffalo Bill Rides Again
Buffalo Rider
Buffalo Stampede
Bugles in the Afternoon
Bull of the West
Bulldog Courage
Bullet for Sandoval
A Bullet for the General
Bullwhip
The Burning Hills
The Bushwackers
Butch and Sundance: The
    Early Days
Butch Cassidy and the
    Sundance Kid
Buzzy Rides the Range
Cahill: United States Marshal
Cain's Cutthroats
Calamity Jane
California Joe
Call of the Canyon
Call of the Forest
Call of the Rockies
Calling Wild Bill Elliott
Captain Apache
The Captive: The Longest
    Drive 2
The Capture
The Caravan Trail

The Cariboo Trail
Carson City Kid
Cattle Queen of Montana
Cavalcade of the West
Cavalier of the West
Cavalry
Cavalry Command
Challenge of McKenna
Charro!
Chato's Land
Check Your Guns
Cheyenne Autumn
Cheyenne Kid
Cheyenne Rides Again
Cheyenne Takes Over
Child of the Prairie
Chino
The Chisholms
Chisum
The Christmas Kid
Chuka
Cimarron
Circle Canyon
Circle of Death
The Cisco Kid
Clearing the Range
Code of the Fearless
Colorado
Colorado Serenade
Colorado Sundown
Colt Comrades
Colt is My Law
Comancheros
Come On, Cowboys
Come On Rangers
Come On Tarzan
Comes a Horseman
Conagher
The Concentratin' Kid
Conquest of Cochise
Copper Canyon
Coroner Creek
Cotter
Courage of the North
Courageous Avenger
Courtin' Wildcats
The Covered Wagon
Covered Wagon Days
Cow Town
Cowboy
Cowboy & the Bandit
Cowboy & the Senorita
Cowboy Commandos
Cowboy Counselor
Cowboy Millionaire
The Cowboys
Cowboys from Texas
Cowboys of the Saturday
    Matinee
Coyote Trails
Crazy Horse and Custer: "The
    Untold Story"
Crooked Trail
Crossfire
Culpepper Cattle Co.
Custer's Last Fight
Custer's Last Stand
Cyclone of the Saddle
Dakota
Dakota Incident
Dan Candy's Law
Danger Ahead
Danger Trails
Daniel Boone
Daniel Boone: Trail Blazer
Dark Command
Dawn on the Great Divide
Dawn Rider
Dawn Rider/Frontier Horizon
Dead for a Dollar
Dead or Alive
Deadly Companions
The Deadly Trackers
Deadwood
Deadwood Pass
Death of a Gunfighter

Westerns

Death Rides the Plains
Death Rides the Range
Death Valley
Death Valley Manhunt
Death Valley Rangers
The Deerslayer
Demon for Trouble
The Denver & Rio Grande
Deputy Marshall
Desert Gold
Desert Guns/Six-Shootin'
 Sheriff
Desert Phantom
Desert Snow
Desert Trail
Desperados
The Desperados
Devil & Leroy Basset
Devil Horse
Devil Riders
Devil's Canyon
The Devil's Mistress
Diamond Trail
Disciple
Distant Drums
Django
Django Shoots First
Dodge City
Don Amigo/Stage to China
Donner Pass: The Road to
 Survival
The Doolins of Oklahoma
Doomed Caravan
Down Dakota Way
Down Mexico Way
Down Texas Way
Draw!
The Drifter
Drum Beat
Drum Taps
Drums Along the Mohawk
Dude Bandit
Dude Ranger
Duel at Diablo
Duel in the Eclipse
Duel in the Sun
Duelo en el Dorado
Duke: The Films of John
 Wayne
Durango Valley Raiders
Dynamite and Gold
Dynamite Pass
Dynamite Ranch
Eagle's Wing
El Ametralladora
El Ciclon
El Condor
El Diablo
El Dorado
El Forastero Vengador
El Fugitivo
El Gallo de Oro
El Gavilan Pollero
El Hombre de la Furia
El Paso Stampede
El Robo al Tren Correo
El Sabor de la Venganza
El Zorro Vengador
The Electric Horseman
Enemy of the Law
Every Man's Law
Extreme Prejudice
Eyes of Texas
False Colors
Fangs of Fate
Far Country
Far Frontier
Fargo Express
Fast Bullets
Fastest Guitar Alive
Feud of the Trail
Feud of the West
$50,000 Reward
Fight for Gold
Fightin' Ranch
Fighting Caballero

Fighting Caravans
Fighting Cowboy
Fighting Fists of Shanghai Joe
Fighting Jack
The Fighting Kentuckian
The Fighting Legion
Fighting Mad
Fighting Parson
Fighting Renegade
The Fighting Stallion
Fighting Texans
Fighting Thru
The Fighting Trooper
Fighting Valley
Fighting Vigilantes
Fighting with Kit Carson
Finger on the Trigger
The First Movie Cowboy
Fistful of Death
Five Card Stud
Flame of the Barbary Coast
Flaming Frontiers
Flaming Lead
Flaming Star
Flamingo Lead
Flesh and the Spur
Forbidden Trails
Forlorn River
Fort Apache
Four Faces West
Four Rode Out
From Broadway to Cheyenne
Frontier Days
Frontier Fugitives
Frontier Horizon
Frontier Justice
Frontier Outlaws
Frontier Pony Express
Frontier Scout
Frontier Vengeance
The Frontiersman
Fuerte Perdido
The Fugitive: Taking of Luke
 McVane
Fugitive Valley
Galloping Dynamite
The Gambling Terror
Gangster's Den
Gangsters of the Frontier
Garringo
The Gatling Gun
The Gay Ranchero
Gene Autry Matinee Double
 Feature #1
Gene Autry Matinee Double
 Feature #2
Gene Autry Matinee Double
 Feature #3
Gentle Savage
The Gentleman from
 California
Gentleman from Texas
The Gentleman Killer
Geronimo
Geronimo's Revenge
Ghost City
Ghost Patrol
Ghost Rider
Ghost Town
Ghost Town Gold
Ghost Town Law
Ghost Town Renegades
Ghost Valley
Ghostriders
Girl from Calgary
Girl of the Golden West
Git Along Little Dogies
God's Gun
The Golden Stallion
Gone with the West
The Good, the Bad and the
 Ugly
Gore Vidal's Billy the Kid
Grand Canyon Trail
The Grand Duel
Grayeagle

Great Day in the Morning
The Great Gundown
Great Jesse James Raid
Great Missouri Raid
The Great Northfield
 Minnesota Raid
Great Treasure Hunt
Gun Code
Gun Fight at Red Sands
Gun Fury
Gun Law
Gun Lords of Stirrup Basin
Gun Play
The Gun Ranger
Gun Riders
Gun Smugglers/Hot Lead
A Gunfight
Gunfight at Sandoval
Gunfight at the O.K. Corral
Gunfighter
The Gunfighters
Gunfire
Gunman from Bodie
Gunners & Guns
Gunplay
Guns for Dollars
Guns in the Dark
Guns of Diablo
Guns of Fury
Guns of Justice
Guns of the Magnificent
 Seven
The Gunslinger
Gunslinger
Gunsmoke: Return to Dodge
Gunsmoke Trail
The Half-Breed
Hands Across the Border
The Hanged Man
The Hanging Tree
Hannie Caulder
Hard Hombre
Harlem on the Prairie
Harlem Rides the Range
Harmony Trail
Harry Tracy
The Harvey Girls
Haunted Ranch
Hawaiian Buckaroo
Hawken's Breed
Headin' for the Rio Grande
Heart of Texas Ryan
Heart of the Golden West
Heart of the Rio Grande
Heart of the Rockies
Heaven's Gate
Hell Fire Austin
Helldorado
Heller in Pink Tights
Hellfire
Hell's Hinges
Helltown
Heritage of the Desert
Heroes of the Alamo
Heroes of the Hills
Heroes of the West
Hidden Gold
Hidden Guns
Hidden Valley
High Lonesome
High Noon
High Noon: Part 2
High Plains Drifter
Hills of Utah
Hired Hand
His Brother's Ghost
His Fighting Blood
His Name was King
Historia de un Gran Amor
Hit the Saddle
Hittin' the Trail
Hombre
Home in Oklahoma
Homesteaders of Paradise
 Valley
Honor of the Range

Hopalong Cassidy
Hopalong Cassidy: Borrowed
 Trouble
Hopalong Cassidy: Dangerous
 Venture
Hopalong Cassidy: False
 Paradise
Hopalong Cassidy: Hoppy's
 Holiday
Hopalong Cassidy: Riders of
 the Deadline
Hopalong Cassidy: Silent
 Conflict
Hopalong Cassidy: Sinister
 Journey
Hopalong Cassidy: The Dead
 Don't Dream
Hopalong Cassidy: The Devil's
 Playground
Hopalong Cassidy: The
 Marauders
Hopalong Cassidy:
 Unexpected Guest
Hoppy Serves a Writ
Horizons West
Hostile Guns
Hour of the Gun
How the West was Won
Hurricane Express
I Shot Billy the Kid
I Shot Jesse James
I Will Fight No More Forever
Idaho
In Old Caliente
In Old California
In Old Cheyenne
In Old Colorado
In Old Montana
In Old New Mexico
In Old Santa Fe
In the Days of the Thundering
 Herd & the Law & the
 Outlaw
The Indian Fighter
Indian Paint
Indian Uprising
Into the Badlands
Invitation to a Gunfighter
The Jayhawkers
Jeremiah Johnson
Jesse James
Jesse James at Bay
Jesse James Meets
 Frankenstein's Daughter
Jesse James Rides Again
Jesse James Under the Black
 Flag
Joe Kidd
John Wayne Anthology: Star
 Packer/Lawless Range
Johnny Guitar
Johnny Reno
Jory
Joshua
Jubal
Jubilee Trail
Judge Roy Bean
Junior Bonner
Justice of the West
Justice Rides Again
Justicia para los Mexicanos
The Kansan
Kansas Pacific
The Kansas Terrors
Keep the Change
Kenny Rogers as the Gambler
Kenny Rogers as the
 Gambler, Part 2: The
 Adventure Continues
Kenny Rogers as the
 Gambler, Part 3: The
 Legend Continues
Kentuckian
Kentucky Rifle
Kid Courageous
Kid from Gower Gulch

Kid Ranger
Kid Vengeance
Kid's Last Ride
The King and Four Queens
King of the Bullwhip
King of the Cowboys
King of the Grizzlies
King of the Pecos
King of the Rodeo
King of the Stallions
King of the Texas Rangers
King of the Wild Horses
Kit Carson
Knights of the Range
La Ley del Revolver
The Lamb
Land of Hunted Men
Land of the Lawless
Land Raiders
Laramie Kid
Last Bullet
The Last Command
Last Days of Frank & Jesse
 James
Last Frontier
Last Gun
Last of the Clintons
Last of the Comanches
The Last of the Mohicans
Last of the Pony Riders
Last of the Warrens
Last of the Wild Horses
The Last Outlaw
Last Outlaw
The Last Ride of the Dalton
 Gang
The Last Tomahawk
Last Train from Gun Hill
The Law and Jake Wade
Law and Lawless
Law and Order
Law of the Land
Law of the Lash
Law of the Pampas
Law of the Saddle
The Law Rides
The Law Rides Again
Law West of Tombstone
Lawless Frontier
Lawless Range
A Lawless Street
Lawman
A Lawman is Born
Lawmen
Leather Burners
The Left-Handed Gun
Legend of Alfred Packer
Legend of Earl Durand
The Legend of Frank Woods
Legend of Frenchie King
The Legend of Jedediah
 Carver
Legend of the Lone Ranger
Legion of the Lawless
The Light of Western Stars
Lightnin' Carson Rides Again
Lightning Bill
Lightning Bill Crandall
Lightning Raiders
Lightning Range
Lightning Strikes West
Lightning Warrior
Lights of Old Santa Fe
Lion's Den
Little Big Horn
Little Big Man
Little Moon & Jud McGraw
Loaded Pistols
The Lone Avenger
Lone Bandit
The Lone Defender
The Lone Ranger
Lone Ranger
The Lone Ranger
Lone Ranger and the Lost
 City of Gold

The Lone Rider in Cheyenne
The Lone Rider in Ghost Town
Lone Star Law Men
The Lone Star Ranger
Lone Wolf McQuade
Lonely are the Brave
Lonely Man
Lonely Trail/Three Texas Steers
Lonesome Dove
Lonesome Trail
The Long Riders
The Longest Drive
Los Apuros de Dos Gallos
Los Asesinos
Los Hermanos Centella
Los Hermanos Diablo
Los Jinetes de la Bruja
Los Sheriffs de la Frontera
Lost Canyon
Love Desperados
Lucky Luke: Daisy Town
Lucky Luke: The Ballad of the Daltons
Lucky Terror
Lucky Texan
Lust for Gold
The Lusty Men
Macho Callahan
MacKenna's Gold
Madron
Magnificent Seven
Major Dundee
A Man Alone
Man & Boy
A Man Called Horse
A Man Called Sledge
Man from Button Willow
Man from Cheyenne
Man from Colorado
The Man from Gun Town
The Man from Hell
Man from Hell's Edges
Man from Laramie
The Man from Music Mountain
The Man from Painted Post
The Man from Snowy River
Man from Texas
Man from the Alamo
Man from Thunder River
Man from Utah
Man of the Forest
Man of the Frontier
Man of the West
Man Who Loved Cat Dancing
The Man Who Shot Liberty Valance
Man Without a Star
Manchurian Avenger
The Manhunt
Manos Torpes
Man's Country
Man's Land
Mariachi
Mark of the Spur
Marked for Murder
Marked Trails
Marshal of Cedar Rock
Marshal of Heldorado
The Marshal's Daughter
Mason of the Mounted
Maverick Queen
Maverick: The Collector's Edition
McCabe & Mrs. Miller
The McMasters
The Meanest Men in the West
Melody Ranch
Melody Trail
Mesquite Buckaroo
Minnesota Clay
Miracle in the Wilderness
Miracle Rider: Vol. 1
Miracle Rider: Vol. 2
Missouri Breaks

Missourians
Mr. Horn
Mohawk
Molly & Lawless John
Montana
Montana Belle
Monte Walsh
Mosby's Marauders
The Mountain Men
Murder on the Yukon
My Darling Clementine
My Heroes Have Always Been Cowboys
My Outlaw Brother
My Pal Trigger
Mysterious Desperado
Mysterious Desperado/Rider From Tucson
The Mysterious Rider
Mystery Man
Mystery Mountain
Mystery of the Hooded Horseman
Mystery Ranch
Mystery Trooper
Naked Hills
Naked in the Sun
The Naked Spur
Narrow Trail
Navajo Joe
'Neath Canadian Skies
'Neath the Arizona Skies
Ned Kelly
Nevada City
Nevada Smith
The Nevadan
The New Frontier
Nido de Aguilas
Night of the Grizzly
Night Rider
Night Riders of Montana
Night Stage to Galveston
Night Time in Nevada
The Nine Lives of Elfego Baca
No Man's Law
No Man's Range
North of the Border
North of the Great Divide
Oath of Vengeance
Oh Susannah
Oklahoma Annie
Oklahoma Badlands
Oklahoma Cyclone
The Oklahoman
Old Barn Dance
Old Corral
On the Night Stage
On the Old Spanish Trail
On Top of Old Smoky
One-Eyed Jacks
100 Rifles
One Little Indian
Only the Valiant
Oregon Trail
Outcast
The Outlaw
Outlaw Express
Outlaw Fury
Outlaw Gang
The Outlaw Josey Wales
Outlaw Justice
Outlaw of the Plains
Outlaw Roundup
Outlaw Rule
The Outlaw Tamer
Outlaw Trail
Outlaw Women
Outlaws of Sonora
Outlaws of the Desert
Outlaws of the Range
Outlaw's Paradise
Overland Mail
Overland Stage Raiders
The Ox-Bow Incident
Painted Desert
The Painted Stallion

Pale Rider
Pals of the Range
Pals of the Saddle
Panamint's Bad Man
Pancho Villa
Pancho Villa Returns
Paroled to Die
Passion
Pat Garrett & Billy the Kid
Pecos Kid
Peter Lundy and the Medicine Hat Stallion
The Phantom Bullet
The Phantom Empire
Phantom of the West
Phantom Patrol
Phantom Ranch
Phantom Ranger
The Phantom Rider
Phantom Thunderbolt
Pinto Canyon
Pinto Rustlers
Pioneer Marshal
Pioneer Woman
The Pioneers
A Place Called Glory
The Plainsman
Pocatello Kid
Pony Express
Pony Express Rider
Posse
Powdersmoke Range
Prairie Badmen
The Prairie King
Prairie Moon
Prairie Pals
The Professionals
The Proud and the Damned
Proud Men
Proud Rebel
Public Cowboy No. 1
Purple Vigilantes
Pursued
The Quick and the Dead
Quigley Down Under
Racketeers of the Range
Radio Ranch
Rage at Dawn
Raiders of Red Gap
Raiders of Sunset Pass
Raiders of the Border
Rainbow Ranch
Rainbow's End
Ramrod
The Ramrodder
Rancho Notorious
Randy Rides Alone
Range Busters
Range Feud
The Range Feud/Two Fisted Law
Range Law
Range Rider
Range Riders
Rangeland Empire
Rangeland Racket
Ranger and the Lady
Ranger's Roundup
Rangers Take Over
The Rare Breed
Rattler Kid
Rawhide
Rawhide Mail
Rawhide Romance
A Reason to Live, A Reason to Die
Red Desert
Red Garters
Red Headed Stranger
Red River
Red River Valley
Red Rock Outlaw
The Red Rope
Red Sun
Renegade Girl

Renegade Ranger/Scarlet River
Renegade Trail
Renfrew of the Royal Mounted
Renfrew on the Great White Trail
The Restless Breed
The Return of a Man Called Horse
Return of Draw Egan
Return of Frank James
Return of Jesse James
The Return of Josey Wales
Return of the Bad Men
Return of the Lash
Return of the Seven
Return of Wildfire
Return to Snowy River
Revenge of the Virgins
The Revenge Rider
Ride 'Em Cowgirl
Ride in the Whirlwind
Ride, Ranger, Ride
Ride the High Country
Ride the Man Down
Ride the Wind
Ride to Glory
Rider from Tucson
Rider of the Law
Riders of Death Valley
Riders of Destiny
Riders of the Desert
Riders of the Range
Riders of the Range/Storm Over Wyoming
Riders of the Rockies
Riders of the Timberline
Riders of the West
Riders of the Whistling Pines
Riders of the Whistling Skull
Ridin' on a Rainbow
Ridin' the California Trail
Ridin' the Lone Trail
Ridin' the Trail
Ridin' Thru
The Riding Avenger
Riding On
Riding Speed
Rim of the Canyon
Rimfire
Rin Tin Tin, Hero of the West
Rio Bravo
Rio Conchos
Rio Diablo
Rio Grande
Rio Grande Raiders
Rio Hondo
Rio Lobo
Rio Rattler
River of No Return
Road Agent
The Roamin' Cowboy
Roamin' Wild
Roarin' Lead
Roaring Guns
Roaring Six Guns
Robbery Under Arms
Robin Hood of Texas
Robin Hood of the Pecos
Rock River Renegades
Rocky Mountain Rangers
Rodeo Girl
Rogue of the Range
Rogue of the Rio Grande
Roll Along Cowboy
Roll on Texas Moon
Roll, Wagons, Roll
Rollin' Plains
Romance on the Range
Rooster Cogburn
Rootin' Tootin' Rhythm
Rose of Rio Grande
Rough Riders of Cheyenne
Rough Riders' Roundup
Rough Riding Rangers

Round-Up Time in Texas
Rounding Up the Law
Run of the Arrow
Running Wild
Rustler's Hideout
Rustler's Paradise
Rustler's Valley
The Sacketts
Sacred Ground
Saddle Buster
Saddle Mountain Round-Up
Saga of Death Valley
Sagebrush Trail
Salute to the "King of the Cowboys," Roy Rogers
San Antonio
San Fernando Valley
Sandflow
Santa Fe Bound
Santa Fe Marshal
Santa Fe Stampede
Santa Fe Trail
Santa Fe Uprising
Santee
Sartana's Here...Trade Your Pistol for a Coffin
Savage Guns
Savage Journey
Scalps
The Searchers
Sergeant Rutledge
Seven Cities of Gold
Seven Sixgunners
Seventh Cavalry
The Shadow Riders
Shadows of Death
Shalako
Shane
She Wore a Yellow Ribbon
Sheriff of Tombstone
Shine on, Harvest Moon
Shoot the Living, Pray for the Dead
Shoot the Sun Down
The Shooting
The Shootist
Shotgun
The Showdown
Showdown
Showdown at Boot Hill
Showdown at Williams Creek
Silent Code
Silent Valley
Silver Bandit
Silver City Kid
Silver Lode
Silver Queen
Silver River
Silver Spurs
Silver Stallion
Silver Star
Silverado
Sing, Cowboy, Sing
Singing Buckaroo
Six Gun Gospel
Six Gun Rhythm
Six Shootin' Sheriff
Sky Bandits
Slaughter Trail
Smoke in the Wind
Smokey Smith
Soldier Blue
The Sombrero Kid
Son of a Gun
Son of God's Country
Son of the Morning Star
Song of Arizona
Song of Nevada
Song of Old Wyoming
Song of Texas
Song of the Gringo
Song of the Trail
Songs and Bullets
Sonora Stagecoach
Sons of Katie Elder
Sons of the Pioneers

Westerns

South of Monterey
South of St. Louis
South of Santa Fe
South of the Border
South of the Rio Grande
Southward Ho!
Spirit of the West
Springtime in the Rockies
Springtime in the Sierras
Spurs
Square Dance Jubilee
Stage to Mesa City
Stagecoach
Stagecoach to Denver
The Stalking Moon
Standing Tall
The Star Packer
Station West
Storm Over Wyoming
Storm Rider
Stormy Trails
Straight Shooter
Straight Shootin'
The Stranger from Pecos
The Stranger Wore a Gun
Stranger's Gold
Strawberry Roan
Sudden Death
Sundance and the Kid
Sundown Fury
Sundown Kid
Sundown Riders
Sundown Saunders
Sunset
Sunset in El Dorado
Sunset on the Desert
Sunset Range
Sunset Serenade
Sunset Trail
Susanna Pass
Sweet Georgia
Swifty
Talion
Tall in the Saddle
The Tall Men
The Tall T
Taste of Death
Tell Them Willie Boy Is Here
Ten Wanted Men
Tennessee's Partner
Tension at Table Rock
Terror of Tiny Town
Terror Trail
Test of Donald Norton
Tex Rides with the Boy
    Scouts
Texas Cyclone
Texas Gunfighter
Texas Guns
Texas John Slaughter:
    Geronimo's Revenge
Texas John Slaughter:
    Stampede at Bitter Creek
Texas Justice
Texas Kid
Texas Lady
Texas Legionnaires
Texas Masquerade
Texas Pioneers
The Texas Rangers
Texas Terror
Texas to Bataan
Texas Trouble
Texas Wildcats
They Died with Their Boots
    On
This Gun for Hire
Thousand Pieces of Gold
Three Bullets for a Long Gun
Three Desperate Men
Three Faces West
Three in the Saddle
3:10 to Yuma
Three Texas Steers
Three Violent People
Three Word Brand

Thunder in God's Country
Thunder in the Desert
Thunder Mountain
Thunder Over Texas
Thunder Pass
Thunder River Feud
Thundering Gunslingers
Thundering Trail
Timber Terrors
Tin Star
To the Last Man
Today We Kill, Tomorrow We
    Die
Toll Gate
Toll of the Desert
Tom Horn
Tom Mix Compilation 1
Tom Mix Compilation 2
Tombstone Canyon
Tombstone Terror
The Tonto Kid
The Tracker
The Trackers
Trail Beyond
Trail Drive
Trail of Robin Hood
Trail of Terror
Trail of the Hawk
Trail of the Mounties
Trail of the Royal Mounted
Trail of the Silver Spurs
Trail Riders
Trail Street
Trailing Double Trouble
Trailing Trouble
Trails West
Train Robbers
Train to Tombstone
The Traitor
Tramplers
Treasure of Pancho Villa
Trigger, Jr.
Trigger Pals
Trigger Trio
Triumphs of a Man Called
    Horse
Trouble Busters
Trouble in Texas
True Grit
Tulsa
Tumbledown Ranch in
    Arizona
Tumbleweed Trail
Tumbleweeds
Twice a Judas
Twilight in the Sierras
Twilight on the Rio Grande
Twilight on the Trail
Two Fisted Justice
Two-Fisted Justice
Two-Fisted Law
Two Gun Man
Two-Gun Man from Harlem
Two-Gun Troubador
Two Mules for Sister Sara
Two Rode Together
Ulzana's Raid
The Undefeated
Under California Stars
Under Nevada Skies
Under Western Stars
Undercover Man
Underground Rustlers
The Unforgiven
Unforgiven
Up River
Utah
Utah Trail
Valdez is Coming
Valley of Fire
Valley of Terror
Valley of the Lawless
Valley of the Sun
Vanishing American
Vanishing Legion
The Vanishing Westerner

Vengeance Valley
Vigilantes of Boom Town
Villa Rides
The Violent Men
Virginia City
The Virginian
Wagon Master
Wagon Trail
Wagon Wheels
Wall Street Cowboy
The Walloping Kid
Wanda Nevada
Wanted: Dead or Alive
War of the Wildcats
The War Wagon
Warlock
Water Rustlers
Way of the West
The Way West
Welcome to Blood City
West of Nevada
West of Pinto Basin
West of the Divide
West of the Law
West to Glory
Western Double Feature 1
Western Double Feature 1:
    Wild Bill & Sunset Carson
Western Double Feature 2
Western Double Feature 2:
    Wayne & Hale
Western Double Feature 3
Western Double Feature 3:
    Rogers & Allen
Western Double Feature 4
Western Double Feature 4:
    Rogers & Evans
Western Double Feature 5
Western Double Feature 5:
    Rogers & Autry
Western Double Feature 6:
    Rogers & Trigger
Western Double Feature 7:
    Wild Bill & Crabbe
Western Double Feature 8:
    Hale & Carradine
Western Double Feature 9:
    LaRue & Beery
Western Double Feature 10:
    Roy, Dale, & Trigger
Western Double Feature 11
Western Double Feature 12
Western Double Feature 13
Western Double Feature 14
Western Double Feature 15
Western Double Feature 16
Western Double Feature 17
Western Double Feature 18
Western Double Feature 19
Western Double Feature 20
Western Double Feature 21
Western Double Feature 22
Western Double Feature 23
Western Double Feature 24
Western Double Feature 25
Western Frontier
Western Justice
Western Mail
Western Pacific Agent
Western Trails
Western Union
The Westerner
Westward Ho
Westward Ho, the Wagons!
When a Man Rides Alone
When the Legends Die
When the West Was Young
Where the North Begins
Where Trails End
Whirlwind Horseman
Whistlin' Dan
Whistling Bullets
White Apache
The White Buffalo
White Comanche
White Eagle

White Gold
The Wild Bunch
Wild Country
The Wild Country
Wild Frontier
Wild Horse
Wild Horse Canyon
Wild Horse Rodeo
Wild Mustang
Wild Times
Wild West
Wild, Wild West Revisited
Wild Women
Wildfire
Will Penny
Winchester '73
The Wind
Winds of the Wasteland
Winners of the West
Winning of the West
With Kit Carson Over the
    Great Divide
Without Honors
Wolf Call
Wolfheart's Revenge
The Woman of the Town
Wrangler
Wyoming Outlaw
The Yellow Rose of Texas
Yodelin' Kid From Pine Ridge
Young Bill Hickok
Young Blood
Young Buffalo Bill
Young Guns
Young Guns 2
Yukon Flight
Yuma
Zachariah
Zandy's Bride
Zorro Rides Again
Zorro's Black Whip
Zorro's Fighting Legion

Wild Kingdom

The Adventures of Tarzan
Africa Texas Style
All Creatures Great and Small
Animal Farm
Bambi
The Barefoot Executive
The Bear
The Bears & I
Beastmaster
Beastmaster 2: Through the
    Portal of Time
Beasts
Bedtime for Bonzo
The Belstone Fox
Black Cobra
Bless the Beasts and Children
Bongo
Born Free
The Brave One
A Breed Apart
Bringing Up Baby
Buffalo Rider
Bugs Bunny Superstar
Call of the Wild
The Carnivores
Catch as Catch Can
Charlie, the Lonesome Cougar
Cheetah
Christian the Lion
The Chronicles of Narnia
Clarence, the Cross-eyed Lion
Courage of the North
A Cry in the Dark
A Cry in the Wild
Daffy Duck Cartoon Festival:
    Ain't That Ducky
Dark Age
Darkest Africa
Day of the Animals
The Day of the Dolphin
Doctor Doolittle

Dot & the Bunny
Dumbo
Eaten Alive
The Electric Horseman
Elephant Boy
Elmer Fudd Cartoon Festival
The Enchanted Journey
Every Which Way But Loose
Eyes of the Panther
The Fifth Monkey
Flight of the Grey Wolf
Flipper
Fraidy Cat
Francis in the Navy
Frasier the Sensuous Lion
Free Willy
Futz
Gaiety
Gentle Giant
Going Ape!
Going Bananas
The Golden Seal
Goldy: The Last of the Golden
    Bears
Goldy 2: The Saga of the
    Golden Bear
Goliathon
Gorilla
Gorillas in the Mist
The Great Adventure
The Great Rupert
Grizzly Adams: The Legend
    Continues
Gus
Harry and the Hendersons
Hatari
Hawmps!
High Country Calling
Himatsuri
In the Shadow of Kilimanjaro
Island of the Blue Dolphins
Jungle
The Jungle Book
Jungle Drums of Africa
King Kung Fu
King of the Grizzlies
Lassie, Come Home
Lassie: The Miracle
The Last Safari
Legend of Lobo
Leonard Part 6
Living Free
Matilda
The Misadventures of Merlin
    Jones
Mr. Kingstreet's War
Monkeys, Go Home!
Monkey's Uncle
Mountain Family Robinson
Mountain Man
Mouse and His Child
Murders in the Rue Morgue
My Sister, My Love
Napoleon and Samantha
Never Cry Wolf
Night of the Grizzly
Nikki, the Wild Dog of the
    North
Once Upon a Forest
Operation Haylift
Pardon My Trunk
Pet Sematary 2
Pippi Longstocking
Planet of the Apes
Project X
Razorback
The Rescuers
The Rescuers Down Under
Ring of Bright Water
Rock-a-Doodle
Rogue Lion
Rub a Dub Dub
The Runaways
Sammy, the Way-Out Seal
Secret of NIMH
Shakma

Blonde Savage
Born in Flames
Buffy the Vampire Slayer
Bury Me an Angel
Business as Usual
China O'Brien 2
Chopper Chicks in
  Zombietown
The Clan of the Cave Bear
Cleopatra
Cleopatra Jones
Colossus and the Amazon
  Queen
Comes a Horseman
Conexion Mexico
Dance of Death
Danger Zone
The Deadly and the Beautiful
Deadly Weapons
Do or Die
The $5.20 an Hour Dream
Get Christie Love!
Girl from Calgary
Golden Lady
Golden Ninja Warrior
Grand Larceny
The Great Texas Dynamite
  Chase
Heartland
Hot Box
Hundra
I Spit on Your Grave
Invincible Barbarian
Kilma, Queen of the Amazons
Kisses for My President
L.A. Crackdown
La Femme Nikita
Lady Scarface
Lethal Woman
The Lost Empire
Mae West
Mame
Mankillers
Marie
Mind Trap
Mission of Justice
Mistress of the Apes
Moonshine County Express
Nancy Drew, Reporter
Night Partners
Not Without My Daughter
Nyoka and the Tigermen
Panther Squad
The Perils of Pauline
Phoenix the Warrior
Point of No Return
Prehistoric Women
Queen Boxer
Queen of the Road
Raiders of Sunset Pass
Resurrection
Roller Blade
Runaway Nightmare
Sara Dane
Savage Beach
The Savage Girl
Savage Streets
See How She Runs
S*H*E
Sheena
She'll Be Wearing Pink
  Pajamas
She's in the Army Now
The Silence of the Lambs
Sister Kenny
Stormquest
Supergirl
Sweet Revenge
Switchblade Sisters
Thor and the Amazon Women
Tiffany Jones
Trapped
Tulsa
Uncaged
Velvet Smooth
Venus the Ninja

Wild Women
The Wild World of Batwoman
Wolfen Ninja
A Woman Rebels
Wrestling Women vs. the
  Aztec Ape
Wrestling Women vs. the
  Aztec Mummy
Zorro's Black Whip

World War I

Ace of Aces
The African Queen
All Quiet on the Western Front
Anzacs: The War Down Under
Arsenal
The Big Parade
Biggles
The Blue Max
The Chaplin Revue
The Charge of the Model T's
Courage Mountain
Crimson Romance
Dark Journey
Dawn Patrol
The Day that Shook the World
Devil in the Flesh
Dr. Mabuse the Gambler
Doughboys
Elizabeth of Ladymead
The End of St. Petersburg
A Farewell to Arms
Fifth Day of Peace
The Fighting 69th
For Me and My Gal
The Four Horsemen of the
  Apocalypse
Gallipoli
Going Home
Grand Illusion
The Great War
Half-Shot at Sunrise
Heart of Humanity
Hearts of the World
Hell's Angels
Hotel Imperial
How Many Miles to Babylon?
An Indecent Obsession
Inside the Lines
The Iron Major
Island
Isn't Life Wonderful
Killing Floor
The King of Hearts
Lafayette Escadrille
Land That Time Forgot
Lawrence of Arabia
The Life and Death of Colonel
  Blimp
Life and Nothing But
The Lighthorseman
The Little American
The Lost Patrol
Man of Legend
Mata Hari
Miracle of Our Lady of Fatima
Nicholas and Alexandra
1918
Nurse Edith Cavell
Paths of Glory
The Patriots
Q Ships
Return of the Soldier
Revolt of the Zombies
She Goes to War
Shout at the Devil
Spy in Black
Suzy
Three Legionnaires
Tomorrow is Forever
Waterloo Bridge
Westfront 1918
What Price Glory?
When the Whales Came
The White Cliffs of Dover

Wilson
Wings
Wings of Eagles
Yankee Doodle in Berlin
Zeppelin

World War II

Above Suspicion
Above Us the Waves
Abroad with Two Yanks
Across the Pacific
Action in Arabia
Action in the North Atlantic
Adventures of Smilin' Jack
Against the Wind
Air Force
Air Raid Wardens
Alan & Naomi
All My Sons
All Through the Night
The Americanization of Emily
And a Nightingale Sang
Angels One Five
Angry Harvest
The Annapolis Story
Another Time, Another Place
Anzio
Arch of Triumph
Armored Command
Around the World
Ashes and Diamonds
The Assault
Assault on Agathon
The Assisi Underground
Attack Force Z
Attack Squadron
The Attic: The Hiding of Anne
  Frank
Au Revoir Les Enfants
Aventure Malgache
Away All Boats
Back to Bataan
Background to Danger
Balkan Express
Bataan
Battle Cry
The Battle of Blood Island
Battle of Britain
Battle of China
The Battle of El Alamein
Battle of Neretva
The Battle of Russia
The Battle of San Pietro
Battle of the Bulge
Battle of the Commandos
Battle of the Eagles
The Battle of the Japan Sea
Battleforce
Battleground
Bear Island
Bedknobs and Broomsticks
Behind Enemy Lines
Berlin Express
The Best Years of Our Lives
Betrayal from the East
Betrayed
Between Heaven and Hell
The Big Lift
The Big Red One
Black Brigade
The Black Dragons
Black Rain
Blockhouse
The Blood of Others
Blood on the Sun
The Boat is Full
Bomb at 10:10
Bombardier
Bon Voyage
Border Street
The Boxer and Death
Brady's Escape
Brass Target
The Brave Bunch
Breakthrough

The Bridge at Remagen
The Bridge on the River Kwai
Bridge to Hell
A Bridge Too Far
Brief Encounter
Bugs & Daffy: The Wartime
  Cartoons
The Burmese Harp
Bye Bye Blues
The Caine Mutiny
Campaign in Poland
A Canterbury Tale
The Canterville Ghost
Captain Newman, M.D.
Captains of the Clouds
Captive Heart
Captive Hearts
Carry On England
Carve Her Name with Pride
Casablanca
Casablanca Express
Catch-22
Caught in the Draft
Chain Lightning
Charlie Grant's War
Chicago Joe & the Showgirl
Children's Island
China Sky
Christ Stopped at Eboli
Christabel
Churchill and the Generals
Class of '44
Cloak and Dagger
The Clock
Closely Watched Trains
Code Name: Emerald
Cold Days
The Colditz Story
Combat Killers
Come and See
Come See the Paradise
Command Decision
Commando Attack
Commando Squad
Commandos
Commandos Strike at Dawn
Conspiracy of Hearts
Convoy
Cornered
Corregidor
Cottage to Let
The Counterfeit Traitor
Cowboy Commandos
The Cranes are Flying
Cross of Iron
Cruel Sea
Cry of Battle
D-Day, the Sixth of June
Dam Busters
Danger UXB
Dangerous Moonlight
Darby's Rangers
Das Boot
David
Dawn Express
The Day and the Hour
A Day in October
The Day Will Dawn
Days of Glory
Deadly Mission
Death is Called Engelchen
Death of a Soldier
The Death of Adolf Hitler
December
December 7th: The Movie
Deep Six
Desert Commandos
The Desert Fox
The Desert Rats
The Desert Tigers
Despair
Desperate Journey
Destination Tokyo
Destroyer
The Devil's Brigade
Diamonds of the Night

The Diary of Anne Frank
The Dirty Dozen
The Dirty Dozen: The Next
  Mission
Dirty Heroes
Distant Thunder
Distant Voices, Still Lives
Dive Bomber
The Dresser
Dressmaker
The Dunera Boys
The Eagle Has Landed
Ebony Dreams
Edge of Darkness
Elizabeth of Ladymead
Elusive Corporal
Empire of the Sun
Enemy Below
Enemy of Women
Enigma Secret
Enola Gay: The Men, the
  Mission, the Atomic Bomb
Ensign Pulver
Era Notte a Roma
Escape from Sobibor
Escape to Athena
Europa, Europa
Every Time We Say Goodbye
The Execution
The Execution of Private
  Slovik
Eye of the Needle
Farewell to the King
Fat Man and Little Boy
Father
Father Goose
Fight for the Title
Fight to the Death
Fighter Attack
Fighting Seabees
The Fighting Sullivans
Films by Peter Thompson
The Final Countdown
Fireball Forward
Fires on the Plain
First Yank into Tokyo
Five for Hell
Flame to the Phoenix
Flat Top
Flying Leathernecks
Flying Tigers
For the Boys
Forbidden
Forbidden Games
Force 10 from Navarone
Foreign Correspondent
The Foreman Went to France
Fortunes of War
The Forty-Ninth Parallel
Forty Thousand Horsemen
Four Bags Full
The Four Horsemen of the
  Apocalypse
Four in a Jeep
Foxtrot
Frieda
From Hell to Victory
From Here to Eternity
G-Men vs. the Black Dragon
The Gallant Hours
Garden of the Finzi-Continis
Geheimakte WB1
General Della Rovere
Generale Della Rovere
A Generation
The Gift Horse
Go for Broke!
The Great Battle
Great Day
The Great Escape
The Great Escape 2: The
  Untold Story
Green for Danger
The Green Glove
Greta
Guadalcanal Diary

Wrestling

Wrong Side of the Tracks

Aaron Loves Angela
Algiers
Alice Adams
Anna Christie
Bachelor Party
Back Door to Heaven
Breaking Away
The Bride Wore Red
Camille
Cannery Row
Captains Courageous
Carbon Copy
Careful, He Might Hear You
Carrie
Cat Ballou
Chains
China Girl
Claudia
Cool As Ice
The Courtney Affair
Courtship
The Crucified Lovers
Cry-Baby
The Dark Side of Love
Diary of a Chambermaid
Dirty Dancing
Dr. Jack/For Heaven's Sake
Eegah!
Far and Away
Fire with Fire
The Flamingo Kid
Foxfire Light
Fresh Horses
Future Kill
Grease
The Great Gatsby
The Hairy Ape
Hearts of Humanity
Historia de un Gran Amor
Iron Maze
It
It Could Happen to You
It Happened One Night
Jungle Fever
King Ralph
The Lacemaker
Last Exit to Brooklyn
Liar's Moon
Little Minister
The Loves of Carmen
Luzia
The Man from Snowy River
Manhattan Melodrama
A Million to One
Min & Bill
My Forbidden Past
My Man Godfrey
Night Beat
Nosotros
Off Beat
Outpost in Morocco
Over the Brooklyn Bridge
The Phantom in the House
Phantom of the Opera
Picnic on the Grass
A Place in the Sun
Pretty in Pink
Primrose Path
Princess Tam Tam
Probation
Pygmalion
Reckless
Reform School Girl
Return to Snowy River
Rich Girl
Riff Raff
Rocky
Room at the Top
Ruby Gentry
Rumble Fish
San Francisco
The Servant

sex, lies and videotape
Show People
Snow Country
Somebody Up There Likes Me
Stay Hungry
The Story of the Late
    Chrysanthemum
Suburbia
The Swan
Sweet Light in a Dark Room
The Tamarind Seed
Tango
This Sporting Life
Tortilla Flat
A Tree Grows in Brooklyn
Under the Boardwalk
Uptown Angel
Valley Girl
Virtue's Revolt
Vivacious Lady
Waterloo Bridge
White Palace
The White Sin
Wild Youth
The World of Suzie Wong
The Young Philadelphians

Yuppie Nightmares

Alice
Almost You
Amos and Andrew
Baby Boom
Bad Influence
Barbarians at the Gate
Bare Essentials
Bedroom Eyes
Beetlejuice
The Big Chill
Blind Date
Blind Side
The Boost
Bright Lights, Big City
Cape Fear
City of Hope
Clara's Heart
Clean and Sober
Consenting Adults
Curly Sue
Desperately Seeking Susan
Diary of a Mad Housewife
Down and Out in Beverly Hills
Drop Dead Fred
Edge of Honor
The End of Innocence
Eye of the Demon
Fatal Attraction
The Fisher King
Folks!
Freefall
Fun with Dick and Jane
The Further Adventures of
    Tennessee Buck
Goodbye, New York
The Guardian
The Hand that Rocks the
    Cradle
The Hard Way
He Said, She Said
Hear No Evil
Heartburn
In the Spirit
Indian Summer
Jungle Fever
Key Exchange
Kicks
L.A. Story
Let's Kill All the Lawyers
Limit Up
Looking for Mr. Goodbar
Lost in America
Love or Money?
Madhouse
Maid to Order
The Malibu Beach Vampires
Micki & Maude

The Mighty Ducks
The Money Pit
Moving
Neighbors
New Year's Day
Night of the Living Babes
Nothing But Trouble
Oasis of the Zombies
The Object of Beauty
Pacific Heights
Perfect Family
Permanent Vacation
Preppies
Private Benjamin
Ransom
Reversal of Fortune
Roadhouse 66
Rude Awakening
Ruthless People
The Secret of My Success
September
sex, lies and videotape
Shattered
Something Wild
Stay Tuned
Straw Dogs
Summer Rental
Taking Care of Business
The Temp
Three Men and a Little Lady
Toxic Avenger, Part 3: The
    Last Temptation of Toxie
Trapped
Unlawful Entry
The Vagrant
Video Americana
Voodoo Dawn
Wall Street
Westworld
What About Bob?
Windy City

Zombies

The Alchemist
Alien Massacre
The Astro-Zombies
Bowery at Midnight
Bride of Re-Animator
Carnival of Souls
Cast a Deadly Spell
Children Shouldn't Play with
    Dead Things
The Chilling
Chopper Chicks in
    Zombietown
C.H.U.D. 2: Bud the Chud
City of the Walking Dead
Counter Destroyer
Creature of the Walking Dead
The Curse of the Aztec
    Mummy
Curse of the Screaming Dead
Dawn of the Dead
Dawn of the Mummy
Day of the Dead
The Dead Don't Die
Dead Heat
Dead Men Don't Die
Dead Pit
Death Becomes Her
The Death Curse of Tartu
Deathdream
Demon Wind
Destroyer
Devil Kiss
Evil Town
The Ghoul
The Hanging Woman
Haunting Fear
Hellgate
The Hereafter
Horror of the Zombies
Horror Rises from the Tomb
The House of Seven Corpses
House of the Dead

I Eat Your Skin
I Walked with a Zombie
Isle of the Dead
The Jitters
King of the Zombies
Kiss Daddy Goodbye
The Last Man on Earth
Messiah of Evil
The Mummy
Mummy & Curse of the Jackal
The Mummy's Revenge
Neon Maniacs
Night Life
Night of Horror
Night of the Comet
Night of the Creeps
Night of the Death Cult
Night of the Ghouls
Night of the Living Babes
Night of the Living Dead
Nightmare Weekend
Ninja Warriors
Oasis of the Zombies
Orgy of the Dead
The Outing
Pet Sematary 2
Plan 9 from Outer Space
Prison
Quatermass 2
The Re-Animator
Redneck Zombies
Return of the Evil Dead
Return of the Living Dead
Return of the Living Dead Part
    2
Revenge of the Dead
Revenge of the Living
    Zombies
Revenge of the Zombies
Revolt of the Zombies
The Robot vs. the Aztec
    Mummy
Seedpeople
Seven Doors of Death
Shock Waves
Sole Survivor
The Stuff
Svengali
Teenage Zombies
Tomb of the Undead
Tombs of the Blind Dead
Torture Chamber of Baron
    Blood
The Vampire's Ghost
Vengeance of the Zombies
Virgin Among the Living Dead
Voodoo Dawn
Voodoo Woman
The White Zombie
Zombie
Zombie High
Zombie Island Massacre
Zombie Lake
Zombie Nightmare
Zombie vs. Ninja
Zombies of Moratau
Zombies of the Stratosphere
Zombies on Broadway
Zombiethon

The **KIBBLES INDEX** presents nearly 300 categories that defy traditional classification—it's a potpourri of movie trivia listing selected authors, playwrights, producers, special effects wizards, and composers, as well as miscellaneous categories like Amy Fisher biopics, top grossing films, four-bone delights, and "the so bad they're almost good" *Woof!* features. Like the category index, the terms are listed alphabetically. Following is a complete list of the categories:

Films Adapted from:
a Book
a Cartoon
a Fairy Tale
a Game
a Play or Musical
a Poem
a Song
a Story
an Article
an Opera
Memoirs or Diaries
Television
the Radio

Books to Film:
Agatha Christie
Alex Haley
Alexandre Dumas
Alice Walker
Alistair MacLean
Ambrose Bierce
Anton Chekhov
Arthur C. Clarke
Arthur Hailey
Astrid Lindgren
Barbara Cartland
Barbara Taylor Bradford
Bram Stoker
Bret Easton Eillis
Charles Dickens
Clive Barker
Clive Cussler
Colleen McCullough
Daniel Defoe
Danielle Steel
Daphne Du Maurier
Dashiell Hammett
Dean R. Koontz

D.H. Lawrence
Dominick Dunne
Edgar Allan Poe
Edgar Rice Burroughs
Edgar Wallace
Edith Wharton
E.L. Doctorow
Elizabeth Groudge
Elmore Leonard
E.M. Forster
Eric Ambler
Ernest Hemingway
Evelyn Waugh
F. Scott Fitzgerald
Fanny Hurst
Frances Hodgson Burnett
Franz Kafka
Frederick Forsyth
Fyodor Dostoyevski
George Eliot
Graham Greene
Gustov Flaubert
Guy de Maupassant
H. Rider Haggard
Hans Christian Andersen
Harlequin Romances
Harold Robbins
Harper Lee
Harriet Beecher Stowe
Henry Fielding
Henry James
Herman Melville
Herman Wouk
H.G. Wells
Howard Fast
H.P. Lovecraft
Ian Fleming
Jack London
Jackie Collins

Jacqueline Susann
James Clavell
James Fenimore Cooper
James Jones
James Joyce
James Michener
James Thurber
Jane Austen
J.M. Barrie
John Cheever
John Irving
John Jakes
John Le Carre
John Steinbeck
John Updike
Jonathan Swift
Joseph Conrad
Joseph Wambaugh
Joyce Carol Oates
J.R.R. Tolkien
Judith Krantz
Judy Blume
Jules Verne
Katherine Anne Porter
Kenneth Grahame
Kurt Vonnegut
Larry McMurtry
Leo Tolstoy
Leon Uris
L.M. Montgomery
Louis L'Amour
Louisa May Alcott
Marcel Pagnol
Mario Puzo
Mark Twain
Mary Higgins Clark
Mary Shelley
Maya Angelou
Michael Chrichton

Miguel de Cervantes
Nathaniel Hawthorne
Neil Simon
Nikolai Gogol
Norman Mailer
O. Henry
Oscar Wilde
Paddy Chayefsky
Pat Conroy
Paul Theroux
Pearl S. Buck
Peter Maas
Ray Bradbury
Raymond Chandler
Robert Bloch
Robert Louis Stevenson
Robert Ludlum
Robin Cook
Rona Jaffe
Rudyard Kipling
Rumer Godden
Scott Turow
S.E. Hinton
Sidney Shelton
Sinclair Lewis
Sir Arthur Conan Doyle
Sir Walter Scott
Stendhal
Stephen Crane
Stephen King
Susan Isaacs
Thomas Hardy
Thornton Wilder
Tom Clancy
Truman Capote
Victor Hugo
Virginia Woolf
Vladimir Nabokov
W. Somerset Maugham
Washington Irving
Willa Cather
William Burroughs
William Faulkner
William Goldman
William Wharton
Zane Grey

Plays to Film:
Beth Henley
Eugune O'Neill
George Bernard Shaw
Horton Foote
Neil Simon
Tennessee Williams
Tom Stoppard
William Shakespeare

Producers:
Andy Warhol
BBC TV Productions
Coppola/American Zoetrope
George Lucas
Hammer Films: Horror
Hammer Films: Sci Fi & Fantasy
Merchant Ivory Productions
Robert Altman
Roger Corman/New World
Steven Spielberg
Troma Films
Val Lewton
William Castle

Musical Score:
Angelo Badalamenti
David Foster
Ennio Morricone
George & Ira Gershwin
Jack Nitzsche
Jerry Goldsmith
John Barry
John Williams
Lerner & Lowe
Menken & Ashman
Rodgers & Hammerstein
Rodgers & Hart

Special Effects:
Special FX Extravaganzas
Special FX Extravaganzas: Make-Up
Anton Furst
Dick Smith
Douglas Trumball
Herschell Gordon Lewis
Ray Harryhausen
Rick Baker
Rob Bottin
Tom Savini

Quality Check:
Classics
Disney Animated Movies
Disney Family Movies
4 Bones
Letterboxed Editions
Modern Shakespeare
Trash
Woofs!

Rip-Offs:
Alien & Rip-Offs
E.T. & Rip-Offs
Gremlins & Rip-Offs
Road Warrior & Rip-Offs

Miscellaneous:
Amy Fisher
Live Action/Animation Combos
Top Grossing Films of 1939-1992

Adapted from a Book

Abduction
About Last Night...
Absolute Beginners
Accident
The Accidental Tourist
Acorn People
Across the Pacific
Act of Passion: The Lost Honor of Kathryn Beck
Adam Had Four Sons
Adorable Julia
The Adventurers
The Adventures of Huck Finn
The Adventures of Huckleberry Finn
The Adventures of Robin Hood
The Adventures of Sadie
The Adventures of Sherlock Holmes: Hound of the Baskervilles
The Adventures of Tom Sawyer
Advise and Consent
The African Queen
After Dark, My Sweet
After Julius
After the Thin Man
The Agency
The Agony and the Ecstasy
Airport
Alan & Naomi
Alice
Alice Adams
Alice in Wonderland
Alice Through the Looking Glass
Alice to Nowhere
Alive
All About Eve
All Creatures Great and Small
All of Me
All Quiet on the Western Front
All the King's Men
All the President's Men
All This and Heaven Too
Allan Quartermain and the Lost City of Gold
Altered States
Amazing Mr. Blunden
The Ambassador
The Ambush Murders

The Americanization of Emily
The Amityville Horror
The Amorous Adventures of Moll Flanders
Anastasia: The Mystery of Anna
Anatomy of a Murder
And Then There Were None
The Anderson Tapes
The Andersonville Trial
The Andromeda Strain
An Angel at My Table
Angel Heart
Angele
Angels with Dirty Faces
Animal Farm
Ann Vickers
Anna Karenina
Anna to the Infinite Power
Anne of Avonlea
Anne of Green Gables
Anthony Adverse
Anzio
Aphrodite
Apocalypse Now
Appointment with Death
The Apprenticeship of Duddy Kravitz
Arch of Triumph
Are You in the House Alone?
Around the World in 80 Days
The Arrangement
Arrowsmith
As Summers Die
Ashes and Diamonds
The Asphalt Jungle
The Assault
At Play in the Fields of the Lord
At Sword's Point
At the Earth's Core
The Atonement of Gosta Berling
The Attic: The Hiding of Anne Frank
Attica
Audrey Rose
Auntie Mame
The Autobiography of Miss Jane Pittman
Avalanche Express
Awakenings
The Bachelor
Back Street
Background to Danger

Bad Day at Black Rock
Bad Ronald
Bambi
Bang the Drum Slowly
Bank Shot
Barabbas
Barbarians at the Gate
Barry Lyndon
The Bastard
The Bat
The Bat Whispers
Battle Beyond the Stars
Battle Cry
The Bawdy Adventures of Tom Jones
Beachcomber
Beaches
The Bear
The Beast Within
Beau Geste
Being There
The Bell Jar
Ben-Hur
Berlin Alexanderplatz
Bernice Bobs Her Hair
The Best Years of Our Lives
Betrayal
The Betsy
Between Friends
Beulah Land
Beyond Innocence
Bhowani Junction
The Bicycle Thief
The Big Fix
The Big Man: Crossing the Line
The Big Sky
The Big Sleep
Big Street
Billionaire Boys Club
Billy Bathgate
Billy Budd
Birdy
The Birth of a Nation
The Bitch
Black Arrow
Black Like Me
The Black Marble
Black Narcissus
Black Robe
The Black Stallion
The Black Stallion Returns
Black Sunday
Blackboard Jungle
Blade Runner

Bless the Beasts and Children
Blockhouse
Blood and Roses
Blood and Sand
Blood Island
The Blood of Others
Blood on the Moon
Blue City
The Blue Max
The Body in the Library
Body Parts
The Body Snatcher
The Bonfire of the Vanities
Bonjour Tristesse
Book of Love
Born Free
Born on the Fourth of July
Borsalino
The Boston Strangler
Botany Bay
The Bourne Identity
Boxcar Bertha
The Boys from Brazil
Bram Stoker's Dracula
Breakheart Pass
Brewster's Millions
The Bride of Frankenstein
The Bridge of San Luis Rey
The Bridge on the River Kwai
The Bridges at Toko-Ri
A Brief History of Time
Bright Lights, Big City
Brighton Rock
Bringing Up Baby
The Brothers Karamazov
Buddy's Song
Bugsy
Bulldog Drummond
Bulldog Drummond's Secret Police
Bullitt
A Bunny's Tale
The Burning Hills
Butterfield 8
Butterfly Ball
Cadence
Camelot
Camille
Cancel My Reservation
Candide
Cannery Row
A Canterbury Tale
The Canterbury Tales
The Canterville Ghost
Cape Fear

Captain Blood
The Captain from Koepenick
Captain Horatio Hornblower
Captain Newman, M.D.
Captains Courageous
The Cardinal
Caroline?
The Carpetbaggers
Carrie
The Case of the Missing Lady
Casino Royale
Cass Timberlane
The Castle
Cat Chaser
Catch-22
Catholics
Catlow
Celebrity
Chamber of Horrors
Champion
Chapayev
Charlotte's Web
Charly
Cheech and Chong's, The Corsican Brothers
Cheers for Miss Bishop
Cheyenne Autumn
Child of Darkness, Child of Light
The Children
Children of Sanchez
Children of the Corn
Children of the Damned
Chilly Scenes of Winter
China Cry
China Seas
China Sky
Chitty Chitty Bang Bang
The Chocolate War
The Choirboys
Christ Stopped at Eboli
Christine
A Christmas Carol
The Christmas Wife
The Chronicles of Narnia
Cinderella
Circle of Two
The Citadel
Citizen Cohn
The City and the Dogs
City of Joy
Civil War Diary
The Clan of the Cave Bear
The Class of Miss MacMichael
The Clergyman's Daughter

Adapted

A Clockwork Orange
Closely Watched Trains
Cold Heaven
Cold Room
The Collector
Colonel Wolodyjowski
The Color Purple
Colossus: The Forbin Project
Columbo: Prescription Murder
Coma
Come Along with Me
Come and Get It
The Comedians
The Comfort of Strangers
Commandos Strike at Dawn
Communion
Compromising Positions
Conagher
Confidentially Yours
A Connecticut Yankee
A Connecticut Yankee in King
   Arthur's Court
Conrack
Consenting Adults
Conspirator
Contempt
Cool Hand Luke
Cop
The Corsican Brothers
Cotton Comes to Harlem
Count Dracula
The Count of Monte Cristo
Coup de Grace
The Courtship of Eddie's
   Father
The Crackler
The Cradle Will Fall
Crainquebille
Crazy in Love
Crime and Punishment
Crimes at the Dark House
Crisis at Central High
Crooked Hearts
Crossing Delancey
The Crucifer of Blood
Crusoe
A Cry for Love
A Cry in the Dark
A Cry in the Night
Cry, the Beloved Country
Cthulhu Mansion
Cujo
The Curse of Frankenstein
Curse of the Demon
Curse of the Headless
   Horseman
Curse of the Yellow Snake
Cyrano de Bergerac
Dad
Daddy Long Legs
The Dain Curse
Damage
Dances with Wolves
Dandy in Aspic
Dangerous Liaisons
Daniel
Dark Age
The Dark Angel
The Dark Half
The Dark Hour
The Dark Secret of Harvest
   Home
Das Boot
David
David and Lisa
David Copperfield
The Day of the Jackal
The Day of the Locust
Day of the Triffids
Dead Calm
Dead Eyes of London
Dead Lucky
Dead Ringers
Dead Solid Perfect
Dead Zone
Deadline at Dawn

Dear Boys
Death Be Not Proud
Death Dreams
Death in Venice
The Death of Richie
Death on the Nile
Death Race 2000
Decoration Day
The Deerslayer
The Deliberate Stranger
Deliverance
Delusions of Grandeur
Dempsey
Desert Bloom
Desert Gold
Desiree
Despair
Desperate Hours
The Detective
The Devil & Daniel Webster
Devil in the Flesh
The Devils
Diamond Head
Diamonds are Forever
Diane
Diary of a Chambermaid
Diary of a Lost Girl
Die Hard
Die Hard 2: Die Harder
Die, Monster, Die!
A Different Kind of Love
Diggstown
Dirty Gertie from Harlem
   U.S.A.
Doc Savage
The Doctor
Doctor Doolittle
Doctor Faustus
Dr. Jekyll and Mr. Hyde
Dr. No
Dr. Seuss' Grinch Grinches
   the Cat in the Hat/Pontoffel
   Pock
Dr. Strangelove, or: How I
   Learned to Stop Worrying
   and Love the Bomb
Doctor Zhivago
Doctors' Wives
Dodsworth
The Dogs of War
The Dollmaker
Don Quixote
Donovan's Brain
Don't Look Back: The Story of
   Leroy "Satchel" Paige
Don't Look Now
Don't Tell Her It's Me
Dorian Gray
Double Indemnity
The Double Negative
Down and Out in Beverly Hills
Dracula
Dracula (Spanish Version)
Dragon: The Bruce Lee Story
A Dream of Kings
Dress Gray
Dressed to Kill
Driver's Seat
The Drowning Pool
Drugstore Cowboy
Drums Along the Mohawk
Dubarry
Dude Ranger
Duel in the Sun
Duel of Hearts
The Duellists
Dune
The Dunwich Horror
Dusty
The Dybbuk
Dynasty
The Eagle Has Landed
East of Eden
East Side, West Side
Easy Living
Ebony Tower

Echo Murders
Echoes in the Darkness
Edge of Darkness
The Education of Sonny
   Carson
Effi Briest
Egg and I
The Eiger Sanction
Eight Men Out
8 Million Ways to Die
El Amor Brujo
Eleanor & Franklin
Eleni
Elmer Gantry
The Elusive Pimpernel
Emil and the Detective
Empire of the Ants
Empire of the Sun
Empty Canvas
Enchanted April
Enchanted Island
Encore
End of August
End of Desire
End of the Road
Endless Love
Endless Night
Endplay
Enemies, a Love Story
Enola Gay: The Men, the
   Mission, the Atomic Bomb
Enormous Changes
Enter Laughing
Erendira
Eric
Escape Me Never
Escape to Witch Mountain
Ethan Frome
Eureka!
The Europeans
Everybody's All American
Everything You Always
   Wanted to Know About
   Sex (But Were Afraid to
   Ask)
The Evil That Men Do
Evil Under the Sun
The Execution of Private
   Slovik
The Executioner's Song
Exodus
Extremities
Eye of the Needle
Eyes Right!
Fahrenheit 451
The Fall of the House of Usher
False Witness
Fanny
Far from the Madding Crowd
A Far Off Place
The Far Pavilions
Farewell, My Lovely
A Farewell to Arms
Fatal Vision
Father Figure
Father of the Bride
Faust
Fellini Satyricon
Field of Dreams
52 Pick-Up
The Fighting Prince of
   Donegal
A Fine Madness
Fine Things
Finessing the King
The Fire in the Stone
The Fire Within
Firestarter
The Firm
The First Deadly Sin
Fitzcarraldo
Five Card Stud
The Five of Me
Five Weeks in a Balloon
The Flame is Love
A Flash of Green

Fletch
Fletch Lives
Flowers in the Attic
Follow That Dream
Food of the Gods: Part 2
For Us, the Living
For Your Eyes Only
Forbidden
Forbidden Passion: The Oscar
   Wilde Movie
Ford: The Man & the Machine
Foreign Affairs
Forever
Forlorn River
The Formula
Fortunes of War
Forty Days of Musa Dagh
The Fountainhead
Four Daughters
The Four Feathers
The Four Horsemen of the
   Apocalypse
The Fourth Protocol
The Franchise Affair
Frankenstein
Frankenstein Unbound
Freaky Friday
Freedom Road
The French Lieutenant's
   Woman
Fried Green Tomatoes
Friendly Persuasion
From Beyond
From the Dead of Night
From the Earth to the Moon
From the Terrace
Fulfillment
Full Metal Jacket
Gabriela
Gal Young 'Un
Gas Food Lodging
General Della Rovere
A Generation
Georgia, Georgia
Georgy Girl
Gervaise
The Getaway
Getting It Right
The Getting of Wisdom
The Ghost and Mrs. Muir
Ghost Story
Giant
Gideon's Trumpet
Gidget
Gigi
Girl Hunters
The Girl in a Swing
Girl in His Pocket
A Girl of the Limberlost
The Girl Who Had Everything
The Glass Key
Glitz
Glory
Gnome-Mobile
Gnomes
Go Tell the Spartans
The Goalie's Anxiety at the
   Penalty Kick
The Godfather
The Godfather 1902-1959:
   The Complete Epic
The Godfather, Part 2
The Godfather, Part 3
God's Little Acre
Golden Demon
The Golden Honeymoon
Golden Rendezvous
The Golden Salamander
Gone with the Wind
The Good Mother
Goodbye Again
Goodbye Columbus
Goodbye, Mr. Chips
Goodbye, My Lady
Goodfellas
Gorky Park

The Graduate
Grambling's White Tiger
Grand Hotel
Grand Isle
The Grapes of Wrath
The Grass is Always Greener
   Over the Septic Tank
Grave of the Fireflies
Graveyard Shift
The Great Escape
Great Expectations
The Great Gabbo
The Great Gatsby
The Great Mouse Detective
The Great Santini
The Great Train Robbery
Greed
The Green Berets
Green Dolphin Street
Green Fields
The Green Man
The Green Room
The Grifters
The Groundstar Conspiracy
The Group
Guadalcanal Diary
The Guardian
A Guide for the Married Man
Gulliver's Travels
The Guns of Navarone
Hail, Hero!
Half a Sixpence
Half Moon Street
The Handmaid's Tale
Hands of a Stranger
The Hands of Orlac
The Happiest Millionaire
Hard Traveling
The Harder They Fall
Harrad Experiment
Harvest
The Haunted Palace
Haunted Summer
Haunted: The Ferryman
The Haunting
The Haunting of Barney
   Palmer
Hawaii
Hazel's People
The Heart is a Lonely Hunter
Heartburn
Hearts & Armour
Heat
Heat and Dust
Heidi
The Heiress
Heller in Pink Tights
Hellraiser 3: Hell on Earth
Helltown
Helter Skelter
A Hero Ain't Nothin' But a
   Sandwich
The Hideaways
The Hiding Place
High & Low
High Sierra
Hiroshima, Mon Amour
His Fighting Blood
The Hitchhiker's Guide to the
   Galaxy
The Hobbit
The Holcroft Covenant
Hollow Triumph
Hombre
The Home and the World
Homecoming: A Christmas
   Story
Honor Thy Father
Hook
Hoppy Serves a Writ
The Horror of Dracula
The Horse's Mouth
Hostage
The Hot Rock
Hotel
Hotel du Lac

Adapted

Transmutations
Transport from Paradise
Treasure Island
Treasure of the Sierra Madre
A Tree Grows in Brooklyn
Trespasser
The Trial
Triple Cross
Tristana
The Triumph of Sherlock Holmes
Trojan Women
Tropic of Desire
True Confessions
True Grit
True West
Tune in Tomorrow
Tunes of Glory
The 27 Day
29th Street
20,000 Leagues Under the Sea
Twice-Told Tales
Twilight's Last Gleaming
Two English Girls
Two Kinds of Love
2001: A Space Odyssey
2010: The Year We Make Contact
Two to Tango
The Two Worlds of Jenny Logan
Ugetsu
The Ugly American
Ulysses
The Unbearable Lightness of Being
The Unbreakable Alibi
Uncle Moses
Uncle Tom's Cabin
Under Capricorn
Under Satan's Sun
Under the Volcano
Underworld
Uneasy Terms
The Unnamable
The Unsinkable Molly Brown
Unsuitable Job for a Woman
Until They Sail
Up the Down Staircase
Users
Valley of the Dolls
Valmont
The Vampire Lovers
Vampyr
The Vanishing
Vanity Fair
A Very Old Man with Enormous Wings
Village of the Damned
Village of the Giants
The Violent Men
The Virgin and the Gypsy
The Virgin Soldiers
The Virginian
Vision Quest
Viva Zapata!
Voyage of the Damned
Voyager
Wages of Fear
Wagon Wheels
Walk on the Wild Side
Walking on Air
Wanderers
War & Love
War and Peace
War & Remembrance, Part 1
War & Remembrance, Part 2
War & Remembrance, Part 3
War & Remembrance, Part 4
War & Remembrance, Part 5
War & Remembrance, Part 6
War & Remembrance, Part 7
War & Remembrance: The Final Chapter, Part 8

War & Remembrance: The Final Chapter, Part 9
War & Remembrance: The Final Chapter, Part 10
War & Remembrance: The Final Chapter, Part 11
War & Remembrance: The Final Chapter, Part 12
War Between the Tates
War Lover
The War of the Worlds
The War Wagon
Warlock
Warriors of the Sung Dynasty
Watchers
Waterland
Watership Down
The Way We Were
The Way West
We the Living
We Think the World of You
Whale for the Killing
What Price Hollywood?
What's Love Got to Do With It?
When the Bough Breaks
When the West Was Young
When the Wind Blows
Where Angels Fear to Tread
Where Are the Children?
Where the Buffalo Roam
Where the Lilies Bloom
Where the Red Fern Grows
Where the Red Fern Grows: Part 2
Where Time Began
Where's Poppa?
Whispers
Whistle Down the Wind
White Fang
White Fang and the Hunter
White Hot: The Mysterious Murder of Thelma Todd
White Lie
White Nights
Who Am I This Time?
Who Framed Roger Rabbit?
Who is Killing the Great Chefs of Europe?
Who'll Stop the Rain?
Why Shoot the Teacher
The Wicked Lady
The Widow
The Wild Country
Wild Times
Wildflower
Will: G. Gordon Liddy
Windom's Way
The Winds of Jarrah
Winter People
Wise Blood
The Witches of Eastwick
Without Reservations
Without Warning: The James Brady Story
Witness for the Prosecution
The Wizard of Loneliness
The Wizard of Oz
Wolf Call
Wolfen
A Woman Called Moses
Woman in the Shadows
A Woman of Substance, Episode 1: Nest of Vipers
A Woman of Substance, Episode 2: The Secret is Revealed
A Woman of Substance, Episode 3: Fighting for the Dream
A Woman Rebels
Women in Love
Wooden Horse
Words by Heart
The World According to Garp

The World is Full of Married Men
The World of Apu
World of Henry Orient
A World of Strangers
The World Owes Me a Living
The Wreck of the Mary Deare
The Wrong Box
The Wrong Move
Wuthering Heights
A Year in Provence
Year of the Dragon
The Yearling
Yentl
Yesterday's Hero
You Only Live Twice
Young at Heart
The Young in Heart
Young Lady Chatterly 2
Young Man with a Horn
Young Winston
Your Ticket Is No Longer Valid
Zandy's Bride
Zatoichi: Master Ichi and a Chest of Gold
Zotzl

Adapted from a Cartoon

The Addams Family
Adventures of Captain Marvel
Adventures of Red Ryder
Adventures of Smilin' Jack
The Amazing Spider-Man
Annie
Asterix vs. Caesar
Batman Returns
The Belles of St. Trinian's
Big Zapper
Brenda Starr
Captain America
Dennis the Menace
Dick Tracy
Dick Tracy vs. Cueball
Dick Tracy's Dilomma
Dr. Strange
Fatty Finn
The Flash
Flash Gordon
Friday Foster
Great St. Trinian's Train Robbery
The Guyver
Hillbilly Blitzkrieg
Howard the Duck
The Incredible Hulk
Kowloon Assignment
Li'l Abner
Little Nemo: Adventures in Slumberland
Little Orphan Annie
Los Caciques
The Perils of Gwendoline
Petit Con
Prince Valiant
The Pure Hell of St. Trinian's
Reg'lar Fellers
The Return of Swamp Thing
The Sad Sack
Superman: The Movie
Superman 2
Superman 3
Superman: The Complete Cartoon Collection
Tales from the Crypt
Teenage Mutant Ninja Turtles: The Movie
Teenage Mutant Ninja Turtles 2: The Secret of the Ooze
Teenage Mutant Ninja Turtles 3
Tom and Jerry: The Movie
Vault of Horror
Wild Palms

The Wild World of Batwoman

Adapted from a Fairy Tale

Adventures of Prince Achmed
Aladdin
Aladdin and His Wonderful Lamp
Alice in Wonderland
Alice's Adventures in Wonderland
Beauty and the Beast
The Boy Who Left Home to Find Out About the Shivers
Butterfly Ball
Cannon Movie Tales: Red Riding Hood
Cannon Movie Tales: Sleeping Beauty
Cannon Movie Tales: Snow White
Cannon Movie Tales: The Emperor's New Clothes
Casey at the Bat
Cinderella
Cinderella/Thumbelina
Cinderella 2000
Cinderfella
The Company of Wolves
The Dancing Princesses
Deadtime Stories
Donkey Skin
Dos Cruces en Danger Pass
Elle Voit des Nains Partout
The Emperor's New Clothes
The Erotic Adventures of Pinocchio
The Fables of Harry Allard Fairytales
Flower Angel
Frog
Fun & Fancy Free
The Glass Slipper
Golden Tales and Legends
Goldilocks & the Three Bears
Hans Christian Andersen
Hansel and Gretel
Happily Ever After
Hello
A Hungarian Fairy Tale
Irish Cinderella
Jack & the Beanstalk
La Petite Sirene
Les Visiteurs du Soir
The Little Match Girl
The Little Mermaid
Little Red Riding Hood
The Magic Fountain
The Magic Legend of the Golden Goose
The Magic Sword
Magical Wonderland
March of the Wooden Soldiers
Mr. Magoo's Storybook
Mother Goose Rock 'n' Rhyme
The NeverEnding Story
The Nightingale
Nutcracker, A Fantasy on Ice
The Nutcracker Prince
Nutcracker: The Motion Picture
Once Upon a Brothers Grimm
Peter and the Wolf and Other Tales
Peter Pan
Pied Piper of Hamelin
The Pied Piper of Hamelin
Pinocchio
Pinocchio's Storybook Adventures
The Princess and the Pea
The Princess and the Swineherd

The Princess Bride
Princess Cinderella
The Princess Who Never Laughed
Puss 'n Boots
Rapunzel
Red Riding Hood
The Red Shoes
Rip van Winkle
Rub a Dub Dub
Rudyard Kipling's Classic Stories
Rumpelstiltskin
The Scalawag Bunch
Sleeping Beauty
Snow Queen
The Snow Queen
Snow Queen
Snow White and the Seven Dwarfs
Snow White and the Three Stooges
Sorcerer's Apprentice
Storytime Classics
The Swan
Swans
The Tale of the Frog Prince
The Three Little Pigs
Thumbelina
tom thumb
The Wacky World of Mother Goose
Who Slew Auntie Roo?
The Wind in the Willows
The Wishmaker
The Witches
Wonderful World of the Brothers Grimm
The Wonders of Aladdin

Adapted from a Game

Clue
Super Mario Bros.
Tag: The Assassination Game

Adapted from a Play or Musical

Abe Lincoln in Illinois
The Adventures of Robin Hood
Age Old Friends
Agnes of God
Ah, Wilderness!
Alfie
Alice
All My Sons
Amadeus
Anastasia
Animal Crackers
The Animal Kingdom
Anna Christie
Annie
Another Country
Any Wednesday
Arsenic and Old Lace
As Is
As You Desire Me
As You Like It
The Avenger
The Awful Truth
Babes in Arms
Babes in Toyland
Baby Doll
Baby, the Rain Must Fall
The Bacchantes
The Bad Seed
The Balcony
The Ballad of the Sad Cafe
Barefoot in the Park
Beatlemania! The Movie
Beau Brummel

Adapted

A Taste of Honey
Tea and Sympathy
Tea for Two
The Teahouse of the August Moon
The Tempest
The Terror
That Championship Season
That's Singing: The Best of Broadway
There's a Girl in My Soup
These Three
They Knew What They Wanted
This Happy Breed
This is the Army
This Property is Condemned
Thoroughly Modern Millie
Those Endearing Young Charms
A Thousand Clowns
Three Men on a Horse
The Three Penny Opera
The Threepenny Opera
Throne of Blood
Tidy Endings
Time Lock
The Time of Your Life
Too Many Girls
Topaze
Torch Song Trilogy
Tough Guy
Toys in the Attic
The Tragedy of King Richard II
The Trip to Bountiful
Troilus & Cressida
The Tunnel of Love
Twelfth Night
Twelve Angry Men
Two Can Play
Two for the Seesaw
Ubu and the Great Gidouille
The Unapproachable
Under Milk Wood
Under the Biltmore Clock
An Unfinished Piece for a Player Piano
Velnio Nuotaka (The Devil's Bride)
Volpone
A Voyage' Round My Father
Wait Until Dark
The War Lord
Watch on the Rhine
Weekend at the Waldorf
We're No Angels
West Side Story
Whales of August
Where Were You When the Lights Went Out?
Whoopee!
Who's Afraid of Virginia Woolf?
Whose Life Is It Anyway?
The Wild Duck
Window Shopping
The Winslow Boy
Winterset
Without Love
The Wiz
The Women
Woyzeck
Woza Albert!
You Can't Take It with You
Young & Willing
You're a Good Man, Charlie Brown
Zoot Suit

Adapted from a Poem

Casey at the Bat
Gunga Din
The Man from Snowy River

Old Ironsides
The Set-Up
Ulysses
The White Cliffs of Dover
Wild Party

Adapted from a Song

Alice's Restaurant
The Baron and the Kid
Born in East L.A.
Convoy
Coward of the County
Frankie and Johnny
Girls Just Want to Have Fun
The Indian Runner
Kenny Rogers as the Gambler
Kenny Rogers as the Gambler, Part 2: The Adventure Continues
Kenny Rogers as the Gambler, Part 3: The Legend Continues
Love Potion #9
My Darlin' Clementine
The Night the Lights Went Out in Georgia
Ode to Billy Joe
Purple People Eater
Single Bars, Single Women
Take This Job & Shove It
Yellow Submarine
You Light Up My Life

Adapted from a Story

ABC Stage 67: Truman Capote's A Christmas Memory
The Adventures of Ichabod and Mr. Toad
The Affair of the Pink Pearl
Alice in Wonderland
Ambassador Bill
Androcles and the Lion
Appointment with Crime
Arizona Bushwackers
As Young As You Feel
The Assassination Bureau
Babette's Feast
The Ballad of the Sad Cafe
Bartleby
The Birds
The Black Abbot
Black Cat
Blackmail
A Boy and His Dog
Breakfast at Tiffany's
Bright Angel
By the Light of the Silvery Moon
Call of the Wild
The Canterville Ghost
Carmilla
Casanova's Big Night
Cat's Eye
Caught in the Draft
Cinderella
Cinderella 2000
College Swing
Country Lovers, City Lovers
Creature with the Blue Hand
Cricket on the Hearth
Dark Eyes
Daughter of the Dragon
David and Bathsheba
A Day in the Country
The Dead
The Decameron
Decameron Nights
Diary of a Madman

The Displaced Person
Dive Bomber
Dr. Seuss' Halloween Is Grinch Night
Door with the Seven Locks
Double Vision
D.P.
The Dropkick
Eat a Bowl of Tea
The Eyes of the Amaryllis
Eyes of the Panther
A Face in the Crowd
Face to Face
The Fighter
Fighting Caravans
Five Days One Summer
The 5000 Fingers of Dr. T
Flirtation Walk
Forger of London
Gangway
Ghost Valley
The Gift of Love
The Glass House
Great Adventure
Gunfight at the O.K. Corral
Guys and Dolls
The Hard Way
Haunting Fear
The Haunting of Morella
Homecoming
Hostile Guns
The House of Usher
How the Grinch Stole Christmas
I'm a Fool
Importance of Being Earnest
The Incredible Sarah
The Indian Scarf
Isle of Forgotten Sins
It's a Date
It's a Dog's Life
Jigsaw
Johnny Eager
Johnny Reno
Jonathan Livingston Seagull
Jungle Book
Kaos
Kim
Kurt Vonnegut's Monkey House
La Chute de la Maison Usher
La Jetee/An Occurrence at Owl Creek Bridge
Lady Killer
The Lady with the Dog
The Lady's Maid's Bell
Late Chrysanthemums
The Lawnmower Man
The Lawrenceville Stories
Le Plaisir
Life on a String
The Little Prince
Love on the Run
The Magic Fountain
The Magic Legend of the Golden Goose
The Magnificent Dope
Main Street to Broadway
Manfish
Marty
Masque of the Red Death
Maximum Overdrive
Mr. Reeder in Room 13
The Most Dangerous Game
Murders in the Rue Morgue
The Murders in the Rue Morgue
My Apprenticeship
My Childhood
My Favorite Blonde
My Mother's Castle
My Universities
The Mysterious Magician
Mystic Circle Murder
Naked Jungle
Nightfall

Nightflyers
No Comebacks
Noon Wine
O Youth and Beauty
Objective, Burma!
The Oblong Box
O.C. and Stiggs
An Occurrence at Owl Creek Bridge
An Occurrence at Owl Creek Bridge/Coup de Grace
On Moonlight Bay
Our Modern Maidens
Our Relations
The Oval Portrait
Paul's Case
Peck's Bad Boy
Peter and the Wolf and Other Tales
The Pied Piper of Hamelin
The Pit and the Pendulum
The Pit & the Pendulum
Play Misty for Me
Pocketful of Miracles
The Possessed
Premature Burial
The Prince and the Pauper
The Princess and the Swineherd
Pudd'nhead Wilson
The Queen of Spades
Quest for Love
Rappaccini's Daughter
Rawhead Rex
Red Balloon/Occurrence at Owl Creek Bridge
The Red Shoes
The Reluctant Dragon
Richie
Ridin' the Lone Trail
Robbers of the Sacred Mountain
Rocket to the Moon
Roman Holiday
Roommate
The Ruggles of Red Gap
Rumpelstiltskin
Sabotage
Salome
Saturday Night Fever
Secret of the Black Trunk
Seven Brides for Seven Brothers
Shadow of a Doubt
Shadow of the Thin Man
Shinbone Alley
The Skull
The Sky is Gray
Sleep of Death
Sleeping Car to Trieste
Smooth Talk
Snow Queen
The Snow Queen
Snow Queen
Snow White and the Seven Dwarfs
The Snows of Kilimanjaro
Somewhere I'll Find You
Song of the Thin Man
Sorrows of Gin
Sorry, Wrong Number
The Southerner
The Spectre of Edgar Allen Poe
Stagecoach
Station West
The Strange Countess
A Summer Story
Swans
Swimmer
Tales from the Darkside: The Movie
Tales of Terror
Tales of the Klondike: In a Far Country

Tales of the Klondike: Race for Number One
Tales of the Klondike: The Scorn of Women
Tales of the Klondike: The Unexpected
The Tell-Tale Heart
Tennessee's Partner
The Thin Man
The Thin Man Goes Home
Three Brothers
The Three Little Pigs
Tomb of Ligeia
Torture Garden
Torture Ship
Trio
Tropical Heat
Twelve Chairs
Two by Forsyth
Two Evil Eyes
Vanina Vanini
Ward Six
Wee Willie Winkie
Who Slew Auntie Roo?
Who's the Man?
The Wind in the Willows
The Window
A Woman Without Love
Women & Men: Stories of Seduction
Women & Men: Stories of Seduction, Part 2
Young at Heart

Adapted from an Article

All Mine to Give
Christiane F.
The Last American Hero
Olivier, Olivier
Streetwise

Adapted from an Opera

Carmen
Carmen Jones
Gypsy Blood
The Magic Flute
Otello

Adapted from Memoirs or Diaries

Celeste
Churchill and the Generals
Danger UXB
The Diary of Anne Frank
The Elegant Criminal
The Flame Trees of Thika
A Free Soul
The Gathering Storm
Gypsy
The Happy Hooker
The Happy Hooker Goes Hollywood
The Happy Hooker Goes to Washington
Heart Beat
Heartland
Henry & June
I Remember Mama
I'll Cry Tomorrow
I'm Dancing as Fast as I Can
Inside the Third Reich
Julia
Meetings with Remarkable Men
Mommie Dearest
Sister Kenny
Stars and Stripes Forever
This Boy's Life

Adapted

What's Love Got to Do With
It?
Wish You Were Here

Adapted from Television

The Addams Family
Boris and Natasha: The Movie
Coneheads
Cooley High
The Crawling Eye
Days of Wine and Roses
Dennis the Menace
The Fugitive
Gunfight at Sandoval
The Key to Rebecca
The Left-Handed Gun
The Naked Gun: From the
Files of Police Squad
Naked Gun 2 1/2: The Smell
of Fear
The Nude Bomb
One Night Stand
Pennies From Heaven
The People Next Door
Queen for a Day
The Saint
Sergeant Ryker
The Untouchables
Wackiest Wagon Train in the
West
Wayne's World

Adapted from the Radio

Big Town
Check & Double Check
Cosmo Jones, Crime Smasher
The Devil's Eye
Dreaming Out Loud
Gang Busters
Gangbusters
Going to Town
Goon Movie
The Great Gildersleeve
Here We Go Again!
Inner Sanctum
International Crime
The Invisible Avenger
Mr. Arkadin
My Friend Irma
Queen for a Day
Renfrew of the Royal
Mounted
The Shadow Strikes
Sorry, Wrong Number
Treacherous Crossing
The War of the Worlds

"Alien" & Rip-Offs

Alien
Alien 3
Alien Prey
Alien Seed
Alien Space Avenger
Aliens
Creature
Deep Space
Deepstar Six
Forbidden World
Galaxy of Terror
Horror Planet
Leviathan
Nightflyers
Predator
Star Crystal
Xtro 2: The Second Encounter

Amy Fisher

The Amy Fisher Story

Casualities of Love: The
"Long Island Lolita" Story
Lethal Lolita—Amy Fisher: My
Story

BBC TV Productions

And a Nightingale Sang
And Now for Something
Completely Different
Candide
Christabel
The Chronicles of Narnia
Danger Man
The Dark Angel
Doctor Who: Cybermen—The
Early Years
Doctor Who: Earthshock
Doctor Who: Shada
Doctor Who: The Caves of
Androzani
Doctor Who: The Curse of
Fenric
Doctor Who: The Five Doctors
Doctor Who: The Hartnell
Years
Doctor Who: The Pertwee
Years
Doctor Who: The Seeds of
Death
Doctor Who: The Talons of
Weng-Chiang
Doctor Who: The Three
Doctors
Doctor Who: The Tom Baker
Years
Doctor Who: The Troughton
Years
Doctor Who: The Twin
Dilemma
Doctor Who: The War Games
Doctor Who: Tomb of the
Cyberman
Edge of Darkness
The Flame Trees of Thika
Fortunes of War
The Hitchhiker's Guide to the
Galaxy
The Lost Language of Cranes
Mansfield Park
Maria's Child
Richard II
Richard III
Robin Hood...The Legend:
Herne's Son
Robin Hood...The Legend:
Robin Hood and the
Sorcerer
Robin Hood...The Legend:
The Swords of Wayland
Robin Hood...The Legend:
The Time of the Wolf
Romeo and Juliet
School for Scandal
The Secret Garden
Sense & Sensibility
Shadowlands
Six Wives of Henry VIII
A Tale of Two Cities
A Year in Provence

Books to Film: Agatha Christie

The Affair of the Pink Pearl
The Alphabet Murders
And Then There Were None
Appointment with Death
The Body in the Library
The Case of the Missing Lady
The Clergyman's Daughter
The Crackler
Death on the Nile

Endless Night
Evil Under the Sun
Finessing the King
The House of Lurking Death
Love from a Stranger
The Man in the Mist
The Mirror Crack'd
Murder Ahoy
Murder at the Gallop
A Murder is Announced
Murder Most Foul
Murder on the Orient Express
Murder She Said
Ordeal by Innocence
A Pocketful of Rye
The Secret Adversary
Ten Little Indians
The Unbreakable Alibi
Witness for the Prosecution

Books to Film: Alex Haley

Malcolm X
Roots
Roots: The Gift
Roots: The Next Generation

Books to Film: Alexandre Dumas

At Sword's Point
Black Magic
Camille
The Corsican Brothers
The Count of Monte Cristo
The Four Musketeers
The Iron Mask
The Man in the Iron Mask
Mountain Fury
The Prince of Thieves
Robin Hood
Sword of Monte Cristo
The Three Musketeers
Three Musketeers

Books to Film: Alice Walker

The Color Purple

Books to Film: Alistair MacLean

Bear Island
Breakheart Pass
Caravan to Vaccares
Force 10 from Navarone
Golden Rendezvous
The Guns of Navarone
Ice Station Zebra
Puppet on a Chain
River of Death
Where Eagles Dare

Books to Film: Ambrose Bierce

Eyes of the Panther
La Jetee/An Occurrence at
Owl Creek Bridge
An Occurrence at Owl Creek
Bridge
An Occurrence at Owl Creek
Bridge/Coup de Grace
Red Balloon/Occurrence at
Owl Creek Bridge

Books to Film: Anton Chekhov

The Lady with the Dog

The Seagull
Ward Six

Books to Film: Arthur C. Clarke

2001: A Space Odyssey
2010: The Year We Make
Contact

Books to Film: Arthur Hailey

Airport
Hotel
Time Lock

Books to Film: Astrid Lindgren

The Land of Faraway
The New Adventures of Pippi
Longstocking
Pippi Goes on Board
Pippi in the South Seas
Pippi Longstocking
Pippi on the Run

Books to Film: Barbara Cartland

Duel of Hearts
The Flame is Love

Books to Film: Barbara Taylor Bradford

Hold the Dream
A Woman of Substance,
Episode 1: Nest of Vipers
A Woman of Substance,
Episode 2: The Secret is
Revealed
A Woman of Substance,
Episode 3: Fighting for the
Dream

Books to Film: Bram Stoker

Count Dracula
Dracula
Dracula (Spanish Version)
The Horror of Dracula
The Lair of the White Worm
Nosferatu
Tomb

Books to Film: Bret Easton Ellis

Less Than Zero

Books to Film: Charles Dickens

An American Christmas Carol
Bleak House
A Christmas Carol
Cricket on the Hearth
David Copperfield
Great Expectations
Great Expectations: The
Untold Story
Little Dorrit, Film 1: Nobody's
Fault
Little Dorrit, Film 2: Little
Dorrit's Story
Mr. Magoo's Christmas Carol
The Muppet Christmas Carol

Nicholas Nickleby
The Old Curiosity Shop
Oliver!
Oliver Twist
The Pickwick Papers
Scrooge
Stingiest Man in Town
A Tale of Two Cities
Tale of Two Cities/In the
Switch Tower

Books to Film: Clive Barker

Candyman
Hellbound: Hellraiser 2
Hellraiser
Hellraiser 3: Hell on Earth
Night Breed
Rawhead Rex
Transmutations
Underworld

Books to Film: Clive Cussler

Raise the Titanic

Books to Film: Colleen McCullough

An Indecent Obsession
The Thorn Birds
Tim

Books to Film: Daniel Defoe

The Amorous Adventures of
Moll Flanders
Crusoe
Man Friday
Robinson Crusoe

Books to Film: Danielle Steel

Fine Things
Now and Forever
The Promise

Books to Film: Daphne Du Maurier

The Birds
Don't Look Now
Jamaica Inn
Rebecca

Books to Film: Dashiell Hammett

After the Thin Man
The Dain Curse
Hammett
The Maltese Falcon
Satan Met a Lady
The Thin Man
Woman in the Shadows

Books to Film: Dean R. Koontz

Servants of Twilight
Watchers
Whispers

Books to Film: D.H. Lawrence

Kangaroo

Books

Classics

Queen Kelly
The Quiet Man
Raging Bull
Ran
Rashomon
Rebel Without a Cause
Red Dust
Red Headed Woman
The Red Pony
Red River
The Red Shoes
Revenge of the Zombies
Ride the High Country
The Rink
Rio Bravo
Romeo and Juliet
Rope
The Ruggles of Red Gap
The Rules of the Game
San Francisco
Sansho the Bailiff
Sawdust & Tinsel
The Scar
Scaramouche
The Scarlet Pimpernel
Scrooge
Seance on a Wet Afternoon
The Searchers
Seven Chances
Seven Samurai
Seven Sixgunners
The Seventh Seal
Shadow of a Doubt
Shane
She Done Him Wrong
She Wore a Yellow Ribbon
The Sheik
Shoeshine
Siegfried
Silk Stockings
The Sin of Madelon Claudet
Singin' in the Rain
The Single Standard
Sleeping Beauty
Sodom and Gomorrah
Son of the Sheik
The Sound of Music
Spies
Spite Marriage
The Spy Who Came in from
    the Cold
Stagecoach
A Star is Born
Star Wars
The Stars Look Down
Steamboat Bill, Jr.
Stella Dallas
Storm Over Asia
Strangers on a Train
Street of Shame
A Streetcar Named Desire
Strike
Student of Prague
A Sunday in the Country
Sunrise
Suspicion
Svengali
Sweet Smell of Success
Tabu: A Story of the South
    Seas
Tarzan, the Ape Man
The Ten Commandments
Ten Days That Shook the
    World
These Three
They Were Expendable
Thief of Baghdad
The Thin Man
The Thing
The Third Man
The Thirteenth Man
Thirty Seconds Over Tokyo
Three Charlies and One
    Phoney!
Three Musketeers
Three on a Match

Throne of Blood
Tin Star
The Tip-Off
To Have & Have Not
To Kill a Mockingbird
Tom Sawyer
Topper
Touch of Evil
Tramp & a Woman
Treasure of the Sierra Madre
True Heart Susie
Tumbleweeds
Twentieth Century
Ugetsu
Un Chien Andalou
Under the Roofs of Paris
The Vagabond
Vampyr
Variety
Vertigo
The Virginian
Wages of Fear
The War of the Worlds
Warning Shadows
Waxworks
Way Down East
Wedding March
West Side Story
Westfront 1918
When Ladies Meet
White Christmas
The White Zombie
The Wild Bunch
The Wild One
Wild Strawberries
The Wind
Wings
The Wizard of Oz
Woman in the Dunes
A Woman of Affairs
Woman of the Year
The World of Apu
Wuthering Heights
Yankee Doodle Dandy
The Yearling
Yojimbo
You Can't Cheat an Honest
    Man
Young Mr. Lincoln
Zero for Conduct
Zvenigora

Disney Animated Movies

Aladdin
Alice in Wonderland
Bambi
Beauty and the Beast
Cinderella
DuckTales the Movie:
    Treasure of the Lost Lamp
Dumbo
Fantasia
The Great Mouse Detective
The Jungle Book
Lady and the Tramp
The Little Mermaid
101 Dalmations
Peter Pan
Pinocchio
The Rescuers
The Rescuers Down Under
Robin Hood
Sleeping Beauty
Snow White and the Seven
    Dwarfs
The Sword in the Stone
The Three Caballeros

Disney Family Movies

The Absent-Minded Professor

The Adventures of Bullwhip
    Griffin
The Adventures of Huck Finn
The Adventures of Ichabod
    and Mr. Toad
Almost Angels
Amy
The Apple Dumpling Gang
The Apple Dumpling Gang
    Rides Again
Babes in Toyland
The Barefoot Executive
The Bears & I
Bedknobs and Broomsticks
Benji the Hunted
Big Red
Black Arrow
The Black Arrow
The Black Hole
Blackbeard's Ghost
The Blue Yonder
Bon Voyage!
Born to Run
Breakin' Through
Candleshoe
The Castaway Cowboy
The Cat from Outer Space
Charley and the Angel
Charlie, the Lonesome Cougar
Cheetah
Child of Glass
The Computer Wore Tennis
    Shoes
Condorman
Darby O'Gill & the Little
    People
Davy Crockett and the River
    Pirates
Davy Crockett, King of the
    Wild Frontier
The Devil & Max Devlin
Diamonds on Wheels
Dr. Syn, Alias the Scarecrow
Emil and the Detective
Escapade in Florence
Escape to Witch Mountain
A Far Off Place
The Fighting Prince of
    Donegal
Flight of the Grey Wolf
Flight of the Navigator
Freaky Friday
Fun & Fancy Free
The Girl Who Spelled
    Freedom
Gnome-Mobile
Gone are the Days
The Great Locomotive Chase
Greyfriars Bobby
Gus
Herbie Goes Bananas
Herbie Goes to Monte Carlo
Herbie Rides Again
Homeward Bound: The
    Incredible Journey
Honey, I Blew Up the Kid
Honey, I Shrunk the Kids
The Horse in the Gray Flannel
    Suit
The Horse Without a Head
Horsemasters
Hot Lead & Cold Feet
In Search of the Castaways
The Incredible Journey
The Island at the Top of the
    World
Johnny Shiloh
Johnny Tremain & the Sons of
    Liberty
The Journey of Natty Gann
Justin Morgan Had a Horse
King of the Grizzlies
The Last Flight of Noah's Ark
Lt. Robin Crusoe, U.S.N.
The Light in the Forest
The Littlest Horse Thieves

The Littlest Outlaw
Lots of Luck
The Love Bug
Love Leads the Way
Mary Poppins
Menace on the Mountain
Mickey's Christmas Carol
Million Dollar Duck
Miracle Down Under
The Miracle of the White
    Stallions
The Misadventures of Merlin
    Jones
Monkeys, Go Home!
Monkey's Uncle
Moon Pilot
Moon-Spinners
Mooncussers
Mosby's Marauders
My Dog, the Thief
Napoleon and Samantha
Never a Dull Moment
Newsies
Night Crossing
Nikki, the Wild Dog of the
    North
The Nine Lives of Elfego Baca
No Deposit, No Return
The North Avenue Irregulars
Now You See Him, Now You
    Don't
Old Yeller
The One and Only, Genuine,
    Original Family Band
One Little Indian
One Magic Christmas
One of Our Dinosaurs Is
    Missing
The Parent Trap
Pete's Dragon
Pollyanna
Return from Witch Mountain
Return to Oz
Ride a Wild Pony
Rob Roy—The Highland
    Rogue
The Rocketeer
Sammy, the Way-Out Seal
Savage Sam
Scandalous John
The Secret of El Zorro
The Shaggy D.A.
The Shaggy Dog
The Sign of Zorro
Smith!
Smoke
Snowball Express
So Dear to My Heart
Son of Flubber
The Story of Robin Hood &
    His Merrie Men
Summer Magic
Superdad
The Swiss Family Robinson
The Sword & the Rose
Ten Who Dared
That Darn Cat
Third Man on the Mountain
Those Calloways
The Three Lives of Thomasina
3 Ninjas
A Tiger Walks
Toby Tyler
Tonka
Treasure Island
The Treasure of Matecumbe
20,000 Leagues Under the
    Sea
The Ugly Dachshund
Undergrads
Unidentified Flying Oddball
Waltz King
Watcher in the Woods
Westward Ho, the Wagons!
White Fang
The Wild Country

Wild Hearts Can't Be Broken
The World's Greatest Athlete

"E.T." & Rip-Offs

E.T.: The Extra-Terrestrial
Mac and Me

4 Bones

Abe Lincoln in Illinois
Adam's Rib
The Adventures of Robin
    Hood
The African Queen
Aladdin
All About Eve
All Quiet on the Western Front
All the King's Men
An American in Paris
Anatomy of a Murder
Andrei Rublev
An Angel at My Table
Angels with Dirty Faces
Annie Hall
Apocalypse Now
The Asphalt Jungle
Au Revoir Les Enfants
The Awful Truth
The Ballad of Narayama
Bambi
The Bank Dick
The Battleship Potemkin
Beauty and the Beast
Ben-Hur
The Best Years of Our Lives
The Bicycle Thief
The Big Parade
The Big Sleep
The Birth of a Nation
The Blue Angel
Breathless
Brian's Song
The Bride of Frankenstein
The Bridge on the River Kwai
Brief Encounter
Bringing Up Baby
The Burmese Harp
Butch Cassidy and the
    Sundance Kid
The Cabinet of Dr. Caligari
The Caine Mutiny
The Cameraman
Casablanca
Cesar
Children of Paradise
Chimes at Midnight
Chinatown
Christ Stopped at Eboli
A Christmas Carol
Citizen Kane
City Lights
The Civil War, Episode 1: The
    Cause—1861
The Civil War, Episode 2: A
    Very Bloody Affair—1862
The Civil War, Episode 3:
    Forever Free—1862
The Civil War, Episode 4:
    Simply Murder—1863
The Civil War, Episode 5: The
    Universe of Battle—1863
The Civil War, Episode 6:
    Valley of the Shadow of
    Death—1864
The Civil War, Episode 7:
    Most Hallowed Ground—
    1864
The Civil War, Episode 8: War
    is All Hell—1865
The Civil War, Episode 9: The
    Better Angels of Our
    Nature—1865
A Clockwork Orange

4

Letterboxed

Musical Score: Jack Nitzsche

Blue Collar
Breathless
Cannery Row
Cruising
The Exorcist
Greaser's Palace
Hardcore
Heart Beat
Heroes
Mermaids
An Officer and a Gentleman
One Flew Over the Cuckoo's Nest
Performance
Personal Best
The Razor's Edge
Starman
Village of the Giants
Windy City
Without a Trace

Musical Score: Jerry Goldsmith

Alien
Ballad of Cable Hogue
Bandolero!
Basic Instinct
Blue Desert
The Blue Max
The Boys from Brazil
Breakheart Pass
Breakout
Cabo Blanco
Capricorn One
The Cassandra Crossing
The Challenge
Chinatown
Coma
Culpepper Cattle Co.
Damien: Omen 2
Damnation Alley
Dennis the Menace
The Detective
The Don is Dead
Escape from the Planet of the Apes
Final Conflict
First Blood
Flim-Flam Man
A Gathering of Eagles
The Great Train Robbery
Gremlins
High Velocity
Hour of the Gun
The Illustrated Man
In Harm's Way
In Like Flint
Islands in the Stream
Justine
Lilies of the Field
The List of Adrian Messenger
Logan's Run
Lonely are the Brave
The Lonely Guy
MacArthur
Magic
Medicine Man
The Mephisto Waltz
Morituri
Night Crossing
The Omen
100 Rifles
One Little Indian
The Other
Our Man Flint
Outland
Papillon
A Patch of Blue
Patton
Planet of the Apes
Players

Poltergeist
The Prize
Psycho 2
Raggedy Man
The Reincarnation of Peter Proud
Rio Lobo
Runaway
The Salamander
The Sand Pebbles
Sebastian
Secret of NIMH
Seven Days in May
Shamus
Star Trek: The Motion Picture
The Stripper
Supergirl
Take a Hard Ride
The Terrorists
Tora! Tora! Tora!
The Trouble with Angels
Twilight Zone: The Movie
Twilight's Last Gleaming
Under Fire
The Vanishing
Von Ryan's Express
Wild Rovers
The Wind and the Lion

Musical Score: John Barry

The Betsy
The Black Hole
Body Heat
Born Free
Chaplin
The Chase
The Cotton Club
Dances with Wolves
The Day of the Locust
The Deep
Diamonds are Forever
Dr. No
A Doll's House
The Dove
Frances
From Russia with Love
Game of Death
Goldfinger
Hammett
Hanover Street
High Road to China
Inside Moves
The Ipcress File
King Kong
King Rat
The Last Valley
Legend of the Lone Ranger
The Lion in Winter
The Little Prince
The Man with the Golden Gun
Midnight Cowboy
Mike's Murder
Monte Walsh
Moonraker
Murphy's War
Never Let Go
Night Games
Octopussy
On Her Majesty's Secret Service
Out of Africa
Petulia
The Quiller Memorandum
Raise the Titanic
Robin and Marian
The Rocky Horror Picture Show
Ruby Cairo
Saturn 3
Seance on a Wet Afternoon
Shampoo
Somewhere in Time
Star Crash

The Tamarind Seed
They Might Be Giants
Thunderball
Touched by Love
Until September
The White Buffalo
The Wrong Box
You Only Live Twice
Zulu

Musical Score: John Williams

Angelo My Love
Black Sunday
Cinderella Liberty
Close Encounters of the Third Kind
Conrack
The Cowboys
Daddy's Gone A-Hunting
The Deer Hunter
Diamond Head
Dracula
Earthquake
The Eiger Sanction
Empire of the Sun
The Empire Strikes Back
E.T.: The Extra-Terrestrial
Family Plot
Far and Away
Fiddler on the Roof
The Fury
Gidget Goes to Rome
Goodbye, Mr. Chips
A Guide for the Married Man
Heartbeeps
Hook
Hot Lead & Cold Feet
Indiana Jones and the Last Crusade
Indiana Jones and the Temple of Doom
Jaws
Jaws 2
Jaws 3
JFK
Jurassic Park
The Killers
The Long Goodbye
Man Who Loved Cat Dancing
Midway
Missouri Breaks
Monsignor
1941
No Deposit, No Return
None But the Brave
The Paper Chase
Pete 'n' Tillie
The Poseidon Adventure
Psychopath
Raiders of the Lost Ark
The Rare Breed
The Reivers
Return of the Jedi
The River
Sergeant Ryker
Star Wars
The Sugarland Express
Superman: The Movie
Superman 2
Superman 3
Superman 4: The Quest for Peace
The Swarm
The Towering Inferno
Valley of the Dolls
Yes, Giorgio

Musical Score: Lerner & Loewe

Brigadoon
Camelot

Gigi
My Fair Lady
Paint Your Wagon

Musical Score: Menken & Ashman

Aladdin
Beauty and the Beast
The Little Mermaid
Little Shop of Horrors

Musical Score: Rodgers & Hammerstein

Carousel
Flower Drum Song
The King and I
Oklahoma!
The Sound of Music
South Pacific
State Fair

Plays to Film: Beth Henley

Crimes of the Heart
Nobody's Fool
True Stories

Plays to Film: Eugene O'Neill

Ah, Wilderness!
Anna Christie
Desire Under the Elms
Emperor Jones
Emperor Jones/Paul Robeson: Tribute to an Artist
The Hairy Ape
Long Day's Journey into Night
The Long Voyage Home
On Borrowed Time
Strange Interlude
Summer Holiday

Plays to Film: George Bernard Shaw

Androcles and the Lion
Caesar and Cleopatra
The Devil's Disciple
Heartbreak House
Major Barbara

Plays to Film: Horton Foote

Baby, the Rain Must Fall
The Chase
Courtship
1918
The Trip to Bountiful

Plays to Film: Neil Simon

Barefoot in the Park
Biloxi Blues
Brighton Beach Memoirs
Broadway Bound
California Suite
Chapter Two
The Cheap Detective
Come Blow Your Horn
The Goodbye Girl
The Heartbreak Kid
I Ought to Be in Pictures

Last of the Red Hot Lovers
Lost in Yonkers
The Marrying Man
Max Dugan Returns
Murder by Death
The Odd Couple
One Trick Pony
Only When I Laugh
The Out-of-Towners
Plaza Suite
Prisoner of Second Avenue
Seems Like Old Times
The Slugger's Wife
Star Spangled Girl
The Sunshine Boys
Sweet Charity

Plays to Film: Tennessee Williams

Baby Doll
Cat on a Hot Tin Roof
The Fugitive Kind
The Glass Menagerie
The Night of the Iguana
Orpheus Descending
Period of Adjustment
Roman Spring of Mrs. Stone
The Rose Tattoo
Senso
A Streetcar Named Desire
Suddenly, Last Summer
Summer and Smoke
Sweet Bird of Youth
This Property is Condemned

Plays to Film: Tom Stoppard

Rosencrantz & Guildenstern Are Dead

Plays to Film: William Shakespeare

Antony and Cleopatra
As You Like It
Carry On Cleo
Hamlet
Henry IV, Part I
Henry IV, Part II
Henry V
Henry VI, Part 3
Henry VIII
Julius Caesar
King Lear
Macbeth
Measure for Measure
A Midsummer Night's Dream
Much Ado About Nothing
Othello
Prospero's Books
Ran
Richard II
Richard III
Romeo and Juliet
The Taming of the Shrew
The Tempest
The Tragedy of King Richard II
Troilus & Cressida
Twelfth Night
West Side Story

Producers: Andy Warhol

Andy Warhol's Bad
Cocaine Cowboys
Flesh
Heat
Trash

Producers

Producers: Coppola/American Zoetrope

American Graffiti
The Black Stallion
The Conversation
Escape Artist
The Godfather, Part 2
Hammett

Producers: George Lucas

The Empire Strikes Back
The Ewok Adventure
More American Graffiti
Raiders of the Lost Ark
Return of the Jedi

Producers: Robert Altman

Buffalo Bill & the Indians
James Dean Story
The Late Show
Nashville
Quintet
Rich Kids
A Wedding
Welcome to L.A.

Producers: Roger Corman/New World

Atlas
Attack of the Giant Leeches
Avalanche
Battle Beyond the Stars
Battle Beyond the Sun
Beyond the Call of Duty
Big Bad Mama
Big Bad Mama 2
The Big Bird Cage
The Big Doll House
Bloodfist
Bloodfist 2
Bloody Mama
Body Waves
Boxcar Bertha
A Bucket of Blood
Caged Heat
Candy Stripe Nurses
Carnival Rock
Cocaine Wars
Cockfighter
Crazy Mama
Daddy's Boys
Death Race 2000
Death Sport
Dementia 13
The Dunwich Horror
Eat My Dust
The Fall of the House of Usher
Fighting Mad
Forbidden World
Futurekick
Galaxy of Terror
Gas-s-s-s!
Grand Theft Auto
The Gunslinger
The Haunted Palace
Humanoids from the Deep
I, Mobster
I Never Promised You a Rose Garden
In the Heat of Passion
It Conquered the World
Jackson County Jail
Lady in Red
The Last Woman on Earth
Little Shop of Horrors
Lords of the Deep

Lumiere
Machine Gun Kelly
Masque of the Red Death
Monster from the Ocean Floor
Munchies
Night of the Blood Beast
Piranha
The Pit and the Pendulum
Premature Burial
Primary Target
Private Duty Nurses
Raiders of the Sun
The Raven
Rock 'n' Roll High School Forever
The St. Valentine's Day Massacre
Ski Troop Attack
Small Change
Smokey Bites the Dust
Stripped to Kill
The Student Nurses
T-Bird Gang
Tales of Terror
Targets
Teenage Caveman
The Terror
Thunder and Lightning
Time Trackers
Tomb of Ligeia
Too Hot to Handle
The Trip
The Undead
Unholy Rollers
Voyage to the Planet of Prehistoric Women
The Wasp Woman
The Wild Angels
The Wild Ride
X: The Man with X-Ray Eyes
The Young Nurses

Producers: Steven Spielberg

Amazing Stories
Amazing Stories, Book 2
Amazing Stories, Book 3
Amazing Stories, Book 4
Amazing Stories, Book 5
An American Tail
An American Tail: Fievel Goes West
Back to the Future
The Color Purple
Empire of the Sun
The Goonies
Gremlins
Honey, I Shrunk the Kids
Innerspace
Jurassic Park
Poltergeist
Twilight Zone: The Movie
Who Framed Roger Rabbit?
Young Sherlock Holmes

Producers: Val Lewton

Bedlam
Cat People
Isle of the Dead

Producers: William Castle

Bug
House on Haunted Hill
Macabre
Riot
Rosemary's Baby
Strait-Jacket
13 Ghosts
Zotz!

"Road Warrior" & Rip-Offs

City Limits
Dead Man Walking
Driving Force
Dune Warriors
Endgame
Escape from Safehaven
Exterminators of the Year 3000
Firefight
Future Hunters
Future Kill
The Killing Edge
Never Too Young to Die
Phoenix the Warrior
Prison Planet
Radioactive Dreams
The Road Warrior
Solarbabies
Steel Dawn
Survival Zone
2020 Texas Gladiators
Ultra Warrior
Warriors of the Apocalypse
Warriors of the Wasteland
Wheels of Fire
World Gone Wild

Special FX Extravaganzas

The Abyss
Aliens
Batman
Beetlejuice
Big Trouble in Little China
The Black Hole
Blithe Spirit
Captain Sinbad
The Ewok Adventure
The Exorcist
Exorcist 2: The Heretic
Fantastic Voyage
Forbidden Planet
Innerspace
Jurassic Park
Lifeforce
Poltergeist
Return of the Jedi
Solar Crisis
Star Trek 2: The Wrath of Khan
Star Trek 4: The Voyage Home
Star Wars
Superman 2
The Terminator
Terminator 2: Judgment Day
The Thing
Total Recall
2001: A Space Odyssey
2010: The Year We Make Contact
Who Framed Roger Rabbit?
Wolfen

Special FX Extravaganzas: Make-Up

An American Werewolf in London
Battle for the Planet of the Apes
Beetlejuice
Beneath the Planet of the Apes
Conquest of the Planet of the Apes
Dawn of the Dead
Day of the Dead

Escape from the Planet of the Apes
The Exorcist
The Fly
The Fly 2
Hocus Pocus
The Howling
The Man Without a Face
Planet of the Apes
Scanners
The Thing

Special FX Wizards: Anton Furst

Alien
Batman
The Company of Wolves
Full Metal Jacket
Moonraker
Star Wars

Special FX Wizards: Dick Smith

Altered States
Amadeus
The Exorcist
Ghost Story
The Godfather
House of Dark Shadows
Little Big Man
Marathon Man
Midnight Cowboy
Scanners
The Sentinel
Spasms
The Sunshine Boys
Taxi Driver
World of Henry Orient

Special FX Wizards: Douglas Trumball

The Andromeda Strain
Blade Runner
Brainstorm
Close Encounters of the Third Kind
Silent Running
Star Trek: The Motion Picture
2001: A Space Odyssey

Special FX Wizards: Herschell Gordon Lewis

Blood Feast
Color Me Blood Red
Gruesome Twosome
Just for the Hell of It
Moonshine Mountain
The Psychic
She-Devils on Wheels
Suburban Roulette
This Stuff'll Kill Ya!
2000 Maniacs
The Wizard of Gore

Special FX Wizards: Ray Harryhausen

The Beast from 20,000 Fathoms
Clash of the Titans
Earth vs. the Flying Saucers
First Men in the Moon
Golden Voyage of Sinbad
It Came from Beneath the Sea
Jason and the Argonauts
Mighty Joe Young
Mysterious Island

The Seventh Voyage of Sinbad
Sinbad and the Eye of the Tiger
The Three Worlds of Gulliver
20 Million Miles to Earth
The Valley of Gwangi

Special FX Wizards: Rick Baker

An American Werewolf in London
Food of the Gods
The Funhouse
The Fury
Greystoke: The Legend of Tarzan, Lord of the Apes
Incredible Melting Man
The Incredible Shrinking Woman
It's Alive
King Kong
Octaman
Schlock
Squirm
Star Wars
Tanya's Island
Track of the Moonbeast
Videodrome

Special FX Wizards: Rob Bottin

Bugsy
Explorers
The Fog
The Howling
Humanoids from the Deep
Innerspace
Legend
RoboCop
Tanya's Island
The Thing
Twilight Zone: The Movie
The Witches of Eastwick

Special FX Wizards: Tom Savini

Creepshow
Dawn of the Dead
Day of the Dead
Deathdream
Deranged
Friday the 13th
Friday the 13th, Part 4: The Final Chapter
Knightriders
Maniac
Martin
Midnight
Monkey Shines
The Prowler
The Ripper
Texas Chainsaw Massacre, Part 2

Top Grossing Films of 1939

Gone with the Wind
The Hunchback of Notre Dame
Jesse James
Mr. Smith Goes to Washington
The Wizard of Oz

Top Grossing Films of 1940

Boom Town

Fantasia
Pinocchio
Rebecca
Santa Fe Trail

Top Grossing Films of 1941

Honky Tonk
The Philadelphia Story
Sergeant York
A Yank in the R.A.F.

Top Grossing Films of 1942

Bambi
Casablanca
Mrs. Miniver
Random Harvest
Yankee Doodle Dandy

Top Grossing Films of 1943

The Outlaw
The Song of Bernadette
Stage Door Canteen
This is the Army

Top Grossing Films of 1944

Going My Way
Meet Me in St. Louis
Since You Went Away
Thirty Seconds Over Tokyo

Top Grossing Films of 1945

Anchors Aweigh
The Bells of St. Mary's
Spellbound
Weekend at the Waldorf

Top Grossing Films of 1946

The Best Years of Our Lives
Duel in the Sun
The Jolson Story

Top Grossing Films of 1947

Egg and I
Life with Father

Top Grossing Films of 1948

Johnny Belinda
On an Island with You
The Paleface
Red River
The Red Shoes
Three Musketeers

Top Grossing Films of 1949

Battleground
Jolson Sings Again
Samson and Delilah
Sands of Iwo Jima

Top Grossing Films of 1950

Cinderella

Father of the Bride
King Solomon's Mines

Top Grossing Films of 1951

Alice in Wonderland
David and Bathsheba
The Great Caruso
Quo Vadis
Show Boat

Top Grossing Films of 1952

The Greatest Show on Earth
Hans Christian Andersen
Ivanhoe
The Snows of Kilimanjaro

Top Grossing Films of 1953

From Here to Eternity
How to Marry a Millionaire
Peter Pan
The Robe
Shane

Top Grossing Films of 1954

The Caine Mutiny
The Glenn Miller Story
Rear Window
20,000 Leagues Under the Sea
White Christmas

Top Grossing Films of 1955

Battle Cry
Lady and the Tramp
Mister Roberts
Oklahoma!

Top Grossing Films of 1956

Around the World in 80 Days
Giant
The King and I
The Ten Commandments

Top Grossing Films of 1957

The Bridge on the River Kwai
Old Yeller
Peyton Place
Raintree County
Sayonara

Top Grossing Films of 1958

Auntie Mame
Cat on a Hot Tin Roof
Gigi
No Time for Sergeants
South Pacific

Top Grossing Films of 1959

Ben-Hur
Darby O'Gill & the Little People
Operation Petticoat

The Shaggy Dog
Sleeping Beauty

Top Grossing Films of 1960

The Alamo
Exodus
Psycho
Spartacus
The Swiss Family Robinson

Top Grossing Films of 1961

The Absent-Minded Professor
El Cid
The Guns of Navarone
West Side Story

Top Grossing Films of 1962

How the West was Won
In Search of the Castaways
Lawrence of Arabia
The Longest Day
The Music Man

Top Grossing Films of 1963

Cleopatra
Irma La Douce
It's a Mad, Mad, Mad, Mad World
The Sword in the Stone
Tom Jones

Top Grossing Films of 1964

The Carpetbaggers
From Russia with Love
Goldfinger
Mary Poppins
My Fair Lady

Top Grossing Films of 1965

Doctor Zhivago
The Sound of Music
That Darn Cat
Those Magnificent Men in Their Flying Machines
Thunderball

Top Grossing Films of 1966

The Bible...In the Beginning
Hawaii
Lt. Robin Crusoe, U.S.N.
A Man for All Seasons
Who's Afraid of Virginia Woolf?

Top Grossing Films of 1967

Bonnie & Clyde
The Dirty Dozen
The Graduate
Guess Who's Coming to Dinner
The Jungle Book

Top Grossing Films of 1968

Bullitt
Funny Girl
The Odd Couple
Romeo and Juliet
2001: A Space Odyssey

Top Grossing Films of 1969

Butch Cassidy and the Sundance Kid
Easy Rider
Hello, Dolly!
The Love Bug
Midnight Cowboy

Top Grossing Films of 1970

Airport
Love Story
M*A*S*H
Patton

Top Grossing Films of 1971

Billy Jack
Diamonds are Forever
Fiddler on the Roof
The French Connection
Summer of '42

Top Grossing Films of 1972

Deliverance
The Godfather
Jeremiah Johnson
The Poseidon Adventure
What's Up, Doc?

Top Grossing Films of 1973

American Graffiti
The Exorcist
Papillon
The Sting
The Way We Were

Top Grossing Films of 1974

Blazing Saddles
Earthquake
The Towering Inferno
The Trial of Billy Jack
Young Frankenstein

Top Grossing Films of 1975

Dog Day Afternoon
Jaws
One Flew Over the Cuckoo's Nest

Top Grossing Films of 1976

All the President's Men
King Kong
Rocky
The Silver Streak
A Star is Born

Top Grossing Films of 1977

Close Encounters of the Third Kind
The Goodbye Girl
Saturday Night Fever
Smokey and the Bandit
Star Wars

Top Grossing Films of 1978

Every Which Way But Loose
Grease
Jaws 2
National Lampoon's Animal House
Superman: The Movie

Top Grossing Films of 1979

Alien
The Jerk
Kramer vs. Kramer
Rocky 2
Star Trek: The Motion Picture

Top Grossing Films of 1980

Airplane!
Any Which Way You Can
The Empire Strikes Back
9 to 5
Stir Crazy

Top Grossing Films of 1981

Arthur
Cannonball Run
On Golden Pond
Stripes
Superman 2

Top Grossing Films of 1982

E.T.: The Extra-Terrestrial
An Officer and a Gentleman
Porky's
Rocky 3

Top Grossing Films of 1983

Return of the Jedi
Superman 3
Terms of Endearment
Trading Places
War Games

Top Grossing Films of 1984

Beverly Hills Cop
Ghostbusters
Gremlins
Indiana Jones and the Temple of Doom
The Karate Kid

Top Grossing Films of 1985

Back to the Future
The Color Purple
Out of Africa
Rambo: First Blood, Part 2

Rocky 4

Top Grossing Films of 1986

Crocodile Dundee
The Karate Kid: Part 2
Platoon
Star Trek 4: The Voyage Home
Top Gun

Top Grossing Films of 1987

Beverly Hills Cop 2
Fatal Attraction
Good Morning, Vietnam
Lethal Weapon
Three Men and a Baby
The Untouchables

Top Grossing Films of 1988

Coming to America
Crocodile Dundee 2
Die Hard
Rain Man
Twins
Who Framed Roger Rabbit?

Top Grossing Films of 1989

Batman
Driving Miss Daisy
Ghostbusters 2
Honey, I Shrunk the Kids
Indiana Jones and the Last Crusade
Lethal Weapon 2

Top Grossing Films of 1990

Dances with Wolves
Dick Tracy
Die Hard 2: Die Harder
Ghost
Home Alone
The Hunt for Red October
Pretty Woman
Teenage Mutant Ninja Turtles: The Movie
Total Recall

Top Grossing Films of 1991

The Addams Family
Backdraft
Boyz N the Hood
City Slickers
Doc Hollywood
Dying Young
Hot Shots!
Naked Gun 2 1/2: The Smell of Fear
New Jack City
101 Dalmations
Robin Hood: Prince of Thieves
The Rocketeer
The Silence of the Lambs
Sleeping with the Enemy
Teenage Mutant Ninja Turtles 2: The Secret of the Ooze
Terminator 2: Judgment Day
What About Bob?

Top Grossing Films of 1992

Aladdin
Alien 3
Basic Instinct
Batman Returns
The Bodyguard
Boomerang
Bram Stoker's Dracula
Fried Green Tomatoes
The Hand that Rocks the Cradle
Home Alone 2: Lost in New York
The Last of the Mohicans
A League of Their Own
Lethal Weapon 3
Patriot Games
Sister Act
Under Siege
Unforgiven
Wayne's World
White Men Can't Jump

Trash

Alien Massacre
Alien Prey
All the Lovin' Kinfolk
The Allnighter
Alone in the T-Shirt Zone
America
American Tickler
And When She Was Bad...
Andy Warhol's Bad
Andy Warhol's Dracula
Andy Warhol's Frankenstein
Angel of H.E.A.T.
Assault of the Killer Bimbos
The Astounding She-Monster
The Astro-Zombies
Attack of the Beast Creatures
Attack of the Giant Leeches
Attack of the Killer Tomatoes
Bad Girls Go to Hell
Baring It All
Barn of the Naked Dead
The Beast of Yucca Flats
Bela Lugosi Meets a Brooklyn Gorilla
The Bellboy and the Playgirls
Best Buns on the Beach
Beverly Hills Bodysnatchers
Beverly Hills Knockouts
The Big Gag
The Bitch
Black Venus
Blazing Stewardesses
Blood Freak
Blood of Ghastly Horror
Bloodlust
Bloodsucking Freaks
Body of Evidence
Bottoms Up
Brain of Blood
Camp Double Feature
Candy Tangerine Man
The Carpetbaggers
Casting Call
The Castle of Fu Manchu
Cheerleader Camp
Cocaine Fiends
Corruption
Creeping Terror
Curse of the Blue Lights
Curse of the Living Dead
Cyborg
Cycle Vixens
Dead Aim
Delinquent School Girls
Demons
Desperate Living
Dolemite 2: Human Tornado
Drop Dead Fred

Drum
Drums O'Voodoo
Eegah!
The Eerie Midnight Horror Show
Escape from Planet Earth
Faces of Death, Part 2
Fat Guy Goes Nutzoid
Female Trouble
Film House Fever
Five Minutes to Love
Flesh and Blood Show
Frankenstein Meets the Space Monster
Fun Down There
Ghoul School
Glen or Glenda
Gore-Met Zombie Chef From Hell
Gun Cargo
Hitchhikers
Hollywood After Dark
Hollywood Chainsaw Hookers
The Hollywood Strangler Meets the Skid Row Slasher
Honkytonk Nights
Horror of Party Beach
The House of Usher
I Spit on Your Grave
I Was a Zombie for the FBI
Ilsa, Harem Keeper of the Oil Sheiks
Ilsa, She-Wolf of the SS
Ilsa, the Tigress of Siberia
Impulse
In the Cold of the Night
Incredibly Strange Creatures Who Stopped Living and Became Mixed-Up Zombies
Invasion of the Bee Girls
Island of Lost Girls
It's Not the Size That Counts
Jail Bait
Jungle Master
Killer Tomatoes Eat France
Killer Tomatoes Strike Back
Kung Fu Vampire Buster
The Last Season
The Lonely Lady
The Loves of Hercules
Man with Two Heads
Manos, the Hands of Fate
Master Blaster
Microwave Massacre
Mind Trap
Mondo Trasho
Motel Hell
Multiple Maniacs
Murder Weapon
The Naked Flame
A Night in Heaven
Night of the Cobra Woman
Night of the Demon
Night of the Ghouls
Nightmare
Oasis of the Zombies
Once is Not Enough
Orgy of the Dead
Out of the Body
The Outcast
Phantasm
Pink Flamingos
Plan 9 from Outer Space
Please Don't Eat My Mother
The Power
The Psychic
Rabid Grannies
Rat Pfink a Boo-Boo
The Rats are Coming! The Werewolves are Here!
Reform School Girl
Return of the Family Man
Return of the Killer Tomatoes
Return to the Blue Lagoon
Revenge of the Virgins

Robot Monster
Rush
Satan's Cheerleaders
Saturday the 14th Strikes Back
Savage Intruder
Screen Test
Sex Madness
She Demons
She-Devils on Wheels
The Sinister Invasion
The Sinister Urge
Slaves in Bondage
Sleazemania III: The Good, the Bad & the Sleazy
Some Call It Loving
Sorority Girl
Space Monster
Streetfight
Sweet Trash
Tarzan, the Ape Man
Teenage Mother
Teenage Strangler
Terror in the Jungle
Texas Layover
They Saved Hitler's Brain
Tomboy
Torture Dungeon
Train Station Pickups
The Trial of Billy Jack
Troma's War
Unholy Rollers
Valley of the Dolls
Victims
The Violent Years
White Pongo
Wild Ones on Wheels
Wild Women of Wongo

Troma Films

Blades
Bloodsucking Freaks
Chopper Chicks in Zombietown
Class of Nuke 'Em High
Class of Nuke 'Em High, Part 2: Subhumanoid Meltdown
Combat Shock
Evil Clutch
Ferocious Female Freedom Fighters
I Married a Vampire
I Was a Teenage TV Terrorist
Monster in the Closet
Rabid Grannies
Redneck Zombies
Sizzle Beach U.S.A.
Splatter University
Squeeze Play
Stuck on You
Student Confidential
Surf Nazis Must Die
Toxic Avenger
Toxic Avenger, Part 2
Toxic Avenger, Part 3: The Last Temptation of Toxie
Troma's War

Woofs!

The Adventurers
Adventures of a Taxi Driver
The Adventures of Ford Fairlane
The Adventurous Knights
After the Fall of New York
Albino
The Alchemist
Alien Contamination
Alien from L.A.
Alien Massacre
Alien Predators
Alien Warrior
Almost Human

The Amazing Transparent Man
The Amazing Transplant
The Ambushers
American Gothic
American Ninja 3: Blood Hunt
American Ninja 4: The Annihilation
Americathon
Amin: The Rise and Fall
Amityville 2: The Possession
The Amityville Curse
Angel 3: The Final Chapter
Angel of Death
Angel of H.E.A.T.
Angels' Wild Women
The Annihilators
A*P*E*
The Appointment
The Astounding She-Monster
Atlas in the Land of the Cyclops
Atom Age Vampire
The Atomic Brain
Ator the Fighting Eagle
Attack from Outer Space
Attack of the Beast Creatures
Attack of the Killer Refrigerator
Attack of the Killer Tomatoes
Attack of the Mayan Mummy
Attack of the Swamp Creature
Auntie
Avenging Angel
Awakening of Candra
Baby Love
Bad Charleston Charlie
Bad Girls Do Cry
Bad Girls from Mars
Bad Girls Go to Hell
Bad Medicine
Balboa
Bananas Boat
Bandera Bandits
Baring It All
Barn of the Naked Dead
Barracuda
Basic Training
Battle of the Bullies
Beachballs
Beaks: The Movie
Beast of the Yellow Night
The Beast of Yucca Flats
The Bees
Beginner's Luck
Bela Lugosi Meets a Brooklyn Gorilla
The Bellboy and the Playgirls
Best Buns on the Beach
Beverly Hills Call Girls
Beyond Atlantis
Beyond Evil
Beyond the Door
Beyond the Door 3
The Big Bust Out
Big Foot
The Bikini Car Wash Company
Birds of Paradise
Birth Right
The Bitch
The Black Cat
Black Cobra
The Black Cobra
Black Gestapo
Black Magic Woman
The Black Maid
Black Shampoo
Black Venus
Blackenstein
Blade of the Ripper
Blastfighter
The Blazing Ninja
Blazing Stewardesses
Blockhouse

Woofs

Mama Dracula
A Man Called Rage
Man from Deep River
Maniac
Mannequin 2: On the Move
Mardi Gras Massacre
A Matter of Time
Maximum Thrust
Maya
Meatballs 3
The Meateater
Mechanical Crabs
The Medal of Honor
Megaforce
Mesa of Lost Women
Meteor
Meteor Monster
Midnight Cabaret
Mistress of the Apes
Mob War
Mondo Trasho
Mongrel
Monsignor
Monster a Go-Go!
Monster Dog
The Monster of Piedras
   Blancas
Moonshine Mountain
Moses
Mountaintop Motel Massacre
Mummy & Curse of the Jackal
Murderer's Keep
Murderlust
Mutant Hunt
Mutants In Paradise
The Mutilator
My African Adventure
My Therapist
Myra Breckinridge
Nail Gun Massacre
Naked Cage
The Naked Flame
Naked Vengeance
Naked Youth
The Narcotics Story
Nathalie Comes of Age
National Lampoon's Class
   Reunion
Naughty Co-Eds
Navy vs. the Night Monsters
Neon Maniacs
The New Gladiators
New Year's Evil
New York Ripper
The Night God Screamed
A Night in Heaven
Night of Dark Shadows
Night of the Bloody Apes
Night of the Bloody Transplant
Night of the Demon
Night of the Ghouls
Night of the Living Babes
Night of the Sharks
Night of the Sorcerers
Night of the Zombies
Night Patrol
Night Train to Terror
Nightmare
Nightmare in Red China
Nightmare Sisters
Nightstalker
Nine Deaths of the Ninja
1990: The Bronx Warriors
Ninja Champion
Ninja Exterminators
Ninja Fantasy
Ninja Hunt
Ninja Terminator
Ninja Wars
No One Cries Forever
Nobody's Perfekt
Nocturna
Norman's Awesome
   Experience
Nude on the Moon
The Occultist

Ocean Drive Weekend
Oddballs
On the Edge: The Survival of
   Dana
One Brief Summer
One Down, Two to Go!
One Russian Summer
The Opposite Sex and How to
   Live With Them
Orca
Orgy of the Dead
The Other Side of Midnight
Parasite
Party Favors
Perfect Timing
Phobia
Pieces
Pink Motel
Plan 9 from Outer Space
Playing the Field
Please Don't Eat My Mother
Police Academy 5:
   Assignment Miami Beach
Prehistoric Women
Pretty Smart
Prettykill
The Prime Time
Private Manoeuvres
The Psychic
Pulsebeat
The Puma Man
Queen of Outer Space
Quick, Let's Get Married
Rabid Grannies
Raise the Titanic
The Rape of the Sabines
Rat Pfink a Boo-Boo
The Rats are Coming! The
   Werewolves are Here!
Rebel Vixens
The Red Menace
The Return
Revenge
Revenge of Doctor X
Ridin' the Lone Trail
The Ripper
The Robot vs. the Aztec
   Mummy
Rocket Attack U.S.A.
Roller Boogie
Rooster: Spurs of Death!
Sahara
Santa Claus
Sasquatch
Satan's Blade
Satan's Cheerleaders
Satan's Touch
Satanwar
Savage!
Savage is Loose
Savage Weekend
Scarlet Spear
Scoring
Scream and Die
Scream Bloody Murder
Scream of the Demon Lover
Screen Test
Secrets of Sweet Sixteen
Senior Week
Sensual Partners
The Sensuous Teenager
The Serpent and the Rainbow
The Severed Arm
Sex Adventures of the Three
   Musketeers
Sex, Drugs, and Rock-n-Roll
The Sex Machine
Sex Madness
Sex on the Run
Sex Surrogate
Sextette
Sharp Fists in Kung Fu
She Came on the Bus
She Demons
She-Devils on Wheels
Sheena

Shriek of the Mutilated
Sidney Sheldon's Bloodline
The Simple Truth
Sincerely Yours
The Sinful Bed
The Sinister Urge
Sinner's Blood
Skinned Alive
Skullduggery
Sky Pirates
Slashdance
The Slasher
The Slaughter of the Vampires
Slaughterhouse
Slaughterhouse Rock
Slave of the Cannibal God
The Slayer
Sledgehammer
Sleepaway Camp 3: Teenage
   Wasteland
The Slime People
Slithis
Sloane
Slugs
Slumber Party Massacre 2
Slumber Party Massacre 3
Smooth Talker
The Snow Creature
Something Weird
Sonny Boy
Sorceress
Sorority House Massacre
Sorority House Massacre 2:
   Nighty Nightmare
Sorority House Scandals
Soul Hustler
South Seas Massacre
Space Monster
Space Riders
Spaced Out
Spare Parts
Spasms
Sphinx
Splatter University
Splitz
Spookies
The Sporting Club
The Squeeze
Squeeze Play
Starlet
Stepsisters
Stewardess School
Stocks and Blondes
Stone Cold
Stormquest
The Strangeness
The Stranger from Venus
Street Hero
Street Hunter
Street People
Street Trash
Street Warriors
Street Warriors, Part 2
Strike Commando
Stroker Ace
Stryker
The Stud
Student Affairs
Student Bodies
Sugar Cookies
Suicide Cult
Summer Camp
Summer Job
Summer School Teachers
Sunnyside
Sunset Strip
Superchick
Superfly T.N.T.
Supersonic Man
Surf 2
Surfacing
Survival Zone
Sweater Girls
Sweet Spirits
Sweet Trash
Switchblade Sisters

Takin' It Off
Tarzan, the Ape Man
Teenage Mother
Teenage Seductress
Teenage Strangler
Teenage Zombies
Teenagers from Outer Space
The Telephone
The Temp
10 Violent Women
Tentacles
Terronauts
The Terror
Terror in Beverly Hills
Terror in the Wax Museum
Terror on Tour
Terrorvision
Test Tube Babies
Texas Chainsaw Massacre,
   Part 2
Texas Layover
They Saved Hitler's Brain
They Went That-a-Way &
   That-a-Way
They're Playing with Fire
Thieves of Fortune
The Thirsty Dead
This Stuff'll Kill Ya!
Three on a Meathook
The Thrill Killers
Throne of Fire
Tintorera...Tiger Shark
TNT Jackson
To All a Goodnight
Tomb of Torture
Tomboy
The Tormentors
Torso
Tower of Evil
Traveling Companions
Treasure of the Moon
   Goddess
The Trial of Billy Jack
Trick or Treats
Troma's War
Tropic Heat
Twice Dead
Twilight People
Two Lost Worlds
2020 Texas Gladiators
Two Women in Gold
The Ultimate Ninja
The Uncanny
Under the Doctor
Under the Rainbow
Undercover Vixens
Underground Aces
The Uninvited
Unknown Island
Unknown Powers
Up Your Anchor
Vampire Raiders—Ninja
   Queen
Vasectomy: A Delicate Matter
Vengeance Is Mine
Venom
Vice Academy 3
Vice Squad
The Video Dead
Video Vixens
Video Wars
Vigilante
Violated
Violent Ones
The Violent Years
Virgins of Purity House
Viva Knievel
Voyage to the Planet of
   Prehistoric Women
Vulcan God of Fire
Wacko
Waitress
Wanted: Babysitter
Warlords from Hell
Warrior of the Lost World
Warriors of the Apocalypse

Warriors of the Wasteland
Weekend with the Babysitter
Werewolves on Wheels
When Lightning Strikes
When Nature Calls
Where the Boys Are '84
White Cannibal Queen
White Gorilla
White Pongo
Wholly Moses!
The Wild Beasts
Wild Guitar
Wild Ones on Wheels
Wild Riders
Wild Wheels
The Wildest Office Party
Wired to Kill
Witchcraft
The Witching
Woman Hunt
Women in Cell Block 7
Women in Fury
Women of the Prehistoric
   Planet
Women Unchained
Women's Prison Massacre
Woodchipper Massacre
The World is Full of Married
   Men
World of the Vampires
The Worm Eaters
Wrestling Racket Girls
Wrestling Women vs. the
   Aztec Ape
Wrestling Women vs. the
   Aztec Mummy
Xanadu
Xtro
The Yesterday Machine
You Light Up My Life
Zandalee
Zero Boys
Zero Pilot
Zombie Nightmare
Zombies of Moratau

The **SERIES INDEX** provides 60 concise listings of major movie series, from James Bond to the Raiders of the Lost Ark to Dirty Harry, as well as recurring and notable cinematic partnerships, including the Three Stooges, Hepburn and Tracy, and Zucker/Abrahams/Zucker. It follows the arrangement of the Category Index, with series names arranged alphabetically. The categories are as follows:

SERIES INDEX

Dracula

Dracula Rising
Dracula (Spanish Version)
Dracula Sucks
Dracula: Up in Harlem
Dracula vs. Frankenstein
Dracula's Daughter
Dracula's Great Love
Dracula's Last Rites
Dracula's Widow
The Horror of Dracula
House of Frankenstein
Hysterical
Love at First Bite
The Monster Squad
Nocturna
Return of the Vampire
The Satanic Rites of Dracula
The Scars of Dracula
The Screaming Dead
Son of Dracula
Taste the Blood of Dracula
To Die for
Transylvania 6-5000
Vampire Circus
Waxwork
Zoltan...Hound of Dracula

Eddy & McDonald

Girl of the Golden West
I Married an Angel
Maytime
Naughty Marietta
New Moon
Rose Marie
Sweethearts

Elvisfilm

Blue Hawaii
Change of Habit
Charro!
Clambake
Double Trouble
Easy Come, Easy Go
Elvis and Me
The Elvis Files
Elvis in the Movies
Elvis Memories
Elvis on Tour
Elvis: One Night with You
Elvis Presley's Graceland
Elvis: Rare Moments with the
   King
Elvis Stories
Elvis: The Echo Will Never Die
Elvis: The Lost Performances
Elvis: The Movie
Flaming Star
Follow That Dream
Frankie and Johnny
Fun in Acapulco
G.I. Blues
Girl Happy
Girls! Girls! Girls!
Harum Scarum
Heartbreak Hotel
Honeymoon in Vegas
It Happened at the World's
   Fair
Jailhouse Rock
Kid Galahad
King Creole
Kissin' Cousins
Live a Little, Love a Little
Love Me Tender
Loving You
Paradise, Hawaiian Style
Rock-a-Doodle
Roustabout
Speedway
Spinout
Stay Away, Joe
This is Elvis
Tickle Me

Top Secret!
The Trouble with Girls (and
   How To Get Into It)
Viva Las Vegas
Wild in the Country

Faerie Tale Theatre

Aladdin and His Wonderful
   Lamp
Beauty and the Beast
The Boy Who Left Home to
   Find Out About the Shivers
Cinderella
The Dancing Princesses
The Emperor's New Clothes
Goldilocks & the Three Bears
Hansel and Gretel
Jack & the Beanstalk
The Little Mermaid
Little Red Riding Hood
The Nightingale
The Pied Piper of Hamelin
Pinocchio
The Princess and the Pea
The Princess Who Never
   Laughed
Puss 'n Boots
Rapunzel
Rip van Winkle
Rumpelstiltskin
Sleeping Beauty
The Snow Queen
Snow White and the Seven
   Dwarfs
The Tale of the Frog Prince
The Three Little Pigs
Thumbelina

The Falcon

The Amityville Curse
The Devil's Cargo
The Falcon in Hollywood
The Falcon in Mexico
Falcon Takes Over/Strange
   Bargain
Falcon's Adventure/Armored
   Car Robbery
The Falcon's Brother

Frankenstein

Abbott and Costello Meet
   Frankenstein
Andy Warhol's Frankenstein
Blackenstein
The Bride
The Bride of Frankenstein
The Curse of Frankenstein
Dr. Frankenstein's Castle of
   Freaks
Dracula vs. Frankenstein
The Evil of Frankenstein
The Flintstones Meet Rockula
   & Frankenstone
Frankenstein
Frankenstein: A Cinematic
   Scrapbook
Frankenstein and the Monster
   from Hell
Frankenstein '80
Frankenstein General Hospital
Frankenstein Island
Frankenstein Meets the Space
   Monster
Frankenstein Meets the
   Wolfman
Frankenstein Unbound
Frankenstein's Daughter
Frankenstein's Great Aunt
   Tillie
Frankenweenie
Gothic
The Horror of Frankenstein

House of Frankenstein
Jesse James Meets
   Frankenstein's Daughter
Lady Frankenstein
Munster's Revenge
Nosferatu
Orlak, the Hell of Frankenstein
Prototype
The Screaming Dead
Son of Frankenstein
Teenage Frankenstein
The Vindicator
Young Frankenstein

Godzilla

Destroy All Monsters
Ghidrah the Three Headed
   Monster
Godzilla, King of the Monsters
Godzilla 1985
Godzilla on Monster Island
Godzilla Raids Again
Godzilla vs. Biollante
Godzilla vs. Gigan
Godzilla vs. Megalon
Godzilla vs. Monster Zero
Godzilla vs. Mothra
Godzilla vs. the Cosmic
   Monster
Godzilla vs. the Sea Monster
Godzilla vs. the Smog
   Monster
Godzilla's Revenge
King Kong Versus Godzilla
Son of Godzilla
Terror of Mechagodzilla

Hallmark Hall of Fame

Caroline?
Decoration Day
Foxfire
Miss Rose White
O Pioneers!
One Against the Wind
Sarah, Plain and Tall
The Secret Garden
Skylark

Hepburn & Tracy

Adam's Rib
Guess Who's Coming to
   Dinner
Hepburn & Tracy
Pat and Mike
State of the Union
Without Love
Woman of the Year

Hopalong Cassidy

Bar-20
Border Patrol
Border Vigilantes
Colt Comrades
Doomed Caravan
False Colors
The Frontiersman
Hopalong Cassidy
Hopalong Cassidy: Borrowed
   Trouble
Hopalong Cassidy: Dangerous
   Venture
Hopalong Cassidy: False
   Paradise
Hopalong Cassidy: Hoppy's
   Holiday
Hopalong Cassidy: Riders of
   the Deadline
Hopalong Cassidy: Silent
   Conflict

Hopalong Cassidy: Sinister
   Journey
Hopalong Cassidy: The Dead
   Don't Dream
Hopalong Cassidy: The Devil's
   Playground
Hopalong Cassidy: The
   Marauders
Hopalong Cassidy:
   Unexpected Guest
Hoppy Serves a Writ
In Old Colorado
Law of the Pampas
Leather Burners
Lost Canyon
Mystery Man
Outlaws of the Desert
Renegade Trail
Riders of the Timberline
Rustler's Valley
Santa Fe Marshal
The Showdown
Texas Masquerade
Twilight on the Trail
Undercover Man

Hope & Crosby

My Favorite Brunette
The Road to Bali
The Road to Hong Kong
The Road to Morocco
The Road to Rio
The Road to Singapore
The Road to Utopia
The Road to Zanzibar

Jack the Ripper

Blade of the Ripper
Cosh Boy
Hands of the Ripper
He Kills Night After Night After
   Night
Jack the Ripper
Jack's Back
The Lodger
The Monster of London City
Murder by Decree
Night Ripper
Phantom Fiend
The Ripper
Room to Let
A Study in Terror
Terror at London Bridge
Terror in the Wax Museum
Time After Time

James Bond

Diamonds are Forever
Dr. No
For Your Eyes Only
From Russia with Love
Goldfinger
License to Kill
Live and Let Die
The Living Daylights
The Man with the Golden Gun
Moonraker
Never Say Never Again
Octopussy
On Her Majesty's Secret
   Service
The Spy Who Loved Me
Thunderball
A View to a Kill
You Only Live Twice

Lassie

Challenge to Lassie
Courage of Lassie
Lassie: Adventures of Neeka
Lassie, Come Home

Lassie: The Miracle
Lassie: Well of Love
Lassie's Great Adventure
Magic of Lassie
The Painted Hills
Son of Lassie

Laurel & Hardy

Air Raid Wardens
Bellhop/The Noon Whistle
Block-heads
Bohemian Girl
Bonnie Scotland
Bullfighters
A Chump at Oxford
The Devil's Brother
A Few Moments with Buster
   Keaton and Laurel and
   Hardy
The Flying Deuces
Golden Age of Comedy
Great Guns
Hollywood Party
Laurel & Hardy and the Family
Laurel & Hardy: Another Fine
   Mess
Laurel & Hardy: At Work
Laurel & Hardy: Be Big
Laurel & Hardy: Below Zero
Laurel & Hardy: Berth Marks
Laurel & Hardy: Blotto
Laurel & Hardy: Brats
Laurel & Hardy: Chickens
   Come Home
Laurel & Hardy Comedy
   Classics, Vol. 1
Laurel & Hardy Comedy
   Classics, Vol. 2
Laurel & Hardy Comedy
   Classics, Vol. 3
Laurel & Hardy Comedy
   Classics, Vol. 4
Laurel & Hardy Comedy
   Classics, Vol. 5
Laurel & Hardy Comedy
   Classics, Vol. 6
Laurel & Hardy Comedy
   Classics, Vol. 7
Laurel & Hardy Comedy
   Classics, Vol. 8
Laurel & Hardy Comedy
   Classics, Vol. 9
Laurel & Hardy: Hog Wild
Laurel & Hardy: Laughing
   Gravy
Laurel & Hardy: Men O'War
Laurel & Hardy: Night Owls
Laurel & Hardy On the Lam
Laurel & Hardy: Perfect Day
Laurel & Hardy Special
Laurel & Hardy Spooktacular
Laurel & Hardy: Stan "Helps"
   Ollie
Laurel & Hardy: The Hoose-
   Gow
Laurel & Hardy, Vol. 1
Laurel & Hardy, Vol. 2
Laurel & Hardy, Vol. 3
Laurel & Hardy, Vol. 4
Movie Struck
Nothing But Trouble
Our Relations
Pack Up Your Troubles
Pardon Us
Pick a Star
Saps at Sea
Silent Laugh Makers, No. 1
Sons of the Desert
Swiss Miss
A Tribute to the Boys
Utopia
Way Out West

Texas

Enemy of the Law
Fighting Valley
Frontier Fugitives
Gangsters of the Frontier
Marked for Murder
Outlaw Roundup
Ranger's Roundup
Rangers Take Over
Three in the Saddle
Wild West

Thin Man

After the Thin Man
Another Thin Man
Shadow of the Thin Man
Song of the Thin Man
The Thin Man
The Thin Man Goes Home

Three Mesquiteers

Come On, Cowboys
Covered Wagon Days
Cowboys from Texas
Frontier Horizon
Ghost Town Gold
Heart of the Rockies
Heroes of the Hills
Hit the Saddle
The Kansas Terrors
Law of the Saddle
Lonely Trail/Three Texas
  Steers
Outlaws of Sonora
Overland Stage Raiders
Pals of the Saddle
Powdersmoke Range
Purple Vigilantes
Riders of the Whistling Skull
Roarin' Lead
Rocky Mountain Rangers
Santa Fe Stampede
Three Texas Steers
Trigger Trio
Wild Horse Rodeo
Wyoming Outlaw

3 Stooges

Dancing Lady
Gold Raiders
Hollywood Party
It's a Mad, Mad, Mad, Mad
  World
The Lost Stooges
Snow White and the Three
  Stooges
Stoogemania
The Stoogephile Trivia Movie
Stooges Shorts Festival
The Stooges Story
Three Stooges Comedy
  Capers: Vol. 1
Three Stooges Comedy
  Classics
Three Stooges: Cookoo
  Cavaliers and Other Nyuks
Three Stooges Festival
Three Stooges: From Nurse to
  Worse and Other Nyuks
Three Stooges: Half-Wit's
  Holiday and Other Nyuks
Three Stooges: Idiots Deluxe
  and Other Nyuks
Three Stooges Meet Hercules
Three Stooges: Nutty but Nice
  and Other Nyuks
Three Stooges: They Stooge
  to Conga and Other Nyuks

Trail Blazers

Arizona Whirlwind
Death Valley Rangers

The Law Rides Again
Outlaw Trail

Turner & Douglas

The Jewel of the Nile
Romancing the Stone
The War of the Roses

Wonderworks
Family Movies

African Journey
Almost Partners
Anne of Avonlea
Anne of Green Gables
The Boy Who Loved Trolls
Bridge to Terabithia
Brother Future
The Canterville Ghost
The Chronicles of Narnia
Clowning Around
Daniel and the Towers
The Fig Tree
Frog
Frogs!
A Girl of the Limberlost
Gryphon
The Haunting of Barney
  Palmer
Hector's Bunyip
Hiroshima Maiden
The Hoboken Chicken
  Emergency
Home at Last
The House of Dies Drear
How to Be a Perfect Person in
  Just Three Days
Jacob Have I Loved
Konrad
Lantern Hill
A Little Princess
Looking for Miracles
Maricela
The Mighty Pawns
Miracle at Moreaux
Necessary Parties
Runaway
Sweet 15
Taking Care of Terrific
Walking on Air
A Waltz Through the Hills
Words by Heart
You Must Remember This

Zucker/Abrahams/
Zucker

Airplane!
Kentucky Fried Movie
More! Police Squad
The Naked Gun: From the
  Files of Police Squad
Naked Gun 2 1/2: The Smell
  of Fear
Police Squad! Help Wanted!
Top Secret!

The **CAST INDEX** lists the video accomplishments of 26,000 actors in a straight alphabetical format by last name (names are presented in a first name, last name format, but alphabetization begins with the last name). Every cast member credited in the main review section is indexed here, creating an intriguing array of videographies for the famous and the not-so-famous. The **Director Index** immediately follows this index.

Beverly Aadland
Assault of the Rebel Girls '59
Raiders of Sunset Pass '43

Lee Aaker
The Atomic City '52
Courage of Rin Tin Tin '83
Rin Tin Tin, Hero of the West '55

Angela Aames
Bachelor Party '84
Basic Training '86
The Lost Empire '83

Willie Aames
Cut and Run '85
Frankenstein '73
Paradise '82
Scavenger Hunt '79
Zapped! '82

Caroline Aaron
Crimes & Misdemeanors '89
Heartburn '86

Judith Abarbanel
The Cantor's Son '37

Diego Abatantuono
Mediterraneo '92

Angelo Abazoglou
Toute Une Nuit '82

Shelly Abblett
Blood Games '90

Bruce Abbott
Bad Dreams '88
Bride of Re-Animator '89
Interzone '88
The Re-Animator '85
Summer Heat '87
Trapped '89

Bud Abbott
Abbott and Costello in Hollywood '45
Abbott and Costello Meet Captain Kidd '52
Abbott and Costello Meet Dr. Jekyll and Mr. Hyde '52
Abbott and Costello Meet Frankenstein '48
Abbott & Costello Meet the Invisible Man '51
Abbott and Costello Meet the Killer, Boris Karloff '49

Abbott and Costello Scrapbook '70s
Africa Screams '49
The Best of Abbott & Costello Live '54
Buck Privates '41
Buck Privates Come Home '47
Classic Comedy Video Sampler '49
Dance with Me, Henry '56
Hey Abbott! '78
Hit the Ice '43
Hold That Ghost '41
Hollywood Clowns '85
Hollywood Goes to War '54
In the Navy '41
Jack & the Beanstalk '52
Keep 'Em Flying '41
Lost in a Harem '44
Mexican Hayride '48
The Naughty Nineties '45
The Noose Hangs High '48
Pardon My Sarong '42
Ride 'Em Cowboy '42
Rio Rita '42
The Time of Their Lives '46
Who Done It? '42
The Wistful Widow of Wagon Gap '47

Diahnne Abbott
Jo Jo Dancer, Your Life is Calling '86
King of Comedy '82
Love Streams '84
New York, New York '77

John Abbott
Adventure Island '47
Cry of the Werewolf '44
Deception '46
The Falcon in Hollywood '44
Humoresque '46
The Merry Widow '52
Pursuit to Algiers '45
The Vampire's Ghost '45

Mike Abbott
Death Code Ninja '87
Hands of Death '88

Phillip Abbott
The Fantastic World of D.C. Collins '84
Hangar 18 '80

Sparky Abbrams
Bottoms Up '87

Kareem Abdul-Jabbar
Airplane! '80
Chuck Berry: Hail! Hail! Rock 'n' Roll '87
The Fish that Saved Pittsburgh '79
Fletch '85
Game of Death '79
Pee-Wee's Playhouse Christmas Special '88
Purple People Eater '88

Paula Abdul
Junior High School '78

Hakeem Abdul-Samad
Ernest Goes to Camp '87

Naoyuki Abe
Gamera vs. Gaos '67

Alan Abel
Is There Sex After Death? '71

Alfred Abel
Dr. Mabuse the Gambler '22
Metropolis '26

Walter Abel
Curley '47
Fabulous Joe '47
Fury '36
Grace Quigley '84
Holiday Inn '42
The Indian Fighter '55
Kid from Brooklyn '46
Law of the Underworld '38
Mirage '66
Mr. Skeffington '44
Prudential Family Playhouse '50
Quick, Let's Get Married '71
Raintree County '57
Silent Night, Bloody Night '73
13 Rue Madeleine '46
Three Musketeers '35
Wake Island '42

Jim Abele
Student Affairs '88
Wimps '87

Ridgely Abele
Master's Revenge '71

Jordan Abeles
South Bronx Heroes '85

Ian Abercrombie
Catacombs '89
Curse 4: The Ultimate Sacrifice '92
Kicks '85
Puppet Master 3: Toulon's Revenge '91

Keith Aberdein
Smash Palace '82
Wild Horses '82

Sivi Aberg
Dr. Death, Seeker of Souls '73

Ric Abernathy
The Squeeze '87

Michael Aberne
The Commitments '91

Abigail
Adventures of Eliza Fraser '76
Breaking Loose '90

William Abney
Flight from Singapore '62

F. Murray Abraham
All the President's Men '76
Amadeus '84
Beyond the Stars '89
The Big Fix '78
The Bonfire of the Vanities '90
An Innocent Man '89
Intimate Power '89
Last Action Hero '93
Madman '79
Mobsters '91
The Name of the Rose '86
National Lampoon's Loaded Weapon 1 '93
Prisoner of Second Avenue '74
The Ritz '76
Scarface '83
Serpico '73
Slipstream '89
The Sunshine Boys '75
They Might Be Giants '71
Third Solution '89

Ken Abraham
Creepozoids '87
Deadly Embrace '88
Marked for Murder '89
Vice Academy '88

Jim Abrahams
Kentucky Fried Movie '77

Klaus Abramowsky
Europa, Europa '91

Michele Abrams
Cool World '92

Andrei Abrikosov
Sword & the Dragon '56

Al Abrikossov
Alexander Nevsky '38

Victoria Abril
After Darkness '85
Caged Heart '85
Esposa y Amante '70s
High Heels '91
L'Addition '85
Lovers: A True Story '90
Moon in the Gutter '84
On the Line '83
Tie Me Up! Tie Me Down! '90

Bella Abzug
Age Isn't Everything '91

Frankie Acciario
Bad Lieutenant '92

Goodman Ace
Two Reelers: Comedy Classics 6 '35

Anna Achdian
A Wedding in Galilee '87

Cristina Ache
Amor Bandido '79

James Acheson
Body Language '92

Tony Acierto
Journey to Spirit Island '92

Sharon Acker
The Hanged Man '74
Off Your Rocker '80
The Stranger '73

MacKenzie Astin
The Garbage Pail Kids Movie
'87

Sean Astin
Encino Man '92
The Goonies '85
Like Father, Like Son '87
Memphis Belle '90
Staying Together '89
Toy Soldiers '91
The War of the Roses '89
Where the Day Takes You '92
White Water Summer '87
The Willies '90

Gertrude Astor
After Midnight '33
The Cat and the Canary '27
The Cheerful Fraud '27
Strong Man '26

Mary Astor
Across the Pacific '42
Beau Brummel '24
Behind Office Doors '31
The Best of Bogart '43
Cass Timberlane '47
Dodsworth '36
Don Juan '26
Don Q., Son of Zorro '25
The Fighting American '24
The Great Lie '41
Hurricane '37
Hush, Hush, Sweet Charlotte '65
The Kennel Murder Case '33
Lady from Nowhere '36
Listen, Darling '38
Little Women '49
The Maltese Falcon '41
Meet Me in St. Louis '44
The Palm Beach Story '42
Prisoner of Zenda '37
Red Dust '32
Return to Peyton Place '61
The Royal Bed '31
This Happy Feeling '58
Thousands Cheer '43

Patti Astor
The Foreigner '78
Underground U.S.A. '84

Pacifico Astrologo
Shoeshine '47

Marianne Astrom-DeFina
Northern Lights '79

Danny Aswatep
After the Fall of Saigon '88

Hooper Atchley
I Can't Escape '34
Midnight Warning '32
Spirit of the West '32

Larry Aten
The Beast of Yucca Flats '61

Roscoe Ates
The Champ '31
Check Your Guns '48
Cheyenne Kid '33
Cimarron '30
Colorado Serenade '46
Freaks '32
Reg'lar Fellers '41
Robin Hood of the Pecos '41
Three Texas Steers '39
Thunder in the Pines '49
West to Glory '47
What! No Beer? '33
Wild Country '47
Wild West '46
Woman in the Shadows '34

William Atherton
Buried Alive '90
Chrome Soldiers '92
Class of '44 '73
The Day of the Locust '75
Die Hard '88
Die Hard 2: Die Harder '90
A Fight for Jenny '90
Ghostbusters '84
Grim Prairie Tales '89
The Hindenburg '75
Intrigue '90
Looking for Mr. Goodbar '77
No Mercy '86
Real Genius '85
The Sugarland Express '74
Tomorrow's Child '82

Harvey Atkin
Meatballs '79
SnakeEater 2: The Drug Buster '89

Christopher Atkins
Beaks: The Movie '87
The Blue Lagoon '80
Child Bride of Short Creek '81
Dracula Rising '93
Fatal Charm '92
King's Ransom '91
Listen to Me '89
Mortuary Academy '91
A Night in Heaven '83
Pirate Movie '82
Secret Weapons '85
Shakma '89

David Atkins
Prick Up Your Ears '87
Squizzy Taylor '84

Eileen Atkins
Bewitched '85
The Dresser '83
I Don't Want to Be Born '75
Let Him Have It '91
The Lost Language of Cranes '92
Oliver Twist '82
The Vision '87

Felicia Atkins
The Errand Boy '61

Jenny Atkins
You're Jinxed, Friend, You've Met Sacramento '70

Suzie Atkins
Secrets of Sweet Sixteen '74

Tom Atkins
Blind Justice '86
Dead Man Out '89
Desperate Lives '82
Halloween 3: Season of the Witch '82
Lethal Weapon '87
Maniac Cop '88
Night of the Creeps '86
Skeezer '82
Special Delivery '76
Tarantulas: The Deadly Cargo '77

Betty Atkinson
Mad Youth '40

Chris Atkinson
Mondo Trasho '70

Don Atkinson
Down Under '86

Jayne Atkinson
Free Willy '93

Rowan Atkinson
Bernard and the Genie '90s
Hot Shots! Part Deux '93
Never Say Never Again '83

The Tall Guy '89
The Witches '90

Farrid El Atrache
Afrita Hanen '47

Richard Attenborough
The Baby and the Battleship '56
The Bliss of Mrs. Blossom '68
Brannigan '75
Brighton Rock '47
Brothers in Law '57
Conduct Unbecoming '75
David Copperfield '70
Doctor Doolittle '67
The Flight of the Phoenix '65
The Gift Horse '52
The Great Escape '63
Guns at Batasi '64
In Which We Serve '43
Jurassic Park '93
League of Gentlemen '60
Loot...Give Me Money, Honey! '70
The Magic Christian '69
Only Two Can Play '66
The Sand Pebbles '66
Seance on a Wet Afternoon '64
S.O.S. Pacific '60
Ten Little Indians '75
10 Rillington Place '71

Elsie Attenoff
Heidi '52

Malcolm Atterbury
Blood of Dracula '57
How to Make a Monster '58
I Was a Teenage Werewolf '57

Mahamed Attifi
Mark of the Scorpion '90

Billy Attmore
The Treasure of Matecumbe '76

Edith Atwater
The Body Snatcher '45
Die Sister, Die! '74
It Happened at the World's Fair '63
The Love Machine '71

Michael Atwell
Buster '88

Roy Atwell
Snow White and the Seven Dwarfs '37

Lionel Atwill
Beggars in Ermine '34
Boom Town '40
Captain America '44
Captain Blood '35
Doctor X '32
Fog Island '45
Frankenstein Meets the Wolfman '42
The Gorilla '39
The Great Waltz '38
High Command '37
The Horror of It All '91
The Hound of the Baskervilles '39
House of Frankenstein '44
Johnny Apollo '40
Lady in Death House '44
Lost City of the Jungle '45
Mystery of the Wax Museum '33
Pardon My Sarong '42
Sherlock Holmes and the Secret Weapon '42
Son of Frankenstein '39

The Sphinx '33
Three Comrades '38
To Be or Not to Be '42
The Vampire Bat '32
The Wrong Road '37

Anat Atzman
Dead End Street '83
Double Edge '92

Robert Atzorn
From the Life of the Marionettes '80

Rene Auberjonois
Brewster McCloud '70
The Dark Secret of Harvest Home '78
Eyes of Laura Mars '78
The Feud '90
Gore Vidal's Billy the Kid '89
King Kong '76
The Little Mermaid '89
M*A*S*H '70
McCabe & Mrs. Miller '71
My Best Friend Is a Vampire '88
Once Upon a Midnight Scary '90
Pete 'n' Tillie '72
Police Academy 5: Assignment Miami Beach '88
A Smoky Mountain Christmas '86
3:15—The Moment of Truth '86
Walker '87
Wild, Wild West Revisited '79
Wildcard '92

Lenore Aubert
Abbott and Costello Meet Frankenstein '48
Abbott and Costello Meet the Killer, Boris Karloff '49
Action in Arabia '44
Having Wonderful Crime '45

Ann Aubrey
Let's Get Married '63

James Aubrey
Bouquet of Barbed Wire '76
Forever Young '85
Home Before Midnight '84
Lord of the Flies '63
Riders of the Storm '88
The Terror '79

Jimmy Aubrey
Aces and Eights '36
Courage of the North '35

Larry Aubrey
Fifth Day of Peace '72

Skye Aubrey
In the Steps of a Dead Man '74

Danielle Aubry
Operation C.I.A. '65

Jacques Aubuchon
Thunder Road '58

Michel Auclair
Beauty and the Beast '46
Manon '50
Murder at 45 R.P.M. '65
The Story of a Love Story '73
Swashbuckler '84

Maxine Audley
A King in New York '57
Peeping Tom '63

Edmund Audran
The Elusive Pimpernel '50

Stephane Audran
Babette's Feast '87
The Big Red One '80
Black Bird '75
The Blood of Others '84
Brideshead Revisited '81
Coup de Torchon '81
The Discreet Charm of the Bourgeoisie '72
Eagle's Wing '79
La Cage aux Folles 3: The Wedding '86
Le Boucher '69
Les Biches '68
Poor Little Rich Girl: The Barbara Hutton Story '87
Silver Bears '78
Ten Little Indians '75
Twist '76
Vincent, Francois, Paul and the Others '76
Violette '78
Wedding in Blood '74

Caroline Audret
Oasis of the Zombies '82

Mischa Auer
And Then There Were None '45
Around the World '43
Arrivederci, Baby! '66
Brewster's Millions '45
The Christmas That Almost Wasn't '66
Condemned to Live '35
Destry Rides Again '39
Drums of Jeopardy '31
Flaming Signal '33
Hold That Ghost '41
I Dream Too Much '35
Inside the Lines '30
Mr. Arkadin '55
The Monster Walks '32
My Man Godfrey '36
Pick a Star '37
The Rage of Paris '38
Seven Sinners '40
Sputnik '61
Sucker Money '34
Sweethearts '38
That Girl from Paris '36
Vogues of 1938 '37
Woman Condemned '33
You Can't Take It with You '38

Claude Aufaure
The Hairdresser's Husband '92

Patrick Auffay
The 400 Blows '59

Claudine Auger
The Associate '82
Bay of Blood '71
Head of the Family '71
The Killing Game '67
Lobster for Breakfast '82
Ricco '74
The Road to Lebanon '60
Secret Places '85
Thunderball '65
Triple Cross '67
Twitch of the Death Nerve '72

Roxanna Augesen
The Video Dead '87

Florrie Augger
Bugsy Malone '76

Lance August
Terror Eyes '87

Robert August
The Endless Summer '66

Nebojsa Bakocevic
Hey, Babu Riba '88

Muhamad Bakri
Beyond the Walls '84
Double Edge '92
Hanna K. '83

Scott Bakula
The Last Fling '86
Necessary Roughness '91
Sibling Rivalry '90

Henry Bal
Angry Joe Bass '76

Bob Balaban
Absence of Malice '81
Altered States '80
Amos and Andrew '93
Bank Shot '74
Close Encounters of the Third Kind '77
Dead Bang '89
End of the Line '88
For Love or Money '93
Girlfriends '78
Midnight Cowboy '69
The Strawberry Statement '70
2010: The Year We Make Contact '84
Whose Life Is It Anyway? '81

Belinda Balaski
The Howling '81
Proud Men '87

Josiane Balasko
Too Beautiful for You '88

Lajos Balaszovits
Hungarian Rhapsody '78

Bill Balbridge
P.O.W. Deathcamp '89

Nick Baldasare
Beyond Dream's Door '88

Rebecca Balding
Silent Scream '80

Renalto Baldini
Four Ways Out '57

Adam Baldwin
Bad Guys '86
Cohen and Tate '88
D.C. Cab '84
Deadbolt '92
Full Metal Jacket '87
Hadley's Rebellion '84
Love on the Run '85
My Bodyguard '80
Next of Kin '89
Ordinary People '80
Predator 2 '90
Radio Flyer '92
Reckless '84
3:15—The Moment of Truth '86
Where the Day Takes You '92

Alan Baldwin
Hillbilly Blitzkrieg '42

Alec Baldwin
The Alamo: Thirteen Days to Glory '87
Alice '90
Beetlejuice '88
Code of Honor '84
Crazy Streets '80s
Dress Gray '86
Forever, Lulu '87
Glengarry Glen Ross '92
Great Balls of Fire '89
The Hunt for Red October '90
Married to the Mob '88
The Marrying Man '91
Miami Blues '90

Prelude to a Kiss '92
She's Having a Baby '88
Talk Radio '88
Working Girl '88

Daniel Baldwin
The Heroes of Desert Storm '91
Knight Moves '93

Janet Baldwin
Gator Bait '73
Humongous '82
Ruby '77

Mary Baldwin
Rock & the Money-Hungry Party Girls '89

Michael Baldwin
Phantasm '79

Peter Baldwin
The Ghost '63

Robert Baldwin
Courageous Dr. Christian '40
Meet Dr. Christian '39

Stephen Baldwin
The Beast '88
Born on the Fourth of July '89
Crossing the Bridge '92
The Lawrenceville Stories '80s
Posse '93

Walter Baldwin
Winter Meeting '48

William Baldwin
Backdraft '91
Flatliners '90
Internal Affairs '90
Internal Affairs '90
Sliver '93
Three of Hearts '93

Christian Bale
Empire of the Sun '87
Henry V '89
The Land of Faraway '87
Newsies '92
Swing Kids '93
Treasure Island '89

Rafael Baledon
La Fuerza Inutil '87
Los Hermanos Diablo '65

John Balee
King Kung Fu '87

Carla Balenda
Outlaw Women '52

Betty Balfour
Champagne '28
Evergreen '34

Michael Balfour
The Canterbury Tales '71
Fiend Without a Face '58
Mania '60
Moulin Rouge '52
Murder on Approval '56
Quatermass 2 '57

Jennifer Balgobin
City Limits '85
Dr. Caligari '89
Repo Man '83
Roadside Prophets '92

Denise Balik
Humanoids from the Deep '80

Ina Balin
Black Orchid '59
Charro! '69
The Children of An Lac '80
Comancheros '61
The Don is Dead '73

From the Terrace '60
Galyon '77
Panic on the 5:22 '74
The Patsy '64
The Projectionist '71
Vasectomy: A Delicate Matter '86

Mireille Balin
Pepe Le Moko '37

Andras Balint
Father '67
Love Film '70
Stalin '92

Eszter Balint
Bail Jumper '89
The Linguini Incident '92
Stranger than Paradise '84

Fairuza Balk
Gas Food Lodging '92
Outside Chance of Maximillian Glick '88
Return to Oz '85
Valmont '89

Geza Balkay
A Hungarian Fairy Tale '87

Dave Balko
Strike Back '80

Angeline Ball
The Commitments '91

Frank Ball
Boothill Brigade '37
Gun Lords of Stirrup Basin '37
When a Man Rides Alone '33

Henry Ball
Ghost Dance '83

Lucille Ball
Abbott and Costello in Hollywood '45
The Affairs of Annabel '38
Annabel Takes a Tour/Maid's Night Out '38
Beauty for the Asking '39
Best Foot Forward '43
Big Street '42
Comedy Classics '35
Dance, Girl, Dance '40
Dark Corner '46
DuBarry Was a Lady '43
Easy Living '49
Fancy Pants '50
Five Came Back '39
Follow the Fleet '36
Forever Darling '56
The Fuller Brush Girl '50
A Girl, a Guy and a Gob '41
A Guide for the Married Man '67
Having Wonderful Time '38
Having Wonderful Time/ Carnival Boat '38
Hedda Hopper's Hollywood '42
Her Husband's Affairs '47
I Dream Too Much '35
Joy of Living '38
The Long, Long Trailer '54
Look Who's Laughing '41
Mame '74
Miss Grant Takes Richmond '49
Next Time I Marry '38
Panama Lady '39
Roberta '35
Roman Scandals '33
Room Service '38
Seven Days' Leave '42
Sorrowful Jones '49
Stage Door '37
That Girl from Paris '36
Thousands Cheer '43

Too Many Girls '40
Top Hat '35
Valley of the Sun '42
Without Love '45
A Woman of Distinction '50
You Can't Fool Your Wife '40
Yours, Mine & Ours '68
Ziegfeld Follies '46

Nicholas Ball
Claudia '85
The House that Bled to Death '81
Lifeforce '85

Vincent Ball
Blood of the Vampire '58
Dead Lucky '60
Demolition '77
A Matter of WHO '62
Not Tonight Darling '72
Terror Ship '54

William Ball
Suburban Commando '91

Carl Ballantine
Hollywood Chaos '89
Revenge of the Cheerleaders '76
Speedway '68
World's Greatest Lover '77

Maxine Ballantyne
Lemora, Lady Dracula '73

Doug Ballard
Sex O'Clock News '85

J.G. Ballard
Empire of the Sun '87

Kaye Ballard
Eternity '90
Fate '90
The Girl Most Likely '57
Modern Love '90
The Ritz '76
Tiger Warsaw '87

Jerry Ballew
Cry from the Mountain '85

Smith Ballew
Gun Cargo '49
Hawaiian Buckaroo '38
Panamint's Bad Man '38
Rawhide '38
Roll Along Cowboy '37

Thomas Balltore
Once Bitten '85

Mario Balmasada
The Last Supper '76

Jean-Francois Balmer
Madame Bovary '91
Window Shopping '86

Joe Balogh
Visions '90

Haydee Balsa
La Nueva Cigarra '86

Martin Balsam
After the Fox '66
Al Capone '59
All the President's Men '76
The Anderson Tapes '71
Bedford Incident '65
Brand New Life '72
Breakfast at Tiffany's '61
Cape Fear '61
Cape Fear '91
The Carpetbaggers '64
Catch-22 '70
Confessions of a Police Captain '72
Death Rage '77

Death Wish 3 '85
The Defender '57
Delta Force '86
Eyes Behind the Stars '72
The Goodbye People '83
Grown Ups '86
Hard Frame '70
Harlow '65
Hombre '67
The House on Garibaldi Street '79
Innocent Prey '88
The Lindbergh Kidnapping Case '76
Little Big Man '70
Little Gloria...Happy at Last '84
Marjorie Morningstar '58
Miles to Go Before I Sleep '74
Mitchell '75
Murder in Space '85
Murder on the Orient Express '74
The People vs. Jean Harris '81
P.I. Private Investigations '87
Psycho '60
Queenie '87
Raid on Entebbe '77
St. Elmo's Fire '85
The Salamander '82
Season for Assassins '71
Silver Bears '78
Spaghetti Western '69
The Stone Killer '73
Summer Wishes, Winter Dreams '73
The Taking of Pelham One Two Three '74
A Thousand Clowns '65
Tora! Tora! Tora! '70
Twelve Angry Men '57
Two Minute Warning '76
The Warning '80

Talia Balsam
Calamity Jane '82
Consenting Adults '85
Crawlspace '86
In the Mood '87
Kent State '81
The Kindred '87
Mass Appeal '84
Nadia '84
On the Edge: The Survival of Dana '79
Private Investigations '87
Sunnyside '79
Trust Me '89

Allison Balson
Best Seller '87

Donna Baltron
Bloodbath in Psycho Town '89

Fernando Balzaretti
The Summer of Miss Forbes '88

Judy Bamber
The Atomic Brain '64

Gerry Bamman
The Chase '91
Lightning Over Water '80
The Ten Million Dollar Getaway '91

Junzaburo Ban
Dodes 'ka-den '70

Alexis Banas
The Haunting of Barney Palmer '90s

Lynn Banashek
Fatal Games '84

Raina Barrett
Oh! Calcutta! '72

Ray Barrett
Rebel '85
Revenge '71
Waterfront '83
Where the Green Ants Dream '84

Rona Barrett
Sextette '78

Roy Barrett
Contagion '87

Tim Barrett
Where the Bullets Fly '66

Victoria Barrett
Three Kinds of Heat '87

Mario Barri
The Steel Claw '61

Amanda Barrie
Carry On Cleo '65

Anthony Barrie
Girlfriend from Hell '89

Barbara Barrie
The Bell Jar '79
Breaking Away '79
Child of Glass '78
End of the Line '88
The Execution '85
Private Benjamin '80
Real Men '87
To Race the Wind '80
Two of a Kind '82

Colin Barrie
Melody '71

Judith Barrie
Party Girls '29

Mona Barrie
Cass Timberlane '47
Dawn on the Great Divide '42
One Night of Love '34
Today I Hang '42

Wendy Barrie
Cash '34
Dead End '37
Five Came Back '39
Follies Girl '43
The Hound of the Baskervilles '39
I Am the Law '38
If I Were Rich '33
The Saint Strikes Back '39
Saint Strikes Back: Criminal Court '46
The Saint Takes Over '40
Vengeance '37
Wedding Rehearsal '32

Edgar Barrier
The Giant Claw '57
Phantom of the Opera '43

Pat Barringer
The Acid Eaters '67
Orgy of the Dead '65

Christopher Barrington-Leigh
Loyalties '86

Pat Barrington
Mantis in Lace '68

Phyliss Barrington
The Drifter '32
Sucker Money '34

Rebecca Barrington
Dance or Die '87

George Barris
Smokey & the Hotwire Gang '79

Seth Barrish
Home Remedy '88

Bill Barron
Alone in the T-Shirt Zone '86

Bob Barron
Ballad of a Gunfighter '64
Song of Old Wyoming '45

John Barron
Whoops Apocalypse '83

Keith Barron
Baby Love '69
Con Man '92
Nothing But the Night '72

Robert Barron
Bill & Ted's Excellent Adventure '89
The Caravan Trail '46
Sea Hound '47
Tank Commando '59

Diana Barrows
My Mom's a Werewolf '89

Barta Barry
Gladiators 7 '62

Bruce Barry
Plunge Into Darkness '77

Donald (Don "Red") Barry
Adventures of Red Ryder '40
Blazing Stewardesses '75
Border Rangers '50
California Joe '43
Frontier Vengeance '40
Gunfire '50
Hard Frame '70
Hostile Guns '67
I Shot Billy the Kid '50
Iron Angel '64
Outlaw Gang '49
Panama Patrol '39
The Purple Heart '44
Red Desert '50
Ringside '49
Saga of Death Valley '39
The Shakiest Gun in the West '68
Sinners in Paradise '38
The Sombrero Kid '42
Square Dance Jubilee '51
Sundown Fury '42
Sundown Kid '43
Texas Layover '75
Tough Assignment '49
Trail of the Mounties '47
Train to Tombstone '50
Western Double Feature 9: LaRue & Beery '40s
Western Double Feature 15 '50
Wyoming Outlaw '39

Dorothy Barry
Sweetie '89

Duece Barry
Werewolves on Wheels '71

Gene Barry
The Adventures of Nellie Bly '81
The Atomic City '52
Back from Eternity '56
China Gate '57
Columbo: Prescription Murder '67
A Cry for Love '80
Maroc 7 '67
Perry Mason: The Case of the Lost Love '87

Red Garters '54
Second Coming of Suzanne '80
Soldier of Fortune '55
Subterfuge '68
Suzanne '80
Thunder Road '58
The 27 Day '57
The War of the Worlds '53

J.J. Barry
Dark August '76

Joan Barry
Rich and Strange '32

Leon Barry
King of the Wild Horses '24
The Three Musketeers '21

Matthew Barry
The Wraith '87

Nat Barry
Police Court '37

Neill Barry
Joey '85
O.C. and Stiggs '87
Old Enough '84

Patricia Barry
Bogie '80
Sammy, the Way-Out Seal '62
Twilight Zone: The Movie '83

Phyllis Barry
Goodbye Love '34
What! No Beer? '33

Raymond J. Barry
Born on the Fourth of July '89
Cop '88
Daddy's Boys '87
K2: The Ultimate High '92
Rapid Fire '92
Year of the Dragon '85

Tony Barry
Goodbye Pork Pie '81
Hard Knocks '80
Little Boy Lost '78
The Quest '86
Shame '87
We of the Never Never '82

Wendy Barry
Knights of the City '85

Wesley Barry
Battling Bunyon '24
The Country Kid '23
Sunny Skies '30

Deborah Barrymore
Bullseye! '90
Lionheart '87

Drew Barrymore
Altered States '80
The Amy Fisher Story '92
Babes in Toyland '86
Cat's Eye '85
A Conspiracy of Love '87
Doppelganger: The Evil Within '90
E.T.: The Extra-Terrestrial '82
Far from Home '89
Firestarter '84
Guncrazy '92
Irreconcilable Differences '84
Motorama '91
Poison Ivy '92
See You in the Morning '89
Sketch Artist '92
Strange Tales/Ray Bradbury Theatre '86

Ethel Barrymore
The Farmer's Daughter '47
Main Street to Broadway '53

Moonrise '48
None But the Lonely Heart '44
The Paradine Case '47
Portrait of Jennie '48
Rasputin and the Empress '32
The Spiral Staircase '46
That Midnight Kiss '49
Young at Heart '54

John Barrymore
Beau Brummel '24
The Beloved Rogue '27
A Bill of Divorcement '32
Bulldog Drummond Comes Back '37
Bulldog Drummond's Peril '38
Bulldog Drummond's Revenge '37
Bulldog Drummond's Revenge/Bulldog Drummond's Peril '38
Dinner at Eight '33
Dr. Jekyll and Mr. Hyde '20
Don Juan '26
Grand Hotel '32
The Great Man Votes '38
The Horror of It All '91
Marie Antoinette '38
Maytime '37
Playmates '41
Rasputin and the Empress '32
Romeo and Juliet '36
State's Attorney '31
Svengali '31
The Tempest '28
The Tempest/The Eagle '27
Topaze '33
Twentieth Century '34

John Barrymore, Jr.
Americana '81
A Game of Crime '60
High Lonesome '50
High School Confidential '58
Never Love a Stranger '58
Smokey Bites the Dust '81

Lionel Barrymore
Ah, Wilderness! '35
America/The Fall of Babylon '24
Camille '36
Captains Courageous '37
David Copperfield '35
Devil Doll '36
Dinner at Eight '33
Dr. Kildare's Strange Case '40
Duel in the Sun '46
Free and Easy '30
A Free Soul '31
The Girl from Missouri '34
The Gorgeous Hussy '36
Grand Hotel '32
A Guy Named Joe '44
It's a Wonderful Life '46
Key Largo '48
Lady Be Good '41
The Little Colonel '35
Main Street to Broadway '53
Mark of the Vampire '35
Mata Hari '32
On Borrowed Time '39
Rasputin and the Empress '32
The Return of Peter Grimm '35
Sadie Thompson '28
Saratoga '37
Short Films of D.W. Griffith, Vol. 2 '09
Since You Went Away '44
Test Pilot '38
Thousands Cheer '43
Treasure Island '34
West of Zanzibar '28
You Can't Take It with You '38

Judith Barsi
Jaws: The Revenge '87
The Land Before Time '88

Vladimir Barsky
The Battleship Potemkin '25

Paul Bartel
Amazon Women on the Moon '87
Baring It All '85
Chopping Mall '86
Desire and Hell at Sunset Motel '92
Eating Raoul '82
Far Out Man '89
Frankenweenie '84
Hollywood Boulevard '76
Into the Night '85
Killer Party '86
Liquid Dreams '92
Mortuary Academy '91
Out of the Dark '88
Piranha '78
The Pope Must Diet '91
Pucker Up and Bark Like a Dog '89
Rock 'n' Roll High School '79
Scenes from the Class Struggle in Beverly Hills '89

Eddie Barth
Twenty Dollar Star '91

John Bartha
Planet on the Prowl '65

Richard Barthelmess
Broken Blossoms '19
The Cabin in the Cotton '32
The Dropkick '27
Heroes for Sale '33
Just Suppose '26
The Love Flower '20
Only Angels Have Wings '39
Ranson's Folly '26
Shore Leave '25
Soul-Fire '25
The Spoilers '42
Spy of Napoleon '36
Tol'able David '21
Way Down East '20

Carl Bartholomew
Cole Justice '89

Freddie Bartholomew
Anna Karenina '35
Captains Courageous '37
David Copperfield '35
Listen, Darling '38
Little Lord Fauntleroy '36
St. Benny the Dip '51
Sepia Cinderella '47
Tom Brown's School Days '40

Scott Bartle
Hector's Bunyip '86

Bennie Bartlett
Clipped Wings '53

Bonnie Bartlett
The Deliberate Stranger '86
Dempsey '83
A Long Way Home '81
Love Letters '83
Rape and Marriage: The Rideout Case '80
Twins '88

Calvin Bartlett
Dudes '87

Martine Bartlett
Sybil '76

Nicola Bartlett
Contagion '87

Richard Bartlett
Silent Raiders '54

Robin Bartlett
If Looks Could Kill '91
Postcards from the Edge '90

Tom Bartlett
Hobgoblins '80s

Robyn Barto
Blue Skies Again '83

Eva Bartok
Blood and Black Lace '64
Crimson Pirate '52
The Gamma People '56
Naked in the Night '58
Norman Conquest '53
Operation Amsterdam '60
S.O.S. Pacific '60
Spaceways '53

Luciano Bartoli
Bizarre '87

Buzz Barton
Apache Kid's Escape '30
The Lone Defender '32
Mystery Trooper '32
Powdersmoke Range '35
The Riding Avenger '36
The Tonto Kid '35

Charles T. Barton
The Fighting Westerner '35

Diana Barton
Body of Influence '93

Gregg Barton
West to Glory '47

James Barton
Here Comes the Groom '51
The Misfits '61
Naked Hills '56
The Time of Your Life '48

Joe Barton
Slaughterhouse '87

Peter Barton
Friday the 13th, Part 4: The Final Chapter '84
Hell Night '81

Laurie Bartrarr
Friday the 13th '80

Brad Bartrum
Twisted Nightmare '87

Billy Barty
Ace Crawford, Private Eye
The Amazing Dobermans '76
Body Slam '87
Cannon Movie Tales: Snow White '89
The Day of the Locust '75
Digging Up Business '91
Foul Play '78
Harum Scarum '65
Legend '86
Life Stinks '91
Masters of the Universe '87
Mickey the Great '39
A Midsummer Night's Dream '35
Night Patrol '85
Roustabout '64
Rumpelstiltskin '86
Under the Rainbow '81
Willow '88
Wishful Thinking '92

Mikhail Baryshnikov
Company Business '91

Dancers '87
That's Dancing! '85
The Turning Point '77
White Nights '85

Anat "Topol" Barzilai
Witchcraft '88

Gary Basaraba
Fried Green Tomatoes '91
One Magic Christmas '85

Dante Basco
Hook '91

Richard Basehart
The Andersonville Trial '70
Being There '79
The Bounty Man '72
The Brothers Karamazov '58
Chato's Land '71
Flood! '76
Great Bank Hoax '78
Hans Brinker '69
He Walked by Night '48
Hitler '62
Island of Dr. Moreau '77
La Strada '54
Marilyn: The Untold Story '80
Mark Twain's A Connecticut Yankee in King Arthur's Court '78
Moby Dick '56
Rage '72
The Rebels '79
Reign of Terror '49
The Swindle '55

Tom Basham
The Pink Angels '71
Psychopath '73

Count Basie
Cinderfella '60
Stage Door Canteen '43

Toni Basil
Angel 3: The Final Chapter '88
Easy Rider '69
Mother, Jugs and Speed '76
Pajama Party '64
Rockula '90
Slaughterhouse Rock '88

Oleg Basilashvili
Autumn Marathon '79

Nadine Basile
Crazy for Love '52

The Basin Street Boys
The Duke is the Tops '38

Kim Basinger
Batman '89
Blind Date '87
Cool World '92
Final Analysis '92
Fool for Love '86
From Here to Eternity '79
Hard Country '81
Killjoy '81
The Man Who Loved Women '83
The Marrying Man '91
My Stepmother Is an Alien '88
Nadine '87
The Natural '84
Never Say Never Again '83
9 1/2 Weeks '86
No Mercy '86

A.W. Baskcomb
Phantom Fiend '35

Elya Baskin
Enemies, a Love Story '89
Moscow on the Hudson '84
The Name of the Rose '86

Spy Trap '92

Marianne Basler
Overseas: Three Women with Man Trouble '90
A Soldier's Tale '91

Lena Basquette
Hard Hombre '31
A Night for Crime '42
Pleasure '31
Rose of Rio Grande '38

Alfie Bass
The Fearless Vampire Killers '67
The Lavender Hill Mob '51
Man on the Run '49

Bobby Bass
The Squeeze '87

Harriet Bass
An Empty Bed '90

Mike Bass
Brotherhood of Death '76

John Bassberger
Thorn '73

Albert Basserman
Foreign Correspondent '40
Madame Curie '43
Melody Master '41
The Moon and Sixpence '43
The Private Affairs of Bel Ami '47
The Red Shoes '48
Reunion in France '42
Rhapsody in Blue '45
The Shanghai Gesture '42
Since You Went Away '44
A Woman's Face '41

Heide Basset
First Turn On '83

Angela Bassett
Boyz N the Hood '91
City of Hope '91
Critters 4 '91
The Heroes of Desert Storm '91
The Jacksons: An American Dream '92
Malcolm X '92
Passion Fish '92
What's Love Got to Do With It? '93

Linda Bassett
Waiting for the Moon '87

Steve Bassett
Spring Break '83

Cynthia Bassinet
Last Dance '91

Paul Bassis
Ganjasaurus Rex '87

Bob Basso
Paradise Motel '84

Christine Basson
Snake Dancer

William Bast
Forever James Dean '88

Alexandra Bastedo
The Blood Spattered Bride '72
Draw! '84
Find the Lady '75
The Ghoul '75
Kashmiri Run '69

Billy Bastiani
Salvation! '87

Fanny Bastien
The Wolf at the Door '87

Michal Bat-Adam
Atalia '85
The House on Chelouche Street '73
I Love You Rosa '72

Sylvia Bataille
The Crime of Monsieur Lange '36
A Day in the Country '46

Alexei Batalov
The Cranes are Flying '57
The Lady with the Dog '59
Moscow Does Not Believe in Tears '80

Nikolai Batalov
Bed and Sofa '27
Mother '26

Pierre Batcheff
Napoleon '27
Un Chien Andalou '28

Anthony Bate
Madhouse Mansion '74
Philby, Burgess and MacLean: Spy Scandal of the Century '84

Natalie Bate
Ground Zero '88

Charles Bateman
The Brotherhood of Satan '71

Jason Bateman
Breaking the Rules '92
Can You Feel Me Dancing? '85
A Taste for Killing '92
Teen Wolf Too '87

Justine Bateman
Can You Feel Me Dancing? '85
The Closer '91
Deadbolt '92
The Fatal Image '90
The Night We Never Met '93
Primary Motive '92
Satisfaction '88

Kent Bateman
Breaking the Rules '92

Alan Bates
Britannia Hospital '82
Club Extinction '89
A Day in the Death of Joe Egg '71
Duet for One '86
An Englishman Abroad '83
The Entertainer '60
Far from the Madding Crowd '67
Georgy Girl '66
The Go-Between '71
Hamlet '90
In Celebration '75
A Kind of Loving '62
The King of Hearts '66
Mr. Frost '89
Nijinsky '80
Prayer for the Dying '87
Quartet '81
Return of the Soldier '84
The Rose '79
Separate Tables '83
The Shout '78
The Story of a Love Story '73
Trespasser '85
An Unmarried Woman '78
A Voyage 'Round My Father '89
We Think the World of You '88
Whistle Down the Wind '62
The Wicked Lady '83

Women in Love '70
Zorba the Greek '64

Barbara Bates
The Caddy '53
The Inspector General '49
June Bride '48
Let's Make it Legal '51
Rhapsody '54

Bill Bates
Ghosts on the Loose '43

Caroline Bates
Grad Night '81

Florence Bates
The Chocolate Soldier '41
Diary of a Chambermaid '46
Heaven Can Wait '43
I Remember Mama '48
The Judge Steps Out '49
Love Crazy '41
Lullaby of Broadway '51
Mexican Spitfire at Sea '42
Mr. Lucky '43
The Moon and Sixpence '43
My Dear Secretary '49
Portrait of Jennie '48
Rebecca '40
Road Show '41
San Antonio '45
The Secret Life of Walter Mitty '47
Since You Went Away '44
The Son of Monte Cristo '41
The Tuttles of Tahiti '42
Winter Meeting '48

Granville Bates
The Great Man Votes '38
Next Time I Marry '38

Jeanne Bates
Eraserhead '78
The Mask of Dijon '46
Mom '89
Sabaka '55
The Strangler '64

Kathy Bates
At Play in the Fields of the Lord '91
Come Back to the Five & Dime Jimmy Dean, Jimmy Dean '82
Dick Tracy '90
Fried Green Tomatoes '91
High Stakes '89
Hostages '93
Men Don't Leave '89
Misery '90
Morning After '86
Murder Ordained '87
Prelude to a Kiss '92
Roe vs. Wade '89
Shadows and Fog '92
Summer Heat '87
Used People '92
White Palace '90

Michael Bates
Bedazzled '68
Patton '70

Paul Bates
Crazy People '90

Ralph Bates
Dr. Jekyll and Sister Hyde '71
Dynasty of Fear '72
The Graveyard '74
The Horror of Frankenstein '70
I Don't Want to Be Born '75
Letters to an Unknown Lover '84
Lust for a Vampire '71
Murder Motel '74
Second Chance '80

Bates ▶cont.

Taste the Blood of Dracula '70

William Bates
Orgy of the Dead '65

Randall Batinkoff
For Keeps '88
The Player '92
School Ties '92
Streetwalkin' '85

Lloyd Batista
Last Plane Out '83

Stiv Bators
Polyester '81
Tapeheads '89

Rick Battaglia
Cold Steel for Tortuga '65
Roland the Mighty '58
'Tis a Pity She's a Whore '73

Jeanette Batti
Four Bags Full '56

Carlo Battista
Umberto D '55

Miriam Battista
Blind Fools '40

Patrick Bauchau
Creepers '85
Double Identity '89
Emmanuelle 4 '84
The Music Teacher '88
The Rapture '91
State of Things '82

Georgette Baudry
Perfumed Nightmare '89

Belinda Bauer
Archer: The Fugitive from the
    Empire '81
Flashdance '83
The Game of Love '90
RoboCop 2 '90
The Rosary Murders '87
Samson and Delilah '84
Servants of Twilight '91
The Sins of Dorian Gray '82
Timerider '83
Winter Kills '79

Bruce Bauer
My Tutor '82

Charita Bauer
The Cradle Will Fall '83

Irv Bauer
Sweet Beat '62

Jamie Lyn Bauer
Mysterious Island of Beautiful
    Women '79

Michelle Bauer
Deadly Embrace '88
Evil Toons '90
Hollywood Chainsaw Hookers
    '88
Phantom Empire '87
Wild Man '89

Steven Bauer
The Beast '88
A Climate for Killing '91
False Arrest '92
Gleaming the Cube '89
Raising Cain '92
Red Shoe Diaries 2: Double
    Dare '92
Running Scared '86
Scarface '83
Sweet Poison '91
Sword of Gideon '86

Thief of Hearts '84
Wildfire '88

Sammy Baugh
King of the Texas Rangers '41

Ricardo Bauleo
Lost Diamond '74

Bruce Baum
Kandyland '87

Andy Bauman
Night of the Kickfighters '91

**Erna Martha
Bauman**
Invasion of the Vampires '61
World of the Vampires '60

**Anne Marie
Baumann**
The Last Days of Pompeii '60

Katherine Baumann
Chrome and Hot Leather '71
Slashed Dreams '74

**Michele
Baumgartner**
The Woman Next Door '81

**Monika
Baumgartner**
The Nasty Girl '90

Harry Baur
Beethoven '36
Crime and Punishment '35
Poil de Carotte '31
Volpone '39

Marc Baur
Ultimate Desires '91

Aurora Bautista
It Happened at Nightmare Inn
    '70

Francis Bavier
The Day the Earth Stood Still
    '51
Horizons West '52
It Started with a Kiss '59
The Lady Says No '51

Jose Baviera
The Exterminating Angel '62

Barbara Baxley
All Fall Down '62
Come Along with Me '84
Countdown '68
Tropic of Desire '80s

David Baxt
Cloud Waltzing '87

Alan Baxter
Abe Lincoln in Illinois '40
Behind Prison Walls '43
Each Dawn I Die '39
It Could Happen to You '37
Saboteur '42
The Set-Up '49
Shadow of the Thin Man '41
She Shoulda Said No '49
Wide Open Faces '38
Wild Weed '49

Anne Baxter
All About Eve '50
Angel on My Shoulder '46
Carnival Story '54
East of Eden '80
The Fighting Sullivans '42
Guest in the House '45
Homecoming '48
I Confess '53
Jane Austen in Manhattan '80
The Magnificent Ambersons
    '42

Masks of Death '86
The North Star '43
The Razor's Edge '46
The Ten Commandments '56
Three Violent People '57
Ticket to Tomahawk '50
Walk on the Wild Side '62

Jane Baxter
The Evil Mind '34

Keith Baxter
Ash Wednesday '73
Berlin Blues '89
Chimes at Midnight '67

Lora Baxter
Before Morning '33

Lynsey Baxter
The French Lieutenant's
    Woman '81
The Girl in a Swing '89
To the Lighthouse '83

Warner Baxter
Adam Had Four Sons '41
Broadway Bill '34
42nd Street '33
Penthouse '33
Stand Up and Cheer '34
Vogues of 1938 '37
West of Zanzibar '28

**Meredith Baxter
Birney**
Ben '72
Beulah Land '80
Bittersweet Love '76
Broken Badge '85
The Family Man '79
The Invasion of Carol Enders
    '74
Jezebel's Kiss '90
The Kissing Place '90
Little Women '78
The Stranger Who Looks Like
    Me '74
Take Your Best Shot '82

Francis Bay
The Attic '80
Critters 3 '91
The Pit & the Pendulum '91

**Sara (Rosalba Neri)
Bay**
Devil's Wedding Night '73
Lady Frankenstein '72
Naked Warriors '73

Susan Bay
Big Mouth '67

Nathalie Baye
Beau Pere '81
Beethoven's Nephew '88
The Green Room '78
Honeymoon '87
La Balance '81
The Man Inside '90
The Return of Martin Guerre
    '83

Gary Bayer
Promised a Miracle '88
Will: G. Gordon Liddy '82

Geoffrey Bayldon
The Bushbaby '70
Madame Sousatzka '88
Porridge '91

Terence Baylor
Macbeth '71

Gene Baylos
The Love Machine '71

Lawrence Bayne
Black Robe '91

A Whisper to a Scream '88

Brenda Bazinet
Self-Defense '88

Brigid Bazlen
The Honeymoon Machine '61

Michael Beach
Cadence '89
In a Shallow Grave '88
Internal Affairs '90
One False Move '91
Weekend War '88

Scott Beach
Out '88

Stephanie Beacham
And Now the Screaming
    Starts '73
The Confessional '75
The Dying Truth '91
Foreign Affairs '93
Horror Planet '80
The Nightcomers '72
Super Bitch '89
Troop Beverly Hills '89

Cindy Beal
Slave Girls from Beyond
    Infinity '87

Crusty Beal
Sinner's Blood '70

John Beal
Amityville 3: The Demon '83
Break of Hearts '35
Double Wedding '37
Edge of Darkness '43
The Firm '93
The Great Commandment '41
I Am the Law '38
The Kid Who Loved Christmas
    '90
Les Miserables '35
Little Minister '34
Ten Who Dared '60

Kay Beal
Torture Train '83

Jennifer Beals
Blood & Concrete: A Love
    Story '90
The Bride '85
Cinderella '84
Club Extinction '89
Flashdance '83
The Gamble '88
In the Soup '92
Indecency '92
Split Decisions '88
Terror Stalks the Class
    Reunion '93
That's Dancing! '85
Vampire's Kiss '88

Lee Ann Beaman
Tropical Heat '93

Dovie Beams
Wild Wheels '75

Christopher F. Bean
Firepower '79

Orson Bean
Anatomy of a Murder '59
The Hobbit '78
Innerspace '87
Instant Karma '90
Lola '69
Movie Maker '86
The Return of the King '80

Rick Bean
Whodunit '82

Robert Bean
Creature from the Haunted
    Sea '60
The Wild Ride '60

Sean Bean
Caravaggio '86
The Field '90
Patriot Games '92
Stormy Monday '88

Hilary Beane
Zapped! '82

Harry Bear
Gods of the Plague '69

**Matthew "Stymie"
Beard**
Broken Strings '40
East of Eden '80
Little Rascals, Book 1 '30s
Little Rascals, Book 2 '30s
Little Rascals, Book 3 '38
Little Rascals, Book 4 '30s
Little Rascals, Book 5 '30s
Little Rascals, Book 6 '30s
Little Rascals, Book 7 '30s
Little Rascals, Book 9 '30s
Little Rascals, Book 16 '30s
Little Rascals: Choo Choo/
    Fishy Tales '32
Little Rascals Christmas
    Special '79
Little Rascals Collector's
    Edition, Vol. 1-6
Little Rascals Comedy
    Classics, Vol. 1
Little Rascals Comedy
    Classics, Vol. 2
Little Rascals: Fish Hooky/
    Spooky Hooky '33
Little Rascals: Honkey
    Donkey/Sprucin' Up '34
Little Rascals: Little Sinner/
    Two Too Young '35
Little Rascals: Mush and Milk/
    Three Men in a Tub '33
Little Rascals: Pups is Pups/
    Three Smart Boys '30
Little Rascals: Readin' and
    Writin'/Mail and Female '31
Little Rascals: Reunion in
    Rhythm/Mike Fright '37
Little Rascals: Spanky/Feed
    'Em and Weep '32
Little Rascals: The Pinch
    Singer/Framing Youth '36
Little Rascals Two Reelers,
    Vol. 1 '29
Little Rascals Two Reelers,
    Vol. 2 '33
Little Rascals Two Reelers,
    Vol. 3 '36
Little Rascals Two Reelers,
    Vol. 4 '30
Little Rascals Two Reelers,
    Vol. 5 '34
Little Rascals Two Reelers,
    Vol. 6 '36
Little Rascals, Vol. 1 '29
Two-Gun Man from Harlem
    '38

Alice Beardsley
Where the Lilies Bloom '74

Nicholas Beardsley
Savage Island '85

Cody Bearpaw
Devil & Leroy Basset '73

Amanda Bearse
Fraternity Vacation '85
Fright Night '85
It's a Bundyful Life '92
Protocol '84

Emmanuelle Beart
Date with an Angel '87
Manon of the Spring '87

Allyce Beasley
Moonlighting '85
Motorama '91
National Lampoon's Loaded
Weapon 1 '93
Silent Night, Deadly Night 4:
Initiation '90

Linda Beatie
The Prodigal Planet '88

Norman Beaton
Growing Pains '82
Playing Away '87

Ann Beattie
Chilly Scenes of Winter '79

Clyde Beatty
Africa Screams '49
Darkest Africa '36
The Lost Jungle '34

Ned Beatty
All God's Children '80
Angel Square '92
Back to School '86
Big Bad John '90
Big Bus '76
The Big Easy '87
Blind Vision '91
Captain America '89
Charlotte Forten's Mission:
Experiment in Freedom '85
Chattahoochee '89
A Cry in the Wild '90
Deliverance '72
Dying Room Only '73
The Execution of Private
Slovik '74
Exorcist 2: The Heretic '77
The Fourth Protocol '87
Friendly Fire '79
Going Under '91
Gray Lady Down '77
Great Bank Hoax '78
The Guyana Tragedy: The
Story of Jim Jones '80
The Haunting of Barney
Palmer '90s
Hear My Song '91
Hopscotch '80
Illusions '91
The Incredible Shrinking
Woman '81
Konrad '90s
The Last American Hero '73
Midnight Crossing '87
Mikey & Nicky '76
Ministry of Vengeance '89
Network '76
1941 '79
Our Town '77
Physical Evidence '89
Pray TV '82
Prelude to a Kiss '92
Promises in the Dark '79
Purple People Eater '88
A Question of Love '78
Repossessed '90
Robert Kennedy and His
Times '90
Rolling Vengeance '87
Rumpelstiltskin '82
Sex and Buttered Popcorn '91
Shadows in the Storm '88
The Silver Streak '76
Sniper '89
Spy '89
Stroker Ace '83
Superman: The Movie '78
Superman 2 '80
Switching Channels '88

The Thief Who Came to
Dinner '73
Time Trackers '88
Touched '82
The Toy '82
Tragedy of Flight 103: The
Inside Story '91
The Trouble with Spies '87
The Unholy '88
White Lightning '73
Wise Blood '79
A Woman Called Golda '82

Robert Beatty
Against the Wind '48
Appointment with Crime '45
Captain Horatio Hornblower
'51
Counterblast '48
The Love of Three Queens '54
Postmark for Danger '56
Postmark for Danger/
Quicksand '56
San Demetrio, London '47
Time Lock '57
Where Eagles Dare '68
Wings of Danger '52

Warren Beatty
All Fall Down '62
Bonnie & Clyde '67
Bugsy '91
Dick Tracy '90
Dollars '71
Heaven Can Wait '78
Ishtar '87
Lilith '64
McCabe & Mrs. Miller '71
Parallax View '74
Promise Her Anything '66
Reds '81
Roman Spring of Mrs. Stone
'61
Shampoo '75
Splendor in the Grass '61

Carolyn Beauchamp
Troma's War '88

Julie Beaulieu
Bridge to Terabithia '85

Hugh Beaumont
Danger Zone '51
The Fallen Sparrow '43
The Human Duplicators '64
The Lady Confesses '45
The Lost Continent '51
The Mole People '56
Money Madness '47
Objective, Burma! '45
Panama Menace '41
Phone Call from a Stranger
'52
Pier 23 '51
Railroaded '47
Roaring City '51
The Seventh Victim '43
To the Shores of Tripoli '42

Kathryn Beaumont
Alice in Wonderland '51
Peter Pan '53

Lucy Beaumont
Condemned to Live '35
The Crowd '28
A Free Soul '31

Nicholas Beauvy
Rage '72
The Toolbox Murders '78

Ellen Beaven
Buster '88

Terry Beaver
Impure Thoughts '86

Louise Beavers
Big Street '42
Bullets or Ballots '38
Coquette '29
Delightfully Dangerous '45
Dixie Jamboree '44
DuBarry Was a Lady '43
General Spanky '36
Goodbye, My Lady '56
In the Money '34
The Jackie Robinson Story
'50
Mr. Blandings Builds His
Dream House '48
Reap the Wild Wind '42
She Done Him Wrong '33
Tammy and the Bachelor '57
Tell It to the Judge '49

George Beban
Italian '15

Claudine Beccaire
Inhibition '86

John C. Becher
Below the Belt '80

Sidney Bechet
Moon Over Harlem '39

Davide Bechini
The Story of Boys & Girls '91

Joan Bechtel
Split '90

William Bechtel
Spite Marriage '29

Bonnie Beck
Merchants of War '90

Jackson Beck
Popeye and Friends in the
South Seas '61

Jeff Beck
The Return of Spinal Tap '92
The Secret Policeman's Other
Ball '82

Jennifer Beck
Tightrope '84

John Beck
Audrey Rose '77
Big Bus '76
A Climate for Killing '91
Deadly Illusion '87
Fire and Rain '89
Great American Traffic Jam
'80
In the Cold of the Night '89
King of the Pecos '36
Lawman '71
The Other Side of Midnight
'77
Paperback Hero '73
Sky Riders '76
Sleeper '73
Three in the Attic '68
Time Machine '78

Julian Beck
Emergency '68
Oedipus Rex '67
Poltergeist 2: The Other Side
'86
Signals Through the Flames
'83

Kimberly Beck
Friday the 13th, Part 4: The
Final Chapter '84
Massacre at Central High '76
Nightmare at Noon '87
Private War '90
Roller Boogie '79

Michael Beck
Blackout '85

Celebrity '85
Deadly Game '91
The Golden Seal '83
Holocaust '78
Madman '79
Megaforce '82
Warlords of the 21st Century
'82
The Warriors '79
Xanadu '80

Stanley Beck
Lenny '74

Thomas Beck
Charlie Chan at the Opera '36
Charlie Chan in Paris '35

Vincent Beck
Santa Claus Conquers the
Martians '64

Graham Beckel
Hazel's People '75
Jennifer 8 '92
The Money '75
The Paper Chase '73
Rising Son '90
Separate But Equal '91

Desiree Becker
Good Morning, Babylon '87

Gerry Becker
Legacy of Lies '92
The Public Eye '92

Gretchen Becker
Firehead '90
Maniac Cop 3 '93

Hartmut Becker
Escape from Sobibor '87
Jenny's War '85

Klaus Becker
The Blum Affair '48

Mary Becker
Mindwarp '91

Pedro Becker
Antonio '73

Tony Becker
Cody '67

Scotty Beckett
Conquest '32
Little Rascals, Book 7 '30s
Nancy Goes to Rio '50

Friedrich Beckhaus
The Wannsee Conference '84

Kate Beckinsale
Much Ado About Nothing '93
One Against the Wind '91

Tony Beckley
Assault '70
The Fiend '71
The Italian Job '69

Henry Beckman
At Sword's Point '51
Family Reunion '88

Reginald Beckwith
Burn Witch, Burn! '62
Men of Sherwood Forest '57

William Beckwith
Escape from Safehaven '88
Prime Evil '88

Rod Bedall
Mona Lisa '86

Don Beddoe
Buck Privates Come Home
'47
The Enforcer '51
Golden Boy '39
Jack the Giant Killer '62

The Narrow Margin '52
Nickel Mountain '85
The Night of the Hunter '55

Bonnie Bedelia
The Big Fix '78
The Boy Who Could Fly '86
Death of an Angel '86
Die Hard '88
Die Hard 2: Die Harder '90
Fat Man and Little Boy '89
The Fire Next Time '93
Heart Like a Wheel '83
Lady from Yesterday '85
Lovers and Other Strangers
'70
Memorial Day '83
Needful Things '93
Presumed Innocent '90
Prince of Pennsylvania '88
A Question of Love '78
Salem's Lot '79
Somebody Has to Shoot the
Picture '90
The Stranger '87
Switched at Birth '91
They Shoot Horses, Don't
They? '69
Violets Are Blue '86
Walking Through the Fire '80
When the Time Comes '91

Rodney Bedell
Just for the Hell of It '68

Barbara Bedford
The Broken Mask '28
Found Alive '34
The Mad Whirl '25
Mockery '27
Tumbleweeds '25

Brian Bedford
Grand Prix '66
Robin Hood '70

Patrick Bedford
Up the Down Staircase '67

Kabir Bedi
Archer: The Fugitive from the
Empire '81
Demon Rage '82
Octopussy '83
Terminal Entry '87

Wendy Bednarz
There's Nothing Out There '90

Guy Bedos
Pardon Mon Affaire '76
Pardon Mon Affaire, Too! '77

Alfonso Bedoya
The Stranger Wore a Gun '53

Janet Beecher
I'd Give My Life '36
The Mark of Zorro '40

David Beecroft
The Rain Killer '90
Shadowzone '90

Holly Beeman
The Legend of Black Thunder
Mountain '79

Steve Beeman
The Legend of Black Thunder
Mountain '79

Daniel Beer
Creepshow 2 '87
Point Break '91

Noah Beery, Jr.
Ace Drummond '36
The Avenging Hand '43
Bad Lands '39
The Bastard '78

Love and the Frenchwoman
'60
Mississippi Mermaid '69
Pierrot le Fou '65
Scoumoune '74
Sois Belle et Tais-Toi '58
Stavisky '74
Stuntwoman '81
Swashbuckler '84
Two Women '61
Un Singe en Hiver '62
A Woman is a Woman '60

Lara Belmonte
Lauderdale '89

Vicki Belmonte
The Grass is Always Greener
Over the Septic Tank '78

Daisy Belmore
Sylvia Scarlett '35

Antoine Belpetre
Le Corbeau '43

Hal Belsoe
The Ghastly Ones '68

Lola Beltran
Duelo en el Dorado

Robert Beltran
Bugsy '91
The Chase '91
Eating Raoul '82
El Diablo '90
Kiss Me a Killer '91
La Pastorela '92
Latino '85
Night of the Comet '84
Scenes from the Class
Struggle in Beverly Hills '89
To Die Standing '91

Mark Beltzman
Mo' Money '92

James Belushi
About Last Night... '86
Best Legs in the 8th Grade
'84
Birthday Boy '85
Curly Sue '91
Diary of a Hitman '91
Homer and Eddie '89
Jumpin' Jack Flash '86
K-9 '89
Last Action Hero '93
Little Shop of Horrors '86
The Man with One Red Shoe
'85
The Masters of Menace '90
Mr. Destiny '90
Mutant Video '76
Once Upon a Crime '92
Only the Lonely '91
The Palermo Connection '91
The Principal '87
Real Men '87
Red Heat '88
Salvador '86
Taking Care of Business '90
Thief '81
Traces of Red '92
Trading Places '83
Wedding Band '89
Who's Harry Crumb? '89
Wild Palms '93

John Belushi
All You Need Is Cash '78
Best of Chevy Chase '87
Best of Dan Aykroyd '86
Best of Gilda Radner '89
Best of John Belushi '85
The Blues Brothers '80
Continental Divide '81
Goin' South '78

National Lampoon's Animal
House '78
Neighbors '81
1941 '79
Old Boyfriends '79
Shame of the Jungle '90

Remy Belvaux
Man Bites Dog '92

Richard Belzer
America '86
The Big Picture '89
Fame '80
Flicks '85
Freeway '88
The Groove Tube '72
Night Shift '82
The Wrong Guys '88

Maggie Bemby
Angels' Wild Women '72

Cliff Bemis
Modern Love '90

Bea Benadaret
The Flintstones '60

Steven Benally, Jr.
The Secret of Navajo Cave
'76

Maurice Benard
Lucy and Desi: Before the
Laughter '91

Pat Benatar
Union City '81

**Gloriella Ruben
Benavides**
El Fin del Tahur '87

Brian Benben
Clean and Sober '88
Gangster Wars '81
I Come in Peace '90
Mortal Sins '90

Peter Benchley
Jaws '75

Robert Benchley
China Seas '35
Foreign Correspondent '40
It's in the Bag '45
The Road to Utopia '46
The Sky's the Limit '43
The Stork Club '45
Weekend at the Waldorf '45
You'll Never Get Rich '41
Young & Willing '42

Andrew Bendarski
Family Sins '87

Don Bendell
The Instructor '83

Russ Bender
The Amazing Colossal Man
'57
Anatomy of a Psycho '61
It Conquered the World '56
Navy vs. the Night Monsters
'66
Suicide Battalion/Hell Squad
'58
The War of the Colossal Beast
'58

Scott Benderer
Great Love Experiment '84

Bruce Benderson
My Father is Coming '91

Michael C. Bendetti
Netherworld '91
Screwball Hotel '88

William Bendix
Abroad with Two Yanks '44
Babe Ruth Story '48
Big Steal '49
Blackbeard the Pirate '52
A Connecticut Yankee in King
Arthur's Court '49
Crashout '55
Dangerous Mission '54
Dark Corner '46
Deep Six '58
Detective Story '51
For Love or Money '63
A Girl in Every Port '52
The Glass Key '42
Guadalcanal Diary '43
The Hairy Ape '44
It's in the Bag '45
Johnny Nobody '61
Lifeboat '44
Macao '51
The Time of Your Life '48
Wake Island '42
Who Done It? '42
Woman of the Year '42

Sherry Bendorf
Slaughterhouse '87

Jitka Bendova
Closely Watched Trains '66

Rikke Bendsen
Memories of a Marriage '90

Miklos Benedek
Bad Guys '79

Nelly Benedetti
The Soft Skin '64

Leonor Benedetto
Con Mi Mujer No Puedo '87
Condemned to Hell '80s

Augusto Benedico
The Exterminating Angel '62

Billy Benedict
Bowery Buckaroos '47
Follow the Leader '44
Ghost Chasers '51
Ghosts on the Loose '43
Hard-Boiled Mahoney '47
Spook Busters '46
Wildcat '42

Brooks Benedict
The Dropkick '27
The Freshman '25
Ranson's Folly '26

Dirk Benedict
Battlestar Galactica '78
Blue Tornado '90
Body Slam '87
Cruise into Terror '78
Follow That Car '80
Georgia, Georgia '72
Mission Galactica: The Cylon
Attack '79
Ruckus '81
Scavenger Hunt '79
Shadow Force '92
Underground Aces '80
W '74

Nick Benedict
Pistol: The Birth of a Legend
'90

Paul Benedict
The Addams Family '91
Babycakes '89
The Chair '87
Cocktail '88
Desperate Moves '86
The Freshman '90
Mandingo '75

Richard Benedict
Beginning of the End '57
Breakdown '53
Omoo Omoo, the Shark God
'49

Armonia Benedito
Strictly Ballroom '92

Michael Benet
Rip-Off '77

Paul Benevictor
Body Parts '91

Yves Beneyton
The Lacemaker '77
Letters to an Unknown Lover
'84
Weekend '67

John Benfield
Hidden Agenda '90

Wilson Benge
The Bat Whispers '30
Robin Hood '22

Norman Bengell
Hellbenders '67
Planet of the Vampires '65

Hubertus Bengsch
Das Boot '81

Jean Benguigui
Buffet Froid '79
Control '87

Joan Benham
The King's Rhapsody '55

Roberto Benigni
Down by Law '86
Night on Earth '91

Francesco Benigno
Forever Mary '89

Annette Bening
Bugsy '91
The Great Outdoors '88
The Grifters '90
Guilty by Suspicion '91
Postcards from the Edge '90
Regarding Henry '91
Valmont '89

Butch Benit
Storyville '74

**Christopher
Benjamin**
Baffled '72
The Plague Dogs '82

Nigel Benjamin
Rocktober Blood '85

Paul Benjamin
Across 110th Street '72
The Deadly Trackers '73
The Education of Sonny
Carson '74
I Know Why the Caged Bird
Sings '79

Richard Benjamin
Catch-22 '70
Diary of a Mad Housewife '70
First Family '80
Goodbye Columbus '69
House Calls '78
How to Beat the High Cost of
Living '80
The Last Married Couple in
America '80
The Last of Sheila '73
Love at First Bite '79
No Room to Run '78
Packin' It In '83
Portnoy's Complaint '72
Saturday the 14th '81

Scavenger Hunt '79
Steagle '71
The Sunshine Boys '75
Westworld '73
Witches' Brew '79

David Bennent
Legend '86
The Tin Drum '79

Heinz Bennent
From the Life of the
Marionettes '80
The Last Metro '80
Nea '78
Possession '81

John Bennes
Black Rainbow '91

Alan Bennett
Fortunes of War '87

Bill Bennett
Robin Hood '22

Bruce Bennett
Before I Hang '40
The Cosmic Man '59
Daniel Boone: Trail Blazer '56
Dark Passage '47
Dragonfly Squadron '54
Hidden Guns '56
I'm from Arkansas '44
Mildred Pierce '45
The More the Merrier '43
The New Adventures of
Tarzan: Vol. 2 '35
The New Adventures of
Tarzan: Vol. 3 '35
The New Adventures of
Tarzan: Vol. 4 '35
Sahara '43
Silver River '48
A Stolen Life '46
Three Violent People '57
Treasure of the Sierra Madre
'48

Constance Bennett
As Young As You Feel '51
Madame X '66
Married? '26
Sin Takes a Holiday '30
Topper '37
Topper Takes a Trip '39
Two-Faced Woman '41
What Price Hollywood? '32

Eloise Bennett
A Tale of Springtime '92

Enid Bennett
Robin Hood '22

Frank Bennett
Reggie Mixes In '16

Hywel Bennett
Deadline '87
Endless Night '71
Loot...Give Me Money, Honey!
'70
Murder Elite '86
The Virgin Soldiers '69

Jill Bennett
For Your Eyes Only '81
Full Circle '77
Hawks '89
I Want What I Want '72
Lust for Life '56
Murders at Lynch Cross '85
The Old Curiosity Shop '75
The Sheltering Sky '90
The Skull '65

Joan Bennett
Bulldog Drummond '29
Colonel Effingham's Raid '45
Disraeli '29

Teresa Blake
Payback '90

Valerie Blake
Blastfighter '85

Whitney Blake
The Stranger Who Looks Like Me '74

Brien Blakely
HauntedWeen '91

Colin Blakely
The Big Sleep '78
The Dogs of War '81
Equus '77
Evil Under the Sun '82
Little Lord Fauntleroy '80
Loophole '83
Love Among the Ruins '75
Murder on the Orient Express '74
Nijinsky '80
Operation Julie '85
The Pink Panther Strikes Again '76
The Private Life of Sherlock Holmes '70
Shattered '72
This Sporting Life '63

Donald Blakely
In the Shadow of Kilimanjaro '86
Short Eyes '79
Strike Force '87

James "Doc" Blakely
Small Town Boy '37

Rubel Blakely
Sepia Cinderella '47

Susan Blakely
Blackmail '91
Broken Angel '88
The Concorde: Airport '79 '79
A Cry for Love '80
Dead Reckoning '89
Dreamer '79
Hiroshima Maiden '88
The Incident '89
Intruders '92
Ladykillers '88
The Lords of Flatbush '74
Make Me an Offer '80
My Mom's a Werewolf '89
Out of Sight, Out of Her Mind '89
Over the Top '86
Report to the Commissioner '74
Savages '72
Secrets '77
The Survivalist '87
The Towering Inferno '74
Wildflower '91

Olive Blakeney
Gangway '37

Ronee Blakley
The Baltimore Bullet '80
Desperate Women '78
The Driver '78
Lightning Over Water '80
Mannikin '77
Murder by Numbers '89
Nashville '75
A Nightmare on Elm Street '84
The Private Files of J. Edgar Hoover '77
Return to Salem's Lot '87
She Came to the Valley '77
Someone to Love '87
Student Confidential '87

Leslie Blalock
Incoming Freshmen '79

Dominique Blanc
May Fools '90

Erika Blanc
The Devil's Nightmare '71
Kill, Baby, Kill '66
Mark of the Devil 2 '72
The Night Evelyn Came Out of the Grave '71
Sartana's Here...Trade Your Pistol for a Coffin '70
Special Forces '68
Sweet Spirits '80s

Mel Blanc
The Best of Warner Brothers, Vol. 2 '30s
Betty Boop '30s
Bugs! '88
Bugs & Daffy's Carnival of the Animals '89
Bugs Bunny: Hollywood Legend '90
Bugs Bunny in King Arthur's Court '89
Bugs Bunny Superstar '75
Bugs Bunny's Comedy Classics '89
Bugs Bunny's Hare-Raising Tales '89
Bugs Bunny's Looney Christmas Tales '79
Bugs Bunny's Wacky Adventures '57
Daffy Duck's Quackbusters '89
The Flintstones '60
The Flintstones: Dino & Juliet '89
Gay Purr-ee '62
Hey There, It's Yogi Bear '64
A Jetson Christmas Carol '89
The Jetsons Meet the Flintstones '88
The Jetsons: Movie '90
Kiss Me, Stupid! '64
Looney Looney Looney Bugs Bunny Movie '81
Neptune's Daughter '49
Phantom Tollbooth '69
Porky Pig Tales '89
Salute to Chuck Jones '60
Salute to Friz Freleng '58
Salute to Mel Blanc '58
Sylvester & Tweety's Crazy Capers '61
Who Framed Roger Rabbit? '88

Michel Blanc
The Favor, the Watch, & the Very Big Fish '92
Menage '86
Monsieur Hire '89
Prospero's Books '91
Uranus '91

Jewel Blanch
Against A Crooked Sky '75
Baffled '72

Dominique Blanchar
L'Avventura '60

Pierre Blanchar
Crime and Punishment '35
La Symphonie Pastorale '46
Man from Nowhere '37

Alan Blanchard
Slithis '78

Felix "Doc" Blanchard
The Spirit of West Point '47

Francois Blanchard
Venus on Fire '84

Keith Blanchard
Portrait of Grandpa Doc '77

Mari Blanchard
Son of Sinbad '55

Susan Blanchard
President's Mistress '78
She's in the Army Now '81

Roland Blanche
Too Beautiful for You '88

Dorothee Blanck
Cleo from 5 to 7 '61
Umbrellas of Cherbourg '64

Sandrine Blancke
Toto le Heros '91

Joyce Bland
Dreaming Lips '37

Peter Bland
Came a Hot Friday '85
Dangerous Orphans '86
Tearaway '87

Clara Blandick
The Adventures of Tom Sawyer '38
Dreaming Out Loud '40
The Girl from Missouri '34
Infamous Crimes '47
Murder at Midnight '31
Romance '30
Small Town Boy '37
The Wizard of Oz '39

Sally Blane
Cross Examination '32
Fighting Mad '39
Heritage of the Desert '33
Law of the Sea '38
Phantom Express '32
Probation '32
The Silver Streak '34
Vagabond Lover '29
Way Down South '39
When the West Was Young '32

Karen Blanguernon
No Survivors, Please '63

Mark Blankfield
Angel 3: The Final Chapter '88
Frankenstein General Hospital '88
Jack & the Beanstalk '83
Jekyll & Hyde...Together Again '82
The Midnight Hour '86
Robin Hood: Men in Tights '93

Billy Blanks
Bloodfist '89
The King of the Kickboxers '91
Talons of the Eagle '92

Arell Blanton
House of Terror '87
Wild Riders '71

Freddie Blassie
My Breakfast with Blassie '83

Barry W. Blaustein
Unlawful Entry '92

Charles Blavette
Toni '34

Hans-Christian Blech
The Blum Affair '48
Dirty Hands '76
The Scarlet Letter '73
The Wrong Move '78

Jonah Blechman
This Boy's Life '93

Tempestt Bledsoe
Dream Date '93

William Bledsoe
Dark Side of the Moon '90

Debra Blee
Beach Girls '82
Malibu Bikini Shop '86
Savage Streets '83
Sloane '84

Brian Blessed
Back in the USSR '92
Flash Gordon '80
Henry V '89
High Road to China '83
The Hound of the Baskervilles '83
I, Claudius, Vol. 1: A Touch of Murder/Family Affairs '91
I, Claudius, Vol. 2: Waiting in the Wings/What Shall We Do With Claudius? '80
I, Claudius, Vol. 3: Poison is Queen/Some Justice '80
King Arthur, the Young Warlord '75
Man of La Mancha '72
Much Ado About Nothing '93
Prisoner of Honor '91
Robin Hood: Prince of Thieves '91
Trojan Women '71
Young Warlord '75

Jack Blessing
The Last of His Tribe '92

Billy Bletcher
Branded Men '31

Brenda Blethyn
A River Runs Through It '92
The Witches '90

Michael Blevins
A Chorus Line '85

Jason Blicker
African Journey '89
American Boyfriends '89

Georg Blickingberg
Walpurgis Night '41

Bernard Blier
Buffet Froid '79
Casanova '70 '65
Catch Me a Spy '71
The Daydreamer '75
Dedee d'Anvers '49
Jenny Lamour '47
Les Miserables '57
The Man in the Raincoat '57
Passion for Life '48
The Tall Blond Man with One Black Shoe '72

Maggie Blinco
The Wicked '89

Hunt Block
Secret Weapons '85

Larry Block
Dead Man Out '89

Dan Blocker
The Errand Boy '61
Lady in Cement '68
Ride the Wind '66

Michael Blodgett
The Ultimate Thrill '74
The Velvet Vampire '71

Joan Blondell
Angel Baby '61
The Baron '88

Blonde Crazy '31
Brother Orchid '40
Bullets or Ballots '38
The Champ '79
The Cincinnati Kid '65
Dames '34
The Dead Don't Die '75
Death at Love House '75
Desk Set '57
Footlight Parade '33
The Glove '78
Gold Diggers of 1933 '33
Hollywood Bloopers '50s
Lady for a Night '42
Millie '31
Night Nurse '31
Opening Night '77
The Opposite Sex '56
Public Enemy '31
The Rebels '79
Stand-In '37
Stay Away, Joe '68
Support Your Local Gunfighter '71
This Could be the Night '57
Three Broadway Girls '32
Three Men on a Horse '36
Three on a Match '32
Topper Returns '41
A Tree Grows in Brooklyn '45
Waterhole #3 '67
The Woman Inside '83

Simone Blondell
Jungle Master '56

Harris Bloodworth
Day of Judgment '81

Anne Bloom
Dirt Bike Kid '86
That's Adequate '90

Bill A. Bloom
Teenage Strangler '64

Brian Bloom
Voyage of Terror: The Achille Lauro Affair '90
Walls of Glass '85

Claire Bloom
Alexander the Great '55
Anastasia: The Mystery of Anna '86
Brideshead Revisited '81
The Brothers Karamazov '58
The Buccaneer '58
Charly '68
Clash of the Titans '81
Crimes & Misdemeanors '89
Deja Vu '84
A Doll's House '89
Ghostwriter '84
Hamlet '79
The Haunting '63
Henry VIII '79
The Illustrated Man '69
Innocents in Paris '53
Intimate Contact '87
Islands in the Stream '77
Limelight '52
Look Back in Anger '58
Queenie '87
Richard III '55
Sammy & Rosie Get Laid '87
Separate Tables '83
Shadow on the Sun '88
Shadowlands '85
Soldier in Love '67
The Spy Who Came in from the Cold '65
This Lightning Always Strikes Twice '85
The Wonderful World of the Brothers Grimm '62

John Bloom
Bachelor Party '84

Three on a Match '32
To Have & Have Not '44
Tokyo Joe '49
Treasure of the Sierra Madre
  '48
The Two Mrs. Carrolls '47
Virginia City '40
We're No Angels '55

Yuri Bogatyrev
An Unfinished Piece for a
  Player Piano '77

Peter Bogdanovich
The Trip '67

**Lucic Bogoljub
Benny**
SS Girls '78

Eric Bogosian
The Caine Mutiny Court
  Martial '88
Last Flight Out: A True Story
  '90
Special Effects '85
Suffering Bastards '90
Talk Radio '88

Kelley Bohanan
Idaho Transfer '73

John Bohn
The Crime of Dr. Crespi '35

Roman Bohnen
The Best Years of Our Lives
  '46
The Hairy Ape '44
Open Secret '48

Jose Bohr
Rogue of the Rio Grande '30

Corinne Bohrer
Dead Solid Perfect '88
Stewardess School '86
Vice Versa '88

Richard Bohringer
Caged Heart '85
Diva '82
L'Addition '85
Le Grand Chemin '87
Peril '85

Jean Boht
The Girl in a Swing '89

Elaine Boies
Legacy of Horror '78

Curt Bois
Bitter Sweet '40
The Boat is Full '81
Boom Town '40
Caught '49
The Great Waltz '38
The Lady in Question '40
The Tuttles of Tahiti '42
Wings of Desire '88

Jocelyne Boisseau
Girls Riot '88

Christine Boisson
Sorceress '88
Unsettled Land '88

Sarel Bok
A Far Off Place '93

Hal Bokar
The Last Reunion '80

James Bolam
Crucible of Terror '72
Dressed for Death '74
In Celebration '75
The Loneliness of the Long
  Distance Runner '62
The Maze '85

Marc Bolan
Born to Boogie '72

Mary Boland
Julia Misbehaves '48
New Moon '40
Nothing But Trouble '44
Pride and Prejudice '40
The Ruggles of Red Gap '35
The Women '39

Cal Bolder
Jesse James Meets
  Frankenstein's Daughter
  '65

Buddy Boles
Reg'lar Fellers '41

John Boles
Craig's Wife '36
Curly Top '35
Frankenstein '31
King of Jazz '30
The Littlest Rebel '35
Sinners in Paradise '38
Stand Up and Cheer '34
Stella Dallas '37
Thousands Cheer '43

Steve Boles
Rockin' Road Trip '85

John Bolger
Parting Glances '86

Ray Bolger
April In Paris '52
Babes in Toyland '61
Daydreamer '66
For Heaven's Sake '79
Four Jacks and a Jill '41
The Great Ziegfeld '36
The Harvey Girls '46
Rosalie '37
The Runner Stumbles '79
Stage Door Canteen '43
Sunny '41
Sweethearts '38
That's Dancing! '85
The Wizard of Oz '39

Elena Bolkan
Acqua e Sapone '83

Florinda Bolkan
Acqua e Sapone '83
Black Lemons '80s
Collector's Item '89
The Day that Shook the World
  '78
The Last Valley '71
Master Touch '74
Ring of Death '72
Some Girls '88
The Word '78

Tiffany Bolling
Bonnie's Kids '73
The Centerfold Girls '74
Ecstasy '84
Kingdom of the Spiders '77
Love Scenes '84
Wild Party '74

Ryan Bollman
Children of the Corn 2: The
  Final Sacrifice '92

Michael Bollner
Willy Wonka & the Chocolate
  Factory '71

Joseph Bologna
Alligator 2: The Mutation '90
Big Bus '76
Blame It on Rio '84
Chapter Two '79
Citizen Cohn '92
Cops and Robbers '73
Coupe de Ville '90

Deadly Rivals '92
Honor Thy Father '73
My Favorite Year '82
One Cooks, the Other Doesn't
  '83
Rags to Riches '87
Torn Between Two Lovers '79
Transylvania 6-5000 '85
The Woman in Red '84

Faye Bolt
Star Crystal '85

Jean Bolt
Arthur's Hallowed Ground '84

Jonathan Bolt
The Eyes of the Amaryllis '82

Pat Bolt
Natas...The Reflection '83

Emily Bolton
Moonraker '79

Heather Bolton
Dark of the Night '85

Bon Jovi
Incident at Channel Q '86

Jon Bon Jovi
Young Guns 2 '90

Sheila Bon
Curse of the Stone Hand '64

Paolo Bonacelli
Christ Stopped at Eboli '79
Henry IV '85
Night on Earth '91
Salo, or the 120 Days of
  Sodom '75

Danny Bonaduce
H.O.T.S. '79

Jacques Bonaffe
First Name: Carmen '83

Brian Bonanno
Sex Appeal '86

Louie Bonanno
Night of the Living Babes '87
Student Affairs '88
Wimps '87

Ivan Bonar
The Haunting Passion '83
MacArthur '77

Deanna Bond
Dogs in Space '87

Derek Bond
Black Tide '56
The Hand '60
Inheritance '47
Nicholas Nickleby '46
Rogue's Yarn '56
Scott of the Antarctic '48
The Stranger from Venus '54
Svengali '55
Tony Draws a Horse '51

Gary Bond
Growing Pains '82

James Bond, III
Def by Temptation '90
The Fish that Saved
  Pittsburgh '79
The Sky is Gray '80

Joy Bond
Sex O'Clock News '85

Lillian Bond
The Old Dark House '32

Renee Bond
Class Reunion '87
Please Don't Eat My Mother
  '72

Richard Bond
Law of the Underworld '38

Steve Bond
Gas Pump Girls '79
H.O.T.S. '79
L.A. Gangs Rising '89
Magdalene '88
Massacre at Central High '76
Picasso Trigger '89
The Prey '80
To Die for '89
To Die for 2 '91

Sudie Bond
Come Back to the Five &
  Dime Jimmy Dean, Jimmy
  Dean '82
I Am the Cheese '83
Tomorrow '83
Where the Lilies Bloom '74

**Tommy "Butch"
Bond**
Little Rascals, Book 15 '30s
Our Gang Comedies '40s
Superman: The Serial, Vol. 1
  '48

Tony Bond
Desert Passion '93

Ward Bond
Big Trail '30
Blowing Wild '54
Born to Be Wild '38
Dakota '45
Dakota Incident '56
Devil Dogs of the Air '35
Drums Along the Mohawk '39
Falcon Takes Over/Strange
  Bargain '49
The Fighting Sullivans '42
Fort Apache '48
The Fugitive '48
Gentleman Jim '42
Gone with the Wind '39
Great Missouri Raid '51
A Guy Named Joe '44
Gypsy Colt '54
Hawaii Calls '38
Heroes for Sale '33
Hitler: Dead or Alive '43
It Happened One Night '34
It's a Wonderful Life '46
Johnny Guitar '53
Kiss Tomorrow Goodbye '50
Kit Carson '40
The Long Gray Line '55
The Making of a Legend:
  "Gone With the Wind" '89
The Maltese Falcon '41
A Man Alone '55
Mister Roberts '55
My Darling Clementine '46
Oklahoma Kid '39
On Dangerous Ground '51
Only the Valiant '50
Prison Break '38
The Quiet Man '52
Rio Bravo '59
The Searchers '56
Sergeant York '41
Tall in the Saddle '44
They Were Expendable '45
Three Godfathers '48
The Time of Your Life '48
Wagon Master '50
White Eagle '32
Wings of Eagles '57
You Only Live Once '37
Young Mr. Lincoln '39

**Natalya
Bondarchuk**
Solaris '72

Sergei Bondarchuk
Battle of Neretva '69
A Summer to Remember '61
War and Peace '68

Beulah Bondi
Back to Bataan '45
Baron of Arizona '51
Breakfast in Hollywood '46
Finishing School '33
The Invisible Ray '36
It's a Wonderful Life '46
Latin Lovers '53
Mr. Smith Goes to
  Washington '39
Moon's Our Home '36
On Borrowed Time '39
Our Town '40
Penny Serenade '41
Rain '32
Sister Kenny '46
The Sisters '38
The Snake Pit '48
So Dear to My Heart '49
The Southerner '45
Street Scene '31
A Summer Place '59
Unholy Wife '57
Vivacious Lady '38
Watch on the Rhine '43
The Wonderful World of the
  Brothers Grimm '62

Ulrikke Juul Bondo
Twist & Shout '84

Christopher Bondy
Deadly Surveillance '91

Priscilla Boner
Red Kimono '25

Peter Bonerz
The Committee '68
How to Break Up a Happy
  Divorce '76
Medium Cool '69
Serial '80
A Session with the Committee
  '69
Your Place or Mine '83

Charles Bonet
Black Dragon's Revenge '75
Death Promise '78
Way of the Black Dragon '81

Lisa Bonet
Angel Heart '87

Nai Bonet
Devil's Angels '67
Fairytales '79
Gangsters '79
Nocturna '79
Soul Hustler '76

Massimo Bonetti
Kaos '85
The Story of Boys & Girls '91

**Helena Bonham
Carter**
Getting It Right '89
Hamlet '90
Howard's End '92
Lady Jane '85
Maurice '87
A Room with a View '86
The Vision '87
Where Angels Fear to Tread
  '91

Hector Bonilla
Narda or The Summer '76

Sandrine Bonnaire
La Puritaine '86
Monsieur Hire '89
A Nos Amours '84

Barbara Bosson
The Committee '68
The Last Starfighter '84
Little Sweetheart '90
A Session with the Committee '69

Cynthia Bostick
Shining Star '75

Barbara Bostock
The Spell '77

Evalyn Bostock
Cowboy Millionaire '35

Matt Boston
Ghosts That Still Walk '77

Barry Bostwick
Fantastic Planet '73
Hitchhiker 3 '87
Jailbait: Betrayed By Innocence '86
Megaforce '82
Movie, Movie '78
Murder by Natural Causes '79
Red Flag: The Ultimate Game '81
The Rocky Horror Picture Show '75
Scruples '80
That's Singing: The Best of Broadway '84
War & Remembrance, Part 1 '88
War & Remembrance, Part 2 '89
Weekend at Bernie's 2 '93
A Woman of Substance, Episode 1: Nest of Vipers '84
A Woman of Substance, Episode 2: The Secret is Revealed '84
A Woman of Substance, Episode 3: Fighting for the Dream '84

Jackson Bostwick
Escape from DS-3 '80s

Charles Boswell
Kiss Me a Killer '91

Connee Boswell
Swing Parade of 1946 '46

Boswell Sisters
Transatlantic Merry-Go-Round '34

Brian Bosworth
Stone Cold '91

Hobart Bosworth
Abraham Lincoln '30
Annapolis '28
The Big Parade '25
The Dark Hour '36
Dubarry '30
The Last of the Mohicans '32
Little Church Around the Corner '23
A Mormon Maid '17
The Nervous Wreck '26
Phantom Express '32
Sea Lion '21
Spangles '26
A Woman of Affairs '28

Wade Boteler
Big News '29
The Green Hornet '40
Let 'er Go Gallegher '28
The Mandarin Mystery '37

Sara Botsford
By Design '82
Deadly Eyes '82
The Gunrunner '84

Jumpin' Jack Flash '86
Murder by Phone '82
Still of the Night '82

Zeinab Botsvadze
Repentance '87

Gritt Bottcher
The Black Abbot '63

Benjamin Bottoms
A Shining Season '79
Stalk the Wild Child '76

Gaye Bottoms
The Abomination '88

Joseph Bottoms
The Black Hole '79
Blind Date '84
Born to Race '88
Celebrity '85
Cloud Dancer '80
Crime & Passion '75
The Dove '74
High Rolling in a Hot Corvette '77
Holocaust '78
Inner Sanctum '91
Intruder Within '81
King of the Mountain '81
Liar's Edge '92
Open House '86
Return Engagement '78
The Sins of Dorian Gray '82
Stalk the Wild Child '76
Surfacing '84
Treacherous Crossing '92

Sam Bottoms
After School '88
Apocalypse Now '79
Bronco Billy '80
Class of '44 '73
Desperate Lives '82
Dolly Dearest '92
East of Eden '80
Gardens of Stone '87
Hearts of Darkness: A Filmmaker's Apocalypse '91
Hunter's Blood '87
In 'n Out '86
The Outlaw Josey Wales '76
Prime Risk '84
Ragin' Cajun '90
Return to Eden '89
Savages '75
Up from the Depths '79
Zandy's Bride '74

Timothy Bottoms
The Drifter '88
East of Eden '80
The Fantasist '89
The Gift of Love '90
Hambone & Hillie '84
High Country '81
Hurricane '79
Husbands, Wives, Money, and Murder '86
In the Shadow of Kilimanjaro '86
Invaders from Mars '86
Istanbul '90
Johnny Got His Gun '71
The Land of Faraway '87
The Last Picture Show '71
Love Leads the Way '84
The Other Side of the Mountain, Part 2 '78
The Paper Chase '73
Rollercoaster '77
The Sea Serpent '85
A Shining Season '79
A Small Town in Texas '76
The Story of David '76
Texasville '90
Tin Man '83

What Waits Below '83
The White Dawn '75

Shiao Bou-Lo
Dance of Death '84

Pegi Boucher
Private Duty Nurses '71

Sherry Boucher
Sisters of Death '76

Barbara Bouchet
Cry of a Prostitute: Love Kills '72
In Harm's Way '65
Mean Machine '73
Rogue '76
Surabaya Conspiracy '75

Patrick Bouchitey
The Best Way '82

Fred Boudin
Summer Job '88

Geoffery Boues
Kidnapping of Baby John Doe '88

Jean-Claude Bouillon
Julia '74

Jean Bouise
Hothead '78
Le Dernier Combat '84
Old Gun '76

Evelyne Bouix
Edith & Marcel '83

Michel Boujenah
Three Men and a Cradle '85

Daniel Boulanger
Breathless '59

Jonathan Bould
Ninja Powerforce '90

Ingrid Boulting
Deadly Passion '85
The Last Tycoon '76

Carol Bouquet
Buffet Froid '79
Dagger Eyes '80s
For Your Eyes Only '81
That Obscure Object of Desire '77
Too Beautiful for You '88

Michel Bouquet
Borsalino '70
The Bride Wore Black '68
Le Complot '73
Mississippi Mermaid '69
Pattes Blanches '49
This Special Friendship '67
Toto le Heros '91

Adrienne Bourbeau
Wild Women of Wongo '59

Whitney Bourne
Flight from Glory '37

Philip Bourneuf
Beyond a Reasonable Doubt '56

Antoine Bourseillor
Cleo from 5 to 7 '61

Bourvil
The Brain '69
Crazy for Love '52
Four Bags Full '56
Les Grandes Gueules '65
Les Miserables '57
Mr. Peek-A-Boo '50
When Wolves Cry '69

Andre Bourvil
The Christmas Tree '69

Kathleen Boutall
The Golden Salamander '51

Genee Boutell
Rawhide Romance '34

Dennis Boutsikaris
The Dream Team '89

Brunella Bova
Miracle in Milan '51
The White Sheik '52

Joe Bova
Roboman '75

Julie Bovasso
Article 99 '92
Gentleman Bandit '81
Moonstruck '87
Willie & Phil '80
Wise Guys '86

Clara Bow
Dancing Mothers '26
Down to the Sea in Ships '22
Free to Love '25
Hula '28
It '27
Mantrap '26
My Lady of Whims '25
Wings '27

Simmy Bow
The Doberman Gang '72

Tui Bow
Frenchman's Farm '87

Dorris Bowdon
Drums Along the Mohawk '39
The Grapes of Wrath '40

Dennis Bowen
Gas Pump Girls '79
Van Nuys Blvd. '79

Harry Bowen
Ghost Valley '32

Lori Bowen
Pumping Iron 2: The Women '85

Michael Bowen
The Abduction of Karl Swenson '87
Casualties of Love: The "Long Island Lolita" Story '93
Echo Park '86
Mortal Passions '90
Night of the Comet '84
Season of Fear '89
The Taking of Beverly Hills '91

Roger Bowen
M*A*S*H '70
What About Bob? '91
Zapped! '82

Sean Bowen
Troma's War '88

Malick Bowens
The Believers '87
Out of Africa '85

Antoinette Bower
Blood Song '82
Die Sister, Die! '74
The Evil That Men Do '84

Tom Bower
Ballad of Gregorio Cortez '83
Family Sins '87
The Lightship '86
Love, Lies and Murder '91
Massive Retaliation '85
Promised a Miracle '88

Raising Cain '92
True Believer '89
Wildrose '85

Bonnie Bowers
There's Nothing Out There '90

John Bowers
The Sky Pilot '21
The White Sin '24

David Bowie
Absolute Beginners '86
Christiane F. '82
The Hunger '83
Into the Night '85
Just a Gigolo '79
Labyrinth '86
The Last Temptation of Christ '88
The Linguini Incident '92
The Man Who Fell to Earth '76
Merry Christmas, Mr. Lawrence '83
Twin Peaks: Fire Walk with Me '92
UHF '89
Yellowbeard '83

Rosemary Bowie
Big Bluff '55

Judi Bowker
Brother Sun, Sister Moon '73
Clash of the Titans '81
East of Elephant Rock '76
The Shooting Party '85

Peter Bowles
A Day in the Death of Joe Egg '71
Endless Night '71
The Offence '73

Dave Bowling
Dark Side of Midnight '86

F.E. Bowling
Oklahoma Bound '81

Don Bowman
Hillbillies in a Haunted House '67

Jessica Bowman
Remote '93

Laura Bowman
Birth Right '39
Drums O'Voodoo '34
Son of Ingagi '40

Lee Bowman
Bataan '43
Cover Girl '44
Love Affair '39
My Dream is Yours '49
Next Time I Marry '38
Smash-Up: The Story of a Woman '47
Tonight and Every Night '45

Loretta L. Bowman
Offerings '89

Ralph Bowman
Flaming Frontiers '38

Riley Bowman
Bloodfist '89

Tina Bowmann
Kill Alex Kill '83

Bruce Boxleitner
The Babe '92
The Baltimore Bullet '80
Diplomatic Immunity '91
Double Jeopardy '92
East of Eden '80
From the Dead of Night '89
Kenny Rogers as the Gambler '80

Carl Bradshaw
The Harder They Come '72
The Lunatic '92

Cathryn Bradshaw
Bert Rigby, You're a Fool '89

David Bradshaw
The Big Hurt '87

Ron Bradsteder
Field of Honor '86

Alice Brady
The Gay Divorcee '34
Gold Diggers of 1935 '35
Her Silent Sacrifice '18
Joy of Living '38
My Man Godfrey '36
Young Mr. Lincoln '39

Bob Brady
Liquid Sky '83

Janelle Brady
Class of Nuke 'Em High '86

Lisa Brady
Kill Slade '89

Pat Brady
Bells of Coronado '50
Call of the Canyon '42
Down Dakota Way '49
The Golden Stallion '49
Song of Texas '43
Sunset on the Desert '42
Texas Legionnaires '43
Trigger, Jr. '50
Twilight in the Sierras '50
Western Double Feature 19 '45

Scott Brady
Arizona Bushwackers '67
Bonnie's Kids '73
Cain's Cutthroats '71
Castle of Evil '66
The China Syndrome '79
Dollars '71
Gun Riders '69
He Walked by Night '48
Johnny Guitar '53
Journey to the Center of Time '67
Kansas City Massacre '75
Loners '72
Maverick Queen '55
Mohawk '56
Montana Belle '52
Party Girls for Sale '54
Port of New York '49
The Restless Breed '58
Satan's Sadists '69
Storm Rider '57
Strange Behavior '81
They Were So Young '55
When Every Day was the Fourth of July '78
White Fire '53

Eric Braeden
The Adultress '77
Aliens Are Coming '80
The Ambulance '90
Colossus: The Forbin Project '70
Death Scream '75
Escape from the Planet of the Apes '71
Happily Ever After '82
Lady Ice '73
The Power Within '79
The Ultimate Thrill '74

Sonia Braga
Dona Flor and Her Two Husbands '78
Gabriela '84
I Love You '81

Kiss of the Spider Woman '85
Lady on the Bus '78
The Last Prostitute '91
The Man Who Broke 1,000 Chains '87
The Milagro Beanfield War '88
Moon Over Parador '88
The Rookie '90

Helen Bragdon
Where the Lilies Bloom '74

Danny Brainin
Xtro '83

Fredrick Braithwaite
Wild Style '83

Wilfrid Brambell
The Adventures of Picasso '80
The Conqueror Worm '68
Sword of the Valiant '83

Rocio Brambilia
La Hija del General '84

William Bramley
Revenge of the Cheerleaders '76

Francisco (Frank) Brana
Crypt of the Living Dead '73
Cthulhu Mansion '91
Graveyard of Horror '71
Street Warriors '87

Kenneth Branagh
Dead Again '91
Fortunes of War '87
Henry V '89
High Season '88
Look Back in Anger '89
A Month in the Country '87
Much Ado About Nothing '93
Peter's Friends '92
Swing Kids '93

Sarah Branch
Sword of Sherwood Forest '60

Armando Brancia
Amarcord '74

Marilia Branco
La Red del Egano '71

Christopher Brand
Voyage to the Prehistoric Planet '65

Larry Brand
The Drifter '88

Neville Brand
The Adventures of Huckleberry Finn '60
The Barbary Coast '74
Birdman of Alcatraz '62
Cahill: United States Marshal '73
The Deadly Trackers '73
Death Stalk '74
Desperados '69
D.O.A. '49
Eaten Alive '76
Evils of the Night '85
The Halls of Montezuma '50
Hi-Riders '77
Kansas City Confidential '52
Lonely Man '57
The Longest Drive '76
Love Me Tender '56
The Mad Bomber '72
Mohawk '56
The Ninth Configuration '79
No Place to Run '72
Only the Valiant '50

The Prodigal '55
Psychic Killer '75
The Return '80
Riot in Cell Block 11 '54
Scarface Mob '62
The Seekers '79
That Darn Cat '65
This is a Hijack '75
Tin Star '57

Klaus Maria Brandauer
Becoming Colette '92
Burning Secret '89
Colonel Redl '84
Hanussen '88
Kindergarten '84
The Lightship '86
Mephisto '81
Never Say Never Again '83
Out of Africa '85
Quo Vadis '85
The Russia House '90
The Salzburg Connection '72
Streets of Gold '86
White Fang '91

Michael Branden
Accomplice '46

Larry Brandenburg
Mo' Money '92
Victimless Crimes '90

Arthur Brander
The Ghost of Rashmon Hall '47

Leslie Brander
Malibu Hot Summer '81
Sizzle Beach U.S.A. '86

Walter Brandi
The Bloody Pit of Horror '65
The Slaughter of the Vampires '62
Terror Creatures from the Grave '66

Jonathan Brandis
Ladybugs '92
The NeverEnding Story 2: Next Chapter '91
Sidekicks '93
Stepfather 2: Make Room for Daddy '89

Jocelyn Brando
Big Heat '53
Nightfall '56
A Question of Love '78
Ten Wanted Men '54

Luisina Brando
Dias de Ilusion '80
The Lion's Share '79

Marlon Brando
Apocalypse Now '79
The Appaloosa '66
Bedtime Story '63
Burn! '70
The Chase '66
Christopher Columbus: The Discovery '92
Desiree '54
A Dry White Season '89
The Formula '80
The Freshman '90
The Fugitive Kind '60
The Godfather '72
The Godfather 1902-1959: The Complete Epic '81
Guys and Dolls '55
Julius Caesar '53
Last Tango in Paris '73
Marlon Brando '85
The Men '50
Missouri Breaks '76
Morituri '65

Mutiny on the Bounty '62
The Nightcomers '72
On the Waterfront '54
One-Eyed Jacks '61
Reflections in a Golden Eye '67
Sayonara '57
A Streetcar Named Desire '51
Superman: The Movie '78
The Teahouse of the August Moon '56
The Ugly American '63
Viva Zapata! '52
The Wild One '54
The Young Lions '58

Richard Brando
Student Bodies '81

Rikki Brando
The Bikini Car Wash Company 2 '92
Buford's Beach Bunnies '92

Clark Brandon
Fast Food '89
My Tutor '82

David Brandon
Beyond Darkness '92
Stagefright '87

Don Brandon
Monsters Crash the Pajama Party '65

Henry Brandon
Drums of Fu Manchu '40
When the North Wind Blows '74

Michael Brandon
A Change of Seasons '80
James Dean '76
Lovers and Other Strangers '70
Promises in the Dark '79
Red Alert '77
Rich and Famous '81

Sharon H. Brandon
Iron Eagle 2 '88

Luis Brandoni
Made in Argentina '86

Carolyn Brandt
The Erotic Adventures of Pinocchio '71
The Hollywood Strangler Meets the Skid Row Slasher '79
Incredibly Strange Creatures Who Stopped Living and Became Mixed-Up Zombies '63
Rat Pfink a Boo-Boo '66
The Thrill Killers '65

Thordis Brandt
The Witchmaker '69

Victor Elliot Brandt
Neon Maniacs '86

Craig Branham
One Last Run '89

Laura Branigan
Mugsy's Girls '85

Paul Branney
Cobra Against Ninja '80s

Marjorie Bransfield
Easy Wheels '89

Betsy Brantley
Another Country '84
Dreams Lost, Dreams Found '87
Five Days One Summer '82
Havana '90

I Come in Peace '90

Timothy Brantley
Brutal Glory '89

Albert Bras
Napoleon '27

Dominick Brascia
Evil Laugh '86

Keefe Brasselle
Skirts Ahoy! '52
Streets of Sin '49

Claude Brasseur
Act of Aggression '73
Band of Outsiders '64
Elusive Corporal '62
Josepha '82
La Boum '81
L'Etat Sauvage '78
Lobster for Breakfast '82
Pardon Mon Affaire '76
Pardon Mon Affaire, Too! '77
A Simple Story '79

Pierre Brasseur
Carthage in Flames '60
Children of Paradise '44
Horror Chamber of Dr. Faustus '59

Benjamin Bratt
Bound by Honor '93
Bright Angel '91
One Good Cop '91

Andre Braugher
The Court Martial of Jackie Robinson '90
Glory '89
Somebody Has to Shoot the Picture '90

Gunther Braun
Terror Beneath the Sea '66

John Braun
S.S. Experiment Camp 2 '86

Pinkas Braun
The Man Outside '68
Mission Stardust '68
Praying Mantis '83

Asher Brauner
American Eagle '90
B.A.D. Cats '80
Living to Die '91
Merchants of War '90
Treasure of the Moon Goddess '88

Jeff Braunstein
One Night Only '84

Arthur Brauss
The Goalie's Anxiety at the Penalty Kick '71

Bart Braverman
The Great Texas Dynamite Chase '76
Hollywood Hot Tubs 2: Educating Crystal '89

Charlie Bravo
Scalps '83

Tony Bravo
Caches de Oro
East L.A. Warriors '89

Hilda Brawner
One Plus One '61

Kriss Braxton
Danger Zone '87

Jim Bray
Roller Boogie '79

Robert Bray
Never Love a Stranger '58

Edward Brayshaw
Unmasked Part 25 '88

Lidia Brazzi
The Christmas That Almost
Wasn't '66

Rossano Brazzi
The Adventurers '70
The Barefoot Contessa '54
Bobo '67
The Christmas That Almost
Wasn't '66
Dr. Frankenstein's Castle of
Freaks '74
The Far Pavilions '84
Fear City '85
Final Conflict '81
Final Justice '84
Formula for a Murder '85
The Italian Job '69
Legend of the Lost '57
Mr. Kingstreet's War '71
One Step to Hell '68
Rome Adventure '62
South Pacific '58
Summertime '55
Third Solution '89
Three Coins in the Fountain
'54
A Time for Miracles '80
We the Living '42
Woman Times Seven '67

Sebastian Breaks
The Big Switch '70

George Breakston
The Return of Peter Grimm
'35

Peter Breck
The Beatniks '60
Benji '74
The Crawling Hand '63
Highway 61 '91
Shock Corridor '63

Mano Breckenridge
Chameleon Street '89

Candice Brecker
Bridge to Silence '89

**Guillermo
Bredeston**
Con Mi Mujer No Puedo '87

Helen Lloyd Breed
Passed Away '92

Larry Breeding
A Matter of Life and Death '81
Street Music '81

Bobby Breen
Breaking the Ice '38
Escape to Paradise '39
Fisherman's Wharf '39
Hawaii Calls '38
It Happened in New Orleans
'36
Let's Sing Again '36
Make a Wish '37
Way Down South '39

Danny Breen
Bill Murray Live from the
Second City '70s

Mary Breen
Honeymoon Killers '70

Patrick Breen
Nobody's Perfect '90
Passed Away '92

Paulette Breen
The Clonus Horror '79
The Wizard of Speed and
Time '88

Thomas E. Breen
The River '51

Edmund Breese
Defenders of the Law '31

Tracy Bregman
The Concrete Jungle '82
Happy Birthday to Me '81

Marie Breillat
Dracula & Son '76

Valerie Breiman
Tale of Two Sisters '89

Jana Brejchova
Fabulous Adventures of
Baron Munchausen '61
Loves of a Blonde '65
The Original Fabulous
Adventures of Baron
Munchausen '61

Jacques Brel
Franz '72

Lucille Bremer
Behind Locked Doors '48
Human Gorilla '48
Meet Me in St. Louis '44
Till the Clouds Roll By '46
Till the Clouds Roll By/A Star
Is Born '46
Yolanda and the Thief '45
Ziegfeld Follies '46

Sylvia Bremer
Narrow Trail '17

El Brendel
The Beautiful Blonde from
Bashful Bend '49
Big Trail '30
I'm from Arkansas '44

Tom Breneman
Breakfast in Hollywood '46

George Brenlin
Fight for the Title '57

Brid Brennan
Four Days in July '84

Claire Brennan
She-Freak '67

Eileen Brennan
Babes in Toyland '86
Blood Vows: The Story of a
Mafia Wife '87
The Cheap Detective '78
Clue '85
Daisy Miller '74
The Death of Richie '76
FM '78
Fourth Wise Man '85
The Funny Farm '82
Great Smokey Roadblock '76
I Don't Buy Kisses Anymore
'92
The Last Picture Show '71
Murder by Death '76
My Father's House '75
My Old Man '79
The New Adventures of Pippi
Longstocking '88
Pandemonium '82
Playmates '72
Private Benjamin '80
Rented Lips '88
Richie '77
Scarecrow '73
Stella '89
Sticky Fingers '88
The Sting '73
Texasville '90
White Palace '90

Kerry Brennan
Terror Squad '87

Michael Brennan
No Trace '50

Stephen Brennan
Eat the Peach '86

Walter Brennan
The Adventures of Tom
Sawyer '38
Along the Great Divide '51
At Gunpoint '55
Bad Day at Black Rock '54
Barbary Coast '35
Best of the Badmen '50
Blood on the Moon '48
Come and Get It '36
The Cowboy and the Lady '38
Dakota '45
Far Country '55
Fury '36
Glory '56
Gnome-Mobile '67
Goodbye, My Lady '56
The Green Promise '49
Home for the Holidays '72
How the West was Won '63
Meet John Doe '41
Moon's Our Home '36
My Darling Clementine '46
The North Star '43
Northwest Passage '40
The One and Only, Genuine,
Original Family Band '68
The Oscar '66
Phantom of the Air '33
The Pride of the Yankees '42
The Princess and the Pirate
'44
The Range Feud/Two Fisted
Law '31
Red River '48
Rio Bravo '59
Sergeant York '41
The Showdown '50
Smoke in the Wind '75
Stanley and Livingstone '39
A Stolen Life '46
The Story of Vernon and Irene
Castle '39
Support Your Local Sheriff '69
Tammy and the Bachelor '57
Texas Cyclone '32
These Three '36
They Shall Have Music '39
Those Calloways '65
Ticket to Tomahawk '50
To Have & Have Not '44
Two-Fisted Law '32
The Westerner '40
Who's Minding the Mint? '67

Barry Brenner
Surf Nazis Must Die '87

Dori Brenner
Altered States '80
For the Boys '91
Sex and the Single Parent '82
Silent Victim '93
Summer Wishes, Winter
Dreams '73

Eve Brenner
The Great Mouse Detective
'86
Torment '85

Jerome Brenner
Sex Appeal '86

Eve Brent
Tarzan and the Trappers '58

Evelyn Brent
Daughter of the Tong '39
Last Command '28
Law West of Tombstone '38
Love 'Em and Leave 'Em '27
Panama Lady '39

The Payoff '43
The President's Mystery '36
Robot Pilot '41
The Seventh Victim '43
Song of the Trail '36
Trapped by the Mormons '22

George Brent
Baby Face '33
Born Again '78
Dark Victory '39
Experiment Perilous '45
FBI Girl '52
Female '33
The Fighting 69th '40
42nd Street '33
The Great Lie '41
In Person '35
In This Our Life '42
Jezebel '38
Lightning Warrior '31
Man Bait '52
Montana Belle '52
The Old Maid '39
Out of the Blue '47
The Painted Veil '34
Silver Queen '42
The Spiral Staircase '46
Tomorrow is Forever '46

Linda Brent
Below the Border '42
Death Valley Rangers '44

Maya Brent
Battle of the Worlds '61

Romney Brent
Adventures of Don Juan '49
Dreaming Lips '37
The Sign of Zorro '60
Under the Red Robe '36
The Virgin Queen '55

Roy Brent
Lightning Raiders '45

Timothy Brent
Escape from the Bronx '85
Sting of the West '76
Tornado '83
Warriors of the Wasteland '83

Amy Brentano
Blood Sisters '86

Gilbert Brenton
Class of Nuke 'Em High '86

Edmund Breon
Dressed to Kill '46
Gaslight '44

Bobbie Bresee
Evil Spawn '87
Ghoulies '85
Mausoleum '83
Surf Nazis Must Die '87

Jimmy Breslin
Pogo for President: "I Go
Pogo" '84

Kevin Breslin
On the Edge: The Survival of
Dana '79

Felix Bressart
Bitter Sweet '40
Blossoms in the Dust '41
Edison the Man '40
Ninotchka '39
Portrait of Jennie '48
The Seventh Cross '44
The Shop Around the Corner
'40
A Song is Born '48
To Be or Not to Be '42
Without Love '45
Ziegfeld Girl '41

Martin Brest
Fast Times at Ridgemont High
'82
Spies Like Us '85

Richard Brestoff
Car Wash '76

Howard Bretherton
Twilight on the Trail '41

Jean Bretonniere
The Green Glove '52
That Naughty Girl '58

Edward Brett
Maniac '78

Jeremy Brett
The Adventures of Sherlock
Holmes: Hound of the
Baskervilles '89
Haunted: The Ferryman '74
The Medusa Touch '78
My Fair Lady '64
One Deadly Owner '74
The Very Edge '63

Jim Brewer
Mission to Death '66

Joe Brewer
Vice Academy 2 '90

Kidd Brewer, Jr.
The Abyss '89

Rowanne Brewer
Round Trip to Heaven '92

Carol Brewster
Cat Women of the Moon '53

Diane Brewster
Courage of Black Beauty '57
Torpedo Run '58

June Brewster
Two Reelers: Comedy
Classics 4 '36

Maia Brewton
Adventures in Babysitting '87

Kevin Breznahan
Alive '93

Tom Breznahan
The Brain '88
Ski School '91
Twice Dead '88

Jean-Claude Brialy
The Bride Wore Black '68
The Burning Court '62
Catherine & Co. '76
Circle of Love '64
Claire's Knee '71
Cleo from 5 to 7 '61
The Cousins '59
The Judge and the Assassin
'75
La Nuit de Varennes '82
Le Beau Serge '58
Paris Belongs to Us '60
Phantom of Liberty '68
Robert et Robert '79
Tonio Kroger '65
A Woman is a Woman '60

David Brian
Ambush at Tomahawk Gap
'53
Beyond the Forest '49
Castle of Evil '66
Confessions of Tom Harris
'72
Flamingo Road '49
Intruder in the Dust '49
Million Dollar Mermaid '52
Pocketful of Miracles '61

Curt Brober
Ninja Mission '84

Lily Broberg
Famous Five Get Into Trouble
'87

Peter Brocco
The Balcony '63
Homebodies '74

Martine Brochard
Eyeball '78

Anne Brochet
Cyrano de Bergerac '90

Alan Brock
Shriek of the Mutilated '74

Anita Brock
People Who Own the Dark '75

Stan Brock
Galyon '77
Return to Africa '89

Terry Ten Brock
Delirium '77

Gerd Brockmann
The Wannsee Conference '84

Roy Brocksmith
Arachnophobia '90
Big Business '88
Bill & Ted's Bogus Journey
'91
Killer Fish '79
King of the Gypsies '78
Nickel & Dime '92
Tales of Ordinary Madness
'83
Total Recall '90

Gladys Brockwell
The Drake Case '29
Oliver Twist '22
Spangles '26

Beth Broderick
Are You Lonesome Tonight
'92
Thousand Pieces of Gold '91

Chris Broderick
Legacy of Horror '78

Helen Broderick
Bride Walks Out '36
The Rage of Paris '38
Swing Time '36
Top Hat '35

James Broderick
Alice's Restaurant '69
Dog Day Afternoon '75
The Group '66
Keeping On '81
The Shadow Box '80
The Taking of Pelham One
Two Three '74

Matthew Broderick
Biloxi Blues '88
Cinderella '84
Family Business '89
Ferris Bueller's Day Off '86
The Freshman '90
Glory '89
Ladyhawke '85
Master Harold and the Boys
'84
Max Dugan Returns '83
The Night We Never Met '93
1918 '85
On Valentine's Day '86
Out on a Limb '92
Project X '87
Torch Song Trilogy '88
War Games '83

Don Brodie
Pinocchio '40

Greer Brodie
Terror Squad '87

Steve Brodie
The Admiral Was a Lady '50
Armored Car Robbery '50
Badman's Territory '47
The Beast from 20,000
Fathoms '53
Blue Hawaii '62
Criminal Court '46
Desperate '47
Donovan's Brain '53
The Giant Spider Invasion '75
Kiss Tomorrow Goodbye '50
Out of the Past '47
Roustabout '64
Saint Strikes Back: Criminal
Court '46
The Steel Helmet '51
Three for Bedroom C '52
Tough Assignment '49
Treasure of Monte Cristo '50
The Wild World of Batwoman
'66
The Wizard of Speed and
Time '88

Adrien Brody
Home at Last '88
King of the Hill '93

Harry Brogan
Broth of a Boy '59
Shake Hands with the Devil
'59

Giulio Brogi
The Spider's Stratagem '70

James Brolin
The Ambush Murders '82
The Amityville Horror '79
Backstab '90
Bad Jim '89
The Boston Strangler '68
Capricorn One '78
Class of '63 '73
Fantastic Voyage '66
Finish Line '89
Gas Food Lodging '92
High Risk '76
Hold the Dream '85
Mae West '84
Night of the Juggler '80
Nightmare on the 13th Floor
'90
Our Man Flint '66
Steel Cowboy '78
Ted & Venus '93
Von Ryan's Express '65
Westworld '73

Josh Brolin
Finish Line '89
The Goonies '85
Thrashin' '86

**J. Edward
Bromberg**
Cloak and Dagger '46
The Mark of Zorro '40
The Missing Corpse '45
Phantom of the Opera '43
Queen of the Amazons '47
Return of Frank James '40
Reunion in France '42
Son of Dracula '43
A Song is Born '48
Strange Cargo '40

John Bromfield
Big Bluff '55
Easy to Love '53
Flat Top '52
Manfish '56

Valri Bromfield
Home is Where the Hart is '88
Mr. Mom '83
Nothing But Trouble '91
Who's Harry Crumb? '89

Sheila Bromley
Nancy Drew, Reporter '39
Torture Ship '39

Sydney Bromley
Crystalstone '88
The NeverEnding Story '84

Eleanor Bron
The Attic: The Hiding of Anne
Frank '88
Bedazzled '68
Help! '65
Turtle Diary '86
Two for the Road '67
Women in Love '70

William Bronder
Flush '81

Henry Bronett
The Mozart Brothers '86

Fritz Bronner
Tax Season '90

Albert Bronski
The 13th Mission '91

Brick Bronsky
Class of Nuke 'Em High, Part
2: Subhumanoid Meltdown
'91

Anthony Bronson
Bruce Lee Fights Back From
the Grave '76

Betty Bronson
Are Parents People? '25
Ben-Hur '26
Medicine Man '30
Naked Kiss '64
Yodelin' Kid From Pine Ridge
'37

Charles Bronson
Act of Vengeance '86
Assassination '87
Battle of the Bulge '65
Borderline '80
Breakheart Pass '76
Breakout '75
Bull of the West '89
Cabo Blanco '81
Chato's Land '71
Chino '73
Cold Sweat '74
Death Hunt '81
Death Wish '74
Death Wish 2 '82
Death Wish 3 '85
Death Wish 4: The
Crackdown '87
The Dirty Dozen '67
Drum Beat '54
The Evil That Men Do '84
The Family '73
Four for Texas '63
From Noon Till Three '76
The Great Escape '63
Guns of Diablo '64
Hard Times '75
Honor Among Thieves '68
House of Wax '53
The Indian Runner '91
Jubal '56
Kid Galahad '62
Kinjite: Forbidden Subjects
'89
Lola '69
Love and Bullets '79
Machine Gun Kelly '58
Magnificent Seven '60

Master of the World '61
The Meanest Men in the West
'76
The Mechanic '72
Messenger of Death '88
Miss Sadie Thompson '53
Mr. Majestyk '74
Murphy's Law '86
Never So Few '59
Once Upon a Time in the West
'68
Pat and Mike '52
Raid on Entebbe '77
Red Sun '71
Rider on the Rain '70
Run of the Arrow '56
St. Ives '76
The Sandpiper '65
Showdown at Boot Hill '58
Someone Behind the Door '71
The Stone Killer '73
Telefon '77
Ten to Midnight '83
This Property is Condemned
'66
Vera Cruz '53
Villa Rides '68
When Hell Broke Loose '58
The White Buffalo '77
Wild West '87

Harry Bronson
The Thief '52

Lillian Bronson
The Next Voice You Hear '50

David Bronstein
My Father is Coming '91

**Charles D. Brook,
III**
Black Sister's Revenge '76

Claudio Brook
The Bees '78
Daniel Boone: Trail Blazer '56
Dr. Tarr's Torture Dungeon
'75
La Mansion de la Locura '87
Neutron and the Black Mask
'61
The Peking Blond '68
Samson in the Wax Museum
'63
Sisters of Satan '75

Clive Brook
Action for Slander '38
Cavalcade '33
Convoy '40
Hula '28
On Approval '44

Doris Brook
Lone Bandit '33

Faith Brook
After Julius '78
Bloodbath
To Sir, with Love '67
Uneasy Terms '48

Irina Brook
Captive '87
The Girl in the Picture '86

Jayne Brook
Kindergarten Cop '90

Elwyn Brook-Jones
Bonnie Prince Charlie '48
The Gilded Cage '54
Rogue's Yarn '58

Lesley Brook
Murder in the Footlights '51

Lyndon Brook
Above Us the Waves '56
Invasion '65

The Spanish Gardener '57

Bunny Brooke
Alison's Birthday '79

Hillary Brooke
Abbott and Costello Meet
Captain Kidd '52
Africa Screams '49
Big Town '47
Big Town After Dark '47
The Enchanted Cottage '45
Heat Wave '54
Jane Eyre '44
The Lost Continent '51
The Man Who Knew Too
Much '56
Never Wave at a WAC '52
Rangeland Racket '41
The Road to Utopia '46
Sherlock Holmes Faces Death
'43
Sherlock Holmes: The Voice
of Terror '42
The Strange Woman '46
To the Shores of Tripoli '42
Underworld Scandal '47
The Woman in Green '45

Paul Brooke
The Lair of the White Worm
'88

Rebecca Brooke
Confessions of a Young
American Housewife '78
Little Girl...Big Tease '75

Sandy Brooke
Crazed Cop '88
Miami Vendetta '87
Star Slammer '87
Terror on Alcatraz '86

Ted Brooke
Ninja Demon's Massacre '80s

Tim Brooke
12 Plus 1 '70

Tyler Brooke
The Divorcee '30

Walter Brooke
Conquest of Space '55
The Return of Count Yorga
'71

Richard Brooker
Deathstalker '83
Friday the 13th, Part 3 '82

Jacqueline Brookes
Hardhat & Legs '80
Naked Gun 2 1/2: The Smell
of Fear '91
Rodeo Girl '80
Silent Witness '85

Aimee Brooks
Critters 3 '91

Albert Brooks
Broadcast News '87
Defending Your Life '91
Lost in America '85
Modern Romance '81
Private Benjamin '80
Real Life '79
Taxi Driver '76
Twilight Zone: The Movie '83
Unfaithfully Yours '84

Avery Brooks
Half Slave, Half Free '85
Roots: The Gift '88
Uncle Tom's Cabin '87

Christopher Brooks
Alabama's Ghost '72

Terror by Night/Meeting at
  Midnight '46
Thunder in the City '37
Treasure Island '34
The Two Mrs. Carrolls '47
The Woman in Green '45

Virginia Bruce
Action in Arabia '44
Born to Dance '36
The Great Ziegfeld '36
Jane Eyre '34
Let 'Em Have It '35
Pardon My Sarong '42
State Department File 649 '49
Strangers When We Meet '60

Jane Brucker
Dirty Dancing '87

Patrick Bruel
Secret Obsession '88

Christopher Brugger
Bloody Moon '83

Eddie Brugman
Katie's Passion '75

Heidi Bruhl
Captain Sinbad '63

Werner Bruhns
1900 '76

Beau Brummel
Three Bullets for a Long Gun
  '73
Village of the Giants '65

Jeremy Brundell
Fortunes of War '87

Bo Brundin
Headless Eyes '83
Russian Roulette '75
Shoot the Sun Down '81

Adrian Brunel
Spitfire '42

Robert Bruning
The Night After Halloween '83

Natja Brunkhorst
Christiane F. '82

Fernando Bruno
Time Out for Love '61
Two Nights with Cleopatra '54

Paul Bruno
Mankillers '87

Philip Bruns
Dead Men Don't Die '91
The Opposite Sex and How to
  Live With Them '93
Return of the Living Dead Part
  2 '88

Dora Bryan
Great St. Trinian's Train
  Robbery '66
My Son, the Vampire '52
No Trace '50
Screamtime '83
Small Hotel '57
A Taste of Honey '61

Jane Bryan
Each Dawn I Die '39
Kid Galahad '37
Marked Woman '37
The Old Maid '39
The Sisters '38

Tonia Bryan
Hot Summer in Barefoot
  County '74

Walter Bryan
The Respectful Prostitute '52

Betty Bryant
Forty Thousand Horsemen
  '41

Bill Bryant
King Dinosaur '55

John Bryant
Courage of Black Beauty '57

Joyce Bryant
Across the Plains '39
East Side Kids '40

Marie Bryant
The Duke is the Tops '38

Michael Bryant
Girly '70
Goodbye, Mr. Chips '69
Sakharov '84

Nana Bryant
Big Town '47
Eyes of Texas '48
Harvey '50
Inner Sanctum '48
Ladies of the Chorus '49
The Possessed '47
Sinners in Paradise '38

Pamela Bryant
Lunch Wagon '81
Tigershark '87

Virginia Bryant
The Barbarians '87
Demons 2 '87

William Bryant
Corvette Summer '78
Mountain Family Robinson '79

Claudia Bryar
Green Eyes '76

Edita Brychta
Fergie & Andrew: Behind
  Palace Doors '93

Jon Bryden
The Deserters '80s

Yul Brynner
Anastasia '56
Battle of Neretva '69
The Brothers Karamazov '58
The Buccaneer '58
Cast a Giant Shadow '66
Catlow '71
Death Rage '77
Futureworld '76
Fuzz '72
Invitation to a Gunfighter '64
The King and I '56
Light at the Edge of the World
  '71
The Madwoman of Chaillot
  '69
The Magic Christian '69
Magnificent Seven '60
Morituri '65
Night Flight from Moscow '73
The Poppy is also a Flower
  '66
Port of New York '49
Return of the Seven '66
Romance of a Horsethief '71
Solomon and Sheba '59
Taras Bulba '62
The Ten Commandments '56
The Testament of Orpheus
  '59
Triple Cross '67
The Ultimate Warrior '75
Villa Rides '68
Westworld '73

Kathleen Bryon
Twins of Evil '71

Leesa Bryte
Senior Week '88

Barry Buchanan
The Loch Ness Horror '82

Cheryl Buchanan
Escape from Galaxy Three '76

Claud Buchanan
Running Wild '27

Edgar Buchanan
Abilene Town '46
The Big Hangover '50
Big Trees '52
Black Arrow '48
Buffalo Bill '44
Coroner Creek '48
Destroyer '43
The Devil's Partner '58
Human Desire '54
It Started with a Kiss '59
Lust for Gold '49
Make Haste to Live '54
Man from Button Willow '65
Man from Colorado '49
MoLintook! '63
Penny Serenade '41
Rage at Dawn '55
Rawhide '50
Ride the High Country '62
The Rounders '65
Shane '53
She Couldn't Say No '52
Silver Star '55
Talk of the Town '42
Texas '41
Yuma '70

Jack Buchanan
The Band Wagon '53
When Knights were Bold '36

Miles Buchanan
Dangerous Game '90
Runaway Island, Part 1
Runaway Island, Part 2
Runaway Island, Part 3
Runaway Island, Part 4

Robert Buchanan
That Sinking Feeling '79

Sherry Buchanan
Emmanuelle & Joanna '86
Eyes Behind the Stars '72

Simone Buchanan
Run, Rebecca, Run '81
Runaway Island, Part 1
Runaway Island, Part 2
Runaway Island, Part 3
Runaway Island, Part 4
Shame '87

Stuart Buchanan
Snow White and the Seven
  Dwarfs '37

West Buchanan
Cosmos: War of the Planets
  '80

Yvette Buchanan
The Malibu Beach Vampires
  '91

Christine Buchegger
From the Life of the
  Marionettes '80

Horst Buchholz
Aces: Iron Eagle 3 '92
Avalanche Express '79
Berlin Tunnel 21 '81
The Catamount Killing '74
Code Name: Emerald '85
Empty Canvas '64
Fanny '61

From Hell to Victory '79
Magnificent Seven '60
One, Two, Three '61
Raid on Entebbe '77
Return to Fantasy Island '77
Sahara '83
The Savage Bees '76
Teenage Wolfpack '57
Tiger Bay '59

Buck
Robinson Crusoe of Clipper
  Island '36

Frank Buck
Jacare '42
Tiger Fangs '43

Buck the Wonder Dog
Fangs of the Wild '54

Andrew Buckland
Hunted '88

Hugh Buckler
The Last of the Mohicans '36

John Buckler
The Black Room '35
Tarzan Escapes '36

Betty Buckley
Another Woman '88
Babycakes '89
Carrie '76
Frantic '88
Tender Mercies '83
Wild Thing '87

Keith Buckley
Half Moon Street '86
The Virgin Witch '70

Tara Buckman
Xtro 2: The Second Encounter
  '91

Parris Buckner
Trading Hearts '87

Susan Buckner
Deadly Blessing '81

Robert Budaska
Ice Pawn '92

Helen Buday
For Love Alone '86
Mad Max Beyond
  Thunderdome '85

Julie Budd
The Devil & Max Devlin '81

John Carl Buechler
Dungeonmaster '85
The Sleeping Car '90

Nancy Buechler
Thinkin' Big '87

Jack Buetel
Best of the Badmen '50
The Half-Breed '51

Vincent Bufano
Hang Tough '89

Marilyn Buferd
Queen of Outer Space '58

David Buff
Cop-Out '91

Buffalo Bill, Jr.
Deadwood Pass '33
Fighting Cowboy '33
Lightning Bill '35
Powdersmoke Range '35
Rawhide Romance '34
Riding Speed '35
Terror Trail '33

Jimmy Buffett
Doctor Duck's Super Secret
  All-Purpose Sauce '85
FM '78

Niall Buggy
The Playboys '92

Joe Bugner
Fatal Bond '91

Valerie Buhagiar
Highway 61 '91
Roadkill '89

Dorothy Buhrman
Starhops '78

Son Hoang Bui
Table for Five '83

Genevieve Bujold
Anne of the Thousand Days
  '69
Another Man, Another Chance
  '77
Choose Me '84
Coma '78
The Dance Goes On '92
Dead Ringers '88
Earthquake '74
False Identity '90
Final Assignment '80
Journey '77
The King of Hearts '66
The Last Flight of Noah's Ark
  '80
The Moderns '88
Monsignor '82
Murder by Decree '79
Obsession '76
Oh, What a Night '92
A Paper Wedding '89
Swashbuckler '76
Tightrope '84
Trojan Women '71
Trouble in Mind '86

Donald Buka
Stolen Identity '53
The Street with No Name '48

Raymond Buktencia
The Adventures of Nellie Bly
  '81
The Jayne Mansfield Story '80
Wait Till Your Mother Gets
  Home '83

Peter Bull
The African Queen '51
A Christmas Carol '51
Doctor Doolittle '67
Dr. Strangelove, or: How I
  Learned to Stop Worrying
  and Love the Bomb '64
Marie Antoinette '38
Second Best Secret Agent in
  the Whole Wide World '65

Richard Bull
Different Story '78
Lawman '71

Elma Bulla
Cat's Play '74

Billy Bullet
Cycle Vixens '79

Perry Bullington
Chatterbox '76

Sandra Bullock
Love Potion #9 '92
The Thing Called Love '93
The Vanishing '93
Who Shot Pat? '92

Joseph Buloff
The Loves of Carmen '48

Delirious '91
Desperate '47
FBI Girl '52
Godzilla, King of the Monsters '56
Godzilla 1985 '85
Great Day in the Morning '56
His Kind of Woman '51
Horizons West '52
Love Happy '50
Love's Savage Fury '79
A Man Alone '55
The Night the City Screamed '80
Out of the Blue '82
The Ox-Bow Incident '55
Party Girls for Sale '54
Passion '54
Perry Mason Returns '85
Perry Mason: The Case of the Lost Love '87
Pitfall '48
A Place in the Sun '51
Rear Window '54
The Return '80
Showdown at Williams Creek '91
Station West '48
They Were So Young '55
Tomorrow Never Comes '77

Robert Burr
Netherworld '91
The Possession of Joel Delaney '72

Matthew Burrill
Where the Lilies Bloom '74

Bonnie Burroughs
Hard to Kill '89

Jackie Burroughs
Anne of Green Gables '85
Final Notice '89
The Grey Fox '83
The Housekeeper '86
John and the Missus '87
Taking Care of Terrific '88
Undergrads '85

William S. Burroughs
Bloodhounds of Broadway '89
Drugstore Cowboy '89
Kerouac '84

Darren E. Burrows
Class of 1999 '90
Cry-Baby '90

Martin Burrows
Sex with the Stars '81

Ellen Burstyn
Act of Vengeance '86
Alex in Wonderland '71
Alice Doesn't Live Here Anymore '74
The Ambassador '84
The Cemetery Club '93
A Dream of Passion '78
Dying Young '91
The Exorcist '73
Grand Isle '92
Hanna's War '88
Harry and Tonto '74
Into Thin Air '85
The King of Marvin Gardens '72
The Last Picture Show '71
The People vs. Jean Harris '81
Providence '77
Resurrection '80
Same Time, Next Year '78
Silence of the North '81
Something in Common '86
Thursday's Game '74
Twice in a Lifetime '85

Benny Burt
Hawaiian Buckaroo '38
Sea Racketeers '37

Clarissa Burt
The NeverEnding Story 2: Next Chapter '91

Chad Burton
In the Spirit '90

Clarence Burton
The Navigator '24

Corey Burton
Galaxy Express '82

Devera Burton
Omoo Omoo, the Shark God '49

Harry Burton
Fortunes of War '87

Jennifer Burton
Truck Stop Women '74

Julian Burton
A Bucket of Blood '59

Kate Burton
Uncle Tom's Cabin '87

LeVar Burton
Acorn People '82
Almos' a Man '78
Billy: Portrait of a Street Kid '77
Grambling's White Tiger '81
The Guyana Tragedy: The Story of Jim Jones '80
The Hunter '80
The Jesse Owens Story '84
The Midnight Hour '86
One in a Million: The Ron LaFlore Story '78
Roots '77
Roots: The Gift '88
The Supernaturals '86

Maggie Burton
Keep It Up, Jack! '75

Norman Burton
Attack of the Mayan Mummy '63
Bad Guys '86
Bloodsport '88
Crimes of Passion '84
Diamonds are Forever '71
Fright '56
Jud '71
Mausoleum '83
Save the Tiger '73
Simon, King of the Witches '71
The Terminal Man '74

Pierre Burton
Love Circles '85

Richard Burton
Absolution '81
Alexander the Great '55
Anne of the Thousand Days '69
Assassination of Trotsky '72
Becket '64
Bluebeard '72
Breakthrough '78
Circle of Two '80
Cleopatra '63
The Comedians '67
The Desert Rats '53
Divorce His, Divorce Hers '72
Doctor Faustus '68
Equus '77
Exorcist 2: The Heretic '77
The Gathering Storm '74
Green Grow the Rushes '51
Hammersmith is Out '72

Ice Palace '60
The Klansman '74
The Last Days of Dolwyn '49
The Longest Day '62
Look Back in Anger '58
Lovespell '79
Massacre in Rome '73
The Medusa Touch '78
The Night of the Iguana '64
1984 '84
Raid on Rommel '71
The Robe '53
The Sandpiper '65
The Spy Who Came in from the Cold '65
The Taming of the Shrew '67
The Tempest '63
Under Milk Wood '73
The V.I.P.'s '63
Wagner: The Complete Epic '85
Wagner: The Movie '85
Where Eagles Dare '68
Who's Afraid of Virginia Woolf? '66
Wild Geese '78

Robert Burton
The Gallant Hours '60
The Girl Who Had Everything '53
Invasion of the Animal People '62
A Man Called Peter '55
A Reason to Live, A Reason to Die '73
The Slime People '63
The Tall T '57
Teenage Frankenstein '58
Trilogy of Terror '75

Tony Burton
Armed and Dangerous '86
Blackjack '78
Mission of Justice '92
Oceans of Fire '86

Tracy Burton
Zombiethon '86

Wendell Burton
East of Eden '80
Fortune and Men's Eyes '71
The Sterile Cuckoo '69

Sean Bury
Friends '71
Paul and Michelle '74

Steve Buscemi
Barton Fink '91
Billy Bathgate '91
Heart '87
In the Soup '92
Parting Glances '86
Reservoir Dogs '92

Dennis Busch
Faster Pussycat! Kill! Kill! '66

Ernst Busch
Kameradschaft '31

Mae Busch
Bohemian Girl '36
Defenders of the Law '31
Foolish Wives '22
Laurel & Hardy Comedy Classics, Vol. 1 '33
Laurel & Hardy Comedy Classics, Vol. 3 '34
Laurel & Hardy Comedy Classics, Vol. 6 '35
Laurel & Hardy Comedy Classics, Vol. 7 '30s
The Mad Monster '42
Marie Antoinette '38
Sons of the Desert '33
Sucker Money '34

The Unholy Three '25
Without Honors '32
Ziegfeld Girl '41

Gary Busey
Act of Piracy '89
Angels Hard as They Come '71
Barbarosa '82
Big Wednesday '78
The Buddy Holly Story '78
Bulletproof '88
Canvas: The Fine Art of Crime '92
Carny '80
Chrome Soldiers '92
Dangerous Life '89
D.C. Cab '84
Didn't You Hear? '83
The Execution of Private Slovik '74
Eye of the Tiger '86
The Firm '92
Foolin' Around '80
Gumball Rally '76
Half a Lifetime '86
Hider in the House '90
Insignificance '85
The Last American Hero '73
Lethal Weapon '87
Let's Get Harry '87
My Heroes Have Always Been Cowboys '91
The Neon Empire '89
The Player '92
Point Break '91
Predator 2 '90
Rookie of the Year '93
The Shrieking '73
Silver Bullet '85
South Beach '92
A Star is Born '76
Straight Time '78
Thunderbolt & Lightfoot '74
Under Siege '92

Timothy Busfield
Field of Dreams '89
Revenge of the Nerds '84
Revenge of the Nerds 2: Nerds in Paradise '87
Sneakers '92
Strays '91

Billy Green Bush
Alice Doesn't Live Here Anymore '74
Amazing Stories, Book 5 '85
Critters '86
Culpepper Cattle Co. '72
The Deliberate Stranger '86
Electra Glide in Blue '73
Elvis and Me '88
Five Easy Pieces '70
The River '84
Tom Horn '80

Chuck Bush
Fandango '85

Grand Bush
Blind Vengeance '90
Colors '88
Freejack '92
Hang Tough '89
Streets of Fire '84

James Bush
Beggars in Ermine '34
Crimson Romance '34
King of the Cowboys '43
The Return of Peter Grimm '35
A Shot in the Dark '35

Jovita Bush
The Cheerleaders '72
Foxstyle '73

Rebecca Bush
Hunk '87

Anthony Bushell
Angel with the Trumpet '50
The Arsenal Stadium Mystery '39
Dark Journey '37
Disraeli '29
The Ghoul '34
The Miniver Story '50
A Night to Remember '58
The Royal Bed '31
The Scarlet Pimpernel '34
The Small Back Room '49
Vanity Fair '32

Joe Bushkin
The Rat Race '60

Francis X. Bushman
Ben-Hur '26
David and Bathsheba '51
Dick Tracy: The Original Serial, Vol. 1 '37
Dick Tracy: The Original Serial, Vol. 2 '37
Dick Tracy: The Spider Strikes '37
Eyes Right! '26
Honky Tonk '41
Last Frontier '32
Midnight Faces '26
The Phantom Planet '61
Sabrina '54
When Lightning Strikes '34

Trent Bushy
American Shaolin: King of the Kickboxers 2 '92

Akosua Busia
The Color Purple '85
The Final Terror '83
The George McKenna Story '86
Native Son '86
The Seventh Sign '88

Marion Busia
Deadline Auto Theft '83
Gone in 60 Seconds '74

Ricky Busker
Big Shots '87

Narciso Busquets
El Gallo de Oro '65
El Hombre Contra el Mundo '87

Raymond Bussieres
Jonah Who Will Be 25 in the Year 2000 '76
Paris When It Sizzles '64

Maria Bustamante
Yanco '64

Sergio Bustamante
Conexion Mexico '87
Lagrimas de Amor '87

Budd Buster
Border Badmen '45
Cowboy Commandos '43
Frontier Outlaws '44
The Lone Rider in Ghost Town '41
Outlaw of the Plains '46
Pinto Canyon '40
Raiders of Sunset Pass '43
Songs and Bullets '38
Thunder in the Desert '38

Range Busters
Texas to Bataan '42

Kim Butcher
Frightmare '74

Brandon Call
The Adventures of Ford
Fairlane '90
For the Boys '91

John Call
Santa Claus Conquers the
Martians '64

R.D. Call
Stephen King's Golden Years
'91
Young Guns 2 '90

James Callahan
Amazing Stories, Book 3 '86
Outlaw Blues '77

K. Callan
Frankie and Johnny '91
A Touch of Class '73
The Unborn '91

Michael Callan
Bon Voyage! '62
The Cat and the Canary '79
Cat Ballou '65
Donner Pass: The Road to
Survival '84
Double Exposure '82
Frasier the Sensuous Lion '73
Freeway '88
Gidget Goes Hawaiian '61
The Interns '62
Lepke '75
Mysterious Island '61
Photographer '75
Tom Edison: The Boy Who Lit
Up the World '78

Kay Callard
Cat Girl '57

Charlie Callas
Big Mouth '67
Pete's Dragon '77

Claire Callaway
Three of Hearts '93

Joseph Calleia
After the Thin Man '36
Algiers '38
Branded '50
The Caddy '53
Deadline at Dawn '46
Five Came Back '39
Gilda '46
The Glass Key '42
Golden Boy '39
Jungle Book '42
The Light in the Forest '58
The Littlest Outlaw '54
Marie Antoinette '38
My Little Chickadee '40
The Noose Hangs High '48
Riff Raff '35
Sundown '41
Touch of Evil '58

Cecilia Callejo
Outlaw Express '38

Simon Callow
Amadeus '84
The Crucifer of Blood '91
Howard's End '92
Maurice '87
Mr. & Mrs. Bridge '91
A Room with a View '86

Cab Calloway
The Blues Brothers '80
The Cincinnati Kid '65
Hi-De-Ho '35
International House '33
The Littlest Angel '69
Manhattan Merry-Go-Round
'37
Sensations of 1945 '44

Stormy Weather '43

Kirk Calloway
Cinderella Liberty '73
Summertree '71

Starr Calloway
Girl from Chicago '32

**Vanessa Bell
Calloway**
What's Love Got to Do With
It? '93

William Calloway
Flush '81

Donald Calthrop
Number Seventeen '32
The Phantom Light '35
Scrooge '35

Lou Calvelli
Sinners '89

Bill Calvert
Body Waves '91
C.H.U.D. 2: Bud the Chud '89
Terror Squad '87

Charles Calvert
Black Tower '50

John Calvert
The Devil's Cargo '48

Phyllis Calvert
Indiscreet '58
Kipps '41
The Man in Grey '45
Man of Evil '48
Mandy '53
Men of Two Worlds '46
The Woman He Loved '88
The Young and the Guilty '58

Corinne Calvet
Apache Uprising '66
Dr. Heckyl and Mr. Hype '80
Far Country '55
Too Hot to Handle '76
What Price Glory? '52

Henry Calvin
The Sign of Zorro '60
Toby Tyler '59

John Calvin
California Dreaming '79
Ghostwarrior '86
Primary Target '89

Armando Calvo
Ni Chana Ni Juana '87
Orlak, the Hell of Frankenstein
'60
Satanik '69
The Witch's Mirror '60

Pablito Calvo
The Man Who Wagged His
Tail '57

Cornelia Calwer
Girls Riot '88

Art Camacho
Chinatown Connection '90

Roberto Camardiel
Guns for Dollars '73

Bill Cambra
Kill Squad '81

Del Cambre
Tundra '36

Adele Cambria
Accatone! '61

Godfrey Cambridge
Cotton Comes to Harlem '70
Friday Foster '75
Gone are the Days '63

The President's Analyst '67
Purlie Victorious '63
Son of Blob '72
Watermelon Man '70
Whiffs '75

Ji Tu Cambuka
Glitch! '88
Mandingo '75

Joan Camden
Stolen Identity '53

Paul Camen
The Student Nurses '70

Juan Jose Camero
El Muerto '75
Far Away and Long Ago '74
Veronico Cruz '87

David Cameron
My First Wife '84

Dean Cameron
Bad Dreams '88
Miracle Beach '92
Rockula '90
Ski School '91

James Cameron
Last Action Hero '93

Jane Cameron
The Unborn '91

Joanna Cameron
How to Commit Marriage '69

Kimberly Cameron
H.O.T.S. '79

Kirk Cameron
The Best of Times '86
Like Father, Like Son '87
Listen to Me '89

Rod Cameron
The Electronic Monster '57
Evel Knievel '72
G-Men vs. the Black Dragon
'43
Jungle '52
The Last Movie '71
Manhunt in the African Jungle
'54
Midnight Auto Supply '78
Psychic Killer '75
Ride the Man Down '53
Salome, Where She Danced
'45
Wake Island '42

Trent Cameron
The Kid Who Loved Christmas
'90

Terry Camillieri
The Cars That Ate Paris '74

Blackie Cammett
The American Scream '80s

Colleen Camp
Apocalypse Now '79
Backfield in Motion '91
Cat in the Cage '68
Cloud Dancer '80
Clue '85
D.A.R.Y.L. '85
Deadly Games '80
Death Game '76
Doin' Time '85
Game of Death '79
Illegally Yours '87
Joy of Sex '84
Lady of the House '78
The Last Porno Flick '74
Midnight Auto Supply '78
Police Academy 2: Their First
Assignment '85

**Police Academy 4: Citizens on
Patrol '87**
Rosebud Beach Hotel '85
Screwball Academy '86
Seducers '77
The Seduction '82
She Devils in Chains
Sliver '93
Smile '75
Smokey and the Bandit, Part
3 '83
The Swinging Cheerleaders
'74
They All Laughed '81
Track 29 '88
Valley Girl '83
Walk Like a Man '87
Wayne's World '92
Wicked Stepmother '89

Hamilton Camp
Arena '88
Casey at the Bat '85
Meatballs 2 '84
Rosebud Beach Hotel '85
Under Fire '83

Philip Campanaro
Sex Appeal '86

Frank Campanella
Blood Red '88
Chesty Anderson USN '76

Joe Campanella
Original Intent '91

Joseph Campanella
Ben '72
Body Chemistry '90
Club Fed '91
Comic Book Kids '82
Down the Drain '89
Hangar 18 '80
Last Call '90
Meteor '79
Murder Once Removed '71
Ninja Dragons '92
No Retreat, No Surrender 3:
Blood Brothers '91
Plutonium Incident '82
The President's Plane is
Missing '71
Return to Fantasy Island '77
The St. Valentine's Day
Massacre '67
Sky Hei$t '75
Steele Justice '87
Terror on the 40th Floor '74

Beatrice Campbell
Last Holiday '50
The Master of Ballantrae '53

Bill Campbell
Bram Stoker's Dracula '92
Crime Story: The Complete
Saga '86
The Night We Never Met '93
The Rocketeer '91

Bruce Campbell
Army of Darkness '92
Crimewave '85
Evil Dead '83
Evil Dead 2: Dead by Dawn
'87
Going Back '83
Lunatics: A Love Story '92
Maniac Cop '88
Maniac Cop 2 '90
Mindwarp '91
Moontrap '89
Sundown '91
Waxwork 2: Lost in Time '91

C. Jutson Campbell
Star Crystal '85

Charlene Campbell
Dance '90

Cheryl Campbell
Chariots of Fire '81
Greystoke: The Legend of
Tarzan, Lord of the Apes
'84
Lillie '79
McVicar '80
The Shooting Party '85

Chip Campbell
Driven to Kill '90

Christina Campbell
Sensuous Summer '93

Colin Campbell
Leather Boys '63

Daphne Campbell
Overlanders '46

**David James
Campbell**
Killzone '85

Douglas Campbell
Oedipus Rex '57

Elizabeth Campbell
Wrestling Women vs. the
Aztec Ape '62

Eric Campbell
Charlie Chaplin Festival '17
Charlie Chaplin: The Early
Years, Vol. 1 '17
Charlie Chaplin: The Early
Years, Vol. 2 '17
Charlie Chaplin: The Early
Years, Vol. 3 '16
Charlie Chaplin: The Early
Years, Vol. 4 '16
Count/Adventurer '17
The Cure '17
The Fireman '16
The Floorwalker/By the Sea
'15
Triple Trouble/Easy Street '18
The Vagabond '16

Glen Campbell
Rock-a-Doodle '92
True Grit '69
Uphill All the Way '85

Graeme Campbell
And Then You Die '88

**Anna Campbell-
Jones**
Secrets '82

Judy Campbell
Bonnie Prince Charlie '48
Convoy '40
Dust to Dust '85
The World Owes Me a Living
'47

Julia Campbell
Livin' Large '91
Opportunity Knocks '90

Kate Campbell
Ghost Valley '32
Monte Carlo Nights '34

Ken Campbell
Letter to Brezhnev '86
Smart Money '88

Louise Campbell
Bulldog Drummond Comes
Back '37
Bulldog Drummond's Peril '38
Bulldog Drummond's
Revenge '37

Bulldog Drummond's
Revenge/Bulldog
Drummond's Peril '38

Naomi Campbell
Cool As Ice '91

Nicholas Campbell
The Big Slice '90
Certain Fury '85
Fast Company '78
Going Home '86
July Group '70s
Knights of the City '85
Rampage '87
Shades of Love: Champagne
for Two '87
The Victory '88

Patrick Campbell
Smokey Bites the Dust '81

Paul Campbell
The Lunatic '92

Peggy Campbell
Big Calibre '35

Rob Campbell
Unforgiven '92

Ron Campbell
Silhouette '91

Stuart Campbell
Gallagher's Travels '87

Tisha Campbell
Boomerang '92
House Party '90
House Party 2: The Pajama
Jam '91
Rags to Riches '87
Rooftops '89
School Daze '88

Torquil Campbell
The Golden Seal '83
Heaven on Earth '89

William Campbell
Battle Circus '53
Dementia 13 '63
Man Without a Star '55
Night of Evil '62
Portrait in Terror '66
Track of the Vampire '66

Frank Campeau
The Man from Painted Post
'17
When the Clouds Roll By '19

Cris Campion
Field of Honor '87
Pirates '86

Liz Campion
Those Glory, Glory Days '83

Wally Campo
The Beast from Haunted Cave
'60
Hell Squad '58
Machine Gun Kelly '58
Suicide Battalion/Hell Squad
'58
Tank Commando '59

Rafael Campos
The Astro-Zombies '67
The Hanged Man '74
Lady in a Cage '64
The Return of Josey Wales
'86
Slumber Party '57 '76
This Could Be the Night '57

Victor Campos
Archer: The Fugitive from the
Empire '81

Rocky Camron
Sonora Stagecoach '44

Robert Canada
Danger Zone '87

Giana Maria Canale
The Devil's Commandment
'56
Evil's Commandment '56
Go for Broke! '51
Hercules '58
Man from Cairo '54
Sins of Rome '54
Tiger of the Seven Seas '62

Maria Canale
Marauder '65

Lee Canalito
The Glass Jungle '88
Paradise Alley '78

David Canary
Johnny Firecloud '75
Melvin Purvis: G-Man '74
Posse '75
Sharks' Treasure '75

Stelio Candelli
A Man Called Rage '84

Candy Candido
The Great Mouse Detective
'86
Peter Pan '53
Rhythm Parade '43

John Candy
Armed and Dangerous '86
Best of Comic Relief '86
The Best of John Candy on
SCTV '80s
The Blues Brothers '80
Boris and Natasha: The Movie
'92
Brewster's Millions '85
Career Opportunities '91
Clown Murders '83
Delirious '91
Find the Lady '75
Going Berserk '83
The Great Outdoors '88
Home Alone '90
Hot to Trot! '88
It Came from Hollywood '82
JFK '91
The Last Polka '84
Little Shop of Horrors '86
Lost and Found '79
The Masters of Menace '90
National Lampoon's Vacation
'83
Nothing But Trouble '91
Once Upon a Crime '92
Only the Lonely '91
Planes, Trains & Automobiles
'87
Really Weird Tales '86
The Rescuers Down Under
'90
Second City Insanity '81
Sesame Street Presents:
Follow That Bird '85
The Silent Partner '78
Spaceballs '87
Speed Zone '88
Splash '84
Stripes '81
Summer Rental '85
Tales of the Klondike: The
Unexpected '87
Tunnelvision '76
Uncle Buck '89
Volunteers '85
Who's Harry Crumb? '89

Charles Cane
Dead Reckoning '47

Lucky Me '54
Native Son '51

Roberto Canedo
Bestia Nocturna '86
Wrestling Women vs. the
Aztec Ape '62

Lina Canelajas
The Garden of Delights '70

Jeff Canfield
Night of Horror '80s

Lee Canfield
Escapes '86

**Mary Grace
Canfield**
South of Reno '87

Enzo Cannavale
Flatfoot '78

James Canning
The Boys in Company C '77

Amanda Cannings
Forbidden '85

David Cannon
The Severed Arm '73

Dyan Cannon
The Anderson Tapes '71
Author! Author! '82
Bob & Carol & Ted & Alice '69
Caddyshack 2 '88
Christmas in Connecticut '92
Coast to Coast '80
Deathtrap '82
Doctors' Wives '70
The End of Innocence '90
Having It All '82
Heaven Can Wait '78
Honeysuckle Rose '80
Jenny's War '85
Lady of the House '78
The Last of Sheila '73
The Love Machine '71
Merlin and the Sword '85
Revenge of the Pink Panther
'78
Shamus '73
The Virginia Hill Story '76

Ed Cannon
Vampire Cop '90

Esma Cannon
Crow Hollow '52

Freddy Cannon
Village of the Giants '65

J.D. Cannon
The Adventures of Nellie Bly
'81
Cool Hand Luke '67
Cotton Comes to Harlem '70
Death Wish 2 '82
Killing Stone '78
Lawman '71
Pleasure Palace '80
Raise the Titanic '80
Scorpio '73
Street Justice '89
Walking Through the Fire '80

Katherine Cannon
High Noon: Part 2 '80
Matters of the Heart '90
Private Duty Nurses '71
The Red Fury '70s
Will: G. Gordon Liddy '82

Mary Cannon
Trucker's Woman '83

Pomeroy Cannon
The Four Horsemen of the
Apocalypse '21

Vince Cannon
The Manhandlers '73

**Jean-Michel
Cannone**
A Fine Romance '92

Gaspar Cano
Hot Blood '89

Anne Canoras
Revenge of the Dead '84

Diana Canova
The First Nudie Musical '75
Night Partners '83

Judy Canova
The Adventures of
Huckleberry Finn '60
Oklahoma Annie '51

Anne Canovos
High Frequency '88

Antonio Cantafora
Gabriela '84

**Luis Aceves
Cantaneda**
Curse of the Aztec Mummy/
Robot vs. the Aztec
Mummy '59
The Robot vs. the Aztec
Mummy '59

Elena Cantarone
Evil Clutch '89

Kieran Canter
Buried Alive '81

Jo Canterbury
Teenage Strangler '64

Cantinflas
Around the World in 80 Days
'56
El Gendarme Desconocido '41

Toni Canto
I'm the One You're Looking
For '88

Eddie Cantor
Glorifying the American Girl
'30
Hollywood Goes to War '54
If You Knew Susie '48
Kid Millions '34
Roman Scandals '33
Show Business '44
Thank Your Lucky Stars '43
Whoopee! '30

Yakima Canutt
Branded a Coward '35
Calling Wild Bill Elliott '43
Circle of Death '36
Cyclone of the Saddle '35
Dawn Rider '35
The Fighting Stallion '26
Gone with the Wind '39
Heart of the Rockies '37
Hit the Saddle '37
The Kansas Terrors '39
King of the Pecos '36
Last Frontier '32
Lucky Texan '34
The Man from Hell '34
Outlaw Rule '36
Overland Stage Raiders '38
The Painted Stallion '37
Paradise Canyon '35
Riders of the Rockies '37
Riders of the Whistling Skull
'37
Sagebrush Trail '33
Santa Fe Stampede '38
The Showdown '50
The Star Packer '34

Trouble in Texas '37
West of the Divide '34
Wild Horse Canyon '25
Winds of the Wasteland '36
Wyoming Outlaw '39

Peter Capaldi
Dangerous Liaisons '88
John & Yoko: A Love Story
'85
The Lair of the White Worm
'88
Local Hero '83

Jad Capelja
Freedom '81
Puberty Blues '81

Barbara Capell
The Werewolf vs. the Vampire
Woman '70

Hedge Capers
The Legend of Hillbilly John
'73

Virginia Capers
The North Avenue Irregulars
'79
White Mama '80

Manuel Capetillo
Passion for Power '85
Vivo o Muerto '87

**Raymundo
Capetillo**
Bestia Nocturna '86

Frank Capizzi
Desert Snow '89

Katie Caple
Shotgun '89

**Carmine
Capobianco**
Galactic Gigolo '87
Psychos in Love '87

John Capodice
The Hard Way '91
Honeymoon in Vegas '92

Lino Capolicchio
Garden of the Finzi-Continis
'71

Nadia Capone
Skull: A Night of Terror '88
A Whisper to a Scream '88

Truman Capote
Murder by Death '76

Carl Capotorto
American Blue Note '89
Mac '93

Patrizia Capparelli
The Decameron '70

Pier Paola Capponi
Man of Legend '71

Piero Cappucilli
Otello '59

Jordanna Capra
Hired to Kill '91

Tony Caprari
River of Diamonds '90

Anna Capri
The Brotherhood of Satan '71
Darker than Amber '70
Payday '72
The Specialist '75

Kate Capshaw
Best Defense '84
Black Rain '89
Code Name: Dancer '87

Carradine ▶cont.

Death Sport '78
Double Trouble '91
Dune Warriors '91
The Dying Truth '91
Evil Toons '90
Field of Fire '92
Future Force '89
Future Zone '90
Gray Lady Down '77
High Noon: Part 2 '80
Jealousy '84
Kung Fu '72
Kung Fu: The Movie '86
Lone Wolf McQuade '83
The Long Goodbye '73
The Long Riders '80
Macho Callahan '70
Martial Law '90
Maybe I'll Be Home in the
    Spring '70
The McMasters '70
Mean Streets '73
Midnight Fear '90
The Misfit Brigade '87
Mr. Horn '79
Night Children '89
Night Rhythms '92
North and South '85
Nowhere to Run '88
Oceans of Fire '86
On the Line '83
The P.O.W. Escape '86
Project: Eliminator '91
Q (The Winged Serpent) '82
Roadside Prophets '92
Safari 3000 '82
The Serpent's Egg '78
Sonny Boy '87
Sundown '91
Think Big '90
Thunder and Lightning '77
Trick or Treats '82
Tropical Snow '88
Violent Ones '68
Warlords '88
The Warrior & the Sorceress
    '84
Wizards of the Lost Kingdom
    2 '89

John Carradine

The Adventures of
    Huckleberry Finn '60
Alien Massacre '67
Around the World in 80 Days
    '56
The Astro-Zombies '67
Autopsy of a Ghost '67
Bad Charleston Charlie '73
The Bees '78
Big Foot '72
Billy the Kid Versus Dracula
    '66
Blood and Sand '41
Blood Legacy '73
Blood of Dracula's Castle '69
Blood of Ghastly Horror '72
Bluebeard '44
The Boogey Man '80
Boogey Man 2 '83
Boxcar Bertha '72
The Bride of Frankenstein '35
Buried Alive '89
The C-Man '49
Cain's Cutthroats '71
Captain Kidd '45
Captains Courageous '37
Casanova's Big Night '54
Cheyenne Autumn '64
The Christmas Coal Mine
    Miracle '77
The Cosmic Man '59
Court Jester '56

Curse of the Stone Hand '64
Daniel Boone '34
Death at Love House '75
Demon Rage '82
Dimples '36
Drums Along the Mohawk '39
The Egyptian '54
Everything You Always
    Wanted to Know About
    Sex (But Were Afraid to
    Ask) '72
Evil Spawn '87
Evils of the Night '85
The Female Jungle '56
Five Came Back '39
Frankenstein Island '81
Gallery of Horror '67
The Garden of Allah '36
The Gatling Gun '72
Golden Rendezvous '77
Goliath Awaits '81
The Grapes of Wrath '40
Gun Riders '69
Half Human '58
Hell Ship Mutiny '57
Hidden Guns '56
Hillbillies in a Haunted House
    '67
Hollywood Ghost Stories '86
The Horror of It All '91
Horror of the Blood Monsters
    '70
Horrors of the Red Planet '64
The Hostage '67
The Hound of the Baskervilles
    '39
House of Frankenstein '44
The House of Seven Corpses
    '73
House of the Black Death '65
House of the Long Shadows
    '82
The Howling '81
Ice Pirates '84
The Incredible Petrified World
    '58
Invasion of the Animal People
    '62
Isle of Forgotten Sins '43
Johnny Guitar '53
Journey into the Beyond '76
Kentuckian '55
Killer Inside Me '76
Last Hurrah '58
The Last Tycoon '76
Les Miserables '35
Mary, Mary, Bloody Mary '76
Mary of Scotland '36
The McMasters '70
Mr. Moto's Last Warning '39
Monster '78
The Monster Club '85
Monster in the Closet '86
Mummy & Curse of the Jackal
    '67
Myra Breckinridge '70
The Nesting '80
Nocturna '79
The Patsy '64
Peggy Sue Got Married '86
The Private Affairs of Bel Ami
    '47
Return of Frank James '40
Return of the Ape Man '44
Reunion in France '42
Revenge '86
Revenge of the Zombies '43
Satan's Cheerleaders '77
Secret of NIMH '82
The Seekers '79
The Sentinel '76
Shinbone Alley '70
Shock Waves '77
The Shootist '76
Showdown at Boot Hill '58
The Shrieking '73

Silent Night, Bloody Night '73
Silver Spurs '43
Stagecoach '39
Star Slammer '87
The Ten Commandments '56
Terror in the Wax Museum '73
To the Last Man '33
Tomb '86
The Trouble with Girls (and
    How To Get Into It) '69
The Unearthly '57
The Vals '85
The Vampire Hookers '78
Waterfront '44
Western Double Feature 8:
    Hale & Carradine '40s
Western Union '41
The White Buffalo '77
Winterset '36

Keith Carradine

An Almost Perfect Affair '79
The Bachelor '93
Backfire '88
The Ballad of the Sad Cafe
    '91
Blackout '85
Capone '89
Chiefs '83
Choose Me '84
Cold Feet '89
Crisscross '92
Daddy's Dyin'...Who's Got the
    Will? '90
The Duellists '78
Eye on the Sparrow '91
The Forgotten '89
A Gunfight '71
Half a Lifetime '86
Idaho Transfer '73
The Inquiry '87
Judgment '90
Kung Fu '72
The Long Riders '80
Lumiere '76
Man on a String '71
Maria's Lovers '84
McCabe & Mrs. Miller '71
The Moderns '88
Murder Ordained '87
Nashville '75
Old Boyfriends '79
Payoff '91
Pretty Baby '78
A Rumor of War '80
The Shrieking '73
Southern Comfort '81
Trouble in Mind '86
Welcome to L.A. '77

Robert Carradine

Aladdin and His Wonderful
    Lamp '84
All's Fair '89
Aloha, Bobby and Rose '74
As Is '85
The Big Red One '80
Blackout '78
Buy & Cell '89
Cannonball '76
Clarence '91
Coming Home '78
Conspiracy: The Trial of the
    Chicago Eight '87
The Cowboys '72
Double-Crossed '91
Heartaches '82
Illusions '91
The Incident '89
Jackson County Jail '76
Joyride '77
Just the Way You Are '84
The Long Riders '80
Massacre at Central High '76
Mean Streets '73
Monte Carlo '86

Number One with a Bullet '87
On the Edge: The Survival of
    Dana '79
The Player '92
Pom Pom Girls '76
Revenge of the Nerds '84
Revenge of the Nerds 2:
    Nerds in Paradise '87
Revenge of the Nerds 3: The
    Next Generation '92
Rude Awakening '89
Somebody Has to Shoot the
    Picture '90
Tag: The Assassination Game
    '82
Tales of the Klondike: In a Far
    Country '83
Wavelength '83

Janice Carraher

Firefight '87

Chris Carrara

Remote '93

Don Carrara

Curse of the Headless
    Horseman '72

Gabriele Carrara

SS Girls '78

Ada Carrasco

Like Water for Chocolate '93

Danny Carrel

Mill of the Stone Women '60

J. Antonio Carreon

Wolf '86

Barbara Carrera

Condorman '81
Embryo '76
I, the Jury '82
Island of Dr. Moreau '77
Lone Wolf McQuade '83
Love at Stake '87
Loverboy '89
Masada '81
Never Say Never Again '83
The Underachievers '88
When Time Ran Out '80
Wicked Stepmother '89
Wild Geese 2 '85

Tia Carrere

Aloha Summer '88
Fatal Mission '89
Rising Sun '93
Showdown in Little Tokyo '91
Wayne's World '92
Zombie Nightmare '86

Tonia Carrero

The Fable of the Beautiful
    Pigeon Fancier '88

Jim Carrey

Club Med '83
Earth Girls are Easy '89
Finders Keepers '84
Once Bitten '85

Monica Carrico

Running Hot '83

Corey Carrier

After Dark, My Sweet '90
Men Don't Leave '89

Matthieu Carriere

The Bay Boy '85
Coup de Grace '78
La Passante '83
Naked Massacre '80s
An Occurrence at Owl Creek
    Bridge/Coup de Grace '62
A Woman in Flames '84

Camille Carrigan

Legion of Iron '90

Elpidia Carrillo

Assassin '89
Beyond the Limit '83
The Border '82
Let's Get Harry '87
The Lightning Incident '91
Predator '87
Salvador '86

Leo Carrillo

American Empire '42
Before Morning '33
Don Amigo/Stage to Chino
    '40s
Fisherman's Wharf '39
Fit for a King '37
The Fugitive '48
Girl of the Golden West '38
History is Made at Night '37
Manhattan Melodrama '34
Pancho Villa Returns '50
Phantom of the Opera '43
Riders of Death Valley '41
Too Hot to Handle '38
Viva Villa! '34

Debbie Lee Carrington

Club Fed '91
Spaced Invaders '90

John Carrol

Mantis in Lace '68

Katja Carrol

Train Station Pickups '70s

Regina Carrol

Angels' Wild Women '72
Blazing Stewardesses '75
Blood of Ghastly Horror '72
Brain of Blood '71
Dracula vs. Frankenstein '71
The Female Bunch '69
Jessie's Girls '75
Satan's Sadists '69
Texas Layover '75

Barbara Carroll

Goliath Against the Giants '63
The Last Days of Pompeii '60

Brandon Carroll

Hell Squad '58
Suicide Battalion/Hell Squad
    '58

Corky Carroll

Under the Boardwalk '89

Diahann Carroll

Carmen Jones '54
Death Scream '75
The Five Heartbeats '91
From the Dead of Night '89
Goodbye Again '61
I Know Why the Caged Bird
    Sings '79
Paris Blues '61
That's Singing: The Best of
    Broadway '84

Erika Carroll

The Fat Albert Halloween
    Special '77

Helen Carroll

The Dead '87

James Carroll

Girls Night Out '83

Janet Carroll

Bluffing It '87
Family Business '89
Memories of Me '88
Risky Business '83

Jean Carroll

The Mermaids of Tiburon '62

Jill Carroll
The Vals '85

Jim Carroll
The Unholy '88

Joan Carroll
Primrose Path '40

John Carroll
The Farmer Takes a Wife '53
Flying Tigers '42
Go West '40
Lady Be Good '41
Only Angels Have Wings '39
Rio Rita '42
Rock, Baby, Rock It '57
Rose of Rio Grande '38
Sunny '41
Susan and God '40
Wolf Call '39
Zorro Rides Again '37

June Carroll
New Faces of 1952 '54

Lane Carroll
The Crazies '73

Leo G. Carroll
Bahama Passage '42
Bulldog Drummond's Secret
    Police '39
A Christmas Carol '38
Father of the Bride '50
First Legion '51
North by Northwest '59
One Plus One '61
The Paradine Case '47
The Parent Trap '61
The Private Lives of Elizabeth
    & Essex '39
The Prize '63
Rebecca '40
The Snows of Kilimanjaro '52
Spellbound '45
Strangers on a Train '51
Suspicion '41
Tarantula '55
The Tower of London '39
Treasure of the Golden
    Condor '53
We're No Angels '55
Wuthering Heights '39

Madeleine Carroll
Bahama Passage '42
The General Died at Dawn '36
Hitchcock Collection '87
My Favorite Blonde '42
My Love For Yours '39
Prisoner of Zenda '37
The Secret Agent '36
The 39 Steps '35

Nancy Carroll
Dance of Life '29
Transatlantic Merry-Go-Round
    '34

Pat Carroll
Brothers O'Toole '73
The Little Mermaid '89
Tropic of Desire '80s
With Six You Get Eggroll '68

Peter Carroll
Cass '78
Who Killed Baby Azaria? '83

Susan Carroll
Stanley '72

Tom Carroll
Mad Wax: The Surf Movie '90

Ric Carrott
Slashed Dreams '74

Ben Carruthers
Riot '69

Julius J. Carry, III
The Last Dragon '85

Charles Carson
Beau Brummel '54
Broken Melody '34
The Courageous Mr. Penn '41
Cry, the Beloved Country '51
Dreaming Lips '37

Crystal Carson
Killer Tomatoes Strike Back
    '90
Kiss and Be Killed '91

Frances Carson
Two-Faced Woman '41

Glen Carson
Ninja Death Squad '87
Ninja Phantom Heroes '87
Warriors of Fire '80s

Hunter Carson
Invaders from Mars '86
Mr. North '88
Paris, Texas '83

Jack Carson
Arsenic and Old Lace '44
The Bride Came C.O.D. '41
Carefree '38
Cat on a Hot Tin Roof '58
Dangerous When Wet '53
Destry Rides Again '39
Gentleman Jim '42
It's a Great Feeling '49
The King of the Roaring '20s:
    The Story of Arnold
    Rothstein '61
Love Crazy '41
Lucky Partners '40
Mildred Pierce '45
Mr. & Mrs. Smith '41
Mr. Smith Goes to
    Washington '39
My Dream is Yours '49
Phffft! '54
Red Garters '54
Romance on the High Seas
    '48
The Saint in New York '38
Stage Door '37
Stand-In '37
A Star is Born '54
Strawberry Blonde '41
Thank Your Lucky Stars '43
Vivacious Lady '38

John Carson
African Dream '90
After Julius '78
Captain Kronos: Vampire
    Hunter '74
Taste the Blood of Dracula '70

John David Carson
The Charge of the Model T's
    '76
Creature from Black Lake '76
Empire of the Ants '77
Savage is Loose '74

Kit Carson
The Walloping Kid '26

L.M. Kit Carson
Running on Empty '88

Nina Carson
Cherry Hill High '76

Rachelle Carson
Killcrazy '89

Shawn Carson
The Funhouse '81

Stacy Carson
Night Vision '87

Sunset Carson
Alias Billy the Kid
Battling Marshal '48
Bells of Rosarita '45
Call of the Rockies
Rio Grande Raiders '46
Rough Riders of Cheyenne
    '45
Stage Door Canteen '43
Western Double Feature 1:
    Wild Bill & Sunset Carson
    '40s
Western Double Feature 17
    '40s

**Terrence "T.C."
Carson**
Livin' Large '91

Peter Carsten
Black Lemons '80s
Secret of the Black Trunk '62
Web of the Spider '70
Zeppelin '71

Margit Carstensen
The Bitter Tears of Petra von
    Kant '72
Chinese Roulette '86
Mother Kusters Goes to
    Heaven '76
Possession '81

Marcelia Cartaxo
Hour of the Star '85

Eric Carte
Space: 1999—Alien Attack
    '79

Michael Cartel
Runaway Nightmare '84

Carmen Cartellieri
The Hands of Orlac '25

Alice Carter
Gross Anatomy '89

Ann Carter
Curse of the Cat People '44
The Two Mrs. Carrolls '47

Ben Carter
Kentucky Blue Streak '35

Benny Carter
The Cosmic Eye '71

Bill Carter
Battle of the Worlds '61
Flatbed Annie and Sweetiepie:
    Lady Truckers '79

Bruce Carter
Laser Moon '92

Dixie Carter
Killing of Randy Webster '81

Finn Carter
How I Got into College '89
Sweet Justice '92
Tremors '89

Gary Carter
Cobra Against Ninja '80s
Ninja Strike Force '88

Georgianna Carter
The Wild Ride '60

Helena Carter
Bugles in the Afternoon '52
Invaders from Mars '53
Kiss Tomorrow Goodbye '50

Jack Carter
Alligator '80
The Amazing Dobermans '76
Arena '88
Deadly Embrace '88
Death Blow '87

The Devil's Daughter '39
Ecstasy '84
The Glove '78
Hambone & Hillie '84
The Happy Hooker Goes to
    Washington '77
Heartbeeps '81
History of the World: Part 1
    '81
In the Heat of Passion '91
Octagon '80
Rainbow '78
Red Nights '87
Resurrection of Zachary
    Wheeler '71
Robo-Chic '89
Sexpot '88
Viva Las Vegas '63

Jake Carter
Soul Vengeance '75

Janis Carter
Flying Leathernecks '51
The Half-Breed '51
I Married an Angel '42
Lady of Burlesque '43
Miss Grant Takes Richmond
    '49

Jim Carter
Haunted Honeymoon '86
Stalin '92

Jimmy Carter
Long Shadows '86

J.K. Carter
Seems Like Old Times '80

Karen Carter
The Big Bust Out '73
The Legend of the Wolf
    Woman '77

Lynda Carter
Bobbie Jo and the Outlaw '76
Hotline '82
I Posed for Playboy '91
Last Song '80
Rita Hayworth: The Love
    Goddess '83

Marsha Carter
Feelin' Screwy '90

Nell Carter
Final Shot: The Hank Gathers
    Story '92
Modern Problems '81
That's Singing: The Best of
    Broadway '84

Nick Carter
Class Reunion Massacre '77

Reggie Carter
The Lunatic '92

Terry Carter
Battlestar Galactica '78
Black Force 2 '78
Foxy Brown '74
Man on the Run '74

Thomas Carter
Monkey Hustle '77
Whose Life Is It Anyway? '81

T.K. Carter
Doctor Detroit '83
He's My Girl '87
Runaway Train '85
Ski Patrol '89
Southern Comfort '81
The Thing '82

Anna Carteret
The Heat of the Day '91

Gabrielle Carteris
Raising Cain '92

Caroline Cartier
Lumiere '76

Miranda Cartledge
Save the Lady '82

Angela Cartwright
High School USA '84
Scout's Honor '80

Lynn Cartwright
Queen of Outer Space '58

Nancy Cartwright
The Little Mermaid '89
The Simpsons Christmas
    Special '89

**Veronica
Cartwright**
Alien '79
Bernice Bobs Her Hair '76
The Birds '63
The Children's Hour '61
Dead in the Water '91
False Identity '90
Flight of the Navigator '86
Goin' South '78
Hitler's Daughter '90
Inserts '76
Invasion of the Body
    Snatchers '78
Kid from Not-So-Big '78
Man Trouble '92
My Man Adam '86
Nightmares '83
Prime Suspect '82
The Right Stuff '83
Robert Kennedy and His
    Times '77
Valentino Returns '88
Wisdom '86
The Witches of Eastwick '87

Anthony Caruso
The Asphalt Jungle '50
Cattle Queen of Montana '54
Claws '77
Drum Beat '54
Legend of Earl Durand '74
Objective, Burma! '45
When Gangland Strikes '56
Zebra Force '76

David Caruso
Blue City '86
China Girl '87
King of New York '90
Mad Dog and Glory '93

Tony Caruso
Grizzly Adams: The Legend
    Continues '90

Britt Carva
The Invisible Dead

Suzanne Carvall
Massacre in Dinosaur Valley
    '85

Suzanne Carvalno
Women in Fury '84

Ursula Carven
Scandalous '88

Brent Carver
Crossbar '79
Millenium '89
One Night Stand '77

Lynne Carver
The Adventures of
    Huckleberry Finn '39
The Bride Wore Red '37
A Christmas Carol '38
Everybody Sing '38
Maytime '37
Sunset on the Desert '42

Hillbillies in a Haunted House '67
House of Frankenstein '44
House of the Black Death '65
I Died a Thousand Times '55
The Indestructible Man '56
The Indian Fighter '55
Johnny Reno '66
Last Frontier '32
A Lion is in the Streets '53
Manfish '56
My Favorite Brunette '47
Not as a Stranger '55
Of Mice and Men '39
One Million B.C. '40
Only the Valiant '50
Overland Mail '41
Passion '54
Renegade Ranger/Scarlet River '38
Riders of Death Valley '41
Saturday Night Serials '40
Sixteen Fathoms Deep '34
Son of Dracula '43
Spider Baby '64
Three Musketeers '33
Undersea Kingdom '36
The Wolf Man '41

Lon Chaney, Sr.
The Bushwackers '52
Flesh and Blood '22
The Horror of It All '91
The Hunchback of Notre Dame '23
Mockery '27
The Monster '25
Nomads of the North '20
Oliver Twist '22
Oubliette '14
Outside the Law '21
Phantom of the Opera '25
The Scarlet Car '17
Shadows '22
The Shock '23
The Trap '22
The Unholy Three '25
The Unholy Three '30
The Unknown '27
West of Zanzibar '28
Where East is East '29

Victoria Chaney
The Abomination '88

Billy Chang
American Shaolin: King of the Kickboxers 2 '92

Chen Chien Chang
Shaolin Temple Strikes Back '72

Ching Ching Chang
Blood on the Sun '75

David Chang
The 7 Brothers Meet Dracula '73

Jeanie Chang
Ninja Checkmate '90

John Chang
Two Wondrous Tigers '79

Lin Chang
Ninja Enforcer '70s

Lisa Chang
The Unbeaten 28 '80s

Sari Chang
China Girl '87

Shwu-Fen Chang
Song of the Exile '90

Sylvia Chang
Mad Mission 3 '84

Carissa Channing
Lurkers '88

Carol Channing
Happily Ever After '93
Shinbone Alley '70
Thoroughly Modern Millie '67

Ruth Channing
The Merry Widow '34

Stockard Channing
The Applegates '89
Big Bus '76
The Cheap Detective '78
Echoes in the Darkness '87
The Fish that Saved Pittsburgh '79
Grease '78
Heartburn '86
The Hospital '71
Married to It '93
The Men's Club '86
Not My Kid '85
Perfect Witness '89
Safari 3000 '82
Silent Victory: The Kitty O'Neil Story '79
Staying Together '89
Table Settings '84
Tidy Endings '88
A Time of Destiny '88
Without a Trace '83

Li Chao
Japanese Connection '82

Rosalind Chao
The Big Brawl '80
Chinese Web '78
Memoirs of an Invisible Man '92
The Terry Fox Story '83
Thousand Pieces of Gold '91
Twirl '81
White Ghost '88

Damian Chapa
Bound by Honor '93

Loyita Chapel
A Legacy for Leonette '85

Billy Chapin
The Night of the Hunter '55
Tobor the Great '54

Jonathan Chapin
Twice Dead '88

Michael Chapin
Murderer's Wife

Miles Chapin
Bless the Beasts and Children '71
French Postcards '79
The Funny Farm '82
Pandemonium '82

Stuart Chapin
Shotgun '89

Tom Chapin
Lord of the Flies '63

Jack Chaplain
Git! '65

Charles Chaplin, Jr.
Fangs of the Wild '54
Girls' Town '59
High School Confidential '58

Charlie Chaplin
The Adventurer '17
The Best of Chaplin '18
Burlesque of Carmen '16
The Champion/His New Job '15
Chaplin: A Character Is Born '79

Chaplin: A Character Is Born/
Keaton: The Great Stone Face
Chaplin Essanay Book 1 '15
The Chaplin Revue '58
Charlie Chaplin Carnival, Four Early Shorts '16
Charlie Chaplin Cavalcade, Mutual Studios Shorts '16
Charlie Chaplin Centennial Collection '10s
Charlie Chaplin Festival '17
Charlie Chaplin Festival '17
Charlie Chaplin: Night at the Show '17
Charlie Chaplin: Rare Chaplin '15
Charlie Chaplin: The Early Years, Vol. 1 '17
Charlie Chaplin: The Early Years, Vol. 2 '17
Charlie Chaplin: The Early Years, Vol. 3 '16
Charlie Chaplin: The Early Years, Vol. 4 '16
Charlie Chaplin...Our Hero! '15
Charlie Chaplin's Keystone Comedies #1 '14
Charlie Chaplin's Keystone Comedies #2 '14
Charlie Chaplin's Keystone Comedies #3 '14
Charlie Chaplin's Keystone Comedies #4 '14
Charlie Chaplin's Keystone Comedies #5 '14
The Circus '19
City Lights '31
The Count '16
Count/Adventurer '17
The Cure '17
Days of Thrills and Laughter '61
Easy Street '16
The Fireman '16
The Floorwalker '17
The Floorwalker/By the Sea '15
The Gold Rush '25
Gold Rush/Payday '25
The Great Dictator '40
His Prehistoric Past/The Bank '15
Hollywood Clowns '85
The Immigrant '17
The Kid '21
The Kid/Idle Class '21
Kid's Auto Race/Mabel's Married Life '15
A King in New York '57
The Knockout/Dough and Dynamite '14
Laughfest '10s
Limelight '52
Man in the Silk Hat '83
Modern Times '36
Monsieur Verdoux '47
One A.M. '16
Pawnshop '16
The Rink '16
Rink/Immigrant '10s
Silent Laugh Makers, No. 1 '15
Slapstick '30s
Story of William S. Hart/Sad Clowns '20s
Three Charlies and One Phoney! '18
Tillie's Punctured Romance '14
Tramp & a Woman '15
Triple Trouble/Easy Street '18
The Vagabond '16
When Comedy was King '59

Woman of Paris/Sunnyside '23
Work/Police '16

Deborah Chaplin
Bruce Lee Fights Back From the Grave '76

Geraldine Chaplin
Bolero '82
Buffalo Bill & the Indians '76
Chaplin '92
The Children '90
Cria '76
Doctor Zhivago '65
Duel of Hearts '92
The Four Musketeers '75
I Killed Rasputin '67
In Memoriam '76
Mama Turns a Hundred '79
The Mirror Crack'd '80
The Moderns '88
Nashville '75
Roseland '77
Three Musketeers '74
A Wedding '78
Welcome to L.A. '77
White Mischief '88
The Word '78
Zero Population Growth '72

Josephine Chaplin
The Canterbury Tales '71
Escape to the Sun '72
Jack the Ripper '80
L'Odeur des Fauves '66
Shadow Man '75

Lita Grey Chaplin
The Devil's Sleep '51

Michael Chaplin
A King in New York '57

Sydney Chaplin
Abdulla the Great '56
The Chaplin Revue '58
Charley's Aunt '25
Land of the Pharaohs '55
Satan's Cheerleaders '77
The Sibling '72
Three Charlies and One Phoney! '18
The Woman Hunter '72

Tamara Chaplin
Shades of Love: The Ballerina & the Blues '87

Alexander Chapman
Princess in Exile '90

Daniel Chapman
Death Collector '89
Exquisite Corpses '88

Edward Chapman
Bhowani Junction '56
Convoy '40
Juno and the Paycock '30
Man on the Run '49
October Man '48
The Young and the Guilty '58

Edythe Chapman
Ten Commandments '23

Graham Chapman
And Now for Something Completely Different '72
The Magic Christian '69
Monty Python and the Holy Grail '75
Monty Python Live at the Hollywood Bowl '82
Monty Python Meets Beyond the Fringe
Monty Python's Life of Brian '79

Monty Python's Parrot Sketch Not Included '90
Monty Python's The Meaning of Life '83
The Odd Job '78
The Secret Policeman's Other Ball '82
Yellowbeard '83

Helen Chapman
Hopalong Cassidy: Borrowed Trouble '48
Outlaw Roundup '44

Judith Chapman
And God Created Woman '88
Dead Space '90
Scalpel '76

Loni Chapman
Alexander: The Other Side of Dawn '77
The China Lake Murders '90
He Who Walks Alone '78
Moving Violation '76
Where the Red Fern Grows '74
Witch Who Came from the Sea '76

Lonny Chapman
52 Pick-Up '86

Marguerite Chapman
The Amazing Transparent Man '60
Charlie Chan at the Wax Museum '40
Coroner Creek '48
Destroyer '43
Flight to Mars '52
The Green Promise '49
Man Bait '52
Spy Smasher Returns '42

Pattee Chapman
Summer and Smoke '61

Sean Chapman
Hellbound: Hellraiser 2 '88
Hellraiser '87

Val Chapman
The Legend of Jedediah Carver '70s

Anna Chappell
Mountaintop Motel Massacre '86

Norman Chappell
Danger UXB '81

Dave Chappelle
Robin Hood: Men in Tights '93

Corynne Charbit
La Chevre '81

Jay Charbonneau
Complex World '92

Patricia Charbonneau
Brain Dead '89
Call Me '88
Desert Hearts '86
K2: The Ultimate High '92
RoboCop 2 '90
Shakedown '88
Stalking Danger '88

Jon Chardiet
Beat Street '84

Cyd Charisse
The Band Wagon '53
Brigadoon '54
Deep in My Heart '54
The Harvey Girls '46
It's Always Fair Weather '55

Coghlan ▶cont.

Kentucky Blue Streak '35
The Last of the Mohicans '32
Let 'er Go Gallegher '28
Little Red Schoolhouse '36
Marked Money '28
Square Shoulders '29
Yankee Clipper '27

Alain Cohen
Two of Us '68

Emma Cohen
Bronson's Revenge '79
Horror Rises from the Tomb '72

Jeff B. Cohen
The Goonies '85

Mitchell Cohen
Toxic Avenger '86

Saskia Cohen Tanugi
Never Say Never Again '83

Stefano Colagrande
Misunderstood '87

Nicholas Colasanto
Fat City '72
Mad Bull '77
Raging Bull '80

Angel Colbert
Women Unchained '70s

Catero Colbert
Sweet Perfection '90
Up Against the Wall '91

Claudette Colbert
Boom Town '40
Cleopatra '34
Drums Along the Mohawk '39
Egg and I '47
Guest Wife '45
I Cover the Waterfront '33
It Happened One Night '34
Let's Make it Legal '51
The Love Goddesses '65
The Palm Beach Story '42
Since You Went Away '44
Texas Lady '56
Three Came Home '50
Tomorrow is Forever '46
Without Reservations '46

Curt Colbert
The Psychotronic Man '91

June Colbourne
Sin You Sinners '63

Anita Colby
Cover Girl '44

Barbara Colby
Memory of Us '74

Albert Cole
The Incredible Two-Headed Transplant '71

Alexandra Cole
Doctor Butcher M.D. '80

Ben Cole
Howling 5: The Rebirth '89

Celea Ann Cole
Bloodstalkers '76

Dallas Cole
Glitch! '88

Dennis Cole
Amateur Night '85
The Barbary Coast '74
The Connection '73

Dead End City '88
Death House
Powder Keg '70
Pretty Smart '87

Gary Cole
Echoes in the Darkness '87
Fatal Vision '84
In the Line of Fire '93
Son of the Morning Star '91

George Cole
The Adventures of Sadie '55
The Belles of St. Trinian's '53
Blue Murder at St. Trinian's '56
A Christmas Carol '51
Cottage to Let '41
Deadline Auto Theft '83
Dr. Syn, Alias the Scarecrow '64
Fright '71
Gone in 60 Seconds '74
The Pure Hell of St. Trinian's '61
Too Many Crooks '59
The Vampire Lovers '70

Jack Cole
Designing Woman '57

Jacqulin Cole
Bad Bunch '76
Satan's Cheerleaders '77

Kay Cole
Dr. Syn, Alias the Scarecrow '64

Michael Cole
Chuka '67
Nickel Mountain '85

Mike "Cobra" Cole
Triple Impact '92

Nat King Cole
Cat Ballou '65
China Gate '57
Killer Diller '48
Small Town Girl '53

Olivia Cole
The Fig Tree '87
North and South '85
The Sky is Gray '80
Some Kind of Hero '82
The Women of Brewster Place '89

Skyler Cole
Adventures Beyond Belief '87

Stephenie Cole
Open All Hours '83

Robert Coleby
The Blue Lightning '86
Great Expectations: The Untold Story '87
Hector's Bunyip '86
Now and Forever '82
Plumber '79

Brian Coleman
The Hand '60

Charles Coleman
Bachelor Apartment '31
Grand Canyon Trail '48

Christian Coleman
South Central '92

Dabney Coleman
Amos and Andrew '93
The Applegates '89
Bad Ronald '74
Bite the Bullet '75
Callie and Son '81
Cinderella Liberty '73
Clifford '93

Cloak & Dagger '84
The Dove '74
Downhill Racer '69
Dragnet '87
Dying Room Only '73
Fist '79
Guilty of Innocence '87
Homeboy '80s
Hot to Trot! '88
The Man with One Red Shoe '85
Melvin and Howard '80
Modern Problems '81
Muppets Take Manhattan '84
Murrow '85
Never Forget '91
9 to 5 '80
North Dallas Forty '79
Nothing Personal '80
On Golden Pond '81
The Other Side of the Mountain '75
Pray TV '80
The President's Plane is Missing '71
The Scalphunters '68
Short Time '90
There Goes the Neighborhood '92
Tootsie '82
The Trouble with Girls (and How to Get Into It) '69
Viva Knievel '77
War Games '83
Where the Heart Is '90
Young Doctors in Love '82

Frank Coleman
Count/Adventurer '17

Gary Coleman
The Fantastic World of D.C. Collins '84
Jimmy the Kid '82
The Kid from Left Field '79
The Kid with the Broken Halo '82
The Kid with the 200 I.Q. '83
On the Right Track '81
Scout's Honor '80

Jimmy Coleman
Riff Raff '92

Kyle Coleman
Run Virgin Run '90

Leo Coleman
The Medium '51

Marilyn Coleman
Which Way Is Up? '77

Nancy Coleman
Desperate Journey '42
Edge of Darkness '43
Kings Row '41

Renee Coleman
After School '89
A League of Their Own '92
Return to Eden '89
Who's Harry Crumb? '89

Sylvia Coleridge
I Met a Murderer '39

Tania Coleridge
The Rain Killer '90

Charles "Honi" Coles
Dirty Dancing '87

Michael Coles
The Satanic Rites of Dracula '73

Mildred Coles
Lady Scarface '41
Oklahoma Badlands '48

Seven Days Ashore/Hurry, Charlie, Hurry '44

Robert Coles
Long Shadows '86

David Coley
Platoon the Warriors '88

John Ford Coley
Scenes from the Goldmine '87

Thomas Coley
Dr. Cyclops '40

John Colicos
Anne of the Thousand Days '69
Battlestar Galactica '78
Doctors' Wives '70
Love and Hate '90
Murder on Approval '56
The Postman Always Rings Twice '81
Raid on Rommel '71
Scorpio '73
Shadow Dancing '88

David Colin, Jr.
Beyond the Door '75
Beyond the Door 2 '79

Gregoire Colin
Olivier, Olivier '92

Ian Colin
Late Extra '35
Never Too Late to Mend '37

Jean Colin
Mad About Money '30

Margaret Colin
Amos and Andrew '93
The Butcher's Wife '91
Like Father, Like Son '87
Martians Go Home! '90
Pretty in Pink '86
Something Wild '86
Three Men and a Baby '87
Traveling Man '89
True Believer '89

Melanie Coll
Lust for Freedom '87

Richard A. Colla
Battlestar Galactica '78

Tony Collado
Feelin' Up '76

Christopher Collet
First Born '84
The Manhattan Project '86
Pigeon Feathers '88
Prayer of the Rollerboys '91
Sleepaway Camp '83

Joris Collet
Daughters of Darkness '71

Toni Collette
The Efficiency Expert '92

Kenneth Colley
And Nothing But the Truth '82
Casanova '87
Firefox '82
The Music Lovers '71
The Rainbow '89
Return to Waterloo '85

Ombretta Colli
Gladiator of Rome '63

Craig Collicott
Northville Cemetery Massacre '76

Constance Collier
Dark Corner '46
Monsieur Beaucaire '46
The Perils of Pauline '47

Rope '48
Thunder in the City '37
Wee Willie Winkie '37

Don Collier
The Last Ride of the Dalton Gang '79

Lois Collier
The Naughty Nineties '45

Marian Collier
Road Racers '59

Patience Collier
Baby Love '69

William Collier, Jr.
Cimarron '30
Phantom Express '32
Street Scene '31

Joe Colligan
Goin' All the Way '82

John Collin
Tess '80

Patricia Collinge
Tender Comrade '43

Anne Collings
The Mask '61
Return to Africa '89

Peter Collingwood
The Wacky World of Wills & Burke '85

Alan Collins
Ark of the Sun God '82
Exterminators of the Year 3000 '83
Hunters of the Golden Cobra '82
The Last Hunter '80
Tiger Joe '85
Tornado '83

Alana Collins
Night Call Nurses '72

Amber Collins
Planet on the Prowl '65

Anne Collins
Seven Alone '75

Bob Collins
Night of the Demon '80

Charles Collins
Dancing Pirate '36

Cora Sue Collins
The Scarlet Letter '34
The World Accuses '35

Doug Collins
Mind Warp '72

Eddie Collins
The Blue Bird '40
Drums Along the Mohawk '39
Young Mr. Lincoln '39

Gary Collins
Hangar 18 '80

Georgie Collins
Ghost Keeper '80

Jackie Collins
Room 43 '58

Joan Collins
The Adventures of Sadie '55
The Bawdy Adventures of Tom Jones '76
The Big Sleep '78
The Bitch '78
The Bravados '58
Cartier Affair '84
Cosh Boy '61
Dark Places '73

Forty Days of Musa Dagh '85
If It's Tuesday, This Must Be Belgium '69
In the Mood '87
Justine '69
Killing in the Sun
The North Avenue Irregulars '79
Prancer '89
Question of Faith '93
The Reivers '69
Say Goodbye, Maggie Cole '72
Silent Rebellion '82

John Conte
Lost in a Harem '44
The Man with the Golden Arm '55
Trauma '62

Michael Conte
Necropolis '87

Richard Conte
Assault on a Queen '66
Big Combo '55
Circus World '64
Explosion '69
The Fighter '52
Full of Life '56
The Godfather '72
The Godfather 1902-1959: The Complete Epic '81
Guadalcanal Diary '43
Hotel '67
House of Strangers '49
I'll Cry Tomorrow '55
Lady in Cement '68
1931: Once Upon a Time in New York '72
Operation Cross Eagles '69
The Purple Heart '44
Race for Life '55
They Came to Cordura '59
13 Rue Madeleine '46
Tony Rome '67
Violent Professionals '82
A Walk in the Sun '46

Steve Conte
Attack of the Mayan Mummy '63
Terror of the Bloodhunters '62

John Content
Death Row Diner '88

Catherine Conti
Cry of the Black Wolves '70s
2069: A Sex Odyssey '78

Tom Conti
American Dreamer '84
Beyond Therapy '86
Deep Cover '88
The Duellists '78
Dumb Waiter '87
Full Circle '77
The Gospel According to Vic '87
Merry Christmas, Mr. Lawrence '83
Miracles '86
The Norman Conquests, Part 1: Table Manners '80
The Norman Conquests, Part 2: Living Together '80
The Norman Conquests, Part 3: Round and Round the Garden '80
The Princess and the Pea '83
The Quick and the Dead '87
Reuben, Reuben '83
Saving Grace '86
Shirley Valentine '89
That Summer of White Roses '90

Ugo Conti
Mediterraneo '92

Vincent Conti
Deadly Impact '84

Dick Contino
Daddy-O '59

Chantal Contouri
The Night After Halloween '83
Thirst '87

Maria Contrera
Brandy Sheriff '78

Patricio Contreras
The Official Story '85
Old Gringo '89

Frank Converse
Alone in the Neon Jungle '87
Anne of Avonlea '87
Brother Future '91
The Bushido Blade '80
Cruise into Terror '78
Danger in the Skies '79
Everybody Wins '90
Home at Last '88
Killer on Board '77
Marilyn: The Untold Story '80
A Movie Star's Daughter '79
Mystery at Fire Island '81
The Pilot '82
Sergeant Matlovich vs. the U.S. Air Force '78
Tales of the Unexpected '91
The Tattered Web '71
Uncle Tom's Cabin '87

William Converse-Roberts
Courtship '87
The Fig Tree '87
1918 '85
On Valentine's Day '86

Bert Convy
A Bucket of Blood '59
Cannonball Run '81
Help Wanted: Male '82
Hero at Large '80
Jennifer '78
The Love Bug '68
The Man in the Santa Claus Suit '79
Racquet '79
Semi-Tough '77

Blake Conway
Ghost Town '88

Gary Conway
American Ninja 2: The Confrontation '87
How to Make a Monster '58
Liberty & Bash '90
Teenage Frankenstein '58

Joseph Conway
Ring of Terror '62

Kevin Conway
F.I.S.T. '78
Homeboy '88
Jennifer 8 '92
Johnny We Hardly Knew Ye '77
Lathe of Heaven '80
One Good Cop '91
Paradise Alley '78
Rage of Angels '83
Rambling Rose '91

Morgan Conway
Bowery at Midnight/Dick Tracy vs. Cueball '42
Dick Tracy, Detective '45
Dick Tracy, Detective/The Corpse Vanishes '42

Dick Tracy Double Feature #1 '45
Dick Tracy Double Feature #2 '47
Dick Tracy: The Spider Strikes '37
Dick Tracy vs. Cueball '46
The Saint Takes Over '40
Sinners in Paradise '38

Pat Conway
Brighty of the Grand Canyon '67
The Deadly Mantis '57
Geronimo '62

Russ Conway
The Screaming Skull '58

Tim Conway
Ace Crawford, Private Eye
The Apple Dumpling Gang '75
The Apple Dumpling Gang Rides Again '79
The Billion Dollar Hobo '78
Cannonball Run II '84
Dorf and the First Games of Mount Olympus '87
Dorf Goes Auto Racing '89
Dorf on Golf '86
Dorf's Golf Bible '89
Gus '76
The Longshot '86
The Private Eyes '80
Prize Fighter '79
The Shaggy D.A. '76
They Went That-a-Way & That-a-Way '78
The World's Greatest Athlete '73

Tom Conway
Bride of the Gorilla '51
Cat People '42
Criminal Court '46
The Falcon in Hollywood '44
The Falcon in Mexico '44
Falcon's Adventure/Armored Car Robbery '50
The Falcon's Brother '42
I Walked with a Zombie '43
Lady Be Good '41
Mrs. Miniver '42
Murder on Approval '56
Norman Conquest '53
One Touch of Venus '48
Peter Pan '53
Rio Rita '42
Saint Strikes Back: Criminal Court '46
The Seventh Victim '43
Tarzan's Secret Treasure '41
Three Stops to Murder '53
Voodoo Woman '57

Sarah Conway Ciminera
Beyond the Door 3 '91

Jackie Coogan
College Swing '38
Dr. Heckyl and Mr. Hype '80
Escape Artist '82
Free and Easy '30
Girl Happy '65
Halloween with the Addams Family '79
High School Confidential '58
Human Experiments '79
The Kid '21
The Kid/Idle Class '21
Lonelyhearts '58
Mesa of Lost Women '52
Oliver Twist '22
Outlaw Women '52
Peck's Bad Boy '21
The Prey '80

The Shakiest Gun in the West '68
Tom Sawyer '30
Varieties on Parade '52

Keith Coogan
Adventures in Babysitting '87
Book of Love '91
Cheetah '89
Cousins '89
Don't Tell Mom the Babysitter's Dead '91
Hiding Out '87
Toy Soldiers '91
Under the Boardwalk '89

Carole Cook
The Incredible Mr. Limpet '64
Sixteen Candles '84

Christopher Cook
A Christmas Carol '54

Clyde Cook
Through the Breakers '28
White Gold '28

Dale "Apollo" Cook
Blood Ring '93
Triple Impact '92

Diana Cook
The Mermaids of Tiburon '62

Donald Cook
Baby Face '33
Confidential '35
Show Boat '36
Viva Villa! '34

Doria Cook
Evil Town '87

Elisha Cook, Jr.
Behave Yourself! '52
The Big Sleep '46
Black Bird '75
Born to Kill '47
Carny '80
The Champ '79
Dark Mountain '44
Dark Waters '44
Dillinger '45
Don't Bother to Knock '52
Drum Beat '54
El Condor '70
Electra Glide in Blue '73
The Great Northfield Minnesota Raid '72
Hammett '82
The Haunted Palace '63
The Indian Fighter '55
The Killing '56
Leave 'Em Laughing '81
The Maltese Falcon '41
Messiah of Evil '74
1941 '79
One-Eyed Jacks '61
Papa's Delicate Condition '63
Platinum High School '60
Plunder Road '57
Rosemary's Baby '68
St. Ives '76
Salem's Lot '79
Shane '53
Stranger on the Third Floor '40
They Won't Forget '37
Wildcat '42

Gary Aron Cook
Kiss the Night '87

Lawrence Cook
The Spook Who Sat By the Door '73

Lisa Cook
Wager of Love '90

Penny Cook
Deadly Possession '88

Peter Cook
Bedazzled '68
Dandy in Aspic '68
Find the Lady '75
Getting It Right '89
The Hound of the Baskervilles '77
The Princess Bride '87
Those Daring Young Men in Their Jaunty Jalopies '69
Whoops Apocalypse '88
Without a Clue '88
The Wrong Box '66
Yellowbeard '83

Sophie Cook
The Chronicles of Narnia '89

Tommy Cook
Missile to the Moon '59
Teenage Crime Wave '55

Tracy Cook
SnakeEater 3: His Law '92

William Cook
I, Madman '89

Alan Cooke
Defenders of the Law '31

Alistair Cooke
The Three Faces of Eve '57

Christopher Cooke
The Unbelievable Truth '90

C.J. Cooke
Nightmare '82

Gregory Cooke
Vietnam War Story 3 '89

Jennifer Cooke
Friday the 13th, Part 6: Jason Lives '86
Gimme an F '85

Keith Cooke
China O'Brien '88
China O'Brien 2 '89
The King of the Kickboxers '91

Steven Cooke
Getting Lucky '89
Wilding '90

Wendy J. Cooke
The Murder of Mary Phagan '87

Peter Cookson
Black Tower '50
Fear '46

Marjorie Cooley
The Great Commandment '41

Spade Cooley
Everybody's Dancin' '50
Kid from Gower Gulch '47
Silver Bandit '47

Rita Coolidge
Club Med '83

Michael Coon
L.A. Crackdown '87

Ray Cooney
The Hand '60

Theresa Cooney
Evil Altar '89

Alice Cooper
Freddy's Dead: The Final Nightmare '91
Monster Dog '82
Roadie '80
Sextette '78

Andrew "Buzz" Cooper
Getting Over '81

Ann Cooper
Blue Sunshine '78

Barrett Cooper
Buford's Beach Bunnies '92

Ben Cooper
The Rose Tattoo '55

Bigelow Cooper
The Broadway Drifter '27

Cami Cooper
The Applegates '89
Shocker '89

Chris Cooper
Guilty by Suspicion '91
Matewan '87
This Boy's Life '93
Thousand Pieces of Gold '91

Clancy Cooper
Girls in Chains '43
Naked Youth '59

Gary Cooper
Along Came Jones '45
Ball of Fire '41
Beau Geste '39
Blowing Wild '54
Cloak and Dagger '46
The Court Martial of Billy
  Mitchell '55
The Cowboy and the Lady '38
Distant Drums '51
A Farewell to Arms '32
Fighting Caravans '31
The Fountainhead '49
Friendly Persuasion '56
The General Died at Dawn '36
Good Sam '48
The Hanging Tree '59
Hedda Hopper's Hollywood
  '42
High Noon '52
It '27
It's a Great Feeling '49
Kings, Queens, Jokers '30s
The Last Outlaw '27
The Lives of a Bengal Lancer
  '35
Love in the Afternoon '57
Man of the West '58
Meet John Doe '41
Mr. Deeds Goes to Town '36
Morocco '30
The Naked Edge '61
The Plainsman '37
The Pride of the Yankees '42
The Real Glory '39
Sergeant York '41
Ten North Frederick '58
They Came to Cordura '59
Vera Cruz '53
The Virginian '29
The Westerner '40
Wings '27
The Wreck of the Mary Deare
  '59

George Cooper
Federal Agent '36
Little Church Around the
  Corner '23
Uptown New York '32

Gladys Cooper
Beware of Pity '47
The Bishop's Wife '47
Homecoming '48
The Iron Duke '34
Kitty Foyle '40
Madame Bovary '49
Mrs. Parkington '44

Mr. Lucky '43
My Fair Lady '64
Nice Girl Like Me '69
Now, Voyager '42
The Pirate '48
Rebecca '40
The Secret Garden '49
Separate Tables '58
The Song of Bernadette '43
That Hamilton Woman '41
The White Cliffs of Dover '44

Harry E. Cooper
The Caddy '53

Inez Cooper
I Married an Angel '42
'Neath Canadian Skies '46
North of the Border '46

Jack Cooper
All Night Long/Smile Please
  '24
Cord & Dischords/Naughty
  Nurse '28

Jackie Cooper
The Abe Lincoln of Ninth
  Avenue '39
The Champ '31
Little Rascals, Book 9 '30s
Little Rascals, Book 10 '30s
Little Rascals, Book 12 '37
Little Rascals, Book 13 '37
The Love Machine '71
Maybe I'll Be Home in the
  Spring '70
The Navy Comes Through '42
Peck's Bad Boy '34
Return of Frank James '40
Superman: The Movie '78
Superman 2 '80
Superman 3 '83
Surrender '87
Treasure Island '34
Ziegfeld Girl '41

James Cooper
The American Scream '80s

Jeanne Cooper
Plunder Road '57
Red Nightmare '62
Shame '61
Sweet Hostage '75

Jeff Cooper
Circle of Iron '78
Fantastic Balloon Voyage '80s

Jeremy Cooper
The Reflecting Skin '91

Maggie Cooper
And Baby Makes Six '79
Death Ray 2000 '81
An Eye for an Eye '81

Marilyn Cooper
Family Business '89

Melville Cooper
The Adventures of Robin
  Hood '38
Around the World in 80 Days
  '56
Dawn Patrol '38
Heartbeat '46
Immortal Sergeant '43
The Lady Eve '41
Let's Dance '50
Murder Over New York '40
Private Life of Don Juan '34
13 Rue Madeleine '46
The Underworld Story '50

Ralph Cooper
The Duke is the Tops '38
Gang War '40

Rosemary Cooper
The Return of Boston Blackie
  '27

Rusty Cooper
Danger Zone 3: Steel Horse
  War '90

Sally Cooper
Moving Out '83

Stan Cooper
Great Treasure Hunt '70s
The Hanging Woman '72
Hell Commandos '69

Tabi Cooper
The Life & Times of the
  Chocolate Killer '88

Ted Cooper
Phantom from Space '53

Terence Cooper
Heart of the Stag '84

Trace Cooper
The Mutilator '85

Trudi Cooper
Spittin' Image '83

Michael Coopet
Night Terror '89

Robert Coote
Alice Through the Looking
  Glass '66
Bad Lands '39
Commandos Strike at Dawn
  '43
The Elusive Pimpernel '50
The Ghost and Mrs. Muir '47
The Horse's Mouth '58
Macbeth '48
The Merry Widow '52
Mr. Moto's Last Warning '39
My Fair Lady '64
Nurse Edith Cavell '39
Othello '52
Scaramouche '52
Three Musketeers '48
Tunes of Glory/Horse's Mouth
  '60
You Can't Fool Your Wife '40

Sylvain Copans
Cross My Heart '91

Kenneth Cope
Carry On at Your
  Convenience '71

Joan Copeland
Her Alibi '88
The Laserman '90
Roseland '77

John Copeland
The Professor '58

Campbell Copelin
Typhoon Treasure '39

Peter Copely
The Golden Salamander '51

Teri Copley
Brain Donors '92
Down the Drain '89
The FBI Murders '88
Frozen Assets '92
I Married a Centerfold '84
Transylvania Twist '89

David Copperfield
Terror Train '80
Three of a Kind '80s

Tyler Coppin
One Night Stand '84

Robin Copping
Alvin Rides Again '74

Robert Copple
Crazy Fat Ethel II '85

Andrea Coppola
Escape from the Bronx '85

Andrew Louis Coppola
White Slave '86

Eleanor Coppola
Hearts of Darkness: A
  Filmmaker's Apocalypse
  '91

Francis Ford Coppola
Hearts of Darkness: A
  Filmmaker's Apocalypse
  '91

Sofia Coppola
The Godfather, Part 3 '90

Jurg Coray
Sex Adventures of the Three
  Musketeers '80s

Benny Corbett
Outlaw's Paradise '39

Glenn Corbett
All the Young Men '60
Chisum '70
The Mountain Road '60
Ride in a Pink Car '74
Shadow Force '92
Shenandoah '65
The Stranger '73
The Violent Years '56

Gretchen Corbett
Jaws of Satan '81
Let's Scare Jessica to Death
  '71
PSI Factor '80
The Savage Bees '76
Secrets of Three Hungry
  Wives '78

Harry H. Corbett
Carry On Screaming '66
Rattle of a Simple Man '64
Silver Dream Racer '83
The Unstoppable Man '59

Jeff Corbett
Talent for the Game '91

Lenora Corbett
Heart's Desire '37

Pamela Corbett
Bad Bunch '76

Ronnie Corbett
The Best of the Two Ronnies
  '70s

Barry Corbin
Ballad of Gregorio Cortez '83
Bitter Harvest '81
Career Opportunities '91
The Chase '91
Conagher '91
Critters 2: The Main Course
  '88
Hard Traveling '85
It Takes Two '88
LBJ: The Early Years '88
My Science Project '85
Prime Suspect '82
Short Time '90
Six Pack '82
Undercover '87
Urban Cowboy '80
What Comes Around '85
Who's Harry Crumb? '89

Virginia Lee Corbin
Bare Knees '28

Chance Michael Corbitt
Cold Heat '90

Ellen Corby
All Mine to Give '56
A Day for Thanks on Walton's
  Mountain '82
The Glass Bottom Boat '66
Homecoming: A Christmas
  Story '71
I Remember Mama '48
Illegal '55
It's a Wonderful Life '46
On Moonlight Bay '51
The Strangler '64
Support Your Local
  Gunfighter '71
Thanksgiving Story '73
Vertigo '58

Donna Corcoran
Don't Bother to Knock '52
Gypsy Colt '54

Kevin Corcoran
Johnny Shiloh '63
Mooncussers '62
Old Yeller '57
Pollyanna '60
Savage Sam '63
The Shaggy Dog '59
A Tiger Walks '64
Toby Tyler '59

Noreen Corcoran
I Love Melvin '53

Alex Cord
The Brotherhood '68
C.I.A.: Code Name Alexa '92
Fire '77
A Girl to Kill for '90
Goliath Awaits '81
Grayeagle '77
Inn of the Damned '74
Jungle Warriors '84
A Minute to Pray, A Second to
  Die '67
Roots of Evil '91
Sidewinder One '77
Stiletto '69
Street Asylum '90
To Be the Best '93
The Uninvited '88

Bill Cord
She Gods of Shark Reef '56

Mara Corday
The Black Scorpion '57
The Giant Claw '57
Tarantula '55

Paula Corday
Because You're Mine '52
Sword of Monte Cristo '51

Rita Corday
The Body Snatcher '45
The Falcon in Hollywood '44
The Leopard Man '43

Cathleen Cordell
Gaslight '39

Chase Cordell
Track of the Moonbeast '76

Melinda Cordell
Bloody Birthday '80

Ricky Cordell
The Singing Nun '66

Shane Cordell
Fiend Without a Face '58

Joaquin Cordero
Dos Esposas en Mi Cama '87
El Libro de Piedra '68

Jack Cowell
A Face in the Fog '36

Bruce Cowling
Battleground '49
Cause for Alarm '51
The Painted Hills '66

Nicola Cowper
Dreamchild '85
Journey to the Center of the Earth '88
Lionheart '87
Transmutations '86
Underworld '85
Winter Flight '84

Alan Cox
Young Sherlock Holmes '85

Bobby Cox
Young Eagles '34

Brian Cox
Hidden Agenda '90
In Celebration '75
The Lost Language of Cranes '92
Manhunter '86
Murder by Moonlight '91
Pope John Paul II '84
Secret Weapon '90
Silent Scream '84

Courteney Cox
Blue Desert '91
Cocoon: The Return '88
Curiosity Kills '90
Down Twisted '89
Masters of the Universe '87
Misfits of Science '85
Mr. Destiny '90
The Opposite Sex and How to Live With Them '93
The Prize Pulitzer '89
Shaking the Tree '92

David Cox
The Last Season '87

Elizabeth Cox
Intruder '88

Gregory Cox
Unmasked Part 25 '88

Mitch Cox
Red Snow '91

Richard Cox
King of the Mountain '81
Street Justice '89
The Vindicator '85
Zombie High '87

Ronny Cox
The Abduction of Kari Swenson '87
The Beast Within '82
Beverly Hills Cop '84
Beverly Hills Cop 2 '87
Bound for Glory '76
Captain America '89
The Connection '73
Deliverance '72
Fallen Angel '81
The FBI Murders '88
Gray Lady Down '77
Harper Valley P.T.A. '78
Hollywood Vice Squad '86
Kavik the Wolf Dog '84
Last Song '80
Loose Cannons '90
Lost Legacy: A Girl Called Hatter Fox '77
Martians Go Home! '90
Mind Snatchers '72
One Man Force '89
The Onion Field '79
Our Town '77

Raw Courage '84
Reckless Disregard '84
RoboCop '87
Scandal in a Small Town '88
Scissors '91
Some Kind of Hero '82
Steele Justice '87
Tangiers '83
Taps '81
Target: Favorite Son '87
Total Recall '90
Two of a Kind '82
Vision Quest '85
When Hell Was in Session '82
Who Is the Black Dahlia? '77

Ruth Cox
The Attic '80
Swap Meet '79

Tony Cox
Spaced Invaders '90

Veanne Cox
National Lampoon's Class of '86 '86

Wally Cox
The Barefoot Executive '71
Bedford Incident '65
The Boatniks '70
A Guide for the Married Man '67
Morituri '65
The One and Only, Genuine, Original Family Band '68
State Fair '62

Walter W. Cox
Deadly Dancer '90

Lane Coyle
Fatal Images '82

Bill Coyne
Suburbia '83

Peter Coyote
Baja Oklahoma '87
Best Kept Secrets '88
The Blue Yonder '86
Crooked Hearts '91
Cross Creek '83
Die Laughing '80
Echoes in the Darkness '87
Endangered Species '82
E.T.: The Extra-Terrestrial '82
Exposure '91
Heart of Midnight '89
Heartbreakers '84
Hitchhiker 2 '85
The Jagged Edge '85
Keeper of the City '92
Legend of Billie Jean '85
A Man in Love '87
The Man Inside '90
Out '88
Outrageous Fortune '87
The People vs. Jean Harris '81
Slayground '84
Southern Comfort '81
Stacking '87
Strangers Kiss '83
Tell Me a Riddle '80
Timerider '83

Cylk Cozart
White Men Can't Jump '92

Paolo Cozza
Demons '86

Buster Crabbe
Alien Dead '85
Arizona Raiders '65
Billy the Kid Trapped '42
Border Badmen '45
Buck Rogers Conquers the Universe '39
Buffalo Stampede '33

Desert Gold '36
Destination Saturn '39
Devil Riders '44
Flash Gordon Conquers the Universe '40
Flash Gordon: Mars Attacks the World '38
Flash Gordon: Rocketship '36
Forlorn River '37
Frontier Outlaws '44
Gangster's Den '45
His Brother's Ghost '45
Jungle Siren '42
King of the Congo '52
The Last of the Redmen '47
Law and Order '42
Lightning Raiders '45
The Mysterious Rider '42
Nabonga '44
Oath of Vengeance '44
The Original Flash Gordon Collection '91
Outlaw of the Plains '46
Pirates of the High Seas '50
Prairie Badmen '46
Red Barry '38
Rocketship '36
Rustler's Hideout '44
Sea Hound '47
Shadows of Death '45
Space Soldiers Conquer the Universe '40
Swamp Fire '46
Swim Team '79
Tarzan the Fearless '33
Thundering Gunslingers '40
To the Last Man '33
Western Double Feature 7: Wild Bill & Crabbe '45
Wild Horse Phantom '44
Wildcat '42

Debra Crable
How U Like Me Now? '92

Buddy Crabtree
Legend of Boggy Creek '75

Jeff Crabtree
Legend of Boggy Creek '75

Ruth Cracknell
Alice to Nowhere '86
Island Trader '71

Omie Craden
Concrete Angels '87

Rita Crafts
Ghosts That Still Walk '77

Daniel Craig
The Power of One '92

Diane Craig
All the Rivers Run '84
The Mango Tree '77
Ned Kelly '70
Roses Bloom Twice '77

Ed Craig
Operation Dames '59

Helen Craig
The Snake Pit '48
They Live by Night '49

James Craig
Cyclops '56
The Devil & Daniel Webster '41
The Devil's Brigade '68
Drums in the Deep South '51
The Human Comedy '43
Kitty Foyle '40
Naked in the Sun '57
Our Vines Have Tender Grapes '45
Seven Miles from Alcatraz/Flight from Glory '43

The Tormentors '80s
Valley of the Sun '42
Winners of the West '40

Michael Craig
Escape 2000 '81
Inn of the Damned '74
The Irishman '78
Lola '69
Mysterious Island '61
Night of the Assassin '77
Ride a Wild Pony '75
Robin Hood...The Legend: Herne's Son '85
Roses Bloom Twice '77
Sapphire '59
The Silent Enemy '58
Vault of Horror '73

Phyllis Craig
Deadtime Stories '86

Wendy Craig
The Servant '63

Yvonne Craig
Digging Up Business '91
It Happened at the World's Fair '63
Kissin' Cousins '64
Mars Needs Women '66

Jeanne Crain
A Letter to Three Wives '49
Man Without a Star '55
Nefertiti, Queen of the Nile '64
The Night God Screamed '80s
State Fair '45

Richard Cram
Mad Wax: The Surf Movie '90

Grant Cramer
Hardbodies '84
Killer Klowns from Outer Space '88

Joey Cramer
Flight of the Navigator '86
Stone Fox '87

John Cramer
The Student Teachers '73

Marc Cramer
First Yank into Tokyo '45
Isle of the Dead '45

Richard Cramer
The Fatal Glass of Beer '33
Frontier Justice '35
Santa Fe Bound '37
Saps at Sea '40

Barbara Crampton
Body Double '84
Chopping Mall '86
Fraternity Vacation '85
From Beyond '86
Kidnapped '87
Puppet Master '89
The Re-Animator '85
Robot Wars '93
Trancers 2: The Return of Jack Deth '91

Brad Crandall
In Search of Historic Jesus '79

Barbara Crane
Sorority Girl '57

Bob Crane
Gus '76
Return to Peyton Place '61
Superdad '73

Fred Crane
The Making of a Legend: "Gone With the Wind" '89

Freya Crane
Scoring '80

Judith Crane
Mantis in Lace '68

Larry Crane
Falling from Grace '92

Norma Crane
Fiddler on the Roof '71
Tea and Sympathy '56
They Call Me Mr. Tibbs! '70

Richard Crane
The Devil's Partner '58
Dynamite '49
Guns Don't Argue '57
Winning of the West '53

Stephen Crane
Cry of the Werewolf '44

William H. Crane
The Saphead '21

Kenneth Cranham
Brother Sun, Sister Moon '73
Chocolat '88
Danger UXB '81
Hellbound: Hellraiser 2 '88
Monkey Boy '90
Prospero's Books '91
Under Suspicion '92

Bryan Cranston
Dead Space '90

Toller Cranston
Snow Queen '82

Emily Cranz
Sexo Y Crimen '87

Rich Crater
Carnal Crimes '91

Nick Cravat
Crimson Pirate '52
The Flame & the Arrow '50
The Scalphunters '68

Noel Cravat
G-Men vs. the Black Dragon '43

Frank Craven
City for Conquest '40
Dreaming Out Loud '40
In This Our Life '42
Jack London '44
Our Town '40
Son of Dracula '43

James Craven
D-Day on Mars '45
Green Archer '40
Sherlock Holmes and the Secret Weapon '42
Today I Hang '42

Matt Craven
Agent on Ice '86
Chattahoochee '89
A Few Good Men '92
Happy Birthday to Me '81
Indian Summer '93
Jacob's Ladder '90
K2: The Ultimate High '92
Palais Royale '88
Smokescreen '90
Till Death Do Us Part '72

Wes Craven
Fangoria's Weekend of Horrors '86

Mozelle Cravens
Raiders of Sunset Pass '43

Kathryn Craviness
Blood of Jesus '41

Andrew Crawford
Dear Murderer '47
The Gay Lady '49

F.I.S.T. '78
Foreign Affairs '93
Foul Play '78
Gladiator '92
Gorky Park '83
Indio '90
The Jericho Mile '79
Johnny We Hardly Knew Ye '77
Killing in a Small Town '90
The Last of the Finest '90
Legal Eagles '86
Lion of Africa '87
The Little Mermaid '84
Little Miss Marker '80
Miles from Home '88
Never Cry Wolf '83
North Dallas Forty '79
Perfect Witness '89
Presumed Innocent '90
A Real American Hero '78
Return to Snowy River '88
Rising Son '90
The River Rat '84
A Rumor of War '80
Semi-Tough '77
Silent Victory: The Kitty O'Nell Story '79
Silverado '85
Split Image '82
Teamster Boss: The Jackie Presser Story '92
10 '79
To Catch a Killer '92
To Love Again '80
Twice in a Lifetime '85

Barbara Dennek
Playtime '67

Barry Dennen
Liquid Dreams '92

Charles Denner
Bluebeard '63
The Holes '72
Les Assassins de L'Ordre '71
Mado '76
The Man Who Loved Women '77
Robert et Robert '79
Two of Us '68
Window Shopping '86
Z '69

Dodo Denney
Willy Wonka & the Chocolate Factory '71

Richard Denning
Adam Had Four Sons '41
An Affair to Remember '57
Alice Through the Looking Glass '66
Black Beauty '46
The Black Scorpion '57
Creature from the Black Lagoon '54
Double Deal '50
Girls in Prison '56
The Glass Key '42
Hangman's Knot '52
Unknown Island '48

John Dennis
Tomb of the Undead '72

Sandy Dennis
Another Woman '88
Come Back to the Five & Dime Jimmy Dean, Jimmy Dean '82
The Execution '85
The Four Seasons '81
God Told Me To '76
The Indian Runner '91
Mr. Sycamore '74
Nasty Habits '77
976-EVIL '88

The Out-of-Towners '70
Parents '89
Splendor in the Grass '61
That Cold Day in the Park '69
Up the Down Staircase '67
Who's Afraid of Virginia Woolf? '66

Winifred Dennis
Die! Die! My Darling! '65

Sabrina Dennison
Santa Sangre '90

Leslie Denniston
Blue Heaven '84

Reginald Denny
Abbott and Costello Meet Dr. Jekyll and Mr. Hyde '52
Anna Karenina '35
Around the World in 80 Days '56
Arrest Bulldog Drummond '38
Assault on a Queen '66
Bulldog Drummond Comes Back '37
Bulldog Drummond Escapes '37
Bulldog Drummond's Bride '39
Bulldog Drummond's Peril '38
Bulldog Drummond's Revenge '37
Bulldog Drummond's Revenge/Bulldog Drummond's Peril '38
Bulldog Drummond's Secret Police '39
California Straight Ahead '25
Captains of the Clouds '42
Cat Ballou '65
The Cheerful Fraud '27
Dancing Man '33
Escape Me Never '47
Escape to Burma '55
The Lost Patrol '34
Madam Satan '30
The Midnight Phantom '35
Mr. Blandings Builds His Dream House '48
My Favorite Brunette '47
Of Human Bondage '34
Parlor, Bedroom and Bath '31
Private Lives '31
Rebecca '40
Sabaka '55
Sherlock Holmes: The Voice of Terror '42
Skinner's Dress Suit '26
We're in the Legion Now '37

Vernon Dent
Baby Face Harry Langdon '26
The Cameraman '28
Extra Girl '23
His First Flame '26
Texas Cyclone '32
Two Reelers: Comedy Classics 10 '31

Christa Denton
Convicted: A Mother's Story '87
The Gate '87
Scandal in a Small Town '88

Donna Denton
Death Blow '87
Glory Years '87
Outlaw of Gor '87
Slaughterhouse Rock '88

Paul Dentzer
They '80s

Bob Denver
Back to the Beach '87
High School USA '84

Wackiest Wagon Train in the West '77
Who's Minding the Mint? '67

John Denver
Fire and Ice '87
Foxfire '87
Oh, God! '77

Manuela Denz
Sugarbaby '85

Elisabeth Depardieu
Jean de Florette '87
Tartuffe '84

Gerard Depardieu
Buffet Froid '79
Camille Claudel '89
Choice of Arms '83
Cyrano de Bergerac '90
Danton '82
1492: Conquest of Paradise '92
Get Out Your Handkerchiefs '78
Going Places '74
Green Card '90
The Holes '72
I Love All of You '83
Jean de Florette '87
La Chevre '81
The Last Metro '80
Les Comperes '83
Loulou '80
Maitresse '76
Menage '86
Mon Oncle D'Amerique '80
Moon in the Gutter '84
1900 '76
One Woman or Two '85
Police '85
The Return of Martin Guerre '83
Stavisky '74
Tartuffe '84
Too Beautiful for You '88
Under Satan's Sun '87
Uranus '91
Vincent, Francois, Paul and the Others '76
The Woman Next Door '81

Brian DePersia
Deadtime Stories '86

Johnny Depp
Benny & Joon '93
Cry-Baby '90
Edward Scissorhands '90
Freddy's Dead: The Final Nightmare '91
A Nightmare on Elm Street '84
Platoon '86
Private Resort '84

Theo Depuay
Gore-Met Zombie Chef From Hell '87

Bo Derek
Bolero '84
A Change of Seasons '80
Fantasies '73
Ghosts Can't Do It '90
Hot Chocolate '92
Orca '77
Tarzan, the Ape Man '81
10 '79

John Derek
All the King's Men '49
Ambush at Tomahawk Gap '53
The Annapolis Story '55
Exodus '60
Knock on Any Door '49
Omar Khayyam '57

Once Before I Die '65
Outcast '54
The Ten Commandments '56

Joe DeRita
It's a Mad, Mad, Mad, Mad World '63
Three Stooges Meet Hercules '61

Edouard Dermithe
Les Enfants Terrible '50
The Testament of Orpheus '59

Anton Dermota
The Life and Loves of Mozart '59

Bruce Dern
After Dark, My Sweet '90
Big Town '87
Black Sunday '77
Bloody Mama '70
The 'Burbs '89
Carolina Skeletons '92
Coming Home '78
The Court Martial of Jackie Robinson '90
The Cowboys '72
Diggstown '92
The Driver '78
Family Plot '76
The Great Gatsby '74
Harry Tracy '83
Hush, Hush, Sweet Charlotte '65
The Incredible Two-Headed Transplant '71
Into the Badlands '92
The King of Marvin Gardens '72
Laughing Policeman '74
Marnie '64
Middle Age Crazy '80
1969 '89
On the Edge '86
Posse '75
Psych-Out '68
Rebel Rousers '69
The St. Valentine's Day Massacre '67
Silent Running '71
Smile '75
Support Your Local Sheriff '69
Tattoo '81
That Championship Season '82
They Shoot Horses, Don't They? '69
Thumb Tripping '72
Toughlove '85
The Trip '67
Twist '76
Uncle Tom's Cabin '87
The War Wagon '67
Waterhole #3 '67
The Wild Angels '66
Will Penny '67
World Gone Wild '88

Laura Dern
Afterburn '92
Blue Velvet '86
Fat Man and Little Boy '89
Foxes '80
Haunted Summer '88
Jurassic Park '93
Mask '85
Rambling Rose '91
Smooth Talk '85
Strange Case of Dr. Jekyll & Mr. Hyde '89
Teachers '84
Wild at Heart '90

Derna-Hazell
The Dummy Talks '43

Enrique DeRosas
Sandflow '37

Richard Derr
Adam at 6 A.M. '70
Castle in the Desert '42
Guilty of Treason '50
The Invisible Avenger '58
Terror is a Man '59
When Worlds Collide '51

Cleavant Derricks
Bluffing It '87
Moscow on the Hudson '84
Off Beat '86

Joe Derrig
Maximum Thrust '87

Dominique Deruddere
Istanbul '85

Jacqueline Derval
Battle of the Worlds '61

Lamya Derval
Howling 4: The Original Nightmare '88

Hal Derwin
Everybody's Dancin' '50

Janos Derzsi
Bad Guys '79

Michael Des Barres
Nightflyers '87
Pink Cadillac '89
Waxwork 2: Lost in Time '91

Jean Desailly
Assassination of Trotsky '72
La Symphonie Pastorale '46
The Soft Skin '64

Stefan DeSalle
Russkies '87

Stanley DeSantis
Candyman '92

Daniel Desanto
Goodnight, Michelangelo '89

Gerard Desarthe
Uranus '91

Hubert Deschamps
The Fire Within '64

Mary Jo Deschanel
The Right Stuff '83
2010: The Year We Make Contact '84

Sandy Descher
The Cobweb '55
The Prodigal '55

Colette Descombes
Paranoia '69

Robert Desiderio
Gross Anatomy '89
Maximum Security '87
Oh, God! You Devil '84

Donna Desmond
Tender Loving Care '73

Florence Desmond
Accused '36

Johnny Desmond
Hawk of the Caribbean '70s

William Desmond
Courage of the North '35
Cowboy & the Bandit '35
Cyclone of the Saddle '35
Phantom of the Air '33
Phantom of the West '31
Powdersmoke Range '35
Tailspin Tommy '34

Desmond ▶cont.

Way of the West '35

Geory Desmouceaux
Small Change '76

Ivan Desny
Berlin Alexanderplatz '80
End of Desire '62
Escapade in Florence '62
Escape from the KGB '87
Lola Montes '55
Madeleine '50
The Marriage of Maria Braun '79
Quicker Than the Eye '88
The Respectful Prostitute '52
Sherlock Holmes and the Deadly Necklace '62
The Snake Hunter Strangler '66
Song Without End '60
Touch Me Not '74

Paul DeSouza
Web of Deceit '90

Masja Dessau
Parallel Corpse '83

Maruschka Detmers
Devil in the Flesh '87
First Name: Carmen '83
Hanna's War '88
The Mambo Kings '92

Tamara DeTreaux
Ghoulies '85

Bruce Detrick
Invasion of the Blood Farmers '72

Geoffrey Deuel
Amateur Night '85
Chisum '70

Beni Deus
Dos Postolas Gemelas '65

Ernst Deutsch
The Golem '20

Patti Deutsch
The Jetsons: Movie '90

William Devane
The Bad News Bears in Breaking Training '77
The Dark '79
Family Plot '76
From Here to Eternity '79
Hadley's Rebellion '84
Honky Tonk Freeway '81
Jane Doe '83
Marathon Man '76
McCabe & Mrs. Miller '71
Missiles of October '74
My Old Man's Place '71
Red Alert '77
Red Flag: The Ultimate Game '81
Rolling Thunder '77
Testament '83
Timestalkers '87
Urge to Kill '84
Vital Signs '90
Yanks '79

Joanna DeVarona
A*P*E* '76

Devin Devasquez
Society '92

Alan Deveau
Loose Screws '85
Recruits '86

Ed Devereaux
Money Movers '78

Helen Devereaux
The Scarlet Clue '45

Shawn Devereaux
Mona's Place '89

Kamala Devi
Geronimo '62

Renee Devillers
The French Touch '54
Heart of a Nation '43
J'Accuse '37

Maurice Devincentis
Moving Out '83

Andy Devine
The Adventures of Huckleberry Finn '60
Around the World in 80 Days '56
Eyes of Texas '48
Far Frontier '48
The Gay Ranchero '42
Grand Canyon Trail '48
How the West was Won '63
The Man Who Shot Liberty Valance '62
Montana Belle '52
Mouse and His Child '77
Myra Breckinridge '70
Never a Dull Moment '50
Night Time in Nevada '48
On the Old Spanish Trail '47
The Red Badge of Courage '51
Robin Hood '73
Slaughter Trail '51
Smoke '70
Springtime in the Sierras '47
Stagecoach '39
A Star is Born '37
Till the Clouds Roll By/A Star Is Born '46
Two Rode Together '61
Under California Stars '48
Western Double Feature 18 '40s
Western Double Feature 25
Whale of a Tale '76
Yellowstone '36
Zebra in the Kitchen '65

Dennis Devine
Lafayette Escadrille '58

George Devine
Tom Jones '63

Loretta Devine
Caged Fear '92

Danny DeVito
Amazing Stories '85
Batman Returns '92
Goin' South '78
Going Ape! '81
Head Office '86
Hoffa '92
Hurry Up or I'll Be Thirty '73
Jack the Bear '93
The Jewel of the Nile '85
Joe Piscopo: New Jersey Special '87
Johnny Dangerously '84
The Money '75
My Little Pony: The Movie '86
One Flew Over the Cuckoo's Nest '75
Other People's Money '91
Ratings Game '84
Romancing the Stone '84
Ruthless People '86
Terms of Endearment '83

Throw Momma from the Train '87
Tin Men '87
Twins '88
The Van '77
The War of the Roses '89
Wise Guys '86

Karla DeVito
Modern Love '90

Francis Devlaeminck
Small Change '76

Alan Devlin
The Lonely Passion of Judith Hearne '87
The Playboys '92

Don Devlin
Operation Dames '59

Joe Devlin
Double Dynamite '51

Devo
Spirit of '76 '91

Gordon Devol
Killings at Outpost Zeta '80

Laura Devon
Red Line 7000 '65

Richard Devon
The Battle of Blood Island '60
The Prodigal '55

Felicity Devonshire
Sex and the Other Woman '79
Whose Child Am I? '75

Dorothy Devore
Silent Movies...Just For the Fun of It! '26
The Tomboy '24

George DeVries
Mission Mars '67

Jon DeVries
Act of Passion: The Lost Honor of Kathryn Beck '83
The 4th Man '79
Grand Isle '92
Lianna '83
Sarah, Plain and Tall '91
Truth or Die '86

Elaine Devry
The Cheyenne Social Club '70
A Guide for the Married Man '67

Eddie Dew
Raiders of Sunset Pass '43
Six Gun Gospel '43

Patrick Dewaere
Beau Pere '81
The Best Way '82
Catherine & Co. '76
The French Detective '75
Get Out Your Handkerchiefs '78
Going Places '74
Heat of Desire '84
Hothead '78

Diane Dewey
The Girl in Blue '74

Rebecca Dewey
The Man Who Guards the Greenhouse '88

Colleen Dewhurst
And Baby Makes Six '79
Anne of Avonlea '87
Anne of Green Gables '85
Annie Hall '77
Bed & Breakfast '92

Between Two Women '86
The Blue and the Grey '85
The Boy Who Could Fly '86
The Cowboys '72
Dead Zone '83
Dying Young '91
Final Assignment '80
A Fine Madness '66
The Glitter Dome '84
The Guyana Tragedy: The Story of Jim Jones '80
Ice Castles '79
Lantern Hill '90
Mary and Joseph: A Story of Faith '79
McQ '74
Medea '59
The Nun's Story '59
Obsessed '88
Silent Victory: The Kitty O'Neil Story '79
The Story of Jacob & Joseph '74
Sword of Gideon '86
Termini Station '91
Third Walker '79
When a Stranger Calls '79
You Can't Take It with You '84

Johana DeWinter
Planet Earth '74

Billy DeWolfe
Billie '65
Dear Wife '49
Frosty the Snowman '69
Lullaby of Broadway '51
The Perils of Pauline '47
Tea for Two '50

Anthony Dexter
Fire Maidens from Outer Space '56
Married Too Young '62

Brad Dexter
Between Heaven and Hell '56
The Las Vegas Story '52
Last Train from Gun Hill '59
Magnificent Seven '60
None But the Brave '65
The Oklahoman '56
Run Silent, Run Deep '58
Secret Ingredient '88
Von Ryan's Express '65
Winter Kills '79

Tony Dexter
The Phantom Planet '61

Susan Dey
Comeback Kid '80
Echo Park '86
First Love '77
L.A. Law '86
Little Women '78
Looker '81
Love Leads the Way '84
Sunset Limousine '83
That's Adequate '90
The Trouble with Dick '88

Cliff DeYoung
Annie Oakley '85
Awakening of Candra '81
Bulldance '88
Code Name: Dancer '87
Dangerous Company '88
Dr. Giggles '92
F/X '86
Fear '88
Flight of the Navigator '86
Forbidden Sun '89
Fourth Story '90
The Hunger '83
Immortal Sins '91
In Dangerous Company '88
Independence Day '83

King '78
The Lindbergh Kidnapping Case '76
Nails '92
Protocol '84
Pulse '88
Reckless '84
Robert Kennedy and His Times '90
Rude Awakening '89
Secret Admirer '85
Shock Treatment '81
The Survivalist '87
To Die Standing '91

Eddie Dezen
Mob Boss '90

Ayesha Dharker
City of Joy '92

Dharmendra
Deadly Thief '78

Bernard Dheran
Bernadette '90

Robert Dhery
Femmes de Paris '53

Danica D'Hondt
The Unkissed Bride '66

Dalia di Lazzaro
Andy Warhol's Frankenstein '74
Creepers '85

Lea di Lea
The Earrings of Madame De... '54

Alice Diabo
Strangers in Good Company '91

Rika Dialina
Black Sabbath '64

Catherine Diamant
The Nun '66

Despo Diamantidou
Love and Death '75

Don Diamond
Borderline. '50

George Diamond
Video Wars '84

Joel Diamond
Crossover Dreams '85

Keith Diamond
Dr. Giggles '92

Marcia Diamond
Deranged '74

Neil Diamond
Jazz Singer '80
The Last Waltz '78

Reed Edward Diamond
Ironclads '90
Memphis Belle '90
O Pioneers! '91

Selma Diamond
All of Me '84
Bang the Drum Slowly '73
Twilight Zone: The Movie '83

John DiAquino
Pumpkinhead '88
Slipping into Darkness '88

Chico Diaz
The Fable of the Beautiful Pigeon Fancier '88

Justino Diaz
Otello '86

Maria Diaz
The Heroes of Desert Storm '91

Sully Diaz
Gryphon '88

Tony Diaz
Hay Muertos Que No Hacen Ruido '47

Vic Diaz
Beast of the Yellow Night '70
The Children of An Lac '80
The Deadly and the Beautiful '73
Deathhead Virgin '74
Flight to Fury '66
Night of the Cobra Woman '72
Savage! '73
Too Hot to Handle '76

Kem Dibbs
Daniel Boone: Trail Blazer '56

Tony DiBenedetto
Someone to Watch Over Me '87

Luigi Diberti
All Screwed Up '74

Louie Dibianco
Mafia Princess '86

Leonardo DiCaprio
Critters 3 '91
This Boy's Life '93

George DiCenzo
The Equalizer: Memories of Manon '88
The Exorcist 3 '90
The Frisco Kid '79
Helter Skelter '76
The New Adventures of Pippi Longstocking '88
The Night the City Screamed '80
Omega Syndrome '87
Sing '89

Bobby DiCicco
Frame Up '91
I Wanna Hold Your Hand '78
The Last Hour '91
Night Shift '82
The Philadelphia Experiment '84
Splash '84
Tiger Warsaw '87

Pier Giorgia DiCicco
Psycho Girls '86

Danny Dick
Dungeonmaster '85

Douglas Dick
The Accused '48
The Oklahoman '56
The Red Badge of Courage '51

Beach Dickerson
Creature from the Haunted Sea '60
T-Bird Gang '59

George Dickerson
After Dark, My Sweet '90
Blue Velvet '86
Cutter's Way '81
Death Warrant '90

James Dickey
Deliverance '72

Lucinda Dickey
Breakin' '84

Breakin' 2: Electric Boogaloo '84
Cheerleader Camp '88
Ninja 3: The Domination '84

Paul Dickey
Robin Hood '22

Angie Dickinson
Big Bad Mama '74
Big Bad Mama 2 '87
Captain Newman, M.D. '63
Cast a Giant Shadow '66
Charlie Chan and the Curse of the Dragon Queen '81
The Chase '66
China Gate '57
Death Hunt '81
Dressed to Kill '80
Fire and Rain '89
Hidden Guns '56
Jealousy '84
The Killers '64
Klondike Fever '79
Lucky Me '54
Ocean's 11 '60
One Shoe Makes It Murder '82
The Outside Man '73
Point Blank '67
The Poppy is also a Flower '66
Pray for the Wildcats '74
Resurrection of Zachary Wheeler '71
Rio Bravo '59
Rome Adventure '62
Texas Guns '90
Thief '71
Treacherous Crossing '92
Wild Palms '93

George Dickson
Ninja Phantom Heroes '87

Lance Dickson
Project: Nightmare

Neil Dickson
Biggles '85
It Couldn't Happen Here '88
The Murders in the Rue Morgue '86

Bo Diddley
Chuck Berry: Hail! Hail! Rock 'n' Roll '87
Hell's Angels Forever '83
Rockula '90

Arlette Didier
Bernadette '90

Dan Diego
Three Way Weekend '81

Gabino Diego
Ay, Carmela! '90

John Diehl
Angel '84
Cool Blue '88
Dark Side of the Moon '90
Glitz '88
Kickboxer 2: The Road Back '90
Madhouse '90
Miami Vice '84
Mikey '92
Mo' Money '92
Motorama '91
Remote '93

John Dierkes
The Daughter of Dr. Jekyll '57
The Haunted Palace '63

Charles Dierkop
Banzai Runner '86
The Fix '84
Roots of Evil '91

Gustav Diesl
Crimes of Dr. Mabuse '32
Das Testament des Dr. Mabuse '33
Westfront 1918 '30

William Dieterle
Backstairs '21
Waxworks '24

Marsha Dietlein
Return of the Living Dead Part 2 '88

Daniel Dietrich
Crossfire '89

Marlene Dietrich
Around the World in 80 Days '56
Blonde Venus '32
The Blue Angel '30
Destry Rides Again '39
The Garden of Allah '36
Jigsaw '49
Judgment at Nuremberg '61
Just a Gigolo '79
Knight Without Armour '37
The Love Goddesses '65
Morocco '30
Paris When It Sizzles '64
Rancho Notorious '52
Seven Sinners '40
The Spoilers '42
Stage Fright '50
Touch of Evil '58
Witness for the Prosecution '57

Frank Dietz
The Jitters '88
Zombie Nightmare '86

Albert Dieudonne
Napoleon '27

Anton Diffring
Black Werewolf '75
Call Him Mr. Shatter '74
Circus of Horrors '60
The Colditz Story '55
Fahrenheit 451 '66
Mark of the Devil 2 '72
Seven Deaths in the Cat's Eye '72
Where Eagles Dare '68
The Winds of War '83
Zeppelin '71

Dudley Digges
China Seas '35
Devotion '31
Emperor Jones '33
Emperor Jones/Paul Robeson: Tribute to an Artist '33
The General Died at Dawn '36
The Invisible Man '33
The Maltese Falcon '31
Mutiny on the Bounty '35

Arthur Dignam
Between Wars '74
The Devil's Playground '76
The Everlasting Secret Family '88
Grendel, Grendel, Grendel '82
King Solomon's Mines '86
The Right Hand Man '87
Strange Behavior '81
We of the Never Never '82
The Wild Duck '84

Alan Dijon
Assignment Outer Space '61

Irasema Dilian
Wuthering Heights '53

Matt Dill
The Boy Who Loved Trolls '84

Victoria Dillard
Deep Cover '92

Denise Dillaway
The Cheerleaders '72

Phyllis Diller
The Bone Yard '90
Boy, Did I Get a Wrong Number! '66
Happily Ever After '93
Mad Monster Party '68
Maniac '34
Minsky's Follies '83
The Nutcracker Prince '91
Pink Motel '82
A Pleasure Doing Business '79
Splendor in the Grass '61
The Worst of Hollywood: Vol. 1 '90

Bradford Dillman
The Amsterdam Kill '78
Black Water Gold '69
The Bridge at Remagen '69
Brother John '70
Bug '75
Death in Deep Water '74
The Enforcer '76
Escape from the Planet of the Apes '71
Force Five '75
Heroes Stand Alone '89
Legend of Walks Far Woman '82
Lords of the Deep '89
Love and Bullets '79
Man Outside '88
Master Mind '73
The Mephisto Waltz '71
Moon of the Wolf '72
Murder or Mercy '74
99 & 44/100 Dead '74
One Away '80
Piranha '78
Resurrection of Zachary Wheeler '71
Running Scared '79
Sergeant Ryker '68
Sudden Impact '83
Suppose They Gave a War and Nobody Came? '70
The Swarm '78
The Treasure of the Amazon '84
The Way We Were '73
The Widow '76

Brandan Dillon
The Killing of Sister George '69

Brendan Dillon, Jr.
Lords of Magick '88

C.J. Dillon
Return of the Killer Tomatoes '88

Edward Dillon
Broadway Melody '29

Kevin Dillon
The Blob '88
The Doors '91
Heaven Help Us '85
Immediate Family '89
A Midnight Clear '92
No Big Deal '83
Platoon '86
Remote Control '88
The Rescue '88
War Party '89
When He's Not a Stranger '89

Matt Dillon
Big Town '87
Bloodhounds of Broadway '89
Drugstore Cowboy '89
The Flamingo Kid '84
Kansas '88
A Kiss Before Dying '91
Liar's Moon '82
Little Darlings '80
My Bodyguard '80
Native Son '86
The Outsiders '83
Over the Edge '79
Rebel '85
Rumble Fish '83
Singles '92
Target '85
Tex '82
Women & Men: Stories of Seduction, Part 2 '91

Melinda Dillon
Absence of Malice '81
Bound for Glory '76
Captain America '89
A Christmas Story '83
Close Encounters of the Third Kind '77
Fallen Angel '81
F.I.S.T. '78
Harry and the Hendersons '87
The Juggler of Notre Dame '84
Marriage is Alive and Well '80
Nightbreaker '89
The Prince of Tides '91
Right of Way '84
The Shadow Box '80
Shattered Spirits '91
Slap Shot '77
Songwriter '84
Spontaneous Combustion '89
Staying Together '89

Mick Dillon
Champions '84

Paul Dillon
The Beat '88
Kiss Daddy Goodnight '87

Stephen Dillon
An Affair in Mind '89
Christabel '89

Tom Dillon
Dressed to Kill '46
Night Tide '63

Joe DiMaggio
Manhattan Merry-Go-Round '37

Joseph Dimambro
Concrete Angels '87

James Dime
Stand and Deliver '28

Richard Dimitri
Johnny Dangerously '84

Dennis Dimster
Olly Olly Oxen Free '78

Ayub Khan Din
Sammy & Rosie Get Laid '87

Alan Dinehart
After Midnight '33
Baby, Take a Bow '34
A Study in Scarlet '33

Mark Dingham
Hamlet '69

Charles Dingle
The Beast with Five Fingers '46
The Court Martial of Billy Mitchell '55

Dingle ▶cont.

Guest Wife '45
If You Knew Susie '48
Johnny Eager '42
The Little Foxes '41
Somewhere I'll Find You '42
A Southern Yankee '48

Ernie Dingo
The Fringe Dwellers '86
Until The End of The World '91
A Waltz Through the Hills '88

Kelly Dingwall
Around the World in 80 Ways '86

Memo Dini
Mediterraneo '92

Jerry Dinome
Tomboy '85

Reece Dinsdale
Threads '85
Winter Flight '84
Young Catherine '91

Franco Diogene
The Bachelor '93

Rose Dione
Salome '22
Suds '20

Silvia Dionisio
The Scalawag Bunch '75

Dyanne DiRosario
Dr. Hackenstein '88

John Disanti
Eyes of a Stranger '81

Alesandro DiSanzo
Forever Mary '89

Michael Disend
Fathers and Sons '92

Bob Dishy
Brighton Beach Memoirs '86
I Wonder Who's Killing Her Now? '76
Kill My Wife...Please!
Lovers and Other Strangers '70
Used People '92

Joe DiSue
Blackenstein '73

Divine
Divine '90
Female Trouble '75
Hairspray '88
I Wanna Be a Beauty Queen '85
Lust in the Dust '85
Mondo Trasho '70
Multiple Maniacs '70
Out of the Dark '88
Pink Flamingos '73
Polyester '81
Trouble in Mind '86

Andrew Divoff
Back in the USSR '92
Interceptor '92
Toy Soldiers '91

Dorothy Dix
Drum Taps '33

Richard Dix
Ace of Aces '33
American Empire '42
Archer: The Fugitive from the Empire '81
Buckskin Frontier '43

Cimarron '30
The Kansan '43
Lost Squadron '32
Lucky Devil '25
Ten Commandments '23
Transatlantic Tunnel '35
Vanishing American '26

Robert Dix
Blood of Dracula's Castle '69
Cain's Cutthroats '71
Deadwood '65
Horror of the Blood Monsters '70
Killers '88
Satan's Sadists '69
Wild Wheels '75

Tommy Dix
Best Foot Forward '43

Phyllis Dixey
Dual Alibi '47

Beth Dixon
The Ballad of the Sad Cafe '91

Carter Dixon
Young Eagles '34

David Dixon
Escort Girls '74

Donna Dixon
Beverly Hills Madam '86
The Couch Trip '87
Doctor Detroit '83
Lucky Stiff '88
Margin for Murder '81
Speed Zone '88
Spies Like Us '85
Wayne's World '92

Ernest Dixon
Freedom Road '79

Ivan Dixon
Car Wash '76
Fer-De-Lance '74
A Patch of Blue '65
A Raisin in the Sun '61
Suppose They Gave a War and Nobody Came? '70

James Dixon
It's Alive '74
It's Alive 3: Island of the Alive '87
Return to Salem's Lot '87

Jean Dixon
Joy of Living '38

Joan Dixon
Gunplay '51

MacIntyre Dixon
Funny Farm '88
Ghostwriter '84

Michael Dixon
Chains '89

Pamela Dixon
Chance '89
C.I.A.: Code Name Alexa '92
Hollywood in Trouble '87
L.A. Crackdown '87
L.A. Crackdown 2 '88
Mayhem '87

Steve Dixon
The Carrier '87

Willie Dixon
Rich Girl '91

Gregg D'Jah
Cheering Section '73

Badja Djola
Mississippi Burning '88

The Serpent and the Rainbow '87
Who's the Man? '93

Ho Chung Do
Fists of Fury 2 '80

Mauricio Do Valle
Amazon Jail '85
Antonio Das Mortes '68

Wong Do
Moonlight Sword & Jade Lion '70s

Heidi Dobbs
Death Journey '76
Jornada de Muerte '80s

James Dobbs
Impulse '74

Valeria D'Obici
Escape from the Bronx '85
Passion of Love '82

Alan Dobie
White Mischief '88

Larry Dobkin
Beastmaster 2: Through the Portal of Time '91

Lawrence Dobkin
Geronimo '62
Patton '70

Gosia Dobrowolska
Around the World in 80 Ways '86
Silver City '84
A Woman's Tale '92

James Dobson
Jet Attack/Paratroop Command '58

Kevin Dobson
All Night Long '81
Code of Honor '84
Dirty Work '92
Hardhat & Legs '80
Margin for Murder '81
Midway '76
Orphan Train '79

Peter Dobson
The Marrying Man '91
Sing '89
Where the Day Takes You '92

Tamara Dobson
The Amazons '84
Chained Heat '83
Cleopatra Jones '73
Cleopatra Jones & the Casino of Gold '75

Vernon Dobtcheff
The Assassination Bureau '69
Nijinsky '80
Pascali's Island '88

Trudi Dochtermann
Down Twisted '89

Leslie Dockery
Eubie! '82

Dr. Dre
Who's the Man? '93

Carol Doda
Honkytonk Nights '70s

Claire Dodd
Ex-Lady '33

Jimmie Dodd
Snuffy Smith, Yard Bird '42

Marilyn Dodd-Frank
Sweet Lies '88

Lorenzo Dodo
The Executioner '78

Jack Dodson
The Getaway '72

John Doe
Great Balls of Fire '89
A Matter of Degrees '90
Pure Country '92
Roadside Prophets '92
Slamdance '87
Without You I'm Nothing '90

Christian Doermer
Teenage Wolfpack '57

Tatiana Dogileva
A Forgotten Tune for the Flute '88

Robert Dogui
Almos' a Man '78

Matt Doherty
So I Married an Axe Murderer '93

Shannen Doherty
Freeze Frame '92
Girls Just Want to Have Fun '85
Heathers '89
Night Shift '82

Lou Doillon
Le Petit Amour '87

Katie Dolan
The Vampire Hookers '78

Michael Dolan
Hamburger Hill '87

Rainbow Dolan
In the Aftermath '87

Thomas Dolby
Rockula '90

Guy Doleman
The Ipcress File '65
Thunderball '65

Jim Dolen
The Virgin of Nuremberg '65

Ami Dolenz
Children of the Night '92
Faith '92
Miracle Beach '92
Stepmonster '92

Mickey Dolenz
Head '68
Night of the Strangler '73

Birgit Doll
Nuclear Conspiracy '85

Dora Doll
Black and White in Color '76
Boomerang '76

Patrick Dollaghan
Circle of Fear '89
Kill Slade '89
Murphy's Fault '88

Neige Dolsky
Tatie Danielle '91

Larry Domasin
Fun in Acapulco '63
Island of the Blue Dolphins '64

Arielle Dombasle
The Boss' Wife '86
Le Beau Mariage '82
Pauline at the Beach '83
Trade Secrets '90s
Twisted Obsession '90

Andrea Domburg
Katie's Passion '75

Faith Domergue
The Atomic Man '56
Blood Legacy '73
The House of Seven Corpses '73
It Came from Beneath the Sea '55
The Sibling '72
This Island Earth '55
Voyage to the Prehistoric Planet '65

Placido Domingo
Otello '86

Berta Dominguez
Maya '82

Arturo Dominici
Black Sunday '60
Hercules '58

Fats Domino
Rock, Rock, Rock '56

Solveig Dommartin
Until The End of The World '91
Wings of Desire '88

Angelica Domrose
Girls Riot '88
The Scorpion Woman '89

Linda Dona
Delta Heat '92
Final Embrace '92

Elinor Donahue
Freddy's Dead: The Final Nightmare '91
Girls' Town '59
High School USA '84
Love is Better Than Ever '52

Mitzi Donahue
Lethal Pursuit '88

Troy Donahue
Assault of the Party Nerds '89
The Chilling '89
Cockfighter '74
Cry-Baby '90
Cyclone '87
Deadly Diamonds '91
Deadly Prey '87
Deadly Spygames '89
Dr. Alien '88
The Godfather 1902-1959: The Complete Epic '81
The Godfather, Part 2 '74
Grandview U.S.A. '84
Hawkeye '88
Hollywood Cop '87
Imitation of Life '59
The Legend of Frank Woods '77
Love Thrill Murders '71
Nudity Required '90
Omega Cop '90
Palm Springs Weekend '63
The Pamela Principle '91
Rome Adventure '62
Sexpot '88
Shock 'Em Dead '90
Sounds of Silence '91
South Seas Massacre
A Summer Place '59
Terminal Force '88
Those Fantastic Flying Fools '67
Tin Man '83
A Woman Obsessed '88

Dorothy Donald
Fangs of Fate '25

James Donald
Beau Brummel '54
The Big Sleep '78

Christopher Eccleston
Let Him Have It '91

Gisela Echevarria
In a Glass Cage '86

Guy Ecker
Devil Wears White '86
Night Terror '89

James Eckhouse
Blue Heaven '84
Leaving Normal '92

Billy Eckstine
Jo Jo Dancer, Your Life is Calling '86
Skirts Ahoy! '52

Barbara Eda-Young
Serpico '73

Helen Jerome Eddy
The Country Kid '23
County Fair '20
Rebecca of Sunnybrook Farm '17
A Shot in the Dark '35

Nelson Eddy
Bitter Sweet '40
The Chocolate Soldier '41
Dancing Lady '33
Girl of the Golden West '38
I Married an Angel '42
Maytime '37
Naughty Marietta '35
New Moon '40
Northwest Outpost '47
Phantom of the Opera '43
Rosalie '38
Rose Marie '36
Sweethearts '38

Alfred Edel
My Father is Coming '91

Gregg Edelman
Green Card '90

Herb Edelman
The Charge of the Model T's '76
Cracking Up '83
A Cry for Love '80
Goin' Coconuts '78
Marathon '80
On the Right Track '81
Special Olympics '78
A Strange and Deadly Occurence '74
Strike Force '81
The Way We Were '73
The Yakuza '75

Barbara Eden
The Amazing Dobermans '76
Chattanooga Choo Choo '84
Five Weeks in a Balloon '62
Flaming Star '60
From the Terrace '60
Harper Valley P.T.A. '78
How to Break Up a Happy Divorce '76
Quick, Let's Get Married '71
Return of the Rebels '81
Ride the Wild Surf '64
Seven Faces of Dr. Lao '63
The Stranger Within '74
Voyage to the Bottom of the Sea '61
The Woman Hunter '72
The Wonderful World of the Brothers Grimm '62

Chana Eden
Holocaust Survivors...Remembrance of Love '83

Elana Eden
The Story of Ruth '60

Jerome Eden
The Defilers '65
2000 Maniacs '64

Mark Eden
The Crimson Cult '68
Seance on a Wet Afternoon '64

Richard Eden
Liberty & Bash '90

Robert Edeson
On the Night Stage '15
Walking Back '26

George Edgely
Common Law Wife '63
Free, White, and 21 '62

Earle Edgerton
Carnival of Blood '71

Walker Edmiston
The Beach Girls and the Monster '65

Jeff Edmond
Getting It On '83

Dale Edmonds
Paisan '46

Elizabeth Edmonds
Experience Preferred... But Not Essential '83
Scrubbers '82

Roy Edmonds
Sniper '92

Ade Edmondson
The Young Ones '88

Adrian Edmondson
Supergrass '87

Lada Edmund
Savage! '73

Marie Edmund
Assault of the Rebel Girls '59

Beatie Edney
The Dark Angel '91
Diary of a Mad Old Man '88
Highlander '86
Mister Johnson '91

Nekohachi Edoya
The Funeral '84

Richard Edson
Do the Right Thing '89
Eight Men Out '88
Good Morning, Vietnam '87
Let It Ride '89
Platoon '86
Stranger than Paradise '84
Super Mario Bros. '93
Tougher than Leather '88

Allan Edwall
Brothers Lionheart '85
Fanny and Alexander '83
The Sacrifice '86

Anthony Edwards
Delta Heat '92
Downtown '89
El Diablo '90
Fast Times at Ridgemont High '82
Going for the Gold: The Bill Johnson Story '85
Gotcha! '85
Hawks '89
Heart Like a Wheel '83
How I Got into College '89
Landslide '92
Miracle Mile '89

Mr. North '88
Pet Sematary 2 '92
Revenge of the Nerds '84
Revenge of the Nerds 2: Nerds in Paradise '87
Summer Heat '87
The Sure Thing '85
Top Gun '86

Barbara Edwards
Another Chance '88
Malibu Express '85

Bill Edwards
First Man into Space '59
Ladies of the Chorus '49
War Lover '62

Blake Edwards
Strangler of the Swamp '46

Bruce Edwards
The Black Widow '47
The Fallen Sparrow '43
Federal Agents vs. Underworld, Inc. '49
Hitler: Dead or Alive '43
The Iron Major '43

Cassandra Edwards
Vasectomy: A Delicate Matter '86

Cliff Edwards
Dance Fools Dance '31
Doughboys '30
Dumbo '41
Girl of the Golden West '38
His Girl Friday '40
Laughing Sinners '31
Parlor, Bedroom and Bath '31
Pinocchio '40
Saratoga '37
The Sin of Madelon Claudet '31

Elizabeth Edwards
The Pink Chiquitas '86

Ella Edwards
Sweet Sugar '72

Gail Edwards
Get Crazy '83

Gene Edwards
Grizzly Adams: The Legend Continues '90

Gerald Edwards
The Fat Albert Christmas Special '77
The Fat Albert Easter Special '82
The Fat Albert Halloween Special '77

Harry Edwards
Baby Face Harry Langdon '26

Henry Edwards
The Golden Salamander '51

Hilton Edwards
Othello '52

Hugh Edwards
Lord of the Flies '63

James Edwards
Home of the Brave '49
Patton '70
Pork Chop Hill '59
The Set-Up '49
The Steel Helmet '51

Jennifer Edwards
All's Fair '89
Heidi '67
The Man Who Loved Women '83
Overexposed '90
Perfect Match '88

Peter Gunn '89
S.O.B. '81
Sunset '88
That's Life! '86

Jimmy Edwards
Innocents in Paris '53

Judy Edwards
The Mermaids of Tiburon '62

Kyle Edwards
Death Weekend '76

Lance Edwards
Peacemaker '90
A Woman, Her Men and Her Futon '92

Luke Edwards
Newsies '92
The Wizard '89

Mark Edwards
The Boldest Job in the West '71
Tower of Evil '72

Meredith Edwards
The Electronic Monster '57

Olga Edwards
Angel with the Trumpet '50

Patty Edwards
Torture Train '83

Paul Edwards
Combat Killers '80

Penny Edwards
Heart of the Rockies '51
North of the Great Divide '50
Trail of Robin Hood '50
Western Double Feature 11 '50
Western Double Feature 15 '50

Rick Edwards
Hearts & Armour '83

Ronnie Clair Edwards
A Day for Thanks on Walton's Mountain '82
Future Cop '76

Sam Edwards
Gang Busters '55

Sebastian Rice Edwards
Hope and Glory '87

Snitz Edwards
Battling Butler '26
Seven Chances '25
The Thief of Baghdad '24

Stacy Edwards
Vietnam War Story 3 '89

Stephanie Edwards
Big Mo '73

Stracker Edwards
Blood on the Mountain '88

Ted Edwards
Maniac '34

Vince Edwards
Andy and the Airwave Rangers '89
Cellar Dweller '87
Death Stalk '74
Desperados '69
The Devil's Brigade '68
Firehouse '72
The Fix '84
The Gumshoe Kid '89
The Killing '56
The Mad Bomber '72

Motorama '91
Original Intent '91
Return to Horror High '87
The Seduction '82
Sno-Line '85
Space Raiders '83
The Three Faces of Eve '57

Walter Edwards
Grit of the Girl Telegrapher/In the Switch Tower '15
Tale of Two Cities/In the Switch Tower '15

Joseph Eero
Igor & the Lunatics '85

Colin Efford
Invitation to Hell '84

Marshall Efron
First Time '82
Is There Sex After Death? '71

Aeryk Egan
Book of Love '91
Keeper of the City '92

Eddie Egan
Badge 373 '73
The French Connection '71

Michael Egan
Rappaccini's Daughter '80

Peter Egan
Hennessy '75
Lillie '79
One Brief Summer '70

Richard Egan
The Amsterdam Kill '78
Blackbeard the Pirate '52
Demetrius and the Gladiators '54
The Hunters '58
Love Me Tender '56
Mission to Glory '80
One Minute to Zero '52
Pollyanna '60
Seven Cities of Gold '55
Split Second '53
A Summer Place '59
Sweet Creek County War '82
Tension at Table Rock '56
Underwater '55

Will Egan
Glitch! '88
Ninja Academy '90

Julie Ege
Craze '74
Creatures the World Forgot '70
The Freakmaker '73
On Her Majesty's Secret Service '69
Rentadick '72
The 7 Brothers Meet Dracula '73

Samantha Eggar
All the Kind Strangers '74
Battleforce '78
The Brood '79
The Collector '65
Curtains '83
Dark Horse '92
Demonoid, Messenger of Death '81
Doctor Dolittle '67
Doctor in Distress '63
Exterminator '80
The Great Battle '79
Hot Touch '80s
Light at the Edge of the World '71
Man of Destiny '73
Molly Maguires '70
A Name for Evil '70

Lui I. Fan
Incredible Master Beggars '82

Nan Kung Fan
Super Kung Fu Kid

Jamaa Fanaka
Penitentiary '79

Mary Fanaro
Demon Queen '80s
Truth or Dare? '86

Bo Fanders
Salem's Lot '79

Lu Fang
Kung Fu Vampire Buster

Paul Fankeur
Jour de Fete '48

Al Fann
Frankie and Johnny '91
Parasite '81

Lou Fant
Amy '81

Ennio Fantastichini
Open Doors '89
The Station '92

Sergio Fantoni
Atom Age Vampire '61
The Giant of Marathon '60
The Prize '63
Von Ryan's Express '65
What Did You Do in the War,
   Daddy? '66

Stephanie Faracy
Blind Date '87
The Great Outdoors '88

Daniel Faraldo
Above the Law '88
Full Fathom Five '90

Amy Farber
Hot Times '74

Arlene Sue Farber
Teenage Mother '67

Violet Farebrother
Easy Virtue '27

Debrah Farentino
Bugsy '91
Capone '89
Mortal Sins '90

James Farentino
The Cradle Will Fall '83
Dead and Buried '81
Ensign Pulver '64
Family Sins '87
The Final Countdown '80
Her Alibi '88
License to Kill '84
Naked Lie '89
The Possessed '77
Psychomania '63
Silent Victory: The Kitty O'Neil
   Story '79
Sins '85
A Summer to Remember '84
The War Lord '65

Antonio Fargas
Across 110th Street '72
The Ambush Murders '82
The Borrower '89
Busting '74
Car Wash '76
Cornbread, Earl & Me '75
Firestarter '84
Florida Straits '87
Foxy Brown '74
Howling 6: The Freaks '90
Huckleberry Finn '75
I'm Gonna Git You Sucka '88

Milo Milo '60s
Night of the Sharks '89
Nurse '80
Pretty Baby '78
Shakedown '88
Streetwalkin' '85

Jillian Fargey
Close to Home '86

Betty Faria
Bye Bye Brazil '79
The Story of Fausta '88

Carolyn Farina
Metropolitan '90

Dennis Farina
Code of Silence '85
Crime Story '86
Crime Story: The Complete
   Saga '86
Drug Wars 2: The Cocaine
   Cartel '92
The Hillside Strangler '89
Manhunter '86
Men of Respect '91
Midnight Run '88
Another Stakeout '93
Street Crimes '92
We're Talkin' Serious Money
   '92

Gabriella Farinon
Assignment Outer Space '61

James Farkas
The Shaman '87

Lynn Farleigh
Lovers of Their Time '85

Albert Farley
Scalps '83

Chris Farley
Coneheads '93

Morgan Farley
Open Secret '48

Teresa Farley
Bad Girls Dormitory '84

Zedna Farley
The Dentist '32

Frances Farmer
Come and Get It '36
South of Pago Pago '40
Toast of New York '37

Gary Farmer
Powwow Highway '89

Ken Farmer
Another Pair of Aces: Three of
   a Kind '91

Marva Farmer
Candy Tangerine Man '75

Mimsy Farmer
Allonsanfan '73
Autopsy '78
The Black Cat '81
Black Cat '86
Codename: Wildgeese '84
Devil's Angels '67
More '69
Road to Salina '68

Suzan Farmer
Death in Deep Water '74
Die, Monster, Die! '65
The Graveyard '74

Ellen Farner
Umbrellas of Cherbourg '64

Alberto Farnese
Conqueror & the Empress '64
The Giants of Thessaly '60
Gladiator of Rome '63

Richard Farnsworth
Anne of Green Gables '85
Chase '85
Comes a Horseman '78
The Fire Next Time '93
The Grey Fox '83
Havana '90
Highway to Hell '92
Independence Day '83
Into the Night '85
Legend of the Lone Ranger
   '81
Misery '90
The Natural '84
Resurrection '80
Rhinestone '84
Ruckus '81
Space Rage '86
Strange New World '75
Sylvester '85
Tom Horn '80
The Two Jakes '90
Waltz Across Texas '83
Witchery '88

Franklin Farnum
Battling with Buffalo Bill '31
Hopalong Cassidy '35
Mark of the Spur '32
Powdersmoke Range '35
Prison Train '38
The Scarlet Car '17

William Farnum
Between Men '35
A Connecticut Yankee '31
Custer's Last Stand '36
The Drifter '32
Dubarry '30
Git Along Little Dogies '37
God's Country '46
Gun Cargo '49
Kid Ranger '36
Law of the Sea '38
Million Dollar Haul '35
Mr. Robinson Crusoe '32
My Dog Shep '46
Painted Desert '31
Powdersmoke Range '35
Public Cowboy No. 1 '37
Santa Fe Stampede '38
The Silver Streak '34
The Spoilers '14
Ten Nights in a Bar-Room '31
Today I Hang '42
Trail of Robin Hood '50
Two Reelers: Comedy
   Classics 8 '33

Derek Farr
Man on the Run '49
Spellbound '41
Truth About Women '58

Felicia Farr
Charley Varrick '73
Jubal '56
Kiss Me, Stupid! '64
Kotch '71
3:10 to Yuma '57

Jamie Farr
Cannonball Run '81
Cannonball Run II '84
Combat Academy '86
Curse 2: The Bite '88
For Love or Money '84
Happy Hour '87
M*A*S*H: Goodbye, Farewell
   & Amen '83
No Time for Sergeants '58
Return of the Rebels '81
Scrooged '88
Speed Zone '88
Who's Minding the Mint? '67

Patricia Farr
Mistaken Identity '36

Tailspin Tommy '34

Yolanda Farr
Gulliver '70s

David Farrar
Beat Girl '60
Black Narcissus '47
Echo Murders '45
Frieda '47
Let's Make Up '55
Meet Sexton Blake '44
The Obsessed '51
Pearl of the South Pacific '55
Sea Chase '55
The Small Back Room '49
The World Owes Me a Living
   '47

Gwen Farrar
She Shall Have Music '36

Tom Farrel
Lightning Over Water '80

Brioni Farrell
The Student Nurses '70

Charles Farrell
Aggie Appleby, Maker of Men
   '33
City Girl '30
Just Around the Corner '38
Moonlight Sonata '38
Night and the City '50
Old Ironsides '26

Glenda Farrell
Bureau of Missing Persons
   '33
Disorderly Orderly '64
Gold Diggers of 1935 '35
Heading for Heaven '47
I Am a Fugitive from a Chain
   Gang '32
Johnny Eager '42
Kissin' Cousins '64
Lady for a Day '33
Little Caesar '30
Mystery of the Wax Museum
   '33
A Night for Crime '42
Prison Break '38
Talk of the Town '42

Mike Farrell
Damien: The Leper Priest '80
Dark River: A Father's
   Revenge '90
Escape from Planet Earth '67
The Graduate '67
Lockdown '90
M*A*S*H: Goodbye, Farewell
   & Amen '83
Memorial Day '83
Prime Suspect '82
Sex and the Single Parent '82
Silent Motive '91
Vanishing Act '88

Sharon Farrell
It's Alive '74
The Love Machine '71
Marlowe '69
Night of the Comet '84
One Man Force '89
The Premonition '75
Rage '80
The Reivers '69

Terry Farrell
Beverly Hills Madam '86
Hellraiser 3: Hell on Earth '92
Off the Mark '87

Timothy Farrell
The Devil's Sleep '51
Gun Girls '56
Jail Bait '54
Test Tube Babies '48

Tom Riis Farrell
Scent of a Woman '92

Tommy Farrell
Kissin' Cousins '64
Pirates of the High Seas '50

Donato Farretta
Tank Commando '59

Debbie Farrington
Black Panther '77

Hugh Farrington
Arizona Heat '87

Kenneth Farrington
Danger UXB '81

Mia Farrow
Alice '90
Another Woman '88
Avalanche '78
Broadway Danny Rose '84
Crimes & Misdemeanors '89
Dandy in Aspic '68
Death on the Nile '78
Full Circle '77
The Great Gatsby '74
Guns at Batasi '64
Hannah and Her Sisters '86
High Heels '72
Hurricane '79
Husbands and Wives '92
The Last Unicorn '82
A Midsummer Night's Sex
   Comedy '82
New York Stories '89
The Purple Rose of Cairo '85
Radio Days '87
Rosemary's Baby '68
Sarah & the Squirrel '83
Secret Ceremony '69
See No Evil '71
September '88
Shadows and Fog '92
Supergirl '84
A Wedding '78
Zelig '83

Tisa Farrow
And Hope to Die '72
Fingers '78
Grim Reaper '81
Initiation of Sarah '78
The Last Hunter '80
Search and Destroy '81
Some Call It Loving '73
Strange Shadows in an Empty
   Room '76
Striking Back '81
Winter Kills '79
Zombie '80

Lena Farugia
The Gods Must Be Crazy 2
   '89

**Rainer Werner
Fassbinder**
Fox and His Friends '75
Kamikaze '89 '83

Nikki Fastinetti
Alien Private Eye '87

Fat Boys
Knights of the City '85
Krush Groove '85

Chow Yung Fat
Triad Savages

Rikki Fataar
All You Need Is Cash '78

**Alexandre
Fatiouchine**
Solo Voyage: The Revenge
   '90

Walter Fenner
The Shanghai Cobra '45

Frank Fenton
The Golden Stallion '49
Isle of Forgotten Sins '43
Mexican Hayride '48
Naked Hills '56

Lance Fenton
Heathers '89
Night of the Demons '88

Leslie Fenton
F.P. 1 '33
Fugitive Road '34
The House of Secrets '37
Lady Killer '33
Marie Galante '34
Murder at Midnight '31
Public Enemy '31

Sarah-Jane Fenton
The Bachelor '93

Simon Fenton
Matinee '92

Colm Feore
Beautiful Dreamers '92
Blades of Courage '88
Personals '90

Scott Feraco
Nasty Hero '89

Maurice Feraudy
Crainquebille '23

Pamelyn Ferdin
Sealab 2020 '72
The Toolbox Murders '78

Tawny Fere
Angel 3: The Final Chapter '88
Night Children '89
Rockula '90

Adam Ferency
The Interrogation '82

Al Ferguson
Laramie Kid '35
Lightning Raiders '45
Roamin' Wild '36
Rose Marie '54
Tarzan the Tiger '29

Andrew Ferguson
Miracle Down Under '87

Casson Ferguson
Cobra '25

J. Don Ferguson
Loveless '83
Running Mates '86

Jane Ferguson
Mystery Mansion '83

Jean Ferguson
Gun Girls '56

Kathleen Ferguson
Nightmare '82

Marlow Ferguson
American Tickler '76

Karen Fergusson
An Angel at My Table '89

John Ferita
Video Murders '87

Lawrence Ferlinghetti
Kerouac '84

Maria Fernanda
Hijazo de Mi Vidaza '70s

Fernandel
Angele '34

Around the World in 80 Days '56
Dressmaker '56
Fernandel the Dressmaker '57
The French Touch '54
Harvest '37
Little World of Don Camillo '51
The Man in the Raincoat '57
Nais '45
Pantaloons '57
Paris Holiday '57
The Sheep Has Five Legs '54
Topaze '51
Well-Digger's Daughter '46

Abel Fernandez
Rose Marie '54

Angel Fernandez
Street Warriors, Part 2 '87

Arturo Fernandez
Sound of Horror '64

Eddie Fernandez
The Vampire People '66

Emilio Fernandez
Bring Me the Head of Alfredo Garcia '74
Duelo en el Dorado

Esther Fernandez
Pancho Villa Returns '50

Evelina Fernandez
American Me '92

Jaime Fernandez
El Forastero Vengador '65
Emiliano Zapata '87
Los Hermanos Centella '65
Samson vs. the Vampire Women '61

Jesus Fernandez
Nazarin '58

Juan Fernandez
The Amazing Transplant '70
Cat Chaser '89
Kinjite: Forbidden Subjects '89
Liquid Dreams '92

Lucia Gil Fernandez
La Ley del Revolver '78

Maribel Fernandez
Bus Station '88

Miguel Fernandez
The Kidnapping of the President '80
Sorry, Wrong Number '89
True Believer '89

Ricardo Fernandez
Y Donde Esta el Muerto? (And... Where Is the Dead) '87

Vicente Fernandez
Tacos al Carbon '87

Wilhelmenia Wiggins Fernandez
Diva '82

Rudolf Fernau
The Invisible Dr. Mabuse '62

Didier Ferney
Toto le Heros '91

Rachid Ferrache
My Other Husband '85

Catherine Ferran
Baxter '89

Sabrina Ferrand
Sinners '89

Tony Ferrandis
Heat of the Flame '82

Tim Ferrante
A Taste for Flesh and Blood '90

Juan Ferrara
La Hija del General '84

Ashley Ferrare
Cyclone '87

Christina Ferrare
Mary, Mary, Bloody Mary '76

Antonio Ferrari
The Tree of Wooden Clogs '78

Nick Ferrari
Baby It's You '82

Sarah Ferrati
The Witch '66

Rebecca Ferratti
Cheerleader Camp '88
Gor '88
Outlaw of Gor '87

Francis Ferre
Bridge to Hell '87

Jamie Ferreira
Danger Zone '87

Taumaturgo Ferreira
Subway to the Stars '87

Conchata Ferrell
Backfield in Motion '91
Deadly Hero '76
Eye on the Sparrow '91
Family Prayers '91
Heartland '81
Lost Legacy: A Girl Called Hatter Fox '77
Portrait of a White Marriage '88
Rape and Marriage: The Rideout Case '80
To Love Again '80
True Romance '93
Where the River Runs Black '86

Tyra Ferrell
Boyz N the Hood '91
Lady Beware '87
Poetic Justice '93
Ulterior Motives '92
White Men Can't Jump '92

Andrea Ferreol
Control '87
Despair '79
The Last Metro '80
The Sleazy Uncle '89
Stroke of Midnight '90
Three Brothers '80
A Zed & Two Noughts '88

Jose Ferrer
The Art of Crime '75
The Being '83
Berlin Tunnel 21 '81
The Big Brawl '80
Big Bus '76
Blood Tide '82
Bloody Birthday '80
The Caine Mutiny '54
Christopher Columbus '85
Cyrano de Bergerac '50
Deep in My Heart '54
Dune '84
Enter Laughing '67
The Evil That Men Do '84
The Fifth Musketeer '79
Gideon's Trumpet '80

The Greatest Story Ever Told '65
Hired to Kill '91
The Horror of It All '91
Joan of Arc '48
Lawrence of Arabia '62
A Life of Sin '92
The Little Drummer Boy '68
A Midsummer Night's Sex Comedy '82
Miss Sadie Thompson '53
Moulin Rouge '52
Natural Enemies '79
Old Explorers '90
Order to Kill '73
Paco '75
Pleasure Palace '80
The Private Files of J. Edgar Hoover '77
Samson and Delilah '84
Seduced '85
The Sentinel '76
Ship of Fools '65
Strange Interlude '90
The Swarm '78
To Be or Not to Be '83
Voyage of the Damned '76
Who Has Seen the Wind? '77
Zoltan...Hound of Dracula '77

Lupita Ferrer
Balboa '82
Children of Sanchez '79

Mel Ferrer
Blood and Roses '61
Born to Be Bad '50
Brannigan '75
City of the Walking Dead '83
Deadly Game '83
Eaten Alive '76
Elena and Her Men '56
Emerald Jungle '80
The Fall of the Roman Empire '64
The Fifth Floor '80
The Great Alligator '81
The Hands of Orlac '60
Hi-Riders '77
Knights of the Round Table '53
Lili '53
The Longest Day '62
Norseman '78
One Shoe Makes It Murder '82
Outrage! '86
Paris When It Sizzles '64
Rancho Notorious '52
Scaramouche '52
Sex and the Single Girl '64
The Tempter '74
The Visitor '80
War and Peace '56

Miguel Ferrer
Deepstar Six '89
Flashpoint '84
The Harvest '93
Hot Shots! Part Deux '93
Lovelines '84
Point of No Return '93
Python Wolf '88
Revenge '90
RoboCop '87
Another Stakeout '93
Star Trek 3: The Search for Spock '84

Tony Ferrer
Blind Rage '78

Marco Ferreri
Bellissimo: Images of the Italian Cinema '87

Martin Ferrero
High Spirits '88

Jurassic Park '93
Planes, Trains & Automobiles '87
Stop! or My Mom Will Shoot '92

Eve Ferret
Foreign Body '86

Diana Ferreti
La Hora 24 '87

Benoit Ferreux
Murmur of the Heart '71

Alessandra Ferri
Dancers '87

Mark Alan Ferri
Getting It On '83

Peter Ferri
Fly with the Hawk

Babette Ferrier
Chloe in the Afternoon '72

Noel Ferrier
Adventures of Eliza Fraser '76
Great Expectations: The Untold Story '87
Return of Captain Invincible '83

Martine Ferriere
Mississippi Mermaid '69

Carla Ferrigno
Black Roses '88
Seven Magnificent Gladiators '84

Lou Ferrigno
All's Fair '89
The Cage '89
Death of the Incredible Hulk '90
Desert Warrior '88
Hercules '83
Hercules 2 '85
The Incredible Hulk '77
The Incredible Hulk Returns '88
Liberty & Bash '90
Pumping Iron '76
Seven Magnificent Gladiators '84
Sinbad of the Seven Seas '89
The Trial of the Incredible Hulk '89

Barbara Ferris
Children of the Damned '63
A Chorus of Disapproval '89
Nice Girl Like Me '69

Irena Ferris
Covergirl '83

John Ferris
Monique '83
Torpedo Attack '72

Loraine Ferris
Cycle Vixens '79

Turi Ferro
Malicious '74

Frank Ferrucci
The Hitman '91

David Ferry
Men of Steel '88
Tales of the Klondike: Race for Number One '87

Gabriel Ferzetti
Angel in a Taxi '59
Appassionata '74
Basileus Quartet '82
Counter Punch '71
Julia and Julia '87
L'Avventura '60

Flynn ►cont.

Against All Flags '52
Assault of the Rebel Girls '59
Captain Blood '35
The Charge of the Light
  Brigade '36
Dawn Patrol '38
Desperate Journey '42
Dive Bomber '41
Dodge City '39
Edge of Darkness '43
Escape Me Never '47
Gentleman Jim '42
Hollywood Bloopers '50s
It's a Great Feeling '49
Kim '50
The King's Rhapsody '55
Let's Make Up '55
The Master of Ballantrae '53
Northern Pursuit '43
Objective, Burma! '45
The Prince and the Pauper '37
The Private Lives of Elizabeth
  & Essex '39
San Antonio '45
Santa Fe Trail '40
The Sea Hawk '40
Silver River '48
The Sisters '38
Thank Your Lucky Stars '43
That Forsyte Woman '50
They Died with Their Boots
  On '41
Virginia City '40
The Warriors '55

Jerome Flynn
Edward II '92

Joe Flynn
The Computer Wore Tennis
  Shoes '69
Gentle Savage '73
Lover Come Back '61
Million Dollar Duck '71
My Dog, the Thief '69
Now You See Him, Now You
  Don't '72
Superdad '73

John Flynn
Split '90

Kelly Flynn
A Patch of Blue '65

Kimberly Flynn
Revolution! A Red Comedy
  '91

Miriam Flynn
18 Again! '88
National Lampoon's
  Christmas Vacation '89

Sean Flynn
Dos Postolas Gemelas '65
Mission to Venice '63
Son of Captain Blood '62

Spiros Focas
The Jewel of the Nile '85
Rambo 3 '88

Nina Foch
An American in Paris '51
Child of Glass '78
Columbo: Prescription Murder
  '67
Cry of the Werewolf '44
Dark Past '49
Dixie Lanes '88
Executive Suite '54
Illegal '55
Jennifer '78
Mahogany '75
Return of the Vampire '43

St. Benny the Dip '51
Salty '73
Scaramouche '52
Skin Deep '89
Sliver '93
A Song to Remember '45
Spartacus '60
The Ten Commandments '56

Brenda Fogarty
Deadly Fieldtrip '74
Fairytales '79

Vladimar Fogel
Bed and Sofa '27
The Girl with the Hat Box '27

Kick Fairbanks Fogg
Alien Space Avenger '91

Erzebet Foldi
All That Jazz '79

Dave Foley
The Best of the Kids in the
  Hall '93

Ellen Foley
Fatal Attraction '87
Married to the Mob '88

Macka Foley
Las Vegas Weekend '85
WarCat '88

Michael Foley
The Divine Enforcer '91
Intent to Kill '92
Prison Planet '92

Sandra Foley
Assault with a Deadly Weapon
  '82

Randy Follet
John and the Missus '87

Megan Follows
Anne of Avonlea '87
Anne of Green Gables '85
Back to Hannibal: The Return
  of Tom Sawyer and
  Huckleberry Finn '90s
The Chase '91
Hockey Night '84
The Nutcracker Prince '91
Silver Bullet '85
Stacking '87
Termini Station '91
A Time of Destiny '88

Megan Folson
Heartland '81

Bridget Fonda
Aria '88
Army of Darkness '92
Doc Hollywood '91
Frankenstein Unbound '90
The Godfather, Part 3 '90
Iron Maze '91
Jacob Have I Loved '88
Leather Jackets '90
Light Years '88
Out of the Rain '90
Point of No Return '93
Scandal '89
Shag: The Movie '89
Single White Female '92
Singles '92
Strapless '90
You Can't Hurry Love '88

Henry Fonda
Advise and Consent '62
Ash Wednesday '73
Battle of the Bulge '65
Battleforce '78
Bernice Bobs Her Hair '76
The Best Man '64

A Big Hand for the Little Lady
  '66
Big Street '42
The Boston Strangler '68
The Cheyenne Social Club '70
City on Fire '78
Clarence Darrow '78
The Displaced Person '76
Drums Along the Mohawk '39
Fail-Safe '64
The Farmer Takes a Wife '35
Fort Apache '48
The Fugitive '48
Gideon's Trumpet '80
Golden Age of Hollywood '77
The Grapes of Wrath '40
The Great Battle '79
Great Smokey Roadblock '76
Home to Stay '79
How the West was Won '63
I Dream Too Much '35
Immortal Sergeant '43
In Harm's Way '65
Jesse James '39
Jezebel '38
Jigsaw '49
The Lady Eve '41
Last Four Days '77
The Longest Day '62
Mad Miss Manton '38
Madigan '68
The Magnificent Dope '42
The Man That Corrupted
  Hadleyburg '80
Meteor '79
Midway '76
Mister Roberts '55
Moon's Our Home '36
My Darling Clementine '46
My Name is Nobody '74
Night Flight from Moscow '73
Oldest Living Graduate '82
On Golden Pond '81
Once Upon a Time in the West
  '68
The Ox-Bow Incident '43
Rappaccini's Daughter '80
The Red Pony '76
Return of Frank James '40
Rollercoaster '77
Roots: The Next Generation
  '79
The Rounders '65
Sex and the Single Girl '64
Sometimes a Great Notion '71
Stage Struck '57
Summer Solstice '81
The Swarm '78
Tentacles '77
That Certain Woman '37
There was a Crooked Man '70
Tin Star '57
Too Late the Hero '70
Twelve Angry Men '57
Wanda Nevada '79
War and Peace '56
Warlock '59
The Wrong Man '56
You Only Live Once '37
Young Mr. Lincoln '39
Yours, Mine & Ours '68

Jane Fonda
Agnes of God '85
Any Wednesday '66
Barbarella '68
Barefoot in the Park '67
California Suite '78
Cat Ballou '65
The Chase '66
The China Syndrome '79
Circle of Love '64
Comes a Horseman '78
Coming Home '78
The Dollmaker '84
A Doll's House '73

The Electric Horseman '79
Fun with Dick and Jane '77
The Game is Over '66
Joy House '64
Julia '77
Klute '71
Morning After '86
9 to 5 '80
Old Gringo '89
On Golden Pond '81
Period of Adjustment '62
Rollover '81
Spirits of the Dead '68
Stanley and Iris '90
Steelyard Blues '73
Tall Story '60
They Shoot Horses, Don't
  They? '69
Walk on the Wild Side '62

Peter Fonda
Cannonball Run '81
Certain Fury '85
Dirty Mary Crazy Larry '74
Easy Rider '69
Fatal Mission '89
Fighting Mad '76
Futureworld '76
Hawken's Breed '87
High Ballin' '78
Hired Hand '71
Hollywood Uncensored '87
The Hostage Tower '80
Jungle Heat '84
Killer Force '75
The Last Movie '71
Lilith '64
Mercenary Fighters '88
92 in the Shade '76
Outlaw Blues '77
Race with the Devil '75
The Rose Garden '89
South Beach '92
Spasms '82
Spirits of the Dead '68
Split Image '82
Tammy and the Doctor '63
The Trip '67
Wanda Nevada '79
The Wild Angels '66

Phil Fondacaro
Ghoulies 2 '88
Meridian: Kiss of the Beast
  '90

Stephanie Fondue
The Cheerleaders '72

Allen Fong
Just Like Weather '86

Au Fong
The White Butterfly Killer

Benson Fong
Charlie Chan in the Secret
  Service '44
The Chinese Cat '44
Conquest of Space '55
Deception '46
Girls! Girls! Girls! '62
His Majesty O'Keefe '53
Kung Fu: The Movie '86
Our Man Flint '66
The Purple Heart '44
The Scarlet Clue '45
The Shanghai Cobra '45

Chee Fong
The White Butterfly Killer

Leo Fong
Blind Rage '78
Enforcer from Death Row '78
Killpoint '84
The Last Reunion '80
Low Blow '85
Ninja Nightmare '88

Samantha Fong
Swindle '92

Alisha Fontaine
French Quarter '78

Jean Fontaine
The Sinister Urge '60

Joan Fontaine
Annabel Takes a Tour/Maid's
  Night Out '38
Beyond a Reasonable Doubt
  '56
The Bigamist '53
Born to Be Bad '50
Casanova's Big Night '54
A Damsel in Distress '37
Decameron Nights '53
Gunga Din '39
Island in the Sun '57
Ivanhoe '52
Jane Eyre '44
Letter from an Unknown
  Woman '48
Maid's Night Out '38
A Million to One '37
Othello '52
Rebecca '40
September Affair '50
Suspicion '41
Until They Sail '57
Voyage to the Bottom of the
  Sea '61
The Women '39

William Fontaine
Hallelujah! '29

Genevieve Fontanel
Grain of Sand '84

Lynn Fontanne
The Guardsman '31

Catherine Fontenoy
Poil de Carotte '31

Guilherme Fontes
Subway to the Stars '87

Hallie Foote
Courtship '87
1918 '85
On Valentine's Day '86

Horton Foote, Jr.
Blood Red '88
1918 '85

Richard Foote
Dangerous Charter '62

Dick Foran
Atomic Submarine '59
Boy Meets Girl '38
Brighty of the Grand Canyon
  '67
Dangerous '35
Deputy Marshall '50
Earthworm Tractors '36
The Fighting 69th '40
Four Daughters '38
Guest Wife '45
The Mummy's Hand '40
My Little Chickadee '40
Petrified Forest '36
Private Buckaroo '42
Ride 'Em Cowboy '42
Riders of Death Valley '41
The Sisters '38
Winners of the West '40

June Foray
Looney Looney Looney Bugs
  Bunny Movie '81
Sabaka '55
Scruffy '80
Who Framed Roger Rabbit?
  '88

Forster ►cont.

Avalanche '78
The Banker '89
The Black Hole '79
The City '76
Committed '91
The Death Squad '73
Delta Force '86
Diplomatic Immunity '91
The Don is Dead '73
Goliath Awaits '81
Hollywood Harry '86
In Between '92
Journey Through Rosebud '72
Medium Cool '69
Once a Hero '88
Peacemaker '90
Satan's Princess '90
The Stalking Moon '69
Standing Tall '78
Stunts '77
Vigilante '83
Walking the Edge '83

Rudolph Forster
The Mad Executioners '65
The Return of Dr. Mabuse '61
The Threepenny Opera '31

Bruce Forsyth
Bedknobs and Broomsticks '71

Rosemary Forsyth
Columbo: Murder By the Book '71
The Gladiator '86
Gray Lady Down '77
My Father's House '75
Shenandoah '65
The War Lord '65
Whatever Happened to Aunt Alice? '69

Tony Forsyth
Wonderland '88

Drew Forsythe
Doctors and Nurses '82
A Test of Love '84
Wrangler '88

Henderson Forsythe
Carolina Skeletons '92
Crisis at Central High '80
Sessions '83

John Forsythe
The Ambassador's Daughter '56
And Justice for All '79
Cruise into Terror '78
Cry Panic '74
Destination Tokyo '43
The Happy Ending '69
In Cold Blood '67
Madame X '66
Murder Once Removed '71
Mysterious Two '82
Scrooged '88
Sizzle '81
Sniper '75
Terror on the 40th Floor '74
A Time for Miracles '80
Topaz '69
The Trouble with Harry '55
Users '78

Stephen Forsythe
Hatchet for the Honeymoon '70

William Forsythe
American Me '92
Career Opportunities '91

Dead Bang '89
Dick Tracy '90
The Gun in Betty Lou's Handbag '92
The Lightship '86
The Long, Hot Summer '86
Out for Justice '91
Patty Hearst '88
Raising Arizona '87
Savage Dawn '84
Stone Cold '91
Torrents of Spring '90
The Waterdance '91
Weeds '87

Fabrizio Forte
Padre Padrone '77

Josef Forte
Pals of the Saddle '38

Marlene Forte
The Bronx War '90

Nick Apollo Forte
Broadway Danny Rose '84

Albert Fortell
Nuclear Conspiracy '85
Scandalous '88
Time Troopers '89

Gregory Fortescue
The Carrier '87

Jane Forth
Trash '70

Nurla Forway
Hawk and Castile

Bob Fosse
Give a Girl a Break '53
Kiss Me Kate '53
The Little Prince '74
My Sister Eileen '55

Nicole Fosse
All That Jazz '79
A Chorus Line '85

Ernie Fosselius
Heat and Sunlight '87

Brigitte Fossey
Blue Country '77
Chanel Solitaire '81
Enigma '82
Forbidden Games '52
Going Places '74
Honor Among Thieves '68
La Boum '81
The Man Who Loved Women '77
Quintet '79
The Wanderer '67

Simche Fostel
Yidl Mitn Fidl '36

Barry Foster
Beyond the Next Mountain '87
Frenzy '72
Quiet Day In Belfast '74
Robbery '67

Charles Foster
Emmanuelle 5 '87

Clayton Foster
Hospital of Terror '78

Dianne Foster
Kentuckian '55
The King of the Roaring '20s: The Story of Arnold Rothstein '61
Last Hurrah '58
The Violent Men '55

Eric Foster
Grandma's House '88

Frances Foster
Enemy Territory '87

Gloria Foster
City of Hope '91
The House of Dies Drear '88
Leonard Part 6 '87
Man & Boy '71
To All My Friends on Shore '71

Helen Foster
Ghost City '32
The Road to Ruin '28
Saddle Buster '32
Young Blood '33

Jodie Foster
The Accused '88
Alice Doesn't Live Here Anymore '74
Backtrack '89
The Blood of Others '84
Bugsy Malone '76
Candleshoe '78
Carny '80
Five Corners '88
Foxes '80
Freaky Friday '76
The Hotel New Hampshire '84
The Little Girl Who Lives Down the Lane '76
Little Man Tate '91
Mesmerized '84
Napoleon and Samantha '72
O'Hara's Wife '82
One Little Indian '73
Shadows and Fog '92
Siesta '87
The Silence of the Lambs '91
Smile, Jenny, You're Dead '74
Sommersby '93
Stealing Home '88
Svengali '83
Taxi Driver '76
Tom Sawyer '73

Julia Foster
F. Scott Fitzgerald in Hollywood '76
Great McGonagall '75
Half a Sixpence '67
Henry VI, Part 3 '82
The Loneliness of the Long Distance Runner '62
Thirteenth Reunion '81

Kimberly Foster
It Takes Two '88

Lewis R. Foster
Laurel & Hardy Comedy Classics, Vol. 8 '30s

Lisa Foster
Blade Master '84

Marvin Foster
Mad Wax: The Surf Movie '90

Meg Foster
Adam at 6 A.M. '70
Backstab '90
Best of the Best 2 '93
Blind Fury '90
Carny '80
Different Story '78
Diplomatic Immunity '91
The Emerald Forest '85
Futurekick '91
James Dean '76
Jezebel's Kiss '90
The Legend of Sleepy Hollow '79
Leviathan '89
Masters of the Universe '87
The Osterman Weekend '83
Project: Shadowchaser '92
Relentless '89

Relentless 2: Dead On '91
Stepfather 2: Make Room for Daddy '89
They Live '88
Things in Their Season '74
Thumb Tripping '72
Ticket to Heaven '81
To Catch a Killer '92
Tripwire '89
The Wind '87

Norman Foster
Journey into Fear '42
Skyscraper Souls '32

Peter Foster
Dangerous Charter '62

Phil Foster
Bang the Drum Slowly '73
Conquest of Space '55
Hail '73

Preston Foster
American Empire '42
Annie Oakley '35
The Big Cat '49
Doctor X '32
Guadalcanal Diary '43
The Harvey Girls '46
I Am a Fugitive from a Chain Gang '32
I Shot Jesse James '49
The Informer '35
Kansas City Confidential '52
Ladies They Talk About '33
Last Days of Pompeii '35
The Last Mile '32
The Marshal's Daughter '53
My Friend Flicka '43
Ramrod '47
Sea Devils '37
Three Desperate Men '50
The Time Travelers '64

Robert Foster
Counterforce '87

Steffen Gregory Foster
Dead Pit '89

Susanna Foster
Phantom of the Opera '43

Andre Fouche
Cesar '36

Byron Foulger
Bells of San Fernando '47
The Devil's Partner '58
Hoppy Serves a Writ '43
The Panther's Claw '42
Prisoner of Zenda '37
Sullivan's Travels '41

Yiorgo Fountas
Stella '55

Alain Foures
Rape of Love '79

Noel Fournier
Fatal Chase '77

Silvia Fournier
World of the Vampires '60

Derek Fowlds
Over the Hill '93

Susannah Fowle
The Getting of Wisdom '77

Blaque Fowler
Tainted '88

Frank Fowler
The Atomic Brain '64

Harry Fowler
Fire Maidens from Outer Space '56

Flight from Singapore '62

Douglas Fowley
Bar-20 '43
Battleground '49
Behind Locked Doors '48
Cat Women of the Moon '53
Colt Comrades '43
Desperate '47
From Noon Till Three '76
It Could Happen to You '39
Lost Canyon '43
Meet the Mob '42
Mr. Wise Guy '42
North of the Border '46
Poor White Trash '57
Rider from Tucson '50
Scared to Death '47
Shake Hands with Murder '44
Sunset on the Desert '42
Susanna Pass '49
Tanks a Million '41
The White Buffalo '77
Wild Country '47

Angel Fox
The Arousers '70

Anne Marie Fox
Rabid Grannies '89

Bernard Fox
Arnold '73
House of the Dead '80
The Private Eyes '80
Zone of the Dead '78

Colin Fox
Beautiful Dreamers '92
My Pleasure Is My Business '74

Edgar Fox
Death Code Ninja '87

Edward Fox
Anastasia: The Mystery of Anna '86
Battle of Britain '69
The Big Sleep '78
The Bounty '84
A Bridge Too Far '77
The Cat and the Canary '79
The Crucifer of Blood '91
The Day of the Jackal '73
A Doll's House '73
The Dresser '83
The Duellists '78
Edward and Mrs. Simpson '80
Force 10 from Navarone '78
Gandhi '82
The Go-Between '71
The Mirror Crack'd '80
Never Say Never Again '83
Portrait of a Lady '67
Road to 1984
Robin Hood '91
Shaka Zulu '83
The Shooting Party '85
Skullduggery '70
Soldier of Orange '78
The Squeeze '77
Wild Geese 2 '85

Erika Fox
Hooch '76

Huckleberry Fox
The Blue Yonder '86
Konrad '90s
Misunderstood '84

Jack Fox
Thunder Score

James Fox
Absolute Beginners '86
Afraid of the Dark '92
The Chase '66
Cheyenne Rides Again '38

David Franklin
Early Frost '84
Rock & Roll Cowboys '92

Diane Franklin
Better Off Dead '85
Last American Virgin '82
Second Time Lucky '84
Terrorvision '86

Don Franklin
Fast Forward '84

Gloria Franklin
Drums of Fu Manchu '40
Without Warning '52

Joe Franklin
Ghoul School '90

John Franklin
The Addams Family '91
Children of the Corn '84

Pamela Franklin
And Soon the Darkness '70
David Copperfield '70
Eleanor & Franklin '76
Flipper's New Adventure '64
Food of the Gods '76
The Horse Without a Head '63
The Legend of Hell House '73
The Prime of Miss Jean
 Brodie '69
Satan's School for Girls '73
Screamer '74
A Tiger Walks '64
The Witching '72

Richard Franklin
Into the Night '85

Sidney Franklin
The Three Musketeers '21

William Franklyn
Quatermass 2 '57
The Satanic Rites of Dracula
 '73
Splitting Heirs '93

Chloe Franks
The House that Dripped Blood
 '71
Ivanhoe '82

Philip Franks
Bleak House '85

Mary Frann
Fatal Charm '92
I'm Dangerous Tonight '90

Fely Franquelli
Back to Bataan '45

Arthur Franz
Abbott & Costello Meet the
 Invisible Man '51
Atomic Submarine '59
Beyond a Reasonable Doubt
 '56
Bogie '80
Dream No Evil '75
Flight to Mars '52
Hellcats of the Navy '57
The Human Factor '75
Invaders from Mars '53
Jungle Patrol '48
The Member of the Wedding
 '52
Sisters of Death '76

Chris Franz
Stop Making Sense '84

Dennis Franz
Blow Out '81
Body Double '84
Die Hard 2: Die Harder '90
Dressed to Kill '80
Kiss Shot '89

The Package '89
Psycho 2 '83

Eduard Franz
The Burning Hills '56
Hollow Triumph '48
The Indian Fighter '55
Latin Lovers '53
One Minute to Zero '52
Outpost in Morocco '49
The Scar '48
Sins of Jezebel '54
The Story of Ruth '60

Filippa Franzen
The Sacrifice '86

Bill Fraser
Alias John Preston '56
Little Dorrit, Film 1: Nobody's
 Fault '88
Little Dorrit, Film 2: Little
 Dorrit's Story '88
Naughty Knights '71
Pirates '86

Brendan Fraser
Dogfight '91
Encino Man '92
School Ties '92

Brent Fraser
Wild Orchid 2: Two Shades of
 Blue '92

Christopher Fraser
Summer City '77

David Fraser
Teenage Mutant Ninja Turtles
 3 '93

Elisabeth Fraser
Ask Any Girl '59
The Man Who Came to Dinner
 '41
A Patch of Blue '65
The Tunnel of Love '58
Two for the Seesaw '62
Young at Heart '54

Hugh Fraser
The Draughtsman's Contract
 '82

John Fraser
Horsemasters '61
Isadora '68
Repulsion '65

Liz Fraser
Adventures of a Taxi Driver
 '76
The Americanization of Emily
 '64
Carry On Cruising '62
Chicago Joe & the Showgirl
 '90
Two-Way Stretch '60

Moyra Fraser
The Boy Friend '71

Phyllis Fraser
Tough to Handle '37
Western Double Feature 3 '36
Winds of the Wasteland '36

Richard Fraser
Bedlam '45
The Cobra Strikes '48
The Private Affairs of Bel Ami
 '47
White Pongo '45

Ronald Fraser
The Killing of Sister George
 '69
Rentadick '72

Sally Fraser
Dangerous Charter '62

Giant from the Unknown '58
It Conquered the World '56
The War of the Colossal Beast
 '58

Stuart Fratkin
Dr. Alien '88
Prehysteria '93
Remote '93
Ski School '91

Charles Frawley
The Devil's Playground '76

William Frawley
Abbott & Costello Meet the
 Invisible Man '51
The Adventures of
 Huckleberry Finn '39
Babe Ruth Story '48
The Bride Came C.O.D. '41
Down to Earth '47
East Side, West Side '49
Fighting Seabees '44
Flame of the Barbary Coast
 '45
The General Died at Dawn '36
Gentleman Jim '42
Harmony Lane '35
The Inner Circle '46
The Lemon Drop Kid '51
Miracle on 34th Street '47
Monsieur Verdoux '47
Rancho Notorious '52
Something to Sing About '36
Whistling in Brooklyn '43
Wildcat '42

Jane Frazee
The Gay Ranchero '42
Grand Canyon Trail '48
Last of the Wild Horses '49
On the Old Spanish Trail '47
Springtime in the Sierras '47
Under California Stars '48

Quincy Frazer
Forgotten Warrior '86

Robert Frazer
Dawn Express '42
Death from a Distance '36
The Drake Case '29
Fighting Parson '35
Fighting Pilot '35
Found Alive '34
Monte Carlo Nights '34
Mystery Trooper '32
Renfrew on the Great White
 Trail '38
Saddle Buster '32
Ten Nights in a Bar-Room '31
Trail of the Royal Mounted '34

Rupert Frazer
The Girl in a Swing '89

Sheila Frazier
Firehouse '72
The Hitter '79
Superfly '72
Superfly T.N.T. '73
Three the Hard Way '74

Sterling Frazier
Starhops '78

Patrick Frbezar
Ninja of the Magnificence '89

Stan Freberg
Amazing Stories, Book 2 '86
Lady and the Tramp '55
Pogo for President: "I Go
 Pogo" '84

Mark Frechette
Zabriskie Point '70

Peter Frechette
No Small Affair '84

Paint It Black '89

**Freddie & the
Dreamers**
Seaside Swingers '65

**Freddie Redd
Quartet**
The Connection '61

Blanche Frederici
A Farewell to Arms '32
Night Nurse '31
Sadie Thompson '28

Lynne Frederick
Amazing Mr. Blunden '72
Phase 4 '74
Prisoner of Zenda '79
Schizo '77
Vampire Circus '71
Voyage of the Damned '76

Pauline Frederick
Smouldering Fires '25

Rick Frederick
Let's Kill All the Lawyers '93

Vicki Frederick
...All the Marbles '81
Body Rock '84
Chopper Chicks in
 Zombietown '91
A Chorus Line '85

Dean Fredericks
The Phantom Planet '61

Nina Fredric
2069: A Sex Odyssey '78

Christa Free
Revealing of Elsie '86

Alan Freed
Go, Johnny Go! '59
Rock, Rock, Rock '56

Bert Freed
The Cobweb '55
Detective Story '51
Evel Knievel '72
The Halls of Montezuma '50
Men of the Fighting Lady '54

Rona Freed
The Penitent '88

Sam Freed
Call Me '88

Danny Freedman
Fortune and Men's Eyes '71

Harry Freedman
Storm '87

Al Freeman, Jr.
The Defense Never Rests '90
The Detective '68
Ensign Pulver '64
Finian's Rainbow '68
Malcolm X '92
My Sweet Charlie '70
Perry Mason Returns '85
Seven Hours to Judgment '88

Eric Freeman
Silent Night, Deadly Night 2
 '87

Howard Freeman
Air Raid Wardens '43
Double Dynamite '51
Million Dollar Mermaid '52
Scaramouche '52

J.E. Freeman
Aces: Iron Eagle '92
Casualties of Love: The
 "Long Island Lolita" Story
 '93
Hard Traveling '85

Memphis '91
Miller's Crossing '90
Wild at Heart '90

Joan Freeman
Fastest Guitar Alive '68
Panic in the Year Zero! '62
The Rounders '65
Roustabout '64
Tower of London '62

John Freeman
Buffalo Rider '78

Jonathan Freeman
Aladdin '92

Kathleen Freeman
Disorderly Orderly '64
The Errand Boy '61
Hollywood Chaos '89
In the Mood '87
Love is Better Than Ever '52
Malibu Bikini Shop '86
The Nutty Professor '63
The Rounders '65
The Willies '90

Mona Freeman
Battle Cry '55
Black Beauty '46
Black Beauty/Courage of
 Black Beauty '57
Branded '50
Copper Canyon '50
Dear Wife '49
Jumping Jacks '52
That Brennan Girl '46
The Way Out '56

Morgan Freeman
Blood Money: The Story of
 Clinton and Nadine '88
The Bonfire of the Vanities '90
Brubaker '80
Clean and Sober '88
Driving Miss Daisy '89
Execution of Raymond
 Graham '85
Eyewitness '81
Glory '89
Harry & Son '84
Johnny Handsome '89
Lean on Me '89
Marie '85
The Power of One '92
Robin Hood: Prince of Thieves
 '91
Roll of Thunder, Hear My Cry
 '78
Street Smart '87
Teachers '84
That Was Then...This Is Now
 '85
Unforgiven '92

Paul Freeman
Aces: Iron Eagle 3 '92
The Dogs of War '81
Eminent Domain '91
Murderers Among Us: The
 Simon Wiesenthal Story '89
Prisoner of Rio '89
Raiders of the Lost Ark '81
The Sender '82
Shanghai Surprise '86
Unsuitable Job for a Woman
 '82
Whose Child Am I? '75
Without a Clue '88
A World Apart '88

Tony Freeman
Invincible Gladiators '64
Ocean Drive Weekend '85

Willie Freeman
Leopard Fist Ninja '80s

The Children's Hour '61
Darby's Rangers '58
Decoration Day '90
Duel at Diablo '66
The Fan '81
Fire in the Sky '93
The Glitter Dome '84
Grand Prix '66
The Great Escape '63
Hour of the Gun '67
How Sweet It Is! '68
A Man Called Sledge '71
Marlowe '69
Murphy's Romance '85
One Little Indian '73
Sayonara '57
Skin Game '71
Sunset '88
Support Your Local Gunfighter '71
Support Your Local Sheriff '69
Tank '83
They Only Kill Their Masters '72
The Thrill of It All! '63
Up Periscope '59
Victor/Victoria '82
The Wheeler Dealers '63

Katrina Garner
Halloween Night '90

Peggy Ann Garner
Betrayal '78
The Big Cat '49
The Cat '66
Eight Witnesses '54
Jane Eyre '44
The Keys of the Kingdom '44
The Lovable Cheat '49
A Tree Grows in Brooklyn '45
A Wedding '78

Gale Garnett
The Children '80
Mr. & Mrs. Bridge '91

James Garnett
Blood Screams '88

Tay Garnett
Challenge To Be Free '76
Strong Man '26

Pauline Garon
The Average Woman '24

Eddie Garr
Varieties on Parade '52

Teri Garr
After Hours '85
The Black Stallion '79
The Black Stallion Returns '83
Close Encounters of the Third Kind '77
The Conversation '74
Escape Artist '82
First Born '84
Full Moon in Blue Water '88
Head '68
The History of White People in America '85
Honky Tonk Freeway '81
Let It Ride '89
Miracles '86
Mr. Mike's Mondo Video '79
Mr. Mom '83
Mom and Dad Save the World '92
Oh, God! '77
Once Upon a Brothers Grimm '77
One from the Heart '82
Out Cold '89
The Player '92
Prime Suspect '82
Short Time '90
Speedway '68

Steve Martin Live '85
The Sting 2 '83
The Tale of the Frog Prince '83
To Catch a King '84
Tootsie '82
Waiting for the Light '90
Witches' Brew '79
Young Frankenstein '74

Martin Garralaga
The Fighter '52
In Old New Mexico '45
South of Monterey '47
Susanna Pass '49

Ivo Garrani
Black Sunday '60
The Day the Sky Exploded '57
The Giant of Marathon '60
Great Leaders of the Bibles '70s
Street People '76
Waterloo '71

Donna Garrat
Diamonds are Forever '71

Betty Garrett
My Sister Eileen '55
Neptune's Daughter '49
On the Town '49
Take Me Out to the Ball Game '49
Words and Music '48

Eliza Garrett
Schlock '73
Terraces '77

Hank Garrett
Blood Frenzy '87
The Boys Next Door '85
Rosebud Beach Hotel '85

Leif Garrett
The Banker '89
Cheerleader Camp '88
Kid Vengeance '75
The Outsiders '83
Party Line '88
Peter Lundy and the Medicine Hat Stallion '77
Shaker Run '85
Skateboard '77
Spirit of '76 '91
Thunder Alley '85
Walking Tall: The Final Chapter '77

Patsy Garrett
Benji '74
For the Love of Benji '77

Roger Garrett
Night of the Cobra Woman '72
The Passing of Evil '70

Barbara Garrick
The Firm '93
Sleepless In Seattle '93

John Garrick
Broken Melody '34
Lily of Killarney '34
Lottery Bride '30
Song O' My Heart '29

Rian Garrick
Mooncussers '62

Barbara Garrison
Courier of Death '84

David Garrison
Homeboys '92

Jim Garrison
JFK '91

Miranda Garrison
Salsa '88

Pat Garrison
The Flying Saucer '50

Riccardo Garrone
Terror Creatures from the Grave '66
Two Nights with Cleopatra '54

Bob Garry
Summer Heat '73

Greer Garson
Blossoms in the Dust '41
Goodbye, Mr. Chips '39
The Happiest Millionaire '67
Invincible Mr. Disraeli '63
Julia Misbehaves '48
Julius Caesar '53
The Little Drummer Boy '68
Little Women '78
Madame Curie '43
The Miniver Story '50
Mrs. Miniver '42
Mrs. Parkington '44
Pride and Prejudice '40
Random Harvest '42
The Singing Nun '66
Sunrise at Campobello '60
That Forsyte Woman '50
When Ladies Meet '41

Willie Garson
Untamed Heart '93

Christopher Gartin
Matters of the Heart '90
No Big Deal '83

Elizabeth Garvie
Pride and Prejudice '85

Anita Garvin
Laurel & Hardy Comedy Classics, Vol. 2 '30

John Garwood
Hell's Angels on Wheels '67
A Taste of Hell '73

Arthur Gary
Catholic Hour '60

Christopher Gary
Planet Earth '74

Lorraine Gary
The Crash of Flight 401 '78
Jaws '75
Jaws 2 '78
Jaws: The Revenge '87
1941 '79
Pray for the Wildcats '74

Miguel Garza
La Montana del Diablo '87

Fernando Garzon
Sex Crimes '92

Jean Gascon
A Man Called Horse '70

Alessandro Gassman
Sacrilege '86

Vittorio Gassman
Big Deal on Madonna Street '58
Bitter Rice '49
Catch as Catch Can '68
The Easy Life '63
The Family '87
The Great War '59
Il Sorpasso '63
Immortal Bachelor '80
Lure of the Sila '49
Mambo '55
The Palermo Connection '91
Quintet '79
Rhapsody '54
Sharky's Machine '81

The Sleazy Uncle '89
Sweet Smell of Woman '75
The Tempest '82
Tiger and the Pussycat '67
12 Plus 1 '70
War and Peace '56
We All Loved Each Other So Much '77
A Wedding '78
Woman Times Seven '67

Lisa Gastoni
The Baby and the Battleship '56
The Great Armored Car Swindle '64
Messalina vs. the Son of Hercules '64
Submission '77
Tharus Son of Attila '87
Wild, Wild Planet '65

Anthony Gates
L.A. Crackdown 2 '88

John W. Gates
Legend of Boggy Creek '75

Larry Gates
Death of a Gunfighter '69
Funny Lady '75
The Henderson Monster '80
The Sand Pebbles '66
Toys in the Attic '63
Underworld, U.S.A. '60

Nancy Gates
The Atomic City '52
Check Your Guns '48
The Great Gildersleeve '43
Master Race '44
The Search for Bridey Murphy '56
Some Came Running '58
Suddenly '54
Torch Song '53

Jimmy Gatherum
Amazing Stories, Book 5 '85

Jerry Gatlin
Train Robbers '73

Jill Gatsby
The Ambulance '90
Return to Salem's Lot '87

Jennifer Gatti
Street Knight '93

Valerie Gaunt
The Curse of Frankenstein '57
The Horror of Dracula '58

Mikkel Gaup
Pathfinder '87

Sara Marit Gaup
Pathfinder '87

Dan Gauthier
Son-in-Law '93
Teen Witch '89

Matt Gauthier
Lords of Magick '88

Dick Gautier
Get Smart: The Movie '89
Glitch! '88
Marathon '80

Jack Gautier
Playtime '67

Cassandra Gava
The Amityville Curse '90

Yula Gavala
Silent Rebellion '82

Erica Gavin
Caged Heat '74

John Gavin
Back Street '61
Breath of Scandal '60
History of the World: Part 1 '81
House of Shadows '83
Imitation of Life '59
Jennifer '78
The Madwoman of Chaillot '69
Midnight Lace '60
Murder for Sale '70
Psycho '60
Sophia Loren: Her Own Story '80
Spartacus '60
Thoroughly Modern Millie '67
A Time to Love & a Time to Die '58

Cassandra Gaviola
The Black Room '82
Conan the Barbarian '82

Peter Gawthorne
Phantom Fiend '35

William Gaxton
Best Foot Forward '43
It's the Old Army Game '26

Arnette Gay
Zombie '80

Gregory Gay
Seven Doors to Death '44

Ramon Gay
The Curse of the Aztec Mummy '59
Curse of the Aztec Mummy/Robot vs. the Aztec Mummy '59
The Robot vs. the Aztec Mummy '59

Annie Gaybis
Hollywood Zap '86

Howard Gaye
Dante's Inferno '24
Flirting with Fate '16

Lisa Gaye
Castle of Evil '66
Class of Nuke 'Em High, Part 2: Subhumanoid Meltdown '91
Night of Evil '62
Shake, Rattle and Rock '57
The Sign of Zorro '60
Toxic Avenger, Part 3: The Last Temptation of Toxie '89

Marvin Gaye
Chrome and Hot Leather '71

Nora Gaye
Dubeat-E-O '84

Jackie Gayle
Bert Rigby, You're a Fool '89
Pepper and His Wacky Taxi '72
Tin Men '87

Monica Gayle
Nashville Girl '76
Switchblade Sisters '75
Undercover Vixens '87

Anna Gaylor
The Killing Game '67

Gerry Gaylor
Queen of Outer Space '58

Mitch Gaylord
American Anthem '86
American Tiger '89
Animal Instincts '92

Raymond Gaylord
Face of the Screaming
Werewolf '59

George Gaynes
Breaking Up Is Hard to Do '79
Dead Men Don't Wear Plaid
'82
It Came Upon a Midnight
Clear '84
Micki & Maude '84
Police Academy '84
Police Academy 2: Their First
Assignment '85
Police Academy 3: Back in
Training '86
Police Academy 4: Citizens on
Patrol '87
Police Academy 5:
Assignment Miami Beach
'88
Police Academy 6: City Under
Siege '89
Stepmonster '92

Janet Gaynor
The Farmer Takes a Wife '35
A Star is Born '37
Sunrise '27
Till the Clouds Roll By/A Star
Is Born '46
The Young in Heart '38

Jock Gaynor
Deathhead Virgin '74

Mitzi Gaynor
Birds & the Bees '56
For Love or Money '63
Les Girls '57
South Pacific '58
There's No Business Like
Show Business '54
We're Not Married '52

Eunice Gayson
Carry On Admiral '57
Dr. No '62
From Russia with Love '63

John Gazarian
Real Bullets '90

Wendy Gazelle
Hot Pursuit '87
Sammy & Rosie Get Laid '87
Triumph of the Spirit '89
Understudy: The Graveyard
Shift 2 '88

Ben Gazzara
Anatomy of a Murder '59
The Bridge at Remagen '69
Control '87
The Death of Richie '76
An Early Frost '85
Fireball Forward '72
High Velocity '76
The Killing of a Chinese
Bookie '76
Lies Before Kisses '92
Neptune Factor '73
Opening Night '77
Passionate Thief '60
Pursuit '72
QB VII '74
Question of Honor '80
Quicker Than the Eye '88
Richie '77
Road House '89
Saint Jack '79
Secret Obsession '88
Shattered Silence '71
Sicilian Connection '74
Sidney Sheldon's Bloodline
'79
Tales of Ordinary Madness
'83
They All Laughed '81

The Trial of Lee Harvey
Oswald '77
Voyage of the Damned '76

Michael Gazzo
Black Sunday '77
Cookie '89
Fingers '78
Gangsters '79
The Godfather 1902-1959:
The Complete Epic '81
The Godfather, Part 2 '74
Kill Castro '80
King of the Gypsies '78
Love and Bullets '79
The Mercenaries '80
Sweet Dirty Tony '81

Luella Gear
Phffft! '54

Valerie Gearon
Invasion '65

Anthony Geary
Crack House '89
Dangerous Love '87
High Desert Kill '90
The Imposter '84
Kicks '85
Night of the Warrior '91
Pass the Ammo '88
Penitentiary 3 '87
Scorchers '92
UHF '89
You Can't Hurry Love '88

Bud Geary
D-Day on Mars '45

Maine Geary
Robin Hood '22

Gordon Gebert
The Narrow Margin '52

Nicholas Gecks
Forever Young '85

Jason Gedrick
Backdraft '91
Crossing the Bridge '92
The Heavenly Kid '85
Iron Eagle '86
Massive Retaliation '85
Promised Land '88
Rooftops '89
Stacking '87
Still Life '92
The Zoo Gang '85

Prunella Gee
Never Say Never Again '83
The Wilby Conspiracy '75
Witching Time '84

Ellen Geer
Babe! '75
Bloody Birthday '80
Hard Traveling '85
Harold and Maude '71
Memory of Us '74
A Shining Season '79
Silence '73

Roman Geer
After the Fall of New York '85

Will Geer
Bandolero! '68
The Billion Dollar Hobo '78
Black Like Me '64
Broken Arrow '50
Brother John '70
Bunco '83
Dear Dead Delilah '72
Executive Action '73
The Hanged Man '74
Hurricane '74
Jeremiah Johnson '72
Lust for Gold '49

Memory of Us '74
Moving Violation '76
My Sister, My Love '78
Napoleon and Samantha '72
The President's Analyst '67
The Reivers '69
Salt of the Earth '54
Silence '73
Thanksgiving Story '73
Unknown Powers '80
The Waltons: The Children's
Carol '78
Winchester '73 '50
A Woman Called Moses '78

Judy Geeson
Adventures of a Taxi Driver
'76
Berserk! '67
Carry On England '76
Danger UXB '81
Doomwatch '72
Dynasty of Fear '72
The Executioner '70
Horror Planet '80
It Happened at Nightmare Inn
'70
Murder on the Midnight
Express '74
The Plague Dogs '82
10 Rillington Place '71
To Sir, with Love '67
Twinsanity '70

Sally Geeson
Cry of the Banshee '70
The Oblong Box '69

Deborah Geffner
Exterminator 2 '84

Martha Gehman
Father of the Bride '91
The Flamingo Kid '84
A Kiss Before Dying '91

Pleasant Gehman
The Runnin' Kind '89
The Running Kind '89

Lou Gehrig
Rawhide '38

William Geiger
Beyond the Door 3 '91

Joe "Corky" Geil
Our Gang Comedies '40s

Bob Geldof
Pink Floyd: The Wall '82
The Secret Policeman's Other
Ball '82

Ruth Geler
Hamsin '83

Daniel Gelin
Is Paris Burning? '68
La Ronde '51
Mademoiselle Striptease '57
The Man Who Knew Too
Much '56
Murmur of the Heart '71
The Testament of Orpheus
'59
A Woman of Rome '56

Manuel Gelin
Oasis of the Zombies '82

Gratien Gelinas
Agnes of God '85

Sarah Gellar
High Stakes '89

Larry Gelman
Chatterbox '76
Slumber Party '57 '76

Rhoda Gemignani
Concrete Beat '84

Giuliano Gemma
Battleforce '78
Blood at Sundown
Corleone '79
Erik, the Viking '72
Goliath and the Sins of
Babylon '64
Master Touch '74
Smugglers '75
Unsane '82
The Warning '80

Julian Gemma
The Opponent '89

Laura Gemser
Ator the Fighting Eagle '83
Black Cobra '83
Caged Women '84
Crime Busters '78
Emmanuelle in the Country
'78
Emmanuelle on Taboo Island
'76
Emmanuelle, the Queen '75
Emmanuelle's Daughter '79
Emperor Caligula: The Untold
Story '80s
Fury '80s
Love Camp '76
Naked Paradise '78
Women's Prison Massacre
'85

Denise Gence
Buffet Froid '79

**Francois-Eric
Gendron**
Boyfriends & Girlfriends '88
Cloud Waltzing '87

Bryan Genesse
California Casanova '89
Loose Screws '85

Sabryn Gene't
Illegal Entry: Formula for Fear
'93

Marcelle Geniat
Crime and Punishment '35

Leo Genn
Circus of Fear '67
Green for Danger '47
Henry V '44
Lady Chatterley's Lover '55
The Longest Day '62
Mackintosh Man '73
The Miniver Story '50
Moby Dick '56
The Snake Pit '48
Strange Case of Dr. Jekyll &
Mr. Hyde '68
Velvet Touch '48
When Thief Meets Thief '37
Wooden Horse '50

Lina Gennari
Umberto D '55

Dick Genola
The Psychic '68

Claude Gensac
Cloud Waltzing '87

Denise Gentile
Netherworld '91

Linda Gentile
To All a Goodnight '80

Nikki Gentile
Traveling Companions '86
Truck Stop

Robert Gentile
Strangers in the City '62

John Gentry
Hard Drivin' '60

Minnie Gentry
Def by Temptation '90
Georgia, Georgia '72

Roger Gentry
Alien Massacre '67
Horrors of the Red Planet '64

Lisa Geoffreion
Disturbance '89

Paul Geoffrey
Excalibur '81
Flame to the Phoenix '85

Stephen Geoffreys
The Chair '87
Fraternity Vacation '85
Fright Night '85
Moon 44 '90
976-EVIL '88

Brian George
Smokescreen '90

Chief Dan George
Americathon '79
The Bears & I '74
Cancel My Reservation '72
Dan Candy's Law '73
Harry and Tonto '74
Little Big Man '70
The Outlaw Josey Wales '76

Christopher George
AngKor: Cambodia Express
'81
Chisum '70
Cruise into Terror '78
Day of the Animals '77
Dixie Dynamite '76
El Dorado '67
Enter the Ninja '81
Exterminator '80
Gates of Hell '83
Graduation Day '81
Grizzly '76
Man on a String '71
Midway '76
Mortuary '81
Pieces '83
Train Robbers '73
Whiskey Mountain '77

Gladys George
The Best Years of Our Lives
'46
Detective Story '51
Flamingo Road '49
House Across the Bay '40
Lullaby of Broadway '51
The Maltese Falcon '41
Marie Antoinette '38
The Roaring Twenties '39

Goetz George
Out of Order '84

Grace George
Johnny Come Lately '43

Heinrich George
Jud Suess '40
Kolberg '45

Jan George
The American Soldier '70

Lynda Day George
Aliens from Spaceship Earth
'77
Ants '77
The Barbary Coast '74
Beyond Evil '80
Casino '80
Cruise into Terror '78

Glaudini ▶cont.

Chameleon '81

Louise Glaum
The Leopard Woman '20
Return of Draw Egan '16
Sex '20
The Three Musketeers '16

Eugene Glazer
Dollman '91

Jackie Gleason
All Through the Night '42
Don't Drink the Water '69
How to Commit Marriage '69
The Hustler '61
Izzy & Moe '85
Mr. Billion '77
Mister Halpren & Mister
    Johnson '83
Nothing in Common '86
Orchestra Wives '42
Papa's Delicate Condition '63
Smokey and the Bandit '77
Smokey and the Bandit, Part
    2 '80
Smokey and the Bandit, Part
    3 '83
Soldier in the Rain '63
Springtime in the Rockies '42
The Sting 2 '83
The Toy '82

James Gleason
Arsenic and Old Lace '44
The Bishop's Wife '47
The Clock '45
The Crooked Circle '32
Down to Earth '47
Ex-Mrs. Bradford '36
Falcon Takes Over/Strange
    Bargain '49
Footlight Serenade '42
Forever Female '53
A Free Soul '31
A Guy Named Joe '44
Here Comes Mr. Jordan '41
I'll See You in My Dreams '51
The Jackpot '50
The Keys of the Kingdom '44
Last Hurrah '58
Loving You '57
Meet John Doe '41
Miss Grant Takes Richmond
    '49
Movie Stuntmen '53
The Night of the Hunter '55
Suddenly '54
Tanks a Million '41
A Tree Grows in Brooklyn '45
Tycoon '47
We're Not Married '52
What Price Glory? '52
The Yellow Cab Man '50

Joanna Gleason
Crimes & Misdemeanors '89
F/X 2: The Deadly Art of
    Illusion '91
For Richer, For Poorer '92
Heartburn '86

Pat Gleason
Criminal Court '46
I Killed That Man '42
Rogue's Gallery '44
Swing It, Professor '37

Paul Gleason
Challenge of a Lifetime '85
Die Hard '88
The Ewoks: Battle for Endor
    '85
Forever, Lulu '87
Fourth Story '90

Ghost Chase '88
He Knows You're Alone '80
Johnny Be Good '88
Maniac Cop 3 '93
Miami Blues '90
Morgan Stewart's Coming
    Home '87
Night Game '89
Private Duty Nurses '71
Rich Girl '91
She's Having a Baby '88
Trading Places '83
Wild Cactus '92

Russell Gleason
All Quiet on the Western Front
    '30
Condemned to Live '35
The Flying Fool '29
I Can't Escape '34

Robert Gleckler
Defenders of the Law '31

Nicholas Gledhill
Careful, He Might Hear You
    '84

Michele Gleizer
Europa, Europa '91

Iain Glen
Fools of Fortune '90
Mountains of the Moon '90
Rosencrantz & Guildenstern
    Are Dead '90

**Candace
Glendenning**
Flesh and Blood Show '73

Cody Glenn
Border Shootout '90

Montgomery Glenn
Castle of Blood '64

Raymond Glenn
The Return of Boston Blackie
    '27

Roy Glenn
Carmen Jones '54
Jungle Drums of Africa '53

Scott Glenn
Angels Hard as They Come
    '71
Apocalypse Now '79
As Summers Die '86
The Baby Maker '70
Backdraft '91
The Challenge '82
Fighting Mad '76
The Hunt for Red October '90
Intrigue '90
The Keep '83
Man on Fire '87
Miss Firecracker '89
More American Graffiti '79
My Heroes Have Always Been
    Cowboys '91
Off Limits '87
Personal Best '82
The Player '92
The Right Stuff '83
The River '84
Shadowhunter '93
She Came to the Valley '77
The Shrieking '73
The Silence of the Lambs '91
Silverado '85
Urban Cowboy '80
Verne Miller '88
Wild Geese 2 '85
Women & Men: Stories of
    Seduction, Part 2 '91

Frank Glennon
Aces and Eights '36

Sharon Gless
The Crash of Flight 401 '78
Hardhat & Legs '80
Hobson's Choice '83
Letting Go '85
Revenge of the Stepford
    Wives '80
The Star Chamber '83
Tales of the Unexpected '91

Stacey Glick
Three O'Clock High '87

Robert Gligorov
Stagefright '87

Greg Glionna
Meet the Parents '91

Brian Glover
Alien 3 '92
An American Werewolf in
    London '81
The Company of Wolves '85
The McGuffin '85

Bruce Glover
Chrome Hearts '70
Diamonds are Forever '71
Ghost Town '88
Killcrazy '89
Stunts '77

Crispin Glover
At Close Range '86
Back to the Future '85
Friday the 13th, Part 4: The
    Final Chapter '84
Little Noises '91
My Tutor '83
Racing with the Moon '84
River's Edge '87
Rubin & Ed '92
Teachers '84
Twister '89
Where the Heart Is '90
Wild at Heart '90

Danny Glover
Bat 21 '88
Chu Chu & the Philly Flash '81
The Color Purple '85
Dead Man Out '89
Escape from Alcatraz '79
Flight of the Intruder '90
Grand Canyon '91
Iceman '84
Keeping On '81
Lethal Weapon '87
Lethal Weapon 2 '89
Lethal Weapon 3 '92
Lonesome Dove '89
Mandela '87
Memorial Day '83
Out '88
Places in the Heart '84
Predator 2 '90
Pure Luck '91
A Rage in Harlem '91
A Raisin in the Sun '89
Silverado '85
Stand-In '85
To Sleep with Anger '90
Witness '85

John Glover
Annie Hall '77
Apology '86
The Chocolate War '88
Dead on the Money '91
Drug Wars 2: The Cocaine
    Cartel '92
An Early Frost '85
El Diablo '90
Ernie Kovacs: Between the
    Laughter '84
The Evil That Men Do '84
52 Pick-Up '86

Gremlins 2: The New Batch
    '90
A Killing Affair '85
The Last Embrace '79
A Little Sex '82
Masquerade '88
Meet the Hollowheads '89
The Mountain Men '80
Rocket Gibraltar '88
Scrooged '88
Something Special '86
Traveling Man '89

Julian Glover
For Your Eyes Only '81
The Fourth Protocol '87
Hearts of Fire '87
Henry VIII '79
Indiana Jones and the Last
    Crusade '89
Ivanhoe '82
Mandela '87
The Secret Garden '87
The Story of Jacob & Joseph
    '74
Theatre of Death '67
Tom Jones '63
Treasure Island '89
Tusks '89

Kara Glover
The Beat '88
Caribe '87

Carlin Glynn
Blood Red '88
Continental Divide '81
Night Game '89
Sixteen Candles '84
The Trip to Bountiful '85

Mary Glynne
Scrooge '35

Mathias Gnaedinger
The Boat is Full '81
Journey of Hope '90

Hiromi Go
MacArthur's Children '85

Harry Goaz
Twin Peaks '90

Tito Gobbi
Musica Proibita '43

George Gobel
Better Late Than Never '79
Birds & the Bees '56
Ellie '84
The Fantastic World of D.C.
    Collins '84
I Married a Woman '56
Rabbit Test '78

Boy Gobert
Kamikaze '89 '83

Justin Gocke
My Grandpa is a Vampire '92

Jean-Luc Godard
Cleo from 5 to 7 '61
First Name: Carmen '83
King Lear '87

John Goddard
Naked Youth '59
Storm Rider '57

Mark Goddard
Blue Sunshine '78
The Death Squad '73
Roller Boogie '79
Strange Invaders '83

Patricia Goddard
Uneasy Terms '48

Paulette Goddard
Diary of a Chambermaid '46

The Ghost Breakers '40
The Great Dictator '40
The Making of a Legend:
    "Gone With the Wind" '89
Modern Times '36
Pot O' Gold '41
Reap the Wild Wind '42
Second Chorus '40
Sins of Jezebel '54
Time of Indifference '64
Unholy Four '54
The Women '39
The Young in Heart '38

Drew Godderis
Evil Spawn '87

Danielle Godet
The Elusive Pimpernel '50

Thomas Godet
Toto le Heros '91

Arthur Godfrey
Angel's Brigade '79
Flatbed Annie and Sweetiepie:
    Lady Truckers '79
The Glass Bottom Boat '66
Great Bank Hoax '78

Derek Godfrey
A Midsummer Night's Dream
    '68

Lynnie Godfrey
Eubie! '82

Terrie Godfrey
The Majorettes '87

Jacques Godin
Double Identity '89
The Man Inside '76
The Victory '88

Hector Godoy
Bring Me the Vampire '61

Vanda Godsell
This Sporting Life '63

Alexander Godunov
Die Hard '88
The Money Pit '86
The Runestone '91
Waxwork 2: Lost in Time '91
Witness '85

Dave Goelz
The Muppet Christmas Carol
    '92

Angela Goethals
Heartbreak Hotel '88
V.I. Warshawski '91

Michael C. Goetz
Deadly Encounter '72
Village of the Damned '60

Peter Michael Goetz
Beer '85
Father of the Bride '91
Jumpin' Jack Flash '86
King Kong Lives '86
Tagget '90

John Goff
The Alpha Incident '76
The Capture of Bigfoot '79
Devil & Leroy Basset '73
Getting Over '81
Night Stalker '87
Party Plane '90

Norris Goff
The Bashful Bachelor '42
Dreaming Out Loud '40

Hiromi Goh
Gonza the Spearman '86

Gila Golan
Catch as Catch Can '68

Our Man Flint '66
The Valley of Gwangi '69

Brandy Gold
Amityville 4 '89

Eleanor Gold
The New Gladiators '87

Tracey Gold
Shoot the Moon '82

Rubin Goldberg
Uncle Moses '32

Whoopi Goldberg
Best of Comic Relief '86
Best of Comic Relief '90 '90
Burglar '87
Clara's Heart '88
The Color Purple '85
Doctor Duck's Super Secret
All-Purpose Sauce '85
Fatal Beauty '87
Ghost '90
Homer and Eddie '89
Jumpin' Jack Flash '86
Kiss Shot '89
The Long Walk Home '89
Made in America '93
Pee-Wee's Playhouse
Christmas Special '88
The Player '92
Sarafina! '92
Sister Act '92
Soapdish '91
The Telephone '87

Harold Goldblatt
Children of the Damned '63

Jeff Goldblum
The Adventures of Buckaroo
Banzai Across the Eighth
Dimension '84
Annie Hall '77
Between the Lines '77
Beyond Therapy '86
The Big Chill '83
Death Wish '74
Deep Cover '92
Earth Girls are Easy '89
Ernie Kovacs: Between the
Laughter '84
Fathers and Sons '92
The Favor, the Watch, & the
Very Big Fish '92
The Fly '86
Framed '90
Into the Night '85
Invasion of the Body
Snatchers '78
Jurassic Park '93
The Legend of Sleepy Hollow
'79
Mr. Frost '89
The Player '92
Rehearsal for Murder '82
The Right Stuff '83
The Sentinel '76
Shooting Elizabeth '92
Silverado '85
Special Delivery '76
Strange Tales/Ray Bradbury
Theatre '86
The Tall Guy '89
Thank God It's Friday '78
The Three Little Pigs '84
Threshold '83
Transylvania 6-5000 '85
Twisted Obsession '90
Vibes '88

Annie Golden
Desperately Seeking Susan
'85
Forever, Lulu '87
Hair '79
Key Exchange '85

Love at Stake '87
National Lampoon's Class of
'86 '86
Streetwalkin' '85

Eddie Golden
Broth of a Boy '59

Marta Golden
Work/Police '16

**Norman D. Golden,
II**
Cop and a Half '93

Devin Goldenberg
Guess What We Learned in
School Today? '70

Martin Goldin
Fun Down There '88

Ricky Paull Goldin
Hyper-Sapien: People from
Another Star '86
Lambada '90
Mirror, Mirror '90

Sidney Goldin
East and West '23

Andrea Goldman
Blue Paradise '86

Danny Goldman
Swap Meet '79

Gary Goldman
Deranged '87

Philippe Goldman
Small Change '76

Lelia Goldoni
Choices '81
The Disappearance of Aimee
'76
Fatal Chase '77
The Spell '77
Theatre of Death '67

Matthew Goldsby
Student Bodies '81

Clio Goldsmith
The Gift '82
Heat of Desire '84
Honey '81
La Cicada '83

Jonathan Goldsmith
Phantom of the Mall: Eric's
Revenge '89

Saul Goldsmith
Mummy & Curse of the Jackal
'67

Allan Goldstein
The Lawrenceville Stories
'80s

Jenette Goldstein
Aliens '86
Near Dark '87
The Presidio '88

Jenney Goldstein
The Two Sisters '37

Michael Goldstein
Green Fields '37

Bob Goldthwait
Burglar '87
Hot to Trot! '88
Little Vegas '90
One Crazy Summer '86
Police Academy 3: Back in
Training '86
Police Academy 4: Citizens on
Patrol '87
Scrooged '88
Shakes the Clown '92

Shawn Goldwater
Rebel High '88

Tony Goldwyn
Ghost '90
Iran: Days of Crisis '91
Kuffs '92
Traces of Red '92

Valeria Golino
Hot Shots! '91
Hot Shots! Part Deux '93
The Indian Runner '91
A Joke of Destiny, Lying in
Wait Around the Corner
Like a Bandit '84
The King's Whore '90
Rain Man '88
Torrents of Spring '90
Year of the Gun '91

Francesco Golisano
Miracle in Milan '51

Alexander Golling
Geheimakte WB1 '42

Liza Golm
Come Back, Little Sheba '52
The Hoodlum '51

Arlene Golonka
Dr. Alien '88
Foxtrap '85
The Gumshoe Kid '89
The Hoboken Chicken
Emergency '84
The In-Laws '79
My Tutor '82

Marina Golovine
Olivier, Olivier '92
The Stolen Children '93

Minna Gombell
Doomed Caravan '41
The Great Waltz '38
I'll See You in My Dreams '51
The Merry Widow '34
Pagan Love Song '50
The Thin Man '34

Carlos Gomez
Silhouette '91

Consuelo Gomez
El Mariachi '93

Fernando Gomez
Gulliver '70s
Mama Turns a Hundred '79
Spirit of the Beehive '73
The Stilts '84

Jose Luis Gomez
In Memoriam '76

Panchito Gomez
Paco '75
Sweet 15 '90

Thomas Gomez
But Not for Me '59
The Conqueror '56
Force of Evil '49
The Magnificent Matador '55
The Merry Widow '52
Sorrowful Jones '49
Stay Away, Joe '68
Summer and Smoke '61

Toco Gomez
La Nueva Cigarra '86

Vincente Gomez
The Snows of Kilimanjaro '52

Mikhail Gomorov
The Battleship Potemkin '25

Milton Goncalves
Subway to the Stars '87

Mascha Gonska
Infernal Trio '74
Tea For Three '84

Dacia Gonzales
El Hombre de la Furia '65
La Hifa Sin Padre '87
Los Hermanos Centella '65

Mary Gonzales
The Lonely Sex '59

Pancho Gonzales
Players '79

Peter Gonzales
Fellini's Roma '72

Will Gonzales
White Slave '86

Carmelita Gonzalez
Mexican Bus Ride '51

**Jose Gonzalez-
Gonzalez**
The Mermaids of Tiburon '62

Christopher Good
Bullshot '83

Constance Good
I Know Why the Caged Bird
Sings '79

Caroline Goodall
Cliffhanger '93
Hook '91

Grant Goodeve
Hot Rod '79
Last Cry for Help '79
Take Two '87

Joan Goodfellow
Buster and Billie '74

Ken Goodlet
Endplay '75

Cuba Gooding, Jr.
Boyz N the Hood '91
A Few Good Men '92
Gladiator '92
Hitz '92

Michael Goodliffe
The Gorgon '64
A Night to Remember '58
To the Devil, A Daughter '76
Up the Creek '58
The Way Out '56

Benny Goodman
A Song is Born '48
Stage Door Canteen '43

Dody Goodman
Bedtime Story '63
Cool As Ice '91
Frozen Assets '92
Magic on Love Island '80
Private Resort '84
Splash '84

George Goodman
Superbug Super Agent '76

John Goodman
Always '89
Arachnophobia '90
The Babe '92
Barton Fink '91
The Big Easy '87
Born Yesterday '93
Burglar '87
C.H.U.D. '84
Eddie Macon's Run '83
Everybody's All American '88
King Ralph '91
Maria's Lovers '84
Matinee '92
Punchline '88

Raising Arizona '87
Revenge of the Nerds '84
Sea of Love '89
Stella '89
Survivors '83
True Stories '86
The Wrong Guys '88

Karen Goodman
The Mermaids of Tiburon '62

Patricia Goodman
Ninja Death Squad '87

Carol Goodner
Mimi '35

Deborah Goodrich
Remote Control '88
Survival Game '87

Garry Goodrow
Cardiac Arrest '74
The Committee '68
The Connection '61
A Session with the Committee
'69

Amanda Goodwin
Working Girls '87

Angela Goodwin
Autopsy '78
Julia and Julia '87

Bill Goodwin
The Atomic Kid '54
Bathing Beauty '44
It's a Great Feeling '49
Jolson Sings Again '49
The Jolson Story '46
Lucky Me '54
Mickey '48
The Stork Club '45
Tea for Two '50

Harold Goodwin
Angels One Five '54
The Cameraman '28
College '27
Suds '20
Tanks a Million '41

**Laura Jane
Goodwin**
Crystalstone '88

Laurel Goodwin
Girls! Girls! Girls! '62
Papa's Delicate Condition '63

Michael Goodwin
Date with an Angel '87
The Dead Pool '88
Deadline Assault '90
Remembrance of Love '82
Sizzle '81

Fred Goodwine
Down to Earth '17

**Bernice Tamara
Goor**
Speak of the Devil '90

Allen Goorwitz
Leave 'Em Laughing '81
One Trick Pony '80

Janos Gorbe
The Round Up '66

Bernard Gorcey
Blues Busters '50
Bowery Buckaroos '47
Clipped Wings '53
Ghost Chasers '51
Hard-Boiled Mahoney '47
Spook Busters '46

David Gorcey
Blues Busters '50
Bowery Buckaroos '47

Friday Foster '75
Greased Lightning '77
Naked Warriors '73
On the Edge '86
The Package '89
Posse '93
Scream Blacula Scream '73
Sheba, Baby '75
Something Wicked This Way
  Comes '83
Stand Alone '85
Tough Enough '87
Twilight People '72
The Vindicator '85

Roosevelt Grier
The Big Push '75
The Glove '78
The Seekers '79
Sophisticated Gents '81
The Treasure of Jamaica Reef
  '74

Charles Gries
Chance '89

Jonathan Gries
Joy Sticks '83
Kill Me Again '89
Pucker Up and Bark Like a
  Dog '89
Real Genius '85
Swap Meet '79

Russ Grieve
The Hills Have Eyes '77

Joe Grifasi
Bad Medicine '85
Benny & Joon '93
Chances Are '89
The Feud '90
Gentleman Bandit '81
On the Yard '79
Presumed Innocent '90
Still of the Night '82

Simone Griffeth
Death Race 2000 '75
Delusion '84
Hot Target '85
Patriot '86
Sixteen '72

Frank Griffin
Teenage Crime Wave '55

Josephine Griffin
The Man Who Never Was '55
Postmark for Danger '56
The Spanish Gardener '57

Lorie Griffin
Aloha Summer '88
Cheerleader Camp '88

Lynne Griffin
Obsessed '88

Merv Griffin
The Lonely Guy '84

Michael Griffin
Sonny Boy '87

Robert Griffin
I Was a Teenage Werewolf
  '57
Monster from Green Hell '58

Tod Griffin
She Demons '58

Tony Griffin
Evil Laugh '86
Robin Hood: Men in Tights '93

Andy Griffith
A Face in the Crowd '57
Fatal Vision '84
From Here to Eternity '79
Hearts of the West '75

Murder in Coweta County '83
Murder in Texas '81
No Time for Sergeants '58
Pray for the Wildcats '74
Return to Mayberry '85
Rustler's Rhapsody '85
Savages '75

Bill Griffith
Whirlwind Horseman '38

Charles B. Griffith
It Conquered the World '56

Corrine Griffith
Dracula/Garden of Eden '28
The Garden of Eden '28

Eva Griffith
Ride a Wild Pony '75
The Turn of the Screw '74

Geraldine Griffith
Experience Preferred... But
  Not Essential '83

Gordon Griffith
Little Annie Rooney '25
Outlaws of the Range '36

Hugh Griffith
The Abominable Dr. Phibes
  '71
Ben-Hur '59
The Big Scam '79
The Canterbury Tales '71
The Counterfeit Traitor '62
Craze '74
Cry of the Banshee '70
Diary of Forbidden Dreams
  '73
Doctor Phibes Rises Again '72
Exodus '60
The Final Programme '73
The Last Days of Dolwyn '49
Legend of the Werewolf '75
Lucky Jim '58
Luther '74
Mutiny on the Bounty '62
Oh Dad, Poor Dad (Momma's
  Hung You in the Closet &
  I'm Feeling So Sad) '67
Oliver! '68
The Passover Plot '75
The Sleeping Tiger '54
Start the Revolution Without
  Me '70
Tom Jones '63
Who Slew Auntie Roo? '71
Wuthering Heights '70

James Griffith
The Amazing Transparent
  Man '60
Bullwhip '58
The Legend of Sleepy Hollow
  '79

Jeff Griffith
The 13th Mission '91

Kenneth Griffith
The Assassination Bureau '69
Circus of Horrors '60
The Final Option '82
Koroshi '67
Night of the Laughing Dead
  '75
Revenge '71

Kristin Griffith
Interiors '78

Melanie Griffith
Body Double '84
The Bonfire of the Vanities '90
Born Yesterday '93
Cherry 2000 '88
The Drowning Pool '75
Fear City '85
Harrad Experiment '73

In the Spirit '90
Joyride '77
The Milagro Beanfield War '88
Night Moves '75
One on One '77
Pacific Heights '90
Paradise '91
She's in the Army Now '81
Shining Through '92
Smile '75
Something Wild '86
Steel Cowboy '78
Stormy Monday '88
A Stranger Among Us '92
Underground Aces '80
Women & Men: Stories of
  Seduction '90
Working Girl '88

Raymond Griffith
All Quiet on the Western Front
  '30
Hands Up '26
The Night Club '25
Paths to Paradise '25

Thomas Ian Griffith
Excessive Force '93
Ulterior Motives '92

Tom Griffith
The Alien Factor '78
Hawk and Castile
Night Beast '83

Tracy Griffith
Fast Food '89
The Finest Hour '91
The First Power '89
Sleepaway Camp 3: Teenage
  Wasteland '89

Linda Griffiths
Lianna '83
Overdrawn at the Memory
  Bank '83
Reno and the Doc '84

Richard Griffiths
Blame It on the Bellboy '92
Naked Gun 2 1/2: The Smell
  of Fear '91
Shanghai Surprise '86
Whoops Apocalypse '83
Withnail and I '87

Susan Griffiths
Calendar Girl '93

Trevor Griffiths
Singing the Blues in Red '87

Jeff Griggs
Eden '92
Eden 2 '93

Ele Grigsby
Invasion of the Girl Snatchers
  '73

Johanna Grika
Vice Academy 3 '91
Visitants '87

John Grillo
Afterward '85

Lucky Grills
Money Movers '78

Dan Grimaldi
Don't Go in the House '80

Eva Grimaldi
The Black Cobra '87

Hugo Grimaldi
Godzilla Raids Again '59

Iliana Grimaldi
The Sword of El Cid '62

Frank Grimes
Crystalstone '88
The Dive '89

Gary Grimes
Cahill: United States Marshal
  '73
Class of '44 '73
Culpepper Cattle Co. '72
Summer of '42 '71

Rebecca Grimes
Rebel '73

Scott Grimes
Critters '86
Critters 2: The Main Course
  '88
Frog '89
Frogs! '90s
It Came Upon a Midnight
  Clear '84
Night Life '90

Tammy Grimes
America '86
The Last Unicorn '82
Mr. North '88
No Big Deal '83
The Runner Stumbles '79

Daniel Grimm
Osa '85

Dick Grimm
Night of the Bloody Transplant
  '86

Herbert Grimwood
Romola '25
When the Clouds Roll By '19

Nikolai Grinko
Andrei Rublev '66
Stalker '79

Alan Grint
The Secret Garden '87

Brad Grinter
Scream, Baby, Scream '69

Randy Grinter, Jr.
Blood Freak '72

Harry Grippe
Great K & A Train Robbery
  '26

Christina Grisanti
A Woman Under the Influence
  '74

Jerry Grisham
Escapes '86

Stephen Grives
Horror Planet '80

George Grizzard
Advise and Consent '62
Attica '80
Bachelor Party '84
Caroline? '90
Comes a Horseman '78
The Deliberate Stranger '86
Embassy '85
False Witness '89
From the Terrace '60
Iran: Days of Crisis '91
Oldest Living Graduate '82
Pueblo Affair '73
Seems Like Old Times '80
The Stranger Within '74
Wrong is Right '82

Kenna Grob
Deadly Diamonds '91

David Grocey
Pride of the Bowery '41

Tomasz Grochoczki
Greta '86

Charles Grodin
Beethoven '92
Catch-22 '70
Clifford '93
The Couch Trip '87
Dave '93
11 Harrowhouse '74
The Grass is Always Greener
  Over the Septic Tank '78
The Great Muppet Caper '81
Grown Ups '86
Heart and Souls '93
The Heartbreak Kid '72
Heaven Can Wait '78
The Incredible Shrinking
  Woman '81
Ishtar '87
It's My Turn '80
Just Me & You '78
King Kong '76
Last Resort '86
The Lonely Guy '84
The Meanest Men in the West
  '76
Midnight Run '88
Movers and Shakers '85
Real Life '79
Rosemary's Baby '68
Seems Like Old Times '80
Sex and the College Girl '64
So I Married an Axe Murderer
  '93
Sunburn '79
Taking Care of Business '90
The Woman in Red '84
You Can't Hurry Love '88

Kathryn Grody
The Lemon Sisters '90
Quick Change '90

Claire Grogan
Gregory's Girl '80

C.P. Grogan
Comfort and Joy '84

David Groh
A Hero Ain't Nothin' But a
  Sandwich '78
Hot Shot '86
Zertigo Diamond Caper '82

Ake Gronberg
Monika '52
Sawdust & Tinsel '53

Herbert Groncmeyer
Das Boot '81
Spring Symphony '86

Ray Gronwold
The Prime Time '60

Sam Groom
The Baby Maker '70
Betrayal '74
Beyond the Bermuda Triangle
  '75
Deadly Eyes '82
Deadly Games '80
Run for the Roses '78

Malcolm Groome
Feelin' Up '76

Gary Groomes
Wired '89

Frank Groothof
In for Treatment '82

Arye Gross
Boris and Natasha: The Movie
  '92
The Couch Trip '87
Coupe de Ville '90

Tito Guizar
The Gay Ranchero '42
On the Old Spanish Trail '47

Clu Gulager
And Now Miguel '66
Chattanooga Choo Choo '84
Force of One '79
The Glass House '72
He Who Walks Alone '78
The Hidden '87
Hit Lady '74
Hunter's Blood '87
The Initiation '84
Into the Night '85
Kenny Rogers as the Gambler '80
Kenny Rogers as the Gambler, Part 2: The Adventure Continues '83
The Killers '64
The Last Picture Show '71
Lies '83
McQ '74
A Nightmare on Elm Street 2: Freddy's Revenge '85
The Offspring '87
The Other Side of Midnight '77
A Question of Love '78
Return of the Living Dead '85
Smile, Jenny, You're Dead '74
Snowblind '78
Tapeheads '89
Teen Vamp '88
Touched by Love '80
The Uninvited '88
Willa '79
Winning '69
Wonderland Cove '75

Dorothy Gulliver
Outlaw Justice '32
Shadow of the Eagle '32
Under Montana Skies '30

Leo Gullotta
Sinbad of the Seven Seas '89

Eisi Gulp
Sugarbaby '85

David Gulpilil
Crocodile Dundee '86
Dark Age '88
The Last Wave '77
Mad Dog Morgan '76

Natalia Gundareva
Autumn Marathon '79

Bill Gunn
Black Vampire '73

Eric Gunn
Blind Faith '89

Judy Gunn
The Private Secretary '35

Moses Gunn
Aaron Loves Angela '75
Amazing Grace '74
Amityville 2: The Possession '82
Certain Fury '85
Charlotte Forten's Mission: Experiment in Freedom '85
Cornbread, Earl & Me '75
Firestarter '84
The Great White Hope '70
Haunts of the Very Rich '72
The Hot Rock '70
The House of Dies Drear '88
Killing Floor '85
Memphis '91
The NeverEnding Story '84
Ragtime '81
Rollerball '75
Shaft '71

Shaft's Big Score '72
Wild Rovers '71
The Women of Brewster Place '89

Paul Gunning
Hollywood Hot Tubs '84

Ted Gunther
The Green Slime '68

Bob Gunton
Cookie '89
Dead Ahead: The Exxon Valdez Disaster '92
Glory '89
Rollover '81
Sinatra '92
Static '87
Wild Palms '93

Robert Gunton
Lois Gibbs and the Love Canal '82

Kamlesh Gupta
Crystalstone '88

Pinaki Sen Gupta
Aparajito '58

Uma Das Gupta
Pather Panchali '54

Alizia Gur
Beast of Morocco '66
From Russia with Love '63

Jack Gurci
Don't Mess with My Sister! '85

Sigrid Gurie
Algiers '38
Enemy of Women '44
Three Faces West '40

Cindy Gurling
Daughter of Death '82

Sharon Gurney
Crucible of Horror '69

Juan Jose Gurrola
Frida '84

Eric Gurry
Bad Boys '83
Mystery at Fire Island '81
Something Special '86
The Zoo Gang '85

Louis Guss
American Blue Note '89
Moonstruck '87
Nitti: The Enforcer '88
Willie & Phil '80

Arlo Guthrie
Alice's Restaurant '69
Roadside Prophets '92

Catherine Guthrie
The Girl in the Picture '86

Tani Phelps Guthrie
Daughters of Satan '72
The Thirsty Dead '74

Tyrone Guthrie
Beachcomber '38

Antonio Gutierrez
Virgin Sacrifice '59

Emilio Gutierrez-Caba
The Hunt '67

Zaide Silvia Gutierrez
El Norte '83

Steve Guttenberg
Amazon Women on the Moon '87
Bad Medicine '85
The Bedroom Window '87
The Boys from Brazil '78
Can't Stop the Music '80
The Chicken Chronicles '77
Cocoon '85
Cocoon: The Return '88
The Day After '83
Diner '82
Don't Tell Her It's Me '90
High Spirits '88
The Man Who Wasn't There '83
Miracle on Ice '81
Pecos Bill '86
Police Academy '84
Police Academy 2: Their First Assignment '85
Police Academy 3: Back in Training '86
Police Academy 4: Citizens on Patrol '87
Short Circuit '86
Surrender '87
Three Men and a Baby '87
Three Men and a Little Lady '90
To Race the Wind '80

Lucy Gutteridge
The Secret Garden '87
Top Secret! '84
The Trouble with Spies '87
Tusks '89
The Woman He Loved '88

Ronald Guttman
Josh and S.A.M. '93

Bertil Guve
Fanny and Alexander '83

DeJuan Guy
Candyman '92

Felicia Guy
The Naked Angels '69

J. Scott Guy
Armed for Action '92

Jasmine Guy
Harlem Nights '89
Runaway '89

Sheila Guyse
Boy! What a Girl '45
Boy! What a Girl '45
Miracle in Harlem '48
Sepia Cinderella '47

Joe Guzaldo
Bingo '91
Smooth Talker '90

Sergio Guzik
La Justicia Tiene Doce Anos '87

Enrique Guzman
The Sinister Invasion '68

Luis Guzman
Guilty as Sin '93
Jumpin' at the Boneyard '92
Q & A '90

Roberto "Flaco" Guzman
Arizona '86
La Hifa Sin Padre '87
Marcados por el Destino '87

Teri Guzman
Escape from Cell Block Three '78
Women Unchained '70s

Margherita Guzzinati
The Witch '66

Jack Gwaltney
Vital Signs '90

Robert Gwaltney
Trading Hearts '87

Edmund Gwenn
The Bigamist '53
Cash '34
Challenge to Lassie '49
Cheers for Miss Bishop '41
The Devil & Miss Jones '41
Doctor Takes a Wife '40
Forever and a Day '43
Green Dolphin Street '47
If I Were Rich '33
It's a Dog's Life '55
Java Head '35
The Keys of the Kingdom '44
Lassie, Come Home '43
Life with Father '47
Miracle on 34th Street '47
Pride and Prejudice '40
Skin Game '31
The Student Prince '54
Sylvia Scarlett '35
Them! '54
The Trouble with Harry '55
A Woman of Distinction '50

David Gwillim
Henry IV, Part I '80
Henry IV, Part II '80
The Island at the Top of the World '74

Jack Gwillim
The Bushbaby '70
Flame Over India '60
Sword of Sherwood Forest '60

Andy Gwyn
Dark Sanity '82

Michael Gwynn
Jason and the Argonauts '63
The Scars of Dracula '70

Anne Gwynne
Adam at 6 A.M. '70
Black Tower '50
Breakdown '53
Fear '46
House of Frankenstein '44
Killer Dill '47
King of the Bullwhip '51
Meteor Monster '57
Ride 'Em Cowboy '42

Fred Gwynne
The Boy Who Could Fly '86
The Cotton Club '84
Day with Conrad Green '80
Disorganized Crime '89
Fatal Attraction '87
Ironweed '87
The Littlest Angel '69
The Man That Corrupted Hadleyburg '80
Munster's Revenge '81
Murder by the Book '87
My Cousin Vinny '92
The Mysterious Stranger '82
Off Beat '86
Pet Sematary '89
Shadows and Fog '92
Simon '80
Vanishing Act '88
Water '85

Michael C. Gwynne
Cherry 2000 '88
Harry Tracy '83
The Last of the Finest '90

Payday '72
Seduced '85
Special Delivery '76
The Streets of L.A. '79

Peter Gwynne
The Dove '74
Puzzle '78
Tim '79

Tibor Gyapjas
Moving Out '83

Agi Gyenes
Just for the Hell of It '68

Kim Gyngell
The Wacky World of Wills & Burke '85

Greta Gynt
The Arsenal Stadium Mystery '39
Dear Murderer '47
The Hooded Terror '38
The Human Monster '39
Mr. Emmanuel '44
Sexton Blake and the Hooded Terror '38

Deanna Haas
Devonsville Terror '83

Hugo Haas
Days of Glory '43
The Fighting Kentuckian '49
Holiday in Mexico '46
King Solomon's Mines '50
My Girl Tisa '48
Northwest Outpost '47
The Private Affairs of Bel Ami '47

Lukas Haas
Alan & Naomi '92
The Lady in White '88
Leap of Faith '92
Music Box '89
Rambling Rose '91
See You in the Morning '89
Shattered Spirits '91
Solarbabies '86
Witness '85
The Wizard of Loneliness '88

Susanna Haavisto
Ariel '89

Sylvie Habault
Therese '86

Matthias Habich
Coup de Grace '78
An Occurrence at Owl Creek Bridge/Coup de Grace '62
The Savage Woman '91
Straight for the Heart '88

Cox Habrema
Question of Silence '83

Shelley Hack
Annie Hall '77
Blind Fear '89
A Casualty of War '90
The Finishing Touch '92
If Ever I See You Again '78
Kicks '85
King of Comedy '82
Single Bars, Single Women '84
The Stepfather '87
Troll '85

George Hackathorne
Merry-Go-Round '23

Joseph Hacker
Little Treasure '85
The Ultimate Imposter '79

First Born '84
License to Drive '88
The Lost Boys '87
Lucas '86
Murphy's Romance '85
Oh, What a Night '92
Prayer of the Rollerboys '91
Secret Admirer '85
Silver Bullet '85
Time to Live '85
Watchers '88

Donald Haines
Flying Wild '41

Eli Haines
Candy Tangerine Man '75

Larry Haines
The Seven-Ups '73

Patricia Haines
Night Caller from Outer Space '66
The Virgin Witch '70

Richard Haines
African Dream '90

Ron Haines
Legend of Alfred Packer '80

William Haines
Free and Easy '30
Little Annie Rooney '25
Show People '28

Judit Halasz
Love Film '70

Alan Hale, Jr.
Action in the North Atlantic '43
Adventures of Don Juan '49
The Adventures of Robin Hood '38
Algiers '38
Big Trees '52
Casey Jones and Fury (Brave Stallion) '57
The Crawling Hand '63
Desperate Journey '42
Destination Tokyo '43
Dick Turpin '25
Dodge City '39
The Fifth Musketeer '79
Gentleman Jim '42
The Giant Spider Invasion '75
Hambone & Hillie '84
Hard Drivin' '60
Home Town Story '51
The Indian Fighter '55
The Inspector General '49
It Happened One Night '34
Johnny Dangerously '84
Last Days of Pompeii '35
The Leatherneck '28
Little Minister '34
The Lost Patrol '34
The Man in the Iron Mask '39
My Girl Tisa '48
Night and Day '46
The North Avenue Irregulars '79
Of Human Bondage '34
Our Relations '36
Power '28
The Prince and the Pauper '37
The Private Lives of Elizabeth & Essex '39
Pursued '47
Rim of the Canyon '49
Robin Hood '22
Santa Fe Trail '40
The Scarlet Letter '34
The Sea Hawk '40
The Sin of Madelon Claudet '31
South of St. Louis '48
The Spirit of West Point '47

Stella Dallas '37
Strawberry Blonde '41
Susan Lenox: Her Fall and Rise '31
Thank Your Lucky Stars '43
There was a Crooked Man '70
They Drive by Night '40
This is the Army '43
To the Shores of Tripoli '42
The Underworld Story '50
Up Periscope '59
The West Point Story '50
When Thief Meets Thief '37
Young at Heart '54

Alan Hale, Sr.
All Mine to Give '56
Captains of the Clouds '42
The Covered Wagon '23
The Fighting 69th '40
The Four Horsemen of the Apocalypse '21
Listen, Darling '38
The Trap '22
Virginia City '40

Barbara Hale
The Boy with the Green Hair '48
Buckskin '68
The Clay Pigeon '49
The Defense Never Rests '90
The Falcon in Hollywood '44
First Yank into Tokyo '45
Flight of the Grey Wolf '76
The Giant Spider Invasion '75
Going to Town '44
The Jackpot '50
Jolson Sings Again '49
Last of the Comanches '52
A Lion is in the Streets '53
The Oklahoman '56
Perry Mason Returns '85
Perry Mason: The Case of the Lost Love '87
Seventh Cavalry '56
The Window '49

Bill Hale
Stakeout '62

Binnie Hale
Love from a Stranger '37
The Phantom Light '35

Creighton Hale
The Cat and the Canary '27
The Marriage Circle '24
Shop Angel '32
Way Down East '20

Doug Hale
Manhunter '83

Elvi Hale
Six Wives of Henry VIII '70s

Frona Hale
Fighting Jack '26

Georgina Hale
The Boy Friend '71
Castaway '87
The Gold Rush '25
Gold Rush/Payday '25
Mahler '74

Jean Hale
In Like Flint '67
Psychomania '63
The St. Valentine's Day Massacre '67

Jonathan Hale
Bringing Up Baby '38
Exiled to Shanghai '37
Hollywood Canteen '44
The Judge '49
The Saint Strikes Back '39
The Saint Takes Over '40

The Saint's Double Trouble '40
Saratoga '37
Silver River '48

Louise Closser Hale
Devotion '31
Platinum Blonde '31

Marcus Hale
Gone to Ground '76

Michael Hale
The Devil Bat's Daughter '46

Monte Hale
Missourians '50
Pioneer Marshal '49
Son of God's Country '48
Trail of Robin Hood '50
The Vanishing Westerner '50
Western Double Feature 2: Wayne & Hale '80s
Western Double Feature 8: Hale & Carradine '40s

Sonnie Hale
Evergreen '34
It's Love Again '36

Jerry Haleva
Hot Shots! Part Deux '93

Jack Haley
George White's Scandals '45
Higher and Higher '44
Moon Over Miami '41
Movie Struck '37
One Body Too Many '44
People Are Funny '46
Pick a Star '37
The Poor Little Rich Girl '36
Rebecca of Sunnybrook Farm '38
Take It Big '44
Treasure of Fear '45
The Wizard of Oz '39

Jackie Earle Haley
The Bad News Bears '76
The Bad News Bears Go to Japan '78
The Bad News Bears in Breaking Training '77
Breaking Away '79
Damnation Alley '77
Dollman '91
Losin' It '82
The Zoo Gang '85

H.B. Halicki
Deadline Auto Theft '83
Gone in 60 Seconds '74
The Junkman '82

Albert Hall
Apocalypse Now '79
Betrayed '88
Hearts of Darkness: A Filmmaker's Apocalypse '91
The Long, Hot Summer '86
Malcolm X '92
Separate But Equal '91
Uncle Tom's Cabin '87

Anthony Hall
Atlantis, the Lost Continent '61

Anthony Michael Hall
The Breakfast Club '85
Edward Scissorhands '90
Into the Sun '92
Johnny Be Good '88
National Lampoon's Vacation '83
Out of Bounds '86
Six Pack '82

Sixteen Candles '84
Weird Science '85

Arch Hall, Jr.
The Choppers '61
Deadwood '65
Eegah! '62
Nasty Rabbit '64
The Sadist '63
Wild Guitar '62

Archie Hall
Border Badmen '45
His Brother's Ghost '45

Arsenio Hall
Amazon Women on the Moon '87
Coming to America '88
Harlem Nights '89

Berta Hall
Port of Call '48

Brad Hall
Best of Eddie Murphy '89
Limit Up '89
Worth Winning '89

Carol E. Hall
Love Your Mama '93

Charlie Hall
A Chump at Oxford '40
Laurel & Hardy Comedy Classics, Vol. 1 '33
Laurel & Hardy Comedy Classics, Vol. 6 '35

Chip Hall
Kiss and Be Killed '91

Cleve Hall
Twisted Nightmare '87

Cliff Hall
Prudential Family Playhouse '50

Lillian Hall-Davies
The Farmer's Wife '28
The Ring '27

Deidre Hall
Special Delivery '76

Delores Hall
Lethal Weapon 3 '92

Dickie Hall
Shadow of the Thin Man '41

Dorothy Hall
The Broadway Drifter '27

Ella Hall
West-Bound Limited '23

Ellen Hall
Raiders of the Border '44

Georgine Hall
Out of the Rain '90

Gita Hall
The Legend of the Sea Wolf '58

Grayson Hall
Adam at 6 A.M. '70
House of Dark Shadows '70
Night of Dark Shadows '71
The Night of the Iguana '64

Harriet Hall
Foxfire '87

Henry Hall
The Ape '40
Lightning Raiders '45
Midnight Warning '32
Rainbow Ranch '33

Huntz Hall
Angels with Dirty Faces '38

Auntie Lee's Meat Pies '92
Blues Busters '50
Bowery Blitzkrieg '41
Bowery Buckaroos '47
Clipped Wings '53
Cyclone '87
Escape Artist '82
Follow the Leader '44
Gas Pump Girls '79
Gentle Giant '67
Ghost Chasers '51
Ghosts on the Loose '43
Hard-Boiled Mahoney '47
Here Come the Marines '52
Junior G-Men '40
Junior G-Men of the Air '42
Kid Dynamite '43
Let's Get Tough '42
Little Tough Guy '38
Million Dollar Kid '44
Mr. Wise Guy '42
'Neath Brooklyn Bridge '42
Pride of the Bowery '41
Smart Alecks '42
Smugglers' Cove '48
Spook Busters '46
Spooks Run Wild '41
Zis Boom Bah '42

James Hall
Hell's Angels '30
Hotel Imperial '27
Millie '31

Jerry Hall
Batman '89
Running Out of Luck '86

John Hall
Midnight '81
Muse Concert: No Nukes '80

Hall Johnson Choir
Way Down South '39

Jon Hall
The Beach Girls and the Monster '65
Deputy Marshall '50
Hell Ship Mutiny '57
Hurricane '37
Kit Carson '40
The Last of the Redmen '47
The Lion Man '36
The Prince of Thieves '48
South of Pago Pago '40
The Tuttles of Tahiti '42

Juanita Hall
Flower Drum Song '61
Paradise in Harlem '40
South Pacific '58

Kevin Peter Hall
Highway to Hell '92
Misfits of Science '85

Lena Hall
Witchcraft 3: The Kiss of Death '90

Lois Hall
Dead Again '91
Kalifornia '93
Pirates of the High Seas '50

Mark Hall
Across the Great Divide '76

Michael Keys Hall
Blackout '88
Flight of Black Angel '91

Nathaniel "Afrika" Hall
Livin' Large '91

Philip Baker Hall
Blue Desert '91
The Last Reunion '80
Secret Honor '85

Porter Hall
The Beautiful Blonde from
  Bashful Bend '49
Bulldog Drummond Escapes
  '37
Bulldog Drummond's Peril '38
Bulldog Drummond's
  Revenge/Bulldog
  Drummond's Peril '38
The Case of the Lucky Legs
  '35
Double Indemnity '44
The General Died at Dawn '36
Going My Way '44
The Great Moment '44
The Half-Breed '51
His Girl Friday '40
Intruder in the Dust '49
Miracle of Morgan's Creek '44
Miracle on 34th Street '47
Mr. Smith Goes to
  Washington '39
Petrified Forest '36
The Plainsman '37
Satan Met a Lady '36
The Story of Louis Pasteur
  '36
Sullivan's Travels '41
They Shall Have Music '39
The Thin Man '34
Weekend at the Waldorf '45
The Woman of the Town '44

Rich Hall
Million Dollar Mystery '87
Rich Hall's Vanishing America
  '86

Ron Hall
Triple Impact '92

Ruth Hall
Between Fighting Men '32
Monkey Business '31
The Return of Casey Jones
  '34
Strawberry Roan '33

Sam Hall
South of Hell Mountain '70

Shannah Hall
Boogey Man 2 '83
The Princess & the Call Girl
  '84

Thurston Hall
The Black Room '35
Call of the Canyon '42
Each Dawn I Die '39
The Great Gildersleeve '43
I Dood It '43
Lady from Nowhere '36
Night Stage to Galveston '52
Rim of the Canyon '49
You Can't Cheat an Honest
  Man '39

Zooey Hall
Fortune and Men's Eyes '71
I Dismember Mama '74

Charles Hallahan
Body of Evidence '92
Margin for Murder '81
Pale Rider '85
The Thing '82
True Believer '89
Vision Quest '85
Wild Palms '93

John Hallam
Dragonslayer '81
The Offence '73
Under Capricorn '82

C.M. Hallard
King of the Damned '36

Jane Hallaren
Lianna '83
A Night in the Life of Jimmy
  Reardon '88

Neil Hallett
The Virgin Witch '70

Tom Hallick
Hangar 18 '80
A Rare Breed '81

Bryant Halliday
Tower of Evil '72

Heather Halliday
Peter Pan '60

John Halliday
Consolation Marriage '31
Finishing School '33

Peter Halliday
Fast Kill '73
Millie '31

Lori Hallier
Blindside '88
The Gunfighters '87
Higher Education '88
My Bloody Valentine '81

William Halligan
Jive Junction '43
Robot Pilot '41
Turf Boy '42

David Hallyday
He's My Girl '87

Martin Halm
Ernesto '79

Billy Halop
Angels with Dirty Faces '38
Junior G-Men '40
Junior G-Men of the Air '42
Little Tough Guy '38
Pride of the Bowery '41

Dina Halpern
The Dybbuk '37

Daria Halprin
Zabriskie Point '70

Luke Halprin
Flipper '63
Flipper's New Adventure '64
Flipper's Odyssey '66
If It's Tuesday, This Must Be
  Belgium '69
Island of the Lost '68
Peter Pan '60
Shock Waves '77

Brett Halsey
Atomic Submarine '59
Black Cat '90
The Crash of Flight 401 '78
Dangerous Obsession '88
The Girl in Lover's Lane '60
Jet Over the Atlantic '59
Magnificent Adventurer '76
Return of the Fly '59
Return to Peyton Place '61
Submarine Seahawk '59
Twice-Told Tales '63

Michael Halsey
Dollman '91
Treasure Island '89
Under the Gun '88

Charles Halton
Across the Pacific '42
Dr. Cyclops '40
Pick a Star '37
Rhapsody in Blue '45

Peter Ham
The Happy Gigolo '70s

Mie Hama
What's Up, Tiger Lily? '66
You Only Live Twice '67

Torahiko Hamada
X from Outer Space '67

Yuko Hamada
Gamera vs. Guiron '69

Stuart Hamblen
King of the Forest Rangers
  '46

John Hamblin
Who Killed Baby Azaria? '83

Veronica Hamel
Cannonball '76
The Gathering '77
The Gathering: Part 2 '79
A New Life '88
Sessions '83
Snowblind '78
Taking Care of Business '90

Gerald Hamer
Scarlet Claw '44

Rusty Hamer
Dance with Me, Henry '56

Jayne Hamil
Vice Academy '88
Vice Academy 2 '90

Dorothy Hamill
Nutcracker, A Fantasy on Ice
  '83
Snow Queen '82

Mark Hamill
The Big Red One '80
Black Magic Woman '91
Britannia Hospital '82
The City '76
Corvette Summer '78
The Empire Strikes Back '80
Eric '75
From "Star Wars" to "Jedi":
  The Making of a Saga '83
The Guyver '91
The Night the Lights Went Out
  in Georgia '81
Return of the Jedi '83
Sleepwalkers '92
Slipstream '89
Star Wars '77
Time Runner '92

Alexa Hamilton
Dragonfight '92

Anthony Hamilton
Howling 4: The Original
  Nightmare '88
Samson and Delilah '84

Antony Hamilton
Mirrors '85

Bernie Hamilton
Bucktown '75
Captain Sinbad '63
The Losers '70
Scream Blacula Scream '73

Carrie Hamilton
Cool World '92
Shag: The Movie '89
Tokyo Pop '88

Dan Hamilton
Opposing Force '87

Dean Hamilton
Rush Week '88

George Hamilton
Angel Baby '61
By Love Possessed '61
The Dead Don't Die '75
Doc Hollywood '91

Evel Knievel '72
Express to Terror '79
From Hell to Victory '79
The Godfather, Part 3 '90
The Happy Hooker Goes to
  Washington '77
Home from the Hill '60
Killer on Board '77
Love at First Bite '79
Medusa '74
Monte Carlo '86
Once is Not Enough '75
Once Upon a Crime '92
Poker Alice '87
The Seekers '79
Sextette '78
Togetherness '70
Two Fathers' Justice '85
Two Weeks in Another Town
  '62
Users '78
Where the Boys Are '60
Zorro, the Gay Blade '81

Guy Hamilton
Barry Lyndon '75

Hale Hamilton
The Champ '31
Murder at Midnight '31
Susan Lenox: Her Fall and
  Rise '31

Jane Hamilton
Bedroom Eyes 2 '89
Bloodsucking Pharoahs of
  Pittsburgh '90
Cleo/Leo '89
Deranged '87
New York's Finest '87
Slammer Girls '87
Wildest Dreams '90

John Hamilton
Fangs of the Living Dead '68
The Fatal Hour '40
I Killed That Man '42
Outcasts of the City '58
Phantom Killer '42
The Saint's Double Trouble
  '40

Josh Hamilton
Alive '93
O Pioneers! '91

Judd Hamilton
Gun Crazy '69
The Last Horror Film '82
Star Crash '78

Kipp Hamilton
War of the Gargantuas '70

**Ellen Hamilton-
Latzen**
Fatal Attraction '87

Linda Hamilton
Beauty and the Beast '87
Beauty and the Beast: Though
  Lovers Be Lost '89
Black Moon Rising '86
Children of the Corn '84
King Kong Lives '86
Mr. Destiny '90
Rape and Marriage: The
  Rideout Case '80
Secret Weapons '85
The Stone Boy '84
Tag: The Assassination Game
  '82
The Terminator '84
Terminator 2: Judgment Day
  '91

Lois Hamilton
Armed Response '86

Mahlon Hamilton
Peg O' My Heart '22

Margaret Hamilton
The Adventures of Tom
  Sawyer '38
The Anderson Tapes '71
Breaking the Ice '38
Brewster McCloud '70
Broadway Bill '34
Daydreamer '66
George White's Scandals '45
Guest in the House '45
Moon's Our Home '36
My Little Chickadee '40
Nothing Sacred '37
The Red Pony '49
The Sin of Harold Diddlebock
  '47
These Three '36
13 Ghosts '60
The Wizard of Oz '39
You Only Live Once '37

Murray Hamilton
The Amityville Horror '79
Anatomy of a Murder '59
The Boston Strangler '68
The Brotherhood '68
Brubaker '80
Casey's Shadow '78
Darby's Rangers '58
The Drowning Pool '75
The FBI Story '59
The Graduate '67
Houseboat '58
If It's Tuesday, This Must Be
  Belgium '69
Jaws '75
Jaws 2 '78
Last Cry for Help '79
The Last Days of Patton '86
Mazes and Monsters '82
1941 '79
No Time for Sergeants '58
No Way to Treat a Lady '68
Papa's Delicate Condition '63
Rona Jaffe's Mazes &
  Monsters '82
Sergeant Ryker '68
Spirit of St. Louis '57
The Tattered Web '71
Too Scared to Scream '85
The Way We Were '73

Neil Hamilton
America/The Fall of Babylon
  '24
The Animal Kingdom '32
The Devil's Hand '61
Hollywood Stadium Mystery
  '38
Isn't Life Wonderful '24
King of the Texas Rangers '41
Laughing Sinners '31
The Patsy '64
The Saint Strikes Back '39
The Sin of Madelon Claudet
  '31
Tarzan and His Mate '34
Tarzan, the Ape Man '32
What Price Hollywood? '32
The White Rose '23
X Marks the Spot '42

Patricia Hamilton
Anne of Avonlea '87
Anne of Green Gables '85
The Christmas Wife '88

Paula Hamilton
Four Days in July '84

Rex Hamilton
More! Police Squad '82

Richard Hamilton
In Country '89

Rusty Hamilton
Rock 'n' Roll Nightmare '85

Shorty Hamilton
On the Night Stage '15

Suzanna Hamilton
Brimstone & Treacle '82
Duel of Hearts '92
1984 '84
Out of Africa '85
Wetherby '85

Suzette Hamilton
Scream Bloody Murder '72

Ted Hamilton
Pirate Movie '82

Tony Hamilton
Fatal Instinct '92
Nocturna '79

Wendy Hamilton
The Scars of Dracula '70

Dilys Hamlett
Bananas Boat '78

Harry Hamlin
Blue Skies Again '83
Clash of the Titans '81
Deceptions '85
Dinner at Eight '89
King of the Mountain '81
L.A. Law '86
Laguna Heat '87
Making Love '82
Maxie '85
Movie, Movie '78
Target: Favorite Son '87

Dan Hamlon
20,000 Leagues Under the
Sea '16

Eric Hamm
Summer '86

Warren Hammack
The Eye Creatures '65

Fritz Hammel
The Scorpion Woman '89

Achim Hammer
Sex Adventures of the Three
Musketeers '80s

Ben Hammer
Crazy People '90
The Execution of Private
Slovik '74
Invasion of the Bee Girls '73
Survival Quest '89

Heidi Hammer
2069: A Sex Odyssey '78

Jon Hammer
Phantom Brother '88

M.C. Hammer
Last Action Hero '93

John Hammil
Crossover Dreams '85

Alicia Hammond
Killers '88

John Hammond
The Blue and the Grey '85
Enforcer from Death Row '78
The Prodigal '83

Kay Hammond
Abraham Lincoln '30
Blithe Spirit '45

Nicholas Hammond
The Amazing Spider-Man '77
Chinese Web '78
The Martian Chronicles: Part 1
'79

The Martian Chronicles: Part 3
'79
Spiderman: The Deadly Dust
'78
Trouble in Paradise '88

**Patricia Lee
Hammond**
Dracula's Last Rites '79

Peter Hammond
The Adventurers '51

Chastity Hammons
White Fury '90

Olivia Hamnett
Deadly Possession '88
Earthling '80
The Last Wave '77
Plunge Into Darkness '77

Lucienne Hamon
Becoming Colette '92

Hally Hamond
Blood at Sundown

Walter Hampden
The Prodigal '55
Reap the Wild Wind '42
Sabrina '54

Susan Hampshire
Baffled '72
Cry Terror '74
David Copperfield '70
The Fighting Prince of
Donegal '66
Living Free '72
The Story of David '76
Those Daring Young Men in
Their Jaunty Jalopies '69
The Three Lives of Thomasina
'63

James Hampton
Amazing Howard Hughes '77
The China Syndrome '79
Condorman '81
Force Five '75
Hangar 18 '80
Hawmps! '76
Teen Wolf '85

Jane Hampton
Iron Cowboy '68

Lionel Hampton
The Benny Goodman Story
'55
Force of Impulse '60

Paul Hampton
Hit! '73
Private Duty Nurses '71
They Came from Within '75

Susie Hampton
Fast Kill '73

Charles Han
Strike of Thunderkick Tiger
'80s

Eagle Han
Shaolin Incredible Ten '70s

Maggie Han
The Last Emperor '87

**Master Bong Soo
Han**
Force: Five '81
Kill the Golden Goose '79

Shotaro Hanayagi
The Story of the Late
Chrysanthemum '39

Yoshiaki Hanayagi
Sansho the Bailiff '54

Herbie Hancock
Round Midnight '86

John Hancock
Archer: The Fugitive from the
Empire '81
In the Custody of Strangers
'82
Traxx '87
Why Me? '90

Lou Hancock
Miracle Mile '89

Sheila Hancock
Buster '88
Hawks '89

Susan Hancock
Finian's Rainbow '68

Irene Handl
Adventures of a Private Eye
'87
Morgan! '66
The Private Life of Sherlock
Holmes '70
Riding High '78
Small Hotel '57
Wonderwall: The Movie '69

Rene Handren-Seals
Powwow Highway '89

Robert Hands
Foreign Affairs '93

James Handy
Bird '88
False Arrest '92

Josef Hanet
Revenge '86

Carol Haney
Pajama Game '57

Daryl Haney
Daddy's Boys '87
Lords of the Deep '89

David Haney
Hootch Country Boys '75

Dorothy Haney
Terror of the Bloodhunters '62

Helen Hanft
Stardust Memories '80
Used People '92

Roger Hanin
My Other Husband '85
Rocco and His Brothers '60

Barry Hankerson
Pipe Dreams '76

Tom Hankerson
Candy Tangerine Man '75

Larry Hankin
Armed and Dangerous '86
Black Magic Woman '91
Out on a Limb '92

Brad Hanks
HauntedWeen '91

Jim Hanks
Buford's Beach Bunnies '92

Steve Hanks
B.A.D. Cats '80

Tom Hanks
Bachelor Party '84
Big '88
The Bonfire of the Vanities '90
The 'Burbs '89
Dragnet '87
Every Time We Say Goodbye
'86
He Knows You're Alone '80
Joe Versus the Volcano '90

A League of Their Own '92
The Man with One Red Shoe
'85
Mazes and Monsters '82
The Money Pit '86
Nothing in Common '86
Punchline '88
Rona Jaffe's Mazes &
Monsters '82
Sleepless In Seattle '93
Splash '84
Turner and Hooch '89
Volunteers '85

Bridget Hanley
Chattanooga Choo Choo '84

Jenny Hanley
Flesh and Blood Show '73
On Her Majesty's Secret
Service '69
The Scars of Dracula '70

Jimmy Hanley
The Blue Lamp '49
Captive Heart '47
Housemaster '38
Room to Let '49
Salute John Citizen '42

Peter Hanley
Best of Ernie Kovacs '56

Robert Hanley
L.A. Bounty '89

Julie Hanlon
I Was a Teenage TV Terrorist
'87

Adam Hann-Byrd
Little Man Tate '91

Daryl Hannah
At Play in the Fields of the
Lord '91
Blade Runner '82
The Clan of the Cave Bear '86
Crazy People '90
Crimes & Misdemeanors '89
The Final Terror '83
The Fury '78
Hard Country '81
High Spirits '88
Legal Eagles '86
Memoirs of an Invisible Man
'92
The Pope of Greenwich
Village '84
Reckless '84
Roxanne '87
Splash '84
Steel Magnolias '89
Summer Lovers '82
Wall Street '87

Page Hannah
After School '88
Creepshow 2 '87
My Man Adam '86
Racing with the Moon '84
Shag: The Movie '89

Will Hannah
Buckeye and Blue '87

John Hannan
Strictly Ballroom '92

Alyson Hannigan
My Stepmother Is an Alien '88

Marilyn Hanold
Frankenstein Meets the Space
Monster '65

Wladyslaw Hanoza
Casimir the Great

Lawrence Hanray
Mimi '35

Wuk Ma No Hans
Bruce's Deadly Fingers '80

Kali Hansa
Night of the Sorcerers '70

Glen Hansard
The Commitments '91

Catherine Hansen
The Magic Fountain '61

Cheryl Hansen
Thou Shalt Not Kill...Except
'87

Gale Hansen
Dead Poets Society '89
The Deadly and the Beautiful
'73
Double Vision '92
The Finest Hour '91
Shaking the Tree '92

Gunnar Hansen
The Demon Lover '77
Hollywood Chainsaw Hookers
'88
The Texas Chainsaw
Massacre '74

Heidi Hansen
Superbug Super Agent '76

James Hansen
Night Ripper '86

Joachim Hansen
Frozen Alive '64
Secret of the Black Trunk '62

Juanita Hansen
Charlie Chase and Ben Turpin
'21

Juliana Hansen
Perfect Family '92

Lory Hansen
Point of Terror '71

Patti Hansen
Hard to Hold '84
They All Laughed '81

William Hansen
Homebodies '74

Rhonda Hansome
Feelin' Up '76

Eleanor Hanson
Flaming Frontiers '38

Jody Hanson
Felicity '83

Kristina Hanson
Dinosaurus! '60

Lars Hanson
The Atonement of Gosta
Berling '24
The Flesh and the Devil '27
Homecoming '28
Walpurgis Night '41
The Wind '28

Peter Hanson
When Worlds Collide '51

Tom Haoff
Summer's Children '84

Setsuko Hara
Early Summer '51
The Idiot '51
Late Spring '49
No Regrets for Our Youth '46
Tokyo Story '53

Daijiro Harada
The Silk Road '92

Ernest Harada
Volunteers '85

Itoko Harada
X from Outer Space '67

Kinako Harada
Days of Hell '84

Meiko Harada
Akira Kurosawa's Dreams '90
Nomugi Pass '79
Ran '85

Haya Harareet
Ben-Hur '59
Hill 24 Doesn't Answer '55
The Interns '62
Journey Beneath the Desert '61

Clement Harari
Flight of the Eagle '82
Monkeys, Go Home! '66

Suzette Harbin
Look Out Sister '48

Christine Harbort
Mephisto '81

Martin Harburg
Hockey Night '84

James Harcourt
The Avenging Hand '43

Diana Hardcastle
Fortunes of War '87

Ernest Harden
The Final Terror '83
White Mama '80

Ernest Harden, Jr.
White Men Can't Jump '92

Jacques Harden
Lola '61

Marcia Gay Harden
Fever '91
Late for Dinner '91
Miller's Crossing '90
Sinatra '92
Used People '92

Crofton Hardester
Devastator '85

Kate Hardie
Conspiracy '89
Mona Lisa '86

Raymond Hardie
Look Back in Anger '80

Jerry Hardin
Blaze '89
The Firm '93
Wanted Dead or Alive '86
Wolf Lake '79

Melora Hardin
Big Man on Campus '89
Lambada '89
The North Avenue Irregulars '79

Rellie Hardin
Bronze Buckaroo '39

Sherry Hardin
Hollywood High '77

Ty Hardin
Bad Jim '89
Battle of the Bulge '65
Berserk! '67
I Married a Monster from Outer Space '58
Merrill's Marauders '62
One Step to Hell '68
Palm Springs Weekend '63
PT 109 '63
Rooster: Spurs of Death! '83

You're Jinxed, Friend, You've Met Sacramento '70

Ann Harding
The Animal Kingdom '32
Devotion '31
Love from a Stranger '37
The Man in the Gray Flannel Suit '56
Promise to Murder '56
Two Weeks with Love '50

Jeff Harding
Blood Tracks '86

John Harding
This Property is Condemned '66

June Harding
The Trouble with Angels '66

Kay Harding
Scarlet Claw '44

Lyn Harding
The Man Who Lived Again '36
Murder at the Baskervilles '37
The Mutiny of the Elsinore '39
Old Spanish Custom '36
Sherlock Holmes: The Silver Blaze '41
The Speckled Band '31

Kadeem Hardison
Beat Street '84
Def by Temptation '90
Dream Date '93
White Men Can't Jump '92

Karl Hardman
Night of the Living Dead '68

Joe Hardt
Blood Cult '85

Derek Hardwick
Among the Cinders '83

Cedric Hardwicke
Around the World in 80 Days '56
Becky Sharp '35
Beware of Pity '46
Botany Bay '53
Commandos Strike at Dawn '43
A Connecticut Yankee in King Arthur's Court '49
The Desert Fox '51
Diane '55
Five Weeks in a Balloon '62
The Ghoul '34
The Green Glove '52
The Howards of Virginia '40
The Hunchback of Notre Dame '39
I Remember Mama '48
The Invisible Man Returns '40
The Keys of the Kingdom '44
King Solomon's Mines '37
Les Miserables '35
The Lodger '44
The Magic Fountain '61
Nicholas Nickleby '46
Nine Days a Queen '34
On Borrowed Time '39
Power '34
Richard III '55
Rope '48
Salome '53
Stanley and Livingstone '39
Sundown '41
Suspicion '41
The Ten Commandments '56
Things to Come '36
Tom Brown's School Days '40
Tycoon '47
Valley of the Sun '42
The White Tower '50

Wilson '44
A Wing and a Prayer '44
The Winslow Boy '48

Edward Hardwicke
The Adventures of Sherlock Holmes: Hound of the Baskervilles '89

Jonathon Hardy
The Devil's Playground '76
Lonely Hearts '82
The Wacky World of Wills & Burke '85

Oliver Hardy
Air Raid Wardens '43
Bakery/Grocery Clerk '21
Bellhop/The Noon Whistle '22
Block-heads '38
Bohemian Girl '36
Bonnie Scotland '35
Bullfighters '45
A Chump at Oxford '40
Comedy Classics '35
Days of Thrills and Laughter '61
The Devil's Brother '33
A Few Moments with Buster Keaton and Laurel and Hardy '63
The Fighting Kentuckian '49
The Flying Deuces '39
Golden Age of Comedy '58
Great Guns '41
Hollywood Clowns '85
Hollywood Party '34
Laurel & Hardy and the Family '33
Laurel & Hardy: Another Fine Mess '30
Laurel & Hardy: At Work '32
Laurel & Hardy: Be Big '31
Laurel & Hardy: Below Zero '30
Laurel & Hardy: Berth Marks '29
Laurel & Hardy: Blotto '30
Laurel & Hardy: Brats '30
Laurel & Hardy: Chickens Come Home '31
Laurel & Hardy Comedy Classics, Vol. 1 '33
Laurel & Hardy Comedy Classics, Vol. 2 '30
Laurel & Hardy Comedy Classics, Vol. 3 '34
Laurel & Hardy Comedy Classics, Vol. 4 '32
Laurel & Hardy Comedy Classics, Vol. 5 '31
Laurel & Hardy Comedy Classics, Vol. 6 '35
Laurel & Hardy Comedy Classics, Vol. 7 '30s
Laurel & Hardy Comedy Classics, Vol. 8 '30s
Laurel & Hardy Comedy Classics, Vol. 9 '30s
Laurel & Hardy: Hog Wild '30
Laurel & Hardy: Laughing Gravy '31
Laurel & Hardy: Men O'War '29
Laurel & Hardy: Night Owls '30
Laurel & Hardy On the Lam '30
Laurel & Hardy: Perfect Day '29
Laurel & Hardy Special
Laurel & Hardy: Stan "Helps" Ollie '33
March of the Wooden Soldiers '34
Movie Struck '37
Music Box/Helpmates '32

No Man's Law '21
Nothing But Trouble '44
Our Relations '36
Pack Up Your Troubles '32
Pardon Us '31
Pick a Star '37
Saps at Sea '40
Silent Laugh Makers, No. 1 '15
Silent Laugh Makers, No. 2 '17
Sons of the Desert '33
Swiss Miss '38
Three Ages '23
Utopia '51
Way Out West '37
The Wizard of Oz '25

Robert Hardy
Blat
Dark Places '73
Demons of the Mind '72
Jenny's War '85
The Shooting Party '85
War & Remembrance, Part 1 '88
War & Remembrance: The Final Chapter, Part 8 '89
The Woman He Loved '88

Sam Hardy
Big News '29
Break of Hearts '35
Powdersmoke Range '35

Sophie Hardy
Erotic Touch of Hot Skin '65
The Mysterious Magician '65

Stephanie Hardy
To Sleep with a Vampire '92

William Hardy
My Sweet Charlie '70

Doris Hare
Nuns on the Run '90

Lumsden Hare
Northwest Passage '40
Rose Marie '54
Shadows on the Stairs '41
That Forsyte Woman '50

Robertson Hare
The Adventures of Sadie '55
Murder on the Campus '52
Things Happen at Night '48

Dorian Harewood
Against All Odds '84
The Ambush Murders '82
An American Christmas Carol '79
Beulah Land '80
The Falcon and the Snowman '85
Full Metal Jacket '87
God Bless the Child '88
Guilty of Innocence '87
The Jesse Owens Story '84
Kiss Shot '89
Pacific Heights '90
Panic in Echo Park '77
Roots: The Next Generation '79
Sparkle '76
Strike Force '81
Tank '83

Mariska Hargitay
Finish Line '89
Ghoulies '85
Welcome to 18 '87

Mickey Hargitay
The Bloody Pit of Horror '65
Lady Frankenstein '72
The Loves of Hercules '60

Doris Hargrave
Last Night at the Alamo '83
The Whole Shootin' Match '79

T.J. Hargrave
The Prince of Central Park '77

Christine Hargreaves
Pink Floyd: The Wall '82

John Hargreaves
Beyond Reasonable Doubt '80
Careful, He Might Hear You '84
Don's Party '76
Great Gold Swindle '84
Killing of Angel Street '81
Little Boy Lost '78
Malcolm '86
My First Wife '84
Sky Pirates '87

Gordon Harker
Champagne '28
The Farmer's Wife '28
Inspector Hornleigh '39
The Phantom Light '35
The Ring '27
Small Hotel '57
Things Happen at Night '48

Susannah Harker
The Crucifer of Blood '91

John Harkins
Absence of Malice '81
Amityville 3: The Demon '83
Birdy '84
City Killer '87
Rampage '87
Slaves of New York '89
This Gun for Hire '90

Paul Harkins
Heartbreak Hotel '88

Percy Harkness
Caged Terror '72

Kenneth Harlan
Dawn Express '42
Death Valley Rangers '44
The Ice Flood '26
Little Church Around the Corner '23
A Million to One '37
Paradise Island '30
Phantom Killer '42
The Primitive Lover '16
Renfrew of the Royal Mounted '37
Santa Fe Marshal '40
Under Montana Skies '30
The Virginian '23

Otis Harlan
I Can't Escape '34
King Kelly of the U.S.A. '34
Mr. Boggs Steps Out '38
Outlaws of Sonora '38
Snow White and the Seven Dwarfs '37

Robin Harlan
Party Animal '83

Willie Harlander
Rosalie Goes Shopping '89

Honey Harlow
Dance Hall Racket '58

Jean Harlow
Bombshell '33
China Seas '35
City Lights '31
Dinner at Eight '33
The Girl from Missouri '34
Golden Age of Comedy '58

Hell's Angels '30
Hold Your Man '33
Libeled Lady '36
The Love Goddesses '65
Personal Property '37
Platinum Blonde '31
Public Enemy '31
Reckless '35
Red Dust '32
Red Headed Woman '32
Riff Raff '35
Saratoga '37
Suzy '26
Wife Versus Secretary '36

Deborah Harmon
Bachelor Party '84
Prince of Bel Air '87
Used Cars '80

Helen Harmon
Where the Lilies Bloom '74

Mark Harmon
After the Promise '87
Beyond the Poseidon
    Adventure '79
Cold Heaven '92
Comes a Horseman '78
The Deliberate Stranger '86
Fourth Story '90
Goliath Awaits '81
Let's Get Harry '87
The Presidio '88
Prince of Bel Air '87
Stealing Home '88
Summer School '87
Till There was You '91
Worth Winning '89

Renee Harmon
The Executioner, Part 2:
    Frozen Scream '84
Lady Street Fighter '86
Night of Terror '87

Tom Harmon
The Spirit of West Point '47

**Raymond
Harmstorf**
Thunder Warrior '85

Elisabeth Harnois
Where Are the Children? '85

Christina Harnos
Denial: The Dark Side of
    Passion '91
The Rescue '88

Ralf Harolde
Baby Face Morgan '42
Behind Locked Doors '48
Hook, Line and Sinker '30
I Killed That Man '42
Night Nurse '31
The Sea Wolf '41

Helen Harp
Tombs of the Blind Dead '72

Shraga Harpaz
Secret of Yolanda '82

Betty Harper
Jigsaw '49

David W. Harper
A Day for Thanks on Walton's
    Mountain '82

Gerald Harper
If It's a Man, Hang Up '75

Jessica Harper
Big Man on Campus '89
Blue Iguana '88
Eat a Bowl of Tea '89
The Evictors '79
Imagemaker '86
Inserts '76

My Favorite Year '82
Pennies From Heaven '81
Phantom of the Paradise '74
Shock Treatment '81
Stardust Memories '80
Suspiria '77

Kay Harper
Afterward '85

Kyra Harper
Buffalo Jump '90

Marjorie Harper
Life & Times of Grizzly Adams
    '74

Paul Harper
Bloody Trail '72
Mona's Place '89

Robert Harper
Final Analysis '92
Held Hostage '91

Ron Harper
Temporada Salvaje '87

Samantha Harper
Oh! Calcutta! '72

Susan Harper
Phantasm '79

Tess Harper
Amityville 3: The Demon '83
Chiefs '83
Crimes of the Heart '86
Criminal Law '89
Daddy's Dyin'...Who's Got the
    Will? '90
Dark River: A Father's
    Revenge '90
Far North '88
Flashpoint '84
Her Alibi '88
The Man in the Moon '91
My Heroes Have Always Been
    Cowboys '91
Reckless Disregard '84
A Summer to Remember '84
Tender Mercies '83

Valerie Harper
Blame It on Rio '84
Chapter Two '79
Don't Go to Sleep '82
Drop-Out Mother '88
The Execution '85
Freebie & the Bean '74
The Last Married Couple in
    America '80
Night Terror '76
The Shadow Box '80
Thursday's Game '74

Roland Harrah, III
Braddock: Missing in Action 3
    '88

Cindy Harrel
The Final Terror '83
Model Behavior '82

Georgia Harrell
First Turn On '83

Jim Harrell
Don't Open the Door! '74

Rebecca Harrell
Prancer '89

Woody Harrelson
Cool Blue '88
Doc Hollywood '91
Eye of the Demon '87
Indecent Proposal '93
White Men Can't Jump '92
Wildcats '86

Nedda Harrigan
Charlie Chan at the Opera '36

William Harrigan
Exiled to Shanghai '37
"G" Men '35
The Invisible Man '33

Richard Harriman
Incoming Freshmen '79

Laura Harring
Rio Diablo '93

Robert Harring
True Heart Susie '19

**Cheryl Francis
Harrington**
Perfume '91

Curtis Harrington
Cult People '89

**Hamtree
Harrington**
The Devil's Daughter '39

Laura Harrington
Maximum Overdrive '86
Vietnam War Story 3 '89

Lisa Jay Harrington
Witchcraft 4: Virgin Heart '92

Pat Harrington
The Affair '73
Easy Come, Easy Go '67
The President's Analyst '67

Aaron Harris
Glory Boys '84

Anita Harris
Follow That Camel '67

Ann Harris
Honeymoon Killers '70

Barbara Harris
Family Plot '76
Freaky Friday '76
Movie, Movie '78
Nashville '75
Nice Girls Don't Explode '87
The North Avenue Irregulars
    '79
Oh Dad, Poor Dad (Momma's
    Hung You in the Closet &
    I'm Feeling So Sad) '67
Peggy Sue Got Married '86
Plaza Suite '71
The Seduction of Joe Tynan
    '79
A Thousand Clowns '65

Bob Harris
The Student Teachers '73

Brad Harris
The Freakmaker '73
The Fury of Hercules '61
Goliath Against the Giants '63
Hercules '83
Island of Lost Girls '73
Jungle Inferno '70s
King of Kong Island '78
The Mad Butcher '72
Rattler Kid '70s
Samson '61
Seven Magnificent Gladiators
    '84

Bud Harris
Moon Over Harlem '39

Cassandra Harris
For Your Eyes Only '81

Connie Harris
Harlem on the Prairie '38

Cynthia Harris
Edward and Mrs. Simpson '80
Izzy & Moe '85
Pancho Barnes '88

Reuben, Reuben '83

Danielle Harris
Halloween 4: The Return of
    Michael Myers '88
Halloween 5: The Revenge of
    Michael Myers '89
The Last Boy Scout '91
Marked for Death '90

David Harris
Badge of the Assassin '85
Undercover '87
Vietnam War Story 1 '88

Ed Harris
The Abyss '89
Alamo Bay '85
Borderline '80
Code Name: Emerald '85
Creepshow '82
The Firm '93
A Flash of Green '85
Glengarry Glen Ross '92
Jacknife '89
Knightriders '81
Last Innocent Man '87
Needful Things '93
Paris Trout '91
Places in the Heart '84
The Right Stuff '83
Running Mates '92
The Seekers '79
State of Grace '90
Sweet Dreams '85
Swing Shift '84
To Kill a Priest '89
Under Fire '83
Walker '87

Eddie Harris
Dynamite Dan '24

Edna Mae Harris
Lying Lips '39
Paradise in Harlem '40

Emmylou Harris
The Last Waltz '78

Fox Harris
Alienator '89
Dr. Caligari '89
Repo Man '83
Warlords '88

Fred Harris
Exterminators of the Year
    3000 '83

Jack Harris
Stakeout '62

Jared Harris
The Public Eye '92

Jim Harris
Waitress '81

Jo Ann Harris
Act of Vengeance '74
Deadly Games '80

John Harris
Carnival of Blood '71

Julie Harris
America at the Movies '76
The Bell Jar '79
The Christmas Wife '88
The Dark Half '91
A Doll's House '59
East of Eden '54
Forever James Dean '88
Gorillas in the Mist '88
Harper '66
The Haunting '63
The Hiding Place '75
Holy Terror '65
Home for the Holidays '72
Housesitter '92
I Am a Camera '55

James Dean: The First
    American Teenager '76
The Last of Mrs. Lincoln '76
The Member of the Wedding
    '52
The People Next Door '70
Reflections in a Golden Eye
    '67
Truth About Women '58
Victoria Regina '61
Voyage of the Damned '76
The Woman He Loved '88
You're a Big Boy Now '66

Julius W. Harris
Black Caesar '73
Crimewave '85
Hell Up in Harlem '73
Live and Let Die '73
Missing Pieces '83
Prayer of the Rollerboys '91
Shaft's Big Score '72
Superfly '72

Lara Harris
Blood Red '88
The Fourth War '90
No Man's Land '87

Leigh Anne Harris
I, the Jury '82
Sorceress '82

Lynette Harris
I, the Jury '82
Sorceress '82

Maxine Harris
Signals Through the Flames
    '83

Mel Harris
Cameron's Closet '89
Desperate Motives '92
K-9 '89
Raising Cain '92
Wanted Dead or Alive '86

Michael Harris
Shriek of the Mutilated '74

Michelle Harris
A Matter of Love '78

Mitchell Harris
Ghost Valley '32

M.K. Harris
Genuine Risk '89
Horseplayer '91
Slumber Party Massacre 3 '90

Neil Patrick Harris
Clara's Heart '88
Cold Sassy Tree '89
Purple People Eater '88

Paul Harris
Jive Turkey '76

Phil Harris
Dreaming Out Loud '40
The Gatling Gun '72
Goodbye, My Lady '56
Here Comes the Groom '51
Melody Cruise '32
The Patsy '64
Robin Hood '73
Rock-a-Doodle '92
The Wheeler Dealers '63

Priscilla Harris
Nights in White Satin '87

Richard Harris
The Bible...In the Beginning
    '66
Camelot '67
The Cassandra Crossing '76
Cromwell '70
The Deadly Trackers '73
The Field '90

Michael Hartson
Terrorgram '90

Masumi Harukawa
Tokyo Pop '88

Elvind Harum
The Shaman '87

Rainbow Harvest
Mirror, Mirror '90
Old Enough '84

Don Harvey
Casualties of War '89
Eight Men Out '88
Gang Busters '55
Prey of the Chameleon '91

Forrester Harvey
Thoroughbreds Don't Cry '37

Harry Harvey
Code of the Fearless '39
I'm from Arkansas '44
In Old Montana '39
The Narrow Margin '52
The Reckless Way '36
Ridin' the Trail '40
Tea for Two '50

Herk Harvey
Carnival of Souls '62

Joan Harvey
Hands of a Stranger '62

Jon Harvey
Pin-Up Girl '44

Laurence Harvey
The Alamo '60
Butterfield 8 '60
Dandy in Aspic '68
Darling '65
Escape to the Sun '72
I Am a Camera '55
Innocents in Paris '53
The Magic Christian '69
Man on the Run '49
The Manchurian Candidate '62
Night Watch '72
Of Human Bondage '64
Romeo and Juliet '54
Room at the Top '59
The Silent Enemy '58
Spy with a Cold Nose '66
Summer and Smoke '61
Truth About Women '58
Walk on the Wild Side '62
The Wonderful World of the Brothers Grimm '62

Lilian Harvey
Congress Dances '31

Marilyn Harvey
The Astounding She-Monster '58

Michael Harvey
Don't Look in the Basement '73

Paul Harvey
April In Paris '52
Helldorado '46
Meet Dr. Christian '39
A Southern Yankee '48
23 1/2 Hours Leave '37
The Yellow Cab Man '50

Rodney Harvey
Five Corners '88
Guncrazy '92
My Own Private Idaho '91
Salsa '88

Russ Harvey
Dungeon of Harrow '64

Terence Harvey
The Phantom of the Opera '89

Tom Harvey
And Then You Die '88

Kazuo Hasegawa
The Crucified Lovers '54
Gate of Hell '54

Joyce Hash
Twisted Brain '74

Hunsija Hasimovic
Time of the Gypsies '90

David Haskell
Body Double '84

Peter Haskell
Child's Play 3 '91
Christina '74
The Cracker Factory '79
Legend of Earl Durand '74
Robot Wars '93

Joan Haskett
Mr. Mike's Mondo Video '79

Dolly Hass
Spy of Napoleon '36

Imogen Hassall
When Dinosaurs Ruled the Earth '70

O.E. Hasse
Above Us the Waves '56
Betrayed '54
The Big Lift '50
Elusive Corporal '62
State of Siege '73

Danny Hassel
A Nightmare on Elm Street 4: Dream Master '88
A Nightmare on Elm Street 5: Dream Child '89

David Hasselhoff
Bail Out '90
Cartier Affair '84
The Final Alliance '89
Fire and Rain '89
Revenge of the Cheerleaders '76
Star Crash '78
Terror at London Bridge '85
Witchery '88

Jenny Hasselquist
The Atonement of Gosta Berling '24

Lee Hassen
Goliathon '79

Marilyn Hassett
The Bell Jar '79
Body Count '87
Messenger of Death '88
The Other Side of the Mountain '75
The Other Side of the Mountain, Part 2 '78
Twenty Dollar Star '91
Two Minute Warning '76

Signe Hasso
A Double Life '47
Heaven Can Wait '43
Johnny Angel '45
Journey for Margaret '42
The Seventh Cross '44

Bob Hastings
Harper Valley P.T.A. '78
Munster's Revenge '81
Shadow Force '92
Snowballing '85

Lynn Hastings
Cherry Hill High '76

Stephanie Hastings
Cheerleaders' Beach Party '77

Richard Hatch
Battlestar Galactica '78
Charlie Chan and the Curse of the Dragon Queen '81
Deadman's Curve '78
Delta Force Commando 2 '90
Ghetto Blaster '89
The Hatfields & the McCoys '75
Heated Vengeance '87
Mission Galactica: The Cylon Attack '79
Party Line '88
Prisoners of the Lost Universe '84

Mary Hatcher
The Big Wheel '49
Holiday in Havana '49
Tales of Robin Hood '52

Teri Hatcher
Dead in the Water '91
Soapdish '91
Straight Talk '92
Tango and Cash '89

Hurd Hatfield
The Boston Strangler '68
Crimes of the Heart '86
Diary of a Chambermaid '46
Dragon Seed '44
El Cid '61
Her Alibi '88
Invincible Mr. Disraeli '63
King David '85
The King of Kings '61
Lamp at Midnight '66
Picture of Dorian Gray '45
Thief '71
The Word '78

Mert Hatfield
The Ballad of the Sad Cafe '91

Kellen Hathaway
Dennis the Menace '93

Noah Hathaway
The NeverEnding Story '84
Troll '85

Ernie Hatrak
Best of Ernie Kovacs '56

Rohini Hattangady
Gandhi '82

Raymond Hatton
Arizona Bound '41
Behind the Front '26
Below the Border '42
Blazing Guns '50
Border Bandits '46
Buffalo Stampede '33
Covered Wagon Days '40
Cowboys from Texas '39
The Crooked Circle '32
Dawn on the Great Divide '42
Desert Gold '36
Down Texas Way '42
Drifting Souls '32
The Fighting American '24
Flesh and the Spur '57
Forbidden Trails '41
Frontier Horizon '39
Gentleman from Texas '46
Ghost Rider '43
Ghost Town Law '42
Girls in Prison '56
Gunman from Bodie '41
Guns of Justice '50
The Kansas Terrors '39
Kentucky Jubilee '51
Lady Killer '33

Land of the Lawless '47
Lawmen '44
The Little American '17
Lonely Trail/Three Texas Steers '39
Male and Female '19
Marshal of Heldorado '50
Motorcycle Gang '57
Northwest Trail '46
Peck's Bad Boy '21
Raiders of the Border '44
Reap the Wild Wind '42
Riders of the West '42
Rocky Mountain Rangers '40
Rogue of the Rio Grande '30
Rolling Home '46
Rough Riders' Roundup '34
Shake, Rattle and Rock '57
Six Gun Gospel '43
The Stranger from Pecos '45
Sudden Death '50
Terror Trail '33
Three Musketeers '33
Uptown New York '32
The Virginian '23
West of the Law '42
Wyoming Outlaw '39

Rondo Hatton
The Brute Man '46
The Pearl of Death '44

Tom Hatton
Spies Like Us '85

Didier Haudepin
This Special Friendship '67

Sabine Haudepin
The Last Metro '80

Aysha Hauer
Witchcraft 5: Dance with the Devil '92

Rutger Hauer
Beyond Justice '92
Blade Runner '82
Blind Fury '90
Blind Side '93
The Blood of Heroes '89
Bloodhounds of Broadway '89
A Breed Apart '84
Buffy the Vampire Slayer '92
Chanel Solitaire '81
Cold Blood '70s
Dandelions '74
Deadlock '91
Escape from Sobibor '87
Eureka! '81
Fatal Error '83
Flesh and Blood '85
Hitcher '85
Inside the Third Reich '82
Katie's Passion '75
Keetje Tippei '75
Ladyhawke '85
Mysteries '84
Nighthawks '81
The Osterman Weekend '83
Past Midnight '92
Soldier of Orange '78
Spetters '80
Split Second '92
Turkish Delights '73
Wanted Dead or Alive '86
The Wilby Conspiracy '75

Angelika Hauff
The Life and Loves of Mozart '59
Tromba, the Tiger Man '52

David Cain Haughton
Emperor Caligula: The Untold Story '80s

Ullrich Haupt
Morocco '30

Cole Hauser
School Ties '92

Fay Hauser
Christmas Lilies of the Field '84
Jimmy the Kid '82
Jo Jo Dancer, Your Life is Calling '86
Marvin & Tige '84

Jerry Hauser
Forbidden Love '82

Patrick Hauser
Weekend Pass '84

Wings Hauser
The Art of Dying '90
Beastmaster 2: Through the Portal of Time '91
Bedroom Eyes 2 '89
Blood Money '91
The Carpenter '89
Code of Honor '84
Coldfire '90
Dead Man Walking '88
Deadly Conspiracy '91
Deadly Force '83
Exiled in America '90
Frame Up '91
Homework '82
Hostage '87
In Between '92
Jo Jo Dancer, Your Life is Calling '86
The Killer's Edge '90
L.A. Bounty '89
Living to Die '91
The Long, Hot Summer '86
Marked for Murder '89
Mind, Body & Soul '92
Mutant '83
Nightmare at Noon '87
No Safe Haven '87
Out of Sight, Out of Her Mind '89
Pale Blood '91
Reason to Die '90
The Siege of Firebase Gloria '89
A Soldier's Story '84
Street Asylum '90
Tough Guys Don't Dance '87
Vice Squad '82
Wilding '90
The Wind '87

Michael Hauserman
Slaughterday '77

David Hausman
Osa '85

Thomas Haustein
Christiane F. '82

Semu Haute
Out '88

Moshe Havazelet
Noa at Seventeen '82

Annette Haven
Dracula Sucks '79
Pleasure Resort '90

Richie Havens
Street Hunter '90
Woodstock '70

June Haver
Love Nest '51

Phyllis Haver
The Balloonatic/One Week '23
The Blacksmith/The Balloonatic '23

Arrowsmith '31
Candleshoe '78
Family Upside Down '78
A Farewell to Arms '32
Herbie Rides Again '74
Main Street to Broadway '53
One of Our Dinosaurs Is
    Missing '75
Riders of the Range '24
The Sin of Madelon Claudet
    '31
Skin Game '31
Spy in Black '39
Stage Door Canteen '43
Third Man on the Mountain
    '59

Isaac Hayes
Counterforce '87
Dead Aim '87
Escape from New York '81
Guilty as Charged '92
I'm Gonna Git You Sucka '88
Jailbait: Betrayed By
    Innocence '86
Nightstick '87
Posse '93
Prime Target '91
Robin Hood: Men in Tights '93
Truck Turner '74

Jerri Hayes
Black Sister's Revenge '76

Kathryn Hayes
357 Magnum '77

Linda Hayes
Danger on the Air '38
South of Santa Fe '42

Maggie Hayes
Girls' Town '59

Margaret Hayes
Blackboard Jungle '55
In Old Colorado '41
Omar Khayyam '57
Sullivan's Travels '41

Mary Hayes
Roaring Six Guns '37

Patricia Hayes
The NeverEnding Story '84
Super Bitch '89
The Terrornauts '67

Peter Lind Hayes
The 5000 Fingers of Dr. T '53
Playmates '41
Seven Days' Leave '42
Zis Boom Bah '42

Stephen K. Hayes
Ninja Vengeance '93

Terry Hayes
Flesh Eating Mothers '89

William Hayes
The Cage '90

Lisa Hayland
Novel Desires '92

Cyd Hayman
After Julius '78
After Julius '78
The Godsend '79

David Hayman
Hope and Glory '87
A Sense of Freedom '78
Sid & Nancy '86

Dick Haymes
Betrayal '74
DuBarry Was a Lady '43
One Touch of Venus '48
St. Benny the Dip '51
State Fair '45

Cal Haynes
Fyre '78
Kemek '88

Daniel L. Haynes
Hallelujah! '29

Linda Haynes
Human Experiments '79
Rolling Thunder '77

Loren Haynes
The Expendables '89

Michael Haynes
Chrome and Hot Leather '71

Roberta Haynes
The Adventurers '70
The Fighter '52
Hell Ship Mutiny '57

Jim Haynie
Bitter Harvest '81
From Hollywood to Deadwood
    '89
Grand Tour: Disaster in Time
    '92
Hard Traveling '85
Jack's Back '87
On the Edge '86
Out '88
Sleepwalkers '92
Too Much Sun '90

Don Hays
The Little Match Girl '84

Hubert Hays
Empire of Spiritual Ninja

Robert Hays
Airplane! '80
Airplane 2: The Sequel '82
California Gold Rush '81
Cat's Eye '85
The Fall of the House of Usher
    '80
Fifty Fifty '93
Homeward Bound: The
    Incredible Journey '93
Honeymoon Academy '90
Hot Chocolate '92
Initiation of Sarah '78
Murder by the Book '87
Running Against Time '90
Scandalous '84
Take This Job & Shove It '81
Touched '82
Trenchcoat '83
Utilities '83

Dennis Haysbert
Love Field '91
Major League '89
Mr. Baseball '92
Navy SEALS '90

John Hayt
Operation C.I.A. '65

James Hayter
Beau Brummel '54
Four Sided Triangle '53
The Pickwick Papers '54
Tom Brown's School Days '51
Trio '50

Chad Hayward
The Killing Game '87
Violent Zone '89

Chris Hayward
In Search of Anna '79

David Hayward
Delusion '84
Thousand Pieces of Gold '91

**John Nugent
Hayward**
Overlanders '46

Louis Hayward
And Then There Were None
    '45
Anthony Adverse '36
Black Arrow '48
The Christmas Kid '68
Chuka '67
Dance, Girl, Dance '40
The Man in the Iron Mask '39
Promise to Murder '56
The Saint in New York '38
The Search for Bridey Murphy
    '56
The Son of Monte Cristo '41
The Strange Woman '46
Terror in the Wax Museum '73

Rachel Hayward
Breaking All the Rules '85

Susan Hayward
Adam Had Four Sons '41
Back Street '61
Beau Geste '39
The Conqueror '56
David and Bathsheba '51
Deadline at Dawn '46
Demetrius and the Gladiators
    '54
Fighting Seabees '44
The Hairy Ape '44
The Honey Pot '67
House of Strangers '49
I Married a Witch '42
I Want to Live! '58
I'll Cry Tomorrow '55
Jack Frost '43
Jack London '44
Lost Moment '47
The Lusty Men '52
Rawhide '50
Reap the Wild Wind '42
Say Goodbye, Maggie Cole
    '72
Smash-Up: The Story of a
    Woman '47
The Snows of Kilimanjaro '52
Soldier of Fortune '55
They Won't Believe Me '47
Tulsa '49
Valley of the Dolls '67
Young & Willing '42

Chris Haywood
Attack Force Z '84
The Clinic '83
Heatwave '83
Man of Flowers '84
The Navigator '88
Newsfront '78
Quigley Down Under '90
Razorback '84
Sweet Talker '91
The Tale of Ruby Rose '87
Waterfront '83
A Woman's Tale '92

Pat Haywood
Getting It Right '89

Carmen Hayworth
Boss '74

Rita Hayworth
Affair in Trinidad '52
Angels Over Broadway '40
Blood and Sand '41
Circus World '64
Cover Girl '44
Down to Earth '47
Fire Down Below '57
Gilda '46
Hit the Saddle '37
The Lady from Shanghai '48
The Lady in Question '40
The Love Goddesses '65
The Loves of Carmen '48
Miss Sadie Thompson '53

Music in My Heart '40
Only Angels Have Wings '39
Pal Joey '57
The Poppy is also a Flower
    '66
Renegade Ranger/Scarlet
    River '38
Road to Salina '68
Salome '53
Separate Tables '58
Strawberry Blonde '41
Susan and God '40
They Came to Cordura '59
Tonight and Every Night '45
Trouble in Texas '37
You Were Never Lovelier '42
You'll Never Get Rich '41

Jonathan Haze
Apache Woman '55
The Gunslinger '56
It Conquered the World '56
Little Shop of Horrors '60
Poor White Trash '57
Rock All Night '57
Track of the Vampire '66
X: The Man with X-Ray Eyes
    '63

Meridith Haze
Death Wish Club '83

Stan Haze
From Noon Till Three '76

Hy Hazell
The Key Man '57

Noni Hazlehurst
Fran '85
Monkey Grip '82
True Colors '87
Waterfront '83

Murray Head
Sunday, Bloody Sunday '71
White Mischief '88

Lena Headey
Waterland '92

Shari Headley
Coming to America '88

Glenne Headly
Dick Tracy '90
Dirty Rotten Scoundrels '88
Doctor Detroit '83
Fandango '85
Grand Isle '92
Making Mr. Right '86
Mortal Thoughts '91
Nadine '87
Paperhouse '89
The Purple Rose of Cairo '85
Seize the Day '86
Stars and Bars '88

Anthony Heald
Postcards from the Edge '90
The Silence of the Lambs '91
Whispers in the Dark '92

Dan Healey
Glorifying the American Girl
    '30

James Healey
Strangers '90

Jeff Healey
Road House '89

Myron Healey
Cavalry Command '63
Claws '77
Down to Earth '47
Gang Busters '55
Guns Don't Argue '57
Pulse '88
Smoke in the Wind '75
The Unearthly '57

Varan the Unbelievable '61

David Healy
The Sign of Four '83
Supergirl '84

Katherine Healy
Six Weeks '82

Mary Healy
The 5000 Fingers of Dr. T '53
Zis Boom Bah '42

Patricia Healy
Sweet Poison '91

Ted Healy
Dancing Lady '33
Hollywood Party '34
Mad Love '35
Reckless '35
Three Stooges Comedy
    Classics '49

John Heard
After Hours '85
Awakenings '90
Beaches '88
Best Revenge '83
Betrayed '88
Between the Lines '77
Big '88
Blown Away '90
Cat People '82
Chilly Scenes of Winter '79
C.H.U.D. '84
Cutter's Way '81
Dead Ahead: The Exxon
    Valdez Disaster '92
Deceived '91
The End of Innocence '90
First Love '77
Gladiator '92
Heart Beat '80
Heaven Help Us '85
Home Alone '90
Home Alone 2: Lost in New
    York '92
Legs '83
The Milagro Beanfield War '88
Mindwalk '91
On the Yard '79
Out on a Limb '87
The Package '89
Radio Flyer '92
Rambling Rose '91
The Seventh Sign '88
The Telephone '87
Too Scared to Scream '85
The Trip to Bountiful '85
Violated '84
Waterland '92

Susan Heard
The Body Beneath '70

George Hearn
A Piano for Mrs. Cimino '82
Sanctuary of Fear '79
See You in the Morning '89
Sneakers '92
Sweeney Todd: The Demon
    Barber of Fleet Street '84
The Vanishing '93

Mary Ann Hearn
Death Driver '78

Richard Hearne
Butler's Dilemma '43

Patty Hearst
Cry-Baby '90

Rick Hearst
Crossing the Line '90

Marla Heasly
Born to Race '88

Thomas Heathcote
Above Us the Waves '56

Sherman Hemsley
Camp Cucamonga: How I
   Spent My Summer
   Vacation '90
Club Fed '91
Combat Academy '86
Ghost Dance '83
Ghost Fever '87
Love at First Bite '79
Mr. Nanny '93

Joseph Henabery
The Birth of a Nation '15

George Henare
The Silent One '86

Richard Hench
Bio Hazard '85

Frederique Hender
The Devil's Nightmare '71

Albert Henderson
Greaser's Palace '72

Bill Henderson
Ace Crawford, Private Eye
City Slickers '91
Get Crazy '83
Movie Maker '86
Murphy's Law '86

Chuck Henderson
Operation Dames '59

Dell Henderson
The Crowd '28
Show People '28

Don Henderson
The Ghoul '75
The Island '80

Douglas Henderson
King Dinosaur '55

Ena Henderson
Fatal Exposure '90

**Florence
Henderson**
Shakes the Clown '92
Song of Norway '70
A Very Brady Christmas '88

Harry Henderson
Scar of Shame '27

Jeff Henderson
Last Witness '88

Jo Henderson
Lianna '83

Maggie Henderson
Indiscreet '88

Marcia Henderson
Naked Hills '56
Thunder Bay '53

Scott A. Henderson
The Milpitas Monster '75

Ty Henderson
The Competition '80
Happy Hour '87

Lauri Hendler
High School USA '84

Martin Hendler
Forbidden Impulse '85

Tony Hendra
This is Spinal Tap '84

Darlene Hendricks
The Narcotics Story '58

Evelyn Hendricks
Night of Bloody Horror '76

Nancy Hendrickson
Mother's Day '80

Elaine Hendrix
Last Dance '91

Jimi Hendrix
Monterey Pop '68
Woodstock '70

Leah Ayres Hendrix
Hot Child in the City '87

Wanda Hendrix
The Admiral Was a Lady '50
My Outlaw Brother '51

Gloria Hendry
Bare Knuckles '77
Black Belt Jones '74
Black Caesar '73
Hell Up in Harlem '73
Live and Let Die '73
Slaughter's Big Ripoff '73

Ian Hendry
The Ditch '78
Captain Kronos: Vampire
   Hunter '74
Captain Kronos: Vampire
   Hunter '74
Children of the Damned '63
Journey to the Far Side of the
   Sun '69
Killer with Two Faces '74
The Passenger '75
Repulsion '65
The Saint '68
Tales from the Crypt '72
Theatre of Blood '73

Sonja Henie
Sun Valley Serenade '41

Anna Henkel
1900 '76

Drewe Henley
When Dinosaurs Ruled the
   Earth '70

Carrie Henn
Aliens '86

Dermot Hennelly
The Deserters '80s

Marilu Henner
Between the Lines '77
Bloodbrothers '78
Cannonball Run II '84
Chains of Gold '92
Grand Larceny
Grown Ups '86
Hammett '82
Johnny Dangerously '84
L.A. Story '91
Ladykillers '88
Love with a Perfect Stranger
   '86
The Man Who Loved Women
   '83
Noises Off '92
Perfect '85
Rustler's Rhapsody '85
Stark '85

Mark Hennessy
Terminal Exposure '89

Eva Henning
Devil's Wanton '49
Three Strange Loves '49

**Astrid Henning-
Jensen**
The Element of Crime '85

Sam Hennings
Seedpeople '92

Paul Henreid
Battle Shock '56
Casablanca '42
Deception '46

Deep in My Heart '54
The Four Horsemen of the
   Apocalypse '62
Goodbye, Mr. Chips '39
Hollow Triumph '48
Joan of Paris '42
The Madwoman of Chaillot
   '69
Never So Few '59
Night Train to Munich '40
Now, Voyager '42
The Scar '48
The Spanish Main '45
A Stolen Face '52
Tall Lie '53

Bobby Henrey
The Fallen Idol '49

Lance Henriksen
Alien 3 '92
Aliens '86
Choke Canyon '86
Comrades in Arms '91
Damien: Omen 2 '78
Deadly Intent '88
Delta Heat '92
Dog Day Afternoon '75
Excessive Force '93
The Hit List '88
The Horror Show '89
The Jagged Edge '85
Jennifer 8 '92
Johnny Handsome '89
Near Dark '87
Nightmares '83
Piranha 2: The Spawning '82
The Pit & the Pendulum '91
Prince of the City '81
Pumpkinhead '88
The Right Stuff '83
Savage Dawn '84
Stone Cold '91
Survival Quest '89
Tales from the Crypt, Vol. 3
   '90
The Terminator '84
The Visitor '80

Anders Henrikson
Miss Julie '50
A Woman's Face '38

Buck Henry
Aria '88
Best of Gilda Radner '89
Best of John Belushi '85
Catch-22 '70
Dark Before Dawn '89
Defending Your Life '91
Eating Raoul '82
Gloria '80
The Graduate '67
Is There Sex After Death? '71
Keep the Change '92
The Linguini Incident '92
The Man Who Fell to Earth '76
Old Boyfriends '79
The Player '92
Rude Awakening '89
Steve Martin Live '85
Tune in Tomorrow '90

Buss Henry
Rolling Home '48

Charlotte Henry
Bowery Blitzkrieg '41
Charlie Chan at the Opera '36
The Mandarin Mystery '37
March of the Wooden Soldiers
   '34

Gloria Henry
Miss Grant Takes Richmond
   '49

Greg Henry
Body Double '84

Fair Game '89
Funny Money '82
Hitchhiker 4 '87
Hot Rod '79
Just Before Dawn '80
The Last of Philip Banter '87
Mean Dog Blues '78
Patriot '86

Justin Henry
Kramer vs. Kramer '79
Martin's Day '85
Sixteen Candles '84
Sweet Hearts Dance '88
Tiger Town '83

Laura Henry
Heavenly Bodies '84

Lenny Henry
Bernard and the Genie '90s
The Suicide Club '88
Three of a Kind '80s
True Identity '91

Martha Henry
Dancing in the Dark '86
White Light '90

Mike Henry
Adios Amigo '75
Smokey and the Bandit '77
Smokey and the Bandit, Part
   2 '80
Smokey and the Bandit, Part
   3 '83

Pat Henry
Lady in Cement '68

**Robert "Buzzy"
Henry**
Buzzy Rides the Range '40
The Great Mike '44
Turf Boy '42
Western Frontier '35
Wild West '46

Terence Henry
The Berlin Conspiracy '91

Tim Henry
The Dawson Patrol '78

William Henry
Dance Hall '41
Marshal of Cedar Rock '53
Movie Stuntmen '53
Tarzan Escapes '36

Jim Henshaw
Snapshot '77

Craig Hensley
Natas...The Reflection '83

Lisa Hensley
The 13th Floor '88

Pamela Hensley
Buck Rogers in the 25th
   Century '79
Doc Savage '75
Double Exposure '82
The Nude Bomb '80
The Rebels '79

Basil Henson
Anatomy of Terror '74

Brad Henson
Warlords from Hell '87

Gladys Henson
Train of Events '49

Jim Henson
Into the Night '85
The Muppet Movie '79
Muppets Take Manhattan '84
Timepiece '65

Nicky Henson
Number 1 of the Secret
   Service '77
Psychomania '73

Torsten Hentes
David '79

Audrey Hepburn
Always '89
Breakfast at Tiffany's '61
Charade '63
The Children's Hour '61
Funny Face '57
The Lavender Hill Mob '51
Love in the Afternoon '57
My Fair Lady '64
The Nun's Story '59
Paris When It Sizzles '64
Robin and Marian '76
Roman Holiday '53
Sabrina '54
Sidney Sheldon's Bloodline
   '79
They All Laughed '81
Two for the Road '67
The Unforgiven '60
Wait Until Dark '67
War and Peace '56

Dee Hepburn
Gregory's Girl '80

Katharine Hepburn
Adam's Rib '50
The African Queen '51
Alice Adams '35
Bacall on Bogart '88
A Bill of Divorcement '32
Break of Hearts '35
Bringing Up Baby '38
Christopher Strong '33
Desk Set '57
Dragon Seed '44
Grace Quigley '84
Guess Who's Coming to
   Dinner '67
Hepburn & Tracy '84
Holiday '38
The Lion in Winter '68
Little Minister '34
Little Women '33
Long Day's Journey into Night
   '62
Love Among the Ruins '75
The Madwoman of Chaillot
   '69
Mary of Scotland '36
Morning Glory '33
Olly Olly Oxen Free '78
On Golden Pond '81
Pat and Mike '52
The Philadelphia Story '40
Quality Street '37
The Rainmaker '56
Rooster Cogburn '75
Spitfire '34
Stage Door '37
Stage Door Canteen '43
State of the Union '48
Storytime Classics '83
Suddenly, Last Summer '59
Summertime '55
Sylvia Scarlett '35
Trojan Women '71
Without Love '45
Woman of the Year '42
A Woman Rebels '36

Bernard Hepton
Eminent Domain '91
Mansfield Park '85

Douglas Herald
Typhoon Treasure '39

Charles Herbert
13 Ghosts '60

Virginia Hey
Obsession: A Taste for Fear '89

Weldon Heyburn
The Chinese Cat '44
Criminals Within '41
Panama Patrol '39
Sea Racketeers '37
The Thirteenth Man '37

Yvette Heyden
Tides of War '90

Louis Jean Heydt
The Big Sleep '46
The Great McGinty '40
Our Vines Have Tender Grapes '45
Thirty Seconds Over Tokyo '44
Zombies on Broadway '44

Herbert Heyes
Behind Locked Doors '48
Calling Wild Bill Elliott '43
The Cobra Strikes '48
Teenage '44

John Heyl
A Separate Peace '73

Barton Heyman
Billy Galvin '86
He Who Walks Alone '78
Let's Scare Jessica to Death '71
Raising Cain '92
Roadside Prophets '92
Valdez is Coming '71

Sean Heyman
The Lost Platoon '89

Anne Heywood
The Brain '62
Carthage in Flames '60
Doctor at Large '57
I Want What I Want '72
Sadat '83
Scenes from a Murder '72
The Shaming '71
The Very Edge '63

Pat Heywood
Girly '70
Rude Awakening '81
Wish You Were Here '87

Ruth Hiatt
Ridin' Thru '35

Barry Hickey
Las Vegas Weekend '85

Brendan Hickey
I Married a Vampire '87

Marguerite Hickey
Mirrors '85

Tom Hickey
Nuns on the Run '90

William Hickey
Any Man's Death '90
The Boston Strangler '68
Bright Lights, Big City '88
Hobo's Christmas '87
Invitation to a Gunfighter '64
Mikey & Nicky '76
Mob Boss '90
My Blue Heaven '90
The Name of the Rose '86
National Lampoon's Christmas Vacation '89
One Crazy Summer '86
Pink Cadillac '89
Prizzi's Honor '85
Puppet Master '89
The Runestone '91
Sea of Love '89

Tales from the Crypt, Vol. 3 '90
Tales from the Darkside: The Movie '90
Walls of Glass '85

Catherine Hickland
Ghost Town '88
Millions '90
Witchery '88

Darryl Hickman
The Devil on Wheels '47
Fighting Father Dunne '48
Geronimo's Revenge '60
Johnny Shiloh '63
Men of Boys Town '41
Tea and Sympathy '56
Texas John Slaughter: Geronimo's Revenge '60

Dwayne Hickman
Cat Ballou '65
Dr. Goldfoot and the Bikini Machine '66
High School USA '84
How to Stuff a Wild Bikini '65
My Dog, the Thief '69

Howard Hickman
Civilization '16

Catherine Hicks
Better Late Than Never '83
Child's Play '88
Death Valley '81
Fever Pitch '85
Garbo Talks '84
Laguna Heat '87
Like Father, Like Son '87
Marilyn: The Untold Story '80
Peggy Sue Got Married '86
The Razor's Edge '84
Running Against Time '90
Secret Ingredient '88
She's Out of Control '89
Souvenir '88
Spy '89
Star Trek 4: The Voyage Home '86

Dan Hicks
Evil Dead 2: Dead by Dawn '87

Greg Hicks
Fortunes of War '87

John Hicks
Free, White, and 21 '62

Kevin Hicks
Blood Relations '87
Final Notice '89
Higher Education '88

Leonard Hicks
Santa Claus Conquers the Martians '64

Russell Hicks
Air Raid Wardens '43
The Bank Dick '40
Blind Fools '40
Devil Dogs of the Air '35
Hitler: Dead or Alive '43
Pick a Star '37
Seventh Cavalry '56
Stanley and Livingstone '39
Tarzan's New York Adventure '42

Seymour Hicks
Fame is the Spur '47
Scrooge '35
The Secret of the Loch '34

Tommy Redmond Hicks
She's Gotta Have It '86

William T. Hicks
Challenge '74
Day of Judgment '81
Death Screams '83
House of Death '82
Order of the Black Eagle '87
Unmasking the Idol '86

Joan Hickson
The Body in the Library '87
A Day in the Death of Joe Egg '71
Doctor in the House '53
Great Expectations '81
A Murder is Announced '87
A Pocketful of Rye '87

Raymundo Hidalgo-Gato
El Super '79

Bokuzen Hidari
The Lower Depths '57

Sachiko Hidari
The Insect Woman '63
She and He '63

Tonpei Hidari
The Ballad of Narayama '83

Chieko Higashiyama
Tokyo Story '53

Mary Jane Higby
Honeymoon Killers '70

Wilbur Higby
Reggie Mixes In '16

Anthony Higgins
The Bride '85
Cold Room '84
The Draughtsman's Contract '82
For Love or Money '93
One Against the Wind '91
Quartet '81
She'll Be Wearing Pink Pajamas '84

Clare Higgins
Hellbound: Hellraiser 2 '88
Hellraiser '87
Wonderland '88

Colin Higgins
Into the Night '85

Joe Higgins
Flipper's New Adventure '64
Milo Milo '60s
Namu, the Killer Whale '66

Joel Higgins
First Affair '83

John Michael Higgins
National Lampoon's Class of '86 '86

Michael Higgins
Born Beautiful '82
The Conversation '74
Courtship '87
Dead Bang '89
Desperate Characters '71
1918 '85
On Valentine's Day '86
Paul's Case '80

Jane Higginson
Devil Wears White '86
Silent Night, Deadly Night 5: The Toymaker '91

Mark High
The Glass Jungle '88

Jennifer Hilary
Miss A & Miss M '86
One Brief Summer '70

Lise Hilboldt
A Married Man '84
Noon Wine '84

Hilde Hildebrand
Die Grosse Freiheit Nr. 7 '45

Charles George Hildebrandt
Return of the Aliens: The Deadly Spawn '83

Mark Hildreth
After the Promise '87

Joel Hile
Visitants '87

Arthur Hill
The Amateur '82
The Andromeda Strain '71
A Bridge Too Far '77
The Champ '79
Churchill and the Generals '81
Death Be Not Proud '75
Dirty Tricks '81
Futureworld '76
The Guardian '84
Harper '66
Judge Horton and the Scottsboro Boys '76
The Killer Elite '75
Love Leads the Way '84
Making Love '82
One Magic Christmas '85
The Ordeal of Dr. Mudd '80
Petulia '68
The Pursuit of Happiness '70
Return of Frank Cannon '80
Revenge of the Stepford Wives '80
Riel '79
Tales of the Unexpected '91
Tomorrow's Child '82
The Ugly American '63

Benny Hill
Benny Hill's Crazy World '74
Chitty Chitty Bang Bang '68
The Italian Job '69
Those Magnificent Men in Their Flying Machines '65
To See Such Fun '81

Bernard Hill
Bellman and True '88
The Bounty '84
Drowning by Numbers '87
Henry VI, Part 3 '82
Mountains of the Moon '90

Charles Hill
Rainbow's End '35

Craig Hill
Adios, Hombre '68
Animal Called Man '87
Black Box Affair '66
Detective Story '51
What Price Glory? '52

Dana Hill
Cross Creek '83
Fallen Angel '81
The $5.20 an Hour Dream '80
The Jetsons: Movie '90
The Member of the Wedding '83
National Lampoon's European Vacation '85
Shoot the Moon '82
Silence of the Heart '84

David Hill
The Raggedy Rawney '90

Dean Hill
Hard Knox '83

Frederick Hill
Wonsan Operation '78

Gloria Davis Hill
Uptown Angel '90

Jack Hill
The Brain Eaters '58
Dance of Death '69
The Female Jungle '56
The Sinister Invasion '68

James Hill
Christian the Lion '76

Jean Hill
Desperate Living '77

Johnnie Hill
Velvet Smooth '76

Julie Hill
The Fix '84

Ken Hill
Mind, Body & Soul '92

Lauryn Hill
King of the Hill '93

Louis Hill
Ninja Force of Assassins '70s

Marianna Hill
The Baby '72
Blood Beach '81
El Condor '70
The Godfather, Part 2 '74
High Plains Drifter '73
The Invisible Strangler '76
The Last Porno Flick '74
Married Too Young '62
Medium Cool '69
Messiah of Evil '74
Paradise, Hawaiian Style '66
Red Line 7000 '65
Roustabout '64
Schizoid '80
Thumb Tripping '72

Mary Hill
The Beast from 20,000 Fathoms '53
Mesa of Lost Women '52

Matt Hill
Teenage Mutant Ninja Turtles 3 '93

Morgan Hill
23 1/2 Hours Leave '37

Nellie Hill
Mistaken Identity '41
Murder with Music '45

Nikki Hill
Game of Survival '85
Game of Survival '89

Peter Murray Hill
House of Mystery '41

Ralston Hill
1776 '72

Richard Hill
Bloodfist 2 '90
Deathstalker '83
Deathstalker 4: Clash of the Titans '91
Devastator '85
Dune Warriors '91
Warrior Queen '87

Roy Hill
Bronson's Revenge '79

Steven Hill
Between Two Women '86
Billy Bathgate '91

Phil Hock
Nudity Required '90

Harriet Hocter
The Great Ziegfeld '36

Douglas Hodge
Salome's Last Dance '88

Kate Hodge
Leatherface: The Texas
  Chainsaw Massacre 3 '89
Love Kills '91
Rapid Fire '92

Patricia Hodge
Betrayal '83
Diamond's Edge '88
Dust to Dust '85
The Heat of the Day '91
Spymaker: The Secret Life of
  Ian Fleming '90
Sunset '88

Horace Hodgers
London Melody '37

Eddie Hodges
The Adventures of
  Huckleberry Finn '60
A Hole in the Head '59
Live a Little, Love a Little '68
Summer Magic '63

Ralph Hodges
Sea Hound '47

Runa Hodges
A Fool There Was '14

Thomas E. Hodges
Lucas '86

Tom Hodges
Amazing Stories, Book 3 '86
The Baby Doll Murders '92
Vietnam War Story 3 '89

Earle Hodgins
Aces and Eights '36
The Bashful Bachelor '42
Colt Comrades '43
Heroes of the Alamo '37
Hoppy Serves a Writ '43
Inside the Law '42
A Lawman is Born '37
Santa Fe Marshal '40

John Hodiak
Across the Wide Missouri '51
Ambush at Tomahawk Gap
  '53
Battleground '49
Command Decision '48
Conquest of Cochise '53
Dragonfly Squadron '54
The Harvey Girls '46
Homecoming '48
Lifeboat '44
Love from a Stranger '47
The Miniver Story '50

Katrina Hodiak
Jane Austen in Manhattan '80

Tobias Hoels
Mines of Kilimanjaro '87

Devin Hoelscher
Wired to Kill '86

Heinz Hoenig
Judgment in Berlin '88

Paul Hoerbiger
The Mozart Story '48

Dennis Hoey
David and Bathsheba '51
House of Fear '45
The Pearl of Death '44
Power '34
Roll on Texas Moon '46

**Sherlock Holmes and the
  Secret Weapon** '42
Spider Woman '44

John Hofeus
Return to Boggy Creek '77

Abbie Hoffman
Born on the Fourth of July '89

Alfred Hoffman
Antonia and Jane '91

Avi Hoffman
The Imported Bridegroom '89

Basil Hoffman
Communion '89
The Double O Kid '92
Lambada '89

Connie Hoffman
Texas Layover '75

David Hoffman
Children in the Crossfire '84
Wolf Lake '79

Dustin Hoffman
Agatha '79
Alfredo, Alfredo '72
All the President's Men '76
Billy Bathgate '91
Death of a Salesman '86
Dick Tracy '90
Family Business '89
The Graduate '67
Hero '92
Hook '91
Ishtar '87
Kramer vs. Kramer '79
Lenny '74
Little Big Man '70
Madigan's Millions '67
Marathon Man '76
Midnight Cowboy '69
Papillon '73
Rain Man '88
Straight Time '78
Straw Dogs '72
Tootsie '82

Elizabeth Hoffman
Fear No Evil '80

Gaby Hoffman
Field of Dreams '89
The Man Without a Face '93
Sleepless In Seattle '93
This is My Life '92

Gertrude Hoffman
The Ape '40

Isabella Hoffman
Tripwire '89

Jane Hoffman
Senior Trip '81
Sybil '76
Up the Sandbox '72

Jon Hoffman
Night Terror '89

Joshua Hoffman
The Legend of Jedediah
  Carver '70s

Philip S. Hoffman
Leap of Faith '92
Scent of a Woman '92

Robert Hoffman
A Black Veil for Lisa '68
Eyes Behind the Stars '72
Joe Panther '76

Roy Hoffman
Skyline '84

Shawn Hoffman
Adventures in Dinosaur City
  '92

Susan Lee Hoffman
Wizards of the Lost Kingdom
  2 '89

Thom Hoffman
The 4th Man '79
Lily was Here '89

Thurn Hoffman
In the Spirit '90

Susanna Hoffs
The Allnighter '87

**Marco
Hofschneider**
Europa, Europa '91

Rene Hofschneider
Europa, Europa '91

Halvart Hoft
Leaves from Satan's Book '19

Ben Hogan
The Caddy '53

Bosco Hogan
James Joyce: A Portrait of the
  Artist as a Young Man '77

Helen Hogan
Dungeon of Harrow '64

Hulk Hogan
Mr. Nanny '93
No Holds Barred '89
Suburban Commando '91

Jack Hogan
Jet Attack/Paratroop
  Command '58

Michael Hogan
Clearcut '92
Lost '86
Smokescreen '90

Pat Hogan
Davy Crockett, King of the
  Wild Frontier '55
Indian Paint '64
Seventh Cavalry '56

Paul Hogan
Almost an Angel '90
Anzacs: The War Down Under
  '85
Crocodile Dundee '86
Crocodile Dundee 2 '88

Robert Hogan
Gone are the Days '84
Memory of Us '74

Susan Hogan
Phobia '80
Title Shot '81
White Fang '91

Ian Hogg
The Legacy '79

James Hogue
The Rejuvenator '88

Kong Hoi
Seven Indignant

Wang Hoi
Twister Kicker '85

**Mary Ellen
Hokanson**
Desperate Characters '71

Fred Holbert
Scream Bloody Murder '72

David Holbrook
Creepshow 2 '87
Return to Salem's Lot '87

Hal Holbrook
All the President's Men '76

Behind Enemy Lines '85
Capricorn One '78
Creepshow '82
Dress Gray '86
The Firm '93
Fletch Lives '89
The Fog '78
The Girl from Petrovka '74
Girls Night Out '83
The Great White Hope '70
The Group '66
Julia '77
The Kidnapping of the
  President '80
Killing in a Small Town '90
Killing of Randy Webster '81
Magnum Force '73
Midway '76
Murder by Natural Causes '79
Natural Enemies '79
North and South '85
Our Town '77
The People Next Door '70
Pueblo Affair '73
Rituals '79
Sorry, Wrong Number '89
The Star Chamber '83
They Only Kill Their Masters
  '72
The Unholy '88
Wall Street '87
When Hell Was in Session '82
Wild in the Streets '68

Tami Holbrook
Hot Moves '84

Victor Holchak
Hughes & Harlow: Angels in
  Hell '77

Kathryn Holcomb
Skag '79

Kimberly Holcomb
Stripper '86

Sarah Holcomb
Caddyshack '80
Happy Birthday, Gemini '80

Diane Holden
Black Starlet '74
Grave of the Vampire '72

Fay Holden
Andy Hardy Gets Spring Fever
  '39
Andy Hardy Meets Debutante
  '40
Andy Hardy's Double Life '42
Andy Hardy's Private
  Secretary '41
The Big Hangover '50
Bitter Sweet '40
Blossoms in the Dust '41
Life Begins for Andy Hardy
  '41
Love Finds Andy Hardy '38
Love Laughs at Andy Hardy
  '46
Samson and Delilah '50
Ziegfeld Girl '41

Gloria Holden
Behind the Rising Sun '43
Dracula's Daughter '36
Hawaii Calls '38
The Life of Emile Zola '37

Jan Holden
Fire Maidens from Outer
  Space '56
One Brief Summer '70

Marjean Holden
Stripped to Kill II: Live Girls '89

Mark Holden
Blue Fire Lady '78

Peter Holden
The Great Man Votes '38

Rebecca Holden
The Sisterhood '88
Twenty Dollar Star '91

Tommy Holden
What's Up Front '63

William Holden
Alvarez Kelly '66
Ashanti, Land of No Mercy '79
Boots Malone '52
Born Yesterday '50
The Bridge on the River Kwai
  '57
The Bridges at Toko-Ri '55
Casino Royale '67
The Christmas Tree '69
The Counterfeit Traitor '62
Country Girl '54
Damien: Omen 2 '78
Dance Fools Dance '31
Dark Past '49
Dear Wife '49
The Devil's Brigade '68
Earthling '80
Escape to Athena '79
Executive Suite '54
Forever Female '53
Golden Boy '39
The Horse Soldiers '59
The Key '58
Love is a Many-Splendored
  Thing '55
Man from Colorado '49
Miss Grant Takes Richmond
  '49
Moon is Blue '53
Network '76
Our Town '40
Paris When It Sizzles '64
Picnic '55
Rachel and the Stranger '48
Sabrina '54
S.O.B. '81
Stalag 17 '53
Sunset Boulevard '50
Texas '41
The Towering Inferno '74
21 Hours at Munich '76
Union Station '50
When Time Ran Out '80
When Wolves Cry '69
The Wild Bunch '69
Wild Rovers '71
The World of Suzie Wong '60
Young & Willing '42

Winifred Holden
Strangers in Good Company
  '91

Chris Holder
Deadly Intruder '84

Geoffrey Holder
Boomerang '92
Doctor Doolittle '67
Everything You Always
  Wanted to Know About
  Sex (But Were Afraid to
  Ask) '72
Live and Let Die '73
Swashbuckler '76

Roy Holder
Loot...Give Me Money, Honey!
  '70

Thomas Holding
The Three Musketeers '21

Judd Holdren
Satan's Satellites '58
Zombies of the Stratosphere
  '52

X Marks the Spot '42

David Homb
The Channeler '89
Street Soldiers '91

Paul Home
The 13th Mission '91

Skip Homeier
The Burning Hills '56
Cry Vengeance '54
Gunfighter '50
The Halls of Montezuma '50
Johnny Shiloh '63
Starbird and Sweet William '73
The Tall T '57
Ten Wanted Men '54
The Voyage of the Yes '72

Charles Homet
Beginner's Luck '84

Oscar Homolka
Ball of Fire '41
The Executioner '70
Funeral in Berlin '66
The House of the Arrow '53
I Remember Mama '48
The Key '58
The Madwoman of Chaillot '69
Mooncussers '62
Rhodes '36
Sabotage '36
Seven Sinners '40
The Seven Year Itch '55
Song of Norway '70
Strange Case of Dr. Jekyll & Mr. Hyde '68
War and Peace '56
The White Tower '50
The Wonderful World of the Brothers Grimm '62

Karl Arne Homsten
Secrets of Women '52

Jean-Marie Hon
Blade in Hong Kong '85

Kam Hon
Samurai Sword of Justice

Shek Hon
Four Robbers '70s

Wah Hon
The White Butterfly Killer

Inoshiro Honda
King Kong Versus Godzilla '63

Germane Honde
Prettykill '87

Mikhael Honesseau
Anita, Dances of Vice '87

James Hong
Bethune '77
Body Trouble '92
The Brotherhood of the Rose '89
Caged Fury '90
Crime Lords '91
Dragonfight '92
The Golden Child '86
The Jitters '88
L.A. Goddess '92
Question of Faith '93
Revenge of the Nerds 2: Nerds in Paradise '87
Shadowzone '90
Talons of the Eagle '92
Tango and Cash '89
Tax Season '90
The Vineyard '89
Yes, Giorgio '82

Kojiro Hongo
Destroy All Planets '68
Gamera vs. Barugon '66
Gamera vs. Gaos '67

Misako Honno
The Go-Masters '82

Andre Honore
The Slumber Party Massacre '82

Darla Hood
The Bat '59
Bohemian Girl '36
Little Rascals, Book 3 '38
Little Rascals, Book 4 '30s
Little Rascals, Book 5 '30s
Little Rascals, Book 6 '30s
Little Rascals, Book 7 '30s
Little Rascals, Book 8 '30s
Little Rascals, Book 9 '30s
Little Rascals, Book 10 '30s
Little Rascals, Book 11 '38
Little Rascals, Book 12 '37
Little Rascals, Book 14 '30s
Little Rascals, Book 16 '30s
Little Rascals, Book 17 '31
Little Rascals: Choo Choo/Fishy Tales '32
Little Rascals Christmas Special '79
Little Rascals Collector's Edition, Vol. 1-6
Little Rascals Comedy Classics, Vol. 1
Little Rascals Comedy Classics, Vol. 2
Little Rascals: Fish Hooky/Spooky Hooky '33
Little Rascals: Honkey Donkey/Sprucin' Up '34
Little Rascals: Little Sinner/Two Too Young '35
Little Rascals: Mush and Milk/Three Men in a Tub '33
Little Rascals on Parade '37
Little Rascals: Pups is Pups/Three Smart Boys '30
Little Rascals: Readin' and Writin'/Mail and Female '31
Little Rascals: Reunion in Rhythm/Mike Fright '37
Little Rascals: Spanky/Feed 'Em and Weep '32
Little Rascals: The Pinch Singer/Framing Youth '36
Little Rascals Two Reelers, Vol. 1 '29
Little Rascals Two Reelers, Vol. 2 '33
Little Rascals Two Reelers, Vol. 3 '36
Little Rascals Two Reelers, Vol. 4 '30
Little Rascals Two Reelers, Vol. 5 '34
Little Rascals Two Reelers, Vol. 6 '36
Little Rascals, Vol. 1 '29
Our Gang Comedies '40s

Don Hood
Absence of Malice '81
Blind Vengeance '90
Marie '85

Miki Hood
Inspector Hornleigh '39

Carla Hoogeveen
Alternative '76

John Lee Hooker
The Blues Brothers '80

Jan Hooks
Batman Returns '92
Coneheads '93

Kevin Hooks
Aaron Loves Angela '75
Can You Hear the Laughter? The Story of Freddie Prinze '79
Sounder '72

Robert Hooks
Aaron Loves Angela '75
The Execution '85
Fast Walking '82
Passenger 57 '92
Sweet Love, Bitter '67
A Woman Called Moses '78
Words by Heart '84

Brett Hool
Steel Dawn '87

Michael Hoole
Psycho Girls '86

Barbara Hooper
The Sisterhood '88

Geraldine Hooper
Cambio de Cara '71

Tobe Hooper
Fangoria's Weekend of Horrors '86
Sleepwalkers '92

Peter Hooten
Deadly Mission '78
Dr. Strange '78
Fantasies '73
Slashed Dreams '74
2020 Texas Gladiators '85

William Hootkins
Hear My Song '91

Phil Hoover
Black Gestapo '75
Policewomen '73

Hoover the Dog
Little Heroes '91

Bob Hope
Boy, Did I Get a Wrong Number! '66
Cancel My Reservation '72
Casanova's Big Night '54
Caught in the Draft '41
College Swing '38
Fancy Pants '50
The Ghost Breakers '40
The Great Lover '49
Here Come the Girls '53
Hollywood Clowns '85
Hollywood Goes to War '54
How to Commit Marriage '69
The Lemon Drop Kid '51
Louisiana Purchase '41
Monsieur Beaucaire '46
The Muppet Movie '79
My Favorite Blonde '42
My Favorite Brunette '47
Off Limits '53
The Oscar '66
The Paleface '48
Paris Holiday '57
The Princess and the Pirate '44
The Road to Bali '53
The Road to Hong Kong '62
The Road to Lebanon '60
The Road to Morocco '42
The Road to Rio '47
The Road to Singapore '40
The Road to Utopia '46
The Road to Zanzibar '41
Scared Stiff '53
The Seven Little Foys '55
Son of Paleface '52
Sorrowful Jones '49
Strictly G.I. '44
They Got Me Covered '43

Two Reelers: Comedy Classics 9 '34

Gary Hope
Big Zapper '73

Harry Hope
Escape from Planet Earth '67

Leslie Hope
The Abduction of Allison Tate '92
The Big Slice '90
Doppelganger: The Evil Within '90
It Takes Two '88
Kansas '88
Men at Work '90
Prep School '81
Sword of Gideon '86
Talk Radio '88

Richard Hope
Antonia and Jane '91
Bellman and True '88
A Casualty of War '90
Singleton's Pluck '84

Vida Hope
Angels One Five '54
Roadhouse Girl '53

William Hope
Hellbound: Hellraiser 2 '88

Jason Hopely
The War Boy '85

Anthony Hopkins
All Creatures Great and Small '74
Arch of Triumph '85
Audrey Rose '77
The Bounty '84
Bram Stoker's Dracula '92
A Bridge Too Far '77
A Change of Seasons '80
Chaplin '92
A Chorus of Disapproval '89
Desperate Hours '90
A Doll's House '89
The Efficiency Expert '92
84 Charing Cross Road '86
The Elephant Man '80
Freejack '92
The Girl from Petrovka '74
The Good Father '87
Great Expectations '89
Hamlet '69
Howard's End '92
Hunchback of Notre Dame '82
International Velvet '78
Juggernaut '74
The Lindbergh Kidnapping Case '76
The Lion in Winter '68
The Looking Glass War '69
Magic '78
A Married Man '84
Mussolini & I '85
One Man's War '90
Othello '82
QB VII '74
The Silence of the Lambs '91
The Tenth Man '88
Young Winston '72

Barrett Hopkins
Firehouse '87

Bo Hopkins
American Graffiti '73
Big Bad John '90
Bounty Hunters '89
Casino '80
Center of the Web '92
Culpepper Cattle Co. '72
The Day of the Locust '75
The Fifth Floor '80
The Final Alliance '89

The Getaway '72
Kansas City Massacre '75
The Killer Elite '75
The Legend of Wolf Mountain '92
Midnight Express '78
More American Graffiti '79
Mutant '83
Nightmare at Noon '87
The Only Way Home '72
Plutonium Incident '82
Posse '75
Rodeo Girl '80
The Runaway Barge '75
A Small Town in Texas '76
A Smoky Mountain Christmas '86
Sweet 16 '81
Tentacles '77
Trapper County War '89
What Comes Around '85
White Lightning '73
The Wild Bunch '69

Harold Hopkins
Demonstrator '71
Fantasy Man '84
Monkey Grip '82
Sara Dane '81

Jermaine Hopkins
Juice '92

Joan Hopkins
Man on the Run '49

Katherine Hopkins
The Capture of Bigfoot '79
Legend of Big Foot '82

Mary Hopkins
Getting Over '81

Miriam Hopkins
Barbary Coast '35
Becky Sharp '35
Carrie '52
The Chase '66
The Children's Hour '61
Dr. Jekyll and Mr. Hyde '31
Fanny Hill: Memoirs of a Woman of Pleasure '64
The Heiress '49
Men are not Gods '37
The Old Maid '39
Savage Intruder '68
These Three '36
Virginia City '40

Rhonda Leigh Hopkins
Cover Girl Models '75
Summer School Teachers '75
Tidal Wave '75

Shirley Knight Hopkins
Secrets '71

Telma Hopkins
The Kid with the Broken Halo '82
Trancers '85
Trancers 3: Deth Lives '92
Vital Signs '90

Maja Hoppe
M'Lady's Court '80s

Marianne Hoppe
The Strange Countess '61

Rolf Hoppe
Mephisto '81
Spring Symphony '86

Dennis Hopper
The American Friend '77
Apocalypse Now '79
Backtrack '89
Black Widow '87

Lamont Jackson
Assault with a Deadly Weapon '82
Class Act '91

Leonard Jackson
Black Vampire '73

Linda Jackson
Black Bikers from Hell '70
The Outlaw Bikers—Gang Wars '70

Mahalia Jackson
The Best Man '64

Marlon Jackson
Student Confidential '87

Mary Jackson
Skinned Alive '89
Terror at Red Wolf Inn '72

Mary Ann Jackson
Little Rascals, Book 1 '30s
Little Rascals, Book 8 '30s
Little Rascals, Book 9 '30s
Little Rascals, Book 10 '30s
Little Rascals, Book 12 '37
Little Rascals, Book 14 '30s
Little Rascals, Book 18 '29

Michael Jackson
The Wiz '78

Mike Jackson
Black King '32

Peter Jackson
Bad Taste '88

Reggie Jackson
The Naked Gun: From the Files of Police Squad '88

Ron Jackson
Play Dead '81

Sam Jackson
Dead Man Out '89
Return of Superfly '90
White Sands '92

Sammy Jackson
Fastest Guitar Alive '68
None But the Brave '65
Shame, Shame on the Bixby Boys '82

Samuel L. Jackson
Amos and Andrew '93
Def by Temptation '90
Fathers and Sons '92
Juice '92
Jumpin' at the Boneyard '92
Jungle Fever '91
Jurassic Park '93
National Lampoon's Loaded Weapon 1 '93
Patriot Games '92
True Romance '93

Selmer Jackson
The Fighting Sullivans '42
The Thirteenth Man '37

Sherry Jackson
The Adventures of Huckleberry Finn '60
Bare Knuckles '77
Cotter '72
Miracle of Our Lady of Fatima '52
Stingray '78
Trouble Along the Way '53

Sonia Jackson
Clifford '93

Stoney Jackson
Knights of the City '85
Roller Boogie '79
Streets of Fire '84

Sweet Perfection '90
Up Against the Wall '91

Victoria Jackson
Casual Sex? '88
Dream a Little Dream '89
Family Business '89
UHF '89

Wilfred Jackson
Alice in Wonderland '51

Catherine Jacob
Tatie Danielle '91

Irene Jacob
Au Revoir Les Enfants '87
The Double Life of Veronique '91

Peter Jacob
Miss Melody Jones '73

Derek Jacobi
Blue Blood '73
Cyrano de Bergerac '85
The Day of the Jackal '73
Dead Again '91
Enigma '82
Hamlet '79
Henry V '89
Hunchback of Notre Dame '82
I, Claudius, Vol. 1: A Touch of Murder/Family Affairs '91
I, Claudius, Vol. 2: Waiting in the Wings/What Shall We Do With Claudius? '80
I, Claudius, Vol. 3: Poison is Queen/Some Justice '80
I, Claudius, Vol. 4: Queen of Heaven/Reign of Terror '80
I, Claudius, Vol. 5: Zeus, By Jove!/Hail Who? '80
I, Claudius, Vol. 6: Fool's Luck/A God in Colchester '80
I, Claudius, Vol. 7: Old King Log '80
Inside the Third Reich '82
Little Dorrit, Film 1: Nobody's Fault '88
Little Dorrit, Film 2: Little Dorrit's Story '88
The Medusa Touch '78
The Odessa File '74
Philby, Burgess and MacLean: Spy Scandal of the Century '84
Richard II '79
The Secret Garden '87
Secret of NIMH '82
The Tenth Man '88

Lou Jacobi
Amazon Women on the Moon '87
Arthur '81
Avalon '90
Better Late Than Never '79
The Boss' Wife '86
Chu Chu & the Philly Flash '81
Cotton Comes to Harlem '70
The Diary of Anne Frank '59
Everything You Always Wanted to Know About Sex (But Were Afraid to Ask) '72
I Don't Buy Kisses Anymore '92
Little Murders '71
The Magician of Lublin '79
My Favorite Year '82
Next Stop, Greenwich Village '76
Off Your Rocker '80
Roseland '77
Song Without End '60

Andre Jacobs
Emissary '89
Prey for the Hunter '92
Pursuit '90

Carolyn Jacobs
Desert Snow '89

Emma Jacobs
Murder on Line One '90

Jake Jacobs
Driven to Kill '90

Jasper Jacobs
The Turn of the Screw '74

Lisa Jacobs
The Attic: The Hiding of Anne Frank '88

Manny Jacobs
Battle of the Bullies '85
The Seventh Sign '88

Mark Jacobs
Blood Hook '86

Olu Jacobs
Pirates '86

Steve Jacobs
Alice to Nowhere '86

Steven Jacobs
Echoes of Paradise '86
Father '90

Howard Jacobsen
Forever Evil '87

Hymie Jacobsen
Der Purimshpiler '37

Peggy Jacobsen
Search and Destroy '88

David Jacobson
The Beat '88

Dean Jacobson
Child's Play 3 '91

Jill Jacobson
Hospital of Terror '78

Ken Jacobson
Eye of the Eagle 2 '89

Ulla Jacobsson
Fox and His Friends '75
Smiles of a Summer Night '55

Billy Jacoby
Beastmaster '82
Bloody Birthday '80
Dr. Alien '88
Just One of the Guys '85
Party Camp '87

Bobby Jacoby
The Applegates '89
Wizards of the Lost Kingdom 2 '89

Dale Jacoby
Bloodmatch '91
Ring of Fire '91
Ring of Fire 2: Blood and Steel '92

Scott Jacoby
Bad Ronald '74
Deadly Rivals '72
The Little Girl Who Lives Down the Lane '76
Midnight Auto Supply '78
Return to Horror High '87
Rivals '72
To Die for '89
To Die for 2 '91

Michael Jacot
Inn of Temptation '86

Maurice Jacquemont
The Return of Martin Guerre '83

Hattie Jacques
Carry On Nurse '59
Carry On 'Round the Bend '72
A Christmas Carol '51
Make Mine Mink '60

Stephen Jacques
Sinner's Blood '70

Gaston Jacquet
Prix de Beaute '30

Roger Jacquet
Red Balloon/Occurrence at Owl Creek Bridge '62

Nicholas Jacquez
Vengeance '80

Jada
Sex with the Stars '81

Claude Jade
Love on the Run '78

Richard Jaeckel
...All the Marbles '81
Awakening of Candra '81
Battleground '49
Black Moon Rising '86
Blood Song '82
Born Innocent '74
Chisum '70
Cold River '81
Come Back, Little Sheba '52
The Dark '79
Day of the Animals '77
Delta Force 2: Operation Stranglehold '90
The Devil's Brigade '68
The Dirty Dozen '67
The Dirty Dozen: The Next Mission '85
The Drowning Pool '75
Firehouse '72
The $5.20 an Hour Dream '80
The Fix '84
Flaming Star '60
The Gallant Hours '60
Ghetto Blaster '89
The Green Slime '68
Grizzly '76
Guadalcanal Diary '43
Herbie Goes Bananas '80
Hoodlum Empire '52
Jaws of Death '76
Jungle Patrol '48
The Kill '73
The King of the Kickboxers '91
Once Before I Die '65
Pacific Inferno '85
Pat Garrett & Billy the Kid '73
Platinum High School '60
Sands of Iwo Jima '49
Sometimes a Great Notion '71
Speedtrap '78
Starman '84
Surabaya Conspiracy '75
3:10 to Yuma '57
Ulzana's Raid '72
Walking Tall: Part 2 '75
When Hell Broke Loose '58
A Wing and a Prayer '44

Elizabeth Jaegen
Barbarian Queen 2: The Empress Strikes Back '89

Frederick Jaeger
Nijinsky '80
Slaughterday '77

Hannes Jaenicke
Out of Order '84

Chapelle Jaffe
Confidential '86
One Night Stand '77

Melissa Jaffe
The Cars That Ate Paris '74

Nicole Jaffe
The Trouble with Girls (and How To Get Into It) '69

Sam Jaffe
The Accused '48
The Asphalt Jungle '50
Barbarian and the Geisha '58
Battle Beyond the Stars '80
Bedknobs and Broomsticks '71
Ben-Hur '59
The Day the Earth Stood Still '51
The Dunwich Horror '70
Gideon's Trumpet '80
A Guide for the Married Man '67
Gunga Din '39
Lost Horizon '37
Night Gallery '69
On the Line '83
13 Rue Madeleine '46

Seth Jaffe
Beverly Hills Bodysnatchers '89
Stark '85

Melissa Jaffer
Weekend of Shadows '77

Madhur Jaffrey
Autobiography of a Princess '75
Shakespeare Wallah '65

Saeed Jaffrey
The Courtesans of Bombay '85
The Deceivers '88
Gandhi '82
Hullabaloo Over Georgie & Bonnie's Pictures '78
The Man Who Would Be King '75
My Beautiful Laundrette '86
The Razor's Edge '84
The Wilby Conspiracy '75

Angelika Jager
Robot Holocaust '87

Bianca Jagger
C.H.U.D. 2: Bud the Chud '89

Dean Jagger
Alligator '80
Bad Day at Black Rock '54
Billy Rose's Jumbo '62
The C-Man '49
The Denver & Rio Grande '51
Elmer Gantry '60
End of the World '77
Evil Town '87
Executive Suite '54
Exiled to Shanghai '37
Game of Death '79
Gideon's Trumpet '80
The Glass House '72
The Hanged Man '74
The Honeymoon Machine '61
Hootch Country Boys '75
I Heard the Owl Call My Name '73
I Live in Grosvenor Square '46
It's a Dog's Life '55
King Creole '58
The Lindbergh Kidnapping Case '77
The North Star '43
The Nun's Story '59
Proud Rebel '58

Pursued '47
Rawhide '50
Revolt of the Zombies '36
The Robe '53
Sister Kenny '46
The Stranger '73
Twelve O'Clock High '49
Valley of the Sun '42
Vanishing Point '71
Visions of Evil '73
Western Union '41
White Christmas '54

Mick Jagger
Burden of Dreams '82
The Compleat Beatles '82
Freejack '92
Ned Kelly '70
The Nightingale '83
Performance '70
Running Out of Luck '86
Sympathy for the Devil '70

Henry Jaglom
Always '85
New Year's Day '89
Psych-Out '68
Sitting Ducks '80
Someone to Love '87

Marine Jahan
Streets of Fire '84

Herbert G. Jahncke
Crypt of Dark Secrets '76

Maggie Jakobson
New Year's Day '89

Robert Louis Jakson
The Vernonia Incident '89

Lisa Jakub
Matinee '92
The Phone Call '89
Rambling Rose '91

Shyamanand Jalan
City of Joy '92

Jan Jalenak
American Autobahn '84

Hassan Jamal
Feelin' Screwy '90

Anthony James
Columbo: Prescription Murder '67
The Last Days of Dolwyn '49
Slow Burn '90
The Teacher '74
Unforgiven '92

Barney James
Sebastiane '79

Billy T. James
Came a Hot Friday '85

Brion James
Another 48 Hrs. '90
Armed and Dangerous '86
Ballad of Gregorio Cortez '83
Beyond the Silhouette '90
Black Magic '92
Blade Runner '82
A Breed Apart '84
Crimewave '85
Dead Man Walking '88
Enemy Mine '85
48 Hrs. '82
The Horror Show '89
Mom '90
Mutator '90
Nightmare at Noon '87
The Player '92
Red Scorpion '89
Rio Diablo '93
Southern Comfort '81

Steel Dawn '87
Street Asylum '90
Tango and Cash '89
Time Runner '92
Ultimate Desires '91

Carole James
The Story of O, Part 2 '87

Cheryl "Salt" James
Who's the Man? '93

Chrissie James
Blood Money '80

Clifton James
The Bad News Bears in Breaking Training '77
Bank Shot '74
Black Like Me '64
The Bonfire of the Vanities '90
Buster and Billie '74
Carolina Skeletons '92
David and Lisa '62
Eight Men Out '88
The Last Detail '73
Live and Let Die '73
The Man with the Golden Gun '74
Rancho Deluxe '75
Sniper '75
Talk to Me '82
Werewolf of Washington '73
Where Are the Children? '85
Will Penny '67

Debbie James
976-EVIL 2: The Astral Factor '91

Elizabeth James
Born Losers '67

Etta James
Chuck Berry: Hail! Hail! Rock 'n' Roll '87

Gennie James
Amazing Stories, Book 5 '85
The Secret Garden '87
A Smoky Mountain Christmas '86

Gerald James
Hope and Glory '87

Geraldine James
The Jewel in the Crown '84
The Tall Guy '89

Gladden James
Paradise Island '30
The Social Secretary '16

Harry James
The Benny Goodman Story '55
Best Foot Forward '43
Private Buckaroo '42
Strictly G.I. '44
Two Girls and a Sailor '44

Hawthorne James
The Five Heartbeats '91

Ida James
The Devil's Daughter '39
Hi-De-Ho '35

Jeff James
The Forbidden Dance '90

Jesse James, Jr.
Jesse James Under the Black Flag '21

Jessica James
I, the Jury '82

Jim James
Kung Fu Avengers '85

Joe James
Demonstrator '71

John James
The Devil Bat's Daughter '46
Lonesome Trail '55
Man from Thunder River '43
Secret Passions '78

Julie James
Night of the Death Cult '75
Terror Beach '80s

Ken James
At Sword's Point '51
Landslide '92

Lee James
Cassandra '87
The Taking of Beverly Hills '91

Michael James
Commando Invasion '87
Warriors of the Apocalypse '85

Richard James
Sebastiane '79

Robin James
Creeping Terror '64

Ron James
The Boogey Man '80
Swinging Wives '79

Samuel H. James
Go Down Death '41

Sidney James
Carry On at Your Convenience '71
Carry On Cleo '65
Carry On Cowboy '66
Carry On Cruising '62
Glass Tomb '55
Heat Wave '54
The Lavender Hill Mob '51
Norman Conquest '53
Quatermass 2 '57
The Silent Enemy '58
What a Carve-Up! '62

Sonny James
Las Vegas Hillbillys '66

Steve James
American Ninja '85
American Ninja 2: The Confrontation '87
American Ninja 3: Blood Hunt '89
Avenging Force '86
The Brother from Another Planet '84
Hero and the Terror '88
I'm Gonna Git You Sucka '88
Johnny Be Good '88
McBain '91
The P.O.W. Escape '86
Python Wolf '88
Riverbend '89
Stalking Danger '88
Street Hunter '90
Weekend at Bernie's 2 '93

Tina James
In Your Face '77

Walter James
Battling Butler '26
The Kid Brother '27
Little Annie Rooney '25

Joyce Jameson
The Balcony '63
The Comedy of Terrors '64
Good Neighbor Sam '64
Hardbodies '84
Pray TV '80
Savage Run '70
Tales of Terror '62

Malcom Jamieson
Meridian: Kiss of the Beast '90

Georges Jamin
Daughters of Darkness '71

Bud Jamison
Charlie Chaplin: Rare Chaplin '15
The Dentist '32
W.C. Fields: Flask of Fields '30

Mikki Jamison-Olsen
Sea Gypsies '78

DeWitt Jan
Harley '90

Lawrence Jan
To Live and Die in Hong Kong '89

Adam Janas
Bottoms Up '87

Tadeusz Janczar
Kanal '56

Krystyna Janda
The Interrogation '82
Man of Marble '76
Mephisto '81

Ivan Jandl
The Search '48

Randy Jandt
Thinkin' Big '87

Topsy Jane
The Loneliness of the Long Distance Runner '62

Conrad Janis
The Buddy Holly Story '78
The Duchess and the Dirtwater Fox '76
Oh, God! Book 2 '80
Sonny Boy '87

Carrie Janisse
Desert Passion '93

Annabel Jankel
Max Headroom, the Original Story '86

Oleg Jankowski
My Twentieth Century '90

Leon Janney
Charly '68
Police Court '37

William Janney
Coquette '29

Rosanna Janni
Sonny and Jed '73

Emil Jannings
The Americano/Variety '25
The Blue Angel '30
Faust '26
Fortune's Fool '21
Last Command '28
The Last Laugh '24
Othello '22
Passion '19
Variety '25
Waxworks '24

Robert Jannucci
Exterminators of the Year 3000 '83

Ellen Janov
The Horse in the Gray Flannel Suit '68

Walter Janovitz
Billy the Kid Versus Dracula '66

Tama Janowitz
Slaves of New York '89

Andre Jansen
A Waltz Through the Hills '88

Gina Jansen
Sensual Partners '87

Horst Janson
Captain Kronos: Vampire Hunter '74
To Catch a King '84

David Janssen
Birds of Prey '72
City in Fear '80
Darby's Rangers '58
Fer-De-Lance '74
Francis in the Navy '55
Generation '69
Golden Rendezvous '77
The Green Berets '68
Hell to Eternity '60
High Ice '80
The King of the Roaring '20s: The Story of Arnold Rothstein '61
Lafayette Escadrille '58
Macho Callahan '70
Marooned '69
Moon of the Wolf '72
Once is Not Enough '75
Pioneer Woman '73
Prisoner in the Middle '74
The Shoes of the Fisherman '68
Smile, Jenny, You're Dead '74
S.O.S. Titanic '79
Stalk the Wild Child '76
Swamp Fire '46
Swiss Conspiracy '77
Two Minute Warning '76
The Word '78

Eilene Janssen
Curley '47

Famke Janssen
Fathers and Sons '92

Walther Jansson
The Mozart Story '48

Lois January
Bulldog Courage '35
Cocaine Fiends '36
Lightning Bill Crandall '37
The Red Rope '37
The Roamin' Cowboy '37

Al Jardine
Beach Boys: An American Band '85

Paully Jardine
Summer's Children '84

Claude Jarman, Jr.
Hangman's Knot '52
Intruder in the Dust '49
Rio Grande '50
The Yearling '46

Jim Jarmusch
American Autobahn '84
Leningrad Cowboys Go America '89
Straight to Hell '87

Marthe Jarnias
Vagabond '85

John Jarratt
Dark Age '88
Next of Kin '82
Sound of Love '77
Summer City '77

Sasha Jensen
Dream Trap '90
A Girl to Kill for '90

Todd Jensen
Prey for the Hunter '92

Jerry Jenson
Ghosts That Still Walk '77

Linda Jenson
Cheerleaders' Beach Party
'77

Roy Jenson
Bandits '73
Crossfire '67

**Roy Cameron
Jenson**
Demonoid, Messenger of
Death '81

Dominic Jephcott
African Dream '90

Helen Jepson
The Goldwyn Follies '38

Adele Jergens
Abbott & Costello Meet the
Invisible Man '51
Armored Car Robbery '50
Big Chase '54
Blues Busters '50
The Cobweb '55
Dark Past '49
Down to Earth '47
Falcon's Adventure/Armored
Car Robbery '50
Fuller Brush Man '48
Girls in Prison '56
Ladies of the Chorus '49
The Prince of Thieves '48
Radar Secret Service '50
Treasure of Monte Cristo '50

Diane Jergens
High School Confidential '58

Ebony Jerido
Just Another Girl on the I.R.T.
'93

Tim Jerome
Billy Bathgate '91

Mary Jerrold
The Queen of Spades '49

Bill Jesse
Riff Raff '92

Dan Jesse
Angels with Dirty Faces '38

George Jessel
Diary of a Young Comic '79
Valley of the Dolls '67

Patricia Jessel
Horror Hotel '60

Michael Jeter
Dead Bang '89

Joan Jett
Dubeat-E-O '84
Light of Day '87

Mark V. Jevicky
The Majorettes '87

Betty Jewel
The Last Outlaw '27

Jimmy Jewel
Arthur's Hallowed Ground '84

Geri Jewell
Two of a Kind '82

Isabel Jewell
The Arousers '70
Blessed Event '32

Ceiling Zero '35
The Leopard Man '43
Lost Horizon '37
Manhattan Melodrama '34
Marked Woman '37
The Seventh Victim '43
Swing It, Sailor! '37
A Tale of Two Cities '35

Zheng Jian
Ju Dou '90

Takeo Jii
Nomugi Pass '79

Penn Jillette
Light Years '88
Miami Vice 2: The Prodigal
Son '85
Penn and Teller Get Killed '90

Ann Jillian
The Ann Jillian Story '88
Convicted: A Mother's Story
'87
Girls of the White Orchid '85
Gypsy '62
Little White Lies '89
Mae West '84
Mr. Mom '83
Sealab 2020 '72

Joyce Jillson
Slumber Party '57 '76
Superchick '71

Yolanda Jilot
Diving In '90

Chrysti Jimenez
Omega Cop '90

Falco Jimenez
La Pastorela '92

Jose Luis Jimenez
Spiritism '61
The Vampire '57

Sergio Jimenez
La Pachange '87
Los Caifanes '87
Los Dos Hermanos '87

**Orlando Jiminez-
Leal**
El Super '79

Maria Rosa Jiminez
Loyola, the Soldier Saint '52

Ma Jingwu
Raise the Red Lantern '91

Betty Jinnette
In the Mood '87

Mike Jittlov
The Wizard of Speed and
Time '88

**Jo Stafford & the
Pied Pipers**
DuBarry Was a Lady '43

Suzy Joachim
Ultimate Desires '91

Keith Joakum
The Witches of Eastwick '87

Robert Joamie
Map of the Human Heart '93

Marlene Jobert
Catch Me a Spy '71
Masculine Feminine '66
Rider on the Rain '70
Swashbuckler '84
Ten Days Wonder '72

Adan Jodorowsky
Santa Sangre '90

Axel Jodorowsky
Santa Sangre '90

Cameron Johann
Spy Trap '92

Zita Johann
The Mummy '32

Ingemar Johannson
48 Hours to Live '60

David Johansen
Candy Mountain '87
Desire and Hell at Sunset
Motel '92
Freejack '92
Let It Ride '89
Light Years '88
Mr. Nanny '93
Scrooged '88
Tales from the Darkside: The
Movie '90

Paul Johansson
Martial Law 2: Undercover '91
Soapdish '91

I.S. Johar
Flame Over India '60
Maya '66

Zizi Johari
The Killing of a Chinese
Bookie '76

Domenick John
Creepshow 2 '87

Elton John
Born to Boogie '72
Tommy '75

Gottfried John
Berlin Alexanderplatz '80
Mata Hari '85
Mother Kusters Goes to
Heaven '76

Karl John
The Lost One '51
The Mysterious Magician '65

**The John Kirby
Sextet**
Sepia Cinderella '47

Robert John
Creatures the World Forgot
'70

Rosamund John
Fame is the Spur '47
Spitfire '42

Alexandra Johnes
Zelly & Me '88

Tom Johnigam
Bad Bunch '76

Anne Johns
Family Enforcer '76

Glynis Johns
The Adventures of Tartu '43
All Mine to Give '56
Another Time, Another Place
'58
Around the World in 80 Days
'56
Court Jester '56
Dear Brigitte '65
Encore '52
The Forty-Ninth Parallel '41
Frieda '47
Land of Fury '55
Mary Poppins '64
Mrs. Amworth '77
Papa's Delicate Condition '63
The Promoter '52
Rob Roy—The Highland
Rogue '53

Shake Hands with the Devil
'59
Sprague '84
The Sundowners '60
The Sword & the Rose '53
Under Milk Wood '73
Vault of Horror '73
Zelly & Me '88

Marion Johns
Gone to Ground '76

Mervyn Johns
Captive Heart '47
A Christmas Carol '51
Counterblast '48
Day of the Triffids '63
Dead of Night '45
The Master of Ballantrae '53
No Love for Johnnie '60
Pink Strings and Sealing Wax
'45
Romeo and Juliet '54
San Demetrio, London '47
Tony Draws a Horse '51

Stratford Johns
A Demon in My View '92
Great Expectations '81
The Lair of the White Worm
'88
Salome's Last Dance '88
Splitting Heirs '93

Tracy C. Johns
New Jack City '91

A.J. Johnson
Double Trouble '91
House Party '90

Alan Johnson
Iced '88

**Anne-Marie
Johnson**
Dream Date '93
Hollywood Shuffle '87
I'm Gonna Git You Sucka '88
Robot Jox '89
True Identity '91

Ariyan Johnson
Just Another Girl on the I.R.T.
'93

Arnold Johnson
My Demon Lover '87
Putney Swope '69

Arte Johnson
Bud and Lou '78
Bunco '83
The Charge of the Model T's
'76
Evil Spirits '91
Evil Toons '90
If Things Were Different '79
Love at First Bite '79
Munchie '92
The Red Raven Kiss-Off '90
Tax Season '90
What Comes Around '85

Ben Johnson
Back to Back '90
Bite the Bullet '75
Breakheart Pass '76
Champions '84
The Chase '91
Cherry 2000 '88
Chisum '70
Dark Before Dawn '89
Dillinger '73
The Getaway '72
Grayeagle '77
Junior Bonner '72
The Last Picture Show '71
Let's Get Harry '87
Major Dundee '65

Mighty Joe Young '49
My Heroes Have Always Been
Cowboys '91
One-Eyed Jacks '61
Radio Flyer '92
The Rare Breed '66
Red Dawn '84
Rio Grande '50
Ruckus '81
The Sacketts '79
The Savage Bees '76
The Shadow Riders '82
Shane '53
She Wore a Yellow Ribbon '49
Soggy Bottom U.S.A. '84
The Sugarland Express '74
The Swarm '78
Terror Train '80
Tex '82
Three Godfathers '48
Tomboy & the Champ '58
Town that Dreaded Sundown
'76
Train Robbers '73
Trespasses '86
The Undefeated '69
Wagon Master '50
Wild Horses '84
Wild Times '79
Will Penny '67

Beverly Johnson
Ashanti, Land of No Mercy '79

Bill Johnson
Texas Chainsaw Massacre,
Part 2 '86

Bobby Johnson
Hollywood's New Blood '88

Brad Johnson
Always '89
Flight of the Intruder '90
The Losers '70
Nam Angels '88

Bruce Johnson
Beach Boys: An American
Band '85

Candy Johnson
Muscle Beach Party '64
Pajama Party '64

Ceepee Johnson
Mystery in Swing '40

Celia Johnson
Brief Encounter '46
Captain's Paradise '53
The Hostage Tower '80
In Which We Serve '43
Les Miserables '78
The Prime of Miss Jean
Brodie '69
Staying On '80
This Happy Breed '47
Unicorn '83

Chic Johnson
All Over Town '37
Country Gentlemen '36

Clark Johnson
The Finishing Touch '92
Personals '90

Don Johnson
Beulah Land '80
Born Yesterday '93
A Boy and His Dog '75
Cease Fire '85
The City '76
Dead Bang '89
G.I. Joe: The Movie '86
Guilty as Sin '93
Harley Davidson and the
Marlboro Man '91
Harrad Experiment '73

Longtime Companion '90
Millenium '89
Miracle at Moreaux '86
Shadows and Fog '92
She's Back '88
The Suicide Club '88
Sword of Gideon '86

Alice Joyce
Dancing Mothers '26
Song O' My Heart '29

Brenda Joyce
The Enchanted Forest '45

Elaine Joyce
Motel Hell '80

Natalie Joyce
Through the Breakers '28

Peggy Hopkins Joyce
International House '33

William Joyce
I Eat Your Skin '64
The Young Nurses '73

Yootha Joyce
Die! Die! My Darling! '65
Horrors of Burke & Hare '71

Odette Joyeux
La Ronde '51
Sylvia and the Phantom '45

Joyzelle Joyner
Whistlin' Dan '32

Kimble Joyner
Spy Trap '92

Mario Joyner
Hangin' with the Homeboys '91

Michelle Joyner
Traces of Red '92

Paul Joynt
Opposing Force '87

Jesus Juarez
Santa Sangre '90

Ruben Juarez
Tango Bar '88

Carolyn Judd
Escape from Cell Block Three '78
Women Unchained '70s

Edward Judd
The Day the Earth Caught Fire '62
First Men in the Moon '64
Invasion '65
Island of Terror '66
The Kitchen Toto '87
Murder Motel '74
Whose Child Am I? '75

Naomi Judd
Rio Diablo '93

Robert Judd
Fight for Your Life '79

Charles Judels
Baby Face Morgan '42
Love on the Run '36
Pinocchio '40
Two Reelers: Comedy Classics 8 '33

Arline Judge
The Crawling Hand '63
Girls in Chains '43
Law of the Jungle '42
Mysterious Mr. Wong '35
Song of Texas '43
Take It Big '44

Wildcat '42

Naomi Judge
Terror Trail '33

Gordon Judges
Busted Up '86

Hernadi Judit
Another Way '82

Arno Juergling
Andy Warhol's Dracula '74

Harald Juhnke
Code Name Alpha '67
Red-Dragon '67

Raul Julia
The Addams Family '91
The Alamo: Thirteen Days to Glory '87
Compromising Positions '85
Death Scream '75
Escape Artist '82
Eyes of Laura Mars '78
Florida Straits '87
Frankenstein Unbound '90
Gumball Rally '76
Havana '90
Kiss of the Spider Woman '85
A Life of Sin '92
Mack the Knife '89
Moon Over Parador '88
Morning After '86
Onassis '88
One from the Heart '82
The Organization '71
Overdrawn at the Memory Bank '83
Panic in Needle Park '75
The Penitent '88
Presumed Innocent '90
Romero '89
The Rookie '90
Stiletto '69
Strong Medicine '84
Tango Bar '88
The Tempest '82
Tequila Sunrise '88
Trading Hearts '87

Janet Julian
Ghostwarrior '86
Humongous '82
King of New York '90
Smokey Bites the Dust '81

Lenny Juliano
Not of This Earth '88

Jorge Juliao
Pixote '81

Max Julien
Getting Straight '70
Mack '73

Montserrat Julio
The Blood Spattered Bride '72

Julissa
Dance of Death '69
The Fear Chamber '68

Ami Julius
Malibu Bikini Shop '86

Sandra Jullien
The Sensuous Teenager '70

Gordon Jump
Dirkham Detective Agency '83
Making the Grade '84
Ransom Money '88

Tito Junco
El Hombre Contra el Mundo '87
Invasion of the Vampires '61
A Woman Without Love '51

Victor Junco
Conexion Mexico '87
Gente Violenta '87

Calvin Jung
American Ninja 3: Blood Hunt '89
In the Shadow of Kilimanjaro '86

Sun Jung-Chi
Monkey Kung Fu '80s

Fabio Junior
Bye Bye Brazil '79

Bernie Junker
Clash of the Ninja '86

Katy Jurado
Arrowhead '53
The Badlanders '58
Barabbas '62
Broken Lance '54
The Brute '52
Bullfighter & the Lady '50
Children of Sanchez '79
El Bruto '52
Fearmaker '89
High Noon '52
Once Upon a Scoundrel '73
One-Eyed Jacks '61
Pat Garrett & Billy the Kid '73
Stay Away, Joe '68
Trapeze '56
Under the Volcano '84

Peter Jurasik
Full Exposure: The Sex Tape Scandals '89
Peter Gunn '89
Problem Child '90

Curt Jurgens
And God Created Woman '57
The Assassination Bureau '69
Battle of Britain '69
Battle of Neretva '69
Battle of the Commandos '71
Breakthrough '78
Cruise Missile '78
The Devil in Silk '56
Dirty Heroes '71
Enemy Below '57
Ferry to Hong Kong '59
French Intrigue
Goldengirl '79
The Inn of the Sixth Happiness '58
The Invincible Six '68
Just a Gigolo '79
The Longest Day '62
Lord Jim '65
The Mephisto Waltz '71
The Miracle of the White Stallions '63
The Mozart Story '48
Murder for Sale '70
Nicholas and Alexandra '71
Sleep of Death '79
The Spy Who Loved Me '77
Tamango '59
This Happy Feeling '58
The Three Penny Opera '62
Twist '76
Vault of Horror '73

Deana Jurgens
Code Name: Zebra '84
Tin Man '83

Melita Jurisic
The Tale of Ruby Rose '87

Rich Jury
Blood on the Mountain '88

Ed Justice
The Vernonia Incident '89

James Robertson Justice
Above Us the Waves '56
Alien Women '69
David and Bathsheba '51
Doctor at Large '57
Doctor at Sea '56
Doctor in Distress '63
Doctor in the House '53
The Lady Says No '51
Land of the Pharaohs '55
Le Repos du Guerrier '62
The Love Factor '69
Murder She Said '62
Rob Roy—The Highland Rogue '53
Spirits of the Dead '68
The Sword & the Rose '53
Whiskey Galore '48

Katherine Justice
Captain America 2: Death Too Soon '79
Columbo: Prescription Murder '67
Five Card Stud '68
Frasier the Sensuous Lion '73
The Stepmother '71

William Justine
The Bride & the Beast '58
Trauma '62

Claude Jutra
Till Death Do Us Part '72

Kaethe Kaack
Baron Munchausen '43

Jeff Kaake
Border Shootout '90

Suzanne Kaaren
The Devil Bat '41
Phantom Ranger '00

Roger Kabler
Alligator Eyes '90

Vladimir Kachpour
Taxi Blues '90

George Kaczender
The Agency '81

Jane Kaczmarek
All's Fair '89
D.O.A. '88
Door to Door '84
Falling in Love '84
The Heavenly Kid '85
Vice Versa '88

Fawzia el Kader
The Battle of Algiers '66

Nicholas Kadi
Navy SEALS '90

Karen Kadler
The Beatniks '60
It Conquered the World '56

Piotr Kadochnikev
Ivan the Terrible, Part 1 '44
Ivan the Terrible, Part 2 '46

Larisa Kadochnikova
Shadows of Forgotten Ancestors '64

Diane Kagan
The Life and Assassination of the Kingfish '76
Mr. & Mrs. Bridge '91

Marilyn Kagan
Foxes '80

Kyoko Kagawa
The Crucified Lovers '54

The Lower Depths '57
Mother '52
Sansho the Bailiff '54

David Kagen
Body Chemistry '90
Conspiracy: The Trial of the Chicago Eight '87
Friday the 13th, Part 6: Jason Lives '86

Saul Kahan
Schlock '73

Steve Kahan
Lethal Weapon '87
Lethal Weapon 2 '89
Lethal Weapon 3 '92

Wolf Kahler
Raiders of the Lost Ark '81

Jonathan Kahn
The Sailor Who Fell from Grace with the Sea '76

Madeline Kahn
The Adventures of Sherlock Holmes' Smarter Brother '78
Best of Dan Aykroyd '86
Best of Gilda Radner '89
Betsy's Wedding '90
Blazing Saddles '74
The Cheap Detective '78
City Heat '84
Clue '85
The Dove '68
First Family '80
For Richer, For Poorer '92
Happy Birthday, Gemini '80
The Hideaways '73
High Anxiety '77
History of the World: Part 1 '81
The Muppet Movie '79
My Little Pony: The Movie '86
Paper Moon '73
Scrambled Feet '83
Simon '80
Slapstick of Another Kind '84
Wanted: The Perfect Guy '90
Wholly Moses! '80
Yellowbeard '83
Young Frankenstein '74

Sajid Kahn
Maya '66

Chia Kai
Dance of Death '84
Empire of the Dragon '80s
Of Cooks and Kung-Fu '80s

Alexander Kaidanovsky
Stalker '79

Khalil Kain
Juice '92

Burt Kaiser
The Female Jungle '56

Caroline Kaiser
Old Explorers '90

Elizabeth Kaitan
Aftershock '88
Roller Blade Warriors: Taken By Force '90
Vice Academy 3 '91

Terrie Kalbus
Phantasm '79

Bonita Kalem
Escape from Cell Block Three '78
Women Unchained '70s

Toni Kalem
Billy Galvin '86
Silent Rage '82

Patricia Kalember
Big Girls Don't Cry...They Get
Even '92

Bernard Kaler
The Rats are Coming! The
Werewolves are Here! '72

Goren Kalezik
Fireballs '90

Jean-Pierre Kalfon
Condorman '81
Weekend '67

Stephan Kalipha
Born of Fire '87

Jacob Kalish
East and West '23

Helena Kallianiotes
Backtrack '89

John Kallo
My Samurai '92

Jagoda Kaloper
WR: Mysteries of the
Organism '71

Alexander Kalyagin
A Slave of Love '78
An Unfinished Piece for a
Player Piano '77

Hung Kam-Bo
Lightning Kung Fu '70s

Rob Kaman
Bloodfist '89

Stan Kamber
Soul Vengeance '75

Danny Kamekona
The Karate Kid: Part 2 '86
Robot Jox '89
Robot Wars '93

Stanley Kamel
Murder by Numbers '89

Milt Kamen
Group Marriage '72

Dan Kamin
Another Pair of Aces: Three of
a Kind '91

Susana Kamini
Sisters of Satan '75

Ida Kaminska
The Shop on Main Street '65

Dana Kaminsky
Super Mario Bros. '93

Kris Kamm
Born to Ride '91

Locs Kamme
Strike Commando '87

Fritz Kampers
Kameradschaft '31
Westfront 1918 '30

Steven Kampmann
A Tiger's Tale '87

Victor Kan
Ping Pong '87

Akiko Kana
The Imperial Japanese Empire
'85

Anna Kanakis
After the Fall of New York '85
Warriors of the Wasteland '83

Steve Kanaly
Balboa '82
Double Trouble '91
Driving Me Crazy '91
Eye of the Eagle 3 '91
Fleshburn '84
Headhunter '89

Sean Kanan
Rich Girl '91

Alden Kane
Prom Night 4: Deliver Us From
Evil '91

Babe Kane
The Dentist '32
Pharmacist '32
W.C. Fields Comedy Bag '33
W.C. Fields: Flask of Fields
'30

Big Daddy Kane
Posse '93

Brad Kane
Aladdin '92

Carol Kane
Annie Hall '77
Baby on Board '92
Burning Rage '84
Carnal Knowledge '71
Casey at the Bat '85
Desperate Characters '71
Dog Day Afternoon '75
Drop-Out Mother '88
Flashback '89
Harry & Walter Go to New
York '76
Hester Street '75
Jumpin' Jack Flash '86
Keeping On '81
The Last Detail '73
The Lemon Sisters '90
License to Drive '88
The Muppet Movie '79
My Blue Heaven '90
My Sister, My Love '78
Norman Loves Rose '82
Over the Brooklyn Bridge '83
Pandemonium '82
The Princess Bride '87
Racing with the Moon '84
Rap Master Ronnie '88
Scrooged '88
The Secret Diary of Sigmund
Freud '84
Sticky Fingers '88
Strong Medicine '84
Transylvania 6-5000 '85
Wedding in White '72
When a Stranger Calls '79
World's Greatest Lover '77

Fernne Kane
Psycho Girls '86

Gail Kane
The White Sister '23

Gordon Kane
Danger UXB '81

Irene Kane
Killer's Kiss '55

Jimmy Kane
Challenge To Be Free '76

Kathleen Kane
Deadly Diamonds '91

Marjorie Kane
Border Romance '30
The Great Gabbo '29
Sunny Skies '30

Michael Kane
The Gunfighters '87

Sharon Kane
Sex, Drugs, and Rock-n-Roll
'84

Stan Kane
Storm '87

Naomi Kaneda
Blood Tracks '86

Chin Kang
Return of the Chinese Boxer
'74

John Kani
African Dream '90
Killing Heat '84
Options '88
Sarafina! '92

Frank Kanig
At Gunpoint '90

Gretchen Kanne
Psychopath '73

Alexis Kanner
Kings and Desperate Men '83
Nightfall '88
Twinsanity '70

Mike Kannon
Rat Pfink a Boo-Boo '66

Vicki Kantenwine
The Mermaids of Tiburon '62

Jennifer Kanter
Maximum Thrust '87

Ivar Kants
Gallagher's Travels '87
Plumber '79
Silver City '84

Aneeta Kanwar
Salaam Bombay! '88

John Kapelos
All's Fair '89
The Boost '88
Man Trouble '92

Gabe Kaplan
Fast Break '79
The Hoboken Chicken
Emergency '84
Nobody's Perfekt '79
Tulips '81

Jonathan Kaplan
Cannonball '76
Hollywood Boulevard '76

Marvin Kaplan
Adam's Rib '50
Fangs '75
The Severed Arm '73

Shammi Kapoor
Deadly Thief '78

Shashi Kapoor
Bombay Talkie '70
The Deceivers '88
Heat and Dust '82
The Householder '63
Sammy & Rosie Get Laid '87
Shakespeare Wallah '65

Valerie Kaprisky
Aphrodite '83
Breathless '83
L'Annee des Meduses '86
The Year of the Jellyfish '84

Mitzi Kapture
Angel 3: The Final Chapter '88
Liberty & Bash '90
Private Road: No Trespassing
'87

Ron Karabatsos
Flashdance '83

Hollywood Heartbreak '89
Missing Pieces '83
Rich Girl '91

Shoji Karada
Fist of Vengeance '70s

**Setsuko
Karamsumarau**
Twilight of the Cockroaches
'90

Diana Karanikas
Dead Girls '90

Mirjana Karanovic
When Father was Away on
Business '85

May Karasun
Lake Consequence '92

Selan Karay
Night of the Zombies '83

James Karen
Billionaire Boys Club '87
The China Syndrome '79
The Closer '91
Cult People '89
Frankenstein Meets the Space
Monster '65
Girlfriend from Hell '89
Hardbodies 2 '86
Hercules in New York '70
The Jagged Edge '85
Lies Before Kisses '92
Poltergeist '82
Return of the Living Dead '85
Return of the Living Dead Part
2 '88
Sam's Son '84
The Unborn '91
Vital Signs '90
The Willies '90

Suzanne Karen
Undercover Man '36

Anna Karin
Body of Influence '93
Wild Cactus '92

Rita Karin
Age Isn't Everything '91
Enemies, a Love Story '89
He Said, She Said '91
Sophie's Choice '82

Anna Karina
Alphaville '65
Band of Outsiders '64
Chinese Roulette '86
Cleo from 5 to 7 '61
Les Carabiniers '63
My Life to Live '62
The Nun '66
Pierrot le Fou '65
Regina '83
The Salzburg Connection '72
Ski Bum '75
A Woman is a Woman '60

Vassilli Karis
Animal Called Man '87
SS Girls '78

Vic Karis
Naked Warriors '73

Toyomi Karita
Warning from Space '56

Olga Karlatos
Purple Rain '84
Zombie '80

John Karlen
American Dream '81
Babycakes '89
Daughters of Darkness '71
Gimme an F '85

Impulse '84
Melvin Purvis: G-Man '74
Native Son '86
Night of Dark Shadows '71
Nightmare on the 13th Floor
'90
Racing with the Moon '84
Rosie: The Rosemary Clooney
Story '82
Trilogy of Terror '75

Boris Karloff
Abbott and Costello Meet Dr.
Jekyll and Mr. Hyde '52
Abbott and Costello Meet the
Killer, Boris Karloff '49
The Ape '40
Bedlam '45
Before I Hang '40
The Black Cat '34
The Black Room '35
Black Sabbath '64
The Body Snatcher '45
The Bride of Frankenstein '35
British Intelligence '40
Cauldron of Blood '67
Charlie Chan at the Opera '36
The Comedy of Terrors '64
Corridors of Blood '58
Criminal Code '31
The Crimson Cult '68
Dance of Death '69
Daydreamer '66
Dick Tracy Double Feature #2
'47
Dick Tracy Meets Gruesome
'47
Die, Monster, Die! '65
Doomed to Die '40
Dynamite Dan '24
The Fatal Hour '40
The Fear Chamber '68
Frankenstein '31
The Ghoul '34
The Haunted Strangler '58
The Horror of It All '91
House of Evil '68
House of Frankenstein '44
How the Grinch Stole
Christmas '65
The Invisible Ray '36
Island Monster '53
Isle of the Dead '45
Juggernaut '36
King of the Kongo '29
The Lost Patrol '34
Mad Monster Party '68
The Man They Could Not
Hang '39
The Man Who Lived Again '36
The Mask of Fu Manchu '32
Mr. Wong, Detective '38
Mr. Wong in Chinatown '39
The Mummy '32
Mystery of Mr. Wong '39
The Old Dark House '32
Old Ironsides '26
The Raven '35
The Raven '63
Sabaka '55
Scarface '31
The Secret Life of Walter
Mitty '47
The Sinister Invasion '68
The Snake People '68
Son of Frankenstein '39
Targets '69
The Terror '63
The Tower of London '39
You'll Find Out '40

John Karlsen
Maciste in Hell '60
Waterfront '83

Oscar Karlweis
Meet Me in Las Vegas '56

Cathy Lacommaro
Splatter University '84

Philippe Lacoste
Hail Mary '85

Denis Lacroix
Running Brave '83

Beatriz Lacy
Graveyard of Horror '71

Jerry Lacy
Play It Again, Sam '72

John Lacy
Wildcard '92

John Ladalski
Chinese Stuntman '70s
Counter Attack '84

Andrea Ladanyi
Gate 2 '92

Alan Ladd
All the Young Men '60
The Badlanders '58
Botany Bay '53
Branded '50
Captain Caution '40
The Carpetbaggers '64
Citizen Kane '41
Deep Six '58
Drum Beat '54
Duel of Champions '61
Gangs, Inc. '41
The Glass Key '42
Hell on Frisco Bay '55
The Howards of Virginia '40
Joan of Paris '42
The McConnell Story '55
My Favorite Brunette '47
Proud Rebel '58
Shane '53
This Gun for Hire '42

Cheryl Ladd
Fulfillment '89
The Hasty Heart '86
Lisa '90
Millenium '89
Now and Forever '82
Poison Ivy '92
Purple Hearts '84
Romance on the Orient
    Express '89
Satan's School for Girls '73
The Treasure of Jamaica Reef
    '74

David Ladd
Catlow '71
A Dog of Flanders '59
Misty '61
The Treasure of Jamaica Reef
    '74

Diane Ladd
Alice Doesn't Live Here
    Anymore '74
All Night Long '81
Carnosaur '93
The Cemetery Club '93
Chinatown '74
Code Name: Chaos '90
Desperate Lives '82
Embryo '76
Father Hood '93
I Married a Centerfold '84
A Kiss Before Dying '91
The Lookalike '90
National Lampoon's
    Christmas Vacation '89
Plain Clothes '88
Rambling Rose '91
Rebel Rousers '69
Something Wicked This Way
    Comes '83
The Wild Angels '66

Wild at Heart '90
Willa '79

Nicole Ladmiral
Diary of a Country Priest '50

Gabriele Lafari
A Woman in Flames '84

John Lafayette
Full Fathom Five '90
White Sands '92

Patricia Laffan
Devil Girl from Mars '54
Quo Vadis '51

Art LaFleur
Jack the Bear '93
Live! From Death Row '92
Rampage '87
Trancers '85
Zone Troopers '85

C.D. LaFleure
Alice Goodbody '74

Bernadette LaFont
Catch Me a Spy '71
Le Beau Serge '58
The Perils of Gwendoline '84
Too Pretty to Be Honest '72
Trop Jolie pour Etre Honette
    '60s
A Very Curious Girl '69
Violette '78

**Jean-Philippe
LaFont**
Babette's Feast '87

Desiree Laforge
Blood on the Badge

Frederic Lagache
Emmanuelle, the Joys of a
    Woman '76

Jocelyn Lagarde
Hawaii '66

Caroline Lagerfelt
Home at Last '88

Sture Lagerwall
Walpurgis Night '41

Valerie Lagrange
A Man and a Woman '66
Morgan the Pirate '60
Weekend '67

Bert Lahr
Just Around the Corner '38
The Night They Raided
    Minsky's '69
Rose Marie '54
Ship Ahoy '42
Sing Your Worries Away '42
Two Reelers: Comedy
    Classics 4 '36
The Wizard of Oz '39

Christine Lahti
And Justice for All '79
Crazy from the Heart '91
The Doctor '91
The Executioner's Song '82
The Fear Inside '92
Funny About Love '90
The Good Fight '92
Gross Anatomy '89
The Henderson Monster '80
Housekeeping '87
Just Between Friends '86
Leaving Normal '92
Miss Firecracker '89
Running on Empty '88
Single Bars, Single Women
    '84
Stacking '87
Swing Shift '84

Whose Life Is It Anyway? '81

Gary Lahti
Knightriders '81

Bruce Lai
Clones of Bruce Lee '80
The Magnificent

Christina Lai
Savage Island '85

Lo Lai
Young Dragon '77

Leah Lail
Body Waves '91

Bill Laimbeer
Hot Shots! '91

Jewell Lain
Suicide Battalion/Hell Squad
    '58

Frankie Laine
Meet Me in Las Vegas '56

Jeff Laine
Cheering Section '73

Jennifer Laine
Caged Fury '80

Jimmy Laine
Driller Killer '74
Ms. 45 '81

Ray Laine
Season of the Witch '73

Marvin Laird
Beyond Reason '77

Oze Lajos
Oh, Bloody Life! '88

Alan Lake
Con Man '92
Don't Open Till Christmas '84

Arthur Lake
Exiled to Shanghai '37
Silent Laugh Makers, No. 1
    '15
The Silver Streak '34
Skinner's Dress Suit '26
23 1/2 Hours Leave '37

Florence Lake
Going to Town '44
Next Time I Marry '38
Quality Street '37
Romance '30
Savage Intruder '68

Michael Lake
Sweetie '89

Ricki Lake
Babycakes '89
The Chase '91
Cookie '89
Cry-Baby '90
Hairspray '88
Last Exit to Brooklyn '90
Where the Day Takes You '92
Working Girl '88

Veronica Lake
Flesh Feast '69
The Glass Key '42
I Married a Witch '42
Ramrod '47
Sullivan's Travels '41
This Gun for Hire '42

Elaine Lakeman
Death Target '83

Joe Lala
The Take '90

Michael Lally
The Nesting '80

Frank Laloggia
The Wizard of Speed and
    Time '88

Donny Lalonde
Boxcar Blues '90

Robert Lalonde
Men of Steel '88

Barry Lam
Rivals of the Silver Fox '80

Debbie Lam
Snake Fist of the Buddhist
    Dragon '70s

Jack Lam
Leopard Fist Ninja '80s

Libertad Lamarque
Una Vez en la Vida '49

Hedy Lamarr
Algiers '38
Boom Town '40
Copper Canyon '50
Dishonored Lady '47
Ecstasy '33
Experiment Perilous '45
The Love of Three Queens '54
Samson and Delilah '50
The Strange Woman '46
Tortilla Flat '42
Ziegfeld Girl '41

Jean LaMarre
Malcolm X '92

Fernando Lamas
The Cheap Detective '78
Dangerous When Wet '53
The Girl Who Had Everything
    '53
The Merry Widow '52
Murder on Flight 502 '75
100 Rifles '69
Powder Keg '70
Rich, Young and Pretty '51
Rose Marie '54
Violent Ones '68

Lorenzo Lamas
Body Rock '84
C.I.A.: Code Name Alexa '92
Final Impact '91
Killing Streets '91
Night of the Warrior '91
SnakeEater '89
SnakeEater 2: The Drug
    Buster '89
SnakeEater 3: His Law '92
The Swordsman '92
Take Down '79

Andrea Lamatsch
Blood Ring '93

Debra Lamb
Beverly Hills Vamp '88
B.O.R.N. '88
Evil Spirits '91
The Invisible Maniac '90
Rock & the Money-Hungry
    Party Girls '89
Stripped to Kill II: Live Girls '89

Gil Lamb
Comedy Festival #2 '30s
Day of the Animals '77

Larry Lamb
Buster '88
Underworld '85

**Anne Louise
Lambert**
The Draughtsman's Contract
    '82
Great Expectations: The
    Untold Story '87

**Christopher
Lambert**
Greystoke: The Legend of
    Tarzan, Lord of the Apes
    '84
Highlander '86
Highlander 2: The Quickening
    '91
Knight Moves '93
Love Songs '85
Priceless Beauty '90
The Sicilian '87
Subway '85
To Kill a Priest '89
Why Me? '90

Henry Lambert
Oasis of the Zombies '82

Jack Lambert
Dick Tracy's Dilemma '47
Hue and Cry '47
Machine Gun Kelly '58
Montana Belle '52
North of the Great Divide '50

Jane Lambert
Crazy Fat Ethel II '85

Janet Lambert
Abroad with Two Yanks '44

Kim Lambert
If Looks Could Kill '86

Paul Lambert
Mama's Dirty Girls '74

Heath Lamberts
To Kill a Clown '72

Ellie Lambetti
Girl in Black '56
A Matter of Dignity '57

Vassili Lambrinos
Last Rites '88

Derek Lamden
Baby Love '69

Karen Lamm
Ants '77
The Hatfields & the McCoys
    '75

Adele Lamont
The Brain That Wouldn't Die
    '63

Duncan Lamont
The Evil of Frankenstein '64
The Golden Coach '52
Murder at the Gallop '63

Molly Lamont
The Awful Truth '37
The Devil Bat's Daughter '46
Somewhere I'll Find You '42

Sonny Lamont
The Adventures of the
    Masked Phantom '38

Pascal Lamorisse
The Red Balloon '56
Red Balloon/Occurrence at
    Owl Creek Bridge '62
Voyage en Balloon '59

Mark Lamos
Longtime Companion '90

John Lamotta
One More Chance '90
We're Talkin' Serious Money
    '92

Dorothy Lamour
Caught in the Draft '41
Creepshow 2 '87
Dixiana '30
Donovan's Reef '63

Johan Leysen
Egg '88
The Music Teacher '88

John Leyton
Guns at Batasi '64
Seaside Swingers '65
Von Ryan's Express '65

Sara Lezana
Gun Fight at Red Sands '63

Thierry Lhermitte
My Best Friend's Girl '84
My New Partner '84
Next Year If All Goes Well '83
Until September '84

Bruce Li
Blind Fists of Bruce '70s
Bruce Li in New Guinea '80
Bruce Li the Invincible '80
Chinese Connection 2 '84
Chinese Stuntman '70s
Counter Attack '84
Edge of Fury '80s
Enter the Panther '79
Enter Three Dragons '81
Fists of Fury 2 '80
Image of Bruce Lee '70s
Iron Dragon Strikes Back '84
Kung Fu Avengers '85
Return of the Tiger '78
Story of the Dragon '82

Chang Li
Black Belt Fury '81
Enter Three Dragons '81
Fight to the Death '83

Gong Li
Ju Dou '90
Raise the Red Lantern '91
Red Sorghum '88

Hwang Cheng Li
Dragon's Claw '80s

John Li
Lightning Kung Fu '70s

Pi Li Lee
Kung Fu Massacre '82

Chou Li Lung
Crack Shadow Boxers '70s

Man Li Peng
Little Big Master '70s

Wang Li
Zombie vs. Ninja

Bruce Liang
The Fist, the Kicks, and the Evils '80
Showdown at the Equator '83

Guo Liang
Young Hero of Shaolin
Young Hero of the Shaolin Part 2

Ko Shou Liang
Ninja Exterminators '81
Renegade Monk '82
Shaolin Ex-Monk '82

Liu Chang Liang
Fighting Ace '80s
Renegade Monk '82

Tan Tao Liang
Dual Flying Kicks '82
Incredible Master Beggars '82

Peter Paul Liapis
Starhops '78

Brian Libby
Platoon Leader '87
Silent Rage '82

Liberace
The Loved One '65
Sincerely Yours '56

Anne Libert
The Demons '74
Girls of Don Juan '70s
Virgin Among the Living Dead '71

Richard Libertini
All of Me '84
And You Thought Your Parents Were Weird! '91
Animal Behavior '89
Big Trouble '86
The Bonfire of the Vanities '90
Deal of the Century '83
Fletch '85
Fletch Lives '89
Fourth Wise Man '85
Going Berserk '83
The In-Laws '79
Popeye '80
Sharky's Machine '81
Soup for One '82
Unfaithfully Yours '84

Mitchell Lichenstein
Streamers '83

Jeremy Licht
Father Figure '80
Lois Gibbs and the Love Canal '82
Next One '84
The Seekers '79
Twilight Zone: The Movie '83

Chung Lick
Super Kung Fu Kid

Gabriella Licudi
The Last Safari '67
The Unearthly Stranger '64

Laura Liddell
Shakespeare Wallah '65

G. Gordon Liddy
Adventures in Spying '92
Camp Cucamonga: How I Spent My Summer Vacation '90
Street Asylum '90
When Nature Calls '85

Anki Liden
My Life as a Dog '85

Leon Liebgold
Yidl Mitn Fidl '36

Harry Liedtke
Passion '19

Chen Hung Lieh
To Subdue the Evil

Lo Lieh
Born Invincible '76
Bruce's Deadly Fingers '80
The Dragon Returns
Fists of Bruce Lee '80s
The Golden Triangle '80
King Boxer '90
Kung Fu from Beyond the Grave
Ninja Massacre '84
The Ninja Pirates '90
The Noble Ninja '90
Shaolin Executioner '80s
Showdown at the Equator '83
The Stranger and the Gunfighter '76

Robert Liensol
Time to Kill '89

Johanna Lier
Alpine Fire '89

Albert Lieven
Beware of Pity '46
Frieda '47
The Life and Death of Colonel Blimp '43
Seventh Veil '46
Sleeping Car to Trieste '45

Enyaw Liew
Machoman '70s

Tina Lifford
Grand Canyon '91

Judith Light
Stamp of a Killer '87

Karl Light
The Lonely Sex '59

Gordon Lightfoot
Harry Tracy '83

Marilyn Lightstone
Anne of Green Gables '85
Grand Tour: Disaster in Time '92
Lies My Father Told Me '75
Surrogate '88
Wild Pony '83

Tom Ligon
Fury on Wheels '71
Judge Horton and the Scottsboro Boys '76

Mitsos Liguisos
Never on Sunday '60

Dennis Lili
Lillie '79

Lili Liliana
The Dybbuk '37

Dennis Lill
Bad Blood '87

Tom Lillard
The Brig '64

Anna Lillian
Where is My Child? '37

Beatrice Lillie
On Approval '44
Thoroughly Modern Millie '67

Sandy Lillingston
Dangerous Game '90

Silvia Lillo
Love in the City '53

Kay Tong Lim
Dragon: The Bruce Lee Story '93

Yvonne Lime
I Was a Teenage Werewolf '57

Dina Limon
Boy Takes Girl '83

Bridget Lin
Jackie Chan's Police Force '85

Kong Lin
Raise the Red Lantern '91

Pearl Lin
Bruce Lee's Ways of Kung Fu '80s

Sinon Lin
Dreadnaught Rivals '80s

Traci Lin
Class of 1999 '90
Fright Night 2 '88
No Secrets '91
Survival Quest '89
A Tiger's Tale '87
Voyager '91

Kay Linaker
Hidden Enemy '40

Peter Linari
Fat Guy Goes Nutzoid '86

Abbey Lincoln
For Love of Ivy '68

Elmo Lincoln
The Adventures of Tarzan '21
Tarzan of the Apes '17
Tarzan's New York Adventure '42
Wyoming Outlaw '39

Fred J. Lincoln
Last House on the Left '72

Lar Park Lincoln
Friday the 13th, Part 7: The New Blood '88
Princess Academy '87

Pamela Lincoln
Anatomy of a Psycho '61

Richard Lincoln
Manny's Orphans '78

Warren Lincoln
The Power '80

Della Lind
Swiss Miss '38

Jenny Lind
Barnum '86

Hala Linda
Legion of Missing Men '37

Kristina Lindberg
Maid in Sweden '83

Sven Lindberg
Face to Face '76

Gunnel Lindblom
Hunger '66
The Seventh Seal '56
The Virgin Spring '59

Jainine Linde
Moving Target '89

Carrie Lindell
Cannibal Campout '88

Doris Linden
Hillbilly Blitzkrieg '42
Snuffy Smith, Yard Bird '42

Eric Linden
Ah, Wilderness! '35
Criminals Within '41
Let 'Em Have It '35
Sweetheart of the Navy '37

Hal Linden
Father Figure '80
How to Break Up a Happy Divorce '76
I Do! I Do! '84
Mr. Inside, Mr. Outside '74
My Wicked, Wicked Ways '84
A New Life '88
Starflight One '83

Jennie Linden
Hedda '75
Women in Love '70

Liane Linden
The Arsenal Stadium Mystery '39

Cec Linder
Deadly Eyes '82
The Devil's Web '74
Goldfinger '64
Heavenly Bodies '84
A Touch of Class '73

Christa Linder
Night of a Thousand Cats '72

Max Linder
Early Cinema Vol. 1 '19
Laugh with Linder! '13
Man in the Silk Hat '15
Man in the Silk Hat '83
Max '22
Pop Goes the Cork '22
Seven Years Bad Luck '20

Viveca Lindfors
Adventures of Don Juan '49
The Ann Jillian Story '88
Bell from Hell '74
The Best Little Girl in the World '81
Cauldron of Blood '67
Child of Darkness, Child of Light '91
Creepshow '82
Exiled in America '90
The Exorcist 3 '90
For Ladies Only '81
Four in a Jeep '51
Girlfriends '78
The Hand '81
Inside the Third Reich '82
The King of Kings '61
Lady Beware '87
The Linguini Incident '92
Marilyn: The Untold Story '80
Mom, the Wolfman and Me '80
Moonfleet '55
Natural Enemies '79
A Question of Guilt '78
Rachel River '89
Secret Weapons '85
Silent Madness '84
The Story of Ruth '60
The Sure Thing '85
The Way We Were '73
A Wedding '78
Welcome to L.A. '77
Zandalee '91

Peter Lindgren
I Am Curious (Yellow) '67

Kristen Lindholm
Twins of Evil '71

Audra Lindley
Best Friends '82
Cannery Row '82
Desert Hearts '86
The Heartbreak Kid '72
Revenge of the Stepford Wives '80
The Spellbinder '88
Stamp of a Killer '87

Delroy Lindo
Bound by Honor '93
Bright Angel '91
Malcolm X '92

Olga Lindo
The Hidden Room '49
Things Happen at Night '48

Betty H. Lindon
I Eat Your Skin '64

Vincent Lindon
A Man in Love '87

Ann Lindsay
Weird World of LSD '67

Carol Lindsay
She Gods of Shark Reef '56

Helen Lindsay
Secrets '82

Margaret Lindsay
Baby Face '33
British Intelligence '40

Cass Timberlane '47
Cavalcade '33
Club Havana '46
Dangerous '35
Devil Dogs of the Air '35
"G" Men '35
Jezebel '38
Lady Killer '33
Please Don't Eat the Daisies '60
The Spoilers '42

Robert Lindsay
Bert Rigby, You're a Fool '89
Strike It Rich '90

Vera Lindsay
Spellbound '41

Stuart Lindsell
Man of Evil '48
Profile '54

George Lindsey
Robin Hood '73

Lance Lindsey
Quiet Fire '91

Clarke Lindsley
The Immortalizer '89

Gunnel Lindstrom
The Silence '63

Helga Line
Horror Rises from the Tomb '72
The Mummy's Revenge '73
Nightmare Castle '65
Pulsebeat '85
The Saga of the Draculas '72
When the Screaming Stops '73

Wci Ping Line
Marvelous Stunts of Kung Fu '83

Richard Lineback
Beyond the Next Mountain '87

Jeannie Linero
Flush '81

Chen Pei Ling
The Furious Avenger '76
Golden Sun '80s

Chia Ling
Against the Drunken Cat Paws '75
Eighteen Jade Arhats '84
The Great Hunter '75
Kung Fu Shadow '85
Ninja Swords of Death '90
Ten Brothers of Shao-lin '80s

Chio Chi Ling
Duel of the Seven Tigers '80

Chu Hai Ling
Taoism Drunkard

Fan Ling
The Furious Avenger '76

Shangkuan Ling-Feng
Fight for Survival '77
Green Dragon Inn '82
Kung Fu Commandos '80
Shaolin Traitor '82

Wendy Lingham
Alien Women '69
Demonstrator '71

Paul Linke
Motel Hell '80
Time Flies When You're Alive '89

Richard Linklater
Slacker '91

Art Linkletter
Champagne for Caesar '50
People Are Funny '46

Mark Linn-Baker
Bare Essentials '91
Ghostwriter '84
Me and Him '89
My Favorite Year '82
Noises Off '92

Rex Linn
Cliffhanger '93

Velta Linne
Rasputin '85

Joanne Linville
Scorpio '73
Secrets '77

Larry Linville
Blue Movies '88
Body Waves '91
Earth Girls are Easy '89
Night Partners '83
Rock 'n' Roll High School Forever '91
School Spirit '85
The Stepmother '71

Lio
Window Shopping '86

Leon M. Lion
Amazing Adventure '37
Number Seventeen '32

Alberto Lionello
Till Marriage Do Us Part '74

Therese Liotard
Oloud Waltzing '87
My Father's Glory '91
My Mother's Castle '91
One Sings, the Other Doesn't '77

Lou Liotta
Severance '88

Ray Liotta
Article 99 '92
Dominick & Eugene '88
Field of Dreams '89
Goodfellas '90
The Lonely Lady '83
Something Wild '86
Unlawful Entry '92
Women & Men: Stories of Seduction, Part 2 '91

Victor Lipari
Futz '69

Kent Lipham
Bikini Summer '91

Eugene Lipinski
Going Home '86
Moonlighting '82
Perfectly Normal '91
Riders of the Storm '88

Michael Lipkin
But Where Is Daniel Wax? '74

Maureen Lipman
Educating Rita '83
A Little Princess '87

Moshe Lipman
The Dybbuk '37

Enrique Liporace
La Casa del Amor '87

Jonathon Lippe
Blood Voyage '77
Green Eyes '76

Renee Lippin
Radio Days '87

Dennis Lipscomb
Eyes of Fire '84
Guilty of Innocence '87
Retribution '88
Sister, Sister '87
Slow Burn '86
Union City '81

Jack Lipson
Cannon Ball/Eyes Have It '15
Flash Gordon: Rocketship '36

Albert Lipton
Mirele Efros '38

Celia Lipton
Calling Paul Temple '48

Gene Lipton
The Brig '64

Lynn Lipton
Max '79

Peggy Lipton
Fatal Charm '92
Kinjite: Forbidden Subjects '89
Mosby's Marauders '66
Purple People Eater '88
Twin Peaks '90
Twin Peaks: Fire Walk with Me '92

Robert Lipton
A Woman, Her Men and Her Futon '92

Natalia Lisenko
Early Russian Cinema, Vol. 10: The End of an Era '17

Joe Lisi
Traces of Red '92

Virna Lisi
Assault on a Queen '66
Bluebeard '72
Casanova '70 '65
The Christmas Tree '69
Christopher Columbus '85
How to Murder Your Wife '64
I Love N.Y. '87
La Cicada '83
Miss Right '81
Night Flight from Moscow '73
The Statue '71
When Wolves Cry '69

Ivan Liska
The Lady of the Camellias '87

Lucille Lisle
Midnight at the Wax Museum '36

Leon Lissek
Adventures of Eliza Fraser '76
Blockhouse '73
Bloodmoon '90

Lissette
El Derecho de Comer '87

Eve Lister
Demon Barber of Fleet Street '36

Moira Lister
The Limping Man '53
Trouble in Store '53
Uneasy Terms '48

Tiny Lister
9 1/2 Ninjas '90
No Holds Barred '89
Posse '93
Prison '88

Giorgio Listuzzi
The Roof '56

John Litel
Boss of Big Town '43
Cass Timberlane '47
The Fighting 69th '40
The Fuller Brush Girl '50
Montana Belle '52
Nancy Drew, Reporter '39
Northwest Trail '46
Outpost in Morocco '49
Pitfall '48
San Antonio '45

Gene Lithgow
Christmas in Connecticut '92

John Lithgow
The Adventures of Buckaroo Banzai Across the Eighth Dimension '84
All That Jazz '79
At Play in the Fields of the Lord '91
Baby Girl Scott '87
The Big Fix '78
Blow Out '81
Cliffhanger '93
The Day After '83
Distant Thunder '88
Footloose '84
The Glitter Dome '84
Goldilocks & the Three Bears '83
Harry and the Hendersons '87
I'm Dancing as Fast as I Can '82
Ivory Hunters '90
The Manhattan Project '86
Memphis Belle '90
Mesmerized '84
Mom, the Wolfman and Me '80
Obsession '76
Oldest Living Graduate '82
Out Cold '89
Raising Cain '92
Rich Kids '79
Ricochet '91
Santa Claus: The Movie '85
Terms of Endearment '83
Traveling Man '89
Twilight Zone: The Movie '83
2010: The Year We Make Contact '84
The World According to Garp '82

Richard Litt
Landlord Blues '87

Ann Little
The Roaring Road '19

Cleavon Little
Blazing Saddles '74
Cotton Comes to Harlem '70
Don't Look Back: The Story of Leroy "Satchel" Paige '81
Double Exposure '82
E. Nick: A Legend in His Own Mind '84
Fletch Lives '89
FM '78
The Gig '85
Greased Lightning '77
High Risk '76
Homecoming: A Christmas Story '71
Jimmy the Kid '82
Murder by Numbers '89
Once Bitten '85
Once Upon a Brothers Grimm '77
The Salamander '82
Scavenger Hunt '79
Separate But Equal '91

The Sky is Gray '80
Surf 2 '84
Toy Soldiers '84
Vanishing Point '71

Sacheen Little Feather
Johnny Firecloud '75
Shoot the Sun Down '81

Mark Little
The Wacky World of Wills & Burke '85
Waterfront '83

Michelle Little
Appointment with Fear '85
Blood Clan '91
Bluffing It '87
My Demon Lover '87
Radioactive Dreams '86

Rich Little
Christmas Raccoons '84
Dirty Tricks '81
Happy Hour '87

Little Richard
Down and Out in Beverly Hills '86
Last Action Hero '93
Pee-Wee's Playhouse Christmas Special '88
Purple People Eater '88
Scenes from the Class Struggle in Beverly Hills '89

Eddie Little Sky
Journey Through Rosebud '72
Savage Run '70

Lucien Littlefield
Bulldog Drummond's Revenge '37
Charley's Aunt '25
The Gladiator '38
Hillbilly Blitzkrieg '42
Hollywood Stadium Mystery '38
Let's Sing Again '36
The Sheik '21
Strangors of the Evening '32
Susanna Pass '49
Tom Sawyer '30
Tumbleweeds '25
Wide Open Faces '38
Zorro's Black Whip '44

Gary Littlejohn
Angels Hard as They Come '71
Bury Me an Angel '71

Mario Litto
The Avenger '60

Carolyn Liu
Do or Die '91

Harrison Liu
Black Robe '91

Jimmy Liu
Dragon's Claw '80s

John Liu
Avenging Ninja '80s
Instant Kung-Fu Man '84
Kung Fu Commandos '80
Ninja in the Claws of the C.I.A. '83
Shaolin Ex-Monk '82
Snuff-Bottle Connection '82

Terry Liu
Infra-Man '76

Boris Livanov
Ten Days That Shook the World '27

Ricky Long
Ghostriders '87

Shelley Long
Caveman '81
The Cracker Factory '79
Don't Tell Her It's Me '90
Frozen Assets '92
Hello Again '87
Irreconcilable Differences '84
Losin' It '82
The Money Pit '86
Night Shift '82
Outrageous Fortune '87
A Small Circle of Friends '80
Troop Beverly Hills '89

Tarng Long
Challenge of the Dragon '82

Walter Long
Blood and Sand '22
Flaming Lead '39
The Little American '17
Little Church Around the Corner '23
Man's Country '38
Moran of the Lady Letty '22
Sea Devils '31
The Sheik '21
Silver Stallion '41
Six Shootin' Sheriff '38
Soul-Fire '25
Yankee Clipper '27

John Longden
Alias John Preston '56
Juno and the Paycock '30
Quatermass 2 '57
Tower of Terror '42

Robert Longden
Danger UXB '81

Terence Longden
Murder on the Campus '52

John Longdon
Blackmail '29

Claudine Longet
The Party '68

Stephen Longhurst
Invitation to Hell '84

Sue Longhurst
Keep It Up, Jack! '75
A Man with a Maid '73
Victorian Fantasies '86

Victoria Longley
Celia: Child Of Terror '89

Alix Longman
The Getting of Wisdom '77

Tony Longo
Bloodhounds of Broadway '89
Prehysteria '93
Remote '93
Suburban Commando '91
Worth Winning '89

Emily Longstreth
American Drive-In '88
The Big Picture '89
Private Resort '84
Rising Son '90
Wired to Kill '86

Tadeusz Loniski
Colonel Wolodyjowski '69

Ray Lonnen
Belfast Assassin '84
Guardian of the Abyss '82

Michael Lonsdale
The Bride Wore Black '68
Enigma '82
Erendira '83
The Holcroft Covenant '85

Is Paris Burning? '68
Les Assassins de L'Ordre '71
Moonraker '79
Murmur of the Heart '71
The Name of the Rose '86
Souvenir '88

Richard Loo
Across the Pacific '42
Back to Bataan '45
Betrayal from the East '44
China Sky '44
The Clay Pigeon '49
First Yank into Tokyo '45
Love is a Many-Splendored Thing '55
The Man with the Golden Gun '74
Mr. Wong in Chinatown '39
The Purple Heart '44
The Steel Helmet '51

Anne Looby
Strangers '90

Michael Lookinland
A Very Brady Christmas '88

Christopher Loomis
The Nesting '80

Deborah Loomis
Hercules in New York '70

Nancy Loomis
Halloween '78

Rod Loomis
Jack's Back '87

Larry Loonin
The Man Who Envied Women '85

Friedl Loor
The Eternal Waltz '59

Silvia Lopel
Hercules Unchained '59

Tanya Lopert
Navajo Joe '67
Tales of Ordinary Madness '83

Angelo Lopez
Street Hitz '92

Estrellita Lopez
Only Once in a Lifetime '83

Ivonne Lopez
Letters from the Park '88

Kamala Lopez
Born in East L.A. '87
Crazy from the Heart '91
Dollman '91
Exiled in America '90

Margo Lopez
El Libro de Piedra '68
Nazarin '58

Perry Lopez
Chinatown '74
McLintock! '63
Taras Bulba '62

Priscilla Lopez
Jesse '88

Sal Lopez
American Me '92
The Fire Next Time '93

Trini Lopez
Antonio '73
The Dirty Dozen '67
The Poppy is also a Flower '66

Laura Lopinski
Dorm That Dripped Blood '82

Gail Lorber
Hot Times '74

Isabel Lorca
Lightning: The White Stallion '86
She's Having a Baby '88

Barbara Lord
The Bloody Brood '59

David Paul Lord
Ninja Vengeance '93

Gayle Lord
Colt Comrades '43

Jack Lord
The Court Martial of Billy Mitchell '55
Dr. No '62
The Doomsday Flight '66
God's Little Acre '58
Man of the West '58

Justine Lord
He Kills Night After Night After Night '70
Skeezer '82

Marjorie Lord
Boy, Did I Get a Wrong Number! '66
Johnny Come Lately '43
Sherlock Holmes in Washington '43

Pauline Lord
Mrs. Wiggs of the Cabbage Patch '34

Phillips Lord
Way Back Home '32

Tamblyn Lord
Vicious '88

Athena Lorde
Dr. Death, Seeker of Souls '73

Traci Lords
Cry-Baby '90
Fast Food '89
Intent to Kill '92
Laser Moon '92
Not of This Earth '88
Raw Nerve '91
Shock 'Em Dead '90
A Time to Die '91

Tony Lorea
The Deadly and the Beautiful '73
Smokey & the Hotwire Gang '79

Mary Lou Loredan
Cheerleaders' Beach Party '77

Donna Loren
Pajama Party '64

Sophia Loren
Angela '77
Arabesque '66
Bellissimo: Images of the Italian Cinema '87
Black Orchid '59
Blood Feud '79
Boccaccio '70 '62
Brass Target '78
Breath of Scandal '60
The Cassandra Crossing '76
Courage '86
Desire Under the Elms '58
El Cid '61
The Fall of the Roman Empire '64
Firepower '79
Get Rita
The Gold of Naples '54

Heller in Pink Tights '60
Houseboat '58
It Started in Naples '60
The Key '58
Lady of the Evening '79
Legend of the Lost '57
Man of La Mancha '72
Marriage Italian Style '64
Operation Crossbow '65
The Pride and the Passion '57
Quo Vadis '51
Running Away '89
Sophia Loren: Her Own Story '80
A Special Day '77
Two Nights with Cleopatra '54
Two Women '61
Yesterday, Today and Tomorrow '64

Tray Loren
The American Angels: Baptism of Blood '89
Gator Bait 2: Cajun Justice '88
Rocktober Blood '85

Jerry Lorenz
The Texas Chainsaw Massacre '74

Livio Lorenzon
Gladiators 7 '62
The Invincible Gladiator '63
Pirates of the Coast '61

Susanne Loret
Atom Age Vampire '61

Virginia Loridans
Video Murders '87

Evan Lorie
Ring of Fire 2: Blood and Steel '92

Lisa Lorient
Pretty Smart '87

Gloria Loring
Convicted: A Mother's Story '87

Lisa Loring
Blood Frenzy '87

Lynn Loring
Journey to the Far Side of the Sun '69
Kansas City Massacre '75

Michael Loring
Postal Inspector '36

Teala Loring
Delinquent Daughters '44
Hard-Boiled Mahoney '47

James Lorinz
Frankenhooker '90
Punch the Clock '90

Diana Loris
Superargo '67

Jon Lormer
Beyond the Next Mountain '87

Marion Lorne
The Graduate '67

George Loros
Apology '86
Shakedown '88

Carrie Lorraine
Dolls '87

Peter Lorre
All Through the Night '42
Around the World in 80 Days '56
Arsenic and Old Lace '44

Background to Danger '43
The Beast with Five Fingers '46
Beat the Devil '53
Casablanca '42
The Chase '46
The Comedy of Terrors '64
Crime and Punishment '35
Daffy Duck & Company '50
Five Weeks in a Balloon '62
F.P. 1 Doesn't Answer '33
Hell Ship Mutiny '57
The Lost One '51
M '31
Mad Love '35
The Maltese Falcon '41
The Man Who Knew Too Much '34
Meet Me in Las Vegas '56
Mr. Moto's Last Warning '39
Mr. Moto's Last Warning/ Meeting at Midnight '44
Muscle Beach Party '64
My Favorite Brunette '47
Passage to Marseilles '44
The Patsy '64
Postmark for Danger/ Quicksand '56
Promise to Murder '56
Quicksand '50
The Raven '63
The Sad Sack '57
The Secret Agent '36
Silk Stockings '57
Strange Cargo '40
Stranger on the Third Floor '40
Tales of Terror '62
20,000 Leagues Under the Sea '54
Voyage to the Bottom of the Sea '61
You'll Find Out '40

Peter Lorre, Jr.
Frasier the Sensuous Lion '73

Joan Lorring
The Corn is Green '45
Good Sam '48

Diana Lorys
Fangs of the Living Dead '68
House of Psychotic Women '73
Lightning Bolt '67

Tilly Losch
The Garden of Allah '36

Marcello Loti
Pool Hustlers '83

Dennis Lotis
Horror Hotel '60

Ney Lotorraco
The Fable of the Beautiful Pigeon Fancier '88

Robert Lott
Chain Gang Women '72

Eb Lottimer
Beyond the Call of Duty '92
The Finest Hour '91
Futurekick '91
Lords of the Deep '89
Quake '92
Quicker Than the Eye '88
Streets '90
Stripped to Kill II: Live Girls '89

Alexander Lou
Mafia vs. Ninja '84
Ninja Condors '87
Ninja in the U.S.A. '88
Ninja the Battalion '90
Ninja vs. the Shaolin '84
Super Dragons/Mafia vs. Ninja

Galaxina '80
Graveyard Shift '90
Killjoy '81
The Monster Squad '87
Trancers 3: Deth Lives '92

Ian MacInnes
Half Moon Street '86

Polly MacIntyre
Jet Benny Show '86

Betty Mack
Fighting Texans '33
Outlaw Rule '36
Toll of the Desert '35

Charles Mack
Dream Street '21

Helen Mack
Fargo Express '32
Fit for a King '37
Melody Cruise '32
Milky Way '36
The Return of Peter Grimm '35
Son of Kong '33
The Wrong Road '37

Kerry Mack
Fair Game '85
Fantasy Man '84
Savage Attraction '83

Marion Mack
The General '27

Michael Mack
Star Quest '89

Wayne Mack
Crypt of Dark Secrets '76
Mardi Gras Massacre '78
Storyville '74

Dorothy Mackaill
Bulldog Drummond at Bay '37
Kept Husbands '31
Ranson's Folly '26
Shore Leave '25

Barry Mackay
Evergreen '34
Gangway '37
The Private Secretary '35
Sailing Along '38

Fulton Mackay
Defense of the Realm '85
Local Hero '83
Nothing But the Night '72
Porridge '91
A Sense of Freedom '78

John MacKay
Alligator Eyes '90
Fat Guy Goes Nutzoid '86
The Rejuvenator '88

John Alexander MacKay
Simple Men '92

Bronwyn MacKay-Payne
Dawn! '83

Helen MacKellar
Bad Boy '39
Delinquent Parents '38

Kenneth MacKenna
Sin Takes a Holiday '30

Ella MacKenzie
Cord & Dischords/Naughty Nurse '28

Evan Mackenzie
Ghoulies 3: Ghoulies Go to College '91

Giselle MacKenzie
Music Shoppe '82
One Minute Before Death '88
The Oval Portrait '88

Jan MacKenzie
The American Angels: Baptism of Blood '89
Gator Bait 2: Cajun Justice '88

Patch MacKenzie
Black Eliminator '70s
Defense Play '88
Goodbye, Norma Jean '75
Graduation Day '81
Isle of Secret Passion '85

Philip Charles MacKenzie
Blind Justice '86

Scott MacKenzsie
Hootch Country Boys '75

Vivian Mackerell
Madhouse Mansion '74

Paul Mackey
People Who Own the Dark '75

Mary Mackie
Alternative '76

Steven Mackintosh
London Kills Me '91

Albert Macklin
Date with an Angel '87

Jim Mackrell
Just Between Friends '86

Janet MacLachlan
Big Mo '73
Darker than Amber '70
Louis Armstrong: Chicago Style '75
Murphy's Law '86
Roll of Thunder, Hear My Cry '78
She's in the Army Now '81
Sounder '72

Kyle MacLachlan
Blue Velvet '86
Don't Tell Her It's Me '90
The Doors '91
Dune '84
The Hidden '87
Rich in Love '93
Twin Peaks '90
Twin Peaks: Fire Walk with Me '92
Where the Day Takes You '92

Shirley MacLaine
All in a Night's Work '61
The Apartment '60
Around the World in 80 Days '56
Artists and Models '55
Ask Any Girl '59
Being There '79
The Bliss of Mrs. Blossom '68
Can-Can '60
Cannonball Run II '84
Career '59
A Change of Seasons '80
The Children's Hour '61
Desperate Characters '71
Gambit '66
Golden Age of Hollywood '77
Hot Spell '58
Irma La Douce '63
Loving Couples '80
Madame Sousatzka '88
The Matchmaker '58
My Geisha '62
Out on a Limb '87

The Possession of Joel Delaney '72
Postcards from the Edge '90
Some Came Running '58
Steel Magnolias '89
Sweet Charity '69
Terms of Endearment '83
That's Dancing! '85
The Trouble with Harry '55
The Turning Point '77
Two for the Seesaw '62
Two Mules for Sister Sara '70
Used People '92
Waiting for the Light '90
Woman Times Seven '67

Barton MacLane
All Through the Night '42
Arizona Bushwackers '67
Big Street '42
Black Fury '35
Bombardier '43
Buckskin '68
Bugles in the Afternoon '52
Bullets or Ballots '38
The Case of the Lucky Legs '35
Ceiling Zero '35
Cry of the Werewolf '44
Drums in the Deep South '51
"G" Men '35
The Geisha Boy '58
The Half-Breed '51
Kansas Pacific '53
Let's Dance '50
The Maltese Falcon '41
Man of the Forest '33
Marine Raiders '43
Melody Ranch '40
Mutiny in the Big House '39
Nabonga '44
Naked in the Sun '57
The Prince and the Pauper '37
Prison Break '38
Silver River '48
Song of Texas '43
The Spanish Main '45
Three Violent People '57
To the Last Man '33
Treasure of Fear '45
Treasure of the Sierra Madre '48
The Underdog '43
Unknown Island '48
Western Union '41
You Only Live Once '37

Fawna MacLaren
Dragonfight '92

Mary MacLaren
A Lawman is Born '37
The New Frontier '35

Ian MacLean
The Arsenal Stadium Mystery '39

Elizabeth MacLellan
Puppet Master 2 '91

Gavin MacLeod
The Love Boat '70s
The Party '68
The Sand Pebbles '66
Scruples '80

Michael MacLiammoir
Othello '52
What's the Matter with Helen? '71

Ellie MacLure
Air Hawk '84
Alvin Purple '73
Heat of the Flame '82

Aline MacMahon
Ah, Wilderness! '35
Back Door to Heaven '39
Dragon Seed '44
The Flame & the Arrow '50
Gold Diggers of 1933 '33
Heroes for Sale '33
I Could Go on Singing '63
I Live My Life '35
Man from Laramie '55
The Search '48

Kenneth MacMillan
Bloodbrothers '78
Eyewitness '81
Three Fugitives '89

Fred MacMurray
Above Suspicion '43
The Absent-Minded Professor '61
Alice Adams '35
The Apartment '60
At Gunpoint '55
Beyond the Bermuda Triangle '75
Bon Voyage! '62
Borderline '50
The Caine Mutiny '54
Charley and the Angel '73
Dive Bomber '41
Double Indemnity '44
Egg and I '47
Follow Me, Boys! '66
The Happiest Millionaire '67
Kisses for My President '64
The Miracle of the Bells '48
My Love For Yours '39
Never a Dull Moment '50
The Shaggy Dog '59
Son of Flubber '63
The Swarm '78
Swing High, Swing Low '37

Pattie MacNamara
Irish Cinderella '22

Alan MacNaughton
The Dark Angel '91

Robert MacNaughton
E.T.: The Extra-Terrestrial '82
I Am the Cheese '83

Patrick Macnee
Battlestar Galactica '78
The Blood Suckers '71
The Bloodsuckers '70
Chill Factor '90
A Christmas Carol '51
Cult People '89
Dead of Night '77
Down Under '86
The Elusive Pimpernel '50
The Howling '81
King Solomon's Treasure '76
Les Girls '57
Lobster Man from Mars '89
Masque of the Red Death '89
Rehearsal for Murder '82
Return of the Man from U.N.C.L.E. '83
Sea Wolves '81
Shadey '87
Sherlock Holmes and the Incident at Victoria Falls '91
Sorry, Wrong Number '89
Spaceship '81
Sweet 16 '81
This is Spinal Tap '84
Transformations '88
A View to a Kill '85
Waxwork '88
Young Doctors in Love '82

Rita MacNeil
Candy Mountain '87

Peter MacNicol
American Blue Note '89
The Boy Who Left Home to Find Out About the Shivers '81
Dragonslayer '81
Ghostbusters 2 '89
Hard Promises '92
Heat '87
Housesitter '92
Sophie's Choice '82

Joseph Macolo
Shaft's Big Score '72

Joe MacPherson
The Bay Boy '85

Albert MacQuarrie
When the Clouds Roll By '19

George MacQuarrie
The Love Flower '20

King MacQueen
Linchamiento '68

Gordon MacRae
By the Light of the Silvery Moon '53
Carousel '56
Danger in the Skies '79
Oklahoma! '55
On Moonlight Bay '51
The Pilot '82
Tea for Two '50
The West Point Story '50

Heather MacRae
Bang the Drum Slowly '73
The Connection '73
Secrets of Three Hungry Wives '78

Meredith MacRae
Husbands, Wives, Money, and Murder '86
Sketches of a Stranger '78
Vultures '84

Michael MacRae
Dear Detective '78
Great Ride '78
Greedy Terror '78
Isle of Secret Passion '85
Madhouse '87

George Macready
Black Arrow '48
Coroner Creek '48
Detective Story '51
The Doolins of Oklahoma '49
Down to Earth '47
Gilda '46
Great Race '65
The Green Glove '52
The Human Duplicators '64
I Beheld His Glory '53
Julius Caesar '53
Knock on Any Door '49
The Nevadan '50
Paths of Glory '57
The Return of Count Yorga '71
The Seventh Cross '44
The Stranger Wore a Gun '53
Taras Bulba '62
Tora! Tora! Tora! '70
Two Weeks in Another Town '62
Vera Cruz '53

Michael Macready
Count Yorga, Vampire '70

Patrick MacVey
Top of the Heap '72

Bill Macy
Bad Medicine '85
Casey at the Bat '85

Margit Makay
Cat's Play '74

Miriam Makeba
Sarafina! '92

Chris Makepeace
Aloha Summer '88
Captive Hearts '87
Last Chase '81
Mazes and Monsters '82
My Bodyguard '80
The Mysterious Stranger '82
Rona Jaffe's Mazes &
    Monsters '82
Savage Hunger '84
The Terry Fox Story '83
Undergrads '85
Vamp '86

Swapan Makerji
The World of Apu '59

**Avtandil
Makharadze**
Repentance '87

Wendy Makkena
Sister Act '92

Mako
Armed Response '86
The Big Brawl '80
Conan the Barbarian '82
Conan the Destroyer '84
An Eye for an Eye '81
Fatal Mission '89
The Island at the Top of the
    World '74
The Killer Elite '75
Kung Fu: The Movie '86
My Samurai '92
The Nightingale '83
Pacific Heights '90
The P.O.W. Escape '86
Rising Sun '93
The Sand Pebbles '66
Sidekicks '93
The Streets of San Francisco
    '72
Taking Care of Business '90
Tucker: The Man and His
    Dream '88
Under the Rainbow '81
An Unremarkable Life '89
The Wash '88

Dragan Maksimovic
Meetings with Remarkable
    Men '79

Thony Maky
Tomb of Torture '65

Mala
Hawk of the Wilderness '38
Robinson Crusoe of Mystery
    Island '36
The Tuttles of Tahiti '42

Ray Mala
Robinson Crusoe of Clipper
    Island '36

Patrick Malahide
Comfort and Joy '84
A Month in the Country '87

**Zygmunt
Malandowicz**
Knife in the Water '62

**Christophe
MaLavoy**
Madame Bovary '91
Peril '85

Henrik Malberg
Ordet '55

Paolo Malco
The House by the Cemetery
    '83

**Christopher
Malcolm**
The Great Riviera Bank
    Robbery '79

Karl Malden
The Adventures of Bullwhip
    Griffin '66
All Fall Down '62
Baby Doll '56
Beyond the Poseidon
    Adventure '79
Billy Galvin '86
Birdman of Alcatraz '62
Blue '68
The Cat o' Nine Tails '71
Cheyenne Autumn '64
The Cincinnati Kid '65
Diplomatic Courier '52
Fatal Vision '84
Fear Strikes Out '57
The Great Impostor '61
Gunfighter '50
Gypsy '62
The Halls of Montezuma '50
The Hanging Tree '59
Hotel '67
How the West was Won '63
I Confess '53
Kiss of Death '47
Meteor '79
Miracle on Ice '81
Murderers' Row '66
Nevada Smith '66
Nuts '87
On the Waterfront '54
One-Eyed Jacks '61
Patton '70
Pollyanna '60
Ricco '74
Ruby Gentry '52
Skag '79
The Sting 2 '83
A Streetcar Named Desire '51
The Streets of San Francisco
    '72
They Knew What They
    Wanted '40
13 Rue Madeleine '46
Urge to Kill '84
Wild Rovers '71

Richard Maldone
Faith '90

Telo Malese
The Silent One '86

Arthur Malet
Beastmaster 2: Through the
    Portal of Time '91
Hook '91

Laurent Malet
Blood Relatives '78
Invitation au Voyage '83
Jacko & Lise '82
Querelle '83
Sword of Gideon '86

Pierre Malet
Basileus Quartet '82

Marina Malfatti
The Night Evelyn Came Out of
    the Grave '71

Art Malik
City of Joy '92
Harem '86
The Jewel in the Crown '84
Year of the Comet '92

Tirlok Malik
Lonely in America '90

Judith Malina
The Addams Family '91
Emergency '68
Enemies, a Love Story '89
Signals Through the Flames
    '83

Luba Malina
Mexican Hayride '48

Ross Malinger
Sleepless In Seattle '93

Sam Malkin
Caribe '87

John Malkovich
Alive '93
American Dream '81
Dangerous Liaisons '88
Death of a Salesman '86
Eleni '85
Empire of the Sun '87
The Glass Menagerie '87
In the Line of Fire '93
Jennifer 8 '92
The Killing Fields '84
Making Mr. Right '86
Miles from Home '88
The Object of Beauty '91
Of Mice and Men '92
Places in the Heart '84
Queens Logic '91
Rocket to the Moon '86
Shadows and Fog '92
The Sheltering Sky '90
True West '86

Korey Mall
Mirror Images '91

George Mallaby
Endplay '75

Aubrey Mallalieu
The Courageous Mr. Penn '41

Emby Mallay
The Touch of Satan '70

Jade Malle
Man on Fire '87

Miles Malleson
Brothers in Law '57
Captain's Paradise '53
A Christmas Carol '51
The Golden Salamander '51
The King's Rhapsody '55
Nine Days a Queen '34
Train of Events '49

Tania Mallet
Goldfinger '64

Perry Mallette
Going Back '83

**Patricia "Boots"
Mallory**
Carnival Lady '33
Powdersmoke Range '35
Sing Sing Nights '35
Wolf Dog '33

Matt Malloy
Surviving Desire '91

Birger Malmsten
Night Is My Future '47
The Silence '63
Summer Interlude '50
Three Strange Loves '49

Gina Malo
Lily of Killarney '34

Clancy Malone
Jail Bait '54

Dorothy Malone
Abduction '75
Artists and Models '55

At Gunpoint '55
Basic Instinct '92
Battle Cry '55
Beach Party '63
The Big Sleep '46
The Bushwackers '52
Day Time Ended '80
The Fast and the Furious '54
The Last Voyage '60
Man of a Thousand Faces '57
The Man Who Would Not Die
    '75
The Nevadan '50
Night and Day '46
Off Your Rocker '80
Rest In Pieces '87
Scared Stiff '53
Sincerely Yours '56
South of St. Louis '48
Tension at Table Rock '56
Torpedo Alley '53
Warlock '59
Winter Kills '79
Written on the Wind '56
Young at Heart '54

Mark Malone, Jr.
Straight Out of Brooklyn '91

Mollie Malone
Battling Bunyon '24
Straight Shootin' '17

Nancy Malone
Fright '56

Patrick Malone
Grand Canyon '91
Rock 'n' Roll High School
    Forever '91

Today Malone
Revolution '69

Michael Maloney
Henry V '89
Sharma & Beyond '84
Truly, Madly, Deeply '91

Rey Malonzo
P.O.W. Deathcamp '89

Leonard Maltin
Bugs & Daffy: The Wartime
    Cartoons '45
The Lost Stooges '33

Leslie Malton
The Unapproachable '82

Valerie Mamches
Children Shouldn't Play with
    Dead Things '72

Robert Mammone
The Crossing '92

Piotr Mamonov
Taxi Blues '90

Mang Yuen Man
Hell's Wind Staff '82

Yuan Man-tzu
Infra-Man '76

Biff Manard
Trancers 2: The Return of
    Jack Deth '91
Zone Troopers '85

Michael Manches
Witchery '88

Melissa Manchester
For the Boys '91
The Great Mouse Detective
    '86

**Ray "Boom Boom"
Mancini**
Backstreet Dreams '90
Oceans of Fire '86

Wishful Thinking '92

Ric Mancini
Penitentiary 3 '87

Nick Mancuso
Blame It on the Night '84
Death of an Angel '86
Death Ship '80
Double Identity '89
Embassy '85
Fatal Exposure '91
Half a Lifetime '86
Heartbreakers '84
The House on Garibaldi Street
    '79
Legend of Walks Far Woman
    '82
Lena's Holiday '91
Lies Before Kisses '92
Maria Chapdelaine '84
Mother Lode '82
Nightwing '79
Rapid Fire '92
Tell Me That You Love Me '84
Ticket to Heaven '81
Wild Palms '93

Robert Mandan
In Love with an Older Woman
    '82
Perry Mason: The Case of the
    Lost Love '87
Return of the Rebels '81
Zapped! '82

Howie Mandel
Best of Comic Relief '86
A Fine Mess '86
Gas '81
Little Monsters '89
The Princess Who Never
    Laughed '84
Walk Like a Man '87

Suzy Mandel
Mistress of the Apes '79

Johnny Mandell
Body Parts '90

Peter Mandell
Xtro '83

Miles Mander
Brighton Strangler '45
The Brighton Strangler/Before
    Dawn '45
Don Quixote '35
Guadalcanal Diary '43
The Little Princess '39
Mad Miss Manton '38
Murder '30
Murder, My Sweet '44
The Pearl of Death '44
Primrose Path '40
Return of the Vampire '43
Scarlet Claw '44
Shadows on the Stairs '41
Stanley and Livingstone '39
Three Musketeers '35
The Tower of London '39
Wuthering Heights '39

Barbara Mandrell
Burning Rage '84
The Concrete Cowboys '79
Ramblin' Man '79

Costas Mandylor
Mobsters '91
Soapdish '91

Doura Mane
L'Etat Sauvage '78

Gianni Manera
Fear in the City '81

Gina Manes
Napoleon '27

Gaspard Manesse
Au Revoir Les Enfants '87

Larry Manetti
The Take '90

John Manfredi
Thou Shalt Not Kill...Except '87

Nino Manfredi
Alberto Express '92
Cafe Express '83
Down & Dirty '76
Head of the Family '71
In the Name of the Pope-King '85
Nudo di Donna '83
Spaghetti House '82
We All Loved Each Other So Much '77

William Mang
The Final Executioner '83

Xiem Mang
The Lover '92

Silvana Mangano
Barabbas '62
Bitter Rice '49
Conversation Piece '75
Dark Eyes '87
Death in Venice '71
The Decameron '70
Dune '84
The Gold of Naples '54
The Great War '59
Lure of the Sila '49
Mambo '55
Oedipus Rex '67
Teorema '68
Ulysses '55

Lata Mangeskar
Mere Jeevan Saathi '65

Alec Mango
The Cosmic Monsters '58

Kate Manheim
Strong Medicine '84

Karin Mani
Alley Cat '84
Avenging Angel '85

Cindy Manion
Preppies '82

Beatrice Manley
Night Terror '76

Dudley Manlove
The Creation of the Humanoids '62

Cecile Mann
Ghostwriter '84

Edward Mann
Jungle Master '56

George Mann
Neptune's Daughter '49

Hank Mann
City Lights '31
Spite Marriage '29

Leonard Mann
Corrupt '84
Night School '81

Lisa Mann
Lilies of the Field '63

Marika Mann
Escort Girls '74

Robert Mann
Assault of the Party Nerds '89

Sam Mann
Hard Rock Zombies '85

Shari Mann
Mausoleum '83
Starlet '87

Terrence Mann
A Chorus Line '85
Critters 2: The Main Course '88
Critters 4 '91
The Ten Million Dollar Getaway '91

Tracey Mann
Fast Talking '86
Hard Knocks '80

Wesley Mann
My Stepmother Is an Alien '88

Yanka Mann
Flesh Feast '69

Guido Mannari
Cop in Blue Jeans '78

Jay Mannering
Waterfront '83

David Manners
A Bill of Divorcement '32
The Black Cat '34
The Death Kiss '33
Dracula '31
The Mummy '32
Three Broadway Girls '32

Sheila Manners
Lawless Range '35
Westward Ho '35

Renate Mannhardt
The Lost One '51

Lucie Mannheim
High Command '37
Hotel Reserve '44
The 39 Steps '35

Ettore Manni
Angel in a Taxi '59
The Battle of Austerlitz '60
The Battle of El Alamein '68
City of Women '81
Giants of Rome '63
Hercules and the Captive Women '63
Heroes in Hell '67
Street People '76
Two Nights with Cleopatra '54

Barbara Manning
See How She Runs '78

Irene Manning
Yankee Doodle Dandy '42

Katya Manning
The Quest '86

Marilyn Manning
Eegah! '62
The Sadist '63
What's Up Front '63

Ned Manning
Dead End Drive-In '86

Patricia Manning
Hideous Sun Demon '59

Roger Manning
The Day It Came to Earth '77

Anthony Mannino
Starhops '78

Elizabeth Mannino
Dead Mate '88

Joe Manno
Night Screams '87

Dinah Manoff
Backfire '88
Bloodhounds of Broadway '89

Child's Play '88
For Ladies Only '81
I Ought to Be in Pictures '82
Ordinary People '80
The Possessed '77
Table Settings '84
Welcome Home, Roxy Carmichael '90

Miki Manojlovic
When Father was Away on Business '85

Manolete
Torero '56

Andreas Manolikakis
Ice House '89

Gloria Manon
The Woman Inside '83

Peter Manoogian
Dungeonmaster '85

Don Manor
Crime Zone '88

Silvia Manriquez
Conexion Mexico '87
Emilio Varela vs. Camelia La Texana '87

Marie Mansert
Two English Girls '72

Jayne Mansfield
Dog Eat Dog '64
The Female Jungle '56
The Girl Can't Help It '56
A Guide for the Married Man '67
Hell on Frisco Bay '55
Illegal '55
It Takes a Thief '59
Las Vegas Hillbillys '66
The Loves of Hercules '60
Panic Button '62
Pete Kelly's Blues '55
Promises! Promises! '63
Single Room Furnished '68
Underwater '55
Wild, Wild World of Jayne Mansfield '68

Martha Mansfield
Dr. Jekyll and Mr. Hyde '20

Leonor Manso
Far Away and Long Ago '74
House of Shadows '83
Made in Argentina '86

Alan Manson
Let's Scare Jessica to Death '71
Whiffs '75

Jean Manson
The Young Nurses '73

Laura Manszky
Sweet Lies '88

Joe Mantegna
Alice '90
Body of Evidence '92
Bugsy '91
Compromising Positions '85
The Comrades of Summer '92
Critical Condition '86
Elvis: The Movie '79
Family Prayers '91
The Godfather, Part 3 '90
Homicide '91
House of Games '87
The Money Pit '86
Off Beat '86
Queens Logic '91
Second Thoughts '83
Suspect '87

Things Change '88
Three Amigos '86
Wait Until Spring, Bandini '90
Weeds '87

Michael Mantell
The Night We Never Met '93

Fernando Soto Mantequilla
Guitarras Lloren Guitarras '47

Hector Manthanda
Warriors from Hell '90

Clive Mantle
Robin Hood...The Legend: Robin Hood and the Sorcerer '83

Randolph Mantooth
The Seekers '79
Terror at London Bridge '85

Paul Mantu
Wolf Lake '79

Mike Manty
Blood Debts '83

Robert Manuel
Rififi '54

Chantal Manz
The 13th Mission '91

Linda Manz
Days of Heaven '78
Orphan Train '79
Out of the Blue '82
The Snow Queen '83
Wanderers '79

Armando Manzanero
Somos Novios '68

Eduardo Manzano
El Aviso Inoportuno '87
Hijazo de Mi Vidaza '70s

Miguel Manzano
The Illusion Travels by Streetcar '53

David Manzy
The Baby '72

Angela Mao
The Association '80s
The Fate of Lee Khan '73
Return of the Tiger '78
Sting of the Dragon Masters '74
When Taekwondo Strikes '83

Adele Mara
Bells of Rosarita '45
The Inner Circle '46
Night Time in Nevada '48
Robin Hood of Texas '47
Twilight on the Rio Grande '41

Mary Mara
Love Potion #9 '92
Mr. Saturday Night '92

Steve Marachuk
Hot Target '85
Piranha 2: The Spawning '82
The Spawning '82
Waikiki '80

Jean Marais
The Battle of Austerlitz '60
Beauty and the Beast '46
Donkey Skin '70
Dos Cruces en Danger Pass '71
Elena and Her Men '56
Eternal Return '43
Girl in His Pocket '62
Orpheus '49

The Rape of the Sabines '61
The Testament of Orpheus '59
White Nights '57

Maria Marais
The Power of One '92

Sam Marais
Playing with Fire '70s

Andree Maranda
Toxic Avenger '86

Evi Marandi
Planet of the Vampires '65

Janna Marangosoff
Men... '85

Cindy Maranne
Provoked '89
Slashdance '89

Richard Marant
On the Third Day '83

Mario Maranzana
Day of the Cobra '84

Pete Maravich
Scoring '80

Peter Marc
Dangerous Love '87

Joss Marcano
Delivery Boys '84

Marcel Marceau
Barbarella '68
Silent Movie '76

Sophie Marceau
La Boum '81
Police '85

Su Carnal Marcelo
Hay Muertos Que No Hacen Ruido '47

Barbara March
The Deserters '80s

Fredric March
Alexander the Great '55
Anna Karenina '35
Anthony Adverse '36
The Barretts of Wimpole Street '34
The Best Years of Our Lives '46
The Bridges at Toko-Ri '55
A Christmas Carol '54
Christopher Columbus '49
Desperate Hours '55
Dr. Jekyll and Mr. Hyde '31
Executive Suite '54
Hombre '67
I Married a Witch '42
Inherit the Wind '60
Les Miserables '35
The Man in the Gray Flannel Suit '56
Mary of Scotland '36
Nothing Sacred '37
Seven Days in May '64
So Ends Our Night '41
A Star is Born '37
Susan and God '40
Till the Clouds Roll By/A Star Is Born '46

Jane March
The Lover '92

Tony March
Shallow Grave '87

Georges Marchal
The French Way '40

Colette Marchand
Moulin Rouge '52

Corinne Marchand
Borsalino '70
Cleo from 5 to 7 '61

Guy Marchand
Coup de Torchon '81
Cousin, Cousine '76
Entre-Nous '83
Heat of Desire '84
Loulou '80
May Wine '90
Petit Con '84

Henri Marchand
A Nous la Liberte '31

Mitchell Marchand
Fathers and Sons '92

Nancy Marchand
The Bostonians '84
Brain Donors '92
The Hospital '71
Killjoy '81
Marty '53
The Naked Gun: From the
    Files of Police Squad '88

Ron Marchini
Death Machines '76
Forgotten Warrior '86
Ninja Warriors '85
Omega Cop '90
Return Fire '91
Wolf '86

David Marciano
Hellbent '90
Kiss Shot '89

Joseph Marco
Gladiators 7 '62

Paul Marco
Night of the Ghouls '59

Silvia Marco
The Man Who Wagged His
    Tail '57

Saverio Marconi
Padre Padrone '77

Andrea Marcovicci
The Concorde: Airport '79 '79
The Devil's Web '74
The Front '76
The Hand '81
Jack the Bear '93
Kings and Desperate Men '83
Packin' It In '83
Someone to Love '87
Spacehunter: Adventures in
    the Forbidden Zone '83
Spraggue '84
The Stuff '85

Deborah Marcus
Cycle Vixens '79

James Marcus
The Broken Mask '28
The Eagle '25
The Lone Avenger '33
Sadie Thompson '28

Richard Marcus
Cannibal Campout '88
Deadly Friend '86
Enemy Mine '85

Theo Marcuse
Harum Scarum '65

Elio Marcuzzo
Ossessione '42

Jordan Marder
Walking on Air '87

Tom Mardirosian
The Dark Half '91

Heinz Marecek
Tea For Three '84

Lynn Maree
Deadly Passion '85

Vera Maretskaya
No Greater Love '43

Simone Marevil
Un Chien Andalou '28

Janie Mareze
La Chienne '31

Arthur Margetson
Juggernaut '37
The Phantom Ship '37
Sherlock Holmes Faces Death
    '43

Lukacs Margit
Oh, Bloody Life! '88

Agi Margittay
Nice Neighbor '79

Margo
Behind the Rising Sun '43
I'll Cry Tomorrow '55
The Leopard Man '43
Lost Horizon '37
Viva Zapata! '52
Who's Got the Action? '63
Winterset '36

Janet Margolin
Annie Hall '77
Buona Sera, Mrs. Campbell
    '68
David and Lisa '62
Distant Thunder '88
Enter Laughing '67
The Game of Love '90
The Last Embrace '79
Morituri '65
Planet Earth '74
Plutonium Incident '82
Pray for the Wildcats '74
Take the Money and Run '69
The Triangle Factory Fire
    Scandal '79

Stuart Margolin
Big Bus '76
Bye Bye Blues '89
Class '83
Days of Heaven '78
Death Wish '74
A Fine Mess '86
Futureworld '76
The Glitter Dome '84
Guilty by Suspicion '91
Iron Eagle 2 '88
Kelly's Heroes '70
Running Hot '83
S.O.B. '81
Women of the Prehistoric
    Planet '66

Mark Margolis
Descending Angel '90

Miriam Margolyes
The Butcher's Wife '91
Little Dorrit, Film 1: Nobody's
    Fault '88
Little Dorrit, Film 2: Little
    Dorrit's Story '88
Orpheus Descending '91
Pacific Heights '90
Stalin '92

Michael Margotta
The Blue Knight '75
Can She Bake a Cherry Pie?
    '83

David Margulies
Dressed to Kill '80
Family Prayers '91

Funny About Love '90
Ghostbusters 2 '89
9 1/2 Weeks '86
Out on a Limb '92
Running on Empty '88

Fiorella Mari
The Day the Sky Exploded '57

Gina Mari
The Slumber Party Massacre
    '82

Angelica Maria
Somos Novios '68
To Kill a Stranger '70s

Ferdinand Marian
Jud Suess '40

Mark Marian
Tomb of Torture '65

Ann Marie
Beneath the Valley of the
    Ultra-Vixens '79

Jeanne Marie
If Looks Could Kill '86
Young Nurses in Love '89

Nadia Marie
Quiet Fire '91

**Jean-Pierre
Marielle**
Coup de Torchon '81
One Wild Moment '78
Uranus '91

Marietto
Angel in a Taxi '59
It Started in Naples '60

Roy Marika
Where the Green Ants Dream
    '84

Wandjuk Marika
Where the Green Ants Dream
    '84

Cheech Marin
After Hours '85
Born in East L.A. '87
Cheech and Chong: Still
    Smokin' '83
Cheech and Chong: Things
    Are Tough All Over '82
Cheech and Chong's Next
    Movie '80
Cheech and Chong's Nice
    Dreams '81
Cheech and Chong's, The
    Corsican Brothers '84
Cheech and Chong's Up in
    Smoke '79
Echo Park '86
Far Out Man '89
Fatal Beauty '87
Ferngully: The Last Rain
    Forest '92
It Came from Hollywood '82
La Pastorela '92
Rude Awakening '89
The Shrimp on the Barbie '90
Yellowbeard '83

Gloria Marin
Bromas S.A. '87
El Gendarme Desconocido '41
Historia de un Gran Amor '57

Jacques Marin
The Island at the Top of the
    World '74

Jason Marin
The Little Mermaid '89

Luis Marin
Great Treasure Hunt '70s

Rikki Marin
Cheech and Chong: Things
    Are Tough All Over '82
Cheech and Chong's, The
    Corsican Brothers '84

Ed Marinaro
Born Beautiful '82
Dead Aim '87
The Diamond Trap '91
The Game of Love '90
Lethal Lolita—Amy Fisher: My
    Story '92
Policewoman Centerfold '83
Queens Logic '91

Barbara Marineau
When Nature Calls '85

Alex Marino
Sex with a Smile '76

Kenny Marino
Alphabet City '84
Prince of the City '81

Beth Marion
Between Men '35
Rip Roarin' Buckaroo '36

George F. Marion
Anna Christie '30
Death from a Distance '36
Hook, Line and Sinker '30

Salverio Marioni
Padre Padrone '77

Mona Maris
The Falcon in Mexico '44
Heartbeat '46
I Married an Angel '42
Love on the Run '36

Richard Maris
Thrilled to Death '88

Silvia Mariscal
La Fuerza Inutil '87

Marisol
Blood Wedding '81

Kensaku Marita
Renegade Ninja '83
War in Space '77

Sari Maritza
Crimson Romance '34
Greek Street '30
International House '33

Robert Marius
The 13th Mission '91
Triple Impact '92

Mary Mark
Voyage to the Planet of
    Prehistoric Women '68

Robert Mark
Superbug Super Agent '76

Jane Marken
Crazy for Love '52
A Day in the Country '46
Dedee d'Anvers '49

Tony Markes
In the Aftermath '87

Enid Markey
Civilization '16
The Fugitive: Taking of Luke
    McVane '15
Tarzan of the Apes '17

Barbara Markham
House of Whipcord '75

Kika Markham
Deep Cover '88
Miss A & Miss M '86
Two English Girls '72

Monte Markham
Counter Measures '80s
Defense Play '88
Ginger in the Morning '73
Guns of the Magnificent
    Seven '69
Hotline '82
Hustling '75
Judgment Day '88
Off the Wall '82
Shame, Shame on the Bixby
    Boys '82

Ted Markland
Angels from Hell '68
Wanda Nevada '79

Stephen Markle
984: Prisoner of the Future
    '84
Perfect Timing '84

Monica Marko
Possession: Until Death Do
    You Part '90

Margaret Markov
Hot Box '72
Naked Warriors '73
Run, Angel, Run! '69

Olivera Markovic
Fury is a Woman '61

Alfred Marks
Antonia and Jane '91
Mission: Monte Carlo '75
Scream and Scream Again '70

Barbara Marks
Teenage Devil Dolls '53

Harrison Marks
Nine Ages of Nakedness '69

Joe E. Marks
Li'l Abner '59

Logena Marks
Secrets in the Dark '83

Michael Marks
The Wasp Woman '49

Sherry Marks
Satan's Cheerleaders '77

Slash Marks
Night of the Cobra Woman '72

Willis Marks
The Jack Knife Man '20

Zoli Marks
No One Cries Forever '85

Winnie Markus
The Devil in Silk '56
The Mozart Story '48

Arnold Marle
Men of Two Worlds '46
The Snake Woman '61

John Marley
Deathdream '72
Framed '75
The Glitter Dome '84
The Godfather '72
The Godfather 1902-1959:
    The Complete Epic '81
The Greatest '77
Hooper '78
It's Alive 2: It Lives Again '78
Jory '72
Kid Vengeance '75
Love Story '70
A Man Called Sledge '71
On the Edge '86
Robbers of the Sacred
    Mountain '83
Threshold '83
Utilities '83

Anne Marlie
Swinging Sorority Girls '70s

Carla Marlier
The Avenger '62
The Big Grab '63
Spirits of the Dead '68
Zazie dans le Metro '61

Lynn Marlin
Perfume '91

Lucy Marlow
My Sister Eileen '55

Alan Marlowe
Deadly Vengeance '81

Hugh Marlowe
All About Eve '50
Birdman of Alcatraz '62
Bugles in the Afternoon '52
Casanova's Big Night '54
Castle of Evil '66
The Day the Earth Stood Still '51
Earth vs. the Flying Saucers '56
Elmer Gantry '60
Illegal '55
Monkey Business '52
Night and the City '50
Rawhide '50
Twelve O'Clock High '49

June Marlowe
Don Juan '26
The Lone Defender '32
The Night Cry '26
Pardon Us '31

Linda Marlowe
Big Zapper '73
The Green Man '91
He Kills Night After Night After Night '70
Night After Night After Night '70
Night Slasher '84

Florence Marly
Dr. Death, Seeker of Souls '73
Planet of Blood '66
Tokyo Joe '49

Percy Marmont
Four Sided Triangle '53
Lady of the Lake '28
Lisbon '56
Mantrap '26
Rich and Strange '32
Young and Innocent '37

Elizabeth Marner-Brooks
I Drink Your Blood '71

Kelli Maroney
Fast Times at Ridgemont High '82
Night of the Comet '84
Servants of Twilight '91
Slayground '84
Zero Boys '86

Carl Marotte
Breaking All the Rules '85
Hang Tough '89
Pick-Up Summer '79
Workin' for Peanuts '85

Christian Marquand
And God Created Woman '57
The Corrupt Ones '67
End of Desire '62

Peter Marquardt
El Mariachi '93

Maria Elena Marques
Across the Wide Missouri '51
Ambush at Tomahawk Gap '53
The Pearl '48

Esteban Marquez
Mexican Bus Ride '51

Evarist Marquez
Burn! '70

Andre Marquis
Paco '75

Margaret Marquis
Brand of the Outlaws '36

Eddie Marr
Hollywood Canteen '44
I Was a Teenage Werewolf '57

Pons Marr
The American Scream '80s

Fred Marratto
The Narcotics Story '58

Moore Marriot
The Flying Scotsman '29
Oh, Mr. Porter '37

David Marriott
Monster High '89

John Marriott
Black Like Me '64

Sylvia Marriott
Crimes at the Dark House '39
Two English Girls '72

Dina Marrone
Quest for the Mighty Sword '90

Eugenia Marruzzo
Alberto Express '92

Kenneth Mars
The Apple Dumpling Gang Rides Again '79
Beer '85
Butch Cassidy and the Sundance Kid '69
Desperate Characters '71
Fletch '85
For Keeps '88
Get Smart: The Movie '89
Goin' Coconuts '78
Illegally Yours '87
The Little Mermaid '89
Misfits of Science '85
Night Moves '75
Parallax View '74
The Producers '68
Protocol '84
Radio Days '87
Rented Lips '88
Shadows and Fog '92
What's Up, Doc? '72
Young Frankenstein '74

Maurice Marsac
Clarence, the Cross-eyed Lion '65
Tarzan and the Trappers '58
Werewolf in a Girl's Dormitory '61

Branford Marsalis
School Daze '88

Marita Marschall
Deadline '87

Beatrice Marsden
The Ghost of Rashmon Hall '47

Carol Marsh
Alice in Wonderland '50
Brighton Rock '47
A Christmas Carol '51
The Horror of Dracula '58

Garry Marsh
A Girl in a Million '46
Just William's Luck '47
Pink Strings and Sealing Wax '45
Someone at the Door '50

Jean Marsh
The Changeling '80
Frenzy '72
Goliath Awaits '81
Horsemasters '61
Return to Oz '85
The Unearthly Stranger '64
Willow '88

Joan Marsh
Champagne for Breakfast '79
Follow the Leader '44
High Gear '33
Manhunt in the African Jungle '54

Linda Marsh
Homebodies '74

Mae Marsh
The Birth of a Nation '15
D.W. Griffith Triple Feature '13
The Fighting Sullivans '42
From the Terrace '60
Gunfighter '50
Home Sweet Home '14
Hoodoo Ann '16
Intolerance '16
Judith of Bethulia '14
Sergeant Rutledge '60
Short Films of D.W. Griffith, Vol. 2 '09
Story of the Silent Serials Girls in Danger
The Tall Men '55
Three Godfathers '48
While the City Sleeps '56
The White Rose '23

Marian Marsh
The Black Room '35
Crime and Punishment '35
House of Errors '42
Svengali '31
When's Your Birthday? '37
Youth on Parole '37

Matthew Marsh
An Affair in Mind '89
In the Secret State

Michele Marsh
Deadly Alliance '78
Evil Town '87

Yvonne Marsh
Little Ballerina '47

Alan Marshal
After the Thin Man '36
Conquest '32
House on Haunted Hill '58
The Howards of Virginia '40
Lydia '41
Tom, Dick, and Harry '41
The White Cliffs of Dover '44

Brenda Marshall
Background to Danger '43
Captains of the Clouds '42
The Sea Hawk '40

Bryan Marshall
Because of the Cats '74
The Long Good Friday '79
Return to Snowy River '88

Darrah Marshall
Teenage Caveman '58

David Anthony Marshall
Another 48 Hrs. '90

Dodie Marshall
Easy Come, Easy Go '67
Spinout '66

Don Marshall
Terminal Island '73

E.G. Marshall
Abduction of St. Anne '75
The Bridge at Remagen '69
Broken Lance '54
The Buccaneer '58
The Caine Mutiny '54
The Chase '66
Consenting Adults '92
Creepshow '82
Eleanor: First Lady of the World '82
Independence '76
Interiors '78
Ironclads '90
Is Paris Burning? '68
Kennedy '83
The Lazarus Syndrome '79
The Left Hand of God '55
The Littlest Angel '69
The Mountain '56
My Chauffeur '86
National Lampoon's Christmas Vacation '89
The Poppy is also a Flower '66
Power '86
Pursuit '72
The Pursuit of Happiness '70
Saigon: Year of the Cat '87
The Silver Chalice '54
Superman 2 '80
13 Rue Madeleine '46
Tora! Tora! Tora! '70
Twelve Angry Men '57

Garry Marshall
Hocus Pocus '93
Jumpin' Jack Flash '86
A League of Their Own '92
Lost in America '85
Soapdish '91
Soapdish '91

Herbert Marshall
Blonde Venus '32
Captain Blackjack '51
Crack-Up '46
Duel in the Sun '46
The Enchanted Cottage '45
The Fly '58
Foreign Correspondent '40
Forever and a Day '43
The Letter '40
The Little Foxes '41
The Moon and Sixpence '43
Murder '30
The Painted Veil '34
The Razor's Edge '46
The Secret Garden '49
Stage Struck '57
The Underworld Story '50
The Virgin Queen '55
When Ladies Meet '41
A Woman Rebels '36

James Marshall
A Few Good Men '92
Gladiator '92
Twin Peaks: Fire Walk with Me '92

Joshua Marshall
Flirting '89

Ken Marshall
Double Exposure: The Story of Margaret Bourke-White '89
Feds '88
Krull '83
Tilt '78

Lee Marshall
The American Angels: Baptism of Blood '89

Meri D. Marshall
Valet Girls '86

Nancy Marshall
Frankenstein Meets the Space Monster '65

Paul Marshall
Ninja Operation: Licensed to Terminate '87

Paula Marshall
Hellraiser 3: Hell on Earth '92

Penny Marshall
Challenge of a Lifetime '85
The Hard Way '91
Hocus Pocus '93
How Come Nobody's On Our Side? '73
Movers and Shakers '85

Peter Marshall
Americathon '79
A Guide for the Married Woman '78
Return of Jesse James '50

Sarah Marshall
The People vs. Jean Harris '81

Sean Marshall
Pete's Dragon '77

Steve Marshall
Night of the Creeps '86

Tony Marshall
I Was a Teenage Werewolf '57

Trudy Marshall
The Fighting Sullivans '42
Joe's Bed-Stuy Barbershop: We Cut Heads '83
Married Too Young '62

Tully Marshall
Behind Prison Walls '43
Big Trail '30
The Cabin in the Cotton '32
The Cat and the Canary '27
Fighting Caravans '31
Hawthorne of the USA '19
Let's Go! '23
Mr. Boggs Steps Out '38
Queen Kelly '29
Smouldering Fires '25
Strangers of the Evening '32
Tom Sawyer '30
Two-Fisted Law '32

William Marshall
Blacula '72
The Boston Strangler '68
Demetrius and the Gladiators '54
The Great Skycopter Rescue '82
Scream Blacula Scream '73
State Fair '45
That Brennan Girl '46
Vasectomy: A Delicate Matter '86

Zena Marshall
Dr. No '62
Terronauts '67
The Terrornauts '67

Walter Mason
Black Like Me '64

John Massari
The Wizard of Speed and Time '88

Lea Massari
Allonsanfan '73
Christ Stopped at Eboli '79
L'Avventura '60
Les Rendez-vous D'Anna '78
Murmur of the Heart '71
The Story of a Love Story '73
The Things of Life '70
Vengeance '86

Michael Massee
My Father is Coming '91

Osa Massen
Background to Danger '43
Cry of the Werewolf '44
Master Race '44
Outcasts of the City '58
Rocketship X-M '50
A Woman's Face '41

Richard Massery
Killzone '85

Anna Massey
Another Country '84
A Doll's House '89
Foreign Body '86
Frenzy '72
Hotel du Lac '86
The Little Drummer Girl '84
Mansfield Park '85
The McGuffin '85
Mountains of the Moon '90
Peeping Tom '63
Sweet William '79
Vault of Horror '73

Daniel Massey
The Cat and the Canary '79
The Entertainer '60
The Incredible Sarah '76
Intimate Contact '87
Love with a Perfect Stranger '86
Stalin '92
Vault of Horror '73
Victory '81

Dick Massey
The Commitments '91

Edith Massey
Desperate Living '77
Female Trouble '75
Multiple Maniacs '70
Mutants In Paradise '88
Pink Flamingos '73
Polyester '81

Gina Massey
Thrillkill '84

Ilona Massey
Holiday in Mexico '46
Love Happy '50
Melody Master '41
Northwest Outpost '47
Rosalie '38

Raymond Massey
Abe Lincoln in Illinois '40
Action in the North Atlantic '43
Arsenic and Old Lace '44
Battle Cry '55
Chain Lightning '50
David and Bathsheba '51
Desperate Journey '42
Dreaming Lips '37
Drums '38
East of Eden '54
Fire Over England '37
The Forty-Ninth Parallel '41

The Fountainhead '49
The Great Impostor '61
How the West was Won '63
Hurricane '37
MacKenna's Gold '69
The Naked and the Dead '58
The Old Dark House '32
Omar Khayyam '57
The Possessed '47
The President's Plane is Missing '71
Prisoner of Zenda '37
Reap the Wild Wind '42
Santa Fe Trail '40
The Scarlet Pimpernel '34
The Speckled Band '31
Things to Come '36
Under the Red Robe '36

Paul Massie
Sapphire '59

Leonide Massine
The Red Shoes '48

Ben Masters
All That Jazz '79
Celebrity '85
The Deliberate Stranger '86
Dream Lover '85
Key Exchange '85
Making Mr. Right '86
Mandingo '75
Running Mates '92
The Shadow Box '80

James Masters
Rip-Off '77

Marie Masters
Scream for Help '86

Sharon Masters
Deadline '82

Fay Masterson
The Man Without a Face '93
The Power of One '92

Mary Stuart Masterson
Amazing Stories, Book 2 '86
At Close Range '86
Benny & Joon '93
Chances Are '89
Fried Green Tomatoes '91
Funny About Love '90
Gardens of Stone '87
Heaven Help Us '85
Immediate Family '89
Mad at the Moon '92
Married to It '93
Mr. North '88
My Little Girl '87
Some Kind of Wonderful '87

Peter Masterson
A Question of Guilt '78

Rod Masterson
Delta Heat '92

Sean Masterson
Fatal Games '84

Mary Elizabeth Mastrantonio
The Abyss '89
Class Action '91
The Color of Money '86
Consenting Adults '92
Fools of Fortune '90
The January Man '89
Robin Hood: Prince of Thieves '91
Scarface '83
Slamdance '87
White Sands '92

Gina Mastrogiacomo
Alien Space Avenger '91

Marcello Mastroianni
Allonsanfan '73
Bellissimo: Images of the Italian Cinema '87
Beyond Obsession '82
Beyond Obsession '89
Big Deal on Madonna Street '58
Blood Feud '79
Casanova '70 '65
City of Women '81
Dark Eyes '87
Diary of Forbidden Dreams '73
Divine Nymph '71
Divorce—Italian Style '62
8 1/2 '63
Everybody's Fine '90
A Fine Romance '92
Gabriela '84
Get Rita
Ginger & Fred '86
Henry IV '85
Intervista '87
La Dolce Vita '60
La Nuit de Varennes '82
Lady of the Evening '79
Lunatics & Lovers '76
Macaroni '85
Marriage Italian Style '64
Massacre in Rome '73
The Poppy is also a Flower '66
Salut l'Artiste '74
Shoot Loud, Louder, I Don't Understand! '66
A Slightly Pregnant Man '79
A Special Day '77
Stay As You Are '78
10th Victim '65
Used People '92
A Very Private Affair '62
We All Loved Each Other So Much '77
Where the Hot Wind Blows '59
White Nights '57
Wifemistress '79
Yesterday, Today and Tomorrow '64

Toru Masuoka
A Taxing Woman Returns '88

Richard Masur
Adam '83
Amazing Stories, Book 3 '86
The Believers '87
Betrayal '78
Burning Bed '85
Cast the First Stone '89
East of Eden '80
Embassy '85
Encino Man '92
Fallen Angel '81
Far from Home '89
The George McKenna Story '86
Heartburn '86
Heaven's Gate '81
Hiroshima Maiden '88
License to Drive '88
The Man Without a Face '93
Mean Season '85
My Science Project '85
Nightmares '83
Rent-A-Cop '88
Risky Business '83
Semi-Tough '77
Shoot to Kill '88
Stephen King's It '90

The Thing '82
Third Degree Burn '89
Timerider '83
Under Fire '83
Walker '87
Walking Through the Fire '80
When the Bough Breaks '86
Who'll Stop the Rain? '78
Wild Horses '84

Gabor Mate
My Twentieth Century '90

Steve Mateo
Vice Academy 3 '91

Julian Mateos
Four Rode Out '69
Hellbenders '67
Kashmiri Run '69

Mahdu Mathen
Children of the Damned '63

Aubrey Mather
Adventures of Don Juan '49
House of Fear '45
Jane Eyre '44
The Lodger '44
Mrs. Miniver '42
The Silent Passenger '35
That Forsyte Woman '50
The Undying Monster '42

George Mather
Ring of Terror '62

James Mathers
Dr. Jekyll's Dungeon of Death '82

Jerry Mathers
Back to the Beach '87
Down the Drain '89
Men of the Fighting Lady '54
The Trouble with Harry '55

Marissa Mathes
Track of the Vampire '66

Judy Matheson
The House that Vanished '73
Scream and Die '74
Twins of Evil '71

Michelle Matheson
Howling 6: The Freaks '90

Tim Matheson
The Apple Dumpling Gang Rides Again '79
Best Legs in the 8th Grade '84
Blind Justice '86
Buried Alive '90
The Captive: The Longest Drive 2 '76
Dreamer '79
Drop Dead Fred '91
Eye of the Demon '87
Fletch '85
How to Commit Marriage '69
Impulse '84
Listen to Your Heart '83
A Little Sex '82
Little White Lies '89
The Longest Drive '76
Magnum Force '73
Mary White '77
National Lampoon's Animal House '78
1941 '79
Quicksand: No Escape '91
The Runaway Barge '75
Solar Crisis '92
Sometimes They Come Back '91
Speed Zone '88
To Be or Not to Be '83
Up the Creek '84
Yours, Mine & Ours '68

Carmin Mathews
Sounder '72

Carole Mathews
Strange Awakening '58

Christopher Mathews
The Seducer '82

George Mathews
Last of the Comanches '52
The Man with the Golden Arm '55

Kerwin Mathews
Battle Beneath the Earth '68
The Devil at 4 O'Clock '61
Jack the Giant Killer '62
Killer Likes Candy '78
Maniac '63
Nightmare in Blood '75
Octaman '71
The Seventh Voyage of Sinbad '58
The Three Worlds of Gulliver '59
Waltz King '63

Oliver Mathews
Devil Kiss '77

Thom Mathews
Alien from L.A. '87
Bloodmatch '91
Down Twisted '89
Friday the 13th, Part 6: Jason Lives '86
Return of the Living Dead Part 2 '88

Darien Mathias
Blue Movies '88

Samantha Mathis
Ferngully: The Last Rain Forest '92
Pump Up the Volume '90
Super Mario Bros. '93
The Thing Called Love '93
This is My Life '92

Jacques Mathou
The Hairdresser's Husband '92
Year of the Comet '92

Steve Matilla
Last Night at the Alamo '83

Doug Matley
Sledgehammer '83

Marlee Matlin
Bridge to Silence '89
Children of a Lesser God '86
Hear No Evil '93
The Linguini Incident '92
The Player '92
Walker '87

Scotty Matraw
Snow White and the Seven Dwarfs '37

John Matshikiza
Dust '85
Mandela '87

Eiko Matsuda
In the Realm of the Senses '76

Yusaku Matsuda
The Family Game '83
Murder in the Doll House '79

Yoko Matsuyama
Watch Out, Crimson Bat! '69

Sharon Matt
Sweet Trash '89

Dietrich Mattausch
The Wannsee Conference '84

Eva Mattes
The Bitter Tears of Petra von Kant '72
Celeste '81
David '79
A Man Like Eva '83
Stroszek '77
Woyzeck '78

Pam Matteson
Punchline '88

Walter Matthau
Atomic Attack '50
The Bad News Bears '76
Buddy Buddy '81
Cactus Flower '69
California Suite '78
Casey's Shadow '78
Charade '63
Charley Varrick '73
The Couch Trip '87
Dennis the Menace '93
Earthquake '74
Ensign Pulver '64
A Face in the Crowd '57
Fail-Safe '64
First Monday in October '81
The Fortune Cookie '66
The Front Page '74
A Guide for the Married Man '67
Hello, Dolly! '69
Hopscotch '80
House Calls '78
I Ought to Be in Pictures '82
The Incident '89
The Indian Fighter '55
JFK '91
Kentuckian '55
King Creole '58
Kotch '71
Laughing Policeman '74
Little Miss Marker '80
Lonely are the Brave '62
Mirage '66
Movers and Shakers '85
A New Leaf '71
The Odd Couple '68
Pete 'n' Tillie '72
Pirates '86
Plaza Suite '71
Secret Life of an American Wife '68
Strangers When We Meet '60
The Sunshine Boys '75
Survivors '83
The Taking of Pelham One Two Three '74
Who's Got the Action? '63

A.E. Matthews
Carry On Admiral '57
The Iron Duke '34
Made in Heaven '52

Al Matthews
American Roulette '88

Brian Matthews
The Burning '82
Red Nights '87

Carole Matthews
Shark River '53
Swamp Women '55

Dakin Matthews
Child's Play 3 '91
In a Stranger's Hand '92
Naked Lie '89
Revolver '92
The Temp '93

Francis Matthews
Bhowani Junction '56

Corridors of Blood '58
The Hellfire Club '61
The McGuffin '85
Murder Ahoy '64
Small Hotel '57

Fritz Matthews
Born Killer '89
Deadly Prey '87
Hell on the Battleground '88

Jessie Matthews
Candles at Nine '44
Evergreen '34
Forever and a Day '43
Gangway '37
The Hound of the Baskervilles '77
It's Love Again '36
Sailing Along '38

John Matthews
A Secret Space '88

Junius Matthews
The Sword in the Stone '63

Lee Matthews
Fu Manchu '56

Lester Matthews
The Raven '35
Werewolf of London '35

Peter Matthey
New York Nights '84

Darlene Mattingly
Women Unchained '70s

Luisa Mattioli
La Bella Lola '87

Robin Mattson
Bonnie's Kids '73
Candy Stripe Nurses '74
Captain America '79
Hot Rod '79
In Between '92
Namu, the Killer Whale '66
Return to Macon County '75
Take Two '88
Wolf Lake '79

Veronika Mattson
Pay Off '89

Victor Mature
After the Fox '66
Androcles and the Lion '52
Betrayed '54
Captain Caution '40
Dangerous Mission '54
Demetrius and the Gladiators '54
Easy Living '49
The Egyptian '54
Footlight Serenade '42
I Wake Up Screaming '41
Kiss of Death '47
The Las Vegas Story '52
The Long Haul '57
Million Dollar Mermaid '52
My Darling Clementine '46
No, No Nanette '40
One Million B.C. '40
The Robe '53
Samson and Delilah '50
Samson and Delilah '84
Seven Days' Leave '42
The Shanghai Gesture '42
Song of the Islands '42

John Matuszak
Caveman '81
Down the Drain '89
Ghost Writer '89
The Goonies '85
Ice Pirates '84
My Darlin' Clementine '86
North Dallas Forty '79

One Man Force '89
Semi-Tough '77

Johanna Matz
The Life and Loves of Mozart '59
Party Girls for Sale '54
They Were So Young '55

Billy Mauch
The Prince and the Pauper '37

Jack Mauck
Greenstone '85

Arthur Maude
The Man from Beyond '22

Joan Maude
Power '34
The Temptress '49

Mary Maude
Crucible of Terror '72

Howard Mauer
Ilsa, the Tigress of Siberia '79

Monica Maughan
Cactus '86
Prisoner Cell Block H '80
A Woman's Tale '92

Bill Mauldin
The Red Badge of Courage '51

Wayne Maunder
Crazy Horse and Custer: "The Untold Story" '90

Sarah Maur-Thorp
Edge of Sanity '89
River of Death '89
Ten Little Indians '89

Carmen Maura
Ay, Carmela! '90
Dark Habits '84
Law of Desire '86
Matador '86
Pepi, Luci, Bom and Other Girls on the Heap '80
What Have I Done to Deserve This? '85
Women on the Verge of a Nervous Breakdown '88

Joshua Maurer
Tour of Duty '87

Peggy Maurer
I Bury the Living '58

Nicole Maurey
Day of the Triffids '63
The Jayhawkers '59
Rogue's Yarn '56

Paco Mauri
Ruby Cairo '92

Jon Maurice
Primal Scream '87

Giovanni Mauriello
Another Time, Another Place '83

Claire Maurier
Back to the Wall '56
The 400 Blows '59
La Cage aux Folles '78
Sweet Ecstasy '62

Toralv Maurstad
Song of Norway '70

Gerda Maurus
Spies '28
Woman in the Moon '29

Derrel Maury
Massacre at Central High '76

Jean Max
J'Accuse '37

Ron Max
Forced Entry '75

Edwin Maxwell
Behind Prison Walls '43
Mystery Liner '34
Swamp Fire '46
The Taming of the Shrew '29
Waterfront '44
Way Down South '39
Woman in Brown '48

Frank Maxwell
The Haunted Palace '63
Lonelyhearts '58
Shame '61

James Maxwell
One Day in the Life of Ivan Denisovich '71

Jane Maxwell
The Black Devils of Kali '55

John Maxwell
Boss of Big Town '43
Honky Tonk '41
The Payoff '43
Prowler '51

Larry Maxwell
Poison '91

Lois Maxwell
Diamonds are Forever '71
Dr. No '62
Eternal Evil '87
For Your Eyes Only '81
From Russia with Love '63
Goldfinger '64
Live and Let Die '73
The Man with the Golden Gun '74
Moonraker '79
On Her Majesty's Secret Service '69
The Spy Who Loved Me '77
Thunderball '65
The Unstoppable Man '59
A View to a Kill '85
You Only Live Twice '67

Marilyn Maxwell
Arizona Bushwackers '67
Champion '49
The Lemon Drop Kid '51
Lost in a Harem '44
Off Limits '53
Summer Holiday '48
Wild Women '70

Paul Maxwell
Cloud Waltzing '87
Going Home '86

Roberta Maxwell
Lois Gibbs and the Love Canal '82
Psycho 3 '86

Angela May
Blackjack '78

April May
Hollywood High, Part 2 '81

Deborah May
Caged Fear '92
Johnny Be Good '88
Rage of Angels '83

Donald May
Bogie '86
Kisses for My President '64

Elaine May
California Suite '78
Enter Laughing '67
In the Spirit '90

Luv '67
A New Leaf '71

Jack May
He Kills Night After Night After Night '70
Night After Night After Night '70
Night Slasher '84

Jodhi May
Eminent Domain '91
The Last of the Mohicans '92
Max and Helen '90
A World Apart '88

Lola May
Civilization '16

Mathilda May
Becoming Colette '92
Letters to an Unknown Lover '84
Lifeforce '85

Rita May
Threads '85

Herschel Mayall
Kismet '20

John Mayall
Sunset Strip '85

Rik Mayall
Drop Dead Fred '91
Little Noises '91
Whoops Apocalypse '83
The Young Ones '88

Anthony Mayans
Heat of the Flame '82
Zombie Lake '84

Gale Mayberrie
Swinging Wives '79

Eddie Mayehoff
Artists and Models '55
How to Murder Your Wife '64

Chip Mayer
Our Family Business '81
Survivor '87

Frederic Mayer
Field of Honor '87

Ray Mayer
Swing It, Sailor! '37

Val Mayerick
The Demon Lover '77

Curtis Mayfield
Short Eyes '79

Peter Mayhew
The Empire Strikes Back '80
Return of the Jedi '83

Ken Maynard
Arizona Terror '31
Arizona Whirlwind '44
Between Fighting Men '32
Branded Men '31
Come On Tarzan '32
Death Rides the Range '40
Death Valley Rangers '44
Desert Guns/Six-Shootin' Sheriff '36
Drum Taps '33
Dynamite Ranch '32
False Faces '32
Fargo Express '32
$50,000 Reward '25
Fightin' Ranch '30
The Fighting Legion '30
Fighting Thru '30
Flaming Lead '39
Flamingo Lead '39
Harmony Trail '44
Hell Fire Austin '32

Kris McKeon
Lovey: A Circle of Children 2
'82

Nancy McKeon
High School USA '84
The Lightning Incident '91
Poison Ivy '85
Scruffy '80

Philip McKeon
Amazing Stories, Book 3 '86
Red Surf '90
Return to Horror High '87

Charles McKeown
The Adventures of Baron
Munchausen '89

Leo McKern
The Adventures of Sherlock
Holmes' Smarter Brother
'78
The Amorous Adventures of
Moll Flanders '65
The Blue Lagoon '80
Candleshoe '77
The Day the Earth Caught Fire
'62
Doctor in Distress '63
The French Lieutenant's
Woman '81
Help! '65
The Horse Without a Head '63
The House on Garibaldi Street
'79
Ladyhawke '85
Massacre in Rome '73
The Mouse That Roared '59
Rumpole of the Bailey:
Rumpole's Return '90
Ryan's Daughter '70
The Shoes of the Fisherman
'68
Travelling North '87

Karen McKevic
The Big Bird Cage '72

Matt McKim
The Little Match Girl '84

Robert McKim
Disciple '15
Hell's Hinges '16

Mary McKinley
California Girls '84

Bill McKinney
Against All Odds '84
Bronco Billy '80
Cannonball '76
The China Lake Murders '90
Deliverance '72
The Gauntlet '77
Heart Like a Wheel '83
The Outlaw Josey Wales '76
Parallax View '74
St. Helen's, Killer Volcano '82
She-Freak '67
The Shootist '76
Tex '82

Kurt McKinney
No Retreat, No Surrender '86

Mark McKinney
The Best of the Kids in the
Hall '93

Mira McKinney
Heart of the Rockies '51

Nina Mae McKinney
The Devil's Daughter '39
Hallelujah! '29

Ray McKinnon
Indecency '92

Jim McKrell
Love at the Top '86

Rod McKuen
Rock, Pretty Baby '56

John McKutcheon
The Thief '52

Andrew V. McLaglen
Since You Went Away '44

Clifford McLaglen
Late Extra '35

Victor McLaglen
Around the World in 80 Days
'56
Broadway Limited '41
Call Out the Marines '42
Devil's Party '38
Forever and a Day '43
Fort Apache '48
Gunga Din '39
The Informer '35
Laughing at Life '33
The Lost Patrol '34
Murder at the Vanities '34
Prince Valiant '54
The Princess and the Pirate
'44
The Quiet Man '52
Rio Grande '50
Sea Devils '37
She Wore a Yellow Ribbon '49
South of Pago Pago '40
Trouble in the Glen '54
The Unholy Three '25
Wee Willie Winkie '37
Whistle Stop '46

Mary McLain
Alligator Eyes '90

Hollis McLaren
Atlantic City '81
Lost and Found '79
Outrageous! '77
Vengeance Is Mine '84

James E. McLarty
Mission to Death '66

Ron McLarty
Enormous Changes '83
The Feud '90
Tiger Town '83
Trumps '88

Bill McLaughlin
Comic Cabby '87
Naked Vengeance '85
Silk '86

Gibb McLaughlin
Bulldog Jack '35
Inspector Hornleigh '39
Mr. Reeder in Room 13 '38
The Old Curiosity Shop '35
Power '34

John McLaughlin
Summer Camp '78
Summer School '77

Sheila McLaughlin
Seduction: The Cruel Woman
'89

David McLean
Death Sport '78
Hughes & Harlow: Angels in
Hell '77
The Strangler '64

Diana McLean
Early Frost '84

Garth McLean
Rockin' Road Trip '85

Jackie McLean
The Connection '61

Jason McLean
Alice in Wonderland '82

Stephanie McLean
Space Riders '83

Rita McLedo
Nazarin '58

Catherine McLeod
I've Always Loved You '46
Sword of Venus '53

Duncan McLeod
Tomb of the Undead '72

Gavin McLeod
The Cary Grant Collection '90
Kelly's Heroes '70
Only with Married Men '74

Gordon McLeod
Meet Sexton Blake '44

Kenneth McLeod
Judgment Day '88

Rona McLeod
The Clinic '83

Sandy McLeod
Variety '83

Allyn Ann McLerie
And Baby Makes Six '79
Calamity Jane '53
Death Scream '75
A Shining Season '79
Someone I Touched '75
They Shoot Horses, Don't
They? '69

John McLiam
The Ambush Murders '82
The Five of Me '81
Freedom Road '79
Showdown '73
Split Decisions '88

Shirley McLine
Curse of the Swamp Creature
'66

Jodie Lynne McLintock
Long Day's Journey into Night
'88

Rachel McLish
Aces: Iron Eagle 3 '92
Pumping Iron 2: The Women
'85

Marshall McLuhan
Annie Hall '77

Ed McMahon
Daughter of Horror '55
Fun with Dick and Jane '77
Great American Traffic Jam
'80
The Incident '67
The Kid from Left Field '79
Slaughter's Big Ripoff '73

Horace McMahon
The Delicate Delinquent '56
Detective Story '51
Melody Ranch '40
My Sister Eileen '55
The Wrong Road '37

Shannon McMahon
Pledge Night '90

Mark McManus
Ned Kelly '70

Michael McManus
Captain America '79
Funland '89

Mr. Bill's Real Life Adventures
'86
Speaking Parts '89

Sharon McManus
Anchors Aweigh '45

John McMartin
Dream Lover '85
Little Sweetheart '90
Private Contentment '83
Roots: The Gift '88
Separate But Equal '91
Sweet Charity '69

Niles McMaster
Bloodsucking Freaks '75

Kenneth McMillan
Acceptable Risks '86
Armed and Dangerous '86
Blue Skies Again '83
Borderline '80
Carny '80
Cat's Eye '85
Chilly Scenes of Winter '79
Concrete Beat '84
Dixie: Changing Habits '85
Dune '84
Heartbeeps '81
Hide in Plain Sight '80
In the Custody of Strangers
'82
Johnny We Hardly Knew Ye
'77
Killing Hour '84
Malone '87
Partners '82
The Pope of Greenwich
Village '84
Protocol '84
Ragtime '81
Reckless '84
Runaway Train '85
Salem's Lot '79
True Confessions '81
Whose Life Is It Anyway? '81

W.G. McMillan
The Crazies '73
The Sister-in-Law '74

Andrew Ian McMillian
Kavik the Wolf Dog '84

Roddy McMillian
Killer with Two Faces '74

Teri McMinn
The Texas Chainsaw
Massacre '74

James McMullan
Extreme Close-Up '73
Sex Through a Window '72

Cliff McMullen
Uptown Angel '90

Sam McMurray
L.A. Story '91
Stone Cold '91

Pamela McMyler
The $5.20 an Hour Dream '80
The Stick-Up '77

Barbara McNair
Change of Habit '69
Dead Right '88
The Organization '71
Stiletto '69
They Call Me Mr. Tibbs! '70
Venus in Furs '70

Kevin McNally
The Berlin Affair '85

Ray McNally
Jack the Ripper '88

Stephen McNally
Air Raid Wardens '43
A Bullet Is Waiting '54
Criss Cross '48
Dear Detective '78
Devil's Canyon '53
Diplomatic Courier '52
For Me and My Gal '42
Hi-Riders '77
Make Haste to Live '54
Split Second '53
Thirty Seconds Over Tokyo
'44
Winchester '73 '50

Billy McNamara
Dream a Little Dream '89

Brian McNamara
Billionaire Boys Club '87
Detective Sadie & Son '84
Mystery Date '91
Short Circuit '86

Ed McNamara
Johnny Come Lately '43
Tramp at the Door '87

Julianne McNamara
Class of Fear '91
Saturday the 14th Strikes
Back '88

Maggie McNamara
The Cardinal '63
Moon is Blue '53
Three Coins in the Fountain
'54

Michael McNamara
Twin Dragon Encounter '80s

William McNamara
The Beat '88
Stealing Home '88
Terror at the Opera '88
Texasville '90
Wildflower '91

Howard McNear
The Errand Boy '61
Follow That Dream '61
Fun in Acapulco '63
Kiss Me, Stupid! '64

Ian McNeice
The Lonely Passion of Judith
Hearne '87
Valmont '89
Year of the Comet '92

Claudia McNeil
Cry Panic '74
A Raisin in the Sun '61
Roll of Thunder, Hear My Cry
'78

Kate McNeil
Amazing Stories, Book 4 '85
Monkey Shines '88

Kathy McNeil
Beach House '82
The House on Sorority Row
'83

Michele McNeil
Driven to Kill '90

Jimmy McNichol
Blinded by the Light '82
Escape from El Diablo '83
Night Warning '82
Smokey Bites the Dust '81

Kristy McNichol
Baby of the Bride '91
Blinded by the Light '82
Dream Lover '85
The End '78
The Forgotten One '89
Just the Way You Are '84

Roy Mehaffey
The Body Shop '72
Doctor Gore '75

Chang Mei
Kung Fu Rebels '80

Lou Mei
Super Ninja

Armin Meier
Mother Kusters Goes to
Heaven '76

Thomas Meighan
The Forbidden City '18
Male and Female '19
Peck's Bad Boy '21
Peck's Bad Boy '34

Mary Meigs
Strangers in Good Company
'91

John Meillon
Billy Budd '62
The Blue Lightning '86
The Cars That Ate Paris '74
Crocodile Dundee '86
The Dunera Boys '85
Fourth Wish '75
Frenchman's Farm '87
Inn of the Damned '74
Ride a Wild Pony '75

Michael Mein
2069: A Sex Odyssey '78

Frederique Meininger
The Lover '92

Kathryn Meisle
Basket Case 2 '90

Gunter Meisner
Between Wars '74
In a Glass Cage '86
Magdalene '88

Karl Meixner
Crimes of Dr. Mabuse '32
Das Testament des Dr.
Mabuse '33

Miguel Aceves Mejia
El Ciclon '47
Los Apuros de Dos Gallos '69
Viva Chihuahua (Long Live
Chihuahua) '47

Alfonso Mejias
Los Olvidados '50
Rio Hondo '47

Isabelle Mejias
The Bay Boy '85
Daughter of Death '82
Fall from Innocence '88
Higher Education '88
Meatballs 3 '87
Scanners 2: The New Order
'91
Unfinished Business '89

Adolfas Mekas
The Brig '64

Mariangela Melato
By the Blood of Others '73
Dancers '87
Love and Anarchy '73
Seduction of Mimi '74
So Fine '81
Summer Night '87
Summer Night with Greek
Profile, Almond Eyes &
Scent of Basil '87
Swept Away... '75
To Forget Venice '79

Lauritz Melchior
Thrill of a Romance '45

Max Meldrum
Death Train '79

Wendel Meldrum
Beautiful Dreamers '92

Annielo Mele
Shoeshine '47

Nicholas Mele
Impulse '90

Asdrubal Melendez
A Very Old Man with
Enormous Wings '88

Sonny Melendrez
The Return of the King '80

Jack Melford
When Thief Meets Thief '37

Lilly Melgar
Midnight Warrior '89

Joe Melia
Privates on Parade '84

Harley Melin
The Russian Terminator '90

Anna Melita
Naked Warriors '73

Joseph Mell
I Was a Teenage Werewolf
'57

Marisa Mell
Danger: Diabolik '68
Hostages '79
Mad Dog '84
Secret Agent Super Dragon
'66

John Cougar Mellencamp
Falling from Grace '92

Sunnyi Melles
'38: Vienna Before the Fall '88

Fuller Mellish, Jr.
Applause '29

Breno Mello
Black Orpheus '58

Douglas Mellor
The Beast of Yucca Flats '61

Robin Meloy
The House on Sorority Row
'83

Frank Melton
Stand Up and Cheer '34
Tanks a Million '41

Sid Melton
Hit! '73
Leave It to the Marines '51
The Lost Continent '51
Sky High '51
The Steel Helmet '51
Stop That Cab '51

Jean-Pierre Melville
Breathless '59

Pauline Melville
Mona Lisa '86

Sam Melville
Roughnecks '80
Twice Dead '88

Winifred Melville
The Greed of William Hart '48

Donnie Melvin
ABC Stage 67: Truman
Capote's A Christmas
Memory '66

Murray Melvin
The Bawdy Adventures of
Tom Jones '76
The Devils '71
Madhouse Mansion '74
A Taste of Honey '61

Steven Memel
Savage Justice '88

George Memmoli
Hot Potato '76

Ben Mendelsohn
Quigley Down Under '90
The Year My Voice Broke '87

Bob Mendelsohn
The Efficiency Expert '92

David Mendenhall
Going Bananas '88
Over the Top '86
Secret of the Ice Cave '89
Space Raiders '83
Streets '90
Witchfire '86

Marcy Mendham
The Groove Tube '72

Bob Mendlesolin
Devil's Gift '84

Mauro Mendonca
Calacan '79
Dona Flor and Her Two
Husbands '79
Love Strange Love '82

Victor Manuel Mendoza
Susana '51

Ramiro Meneses
Rodrigo D.: No Future '91

Bernard Menez
Dracula & Son '76

John Mengatti
Knights of the City '85
Meatballs 2 '84

Jon Menick
Easy Wheels '89

Adolphe Menjou
Across the Wide Missouri '51
The Ambassador's Daughter
'56
Are Parents People? '25
Bundle of Joy '56
A Farewell to Arms '32
The Front Page '31
Gold Diggers of 1935 '35
Golden Boy '39
The Goldwyn Follies '38
The Grand Duchess and the
Waiter '26
Heartbeat '46
Hi Diddle Diddle '43
The Hucksters '47
I Married a Woman '56
The King on Main Street '25
Letter of Introduction '38
Little Miss Marker '34
The Marriage Circle '24
Milky Way '36
Morning Glory '33
Morocco '30
My Dream is Yours '49
Paths of Glory '57
Pollyanna '60
Road Show '41
The Sheik '21

The Sorrows of Satan '26
Stage Door '37
A Star is Born '37
State of the Union '48
Step Lively '44
The Swan '25
Till the Clouds Roll By/A Star
Is Born '46
Woman of Paris/Sunnyside
'23
You Were Never Lovelier '42

Shepard Menken
The Red Menace '49

Tinka Menkes
Queen of Diamonds '91

Vladimir Mensik
All My Good Countrymen '68

Narciso Ibanez Menta
The Saga of the Draculas '72

Heather Menzies
Captain America '79
Piranha '78
Red, White & Busted '75
The Sound of Music '65

Robert Menzies
Cactus '86

Christian Meoli
Alive '93

Doro Merande
Kiss Me, Stupid! '64
The Man with the Golden Arm
'55
The Russians are Coming, the
Russians are Coming '66
The Seven Year Itch '55

Maria Mercader
Musica Proibita '43

Beryl Mercer
All Quiet on the Western Front
'30
Cavalcade '33
Jane Eyre '34

Frances Mercer
Beauty for the Asking '39
Hunt the Man Down/
Smashing the Rackets '50

Jack Mercer
Popeye and Friends in the
South Seas '61

Mae Mercer
Frogs '72

Marian Mercer
Out on a Limb '92

Nicholas Mercer
Deadly Diamonds '91

Vivien Merchant
Accident '67
Alfie '66
Frenzy '72
The Offence '73
Under Milk Wood '73

Chantal Mercier
Small Change '76

Michele Mercier
Black Sabbath '64
Call of the Wild '72
Casanova '70 '65
Oldest Profession '67
Web of the Spider '70

Melina Mercouri
A Dream of Passion '78
Nasty Habits '77
Never on Sunday '60

Once is Not Enough '75
Stella '55
Topkapi '64
Where the Hot Wind Blows
'59

Jean Mercure
Baxter '89

Marthe Mercure
The Victory '88

Monique Mercure
The Odyssey of the Pacific '82
Tramp at the Door '87
Two Women in Gold '70

Gus Mercurio
All the Rivers Run '84

Paul Mercurio
Strictly Ballroom '92

Burgess Meredith
Advise and Consent '62
Batman '66
A Big Hand for the Little Lady
'66
Burnt Offerings '76
The Cardinal '63
Clash of the Titans '81
The Day of the Locust '75
Diary of a Chambermaid '46
Final Assignment '80
Foul Play '78
Full Moon in Blue Water '88
G.I. Joe: The Movie '86
Golden Rendezvous '77
Great Bank Hoax '78
The Hindenburg '75
Idiot's Delight '39
In Harm's Way '65
Jigsaw '49
Johnny We Hardly Knew Ye
'77
King Lear '87
Last Chase '81
MacKenna's Gold '69
Madame X '66
Magic '78
Man on the Eiffel Tower '48
The Manitou '78
Mine Own Executioner '47
Mr. Corbett's Ghost '90
92 in the Shade '76
Oddball Hall '91
Of Mice and Men '39
Outrage! '86
Probe '72
Rocky '76
Rocky 2 '79
Rocky 3 '82
Rocky 5 '90
Santa Claus: The Movie '85
Second Chorus '40
The Sentinel '76
Son of Blob '72
State of Grace '90
Stay Away, Joe '68
That Uncertain Feeling '41
There was a Crooked Man '70
Thumbelina '82
Tom, Dick, and Harry '41
Torture Garden '67
True Confessions '81
Twilight Zone: The Movie '83
Wet Gold '84
When Time Ran Out '80
Winterset '36
Yin & Yang of Mr. Go '71

Don Meredith
Express to Terror '79
The Night the City Screamed
'80
Sky Hei$t '75
Terror on the 40th Floor '74

Lorraine Miller
Ambush Trail '46
Border Badmen '45
Frontier Fugitives '45
Lonesome Trail '55
White Gorilla '47

Lydia Miller
Backlash '86

Lynn Miller
Poor Girl, A Ghost Story '74

Mandy Miller
Mandy '53

Marjorie Miller
Party Favors '89

Mark Miller
Ginger in the Morning '73
Savannah Smiles '82

Mark Thomas Miller
Blue De Ville '86
Misfits of Science '85
Mom '89

Martin Miller
Bergonzi Hand '70
Frenzy '46
Hotel Reserve '44
Man on the Run '49

Marvin Miller
Dead Reckoning '47
Kiss Daddy Goodbye '81
Off Limits '53

Mary Louise Miller
The Night Cry '26

Michael B. Miller
One Summer Love '76

Mindi Miller
Sacred Ground '83

Mirta Miller
Icebox Murders '80s

Patsy Ruth Miller
Headwinds '28
The Hunchback of Notre Dame '23
Lonely Wives '31
The Sheik '21
So This is Paris '26

Penelope Ann Miller
Adventures in Babysitting '87
Awakenings '90
Big Top Pee Wee '88
Biloxi Blues '88
Chaplin '92
Dead Bang '89
Downtown '89
The Freshman '90
The Gun in Betty Lou's Handbag '92
Kindergarten Cop '90
Miles from Home '88
Other People's Money '91
Year of the Comet '92

Rebecca Miller
Consenting Adults '92
The Murder of Mary Phagan '87
Wind '92

Roger Miller
Robin Hood '73

Roosevelt Miller, Jr.
Game of Survival '85
Game of Survival '89

Sam Miller
Fergie & Andrew: Behind Palace Doors '93

Sherie Miller
Goin' All the Way '82

Sidney Miller
Boys Town '38
Men of Boys Town '41

Stephen E. Miller
Home is Where the Hart is '88
Jane Doe '83

Tony Miller
T-Bird Gang '59

Walter Miller
Blessed Event '32
Ghost Patrol '36
The Lone Defender '32
Tailspin Tommy '34

Andra Millian
Nightfall '88
Stacy's Knights '83

James Millican
The Adventures of Gallant Bess '48
Man from Colorado '49
Rimfire '49
The Winning Team '52

Spike Milligan
The Case of the Mukkinese Battle Horn '56
Digby, the Biggest Dog in the World '73
Down Among the Z Men '52
Ghost in the Noonday Sun '74
Goon Movie '53
Great McGonagall '75
The Hound of the Baskervilles '77
The Magic Christian '69
Rentadick '72
To See Such Fun '81

Alley Mills
Rape and Marriage: The Rideout Case '80

Barbara Mills
Chain Gang Women '72

Brooke Mills
The Big Doll House '71
Dream No Evil '75
The Student Teachers '73

Danny Mills
Female Trouble '75
Pink Flamingos '73

Donna Mills
Beyond the Bermuda Triangle '75
Bunco '83
Curse of the Black Widow '77
False Arrest '92
Fire '77
Haunts of the Very Rich '72
The Hunted Lady '77
The Incident '67
Killer with Two Faces '74
Live a Little, Steal a Lot '75
Murph the Surf '75
One Deadly Owner '74
Play Misty for Me '71
Waikiki '80
The World's Oldest Living Bridesmaid '92

Grace Mills
Night of the Howling Beast '75

Hayley Mills
Africa Texas Style '67
Appointment with Death '88
Bananas Boat '78

The Chalk Garden '64
Deadly Strangers '82
Endless Night '71
The Flame Trees of Thika '80s
In Search of the Castaways '62
Kingfisher Caper '76
Moon-Spinners '64
The Parent Trap '61
Pollyanna '60
Summer Magic '63
That Darn Cat '65
Tiger Bay '59
The Trouble with Angels '66
Whistle Down the Wind '62

Jacob Mills
The Islander '88

Jed Mills
New Year's Evil '78

Jenny Mills
Ninja Fantasy '86

John Mills
Above Us the Waves '56
Africa Texas Style '67
Around the World in 80 Days '56
The Baby and the Battleship '56
The Big Sleep '78
A Black Veil for Lisa '68
The Chalk Garden '64
Choice of Weapons '76
Chuka '67
The Colditz Story '55
Cottage to Let '41
Dr. Strange '78
Escapade '55
Gandhi '82
The Ghost Camera '33
Goodbye, Mr. Chips '39
Great Expectations '46
Hobson's Choice '53
The Human Factor '75
In Which We Serve '43
King Rat '65
Lady Caroline Lamb '73
Masks of Death '86
Nine Days a Queen '34
October Man '48
O.H.M.S. '37
Oklahoma Crude '73
Operation Crossbow '65
Quatermass Conclusion '79
Ryan's Daughter '70
Sahara '83
Scott of the Antarctic '48
The Swiss Family Robinson '60
A Tale of Two Cities '91
The Thirty-Nine Steps '79
This Happy Breed '47
Tiara Tahiti '62
Tiger Bay '59
Tunes of Glory '60
Tunes of Glory/Horse's Mouth '60
The Vicious Circle '57
War and Peace '56
We Dive at Dawn '43
When the Wind Blows '86
Who's That Girl? '87
The Wrong Box '66
Young Winston '72
Zulu Dawn '79

Juliet Mills
Alexander: The Other Side of Dawn '77
Barnaby and Me '77
Beyond the Door '75
The Cracker Factory '79
Jonathan Livingston Seagull '73
October Man '48

QB VII '74
The Rare Breed '66

Riley Mills
I Drink Your Blood '71

Samantha Mills
Prehysteria '93

Tom Mills
Luther the Geek '90

Leslie Milne
Vampire at Midnight '88

Martin Milner
Columbo: Murder By the Book '71
Flood! '76
Francis in the Navy '55
The Halls of Montezuma '50
Hurricane '74
Life with Father '47
Nashville Beat '89
Pete Kelly's Blues '55
The Seekers '79
Sweet Smell of Success '57
13 Ghosts '60
Valley of the Dolls '67
Zebra in the Kitchen '65

Sandra Milo
Bang Bang Kid '67
Dead for a Dollar '70s
8 1/2 '63
General Della Rovere '60
Generale Della Rovere '60
Herod the Great '60
Vanina Vanini '61

Ana Milosavljevic
Innocence Unprotected '68

F.A. Milovich
The Legend of Black Thunder Mountain '79

Josh Milrad
Beastmaster '82

Helge Milsen
Leaves from Satan's Book '19

Ernest Milton
Alice in Wonderland '50

James Milton
Escape from Galaxy Three '76

Nadia Milton
El Hombre Contra el Mundo '87
Los Dos Hermanos '87
Sin Salida '87
Tacos al Carbon '87

John Omirah Miluwi
Gorillas in the Mist '88

Aiko Mimasu
Street of Shame '56

Yvette Mimieux
The Black Hole '79
Brainwash '82
Caper of the Golden Bulls '67
Devil Dog: The Hound of Hell '78
Diamond Head '62
Forbidden Love '82
The Four Horsemen of the Apocalypse '62
Hit Lady '74
Jackson County Jail '76
Journey into Fear '74
Legend of Valentino '75
Monkeys, Go Home! '66
Neptune Factor '73
Night Partners '83
Obsessive Love '84
Outside Chance '78
Platinum High School '60

Snowbeast '77
Three in the Attic '68
The Time Machine '60
Toys in the Attic '63
Where the Boys Are '60
The Wonderful World of the Brothers Grimm '62

Peggy Min
Secret Executioners '70s

Michio Minami
The Human Condition: Road to Eternity '59

Yoko Minamida
The Crucified Lovers '54

Nico Minardos
Assault on Agathon '75

Ester Minciotti
Full of Life '56
Marty '55

Sal Mineo
Cheyenne Autumn '64
Dino '57
Escape from the Planet of the Apes '71
Exodus '60
The Gene Krupa Story '59
Giant '56
James Dean: The First American Teenager '76
The Longest Day '62
Rebel Without a Cause '55
Rock, Pretty Baby '56
Somebody Up There Likes Me '56
Tonka '58

Jan Miner
Lenny '74
Mermaids '90
Willie & Phil '80

Mike Minett
Bad Taste '88

Bernard Minetti
Tiefland '44

Bobby Ming
Dynasty '77

Lau Siu Ming
Eat a Bowl of Tea '89

Li Tang Ming
Incredible Master Beggars '82

Wu Ming-Tsai
Japanese Connection '82

Liza Minnelli
Arthur '81
Arthur 2: On the Rocks '88
Cabaret '72
Golden Age of Hollywood '77
Hedda Hopper's Hollywood '42
In the Good Old Summertime '49
King of Comedy '82
A Matter of Time '76
Muppets Take Manhattan '84
New York, New York '77
The Princess and the Pea '83
Rent-A-Cop '88
Silent Movie '76
Stepping Out '91
The Sterile Cuckoo '69
That's Dancing! '85
Time to Live '85

Dani Minnick
The Sleeping Car '90

Byron Keith Minns
South Central '92

Bob Minos
Black Eliminator '70s
Delinquent School Girls '84

Alexis Minotis
Land of the Pharaohs '55

Kelly Jo Minter
A Nightmare on Elm Street 5:
Dream Child '89
Pilot '84
Popcorn '89

Kristin Minter
Cool As Ice '91

Mary Miles Minter
Eyes of Julia Deep '18

Emil Minty
The Road Warrior '82

Fabrizio Mioni
Hercules '58

Miou-Miou
Dog Day '83
Entre-Nous '83
Going Places '74
Jonah Who Will Be 25 in the
Year 2000 '76
Josepha '82
La Lectrice '88
May Fools '90
Menage '86
My Other Husband '85
No Problem '70s
Roads to the South '78

Joelle Miquel
Four Adventures of Reinette
and Mirabelle '89

Brigitte Mira
Ali: Fear Eats the Soul '74
Berlin Alexanderplatz '80
Chinese Roulette '86
Mother Kusters Goes to
Heaven '76

Irene Miracle
In the Shadow of Kilimanjaro
'86
Inferno '78
The Last of Philip Banter '87
Puppet Master '89

Evan Mirand
Brotherhood of Justice '86
My Best Friend Is a Vampire
'88
Weekend War '88

Althea Miranda
Kickboxer 3: The Art of War
'92

Aurora Miranda
The Three Caballeros '45

Carmen Miranda
Copacabana '47
A Date with Judy '48
Doll Face '46
Down Argentine Way '40
Gotta Dance, Gotta Sing '84
Hollywood Goes to War '54
Nancy Goes to Rio '50
Scared Stiff '53
Springtime in the Rockies '42

Isa Miranda
Bay of Blood '71
Dog Eat Dog '64
La Ronde '51
La Signora di Tutti '34
The Night Porter '74
Seven Deadly Sins '53

Isabelle Miranda
Just Another Pretty Face '58

Juan Miranda
El Zorro Blanco '87

Mark Miranda
Lassie: Adventures of Neeka
'68

Robert Miranda
Lost in Yonkers '93
Sister Act '92

Soledad Miranda
Count Dracula '71
Sound of Horror '64

Vasco Mirandola
Mediterraneo '92

Jaime Miravilles
Un Chien Andalou '28

Veronica Miriel
Street Warriors, Part 2 '87

Olga Mironova
Come and See '85

Helen Mirren
As You Like It '79
Cal '84
Caligula '80
The Comfort of Strangers '91
The Cook, the Thief, His Wife
& Her Lover '90
Excalibur '81
The Fiendish Plot of Dr. Fu
Manchu '80
The Gospel According to Vic
'87
Hussy '80
The Little Mermaid '84
The Long Good Friday '79
The Long Goodbye '73
A Midsummer Night's Dream
'68
A Midsummer Night's Dream
'82
The Mosquito Coast '86
O Lucky Man '73
Pascali's Island '88
Priest of Love '81
Red King, White Knight '89
S.O.S. Titanic '79
2010: The Year We Make
Contact '84
When the Whales Came '89
Where Angels Fear to Tread
'91
White Nights '85

Laura Misch
Mardi Gras Massacre '78

Martha Mischon
Flesh Feast '69

Yukio Mishima
Black Lizard '68

Karen Mistal
Cannibal Women in the
Avocado Jungle of Death
'89
Return of the Killer Tomatoes
'88

Mr. T
D.C. Cab '84
Penitentiary 2 '82
Rocky 3 '82
Straight Line '88

Fernanda Mistral
The Lion's Share '79

George Mistral
The Sword and the Cross '58

Jorge Mistral
Camelia
La Justicia Tiene Doce Anos
'87

Ivan Mistrik
Sweet Light in a Dark Room
'60

Stacy Mistysyn
Princess in Exile '90

Ann Mitchell
Paper Marriage '93

Belle Mitchell
Crazed '82
Slipping into Darkness '88

Cameron Mitchell
Action U.S.A. '89
The Adventures of Gallant
Bess '48
All Mine to Give '56
The Andersonville Trial '70
Autopsy of a Ghost '67
The Bastard '78
Blood and Black Lace '64
Bloodlink '86
Buck and the Preacher '72
Carousel '56
Cataclysm '81
Code of Honor '88
Codename: Vengeance '87
Conquest of the Normans '62
Crossing the Line '90
Cult People '89
Deadly Prey '87
The Demon '81
Desiree '54
Dog Eat Dog '64
Easy Kill '89
El Sabor de la Venganza '65
Enforcer from Death Row '78
Escapade in Japan '57
Flight to Mars '52
Flood! '76
Frankenstein Island '81
Go for the Gold '84
The Guns and the Fury '83
The Hanged Man '74
Haunts '77
Hollywood Cop '87
Hombre '67
Homecoming '48
How to Marry a Millionaire '53
The Invaders '63
It's Called Murder, Baby '82
Kill Squad '81
Killer Commandos
Killers '88
Killpoint '84
The Klansman '74
Last Gun '64
The Last Reunion '80
The Longest Drive '76
Love Me or Leave Me '55
Low Blow '85
Medusa '74
Memorial Valley Massacre '88
The Messenger '87
Minnesota Clay '65
Mission to Kill '85
My Favorite Year '82
Night Train to Terror '84
Nightforce '86
Nightmare in Wax '69
The Offspring '87
The Ox-Bow Incident '55
Prince Jack '83
Rage to Kill '88
Raw Force '81
Rebel Rousers '69
Return to Fantasy Island '77
Ride in the Whirlwind '67
Scalp Merchant '77
Silent Scream '80
Slaughter '72
Slavers '77
Space Mutiny '88
The Stranger '73

Wuthering Heights '53

Camille Mitchell
Laboratory '80

Channing Mitchell
Texas Lightning '81

**Chuck "Porky"
Mitchell**
Ghost Chase '88
Goodbye Cruel World '82
Hollywood Zap '86
Porky's Revenge '85
Swift Justice '88

Don Mitchell
Scream Blacula Scream '73

Donna Mitchell
The Portrait '93
Psycho 4: The Beginning '90

Duke Mitchell
Bela Lugosi Meets a Brooklyn
Gorilla '52
The Executioner '78

Eddy Mitchell
Coup de Torchon '81

Eric Mitchell
The Foreigner '78
Rome '78 '78
Underground U.S.A. '84

Gordon Mitchell
Battle of Valiant '63
Beyond the Law '68
The Big Bust Out '73
Commando Invasion '87
Erik, the Viking '72
Fighting Fists of Shanghai Joe
'65
Frankenstein '80 '79
The Giant of Metropolis '61
Linchamiento '68
Mafia la Ley Que Non
Perdona '72
Mines of Kilimanjaro '87
Operation Orient
Rush '84
Slaughterday '77
Suicide Patrol '70s
Vulcan God of Fire

Grant Mitchell
Conflict '45
Gold Diggers of 1935 '35
The Grapes of Wrath '40
The Great Lie '41
Heroes for Sale '33
In Person '35
Laura '44
The Man Who Came to Dinner
'41
No Man of Her Own '32
Three on a Match '32

Guy Mitchell
Red Garters '54

Heather Mitchell
The Everlasting Secret Family
'88
Proof '91

Supersonic Man '78
The Swarm '78
Swift Justice '88
The Tall Men '55
Tension at Table Rock '56
Terror in Beverly Hills '90
Texas Detour '77
Texas Lightning '81
They Were Expendable '45
Thief '71
Tomb '86
The Toolbox Murders '78
The Unstoppable Man '59
Viking Massacre '70s
Viva Knievel '77

Ian Mitchell
Secret Weapon '90

**John Cameron
Mitchell**
Book of Love '91

Joni Mitchell
The Last Waltz '78

Julien Mitchell
Hotel Reserve '44

Keith Mitchell
Bergonzi Hand '70
The Executioner '70
Julius Caesar '79
Memorial Day '83
Tenth Month '79

Knolly Mitchell
Black King '32

Laurie Mitchell
Missile to the Moon '59
Queen of Outer Space '58

Leigh Mitchell
Scream Bloody Murder '72

Margaret Mitchell
The Making of a Legend:
"Gone With the Wind" '89

Mary Mitchell
Panic in the Year Zero! '62
A Swingin' Summer '65
Toga Party '79

Millard Mitchell
A Double Life '47
Gunfighter '50
Here Come the Girls '53
The Naked Spur '53
Singin' in the Rain '52
Twelve O'Clock High '49
Winchester '73 '50

Red Mitchell
Forever Evil '87

Rhea Mitchell
On the Night Stage '15

Sandford Mitchell
The Corpse Grinders '71

Sasha Mitchell
Kickboxer 2: The Road Back
'90
Kickboxer 3: The Art of War
'92
Spike of Bensonhurst '88

Scoey Mitchell
Jo Jo Dancer, Your Life is
Calling '86
The Voyage of the Yes '72

Ilan Mitchell-Smith
The Chocolate War '88
How to Be a Perfect Person in
Just Three Days '84
Identity Crisis '90
Journey to the Center of the
Earth '88
Weird Science '85

Steve Mitchell
The Sibling '72
Submarine Seahawk '59

Thomas Mitchell
Angels Over Broadway '40
Bataan '43
The Big Wheel '49
Buffalo Bill '44
By Love Possessed '61
Dark Mirror '46
Dark Waters '44
The Fighting Sullivans '42
Gone with the Wind '39
High Noon '52

Alison Moir
Johnny Suede '92

Richard Moir
Heatwave '83
In Search of Anna '79
Panic Station '82
Remember Me '85
Wrangler '88

Zakes Mokae
Body Parts '91
The Comedians '67
Dad '89
A Dry White Season '89
Gross Anatomy '89
A Rage in Harlem '91
The Serpent and the Rainbow '87
A World of Strangers '62

Albert Mol
Dear Boys '80

Karin Molander
Thomas Graal's Best Film '17
Thomas Graal's First Child '18

Jeff Moldovan
Master Blaster '85

Jerry Molen
Rain Man '88

Alberto Molina
Portrait of Teresa '79

Alfred Molina
American Friends '93
Blat
Enchanted April '92
Not Without My Daughter '90
Prick Up Your Ears '87

Angela Molina
Camorra: The Naples Connection '85
Demons in the Garden '82
The Eyes, the Mouth '83
1492: Conquest of Paradise '92
Half of Heaven '86
That Obscure Object of Desire '77

Anya Molina
Bloodmoon '90

Stefano Molinari
Evil Clutch '89

Richard Molinos
Strange Awakening '58

Charles Moll
Cataclysm '80
Combat Academy '86
Night Train to Terror '84

Georgia Moll
Contempt '64
Thief of Baghdad '61
What a Way to Die '70

Richard Moll
Dream Date '93
Driving Me Crazy '91
Dungeonmaster '85
Hard Country '81
House '86
Metalstorm '83
National Lampoon's Loaded Weapon 1 '93
Savage Journey '83
Sidekicks '93
Survivor '80
Sword & the Sorcerer '82
Think Big '90
Wicked Stepmother '89

Flemming Quist Moller
Ladies on the Rocks '83

Clifford Mollison
A Christmas Carol '51

Darbnia Molloy
Paddy '70

Patrick Molloy
Phantom Brother '88
Plutonium Baby '87

Tibor Molnar
The Round Up '66

Steve Molone
The Big Sweat '90

Alessandro Momo
Malicious '74

Ghislaine Mona
Therese '86

Marjorie Monaghan
Nemesis '93

Dan Monahan
Porky's '82
Porky's 2: The Next Day '83
Porky's Revenge '85

Maria Monay
Flesh and the Spur '57

Dick Monda
Body Parts '90

Jorge Mondragon
The New Invisible Man '58
Spiritism '61

Pierre Mondy
The Gift '82

Paul Mones
Tuff Turf '85

Richard Monette
Big Zapper '73
Far Cry from Home '70s
Hello Mary Lou: Prom Night 2 '87
Higher Education '88
Murder by Night '89

Corbett Monica
The Passing of Evil '70

Louisa Monk
Dreadnaught Rivals '80s

Yvonne Monlaur
The Brides of Dracula '60
Circus of Horrors '60
Hawk of the Caribbean '70s
License to Kill '64

Valentine Monnier
After the Fall of New York '85

Lawrence Monoson
Dangerous Love '87
Last American Virgin '82
Mask '85

Cinzia Monreale
Buried Alive '81

Louise Monroe
Alien Contamination '81

Marilyn Monroe
All About Eve '50
As Young As You Feel '51
The Asphalt Jungle '50
Bus Stop '56
Clash by Night '52
Don't Bother to Knock '52
Gentlemen Prefer Blondes '53
Hollywood Home Movies '87
Hollywood Outtakes & Rare Footage '83

Home Town Story '51
How to Marry a Millionaire '53
Ladies of the Chorus '49
Let's Make it Legal '51
Let's Make Love '60
The Love Goddesses '65
Love Happy '50
Love Nest '51
The Misfits '61
Monkey Business '52
Niagara '52
The Prince and the Showgirl '57
River of No Return '54
The Seven Year Itch '55
Some Like It Hot '59
There's No Business Like Show Business '54
We're Not Married '52

Jacques Monseau
The Devil's Nightmare '71

Renzo Montagnani
A Joke of Destiny, Lying in Wait Around the Corner Like a Bandit '84

Bruce Montague
Whoops Apocalypse '83

Lee Montague
Brother Sun, Sister Moon '73
Mahler '74

Monte Montague
Courtin' Wildcats '29
King of the Rodeo '28
Radio Patrol '37

Carlos Montalban
Bananas '71

Ricardo Montalban
Across the Wide Missouri '51
Alice Through the Looking Glass '66
Battleground '49
Black Water Gold '69
Blue '68
Cannonball Run II '84
Cheyenne Autumn '64
Conquest of the Planet of the Apes '72
Escape from the Planet of the Apes '71
Fantasy Island '76
Fireball Forward '72
Iron Cowboy '68
Joe Panther '76
Latin Lovers '53
Madame X '66
Mission to Glory '80
The Naked Gun: From the Files of Police Squad '88
Neptune's Daughter '49
Nosotros '44
On an Island with You '48
Pirate Warrior '64
Return to Fantasy Island '77
Ride to Glory '71
Sayonara '57
The Singing Nun '66
Star Trek 2: The Wrath of Khan '82
Sweet Charity '69
Train Robbers '73
Two Weeks with Love '50

Celia Montalvan
Toni '34

Karla Montana
La Pastorela '92
Sweet 15 '90

Monte Montana
Circle of Death '36
Down Dakota Way '49

Silvia Montanari
Deadly Revenge '83

Yves Montand
Cesar & Rosalie '72
Choice of Arms '83
Delusions of Grandeur '76
Goodbye Again '61
Grand Prix '66
Is Paris Burning? '68
Jean de Florette '87
Let's Make Love '60
Lovers Like Us '75
Manon of the Spring '87
My Geisha '62
Napoleon '55
On a Clear Day You Can See Forever '70
Roads to the South '78
State of Siege '73
Vincent, Francois, Paul and the Others '76
Wages of Fear '55
Where the Hot Wind Blows '59
Z '69

Lew Montania
Wonsan Operation '78

Arlene Montano
Furious '83

Lane Montano
Ricky 1 '88

Marlo Monte
Soul Vengeance '75

Elias Monteiro da Silva
Medicine Man '92

Caroline Monteith
Novel Desires '92

Kelly Monteith
Hollywood Boulevard 2 '89
Screwball Hotel '88

Carmen Montejo
El Rey '87
Ni Chana Ni Juana '87
The Vampire '57

Lisa Montell
The Nine Lives of Elfego Baca '58
She Gods of Shark Reef '56

Mario Montenegro
Brides of the Beast '68

Sasha Montenegro
Bellas de Noche
Los Vampiros de Coyacan '87
Passion for Power '85

Elsa Montero
Death of a Bureaucrat '66

John Montero
Blood Frenzy '87

Zully Montero
El Super '79

Rosenda Monteros
Cauldron of Blood '67
Tiara Tahiti '62
The White Orchid '54

Enrico Monterrano
Sex with a Smile '76

Elisa Montes
As If It Were Raining '63

Fernando Montes
The Diabolical Dr. Z '65

Enrico Montesano
Lobster for Breakfast '82 ·
Sotto, Sotto '85

Jorge Montesi
Death Target '83

Liliane Montevecchi
Meet Me in Las Vegas '56

Eva Montez
The Vampire People '66

Belinda J. Montgomery
Blackout '78
The Man from Atlantis '77
Silent Madness '84
Stone Cold Dead '80
Stone Fox '87
Tell Me That You Love Me '84
The Todd Killings '71

Douglass Montgomery
Harmony Lane '35

Elizabeth Montgomery
Amos '85
The Court Martial of Billy Mitchell '55
Deadline Assault '90
Missing Pieces '83

Eve Montgomery
Demon Possessed '90s

George Montgomery
Battle of the Bulge '65
Bomb at 10:10 '67
From Hell to Borneo '64
Hallucination '67
Hostile Guns '67
Indian Uprising '51
Orchestra Wives '42
Rough Riders' Roundup '34
Samar '62
Satan's Harvest '65
The Steel Claw '61
Sword of Monte Cristo '51
The Texas Rangers '51
War Kill '68
Warkill '65

Jeff Montgomery
Oasis of the Zombies '82

Julia Montgomery
Girls Night Out '83
Revenge of the Nerds '84
Revenge of the Nerds 3: The Next Generation '92
Savage Justice '88
South of Reno '87
Stewardess School '86
Up the Creek '84

Lee Montgomery
Ben '72
Girls Just Want to Have Fun '85
Into the Fire '88
The Midnight Hour '86
Mutant '83
Pete 'n' Tillie '72
Prime Risk '84
Savage is Loose '74

Richard Montgomery
The Legend of Jedediah Carver '70s

Robert Montgomery
The Divorcee '30
Eye Witness '49
Forsaking All Others '35
Free and Easy '30
Here Comes Mr. Jordan '41
Hide-Out '34

ffolkes '80
Fiction Makers '67
Fire, Ice and Dynamite '91
Five Miles to Midnight '80
For Your Eyes Only '81
Happy Anniversary 007: 25
    Years of James Bond '87
The Last Time I Saw Paris '54
Live and Let Die '73
The Man Who Haunted
    Himself '70
The Man with the Golden Gun
    '74
Mission: Monte Carlo '75
Moonraker '79
The Naked Face '84
Octopussy '83
Overture '75
Panama Hattie '42
The Persuaders '71
The Rape of the Sabines '61
The Saint '68
Sea Wolves '81
Shout at the Devil '76
The Spy Who Loved Me '77
Street People '76
That Lucky Touch '75
Vendetta for the Saint '68
A View to a Kill '85
Wild Geese '78

Rudy Ray Moore
Avenging Disco Godfather '76
Devil's Son-in-Law '77
Dolemite '75
Dolemite 2: Human Tornado
    '76
Monkey Hustle '77

Sam Moore
Tapeheads '89

Stephen Moore
Clockwise '86

Terry Moore
Beneath the 12-Mile Reef '53
Between Heaven and Hell '56
Beverly Hills Brats '89
Come Back, Little Sheba '52
Daddy Long Legs '55
Death Blow '87
Gaslight '44
The Great Rupert '50
Hellhole '85
Kill Factor
Mighty Joe Young '49
Peyton Place '57
Platinum High School '60
Postmark for Danger '56
Postmark for Danger/
    Quicksand '56
Shack Out on 101 '55
Since You Went Away '44

Thomas Moore
Escape from the Bronx '85
Feast for the Devil '70s

Tim Moore
Boy! What a Girl '45

Tom Moore
Mystery in Swing '40

Victor Moore
Louisiana Purchase '41
The Seven Year Itch '55
Swing Time '36
We're Not Married '52
Ziegfeld Follies '46

Agnes Moorehead
Adventures of Captain Fabian
    '51
Alice Through the Looking
    Glass '66
The Bat '59
Big Street '42

Captain Blackjack '51
Charlotte's Web '79
Citizen Kane '41
The Conqueror '56
Dark Passage '47
Dear Dead Delilah '72
Dragon Seed '44
How the West was Won '63
Hush, Hush, Sweet Charlotte
    '65
Jane Eyre '44
Johnny Belinda '48
Journey into Fear '42
The Left Hand of God '55
Lost Moment '47
The Magnificent Ambersons
    '42
Magnificent Obsession '54
Main Street to Broadway '53
Meet Me in Las Vegas '56
Mrs. Parkington '44
The Opposite Sex '56
Our Vines Have Tender
    Grapes '45
Pollyanna '60
Raintree County '57
The Seventh Cross '44
Show Boat '51
Since You Went Away '44
The Singing Nun '66
Station West '48
Summer Holiday '48
What's the Matter with Helen?
    '71

Jean Moorehead
The Violent Years '56

Natalie Moorhead
Dancing Man '33
Hook, Line and Sinker '30
Morals for Women '31
Murder on the High Seas '32
The Thin Man '34

Elizabeth Moorman
Eliza's Horoscope '70

Margarita Mora
El Ametralladora '65

Norma Mora
Samson in the Wax Museum
    '63
Viva Chihuahua (Long Live
    Chihuahua) '47

Angelica Morales
Virgin Sacrifice '59

Benito Morales
Borderline '80

Brooks Morales
Feelin' Screwy '90

Esai Morales
Bad Boys '83
Bloodhounds of Broadway '89
Freejack '92
Great Love Experiment '84
L.A. Bad '85
La Bamba '87
On Wings of Eagles '86

Gonzalo Morales
Veronico Cruz '87

Ines Morales
House of Psychotic Women
    '73

Santos Morales
Hot to Trot! '88

Dolores Moran
The Horn Blows at Midnight
    '45
To Have & Have Not '44

Erin Moran
Galaxy of Terror '81

How Sweet It Is! '68
Twirl '81
Watermelon Man '70

Frank Moran
Return of the Ape Man '44
Ships in the Night '28

Jackie Moran
The Adventures of Tom
    Sawyer '38
Buck Rogers Conquers the
    Universe '39
The Gang's All Here '41
Let's Go Collegiate '41
Old Swimmin' Hole '40
Tomboy '40

Lee Moran
High Gear '33
My Lady of Whims '25
The Tomboy '24

Lois Moran
Just Suppose '26

Manolo Moran
Como Dos Gotas de Agua
    '70s

Patsy Moran
Children of the Wild '37

Peggy Moran
The Mummy's Hand '40

Polly Moran
Adam's Rib '50
Hollywood Party '34
Kings, Queens, Jokers '30s

Morando Morandini
Before the Revolution '65

Jacqueline Morane
Picnic on the Grass '59

Rick Moranis
The Best of John Candy on
    SCTV '80s
Brewster's Millions '85
Club Paradise '86
Ghostbusters '84
Ghostbusters 2 '89
Head Office '86
Hockey Night '84
Honey, I Blew Up the Kid '92
Honey, I Shrunk the Kids '89
The Last Polka '84
Little Shop of Horrors '86
My Blue Heaven '90
Parenthood '89
Spaceballs '87
Splitting Heirs '93
Strange Brew '83
Streets of Fire '84
The Wild Life '84

Richard Morant
John & Yoko: A Love Story
    '85
Mahler '74

Laura Morante
The Tragedy of a Ridiculous
    Man '81

Milburn Morante
Ghost Rider '43
Sherlock's Rivals & Where's
    My Wife '27

Morasi
Scarlet Spear '54

Yvonne Moray
Terror of Tiny Town '38

Nonna Mordyukova
Commissar '68

Camilla More
Dark Side of the Moon '90

Kenneth More
The Adventures of Sadie '55
Battle of Britain '69
Doctor in the House '53
Flame Over India '60
Genevieve '53
Leopard in the Snow '78
The Longest Day '62
Man on the Run '49
A Night to Remember '58
Reach for the Sky '56
The Rocking Horse Winner
    '50
Scott of the Antarctic '48
Scrooge '70
Sink the Bismarck '60
A Tale of Two Cities '80
Unidentified Flying Oddball '79
Where Time Began '77

Jeanne Moreau
Alberto Express '92
Alex in Wonderland '71
Back to the Wall '56
The Bride Wore Black '68
Chimes at Midnight '67
Dangerous Liaisons '60
Diary of a Chambermaid '64
Frantic '58
Going Places '74
Heat of Desire '84
Jules and Jim '62
La Femme Nikita '91
La Truite '83
The Last Tycoon '76
The Little Theatre of Jean
    Renoir '71
The Lovers '59
Lumiere '76
Map of the Human Heart '93
Mr. Klein '75
Monte Walsh '70
Oldest Profession '67
Querelle '83
The Train '65
The Trial '63
Until The End of The World
    '91
Your Ticket Is No Longer Valid
    '84

Marsha Moreau
Miracle at Moreaux '86

Nathaniel Moreau
George's Island '91

Yolanda Moreau
Vagabond '85

Sam Moree
God's Bloody Acre '75

Elizabeth Morehead
Interceptor '92

Mantan Moreland
Charlie Chan in the Secret
    Service '44
The Chinese Cat '44
Cosmo Jones, Crime Smasher
    '43
Footlight Serenade '42
Frontier Scout '38
The Gang's All Here '41
Harlem on the Prairie '38
The Jade Mask '45
Juke Joint '47
King of the Zombies '41
Law of the Jungle '42
Let's Go Collegiate '41
Meeting at Midnight '44
Mr. Moto's Last Warning/
    Meeting at Midnight '44
Next Time I Marry '38
Phantom Killer '42
Pin-Up Girl '44
Revenge of the Zombies '43

The Scarlet Clue '45
The Shanghai Cobra '45
Spider Baby '64
The Spirit of Youth '37
Tall, Tan and Terrific '46
Two-Gun Man from Harlem
    '38
Up in the Air '40
The Young Nurses '73

Andre Morell
The Baby and the Battleship
    '56
The Hound of the Baskervilles
    '59
The Man Who Never Was '55
A Stolen Face '52
10 Rillington Place '71

Antonio Moreno
Creature from the Black
    Lagoon '54
Gaiety '43
It '27
Rose of Rio Grande '38
Valley of the Sun '42

Jaime Moreno
El Fin del Tahur '87
La Hifa Sin Padre '87

Jose Elias Moreno
Night of the Bloody Apes '68
Santa Claus '59

Lisa Moreno
From Hell to Borneo '64

Rita Moreno
Age Isn't Everything '91
Anatomy of a Seduction '79
Boss' Son '79
Carnal Knowledge '71
Cry of Battle '63
The Four Seasons '81
Happy Birthday, Gemini '80
The King and I '56
Marlowe '69
Pagan Love Song '50
Popi '69
Portrait of a Showgirl '82
The Ring '52
The Ritz '76
Seven Cities of Gold '55
Singin' in the Rain '52
Summer and Smoke '61
The Toast of New Orleans '50
West Side Story '61

Leon Morenzie
Caged Terror '72

Gina Moret
Night of the Bloody Apes '68

Sandro Moretti
The Sword of El Cid '62

Abraham Morewski
The Dybbuk '37

Bill Morey
Whitcomb's War '88

George Morfogen
Deadly Business '86
Deadly Matrimony '92
Yuri Nosenko, KGB '86

Audrey Morgan
Love Your Mama '93

Chesty Morgan
Deadly Weapons '70

Cindy Morgan
Tron '82

Debbi Morgan
Guilty of Innocence '87
The Jesse Owens Story '84
Monkey Hustle '77

Aubrey Morris
Lifeforce '85
Night Caller from Outer Space
    '66

Barboura Morris
Atlas '60
A Bucket of Blood '59
Machine Gun Kelly '58
The Wasp Woman '49

Brad Morris
American Kickboxer 1 '91

Chester Morris
The Bat Whispers '30
Corsair '31
The Divorcee '30
Five Came Back '39
Flight from Glory '37
Frankie and Johnny '36
Gambler's Choice '44
The Great White Hope '70
Hunt the Man Down/
    Smashing the Rackets '50
Law of the Underworld '38
Red Headed Woman '32
Seven Miles from Alcatraz/
    Flight from Glory '43
Tomorrow at Seven '33

Colleen Morris
Crossing the Line '90
Prehysteria '93

Dorothy Morris
Club Havana '46

Frances Morris
Boss Cowboy '35

Garrett Morris
The Anderson Tapes '71
Best of Chevy Chase '87
Best of Gilda Radner '89
Best of John Belushi '85
Cooley High '75
Husbands, Wives, Money, and
    Murder '86
Motorama '91
Severed Ties '92
The Stuff '85
The Underachievers '88

Glenn Morris
Tarzan's Revenge '38

Greg Morris
Vegas '78

Haviland Morris
For Love or Money '88
Love or Money? '88
Sixteen Candles '84
Who's That Girl? '87

Howard Morris
End of the Line '88
High Anxiety '77
History of the World: Part 1
    '81
Life Stinks '91
Munster's Revenge '81
The Nutty Professor '63
Portrait of a Showgirl '82
Splash '84

Jane Morris
Frankie and Johnny '91

Jeff Morris
Payday '72

Jim Morris
Rap Master Ronnie '88

John Morris
Beyond Innocence '87

Judy Morris
Best Enemies '86
Between Wars '74

Cass '78
In Search of Anna '79
Phar Lap '84
Plumber '79
Razorback '84

Kirk Morris
Devil of the Desert Against the
    Son of Hercules '62
Maciste in Hell '60
Terror of the Steppes '64
Triumph of the Son of
    Hercules '63
The Witch's Curse '62

Lana Morris
The Gay Lady '49

Marianne Morris
Vampyres '74

Mary Morris
Pimpernel Smith '42
Train of Events '49

Mercury Morris
The Black Six '74

Robert Morris
One Deadly Owner '74

Wayne Morris
The Bushwackers '52
Kid Galahad '37
Paths of Glory '57
Plunder Road '57

E.G. Morrison
The Last Chance '45

Ernie Morrison
Return of Our Gang '25

Kenny Morrison
The NeverEnding Story 2:
    Next Chapter '91
The Quick and the Dead '87

Sammy Morrison
Flying Wild '41
Follow the Leader '44
Ghosts on the Loose '43
Let's Get Tough '42
'Neath Brooklyn Bridge '42
Spooks Run Wild '41

Shelly Morrison
Castle of Evil '66
Devil Times Five '74

Steven Morrison
Last House on Dead End
    Street '77

Tom Morrison
Rocky 5 '90

Van Morrison
The Last Waltz '78

Billy Morrissette
Severed Ties '92

Eamon Morrissey
Eat the Peach '86

Nani Morrissey
The Mermaids of Tiburon '62

Bruce Morrow
Dirty Dancing '87

Doretta Morrow
Because You're Mine '52

Jeff Morrow
The Giant Claw '57
Hour of Decision '57
Kronos '57
Octaman '71
The Robe '53
The Story of Ruth '60
This Island Earth '55

Jo Morrow
Dr. Death, Seeker of Souls '73
13 Ghosts '60
The Three Worlds of Gulliver
    '59

Patricia Morrow
Surf Party '64

Rob Morrow
Private Resort '84

Scotty Morrow
The Cosmic Man '59

Susan Morrow
Cat Women of the Moon '53

Vic Morrow
The Adventures of Tom
    Sawyer '73
B.A.D. Cats '80
The Bad News Bears '76
Blackboard Jungle '55
Curse of the Black Widow '77
Death Stalk '74
Dirty Mary Crazy Larry '74
The Evictors '79
Express to Terror '79
Funeral for an Assassin '77
The Glass House '72
God's Little Acre '58
Humanoids from the Deep '80
King Creole '58
Men in War '57
1990: The Bronx Warriors '83
The Seekers '79
The Treasure of Matecumbe
    '76
Twilight Zone: The Movie '83
Wanted: Babysitter '75
Wild & Wooly '78

Barry Morse
Asylum '72
Destination Moonbase Alpha
    '75
Glory! Glory! '90
Love at First Sight '76
The Martian Chronicles: Part 2
    '79
The Martian Chronicles: Part 3
    '79
No Trace '50
Power Play '81
Sadat '83
Space: 1999—Alien Attack
    '79
A Tale of Two Cities '80
Welcome to Blood City '77
Whoops Apocalypse '83

David Morse
The Brotherhood of the Rose
    '89
Dead Ahead: The Exxon
    Valdez Disaster '92
Desperate Hours '90
The Indian Runner '91
Inside Moves '80
Prototype '83
Shattered Vows '84

Helen Morse
Agatha '79
Caddie '81
Far East '85
Iris '83
Picnic at Hanging Rock '75
A Town Like Alice '85

Natalie Morse
The Little Match Girl '87

Robert Morse
The Boatniks '70
Cannon Movie Tales: The
    Emperor's New Clothes '89
A Guide for the Married Man
    '67

**How to Succeed in Business
    without Really Trying '67**
The Loved One '65
The Matchmaker '58
Oh Dad, Poor Dad (Momma's
    Hung You in the Closet &
    I'm Feeling So Sad) '67
That's Singing: The Best of
    Broadway '84
Where Were You When the
    Lights Went Out? '68
Wild Palms '93

Robin Morse
Rock All Night '57

Terry Morse
Fog Island '45

Glen Morshower
Drive-In '76
84 Charlie Mopic '89

Clara Mortensen
Pin Down Girls '51

Viggo Mortensen
Boiling Point '93
The Indian Runner '91
Prison '88
The Reflecting Skin '91
Ruby Cairo '92
Salvation! '87

Jane Mortifee
My American Cousin '85

Janne Mortil
Nightmare at Bittercreek '91

Caroline Mortimer
The Death of Adolf Hitler '84

Clive Morton
A Matter of WHO '62
The Moonraker '58

Gregory Morton
The Adultress '77

Joe Morton
Alone in the Neon Jungle '87
The Brother from Another
    Planet '84
City of Hope '91
Crossroads '86
Forever Young '92
Legacy of Lies '92
Of Mice and Men '92
Tap '89
Terminator 2: Judgment Day
    '91
Trouble in Mind '86

Phil Morton
Monster a Go-Go! '65

Randy Morton
Dirkham Detective Agency '83

Rocky Morton
Max Headroom, the Original
    Story '86

Tom Morton
Main Street to Broadway '53

Walter Morton
The Wishing Ring '14

Jonas Moscartolo
Ernest Scared Stupid '91

Gastone Moschin
The Conformist '71
A Joke of Destiny, Lying in
    Wait Around the Corner
    Like a Bandit '84
Mr. Superinvisible '73

Maurice Moscovich
The Great Commandment '41

David Moscow
Big '88
Newsies '92

Bill Moseley
Crash and Burn '90
Fair Game '89
Osa '85
Silent Night, Deadly Night 3:
    Better Watch Out! '89

Page Moseley
Edge of the Axe '89

Sonia Moser
Legend of the Lost '57

David Moses
Daring Dobermans '73
Scared to Death '80

Ethel Moses
Birth Right '39

Harry Moses
Sweater Girls '78
The Van '77

Lucia Lynn Moses
Scar of Shame '27

Marian Moses
Buona Sera, Mrs. Campbell
    '68
Dead Heat on a Merry-Go-
    Round '66

Mark Moses
Dead Men Don't Die '91
Hollywood Heartbreak '89
The Tracker '88

Rick Moses
Avalanche '78

William R. Moses
Alien from L.A. '87
Mystic Pizza '88

Odeardo Mosini
The Last Chance '45

Ivan Mosjoukine
Early Russian Cinema, Vol. 5:
    Chardynin's Pushkin '13
Early Russian Cinema, Vol.
    10: The End of an Era '17

Roger E. Mosley
Attica '80
Darktown Strutters '74
The Greatest '77
I Know Why the Caged Bird
    Sings '79
The Jericho Mile '79
Mack '73
Pray TV '80
The River Niger '76
Steel '80
Unlawful Entry '92

Arnold Moss
The Fool Killer '65
The Loves of Carmen '48
Reign of Terror '49
The 27 Day '57
Viva Zapata! '52

Bertha Moss
Invasion of the Vampires '61

George Moss
Riff Raff '92

Ron Moss
Hard Ticket to Hawaii '87
Hearts & Armour '83

Stewart Moss
The Bat People '74
Dr. Death, Seeker of Souls '73

Warwick Moss
Kiss the Night '87

Donny Most
Huckleberry Finn '75

Josh Mostel
Almost You '85
Animal Behavior '89
City Slickers '91
Compromising Positions '85
Deadly Hero '75
Harry and Tonto '74
Jesus Christ, Superstar '73
The King of Marvin Gardens '72
The Money Pit '86
Radio Days '87
Sophie's Choice '82
Star 80 '83
Stoogemania '85
Windy City '84

Zero Mostel
DuBarry Was a Lady '43
The Enforcer '51
Foreplay '75
The Front '76
A Funny Thing Happened on the Way to the Forum '66
The Hot Rock '70
Journey into Fear '74
Marco '73
Master Mind '73
Once Upon a Scoundrel '73
Panic in the Streets '50
The Producers '68
Sirocco '51

Lloyd B. Mote
Night Terror '89

Collin Mothupi
Cheetah '89

Motley Crue
Incident at Channel Q '86

Zeze Motta
Quilombo '84

Antoine John Mottet
The Executioner, Part 2: Frozen Scream '84

Judy Motulsky
Slithis '78

Catherine Mouchet
Therese '86

Prentiss Moulden
Hospital of Terror '78

John Moulder-Brown
Deep End '70
First Love '70
Killing Heat '84
King, Queen, Knave '74
Rumpelstiltskin '86
Vampire Circus '71

Jean-Paul Moulinot
The Fire Within '64

Buck Moulton
Ghost Valley '32

Charles Moulton
The Baker's Wife '33

Katherine Mousseau
In Trouble '67

Irina Movila
Subspecies '91

Lisbeth Movin
Day of Wrath '43

Movita
Panic in Echo Park '77
Rose of Rio Grande '38

Tower of Terror '42
Wolf Call '39

Alan Mowbray
Abbott and Costello Meet the Killer, Boris Karloff '49
The Girl from Missouri '34
I Wake Up Screaming '41
In Person '35
It Happened in New Orleans '36
The King and I '56
The Lovable Cheat '49
The Man Who Knew Too Much '56
Mary of Scotland '36
Music in My Heart '40
My Dear Secretary '49
Panama Hattie '42
The Phantom of 42nd Street '45
The Prince of Thieves '48
So This is Washington '43
Stand-In '37
A Study in Scarlet '33
That Hamilton Woman '41
That Uncertain Feeling '41
Topper Takes a Trip '39
The Villain Still Pursued Her '41
Vogues of 1938 '37
Way Down South '39

Jack Mower
Mystery Squadron '33
Ships in the Night '28

Patrick Mower
The Bloodsuckers '70
Carry On England '76
Catch Me a Spy '71
Cry of the Banshee '70

John Mowod
Revenge of the Living Zombies '88

John Llewellyn Moxey
No Place to Hide '81

Wood Moy
Chan is Missing '82

Pat Moya
In the Soup '92

Allan Moyle
Outrageous! '77

Rodolpho Moyos
The Brave One '56

Sandra Mozar
Terror Beach '80s

Sandra Mozarowsky
Night of the Death Cult '75

George Mozart
Song of Freedom '38

Mr. Stubbs
Toby Tyler '59

Mr. Wizard
Starlight Hotel '90

Chen Mu-Chuan
Monkey Kung Fu '80s

Carlo Mucari
Obsession: A Taste for Fear '89

David Mucci
Unforgiven '92

Richard Much
Inn on the River '62

Leonard Mudie
British Intelligence '40

Cookie Mueller
Female Trouble '75

Julia Mueller
The Unbelievable Truth '90

Maureen Mueller
In a Shallow Grave '88

Armin Mueller-Stahl
Angry Harvest '85
Avalon '90
Colonel Redl '84
Forget Mozart '85
Lethal Obsession '87
A Love in Germany '84
Midnight Cop '88
Music Box '89
Night on Earth '91
The Power of One '92

Lola Muethel
From the Life of the Marionettes '80

Amanda Muggleton
Queen of the Road '84

Alfonso Muguia
Furia Pasional

Nino Muhlach
The Boy God '86

Anita Mui
Rouge '87

David Muir
Dr. Hackenstein '88

Donald Muir
Ninja's Extreme Weapons '90

Esther Muir
Racing Luck '35

Gavin Muir
Abbott & Costello Meet the Invisible Man '51
House of Fear '45
Mary of Scotland '36
Night Tide '63
Sherlock Holmes Faces Death '43

Geraldine Muir
Hope and Glory '87

Barbara Mujica
Mayalunta '86

Karl Muka
Mad Mission 3 '84

Romesh Mukerji
Distant Thunder '73

Diana Muldaur
Beyond Reason '77
Master Ninja 3 '83
McQ '74
The Other '72
Planet Earth '74
Return of Frank Cannon '80

Deborah Muldowney
Cellar Dweller '87

Gary Muledeer
Diary of a Young Comic '79

Matt Mulern
Biloxi Blues '88

Nancy Mulford
Skeleton Coast '89

Kate Mulgrew
Lovespell '81
The Manions of America '81
Remo Williams: The Adventure Begins '85

Roots: The Gift '88
Round Numbers '91
A Stranger is Watching '82
Throw Momma from the Train '87
A Time for Miracles '80
The Word '78

Jack Mulhall
Burn 'Em Up Barnes '34
The Clutching Hand '36
Custer's Last Stand '36
Dawn Express '42
Desperate Cargo '41
A Face in the Fog '36
Hell's Headquarters '32
I Killed That Man '42
Mr. Wise Guy '42
Murder on the High Seas '32
Mystery Squadron '33
'Neath Canadian Skies '46
North of the Border '46
Outlaws of Sonora '38
Skull & Crown '38

Edward Mulhare
Hill 24 Doesn't Answer '55
Megaforce '82
Our Man Flint '66
Von Ryan's Express '65

Michael Mulheren
Johnny Suede '92

Mark Mulholland
No Surrender '86

Chris Mulkey
Dangerous Company '88
Deadbolt '92
Heartbreak Hotel '88
In Dangerous Company '88
K-9000 '89
Patti Rocks '88
Roe vs. Wade '89
The Silencer '92
Tricks of the Trade '88
Write to Kill '91

Randy Mulkey
Natas...The Reflection '83

Martin Mull
Bad Manners '84
The Boss' Wife '86
Clue '85
Cutting Class '89
Dance with Death '91
Far Out Man '89
Flicks '85
FM '78
The History of White People in America '85
The History of White People in America: Vol. 2 '85
Home is Where the Hart is '88
Lots of Luck '85
Miracle Beach '92
Mr. Mom '83
My Bodyguard '80
O.C. and Stiggs '87
Pecos Bill '86
The Player '92
Portrait of a White Marriage '88
Rented Lips '88
Serial '80
Ski Patrol '89
Take This Job & Shove It '81
Think Big '90

Jack Mullaney
George! '70
The Honeymoon Machine '61
Spinout '66
Tickle Me '65

Greg Mullavey
Body Count '87

Chrome Hearts '70
Deadly Conspiracy '91
Husbands, Wives, Money, and Murder '86
I Dismember Mama '74
The Love Machine '71

Patty Mullen
Doom Asylum '88
Frankenhooker '90

Harrison Muller
The Final Executioner '83
Miami Cops '89
She '83
2020 Texas Gladiators '85
Violent Breed '83

Katrin Muller
Perfumed Nightmare '89

Paul Muller
The Black Devils of Kali '55
The Devil's Commandment '56
Fangs of the Living Dead '68
Four Ways Out '57
Goliath and the Sins of Babylon '64
Lady Frankenstein '72
Naked Warriors '73
Nightmare Castle '65
Two Nights with Cleopatra '54
Virgin Among the Living Dead '71

Peter Muller
25 Fireman's Street '73

Richard Mulligan
Babes in Toyland '86
Big Bus '76
Doin' Time '85
A Fine Mess '86
The Group '66
The Heavenly Kid '85
The Hideaways '73
Little Big Man '70
Meatballs 2 '84
Micki & Maude '84
Poker Alice '87
Pueblo Affair '73
Scavenger Hunt '79
S.O.B. '81
Teachers '84

Rod Mullinar
Breakfast in Paris '81
Echoes of Paradise '86
Patrick '78

Michael Mullins
Pom Pom Girls '76

Dermot Mulroney
Bright Angel '91
Career Opportunities '91
Longtime Companion '90
Point of No Return '93
Samantha '92
Staying Together '89
Sunset '88
Survival Quest '89
The Thing Called Love '93
Where the Day Takes You '92
Young Guns '88

Kieran Mulroney
Career Opportunities '91
Nowhere to Run '88

Billy Mumy
Bless the Beasts and Children '71
Dear Brigitte '65
Sammy, the Way-Out Seal '62
Twilight Zone: The Movie '83

Mary Munday
Pressure Point '62

George Murray
Love at First Sight '76

Guillermo Murray
El Cuarto Chino '71
World of the Vampires '60

James Murray
Baby Face '33
The Crowd '28
High Gear '33
Skull & Crown '38

Jan Murray
Which Way to the Front? '70

Joel Murray
Elvis Stories '89

John Murray
Moving Violations '85

Ken Murray
Follow Me, Boys! '66
Hollywood My Hometown
The Marshal's Daughter '53

Mae Murray
A Mormon Maid '17

Stephen Murray
Alice in Wonderland '50
Four Sided Triangle '53

Tom Murray
The Gold Rush '25
Stuckey's Last Stand '78

Milton Raphiel Murrill
Mutator '90

Christina Murrull
The Kid with the 200 I.Q. '83

Kate Murtagh
Doctor Detroit '83

Lionel Murton
Carry On Admiral '57
Meet the Navy '46

Christopher Murvey
Maximum Overdrive '86

Tony Musante
The Bird with the Crystal
   Plumage '70
Breaking Up Is Hard to Do '79
Collector's Item '89
The Detective '68
Fatal Chase '77
The Grissom Gang '71
High Ice '80
The Incident '67
The Pope of Greenwich
   Village '84

Clarence Muse
The Black Stallion '79
Broken Strings '40
A Dream for Christmas '73
Prison Train '38
That Gang of Mine '40
Way Down South '39

Pip Mushin
Strictly Ballroom '92

Al Music
California Girls '84

Lorenzo Music
Here Comes Garfield '90

Bernard Musson
Sweet Young Thing

Minor Mustain
SnakeEater 3: His Law '92

Ornella Muti
Appassionata '74
Casanova '87

Flash Gordon '80
Hitchhiker 3 '87
Leonor '75
Life is Beautiful '79
Once Upon a Crime '92
Oscar '91
Summer Affair '79
Swann in Love '84
Tales of Ordinary Madness
   '83
The Violation of Laura '72

Klaus Mutter
Clash of the Ninja '86
Thundering Ninja '80s

Roger Mutton
The Girl on a Motorcycle '68

Franz Muxeneder
All the Way Down '87
Faraway Fantasy '87
Has Anyone Seen My Pants?

Melvin Muza
Street Hitz '92

Paul Muzzcat
Gator Bait 2: Cajun Justice
   '88

Linda Mvusi
A World Apart '88

Bruce Myers
The Mahabharata '89

Carmel Myers
Beau Brummel '24
Ben-Hur '26
Chinatown After Dark '31
Pleasure '31

Diwaldo Myers
Savages from Hell '68

Harry Myers
City Lights '31
Convicted '32
The Marriage Circle '24
The Savage Girl '32

Kim Myers
A Nightmare on Elm Street 2:
   Freddy's Revenge '85

Mike Myers
So I Married an Axe Murderer
   '93
Wayne's World '92

Susan Myers
Desperate Women '78
The Spell '77

Jessica Myerson
A Session with the Committee
   '69

Billy Myles
Sweet Beat '62

Bruce Myles
A Cry in the Dark '88
Sweet Talker '91

Ray Myles
Blood Orgy of the She-Devils
   '74

John Mylong
The Mermaids of Tiburon '62

Jim Nabors
The Best Little Whorehouse in
   Texas '82
Cannonball Run II '84
Stroker Ace '83

Troy Nabors
Apache Blood '75

Mia Nadasi
Visitor from the Grave '81

Mikola Nademsy
Earth '30
Zvenigora '28

George Nader
Away All Boats '56
Beyond Atlantis '73
Carnival Story '54
The House of 1000 Dolls '67
The Human Duplicators '64
Robot Monster '53
Sins of Jezebel '54

Michael Nader
The Finishing Touch '92
The Flash '90
Lady Mobster '88
Nick Knight '80s

Aldo Nadi
Tournament '29

Lycia Naff
Chopper Chicks in
   Zombietown '91

Hiroyuki Nagaes
The Insect Woman '63

Mieko Nagai
Warning from Space '56

Masatoshi Nagase
Mystery Train '89

Eiko Nagashima
Human Beasts '80

Anne Nagel
Dawn Express '42
Don Winslow of the Navy '43
Gang Bullets '38
The Green Hornet '40
The Mad Monster '42
The Spirit of West Point '47
Three Legionnaires '37
Winners of the West '40

Conrad Nagel
Ann Vickers '33
The Divorcee '30
Dubarry '30
The Kiss '29
The Michigan Kid '28
The Mysterious Lady '28
Woman in Brown '48
Yellow Cargo '36

Alan Naggar
Cleo/Leo '89
New York's Finest '87

Mayumi Nagisa
Tattooed Hit Man '76

Austin Nagler
Ernest Scared Stupid '91

Morgan Nagler
Bird '88

Nickolas Nagurney
Fun Down There '88

Christina Nagy
Formula for a Murder '85

Ajay Naidu
Touch and Go '86
Where the River Runs Black
   '86

Leela Naidu
The Householder '63

Jimmy Nail
Crusoe '89
Morons from Outer Space '85

Joanne Nail
Switchblade Sisters '75
The Visitor '80

Johnny Nainam
King Boxers '80

Mira Nair
Mississippi Masala '92

J. Carroll Naish
Across the Wide Missouri '51
The Beast with Five Fingers
   '46
Beau Geste '39
Behind the Rising Sun '43
Beneath the 12-Mile Reef '53
Black Fury '35
The Black Hand '50
Blood and Sand '41
Captain Blood '35
The Charge of the Light
   Brigade '36
Clash by Night '52
Confidential '35
The Corsican Brothers '42
The Denver & Rio Grande '51
Down Argentine Way '40
Dracula vs. Frankenstein '71
Dragon Seed '44
Fighter Attack '53
Force of Impulse '60
The Fugitive '48
Hit the Deck '55
House of Frankenstein '44
Humoresque '46
The Last Command '55
The Monster Maker '44
Mystery Squadron '33
Rage at Dawn '55
Rio Grande '50
The Royal Bed '31
Sahara '43
Sea Racketeers '37
The Southerner '45
That Midnight Kiss '49
This Could Be the Night '57
The Toast of New Orleans '50
Waterfront '44
The World Gone Mad '33

Laurence Naismith
Amazing Mr. Blunden '72
The Bushbaby '70
Carrington, V.C. '54
Diamonds are Forever '71
Greyfriars Bobby '61
Jason and the Argonauts '63
The Man Who Never Was '55
Mission: Monte Carlo '75
A Night to Remember '58
The Prince and the Pauper '62
Quest for Love '71
Robbery Under Arms '57
Room to Let '49
Sink the Bismarck '60
Third Man on the Mountain
   '59
Train of Events '49
The Valley of Gwangi '69
Village of the Damned '60
The World of Suzie Wong '60

Rick Najera
Red Surf '90

Kathy Najimy
Hocus Pocus '93
Sister Act '92
Soapdish '91

Machiko Naka
Godzilla's Revenge '69

Tatsuya Nakadai
Face of Another '66
High & Low '62
The Human Condition: A
   Soldier's Prayer '61
The Human Condition: No
   Greater Love '58

The Human Condition: Road
   to Eternity '59
Hunter in the Dark '80
Kagemusha '80
Kojiro '67
Phoenix '78
Ran '85
Sanjuro '62
Sword of Doom '67
Today We Kill, Tomorrow We
   Die '71
When a Woman Ascends the
   Stairs '60
The Wolves '82

Anna Nakagawa
The Silk Road '92

Ken Nakagawa
Living on Tokyo Time '87

Roger Nakagawa
Escapade in Japan '57

Aio Nakajima
In the Realm of the Senses
   '76

Atsuo Nakamura
The Highest Honor '84

Ganjiro Nakamura
Drifting Weeds '59
The Lower Depths '57
Odd Obsession '60

Kichiemon Nakamura
Double Suicide '69

Kinnosuke Nakamura
Swords of Death '71

Ryuzaburo Nakamura
Traitors of the Blue Castle '58

Satoshi Nakamura
The Manster '59

Tadao Nakamura
The Secret of the Telegian '61

Takeya Nakamura
A Taxing Woman Returns '88

Tamao Nakamura
The Human Condition: A
   Soldier's Prayer '61

Yoshiko Nakana
Love and Faith '78

Lane Nakano
Go for Broke! '51

Miyuki Nakano
Summer Vacation: 1999 '87

Rodion Nakhapetov
A Slave of Love '78

Daniel Nalbach
The Gig '85

Reggie Nalder
The Day and the Hour '63
Dracula Sucks '79
Mark of the Devil '69
Mark of the Devil 2 '72
Salem's Lot '79
Zoltan...Hound of Dracula '77

Nita Naldi
Blood and Sand '22
Cobra '25
Dr. Jekyll and Mr. Hyde '20

James Nam
Jaws of the Dragon '76

Kenny Nam
Jaws of the Dragon '76

**Corin "Corky"
Nemec**
Solar Crisis '92

Jiri Nemec
The Report on the Party and
the Guests '66

Henry Nemo
The Plot Against Harry '69

Stacey Nemour
Computer Beach Party '88

Tien Ner
The Golden Triangle '80

Nadia Neri
Emmanuelle's Daughter '79

**Rosalba (Sara Bay)
Neri**
The Castle of Fu Manchu '68
Conquest of Mycene '63
The Seducers '70
Slaughter Hotel '71

Tommaso Neri
The Battle of Algiers '66

David Nerman
The Scorpio Factor '90

Franco Nero
Battle of Neretva '69
The Bible...In the Beginning
'66
Blood Brothers '74
Camelot '67
Challenge to White Fang '86
Confessions of a Police
Captain '72
Day of the Cobra '84
Devil's Crude '71
Die Hard 2: Die Harder '90
Django '68
Enter the Ninja '81
Falcon '74
Fifth Day of Peace '72
Force 10 from Navarone '78
The Girl '86
High Crime '73
Last Four Days '77
Legend of Valentino '75
Magdalene '88
The Man with Bogart's Face
'80
Querelle '83
Redneck '73
Ring of Death '72
The Salamander '82
Sardinia Kidnapped '75
Shark Hunter '84
Spaghetti Western '69
Street Law '79
Submission '77
Sweet Country '87
Tristana '70
21 Hours at Munich '76
The Virgin and the Gypsy '70
Wagner: The Movie '85
Wild, Wild Planet '65
Windmills of the Gods '88
Young Catherine '91

Toni Nero
No Dead Heroes '87
Silent Night, Deadly Night '84

Cathleen Nesbitt
An Affair to Remember '57
Desiree '54
Man of Evil '48
Men of Two Worlds '46
Nicholas Nickleby '46
The Passing of the Third Floor
Back '36
Promise Her Anything '66
Separate Tables '58

Derren Nesbitt
Funny Money '82
Horrors of Burke & Hare '71

Lynn Nesbitt
Bullseye! '90

Vickie Nesbitt
The Hanging Woman '72

Michael Nesmith
Doctor Duck's Super Secret
All-Purpose Sauce '85
Head '68

Helen Ness
Northern Lights '79

Ray Ness
Northern Lights '79

Peter Nestler
The Magic Fountain '61

Jinpachi Nesu
Ran '85

Hugo Netsers
Dear Boys '80

John Nettelton
And Soon the Darkness '70

Lois Nettleton
The Bamboo Saucer '68
The Best Little Whorehouse in
Texas '82
Brass '85
Butterfly '82
Deadly Blessing '81
Manhunt for Claude Dallas '86
Period of Adjustment '62
Soggy Bottom U.S.A. '84

Jack Neubeck
Invasion of the Blood Farmers
'72

Jenny Neumann
Delos Adventure '86
Hell Night '81
Mistress of the Apes '79
Stage Fright '83
Swim Team '79

John Neumeier
The Lady of the Camellias '87

Bebe Neuwirth
Bugsy '91
Green Card '90
Wild Palms '93

Peter Nevargic
Lady Beware '87

Suzanne Neve
Portrait of a Lady '67

Aaron Neville
Zandalee '91

John Neville
The Adventures of Baron
Munchausen '89
Billy Budd '62
A Study in Terror '66
The Unearthly Stranger '64

Robyn Nevin
Careful, He Might Hear You
'84
Fourth Wish '75
The Irishman '78

Claudette Nevins
Child of Darkness, Child of
Light '91
The Mask '61
The Possessed '77
Sleeping with the Enemy '91
Take Your Best Shot '82

Derek Newark
Bellman and True '88
The Offence '73

George Newbern
Adventures in Babysitting '87
Doppelganger: The Evil Within
'90
Father of the Bride '91
It Takes Two '88
Paramedics '88

**Phineas Newborn,
III**
Breakin' '84

Anthony Newcastle
Captive Planet '78
Metallica '85

Jamie Newcomb
Lone Wolf '88

Billy Newell
Bulldog Edition '36

Carol Irene Newell
The Alpha Incident '76

**Cheri Cameron
Newell**
Sunset Strip '85

Patrick Newell
The Unearthly Stranger '64

William Newell
Doctor Satan's Robot '40
The Invisible Killer '40
The Mandarin Mystery '37

Sam Newfield
Ghost Patrol '36

Bob Newhart
Catch-22 '70
Cold Turkey '71
First Family '80
Hell is for Heroes '62
Little Miss Marker '80
Marathon '80
On a Clear Day You Can See
Forever '70
The Rescuers Down Under
'90
Thursday's Game '74

Sarah Newhouse
The House on Tombstone Hill
'92

Sheila Newhouse
Lost '83

James Newill
Boss of Rawhide '44
Danger Ahead '40
Fighting Mad '39
Fighting Valley '43
The Great American
Broadcast '41
Murder on the Yukon '40
Outlaw Roundup '44
Rangers Take Over '43
Renfrew of the Royal
Mounted '37
Renfrew on the Great White
Trail '37
Sky Bandits '40
Yukon Flight '40

Mary Newland
The Silent Passenger '35

Anthony Newlands
Circus of Fear '67
Scream and Scream Again '70

Anthony Newley
Above Us the Waves '56
Blade in Hong Kong '85

Boris and Natasha: The Movie
'92
Doctor Doolittle '67
Fire Down Below '57
The Garbage Pail Kids Movie
'87
Let's Get Married '63
Little Ballerina '47
The Old Curiosity Shop '75
Oliver Twist '48
Outrage! '86
Stagecoach '86

A.R. Newman
Visions '90

Barry Newman
Amy '81
City on Fire '78
Deadline '81
Fatal Vision '84
Having It All '82
The Salzburg Connection '72
Vanishing Point '71

James Newman
Silent Night, Deadly Night 2
'87

Laraine Newman
Best of Chevy Chase '87
Best of Dan Aykroyd '86
Best of Gilda Radner '89
Best of John Belushi '85
Coneheads '93
Her Life as a Man '83
Invaders from Mars '86
Mr. Mike's Mondo Video '79
Perfect '85
Problem Child 2 '91
Tunnelvision '76
Wholly Moses! '80

Lissy Newman
See How She Runs '78

Nanette Newman
Long Ago Tomorrow '71
The Madwoman of Chaillot
'69
The Wrong Arm of the Law
'63

Paul Newman
Absence of Malice '81
Bang the Drum Slowly '56
Blaze '89
Buffalo Bill & the Indians '76
Butch Cassidy and the
Sundance Kid '69
Cat on a Hot Tin Roof '58
The Color of Money '86
Cool Hand Luke '67
The Drowning Pool '75
Exodus '60
Fat Man and Little Boy '89
Fort Apache, the Bronx '81
From the Terrace '60
Harper '66
Harry & Son '84
Hombre '67
Hud '63
The Hustler '61
The Left-Handed Gun '58
Life & Times of Judge Roy
Bean '72
The Long, Hot Summer '58
Mackintosh Man '73
Mr. & Mrs. Bridge '91
A New Kind of Love '63
Paris Blues '61
Pocket Money '72
The Prize '63
Quintet '79
The Secret War of Harry Frigg
'68
Silent Movie '76
The Silver Chalice '54
Slap Shot '77

Somebody Up There Likes Me
'56
Sometimes a Great Notion '71
The Sting '73
Sweet Bird of Youth '62
Torn Curtain '66
The Towering Inferno '74
Until They Sail '57
The Verdict '82
When Time Ran Out '80
Winning '69
The Young Philadelphians '59

Phyllis Newman
Follies in Concert '85
Picnic '55
A Secret Space '88

Randy Newman
Three Amigos '86

Scott Newman
The Great Waldo Pepper '75

Stephen D. Newman
Sophie's Choice '82
Yuri Nosenko, KGB '86

**Susan Kendall
Newman**
I Wanna Hold Your Hand '78

Julie Newmar
Deep Space '87
Ecstasy '84
Evils of the Night '85
For Love or Money '63
Hysterical '83
Li'l Abner '59
MacKenna's Gold '69
Nudity Required '90
Robo-Chic '89
Seven Brides for Seven
Brothers '54
Streetwalkin' '85
Terraces '77

Carmen Newsome
Birth Right '39
Lying Lips '39

Bart Newton
Fatty Finn '84

**John Haymes
Newton**
Alive '93
Desert Kickboxer '92

Olivia Newton-John
Grease '78
Two of a Kind '83
Xanadu '80

Margie Newton
The Bronx Executioner '86

**Margit Evelyn
Newton**
The Last Hunter '80
Night of the Zombies '83

Robert Newton
Androcles and the Lion '52
Around the World in 80 Days
'56
Beachcomber '38
Blackbeard the Pirate '52
The Desert Rats '53
Epic That Never Was '65
Henry V '44
The Hidden Room '49
Jamaica Inn '39
Long John Silver '53
Odd Man Out '47
Oliver Twist '48
This Happy Breed '47
Tom Brown's School Days '51
Treasure Island '50

The Night Stalker: Two Tales
of Terror '74
On a Clear Day You Can See
Forever '70
Psycho '60
The Rise and Fall of Legs
Diamond '60
The Sand Pebbles '66
Tony Rome '67
West Side Story '61

Vivien Oakland
Roaring Speedboats '37

Wheeler Oakman
Aces and Eights '36
The Broken Mask '28
Death from a Distance '36
Frontier Days '34
Ghost Patrol '36
In Old Santa Fe '34
The Man from Gun Town '36
Meet the Mob '42
Outside the Law '21
Peck's Bad Boy '21
Roaring Guns '36
Slaves in Bondage '37
Song of the Trail '36
The Spoilers '14
Teenage '44
Texas Cyclone '32
Two-Fisted Law '32
Wolf Call '39

Simon Oates
Doomwatch '72
Terronauts '67
The Terronauts '67

Warren Oates
And Baby Makes Six '79
Badlands '74
The Blue and the Grey '85
Blue Thunder '83
The Border '82
Bring Me the Head of Alfredo
Garcia '74
Brink's Job '78
Cockfighter '74
Crooks & Coronets '69
Dillinger '73
Dixie Dynamite '76
Drum '76
East of Eden '80
Gunfire '78
Hired Hand '71
In the Heat of the Night '67
My Old Man '79
1941 '79
92 in the Shade '76
Prime Time '80
Race with the Devil '75
Return of the Seven '66
Ride the High Country '62
The Shooting '66
Sleeping Dogs '82
Stripes '81
There was a Crooked Man '70
The Thief Who Came to
Dinner '73
Tom Sawyer '73
Tough Enough '87
The White Dawn '75
The Wild Bunch '69

Patti Oatman
Slipstream '72

Dan O'Bannon
Dark Star '74

Philip Ober
Come Back, Little Sheba '52
Escapade in Japan '57
From Here to Eternity '53
The Mating Game '59
Never a Dull Moment '50

Elan Oberon
Farewell to the King '89

Merle Oberon
Beloved Enemy '36
Berlin Express '48
Broken Melody '34
The Cowboy and the Lady '38
Dark Waters '44
Deep in My Heart '54
Desiree '54
The Divorce of Lady X '38
Epic That Never Was '65
Forever and a Day '43
Hotel '67
Interval '73
The Lion Has Wings '40
The Lodger '44
Lydia '41
The Oscar '66
Private Life of Don Juan '34
The Private Life of Henry VIII
'33
The Scarlet Pimpernel '34
A Song to Remember '45
Stage Door Canteen '43
That Uncertain Feeling '41
These Three '36
Wedding Rehearsal '32
Wuthering Heights '39

Anna Obregon
Bolero '84
Car Crash
Treasure of the Four Crowns
'82

Rodrigo Obregon
Hard Hunted '92
Savage Beach '89
Tides of War '90

Hugh O'Brian
Africa Texas Style '67
Broken Lance '54
Cruise into Terror '78
Doin' Time on Planet Earth '88
Fantasy Island '76
In Harm's Way '65
Little Big Horn '51
Love has Many Faces '65
Murder on Flight 502 '75
Probe '72
Return of Jesse James '50
Rocketship X-M '50
The Seekers '79
The Shootist '76
There's No Business Like
Show Business '54
Twins '88
Vengeance Valley '51
Wild Women '70

Seamus O'Brian
Bloodsucking Freaks '75

Austin O'Brien
Last Action Hero '93
Prehysteria '93

Clay O'Brien
One Little Indian '73

Dave O'Brien
Boss of Rawhide '44
Bowery at Midnight '42
Buzzy Rides the Range '40
Camp Double Feature '39
Danger Ahead '40
Daughter of the Tong '39
Dead or Alive '41
The Devil Bat '41
Enemy of the Law '45
Fighting Valley '43
Frontier Fugitives '45
Gangsters of the Frontier '44
King of the Stallions '42
Lightning Bill Crandall '37
Lion's Den '36

Marked for Murder '45
Murder on the Yukon '40
The Phantom of 42nd Street
'45
Rangers Take Over '43
Reefer Madness '38
Sky Bandits '40
Spooks Run Wild '41
That Gang of Mine '40
Three in the Saddle '45
Water Rustlers '39
Yukon Flight '40

Donald O'Brien
Doctor Butcher M.D. '80
The Master Killers '73
Quest for the Mighty Sword
'90
Trap Them & Kill Them '84

Edmond O'Brien
The Admiral Was a Lady '50
The Barefoot Contessa '54
The Bigamist '53
Birdman of Alcatraz '62
D-Day, the Sixth of June '56
The Denver & Rio Grande '51
D.O.A. '49
The Doomsday Flight '66
A Double Life '47
Dream No Evil '75
Fantastic Voyage '66
A Girl, a Guy and a Gob '41
The Girl Can't Help It '56
The Great Impostor '61
The Hitch-Hiker '53
The Hunchback of Notre
Dame '39
Jigsaw '71
Julius Caesar '53
The Last Voyage '60
The Longest Day '62
Lucky Luciano '74
The Man Who Shot Liberty
Valance '62
Moon Pilot '62
99 & 44/100 Dead '74
Pete Kelly's Blues '55
Rio Conchos '64
Seven Days in May '64
Stopover Tokyo '57
They Only Kill Their Masters
'72
Up Periscope '59
White Heat '49
The Wild Bunch '69

Edna O'Brien
Hard Way '80

Eugene O'Brien
Rebecca of Sunnybrook Farm
'17

Florence O'Brien
Double Deal '39

George O'Brien
Cheyenne Autumn '64
Cowboy Millionaire '35
Daniel Boone '34
Don Amigo/Stage to Chino
'40s
Dude Ranger '34
Gold Raiders '51
Legion of the Lawless '40
The Lone Star Ranger '39
Mystery Ranch '34
Painted Desert '31
Racketeers of the Range '39
Renegade Ranger/Scarlet
River '38
She Wore a Yellow Ribbon '49
Sunrise '27
Thunder Mountain '35
Windjammer '31

Jeanne O'Brien
Dirty Laundry '87

Jimmy O'Brien
Yes, Sir, Mr. Bones '51

Joan O'Brien
It Happened at the World's
Fair '63
Operation Petticoat '59
Samar '62

Kieran O'Brien
Bellman and True '88

Liam O'Brien
Spirit of '76 '91

Margaret O'Brien
Amy '81
The Canterville Ghost '44
Glory '56
Heller in Pink Tights '60
Jane Eyre '44
Journey for Margaret '42
Little Women '49
Meet Me in St. Louis '44
Our Vines Have Tender
Grapes '45
The Secret Garden '49
Thousands Cheer '43

Maria O'Brien
Escort Girls '74
In a Stranger's Hand '92
Promised a Miracle '88

Mary O'Brien
Battling Butler '26

Niall O'Brien
Lovespell '79

Pat O'Brien
Angels with Dirty Faces '38
Bombardier '43
Bombshell '33
Boy Meets Girl '38
The Boy with the Green Hair
'48
Bureau of Missing Persons
'33
Ceiling Zero '35
Consolation Marriage '31
Crack-Up '36
Devil Dogs of the Air '35
The Devil Thumbs a Ride/
Having Wonderful Crime
'47
Doomed Caravan '41
The End '78
Fighting Father Dunne '48
The Fighting 69th '40
Flirtation Walk '34
The Front Page '31
Having Wonderful Crime '45
Hawaiian Buckaroo '38
Hell's House '32
The Iron Major '43
Jubilee Trail '54
Knute Rockne: All American
'40
Last Hurrah '58
Marine Raiders '43
The Navy Comes Through '42
Ragtime '81
Riff-Raff '47
Scout's Honor '80
Slightly Honorable '40
Some Like It Hot '59
The World Gone Mad '33

Peter O'Brien
The Grand Duel '73
A Kink in the Picasso '90

Richard O'Brien
Robin Hood...The Legend:
The Time of the Wolf '85
The Rocky Horror Picture
Show '75
Shock Treatment '81

Tex O'Brien
Outlaw Roundup '44

**Timothy Eric
O'Brien**
Suburbia '83

Tom O'Brien
The Big Parade '25

Virginia O'Brien
Big Store '41
DuBarry Was a Lady '43
The Harvey Girls '46
Lady Be Good '41
Panama Hattie '42
Ship Ahoy '42
Thousands Cheer '43
Till the Clouds Roll By '46
Till the Clouds Roll By/A Star
Is Born '46
Two Girls and a Sailor '44

Jeffrey Obrow
The Power '80

Karyn O'Bryan
Private Resort '84

Melody O'Bryan
Melody in Love '78

Pat O'Bryan
976-EVIL '88
976-EVIL 2: The Astral Factor
'91
Relentless '89

Ric Ocasek
Made in Heaven '87

Andrea Occhipinti
A Blade in the Dark '83
Bolero '84
Conquest '83
Control '87
El Barbaro '84
Running Away '89

Kevin Och
Fun Down There '88

**Manuel Lopez
Ochoa**
Crossfire '67
El Tesoro de Chucho el Roto
'47
Los Tres Calaveras '64

Uwe Ochsenknecht
Fire, Ice and Dynamite '91
Men... '85

Arthur O'Connell
Anatomy of a Murder '59
Ben '72
Bus Stop '56
Fantastic Voyage '66
Follow That Dream '61
Gidget '59
The Great Impostor '61
The Hiding Place '75
Huckleberry Finn '74
Kissin' Cousins '64
The Last Valley '71
Law of the Jungle '42
The Man in the Gray Flannel
Suit '56
Man of the West '58
Misty '61
Monkey's Uncle '65
Open Secret '48
Operation Petticoat '59
Picnic '55
Pocketful of Miracles '61
Seven Faces of Dr. Lao '64
There was a Crooked Man '70
They Only Kill Their Masters
'72

Davie Orange
When Nature Calls '85

Alessio Orano
The Count of Monte Cristo '74

Jerry Orbach
Beauty and the Beast '91
Brewster's Millions '85
Broadway Bound '92
California Casanova '89
Crimes & Misdemeanors '89
Dead Women in Lingerie '90
Delirious '91
Delusion '91
Dirty Dancing '87
F/X '86
Foreplay '75
I Love N.Y. '87
Imagemaker '86
Last Exit to Brooklyn '90
Mr. Saturday Night '92
Out for Justice '91
Out on a Limb '87
Prince of the City '81
Someone to Watch Over Me '87
Straight Talk '92
Toy Soldiers '91
24 Hours in a Woman's Life '61
Underground Aces '80
Universal Soldier '92

Roy Orbison
Chuck Berry: Hail! Hail! Rock 'n' Roll '87
Fastest Guitar Alive '68
Roadie '80

Pierre Orcel
Marianela '70s

Murray Ord
Ghost Keeper '80

Orlando Ordaneta
Macho y Hembra '85

Beryl Orde
The Dummy Talks '43

Liane Ordeyne
Gangway '37

Cyril O'Reilly
Dance of the Damned '88
Navy SEALS '90
On Wings of Eagles '86
Porky's '82
Porky's 2: The Next Day '83
Purple Hearts '84

Liana Orfei
The Avenger '62
Casanova '70 '65
The Giant of Metropolis '61
Mill of the Stone Women '60
Nefertiti, Queen of the Nile '64
Pirate Warrior '64
Pirates of the Coast '61

Moira Orfei
Ursus in the Valley of the Lions '62

Cait O'Riordan
The Courier '88

William Orlamond
The Wind '28

Felice Orlandi
The Outside Man '73

Tony Orlando
Rosie: The Rosemary Clooney Story '82

Tom Ormeny
Agent on Ice '86

Julia Ormond
Stalin '92
Young Catherine '91

Tim Ormond
The Girl from Tobacco Row '66

Alan Ormsby
Children Shouldn't Play with Dead Things '72

Anya Ormsby
Children Shouldn't Play with Dead Things '72

Luigi Ornaghi
The Tree of Wooden Clogs '78

Babro Ornas
Brink of Life '57

Moon Orona
Salsa '88

Ed O'Ross
Another 48 Hrs. '90
The Hidden '87
Play Nice '92
Red Heat '88
Tailspin: Behind the Korean Airline Tragedy '89
Universal Soldier '92

Heather O'Rourke
Poltergeist '82
Poltergeist 2: The Other Side '86
Poltergeist 3 '88

Heidi O'Rourke
Funny Lady '75

Marina Orsini
Battle of the Worlds '61
Eddie and the Cruisers 2: Eddie Lives! '89

Umberto Orsini
Cesar & Rosalie '72
Emmanuelle, the Joys of a Woman '76
The Outside Man '73

Palito Ortega
Somos Novios '68

Dyana Ortelli
Alienator '89

Bruno Ortensi
Shoeshine '47

Frank Orth
The Great Rupert '50

Humberto Ortiz
Dollman '91

Joe Ortiz
Black Shampoo '76

Rossana Ortiz
Savage! '73

Kid Ory
The Benny Goodman Story '55

Jay O'Saunders
The Revolt of Mother '88

Andrew Osborn
Spaceways '53
Three Stops to Murder '53

Lyn Osborn
The Amazing Colossal Man '57

Ted Osborn
Buried Alive '39
Charlie Chan at the Wax Museum '40

Bud Osborne
Across the Plains '39
Border Badmen '45
Border Bandits '46
The Caravan Trail '46
Dead or Alive '41
Deadwood Pass '33
Death Rides the Range '40
Diamond Trail '33
The Fighting Stallion '26
His Brother's Ghost '45
Mark of the Spur '32
Outlaw of the Plains '46
Ridin' Thru '35
Rustler's Hideout '44
Six Gun Gospel '43
When a Man Rides Alone '33
Wild Horse Phantom '44
Wild West '46

John Osborne
The Power of One '92

Scott Osborne
Nature's Playmates '62

Vivienne Osborne
Captain Caution '40
Let's Sing Again '36
The Phantom Broadcast '33
Primrose Path '40
Tomorrow at Seven '33

Ozzy Osbourne
Trick or Treat '86

Henry Oscar
The Courageous Mr. Penn '41
The Greed of William Hart '48
Postmark for Danger '56
The Spaniard's Curse '58
The Terror '38

Per Oscarsson
Blockhouse '73
Dandy in Aspic '68
The Doll '62
Endless Night '71
Hunger '66
The Last Valley '71
The Night Visitor '70
Secrets '71
Sleep of Death '79

Bill Osco
Copkillers '77

Brian O'Shaughnessy
Claws '85
Mr. Kingstreet's War '71

Amber O'Shea
Intimate Power '89
The Pilot '82

Daniel O'Shea
Hamburger Hill '87

Kevin O'Shea
The Purple Heart '44
A Wing and a Prayer '44

Michael O'Shea
The Big Wheel '49
Jack Frost '43
Jack London '44
Lady of Burlesque '43
Lady Scarface/The Threat '49
The Last of the Redmen '47
Parole, Inc. '49
Threat '49
The Underworld Story '50

Milo O'Shea
Barbarella '68
Danger in the Skies '79
The Dream Team '89
Loot...Give Me Money, Honey! '70
No Comebacks '85

Once a Hero '88
Only the Lonely '91
Opportunity Knocks '90
Paddy '70
Peter Lundy and the Medicine Hat Stallion '77
The Playboys '92
Portrait of a Rebel: Margaret Sanger '82
The Purple Rose of Cairo '85
Romeo and Juliet '68
Sacco & Vanzetti '71
Theatre of Blood '73
A Time for Miracles '80
Two by Forsyth '86
Ulysses '67
The Verdict '82

Paul O'Shea
Among the Cinders '83

Tessie O'Shea
The Russians are Coming, the Russians are Coming '66

Nagisa Oshima
The Empire of Passion '76

William Osler
The Girl in Blue '74

K.T. Oslin
The Thing Called Love '93

Cliff Osmond
The Adventures of Nellie Bly '81
The Fortune Cookie '66
Hangar 18 '80
In Search of a Golden Sky '84
Invasion of the Bee Girls '73
Joe Panther '76
Kiss Me, Stupid! '64
Mountain Man '77
Sharks' Treasure '75
Sweet Sugar '72

Donny Osmond
Goin' Coconuts '78

Marie Osmond
The Gift of Love '90
Goin' Coconuts '78
Hugo the Hippo '76

Sam O'Steen
Queen of the Stardust Ballroom '75

Jeffery Osterhage
Buckeye and Blue '87
Dark Before Dawn '89
Masque of the Red Death '89
The Sacketts '79
Sex Crimes '92
The Shadow Riders '82
South of Reno '87

Robert Osterloh
One Minute to Zero '52

Georg Osterman
Revolution! A Red Comedy '91

Bibi Osterwald
Bank Shot '74

Robert Osth
Don't Go in the House '80

William Ostrander
Fire and Ice '83
Mike's Murder '84
Red Heat '85

Pamela Ostrer
Power '34

Peter Ostrum
Willy Wonka & the Chocolate Factory '71

Brian O'Sullivan
Men of Ireland '38

James O'Sullivan
Flight of Black Angel '91

Maureen O'Sullivan
Anna Karenina '35
The Barretts of Wimpole Street '34
A Connecticut Yankee '31
David Copperfield '35
A Day at the Races '37
Devil Doll '36
Hannah and Her Sisters '86
Hide-Out '34
Peggy Sue Got Married '86
Pride and Prejudice '40
Skyscraper Souls '32
Song O' My Heart '29
Stranded '87
Strange Interlude '32
The Tall T '57
Tarzan and His Mate '34
Tarzan Escapes '36
Tarzan Finds a Son '39
Tarzan, the Ape Man '32
Tarzan's New York Adventure '42
Tarzan's Secret Treasure '41
The Thin Man '34
Too Scared to Scream '85

Sheila O'Sullivan
Ulysses '67

Claudia Osuna
Cancion en el Alma

Shinobu Otake
Nomugi Pass '79

Shoji Otake
The Funeral '84
Tampopo '86

Tomoko Otakra
Summer Vacation: 1999 '88

Gabi Oterman
I Love You Rosa '72

Carre Otis
Wild Orchid '90

Annette O'Toole
Best Legs in the 8th Grade '84
Bridge to Terabithia '85
Cat People '82
Cross My Heart '88
Foolin' Around '80
48 Hrs. '82
A Girl of the Limberlost '90
King of the Gypsies '78
Love at Large '89
One on One '77
Smile '75
Stephen King's It '90
Superman 3 '83
White Lie '91

Peter O'Toole
Becket '64
The Bible...In the Beginning '66
Caligula '80
Casino Royale '67
Club Paradise '86
Creator '85
The Dark Angel '91
Foxtrot '76
Goodbye, Mr. Chips '69
High Spirits '88
Kidnapped '60
King Ralph '91
The Last Emperor '87
Lawrence of Arabia '62
The Lion in Winter '68
Lord Jim '65

Stuart Pankin
Betrayal of the Dove '92
Dirt Bike Kid '86
Fatal Attraction '87
Life Stinks '91
Love at Stake '87
Mannequin 2: On the Move
'91
Second Sight '89
That's Adequate '90
The Vagrant '92

John Pankow
Johnny Be Good '88
Monkey Shines '88
Mortal Thoughts '91
A Stranger Among Us '92
Talk Radio '88
To Live & Die in L.A. '85
Year of the Gun '91

Gerulf Pannach
Singing the Blues in Red '87

Joe Pantoliano
Calendar Girl '93
Downtown '89
Eddie and the Cruisers '83
Empire of the Sun '87
The Final Terror '83
The Fugitive '93
Idolmaker '80
The In Crowd '88
La Bamba '87
The Last of the Finest '90
Mean Season '85
Midnight Run '88
Risky Business '83
Running Scared '86
Scenes from the Goldmine '87
Short Time '90
The Squeeze '87
Tales from the Crypt '89
Three of Hearts '93
Used People '92
Zandalee '91

Anny Papa
A Blade in the Dark '83

**Nicols
Papaconstantinou**
The Enchantress '85

**Tatiana
Papamoskou**
Iphigenia '77

Joe Paparone
Mac '93

Helen Papas
Graveyard Shift '87

Irene Papas
Anne of the Thousand Days
'69
The Assisi Underground '84
The Brotherhood '68
Christ Stopped at Eboli '79
A Dream of Kings '69
Erendira '83

Patrick Pankhurst
Whitcomb's War '88

The Guns of Navarone '61

Kay Parker
Dracula Sucks '79
Pleasure Resort '90

Kim Parker
Fiend Without a Face '58
Fire Maidens from Outer
  Space '56

Lara Parker
Foxfire Light '84
Hi, Mom! '70
Night of Dark Shadows '71
Race with the Devil '75
The Solitary Man '82

Leila Parker
Frankenstein '80 '79

Luana Parker
Home from the Hill '60

Mary Louise Parker
Fried Green Tomatoes '91
Grand Canyon '91
Longtime Companion '90

Melanie Parker
Monkey Shines '88

Michael Parker
Kill Line '91
My Own Private Idaho '91

Monica Parker
Coming Out Alive '84
Improper Channels '82

Noelle Parker
Ernest Saves Christmas '88
Lethal Lolita—Amy Fisher: My
  Story '92
Twisted '86

Norman Parker
Killing Hour '84
Question of Faith '93

Ray Parker, Jr.
Enemy Territory '87

Sachi Parker
The Dancing Princesses '84
Riders to the Seas '88
Welcome Home, Roxy
  Carmichael '90

Sage Parker
Dirt Bike Kid '86

**Sarah Jessica
Parker**
Almost Royal Family '84
First Born '84
Flight of the Navigator '86
Footloose '84
Girls Just Want to Have Fun
  '85
Going for the Gold: The Bill
  Johnson Story '85
Hocus Pocus '93
Honeymoon in Vegas '92
L.A. Story '91
Somewhere Tomorrow '85

Scott Parker
The Milpitas Monster '75

Sunshine Parker
Cannery Row '82
Spittin' Image '83

Suzy Parker
Funny Face '57
The Interns '62
Ten North Frederick '58

Ursula Parker
Lightning Bolt '67

Wes Parker
Cry from the Mountain '85

Willard Parker
Bandit Queen '51
Great Jesse James Raid '49
Hunt the Man Down/
  Smashing the Rackets '50

Dean Parkin
The War of the Colossal Beast
  '58

Barbara Parkins
Asylum '72
Bear Island '80
Breakfast in Paris '81
Christina '74
The Deadly Trap '71
Law of the Land '76
The Mephisto Waltz '71
Puppet on a Chain '72
Shout at the Devil '76
Snatched '72
To Catch a King '84
Valley of the Dolls '67

Michael Parkinson
Madhouse '74

Barbara Parks
California Girls '84

Bert Parks
The Freshman '90
Shining Star '75

Catherine Parks
Body of Influence '93

Larry Parks
Down to Earth '47
Jolson Sings Again '49
The Jolson Story '46
Love is Better Than Ever '52
You Were Never Lovelier '42

Michael Parks
Arizona Heat '87
Breakthrough '78
Chase '85
The China Lake Murders '90
Club Life '86
The Evictors '79
ffolkes '80
French Quarter Undercover
  '85
Gore Vidal's Billy the Kid '89
Hard Country '81
The Hitman '91
Midnight Auto Supply '78
Night Cries '78
The Private Files of J. Edgar
  Hoover '77
The Return of Josey Wales
  '86
The Savage Bees '76
Savannah Smiles '82
Sidewinder One '77
Stamp of a Killer '87
Storyville '92
Welcome to Spring Break '88

Patricia Parks
Fresh Kill '87

Tom Parks
Ladybugs '92

Tricia Parks
L.A. Crackdown '87

Trina Parks
Darktown Strutters '74
Diamonds are Forever '71
The Muthers '76

Dita Parlo
Grand Illusion '37
Homecoming '28
L'Atalante '34

Emory Parnell
Man of the West '58

Miracle of Morgan's Creek '44
Trail of Robin Hood '50

Rick Parnell
The Return of Spinal Tap '92

Richard Parnes
Enrapture '90

Oliver Parniere
36 Fillete '88

Blake Parrish
Three Way Weekend '81

Helen Parrish
Big Trail '30
Little Tough Guy '38
Overland Mail '41
Sunset Serenade '42
X Marks the Spot '42
You'll Find Out '40

John Parrish
Hopalong Cassidy: The Dead
  Don't Dream '48

Julie Parrish
The Doberman Gang '72
Paradise, Hawaiian Style '66

Leslie Parrish
For Love or Money '63
The Giant Spider Invasion '75
The Invisible Strangler '76
Li'l Abner '59
The Manchurian Candidate
  '62
Sex and the Single Girl '64

Steve Parrish
Midnight '89
Scanners 3: The Takeover '92

James Parrott
Laurel & Hardy Comedy
  Classics, Vol. 8 '30s

Paul Parrott
Early Cinema Vol. 1 '19

David Parry
Auntie Lee's Meat Pies '92
Dr. Caligari '89
The Lost Platoon '89

George Parry
Special Olympics '78

Nastasha Parry
Crow Hollow '52
Haunted: The Ferryman '74

Tom Parsekian
Club Life '86
Hot Resort '85

Frederick Parslow
The Last Wave '77
Wrangler '88

Estelle Parsons
Bonnie & Clyde '67
Come Along with Me '84
Dick Tracy '90
Don't Drink the Water '69
For Pete's Sake '74
Foreplay '75
Gentleman Bandit '81
I Never Sang For My Father
  '70
A Private Matter '92
Rachel, Rachel '68
Watermelon Man '70

Julie Parsons
Sweater Girls '78

Karyn Parsons
Class Act '91

Louella Parsons
Without Reservations '46

Nancy Parsons
Ladybugs '92
Motel Hell '80
Porky's Revenge '85

Percy Parsons
Dangerous Moonlight '41
Power '34
Rhodes '36

Paul A. Partain
The Texas Chainsaw
  Massacre '74

Dolly Parton
The Best Little Whorehouse in
  Texas '82
9 to 5 '80
Rhinestone '84
A Smoky Mountain Christmas
  '86
Steel Magnolias '89
Straight Talk '92

Julia Parton
Vice Academy 3 '91

William Parton
The Lady of the Camellias '87

Kimberly Partridge
Better Late Than Never '83

Christine Pascal
The Best Way '82
The Clockmaker '76
Le Grand Chemin '87
Sincerely Charlotte '86

Mary Ann Pascal
Lethal Lolita—Amy Fisher: My
  Story '92
Writer's Block '91

Olivia Pascal
Bloody Moon '83
C.O.D. '83
Summer Night Fever '79

Pat Pascal
Summer Heat '73

Nadine Pascale
Zombie Lake '84

Natalie Pascaud
Mr. Hulot's Holiday '53

Isabelle Pasco
High Frequency '88
Prospero's Books '91

Richard Pasco
As You Like It '79
The Gorgon '64
Julius Caesar '79
Sword of Sherwood Forest
  '60

Christina Pascual
Dark Habits '84

Adrian Pasdar
Cookie '89
Grand Isle '92
The Lost Capone '90
Made in USA '88
Near Dark '87
Streets of Gold '86
Torn Apart '89
Vital Signs '90

Encarna Paso
Demons in the Garden '82

Pier Paolo Pasolini
Bellissimo: Images of the
  Italian Cinema '87
The Canterbury Tales '71
The Decameron '70
Oedipus Rex '67

Susanna Pasolini
Gospel According to St.
  Matthew '64

Cyndi Pass
Bikini Island '91
Deadbolt '92
Desperate Motives '92
Mission of Justice '92

Dira Pass
The Emerald Forest '85

Mary Kay Pass
Hospital of Terror '78

Antonio Passallia
Le Boucher '69

Lars Passgard
Through a Glass Darkly '61

Earl Pastko
Highway 61 '91

Julian Pastor
Patsy, Mi Amor '87

Louis Pastore
Agent on Ice '86

Raimundo Pastore
Una Vez en la Vida '49

Vinny Pastore
True Love '89

Robert Pastorelli
Dances with Wolves '90
Folks! '92

Dan Pastorini
The Florida Connection '74

Willie Pastrano
Alligator Alley '72
Wild Rebels '71

Franca Pasut
Accatone! '61

Patachou
French Can-Can '55

Andre Pataczek
Sweetie '89

Michael Pataki
The Amazing Spider-Man '77
American Anthem '86
The Baby '72
The Bat People '74
Dead and Buried '81
Delinquent School Girls '84
Dirt Gang '71
Grave of the Vampire '72
Halloween 4: The Return of
  Michael Myers '88
The Last Porno Flick '74
The Last Word '80
On the Edge: The Survival of
  Dana '79
One More Chance '90
The Pink Angels '71
Rocky 4 '85
The Underachievers '88
When Every Day was the
  Fourth of July '78
Zoltan...Hound of Dracula '77

Wally Patch
Calling Paul Temple '48
Cottage to Let '41
Don Quixote '35
Inspector Hornleigh '39

Christopher Pate
The Mango Tree '77

Michael Pate
Face to Face '52
Houdini '53
Howling 3: The Marsupials '87
Julius Caesar '53

Pate ▶cont.

A Lawless Street '55
McLintock! '63
The Oklahoman '56
Return of Captain Invincible '83
Seventh Cavalry '56
The Singing Nun '66
Tower of London '62

Nana Patekar
Salaam Bombay! '88

Daniela Patella
Alfredo, Alfredo '72

Bill Paterson
The Adventures of Baron Munchausen '89
Comfort and Joy '84
Coming Up Roses '87
Defense of the Realm '85
Dutch Girls '87
Hidden City '87
The Killing Fields '84
The Object of Beauty '91
The Ploughman's Lunch '83
A Private Function '84
The Rachel Papers '89
Traffik '90s
Truly, Madly, Deeply '91
The Witches '90

Smita Patil
Spices '86

Mandy Patinkin
Alien Nation '88
The Big Fix '78
Daniel '83
Dick Tracy '90
The Doctor '91
Follies in Concert '85
French Postcards '79
The House on Carroll Street '88
Impromptu '90
The Last Embrace '79
Maxie '85
Night of the Juggler '80
The Princess Bride '87
Ragtime '81
Sunday in the Park with George '86
True Colors '91
Yentl '83

Jorge Patino
La Venganza del Rojo '87

Angela Paton
Groundhog Day '93

Charles Paton
Blackmail '29

Laurie Paton
The Amy Fisher Story '92
Norman's Awesome Experience '88

Jason Patric
After Dark, My Sweet '90
The Beast '88
Denial: The Dark Side of Passion '91
Frankenstein Unbound '90
The Lost Boys '87
Rush '91
Solarbabies '86
Toughlove '85

Cynthia Patrick
The Mole People '56

David Patrick
Hide and Seek '77

Dennis Patrick
Choices '81
Dear Dead Delilah '72
Joe '70
The Time Travelers '64

Dorothy Patrick
Follow Me Quietly '49
Torch Song '53

Gail Patrick
Badmen of Nevada '33
Brewster's Millions '45
Doctor Takes a Wife '40
Love Crazy '41
My Favorite Wife '40
My Man Godfrey '36
The Mysterious Rider '33
The Phantom Broadcast '33
Stage Door '37
To the Last Man '33
Wagon Wheels '34
Wives Under Suspicion '38

Gregory Patrick
Sexpot '88
A Woman Obsessed '88

Joan Patrick
The Astro-Zombies '67

Lee Patrick
Black Bird '75
Fisherman's Wharf '39
The Fuller Brush Girl '50
Gambler's Choice '44
In This Our Life '42
Inner Sanctum '48
Law of the Underworld '38
The Maltese Falcon '41
Mrs. Parkington '44
Pillow Talk '59
Seven Faces of Dr. Lao '63
Somewhere I'll Find You '42
Summer and Smoke '61

Nigel Patrick
Battle of Britain '69
The Browning Version '51
Encore '52
The Executioner '70
Johnny Nobody '61
League of Gentlemen '60
Mackintosh Man '73
The Pickwick Papers '54
Raintree County '57
Sapphire '59
Trio '50
The Virgin Soldiers '69

Randal Patrick
Fast Food '89

Robert Patrick
Behind Enemy Lines '85
Die Hard 2: Die Harder '90
Eye of the Eagle '87
Fire in the Sky '93
Future Hunters '88
Last Action Hero '93
Terminator 2: Judgment Day '91

Tom Patricola
Two Reelers: Comedy Classics 8 '33

Stefano Patrizi
The Hurried Man '77

Jean-Marie Patte
The Rise of Louis XIV '66

Luanna Patten
Follow Me, Boys! '66
Johnny Tremain & the Sons of Liberty '58
Rock, Pretty Baby '56
So Dear to My Heart '49

Chuck Patterson
The Five Heartbeats '91

David Patterson
The Secret Garden '84

Elizabeth Patterson
A Bill of Divorcement '32
Hide-Out '34
Hold Your Man '33
Intruder in the Dust '49
No Man of Her Own '32
The Sky's the Limit '43

Frank Patterson
The Dead '87

George Patterson
I Drink Your Blood '71

Jay Patterson
Double Exposure: The Story of Margaret Bourke-White '89
Heaven Help Us '85
McBain '91
Street Smart '87

J.G. Patterson
Doctor Gore '75

John D. Patterson
Forlorn River '37

Lee Patterson
Above Us the Waves '56
Bullseye! '90
Chato's Land '71
He Lives: The Search for the Evil One '88
Jack the Ripper '60
The Key Man '57
The Spaniard's Curse '58
Time Lock '57

Lorna Patterson
The Imposter '84

Melody Patterson
The Immortalizer '89

Neva Patterson
An Affair to Remember '57
David and Lisa '62
Desk Set '57
The Runaways '75
Women of Valor '86

Pat Patterson
The Body Shop '72
Gas-s-s-s! '70
Moonshine Mountain '64

Robert Patterson
Nuns on the Run '90

Rocky Patterson
Armed for Action '92
Blood on the Badge '92
Nail Gun Massacre '86

Sarah Patterson
The Company of Wolves '85

Brigitta Pattersson
The Virgin Spring '59

Jeremy Pattnosh
Certain Sacrifice '80

Bart Patton
Dementia 13 '63

Bill Patton
Fangs of Fate '25

Maggie Patton
Let's Kill All the Lawyers '93

Mark Patton
Anna to the Infinite Power '84
A Nightmare on Elm Street 2: Freddy's Revenge '85

Will Patton
Belizaire the Cajun '86
Chinese Boxes '84
Cold Heaven '92
Deadly Desire '91
Everybody Wins '90
In the Soup '92
No Way Out '87
The Rapture '91
A Shock to the System '90
Signs of Life '89
Stars and Bars '88
Variety '83
Wildfire '88

Henrik Pauer
Time Stands Still '82

Adrian Paul
Masque of the Red Death '89

Alexandra Paul
American Flyers '85
American Nightmare '81
Christine '84
8 Million Ways to Die '85
Getting Physical '84
In Between '92
Just the Way You Are '84
Millions '91
Prey of the Chameleon '91
Sunset Grill '92

David Paul
The Barbarians '87
Double Trouble '91
Ghost Writer '89
Think Big '90

Don Michael Paul
Alien from L.A. '87
Aloha Summer '88
Brotherhood of Justice '86
The Heart of Dixie '89
Lovelines '84
Rich Girl '91
Robot Wars '93
Rolling Vengeance '87
Winners Take All '87

Jean Paul
Full Metal Ninja '89

John Paul
Doomwatch '72

Lee Paul
The Children of An Lac '80

Nancy Paul
Lifeforce '85

Peter Paul
The Barbarians '87
Double Trouble '91
Ghost Writer '89
Think Big '90

Rene Paul
The C-Man '49

Richard Paul
Bloodfist 3: Forced to Fight '91
Not for Publication '84
Princess Academy '87

Richard Joseph Paul
Under the Boardwalk '89

Ricky Paul
Piranha 2: The Spawning '82

Rosemary Paul
Dead Easy '82

Stuart Paul
Emanon '86
Fate '90

Talia Paul
Anguish '88

Scott Paulin
Captain America '89
From Hollywood to Deadwood '89
Grim Prairie Tales '89
The Last of Philip Banter '87
Pump Up the Volume '90
The Right Stuff '83
A Soldier's Story '84
Teen Wolf '85
Tricks of the Trade '88
Turner and Hooch '89
Weekend War '88

Morgan Paull
Surf 2 '84

Albert Paulsen
The Arab Conspiracy '76

Pat Paulsen
Auntie Lee's Meat Pies '92
Ellie '84
Foreplay '75
Harper Valley P.T.A. '78
Night Patrol '85
They Still Call Me Bruce '86
Where Were You When the Lights Went Out? '68

Rob Paulsen
Eyes of Fire '84
Perfect Match '88

George Paulsin
Simon, King of the Witches '71

Marisa Pavan
Diane '55
Drum Beat '54
The Man in the Gray Flannel Suit '56
The Rose Tattoo '55
Solomon and Sheba '59
What Price Glory? '52

Anna Pavane
Portrait in Terror '66

Luciano Pavarotti
Yes, Giorgio '82

Maria Pavelle
The Prime Time '60

Lucy Pavey
The Fall of the House of Usher '52

Johanna Pavlis
Until September '84

Nadia Pavlova
Murder She Said '62

Drina Pavlovic
Games Girls Play '75

Pavel Pavlovsky
All My Good Countrymen '68

Muriel Pavlow
Doctor at Large '57
Doctor in the House '53
Malta Story '53

Janet K. Pawlak
Ninja Vengeance '93

Lennox Pawle
Sylvia Scarlett '35

Adam Pawlikowski
Ashes and Diamonds '58

James Pax
In Love and War '91

Katina Paxinou
Inheritance '47

Gil Peterson
The Brain Machine '72
Mind Warp '72

Nan Peterson
Hideous Sun Demon '59

Sarah Peterson
Cannon Movie Tales: Snow White '89

Shelly Peterson
The Housekeeper '86

Stewart Peterson
Against A Crooked Sky '75
Pony Express Rider '76
Seven Alone '75
Where the Red Fern Grows '74

Vidal Peterson
Wizards of the Lost Kingdom '85

Edward Petherbridge
Lovers of Their Time '85
Strange Interlude '90

Pascale Petit
End of Desire '62

Victor Petit
Night of the Death Cult '75
Street Warriors '87
Terror Beach '80s

Gio Petre
The Doll '62
Gorilla '56

Ian Petrella
A Christmas Story '83

Alexei Petrenko
Rasputin '85

Marcella Petri
Nathalie Comes of Age '86

Mario Petri
Conqueror & the Empress '64

Anne Petrie
Close to Home '86

Hay Petrie
A Canterbury Tale '44
Crimes at the Dark House '39
The Old Curiosity Shop '35
Spellbound '41
Spy in Black '39

Susan Petrie
Snapshot '77

Sammy Petrillo
Bela Lugosi Meets a Brooklyn Gorilla '52

Sonia Petrovna
The Fatal Image '90

Joanna Pettet
Blue '68
Casino Royale '67
Cry of the Innocent '80
Double Exposure '82
The Evil '78
The Group '66
A Killer in Every Corner '74
Night of the Generals '67
Pioneer Woman '73
Return of Frank Cannon '80
Robbery '67
Sweet Country '87
Terror in Paradise

Valarie Pettiford
Street Hunter '90

Frank Pettingell
Gaslight '39

Lori Petty
Cadillac Man '90
Free Willy '93
A League of Their Own '92
Point Break '91

Richard Petty
Richard Petty Story '72
Speedway '68

Ross Petty
The Housekeeper '86

Tom Petty
Made in Heaven '87

Angelique Pettyjohn
Bio Hazard '85
Confessions of Tom Harris '72
G.I. Executioner '71
The Lost Empire '83
Repo Man '83
Revenge of Doctor X '80s
Takin' It Off '84
The Wizard of Speed and Time '88

Joseph Pevney
Nocturne '46
The Street with No Name '48

Penny Peyser
The Frisco Kid '79
The In-Laws '79
Messenger of Death '88

Claudia Peyton
Bloodbeat '85

Christian Pezy
Sweet Ecstasy '62

Ben Pfeifer
Kill Line '91

Dedee Pfeiffer
Brothers in Arms '88
The Horror Show '89
King's Ransom '91
The Midnight Hour '86
Red Surf '90
Toughlove '85

James Pfeiffer
Firefight '87

Michelle Pfeiffer
Amazon Women on the Moon '87
B.A.D. Cats '80
Batman Returns '92
Callie and Son '81
Charlie Chan and the Curse of the Dragon Queen '81
Dangerous Liaisons '88
The Fabulous Baker Boys '89
Falling in Love Again '80
Frankie and Johnny '91
Grease 2 '82
Into the Night '85
Ladyhawke '85
Love Field '91
Married to the Mob '88
Power, Passion & Murder '83
The Russia House '90
Scarface '83
The Solitary Man '82
Sweet Liberty '86
Tequila Sunrise '88
The Witches of Eastwick '87

Welsey Pfenning
Circle of Fear '89

JoAnn Pflug
Catlow '71
The Day the Women Got Even '80
M*A*S*H '70

Douglas Phair
The Rats are Coming! The Werewolves are Here! '72

Joe Phelan
Fatal Pulse '88
South of Reno '87
Terminal Exposure '89
Zero Boys '86

Buster Phelps
Little Orphan Annie '32

Peter Phelps
Breaking Loose '90
The Lighthorseman '87
Rock & Roll Cowboys '92
Starlight Hotel '90

Michael Phenicie
9 1/2 Ninjas '90

John Philbin
Martians Go Home! '90
North Shore '87
Shy People '87

Joy Philbin
Night and the City '92

Mary Philbin
Human Hearts '22
The Man Who Laughs '27
Merry-Go-Round '23
Phantom of the Opera '25

Phil Philbin
Flesh Feast '69

Regis Philbin
Night and the City '92

James Philbrook
Finger on the Trigger '65
Last Day of the War '69
Sound of Horror '64

Robert Philip
Adios Amigo '75
Children Shouldn't Play with Dead Things '72

Gerard Philippe
Dangerous Liaisons '60
Devil in the Flesh '46
Fever Mounts at El Pao '59
La Ronde '51
The Red and the Black '57

Mary Philips
A Farewell to Arms '32
Prince Valiant '54

Barney Phillips
I Was a Teenage Werewolf '57
Savage Run '70

Barry Phillips
Dr. Caligari '89

Britta Phillips
Satisfaction '88

Chynna Phillips
Caddyshack 2 '88
The Invisible Kid '88
The Prize Pulitzer '89

Conrad Phillips
Murder She Said '62

Dorothy Phillips
Heart of Humanity '18

E.D. Phillips
Welcome Back Mr. Fox '83

Eddie Phillips
Phantom Patrol '36
Probation '32

Emo Phillips
Meet the Parents '91

Ethan Phillips
Bloodhounds of Broadway '89
Green Card '90

Frank Phillips
Battle of the Eagles '81

Gary Phillips
Whodunit '82

Grace Phillips
All the Vermeers in New York '91

Howard Phillips
The Last Mile '32

James Phillips
Prison Planet '92

Jean Phillips
Outlaws of the Desert '41

John Phillips
Max and Helen '90

Joseph C. Phillips
Strictly Business '91

Julianne Phillips
Fletch Lives '89
Seven Hours to Judgment '88
Skin Deep '89
Summer Fantasy '84
Sweet Lies '88

Lawrence King Phillips
Abducted '86

Lee Phillips
The Hunters '58
Peyton Place '57
Psychomania '63

Leo Phillips
Wedding in White '72

Leslie Phillips
Empire of the Sun '87
The Limping Man '53
Maroc 7 '67
Mountains of the Moon '90
The Smallest Show on Earth '57
Train of Events '49

Lou Diamond Phillips
Ambition '91
Dakota '88
Disorganized Crime '89
The First Power '89
Harley '90
La Bamba '87
Renegades '89
Shadow of the Wolf '92
A Show of Force '90
Stand and Deliver '88
Trespasses '86
Young Guns '88
Young Guns 2 '90

MacKenzie Phillips
American Graffiti '73
Eleanor & Franklin '76
Love Child '82
Miles to Go Before I Sleep '74
More American Graffiti '79
Rafferty & the Gold Dust Twins '75

Meredith Phillips
Sky Pirates '87

Michelle Phillips
American Anthem '86
Assault and Matrimony '87
The Death Squad '73
Dillinger '73
Let It Ride '89
Scissors '91

Secrets of a Married Man '84
Sidney Sheldon's Bloodline '79

Peg Phillips
Dogfight '91

Robert Phillips
The Killing of a Chinese Bookie '76

Sian Phillips
The Carpathian Eagle '81
Clash of the Titans '81
The Doctor and the Devils '85
Dune '84
The Ewoks: Battle for Endor '85
Goodbye, Mr. Chips '69
I, Claudius, Vol. 1: A Touch of Murder/Family Affairs '91
I, Claudius, Vol. 2: Waiting in the Wings/What Shall We Do With Claudius? '80
I, Claudius, Vol. 3: Poison is Queen/Some Justice '80
I, Claudius, Vol. 4: Queen of Heaven/Reign of Terror '80
Murphy's War '71
Nijinsky '80
Valmont '89

Sydney Coale Phillips
Maximum Breakout '91

Wendy Phillips
Bugsy '91
Death Be Not Proud '75

Bill Phipps
Cat Women of the Moon '53

Max Phipps
The Blue Lightning '86
Dark Age '88
Nate and Hayes '83
Return of Captain Invincible '83
Sky Pirates '87

Nicholas Phipps
Captain's Paradise '53
Elizabeth of Ladymead '48
Maytime in Mayfair '52

William Phipps
Cavalry Command '63
Cinderella '50
The Vanishing Westerner '50

Leaf Phoenix
Parenthood '89
Russkies '87
SpaceCamp '86

River Phoenix
Dogfight '91
Explorers '85
I Love You to Death '90
Indiana Jones and the Last Crusade '89
Little Nikita '88
The Mosquito Coast '86
My Own Private Idaho '91
A Night in the Life of Jimmy Reardon '88
Running on Empty '88
Sneakers '92
Stand By Me '86
The Thing Called Love '93

Edith Piaf
French Can-Can '55

Maurice Pialat
A Nos Amours '84
Under Satan's Sun '87

Joseph Piantadosi
Schlock '73

You Only Live Twice '67

John Pleshette
Burning Rage '84
The Kid with the Broken Halo '82
Lies of the Twins '91
The Trial of Lee Harvey Oswald '77

Suzanne Pleshette
The Adventures of Bullwhip Griffin '66
Alone in the Neon Jungle '87
The Birds '63
Blackbeard's Ghost '67
Dixie: Changing Habits '85
For Love or Money '84
The Geisha Boy '58
Hard Frame '70
Help Wanted: Male '82
Hot Stuff '80
If It's Tuesday, This Must Be Belgium '69
If Things Were Different '79
Kojak: The Belarus File '85
Legend of Valentino '75
Nevada Smith '66
Oh, God! Book 2 '80
One Cooks, the Other Doesn't '83
The Queen of Mean '90
Rome Adventure '62
The Shaggy D.A. '76
Support Your Local Gunfighter '71
Suppose They Gave a War and Nobody Came? '70
The Ugly Dachshund '65

Jacqueline Plessis
Seven Deadly Sins '53

George Plimpton
Easy Wheels '89
Reds '81
Rio Lobo '70
Volunteers '85

Martha Plimpton
Another Woman '88
The Goonies '85
Josh and S.A.M. '93
The Mosquito Coast '86
Parenthood '89
The River Rat '84
Rollover '81
Running on Empty '88
Samantha '92
Shy People '87
Silence Like Glass '90
Stanley and Iris '90
Stars and Bars '88

Shelley Plimpton
Glen and Randa '71

Melinda Plowman
Billy the Kid Versus Dracula '66
Home Town Story '51

Joan Plowright
And a Nightingale Sang '91
Avalon '90
Brimstone & Treacle '82
Britannia Hospital '82
A Dedicated Man '86
Dennis the Menace '93
Dressmaker '89
Drowning by Numbers '87
Enchanted April '92
The Entertainer '60
Equus '77
I Love You to Death '90
Last Action Hero '93
Revolution '85
School for Scandal '65
Stalin '92

Erika Pluhar
The Goalie's Anxiety at the Penalty Kick '71

Eve Plumb
Alexander: The Other Side of Dawn '77
Force of Evil '77
I'm Gonna Git You Sucka '88
Little Women '78
Secrets of Three Hungry Wives '78
A Very Brady Christmas '88

Amanda Plummer
Courtship '87
Daniel '83
The Dollmaker '84
The Fisher King '91
Freejack '92
Gryphon '88
The Hotel New Hampshire '84
Joe Versus the Volcano '90
Made in Heaven '87
Miss Rose White '92
Needful Things '93
Prisoners of Inertia '89
Riders to the Seas '88
So I Married an Axe Murderer '93
Static '87
The World According to Garp '82

Christopher Plummer
The Amateur '82
The Assignment '78
Battle of Britain '69
The Boss' Wife '86
Boy in Blue '86
Conduct Unbecoming '75
The Day that Shook the World '78
Disappearance '81
A Doll's House '59
Dragnet '87
Dreamscape '84
Eyewitness '81
The Fall of the Roman Empire '64
Firehead '90
Hanover Street '79
Highpoint '80
I Love N.Y. '87
Inside Daisy Clover '65
International Velvet '78
Liar's Edge '92
Light Years '88
Lily in Love '85
Little Gloria...Happy at Last '84
The Man Who Would Be King '75
Many Faces of Sherlock Holmes '86
Mindfield '89
Murder by Decree '79
Night of the Generals '67
Ordeal by Innocence '84
Prototype '83
The Pyx '73
Red Blooded American Girl '90
Return of the Pink Panther '74
Riel '79
Rock-a-Doodle '92
The Scarlet & the Black '83
The Shadow Box '80
Shadow Dancing '88
Sherlock Holmes: The Silver Blaze '77
The Silent Partner '78
Somewhere in Time '80
The Sound of Music '65
Souvenir '88

Spiral Staircase '75
Stage Struck '57
Star Crash '78
Star Trek 6: The Undiscovered Country '91
The Thorn Birds '83
Triple Cross '67
Waterloo '71
Where the Heart Is '90
Young Catherine '91

Glenn Plummer
Pastime '91
South Central '92

Shum Shim Po
Fists of Fury 2 '80

Werner Pochat
Flatfoot '78
Thunder Warrior 3 '88

Rick Podell
Lunch Wagon '81
World Gone Wild '88

Rossana Podesta
Alone Against Rome '62
Homo Eroticus/Man of the Year '71
The Sensual Man '74
Sodom and Gomorrah '62
Ulysses '55
The Virgin of Nuremberg '65

Cathy Podewell
Night of the Demons '88

Alexander Podorozhny
Zvenigora '28

Harlan Cary Poe
Stigma '73

Benoit Poelvoorde
Man Bites Dog '92

Judith Pogany
A Hungarian Fairy Tale '87

Kathryn Pogson
Over Indulgence '87

Ken Pogue
Blind Man's Bluff '91
Crazy Moon '87
Dead of Winter '87
The Grey Fox '83
The Hitman '91
Keeping Track '86
Miracle at Moreaux '86
Run '91

Klaus Pohl
Woman in the Moon '29

Christopher Pohlad
Old Explorers '90

William M. Pohlad
Old Explorers '90

Eric Pohlmann
The Belles of St. Trinian's '53
Blackout '50
Glass Tomb '55
Moulin Rouge '52
Terror Street '54
Three Stops to Murder '53
Tiffany Jones '75

Larry Poindexter
American Ninja 2: The Confrontation '87
Blue Movies '88

Priscilla Pointer
Archer: The Fugitive from the Empire '81
The Competition '80
Disturbed '90
Honeysuckle Rose '80

Mysterious Two '82
A Nightmare on Elm Street 3: Dream Warriors '87
Rumpelstiltskin '86

Jean Poiret
The Elegant Criminal '92
The Last Metro '80

Cyril Poitier
Savages from Hell '68

Sidney Poitier
All the Young Men '60
Bedford Incident '65
Blackboard Jungle '55
Brother John '70
Buck and the Preacher '72
Cry, the Beloved Country '51
The Defiant Ones '58
Duel at Diablo '66
Emperor Jones/Paul Robeson: Tribute to an Artist '33
For Love of Ivy '68
Goodbye, My Lady '56
The Greatest Story Ever Told '65
Guess Who's Coming to Dinner '67
In the Heat of the Night '67
Let's Do It Again '75
Lilies of the Field '63
Little Nikita '88
The Mark of the Hawk '57
The Organization '71
Paris Blues '61
A Patch of Blue '65
Piece of the Action '77
Pressure Point '62
A Raisin in the Sun '61
Separate But Equal '91
Shoot to Kill '88
The Slender Thread '65
Sneakers '92
Something of Value '57
They Call Me Mr. Tibbs! '70
To Sir, with Love '67
Uptown Saturday Night '74
The Wilby Conspiracy '75

Hanna Pola
Ninja Mission '84

Isa Pola
The Children Are Watching Us '44

Diana Polakov
Supersonic Man '78

Anna Maria Polani
Hercules Against the Moon Men '64

Roman Polanski
Andy Warhol's Dracula '74
Back in the USSR '92
Chinatown '74
Ciao Federico! Fellini Directs Satyricon '69
Diary of Forbidden Dreams '73
The Fearless Vampire Killers '67
A Generation '54
The Magic Christian '69
The Tenant '76

Maurice Poli
Gangster's Law '86

Jon Polito
Barton Fink '91
Deadly Business '86
The Equalizer: Memories of Manon '88
Fire with Fire '86
The Freshman '90
Highlander '86

Leather Jackets '90
Miller's Crossing '90

Lina Polito
All Screwed Up '74
Blood Brothers '74

Bridgit Polk
Watched '73

Oscar Polk
Green Pastures '36

Ben Pollack
The Benny Goodman Story '55
The Glenn Miller Story '54

Kevin Pollack
L.A. Story '91
The Opposite Sex and How to Live With Them '93

Sydney Pollack
Death Becomes Her '92
Husbands and Wives '92
The Player '92

Cheryl Pollak
Crossing the Bridge '92
My Best Friend Is a Vampire '88
Night Life '90
Pump Up the Volume '90
Swimsuit: The Movie '89

Kevin Pollak
Avalon '90
A Few Good Men '92
Indian Summer '93
Ricochet '91

Tracy Pollan
The Abduction of Kari Swenson '87
Baby It's You '82
Bright Lights, Big City '88
Fine Things '90
Great Love Experiment '84
Promised Land '88
A Stranger Among Us '92
The Tender Age '84

Daphne Pollard
Bonnie Scotland '35
Laurel & Hardy Comedy Classics, Vol. 7 '30s
Our Relations '36

Michael J. Pollard
America '86
American Gothic '88
The Arrival '90
The Art of Dying '90
Between the Lines '77
Bonnie & Clyde '67
Dick Tracy '90
Enter Laughing '67
Fast Food '89
Heated Vengeance '87
I Come in Peace '90
Legend of Frenchie King '71
Melvin and Howard '80
Motorama '91
Next of Kin '89
Night Visitor '89
Patriot '86
Riders of the Storm '88
Roxanne '87
Scrooged '88
Season of Fear '89
Sleepaway Camp 3: Teenage Wasteland '89
Split Second '92
Tango and Cash '89
Vengeance Is Mine '84
Why Me? '90
The Wild Angels '66

Snub Pollard
Arizona Days '37

Hell on the Battleground '88
Jungle Assault '89
Killzone '85
Raw Nerve '91
Sledgehammer '83

Albert Priscoe
The Prairie King '27

David Pritchard
Slashed Dreams '74

Michael Pritchard
Lightblast '85
Massive Retaliation '85

Stanton Pritchard
Revenge of the Virgins '62

Lucien Prival
Hell's Angels '30
Panama Menace '41
Party Girls '29

Gilles Privat
Mama, There's a Man in Your Bed '89

Juergen Prochnow
Beverly Hills Cop 2 '87
Body of Evidence '92
The Cop & the Girl '86
Das Boot '81
A Dry White Season '89
Dune '84
The Fire Next Time '93
Forbidden '85
The Fourth War '90
Hurricane Smith '92
Interceptor '92
The Keep '83
Kill Cruise '90
Killing Cars '85
The Loot Honor of Katharina Blum '75
The Man Inside '90
My Sweet Victim '85
Robin Hood '91
The Seventh Sign '88

Anna Proclemer
A Matter of Time '76

Marland Proctor
Terrorists '83

Phil Proctor
Firesign Theatre Presents Nick Danger in the Case of the Missing Yolks '83
J-Men Forever! '79

Luis Procuna
Torero '56

Shanna Prokhorenko
Ballad of a Soldier '60

Paul Prokop
The Velvet Vampire '71

Melissa Prophet
Better Late Than Never '83
Invasion U.S.A. '85
Van Nuys Blvd. '79

Robert Prosky
Age Isn't Everything '91
Big Shots '87
Broadcast News '87
Christine '84
Far and Away '92
From the Dead of Night '89
Funny About Love '90
Green Card '90
Hoffa '92
Into Thin Air '85
The Keep '83
Last Action Hero '93
The Lords of Discipline '83

The Murder of Mary Phagan '87
The Natural '84
Thief '81
Things Change '88

Jean-Marie Proslier
Charles et Lucie '79

Brian Protheroe
Richard III '82

Jed Prouty
Broadway Melody '29
Danger on the Air '38
Ella Cinders '26
Remedy for Riches '40
Small Town Boy '37
Two Reelers: Comedy Classics 3 '33

Victoria Prouty
American Tiger '89

David Proval
Innocent Blood '92
Mean Streets '73
Vice Versa '88

Paul Provenza
Survival Quest '89

Dorothy Provine
Good Neighbor Sam '64
It's a Mad, Mad, Mad, Mad World '63
Never a Dull Moment '68
That Darn Cat '65
30-Foot Bride of Candy Rock '59
Who's Minding the Mint? '67

Guy Provost
The Klutz '73

Jon Provost
All Mine to Give '56
Escapade in Japan '57
Lassie's Great Adventure '62
This Property is Condemned '66

David Prowse
A Clockwork Orange '71
The Empire Strikes Back '80
Frankenstein and the Monster from Hell '74
From "Star Wars" to "Jedi": The Making of a Saga '83
The Horror of Frankenstein '70
Return of the Jedi '83
Star Wars '77
Vampire Circus '71

Haydon Prowse
The Secret Garden '93

Juliet Prowse
Can-Can '60
Dingaka '65
G.I. Blues '60

Anna Prucnall
City of Women '81

Cameron Prudhomme
The Rainmaker '56

Harold Pruett
Spellcaster '91
Summer Camp Nightmare '86

Jeanne Pruett
Sweet Country Road '81

Jonathan Pryce
The Adventures of Baron Munchausen '89
Barbarians at the Gate '93
Brazil '85
Breaking Glass '80

Consuming Passions '88
The Doctor and the Devils '85
Glengarry Glen Ross '92
Haunted Honeymoon '86
Jumpin' Jack Flash '86
Loophole '83
Man on Fire '87
The Ploughman's Lunch '83
Praying Mantis '83
The Rachel Papers '89
Something Wicked This Way Comes '83

Maureen Pryor
The Music Lovers '71

Nicholas Pryor
Brain Dead '89
East of Eden '80
The Fish that Saved Pittsburgh '79
The $5.20 an Hour Dream '80
Force Five '75
Gumball Rally '76
The Happy Hooker '75
Hoffa '92
Last Song '80
The Life and Assassination of the Kingfish '76
Morgan Stewart's Coming Home '87
Night Terror '76
Nightbreaker '89
Pacific Heights '90
Risky Business '83
Smile '75

Richard Pryor
Adios Amigo '75
Another You '91
Best of Chevy Chase '87
Bingo Long Traveling All-Stars & Motor Kings '76
Black Brigade '69
Blue Collar '78
Brewster's Millions '85
Bustin' Loose '81
California Suite '78
Car Wash '76
Critical Condition '86
Greased Lightning '77
Harlem Nights '89
Hit! '73
Jo Jo Dancer, Your Life is Calling '86
Lady Sings the Blues '72
Mack '73
Moving '88
Richard Pryor: Here and Now '83
Richard Pryor: Live and Smokin' '71
Richard Pryor: Live in Concert '79
Richard Pryor: Live on the Sunset Strip '82
See No Evil, Hear No Evil '89
The Silver Streak '76
Some Call It Loving '73
Some Kind of Hero '82
Stir Crazy '80
Superman 3 '83
The Toy '82
Uptown Saturday Night '74
Which Way Is Up? '77
Wholly Moses! '80
Wild in the Streets '68
The Wiz '78

Roger Pryor
Headline Woman '35
Identity Unknown '45
Kid Sister '45
Lady by Choice '34
The Man They Could Not Hang '39
Meet the Mob '42

Panama Menace '41

Roger Pryor, Jr.
Smart Alecks '42

Geof Pryssir
Hot Child in the City '87

Lenita Psillakis
Girl-Toy '84

Wojciech Pszoniak
Angry Harvest '85
Danton '82

Robert Pucci
The Last Hour '91

Vladimir Pucholt
Loves of a Blonde '65

Vsevolod Pudovkin
The Extraordinary Adventures of Mr. West in the Land of the Bolsheviks '24

Tito Puente
The Mambo Kings '92

David Pugh
The Love Pill '71

Robert Pugh
Danger UXB '81

Willard Pugh
Ambition '91
The Color Purple '85

William E. Pugh
Traxx '87

Frank Puglia
The Black Hand '50
Bulldog Drummond's Revenge '37
The Fatal Hour '40
Romola '25
20 Million Miles to Earth '57
Viva Villa! '34
Without Reservations '46

Al Pugliese
Quicksand: No Escape '91

Aldo Puglisi
Marriage Italian Style '64
Seduced and Abandoned '64

Bill Pullman
The Accidental Tourist '88
Brain Dead '89
Bright Angel '91
Cold Feet '89
Crazy in Love '92
Going Under '91
A League of Their Own '92
Liebestraum '91
Newsies '92
Rocket Gibraltar '88
Ruthless People '86
The Serpent and the Rainbow '87
Sibling Rivalry '90
Sleepless In Seattle '93
Sommersby '93
Spaceballs '87

Lilo (Liselotte) Pulver
The Nun '66
A Time to Love & a Time to Die '58

Kong Pun
Ninja Swords of Death '90
Samurai Blood, Samurai Guts
Soul of Samurai

Ng Pun
Samurai Blood, Samurai Guts

Bernard Punsley
Angels with Dirty Faces '38

Henri Puopon
Angele '34

Dick Purcell
The Abe Lincoln of Ninth Avenue '39
Captain America '44
Heroes in Blue '39
Irish Luck '39
King of the Zombies '41
Phantom Killer '42
Timber Queen '44
Tough Kid '39
X Marks the Spot '42

James Purcell
Playroom '90
White Light '90

Lee Purcell
Adam at 6 A.M. '70
Amazing Howard Hughes '77
Big Wednesday '78
Eddie Macon's Run '83
Homework '82
The Incredible Hulk Returns '88
Jailbait: Betrayed By Innocence '86
Kenny Rogers as the Gambler '80
Killing at Hell's Gate '81
Mr. Majestyk '74
Space Rage '86
Stir Crazy '80
The Witching '72

Noel Purcell
Encore '52
Land of Fury '55
Lust for Life '56

Richard Purcell
The Bank Dick '40

Nathan Purdee
Return of Superfly '90

Reginald Purdell
Brighton Rock '47
Candles at Nine '44
The Old Curiosity Shop '35

Edmund Purdom
After the Fall of New York '85
Athena '54
Ator the Fighting Eagle '83
Big Boss '77
Dr. Frankenstein's Castle of Freaks '74
Don't Open Till Christmas '84
The Egyptian '54
Herod the Great '60
Mr. Scarface '77
Nefertiti, Queen of the Nile '64
The Prodigal '55
Rulers of the City '71
The Student Prince '54

Carolyn Purdy-Gordon
Dolls '87

Amrish Puri
Indiana Jones and the Temple of Doom '84

Om Puri
City of Joy '92

Linda Purl
The Adventures of Nellie Bly '81
Body Language '92
Crazy Mama '75
Eleanor & Franklin '76
The Flame is Love '79
High Country '81
Last Cry for Help '79
Little Ladies of the Night '77

Marie Quillen
Campus Knights '29
Saddle Buster '32

Denis Quilley
Foreign Body '86
Mister Johnson '91
Murder of a Moderate Man
   '70s
Privates on Parade '84

Veronica Quilligan
Danny Boy '84

David Quilter
Charles & Diana: A Palace
   Divided '93

Barry Quin
Prisoner Cell Block H '80
Sara Dane '81

**Umberto P.
Quinavalle**
Salo, or the 120 Days of
   Sodom '75

Dan Quine
Clayton County Line '80s

Richard Quine
Babes on Broadway '41
For Me and My Gal '42

Kathleen Quinlan
Airport '77 '77
American Graffiti '73
Blackout '85
Clara's Heart '88
The Doors '91
Dreams Lost, Dreams Found
   '87
Hanky Panky '82
I Never Promised You a Rose
   Garden '77
Independence Day '83
The Last Winter '84
Lifeguard '75
Man Outside '88
The Promise '78
The Runner Stumbles '79
She's in the Army Now '81
Strays '91
Sunset '88
Trapped '89
Twilight Zone: The Movie '83
Warning Sign '85
Where Have All the People
   Gone? '74
Wild Thing '87

Aidan Quinn
All My Sons '86
At Play in the Fields of the
   Lord '91
Avalon '90
Benny & Joon '93
Crusoe '89
Desperately Seeking Susan
   '85
An Early Frost '85
The Handmaid's Tale '90
The Lemon Sisters '90
Lies of the Twins '91
The Mission '86
Perfect Witness '89
The Playboys '92
A Private Matter '92
Reckless '84
Stakeout '87

Aileen Quinn
Annie '82

Anthony Quinn
Across 110th Street '72
African Rage '78
Against All Flags '52
Back to Bataan '45
Barabbas '62

Behold a Pale Horse '64
Black Orchid '59
Blood and Sand '41
Blowing Wild '54
Buffalo Bill '44
Children of Sanchez '79
China Sky '44
City for Conquest '40
The Con Artists '80
The Destructors '74
The Don is Dead '73
A Dream of Kings '69
The Ghost Breakers '40
Ghosts Can't Do It '90
The Greek Tycoon '78
Guadalcanal Diary '43
The Guns of Navarone '61
Heller in Pink Tights '60
High Risk '76
Hot Spell '58
The Inheritance '76
Jesus of Nazareth '77
Jungle Fever '91
La Strada '54
Last Action Hero '93
Last Train from Gun Hill '59
Lawrence of Arabia '62
Lion of the Desert '81
The Lost Command '66
Lust for Life '56
The Magnificent Matador '55
A Man of Passion '90s
Mobsters '91
Mohammed: Messenger of
   God '77
Onassis '88
Only the Lonely '91
The Ox-Bow Incident '43
The Plainsman '37
Regina '83
Revenge '90
The Road to Morocco '42
The Road to Singapore '40
R.P.M.* (*Revolutions Per
   Minute) '70
The Salamander '82
Seven Cities of Gold '55
The Shoes of the Fisherman
   '68
Sinbad the Sailor '47
The Switch '89
They Died with Their Boots
   On '41
Tigers Don't Cry '81
Tycoon '47
Ulysses '55
Viva Zapata! '52
Walk in the Spring Rain '70
Warlock '59
Zorba the Greek '64

Bill Quinn
Big Calibre '35
Bustin' Loose '81
Dead and Buried '81
Twilight Zone: The Movie '83

B.J. Quinn, Jr.
Rip Roarin' Buckaroo '36

Colin Quinn
Who's the Man? '93

Francesco Quinn
Dead Certain '92
Deadly Rivals '92
Indio '90
Platoon '86
Priceless Beauty '90
Quo Vadis '85

Glenn Quinn
Dr. Giggles '92

James Quinn
Joey '85

James W. Quinn
Witchboard '87

WitchTrap '89

J.C. Quinn
The Abyss '89
All-American Murder '91
The Babe '92
Barfly '87
Crisscross '92
Megaville '91
Prayer of the Rollerboys '91
Turner and Hooch '89
Twisted '86
Violated '84

Lorenzo Quinn
Onassis '88

Louis Quinn
Superchick '71
Unholy Rollers '72

Martha Quinn
Bad Channels '92
Motorama '91
The Return of Spinal Tap '92
Tapeheads '89

Pat Quinn
Alice's Restaurant '69
Clean and Sober '88
Zachariah '70

Patricia Quinn
Shock Treatment '81
Witching Time '84

Sally Quinn
Born Yesterday '93

Tandra Quinn
Mesa of Lost Women '52

Terry Quinn
Prisoners of the Sun '91

**Adolfo "Shabba
Doo" Quinones**
Breakin' 2: Electric Boogaloo
   '84

**Lee George
Quinones**
Wild Style '83

Elvira Quintana
Los Amores de Marieta '87

Rosita Quintana
Susana '51

Gene Quintano
Treasure of the Four Crowns
   '82

Lorenzo Quinteros
Man Facing Southeast '86

Frederic Quiring
Olivier, Olivier '92

Beulah Quo
The Children of An Lac '80
Girls! Girls! Girls! '62

Marianne Quon
Charlie Chan in the Secret
   Service '44

Elie Raab
The Fabulous Baker Boys '89

Kurt Raab
Fox and His Friends '75
Parker '84
Tricheurs '84

Catarina Raacke
Forget Mozart '85

Amy Raasch
Hellmaster '92

Francisco Rabal
Bloody Che Contra

Camorra: The Naples
   Connection '85
City of the Walking Dead '83
Diary of a Rebel '84
The Eclipse '66
El Muerto '75
Exorcism's Daughter '74
The Holy Innocents '84
Nazarin '58
The Nun '66
Reborn '78
Sorcerer '77
Stay As You Are '78
The Stilts '84
Tie Me Up! Tie Me Down! '90
A Time of Destiny '88
Viridiana '61

Alessandro Rabelo
Where the River Runs Black
   '86

Catherine Rabett
Frankenstein Unbound '90
Livin' the Life '84

Hugo Race
In Too Deep '90

Francine Racette
Au Revoir Les Enfants '87
Lumiere '76

Thom Rachford
The Prodigal Planet '88

Alan Rachins
Heart Condition '90
L.A. Law '86
Mistress '87

Victoria Racimo
Ernest Goes to Camp '87
G.I. Executioner '71
Green Eyes '76
Prophecy '79
Roanoak '86
Search for the Gods '75

Kurt Rackelmann
First Spaceship on Venus '60

Marty Rackham
Body Trouble '92

Steve Rackman
The Kick Fighter '91

Sudhir Rad
Morgan Stewart's Coming
   Home '87

Goran Radakovic
Hey, Babu Riba '88

Rosemary Radcliffe
Anne of Green Gables '85

Claudia Rademaker
Lady Terminator '89

Fons Rademakers
Daughters of Darkness '71

Sascha Radetsky
Home at Last '88

Basil Radford
Captive Heart '47
Dead of Night '45
The Lady Vanishes '38
Passport to Pimlico '49
Whiskey Galore '48
The Winslow Boy '48

Natalie Radford
Tomcat: Dangerous Desires
   '93

Radha
The River '51

Ken Radley
Sniper '92

Gilda Radner
All You Need Is Cash '78
Best of Chevy Chase '87
Best of Dan Aykroyd '86
Best of Gilda Radner '89
Best of John Belushi '85
First Family '80
Hanky Panky '82
Haunted Honeymoon '86
It Came from Hollywood '82
The Last Detail '73
Mr. Mike's Mondo Video '79
Movers and Shakers '85
The Woman in Red '84

Jerzy Radziwilowicz
Man of Marble '76

Charlotte Rae
Bananas '71
The Hot Rock '70
Jenny '70
Queen of the Stardust
   Ballroom '75
Sidewinder One '77
The Triangle Factory Fire
   Scandal '79
Words by Heart '84

Rafael
The Life & Loves of a Male
   Stripper '87

Bob Rafelson
Always '85

Erika Raffael
The Big Switch '70

Chips Rafferty
The Desert Rats '53
Double Trouble '67
Eureka Stockade '49
Forty Thousand Horsemen
   '41
Overlanders '46
Skullduggery '70
The Sundowners '60
Wackiest Ship in the Army '61
Walk into Hell '57

Frances Rafferty
Abbott and Costello in
   Hollywood '45
Curley '47
Mrs. Parkington '44
Money Madness '47

Deborah Raffin
Claudia '85
Death Wish 3 '85
The Dove '74
For the Love of It '80
Forty Carats '73
God Told Me To '76
Hanging on a Star '78
How to Pick Up Girls '78
Jungle Heat '84
Killing at Hell's Gate '81
Maniac '78
Night of the Fox '90
Nightmare in Badham County
   '76
Once is Not Enough '75
Ransom '84
Scanners 2: The New Order
   '91
Snowblind '78
Touched by Love '80
Willa '79

George Raft
Around the World in 80 Days
   '56
Background to Danger '43
The Best of Abbott & Costello
   Live '54
Casino Royale '67
Each Dawn I Die '39

Raft ▶cont.

Five Golden Dragons '67
House Across the Bay '40
I'll Get You '53
Jet Over the Atlantic '59
Johnny Angel '45
Loan Shark '52
Man from Cairo '54
Mr. Ace '46
Nocturne '46
Outpost in Morocco '49
Scarface '31
Sextette '78
Some Like It Hot '59
Stage Door Canteen '43
They Drive by Night '40
Whistle Stop '46

Jerry Rages
Machoman '70s

Rags Ragland
The Canterville Ghost '44
DuBarry Was a Lady '43
Panama Hattie '42
Whistling in Brooklyn '43
Whistling in the Dark '41

Floyd Ragner
The Vernonia Incident '89

Joe Ragno
The Babe '92

William Ragsdale
Fright Night '85
Fright Night 2 '88
Mannequin 2: On the Move '91

Ramona Rahman
Fifty Fifty '93

Umberto Raho
Aladdin '86
The Night Evelyn Came Out of the Grave '71
Satanik '69

Steve Railsback
Alligator 2: The Mutation '90
Angela '77
Armed and Dangerous '86
Assassin '89
Blue Monkey '87
Deadly Games '80
Deadly Intent '88
Distortions '87
Escape 2000 '81
The Forgotten '89
From Here to Eternity '79
The Golden Seal '83
Helter Skelter '76
Lifeforce '85
Quake '92
Scenes from the Goldmine '87
Scissors '91
The Stunt Man '80
Sunstroke '92
The Survivalist '87
Torchlight '85
Trick or Treats '82
The Wind '87

Lucien Raimbourg
The Devil's Nightmare '71

Sam Raimi
Indian Summer '93
Thou Shalt Not Kill...Except '87

Theodore Raimi
The Finishing Touch '92
Lunatics: A Love Story '92

Ruggero Raimondi
La Truite '83

Raimu
The Baker's Wife '33
Cesar '36
Fanny '32
Heart of a Nation '43
Marius '31
Well-Digger's Daughter '46

Douglas Rain
Oedipus Rex '57

Joe Rainer
Final Cut '88

Luise Rainer
The Good Earth '37
The Great Waltz '38
The Great Ziegfeld '36
Tiefland '44

Beth Raines
Forever '78

Christina Raines
The Duellists '78
Livin' the Life '84
Nashville '75
Nightmares '83
North Shore '87
Quo Vadis '85
Russian Roulette '75
The Sentinel '76
The Shrieking '73
Silver Dream Racer '83
Stacey '73
Touched by Love '80

Ella Raines
Hail the Conquering Hero '44
Impact '49
Ride the Man Down '53
The Senator was Indiscreet '47
The Strange Affair of Uncle Harry '45
Tall in the Saddle '44

Frances Raines
The Mutilator '85

Lisa Raines
Fanny Hill '83

Ford Rainey
Babe! '75
The Cellar '90
Mountain Man '77
My Sweet Charlie '70
Sixteen '72
Strange New World '75
Strangers: The Story of a Mother and Daughter '79

Shugfoot Rainey
Common Law Wife '63

Claude Rains
The Adventures of Robin Hood '38
Angel on My Shoulder '46
Anthony Adverse '36
Battle of the Worlds '61
Caesar and Cleopatra '46
Casablanca '42
Deception '46
The Evil Mind '34
Forever and a Day '43
Four Daughters '38
The Greatest Story Ever Told '65
Here Comes Mr. Jordan '41
The Invisible Man '33
Juarez '39
Kings Row '41
Lawrence of Arabia '62
Lisbon '56
Mr. Skeffington '44
Mr. Smith Goes to Washington '39
Notorious '46

Now, Voyager '42
Paris Express '53
Passage to Marseilles '44
Phantom of the Opera '43
Pied Piper of Hamelin '57
The Prince and the Pauper '37
The Sea Hawk '40
They Made Me a Criminal '39
They Won't Forget '37
The White Tower '50
The Wolf Man '41

Bonnie Raitt
Muse Concert: No Nukes '80

John Raitt
Pajama Game '57

Tommy Rall
Dancers '87
Kiss Me Kate '53
My Sister Eileen '55
Seven Brides for Seven Brothers '54

Giovanna Ralli
Caper of the Golden Bulls '67
General Della Rovere '60
Sex with a Smile '76
What Did You Do in the War, Daddy? '66

Paul Ralli
Show People '28

Steve Rally
Overkill '86

Jessie Ralph
After the Thin Man '36
The Bank Dick '40
The Blue Bird '40
Double Wedding '37
Drums Along the Mohawk '39
I Live My Life '35
The Last of Mrs. Cheyney '37
Little Lord Fauntleroy '36
One Night of Love '34
San Francisco '36

Sheryl Lee Ralph
Codename: Foxfire '85
The Distinguished Gentleman '92
Mistress '91

David Ralphe
Heaven's Heroes '88

Darla Ralston
Thinkin' Big '87

Esther Ralston
$50,000 Reward '25
Lonely Wives '31
Lucky Devil '25
Old Ironsides '26
Oliver Twist '22
Shadows of the Orient '37
To the Last Man '33
We're in the Legion Now '37

James Ralston
Night of the Strangler '73

Jobyna Ralston
Dr. Jack/For Heaven's Sake '26
For Heaven's Sake '26
The Freshman '25
Girl Shy '24
The Kid Brother '27

Vera Ralston
Dakota '45
The Fighting Kentuckian '49
Hoodlum Empire '52
Jubilee Trail '54

Cecil Ramage
King of the Damned '36

Elba Ramalho
Opera do Malandro '87

Gordon Raman
Headless Eyes '83

Enrique Rambal
The Exterminating Angel '62
The Man and the Monster '65
Para Servir a Usted '87
Sexo Y Crimen '87

Marjorie Rambeau
Forever Female '53
Laughing Sinners '31
A Man Called Peter '55
Man of a Thousand Faces '57
Min & Bill '30
Primrose Path '40
Santa Fe Marshal '40
Torch Song '53

Dack Rambo
Hit Lady '74
River of Diamonds '90
The Spring '89
Ultra Warrior '90s
Waikiki '80

Emil Rameau
Gaslight '44

Henry Ramer
The Big Slice '90
Hockey Night '84
My Pleasure Is My Business '74
Reno and the Doc '84
Starship Invasions '77

Carlos Ramirez
Anchors Aweigh '45
Bathing Beauty '44
Two Girls and a Sailor '44

Frank Ramirez
Miracle in Rome '88
Smith! '69

Luis Alberto Ramirez
A Very Old Man with Enormous Wings '88

Luis Fernando Ramirez
Cancion en el Alma

Lyota Ramirez
Street Hitz '92

Paul Ramirez
Street Warriors, Part 2 '87

Raul Ramirez
El Ciclon '47

Harold Ramis
Baby Boom '87
Best of Comic Relief '86
The Best of John Candy on SCTV '80s
Ghostbusters '84
Ghostbusters 2 '89
Stealing Home '88
Stripes '81

Rayak Ramnate
After the Fall of Saigon '88

Juan Ramon
Lost Diamond '74

Bob Ramos
Weapons of Death '83

Rudy Ramos
Colors '88
Open House '86
Quicksilver '86

Sergio Ramos
Bus Station '88

Tacos al Carbon '87

Charlotte Rampling
Angel Heart '87
Caravan to Vaccares '74
The Damned '69
D.O.A. '88
Farewell, My Lovely '75
Foxtrot '76
Georgy Girl '66
Mascara '87
The Night Porter '74
Orca '77
The Purple Taxi '77
Sardinia Kidnapped '75
Ski Bum '75
Stardust Memories '80
'Tis a Pity She's a Whore '73
The Verdict '82
Zardoz '73

Anne Elizabeth Ramsay
A League of Their Own '92

Bruce Ramsay
Alive '93

Remak Ramsay
The Dining Room '86
Mr. & Mrs. Bridge '91

John Ramsbottom
Kill and Kill Again '81

Frances Ramsden
The Sin of Harold Diddlebock '47

Anne Ramsey
Another Chance '88
The Boy in the Plastic Bubble '76
Deadly Friend '86
Dr. Hackenstein '88
Goin' South '78
The Goonies '85
Marilyn: The Untold Story '80
Meet the Hollowheads '89
A Small Killing '81
Throw Momma from the Train '87
Weeds '87
White Mama '80

Logan Ramsey
Confessions of Tom Harris '72
Conspiracy of Terror '75
Dr. Hackenstein '88
Fury on Wheels '71
Say Yes! '86

Marion Ramsey
Police Academy 3: Back in Training '86
Police Academy 5: Assignment Miami Beach '88
Police Academy 6: City Under Siege '89

Thea Ramsey
Maniac '34

Ward Ramsey
Dinosaurus! '60

Nick Ramus
Journey to Spirit Island '92

Peter Ramwa
After the Fall of Saigon '88

Frederica Ranchi
Son of Samson '62

Renee Rancourt
Beyond the Door 3 '91

The Wreck of the Mary Deare
'59

Vanessa Redgrave
Agatha '79
The Ballad of the Sad Cafe
'91
Bear Island '80
Blow-Up '66
The Bostonians '84
Camelot '67
Consuming Passions '88
The Devils '71
Howard's End '92
Isadora '68
Julia '77
A Man for All Seasons '88
Morgan! '66
Murder on the Orient Express
'74
Orpheus Descending '91
Out of Season '75
Peter the Great '86
Playing for Time '80
Prick Up Your Ears '87
The Seven Percent Solution
'76
Snow White and the Seven
Dwarfs '83
Steaming '86
Three Sovereigns for Sarah
'85
Trojan Women '71
Wagner: The Complete Epic
'85
Wagner: The Movie '85
Wetherby '85
Yanks '79
Young Catherine '91

Juli Reding
Mission in Morocco '59
Tormented '60

Nick Reding
Mister Johnson '91

Richard Redlin
Victimless Crimes '90

Amanda Redman
Richard's Things '80

Joyce Redman
A Different Kind of Love '85
Tom Jones '63

Charles Redmond
Ocean Drive Weekend '85

Liam Redmond
Devil on Horseback '54
The Last Safari '67

Marge Redmond
Adam at 6 A.M. '70

Siobhan Redmond
Look Back in Anger '89

Eric Redner
Challenge the Ninja '80s

Joe Redner
Clash of the Ninja '86
Thundering Ninja '80s

Emiliano Redondo
Black Venus '83

Bill Redvers
Wardogs '87

Brian Reece
Carry On Admiral '57

Alaina Reed
Eubie! '82

Alan Reed
Actors and Sin '52
Days of Glory '43
The Flintstones '60

The Flintstones: Dino & Juliet
'89
Lady and the Tramp '55
The Postman Always Rings
Twice '46
Shinbone Alley '70

Alyson Reed
A Chorus Line '85
Skin Deep '89

Diana Reed
Jesse James Under the Black
Flag '21

Dolly Reed
Beyond the Valley of the Dolls
'70

Donna Reed
The Benny Goodman Story
'55
The Caddy '53
From Here to Eternity '53
Green Dolphin Street '47
Gun Fury '53
Hangman's Knot '52
The Human Comedy '43
It's a Wonderful Life '46
The Last Time I Saw Paris '54
Picture of Dorian Gray '45
Shadow of the Thin Man '41
They Were Expendable '45
Thousands Cheer '43
Trouble Along the Way '53

Gavin Reed
The Body Beneath '70

George Reed
Green Pastures '36
Strange Illusion '45

Hal Reed
The Zodiac Killer '71

James Reed
Eight Men Out '88

Jerry Reed
Bat 21 '88
The Concrete Cowboys '79
Gator '83
High Ballin' '78
Hot Stuff '80
Ramblin' Man '79
Smokey and the Bandit '77
Smokey and the Bandit, Part
2 '80
Smokey and the Bandit, Part
3 '83
Survivors '83
What Comes Around '85

Joel M. Reed
Night of the Zombies '81

Lady Reed
Avenging Disco Godfather '76
Dolemite 2: Human Tornado
'76

Lou Reed
Get Crazy '83
One Trick Pony '80

Maxwell Reed
Blackout '50
Dear Murderer '47
Night Beat '48
Roadhouse Girl '53
Sea Devils '53

Miriam Reed
Ruby Cairo '92

Oliver Reed
The Adventures of Baron
Munchausen '89
The Assassination Bureau '69
Beat Girl '60
The Big Sleep '78

The Black Arrow '84
Blood Island '68
Blue Blood '73
The Brood '79
Burnt Offerings '76
Captive '87
Captive Rage '88
Castaway '87
Christopher Columbus '85
The Class of Miss MacMichael
'78
Condorman '81
The Curse of the Werewolf
'61
Dante's Inferno: Life of Dante
Gabriel Rossetti '69
The Devils '71
Dr. Heckyl and Mr. Hype '80
Dragonard '88
Fanny Hill '83
The Four Musketeers '75
Gor '88
Great Scout & Cathouse
Thursday '76
Hired to Kill '91
The House of Usher '88
Lion of the Desert '81
Maniac '78
Master of Dragonard Hill '89
The Misfit Brigade '87
No Love for Johnnie '60
Oliver! '68
One Russian Summer '73
The Pit & the Pendulum '91
The Prince and the Pauper '78
Prisoner of Honor '91
Rage to Kill '88
Ransom '84
The Revenger '90
Sell Out '76
Severed Ties '92
Skeleton Coast '89
Spasms '82
The Sting 2 '83
Sword of Sherwood Forest
'60
Ten Little Indians '75
Three Musketeers '74
Tommy '75
Tomorrow Never Comes '77
Trap '66
Treasure Island '89
Triple Echo '77
Two of a Kind '83
Venom '82
Women in Love '70
Zero Population Growth '72

Pamela Reed
The Best of Times '86
Cadillac Man '90
Caroline? '90
Chattahoochee '89
The Clan of the Cave Bear '86
Eyewitness '81
The Goodbye People '83
Kindergarten Cop '90
The Long Riders '80
Melvin and Howard '80
Passed Away '92
Rachel River '89
The Right Stuff '83
Tanner '88 '88
Young Doctors in Love '82

Patricia Reed
Scandal '80s

Penelope Reed
Amazons '86
Hired to Kill '91

Philip Reed
Bandit Queen '51
Big Town '47
Big Town After Dark '47
Female '33

Song of the Thin Man '47
Underworld Scandal '47
Unknown Island '48

Ralph Reed
Reform School Girl '57

Rex Reed
Myra Breckinridge '70

Ricky Addison Reed
Return to Salem's Lot '87

Robert Reed
Bloodlust '59
The Boy in the Plastic Bubble
'76
Bud and Lou '78
Casino '80
Death of a Centerfold '81
Haunts of the Very Rich '72
The Hunted Lady '77
The Love Bug '68
Love's Savage Fury '79
Nightmare in Badham County
'76
No Prince for My Cinderella
'78
Nurse '80
Prime Target '91
The Seekers '79
Snatched '72
A Very Brady Christmas '88

Shanna Reed
The Banker '89
Legs '83

Suzanne Reed
Beyond the Bermuda Triangle
'75
Up from the Depths '79

Tracy Reed
No Way Back '74
Piece of the Action '77

Walter Reed
Government Agents vs.
Phantom Legion '51
How to Make a Monster '58
Macumba Love '60
Seven Days' Leave '42

William Reed
Necropolis '87

Karen Reel
Thunder Warrior 2 '85

Harry Reems
Deadly Weapons '70
R.S.V.P. '84

Angharad Rees
Hands of the Ripper '71

Betty A. Rees
Unholy Rollers '72

Donough Rees
Starship '87

Lannie Rees
My Dog Shep '46

Roger Rees
Charles & Diana: A Palace
Divided '93
Ebony Tower '86
If Looks Could Kill '91
Mountains of the Moon '90
Robin Hood: Men in Tights '93
Star 80 '83
Stop! or My Mom Will Shoot
'92

Della Reese
Harlem Nights '89
The Kid Who Loved Christmas
'90
Nightmare in Badham County
'76

Psychic Killer '75
The Voyage of the Yes '72

Michelle Reese
Night Stalker '87

Tom Reese
The Hollywood Detective '89

Christopher Reeve
Anna Karenina '85
The Aviator '85
The Bostonians '84
Death Dreams '92
Deathtrap '82
Gray Lady Down '77
The Great Escape 2: The
Untold Story '88
Monsignor '82
Mortal Sins '92
Noises Off '92
The Rose and the Jackal '90
Sleeping Beauty '83
Somewhere in Time '80
Street Smart '87
Superman: The Movie '78
Superman 2 '80
Superman 3 '83
Superman 4: The Quest for
Peace '87
Switching Channels '88

Geoffrey Reeve
Puppet on a Chain '72

George Reeves
Bar-20 '43
Blood and Sand '41
Border Patrol '43
Bugles in the Afternoon '52
Colt Comrades '43
The Fighting 69th '40
Forever Female '53
From Here to Eternity '53
Gone with the Wind '39
The Great Lover '49
Hoppy Serves a Writ '43
Jungle Goddess '49
Leather Burners '43
Lydia '41
The Making of a Legend:
"Gone With the Wind" '89
Rancho Notorious '52
Stamp Day for Superman '53
Strawberry Blonde '41
Superman & the Mole Men '51
Thunder in the Pines '49
Westward Ho, the Wagons!
'56

Keanu Reeves
Babes in Toyland '86
Bill & Ted's Bogus Journey
'91
Bill & Ted's Excellent
Adventure '89
Bram Stoker's Dracula '92
Brotherhood of Justice '86
Dangerous Liaisons '88
Dream to Believe '85
I Love You to Death '90
Much Ado About Nothing '93
My Own Private Idaho '91
The Night Before '88
Parenthood '89
Permanent Record '88
Point Break '91
Prince of Pennsylvania '88
River's Edge '87
Tune in Tomorrow '90
Youngblood '86

Lisa Reeves
The Chicken Chronicles '77
Pom Pom Girls '76
Snowblind '78

Martha Reeves
Fairytales '79

Rijn ▶cont.

Special Effects '85

Lineke Rijxman
Broken Mirrors '85

Robin Riker
Alligator '80
Body Chemistry 2: Voice of a
   Stranger '91
Stepmonster '92

**Bridgett "Baby
Doll" Riley**
Triple Impact '92

Elaine Riley
Clipped Wings '53
Hopalong Cassidy: Borrowed
   Trouble '48
Hopalong Cassidy: The Devil's
   Playground '46
Rider from Tucson '50

Gary Riley
Amazing Stories, Book 5 '85

Jack Riley
Night Patrol '84
Portrait of a White Marriage
   '88

Jeannine Riley
Big Mouth '67
The Comic '69
Electra Glide in Blue '73
Wackiest Wagon Train in the
   West '77

John Riley
Greenstone '85

Larry Riley
Crackers '84
Dead Solid Perfect '88
A Soldier's Story '84

Michael Riley
Perfectly Normal '91
To Catch a Killer '92

Rob Riley
Mutant Video '76

Eli Rill
Slipstream '72

Walter Rilla
Black Eyes '39
Frozen Alive '64
The Gamma People '56
The Golden Salamander '51
House of Mystery '41
Mr. Emmanuel '44

Shane Rimmer
The People That Time Forgot
   '77
S*P*Y*S '74

Rin Tin Tin Jr
The Adventures of Rex &
   Rinty '35
Lightning Warrior '31

Susan Rinell
Pals '87

Blanche Ring
It's the Old Army Game '26

Erica Ringston
Last Dance '91

Molly Ringwald
Betsy's Wedding '90
The Breakfast Club '85
Face the Music '92
For Keeps '88
Fresh Horses '88
Johnny Appleseed '86

King Lear '87
Packin' It In '83
The Pick-Up Artist '87
P.K. and the Kid '85
Pretty in Pink '86
Sixteen Candles '84
Spacehunter: Adventures in
   the Forbidden Zone '83
Strike It Rich '90
The Tempest '82
Women & Men: Stories of
   Seduction '90

Brad Rinn
Smithereens '84

Lisa Rinna
Robot Wars '93

Dante Rino
The Golden Coach '52

David Rintoul
Legend of the Werewolf '75
Pride and Prejudice '85

Nicole Rio
Sorority House Massacre '86
Visitants '87
Zero Boys '86

Marjorie Riordan
The Hoodlum '51
Pursuit to Algiers '45
South of Monterey '47
Stage Door Canteen '43

Guillermo Rios
Old Gringo '89

Genevieve Rioux
The Decline of the American
   Empire '86

Michael Ripper
The Curse of the Werewolf
   '61
Dead Lucky '60
Dracula Has Risen from the
   Grave '68
Eye Witness '49
Girly '70
Quatermass 2 '57
The Scars of Dracula '70
Where the Bullets Fly '66

Frank Ripploh
Taxi zum Klo '81

Leon Rippy
Eye of the Storm '91
Jesse '88
Kuffs '92
Track 29 '88

Carlos Riquelme
The Milagro Beanfield War '88

Elisabeth Risdon
Crime and Punishment '35
Down Dakota Way '49
The Great Man Votes '38
Guilty of Treason '50
Mannequin '37
Mexican Spitfire at Sea '42
Reap the Wild Wind '42
Scaramouche '52

Miriam Riselle
The Singing Blacksmith '38
Tevye '39

Jeff Risk
Kill Squad '81

Jacques Rispal
Le Chat '75

Roberto Risso
Gladiator of Rome '63

Gary Rist
The Young Graduates '71

Robbie Rist
He is My Brother '75
Teenage Mutant Ninja Turtles:
   The Movie '90

Cyril Ritchard
Blackmail '29
The First Christmas '75
Half a Sixpence '67
Hans Brinker '69
Peter Pan '60

Bruce Ritchey
A Child is Waiting '63

Clint Ritchie
Against A Crooked Sky '75
Peacekillers '71
The St. Valentine's Day
   Massacre '67

June Ritchie
A Kind of Loving '62
The Three Penny Opera '62

Kristen Riter
Student Bodies '81

Jennifer Riter
The Young Graduates '71

Martin Ritt
Conrack '74
The Slugger's Wife '85

Brent Ritter
Curse of the Blue Lights '88

John Ritter
Americathon '79
The Barefoot Executive '71
Comeback Kid '80
Flight of Dragons '82
Hero at Large '80
In Love with an Older Woman
   '82
The Last Fling '86
Letting Go '85
Noises Off '92
The Other '72
Pray TV '82
Problem Child '90
Problem Child 2 '91
Real Men '87
Skin Deep '89
A Smoky Mountain Christmas
   '86
Stay Tuned '92
Stephen King's It '90
The Stone Killer '73
Sunset Limousine '83
They All Laughed '81
Tricks of the Trade '88
Unnatural Causes '86
Wholly Moses! '80

Tex Ritter
Arizona Days '37
Cowboy '54
Cowboys of the Saturday
   Matinee '84
Dead or Alive '41
Enemy of the Law '45
Frontier Fugitives '45
Gangsters of the Frontier '44
The Girl from Tobacco Row
   '66
Headin' for the Rio Grande '36
Hittin' the Trail '37
Holiday Rhythm '50
Man from Texas '39
Marked for Murder '45
The Marshal's Daughter '53
Mystery of the Hooded
   Horseman '37
The Pioneers '41
Riders of the Rockies '37
Roll, Wagons, Roll '39
Rollin' Plains '38
Sing, Cowboy, Sing '37

Song of the Gringo '36
Take Me Back to Oklahoma
   '40
Tex Rides with the Boy
   Scouts '37
Three in the Saddle '45
Trouble in Texas '37
Utah Trail '38

Thelma Ritter
All About Eve '50
As Young As You Feel '51
Birdman of Alcatraz '62
Boeing Boeing '65
Daddy Long Legs '55
The Farmer Takes a Wife '53
For Love or Money '63
A Hole in the Head '59
How the West was Won '63
The Incident '67
A Letter to Three Wives '49
Miracle on 34th Street '47
The Misfits '61
A New Kind of Love '63
Pickup on South Street '53
Pillow Talk '59
Rear Window '54

The Ritz Brothers
Blazing Stewardesses '75
The Goldwyn Follies '38

Harry Ritz
Silent Movie '76
Texas Layover '75

Jimmy Ritz
Texas Layover '75

Emmanuelle Riva
Hiroshima, Mon Amour '59
Kapo '59
Leon Morin, Priest '61

Sandra Riva
The Green Wall '70

Carlos Rivas
The Black Scorpion '57
El Cuarto Chino '71
The King and I '56

Guillermo Rivas
Bus Station '88
Los Hermanos Centella '65

Sonia Rivas
Lost Diamond '74

Amparo Rivelles
Anita de Montemar '60s
El Fugitivo '65

Luisa Rivelli
A Game of Crime '60

Gabriel River
Ecstasy Inc. '87

Cecilia Rivera
Aguirre, the Wrath of God '72

Chita Rivera
Mayflower Madam '87
Once Upon a Brothers Grimm
   '77
Pippin '81
Sweet Charity '69
That's Singing: The Best of
   Broadway '84

Kirk Rivera
Body Moves '90

Patricia Rivera
La Fuga del Rojo '87

George Rivero
Bordello '79
Counterforce '87
Fist Fighter '88
Target Eagle '84

Jorge Rivero
Bellas de Noche
Conquest '83
Day of the Assassin '81
El Hombre Contra el Mundo
   '87
La Montana del Diablo '87
Los Caciques '87
Los Dos Hermanos '87
Priest of Love '81
Rio Lobo '70
Sin of Adam & Eve '72
Sin Salida '87
Soldier Blue '70
Volver, Volver, Volver! '87

Julian Rivero
Arizona Gangbusters '40
Heroes of the Alamo '37
Man from Hell's Edges '32
Phantom Patrol '36
Ridin' the Lone Trail '37

Joan Rivers
Les Patterson Saves the
   World '90
Muppets Take Manhattan '84
Pee-Wee's Playhouse
   Christmas Special '88
Spaceballs '87

Michael Rivers
La Ley del Revolver '78

Victor Rivers
Black Magic Woman '91
Bound by Honor '93

Catherine Rivet
Emmanuelle, the Joys of a
   Woman '76

Jean Riveyre
Diary of a Country Priest '50

George Riviere
Castle of Blood '64
Journey Beneath the Desert
   '61
The Virgin of Nuremberg '65

Isabelle Riviere
Summer '86

Marie Riviere
Summer '86

Lucille Rivin
Home Free All '84

Cheryl Rixon
Swap Meet '79

Gianni Rizzo
Desert Commandos '60s
Mission Stardust '68

Bert Roach
The Crowd '28
The Great Waltz '38

Bruce Roach
Things '80s

Pat Roach
Willow '88

Rickey Roach
Black Devil Doll from Hell '84

Shula Roan
Sinthia: The Devil's Doll '70

Adam Roarke
Beach Girls '82
Dirty Mary Crazy Larry '74
Four Deuces '75
Frogs '72
Hell's Angels on Wheels '67
How Come Nobody's On Our
   Side? '73
Hughes & Harlow: Angels in
   Hell '77

The Losers '70
The Savage Seven '68
This is a Hijack '75
Trespasses '86
Women of the Prehistoric
  Planet '66

John Roarke
Mutant on the Bounty '89

Jason Robards, Sr.
Bedlam '45
Crimson Romance '34
Desperate '47
The Fatal Hour '40
Fighting Marines '36
Mademoiselle Fifi '44
Riff-Raff '47
Rimfire '49
Stunt Pilot '39
Sweetheart of the Navy '37
Wayne Murder Case '38
Western Pacific Agent '51
White Eagle '32

Jason Robards, Jr.
The Adventures of Huck Finn
  '93
All the President's Men '76
Any Wednesday '66
Ballad of Cable Hogue '70
A Big Hand for the Little Lady
  '66
Black Rainbow '91
A Boy and His Dog '75
Breaking Home Ties '87
Bright Lights, Big City '88
Burden of Dreams '82
By Love Possessed '61
Cabo Blanco '81
A Christmas to Remember '78
The Christmas Wife '88
Comes a Horseman '78
The Day After '83
A Doll's House '59
Dream a Little Dream '89
Final Warning '90
Fools '70
The Good Mother '88
Hour of the Gun '67
A House without a Christmas
  Tree '72
Hurricane '79
An Inconvenient Woman '91
Isadora '68
Johnny Got His Gun '71
Julia '77
Julius Caesar '70
Laguna Heat '87
Legend of the Lone Ranger
  '81
Long Day's Journey into Night
  '62
The Long, Hot Summer '86
Mark Twain and Me '91
Max Dugan Returns '83
Melvin and Howard '80
Mr. Sycamore '74
Murders in the Rue Morgue
  '71
The Night They Raided
  Minsky's '69
Once Upon a Time in the West
  '68
Parenthood '89
Quick Change '90
Raise the Titanic '80
Return of the Bad Men '48
Reunion '88
The St. Valentine's Day
  Massacre '67
Sakharov '84
Something Wicked This Way
  Comes '83
Square Dance '87
Storyville '92
A Thousand Clowns '65

Tora! Tora! Tora! '70
Trail Street '47
You Can't Take It with You
  '84

Sam Robards
Fandango '85
Into Thin Air '85
Not Quite Paradise '86
Pancho Barnes '88
The Tempest '82

Willis Robards
The Three Musketeers '21

Barbra Robb
Young Nurses in Love '89

David Robb
The Flame Trees of Thika '80s

Michael Robbin
Rock House '92

Brian Robbins
Cellar Dweller '87
C.H.U.D. 2: Bud the Chud '89

Christmas Robbins
The Demon Lover '77

Cindy Robbins
I Was a Teenage Werewolf
  '57

Gale Robbins
The Barkleys of Broadway '49
The Belle of New York '52
The Fuller Brush Girl '50
My Girl Tisa '48
Parasite '81
Three Little Words '50

Gary Robbins
Ring of Fire 2: Blood and Steel
  '92

Jessie Robbins
The Fearless Vampire Killers
  '67

Marty Robbins
Ballad of a Gunfighter '64
Hell on Wheels '67
Road to Nashville '67

Oliver Robbins
Poltergeist '82
Poltergeist 2: The Other Side
  '86

**Skeeter Bill
Robbins**
Fighting Parson '35
Hard Hombre '31
Man's Land '32

Tim Robbins
Bob Roberts '92
Bull Durham '88
Cadillac Man '90
Erik the Viking '89
Five Corners '88
Fraternity Vacation '85
Howard the Duck '86
Jacob's Ladder '90
Miss Firecracker '89
No Small Affair '84
The Player '92
The Sure Thing '85
Tapeheads '89
Top Gun '86
Toy Soldiers '84

Tom Robbins
Made in Heaven '87

Paul Robeling
Carolina Skeletons '92

Miguel Robelo
Only Once in a Lifetime '83

Richard Rober
Jet Pilot '57
The Well '51

Sean Roberge
Straight Line '88

Allene Roberts
The Hoodlum '51
The Red House '47
Union Station '50

Arthur Roberts
Deadly Vengeance '81
Illegal Entry: Formula for Fear
  '93
Not of This Earth '88

Beverly Roberts
Buried Alive '39

Bill Roberts
Bongo '47

Carol Roberts
Commando Invasion '87

Christian Roberts
The Adventurers '70
Desperados '69
To Sir, with Love '67

Conrad Roberts
The Mosquito Coast '86
The Serpent and the Rainbow
  '87

Daryll Roberts
How U Like Me Now? '92

Des Roberts
Black Bikers from Hell '70
The Outlaw Bikers—Gang
  Wars '70

Doris Roberts
The Fig Tree '87
Hester Street '75
Honeymoon Killers '70
National Lampoon's
  Christmas Vacation '89
The Night We Never Met '93
Ordinary Heroes '85
Simple Justice '89
Used People '92

Edith Roberts
Man from Headquarters '28
The Taxi Mystery '26

Eric Roberts
The Ambulance '90
Best of the Best '89
Best of the Best 2 '93
Blood Red '88
The Coca-Cola Kid '84
Descending Angel '90
A Family Matter '91
Final Analysis '92
King of the Gypsies '78
Lonely Hearts '91
The Lost Capone '90
Nobody's Fool '86
Options '88
Paul's Case '80
The Pope of Greenwich
  Village '84
Raggedy Man '81
Rude Awakening '89
Runaway Train '85
Slow Burn '86
Star 80 '83
To Heal a Nation '88

Florence Roberts
Harmony Lane '35
Kept Husbands '31
Sons of Steel '35

Francesca Roberts
The Heart of Dixie '89

Glenn Roberts
The Crater Lake Monster '77

Ian Roberts
The Power of One '92

Jason Roberts
Claws '85

Jay Roberts, Jr.
Aftershock '88
White Phantom: Enemy of
  Darkness '87

J.H. Roberts
The Courageous Mr. Penn '41

Joe Roberts
Our Hospitality '23

Julia Roberts
Baja Oklahoma '87
Blood Red '88
Dying Young '91
Flatliners '90
Hook '91
Mystic Pizza '88
The Player '92
Pretty Woman '90
Satisfaction '88
Sleeping with the Enemy '91
Steel Magnolias '89

Ken Roberts
Fatal Pulse '88
The Great Land of Small '86

Larry Roberts
Lady and the Tramp '55

Lee Roberts
Battling Marshal '48

Luanne Roberts
Weekend with the Babysitter
  '70

**Lynn (Mary Hart)
Roberts**
Billy the Kid Returns '38
Dynamite Pass '50
Eyes of Texas '48
Frolics on Ice '40
Heart of the Rockies '37
Hollywood Stadium Mystery
  '38
Hunt the Man Down '50
Hunt the Man Down/
  Smashing the Rackets '50
In Old Caliente '39
Robin Hood of Texas '47
Rough Riders' Roundup '34
Shine on, Harvest Moon '38
Sioux City Sue '46

Mariwin Roberts
Enforcer from Death Row '78
Jokes My Folks Never Told
  Me '77

Mark Roberts
Posse '75

Marty Roberts
Alien Space Avenger '91

Michael D. Roberts
Heartbreaker '83
Ice Pirates '84
Live! From Death Row '92
Rain Man '88

Pascale Roberts
Friends '71
Le Grand Chemin '87
The Peking Blond '68

Pernell Roberts
The Errand Boy '61
Four Rode Out '69
High Noon: Part 2 '80
Hot Rod '79

Kashmiri Run '69
Magic of Lassie '78
The Night Train to Kathmandu
  '88
Paco '75
Sniper '75

Rachel Roberts
Alpha Beta '73
Baffled '72
The Belstone Fox '73
Charlie Chan and the Curse of
  the Dragon Queen '81
Doctors' Wives '70
Foul Play '78
The Hostage Tower '80
Murder on the Orient Express
  '74
O Lucky Man '73
Picnic at Hanging Rock '75
Sorrows of Gin '79
This Sporting Life '63
When a Stranger Calls '79
Wild Rovers '71
Yanks '79

Ray Roberts
Alien Dead '85
Force of Evil '49

Roy Roberts
Borderline '50
The Enforcer '51
The Fighting Sullivans '42
Guadalcanal Diary '43
He Walked by Night '48
The King and Four Queens
  '56
Second Chance '53

Tanya Roberts
Almost Pregnant '91
Beastmaster '82
Body Slam '87
California Dreaming '79
Fingers '78
Forced Entry '75
Hearts & Armour '83
Inner Sanctum '91
Legal Tender '90
Night Eyes '90
Purgatory '89
Racquet '79
Sheena '84
Sins of Desire '92
Tourist Trap '79
A View to a Kill '85
The Yum-Yum Girls '78

Teal Roberts
Hardbodies '84

Thayer Roberts
This is Not a Test '62

Theodore Roberts
The Roaring Road '19
Suds '20
Ten Commandments '23

Tony Roberts
Amityville 3: The Demon '83
Annie Hall '77
18 Again! '88
Hannah and Her Sisters '86
If Things Were Different '79
Just Tell Me What You Want
  '80
Key Exchange '85
The Lindbergh Kidnapping
  Case '76
Lovers Like Us '75
A Midsummer Night's Sex
  Comedy '82
Million Dollar Duck '71
Packin' It In '83
Play It Again, Sam '72
Popcorn '89
Question of Honor '80

Reckless '35
Red Headed Woman '32
A Star is Born '37
Strange Interlude '32
Wife Versus Secretary '36

Wayne Robson
And Then You Die '88
Bye Bye Blues '89
The Grey Fox '83
Mania '80s

Patricia Roc
Captain Blackjack '51
Johnny Frenchman '46
Man on the Eiffel Tower '48
The Wicked Lady '45

Pascale Rocard
Field of Honor '87

Daniela Rocca
Divorce—Italian Style '62
The Giant of Marathon '60

Luigina Rocchi
Arabian Nights '74

Alex Rocco
Badge of the Assassin '85
Blood Mania '70
The Blue Knight '75
Bonnie's Kids '73
Boris and Natasha: The Movie '92
Detroit 9000 '73
Dream a Little Dream '89
The Entity '83
The Godfather '72
The Godfather 1902-1959: The Complete Epic '81
Gotcha! '85
The Grass is Always Greener Over the Septic Tank '78
Herbie Goes Bananas '80
Hustling '75
The Lady in White '88
Motor Psycho '65
P.K. and the Kid '85
The Pope Must Diet '91
A Question of Guilt '78
Rabbit Test '78
Return to Horror High '87
Scenes from the Goldmine '87
Slither '73
Stanley '72
The Stunt Man '80
Three the Hard Way '74
Wild Riders '71
Wired '89

Glauce Rocha
Earth Entranced '66

Catherine Roche
Strangers in Good Company '91

Eugene Roche
Corvette Summer '78
Cotton Comes to Harlem '70
Eternity '90
Foul Play '78
The Late Show '77
Newman's Law '74
Oh, God! You Devil '84
The Possessed '77
Rape and Marriage: The Rideout Case '80
Slaughterhouse Five '72
They Might Be Giants '71
W '74
Winds of Kitty Hawk '78

Frank Roche
The Prime Time '60

Gene Roche
The Juggler of Notre Dame '84

Suzzy Roche
Almost You '85
Crossing Delancey '88

Jean Rochefort
Birgitt Haas Must Be Killed '83
The Clockmaker '76
Dirty Hands '76
The Hairdresser's Husband '92
I Sent a Letter to My Love '81
Le Cavaleur '78
Le Complot '73
Le Crabe Tambour '77
Mean Frank and Crazy Tony '75
My Wonderful Life '90
Pardon Mon Affaire '76
Pardon Mon Affaire, Too! '77
Return of the Tall Blond Man With One Black Shoe '74
Salut l'Artiste '74
The Tall Blond Man with One Black Shoe '72
Till Marriage Do Us Part '74
Who is Killing the Great Chefs of Europe? '78

Claire Rochelle
Boothill Brigade '37
Code of the Fearless '39
Guns in the Dark '37
Harvest Melody '43
Ridin' the Lone Trail '37
Shake Hands with Murder '44
Texas Justice '42
Two-Gun Troubador '37

Chris Rock
Boomerang '92
CB4: The Movie '93
Coneheads '93
New Jack City '91

Michael Rock
The Islander '88

Marilyn Rockafellow
The Perfect Bride '91

Charles Rocket
Dances with Wolves '90
Delirious '91
Down Twisted '89
Earth Girls are Easy '89
Fraternity Vacation '85
How I Got into College '89
Miracles '86
Wild Palms '93

Kathy Rockmeier
Getting It On '83

Bradley Rockwell
Presumed Guilty '91

Jack Rockwell
Brand of the Outlaws '36
The Man from Hell '34
Outlaw Rule '36
Raiders of Sunset Pass '43
Renegade Trail '39
The Tonto Kid '35
Tumbleweed Trail '42
Twilight on the Trail '41

Rick Rockwell
Killer Tomatoes Strike Back '90

Robert Rockwell
Lassie: Adventures of Neeka '68
The Red Menace '49

Sam Rockwell
Clown House '88

Benbol Roco
Fight for Us '89

Ziva Rodann
The Giants of Thessaly '60
Last Train from Gun Hill '59
Macumba Love '60
Samar '62

Marcia Rodd
Citizens Band '77
How to Break Up a Happy Divorce '76
Keeping On '81
Little Murders '71

Allison Roddan
Monsieur Verdoux '47

Ebbe Rode
Babette's Feast '87
Gertrud '64
Topsy Turvy '84

Nina Pens Rode
Gertrud '64

Thierry Rode
Hail Mary '85

Anton Rodgers
Impromptu '90
Lillie '79

Jon Rodgers
Sea of Dreams '90

Marie Antoinette Rodgers
Journey to Spirit Island '92

Marilyn Rodgers
Felicity '83

Jack Rodman
Ninja Fantasy '86

John Rodney
Pursued '47

Madeleine Rodrigue
The Crazy Ray '22

Agustin Rodriguez
Final Analysis '92

Dagoberto Rodriguez
Los Hermanos Centella '65
Mision Suicida '87

Estelita Rodriguez
The Gay Ranchero '42
The Golden Stallion '49
Susanna Pass '49
Twilight in the Sierras '50

Johnny Rodriguez
Nashville Girl '76

Jose Antonio Rodriguez
The Last Supper '76

Marco Rodriguez
Internal Affairs '90
The Rookie '90

Milton Rodriguez
Los Cacos '87

Paul Rodriguez
Born in East L.A. '87
La Pastorela '92
Made in America '93
Miracles '86
Quicksilver '86
The Whoopee Boys '86

Rosa Ma Rodriguez
The Blood Spattered Bride '72

Mario Alberto Rodriquez
Los Caciques '87

Ben Rodska
Oliver Twist '85

Norman Rodway
Chimes at Midnight '67

Matt Roe
Last Call '90

Paul Roebling
End of August '82

Daniel Roebuck
Cave Girl '85
Disorganized Crime '89
Dudes '87
The Killing Mind '90
Miles from Home '88
River's Edge '87
Terror Eyes '87

William Roebuck
The Big Sweat '90

Adriana Roel
Diamante, Oro y Amor '87

Gabriela Roel
Old Gringo '89

William Roerick
The Love Machine '71
A Separate Peace '73
The Wasp Woman '49

Maurice Roeves
The Big Man: Crossing the Line '91
Danger UXB '81
Hidden Agenda '90
The Last of the Mohicans '92
Ulysses '67

Beth Rogan
Mysterious Island '61

Michael Rogan
Doom Asylum '88
Punch the Clock '90

Roger-Pierre
Mon Oncle D'Amerique '80

Alva Rogers
Daughters of the Dust '92

Bill Rogers
Shanty Tramp '67

Cecile Rogers
Athena '54

Charles "Buddy" Rogers
Mexican Spitfire at Sea '42
My Best Girl '27
Wings '27

Dinah Anne Rogers
A Legacy for Leonette '85

Doris Rogers
Gangway '37

Gil Rogers
The Children '80

Ginger Rogers
Bachelor Mother '39
The Barkleys of Broadway '49
Carefree '38
Cinderella '64
Fifth Avenue Girl '39
Finishing School '33
Flying Down to Rio '33
Follow the Fleet '36
Forever Female '53
42nd Street '33
The Gay Divorcee '34
Gold Diggers of 1933 '33
Gotta Dance, Gotta Sing '84
Having Wonderful Time '38
Having Wonderful Time/Carnival Boat '38

Heartbeat '46
In Person '35
Irving Berlin's America '86
Kitty Foyle '40
Lucky Partners '40
Monkey Business '52
Once Upon a Honeymoon '42
Primrose Path '40
Quick, Let's Get Married '71
Roberta '35
Romance in Manhattan '34
Shall We Dance '37
Shriek in the Night '33
Stage Door '37
Star of Midnight '35
The Story of Vernon and Irene Castle '39
Swing Time '36
Tender Comrade '43
That's Dancing! '85
13th Guest '32
The Tip-Off '31
Tom, Dick, and Harry '41
Top Hat '35
Vivacious Lady '38
Weekend at the Waldorf '45
We're Not Married '52

Ina Rogers
Buford's Beach Bunnies '92

Ivan Rogers
Ballbuster
Crazed Cop '88
Slow Burn '90
Two Wrongs Make a Right '89

Jean Rogers
Ace Drummond '36
Flash Gordon: Mars Attacks the World '38
Flash Gordon: Rocketship '36
Rocketship '36
Squadron of Doom '36
Whistling in Brooklyn '43

Jimmy Rogers
False Colors '43
Hopalong Cassidy: Riders of the Deadline '43
Mystery Man '44
Texas Masquerade '44

Kasey Rogers
The Naked Flame '68

Kenny Rogers
Coward of the County '81
Kenny Rogers as the Gambler '80
Kenny Rogers as the Gambler, Part 2: The Adventure Continues '83
Kenny Rogers as the Gambler, Part 3: The Legend Continues '87
The Return of Spinal Tap '92
Rio Diablo '93
Six Pack '82
Wild Horses '84

Maggie Rogers
The Ghastly Ones '68

Melanie Rogers
Striker '88

Melody Rogers
Hooch '76

Mimi Rogers
Blue Skies Again '83
Dark Horse '92
Deadlock '92
Desperate Hours '90
Embassy '85
Fourth Story '90
Gung Ho '85
Hider in the House '90
Ladykiller '92

Cherie Romaors
The Malibu Beach Vampires '91

Anatoly Romashin
Rasputin '85

Lina Romay
Gemidos de Placer '70s
Ilsa, the Wicked Warden '78
Love Laughs at Andy Hardy '46
The Loves of Irina '80s

Luis Romay
Death of a Bureaucrat '66

Sindi Rome
Knock Outs '92
Swift Justice '88

Sydne Rome
Diary of Forbidden Dreams '73
Just a Gigolo '79
Order to Kill '73
The Puma Man '80
That Lucky Touch '75
Twist '76
Wanted: Babysitter '75

Rachel Romen
The Girl from Tobacco Row '66
Ransom Money '88

Fred Romer
Great Adventure '75

Kim Romer
A Day in October '92

Cesar Romero
Americano '55
Around the World in 80 Days '56
Batman '66
The Beautiful Blonde from Bashful Bend '49
The Big Push '75
The Computer Wore Tennis Shoes '69
Crooks & Coronets '69
Dance Hall '41
Donovan's Reef '63
FBI Girl '52
The Great American Broadcast '41
Gun Crazy '69
Happy Go Lovely '51
Judgment Day '88
Julia Misbehaves '48
Jungle '52
The Little Princess '39
The Lost Continent '51
Lust in the Dust '85
Madigan's Millions '67
Mission to Glory '80
Mortuary Academy '91
Now You See Him, Now You Don't '72
Orchestra Wives '42
The Proud and the Damned '72
The Racers '55
Scotland Yard Inspector '52
The Shadow Man '53
Show Them No Mercy '35
Simple Justice '89
The Spectre of Edgar Allen Poe '73
Springtime in the Rockies '42
The Thin Man '34
Vera Cruz '53
Wee Willie Winkie '37

Chanda Romero
The Last Reunion '80
Olongape: The American Dream '89

David Romero
Over the Summer '85

Joanelle Romero
Lost Legacy: A Girl Called Hatter Fox '77

Ned Romero
Children of the Corn 2: The Final Sacrifice '92
The Deerslayer '78
House 4: Home Deadly Home '91
I Will Fight No More Forever '75
The Last of the Mohicans '85

Tina Romero
Sisters of Satan '75

Daniela Romo
Frontera

John Romo
Dead Women in Lingerie '90

Danny Ronan
Nightmare '82

Clelia Rondinelli
Where's Piccone '84

Maurice Ronet
Beau Pere '81
Besame '87
The Deadly Trap '71
The Fire Within '64
Frantic '58
How Sweet It Is! '68
The Lost Command '66
L'Odeur des Fauves '66
Scandal Man '67
Sidney Sheldon's Bloodline '79
Sphinx '81
Swimming Pool '70
Time Out for Love '61
Without Warning '52
The Women '69

John Roney
Barnum '86

Linda Ronstadt
Chuck Berry: Hail! Hail! Rock 'n' Roll '87
FM '78
La Pastorela '92
The Pirates of Penzance '83

Michael Rooker
Afterburn '92
Cliffhanger '93
The Dark Half '91
Days of Thunder '90
Eight Men Out '88
Henry: Portrait of a Serial Killer '90
JFK '91
Mississippi Burning '88
Music Box '89
Sea of Love '89

Charles Rooner
The Pearl '48

Mickey Rooney
Ace of Hearts '85
The Adventures of Huckleberry Finn '39
Ah, Wilderness! '35
Andy Hardy Gets Spring Fever '39
Andy Hardy Meets Debutante '40
Andy Hardy's Double Life '42
Andy Hardy's Private Secretary '41
The Atomic Kid '54
Babes in Arms '39
Babes on Broadway '41

The Big Wheel '49
Bill '81
Bill: On His Own '83
The Black Stallion '79
Boys Town '38
Breakfast at Tiffany's '61
The Bridges at Toko-Ri '55
Captains Courageous '37
The Care Bears Movie '84
The Comic '69
The Dark Side of Love '79
The Domino Principle '77
Erik the Viking '89
Find the Lady '75
Girl Crazy '43
Healer '36
Hide-Out '34
Home for Christmas '90
How to Stuff a Wild Bikini '65
The Human Comedy '43
It Came Upon a Midnight Clear '84
It's a Mad, Mad, Mad, Mad World '63
The King of the Roaring '20s: The Story of Arnold Rothstein '61
Leave 'Em Laughing '81
The Legend of Wolf Mountain '92
Life Begins for Andy Hardy '41
Lightning: The White Stallion '86
Little Lord Fauntleroy '36
Love Finds Andy Hardy '38
Love Laughs at Andy Hardy '46
Magic of Lassie '78
Manhattan Melodrama '34
Manipulator '71
Maximum Force '92
Men of Boys Town '41
Mickey Rooney in the Classic Mickey McGuire Silly Comedies
Mickey the Great '39
A Midsummer Night's Dream '35
My Heroes Have Always Been Cowboys '91
My Outlaw Brother '51
National Velvet '44
The Odyssey of the Pacific '82
Off Limits '53
Pete's Dragon '77
Platinum High School '60
Postmark for Danger/ Quicksand '56
Pulp '72
Quicksand '50
Rachel's Man '75
Riff Raff '35
Rudolph & Frosty's Christmas in July '82
Santa Claus is Coming to Town '70
Senior Trip '81
Silent Night, Deadly Night 5: The Toymaker '91
Strike Up the Band '40
Summer Holiday '48
Sweet Justice '92
Thoroughbreds Don't Cry '37
Thousands Cheer '43
Thunder County '74
Women's Prison Escape
Words and Music '48

Pat Rooney, Jr.
Two Reelers: Comedy Classics 7 '38

Tim Rooney
Storyville '74

Thorkild Roose
Day of Wrath '43

Andre Roosevelt
Beyond the Carribean '32

Buddy Roosevelt
Boss Cowboy '35
Circle Canyon '33
Lightning Range '33
Powdersmoke Range '35
Range Riders '35

Stephen Root
Monkey Shines '88

Brian Roper
The Secret Garden '49

Gil Roper
Basket Case 3: The Progeny '92

Nocl Roquevort
Le Corbeau '43

Hayden Rorke
The Night Walker '64

Robby Rosa
Salsa '88

Donna Rosae
Master Blaster '85

Rosa Rosal
Ethan '71

Tom Rosales
Bail Out '90

Marion Rosamond
I Married an Angel '42

Bert Rosario
Cold Justice '89

Tony Rosato
Busted Up '86
City of Shadows '86
Hog Wild '80

Francoise Rosay
Bizarre Bizarre '39
Carnival in Flanders '35
Johnny Frenchman '46
The Pedestrian '73
September Affair '50
Seven Deadly Sins '53

Bartholomew Rose
Flirting '89

Clifford Rose
Marat/Sade '66

Cristine Rose
Singing the Blues in Red '87

Deborah Rose
The Bone Yard '90

Felissa Rose
Sleepaway Camp '83

Gabrielle Rose
The Adjuster '92
Family Viewing '88

George Rose
The Devil's Disciple '59
The Hideaways '73
Jack the Ripper '60
Mania '60
A New Leaf '71
A Night to Remember '58
The Pirates of Penzance '83
You Can't Take It with You '84

Jamie Rose
Chopper Chicks in Zombietown '91
Heartbreakers '84

In Love with an Older Woman '82
Playroom '90
Rebel Love '85
Tightrope '84
To Die Standing '91
Twirl '81

Laurie Rose
Blood Voyage '77
Hot Box '72
Woman Hunt '72
Working Girls '75

Rose Marie
Bruce's Deadly Fingers '80
Cheaper to Keep Her '80
Dead Heat on a Merry-Go-Round '66
Ghetto Blaster '89
Man from Clover Grove '78
Memory of Us '74
Witchboard '87

Pauline Rose
Hot T-Shirts '79

Robin Pearson Rose
Lucy and Desi: Before the Laughter '91

Roger Rose
Ski Patrol '89

Sherrie Rose
Double Threat '92
Martial Law 2: Undercover '91
Maximum Force '92
Summer Job '88

Steve Rose
Summer School '77

Will Rose
Red Desert Penitentiary '83

Ben Roseman
Daughter of Horror '55

Daniela Rosen
Sin Salida '87

Eric Rosen
Dollar '38

Neal Rosen
Flesh Eating Mothers '89

Alan Rosenberg
After Midnight '89
Happy Birthday, Gemini '80
In a Stranger's Hand '92
White of the Eye '88

Michael Rosenberg
His Wife's Lover '31
Mirele Efros '38
The Two Sisters '37

Maxie Rosenbloom
Cooking Up Trouble '44
Each Dawn I Die '39
Ghost Crazy '44
Here Comes Kelly '43
Hollywood or Bust '56
I Married a Monster from Outer Space '58
Louisiana Purchase '41
To the Shores of Tripoli '42

Zachary Rosencrantz
Hard to Kill '89

Rick Rosenthal
Distant Thunder '88

Ron Rosenthal
Black Rainbow '91

Rosette
Pauline at the Beach '83

Sandrelli ▶cont.

The Sleazy Uncle '89
We All Loved Each Other So
   Much '77

Luis Sandrini
El Profesor Hippie '69

Billy Sands
Harrad Experiment '73

Diana Sands
Doctors' Wives '70
Georgia, Georgia '72
Honeybaby '74
A Raisin in the Sun '61
Three Days in Beirut '83

Julian Sands
After Darkness '85
Arachnophobia '90
Crazy in Love '92
The Doctor and the Devils '85
Gothic '87
Grand Isle '92
Harem '86
Husbands and Lovers '91
Impromptu '90
The Killing Fields '84
Murder by Moonlight '91
Naked Lunch '91
Oxford Blues '84
Privates on Parade '84
The Room '87
A Room with a View '86
Siesta '87
The Turn of the Screw '92
Vibes '88
Warlock '91

Peggy Sands
Phoenix the Warrior '88

Ran Sands
Blood Screams '88

Sonny Sands
The Bellboy '60

Tommy Sands
Babes in Toyland '61
None But the Brave '65

Ellen Sandweiss
Evil Dead '83

Gary Sandy
Hail '73
Troll '85

Erskine Sanford
Citizen Kane '41
Crack-Up '46
The Lady from Shanghai '48
The Magnificent Ambersons
   '42

Garwin Sanford
Quarantine '89

Isabel Sanford
Desperate Moves '86
Love at First Bite '79

Ralph Sanford
A Night for Crime '42

Barbara Sanon
Straight Out of Brooklyn '91

Carmen Santa Maria
Bikini Summer '91

Dolores Santamaria
Perfumed Nightmare '89

Jose Santamaria
Pirates '86

Carlos Santana
Woodstock '70

Walter Santesso
La Dolce Vita '60

Sabrina Santi
2020 Texas Gladiators '85

Rubin Santiago
A Taste for Flesh and Blood
   '90

Saundra Santiago
Beat Street '84
Miami Vice '84

**Ruben Santiago-
Hudson**
Which Way Home '90

Pierre Santini
Dirty Dishes '82

Santo
Invasion of the Zombies '61
Mision Suicida '87
Samson in the Wax Museum
   '63
Samson vs. the Vampire
   Women '61

Vincent Santo
2000 Maniacs '64

Penny Santon
Love with the Proper Stranger
   '63

Espartaco Santoni
Exorcism's Daughter '74

Reni Santoni
Anzio '68
Bad Boys '83
Cobra '86
Dead Men Don't Wear Plaid
   '82
Dirty Harry '71
Enter Laughing '67
Guns of the Magnificent
   Seven '69
The Package '89
The Student Nurses '70

Gaston Santos
Black Pit of Dr. M '58
The Living Coffin '58
Misterios de Ultratumba '47
Swamp of the Lost Monster
   '65

Joe Santos
Deadly Desire '91
Fear City '85
Mo' Money '92
Revenge '90
Shaft's Big Score '72
Sinatra '92
Zandy's Bride '74

Thomas Santschi
Paradise Island '30
Paths to Paradise '25
Phantom of the West '31
The Spoilers '14
Ten Nights in a Bar-Room '31

Michael Sanville
Dreams Come True '84
First Turn On '83

Ita Sanvina
Private Life '82

Jorge Sanz
Lovers: A True Story '90

Ade Sapara
Crusoe '89

Jean Sapienza
The American Scream '80s

Peter Sapienza
Don't Mess with My Sister!
   '85

Alice Sapritch
Delusions of Grandeur '76

Vicki Saputo
Devil's Gift '84

Mia Sara
Any Man's Death '90
Apprentice to Murder '88
A Climate for Killing '91
Ferris Bueller's Day Off '86
Legend '85
Queenie '87
Shadows in the Storm '88
A Stranger Among Us '92

Richard Sarafian
Bugsy '91
Ruby '92

Chris Sarandon
Child's Play '88
Collision Course '89
Cuba '79
Dog Day Afternoon '75
Forced March '90
Fright Night '85
Lipstick '76
Mayflower Madam '87
The Osterman Weekend '83
The Princess Bride '87
Protocol '84
The Resurrected '91
The Sentinel '76
Slaves of New York '89
Tailspin: Behind the Korean
   Airline Tragedy '89
A Tale of Two Cities '80
Whispers '89

Susan Sarandon
Atlantic City '81
Beauty and the Beast '83
The Buddy System '83
Bull Durham '88
Compromising Positions '85
A Dry White Season '89
The Front Page '74
Great Smokey Roadblock '76
The Great Waldo Pepper '75
The Hunger '83
The January Man '89
Joe '70
King of the Gypsies '78
Light Sleeper '92
Lorenzo's Oil '92
Loving Couples '80
Mussolini & I '85
One Summer Love '76
The Other Side of Midnight
   '77
The Player '92
Pretty Baby '78
The Rocky Horror Picture
   Show '75
Something Short of Paradise
   '79
Sweet Hearts Dance '88
The Tempest '82
Thelma & Louise '91
White Palace '90
Who Am I This Time? '82
The Witches of Eastwick '87
Women of Valor '86

Lane Sarasohn
The Groove Tube '72

Martine Sarcey
One Wild Moment '78
Pardon Mon Affaire '76

Kate Sarchet
Sweater Girls '78

**Frank Sarcinello,
Sr.**
Death Row Diner '88

Fernand Sardou
The Little Theatre of Jean
   Renoir '71
Picnic on the Grass '59

**Leilani Sarelle
Ferrer**
Barbarians at the Gate '93
Basic Instinct '92
The Harvest '93
Neon Maniacs '86

Dick Sargent
Billie '65
Body Count '87
The Clonus Horror '79
Fantasy Island '76
Frame Up '91
Hardcore '79
Live a Little, Love a Little '68
Melvin Purvis: G-Man '74
Murder by Numbers '89
Teen Witch '89
That Touch of Mink '62
Twenty Dollar Star '91

Kenny Sargent
Thinkin' Big '87

Lewis Sargent
The New Adventures of
   Tarzan: Vol. 1 '35

Richard Sargent
For Love or Money '63
Tanya's Island '81

Michael Sarne
Cult People '89
Head Over Heels '67
Seaside Swingers '65

Michael Sarrazin
Beulah Land '80
Captive Hearts '87
The Double Negative '80
Fighting Back '82
Flim-Flam Man '67
For Pete's Sake '74
The Groundstar Conspiracy
   '72
Gumball Rally '76
Joshua Then and Now '85
Keeping Track '86
Lena's Holiday '91
Loves & Times of
   Scaramouche '76
Malarek '89
Mascara '87
The Phone Call '89
The Pursuit of Happiness '70
The Reincarnation of Peter
   Proud '75
The Seduction '82
Sometimes a Great Notion '71
They Shoot Horses, Don't
   They? '69
The Train Killer '83

Gailard Sartain
Blaze '89
Ernest Goes to Camp '87
Ernest Goes to Jail '90
Fried Green Tomatoes '91
The Grifters '90
Guilty by Suspicion '91
Hard Country '81
Leader of the Band '87
Mississippi Burning '88
Roadie '80
Stop! or My Mom Will Shoot
   '92

Katsuhiko Sasakai
Godzilla vs. Megalon '76

Terror of Mechagodzilla '78

Sumie Sasaki
The Insect Woman '63

Nicole Sassaman
Witchcraft 5: Dance with the
   Devil '92

Jacqueline Sassard
Accident '67
Les Biches '68
Pirates of the Seven Seas '62

Oley Sassone
Storyville '74

Catya Sassoon
Dance with Death '91
Tuff Turf '85

Lina Sastri
Goodnight, Michelangelo '89
The Inquiry '87
Where's Piccone '84

Tura Satana
The Astro-Zombies '67
The Doll Squad '73
Faster Pussycat! Kill! Kill! '66

Kei Sato
Onibaba '64
Zatoichi: The Blind
   Swordsman's Vengeance
   '66

Koichi Sato
The Silk Road '92

Tomomi Sato
Body Snatcher from Hell '69

Jaroslav Satoransky
Larks on a String '68

Barry Sattels
Dawn of the Mummy '82

Paul Satterfield
Arena '88

Lou Satton
Space: 1999—Alien Attack
   '79

Ludwig Satz
His Wife's Lover '31

Mo Man Sau
The Four Hands of Death:
   Wily Match

Rick Saucedo
Elvis Stories '89

Jennifer Saunders
Supergrass '87

Justine Saunders
The Fringe Dwellers '86

Lori Saunders
Track of the Vampire '66

Mary Jane Saunders
Sorrowful Jones '49

Pamela Saunders
Alien Warrior '85

Rebecca Saunders
Tearaway '87

Terry Saunders
The King and I '56

Tom Saunders
Tainted Image '91

Ann Savage
Detour '46
The More the Merrier '43
Pier 23 '51
Renegade Girl '46
Treasure of Fear '45

Archie Savage
Assignment Outer Space '61

Ben Savage
Big Girls Don't Cry...They Get Even '92
Little Monsters '89
Wild Palms '93

Fred Savage
The Boy Who Could Fly '86
Convicted: A Mother's Story '87
Little Monsters '89
The Princess Bride '87
Vice Versa '88
The Wizard '89

Houston Savage
The Losers '70

John Savage
All the Kind Strangers '74
The Amateur '82
Any Man's Death '90
Bad Company '72
The Beat '88
Brady's Escape '84
Caribe '87
Coming Out of the Ice '82
The Deer Hunter '78
Do the Right Thing '89
Eric '75
The Godfather, Part 3 '90
Hair '79
Hotel Colonial '88
The Hunting '92
Inside Moves '80
The Killing Kind '73
Maria's Lovers '84
Nairobi Affair '88
The Onion Field '79
Primary Motive '92
Salvador '86
Silent Witness '85
The Sister-in-Law '74
Soldier's Revenge '70s
Steelyard Blues '73
The Tender Age '84

Rick Savage
Sensations '87

Vic Savage
Creeping Terror '64

Dany Saval
Boeing Boeing '65
Moon Pilot '62

George Savalas
Kojak: The Belarus File '85

Telly Savalas
The Assassination Bureau '69
Bandera Bandits
Battle of the Bulge '65
Beyond Reason '77
Beyond the Poseidon Adventure '79
Birdman of Alcatraz '62
Buona Sera, Mrs. Campbell '68
Cannonball Run II '84
Cape Fear '61
Capricorn One '78
Cartier Affair '84
Crooks & Coronets '69
The Dirty Dozen '67
Escape to Athena '79
Fake Out '82
The Family '73
The Greatest Story Ever Told '65
The Hollywood Detective '89
Horror Express '72
Inside Out '75
The Interns '62
Kelly's Heroes '70

Killer Force '75
Kojak: The Belarus File '85
Land Raiders '69
Lisa and the Devil '75
MacKenna's Gold '69
The Muppet Movie '79
New Mafia Boss '72
On Her Majesty's Secret Service '69
Pancho Villa '72
A Reason to Live, A Reason to Die '73
Redneck '73
The Scalphunters '68
Scenes from a Murder '72
Silent Rebellion '82
The Slender Thread '65
Sonny and Jed '73
A Town Called Hell '72

Doug Savant
Maniac Cop 3 '93
Masquerade '88
Paint It Black '89
Red Surf '90
Shaking the Tree '92

Lyudmila Savelyeva
The Seagull '71
War and Peace '68

Josh Saviano
Camp Cucamonga: How I Spent My Summer Vacation '90

John Savident
Brain Donors '92

Krung Savilai
H-Bomb '71

Tom Savini
Creepshow 2 '87
Knightriders '81
Maniac '80

Joe Savino
The Crying Game '92

Jessica Savitch
Nasty Habits '77

Suzanne Savoy
The Cellar '90

Iya Savvina
The Lady with the Dog '59

Kenji Sawada
Mishima: A Life in Four Chapters '85

Yasuka Sawaguchi
Godzilla 1985 '85

Sadako Sawahura
Late Chrysanthemums '54

Joe Sawyer
As You Were '51
Fighting Father Dunne '48
Indian Uprising '51
The Killing '56
Melody Ranch '40
Mr. Walkie Talkie '52
The Naughty Nineties '45
Tanks a Million '41

Joseph Sawyer
Ace of Aces '33
The Informer '35

Marie Sawyer
Sex Appeal '86

Anne Saxon
The Sister-in-Law '74

John Saxon
Aftershock '88
Animal Instincts '92
The Appaloosa '66

The Arrival '90
The Baby Doll Murders '92
Battle Beyond the Stars '80
The Bees '78
Beyond Evil '80
Big Score '83
Black Christmas '75
Blackmail '91
Blood Beach '81
Blood Salvage '90
The Cardinal '63
Criminal Act '88
Crossing the Line '90
Deadly Conspiracy '91
Deadly Thief '78
Death House
Death of a Gunfighter '69
The Doomsday Flight '66
The Electric Horseman '79
Enter the Dragon '73
Fast Company '78
Fever Pitch '85
The Final Alliance '89
The Glove '79
Half Slave, Half Free '85
Hands of Steel '86
Hellmaster '92
Invasion of the Flesh Hunters '82
Joe Kidd '72
Maximum Force '92
Mr. Hobbs Takes a Vacation '62
Mr. Kingstreet's War '71
Mitchell '75
Moonshine County Express '77
My Mom's a Werewolf '89
Night Caller from Outer Space '66
A Nightmare on Elm Street '84
A Nightmare on Elm Street 3: Dream Warriors '87
Payoff '91
Planet Earth '74
Planet of Blood '66
Prisoners of the Lost Universe '84
Raid on Entebbe '77
The Reluctant Debutante '58
Rock, Pretty Baby '56
Running Scared '79
Scorpion with Two Tails '82
Snatched '72
Strange New World '75
Strange Shadows in an Empty Room '76
This Happy Feeling '58
The Unforgiven '60
Unsane '82
Welcome to Spring Break '88
Wrong is Right '82

Vin Saxon
Rat Pfink a Boo-Boo '66

Glen Saxson
Django Shoots First '74
Linchamiento '68
Scandal '80s

Diane Sayer
The Strangler '64

Philip Sayer
Green Horizon '83
Slayground '84
Xtro '83

Jo Ann Sayers
The Light of Western Stars '40

Alexei Sayle
Siesta '87
Whoops Apocalypse '83
The Young Ones '88

John Sayles
The Brother from Another Planet '84
City of Hope '91
Eight Men Out '88
Hard Choices '84
Lianna '83
Little Vegas '90
Matinee '92
Something Wild '86
Straight Talk '92

Syd Saylor
Ambush Trail '46
Arizona Days '37
Forlorn River '37
Harvest Melody '43
Headin' for the Rio Grande '36
The Light of Western Stars '30
Sea Racketeers '37

Carmela Sazio
Paisan '46

Raphael Sbarge
Back to Hannibal: The Return of Tom Sawyer and Huckleberry Finn '90s
Billionaire Boys Club '87
Carnosaur '93
Murder 101 '91
My Man Adam '86
My Science Project '85
Risky Business '83

Mattia Sbragia
Dial Help '88

Greta Scacchi
Burke & Wills '85
The Coca-Cola Kid '84
Defense of the Realm '85
Ebony Tower '86
Fires Within '91
Good Morning, Babylon '87
Heat and Dust '82
A Man in Love '87
The Player '92
Presumed Innocent '90
Shattered '91
Watertront '83
White Mischief '88

Frank Scala
The Glass Jungle '88

Gia Scala
The Tunnel of Love '58

Franco Scaldati
Kaos '85

Prunella Scales
A Chorus of Disapproval '89
Consuming Passions '88
Howard's End '92
The Lonely Passion of Judith Hearne '87
The Wicked Lady '83

Jack Scalia
After the Shock '90
The Amazons '84
Casualities of Love: The "Long Island Lolita" Story '93
Deadly Desire '91
Devlin Connection '82
Endless Descent '90
Fear City '85
Illicit Behavior '91

Valentina Scalici
The Stolen Children '93

David Scammell
Revenge of the Radioactive Reporter '91

Carlo Scandiuzzi
Red Snow '91
Shredder Orpheus '89

Sean Scanlan
A Sense of Freedom '78

Michelle Scarabelli
Age Old Friends '89
Deadbolt '92
Perfect Timing '84
SnakeEater 2: The Drug Buster '89

Tecla Scarano
Marriage Italian Style '64

Don Scardino
He Knows You're Alone '80
Squirm '76

Alan Scarfe
The Bay Boy '85
Cathy's Curse '77
The Deserters '80s
Iron Eagle 2 '88
Keeping Track '86
Python Wolf '88

Roberto Scaringelli
Accatone! '61

Diana Scarwid
After the Promise '87
Brenda Starr '86
A Bunny's Tale '85
Desperate Lives '82
Extremities '86
Forever '78
Inside Moves '80
Ladies Club '86
Mommie Dearest '81
The Possessed '77
Pretty Baby '78
Psycho 3 '86
Rumble Fish '83
Silkwood '83
Strange Invaders '83

James Scay
Killers from Space '54

Frank Schaafsma
Army Brats '84

Wendy Schaal
Creature '85
Going Under '91
Innerspace '87
When the Time Comes '91
Where the Boys Are '84 '84

Sam Schacht
A Secret Space '88

Felice Schachter
Zapped! '82

Floyd Schackleford
The Savage Girl '32

Laura Schaefer
Catacombs '89
Curse 4: The Ultimate Sacrifice '92
Ghost Town '88

Anthony Schaeffer
Gunpowder '84

Mary Schaeffer
Maxim Xul '91

Rebecca Schaeffer
The End of Innocence '90
Scenes from the Class Struggle in Beverly Hills '89
Voyage of Terror: The Achille Lauro Affair '90

Natalie Schafer
Caught '49
Forever Darling '56

Schafer ▶cont.

The Time of Your Life '48

Paul Schaffer
Light Years '88
Mr. Mike's Mondo Video '79
This is Spinal Tap '84

William Schallert
The Computer Wore Tennis Shoes '69
Death Sentence '74
Held Hostage '91
The Incident '89
Innerspace '87
Man on a String '71
Speedway '68
Sword of Venus '53
Trial of the Catonsville Nine '72
Twilight Zone: The Movie '83
War & Remembrance, Part 1 '88
War & Remembrance: The Final Chapter, Part 8 '89

Carina Schally
The Dolls '83

Tom Schanley
Nothing Underneath '85

Sabrina Scharf
Hell's Angels on Wheels '67
Hunter '73

Svein Scharffenberg
Pathfinder '87

Lynday Scharnott
The Instructor '83

Roger Schauer
The Inheritors '85

Magilla Schaus
Tainted '88

Ann Schedeen
Embryo '76

Rich Scheeland
Buffalo Rider '78

Roy Scheider
All That Jazz '79
Blue Thunder '83
Cohen and Tate '88
Curse of the Living Corpse '64
52 Pick-Up '86
The Fourth War '90
The French Connection '71
Jaws '75
Jaws 2 '78
Klute '71
The Last Embrace '79
Listen to Me '89
Marathon Man '76
The Men's Club '86
Mishima: A Life in Four Chapters '85
Naked Lunch '91
Night Game '89
The Outside Man '73
Paper Lion '68
The Russia House '90
The Seven-Ups '73
Somebody Has to Shoot the Picture '90
Sorcerer '77
Stiletto '69
Still of the Night '82
Tiger Town '83
2010: The Year We Make Contact '84

Loren Schein
Microwave Massacre '83

Ellen Scheirs
The Invisible Terror '63

Clemens Scheitz
Stroszek '77

Carl Schell
Quick, Let's Get Married '71
Werewolf in a Girl's Dormitory '61

Catherine Schell
Gulliver's Travels '77
On Her Majesty's Secret Service '69
On the Third Day '83
Return of the Pink Panther '74

Maria Schell
Angel with the Trumpet '50
The Brothers Karamazov '58
Christmas Lilies of the Field '84
End of Desire '62
Gervaise '56
The Hanging Tree '59
Inside the Third Reich '82
Just a Gigolo '79
La Passante '83
The Mark '61
Napoleon '55
99 Women '69
The Odessa File '74
Samson and Delilah '84
Twist '76
Voyage of the Damned '76
White Nights '57

Maximilian Schell
The Assisi Underground '84
Avalanche Express '79
The Black Hole '79
The Castle '68
Cross of Iron '76
The Day that Shook the World '78
A Far Off Place '93
First Love '70
The Freshman '90
Heidi '67
Judgment at Nuremberg '61
Julia '77
Miss Rose White '92
The Odessa File '74
The Pedestrian '73
Peter the Great '86
Players '79
The Rose Garden '89
St. Ives '76
Simon Bolivar '69
Stalin '92
Together '79
Topkapi '64
Young Catherine '91
The Young Lions '58

Ronnie Schell
Gus '76
The Jetsons: Movie '90

Tom Schell
Death Row Diner '88

August Schellenberg
Black Robe '91
Confidential '86
Free Willy '93
Mark of Cain '84
Striker's Mountain '87
Tramp at the Door '87

Erich Schellow
The Captain from Koepenick '56

Sandy Schemmel
Dark Side of Midnight '86

Earl Schenck
Salome '22

Wolfgang Schenck
Effi Briest '74

Robert Schenkkan
Act of Vengeance '86
The Manhattan Project '86

Sally Schermerhorn
Satanwar '79

Paul Scherrer
Children of the Corn 2: The Final Sacrifice '92

Karl Scheydt
The American Soldier '70

Rosanna Schiaffino
Arrivederci, Baby! '66
Code Name Alpha '67
Red-Dragon '67
Simon Bolivar '69
Two Weeks in Another Town '62
The Witch '66

Vincent Schiavelli
The Adventures of Buckaroo Banzai Across the Eighth Dimension '84
Amadeus '84
Batman Returns '92
Fast Times at Ridgemont High '82
Ghost '90
Miracle Beach '92
Playroom '90
The Return '80
Valmont '89
Waiting for the Light '90

Ralph Schicha
Savage Attraction '83

Ben Schick
Shooters '89

Stephanie Schick
Do or Die '91

Eric Schiff
Toughlove '85

Joseph Schildkraut
Cleopatra '34
The Diary of Anne Frank '59
Flame of the Barbary Coast '45
The Garden of Allah '36
King of Kings '27
The Life of Emile Zola '37
The Man in the Iron Mask '39
Marie Antoinette '38
Monsieur Beaucaire '46
Orphans of the Storm '21
The Road to Yesterday '25
Road to Yesterday/The Yankee Clipper '27
The Shop Around the Corner '40
Viva Villa! '34
Wandering Jew '20

Rudolf Schildkraut
Wandering Jew '20

Charles Schillaci
Hot Chili '85

Norbert Schiller
Outcasts of the City '58

Gus Schilling
Citizen Kane '41
The Lady from Shanghai '48

Vivian Schilling
The Legend of Wolf Mountain '92
Project: Eliminator '91

Soultaker '90
Terror Eyes '87

Tom Schioler
Maniac Warriors '90s
Storm '87

Daniel Schlachet
Swoon '91

Sharon Schlarth
Dead as a Doorman '85
Eat and Run '86

Charlie Schlatter
All-American Murder '91
Bright Lights, Big City '88
18 Again! '88
Heartbreak Hotel '88
Sunset Heat '92

Guylaine Schlumberger
My Life to Live '62

Dan Schmale
Fatal Exposure '90

Walter Schmidinger
From the Life of the Marionettes '80
Hanussen '88

Christine Schmidt
Linchamiento '68

Helmut Schmidt
The Head '59

Joseph Schmidt
My Song Goes Round the World '34

Lisa Schmidt
Assault of the Killer Bimbos '87
Cemetery High '89

Lou Ann Schmidt
Ranch '88

Marlene Schmidt
Dr. Minx '75
Scorchy '76
The Stepmother '71

Nathalie Schmidt
Europa, Europa '91

Phoebe Schmidt
Summer School '77

Rick Schmidt
Club Fed '91

Stan Schmidt
Kill and Kill Again '81

Christianne Schmidtmer
The Big Doll House '71
Boeing Boeing '65
The Giant Spider Invasion '75

Timothy B. Schmit
Scenes from the Goldmine '87

Gae Schmitt
Night of Horror '80s

Sybille Schmitz
Diary of a Lost Girl '29
F.P. 1 Doesn't Answer '33
Vampyr '31

David Schmoeller
The Arrival '90

Benjamin Schmoll
Daughter of Death '82

August Schmolzer
Requiem for Dominic '91

Stefan Schnabel
Houdini '53

The 27 Day '57
Two Weeks in Another Town '62

Monika Schnarre
The Death Merchant '91
Waxwork 2: Lost in Time '91

Betty Schneider
Paris Belongs to Us '60

Bonnie Schneider
Mama Dracula '80
Murderlust '86

Dan Schneider
Better Off Dead '85
Happy Together '89

Dawn Schneider
Free Ride '86

Fred Schneider
A Matter of Degrees '90

Helmut Schneider
Captain Sinbad '63
Fifth Day of Peace '72

John Schneider
Christmas Comes to Willow Creek '87
Cocaine Wars '86
The Curse '87
Eddie Macon's Run '83
Ministry of Vengeance '89
Speed Zone '88
Stagecoach '86

Maria Schneider
Crime of Honor '85
Last Tango in Paris '73
Mama Dracula '80
The Passenger '75
Wanted: Babysitter '75

Michael Schneider
Double Edge '92

Rob Schneider
Home Alone 2: Lost in New York '92

Romy Schneider
Assassination of Trotsky '72
Boccaccio '70 '62
Cesar & Rosalie '72
Death Watch '80
Dirty Hands '76
Good Neighbor Sam '64
The Hero '71
Infernal Trio '74
La Passante '83
The Last Train '74
Mado '76
Old Gun '76
Sidney Sheldon's Bloodline '79
A Simple Story '79
Swimming Pool '70
The Things of Life '70
The Trial '63
Triple Cross '67
What's New Pussycat? '65

Michael Schnider
The Last Winter '84

Andrea Schober
The Merchant of Four Seasons '71

Barbara Schock
From Hollywood to Deadwood '89

Michael Schoeffling
Belizaire the Cajun '86
Let's Get Harry '87
Longtime Companion '90
Mermaids '90
Sixteen Candles '84

Sylvester '85
Vision Quest '85
Wild Hearts Can't Be Broken '91

Jill Schoelen
Adventures in Spying '92
Babes in Toyland '86
Billionaire Boys Club '87
Curse 2: The Bite '88
Cutting Class '89
D.C. Cab '84
Hot Moves '84
The Phantom of the Opera '89
Popcorn '89
Rich Girl '91
The Stepfather '87
That Was Then...This Is Now '85
Thunder Alley '85

Ingrid Schoeller
Psychopath '68
They Paid with Bullets: Chicago 1929 '70s

Margareta Schoen
Kriemhilde's Revenge '24
Siegfried '24

Reiner Schoene
The Gunfighters '87

Ingeborg Schoener
Cold Steel for Tortuga '65
Mark of the Devil '69
Mr. Superinvisible '73

Dietmar Schoenherr
Journey of Hope '90
The Monster of London City '64

Annabel Schofield
Dragonard '88
Solar Crisis '92

Neil Schofield
Puberty Blues '81

Christina Schollin
Song of Norway '70

Eva Scholtz
The Black Abbot '63

Horts Schon
Thunder Warrior 3 '88

Inge Schoner
George! '70

Bill Schoppert
The Personals '83

Evald Schorm
The Report on the Party and the Guests '66

Bob Schott
Future Hunters '88

Paul Schrader
American Gigolo '79

Lisa Schrage
China White '91
Food of the Gods: Part 2 '88
Hello Mary Lou: Prom Night 2 '87

Bitty Schram
A League of Their Own '92

Max Schreck
Dracula/Garden of Eden '28
Nosferatu '22

Avery Schreiber
Galaxina '80
Hunk '87
Saturday the 14th Strikes Back '88

Silent Scream '80

Tell Schreiber
Keeper '84

Tom Schreir
The Ripper '86

Rick Schroder
Across the Tracks '89
The Champ '79
Earthling '80
Hansel and Gretel '82
The Last Flight of Noah's Ark '80
Little Lord Fauntleroy '80
Lonesome Dove '89
Two Kinds of Love '85

Arnulf Schroeder
The Eternal Waltz '59

Greta Schroeder
Nosferatu '22

Hannelore Schroth
The Captain from Koepenick '56

Pete Schrum
Demonic Toys '91

Karin Schubert
Black Emmanuelle '76
Delusions of Grandeur '76
Till Marriage Do Us Part '74
Under the Sheets '86

Viktoria Schubert
Requiem for Dominic '91

John Schuck
Blade '72
Brewster McCloud '70
Butch and Sundance: The Early Days '70
M*A*S*H '70
McCabe & Mrs. Miller '71
My Mom's a Werewolf '89
The New Adventures of Pippi Longstocking '88
Second Sight '89

Al Schuerman
Presumed Guilty '91

Dwight Schultz
Alone in the Dark '82
Fat Man and Little Boy '89
The Long Walk Home '89
The Temp '93
When Your Lover Leaves '83

Frank Schultz
Sky High '84

Gregg Schultz
Clayton County Line '80s

Jeff Schultz
Buying Time '89

Mary Schultz
Landlord Blues '87

Maurice Schultz
The Passion of Joan of Arc '28

Brian Schulz
Thou Shalt Not Kill...Except '87

Charles M. Schulz
Play It Again, Charlie Brown '70

Hans Schumm
Spy Smasher Returns '42

Reinhold Schunzel
Fortune's Fool '21
The Threepenny Opera '31
Woman in Brown '48

Melinda Schurcher
The Love Pill '71

Erna Schurer
Specters '87

Angelica Schutz
Requiem for Dominic '91

Ivyann Schwan
Problem Child 2 '91

Ellen Schwannecke
Maedchen in Uniform '31

Bill Schwartz
King Kung Fu '87

Jennifer Schwartz
Desperate Teenage Lovedolls '84

Maurice Schwartz
Salome '53
Tevye '39
Uncle Moses '32

Sam Schwartz
The Cemetery Club '93

Scott Schwartz
Kidco '83
Time to Live '85

Stephen Schwartz
Music Shoppe '82

Arnold Schwarzenegger
Commando '85
Conan the Barbarian '82
Conan the Destroyer '84
Dave '93
Hercules in New York '70
The Jayne Mansfield Story '80
Kindergarten Cop '90
Last Action Hero '93
The Long Goodbye '73
Predator '87
Pumping Iron '76
Raw Deal '86
Red Heat '88
Red Sonja '85
The Running Man '87
Stay Hungry '76
The Terminator '84
Terminator 2: Judgment Day '91
Total Recall '90
Twins '88
The Villain '79

Klaus Schwarzkopf
For Your Love Only '79

Lisa Schwedop
Revenge of the Teenage Vixens from Outer Space '86

Eric Schweig
The Last of the Mohicans '92

Hanna Schygulla
Barnum '86
Berlin Alexanderplatz '80
The Bitter Tears of Petra von Kant '72
Casanova '87
Dead Again '91
Delta Force '86
Effi Briest '74
Forever, Lulu '87
Gods of the Plague '69
La Nuit de Varennes '82
A Love in Germany '84
The Marriage of Maria Braun '79
The Merchant of Four Seasons '71
Sheer Madness '84

The Summer of Miss Forbes '88
The Wrong Move '78

Annabella Sciorra
Cadillac Man '90
The Hand that Rocks the Cradle '92
The Hard Way '91
Internal Affairs '90
Jungle Fever '91
The Night We Never Met '93
Prison Stories: Women on the Inside '91
Reversal of Fortune '90
True Love '89
Whispers in the Dark '92

Edith Scob
The Burning Court '62
Horror Chamber of Dr. Faustus '59
The Milky Way '68

Paul Scofield
Anna Karenina '85
The Attic: The Hiding of Anne Frank '88
Bartleby '70
Carve Her Name with Pride '58
The Curse of King Tut's Tomb '80
Hamlet '90
Henry V '89
King Lear '71
A Man for All Seasons '66
Mr. Corbett's Ghost '90
Scorpio '73
The Train '65
When the Whales Came '89

Donna Scoggins
Rocktober Blood '85

Tracy Scoggins
Alien Intruder '93
Beyond the Silhouette '90
Dangerous Company '88
Demonic Toys '91
The Gumshoe Kid '89
In Dangerous Company '88
One Last Run '89
Play Murder for Me '91
The Red Raven Kiss-Off '90
Timebomb '91
Toy Soldiers '84
Twirl '81
Ultimate Desires '91
Watchers 2 '90

Maria Scola
El Barbaro '84

Peter Scolari
Corporate Affairs '90
Mr. Bill's Real Life Adventures '86
Rosebud Beach Hotel '85

Zvee Scooler
Trumps '88

Martin Scorsese
Cannonball '76
Guilty by Suspicion '91
Round Midnight '86

Alex Scott
The Abominable Dr. Phibes '71
The Asphyx '72
Next of Kin '82
The Persuaders '71
Peter's Friends '92

Amber Scott
Hook '91

Bainbridge Scott
Death Chase '87

Hell Squad '85

Barry Scott
Ernest Goes to Jail '90

Brenda Scott
Johnny Tiger '66
Simon, King of the Witches '71

Campbell Scott
Dead Again '91
Dying Young '91
The Ghost of Fletcher Ridge '80s
Longtime Companion '90
The Sheltering Sky '90
Singles '92

Carey Scott
Diving In '90
Making the Grade '84

Carl Scott
Kung Fu Avengers '85

Chad Scott
Sea of Dreams '90

Chuck Scott
Moonshine Mountain '64

Cliff Scott
The Ghosts of Hanley House '68

Colleen Scott
The Lady of the Camellias '87

Connie Scott
Flipper '63

Dan Scott
Spookies '85

Deborah Scott
Witchcraft '88

Debralee Scott
Deathmoon '78
Incoming Freshmen '79
Just Tell Me You Love Me '80
Police Academy '84

Donovan Scott
Goldilocks & the Three Bears '83
Savannah Smiles '82
Sheena '84

Eric Scott
Children's Carol '80
A Day for Thanks on Walton's Mountain '82

Evelyn Scott
Devil Kiss '77

Fred Scott
Code of the Fearless '39
In Old Montana '39
Ranger's Roundup '38
Ridin' the Trail '40
The Roamin' Cowboy '37
Singing Buckaroo '37
Songs and Bullets '38
Two-Gun Troubador '37

Geoffrey Scott
First & Ten '85
First & Ten: The Team Scores Again '85
Morning After '86

George C. Scott
Anatomy of a Murder '59
Bank Shot '74
The Bible...In the Beginning '66
The Changeling '80
The Day of the Dolphin '73
Descending Angel '90

Joe Sharkey
Bloodsucking Pharoahs of
  Pittsburgh '90

Ray Sharkey
Act of Piracy '89
Behind Enemy Lines '85
Body Rock '84
Caged Fear '92
Capone '89
Chrome Soldiers '92
Cop and a Half '93
Dubeat-E-O '84
Heart Beat '80
Hellhole '85
Idolmaker '80
The Neon Empire '89
No Mercy '86
Private Investigations '87
The Rain Killer '90
Regina '83
Relentless 2: Dead On '91
Round Trip to Heaven '92
Scenes from the Class
  Struggle in Beverly Hills '89
Some Kind of Hero '82
The Take '90
Who'll Stop the Rain? '78
Willie & Phil '80
Wired '89
Wise Guys '86
Zebrahead '92

Sailor Sharkey
Fighting Jack '26

Chanda Sharma
Salaam Bombay! '88

Anthony Sharp
The Confessional '75

John Sharp
Misunderstood '87

Sally Sharp
End of August '82

Albert Sharpe
Darby O'Gill & the Little
  People '59

Cornelia Sharpe
The Arab Conspiracy '76
Busting '74
The Reincarnation of Peter
  Proud '75
Serpico '73
S*H*E '79
Venom '82

David Sharpe
The Adventurous Knights '35
Colorado Serenade '46
Haunted Ranch '43
Roaring Roads '35
Silver Stallion '41
Social Error '35
Texas to Bataan '42
Trail Riders '42
Two-Fisted Justice '43

Michael Sharrett
Deadly Friend '86

Melanie Shatner
Cthulhu Mansion '91
Syngenor '90

William Shatner
Airplane 2: The Sequel '82
The Andersonville Trial '70
The Babysitter '80
The Barbary Coast '74
The Bastard '78
Big Bad Mama '74
Bill & Ted's Bogus Journey
  '91
Broken Angel '88
The Brothers Karamazov '58

The Crash of Flight 401 '78
The Defender '57
Devil's Rain '75
Impulse '74
Judgment at Nuremberg '61
The Kidnapping of the
  President '80
Kingdom of the Spiders '77
Little Women '78
National Lampoon's Loaded
  Weapon 1 '93
The People '71
Pioneer Woman '73
Pray for the Wildcats '74
Riel '79
Secrets of a Married Man '84
Shame '61
Star Trek: The Motion Picture
  '80
Star Trek 2: The Wrath of
  Khan '82
Star Trek 3: The Search for
  Spock '84
Star Trek 4: The Voyage
  Home '86
Star Trek 5: The Final Frontier
  '89
Star Trek 6: The
  Undiscovered Country '91
Star Trek Bloopers '69
Third Walker '79
Visiting Hours '82
Whale of a Tale '76
White Comanche '67

Shari Shattuck
Arena '88
Desert Warrior '88
Hot Child in the City '87
Mad About You '90
Naked Cage '86
The Spring '89
Tainted '88
The Uninvited '88

Grant Shaud
The Distinguished Gentleman
  '92

**Mickey
Shaughnessy**
The Adventures of
  Huckleberry Finn '60
Conquest of Space '55
Designing Woman '57
From Here to Eternity '53
Jailhouse Rock '57
The King of the Roaring '20s:
  The Story of Arnold
  Rothstein '61
Last of the Comanches '52
My Dog, the Thief '69
Pocketful of Miracles '61
Primal Scream '87

Helen Shaver
Amazing Stories, Book 4 '85
The Amityville Horror '79
The Believers '87
Best Defense '84
The Color of Money '86
Coming Out Alive '84
Desert Hearts '86
Gas '81
Harry Tracy '83
High Ballin' '78
In Praise of Older Women '78
Innocent Victim '90
The Land Before Time '88
Lost '86
Off Your Rocker '80
The Osterman Weekend '83
Outrageous! '77
The Park is Mine '85
Shoot '85
Starship Invasions '77
The War Boy '85

Who Has Seen the Wind? '77

Anabel Shaw
Gun Crazy '49
Shock! '46

Artie Shaw
Second Chorus '40

Bill Shaw
Ghostriders '87

Bob Shaw
Cinema Shrapnel '87

Bobbi Shaw
Pajama Party '64

Chris Shaw
Split '90

Crystal Shaw
Hardbodies '84
Laser Moon '92

Fiona Shaw
London Kills Me '91
Maria's Child '93
Mountains of the Moon '90
My Left Foot '89
Super Mario Bros. '93

Huang Hsing Shaw
Renegade Monk '82
Shaolin Ex-Monk '82

Jack Shaw
Dick Barton, Special Agent
  '48

Leona Shaw
Three Men and a Little Lady
  '90

Martin Shaw
Golden Voyage of Sinbad '73
The Hound of the Baskervilles
  '83
Intrigue '90
Macbeth '71
Professionals '76
Richard III '82

Maxwell Shaw
The Oblong Box '69

Montague Shaw
Square Shoulders '29

Oscar Shaw
The Cocoanuts '29

Patty Shaw
Death Driver '78

Reta Shaw
All Mine to Give '56
Pajama Game '57
Picnic '55

Robert Shaw
Adam Had Four Sons '41
Avalanche Express '79
Battle of Britain '69
Battle of the Bulge '65
Black Sunday '77
The Deep '77
Diamonds '72
Force 10 from Navarone '78
From Russia with Love '63
Jaws '75
A Man for All Seasons '66
A Reflection of Fear '72
Robin and Marian '76
The Sting '73
Swashbuckler '76
The Taking of Pelham One
  Two Three '74
A Town Called Hell '72
Young Winston '72

Sebastian Shaw
High Season '88

A Midsummer Night's Dream
  '68
Reilly: Ace of Spies '87
Spy in Black '39
The Squeaker '37

Stan Shaw
Billionaire Boys Club '87
Bingo Long Traveling All-Stars
  & Motor Kings '76
Body of Evidence '92
The Boys in Company C '77
Busted Up '86
The Court Martial of Jackie
  Robinson '90
Dirkham Detective Agency '83
D.P. '85
Fear '90
Fried Green Tomatoes '91
The Gladiator '86
Roots: The Next Generation
  '79
Runaway '84
Samaritan: The Mitch Snyder
  Story '86
Tough Enough '87

Steve Shaw
Child of Glass '78

Susan Shaw
Fire Maidens from Outer
  Space '56
The Junkman '82
Train of Events '49

**Susan Damante
Shaw**
The Adventures of the
  Wilderness Family '76
Further Adventures of the
  Wilderness Family, Part 2
  '77
Image of Passion '86
Mountain Family Robinson '79
The Student Teachers '73

Vanessa Shaw
Horror Hospital '73

Victoria Shaw
The Eddy Duchin Story '56

Vinessa Shaw
Hocus Pocus '93
Ladybugs '92

Wini Shaw
Gold Diggers of 1935 '35

Yasin Shawap
Hamsin '83

Joan Shawlee
The Apartment '60
Buck Privates Come Home
  '47
Prehistoric Women '50

Dick Shawn
Angel '84
Beer '85
Check is in the Mail '85
The Emperor's New Clothes
  '84
Goodbye Cruel World '82
The Happy Ending '69
It's a Mad, Mad, Mad, Mad
  World '63
Love at First Bite '79
Maid to Order '87
The Producers '68
Rented Lips '88
The Secret Diary of Sigmund
  Freud '84
What Did You Do in the War,
  Daddy? '66
Young Warriors '83

Wallace Shawn
All That Jazz '79
The Bedroom Window '87
The Bostonians '84
Crackers '84
Deal of the Century '83
The Double O Kid '92
First Time '82
Heaven Help Us '85
The Hotel New Hampshire '84
How to Be a Perfect Person in
  Just Three Days '84
A Little Sex '82
Manhattan '79
Micki & Maude '84
The Moderns '88
Mom and Dad Save the World
  '92
My Dinner with Andre '81
Nice Girls Don't Explode '87
Nickel & Dime '92
Prick Up Your Ears '87
The Princess Bride '87
Radio Days '87
Scenes from the Class
  Struggle in Beverly Hills '89
Shadows and Fog '92
She's Out of Control '89
Simon '80
Strange Invaders '83
Strong Medicine '84

Christi Shay
Motown's Mustang '86

John Shay
The Missing Corpse '45

Luke Shay
Blood Games '90

Konstantin Shayne
The Stranger '46

Robert Shayne
Christmas in Connecticut '45
The Giant Claw '57
Marshal of Cedar Rock '53
Rhapsody in Blue '45
The Spirit of West Point '47
Stamp Day for Superman '53

Tamara Shayne
The Jolson Story '46
Somewhere I'll Find You '42

Elizabeth She
Howling 5: The Rebirth '89

Gloria Shea
Dude Bandit '32
Last Days of Pompeii '35
Phantom of the Air '33

Jack Shea
Lucky Me '54

John Shea
A Case of Deadly Force '86
The Dining Room '86
Freejack '92
Honey, I Blew Up the Kid '92
Honeymoon '87
Hussy '80
The Impossible Spy '87
Kennedy '83
Ladykiller '92
Light Years '88
Missing '82
Nativity '78
A New Life '88
Small Sacrifices '89
Stealing Home '88
Unsettled Land '88
Windy City '84

Patrick Shea
Corruption '89

Tom Shea
Somewhere Tomorrow '85

Joseph Sheahan
Invitation to Hell '84

Al Shear
The Great Waltz '38
It Could Happen to You '37
San Francisco '36
Tim Tyler's Luck '37
Ziegfeld Girl '41

Rhonda Shear
Basic Training '86

Alan Shearer
Rock House '92

Harry Shearer
One Trick Pony '80
Portrait of a White Marriage
'88
Pure Luck '91
The Return of Spinal Tap '92
The Right Stuff '83
The Simpsons Christmas
Special '89
This is Spinal Tap '84

Moira Shearer
Peeping Tom '63
The Red Shoes '48
The Tales of Hoffman '51

Norma Shearer
The Barretts of Wimpole
Street '34
The Divorcee '30
A Free Soul '31
Idiot's Delight '39
Marie Antoinette '38
Private Lives '31
Romeo and Juliet '36
Strange Interlude '32
The Student Prince in Old
Heidelberg '27
Two Reelers: Comedy
Classics 10 '31
The Women '39

Alan Shearman
Bullshot '83
Footlight Frenzy '84

Ally Sheedy
Bad Boys '83
The Best Little Girl in the
World '81
Betsy's Wedding '90
Blue City '86
The Breakfast Club '85
Fear '90
The Heart of Dixie '89
The Lost Capone '90
Maid to Order '87
Only the Lonely '91
Oxford Blues '84
St. Elmo's Fire '85
Short Circuit '86
Twice in a Lifetime '85
War Games '83
We are the Children '87

Doug Sheehan
The FBI Murders '88

John Sheehan
Criminal Code '31

Charlie Sheen
Amazing Stories, Book 3 '86
Backtrack '89
The Boys Next Door '85
Cadence '89
Courage Mountain '89
Eight Men Out '88
Ferris Bueller's Day Off '86
Hot Shots! '91
Hot Shots! Part Deux '93

Lucas '86
Major League '89
Men at Work '90
National Lampoon's Loaded
Weapon 1 '93
Navy SEALS '90
Never on Tuesday '88
No Man's Land '87
Platoon '86
Red Dawn '84
The Rookie '90
Silence of the Heart '84
Tale of Two Sisters '89
Three for the Road '87
Wall Street '87
The Wraith '87
Young Guns '88

Lucy Sheen
Ping Pong '87

Martin Sheen
The Andersonville Trial '70
Apocalypse Now '79
Badlands '74
The Believers '87
Beverly Hills Brats '89
Beyond the Stars '89
Blind Ambition '82
Cadence '89
The Cassandra Crossing '76
Catch-22 '70
Catholics '73
Cold Front '89
Consenting Adults '85
Conspiracy: The Trial of the
Chicago Eight '87
Da '88
Dead Zone '83
Eagle's Wing '79
Enigma '82
The Execution of Private
Slovik '74
The Final Countdown '80
Firestarter '84
Fourth Wise Man '85
Gandhi '82
The Guardian '84
Hear No Evil '93
Hearts of Darkness: A
Filmmaker's Apocalypse
'91
Hot Shots! Part Deux '93
In the Custody of Strangers
'82
In the King of Prussia '83
The Incident '67
Judgment in Berlin '88
Kennedy '83
Legend of Earl Durand '74
The Little Girl Who Lives
Down the Lane '76
Loophole '83
The Maid '90
Man, Woman & Child '83
Missiles of October '74
News at Eleven '86
Nightbreaker '89
No Drums, No Bugles '71
Original Intent '85
Out of the Darkness '85
Pursuit '72
Rage '72
Samaritan: The Mitch Snyder
Story '86
Shattered Spirits '91
Siesta '87
Sweet Hostage '75
That Championship Season
'82
Wall Street '87
When the Line Goes Through
'71
Where the Eagle Flies '72

Ramon Sheen
A Man of Passion '90s

Ruth Sheen
High Hopes '89

Barry Sheene
Space Riders '83

John Sheerin
Robbery '85

Chad Sheets
Dirt Bike Kid '86

Craig Sheffer
Babycakes '89
Blue Desert '91
Eye of the Storm '91
Fire in the Sky '93
Fire with Fire '86
Instant Karma '90
Night Breed '90
A River Runs Through It '92
Some Kind of Wonderful '87
Split Decisions '88
That Was Then...This Is Now
'85
Voyage of the Rock Aliens '87

Johnny Sheffield
Tarzan Finds a Son '39
Tarzan's New York Adventure
'42
Tarzan's Secret Treasure '41

Maceo B. Sheffield
Gang War '40
Harlem on the Prairie '38
Look Out Sister '48

Reginald Sheffield
Second Chance '53

Mark Sheffler
Last House on the Left '72

Sheila E
The Adventures of Ford
Fairlane '90
Krush Groove '85

David S. Sheiner
News at Eleven '86

LaRita Shelby
South Central '92

Gene Sheldon
The Sign of Zorro '60
Toby Tyler '59

Jack Sheldon
For the Boys '91

Lorell Sheldon
The Missing Corpse '45

Nancy Sheldon
Sinner's Blood '70

Valerie Sheldon
Berserker '87

Irit Sheleg
Fictitious Marriage '88

Tom Shell
Surf Nazis Must Die '87

Kalei Shellabarger
The Invisible Maniac '90

Stephen Shellan
Casual Sex? '88
Damned River '89
Gimme an F '85
Murder One '88
A River Runs Through It '92
Still Life '92
Talking Walls '85
Victim of Beauty '91

Barbara Shelley
Blood of the Vampire '58
Cat Girl '57
The Dark Angel '91

The Gorgon '64
Madhouse Mansion '74
Village of the Damned '60

Carol Shelley
Robin Hood '73

Dave Shelley
The Jayne Mansfield Story '80

Adrienne Shelly
Big Girls Don't Cry...They Get
Even '92
Hexed '93
Trust '91
The Unbelievable Truth '90

Deborah Shelton
Blind Vision '91
Body Double '84
Hunk '87
Mysterious Island of Beautiful
Women '79
Perfect Victims '87

John Shelton
Ghost City '32
The Time of Their Lives '46

Joy Shelton
Impulse '55
Norman Conquest '53
Uneasy Terms '48

Maria Shelton
Escape to Paradise '39
The Phantom Rider '37

Marlee Shelton
The Sandlot '93

Reid Shelton
Breakin' Through '84
First & Ten '85
First & Ten: The Team Scores
Again '85

Carole Shelyne
Dark August '76

Chang Shen
Five Fighters from Shaolin
'70s

Paul Shenar
The Bedroom Window '87
Best Seller '87
The Big Blue '88
Brass '85
Deadly Force '83
Dream Lover '85
Man on Fire '87
Raw Deal '86
Scarface '83
The Tragedy of King Richard II
'82

Chien Yueh Sheng
Buddha Assassinator '82

Li Hai Sheng
Incredible Master Beggars '82

Lu Sheng
Infra-Man '76

Elaine Shepard
Darkest Africa '36

Hilary Shepard
Peacemaker '90

Jewel Shepard
Hollywood Hot Tubs '84
Hollywood Hot Tubs 2:
Educating Crystal '89
My Tutor '82
Return of the Living Dead '85
Scenes from the Goldmine '87

O-Lan Shepard
Out '88

Patty Shepard
Crypt of the Living Dead '73
Curse of the Devil '73
Dracula vs. Frankenstein '69
El Monte de las Brujas '70s
The Stranger and the
Gunfighter '76
Surprise Attack '70s
The Werewolf vs. the Vampire
Woman '70
Witches' Mountain '71

Sam Shepard
Baby Boom '87
Bright Angel '91
Country '84
Crimes of the Heart '86
Days of Heaven '78
Defenseless '91
Fool for Love '86
Frances '82
Raggedy Man '81
Resurrection '80
The Right Stuff '83
Steel Magnolias '89
Thunderheart '92
Voyager '91

Karen Lee Sheperd
Shinobi Ninja '84

Cybill Shepherd
Alice '90
Chances Are '89
Daisy Miller '74
Elvis Memories '85
A Guide for the Married
Woman '78
The Heartbreak Kid '72
Lady Vanishes '79
The Last Picture Show '71
The Long, Hot Summer '86
Married to It '93
Memphis '91
Moonlighting '85
Once Upon a Crime '92
The Return '80
Secrets of a Married Man '84
Seduced '85
Silver Bears '78
Special Delivery '76
Taxi Driver '76
Texasville '90
Which Way Home '90

Elizabeth Shepherd
The Double Negative '80
Invitation to the Wedding '73
Phoenix Team '80
Tomb of Ligeia '64

Jack Shepherd
Escape from Sobibor '87
Twenty-One '91
The Virgin Soldiers '69

John Shepherd
Banzai Runner '86
Friday the 13th, Part 5: A New
Beginning '85
Thunder Run '86

Simon Shepherd
Fire, Ice and Dynamite '91
Murder on Line One '90

**W. Morgan
Shepherd**
Elvira, Mistress of the Dark
'88

Michael Shepley
Housemaster '38
Mine Own Executioner '47
The Private Secretary '35
A Shot in the Dark '33

Delia Sheppard
Animal Instincts '92

Mirror Images '91
Night Rhythms '92
Roots of Evil '91
Secret Games '92
Sins of Desire '92
Witchcraft 2: The Temptress '90

Paula Sheppard
Alice Sweet Alice '76
Liquid Sky '83

Anthony Sher
Erik the Viking '89
Moliere '84
Shadey '87
Tartuffe '90

Maurice Sherbanee
Jud '71

Ann Sheridan
Angels with Dirty Faces '38
Appointment in Honduras '53
City for Conquest '40
Dodge City '39
Edge of Darkness '43
The Fighting Westerner '35
George Washington Slept Here '42
Good Sam '48
Kings Row '41
Letter of Introduction '38
The Man Who Came to Dinner '41
The Opposite Sex '56
Silver River '48
Thank Your Lucky Stars '43
They Drive by Night '40
They Made Me a Criminal '39

Dinah Sheridan
Blackout '50
Calling Paul Temple '48
Genevieve '53
No Trace '50
Railway Children '70
Salute John Citizen '42
Thirteenth Reunion '81

Jamey Sheridan
All I Want for Christmas '91
Jumpin' Jack Flash '86
Stanley and Iris '90
A Stranger Among Us '92
Whispers in the Dark '92

Jim Sheridan
Way of the West '35

Margaret Sheridan
One Minute to Zero '52
The Thing '51

Nicolette Sheridan
Deceptions '90
Noises Off '92
The Sure Thing '85

Louise Sherill
Speak of the Devil '90

Alan Sherman
Pepper and His Wacky Taxi '72

Bobby Sherman
He is My Brother '75

Didi Sherman
Green Inferno '80s

Editta Sherman
Ms. 45 '81

Ellen Sherman
Dr. Tarr's Torture Dungeon '75
La Mansion de la Locura '87

Jenny Sherman
Mean Johnny Barrows '75

Kerry Sherman
Satan's Cheerleaders '77

Lowell Sherman
Bachelor Apartment '31
False Faces '32
The Garden of Eden '28
Monsieur Beaucaire '24
The Royal Bed '31
Three Broadway Girls '32
Way Down East '20
What Price Hollywood? '32

Ransom Sherman
Winter Meeting '48

Robert Sherman
Tall Lie '53

Wendy Sherman
Million Dollar Mystery '87

Tudor Sherrard
Heartbreak Hotel '88

Kid Sherrif
The Amsterdam Connection '70s

Martha Sherrill
Call of the Forest '49

J. Barney Sherry
The White Sister '23

David Sherwood
River of Diamonds '90

Gale Sherwood
Blonde Savage '47

Madeline Sherwood
Pendulum '69
Sweet Bird of Youth '62
Teachers '84

Robin Sherwood
Love Butcher '82
Tourist Trap '79

Vladek Sheybal
The Boy Friend '71
Scorpio '73
S*P*Y*S '74

Toshio Shibaki
Godzilla vs. the Smog Monster '72

Mihoko Shibata
A Taxing Woman Returns '88

Arthur Shields
The Corn is Green '45
The Daughter of Dr. Jekyll '57
Drums Along the Mohawk '39
Enchanted Island '58
The Fabulous Dorseys '47
Fighting Father Dunne '48
Gentleman Jim '42
The Keys of the Kingdom '44
The King and Four Queens '56
The Quiet Man '52
The River '51
The White Cliffs of Dover '44

Brooke Shields
Alice Sweet Alice '76
Backstreet Dreams '90
The Blue Lagoon '80
Brenda Starr '86
The Diamond Trap '91
Endless Love '81
King of the Gypsies '78
Muppets Take Manhattan '84
Pretty Baby '78
The Prince of Central Park '77
Sahara '83
Speed Zone '88
Tilt '78
Wanda Nevada '79
Wet Gold '84

Gordon Shields
Vigil '84

Nicholas Shields
Liar's Edge '92
Lost in the Barrens '91
Princess in Exile '90

Dhiu Min Shien
Five Fighters from Shaolin '70s

James Shigeta
The Cage '89
China Cry '91
Die Hard '88
Enola Gay: The Men, the Mission, the Atomic Bomb '80
Flower Drum Song '61
Paradise, Hawaiian Style '66
Tomorrow's Child '82

Marion Shilling
Captured in Chinatown '35
Cavalcade of the West '36
Gun Play '36
I'll Name the Murderer '36
Inside Information '34
Man's Land '32
Rio Rattler '35
Shop Angel '32
A Shot in the Dark '35
Thunder Over Texas '34

Shmuel Shilo
Double Edge '92
Goodbye, New York '85
Noa at Seventeen '82

Yoseph Shiloah
I Love You Rosa '72
Private Manoeuvres '83

Joseph Shiloal
Eagles Attack at Dawn '74
Lion of Africa '87

Yoko Shimada
My Champion '84
Shogun '80

Armin Shimerman
Arena '88

Dalia Shimko
Noa at Seventeen '82

Joanna Shimkus
The Virgin and the Gypsy '70

Sab Shimono
Come See the Paradise '90
Gung Ho '85
Presumed Innocent '90
Teenage Mutant Ninja Turtles 3 '93
The Wash '88

Takashi Shimura
The Bad Sleep Well '60
Drunken Angel '48
Godzilla, King of the Monsters '56
I Live in Fear '55
Ikiru '52
Love and Faith '78
The Mysterians '58
Sanshiro Sugata '43
Seven Samurai '54
Stray Dog '49
Throne of Blood '57

Eitaro Shindo
The Crucified Lovers '54
Sansho the Bailiff '54

Chen Shing
The Amsterdam Connection '70s
Snake in the Eagle's Shadow 2 '83

The Two Great Cavaliers '73

Li Tai Shing
Hurricane Sword '70s

Mo Si Shing
Samurai Sword of Justice

Sung Kam Shing
Kung Fu from Beyond the Grave

Tony Wai Shing
Duel of the Brave Ones '80

Christine Shinn
White Fury '90

Hiroko Shino
Murder in the Doll House '79

Saburo Shinoda
The Imperial Japanese Empire '85

Sue Shiomi
Dragon Princess '70s
Shogun's Ninja '83
The Street Fighter's Last Revenge '79

Toshi Shioya
Mr. Baseball '92
Prisoners of the Sun '91

John Wesley Shipp
Baby of the Bride '91
The Flash '90
The NeverEnding Story 2: Next Chapter '91

Yumi Shirakawa
H-Man '59
The Mysterians '58
Rodan '56
The Secret of the Tologian '61

Talia Shire
Bed & Breakfast '92
Blood Vows: The Story of a Mafia Wife '87
Cold Heaven '92
For Richer, For Poorer '92
Gas-s-s-s! '70
The Godfather '72
The Godfather 1902-1959: The Complete Epic '81
The Godfather, Part 2 '74
The Godfather, Part 3 '90
Hyper-Sapien: People from Another Star '86
Lionheart '87
Mark Twain and Me '91
Murderer's Keep '88
New York Stories '89
Old Boyfriends '79
Prophecy '79
Rad '86
Rip van Winkle '85
Rocky '76
Rocky 2 '79
Rocky 3 '82
Rocky 4 '85
Rocky 5 '90
Windows '80

Bill Shirk
Ballbuster
Escapist '83

Anne Shirley
Anne of Green Gables '34
Bombardier '43
The Devil & Daniel Webster '41
Four Jacks and a Jill '41
Law of the Underworld '38
Murder, My Sweet '44
Rasputin and the Empress '32
Stella Dallas '37

Bill Shirley
Abbott and Costello Meet Captain Kidd '52
I Dream of Jeannie '52

Cathie Shirriff
Covergirl '83
Star Trek 3: The Search for Spock '84

Tiki Shirtee
Ninja Massacre '84

Stephan Shkurat
Earth '30

Sallie Shockley
The Tattered Web '71

William Shockley
Howling 5: The Rebirth '89

Ingrid Sholder
Mission Phantom '79

Pamela Shoop
One Man Jury '78

Dan Shor
Bill & Ted's Excellent Adventure '89
Daddy's Boys '87
Mesmerized '84
Mike's Murder '84
A Rumor of War '80
Strange Behavior '81
Strangers Kiss '83
Tron '82

Dinah Shore
Fun & Fancy Free '47
Hollywood Goes to War '54
Oh, God! '77
Pee-Wee's Playhouse Christmas Special '88
Thank Your Lucky Stars '43
Till the Clouds Roll By '46
Till the Clouds Roll By/A Star Is Born '46
Up in Arms '44

Pauly Shore
Dream Date '93
Encino Man '92
Son-in-Law '93

Bobby Short
For Love or Money '93
Hardhat & Legs '80

Dorothy Short
Brothers of the West '37
Camp Double Feature '39
Daughter of the Tong '39
Reefer Madness '38
Savage Fury '33
Trail of the Silver Spurs '41
Wild Horse Canyon '39

Florence Short
The Love Flower '20

Martin Short
Best of Comic Relief '86
The Best of John Candy on SCTV '80s
The Big Picture '89
Captain Ron '92
Clifford '93
Cross My Heart '88
The Family Man '79
Father of the Bride '91
Innerspace '87
Johnny Appleseed '86
Lost and Found '79
Pure Luck '91
Really Weird Tales '86
The Return of Spinal Tap '92
Sunset Limousine '83
Three Amigos '86
Three Fugitives '89

Shorter

Ken Shorter
Ned Kelly '70

Robin Shou
Honor and Glory '92

Grant Show
Treacherous Crossing '92
A Woman, Her Men and Her Futon '92

Max Showalter
Racing with the Moon '84
Sixteen Candles '84

Kathy Shower
Bedroom Eyes 2 '89
Commando Squad '87
Frankenstein General Hospital '88
The Further Adventures of Tennessee Buck '88
L.A. Goddess '92
Out on Bail '89
Robo-Chic '89
Wild Cactus '92

Herb Shriner
Main Street to Broadway '53

Kin Shriner
Angel 3: The Final Chapter '88
Escape '90
Obsessive Love '84
Vendetta '85

Will Shriner
Time Trackers '88

Tsen Shu-yi
Infra-Man '76

Katharine Shubeck
Wanda, The Sadistic Hypnotist '67

Karin Shubert
Cold Eyes of Fear '70s

Elisabeth Shue
Adventures in Babysitting '87
Back to the Future, Part 2 '89
Back to the Future, Part 3 '90
Call to Glory '84
Cocktail '88
Heart and Souls '93
The Karate Kid '84
Link '86
The Marrying Man '91
Soapdish '91

Lee Shue
Samurai Blood, Samurai Guts
Samurai Sword of Justice

Stephanie Shuford
Dreams Come True '84

Richard B. Shull
Big Bus '76
Cockfighter '74
Dreamer '79
Hail '73
Housesitter '92
The Pack '77
Slither '73
Splash '84
Unfaithfully Yours '84

Yisroel Shumacher
The Jolly Paupers '38

Yuen Shun-Yee
Dreadnaught

Antonina Shuranova
An Unfinished Piece for a Player Piano '77
War and Peace '68

Ethel Shutta
Whoopee! '30

Jin Shuyuan
Raise the Red Lantern '91

A. Shvorin
The Cranes are Flying '57

Ting Shan Si
La Venganza del Kung Fu '87

Yeung Si
Super Kung Fu Kid

Sabrina Siami
Throne of Fire '82

Ryp Siani
Robby '68

Sabrina Siani
Ator the Fighting Eagle '83
Conquest '83

Stefano Sibaldi
Mondo Cane '63

Jane Sibbet
The Resurrected '91

John Sibbit
Love Circles '85

Nadia Sibirskaia
The Crime of Monsieur Lange '36

Joseph R. Sicari
Night School '81

George Sidney
Manhattan Melodrama '34

Sylvia Sidney
Beetlejuice '88
Blood on the Sun '45
Come Along with Me '84
Corrupt '84
Damien: Omen 2 '78
Dead End '37
Death at Love House '75
An Early Frost '85
Finnegan Begin Again '84
Fury '36
God Told Me To '76
Hammett '82
Having It All '82
I Never Promised You a Rose Garden '77
Love from a Stranger '47
Mr. Ace '46
One Third of a Nation '39
Pals '87
Raid on Entebbe '77
Sabotage '36
The Shadow Box '80
A Small Killing '81
Snowbeast '77
Street Scene '31
Summer Wishes, Winter Dreams '73
Used People '92
You Only Live Once '37

Charles Siebert
Blue Sunshine '78
A Cry for Love '80
Tarantulas: The Deadly Cargo '77

Oliver Siebert
The White Rose '83

Paul Siederman
Deranged '87

Jim Siedow
The Texas Chainsaw Massacre '74
Texas Chainsaw Massacre, Part 2 '86

Don Siegel
Into the Night '85

Invasion of the Body Snatchers '56
Invasion of the Body Snatchers '78
Play Misty for Me '71

Harvey Siegel
Enrapture '90

Mark Siegel
The Crater Lake Monster '77

George Siegmann
Hotel Imperial '27
The Man Who Laughs '27
Oliver Twist '22
The Three Musketeers '21

Casey Siemaszko
Amazing Stories '85
Back to the Future '85
Back to the Future, Part 2 '89
The Big Slice '90
Biloxi Blues '88
Breaking In '89
The Chase '91
Class '83
Gardens of Stone '87
Miracle of the Heart: A Boys Town Story '86
Near Misses '91
Of Mice and Men '92
Secret Admirer '85
Stand By Me '86
Three O'Clock High '87
Young Guns '88

Nina Siemaszko
Bed & Breakfast '92
Sinatra '92
Wild Orchid 2: Two Shades of Blue '92

Tom Sierchio
Delivery Boys '84

Gregory Sierra
The Clones '73
Code Name: Dancer '87
Deep Cover '92
Dynamite and Gold '88
Let's Get Harry '87
Mean Dog Blues '78
Miami Vice '84
Pocket Money '72
The Thief Who Came to Dinner '73

Miguel Sierra
The Bronx War '90

Asha Siewkumar
Tropical Heat '93

Everett Sifuentes
The Return of Josey Wales '86

Elsbeth Sigmund
Heidi '52

Tom Signorelli
Crossover Dreams '85
The Last Porno Flick '74

Simone Signoret
Against the Wind '48
The Day and the Hour '63
Dedee d'Anvers '49
Diabolique '55
I Sent a Letter to My Love '81
Is Paris Burning? '68
La Ronde '51
Le Chat '75
Madame Rosa '77
Room at the Top '59
Ship of Fools '65
Widow Couderc '74

Caroline Sihol
Confidentially Yours '83

Huang Ing Sik
When Taekwondo Strikes '83

Lung Sikar
The Unbeaten 28 '80s

Cynthia Sikes
Goodbye Cruel World '82
Love Hurts '91
The Man Who Loved Women '83
Oceans of Fire '86

James B. Sikking
Black Force 2 '78
The Brotherhood of the Rose '89
Charro! '69
The Competition '80
Dress Gray '86
Final Approach '91
Man on the Run '74
Morons from Outer Space '85
Narrow Margin '90
The Night God Screamed '80s
Ordinary People '80
Outland '81
Scorpio '73
Star Trek 3: The Search for Spock '84
The Terminal Man '74
Up the Creek '84

Tom Silardi
Fury to Freedom: The Life Story of Raul Ries '85

Vic Silayan
The Last Reunion '80

Adam Silbar
Hot Moves '84

Tusse Silberg
The Company of Wolves '85
Hidden City '87

Vira Silenti
Atlas in the Land of the Cyclops '61
Maciste in Hell '60
Son of Samson '62

Karen Sillas
Simple Men '92

Allison Silva
Bridge to Silence '89

David Silva
El Aviador Fenomeno '47
Senora Tentacion '49
Sisters of Satan '75

Franco Silva
The Mongols '60

Geno Silva
Drug Wars 2: The Cocaine Cartel '92
Night Eyes 2 '91

Henry Silva
Above the Law '88
Alligator '80
Almost Human '79
The Bravados '58
Buck Rogers in the 25th Century '79
Bulletproof '88
Cannonball Run II '84
Chained Heat '83
Cinderfella '60
Code of Silence '85
The Colombian Connection '91
Crimebusters '79
Cry of a Prostitute: Love Kills '72
Day of the Assassin '81
Deadly Sting '82

The Desperados '80s
Escape from the Bronx '85
A Gathering of Eagles '63
The Harvest '93
Hired to Kill '73
Hit Men '73
The Italian Connection '73
The Jayhawkers '59
Killer '70s
Killing in the Sun
The Law and Jake Wade '58
Love and Bullets '79
Lust in the Dust '85
Man & Boy '71
The Manchurian Candidate '62
Manhunt '73
Megaforce '82
Never a Dull Moment '68
Sharky's Machine '81
Shoot '85
The Tall T '57
Thirst '87
Three Days to a Kill '91
Violent Breed '83
Wrong is Right '82

Maria Silva
Curse of the Devil '73
The Mummy's Revenge '73

Rebeca Silva
Gente Violenta '87

Simone Silva
Big Deadly Game '54
The Shadow Man '53

Trinidad Silva
Colors '88
Crackers '84
The Night Before '88

Silvagni
The Rise of Louis XIV '66

Aldo Silvani
La Strada '54

Alvin Silver
Nudity Required '90

Borah Silver
Elves '89

Christine Silver
Room to Let '49

Cindy Silver
Hardbodies '84

Fawn Silver
Orgy of the Dead '65
Terror in the Jungle '68

Jeanne Silver
Sex, Drugs, and Rock-n-Roll '84

Joan Micklin Silver
How to Be a Perfect Person in Just Three Days '84

Joe Silver
Almost You '85
The Apprenticeship of Duddy Kravitz '74
The Gig '85
Mr. Nice Guy '86
Rabid '77
Raggedy Ann and Andy: A Musical Adventure '77
They Came from Within '75

Ron Silver
Best Friends '82
Betrayal '78
Billionaire Boys Club '87
Blind Side '93
Blue Steel '90
Eat and Run '86
Enemies, a Love Story '89

Dwan Smith
Sparkle '76

Ebbe Roe Smith
The Big Easy '87

Elwood Smith
Boy! What a Girl '45

Ethel Smith
Bathing Beauty '44

Forry Smith
Black Cobra 3: The Manila
Connection '90

G. Michael Smith
Offerings '89

Garnett Smith
Laboratory '80
Whitcomb's War '88

Geraldine Smith
Flesh '68
Mixed Blood '84

Grace Smith
Girl from Chicago '32

Howard Smith
State of the Union '48

Howard K. Smith
Nasty Habits '77

J. Smith
Gal Young 'Un '79

J. Augustus Smith
Drums O'Voodoo '34

Jaclyn Smith
The Adventurers '70
The Bourne Identity '88
Deja Vu '84
Goodbye Columbus '69
Jacqueline Bouvier Kennedy
'81
Lies Before Kisses '92
The Night They Saved
Christmas '87
Nightkill '80
Probe '72
Rage of Angels '83
Rage of Angels: The Story
Continues '86
Users '78
Windmills of the Gods '88

Jamie Smith
Killer's Kiss '55

Jayne Smith
R.O.T.O.R. '88

John W. Smith
Hot Rod Girl '56
Star Crystal '85

J. Walter Smith
In Your Face '77

Karen Smith
The Erotic Adventures of
Pinocchio '71

Kate Smith
Irving Berlin's America '86
This is the Army '43

Keely Smith
Thunder Road '58

Keith Smith
Beyond Innocence '87

Kelly Shaye Smith
The Opponent '89

Ken Smith
Santa Claus '59

Kent Smith
The Affair '73
Back Door to Heaven '39

The Badlanders '58
The Balcony '63
Cat People '42
Curse of the Cat People '44
Die Sister, Die! '74
Magic Town '47
Party Girl '58
Pete 'n' Tillie '72
Probe '72
The Spiral Staircase '46
Strangers When We Meet '60

Kurtwood Smith
Company Business '91
The Crush '93
Dead Poets Society '89
The Heart of Dixie '89
The Nightmare Years '89
Rambo 3 '88
RoboCop '87
Shadows and Fog '92
True Believer '89

Lane Smith
Air America '90
Blind Vengeance '90
The Displaced Person '76
The Distinguished Gentleman
'92
Dress Gray '86
Duplicates '92
False Arrest '92
The Mighty Ducks '92
My Cousin Vinny '92
Night Game '89
Prime Suspect '82
Prison '88
The Solitary Man '82
Son-in-Law '93
Weeds '87

Lewis Smith
The Adventures of Buckaroo
Banzai Across the Eighth
Dimension '84
Diary of a Hitman '91
The Final Terror '83
Fulfillment '89
The Heavenly Kid '85

Linda Smith
The Phone Call '89

Liz Smith
Apartment Zero '88
A Private Function '84
We Think the World of You
'88

Lois Smith
Five Easy Pieces '70
Fried Green Tomatoes '91
Green Card '90
Hard Promises '92
Keep the Change '92
Reckless '84
Reuben, Reuben '83
Skylark '93
Switched at Birth '91
Twisted '86

Loring Smith
Shadow of the Thin Man '41

Louise Smith
Working Girls '87

Madeleine Smith
Frankenstein and the Monster
from Hell '74
Live and Let Die '73
The Vampire Lovers '70

Madolyn Smith
All of Me '84
The Caller '87
Ernie Kovacs: Between the
Laughter '84
Final Approach '91
Funny Farm '88

Pray TV '82
Rehearsal for Murder '82
The Rose and the Jackal '90
Sadat '83
The Super '91
2010: The Year We Make
Contact '84
Urban Cowboy '80

Maggie Smith
Better Late Than Never '83
California Suite '78
Clash of the Titans '81
Death on the Nile '78
Evil Under the Sun '82
The Honey Pot '67
Hook '91
Lily in Love '85
The Lonely Passion of Judith
Hearne '87
The Missionary '82
Mrs. Silly '85
Murder by Death '76
The Prime of Miss Jean
Brodie '69
A Private Function '84
Quartet '81
A Room with a View '86
The Secret Garden '93
Sister Act '92
Travels with My Aunt '72
The V.I.P.'s '63

Mamie Smith
Paradise in Harlem '40

Mark Clifford Smith
An Empty Bed '90

Marty Smith
Let's Kill All the Lawyers '93

Maurice Smith
Bloodfist 2 '90

Mel Smith
Brain Donors '92
The Misadventures of Mr. Wilt
'90
Morons from Outer Space '85
The Princess Bride '87
Slayground '84

Melanie Smith
The Baby Doll Murders '92
Trancers 3: Deth Lives '92

Michael Smith
C.I.A.: Code Name Alexa '92

Mike Smith
Time is Running Out '52

Oliver Smith
Hellbound: Hellraiser 2 '88
Hellraiser '87

Pam Smith
Misty '61

Patricia Smith
Save the Tiger '73
Spirit of St. Louis '57

Paul Smith
Caged Fury '90
Crimewave '85
Crossing the Line '90
Death Chase '87
Desert Kickboxer '92
Dune '84
The Fire in the Stone '85
Gor '88
Haunted Honeymoon '86
Jungle Warriors '84
Madron '70
Midnight Express '78
Mortuary '81
Outlaw Force '87
Pieces '83
Platypus Cove '86

Popeye '80
Raiders in Action '71
Red Sonja '85
Return of the Tiger '78
The Salamander '82
Sno-Line '85
Sonny Boy '87

Pete Smith
A Few Moments with Buster
Keaton and Laurel and
Hardy '63

Peter Smith
The Quiet Earth '85

Putter Smith
Diamonds are Forever '71

Queenie Smith
The Great Rupert '50

Reid Smith
Teenager '74

Rex Smith
The Pirates of Penzance '83
Shades of Love: The Ballerina
& the Blues '87
Snow White and the Seven
Dwarfs '83
Sooner or Later '78
Street Hawk '84
Transformations '88
The Trial of the Incredible Hulk
'89

Robert Smith
Call Out the Marines '42

**Robert Guenveur
Smith**
Deep Cover '92

Roger Smith
Auntie Mame '58
Man of a Thousand Faces '57

Savannah Smith
Code of Honor '84
Everybody's All American '88
The Long Riders '80

Sharon Smith
Nightmare '82

Shawn Smith
It! The Terror from Beyond
Space '58
The River Rat '84

Shawnee Smith
The Blob '88
Summer School '87
Who's Harry Crumb? '89

Shelley Smith
The Fantastic World of D.C.
Collins '84
National Lampoon's Class
Reunion '82
The Night the City Screamed
'80

Sinjin Smith
Side Out '90

Stuart Smith
Ninja Destroyer '70s
Ninja Hunt '80s
Ninja Kill '87
The Ultimate Ninja '85

Terri Susan Smith
Basket Case '82

Tracy N. Smith
Hot Dog...The Movie! '83

Will Smith
Made in America '93
Where the Day Takes You '92

William Smith
Action U.S.A. '89
Angels Die Hard '84
At Sword's Point '51
Blackjack '78
B.O.R.N. '88
Boss '74
Chrome and Hot Leather '71
Chrome Hearts '70
Commando Squad '87
Conan the Barbarian '82
Darker than Amber '70
Deadly Breed '89
The Deadly Trackers '73
Dr. Minx '75
East L.A. Warriors '89
Emperor of the Bronx '89
Evil Altar '89
Eye of the Tiger '86
Fast Company '78
Fever Pitch '85
The Frisco Kid '79
Gentle Savage '73
Grave of the Vampire '72
Hell on the Battleground '88
Hollywood Man '76
Invasion of the Bee Girls '73
Jungle Assault '89
L.A. Vice '89
The Last Riders '90
The Losers '70
Maniac Cop '88
Mean Season '85
Memorial Valley Massacre '88
Moon in Scorpio '86
Platoon Leader '87
The Rebels '79
Red Dawn '84
Run, Angel, Run! '69
Scorchy '76
Seven '79
Slow Burn '90
A Taste of Hell '73
Terror in Beverly Hills '90
The Ultimate Warrior '75

Willie E. Smith
Legend of Boggy Creek '75

Yeardley Smith
City Slickers '91
Ginger Ale Afternoon '89
Heaven Help Us '85
Legend of Billie Jean '85
Maximum Overdrive '86
The Simpsons Christmas
Special '89

**Jamie Smith-
Jackson**
Satan's School for Girls '73

Jan Smithers
Mr. Nice Guy '86
Where the Lilies Bloom '74

William Smithers
Death Sport '78
Scorpio '73

Bill Smitrovich
Crazy People '90
Crime Story: The Complete
Saga '86
A Killing Affair '85
Renegades '89

Jimmy Smits
The Believers '87
Fires Within '91
Glitz '88
L.A. Law '86
Old Gringo '89
Running Scared '86
Stamp of a Killer '87
Switch '91
Vital Signs '90

Sonja Smits
Hitchhiker 4 '87
The Pit '81
That's My Baby! '88
Videodrome '83
War Brides '80s

Rinaldo Smordoni
Shoeshine '47

Dick Smothers
Rap Master Ronnie '88
Speed Zone '88
Tales of the Unexpected '91

Tom Smothers
Alice Through the Looking
  Glass '66
Pandemonium '82
A Pleasure Doing Business
  '79
Rap Master Ronnie '88
Serial '80
Silver Bears '78
Speed Zone '88

Josephine Smulders
The Gold & Glory '88

David Smulker
Mark of the Beast

Dana Smutna
Sweet Light in a Dark Room
  '60

Ann Smyrner
Beyond the Law '68
The House of 1000 Dolls '67

Sam Snead
The Caddy '53

Brian Sneagle
Deranged '74

Susan Sneers
Tiffany Jones '75

Gerti Sneider
2069: A Sex Odyssey '78

Mike Snell
Derby '71

Helmut Snider
Kemek '88

Wesley Snipes
Boiling Point '93
Jungle Fever '91
King of New York '90
Major League '89
Mo' Better Blues '90
New Jack City '91
Passenger 57 '92
Rising Sun '93
Streets of Gold '86
Vietnam War Story 2 '88
The Waterdance '91
White Men Can't Jump '92
Wildcats '86

Carrie Snodgress
Across the Tracks '89
The Attic '80
Blueberry Hill '88
Chill Factor '90
Diary of a Mad Housewife '70
The Fury '78
L.A. Bad '85
Mission of the Shark '91
Murphy's Law '86
Nadia '84
A Night in Heaven '83
Pale Rider '85
The Rose and the Jackal '90
Silent Night, Lonely Night '69
The Solitary Man '82
Trick or Treats '82

Peter Snook
Fly with the Hawk

Marguerite Snow
With Kit Carson Over the
  Great Divide '25

Rhonda Snow
American Drive-In '88

Victoria Snow
Buffalo Jump '90
Love and Hate '90

Jane Snowdon
The French Lesson '86

Arlen Dean Snyder
Deadly Force '83
Dear Detective '78
Heartbreak Ridge '86
Marked for Death '90
Night Partners '83
No Place to Hide '81
Red Flag: The Ultimate Game
  '81
Scalpel '76
Wheels of Terror '90
Yanks '79
Young Love, First Love '79

Drew Snyder
Dance with Death '91
Firestarter '84
Night School '81
Project: Eliminator '91

Gladys Snyder
Gang War '40

Nancy Snyder
The Kirlian Witness '78

Sandy Snyder
Murder-in-Law '92

Suzanne Snyder
Killer Klowns from Outer
  Space '88
The Night Before '88
Prettykill '87
Retribution '88

Sammy Snyders
The Pit '81

Barry Sobel
Martians Go Home! '90
Punchline '88

Maria Socas
Deathstalker 2: Duel of the
  Titans '87
The Warrior & the Sorceress
  '84

Kristina Soderbaum
Jud Suess '40
Kolberg '45

Lars Soderdahl
Brothers Lionheart '85

Camilla Soeberg
Twist & Shout '84

Abraham Sofaer
Bhowani Junction '56
Calling Paul Temple '48
Captain Sinbad '63
Demon with a Glass Hand '64
Dual Alibi '47
Elephant Walk '54
Naked Jungle '54
Quo Vadis '51

Elena Sofonova
Dark Eyes '87

Ika Sohar
I Don't Give a Damn '88

Hans Sohnker
The Phantom of Soho '64

Sherlock Holmes and the
  Deadly Necklace '62

Sojin
The Thief of Baghdad '24

Ruzica Sokic
The Love Affair, or The Case
  of the Missing Switchboard
  Operator '67

Marilyn Sokol
The Goodbye Girl '77
Something Short of Paradise
  '79

Vladimir Sokoloff
Baron of Arizona '51
Beyond the Time Barrier '60
Cloak and Dagger '46
Conquest '32
I Was a Teenage Werewolf
  '57
The Lower Depths '36
The Road to Morocco '42
Taras Bulba '62

Andrei Sokolov
Little Vera '88

Miguel Angel Sola
Funny, Dirty Little War '83
Mayalunta '86

Silvia Solar
As If It Were Raining '63
Finger on the Trigger '65
The Gentleman Killer '78
Night of the Howling Beast '75

**Augustin Martinez
Solares**
Night of the Bloody Apes '68

Suzanne Solari
Roller Blade '85

Andres Soler
The Brute '52
El Bruto '52
El Ceniciento '47
Orlak, the Hell of Frankenstein
  '60

Domingo Soler
The Illusion Travels by
  Streetcar '53

Fernando Soler
Anita de Montemar '60s
The Great Madcap '49
Susana '51

Paul Soles
Beethoven Lives Upstairs '92
The Gunrunner '84

P.J. Soles
Alienator '89
B.O.R.N. '88
Halloween '78
Innocent Prey '88
The Possessed '77
Rock 'n' Roll High School '79
Saigon Commandos '88
Soldier's Fortune '91
Stripes '81

Javier Solis
El Hombre de la Furia '65
Los Tres Calaveras '64

Madeleine Sologne
Eternal Return '43

Jonathan Soloman
Body Trouble '92

Yuri Solomin
Dersu Uzala '75

Bruce Solomon
Children Shouldn't Play with
  Dead Things '72
Foul Play '78

Charles Solomon
The Channeler '89
Witchcraft 2: The Temptress
  '90
Witchcraft 3: The Kiss of
  Death '90
Witchcraft 4: Virgin Heart '92

Todd Solondz
Fear, Anxiety and Depression
  '89

Anatoli Solonitzin
Andrei Rublev '66
Stalker '79

Elena Solovei
Oblomov '80
A Slave of Love '78
An Unfinished Piece for a
  Player Piano '77

Bertalan Solti
Hungarian Rhapsody '78

Ollie Soltoft
Victorian Fantasies '86

Jack Somack
Desperate Characters '71

Yanti Somer
Cosmos: War of the Planets
  '80
Reactor '85

Kristi Somers
Hardbodies '84
Tomboy '85

Suzanne Somers
American Graffiti '73
Ants '77
Happily Ever After '82
Nothing Personal '80
Sky Hei$t '75
Yesterday's Hero '79

**Gretschen
Somerville**
Fun Down There '88

Julie Sommars
Herbie Goes to Monte Carlo
  '77
I'm the Girl He Wants to Kill
  '74
Sex and the Single Parent '82

Elke Sommer
Adventures Beyond Belief '87
Anastasia: The Mystery of
  Anna '86
The Big Scam '79
Boy, Did I Get a Wrong
  Number! '66
Carry On Behind '75
The Corrupt Ones '67
The Double McGuffin '79
Fantastic Seven '82
Inside the Third Reich '82
The Invincible Six '68
The Invisible Strangler '76
It's Not the Size That Counts
  '74
Jenny's War '85
Left for Dead '78
Lily in Love '85
Lisa and the Devil '75
No One Cries Forever '85
One Away '80
The Oscar '66
Prisoner of Zenda '79
The Prize '63
Probe '72
Severed Ties '92

A Shot in the Dark '64
Sweet Ecstasy '62
Ten Little Indians '75
Torture Chamber of Baron
  Blood '72
The Treasure Seekers '79
Zeppelin '71

Josef Sommer
Absence of Malice '81
Bloodhounds of Broadway '89
Bridge to Silence '89
Chances Are '89
Dracula's Widow '88
Execution of Raymond
  Graham '85
Forced March '90
Hide in Plain Sight '80
Hostages '93
Iceman '84
Independence Day '83
The Mighty Ducks '92
Rods '81
Rollover '81
The Rosary Murders '87
Shadows and Fog '92
Silkwood '83
Still of the Night '82
Target '85
Witness '85
Yuri Nosenko, KGB '86

Helga Sommerfeld
Code Name Alpha '67
The Phantom of Soho '64

Josef Somr
Closely Watched Trains '66

Gale Sondergaard
Anthony Adverse '36
The Blue Bird '40
East Side, West Side '49
Echoes '83
Isle of Forgotten Sins '43
Juarez '39
The Letter '40
The Life of Emile Zola '37
The Mark of Zorro '40
My Favorite Blonde '42
A Night to Remember '42
The Return of a Man Called
  Horse '76
The Road to Rio '47
Savage Intruder '68
Spider Woman '44
The Time of Their Lives '46

Jiro Soneya
The Mutiny of the Elsinore '39

Yang Song
Super Ninja

Keisuke Sonoi
X from Outer Space '67

Gerry Sont
Girl-Toy '84

Susan Sontag
Zelig '83

Michael Sonye
Surf Nazis Must Die '87

Jack Soo
Flower Drum Song '61
Return from Witch Mountain
  '78

Park Jong Soo
Search and Destroy '81
Striking Back '81

Jonathan Soper
Ninja Brothers of Blood '89

Mark Soper
Understudy: The Graveyard
  Shift 2 '88

Mike Soper
Blood Rage '87

Michael Sopkiw
After the Fall of New York '85
Blastfighter '85
Massacre in Dinosaur Valley '85

Agnes Soral
Killing Cars '85
One Wild Moment '78
Tchao Pantin '84

Elga Sorbas
The American Soldier '70

Alberto Sordi
The Great War '59
I Vitelloni '53
Those Magnificent Men in Their Flying Machines '65
Two Nights with Cleopatra '54
The White Sheik '52

Guy Sorel
Honeymoon Killers '70

Jean Sorel
Paralyzed '70s

Louise Sorel
Get Christie Love! '74
Mazes and Monsters '82
Plaza Suite '71
The President's Plane is Missing '71
Rona Jaffe's Mazes & Monsters '82
When Every Day was the Fourth of July '78

Ted Sorel
Basket Case 2 '90
From Beyond '86

Linda Sorensen
Family Reunion '88
Kavik the Wolf Dog '84
Stone Cold Dead '80

Paul Sorenson
The Day the Earth Froze '59

Ricky Sorenson
The Sword in the Stone '63
Tarzan and the Trappers '58

Sylvia Sorente
Castle of Blood '64

Adam Sorg
Moonshine Mountain '64

Charo Soriano
Dracula's Great Love '72
The Garden of Delights '70
Orgy of the Vampires '73

Judie Soriano
Black Force '75

Jim Soriero
Delivery Boys '84

Louis Sorin
Animal Crackers '30

Arleen Sorkin
From Here to Maternity '85

Janet Sorley
Last House on Dead End Street '77

Jason Sorokin
Oddballs '84

Paul Sorvino
Age Isn't Everything '91
Almost Partners '87
Bloodbrothers '78
Brink's Job '78
Chiefs '83

Cruising '80
Cry Uncle! '71
The Day of the Dolphin '73
Dick Tracy '90
A Fine Mess '86
Fury on Wheels '71
The Gambler '74
Goodfellas '90
I, the Jury '82
I Will, I Will for Now '76
Jailbait: Betrayed By Innocence '86
Lost and Found '79
Melanie '82
My Mother's Secret Life '84
Off the Wall '82
Oh, God! '77
Panic in Needle Park '75
Question of Honor '80
Reds '81
The Rocketeer '91
The Stuff '85
Tell Me Where It Hurts '74
That Championship Season '82
A Touch of Class '73
Turk 182! '85
Vasectomy: A Delicate Matter '86
Very Close Quarters '84

Sander Soth
Time Stands Still '82

Ann Sothern
The Best Man '64
Crazy Mama '75
The Judge Steps Out '49
Kid Millions '34
The Killing Kind '73
Lady Be Good '41
Lady in a Cage '64
A Letter to Three Wives '49
Little Dragons '80
The Manitou '78
Mexican Spitfire/Smartest Girl in Town '40
Nancy Goes to Rio '50
Panama Hattie '42
Whales of August '87
Words and Music '48

Hugh Sothern
Fighting Devil Dogs '43

Carmen Sotir
Moonshine Mountain '64

Fernando Soto
Boom in the Moon '46
El Hombre de la Furia '65
The Illusion Travels by Streetcar '53
Invasion of the Vampires '61

Hugo Soto
Man Facing Southeast '86
Times to Come '81

Luchy Soto
The Garden of Delights '70

Talisa Soto
Hostage '92
License to Kill '89
The Mambo Kings '92
Prison Stories: Women on the Inside '91
Silhouette '91
Spike of Bensonhurst '88

Miao Ko Sou
Samurai Death Bells

Alain Souchon
One Deadly Summer '83

Christine Souder
Street Girls '75

David Soul
Appointment with Death '88
Dog Pound Shuffle '75
The FBI Murders '88
Grave Secrets: The Legacy of Hilltop Drive '92
Hanoi Hilton '87
Homeward Bound '80
In the Cold of the Night '89
The Key to Rebecca '85
Little Ladies of the Night '77
Magnum Force '73
The Manions of America '81
Rage '80
Salem's Lot '79
The Stick-Up '77
Through Naked Eyes '87
Tides of War '90
World War III '86

Stephen Soul
Silent Killers

Renee Soutendijk
Cold Room '84
Eve of Destruction '90
Forced March '90
The 4th Man '79
Grave Secrets '89
Inside the Third Reich '82
Keeper of the City '92
Murderers Among Us: The Simon Wiesenthal Story '89
Out of Order '84
Second Victory '87
Spetters '80

Eve Southern
Morocco '30

Linda Southern
The Amazing Transplant '70

Tom Southern
Harlem Rides the Range '39

Charles Southwood
Guns for Dollars '73
Sartana's Here...Trade Your Pistol for a Coffin '70

Ben Soutten
The Crimes of Stephen Hawke '36
The Mutiny of the Elsinore '39

George Sowards
Backfire '22

Jack Sowards
Tank Commando '59

Doris Anne Soyka
Dead Silence '90

Agnes Spaak
Dr. Orloff's Monster '64

Catherine Spaak
The Cat o' Nine Tails '71
Circle of Love '64
Counter Punch '71
The Easy Life '63
Empty Canvas '64
Honey '81
Hotel '67

Arthur Space
Miss Grant Takes Richmond '49
Riot Squad '41
A Southern Yankee '48
Terror at Red Wolf Inn '72
The Vanishing Westerner '50

Sissy Spacek
Badlands '74
Carrie '76
Coal Miner's Daughter '80
Crimes of the Heart '86
Ginger in the Morning '73

The Girls of Huntington House '73
Hard Promises '92
Heart Beat '80
JFK '91
Katherine '75
The Long Walk Home '89
The Man with Two Brains '83
Marie '85
Missing '82
'night, Mother '86
Prime Cut '72
A Private Matter '92
The Radical '75
Raggedy Man '81
The River '84
Violets Are Blue '86
Welcome to L.A. '77

Kevin Spacey
Consenting Adults '92
Dad '89
Glengarry Glen Ross '92
Henry & June '90
Long Day's Journey into Night '88
The Murder of Mary Phagan '87

Odoardo Spadaro
The Golden Coach '52

David Spade
Coneheads '93

James Spader
Baby Boom '87
Bad Influence '90
Endless Love '81
Family Secrets '84
Jack's Back '87
Less Than Zero '87
Mannequin '87
The New Kids '85
Pretty in Pink '86
The Rachel Papers '89
sex, lies and videotape '89
Storyville '92
True Colors '91
Tuff Turf '85
Wall Street '87
White Palace '90

Pasquale Spadola
Kaos '85

Merrie Spaeth
World of Henry Orient '64

Fay Spain
Al Capone '59
Dragstrip Girl '57
Flight to Fury '66
The Godfather, Part 2 '74
Hercules and the Captive Women '63

Roda Spain
Rebel Vixens '85

B.J. Spalding
Bail Jumper '89

Kim Spalding
It! The Terror from Beyond Space '58

Timothy Spall
Crusoe '89
Dutch Girls '87
Gothic '87
Life is Sweet '91
The Sheltering Sky '90
White Hunter, Black Heart '90

Laurette Spang
Battlestar Galactica '78

Joe Spano
American Graffiti '73
Brotherhood of Justice '86

Brujo Luna
Cast the First Stone '89
The Dunera Boys '85
Fever '91
Northern Lights '79
Terminal Choice '85
Warlock Moon '73

Vincent Spano
Afterburn '92
Alive '93
Alphabet City '84
And God Created Woman '88
Baby It's You '82
The Black Stallion Returns '83
Blood Ties '87
City of Hope '91
Creator '85
The Double McGuffin '79
Good Morning, Babylon '87
High Frequency '88
Indian Summer '93
Maria's Lovers '84
Over the Edge '79
Rumble Fish '83
Senior Trip '81

Adrian Sparks
My Stepmother Is an Alien '88
Roanoak '86

Don Sparks
Fairytales '79

Ned Sparks
Bride Walks Out '36
Corsair '31
Going Hollywood '33
Gold Diggers of 1933 '33
Hawaii Calls '38
Kept Husbands '31
Lady for a Day '33
Marie Galante '34
Sweet Adeline '35

Krao Spartacus
After the Fall of Saigon '88

George Spartels
Mad Max Beyond Thunderdome '85

Camilla Sparv
Dead Heat on a Merry-Go-Round '66
Downhill Racer '69
Survival Zone '84

Dan Speaker
Glitch! '88

Jeff Speakman
The Perfect Weapon '91
Street Knight '93

Bernard Spear
Yentl '83

Robert Egon Spechtenhauser
Bizarre '87

Lynda Speciale
Screwballs '83

Carol Speed
Avenging Disco Godfather '76
The Big Bird Cage '72
Bummer '73
Mack '73
Savage! '73

Hermann Speelmanns
Baron Munchausen '43
F.P. 1 Doesn't Answer '33

Martin Speer
The Dark Ride '84
The Hills Have Eyes '77

Blaze Starr
On the Block '91

Dolores Starr
Athena '54

Emerald Starr
Men in Love '90

Kay Starr
Pied Piper of Hamelin '57

Mike Starr
Billy Bathgate '91
The Bodyguard '92
Mad Dog and Glory '93
Mardi Gras for the Devil '93
Nasty Hero '89

Ringo Starr
Born to Boogie '72
Caveman '81
The Compleat Beatles '82
Give My Regards to Broad
  Street '84
Hard Day's Night '64
Help! '65
Let It Be '70
Lisztomania '75
The Magic Christian '69
Magical Mystery Tour '67
The Point '71
Princess Daisy '83
Sextette '78
That'll Be the Day '73
200 Motels '71
Water '85
Yellow Submarine '68

Ronald Starr
Ride the High Country '62

Wanda Starr
The Guy from Harlem '77

Charles Starrett
Dangerous Appointment '34
Jungle Bride '33
Make a Million '35
The Mask of Fu Manchu '32
Mr. Skitch '33
The Return of Casey Jones
  '34
A Shot in the Dark '35
The Silver Streak '34
Sons of Steel '35

Jack Starrett
Angels from Hell '68
Brothers in Arms '88
Death Chase '87
First Blood '82
Mr. Horn '79
Nightwish '89

Valerie Starrett
Run, Angel, Run! '69

Herbert Stass
The Invisible Terror '63

Dina Stat
The Fable of the Beautiful
  Pigeon Fancier '88

Jim Stathis
The Black Room '82

Lynn Statten
The 7th Commandment '61

Joseph Stauch, Jr.
Heart of the Rio Grande '42

Imelda Staunton
Antonia and Jane '91
Much Ado About Nothing '93
Peter's Friends '92

Mary Stavin
Open House '86
The Opponent '89

Eddie Stazak
Day of the Panther '88
Fists of Blood '87

Alison Steadman
Abigail's Party '77
The Adventures of Baron
  Munchausen '89
Blame It on the Bellboy '92
Champions '84
Clockwise '86
Kipperbang '82
Life is Sweet '91
The Misadventures of Mr. Wilt
  '90
Nuts in May '76
Shirley Valentine '89
Tartuffe '90

John Steadman
The Hills Have Eyes '77
Poco '77

Red Steagall
Benji the Hunted '87
Dark Before Dawn '89

Michael Stearns
Chain Gang Women '72
Chrome and Hot Leather '71

Speed Stearns
Joy Ride to Nowhere '78

Leonard Steckel
Secret of the Black Trunk '62

Ray Dennis Steckler
Las Vegas Weekend '85

Myrtle Stedman
In the Days of the Thundering
  Herd & the Law & the
  Outlaw '14
The Mad Whirl '25
Sex '20

Ted Steedman
Bill & Ted's Excellent
  Adventure '89

Inga Steeger
Sex Adventures of the Three
  Musketeers '80s

Alan Steel
The Fury of Hercules '61
Hercules Against the Moon
  Men '64
Samson '61
Samson and His Mighty
  Challenge '64

Amy Steel
Friday the 13th, Part 2 '81
Walk Like a Man '87

Anthony Steel
48 Hours to Live '60
Harry Black and the Tiger '58
I'm the Girl He Wants to Kill
  '74
Malta Story '53
Massacre in Rome '73
The Master of Ballantrae '53
Perfect Crime '78
The Story of O '75
Tiger of the Seven Seas '62
Wooden Horse '50

Don Steel
Into the Night '85

Adrian Steele
The Mosquito Coast '86

Anthony Steele
Revenge of the Barbarians '64

Barbara Steele
An Angel for Satan '66
Black Sunday '60
Caged Heat '74

Castle of Blood '64
The Crimson Cult '68
8 1/2 '63
The Ghost '63
The Horrible Dr. Hichcock '62
La Dolce Vita '60
The Monocle '64
Nightmare Castle '65
Piranha '78
The Pit and the Pendulum '61
Pretty Baby '78
The She-Beast '65
Silent Scream '80
Terror Creatures from the
  Grave '66
They Came from Within '75
The Winds of War '83

Bob Steele
Alias John Law '35
Ambush Trail '46
Arizona Gunfighter '37
Arizona Whirlwind '44
Atomic Submarine '59
Battling Outlaws '40s
Big Calibre '35
The Big Sleep '46
Billy the Kid in Texas '40
Border Phantom '37
Brand of Hate '34
Brand of the Outlaws '36
Breed of the Border '33
Cavalry '36
City for Conquest '40
Death Valley Rangers '44
Demon for Trouble '34
Durango Valley Raiders '38
El Diablo Rides '39
The Enforcer '51
Giant from the Unknown '58
Gun Lords of Stirrup Basin '37
The Gun Ranger '34
Hidden Valley '32
Kid Courageous '35
Kid Ranger '36
Last of the Warrens '36
The Law Rides '36
Lightning Bill Crandall '37
Man from Hell's Edges '32
Marked Trails '44
Mesquite Buckaroo '39
Mystery Squadron '33
No Man's Range '35
Northwest Trail '46
Of Mice and Men '39
Oklahoma Cyclone '30
Outlaw Trail '44
Paroled to Die '37
Pinto Canyon '40
Pork Chop Hill '59
Powdersmoke Range '35
The Red Rope '37
Rider of the Law '35
Riders of the Desert '32
Ridin' the Lone Trail '37
Rio Bravo '59
Rio Grande Raiders '46
Smokey Smith '36
Sonora Stagecoach '44
South of Santa Fe '32
Sundown Saunders '36
Texas Trouble '30s
Thunder in the Desert '38
Tombstone Terror '34
Trail of Terror '35
Trails West '40s
Twilight on the Rio Grande '41
Western Double Feature 6:
  Rogers & Trigger '50
Western Justice '35
Wildfire '45
Young Blood '33

Fred Steele
Demolition '77

George Steele
Tall Texan '53

Henry Steele
Ninja Connection '90

Jadrien Steele
The Secret Garden '87

Karen Steele
Bail Out at 43,000 '57
Marty '55
The Rise and Fall of Legs
  Diamond '60
Trap on Cougar Mountain '72

Marjorie Steele
Face to Face '52
Tough Assignment '49

Pippa Steele
Lust for a Vampire '71
The Vampire Lovers '70

Tommy Steele
Finian's Rainbow '68
G-Men Never Forget '48
Half a Sixpence '67
The Happiest Millionaire '67

Irving Steen
The Fall of the House of Usher
  '52

Jessica Steen
John and the Missus '87
Sing '89
Still Life '92

Stuart Steen
Ninja Connection '90
Ninja in Action '80s

Mary Steenburgen
The Attic: The Hiding of Anne
  Frank '88
Back to the Future, Part 3 '90
The Butcher's Wife '91
Clifford '93
Cross Creek '83
Dead of Winter '87
End of the Line '88
Goin' South '78
Little Red Riding Hood '83
Melvin and Howard '80
A Midsummer Night's Sex
  Comedy '82
Miss Firecracker '89
One Magic Christmas '85
Parenthood '89
Ragtime '81
Romantic Comedy '83
Time After Time '79
Whales of August '87

Jessica Steer
Workin' for Peanuts '85

Yvette Stefens
Carnal Crimes '91

Anthony Steffen
An Angel for Satan '66
Escape from Hell '89
Garringo '69
The Gentleman Killer '78
The Last Tomahawk '65
The Night Evelyn Came Out of
  the Grave '71
On the Edge '82
Savage Island '85
Stranger in Paso Bravo '73

Michael Stefoni
Trancers '85

Bernice Stegers
City of Women '81
Frozen Terror '80
The Girl '86
Xtro '83

Renate Steiger
The Boat is Full '81

Rod Steiger
Across the Bridge '57
Al Capone '59
American Gothic '88
The Amityville Horror '79
Back from Eternity '56
The Ballad of the Sad Cafe
  '91
The Big Knife '55
Breakthrough '78
Catch the Heat '87
The Court Martial of Billy
  Mitchell '55
Dirty Hands '76
Doctor Zhivago '65
F.I.S.T. '78
A Fistful of Dynamite '72
Glory Boys '84
Guilty as Charged '92
The Harder They Fall '56
Hennessy '75
The Illustrated Man '69
In the Heat of the Night '67
The January Man '89
Jubal '56
The Kindred '87
Klondike Fever '79
The Last Contract '86
Last Four Days '77
Lion of the Desert '81
The Longest Day '62
Love and Bullets '79
The Loved One '65
Lucky Luciano '74
The Mark '61
Marty '53
The Naked Face '84
No Way to Treat a Lady '68
Oklahoma! '55
On the Waterfront '54
Pawnbroker '65
The Player '92
Portrait of a Hitman '77
Run of the Arrow '56
Seven Thieves '60
Sinatra '92
Sword of Gideon '86
That Summer of White Roses
  '90
Time of Indifference '64
Unholy Wife '57
Waterloo '71
Wolf Lake '79

Chris Stein
Men of Respect '91

David Stein
The Amityville Curse '90

**Margaret Sophie
Stein**
Enemies, a Love Story '89
Sarah, Plain and Tall '91
Skylark '93

Ingeborg Steinbach
Train Station Pickups '70s

Victor Steinbach
Quiet Thunder '87

David Steinberg
The End '78
The Marx Brothers in a
  Nutshell '90
Something Short of Paradise
  '79

Heidi Steindorsottir
Running Blind '70s

John Steiner
Ark of the Sun God '82
Beyond the Door 2 '79
Blood and Guns '79

Morgan Stevens
Survival Zone '84
Up River '79

Onslow Stevens
Angel on My Shoulder '46
The Creeper '48
Fangs of the Wild '54
Flight from Glory '37
Hands Across the Border '43
I Can't Escape '34
A Lion is in the Streets '53
One Too Many '51
Seven Miles from Alcatraz/
  Flight from Glory '43
Them! '54
Three Musketeers '35

Paul Stevens
Exodus '60
Get Christie Love! '74
Hercules and the Princess of
  Troy '65
The Mask '61

Peter Stevens
Dangerous Orphans '86

Ray Stevens
Ramblin' Man '79

Rise Stevens
The Chocolate Soldier '41
Going My Way '44

Shadoe Stevens
Traxx '87

Shawn Stevens
The Vernonia Incident '89

Stella Stevens
Adventures Beyond Belief '87
The Amazons '84
Arnold '73
Ballad of Cable Hogue '70
Chained Heat '83
Cleopatra Jones & the Casino
  of Gold '75
The Courtship of Eddie's
  Father '62
Cruise into Terror '78
Down the Drain '89
Exiled in America '90
Express to Terror '79
Girls! Girls! Girls! '62
Las Vegas Lady '76
Last Call '90
Li'l Abner '59
The Longshot '86
Make Me an Offer '80
The Manitou '78
Mom '89
Monster in the Closet '86
The Nutty Professor '63
Power, Passion & Murder '83
Slaughter '72
The Terror Within 2 '91
A Town Called Hell '72
Twirl '81
Wacko '83

Warren Stevens
Forbidden Planet '56
Shark River '53

Cynthia Stevenson
The Player '92
Watch It '93

Doug Stevenson
Iced '88

Juliet Stevenson
Drowning by Numbers '87
Truly, Madly, Deeply '91

McLean Stevenson
The Cat from Outer Space '78
Win, Place, or Steal '72

Parker Stevenson
Are You Lonesome Tonight
  '92
Lifeguard '75
A Separate Peace '73
Shooting Stars '85
Stitches '85
Stroker Ace '83

Robert Stevenson
Fangs of the Wild '54
One of Our Dinosaurs Is
  Missing '75

Tom Stevenson
Gaslight '44

Venetia Stevenson
Darby's Rangers '58
Horror Hotel '60

Brad Steward
The Legend of Frank Woods
  '77

Stephen Steward
Vice Academy '88

Deon Stewardson
Warriors from Hell '90

Joe Stewardson
City of Blood '88
Flatfoot '78
Follow That Rainbow '66

Alexandra Stewart
The Agency '81
Because of the Cats '74
The Destructors '74
Exodus '60
In Praise of Older Women '78
Intimate Moments '82
Kemek '88
Last Chase '81
Zeppelin '71

Amy Stewart
Mark Twain and Me '91

Andy Stewart
Battle Beyond the Sun '63

Ann Stewart
South of Hell Mountain '70

April Stewart
Valet Girls '86

Athole Stewart
Accused '36
The Speckled Band '31

Byron Stewart
Grambling's White Tiger '81
How U Like Me Now? '92

**Catherine Mary
Stewart**
The Apple '80
Cafe Romeo '91
Dudes '87
The Last Starfighter '84
Mischief '85
Murder by the Book '87
Night of the Comet '84
Nightflyers '87
Nighthawks '81
Psychic '91
Scenes from the Goldmine '87
Sins '85
Weekend at Bernie's '89
World Gone Wild '88

Charles Stewart
The War of the Colossal Beast
  '58

Charlotte Stewart
Eraserhead '78

David J. Stewart
Carnival Rock '57

Dennis Stewart
Demon Queen '80s

Don Stewart
Lost '83

Elaine Stewart
Meet Me in Las Vegas '56
Riders of the Timberline '41
The Rise and Fall of Legs
  Diamond '60

Eleanor Stewart
Arizona Days '37
Fighting Devil Dogs '43
Flaming Lead '39
The Gun Ranger '34
Headin' for the Rio Grande '36
Mystery Man '44

Evelyn Stewart
Adios Gringo '65
Blood for a Silver Dollar '66
Django Shoots First '74
Murder Mansion '70
The Psychic '78
The Scorpion's Tail '71

Frank Stewart
Cemetery High '89
Galactic Gigolo '87
Psychos in Love '87
Sensations '87
Sexpot '88

James Stewart
After the Thin Man '36
Airport '77 '77
An American Tail: Fievel Goes
  West '91
Anatomy of a Murder '59
Bandolero! '68
Bell, Book and Candle '58
Bend of the River '52
The Big Sleep '78
Born to Dance '36
Broken Arrow '50
Cheyenne Autumn '64
The Cheyenne Social Club '70
Dear Brigitte '65
Destry Rides Again '39
Far Country '55
The FBI Story '59
The Flight of the Phoenix '65
The Glenn Miller Story '54
The Gorgeous Hussy '36
The Greatest Show on Earth
  '52
Green Horizon '83
Harvey '50
Hollywood Bloopers '50s
How the West was Won '63
It's a Wonderful Life '46
The Jackpot '50
Made for Each Other '39
Magic of Lassie '78
Magic Town '47
Man from Laramie '55
The Man Who Knew Too
  Much '56
The Man Who Shot Liberty
  Valance '62
Mr. Hobbs Takes a Vacation
  '62
Mr. Smith Goes to
  Washington '39
The Mountain Road '60
The Naked Spur '53
The Philadelphia Story '40
Pot O' Gold '41
The Rare Breed '66
Rear Window '54
Right of Way '84
Rope '48
Rose Marie '36
Shenandoah '65
The Shootist '76

The Shop Around the Corner
  '40
Spirit of St. Louis '57
Strategic Air Command '55
Thunder Bay '53
Two Rode Together '61
Vertigo '58
Vivacious Lady '38
War in the Sky '82
Wife Versus Secretary '36
Winchester '73 '50
You Can't Take It with You
  '38
Ziegfeld Girl '41

John Stewart
Boots Malone '52
Last of the Comanches '52

**Kate McGregor
Stewart**
Father of the Bride '91

Marland T. Stewart
357 Magnum '77

Martha Stewart
Doll Face '46

Mel Stewart
The Kid with the 200 I.Q. '83

Melvin Stewart
Scorpio '73
A Session with the Committee
  '69

Patrick Stewart
Code Name: Emerald '85
The Doctor and the Devils '85
Excalibur '81
Hamlet '79
Hedda '75
L.A. Story '91
Lady Jane '85
Lifeforce '85
The Plague Dogs '82

Paul Stewart
Bite the Bullet '75
Citizen Kane '41
The Cobweb '55
Easy Living '49
How to Commit Marriage '69
Joe Louis Story '53
King Creole '58
Kiss Me Deadly '55
Mr. Lucky '43
Murph the Surf '75
Opening Night '77
Seduced '85
The Tempest '82
Twelve O'Clock High '49
Walk Softly, Stranger '50

Peggy Stewart
The Black Lash '52
Rough Riders of Cheyenne
  '45
Son of Zorro '47
Stagecoach to Denver '46
The Vampire's Ghost '45
Vigilantes of Boom Town '46

Penelope Stewart
Vigil '84

Richard Stewart
Terror Ship '54
Watch Me When I Kill '81

Robin Stewart
The 7 Brothers Meet Dracula
  '73

Roy Stewart
Live and Let Die '73
Sparrows '26
With Kit Carson Over the
  Great Divide '25

Sandy Stewart
Go, Johnny Go! '59

Sophie Stewart
Devil Girl from Mars '54
Murder in the Old Red Barn
  '36

Steven Stewart
The Young Graduates '71

Susan Stewart
Mantis in Lace '68

Trish Stewart
Breaking Up Is Hard to Do '79
Wild Times '79

Yvonne Stewart
Satan's Sadists '69

Pat Stich
Loners '72

Dorothy Stickney
I Never Sang For My Father
  '70

Phyllis Stickney
Talkin' Dirty After Dark '91
What's Love Got to Do With
  It? '93

Ted Stidder
Home is Where the Hart is '88

David Ogden Stiers
The Accidental Tourist '88
Another Woman '88
The Bad Seed '85
Beauty and the Beast '91
Better Off Dead '85
Breaking Up Is Hard to Do '79
Creator '85
Damien: The Leper Priest '80
Doc Hollywood '91
Final Notice '89
The First Olympics: Athens
  1896 '84
Harry's War '84
The Innocents Abroad '84
J. Edgar Hoover '87
The Kissing Place '90
The Last of His Tribe '92
The Man with One Red Shoe
  '85
M*A*S*H: Goodbye, Farewell
  & Amen '83
North and South '85
Oh, God! '77
Oldest Living Graduate '82
Perry Mason: The Case of the
  Lost Love '87
Sergeant Matlovich vs. the
  U.S. Air Force '78

Hugo Stiglitz
City of the Walking Dead '83
Counterforce '87
Fantastic Balloon Voyage '80s
Night of a Thousand Cats '72
Robinson Crusoe & the Tiger
  '72

Ryan Stiles
Hot Shots! Part Deux '93

Shannon Stiles
Bikini Island '91

Victor Stiles
Santa Claus Conquers the
  Martians '64

Robin Stille
American Ninja 4: The
  Annihilation '91
The Slumber Party Massacre
  '82

Ben Stiller
Elvis Stories '89

Basic Instinct '92
Beyond the Stars '89
Blood and Sand '89
Cold Steel '87
Deadly Blessing '81
Diary of a Hitman '91
He Said, She Said '91
Irreconcilable Differences '84
King Solomon's Mines '85
Las Vegas Strip War '84
Last Action Hero '93
Police Academy 4: Citizens on Patrol '87
Scissors '91
Sliver '93
Total Recall '90
The Vegas Strip Wars '84
War & Remembrance, Part 1 '88
War & Remembrance: The Final Chapter, Part 8 '89
Where Sleeping Dogs Lie '91
Year of the Gun '91

Stuart Stone
Heavenly Bodies '84

Tammy Stone
Neurotic Cabaret '90

Sherri Stoner
Impulse '84
Lovelines '84
Reform School Girls '86

Paolo Stoppa
The Gold of Naples '54
Miracle in Milan '51
Seven Deadly Sins '53
Where the Hot Wind Blows '59

Franca Stoppi
Buried Alive '81

Larry Storch
Adventures Beyond Belief '87
The Adventures of Huckleberry Finn '78
Better Late Than Never '79
Captain Newman, M.D. '63
Hard Frame '70
I Don't Buy Kisses Anymore '92
The Incredible Rocky Mountain Race '77
Sex and the Single Girl '64
S.O.B. '81
Sweet 16 '81
The Woman Hunter '72

June Storey
Dance Hall '41
The Strange Woman '46

Veronica Stork
Combat Shock '84

Adam Storke
Death Becomes Her '92
Highway to Hell '92
Mystic Pizza '88

Gale Storm
Let's Go Collegiate '41
Lure of the Islands '42
Man from Cheyenne '42
Revenge of the Zombies '43
Rhythm Parade '43
Smart Alecks '42
Swing Parade of 1946 '46
The Texas Rangers '51
The Underworld Story '50

James Storm
Ants '77
Night of Dark Shadows '71

Peter Stormare
Damage '92

Ludwig Stossel
Cloak and Dagger '46
G.I. Blues '60

George Stover
Deadly Neighbor '91
Fiend '83

Madeleine Stowe
The Amazons '84
Closet Land '90
Gangster Wars '81
The Last of the Mohicans '92
Nativity '78
Revenge '90
Stakeout '87
Another Stakeout '93
Tropical Snow '88
The Two Jakes '90
Unlawful Entry '92
Worth Winning '89

Scott Strader
Jocks '87

Rose Stradner
The Keys of the Kingdom '44

Joseph R. Straface
Virgin Queen of St. Francis High '88

Beatrice Straight
The Dain Curse '78
Endless Love '81
The Formula '80
Killer on Board '77
Network '76
The Nun's Story '59
Patterns '56
Poltergeist '82
Power '86
The Princess and the Pea '83
The Promise '78
Robert Kennedy and His Times '90
Sidney Sheldon's Bloodline '79
Two of a Kind '83

Julie Strain
Mirror Images '91
Night Rhythms '92
The Unnamable 2: The Statement of Randolph Carter '92
Witchcraft 4: Virgin Heart '92

George Strait
Pure Country '92

Ralph Strait
Halloween 3: Season of the Witch '82

Sharon Strand
The Narcotics Story '58

Harry Strang
The Fighting Sullivans '42
Phantom Ranger '38

Derrick Strange
Revenge of the Radioactive Reporter '91

Glenn Strange
Abbott and Costello Meet Frankenstein '48
Across the Plains '39
Billy the Kid Trapped '42
The Black Raven '43
Boot Hill Bandits '42
Fugitive Valley '41
Hard Hombre '31
House of Frankenstein '44
Jailhouse Rock '57
Law of the Pampas '39
The Mad Monster '42
Sonora Stagecoach '44
Sunset on the Desert '42

The Wistful Widow of Wagon Gap '47

Robert Strange
The Saint Strikes Back '39

Lee Strasberg
And Justice for All '79
The Cassandra Crossing '76
The Godfather 1902-1959: The Complete Epic '81
The Godfather, Part 2 '74
Going in Style '79

Susan Strasberg
Bloody Birthday '80
The Brotherhood '68
The Cobweb '55
Delta Force '86
Frankenstein '73
In Praise of Older Women '78
Kapo '59
The Legend of Hillbilly John '73
The Light in the Jungle '91
The Manitou '78
Mazes and Monsters '82
Picnic '55
Prime Suspect '88
Psych-Out '68
Rollercoaster '77
Rona Jaffe's Mazes & Monsters '82
The Runnin' Kind '89
Scream of Fear '61
The Sibling '72
Stage Struck '57
Sweet 16 '81
The Trip '67

Morris Strassberg
Where is My Child? '37

Robin Strasser
Glitz '88

Marcia Strassman
And You Thought Your Parents Were Weird! '91
The Aviator '85
Changes '69
Fast Getaway '91
Honey, I Blew Up the Kid '92
Honey, I Shrunk the Kids '89
Soup for One '82
Another Stakeout '93

Willie Stratford, Jr.
The Bone Yard '90

David Strathairn
Big Girls Don't Cry...They Get Even '92
The Brother from Another Planet '84
City of Hope '91
Eight Men Out '88
Enormous Changes '83
The Feud '90
The Firm '93
Iceman '84
Judgment '90
A League of Their Own '92
Lost in Yonkers '93
Matewan '87
Memphis Belle '90
O Pioneers! '91
Passion Fish '92
Return of the Secaucus 7 '80
Silkwood '83
Sneakers '92
Without Warning: The James Brady Story '91

Elana Stratheros
The Vals '85

Dorothy Stratten
Autumn Born '79
Galaxina '80

They All Laughed '81

Charles Stratton
Munchies '87
Summer Camp Nightmare '86

John Stratton
Frankenstein and the Monster from Hell '74

Christopher Strauli
Measure for Measure '79

Jessica Straus
The Weirdo '89

Eduard Strauss, Jr.
The Eternal Waltz '59

Peter Strauss
Angel on My Shoulder '80
The Brotherhood of the Rose '89
Flight of Black Angel '91
Hail, Hero! '69
The Jericho Mile '79
The Last Tycoon '76
Man of Legend '71
Masada '81
Penalty Phase '86
Peter Gunn '89
Proud Men '87
Secret of NIMH '82
Soldier Blue '70
Spacehunter: Adventures in the Forbidden Zone '83
Trial of the Catonsville Nine '72
Whale for the Killing '81

Robert Strauss
The Atomic Kid '54
The Bridges at Toko-Ri '55
Family Jewels '65
The 4D Man '59
Frankie and Johnny '65
Girls! Girls! Girls! '62
Here Come the Girls '53
I, Mobster '58
Jumping Jacks '52
The Man with the Golden Arm '55
The Seven Year Itch '55
Stalag 17 '53

Meryl Streep
A Cry in the Dark '88
Death Becomes Her '92
The Deer Hunter '78
Defending Your Life '91
Falling in Love '84
The French Lieutenant's Woman '81
Heartburn '86
Holocaust '78
Ironweed '87
Julia '77
Kramer vs. Kramer '79
Manhattan '79
Out of Africa '85
Plenty '85
Postcards from the Edge '90
The Seduction of Joe Tynan '79
She-Devil '89
Silkwood '83
Sophie's Choice '82
Still of the Night '82

David Street
Holiday Rhythm '50

Elliot Street
Harrad Experiment '73
Melvin Purvis: G-Man '74
Paper Man '71

Russell Streiner
Night of the Living Dead '68

Barbra Streisand
All Night Long '81
For Pete's Sake '74
Funny Girl '68
Funny Lady '75
Hello, Dolly! '69
The Main Event '79
Nuts '87
On a Clear Day You Can See Forever '70
The Owl and the Pussycat '70
The Prince of Tides '91
A Star is Born '76
Up the Sandbox '72
The Way We Were '73
What's Up, Doc? '72
Yentl '83

Melissa Stribling
Crow Hollow '52
The Horror of Dracula '58

Connie Strickland
Act of Vengeance '74
Bummer '73

Gail Strickland
Eleanor: First Lady of the World '82
The Gathering '77
The Gathering: Part 2 '79
Hyper-Sapien: People from Another Star '86
Lies '83
The Man in the Moon '91
A Matter of Life and Death '81
One on One '77
Oxford Blues '84
Protocol '84
Rape and Marriage: The Rideout Case '80
Snowbling '78
Three of Hearts '93
Who'll Stop the Rain? '78

John Stride
Henry VIII '79

Karen Stride
The Vampire Hookers '78

Hal Strieb
Maxim Xul '91

Anita Strindberg
The Scorpion's Tail '71
The Tempter '74
Women in Cell Block 7 '77

Elaine Stritch
Follies in Concert '85
Perfect Furlough '59
Providence '77
September '88
Three Violent People '57

Axel Strobye
Pelle the Conqueror '88

Woody Strode
Boot Hill '69
The Final Executioner '83
The Gatling Gun '72
Hired to Kill '73
Hit Men '73
The Italian Connection '73
Jaguar Lives '79
Jungle Warriors '84
Kill Castro '80
Kingdom of the Spiders '77
The Last Voyage '60
Loaded Guns '75
Lust in the Dust '85
The Man Who Shot Liberty Valance '62
Manhunt '73
The Mercenaries '80
Oil '78
Once Upon a Time in the West '68

Hideko Takamine
Mistress '53
Twenty-Four Eyes '54
When a Woman Ascends the
    Stairs '60

Aya Takanashi
Mr. Baseball '92

Akira Takarada
Godzilla vs. Mothra '64
Half Human '58
Last War '68

Minoru Takashima
Godzilla on Monster Island '72
Godzilla vs. Gigan '72

Tadao Takashima
King Kong Versus Godzilla '63
Son of Godzilla '66

Toru Takatsuka
Destroy All Planets '68

George Takei
The Green Berets '68
Ice Palace '59
Prisoners of the Sun '91
Red Line 7000 '65
Star Trek: The Motion Picture
    '80
Star Trek 2: The Wrath of
    Khan '82
Star Trek 3: The Search for
    Spock '84
Star Trek 4: The Voyage
    Home '86
Star Trek 5: The Final Frontier
    '89
Star Trek 6: The
    Undiscovered Country '91
Star Trek Bloopers '69

Takeshi
Merry Christmas, Mr.
    Lawrence '83

Yusuke Takita
Double Suicide '69

Osamu Takizawa
Fires on the Plain '59
Zatoichi vs. Yojimbo '70

Sharyn Talbert
Stepsisters '85

Jay Talbet
Wild Horse Canyon '25

Brad Talbot
Finger on the Trigger '65

Helen Talbot
California Joe '43
King of the Forest Rangers
    '46

Kate Talbot
Beginner's Luck '84

Lyle Talbot
Border Rangers '50
The Case of the Lucky Legs
    '35
Clipped Wings '53
The Devil's Cargo '48
Gambler's Choice '44
Glen or Glenda '53
Gold Raiders '51
High School Confidential '58
Highway 13 '48
Jail Bait '54
Ladies They Talk About '33
Mesa of Lost Women '52
A Night for Crime '42
North of the Border '46
One Body Too Many '44
One Night of Love '34
One Too Many '51
Our Little Girl '35

Parole, Inc. '49
Plan 9 from Outer Space '56
Sensations of 1945 '44
She Shoulda Said No '49
Shriek in the Night '33
Song of Arizona '46
Sunrise at Campobello '60
13th Guest '32
Three Legionnaires '37
Three on a Match '32
Thunder in the Pines '49
Torture Ship '39
Up in Arms '44
Vengeance '37
Wild Weed '49

Nita Talbot
Amityville 1992: It's About
    Time '92
Chained Heat '83
The Concrete Jungle '82
Fraternity Vacation '85
Frightmare '83
Girl Happy '65
I Married a Woman '56
Night Shift '82
Puppet Master 2 '91
Sweet Creek County War '82
Take Two '87
Who's Got the Action? '63

Patty Talbot
Shades of Love: Echoes in
    Crimson '87

Gloria Talbott
Arizona Raiders '65
Cyclops '56
The Daughter of Dr. Jekyll '57
Girls' Town '59
I Married a Monster from
    Outer Space '58
The Oklahoman '56

Michael Talbott
Miami Vice '84
Racing with the Moon '84

Alberto Talegalli
Two Nights with Cleopatra '54

Hal Taliaferro
Border Vigilantes '41
Hoppy Serves a Writ '43
Leather Burners '43
Riders of the Timberline '41

Maria Tallchief
Million Dollar Mermaid '52

Margaret Tallichet
Stranger on the Third Floor
    '40

Patricia Tallman
Night of the Living Dead '90

Luana Talltree
Angels from Hell '68

**Constance
Talmadge**
America/The Fall of Babylon
    '24
The Babylon Story from
    "Intolerance" '16
Intolerance '16
Matrimaniac '16
The Primitive Lover '16

Natalie Talmadge
Our Hospitality '23

Norma Talmadge
Dubarry '30
The Forbidden City '18
The Social Secretary '16
Tale of Two Cities/In the
    Switch Tower '15

Richard Talmadge
Fighting Pilot '35
Let's Go! '23
The Live Wire '34

Lloyd Talman
Robin Hood '22

William Talman
Armored Car Robbery '50
Crashout '55
Falcon's Adventure/Armored
    Car Robbery '50
The Hitch-Hiker '53
One Minute to Zero '52

Vera Talqui
Little World of Don Camillo '51

Alix Talton
The Deadly Mantis '57

Tetsuro Tamba
Hunter in the Dark '80
The Imperial Japanese Empire
    '85
One-Eyed Swordsman '63
A Taxing Woman Returns '88
Tokyo Pop '88
You Only Live Twice '67
Zero '84

Carlo Tamberlani
The Fury of Hercules '61

Russ Tamblyn
Aftershock '88
B.O.R.N. '88
Commando Squad '87
Cyclone '87
Dracula vs. Frankenstein '71
Father of the Bride '50
Father of the Bride '50
Father's Little Dividend '51
The Female Bunch '69
Free Grass '69
The Haunting '63
High School Confidential '58
Hit the Deck '55
How the West was Won '63
The Last Movie '71
Necromancer: Satan's
    Servant '88
Peyton Place '57
Phantom Empire '87
Retreat, Hell! '52
Running Mates '92
Satan's Sadists '69
Seven Brides for Seven
    Brothers '54
tom thumb '58
Twin Peaks '90
War of the Gargantuas '70
West Side Story '61
The Winning Team '52
The Wonderful World of the
    Brothers Grimm '62

Jeffrey Tambor
Article 99 '92
Brenda Starr '86
City Slickers '91
Crossing the Bridge '92
Desert Hearts '86
A Gun in the House '81
Life Stinks '91
Lisa '90
The Man Who Wasn't There
    '83
Mr. Mom '83
Pastime '91
Sadat '83
Take Your Best Shot '82
Tales from the Crypt, Vol. 3
    '90

Jenny Tamburi
Bloody Avenger '80s
Women in Cell Block 7 '77

Zoe Tamerlis
Ms. 45 '81
Special Effects '85

Akim Tamiroff
Alphaville '65
Anastasia '56
The Bacchantes '63
Battle Hell '56
Black Magic '49
The Bridge of San Luis Rey
    '44
The Corsican Brothers '42
Deadly Sanctuary '68
Dragon Seed '44
The General Died at Dawn '36
The Great McGinty '40
Lt. Robin Crusoe, U.S.N. '66
Lord Jim '65
The Merry Widow '34
Miracle of Morgan's Creek '44
Mr. Arkadin '55
My Girl Tisa '48
Outpost in Morocco '49
Panic Button '62
The Story of Louis Pasteur
    '36
Topkapi '64
Tortilla Flat '42
Touch of Evil '58
The Trial '63
Vulture '67

Jiro Tamiya
Professional Killers 1 '73
Sword of Fury I '73
Sword of Fury II '73

Mary Tamm
The Assassination Run '80
The Odessa File '74
Tales That Witness Madness
    '73

Takahiro Tamura
The Empire of Passion '76
In the Realm of Passion '80

Birke Tan
Stripped to Kill II: Live Girls '89

Lawrence Tan
Heroes Three '84

Tin Tan
El Ceniciento '47
Musico, Poeta y Loco '47

Turia Tan
Prisoner in the Middle '74

Haruo Tanaka
The Pornographers '66

Ken Tanaka
Godzilla 1985 '85

Kinuyo Tanaka
Equinox Flower '58
Life of Oharu '52
Mother '52
Sandakan No. 8 '74
Sansho the Bailiff '54
Ugetsu '53

Shinji Tanaka
The Island '61

Sony Tanaka
The Blazing Ninja

Toru Tanaka
Tax Season '90
3 Ninjas '92

Yoshiko Tanaka
Black Rain '88

Jessica Tandy
*batteries not included '87
Best Friends '82
The Birds '63

The Bostonians '84
Cocoon '85
Cocoon: The Return '88
The Desert Fox '51
Driving Miss Daisy '89
Foxfire '87
Fried Green Tomatoes '91
Gin Game '84
The House on Carroll Street
    '88
The Light in the Forest '58
September Affair '50
The Seventh Cross '44
Still of the Night '82
Used People '92
The World According to Garp
    '82

Mark Tandy
Maurice '87
The Railway Station Man '92

Ronald Tanet
Crypt of Dark Secrets '76

Alan Tang
The Bloody Fight '70s

Tang-Hua-Ta
First Spaceship on Venus '60

Kiyoko Tange
Dodes 'ka-den '70

Yoko Tani
First Spaceship on Venus '60
Invasion '65
Koroshi '67
Samson and the 7 Miracles of
    the World '62

Tracey Tanish
Frenchman's Farm '87

Julius Tannen
Miracle of Morgan's Creek '44

William Tannen
Jupiter's Darling '55
Whistling in the Dark '41

Joy Tanner
Prom Night 4: Deliver Us From
    Evil '91

Sherry Tansey
Wild Horse Canyon '39

Warhawk Tanzania
Black Force '75
Gang Wars '75

Chinag Tao
Kung Fu Zombie '82

David Tao
Ninja Supremo '90

Ho Chung Tao
Chinese Stuntman '70s

Wang Tao
The Hot, the Cool, and the
    Vicious '80s
Ninja Thunderbolt '85
Snake in the Eagle's Shadow
    2 '83
Ten Brothers of Shao-lin '80s
Two Assassins in the Dark
    '80s

Faviola Tapia
Santa Sangre '90

Quentin Tarantino
Reservoir Dogs '92

Georgi Taratorkin
Crime and Punishment '70

Le Tari
Brotherhood of Death '76

Rockne Tarkington
Black Starlet '74

Noah Taylor
Flirting '89
The Year My Voice Broke '87

Ray Taylor
Robinson Crusoe of Mystery
Island '36

Renee Taylor
Delirious '91
The Errand Boy '61
Last of the Red Hot Lovers
'72
That's Adequate '90

Rip Taylor
Cheech and Chong: Things
Are Tough All Over '82
Indecent Proposal '93
Minsky's Follies '83

Robert Taylor
Bataan '43
Beat Street '84
Broadway Melody of 1936 '35
Broadway Melody of 1938 '37
Camille '36
Conspirator '49
D-Day, the Sixth of June '56
The Gorgeous Hussy '36
The Hot Line '69
I Love Melvin '53
Ivanhoe '52
Johnny Eager '42
Johnny Tiger '66
Knights of the Round Table
'53
The Law and Jake Wade '58
The Miracle of the White
Stallions '63
The Night Walker '64
Party Girl '58
Personal Property '37
Quo Vadis '51
Three Comrades '38
Waterloo Bridge '40
When Ladies Meet '41

Rochelle Taylor
Murderlust '86

Rod Taylor
Ask Any Girl '59
The Birds '63
The Catered Affair '56
Chuka '67
Colossus and the Amazon
Queen '64
Cry of the Innocent '80
Darker than Amber '70
The Deadly Trackers '73
A Gathering of Eagles '63
Germicide '74
Giant '56
The Glass Bottom Boat '66
Hell River '75
Hotel '67
Jacqueline Bouvier Kennedy
'81
Long John Silver '53
Man Who Had Power Over
Women '70
Marbella '85
Nowhere to Hide
101 Dalmations '61
Powder Keg '70
Raintree County '57
Separate Tables '58
The Time Machine '60
Time to Die '83
Train Robbers '73
The Treasure Seekers '79
The V.I.P.'s '63
Zabriskie Point '70

Russi Taylor
The Jetsons: Movie '90

Stuart Taylor
Malibu High '79

Tammy Taylor
Lovelines '84
Meatballs 2 '84

Terry Taylor
The Great Skycopter Rescue
'82

Tom Taylor
Visions '90

Tyrone Taylor
Redneck Zombies '88

Vaughn Taylor
Jailhouse Rock '57

Wally Taylor
Shaft's Big Score '72

William Taylor
S*H*E '79

Zack Taylor
Group Marriage '72
The Young Nurses '73

Leigh Taylor-Young
Accidents '89
The Adventurers '70
Can't Stop the Music '80
Devlin Connection '82
Honeymoon Academy '90
Horsemen '70
I Love You, Alice B. Toklas
'68
The Jagged Edge '85
Looker '81
Marathon '80
Secret Admirer '85
Soylent Green '73

Jun Tazaki
Destroy All Monsters '68

Ivan Tchenko
Isadora '68

Ludmila Tcherina
Sins of Rome '54

Kiri Te Kanawa
Meeting Venus '91
Otello '82
The Ring '52

Phil Tead
Fangs of the Wild '54
Music in My Heart '40

Anthony Teague
How to Succeed in Business
without Really Trying '67
The Trouble with Girls (and
How To Get Into It) '69

Lewis Teague
Alligator '80

Marshall Teague
Road House '89
The Shadow Riders '82

Darien Teakle
The Lost Tribe '89

Ray Teal
Ambush at Tomahawk Gap
'53
Carrie '52
Distant Drums '51
Hollywood Canteen '44
Jumping Jacks '52
Lucky Me '54
Montana Belle '52

Conway Tearle
Desert Guns/Six-Shootin'
Sheriff '36
Headline Woman '35
Held for Murder '32

Hurricane Express '32
Lost Zeppelin '29
Morals for Women '31
Pleasure '31
Sing Sing Nights '35
Stella Maris '18
Vanity Fair '32

Godfrey Tearle
One of Our Aircraft Is Missing
'41
The 39 Steps '35

Verree Teasdale
Goodbye Love '34
Milky Way '36
Skyscraper Souls '32

Steven Tedd
Rough Justice '87

Paolo Tedesco
New Mafia Boss '72

Irene Tedrow
Special Olympics '78
The Two Worlds of Jenny
Logan '79

Maureen Teefy
Legs '83
Star Time '92
Supergirl '84

Tom Teeley
Beatlemania! The Movie '81

Blair Tefkin
Sinful Life '89

Susanne Tegman
Mankillers '87

Aaron Teich
Bloodspell '87
Darkroom '90

Virgilio Teixeira
Tricheurs '84

Leszek Teleszynski
Leper '76

Izabella Telezynska
The Music Lovers '71

Lou Tellegen
Salome/Queen Elizabeth '23

Teller
Penn and Teller Get Killed '90

**Vladimir
Temelianov**
Planet Burg '62

Marie Tempest
Moonlight Sonata '38

Grant Temple
Ninja Operation: Licensed to
Terminate '87

Julien Temple
Secret Policeman's Private
Parts '81

Shirley Temple
Baby, Take a Bow '34
The Bachelor and the Bobby-
Soxer '47
The Blue Bird '40
Bright Eyes '34
Captain January '36
Comedy Festival #3 '30s
Curly Top '35
Dimples '36
Fort Apache '48
Gotta Dance, Gotta Sing '84
Heidi '37
Just Around the Corner '38
Kid 'n' Hollywood and Polly
Tix in Washington '33
The Little Colonel '35

Little Miss Broadway '38
Little Miss Marker '34
The Little Princess '39
The Littlest Rebel '35
Miss Annie Rooney '42
Our Little Girl '35
The Poor Little Rich Girl '36
Rebecca of Sunnybrook Farm
'38
Shirley Temple Festival '33
Since You Went Away '44
Stand Up and Cheer '34
The Story of Seabiscuit '49
Stowaway '36
Susannah of the Mounties '39
To the Last Man '33
Wee Willie Winkie '37

Paul Temps
A Day in the Country '46

Aimee Tenalia
The Night Brings Charlie '90

Kay Tendeter
The Fall of the House of Usher
'52

Stacey Tendeter
Two English Girls '72

Hedi Tenessy
The Revolt of Job '84

Brigit Tengroth
Three Strange Loves '49

Neil Tennant
It Couldn't Happen Here '88

Victoria Tennant
All of Me '84
Best Seller '87
Chiefs '83
Dempsey '83
The Dogs of War '81
Flowers in the Attic '87
The Handmaid's Tale '90
The Holcroft Covenant '85
Horror Planet '80
L.A. Story '91
Little Lord Fauntleroy '80
Strangers Kiss '83
War & Remembrance, Part 1
'88
War & Remembrance, Part 2
'89
War & Remembrance, Part 3
'88
War & Remembrance, Part 4
'88
War & Remembrance, Part 5
'88
War & Remembrance, Part 6
'88
War & Remembrance, Part 7
'88
War & Remembrance: The
Final Chapter, Part 8 '89
War & Remembrance: The
Final Chapter, Part 9 '89
War & Remembrance: The
Final Chapter, Part 10 '89
War & Remembrance: The
Final Chapter, Part 11 '89
War & Remembrance: The
Final Chapter, Part 12 '89
Whispers '89
The Winds of War '83

**Tennessee
Ramblers**
Yodelin' Kid From Pine Ridge
'37

Jon Tenney
Watch It '93

Julius Tennon
Riverbend '89

Judy Tenuta
White Hot '88

Oded Teomi
They Were Ten '61

William Tepper
Bachelor Party '84
Miss Right '81

Johanna Ter Steege
Meeting Venus '91
The Vanishing '88
Vincent & Theo '90

Akira Terao
Akira Kurosawa's Dreams '90
Ran '85

**Margarita
Terekhova**
The Mirror '75

Max Terhune
Arizona Stagecoach '42
Black Market Rustlers '43
Boot Hill Bandits '42
Cowboy Commandos '43
Fugitive Valley '41
Ghost Town Gold '36
Haunted Ranch '43
Heart of the Rockies '37
Heroes of the Hills '38
Hit the Saddle '37
Kid's Last Ride '41
Land of Hunted Men '43
Outlaws of Sonora '38
Overland Stage Raiders '38
Pals of the Saddle '38
Purple Vigilantes '38
Range Busters '40
Ride, Ranger, Ride '36
Riders of the Whistling Skull
'37
Roarin' Lead '37
Saddle Mountain Round-Up
'41
Santa Fe Stampede '38
Texas to Bataan '42
Three Texas Steers '39
Thunder River Feud '42
Trail of the Silver Spurs '41
Trail Riders '42
Trailing Double Trouble '40
Trigger Trio '37
Tumbledown Ranch in
Arizona '41
Two-Fisted Justice '43
Underground Rustlers '41
West of Pinto Basin '40

Studs Terkel
Eight Men Out '88
Long Shadows '86

John Terlesky
The Allnighter '87
Chopping Mall '86
Damned River '89
Deathstalker 2: Duel of the
Titans '87
When He's Not a Stranger '89

Leonard Termo
Year of the Dragon '85

Micha Terr
Nasty Rabbit '64

Hal Terrance
Kid Colter '85

John Terrance
Evil Spawn '87

Greg Terrell
Two Fathers' Justice '85

Steven Terrell
Dragstrip Girl '57
Motorcycle Gang '57

Jameson Thomas
Beggars in Ermine '34
Convicted '32
The Farmer's Wife '28
Jane Eyre '34
Night Life in Reno '31
Sing Sing Nights '35

Jay Thomas
Straight Talk '92

Kevin Thomas
Cleo/Leo '89

Kurt Thomas
Gymkata '85

Larry Thomas
Night Ripper '86

Leonard Thomas
Bad Lieutenant '92

Mark Thomas
Working Girls '75

Marlo Thomas
Act of Passion: The Lost
    Honor of Kathryn Beck '83
Consenting Adults '85
Held Hostage '91
In the Spirit '90
Jenny '70

Philip Michael Thomas
Death Drug '83
False Witness '89
A Fight for Jenny '90
Homeboy '80s
Miami Vice '84
Miami Vice 2: The Prodigal
    Son '85
Sparkle '76
Stigma '73
Streetfight '75
The Wizard of Speed and
    Time '88

Richard Thomas
All Quiet on the Western Front
    '79
Andy and the Airwave
    Rangers '89
Battle Beyond the Stars '80
Berlin Tunnel 21 '81
Cactus in the Snow '72
A Doll's House '59
Glory! Glory! '90
Hobson's Choice '83
Homecoming: A Christmas
    Story '71
Johnny Belinda '82
Last Summer '69
Mission of the Shark '91
Roots: The Next Generation
    '79
September 30, 1955 '77
Stephen King's It '90
Thanksgiving Story '73
The Todd Killings '71
The Waltons: The Children's
    Carol '78
Winning '69

Robin Thomas
From the Dead of Night '89
Memories of Murder '90
Personals '90

Ron Thomas
The Big Bet '85
Night Screams '87

Scott Thomas
Guns of the Magnificent
    Seven '69

Tressa Thomas
The Five Heartbeats '91

Howard Thomashefsky
America '86

William Thomason
The Devil's Sleep '51
Test Tube Babies '53

Lee Thomburg
Hollywood High, Part 2 '81

Tim Thomerson
Air America '90
Cherry 2000 '88
Dollman '91
Fade to Black '80
Glory Years '87
The Harvest '93
Intimate Stranger '91
Iron Eagle '85
Jekyll & Hyde...Together
    Again '82
The Legend of Sleepy Hollow
    '86
Metalstorm '83
Near Dark '87
Nemesis '93
Rhinestone '84
Terraces '77
A Tiger's Tale '87
Trancers '85
Trancers 2: The Return of
    Jack Deth '91
Trancers 3: Deth Lives '92
Uncommon Valor '83
Vietnam, Texas '90
Volunteers '85
Who's Harry Crumb? '89
The Wrong Guys '88
Zone Troopers '85

Beatrix Thompson
The Old Curiosity Shop '35

Blue Thompson
The Abomination '88

Brian Thompson
Commando Squad '87
Doctor Mordrid: Master of the
    Unknown '92
Hired to Kill '91
Lionheart '90
Rage and Honor '92

Carolyn Thompson
Three on a Meathook '72

Cindy Ann Thompson
Cave Girl '85

Derek Thompson
Belfast Assassin '84
The Long Good Friday '79

Dorri Thompson
Chesty Anderson USN '76

Edward Thompson
Double Deal '39

Elizabeth Thompson
Metropolitan '90

Emma Thompson
Dead Again '91
Fortunes of War '87
Henry V '89
Howard's End '92
Impromptu '90
Look Back in Anger '89
Much Ado About Nothing '93
Peter's Friends '92
The Tall Guy '89

Eric Thompson
One Day in the Life of Ivan
    Denisovich '71

Ernest Thompson
Malcolm X '92

Fred Dalton Thompson
Aces: Iron Eagle 3 '92
Barbarians at the Gate '93
Born Yesterday '93
Cape Fear '91
Curly Sue '91
Days of Thunder '90
Die Hard 2: Die Harder '90
Feds '88
The Hunt for Red October '90
In the Line of Fire '93
Keep the Change '92
Marie '85
Thunderheart '92
White Sands '92

Hal Thompson
Animal Crackers '30
Lassie from Lancashire '38

Jack Thompson
Bad Blood '87
Breaker Morant '80
Burke & Wills '85
Caddie '81
The Club '81
Earthling '80
A Far Off Place '93
Ground Zero '88
Jock Petersen '74
The Man from Snowy River
    '82
Merry Christmas, Mr.
    Lawrence '83
Ruby Cairo '92
Shadow on the Sun '88
Sunday Too Far Away '74
Trouble in Paradise '88
Waterfront '83
Wind '92

Jeffrey V. Thompson
Eubie! '82

Katheryn Thompson
Challenge '74

Kay Thompson
Funny Face '57
Manhattan Merry-Go-Round
    '37

Kevin Thompson
Spaced Invaders '90

Larry Thompson
King of the Forest Rangers
    '46

Lea Thompson
All the Right Moves '83
Article 99 '92
Back to the Future '85
Back to the Future, Part 2 '89
Back to the Future, Part 3 '90
Casual Sex? '88
Dennis the Menace '93
Going Undercover '88
Howard the Duck '86
Jaws 3 '83
Montana '90
Nightbreaker '89
Red Dawn '84
Some Kind of Wonderful '87
SpaceCamp '86
The Wild Life '84
The Wizard of Loneliness '88

Marshall Thompson
Battleground '49
Bog '84
The Caddy '53

Clarence, the Cross-eyed Lion
    '65
The Clock '45
Crashout '55
East of Kilimanjaro '59
Fiend Without a Face '58
First Man into Space '59
George! '70
It! The Terror from Beyond
    Space '58
Mighty Jungle '64
The Purple Heart '44
They Were Expendable '45
To Hell and Back '55
To the Shores of Hell '65
The Turning Point '77
Words and Music '48

Peter Thompson
The Wistful Widow of Wagon
    Gap '47

Rex Thompson
All Mine to Give '56
The Eddy Duchin Story '56
The King and I '56

R.H. Thompson
And Then You Die '88
Charlie Grant's War '80
Ford: The Man & the Machine
    '87
Heaven on Earth '89
If You Could See What I Hear
    '82
Surfacing '84
Ticket to Heaven '81

Ross Thompson
Chain Reaction '80

Sada Thompson
The Adventures of
    Huckleberry Finn '85
Desperate Characters '71
Our Town '77

Scott Thompson
The Best of the Kids in the
    Hall '93

Sophie Thompson
Twenty-One '91

Victoria Thompson
Harrad Experiment '73
Harrad Summer '74

Weyman Thompson
Hot Shot '86

William Thompson
Test Tube Babies '48

Deborah Thompson-Carlin
Prison Planet '92

Greg Gomez Thomsen
Crack House '89

Gregg Thomsen
Soultaker '90

Pat Thomsen
Strictly Ballroom '92

Anna Thomson
Unforgiven '92

Gordon Thomson
Explosion '69

Helen Thomson
Bloodmoon '90

Jimmy Thomson
The Caddy '53

Kenneth Thomson
Broadway Melody '29
Held for Murder '32

Hopalong Cassidy '35
In Old Santa Fe '34
White Gold '28

Kim Thomson
Murder 101 '91
Stealing Heaven '88

Scott Thomson
Fast Times at Ridgemont High
    '82
Ghoulies '85

Jon Mikl Thor
Rock 'n' Roll Nightmare '85
Zombie Nightmare '86

June Thorburn
Broth of a Boy '59

Kelly Thordsen
The Ugly Dachshund '65

Frankie Thorn
Bad Lieutenant '92
Liquid Dreams '92

Bill Thornbury
Phantasm '79

Russell Thorndike
A Shot in the Dark '33

Sybil Thorndike
Major Barbara '41
Nicholas Nickleby '46
Nine Days a Queen '34
The Prince and the Showgirl
    '57
Shake Hands with the Devil
    '59
Stage Fright '50

Angela Thorne
Poor Girl, A Ghost Story '74

Dyanne Thorne
The Erotic Adventures of
    Pinocchio '71
Hellhole '85
Ilsa, Harem Keeper of the Oil
    Sheiks '76
Ilsa, She-Wolf of the SS '74
Ilsa, the Tigress of Siberia '79
Ilsa, the Wicked Warden '78
Point of Terror '71

William Thorne
Silent Night, Deadly Night 5:
    The Toymaker '91

Courtney Thorne-Smith
Lucas '86
Revenge of the Nerds 2:
    Nerds in Paradise '87
Side Out '90
Summer School '87
Welcome to 18 '87

Billy Bob Thornton
Indecent Proposal '93
One False Move '91

David Thornton
Diamond Run '90

Edith Thornton
Virtue's Revolt '24

Noley Thornton
Fine Things '90

Sigrid Thornton
All the Rivers Run '84
Best Enemies '86
Great Expectations: The
    Untold Story '87
The Lighthorseman '87
The Man from Snowy River
    '82
Nevil Shute's The Far Country
    '85

Wanted: Babysitter '75
The Woman Hunter '72
The Young Philadelphians '59

Marcus Vaughter
Visitants '87

Natalie Vavilova
Moscow Does Not Believe in Tears '80

Ron Vawter
Internal Affairs '90
King of the Hill '93
sex, lies and videotape '89
Sudden Death '77
Swoon '91

Selma Vaz Dias
The Tell-Tale Heart '62

Bruno Ve Sota
Attack of the Giant Leeches '59
The Choppers '61
Creature of the Walking Dead '60
Daughter of Horror '55
The Gunslinger '56
The Wasp Woman '49

Edward Vedder
The Mozart Story '48

Deeann Veeder
Carnage '84

Isela Vega
Barbarosa '82
Bordello '79
Bring Me the Head of Alfredo Garcia '74
Drum '76
El Sabor de la Venganza '65
Fin de Fiesta '71
Joshua '76
Temporada Salvaje '87

Misa Vehara
The Hidden Fortress '58

Conrad Veidt
Above Suspicion '43
All Through the Night '42
The Beloved Rogue '27
The Cabinet of Dr. Caligari '19
Casablanca '42
Congress Dances '31
Dark Journey '37
F.P. 1 '33
The Hands of Orlac '25
King of the Damned '36
The Man Who Laughs '27
The Passing of the Third Floor Back '36
Power '34
Spy in Black '39
Thief of Baghdad '40
Under the Red Robe '36
Waxworks '24
Whistling in the Dark '41
A Woman's Face '41

Ofra Veingarten
Fictitious Marriage '88

Harry Vejar
West to Glory '47

Reginald Vel Johnson
Die Hard '88
Die Hard 2: Die Harder '90

Paco Vela
The Return of Josey Wales '86

Maria Elena Velasco
Ni Chana Ni Juana '87

Andres Velasquez
The Littlest Outlaw '54

Jaime Velasquez
Semaforo en Rojo '47

Lorena Velasquez
Mision Suicida '87
Samson vs. the Vampire Women '61
Wrestling Women vs. the Aztec Ape '62
Wrestling Women vs. the Aztec Mummy '59

Pilar Velasquez
Ace of Hearts '85
Manos Torpes '65
Sex on the Brain

Teresa Velasquez
Dos Esposas en Mi Cama '87
Night of a Thousand Cats '72

Henri Velbert
Letters from My Windmill '54

Hans Man Int Veld
In for Treatment '82

Eddie Velez
Doin' Time '85
Romero '89
Rooftops '89
Split Decisions '88
Women's Club '87

Lupe Velez
Hell Harbor '30
Hell's Harbor '34
Hollywood Party '34
Mad About Money '30
Mexican Spitfire at Sea '42
Mexican Spitfire/Smartest Girl in Town '40
Palooka '34
Playmates '41
Stand and Deliver '28
Where East is East '29

John Vella
Wild Rebels '71

Charles Veltman
Revenge of the Virgins '62

Sophia Vembo
Stella '55

Evelyn Venable
Alice Adams '35
The Frontiersman '38
Harmony Lane '35
Hollywood Stadium Mystery '38
The Little Colonel '35
Mrs. Wiggs of the Cabbage Patch '34
Pinocchio '40

Luca Venantini
Aladdin '86

Shirley Venard
Satan's Touch '84

Amy Veness
Man of Evil '48

Marijke Vengelers
Egg '88

Ingrid Veninger
Hide and Seek '77

Chick Vennera
Double Threat '92
Kidnapped '87
Last Rites '88
The Milagro Beanfield War '88
The Terror Within 2 '91
Thank God It's Friday '78
Yanks '79

Diane Venora
Bird '88
The Cotton Club '84
F/X '86
Ironweed '87
Terminal Choice '85
Wolfen '81

John Ventantonio
Private Parts '72

Wanda Ventham
Blood Beast Terror '67
Captain Kronos: Vampire Hunter '74

Clyde Ventura
Bury Me an Angel '71
Gator Bait '73

Jesse Ventura
Abraxas: Guardian of the Universe '90
Boxcar Blues '90
Predator '87
Repossessed '90
Ricochet '91
The Running Man '87
Thunderground '89

Lino Ventura
The French Detective '75
Happy New Year '74
Jailbird's Vacation '65
Les Grandes Gueules '65
The Medusa Touch '78
Mistress of the World '59
Pain in the A— '77
The Slap '76
Sword of Gideon '86
The Three Penny Opera '62

Viviane Ventura
Battle Beneath the Earth '68

Richard Venture
The Effect of Gamma Rays on Man-in-the-Moon Marigolds '73
Missing '82
Scent of a Woman '92
Street Hawk '84

Silvana Venturelli
Erotic Illusion '86
The Lickerish Quartet '70

Massimo Venturiello
My Wonderful Life '90
Rorret '87

Billy Vera
Finish Line '89

Victoria Vera
A Man of Passion '90s
Monster Dog '82

Vera-Ellen
The Belle of New York '52
Happy Go Lovely '51
Love Happy '50
On the Town '49
Three Little Words '50
White Christmas '54
Wonder Man '45
Words and Music '48

Gwen Verdon
Alice '90
Cocoon '85
Cocoon: The Return '88
The Cotton Club '84
Damn Yankees '58
Legs '83
Nadine '87

Carlo Verdone
Acqua e Sapone '83

Maribel Verdu
Lovers: A True Story '90

Elena Verdugo
The Big Sombrero '49
Cyrano de Bergerac '50
House of Frankenstein '44
The Moon and Sixpence '43

Noah Verduzco
Kickboxer 3: The Art of War '92

Ben Vereen
All That Jazz '79
Breakin' Through '84
Buy & Cell '89
Funny Lady '75
Gas-s-s-s! '70
Intruders '92
The Jesse Owens Story '84
The Kid Who Loved Christmas '90
Louis Armstrong: Chicago Style '75
Once Upon a Forest '93
Pippin '81
Puss 'n Boots '84
Roots '77
The Zoo Gang '85

Alicia Vergel
Cavalry Command '63

Betty Verges
Dracula Blows His Cool '82
Summer Night Fever '79

Tom Verica
Die Hard 2: Die Harder '90

Bernard Verley
Chloe in the Afternoon '72
The Milky Way '68

Francoise Verley
Chloe in the Afternoon '72

Renaud Verley
Bell from Hell '74

Karen Verlier
Charlie Bravo '80s

Melanie Verliin
Midnight '81

Arpad Vermes
A Hungarian Fairy Tale '87

Harold Vermilyea
Sorry, Wrong Number '48

Denise Vernac
The Mask of Dijon '46

Denise Vernanc
Unnatural '52

Karen Verne
All Through the Night '42
Kings Row '41
The Seventh Cross '44
Sherlock Holmes and the Secret Weapon '42

Ines Vernengo
Man Facing Southeast '86

Guy Verney
Fame is the Spur '47
Martin Luther '53

Pierre Vernier
Mama, There's a Man in Your Bed '89

Anne Vernon
Therese & Isabelle '68
Umbrellas of Cherbourg '64

Bobby Vernon
A Hash House Fraud/The Sultan's Wife '15

Teddy at the Throttle '16
Teddy at the Throttle/Speeding Along '17

Glenn Vernon
Bedlam '45
Hollywood Varieties '50

Howard Vernon
Castle of the Creeping Flesh '68
The Diabolical Dr. Z '65
Dr. Orloff's Invisible Horror '72
The Invisible Dead
Revenge in the House of Usher '82
The Screaming Dead '72
Triple Cross '67
Virgin Among the Living Dead '71
Zombie Lake '84

Jackie Vernon
Frosty the Snowman '69
Microwave Massacre '83
Rudolph & Frosty's Christmas in July '82

John Vernon
Angela '77
Bail Out '90
The Barbary Coast '74
The Black Windmill '74
The Blood of Others '84
Blue Monkey '87
Border Heat '88
Brannigan '75
Chained Heat '83
Charley Varrick '73
Curtains '83
Deadly Stranger '88
Dirty Harry '71
Dixie Lanes '88
Doin' Time '85
Ernest Goes to Camp '87
Fraternity Vacation '85
Golden Rendezvous '77
Herbie Goes Bananas '80
Hunter '73
Journey '77
Jungle Warriors '84
Justine '69
Killer Klowns from Outer Space '88
Mob Story '90
National Lampoon's Animal House '78
Nightstick '87
The Outlaw Josey Wales '76
Savage Streets '83
Tell Them Willie Boy Is Here '69
Terminal Exposure '89
The Virginia Hill Story '76
W '74
War Bus Commando '89

Kate Vernon
Alphabet City '84
Hostile Takeover '88
The Last of Philip Banter '87
Malcolm X '92
Mob Story '90
Roadhouse 66 '84

Richard Vernon
The Satanic Rites of Dracula '73

Sherri Vernon
10 Violent Women '79

Wally Vernon
Broadway Serenade '39
Gunfire '50
Square Dance Jubilee '51

Gennadi Vernov
Planet Burg '62

Michael Visaroff
Charlie Chan at the Wax
Museum '40

Sal Viscuso
Spaceballs '87

Giovanni Visentin
Hearts & Armour '83

Angela Visser
Hot Under the Collar '91

Alex Vitale
Beyond the Door 3 '91
Urban Warriors '75

Antonella Vitale
Terror at the Opera '88

Joseph Vitale
The Stranger Wore a Gun '53
Zombies on Broadway '44

Mario Vitale
Stromboli '50

Milly Vitale
The Seven Little Foys '55

Keith Vitali
American Kickboxer 1 '91
No Retreat, No Surrender 3:
Blood Brothers '91

Mike Vitar
The Sandlot '93

Antoine Vitez
My Night at Maud's '69

Hansa Vithal
Salaam Bombay! '88

Michel Vitold
Basileus Quartet '82

Ray Vitte
Grambling's White Tiger '81
Sky Hei$t '75

Monica Vitti
An Almost Perfect Affair '79
Bellissimo: Images of the
Italian Cinema '87
Blonde in Black Leather '77
The Eclipse '66
Girls of Don Juan '70s
Immortal Bachelor '80
L'Avventura '60
Phantom of Liberty '68
The Red Desert '64
Tigers in Lipstick '80

Viva
Edie in Ciao! Manhattan '72
Forbidden Zone '80
Play It Again, Sam '72
State of Things '82

Giana Vivaldi
Kill, Baby, Kill '66

Ruth Vivian
The Man Who Came to Dinner
'41

Sonia Viviani
Hercules 2 '85

Sal Viviano
Black Roses '88
The Jitters '88

Floyd Vivino
Crazy People '90

Richard Vlacia
Mixed Blood '84

Marina Vlady
Chimes at Midnight '67
Double Agents '59

Michael Vlastas
Blackbelt 2: Fatal Force '92

Emmett Vogan
Down Dakota Way '49
The Lady Confesses '45
Robot Pilot '41

Jack Vogel
Lock and Load '90
Presumed Guilty '91

Mitch Vogel
Texas Detour '77

Nikolas Vogel
Dangerous Liaisons '60
The Inheritors '85

Peter Vogel
The Phantom of Soho '64

Ruediger Vogler
Alice in the Cities '74
Kings of the Road—In the
Course of Time '76
Until The End of The World
'91
The Wrong Move '78

Joan Vohs
As You Were '51
Cry Vengeance '54

Jon Voight
Catch-22 '70
The Champ '79
Coming Home '78
Conrack '74
Deliverance '72
Desert Bloom '86
Eternity '90
Final Warning '90
Hour of the Gun '67
The Last of His Tribe '92
Lookin' to Get Out '82
Midnight Cowboy '69
The Odessa File '74
Runaway Train '85
Table for Five '83

Vicki Volante
Angels' Wild Women '72
Blood of Dracula's Castle '69
Brain of Blood '71
Horror of the Blood Monsters
'70

Ingrid Vold
To Sleep with a Vampire '92

**Merete
Voldstedlund**
The Wolf at the Door '87

Claudio Volonte
Bay of Blood '71

Gian Marie Volonte
A Bullet for the General '68
Christ Stopped at Eboli '79
A Fistful of Dollars '64
For a Few Dollars More '65
Journey Beneath the Desert
'61
Lucky Luciano '74
Open Doors '89
Sacco & Vanzetti '71
The Witch '66

Julian Voloshin
Aladdin '86

Phillipe Volter
Cyrano de Bergerac '90
The Double Life of Veronique
'91
The Music Teacher '88

**Ferdinand von
Alten**
Champagne '28

Brad von Beltz
Kill the Golden Goose '79

Christina von Blanc
Virgin Among the Living Dead
'71

**William von
Brinken**
Hidden Enemy '40
International Crime '37
King Kelly of the U.S.A. '34

**Michael von der
Goltz**
American Autobahn '84

Lenny Von Dohlen
Billy Galvin '86
Blind Vision '91
Dracula's Widow '88
Electric Dreams '84
Eyes of the Beholder '92
Leaving Normal '92
Love Kills '91
Under the Biltmore Clock '85

Sholto Von Douglas
Boogey Man 2 '83

Theodore von Eltz
Confidential '35
Drifting Souls '32
High Gear '33
No Man's Law '21
Strangers of the Evening '32

Loni von Friedl
Journey to the Far Side of the
Sun '69

Paul von Hauser
Demons of Ludlow '75

**Wilhelm von
Homburg**
Ghostbusters 2 '89

Annette Von Klier
The Cop & the Girl '86

Hunter von Leer
Under the Boardwalk '89

**Irene von
Meyendorf**
The Mozart Story '48

Rik von Nutter
Assignment Outer Space '61
Tharus Son of Attila '87
Thunderball '65

Joel von Ornsteiner
Robot Holocaust '87
Slashdance '89

Heidi von Palleske
Blind Fear '89
Dead Ringers '88
White Light '90

Akos Von Rathony
Cave of the Living Dead '65

Hans von Schlettow
Isn't Life Wonderful '24

**Gustav von
Seyffertitz**
Don Juan '26
Down to Earth '17
The Mysterious Lady '28
Mystery Liner '34
Rasputin and the Empress '32
Sparrows '26

Josef von Sternberg
Epic That Never Was '65

Erich von Stroheim
As You Desire Me '32
The Birth of a Nation '15
Blind Husbands '19
The Crime of Dr. Crespi '35

Crimson Romance '34
Foolish Wives '22
Fugitive Road '34
Grand Illusion '37
Great Flamarion '45
The Great Gabbo '29
Heart of Humanity '18
Hearts of the World '18
Intolerance '16
Lost Squadron '32
The Mask of Dijon '46
Napoleon '55
The North Star '43
So Ends Our Night '41
Sunset Boulevard '50
Unnatural '52
Wedding March '28
The Worst of Hollywood: Vol.
2 '90

Max von Sydow
Awakenings '90
The Bachelor '93
Brass Target '78
Brink of Life '57
Christopher Columbus '85
Code Name: Emerald '85
Conan the Barbarian '82
Death Watch '80
Dreamscape '84
Duet for One '86
Dune '84
Embassy '72
The Exorcist '73
Exorcist 2: The Heretic '77
Father '90
Flash Gordon '80
Flight of the Eagle '82
Foxtrot '76
The Greatest Story Ever Told
'65
Hannah and Her Sisters '86
Hawaii '66
Hiroshima: Out of the Ashes
'90
Hour of the Wolf '68
Hurricane '79
A Kiss Before Dying '91
Kojak: The Belarus File '85
The Magician '58
March or Die '77
Needful Things '93
Never Say Never Again '83
The Night Visitor '70
The Ox '91
The Passion of Anna '70
Pelle the Conqueror '88
The Quiller Memorandum '66
Quo Vadis '85
Red King, White Knight '89
Samson and Delilah '84
Second Victory '87
The Seventh Seal '56
The Shame '68
Soldier's Tale '84
Steppenwolf '74
Strange Brew '83
Target Eagle '84
Three Days of the Condor '75
Through a Glass Darkly '61
The Touch '71
The Ultimate Warrior '75
Until The End of The World
'91
Victory '81
The Virgin Spring '59
Voyage of the Damned '76
Wild Strawberries '57
The Winter Light '62
The Wolf at the Door '87
Zentropa '92

Hanz von Teuffen
The Flying Saucer '50

**Margarethe von
Trotta**
Coup de Grace '78
An Occurrence at Owl Creek
Bridge/Coup de Grace '62

**Hans von
Twardowski**
Dawn Express '42

**Gustav von
Wagenheim**
Nosferatu '22
Woman in the Moon '29

Harry von Zell
Son of Paleface '52
The Strange Affair of Uncle
Harry '45

**Danielle von
Zernaeck**
Dangerous Curves '88
La Bamba '87
My Science Project '85
Under the Boardwalk '89

Kurt Vonnegut, Jr.
Back to School '86

Zandor Vorkov
Brain of Blood '71
Dracula vs. Frankenstein '71

George Voskovec
The Boston Strangler '68
The Bravados '58
Twelve Angry Men '57
The 27 Day '57

Arnold Vosloo
The Finishing Touch '92
Living to Die '91
Reason to Die '90
Red Shoe Diaries 2: Double
Dare '92
The Rutanga Tapes '90

Frank Vosper
Power '34

Andreas Voutsinas
A Dream of Passion '78

Yorgo Voyagis
The Adventurers '70
The Bourne Identity '88
Courage Mountain '89
Frantic '88
The Little Drummer Girl '84

Vlasta Vrana
Deadly Surveillance '91
Keeping Track '86
Scanners 2: The New Order
'91

Irene Vrkijan
David '79

Frederick Vroom
The Navigator '24

Eric Vu-An
The Sheltering Sky '90

Olivera Vuco
Mark of the Devil '69

Vuillemin
The Mystery of Alexina '86

Tito Vuolo
The Enforcer '51

Murvyn Vye
Al Capone '59
A Connecticut Yankee in King
Arthur's Court '49
Pickup on South Street '53
River of No Return '54
The Road to Bali '53

Stage Door Canteen '43

Christopher Walker
Echo Park '86

Clint Walker
Baker's Hawk '76
The Bounty Man '72
Deadly Harvest '72
The Dirty Dozen '67
Maya '66
Mysterious Island of Beautiful Women '79
Night of the Grizzly '66
None But the Brave '65
Pancho Villa '72
Snowbeast '77
The White Buffalo '77
Yuma '70

Denis Walker
The Fringe Dwellers '86

Dominic Walker
The Power of One '92

Eric Walker
The Ewok Adventure '84
The Ewoks: Battle for Endor '85

Fiona Walker
The Asphyx '72

Helen Walker
Abroad with Two Yanks '44
Big Combo '55
Brewster's Millions '45
People Are Funny '46

Jeffrey Walker
Proof '91

Jimmie Walker
B.A.D. Cats '80
The Concorde: Airport '79 '79
Doin' Time '85
Going Bananas '88
Let's Do It Again '75
My African Adventure '87
Water '85

Johnnie Walker
Baro Knees '28

Jonathan Walker
American Blue Note '89

Junior Walker
Tapeheads '89

Kathryn Walker
Blade '72
Dangerous Game '90
The Murder of Mary Phagan '87
Neighbors '81
O Youth and Beauty '79
Private Contentment '83
Rich Kids '79
Special Bulletin '83
Uncle Tom's Cabin '87
Whale for the Killing '81
Winds of Kitty Hawk '78

Kim Walker
Deadly Weapon '88
Heathers '89

Liza Walker
Twisted Obsession '90

Maggie Walker
Scream and Die '74

Mark Walker
Disconnected '87

Martin Walker
Mimi '35

Matthew Walker
Child's Play 3 '91

Michael Walker, Jr.
Gone with the West '72

Nancy Walker
Best Foot Forward '43
Broadway Rhythm '44
Death Scream '75
Forty Carats '73
Girl Crazy '43
Lucky Me '54
Murder by Death '76
Thursday's Game '74

Pete Walker
Osa '85

Polly Walker
Enchanted April '92
Patriot Games '92
Sliver '93

Ray Walker
Bulldog Edition '36
The Dark Hour '36
Goodbye Love '34
House of Errors '42
Rogue's Gallery '44

Robert Walker
Bataan '43
The Clock '45
Madame Curie '43
One Touch of Venus '48
Since You Went Away '44
Strangers on a Train '51
Thirty Seconds Over Tokyo '44
Till the Clouds Roll By '46
Till the Clouds Roll By/A Star Is Born '46
Vengeance Valley '51

Robert Walker, Jr.
AngKor: Cambodia Express '81
Devonsville Terror '83
Easy Rider '69
Ensign Pulver '64
Evil Town '87
Hambone & Hillie '84
Olivia '83
Road to Salina '68
The Savage Seven '68
The Shrieking '73
Son of Blob '72
The Spectre of Edgar Allen Poe '73
The War Wagon '67

Sarah Walker
Housekeeping '87
Man of Flowers '84

Stacy Walker
Infamous Daughter of Fanny Hill '87

Sydney Walker
Prelude to a Kiss '92

Terry Walker
Delinquent Parents '38
Renfrew on the Great White Trail '38
Take Me Back to Oklahoma '40
23 1/2 Hours Leave '37

Tippy Walker
The Jesus Trip '71
World of Henry Orient '64

Walter Walker
Sons of Steel '35

Will Walker
Death Sport '78

Zena Walker
The Dresser '83

Max Wall
Jabberwocky '77
A Killer in Every Corner '74
Little Dorrit, Film 1: Nobody's Fault '88
Little Dorrit, Film 2: Little Dorrit's Story '88
Strike It Rich '90
We Think the World of You '88

Anzac Wallace
Utu '83

Basil Wallace
Marked for Death '90

Beryl Wallace
Sunset on the Desert '42

Bill Wallace
Force of One '79
Manchurian Avenger '84
Ninja Turf '86

Chris Wallace
New Year's Evil '78

Coley Wallace
Joe Louis Story '53

David Wallace
The Babysitter '80
Humongous '82
Mazes and Monsters '82
Money to Burn '83

Gary Wallace
The Jar '84

George Wallace
Forbidden Planet '56
Radar Men from the Moon '52

Jack Wallace
Assignment Outer Space '61
The Bear '89

Jean Wallace
Big Combo '55
Jigsaw '49
Native Son '51
Sword of Lancelot '63

J.T. Wallace
Terrorgram '90

Julie T. Wallace
The Lunatic '92

Linda Wallace
Charlie, the Lonesome Cougar '67

Marcia Wallace
My Mom's a Werewolf '89
Pray TV '80

May Wallace
Laurel & Hardy Comedy Classics, Vol. 1 '33

Morgan Wallace
Confidential '35
Delinquent Parents '38
Gang Bullets '38
Honky Tonk '41
The House of Secrets '37
In Old Colorado '41
Star Reporter '39

Paul Wallace
Gypsy '62

Royce Wallace
Green Eyes '76

Sue Wallace
Experience Preferred... But Not Essential '83

Eli Wallach
Ace High '68
Article 99 '92

Baby Doll '56
The Brain '69
Christopher Columbus '85
Cinderella Liberty '73
Circle of Iron '78
The Deep '77
The Domino Principle '77
Embassy '85
The Executioner's Song '82
A Family Matter '91
Girlfriends '78
The Godfather, Part 3 '90
The Good, the Bad and the Ugly '67
How the West was Won '63
The Hunter '80
The Impossible Spy '87
Independence '76
Kisses for My President '64
Legacy of Lies '92
Lord Jim '65
MacKenna's Gold '69
Magnificent Seven '60
The Misfits '61
Mistress '91
Moon-Spinners '64
Movie, Movie '78
Nasty Habits '77
Night and the City '92
Nuts '87
The People Next Door '70
The Poppy is also a Flower '66
Pride of Jesse Hallum '81
Rocket to the Moon '86
Romance of a Horsethief '71
The Salamander '82
Sam's Son '84
Seven Thieves '60
Something in Common '86
Stateline Motel '75
Teamster Boss: The Jackie Presser Story '92
Tough Guys '86
The Two Jakes '90
Winter Kills '79

Roberta Wallach
The Effect of Gamma Rays on Man-in-the-Moon Marigolds '73

Sigurd Wallen
Swedenhielms '35

Eddy Waller
El Paso Stampede '53
Marshal of Cedar Rock '53

Fats Waller
Stormy Weather '43

Deborah Walley
Benji '74
Bon Voyage! '62
Dr. Goldfoot and the Bikini Machine '66
Gidget Goes Hawaiian '61
The Severed Arm '73
Spinout '66
Summer Magic '63

Richard Walling
Walking Back '26

William Walling
Great K & A Train Robbery '26
Range Feud '31

Jimmy Wallington
Hollywood Stadium Mystery '38

Shani Wallis
Arnold '73
Oliver! '68
Round Numbers '91

Frika Wallner
Esposa y Amante '70s

Samuel Walls
Enter Three Dragons '81

Tom Walls
Johnny Frenchman '46
Maytime in Mayfair '52
While I Live '47

Tom Walls, Jr.
Maytime in Mayfair '52

Jon Walmsley
Children's Carol '80
A Day for Thanks on Walton's Mountain '82

Louis Walser
Last Mercenary '84

Angela Walsh
Distant Voices, Still Lives '88

Dale Walsh
The New Adventures of Tarzan: Vol. 1 '35

Dermot Walsh
Ghost Ship '53
The Great Armored Car Swindle '64
Mania '60
Murder on the Campus '52
The Tell-Tale Heart '62

Ed Walsh
Let It Ride '89

George Walsh
American Pluck '25
The Broadway Drifter '27
The Live Wire '34
Test of Donald Norton '26

Gwynyth Walsh
Blue Monkey '87
The Crush '93

Joey Walsh
Hans Christian Andersen '52

Johnny Walsh
Body Parts '91
Wild Women of Wongo '59

J.T. Walsh
Backdraft '91
The Big Picture '89
Crazy People '90
Dad '89
Defenseless '91
A Few Good Men '92
The Grifters '90
Hard Choices '84
Hoffa '92
House of Games '87
Iron Maze '91
Narrow Margin '90
National Lampoon's Loaded Weapon 1 '93
Power '86
The Russia House '90
Sniper '92
Tequila Sunrise '88
Why Me? '90
Wired '89

Kay Walsh
Encore '52
Greyfriars Bobby '61
The Horse's Mouth '58
In Which We Serve '43
Last Holiday '50
October Man '48
Oliver Twist '48
Stage Fright '50
This Happy Breed '47
Tunes of Glory '60
Tunes of Glory/Horse's Mouth '60

Jumpin' Jack Flash '86

Davina Whitehouse
Night Nurse '77

Billie Whitelaw
Dressmaker '89
Duel of Hearts '92
Frenzy '72
Gumshoe '72
The Krays '90
Leopard in the Snow '78
Make Mine Mink '60
Mania '60
Murder Elite '86
Night Watch '72
No Love for Johnnie '60
The Omen '76
The Secret Garden '87
Shadey '87
Slayground '84
Small Hotel '57
Start the Revolution Without
Me '70
Strange Case of Dr. Jekyll &
Mr. Hyde '80
A Tale of Two Cities '80
Unsuitable Job for a Woman
'82
Water Babies '79

Arkie Whiteley
Razorback '84

Jon Whiteley
Moonfleet '55
The Spanish Gardener '57

Paul Whiteman
The Fabulous Dorseys '47
King of Jazz '30
Strike Up the Band '40

Ray Whiteside
Davy Crockett, King of the
Wild Frontier '55

Lynn Whitfield
Doctor Detroit '83
The George McKenna Story
'86
Johnnie Gibson F.B.I. '87
The Josephine Baker Story
'90

Mitchell Whitfield
Dogfight '91
My Cousin Vinny '92

Bradley Whitford
Dead as a Doorman '85
Scent of a Woman '92
Vital Signs '90

Peter Whitford
Dead End Drive-In '86
Strictly Ballroom '92
Warm Nights on a Slow-
Moving Train '87

Barbara Whiting
Beware, My Lovely '52

Jack Whiting
Sailing Along '38

Leonard Whiting
Rachel's Man '75
Romeo and Juliet '68
Say Hello to Yesterday '71

Margaret Whiting
Sinbad and the Eye of the
Tiger '77
Trespasser '85

Ray Whitley
Hittin' the Trail '37
Racketeers of the Range '39
Renegade Ranger/Scarlet
River '38

Lloyd Whitlock
Diamond Trail '33
The Michigan Kid '28
West of the Divide '34

Jill Whitlow
Adventures Beyond Belief '87
Ghost Chase '88
Night of the Creeps '86
Thunder Run '86
Twice Dead '88

Ernest Whitman
Blonde Savage '47

Kari Whitman
Phantom of the Mall: Eric's
Revenge '89

Kipp Whitman
Bummer '73

Stuart Whitman
Butterfly '82
Call Him Mr. Shatter '74
Captain Apache '71
Comancheros '61
Crazy Mama '75
Darby's Rangers '58
The Day and the Hour '63
Deadly Reactor '89
Delta Fox '77
Demonoid, Messenger of
Death '81
Eaten Alive '76
First Strike '85
Fury '80s
Hostages '79
The Invincible Six '68
Kill Castro '80
Las Vegas Lady '70
The Longest Day '62
Maniac '78
The Mark '61
Mean Johnny Barrows '75
The Mercenaries '80
Mob Boss '90
The Monster Club '85
Moving Target '89
Oil '78
Omega Cop '90
Ransom '84
Rio Conchos '64
Ruby '77
Run for the Roses '78
The Seekers '79
Silver Lode '54
Smooth Talker '90
The Story of Ruth '60
Strange Shadows in an Empty
Room '76
Sweet Dirty Tony '81
Ten North Frederick '58
Those Magnificent Men in
Their Flying Machines '65
The Treasure of the Amazon
'84
The Treasure Seekers '79
Vultures '84
The White Buffalo '77
The Woman Hunter '72

Walt Whitman
The Three Musketeers '16

Steve Whitmire
The Muppet Christmas Carol
'92

James Whitmore
The Adventures of Mark
Twain '85
All My Sons '86
The Asphalt Jungle '50
Battle Cry '55
Battleground '49
Because You're Mine '52
Black Like Me '64
Chato's Land '71

Chuka '67
Deep Six '58
Don't Cry, It's Only Thunder
'82
The Eddy Duchin Story '56
The First Deadly Sin '80
The Girl Who Had Everything
'53
Give 'Em Hell, Harry! '75
Glory! Glory! '90
Guns of the Magnificent
Seven '69
Harrad Experiment '73
High Crime '73
I Will Fight No More Forever
'75
Kiss Me Kate '53
Madigan '68
The McConnell Story '55
The Next Voice You Hear '50
Nuts '87
Oklahoma! '55
Old Explorers '90
Planet of the Apes '68
Rage '80
The Serpent's Egg '78
Target: Favorite Son '87
Them! '54
Tora! Tora! Tora! '70
Waterhole #3 '67
Where the Red Fern Grows
'74
The Word '78

**James Whitmore,
Jr.**
The Five of Me '81
The Gypsy Warriors '78
The Long Riders '80
Tricks of the Trade '88

Claire Whitney
Blind Fools '40

Grace Lee Whitney
Star Trek 3: The Search for
Spock '84

Helene Whitney
The Saint's Double Trouble
'40

Peter Whitney
Destination Tokyo '43
Rio Rita '42
Valley of the Sun '42

Susan Whitney
Miracle of Our Lady of Fatima
'52

Taylor Whitney
Curse of the Queerwolf '87

Stephen Whittaker
Bury Me an Angel '71

Frank Whitten
Vigil '84

Marguerite Whitten
Mystery in Swing '40
Two-Gun Man from Harlem
'38

Paul Whitthorne
Critters 4 '91

Brenton Whittle
Sara Dane '81

Margaret Whitton
The Best of Times '86
Big Girls Don't Cry...They Get
Even '92
Ironweed '87
Little Monsters '89
Major League '89
The Man Without a Face '93
9 1/2 Weeks '86
The Secret of My Success '87

William Whitton
Lemora, Lady Dracula '73

May Whitty
Conquest '32
Gaslight '44
The Lady Vanishes '38
Lassie, Come Home '43
Madame Curie '43
Mrs. Miniver '41
Suspicion '41
The White Cliffs of Dover '44

James Whitworth
Black Bikers from Hell '70
The Hills Have Eyes '77
Mona's Place '83
Planet of the Dinosaurs '80
357 Magnum '77

Kit Wholihan
The Islander '88

Richard Whorf
Chain Lightning '50
Midnight '34
Yankee Doodle Dandy '42

James Whylie
Place of Weeping '86

Anna Wiazemsky
Teorema '68

Leslie Ann Wick
Revenge of the Living
Zombies '88

Tom Wicker
Long Shadows '86

Mary Wickes
Almost Partners '87
By the Light of the Silvery
Moon '53
The Canterville Ghost '91
Dance with Me, Henry '56
How to Murder Your Wife '64
I'll See You in My Dreams '51
June Bride '48
The Man Who Came to Dinner
'41
On Moonlight Bay '51
Postcards from the Edge '90
Private Buckaroo '42
Sister Act '92
Who Done It? '42

Bernhard Wicki
Crime & Passion '75
The Eternal Waltz '59

Sidney Wicks
Coach '78

Kathleen Widdoes
The Group '66
Mafia Princess '86
The Mephisto Waltz '71
Savages '72

Olaf Widgren
June Night '40

Susanne Widl
Invisible Adversaries '77

Ellen Widmann
M '31

Richard Widmark
Against All Odds '84
The Alamo '60
All God's Children '80
Alvarez Kelly '66
Bear Island '80
Bedford Incident '65
Blackout '85
Broken Lance '54
Cheyenne Autumn '64
The Cobweb '55
Cold Sassy Tree '89

Coma '78
Death of a Gunfighter '69
The Domino Principle '77
Don't Bother to Knock '52
The Final Option '82
Gun Crazy '69
The Halls of Montezuma '50
Hanky Panky '82
How the West was Won '63
Judgment at Nuremberg '61
Kiss of Death '47
The Law and Jake Wade '58
Madigan '68
Mr. Horn '79
Murder on the Bayou '91
Murder on the Orient Express
'74
National Lampoon Goes to the
Movies '81
Night and the City '50
Panic in the Streets '50
Pickup on South Street '53
Road House '48
Rollercoaster '77
Saint Joan '57
Sell Out '76
The Street with No Name '48
The Swarm '78
Texas Guns '90
To the Devil, A Daughter '76
The Trap '59
True Colors '91
The Tunnel of Love '58
Twilight's Last Gleaming '77
Two Rode Together '61
Warlock '59
The Way West '67
Whale for the Killing '81
When the Legends Die '72

Robert Widmark
Perfect Killer '77

Bud Widom
The Green Slime '68

Dorothea Wieck
Maedchen in Uniform '31

Jane Wiedlin
Clue '85

David Wieland
Flirting '89

Matthias Wieman
The Blue Light '32

Elisabeth Wiener
Marry Me, Marry Me '69

Lynda Wiesmeier
Preppies '82
R.S.V.P. '84
Wheels of Fire '84

Dianne Wiest
Bright Lights, Big City '88
Cookie '89
Edward Scissorhands '90
Falling in Love '84
Footloose '84
Hannah and Her Sisters '86
Independence Day '83
It's My Turn '80
Little Man Tate '91
The Lost Boys '87
Parenthood '89
The Purple Rose of Cairo '85
Radio Days '87
September '88

Naima Wifstrand
The Magician '58
Night Is My Future '47

Chris Wiggins
Babar: The Movie '88
The Bay Boy '85

Wiggins

Wiggins ►*cont.*

Ford: The Man & the Machine '87
Kavik the Wolf Dog '84
King of the Grizzlies '69
Why Shoot the Teacher '79

Tudi Wiggins
Tropic Heat '84

Dawna Wightman
The Amityville Curse '90

Robert Wightman
A Day for Thanks on Walton's Mountain '82
Opposing Force '87
Stepfather 3: Father's Day '92

Carlton Wilborn
Dance '90

Claire Wilbur
Score '73

James Wilby
Conspiracy '89
A Handful of Dust '88
Howard's End '92
Maurice '87
A Summer Story '88

Frank Wilcox
Infamous Crimes '47
Seventh Cavalry '56

Larry Wilcox
The Dirty Dozen: The Next Mission '85
The Last Ride of the Dalton Gang '79
Mission Manila '87
National Lampoon's Loaded Weapon 1 '93
Sky Hei$t '75

Lisa Wilcox
A Nightmare on Elm Street 4: Dream Master '88
A Nightmare on Elm Street 5: Dream Child '89

Mary Wilcox
Beast of the Yellow Night '70
Love Me Deadly '76

Ralph Wilcox
Megaforce '82

Robert Wilcox
Buried Alive '39
Doctor Satan's Robot '40
Dreaming Out Loud '40
The Man They Could Not Hang '39
Mysterious Doctor Satan '40

Shannon Wilcox
Hollywood Harry '86
When Your Lover Leaves '83

Sophie Wilcox
The Chronicles of Narnia '89

Toyah Wilcox
Ebony Tower '86
Jubilee '78
Murder: Ultimate Grounds for Divorce '85

Collin Wilcox-Horne
The Baby Maker '70
Fury on Wheels '71

Henry Wilcoxon
Cleopatra '34
A Connecticut Yankee in King Arthur's Court '49
The Corsican Brothers '42

Enola Gay: The Men, the Mission, the Atomic Bomb '80
Escape from Planet Earth '67
Jericho '38
The Last of the Mohicans '36
Man in the Wilderness '71
Mrs. Miniver '42
Pony Express Rider '76
The President's Mystery '36
Samson and Delilah '50
Scaramouche '52
Tarzan Finds a Son '39
The Ten Commandments '56
That Hamilton Woman '41
The Two Worlds of Jenny Logan '79
The War Lord '65
When Every Day was the Fourth of July '78

Christopher Wild
Knights & Emeralds '87

Jack Wild
Melody '71
Oliver! '68
Robin Hood: Prince of Thieves '91

Katy Wild
The Evil of Frankenstein '64

Wild Samoan
Body Slam '87

Andrew Wilde
Murder on Line One '90
1984 '84
Pete Townsend: White City '85

Cornel Wilde
At Sword's Point '51
Big Combo '55
The Comic '69
The Fifth Musketeer '79
The Greatest Show on Earth '52
High Sierra '41
Main Street to Broadway '53
The Naked Prey '66
Norseman '78
Omar Khayyam '57
Passion '54
Road House '48
Sharks' Treasure '75
A Song to Remember '45
Sword of Lancelot '63
Treasure of the Golden Condor '53

Heather Wilde
The Undying Monster '42

Lois Wilde
Brothers of the West '37

Gene Wilder
The Adventures of Sherlock Holmes' Smarter Brother '78
Another You '91
Blazing Saddles '74
Everything You Always Wanted to Know About Sex (But Were Afraid to Ask) '72
The Frisco Kid '79
Funny About Love '90
Hanky Panky '82
Haunted Honeymoon '86
The Little Prince '74
The Producers '68
Quackser Fortune Has a Cousin in the Bronx '70
See No Evil, Hear No Evil '89
The Silver Streak '76

Start the Revolution Without Me '70
Stir Crazy '80
Thursday's Game '74
Willy Wonka & the Chocolate Factory '71
The Woman in Red '84
World's Greatest Lover '77
Young Frankenstein '74

Glenn Wilder
Zebra Force '76

James Wilder
Murder One '88
Prey of the Chameleon '91
Scorchers '92
Zombie High '87

Yvonne Wilder
Honeyboy '82
The Return of Count Yorga '71

Michael Wilding
Convoy '40
Cottage to Let '41
The Courtney Affair '47
The Egyptian '54
The Glass Slipper '55
Kipps '41
Late Extra '35
Maytime in Mayfair '52
The Naked Edge '61
Stage Fright '50
Torch Song '53
Under Capricorn '49
Waterloo '71
The World of Suzie Wong '60

John Wildman
American Boyfriends '89
Lethal Pursuit '88
My American Cousin '85
Sorority Babes in the Slimeball Bowl-A-Rama '87

Valerie Wildman
Inner Sanctum '91
Neon City '91

Dawn Wildsmith
Alienator '89
Cyclone '87
Evil Spawn '87
Phantom Empire '87
Surf Nazis Must Die '87
Terminal Force '88
Warlords '88

Jean Wiles
The King and Four Queens '56

Mike Wiles
Cole Justice '89
Terror at Tenkiller '86

Bill Wiley
Porky's 2: The Next Day '83

Jane Wiley
Dawn on the Great Divide '42
Jive Junction '43
Master Key '44
Rhythm Parade '43
The Underdog '43

John Wilford
Death Code Ninja '87
Ninja: American Warrior '90
Ninja Death Squad '87

Dian Wilhite
Flesh Feast '69

Kathleen Wilhoite
Bad Influence '90
Campus Man '87
Everybody Wins '90
Lorenzo's Oil '92
Morning After '86

Murphy's Law '86
Private School '83
Undercover '87
Witchboard '87

Robert J. Wilke
20,000 Leagues Under the Sea '54

Catherine Wilkening
Jesus of Montreal '89

Jose Wilker
Bye Bye Brazil '79
Dona Flor and Her Two Husbands '78
Medicine Man '92

Guy Wilkerson
Dead or Alive '41
Fighting Valley '43
Frontier Fugitives '45
Man of the West '58
Marked for Murder '45
Outlaw Roundup '44

Jacen Wilkerson
The Jacksons: An American Dream '92

Donna Wilkes
Angel '84
Blood Song '82
Fyre '78
Grotesque '87
Hard Knocks

Elaine Wilkes
Killer Party '86
Roommate '84

Keith Wilkes
Cornbread, Earl & Me '75

Barbara Wilkin
The Flesh Eaters '64

Martin Wilkins
Law of the Jungle '42

Charles Wilkinson
Quarantine '89

June Wilkinson
The Bellboy and the Playgirls '62
The Florida Connection '74
Frankenstein's Great Aunt Tillie '83
Macumba Love '60
Sno-Line '85
Vasectomy: A Delicate Matter '86

Tom Wilkinson
Sylvia '86

Lee Wilkof
Chattahoochee '89

Edmund Willard
The Mystery of the Mary Celeste '37

Fred Willard
Americathon '79
Chesty Anderson USN '76
The History of White People in America '85
Lots of Luck '85
Moving Violations '85
Portrait of a White Marriage '88
Roxanne '87
Salem's Lot '79
Second City Insanity '81

Dave Willcock
Queen of Outer Space '58

Jack Willcox
Prison Planet '92

Pete Willcox
Dudes '87

Jo Ann Willette
Welcome to 18 '87

Noel William
Across the Bridge '57

Warren William
The Case of the Lucky Legs '35
Cleopatra '34
Employees' Entrance '33
Fear '46
The Firefly '37
Lady for a Day '33
The Private Affairs of Bel Ami '47
Satan Met a Lady '36
Skyscraper Souls '32
Strange Illusion '45
Three on a Match '32
Wives Under Suspicion '38
The Wolf Man '41

Adam Williams
The Badlanders '58
Fear Strikes Out '57
Queen for a Day '51
Without Warning '52

Allen Williams
Scorpion '86
The Two Worlds of Jenny Logan '79

Anson Williams
I Married a Centerfold '84

Arnold Williams
The King of Marvin Gardens '72

Barbara Williams
City of Hope '91
Indecency '92
Jo Jo Dancer, Your Life is Calling '86
Oh, What a Night '92
Peter Gunn '89
Tell Me That You Love Me '84
Thief of Hearts '84
Tiger Warsaw '87
Watchers '88

Barry Williams
A Very Brady Christmas '88

Bernadette Williams
Caged Fury '80

Bill Williams
Buckskin '68
The Cariboo Trail '50
The Clay Pigeon '49
Deadline at Dawn '46
Flight of the Grey Wolf '76
The Giant Spider Invasion '75
Operation Haylift '50
Son of Paleface '52
Storm Rider '57
Till the End of Time '46
Torpedo Alley '53
A Woman's Secret '49

Billy Dee Williams
Alien Intruder '93
Batman '89
Bingo Long Traveling All-Stars & Motor Kings '76
Black Brigade '69
Brian's Song '71
Chiefs '83
Children of Divorce '80
Christmas Lilies of the Field '84
Courage '86
Deadly Illusion '87

Alvaro Zermeno
Caches de Oro

Gene Zerna
Dr. Caligari '89

Maria Louise Zetha
Love Lessons '85

Mai Zetterling
Frieda '47
Hidden Agenda '90
Night Is My Future '47
Only Two Can Play '62
Truth About Women '58
The Witches '90

Esther Zevko
But Where Is Daniel Wax? '74

Yu Zhang
Girl from Hunan '86

Ye Zharikov
My Name is Ivan '62

Stacia Zhivago
Sorority House Massacre 2:
   Nighty Nightmare '92

Nick Zickefoose
Cole Justice '89

Howard Zieff
Flesh Gordon '72

Sonja Ziemann
Made in Heaven '52
A Matter of WHO '62

Chip Zien
Grace Quigley '84

Paul Ziller
Pledge Night '90

Madeline Zima
The Hand that Rocks the
   Cradle '92
Mr. Nanny '93

Efrem Zimbalist, Jr.
Airport '75 '75
By Love Possessed '61
Deep Six '58
Family Upside Down '78
The Gathering: Part 2 '79
Hot Shots! '91
House of Strangers '49
Scruples '80
Shooting Stars '85
Terror Out of the Sky '78
Wait Until Dark '67
Who Is the Black Dahlia? '75

Stephanie Zimbalist
Awakening '80
The Babysitter '80
Caroline? '90
Forever '78
The Gathering '77
The Killing Mind '90
Long Journey Back '78
Love on the Run '85
Magic of Lassie '78
Personals '90
Tomorrow's Child '82
The Triangle Factory Fire
   Scandal '79

Marlene Zimmerman
Kill Line '91

Patric Zimmerman
The Jetsons: Movie '90

Terri Zimmern
The Manster '59

Karl Zinny
Demons '86

Victoria Zinny
Beyond the Door 3 '91
Viridiana '61

Amanda Zinsser
Covert Action '88

William Zipp
Death Chase '87
Future Force '89
Jungle Assault '89
Mankillers '87

August Zirner
Voyager '91

Hanns Zischler
Kings of the Road—In the
   Course of Time '76
Les Rendez-vous D'Anna '78
A Woman in Flames '84

Dan Ziskie
Twisted '86
Zebrahead '92

Adrian Zmed
Bachelor Party '84
The Final Terror '83
For the Love of It '80
Grease 2 '82

Moses Znaimer
Best Revenge '83

Istvan Znamenak
Time Stands Still '82

Richard Zobel
To Sleep with a Vampire '92

Arlene Zoellner
Gamera vs. Zigra '71

Gloria Zoellner
Gamera vs. Zigra '71

Jean-Pierre Zola
Mon Oncle '58

Aldo Zollo
Romeo and Juliet '54

Bezeredi Zoltan
Oh, Bloody Life! '88

Michael Zorek
Hot Moves '84
Private School '83

Louis Zorich
Cheap Shots '91
Death of a Salesman '86
Newman's Law '74

Vera Zorina
The Goldwyn Follies '38
Louisiana Purchase '41

Zouzou
Chloe in the Afternoon '72
S*P*Y*S '74

Rod Zuanic
Fast Talking '86
Mad Max Beyond
   Thunderdome '85

Olga Zubarry
Desde el Abismo
La Nueva Cigarra '86
Somos Novios '68

Valentin Zubkov
My Name is Ivan '62

George Zucco
The Adventures of Sherlock
   Holmes '39
Arrest Bulldog Drummond '38
The Black Raven '43
The Bride Wore Red '37
Bulldog Drummond in Africa/
   Arrest Bulldog Drummond
   '38

David and Bathsheba '51
Dead Men Walk '43
The Devil Thumbs a Ride/
   Having Wonderful Crime
   '47
The Firefly '37
Fog Island '45
Having Wonderful Crime '45
House of Frankenstein '44
The Hunchback of Notre
   Dame '39
The Mad Monster '42
Madame Bovary '49
Marie Antoinette '38
The Mummy's Hand '40
My Favorite Blonde '42
The Pirate '48
Return of the Ape Man '44
Saratoga '37
Scared to Death '47
Scared to Death/Dick Tracy's
   Dilemma '47
The Seventh Cross '44
Sherlock Holmes in
   Washington '43
Three Comrades '38
A Woman's Face '41

David Zucker
Kentucky Fried Movie '77

Jerry Zucker
Kentucky Fried Movie '77

Miriam Zucker
Street Trash '87

Ralph Zucker
The Bloody Pit of Horror '65

Joshua Zuehlke
Amazing Grace & Chuck '87

Zulu
Code Name: Diamond Head
   '77

Daphne Zuniga
Eyes of the Panther '90
The Fly 2 '89
Gross Anatomy '89
The Initiation '84
Last Rites '88
Modern Girls '86
Prey of the Chameleon '91
Quarterback Princess '85
Spaceballs '87
Staying Together '89
The Sure Thing '85
Vision Quest '85

Idit Zur
Noa at Seventeen '82

Dianik Zurakowska
Cauldron of Blood '67
Orgy of the Vampires '73

Carey Zuris
Bad Girls Dormitory '84

Martin Zurla
South Bronx Heroes '85

Yoshitaka Zushi
Dodes 'ka-den '70

Brad Zutaut
Hardbodies 2 '86
Knock Outs '92
Nudity Required '90

Dor Zweigenbom
Late Summer Blues '87

Darrell Zwerling
Chinatown '74

Noam Zylberman
Love and Hate '90
Outside Chance of Maximillian
   Glick '88

DIRECTOR INDEX

The **DIRECTOR INDEX** lists the video accomplishments of nearly 6,000 directors, arranged in a straight alphabetical format by last name (names are presented in a first name, last name format, but alphabetization begins with the last name). Every director cited in the main review section is included in the index, presenting a surefire locator for hard-to-find directors and their movies. The **Cast Index** immediately precedes this index.

Paul Aaron
Deadly Force '83
Different Story '78
Force of One '79
Imperial Navy '80s
In Love and War '91
Maxie '85
The Miracle Worker '79

Charles Abbott
The Adventures of the
  Masked Phantom '38

George Abbott
Damn Yankees '58
Pajama Game '57
Too Many Girls '40

Alan Abel
Is There Sex After Death? '71

Jeanne Abel
Is There Sex After Death? '71

Robert Abel
Elvis on Tour '72

Lewis Abernathy
House 4: Home Deadly Home
  '91

Derwin Abrahams
Border Vigilantes '41
Northwest Trail '46

Jim Abrahams
Airplane! '80
Big Business '88
Hot Shots! '91
Hot Shots! Part Deux '93
Police Squad! Help Wanted!
  '82
Ruthless People '86
Top Secret! '84
Welcome Home, Roxy
  Carmichael '90

Tenghiz Abuladze
Repentance '87

Jovan Acin
Hey, Babu Riba '88

Rodney Ackland
Thursday's Child '43

David Acomba
Night Life '90

Catlin Adams
Sticky Fingers '88

Daniel Adams
Primary Motive '92

Doug Adams
Blackout '88

Al Adamson
Angels' Wild Women '72
Black Samurai '77
Blazing Stewardesses '75
Blood of Dracula's Castle '69
Blood of Ghastly Horror '72
Brain of Blood '71
Cinderella 2000 '78
Dracula vs. Frankenstein '71
The Female Bunch '69
Gun Riders '69
Horror of the Blood Monsters
  '70
Hospital of Terror '78
I Spit on Your Corpse '74
Jessie's Girls '75
Satan's Sadists '69
Texas Layover '75

Victor Adamson
Boss Cowboy '35
Rawhide Romance '34

Pierre Adidge
Elvis on Tour '72

Joseph Adler
Scream, Baby, Scream '69
Sex and the College Girl '64

Lou Adler
Cheech and Chong's Up in
  Smoke '79

Percy Adlon
Bagdad Cafe '88
Celeste '81
The Last Five Days '82
Rosalie Goes Shopping '89
Sugarbaby '85

Ed Adlum
Invasion of the Blood Farmers
  '72

Frank Agrama
Dawn of the Mummy '82

Joseph Louis Agraz
Treasure of the Moon
  Goddess '88

Javier Aguirre
Dracula's Great Love '72
The Rue Morgue Massacres
  '73

Agust Agustsson
Maya '82

Charlie Ahearn
Wild Style '83

Mac Ahlberg
Gangsters '79

Chantal Akerman
Akermania, Vol. 1 '92
Je Tu Il Elle '74
Les Rendez-vous D'Anna '78
News from Home '76
Toute Une Nuit '82
Window Shopping '86

Moustapha Akkad
Lion of the Desert '81
Mohammed: Messenger of
  God '77

Pat Alan
Shootfighter: Fight to the
  Death '93

Benito Alazraki
Invasion of the Zombies '61
Spiritism '61

Rafael Morena Alba
Exorcism's Daughter '74

**Jean-Gabriel
Albicocco**
The Wanderer '67

Hans Albin
No Survivors, Please '63

Carlton J. Albright
Luther the Geek '90

Alan Alda
Betsy's Wedding '90
The Four Seasons '81
A New Life '88
Sweet Liberty '86

Thomas Alderman
The Severed Arm '73

Will Aldis
Stealing Home '88

Adell Aldrich
The Kid from Left Field '79

Robert Aldrich
...All the Marbles '81
Apache '54
Autumn Leaves '56
The Big Knife '55
The Choirboys '77
The Dirty Dozen '67
The Flight of the Phoenix '65
Four for Texas '63
The Frisco Kid '79
The Grissom Gang '71
Hush, Hush, Sweet Charlotte
  '65
Hustle '75
The Killing of Sister George
  '69
Kiss Me Deadly '55
The Longest Yard '74
Sodom and Gomorrah '62
Too Late the Hero '70
Twilight's Last Gleaming '77
Ulzana's Raid '72
Vera Cruz '53
What Ever Happened to Baby
  Jane? '62

**Thomas Gutierrez
Alea**
Death of a Bureaucrat '66
Memories of
  Underdevelopment '68

**Goffredo
Alessandrini**
We the Living '42

Ottavio Alessi
The Seducers '70

Bill Alexander
Moliere '84
Tartuffe '90

Max Alexander
Flaming Lead '39

Grigori Alexandrov
Que Viva Mexico '32
Ten Days That Shook the
  World '27

James Algar
The Adventures of Ichabod
  and Mr. Toad '49
The Legend of Sleepy Hollow
  '49
Secrets of Life '56
Vanishing Prairie '54

Sidney Algier
Wild Horse '31

Marcello Aliprandi
Vatican Conspiracy '81

Howard Alk
Janis: A Film '74

Marc Allegret
Fanny '32
Lady Chatterley's Lover '55
The Love of Three Queens '54
Mademoiselle Striptease '57
Sois Belle et Tais-Toi '58
Zou Zou '34

Yves Allegret
Dedee d'Anvers '49
Johnny Apollo '40
Seven Deadly Sins '53

A.K. Allen
Ladies Club '86

Corey Allen
The Ann Jillian Story '88
Avalanche '78
Brass '85
Codename: Foxfire '85
The Erotic Adventures of
  Pinocchio '71
The Last Fling '86
The Man in the Santa Claus
  Suit '79
Return of Frank Cannon '80
Thunder and Lightning '77

David Allen
Puppet Master 2 '91

Fred Allen
Ghost Valley '32
The Mysterious Rider '33
Saddle Buster '32

Irving Allen
Slaughter Trail '51

Adolfo Aristarain
The Stranger '87
Time for Revenge '82

Alan Arkin
Little Murders '71

Robert Arkless
The Man Who Would Not Die '75

Allan Arkush
Caddyshack 2 '88
Death Sport '78
Get Crazy '83
Heartbeeps '81
Hollywood Boulevard '76
Rock 'n' Roll High School '79

Leslie Arliss
A Man About the House '47
The Man in Grey '45
The Night Has Eyes '42

George Armitage
Hot Rod '79
Miami Blues '90
Private Duty Nurses '71

Gillian Armstrong
Fires Within '91
High Tide '87
The Last Days of Chez Nous '92
Mrs. Soffel '85
My Brilliant Career '79
Starstruck '82

Karl Armstrong
Ninja Vengeance '93

Michael Armstrong
Mark of the Devil '69

Moira Armstrong
How Many Miles to Babylon? '82

Robin B. Armstrong
Pastime '91

Gwen Arner
A Matter of Principle '83
Necessary Parties '88

Eddie Arno
Murder Story '89

Frank Arnold
A Waltz Through the Hills '88

Jack Arnold
Boss '74
Creature from the Black Lagoon '54
Games Girls Play '75
High School Confidential '58
The Incredible Shrinking Man '57
It Came From Outer Space '53
Marilyn: The Untold Story '80
The Mouse That Roared '59
Swiss Conspiracy '77
Tarantula '55

Newton Arnold
Bloodsport '88
Hands of a Stranger '62

Fernando Arrabal
The Odyssey of the Pacific '82

Karen Arthur
Bridge to Silence '89
Broken Badge '85
A Bunny's Tale '85
The Jacksons: An American Dream '92
Lady Beware '87
My Sister, My Love '78

Raul Artigot
Witches' Mountain '71

Ami Artzi
Purgatory '89

Dorothy Arzner
The Bride Wore Red '37
Christopher Strong '33
Craig's Wife '36
Dance, Girl, Dance '40

Anthony Ascot
Guns for Dollars '73
Gunslinger '70s

Hal Ashby
Being There '79
Bound for Glory '76
Coming Home '78
8 Million Ways to Die '85
Harold and Maude '71
The Last Detail '73
Lookin' to Get Out '82
Shampoo '75
The Slugger's Wife '85

Ronnie Ashcroft
The Astounding She-Monster '58

Richard Ashe
Track of the Moonbeast '76

Robert Asher
Make Mine Mink '60

William Asher
Beach Blanket Bingo '65
Beach Party '63
Bikini Beach '64
How to Stuff a Wild Bikini '65
Movers and Shakers '85
Muscle Beach Party '64
Night Warning '82

Melvin Ashford
Mondo Magic '76

Alexander Askoldov
Commissar '68

John Aslanian
Torment '85

Anthony Asquith
The Browning Version '51
Carrington, V.C. '54
Cottage to Let '41
The Demi-Paradise '43
I Stand Condemned '36
Importance of Being Earnest '52
Man of Evil '48
Pygmalion '38
The V.I.P.'s '63
We Dive at Dawn '43
The Winslow Boy '48

Ovidio G. Assonitis
Madhouse '87

Alexandre Astruc
End of Desire '58

Thomas Atcheson
Deadly Diamonds '91

J.D. Athens
Cannibal Women in the Avocado Jungle of Death '89

Thomas Atkins
The Silver Streak '34

Richard Attenborough
A Bridge Too Far '77
Chaplin '92
A Chorus Line '85

Cry Freedom '87
Gandhi '82
Magic '78
Young Winston '72

Daniel Attias
Silver Bullet '85

Bobby A. Auarez
One Armed Executioner '80

Pascal Aubier
Death of the Rat '75

Guillaume Martin Aucion
Oh! Calcutta! '72

Michael Audley
The Mark of the Hawk '57

John H. Auer
City That Never Sleeps '53
The Crime of Dr. Crespi '35
Wheel of Fortune '41

Lee Auerbach
Jupiter Menace '82

Bille August
Pelle the Conqueror '88
Twist & Shout '84

Carlos Aured
Curse of the Devil '73
Horror Rises from the Tomb '72
House of Psychotic Women '73
The Mummy's Revenge '73

Carl Ausino
Don't Look in the Attic '81

Sam Auster
Screen Test '85

Ray Austin
House of the Living Dead '73
Return of the Man from U.N.C.L.E. '83
The Virgin Witch '70
The Zany Adventures of Robin Hood '84

Claude Autant-Lara
Devil in the Flesh '46
Four Bags Full '56
Oldest Profession '67
The Red and the Black '57
Seven Deadly Sins '53
Sylvia and the Phantom '45

Igor Auzins
Death Train '79
High Rolling in a Hot Corvette '77
Night Nurse '77
We of the Never Never '82

Aram Avakian
Cops and Robbers '73
11 Harrowhouse '74
End of the Road '70

Marcello Avallone
Specters '87

Pupi Avati
Revenge of the Dead '84
The Story of Boys & Girls '91

Hikmet Avedis
Dr. Minx '75
Scorchy '76
The Specialist '75
The Stepmother '71
The Teacher '74
Texas Detour '77

Howard Avedis
The Fifth Floor '80
Kidnapped '87

Mortuary '81
Separate Ways '82
They're Playing with Fire '84

Hy Averback
A Guide for the Married Woman '78
I Love You, Alice B. Toklas '68
She's in the Army Now '81
Suppose They Gave a War and Nobody Came? '70
Where the Boys Are '84 '84
Where Were You When the Lights Went Out? '68

Tex Avery
All This and Tex Avery, Too! '92
Bugs Bunny & Elmer Fudd Cartoon Festival '44
Cartoon Moviestars: Porky! '47
Daffy Duck: The Nuttiness Continues... '56
Tex Avery's Screwball Classics, Vol. 1 '40s
Tex Avery's Screwball Classics, Vol. 2 '40s

John G. Avildsen
Cry Uncle '71
For Keeps '88
Foreplay '75
The Formula '80
Guess What We Learned in School Today? '70
Happy New Year '87
Joe '70
The Karate Kid '84
The Karate Kid: Part 2 '86
The Karate Kid: Part 3 '89
Lean on Me '89
Neighbors '81
A Night in Heaven '83
The Power of One '92
Rocky '76
Rocky 5 '90
Save the Tiger '73

Tom Avildsen
Cheech and Chong: Things Are Tough All Over '82

Meiert Avis
Far from Home '89

Jon Avnet
Fried Green Tomatoes '91

Gabriel Axel
Babette's Feast '87

George Axelrod
Secret Life of an American Wife '68

Fernando Ayala
El Profesor Hippie '69

Dan Aykroyd
Nothing But Trouble '91

Julian Aymes
Jane Eyre '83

Mario Azzopardi
Deadline '82
Nowhere to Hide '87

Beth B
Salvation! '87
Vortex '81

Scott B
Vortex '81

Hector Babenco
At Play in the Fields of the Lord '91
Ironweed '87
Kiss of the Spider Woman '85

Pixote '81

Gideon Bachmann
Ciao Federico! Fellini Directs Satyricon '69

Lloyd Bacon
Action in the North Atlantic '43
Boy Meets Girl '38
Brother Orchid '40
Devil Dogs of the Air '35
The Fighting Sullivans '42
Footlight Parade '33
42nd Street '33
The French Line '54
The Fuller Brush Girl '50
Kept Husbands '31
Knute Rockne: All American '40
Marked Woman '37
Miss Grant Takes Richmond '49
Oklahoma Kid '39
She Couldn't Say No '52
Silver Queen '42

Peter Bacso
Oh, Bloody Life! '88

Randall Badat
Surf 2 '84

Clarence Badger
Hands Up '26
It '27
Paths to Paradise '25
Teddy at the Throttle '16

Phillip Badger
The Forgotten One '89

John Badham
American Flyers '85
Bingo Long Traveling All-Stars & Motor Kings '76
Bird on a Wire '90
Blue Thunder '83
Dracula '79
The Hard Way '91
Point of No Return '93
Reflections of Murder '74
Saturday Night Fever '77
Short Circuit '86
Stakeout '87
Another Stakeout '93
War Games '83
Whose Life Is It Anyway? '81

Reza Badiyi
Blade in Hong Kong '85
Of Mice and Men '81
Policewoman Centerfold '83

Max Baer
Hometown U.S.A. '79
Ode to Billy Joe '76

Milton Bagby, Jr.
Rebel Love '85

King Baggott
Tumbleweeds '25

James Bagle
Stones of Death '88

Fax Bahr
Hearts of Darkness: A Filmmaker's Apocalypse '91

Chuck Bail
Choke Canyon '86
Cleopatra Jones & the Casino of Gold '75
Gumball Rally '76

Patrick Bailey
Door to Door '84

Richard Bailey
Win, Place, or Steal '72

Timothy Bond
Deadly Harvest '72
One Night Only '84

Sergei Bondarchuk
War and Peace '68
Waterloo '71

Peter Bonerz
Nobody's Perfekt '79
Police Academy 6: City Under Siege '89

George Bonge
The Master Killers '73

Mario Bonnard
The Last Days of Pompeii '60

Lee Bonner
Adventure of the Action Hunters '87

Rene Bonniere
Perfect Timing '84

Miguel Iglesias Bonns
Night of the Howling Beast '75

Andre Bonzel
Man Bites Dog '92

John Boorman
Deliverance '72
The Emerald Forest '85
Excalibur '81
Exorcist 2: The Heretic '77
Hell in the Pacific '69
Hope and Glory '87
Point Blank '67
Where the Heart Is '90
Zardoz '73

H. Gordon Boos
Red Surf '90

Walter Boos
Train Station Pickups '70s

Jose Luis Borau
On the Line '83

Donald P. Borchers
Grave Secrets '89

Lizzie Borden
Born in Flames '83
Love Crimes '92
Working Girls '87

Bernard Borderie
Your Turn Darling '63

Michael Bordon
The Ghost of Fletcher Ridge '80s

Robert Boris
Buy & Cell '89
Oxford Blues '84
Steele Justice '87

Walerian Borowczyk
Emmanuelle 5 '87

Clay Borris
The Gunfighters '87
Prom Night 4: Deliver Us From Evil '91
Quiet Cool '86

Phillip Borsos
The Grey Fox '83
Mean Season '85
One Magic Christmas '85

Michael Bortman
Crooked Hearts '91

Frank Borzage
A Farewell to Arms '32
Flirtation Walk '34

History is Made at Night '37
I've Always Loved You '46
Journey Beneath the Desert '61
Mannequin '37
Moonrise '48
The Shining Hour '38
Smilin' Through '41
Song O' My Heart '29
The Spanish Main '45
Stage Door Canteen '43
Strange Cargo '40
Three Comrades '38

Juan Bosch
Exorcism '74

John Boskovich
Without You I'm Nothing '90

John Boulting
Brighton Rock '47
Heavens Above '63
I'm All Right Jack '59
Lucky Jim '58

Roy Boulting
Brothers in Law '57
Carlton Browne of the F.O. '59
Fame is the Spur '47
Heavens Above '63
There's a Girl in My Soup '70

Serge Bourguignon
A Coeur Joie '67
Head Over Heels '67
Sundays & Cybele '62

Robert Bouvier
City in Panic '86

Haim Bouzaglo
Fictitious Marriage '88

John Bowab
Love at the Top '86

Jenny Bowen
Street Music '81
The Wizard of Loneliness '88

John Bowen
Knock Outs '92
Lethal Games '90

Dallas Bower
Alice in Wonderland '50

Anthony Bowers
Shame, Shame on the Bixby Boys '82

Geoffrey G. Bowers
Danger Zone 2 '89

George Bowers
Body & Soul '81
The Hearse '80
My Tutor '82
Private Resort '84

John R. Bowey
Mutator '90

John Bown
Nudity Required '90

Kenneth Bowser
In a Shallow Grave '88

Muriel Box
Rattle of a Simple Man '64
Truth About Women '58

Daniel Boyd
Chillers '88
Invasion of the Space Preachers '90

Don Boyd
East of Elephant Rock '76
Twenty-One '91

Julianne Boyd
Eubie! '82

Jean Boyer
Dressmaker '56
Fernandel the Dressmaker '57
The French Touch '54
Mr. Peek-A-Boo '50

Pat Boyette
Dungeon of Harrow '64

Bruno Bozzetto
Allegro Non Troppo '76
Mr. Rossi's Dreams '83
Mr. Rossi's Vacation '83
Vip, My Brother Superman '90
West and Soda '90

Charles Brabant
The Respectful Prostitute '52

Charles Brabin
The Mask of Fu Manchu '32
The Raven '15

Robert North Bradbury
Alias John Law '35
Between Men '35
Big Calibre '35
Blue Steel '34
Brand of the Outlaws '36
Breed of the Border '33
Cavalry '36
Dawn Rider '35
Dawn Rider/Frontier Horizon '39
Desert Trail '35
Forbidden Trails '41
Headin' for the Rio Grande '36
Hidden Valley '32
Hittin' the Trail '37
John Wayne Anthology: Star Packer/Lawless Range '34
Kid Ranger '36
Lawless Frontier '35
Lawless Range '35
Lucky Texan '34
Man from Hell's Edges '32
Man from Utah '34
Riders of Destiny '33
Riders of the Rockies '37
Smokey Smith '36
The Star Packer '34
Sundown Saunders '36
Trail Beyond '34
Trouble in Texas '37
Valley of the Lawless '36
West of the Divide '34
Western Double Feature 2 '33
Western Double Feature 5 '35
Western Justice '36
Westward Ho '35

Samuel Bradford
Teen Vamp '88

Al Bradley
Bloody Avenger '80s
Captive Planet '78
Cosmos: War of the Planets '80
Cross Mission '89
Iron Warrior '87
Metallica '85
Miami Cops '89

David Bradley
They Saved Hitler's Brain '64

John Bradshaw
The Big Slice '90
That's My Baby! '88

Randy Bradshaw
Blades of Courage '88

Carlo L. Bragaglia
The Loves of Hercules '60

The Sword and the Cross '58

John Brahm
Face to Face '52
Guest in the House '45
The Lodger '44
Miracle of Our Lady of Fatima '52
The Undying Monster '42

Stan Brakhage
Dog Star Man '64

Bill Brame
Ebony Dreams '80
Jive Turkey '76
Miss Melody Jones '73

Kenneth Branagh
Dead Again '91
Henry V '89
Much Ado About Nothing '93
Peter's Friends '92

Larry Brand
The Drifter '88
Masque of the Red Death '89
Overexposed '90

Timothy Brand
Till Death Do Us Part '72

Richard Brander
Sizzle Beach U.S.A. '86

Marlon Brando
One-Eyed Jacks '61

Michael Brandon
Queen of the Stardust Ballroom '75

Charlotte Brandstrom
Road to Ruin '91
Sweet Revenge '90

Fred Brannon
The Crimson Ghost '46
Cyclotrode "X" '46
D-Day on Mars '45
Federal Agents vs. Underworld, Inc. '49
G-Men Never Forget '48
The Invisible Monster '50
Jesse James Rides Again '47
Jungle Drums of Africa '53
King of the Rocketmen '49
Lost Planet Airmen '49
Radar Men from the Moon '52
Satan's Satellites '58
Zombies of the Stratosphere '52

Dominick Brascia
Evil Laugh '86

Enrique Braso
In Memoriam '76

Tinto Brass
Caligula '80

Keefe Brasselle
If You Don't Stop It...You'll Go Blind '77

Michel Brault
A Paper Wedding '89

Joseph Braunstein
Edge of the Axe '89
Rest In Pieces '87

Charles Braverman
Brotherhood of Justice '86
Hit & Run '82
Prince of Bel Air '87

Bob Bravler
Rush Week '88

John Bravman
Zombie Nightmare '86

William Brayne
Cold War Killers '86
Flame to the Phoenix '85

Rossano Brazzi
The Christmas That Almost Wasn't '66

George Breakston
Scarlet Spear '54
White Huntress '57

Gil Brealey
A Test of Love '84

Richard L. Breen
Stopover Tokyo '57

Catherine Breillat
36 Fillete '88

Jacques Brel
Franz '72

Milton Bren
Three for Bedroom C '52

Herbert Brenon
Black Eyes '39
Dancing Mothers '26
Housemaster '38

Alfonso Brescia
White Fang and the Hunter '85

Robert Bresson
Diary of a Country Priest '50
A Man Escaped '57
Mouchette '60
Pickpocket '59

Martin Brest
Beverly Hills Cop '84
Going in Style '79
Midnight Run '88
Scent of a Woman '92

Howard Bretherton
Below the Border '42
Boy's Reformatory '39
Dawn on the Great Divide '42
Down Texas Way '42
Ghost Town Law '42
Hidden Enemy '40
Hopalong Cassidy '35
In Old Colorado '41
Ladies They Talk About '33
Midnight Limited '40
Outlaws of the Desert '41
The Prince of Thieves '48
Rhythm Parade '43
Riders of the West '42
The Showdown '40
Star Reporter '39
Tough Kid '39
Up in the Air '40
West of the Law '42

Beth Brickell
Death Game '76

Jules Bricken
Explosion '69

Marshall Brickman
Lovesick '83
The Manhattan Project '86
Simon '80

Paul Brickman
Risky Business '83

Alan Bridges
Invasion '65
Out of Season '75
Pudd'nhead Wilson '87
Return of the Soldier '84
The Shooting Party '85

Beau Bridges
Seven Hours to Judgment '88
The Wild Pair '87

William Forest Crouch
Reet, Petite and Gone '47

Avery Crounse
Eyes of Fire '84
The Invisible Kid '88

Dean Crow
Backwoods '87

Cameron Crowe
Say Anything '89
Singles '92

Christopher Crowe
Off Limits '87
Whispers in the Dark '92

James Cruze
The Covered Wagon '23
The Great Gabbo '29
Hawthorne of the USA '19
I Cover the Waterfront '33
Mr. Skitch '33
Old Ironsides '26
The Roaring Road '19
The Wrong Road '37

Billy Crystal
Mr. Saturday Night '92

George Cukor
Adam's Rib '50
Bhowani Junction '56
A Bill of Divorcement '32
Born Yesterday '50
Camille '36
David Copperfield '35
Dinner at Eight '33
A Double Life '47
Gaslight '44
Heller in Pink Tights '60
Holiday '38
It Should Happen to You '54
Justine '69
Les Girls '57
Let's Make Love '60
A Life of Her Own '50
Little Women '33
Love Among the Ruins '75
My Fair Lady '64
Pat and Mike '52
The Philadelphia Story '40
Rich and Famous '81
Romeo and Juliet '36
Song Without End '60
A Star is Born '54
Susan and God '40
Sylvia Scarlett '35
Travels with My Aunt '72
Two-Faced Woman '41
What Price Hollywood? '32
A Woman's Face '41
The Women '39

Mark Cullingham
Cinderella '84
Dead on the Money '91
Gryphon '88

Howard Cummings
Courtship '87

Irving Cummings
Curly Top '35
Double Dynamite '51
Down Argentine Way '40
Flesh and Blood '22
Just Around the Corner '38
Little Miss Broadway '38
Louisiana Purchase '41
The Poor Little Rich Girl '36
Springtime in the Rockies '42
Vogues of 1938 '37

James Cummins
The Bone Yard '90

Richard Cunha
Frankenstein's Daughter '58
Giant from the Unknown '58
Missile to the Moon '59
She Demons '58

Curtis Cunningham
Mata Hari '85

Sean S. Cunningham
Deepstar Six '89
Friday the 13th '80
Manny's Orphans '78
The New Kids '85
Spring Break '83
A Stranger is Watching '82

Frederick Curiel
Genie of Darkness '60
The Monster Demolisher '60
Neutron and the Black Mask '61
Neutron vs. the Amazing Dr. Caronte '61
Neutron vs. the Death Robots '62

Pauline Curley
The Walloping Kid '26

Anthony Currie
The Pink Chiquitas '86

Dan Curtis
Burnt Offerings '76
Curse of the Black Widow '77
Dead of Night '77
Dracula '73
Express to Terror '79
House of Dark Shadows '70
Intruders '92
Kansas City Massacre '75
The Last Ride of the Dalton Gang '79
The Long Days of Summer '80
Melvin Purvis: G-Man '74
Mrs. R's Daughter '79
Night of Dark Shadows '71
Trilogy of Terror '75
The Turn of the Screw '74
War & Remembrance, Part 1 '88
War & Remembrance, Part 2 '89
War & Remembrance, Part 3 '88
War & Remembrance, Part 4 '88
War & Remembrance, Part 5 '88
War & Remembrance, Part 6 '88
War & Remembrance, Part 7 '88
War & Remembrance: The Final Chapter, Part 8 '89
War & Remembrance: The Final Chapter, Part 9 '89
War & Remembrance: The Final Chapter, Part 10 '89
War & Remembrance: The Final Chapter, Part 11 '89
War & Remembrance: The Final Chapter, Part 12 '89
When Every Day was the Fourth of July '78
The Winds of War '83

Douglas Curtis
The Campus Corpse '77
The Sleeping Car '90

Jack Curtis
The Flesh Eaters '64

Michael Curtiz
The Adventures of Huckleberry Finn '60
The Adventures of Robin Hood '38
Angels with Dirty Faces '38
Black Fury '35
Breath of Scandal '60
The Cabin in the Cotton '32
Captain Blood '35
Captains of the Clouds '42
Casablanca '42
The Charge of the Light Brigade '36
Comancheros '61
Dive Bomber '41
Doctor X '32
Dodge City '39
The Egyptian '54
Female '33
Flamingo Road '49
Four Daughters '38
I'll See You in My Dreams '51
Jim Thorpe: All American '51
The Kennel Murder Case '33
Kid Galahad '37
King Creole '58
Life with Father '47
Mildred Pierce '45
My Dream is Yours '49
Mystery of the Wax Museum '33
Night and Day '46
Passage to Marseilles '44
The Private Lives of Elizabeth & Essex '39
Proud Rebel '58
Santa Fe Trail '40
The Sea Hawk '40
The Sea Wolf '41
This is the Army '43
Trouble Along the Way '53
Virginia City '40
We're No Angels '55
White Christmas '54
Yankee Doodle Dandy '42
Young Man with a Horn '50

Ralph Cushman
Secret File of Hollywood '62

Rudolph Cusumano
Wild Ones on Wheels '62

Paul Czinner
As You Like It '36
Catherine the Great '34
Dreaming Lips '37

Renee Daalder
Massacre at Central High '76

Morton DaCosta
Auntie Mame '58
The Music Man '62

Dimis Dadiras
The Mediterranean in Flames '72

John Dahl
Kill Me Again '89

Bob Dahlin
Monster in the Closet '86

Reno Dakota
American Fabulous '92

Tom Daley
The Outing '87

Salvador Dali
Un Chien Andalou '28

Massimo Dallamano
A Black Veil for Lisa '68
Dorian Gray '70
Super Bitch '89

Neville D'Almedia
Lady on the Bus '78

Robert Dalva
The Black Stallion Returns '83

William Robert Daly
Uncle Tom's Cabin '14

Joe D'Amato
Buried Alive '81
Grim Reaper '81

Damiano Damiani
Amityville 2: The Possession '82
A Bullet for the General '68
Confessions of a Police Captain '72
Empty Canvas '64
The Inquiry '87
The Warning '80
The Witch '66

Charles Damic
Bomb at 10:10 '67

Mel Damski
American Dream '81
Badge of the Assassin '85
For Ladies Only '81
Happy Together '89
Legend of Walks Far Woman '82
Long Journey Back '78
Mischief '85
Murder by the Book '87
Wildcard '92
Yellowbeard '83

Anthony D'Andrea
Thrillkill '84

Lawrence Dane
Heavenly Bodies '84

Rod Daniel
K-9 '89
Like Father, Like Son '87
The Super '91
Teen Wolf '85

Georgi Daniela
Autumn Marathon '79

Godfrey Daniels
Cassie '87

Harold Daniels
House of the Black Death '65
Poor White Trash '57
Sword of Venus '53
Terror in the Haunted House '58

Marc Daniels
Planet Earth '74
Vengeance '89

Tage Danielsson
The Adventures of Picasso '80

Claude D'Anna
Salome '85

Danniel Danniel
Egg '88

Herbert Danska
Sweet Love, Bitter '67

Joe Dante
Amazon Women on the Moon '87
The 'Burbs '89
Explorers '85
Gremlins '84
Gremlins 2: The New Batch '90
Hollywood Boulevard '76
The Howling '81
Innerspace '87
Matinee '92
Piranha '78
Twilight Zone: The Movie '83

Ray Danton
Crypt of the Living Dead '73
Psychic Killer '75
Tales of the Unexpected '91

Phil D'Antoni
The Seven-Ups '73

Frank Darabont
Buried Alive '90

Joan Darling
Check is in the Mail '85
First Love '77
Hiroshima Maiden '88
Willa '79

David Darlow
Tailspin: Behind the Korean Airline Tragedy '89

Harry D'Abbadie D'Arrast
Topaze '33

Julie Dash
Daughters of the Dust '92

Jules Dassin
The Canterville Ghost '44
Circle of Two '80
A Dream of Passion '78
The Naked City '48
Never on Sunday '60
Night and the City '50
Reunion in France '42
Rififi '54
Topkapi '64
Where the Hot Wind Blows '59

Tony Zarin Dast
Cat in the Cage '68

Herschel Daugherty
The Light in the Forest '58

Darrell Davenport
Shadow Force '92

Harry Bromley Davenport
Xtro '83
Xtro 2: The Second Encounter '91

Delmer Daves
The Badlanders '58
Broken Arrow '50
Dark Passage '47
Demetrius and the Gladiators '54
Destination Tokyo '43
Drum Beat '54
The Hanging Tree '59
Hollywood Canteen '44
Jubal '56
Kings Go Forth '58
The Red House '47
Rome Adventure '62
A Summer Place '59
3:10 to Yuma '57
Treasure of the Golden Condor '53

Allan David
The Magic Fountain '61

Boaz Davidson
Dutch Treat '86
Going Bananas '88
Hospital Massacre '81
Last American Virgin '82
Salsa '88

Miguel M. Delgado
El Gendarme Desconocido '41

Sean Delgado
Alexa: A Prostitute's Own Story '88

Bill D'Elia
The Feud '90

Francis Delia
Freeway '88

Bert Deling
Dead Easy '82

Jeffrey Dell
Carlton Browne of the F.O. '59

Jeffrey Delman
Deadtime Stories '86

Nathalie Delon
Sweet Lies '88

Robert Deltano
Gun Girls '56

Rudy DeLuca
Transylvania 6-5000 '85

Dom DeLuise
Hot Stuff '80

Michael DeLuise
Almost Pregnant '91

Richard Dembo
Dangerous Moves '84

Eames Demetrios
Mind Trap '91

Tulio Demicheli
Dracula vs. Frankenstein '69
Son of Captain Blood '62

Cecil B. DeMille
The Cheat '15
Cleopatra '34
The Greatest Show on Earth '52
King of Kings '27
Madam Satan '30
Male and Female '19
The Plainsman '37
Reap the Wild Wind '42
The Road to Yesterday '25
Road to Yesterday/The Yankee Clipper '27
Samson and Delilah '50
Ten Commandments '23
The Ten Commandments '56

Jonathan Demme
Caged Heat '74
Citizens Band '77
Crazy Mama '75
Fighting Mad '76
The Last Embrace '79
Married to the Mob '88
Melvin and Howard '80
The Silence of the Lambs '91
Something Wild '86
Stop Making Sense '84
Swimming to Cambodia '87
Swing Shift '84
Who Am I This Time? '82

Ted Demme
Who's the Man? '93

Rene Demoulin
Charlie Bravo '80s

Jacques Demy
Donkey Skin '70
Dos Cruces en Danger Pass '71
Lola '61
A Slightly Pregnant Man '79
Umbrellas of Cherbourg '64

Drew Denbaum
Nickel Mountain '85

Reginald Denham
The Silent Passenger '35

Claire Denis
Chocolat '88

Jean-Pierre Denis
Field of Honor '87

Charles Dennis
Reno and the Doc '84

Pen Densham
The Kiss '88
The Zoo Gang '85

Ruggero Deodato
The Barbarians '87
Dial Help '88
House on the Edge of the Park '84
The Lone Runner '88
Phantom of Death '87

Brian DePalma
Blow Out '81
Body Double '84
The Bonfire of the Vanities '90
Carrie '76
Casualties of War '89
Dressed to Kill '80
The Fury '78
Greetings '68
Hi, Mom! '70
Home Movies '79
Obsession '76
Phantom of the Paradise '74
Raising Cain '92
Scarface '83
Sisters '73
The Untouchables '87
The Wedding Party '69
Wise Guys '86

Gerard Depardieu
Tartuffe '84

Jacques Deray
Borsalino '70
The Outside Man '73
Swimming Pool '70

John Derek
Bolero '84
Confessions of Tom Harris '72
Fantasies '73
Ghosts Can't Do It '90
Once Before I Die '65
Tarzan, the Ape Man '81

Dominique Deruddere
Wait Until Spring, Bandini '90

Hugues des Roziers
Blue Jeans '78

Caleb Deschanel
Crusoe '89
Escape Artist '82

Henri Desfontaines
Salome/Queen Elizabeth '23

James Desmond
Monterey Pop '68

Brian Desmond-Hurst
A Christmas Carol '51

Robert Deubel
Girls Night Out '83

Howard Deutch
Article 99 '92
The Great Outdoors '88
Pretty in Pink '86

Some Kind of Wonderful '87
Tales from the Crypt, Vol. 3 '90

Ross Devenish
Bleak House '85
Over Indulgence '87

Michel DeVille
La Lectrice '88
La Petite Bande '84
Peril '85

Dirk DeVilliers
Kingfisher Caper '76
Snake Dancer

David Devine
Beethoven Lives Upstairs '92

Dennis Devine
Dead Girls '90

Danny DeVito
Amazing Stories '85
Hoffa '92
Ratings Game '84
Throw Momma from the Train '87
The War of the Roses '89

Tom Dewier
Death by Dialogue '88

Peter Dews
The Taming of the Shrew '81

John Dexter
I Want What I Want '72
The Virgin Soldiers '69

Maury Dexter
Surf Party '64

Bernard Deyries
Here Come the Littles: The Movie '85

Fernando Di Leo
The Italian Connection '73
Kidnap Syndicate '76
Loaded Guns '75
Mr. Scarface '77
Slaughter Hotel '71
Violent Breed '83

Mario Di Leo
The Final Alliance '89

Victor Di Mello
Her Summer Vacation

Rino Di Silvestro
Women in Cell Block 7 '77

Jose Diaz Morales
Loyola, the Soldier Saint '52

Tom DiCillo
Johnny Suede '92

Nigel Dick
Deadly Intent '88
Private Investigations '87

Ernest R. Dickerson
Juice '92

Thorold Dickinson
The Arsenal Stadium Mystery '39
Gaslight '39
High Command '37
Hill 24 Doesn't Answer '55
Men of Two Worlds '46
The Queen of Spades '49

Lance Dickson
Hollywood Heartbreak '89

Marc Didden
Istanbul '85

Samuel Diege
Ride 'Em Cowgirl '41

Water Rustlers '39

Carlos Diegues
Bye Bye Brazil '79
Quilombo '84
Subway to the Stars '87

Baruch Dienar
They Were Ten '61

William Dieterle
The Accused '48
Boots Malone '52
The Devil & Daniel Webster '41
Elephant Walk '54
Fashions of 1934 '34
Female '33
The Hunchback of Notre Dame '39
Juarez '39
The Life of Emile Zola '37
A Midsummer Night's Dream '35
Mistress of the World '59
Omar Khayyam '57
Portrait of Jennie '48
Quick, Let's Get Married '71
Salome '53
Satan Met a Lady '36
September Affair '50
The Story of Louis Pasteur '36

Eric Dignam
Denial: The Dark Side of Passion '91

Jack Dillon
Suds '20

John Francis Dillon
Millie '31

Dennis Dimster
Mikey '92

Michael Dinner
Heaven Help Us '85
Hot to Trot! '88
Off Beat '86

Carlo DiPalma
Blonde in Black Leather '77

John Dirlam
Fatal Instinct '92

Mark DiSalle
Kickboxer '89
The Perfect Weapon '91

Denver Dixon
Fighting Cowboy '33

Ivan Dixon
The Spook Who Sat By the Door '73

Ken Dixon
Slave Girls from Beyond Infinity '87

Edward Dmytryk
Alvarez Kelly '66
Anzio '68
Back to Bataan '45
Behind the Rising Sun '43
Bluebeard '72
Broken Lance '54
The Caine Mutiny '54
The Carpetbaggers '64
Cornered '45
Crossfire '47
He is My Brother '75
The Hidden Room '49
Hitler's Children '43
The Human Factor '75
The Left Hand of God '55
Mirage '66
The Mountain '56
Murder, My Sweet '44

Mutiny '52
Raintree County '57
Seven Miles from Alcatraz/Flight from Glory '43
Shalako '68
Soldier of Fortune '55
Tender Comrade '43
Till the End of Time '46
Trail of the Hawk '37
Walk on the Wild Side '62
Warlock '59
The Young Lions '58

Tony B. Dobb
Blue Tornado '90

Frank Q. Dobbs
Uphill All the Way '85

Lawrence Dobkin
Children's Carol '80
Sixteen '72

Kevin Dobson
Demolition '77
Image of Death '77
The Mango Tree '77
Miracle in the Wilderness '91
Squizzy Taylor '84

James Dodson
Deadly Rivals '92

Donald M. Dohler
The Alien Factor '78
Deadly Neighbor '91
Fiend '83

Jacques Doillon
La Vengeance d'une Femme '89

Lou Doillon
La Puritaine '86

Martin Dolman
After the Fall of New York '85
American Tiger '89
Hands of Steel '86

Roger Donaldson
The Bounty '84
Cadillac Man '90
Cocktail '88
Marie '85
No Way Out '87
Nutcase '83
Sleeping Dogs '82
Smash Palace '82
White Sands '92

Vincent J. Donehue
Lonelyhearts '58
Peter Pan '60
Sunrise at Campobello '60

Stanley Donen
Arabesque '66
Bedazzled '68
Blame It on Rio '84
The Cary Grant Collection '90
Charade '63
Damn Yankees '58
Deep in My Heart '54
Funny Face '57
Give a Girl a Break '53
The Grass is Greener '61
Indiscreet '58
It's Always Fair Weather '55
The Little Prince '74
Love is Better Than Ever '52
Movie, Movie '78
On the Town '49
Pajama Game '57
Royal Wedding '51
Saturn 3 '80
Seven Brides for Seven Brothers '54
Singin' in the Rain '52
Two for the Road '67

Walter Doniger
Mad Bull '77

Dennis Donnelly
The Toolbox Murders '78

Tom Donnelly
Quicksilver '86

Clive Donner
Babes in Toyland '86
Charlie Chan and the Curse of
the Dragon Queen '81
Luv '67
Merlin and the Sword '85
The Nude Bomb '80
Oliver Twist '82
The Scarlet Pimpernel '82
Stealing Heaven '88
The Thief of Baghdad '78
To Catch a King '84
What's New Pussycat? '65

Richard Donner
The Goonies '85
Inside Moves '80
Ladyhawke '85
Lethal Weapon '87
Lethal Weapon 2 '89
Lethal Weapon 3 '92
Lola '69
The Omen '76
Radio Flyer '92
Scrooged '88
Superman: The Movie '78
Tales from the Crypt '89
The Toy '82

**Mary Agnes
Donoghue**
Paradise '91

Jack Donohue
Assault on a Queen '66
Babes in Toyland '61
Lucky Me '54
Watch the Birdie '50
The Yellow Cab Man '50

Martin Donovan
Apartment Zero '88
Death Dreams '92
Mad at the Moon '92

Paul Donovan
Def-Con 4 '85
George's Island '91
Norman's Awesome
Experience '88

Tom Donovan
Lovespell '79

Mark Donskoi
My Apprenticeship '39
My Childhood '38
My Universities '40

Lee Doo-yong
Silent Assassins '88

Thomas Doran
Spookies '85

Jacques Dorfman
Shadow of the Wolf '92

Robert Dornhelm
Cold Feet '89
Echo Park '86
Requiem for Dominic '91

Doris Dorrie
Me and Him '89
Men... '85

Shimon Dotan
The Finest Hour '91

**Russell S.
Doughten, Jr.**
The Hostage '67

Whitcomb's War '88

Gordon Douglas
Black Arrow '48
Broadway Limited '41
Chuka '67
The Detective '68
Dick Tracy vs. Cueball '46
The Doolins of Oklahoma '49
The Falcon in Hollywood '44
First Yank into Tokyo '45
Follow That Dream '61
Girl Rush '44
The Great Gildersleeve '43
Great Missouri Raid '51
Harlow '65
If You Knew Susie '48
In Like Flint '67
Kiss Tomorrow Goodbye '50
Lady in Cement '68
The McConnell Story '55
The Nevadan '50
Only the Valiant '50
Rio Conchos '64
Robin and the Seven Hoods
'64
Saps at Sea '40
Sincerely Yours '56
Skullduggery '70
Slaughter's Big Ripoff '73
Them! '54
They Call Me Mr. Tibbs! '70
Tony Rome '67
Up Periscope '59
Viva Knievel '77
Young at Heart '54
Zombies on Broadway '44

Kirk Douglas
Posse '75

Neil Douglas
Sinner's Blood '70

Peter Douglas
A Tiger's Tale '87

Lorenzo Doumani
Mad About You '90

**Alexander
Dovzhenko**
Arsenal '29
Earth '30
Zvenigora '28

Kathleen Dowdey
Blue Heaven '84

Robert Downey
America '86
Greaser's Palace '72
Putney Swope '69
Rented Lips '88
Too Much Sun '90
Up the Academy '80

Michael Drach
Les Violons du Bal '74

Mircea Dragan
Oil '78

Bert L. Dragin
Summer Camp Nightmare '86
Twice Dead '88

Stan Dragoti
Love at First Bite '79
The Man with One Red Shoe
'85
Mr. Mom '83
Necessary Roughness '91
She's Out of Control '89

Jim Drake
Mr. Bill's Real Life Adventures
'86
Police Academy 4: Citizens on
Patrol '87
Speed Zone '88

Oliver Drake
Battling Marshal '48
Fighting Valley '43
Mummy & Curse of the Jackal
'67
Today I Hang '42

Tom Drake
Keeper '84

Tony Drazan
Zebrahead '92

Arthur Dreifuss
Baby Face Morgan '42
Boss of Big Town '43
Double Deal '39
Mystery in Swing '40
The Payoff '43
Reg'lar Fellers '41

Fred Dresch
My Samurai '92

Jean Dreville
Seven Deadly Sins '53
Sputnik '61

Di Drew
The Right Hand Man '87
Trouble in Paradise '88

**Carl Theodor
Dreyer**
Day of Wrath '43
Gertrud '64
Leaves from Satan's Book '19
Master of the House '25
Ordet '55
The Passion of Joan of Arc
'28
Vampyr '31

Richard Driscoll
The Comic '85

Sara Driver
Sleepwalk '88

Antonio Drove
The Tunnel '89

David Drury
Defense of the Realm '85
Forever Young '85
Intrigue '90
Split Decisions '88

Mihael Dryhurst
Hard Way '80

Lee Drysdale
Leather Jackets '90

Charles S. Dubin
Cinderella '64
Drop-Out Mother '88
The Gathering: Part 2 '79
The Manions of America '81
Moving Violation '76
Murder Once Removed '71

Jay Dubin
Rap Master Ronnie '88

Jean-Claude Dubois
The Evil Below '87

Arthur Dubs
Vanishing Wilderness '73

Roger Duchonwny
Camp Cucamonga: How I
Spent My Summer
Vacation '90

Peter Duffell
Experience Preferred... But
Not Essential '83
The Far Pavilions '84
The House that Dripped Blood
'71
Inside Out '75

Letters to an Unknown Lover
'84

Dennis Dugan
Brain Donors '92
Problem Child '90

Michael Dugan
Mausoleum '83
Super Seal '77

George Dugdale
Slaughter High '86

Christian Duguay
Live Wire '92
Scanners 2: The New Order
'91
Scanners 3: The Takeover '92

John Duigan
Far East '85
Flirting '89
One Night Stand '84
Romero '89
The Winter of Our Dreams '82
The Year My Voice Broke '87

Bill Duke
The Cemetery Club '93
Deep Cover '92
Johnnie Gibson F.B.I. '87
Maximum Security '87
A Rage in Harlem '91
A Raisin in the Sun '89

Daryl Duke
Griffin and Phoenix: A Love
Story '76
Hang Tough '89
I Heard the Owl Call My Name
'73
Payday '72
The President's Plane is
Missing '71
The Silent Partner '78
Tai-Pan '86
The Thorn Birds '83

William Duke
Killing Floor '85

Germaine Dulac
Smiling Madame Beudet/The
Seashell and the
Clergyman '28

Georges Dumoulin
Nous N'Irons Plus au Bois '69
We Will Not Enter the Forest
'79

Patrick Duncan
84 Charlie Mopic '89
Live! From Death Row '92

Duwayne Dunham
Homeward Bound: The
Incredible Journey '93

Scott R. Dunlap
Irish Luck '39

Paul Dunlop
Twin Dragon Encounter '80s

Philip Dunne
Ten North Frederick '58
Wild in the Country '61

George Dunning
Yellow Submarine '68

E.A. Dupont
The Americano/Variety '25
Variety '25

Michael DuPont
Ethan '71

William Duprey
Uncaged '91

Ciro Duran
Tropical Snow '88

Fernando Duran
La Hora 24 '87

Rudy Durand
Tilt '78

John Durst
One Wish Too Many '55

David E. Durston
I Drink Your Blood '71
Stigma '73

Robert Duvall
Angelo My Love '83

Julien Duvivier
Anna Karenina '48
Captain Blackjack '51
Diabolically Yours '67
The Great Waltz '38
Little World of Don Camillo '51
Lydia '41
The Man in the Raincoat '57
Maria Chapdelaine '34
Panique '47
Pepe Le Moko '37
Poil de Carotte '31

Allan Dwan
Abroad with Two Yanks '44
Around the World '43
Brewster's Millions '45
Cattle Queen of Montana '54
Enchanted Island '58
Escape to Burma '55
The Gorilla '39
Heidi '37
Here We Go Again! '42
Hollywood Party '34
I Dream of Jeannie '52
The Iron Mask '29
Look Who's Laughing '41
Montana Belle '52
Northwest Outpost '47
Passion '54
Pearl of the South Pacific '55
Rebecca of Sunnybrook Farm
'38
The Restless Breed '58
Robin Hood '22
Sands of Iwo Jima '49
Silver Lode '54
Slightly Scarlet '56
Tennessee's Partner '55

H. Kaye Dyal
Memory of Us '74
Project: Eliminator '91

Robert Dyke
Moontrap '89

Boris Eagle
The Tormentors '80s

B. Reeves Eason
The Adventures of Rex &
Rinty '35
The Coast Patrol '25
Fighting Marines '36
Hollywood Mystery '34
The Last of the Mohicans '32
Man of the Frontier '36
Mystery Mountain '34
North of the Border '46
Red River Valley '36
Rimfire '49
Test of Donald Norton '26
Undersea Kingdom '36
Vanishing Legion '31

Walter B. Eason
Sea Hound '47

Allan Eastman
Crazy Moon '87

Ferdinand Fairfax
Nate and Hayes '83
The Rescue '88
Spymaker: The Secret Life of
Ian Fleming '90

Feliks Falk
Hero of the Year '85

Harry Falk
Abduction of St. Anne '75
Beulah Land '80
The Death Squad '73
High Desert Kill '90
The Night the City Screamed
'80
Sophisticated Gents '81

Jamaa Fanaka
Black Sister's Revenge '76
Penitentiary '79
Penitentiary 2 '82
Penitentiary 3 '87
Soul Vengeance '75

Jacques Fansten
Cross My Heart '91

James Fargo
Born to Race '88
The Enforcer '76
Every Which Way But Loose
'78
Forced Vengeance '82
Game for Vultures '86
Voyage of the Rock Aliens '87

Ernest Farino
Steel and Lace '90

W. Farkas
Prime Risk '84

Donald Farmer
Demon Queen '80s
Scream Dream '89

Anthony Farrar
Sin You Sinners '63

John Farris
Dear Dead Delilah '72

John Farrow
Back from Eternity '56
Botany Bay '53
A Bullet Is Waiting '54
Commandos Strike at Dawn
'43
Copper Canyon '50
Five Came Back '39
His Kind of Woman '51
The Saint Strikes Back '39
Saint Strikes Back: Criminal
Court '46
Sea Chase '55
Unholy Wife '57
Wake Island '42

Andre Farwagi
Boarding School '83

John Fasano
Black Roses '88
The Jitters '88
Rock 'n' Roll Nightmare '85

**Rainer Werner
Fassbinder**
Ali: Fear Eats the Soul '74
The American Soldier '70
Berlin Alexanderplatz '80
The Bitter Tears of Petra von
Kant '72
Chinese Roulette '86
Despair '79
Effi Briest '74
Fox and His Friends '75
Gods of the Plague '69
The Marriage of Maria Braun
'79

**The Merchant of Four
Seasons '71**
Mother Kusters Goes to
Heaven '76
Querelle '83
The Tin Drum '79
Veronika Voss '82

William C. Faure
Shaka Zulu '83

Neill Fearnley
Black Ice '92

Linda Feferman
Seven Minutes in Heaven '86

Xie Fei
Girl from Hunan '86

**Beda Ocampo
Feijoo**
Under the Earth '86

Felix Feist
Big Trees '52
Deluge '33
The Devil Thumbs a Ride '47
The Devil Thumbs a Ride/
Having Wonderful Crime
'47
Donovan's Brain '53
George White's Scandals '45
Guilty of Treason '50
Threat '49

Dennis Feldman
Real Men '87

Gene Feldman
Danny '79

John Feldman
Alligator Eyes '90

Marty Feldman
The Last Remake of Beau
Geste '77

Federico Fellini
Amarcord '74
And the Ship Sails On '83
Boccaccio '70 '62
City of Women '81
The Clowns '71
8 1/2 '63
Fellini Satyricon '69
Fellini's Roma '72
Ginger & Fred '86
I Vitelloni '53
Intervista '87
Juliet of the Spirits '65
La Dolce Vita '60
La Strada '54
Love in the City '53
Nights of Cabiria '57
Spirits of the Dead '68
The Swindle '55
Variety Lights '51
The White Sheik '52

Georg Fenady
Arnold '73
Terror in the Wax Museum '73

Huang Feng
Sting of the Dragon Masters
'74

Philip Fently
The Baron '88

Claude Feraldo
Trade Secrets '90s

Rene Feret
The Mystery of Alexina '86

Michael Ferguson
Glory Boys '84

Emilio Fernandez
Flor Silvestre '58

La Choca '73
Maria Candelaria '46
The Pearl '48

Abel Ferrara
Bad Lieutenant '92
Cat Chaser '90
China Girl '87
Crime Story '86
Driller Killer '74
Fear City '85
The Gladiator '86
King of New York '90
Ms. 45 '81

Romano Ferrara
Planets Against Us '61

Jeff Ferrell
Revenge of the Teenage
Vixens from Outer Space
'86

Jose Ferrer
Return to Peyton Place '61
State Fair '62

Marco Ferreri
El Cochecito '60
L'Udienza '71
Tales of Ordinary Madness
'83

Robert A. Ferretti
Fear '88

Frank Ferrin
Sabaka '55

Stan Ferris
Tulips '81

George Ferron
The Scalawag Bunch '75

Giorgio Ferroni
The Bacchantes '63
Conquest of Mycene '63
Mill of the Stone Women '60

Jacques Feyder
Carnival in Flanders '35
Crainquebille '23
The Kiss '29
Knight Without Armour '37

Leonard Fields
King Kelly of the U.S.A. '34

Michael Fields
Bright Angel '91
Noon Wine '84

Steven Fierberg
Voodoo Dawn '89

Douglas Fifthian
Touch Me Not '74

Mike Figgis
Internal Affairs '90
Liebestraum '91
Stormy Monday '88
Women & Men: Stories of
Seduction, Part 2 '91

Charles Finch
Priceless Beauty '90
Where Sleeping Dogs Lie '91

David Fincher
Alien 3 '92

Michael Findlay
Shriek of the Mutilated '74

Roberta Findlay
Blood Sisters '86
Lurkers '88
The Oracle '85
Prime Evil '88

John P. Finegan
Girls School Screamers '86

B.P. Fineman
Beauty for the Asking '39

Janace Fink
Velvet Smooth '76

Michael Fink
Black Force '75

Ken Finkleman
Airplane 2: The Sequel '82
Head Office '86

Joe Finley
Barbarian Queen 2: The
Empress Strikes Back '89

Edward Finney
King of the Stallions '42
Riot Squad '41
Silver Stallion '41

Rex Firlin
The Death of Adolf Hitler '84

Sam Firstenberg
American Ninja '85
American Ninja 2: The
Confrontation '87
American Samurai '92
Avenging Force '86
Breakin' 2: Electric Boogaloo
'84
Delta Force 3: The Killing
Game '91
My African Adventure '87
Ninja 3: The Domination '84
One More Chance '83
Revenge of the Ninja '83
Riverbend '89

Michael Firth
Heart of the Stag '84
Sylvia '86

Michael Fischa
Crack House '89
Death Spa '87
My Mom's a Werewolf '89

Max Fischer
Killing 'em Softly '85

David Fisher
Liar's Moon '82
Toy Soldiers '84

Jack Fisher
Torn Apart '89

Mary Ann Fisher
Lords of the Deep '89

Terence Fisher
Blackout '54
The Brides of Dracula '60
The Curse of Frankenstein '57
The Curse of the Werewolf
'61
Four Sided Triangle '53
Frankenstein and the Monster
from Hell '74
The Gorgon '64
The Horror of Dracula '58
The Hound of the Baskervilles
'59
Island of Terror '66
Island of the Burning Doomed
'67
Man Bait '52
The Mummy '59
Race for Life '55
Robin Hood: The Movie '55
Sherlock Holmes and the
Deadly Necklace '62
Spaceways '53
A Stolen Face '52
Sword of Sherwood Forest
'60
Three Stops to Murder '53
Unholy Four '54

Tom Fisher
Cannibal Campout '88

Bill Fishman
Tapeheads '89

Jack Fisk
Daddy's Dyin'...Who's Got the
Will? '90
Final Verdict '91
Raggedy Man '81
Violets Are Blue '86

**Christopher
Fitchett**
Blood Money '80
Fair Game '85

George Fitzmaurice
As You Desire Me '32
The Last of Mrs. Cheyney '37
Mata Hari '32
Son of the Sheik '26
Suzy '26

**James A.
Fitzpatrick**
Lady of the Lake '28

Robert S. Fiveson
The Clonus Horror '79

Paul Flaherty
Billy Crystal: Midnight Train to
Moscow '89
Clifford '93
18 Again! '88
Who's Harry Crumb? '89

Robert Flaherty
Elephant Boy '37
Louisiana Story '48
Man of Aran '34
Moana, a Romance of the
Golden Age '26
Tabu: A Story of the South
Seas '31

Dave Fleischer
Best of Betty Boop '35
Betty Boop Special Collector's
Edition, Vol. 1 '35
Gulliver's Travels '39
Hoppity Goes to Town '41

Max Fleischer
Betty Boop Cartoon Festival
'30s
Betty Boop Festival, Vol. 1
'30s
Betty Boop Festival, Vol. 2
'30s
Betty Boop Festival, Vol. 3
'30s
Betty Boop Program '30s
Betty Boop Special Collector's
Edition, Vol. 1 '35
Koko Cartoons: No. 1 '27
Max Fleischer's Documentary
Features '23
Max Fleischer's Popeye
Cartoons '39

Richard Fleischer
Amityville 3: The Demon '83
Armored Car Robbery '50
Ashanti, Land of No Mercy '79
Barabbas '62
Between Heaven and Hell '56
The Boston Strangler '68
The Clay Pigeon '49
Conan the Destroyer '84
Doctor Doolittle '67
The Don is Dead '73
Fantastic Voyage '66
Follow Me Quietly '49
The Incredible Sarah '76
Jazz Singer '80
Mandingo '75

Fleischer ▶cont.

Million Dollar Mystery '87
Mr. Majestyk '74
The New Centurions '72
The Prince and the Pauper '78
Red Sonja '85
See No Evil '71
Soylent Green '73
10 Rillington Place '71
Tora! Tora! Tora! '70
Tough Enough '87
Trapped '49
20,000 Leagues Under the
   Sea '54
The Vikings '58

Andrew Fleming
Bad Dreams '88

Edward Fleming
Topsy Turvy '84

Victor Fleming
Bombshell '33
Captains Courageous '37
Dr. Jekyll and Mr. Hyde '41
The Farmer Takes a Wife '35
Gone with the Wind '39
A Guy Named Joe '44
Hula '28
Joan of Arc '48
Mantrap '26
Reckless '35
Red Dust '32
Test Pilot '38
Tortilla Flat '42
Treasure Island '34
The Virginian '29
When the Clouds Roll By '19
The Wizard of Oz '39

Gordon Flemyng
Cloud Waltzing '87
Daleks—Invasion Earth 2150
   A.D. '66
Doctor Who and the Daleks
   '65
Philby, Burgess and MacLean:
   Spy Scandal of the Century
   '84

Rodman Flender
In the Heat of Passion '91
The Unborn '91

Theodore J. Flicker
Playmates '72
The President's Analyst '67
Soggy Bottom U.S.A. '84
Three in the Cellar '70

James T. Flocker
Ghosts That Still Walk '77
Ground Zero '88
The Secret of Navajo Cave
   '76

John Florea
Computer Wizard '77
The Invisible Strangler '76
Island of the Lost '68
Where the Eagle Flies '72
Where's Willie? '77

Isaac Florentine
Desert Kickboxer '92

John Flores
Hot Child in the City '87

Robert Florey
The Beast with Five Fingers
   '46
The Cocoanuts '29
Ex-Lady '33
Murders in the Rue Morgue
   '32
Outpost in Morocco '49

Aldo Florio
Five Giants from Texas '66

Calvin Floyd
Sleep of Death '79

Drago Floyd
Troll 2 '92

John Flynn
Best Seller '87
Defiance '79
Lock Up '89
Marilyn: The Untold Story '80
Nails '92
Rolling Thunder '77
Touched '82

Tom Flynn
Watch It '93

Helmut Foernbacher
What a Way to Die '70

Lawrence Foldes
Curse of the Living Dead '89
The Great Skycopter Rescue
   '82
Nightforce '86
Young Warriors '83

Peter Foleg
The Unseen '80

James Foley
After Dark, My Sweet '90
At Close Range '86
Glengarry Glen Ross '92
Reckless '84
Who's That Girl? '87

Peter Fonda
Hired Hand '71
Idaho Transfer '73
Wanda Nevada '79

Marcello Fondato
Immortal Bachelor '80

Allen Fong
Just Like Weather '86

Leo Fong
Hawkeye '88
24 Hours to Midnight '92

Angelino Fons
Marianela '70s

Jorge Fons
Jory '72

Lloyd Fonvielle
Gotham '88

Bryan Forbes
Better Late Than Never '83
International Velvet '78
King Rat '65
Long Ago Tomorrow '71
The Madwoman of Chaillot
   '69
The Naked Face '84
Seance on a Wet Afternoon
   '64
Whistle Down the Wind '62
The Wrong Box '66

Lewis J. Force
Night After Night After Night
   '70

Francis Ford
Custer's Last Fight '12

Greg Ford
Daffy Duck's Quackbusters
   '89

John Ford
Arrowsmith '31
Cheyenne Autumn '64
December 7th: The Movie '91

Donovan's Reef '63
Drums Along the Mohawk '39
Fort Apache '48
The Fugitive '48
The Grapes of Wrath '40
The Horse Soldiers '59
How Green was My Valley '41
How the West was Won '63
Hurricane '37
The Informer '35
Judge Priest '34
Last Hurrah '58
The Long Voyage Home '40
The Lost Patrol '34
The Man Who Shot Liberty
   Valance '62
Mary of Scotland '36
Mister Roberts '55
Mogambo '53
My Darling Clementine '46
The Quiet Man '52
Rio Grande '50
The Searchers '56
Sergeant Rutledge '60
She Wore a Yellow Ribbon '49
Stagecoach '39
Straight Shootin' '17
The Sun Shines Bright '53
They Were Expendable '45
Three Godfathers '48
Two Rode Together '61
Wagon Master '50
Wee Willie Winkie '37
What Price Glory? '52
Wings of Eagles '57
Young Mr. Lincoln '39

Philip Ford
The Inner Circle '46
The Vanishing Westerner '50

Eugene Forde
Inspector Hornleigh '39

Walter Forde
Bulldog Jack '35
The Ghost Train '41
King of the Damned '36
The Secret Four '40

Richard Foreman
Sudden Death '77

Milos Forman
Amadeus '84
The Firemen's Ball '68
Hair '79
Loves of a Blonde '65
One Flew Over the Cuckoo's
   Nest '75
Ragtime '81
Valmont '89

Tom Forman
The Fighting American '24
The Virginian '23

Rolf Forsberg
Beyond the Next Mountain
   '87

Robert Forster
Hollywood Harry '86

Bill Forsyth
Breaking In '89
Comfort and Joy '84
Gregory's Girl '80
Housekeeping '87
Local Hero '83
That Sinking Feeling '79

Ed Forsyth
Chesty Anderson USN '76
Inferno in Paradise '88
Superchick '71

Bob Fosse
All That Jazz '79
Cabaret '72

Lenny '74
Star 80 '83
Sweet Charity '69

Giles Foster
Consuming Passions '88
Dutch Girls '87
Hotel du Lac '86
Innocent Victim '90
Silas Marner '85

Jodie Foster
Little Man Tate '91

Lewis R. Foster
Crashout '55
Dakota Incident '56
The Sign of Zorro '60
Tonka '58

Norman Foster
Brighty of the Grand Canyon
   '67
Davy Crockett and the River
   Pirates '56
Davy Crockett, King of the
   Wild Frontier '55
Indian Paint '64
Journey into Fear '42
Mr. Moto's Last Warning '39
The Nine Lives of Elfego Baca
   '58
Rachel and the Stranger '48
The Sign of Zorro '60
Tell It to the Judge '49

Claude Fournier
Dan Candy's Law '73
Tales of the Klondike: The
   Scorn of Women '87

Gene Fowler
I Married a Monster from
   Outer Space '58
I Was a Teenage Werewolf
   '57
The Rebel Set '59
Showdown at Boot Hill '58

Robert Fowler
Below the Belt '80

Douglas Fowley
Macumba Love '60

Emerson Fox
Shocking Asia '75

Erika Fox
Dead Women in Lingerie '90

Marilyn Fox
Codename: Icarus '85

Wallace Fox
Bowery at Midnight '42
Bowery Blitzkrieg '41
The Corpse Vanishes '42
Ghost Rider '43
The Great Mike '44
Kid Dynamite '43
Let's Get Tough '42
Million Dollar Kid '44
'Neath Brooklyn Bridge '42
Powdersmoke Range '35
Smart Alecks '42

William A. Fraker
Legend of the Lone Ranger
   '81
Monte Walsh '70
A Reflection of Fear '72

Comedie Francaise
Le Bourgeois Gentilhomme
   '58

Gianni Franciolini
Pardon My Trunk '52

Coleman Francis
The Beast of Yucca Flats '61

Freddie Francis
The Brain '62
Craze '74
The Creeping Flesh '72
The Doctor and the Devils '85
Dr. Terror's House of Horrors
   '65
Dracula Has Risen from the
   Grave '68
The Evil of Frankenstein '64
The Ghoul '75
Girly '70
Hysteria '64
Legend of the Werewolf '75
The Skull '65
Tales from the Crypt '72
Tales That Witness Madness
   '73
They Came from Beyond
   Space '67
Torture Garden '67
The Vampire Happening '71

Karl Francis
And Nothing But the Truth '82

Pietro Francisci
Hercules '58
Hercules Unchained '59

Jess (Jesus) Franco
Angel of Death '86
Attack of the Robots '66
Bloody Moon '83
The Castle of Fu Manchu '68
Count Dracula '71
Deadly Sanctuary '68
The Diabolical Dr. Z '65
Dr. Orloff's Monster '64
Ilsa, the Wicked Warden '78
The Invisible Dead
Jack the Ripper '80
Kiss and Kill '68
The Loves of Irina '80s
99 Women '69
Revenge in the House of
   Usher '82
The Screaming Dead '72
Venus in Furs '70
Virgin Among the Living Dead
   '71

Richardo Franco
Berlin Blues '89

Georges Franju
Horror Chamber of Dr.
   Faustus '59
Judex '64

A.M. Frank
Oasis of the Zombies '82

Carol Frank
Sorority House Massacre '86

Charles Frank
Inheritance '47

Christopher Frank
Josepha '82
The Year of the Jellyfish '84

Hubert Frank
The Dolls '83
Melody in Love '78

Melvin Frank
Buona Sera, Mrs. Campbell
   '68
Court Jester '56
The Duchess and the
   Dirtwater Fox '76
The Jayhawkers '59
Li'l Abner '59
Lost and Found '79
Prisoner of Second Avenue
   '74
A Touch of Class '73
Walk Like a Man '87

Robert Frank
Candy Mountain '87

T.C. Frank
Billy Jack '71
Born Losers '67

Cyril Frankel
Devil on Horseback '54
Make Me an Offer '55
Permission To Kill '75
The Very Edge '63

John Frankenheimer
All Fall Down '62
Birdman of Alcatraz '62
Black Sunday '77
The Challenge '82
Days of Wine and Roses '58
Dead Bang '89
52 Pick-Up '86
The Fourth War '90
French Connection 2 '75
Grand Prix '66
The Holcroft Covenant '85
Horsemen '70
The Manchurian Candidate '62
99 & 44/100 Dead '74
Prophecy '79
Seven Days in May '64
The Story of a Love Story '73
The Train '65
Year of the Gun '91

Carl Franklin
Eye of the Eagle 2 '89
Full Fathom Five '90
Nowhere to Run '88
One False Move '91

Chester M. Franklin
Vanity Fair '02

Howard Franklin
The Public Eye '92

Jimmy Franklin
Ripping Yarns '75

Richard Franklin
Cloak & Dagger '84
F/X 2: The Deadly Art of Illusion '91
Link '86
Patrick '78
Psycho 2 '83
Road Games '81

Roger Franklin
Raiders of Atlantis '83

Sidney Franklin
The Barretts of Wimpole Street '34
The Forbidden City '18
The Good Earth '37
The Guardsman '31
The Primitive Lover '16
Private Lives '31
Wild Orchids '28

Harry Fraser
Aces Wild '37
Ambush Trail '46
Broadway to Cheyenne '32
Cavalcade of the West '36
Chained for Life '51
Diamond Trail '33
Enemy of the Law '45
Fighting Parson '33
From Broadway to Cheyenne '32
Frontier Fugitives '45
Galloping Dynamite '37
Ghost City '32
Ghost Town '37
Heroes of the Alamo '37
'Neath the Arizona Skies '34

Outlaw Roundup '44
Rainbow Ranch '33
Randy Rides Alone '34
Rustler's Paradise '35
The Savage Girl '32
Six Shootin' Sheriff '38
Three in the Saddle '45
The Tonto Kid '35
Wagon Trail '35
Wild Mustang '35
Wolf Dog '33

James Frawley
Assault and Matrimony '87
Big Bus '76
Fraternity Vacation '85
Great American Traffic Jam '80
Hansel and Gretel '82
The Muppet Movie '79
Spies, Lies and Naked Thighs '91

Stephen Frears
Dangerous Liaisons '88
The Grifters '90
Gumshoe '72
Hero '92
The Hit '85
My Beautiful Laundrette '86
Prick Up Your Ears '87
Saigon: Year of the Cat '87
Sammy & Rosie Get Laid '87

Riccardo Freda
Devil of the Desert Against the Son of Hercules '62
The Devil's Commandment '56
Evil's Commandment '56
The Giants of Thessaly '60
The Horrible Dr. Hichcock '62
Les Miserables '52
Maciste in Hell '60
The Mongols '60
Samson and the 7 Miracles of the World '62
Sins of Rome '54
The Witch's Curse '62

Herb Freed
Beyond Evil '80
Graduation Day '81
Haunts '77
Survival Game '87
Tomboy '85

Mark Freed
Shock 'Em Dead '90

Jerrold Freedman
Best Kept Secrets '88
Borderline '80
Family Sins '87
He Who Walks Alone '78
Legs '83
Native Son '86
Seduced '85
The Streets of L.A. '79
Thompson's Last Run '90

Robert Freedman
Goin' All the Way '82

Thornton Freeland
Accused '36
Flying Down to Rio '33
Jericho '38
Whoopee! '30

Hal Freeman
Blood Frenzy '87

Joan Freeman
Satisfaction '88
Streetwalkin' '85

Warwick Freeman
Demonstrator '71

Paul Frees
The Beatniks '60

Hugo Fregonese
Blowing Wild '54
Decameron Nights '53
Dracula vs. Frankenstein '69
Harry Black and the Tiger '58

Friz Freleng
The Best of Warner Brothers, Vol. 1 '40s
The Best of Warner Brothers, Vol. 2 '40s
Bugs & Daffy: The Wartime Cartoons '45
Bugs Bunny & Elmer Fudd Cartoon Festival '44
Bugs Bunny Cartoon Festival '44
Bugs Bunny Cartoon Festival: Little Red Riding Rabbit '43
Bugs Bunny Superstar '75
Bugs Bunny's Looney Christmas Tales '79
Bugs Bunny's 3rd Movie: 1,001 Rabbit Tales '82
Bugs Bunny's Wacky Adventures '57
Bugs vs. Elmer '53
Cartoon Classics in Color, No. 2 '40s
Cartoon Classics in Color, No. 3 '43
Cartoon Classics in Color, No. 4 '48
Cartoon Classics, No. 4: Cobweb Hotel
Cartoon Collection, No. 3: Coal Black & de Sebben Dwarfs '40s
Cartoon Moviestars: Bugs! '48
Cartoon Moviestars: Elmer! '48
Cartoon Moviestars: Porky! '47
Cartoon Parade, Vol. 1 '40s
Daffy Duck & Company '50
Daffy Duck Cartoon Festival: Ain't That Ducky '40s
Daffy Duck's Movie: Fantastic Island '83
Elmer Fudd Cartoon Festival '40s
Elmer Fudd's Comedy Capers '55
Foghorn Leghorn's Fractured Funnies '52
Just Plain Daffy '48
Looney Looney Looney Bugs Bunny Movie '81
Looney Tunes Video Show, Vol. 1
Looney Tunes Video Show, Vol. 2
Looney Tunes Video Show, Vol. 3
Looney Tunes Video Show, Vol. 4
Looney Tunes Video Show, Vol. 5
Looney Tunes Video Show, Vol. 6
Looney Tunes Video Show, Vol. 7
Porky Pig and Company '48
Porky Pig Cartoon Festival '45
Porky Pig Cartoon Festival: Tom Turk and Daffy Duck '44
Porky Pig's Screwball Comedies '52
Salute to Friz Freleng '58
Salute to Mel Blanc '58
Starring Bugs Bunny! '48

Sylvester & Tweety's Crazy Capers '61
Tweety & Sylvester '48
Warner Brothers Cartoon Festival 1 '40s
Warner Brothers Cartoon Festival 2 '40s
Warner Brothers Cartoon Festival 3 '40s
Warner Brothers Cartoon Festival 4 '40s

Harold French
The Day Will Dawn '42
Encore '52
Paris Express '53
Rob Roy—The Highland Rogue '53
Trio '50

Charles Frend
Cruel Sea '53
The Foreman Went to France '42
Johnny Frenchman '46
San Demetrio, London '47
Scott of the Antarctic '48
The Third Key '57

Karl Freund
Mad Love '35
The Mummy '32

Randall Fried
Heaven is a Playground '91

Rick Friedberg
Off the Wall '82
Pray TV '80

Richard Friedenberg
The Adventures of Frontier Fremont '75
The Deerslayer '78
Life & Times of Grizzly Adams '74

William Friedkin
The Boys in the Band '70
Brink's Job '78
Cruising '80
Deal of the Century '83
The Exorcist '73
The French Connection '71
The Guardian '90
The Night They Raided Minsky's '69
Python Wolf '88
Rampage '87
Sorcerer '77
Stalking Danger '88
To Live & Die in L.A. '85

Adam Friedman
Erotica: Fabulous Female Fantasies '86
To Sleep with a Vampire '92

Anthony Friedman
Bartleby '70

David Friedman
The Defilers '65

Ken Friedman
Made in USA '88

Richard S. Friedman
Deathmask '69
Doom Asylum '88
Phantom of the Mall: Eric's Revenge '89
Scared Stiff '87

Seymour Friedman
I'll Get You '53
Loan Shark '52

Gunther Fritsch
Stolen Identity '53

Bill Froechlich
Return to Horror High '87

Lee Frost
Chain Gang Women '72
Chrome and Hot Leather '71
Dixie Dynamite '76
Policewomen '73

Mark Frost
Storyville '92

William Fruet
Bedroom Eyes '86
Blue Monkey '87
Death Weekend '76
Funeral Home '82
Killer Party '86
Search and Destroy '81
Spasms '82
Striking Back '81
Wedding in White '72

E. Max Frye
Amos and Andrew '93

Robert Fuest
The Abominable Dr. Phibes '71
And Soon the Darkness '70
Aphrodite '83
Devil's Rain '75
Doctor Phibes Rises Again '72
The Final Programme '73
Island '77
A Movie Star's Daughter '79
Revenge of the Stepford Wives '80
Wuthering Heights '70

Kinji Fukasaku
Black Lizard '68
The Green Slime '68
Samurai Reincarnation '81
Tora! Tora! Tora! '70
Virus '82

Jun Fukuda
Godzilla on Monster Island '72
Godzilla vs. Gigan '72
Godzilla vs. Megalon '76
Godzilla vs. the Cosmic Monster '74
Godzilla vs. the Sea Monster '66
The Secret of the Telegian '61
Son of Godzilla '66

Lucio Fulci
The Black Cat '81
Black Cat '86
Challenge to White Fang '86
Conquest '83
Contraband '86
Dangerous Obsession '88
Gates of Hell '83
The House by the Cemetery '83
Manhattan Baby '82
The New Gladiators '87
New York Ripper '82
The Psychic '78
Zombie '80

Fleming Fuller
Prey of the Chameleon '91

Louis Fuller
Seven Doors of Death '82

Samuel Fuller
Baron of Arizona '51
The Big Red One '80
China Gate '57
I Shot Jesse James '49
The Meanest Men in the West '76

Robert Ginty
Bounty Hunters '89
Vietnam, Texas '90

Christian Gion
Here Comes Santa Claus '84

Jose Giovanni
Boomerang '76
Gypsy '75

Buddy Giovnazzo
Combat Shock '84

Bob Giraldi
Club Med '83
Hiding Out '87

Franco Giraldi
A Minute to Pray, A Second to Die '67

Andre Girard
Qui Etes Vous, Mr. Sorge? '61

Bernard Girard
Dead Heat on a Merry-Go-Round '66
Hard Frame '70
Little Moon & Jud McGraw '78
Mind Snatchers '72
A Name for Evil '70

Michael Paul Girard
Getting Lucky '89

Bernard Giraudeau
Gone with the West '72

William Girdler
Asylum of Satan '72
Day of the Animals '77
Grizzly '76
The Manitou '78
Sheba, Baby '75
Three on a Meathook '72

Francis Girod
The Elegant Criminal '92
Infernal Trio '74
L'Etat Sauvage '78

Paul Michael Glaser
Amazing Stories, Book 4 '85
The Amazons '84
Band of the Hand '86
The Cutting Edge '92
The Running Man '87

Lesli Linka Glatter
Amazing Stories, Book 3 '86
Amazing Stories, Book 5 '85
Into the Homeland '87

Michie Gleason
Summer Heat '87

John Glen
Aces: Iron Eagle 3 '92
Christopher Columbus: The Discovery '92
For Your Eyes Only '81
License to Kill '89
The Living Daylights '87
Octopussy '83
A View to a Kill '85

John Glenister
After Julius '78

Bert Glennon
Paradise Island '30
South of Santa Fe '32

Peter Glenville
Becket '64
The Comedians '67
The Prisoner '55
Summer and Smoke '61

James Glickenhaus
Exterminator '80

McBain '91
Protector '85
Shakedown '88
The Soldier '82

Paul Glickler
The Cheerleaders '72
Running Scared '79

Arne Glimcher
The Mambo Kings '92

Greg Glionna
Meet the Parents '91

Wolfgang Gluck
'38: Vienna Before the Fall '88

Tom Gniazdowski
Death Collector '89

Constantine S. Gochis
The Redeemer '76

Jean-Luc Godard
Alphaville '65
Aria '88
Band of Outsiders '64
Breathless '59
Contempt '64
First Name: Carmen '83
France/Tour/Detour/Deux/Enfants '78
Godard/Truffaut Shorts '58
Hail Mary '85
The Joy of Knowledge '65
King Lear '87
Les Carabiniers '63
A Married Woman '65
Masculine Feminine '66
My Life to Live '62
Nouvelle Vague '90
Oldest Profession '67
Pierrot le Fou '65
Scenario du Film Passion '82
Six Fois Deux/Sur et Sous la Communication '76
Soft and Hard '85
Sympathy for the Devil '70
Weekend '67
A Woman is a Woman '60

Gary Goddard
Masters of the Universe '87

Jim Goddard
The Impossible Spy '87
Reilly: Ace of Spies '87
Shanghai Surprise '86
A Tale of Two Cities '80

Peter Godfrey
Christmas in Connecticut '45
Escape Me Never '47
The Two Mrs. Carrolls '47

Jill Godmilow
Waiting for the Moon '87

Alex E. Goiten
Cheerleaders' Beach Party '77
Cherry Hill High '76

Menahem Golan
The Apple '80
Delta Force '86
Diamonds '72
Enter the Ninja '81
Escape to the Sun '72
Hanna's War '88
Hit the Dutchman '92
Lepke '75
Lupo '70
Mack the Knife '89
The Magician of Lublin '79
Operation Thunderbolt '77
Over the Brooklyn Bridge '83
Over the Top '86
Silent Victim '92

Greg Gold
House of the Rising Sun '87

Jack Gold
Catholics '73
Escape from Sobibor '87
Little Lord Fauntleroy '80
Man Friday '76
The Medusa Touch '78
Murrow '85
The Naked Civil Servant '75
Praying Mantis '83
Roboman '75
The Rose and the Jackal '90
Sakharov '84
The Tenth Man '88

Myron G. Gold
Frankenstein's Great Aunt Tillie '83

Willis Goldbeck
Between Two Women '86
Love Laughs at Andy Hardy '46

Dan Goldberg
Feds '88

Gary David Goldberg
Dad '89

Mark Goldblatt
Dead Heat '88
The Punisher '90

Dan Golden
Naked Obsession '91

John Golden
Fat Guy Goes Nutzoid '86

Murray Golden
Haunting of Harrington House '82

Sidney Goldin
East and West '23
His Wife's Lover '31
Uncle Moses '32

Paul Golding
Pulse '88

Jim Goldman
Desert Warrior '88

Martin Goldman
Dark August '76

Stuart Goldman
Senior Week '88

John Goldschmidt
Crime of Honor '85
She'll Be Wearing Pink Pajamas '84

Allan Goldstein
Common Bonds '91
The Dining Room '86
The House of Dies Drear '88
Outside Chance of Maximillian Glick '88
The Phone Call '89
True West '86

Amy Goldstein
The Silencer '92

Scott Goldstein
Ambition '91
Walls of Glass '85

James Goldstone
Brother John '70
Calamity Jane '82
Cry Panic '74
Eric '75
Kent State '81
Rita Hayworth: The Love Goddess '83

Rollercoaster '77
Swashbuckler '76
They Only Kill Their Masters '72
Things in Their Season '74
When Time Ran Out '80
Winning '69

Bob Goldthwait
Shakes the Clown '92

Steve Gomer
Sweet Lorraine '87

Nick Gomez
Laws of Gravity '92

Vasilii Goncharov
Early Russian Cinema, Vol. 2: Folklore & Legend '12
Early Russian Cinema, Vol. 6: Class Distinctions '14

Regelio A. Gonzalez, Jr.
The Oval Portrait '88

Servando Gonzalez
The Fool Killer '65

Gregory Goodell
Human Experiments '79

Saul Goodkind
Buck Rogers Conquers the Universe '39

Fred Goodwin
Curse 2: The Bite '88

Leslie Goodwins
Day the Bookies Wept '39
Mexican Spitfire at Sea '42
Pop Always Pays '40

Bert I. Gordon
The Amazing Colossal Man '57
Beginning of the End '57
The Big Bet '85
Cyclops '56
Earth vs. the Spider '58
Empire of the Ants '77
Food of the Gods '76
The Mad Bomber '72
The Magic Sword '62
Picture Mommy Dead '66
Satan's Princess '90
Tormented '60
Village of the Giants '65
The War of the Colossal Beast '58
The Witching '72

Bette Gordon
Variety '83

Bryan Gordon
Career Opportunities '91

Keith Gordon
The Chocolate War '88
A Midnight Clear '92

Michael Gordon
Cyrano de Bergerac '50
For Love or Money '63
Pillow Talk '59

Robert Gordon
The Gatling Gun '72
It Came from Beneath the Sea '55

Steve Gordon
Arthur '81

Stuart Gordon
Dolls '87
From Beyond '86
The Pit and Pendulum '91
The Re-Animator '85
Robot Jox '89

Berry Gordy
Mahogany '75

Serif Goren
Yol '82

Claude Goretta
The Lacemaker '77

Vladimir Gorikker
The Tsar's Bride '66

Charles Gormley
The Gospel According to Vic '87

Michael Gornick
Creepshow 2 '87

Morleen Gorris
Broken Mirrors '85
Question of Silence '83

Hideo Gosha
Hunter in the Dark '80
The Wolves '82

Jurgen Goslar
Albino '76
Slavers '77

Peter Gothar
Time Stands Still '82

Toshio Goto
Forest of Little Bear '79

Carl Gottlieb
Amazon Women on the Moon '87
Caveman '81

Franz Gottlieb
The Black Abbot '63
Curse of the Yellow Snake '63
The Phantom of Soho '64

Lisa Gottlieb
Just One of the Guys '85

Michael Gottlieb
Mannequin '87
Mr. Nanny '93

Robert Gottschalk
Dangerous Charter '62

Siggi Gotz
Summer Night Fever '79

Heywood Gould
One Good Cop '91

Alfred Goulding
A Chump at Oxford '40
Dick Barton, Special Agent '48

Edmund Goulding
Dark Victory '39
Dawn Patrol '38
Forever and a Day '43
Grand Hotel '32
The Great Lie '41
The Old Maid '39
The Razor's Edge '46
Reaching for the Moon '31
That Certain Woman '37
We're Not Married '52

Richard Governor
Ghost Town '88

Bruce Gowers
Eddie Murphy "Delirious" '83

William Grace
Tomb of Torture '65

Marc Gracie
A Kink in the Picasso '90

Roger Graef
Secret Policeman's Private Parts '81

Nikolai Gubenko
Orphans '83

Robert Guenette
Here's Looking at You, Warner Bros. '93

James W. Guercio
Electra Glide in Blue '73

Ruy Guerra
Erendira '83
The Fable of the Beautiful Pigeon Fancier '88
Opera do Malandro '87

Juan Guerreo
Narda or The Summer '76

Romolo Guerrieri
The Final Executioner '83

Mino Guerrini
Mines of Kilimanjaro '87

Christopher Guest
The Big Picture '89

Cliff Guest
Disturbance '89

Robert Guest
Fatal Confinement '64

Val Guest
Carry On Admiral '57
Casino Royale '67
The Day the Earth Caught Fire '62
Just William's Luck '47
Killer Force '75
Men of Sherwood Forest '57
Quatermass 2 '57
The Quatermass Experiment '56
The Runaway Bus '54
Up the Creek '58
When Dinosaurs Ruled the Earth '70

John Guillermin
The Blue Max '66
The Bridge at Remagen '69
Crossover '82
Death on the Nile '78
El Condor '70
Guns at Batasi '64
King Kong '76
King Kong Lives '86
Never Let Go '60
Sheena '84
The Towering Inferno '74
The Tracker '88
Waltz of the Toreadors '62

Fred Guiol
Mr. Walkie Talkie '52
Tanks a Million '41

Sacha Guitry
Napoleon '55

Yilmaz Guney
Baba '73
The Wall '83

Bill Gunn
Black Vampire '73

Gilbert Gunn
The Cosmic Monsters '58

Hrafn Gunnlaugsson
Revenge of the Barbarians '85

Tyrone Guthrie
Oedipus Rex '57

Nathaniel Gutman
Deadline '87

Andre Guttfreund
Femme Fatale '90

Amos Guttman
Drifting '82

Claudio Guzman
Antonio '73
The Hostage Tower '80
Willa '79

Stephen Gyllenhaal
The Abduction of Kari Swenson '87
Certain Fury '85
Killing in a Small Town '90
Paris Trout '91
Promised a Miracle '88
Question of Faith '93
Waterland '92

Imre Gyongyossy
The Revolt of Job '84

Charles Haas
Girls' Town '59
Platinum High School '60

Herve Hachuel
The Last of Philip Banter '87

Taylor Hackford
Against All Odds '84
Bound by Honor '93
Chuck Berry: Hail! Hail! Rock 'n' Roll '87
Everybody's All American '88
Idolmaker '80
An Officer and a Gentleman '82
White Nights '85

Rolf Haedrich
Among the Cinders '83

Petra Hafter
A Demon in My View '92

Ross Hagen
B.O.R.N. '88
The Glove '78

Mark Haggard
The First Nudie Musical '75

Piers Haggard
The Blood on Satan's Claw '71
The Fiendish Plot of Dr. Fu Manchu '80
Fulfillment '89
Quatermass Conclusion '79
A Summer Story '88
Venom '81

Larry Hagman
Son of Blob '72

Stuart Hagmann
The Strawberry Statement '70
Tarantulas: The Deadly Cargo '77

Steven Hahn
Starchaser: The Legend of Orin '85

Weng Yao Hai
Crack Shadow Boxers '70s

Fred Haines
Steppenwolf '74

Randa Haines
Children of a Lesser God '86
The Doctor '91

Richard W. Haines
Alien Space Avenger '91
Class of Nuke 'Em High '86
Splatter University '84

John Halas
Animal Farm '55

Don Haldane
Nikki, the Wild Dog of the North '61
The Reincarnate '71

Alan Hale, Jr.
Risky Business '28

Billy Hale
Harem '86
The Murder of Mary Phagan '87
Red Alert '77
S.O.S. Titanic '79

Sonnie Hale
Gangway '37
Sailing Along '38

William Hale
Murder in Texas '81
One Shoe Makes It Murder '82
Stalk the Wild Child '76

Jack Haley, Jr.
The Love Machine '71
That's Dancing! '85
That's Entertainment '74

H.B. Halicki
Deadline Auto Theft '83
Gone in 60 Seconds '74
The Junkman '82

Alexander Hall
Because You're Mine '52
Doctor Takes a Wife '40
Down to Earth '47
Forever Darling '56
The Great Lover '49
Here Comes Mr. Jordan '41
I Am the Law '38
Little Miss Marker '34

Godfrey Hall
Honor and Glory '92

Ivan Hall
Funeral for an Assassin '77
Kill and Kill Again '81
Kill or Be Killed '80

Jon Hall
The Beach Girls and the Monster '65

Kenneth J. Hall
Evil Spawn '87
Ghost Writer '89

Peter Hall
A Midsummer Night's Dream '68

Daniel Haller
Buck Rogers in the 25th Century '79
Devil's Angels '67
Die, Monster, Die! '65
The Dunwich Horror '70
Follow That Car '80
Margin for Murder '81
Paddy '70

Todd Hallowell
Love or Money? '88

Lasse Hallstrom
My Life as a Dog '85
Once Around '91

Victor Halperin
Buried Alive '39
I Conquer the Sea '36
Party Girls '29
Revolt of the Zombies '36
Torture Ship '39
The White Zombie '32

Glenda Hambly
Fran '85

Robert Hamer
Dead of Night '45
The Detective '54
Kind Hearts and Coronets '49
Pink Strings and Sealing Wax '45
To Paris with Love '55

David Hamilton
Bilitis '77

Guy Hamilton
Battle of Britain '69
The Colditz Story '55
The Devil's Disciple '59
Diamonds are Forever '71
Evil Under the Sun '82
Force 10 from Navarone '78
Funeral in Berlin '66
Goldfinger '64
Live and Let Die '73
The Man with the Golden Gun '74
The Mirror Crack'd '80
Remo Williams: The Adventure Begins '85

Strathford Hamilton
Betrayal of the Dove '92
Blueberry Hill '88
Diving In '90

Robert Hammer
Don't Answer the Phone '80

Peter Hammond
The Dark Angel '91

Robert Hampton
The Ghost '63
The Horrible Dr. Hichcock '62

Victor Hanbury
The Avenging Hand '43
Hotel Reserve '44

John Hancock
Bang the Drum Slowly '73
California Dreaming '79
Let's Scare Jessica to Death '71
Prancer '89
Steal the Sky '88
Weeds '87

David Hand
Bambi '42
Snow White and the Seven Dwarfs '37

Richard Handford
Second Chance '80

Alan Handley
Alice Through the Looking Glass '66

Ken Handley
Delivery Boys '84

Susumu Hani
Nanami, First Love '68
She and He '63

William Hanna
Hey There, It's Yogi Bear '64
The Jetsons: Movie '90

Ken Hannam
The Assassination Run '80
Sunday Too Far Away '74

Brian Hannant
The Time Guardian '87

Izhak Hanooka
Red Nights '87

Marion Hansel
Dust '85

Ed Hansen
The Bikini Car Wash Company '90
Party Favors '89
Party Plane '90
Takin' It All Off '87

Rolf Hansen
The Devil in Silk '56

Curtis Hanson
The Arousers '70
Bad Influence '90
The Bedroom Window '87
The Children of Times Square '86
The Hand that Rocks the Cradle '92
Little Dragons '80
Losin' It '82

John Hanson
Northern Lights '79
Wildrose '85

Tom Hanson
The Zodiac Killer '71

Richard Harbinger
T-Bird Gang '59

Cedric Hardwicke
Forever and a Day '43

Joseph Hardy
Love's Savage Fury '79
Return Engagement '78
To Love Again '80
Users '78

Robin Hardy
The Fantasist '89
The Wicker Man '75

Rod Hardy
Sara Dane '81
Thirst '87
Under Capricorn '82

David Hare
Strapless '90
Wetherby '85

Dean Hargrove
Dear Detective '78

Veit Harlan
Jud Suess '40
Kolberg '45

Renny Harlin
The Adventures of Ford Fairlane '90
Born American '86
Cliffhanger '93
Die Hard 2: Die Harder '90
A Nightmare on Elm Street 4: Dream Master '88
Prison '88

John Harlow
Appointment with Crime '45
Candles at Nine '44
Meet Sexton Blake '44
Spellbound '41
While I Live '47

Robert Harmon
Hitcher '85
Nowhere to Run '93

Curtis Harrington
The Dead Don't Die '75
Devil Dog: The Hound of Hell '78
The Killing Kind '73
Night Tide '63
Planet of Blood '66
Ruby '77
What's the Matter with Helen? '71
Who Slew Auntie Roo? '71

Daniel Boone '34
Hollywood Stadium Mystery '38
In Old Santa Fe '34
Mystery Ranch '34
Renegade Ranger/Scarlet River '38

Leslie Howard
Pimpernel Smith '42
Pygmalion '38
Spitfire '42

Paul Howard
Night Terror '89

Ron Howard
Backdraft '91
Cotton Candy '82
Far and Away '92
Grand Theft Auto '77
Gung Ho '85
Night Shift '82
Parenthood '89
Splash '84
Willow '88

William K. Howard
Back Door to Heaven '39
Fire Over England '37
Johnny Come Lately '43
White Gold '28

John Howley
Happily Ever After '93

Frank Howson
The Hunting '92

Harry Hoyt
The Lost World '25
The Return of Boston Blackie '27

Talun Hsu
Witchcraft 5: Dance with the Devil '92

VV Dachin Hsu
Pale Blood '91

Hua-Shan
Infra-Man '76

Daniel Hubenbecker
Wardogs '87

Jean-Loup Hubert
Le Grand Chemin '87
Next Year If All Goes Well '83

Faith Hubley
The Cosmic Eye '71

John Huckert
The Passing '88

Reginald Hudlin
Boomerang '92
House Party '90

Gary Hudson
Thunder Run '86

Hugh Hudson
Chariots of Fire '81
Greystoke: The Legend of Tarzan, Lord of the Apes '84
Lost Angels '89
Revolution '85

P.J. Huemer
Kiss Daddy Goodnight '87

Mark Huestis
Men in Love '90

Roy Huggins
Hangman's Knot '52

R. John Hugh
Deadly Encounter '78

The Meal '75
Naked in the Sun '57
Yellowneck '55

David Hughes
Missing Link '88

Howard Hughes
Hell's Angels '30
The Outlaw '43
Power '28

John Hughes
The Breakfast Club '85
Curly Sue '91
Ferris Bueller's Day Off '86
Home Alone '90
Home Alone 2: Lost in New York '92
Planes, Trains & Automobiles '87
She's Having a Baby '88
Sixteen Candles '84
Uncle Buck '89
Weird Science '85

Ken Hughes
Arrivederci, Baby! '66
The Atomic Man '56
Casino Royale '67
Chitty Chitty Bang Bang '68
Cromwell '70
Heat Wave '54
Internecine Project '73
The Long Haul '57
Night School '81
Of Human Bondage '64
Oh, Alfie '75
Sextette '78

Robert C. Hughes
Down the Drain '89
Hunter's Blood '87
Memorial Valley Massacre '88

Terry Hughes
The Butcher's Wife '91
For Love or Money '84
Monty Python Live at the Hollywood Bowl '82
Ripping Yarns '75
Sunset Limousine '83

Ann Hui
Song of the Exile '90

Don Hulette
Breaker! Breaker! '77
Great Ride '78

Steven A. Hull
Devil Wears White '86

H. Bruce Humberstone
Charlie Chan at the Opera '36
The Crooked Circle '32
Happy Go Lovely '51
I Wake Up Screaming '41
Pin-Up Girl '44
Strangers of the Evening '32
Sun Valley Serenade '41
Tarzan and the Trappers '58
Ten Wanted Men '54
To the Shores of Tripoli '42
Wonder Man '45

Humphrey Humbert
Ghosthouse '88

Chieng Hung
Tough Guy '70s

Hsu Tseng Hung
Invincible Sword '78

David Hunt
Triple Impact '92

Edward Hunt
Alien Warrior '85
Bloody Birthday '80
The Brain '88
Starship Invasions '77

Paul Hunt
The Clones '73
The Great Gundown '75
Twisted Nightmare '87

Peter Hunt
The Adventures of Huckleberry Finn '84
The Adventures of Huckleberry Finn '85
Assassination '87
Death Hunt '81
Gulliver's Travels '77
Hyper-Sapien: People from Another Star '86
It Came Upon a Midnight Clear '84
The Mysterious Stranger '82
On Her Majesty's Secret Service '69
1776 '72
Shout at the Devil '76
Skeezer '82
Smart-Aleck Kill '85
Wild Geese 2 '85

Max (Massimo Pupillo) Hunter
The Bloody Pit of Horror '65

T. Hayes Hunter
The Ghoul '34

Tim Hunter
Lies of the Twins '91
Paint It Black '89
River's Edge '87
Sylvester '85
Tex '82

Lawrence Huntington
The Franchise Affair '52
Man on the Run '49
Tower of Terror '42
Vulture '67

Caroline Huppert
Sincerely Charlotte '86

Brian Desmond Hurst
Dangerous Moonlight '41
The Gay Lady '49
The Lion Has Wings '40
Malta Story '53
Playboy of the Western World '62
Simba '55

William T. Hurtz
Little Nemo: Adventures in Slumberland '92

Harry Hurwitz
The Projectionist '71
Rosebud Beach Hotel '85
Safari 3000 '82
That's Adequate '90

Waris Hussein
And Baby Makes Six '79
Arch of Triumph '85
Callie and Son '81
Coming Out of the Ice '82
Divorce His, Divorce Hers '72
Edward and Mrs. Simpson '80
The Henderson Monster '80
Intimate Contact '87
Little Gloria...Happy at Last '84
Melody '71
Onassis '88

The Possession of Joel Delaney '72
Princess Daisy '83
Quackser Fortune Has a Cousin in the Bronx '70
Switched at Birth '91
When the Bough Breaks '86

Danny Huston
Becoming Colette '92
Mr. North '88

Jimmy Huston
Death Driver '78
Final Exam '81
My Best Friend Is a Vampire '88

John Huston
Across the Pacific '42
The African Queen '51
Annie '82
The Asphalt Jungle '50
Barbarian and the Geisha '58
Beat the Devil '53
The Bible...In the Beginning '66
Casino Royale '67
The Dead '87
Fat City '72
In This Our Life '42
Independence '76
Life & Times of Judge Roy Bean '72
The List of Adrian Messenger '63
Mackintosh Man '73
The Maltese Falcon '41
The Man Who Would Be King '75
The Misfits '61
Moby Dick '56
Moulin Rouge '52
The Night of the Iguana '64
Phobia '80
Prizzi's Honor '85
The Red Badge of Courage '51
Reflections in a Golden Eye '67
Treasure of the Sierra Madre '48
Under the Volcano '84
The Unforgiven '60
Victory '81
Wise Blood '79

Zoltan Huszarik
Sinbad '71

Charles Hutchinson
Found Alive '34
Phantom Patrol '36

Harold Huth
Night Beat '48

Brian G. Hutton
The First Deadly Sin '80
High Road to China '83
Kelly's Heroes '70
Night Watch '72
Where Eagles Dare '68
X, Y & Zee '72

Robert Hutton
The Slime People '63

Willard Huyck
Best Defense '84
French Postcards '79
Howard the Duck '86
Messiah of Evil '74

Chen Che Hwa
Young Dragons: The Kung Fu Kids 2 '89

Jacky Hwong
Ninja vs. the Shaolin '84

Nessa Hyams
Leader of the Band '87

Peter Hyams
Amazing Stories, Book 3 '86
Busting '74
Capricorn One '78
Death Target '83
Hanover Street '79
Narrow Margin '90
Outland '81
The Presidio '88
Running Scared '86
The Star Chamber '83
Stay Tuned '92
2010: The Year We Make Contact '84

Chang Shinn I
Snake in the Eagle's Shadow 2 '83

Juan Ibanez
Dance of Death '69
The Fear Chamber '68
House of Evil '68
The Sinister Invasion '68

Leon Ichaso
Crossover Dreams '85
El Super '79
The Fear Inside '92
Power, Passion & Murder '83
The Take '90

Kon Ichikawa
The Burmese Harp '56
Fires on the Plain '59
The Makioka Sisters '83
Odd Obsession '60
Revenge of a Kabuki Actor '63
Tokyo Olympiad '66

Eric Idle
All You Need Is Cash '78
The Tale of the Frog Prince '83

Miguel Iglesias
The Sword of El Cid '62

Kazuo Ikehiro
Zatoichi: Master Ichi and a Chest of Gold '64

Shohei Imamura
The Ballad of Narayama '83
Black Rain '88
Eijanaika '81
The Insect Woman '63
The Pornographers '66
Vengeance Is Mine '79

Shmuel Imberman
I Don't Give a Damn '88

Markus Imhoof
The Boat is Full '81

Hiroshi Inagaki
Kojiro '67
Rikisha-Man '58
Samurai 1: Musashi Miyamoto '55
Samurai 2: Duel at Ichijoji Temple '55
Samurai 3: Duel at Ganryu Island '56

Thomas Ince
Civilization '16
The Three Musketeers '16

Franco Indovina
Catch as Catch Can '68
Oldest Profession '67

Lloyd Ingraham
American Aristocracy '17
Eyes of Julia Deep '18

Rex Ingram
The Four Horsemen of the
Apocalypse '21

Boris Ingster
The Judge Steps Out '49
Stranger on the Third Floor
'40

**J. Christian
Ingvordsen**
Comrades in Arms '91
Covert Action '88
Firehouse '87
Hangmen '87
Mob War '88
Search and Destroy '88

Markus Innocenti
Murder Story '89

John Ireland
The Fast and the Furious '54

O'Dale Ireland
Date Bait '60
High School Caesar '56

John Irvin
Champions '84
The Dogs of War '81
Eminent Domain '91
Ghost Story '81
Hamburger Hill '87
Haunted: The Ferryman '74
Next of Kin '89
Raw Deal '86
Robin Hood '91
Turtle Diary '86

Sam Irvin
Guilty as Charged '92

Kevin Irvine
Greenstone '85

David Irving
Cannon Movie Tales: Sleeping
Beauty '89
Cannon Movie Tales: The
Emperor's New Clothes '89
C.H.U.D. 2: Bud the Chud '89
Goodbye Cruel World '82
Night of the Cyclone '90
Rumpelstiltskin '82
Rumpelstiltskin '86

Richard Irving
The Art of Crime '75
Columbo: Prescription Murder
'67
The Jesse Owens Story '84

James Isaac
The Horror Show '89

Ronnie Isaacs
Warriors from Hell '90

Antonio Isasi
Ricco '74
Vengeance '74

Robert Iscove
The Lawrenceville Stories
'80s
The Little Mermaid '84
Mission of the Shark '91
Puss 'n Boots '84

Gerald I. Isenberg
Seizure: The Story of Kathy
Morris '82

Wayne Isham
For Those About to Rock:
Monsters in Moscow '91

Neal Israel
Americathon '79
Bachelor Party '84
Breaking the Rules '92

'Combat Academy '86
Moving Violations '85
Tunnelvision '76

Peter Israelson
Side Out '90

Juzo Itami
The Funeral '84
Tampopo '86
A Taxing Woman '87
A Taxing Woman Returns '88

James Ivory
Autobiography of a Princess
'75
Bombay Talkie '70
The Bostonians '84
The Europeans '79
Heat and Dust '82
The Householder '63
Howard's End '92
Hullabaloo Over Georgie &
Bonnie's Pictures '78
Jane Austen in Manhattan '80
Maurice '87
Mr. & Mrs. Bridge '91
Quartet '81
A Room with a View '86
Roseland '77
Savages '72
Shakespeare Wallah '65
Slaves of New York '89
Wild Party '74

Arnaldo Jabor
I Love You '81

Fred Jackman
No Man's Law '21

Donald G. Jackson
The Demon Lover '77
Roller Blade '85

Douglas Jackson
Whispers '89

George Jackson
House Party 2: The Pajama
Jam '91

Horace Jackson
The Bus Is Coming '72

Jalil Jackson
Lady Terminator '89

Larry Jackson
Bugs Bunny Superstar '75

Lewis Jackson
Terror in Toyland '85

Mick Jackson
The Bodyguard '92
Chattahoochee '89
L.A. Story '91
Threads '85
Yuri Nosenko, KGB '86

Mike Jackson
Blood Tracks '86

Pat Jackson
Encore '52
King Arthur, the Young
Warlord '75
What a Carve-Up! '62

Peter Jackson
Bad Taste '88

Wilfred Jackson
Cinderella '50

Harry Jacobs
Rebel High '88

John Jacobs
Rocket to the Moon '86

Werner Jacobs
Heidi '65

Irving Jacoby
Snow Treasure '67

Joseph Jacoby
Great Bank Hoax '78
Hurry Up or I'll Be Thirty '73

Gualtiero Jacopetti
Mondo Cane '63
Mondo Cane 2 '64

Just Jaeckin
Emmanuelle '74
The French Woman '79
Lady Chatterley's Lover '81
The Perils of Gwendoline '84
The Story of O '75

Stanley R. Jaffe
Without a Trace '83

Henry Jaglom
Always '85
Can She Bake a Cherry Pie?
'83
Eating '90
New Year's Day '89
Sitting Ducks '80
Someone to Love '87
Tracks '76

Sam Jaimes
Good Grief, Charlie Brown '83
Happy New Year, Charlie
Brown '82

Patrick Jamain
Honeymoon '87

Alan James
Fargo Express '32
Lucky Terror '36
Phantom Thunderbolt '33
Red Barry '38

Bob James
Alien Seed '89

Jerry Jameson
The Bat People '74
Cowboy & the Ballerina '84
Dirt Gang '71
Fire and Rain '89
High Noon: Part 2 '80
Hotline '82
Hurricane '74
Killing at Hell's Gate '81
Raise the Titanic '80
Sniper '75
Starflight One '83
Terror on the 40th Floor '74

Miklos Jancso
Hungarian Rhapsody '78
The Red and the White '68
The Round Up '66

Gerhard Janda
Tea For Three '84

Zoran Janjic
A Connecticut Yankee in King
Arthur's Court '70

Annabel Jankel
D.O.A. '88
Super Mario Bros. '93

Stole Jankovic
Hell River '75

Victor Janos
Last House on Dead End
Street '77

Christian Jaque
Legend of Frenchie King '71

Derek Jarman
Aria '88
Caravaggio '86
Edward II '92
The Last of England '87

Sebastiane '79

Jim Jarmusch
Down by Law '86
Mystery Train '89
Night on Earth '91
Stranger than Paradise '84

Charles Jarrott
The Amateur '82
Boy in Blue '86
Condorman '81
The Dove '74
The Last Flight of Noah's Ark
'80
The Littlest Horse Thieves '76
Lucy and Desi: Before the
Laughter '91
Night of the Fox '90
The Other Side of Midnight
'77
Poor Little Rich Girl: The
Barbara Hutton Story '87
Strange Case of Dr. Jekyll &
Mr. Hyde '68
The Woman He Loved '88

Vojtech Jasny
All My Good Countrymen '68
The Great Land of Small '86

Leigh Jason
Bride Walks Out '36
The Choppers '61
High Gear '33
Lady for a Night '42
Lost Honeymoon '47
Mad Miss Manton '38
Out of the Blue '47
That Girl from Paris '36

Will Jason
Everybody's Dancin' '50

Roland S. Jefferson
Perfume '91

Tom Jeffrey
The Odd Angry Shot '79

Lionel Jeffries
Amazing Mr. Blunden '72
Railway Children '70
Water Babies '79
Wombling Free '77

Andras Jeles
The Little Valentino '79

Tom Jelfry
Weekend of Shadows '77

Michael Jenkins
Rebel '85
Sweet Talker '91

Patrick Jenkins
The Gambler & the Lady '52

**Astrid Henning
Jensen**
Boy of Two Worlds '70

Alain Jessua
The Killing Game '67

Jean-Marie Jeunet
Delicatessen '92

Norman Jewison
Agnes of God '85
And Justice for All '79
Best Friends '82
The Cincinnati Kid '65
Fiddler on the Roof '71
F.I.S.T. '78
In Country '89
In the Heat of the Night '67
Jesus Christ, Superstar '73
Moonstruck '87
Other People's Money '91
Rollerball '75

The Russians are Coming, the
Russians are Coming '66
Send Me No Flowers '64
A Soldier's Story '84
Thomas Crown Affair '68
The Thrill of It All! '63

Neal Jimenez
The Waterdance '91

Robert Jiras
I Am the Cheese '83

Duan Jishun
The Go-Masters '82

Mike Jittlov
The Wizard of Speed and
Time '88

Leo Joannon
Utopia '51

Phil Joanou
Final Analysis '92
State of Grace '90
Three O'Clock High '87
Wild Palms '93

Dickie Jobson
Countryman '83

**Alejandro
Jodorowsky**
Santa Sangre '90

Steve Jodrell
Shame '87

Michael Joens
My Little Pony: The Movie '86

Alfred Joffe
Harem '85

Arthur Joffe
Alberto Express '92

Mark Joffe
The Efficiency Expert '92
Grievous Bodily Harm '89
Night Master '87

Roland Joffe
City of Joy '92
Fat Man and Little Boy '89
The Killing Fields '84
The Mission '86

Alan Johnson
Solarbabies '86
To Be or Not to Be '83

Emory Johnson
Phantom Express '32

Floch Johnson
Maid in Sweden '83

Irvin Johnson
Blood Ring '93

Jed Johnson
Andy Warhol's Bad '77

John H. Johnson
Curse of the Blue Lights '88

Kenneth Johnson
The Incredible Hulk '77
Senior Trip '81
Short Circuit 2 '88

Lamont Johnson
Crisis at Central High '80
Ernie Kovacs: Between the
Laughter '84
Escape '90
The Execution of Private
Slovik '74
FM '78
The Groundstar Conspiracy
'72
A Gunfight '71
Jack & the Beanstalk '83

Sarah Kernochan
Marjoe '72

Irvin Kershner
The Empire Strikes Back '80
Eyes of Laura Mars '78
A Fine Madness '66
Flim-Flam Man '67
Never Say Never Again '83
Raid on Entebbe '77
The Return of a Man Called
    Horse '76
RoboCop 2 '90
S*P*Y*S '74
Traveling Man '89
Up the Sandbox '72

Emmanuel Kervyn
Rabid Grannies '89

Harry Kerwin
Barracuda '78
Cheering Section '73
God's Bloody Acre '75

Alek Keshishian
Truth or Dare '91

Bruce Kessler
Angels from Hell '68
Cruise into Terror '78
Deathmoon '78
Simon, King of the Witches
    '71

Kliff Keuhl
Murder Rap '87

Michael Keusch
Lena's Holiday '91

Riffat A. Khan
Feelin' Screwy '90

Michel Khleifi
A Wedding in Galilee '87

Kim Ki-dak
Yongkari Monster of the Deep
    '67

Beeban Kidron
Antonia and Jane '91
Used People '92

Fritz Kiersch
Children of the Corn '84
Gor '88
Into the Sun '92
Tuff Turf '85
Under the Boardwalk '89
Winners Take All '87

**Krzysztof
Kieslowski**
The Double Life of Veronique
    '91

Gerard Kikione
Buried Alive '89
Dragonard '88
Edge of Sanity '89
Frank and I '83

Jon Killough
Skinned Alive '89

Edward Killy
Don Amigo/Stage to Chino
    '40s

Richard H. Kim
Kill Line '91

Clinton Kimbrough
The Young Nurses '73

Bruce Kimmel
Spaceship '81

Anthony Kimmins
Bonnie Prince Charlie '48
Captain's Paradise '53
Mine Own Executioner '47

John Kincade
Back to Back '90
Terminal Entry '87

Tim Kincaid
Bad Girls Dormitory '84
Mutant Hunt '87
Robot Holocaust '87
She's Back '88

Allan Winton King
Silence of the North '81

Allen King
Termini Station '91

Burton King
The Adorable Cheat '28
The Man from Beyond '22

George King
The Case of the Frightened
    Lady '39
Crimes at the Dark House '39
The Crimes of Stephen
    Hawke '36
Demon Barber of Fleet Street
    '36
The Face at the Window '39

Henry King
The Bravados '58
Carousel '56
David and Bathsheba '51
Gunfighter '50
Hell Harbor '30
Jesse James '39
Love is a Many-Splendored
    Thing '55
Marie Galante '34
Romola '25
She Goes to War '29
The Snows of Kilimanjaro '52
The Song of Bernadette '43
Stanley and Livingstone '39
Tol'able David '21
Twelve O'Clock High '49
The White Sister '23
Wilson '44
A Yank in the R.A.F. '41

Louis King
Bulldog Drummond Comes
    Back '37
Bulldog Drummond's
    Revenge '37
Dangerous Mission '54
Drifting Souls '32
Sabre Jet '53

Rick King
Forced March '90
Hard Choices '84
Hot Shot '86
Kickboxer 3: The Art of War
    '92
The Killing Time '87
Prayer of the Rollerboys '91

Stephen King
Maximum Overdrive '86

Zalman King
Red Shoe Diaries '92
Red Shoe Diaries 2: Double
    Dare '92
Two Moon Junction '88
Wild Orchid '90
Wild Orchid 2: Two Shades of
    Blue '92
Wildfire '88

Alan Kingsberg
Almost Partners '87

Jack Kinney
Bongo '4
The Legend of Sleepy Hollow
    '49

Keisuke Kinoshita
Twenty-Four Eyes '54

Teinosuke Kinugasa
Gate of Hell '54

Alex Kirby
The Chronicles of Narnia '89

Robert Kirk
Destroyer '88

David Kirkland
The Tomboy '24

John Kirkland
Curse of the Headless
    Horseman '72

Klaus Kirschner
Mozart: A Childhood
    Chronicle '76

John Kirsh
Jesus '79

Ephraim Kishon
Sallah '63

Lek Kitiparaporn
AngKor: Cambodia Express
    '81

Carl Kitt
Up River '79

Robert J. Kizer
Death Ring '93
Godzilla 1985 '85
Hell Comes to Frogtown '88

Alf Kjellin
The Girls of Huntington House
    '73
The McMasters '70

Robert Klane
Thank God It's Friday '78
Weekend at Bernie's 2 '93

Damian Klaus
Futurekick '91

Dennis Klein
One More Saturday Night '86

Randal Kleiser
Big Top Pee Wee '88
The Blue Lagoon '80
The Boy in the Plastic Bubble
    '76
Flight of the Navigator '86
The Gathering '77
Getting It Right '89
Grandview U.S.A. '84
Grease '78
Honey, I Blew Up the Kid '92
Summer Lovers '82
White Fang '91

Max Kleven
Bail Out '89
Border Heat '88
Deadly Stranger '88
Ruckus '81

Roland Klick
Let It Rock '86

Elem Klimov
Come and See '85
Rasputin '85

Leon Klimovsky
The Devil's Possessed '74
Dr. Jekyll and the Wolfman
    '71
Orgy of the Vampires '73
The Saga of the Draculas '72
Vengeance of the Zombies
    '72
The Werewolf vs. the Vampire
    Woman '70

Ben Kline
Lightning Warrior '31

Herbert Kline
The Fighter '52

Tony Klinger
Butterfly Ball '76

Werner Klingler
Secret of the Black Trunk '62

Elmar Klos
Death is Called Engelchen '63
The Shop on Main Street '65

Steven Kloves
The Fabulous Baker Boys '89

Pavel Klushantsev
Planet Burg '62

Castleton Knight
The Flying Scotsman '29

Robert Knights
A Dedicated Man '86
Double Vision '92
Ebony Tower '86
Lovers of Their Time '85

Edwin H. Knopf
The Light of Western Stars
    '30

Bernard Knowles
Frozen Alive '64
Murder on Approval '56
Norman Conquest '53

Werner Knox
Scalps '83

Philip Ko
Platoon the Warriors '88

Masaki Kobayashi
The Human Condition: A
    Soldier's Prayer '61
The Human Condition: No
    Greater Love '58
The Human Condition: Road
    to Eternity '59
Kwaidan '64

Howard W. Koch
Badge 373 '73
Girl in Black Stockings '57

Philip Koch
Pink Nights '87

Pancho Kohner
Mr. Sycamore '74

Marja Kok
In for Treatment '82

Amos Kollek
Crazy Streets '80s
Double Edge '92
Forever, Lulu '87
Goodbye, New York '85
High Stakes '89

Xavier Koller
Journey of Hope '90

James Komack
Porky's Revenge '85

Sergei Komarov
A Kiss for Mary Pickford '27

**Kazuo
Komatsubara**
Warriors of the Wind '85

**Andrei
Konchalovsky**
Duet for One '86
Homer and Eddie '89
The Inner Circle '91
Maria's Lovers '84
Runaway Train '85

Shy People '87
Tango and Cash '89

Jackie Kong
The Being '83
Blood Diner '87
Night Patrol '85
The Underachievers '88

Joseph Kong
Clones of Bruce Lee '80
Thundering Ninja '80s

Barbara Kopple
Harlan County, U.S.A. '76
Keeping On '81

Alexander Korda
Marius '31
Private Life of Don Juan '34
The Private Life of Henry VIII
    '33
Rembrandt '36
That Hamilton Woman '41
Wedding Rehearsal '32

Zoltan Korda
Cash '34
Cry, the Beloved Country '51
Drums '38
Elephant Boy '37
The Four Feathers '39
Jungle Book '42
Sahara '43
Sanders of the River '35

John Korty
The Autobiography of Miss
    Jane Pittman '74
Cast the First Stone '89
A Christmas Without Snow
    '80
Class of '63 '73
Deadly Business '86
The Ewok Adventure '84
Eye on the Sparrow '91
Forever '78
The Haunting Passion '83
Oliver's Story '78
The People '71
Silence '73

**Waldemar
Korzenioswsky**
The Chair '87

Grigori Kosintsev
Don Quixote '57

Henry Koster
The Bishop's Wife '47
D-Day, the Sixth of June '56
Dear Brigitte '65
Desiree '54
Flower Drum Song '61
Harvey '50
The Inspector General '49
A Man Called Peter '55
Mr. Hobbs Takes a Vacation
    '62
The Rage of Paris '38
The Robe '53
The Singing Nun '66
Stars and Stripes Forever '52
The Story of Ruth '60
The Virgin Queen '55

Tom Kotani
The Bushido Blade '80

Ted Kotcheff
The Apprenticeship of Duddy
    Kravitz '74
First Blood '82
Folks! '92
Fun with Dick and Jane '77
Joshua Then and Now '85
North Dallas Forty '79
Split Image '82
Switching Channels '88

Michael Landon
It's Good to Be Alive '74
Killing Stone '78
Little House on the Prairie,
Vol. 1 '74
The Loneliest Runner '76
Sam's Son '84

Paul Landres
Flipper's Odyssey '66
Go, Johnny Go! '59
Square Dance Jubilee '51

Alan Landsburg
Black Water Gold '69

Andrew Lane
Desperate Motives '92
Jake Speed '86
Mortal Passions '90

Charles Lane
True Identity '91

Rocky Lane
All's Fair '89

Eric Laneuville
The George McKenna Story
'86
The Mighty Pawns '87

Sidney Lanfield
The Hound of the Baskervilles
'39
The Lemon Drop Kid '51
My Favorite Blonde '42
Skirts Ahoy! '52
Sorrowful Jones '49
Station West '48
You'll Never Get Rich '41

Fritz Lang
Beyond a Reasonable Doubt
'56
Big Heat '53
Clash by Night '52
Cloak and Dagger '46
Crimes of Dr. Mabuse '32
Das Testament des Dr.
Mabuse '33
Dr. Mabuse the Gambler '22
Fury '36
Human Desire '54
Journey to the Lost City '58
Kriemhilde's Revenge '24
Liliom '35
M '31
Metropolis '26
Moonfleet '55
Rancho Notorious '52
Return of Frank James '40
Scarlet Street '45
Secret Beyond the Door '48
Siegfried '24
Spiders '18
Spies '28
The Thousand Eyes of Dr.
Mabuse '60
Western Union '41
While the City Sleeps '56
Woman in the Moon '29
You Only Live Once '37

Krzysztof Lang
Paper Marriage '93

Michael Lang
The Gift '82
Holiday Hotel '77

Perry Lang
Little Vegas '90

Richard Lang
A Change of Seasons '80
Christmas Comes to Willow
Creek '87
Don't Go to Sleep '82
Fantasy Island '76

Force of Evil '77
The Hunted Lady '77
Kung Fu: The Movie '86
The Mountain Men '80
Night Cries '78
Shooting Stars '85
Strike Force '81
Vegas '78

Rocky Lang
Race for Glory '89

Walter Lang
The Blue Bird '40
But Not for Me '59
Can-Can '60
Desk Set '57
The Jackpot '50
The King and I '56
The Little Princess '39
The Magnificent Dope '42
Moon Over Miami '41
Red Kimono '25
Snow White and the Three
Stooges '61
Song of the Islands '42
State Fair '45
There's No Business Like
Show Business '54

Declan Langan
Erotic Images '85

Noel Langley
The Adventures of Sadie '55
The Pickwick Papers '54
The Search for Bridey Murphy
'56
Svengali '55

Chris Langman
Moving Targets '87

Murray Langston
Wishful Thinking '92

Simon Langton
Act of Passion: The Lost
Honor of Kathryn Beck '83
Anna Karenina '85
Casanova '87
Laguna Heat '87
The Whistle Blower '87

Anthony M. Lanza
The Glory Stompers '67
The Incredible Two-Headed
Transplant '71

James Lapine
Impromptu '90
Life With Mikey '93
Sunday in the Park with
George '86

Joseph Larraz
Golden Lady '79
The House that Vanished '73
Scream and Die '74
Vampyres '74

Sheldon Larry
Behind Enemy Lines '85
Terminal Choice '85

Keith Larsen
Mission Batangas '69
Trap on Cougar Mountain '72
Young & Free '78

Robert W. Larsen
The Narcotics Story '58

Eric Larson
Sleeping Beauty '59

Larry Larson
Deadly Passion '85

J.A. Laser
Zombie Lake '84

Stan Lathan
Amazing Grace '74
Beat Street '84
The Sky is Gray '80
Uncle Tom's Cabin '87

John Latos
The Voyage of Tanai '75

Alberto Lattuada
Christopher Columbus '85
La Cicada '83
Love in the City '53
Stay As You Are '78
Variety Lights '51

S.H. Lau
Heroes Three '84

Frank Laudner
I See a Dark Stranger '46

Frank Laughlin
The Trial of Billy Jack '74

Michael Laughlin
Mesmerized '84
Strange Behavior '81
Strange Invaders '83

Charles Laughton
The Night of the Hunter '55

Frank Launder
The Belles of St. Trinian's '53
Blue Murder at St. Trinian's
'56
Great St. Trinian's Train
Robbery '66
The Pure Hell of St. Trinian's
'61

Dale Launer
Love Potion #9 '92

Fabrizio Laurenti
Witchery '88

George Lauris
Buffalo Rider '78

Fernand Lauterier
Nais '45

Georges Lautner
Icy Breasts '75
La Cage aux Folles 3: The
Wedding '86
My Other Husband '85
Road to Salina '68

Linda Lautrec
My Breakfast with Blassie '83

Gerard Lauzier
Petit Con '84

Jean-Claude Lauzon
Night Zoo '87

Arnold Laven
Geronimo '62
The Monster that Challenged
the World '57
Without Warning '52

Martin Lavut
Palais Royale '88
Smokescreen '90

Albert Law
Cold Blooded Murder

Clara Law
The Reincarnation of Golden
Lotus '89

George Law
Torpedo Attack '72

Tom Law
Tax Season '90

Denny Lawrence
Archer's Adventure '85

John Lawrence
Savage Abduction '73

Marc Lawrence
Pigs '73

Quentin Lawrence
The Crawling Eye '58

Ray Lawrence
Bliss '85

Jennifer Lax
Max '79

Joe Layton
Richard Pryor: Live on the
Sunset Strip '82

Pedro Lazaga
Gladiators 7 '62

Ashley Lazarus
Golden Rendezvous '77

**Jean-Paul Le
Chanois**
L'Ecole Buisoniere '51

Wilford Leach
The Pirates of Penzance '83
The Wedding Party '69

Philip Leacock
Angel City '80
Baffled '72
The Curse of King Tut's Tomb
'80
Dying Room Only '73
Escapade '55
Killer on Board '77
Shattered Silence '71
The Spanish Gardener '57
Thanksgiving Story '73
Three Sovereigns for Sarah
'85
War Lover '62
Wild & Wooly '78

Anton Leader
Children of the Damned '63

Paul Leaf
Sergeant Matlovich vs. the
U.S. Air Force '78

Louis Leahman
South of Hell Mountain '70

David Lean
Blithe Spirit '45
The Bridge on the River Kwai
'57
Brief Encounter '46
Doctor Zhivago '65
Great Expectations '46
Hobson's Choice '53
In Which We Serve '43
Lawrence of Arabia '62
Madeleine '50
Oliver Twist '48
A Passage to India '84
Ryan's Daughter '70
Summertime '55
This Happy Breed '47

Norman Lear
Cold Turkey '71

Timothy Leary
Cheech and Chong's Nice
Dreams '81
Shocker '89

Maria Lease
Dolly Dearest '92

Don Leaver
Witching Time '84

Reginald LeBorg
Diary of a Madman '63
G.I. Jane '51

Great Jesse James Raid '49
House of the Black Death '65
The Sibling '72
Sins of Jezebel '54
The White Orchid '54

**Jean-Paul
LeChanois**
Le Cas du Dr. Laurent '57
Les Miserables '57
Passion for Life '48

Patrice Leconte
The Hairdresser's Husband
'92

Paul Leder
The Abduction of Allison Tate
'92
A*P*E* '76
The Baby Doll Murders '92
Body Count '87
Deadly Conspiracy '91
Exiled in America '90
Frame Up '91
I Dismember Mama '74
Murder by Numbers '89
Sketches of a Strangler '78
Twenty Dollar Star '91
Vultures '84

Charles Lederer
Monkey Business '52
Never Steal Anything Small
'59

Ross Lederman
Phantom of the West '31
Racketeers of the Range '39
Range Feud '31
The Range Feud/Two Fisted
Law '31
Shadows on the Stairs '41
Tarzan's Revenge '38
Two-Fisted Law '32

Paul Leduc
Frida '84

Bruce Lee
Fists of Bruce Lee '80s
Return of the Dragon '73

Charles Lee
Full Metal Ninja '89
Ninja of the Magnificence '89

Damian Lee
Boxcar Blues '90
Food of the Gods: Part 2 '88
Last Man Standing '87
Ski School '91

DeWitt Lee
The Legend of Jedediah
Carver '70s
Ransom Money '88

Jack Lee
The Captain's Table '60
Robbery Under Arms '57
Wooden Horse '50

Joanna Lee
Children of Divorce '80

Joe Lee
The Courier '88

Norman Lee
Bulldog Drummond at Bay '37
Chamber of Horrors '40

Rowland V. Lee
The Bridge of San Luis Rey
'44
Captain Kidd '45
The Count of Monte Cristo '34
Love from a Stranger '36
One Rainy Afternoon '36
Son of Frankenstein '39
The Son of Monte Cristo '41

Lee ►*cont.*

Three Musketeers '35
Toast of New York '37
The Tower of London '39

Spike Lee
Do the Right Thing '89
Joe's Bed-Stuy Barbershop:
　We Cut Heads '83
Jungle Fever '91
Malcolm X '92
Mo' Better Blues '90
School Daze '88
She's Gotta Have It '86

David Leeds
Shoot the Sun Down '81

Abraham Leff
Where is My Child? '37

Johnny Legend
My Breakfast with Blassie '83

Gary Legon
My Therapist '84

Francosis Legrand
Sex on the Run '78

Ernest Lehman
Portnoy's Complaint '72

Lew Lehman
The Pit '81

Michael Lehmann
The Applegates '89
Heathers '89
Hudson Hawk '91

Peter Lehner
Megaville '91

Arnold Leibovit
The Puppetoon Movie '87

Neil Leifer
Trading Hearts '87
Yesterday's Hero '79

Mike Leigh
Abigail's Party '77
Four Days in July '84
High Hopes '89
Life is Sweet '91
Nuts in May '76

Warren Leight
The Night We Never Met '93

Mitchell Leisen
The Girl Most Likely '57
Murder at the Vanities '34
Swing High, Swing Low '37

Erwin Leiser
Mein Kampf '60

Christopher Leitch
Courage Mountain '89
The Hitter '79
Teen Wolf Too '87

David Leland
The Big Man: Crossing the
　Line '91
Checking Out '89
Wish You Were Here '87

Claude Lelouch
And Now My Love '74
Another Man, Another Chance
　'77
Bolero '82
Cat and Mouse '78
Edith & Marcel '83
Happy New Year '74
A Man and a Woman '66
A Man and a Woman: 20
　Years Later '86

Robert et Robert '79

Alan LeMay
High Lonesome '50

James Lemmo
Heart '87
Tripwire '89
We're Talkin' Serious Money
　'92

Jack Lemmon
Kotch '71

Rusty Lemorande
Journey to the Center of the
　Earth '88

Paul Leni
The Cat and the Canary '27
The Man Who Laughs '27
Waxworks '24

Jan Lenica
Ubu and the Great Gidouille
　'79

Terry Lennon
Daffy Duck's Quackbusters
　'89

Miklos Lente
Oddballs '84

Umberto Lenzi
Almost Human '79
Battle of the Commandos '71
Battleforce '78
Bridge to Hell '87
Bruce Lee Fights Back From
　the Grave '76
City of the Walking Dead '83
Emerald Jungle '80
Eyeball '78
From Hell to Victory '79
Man from Deep River '77
Messalina vs. the Son of
　Hercules '64
Paranoia '69
Pirates of the Seven Seas '62

Malcolm Leo
Beach Boys: An American
　Band '85
It Came from Hollywood '82
This is Elvis '81

Arthur Leonard
Boy! What a Girl '45

Brett Leonard
Dead Pit '89
The Lawnmower Man '92

Leo Leonard
Omoo Omoo, the Shark God
　'49

Robert Z. Leonard
Broadway Serenade '39
Clown '53
Dancing Lady '33
The Divorcee '30
Duchess of Idaho '50
The Firefly '37
Girl of the Golden West '38
The Great Ziegfeld '36
In the Good Old Summertime
　'49
Maytime '37
A Mormon Maid '17
Nancy Goes to Rio '50
New Moon '40
Pride and Prejudice '40
Strange Interlude '32
Susan Lenox: Her Fall and
　Rise '31
Weekend at the Waldorf '45
When Ladies Meet '41
Ziegfeld Girl '41

Terry J. Leonard
Death Before Dishonor '87

**Jordan
Leondopoulos**
The Swap '71

John Leone
Great Smokey Roadblock '76

Sergio Leone
A Fistful of Dollars '64
A Fistful of Dynamite '72
For a Few Dollars More '65
The Good, the Bad and the
　Ugly '67
Once Upon a Time in America
　'84
Once Upon a Time in the West
　'68

Po Chich Leong
Ping Pong '87

Antonio Leonuiola
Atlas in the Land of the
　Cyclops '61
Tor '64

Reymond LePlont
La Balance '82

Carl Lerner
Black Like Me '64

Irving Lerner
Cry of Battle '63
Studs Lonigan '60

Joseph Lerner
The C-Man '49

Richard Lerner
Revenge of the Cheerleaders
　'76

Mervyn LeRoy
Anthony Adverse '36
The Bad Seed '56
Blossoms in the Dust '41
The Devil at 4 O'Clock '61
East Side, West Side '49
The FBI Story '59
Gold Diggers of 1933 '33
Gypsy '62
Homecoming '48
I Am a Fugitive from a Chain
　Gang '32
Johnny Eager '42
Latin Lovers '53
Little Caesar '30
Little Women '49
Lovely to Look At '52
Madame Curie '43
Million Dollar Mermaid '52
Mister Roberts '55
No Time for Sergeants '58
Quo Vadis '51
Random Harvest '42
Rose Marie '54
Sweet Adeline '35
They Won't Forget '37
Thirty Seconds Over Tokyo
　'44
Three Men on a Horse '36
Three on a Match '32
Waterloo Bridge '40
Without Reservations '46

Bill Lesley
Nail Gun Massacre '86

Mark L. Lester
Armed and Dangerous '86
Bobbie Jo and the Outlaw '76
Class of 1984 '82
Class of 1999 '90
Commando '85
Firestarter '84
Gold of the Amazon Women
　'79

Roller Boogie '79
Showdown in Little Tokyo '91
Steel Arena '72
Stunts '77
Truck Stop Women '74

Richard Lester
Butch and Sundance: The
　Early Days '79
Cuba '79
Finders Keepers '84
The Four Musketeers '75
A Funny Thing Happened on
　the Way to the Forum '66
Hard Day's Night '64
Help! '65
How I Won the War '67
Juggernaut '74
Petulia '68
The Ritz '76
Robin and Marian '76
Superman 2 '80
Superman 3 '83
Three Musketeers '74

Sheldon Lettich
Double Impact '91
Lionheart '90

Brian Levant
Beethoven '92
Problem Child 2 '91

Joseph Levering
Defenders of the Law '31
Sea Devils '31

Michel Levesque
Sweet Sugar '72
Werewolves on Wheels '71

Jay Levey
UHF '89

William A. Levey
Blackenstein '73
Committed '91
The Happy Hooker Goes to
　Washington '77
Hellgate '89
Lightning: The White Stallion
　'86
Slumber Party '57 '76
To Be a Rose '74

Alan J. Levi
Blood Song '82
Last Song '80
Riding with Death '76

Henry Levin
The Ambushers '67
Cry of the Werewolf '44
Desperados '69
The Farmer Takes a Wife '53
Jolson Sings Again '49
Journey to the Center of the
　Earth '59
Lonely Man '57
Man from Colorado '49
Murderers' Row '66
Run for the Roses '78
Scout's Honor '80
The Warriors '55
Where the Boys Are '60
The Wonderful World of the
　Brothers Grimm '62
The Wonders of Aladdin '61

Peter Levin
Comeback Kid '80
Rape and Marriage: The
　Rideout Case '80
Washington Mistress '81

Jack Levine
Ghost Rider '35

Barry Levinson
Avalon '90
Bugsy '91

Diner '82
Good Morning, Vietnam '87
The Natural '84
Rain Man '88
Tin Men '87
Toys '92
Young Sherlock Holmes '85

Fred Levinson
Hail '73

**Israeli Nadav
Levitan**
Intimate Story '81
The Seventeenth Bride '84

Abe Levitow
Bugs Bunny's Hare-Raising
　Tales '89
Gay Purr-ee '62

Gene Levitt
Magee and the Lady '78

Bob Levy
If You Don't Stop It...You'll Go
　Blind '77

Edmond Levy
Mom, the Wolfman and Me
　'80

Eugene Levy
Once Upon a Crime '92

Gerry Levy
Invasion of the Body Stealers
　'69

I. Robert Levy
Can I Do It...Till I Need
　Glasses? '77

Louis Levy
The Wicked Lady '45

Ralph Levy
Bedtime Story '63

Shuki Levy
Blind Vision '91
Perfect Victims '87

Eric Lewald
Incoming Freshmen '79

Stephen Lewicki
Certain Sacrifice '80

Albert Lewin
The Moon and Sixpence '43
Picture of Dorian Gray '45
The Private Affairs of Bel Ami
　'47

Ben Lewin
The Favor, the Watch, & the
　Very Big Fish '92

Sam Lewin
The Dunera Boys '85

Al Lewis
Our Miss Brooks '56

Christopher Lewis
The Red Raven Kiss-Off '90
Revenge '86
The Ripper '86

David Lewis
Dangerous Curves '88

**Herschell Gordon
Lewis**
Blood Feast '63
Color Me Blood Red '64
Gruesome Twosome '67
Just for the Hell of It '68
Monster a Go-Go! '65
Moonshine Mountain '64
Nature's Playmates '62
The Prime Time '60
The Psychic '68

She-Devils on Wheels '68
Something Weird '68
Suburban Roulette '67
This Stuff'll Kill Ya! '71
2000 Maniacs '64
The Wizard of Gore '70

Jay Lewis
The Baby and the Battleship '56

Jerry Lewis
The Bellboy '60
Big Mouth '67
Cracking Up '83
The Errand Boy '61
Family Jewels '65
Hardly Working '81
The Ladies' Man '61
The Nutty Professor '63
The Patsy '64
Which Way to the Front? '70

Joseph H. Lewis
Big Combo '55
Boys of the City '40
Criminals Within '41
Gun Crazy '49
The Invisible Ghost '41
A Lawless Street '55
Pride of the Bowery '41
Retreat, Hell! '52
Seventh Cavalry '56
That Gang of Mine '40

Robert Lewis
Child Bride of Short Creek '81
City Killer '87
Dead Reckoning '89
Desperate Lives '82
Embassy '85
Fallen Angel '81
If Things Were Different '79
Ladykillers '88
Memories of Murder '90
No Room to Run '78
Pray for the Wildcats '74
S*H*E '79
A Summer to Remember '84

Stanley Lewis
Punk Vacation '90

Denis Lewiston
Hot Target '85

Bruce Li
Counter Attack '84

Liu Chia Liang
Master Killer '84

Yu Lianqi
Kung Fu Hero 2 '90

Carlo Liconti
Goodnight, Michelangelo '89

Jeff Lieberman
Blue Sunshine '78
Just Before Dawn '80
Remote Control '88
Squirm '76

Robert Lieberman
All I Want for Christmas '91
Fire in the Sky '93
Table for Five '83
Will: G. Gordon Liddy '82

Lo Lieh
Fists of the White Lotus '80s

Mike Light
Flesh Gordon '72

Ralph M. Like
Chinatown After Dark '31

Peter Lilienthal
David '79
The Uprising '81

Walter Lima, Jr.
The Dolphin '87

Fred J. Lincoln
Wild Man '89

Per Lindberg
June Night '40

Mitchell Linden
The American Scream '80s

Maud Linder
Man In the Silk Hat '15

Max Linder
Early Cinema Vol. 1 '19

Lance Lindsay
Real Bullets '90
Star Crystal '85

Michael Lindsay-Hogg
Annie Oakley '85
As Is '85
Brideshead Revisited '81
Let It Be '70
The Little Match Girl '87
Master Harold and the Boys '84
Murder by Moonlight '91
Nasty Habits '77
The Object of Beauty '91
Running Mates '92
Strange Case of Dr. Jekyll & Mr. Hyde '89
Thumbelina '82

Leopold Lindtberg
Four in a Jeep '51
The Last Chance '45

Liou-Xiao Ling
Challenge of the Dragon '82

John F. Link
Call of the Forest '49
The Devil's Cargo '48

Ron Link
Zombie High '87

Richard Linklater
Slacker '91

Art Linson
Whore the Buffalo Roam '80
The Wild Life '84

Aaron Lipstadt
Android '82
City Limits '85
The Slumber Party Massacre '82

Steven Lisberger
Hot Pursuit '87
Slipstream '89
Tron '82

David Lister
Hunted '88
The Rutanga Tapes '90

Miguel Littin
Alsino and the Condor '82

Dwight Little
Bloodstone '88
Getting Even '86
Halloween 4: The Return of Michael Myers '88
Marked for Death '90
The Phantom of the Opera '89
Rapid Fire '92

Lynne Littman
Testament '83

Anatole Litvak
All This and Heaven Too '40
Anastasia '56
City for Conquest '40

Goodbye Again '61
Mayerling '36
Night of the Generals '67
The Sisters '38
The Snake Pit '48
Sorry, Wrong Number '48

Gerry Lively
Body Moves '90

Jennie Livingston
Paris is Burning '91

Carlo Lizzani
House of the Yellow Carpet '84
Last Four Days '77
Love in the City '53

Julio Ruiz Llaneza
By Hook or Crook '85

Luis Llosa
Crime Zone '88
Hour of the Assassin '86
Sniper '92

Frank Lloyd
Blood on the Sun '45
Cavalcade '33
Forever and a Day '43
The Howards of Virginia '40
The Last Command '55
Mutiny on the Bounty '35
Oliver Twist '22

Harold Lloyd
Early Cinema Vol. 1 '19
His Royal Slyness/Haunted Spooks '20
I'm on My Way/The Non-Stop Kid '18

Norman Lloyd
Tales of the Unexpected '91

Ken Loach
Family Life '71
Hidden Agenda '90
Riff Raff '92
Singing the Blues in Red '87

Tony LoBianco
Too Scared to Scream '85

Victor Lobl
Eden '92

Sondra Locke
Impulse '90
Ratboy '86

Roy Lockwood
The Mutiny of the Elsinore '39

Bob Logan
Meatballs 4 '92
Repossessed '90
Up Your Alley '89

Bruce Logan
Vendetta '85

Joshua Logan
Bus Stop '56
Camelot '67
Ensign Pulver '64
Fanny '61
Paint Your Wagon '69
Picnic '55
Sayonara '57
South Pacific '58
Tall Story '60

Stanley Logan
The Falcon's Brother '42

Tom Logan
Dream Trap '90
The Night Brings Charlie '90

Dimitri Logothetis
The Closer '91
Pretty Smart '87

Slaughterhouse Rock '88

J. Anthony Loma
Counterforce '87
A Man of Passion '90s
Target Eagle '84

Joseph Loman
The Boldest Job in the West '71
Surprise Attack '70s

Francisco J. Lombardi
La Boca del Lobo '89

Lou Lombardo
P.K. and the Kid '85
Russian Roulette '75

Ulli Lommel
The Big Sweat '90
The Boogey Man '80
Brainwaves '82
Cocaine Cowboys '79
Cold Heat '90
Devonsville Terror '83
Olivia '83
Overkill '86
Strangers in Paradise '86
Warbirds '88

Richard Loncraine
Bellman and True '88
Brimstone & Treacle '82
Deep Cover '88
Full Circle '77
The Missionary '82

Jerry London
Chiefs '83
Father Figure '80
Haunting of Sarah Hardy '89
Kiss Shot '89
Manhunt for Claude Dallas '86
Rent-A-Cop '88
The Scarlet & the Black '83
Shogun '80
Victim of Love '91

Roy London
Diary of a Hitman '91

Richard Long
The Word '78

Stanley Long
Adventures of a Private Eye '87
Adventures of a Taxi Driver '76

Humphrey Longan
The Great Battle '79

Temistocles Lopez
Exquisite Corpses '88

Del Lord
Vengeance '37

Jean-Claude Lord
Covergirl '83
Eddie and the Cruisers 2: Eddie Lives! '89
Landslide '92
Mindfield '89
Toby McTeague '87
The Vindicator '85
Visiting Hours '82

Ken Loring
Combat Killers '80

Peter Lorre
The Lost One '51

Joseph Losey
Accident '67
Assassination of Trotsky '72
The Boy with the Green Hair '48
A Doll's House '73

The Go-Between '71
La Truite '83
Mr. Klein '75
Roads to the South '78
Romantic Englishwoman '75
Secret Ceremony '69
The Servant '63
The Sleeping Tiger '54
Steaming '86

Pavel Lounguine
Taxi Blues '90

John Lounsbery
The Rescuers '77

Eugene Lourie
The Beast from 20,000 Fathoms '53
Gorgo '61

Eric Louzil
Lust for Freedom '87
Wilding '90

Horace Love
Playing Away '87

Charles Loventhal
First Time '82
My Demon Lover '87

Bert Lovitt
Prince Jack '83

Steven Lovy
Circuitry Man '90

Lucas Lowe
American Shaolin: King of the Kickboxers 2 '92
The King of the Kickboxers '91

William Lowe
Slaughter in San Francisco '81

Richard Lowenstein
Dogs in Space '87
Pete Townsend: White City '85

Dick Lowry
Coward of the County '81
The FBI Murders '88
The Jayne Mansfield Story '80
Kenny Rogers as the Gambler '80
Kenny Rogers as the Gambler, Part 2: The Adventure Continues '83
Kenny Rogers as the Gambler, Part 3: The Legend Continues '87
Smokey and the Bandit, Part 3 '83
Wet Gold '84
Wild Horses '84

David Loxton
Lathe of Heaven '80

Nanni Loy
Cafe Express '83
Head of the Family '71
Where's Piccone '84

Arthur Lubin
Buck Privates '41
Delightfully Dangerous '45
Escapade in Japan '57
Francis in the Navy '55
Hold That Ghost '41
Impact '49
In the Navy '41
The Incredible Mr. Limpet '64
Keep 'Em Flying '41
Phantom of the Opera '43
Queen for a Day '51
Ride 'Em Cowboy '42
Thief of Baghdad '61
Yellowstone '36

Ernst Lubitsch
Gypsy Blood '18
Heaven Can Wait '43
Lady Windermere's Fan '26
The Marriage Circle '24
The Merry Widow '34
Ninotchka '39
One Arabian Night '21
Passion '19
The Shop Around the Corner '40
So This is Paris '26
The Student Prince in Old Heidelberg '27
That Uncertain Feeling '41
To Be or Not to Be '42

S. Roy Luby
Arizona Badman '42
Arizona Stagecoach '42
Black Market Rustlers '43
Boot Hill Bandits '42
Border Phantom '37
Cowboy Commandos '43
Fugitive Valley '41
Kid's Last Ride '41
Outlaw Rule '36
The Red Rope '37
Tough to Handle '37
Trail of the Silver Spurs '41
Tumbledown Ranch in Arizona '41
Underground Rustlers '41

George Lucas
American Graffiti '73
From "Star Wars" to "Jedi": The Making of a Saga '83
Star Wars '77
THX 1138 '71

Leandro Lucchetti
Getting Even '92

Francesco Lucente
Virgin Queen of St. Francis High '88

Maurizio Lucidi
Stateline Motel '75
Street People '76

William Lucking
Humanoid Defender '85

Larry Ludman
Deadly Impact '84
The Manhunt '86
Operation 'Nam '85
Overthrow '82
Thunder Warrior '85
Thunder Warrior 2 '85
Thunder Warrior 3 '88

Edward Ludwig
Big Jim McLain '52
The Big Wheel '49
The Black Scorpion '57
Fighting Seabees '44
Flame of the Islands '55
Wake of the Red Witch '49

Baz Luhrmann
Strictly Ballroom '92

Sidney Lumet
The Anderson Tapes '71
Daniel '83
Deathtrap '82
Dog Day Afternoon '75
Equus '77
Fail-Safe '64
Family Business '89
The Fugitive Kind '60
Garbo Talks '84
The Group '66
Guilty as Sin '93
Just Tell Me What You Want '80

Long Day's Journey into Night '62
Morning After '86
Murder on the Orient Express '74
Network '76
The Offence '73
Pawnbroker '65
Power '86
Prince of the City '81
Q & A '90
Running on Empty '88
Serpico '73
Stage Struck '57
A Stranger Among Us '92
Twelve Angry Men '57
The Verdict '82
The Wiz '78

Auguste Lumiere
The Great Train Robbery: Cinema Begins '03

Bigas Luna
Anguish '88

Ida Lupino
The Bigamist '53
The Hitch-Hiker '53
The Trouble with Angels '66

Michele Lupo
Goliath and the Sins of Babylon '64
Master Touch '74
Mean Frank and Crazy Tony '75

Hamilton Luske
Lady and the Tramp '55
101 Dalmations '61
Peter Pan '53

William Lustig
The Hit List '88
Maniac '80
Maniac '80
Maniac Cop '88
Maniac Cop 2 '90
Maniac Cop 3 '93
Relentless '89
Vigilante '83

Salvo Luther
Forget Mozart '85

David Lynch
Blue Velvet '86
Dune '84
The Elephant Man '80
Eraserhead '78
Twin Peaks '90
Twin Peaks: Fire Walk with Me '92
Wild at Heart '90

Paul Lynch
At Sword's Point '51
Blindside '88
Bullies '86
Cross Country '83
Humongous '82
Murder by Night '89
Prom Night '80
Victim of Beauty '91

Paul Lynde
Dream to Believe '85

Adrian Lyne
Fatal Attraction '87
Foxes '80
Indecent Proposal '93
Jacob's Ladder '90
9 1/2 Weeks '86

Harry Lynn
Where is My Child? '37

Jonathan Lynn
Clue '85

The Distinguished Gentleman '92
My Cousin Vinny '92
Nuns on the Run '90

Francis D. Lyon
Bail Out at 43,000 '57
Castle of Evil '66
The Great Locomotive Chase '56
The Oklahoman '56
Tomboy & the Champ '58

Dick Maas
Amsterdamned '88
The Lift '85

Byron Mabe
She-Freak '67

Kurt MacCarley
Rock & the Money-Hungry Party Girls '89

David MacDonald
The Adventurers '51
Alias John Preston '56
Christopher Columbus '49
Devil Girl from Mars '54
The Moonraker '58
Never Too Late to Mend '37
Small Hotel '57

Peter Macdonald
Mo' Money '92

Hamilton MacFadden
Inside the Law '42
Sea Racketeers '37
Stand Up and Cheer '34

Mike MacFarland
Hanging on a Star '78
Pink Motel '82

Gustav Machaty
Ecstasy '33

Brice Mack
Jennifer '78
Swap Meet '79

Roy Mack
Hillbilly Blitzkrieg '42

Russell Mack
Lonely Wives '31

Yvonne Mackay
The Silent One '86

Alexander MacKendrick
Ladykillers '55
Man in the White Suit '51
Mandy '53
Sweet Smell of Success '57
Whiskey Galore '48

John MacKenzie
Act of Vengeance '86
Beyond the Limit '83
The Fourth Protocol '87
The Last of the Finest '90
The Long Good Friday '79
One Brief Summer '70
Ruby '92
A Sense of Freedom '78

Peter M. MacKenzie
Merchants of War '90

Will MacKenzie
Hobo's Christmas '87
Worth Winning '89

Gilles Mackinnon
The Playboys '92

Duncan Maclachlan
Scavengers '87

Stephen MacLean
Around the World in 80 Ways '86

Norman Z. MacLeod
Horse Feathers '32
It's A Gift '34
Kid from Brooklyn '46
The Paleface '48
The Road to Rio '47
The Secret Life of Walter Mitty '47
Topper '37
Topper Takes a Trip '39

Henry MacRae
King of the Rodeo '28
Mystery of the Riverboat '44
Tarzan the Tiger '29

William H. Macy
Lip Service '88

John Madden
Ethan Frome '92

Lee Madden
Hell's Angels '69 '69
The Manhandlers '73
Night Creature '79
The Night God Screamed '80s

Paul Madden
Summer Job '88

Miguel Madrid
Graveyard of Horror '71

Kenneth Madsen
A Day in October '92

Jose Maesso
Order to Kill '73

Kurt Maetzig
First Spaceship on Venus '60

Guy Magar
Retribution '88
Stepfather 3: Father's Day '92

Constantino Magnatta
The Darkside '87

Luigi Magni
In the Name of the Pope-King '85

Albert Magnoli
American Anthem '86
Atom Age Vampire '61
Purple Rain '84
Street Knight '93

Dezso Magyar
King of America '80
No Secrets '91
Rappaccini's Daughter '80

Anthony Maharaj
Crossfire '89
The Kick Fighter '91

Barry Mahon
Assault of the Rebel Girls '59
Rocket Attack U.S.A. '58
Violent Women '59

Bob Mahoney
Operation Julie '85

Norman Mailer
Tough Guys Don't Dance '87

George Maitland
Invasion Earth: The Aliens Are Here! '87

Lech Majewski
Prisoner of Rio '89

Dusan Makavejev
The Coca-Cola Kid '84

Innocence Unprotected '68
The Love Affair, or The Case of the Missing Switchboard Operator '67
Man is Not a Bird '65
Montenegro '81
Sweet Movie '75
WR: Mysteries of the Organism '71

Karoly Makk
Another Way '82
Cat's Play '74
Deadly Game '83
Lily in Love '85
Love '72

Guido Malatesta
Goliath Against the Giants '63

Roberto Malenotti
Slave Trade in the World Today '64

Terence Malick
Badlands '74
Days of Heaven '78

Louis Malle
Alamo Bay '85
Atlantic City '81
Au Revoir Les Enfants '87
Crackers '84
Damage '92
The Fire Within '64
Frantic '58
The Lovers '59
May Fools '90
Murmur of the Heart '71
My Dinner with Andre '81
Pretty Baby '78
Spirits of the Dead '68
A Very Private Affair '62
Zazie dans le Metro '61

Matthew Mallinson
Fist of Fear, Touch of Death '77

James Mallon
Blood Hook '86

Bruce Malmuth
Foreplay '75
Hard to Kill '89
The Man Who Wasn't There '83
Nighthawks '81
Where Are the Children? '85

William Malone
Creature '85
Scared to Death '80

Paul Maloney
I Live with Me Dad '86

David Mamet
Homicide '91
House of Games '87

Yurii Mamin
Sideburns '91

Rouben Mamoulian
Applause '29
Becky Sharp '35
Blood and Sand '41
Dr. Jekyll and Mr. Hyde '31
Golden Boy '39
The Mark of Zorro '40
Queen Christina '33
Silk Stockings '57
Summer Holiday '48

Janine Manatis
Tales of the Klondike: In a Far Country '87

Mario Mancini
Frankenstein '80 '79

Kevin Mancuso
2020 Texas Gladiators '85

Jeffrey Mandel
Elves '89

Robert Mandel
Big Shots '87
F/X '86
Independence Day '83
Perfect Witness '89
School Ties '92
Touch and Go '86

Luis Mandoki
Born Yesterday '93
Gaby: A True Story '87
Murderer in the Hotel '83
White Palace '90

Joseph Manduke
Beatlemania! The Movie '81
Cornbread, Earl & Me '75
The Gumshoe Kid '89
Kid Vengeance '75
Omega Syndrome '87

Gianni Manera
Fear in the City '81

Nino Manfredi
Nudo di Donna '83

Joseph Mangine
Neon Maniacs '86

Francis Mankiewicz
And Then You Die '88
Les Bons Debarras '81
Love and Hate '90

**Joseph L.
Mankiewicz**
All About Eve '50
The Barefoot Contessa '54
Cleopatra '63
The Ghost and Mrs. Muir '47
Guys and Dolls '55
The Honey Pot '67
House of Strangers '49
Julius Caesar '53
A Letter to Three Wives '49
Sleuth '72
Suddenly, Last Summer '59
There was a Crooked Man '70

Tom Mankiewicz
Delirious '91
Dragnet '87

Henry Mankiewirk
Hell's Brigade: The Final
   Assault '80

Abby Mann
King '78

Anthony Mann
Bend of the River '52
Dandy in Aspic '68
Desperate '47
El Cid '61
The Fall of the Roman Empire
   '64
Far Country '55
The Glenn Miller Story '54
God's Little Acre '58
Great Flamarion '45
He Walked by Night '48
Man from Laramie '55
Man of the West '58
Men in War '57
The Naked Spur '53
Railroaded '47
Reign of Terror '49
Strategic Air Command '55
T-Men '47
Thunder Bay '53
Tin Star '57
Winchester '73 '50

Daniel Mann
Big Mo '73
Butterfield 8 '60
Come Back, Little Sheba '52
A Dream of Kings '69
For Love of Ivy '68
Hot Spell '58
I'll Cry Tomorrow '55
Interval '73
Journey into Fear '74
The Last Angry Man '59
The Man Who Broke 1,000
   Chains '87
Matilda '78
The Mountain Road '60
Our Man Flint '66
Playing for Time '80
The Rose Tattoo '55
The Teahouse of the August
   Moon '56
Who's Got the Action? '63
Willard '71

Delbert Mann
All Quiet on the Western Front
   '79
The Birch Interval '78
Breaking Up '78
David Copperfield '70
Desire Under the Elms '58
Francis Gary Powers: The
   True Story of the U-2 Spy
   '76
A Gathering of Eagles '63
Heidi '67
Home to Stay '79
Ironclads '90
The Last Days of Patton '86
Love Leads the Way '84
Lover Come Back '61
Marty '53
Marty '55
The Member of the Wedding
   '83
Night Crossing '81
No Place to Run '72
Separate Tables '58
She Waits '71
That Touch of Mink '62
Torn Between Two Lovers '79

Edward Mann
Cauldron of Blood '67
Hallucination '67
Hooch '76

Michael Mann
The Jericho Mile '79
The Keep '83
The Last of the Mohicans '92
Manhunter '86
Thief '81

Kim Manners
K-9000 '89

Michelle Manning
Blue City '86

Peter Manoogian
Arena '88
Demonic Toys '91
The Eliminators '86
Enemy Territory '87
Seedpeople '92

Mark Manos
Liquid Dreams '92

**Manoussos
Manoussakis**
The Enchantress '85

Duncan Mansfield
Sweetheart of the Navy '37

Scott Mansfield
Deadly Games '80

Guido Manuli
Volere Volare '92

Ray Manzarek
The Doors: Soft Parade, a
   Retrospective '69

Robert Marcarelli
I Don't Buy Kisses Anymore
   '92
Original Intent '91

Terry Marcel
Hawk the Slayer '81
Jane & the Lost City '87
Prisoners of the Lost Universe
   '84

Siro Marcellini
Gangster's Law '86

Alex March
Firehouse '72
Master Mind '73
Paper Lion '68

**Rafael Romero
Marchent**
Garringo '69

David Marconi
The Harvest '93

James Marcus
Double Cross '92

Philip Marcus
Terror on Alcatraz '86

Andreas Marfori
Evil Clutch '89

Antonio Margheriti
Assignment Outer Space '61
Wild, Wild Planet '65

Stuart Margolin
The Glitter Dome '84
Paramedics '88
A Shining Season '79

Jeff Margolis
Richard Pryor: Live in Concert
   '79

Cheech Marin
Born in East L.A. '87

Edwin L. Marin
Abilene Town '46
The Cariboo Trail '50
A Christmas Carol '38
The Death Kiss '33
Everybody Sing '38
I'd Give My Life '36
Johnny Angel '45
Listen, Darling '38
Miss Annie Rooney '42
Mr. Ace '46
Nocturne '46
Show Business '44
A Study in Scarlet '33
Tall in the Saddle '44

Lex Marinos
An Indecent Obsession '85
Remember Me '85

Peter Maris
Delirium '77
Diplomatic Immunity '91
Hangfire '91
Land of Doom '84
Terror Squad '87
True Blood '89
Viper '88

Chris Marker
La Jetee/An Occurrence at
   Owl Creek Bridge '64
Le Joli Mai '62
Sans Soleil '82

Russ Marker
The Yesterday Machine '63

Anthony Markes
Last Dance '91

Tony Markes
Bikini Island '91

David Markey
Desperate Teenage Lovedolls
   '84

Monte Markham
Defense Play '88
Neon City '91

Kelly Markin
Tiger Claws '91

Gabriel Markiw
Mob Story '90

Jancarlo Markiw
Mob Story '90

Fletcher Markle
The Incredible Journey '63
Jigsaw '49

Peter Markle
Bat 21 '88
El Diablo '90
Hot Dog...The Movie! '83
Nightbreaker '89
The Personals '83
Youngblood '86

Murray Markowitz
Left for Dead '78

Robert Markowitz
Afterburn '92
Decoration Day '90
Kojak: The Belarus File '85
A Long Way Home '81
Love, Lies and Murder '91
My Mother's Secret Life '84
Pray TV '82

Arthur Marks
Bonnie's Kids '73
Bucktown '75
Detroit 9000 '73
Friday Foster '75
J.D.'s Revenge '76
Monkey Hustle '77
Togetherness '70

Morley Markson
Off Your Rocker '80

**Malcolm
Marmorstein**
Dead Men Don't Die '91

Richard Marquand
Eye of the Needle '81
Hearts of Fire '87
The Jagged Edge '85
The Legacy '79
Return of the Jedi '83
Until September '84

Jacques Marquette
Meteor Monster '57

Charles Marquis
Tension at Table Rock '56

Leon Marr
Dancing in the Dark '86

Roberto Marrtero
Thirty-Six Hours of Hell '77

David Marsh
Lords of Magick '88

Ray Marsh
The Last Porno Flick '74

Philip Marshak
Cataclysm '81

Dracula Sucks '79

Frank Marshall
Alive '93
Arachnophobia '90

Garry Marshall
Beaches '88
The Flamingo Kid '84
Frankie and Johnny '91
Nothing in Common '86
Overboard '87
Pretty Woman '90
Young Doctors in Love '82

George Marshall
Boy, Did I Get a Wrong
   Number! '66
Destry Rides Again '39
Fancy Pants '50
The Ghost Breakers '40
The Goldwyn Follies '38
Houdini '53
How the West was Won '63
It Started with a Kiss '59
The Mating Game '59
Monsieur Beaucaire '46
My Friend Irma '49
Never a Dull Moment '50
Off Limits '53
Pack Up Your Troubles '32
The Perils of Pauline '47
Pot O' Gold '41
Red Garters '54
The Sad Sack '57
Scared Stiff '53
Show Them No Mercy '35
Texas '41
Valley of the Sun '42
You Can't Cheat an Honest
   Man '39

Penny Marshall
Awakenings '90
Big '88
Jumpin' Jack Flash '86
A League of Their Own '92

William Marshall
Adventures of Captain Fabian
   '51
The Phantom Planet '61

Charles Martin
Death of a Scoundrel '56
My Dear Secretary '49
One Man Jury '78

D'Urville Martin
Dolemite '75
Fass Black '77

Eugenio Martin
It Happened at Nightmare Inn
   '70
Pancho Villa '72

Frank Martin
Doctor Butcher M.D. '80

Gene Martin
Bad Man's River '72
Horror Express '72

James Aviles Martin
Flesh Eating Mothers '89

Arturo Martinez
La Marchanta '73

Chuck Martinez
Nice Girls Don't Explode '87

Rene Martinez, Jr.
The Guy from Harlem '77

Richard Martini
Limit Up '89
You Can't Hurry Love '88

Raymond Martino
DaVinci's War '92

Sergio Martino
Casablanca Express '89
The Cheaters '76
Day of the Maniac '77
The Great Alligator '81
Next Victim '71
The Opponent '89
The Scorpion's Tail '71
Screamers '80
Sex with a Smile '76
Slave of the Cannibal God '79
Torso '73
Violent Professionals '82

Leslie Martinson
The Atomic Kid '54
Batman '66
The Fantastic World of D.C. Collins '84
Hot Rod Girl '56
The Kid with the Broken Halo '82
The Kid with the 200 I.Q. '83
PT 109 '63
Return to Africa '89

Andrew Marton
Africa Texas Style '67
Around the World Under the Sea '65
Clarence, the Cross-eyed Lion '65
Gypsy Colt '54
Men of the Fighting Lady '54

Mike Marvin
Hamburger...The Motion Picture '86
The Wraith '87

Joseph Mascelli
The Atomic Brain '64

Francesco Maselli
Love in the City '53
Time of Indifference '64

Claudio Masenza
James Dean '85
Marlon Brando '85

Giuseppe Masini
Journey Beneath the Desert '61

Herbert Mason
Lady in Distress '39

Noel Mason
Fighting Pilot '35

Francesco Massaro
Private Affairs '89

Ivana Massetti
Domino '88

Joe Massot
Space Riders '83
Wonderwall: The Movie '69

Quentin Masters
Dangerous Summer '82
PSI Factor '80
The Stud '78
Thumb Tripping '72

Peter Masterson
Blood Red '88
Full Moon in Blue Water '88
Night Game '89
The Trip to Bountiful '85

Nico Mastorakis
Blind Date '84
Glitch! '88
Hired to Kill '91
In the Cold of the Night '89
Next One '84
Nightmare at Noon '87
Ninja Academy '90
Sky High '84

Terminal Exposure '89
The Wind '87
Zero Boys '86

Camillo Mastrocinque
Full Hearts & Empty Pockets '63

Armand Mastroianni
Cameron's Closet '89
Distortions '87
Double Revenge '89
He Knows You're Alone '80
Killing Hour '84
The Supernaturals '86

Toshio Masuda
Tora! Tora! Tora! '70
Zero '84

Orestes Matacena
Tainted '88

Eddy Matalon
Blackout '78
Cathy's Curse '77

Vivian Matalon
Private Contentment '83

Rudolph Mate
Branded '50
Dark Past '49
Deep Six '58
D.O.A. '49
The Green Glove '52
Second Chance '53
Three Violent People '57
Union Station '50
The Violent Men '55
When Worlds Collide '51

Shue Matsubayashi
Last War '68

Bruno Mattei
Night of the Zombies '83
Seven Magnificent Gladiators '84

Marius Mattei
Moving Target '89

Charles Matthau
Doin' Time on Planet Earth '88

Burny Mattinson
The Great Mouse Detective '86

Frank S. Mattison
With Kit Carson Over the Great Divide '25

Sally Mattison
Slumber Party Massacre 3 '90

Mario Mattoli
Two Nights with Cleopatra '54

Walt Mattox
Scared to Death '47

Arne Mattson
The Doll '62
The Girl '86

Peter Matulavich
Jupiter Menace '82

Robert Mauri
Invincible Gladiators '64
The Slaughter of the Vampires '62

Paul Maxwell
Superargo '67

Peter Maxwell
The Highest Honor '84
Platypus Cove '86
Plunge Into Darkness '77

Run, Rebecca, Run '81
Touch & Go '80

Ronald F. Maxwell
Kidco '83
Little Darlings '80
The Night the Lights Went Out in Georgia '81

Bradford May
Mortal Sins '92

Elaine May
The Heartbreak Kid '72
Ishtar '87
Mikey & Nicky '76
A New Leaf '71

Joe May
Homecoming '28
The Invisible Man Returns '40

Paul May
Dr. Mabuse vs. Scotland Yard '64

Russ Mayberry
Challenge of a Lifetime '85
Fer-De-Lance '74
The $5.20 an Hour Dream '80
The Jesus Trip '71
Marriage is Alive and Well '80
A Matter of Life and Death '81
Probe '72
The Rebels '79
Unidentified Flying Oddball '79

Gerald Mayer
The Man Inside '76

Paul Mayersberg
Captive '87
Nightfall '88

Les Mayfield
Encino Man '92

Tony Maylam
The Burning '82
The Riddle of the Sands '84
The Sins of Dorian Gray '82
Split Second '92

Ken Maynard
Honor of the Range '34
Strawberry Roan '33

Archie Mayo
Angel on My Shoulder '46
The Case of the Lucky Legs '35
The Great American Broadcast '41
House Across the Bay '40
A Night in Casablanca '46
Orchestra Wives '42
Petrified Forest '36
Svengali '31
They Shall Have Music '39

Al Maysles
Grey Gardens '76

David Maysles
Grey Gardens '76

Michael Mazo
Possession: Until Death Do You Part '90
Time Runner '92

Paul Mazursky
Alex in Wonderland '71
Blume in Love '73
Bob & Carol & Ted & Alice '69
Down and Out in Beverly Hills '86
Enemies, a Love Story '89
Harry and Tonto '74
Moon Over Parador '88
Moscow on the Hudson '84

Next Stop, Greenwich Village '76
Scenes from a Mall '91
The Tempest '82
An Unmarried Woman '78
Willie & Phil '80

Joseph Mazzuca
Sisters of Death '76

Don McBrearty
American Nightmare '81
Child's Christmas in Wales '88

Jim McBride
The Big Easy '87
Breathless '83
Glen and Randa '71
Great Balls of Fire '89
Hot Times '74

Jon McBride
Cannibal Campout '88
Woodchipper Massacre '89

Gene McCabe
Follow Me '69

James McCalmont
Escape from Safehaven '88
Underground Terror '88

Leo McCarey
The Awful Truth '37
The Bells of St. Mary's '45
Duck Soup '33
Going My Way '44
Good Sam '48
Indiscreet '31
Love Affair '39
Milky Way '36
Once Upon a Honeymoon '42
The Ruggles of Red Gap '35

Ray McCarey
Devil's Party '38
The Mystery Man '35
You Can't Fool Your Wife '40

John P. McCarthy
Cavalier of the West '31
Oklahoma Cyclone '30
The Return of Casey Jones '34
Song of the Gringo '36

Michael McCarthy
Crow Hollow '52
Operation Amsterdam '60

John McCauley
Rattlers '76

Gregory McClatchy
Vampire at Midnight '88

Arn McConnell
Shock! Shock! Shock! '87

Bret McCormick
Blood on the Badge
Tabloid! '88

George McCowan
Frogs '72
Murder on Flight 502 '75
Return to Fantasy Island '77
Savage Run '70

Peter McCubbin
Home for Christmas '90

Jim McCullough
The Aurora Encounter '85
The Charge of the Model T's '76
Mountaintop Motel Massacre '86

Bruce McDonald
Highway 61 '91
Roadkill '89

Frank McDonald
Apache Chief '50
Bells of Rosarita '45
The Big Sombrero '49
Gambler's Choice '44
My Pal Trigger '46
One Body Too Many '44
Song of Arizona '46
Take It Big '44
Timber Queen '44
Treasure of Fear '45
Twilight on the Rio Grande '41
Under Nevada Skies '46
Wildcat '42

Peter McDonald
Rambo 3 '88

Rodney McDonald
Night Eyes 2 '91

Donald McDougall
Chinese Web '78

Bernard McEveety
The Bears & I '74
The Broadway Drifter '27
The Brotherhood of Satan '71
Napoleon and Samantha '72
One Little Indian '73
Roughnecks '80

Vincent McEveety
Amy '81
The Apple Dumpling Gang Rides Again '79
The Castaway Cowboy '74
Charley and the Angel '73
Gunsmoke: Return to Dodge '87
Gus '76
Herbie Goes Bananas '80
Herbie Goes to Monte Carlo '77
Million Dollar Duck '71
Smoke '70
Superdad '73
The Treasure of Matecumbe '76

Bruce McFarlane
Kill Slade '89

William F. McGaha
Iron Horsemen '71

William McGann
American Empire '42
Dr. Christian Meets the Women '40
In Old California '42

Darren McGavin
Run, Stranger, Run '73

Robert McGinley
Shredder Orpheus '89

Dorrell McGowan
The Showdown '50

J.P. McGowan
Below the Deadline '29
Deadwood Pass '33
Drum Taps '33
Hurricane Express '32
Lone Bandit '33
Mark of the Spur '32
The Outlaw Tamer '33
Red Signals '27
Road Agent '26
When a Man Rides Alone '33

Robert McGowan
Frontier Justice '35
Old Swimmin' Hole '40

Stuart E. McGowan
The Billion Dollar Hobo '78
The Showdown '50

Ombra

▲ 1483 • DIRECTOR INDEX

John H. Parr
Prey for the Hunter '92
Pursuit '90

Larry Parr
A Soldier's Tale '91

James D. Parriott
Heart Condition '90

Robert Parrish
Bobo '67
Casino Royale '67
Cry Danger '51
The Destructors '74
Fire Down Below '57
Journey to the Far Side of the Sun '69
A Town Called Hell '72

James Parrott
Pardon Us '31

Gordon Parry
Innocents in Paris '53
Tom Brown's School Days '51

John Parsons
Watched '73

Gabriel Pascal
Caesar and Cleopatra '46
Major Barbara '41

Pier Paolo Pasolini
Accatone! '61
Arabian Nights '74
The Canterbury Tales '71
The Decameron '70
Gospel According to St. Matthew '64
The Hawks & the Sparrows '67
Love Meetings '64
Notes for an African Orestes '70
Oedipus Rex '67
Salo, or the 120 Days of Sodom '75
Teorema '68

Ivan Passer
Born to Win '71
Creator '85
Crime & Passion '75
Cutter's Way '81
Fourth Story '90
Haunted Summer '88
Law and Disorder '74
The Nightingale '83
Silver Bears '78
Stalin '92

Giovanni Pastrone
Cabiria '14
Salammbo '14

Franca Pasut
Flashdance '83

Michael Pataki
Cinderella '77

Tom Patchett
Best Legs in the 8th Grade '84

Michael Pate
Tim '79

Raju Patel
In the Shadow of Kilimanjaro '86

Sharad Patel
Amin: The Rise and Fall '82

Stuart Paton
20,000 Leagues Under the Sea '16

Michael Patrick
Hider in the House '90

Nigel Patrick
Johnny Nobody '61

Robert Patrick
Road to Nashville '67

John D. Patterson
Deadly Innocence '88
Grave Secrets: The Legacy of Hilltop Drive '92
Legend of Earl Durand '74
The Spring '89

Pat Patterson
The Body Shop '72
Doctor Gore '75

Ray Patterson
The Good, the Bad, and Huckleberry Hound '88
Yogi's First Christmas '80

Richard Patterson
J-Men Forever! '79

Willi Patterson
Dreams Lost, Dreams Found '87

Michael Pattinson
...Almost '90
Ground Zero '88
Moving Out '83

Peter Patzak
Lethal Obsession '87
Midnight Cop '88
Slaughterday '77

Byron Paul
Lt. Robin Crusoe, U.S.N. '66

Steven Paul
Eternity '90
Falling in Love Again '80
Slapstick of Another Kind '84

Stuart Paul
Emanon '86
Fate '91

David Paulsen
Schizoid '80

George Pavlou
Rawhead Rex '87
Transmutations '86
Underworld '85

Alain Payet
Helltrain '80

Clark Paylow
Ring of Terror '62

Barry Peak
The Big Hurt '87

Michael Pearce
James Joyce's Women '85

Richard Pearce
Country '84
Dead Man Out '89
Heartland '81
Leap of Faith '92
The Long Walk Home '89
No Mercy '86
Sessions '83
Threshold '83

Robert E. Pearso
Devil & Leroy Basset '73

George Pearson
Midnight at the Wax Museum '36
A Shot in the Dark '33

Peter Pearson
Paperback Hero '73
Tales of the Klondike: The Unexpected '87

Max Pecas
Erotic Touch of Hot Skin '65
The Sensuous Teenager '70
Sweet Ecstasy '62

Brian Peck
The Willies '90

Sam Peckinpah
Ballad of Cable Hogue '70
Bring Me the Head of Alfredo Garcia '74
Convoy '78
Cross of Iron '76
Deadly Companions '61
The Getaway '72
Junior Bonner '72
The Killer Elite '75
Major Dundee '65
The Osterman Weekend '83
Pat Garrett & Billy the Kid '73
Ride the High Country '62
Straw Dogs '72
The Wild Bunch '69

Larry Peerce
Ash Wednesday '73
The Bell Jar '79
The Court Martial of Jackie Robinson '90
Elvis and Me '88
Goodbye Columbus '69
Hard to Hold '84
The Incident '67
Love Child '82
The Neon Empire '89
The Other Side of the Mountain '75
The Other Side of the Mountain, Part 2 '78
Queenie '87
A Separate Peace '73
The Sporting Club '72
The Stranger Who Looks Like Me '74
Two Minute Warning '76
Wired '89

Barbara Peeters
Bury Me an Angel '71
Humanoids from the Deep '80
Starhops '78
Summer School Teachers '75

Antonio Pelaez
Crystalstone '88

Anthony Pelissier
Encore '52

Scott Pembroke
Medicine Man '30

Nettie Pena
Home Sweet Home '80

Maurice Penczner
I Was a Zombie for the FBI '82

Chang Peng-I
Shaolin Kung Fu Mystagogue '84

Sze Ma Peng
Venus the Ninja '80s

Arthur Penn
Alice's Restaurant '69
Bonnie & Clyde '67
The Chase '66
Dead of Winter '87
Four Friends '81
The Left-Handed Gun '58
Little Big Man '70
The Miracle Worker '62
Missouri Breaks '76
Night Moves '75
Penn and Teller Get Killed '90
The Portrait '93
Target '85

Leo Penn
The Dark Secret of Harvest Home '78
Judgment in Berlin '88
A Man Called Adam '66

Sean Penn
The Indian Runner '91

D.A. Pennebaker
Don't Look Back '67

Eagle Pennell
Ice House '89
Last Night at the Alamo '83
The Whole Shootin' Match '79

David Peoples
The Blood of Heroes '89

Richard Pepin
Fist of Honor '92

Clare Peploe
High Season '88

Mark Peploe
Afraid of the Dark '92

Frank Peregini
Scar of Shame '27

Miguel Pereira
Veronico Cruz '87

Hope Perello
Howling 6: The Freaks '90

Antonio Perez
The 13th Mission '91

Etienne Perier
The Hot Line '69
Investigation '79
Murder at 45 R.P.M. '65
Zeppelin '71

Anthony Perkins
Lucky Stiff '88
Psycho 3 '86

Paul Perri
Revenge of the Virgins '62

Frank Perry
ABC Stage 67: Truman Capote's A Christmas Memory '66
Compromising Positions '85
David and Lisa '62
Diary of a Mad Housewife '70
Hello Again '87
Last Summer '69
Mommie Dearest '81
Monsignor '82
Rancho Deluxe '75
Skag '79
Swimmer '68

Peter Perry
Cycle Vixens '79

Bill Persky
How to Pick Up Girls '78
Serial '80
Wait Till Your Mother Gets Home '83

Francisco J. Lombardi Pery
The City and the Dogs '85

P.J. Pesce
Body Waves '91

Bonny Peters
Sandstone '74

Brooke L. Peters
Anatomy of a Psycho '61
The Unearthly '57

Charlie Peters
Passed Away '92

Wolfgang Petersen
Das Boot '81
Enemy Mine '85
For Your Love Only '79
In the Line of Fire '93
The NeverEnding Story '84
Shattered '91

Daniel M. Peterson
Girlfriend from Hell '89

Kristine Peterson
Body Chemistry '90
Critters 3 '91
Deadly Dreams '88
Eden 2 '93
Lower Level '91

Christopher Petit
Chinese Boxes '84
Unsuitable Job for a Woman '82

Elio Petri
10th Victim '65

Daniel Petrie
The Bay Boy '85
The Betsy '78
Buster and Billie '74
Cocoon: The Return '88
The Dollmaker '84
Eleanor & Franklin '76
Execution of Raymond Graham '85
Fort Apache, the Bronx '81
Lifeguard '75
Moon of the Wolf '72
Mystic Pizza '88
Neptune Factor '73
A Raisin in the Sun '61
Resurrection '80
Rocket Gibraltar '88
Silent Night, Lonely Night '69
Six Pack '82
Spy with a Cold Nose '66
Square Dance '87
Sybil '76
Toy Soldiers '91

Donald Petrie
Amazing Stories, Book 4 '85
Opportunity Knocks '90

Boris L. Petroff
Hats Off '37
Outcasts of the City '58

Giulio Petroni
Blood and Guns '79

Vladimir Petrov
The Inspector General '54
Peter the First: Part 1 '37
Peter the First: Part 2 '38

Joseph Pevney
Away All Boats '56
Man of a Thousand Faces '57
Mysterious Island of Beautiful Women '79
Night of the Grizzly '66
Tammy and the Bachelor '57
Torpedo Run '58
Who Is the Black Dahlia? '75

John Peyser
The Centerfold Girls '74
Four Rode Out '69
Kashmiri Run '69

Scott Pfeiffer
Firefight '87

Michael Pfleghar
Oldest Profession '67

Will Phelps
North Shore '87

Lee Philips
Barnum '86

John Prescott
Bootleg '89

Emeric Pressburger
Black Narcissus '47
A Canterbury Tale '44
The Elusive Pimpernel '50
The Life and Death of Colonel
  Blimp '43
Night Ambush '57
One of Our Aircraft Is Missing
  '41
The Tales of Hoffman '51

Michael Pressman
The Bad News Bears in
  Breaking Training '77
Boulevard Nights '79
Doctor Detroit '83
The Great Texas Dynamite
  Chase '76
The Imposter '84
Quicksand: No Escape '91
Secret Passions '78
Some Kind of Hero '82
Teenage Mutant Ninja Turtles
  2: The Secret of the Ooze
  '91
Those Lips, Those Eyes '80

Gaylene Preston
Dark of the Night '85

Ruben Preuss
Blackmail '91
Dangerous Company '88
In Dangerous Company '88
Write to Kill '91

Pierre Prevert
Voyage-Suprise '46

Steve Previn
Almost Angels '62
Escapade in Florence '62
Waltz King '63

B. Lawrence Price
Teenage Devil Dolls '53

David F. Price
Children of the Corn 2: The
  Final Sacrifice '92
To Die for 2 '91

Will Price
Rock, Rock, Rock '56

Joseph Prieto
Savages from Hell '68
Shanty Tramp '67

Barry Primus
Mistress '91

Prince
Graffiti Bridge '90
Under the Cherry Moon '86

Harold Prince
A Little Night Music '77
Something for Everyone '70
Sweeney Todd: The Demon
  Barber of Fleet Street '84

Ian Pringle
Panic Station '82

David A. Prior
Center of the Web '92
Deadly Prey '87
Death Chase '87
Double Threat '92
Future Zone '90
Hell on the Battleground '88
Invasion Force '90
Jungle Assault '89
Killzone '85
Lock and Load '90
The Lost Platoon '89
Mankillers '87
Mardi Gras for the Devil '93

Night Wars '88
Rapid Fire '89
White Fury '90

Vincent J. Privitera
Witchfire '86

Franco Prosperi
Counter Punch '71
Throne of Fire '82
The Wild Beasts '85

Iakov Protazanov
Aelita: Queen of Mars '24
Early Russian Cinema, Vol. 8:
  Iakov Protazanov '16

A.J. Prowse
Driving Force '88

Andrew Prowse
Demonstone '89

Craig Pryce
Revenge of the Radioactive
  Reporter '91

Richard Pryor
Jo Jo Dancer, Your Life is
  Calling '86
Richard Pryor: Here and Now
  '83

Alexander Ptushko
The Magic Voyage of Sinbad
  '52
Sword & the Dragon '56

Vsevolod Pudovkin
The End of St. Petersburg '27
Mother '26
Mystery of the Leaping Fish/
  Chess Fever '25
Storm Over Asia '28

Luis Puenzo
The Official Story '85
Old Gringo '89

Evelyn Purcell
Nobody's Fool '86

Joseph Purcell
Delos Adventure '86

Edmund Purdom
Don't Open Till Christmas '84

Manfred Purzer
Girls Riot '88

Dorothy Ann Puzo
Cold Steel '87

Joe Pytka
Let It Ride '89

Albert Pyun
Alien from L.A. '87
Bloodmatch '91
Captain America '89
Cyborg '89
Dangerously Close '86
Dollman '91
Down Twisted '89
Kickboxer 2: The Road Back
  '90
Nemesis '93
Radioactive Dreams '86
Sword & the Sorcerer '82

Mohy Quandour
The Spectre of Edgar Allen
  Poe '73

John Quested
Loophole '83

George P. Quigley
Murder with Music '45

Thomas Quillen
Apache Blood '75

Richard Quine
Bell, Book and Candle '58
Full of Life '56
Gun Crazy '69
Hotel '67
How to Murder Your Wife '64
My Sister Eileen '55
Oh Dad, Poor Dad (Momma's
  Hung You in the Closet &
  I'm Feeling So Sad) '67
Paris When It Sizzles '64
Prisoner of Zenda '79
Sex and the Single Girl '64
Strangers When We Meet '60
W '74
The World of Suzie Wong '60

Anthony Quinn
The Buccaneer '58

James Quinn
Blind Man's Bluff '91

John Quinn
Cheerleader Camp '88
Total Exposure '91

Gene Quintano
Honeymoon Academy '90
National Lampoon's Loaded
  Weapon 1 '93
Why Me? '90

Jose Quintero
Medea '59
Roman Spring of Mrs. Stone
  '61

Byron Quisenberry
Scream '83

**Arthur Maria
Rabenalt**
Unnatural '52

Fons Rademakers
The Assault '86
Because of the Cats '74
The Rose Garden '89

Peter Rader
Grandma's House '88
Hired to Kill '91

Michael Radford
Another Time, Another Place
  '83
1984 '84
White Mischief '88

Bob Radler
Best of the Best '89
Best of the Best 2 '93

Michael Raeburn
Killing Heat '84

Bob Rafelson
Black Widow '87
Five Easy Pieces '70
Head '68
The King of Marvin Gardens
  '72
Man Trouble '92
Mountains of the Moon '90
The Postman Always Rings
  Twice '81
Stay Hungry '76

Piccio Raffanini
Obsession: A Taste for Fear
  '89

Kevin Rafferty
The Atomic Cafe '82

Stewart Raffill
Across the Great Divide '76
The Adventures of the
  Wilderness Family '76
High Risk '76
Ice Pirates '84

Mac and Me '88
Mannequin 2: On the Move
  '91
The Philadelphia Experiment
  '84
Sea Gypsies '78
The Tender Warrior '71
When the North Wind Blows
  '74

Alan Rafkin
The Shakiest Gun in the West
  '68

Ubaldo Ragona
The Last Man on Earth '64

Ed Ragozzini
Sasquatch '78

Ken Raich
Hollywood Hot Tubs 2:
  Educating Crystal '89

Sam Raimi
Army of Darkness '92
Crimewave '85
Darkman '90
Evil Dead '83
Evil Dead 2: Dead by Dawn
  '87

Yvonne Rainer
The Man Who Envied Women
  '85

Alvin Rakoff
City on Fire '78
Death Ship '80
Dirty Tricks '81
The First Olympics: Athens
  1896 '84
King Solomon's Treasure '76
Mrs. Amworth '77
Mister Halpren & Mister
  Johnson '83
Room 43 '58
Say Hello to Yesterday '71
A Voyage' Round My Father
  '89

Alexander Ramati
The Assisi Underground '84

Vittoria Rambaldi
Primal Rage '90

Harold Ramis
Caddyshack '80
Club Paradise '86
Groundhog Day '93
National Lampoon's Vacation
  '83
Untamed Heart '93

Patrick Rand
Mom '89

Addison Randall
Chance '89
East L.A. Warriors '89
The Killing Zone '90

Tony Randel
Amityville 1992: It's About
  Time '92
Children of the Night '92
Hellbound: Hellraiser 2 '88

Arthur Rankin, Jr.
The Ballad of Paul Bunyan '72
Flight of Dragons '82
Frosty the Snowman '69
The Hobbit '78
The Return of the King '80
Santa Claus is Coming to
  Town '70

Lazlo Ranody
Nobody's Daughter '76

Frederic Raphael
Women & Men: Stories of
  Seduction '90

Joel Rapp
The Battle of Blood Island '60

**Jean-Paul
Rappeneau**
Cyrano de Bergerac '90
Lovers Like Us '75
Swashbuckler '84

Irving Rapper
Born Again '78
The Brave One '56
The Corn is Green '45
Deception '46
Forever Female '53
Joseph & His Brethren '60
Marjorie Morningstar '58
Now, Voyager '42
Rhapsody in Blue '45

Steve Rash
The Buddy Holly Story '78
Can't Buy Me Love '87
Queens Logic '91
Rich Hall's Vanishing America
  '86
Son-in-Law '93
Under the Rainbow '81

Jay Raskin
I Married a Vampire '87

Daniel Raskov
The Masters of Menace '90
Wedding Band '89

Tina Rathborne
Zelly & Me '88

Gregory Ratoff
Abdulla the Great '56
Adam Had Four Sons '41
Black Magic '49
The Corsican Brothers '42
Footlight Serenade '42
Intermezzo '39

Jans Rautenbach
No One Cries Forever '85

Max Raven
The Abomination '88

Ousama Rawi
The Housekeeper '86

John Rawlins
Dick Tracy Meets Gruesome
  '47
Dick Tracy's Dilemma '47
Shark River '53
Sherlock Holmes: The Voice
  of Terror '42

Albert Ray
Dancing Man '33
Shriek in the Night '33
13th Guest '32
Undercover Man '36

Bernard B. Ray
Broken Strings '40
Buffalo Bill Rides Again '47
House of Errors '42
Movie Stuntmen '53
Rio Rattler '35
Roamin' Wild '36

Fred Olen Ray
Alien Dead '85
Alienator '89
Armed Response '86
Bad Girls from Mars '90
Beverly Hills Vamp '88
Bio Hazard '85
Commando Squad '87
Cyclone '87

Ray ▶cont.

Deep Space '87
Evil Toons '90
Haunting Fear '91
Hollywood Chainsaw Hookers '88
Inner Sanctum '91
Mob Boss '90
Phantom Empire '87
Spirits '90
Star Slammer '87
Terminal Force '88
Tomb '86
Warlords '88

Nicholas Ray
Born to Be Bad '50
55 Days at Peking '63
Flying Leathernecks '51
In a Lonely Place '50
Johnny Guitar '53
The King of Kings '61
Knock on Any Door '49
The Lusty Men '52
On Dangerous Ground '51
Party Girl '58
Rebel Without a Cause '55
They Live by Night '49
A Woman's Secret '49

Satyajit Ray
The Adversary '71
Aparajito '58
Days and Nights in the Forest '70
Devi '60
Distant Thunder '73
The Home and the World '84
Pather Panchali '54
Two Daughters '61
The World of Apu '59

Michael Raye
Laserblast '78

Herman C. Raymaker
The Night Cry '26

Bill Raymond
Bolo '70s

Jack Raymond
The Speckled Band '31

Tom Raymonth
Battle of the Eagles '81

Spiro Razatos
Fast Getaway '91

Bill Rebane
The Alpha Incident '76
The Capture of Bigfoot '79
The Giant Spider Invasion '75

Eric Red
Body Parts '91
Cohen and Tate '88

Robert Redford
The Milagro Beanfield War '88
Ordinary People '80
A River Runs Through It '92

Carol Reed
The Agony and the Ecstasy '65
The Fallen Idol '49
Immortal Battalion '44
The Key '58
Kipps '41
Night Train to Munich '40
Odd Man Out '47
Oliver! '68
The Stars Look Down '39
The Third Man '49
Trapeze '56

Unicorn '83

James Reed
Mission Phantom '79

Jerry Reed
What Comes Around '85

Joel M. Reed
Bloodsucking Freaks '75
G.I. Executioner '71
Night of the Zombies '81

Luther Reed
Dixiana '30

Roland D. Reed
The House of Secrets '37

William Reed
Scorpion '86

Clive Rees
Blockhouse '73
When the Whales Came '89

Jerry Rees
The Marrying Man '91

Geoffrey Reeve
Caravan to Vaccares '74
Puppet on a Chain '72
Souvenir '88

Michael Reeves
The Conqueror Worm '68
The She-Beast '65

Thomas G. Reeves
Angry Joe Bass '76

Patrick Regan
Kiss Daddy Goodbye '81

Godfrey Reggio
Koyaanisqatsi '83
Powaqqatsi: Life in Transformation '88

Mark Reichart
Union City '81

Alastair Reid
Baby Love '69
Shattered '72
Teamster Boss: The Jackie Presser Story '92

Dorothy Reid
Sucker Money '34

Max Reid
Wild Thing '87

Tim Reid
The Little Mermaid '78

William Reilly
Men of Respect '91

Carl Reiner
All of Me '84
Bert Rigby, You're a Fool '89
The Comic '69
Dead Men Don't Wear Plaid '82
Enter Laughing '67
Fatal Instinct '93
The Jerk '79
The Man with Two Brains '83
Oh, God! '77
The One and Only '78
Sibling Rivalry '90
Summer Rental '85
Summer School '87
Where's Poppa? '70

Jeff Reiner
Blood & Concrete: A Love Story '90
Trouble Bound '92

Lucas Reiner
Spirit of '76 '91

Rob Reiner
A Few Good Men '92
Misery '90
The Princess Bride '87
Stand By Me '86
The Sure Thing '85
This is Spinal Tap '84
When Harry Met Sally '89

Gottfried Reinhardt
Betrayed '54

John Reinhardt
Open Secret '48

Max Reinhardt
A Midsummer Night's Dream '35

Lotte Reiniger
Adventures of Prince Achmed '27

Harald Reinl
Fight for Gold '86
Forger of London '61
The Invisible Dr. Mabuse '62
The Return of Dr. Mabuse '61
The Torture Chamber of Dr. Sadism '69

Irving Reis
The Bachelor and the Bobby-Soxer '47
Big Street '42
Crack-Up '46
Falcon Takes Over/Strange Bargain '49
Three Husbands '50

Walter Reisch
Men are not Gods '37

Allen Reisner
All Mine to Give '56

Charles F. Reisner
The Cobra Strikes '48
Train to Tombstone '50

Karel Reisz
Everybody Wins '90
The French Lieutenant's Woman '81
The Gambler '74
Isadora '68
Morgan! '66
Sweet Dreams '85
Who'll Stop the Rain? '78

Wolfgang Reitherman
The Rescuers '77
Robin Hood '73
Sleeping Beauty '59
The Sword in the Stone '63
The Wind in the Willows '49

Ivan Reitman
Dave '93
Ghostbusters '84
Ghostbusters 2 '89
Kindergarten Cop '90
Legal Eagles '86
Meatballs '79
Stripes '81
Twins '88

Norman Rene
Longtime Companion '90
Prelude to a Kiss '92

Jean Renoir
Boudu Saved from Drowning '32
Charleston '26
The Crime of Monsieur Lange '36
A Day in the Country '46
Diary of a Chambermaid '46
Elena and Her Men '56

Elusive Corporal '62
French Can-Can '55
The Golden Coach '52
Grand Illusion '37
La Bete Humaine '38
La Chienne '31
La Marseillaise '37
The Little Theatre of Jean Renoir '71
The Lower Depths '36
Madame Bovary '34
Picnic on the Grass '59
Renoir Shorts '27
The River '51
The Rules of the Game '39
The Southerner '45
The Testament of Dr. Cordelier '59
This Land is Mine '43
Toni '34
Tournament '29
Zero for Conduct/Taris/A Propos de Nice '91

Alain Resnais
Hiroshima, Mon Amour '59
Last Year at Marienbad '61
Mon Oncle D'Amerique '80
Muriel '63
Providence '77
Stavisky '74

Robert Resnikoff
The First Power '89

Harry Revier
Child Bride '39
The Lost City '34

Bernard Revon
The Rascals '81

Buddy Reyes
Night of the Kickfighters '91

Burt Reynolds
The End '78
Gator '76
Sharky's Machine '81
Stick '85

C.D.H. Reynolds
Day of Judgment '81

Christopher Reynolds
Offerings '89

Don Reynolds
His Name was King '85

Gene Reynolds
Truth or Die '86

Kevin Reynolds
The Beast '88
Fandango '85
Robin Hood: Prince of Thieves '91

Norman Reynolds
Amazing Stories, Book 5 '85

Ursi Reynolds
Ganjasaurus Rex '87

Mark Rezyka
South of Reno '87

Michael Rhodes
The Killing Mind '90
Matters of the Heart '90

Tonino Ricci
Great Treasure Hunt '70s
Rush '84

Bill Rice
The Vineyard '89

David Rice
Quiet Thunder '87

David Lowell Rich
Chu Chu & the Philly Flash '81
The Concorde: Airport '79 '79
Convicted '86
Enola Gay: The Men, the Mission, the Atomic Bomb '80
Family Upside Down '78
The Hearst and Davies Affair '85
Little Women '78
Madame X '66
Northeast of Seoul '72
Nurse '80
Satan's School for Girls '73

John Rich
Boeing Boeing '65
Clarence Darrow '78
Easy Come, Easy Go '67
Roustabout '64

Matty Rich
Straight Out of Brooklyn '91

Jef Richard
Berserker '87

Jefferson Richard
In Search of a Golden Sky '84

Pierre Richard
The Daydreamer '75
Too Shy to Try '82

C. Pennington Richards
Hour of Decision '57

Dick Richards
Culpepper Cattle Co. '72
Death Valley '81
Farewell, My Lovely '75
Man, Woman & Child '83
March or Die '77
Rafferty & the Gold Dust Twins '75

Lloyd Richards
Paul Robeson '70s

R.M. Richards
Heat '87

John Richardson
Dusty '85

Peter Richardson
Eat the Rich '87
The Pope Must Diet '91
Supergrass '87

Tony Richardson
The Border '82
The Entertainer '60
Hamlet '69
The Hotel New Hampshire '84
Joseph Andrews '77
The Loneliness of the Long Distance Runner '62
Look Back in Anger '58
The Loved One '65
Ned Kelly '70
Penalty Phase '86
Shadow on the Sun '88
A Taste of Honey '61
Tom Jones '63
Women & Men: Stories of Seduction '90

William Richert
A Night in the Life of Jimmy Reardon '88
Winter Kills '79

Anthony Richmond
Days of Hell '84
Deja Vu '84
A Man Called Rage '84
Night of the Sharks '89

Ota Richter
Skullduggery '79

W.D. Richter
The Adventures of Buckaroo
Banzai Across the Eighth
Dimension '84
Late for Dinner '91

James Ricketson
Kiss the Night '87

Tom Rickman
The River Rat '84

Philip Ridley
The Reflecting Skin '91

Leni Riefenstahl
The Blue Light '32
Tiefland '44
Triumph of the Will '34

Charles Riesner
Big Store '41
Lost in a Harem '44
Manhattan Merry-Go-Round
'37
Steamboat Bill, Jr. '28

Dean Riesner
Bill and Coo '47

Vladmir Rif
Very Close Quarters '84

J. Riffel
The House on Tombstone Hill
'92

Adam Rifkin
The Dark Backward '91
Never on Tuesday '88

Gennaro Righelli
Peddlin' in Society '47

Eran Riklis
Cup Final '92

Wolf Rilla
Bachelor of Hearts '58
Roadhouse Girl '53
Village of the Damned '60

Carlo Rim
Seven Deadly Sins '53

Taro Rin
Galaxy Express '82

Arthur Ripley
The Chase '46
Thunder Road '58

Frank Ripploh
Taxi zum Klo '81

Arturo Ripstein
Foxtrot '76

Michael Rischa
Delta Heat '92

Dino Risi
The Easy Life '63
How Funny Can Sex Be? '76
Il Sorpasso '63
Love in the City '53
Running Away '89
Sweet Smell of Woman '75
Tiger and the Pussycat '67

Marco Risi
Forever Mary '89

Michael Rissi
Soultaker '90

Michael Ritchie
An Almost Perfect Affair '79
The Bad News Bears '76
The Candidate '72
The Couch Trip '87
Diggstown '92

Divine Madness '80
Downhill Racer '69
Fletch '85
Fletch Lives '89
The Golden Child '86
The Island '80
The Positively True
Adventures of the Alleged
Texas Cheerleader-
Murdering Mom '93
Prime Cut '72
Semi-Tough '77
Smile '75
Survivors '83
Wildcats '86

Viktors Ritelis
Crucible of Horror '69

Martin Ritt
Back Roads '81
Black Orchid '59
The Brotherhood '68
Casey's Shadow '78
Conrack '74
Cross Creek '83
The Front '76
The Great White Hope '70
Hombre '67
Hud '63
The Long, Hot Summer '58
Molly Maguires '70
Murphy's Romance '85
Norma Rae '79
Nuts '87
Paris Blues '61
Pete 'n' Tillie '72
Sounder '72
The Spy Who Came in from
the Cold '65
Stanley and Iris '90

Giorgio Rivalta
The Avenger '62

Fernando A. Rivero
Nosotros '44

Joan Rivers
Rabbit Test '78

Jacques Rivette
The Nun '66
Paris Belongs to Us '60

Chris Roach
The 13th Floor '88

Frank Roach
Nomad Riders '81

Hal Roach
The Devil's Brother '33
One Million B.C. '40
Road Show '41

Hal Roach, Jr.
One Million B.C. '40

Seymour Robbie
Chrome Hearts '70
Marco '73

Jerome Robbins
West Side Story '61

Matthew Robbins
*batteries not included '87
Bingo '91
Corvette Summer '78
Dragonslayer '81
Legend of Billie Jean '85

Tim Robbins
Bob Roberts '92

Mike Robe
Child in the Night '90
Murder Ordained '87
News at Eleven '86
Son of the Morning Star '91
Urge to Kill '84

Jim Roberson
Legend of Alfred Packer '80

Syd Roberson
Robin Hood...The Legend:
The Time of the Wolf '85

Genevieve Robert
Casual Sex? '88

Yves Robert
My Father's Glory '91
My Mother's Castle '91
Pardon Mon Affaire '76
Pardon Mon Affaire, Too! '77
Return of the Tall Blond Man
With One Black Shoe '74
Salut l'Artiste '74
The Tall Blond Man with One
Black Shoe '72

Alan Roberts
The Happy Hooker Goes
Hollywood '80
Round Trip to Heaven '92
Young Lady Chatterly 2 '85

Daryll Roberts
How U Like Me Now? '92

Deborah Roberts
Frankenstein General Hospital
'88

Edward Roberts
The Adventurous Knights '35

Stephen Roberts
Ex-Mrs. Bradford '36
Star of Midnight '35

Cliff Robertson
Danger in the Skies '79
The Pilot '82

David Robertson
Firebird 2015 A.D. '81

Doug Robertson
HauntedWeen '91

John S. Robertson
Dr. Jekyll and Mr. Hyde '20
Little Orphan Annie '32
Our Little Girl '35
Shore Leave '25
The Single Standard '29
Soul-Fire '25

Joseph F. Robertson
Auntie Lee's Meat Pies '92

Herb Robins
The Worm Eaters '77

John Robins
Hot Resort '85

Arthur Robinson
Warning Shadows '23

Bruce Robinson
How to Get Ahead in
Advertising '89
Jennifer 8 '92
Withnail and I '87

Chris Robinson
Sunshine Run '79
Women's Prison Escape

John Mark Robinson
Kid '90
Roadhouse 66 '84

Lee Robinson
Walk into Hell '57

Phil Alden Robinson
Field of Dreams '89

In the Mood '87
Sneakers '92

Richard Robinson
Bloody Trail '72
Poor Pretty Eddie '73

Armando Robles
The Green Wall '70

Mark Robson
Avalanche Express '79
Bedlam '45
The Bridges at Toko-Ri '55
Champion '49
Daddy's Gone A-Hunting '69
Earthquake '74
From the Terrace '60
The Harder They Fall '56
Home of the Brave '49
The Inn of the Sixth
Happiness '58
Isle of the Dead '45
The Lost Command '66
Peyton Place '57
Phffft! '54
The Prize '63
The Seventh Victim '43
Valley of the Dolls '67
Von Ryan's Express '65

Marc Rocco
Dream a Little Dream '89
Scenes from the Goldmine '87
Where the Day Takes You '92

Glauce Rocha
Antonio Das Mortes '68
Black God & White Devil '64
Earth Entranced '66

Eric Rochant
The Fifth Monkey '90
Love Without Pity '91

Sean Roche
Chasing Dreams '81

Sheldon Rochlin
Signals Through the Flames
'83

Joe Rock
Cotton Queen '37

Alexandre Rockwell
In the Soup '92

Franc Roddam
Aria '88
The Bride '85
K2: The Ultimate High '92
The Lords of Discipline '83
Quadrophenia '79
War Party '89

Ismael Rodriguez
Daniel Boone: Trail Blazer '56

Robert Rodriguez
El Mariachi '93

Nicolas Roeg
Aria '88
Castaway '87
Cold Heaven '92
Don't Look Now '73
Eureka! '81
Insignificance '85
The Man Who Fell to Earth '76
Performance '70
Track 29 '88
The Witches '90

Larry Roemer
Rudolph the Red-Nosed
Reindeer '64

Michael Roemer
Pilgrim, Farewell '82
The Plot Against Harry '69

Rick Roessler
Slaughterhouse '87

Koos Roets
Brutal Glory '89

Julian Roffman
The Mask '61

Albert Rogell
The Admiral Was a Lady '50
Cyclone Cavalier '25
Li'l Abner '40
The Tip-Off '31
War of the Wildcats '43

Charles "Buddy" Rogers
The Devil's Brother '33
March of the Wooden Soldiers
'34

Maclean Rogers
Calling Paul Temple '48
Down Among the Z Men '52

Cliff Roguemore
Devil's Son-in-Law '77

Eric Rohmer
Boyfriends & Girlfriends '88
Chloe in the Afternoon '72
Claire's Knee '71
Four Adventures of Reinette
and Mirabelle '89
Full Moon in Paris '84
Le Beau Mariage '82
My Night at Maud's '69
Pauline at the Beach '83
Summer '86
A Tale of Springtime '92

Sutton Roley
Loners '72
Snatched '72

Bernie Rollins
Getting Over '81

Phil Roman
Be My Valentine, Charlie
Brown '75
A Charlie Brown Thanksgiving
'81
Good Grief, Charlie Brown '83
It's a Mystery, Charlie Brown
'87
It's Magic, Charlie Brown/
Charlie Brown's All Star '81
It's Three Strikes, Charlie
Brown '86
It's Your First Kiss, Charlie
Brown/Someday You'll
Find Her, Charlie Brown '77
Life is a Circus, Charlie
Brown/You're the Greatest,
Charlie Brown '80
She's a Good Skate, Charlie
Brown '80

Mark Romanek
Static '87

Eddie Romero
Beast of the Yellow Night '70
Beyond Atlantis '73
Brides of the Beast '68
Cavalry Command '63
Twilight People '72
WhiteForce '88
Woman Hunt '72

George A. Romero
The Crazies '73
Creepshow '82
The Dark Half '91
Dawn of the Dead '78
Day of the Dead '85
Knightriders '81
Martin '77
Monkey Shines '88

Aaron Russo
Rude Awakening '89

John Russo
The Majorettes '87
Midnight '81

Mardi Rustam
Evils of the Night '85

Mark Rutland
Prime Suspect '88

Todd Rutt
Shock! Shock! Shock! '87

Frank Ryan
Call Out the Marines '42

Edgar Ryazanov
A Forgotten Tune for the Flute '88
Private Life '82

Mark Rydell
Cinderella Liberty '73
The Cowboys '72
For the Boys '91
Harry & Walter Go to New York '76
On Golden Pond '81
The Reivers '69
The River '84
The Rose '79

Stellan Rye
Student of Prague '13

Judy Rymer
Who Killed Baby Azaria? '83

William Sachs
Galaxina '80
Hot Chili '85
Incredible Melting Man '77
The Last Hour '91
South of Hell Mountain '70
Van Nuys Blvd. '79

Alan Sacks
Dubeat-E-O '84

James Sadwith
Bluffing It '87
Sinatra '92

Eddie Saeta
Dr. Death, Seeker of Souls '73

Henri Safran
Norman Loves Rose '82
The Wild Duck '84

Boris Sagal
Angela '77
Girl Happy '65
Guns of Diablo '64
Masada '81
Night Gallery '69
Omega Man '71
The Runaway Barge '75

Leontine Sagan
Maedchen in Uniform '31

Malcolm St. Clair
The Bashful Bachelor '42
Bullfighters '45
The Grand Duchess and the Waiter '26

Christopher St. John
Top of the Heap '72

Gene Saks
Barefoot in the Park '67
Brighton Beach Memoirs '86
Cactus Flower '69
Last of the Red Hot Lovers '72
Mame '74
The Odd Couple '68

Henry Sala
Nightmare Weekend '86

Richard Sale
Let's Make it Legal '51
Ticket to Tomahawk '50

Sidney Salkow
The Last Man on Earth '64
Twice-Told Tales '63

Mikael Salomon
A Far Off Place '93

Victor Salva
Clown House '88

Jaime Salvador
Boom in the Moon '46

Gabriele Salvatores
Mediterraneo '92

Salvatore Samperi
Ernesto '79
Malicious '74
Submission '77

Edwards Sampson
The Fast and the Furious '54

Samson & Hopkins
Torment '85

Barry Samson
Ice Pawn '92

Fang Mui San
The Amsterdam Connection '70s

Denis Sanders
Invasion of the Bee Girls '73

Clifford Sandforth
Murder by Television '35

Jay Sandrich
For Richer, For Poorer '92
Seems Like Old Times '80

Mark Sandrich
Aggie Appleby, Maker of Men '33
Carefree '38
Cockeyed Cavaliers '34
Follow the Fleet '36
The Gay Divorcee '34
Hips, Hips, Hooray '34
Holiday Inn '42
Melody Cruise '32
Shall We Dance '37
Top Hat '35
A Woman Rebels '36

Helen Sanford
Angel of H.E.A.T. '82

Luk Pak Sang
Tattoo Connection '78

Jonathan Sanger
Code Name: Emerald '85

Jimmy Sangster
Dynasty of Fear '72
The Horror of Frankenstein '70
Lust for a Vampire '71

Erick Santamaria
Playgirl Killer '66

Alfred Santell
The Hairy Ape '44
Having Wonderful Time '38
Jack London '44
That Brennan Girl '46
Winterset '36

Cirio H. Santiago
Caged Fury '80
Cover Girl Models '75
Death Force '78
Demon of Paradise '87

Devastator '85
Dune Warriors '91
Equalizer 2000 '86
The Expendables '89
Eye of the Eagle '87
Fighting Mad '77
Future Hunters '88
The Muthers '76
Naked Vengeance '85
Raiders of the Sun '92
Savage! '73
She Devils in Chains
Silk '86
Silk 2 '89
The Sisterhood '88
Stryker '83
TNT Jackson '75
The Vampire Hookers '78
Wheels of Fire '84

Pablo Santiago
South Seas Massacre

Joseph Santley
Call of the Canyon '42
The Cocoanuts '29
Down Mexico Way '41
Harmony Lane '35
Melody Ranch '40
Music in My Heart '40

Damon Santostefano
Severed Ties '92

David Saperstein
Beyond the Stars '89
A Killing Affair '85

Deran Sarafian
Alien Predators '80
Back in the USSR '92
Death Warrant '90
To Die for '89

Richard Sarafian
The Arab Conspiracy '76
Eye of the Tiger '86
Gangster Wars '81
Man in the Wilderness '71
Man Who Loved Cat Dancing '73
Street Justice '89
Sunburn '79
Vanishing Point '71

Joseph Sargent
Amber Waves '82
Caroline? '90
Coast to Coast '80
Colossus: The Forbin Project '70
Freedom '81
Goldengirl '79
Hustling '75
Ivory Hunters '90
Jaws: The Revenge '87
MacArthur '77
Man on a String '71
The Manions of America '81
Maybe I'll Be Home in the Spring '71
Memorial Day '83
Miss Rose White '92
Never Forget '91
Nightmares '83
Passion Flower '86
Skylark '93
The Taking of Pelham One Two Three '74
Tomorrow's Child '82
Tribes '70
White Lightning '73

Marina Sargenti
Child of Darkness, Child of Light '91
Mirror, Mirror '90

Dick Sarin
Family Reunion '88

Vic Sarin
Cold Comfort '90

Maurice Sarli
The Bodyguard '76

Michael Sarne
Myra Breckinridge '70

Jonathan Sarno
The Kirlian Witness '78

Peter Sasdy
The Devil's Undead '75
Doomwatch '72
Hands of the Ripper '71
I Don't Want to Be Born '75
King Arthur, the Young Warlord '75
The Lonely Lady '83
Nothing But the Night '72
Rude Awakening '81
Taste the Blood of Dracula '70
Thirteenth Reunion '81
The Two Faces of Evil '82
Young Warlord '75

Barbara Sass
Without Love '80

Oley Sassone
Bloodfist 3: Forced to Fight '91
Final Embrace '92

Ron Satlof
Perry Mason Returns '85
Perry Mason: The Case of the Lost Love '87
Spiderman: The Deadly Dust '78
Waikiki '80

Buichi Sato
Baby Cart 4: Heart of a Parent...Heart of a Child '72

Hajime Sato
Body Snatcher from Hell '69
Terror Beneath the Sea '66

Junya Sato
The Go-Masters '82
The Silk Road '92

Carlos Saura
The Hunt '67

Claude Sautet
Cesar & Rosalie '72
Mado '76
A Simple Story '79
The Things of Life '70
Vincent, Francois, Paul and the Others '76

Derek Savage
The Meateater '79

Telly Savalas
Beyond Reason '77

Igor Savchenko
Guerilla Brigade '39

Brian Savegar
The Inheritor '90

Philip Saville
Fellow Traveler '89
Mandela '87
Max and Helen '90
Secrets '71
Shadey '87
Those Glory, Glory Days '83
Wonderland '88

Victor Saville
Conspirator '49

Dark Journey '37
Evergreen '34
Forever and a Day '43
Green Dolphin Street '47
The Iron Duke '34
It's Love Again '36
Kim '50
The Silver Chalice '54
Storm in a Teacup '37
Tonight and Every Night '45

Tom Savini
Night of the Living Dead '90

Nancy Savoca
Dogfight '91
True Love '89

Leopoldo Savona
The Mongols '60

Carlos Savrat
Ay, Carmela! '90
Blood Wedding '81
Carmen '83
Cria '76
El Amor Brujo '86
The Garden of Delights '70
Mama Turns a Hundred '79
The Stilts '84

Stephen Sayadian
Dr. Caligari '89

Eric Sayers
Common Law Wife '63

John Sayles
Baby It's You '82
The Brother from Another Planet '84
City of Hope '91
Eight Men Out '88
Lianna '83
Matewan '87
Passion Fish '92
Return of the Secaucus 7 '80
Unnatural Causes '86

James Sbardellati
Under the Gun '88

Joseph L. Scanlan
Nightstick '87
Spring Fever '81
The World's Oldest Living Bridesmaid '92

Umberto Scarpelli
The Giant of Metropolis '61

Romano Scavolini
Nightmare '82

Armand Schaefer
Exiled to Shanghai '37
Fighting Texans '33
Fighting with Kit Carson '33
Hurricane Express '32
Lightning Warrior '31
Miracle Rider: Vol. 1 '35
Miracle Rider: Vol. 2 '35
Outlaw Justice '32
Sagebrush Trail '33
Sixteen Fathoms Deep '34
Terror Trail '33

George Schaefer
Barefoot in Athens '66
Children in the Crossfire '84
Deadly Game '82
Doctors' Wives '70
Elizabeth, the Queen '68
Generation '69
Holy Terror '65
In This House of Brede '75
Invincible Mr. Disraeli '63
Lamp at Midnight '66
Lost Legacy: A Girl Called Hatter Fox '77
Once Upon a Scoundrel '73

A Time to Love & a Time to Die '58
Written on the Wind '56

Marlon Sirko
Perfect Killer '77

Hal Sitowitz
Last Cry for Help '79

Yuri Sivo
Mortal Sins '90

Alf Sjoberg
Miss Julie '50
Torment '44

Vilgot Sjoman
I Am Curious (Yellow) '67

Victor Sjostrom
The Outlaw and His Wife '17
The Phantom Chariot '20
Under the Red Robe '36
The Wind '28

Calvin Skaggs
The Fig Tree '87

Jerzy Skolimowski
Deep End '70
Hands Up '81
King, Queen, Knave '74
The Lightship '86
Moonlighting '82
The Shout '78
Success is the Best Revenge '85
Torrents of Spring '90

Guy Slater
A Pocketful of Rye '87

Bob Slatzer
Big Foot '72
Hellcats '68

John Sledge
The Invisible Avenger '58
New Orleans After Dark '58

Wladyslaw Slesicki
In Desert and Wilderness '73

Paul Sloane
The Coming of Amos '25
Consolation Marriage '31
Half-Shot at Sunrise '30
Made for Love '26

Rick Sloane
Hobgoblins '80s
Marked for Murder '89
Mind, Body & Soul '92
Vice Academy '88
Vice Academy 2 '90
Vice Academy 3 '91
Visitants '87

Edward Sloman
Lost Zeppelin '29

George Sluizer
Red Desert Penitentiary '83
The Vanishing '88
The Vanishing '93

John Smallcombe
African Dream '90

Ralph Smart
Curtain Up '53
Robin Hood: The Movie '55

Robert J. Smawley
American Eagle '90
Murphy's Fault '88
River of Diamonds '90

Jack Smight
Airport '75 '75
Airport '77 '77
Damnation Alley '77
Fast Break '79

Harper '66
Holocaust Survivors...Remembrance of Love '83
The Illustrated Man '69
Intimate Power '89
Loving Couples '80
Midway '76
No Way to Treat a Lady '68
Number One with a Bullet '87
Remembrance of Love '82
Roll of Thunder, Hear My Cry '78
The Secret War of Harry Frigg '68

Bruce Smith
Bebe's Kids '92

Bud Smith
Johnny Be Good '88

Charles Martin Smith
Boris and Natasha: The Movie '92
Fifty Fifty '93
Trick or Treat '86

Clive A. Smith
Rock & Rule '83

Howard Smith
Gizmo! '77
Marjoe '72

Kent Smith
Forever and a Day '43

Kiki Smith
Cave Girls '82

Mel Smith
The Tall Guy '89

Peter Smith
No Surrender '86

Richard Smith
Trident Force '88

Alan Smithee
Appointment with Fear '85
Bloodsucking Pharoahs of Pittsburgh '90
City in Fear '80
Fatal Charm '92
Ghost Fever '87
I Love N.Y. '87
The Indiscreet Mrs. Jarvis
Iron Cowboy '68
Let's Get Harry '87
Morgan Stewart's Coming Home '87
The Shrimp on the Barbie '90
Stitches '85

Stephen Smoke
Final Impact '91
Street Crimes '92

Phil Smoot
The Dark Power '85

Skott Snider
Miracle Beach '92

Michael Snyder
Caged in Paradiso '89

Michele (Michael) Soavi
The Church '90
The Devil's Daughter '91
Stagefright '87

Mark Sobel
Access Code '84
Sweet Revenge '87

Steven Soderberg
Kafka '91
King of the Hill '93

sex, lies and videotape '89

Hugo Sofovich
Departamento Compartido '85

Joel Soisson
Maniac Cop 3 '93

Peter Solan
The Boxer and Death '63

Gilberto Martinez Solares
Face of the Screaming Werewolf '59

Russell Solberg
Payback '90

Giovanni Soldati
The Lie '84

Alfred Sole
Alice Sweet Alice '76
Pandemonium '82
Tanya's Island '81

Sergio Sollima
The Family '73

Todd Solondz
Fear, Anxiety and Depression '89

Ola Solum
Turnaround '87

Paul Solvay
Devil's Wedding Night '73

Josef Sommer
Thoughts are Free '84

Stephen Sommers
The Adventures of Huck Finn '93
Catch Me...If You Can '89

Barry Sonnenfeld
The Addams Family '91
For Love or Money '93

Dimitri Sotirakis
Beverly Hills Brats '89

Jim Sotos
Forced Entry '75
Hot Moves '84
Sweet 16 '81

Colin South
In Too Deep '90

Larry Spangler
Joshua '76

Hans A. Spanuth
The Great Train Robbery: Cinema Begins '03

Teresa Sparks
Over the Summer '85

Robert Sparr
A Swingin' Summer '65

Shane Spaulding
Armed for Action '92

Martin Speer
The Hasty Heart '86

Michael Spence
Edge of Honor '91

Alan Spencer
Hexed '93

Jane Spencer
Little Noises '91

Josh Spencer
Easy Kill '89

Norman Spencer
Rainbow's End '35

Robert Spera
Witchcraft '88

Penelope Spheeris
The Boys Next Door '85
Decline of Western Civilization 1 '81
Decline of Western Civilization 2: The Metal Years '88
Dudes '87
Hollywood Vice Sqaud '86
Prison Stories: Women on the Inside '91
Suburbia '83
Thunder & Mud '89
Wayne's World '92

Larry Spiegel
Survival Run '80

Scott Spiegel
Intruder '88

Steven Spielberg
Always '89
Amazing Stories '85
Close Encounters of the Third Kind '77
The Color Purple '85
Columbo: Murder By the Book '71
Duel '71
Empire of the Sun '87
E.T.: The Extra-Terrestrial '82
Hook '91
Indiana Jones and the Last Crusade '89
Indiana Jones and the Temple of Doom '84
Jaws '75
Jurassic Park '93
Night Gallery '69
1941 '79
Raiders of the Lost Ark '81
The Sugarland Express '74
Twilight Zone: The Movie '83

Alan Spires
Little Boy Lost '78

Murray Douglas Sporup
Rock, Baby, Rock It '57

Roger Spottiswoode
Air America '90
The Best of Times '86
Last Innocent Man '87
The Pursuit of D.B. Cooper '81
Shoot to Kill '88
Stop! or My Mom Will Shoot '92
Terror Train '80
Third Degree Burn '89
Time Flies When You're Alive '89
Turner and Hooch '89
Under Fire '83

G.D. Spradlin
The Only Way Home '72

Tim Spring
Reason to Die '90

R.G. Springsteen
Apache Uprising '66
Arizona Cowboy '49
Hellfire '48
Hostile Guns '67
Johnny Reno '66
Oklahoma Annie '51
The Red Menace '49
Stagecoach to Denver '46
Vigilantes of Boom Town '46
When Gangland Strikes '56

Robin Spry
A Cry in the Night '93

Drying Up the Streets '76
Keeping Track '86
Obsessed '88

Pasquale Squitieri
Blood Brothers '74
Corleone '79
Third Solution '89

Stephen Stafford
I Posed for Playboy '91

Juan Bautista Stagnaro
Under the Earth '86

Eric Steven Stahl
Final Approach '91

John M. Stahl
Immortal Sergeant '43
The Keys of the Kingdom '44
Letter of Introduction '38

Roy Stahl
Scarlet Spear '54

Sylvester Stallone
Paradise Alley '78
Rocky 2 '79
Rocky 3 '82
Rocky 4 '85
Staying Alive '83

John Stanley
Nightmare in Blood '75

Michael Stanley
Attack of the Beast Creatures '85

Paul Stanley
Cotter '72
The Ultimate Imposter '79

Richard Stanley
Hardware '90

David L. Stanton
Chill Factor '90

Richard Stanton
American Pluok '25

Jeff Stanzler
Jumpin' at the Boneyard '92

George Stapleford
Mountain Charlie '80

Wladislaw Starewicz
Early Russian Cinema, Vol. 3: Starewicz's Fantasies '15

Bruce Starr
Boogey Man 2 '83

Ringo Starr
Born to Boogie '72

Jack Starrett
Cleopatra Jones '73
Fatal Chase '77
Hollywood Man '76
Kiss My Grits '82
The Losers '70
Mr. Horn '79
On the Edge: The Survival of Dana '79
Race with the Devil '75
Run, Angel, Run! '69
Slaughter '72
A Small Town in Texas '76
Walking Tall: The Final Chapter '77

Ralph Staub
Country Gentlemen '36
Danger Ahead '40
Gene Autry Matinee Double Feature #3 '53
The Mandarin Mystery '37

Ray Dennis Steckler
The Hollywood Strangler
Meets the Skid Row
Slasher '79
Incredibly Strange Creatures
Who Stopped Living and
Became Mixed-Up Zombies
'63
Rat Pfink a Boo-Boo '66
Sinthia: The Devil's Doll '70
The Thrill Killers '65
Wild Guitar '62

David Steensland
Escapes '86

Giorgio Stegani
Beyond the Law '68

Herbert Stein
Escape to Love '82

Ken Stein
The Rain Killer '90

Paul Stein
Counterblast '48
Heart's Desire '37
Lottery Bride '30
Mimi '35
Sin Takes a Holiday '30

Sandor Stein
Glitz '88

David Steinberg
Casey at the Bat '85
Going Berserk '83
Paternity '81

**David Max
Steinberg**
Severance '88

Michael Steinberg
The Waterdance '91

Ziggy Steinberg
The Boss' Wife '86

Danny Steinmann
Friday the 13th, Part 5: A New
Beginning '85
Savage Streets '83

Jos Stelling
The Pointsman '86
Rembrandt—1669 '77

Steno
Flatfoot '78

Frederick Stephani
Flash Gordon: Rocketship '36

A.C. Stephen
Lady Godiva Rides '68
Orgy of the Dead '65
Saturday Night Sleazies, Vol.
1 '66

Daniel Stern
Rookie of the Year '93

David Hillard Stern
Miracle on Ice '81

Noah Stern
Pyrates '91

Sandor Stern
Amityville 4 '89
Assassin '86
Dangerous Pursuit '89
Duplicates '92
John & Yoko: A Love Story
'85
Pin '88
Web of Deceit '90

**Steven Hilliard
Stern**
The Ambush Murders '82

Anatomy of a Seduction '79
The Devil & Max Devlin '81
Draw! '81
Final Notice '89
Forbidden Love '82
Getting Physical '84
Harrad Summer '74
I Wonder Who's Killing Her
Now? '76
Kill My Wife...Please! '91
Love & Murder '91
Mazes and Monsters '82
Murder in Space '85
Obsessive Love '84
The Park is Mine '85
Personals '90
Portrait of a Showgirl '82
Rolling Vengeance '87
Rona Jaffe's Mazes &
Monsters '82
A Small Killing '81
Undergrads '85
Weekend War '88
Young Love, First Love '79

Andrew Stevens
The Terror Within 2 '91

Arnold Stevens
Attack of the Swamp Creature
'75

David Stevens
The Clinic '83
Kansas '88
Roses Bloom Twice '77
A Town Like Alice '85

George Stevens
Alice Adams '35
Annie Oakley '35
A Damsel in Distress '37
The Diary of Anne Frank '59
Giant '56
The Greatest Story Ever Told
'65
Gunga Din '39
I Remember Mama '48
Kentucky Kernels '34
The More the Merrier '43
Penny Serenade '41
A Place in the Sun '51
Quality Street '37
Separate But Equal '91
Shane '53
Swing Time '36
Talk of the Town '42
Vivacious Lady '38
Woman of the Year '42

Leslie Stevens
Three Kinds of Heat '87

Mark Stevens
Cry Vengeance '54

Robert Stevens
Never Love a Stranger '58

Stella Stevens
Ranch '88

Robert Stevenson
The Absent-Minded Professor
'61
Bedknobs and Broomsticks
'71
Blackbeard's Ghost '67
Darby O'Gill & the Little
People '59
Dishonored Lady '47
Forever and a Day '43
Gnome-Mobile '67
Herbie Rides Again '74
In Search of the Castaways
'62
The Island at the Top of the
World '74
Jane Eyre '44

Joan of Paris '42
Johnny Tremain & the Sons of
Liberty '58
Kidnapped '60
King Solomon's Mines '37
The Las Vegas Story '52
The Love Bug '68
The Man Who Lived Again '36
Mary Poppins '64
The Misadventures of Merlin
Jones '63
Monkey's Uncle '65
My Dog, the Thief '69
My Forbidden Past '51
Nine Days a Queen '34
Non-Stop New York '37
Old Yeller '57
One of Our Dinosaurs Is
Missing '75
The Shaggy D.A. '76
Son of Flubber '63
That Darn Cat '65
Tom Brown's School Days '40
Walk Softly, Stranger '50

Alan L. Stewart
Ghetto Blaster '89
Ghostriders '87

**Douglas Day
Stewart**
Listen to Me '89
Thief of Hearts '84

John Stewart
Action U.S.A. '89
Hidden Obsession '92

Larry Stewart
The Initiation '84

Peter Stewart
Adventure Island '47
Arizona Gangbusters '40
Gun Code '40
State Department File 649 '49

Robert Stewart
Mark of the Beast
Rock & Roll Cowboys '92

Mauritz Stiller
The Atonement of Gosta
Berling '24
Hotel Imperial '27
Thomas Graal's Best Film '17
Thomas Graal's First Child '18
Treasure of Arne '19

Whit Stillman
Metropolitan '90

Alexander Stitt
Grendel, Grendel, Grendel '82

Mark Stock
Midnight Movie Massacre '88

John Stockwell
Undercover '87

Ben Stoloff
The Affairs of Annabel '38
It's a Joke, Son! '47
Palooka '34
Sea Devils '37
Transatlantic Merry-Go-Round
'34

Victor Stoloff
Washington Affair '77

Andrew L. Stone
The Girl Said No '37
Hell's Headquarters '32
Hi Diddle Diddle '43
The Last Voyage '60
Sensations of 1945 '44
Song of Norway '70
Stormy Weather '43

Norman Stone
Shadowlands '85
The Vision '87

Oliver Stone
Born on the Fourth of July '89
The Doors '91
The Hand '81
JFK '91
Platoon '86
Salvador '86
Seizure '74
Wall Street '87

Virginia Stone
Money to Burn '83

**Virginia Lively
Stone**
Run If You Can '87
The Treasure of Jamaica Reef
'74

Tom Stoppard
Rosencrantz & Guildenstern
Are Dead '90

Esben Storm
In Search of Anna '79

Howard Storm
Once Bitten '85
The Three Little Pigs '84

Jerome Storm
Courtin' Wildcats '29
Sweet Adeline '26

Mark Story
Odd Jobs '85

Thomas L. Story
Last Frontier '32

Larry N. Stouffer
Twisted Brain '74

Mark Stouffer
Man Outside '88

**Louis Clyde
Stouman**
Operation Dames '59

Frank Strayer
Condemned to Live '35
Death from a Distance '36
Fugitive Road '34
The Ghost Walks '34
In the Money '34
The Monster Walks '32
Murder at Midnight '31
The Vampire Bat '32

Barbra Streisand
The Prince of Tides '91
Yentl '83

Joseph Strick
The Balcony '63
Ulysses '67

Herbert L. Strock
Blood of Dracula '57
The Crawling Hand '63
How to Make a Monster '58
Man on the Run '74
Monster '78
Teenage Frankenstein '58
Witches' Brew '79

**William R.
Stromberg**
The Crater Lake Monster '77

Jonathan Stryker
Curtains '83

Brian Stuart
Sorceress '82

Mel Stuart
The Chisholms '79

Happy Anniversary 007: 25
Years of James Bond '87
I Love My...Wife '70
If It's Tuesday, This Must Be
Belgium '69
Mean Dog Blues '78
Sophia Loren: Her Own Story
'80
The Triangle Factory Fire
Scandal '79
Willy Wonka & the Chocolate
Factory '71

John Sturges
Alice Goodbody '74
Bad Day at Black Rock '54
By Love Possessed '61
The Capture '50
Chino '75
The Eagle Has Landed '77
The Great Escape '63
Gunfight at the O.K. Corral '57
The Hallelujah Trail '65
Hour of the Gun '67
Ice Station Zebra '68
Joe Kidd '72
Last Train from Gun Hill '59
The Law and Jake Wade '58
Magnificent Seven '60
Marooned '69
McQ '74
Never So Few '59
Underwater '55

Preston Sturges
The Beautiful Blonde from
Bashful Bend '49
Christmas in July '40
The Great McGinty '40
The Great Moment '44
Hail the Conquering Hero '44
Hail the Conquering Hero '44
The Lady Eve '41
Miracle of Morgan's Creek '44
The Palm Beach Story '42
The Sin of Harold Diddlebock
'47
Sullivan's Travels '41
Unfaithfully Yours '48

Charles Sturridge
Aria '88
Brideshead Revisited '81
A Handful of Dust '88
Where Angels Fear to Tread
'91

Richard Styles
Escape '90
Shallow Grave '87

Bobby Suarez
American Commandos '84
Pay or Die '83
Warriors of the Apocalypse
'85

Eliseo Subiela
Man Facing Southeast '86

Arne Sucksdorff
The Great Adventure '53

L. Sudjio
Black Magic Terror '79

Andrew Sugarman
Basic Training '86

Toshio Sugie
Saga of the Vagabond '59

Terrence Sul
Wonsan Operation '78

Fred G. Sullivan
Cold River '81

Jack Sullivan
The Charge of the Light
Brigade '36

Kevin Sullivan
Anne of Avonlea '87
Anne of Green Gables '85
Lantern Hill '90
Wild Pony '83

Jeremy Summers
Five Golden Dragons '67
The House of 1000 Dolls '67

Walter Summers
House of Mystery '41
The Human Monster '39

Shirley Sun
Iron & Silk '91

Cedric Sundstrom
American Ninja 3: Blood Hunt '89
American Ninja 4: The Annihilation '91
Captive Rage '88
The Revenger '90

Neal Sundstrom
Howling 5: The Rebirth '89

Jack A. Sunseri
The Chilling '89

Fred Surin
The Bride Is Much Too Beautiful '58

Henry Suso
Death Sport '78

Jean-Claude Sussfeld
Elle Voit des Nains Partout '83

Edward Sutherland
Behind the Front '26
Beyond Tomorrow '40
The Devil Thumbs a Ride/ Having Wonderful Crime '47
The Flying Deuces '39
Having Wonderful Crime '45
International House '33
It's the Old Army Game '26
Mr. Robinson Crusoe '32
The Navy Comes Through '42
Sing Your Worries Away '42

Hal Sutherland
The Fat Albert Christmas Special '77
The Fat Albert Halloween Special '77

Noribumi Suzuki
Shogun's Ninja '83

Jan Svankmajer
Alice '88

Peter Svatek
Mystery of the Million Dollar Hockey Puck '80s

E.W. Swackhamer
The Amazing Spider-Man '77
Are You Lonesome Tonight '92
The Dain Curse '78
Death at Love House '75
Death Sentence '74
Man & Boy '71
Night Terror '76
Perfect Family '92
The Rousters '90
The Secret Passion of Robert Clayton '92
Terror at London Bridge '85
Winds of Kitty Hawk '78

Bob Swaim
Half Moon Street '86
Masquerade '88

Don Swan
Gore-Met Zombie Chef From Hell '87

Bob Sweeney
Return to Mayberry '85

Charles Swenson
Little Rascals Christmas Special '79

Arthur Swerdloff
Road Racers '59

David Swift
Good Neighbor Sam '64
How to Succeed in Business without Really Trying '67
The Interns '62
The Parent Trap '61
Pollyanna '60

Saul Swimmer
Mrs. Brown, You've Got a Lovely Daughter '68

Michael Switzer
Fergie & Andrew: Behind Palace Doors '93
The Lightning Incident '91
Nitti: The Enforcer '88

Ron Switzer
Science Crazed

Peter Sykes
Demons of the Mind '72
Jesus '79
Night of the Laughing Dead '75
To the Devil, A Daughter '76

Paul Sylbert
Steagle '71

Istvan Szabo
Colonel Redl '84
Father '67
Hanussen '88
Love Film '70
Meeting Venus '91
Mephisto '81
25 Fireman's Street '73

William Szarka
Phantom Brother '88
South Bronx Heroes '85

Andras Szirtes
After the Revolution '90

Samy Szlingerbaum
Brussels Transit '80

Gyorgy Szomjas
Bad Guys '79

Boris Szulzinger
Mama Dracula '80
Shame of the Jungle '90

Jeannot Szwarc
Bug '75
Code Name: Diamond Head '77
Enigma '82
Extreme Close-Up '73
Jaws 2 '78
The Murders in the Rue Morgue '86
Santa Claus: The Movie '85
Sex Through a Window '72
Somewhere in Time '80
Supergirl '84

Sylvio Tabet
Beastmaster 2: Through the Portal of Time '91

Carlos Enrique Taboada
El Libro de Piedra '68

Jean-Charles Tacchella
Cousin, Cousine '76
The Last Winters '71

Gene Taft
Blame It on the Night '84

Kidlat Tahimik
Perfumed Nightmare '89
Turumba '84

Robert Taicher
Inside Out '91

Tibor Takacs
The Gate '87
Gate 2 '92
I, Madman '89
Red Shoe Diaries 2: Double Dare '92

Isao Takahata
Grave of the Fireflies '88

Rachel Talalay
Freddy's Dead: The Final Nightmare '91

Greg Tallas
Assignment Skybolt '80s
Cataclysm '81
Prehistoric Women '50

Richard Talmadge
Detour to Danger '45
Devil Horse '32
Project Moon Base '53

Harry Tampa
Fairytales '79
Nocturna '79

Shigeo Tanaka
Gamera vs. Barugon '66

Tokuzo Tanaka
Zatoichi: The Blind Swordsman's Vengeance '66

Senkichi Taniguhi
The Gambling Samurai '60
What's Up, Tiger Lily? '66

Terrell Tannen
Shadows in the Storm '88

William Tannen
Deadly Illusion '87
Flashpoint '84
Hero and the Terror '88

Alain Tanner
In the White City '83
Jonah Who Will Be 25 in the Year 2000 '76

Robert Tanos
Fly with the Hawk

Robert Tansey
Arizona Roundup '42
Death Valley Rangers '44
God's Country '46
Haunted Ranch '43
Lone Star Law Men '42
Outlaw Trail '44
Song of Old Wyoming '45
Sonora Stagecoach '44
Texas to Bataan '42
Western Mail '42
Where Trails End '42
Wild West '46
Wildfire '45

Daniel Taplitz
Black Magic '92
Nightlife '90

Michael Tarantini
Crimebusters '79

Quentin Tarantino
Reservoir Dogs '92

Andrei Tarkovsky
Andrei Rublev '66
The Mirror '75
My Name is Ivan '62
The Sacrifice '86
Solaris '72
Stalker '79

Max Tash
The Runnin' Kind '89
The Running Kind '89

Frank Tashlin
The Alphabet Murders '65
Artists and Models '55
Bugs vs. Elmer '53
Cartoon Moviestars: Porky! '47
Cinderfella '60
Disorderly Orderly '64
Fuller Brush Man '48
The Geisha Boy '58
The Girl Can't Help It '56
The Glass Bottom Boat '66
Hollywood or Bust '56
Just Plain Daffy '48
Son of Paleface '52
Susan Slept Here '54

Nadia Tass
Malcolm '86
Pure Luck '91
Rikky and Pete '88

Jacques Tati
Jour de Fete '48
Mr. Hulot's Holiday '53
Mon Oncle '58
Parade '74
Playtime '67

Norman Taurog
The Adventures of Tom Sawyer '38
Birds & the Bees '56
Blue Hawaii '62
Boys Town '38
Broadway Melody of 1940 '40
Bundle of Joy '56
The Caddy '53
Dr. Goldfoot and the Bikini Machine '66
Double Trouble '67
G.I. Blues '60
Girl Crazy '43
Girls! Girls! Girls! '62
Hold 'Em Jail '32
It Happened at the World's Fair '63
Jumping Jacks '52
Little Nellie Kelly '40
Live a Little, Love a Little '68
Men of Boys Town '41
Mrs. Wiggs of the Cabbage Patch '34
Palm Springs Weekend '63
Presenting Lily Mars '43
Rich, Young and Pretty '51
Speedway '68
Spinout '66
Sunny Skies '30
That Midnight Kiss '49
Tickle Me '65
The Toast of New Orleans '50
Words and Music '48

Bertrand Tavernier
Beatrice '88
The Clockmaker '76
Coup de Torchon '81
Death Watch '80
The Judge and the Assassin '75
Life and Nothing But '89
Round Midnight '86

A Sunday in the Country '84

Paolo Taviani
Allonsanfan '73
Good Morning, Babylon '87
Kaos '85
Night of the Shooting Stars '82
Padre Padrone '77

Vittorio Taviani
Good Morning, Babylon '87
Kaos '85
Night of the Shooting Stars '82
Padre Padrone '77

Baz Taylor
Near Misses '91

Don Taylor
Damien: Omen 2 '78
Escape from the Planet of the Apes '71
The Final Countdown '80
Going for the Gold: The Bill Johnson Story '85
Great Scout & Cathouse Thursday '76
Island of Dr. Moreau '77
Listen to Your Heart '83
My Wicked, Wicked Ways '84
Red Flag: The Ultimate Game '81
Ride the Wild Surf '64
Secret Weapons '85
September Gun '83
Tom Sawyer '73
Wild Women '70

Judd Taylor
The Christmas Coal Mine Miracle '77
Foxfire '87
Future Cop '76
License to Kill '84
Lovey: A Circle of Children 2 '82
Mary White '77
Out of the Darkness '85
Packin' It In '83
Question of Honor '80
Return to Earth '76
Say Goodbye, Maggie Cole '72
Search for the Gods '75

Ray Taylor
Adventures of Smilin' Jack '43
The Adventures of the Flying Cadets '44
Border Feud '47
Check Your Guns '48
Cheyenne Takes Over '47
Dick Tracy: The Original Serial, Vol. 1 '37
Dick Tracy: The Original Serial, Vol. 2 '37
Don Winslow of the Coast Guard '43
Don Winslow of the Navy '43
Fighting Vigilantes '47
Flaming Frontiers '38
Ghost Town Renegades '47
Hawaiian Buckaroo '37
Lost City of the Jungle '45
Mystery of the Hooded Horseman '37
The Painted Stallion '37
Panamint's Bad Man '38
The Perils of Pauline '34
Phantom of the Air '33
Rawhide '38
Return of Chandu '34
Return of the Lash '47
Riders of Death Valley '41
Stage to Mesa City '48
The Vigilantes are Coming '36

Ivan Tors
Zebra in the Kitchen '65

Bruce Toscano
The Jar '84

Robert Totten
Dark Before Dawn '89
Huckleberry Finn '75
Pony Express Rider '76
The Red Pony '76
The Sacketts '79
The Wild Country '71

Mikhail Toumanichulli
Solo Voyage: The Revenge '90

Jacques Tourneur
Appointment in Honduras '53
Berlin Express '48
Cat People '42
The Comedy of Terrors '64
Curse of the Demon '57
Days of Glory '43
Easy Living '49
Experiment Perilous '45
The Flame & the Arrow '50
The Giant of Marathon '60
Great Day in the Morning '56
I Walked with a Zombie '43
The Leopard Man '43
Nightfall '56
Out of the Past '47

Maurice Tourneur
A Girl's Folly '17
A Poor Little Rich Girl '17
Pride of the Clan '18
Trilby '17
Volpone '39
The Wishing Ring '14

Robert Towne
Personal Best '82
Tequila Sunrise '88

Bud Townsend
Coach '78
Nightmare in Wax '69
Terror at Red Wolf Inn '72

Patrice Townsend
Beach Girls '82

Robert Townsend
Eddie Murphy: Raw '87
The Five Heartbeats '91
Hollywood Shuffle '87
The Meteor Man '93

Ian Toynton
The Maid '90

Shiro Toyoda
Mistress '53
Snow Country '57

Benno Trachtmann
The Jumper '85

Jean-Claude Tramont
All Night Long '81
As Summers Die '86

Alfred Travers
Dual Alibi '47

Bill Travers
Christian the Lion '76

Stephen Traxler
Slithis '78

Peter S. Traynor
Death Game '76
Seducers '77

Norma Trelvar
A Nation Aflame '37

Brian Trenchard-Smith
BMX Bandits '83
Day of the Assassin '81
Day of the Panther '88
Dead End Drive-In '86
Escape 2000 '81
Fists of Blood '87
Out of the Body '88
The Quest '86
The Siege of Firebase Gloria '89

John Trent
Best Revenge '83
The Bushbaby '70
Crossbar '79
Find the Lady '75
Middle Age Crazy '80
Vengeance Is Mine '84

Georg Tressier
Teenage Wolfpack '57

Monika Treut
My Father is Coming '91
Seduction: The Cruel Woman '89

Dale Trevillion
Las Vegas Weekend '85
One Man Force '89

Gus Trikonis
Dempsey '83
The Evil '78
First Affair '83
Jungle Heat '84
Love on the Run '85
Miss All-American Beauty '82
Moonshine County Express '77
Nashville Girl '76
The Rumor Mill '86
She's Dressed to Kill '79
Take This Job & Shove It '81
Touched by Love '80
Twirl '81

Nadine Trintignant
Next Summer '84

Victor Trivas
The Head '59

Jan Troell
Flight of the Eagle '02
Hurricane '79
Zandy's Bride '74

Tzipi Trope
Tell Me That You Love Me '84

Gary Trousdale
Beauty and the Beast '91

Gary A. Troy
Computer Beach Party '88

Fernando Trueba
Twisted Obsession '90

Francois Truffaut
The Bride Wore Black '68
Confidentially Yours '83
Day for Night '73
Fahrenheit 451 '66
The 400 Blows '59
Godard/Truffaut Shorts '58
The Green Room '78
Jules and Jim '62
The Last Metro '80
Les Mistons '57
Love on the Run '78
The Man Who Loved Women '77
Mississippi Mermaid '69
Shoot the Piano Player '62
Small Change '76
The Soft Skin '64
Stolen Kisses '68

Story of Adele H. '75
Two English Girls '72
The Wild Child '70
The Woman Next Door '81

Michael Truman
Koroshi '67

Dalton Trumbo
Johnny Got His Gun '71

Douglas Trumbull
Brainstorm '83
Silent Running '71

Glenn Tryon
Law West of Tombstone '38
Small Town Boy '37

Manolis Tsafos
Rip-Off '77

Chan Tsi-liang
Lai Shi: China's Last Eunuch '88

Shinya Tsukamoto
Tetsuo: The Iron Man '92

Slava Tsukerman
Liquid Sky '83

Michael Tuchner
Adam '83
Amos '85
Hunchback of Notre Dame '82
The Misadventures of Mr. Wilt '90
Mistress '87
Not My Kid '85
The Old Curiosity Shop '75
The Summer of My German Soldier '78
Trapped in Silence '86
Trenchcoat '83

David Tucker
A Year in Provence '92

George Tucker
Traffic in Souls '13

Phil Tucker
Dance Hall Racket '58
Robot Monster '53

Roger Tucker
Deadly Recruits '86

Richard Tuggle
Out of Bounds '86
Tightrope '84

Montgomery Tully
Battle Beneath the Earth '68
Dead Lucky '60
The Electronic Monster '57
Glass Tomb '55
The House in Marsh Road '60
The Key Man '57
Paid to Kill '54
Strange Awakening '58
Terronauts '67
The Terronauts '67
The Way Out '56

Sandy Tung
Across the Tracks '89

Saul J. Turell
The Love Goddesses '65

Sophia Turkiewicz
Silver City '84

Rosemarie Turko
Dungeonmaster '85
Scarred '84

Zygmund Turkow
The Jolly Paupers '38

Lawrence Turman
Second Thoughts '83

Ann Turner
Celia: Child Of Terror '89

Chester Turner
Black Devil Doll from Hell '84

Kenneth Turner
The Love Pill '71

Jon Turteltaub
Driving Me Crazy '91
3 Ninjas '92

John Turturro
Mac '93

Frank Tuttle
Hell on Frisco Bay '55
Love 'Em and Leave 'Em '27
Lucky Devil '25
Roman Scandals '33
This Gun for Hire '42

Derek Twist
Green Grow the Rushes '51

David N. Twohy
Grand Tour: Disaster in Time '92

Jean Tych
Great Expectations '83

Tomu Uchida
Swords of Death '71

Seiichiro Uchikawa
One-Eyed Swordsman '63

Edgar G. Ulmer
The Amazing Transparent Man '60
Beyond the Time Barrier '60
The Black Cat '34
Bluebeard '44
Club Havana '46
The Daughter of Dr. Jekyll '57
Detour '46
Girls in Chains '43
Isle of Forgotten Sins '43
Jive Junction '43
Journey Beneath the Desert '61
The Light Ahead '39
Moon Over Harlem '39
Naked Venus '58
St. Benny the Dip '51
The Singing Blacksmith '38
Strange Illusion '45
The Strange Woman '46
Thunder Over Texas '34

Ron Underwood
City Slickers '91
Heart and Souls '93
Tremors '89

Lawrence Unger
Novel Desires '92

Michael Toshiyuki Uno
The Wash '88
Without Warning: The James Brady Story '91

Jeff Ureles
Cheap Shots '91

Frank Urson
The Night Club '25

Chano Urueto
The Living Head '59
The Witch's Mirror '60

Peter Ustinov
Billy Budd '62
Hammersmith is Out '72

Jamie Uys
Dingaka '65
The Gods Must Be Crazy '84

The Gods Must Be Crazy 2 '89

Jack Vacek
Rock House '92

Roger Vadim
And God Created Woman '57
And God Created Woman '88
Barbarella '68
Beauty and the Beast '83
Blood and Roses '61
Circle of Love '64
Dangerous Liaisons '60
The Game is Over '66
Game of Seduction '86
Le Repos du Guerrier '62
Night Games '80
Spirits of the Dead '68

Steve Vagnino
A Pleasure Doing Business '79

Ladislao Vajda
The Man Who Wagged His Tail '61

Luis Valdez
La Bamba '87
La Pastorela '92
Zoot Suit '81

Frank Valenti
Delta Force Commando 2 '90
War Bus Commando '89

Jon Valentine
Night of the Living Babes '87

Jean Valere
Time Out for Love '61

Tonino Valerii
My Name is Nobody '74
A Reason to Live, A Reason to Die '73

Robert Van Ackeren
A Woman in Flames '84

Jaco Van Dormael
Toto le Heros '91

Bruce Van Dusen
Cold Feet '84

Woodbridge S. Van Dyke
After the Thin Man '36
Andy Hardy Gets Spring Fever '39
Another Thin Man '39
Bitter Sweet '40
Forsaking All Others '35
Hide-Out '34
I Live My Life '35
I Love You Again '40
I Married an Angel '42
Journey for Margaret '42
Love on the Run '36
Manhattan Melodrama '34
Marie Antoinette '38
Naughty Marietta '35
Penthouse '33
Personal Property '37
The Prizefighter and the Lady '33
Rosalie '38
Rose Marie '36
San Francisco '36
Shadow of the Thin Man '41
Sweethearts '38
Tarzan, the Ape Man '32
The Thin Man '34
White Shadows in the South Seas '28

Ruud Van Hemert
Army Brats '84

Flesh and Blood Show '73
Frightmare '74
Home Before Midnight '84
House of the Long Shadows '82
House of Whipcord '75
Man of Violence '71
Schizo '77
Tiffany Jones '75

Stuart Walker
Werewolf of London '35

Gary Walkow
The Trouble with Dick '88

Richard Wallace
Bombardier '43
Captain Caution '40
The Fallen Sparrow '43
A Girl, a Guy and a Gob '41
It's in the Bag '45
Little Minister '34
A Night to Remember '42
Sinbad the Sailor '47
Tycoon '47
The Young in Heart '38

Rick Wallace
Acceptable Risks '86
California Girls '84
Time to Live '85

Stephen Wallace
For Love Alone '86
Prisoners of the Sun '91

Tommy Lee Wallace
Aloha Summer '88
The Comrades of Summer '92
Fright Night 2 '88
Halloween 3: Season of the Witch '82
Stephen King's It '90

Herb Wallerstein
Snowbeast '77

Hal B. Wallis
Anne of the Thousand Days '69

Raoul Walsh
Along the Great Divide '51
Battle Cry '55
Big Trail '30
Blackbeard the Pirate '52
Captain Horatio Hornblower '51
College Swing '38
Dark Command '40
Desperate Journey '42
Distant Drums '51
The Enforcer '51
Gentleman Jim '42
Gun Fury '53
High Sierra '41
The Horn Blows at Midnight '45
The King and Four Queens '56
A Lion is in the Streets '53
The Naked and the Dead '58
Northern Pursuit '43
Objective, Burma! '45
O.H.M.S. '37
Pursued '47
The Roaring Twenties '39
Sadie Thompson '28
Sea Devils '53
Silver River '48
Strawberry Blonde '41
The Tall Men '55
They Died with Their Boots On '41
They Drive by Night '40
The Thief of Baghdad '24
When Thief Meets Thief '37

White Heat '49

Walter Walsh
Going Hollywood '33

Charles Walters
Ask Any Girl '59
The Barkleys of Broadway '49
The Belle of New York '52
Billy Rose's Jumbo '62
Dangerous When Wet '53
Easter Parade '48
Easy to Love '53
The Glass Slipper '55
Good News '47
High Society '56
Lili '53
Please Don't Eat the Daisies '60
Summer Stock '50
The Tender Trap '55
Texas Carnival '51
Three Guys Named Mike '51
Torch Song '53
The Unsinkable Molly Brown '64
Walk, Don't Run '66

Fred Walton
April Fool's Day '86
Hadley's Rebellion '84
Homewrecker '92
The Rosary Murders '87
Trapped '89
When a Stranger Calls '79

Sam Wanamaker
Catlow '71
The Executioner '70
Killing of Randy Webster '81
Sinbad and the Eye of the Tiger '77

Peter Wang
A Great Wall '86
The Laserman '90

Steve Wang
The Guyver '91

Wayne Wang
Chan is Missing '82
Dim Sum: A Little Bit of Heart '85
Eat a Bowl of Tea '89
A Man, a Woman and a Killer
Slamdance '87

Orville Wanzer
The Devil's Mistress '68

Grzegorz Warchol
I Like Bats '85

Bill Ward
Ballad of a Gunfighter '64

David S. Ward
Cannery Row '82
King Ralph '91
Major League '89

Richard Ward
Sakura Killers '86

Vincent Ward
Map of the Human Heart '93
The Navigator '88
Vigil '84

Clyde Ware
Bad Jim '89
The Hatfields & the McCoys '75
No Drums, No Bugles '71

Chris Warfield
Little Miss Innocence '73

Ed Warnick
Manchurian Avenger '84

Charles Marquis Warren
Arrowhead '53
Charro! '69
Little Big Horn '51
Red Desert '50

Deryn Warren
Black Magic Woman '91
Bloodspell '87

Hal P. Warren
Manos, the Hands of Fate '66

Jerry Warren
Attack of the Mayan Mummy '63
Creature of the Walking Dead '60
Curse of the Stone Hand '64
Face of the Screaming Werewolf '59
Frankenstein Island '81
The Incredible Petrified World '58
Invasion of the Animal People '62
Man Beast '55
Teenage Zombies '58
Terror of the Bloodhunters '62
The Wild World of Batwoman '66

Joseph Warren
Urban Warriors '75

Norman J. Warren
Alien Prey '83
Bloody New Year '87
Horror Planet '80
Spaced Out '80
The Terror '79

Michal Waszynski
The Dybbuk '37

John Waters
Cry-Baby '90
Desperate Living '77
Divine '90
Female Trouble '75
Hairspray '88
Mondo Trasho '70
Multiple Maniacs '70
Pink Flamingos '73
Polyester '81

Peter Watkins
The Gladiators '70

James C. Watson
Night of the Demon '80

John Watson
Deathstalker '83
The Zoo Gang '85

William Watson
Heroes in Blue '39

Harry Watt
Eureka Stockade '49
Overlanders '46

Nate Watt
Law of the Pampas '39
Rustler's Valley '37

Roy Watts
Hambone & Hillie '84

Al Waxman
My Pleasure Is My Business '74
White Light '90

Ron Way
Frenchman's Farm '87

Keenan Ivory Wayans
I'm Gonna Git You Sucka '88

John Wayne
The Alamo '60
The Green Berets '68

Michael Weaver
Night Terror '89

Harry S. Webb
Laramie Kid '35
The Live Wire '34
Mesquite Buckaroo '39
Ridin' Thru '35
Riding On '37
Santa Fe Bound '37

Jack Webb
D.I. '57
Dragnet '54
Pete Kelly's Blues '55

Kenneth Webb
Just Suppose '26

Millard Webb
The Dropkick '27
Glorifying the American Girl '30

Peter Webb
Give My Regards to Broad Street '84

Robert D. Webb
Beneath the 12-Mile Reef '53
Love Me Tender '56
Seven Cities of Gold '55

William Webb
The Banker '89
Dirty Laundry '87
Party Line '88
Under Siege '92

Billy Weber
Josh and S.A.M. '93

Lois Weber
The Blot '21
Chapter in Her Life '23
Discontent '16
Too Wise Wives '21

D.J. Webster
Dark Side of the Moon '90

Nicholas Webster
Gone are the Days '63
Mission Mars '67
Purlie Victorious '63
Santa Claus Conquers the Martians '64

David Wechter
Malibu Bikini Shop '86
Midnight Madness '80

Stephen Weeks
Madhouse Mansion '74
Sword of the Valiant '83

Paul Wegener
The Golem '20
Student of Prague '13

Lo Wei
Chinese Connection '73
Fists of Fury '73
Shaolin Wooden Men
Tattooed Dragon '82

Alfred Weidenmann
Adorable Julia '62

Ken Weiderhorn
Return of the Living Dead Part 2 '88

Samuel Weil
First Turn On '83
Squeeze Play '79
Stuck on You '84
Troma's War '88
Waitress '81

Paul Weiland
Leonard Part 6 '87

Claudia Weill
Girlfriends '78
It's My Turn '80
Once a Hero '88

Chuck Wein
Rainbow Bridge '71

Bob Weinstein
Playing for Keeps '86

Harvey Weinstein
Light Years '88

Sandra Weintraub
The Deadliest Art: The Best of the Martial Arts Films '90
Women's Club '87

Peter Weir
The Cars That Ate Paris '74
Dead Poets Society '89
Gallipoli '81
Green Card '90
The Last Wave '77
The Mosquito Coast '86
Picnic at Hanging Rock '75
Plumber '79
Witness '85
The Year of Living Dangerously '82

Bob Weis
The Wacky World of Wills & Burke '85

Don Weis
Billie '65
The Gene Krupa Story '59
I Love Melvin '53
Munster's Revenge '81
Pajama Party '64
Zero to Sixty '78

Gary Weis
Diary of a Young Comic '79

Jack Weis
Crypt of Dark Secrets '76
Mardi Gras Massacre '78
Storyville '74

Straw Weisman
Dead Mate '88

Adrian Weiss
The Bride & the Beast '58

Gary Weiss
Wholly Moses! '80

Helmut Weiss
Tromba, the Tiger Man '52

Jiri Weiss
Sweet Light in a Dark Room '60

Robert Weiss
Amazon Women on the Moon '87

Mel Welles
Lady Frankenstein '72

Orson Welles
Chimes at Midnight '67
Citizen Kane '41
The Lady from Shanghai '48
Macbeth '48
The Magnificent Ambersons '42
Mr. Arkadin '55
Othello '52
The Stranger '46
Touch of Evil '58
The Trial '63

David Wellington
The Carpenter '89

My Girl '91
Private Benjamin '80
Slither '73
Unfaithfully Yours '84

Paul Ziller
Deadly Surveillance '91

Vernon Zimmerman
Fade to Black '80
Unholy Rollers '72

Fred Zinneman
Behold a Pale Horse '64
The Day of the Jackal '73
Five Days One Summer '82
From Here to Eternity '53
High Noon '52
Julia '77
A Man for All Seasons '66
The Member of the Wedding '52
The Men '50
The Nun's Story '59
Oklahoma! '55
The Search '48
The Seventh Cross '44
The Sundowners '60

Peter Zinner
The Salamander '82

Joseph Zito
Abduction '75
Friday the 13th, Part 4: The Final Chapter '84
Invasion U.S.A. '85
Missing in Action '84
Prowler '51
The Prowler '81
Red Scorpion '89

Vilmos Zsigmond
The Two Jakes '90

David Zucker
Naked Gun 2 1/2: The Smell of Fear '91
Police Squad! Help Wanted! '82
Ruthless People '86
Top Secret! '84

Jerry Zucker
Airplane! '80
Ghost '90
Police Squad! Help Wanted! '82
Top Secret! '84

Ralph Zucker
Terror Creatures from the Grave '66

Andrzej Zulawski
Possession '81

Frank Zuniga
Fist Fighter '88
Further Adventures of the Wilderness Family, Part 2 '77
The Golden Seal '83
Heartbreaker '83

Marcos Zurinaga
Tango Bar '88

Guido Zurli
Psychopath '68

John Zuru
The Mad Butcher '72

Martin Zweiback
Cactus in the Snow '72

Edward Zwick
About Last Night... '86
Glory '89
Having It All '82

Leaving Normal '92
Special Bulletin '83

Joel Zwick
Second Sight '89

Karl Zwicky
Contagion '87
Vicious '88

MUSIC VIDEO GUIDE

The **MUSIC INDEX GUIDE** alphabetically lists the titles of more than 4,000 music videos and music performance recordings. These videos are typically prefaced by the name of the artist for quick identification. Due to space limitations and the remarkable sameness of most of the reviews (Music star sings, dances, songs include...), these videos are not covered elsewhere in the book. Three-letter distributor codes immediately follow the video title. These codes refer to the distributors listed in the Distributor Guide at the back of the book. There, you'll find full contact information.

Music Video

ABBA *MVD, MON, TVC*
ABBA: Again *MVD, MON, TVC*
ABBA Gold: Greatest Hits *PGV*
ABBA: In Concert *NO*
ABBA: Story (1974-1982) *MVD*
ABBA: Waterloo *MCA*
Abbey Lincoln: You Gotta Pay the Band *PGV, MVD*
ABC: Absolutely ABC *MVD, PGV*
ABC: Mantrap *MVD, COL*
Abrasive Wheels *MVD*
AC/DC: Clipped *AVE, FFF*
AC/DC: Fly on the Wall *MVD, AVE, FFF*
AC/DC: Let There Be Rock *MVD, WAR*
AC/DC: Live at Donington *MVD, AVE, FFF*
AC/DC: The Interview Sessions *MVD*
AC/DC: Who Made Who *MVD, AVE, FFF*
A.C. Jobim/Gal Costa: Rio Revisited *MVD*
Acoustic Sounds from Africa
Adam and the Ants *FOX*
Adam and the Ants: Prince Charming Revue *FOX*
Adam Ant: Antics in the Forbidden Zone *MVD, SMV*
Aerosmith: The Making of ''Pump'' *MVD, SMV, IME*
Aerosmith: Things That Go Pump in the Night *MVD*
Aerosmith: 3 x 5 *MVD*
Aerosmith: Video Scrapbook *MVD, FOX*
Afrika Bambaataa & Family: Electric Dance Hop *MVD, MPI*
Agent Steel: Mad Locust Rising *MVD*
Agony *MVD*
A-Ha: The Hits *MVD*
Aida *HMV, HBO, ING*
Aim High America *TGV*
Air Supply: Live in Hawaii *MVD*

Al Green: Gospel According to Al Green *MVD, IME, FCT*
Al Green: On Fire in Tokyo *MVD, XVC, FCT*
Al Jarreau in London *MVD, WRV, PIA*
Alabama: Greatest Hits Video *MVD, COL, PIA*
Alabama: Pass It on Down *MVD, BMG, PIA*
Alan Holdsworth: Tokyo Dream *MVD*
Alan T.D. Wiggins & Band in Concert *PRH, MVD*
Alannah Myles *MVD, AVE, FFF*
The Alarm: Blaze of Glory—Greatest Hits Live in Concert *SVI, MVD*
Alarm: Spirit of '86 *MCA, MVD*
Alarm: Standards *MVD*
Alberta Hunter *CMR*
Alcatraz: Metallic Live '84 in Japan *MVD*
Alcatraz: Power Live *MVD*
Alejandra Guzman: La Diva del Rock *MVD*
Alejandra Guzman: Lo Mejor de Alejandra Guzman *MVD*
Alexander O'Neal: Live in London *MVD, SMV*
Alice Cooper & Friends *MED*
Alice Cooper: The Nightmare Returns *MCA, MVD*
Alice Cooper: Trash These Videos *MVD, SMV*
Alice Cooper Trashes the World *MVD, SMV*
Alice Cooper: Welcome to My Nightmare *MVD, RHI, VTK*
Alice in Chains: Live Facelift *SMV*
Alien Sex Fiend: A Purple Glistener *MVD*
Alien Sex Fiend: Edit *MVD*
Alien Sex Fiend: Overdose *MVD*
All Aboard: A Collection of Music Videos for Children
All Soul's Day Concert 1983 *NO*
All Soul's Day Concert 1985 *NO*

All-Star Country Music Fair *BMG, MVD*
All-Star Gospel Session *MVD, AVE, HBO*
The All-Star Reggae Session *HBO, MVD, IME*
All-Star Swing Festival *MVD, VES, VTK*
All Strings Attached *MVD*
The Allman Brothers Band: Brothers of the Road *MVD, COL, PIA*
Almighty: Soul Destruction Live *MVD*
Alyssa Milano: Look in My Heart *MVD*
Amazing Grace with Bill Moyers *PBS, PAV, KAR*
Amazon Dreams *MTX, KAR*
America Live in Central Park *PIA*
American Patchwork: Land Where Blues Began *PBS, PAV, TVC*
American Suite *SVS, KAR*
America's Music: Chicago and All That Jazz *MVD, CTY*
America's Music, Vol. 2: Country & Western 2 *MVD, CTY*
America's Music, Vol. 3: Blues 1 *CTY, MVD*
America's Music, Vol. 4: Blues 2 *CTY, MVD, FCT*
America's Music, Vol. 5: Rhythm and Blues 1 *CTY, MVD, FCT*
America's Music, Vol. 6: Rhythm and Blues 2 *CTY, MVD, FCT*
America's Music, Vol. 7: Folk 1 *MVD, CTY*
America's Music, Vol. 8: Folk 2 *MVD, CTY*
America's Music, Vol. 9: Jazz Then Dixieland 1 *MVD, CTY*
America's Music, Vol. 10: Dixieland 2 *CTY, MVD*
America's Music, Vol. 11: Soul 1 *CTY, MVD, FCT*
America's Music, Vol. 12: Soul 2 *CTY, MVD, FCT*
America's Music, Vol. 13: Gospel 1 *MVD, CTY, FCT*

America's Music, Vol. 14: Gospel 2 *MVD, CTY, FCT*
America's Music, Vol. 15: Rock 'n Roll 1 *MVD*
America's Music, Vol. 16: Rock 'n Roll 2 *MVD*
Amy Grant: Age to Age *MVD, A&M, COL*
Amy Grant: Find a Way *A&M, COL, MVD*
Amy Grant: Heart in Motion *A&M, MVD*
Amy Grant's Old Fashioned Christmas *PGV*
Anasa Briggs: Gospel Festival *NO*
Anderson, Bruford, Wakeman and Howe: In the Big Dream *SWH, MVD, PIA*
Andre Walton: Arise Skates *SPW*
Andrew Lloyd Webber: Requiem *HMV, KUL, MVD*
Andrew Lloyd Webber: The Premiere Collection Encore *PGV*
Angelic Gospel Singers: Gospel in Motion *MVD*
Animotion. Video EP *MVD*
Anita Baker: One Night of Rapture *MVD*
Anita O'Day: Live at Ronnie Scotts *MVD*
Anna Russell: The (First) Farewell Concert *BFS, MVD, HMV*
Anna Russell's Farewell Special *MTP*
Annie Lennox: Diva *BMG, MVD*
Anthrax: Attack of the Killer Videos *PGV*
Anthrax: Live Noize *PGV, MVD*
Anthrax: Oidivnikufesin (N.F.V.) *NO*
Anthrax: Through Time P.O.V. *PGV, MVD*
Any Child is My Child *CIG*
April Wine *SVS*
April Wine: Live in London *HBO, PIA*
Arabella *MVD, PGV*
Arcadia *MVD*

''Are My Ears on Wrong?''— A Profile of Charles Ives
Aretha Franklin: Ridin' on the Freeway *MVD, COL*
Aretha Franklin: The Queen of Soul *PAV, AVE, MVD*
Arlen Roth Band: Live in England *MVD*
Armored Saint: A Trip Thru Red Times *MVD, WRV*
A.R.M.S. Concert: Complete *MVD*
A.R.M.S. Concert: Part 1 *MVD, MED*
A.R.M.S. Concert: Part 2 *MVD, MED*
Arrested Development: Home Video *MVD*
Art Blakey & The Jazz Messengers: Japan 1961 *MVD*
Art Blakey: The Jazz Life *MVD*
Art Ensemble of Chicago: Live from the Jazz Showcase *MVD, RHP, KIV*
The Art of Noise: In Visible Silence *MVD*
Arthur Rubinstein: Last Recital for Israel *MVD, BMG*
Artur Rubinstein *KUL, MVD*
Arvis Strickling Jones: From the Inside Out *PRH, MVD*
Ashford and Simpson *HBO, PIA*
Asia in Asia *MVD, VES, PIA*
Asia: Live in Moscow *MOV, RHI, MVD*
Asia: Live in Moscow, 1990 *MVD*
Asia: Live in the UK, 1990 *MVD*
Aswad: Always Wicked *MVD*
Aswad & Pablo Moses: Reggae in the Hills *MVD*
Aswad: Distant Thunder Live *MVD*
Aswad: Live at Light House Studio *MVD*
Atlantic Starr: As the Band Turns...The Video *A&M*
Auf der schwaeb'sche Eise'bahne *GLV*

Aurex Jazz Festival Fusion Super Jam *MVD*
Australia Now *MVD, MED*
Avengers *MVD*
Average White Band Shine *NO*
B-52s: 1979-1989 *MVD*
Babalu Music! I Love Lucy's Greatest Hits *FXV*
Baby Snakes: The Complete Version *MVD, MPI*
Babyface: Tender Lover *MVD, SMV*
Bach: All That Bach—A Celebration *MVD, VAI, VYG*
Bach: Magnificat *MVD*
Bach: St. John Passion *MVD, IME*
Back to the 50's, Vol. 1 *SIM*
Bad English *MVD, SMV*
Bad News Tour *MVD, RHI*
Bad Religion: Along the Way *MVD*
B.A.L.L. *MVD*
Bananarama: And That's Not All... *SVS, MVD*
Bananarama: The Greatest Hits Collection *MVD, PGV*
Bananarama: True Confessions *MVD*
The Band: Japan Tour '83 *MVD*
The Band Reunion *MED*
Band Together at CBGB's *MVD*
Banda Vallarta: Banda Vallarta Show *MVD*
Bangles Greatest Hits *MVD, SMV*
Banjo Feedback *WMM*
The Barber of Seville *PIA, HMV, MVD*
Barbra Streisand: A Happening in Central Park *FOX, MVD, PIA*
Barbra Streisand: Color Me Barbra *MVD, FOX*
Barbra Streisand: My Name is Barbra *MVD, FOX*
Barbra Streisand: One Voice *FOX, MVD, PIA*
Barbra Streisand: Putting It Together *FOX, MVD, PIA*
Barnes and Barnes: Zabagabee *MVD, RHI*
Barney in Concert *LGV*
Barrington Levy *MVD*
Barry Gibb: Now Voyager *MCA, MVD*
Barry Manilow: Because It's Christmas *BMG, SWH*
Barry Manilow: First Special *MGM*
Barry Manilow: Live at the Greek *NO*
Barry Manilow: Live on Broadway *MVD, BMG, PIA*
Barry Manilow: Making of 2 A.M. Paradise Cafe *MVD, COL, BMG*
Barry Manilow: The Concert at Blenheim Palace *MVD, RCA, PIA*
Baryshnikov: The Dancer and the Dance *MVD, VTK, HMV*
Basia: Prime Time TV *MVD, SMV*
Batouka: 1st International Festival of Percussion *RHP, FCT*
Bauhaus: Archive *MVD*
Bauhaus/Chrome: Compilation *MVD*
Bauhaus: Shadow of Light *MVD*

Bay City Rollers: Japan Tour, 1976 *MVD*
B.B. King and Friends: A Night of Red Hot Blues *HBO, AVE, MVD*
B.B. King: Blues Master #1 *MVD*
B.B. King: Live at Nick's *SVS, VTK*
B.B. King: Live at the Apollo *GRP, MVD*
B.B. King: Live in Africa *HBO, MVD, FCT*
B.B. King: Memories of Greatness Live *MVD*
Beast of I.R.S., Vol. 1
The Beastie Boys *MVD, FOX*
The Beastie Boys: The Skills to Pay the Bills *EMI, MVD*
Beat of the Live Drum *COL*
Beatlemania! The Movie *IME*
The Beatles: Live at Budokan *MVD*
Beatles Live: Ready, Steady, Go *VTK, MVD, KAR*
The Beatles: The Mystery Trip *MVD*
Beats Go On: Percussion from Pleistocene to Paradiddle *CHI*
Bebe Cece Winans! *CTL, MVD*
The Bee Gees: Music Biography *MVD*
Bee Gees: One for All Tour, Vol. 1 *MVD, MPI*
Bee Gees: One for All Tour, Vol. 2 *MVD, MPI*
Beethoven *IFB*
Beethoven and His Music *MTI*
Beethoven Cycle *PRS, PIA*
Beethoven: Ordeal and Triumph
Beethoven Piano Concerti *MVD, HMV*
Beethoven: Piano Concerti 3 & 4 *MVD, PGV*
Beethoven: Piano Concerto No. 3 *MVD*
Beethoven: Piano Concerto No. 5 "Emperor" *MVD, PGV*
Beethoven: Symphony No. 5 *MVD, KUL*
Beethoven: Symphony No. 5—Concert Aid *MVD, KUL*
Beethoven Symphony No. 6 "Pastoral" *VVV*
Beethoven: Symphony No. 9 *PGV*
Beethoven, the Cello, and Paul Tortelier
Beggar's Opera *MVD, HMV, FCT*
Behind the Scenes *CMR, NYS*
Bela Fleck and the Flecktones: Flight of the Cosmic Hippo *WRV*
Belinda *MCA, MVD*
Belinda Carlisle: Belinda Live *MVD, MCG*
Belinda Carlisle: Runaway Live *MCA, MVD*
Belinda Carlisle: Runaway Videos *MVD, MCA, PIA*
Bell Biv Devoe: Mental Videos *MVD*
Bell Biv Devoe: Word to the Mutha! *MCA, MVD*
Bellini: La Sonnambula *MVD, VWV*
The Beloved: Happiness *MVD, AVE, FFF*
Ben Vereen: Sing Along Live with the Peter Pan Kids *PPI, MVD*

Ben Webster/Dexter Gordon: Top Tenors *MVD*
Benefit Concert 1
Benefit Concert 2
Benko of Hungary Jazz Band *NO*
Benny Golson/Tubby Hayes *MVD*
Benny Goodman: 1980 Aurex Jazz Festival *MVD*
Benny Goodman: Live *MVD*
Berlin *SVS*
Berlin Dream *MVD*
Bernadette Peters in Concert *MCA, PIA*
Bernstein: Candide *MVD*
Bernstein Conducts Beethoven: Program 1 *FLI*
Bernstein Conducts Beethoven: Program 2 *FLI*
Bernstein Conducts Beethoven: Program 3 *FLI*
Bernstein Conducts Beethoven: Program 4 *FLI*
Bernstein Conducts Beethoven: Program 5 *FLI*
Bernstein Conducts Beethoven: Program 6 *FLI*
Bernstein Conducts Beethoven: Program 7 *FLI*
Bernstein Conducts Beethoven: Program 8 *FLI*
Bernstein Conducts Beethoven: Program 9 *FLI*
Bernstein Conducts Beethoven: Program 10 *FLI*
Bernstein In Berlin: Ode to Freedom, Beethoven's Symphony No. 9 *MVD*
Bernstein on Beethoven: A Tribute *BFA*
Bernstein on Beethoven: Fidelio *BFA*
Bernstein on Beethoven: Ode to Joy *BFA*
Bernstein on Beethoven Series *BFA*
Bernstein: West Side Story *MVD*
Bessie Smith and Friends *MVD, AFR*
Best of Berlin Independence Days *MVD*
Best of Blondie *MVD, PAV*
Best of Elvis Costello and the Attractions *MVD, FOX*
Best of Judy Garland *COL, OM*
The Best of MTV's 120 Minutes *RHI*
Best of New Faces *VDM*
The Best of New Orleans Live *MVD*
The Best of New Wave Theatre, Vol. 1 *MVD, RHI*
The Best of New Wave Theatre, Vol. 2 *MVD, RHI*
The Best of Perry Como *TVC*
The Best of Prince's Trust *MVD*
Best of Reggae Sunsplash, Part 1 *SMV, FCT*
Best of Reggae Sunsplash, Part 2 *MVD*
Best of Spike Jones, Vol. 1 *PAR*
Best of Spike Jones, Vol. 2 *PAR*
Best of the Cutting Edge, Vol. 1 *RHI, IME*
Best of the Cutting Edge, Vol. 2 *RHI, IME*
The Best of the Fest: New Orleans Jazz & Heritage Festival *MVD*

Best of Videophile *MVD*
Best of West Coast Rock, Vol. 1 *MVD*
Best of West Coast Rock, Vol. 2 *MVD*
Best of West Coast Rock, Vol. 3 *MVD*
Bette Midler: Art or Bust *VES, LIV*
Bette Midler: Mondo Beyondo *MVD, HBO*
Bette Midler Show *SUE, OM*
Beverly Sills in La Traviata
Big Audio Dynamite: BAD 1 & 2 *SMV, MVD*
Big Bands at Disneyland (3 volume set) *DIS, OM*
Big Bands, Vol. 101 *VTK*
Big Bands, Vol. 102 *KRT*
Big Bands, Vol. 103 *KRT*
Big Bands, Vol. 104 *KRT*
Big Bands, Vol. 105 *KRT*
Big Bands, Vol. 106 *KRT*
Big Bands, Vol. 107 *MVD, KRT, VTK*
Big Bands, Vol. 108 *KRT*
Big Bands, Vol. 109 *KRT*
Big Bands, Vol. 110 *KRT*
Big Bands, Vol. 111 *KRT*
Big Black: Live Video *MVD*
Big Black: Pigpile *MVD*
Big Black: The Last Blast *MVD*
Big Brother and the Holding Company: Ball and Chain *MVD, RHI*
Big Country Live *MVD, MED*
Big Country: Live in New York *MVD*
Big Daddy Kane: Chocolate City *MVD, WRV*
Big Pig—Bonk: The Videos *A&M*
The Biggest Band Show in the World *TVC*
Bill Bruford: Bruford and the Beat *MVD*
Bill Evans *CMR*
Bill Evans: Live at the Maintenance Shop, 1979 *MVD*
Bill Evans: Universal Mind *FCT*
Bill Harley: Who Made this Mess *PGV, MVD*
Bill Watrous *SVS*
Bill Wyman *SVS*
Bill Wyman: Digital Dreams *MVD, MED*
Billy Bragg Goes to Moscow & Norton, Virginia Too *MVD*
Billy Dean: Video Hits *MVD*
Billy Eckstine/Dizzy Gillespie Be-Bop Big Bands *MVD*
Billy Idol: The Charmed Life Videos *MVD*
Billy Idol: Vital Idol *MVD, VES, LIV*
Billy Joe Royal *MVD, AVE, FFF*
Billy Joel: Eye of the Storm *SMV*
Billy Joel Live at Yankee Stadium *MVD, SMV*
Billy Joel Live from Long Island *MVD, FOX*
Billy Joel: Stormfront *MVD*
Billy Joel: The Video Album, Vol. 1 *MVD, FOX*
Billy Joel: The Video Album, Vol. 2 *MVD, FOX*
Billy Ocean: In London *MVD, COL*
Billy Ocean: Tear Down These Hits *MVD, COL*
Billy Ray Cyrus *PGV, MVD*

Billy Ray Cyrus: Live *PGV*
Billy Squier *HBO, PIA*
Bing Crosby: The Magic of Bing Crosby, Part 1 *AVE, MVD, FFF*
Bingoboys: How To Dance (The Extended Dance Version) *MVD, AVE, FFF*
Birthday Party: Pleasure Heads Must Burn *MVD*
Bizarre Music Television *MVD, RHI*
Black & Tan/St. Louis Blues *CCB*
Black Box: Video Dreams 1991 *BMG*
Black Crowes: Who Killed That Bird Out On Your Window Sill...The Movie *MVD*
Black Diamond Jazz Band *NO*
Black Eagle Jazz Band *NO*
Black Expo Gospel Explosion #4 *BMG, MVD*
Black Flag: Live in San Francisco *MVD*
Black Flag: Six Pack *MVD*
Black Flag: T.V. Party *NO*
Black Jazz & Blues *MVD, VYY, FCT*
Black Music in America: The Seventies *LCA*
Black Sabbath Live: Never Say Die *MVD*
Black Sabbath: Live 1978 *MVD*
Black Sabbath: The Black Sabbath Story, Vol. 1, 1970-1978 *WEA, MVD*
Black Sabbath: The Black Sabbath Story, Vol. 2, 1978-1992 *WRV, MVD*
Black Uhuru and Steel Pulse: Tribute to Bob Marley *MVD*
Black Uhuru: Tear It Up Live *PGV, MVD*
Blanche Thebom in Opera and Song *MVD, VAI, FCT*
Blancmange *SVS*
Blondie: Eat to the Beat *MVD, WAR*
Blondie Live! *MCA, MVD*
Blood on the Cats III...For a Few Pussies More *MVD*
Blood Sweat and Tears: 1973 *BST MVD*
Blotto *SVS, OM*
Blow Monkeys: Digging Your Video *MVD, COL*
Blow Monkeys: Video LP *MVD*
Blue Note I *SVS*
Blue Oyster Cult: Live '76 *MVD*
The Blue Sky Awards Music Videos: A Clean Air Celebration *MPI,*
Blue Suede Shoes: A Rockabilly Session with Carl Perkins and Friends *MVD, MCA, PIA*
Bluebeard's Castle *MVD, PGV, PME*
The Blues *MVD*
The Blues Accordin' to Lightnin' Hopkins *MVD, FFM, FCT*
Blues Alive *BMG, MVD, COL*
Blues Like Showers of Rain *MVD, RHP, FCT*
The Bluffers: Music Video *JFK, WTA*
Bo Diddley and the All Star Jam Show *PGV, MVD, FCT*

Bob Dylan, Tom Petty & the Heartbreakers: Hard to Handle *FOX*

Bob James Live *VWV, MVD, MBP*

Bob Marley and the Wailers *HBO, COL*

Bob Marley and the Wailers: Live at the Rainbow *MVD, COL*

Bob Marley and the Wailers: Live from the Santa Barbara *PIA*

Bob Marley: Legend *MVD, COL, FCT*

The Bob Marley Story: Caribbean Nights *FCT, MVD*

Bobby and the Midnites *VWV*

Bobby Brown: Bobby Bobby Bobby *MCA*

Bobby Brown: His Prerogative *MVD, PIA*

Bobby Brown: Humpin' Around *MCA, MVD*

Bobby Caldwell: Live in Tokyo 1991 *MVD*

Bobby Darin: The Darin Invasion *VWV, MVD, MBP*

Bobby McFerrin: Spontaneous Inventions *MVD, HBO, PIA*

Bobby Short & Friends *MVD, MGM*

Bobby Short at the Cafe Carlyle *MVD, VWV, MBP*

Bobby Vinton *RKO*

Body Music *SVS*

Bolshoi Ballet: Les Sylphides *VWV, MBP, STS*

Bon Jovi: Access All Areas *MVD, PGV, BTV*

Bon Jovi: Breakout *SVS, PIA, MVD*

Bon Jovi: Keep the Faith, an Evening with Bon Jovi *PGV, MVD*

Bon Jovi: New Jersey—The Videos *MVD, PGV*

Bon Jovi: Slippery When Wet *MVD*

Bon Jovi: The Interview Sessions *MVD*

Bon Jovi: Tokyo Road *MVD*

Bones

Bonnie Raitt: The Video Collection *CAP, MVD*

Boogie-Doodle *IFB*

Boogie Down Productions: Edutainment *MVD*

Boogie Down Productions Live *MVD, BMG*

Born to Boogie *MPI, MVD*

Born to Rock: The T.A.M.I.-T.N.T. Show *MVD, MED, FCT*

Born to Swing: The Count Basie Alumni *MVD, KIV, FCT*

Boulez on Varese *CMR, NYS*

Boulez X 3 *CMR, NYS*

Boy George: Sold *MVD*

The Boys: Crazy *MVD*

The Boys: Video Messages *MVD, PIA*

Brahms and His Music *MTI*

Brahms: Concerto in ''A'' for Violin & Cello *MVD*

Brahms: Piano Concerto No. 1 *VWV*

Brahms: Symphonies 3 & 4 *MVD, PGV*

Brahms: Symphony No. 1 *MVD*

Branford Marsalis: Steep *MVD, FOX, FCT*

Branford Marsalis: The Music Tells You *SMV, MVD*

The Brass Menagerie *FVL*

Brazilian Knights & A Lady *MVD*

Breakin' Metal *SVS, MVD*

Breakin' Metal Special *MVD*

Breathe: All That Jazz *MVD*

Brecker Brothers: Return of the Brecker Brothers *GRP*

Brenda Lee: An Evening with Brenda Lee *SIM, MVD*

Brian Eno: Excerpt from the Khumba Nela *MVD*

Brian Eno: Imaginary Landscapes *MFV, FCT*

Brian Eno: Thursday Afternoon *SVS, MVD*

British Big Beat: The Invasion *MVD, RHI*

British Rock: The Legends of Punk & New Wave *MVD, VES, LIV*

Britny Fox: Year of the Fox *MVD, SMV*

Britten, the Voice, and Peter Pears

Broken Bones: Live at Leeds *MVD*

Brooks & Dunn: Pardners—The Brand New Man Videos *SWH*

Bruce Dickinson: Dive! Dive! Live *MVD, SMV*

Bruce Hornsby and the Range: A Night on the Town *MVD, COL, BMG*

Bruce Springsteen and Friends *MVD*

Bruce Springsteen in Concert: MTV Plugged *SMV*

Bruce Springsteen Video Anthology: 1978-88 *MVD, SMV*

Bruce Willis: Return of Bruno *MVD, HBO*

Bruckner: Symphony No. 7 *MVD, PGV*

Bryan Adams: Reckless *MVD, A&M, CCL*

Bryan Adams: Waking Up the Neighbors Videos *PGV*

Bryan Ferry: New Town *MVD*

Buck Creek Jazz Band No. 1 *NO*

Buck Creek Jazz Band No. 2 *NO*

Buckwheat Zydeco: Taking it Home *MVD, PGV*

Bud Powell *MVD*

Buddy Barnes: Live from Studio B *SVS, MVD, FCT*

Buddy Rich *SVS, MVD*

Buddy Rich Memorial Scholarship Concert *MVD, MPI*

Buffalo Jazz Fest *NO*

BulletBoys: Pigs in Mud *MVD, WRV*

Buried Treasures, Vol. 1: The Directors *MVD*

Buried Treasures, Vol. 2: Reggae Classics *PGV, MVD, FCT*

Burning Spear: Live in Paris *MVD*

Buzzcocks: Auf Wiedersehen *MVD*

The Buzzcocks: Playback *MVD*

C/Z Records: We've Come For Your Daughters, Vol. 1 *MVD*

Cab Calloway and His Orchestra *MVD*

Cabaret Voltaire: Gasoline in Your Eye *SVS, OM*

The California Raisins 2: Raisins, Sold Out *TMG, WTA*

California to New York Island *CMR, NYS*

Camel: Pressure Points Live in Concert *MVD*

Cameo: Video EP *SVS, MVD*

Cameo: Word Up *PGV, MVD*

Canadian Reggae Music Awards '88 *MVD, FCT*

Cancion Romantica *NJN*

Canciones de Mi Tierra *MVD*

C&C Music Factory: Everbody Dance Now *SMV*

Canned Heat: Boogie Assault *MVD,, MON*

Cannonball Adderly: 1983 Live *MVD*

Caribbean Music and Dance *MUS, FCT*

Carla Bley Band: Joyful Noise *MVD*

Carly Simon: Live from Martha's Vineyard *MVD, HBO, FFF*

Carly Simon: My Romance in Concert *MVD, PIA, BMG*

Carman: Coming on Strong (Live in Concert) *MVD, SMV*

Carmen *ING, COL, HMV*

Carmen McRae Live *MVD, HMV, FCT*

Carmina Burana *FCT, KUL*

Carnegie Hall at 100: A Place of Dreams *BMG, FCT*

Carnival of the Animals *CMR, NYS*

Carol Jo Brown: Turn It Up *NO*

Carole King: One to One *MVD, MGM, PIA*

Carols for Christmas *HMV, HBO*

Carreras, Domingo, Pavarotti: Three Tenors in Concert *MVD, PGV*

The Cars: Heartbeat City *MVD, WAR, PIA*

The Cars: 1984-1985—Live *MVD, VES*

Casey Kasem's Rock 'n Roll Goldmine: The San Francisco Sound *VES, MOV, MVD*

Casey Kasem's Rock 'n Roll Goldmine: The Sixties *VES, MOV, MVD*

Casey Kasem's Rock 'n Roll Goldmine: The Soul Years *VES, MOV, MVD*

Casiopea: Made in Melbourne *MVD*

Cassandra Wilson Live *PGV, MVD*

Catch a Rising Star's 10th Anniversary *COL, PIA*

Cathy Dennis: Touch Me *MVD*

Cavalcade of Stars, Vol. 2 *NOS*

Cavalleria Rusticana *MVD, VAI, FCT*

Cecil Taylor: Burning Poles *MFV, FCT*

A Celebration *MVD, MON*

Celine Dion: Unison *SMV*

Celtic Frost: Live at the Hammersmith Odeon *MVD*

Central Ohio Hot Jazz Fest *NO*

Chaconne for Traditional Japanese Instruments

Chaka Khan Live *NO*

Chaka Khan: My Night *PIA*

Chamber Music: The String Quartet *NO*

The Chameleons: Live at Camden Palace *MVD*

Chant a Capella *EAI*

Charles Aznavour: Memories of Greatness Live *MVD*

Charles Haughey's Ireland *RGO*

Charles Johnson & the Revivers: One Night Revival *XVC*

Charles Mingus: Live in Norway, 1964 *MVD*

Charles Trenet: Chansons *MVD*

Charley Pride: Live! *LTY, BMG*

Charlie Byrd: Live in New Orleans *MVD,*

The Charlie Daniels Band: Saratoga Concert *MVD, FOX*

Charlie Daniels: Homefolks and Highways *MVD, CAF*

Charlie Peacock

Charlie Pride: An Evening with Charlie Pride *SIM, MVD*

Chartbusters from Kids Incorporated *QNE*

Chase the Devil: Religious Music of the Appalachians *MVD, FCT, SHR*

Cheap Trick: Every Trick in the Book *SMV, MVD, IME*

Cheech and Chong: Get Out of My Room *MCA*

Cheetahchrome: M°S (Live) *MVD*

Chemical People: Live *MVD*

Chen and China's Symphony *CIG*

Cher: Extravaganza: Live at the Mirage *BMG, MVD*

Cherry Bombz *MVD*

Cheryl Ladd: Fascinated *HBO, OM*

Chess Moves *COL*

Chet Atkins and Friends: Music from the Heart *MVD, AVE, HBO*

Chet Baker: Candy *MVD*

Chet Baker/Elvis Costello: Live at Ronnie Scott's *MVD*

Chet Baker: My Funny Valentine *MVD*

Chicago: And the Band Played On *WRV, MVD*

Chicago Basketball: A Musical Celebration *MPI*

Chicago Bears: Super Bowl Shuffle *VTK, MVD*

Chicago Beat: Rock Lobster *MVD*

Chicago Blues *MVD, RHP, TLF*

Chicago: Chicago 17 *PIA*

Chicago Rhythm *NO*

Chicago Six Jazz Band *NO*

Chick Corea *SVS*

Chick Corea: A Very Special Concert *MVD*

Chick Corea & Gary Burton: Live in Tokyo *MVD, PAV, PIA*

Chick Corea Elektric Band: Inside Out *MVD*

Chick Corea: In Madrid *MVD*

Chico Hamilton: The Jazz Life *SVS, MVD, FCT*

The Chieftains: An Irish Evening *BMG, MVD*

The Chieftains: Another Country *BMG*

The Chieftains in China *SHR*

The Chieftains: The Bells of Dublin *BMG*

Children's Songs & Stories with the Muppets *FOX*

Children's Songs Around the World

Choices for the Future *WSH*

Chopi Music of Mozambique/Banguza Timbila *FFM, ICA, FCT*

Chopin/Schubert Recital: Zimerman (laserdisc) *MVD, PGV*

Chris de Burgh: Live from Dublin *MVD*

Chris Isaak: Wicked Game *MVD, WRV*

Christian Death: The Heretics Alive *MVD*

Christians: The Collection *MVD*

Christine McVie: The Video Album *MVD, LIV, VES*

Christmas at Ripon Cathedral *HMV, VYG*

The Christmas Carol Video *NO*

Christmas Carols from England *KUL*

Christmas Classics 3 *NO*

Christmas from St. Patrick's Cathedral *HMV*

The Christmas Oratorio *MVD, FHS*

Christmas Video Sing-Along *SMV, MVD*

Christmas with Eleanor Steber *VAI, FCT*

Christmas with Flicka *VWV, MVD, IME*

Christmas with Luciano Pavarotti *MVD, VTR*

Christmas with the Westminster Choir *NJN*

Christopher Tree *FFM*

Chronos *BMG, MVD, TVC*

Chrysanthemum Ragtime Band *NO*

Chuck Berry: Hail! Hail! Rock 'n' Roll *MCA, MVD, FCT*

Chuck Berry: Rock & Roll Music *WRV, MVD, FCT*

Chuck's Choice Cuts *AOV*

The Church: Goldfish (Jokes, Magic & Souvenirs) *MVD, BMG, PIA*

Cinderella: Heartbreak Station Video Collection *PGV*

Cinderella: Night Songs *MVD, PGV*

Cinderella: Tales from the Gypsy Road *MVD, PGV*

Circuit Rider With Noel Paul Stookey *TMP*

Cissy Houston: Sweet Inspiration *CIG*

Clancy Brothers and Tommy Makem: Reunion Concert *SHR*

Clannad: Pastpresent *MVD, BMG*

Clark Sisters in Concert *XVC, FCT*

The Clash: Rude Boy *MVD, FOX, SMV*

The Clash: This is Video Clash *MVD, FOX*

Classic Jazz *MVD*

Classic Performances *HBO*

A Classical Christmas *MVD*

Claude Bolling: Concerto for Classic Guitar & Jazz Piano *PIA*

Claudio Abbado: Music for Europe *MVD*

Claudio Arrau Signature Performance Series *VAI*
Cliff Richard: Private Collection
Cliff Richard: The Event
Cliff Richard: The Video Connection
Cliff Richard: Together with Cliff Richard *MVD*
Clifton Chenier: The King of Zydeco *MVD, FFM*
Climax Blues Band: Live from London *COL*
Climie Fisher: The Best of Everything *MVD*
Clint Black: Put Yourself in My Shoes *MVD, BMG, PIA*
Clouds *NOR*
Club Date: Milt Jackson *NO*
Club MTV Party to Go *MVD*
Club MTV Party to Go, Vol. 2 *WEA, MVD*
Cobham Meets Bellson *VWV, MBP*
Cold Cut: Doctor in the Video *MVD*
Coleman Hawkins/Harry Edison Quintet *MVD*
Colombian Volcano Concert *MVD*
Color Me Badd: Video Scrapbook 1991 *WRV*
Coloratura Mad Scenes *CMR, NYS*
Combat Tour Live *MVD*
Comedy in Music *VYY*
Comedy Music Videos *VES*
Comedy Videos *VES*
Coming Home for Friends *MVD*
Commissioned in Concert *XVC, MVD*
Communards: Live at Full House *MVD*
Community Three Records: Comm3TV, Vol. 1 *MVD*
The Compleat Beatles *MVD, MGM*
The Complete Claudio Arrau Video Collection *NO*
Completely Country: Various Artists *MVD, WRV*
Concerning the French Horn *CMR, NYS*
Concert Aid *NO*
Concert for Bangladesh *MVD, HBO*
Concert for Planet Earth *SMV*
Concerto at Work *CIG*
Concerto! Claude Frank, Soloist
Concrete Blonde: 12/16/86 - 9/17/90 *MVD*
Concrete Blonde: Mid Life Crisis *EMI, MVD*
Coney Hatch *SVS*
Conjunto Nuestro: Salsa *NJN*
Connie Francis: A Legend in Concert *MVD, MPI*
Contraband *MVD*
Contraband: All the Way from Memphis *MCA*
Conway Twitty: #1 Hits *SIM*
Conway Twitty: King of Hits *SIM*
Cool Cats: 25 Years of Rock 'n' Roll Style *MVD, MGM*
Cool Runnings: The Reggae Movie *MVD, TPV, FCT*
Coroner: No More Color Tour '90 *MVD, SVI*
Costume Party *FCT,*
Cottonmouth D'Arcy's Jazz Vipers *NO*
Count Basie & Friends *MVD*
Count Basie: In Concert *MVD*

Count Basie: In England, 1965 *MVD*
Count Basie Live at the Hollywood Palladium *NO*
Count Basie: Live in Berlin, 1968 *MVD*
Countrified *MVD*
Country *MVD*
Country Christmas *BMG*
Country Comes Alive *MVD, COL, FFM*
Country Gold, Vol. 1 *UND, MVD*
Country Gold, Vol. 2 *RHI, MVD*
Country Ladies: Live *MVD*
Country Love Songs *MVD*
Country Music Classics *SHR*
Country Music Jamboree *NOS, DVT*
Country Music Video Magazine, Vol. 4 *BMG*
Country Music with the Muppets *FOX*
Country Outlaws: Live *MVD*
Country Stars: A New Tradition *MVD, AVE, HBO*
Country Video Hall of Fame, Vol. 1 *QVD, MVD*
Country Video Hall of Fame, Vol. 2 *QVD, MVD*
Country Video Hall of Fame, Vol. 3 *QVD, MVD*
Country Video Hall of Fame, Vol. 4 *QVD, MVD*
Country-Western All-Stars *NOS, DVT*
The Cramps: Live at Napa State Mental Hospital *MVD*
Crash & Burn Rock! *MVD*
Cream Farewell Concert *NOS, DVT, MLB*
The Creation *NO*
Creation Compilation *MVD*
Creation Compilation, Vol. 1 *MVD*
Creation Compilation, Vol. 2 *MVD*
Critical Art Ensemble *MWF*
Crosby, Stills & Nash: Daylight Again *MVD, MCA*
Crosby, Stills & Nash: Long Time Comin' *MVD, MPI*
Crucifix & M.D.C.: Compilation *MVD*
Cruisin' *SIM*
Cruisin' through the 50's *SIM*
Cruisin' through the 50's, Vol. 2 *SIM*
Cruisin' thru the 60's *SIM*
The Crusaders: Live! Midnight Triangle *MCA, MVD*
The Crusaders: Live Tokyo Superjam *MVD*
Crystal Gayle Live *PSM*
Cuban Charanga Music *NJN*
Cuban Music: Marco Rizo *NJN*
Cubik Rave *MVD*
CUD: When at Home Film Me *MVD*
The Cult: Dream Time Live at the Lyceum *MVD*
The Cult: Electric Love *MVD*
The Cult: Sonic Ceremony *MVD*
Culture Club: Kiss Across the Ocean *FOX*
Culture Club: This Time *MVD*
The Cure: Live in Japan *MVD*
The Cure: Picture Show *MVD*
The Cure: Play Out *MVD*
The Cure: Staring at the Sea—Images *MVD*
Curiosity Killed the Cat: Running the Distance *MVD*

A Currier & Ives Christmas *REP*
Curtain Call: USA *UHV*
Curtis Mayfield: Live at Ronnie Scott's *RHI, MVD*
Cutting Crew *MVD*
Cutting Crew: Live at Full House *MVD*
Cutting Edge *RHI*
Cyndi Lauper in Paris *MVD, FOX*
Czech Polkas
Czech Polkas and Songs
Czech Polkas and Waltzes
D-Mob: A Little Bit of This, a Little Bit of That *MVD, PGV*
Daily Intonalization Studies *NO*
Damn Yankees *WRV*
Damn Yankees: Uprising *WRV*
The Damned: Final Damnation *BMG, PGV, MVD*
The Damned: Live 79 *MVD*
Dan Fogelberg: Greetings from the West *SMV, MVD*
Dance Hall Report *MVD*
Dance Hall Sizzling in Tokyo *MVD*
Dance Hall Stage Show '86 *MVD, KRV*
Dance Now *MVD*
Dance Traxx *AVE*
Dance Traxx, Vol. 2 *WAR, OM*
Daniel Lanois: Rocky World *WRV*
Danspak *SVS, OM*
Danspak 2 *SVS, OM*
Danspak 3: Future Pop *NO*
Danzig *MVD, WRV*
Danzig 2: Lucifuge the Video *WRV, MVD*
Dark Ages: Video Collection *MVD, FCT*
Darwyn Apple: Darwyn Apple, Violinist *NET*
Daryl Coley: Live *MVD, SPW*
Daryl Hall and John Oates: Live at the Apollo *MVD, COL*
Daryl Hall and John Oates: Rhythm & Blues *MVD*
Daryl Hall and John Oates: Rock 'n Soul Live *MVD, COL*
Daryl Hall and John Oates: The Liberty Concert *MVD, RCA*
Daryl Hall and John Oates Video Collection: 7 Big Ones *MVD, COL, LTY*
Das EFX: Straight from da Sewer *MVD*
Das Konzert November 1989 *NO*
Das Rheingold *PGV, PME*
Date with Dizzy *FLI*
Dave Grusin and the New York/L.A. Dream Band *MVD, MCA*
Dave Holland Quintet: Freiburg Music Festival '85 *MVD*
Dave Koz & Phil Perry: Live at the Strand *EMI, MVD*
Dave Mason in Concert *MON, MVD,*
Dave Mason: Live at Perkins Palace *PIA*
Dave Stewart & the Spiritual Cowboys *MVD*
David Bowie *MVD, SVS, PIA*
David Bowie: Day In Day Out *MVD*

David Bowie: Jazzin for Blue Jean *PIA*
David Bowie: Love You Till Tuesday *MVD, PGV*
David Bowie: Ricochet *NO*
David Bowie: Serious Moonlight *MED, PIA*
David Bowie: The Glass Spider Tour *MVD, MPI*
David Bowie: Ziggy Stardust & the Spiders from Mars *MVD, LTY*
David Gilmour: In Concert *MVD, FOX*
David Jack Live! Makin' Music, Makin' Friends *NO*
David Lee Roth *MVD, WRV*
David Oistrakh: Remembering a Musician *MVD, KUL, ING*
David Sanborn: Love and Happiness *MVD, WRV, PIA*
David Stout: Lover's Cell *FCT*
David Sylvian: Special *MVD*
Dazzle Dancing: Let's Go Dancing *LIV*
Dead Kennedys: Documentary *MVD*
Dead Kennedys Live *RHI, MVD*
Dead Kennedys: Live 1978-1986 *MVD*
Dead Kennedys: Part 1 *NO*
Dead or Alive: Rip It Up *MVD*
Dead or Alive: Rip It Up Live! *MVD, SMV*
Debbie Gibson: Live Around the World *MVD, AVE, FFF*
Debbie Gibson: Live in Concert *MVD, AVE, PIA*
Debbie Gibson: Out of the Blue *MVD, AVE, FFF*
Debussy/Ravel *MVD, FCT*
Decline of Western Civilization 1 *MVD, MED*
Decline of Western Civilization 2: The Metal Years *COL, MVD, FCT*
Decoder *MVD*
Deep Heat *MVD*
Deep Purple: Live at Budokan '75 *MVD*
Deep Purple: Machine Head Live 1972 *MVD*
Deep Purple: The Videosingles *MVD, PGV*
Def Hype Clips *MVD, MCA*
Def Jam Classics: Vols. 1 and 2 *MVD, SMV*
Def Leppard: Historia *MVD, PGV*
Def Leppard: In the Round - In Your Face - Live *PGV, MVD, WAR*
Deja View *MVD, LHV, WAR*
Deleon Richards in Concert *MVD*
Dennis Brown: Superfest '89 *MVD*
Dennis Chambers: Serious Moves *MVD*
Dennis De Young: Three Piece Suite *A&M*
Depeche Mode: 101 *MVD, WRV*
Depeche Mode: Some Great Videos *WRV, MVD*
Depeche Mode: Strange *MVD, WRV*
Depeche Mode: Strange Too *MVD, WRV*
Depeche Mode: The World We Live in and Live at Hamburg *MVD, WRV*
Der Rosenkavalier *HMV, MVD*
Derrick Harriott Live *KRV*
Desde Monterey con Sabor a Mexico *MVD*

Destination: Mozart: A Night at the Opera with Peter Sellars *KUL, FCT, MVD*
Destination: Universe *BMG, MVD, FHF*
Deutsche Weihnacht mit Heino *GLV*
Devo *SVS*
Devo: The Men Who Make the Music *MVD, WAR*
Devo: We're All Devo *MVD, WAR*
Dexy's Midnight Runners: The Bridge *MVD, BMG, COL*
DFW Mass Choir: I Will Let Nothing Separate Me *MLC, MVD*
Dharma Bums: Live *MVD*
Diamanda Galas: The Litanies of Satan *MVD*
Diana Ross in Concert *COL, PIA*
Diana Ross: The Lady Sings...Jazz & Blues *PGV, MVD*
Diana Ross: Visions of Diana Ross *MVD, COL, PIA*
Diane Reeves: The New Orleans Concert *MVD*
Diane Schuur and the Count Basie Orchestra *GRP*
Diane Schuur & the Count Basie Orchestra *MVD, PIA*
Diane Schuur: Live in Japan 1991 *MVD*
Dick Clark's Best of Bandstand *MVD, LIV, VES*
Dick Clark's Best of Bandstand: The Superstars *MVD, LIV, VTK*
Dick Clark's Golden Greats *MPI*
The Dicks: Fun with Dick and Jane *MVD*
Didjits: Knocked Up *MVD*
Die Fledermaus, Vol. 1 & 2 *MVD, HMV*
Die Ganze Welt ist Himmelblau *GLV*
Die Musik kommt... *GLV*
Die Super Hit-Parade der Volksmusik *GLV*
Dino: "Dino" *MVD*
Dio: A Special from the Spectrum *MVD, WRV*
Dio: Diamonds—The Best of Dio *MVD*
Dio: Live Super Rock 1985 *MVD*
Dio: Sacred Heart Video *MVD, WRV*
Dio: Time Machine *MVD, WRV*
Dionne Warwick: In London *MVD, IME*
Dionne Warwick Live *MVD, PSM*
Dire Straits *WAR, OM*
Dire Straits: Alchemy Live *MED, MVD, IME*
Dire Straits: Brothers in Arms *MVD, WRV*
Dire Straits: On the Night *WAR*
Dire Straits: The Videos *WAR*
The Dirt Band Tonight *HBO, OM*
Dirty Dancing: Live in Concert *LIV, VES*
Divine Madness *WAR*
Dizzy Gillespie *SVS, OM*
Dizzy Gillespie: A Night in Tunisia *VWV, MVD, KAR*
The Dizzy Gillespie Ages *MVD*

Dizzy Gillespie: Diz & Bird & Hawk *MVD*

Dizzy Gillespie: In Redondo Beach *MVD*

Dizzy Gillespie's Dream Band *SVS, AFR*

DJ Jazzy Jeff & the Fresh Prince: Summertime (and Other Hits) *BMG*

Django Reinhardt: Gypsy Guitar—The Legacy of Django Reinhardt *MVD, SHR*

Do They Know It's Christmas? *VES, OM*

D.O.A.: A Night at the Assassination Club *MVD*

D.O.A.: A Right of Passage *VES, LIV, MVD*

D.O.A.: At the Stone *MVD*

D.O.A.: The End *MVD*

Doc & Merle Watson: Live Ramblin' *MVD, SHR, PMS*

Doc Mo She *MVD*

Doc Watson *MVD*

Dr. Demento's 20th Anniversary Collection *MVD, RHI, FCT*

Dr. Feelgood *MVD*

Dr. John & Friends: New Orleans Swamp *MVD*

Dr. John: Live at the Marquee *MVD,*

Dr. Mattie Moss Clark and Friends *PRH, MVD*

Doggy Style: A Hard Dog's Night *MVD*

Dokken: Unchain the Night *MVD, CAN*

Dolly in London *COL, PIA*

Domingo/Pavarotti/Carreras: The Three Tenors—Encore *MVD, IME*

Don Carlo *HMV, PAR, PIA*

Don Giovanni *BFS, HMV, VTK*

Don Johnson: Heartbeat *MVD, FOX*

Don McLean: Live in Concert *MVD*

Don Menza: Live in New Orleans *MVD,*

Don Williams Live! *MVD, BMG*

Donna Summer: A Hot Summer Night *MVD, PIA*

Donnie Harper & New Jersey Mass Choir: I'll Tell It *PRH, MVD*

Donnie Iris and the Cruisers *SVS*

Don't Watch That, Watch This! *SVS, OM*

Don't Watch That, Watch This! Vol. 2 *SVS*

Doobie Brothers: Cycle Tour in Hawaii '90 *MVD*

Doobie Brothers: Farewell Live '82 *MVD*

Doobie Brothers: Listen to the Music *MVD, LIV, VES*

Doomsday News: Cutting Edge Metal *MVD*

Doomsday News: More Cutting Edge Metal *MVD, SVI*

The Doors: A Tribute to Jim Morrison *MVD, WAR, FCT*

The Doors: Dance on Fire *MCA, PIA, MVD*

The Doors: Doors are Open *MVD, VMK*

The Doors: Light My Fire *MVD, AVE, FFF*

The Doors: Live at the Hollywood Bowl *MCA, MVD*

The Doors: Live in Europe, 1968 *MVD, AVE, HBO*

The Doors: Soft Parade, a Retrospective *MCA, PIA*

Dope, Guns & F———g in the Street *MVD*

Dope, Guns & F———g Up Your Videodeck, Vol. 2 *MVD*

Doug Stone: A Video Jukebox *SMV, MVD*

The Dream Academy *WRV*

The Dream Syndicate: Weathered and Torn *MVD*

Dream Warriors *MVD*

D.R.I.: Live at the Ritz *PGV, MVD, IME*

The Drifters: There Goes My Baby *MVD*

Drivin N Cryin: Live On Fire *PGV, MVD*

Drums in the City *NJN*

DTV: Golden Oldies *DIS, OM*

DTV: Groovin' for a '60s Afternoon *DIS, OM*

DTV: Love Songs *DIS, OM*

DTV: Pop & Rock *DIS*

DTV: Rock, Rhythm and Blues *DIS, OM*

Dubliners Live *RGO, PPI*

Duets: Aaron Neville/Lou Reed *MVD, MPI*

Duke Ellington & His Orchestra: 1929-1952 *MVD, AFE, AFR*

Duke Ellington: In Europe, 1963-64 *MVD*

Duke Ellington: Memories of Duke *MVD, AVE, AFR*

Duke Ellington: 1962 *MVD*

Duke Ellington: Solitude *MVD*

Dukes of Dixieland and Friends *MVD,, FCT*

Dukes of Dixieland: Tribute to Jelly Roll Morton *MVD*

Duran Duran *HBO, PIA*

Duran Duran: Arena *MVD, HBO*

Duran Duran: Dancing on the Valentine *PIA*

Duran Duran: Decade *MVD, HBO, PIA*

Duran Duran: Girls on Film/ Hungry Like the Wolf *MVD, SVS*

Duran Duran: Making of Arena *MVD*

Duran Duran: Sing Blue Silver *HBO, IME*

Duran Duran: Three to Get Ready *MVD*

Duran Duran: Working for the Skin Trade *MVD*

Dvorak: Symphony No. 8 *MVD, BMG*

Dvorak's Slavic Dance *NO*

Dwight Yoakam: Just Lookin' for a Hit *MVD, WRV*

Dynamite Chicken *NO*

Earl Hines & Coleman Hawkins: Jazz *MVD, KIV, RHP*

Earl Thomas Conley: Greatest Video Hits *MVD, COL, LTY*

Early American Song *CMR, NYS*

Early Elvis *NO*

Early Music from Chicago *MVD*

Earth Dreaming *WSH, MVD, LUM*

Earth, Wind & Fire in Concert *MVD, VES, PIA*

Earth, Wind & Fire: The Eternal Vision *SMV*

Earthrise: The Rainforest Video *MVD*

Easter with Fred Waring *VAI, FCT*

EBN: Commercial Entertainment Product *MVD*

Echo & the Bunnymen: The Pictures on My Wall *MVD*

Echoes of Ellington, Vol. 1 *MVD, PGV*

Echoes of Ellington, Vol. 2 *MVD*

Eddie Jefferson: Live from the Jazz Showcase *MVD, RHP, KIV*

Eddie Money: Picture of Money *MVD, SMV*

Eddie "Son" House, Jr. & Buddy Guy *CMR*

Edinburgh Military Tattoo 1987 *PME, FUS*

Edinburgh Military Tattoo 1988 *HMV, PME*

Edith Piaf: Chansons *MVD*

Edith Piaf: La Vie en Rose *MVD, FHS, APD*

Edvard Grieg: The Man and His Music *AIM*

Edwyn Collins: Phantasmagoria *MVD*

Egberto Gismonti *MVD, PRS*

1812 Overture *BFA*

El Maestro: Primitivo Santos *NJN*

Eleanor Steber in Opera and Oratorio *VAI, FCT*

Eleanor Steber in Opera and Song *MVD, VAI, CTH*

Eleanor Steber in Opera and Song, Vol. 2 *MVD, VAI, FCT*

Electric Light Orchestra Live at Wembly *MVD, FOX*

Electric Light Orchestra Part 2: Live *BMG, MVD*

Elektra *PAR, VTK, FCT*

11th & B *MWF*

Ella Fitzgerald: J.A.T.P. *MVD*

Ella Jenkins: For the Family *MVD*

Ella Jenkins Live! at the Smithsonian *AFR*

Ellyn Rucker: Live in New Orleans *MVD*

Elton John *SVS*

Elton John: Breaking Hearts Tour *MVD, LIV, VES*

Elton John: Live *MVD, AVE, FFF*

Elton John: Live in Australia *MVD, JTC*

Elton John: Live in Central Park *PIA, OM*

Elton John: Night & Day-The Nighttime Concert *MVD, LIV, VES*

Elton John: The Last Song *MCA, MVD*

Elton John: The Very Best *MVD*

Elton John: To Russia...With Elton *MVD, FOX*

Elton John: Visions *SUE, OM*

Elton John: World Tour 1992 *AVE*

Elvin Jones: A Different Drummer *MVD,*

Elvis *SIM, SPN*

Elvis: Aloha from Hawaii *BMG, MED, MVD*

Elvis Costello and The Brodsky Quartet: The Juliet Letters *WRV, MVD*

Elvis in Concert 1968 *NOS, DVT*

Elvis in the '50s *BTV, DVT*

Elvis on Television *DVT*

Elvis on Tour *MGM*

Elvis: One Night with You *MVD, MED, VTK*

Elvis Presley: 27 Songs That Shook the World *BVV*

Elvis: '68 Comeback Special *BMG, MED, VTK*

Elvis: That's the Way It Is *MVD, MED*

Elvis: The Great Performances, Vol. 1: Center Stage *MVD, BVV, RDG*

Elvis: The Great Performances, Vol. 2: Man & His Music *MVD, BVV, RDG*

Elvis: The Lost Elvis *MVD*

Elvis: The Lost Performances *WAR*

Emerson, Lake and Palmer: Pictures at an Exhibition *MVD, IMF*

Emerson, Lake & Palmer: Welcome Back *SVI, MVD*

EMF: Smoke the Banger *EMI, MVD*

EMI Video Series, Vol. 1: Between Us *MVD*

EMI Video Series, Vol. 2: Breakthrough Video *MVD*

Emmylou Harris and the Nash Ramblers at the Ryman *WRV, MVD*

An Emotional Fish *MVD, AVE, FFF*

An Emperor's Music *FVL*

En Vogue: Born to Sing *MVD, AVE, PIA*

En Vogue: Funky Divas *AVE, MVD, FFF*

Engelbert Humperdinck in Concert *MVD, VES, VTK*

Engelbert Humperdinck Live *QVD*

The Enid *MVD*

Enigma: The Videos, Part 1 *WRV*

Enigma: Vision of Sadness *MVD*

Entertaining the Troops *SVS, COL*

Enuff Z'Nuff *MVD, AVE, FFF*

Enya: Moon Shadows *WRV, MVD*

Erasure: ABBA-Esque *MVD*

Erasure: Live—Wild *WRV, MVD, LUM*

Erasure: Pop—The First 20 Hits *WRV, MVD*

Eric B. & Rakim: Let the Rhythm Hit 'em *MVD, MCA*

Eric Burdon and the Animals: Finally *MVD, FFF*

Eric Clapton & Friends *MVD, LIV, VES*

Eric Clapton: Live '85 *VES, MVD*

Eric Clapton: On the Whistle Test *WRV*

Eric Clapton: The Cream of Eric Clapton *MVD, PGV*

Eric Clapton: 24 Nights *WRV, PIA*

Eric Clapton: Unplugged *WRV, MVD*

Erick Friedman Plays Fritz Kreisler *KUL*

Ernani *HMV, PAR, VTK*

Ernest Tubb: "Thanks Troubadour, Thanks" *CAF, VTK*

Erroll Garner: London/ Copenhagen *MVD*

The Escape Club: Dollars, Sex & Wild, Wild West *AVE, FFF*

Essential Opera *MVD, PME*

Estrellas de la Cancion Nortena *MVD*

Eugene Onegin: Tchaikovsky *MVD, PME*

Europe in America #1 *MVD*

Europe in America #2 *MVD*

Europe: Live *MVD*

Europe: Live in Stockholm, 1986 *MVD*

Europe: The Final Countdown World Tour *MVD, SMV*

Eurythmics: Greatest Hits *MVD, SWH*

Eurythmics Live *MVD, PGV*

Eurythmics: Savage *MVD*

The Eurythmics: Sweet Dreams, the Video Album *MVD, COL, BMG*

Eurythmics: We Two Are One Too *MVD, SWH, BMG*

Eva Marton in Concert *HMV, FCT, PME*

The Eve *NO*

Evelyn Glennie *MVD*

An Evening with Danny Kaye *PAR, HMV, PME*

An Evening with Kiri Te Kanawa *MVD, HMV*

An Evening with Liza Minnelli *FOX*

An Evening with Marlene Dietrich *GLV*

An Evening with Paul Anka *PIA*

An Evening with Ray Charles *MCA, MVD*

An Evening with Sammy Davis Jr. and Jerry Lewis *VES, LIV*

An Evening with Sister Sledge *VHE*

Everly Brothers Album: Flash *SVS*

The Everly Brothers Reunion Concert *MVD, MGM, FFF*

The Everly Brothers: Rock 'n' Roll Odyssey *AVE, MGM, MVD*

Evolutionary Spiral *SVS*

Evviva Belcanto *MCA, ING*

Exile in Concert *MED*

Expanding Visions: An Introduction to the New Age

The Exploited *MVD*

The Exploited: Live at Palm Grove *MVD*

The Exploited: Sexual Favours *MVD*

Expose: Video Exposure *MVD, BMG*

Extreme Art, Vol. 1 *MVD*

Extreme Art, Vol. 2 *MVD*

Extreme Noise Terror: From One Extreme to Another *MVD*

Extreme: Photograffiti *MVD*

Fabulous Thunderbirds: Hot Stuff—The Greatest Hits *MVD*

Fabulous Thunderbirds: Live from London *COL*

Fabulous Thunderbirds: Play It Tough & Play It Live *MVD*

Face/Other Titles

Fact Shorts *MVD*

A Factory Video *MVD*

Factrix: Night of the Succubus *MVD*

The Facts of Life

Fairport Convention: It All Comes Around Again *MVD, IME*

Faith No More: Live at the Brixton Academy *MVD, WRV*

Faith No More: Video Croissant *WRV, MVD*

Falco: Rock Me Falco *A&M, OM*

The Fall: Perverted by Language *MVD*

Falstaff *HMV, VAI, MVD*

Fantastic All-Electric Music Movie *GEM*

The Farm: Spartakus Live *MVD*

Fast Forward, Vol. 1 *MVD*

Fast Forward, Vol. 2 *MVD*

Faster than Lightning *MVD*

Fat Boys on Video: Brrr, Watch 'Em! *MCA, MVD*

Fat Boys: 3 x 3 *MVD*

Father M.C.: Quick Pix *MVD*

Fats Domino and Friends *MVD, AVE, HBO*

Fats Domino: 15 Greatest Hits Live *MVD, SIM*

Fats Domino Live! *MCA, MVD*

Fats Waller *CMR*

Fats Waller and Friends *MVD*

Fela: A Concert *MVD, VWV, MBP*

Fela Anikulapo Kuti: Teacher Don't Teach Me Nonsense *MVD*

Fela Live! *SHR*

Ferruccio Tagliavini in Opera and Song *VAI, FCT*

Fidelio *MVD, HMV, VAI*

Fields of the Nephilim *MVD*

Fields of the Nephilim: Morphic Fields *MVD*

The 5th Dimension Travelling Sunshine Show *VWV*

Fine Young Cannibals: Live at the Paramount *MVD, PGV*

The Firebirds: Rockin' at the Ritz *MVD*

Firehouse: Rock on the Road *SMV*

First Ladies of Opera *MVD, KAR*

The Fishbone: Reality of My Surroundings *SMV*

Five Star: Luxury of Life *MVD, COL*

The Fixx: Live in the USA *MCA, MVD*

Flamenco Greats *MVD*

Flaming Lips: Live *MVD*

Fleetwood Mac: Documentary & Live Concert *MCA*

Fleetwood Mac in Concert: Mirage Tour 1982 *MVD, PIA, COL*

Fleetwood Mac: Tango in the Night *MVD, PIA, WRV*

Flesh for Lulu: Live from London *MVD,*

Flipper *MVD*

Flipside Video, Vol. 1 *MVD*

Flipside Video, Vol. 2 *MVD*

Flipside Video, Vol. 3 *MVD*

Flipside Video, Vol. 4 *MVD*

Flipside Video, Vol. 5 *MVD*

Flipside Video, Vol. 6 *MVD*

Flipside Video, Vol. 7 *MVD*

Flipside Video, Vol. 8 *MVD*

Flipside Video, Vol. 9 *MVD*

Flipside Video, Vol. 10 *MVD*

The Floating World *FHF, LUM*

A Flock of Seagulls *SVS*

Flora Purim & Airto: Latin Jazz All-Stars *VWV, MVD, MBP*

Florida Mass Choir: Higher Hope *MVD*

Florida Mass Choir: Now I Can See *MLC, MVD*

A Flower Out of Place *MED*

The Flying Dutchman *MVD*

Flying Nun: In Love with These Times *MVD*

Folk City 25th Anniversary *MVD, RHI, FCT*

The Folk Music Reunion *VTK*

Fools: World Dance Party *NO*

For Our Children: The Concert *BVV*

Ford Star Jubilee Salute to Cole Porter *NOS, DVT*

Ford Star Jubilee: "Together with Music" *NOS, DVT*

The Foreigner Story: Feels Like the Very First Time *MVD, AVE, FFF*

Foreigner: Super Rock '85 *MVD*

The Forester Sisters: Talkin' 'Bout Men *MVD, WRV*

40 Pop Rock Video Hits *MVD*

Foster & Lloyd: Version of the Truth *MVD, BMG*

The Four Seasons *AIM*

The Four Tops Live *NO*

Frank Cappelli: All Aboard the Train and Other Favorites *A&M*

Frank, Liza and Sammy: The Ultimate Event *WKV*

Frank Patterson: Ireland's Golden Voice *RGO, PPI*

Frank Sinatra: A Man and His Music *WRV, MVD, RDG*

Frank Sinatra: A Man and His Music Ella Jobim *WRV, MVD, RDG*

Frank Sinatra: A Man and His Music, Part 2 *WRV, MVD*

Frank Sinatra: A Man and His Music with the Count Basie Orchestra *WRV, MVD*

Frank Sinatra: Francis Albert Sinatra Does His Thing *WRV, MVD*

Frank Sinatra in Concert at Royal Festival Hall *WRV*

Frank Sinatra: Ol' Blue Eyes Is Back *WRV, MVD, RDG*

Frank Sinatra: Reprise Collection, Vol. 1 *MVD, WRV*

Frank Sinatra: Reprise Collection, Vol. 2 *MVD, WRV*

Frank Sinatra: Reprise Collection, Vol. 3 *MVD, WRV, PIA*

Frank Sinatra Show *NOS, DVT*

Frank Sinatra: Sinatra *WRV*

Frank Sinatra: Sinatra, the Main Event *WRV*

Frank Zappa Presents: The Amazing Mr. Bickford *MVD, MPI*

Frank Zappa: Video from Hell *MVD, MPI*

Frank Zappa's Does Humor Belong in Music? *MVD, MPI*

Frankie Goes to Hollywood: Wasteland...Paradise *COL*

Frankie Valli: Hits From the 60's *MVD, PSM*

Freddie Hubbard *SVS, PIA, MVD*

Freddie Jackson: You Are My Lady *SVS, MVD*

Freddie King: Blues Band Live *MVD*

Freddie Mercury: Story *MVD*

The Freddie Mercury Tribute Concert *BVV*

Frederica von Stade: Christmas *MVD, PME*

Free for All *MVD*

Free: The Best of Free *MVD*

Freedom Beat: The Video *PAV, WRV, IME*

Frehley's Comet: Live 4 *MVD, AVE, FFF*

French Singers *ING, DVT, HEG*

Fresh 89, Part 1 *KRV, MVD, PPI*

Fresh 89, Part 2 *KRV, MVD, PPI*

Fresh 89, Part 2: Vol. 1 *KRV, MVD*

Fresh 89, Part 2: Vol. 2 *KRV, MVD*

Fresh 89, Part 3 *KRV, MVD*

Frightwig: Strip for Frightwig *MVD*

From Mao to Mozart: Isaac Stern in China *WAR, VTK, IME*

From the New World *NO*

Front Row with Charlie Peacock *SPW*

Front Row with Margaret Becker *SPW*

Front Row with Michael Card *SPW*

Front Row with Steve Curtis Chapman *SPW*

Front 242: Integration 8 X 10 *SMV, MVD*

Frontier Records' Picture Book *MVD*

Frontline Music Festival *WKV, MVD, KAR*

Frozen Ghosts *MVD*

Fullerton College Jazz Bands *NO*

Fulton Street #1 *NO*

Fulton Street #2 *NO*

Further on Down the Road *MVD,*

Futurama 6 *MVD*

G. Lewis and D. Ewart Play Music by D. Ewart and G. Lewis

The Gadd Gang Live *MVD, HMV, MBP*

Gala Concert *NO*

Gala Lirica *BMG, MVD*

Gallon Drunk: One for the Ladies *MVD*

A Galway Christmas *HMV*

Gamma Ray: Heading For the East *MVD*

Gang Starr: Step in the Arena *EMI, MVD*

Gap Band Video Train *SVS*

Garden Avenue Seven #2 *NO*

Garth Brooks: This is Garth Brooks *EMI, MVD*

Gary Glitter's Gangshow: The Gang, the Band, the Leader *MVD*

Gary Moore and the Midnight Blues Band: An Evening of the Blues *MVD, WEA*

Gary Numan: Berserker *MVD, COL*

Gary Numan: The Touring Principal '79 *WAR, OM*

Gatemouth Brown *BFA*

G.B.H.: Brit Boys Attacked by Rats *MVD*

G.B.H.: Live *MVD*

G.B.H.: Live in Japan, 1991 *MVD*

Genesis: Invisible Touch Tour *MVD*

Genesis Live: The Mama Tour *MVD, AVE, VTK*

Genesis: The Way We Walk in Concert *PGV*

Genesis: Three Sides Live *BMG, HBO*

Genesis: Videos, Vol. 1 *MVD, AVE, FFF*

Genesis: Videos, Vol. 2 *MVD, AVE, FFF*

Genesis: Visible Touch *MVD, AVE, FFF*

George Brassens Live *MVD*

George Clinton: Parliament/ Funkadelic *SVS, OM*

George Jones: Living Legend in Concert *MED*

George Jones/Tammy Wynette: In Concert *MVD*

George Michael *SMV, MVD, IME*

George Michael: Faith *MVD, FOX, SMV*

George Shearing: Lullaby of Birdland *VWV*

George Strait Live! *MCA, PIA, MVD*

George Thorogood & the Destroyers: Live *NO*

George Thorogood: Born to Be Bad *MVD, EMI*

Georgia Mass Choir: Hold On, Help is on the Way *MVD*

Gerardo: Behind the Scenes with the Latin King *AVE, MVD, FFF*

Gerardo: Rico Suave *MVD, AVE, FFF*

Gerry Mulligan *CMR*

Gerry Mulligan: Live at Eric's *MVD*

The Geto Boys: Uncut Dope *MVD*

Gibson Jazz Concert *SVS, KAR, COL*

Gil Bailey's 19th Anniversary Radio Show *MVD*

Gil Evans *MVD*

Gil Evans and His Orchestra *MVD, VWV, MBP*

Gil Scott-Heron: Black Wax *SMV, VTK, MVD*

Gil Scott-Heron: Tales of Gil *MVD*

Gilbert & Sullivan Present Their Greatest Hits *MVD, LIV, VES*

Gilbert and Sullivan: Their Greatest Hits *VWV*

Gilbert Becaud Live *MVD*

Gimme Shelter *COL, MVD*

Gino Vannelli *WAR, OM*

Giorno Video Pak 3 *MVD*

Gipsy Kings: Fuego! The Videos *MVD*

Girl Groups: The Story of a Sound *MVD, MGM*

Girls Bite Back *MVD*

Girlschool *SVS*

Giulio Cesare *PGV, MVD, PME*

Give Peace a Chance *MVD*

Gladys Knight & the Pips & Ray Charles in Concert *VES*

Glam Rock *MVD*

Glam Rock, Vol. 2 *MVD*

Glen Campbell: Live in London *MVD, PSM*

Glenn Branca: Symphony No. 4 *MWF*

Glenn Frey: Strange Weather Live in Dublin *MCA, MVD*

Glenn Gould: A Portrait *KUL, MVD, HMV*

Glenn Medeiros, Vol. 1 *MVD, MCA*

Glenn Miller: A Moonlight Serenade *NO*

Gloria Estefan & the Miami Sound Machine: Evolution *MVD, SMV*

Gloria Estefan & the Miami Sound Machine: Homecoming *MVD, SMV*

Gloria Estefan: Coming Out of the Dark *SMV, MVD*

Gloria Estefan: Into the Light World Tour *SMV, MVD*

The Glory of Spain *MVD, VAI, APD*

The Go-Betweens: Video Singles *MVD*

Go Go Big Beat *RHI*

Go-Go's: Live at the Capitol Center *MVD*

Go-Go's: Prime Time *MVD, BMG*

Go-Go's: Totally Go-Go's *HBO*

Go-Go's: Wild at the Greek *MVD, COL*

God Bullies: Live *MVD*

Godley & Creme: History Mix *MVD, LIV, VES*

Golden Earring *SVS*

Golden Earring: Live from the Twilight Zone *MVD, COL, PIA*

The Golden Ring: The Making of Solti's "Ring" *MVD, PGV, PME*

Gong Maison *MVD*

Good Mornin' Blues *SHR, PBS, MVD*

Goodtime Rock 'n' Roll *MCA*

Goodyear Jazz Concert with Bobby Hackett *MVD, VYY, DVT*

Goodyear Jazz Concert with Duke Ellington *VYY, DVT*

Goodyear Jazz Concert with Eddie Condon *MVD, VYY, DVT*

Goodyear Jazz Concert with Louis Armstrong *DVT*

Gospel *MVD, MON, VTK*

Gospel from the Holy Land

Gospel Keynotes: Live at Jackson State University *MVD*

Gotta Make This Journey: Sweet Honey in the Rock

Grace Jones: One Man Show *VES, MVD*

Grace Jones: State of Grace *COL*

Graham Parker *SVS*

Gran Temas de la Fiesta Charra *MVD*

Grand Dominion Jazz Band *NO*

Grand Funk: The American Band Live *MVD*

Grand Ole Opry Country Music Celebration *MVD, SIM*

Grand Ole Opry Stars of the Fifties, Vol. 1 *MVD*

Grand Ole Opry Stars of the Fifties, Vol. 2 *MVD*

Grand Ole Opry Stars of the Fifties, Vol. 3 *MVD*

Grand Ole Opry Stars of the Fifties, Vol. 4 *MVD*

Grand Ole Opry Stars of the Fifties, Vol. 5 *MVD*

Grand Ole Opry Stars of the Fifties, Vol. 6 *MVD*

Grand Ole Opry Stars of the Fifties, Vol. 7 *MVD*

Grand Ole Opry Stars of the Fifties, Vol. 8 *MVD*

Grand Ole Opry Stars of the Fifties, Vol. 9 *MVD*

Grand Ole Opry Stars of the Fifties, Vol. 10 *MVD*

Grand Ole Opry Stars of the Fifties, Vol. 11 *MVD*

Grand Ole Opry Stars of the Fifties, Vol. 12 *MVD*

Grand Ole Opry Time *VDM*

Grand Ole Opry Time: Vol. 2 *VDM*

Grand Ole Opry's Classic Country Tributes *AMR*

Grapes of Wrath: Those Days *MVD*

The Grateful Dead: Backstage Pass Video *MVD*

The Grateful Dead: Dead Ahead *PIA*

The Grateful Dead: Making of the ''Touch of Grey'' Video *MVD, SWH, BMG*

The Grateful Dead Movie *MON, VTK, MVD*

Grateful Dead: So Far *MVD, BMG, PIA*

Great American Gospel Sound, Vol. 1 *VTK*

Great American Gospel Sound, Vol. 2 *VTK*

Great American Gospel Sound, Vol. 3 *NO*

Great American Gospel Sound, Vol. 4 *NO*

Great American Jazz Band *NO*

Great Jazz Bands of the '30s *DVT*

Great Music from Chicago *VYY, FCT*

Great Video Hits, Vol. 1 *MVD, BMG*

Great Video Hits, Vol. 2 *MVD, BMG*

Great Video Hits, Vol. 3 *MVD, BMG*

Great White: My...My...My... *CTL, MVD*

Great White: Videos *MVD, LIV*

Greatest Rock n' Roll Hits of the '50s and '60s *RHI*

The Greatest Sound in Gospel: Vol. 1 - 4 *MVD*

The Greatest Week in Gospel *MVD, XVC, HHE*

Greatest Week in Gospel, Part 1 *MVD, XVC, HHE*

Greatest Week in Gospel, Part 2 *MVD, XVC, HHE*

Greatest Week in Gospel, Part 3 *MVD, XVC, HHE*

Greatest Week in Gospel, Part 4 *MVD, XVC, HHE*

The Greatest Years in Rock *MVD*

Green Jelly: Cereal Killer *BMG*

Greenpeace Non-Toxic Video Hits *PIA, VES*

Greg Giuffria: Live in Japan '85 *MVD*

Gregg Allman: One Way Out *MVD*

Gregory Isaacs: Maestro Meets the Cool Ruler *MVD*

Gregory Issacs Live *MVD, KRV*

Grim Tales *MVD*

Grok Gazer *LVI*

Grover Washington, Jr. in Concert *PIA, VWV*

GRP All-Star Big Band *UND, MVD, GRP*

GRP Christmas Collection *GRP, MVD, PIA*

GRP Live in Session *GRP*

GRP Superlive in Concert *GRP, MVD, PIA*

GRP Video Collection *GRP, MVD, PIA*

GTR: The Making of GTR *MVD, COL*

Guarneri String Quartet *VTK*

The Guess Who Reunion *MVD, MED*

Guess Who: Together Again *PIA*

Guitar from Three Centuries *CMR, NYS*

Guitar Men *SVS, MVD*

Gun: Taking on the World *MVD, A&M*

Guns & Roses: Use Your Illusion, Vol. 1 *MCA, MVD, PMS*

Guns & Roses: Use Your Illusion, Vol. 2 *MCA, MVD, PMS*

Guys Next Door *MVD,*

GWAR: Live from Antarctica *MVD, WRV*

GWAR: Phallus in Wonderland *WRV, MVD*

GWAR: Tour De Scum *WRV*

Gypsy Kings: U.S. Tour '90 *MVD*

Haggadah: A Search for Freedom *NJN*

Hail to the Chieftains *CMR, NYS*

Hal Ketchum: Past the Point of Rescue *EMI, MVD*

Hal Smith Trio *NO*

Hal Smith's Rhythmakers *NO*

Hallelujah: A Gospel Celebration *XVC, FCT, MVD*

Hammer: Hammerin' Home the Legit Hits *CTL, MVD*

Hampton Hawes: All Stars *MVD, FCT*

Handel: Messiah Choruses *MVD, LUM*

Hank Williams, Jr. *VTK*

Hank Williams, Jr.: A Star-Spangled Country Party *PAV, MVD*

Hank Williams, Jr.: Full Access *MVD, CAF*

Hank Williams, Jr.: Greatest Video Hits *WRV, MVD*

Hank Williams, Jr.: Pure Hank *NO*

Hank Williams, Sr.: The Show He Never Gave *FFF, MVD*

Hanoi Rocks: The Nottingham Tapes *MVD*

Hanoi Rocks: Video LP *SVS*

Hansel and Gretel *HMV, PAR, FCT*

Happy Hour with the Humans *PAV*

Happy Mondays: Party Live at the G-Mex *MVD*

Happy Traum: Happy Traum in Concert *MVD, SHR*

Hard 'n Heavy: Grindcore Special *AVE, MVD, FFF*

Hard 'n' Heavy: Thrash Metal Speed *MPI*

Hard 'n' Heavy, Vol. 1 *MPI, MVD*

Hard 'n' Heavy, Vol. 2 *MPI, MVD*

Hard 'n' Heavy, Vol. 3 *MPI, MVD*

Hard 'n' Heavy, Vol. 4 *MPI, MVD*

Hard 'n' Heavy, Vol. 5 *MPI, MVD*

Hard 'n' Heavy, Vol. 6 *MPI, MVD*

Hard 'n' Heavy, Vol. 7 *MPI, MVD*

Hard 'n' Heavy, Vol. 8 *MPI, MVD*

Hard 'n' Heavy, Vol. 9 *MPI, MVD*

Hard 'n' Heavy, Vol. 10 *MPI, MVD*

Hard 'n' Heavy, Vol. 11 *MPI, MVD*

Hard 'n' Heavy, Vol. 12 *MPI, MVD*

Hard 'n' Heavy, Vol. 15 *MVD, FFF*

Hard 'n' Heavy, Vol. 16 *MVD*

Hard 'n' Heavy, Vol. 17 *MVD*

Hard 'n' Heavy, Vol. 18 *MVD*

Hard Time '77 *KRV*

Hardcore *MVD*

Hardcore, Vol. 1 *MVD*

Hardcore, Vol. 2 *MVD*

Hardcore, Vol. 3 *MVD*

Harlem Harmonies, Vol. 1 *MVD*

Harlem Harmonies, Vol. 2 *MVD*

Harlem Jazz Festival *VDM*

Harmony *PUL*

Harry Belafonte: Don't Stop the Carnival *HBO, FFF*

Harry Belafonte's Global Carnival *WKV, MVD, KAR*

Harry Chapin: The Final Concert *FOX*

Harry Connick, Jr.: Do You Know What It Means to Miss New Orleans? *KAR*

Harry Connick, Jr.: New York Big Band Concert *COL*

Harry Connick, Jr.: Singin' & Swingin' *SMV, IME, MVD*

Harry Connick, Jr.: Swingin' Out Live *SMV, IME, MVD*

Harry James: One Night Stand *MVD*

Harry Owens and His Royal Hawaiians *NO*

Harvest Jazz Series *SVS*

Harvest Jazz Series: Alto Madness *FCT*

Hawkwind: Chronicle of the Black Sword *COL*

Hawkwind: Live *MVD*

Hawkwind: Night of the Hawks *MVD*

Haydn: The Creation *MVD*

HBTV Music Videos *WOV*

H.E.A.L.: Heal Yourself *WEA, MVD*

Healing Yourself

Heart & Soul *RHI*

Heart: If Looks Could Kill *MVD, MPI*

Heart of Rock *BHV, MVD*

Heart: Video 45 *SVS, MVD*

Heartstrings: Peter, Paul and Mary in Central America *ICA*

Heavenly Host and the Sons of Calvary *MVD*

Heavy D. & the Boyz: The Journey Continues *MCA, MVD*

Heavy D. & the Boyz: We Got Our Own Thang *MVD, MCA*

Heavy Metal *MVD*

Heifetz & Piatigorsky *MVD, HMV, KUL*

Heimat, deine Lieder 2 *GLV*

Helix *KRT*

Henry Mancini and Friends with Robert Goulet and Vicki Carr *SVS, MVD*

Herbie Hancock and the Rockit Band *MVD, FOX*

Herbie Hancock: Jazz Africa *PGV, MVD, FCT*

Herbie Hancock: Rockit Band Live in Tokyo *MVD*

Herbie Hancock Trio: Hurricane! *VWV, FCT*

Here it is, Burlesque *VES*

Heroes and Villains *MVD*

He's Right on Time - Live From Los Angeles *SPW*

Hi-Five: The Video Hits *BMG*

High Fidelity: The Adventures of the Guarneri String Quartet *NYF, FCT*

High School Yearbook: The '50s and the Early '60s *NO*

High Society Jazz Band #1 *NO*

High Society Jazz Band #2 *NO*

Highway 101: Greatest Hits (1987-1990) *WRV*

Highwaymen Live *MVD, SMV*

Hijas #90: Un Videocassette Super Sexy *MVD*

His Legacy for Home Video Series *NO*

The Historic Debt *MVD*

History Never Repeats—The Best of Split Enz *A&M*

The History of Joan Jett & the Blackhearts *MVD*

History of Rock 1978 *MVD*

History of Rock 1979 *MVD*

History of Rock 1980 *MVD*

Hits Live from London *MVD*

The Hoffnung Festival Concert *MVD, PRS, HMV*

Holiday Sing Along With Mitch *MGM*

Holly Dunn: Milestones - Greatest Hits *WRV*

Hollywood Goes to War *NO*

Holst: The Planets *MVD, BMG*

Homage to Verdi *NO*

Homecoming *MLC, MVD*

Homemade American Music *NO*

Hooters: Nervous Night *MVD, FOX*

Horowitz in London *SVS, PIA, KAR*

Horowitz in Moscow *MVD, PIA, MGM*

Horowitz in Vienna *PGV, FCT, MVD*

Hot Antic Jazz Band *NO*

Hot Frogs Jumping Jazz Band #1 *NO*

Hot Frogs Jumping Jazz Band #2 *NO*

Hot Guitarist Video Magazine, Vol. 1 *MVD*

Hot Guitarist Video Magazine, Vol. 2 *MVD*

Hot 'n' Heavy *MVD*

Hot Rock Videos, Vol. 1 *MVD, COL, PIA*

Hot Rock Videos, Vol. 2 *MVD, COL, PIA*

Hot Shop '89 *KRV, MVD*

Hot Shot '91, Vol. 1 *MVD, FCT*

Hot Summer Night...with Donna *COL*

Hothouse Flowers: Take a Last Look at the Sun *PGV, MVD*

How Many Fingers? *VDO*

Howard Jones: Last World Dream *MVD,*

Howard Jones: Like to Get to Know You Well *MVD, WAR*

Howard Jones: Live in Japan *MVD*

The Huberman Festival *PAV, PIA, KUL*

Huey Lewis & the News *FOX*

Huey Lewis & the News: All the Way Live *MVD*

Huey Lewis & the News: Fore and More *MVD, FOX*

Huey Lewis & the News: Live *MVD*

Huey Lewis & the News: The Heart of Rock n' Roll *PIA*

Huey Lewis & the News: Video Hits *MVD, FOX*

Hugh Masekela: Notice to Quit (The Lion Never Sleeps) *MVD*

Hugh Shannon: Saloon Singer *MVD, VWV, MBP*

Hulk Hogan Real American *CSM*

Hullabaloo, Vol. 1 *NOS, DVT*

Human League: Greatest Hits *MVD*

Humans: Happy Hour *PAV*

Hungry i Reunion *PAV*

Hurricane Irene *MVD, VMK*

Husker Du: Makes No Sense *MVD*

The Hutchinson Family Singers *CMR, NYS*

Hymn of the Nations *NOS, VYY, CCB*

I Lombardi Alla Prima Crociata *PIA, HMV, HBO*

Ian and Sylvia *CMR, NYS*

Ian Gillan: Live *MVD*

Ian Gillan: Live at the Rainbow *MVD*

Ian Hunter Rocks *MVD*

Iasos: Crystal Visa *MVD*

Ice Cube: True to the Game *MVD*

Ice-T: Iceberg *MVD*

Ice-T: O.G. The Original Gangster Video *WRV*

I.D.F.: Dark Arts (Live Treatment) *MVD*

Idomeneo *HMV, PAR, VTK*

Iggy Pop: Kiss My Blood *MVD*

Igor Gorin in Opera and Song *MVD*

Illumination *NEM, VTK, WSH*

Im Land der Lieder *GLV*

Imagine the Sound *FCT*

Immortal Canvas: Nettwerk Video Compilation #2 *MVD*

Impact Video Magazine *MVD, MPI*

Imperials: 20th Anniversary Concert *WRD*

The Impressions Series *WSH*

In a Dance All Style: New Yorker, New Yorker in Jamaica *KRV*

In Celebration of the Piano *MVD, VAI, FCT*

In Concert *DCC*

In Love with These Times *MVD*

In mir klingt ein Lied *GLV*

In Our Hands *NO*

In Performance: David Shifrin, Clarinet *FVL*

In the Country *KRT*

In the Silence of the Night *FCT*

Incantation: The Best of Incantation *NO*

Indecent Obsession *MVD*

The Indestructible Beat of Soweto *MVD*
Indie Top Video, Take 4 *MVD*
Indie Top Video, Take 5 *MVD*
Indigo Girls: Live at the Uptown Lounge *MVD, FOX, SMV*
Indoor Cycling
Industria del Amor: Des el Palace de Hollywood *MVD*
The Industrial Symphony No. 1: Dream of the Broken Hearted *MVD, WRV*
Infantasia *NO*
Infantastic Lullabyes on Video *VWV, KAR, MBP*
Infrared Settings *IME*
Inside Country Music, Vol. 1: Edition 2 *MVD*
The International Choral Festival Film *BFA*
Invitation to Paris *NOS, DVT*
INXS: Greatest Video Hits (1980-1990) *MVD, PIA, AVE*
INXS: In Search of Excellence *MVD, PGV*
INXS: Kick the Video Flick *MVD, AVE, FFF*
INXS: Live Baby Live *AVE, FFF*
INXS: Living *MVD, MGM*
INXS: What You Need *MVD, AVE, FFF*
Irene Cara: Live in Japan *MVD*
Irish Magic, Irish Music *RGO*
Iron Maiden: Behind the Iron Curtain *SVS, MVD*
Iron Maiden: From There to Eternity *MVD*
Iron Maiden: Live After Death *SVS, MVD*
Iron Maiden: Live in London *MVD*
Iron Maiden: Maiden England *MVD, SMV, PIA*
Iron Maiden: 12 Wasted Years *MVD, MPI, PIA*
Iron Maiden: Video Pieces *NO*
Isaac Hayes: Black Moses of Soul *FCT, MVD*
Isaac Stern in Jerusalem: A Musical Celebration *MVD, HMV*
Isaac Stern, Itzhak Perlman, Pinchas Zukerman *HMV*
Island Reggae Greats *COL*
Israel in Dance *ERG*
Israel on Parade: A Variety Show *ERG*
Israel Philharmonic Orchestra Welcomes Berliner Philharmoniker *NO*
It's Clean, It Just Looks Dirty *FCT*
It's in Every One of Us *NEM, WSH*
Itzhak Perlman *KUL, HBO, PIA*
Itzhak Perlman, Pinchas Zukerman *MVD*
Ivo Perelman: Live in New York *MVD, VAI, FCT*
Ivo Pogorelich *NO*
Ivo Pogorelich in Villa Contarini *FCT*
J. Geils Band *SVS*
Jack Jones: An Evening with Jack Jones *MVD*
Jack Ruby's 25th Anniversary Dance *MVD*
Jack Sheldon in New Orleans *MVD,*
Jackie McLean: Dynasty *MVD*

Jackie Patterson: Hip Hop Dance *MVD*
The Jackson Southernaires: Live at Jackson State University *MVD*
The Jacksons *MVD*
Jacqueline Du Pre and the Elgar Cello Concerto (A Christopher Nupen Film) *NO*
J'ai Ete au Bal *MVD, FFM, BTV*
Jam: The Trans-Global Unity Express *SVS, MVD*
Jam: The Video Snap! *MVD, MED*
James Brown & Friends: Set Fire to the Soul *HBO, AVE, MVD*
James Brown: Cold Sweat - In Japan *MVD*
James Brown Live in America *MVD, RHI, FCT*
James Brown Live in Berlin *MVD, PGV, WAX*
James Brown Live in Concert *MVD, MED*
James Brown Live in London *SVS*
James Brown: Soulful Night in L.A. *MVD*
James Brown: Story 1956 - 1976 *MVD*
James Brown: The Lost James Brown Tapes *WRV, MVD, FCT*
James Cleveland & the Northern and Southern California Choirs: Breathe on Me *MVD*
James Cleveland: Down Memory Lane *MVD*
James Galway & the Chieftains in Ireland *MVD*
James Galway in Concert *MVD, PRS*
James Galway's Christmas Carol *BMG*
James Moore & the Mississippi Mass Choir *MVD*
The James: Seventh Live *MVD*
James Taylor in Concert *SMV, FOX, MVD*
James Taylor: Squibnocket *SMV*
Jan Peerce Anniversary *CMR, NYS*
Jan Peerce: If I Were a Rich Man *MVD, PRS*
Jan Pietrzak: Mr. Censor *FCT*
Jane's Addiction: The Fan's Video - Soul Kiss *MVD, WRV*
Janet Jackson: Control—The Videos *MVD, A&M, PIA*
Janet Jackson: Control—The Videos, Part II *MVD, A&M*
Janet Jackson: The Rhythm Nation Compilation *MVD, PGV, BTV*
Janet Jackson's Rhythm Nation *MVD, A&M*
Janis: A Film *MVD, MCA, FCT*
Janis Joplin: Comin' Home *MVD*
Jansen/Barbieri: The World's in a Small Room *MVD*
Japan: Instant Pictures *MVD*
Japan: Oil on Canvas *MVD*
Jaques Brel: Chansons *MVD*
Jason Donovan: The Videos, Vol. 2 *MVD*
Jazz at Ronnie's *MVD*

Jazz at the Smithsonian: Alberta Hunter *SVS, MVD, KUL*
Jazz at the Smithsonian: Bob Wilber *SVS, MVD, KUL*
Jazz at the Smithsonian: Joe Lewis *KUL*
Jazz at the Smithsonian: Joe Williams *SVS, MVD, KUL*
Jazz at the Smithsonian: Mel Lewis *SVS, MVD, KUL*
Jazz at the Smithsonian: Red Norvo *SVS, MVD, KUL*
Jazz from Studio 61 *MVD*
Jazz in America *COL, NLC, SUE*
Jazz in America: Dizzy Gillespie *NLC, MOV*
Jazz in America: Max Roach in Washington D.C. *NLC, MOV*
Jazz in America: Starring Gerry Mulligan *NLC, NLC, MOV*
Jazz Legends, Part 1 *MVD*
Jazz Legends, Part 2 *MVD*
Jazz Legends, Part 3 *MVD*
Jazz Legends, Part 4 *MVD*
Jazz on a Summer's Day *NYF, FCT, MVD*
Jazz Shorts *MVD, RHP, FCT*
Jazz Summit *ICA*
Jazz Vocal Special *MVD*
Jazzvisions: Implosions *PGV*
JB Horns with Fred Wesley & Maceo Parker *MVD*
Jeff Healy Band: See the Light *MVD, SWH, PIA*
Jefferson Starship: Live *MVD, PIA*
Jefferson Starship: The Definitive Concert *LTY, BMG*
Jellyfish: Gone Jellyfishin' *WEA, MOV*
Jermaine Jackson: Dynamite Videos *MVD, COL, PIA*
Jermaine Stewart: Frantic Romantic *MVD, COL*
Jerome Hines in Opera and Song *MVD, VAI*
Jerry Lee Lewis & Friends *MVD*
Jerry Lee Lewis: I Am What I Am *JTC, IME, MVD*
Jerry Lee Lewis: Live at the Arena *MVD*
Jerry Lee Lewis Live in London *MVD, FOX*
Jerry Lee Lewis: The Story of Rock and Roll *MVD*
Jerusalem: A Musical Celebration *HMV*
Jesse Rae: Rusha/ D.E.S.I.R.E. *SVS*
Jessy Dixon: I Know What Prayer Can Do *BMG, MVD*
Jessye Norman at Notre Dame *MVD, PME*
Jesus and Mary Chain: Chain Reaction *MVD*
Jesus & Mary Chain: Videos: (1985-1989) *MVD, WRV*
Jethro Tull: Slipstream *MVD, PAV, VTK*
Jethro Tull: The First Twenty Years *MVD*
The Jets: Airplay *MVD, PIA*
The Jickets: Direct Art *MWF*
Jim & Jesse: West Virginia Boys *MVD*
Jim McCann & the Morrisseys *RGO*
Jimi Hendrix: At the Isle of Wight *MVD*

Jimi Hendrix: Atlanta Pop Festival *MVD*
Jimi Hendrix Live *EMI, PIA*
Jimi Hendrix: Berkeley May 1970 *MVD, WRV, VES*
Jimi Hendrix Concerts Videogram *NO*
Jimi Hendrix: Experience *WRV, MVD, FCT*
Jimi Hendrix: Johnny B. Goode *SVS*
Jimi Hendrix: Live in Monterey, 1967 *MVD, HBO*
Jimi Hendrix: Rainbow Bridge *MVD, RHI*
Jimi Hendrix: Rarities *MVD*
Jimi Hendrix: Story *MVD, WAR*
Jimmy Buffett: Live by the Bay *MCA, MVD, PIA*
Jimmy Cliff: Bongo Man *MVD*
Jimmy Smith: Midnight Special *MVD*
Jimmy Somerville: Video Collection 1984-90 *MVD, PGV*
Jive's Greatest Rap Hits *BMG, MVD*
Jivin' in Bebop *MVD, HHT, DVT*
J.J. Johnson & Kai Windig All Stars *MVD*
Joan Armatrading: Track Record *MVD, A&M*
Jodeci *MCA, MVD*
Jody Watley: Video Classics, Vol. 1 *MVD, PIA*
Joe Cocker: Live from Tokyo *TWE*
Joe Cocker: Mad Dogs *PIA*
Joe Cocker: Mad Dogs & Englishmen *COL*
Joe Cocker: Shelter Me *MVD*
Joe Cool Live *MVD, HMV*
Joe Ely: Live From Texas *MVD,*
Joe Jackson: Laughter and Lust, Live *AVE, MVD, FFF*
Joe Jackson Live in Tokyo *MVD, A&M*
Joe Jackson: The Big World Sessions *MVD, A&M, PIA*
Joe Satriani: The Satch Tapes *MVD*
Joe Scruggs in Concert *MVD*
Joe Williams: A Song is Born *VWV, FCT*
John Abercrombie: Live at the Village Vanguard *PIA*
John Anderson: Seminole Wind *MVD, BMG*
John Carter & Bobby Bradford: The New Music *MVD, KIV*
John Cougar Mellencamp: Ain't That America *MVD, COL, PIA*
John Hammond: Bessie Smith to Bruce Springsteen *MVD, SMV*
John Hartford: Learning to Smile All Over Again *MVD*
John Lee Hooker & Charlie Musselwhite *MVD, RHP*
John Lee Hooker: Blue Monday Party *KIV*
John Lennon: A Tribute *MVD*
John Lennon and the Plastic Ono Band: Live Peace in Toronto, 1969 *MVD, HBO*
John Lennon Live in New York City *SVS, PIA, MVD*
John Lennon: The John Lennon Video Collection *MVD*
John Lennon/Yoko Ono: Then and Now *MVD, MED, PIA*

John Renbourn: In Concert *MVD*
John Scofield Live *EMI, PIA*
John Scofield: Live Three Ways *MVD, CTL, PIA*
John Waite: No Brakes Live *MVD, COL, PIA*
Johnnie Taylor: Live in Dallas *MVD*
Johnny Cash: Live in London *NWV*
Johnny Cash: Ridin' the Rails *SVS, VTK, KAR*
Johnny Gill: Video Hits *MVD, MCA*
Johnny Griffin: The Jazz Life *SVS, MVD, FCT*
Johnny Maddox Plays Ragtime *KRT*
Johnny Mathis: Chances Are *MVD, SMV, RDG*
Johnny Mathis: Greatest Hits *PSM*
Johnny Mathis: Home for Christmas *SMV, MVD, IME*
Johnny Mathis: 25th Anniversary Concert *MVD, VES*
Johnny McEvoy: In Concert *RGO*
Johnny Thunders and the Heartbreakers: Dead or Alive *MVD*
Johnny Winter Live *MED, PIA*
Jonathan Butler: Heal Our Land *MVD, BMG*
Joni Mitchell *AIP*
Joni Mitchell: Refuge of Roads *MVD,, PIA*
Joni Mitchell: Shadows & Light *WAR, PIA, MVD*
Jose Carreras: A Life Story *PGV*
Jose Carreras & Friends: Charity Concert *MVD*
Jose Carreras: Silent Night *MVD, KUL, PME*
Jose Greco in Performance *MVD, VAI, FCT*
Jose' Jose' en Acapulco *MCA*
Jose Maria Napoleon: Aqui Entre Nous *MVD*
Jose Serebrier *NO*
Journey: Frontiers and Beyond *MED, VTK*
Joy Division: Here are the Young Men *MVD*
The Joy of Bach *IGP, GFV, KAR*
Joyful Gospel Christmas *MTP*
Joyous Sounds of Christmas *BUP*
Ju Ju *MVD*
Juan Gabriel: Natural *MVD*
Juanita Hall *CMR*
Jubilee U.S.A. *NO*
Judas Priest: Fuel for Life *MVD, FOX*
Judas Priest Live *MVD, MED, FOX*
Judas Priest: Pain Killer *NO*
The Judds: Across the Heartland *PIA, MVD, KAR*
The Judds: Greatest Video Hits *MVD, BMG*
The Judds: Love Can Build a Bridge *MVD, MPI, RDG*
The Judds: Their Final Concert *MPI, MVD, TVC*
Judy Collins: Live *MVD*
Judy Garland (General Electric Theatre) *VYY, PIA*
Judy Garland in Concert, Vol. 1 *RKO, PIA*

Judy Garland in Concert, Vol. 2 *RKO*
Judy Garland: Judy Garland & Friends *WRV, MVD*
Judy Garland Scrapbook *DVT*
The Judy Garland Show *NO*
Juju Music *RHP, FCT, KIV*
Juke Box Saturday Night: All Star Golden Classics *NO*
Julia Fordham: Porcelain *MVD*
Julian Cope: Copelation *MVD*
Julian Lennon: Live in Japan, 1986 *MVD*
Julian Lennon: Stand By Me *MCA, MVD, PIA*
Julie Andrews: In Concert *MVD*
Julie Andrews Sings Her Favorite Songs *QHV, TVC, MVD*
Julie London: In Japan 1964 *MVD*
Juliette Greco Live *MVD*
Julio Iglesias in Spain *MVD, FOX, SMV*
Julio Iglesias: Starry Night *MVD, MOV, SMV*
Jump the Blues Away *MVD, PGV*
Just Say Yes, the Video: Vol. 1 *WRV*
Just Say Yes, the Video: Vol. 2 *WRV*
Justice League: Hyp Existance *MVD*
The JVC Video Anthology of World Music and Dance *BTV*
Kajagoogoo *SVS*
Kansas *SVS*
Kansas City Jazz *NET*
KAOMA Worldbeat: The Lambada Videos *MVD, SMV*
Karajan Conducts *MVD*
Karajan: The Best on Video *PGV*
Karen Akers: On Stage at Wolf Trap *VWV, MVD, IME*
Karpatski Akvareli
Kate Bush: Live at Hammersmith *MVD, HBO*
Kate Bush: Single File *MVD*
Kate Bush: The Sensual World (The Videos) *MVD, SMV*
Kate Bush: The Whole Story *PIA, MVD*
Kathleen Battle at the Metropolitan Museum *PME*
Kathleen Battle in The Magic Flute
Kathy Mattea: From the Heart Hits *MVD, PGV*
Katrina and the Waves *SVS*
K.C. and the Sunshine Band in Concert *MVD, RHI*
k.d. lang: Harvest of Seven Years (Cropped and Chronicled) *WRV*
Kee Marcello: Guitar Instruction *MVD*
Keith Jarrett: Last Solo *SVS, PIA, HMV*
Keith Jarrett: Standards *PIA, MVD*
Keith Jarrett: Standards, Vol. 2 *MVD*
Keith Jarrett: Tokyo Live '85 *MVD*
Keith Richards & the X-Pensive Winos: Live at the Hollywood Palladium *NO*

Keith Whitley: I Wonder, Do You Think of Me? *MVD, BMG*
Kenny Drew: Live in Europe 1992 *MVD*
Kenny G Live *MVD, SWH, BMG*
Kenny Garrett: Computer G *MVD*
Kenny Loggins Alive *FOX, PIA*
Kenny Loggins: Live from the Grand Canyon *SMV*
Kenny Rogers and the First Edition *VWV, MVD*
Kenny Rogers/Dolly Parton: Real Love *MVD, COL, PIA*
Kenny Rogers: Great Video Hits *MVD, BMG*
Kentucky Headhunters: Pickin' on Nashville *MVD, PGV*
Kerrang! *MVD*
Kid Creole & the Coconuts Live *SUE*
Kid Creole & the Coconuts: Live at the Ritz *MVD*
Kid Creole & the Coconuts: The Leisure Tour 1985 *NLC, COL, MVD*
Kid Creole & the Coconuts: The Lifeboat *MVD*
Kid 'n Play: The Video *MVD*
Kid Punch Miller: 'Til the Butcher Cuts Him Down *MVD, RHP*
The Kids are Alright *MVD, HBO*
Killdozer *MVD*
Kids from Fame *MGM*
Kim Carnes *SVS, PIA*
Kim Wilde *SVS*
Kim Wilde: You Keep Me Hangin' On *MVD*
King Crimson: The Noise *NO*
King Crimson: Three of a Perfect Pair *MVD*
King Sunny Ade: Authority of Your Ticket *MVD*
King Sunny Ade: Concert in the Park *MVD*
King Sunny Ade: Juju Music *FCT*
King Sunny Ade: Montreux '83 *MVD*
King Sunny Ade: With His African Beats *MVD*
King's Christmas *PRS, HMV*
Kings of Independence *MVD*
The King's Singers Christmas *MVD*
The King's Singers in Concert *MVD, PRS*
King's X: Chronicles *MVD, AVE, FFF*
The Kingston Trio: An Evening with the Kingston Trio *MVD*
Kingston Trio & Friends: Reunion *CMR*
Kinks: Come Dancing *MVD, RCA, LTY*
Kinks: One for the Road *VES*
Kiri Te Kanawa at Christmas *VWV, MVD, IME*
Kiri Te Kanawa Sings Mozart *MVD*
Kirkpatrick Plays Bach *FHS*
KISS: Animalized Live & Uncensored *MVD, COL, PIA*
KISS: Crazy Nights *MVD, PGV*
KISS: Exposed *MVD, PGV*
KISS: Exposed 2 *PGV, PMS*
KISS Meets the Phantom of the Park *MVD, WOV*

KISS: The Interview Sessions *MVD*
KISS: X-Treme Close-Up *PGV*
Kitaro: Light of the Spirit *NO*
Kitaro: Live *MVD*
Kix: Blow My Fuse - The Videos *MVD, AVE, FFF*
KLF: The Stadium House Trilogy *SWH*
K.M.C. Kru: Home Video *EMI, MVD*
KMFDM: Live *MVD*
Knack: Live at Carnegie Hall *PIA*
Koko Taylor: Queen of the Blues *MPI, MVD, FCT*
Komm mit ins Land der Lieder *GLV*
Kooky Classics *MGM*
Kool and the Gang in Concert *NO*
Kool & the Gang: Tonight! *MVD, PIA*
Kool Moe Dee: Funke, Funke Wisdom *MOV*
Kreator: Hallucinative Comas *MVD*
Krewmen: Live at Billy's *MVD*
Kriss Kross: A Totally Krossed Out World *SMV, MVD*
Kriss Kross: Jump Video Snapshot *SMV*
Krokus: Screaming in the Night *MVD, COL*
Krokus: The Video Blitz *MVD, COL, PIA*
K.T. Oslin: Love in a Small Town *BMG, PIA, MVD*
Kylie Minogue: Live at Dublin *MVD*
Kylie Minogue: On the Go - Live in Japan *MVD*
Kylie Minogue: The Video *MVD*
Kyoto Vivaldi: The Four Seasons *KUL, SVS, VTK*
L.A. All Stars: Big Joe Turner and Hampton Hawes *RHP*
La Bamba Party *GHV*
La Explosion del Video Musical *MVD*
L.A. Guns: Love, Peace & Geese *MVD, PGV*
L.A. Guns: One More Reason *MVD*
La Scala di Seta *MVD, PME*
La Sombria: Concierto en Vivo!! *MVD*
La Toya Jackson *MVD, LIV*
La Traviata *MVD, PME*
Labor Songs *FVL*
The Ladies Sing the Blues *VWV, MVD, KAR*
Lady Day: The Many Faces of Billie Holiday *KUL, FCT, MVD*
Laibach: Live *MVD*
Lambada Dance Party *MVD, SMV*
Larry Carlton: Live *MVD, PIA*
Larry Coryell: Live From Bahia *MVD*
Larry Coryell: Live from Bahia 1991 *HMV*
The LaSalle String Quartet *NET*
The Last of the Blue Devils *MVD, DCL, RHP*
The Last Polka *LIV, VES*
The Last Rally *EAI*
Last Romantic *MGM*
The Last Waltz *MVD, MGM*
Late Night Romantics *MVD, SVS*
Latina Familia *MVD*

Latino Sessions *RHI*
LaTour: People are Still Having Sex *NO*
Laura Branigan: Self Control *MVD, PIA*
Laurie Anderson: Collected Videos *MVD, WRV, FCT*
Laurie Anderson: Home of the Brave *MVD*
Lawrence Welk: America, What it Used to Be/Armed Forces Day *VTK*
Lawrence Welk: Carnival/Fashions & Hits Through the Years *VTK*
Lawrence Welk: Country and Western Show/Salute to New York City *VTK*
Lawrence Welk: Halloween Party/Thanksgiving *VTK*
Lawrence Welk: Love Songs/History of American Musical Entertainment *VTK*
Lawrence Welk: 1985 Christmas Reunion Special/New Year's Party *VTK*
Lawrence Welk on Tour, Vol. 1 & 2 *NO*
Lawrence Welk: Riverboat Show/The Norma Zimmer Show *VTK*
Lawrence Welk: St. Patrick's Day Show/Easter Show *VTK*
Lawrence Welk: Salute to Swing Bands/Tribute to George Gershwin *VTK*
Lawrence Welk: Salute to the Ladies/Spotlight on Our Musical Family *VTK*
Lawrence Welk: Songs from the Movies/South of the Border *VTK*
Lawrence Welk: Summer/Vaudeville *VTK*
Lawrence Welk: The Early Years Collector Series, Vol. 1 *VTK*
Lawrence Welk: The Roaring Twenties/Sights and Sounds of L.A. *VTK*
Le 'El Palm: Pull Back the Covers *NO*
Le Grandi Primadonne *MCA*
Le Nozze di Figaro *PGV, PME*
Le Piano Vivant *CMR, NYS*
The Leaders: Jazz in Paris 1988 *MVD, RHP, KIV*
Led Zeppelin: The Song Remains the Same *MVD, WAR, VTK*
Lee Aaron Live *NLC, MVD, SUE*
Lee Greenwood: God Bless the U.S.A. *MVD, MCA*
Lee Konitz: Portrait of the Artist as Saxophonist *MVD, RHP, KIV*
Lee Ritenour & Dave Grusin: Live from the Record Plant *MVD, HMV, PIA*
Lee Ritenour & Friends: Live from the Coconut Grove, Vol. 1 *HMV*
Lee Ritenour & Friends: Live from the Coconut Grove, Vol. 2 *HMV*
Lee Ritenour: Rit Special *SVS, MVD*
Lee Ritenour: Village, Live *PIA*
Legendary Ladies of Rock & Roll *MVD, HBO, FFF*
Legendary Pink Dots: Live *MVD*

Legends of Rock & Roll *MVD, HBO, FFF*
Legs Diamond *MVD*
Leise flehen meine Lieder *GLV*
L'Elisir d'Amore *PAR*
Lena Horne: The Lady & Her Music *RKO, IME*
Lennon: A Tribute *SMV*
Lenny Kravitz: Video Retrospective *AVE, MVD*
Leo Ferre: Chansons *MVD*
Leo Kottke: Home and Away *MVD, BMG*
Leo Sayer: The Very Best of Leo Sayer *PGV*
Leon Russell: Best of the Festivals Live *MVD*
Leon Russell/Edgar Winter: Main Street Cafe *MVD*
Leonard Cohen: Songs from the Life of Leonard Cohen *SMV*
Leonid Kogan: Interpretations *MVD, KUL*
Les Blues de Balfa *FFM*
Les Contes D'Hoffman *HBO, PME*
Les McCann: Live in New Orleans *MVD, FCT*
Les McCann Trio *MVD, RHP, FCT*
Les Paul & Friends: He Changed the Music *MVD, HBO, AVE*
Les Paul: The Living Legend of the Electric Guitar *BMG*
Lester Young & Billie Holiday *MVD*
Leszek Dlugosz: It Can Be You *FCT*
Let the Good Times Roll *PGV, MVD*
Let's Cotton Together *FCT*
Let's Have an Irish Party *RGO, PPI*
Lettermen: Christmas Reflections *NO*
Level 42: Family of Five *MVD, PGV*
Level 42: Guaranteed Live *MVD*
Level 42: Level Best *MVD, PGV*
Level 42: Live and More *MVD*
Level 42: Live at Wembley *MVD, PGV*
Liberace *MPI, MVD, TVC*
Liberace in Las Vegas *WAR, OM*
Liberace Live *MVD, LIV, VTK*
The Liberace Show *SHO, DVT*
Liberace Show Vol. 2 *MPI*
Lieder, die vom Herzen Kommen *GLV*
Lietuviskos Dainos Suente *IHF*
Lietuvos Dainu Svente *IHF*
Life, Sex & Death: The Invisible Majority *MVD*
Lifers Group: World Tour "Rahway Prison, That's It" *MVD*
Lifestreams Video *WSH*
Light of the Spirit *WSH*
Lightnin' Hopkins: Live in the Late '60s *MVD*
Lightning Seeds *MVD*
Lincoln Center's Mostly Mozart *PAR*
Linda Arnold's World of Make Believe *A&M*
Linda Ronstadt/Nelson Riddle "What's New" *MVD, LIV, VTK*
Lindisfarne: Live *MVD*

Line Dancing With Christy Lane BHV, MVD

Lionel Hampton SVS, FCT

Lionel Hampton: Gypsy in My Soul MVD

Lionel Hampton's One Night Stand NO

Lionel Richie: All Night Long MVD, PIA

Lionel Richie: Making of Dancing on the Ceiling MVD, LHV

Lionel Richie: Super Live 1987 MVD

Lisa Stansfield: Real Life SWH, BMG, MVD

Liszt in Mid-Life at Mid-Century CMR, NYS

Lita Ford: A Midnight Snack BMG, PIA, MVD

Lita Ford: Dangerous Videos, Vol. 1 RCA, MVD

Lita Ford: Lita MVD, BMG, PIA

Lita Ford: Wembley PIA

The Lithuanian Ethnographic Ensemble IHF

Little Richard: Keep on Rockin' WRV, MVD, FCT

Little River Band HBO, PIA

Live & Red Hot KRV

Live at CBGB's MVD

Live at Target MVD

Live at the Biltmore Ballroom MVD

Live at the Village Vanguard, Vol. 1 MVD, VAI

Live at the Village Vanguard, Vol. 2 MVD, VAI

Live at the Village Vanguard, Vol. 3 MVD, VAI

Live at the Village Vanguard, Vol. 4 MVD, VAI

Live at the Village Vanguard, Vol. 5 MVD, VAI

Live at the Village Vanguard, Vol. 6 MVD, VAI

Live from New York City MVD

Live from the Met Highlights, Vol. 1 MVD, HMV, PIA

Live Skull: Live MVD

Live Skull: Live from Ohio MVD

Living Colour: Primer MVD, SMV

Living Colour: Time Tunnel MVD, SMV

Liza in Concert PIA

Liza Minnelli: Live from Radio City Music Hall SMV, PMS

Liza Minnelli: Visible Results MVD, SMV

Lizzy Borden: Live Murderous Row Show MVD

L.L. Cool J: Future of the Funk MVD, SMV

Lo Mejor de Noches Tapatias I MVD

Lohengrin PAR, PIA, FCT

London Beat: Quick Pix MOV

London Rock and Roll Show MVD

Londonbeat: Quick Pix MVD

Lone Justice: Live MVD

Lonely is an Eyesore MVD

Lords of the New Church: Live from London MVD, COL

Loretta Lynn: An Evening with Loretta Lynn SIM, MVD

Loretta Lynn: Honky Tonk Girl NO

Loretta Lynn in Concert MCA, MVD

Lorrie Morgan: Great Video Hits COL

Los Angeles Raiders: The Silver & Black Attack MPI

Los Invasores de Nuevo Leon: The Video MVD

Los Joao NO

Los Yonics MVD

Lou Rawls: An Evening with Lou Rawls MVD, SIM

Lou Rawls with Duke Ellington VWV, MVD, MBP

Lou Reed: A Night with Lou Reed MVD, COL, PIA

Lou Reed & John Cale: Songs for Drella MVD, WRV, LUM

Lou Reed: Coney Island Baby MVD, LIV, VES

Lou Reed: Magic and Loss—Live in Concert WEA, MVD

Lou Reed: The New York Album MVD, WRV

Loudness: Eurobunds MVD

Loudness: In Tokyo MVD

Loudness: Live in Tokyo/Lightning Strikes MVD

Loudness: Once for All MVD

Loudness: Thunder in the East (Complete Version) MVD

Loudness: Video Loudest MVD

Louie Bellson & His Big Band VWV

Louie Bluie MVD, PAV, FCT

Louis Armstrong & His Orchestra: 1942-1965 MVD, AFR

Louis Armstrong: Live in France, 1967 MVD

Louis Armstrong: 1963 MVD

Louis Armstrong: Satchmo MVD, SMV, PTB

Louis Bellson and His Big Band MVD, MBP

Louis Bellson Meets Billy Cobham MVD, MBP

Louis Jordan & Friends MVD

Louis Jordan and His Tympany Five BMG, MVD

Love & Napalm: The Video

Love and Rockets: The Haunted Fish Tank MVD, BMG, PIA

Love Lion MFV, FCT

Love of Destiny KUL, MVD

Loverboy: Any Way You Look At It MVD, FOX

Loverboy: Rock & Roll LIV, VES, PIA

Love's Awakening

Lowell Fulsom/Percy Mayfield: Mark Naftalin's Blue Monday Party MVD, KIV

Lucia di Lammermoor MVD, HMV, KUL

Luciano Pavarotti Gala Concert MVD, HMV, KUL

Luciano Pavarotti: Pavarotti in Hyde Park PGV, MVD

Luciano Pavarotti: The Event MCA, MVD, FCT

Luciano Pavarotti: 30th Anniversary Gala Concert MVD, PGV, PME

Luis Miguel: Un Ano de Conciertos en Vivo MVD

The Lute and the Sword CMR, NYS

Luther Vandross: Live at Wembley MVD, MVD

Luther Vandross: The Best of Luther Vandross SMV

Livivski Muzyky

Lynyrd Skynyrd: Tribute Tour MVD, CAF

M/W/F Music Video One NO

Ma Vlast NO

Mabel Mercer CMR, NYS, FCT

Mabel Mercer: A Singer's Singer MVD, VWV, MBP

Mabel Mercer: Cabaret Artist "Forever and Always" VWV, MVD, MBP

Macbeth HMV, VAI, MVD

Madama Butterfly HMV, HBO, MVD

Madonna and Dance Music MVD

Madonna: Blond Ambition MVD, PIA

Madonna: Ciao Italia MVD, WRV, PIA

Madonna: Immaculate Collection MVD, WRV

Madonna: Justify My Love MVD, WRV

Madonna: Like a Virgin MVD, WRV, PIA

Madonna Live: The Virgin Tour MVD, WRV, PIA

Madonna Live: Who's That Girl? MVD

The Maestro and the Diva MVD

Maestros in Moscow WKV, KAR

Maggie Staton Peebles: Born Again MVD

The Magic Flute MVD, PGV, PME

Magnolia Jazz Band NO

Magnum: Live NLC, MVD, SUE

Magnum: Live at Hammersmith Odeon, 1988 MVD

Mahalia Jackson: Give God the Glory MVD, PTB

Mahler: Song Cycles with Orchestra MVD

Mahler: Symphony No. 1 MVD, PGV

Mahler: Symphony No. 7 MVD

Making Michael Jackson's Thriller VES

Making Music: The Symphony Orchestra

Making of "Teenage Mutant Ninja Turtles: Coming Out of Their Shell Tour" GKK

The Making of "Will the Circle Be Unbroken," Vol. 2 CAF, MVD

Mal Waldron/Jackie MacLean: Left Alone '86 MVD

Malcolm McLaren: Duck Rock COL

Man: Bananas MVD

Manhattan Jazz Quartet MVD

Manhattan Jazz Quartet: Live in Japan MVD

Manhattan Project MVD, CAP, PIA

The Manhattan Transfer CMR

The Manhattan Transfer in Concert PIA

The Manhattan Transfer: Vocalese MVD, ATV, PIA

The Manhattan Transfer: Vocalese Live 1986 FFF

Mannheim Steamroller Video Sampler 1 & 2 WSH

Manon Lescaut HMV, HBO, MVD

Manu Dibango: King Makossa MVD, VWV, MBP

Many Faces of Bird MVD

Marc Bolan: Story, Vol. 1 (1968-1973) MVD

Marc Bolan: Story, Vol. 2 (1973-1977) MVD

Marcia Griffiths/Yellowman: Caribbean Night MVD

Marcus Roberts: Deep in the Shed MVD, BMG, PIA

Margaret Becker NO

Maria Callas: Her Paris Debut MVD

Maria Callas 1962 Hamburg Concert MVD, HMV, KUL

Mariah Carey: The First Vision MVD, SMV

Mariah Carey: Unplugged 3 SMV

Marian Anderson PBS, PTB

Marianne Faithful: Blazing Away MVD, PGV

Marillion: From Stoke Row to Ipanema MVD,

Marillion: Live from Loreley MVD

Marillion: Six of One Half Dozen of the Other EMI, MVD

Marillion: The Videos 1982-1986 MVD

Mark Naftalin's Blue Monday Party: John Lee Hooker RHP

Mark Naftalin's Blue Monday Party: Lowell Fulson & Percy Mayfield RHP

Marky Mark & the Funky Bunch: Music for the People WAR, MVD, FFF

The Marriage of Figaro BFS, MVD, HMV

The Marshall Tucker Band: Live PGV

Martin Briley: Dangerous Moments NO

Marvin Gaye MVD, FRH

Marvin Gaye: Greatest Hits Live MVD, FRH, SMV

Mary J. Blige: 411 Videos MCA

Mary Lou's Mass NJN

Mary's Danish: Live Foxey Lady MVD

Maurice Bejart: Art of the Twentieth Century Ballet MVD

Maurice Jarre: Lean By Jarre MVD, BMG

Max Roach: In Concert/In Session MVD,

Max Roach: In Washington D.C. MVD

Max Roach: Jazz in America - Video 45 MVD, SVS, FCT

Maxi Priest: Maxi MVD

Maynard Ferguson: Big, Bold, & Brassy MVD, MCG

Maze SVS, OM

Maze Featuring Frankie Beverly PIA

M.C. Hammer: 2 Legit 2 Quit CTL, MVD

M.C. Hammer: Addams Groove CTL, MVD

M.C. Hammer: Hammer Time MVD, CAP

M.C. Hammer: Here Comes the Hammer MVD, CAP

M.C. Hammer: Please Hammer Don't Hurt 'Em MVD, CAP

M.C. Lyte: The Lyte Years AVE, MVD, FFF

McCoy Tyner MVD, SVS

The McDonald's Gospelfest: Vol. 1 MVD, PRH

The McDonald's Gospelfest: Vol. 2 MVD, PRH

Meat Loaf: Hits Out of Hell SMV

Meat Loaf Live! VES

Meatloaf: Live BMG, MVD

Media: Zbig Rybczynski, a Collection NO

Medieval Music Performed on Antique Instruments CMR, NYS

Mefistofele FCT, PIA, HMV

Megadeth: Exposure of a Dream MVD

Megadeth: Rusted Pieces MVD

Mel Lewis & His Big Band MVD, VWV, MBP

Mel Torme SVS

Mel Torme & Della Reese in Concert MCA

Mel Torme Special SVS, MVD

Melody Magic GKK

Melody Maker: MMV Vol. 1 MVD

The Melvins: Salad of a Thousand Delights MVD

The Memories: Music from the Yank Years, Vol. 1 PPI

The Memories: Music from the Yank Years, Vol. 2 PPI

Memphis Slim at Ronnie Scott's MVD, PGV

Men at Work: Live in San Francisco...or Was It Berkeley? MVD, FOX

The Men in the Blue Suits IRP

The Mentors: A Piece of Sinema MVD

The Mentors: Tour de Max MVD

Menudo: Live in Concert COL

Menudo: No Me Corten el Pelo MVD

Menudo: Video Explosion MVD, BMG

Meredith Monk MVD

Merengue: Music from the Dominican Republic NJN

Merle Haggard: Live in Concert BHV, MVD

Merle Haggard: Poet of the Common Man MVD, BHV

Messiah NO

The Messiah HMV, HBO, PIA

Messiah MVD

Messin' with the Blues MVD, RHI, FCT

Metal Edge: Heavy Metal Superstars MVD

Metal Hammer Video Magazine: Vol. 3 MVD

Metal Hammer Video Magazine: Vol. 5 MVD

Metal Hammer Video Magazine: Vol. 6 MVD

Metal Mania SVS, MVD

Metal Masters MVD

Metal Variations: Enigma Metal/Hard Rock Videos MVD

Metallica: A Year and a Half in the Life, Part 2

Metallica: Cliff 'em All MVD,

Metallica: Two of One MVD

The Meteors: Attack of the Chainsaw Mutants MVD

The Meteors: Video Nasty MVD

Metro Media vs. Inna City, Part 1 KRV

Metro Media vs. Inna City, Part 2 KRV

The Metropolitan Opera Gala 1991 SIG, PGV, TVC

Mica Paris PGV, MVD

Michael Bolton: Soul and Passion SMV

Michael Bolton: Soul Provider MVD, SMV

Michael Bolton: This is Michael Bolton *SMV*

Michael Damian: Rock On *MVD, A&M*

Michael Feinstein & Friends *KUL, MVD*

Michael Jackson: Moonwalker *MVD, SMV*

Michael Jackson's Thriller *MVD, VTK*

Michael Monroe: Rock Like XXXX-Live at the Whiskey A Go Go 2 *MVD*

Michael Nesmith: Nesmith Live *PAV, MVD*

Michael Nesmith: Nezmuzic *MVD, PAV*

Michael Nesmith: Rio/ Cruisin' *MVD*

Michael Prophet *KRV*

Michael Schenker Group: Rock Will Never Die *MVD, VES*

Michael Stanley Band *SVS*

Michael W. Smith: Big Picture Tour *MVD*

Michael W. Smith: Concert Video *MVD*

Michel Beroff Plays Olivier Messiaen *CMR, NYS*

Michel Petrucciani: Live at the Village Vanguard *PIA*

Michel Petrucciani: Power of Three Video *MVD, CTL*

Michel'le *MVD, AVE, FFF*

Michelle Shocked: Captain Swing Revue *MVD, PGV*

Michelle Shocked: The Texas Campfire Video *MVD*

Michigan Nighthawks Jazz Band #1 *NO*

Michigan Nighthawks Jazz Band #2 *NO*

Michigan Nighthawks Jazz Band #3 *NO*

Midnight Oil: Black Rain Falls *MVD, SMV*

Midori: Live at Carnegie Hall *NO*

A Midsummer Night's Dream *HMV, PIA*

Mighty Clouds of Joy in Concert *MVD, XVC*

The Mighty Sparrow: Live *MVD*

The Mikado *HBO, MVD*

Mike & the Mechanics: A Closer Look *MVD, AVE, FFF*

Mike Mainieri: The Jazz Life *SVS, MVD*

Mike Oldfield: Essential *MVD*

Mike Oldfield: Tubular Bells 2 *MVD*

Mildred Dilling: Memoirs of a Harp Virtuoso

Miles Davis/John Coltrane: Miles & Trane *MVD*

Miles Davis: Live '85 *MVD*

Miles Davis: The Sound of Miles Davis *MVD*

Milli Vanilli: In Motion *MVD, SWH, MVD*

The Mills Brothers Story *TVC, FCT, KUL*

Milton Berle, the Second Time Around: Legends *WKV, KAR*

Milton Brunson & the Thompson Community Singers: Rise Up and Walk *MVD, SMV*

Mingus: Charlie Mingus *MVD, KIV, FCT*

Ministry: In Case You Didn't Feel Like Showing Up *MVD, PIA, LUM*

Ministry: Live 1-28-90 *MVD*

Minor Detail *SVS*

Minor Threat: Live *MVD*

Misbehavin' Jazz Band *NO*

Missa Luba *MVD, PGV, FCT*

Missing Persons *SVS*

Mission: Crusade *MVD*

Mission: Dawn to Dusk *MVD*

Mission of Burma: Live at the Bradford *MVD*

The Mission U.K.: Waves Upon the Sand *MVD*

Mississippi Mass Choir: God Gets the Glory *MLC, MVD*

Mississippi Mass Choir: Live in Jackson, MS *MVD*

Mississippi Six Dixieland Band *NO*

Mr. Big *AVE*

Mr. Big: A Group Portrait *BHV*

Mr. Big: Lean into It *MVD, AVE, FFF*

Mr. Big: Live *AVE, MVD, FFF*

Mr. Charlie *JEF*

Mr. Mister: Videos from the Real World *COL*

Mit Musik durch Stadt und Land *GLV*

Mitch Ryder: Live in Ann Arbor *MVD*

Mitsou *MVD*

Modern British Live! *MVD*

The Modern Jazz Quartet *CMR, NYS*

Modern Jazz Quartet and the Juillard String Quartet *CMR, NYS*

The Moistro Meet the Cool Ruler *KRV*

Moliendo Vidrio *NJN*

Money Madness *FOX*

Monkees: Heart & Soul *MVD, RHI*

Monkees, Vol. 1 *MVD, COL*

Monkees, Vol. 2 *MVD, COL*

Monkees, Vol. 3 *MVD, COL*

Monkees, Vol. 4 *MVD, COL*

Monkees, Vol. 5 *MVD, COL*

Monkees, Vol. 6 *MVD, COL*

Monster TV Rap Hits *MVD*

Monterey Jazz Festival *SMV, MVD, FCT*

Monterey Pop *SVS, VTK, VYG*

Moody Blues: A Night at Red Rocks with the Colorado Symphony Orchestra *PGV, MVD*

Mordred: In This Live Video *MVD*

More Baby Songs *MLT*

More of Jive's Greatest Rap Video Hits *MVD, BMG*

More Than the Music *CFV*

More Women in Rock *MVD*

The Mormon Tabernacle Choir Christmas *LIV, VES*

The Mormon Tabernacle Choir Greatest Hits *MVD, VES*

Morrissey: Hulmerist *MVD, WRV*

Morrissey: Live in Dallas *WRV, MVD*

Moscow Rock Laboratory *MVD*

The Moscow Sax Quintet: Jazznost Tour *VWV, MVD*

Motels: Shock *SVS, MVD*

Mother Mallard's Portable Masterpiece Company *EAI*

Motley Crue: Dr. Feelgood- The Videos *MVD*

Motley Crue: Uncensored *MVD,*

Motorhead: Another Perfect Day *NO*

Motorhead: Deaf Not Blind *MVD*

Motorhead: 1916 Live...And It Serves You Right! *SMV*

Motorhead: The Best of Motorhead *MVD*

Motorhead: The Birthday Party *MVD*

Motown Returns to the Apollo *MVD*

Motown Sounds *MVD*

Motown Time Capsule: The '60s *MCA, PIA, MVD*

Motown Time Capsule: The '70s *MCA, PIA, MVD*

Motown 25: Yesterday, Today, Forever *MVD, MGM*

Moussorgsky: Pictures at an Exhibition *PGV*

Mouthful of Sweat Compilation *MVD*

Movie Memories Series *MVD*

Mozart *SVS*

Mozart/Barenboim Vol. 1 *NO*

Mozart/Barenboim Vol. 2 *NO*

Mozart No End and the Paradise Band *NO*

Mozart on Tour, Vol. 5 *MVD*

Mozart on Tour, Vol. 6: Munich a Staging Post *MVD, PGV*

Mozart on Tour, Vol. 7: Vienna, The Best City for My Metier *MVD, PGV*

Mozart/Smetana/Dvorak *KUL, SVS*

Mozart Under a Microscope *CMR, NYS*

Mozart's Requiem with Colin Davis *HMV, MVD*

MTV: Best of 120 Minutes *MVD*

MTV Closet Classics *MVD, LIV, VES*

MTV Collection: 3rd Annual Video Music Awards *MVD, WRV*

Muddy Waters & Friends: Blues Summit in Chicago *MVD*

Muse Concert: No Nukes *FOX*

Music and Comedy Masters Series *DVT, FCT*

Music and Dance of Pakistan *CMR, NYS*

Music at Large—The Manhattan Percussion Ensemble *NYS*

Music Classics *MPI, MVD*

Music Court *MVD*

Music for Wilderness Lake *BUL*

Music in the Midnight Sun *BUL*

Music in the 12th Century *IFB*

Music in Time *FHS*

The Music of Melissa Manchester *PIA*

Music of the Baroque *CMR, NYS*

Music of the Night: Carreras Sings Andrew Lloyd Webber *MCA*

Music? or Else *CMR, NYS*

Music Video From "Streets of Fire" *MCA*

Musica Latina: "Hot" *APD*

Musica Tipica *NJN*

Musical Personalities No. 1 *NO*

Musicourt *PAV*

Musik aus allen Himmelsrichtungen *GLV*

Musik geht um die Welt, Part 1 *GLV*

Musik geht um die Welt, Part 2 *GLV*

Musik kennt keine Grenzen #1 *GLV*

Musik kennt keine Grenzen #2 *GLV*

Musik kennt keine Grenzen #3 *GLV*

Musik Laden, Part 1: Beat Club *MVD*

Musik Laden, Part 2: Beat Club *MVD*

Musik liegt in der Luft *GLV*

Mutabaruka: Live *MVD*

Mute Exhibit: Visible Evidence, Vol. 1 *MVD*

Mute Exhibit: Visible Evidence, Vol. 2 *MVD*

My Free Ukraine: Independence of Ukraine *MVD*

My Ukraine 1: Ukraine Dancing Songs

My Ukraine 2: New Year in Kiev

My Ukraine 3: Folk Songs

My Ukraine 4: Most Popular Songs from the Ukraine

My Ukraine 5: Festival in Chernivce

My Ukraine 6: Ukraine Popular Songs

My Ukraine 7: Christmas Story

My Ukraine 8: Spring Dances

My Ukraine 9: New Years Eve in Kiev

My Ukraine 10: Childrens Stories

My Ukraine 11: Sokoly

My Ukraine 12: Songs of Sitch Riflemen

My Ukraine 14: Transcarpatian Dances

Mylene Farmer: Les Videos *MVD*

Mylon & Broken Heart: Crank It Up! *MVD*

Myrna Summers & the Myrna Summers Workshop Choir of Washington D.C. *MVD*

Myrna Summers: We're Going to Make It Live *MVD*

Nabucco *HMV, HBO, PIA*

Naked Eyes *SVS*

The Naked Gershwin *NO*

Nana Mouskouri: Live at Herod Atticus *MVD*

Nanci Griffith: One Fair Summer Evening *MVD, MCA*

Nancy Wilson *SVS, VTK, MVD*

Nancy Wilson at Carnegie Hall *VWV, MBP, KAR*

Napalm Death: Live Corruption *MVD, SVI*

Napoli *HMV, MVD*

Nashville Bluegrass Band *MVD*

Nashville Goes International *MVD, CAF*

Nashville Story *NO*

The Nat "King" Cole Story *KAR, AVD, FCT*

Nat "King" Cole: The Incomparable Nat "King" Cole *WRV, PIA*

Nat "King" Cole/The Mills Brothers/The Delta Rhythm *MVD, AFR*

Natalie Cole: Everlasting *MVD, EMI*

Natalie Cole: The Unforgettable Concert *WEA, MVD*

Natasha: A Dance Entertainment *MVD, PBC, KUL*

Natural Light: Windance *MVD, WSH, LUM*

Nazareth: Live! *MVD,*

Ned's Atomic Dustbin: Nothing Is Cool *SMV, MVD*

Neil Diamond: Greatest Hits Live *MVD, SMV, RDG*

Neil Diamond: I'm Glad You're Here With Me Tonight *LIV, VTK, VES*

Neil Diamond: Love at the Greek *MVD, LIV, VTK*

Neil Sedaka in Concert *MVD, MCA, SIM*

Neil Sedaka: Timeless In Concert *BMG*

Neil Young and Crazy Horse: Ragged Glory *MVD, WRV*

Neil Young: Freedom *MVD*

Neil Young in Berlin *MVD, VID*

Neil Young: Rust Never Sleeps *VES, VTK*

Neil Young: Solo Trans *PIA*

Neil Young: Unplugged *WRV*

Neil Young: Weld *WRV, MVD*

Nelson Mandela 70th Birthday Tribute *MVD, SMV, FCT*

Neneh Cherry: The Rise of Neneh Cherry *MVD, BMG*

Neptune's Garden *MTX, KAR*

Neville Brothers & Friends: Tell It Like It Is *MVD, HBO, FFF*

Neville Marriner *MVD, KUL*

New Born King *MVD, VAI*

New Edition: Past and Present *MVD, PIA*

New from London, Vol. 1 *SVS, MVD*

New Kids on the Block: Hangin' Tough *MVD, SMV*

New Kids on the Block: Hangin' Tough Live *MVD, SMV*

New Kids on the Block: Step by Step *MVD, SMV*

New Model Army: History— The Videos 1985- 1990 *MVD*

New Order: Substance *MVD*

New Orleans Live: Cajun & Zydeco *MVD*

New Orleans Live: The Best of Blues *MVD*

New Orleans Live: The Best of Roots & Rock *MVD*

New Sousa Band: On Stage at Wolf Trap *MVD, PRS, HMV*

New Stars on Video *MVD, CAP*

New Year's Concert 1992 *MVD*

New York City: Performance *MVD*

New York Dolls: Live in a Doll's House *MVD*

New York Giants: We're the New York Giants *CSM*

New Yorker, New Yorker *MVD*

NFL Country *PGV, MVD*

NFL Goes Motown: Songs From The Big Thrill *PGV*

NFL Rocks *PGV, MVD*

Nicko McBrain: Rhythms of the Beast *MVD*

Nico: Velvet Memories— Tokyo 1986 *MVD*

Nicolai Ghiaurov: Tribute to the Great Basso *MVD, VWV, MBP*

Nigel Kennedy: The Four Seasons *EMI, MVD*

Night of the Guitar 2, Vol. 1 *MVD*

Night of the Guitar 2, Vol. 2 *MVD*

Night of the Guitar, Vol. 1 *MVD, A&M*

Night of the Guitar, Vol. 2 *MVD*

Night of the Long Knives *MVD*

Night Ranger: Japan in Motion *MVD*

Night Ranger: Japan Tour *MVD*

Night Ranger: 7 Wishes Tour *MCA, MVD*

Nightblooming Jazzmen 1 *NO*

Nightblooming Jazzmen 2 *NO*

Nightblooming Jazzmen 3 *NO*

Nina Simone *CMR*

Nina Simone: Live at Ronnie Scotts *MVD*

999: Feelin' Alright with the Crew *MVD*

Nitty Gritty Dirt Band: Twenty Years of Dirt *WRV, MVD*

Nocturna *MED*

Nocturnal Emissions: Bleed *MVD*

Norman and Nancy Blake: Planet Riders *MVD*

Nostalgia for the '90s *NO*

Now That's What I Call Music *SVS*

Nuclear Assault: Handle with Care *MVD*

Nugget Hotel Jazz Fest *NO*

Nugget Jazz Fest (Hymn-a-Long) *NO*

N.W.A.: Niggaz4life *MVD*

Odyssey: Ron Hays' Music Image *FOX*

Of Men and Music *IVY*

Ofra Haza: From Sunset till Dawn *ERG*

Oh Happy Day *MVD, MON, VTK*

Oingo Boingo: Skeletons in the Closet *MVD, A&M*

Oktoberfest 1 - 2 - g'suffa *GLV*

Oktoberfest Stimmungsvideo *GLV*

Olatunji and His Drums of Passion *MVD*

Old-Fashioned Christmas *MVD, ING*

Oliver Samuels: Front Room *PPI*

Olivia *MCA*

Olivia in Concert *MCA, MVD*

Olivia: Physical *MCA, MVD*

Olivia: Soul Kiss *MCA, MVD*

Olivia: Twist of Fate *MVD, MCA*

One Last Time: The Beatles' Final Concert *TEL*

One Little Indian Compilation *MVD*

One Night With Blue Note Preserved *VTK*

One Voice, One Guitar *NJN*

One World, One Voice *BMG, MVD*

Onegin *HMV*

Opening Concert Berlin: 750 Years *NO*

The Operas of Thomas Pasatieri *CMR, NYS*

Operation Rock 'n' Roll: The Home Video *SMV*

The Orb *MVD*

Orchestral Manoeuvres in the Dark: Crush, the Movie *SVS*

An Orchestral Tribute to the Beatles *SVS, MVD, COL*

Oregon *MVD, PRS*

Oregon: Live at 87 Freiburg *VTK*

Orfeo ed Euridice *MVD, HMV, PME*

Orleans: Live in Japan 1991 *MVD*

Ornette Coleman: Ornette Made in America *MVD*

Oscar Peterson: Quartet Live *MVD*

Osibisa: Warrior *MVD*

The Other Side of Nashville *MVD, MGM*

Otis Day and the Knights: Otis My Man! *MVD, MCA*

Otis Redding: Live in Monterey, 1967 *MVD, HBO*

Otis Redding: Ready, Steady, Go! *SVS, VTK, MVD*

Outlaws *SVS*

Overkill: Videoscope *AVE, MVD, FFF*

Oyster Band *MVD*

Ozzy Osbourne: Bark at the Moon *MVD*

Ozzy Osbourne: Don't Blame Me *SMV*

Ozzy Osbourne: The Ultimate Ozzy *MVD, FOX*

Ozzy Osbourne: Wicked Videos *MVD, SMV*

Paddy Reilly Live *RGO, PPI*

Pain Teens: Live *MVD*

Palm Springs Yacht Club *NO*

Pantera: Cowboys from Hell *MVD, AVE, FFF*

The Paris Reunion Band *MVD, PRS*

Party Tillyadrop Tour Video *BVV*

Pat Benatar Hit Videos *MVD, COL, PIA*

Pat Benatar in Concert *MVD, COL, PIA*

Pat Benatar: The Visual Music Collection *MVD, VES*

Pat Metheney: At Cyclorama Hall *MVD*

Pat Travers: Boom Boom *MVD*

Pat Travers: Just Another Killer Day *MVD, COL, PIA*

Patrice Munsel in Opera and Song *MVD*

Patti La Belle: Live at the Apollo Theater *MCA, MVD*

Patti La Belle: Look to the Rainbow Tour *MVD, PIA, VTK*

Patti Page Video Songbook *KRT, VWV, MVD*

Paul Brady: Echoes and Extracts *MVD*

Paul Dresher Ensemble: "Slowfire" *MVD*

Paul Dresher: Was Are/Will Be *MVD*

Paul McCartney: Liverpool Oratorio *EMI, MVD*

Paul McCartney: Once Upon a Video *MVD*

Paul McCartney: Put It There *MVD, PGV*

Paul McCartney: Rupert and the Frog Song *MVD, PIA*

Paul McCartney's Get Back *VES, LIV, MVD*

Paul Revere and the Raiders: The Last Mad Man of Rock and Roll *MCA, MVD*

Paul Simon: Born at the Right Time *WRV, MVD*

Paul Simon: Concert in Central Park *WRV, MVD*

Paul Simon: Graceland *MVD*

Paul Simon: Graceland, the African Concert *MVD, WRV*

Paul Simon in Concert *MVD, WAR, MVD*

Paul Simon Special *MVD, PAV*

Paul Taylor Dance Co.: Speaking in Tongues *MVD*

Paul Winter: Canyon Consort *MVD, A&M, PIA*

Paul Young: From Time to Time *MVD*

Paul Young: The Video Singles *MVD, FOX*

Paula Abdul: Captivated Video Collection '92 *AVE, MVD*

Paula Abdul: Straight Up *MVD*

Paula Abdul: Under My Spell *PGV*

Pavarotti *TWE*

Pavarotti & Friends *PGV*

Pavarotti & Levine In Recital *MVD, FCT, HMV*

Pavarotti in London *COL, PIA*

P.D.Q. Bach: The Abduction of Figaro *BFS, VAI, MVD*

Peace/Allelujah *PUL*

The Peace Concert *WSH*

Peace on Earth: A Bavarian Christmas *BMG, MVD*

The Peace Tapes *MPI, MVD*

Peerce, Anderson and Segovia *MVD, KUL, PME*

Peggy Lee: The Quintessential Peggy Lee *MVD, PIA*

Penelope Houston: Dash-30-Dash *MVD*

Pentecostal Community Choir with Minister Keith Pringle: No Greater Love *MVD*

Perfect Gentlemen: Rated PG *MVD, SMV*

Perfect Harmony: The Whiffenpoofs in China *DCL*

The Perfumed Handkerchief *KUL*

Personal Property *SVS*

Pet Shop Boys: Actually *MVD*

Pet Shop Boys: Highlights *MVD*

Pet Shop Boys: Performance *MVD*

Pet Shop Boys: Television *MVD, LIV*

The Pet Shop Boys: Videography *EMI, MVD*

Pete Townshend *SVS*

Pete Townshend: Deep End Live *MVD, FFF*

Pete Townshend: Video EP *MVD*

Peter Allen and the Rockettes *FOX*

Peter & the Test Tube Babies: Cattle and Bum *MVD*

Peter and the Wolf *PBS*

Peter and the Wolf: Natalia Sats *MVD, PRS, FCT*

Peter Gabriel: Compilation Video *MVD*

Peter Gabriel: POV *MVD*

Peter Hammill: In the Passionskirche *MVD*

Peter Metro: Live & Hot *MVD*

Peter, Paul and Mary: Holiday Concert *MVD, RHI*

Peter, Paul and Mary: Peter, Paul and Mommy, Too *WRV, MVD*

Peter, Paul and Mary: 25th Anniversary Concert *MVD, RHI*

Peter Tosh Band with Andrew Tosh: Live *MVD*

Peter Tosh: Live *PIA, MVD*

Peter Tosh: Live in Africa *SVS*

Petra: Backstage Pass *SMV, MVD*

Petra: Beyond Belief Video Album *MVD, SMV*

Phantom Empire *COL*

Phil Collins *PIA*

Phil Collins: But Seriously...The Videos *AVE, MVD, FFF*

Phil Collins: Live at Perkins Palace *HBO, PIA*

Phil Collins: No Jacket Required *MVD, AVE, FFF*

Phil Collins: No Ticket Required *MVD, FFF*

Phil Collins: Seriously Live *MVD, AVE, FFF*

Phil Collins: The Singles Collection *MVD, AVE, PIA*

Phil Coulter: A Touch of Tranquility *SHR*

Phil Woods in Concert *VWV, MVD, MBP*

Philip Glass *MVD*

Photonos *VCD*

Pia Zadora's American Songbook *MVD, FOX*

Piano Players Rarely Ever Play Together *SPI, MVD*

Picture Music *MVD, VES*

Pigface: Glitch *MVD*

P.I.L.: '83 *MVD*

P.I.L.: Live in 1985 - The Anarchy Tour *MVD*

Piledriver: The Wrestling Album 2 *COL*

Pilgrim Jubilees: Live in Jackson *MVD*

Pillows and Prayers *MVD*

Pinchers Live: Jumbo *KRV*

Pink Floyd at Pompeii *MVD, VES*

Pink Floyd in Concert: Delicate Sound of Thunder *MVD, SMV*

Pink Floyd: La Carrera Panamericana *SMV, MVD*

Pink Floyd's David Gilmour *FOX*

Pirates of Panasonic *MVD*

Pirates of the Mississippi *MVD*

Placido: A Year in the Life of Placido Domingo *MVD, HMV, KUL*

Placido Domingo: An Evening with Placido *MVD, HMV, KUL*

Placido Domingo: In Person *MVD*

Placido Domingo: Songs of Mexico, Vol. 1 *MVD, PPI*

The Platters/The Coasters: In Concert *MVD*

Playboy Jazz Festival, Vol. 1 *BMG, COL*

Playboy Jazz Festival, Vol. 2 *COL*

Playboy's Girls of Rock & Roll *FOX*

P.M. Dawn: Of the Heart, of the Soul and of the Cross *PGV*

The Pogues: Live at the Town and Country *MVD, PGV*

The Pogues: Poguevision *MVD*

Pointer Sisters: Live in Africa *MVD, HBO, FCT*

Pointer Sisters: So Excited *MVD, COL, PIA*

Poison: Flesh, Blood & Videotape *EMI, MVD*

Poison Idea: Mating Walruses *MVD*

Poison: Sight for Sore Ears *MVD, PGV, PIA*

Police: Around the World *MVD, A&M*

Police: Every Breath You Take (The Videos) *MVD, A&M, PIA*

The Police: Greatest Hits *MVD*

Police: The Synchronicity Concert *MVD, A&M, COL*

Polish Chamber Orchestra, Conducted by Jerzy Maksy *KUL*

Polish Christmas Carols *FCT*

A Portrait of Beverly Sills *MVD*

Power Station: Video EP *MVD, SVS*

Praisin' His Name: The Gospel Soul Children of New Orleans *NO*

Prefab Sprout: The Best of Prefab Sprout—A Life of Surprises *SMV, MVD*

Presenting Joan Sutherland *CTH, FCT, MVD*

The Pretenders: The Singles *MVD, WRV*

Pretty Woman: The Music Videos *MVD, EMI*

Priest Live *FOX*

Primal Scream: Scremadelica *MVD*

Primal Sounds from N.Y.C. *MVD*

Prime Cuts *MVD, FOX*

Prime Cuts: Heavy Metal *MVD, FOX*

Prime Cuts: Jazz and Beyond *MVD, FOX*

Prime Cuts: Red Hots *MVD, FOX*

Primus: Cheesy Home Video *AVE, MVD, FFF*

Prince & the New Power Generation *MVD*

Prince & the New Power Generation: Diamonds & Pearls *WRV*

Prince & the New Power Generation: Sexy MF *WRV, MVD*

Prince and the Revolution: Live *MVD, WRV, PIA*

Prince Jammy *MVD, KRV*

Prince: Nothing Can Stop...Prince and the New Power Generation: Gett Off *WRV*

Prince: Sign O' the Times *MCA, MVD, FCT*

Prince's Trust All-Star Rock Concert *MVD, MGM*

Prince's Trust Rock Gala *LIV*

Private Music Video Collection *MVD, NOR*

Professor Don Burns *NO*

Professor Plum's Jazz *NO*

Prokofiev: Classical Symphony *MVD*

Prokofiev: Romeo & Juliet Suite *MVD*

Propaganda Videozine, Vol. 2 *MVD*

Psychedelic Furs: All of This and Nothing *MVD, SMV*

Psychedelic Rock *MVD*

Psychic T.V.: Black *MVD*

Psychic T.V.: 8Transmissions8 *MVD*

Psychic T.V.: Joy *MVD*

Psychic T.V.: Maple Syrup *MVD*

Public Enemy: Enemy Strikes...Live *SMV*

Public Enemy: The Fight Power—Live *MVD, SMV*

Public Enemy: Tour of a Black Planet *SMV, MVD*

Puerto Rican Danza *NJN*

Puerto Rican Plena *NJN*

Pulcinella Ballet/Histoire du Soldat *MVD*

Punk and Its Aftershocks *MVD*

Punk in London *MVD*

Punk Pioneers *MVD*

Punk Rock Movie *MVD, SUN*

Punk Special *NO*

P.U.N.K.: Various Artists *MVD*

Puro Bronco: 12 Exitos en Video *MVD*

Pussy Galore: Live *MVD*

Pussy Galore: Maximum Penetration *MVD*

Queen: Classic Queen *MVD*

Queen: Greatest Hits *HHE, MVD*

Queen: Live at Budapest *MVD, MPI*

Queen: Live at Wembley '86 *MVD*

Queen: Live in Japan *MVD*

Queen: Live in Rio *SVS, PIA, MVD*

Queen of Spades: Bolshoi Opera *HMV, KUL, PME*

Queen: The Magic Years, Vol. 1 *MVD, MPI, PIA*

Queen: The Magic Years, Vol. 2 *MVD, MPI*

Queen: The Magic Years, Vol. 3 *MVD, MPI*

Queen: The Works *SVS, MVD*

Queen: We are the Champions *MVD*

Queen: We Will Rock You *MVD, VES, SVI*

Queensryche: Building Empires *MVD*

Queensryche: Live in Tokyo *SVS*

Queensryche: Operation Livecrime *EMI*

Queensryche: Video:Mindcrime *MVD, EMI*

Quiet Riot: Bang Thy Head *MVD, FOX*

Quiet Riot: Bang Thy Head (long play version) *NO*

Quincy Jones: A Celebration *VHE, HHE*

Quincy Jones: Live in Hawaii *MVD*

Quincy Jones: Reflections *MVD*

Raccoons: Let's Dance *SUE, NLC*

Radiance/Celebration *NEM, WSH*

Rafael en Raphael *NO*

Raffi in Concert with the Rise & Shine Band *WSH, MVD, PGV*

Raffi: Young Children's Concert with Raffi *WSH, MVD, A&M*

Raggamuffin Tek' Over *KRV*

Rahsaan Roland Kirk/John Cage: Music *MVD*

Rainbow Bridge *RHI, FCT*

Rainbow Goblins Story *PAR*

Rainbow: Japan Tour '84 *MVD*

Rainbow: Live Between the Eyes *MVD, COL, PIA*

Rainbow: Live '82 *MVD*

Rainbow: The Final Cut *MVD, COL*

Rainier Jazz Band *NO*

The Rake's Progress *MVD, HMV, VAI*

Ralph Kirkpatrick Plays Bach *MVD, FHS*

Ralph Tresvant: Stone Cold *MVD*

Ramblin' Jack Elliot *MVD, SHR*

Ramblin' Video Series *SHR*

Ramones: Lifestyles of the Ramones *MVD, LUM*

Ramones: Lifestyles of the Rich and Ramones *MVD, WRV*

Randy Newman Live at the Odeon *MVD, PIA*

Randy Stonehill: One Night in Twenty Years *MVD*

Randy Travis: Forever and Ever *WRV*

Rank & File: Live *MVD*

Rap Classics *MVD*

Rap from Atlantic Street *MVD, AVE, FFF*

Ratt: Detonator: Videoaction 1991 *MVD, AVE, FFF*

Ratt: The Video *MVD, AVE, PIA*

Ravi Shankar: Raga *MFV, FCT*

Raw and Rough Pinchers *KRV*

Raw Talent *AHV*

Ray Charles Live 1991: A Romantic Evening at the McCallum Theatre *MVD, AVE, FFF*

Ray Davies: Return to Waterloo *MVD, COL, PIA*

Ray Manzarek/Michael McClure: Love Lion *MFV, MVD*

RCA's All-Star Country Music Fair *COL*

Reader's Digest: Nature's Symphony *IVN, LUM*

Ready Steady Go, Vol. 2 *HBO, OM*

Ready Steady Go, Vol. 3 *HBO, OM*

Real Country *WRV, MVD*

Reba McEntire *PIA*

Reba McEntire: For My Broken Heart *MCA, MVD*

Red, Hot & Blue *MVD, SWH*

Red Hot Chili Peppers: Funky Monks *WRV*

Red Hot Chili Peppers: Positive Mental Octopus *MVD, EMI, PIA*

Red Hot Chili Peppers: Psychedelic Sexfunk Live from Heaven *EMI, MVD*

Red Hot Chili Peppers: Red Hot Skate Rock *EMI*

Red Hot Chili Peppers: Various States of Undress *EMI, MVD*

Red Hot Dance *SMV, MVD*

Red Hot Rock *MVD, VES*

Red Rose Ragtime Band *NO*

Red Star Army Chorus and Dance Ensemble *MVD*

Reggae Dance Hall Clash Video *MVD*

Reggae Fest '90 *MVD*

Reggae in Babylon *MVD*

Reggae Music Awards *MVD*

Reggae Refreshers *MVD*

Reggae Stars in Concert *MVD*

Reggae Sting '85 *MVD, KRV*

Reggae Sting '89: Vol. 1 *MVD*

Reggae Sting '89: Vol. 2 *MVD*

Reggae Sting '89: Vol. 3 *MVD*

Reggae Sting '89: Vol. 4 *MVD*

Reggae Sting '91 *MVD*

Reggae Sunsplash *SVS*

Reggae Sunsplash: Dance Hall 1987 *MVD*

Reggae Sunsplash: Dance Hall 1988 *MVD*

Reggae Sunsplash: Dance Hall 1989 *MVD*

Reggae Sunsplash: Dance Hall 1991 *AVE, MVD, FFF*

Reggae Sunsplash Music Festival Collector's Edition *AVE, MVD, FFF*

Reggae Sunsplash '90: Dance Hall Night *MVD*

Reggae Sunsplash '90: Singer's Night *MVD*

Reggae Sunsplash '90: Vintage Night *MVD*

Reggae Sunsplash '91: Best of Sunsplash *AVE, MVD, FFF*

Reggae Sunsplash: Variety Night *MVD*

Reggae Superstars in Concert *MVD*

Reggae Time *MVD, KRV*

Reggae Tribute: A Tribute to Bob Marley *SVS, MVD, FCT*

Rehearsal *VYY*

Reinaldo Jorge: Parts 1 & 2 *NJN*

R.E.M.: Pop Screen *MVD, WRV*

R.E.M.: Selected Videos *NO*

R.E.M.: Succumbs *MVD, A&M, PIA*

R.E.M.: This Film Is On *WRV, PIA*

R.E.M.: Tourfilm *MVD, WRV*

Renata Scotto: Prima Donna in Recital *MVD, HMV, VAI*

Renee & Angela: The Video Singles *MVD, PGV*

Rent Party Revellers *NO*

REO Speedwagon: Live Infidelity *MVD, FOX*

REO Speedwagon: Video Anthology 1978-1990 *SMV, MVD*

REO Speedwagon: Wheels Are Turnin' *MVD, FOX*

The Residents: Moleshow/ Whatever Happened to Vileness Fats *MVD*

The Residents: The Eyes Scream *MVD*

The Residents: Video Voodoo *MVD*

Restless Heart: Big Dreams in a Small Town *MVD*

Restless Heart: Fast Moving Train *MVD, BMG*

The Return of Ruben Blades *SMV, MVD, COL*

The Return of Spinal Tap *MPI, MVD*

Return of the Goddess for the New Millenium *MVD,, FCT*

Return of Ulysses *MVD, VAI*

Rev. James Cleveland and the L.A. Gospel Messengers *MLC, MVD*

Revival Temple Mass Choir *MVD*

Revolting Cocks: You Goddam Sonofabitch *MVD*

Rhythm & Blues Review *GVV*

Rhythms of the World Anthology *MVD*

Richard Clayderman: Live In Concert *QVD*

Richard Marx: Hold On to the Nights *MVD, MPI*

Richard Marx, Vol. 1 *MVD, EMI, PIA*

Richard Smallwood Singers: Video Celebration *MVD, PGV*

Richard Thompson *SVS*

Rick Astley: Best Video Hits *MVD*

Rick Derringer *SVS*

Rick Springfield: Platinum Videos *COL, PIA*

Rick Springfield: The Beat of a Live Drum *MVD, PIA*

Rickie Lee Jones: Live at the Wiltern Theatre *PIA*

The Ricky Grundy Chorale *MVD*

Ricky Lee Jones: Live 1992 *MVD*

Ricky Nelson in Concert *MCA, MVD*

Ricky Nelson: Special Memories *MVD*

Ricky Skaggs: Live in London *MVD, FOX*

Ricky van Shelton: RVS...To Be Continued *SMV, MVD*

Ride: Live at Brixton Academy, 1992 *MVD*

Ride: Today Forever *MVD*

The Right Stuff *MTX, KAR*

Rigoletto *HMV, HBO, MVD*

Ringo Starr and His All-Star Band *MVD, PGV, PIA*

Rio Revisited *MVD*

Rise Stevens in Opera and Song, Vol. 2 *VAI, MVD, FCT*

Rita MacNeil in Concert *MVD*

Rob McConnell & the Boss Brass *MVD, MVD*

Robert Cray: Collection *MVD*

Robert Fripp: Careful with that Axe *MVD*

Robert Fripp: Careful with that Axe, Vol. 2 *MVD*

Robert Lockwood, Jr.: Annie's Boogie *MVD*

Robert Palmer: Ridin' High *MVD*

Robert Palmer: Riptide *MVD, COL*

Robert Palmer: Super Nova *MVD, EMI, PIA*

Robert Palmer: Video Addictions *PGV, MVD*

Robert Plant: Mumbo Jumbo *MVD, AVE, FFF*

Robert (Ragtime Bob) Darch *NO*

Roberta Flack: An Evening with Roberta Flack *SIM, MVD*

Roberta Peters in Opera and Song, Vol. 2 *MVD*

Robyn Hitchcock: Brenda of the Lightbulb Eyes *MVD, A&M*

Robyn Hitchcock: Gotta Let this Hen Out *MVD*

The Roches: Live Nude Review *MCA*

Rocio Banquells, Video 1 *NO*

Rock Aid Armenia: The Earth Hour Video *MVD*

Rock Aid Armenia: The Making of "Smoke on the Water" *MVD*

Rock & Read *MCA*

Rock & Roll Call *MVD, LIV*

Rock & Roll Review *GVV*

Rock & Roll Wrestling Music Television *RHI*

Rock & Roll Wrestling Music Television: The Special Edition *RHI*

Rock Bottom Remainders *BMG, MVD*

Rock Classix *MVD*

Rock Classix: Heavy Metal *MVD*

Rock Encyclopedia: 1973 *MVD*

Rock Encyclopedia: 1974 *MVD*

Rock Encyclopedia: 1975 *MVD*

Rock Music with the Muppets *FOX*

Rock n' Roll #3: Sexy Girls & Sexy Guns *MOV*

Rock 'N Roll Classics, Vol. 1 *MVD*

Rock 'N Roll Classics, Vol. 2 *MVD*

Rock 'N Roll Classics, Vol. 3 *MVD*

Rock 'N Roll Classics, Vol. 4 *MVD*

Rock 'N Roll Classics, Vol. 5 *MVD*

Rock 'N Roll Classics, Vol. 6 *MVD*

Rock 'n' Roll Heaven *MGM*

Rock 'n' Roll History: American Rock, the '60s *MVD, GKK*

Rock 'n' Roll History: English Invasion, the '60s *MVD, GKK*

Rock 'n' Roll History: Fabulous Fifties *MVD, GKK*

Rock 'n' Roll History: Girls of Rock 'n' Roll *MVD, GKK*

Rock 'n' Roll History: Rock 'n' Soul Heaven *MVD, GKK*

Rock 'n' Roll History: Rockabilly Rockers *MVD, GKK*

Rock 'n' Roll History: Sixties Soul *MVD, GKK*

Rock 'n Roll Meltdown *MVD, PGV*

Rock 'n' Roll: The Early Days *MVD, PIA*

Rock 'n' Roll: The Greatest Years 1963 *SVI, MVD*

Rock 'n' Roll: The Greatest Years 1964 *SVI, MVD*

Rock 'n' Roll: The Greatest Years 1965 *SVI, MVD*

Rock 'n' Roll: The Greatest Years 1966 *SVI, MVD*

Rock Video Girls 2 *PGV, MVD*

Rock Video Girls 3 *PGV, MVD*

Rockcats: Raw in Japan 1992 *MVD*

Rockers *MVD*

Rockers '87 *KRV*

Rockin' Reindeer Christmas *GKK*

Rockin' the '50s *SIM, KAR*

Rockin' the Night Away *MVD, SIM*

Rock's Rebel Yell *BHV, MVD*

Rockshow *HBO, OM*

Rod Stewart *SVS*

Rod Stewart & the Faces: Videography 1969-1974 MVD
Rod Stewart Concert Video MVD, LHV, WAR
Rod Stewart Live at the L.A. Forum WAR, OM
Rod Stewart: Storyteller 1984-1991 WRV
Rod Stewart: Tonight He's Yours SUE
Rod Stewart: Vagabond Heart Tour WEA, MVD
Rodeo: The Music Video CAF
Roger Daltrey: Ride a Rock Horse MVD
Roger McGuinn/Nitty Gritty Dirt Band: Live! MVD
Roger Waters: Radio K.A.O.S. MVD, SMV
Roger Waters: What God Wants SMV, MVD
Roger Whittaker SVS, MVD
Roll Over Alice
Rolling Stone Presents Twenty Years of Rock & Roll MVD, MGM
The Rolling Stones: Let's Spend the Night Together MVD, SUE, NLC
The Rolling Stones: Live In Hyde Park MVD
The Rolling Stones: Rolling On SIM
The Rolling Stones: Video Rewind-Great Video Hits MVD, VES
Romeo and Juliet (Bolshoi Anniversary) KUL
Romeo and Juliet in Kansas City PYR
Ron Carter & Art Farmer: Live at Sweet Basil VWV, FCT
Ron Carter: Live Double Bass HMV, MVD
Ronnie Milsap: Golden Video Hits MVD, UHV, PIA
Ronnie Milsap: Greatest Video Hits MVD
The Roots of Gospel XVC, HHE
The Roots of Gospel: Part 2 XVC, HHE
Roots, Rock and Reggae: Inside the Jamaican Music Scene MVD, SHR, VTK
Roots/Salute the Saxophone MVD, HMV
Rosanne Cash: Retrospective MVD, FOX, SMV
Rosanne Cash: The Interiors Tour MVD, SMV
Rossini: Gala Concert MVD
Rossini/Strauss/Liszt MVD, PGV
Roxette: Live-ism MVD
Roxette: Look Sharp Live MVD, EMI
Roxette: The Video Hits MVD
Roxy Music: The High Road MVD, COL, PIA
Roxy Music: Total Recall MVD
Roy Acuff's Open House: Vol. 1 NOS, DVT
Roy Acuff's Open House: Vol. 2 NOS, DVT
Roy Ayers: In London 1992 MVD
Roy Ayers: Live at Ronnie Scott's MVD
Roy Brown: Aires Bucaneros NJN
Roy Orbison SIM, MVD

Roy Orbison & Friends: A Black and White Night MVD, HBO, FFF
Roy Orbison: I Drove All Night UND, MVD
Royal Society Jazz Orchestra NO
Royal Tournament Highlights: The Royal Air Force Years TVC
RRRecords Compilation Testament MVD
Rubber Rodeo SVS
Rudolf Schock: Auf Schusters Rappen GLV
Ruff House Presents... SMV, MVD
Run D.M.C. MVD
Run D.M.C.: The Video PFV
Running Wild: Death or Glory Tour Live MVD, SVI
Rush: A Show of Hands MVD, PGV
Rush: Chronicles MVD, PGV, BTV
Rush: Exit...Stage Left COL, PIA
Rush: Grace Under Pressure Tour MVD, COL
Rush: Through the Camera Eye MVD, BMG, COL
Russ Carlyle: Story MVD
Russ Taff: A Christmas Song SPW
Russian Dances
Russian Fantasy: Songs and Dances
Russian Folk Song & Dance VTK, KUL, APD
Ryuichi Sakamoto: Beauty MVD
Ryuichi Sakamoto: Media Ban Live MVD
Ryuichi Sakamoto: Neo Geo MVD
Ryuichi Sakamoto: Tokyo Melody MVD
Sabbat: End of the Beginning MVD
The Sacred Music of Duke Ellington MGM
Sadao Watanabe: Mysha MVD
Sade: Diamond Life Video MVD, FOX
The St. John Passion MVD, FHS
St. Louis Blues CIG
St. Louis Ragtimers NO
St. Matthew Passion MVD, FHS
Salif Keita: Destiny of a Noble Outcast PGV, FCT
Salute to the Edinburgh Tattoo PME, SIG, TVC
Sam Kinison: Banned MVD, WRV
Samantha Fox: Just One Night MVD, BMG
Samantha Fox: Making Music MVD
Samantha Fox: The Music Video MVD, BMG
Sammy Kershaw: Cadillac Style PGV, MVD
San Francisco Blues Festival SVS, MVD, FCT
Sandi Patti: Let There Be Praise (Concert Video) MVD, A&M
Sandi Patti: Live VBL
Santana: Viva Santana (A Conversation with Carlos) MVD, SMV
Sarah Vaughan: Live from Monterey SMV, MVD, FCT

Sarah Vaughan: Live in Tokyo MVD
Sarah Vaughan/Mel Torme: The Nearness of You MVD
Sass & Brass: A Jazz Session MVD, HBO
Savage Republic: Disarmament MVD
Sawyer Brown: Greatest Hits MVD
Sawyer Brown: Shakin' SVS, MVD
Saxon: Live MVD
Scarlatti/Debussy/Ravel KUL, SVS
Scenic Harvest from the Kingdom of Kansas
Schubert: Piano Trio Op. 100, Piano Trio D. 897 MVD, LUM
Schubert: Schwanengesang MVD
Schubert: Symphony No. 9 MVD
Schubert: 3 Piano Sonatas MVD, PGV
Scorpions SVS
Scorpions: Crazy World Tour Live - Berlin 1991 PGV
Scorpions: First Sting PIA, MVD
Scorpions: To Russia With Love MVD, PGV
Scorpions: World Wide Live MVD, COL, PIA
Scott Joplin, 1868-1917 CMR, NYS
Scott Joplin Ragtime Music CMR
Screamers: Live in San Francisco, 1978 MVD
Scritti Politti MVD
Scruggs FOX
The Sea: A Classical Music Video BMV
Seal WRV, MVD
Seal: Live at the Point MVD
Seascapes 2 BMV
The Secret Policeman's Other Ball MGM
Secret Policeman's Private Parts MED
Sensational Nightingales: Ministry in Song MVD
Sepultura: Under Siege MVD
Serge Gainsbourg: Chansons MVD
Sermon on the Mount VYY
Seventeenth Annual Telluride Bluegrass Festival MVD
'70s Revival NO
Severed Heads: Overhead MVD
The Sex Pistols: Bollocks to Everyone MVD
Sex Pistols: Buried Alive MVD
Sex Pistols: Decade MVD
Sex Pistols: Filth & the Fury MVD
Sex Pistols: Last Winterland Concert MVD
Sex Pistols Live NO
Sex Pistols: The Great Rock & Roll Swindle MVD, WRV
Sha Na Na Rock 'n' Roll Concert and Party Video MVD
Shabba Ranks: Naked and Ready SMV
Shabba Ranks: Talk of the Town MVD
Shabba Ranks vs. Ninja Man: Super Clash Round MVD
Shadows on the Grass NET
Shai: Video Personification 1 MCA

Shakespear's Sister: Hormonally Yours PGV, MVD
Sham 69: Live in Japan '91 MVD
Shari Lewis: Lambchop's Play-Along PGV, MLT
Sharing...a Visual Musical Experience VBL
Sheena Easton SVS
Sheena Easton: Act One MVD, PSM
Sheena Easton: Live at the Palace, Hollywood HBO, PIA
Sheena Easton: Private Heaven PIA, VTK, MVD
Sheila E.: Live Romance 1600 MVD, WRV
Sheila Walsh: "Shadowlands" in Concert MVD
Shelley Duvall's Rock 'n' Rhymeland MVD
Shelly Manne Quartet MVD, RHP
Shenandoah: Greatest Video Hits SMV
Sherrill Milnes: Homage to Verdi MVD, HMV, KUL
Shimmy-Disc Compilation, Vol. 1 MVD
Shimmy-Disc Compilation, Vol. 2 MVD
Shimmy Disc Compilation, Vol. 3 MVD
Shindig! Presents British Invasion, Vol. 1 MOV, RHI, MVD
Shindig! Presents British Invasion, Vol. 2 RHI, MVD
Shindig! Presents Frat Party RHI, FCT
Shindig! Presents Groovy Gals RHI, FCT
Shindig! Presents Jackie Wilson RHI, FCT
Shindig! Presents Legends of Rock 'n Roll RHI, MVD
Shindig! Presents Motor City Magic RHI, FCT
Shindig! Presents Soul RHI, FCT
Shindig! Presents the Kinks MOV, RHI, MVD
Shindig! Presents the Righteous Brothers: Unchained Melody RHI, PIA, MVD
Shining Time Station: Singsongs, Vol. 1 FFF, FFF
Shirley Bassey: You Ain't Heard Nothin' Yet: Live MVD
Shirley Caesar: Hold My Mule (Live in Memphis) MVD, AVE, XVC
Shirley Caesar: I Remember Mama MVD, WRD, SMV
Shirley Horn Sings and Plays Here's to Life PGV
Shock Out With Metromedia MVD, KRV
Shockwave MVD, LIV, VES
Short Pieces MWF
Shorty Rogers: West Coast Giants MVD
Shout!: The Story of Johnny O'Keefe FRH
Show My People BUP
Showdown at the Hoedown
Showdown 1 PPI
Siam Odyssey VTK
Simon and Garfunkel: The Concert in Central Park MVD, FOX
Simon Boccanegra HMV, PAR

Simon Phillips MVD
Simple Minds: Verona MVD
Simply Red: A Starry Night With Simply Red MVD
Simply Red: Let Me Take You Home MVD
Simply Red: Moving Picture Book AVE, MVD, FFF
Simultaneous FCT
Sinead O'Connor: Nothing Compares 2 U MVD
Sinead O'Connor: The Value of Ignorance MVD, PGV
Sinead O'Connor: Year of the Horse MOV
Sing Along with Israel ERG
Sing mir das Lied noch einmal GLV
Sing mit Heino GLV
Sing mit Mir, Tanz mit Mir GLV
Singer Presents "Elvis" (The 1968 Comeback Special) NOS, DVT
Singing French Songs for Children FCT
Siouxsie and the Banshees SVS
Siouxsie & the Banshees: Nocturne MVD, MED
Siouxsie & the Banshees: Once Upon a Time NO
Sir George Solti Conducts the Chicago Symphony Orchestra in Tokyo, 1990 NO
Sir Mix-A-Lot: Baby Got Back WRV, MVD
Sir Mix-A-Lot: Maconomics WRV
Sisters of Mercy: Live MVD
Ska Beatz MVD
Ska Explosion MVD
Skid Row: Oh Say, Can You Scream? MVD, AVE, FFF
Skin Deep: The Men NO
Skin Deep: The Women NO
Skinny Puppy: Ain't It Dead Yet? MVD
Sky Cries Mary: Until the Grinders Cease MVD
Slammin' Rap Video Magazine, Vol. 1 MVD, GKK
Slammin' Rap Video Magazine, Vol. 2 MVD, BMG, BTV
Slammin' Rap Video Magazine, Vol. 3 MVD, BMG
Slammin' Rap Video Magazine, Vol. 4 BMG
Slaughter: From the Beginning MVD, CAP
Slaughter: The Wild Life Home Video EMI, MVD
Slayer: Live at Wembley MVD
Slipping Through the Cracks MVD
Slovak Dancing Songs 1
Slovak Dancing Songs 2
Slovak Dancing Songs 3
Slovak Dancing Songs 4
Small Faces: Big Hits MVD
Smashin' the Palace '84 NO
Smithereens: Smithereens 10 MVD, CAP, PIA
The Smiths: The Complete Picture MVD, WRV
Snap: World Power—The Videos MVD, BMG
Snub TV, Vol. 2 MVD
So Proudly We Hail: A Salute to American Patriotism FOX

So Schoen wie Heut, so Muesst es Bleiben (Schlager, die Man nie Vergisst) *GLV*

S.O.D.: Live at Budokan, the Home Video *PGV, MVD*

Soft Cell *HBO*

Soft Cell/Marc Almond: Memorabilia—Video Singles *PGV*

Soldiers of Music: Rostropovich Returns to Russia *NO*

Solo Tribute to Keith Jarrett *HMV, FCT*

Sondheim: A Celebration at Carnegie Hall *BMG*

A Song for Ireland *RGO*

Songs from Papua New Guinea

Songs from the Soul: The Negro Spiritual *FVL*

Sonic Youth: Goo *MOV*

Sonny & Cher Nitty Gritty Hour *VWV, MOV*

Sonny Rollins: Live *MVD, RHP, TLF*

Sonny Rollins: Montreux Jazz Festival *MVD*

Sonny Rollins: Saxaphone Colossus *SVS, MVD*

Sonny Terry: Shoutin' the Blues *NO*

Sophisticated Ladies *JTC, FCT, MVD*

Soul Classix *MVD*

Soul Experience *NO*

The Soul of R & B *MVD, LIV*

Soul to Soul *VTK*

Sound?? *RHP, FCT, KIV*

Sound of Jazz *MVD*

Soundgarden: Louder Than Live *MVD, A&M*

Soundgarden: Motorvision *PGV*

Soundies, Vol. 1: 1940's Music Machine *AHV*

Soundies, Vol. 2: Singing Stars of Swing Era *NO*

Soundies, Vol. 3: Big Band Swing *NO*

Soundies, Vol. 4: Harlem Highlights *NO*

Sounds of Motown *SVS, VTK, PIA*

Sounds of Scotland *TVC*

South Market Street Jazz Band: 1 *NO*

South Market Street Jazz Band: 2 *NO*

South Pacific: The London Sessions *FOX*

Southern Comfort Jazz Band #1 *NO*

Southern Comfort Jazz Band #2 *NO*

Southern Comfort Jazz Band #3 *NO*

Southside Johnny & the Asbury Jukes: Having a Party *MCA, UND, MVD*

Soviet Army Chorus, Band, and Dance Ensemble *KUL, VTK*

Space Dreaming *MVD, LUM*

Space Music *BMG, MVD*

Spandau Ballet: Live Hits *MVD*

Spandau Ballet: Over Britain *MVD, LIV, VES*

Spartacus (Bolshoi Ballet) *HMV, HBO, PIA*

Spike Lee & Co.: Do It A Cappella *MVD*

Spinal Tap: Break Like the Wind the Videos *MCA, MVD*

The Spirit Travels: Immigrant Music in America *CIG*

Spirituals in Concert *PGV, FCT, MVD*

S.P.K.: Despair *MVD*

S.P.K.: 2 Autopsy Films *MVD*

Splashin' the Palace '84 *MVD, MUS,*

Split Enz: History Never Repeats—The Best of Split Enz *MVD, SVS*

Split Enz: Live *MVD*

Sprout Wings and Fly *FFM*

Spyro Gyra *WAR, OM*

Spyro Gyra: Graffiti *MVD, MCA*

Squeeze: A Round & a Bout *MVD, MCA*

Squeeze: Greatest Hits *MVD*

Squeeze Play: The Videos 1978-1987 *MVD, A&M*

Stage Show *VYY*

Stage Show with the Dorsey Brothers *VYY*

Stamping Ground *MVD*

Stan Getz with Richie Cole *MVD*

Stan Kenton & His Orchestra: London, 1970 *MVD*

Stan Kenton: In the USA *MVD*

Stand and Be Proud: Voice of the City *BMG, MVD*

Stand By Me: AIDS Day Benefit Concert *MVD, LIV*

Standards II with Keith Jarrett, Gary Peacock and Jack DeJohnette *HMV, FCT*

Stanley Jordan: Cornucopia *MVD*

Stanley Jordan: Magic Touch *SVS, MVD, FCT*

Stanley Jordan: The Blue Note Concert *CAP, PIA*

Stanley Turrentine: In Concert *MVD, KUL, FCT*

Star Flight

Star Licks *NO*

Star Licks All-Star Bass Video Series *MVD*

Star Spangled Banner 1 *NO*

Star Spangled Video: Operation Desert Storm Welcome Home *TGV*

Stars on 45 *MCA*

Starship: Greatest Hits (Ten Years and Change 1979-1991) *MVD, BMG*

Starship: Video Hoopla *MVD, COL*

State of the Arts Performance Special: A Festival *NJN*

The Statler Brothers: Brothers in Song *MVD, COL*

Status Quo: Anniversary Waltz *MVD*

Status Quo: Rockin' All Over the Years *MVD*

Steel Pulse *MVD, IME*

Steeleye Span: A 20th Anniversary Celebration *SHR*

Steelheart: Quick Pix *MVD*

Stephan Kates, Cellist *CMR, NYS*

Stephane Grappelli in New Orleans *MVD,*

Stephane Grappelli: Live in San Francisco *MVD, RHP, KIV*

Stephanie Mills: Home is Where the Heart is *MCA, MVD*

Stephanie Mills: Television Medicine *NO*

Steps Ahead: Live in Japan *MVD*

Steve and Annie Chapman: The Greatest Gift *NO*

Steve Gadd: In Session *MVD, MVD*

Steve Green: Hymns—A Portrait of Christ *MVD, SPW*

Steve Hackett: Live '89 *MVD*

Steve Miller Band *HBO, PIA*

Steve Miller: Blues in the 20th Century *EMI, MVD*

Steven Curtis Chapman: The Great Adventure Home Video *SPW, MVD*

Stevie Nicks & Friends *MVD*

Stevie Nicks: I Can't Wait *MVD, COL, PIA*

Stevie Nicks in Concert *FOX, PIA, MVD*

Stevie Nicks: Live at Red Rocks *SMV, PIA, MVD*

Stevie Ray Vaughan and Double Trouble: Live at the El Mocombo 1983 *SMV*

Stevie Ray Vaughn and Double Trouble: Pride & Joy *MVD, SMV*

Stewart Copeland: Rhythmatist *COL*

Sting: Bring on the Night *MVD, LHV, WAR*

Sting: Nothing Like the Sun: The Videos *MVD, A&M*

Sting: Ten Summoner's Tales *PGV, MVD*

Sting: The Soul Cages Concert *A&M*

Sting: The Soul Cages Video *MVD, A&M*

Sting: The Videos Part 1 *MVD, PGV, BTV*

Sting: Unplugged *PGV*

The Stone Roses: Blackpool Live *MVD*

Stonehenge '84 *MVD*

Stop Making Sense *MVD, COL*

Stop Sellafield: The Concert *MCA, MVD*

Stop the Violence Movement: Self Destruction *BMG, MVD*

The Story of Creation *WRV, MVD*

Story of Hands Across America *LHV*

The Story of the Clancy Brothers and Tommy Makem *SHR*

Straight from the Hood *MVD*

The Stranglers *MVD*

Stratasphere: Portrait of Teresa Stratas *MVD, KUL, PME*

Stray Cats *PIA*

Stray Cats: Bring It Back Again *MVD, EMI*

Stray Cats: Paris *MVD*

Stray Cats: Rock Detroit *MVD*

Stray Cats Rock Tokyo *BMG, MVD*

Streisand Collection *NO*

Strictly for the Beat *PGV, WAX, MVD*

String Trio of New York: Built by Hand *KIV*

Structures from Silence *NEM, WSH*

Stryper: Against the Law *MVD*

Stryper: In the Beginning *MVD, PGV*

Stryper: Live In Japan *MVD*

Style Council: Far East & Far Out *MED*

Style Council: Jerusalem *MVD, PGV*

Style Council: Live at Full House *MVD*

Style Council: Showbiz *MVD*

Style Council: What We Did On Our Holiday *MVD*

Styx: Caught in the Act *MVD, A&M, COL*

Subbulakshmi: Queen of Song *CMR, NYS*

The Sugar Cubes: Live Zabor

Sugar Minott: Dance Hall Video *NO*

Sugarcubes: Live Zabor *MVD, WAR*

Suicidal Tendencies: Lights...Camera...Suicidal *MVD, SMV*

Summerwind *WSH*

Sun City *LHV,*

Sun, Moon & Feather *CIG*

Sun Ra: Mystery, Mr. Ra *MVD, RHP, KIV*

Sunday Mornin' Country *VBL*

Super Drumming *MVD*

Super Jam 3: Stone Love vs. Metromedia *KRV, MVD*

Super Jam '87 *KRV*

Super Rock '85 *MVD*

Superchunk: Take the Tube *MVD*

Superdrumming *MVD, PRS*

Supershow *MVD*

Superstars in Concert *MVD*

Supertramp: Brother Where You Bound *MVD, A&M, COL*

Supertramp: The Story So Far *MVD*

Surfing Beach Party *MED*

Survivor: Live in Japan *MVD*

Survivors: The Blues Today *MVD*

Suzanne Vega *MVD*

Suzuki Violin Concert Series *NO*

Sweet Baby: Live *MVD*

Sweet Sensation: Sweet Sensation *MVD, AVE, FFF*

Swing Out Sister: And Why Not? *MVD*

Swing Out Sister: Best Videos *MVD*

Swing Out Sister: Kaleidoscope World *MVD, PGV*

Swing: The Best of the Big Bands *MCA, VTK*

Swinging Singing Years *MVD, NOS, DVT*

Swinging U.K. *JEF*

The Swingle Singers in Concert *MVD, PRS, HMV*

Swingtime Video *MVD*

Sylvia Plath, Part 2: Getting There *CMR, NYS*

Sympathy for the Devil *FOX, OM*

Symphony of Swing *MVD*

T. Rex: Solid Gold *MVD*

T. Rex: T-Rexmas *MVD*

T. Rex: The Essential Video Collection *MVD*

Taj Mahal: Live at Ronnie Scott's *MVD*

Takanaka: World *PAR*

Take 6: All Access *WRV, MVD*

The Tales of Hoffman *HMV, PME*

Talk Talk *SVS*

Talk Talk: Natural History *MVD*

Talking Heads: Storytelling Giants *MVD, WRV*

Tam Tam: Do It Tam Tam *NO*

The T.A.M.I. Show *MED*

Tammy Wynette in Concert *MVD, LIV, VTK*

Tanita Tikaram: Ancient Heart *MVD, WRV*

Tankard: Open All Night—Live at the Berlin Wall *MVD*

Tannhaeuser *HMV, PAR, VTK*

Tanya Tucker: Live *MVD*

Tanya Tucker: Video Hits *MVD*

Taylor Dayne: Twists of Fate *MVD, BMG, PIA*

Tchaikovsky Competition: Violin & Piano *MAS, VTK, MVD*

Tchaikovsky Gala in Leningrad *BMG*

Tchaikovsky: Piano Concerto #1 *MVD*

Tchaikovsky/Prokofiev Violin Concertos *BMG, MVD*

Tchaikovsky: Symphonies 4 & 5 *MVD*

Tear In My Beer & Other Great Country Videos *WRV, MVD*

Tears For Fears *SVS, PIA, MVD*

Tears For Fears: Going to California *MVD, PGV*

Tears For Fears: In My Mind's Eye *MVD, MED*

Tears for Fears: Live in London *MVD*

Tears For Fears: Scenes From the Big Chair *PIA*

Tears For Fears: Sowing the Seeds *MVD, PGV*

Tears for Fears: Tears Roll Down (Greatest Hits 82-92) *PGV, MVD*

Teatro Alla Scala: Adrianna Lecouvrer *HMV*

Technotronic: Trip on This—The Videos *MVD,*

Ted Nugent's New Year's Eve Whiplash Bash *MVD, AVE, FFF*

Teddy Pendergrass: Live in London *FOX*

Teenage Mutant Ninja Turtles: Coming Out of Their Shells Tour *GKK*

Teenage Mutant Ninja Turtles: Music Videos *MVD,*

Teenage Mutant Ninja Turtles: The Gettin' Down in Your Town Tour *RAN*

TeenVid Video Magazine, Vol. 1 *MVD, BMG*

TeenVid Video Magazine, Vol. 2 *MVD*

TeenVid Video Magazine, Vol. 3 *BMG, MVD*

The Temps and the Tops *FRH*

Temptations & Four Tops *MVD*

Temptations: Get Ready *MPI*

Temptations: Live in Concert *IME, FCT*

Ten Years After: Going Home *MVD*

10CC: Changing Faces *MVD*

10,000 Maniacs: Time Capsule 1982-1990 *MVD*

Terence Trent D'Arby: Introducing the Hardline... Live *SMV, MVD*

Tesla: Five Man Video Band *MVD, BTV*

Test Department: Program for Progress *SVS, MVD*

Testament: Seen Between the Lines *AVE, FFF*

Tex Wyndham's Red Lion Jazz Band *NO*

Texaco's Swing into Spring *NOS, DVT*

Texas: Southside *MVD*

Texas Style *NO*

That Was Rock (The TAMI/TNT Show) *MVD, MED*

That'll Be the Day *HBO*

The The: Infected *SMV, MVD*

The The: Versus the World *MVD, SMV*

Thelonious Monk: Monk in Europe *MVD*

Thelonious Monk: Music in Monk's Time *MVD*

Thelonious Monk: Portrait of... *MVD*

Thelonious Monk: '63 in Japan *MVD*

Thelonious Monk: Straight, No Chaser *MVD, WAR, TTC*

Thelonious Sphere Monk: Celebrating a Jazz Master *PIA*

There But For Fortune *NO*

There was No Room for You *FCT*

There's a Meetin' Here Tonight *PIA*

They Might Be Giants: The Videos 1986-1989 *MVD, PGV*

They Might Be Giants: Video Compilation *BMG*

Thin Lizzy: Dedication *MVD, PGV*

Thin Lizzy: Live & Dangerous *MVD, AIP*

Thin White Rope: The Axis Calls *BMG*

3rd Bass: The Cactus Vidie/Yo *MVD, SMV*

Third World: Live in Japan '85 *MVD*

Third World: Prisoner in the Street *MVD*

38 Special: Wild Eyed and Live *MVD, A&M, COL*

Thomas Dolby: Live Wireless *HBO*

Thomas Dolby: The Golden Age of Video *MVD, EMI, PIA*

Thomas Dolby: Video 45 *MVD, SVS*

Thompson Twins: Into the Gap Live *MVD, MCA*

Thompson Twins: Live at Liverpool *HBO*

Thompson Twins: Single Vision *MVD, COL*

Three Dog Night: Video Hits *MVD*

Three Tenors: Encore *NLC, COL, MVD*

3-Way Thrash *MVD*

The Thrill of the Orchestra

Throbbing Gristle: Destiny *MVD*

Throbbing Gristle: Live at Kezar *MVD*

Thunder: Backstreet Symphony *MVD*

Thunders, Kane, Nolan: Live on the Sunset Strip *MVD*

Tiffany: Live in Japan *MVD*

Tiger *KRV*

Tiger: Spectacular *MVD*

Tigertailz: Bezerk Live '90 *MVD*

'Til Tuesday *MVD, FOX*

Tim Blake *MVD*

Timbuk 3 *MVD, MCA*

Timbuk 3: Greetings from Eden Alley *MCA*

Time Groove *MVD, VAI, FCT*

Timeless *MVD*

Timex Watch Hour *VDM*

Timmy T. *QVD*

Tin Machine: Live in Hamburg 1991 *MVD*

Tina Turner: Break Every Rule *MVD, HBO, PIA*

Tina Turner: Do You Want Some Action! *MVD, PGV*

Tina Turner: Foreign Affair *EMI*

Tina Turner: Live in Rio *MVD, PGV*

Tina Turner: Live, Nice 'n' Rough *HBO, SVS*

Tina Turner: Live, Private Dancer Tour *PIA*

Tina Turner: Private Dancer *SVS, PIA*

Tina Turner: Queen of Rock & Roll *NO*

Tina Turner: Simply the Best *CTL, MVD*

Tino Rossi: Thanks to Dear Friends—Live *MVD*

Tiny and Ruby: Hell Divin' Women *CIG*

TLC: Oooooooohhh...on the TLC Video Tip *BMG, MVD*

Toad the Wet Sprocket: Seven Songs Seldom Seen *SMV, MVD*

Todd Rundgren: Grok Gazer, Visual Concert Hall *MVD*

Todd Rundgren: Live in Japan *RHI*

Todd Rundgren: Nearly Human—Live in Japan *MVD, RHI*

Todd Rundgren: 2nd Wind Live Recording Sessions *RHI, FCT*

Todd Rundgren: Videosyncracy *BMG*

Tom Chapin: This Pretty Planet *SMV, FFF*

Tom Jones: Live at This Moment *MVD, BMG*

Tom Jones: Live in Las Vegas *FHE, OM*

Tom Paxton: In Concert *MVD, SHR*

Tom Petty: A Bunch of Videos & Some Other Stuff *MVD, MPI*

Tom Petty & the Heartbreakers: Pack Up the Plantation Live! *MVD, MCA*

Tom Petty: Full Moon Fever, the Videos *MVD, MPI*

Tom Petty: Take the Highway *MCA, MVD*

Tom Waits: Big Time *MVD, FRH*

Tommy *COL, MVD, WME*

Tommy Page: I'll Be Your Everything *MVD, WRV*

Tommy Puett: Heart Attack *MVD, BMG*

Tonadillas of Granados *CMR, NYS*

Toni Basil: Word of Mouth *MVD, PAV*

Toni Childs: The Videos *MVD, A&M*

Tony Bennett Live: Watch What Happens *SMV*

Tony Bennett Sings *SVS, MVD*

The Tony Marshall Show *GLV*

Tony Powers *SVS*

Tony! Toni! Tone! *MVD, PGV*

Tony Williams: New York Live Video *MVD, CTL, PIA*

Too Short: Short Dog's in the House *MVD*

Too Short: Shorty the Pimp at the Player's Ball *BMG*

Toots and the Maytals Live from New Orleans *PGV*

Toots Thielemans in New Orleans *MVD*

Tori Amos: Little Earthquakes *MVD, AVE, VMI*

Tori Amos: Tori Amos *AVE, MVD*

Tosca *HMV, HBO*

Toscanini: The Maestro/Hymn of the Nations *MVD, HMV*

Toscanini: The Television Concerts *BMG*

Toshiko Akiyoshi: Jazz is My Native Language *MVD*

Toto: Past to Present *MVD, SMV*

Tout Ecartille *NFC*

Toxic Reasons *MVD*

Toy Dolls *MVD*

Toy Dolls: Idle Gossip *MVD*

Toy Dolls: Live in Japan 1991 *MVD*

Traffic: Live at Santa Monica *RCA, MVD*

Tramaine Hawkins: Bring it Home, Live *MVD, SPW*

Transformation is Our Secret *MWF, FCT*

Travis Tritt: A Celebration: A Musical Tribute to the Spirit of the American Disabled Veteran *WRV*

Travis Tritt: It's All About to Change *WRV*

Tribal Area No. 1 *MVD*

Tribal Area No. 2 *MVD*

Tribal Area No. 3 *MVD*

Tribal Area No. 4 *MVD*

Tribal Area No. 5 *MVD*

A Tribe Called Quest: The Art of Moving Butts *MVD*

A Tribute to Bill Evans *MVD, HMV*

Tribute to John Coltrane *HMV, MVD*

Tribute to Ricky Nelson *RHI*

The Triplets: Video Triple Single *PGV*

Triumph: A Night of Triumph *MVD,, AIP*

Triumph: Live at the US Festival *MVD, MCA*

The Triumph of Charlie Parker: Celebrating Bird *KUL, SVS, PIA*

Trixter *MVD*

TROOP: Attitude *MVD, AVE, FFF*

The Tropicana Music Bowl 3 *NJN*

Troy Game *MVD, HMV*

True North *BMG*

True Story of 200 Motels *MVD, MPI*

Truth or Dare *LIV, FCT, PIA*

Tubes: Live at the Greek *MVD,, MON*

The Tubes Video *HBO, OM*

Turandot *HMV, HBO, MVD*

Turn Up the Volume, Vol. 1 & 2 *BHV*

Turn Up the Volume, Vol. 3 *BHV, MVD*

Turn Up the Volume, Vol. 4 *BHV, MVD*

Turn Up the Volume, Vol. 5 *BHV*

Turnpike Cruisers: Cable T.V. Show *MVD*

The Turtles: Happy Together *MVD, RHI*

Tuxedomoon: Four Major Events *MVD*

TV/ARM Video Magazine *MVD*

Twelve O'Clock High Video Compilation *MVD*

25 ''Roots of Rap'' Videos *MVD*

Twisted Sister: Come Out and Play *MVD, AVE, FFF*

Twisted Sister's Stay Hungry *MVD, SUE, PIA*

Two Fiddles, No Waiting *MVD*

2-Kut: Rock That *MVD*

2 Live Crew: Banned in the USA *MVD, AVE, FFF*

2 Live Crew: Pop That Coochie *MVD, FFF, AVE*

2 Sound Clash Dance Hall *MVD, KRV*

Two X 4 *MVD*

200 Motels *MVD, MGM*

UB40: CCCP (The Video Mix) *MVD, A&M, PIA*

UB40: Family Affair *MVD*

UB40: Labour of Love 2 *MVD, WAR*

UB40: The Best of UB40 *MVD*

U.F.O.: History of U.F.O. *MVD*

U.F.O. Live *NLC, MVD, SUE*

Ugly American Overkill *MVD*

Ugly Kid Joe: America's Least Wanted Tour '92 *MVD*

U.K./D.K. *MVD*

U.K. Subs: Down Amongst the Dead Men *MVD*

U.K. Subs: Grossout *U.K. MVD*

Ultimate Revenge 2 *MVD*

Ultimate Rock *MVD, SPW*

Ultravox: The Collection *MVD, LIV, VES*

Un Ballo in Maschera *MVD, PGV, PME*

Una Aventura Llamada Menudo *SUE*

Uncle Floyd's Nostalgic Music Special *NJN*

Uncle Meat *MVD, MPI*

Und weiter geht's *GLV*

Underground Forces Volumes 1-8 *MVD*

Underground U.S.A. Vol. 1: Music Magazine *MVD*

Underground U.S.A. Vol. 2: Hardcore *MVD*

Underground U.S.A. Vol. 3: Heavy Metal *MVD*

Underground U.S.A. Vol. 4: New Music *MVD*

Underground U.S.A. Vol. 5: New Music *MVD*

Underground U.S.A. Vol. 6: Heavy Metal 2 *MVD*

Underground U.S.A. Vol. 7 *MVD*

Underground U.S.A. Vol. 8 *MVD*

Underground U.S.A. Vol. 9: Son of Heavy Metal *MVD*

Underground U.S.A. Vol. 10: Rap Rap Rap *MVD*

Underground U.S.A. Vol. 11: Rap Rap Rap *MVD*

Underground U.S.A. Vol. 12: Rap Rap Rap *MVD*

Underground U.S.A. Vol. 13: Heavy Metal *MVD*

Underground U.S.A. Vol. 14 *MVD*

Underground U.S.A. Vol. 15 *MVD*

Underground U.S.A. Vol. 16 *MVD*

Underground U.S.A. Vol. 17 *MVD*

Underground U.S.A. Vol. 18 *MVD*

Universal Congress Of: Live *MVD*

Unser kleines Platzkonzert 1 *GLV*

Unser kleines Platzkonzert 2 *GLV*

Unsere schoensten volkstuemlichen Lieder *GLV*

Upper Dallas Jazz Band *NO*

Urban Dance Squad: Mental Floss for the Globe *MVD, SWH*

URGH! A Music War *MVD, FOX*

Uriah Heep: Gypsy *MVD*

Ute Lemper: Illusions *PGV, PMS, PME*

Utopia: A Retrospective 1977-1984 *BMG*

Utopia: An Evening with Utopia *MCA, MVD*

Utopia: Live at the Royal Oak *BMG*

Utopia Redux '92: Live in Japan *BMG*

The Utopia Sampler *SVS*

U2: Achtung Baby *PGV*

U2: Live at Red Rocks ''Under A Blood Red Sky'' *COL, MVD*

U2: Rattle and Hum *MVD, PAR*

U2: The Unforgettable Fire Collection *PGV, COL, MVD*

Van Halen: Live Right Here, Right Now *WRV, MVD*

Van Halen: Live Without a Net *MVD, WRV, VTK*

Van Morrison in Ireland *MVD*

Van Morrison: The Concert *MVD, PGV*

Vancouver New Music 1978-80 *VDO*

Vandenburg: Live in Japan *MVD*

Vanessa Williams: De Right Stuff Collection *MVD, PGV*

Vanessa Williams: The Comfort Zone Collection *PGV, MVD*

Vanilla Ice: Ninja Rap *MVD*

Vanilla Ice: Play That Funky Music, White Boy *MVD*

Vassar Clements: Dobro Summit *MVD*

Vassar Clements: The Fiddle According to Vassar *MVD*

Venom: Alive in '85! *NLC, SUE, MVD*

Venom: Live at Hammersmith Odeon *SVS*

Venom: Live '90 *MVD, SVI*

The Ventures: Live in Japan '84 *MVD*

The Ventures: Live in Japan '90 *MVD*

The Ventures: Live in L.A. '81 *MVD*

Verdi Compilation *MVD*

Verdi: Requiem *HBO, HMV*

Vespers of the Blessed Virgin *FCT*

VH-1 '60s Music Video Album *WKV*

VH-1 '70s Music Video Album *WKV*

Vico Torriani's Internationale Schlager-Revue *GLV*

Victor Borge: 80th Birthday Gala *SIG, TVC*

Victor Borge in London *KUL, SIG, TVC*

Victor Borge: On Stage with Audience Favorites *SIG, TVC*

Victory Over the Sun: A Futuristic Opera *AAI*

Video a Go-Go: Vol. 1 *MVD, COL*

Video a Go-Go: Vol. 2 *MVD, COL*

Video Aid *SVS, MVD*

Video Band: War Dance *MWF*

A Video Christmas Card *NO*

Video Love Songs *MVD, COL, PIA*

Video Meltdown *BMG, MVD*

Video Rap Pack *MVD*

Video Sheet Metal *WRV*

Video Sheet Metal, Vol. 2 *WRV*

Video Void *MWF*

Videotomy, Vol. 1 *SIM, MVD*

Videotomy, Vol. 2 *SIM, MVD*

Vietnam Experience

Vince Gill: I Still Believe in You *MCA, MVD*

Virgin Prunes: The Sons Find Devils *MVD*

Vision Shared: A Tribute to Woody Guthrie & Leadbelly *MVD, SMV*

Vivaldi: The Four Seasons *MVD, PGV*

Vixen: Revved Up *MVD*

Vocomotion: Best of the '50s & '60s *NO*

Vocomotion: Classic Country *NO*

Vocomotion: Famous Star Classic Series *NO*

Vocomotion: Favorite Standards *NO*

Vocomotion: Holiday Favorites *NO*

Vocomotion: Spotlighting the '70s & '80s *NO*

A Voice from Soviet Russia *CMR, NYS*

Voice of the Whale *KIV*

Voices of Firestone Classic Performances *VAI, CTH, MVD*

Voices of Sarafina *NYF, FCT*

Voices that Care *MVD, WRV*

Volkstuemliches Europa *GLV*

Vow Wow: Live *MVD*

The Voyager Odyssey *MVD*

Wagner: Concert in Leipzig *MVD, KUL*

Wagner: The Ring *SIG*

The Wall: Live in Berlin *MVD, PGV, BTV*

Walt Whitman & the Soul Children: Live and Blessed *MVD*

Walter Hawkins & the Love Alive Choir 4 *MVD*

Wanda Butler Nero: New Born Soul *PRH, MVD*

War Requiem *ING, MFV, MVD*

Warfare: A Concept of Hatred *MVD*

Warlock: Live from London *MVD, AIP,*

Warrant: Blood, Sweat & Beers *MVD*

Warrant: Cherry Pie *MVD, SMV*

Warrant: Dirty Rotten Filthy Stinking Rich Live *MVD, SMV*

Warren Zevon *SVS*

W.A.S.P. *SVS*

W.A.S.P.: Live at the Lyceum *MVD*

W.A.S.P.: Videos in the Raw *MVD, LIV*

Wax Trax: Video Compilation 1 in Stereo *MVD*

Waylon Jennings: America *MVD, COL, LTY*

Waylon Jennings: The Lost Outlaw Performance *NO*

Waylon Jennings: Waylon. Renegade. Outlaw. Legend. *NO*

Wayne Newton at the London Palladium *MGM*

We are the World: The Video Event *COL, OM*

We Like the Blues, Vol. 1 *MVD*

We Like the Blues, Vol. 2 *MVD*

Weather Report: Domino Theory *MVD*

Weavers: Wasn't That a Time! *WRV, MGM, MVD*

The Wedding Present: Punk *BMG*

Weird Al Yankovic: This is Life *MVD*

Weird Al Yankovic: Video Library *SWH, MVD*

Welt der Oper *GLV*

Wendy O. Williams: Live *NLC, SUE, MVD*

We're All Devo *RHI*

West End Jazz Band #1 *NO*

West End Jazz Band #2 *NO*

West End Jazz Band #3 *NO*

West End Jazz Band #4 *NO*

Wet, Wet, Wet *MVD*

Wha Dat Disco *MVD, KRV*

Whalesong *BUL*

Wham! in China: Foreign Skies *MVD, FOX*

Wham! The Final *MVD, FOX*

Wham! The Video *MVD, FOX*

What the F**k *MVD*

When the Music's Over *MVD*

White Lion: Escape from Brooklyn *AVE, MVD, FFF*

Whitesnake *NO*

Whitesnake: Live at Donnington *MVD*

Whitesnake: Live at the Monsters of Rock Festival *MVD*

Whitesnake: Live Commandos *MVD*

Whitesnake: Trilogy *MVD*

Whitney Houston: #1 Video Hits *MVD, COL, PIA*

Whitney Houston: The Star Spangled Banner *MVD, SWH, BMG*

Whitney Houston: Welcome Home Heroes *MVD, SWH*

The Who: Rocks America, 1982 American Tour *FOX*

The Who: The Kids are Allright *BMG*

The Who: The Who Live! Tommy *MVD, FOX, SMV*

The Who: Who's Better, Who's Best *MVD, PGV*

Whodini: Back in Black *MVD, COL*

Whodini: Greatest Rap Hits *MVD, BMG*

Widespread Panic: Live from the Georgia Theatre *WRV, MVD*

The Williams Brothers: I'm Just a Nobody *MVD*

Willie & the Poor Boys *NO*

Willie Banks & the Messengers: In Concert *MVD*

Willie N. Johnson & the New Gospel Keynotes *MVD, MLC*

Willie Nelson & Family in Concert *MVD, FOX*

Willie Nelson in Concert *SIM*

Willie Nelson: Live at Budokan *MVD*

Willie Nelson: On the Road Again *SIM*

Willie Nelson: Some Enchanted Evening *MVD, CAF*

Willie Nelson Special with Ray Charles *MVD, SUE, VTK*

Willie Nelson's Greatest Hits: Live *MVD, LIV, VES*

Wilson Phillips *MVD,, PIA*

Wilson Phillips: Shadows and Light *EMI, MVD*

The Winans: Live in Concert *MVD, XVC*

The Winans: Return *MVD, SPW*

Windham Hill in Concert *MVD, PAR, VTK*

Windham Hill Music Video Series *PAR, VTK, WSH*

Winger: In the Heart of the Young *MVD, AVE, FFF*

Winger: In the Heart of the Young, Part 2 *MVD, AVE, FFF*

Winger: Live in Tokyo *MVD*

Winger: The Videos, Vol. 1 *MVD, AVE, FFF*

Wir lassen uns das Singen nicht verbieten *GLV*

Wishbone Ash *MVD*

Wishbone Ash: Phoenix *MVD*

Wojceich Mlynarski: Lyrical Evening *FCT*

Wolf Trap Salutes Dizzy Gillespie: An All Star Tribute to the Jazz Master *MVD*

The Wolfe Tones: 25th Anniversary Concert *MVD*

Women in Rock *MCA, MVD, FFF*

Women in Rock: The Women of Heavy Metal *MVD*

The Wonder Stuff: Seven Appalling Promos *MVD*

The Wonder Stuff: Welcome to the Cheap Seats *PGV, MVD*

The Wonderful Planet *NO*

Woodstock *MVD, WAR, VTK*

Woodstock: The Lost Performances *WAR*

Woody Guthrie: Hard Travelin' *MVD, MGM*

Woody Herman: Live Thunder *MVD, MCG*

Woody Herman: 1982 Aurex Jazz Festival *MVD*

Word Rap Video Compilation, Vol. 1 *MVD, BMG*

Word Up: The Best *MVD*

The Work of Sefan Wolpe *CMR, NYS*

World Drums *BUL*

The World of Music *NYS*

World War II: The Music Video, Vol. 1 *NEG, KAR*

World War II: The Music Video, Vol. 2 *NEG, KAR*

The Worship of Music: The Dagar Singers of India *CMR, NYS*

Wozzeck *HMV, PME*

Wrathchild: Live from London *MVD, AIP*

Wreckx-N-Effect: Hard or Smooth Videos *MCA*

Wrestling Music Television: Born to Bleed *RHI*

Wynton Marsalis: Blues & Swing *MVD, FOX, PIA*

XL Recording: the Video Chaptor *MVD*

XTC: Look Look *MVD*

Y & T Live at the San Francisco Civic *MVD, A&M, COL*

Y & T: Summertime Girls & All American Boys - The Videos *MVD, A&M*

Yakety Yak: Take It Back *MVD, AVE, FFF*

Yankee Air Pirates *NO*

Yankee Doodle's Odyssey *NJN*

The Yardbirds: For Your Love *AVE, MVD*

Yehudi Menuhin: Brahms Violin Concerto in D, Opus 7 *KUL*

Yehudi Menuhin: Concert for the Pope *MVD, VWV, MBP*

Yehudi Menuhin: Tribute to J.S. Bach *VWV, MBP*

Yello: The Yello Video Show *MVD*

Yellow Magic Orchestra: Computer Game *MVD*

Yellow Magic Orchestra: Hurrah *MVD*

Yellow Magic Orchestra: Live '81 *MVD*

Yellow Magic Orchestra: Propaganda *MVD*

Yellow Magic Orchestra: YMO Live in L.A. *MVD*

Yellowman: Live at Woodbury *MVD*

Yellowman: Raw & Rough *MVD, KRV*

Yes *VDO*

Yes: Greatest Video Hits *AVE, MVD, FFF*

Yes: 9012 Live *MVD, AVE, FFF*

Yessongs *MVD, VTK, VID*

The Yngwie Malmsteen Collection *PGV, MVD*

Yngwie Malmsteen: Rising Force - Live '85 *MVD, PGV*

Yngwie Malmsteen: Trial By Fire/Live in Leningrad *MVD, PGV*

Yo-Yo Ma: At Tanglewood *MVD*

A Young Children's Concert with Raffi *MLT, A&M*

The Young Composer *CMR, NYS*

Young Country *MVD, WAR*

Young M.C.: Bustin' Moves *MVD, PGV*

You're the Top: The Cole Porter Story *MVD, FCT*

Youri Vamos: Der Nussknacker - Eine Weihnachtsgeschichte *NO*

Yukihiro Takahashi: Boys Will Be Boys *MVD*

Yuletide TV Treats 2 *SHO*

Yumi Matsutoya: Train of Thought *SVS, COL*

Yves Montand Live *MVD*

Zbigniew Rybezynski: A Collection *NO*

Zenon Laskowik's Benefit: By the Back Door *FCT*

Zev: Six Examples *NO*

Ziggy Marley and the Melody Makers: Conscious Party Live at the Palladium *MVD*

Zildjian Day in New York *MVD,*

Zoot Sims *MVD*

Zoot Sims Quartet *MVD, RHP*

Zydeco *FFM, MVD*

Zydeco Gumbo *RHP*

Zydeco: Night 'n' Day *PGV, MOV, FCT*

ZZ Top Greatest Hits: The Video Collection *WRV, MVD*

DISTRIBUTOR INDEX

DISTRIBUTOR GUIDE

The **DISTRIBUTOR GUIDE** alphabetically lists the full address and phone, toll-free, and fax numbers of 360 distributors. Each video in the main section has at least one and as many as three distributor codes located immediately before the critical rating at the bottom of the review; the key to the codes precedes this guide. Those reviews with the code **OM** are on moratorium (distributed at one time, though not currently). Since a title enjoying such status was once distributed, it may well linger on your local video store shelf. When the distributor is not known, the code **NO** appears in the review. For new releases to the theater that have not yet made it to video (but likely will in the coming year), the code **NYR** (not yet released) appears.

A & E HOME VIDEO (AAE)
c/o New Video Group
250 Park Ave., S.
New York, NY 10010
212-582-9000
800-229-9994
Fax: 212-982-0572

ABC VIDEO (ABC)
Dist. by WEA Corp.
9451 LBJ Fwy., Ste. 107
Dallas, TX 75243
214-234-6200

ACADEMY ENTERTAINMENT (ACA)
1 Pine Haven Shore Rd.
PO Box 788
Shelburne, VT 05482
802-905-2060
Fax: 802-985-3403

ACADEMY VIDEOS (ACD)
Box 5224
Sherman Oaks, CA 91423-5224
818-788-6662
800-423-2397

ACE VIDEO (ACE)
19749 Dearborn St.
Chatsworth, CA 91311
818-718-1116
Fax: 818-718-9109

ACORN VIDEO (ACN)
c/o Academy Entertainment
1 Pine Haven Shore Rd.
PO Box 788
Shelburne, VT 05482
802-985-2060
Fax: 802-985-3403

ACTIVE HOME VIDEO (AHV)
12121 Wilshire Blvd.
Los Angeles, CA 90025
310-447-6131
800-824-6109
Fax: 310-207-0411

ADMIT ONE VIDEO (AOV)
PO Box 66, Sta. O
Toronto, ON, Canada M4A 2M8
416-463-5714

AEF/CAPITAL COMMUNICATIONS (AFC)
3807 Dickerson Rd.
Nashville, TN 37207
615-868-2040
800-822-5678
Fax: 615-868-5239

AFRO-AM DISTRIBUTING COMPANY (AFR)
407 E. 25th St., Ste. 600
Chicago, IL 60616
312-791-1611
Fax: 312-791-0921

AIMS MEDIA (AIM)
9710 DeSoto Ave.
Chatsworth, CA 91311-4409
818-773-4300
800-367-2467
Fax: 818-341-6700

A.I.P. HOME VIDEO, INC. (AIP)
10726 McCune Ave.
Los Angeles, CA 90034
800-456-2471
Fax: 213-559-8849

ALDEN FILMS (ALD)
PO Box 449
Clarksburg, NJ 08510
908-462-3522
Fax: 908-294-0330

ALLIED ARTISTS (ALL)
3415 S. Sepulveda Blvd., Ste. 630
Los Angeles, CA 90034
310-390-6161
Fax: 310-390-6031

ALLIED VIDEO CORP. (AVC)
PO Box 702618
Tulsa, OK 74170
918-496-3332
800-926-5892
Fax: 918-496-0292

AMBROSE VIDEO PUBLISHING, INC. (AMB)
1290 Avenue of the Americas, Ste. 2245
New York, NY 10104

212-265-7272
800-526-4663
Fax: 212-265-8088

AMERICAN FILM FOUNDATION (AFF)
PO Box 2000
Santa Monica, CA 90406
310-394-5689

AMERICAN VIDEO TAPE (AVT)
1116 Edgewater Ave.
Ridgefield, NJ 07657

APPALSHOP FILMS (APL)
306 Madison St.
Whitesburg, KY 41858
606-633-0108
800-545-7467
Fax: 606-633-1009

APPLAUSE PRODUCTIONS, INC. (APD)
85 Longview Rd.
Port Washington, NY 11050
516-883-2825
Fax: 516-883-7460

APPLAUSE THEATRE AND CINEMA (APP)
211 W. 71st St.
New York, NY 10023
212-496-7511
Fax: 212-721-2856

APPLE TREE PRODUCTIONS (ATP)
5200 N. Sawyer
Boise, ID 83714-1491
208-322-6155

ARTEC (ART)
1 Pine Haven Shore Rd.
Shelburne, VT 05482
802-985-9411
800-451-5180
Fax: 802-985-3403

ARTS AMERICA, INC. (AAI)
12 Havermeyer Pl.
Greenwich, CT 06830
203-869-4693
Fax: 203-661-1174

ATLANTIC VIDEO (ATV)
75 Rockefeller Plaza
New York, NY 10019
212-275-2000

ATLANTIC VIDEO (ATV)
150 S. Gordon St.
Alexandria, VA 22304
703-823-2800
Fax: 703-370-6748

ATLAS ENTERTAINMENT CORPORATION (ATL)
1 Jocama Blvd., Ste. 2E
Old Bridge, NJ 08857
908-591-1155
Fax: 908-591-0660

ATLAS VIDEO INC. (ATL)
4915 St. Elmo Ave., Ste. 305
Bethesda, MD 20814
301-907-0030
800-999-0212
Fax: 301-907-9049

ATOMIC PICTURES (ATM)
PO Box 15824
North Hollywood, CA 91615-5824

AUDIO-FORUM (AUD)
96 Broad St.
Guilford, CT 06437
203-453-9794
800-243-1234
Fax: 203-453-9774

AVIATION VIDEO LIBRARY (AVL)
730 Washington St.
Marina del Rey, CA 90292
310-821-3329
800-733-8862

BAKER & TAYLOR VIDEO (BTV)
501 S. Gladiolus
Momence, IL 60954
800-775-2300
Fax: 800-775-3500

BANDERA ENTERPRISES, INC. (BEI)
Box 1107
Studio City, CA 91614
818-985-5050

BARR ENTERTAINMENT (KRT)
12801 Schabarum Ave.
Irwindale, CA 91706
818-338-7878
800-582-2000
Fax: 818-814-2672

BENNETT MARINE VIDEO (BMV)
730 Washington St.
Marina del Rey, CA 90292
213-821-3329
800-262-8862
Fax: 213-306-3162

BENNETT VIDEO GROUP (BVG)
730 Washington St.
Marina del Rey, CA 90292
310-821-3329
800-262-8862
Fax: 310-306-3162

BEST FILM & VIDEO CORPORATION (BFV)
108 New South Rd.
Hicksville, NY 11801-5223
516-931-6969

BEST VIDEO (BST)
10580 Newkirk, Ste. 100
Dallas, TX 75220
214-869-9641
800-541-1008
Fax: 214-556-1686

BFS VIDEO (BFS)
350 Newkirk Rd., N.
Richmond Hill, ON, Canada L4C 367
416-884-2323
Fax: 416-884-8292

BMG (BMG)
6363 Sunset Blvd., 6th Fl.
Hollywood, CA 90028-7318
213-468-4067

BONNIE BUSINESS FORMS (BBF)
2691 Freewood
Dallas, TX 75220
214-357-3956

Bookpeople

BOOKPEOPLE *(BOK)*
7900 Edgewater Dr.
Oakland, CA 94621
510-632-4700

BOSKO VIDEO *(BSV)*
3802 E. Cudahy Ave.
Cudahy, WI 53110-1234

**BRIDGESTONE
PRODUCTION GROUP** *(BPG)*
1979 Palomar Oaks Way
Carlsbad, CA 92009-1307
619-431-9888
800-523-0988
Fax: 619-431-0489

BRITANNICA FILMS *(BRT)*
310 S. Michigan Ave.
Chicago, IL 60604
312-347-7958
Fax: 312-347-7966

BUENA VISTA HOME VIDEO
(BVV)
500 S. Buena Vista St.
Burbank, CA 91521
818-562-3560
Fax: 818-567-6464

BULLFROG FILMS, INC. *(BUL)*
PO Box 149
Oley, PA 19547
215-779-8226
800-543-3764
Fax: 215-370-1978

**CABIN FEVER
ENTERTAINMENT** *(CAF)*
100 W. Putnam Ave.
Greenwich, CT 06830
203-863-5200
Fax: 203-863-5258

CABLE FILMS & VIDEO *(CAB)*
Country Club Sta.
PO Box 7171
Kansas City, MO 64113
816-362-2804
Fax: 816-341-7365

CALIFORNIA NEWSREEL
(CAL)
149 Ninth St., Ste. 420
San Francisco, CA 94103
415-621-6196
Fax: 415-621-6522

**CAMERA THREE
PRODUCTIONS, INC.** *(CMR)*
PO Box 994
Kent, CT 06757
203-927-1964
Fax: 203-927-1965

CANNON VIDEO *(CAN)*
8200 Wilshire Blvd., 3rd Fl.
Beverly Hills, CA 90211
213-966-5600
Fax: 213-653-5485

CAPITOL HOME VIDEO *(CTL)*
4818 Yuma St. NW
Washington, DC 20016
202-363-8800
Fax: 202-363-4680

**CAPITOL VIDEO
COMMUNICATIONS, INC.**
(CAP)
2121 Wisconsin Ave. NW
Washington, DC 20007
202-965-7800

CAROUSEL FILM & VIDEO
(CFV)
260 5th Ave., Rm. 405

New York, NY 10001
212-683-1660
Fax: 212-683-1662

CBS/FOX VIDEO *(FOX)*
1330 Avenue of the Americas,
5th Fl.
New York, NY 10019
212-373-4800
800-800-2369
Fax: 212-373-4802

**CELEBRITY HOME
ENTERTAINMENT** *(CEL)*
22025 Ventura Blvd.
PO Box 4112
Woodland Hills, CA 91365-
4112
818-595-0666
Fax: 818-716-0168

**CENTER FOR HUMANITIES,
INC.** *(CHI)*
Communications Park
Box 1000
Mount Kisco, NY 10549
914-666-4100
800-431-1242
Fax: 914-666-5319

**CENTRAL PARK MEDIA/U.S.
MANGA CORPS** *(CPM)*
250 W. 57th St., Ste. 317
New York, NY 10107
212-977-7456
Fax: 212-977-8709

CENTRE COMMUNICATIONS
(CEN)
1800 30th St., Ste. 207
Boulder, CO 80301
303-444-1166
800-886-1166
Fax: 303-444-1168

**CENTURY HOME VIDEO,
INC.** *(CTY)*
PO Box 34727
Los Angeles, CA 90034-0727
Fax: 213-848-2343

CENTURY PRODUCTIONS
(CTP)
PO Box 1156
Sandy, UT 84091-1156
801-571-5161
Fax: 801-571-5161

CHURCHILL MEDIA *(CHF)*
12210 Nebraska Ave.
Los Angeles, CA 90025
310-207-6600
Fax: 310-207-1330

CINEGLOBE VIDEO INC.
(CGV)
93 Skyway Ave., Ste. 203
Etobicoke, ON, Canada M9W
6C7
416-609-1891
Fax: 416-609-1894

**CINEMA GROUP HOME
VIDEO** *(CGH)*
2320 Cotner
Los Angeles, CA 90064

CINEMA GUILD *(CIG)*
1697 Broadway, Ste. 802
New York, NY 10019
212-246-5522
Fax: 212-246-5525

**CINEMA INTERNATIONAL
CANADA** *(CIC)*
8275 Mayrand

Montreal, PQ, Canada H4P
2C8
514-342-2340
Fax: 514-342-1922

CINEMACABRE VIDEO *(CNM)*
PO Box 10005-D
Baltimore, MD 21285-0005

CINEPLEX, INC. *(CPL)*
8275 Mayrand
Montreal, PQ, Canada H4P
2C8
514-342-2340

CINEVISTA *(CCN)*
560 W. 43rd, No. 8J
New York, NY 10036
212-947-4373
Fax: 212-947-0644

COAST TO COAST VIDEO
(CTC)
148 Lafayette St., 5th Fl.
New York, NY 10013
212-431-3890
800-221-3420

COLISEUM VIDEO *(CSM)*
430 W. 54th St.
New York, NY 10019
212-489-8130
800-288-8130
Fax: 212-582-5690

**COLUMBIA TRISTAR HOME
VIDEO** *(COL)*
3400 Riverside Dr.
Burbank, CA 91505-4627
818-972-8193
Fax: 818-972-0937

CONCORD VIDEO *(CCV)*
7506 N. Broadway Ext., Ste.
505
Oklahoma City, OK 73116
405-840-6031
800-222-2811
Fax: 405-848-3960

CONDOR VIDEO *(CVS)*
c/o Jason Films
2825 Wilcrest, Ste. 670
Houston, TX 77042
713-266-3097

**CONNOISSEUR VIDEO
COLLECTION** *(CVC)*
1543 7th St., Ste. 202
Santa Monica, CA 90401-
2636
310-393-9000

**CONSUMER VIDEO
DISTRIBUTERS** *(CVD)*
1427 Woodhurst St.
Bowling Green, KY 42104
502-843-8300

CONTINENTAL VIDEO *(CON)*
2320 Cotner
Los Angeles, CA 90064
800-821-3427

CORINTH VIDEO *(CTH)*
34 Gansevoort St.
New York, NY 10014
212-463-0305
800-221-4720

**CORONET/MTI FILM &
VIDEO** *(MTI)*
108 Wilmot Rd.
Deerfield, IL 60015
708-940-1260
800-777-8100
Fax: 708-940-3640

COVENANT VIDEO *(COV)*
3200 W. Foster Ave.
Chicago, IL 60625
312-478-4676
800-621-1290
Fax: 312-478-2622

COYOTE HOME VIDEO *(CHV)*
c/o Hemdale Home Video
7966 Beverly Blvd.
Los Angeles, CA 90048
213-966-3158
Fax: 213-651-3107

CRITERION COLLECTION
(CRC)
1351 Pacific Coast Hwy.
Santa Monica, CA 90401
800-446-2001

**CRITICS' CHOICE VIDEO,
INC.** *(CCB)*
PO Box 549
Elk Grove Village, IL 60009
800-367-7765
Fax: 800-544-9852

CROWN VIDEO *(CRV)*
225 Park Ave., S.
New York, NY 10003
212-254-1600

CRYSTAL PRODUCTIONS
(CRY)
1812 Johns Dr.
Box 2159
Glenview, IL 60025
708-657-8144
800-255-8629
Fax: 708-657-8149

DIRECT CINEMA LIMITED
(DCL)
PO Box 10003
Santa Monica, CA 90410
310-396-4774
800-525-0000
Fax: 310-396-3233

**DISCOUNT VIDEO TAPES,
INC.** *(DVT)*
PO Box 7122
Burbank, CA 91510
818-843-3366
Fax: 818-843-3821

**DISNEY EDUCATIONAL
PRODUCTIONS** *(DSN)*
500 S. Buena Vista St.
Burbank, CA 91521
800-621-2131

**DONNA MICHELLE
PRODUCTIONS** *(DMP)*
6253 Hollywood Blvd., Ste.
818
Hollywood, CA 90028
213-469-0672
800-356-4386

**DUSTY WOODS
ENTERTAINMENT** *(DWE)*
6003 Castor Ave.
Philadelphia, PA 19149

EASYRIDERS *(EAS)*
28210 Dorothy Dr.
Agoura Hills, CA 91301
818-889-8740
Fax: 818-889-4726

ECUFILM *(ECU)*
810 Twelfth Ave., S.
Nashville, TN 37203
615-242-6277
800-251-4091

EDDE ENTERTAINMENT
(EDV)
19749 Dearborn St.
Chatsworth, CA 91311
800-727-2229

ELECTRIC PRODUCTIONS
(ELE)
8700 Reseda Blvd.
Ste. 214
Northridge, CA 91325
818-993-1787

ELECTRIC VIDEO *(ELV)*
PO Box 784
Tiffin, OH 44883
419-447-0110

**ELECTRONIC ARTS
INTERMIX** *(EAI)*
536 Broadway, 9th Fl.
New York, NY 10012
212-966-4605

ELECTRONIC BOOKSHELF
(CAR)
5276 S. Clinton County 700
W.
Frankfort, IN 46041-8113
317-324-2182
Fax: 317-324-2183

**EMBASSY HOME
ENTERTAINMENT** *(EMB)*
335 N. Maple Dr., Ste. 350
Beverly Hills, CA 90210
310-285-6000

EMI VIDEO *(EMI)*
1290 Ave. of the Americas,
42nd Fl.
New York, NY 10104
212-492-1200

ERGO MEDIA INC. *(ERG)*
668 Front St.
PO Box 2037
Teaneck, NJ 07666
201-692-0404
800-695-3746
Fax: 201 692-0663

**EUROPEAN VIDEO
DISTRIBUTOR** *(EVD)*
2321 W. Olive Ave., Ste. A
Burbank, CA 91506
818-848-5902
800-423-6752
Fax: 818-848-1965

**EXPANDED
ENTERTAINMENT** *(EXP)*
2222 S. Barrington Ave.
Los Angeles, CA 90064
310-473-6701
Fax: 310-444-9850

FACETS MULTIMEDIA, INC.
(FCT)
1517 W. Fullerton Ave.
Chicago, IL 60614
312-281-9075

**FAMILY HOME
ENTERTAINMENT** *(FHE)*
c/o Live Home Video
15400 Sherman Way
PO Box 10124
Van Nuys, CA 91410-0124
818-499-5827

FAST FORWARD *(FFF)*
3420 Ocean Park Blvd., Ste.
3075
Santa Monica, CA 90405

310-396-4434
Fax: 310-396-2292

FERDE GROFE FILMS *(FGF)*
PO Box 399
Union Washington
Union, WA 98592
206-898-8080
Fax: 206-898-8081

FESTIVAL FILMS *(FST)*
2841 Irving Ave., S.
Minneapolis, MN 55408
612-870-4744
Fax: 612-874-8520

FILMAKERS LIBRARY, INC.
(FLL)
124 E. 40th
New York, NY 10016
212-808-4980

**FILMS FOR THE
HUMANITIES & SCIENCES**
(FHS)
PO Box 2053
Princeton, NJ 08543
609-452-1128
800-257-5126
Fax: 609-275-3767

FILMS INC. VIDEO *(FLI)*
5547 N. Ravenswood Ave.
Chicago, IL 60640-1199
312-878-2600
800-323-4222

**FINLEY-HOLIDAY FILM
CORPORATION** *(FHF)*
PO Box 619
Whittier, CA 90601
310-945-3325
800-345-6707
Fax: 310-693-4756

FIRST RUN/ICARUS FILMS
(ICA)
153 Waverly Pl.
New York, NY 10014
212-727-1711
800-876-1710
Fax: 212-989-7649

FIRST RUN VIDEO *(FRV)*
3620 Overland Ave.
Los Angeles, CA 90034
310-202-8990
Fax: 310-838-5212

FLOWER FILMS *(FFM)*
10341 San Pablo Ave.
El Cerrito, CA 94530
510-525-0942
800-572-7618
Fax: 510-525-1204

FOCUS ON ANIMALS *(FOC)*
PO Box 150
Trumbull, CT 06611
203-377-1116

FORMAT INTERNATIONAL
(FMT)
3921 N. Meridian St.
Indianapolis, IN 46208-4011
317-924-5163

FOX/LORBER HOME VIDEO
(FXL)
419 Park Ave., S., 20th Fl.
New York, NY 10019
212-532-3392
800-229-9994
Fax: 212-685-2625

FOXVIDEO *(FXV)*
2121 Avenue of the Stars,
25th Fl.
Los Angeles, CA 90067
310-203-3900
800-800-2FOX
Fax: 310-774-5811

FRIES HOME VIDEO *(FRH)*
6922 Hollywood Blvd., 12th
Fl.
Hollywood, CA 90028
213-466-2266
Fax: 213-466-2126

FRIGHT VIDEO *(FRG)*
PO Box 179
Billerica, MA 01821
508-663-2510

FUSION VIDEO *(FUS)*
100 Fusion Way
Country Club Hills, IL 60478
708-799-2073
800-338-7710
Fax: 708-799-8375

**GATEWAY FILMS/VISION
VIDEO** *(GFV)*
2030 Wentz Church Rd.
Box 540
Worcester, PA 19490-0540
215-584-1893
800-523-0226
Fax: 215-584-4610

GENESIS HOME VIDEO *(GHV)*
15820 Arminta St.
Van Nuys, CA 91406
818-787-0660
800-344-1060

**GERMAN LANGUAGE VIDEO
CENTER** *(GLV)*
7625 Pendleton Pike
Indianapolis, IN 46226-5298
317-547-1257
800-252-1957
Fax: 317-547-1263

GLENN VIDEO VISTAS, LTD.
(GVV)
6924 Canby Ave., Ste. 103
Reseda, CA 91335
818-881-8110
Fax: 818-981-5506

**GOODTIMES/KIDS
KLASSICS DISTRIBUTION
CORPORATION**(GKK)
401 5th Ave.
New York, NY 10016
212-889-0044
Fax: 212-213-9319

GORGON VIDEO *(GRG)*
6525 Sunset Blvd., Ste. 706
Hollywood, CA 90028
213-505-1981
800-367-3845
Fax: 213-464-8920

GRAPEVINE VIDEO *(GPV)*
PO Box 46161
Phoenix, AZ 85063
602-245-0210

HBO HOME VIDEO *(HBO)*
1114 6th Ave.
New York, NY 10036
212-512-7400

HEMDALE HOME VIDEO *(HMD)*
7966 Beverly Blvd.
Los Angeles, CA 90048

213-966-3758
Fax: 213-651-3107

HEN'S TOOTH VIDEO *(HTV)*
1124 S. Solano Dr.
Las Cruces, NM 88001
505-525-8233

HENWOOD CINEMA VIDEO
(HCV)
PO Box 376
Jamison, PA 18929-0376
215-552-8584

**HIGH/SCOPE EDUCATIONAL
RESEARCH FOUNDATION**
(HSE)
600 N. River St.
Ypsilanti, MI 48198-2898
313-485-2000
Fax: 313-485-0704

**HOLLYWOOD HOME
ENTERTAINMENT** *(HHE)*
1747 Van Buren St., Ste. 700
Hollywood, FL 33020
305-925-2709
800-333-2709
Fax: 305-925-5655

**HOLLYWOOD HOME
THEATRE** *(HHT)*
1540 N. Highland Ave., Ste.
110
Hollywood, CA 90028
213-466-0127

**HOLLYWOOD PICTURES
HOME VIDEO** *(HPH)*
Fairmont Bldg. 526
500 S. Buena Vista St.
Burbank, CA 91505-9842

HOME VISION CINEMA *(IIMV)*
5547 N. Ravenswood Ave.
Chicago, IL 60640-1199
312-878-2600
800-826-3456
Fax: 312-878-8648

HORIZON ENTERTAINMENT
(HEG)
45030 Trevor Ave.
Lancaster, CA 93534
805-940-1040
800-323-2061
Fax: 805-940-8511

IGNATIUS PRESS *(IGP)*
15 Oakland Ave.
Harrison, NY 10528-9974
914-835-4216
Fax: 914-835-8406

IMAGE ENTERTAINMENT
(IME)
9333 Oso Ave.
Chatsworth, CA 91311
818-407-9100

**IMAGE MAGNETIC
ASSOCIATES** *(ISS)*
1525 Saltair, No. 107
West Los Angeles, CA 90025

**IMPERIAL ENTERTAINMENT
CORPORATION** *(IMP)*
4640 Lankershim Blvd., 4th Fl.
North Hollywood, CA 91602
818-762-0005

**INCREASE/SILVERMINE
VIDEO** *(INC)*
6860 Canby Ave., Ste. 118
Reseda, CA 91335

818-342-2880
800-233-2880
Fax: 818-342-4029

INGRAM ENTERTAINMENT
(ING)
1123 Heil Quaker Blvd.
La Vergne, TN 37086
615-793-5000
800-759-5000
Fax: 615-793-3875

**INGRAM INTERNATIONAL
FILMS** *(TAM)*
10990 E. 55th Ave.
Denver, CO 80239
303-373-4583
800-356-3577

INTERAMA, INC. *(INT)*
301 W. 53rd St., Ste. 19E
New York, NY 10019
212-977-4830

**INTERNATIONAL FILM
BUREAU, INC.** *(IFB)*
332 S. Michigan Ave.
Chicago, IL 60604-4382
312-427-4545

**INTERNATIONAL HISTORIC
FILMS, INC. (IHF)** *(IHF)*
PO Box 29035
Chicago, IL 60629
312-927-2900
Fax: 312-927-9211

**INTERNATIONAL VIDEO
ENTERTAINMENT (IVE)** *(IVE)*
15400 Sherman Way, Ste.
500
Van Nuys, CA 91406
818-908-0303
800-423-7455
Fax: 818-778-3259

INTERURBAN FILMS *(IUF)*
PO Box 6444
Glendale, CA 91225-0444
818-240-9130

IVY FILM/VIDEO *(IVY)*
725 Providence Rd.
Charlotte, NC 28207
704-333-3991
Fax: 704-335-0672

J2 COMMUNICATIONS *(JTC)*
10850 Wilshire Blvd., Ste.
1000
Los Angeles, CA 90024
310-474-5252
800-521-8273
Fax: 310-474-1219

**JAMES AGEE FILM
PROJECT** *(JAF)*
316 1/2 E. Main St.
Johnson City, TN 37601
615-926-8637
800-352-5111

JEF FILMS, INC. *(JEF)*
Film House
143 Hickory Hill Circle
Osterville, MA 02655-1322
508-428-7198

JIM HENSON VIDEO *(JHV)*
500 S. Buena Vista St.
Burbank, CA 91521
818-562-3883
Fax: 818-567-6466

JOURNAL FILMS, INC. *(JOU)*
5160 Sherman Ave., Ste. 100
Evanston, IL 60201

708-328-6700
800-323-5448
Fax: 708-328-6706

**JUDAICA CAPTIONED FILM
CENTER, INC.** *(JCF)*
PO Box 21439
Baltimore, MD 21208-0439
410-655-6767

**JUST FOR KIDS HOME
VIDEO** *(JFK)*
6320 Canoga Ave.,
Penthouse Ste.
PO Box 4112
Woodland Hills, CA 91365-
4112
818-715-1980
800-445-8210
Fax: 818-716-0168

K-BEECH VIDEO, INC. *(KBE)*
8847 Wilbur
Northridge, CA 91324
818-772-4201
800-255-5923
Fax: 818-772-4245

KAROL VIDEO *(KAR)*
PO Box 7600
Wilkes Barre, PA 18773
717-822-8899

KEEP THE FAITH INC. *(KEP)*
PO Box 1069
141 Main
Clifton, NJ 07014-1065
201-471-7494
800-221-1564
Fax: 201-471-7584

**KET, THE KENTUCKY
NETWORK ENTERPRISE
DIVISION** *(KET)*
560 Cooper Dr.
Lexington, KY 40502-2279
606-258-7000

KINO ON VIDEO *(KIV)*
333 W. 39th St., Ste. 503
New York, NY 10018
212-629-0871
800-562-3330
Fax: 212-714-0871

KIT PARKER VIDEO *(KIT)*
c/o Central Park Media
301 W. 53rd St., 13th Fl.
New York, NY 10019
212-977-7456
800-833-7456
Fax: 212-977-8709

**KNOWLEDGE UNLIMITED,
INC.** *(KUI)*
Box 52
Madison, WI 53701-0052
608-836-6660
800-356-2303
Fax: 608-831-1570

KULTUR VIDEO *(KUL)*
121 Hwy. No. 36
West Long Branch, NJ 07764
908-229-2343
800-458-5887
Fax: 908-229-0066

LB DISTRIBUTORS, INC.
(LBD)
3186 Doolittle Dr.
Northbrook, IL 60062
800-950-0255
Fax: 800-564-8656

LD VIDEO (LDV)
6911 Topanga Canyon Blvd.,
Ste. 209
Canoga Park, CA 91303
800-238-2302
Fax: 818-999-2731

**LEARNING CORPORATION
OF AMERICA** (LCA)
c/o Coronet/MTI
108 Wilmot Rd.
Deerfield, IL 60015
708-940-1260
800-621-2131
Fax: 708-940-3600

**LIBERTY PUBLISHING
COMPANY, INC.** (LPC)
440 S. Federal Hwy., Ste. 202
Deerfield Beach, FL 33441

LIGHT RAIN PRODUCTIONS
(LRP)
1927 NW Kearney
Portland, OR 97209
503-224-4080
Fax: 503-224-4180

LIGHTNING VIDEO (LTG)
60 Long Ridge Rd.
PO Box 4000
Stamford, CT 06907

**LIGHTYEAR
ENTERTAINMENT** (LTY)
350 5th Ave., Ste. 5101
New York, NY 10118
212-563-4610
800-229-7867
Fax: 212-563-1932

LIVE HOME VIDEO (LIV)
15400 Sherman Way
PO Box 10124
Van Nuys, CA 91410-0124
818-988-5060

LOONIC VIDEO (LOO)
2022 Taraval St., Ste. 6427
San Francisco, CA 94116
510-526-5681

LORIMAR HOME VIDEO (LHV)
15838 N. 62nd St., Ste. 100
Scottsdale, AZ 85254
800-345-1441

LSVIDEO, INC. (LSV)
PO Box 415
Carmel, IN 46032

LUCERNE MEDIA (LME)
37 Ground Pine Rd.
Morris Plains, NJ 07950
201-538-1401
800-341-2293
Fax: 201-538-0855

LUMIVISION CORPORATION
(LUM)
1490 Lafayette St., Ste. 407
Denver, CO 80218
303-860-0400
800-776-5864
Fax: 303-860-0425

MADERA CINEVIDEO (MAD)
525 E. Yosemite Ave.
Madera, CA 93638
209-661-6000
800-624-2204

MAGIC HOUR FILMS (MHF)
55 Bell St., Ste. 202
Seattle, WA 98121
206-443-9818

MAGNA SYSTEMS, INC.
(MGS)
W. Countyline 95
Barrington, IL 60010
708-382-6477
Fax: 708-250-0038

**MANAGEMENT COMPANY
ENTERTAINMENT GROUP
(MCEG), INC.** (MCG)
2121 Avenue of the Stars,
Ste. 2630
Los Angeles, CA 90067
310-282-0871
Fax: 310-315-7850

**MARK IV PICTURES FILM &
VIDEO** (MIV)
5907 Meredith Dr.
Des Moines, IA 50322
515-278-4737
800-247-3456
Fax: 515-278-4738

**MARYLAND PUBLIC
TELEVISION** (MTP)
11767 Owings Mills Blvd.
Owings Mills, MD 21117-1499
410-356-5600
800-873-6154
Fax: 410-581-4338

MASTERVISION, INC. (MAS)
969 Park Ave.
New York, NY 10028
212-879-0448
Fax: 212-744-3560

**MCA/UNIVERSAL HOME
VIDEO** (MCA)
70 Universal City Plaza
Universal City, CA 91608-
9955
818-777-6419
Fax: 818-733-0226

MGM/UA HOME VIDEO, INC.
(MGM)
10000 W. Washington Blvd.
Culver City, CA 90232
310-280-6212

MIKE LEBELL'S VIDEO (MLB)
75 Freemont Pl.
Los Angeles, CA 90005
213-938-3333
Fax: 213-938-3334

MILESTONE FILM & VIDEO
(MIL)
275 W. 96th St., Ste 28C
New York, NY 10025
212-865-7449
Fax: 212-222-8952

**MNTEX ENTERTAINMENT,
INC.** (MTX)
PO Box 667
Prior Lake, MN 55372-0667
612-440-6028
Fax: 612-447-8173

**MODERN SOUND PICTURES,
INC.** (MSP)
1402 Howard St.
Omaha, NE 68102
402-341-8476
800-228-9584
Fax: 402-341-8487

MONARCH HOME VIDEO
(MNC)
1123 Heil Quaker Blvd.
La Vergne, TN 37086-7006

615-793-5000
800-759-5000
Fax: 615-793-3875

**MONDAY/WEDNESDAY/
FRIDAY VIDEO** (MWF)
c/o Moore
73 E. Houston St.
New York, NY 10012
212-219-0765
Fax: 212-966-6680

MONTEREY HOME VIDEO
(MON)
28038 Dorothy Dr., Ste. 1
Agoura Hills, CA 91301
818-597-0047
800-424-2593
Fax: 818-597-0105

MOORE VIDEO (MRV)
PO Box 5703
Richmond, VA 23220
804-745-9785
Fax: 804-745-9785

MORRIS VIDEO (MOR)
2730 Monterey St., No. 105
Monterey Business Park
Torrance, CA 90503
310-533-4800
800-843-3606

MOVIECRAFT, INC. (MVC)
PO Box 438
Orland Park, IL 60462
708-460-9082
Fax: 708-460-9099

MOVIES UNLIMITED (MOV)
6736 Castor Ave.
Philadelphia, PA 19149
215-722-8298
800-523-0823

MPI HOME VIDEO (MPI)
15825 Rob Roy Dr.
Oak Forest, IL 60452
708-687-7881
Fax: 708-687-3797

MTI HOME VIDEO (MTH)
14216 SW 136th St.
Miami, FL 33186
305-255-8684
800-821-7461
Fax: 305-233-6943

MTI TELEPROGRAMS, INC.
(MTT)
108 Wilmot Rd.
Deerfield, IL 60015-9990
708-940-1260
800-621-2131

MUSIC FOR LITTLE PEOPLE
(MLT)
Box 1460
Redway, CA 95560
707-923-3991
800-346-4445
Fax: 707-923-3241

**MUSIC VIDEO
DISTRIBUTORS** (MVD)
O'Neill Industrial Center
1210 Standbridge St.
Norristown, PA 19403
215-272-7771
800-888-0486
Fax: 215-272-6074

MYSTIC FIRE VIDEO (MFV)
PO Box 1092
Cooper Sta.
New York, NY 10276
212-941-0999
Fax: 212-941-1443

**NATIONAL CENTER FOR
JEWISH FILM** (NCJ)
Brandeis University
Lown Bldg. 102
Waltham, MA 02254-9110
617-899-7044
Fax: 617-736-2070

**NATIONAL
ENTERTAINMENT GROUP,
INC.** (NEG)
90 Lake View Dr.
Lake Naomi
Pocono Pines, PA 18350
717-643-4212
800-847-8273
Fax: 717-646-3039

**NATIONAL FILM BOARD OF
CANADA** (NFC)
1251 Avenue of the Americas,
16th Fl.
New York, NY 10020-1173
212-586-5131

**NEW HORIZONS HOME
VIDEO** (NHO)
2951 Flowers Rd., S., Ste.
237
Atlanta, GA 30341
404-458-3488
800-854-3323
Fax: 404-458-2679

NEW JERSEY NETWORK
(NJN)
1573 Parkside Ave.
Trenton, NJ 08625
609-530-5252

NEW LINE HOME VIDEO
(NLC)
116 N. Robertson Blvd.
Los Angeles, CA 90048
310-967-6670
Fax: 310-854-0602

**NEW WORLD
ENTERTAINMENT** (NWV)
1440 S. Sepulveda Blvd.
Los Angeles, CA 90025
310-444-8100

**NEW YORK STATE
EDUCATION DEPARTMENT**
(NYS)
Bureau of Technology
Applications
Rm. C-7 - CEC
Empire State Plaza
Albany, NY 12230
518-474-3168

NEW YORKER VIDEO (NYF)
16 W. 61st St., 11th Fl.
New York, NY 10023
212-247-6110
800-447-0196
Fax: 212-307-7855

NEWSBANK, INC. (NBI)
58 Pine St.
New Canaan, CT 06840
203-966-1100
800-243-7694

NOSTALGIA FAMILY VIDEO
(NOS)
PO Box 606
Baker City, OR 97814
503-523-9034

OCEAN VIDEO (OCE)
2550 Corporate Pl., Ste. C-
103

Monterey Park, CA 91754
213-881-0732

**OHLMEYER
COMMUNICATIONS** (OHC)
962 N. La Cienega Blvd.
Los Angeles, CA 90069
310-659-8557
Fax: 310-659-8923

ORION HOME VIDEO (ORI)
1888 Century Park E.
Los Angeles, CA 90067
310-282-0550

PACIFIC ARTS VIDEO (PAV)
11858 La Grange
Los Angeles, CA 90025
310-820-0991
800-538-5856
Fax: 310-826-4779

PACIFIC COAST VIDEO (PCV)
635 1/2 Chapala St.
Santa Barbara, CA 93101
805-965-5015

**PALISADES
ENTERTAINMENT** (PEV)
1875 Century Park, E., 3rd Fl.
Los Angeles, CA 90067

**PARAGON VIDEO
PRODUCTIONS** (PGN)
PO Box 3478
San Mateo, CA 94403
415-362-2520

PARAMOUNT HOME VIDEO
(PAR)
5555 Melrose Ave.
Los Angeles, CA 90038-3197
213-956-5000

PAULIST PRODUCTIONS
(PAU)
PO Box 1057
Pacific Palisades, CA 90272
310-454-0688
800-624-8613
Fax: 310-459-6549

PBS VIDEO (PBS)
1320 Braddock Pl.
Alexandria, VA 22314-1698
703-739-5380
800-344-3337
Fax: 703-739-5269

PEERLESS FILMS, INC. (PII)
1810 Johns Dr.
Glenview, IL 60025
708-729-8160

PENTREX VIDEO (PEN)
PO Box 94911
Pasadena, CA 91109
818-793-3400
800-950-9333
Fax: 818-793-3797

PETER PAN INDUSTRIES
(PPI)
88 Saint Frances St.
Newark, NJ 07105
201-344-4214
Fax: 201-344-0465

PHOENIX/BFA FILMS (BFA)
468 Park Ave., S.
New York, NY 10016
212-684-5910
800-221-1274

PHOENIX DISTRIBUTERS
(PHX)
6253 Hollywood Blvd., No.
818

Hollywood, CA 90028
800-356-4386
Fax: 213-469-7041

PICTURE START (PIC)
1727 W. Catalpa
Chicago, IL 60640
312-769-2489
800-528-TAPE
Fax: 312-769-4467

PIONEER ARTISTS, INC. (PIA)
200 W. Grand Ave.
Montvale, NJ 07645

**PM ENTERTAINMENT
GROUP, INC.** (PMH)
9450 Chivers Ave.
Sun Valley, CA 91352
818-504-6332
800-934-2111
Fax: 818-504-6380

POLYGRAM VIDEO (PV)
(PGV)
825 8th Ave.
New York, NY 10019
212-333-8000
800-825-7781
Fax: 212-603-7960

POWER SPORTS VIDEO
(PSV)
8444 Reseda Bvld., No. M
Northridge, CA 91324-4626
818-407-0590

PREMIERE HOME VIDEO
(PMR)
755 N. Highland
Hollywood, CA 90038
213-934-8903
Fax: 213-934-8910

PRIME VIDEO (PRV)
19749 Dearborn St.
Chatsworth, CA 91311-6510
818-718-1116

**PRINCETON BOOK
COMPANY PUBLISHERS**
(PBC)
PO Box 57
Pennington, NJ 08534
609-737-8177
800-326-7149
Fax: 609-737-1869

PRISM ENTERTAINMENT
(PSM)
1888 Century Park, E., Ste.
1000
Los Angeles, CA 90067
310-277-3270
Fax: 310-203-8036

**PROFESSIONAL MEDIA
SERVICE CORP.** (PMS)
19122 S. Vermont Ave.
Gardena, CA 90248
310-532-9024
800-223-7672
Fax: 800-253-8853

PROUD TO BE**A BLACK
VIDEO COLLECTION** (PTB)
1235-E East Blvd., Ste. 209
Charlotte, NC 28203
704-523-2227

PUBLIC MEDIA VIDEO (PME)
5547 N. Ravenswood Ave.
Chicago, IL 60640-1199
312-878-2600
800-826-3456
Fax: 312-878-8406

PYRAMID FILM & VIDEO
(PYR)
Box 1048
2801 Colorado Ave.
Santa Monica, CA 90406
310-828-7577
800-421-2304
Fax: 310-453-9083

QUALITY VIDEO (QVD)
7399 Bush Lake Rd.
Minneapolis, MN 55439-2027
612-893-0903
Fax: 612-893-1585

QUESTAR HOME VIDEO
(QHV)
PO Box 11345
Chicago, IL 60611
312-266-9400
800-544-8422
Fax: 312-266-9523

QUINTEX ENTERTAINMENT
(QNE)
345 N. Maple Dr., Ste. 358
Beverly Hills, CA 90210
310-281-2600
Fax: 310-273-9453

RAEDON ENTERTAINMENT
(RAE)
8707-D Lindley Ave., Ste. 173
Northridge, CA 91325
818-582-2550
Fax: 818-773-9770

RANDOM HOUSE MEDIA
(RHU)
400 Hahn Rd.
Westminster, MD 21157
410-848-1900
800-492-0782
Fax: 410-857-1948

RAP ENTERTAINMENT INC.
(RAP)
932-17 Ave. SW, Ste. 310
Calgary, AB, Canada T2T 0A2
403-244-7000
800-565-7777
Fax: 403-245-0511

RCA VIDEO (RCA)
c/o Columbia TriStar Home
Video
3400 Riverside Dr.
Burbank, CA 91505
818-972-8686

**READER'S DIGEST HOME
VIDEO** (RDG)
Reader's Digest Rd.
Pleasantville, NY 10570
800-776-6868

REGENCY HOME VIDEO
(RHV)
9911 W. Pico Blvd.
Los Angeles, CA 90035
310-552-2431
Fax: 310-552-9039

**REPUBLIC PICTURES HOME
VIDEO** (REP)
12636 Beatrice St.
Los Angeles, CA 90066-0930
310-306-4040

REX MILLER (RXM)
Rte. 1, Box 457-D
East Prairie, MO 63845
314-649-5048

RHAPSODY FILMS (RHP)
PO Box 179

New York, NY 10014
212-243-0152
Fax: 212-645-9250

RHINO HOME VIDEO (RHI)
2225 Colorado Ave.
Santa Monica, CA 90404
310-828-1980
800-843-3670
Fax: 310-453-5529

RKO PICTURES (RKO)
1801 Avenue of the Stars,
Ste. 448
Los Angeles, CA 90067
310-277-0707

RM FILMS, INC. (RMF)
Box 3748
Los Angeles, CA 90078
213-466-7791
Fax: 213-461-4152

**SAN FRANCISCO RUSH
VIDEO** (SFR)
1576 Fell St., Ste. 1
San Francisco, CA 94117
415-921-8273
Fax: 415-921-8273

**SATURN PRODUCTIONS,
INC.** (SAT)
575 Madison Ave., Ste. 1006
New York, NY 10022
212-472-4700
800-228-1717
Fax: 212-472-6249

SCHOOLMASTERS VIDEO
(SCH)
745 State Circle
PO Box 1941
Ann Arbor, MI 48106
313-761-5175
800-521-2832
Fax: 313-761-8711

SGE HOME VIDEO (SGE)
Div. of Shapiro Glickenhaus
Entertainment
12001 Ventura Pl., 4th Fl.
Studio City, CA 91604
818-766-8500

SHOKUS VIDEO (SHO)
PO Box 3125
Chatsworth, CA 91313
818-704-0400
800-325-6800
Fax: 818-701-0560

SIGNALS (SIG)
PO Box 64428
St. Paul, MN 55164-0428
800-669-5225
Fax: 612-659-4320

SIMITAR ENTERTAINMENT
(SIM)
3850 Annapolis Ln.
Plymouth, MN 55447
612-559-6660
Fax: 612-559-0210

**SIMON WIESENTHAL
CENTER** (SWC)
9760 W. Pico Blvd.
Los Angeles, CA 90035-4792
310-553-9036
Fax: 310-553-8007

SINISTER CINEMA (SNC)
PO Box 4369
Medford, OR 97501-0168
503-773-6860

**SNOOPY'S HOME VIDEO
LIBRARY** (SHV)
c/o Media Home
Entertainment
510 W. 6th St., Ste. 1032
Los Angeles, CA 90014-1311
213-236-1336

SOMETHING WEIRD VIDEO
(SMW)
c/o Mike Vraney
PO Box 33664
Seattle, WA 98133
206-361-3759
Fax: 206-364-7526

**SONY MUSIC VIDEO
ENTERPRISES** (SMV)
550 Madison Ave.
New York, NY 10022
212-833-7095
Fax: 212-833-8620

**SONY VIDEO SOFTWARE
(SVS, INC.)** (SVS)
1700 Broadway
New York, NY 10019
518-757-4990
800-832-2422
Fax: 518-953-3792

SPARROW DISTRIBUTION
(SPW)
101 Winners Circle
Brentwood, TN 37027
800-877-4443
Fax: 615-371-6909

STAGESTEP (STS)
PO Box 328
Philadelphia, PA 19105
215-829-9800
800-523-0961
Fax: 215-829-0508

**STARMAKER
ENTERTAINMENT, INC.** (STE)
151 Industrial Way, E.
Eatontown, NJ 07724
908-389-1020
800-233-3730
Fax: 908-389-1021

**STRAND/VCI
ENTERTAINMENT** (SVI)
3350 Ocean Park Blvd., Ste.
205
Santa Monica, CA 90405
310-396-7011
Fax: 310-392-2472

STREAMLINE PICTURES
(STP)
971 N. La Cienega, Ste. 209
Los Angeles, CA 90069
310-657-8559
Fax: 310-657-8642

**STUDIO VIDEO
PRODUCTIONS** (STV)
793 Foothills Blvd.
San Luis Obispo, CA 93405
805-543-0707
800-541-1843
Fax: 805-549-0352

SULTAN ENTERTAINMENT
(SUE)
335 N. Maple Dr., Ste. 351
Beverly Hills, CA 90210-3899
310-285-6000

SUMMIT MEDIA COMPANY
(SUM)
25510 Avenue Stanford

Valencia, CA 91355
805-295-0675
Fax: 805-295-0680

SUN VIDEO (SUN)
15 Donnybrook
Demarest, NJ 07627
201-784-0662
Fax: 201-784-0665

SUPER SITTERS, INC. (SSI)
10503 N. Cedarburg Rd.
PO Box 218
Mequon, WI 53092
800-323-3431

SUPER SOURCE (SUP)
PO Box 410777
San Francisco, CA 94141
415-777-1964
800-331-6304
Fax: 415-777-0187

**TAPEWORM VIDEO
DISTRIBUTORS** (TPV)
12420 Montague St., Ste. B
Arleta, CA 91331
818-896-8899
800-367-8437
Fax: 818-896-3855

**THOMSON PRODUCTIONS,
INC.** (TPI)
PO Box 1225
Orem, UT 84059
801-226-0155
800-228-8491

3M AUDIO VISUAL DIVISION
(THA)
Bldg. 223-15-02
St. Paul, MN 55144
612-736-2964
800-328-1371
Fax: 612-736-7479

**TIME-LIFE VIDEO AND
TELEVISION** (TLF)
1450 E. Parham Rd.
Richmond, VA 23280
804-266-6330
800-621-7026

TIMELESS VIDEO INC. (TIM)
10010 Canoga Ave., Ste. B2
Chatsworth, CA 91311
818-773-0284

TOUCHSTONE HOME VIDEO
(TOU)
500 S. Buena Vista St.
Burbank, CA 91521
818-562-3883

**TRANS-WORLD
ENTERTAINMENT** (TWE)
3330 Cahuenga Blvd., W.,
Ste. 500
Los Angeles, CA 90068
213-969-2800

**TRIBORO ENTERTAINMENT
GROUP** (TRI)
12 W. 27th St., 15th Fl.
New York, NY 10001
212-686-6116
Fax: 212-686-6178

**TURNER HOME
ENTERTAINMENT
COMPANY** (TTC)
1 CNN Center
N. Tower, 12th Fl.
Atlanta, GA 30348
404-827-2000

20TH CENTURY FOX FILM CORPORATION (*TCF*)
PO Box 900
Beverly Hills, CA 90213
310-277-2211

21ST GENESIS HOME VIDEO
(*GNS*)
15820 Arminta St.
Van Nuys, CA 91406
818-787-0660
800-344-1060

UAV CORPORATION (*UAV*)
PO Box 7647
Charlotte, NC 28241
704-548-7300
Fax: 704-548-3335

UNI DISTRIBUTION (*UND*)
60 Universal City Plaza
Universal City, CA 91608

UNICORN VIDEO, INC. (*UNI*)
9811 Independence Ave.
Chatsworth, CA 91311
818-407-1333
800-528-4336
Fax: 818-407-8246

UNIVERSITY OF WASHINGTON INSTRUCTIONAL MEDIA SERVICES (*UWA*)
Kane Hall, DG-10
Seattle, WA 98195
206-543-9909
Fax: 206-685-7892

VALENCIA ENTERTAINMENT CORPORATION (*VEC*)
45030 Trevor Ave.
Lancaster, CA 93534-2648
805-940-1040
800-323-2061
Fax: 805-940-8511

VANGUARD VIDEO (*VGD*)
436 Creamery Way, Ste. D
Exton, PA 19341
800-323-7432

VANTAGE COMMUNICATIONS, INC.
(*VAN*)
PO Box 546-G
Nyack, NY 10960
914-268-0715
800-872-0068
Fax: 914-268-3429

VCII HOME ENTERTAINMENT, INC. (*VHE*)
13418 Wyandotte St.
North Hollywood, CA 91605
818-764-1777
800-350-1931
Fax: 818-764-0231

VESTRON VIDEO (*VES*)
c/o Live Home Video
15400 Sherman Way
PO Box 10124
Van Nuys, CA 91410-0124
818-988-5060

VICTORY VIDEO (*VIC*)
4466 Jeff
Toney, AL 35773
205-852-0198
Fax: 205-859-8946

VIDAMERICA, INC. (*VID*)
231 E. 55th St.
New York, NY 10022

212-685-1300
800-843-1994

VIDCREST (*VDC*)
PO Box 69642
Los Angeles, CA 90069
213-650-7310
Fax: 213-654-4810

VIDEO ACTION (*VDA*)
708 W. 1st St.
Los Angeles, CA 90012
213-687-8262
800-422-2241
Fax: 213-687-8425

VIDEO ARTISTS INTERNATIONAL, INC. (*VAI*)
158 Linwood Plaza, Ste. 301
Fort Lee, NJ 07024
201-944-0099
800-477-7146
Fax: 201-947-8850

VIDEO BIBLE LIBRARY, INC.
(*VBL*)
Box 17515
Portland, OR 97217
503-892-7707
Fax: 503-254-8318

THE VIDEO CATALOG (*TVC*)
PO Box 64428
Saint Paul, MN 55164-0428
612-659-4312
800-733-6656
Fax: 612-659-4320

VIDEO CITY PRODUCTIONS
(*VCD*)
4266 Broadway
Oakland, CA 94611
510-428-0202
800-847-8400
Fax: 510-654-7802

VIDEO COMMUNICATIONS, INC. (*UHV*)
6535 E. Skelley Dr.
Tulsa, OK 74145
918-622-6460
800-331-4077
Fax: 918-665-6256

VIDEO CONNECTION (*VCN*)
3123 Sylvania Ave.
Toledo, OH 43613
419-472-7727

VIDEO DIMENSIONS (*VDM*)
322 8th Ave., 4th Fl.
New York, NY 10011
212-929-6135

VIDEO GEMS (*GEM*)
12228 Venice Blvd., No. 504
Los Angeles, CA 90066

VIDEO PLACEMENT INTERNATIONAL (*VPL*)
240 E. 27th St., Ste. 81
New York, NY 10016
212-696-9207

VIDEO PRESENTATIONS, INC. (*VPR*)
6th & Battery Bldg.
2326 6th Ave., Ste. 230
Seattle, WA 98121
206-728-9241
800-458-5335

VIDEO RAILS (*VRL*)
PO Box 80001
San Diego, CA 92138
619-581-6226
800-262-2776
Fax: 619-581-0131

VIDEO RESOURCES (*VRS*)
220 W. 71st St.
New York, NY 10023
212-724-7055
Fax: 212-595-0189

VIDEO SEARCH OF MIAMI
(*VSM*)
PO Box 161917
Miami, FL 33116
305-387-6807

VIDEO TREASURES (*VTR*)
2001 Glenn Pkwy.
Batavia, OH 45103
513-732-2790
Fax: 513-732-2611

VIDEO VIDEO (*VDE*)
1376 Soquel Ave.
Santa Cruz, CA 95062
408-427-2282

VIDEO VISA (*VVC*)
12901 Coral Tree Pl.
Los Angeles, CA 90066
310-827-7222

VIDEO YESTERYEAR (*VYY*)
Box C
Sandy Hook, CT 06482
203-426-2574
800-243-0987
Fax: 203-797-0819

VIDEOGRAF (*VGR*)
144 W. 27th St.
New York, NY 10001
212-242-7871

VIDEOTAKES (*VTK*)
187 Parker Ave.
Rte. 71
Manasquan, NJ 08736
201-528-5000
800-526-7002

VIDEOVISION, INC. (*VVI*)
37 E. Washington St.
Hagerstown, MD 21740
301-791-3496

VIDMARK ENTERTAINMENT
(*VMK*)
2644 30th St.
Santa Monica, CA 90405-3009
310-314-2000

VIP VIDEO (*VIP*)
c/o JEF Films
Film House
143 Hickory Hill Circle
Osterville, MA 02655-1322
508-428-7198

VIRGIN VISION (*VIR*)
6100 Wilshire Blvd., 16th Fl.
Los Angeles, CA 90048

VISION VIDEO (*VIS*)
2030 Wentz Church Rd.
Box 540
Worcester, PA 19490
215-584-1893
800-523-0226
Fax: 215-584-4610

VOYAGER COMPANY (*VYG*)
1351 Pacific Coast Hwy.
Santa Monica, CA 90401
310-451-1383
800-446-2001
Fax: 310-394-2156

WADE WILLIAMS PRODUCTIONS, INC. (*MWP*)
9840 Wornall Rd.

Kansas City, MO 64114-3907
816-241-6684
Fax: 816-941-7055

WALT DISNEY HOME VIDEO
(*DIS*)
500 S. Buena Vista St.
Burbank, CA 91521
818-562-3560

WARNER/ELEKTRA/ ATLANTIC (WEA) CORPORATION (*WEA*)
9451 LBJ Fwy., Ste. 107
Dallas, TX 75243
214-234-6200

WARNER HOME VIDEO, INC.
(*WAR*)
4000 Warner Blvd.
Burbank, CA 91522
818-954-6000

WARNER REPRISE VIDEO
(*WRV*)
3300 Warner Blvd.
Burbank, CA 91505-4694
818-846-9090
Fax: 818-953-3329

WARREN MILLER ENTERTAINMENT (*WME*)
505 Pier Ave.
Hermosa Beach, CA 90254
310-376-2494

WATER BEARER FILMS
(*WBF*)
205 West End Ave., Ste. 24H
New York, NY 10023
212-580-8185
Fax: 212-787-5455

WAXWORKS (*WAX*)
325 E. 3rd St.
Owensboro, KY 42303
502-926-0008
800-825-8558

WEISS GLOBAL ENTERPRISES (*WGE*)
2055 Saviers Rd., Ste. 12
Oxnard, CA 93030
805-486-4495

WESTERN FILM & VIDEO, INC. (*WFV*)
30941 Agoura Rd., Ste. 302
Westlake Village, CA 91361
818-889-7350

WESTERN L.A. FILM PRODUCTIONS, INC. (*WLA*)
7425 Clinton St.
Los Angeles, CA 90036-5703

WESTERNWORLD VIDEO, INC. (*WWV*)
10523-45 Burbank Blvd.
North Hollywood, CA 91601
818-753-3000

WHITE STAR (*WST*)
121 Hwy. 36
West Long Branch, NJ 07764
908-229-2343
800-458-5887
Fax: 908-229-0066

WHOLE TOON CATALOGUE
(*WTA*)
PO Box 369
Issaquah, WA 98027-0369
206-391-8747
Fax: 206-391-9064

WNET/THIRTEEN NON-BROADCAST (*WNE*)
356 W. 58th St.
New York, NY 10019
212-560-3045

WOMBAT FILM AND VIDEO
(*WOM*)
930 Pitner
Evanston, IL 60202
708-328-6700
800-323-5448
Fax: 708-328-6706

WOOD KNAPP & COMPANY, INC. (*WKV*)
Knapp Press
5900 Wilshire Blvd.
Los Angeles, CA 90036
213-965-3500
800-521-2666
Fax: 213-930-2742

WORLD ARTISTS HOME VIDEO (*WAC*)
135 N. Detroit St.
PO Box 36788
Los Angeles, CA 90036
213-933-7057
800-821-1205
Fax: 213-933-2356

WORLD VIDEO ENTERPRISES, INC. (*WVE*)
150 Executive Park Blvd., No. 1600
San Francisco, CA 94134-3303
415-468-6218

WORLDVISION HOME VIDEO, INC. (*WOV*)
1700 Broadwaay
New York, NY 10019-5905
212-261-2700

WORLDWIDE ENTERTAINMENT MARKETING, INC. (*WEM*)
196 Holt St.
PO Box 1070
Hackensack, NJ 07602
201-996-9343
Fax: 201-996-9345

XENON (*XVC*)
211 Arizona Ave.
Santa Monica, CA 90401
800-468-1913

YANKEE-ORIOLE COMPANY
(*YOC*)
21-12 33rd Ave.
Astoria, NY 11106
718-721-0724

ZEITGEIST FILMS (*ZBI*)

VideoHound's VideoDiary
(Notes on Tracking the *Wild Video*)